Empires of the 6th Century BC

EERDMANS
COMMENTARY *on the* BIBLE

EERDMANS COMMENTARY

WILLIAM B. EERDMANS PUBLISHING COMPANY

on the BIBLE

James D. G. Dunn
General Editor
Editor of the New Testament

John W. Rogerson
Editor of the Old Testament and Apocrypha

GRAND RAPIDS, MICHIGAN / CAMBRIDGE, U.K.

Wm. B. Eerdmans Publishing Co.
255 Jefferson Ave. S.E., Grad Rapids, Michigan 49503 /
P.O. Box 163, Cambridge CB3 9PU U.K.
www.eerdmans.com

Printed in the United States of America

08 07 06 05 04 03   7 6 5 4 3 2 1

ISBN 0-8028-3711-5

Contents

Preface

No one familiar with the Bible in any degree needs to be told that it is a remarkable volume. Its documents and traditions span a period of at least a thousand years. It contains the sacred scriptures of two of the world's major religions, Judaism (what Christians call "the Old Testament") and Christianity, and is the lifeblood of each. In and through its words hundreds of thousands have heard, and still hear, the Word of God addressing them personally. The Bible has informed and infused Western culture to such an extent that the foundations, formative traditions, character, and values of Western society cannot be understood without it. Nations have been built on foundational principles drawn from it. Much of the world's greatest art, music, and literature cannot be adequately appreciated without a good knowledge of the Bible. It has been the source and inspiration for countless acts of quiet heroism and lives of sacrificial service — though, paradoxically, many of its texts have also been used to justify acts of unimaginable horror and systems of barbarous intolerance. And in many parts of the world, particularly in Africa and South America, where the Christian churches are growing rapidly, the Bible is being rediscovered and read in new and exciting ways.

A striking and equally familiar feature of the Bible is the rich diversity of types of writing within it — law codes, historical narratives, poetry, psalms and proverbs, prophetic oracles, apocalyptic visions, gospels, and epistles. Each of these genres requires detailed study to unfold its riches, and all of the sixty-six individual writings — not to mention the Apocrypha and Pseudepigrapha — have given rise to numerous commentaries and special studies. Indeed, a further measure of the Bible's importance is that it has resulted in far more secondary literature than has any other single or composite volume in history. In consequence, the beginning student or study group that wants to give the Bible serious attention can quickly be overwhelmed by such an embarrassing abundance of riches. The sheer disparity between the Bible's one volume and all that has been written about it is mind-boggling. At the same time, many briefer treatments of biblical books and themes are written at an overly simplistic level; they neither wrestle with the complexity of many texts, nor penetrate very far into the profundity of others, nor show enough awareness of the diversity of interpretations possible at many points or of the challenges and benefits of much modern scholarship. Despite its age, biblical studies is a fast-moving discipline with new discoveries, angles of approach, and insights constantly calling for fresh assessment of older assumptions simply taken for granted, whether at a fine-detail or whole-picture level.

It is essential, then, that each new generation should have a guide enabling serious students of the Bible to see the forest without getting lost in the trees. Since the Bible too easily becomes the province only of the technical expert, it is desirable that a single volume should sum up the best of modern scholarship and direct interested readers to appropriate further reading. And since the twentieth century witnessed huge strides in the way the Bible is read and heard, with many new translations and ways of approaching the Bible under constant discussion, it is appropriate that students of the Bible should have a handbook which provides authoritative summing up of the best fruits of the last century's scholarship and clear guidance on into the twenty-first century.

The *Eerdmans Commentary on the Bible* is just such a volume.

- It draws on and encapsulates the best of modern and international scholarship on the books of the Bible.
- It is the only one-volume Bible commentary to cover all the texts (including the Apocrypha and *1 Enoch*) regarded by one or more Christian churches as canonical.
- It deals with the text in nontechnical language, and provides both reader-friendly treatments for beginning use of the Bible and succinct summaries of the essence or thrust of each section for those further along the way.
- It focuses on the principal unit of meaning — narrative, prophetic oracle, parable, section of argument, etc. — rather than attempting verse-by-verse analysis.
- The primary objective is to clarify the meaning (and possible meanings) of each unit and to bring out its interconnectedness with the rest of the text.
- It thus avoids the problems (common in many commentaries) either of losing the reader in a mass of detail, or of simply rephrasing what the text itself says.
- It summarizes succinctly major issues unable to be discussed in full detail and refers the reader to fuller discussions.
- The Editors provide two major context-setting articles — "The History of the Tradition: Old Testament and Apocrypha" and "The History of the Tradition: New Testament."
- The commentary includes several "behind the text" and "in front of the text" articles, on background and interpretation, and overview articles which enable the reader to maintain perspective.

The sixty-seven contributors include world-class scholars from a wide variety of backgrounds and faith traditions. Their contributions stand out either for their fresh interpretations of the evidence, or for their way of asking new questions of the text, or for their new angles of approach, or for taking what was once the province of the technical expert and making it manageable for the busy pastor, teacher, student, or layperson. While the translation of choice is the New Revised Standard Version, many of the contributors offer their own vivid translations of the original Hebrew or Greek.

The project has been long in the making. The volume now goes forth with our heartfelt desire and prayer that it may open the windows of many minds and may reward attentive hearing with many fresh insights and a new appreciation of the Bible's manifold riches.

JAMES D. G. DUNN
General Editor
and New Testament Editor

JOHN W. ROGERSON
Editor of the Old Testament
and Apocrypha

Contributors

Philip S. Alexander
Professor of Post-Biblical Literature
Co-Director, Center for Jewish Studies
University of Manchester
Manchester, England
3 Maccabees

Deborah A. Appler
Assistant Professor of Old Testament
Moravian Theological Seminary
Bethlehem, Pennsylvania
Syro-Palestinian and Biblical Archeology

Graeme Auld
Professor of Hebrew Bible
University of Edinburgh
Edinburgh, Scotland
1 and 2 Samuel

David L. Balch
Professor of New Testament
Interim Director of Ph.D. Studies
Brite Divinity School
Texas Christian University
Fort Worth, Texas
Luke

John Barclay
Lightfoot Professor of Divinity
University of Durham
Durham, England
2 Corinthians

Margaret Barker
Independent Scholar
Former President of the Society for Old Testament Study
Derbyshire, England
Isaiah

John R. Bartlett
Fellow Emeritus
Trinity College
Dublin, Republic of Ireland
1 and 2 Maccabees

Stephen C. Barton
Reader in New Testament
Department of Theology
University of Durham
Durham, England
1 Corinthians

Richard Bauckham
Professor of New Testament and
Bishop Wardlaw Professor
St. Mary's College
University of St. Andrews
St. Andrews, Scotland
James

Julye Bidmead
Assistant Professor of Biblical Studies
Department of Religion and Philosophy
James Madison University
Harrisonburg, Virginia
Syro-Palestinian and Biblical Archeology

Philip J. Budd
Formerly Senior Lecturer
The Westminster Institute of Education
Oxford Brookes University
Oxford, England
Numbers

M. Daniel Carroll R. (Rodas)
Professor of Old Testament
Denver Seminary
Denver, Colorado
Adjunct Professor of Old Testament
Seminario Teológico Centroamericano
Guatemala City, Guatemala
Amos and *Malachi*

Ronald E. Clements
Emeritus Professor of Old Testament Studies
King's College
University of London
London, England
Proverbs

David J. A. Clines
Research Professor
Department of Biblical Studies
University of Sheffield
Sheffield, England
Lamentations

CONTRIBUTORS

RICHARD J. COGGINS
Formerly Senior Lecturer in Old Testament Studies
King's College
University of London
London, England
1 and 2 Chronicles

SIDNIE WHITE CRAWFORD
Professor of Hebrew and
Chair, Classics and Religious Studies
University of Nebraska-Lincoln
Lincoln, Nebraska
Esther

PHILIP R. DAVIES
Professor of Biblical Studies
University of Sheffield
Sheffield, England
Prayer of Manasseh

KATHARINE J. DELL
Senior Lecturer
University of Cambridge and
Fellow
St. Catharine's College
Cambridge, England
Job

DAVID A. DESILVA
Professor of New Testament and Greek
Ashland Theological Seminary
Ashland, Ohio
4 Maccabees

A. R. PETE DIAMOND
Educational Consultant
Santa Barbara, California
Jeremiah

JAMES D. G. DUNN
Lightfoot Professor Emeritus of Divinity
University of Durham
Durham, England
GENERAL EDITOR AND NEW TESTAMENT EDITOR
Preface and *The History of the Tradition: New Testament*

GRACE I. EMMERSON
Visiting Lecturer in Theology
University of Birmingham
Birmingham, England
Hosea

CRAIG A. EVANS
Payzant Professor of New Testament
Acadia Divinity School
Wolfville, Nova Scotia, Canada
Mark

DAVID NOEL FREEDMAN
Endowed Chair for Hebrew Biblical Studies
University of California, San Diego
La Jolla, California
The Pentateuch

VICTOR P. FURNISH
University Distinguished Professor Emeritus of New Testament
Perkins School of Theology
Southern Methodist University
Dallas, Texas
Letters in the New Testament

BEVERLY R. GAVENTA
Helen H. P. Manson Professor of New Testament Literature and Exegesis
Princeton Theological Seminary
Princeton, New Jersey
Galatians

ANTHONY GELSTON
Emeritus Reader in Theology
University of Durham
Durham, England
Joel, Obadiah, Habakkuk, and *Zephaniah*

JOHN A. GOLDINGAY
David Allan Hubbard Professor of Old Testament
Fuller Theological Seminary
Pasadena, California
Premodern, Modern, and Postmodern in Old Testament Study and *Ezekiel*

LESTER L. GRABBE
Professor of Hebrew Bible and Early Judaism
University of Hull
Hull, England
Ezra, Nehemiah, and *Tobit*

JOEL B. GREEN
Dean of Academic Affairs and
Professor of New Testament Interpretation
Asbury Theological Seminary
Wilmore, Kentucky
Hermeneutical Approaches to the New Testament Tradition

P. DERYN GUEST
Lecturer in Biblical Hermeneutics
University of Birmingham
Birmingham, England
Judges

DAVID GUNN
A. A. Bradford Chair of Religion
Texas Christian University
Fort Worth, Texas
Jonah

Daniel C. Harlow
Assistant Professor of Religion
Calvin College
Grand Rapids, Michigan
The Hebrew Bible in the Dead Sea Scrolls and
The Dead Sea Scrolls and the New Testament

A. Peter Hayman
Senior Lecturer in Hebrew and Jewish Studies
School of Divinity
University of Edinburgh
Edinburgh, Scotland
Wisdom of Solomon

Morna D. Hooker
Lady Margaret's Professor of Divinity Emerita
University of Cambridge
Life Fellow
Robinson College
Cambridge, England
Colossians and *Philemon*

Walter J. Houston
Chaplain Fellow and Director of Ministerial Training
Mansfield College
Oxford, England
Leviticus

John Jarick
Old Testament Tutor
St. Stephen's House
Oxford, England
Ecclesiastes and Greek Esther

Robert K. Jewett
Guest Professor of New Testament
University of Heidelberg
Heidelberg, Germany
1 and 2 Thessalonians

William D. Johnstone
Professor Emeritus of Hebrew and Semitic Languages
University of Aberdeen
Aberdeen, Scotland
Exodus

I. Howard Marshall
Honorary Research Professor of New Testament
University of Aberdeen
Aberdeen, Scotland
Ephesians

Scot McKnight
Karl A. Olsson Professor in Religious Studies
North Park Seminary
Libertyville, Illinois
2 Peter and *Jude*

James R. Mueller
Associate Professor of Religion
University of Florida
Gainesville, Florida
Introduction to the Pseudepigrapha

Daniel C. Olson
Doctoral Student
Graduate Theological Union
Berkeley, California
1 Enoch

John Painter
Professor of Theology
St. Mark's National Theological Centre
Charles Sturt University, Canberra Campus
Barton, Australian Capital Territory
1, 2, and 3 John

Pheme Perkins
Professor of New Testament
Boston College
Boston, Massachusetts
1 and 2 Timothy and *Titus*

Willem S. Prinsloo (deceased)
Dean and Head of the Department of Old Testament
Theology and Exegesis
Faculty of Theology
University of Pretoria, South Africa
Psalms

Iain Provan
Professor of Old Testament
Regent College
Vancouver, British Columbia
Canada
Daniel

Paul L. Redditt
Chair, Department of Religion
Georgetown College
Georgetown, Kentucky
Introduction to Prophetic Literature

John Reumann
Ministerium of Pennsylvania and
Professor Emeritus of New Testament
Lutheran Theological College
Philadelphia, Pennsylvania
Romans

John W. Rogerson
Professor Emeritus of Biblical Studies
University of Sheffield
Sheffield, England
Editor of the Old Testament and Apocrypha
Preface, The History of the Tradition: Old Testament and Apocrypha, Deuteronomy, Song of Songs, Micah, Nahum, Haggai, Zechariah, and *Additions to Daniel*

CONTRIBUTORS

ANTHONY J. SALDARINI (DECEASED)
Professor of Theology
Boston College
Boston, Massachusetts
Matthew

ALISON SALVESEN
Hebrew Centre Lecturer
The Oriental Institute
University of Oxford
Oxford, England
Psalm 151

JOHN J. SCHMITT
Associate Professor of Biblical Studies
Marquette University
Milwaukee, Wisconsin
Baruch and *2 Esdras*

J. MARTIN C. SCOTT
Senior Vocational Guidance Officer
Board of Ministry
Church of Scotland
Edinburgh, Scotland
John

JOHN SNAITH
Formerly Lecturer in Hebrew and Aramaic
University of Cambridge
Cambridge, England
Sirach (Ecclesiasticus)

JOHN T. SQUIRES
Academic Dean and Lecturer in Biblical Studies
United Theological College
School of Theology
Charles Sturt University
Australia
Acts

GRAHAM N. STANTON
Lady Margaret's Professor of Divinity
University of Cambridge
Cambridge, England
1 Peter

LOREN T. STUCKENBRUCK
Professor of New Testament
University of Durham
Durham, England
Revelation

ANTHONY C. THISELTON
Emeritus Professor of Christian Theology in Residence
University of Nottingham, and
Canon Theologian of Leicester Cathedral
and of Southwell Minster
Nottingham, England
Hebrews

ROGER TOMES
Honorary Research Fellow
University of Manchester
Manchester, England
1 and 2 Kings

CHRISTOPHER M. TUCKETT
Professor of New Testament Studies
University of Oxford
Oxford, England
Introduction to the Gospels

ROBERT E. VAN VOORST
Professor of New Testament
Western Theological Seminary
Holland, Michigan
New Testament Apocrypha

CHARLES A. WANAMAKER
Associate Professor of Religious Studies
University of Cape Town
Cape Town, South Africa
Philippians

GORDON J. WENHAM
Professor of Old Testament
University of Gloucestershire
Gloucestershire, England
Genesis

GERALD WEST
Head of the School of Theology
Director of the Institute for the Study of the Bible
and Worker Ministry Project
Pietermaritzburg, South Africa
Ruth and *Judith*

HUGH G. M. WILLIAMSON
Regius Professor of Hebrew
University of Oxford
Oxford, England
1 Esdras

K. LAWSON YOUNGER JR.
Professor of Old Testament, Semitic Languages, and
Ancient Near Eastern History
Trinity International University — Divinity School
Deerfield, Illinois
Joshua

Abbreviations

PERIODICALS, REFERENCE WORKS, AND SERIALS

AB	Anchor Bible
ABD	D. N. Freedman (ed.), *Anchor Bible Dictionary*
ABRL	Anchor Bible Reference Library
ADPV	Abhandlungen des deutschen Palästina-Vereins
AGJU	Arbeiten zur Geschichte des antiken Judentums und des Urchristentums
AJA	*American Journal of Archaeology*
AJBI	*Annual of the Japanese Biblical Institute*
AJP	*American Journal of Philology*
AJT	*American Journal of Theology*
AnBib	Analecta biblica
ANEP	J. B. Pritchard (ed.), *Ancient Near East in Pictures*
ANET	J. B. Pritchard (ed.), *Ancient Near Eastern Texts*
ANRW	*Aufstieg und Niedergang der römischen Welt*
ANTC	Abingdon New Testament Commentary
AOAT	Alter Orient und Altes Testament
APOT	R. H. Charles (ed.), *Apocrypha and Pseudepigrapha of the Old Testament*
ASV	American Standard Version
ATANT	Abhandlungen zur Theologie des Alten und Neuen Testaments
ATD	Das Alte Testament Deutsch
ATDA	Das Alte Testament Deutsch Apokryphen
ATLAMS	American Theological Library Association Monograph Series
ATR	*Anglican Theological Review*
AusBR	*Australian Biblical Review*
AV	Authorized Version
BA	*Biblical Archaeologist*
BAGD	W. Bauer, W. F. Arndt, F. W. Gingrich, and F. W. Danker, *Greek-English Lexicon of the New Testament*
BAR	*Biblical Archaeology Review*
BASOR	*Bulletin of the American Schools of Oriental Research*
BBB	Bonner biblische Beiträge
BBR	Bulletin for Biblical Research
BDB	F. Brown, S. R. Driver, and C. A. Briggs, *Hebrew and English Lexicon of the Old Testament*
BETL	Bibliotheca ephemeridum theologicarum lovaniensium
BHS	*Biblia hebraica stuttgartensia*
Bib	*Biblica*
BibRev	*Bible Review*
BJRL	*Bulletin of the John Rylands University Library of Manchester*
BJS	Brown Judaic Studies
BKAT	Biblischer Kommentar: Altes Testament
BNTC	Black New Testament Commentary
BR	*Biblical Research*
BT	*The Bible Translator*
BTB	*Biblical Theology Bulletin*
BWANT	Beiträge zur Wissenschaft vom Alten und Neuen Testament
BZ	*Biblische Zeitschrift*
BZAW	Beihefte zur *ZAW*
BZNW	Beihefte zur *ZNW*
CBC	Cambridge Bible Commentary
CBQ	*Catholic Biblical Quarterly*
CBQMS	Catholic Biblical Quarterly — Monograph Series
CBSC	Cambridge Bible for Schools and Colleges
CIG	*Corpus inscriptionum graecarum*
CNT	Commentaire du Nouveau Testament
ConBNT	Coniectanea biblica, New Testament
ConBOT	Coniectanea biblica, Old Testament
CP	*Classical Philology*
CPJ	*Corpus Papyrorum Judaicarum*
CR:BS	*Currents in Research: Biblical Studies*
CRINT	Compendia rerum iudaicarum ad novum testamentum
DJD	Discoveries in the Judaean Desert
DLNTD	*Dictionary of the Later New Testament and Its Developments*
DOTT	D. W. Thomas (ed.), *Documents from Old Testament Times*
DPL	*Dictionary of Paul and His Letters*
Ebib	Etudes bibliques
EDNT	*Exegetical Dictionary of the New Testament*
EKKNT	Evangelisch-katholischer Kommentar zum Neuen Testament
ErIsr	Eretz Israel
EstBíb	*Estudios bíblicos*
ESV	English Standard Version
ETL	*Ephemerides theologicae lovanienses*
EvQ	*Evangelical Quarterly*
EvT	*Evangelische Theologie*
ExpTim	*Expository Times*
FAT	Forschungen zur Altes Testament
FOTL	Forms of the Old Testament Literature

FRLANT	Forschungen zur Religion und Literatur des Alten und Neuen Testaments
GNB	Good News Bible
GNS	Good New Studies
HAR	*Hebrew Annual Review*
HAT	Handbuch zum Alten Testament
HBT	*Horizons in Biblical Theology*
HDR	Harvard Dissertations in Religion
HeyJ	*Heythrop Journal*
HNT	Handbuch zum Neuen Testament
HNTC	Harper's New Testament Commentaries
HR	*History of Religions*
HSM	Harvard Semitic Monographs
HSS	Harvard Semitic Studies
HTKNT	Herders theologischer Kommentar zum Neuen Testament
HTR	*Harvard Theological Review*
HTS	Harvard Theological Studies
HUT	Hermeneutische Untersuchungen zur Theologie
IB	*Interpreter's Bible*
IBC	Interpretation: A Bible Commentary for Teaching and Preaching
IBS	*Irish Biblical Studies*
ICC	International Critical Commentary
IDB	G. A. Buttrick (ed.), *Interpreter's Dictionary of the Bible*
IDBSup	Supplementary volume to *IDB*
IEJ	*Israel Exploration Journal*
Int	*Interpretation*
ITC	International Theological Commentary
ITQ	*Irish Theological Quarterly*
JAC	Jahrbuch für Antike und Christentum
JANESCU	*Journal of the Ancient Near Eastern Society of Columbia University*
JAOS	*Journal of the American Oriental Society*
JB	A. Jones (ed.), *Jerusalem Bible*
JBC	R. E. Brown et al. (eds.), *The Jerome Biblical Commentary*
JBL	*Journal of Biblical Literature*
JEA	*Journal of Egyptian Archaeology*
JETS	*Journal of the Evangelical Theological Society*
JIGRE	*Jewish Inscriptions in Greco-Roman Egypt*
JJS	*Journal of Jewish Studies*
JNES	*Journal of Near Eastern Studies*
JOTTL	*Journal of Translation and Textlinguistics*
JPS	Jewish Publication Society
JR	*Journal of Religion*
JSHRZ	Jüdische Schriften aus hellenistisch-römischer Zeit
JSJ	*Journal for the Study of Judaism in the Persian, Hellenistic, and Roman Period*
JSJSup	Journal for the Study of Judaism Supplement Series
JSNT	*Journal for the Study of the New Testament*
JSNTSup	Journal for the Study of the New Testament — Supplement Series
JSOT	*Journal for the Study of the Old Testament*
JSOTSup	Journal for the Study of the Old Testament — Supplement Series
JSP	*Journal for the Study of the Pseudepigrapha*
JSS	*Journal of Semitic Studies*
JTC	*Journal for Theology and the Church*
JTS	*Journal of Theological Studies*
KAT	Kommentar zum Alten Testament
KJV	King James Version
KS	*Kirjath-Sepher*
LCC	Library of Christian Classics
LEC	Library of Early Christianity
MNTC	Moffatt New Testament Commentary
NAB	New American Bible
NAC	New American Commentary
NASB	New American Standard Bible
NCB	New Century Bible
NCBC	New Century Bible Commentary
NEB	New English Bible
Neot	*Neotestamentica*
NIBC	New International Biblical Commentary
NICNT	New International Commentary on the New Testament
NICOT	New International Commentary on the Old Testament
NIDNTT	*New International Dictionary of New Testament Theology*
NIDOTTE	*New International Dictionary of Old Testament Theology and Exegesis*
NIGTC	The New International Greek Testament Commentary
NIV	New International Version
NIVAC	New International Version Application Commentary
NJB	H. Wansbrough (ed.), *New Jerusalem Bible*
NJBC	R. E. Brown et al. (ed.), *The New Jerome Biblical Commentary*
NJPS	New Jewish Publication Society
NovT	*Novum Testamentum*
NovTSup	Novum Testamentum, Supplements
NRSV	New Revised Standard Version
NTD	Das Neue Testament Deutsch
NTG	New Testament Guides
NTM	Norsk tidsskrift for misjon
NTS	*New Testament Studies*
NTSup	New Testament Supplements
OBO	Orbis biblicus et orientalis
OBT	Overtures to Biblical Theology
ÖTKNT	Ökumenischer Taschenbuchkommentar zum Neuen Testament
OTL	Old Testament Library
OTP	J. H. Charlesworth (ed.), *The Old Testament Pseudepigrapha*
PEQ	*Palestine Exploration Quarterly*
PNTC	Pillar New Testament Commentary
QD	Quaestiones disputatae
QL	Qumran Literature
RB	*Revue biblique*
REB	Revised English Bible
RelSRev	*Religious Studies Review*

ResQ	*Restoration Quarterly*
RevQ	*Revue de Qumran*
RNT	Regensburger Neues Testament
RSV	Revised Standard Version
RTP	*Revue de théologie et de philosophie*
RTR	*Reformed Theological Review*
SacPag	Sacra pagina
SBFLA	*Studii biblici Franciscani liber annuus*
SBLDS	SBL Dissertation Series
SBLEJL	SBL Early Judaism and Its Literature
SBLMS	SBL Monograph Series
SBLRBS	SBL Resources for Biblical Study
SBLSBS	SBL Sources for Biblical Study
SBLSCS	SBL Septuagint and Cognate Studies
SBLSP	SBL Seminar Papers
SBLSS	SBL Symposium Series
SBT	Studies in Biblical Theology
ScEs	*Science et esprit*
SD	Studies and Documents
Sem	*Semitica*
SIG	*Sylloge Inscriptionum Graecarum*
SJLA	Studies in Judaism in Late Antiquity
SJT	*Scottish Journal of Theology*
SNT	Studien zum Neuen Testament
SNTSMS	Society for New Testament Studies Monograph Series
SO	Symbolae osloenses
SOTSMS	Society for Old Testament Study Monograph Series
SPB	Studia postbiblica
SPS	Salzburger patristische Studien
ST	*Studia theologica*
StudBib	Studia Biblica
SUNT	Studien zur Umwelt des Neuen Testaments
SVTP	Studia in Veteris Testamenti pseudepigrapha
TBu	Theologische Bücherei
TCGNT	B. M. Metzger, *A Textual Commentary on the Greek New Testament*
TDNT	G. Kittel and G. Friedrich (eds.), *Theological Dictionary of the New Testament*
TLNT	*Theological Lexicon of the New Testament*
TNTC	Tyndale New Testament Commentaries
TOTC	Tyndale Old Testament Commentaries
TS	*Theological Studies*
TTZ	*Trierer theologische Zeitschrift*
TU	Texte und Untersuchungen
TynBul	*Tyndale Bulletin*
UF	*Ugarit-Forschungen*
USQR	*Union Seminary Quarterly Review*
VC	*Vigiliae christianae*
VT	*Vetus Testamentum*
VTSup	Vetus Testamentum, Supplements
WA	M. Luther, Kristische Gesamtausgabe (= "Weimar" edition)
WBC	Word Biblical Commentary
WMANT	Wissenschaftliche Monographien zum Alten und Neuen Testament
WTJ	*Westminster Theological Journal*
WUNT	Wissenschaftliche Untersuchungen zum Neuen Testament
WWSup	*Word and World Supplement*
ZAW	*Zeitschrift für die alttestamentliche Wissenschaft*
ZBKNT	Zürcher Bibelkommentare, Neuen Testament
ZNW	*Zeitschrift für die neutestamentliche Wissenschaft*
ZTK	*Zeitschrift für Theologie und Kirche*

GENERAL

AD	*anno Domini,* in the year of our Lord
Aram.	Aramaic
b.	born
b.	Babylonian Talmud
BC	before Christ
c.	*circa,* around
cent.	century
cf.	*confer,* compare
ch(s).	chapter(s)
col.	column
d.	died
diss.	dissertation
DSS	Dead Sea Scrolls
ed.	editor, edition
e.g.	*exempli gratia,* for example
esp.	especially
ET	English Translation
etc.	*et cetera,* and the others
frg.	fragment
Gk.	Greek
HB	Hebrew Bible
Heb.	Hebrew
i.e.	*id est,* that is
km.	kilometer
lit.	literally
LXX	Septuagint
m.	Mishnah
mg.	margin
mss.	manuscripts
Mt.	Mount
MT	Masoretic Text
NT	New Testament
OT	Old Testament
p.	Palestinian (Talmud)
par.	parallel
para(s).	paragraph(s)
pp.	pages (used only when necessary)
pt.	part
Q	Quelle ("sayings") source for the Synoptic Gospels
repr.	reprinted
rev.	revised
t.	Tosefta
trans.	translated by

v. (vv.)	verse, verses
Vg	Vulgate
vs.	versus

BIBLICAL BOOKS (WITH THE APOCRYPHA)

Gen	Genesis
Exod	Exodus
Lev	Leviticus
Num	Numbers
Deut	Deuteronomy
Josh	Joshua
Judg	Judges
1-2 Sam	1-2 Samuel
1-2 Kgs	1-2 Kings
Isa	Isaiah
Jer	Jeremiah
Ezek	Ezekiel
Hos	Hosea
Joel	Joel
Amos	Amos
Obad	Obadiah
Jonah	Jonah
Mic	Micah
Nah	Nahum
Hab	Habakkuk
Zeph	Zephaniah
Hag	Haggai
Zech	Zechariah
Mal	Malachi
Ps (*pl.:* Pss)	Psalm(s)
Job	Job
Prov	Proverbs
Ruth	Ruth
Cant	Canticles
Eccl (*or* Qoh)	Ecclesiastes (*or* Qoheleth)
Lam	Lamentations
Esth	Esther
Dan	Daniel
Ezra	Ezra
Neh	Nehemiah
1-2 Chr	1-2 Chronicles
1-2-3-4 Kgdms	1-2-3-4 Kingdoms
Add Esth	Additions to Esther
Bar	Baruch
Bel	Bel and the Dragon
1-2 Esdr	1-2 Esdras
4 Ezra	4 Ezra
Jdt	Judith
Ep Jer	Epistle of Jeremiah
1-2-3-4 Macc	1-2-3-4 Maccabees
Pr Azar	Prayer of Azariah
Pr Man	Prayer of Manasseh
Sir	Sirach
Sus	Susanna
Tob	Tobit
Wis	Wisdom of Solomon
Matt	Matthew
Mark	Mark
Luke	Luke
John	John
Acts	Acts
Rom	Romans
1-2 Cor	1-2 Corinthians
Gal	Galatians
Eph	Ephesians
Phil	Philippians
Col	Colossians
1-2 Thess	1-2 Thessalonians
1-2 Tim	1-2 Timothy
Titus	Titus
Phlm	Philemon
Heb	Hebrews
Jas	James
1-2 Pet	1-2 Peter
1-2-3 John	1-2-3 John
Jude	Jude
Rev	Revelation

ANCIENT WORKS

Pseudepigraphical Books

Apoc. Abr.	*Apocalypse of Abraham*
2-3 *Apoc. Bar.*	Syrian, Greek *Apocalypse of Baruch*
Apoc. Elijah	*Apocalypse of Elijah*
Apoc. Mos.	*Apocalypse of Moses*
Apoc. Zeph.	*Apocalypse of Zephaniah*
As. Mos.	*Assumption of Moses*
Asc. Isa.	*Ascension of Isaiah*
1-2-3 *Enoch*	Ethiopic, Slavonic, Hebrew Enoch
Ep. Arist.	*Epistle of Aristeas*
Jos. Asen.	*Joseph and Aseneth*
Jub.	*Jubilees*
Mart. Isa.	*Martyrdom of Isaiah*
Para. Jer.	*Paraleipomena Jeremiah*
Pss. Sol.	*Psalms of Solomon*
Sib. Or.	*Sibylline Oracles*
T. Job	*Testament of Job*
T. Moses	*Testament of Moses*
T. 12 Patr.	*Testaments of the Twelve Patriarchs*
T. Ash.	*Testament of Asher*
T. Benj.	*Testament of Benjamin*
T. Dan	*Testament of Dan*
T. Iss.	*Testament of Issachar*
T. Jos.	*Testament of Joseph*
T. Jud.	*Testament of Judah*
T. Levi	*Testament of Levi*
T. Naph.	*Testament of Naphtali*
T. Reub.	*Testament of Reuben*
T. Sol.	*Testament of Solomon*

Early Patristic Books

Apost. Const.	*Apostolic Constitutions*
Barn.	*Barnabas*
Clem.	Clement
Strom.	*Stromateis*
1-2 Clem.	*1-2 Clement*
Did.	*Didache*
Diogn.	*Diognetus*

Ep. ad Flor.	*Letter to Florinus*
Eusebius	Eusebius
Hist. Eccl.	*Historia ecclesiastica*
Praep. Evang.	*Praeparatio evangelica*
Gos. Naz.	*Gospel of the Nazarenes*
Herm.	Hermas
Sim.	*Similitude(s)*
Ign.	Ignatius
Eph.	*Letter to the Ephesians*
Magn.	*Letter to the Magnesians*
Phld.	*Letter to the Philadelphians*
Pol.	*Letter to Polycarp*
Trall.	*Letter to the Trallians*
Iren.	Irenaeus
Adv. Haer.	*Adversus haereses*
Justin	Justin
Dial. Tryph.	*Dialogus contra Tryphonem*
1 Apol.	*First Apology*
Origen	Origen
In Jerem. hom. Lat.	*Latinae homiliae in Jeremiam*
Pol.	Polycarp
Phil.	*Letter to the Philippians*
Ps.-Clem.	*Pseudo-Clementine Recognitions*
Ps.-Philo	Pseudo-Philo
Bib. Ant.	*Biblical Antiquities*
Tertullian	Tertullian
Adv. Marc.	*Adversus Marcionum*

Dead Sea Scrolls and Related Texts

CD	Cairo (Genizah text of the) *Damascus (Document)*
1Q, 2Q, 3Q, etc.	Numbered caves of Qumran, yielding written material; followed by abbreviation of biblical or apocryphal book
1QapGen	*Genesis Apocryphon* of Qumran Cave 1
1QH	*Hodayot (Thanksgiving Hymns)* from Qumran Cave 1
1QIsa[a]	First copy of Isaiah from Qumran Cave 1
1QIsa[b]	Second copy of Isaiah from Qumran Cave 1
1QpHab	*Pesher on Habakkuk* from Qumran Cave 1
1QM	*Milḥamah (War Scroll)*
1QS	*Serek hayyahad (Rule of the Community, Manual of Discipline)*
1QSa	Appendix A *(Rule of the Congregation)* to 1QS
4QDibHam	*Words of the Luminaries* from Qumran Cave 4
4QFlor	*Florilegium* (or *Eschatological Midrashim*) from Qumran Cave 4
4QMMT	*Miqṣat Maʿase ha-Torah* from Qumran Cave 4
4QpHab	*Pesher on Habakkuk* from Qumran Cave 4
4QPrNab	*Prayer of Nabonidus* from Qumran Cave 4
4QpsDan ar[a]	*Apocryphon of Daniel*
11QMelch	*Melchizedek* text from Qumran Cave 11
11QTemple	*Temple Scroll* from Qumran Cave 11
11QPs[a]	*Psalms Scroll* from Qumran Cave 11

Targumic Material

Tg. Neb.	*Targum of the Prophets*
Tg. Neof.	*Targum* Neofiti
Tg. Isa	*Targum of Isaiah*
Tg. Hos	*Targum of Hosea*
Tg. Ps.-Jon.	*Targum of Pseudo-Jonathan*

Orders and Tractates in Mishnaic and Related Literature

ʾAbot	*ʾAbot*
B. Bat.	*Baba Batra*
Ber.	*Berakhot*
ʿEd.	*ʿEduyyot*
ʿErub.	*ʿErubin*
Giṭ.	*Giṭṭin*
Ḥag.	*Ḥagigah*
Hor.	*Horayot*
Kelim	*Kelim*
Ker.	*Keritot*
Maʿas.	*Maʿaserot*
Mak.	*Makkot*
Meg.	*Megillah*
Ned.	*Nedarim*
Nid.	*Niddah*
Pesaḥ.	*Pesaḥim*
Sanh.	*Sanhedrin*
Shab.	*Shabbat*
Sheqal.	*Sheqalim*
Soṭa	*Soṭa*
Suk.	*Sukkah*
Taʿan	*Taʿanit*
Ṭohar.	*Ṭoharot*
Yoma	*Yoma*

Other Rabbinic Works

ʾAbot R. Nat.	*ʾAbot de-Rabbi Nathan*
Mek.	*Mekilta*
Midr.	*Midrash*
Pesiq. R.	*Pesiqta Rabbati*
Pesiq. Rab. Kah.	*Pesiqta de Rab Kahana*
Pirqe R. El.	*Pirqe Rabbi Eliezer*
Rab.	*Rabbah*
Sipre	*Sipre*

Other Ancient Works

Aeschylus	
Agam.	*Agamemnon*
Aristotle	
Nic. Eth.	*Nicomachean Ethics*
Rhet.	*On Rhetoric*
Cicero	
Tusc. disp.	*Tusculanae disputationes*
Demosthenes	
Orat.	*Orations*
Dio Chrysostom	
Ep.	*Epistles*
Orat.	*Orations*
Dionysius of Halicarnassus	
Rom. Ant.	*Antiquitates Romanae*
Epictetus	
Disc.	*Discourses*

Diss.	*Dissertations*
Epimenides	
Strom.	*Stromateis*
Herodotus	
Hist.	*Histories*
Josephus	
Ag. Ap.	*Against Apion*
Ant.	*Antiquities*
J.W.	*Jewish Wars*
Life	*Life of Flavius Josephus*
Juvenal	
Sat.	*Satires*
Livy	
Hist.	*Histories*
Lucian	
Peregr.	*The Passing of Peregrinus*
Musonius	
Orat.	*Orations*
Philo	
Abr.	*De Abrahamo*
Agr.	*De agricultura*
Cher.	*De cherubim*
Conf. ling.	*De confusione linguarum*
Congr.	*De congressu eruditionis gratia*
Decal.	*De decalogo*
Det. pot. ins.	*Quod deterius potiori insidiari soleat*
Ebr.	*De ebrietate*
Flacc.	*In Flaccum*
Fug.	*De fuga et inventione*
Gig.	*De gigantibus*
Her.	*Quis rerum divinarum heres sit*
Hypoth.	*Hypothetica*
Leg. all.	*Legum allegoriae*
Legat.	*Legatio ad Gaium*
Migr. Abr.	*De migratione Abrahami*
Mut. nom.	*De mutatione nominum*
Opif.	*De opificio mundi*
Post.	*De posteritate Caini*
Prob.	*Quod omnis probus liber sit*
Quaest. Exod.	*Quaestiones et solutiones in Exodum*
Quaest Gen.	*Quaestiones et solutiones in Genesim*
Sacr.	*De sacrificiis Abelis et Caini*
Somn.	*De somniis*
Spec. leg.	*De specialibus legibus*
Virt.	*De virtutibus*
Vit. Mos.	*De vita Mosis*
Philostratus	
Vita Ap.	*Vita Apollonius*
Plato	
Apol.	*Apology*
Gorg.	*Gorgias*
Rep.	*Republic*
Sym.	*Symposium*
Pliny	
Ep.	*Epistles*
Nat. Hist.	*Natural History*
Plutarch	
Mor.	*Moralia*
Polybius	
Hist.	*History*
Quintilian	
Inst.	*Institutio oratoria*
Rhet. Her.	*Rhetorica ad Herennium*
Seneca	
Benef.	*De beneficiis*
Ep. Mor.	*Epistulae morales*
Strabo	
Geog.	*Geography*
Tacitus	
Ann.	*Annales*
Hist.	*Historiae*
Thucydides	
Hist.	*Histories*
Xenophon	
Apol.	*Apologia Socratis*
Cyr.	*Cyropaedia*
Mem.	*Memorabilia*
Symp.	*Symposium*

The History of the Tradition: Old Testament and Apocrypha

John W. Rogerson

1. The History and Purpose of the Old Testament and Apocrypha

How, when, and why were the Old Testament (OT) and the Apocrypha written? The obvious place to look for answers to these questions is in the texts themselves. Exod 24:7 refers to "the book of the covenant" which Moses read to the people at Mt. Sinai, while Exod 34:28 reports that Moses wrote "the words of the covenant, the ten commandments" on stone tablets according to God's instructions. Many of the regulations concerning priesthood and sacrifice in Leviticus and Numbers begin with the formulae "the LORD said/spoke to Moses/Aaron," implying their divine origin as well as their mediation through Moses and Aaron. Deuteronomy is an address by Moses to the Israelites gathered in the plains of Moab. In 1 Sam 10:25 Samuel writes in a book "the rights and duties of the kingship," while 1 Kgs 4:32 attributes 3,000 proverbs and 1,005 songs to Solomon. The prophet Isaiah is told to seal the testimony and the teaching (i.e., to write them down) among his disciples, while Jeremiah dictates two sets of prophecies to Baruch, the first of which is destroyed by King Jehoiakim (Jeremiah 36). In the Apocrypha the grandson of the author of the original Hebrew of Sirach (Ecclesiasticus) and its translator into Greek tells us something about himself and his grandfather (Sirach, Prologue), while Bar 1:1-2 claims as its author the Baruch who was Jeremiah's scribe. The Letter of Jeremiah (Baruch 6) is "a copy of a letter that Jeremiah sent . . . ." 2 Maccabees describes itself as a condensation of a five-volume work by Jason of Cyrene (2 Macc 2:23), while 2 Esdras claims to be the work of Ezra (2 Esdr 1:1-3).

In the history of interpretation far more attention has been paid to the claims made about authorship in the OT than in the Apocrypha; indeed, in Protestant circles that rejected the Apocrypha as Scripture some of the claims to authorship in the Apocrypha were subjected to critical scrutiny in order to show that they were false and that the Apocrypha were therefore discredited. Out of the hints found in the OT a view of its authorship emerged perhaps as early as the second century AD and was recorded in *b. B. Bat.* 14b-15a. Those who held this view attributed "his book" (presumably most of Genesis to Deuteronomy) and Job to Moses, the book of Joshua and eight verses of the Torah (presumably Deut 34:5-12, recording the death of Moses) to Joshua, the books of Judges, Ruth, and 1 and 2 Samuel to Samuel, and the Psalms to David assisted by ten elders, including the first Adam, Melchizedek, and Abraham. Jeremiah was credited with 1 and 2 Kings, Jeremiah, and Lamentations, and Hezekiah and his helpers (cf. Prov 25:1) with Isaiah, Proverbs, Canticles, and Ecclesiastes. The remainder were attributed to the "Men of the Great Synagogue" and Ezra.

Positions similar to, but not identical with, these were to establish themselves in Christian scholarship and to last into the nineteenth century. They can still be found in the young churches of the developing world which are innocent of biblical criticism. The traditional views of authorship had two strengths. First, they provided a clear account of the origin of the faith of Israel. It was divine revelation communicated directly to individuals such as Moses. Secondly, if the authors of OT books were known, it became possible to regard them as writers inspired by God. The seemingly neutral question, "Who wrote this book?" became closely tied up with theories about the authority and inspiration of the OT such that to question traditional views of the authorship of a book could be regarded as an attack on that book's status as inspired Scripture. This difficulty is still felt by Christians who are not necessarily "fundamentalists."

This is not the place to describe how and why the traditional positions on authorship were abandoned from the late eighteenth century onward. This abandonment did, however, have serious consequences for the study of the OT. The traditional views accounted for the origin of the faith of Israel. Where, however, did this faith come from if it was no longer possible to accept at face value statements such as "the LORD spoke to Moses, saying. . . ?" If, as is often maintained, much of the priestly and sacrificial legislation in Leviticus and Numbers is a late development rather than something revealed to Israel at the outset, how is the history of Israel's faith to be reconstructed?

This question must now be addressed because it is fundamental to any attempt to sketch the origin and formation of the traditions and books that make up the OT and Apocrypha; and it must be said at the outset that only some broad indications can be given. As a first step, we will consider several attempts to account for the origin of the faith of Israel and the traditions witnessing to it. Some or all of them may be familiar to readers, and their strengths and weaknesses are informative.

A consensus that emerged in the latter part of the nineteenth century was that the prophets of Israel, especially those of the eighth century (Isaiah of Jerusalem,

Hosea, Amos, and Micah), were the main force behind the formation of Israel's faith. Reacting to Canaanite fertility cults and despotic rulers, the prophets proclaimed ethical monotheism and social justice and challenged Israel to look beyond national interests to God's universal rule. Failure to respond to these challenges would bring divine punishment upon the people, who had been chosen by God for responsibility and not for complacency. The sixth-century prophets (Jeremiah, Ezekiel, and Deutero-Isaiah) enabled Judah to survive the Babylonian captivity and to learn new and deeper lessons about sin, punishment, and vicarious suffering. Some of these insights were consolidated into the developing sacrificial rituals of the postexilic Jerusalem temple with its emphasis on expiation. At the same time, personal piety found expression in the composition and use of the Psalms, while contact with Hellenism from the late fourth century resulted in the OT "wisdom" traditions (Proverbs, Job, and Ecclesiastes), including those in the Apocrypha (Wisdom of Solomon and Sirach).

This consensus was set in the context of various developmental and evolutionary schemes. One approach, influential in Britain, traced in the OT a progressive development of religious belief from animism, polytheism, and henotheism (belief that the God of Israel was supreme among the gods) to monotheism (belief that the God of Israel was the only God). It also held that Israel had experienced a progressive moral and ethical development. The OT thus became the record of a progressive revelation or education. Other approaches focused on Israel's social development: from a "nomadic" people to one surrounded by fertility cults in a settled land; from a loose association of tribes to a dynastic state ruling other small states. A popular source for Israel's faith was the supposed clarity and purity of the desert in which there were no shades of grey and where God's moral being and ethical demands could be more readily apprehended than elsewhere.

A major factor highlighted by this consensus was that if appeal was no longer made to divine revelation communicated to known individuals as the origin of the faith of Israel, alternative explanations had to be found; and these were likely to be taken from secular theories that were popular at the time, such as those influenced by social Darwinism.

In the twentieth century two notable attempts were made to correct or modify the nineteenth-century consensus and to offer alternative explanations of the origins of Israel's faith. The first, associated with W. F. Albright and his students John Bright and G. E. Wright, believed that archeology supported a mildly critical, traditional reading of the OT. The ancestors (Abraham, Isaac, and Jacob) were located in second-millennium Mesopotamia and Syria/Palestine, and the exodus was dated in the thirteenth century. The faith of Israel derived from acts of God in history such as the exodus, events which could be dated and reconstructed with the aid of historical and archeological research but which inspired witnesses who experienced them had perceived to be acts of God. Wright's books *Biblical Archaeology* and *God Who Acts: Biblical Theology as Recital* were classic statements of this position.

The second approach, that of G. von Rad, was more skeptical about what could be known about figures such as Moses and the ancestors and events associated with them in the biblical record. It did not so much search for the origins of Israel's faith as concern itself with proclamations of that faith which were held to be connected with two great festivals, one which celebrated the occupation of the land and one which celebrated the giving of the law at Mt. Sinai. The datum, in other words, was the faith that was confessed rather than the revelations or events that gave rise to the faith. Those parts of the confession that referred to revelatory events such as the exodus referred to happenings beyond the scope of historical research, either because the necessary evidence was not available or because theological reflection on the events and the celebratory retelling of them had altered them beyond recognition in the tradition. According to von Rad, the core of the Pentateuch was to be found in the "creed" recited at the festival of first fruits, according to Deut 26:5-9:

> "A wandering Aramean was my ancestor; he went down into Egypt and lived there as an alien, few in number, and there he became a great nation, mighty and populous. When the Egyptians treated us harshly and afflicted us, by imposing hard labor on us, we cried to the LORD, the God of our ancestors; the LORD heard our voice and saw our affliction, our toil, and our oppression. The LORD brought us out of Egypt with a mighty hand and an outstretched arm, with a terrifying display of power, and with signs and wonders; and he brought us into this place. . . ."

Two other features of von Rad's position were important: belief in the "Solomonic Enlightenment," a period in the tenth century during the reign of Solomon in which the traditions relating to Israel's faith began to be written down; and acceptance of A. Alt's attempt to identify the "God of the fathers" (i.e., the ancestors) by means of comparative studies. According to Alt, the "God of the fathers" (a common phrase in the tradition) identified a manifestation of the divine to a particular person, whose descendants then worshiped that manifestation as, for example, the God of Abraham or the God of Nahor (Gen 31:53), Abraham and Nahor being the names of ancestors to whom, it was believed, the deity had been manifested. This accounted for the traditions about Abraham and the other ancestors.

Since the work of Wright and von Rad (both of whom died in the early 1970s) OT studies have undergone a transformation in radical directions which has completely changed the landscape of the discipline. New literary-critical study of the Pentateuch and the "historical" books (Joshua to 2 Kings) has suggested later dates for their composition. The nineteenth-century consensus dated the sources for these books from the tenth/ninth to the seventh/sixth centuries. There is now a tendency to regard all of them as postexilic. Von Rad's "Solomonic Enlightenment" has been abandoned. At the same time, archeological research has produced an account of the history of Syria/Palestine that suggests that Israel, Judah, Moab, Ammon, and Edom did not begin to emerge as "states" until the ninth-eighth centuries BC. The biblical accounts of the empires of David and Solomon hardly fit in with this picture, although it is going too far to deny the existence of David and Solomon. Events such as the exodus or the time of the ancestors are now so remote compared with the proposed dates for the traditions about them that they have become invisible as far as any historical attempt to recover them is concerned. At the same time, much more has become known about the popular religion of Israel thanks to the researches of Othmar Keel and his associates on cylinder seals, amulets, and the like.

The task not only of writing a history of Israel but also of accounting for the faith of Israel and the origin and growth of the OT traditions has become more formidable than ever. OT specialists are faced with accounting for a faith that developed within a nation, in circles that often came into conflict with the rulers and ordinary people of that nation. Furthermore, the "history" of the nation that these circles produced was not a history in the modern sense. Although the writers used historical sources such as royal chronicles, their aim was not to present a chronological account of the nation's fortunes but to write what has been called a "decision history" — a story containing incidents with outcomes that would challenge readers/hearers to faith in God. Also, the religious beliefs and practices of the postexilic community were explained in terms of an overall story that was projected back to the creation of the world. In what follows, we will attempt to sketch the origins of Israel's faith and the growth of its Scripture in the light of present OT studies, while taking into account the dynamics indicated in the preceding sentences.

"Israel is laid waste, its seed is no more." These words from the twenty-seventh line of an inscription from the reign of the Egyptian pharaoh Merneptah (variously dated 1224 to 1214 or 1212 to 1202) are the earliest known reference to Israel or an Israel. Through its determinative (a sign that precedes a name and indicates whether the name is that of a god, a person, or a country) the name indicates a group organized along tribal lines. Thus, toward the end of the thirteenth century BC there existed, probably in ancient Palestine (see Görg 1997: 60), a people that was sufficiently distinct for it to be recognized and named by a foreign invader. To what extent this Israel corresponded to a later group or groups bearing the same name has become a battleground of recent OT scholarship.

It is interesting that, however the first part of the name "Israel" is to be understood (it has been connected with *sara'*, "to fight," "to rule," or "to heal" or with *yashar*, "upright"), the second part is "El," the common Semitic word for God. The group is thus named according to the general Semitic term for God rather than the distinctive name for the God of Israel, YHWH, thought to have been pronounced Yahweh. The earliest nonbiblical reference to Yahweh in connection with Israel is in the Inscription of Mesha, king of Moab in the first half of the ninth century BC. Lines 17 and 18 read, "I took from there [i.e., Nebo] the [vessels of] Yhwh." This indicates that the kingdom of Israel ruled by Omri (who is named in the inscription in lines 4-5) had outposts in Transjordan, with holy places at which Yahweh was worshiped.

To the question "How and when did Yahweh become the God of Israel?" no definite answer can be given if appeal is made to nonbiblical sources only. However, attention has been drawn to the occurrence of what is probably a shortened form of the name, Yhw, in Egyptian sources from the time of Amenophis III (1391-1353) (Knauf 1988: 46), one reference being to "Yhw in *Shasu*-land." This may be a reference to a sacred mountain or mountain god, which has been tentatively located in Seir or ancient Edom. The mention of *shasu* draws attention to a nomadic people living in this and other regions. This information can be compared with the OT claims that the name Yahweh was revealed to Moses at the mountain of God in the Sinai wilderness (Exod 3:1-12) as well as with references in poetic parts of the OT to a "coming" of Yahweh from Seir. Thus the "Song of Deborah" states, "LORD [i.e., Yahweh], when you went out from Seir, when you marched from the region of Edom, the earth trembled. . . ." (Judg 5:4; cf. Ps 68:7-8).

Comparisons of biblical texts with extrabiblical evidence must be handled carefully. They do not prove that the biblical texts are "true" in a strictly historical sense. Exod 3:1-12 is no doubt a postexilic and sophisticated theoretical reflection in its present form. The comparisons do, however, provide a plausible, and necessarily provisional, larger context into which biblical texts can be placed. On the basis of the above and similar comparisons as well as recent archeological research we can sketch a tentative picture of Israel's origins and faith as follows.

In the second half of the thirteenth century BC there was a migration of peoples from northern Transjordan to the central hill country of Palestine, the area of the later Northern Kingdom, Israel. The reasons for the migration are unknown; they may have had political or environmental causes, or both. The migratory groups could well have included the entity, or part of it, that is mentioned as Israel in the Merneptah Stele of 1219 or 1207. This group may then have been joined by a group of *shasu* (see Görg: 61, where objections to this view are considered but not regarded as decisive) who brought with them faith in a God, Yahweh, who had helped them to escape from Egyptian slavery. Faith in Yahweh as the God of Israel then became one of the distinguishing features of Israel as it struggled for survival with the Canaanites and the Philistines in Palestine and with neighboring peoples in Transjordan.

An important moment of crisis in the formation of the people came with the arrival of the Philistines, who established themselves in the coastal plain in southern Palestine, probably in the last third of the twelfth century BC. They were part of the larger movement of "sea peoples" who migrated by sea and land from somewhere in the northeastern Mediterranean region and who are mentioned in Egyptian sources from Ramesses III. Toward the end of the eleventh century they began to expand into the central hill country of Palestine, at the expense of the tribes there who constituted Israel.

At this point another puzzle presents itself. No mention has been made so far of Judah, the kingdom whose first king was David and whose capital, Jerusalem, became the capital of the United Kingdom under David and Solomon — the kingdom which, in effect, became Israel after the destruction of the Northern Kingdom of that name by the Assyrians in 722/721 BC. The origin, exact form, and meaning of the name Judah are unknown. Biblical and extrabiblical texts vary the form between *Yehud* and *Yehudah,* among others. Whether the name is a personal name or a place name is disputed; suggested meanings range from "praise" (Gen 29:35; 49:8) to "may Yahweh be victorious." According to the present state of archeological research, it appears that Judah (i.e., the southern hill country) was settled later and less densely than the northern hill country and Galilee, where Israel was established. There are good environmental reasons for this. Rainfall increases in Palestine as one goes northward, and Judah lacks the fertile valleys that become increasingly evident the farther north one goes toward the Jezreel valley. It is true that the Shephelah, or lowlands, a transitional set of hills between the coastal plain and the Judean hills, is a much more fertile region; but the Philistines bordered, and no doubt controlled, this area. A major puzzle is how, if the biblical account is correct, this small, less favored region came, under David and Solomon, to dominate the much larger and potentially more powerful kingdom of Israel. It may be possible for us to give an answer if we handle the biblical material carefully.

In 1 Samuel the Philistine attempt to expand into the central hill country is given as the reason for the institution of kingship, with Saul as the first king. Although this connection is no doubt too simple (Saul may have been more of a paramount chief than a king and the Philistine threat only the sufficient cause), it will serve here. The Philistine expansion destabilized the area of Judah and Israel and united the Israelites against the invader. The emergence of a national leader from the territory most immediately threatened (Benjamin) was a natural consequence. However, an interesting feature of the narrative in 1 Samuel is its insistence that Saul had the backing of, or was even a member of, ecstatic prophetic groups that were zealous in their devotion to Yahweh. Twice comes the proverb "Is Saul also among the prophets?" (1 Sam 10:11-12; 19:24), and Samuel, the apparent leader of the prophets, is instrumental in promoting and deposing Saul as king. In the final form of the tradition, Samuel has become a composite figure combining the features of priest and judge with that of ecstatic prophet. It is arguable, however, that the latter role brings us closest to the historical figure of Samuel. If the association of ecstatic prophetic activity with the appointment of Saul is correct, the rise of the kingship must be seen as more than a political response to the threat of an invader. There was a strong religious element also; and the tradition in 1 and 2 Samuel, which is not exactly sympathetic to Saul in its final form, retains evidence that Saul had tried to carry out religious reforms during his reign (1 Sam 28:3b; 2 Sam 21:1-2).

David, who succeeded where Saul failed, is an enigmatic figure. If the genealogy of 2 Sam 17:24 and other pieces of information (2 Sam 10:1-2) are authentic, David's mother would seem to have been at one time the wife of the Ammonite king Nahash. Certainly David seems to have taken advantage of the Philistine crisis to establish himself as a kind of freebooter heading a group of adventurers who were fiercely loyal to his charismatic leadership. Temporarily allied with Saul, David aroused the latter's suspicions and was forced by his active hostility to desert to the Philistines. While confined to the area of southern Judah, David adopted the dual strategy of forging diplomatic links with the villagers of Judah while raiding the Amalekites in the Negev. After Saul had been defeated by the Philistines, David became king of Judah and then of Israel before defeating the Philistines and setting up his capital in Jerusalem (2 Samuel 5).

These processes can best be understood if we set them in the context of a world where borders between states were not lines drawn on maps, and where rulers had little centralized control over the areas that they claimed to rule. Philistine "control" of Israel would have amounted to the occupation of frontier and strategic cities from which demands for food and labor could be imposed upon the surrounding villages (cf. 1 Sam 13:17). Nonetheless, this was an affront to the Israelites and especially to the ecstatic prophetic groups. Since warfare was essentially battle for control of border or strategic towns, a charismatic leader with a brave and accomplished army could dislodge an enemy from these sites within his own country and even seek to expand beyond it by capturing the key cities of neighboring peoples. If David did indeed create a small "empire," it was in the sense of capturing border and strategic towns that enabled him to claim authority over a whole territory. The actual control of such territory would be strictly limited.

This historical sketch has been a necessary diversion from the religious questions that this introduction is seeking to address. It has drawn attention to the ecstatic prophetic groups; now we must ask what can be guessed about the religion of David. The tradition in 2 Samuel 6 credits David with bringing to Jerusalem the ark of the covenant, a cult object that had apparently at one point been captured by the Philistines. In 1 Sam 4:4 the ark is called the "ark of the covenant of the LORD of hosts," and in Num 10:35-36 it is associated with the earthly and heavenly armies of Yahweh by way of words that also occur in Psalm 68, which, as mentioned earlier, speak of Yahweh coming in a warlike manner from the south. The words are:

> "Arise, O LORD, let your enemies be scattered,
> and your foes flee before you."
> (Num 10:35-36; cf. Ps 68:1)

The ark was therefore possibly a visible symbol of the warlike presence of Yahweh among his people, which had been brought to Palestine by *shasu* groups who settled in Israel. Indeed, the adoption of Yahweh by Israel may have resulted from the belief that the ark had assisted them in their struggles with their neighbors to establish their independence. That David should have reinstated this cult object that had temporarily failed the people is perhaps an indication that his own faith was a soldier's belief in a God who was his helper in war. At any rate, the stories of Saul and the ecstatic prophets, and of David and the ark, established two features that were to be formative in the development of Israel's faith and thus in the production of the OT: a northern prophetic element, and the establishment of the worship of Yahweh in Jerusalem.

We have suggested that when David captured Jerusalem he found there an established priesthood in the person of Zadok and a cult that contained "Canaanite" elements. Hints of this preexisting religion have been found in psalms such as 110, where the king is made a priest "after the order of Melchizedek," and 91, where God is named "the Most High" and "the Almighty" as well as Yahweh. Psalm 46, which speaks of the river that flows beneath the city of God, is another possible allusion to "Canaanite" beliefs. It should, however, be noted that current scholarship is divided about how much of the city of Jerusalem existed at the time of David, while Niehr has argued that the "Canaanite" features of the Jerusalem cult are late developments rather than beliefs and practices that Israelite faith incorporated from a pre-Davidic Jerusalem cult. Only time will tell which of these views is more likely to be correct.

The delineation of the ecstatic prophets in the north and the Jerusalem cult in the south is only a preliminary step in tracing the faith of Israel. The prophetic groups lived on the margins of society, while the Jerusalem cult was that of a royal rather than a national temple. To discover the religious situation of the people in general, we must consider the evidence from personal names, extrabiblical inscriptions, and artistic representations on seals and amulets. The evidence from personal names is not easy to handle because of textual variations between parallel passages (King Abijam in 1 Kgs 14:31; 15:1, etc. is Abijah in the parallel account in 2 Chr 12:16; 13:1, etc.) and differences between the Hebrew and the Septuagint (LXX). The list of names of the thirty heroes of David in 2 Sam 23:24-39 bristles with such difficulties. Bearing all these problems in mind, we nevertheless find it striking that the recorded names of the kings of Israel and Judah begin by having no element of the name Yahweh, and that this element develops only gradually. The first northern king whose name has an element of Yahweh is Ahaziah (853-852 BC), and the first southern king (assuming that Abijam rather than Abijah is correct) is Jehoshaphat (871-848). Of the nineteen kings of the Northern Kingdom, Israel, only seven contain an element of Yahweh, while of the twenty kings of Judah (not counting David and Solomon) fourteen contain this element. The greater presence of Yahweh elements in Judah is probably due to the close connection between the king and the cult of Yahweh in Jerusalem, while of the seven names with Yahweh elements in the Northern Kingdom, five follow one after the other from 853 to 782, the period of major political activity of the prophetic groups led by Elijah and Elisha which resulted in a coup d'état by the Yahweh loyalist Jehu.

Hebrew inscriptions, bearing in mind that their survival and discovery is haphazard, indicate the presence of personal names combined with Yahweh from the eighth century onward (practically no Hebrew inscriptions are known from before this time). From the information in Davies 1991, there are roughly thirteen such names from sites in Judah in the eighth century, eight from the seventh century, and twenty from the late seventh to early sixth centuries. (These figures do not include names ending in *-yah* or *-iyah.*) On the other hand, the Samaria Ostraca, dating from the second half of the eighth century (see Renz and Röllig 1995: 79-109), contain seven personal names with the element *ba'al,* the name of the "Canaanite" god of the storm. This supports the view presented in the books of Kings that the Northern Kingdom, Israel, or at any rate its capital Samaria (the Samaria Ostraca derive from places close to, and linked to, Samaria), was open to Canaanite influences.

Much interest has been aroused by the discovery in 1975/76 of two inscribed jars at Kuntillet-Ajrud, a kind of caravansary fifty kilometers south of Kadesh-barnea, in the Negev. Dated around 800 BC, they were evidently written and painted on by travelers (see Renz and Röllig 1995: 48-50), and among the inscriptions are references to "Yahweh of Samaria," "Yahweh of Teman," and "Yahweh and his Asherah." The references seem to indicate that, for the travelers at any rate, Yahweh was worshiped as a localized deity in Samaria and in the south of Edom (see above for the connection between Yahweh and this region). The reference to Yahweh's Asherah is probably to the sacred pole or tree that represented Asherah because it is not possible (as far as it is known) to add a suffix with the meaning "his" to a proper name in Hebrew in the way that "his" is added to "Asherah" in the inscription. What this indicates is that popular religion associated a fertility symbol, the Asherah pole or tree, with the worship of Yahweh, a practice strongly condemned in the OT (1 Kgs 15:13). The iconography of Israel and Judah shows the influence of Egyptian and Assyrian religious symbols on Israelite popular religion; but it also shows that, at the end of the seventh century, officials in Judah put forth a strenuous effort to avoid "pagan" symbols. The seals from around this time are without idols and contain simply the names of officials concerned (see Keel: 410-14). Their presence confirms the account of the cultic reform carried out by Josiah from 622 BC onward (2 Kings 22–23).

The consideration of such things as personal names, inscriptions, and iconography (for the latter see above all Keel) generally confirms the picture given in the books of Kings, according to which the religion of Israel in the period 950-587 BC was syncretistic. The worship of Yahweh was carried on at many sites called, derogatively, "high places" in the OT; but other deities were worshiped, including Baal, and fertility practices were associated with Yahweh in the form of the Asherah pole or tree. The situation in Israel and Judah can be described in terms of three interacting levels of religion: those of official Yahwism (the religion of the court), popular Yahwism (the religion of the ordinary people), and prophetic Yahwism (the religion of prophetic groups probably on the margins of society). However, there were no doubt important differences between Israel and Judah.

Israel was more open to syncretism at the level of official religion, with the result that the prophetic groups frequently clashed with the kings of Israel and encouraged soldiers and administrators with prophetic sympathies either to subvert official policies or to attempt coups d'état. An instance of the former is the high official Obadiah's concealment of prophets during the reign of Ahab (873-853) when the king's foreign-born wife promoted her own religion and tried to eliminate the Yahweh prophets (1 Kgs 18:3-4). An instance of the latter is the coup d'état of Jehu (841-813) instigated by Elisha (2 Kings 9).

In Judah, which was much smaller territorially and where Jerusalem's influence became increasingly dominant, prophets such as Hosea and Amos directed their attention to Israel. However, Micah was bitterly critical of Jerusalem toward the end of the eighth century, as were Jeremiah and Ezekiel just over a century later. The two slightly different manifestations of Yahwism, in Israel and Judah at the royal and prophetic levels, were brought together following the destruction of the Northern Kingdom, Israel, by the Assyrians in 722/721 BC. Royal chronicles and other written or oral traditions were brought from the north to Judah by groups, including prophetic groups, seeking refuge in the one remaining country where Yahweh was officially worshiped.

It was most likely at this time, during the reign of Hezekiah (727-698 BC), that the first steps were taken toward the production of the OT as we know it. Hezekiah had the necessary scribal resources (Jamieson-Drake 1991; cf. Prov 25:1) and motivation (the presence of the northern prophetic groups plus a desire to resist Assyria and extend his jurisdiction over as much of the former Northern Kingdom as possible) to put in train the production of the initial account of the history of the people from the time of Abraham onward. His scribes made use of royal chronicles, stories emanating from prophetic groups, and stories of local and popular heroes and heroines. Abraham and Isaac were most likely Judahite heroes, their stories being set in southern Judah (Hebron) and the Negev, while Jacob was a northern hero, his story centering in Bethel, Shechem, Transjordan, and Haran. The fact that the Judahite Abraham precedes the Israelite Jacob, whose name is changed to Israel and who becomes the ancestor of the twelve tribes (Gen 29; 32:22-32), is best explained by the supposition that the stories were put together when Judah was the predominant political force.

How the overall story was continued down to Hezekiah's time can only be guessed at. We are on firmest ground with the royal chronicles, described in the books of Kings as the "Book of the Annals of the Kings of Judah/Israel" (see 1 Kgs 14:19, 29). Their general accuracy can be checked against Egyptian and Assyrian records from time to time, from the invasion by Sheshonq I of Egypt in 925 BC (cf. 1 Kgs 14:25-28; Görg: 90-91) through the mention of Omri (in the Inscription of Mesha; see above), Ahab (*ANET,* 279), Jehu (*ANET,* 280-81), and Azariah (Uzziah; *ANET,* 282-83) to Hezekiah himself (*ANET,* 287-88). This does not mean, of course, that every detail is correct from a modern historical point of view. The stories of Elijah and Elisha, which dominate the books of Kings from 1 Kings 17 to 2 Kings 10, contain legendary elements and narratives that sometimes cannot be fitted into the historical scheme; but the general framework can be trusted. What cannot be known is how much of the story from Jacob to the time of David existed in this initial draft. Because tradition abhors a vacuum, it is likely that the story included the exodus (cf. Hos 11:1), Moses, Joshua, and some or most of the "judges," ending with Samuel and Saul. The difficulty is that it is almost impossible to work back from the final forms of these accounts to the form that they might have had in the initial version.

This initial version was the product of official Yahwism as represented in Jerusalem under the patronage of a king (Hezekiah) who allowed himself to be advised by a prophet, Isaiah. Its aim was to legitimize Jerusalem and its Davidic dynasty as chosen by Yahweh, as well as to assert that the whole land of Israel, north and south, had been promised to the descendants of the Judahite ancestor, Abraham. However, the account also no doubt stressed the importance of loyalty to Yahweh over against other deities and used stories as object lessons to point out the consequences of disloyalty. It is also likely that the reign of Hezekiah was the time in which the laws found in Exodus 21–23 were officially promulgated. These restricted the period of slavery to six years and were generally supportive of the poor and disadvantaged (e.g., Exod 22:21-27).

The promise of Hezekiah's reign was cruelly disappointed. Invaded by the Assyrian king Sennacherib in 701, Judah was devastated and Hezekiah was forced to pay tribute (2 Kgs 18:13-16). For the next sixty years Judah was a vassal state of Assyria and "pagan" religion flourished at the official and popular levels (Keel 1992: 322-406). In 640, by which time Assyrian power had declined to the point of no return (the Assyrian Empire would last for no more than a further thirty years), parties favorable to prophetic Yahwism were able to intervene in the politics of Judah and place on the throne the eight-year-old Josiah (2 Kgs 21:19–22:2). His reign (640-609 BC) produced a religious reorganization in Judah that turned Jerusalem from a royal to a national sanctuary. All other sanctuaries were closed down, and all traces of "paganism" were purged from the Jerusalem cult. The Passover was declared to be a national festival, to be observed only at the national sanctuary, Jerusalem. In terms of the threefold distinction between official, popular, and prophetic religion, we can say that official religion, inspired by the prophetic, sought to control popular religion as never before in Judah or Israel, a move made possible by the increasing administrative control of Jerusalem over Judah. This controlling of popular religion is instanced in making the Passover a national festival to be observed only in Jerusalem. The origins of the Passover are obscure and its exact form of observance prior to Josiah unknown; but it was probably a local or family observance of some kind, originating in the Northern Kingdom.

Josiah's reform had a major impact on the formation of the OT. It was inspired by or gave rise to the Deuteronomistic movement, a combination of high official and prophetic circles. These produced a first draft of Deuteronomy and edited the existing story of Israel from the time of Abraham, bringing it down to the time of Josiah (2 Kgs 23:24-25) and adding Deuteronomistic frameworks to books such as Judges. Deuteronomy was probably modeled on the types of vassal treaty that were current in the Near East at the time. These contained a historical prologue setting the context for the treaty (cf. Deut 4:44–11:31), stipulations required to be observed by the vassal (cf. Deuteronomy 12–26), and details of penalties that would be exacted if the vassal was disloyal (cf. Deuteronomy 28, with interesting parallels with the vassal treaties of the Assyrian king Esarhaddon from 681 to 669 BC; see especially Steymans). One of the features of Deuteronomistic theology deriving from the vassal treaty scheme was a recasting of past history to show that disasters that had befallen Israel were divine punishments resulting from disloyalty to Yahweh. In particular, disloyalty to Yahweh was understood in terms of worshiping other gods.

Another feature of the Deuteronomic reform was the introduction of new social measures to counteract poverty and to support the officials whose shrines had been closed down. For example, a three-year tithe was enjoined whose produce was to be distributed locally to Levites (dispossessed local cultic officials) and to the disadvantaged (Deut 14:28-29). Further, a seven-year system of release was commanded in which loans (or the interest on loans) to fellow Israelites were written off (Deut 15:1-6). Women slaves were given the same right of release as men slaves (Deut 15:12-18; cf. Exod 21:7-11, where women slaves do not have this right).

The Deuteronomic reform was brought to an end by Josiah's death in 609 BC at the hands of the Egyptian pharaoh Necho II, and for the remainder of the existence of Judah (to 587) the kingdom was in effect a vassal state, first to Egypt and then to Babylonia. These reverses allowed popular religion to be freed from official control. The books of Jeremiah and Ezekiel contain abundant evidence that ordinary people turned to pagan deities and away from the austere official and prophetic Yahwism that had apparently failed, given Judah's loss of independence.

From the destruction of the temple in 587 BC to the end of the Persian period (333 BC) Israelite history enters a phase about which little information has survived and yet in which the OT and its faith came near to reaching the forms in which we know them. It can be surmised that in this period, priestly, scribal, and prophetic interests combined in the context of a small, temple-based community in Jerusalem to consolidate trends that had been apparent for a considerable amount of time. However, the loss of the Jerusalem temple and the Babylonian exile made a lasting impression on this closing stage of the formulation of the faith and its writings.

In the first place, in the absence of political rule (the last Davidic king was Jehoiachin, who died sometime after 560 BC), religious rule by priests took on new importance, while prophetic activity became primarily concerned with the editing and expanding of teaching deriving from the prophets of earlier generations. Secondly, there was much less scope for popular religion in a temple-based community centered in a Judah that was now smaller than it had been up to 587. The southern part of Judah, for example, had been occupied by Edomites. Thirdly, official religion in the sense of the religion of the court no longer existed, nor did prophetic religion in the sense of the religion of marginal groups fiercely loyal to Yahweh who intervened in politics from time to time. In fact, religion in Judah was now well on the way to becoming a faith based on writings that were regarded as Scripture.

To the Persian period (539-333 BC) can be assigned the editing of the Pentateuch into its final form and the substantial completion of the prophets, which included the books of Joshua, Judges, Samuel, and Kings as well as Isaiah, Jeremiah, Ezekiel, and the twelve Minor Prophets. The story beginning with Abraham was prefaced by the primeval history (Genesis 1–11) and supplemented by the ritual and priestly material now found in Exodus, Leviticus, and Numbers. In the former prophets (Joshua to Kings) the story was brought down to the destruction of the temple and the release from prison of the last king, Jehoiachin, in 560 (2 Kgs 25:27-30). In addition, sections were edited or expanded to meet situations arising from the destruction of the temple in 587 and the Babylonian exile. For example, Solomon's prayer of dedication of the temple in 1 Kings contains sections which imply that there are Jews in the diaspora (i.e., not living in Palestine) for whom the temple will be a place toward which they pray (1 Kgs 8:46-53). It says nothing about the temple as a place of sacrifice. A good example of the work on the latter prophets is Isaiah, where sayings deriving from at least three prophets, Isaiah of Jerusalem (8th cent.), Deutero-Isaiah (mid-6th cent.), and Trito Isaiah (late 6th cent.) were brought together, along with attempts to give the work some unity by thematically linking the closing chapters with the opening ones.

The third section of the Hebrew Bible, the Writings, was less complete by the end of the Persian period. The Psalms, some of which dated from the First Temple period, were probably in their present form as far as Psalm 106. The Proverbs, many of which dated from the time of Hezekiah or earlier, were prefaced by chs. 1–9, which set them in an explicitly Yahwistic theological framework, albeit one which was closer to official Yahwism than to prophetic Yahwism. Also complete by the middle of the fourth century BC were the so-called Chronicler's history (Chronicles, Ezra, and Nehemiah — not necessarily by the same author) and books such as Lamentations (most likely occasioned by the destruction of Jerusalem) and Ruth. It is difficult to determine whether works such as Job, Ecclesiastes, Canticles (the Song of Songs), and Esther were complete by 333 BC.

This uncertainty stems mostly from lack of knowledge about social conditions in Judah in the first half of the fourth century BC and whether changes were beginning to occur before Alexander the Great defeated the Persians and incorporated Syria/Palestine into the Hellenistic environment that would profoundly affect it up to and well beyond the coming of Roman rule in 63 BC. Certainly, the advent of the Greek language, the founding of free Greek cities, especially in Transjordan, and the general spread of Greek culture had a noticeable effect upon the last stages of the genesis of the OT, and of the writing of the Apocrypha. Returning for a moment to Job, Ecclesiastes, and Canticles, while these could all have been written in the fourth or even fifth centuries, a case can be made for saying that Job and Ecclesiastes, at any rate, were produced in response to a skepticism that developed in Judah from the end of the fourth century onward. This skepticism was produced not only by the need to respond to Greek philosophy but by a growing individualism among members of an aristocracy that lacked power and a questioning of aspects of official Yahwism. It has also been argued that Canticles draws upon elements of "pagan" mythology, which became increasingly popular with Hellenization (Müller 1976).

Whatever the truth of these arguments, Hellenization was responsible for the need to translate the OT into Greek from the mid-third century BC, for the benefit of Jews living in Egypt. There was also the clash with Hellenism which resulted in the Maccabean revolt against the Seleucid ruler of Judah, Antiochus IV, from 168/167 to 164. This resulted in the writing of the book of Daniel (in Hebrew and Aramaic) and the production of the books of 1 and 2 Maccabees, the former in Hebrew and the latter in Greek.

If the content of the Apocrypha is compared with that of the OT, the trend toward individualism and toward Greek is clearly discernible. The Apocrypha has no prophetic books, only one psalm, and proportionately more novelistic writings than the OT, in the form of Tobit, Judith, and Additions to Daniel (Susanna and Bel and the Dragon). Works originally composed in Greek include 2-4 Maccabees, Wisdom of Solomon, and Additions to Esther and Daniel.

The Apocrypha also demonstrates that what was said above about the OT books being completed in the Persian period needs to be qualified, while the Additions to Daniel and Esther show how the tradition could be supplemented. The Apocrypha contains 1 Esdras, a work based on part of 2 Chronicles 35–36, Ezra 1:1–10:44, and Neh 7:72–8:13a, but evidently using a Hebrew text differing from that which has become traditional for those books. 1 Esdras also contains two sections (1:23-24 and 3:1–5:6) which have no parallel in the OT. Overall, it provides a more integrated and interesting version of material, most of which is in the OT. The Additions to Esther have the effect of making it a much more "religious" book, with prayers added at crucial points in the story in a book which, notoriously in its Hebrew version, does not mention God. The Additions to Daniel add both hymns and prayers (Greek Daniel 3:24-91) and stories to supplement those about Daniel in the opening chapters of the Hebrew.

It is now time to compare the point which we have reached with what we said in the opening pages. There we pointed out that the OT's view of how Israel's faith originated is that it was revealed by God supremely to Moses but also to other people such as Abraham and the prophets. The outline we have given above has indicated something much more complicated — a series of interactions between official, popular, and prophetic Yahwism in the context of the historical ups and downs of a small people surrounded by, and often victim to, the ambitions of powerful empires. Also, our brief consideration of the Apocrypha has indicated that the processes of formation and development of Israel's faith and the production of its Scriptures was ongoing. The discovery of the Dead Sea Scrolls, for example, has shown how, in the first century BC, there were diverse and competing strands within the broad stream of the Judaism of the time. In a way, the Qumran group might be compared with the prophetic religion of earlier times, seeing that it lived on the margins of society and was fiercely critical of the official Judaism of the time.

The Qumran group is also instructive with regard to its attitudes to Scripture. On the assumption that the *Temple Scroll* and the biblical commentaries were the work of the same group, the Qumran sectarians regarded certain works as sacred and therefore susceptible of interpretation. This is seen in the commentaries on books such as Habakkuk and Nahum, the prophecies of which are interpreted in terms of the group's history and leaders. On the other hand, the *Temple Scroll* is an attempt to fill a gap in the Bible. There is no record in the OT of explicit instructions from God about the form and dimensions of the Jerusalem temple. Exodus 35–40 contain an account of God's instructions for the construction of the portable tabernacle which served the Israelites in the wilderness. 1 Kings 6–7 describe how Hiram built the Jerusalem temple for Solomon. No doubt the description of the tabernacle in Exodus is dependent on the later Second Temple. The point is that the OT contains no specific instructions from God about the construction of the Jerusalem temple; and it is this lack which the *Temple Scroll* remedies, in the form of a direct address of God to Moses about the building of a temple. Thus, as late as the first century BC there was a group within Judaism that claimed and attributed revelations of God to Moses regarding vital matters of religion.

If modern scholarship proposes a gradual development of the faith of Israel as opposed to an initial revelation to a founder such as Moses, this does not mean that we are left with vagaries. However the faith of Israel may have developed (and subsequent research and discoveries may modify or alter the sketch we have proposed in this introduction), the end result was that the texts that were produced and the faith that they implied had what has been called a family likeness. The main features of this "family likeness" were:

- belief in Yahweh as the God of Israel and as the only God, the creator of the universe
- belief in Israel as the people chosen and called by Yahweh to service and obedience, which would lead to Yahweh being acknowledged by the other nations
- belief in Jerusalem as the place chosen by Yahweh for a temple to honor his name, and belief in Yahweh's choice of the house of David to rule over Israel
- belief in Yahweh's laws as revealed to Moses
- belief in a re-creation of the heavens and the earth when Yahweh would establish a peace and justice longed for by the nations.

Not all of these features are to be found in every book of the OT, but they are implied. Ecclesiastes, for example, always uses the general Hebrew word for God rather than the name Yahweh and makes no mention of Israel or of its being specially chosen and commissioned by Yahweh. But its view, that humans live in a world created by God, who is also the creator of individual humans and to whom their spirits return at death, would be impossible without the general background of belief outlined above. Indeed, the skepticism in Ecclesiastes and Job comes precisely from the problems arising from the need to relate Israelite monotheism to the sufferings of innocent people and the many injustices that go unpunished, at a time when Israelite monotheism had not yet developed a belief in the afterlife. Again, a book such as Esther, which in its Hebrew version notoriously fails to mention God, nonetheless depicts the Jews as a distinct entity singled out for hatred and destruction by Haman, thus implying a unique Jewish national self-consciousness and praxis which could arouse hostile feelings against the Jewish people.

Readers of the list of features making up the "family likeness" may be surprised by the omission of belief in the coming of the Messiah. Of course, by the beginning of the common era various types of messianic belief had developed, including the coming of a "prophet like unto Moses" (Deut 18:15), a return of Elijah (Mal 4:5), and a royal (Davidic) or priestly anointed one (which is what "Messiah" means). However, in the OT and Apocrypha only the elements of these later expectations are present, and they are subordinate to the view that God himself will redeem his people and renew the created order.

2. Methods in the Study of the Old Testament and Apocrypha

The attempted reconstruction of the origins of the faith of Israel and its Scriptures in this introduction has depended on the methods of historical criticism. In their modern form these methods go back to the second half of the eighteenth century; but they are based in turn upon observations about the OT in particular that go back much earlier than the eighteenth century. A good example is the apparent discrepancy in regulations about observing the Passover in Exod 12:1-49 as compared with Deut 16:1-8. In the former text the Passover is observed in Egypt in the houses of the Israelites, one of the main purposes of the ritual being that the blood of the Passover lamb sprinkled upon the lintel and doorposts of the Israelite houses will protect them from the divine destroyer when he comes to kill the firstborn males and animals. Exod 12:24-27 implies that the Passover will continue to be observed in this way in the following generations. However, in Deut 16:1-8 the Passover lamb can be killed only at the central sanctuary (i.e., Jerusalem, which is not, however, mentioned in Deuteronomy), to which families must travel if they wish to observe the festival; in that case it becomes impossible to sprinkle the lamb's blood on the lintel and doorposts of houses far away from the central sanctuary, something that is in any case not enjoined by Deut 16:1-8. Jewish scholarship has long since been aware of these and other discrepancies, and explained them in various ways, including making a distinction between the Passover of Egypt and the Passover of the land. Modern biblical criticism developed out of the wrongly called precritical era of scholarship when scholars abandoned the various theological schemes that had protected the Bible from historical investigation "like any other book."

Modern methods can be divided into two groups: (a) those that are concerned with the historical and social background in which the OT and Apocrypha originated, and the methods of composition used in the production of the texts; and (b) methods that are primarily concerned with interpreting the texts. This latter category can be subdivided into methods that investigate how the texts were interpreted in ancient times and how they can be interpreted today. However, any attempt to isolate and classify methods of study is artificial and arbitrary. In practice, methods overlap and slide in and out of each other.

Category (a) methods begin with those which are exterior to the text — archeological explorations, the study of extrabiblical inscriptions and iconography, the study of the history and religion of Israel's neighbors, especially Egypt, Syria, and Mesopotamia, and the study of social and anthropological theory. They then pass to dealing with the texts themselves: establishing the best textual tradition where words or phrases make little sense and there are divergences between the Hebrew tradition and the ancient translations of the Hebrew into Greek, Latin, and Syriac. This also involves the study of ancient Semitic languages akin to Hebrew, such as Aramaic, Akkadian, Ugaritic, and classical Arabic.

Source criticism inquires whether the biblical writers based their work on existing sources. In one case, it is widely, although not universally, accepted that the writer(s) of the books of Chronicles used Samuel and Kings as a source. In other cases, such as the Pentateuch, priestly sources can be separated from non-priestly sources by the identification of distinctive vocabulary and subject matter. Form criticism inquires about the types of literary form and genre used in the literature. The most easily identifiable are two-line proverbs in the book of Proverbs; but in the Psalms, recurring structural features can be found in psalms of lament, such as Psalms 3–7, where an opening address to God detailing the complaint or distress of the psalmist ends with an affirmation of confidence and trust. Prophetic oracles are sometimes highly schematized, beginning with the identification of the speaker (Yahweh), the ground of complaint or praise, and either a threat of judgment or a promise of deliverance. A good example is Jer 35:12-19, which combines praise and promise for the Rechabites with condemnation and judgment on the people of Judah and Jerusalem. Other forms found in prophetic literature include funeral dirges (Amos 5:1-3) and love songs (Isa 5:1-7). Redaction criticism is a method that tries to gain an idea of the overall intention or purpose of a work by examining key passages or concluding formulae. In the so-called Deuteronomistic History, for example (Joshua to 2 Kings), there are key speeches or passages in Joshua 24, 1 Samuel 12, and 2 Kings 17 and 21:10-15 which give an indication of the tenor of the work in its final form.

The first branch of category (b) methods, those dealing with ancient interpretation, concern themselves objectively with the ancient translations of the Hebrew Bible (HB) into Greek and Aramaic in particular. They also deal with ancient works which interpreted or expanded the HB.

Although the Septuagint (LXX) is a translation of the HB into Greek, it is also sometimes an interpretation, making theological points and expanding the text to make it more understandable. Two examples can be given. The Hebrew of Exod 24:10 says that Moses, Aaron, Nadab, Abihu, and seventy elders, having ascended the mountain, "saw the God of Israel." The translators into Greek softened this bold statement into "they saw the place where the God of Israel stood," no doubt bearing in mind the statement that no one can see God and live (Exod 33:20). In Isa 40:1, commands are given that God's people should be comforted, but there is no indication as to who is being told to give these commands. The Greek version adds the word "priests" before "speak tenderly to Jerusalem" in order to meet this difficulty. An example of expansion and interpretation in the Aramaic targums can be found at Ezek 16:2-3. The Hebrew has, speaking of Jerusalem, "Your origin and your birth are of the land of the Canaanites; your father was a Amorite, and your mother a Hittite." The targum has, "Your origin and your birth are from the land of the Canaanites. There I revealed myself to Abraham your father between the pieces [of the covenant; cf. Gen 15:17] and made known to him that you would go down to Egypt. With an uplifted arm I redeemed you, and for the sake of your fathers I drove out from before you the Amorites and destroyed the Hittites."

However, examination of translations, especially the Greek, provides information not only about how passages were interpreted in antiquity; they also give indications of how the biblical books were composed. The Greek version of Jeremiah is *shorter* than the Hebrew versions, the additions in the Hebrew amounting to amplifications and clarifications. A good example is Jeremiah 27:19-22 (ch. 34:19-22 in the Greek). In what follows, material common to both versions is in normal type; what is found in the Hebrew only is in italics:

> 19. For thus says the LORD *of hosts concerning the pillars, the sea, the stands,* and the rest of the vessels that are left in this city, 20. which *Nebuchadnezzar* king of Babylon did not take away when he took into exile from Jerusalem *to Babylon* Jeconiah *the son of Jehoiakim, king of Judah, and all the nobles of Judah and Jerusalem — 21. thus says the LORD of hosts, the God of Israel, concerning the vessels which are left in the house of the LORD, in the house of the king of Judah, and in Jerusalem:* 22. They shall be carried to Babylon *and remain there until the day when I give attention to them,* says the LORD. *Then I will bring them back and restore them to this place.*

This example shows how the biblical tradition grew by expansion and interpretation, and some recent work on the OT, especially the prophets, has assumed that prophecies have been subjected to what is called "inner biblical interpretation."

Turning to other texts, the Apocrypha provides evidence of early biblical interpretation. We have already pointed out that 1 Esdras is a version of the conclusion of 2 Chronicles and of material from Ezra and Nehemiah that adds material and makes the action more coherent. The Additions to Esther make that book more overtly religious, while the Prayer of Manasseh fills the gap left by 2 Chr 33:19, which refers in passing to Manasseh's prayer, "and how God heard his entreaty."

Works outside the Apocrypha that interpret the OT include the commentaries found at Qumran and works such as *Jubilees.* An interesting text is the *Genesis Apocryphon* (1QapGen), found in Cave 1 at Qumran. The beginning, which is lost, apparently dealt with the creation and the story of Adam and Eve. What survives begins with Noah and goes as far as Genesis 15. At one point it seeks to justify Abraham's "deceit" in saying that his wife Sarah was his sister when they went down to Egypt. Abraham feared that he would be killed and that Sarah would be taken for the pharaoh's harem on account of her beauty. Her beauty is described in the *Genesis Apocryphon* in extravagant terms (see Vermes 1997: 454), while Abraham's action is justified in terms of a dream that he has and which Sarah interprets. The text goes on to describe Abraham's anguish when Sarah is taken into the harem, and records the prayer that he prays to God regarding the matter.

The study of ancient interpretation rarely helps modern interpretation directly, for all that it is of interest in itself. However, it indicates that ancient interpreters were aware of moral and other difficulties contained in the text. The same is true of later interpreters such as Augustine (AD 354-430) or the great Jewish scholar Maimonides (AD 1135-1204). Their critical acumen was at least as great as that of modern scholars and gives the lie to the belief that biblical criticism is a recent invention.

Methods of interpretation that try to relate the text to today's world can broadly be divided into two groups, bearing in mind the warning above that such divisions are arbitrary and sometimes misleading. First, there are methods that use the tools of historical criticism to reconstruct social and political conditions in ancient Israel in order to make persuasive analogies with today's world. Second, there are methods which are primarily literary and which read OT texts from the standpoint of various literary strategies.

A pioneering instance of the first group is Norman Gottwald's *The Tribes of Yahweh* (1979). Gottwald reconstructed the origins of ancient Israel and its faith in terms of a peasant revolt against Canaanite urban centers, from which emerged an egalitarian tribal society in the thirteenth to eleventh centuries BC. His work demonstrates both the strengths and weaknesses of such approaches. On the one hand, *The Tribes of Yahweh* uses anthropological and social theory to consider issues that have not usually been considered in such depth in OT studies. On the other hand, it is hostage to progress in research in the discipline, especially to the recent skepticism about what can be known of Israel's earliest history, and it privileges a particular type of social organization (an egalitarian segmentary society) over other forms of social organization in ancient Israel (e.g., the monarchy) in seeking to suggest what might be appropriate for today's world. To be fair to Gottwald, it must be pointed out that the OT itself contains strands that are hostile to monarchy (e.g., 1 Sam 8:10-17), and that other approaches that try to draw examples from ancient Israel for today's world are open to the same criticisms. An example from a scholar representing an evangelical position would be Christopher Wright's *Walking in the Ways of the Lord* (1995), which contrasts Israelite society favorably with Canaanite society from the point of view of social justice and compassion. That such methods share the weaknesses that their reconstructions of ancient Israel can be challenged and that hermeneutical justification is needed for privileging certain types of social organization over others does not mean that writers should not use the OT in this way. Such approaches contribute valuable insights to the understanding of ancient Israel and, by emphasizing positive aspects of OT laws and prophetic witness, counter the common view that the OT is a text about a barbaric people who believed in a wrathful and capricious God.

Probably the best-known exponents of this kind of approach are liberation theologians and some of the feminist interpreters, and it needs to be recognized that, underlying their work, are widely differing agendas (Schottroff/Schroer/Wacker). Some liberationists and feminists see the OT as an essentially oppressive text both in itself and in the way that it has been used in general and ecclesiastical history; and it is undeniable that the OT has been used to support the institution of slavery and the superiority of men over women. Other liberationists and feminists believe that the OT can contribute powerfully to their cause, and, in particular, liberationists have drawn on the story of the exodus to advance the view that redemption should involve economic and social emancipation, and not just the promise of a better life in the hereafter. Feminist and liberation scholarship has concentrated on reconstructing the social position of women and the poor in ancient Israel, to the great benefit of scholarship in general.

The employment of reading strategies from modern literary and philosophical studies has been the other main trend in the contemporary interpretation of the OT (Clines 1998). This approach has shifted attention away from concentration on the text and more toward its readers/users. Reader-response criticism, for example, has emphasized the subjective element supplied by the situatednesses of readers and the interests that they represent. It has led in turn to a twofold examination of the ideological factors in interpretation — those of the interpreters and those of the writers of the texts. The term "ideological" is notoriously difficult to define, ranging in meaning from the leading ideas of a text to a concealed and perhaps unrecognized position which blinds interpreters and writers to their "real" interests (Clines 1995). In modern OT study "ideological" is used in a number of different ways (see the criticism of Barr 2000), with the sternest criticism often being reserved for the biblical writers and their supposed deliberate or innocent veiling of their class, gender, or theological interests.

Other uses of literary methods have included the formal study of Hebrew poetry, the use of plot, character, and narrative structure in texts (Berlin 1983), and "deconstruction" — a modified version of the theory that texts contain elements that contradict and undermine their apparent communicative intention. As in the case of liberation and feminist hermeneutics, many and varied agendas are in operation when literary methods are used, from positive attempts to value OT poetry and narrative as artistic achievements to barely concealed antitheological attempts to undermine the OT as a text to which due regard might be paid.

The advent of literary methods has also raised the question whether traditional historical-critical methods which are concerned with discovery, where possible, of the original intentions of the OT writers/editors should continue to occupy the predominant place in OT studies, or whether literary methods, some of which deny that texts have meanings intended by authors, should be regarded as primary.

A convincing answer to this discussion is provided by sociologist Anthony Giddens, who argues that all acts of communication, including written texts (the present introduction included!), have a communicative intention within a set of nonlinguistic conventions that also affect the communication. Where speakers/writers are available, they can be questioned about what they meant and can argue that they have been misunderstood. Where they are not available, the techniques of historical-critical study can attempt to recover the original communicative intention.

As texts become separated in time and space from their original milieu of production, the closure that they originally possessed (their communicative intention) is supplemented by an openness to legitimate interpretations of their latent meaning that may involve understandings never envisaged by the writers/editors. A good example of this in the OT would be Isa 52:13–53:12, the so-called Fourth Servant Song. Here an unnamed chorus, using the personal pronoun "we," describes how the sufferings of the Servant in some way became the vicarious bearing of their burdens, which led to their healing. The writer of Isa 52:13–53:12 no doubt had in mind something that had happened in the world of his experience. Centuries later, Christian interpretation of this passage saw it as a prophecy of the sufferings of Christ.

A proper appreciation of the relationship between the original communicative intention of a text and the legitimate ways in which it may be used when separated from its original milieu of production is necessary to address the subjects of OT Theology and Biblical Theology. For much of the history of the Christian interpretation of the OT, the OT was part of an agenda that derived from the NT. It played an important role in sustaining Christian theology because it was believed to prove the inspiration of the Bible by containing prophecies that were fulfilled in the NT and which could only have been given, centuries before Christ, by divine inspiration. An example has already been given from Isa 52:13–53:12. Another important example is Isa 7:14, which was understood in Matt 1:22-23 to be a prophecy of the virgin birth of Jesus.

The rise of modern historical criticism from the mid-eighteenth century progressively destroyed the theological scheme that united the OT and NT, divorcing the Bible from subservience to dogmatic theology and raising the question how OT Theology and Biblical Theology could be attempted. Three answers can be given to this question, along the lines laid down by Giddens's general view of the production of texts and their subsequent use. First, OT theology can be descriptive in the sense that it attempts to portray the beliefs that were held by the writers of the OT texts. These beliefs will be set in their social and historical contexts, and their development and divergences will be explored. Some writers would prefer to call this a history of Israelite religion or even the ideology of the OT rather than OT Theology.

A second method would involve dealing with some of the questions raised by the first method but would tackle the matter more formally by addressing to the OT questions that would not have been in the mind of the OT writers in precisely these forms. Thus it would assemble material about the nature and being of God or about human fallibility into sections entitled "Doctrine of God" or "Theological Anthropology." It has been objected that this type of procedure imposes alien structures on the OT, but this objection is valid only if texts possess only an original communicative intention and no latent meaning. The fact that texts can be legitimately understood in ways not envisaged by their original authors/editors is a way in to using the OT theologically to address matters that concern today's world. This is not, of course, the only way to link the OT and today's world, as liberation and feminist scholarship has shown.

A third way of doing theology would be to read the OT and NT together in the light of a theological principle that was not derived from the texts themselves but which legitimately illuminated them. Thus, from a Christian trinitarian perspective, the Psalms could be interpreted in terms of the assumption that the God of the psalmist was the God ultimately revealed as Father, Son, and Holy Spirit. This would not involve an explicit reading back of Christian ideas into the Psalms; but it would involve understanding the spiritual experiences and language found in the Psalms from a Christian perspective, and would be a way into constructing a theology of both Testaments.

Readers will have noticed that the Apocrypha has been conspicuously absent from the last few pages. This is because, apart from treatments such as the use of the story of Judith and Holofernes or of Susanna and the elders in art, the Apocrypha has not yet been subjected to the degree of modern literary or hermeneutical study that the OT has, but has remained much more the province of historical-critical scholarship. No doubt this derives from the fact that, until the end of the last century, Roman Catholic scholars were not encouraged to engage in historical-critical research. Biblical scholarship was thus a Protestant preserve, with its traditional downgrading of the Apocrypha. It remains to be seen whether the creative contribution to contemporary scholarship made by Catholic scholars will bring the Apocrypha into the arena of liberation and feminist hermeneutics or the deployment of modern literary strategies. Perhaps the inclusion of the enlarged Apocrypha in this commentary, including *Enoch,* will set a trend.

Bibliography. Alt, A. 1959, "Der Gott der Väter," in Alt, *Kleine Schriften zur Geschichte des Volkes Israel,* Munich: Beck, 1:1-78 • *ANET,* 1955, *Ancient Near Eastern Texts Relating to the Old Testament,* ed. J. B. Pritchard, Princeton: Princeton University • Barr, J. 2000, *History and Ideology in the Old Testament: Biblical Studies at the End of a Millennium,* Oxford: Oxford University • Berlin, A. 1983, *Poetics and Interpretation of Biblical Narrative,* Sheffield: Almond • Clines, D. J. A. 1995, *Interested Parties: The Ideology of Writers and Readers of the Hebrew Bible,* JSOTSup 205, Sheffield: Sheffield Academic • Clines, D. J. A. 1998, "Methods in Old Testament Study," in J. W. Rogerson, *Beginning Old Testament Study,* London: SPCK, 25-48 • Davies, G. I. 1991, *Ancient Hebrew Inscriptions: Corpus and Concordance,* Cambridge: Cambridge University • Finkelstein, I., and N. Na'aman, eds. 1994, *From Nomadism to Monarchy: Archaeological and Historical Aspects of Early Israel,* Jerusalem: Israel Exploration Society • Giddens, A. 1987, "Structuralism, Poststructuralism and the Production of Culture," in A. Giddens and J. Turner, eds., *Social Theory Today,* Cambridge: Polity, 195-223 • Görg, M. 1997, *Die Beziehungen zwischen dem Alten Israel und Ägypten, von den Anfängen bis zum Exil,* Darmstadt: Wissenschaftliche Buchgesellschaft • Gottwald, N. 1979, *The Tribes of Yahweh: A Sociology of Liberated Israel, 1250-1050 B.C.E.,* London: SCM • Gutiérrez, G. 1974, *A Theology of Liberation: History, Politics and Salvation,* London: SCM • Jamieson-Drake, D. W. 1991, *Scribes and Schools in Monarchic Judah: A Socio-Historical Approach,* JSOTSup 109, Sheffield: Almond • Keel, O. 1992, *Göttinnen, Götter und Gottessymbole: Neue Erkentnisse zur Religionsgeschichte Kanaans und Israels aufgrund bislang unerschlossener ikonographischer Quellen,* QD 134, Freiburg: Herder • Knauf, E. A. 1988, *Midian: Untersuchungen zur Geschichte Palästinas und Nordarabiens am Ende des 2. Jahrtausends v. Chr.,* ADPV, Wiesbaden: Harrassowitz • Müller, H.-P. 1976, "Die lyrische Reproduktion des Mythischen im Hld," *ZTK* 73:23-41 • Niehr, H. N. 1990, *Der höchste Gott: Alttestamentlicher JHWH-Glaube im Kontext syrisch-kanaanäischer Religion des 1. Jahrtausends v. Chr.,* BZAW 190, Berlin: W. de Gruyter • Renz, J., and W. Röllig. 1995, *Handbuch der Althebräischen Epigraphik I,* Darmstadt: Wissenschaftliche Buchgesellschaft • Rogerson, J. W. 1998, *Beginning Old Testament Study,* London: SPCK and St. Louis: Chalice • Rogerson, J. W. 1998, "An Outline of the History of Old Testament Study," in Rogerson, *Beginning Old Testament Study,* 6-24 • Schottroff, L. et al. 1998, *Feminist Interpretation: The Bible in Women's Perspective,* Minneapolis: Fortress • Steymans, H. U. 1995, *Deuteronomium 28 und die* adê *zur Thronfolgeregelung; Asarhaddons. Segen und Fluch im Alten Orient und in Israel,* OBO 145, Freiburg: Universitäts and Göttingen: Vandenhoeck & Ruprecht • von Rad, G. 1958, "Das formgeschichtliche Problem des Hexateuch," in von Rad, *Gesammelte Studien zum Alten Testament,* TBü 8, Munich: Kaiser, 9-86 • Vermes, G. 1997, *The Complete Dead Sea Scrolls in English,* London: Allen Lane • Wright, C. C. J. 1995, *Walking in the Ways of the Lord: The Ethical Authority of the Old Testament,* Leicester: Inter-Varsity • Wright, G. E. 1952, *God Who Acts: Biblical Theology as Recital,* SBT 8, London: SCM • Wright, G. E. 1962, *Biblical Archaeology,* Philadelphia: Westminster and London: Duckworth.

Premodern, Modern, and Postmodern in Old Testament Study

John A. Goldingay

G. W. F. Hegel suggested a three-stage model for understanding the history of thought. Some theory or thesis is accepted. Subsequently, a counterthesis or antithesis gains acceptance. Then a synthesis combines the truths in the first two. Current conventional wisdom implies a Hegelian understanding of the history of biblical interpretation. In the first millennium there was premodern interpretation, the second millennium saw the development of modern interpretation, and in the third there is postmodern interpretation. Calling this the conventional wisdom implies a recognition that it may look silly in a few years' time. Associating it with Hegel implies a recognition that it imposes categories on the history — for instance, we will see that some aspects of Jewish interpretation in the first millennium had features in common with the modern as well as the premodern. Using Hegel's scheme also reflects our need to understand matters in a way that provides them with structure and provides history with closure. But it is still a helpful framework. I want to consider aspects of the way these three ages approach the nature of the OT text, its origin, its historical reference, and its exegesis, and to suggest ways our postmodern context might change our aims and practice in OT study and enable us to appropriate the strengths of the premodern and modern stages while sidestepping their respective weaknesses.

Premodern

Text

The NT illustrates the nature of premodern attitudes to the text of the OT. While assuming that these Scriptures are the inspired words of God, it quotes them in ways that show that it did not infer a need to be inflexible over the details of the text.

The NT's first two quotations illustrate the point. Isaiah 7:14 says, "There, the maiden is pregnant and is giving birth to a son, and you are to call his name 'God-is-with-us.'" The verb is second person singular — that is, the prophet is there addressing the woman (other aspects of the translation and interpretation of Isaiah's words of course raise issues, but we can leave these for the moment). Matthew's text (1:23) corresponds to the fairly literal LXX version except for reading "they will call." In his second quotation (2:6) Matthew says that it stands written, "You, Bethlehem in the land of Judah, are by no mean least among the rulers of Judah, for from you will come out a ruler who will shepherd my people Israel." Mic 5:2 (MT 1) itself says, "You, Bethlehem in Ephrathah, small to be in the clans of Judah, from you will come out for me one to be ruler in Israel." The LXX again translates fairly literally. Matthew's change from "clans" to "rulers" could indicate free translation or a different reading of an ambiguous text, but this is not true of the replacement of Ephrathah by Judah, nor of the addition of "my people." Further, Matthew reverses Micah's point about Bethlehem's insignificance and adds the "for" that reworks the link between Micah's clauses.

These opening NT quotations illustrate how it can quote the scriptural text with relative precision, or with small changes, or with far-reaching adaptations. It can be translated from the original or quoted from an existing Greek translation. The NT shows no concern to quote Scripture with precision.

The textual data presented by the NT may be compared with those presented by the Qumran scrolls. One Isaiah scroll, for instance (1QIsa[b]) presents a text very close to the Masoretic, but another (1QIsa[a]) presents a text with many more detailed differences. None of these differences changes the nature of the gospel; in substance the texts are the same. But they are different in many details. The Qumran community, like the early Christian community, did not sense that their commitment to the Scriptures entailed a concern for a single text form.

Origin

Premodern works may be explicit about their authorship, or may be anonymous, or may be pseudonymous. Paul and John include their names in letters and in Revelation. Genesis–Kings and at least two of the Gospels are anonymous, though the communities that treasured these works came to link them with famous names. The Pentateuch became the Five Books of Moses, and two anonymous Gospels came to be associated with Matthew and Mark, while Hebrews came to be Paul's. There are thus a number of pseudonymous works and no anonymous works in the King James Version of the NT.

What was going on here? Why should the authorship of a work be of interest? First, it may buttress the work's authority. The authority of Paul's writings derives in part from his being an apostle and from his specific relationship with churches he founded. Second, it can put flesh on the bones of a document. We can imagine Solomon contemplating his achievements and possessions in the testimony in Ecclesiastes, and imagine Paul interacting with the churches he visited. The instincts that made people associate anonymous works with a known person will have had a similar background, though the logic or dynamic was different. Hebrews became an authoritative document because of its contents; attributing it to Paul then buttressed or symbolized its authority. Moses, Joshua, and Matthew were in a position to tell the story of the exodus, the conquest of Canaan, and the story of Jesus, so they were appropriate people to link with works that were already authoritative. Papias's story about Mark writing down Jesus' story as Peter told it also undergirds that Gospel's authority, while additionally providing readers with a vivid and attractive picture of the Gospel's origin. One attributes a document to someone whose name will enhance it; choosing an unknown person would defeat the object of the exercise. Readers can feel that the Bible came from important people who had lived close to God and could speak reliably about God's ways. Thus Jeremiah becomes the author of Lamentations and Solomon of the Song of Songs, Proverbs, and Ecclesiastes. First books gain the community's assent and recognition as the word of God; then they are linked with an appropriate human author.

I imagine that the same instincts had earlier led to material becoming pseudonymous in the form in which it appears within Scripture. The authors of the Book of the Covenant, the Priestly Code, and the Deuteronomic Code saw these as expounding the significance of Mosaic faith for their various times. When the Qumran community attributed a document to Moses, it was declaring the conviction that it had Mosaic authority. While its authors might have been making a cynical claim, more likely they, too, believed their work expressed Mosaic faith. In the ancient world there were, in fact, a variety of reasons for attributing a work to someone different from the person who wrote it (see Metzger 1972). It is difficult to be sure of the original significance of the expression *l^e^dawid* in the headings to certain psalms, but it came to be understood as an indication of authorship, and this made it possible to imagine David writing individual psalms in concrete situations in which he needed to reach out to God. Convictions about authorship thus become hermeneutical keys to understanding the books. A further conviction can also be involved. Why did second-century visionaries ascribe their visions to Daniel, a figure from centuries before them? The link of content suggests that Daniel's visions had inspired theirs. The Holy Spirit brought into being the visions in Daniel 7–12 by inspiring people's reflection on Daniel's own vision in Daniel 2 and on other scriptures. Something similar is true about the inclusion in the book of Isaiah of much material that did not issue from Isaiah ben Amoz. There, too, the Holy Spirit inspired much of that material by encouraging people to reflect on the oracles of Isaiah to see what God had to say to later centuries in light of what Isaiah said.

Reference

Until the eighteenth century, readers understood the OT narratives in a "realistic" way, treating them as true accounts of God's involvement in Israel's life over the centuries, though they did this unreflectively. They took for granted that the biblical story corresponds to what actually happened, as well as to the story of their own lives, in the sense that they judged the story of their lives by the Bible's story. In the eighteenth century both of these assumptions came apart (see Frei 1974). People now evaluated the Bible's story by their own story, as they still do, asking whether it is relevant, not whether we are. In addition, they became preoccupied with the difference between the history of Israel and the story the OT tells. It requires some effort of the imagination to put ourselves back into a context where this was not so. Today when someone says, "Jonah was three days and nights in the sea monster's belly," he or she will have a view on whether the statement refers to something that happened historically or that happened in a story. When Jesus said those words, neither he nor his hearers need have worked with that antithesis.

The etymology of the words "history" and "story" tells an instructive tale in this connection. Both derive from a Greek root that provides parts of the defective verb *oida,* "to know" (e.g., *iste* "you know"). A *histor* is a person who knows, a wise person, *historein* refers to learning by investigating something and then to narrating what one has learned, and *historia* is an inquiry or its results, specifically a narrative. The biblical narratives are thus instances of *historia.* They offer insight in narrative form that results from inquiry. That itself might suggest that the material their authors have investigated includes factual material but need not be confined to that. And this corresponds to the nature of history writing in the ancient world.

The point may be illustrated further by considering the nature of much of the scriptural story as midrash — Chronicles being in part a midrash on Kings, and Matthew on Mark and Chronicles. As midrash it retells a story to show what it now means for people, in light of other scriptures and other convictions regarding God's word to people now. When this retelling involved changing words attributed to Solomon or Jesus, the authors presumably realized that what they were writing was not actual history. They and their readers could apparently live happily with that — perhaps rather like Shakespeare and the people who watch his plays, or the scriptwriter and viewers of (say) *Erin Brokovitch* or *A Beautiful Mind.*

Exegesis

Actual interpretation, interaction with the text's meaning, in the premodern period is again conveniently illustrated for us by the NT's interpretation of the OT. The OT scriptures decisively shaped and resourced Jesus' self-understanding and the early Christians' understanding of Jesus and of the church, in an imaginative and intuitive rather than an analytic and systematic fashion. Matthew wants to understand the surprising story of Jesus' birth and early life, and does so by putting verses from the scriptures alongside incidents within the story of Jesus in such a way as to give him and his community some insight regarding what on earth that was about and what it meant (see Matt 1:18–2:23). Paul wants to provide a rationale for the material support of apostles or to shake a congregation into living more uprightly or to underline how Jesus must reign over everything, and one of the ways he does so is by incorporating passages from the scriptures into his argument (see 1 Cor 9:9; 10:1-13; 15:27). Premodern interpretation can thus generate powerful application of scripture directly addressing new contexts and the questions arising there. The understanding of Jesus and of the church that we derive from the NT could not have existed without this use of the scriptures. God used it to mediate key insights for Jesus himself as his Father addressed him in words from Psalm 2, Genesis 22, and Isaiah 42, "You are my Son, my Beloved, with whom I am well pleased" (Mark 1:11), to set before him crucial insights on his identity and vocation.

Such use of scripture suggests some theological principles: the Scriptures are the Spirit-inspired words of God to Israel, Jesus is the climax of Israel's story, and a Christian congregation is a local embodiment of what Israel was called to be. But this use of Scripture did not emerge from such a conscious hermeneutical/theological framework since it did not emerge from exegetical principles. Premodern interpretation was intuitive. It started from present context and faith convictions and moved back to the Scriptures. The serendipitous way in which the NT quotes from the text, to which I have already referred, is one of the symbols of that. The writers' angle of vision did not predetermine what people saw there, though it did determine the *kind* of thing they saw. And it meant that their interpretation would hardly convince someone who did not accept their starting point — it was not designed to do that. It was part of the whole picture of Jesus.

New Testament interpretation of Genesis 1–3 provides many examples of the interpretation of Scripture in light of current issues and convictions and sometimes troubles Christians, particularly those of a feminist persuasion. Most notoriously, 1 Timothy 2 supports the requirement that women should keep silent in church with a reference to the fact that Adam was formed before Eve and that it was Eve, not Adam, who was deceived and became the transgressor. The passage "uses data from Genesis 2–3 selectively to suit the needs of the argument at hand" (Scholer 1986: 211). It does not work within a modern framework.

Modern

Modern interpretation came into existence in the West through the collocation of the Renaissance, the Reformation, and the Enlightenment. The Renaissance gave birth to an interest in the human side of texts from the past and to a desire to understand them in their own right. The Reformation took up this emphasis and declined to allow the interpretation of Scripture to be determined from outside itself — specifically, by the authority of the church. The Enlightenment urged that nothing be accepted on the basis of tradition. Everything should be tested and can be questioned.

Text

Whereas the Qumran community happily treasured manuscripts that differed from each other (see, e.g., 1QIsa[a] and 1QIsa[b]), during the first millennium the Masoretes made it their business to establish *the* one true text of Scripture. The premodern context of this work was reflected in their assumption that the true text was the one that truly represented the tradition — the "Masoretes" *were* the "traditioners." With the Renaissance, this concern for the true text took a new form when scholars came to assume that the *true* text was the *original* text. Seeking to establish the original text became the first stage of critical study of the OT.

This concern gained an extra level of theological importance for evangelicals in the context of the novel development of the doctrine of Scripture by Charles Hodge and B. B. Warfield in the form of their doctrine of Scripture's inerrancy (they actually used the word "infallibility," but "inerrancy" is the more recent equivalent). One of their strategies for coping with apparent mistakes in Scripture was to attribute infallibility to Scripture "as originally given," to the original text that textual criticism sought to establish. Evangelical study thus accepted the same aim as liberal study, and added another level of theological importance to it.

Origin

With the development of modernity biblical critics asked what was the evidence, for example, for the tradition that Moses wrote the Pentateuch, and concluded that it was poor. The books make no statement about authorship, and it is almost a thousand years after Moses' day that he comes to be connected with them. They refer to circumstances from centuries after Moses' day and manifest repetitions and changes in the way they handle questions that suggest that they were compiled from several successive versions rather than written by one person over a short period. So scholarship looked for alternative understandings of the books' origin and eventually settled into a consensus that held until the late twentieth century, that they issued from the interweaving of several versions of the story of Israel's origins from the early monarchy, the seventh century, and the exile or later. This provided a more coherent account of the data, one that corresponds to the way we know books such as Tatian's "Harmony of the Gospels" were written. It sometimes made it possible to link the Torah with specific historical contexts. And it provided grounds for dating the material that did not depend on faith.

The study of the prophetic books went through a parallel process, operating on the assumption that their authority stemmed from links with great figures such as Isaiah and Jeremiah. Study therefore focused on getting behind the books to the words of the prophets themselves, where authority lay. As an undergraduate I remember being puzzled by the random-looking choice of chapters in Isaiah for exegetical study, eventually realizing that they were chapters that some professor had thought really came from Isaiah ben Amoz. The link with the prophet himself made them of paramount importance. Modern evangelical study believed with liberalism that the books' authority was tied up with their being written by the people tradition said, and therefore it tried to find evidence that it was still reasonable to believe that. It thus added another level of theological importance to research into authorship and sought to use modern methods to support premodern convictions.

Reference

Perceiving the difference between the history the OT tells and the actual history of Israel presented scholarship with a fateful choice. In which history would it now interest itself? In the context of modernity there was no contest. "History is God nowadays" (Reumann 1966-67: 147). Scholarship abandoned the history the OT tells in order to investigate the history behind it. In some sense the theology of the OT story depends on its historical factuality, and the critical approach opened up the possibility of establishing historical factuality without presupposing faith, though in practice the results of the venture were discouraging. Modern evangelical study thus agreed with modern liberal study that the historical nature of the OT was vital to its authority, and tried to find evidence that it was still reasonable to believe that the narrative itself was thoroughly historical.

Exegesis

Modern interpretation further assumed that the key to understanding the meaning of Scripture was to project oneself back into the time of its authors. The meaning of Scripture lay in what the authors intended to say. Biblical criticism declined to be bound by the church's tradition regarding Scripture's meaning, whether this was more Catholic tradition or more Protestant/evangelical tradition. That opened up new possibilities of entering into what was going on between (say) Jeremiah and God and of escaping from the interpretations of the Christian tradition that had overlaid God's word, especially in the OT.

It also took further a Reformation principle, for the Reformation was, among other things, an argument about the interpretation of Scripture. The Reformation did not take place against the background of the church's ignoring Scripture. Rather, the Reformers thought the church misinterpreted it, treating it as if it had a wax nose that could be twisted to any shape you wanted (so Luther). They affirmed that it must be read in accordance with its intrinsic meaning. The Reformation thus brought into focus the problem of conflicts of interpretation — what happens when people disagree on the meaning of texts, as Catholics, Protestants, and Anabaptists did?

Postmodern

"Postmodern" is of course a notoriously polyvalent term. I am not here concerned with the broader postmodernity of which "deconstruction" is a "virtual synonym" (Brummitt and Sherwood 2002: 5) but with postmodern attitudes to the areas already outlined. Postmodern attitudes are formulated in reaction to modern ones. They start from the difficulties of modern attitudes even as modern attitudes had started from the difficulties of premodern ones. They remain aware of the difficulties of premodern views, so they do not imply a reversion to premodern ones as if those were right all along and what we need to do is forget the aberration that comprises modernity. Postmodern study starts from the fact that liberal modern study cannot find any alternative answers to the questions that emerge from premodernity, only more and more questions, and that evangelical modern study cannot find any more evidence for its convictions but can only reassure you that traditional views are as good as any other. Postmodern study seeks to combine premodernity and modernity in a new way. It recognizes that one of the traditions of which we now need to be critical is the tradition of the academy, which is part of modernity. A commitment to "believing criticism" can now be seen as involving the attempt to be pre-modern and modern at the same time, which is easier now that postmodernity has dawned. The "believing" part implies the premodern conviction that the whole of the Bible is true, the whole of it is given by God, and the whole of it makes demands on us. The "criticism" part implies recognition that the church's interpretation of Scripture and the academy's interpretation of Scripture are fallible and that we should never assume that what we have been told about the Bible by the church or by scholars is right. We are critical about what anyone says the Bible says.

Text

In the third millennium the aim of textual criticism neither need nor can be the establishing of the original text of the Scriptures.

The discovery of the Qumran scrolls had paradoxically conflicting implications for textual criticism. It reinforced the conviction that nothing too disastrous had happened to the text of the Masoretic tradition in the thousand years between the copying of the scrolls and the production of the great Masoretic codices around AD 1000. In 1945 our oldest complete Hebrew texts were only a thousand years old and were thus nearer to us in age than to anyone who lived in OT times. In 1950 we had substantial texts of Isaiah and other books that were two thousand years old and were thus nearer to their authors' age than to us, and these texts are substantially the same as the Masoretic texts. But the many small differences between, for example, 1QIsa[a] and 1QIsa[b] also reinforced the suspicion that since pre-Christian times there have been several textual traditions. We have no basis for guessing whether any of them is closer to the original text.

Indeed, it has become unclear what we mean by the original text of an OT book. Textual history collapses into redactional history. What do we mean by the original text of Isaiah? More pressingly, what do we mean by the original text of Jeremiah, given the possibility that the shorter LXX text is older than the longer MT text? Should we see the authoritative form of the text as the canonical one (virtually a tautology, that) (see Childs 1979: 84-106; 1984: 518-30)? If Roger Beckwith is right and we define the canonical Scriptures as the works deposited in the temple (Beckwith 1985), is this the text that textual criticism seeks to establish? But how would we know what that text was? It would be wonderful if the temple scrolls were the ones taken up in the Masoretic tradition, but is there any evidence that this was so? And in trying to identify such a single tradition, are we imposing categories on the process? Further, we are ignoring the implication in the NT that there is no need to reckon that the OT's authority requires that there be only one text-form.

A postmodern attitude to textual criticism will be quite at home with pluralism, as we are at home with a plurality of translations. The implication of the NT's attitude is that the Holy Spirit could be involved in the process whereby different texts of the Scriptures developed, as the Holy Spirit was involved in generating the first versions of stories, psalms, sayings, and oracles, and then in the redactional process whereby they were collected, supplemented, and updated. We have no basis for determining what is the one text of the OT, nor any need to do so. We can treat both MT Jeremiah and LXX Jeremiah as inspired and look for edification in each. Instead of being either-or people, we can be both-and people.

I do not think that this argument points toward recognition of the LXX canon; while some NT writers have read and been influenced by books in the longer canon, they never refer to them as Scripture or quote them. Nor does it imply accepting all textual variants as equally valid, as we do not accept all prophecy as equally valid. The question is, Where may we see the Holy Spirit's work in the development of the text? That may lie in deliberate reworking or in misunderstandings and mistakes that generate edifying readings. Alongside a premodern openness to seeing divine involvement in textual development we will maintain a modern spirit that asks questions about the nature of this development. Textual criticism thus remains a critical task, one that involves spiritual discernment. Its critical principles include, for example, what is oldest and what makes sense to the modern critical scholar, but also, for example, Augustine's interpretive criterion, what encourages love?

Here are examples. In Ps 1:5, the MT declares that the faithless will not stand in the judgment when the "company of the true" assembles. It apparently refers to an event in the present life of the community. But in the LXX people will not rise *again* at the judgment, so that the LXX refers the psalm to the Last Judgment. Ps 5:8 MT prays, "Direct your way before me," be purposeful and focused in your action, while in some LXX mss. the psalm prays, "Direct *my* way before *you*. Ps 7:11 MT declares that God is always expressing anger, which is good news because it means that God consistently acts against oppressors, while the LXX declares that God is *not* always expressing anger, which is good news because it means that God is merciful to us. In each case the LXX says something edifying and encouraging or appropriately challenging within the readers' framework. One can see the Holy Spirit's work in that. On the other hand, precisely in doing that, in each case it conforms the text to its readers' expectations. It makes it say something they would be less likely to find surprising. This does not sound like the work of the Holy Spirit because being surprising is one of the Spirit's characteristics. We do not need the Holy Spirit to say things we would have thought of anyway. Postmodern textual criticism is simultaneously affirming and questioning.

Origin

Modern study was predicated on the assumption that we could discover when books were written. We now have to face the fact that there are virtually no assured results of modern criticism. We know very little about the dating of most OT books. Opinions differ, and presuppositions and fashion are very influential on what scholars think. Scholarly writing makes much use of statements such as "it seems likely," implying "there is no hard evidence for this," and of statements such as "most scholars think," implying "this is a view that will soon be outdated." Current interest in interpreting the OT against its sociological background only relocates the problem since we have no more basis for knowledge about the sociological than about the historical. Current interest in interpreting the OT against the historical and social background of the Persian period raises similar questions since we know very little of either and there is no more evidence for dating the books against this background than there was against the alleged "Solomonic enlightenment."

I say "virtually no assured results" because I must not exaggerate the point. In particular, there is a difference between the Prophets and the other books. It is an assured result of modern criticism that Isaiah 40–55 needs interpreting against the background of the late sixth century as well as that Daniel's visions need interpreting against the background of the second century, and I still enjoy inviting students to read Genesis 1 against the background of the exile. But we do not know when most of the OT was written, *and we never will know*. Another recurrent word in scholarly writing is "yet," as in "we are not yet clear," "scholars are not yet sure." This gives the impression that OT research is like medical research and that one day we will know the answers to questions that currently puzzle us. There are grounds for this confidence in medical research; this process has happened in the past. There are virtually no such grounds in OT research. None of the major problems that scholars discussed in the nineteenth century has been solved.

This does not mean that readers can revert to premodern views because the data that led to the modern theories are still there. We can know that Moses did not write the Torah and that there are several collections of teaching and compilations of stories brought together there that represent ways God guided people over the centuries. But we can have no theory about the nature of this process to replace the premodern one that Moses wrote it, or the modern Wellhausenian consensus. And we thus cannot build OT interpretation on convictions about date and authorship. We do not make progress by trying to understand Job, Jonah, or Ruth against their historical context or in light of their author's intentions, except insofar as talking about the author's intentions is another way of talking about the actual content of the books (what the author intended was to say what the book says). And apparently the same is true about, for example, the Pentateuch. The communities that generated and preserved the Scriptures declined to incorporate the kind of data that would help us fix them historically. Modernity thought we needed this, but God does not seem to have agreed.

So postmodern study concludes that in general the question about authorship and dating must be the wrong question. In the postmodern era we simply (?) read the books without knowing who wrote them or when. We thus focus on what can be known from the text rather than on questions that run into the sand.

But with modernity, we do not take for granted that we know what the text says and that it says what we have been told it says. In this sense we approach it critically. We seek to read it with open eyes; we do not revert to what tradition says it says. This aspect of criticism is at least as important as it ever was. We use whatever keys seem to unlock aspects of the text, trying different ones until one opens the lock without forcing it.

Reference

In the aftermath of the Enlightenment, "history" and "story" with their common etymology separated. "History" came to refer to the facts, the events that (might) lie behind a narrative. "Story" came to refer to the narrative, with the implication that it had little value except insofar as it spoke of events that did happen. It was history that now came to count, so that Thucydides and Exodus were valued only for the factual material they contained. Liberals and evangelicals agreed that if Exodus is not factual, its authenticity or value disappears.

Modern historical study has presupposed that we are in a better position to determine where the facts lie than the authors of the narratives were, as well as having the motivation to do that, but this other aspect of a historical approach to the OT also produces disappointing results. It would be pleasant to think that current skepticism about Israelite history issued from end-of-millennium malaise and/or postmodern convictions and that in a decade or two things will settle down (cf Zevit 2001: 1-80; Dever 2001: 245-62 — though even Dever is skeptical about Israel's ancestors and the exodus; his confidence starts only with David). But more likely OT study went through a loss of (false) innocence at the end of the second millennium. In seeking to discover the events that lie behind the story, we are again asking questions the text will not answer. If end-of-millennium malaise allowed this fact to emerge, now that it has emerged, it cannot be evaded. This is not just a temporary problem. The twentieth-century consensus was always just a consensus. Once the boy has commented that the emperor has no clothes, the clothes can never be restored. We cannot abandon the idea that the OT story needs to be basically historical. But we have to trust God that it has the historical value it needs to have, on the basis, for instance, that Jesus would hardly have relied on this book as he did if it did not have the historical value it needed to have, and would hardly have therefore encouraged us to base our thinking and lives on it. But we cannot prove that this is so by using critical methods.

Ziony Zevit defines history as "a true story about the past" of the kind that a law court seeks to establish, concerned with facts (Zevit 2001: 27). This definition fits the history Zevit seeks to write. But for the OT "histories," Jan Huizinga's definition is more illuminating: "History is the intellectual form in which a civilization renders account to itself of its past" (Huizinga 1936: 9; as quoted by Hallo 1999: 83; I do not think it matters if the way people use Huizinga's definition does not exactly correspond to its meaning in the context of his work, as Lawson Younger Jr. 1990: 26-27 implies). Such an account of the past needs to have some relationship with historical events, but a civilization's "past" includes more than the events in which it has been involved, and "giving account of the past" has naturally included — indeed, focused on — the passing on of its traditions in general, which have varied relationships to actual events. Like Western dramatists and scriptwriters, even when telling the story of a historical person ancient "historians" were at home including material of a "fictional" kind — both traditional material ("legends") and material newly created by the author. Genesis 1 is not the last piece of true imaginative fiction in the Bible. The inclusion of such imaginative fictions fits with the nature of history writing in the ancient world. God's inspiring the biblical historians did not make them write as if they were modern historians but write as really good ancient historians.

There is then a paradox here. Moderns and postmoderns are quite happy with the interweaving of fact and fiction in Shakespeare and in movies, and as theatergoers we are not so different from premodern readers. Conversely, perhaps premodern reading of Scripture was not so different from our own. Some readers would assume that narratives indeed related what actually happened, like viewers assuming that soap opera characters are real people. Other readers would know that there was probably some difference between the narrative and the actual events and might sometimes be able to guess where it lay, but would mostly focus on the narrative, like a theatergoer watching a Shakespeare play or a film based on facts. It was the context of modernity that made Gerhard von Rad describe the substantial divergence between the OT narrative and the actual course of Israel's history as a grievous burden (von Rad 1962: 108). In a postmodern context, that seems an understandable but extreme view. The considerations about the nature of history writing I have just pointed to do not eliminate the burden but they do reduce it so that it becomes bearable.

There are disadvantages to our uncertainty about the precise historical value of the OT, but it also brings such significant advantages that I might be prepared to see it as a result of divine providence rather than divine oversight. If we cannot establish what events lie behind the OT, that pushes us to focus more on the text itself. Adopting modernity's understanding of history as the privileged lens through which to view the OT has skewed the perceptions of both liberal and evangelical study. Even if we could establish exactly what actually happened in these events, and even if these were identical with the text itself, the proper subject of OT study would still be the OT, not the history. It would still be the text with its selectivity and arrangement. The narrative gives us the truth and not merely the facts.

In the premodern era the church believed that it lived its life in the context of God's story with Israel, and in the modern era scholarship invited readers to be critical of the tradition of interpretation they had received. Evangelical tradition says it is really important that the events of OT history happened but that they are then of no further relevance to our thinking or life today. What matters is that God is involved in my personal life. Modern interpretation supported this view by seeing biblical narrative as history, with the high boredom potential of that designation. Postmodern interpretation assumes that biblical narrative is story, and mostly the story of a community, and that we need to enter into it as story, into the life of the community, the lives of the characters and the unfolding of the scene, and find our own corporate and individual place there. It invites the church to be self-critical about its assumption that we evaluate the relevance of the OT story by our story and to start living by the OT story.

Exegesis

Premodernity and modernity made two quite different assumptions about the way a text comes to speak to people. It was not quite that one was intuitive, and the other rational; both involved the intuitive and the rational. Premodernity assumed that the royal road to good interpretation was the assumption that the text spoke to our current concerns. It then found that it did so, though it was limited to seeing what spoke to its existent concerns, and its nature did not encourage the broadening out of these so that they matched the text's concerns. Modernity assumed that the royal road to good interpretation was the setting aside of our concerns in order to focus on the text's, but there were problems with its practice. To begin with, it did not work, as countless dull biblical commentaries by both liberal and evangelical writers testify. And one reason was that modernity did not live by its own principles. The text was concerned to feed a community's self-understanding by reminding it of God's involvement with it, but modernity was preoccupied with questions about history that it naively treated as if they were also the text's preoccupation. It never reached the text's agenda.

Perhaps it is partly as a consequence that premodern interpretation persists and is still the dominant form of interpretation in the church, which is virtually unscathed by critical interpretation. This appears in the use of Scripture in lectionaries and in the proof-text approach to Scripture in ecumenical documents. It appears in the use of the Bible in preaching and in people's spiritual reading. Worse, God uses Scripture that way. As an ordinand I went through a period of spiritual uncertainty — not over whether the Christian faith was true but over whether it applied to me. I was no longer sure whether I belonged to the elect. What brought me reassurance was the impact of the reading of Deuteronomy 17 in chapel one day, in particular the phrase relating to the Israelites' having come out of Egypt: "You shall not return that way again." That came to me as a promise that God had taken hold of me and would not let me go. The irony is that in context it is a challenge not a promise. God used the text unhistorically, atomistically, and directly. God had no need to do that and could have given me this reassurance via the intrinsic meaning of some other passage of Scripture. God's using Scripture that way implies that when texts become part of Scripture as a whole they become semi-independent of the historical and literary specificity of their origin. They are open to being read as part of this larger whole and as having a meaning that derives from that larger whole. They have a new level of literal meaning. And they speak to people without going by way of an analytic process.

Modernity's understandable mistake was to attempt to sideline this form of interpretation in order to promote its own. But sidelining simply drove it underground (and not very far underground). Paradoxically, if we want the positive aspects of modern interpretation to have an impact on regular Christian interpretation, we need also to work with premodern interpretation and not against it. The prospect and the challenge of postmodern interpretation are to bring together the strengths of premodern and modern in such a way as to sidestep the limitations of each. We are the victims of a split between academic study and person-involving study. Our postmodern context gives us the opportunity to put these two back together.

Postmodern interpretation will be enthusiastic over the way the Holy Spirit inspires imaginative leaps in the use of Scripture that give the words a significance that may have little to do with their meaning in their grammatical and historical context. But it will not make that a default assumption about the nature of interpretation, for reasons that emerged in the context of the Reformation and the Enlightenment. Such use of Scripture can be a means of making affirmations that are actually unscriptural, and we need ways of being able to argue about whether what someone says is indeed a word from the Lord. If it does not correspond to the text's original meaning, we need to treat it again as we would a purported prophecy — be open to the possibility that it came from the Spirit, but not assume that this is so. We also need to keep in mind that most prophecy is either false or trivial. A bigger problem with "free" interpretation is that it often simply confirms us in what we already believe rather than allowing God to break through. Studying Scripture in a modern way is extremely important because we need to distance ourselves from Scripture as we are familiar with it, in order to let it say what it has to say in its own terms. Our present understanding is probably wrong at some points, and we need to be delivered from our framework of interpretation. We need to understand Scripture historically. But we also need to be open to leaps of inspired imagination.

Bibliography. I adapted some of the above paragraphs from *An Ignatian Approach to Reading the Old Testament* (Cambridge, U.K.: Grove, 2002): 3-7 and from *Old Testament Theology,* vol. 1 (Downers Grove, Ill.: InterVarsity, 2003). See also Beckwith, R. 1985 and 1986, *The Old Testament Canon of the New Testament Church and Its Background in Early Judaism,* London: SPCK/ Grand Rapids: Eerdmans • Brummitt, M., and Sherwood, Y. 2002, "The Tenacity of the Word," in *Sense and Sensitivity,* Robert Carroll Memorial Volume, ed. A. G. Hunter and P. R. Davies, JSOTSup 348, London/New York: Sheffield Academic, • Childs, B. S. 1979, "Text and Canon," in *Introduction to the Old Testament as Scripture,* London: SCM/Philadelphia: Fortress, 84-106 • Childs, B. S. 1984 and 1985, "The Hermeneutical Problem of New Testament Criticism," in *The New Testament as Canon,* London: SCM/Philadelphia: Fortress, 518-30 • Dever, W. G. 2001, *What Did the Biblical Writers Know and When Did They Know It?* Grand Rapids/Cambridge: Eerdmans, 2001 • Frei, H. 1974, *The Eclipse of Biblical Narrative,* New Haven/London: Yale University • Hallo, W. W. 1999, "Biblical History in Its Near Eastern Setting," in *Israel's Past in Present Research,* ed. V. P. Long, Winona Lake, Ind.: Eisenbrauns, 77-97 • Huizinga, J. 1936, "A Definition of the Concept of History," in *Philosophy and History: Essays Presented to Ernst Cassirer,* ed. R. Klibansky and H. J. Paton, Oxford: Oxford University, 1-10 • Younger, Y. L. 1990, *Ancient Conquest Accounts,* JSOTSup 98, Sheffield: Sheffield Academic • Metzger, B. 1972, "Literary Forgeries and Canonical Pseudepigrapha," *JBL* 91:3-25 • Reumann, J. 1966-67, *"Oikonomia-*Terms in Paul in Comparison with Lucan *Heilsgeschichte," NTS* 13:147-67 • Scholer, D. M. 1986, "1 Timothy 2:9-15 and the Place of Women in the Church's Ministry," in *Women, Authority and the Bible,* ed. A. Mickelsen, Downers Grove, Ill.: InterVarsity, 193-219 • von Rad, G. 1962 and 1965, *Old Testament Theology,* 2 vols., Edinburgh: Oliver and Boyd/New York: Harper • Zevit, Z. 2001, *The Religions of Ancient Israel,* London/New York: Continuum.

Syro-Palestinian and Biblical Archeology

Deborah A. Appler and Julye Bidmead

William Dever defines an archeologist as an "anthropologist who deals with the ethnicity of the dead" (2001: 54). In essence, archeologists dig beneath the dirt to uncover the material culture (architecture, pottery, bones, tools, jewelry, religious artifacts) of an ancient society in order to reconstruct its history and culture. Syro-Palestinian archeologists limit their research to the geographic area that encompasses the lands of the Bible, which include the modern state of Israel (including the West Bank and Gaza), Jordan, Syria, and Lebanon. Related disciplines, which also shed light on the biblical text, cover ancient Egypt, Mesopotamia, and the Mediterranean.

Recent land disputes between the Israelis and Palestinians have caused practitioners of Syro-Palestinian archeology to seek an alternative name for the discipline that is less politically charged (see Dever 2003). However, as of now no new name has been universally embraced.

The area of Syro-Palestine has been politically charged ever since the United Nations created the state of Israel in 1948. Archeology and politics have continued to coincide. For example, Yigael Yadin not only served as an officer in the Israeli army but he also made a career out of archeology and excavated such historically relevant sites as Qumran and Megiddo. These discoveries provided modern Israelis with a link to their ancestors who earlier dominated the land. Lawrence protected the British and Arabs from the Ottoman Turks while simultaneously excavating ancient Egypt. In the late twentieth century when Palestinian territories received autonomy from Israel, they made the creation of a department of archeology a priority so that they, too, could establish a link to their ancestors in the land that they hoped to reclaim. Consequently, Albert Glock (1925-92) created such a department at Birzeit University. This program remains a stronghold for Palestinian archeology.

Though Syro-Palestinian archeology concerns itself with territories contained in the Hebrew and Christian Scriptures, this discipline should not be confused with the subdiscipline "Biblical Archeology," a primarily U.S. endeavor spearheaded by William Foxwell Albright of Johns Hopkins University during the middle of the twentieth century. While Syro-Palestinian archeology is a secular endeavor that, in theory, relies on material culture alone to reconstruct ancient societies, Biblical Archeology unabashedly treats the biblical text as further data for these same reconstructions. The majority of archeologists presently excavating in "biblical regions," regardless of religious orientation, seek to collect and interpret their data as impartial scientists. Yet this field finds its roots with those scholars who sought a connection between the biblical text and artifacts.

Roots of the Discipline

While interest in biblical sites existed long before the nineteenth century, first evidenced by the biblical writer describing the ruins of Ai (Josh 8:28) and later by Queen Helena's quest to preserve sites associated with Jesus Christ (AD 326-328) and Napoleon's search for ancient Egypt (eighteenth century), archeology as a modern discipline is a recent phenomenon. The emergence of the Enlightenment led many nineteenth-century biblical scholars to apply new historical-critical methods to the Bible, with results that often challenged the historicity of the text. Consequently, the new discipline of Biblical Archeology emerged, whose earliest proponents sought to verify the "truth" of the Bible by producing scientific data (artifacts and material culture) that corroborated the content of this text. With this goal in mind, Edward Robinson, an expert in biblical Hebrew and history, and Eli Smith (1838), versed in the Arabic language, set off for Palestine and identified over a hundred biblical sites. However, it was Sir William Flinders Petrie's work at Tell el-Hesi (biblical Eglon) in the 1880s that initiated a methodical study of the holy lands.

Petrie was the first to recognize the importance of the mounds dotting Syria, Palestine, and Jordan, which he identified as "tells" (Arabic; *tel* in Hebrew) from the Hebrew and Akkadian *(tillu)* meaning "ruin," or "heap." A tell is a mound or small hill that has been built up over several centuries of occupation. It is formed through the accumulation of remains of repeated building activities. As towns and villages were built, destroyed, and then rebuilt, each new settlement placed its foundation on top of what the earlier dwellers left behind. As Petrie dug through these tells, he noticed that pottery changed over time and could be used to establish a chronology for dating each of these layers of occupation (stratum). Relative dating based on pottery typology continues to be the archeologist's best method for establishing chronology. Later William Foxwell Albright would refine this methodology and provide a more exact pottery chronology for the time periods associated with the biblical material.

Archeological Method

Choosing a Site

The choice of an excavation site often results from regional surveys in which archeologists sweep a geographical area, collect and sort its surface pottery, and note architectural remains and other signs that the area was occupied during their historical period of interest. Some archeologists choose to conduct small-scale excavations (probes) to further determine if the site has potential for a full-scale excavation. With the advent of new technology, some excavated sites, such as Megiddo, are reexcavated to verify or correct previous results. Other tools an archeologist might employ to find a good site include the Proton Magnetometer, which works like a metal detector to identify magnetic activity that might be emitted from buried objects, and Soil Sounding Radar, which bounces radio waves off these same items. Yet in Syro-Palestine where sites abound, the place of preference is the tell, because it is often identified with a biblical site and is located at a strategic geographical point.

In ancient times, just as in rural areas today, people want to live in areas with easy access to water, a favorable climate, good agricultural conditions, close proximity to trade routes, and a good location for defense. In sites with these ideal conditions, settlements grew and then were attacked, conquered, destroyed, or simply abandoned. New peoples arrived and built their own cities on this site using materials such as foundations, building stones, fortifications, and walls from the previous occupiers. In this way tells were gradually built up over the centuries. Megiddo, for example, has approximately twenty identifiable occupation levels ("strata") spanning more than six millennia (7,000 to 500 BC).

Excavations focused on tells are more easily funded because these mounds tend to yield the artifacts and architecture that encourage further donations. Recently, however, the focus on tell archeology has come under fire by such archeologists as Carol Meyers, who argues that tells represented the world of rich and urban dwellers, roughly 10 percent of the population (1988: 24-46). Therefore, the material culture of those in rural areas, who made up the majority of the people in the region, was often ignored. Moreover, tells were predominantly occupied by monarchs and other political heavyweights who made up the male elite. This focus on military prowess and political structures often leads archeologists to conclude erroneously that men were the only major agents in the ancient world (Meyers 1997: 274-76). To remedy such tunnel vision, archeologists are supplementing tells with regional surveys, settlement patterns, comparative site analysis, and a focus on agrarian domestic rather than monumental urban settlements.

How to Pick a Site

Since tells are large areas, archeologists employ both science and art to determine where to place the first pickax. As a scientist, an archeologist does some of the following: incorporates the discoveries from the survey and begins where the largest concentration of pottery and evidence of architecture exists, examines aerial photographs including infrared and satellite imagery that may reveal architecture and other areas of interest not easily detected by the naked eye, or employs comparative site analysis. For instance, city gates are traditionally located on the east side of the tell, usually facing a road or a water source, whereas dumps are almost always located downwind and lower on the mound. Yet most archeologists, perhaps from years of experience, tend to rely on their gut instinct and know just where to dig.

Site Preparation

Most preparation is done in the weeks and months prior to the excavation. For example, funds must be secured, the professional staff must be assembled, and logistics, such as living quarters and an educational program, must be planned. The team usually consists of some or all of the following: a botanist, a paleobotanist, ceramicists, a bone expert, a surveyor, a draftsperson, an architect, a photographer, an epigrapher, a small finds expert, a registrar (to record artifacts), a team member coordinator, a computer expert, a physicist, a chemist, an art historian, historians, biblical scholars, geologists, and social scientists. All of these staff members work interdisciplinarily to arrive at more accurate results.

When the excavation site is located, one of the first steps is to map out the site and establish a grid on the surface (X and Y coordinates to mark geographic location). Prior to the excavation, surveyors prepare topographical maps that show elevation contours and divide the tell into fields or areas that are given alpha or numeric designations. Areas are separated into squares, most commonly five meters by five meters, that are numbered on an X Y axis. Archeologists determine how many squares are dug in any given area based on the personnel, seasonal goals, and other factors that enter in for them.

Hitting the Dirt

While the media tend to paint a romantic picture of the archeologist who goes to a site and sweeps great artifacts off the floor as the enemy attacks (Indiana Jones and Laura Croft come to mind!), the real work is a little more taxing. Archeologists and their team members move piles of dirt, often with little to elicit excitement. Common tools for such endeavors are pickaxes, to break up larger amounts of dirt, hoes to scrape it up, and buckets to haul the dirt away. Smaller tools — small pickaxes trowels, brushes, dustpans, and dental tools — are used to excavate and define installations (e.g., walls, buildings, ovens, floors, skeletons). Sifters are used to uncover small artifacts, such as beads, scarabs, and seeds.

The very act of digging a site destroys it for future generations. Therefore, archeologists take great pains to record every detail in order that any archeologist can reconstruct the original mound. For example, each area supervisor has a map of the dig area with the grid superimposed on it that will serve as the initial top plan, a daily schematic diagram drawn to scale (anywhere between 1:25 to 1:100) that records the architecture and artifacts unearthed. To measure the location of artifacts, architecture, and how much dirt was removed, precise measurements must be taken and recorded based on a predetermined specific coordinate, the benchmark, which will serve as a point of reference from which all future coordinates will be measured. The top plan records the exact location of architecture, artifacts, and pottery baskets, serving as a visual daily diary for any archeologist to reconstruct the site.

As archeologists excavate vertically in a particular area or square, an artificial wall, called a baulk/balk, is left around the perimeter of the square. The balk is one of the most crucial tools for archeological interpretation because it keeps track of finds by providing a visual record of the strata, which are the discernible layers of occupation. The analysis of the sequence of strata in the formation of the tell is called stratigraphy. The tell's stratigraphy is recorded in the face of the balk, also known as a section. This section is measured precisely, both horizontally and vertically, and is carefully photographed and drawn to show all significant features, such as changes in dirt texture and color. The earliest biblical excavators practiced a wide-scale exposure technique in which they dug horizontally across large areas of the tell. One major drawback of this technique was that all evidence of the different strata disappeared, leaving no point of reference. Consequently, Kathleen Kenyon developed a new method that incorporated the wide-scale technique (horizontal) that allowed architecture to be exposed, juxtaposed with the balk technique (vertical) that preserved the stratigraphy. This method, known as the Wheeler-Kenyon method, takes its name from Kenyon and her mentor, Mortimer Wheeler, and is the method of choice for most Syro-Palestinian archeologists.

Each square has at least one locus. A locus is an arbitrary working area defined by some noticeable change of soil, features (walls, architecture, ovens), or any unit that the archeologist wishes to isolate from the larger square in order to determine whether it is a new stratum. Information in each locus is individually tracked and recorded as each locus receives its own pottery bucket and artifact record. It is not unusual to have four or five loci open simultaneously in any given square because it is easier, when information is being interpreted, to combine the information of the various loci than to try to separate one locus into several components (or occupation levels). Each pottery bucket has a tag that notes the area, square, locus, date, and bucket number for the pottery. Each bucket also contains a ventilated bag for bones, another for flint, and one for seeds, and a piece of foil to wrap charcoal. All information on the tag is also recorded in the registrar's notebook or palm pilot to be entered into the archeologist's data base.

The most common artifact found is a potsherd. A potsherd is a broken piece of pottery that can tell archeologists a good deal about a site. As Petrie and Albright showed us, pottery is one of the most useful finds in archeology. Found in the poorest of homes as well as in the richest of palaces and temple, its use in ancient Israel was commonplace and indispensable. Although pottery vessels are themselves fragile and easily broken, the hardened clay out of which they are made does not deteriorate and so can endure for thousands of years. Probably the most important use of pottery, however, is in dating the stratum with which it is associated. This is so because articles made of pottery, like oil lamps, have very distinct sizes, shapes, and decorations, which can be closely related to specific time periods. These subtle changes have now been charted for pottery as early as the Neolithic Period (6,000 to 5,000 BC). Archeologists are able to determine simply from looking at the broken sherds from which time period they arise. Pottery reading and reconstruction is analogous to putting together a complicated jigsaw puzzle — at first all the tiny pieces look identical, but eventually one is able to distinguish color patterns, shapes, and forms from the different fragments. Though this task is not as simplistic as a jigsaw puzzle, ceramic experts do have basic criteria for analyzing sherds.

The form and function of a vessel is one of its first differentiating features; a cooking pot looks different from an oil lamp, for example. The pieces of the sherd are shaped differently. Other forms, such as jugs, vessels, chalices, pitchers, storage jars, plates, and vessels for storing oil, are all found in sites. Once the form of the pottery is determined, the variants are noted. Decoration on pottery also varies with time. During some periods the pottery was burnished or painted; in other periods decoration was completely lacking. Painting can also reveal cultural differences; for instance, Philistine pottery is often decorated with red-and-black paint, spirals, and other unique designs. How the pottery was manufactured is also a significant feature in dating. In the early periods pottery was handmade; later the potter's wheel was used. Differences in material, types of clay, and firing techniques can reveal much about the period and location in which it was manufactured.

Other artifacts and features discovered on a typical dig are grinding stones, loom weights, tools, jewelry, flint, bones (mostly animal), and cultic objects. These finds help to illuminate these ancient cultures by offering clues as to how the ancients created textiles, prepared food, ate, used weapons, and so on. Architectural remains shed light on the economic, religious, and political systems that existed. If an artifact is significant (like a seal, cymbals, tablets, and so forth), a photograph and a drawing may be made of the find *in situ* (in its preremoval state). However, for most artifacts simple measurements will suffice. After measuring the location, the level (height) of the artifact is taken using a transit and meter stick. Each layer, find, feature, and artifact is given a level number.

Relationship between Archeology and Biblical Studies

Though archeology and biblical studies are two separate disciplines, to some degree they rely on each other. Archeology can illuminate the culture and historical setting of the world of ancient Israel. It can also give us information about the cultural, geographic, and material setting in which the stories of the Bible were written down and recorded and help us understand the environment and the life settings of these stories. Archeology provides the background of the biblical world. In other words, archeology can shed light on the material culture of ancient Israel as well as on the events described in the Bible.

Archeological finds and artifacts cannot be understood in isolation. Like many other scientific disciplines, archeology must work in tandem with other disciplines such as history, chemistry, botany, geology, anthropology, epigraphy, and biblical studies to develop the fullest picture of the ancient world. Though most modern archeologists will not use the Bible as a guide as often was the case in earlier expeditions, the biblical text can provide helpful information. The Bible, therefore, can act as a cultural artifact in conjunction with archeology to illuminate both disciplines.

Archeological Finds and the Bible

Many artifacts relating to the Bible have come from Mesopotamian archeology. Early Mesopotamian archeologists such as T. Botta (1842) and A. Laynard identified and excavated Nineveh, one of the capital cities of the ancient Assyrian Empire, unearthing over twenty thousand cuneiform tablets from the library of Assyrian king Ashurbanipal. Other Mesopotamian sites were subsequently excavated, revealing elaborate palaces and temples laden with carved monuments, reliefs, and numerous statues. Since many of the Mesopotamian cities were known previously only from the biblical texts, public and scholarly interest in the excavations of Mesopotamia fueled. The decipherment of cuneiform texts generated the most attention. When one of the cuneiform tablets from Nineveh contained an account of a flood similar to that of Genesis 6–9, even greater public interest was aroused. Leonard Woolley (1929) later claimed to have found evidence of the flood at Ur in southern Mesopotamia. Excavations throughout the ancient Near East at cities such as Mari, Nuzi, and Ebla also produced tablets that illuminated customs and traditions in the biblical ancestral period. The Code of Hammurapi, an eight-foot black diorite stele from eighteenth century BC, records 282 case laws that often parallel the biblical laws. Annals and victory stelae from Assyrian and Babylonian kings Shalmaneser III, Sennacherib, Nebuchadrezzar, and Nabonidus mention various Israelite kings and biblical events. Despite the fervor to "prove the Bible" among many early Mesopotamian archeological expeditions, the discovery of the artifacts and cuneiform texts has proved a valuable source in biblical studies.

Similar royal dedicatory inscriptions have been found in the Transjordan. The Moabite stele of King Mesha (c. 850 BC), a thirty-four-line inscription, honors the Moabite deity Chemosh and commemorates the king's victory over the Israelite king. In 1994 excavators at Tell Dan in northern Israel discovered an inscribed basalt stele that has generated controversy among archeologists and biblical scholars. One line of the thirteen-line Aramaic inscription reads "btdvd." If read as "the house of David," the Tell Dan stele could be the earliest extrabiblical evidence of the mention of King David. Scholars, however, debate this translation. Some other significant finds are the Gezer Calendar, a small limestone tablet dated to approximately 925 BC that gives an early picture of agricultural practices in ancient Israel. The Lachish ostraca, discovered in the 1930s, are a collection of twenty-one letters written on pottery sherds that record correspondence between military commanders. These letters were written just before the city of Lachish fell to the Babylonians (c. 588 BC). Many important archeological finds relating to the Bible have been discovered accidentally. The Dead Sea Scrolls, found by a bedouin in 1947 outside of Qumran on the Dead Sea, have produced the oldest copies of most of the texts of the Hebrew Bible, as well as valuable documents that reveal societal concerns and structures of first-century Palestine and early Judaism.

Bibliography. Dever, W. 2001, *What Did the Biblical Writers Know and When Did They Know It?* Grand Rapids: Eerdmans • Dever, W. 2003, "Whatchamacallit: Why It's So Hard to Name Our Field," *BAR* 29/4: 56-61 • Meyers, C. 1988, *Discovering Eve: Ancient Israelite Women in Context,* New York: Oxford University • Meyers, C. 1997, "Recovering Objects, Re-Visioning Subjects: Archaeology and Feminist Biblical Study," in *Reading the Bible: Approaches, Methods, and Strategies,* ed. A. Brenner and C. Fontaine, Sheffield: Sheffield Academic, 270-84 • Gilchrist, R. 1999, "Gender Archaeology: Contesting the Past," London: Routledge • Kapitan, T., ed. 1999, *Archaeology, History and Culture in Palestine and the Near East,* Atlanta: Scholars.

The Pentateuch

David Noel Freedman

Introduction

The Pentateuch, also known as the Torah or Five Books of Moses, constitutes the first and most important division of the Hebrew Bible (Old Testament). It holds pride of place in the Jewish canon, and was regarded as having the highest authority, higher even than that of the Prophets and the Writings, since it was traditionally thought to be the work of Moses, who alone of the biblical heroes spoke with God face-to-face (cf. Exod 33:11; Deut 34:10-12).

The Pentateuch itself is the first part of a larger literary complex which we may designate the Primary History. This comprises the books from Genesis through 2 Kings but omits Ruth (which in the Hebrew Bible is to be found among the Writings). The Primary History recounts the story of Israel in the context of the total human experience from the beginning (i.e., creation) to the collapse of the kingdom of Judah and the Babylonian exile. It is to be distinguished from the Chronicler's history (1 and 2 Chronicles—Ezra–Nehemiah), which, while covering the same general subject matter, omits most of the earlier narratives and focuses on the kingdom of David and Solomon and their successors. It continues down to the Persian period and the reconstitution of the Jewish community under the leadership of Ezra and Nehemiah. It is apparent from an examination of the two histories that they not only reflect drastically different points of view but are also products of vastly different periods in Israel's history. The inconclusive endings point toward a date of composition shortly after the events with which the story closes (i.e., before the next significant occurrence). Thus it is difficult to suppose that the return from Babylon would not have been mentioned had the Primary History been completed subsequent to that momentous event. By contrast, the Chronicler's account includes this datum and brings the narrative down to the reforms of Ezra and Nehemiah (late fifth century BC). Since his story ends at this point somewhat inconclusively, it is a reasonable inference that the Chronicler's history was compiled about this time, or in any case not later than the early fourth century.

Composition

The date of composition of the Primary History may be fixed by the final entry in 2 Kings, itself a footnote to the story of the fall of Jerusalem and the exile. This note refers to the favor shown the shadow-king Jehoiachin by Evil-merodach, the Babylonian emperor, in the year 561 BC. Since the death of Jehoiachin is hinted at in these verses (2 Kgs 25:29-30), we may date the work of the editor (R_{PH}) in the decade following. By 550 the Primary History in substantially its present form was completed.

The compilation of this sacred history was itself a remarkable achievement. It reflected the determination of the exilic community to remain alive and to retain its identity as the people of God in spite of a series of catastrophic blows culminating in the loss of king and land, temple and priesthood. Nor could they minimize the significance of the disaster by attributing it to a hostile fate, or the changing fortunes of war, or the superiority of alien gods or peoples; rather, it was a deliberate act of judgment by their own God, the covenant God of Israel, who was Lord of heaven and earth and the disposer of the affairs of men. Soberly the exiles reviewed their history in order to discern the meaning of their fate: What had happened between God and his people in the past, from the start? How had they come to their present unhappy state, and what, if anything, might the future hold for them? They could delineate throughout the course of history a consistent pattern of divine grace and favor: a special commitment by God to Abraham and his descendants, fulfilled in the mighty deeds of exodus and conquest surrounding the covenant-making mystery of Sinai, wherein God had declared Israel to be his people and they had claimed him as their God. Successive generations saw the unfolding of this relationship of promise and demand, of grace and obligation, of hope and threat, through the tumultuous period of the judges until it reached fruition in the kingdom of David and Solomon. At the same time the unity and cohesion of the nation were flawed by disobedience to the terms of the covenant and defiance of the will of God, so that the state divided under pressure from within and finally collapsed in ruins from the attacks of foreigners. Thus had a singularly blessed, but persistently sinful, people reaped an inevitable judgment. Nevertheless, the end was not the end. Before and beyond the law of sin and death, there was an unconditional commitment and an eternal relationship of love (cf. Jer 31:3). The God who had summoned Abraham from the east would call his seed to a new pilgrimage westward. And the God who had saved his people from Pharaoh would deliver them again from bondage. Out of the momentous past, and in view of the present agony, the serious student could read sobering lessons for himself and his people. This history was not only a record of what had happened but also words of life and hope for today and tomorrow.

Here was Israel's legacy to Israel: the remains of the old age and a foundation for the new. Old Israel perished in the furnace of exile, but a new Israel was to emerge. The authoritative guide of postexilic Judaism was the Pentateuch. The division of the Primary History into Pentateuch and Former Prophets (Joshua–2 Kings) was occasioned by the needs and insights of the postexilic community: the law of Moses and the social and cultic pattern of the wilderness society were to be normative for the Persian province of Judea. It may well have been Ezra who permanently fixed the authority of the Pentateuch in the Jewish community, although the books themselves had long since been written. There can be little doubt as to the relative antiquity of the text of the Pentateuch (and the Former Prophets) as compared with the other books of the HB. Not only do we have distinct recensions — for example, the Masoretic Text (MT), the Greek Septuagint (LXX), the Samaritan Pentateuch (Sam) — but also a long, traceable history of textual transmission. The Hebrew source of the LXX text goes back at least to the third century BC, and almost certainly to the fourth, while the Samaritan is almost as old. The MT, on the other hand, may be even older. All three are represented in ancient manuscripts from Qumran.

If the Pentateuch was a finished product by the fifth century BC (probably it was already complete in the sixth century BC, as part of the Primary History), is it possible to trace the earlier history of this great work and the sources which contributed to its compilation? Such questions have exercised the minds of biblical scholars for hundreds of years, and the results of their inquiries have varied considerably. While there is as yet no consensus, and the "assured results" of critical analysis are no longer so sure, certain conclusions may be regarded as highly probable, and others as likely. The documentary hypothesis, commonly associated with the name of Julius Wellhausen but actually the product of the labor of many eminent biblical scholars of the past two hundred years, remains the point of departure for the scientific study of the Pentateuch. Its minute source analysis, which was one of the crowning achievements of nineteenth-century biblical criticism, grew out of repeated efforts to deal with the difficulties apparent in the received text. Inconsistencies in content, duplicate or parallel narratives, and significant variations in diction and style militated against the traditional view of unity of authorship. Obvious anachronisms and shifts in the historical and geographical perspective likewise indicated that a Mosaic date for the composition of the Pentateuch was untenable.

In its standard form the documentary hypothesis rested on arguments of two kinds: those based on literary and linguistic evidence, which resulted in the division of the Pentateuchal material into various written sources; and those based on historical evidence for the evolution of religious institutions and ideas in Israel, which produced an analytical description of the interrelationships among the documents and a chronological arrangement to account for them. Literary investigation isolated four primary written sources: J, E, D, and P. D was the simplest to identify since it stands out as a literary unit (i.e., the bulk of the book of Deuteronomy — hence the designation D), with a distinctive style and viewpoint. The separation of P (for "Priestly document") from the remaining narrative material was also a comparatively routine undertaking, and scholars have achieved practical unanimity in defining the contents of this work. It consists chiefly of archival and institutional data spread out on an elaborate genealogical framework. What remains is the general narrative, itself manifestly composite. Thus the separation of the two creation stories in Genesis (1:1–2:4a; 2:4b–3) and the assignment of the former, with its schematized and formulaic pattern, to P and the latter to the narrative source (in this case J) are easily seen. On the other hand, the disentanglement of the narrative strands has proved much more difficult. The Joseph story (Genesis 37; 39–50) is clearly composite. In the episode describing the brothers' treachery against Joseph (37:12-36), there are two accounts of what happened, which have been blended into confusion. In one, Joseph was thrown into a pit and left there to die. He was found by Midianites, brought to Egypt, and sold there. In the other, he was sold to a passing band of Ishmaelites. Reuben figures prominently as the intercessor for Joseph in one, Judah in the other. Only such a separation offers an intelligible account of the episode.

Two principal narrative sources were identified: J (so-called because of its standard use of the name Jehovah [YHWH] for God; it has also been associated with the Southern Kingdom, Judah) and E (because of its use of Elohim for God, though with less consistency beyond the book of Genesis; it has been connected with the Northern Kingdom, Ephraim). The details of the division are not nearly so certain as in the case of D and P; in many passages where J and E have been fused, the analysis is disputed (e.g., Exodus 32–34). Sometime before they were integrated into the Primary History, J and E were combined into a single narrative (JE).

D was the starting point in the determination of the chronological relationships of the sources among themselves and with respect to the history of Israel. D was identified with the law code discovered in the Jerusalem temple in the eighteenth year of Josiah (622 BC); its composition has generally been dated in the seventh century. With regard both to narrative and to legal material, D proved to be later than and dependent upon JE; JE therefore belonged to the monarchic period (tenth-eighth centuries). More precise examination of JE established the priority of J tenth-ninth centuries perhaps) over E (ninth-eighth centuries). This decision was based in part on the opinion that J was more primitive in his theology (i.e., grossly anthropomorphic), but more exuberant and naive in his storytelling. E, on the other hand, was more subtle and sophisticated, and therefore of a later date. Traditionally D has been considered independent of and prior to P, and many still assign P to the exilic period or later. However, a growing number of scholars are arguing for a preexilic P, its earliest editions coming even before D.

The major conclusions of the documentary hypothesis with regard to source analysis and the relative dating of the documents stand fairly firm. Some of the premises are less certain, particularly the theory of a simple evolutionary development of Israel's religious institutions and ideas. And the details of the analysis are open to question in a number of instances. In addition, important new areas of interest have been opened up in the continuing quest for knowledge about the Pentateuch. (See the bibliography.)

A synthesis of what appear to be the soundest insights of scholars who have worked and are now working in the field follows:

J and E

J and E, the familiar narrative sources of classic Pentateuchal analysis, are prose compositions, probably derived from older oral and written sources, but with a significant amount of original material as well. In the Tetrateuch at least, J and E follow the same basic pattern and order of events, and thus presuppose a common source. At the same time they are distinct compositions, with diverging concerns and attitudes, and they differ strikingly in numerous details. On the basis of a minute analysis of these sources, as far as they can be extricated from the Hexateuch, scholars have concluded that J has a southern orientation, as against E, which is northern; that J is concerned with David as king and with his dynasty, while E has marked affinities with and interest in the prophetic movement, especially as it was related to political developments in the north. In general, J has been regarded as a product of the United Monarchy (c. tenth century), and E of the Northern Kingdom (c. ninth-eighth centuries). Subsequent editions (e.g., J_2 and E_2) would be dated still later.

The distinctive historical character of Israel's religion made it inevitable that the story would be rewritten repeatedly so as to include the most recent events which resulted from Yahweh's dealings with his people. Unlike pagan myth, which was timeless and self-completing, and which required only to be rehearsed and reenacted in the cult, Israelite traditions could not finally be contained in this fashion; and reenactment did not exhaust the historical significance or future possibilities of the tradition. In like manner the pagan epic was a self-enclosed entity describing a distinct era of the past: the age of the heroes and their great deeds. But Israel, even with an "epic" tradition, could not simply look back to the glorious past, but was concerned with the continuing actions of God.

While scholarly agreement on the scope of J and E has never been reached, and end points for both have been fixed all the way from the end of Numbers on into Samuel and Kings, it is likely that the end point is determined roughly by the date of the writer. The interpretation herein adheres to the common, if somewhat conservative, view that J dates from the United Monarchy (i.e., tenth century), and that E is northern and is to be dated in the late ninth or early eighth century. This means that both J and E are not simply prose abstracts of an earlier tradition, but rather separate historical accounts based on that tradition, carrying the story beyond its original limits to their own time. Thus J finds the complete fulfillment of the promise to the fathers not in the original settlement under Joshua but in the conquests and kingdom of David. Without attempting to pin down precisely the J material in Judges and Samuel, one may nevertheless point to the two sources of 1 Samuel and identify the earlier, pro-monarchy source with J. The transference of the Abrahamic covenant (Genesis 15 — and old tradition) to David and his house (2 Samuel 7) is also to be attributed to J. Whether J extends beyond this point is debatable (the so-called Court History — 2 Samuel 9–20; 1 Kings 1–2 — may or may not be a separate source); its possible ending, which would put it in the reign of Solomon, could be 1 Kgs 4:20-21 (Heb. 4:20–5:1): "Judah and Israel were as many as the sand by the sea; they ate and drank and were happy. Solomon ruled over all the kingdoms from the Euphrates to the land of the Philistines and to the border of Egypt; they brought tribute and served Solomon all the days of his life." Subsequent editions of J may well have carried further the story of the fortunes of the house of David and the kingdom of Judah.

E is more difficult to fix as to date and extent. On the basis of a northern provenience and demonstrable interest in the prophetic movement, E may be regarded as a product of the religious enthusiasm stimulated by Elijah and Elisha, and his work may be placed in the age of Jehu and his successors (c. 842-745 BC). A clue to the character of E may be found in the evaluation of Jehu's revolution in 2 Kgs 10:28, 30: "Thus Jehu wiped out Baal from Israel. . . . And the LORD said to Jehu, 'Because you have done well in carrying out what is right in my eyes, and have done to the house of Ahab according to all that was in my heart, your sons of the fourth generation shall sit on the throne of Israel.'" This material is embedded in a typically hostile Deuteronomic estimate of the same king (vv. 29, 31) and must therefore derive from a different, and sympathetic, northern source. The reference to the descendants of Jehu to the fourth generation would bring us down to Jeroboam II, whose dominion might be regarded more suitably as a fulfillment both of promise and of prophecy. The assertion that Jeroboam's victories were achieved as fulfillment of the word of the prophet (Jonah son of Amittai) is particularly instructive: "He restored the border of Israel from the entrance of Hamath as far as the Sea of the Arabah, according to the word of the LORD, the God of Israel, which he spoke by his servant Jonah the son of Amittai, the prophet" (2 Kgs 14:25). E reconstructed the story of Israel in the light of the prophetic movement, beginning with Abraham, anachronistically described (by E) as a prophet and similarly identifying Miriam, Deborah(?), Samuel, and other ancient figures by the same term. If we remove the Deuteronomic framework and commentary, what remains of Kings (through 2 Kings 14, essentially E) is predominantly the story of the prophets and their impact on the history of the Northern Kingdom; for it was the prophets who were the successors to the judges and the Northern Kingdom which inherited the traditions of the tribal league and its cult center. Thus E was the defender of the older tradition against the claims of the Davidic dynasty. It may be concluded that E was composed in the eighth century BC, in the north, and represented an attempt, in the prophetic tradition, to relate the ancient traditions to the history of the Northern Kingdom and to establish the latter's claim to be the true successor and heir of "all Israel."

JE is the product of a literary merger. At some time after the completion of J and E as separate entities, they were blended into a continuous narrative by an editor or redactor, R_{JE}. Analysis of the surviving material in the Pentateuch indicates that the editor used a variety of methods in weaving the narratives together. First, the dominant strand is clearly J, which, in fact, formed the basic narrative. E has actually been broken up and inserted piecemeal into the overall structure of J. On occasion there are parallel accounts (J and E) of the same episode; sometimes one version has been suppressed in favor of the other (where apparently they were practically identical); elsewhere they have been woven together into a single narrative. On the face of it, JE is the work of a southern (Judahite or Jerusalemite) editor whose object was to preserve the traditions of the north and to harmonize them with the J narrative to form a single composite history of the people of God. The logical occasion for this work would have been the destruction of Samaria and the collapse of the Northern Kingdom (722-721 BC). Its purpose was to win the surviving population of Ephraim to allegiance to the temple in Jerusalem and the Davidic king of Judah. Since this was the announced policy of Hezekiah, according to the account in 2 Chr 30:1–31:1, in which a determined effort was made to establish Jerusalem as the center of worship for northerners as well as southerners, we may plausibly connect the compilation of JE with the movement toward religious reunion initiated by Hezekiah. We may date R_{JE} in the early seventh century BC and hold that his work included the major part of J and selected material from E, and closed with the reformation of Hezekiah and the attempt to unite "all Israel" in the worship at Jerusalem.

D and DH

The next major subdivision in the classic analysis of the Pentateuch is D, identified with the document found in the temple in the eighteenth year of Josiah (622 BC) and corresponding roughly to the present book of Deuteronomy (perhaps chs. 5–26; 28). Scholars have been divided on the questions of the date of composition and provenience of this document, though there is increasing agreement that D, like E, has northern affinities, and that it was composed during the century preceding its discovery. Its nucleus is a legal corpus, preserving many ancient laws and customs derived from the days of the confederation (e.g., the law of holy war) and reflecting the traditions of the cult center at Shechem and its priesthood. In their present form, chs. 5–26; 28 constitute a series of warnings and exhortations uttered by Moses just before his death. A date of composition in the reign of Hezekiah or later is practically required by the emphasis on centralization of worship in a single sanctuary, presumably the temple at Jerusalem. The tradition of the central sanctuary is very old, going back to the premonarchic period. But the principle of exclusiveness — that is, the single, central sanctuary — is new. It reflects the circumstances of Hezekiah's time: the fall of the Northern Kingdom and the emergence of the Jerusalem temple as the only "independent" cult center. The temple at Bethel apparently survived, but it was under constant attack from the south as heterodox and had suffered considerable loss of prestige with the fall of Samaria. It was finally wrecked by Josiah (cf. 2 Kgs 23:15ff.). Furthermore, the sermonic addresses anticipate or more probably presuppose the destruction of the Northern Kingdom and the captivity of its inhabitants, thus pointing likewise to a date c. 700. A date in the reign of Manasseh is also possible but less likely, while the idea that D was composed in the reign of Josiah and deliberately planted in the temple in order to be discovered there may be dismissed as a fantasy.

The principal concern of D is the Horeb (Sinai) covenant and its significance for the life of Israel. The covenant is a guarantee of life to those who obey its stipulations (the Ten Commandments and subsequent legislation), but for those who forget, ignore, or defy its demands there is certain disaster. Placed in the mouth of Moses, these sermons are not only a reminder of the solemn bond between God and Israel — an explanation of the requirements of the covenant, with its promise of security and threat of destruction — but also a prophetic anticipation of the culmination of Israel's history. For D, Moses is the true prophet (18:15ff.; cf. 34:9-10, which is secondary), who, long before the great prophets of more recent times, foresaw the threatened catastrophe of military invasion and conquest, intensified by that peculiarly inhuman practice of mass deportation. The only hope of Israel, or what survived of it, lay in strict adherence to the covenant obligations beginning with the first commandment, which requires the exclusive worship of Yahweh, and which, on the Deuteronomist's reasoning, restricts worship to the one place he has chosen for his name.

The effect on Josiah and Judah of the discovery of D in the temple is familiar to all. The great reformation of national life and religion is described in detail in 2 Kgs 22:3–23:25 (cf. 2 Chr 34:8–35:19). The so-called Deuteronomic History (DH) probably owes its inspiration and composition to the reformation stimulated by the discovery of D. It is a single work including the books from Deuteronomy through 2 Kings. Beginning with the Mosaic sermons (to which he has prefixed an introduction, Deuteronomy 1–4), the Deuteronomic Historian has traced the Horeb covenant through the history of Israel, interpreting it in the light of the covenant requirements and evaluating kings and people according to their adherence or defiance of them. He has incorporated much older material practically untouched, while providing for the whole a chronological and theological framework. Thus in the book of Judges he has organized chronologically and classified theologically a heterogeneous group of ancient heroes and the folk tales handed down about them. In the books of Kings he has inserted from the official court records the necessary chronological data of accessions, reigns, deaths, and successions; he has also interspersed a theological commentary grading each king in relation to his good or evil deeds.

It used to be thought that the Deuteronomic History was compiled during the exile (i.e., after the last date in 2 Kings), but more recently scholars have argued cogently that the first edition of this work was issued earlier, during the reign of Josiah. Clearly the description of the Josianic reform in 2 Kings 22–23 is the climax of this history, while what follows is a melancholy epilogue. Note especially the fulfillment of the prophecy concerning Bethel (from 1 Kgs 13:1-3) in 2 Kgs 23:15-18, with particular reference to the name of Josiah (which is anticipated in the prophecy), and the conclusion in 23:25: "Before him there was no king like him, who turned to the LORD with all his heart and with all his soul and with all his might, according to all the law of Moses; nor did any like him arise after him." This, together with the formal summary of his reign in v. 28, looks like the original ending of the historical work. It is interesting that the notice of his defeat and death at Megiddo follows the summary.

The Deuteronomic Historian was inspired by the conviction that Josiah was the long-awaited scion of David, who in his work and life would fulfill the ideals of kingship, restore the empire of his illustrious ancestor, and lead his people to renewal of life in obedience to the terms of the ancient Mosaic covenant. The entire history aims at this conclusion, the happy climax of the biblical story. At the same time the Deuteronomic discourses of Moses and the disastrous experience of the Northern Kingdom served as a warning of another denouement, so that the catastrophe which actually ensued was not entirely unprepared. All along there had been two possibilities. With the tragic death of Josiah, it became clearer which alternative was the more likely. It is probable that the Deuteronomic History originally ended with the successful reformation of Josiah, and was subsequently revised to accord with the somber facts of history (cf. the pathetic attempt at reinterpretation, 2 Kgs 23:26: "Still the LORD did not turn from the fierceness of his great wrath, by which his anger was kindled against Judah, because of all the provocations with which Manasseh had provoked him").

Concerning the scope of DH, the question must be raised whether Deuteronomy 1 actually constitutes the beginning. In other words, does Deuteronomy 1–4 serve simply as an introduction to DH, or is it rather a bridge between the narrative of the Tetrateuch (JE) and DH? When it is remembered that D is explicitly attributed to Moses, then the necessity for placing these addresses in the context of the JE narrative becomes clear. Unless JE is to be cut off at the end of Numbers plus a few verses on the death of Moses, it is not possible to argue that DH is an entirely independent work. Not only does such a view leave JE a hopeless torso in the Tetrateuch, but it offers no explanation for the beginning of DH in the fortieth year of the wanderings. If, in the course of D, Moses actually reviewed the previous sequence of mighty deeds, then we could recognize here an imitation of epic style. But there is specific recapitulation only as far back as the Horeb (Sinai) experience, while the antecedent history is dealt with in the vaguest possible way. In short, JE is assumed because it was attached. If J and E actually carried the story down into the period of the monarchy, then DH must have used them, as he used D and other sources. And if he made use of JE for the post-Mosaic period, he could hardly have dismissed or ignored it in the pre-Mosaic and Mosaic eras.

It is likely, therefore, that DH compiled his history along the same lines as J and E (or JE, which is presumably all that was available to him) — that is, he began with Genesis and carried the story down to the reign and reformation of Josiah. However, the fulcrum of his account was the major prophetic exhortations of Moses, the new document, D, found in the temple. DH had little or nothing to add to the JE narrative in the Tetrateuch, though there may be traces of his work there. His creative enterprise begins with Deuteronomy 1–4, which constitutes an introduction to the history which follows but also serves as a bridge connecting it with what has gone before. It is clear that DH did not think that Israelite history began with Moses, whatever may be the opinion of scholars since Wellhausen.

We conclude that the Deuteronomic History was originally composed before the fall of Jerusalem, and that it consisted of JE and D, plus other materials of a narrative and archival nature, covering the period from creation down to the reign and reformation of Josiah.

P

It remains to deal with P, the last of the sources identified in classic Pentateuchal analysis. P consists mainly of archival data of different kinds: genealogical tables, tribal lists, including a pair of census tabulations, and priestly data and regulations — concerning, for example, the tabernacle, the priesthood, sacrifices, and questions of clean and unclean. Embedded in P are also legal prescriptions which form part of the complex legal corpus of the Pentateuch (e.g., the Book of the Covenant and Exodus 34, usually associated with JE; the law code in D; and H, the so-called Holiness Code of Leviticus 17–26). The principal questions concerning P are: (a) Is P an independent source, or is it merely supplemental to JE in the Hexateuch (or Tetrateuch)? Put another way, is P himself the compiler of the Pentateuch, incorporating into the narrative such archival data as seemed desirable? (b) What is the extent of P? It is generally agreed that P is to be found in the books through Numbers, and not in Deuteronomy (except for a couple of verses). But what about Joshua?

The two questions are linked, and the answer given to one will influence one's view of the other. It would seem that the meticulous analysis of earlier scholars and their conclusions concerning the nature of P have not been overthrown by more recent advocates. It still appears that the case for P as an independent source is stronger than the case against it. If P was a self-contained entity, what were its character and scope? That P in Exodus-Numbers is primarily concerned to fix in detail the cultic practice of the wilderness encampment and to establish it as a permanent norm for Israel through the unquestioned authority of Moses is clear. Here there is essentially a static treatment of ancient materials, with a concern, not, as in the older sources, for the movement of God in history, but for the original pattern of worship, which is binding forever. The particular historical event has partly given way to the timeless and unchangeable pattern of heavenly things. If P were limited to Exodus-

Numbers, then the question of its independent status would not figure seriously, and its incorporation into the narrative as essentially supplementary data would be understandable. But the presence of P in Genesis, where it provides the chronological framework and some narrative details, suggests a broader, at least partly historical, concern. If this is true, and it can hardly be doubted, then we must recognize in P the old traditions present in the other historical works and preserved in the festivals which are a principal interest of P. P's interest in the patriarchs, however, requires a corresponding concern with the settlement in the promised land. While Moses and the pattern of life and worship in the wilderness are central to P, the prelude in Genesis can be balanced only by the fulfillment in Numbers and Joshua; but it is only in Joshua that the specific expectations of P in the patriarchal narratives are fulfilled. In no way can Moses and the wanderings or even Sinai be regarded as the resolution of patriarchal anticipation. The divine promise can be realized only in the occupation of the land (which is explicitly not Transjordan and for P does not even include it). Therefore, if P is an independent source, and is found in Genesis as well as in Exodus-Numbers, then we should expect to find it in Joshua also.

It is probable that P was incorporated by the final redactor (R_{PH}) into the so-called Deuteronomic History (including JE, as already pointed out) during the exile. Apparently R_{PH} added the final reference to Jehoiachin, and this points to the completion of the work in the decade 560-550 BC. Thus by the middle of the sixth century the Primary History was complete, and it has been preserved substantially without change. Subsequent to the completion of this work, the Pentateuch was abstracted, and not later than the time of Ezra it was firmly established as the Holy Scripture of Israel.

Form and Contents

The separation of the Pentateuch from the Primary History, and its assignment to a unique place of honor and authority in Israel, was a development of the greatest importance. The factors responsible for the division between Deuteronomy and Joshua were neither literary nor historical, but primarily theological; they arose out of the concerns and needs of the exilic community. Classic critical scholarship identified the Hexateuch as the basic literary compilation, recognizing the close connection between the occupation of the land described in Joshua and the preceding stories of the Pentateuch. More recent scholarship has identified the Deuteronomic History as a single literary work, thus dividing the Primary History at the end of the book of Numbers and connecting Deuteronomy with the following books. It will be seen that neither approach allows for a normal break at the end of Deuteronomy. At the same time, the ultimate sources, oral and documentary, cut across the same dividing line. The conclusion seems inescapable that the isolation of the Pentateuch from the Primary History was the last stage in the process, and that it was occasioned by the special interest of the exilic community in the person of Moses and the experience of Israel in the wilderness. A subtle shift in emphasis from the historical pattern of the older sources to the more static pattern of P is discernible in the new arrangement. Where the Primary History is essentially the record of God's dealings with his people and their experience together through more than twelve hundred years, the Pentateuch, while retaining a chronological framework and, of course, sharing the same narrative for the first half of this era, nevertheless has its central interest not in the mighty deeds of God, nor in the historical vicissitudes of Israel, but rather in the description of an eternal, perfect, and unchangeable pattern of community life, first and fully revealed at Sinai and successfully achieved by Israel in the wilderness. For the Pentateuch, the desert encampment governed by all the laws, civil and criminal, cultic and dietary, was the first true realization of the anticipations outlined in Genesis and the embodiment of the kingdom of God. The pattern of the desert constituted the authoritative example and model for the postexilic community. History has been subordinated to revelation, and mighty deeds to eternal words. Essentially what was required of Israel was conformity to the Sinai pattern; in this would be found the guarantee of its survival and the promise of its security. To a considerable extent, the Pentateuch defined and also restricted the future hope of the postexilic community. While Pentateuchal passages could be pressed into service for messianic purposes, such expectations were more at home in the prophetic literature. The themes of a second Moses, a second exodus, and the perfect realization of the Sinai pattern reflect the shadow cast by the Pentateuch on all hopes and speculations about the future. Alongside the controlling pattern of community life is the figure of Moses, who dominates the Pentateuch. His life constitutes the frame and thread of the story from the beginning of Exodus to the end of Deuteronomy (to which may be added the traditional view that he was the author of all five books). Not only is he the charismatic hero of the JE narrative, but he is also the prophet "nonpareil" of D and Israel's sole lawgiver of P. Thus all the sources and strands of the four latter books of the Pentateuch are drawn together around the superhuman figure of Moses (cf. Exod 34:29-35), while Genesis serves as prologue to the great drama. The chief emphases of the Pentateuch are on the intricate but ultimate pattern of laws governing the life of the people of God, and the mediator of these laws, Moses, who at the same time receives a full biographical treatment.

Select Bibliography. Bentzen, A. 2d ed. 1952, *Introduction to the Old Testament,* Copenhagen: Gad • Blenkinsopp, J. 1992, *The Pentateuch: An Introduction to the First Five Books of the Bible,* New York: Doubleday • Campbell, A. F., and M. A. O'Brien. 1973, *Sources of the Pentateuch: Texts, Introductions, Annotations,* Minneapolis: Fortress • Carpenter, J. E., and G. Harford-Battersby. 1900, *The Hexateuch According to the Revised Version,* 2 vols., London: Longmans, Green • Driver, S. R. 9th ed. 1913, *Introduction to the Literature of the Old Testament,* Edinburgh: T&T Clark • Eissfeldt, O. 2d ed. 1956, *Einleitung in das Alte Testament,* Tübingen: Mohr; ET 1965, *The Old Testament: An Introduction,* trans. P. R. Ackroyd, New York: Harper &

Row • Friedman, R. E. 1981, *The Exile and Biblical Narrative: The Formation of the Deuteronomistic and Priestly Works,* Chico, Calif.: Scholars • Friedman, R. E. 1992, "Torah (Pentateuch)," *ABD,* 6:605-22 • Friedman, R. E. rev. ed. 1997, *Who Wrote the Bible?* San Francisco: HarperSanFrancisco • Friedman, R. E. 1998, *The Hidden Book in the Bible,* San Francisco: HarperSanFrancisco • Hahn, H. F. 1954, *The Old Testament in Modern Research,* Philadelphia: Muhlenberg • Hayes, J. H. 1979, *An Introduction to Old Testament Study,* Nashville: Abingdon • Hölscher, G. 1942, *Die Anfänge der hebräischen Geschichtsschreibung,* Heidelberg: Winter • Hölscher, G. 1952, *Geschichtsschreibung in Israel,* Lund: Gleerup • Kaufmann, Y. 1960, *The Religion of Israel, from Its Beginnings to the Babylonian Exile,* Chicago: University of Chicago • Nicholson, E. 1998, *The Pentateuch in the Twentieth Century: The Legacy of Julius Wellhausen,* Oxford: Clarendon • North, C. R. 1951, "Pentateuchal Criticism," in *The Old Testament and Modern Study,* ed. H. H. Rowley, Oxford: Clarendon, 48-83 • Noth, M. 1943, *Überlieferungsgeschichtliche Studien,* vol. 1, Halle; ET 1981,*The Deuteronomistic History,* Sheffield: JSOT • Noth, M. 1948, *Überlieferungsgeschichte des Pentateuch,* Stuttgart: Kohlhammer; ET, 1972, *A History of Pentateuchal Traditions,* trans. B. W. Anderson, Englewood Cliffs, N.J.: Prentice-Hall • Pedersen, J. 1931, "Die Auffassung vom Alten Testament," *ZAW* 49: 161-81 • Pedersen, J. 1926-40, *Israel: Its Life and Culture,* 2 vols., London: Oxford University • Pfeiffer, R. H. 2nd ed. 1953, *Introduction to the Old Testament,* London: Black • Propp, W. H. C. 1997, "The Priestly Source Recovered Intact?" *VT* 46:458-78 • Rofe, A. 1999, *Introduction to the Composition of the Pentateuch,* trans. H. N. Bock, Sheffield: Sheffield Academic • Rudolph, W. 1938, *Der "Elohist" von Exodus bis Josua,* BZAW 68, Berlin: A. Topelmann • Volz, P., and W. Rudolph. 1933, *Der Elohist als Erzähler: Ein Irrweg der Pentateuchkritik?* BZAW 63 • von Rad, G. 1934, *Die Priesterschrift im Hexateuch,* BWANT 13, Stuttgart: Kohlhammer • von Rad, G. 1938, *Das formgeschichtliche Problem des Hexateuchs,* BWANT 26(78), Stuttgart: Kohlhammer; ET, 1984, *The Problem of the Hexateuch,* London: SCM • von Rad, G. 1953, *Studies in Deuteronomy,* trans. D. M. G. Stalker, SBT 9, London: SCM • von Rad, G. 1953, *Das erste Buch Mose: Genesis,* ATD 2/4, Göttingen: Vandenhoeck & Ruprecht • von Rad, G. 1972, *Genesis: A Commentary,* trans. J. H. Marks, London: SCM • Wellhausen, J. 1885, *Prolegomena to the History of Ancient Israel,* trans. J. S. Black and A. Menzies, Edinburgh: Black • Wellhausen, J. 3d ed. 1899, *Die Composition des Hexateuchs und der historischen Bücher des Altes Testaments,* Berlin • Whybray, R. N. 1987, *The Making of the Pentateuch. A Methodological Study,* JSOTSup 53, Sheffield: Sheffield Academic • Zevit, Z. 1982, "Converging Lines of Evidence Bearing on the Date of P," *ZAW* 94:502-9.

Genesis

Gordon J. Wenham

INTRODUCTION

The Problem of Interpretation

The interpretation of Genesis should be straightforward. Most readers of this commentary will be familiar with the contents of Genesis and will come to the text with a pre-understanding that they have acquired in church, Sunday school, or at their mother's knee. They will therefore think that they know what the text means, and will tend to consult a commentary only regarding points they feel unsure about or to discover what modern scholars are saying about this ancient text.

Now some pre-understanding is necessary for reading any text. But it can also be dangerous: prejudice, especially unconscious prejudice, may distort or even obscure understanding. We often meet this problem in ordinary communication, and we try to eliminate it. However, with Genesis we are on sensitive ground. It is the first book of the Bible, and is therefore regarded by both Jews and Christians as in some sense the Word of God and therefore authoritative for both faith and practice. In Genesis we therefore hope to find our beliefs and moral stances endorsed or at least not contradicted. But because believers' convictions vary, so do their interpretations of Genesis.

Ultimately there is no escape from the reader's input to the interpretation of a text. We decide the questions that we put to the text. Yet we need to ask ourselves whether the questions we are posing are fair. Is it reasonable to look for solutions to problems raised by modern science or ideologies in a three-thousand-year-old text? The text was written at a particular time with a specific readership in mind. So the traditional approach of the commentator has been to attempt to read the text as the presumed first readers did, or, even better, as the author meant it. The recovery of the original sense of the text was the basic duty of the commentator. It is now universally recognized that there are many obstacles to achieving that goal. We know little about the circumstances in which the biblical texts were written, or who their authors were. Interpretation is also dependent on the wider context, as well as on the assumptions and interests of the interpreter.

These factors make interpretation far from straightforward. Nevertheless, this commentary endeavors to make its first priority the recovery of the earliest meaning of the text, however uncertain that may seem to be, and hopefully to let its voice speak. The alternative is to let our personal interests have free rein and impose our own views on the text however contrary they may be to the writer's. Such a capricious approach may be interesting or dull, but it is certainly of passing value.

The believing Christian or Jewish reader will not be satisfied with recovering the original meaning of the text, however. They will want to relate the message of Genesis to their current situation. Here a commentary cannot offer as much because readers differ so much in the situations they face. Yet very often Genesis seems to address issues of perennial concern, so that readers of this commentary should be able to apply its message themselves.

To discover the primary meaning of Genesis we need to look at the following issues: Arrangement, Theme, Sources, Date, and Authorship.

Arrangement

The book of Genesis consists of an introduction (1:1–2:3) followed by ten sections, each of which is headed by the title "These are the descendants of . . ." (2:4; 5:1; 6:8; 10:1; 11:10, 27; 25:12, 19; 36:1; 37:2). Though the Hebrew is the same in 2:4 and 37:2, the NRSV translates the word differently in these passages, "generations" (2:4) and "story of the family" (37:2). This highlights the problem of translation: "descendants" does not fit the context here. Literally the Hebrew term *toledot* means "what comes forth" or "what is generated," so something like "subsequent history" would fit all the contexts reasonably well. Chapter 1 tells of the creation of the heavens and the earth, so 2:4 begins a section about the "subsequent history" of the heavens and earth. Chapters 2–4 introduce us to Adam and his family, so 5:1 tells of the subsequent history of that family. Similarly, Noah is introduced in 5:29, and 6:8 opens a section describing his subsequent life much more fully.

Furthermore, these headings sometimes introduce just a short section like a genealogy (e.g., 25:12) and sometimes a full narrative (e.g., 25:19). Usually short and long sections alternate: 2:4 (heaven and earth) long, 5:1 (Adam) short, 6:8 (Noah) long, 10:1 (sons of Noah) long, 11:10 (Shem) short, 11:27 (Terah) long, 25:12 (Ishmael) short, 25:19 (Isaac) long, 36:1 (Esau) short, and 37:2 (Jacob) long. The last forty chapters of Genesis consist of three long sections (Terah, Isaac, and Jacob), separated by the short genealogies of Ishmael and Esau. Isaac and Ishmael were brothers, as were Jacob and Esau. In each case the genealogy of the nonelect brother precedes the long account of the chosen brother.

This pattern shows the chief interest of the author of Genesis: he wants to trace the origins of the family of Jacob, the ancestor of the nation of Israel. He barely mentions insignificant offshoots of this family (e.g., Ishmael and his descendants or Esau's descendants), but records the acts of Jacob, his sons, and his father and grandfather rather fully. Chapters 1–11, which often attract the most attention of modern writers because of their universal vision, are quite short in comparison with the patriarchal stories and were obviously of less moment to the author of Genesis. They simply serve to set the scene for the emergence of the nation of Israel and its twelve tribes, the sons of Jacob.

Thus consideration of the arrangement of the book helps us to grasp its focus of interest. The title of the book, "Genesis," means "origin," and this sums up its central concern: to trace the origin of the people of Israel and its twelve tribes and their earliest settlement in the land of Canaan. The short genealogies which link the main patriarchal stories show the relationship of Israel to its nearest neighbors, Edom (ch. 36) and desert tribesmen (Ishmael, 25:12-18), while the Table of Nations (ch. 10) locates Israel's position among the seventy peoples known to them in surrounding lands. The author of Genesis is thus an Israelite historian looking out on the world he knows and looking back into the past with a view to explaining his nation's place in world history.

There are two problems with calling the author of Genesis a historian. First, he includes in his narrative not merely human actors but God, and he explains events not simply by reference to human decisions or natural circumstances but by relating them to the will of God. But modern historians, whether they believe in God or not, would not introduce him into their accounts of the past or invoke his will as an explanation of events. They adopt a secular approach to writing history not claiming to be able to relate events on earth to the mind of God in heaven.

But this divide between secular and religious writing was much less marked in ancient times than today. Many ancient Near Eastern texts, from building inscriptions to royal annals, mention the gods as active in history and determining its direction. So while divine explanations may be out of place in modern histories, it by no means follows that their presence in ancient texts means that they cannot be regarded as historical records.

However, this raises the second problem with regarding Genesis as history: Is the author close enough to the events he mentions for his account to be regarded as history, or is it largely or wholly the product of his or others' imaginations? Scholarly opinion on this issue has seesawed dramatically in recent years; we shall discuss it further under "Sources" and "Authorship" below.

Theme

Genesis may therefore be described as a theological history of Israel's origins. But why was the author so interested in the emergence of Israel? What was so significant about it? D. J. A. Clines (1978: 29) has given what is perhaps the best answer: "The theme of the Pentateuch is the partial fulfilment . . . of the promise to or blessing of the patriarchs." Gen 12:1-3 is the first time the promise is made. It comprises four elements. First, it promises Abraham that he will have a land: "Go to the land . . . I will show you"; second, that he will have numerous descendants: "I will make of you a great nation"; third, that he will enjoy God's protection and blessing: "I will bless those who bless you, and the one who curses you I will curse"; and fourth, that other nations will be blessed because of him: "in you all the families of the earth shall be blessed."

The promises are repeated throughout the book. They are not simply repeated, however, but are modified in subtle ways each time, making them more precise or wide-reaching. For example, "the land that I will show you" (12:1) becomes "this land" in 12:7, "all the land that you see" in 13:15, and "all the land of Canaan for a perpetual holding" in 17:8. All the promise passages in Genesis must therefore be read very carefully to see how the different aspects of the promise are progressively developed and made more emphatic (see 12:1-3, 7; 13:14-17; ch. 15; 16:10; ch. 17; 18:10; 21:12-13; 22:16-18; 25:23; 26:2-5, 24; 28:13-15; 35:11-12; 46:3-4). These promises set out the divine program for the family of Abraham and imply that its history is not merely of significance to Israelites but to the whole world.

The promises themselves, however, occupy a very small proportion of Genesis. Most of the book is narrative, stories about the patriarchs and their doings. These episodes are selected, indeed slanted, to show how the promises were gradually fulfilled. In Genesis the greatest amount of attention is devoted to the promise of descendants. The promise is first made to Abram and Sarai, an elderly and infertile couple, so it is not surprising that its fulfillment is difficult. In ch. 16 they resort to surrogate marriage so that Hagar, Sarai's maid, can bear a child for them. But 17:16ff. makes clear that this is not God's way, but that Sarah herself will bear a son. Again, however, it is a while before the promise is realized with the birth of Isaac in 21:1. In due course Isaac marries, but it is twenty years before his wife Rebekah manages to conceive. It is only with Jacob that a patriarch succeeds in fathering several sons, albeit by four different women, and he goes down to Egypt with almost seventy descendants. He is by no means the great nation promised to Abraham, but at least the hope is gradually being realized.

Similarly, the patriarchs are promised divine protection. The LORD says to Abram, "I will bless those who bless you, and the one who curses you I will curse," and to Isaac and Jacob he adds: "I will be with you" (12:3; 26:3; 28:15). The stories illustrate this divine protection in many different situations. When Abraham enters Egypt and fears for his life, while Sarah may have found herself in a difficult situation, both of them escape greatly enriched (12:10-20). Isaac and Rebekah escape from a potentially similar situation in Gerar (26:6-11). Jacob, though he flees from the murderous wrath of his brother into the arms of his rapacious uncle Laban, returns home eventually with two of Laban's daughters as wives and large herds acquired from Laban, to be greeted by a forgiving embrace from his brother. Finally, even when sold into Egyptian slavery and imprisoned there, Joseph experiences that the LORD is with him, as is demonstrated by his rise to be ruler of all Egypt (39:2, 21). There is thus progression within Genesis: each cycle shows its patriarch being more richly blessed and enjoying greater divine protection than the previous one.

Progression is even more marked in the fulfillment of the promise that "in you all the families of the earth shall be blessed." Apart from his rescue of the kings of the plain in ch. 14 and his attempt to intercede for Sodom (ch. 18), other nations do not appear to enjoy much blessing through Abraham. Through Jacob's faithful husbandry of Laban's flocks and herds, the latter was enriched (30:30), but through Joseph all the world was able to come to Egypt to buy grain and the Egyptians themselves were saved from utter destitution (41:57; 47:13-26).

These passages all illustrate how the patriarchal promises are gradually fulfilled. But how do the opening chapters (1–11) relate to this theme of the fulfillment of promises? On first reading they do not appear to have much to do with the promises. Whereas later in Genesis the promises are at least partially fulfilled and the sky brightens, the opening chapters paint a different picture. From the glorious conclusion of ch. 1, "God saw everything that he had made, and, indeed, it was very good," things go rapidly downhill, so that in 6:7 God says, "I am sorry that I have made them." After the flood there is a new start for mankind. Noah is presented as a second Adam, the new father of the human race, but he succumbs to drink; and with the tower of Babel the whole world again suffers judgment. Without a fresh breath of divine grace the prospects for his creation seem bleak. Mankind's failure, so eloquently described in the opening chapters of Genesis, is thus the backdrop to the promises to Abraham and gives these apparently narrow words universal significance.

But there is a tighter link between the opening chapters and the theme of Genesis than this. God's original commands to mankind, to multiply and to subdue the earth, and the creation of humans in God's image, foreshadow the promises of descendants, land, and divine protection in Genesis 12. In Clines' words (1978: 29), the patriarchal promises are "a re-affirmation of the primal divine intentions for man." God's plans for the whole human race enunciated in Genesis 1 will eventually be realized through Abraham and his descendants.

Sources

Unlike some parts of the Bible, especially the books of Kings and Chronicles, Genesis makes almost no reference to the sources it is using. "This is the *list* of the descendants of Adam" (5:1) may be a reference to a source, but this is not clear. This has led to a variety of suggestions about how the book was written.

The oldest view is that Moses was the author of the entire Pentateuch, so that in some Bible translations Genesis is called "The First Book of Moses." Whereas Moses could have been an eyewitness of most of the events described in the later books, however, this is clearly not the case with Genesis, which tells both about the patriarchs who lived half a millennium before Moses and about primordial events such as creation and the flood. How did Moses know about these things? Traditional commentators were not very interested in such questions: insofar as they considered them, they supposed that either Moses learned the stories of Genesis by direct inspiration or orally from his parents or other Israelite storytellers.

Serious modern critical discussion began with J. Astruc's *Conjectures on the Sources Moses May Have Used to Compile Genesis* (1753). In this work he observes that there is duplication in Genesis, for example, in recounting the creation and the flood. He also notes that there are two main designations for God in Genesis, "God" *(Elohim)* and "the LORD" *(Yahweh)*. Using these two criteria, he was able to split Genesis into two main sources: the one using the word "God" was the original, which was later supplemented by the source using the word "LORD." He identified shorter independent sources as well. The phenomena of different divine names and doublets which Astruc highlighted have remained the foundation of critical theory about Genesis, though his belief that Moses was the final editor has almost entirely been abandoned. For the moment we shall defer discussion of the date of the sources and their redaction and focus on the different types of source analysis that have been propounded.

In the early nineteenth century there were three major models of the growth of Genesis. The first was the fragmentary model, which holds that Genesis was compiled out of a variety of relatively short, independent sources, or fragments, that were used by one editor at one time. It did not undergo a prolonged period of growth during which the material was added to or the story line modified. It was put together by one author drawing on various sources in one fell swoop.

Another model of growth was the supplementary. This postulates that there was once a short version of Genesis, but that it went through a series of editions. Each time more material was added, until the present text of Genesis was created.

The third model was the documentary. This holds that Genesis is made up of three main sources which were originally independent, and each covered much the same history, though from different perspectives. The longest source is the Yahwistic source (J), which includes material from Genesis 2 to Genesis 50. The next longest source is the Elohistic (E), which comprises material found in Genesis 15 to 50. The shortest source, the Priestly (P), includes material found throughout Genesis. According to the commonest form of the documentary hypothesis J, the oldest source, after circulating on its own for about a century, was then combined with E to form a new text. Then after another couple of centuries this combined JE document was edited with P to form the present book of Genesis. (Here it may be pointed out that these sources are generally supposed to continue through the other books of the Pentateuch.)

In the early nineteenth century defenders of all three models of the composition of Genesis could be found. But by the end of the century most scholars had been persuaded that the documentary hypothesis best explained the data. This consensus persisted till the late 1970s, when scholars again canvassed fresh alternatives. There is now a strong school of thought represented by J. Van Seters, R. Rendtorff, and E. Blum, among others, that holds that a supplementary hypothesis best explains Genesis. This is not to say that they each describe the growth of the book in exactly the same way, but they do agree that it grew by a series of editions, each of which expanded the previous one. R. N. Whybray, by contrast, has argued for a fragmentary hypothesis: he believes Genesis was written by a single author using a variety of sources.

Most of these writers challenging the documentary hypothesis also agree that the usual criteria for distinguishing between sources, divine names, repetition, style, and vocabulary are not always cogent. A single author may vary his style, use repetition, or employ different names of God for theological or personal reasons. These phenomena, first identified by Astruc as marks of different authorship, may not indicate any such thing. In other words, the scholarly consensus about the sources is not as solid as it used to be. This makes the writing of a brief commentary more problematic: the old consensus cannot be taken for granted, but spelling out all the modern alternatives would be too lengthy. For religious readers the uncertainties of source criticism do not matter much: it has always been the final text that has had canonical authority and been the focus of interpretation. This commentary will focus on the present text of Genesis, not its hypothetical precursors, but by use of the sigla J, E, and P we shall note to which source mainline critical theory has assigned the different parts of Genesis.

Date

It would be possible to believe in a fragmentary, supplementary, or documentary source explanation of Genesis and in Mosaic authorship, just as Astruc did. But as different explanations of the growth of Genesis were advanced, so were different dates of the sources and their progressive amalgamation. With the establishment of the documentary hypothesis as the scholarly solution to the source division went widespread agreement about the date and origin of the sources. J originated in Jerusalem in the late tenth or the ninth century. E was a document from the Northern Kingdom produced about a century later. P is usually supposed to have originated shortly before 500 BC, and the whole was combined into a single book soon afterward.

These dates have been arrived at by reading the sources against the background of these eras. For example, J reflects the power and interests of the Davidic or Solomonic empire. Its picture of worship with patriarchs patronizing a variety of shrines matches the ethos of the period of the early monarchy, when worship was not confined to Jerusalem. P, on the other hand, with its concerns about sabbath observance and circumcision, fits the postexilic era when the importance of religious loyalty had become paramount. Though the postulated backgrounds for the different sources are quite possible, they are not compelling. Rendtorff noted that the dates traditionally assigned to pentateuchal sources rested more on scholarly consensus than on objective criteria. Among those rejecting the traditional documentary theory of the Pentateuch, there is often a preference for holding that the first major edition of Genesis (approximately the J material) dates not from the tenth century BC but from the sixth century. It is argued that the promise of land, for example, is relevant to Israel in exile and that the movements of the patriarchs fit the archeological data of this later period. On this model the P material would have been incorporated into Genesis quite soon after the first edition. On the other hand, there are those who argue that P actually reflects not the religion of the postexilic period but that of the tabernacle, or first temple. These very diverse assessments of the date of the material in Genesis show how much depends on the interpretive input of the historical scholar. Hard data requiring a specific conclusion are unusual in biblical scholarship.

In the midst of this Babel of conflicting views R. W. L. Moberly (1992a) has made some pertinent observations. The Pentateuch as a whole presupposes the normativeness of Mosaic Yahwism with its emphasis on exclusive loyalty to Yahweh, the abolition of foreign gods, and the demand for holiness. Yet Genesis, while tacitly acknowledging these norms, portrays the patriarchs as disregarding them at many points, worshiping at a variety of shrines, living fairly peaceably with the Canaanites, and apparently not concerned about the sabbath, the food laws, and some of the marriage laws. Though scholars have tended to read these patriarchal stories as oblique descriptions of the unorthodox religious and moral practices of later ages, Moberly argues that this is to misread Genesis. The author of Genesis disapproves of much of what the patriarchs do, but he records it nonetheless because it is part of the tradition which has been passed down to him. For Moberly the heterodoxy of the patriarchs is an indication of the great age of the stories about them.

There are many other signs in Genesis that we are dealing with old material that has been modernized to make it intelligible for a later age. Genesis 14 contains a number of glosses to help later readers, for example, "Bela (that is Zoar), . . . Siddim (that is, the Dead Sea)" (14:2, 3). Names of places and peoples, such as Dan, Ur of the Chaldees, and Philistines, and job descriptions like lord "over my house" (41:40) seem to be updated for the benefit of first-millennium readers. But these modernisms occur alongside archaisms, such as the names of the patriarchs themselves, the descriptions of Joseph's role and investiture, and obsolete social customs, as well as ancient parallels to Genesis 1–11 which would appear to be more at home in the second than in the first millennium BC. Putting all these clues together, I would conclude that Genesis was compiled out of materials originating in the second millennium, which received its final revision in the period of the early monarchy.

Authorship

The brilliantly told narratives and tight structure of the book of Genesis make it difficult to believe that it simply evolved out of oral tradition or was the compilation of a mere editor. It bears the stamp of a powerful creative author, but who that was we cannot know. If Moses was as significant as biblical tradition paints him, we may credit him with the first draft of the book. On the other hand, we may suppose that it was composed by some unknown in the period of David and Solomon, which was clearly a high point of Israelite literary culture. Others may prefer to posit a postexilic author writing the first volume of Israel's history, which concluded with the Kings account of the fall of Jerusalem. But whoever wrote Genesis penned one of the greatest and most influential works of world literature.

Bibliography. Commentaries. Cassuto, U. (1961, 1964) • Rad, G. von (1972) • Sarna, N. M. (1989) • Wenham, G. J. (1987, 1994) • Westermann, C. (1984, 1986).

Introductory Issues. Moberly, R. W. L. 1992a, *The Old Testament of the Old Testament,* Minneapolis: Fortress • Moberly, R. W. L. 1992b, *Genesis 12–50,* Old Testament Guide, Sheffield: Sheffield Academic • Rogerson, J. W. 1991, *Genesis 1–11,* Old Testament Guide, Sheffield: Sheffield Academic • Wenham, G. J. 1999, "Pondering the Pentateuch," in D. W. Baker and B. T. Arnold, eds., *The Face of the Old Testament,* Grand Rapids: Baker, 116-44 • Whybray, R. N. 1987, *The Making of the Pentateuch,* Sheffield: JSOT.

Theology. Alexander, T. D. 1997, *From Paradise to Promised Land,* Carlisle: Paternoster • Clines, D. J. A. 1978, *The Theme of the Pentateuch,* Sheffield: JSOT.

Near Eastern Parallels to Genesis 1–11

To appreciate the impact that Genesis 1–11 made on its earliest readers, it is necessary to understand the ideas about world origins and mankind's earliest history that were current in the era in which Genesis was written. The creation and the flood are mentioned in many texts from the ancient world, for example, from Egypt, Ugarit, and Greece, but the accounts which seem closest to the biblical story come from Mesopotamia in the early second millennium BC.

The Sumerian King List (c. 1900 BC) tells of eight or ten kings who ruled before the flood, each for tens of thousands of years. Then, says the List, the flood swept over the earth, and afterward kingship was again lowered from heaven. Subsequent kings reigned over Mesopotamia for merely hundreds of years. This pattern of reigns finds parallels in Genesis 5 and 11. Genesis 5 tells of ten figures who lived nearly a thousand years each before the flood, whereas Genesis 11 tells of the postdiluvians who lived only a few hundred years each. Genesis 4 relates how the descendants of Cain developed arts and crafts such as music, agriculture, city building, and metal working. This seems to echo Babylonian and Phoenician traditions about seven *apkallus* (sages) who in earliest time taught man the arts of civilization. Indeed, the first of these sages, Adapa, has a name akin to Adam.

Three texts show even closer parallels to Genesis. The Sumerian Flood Story as reconstructed by Jacobsen (1981) recounts the history of the world from the creation of man to the flood. It describes first the plight of mankind with no fixed abode, no irrigation canals, and no clothes (cf. Genesis 2–3). The goddess Nintur plans to end human nomadism, but this is a failure (cf. Gen 4:1-16). However, the establishment of kingship leads to the building of the first cities (Gen 4:17-18) and the introduction of worship (Gen 4:26). Then follow a list of kings who reigned before the flood (cf. Genesis 5), a description of the noise that prompted the flood, and an account of the flood itself (Gen 6:1–9:29). The parallels between Genesis and the Sumerian Flood Story are not so close as to lead to the conclusion that either text knows the other. Rather, they both reflect beliefs about earliest times that were widespread in the ancient orient.

This conclusion is supported by a comparison of Genesis with the other two texts, the Atrahasis Epic and Gilgamesh Epic Tablet 11, whose account of the flood was probably drawn from the Atrahasis Epic. This begins with the lesser gods toiling away digging the canals and the ground to provide food for the great gods. But one day the lesser gods went on strike, depriving the great gods of their food. To break the strike the great gods created seven human couples out of clay and the blood of a dead god. However, the increase of human population on earth disturbed the tranquility of heaven. The gods, therefore, tried to destroy mankind by sending a plague and a drought. Both schemes were thwarted by a man offering a sacrifice to the plague god or the rain god. So the gods all agreed to wipe out the human race with a flood. However, one god, Ea, tipped off his worshiper (Atrahasis or Utnapishtim) to build an ark. He did so, and duly embarked with friends, animals, and valuables. Like the biblical Noah, Atrahasis sent out birds to check the flood level, and he eventually emerged from the ark. Then he offered a sacrifice, around which all the gods crowded hungry after the cessation of sacrifices during the flood, and Atrahasis was eventually granted immortality by the gods. (His other name, Utnapishtim, means "finder of life").

Modern readers encountering the Mesopotamian stories for the first time are most often struck by the similarities between them and Genesis. However, if we are to appreciate the impact of Genesis on its first readers, we need to read them as background to Genesis and not as the reverse. These Mesopotamian texts come from the Old Babylonian period (1900-1600 BC), which on any view is earlier than Genesis. These Mesopotamian texts reflect the typical beliefs about origins current throughout the ancient world in the second millennium BC and probably later. They would not have been seen as unusual then, whereas Genesis 1–11 stands out as distinctive. Its first readers then would not have noted the similarities between Genesis and other accounts so much as the differences.

These first readers would have been struck that Genesis mentions only one God and no goddesses. There is no theogony whereby a whole tribe of gods came into being through sexual relations between the gods and goddesses, or even through divine masturbation. This one God, unlike other oriental deities, is sovereign in power and omniscient. He speaks and light, dry land, plants, and animals appear at once. Even the sun, moon, and stars, often regarded as powerful gods in their own right in the ancient orient, are just creatures, according to Genesis. Though in some Egyptian texts a god creates by his mere word, creation often involves a great struggle. And the great gods of Mesopotamia are not always in control. After unleashing the flood they "cower in the corner like dogs," whereas in Genesis it is when God remembers Noah that the flood starts to recede. After the flood Enlil, one of the three top gods, came to the sacrifice offered by Utnapishtim and was astonished to find human beings still alive. Unlike the God of Genesis Mesopotamian deities did not know everything that happened on earth.

It is not just that Genesis has only one God, who is both sovereign and omnipotent, but his relationship with mankind is quite different. Other cultures recognized that humans were both physical (from the clay or dust) and spiritual (containing the blood of a dead god, or breathed into by God), and believed that kings at least were the image of the god representing and ruling for him on earth. But Genesis affirms that every human being, male and female, is created in God's image to represent him and exercise dominion on his behalf. What is more, far from mankind being a mere afterthought or even a stopgap in the divine plan, Genesis portrays the creation of man as the climax of creation. The works of the preceding five days all prepare the environment for man, and then when the human race itself is created all the angels are invited to participate in this master stroke of creation, as the Creator announces, "Let us make humankind in our image." And whereas according to the Atrahasis epic man was created to provide the gods with food, Genesis notes that God supplied man with food: "See, I have given you every plant . . . for food" (1:29). This theme of God's concern for human welfare is reemphasized in ch. 2, where God provides a garden full of fruit trees, animals as companions, and finally a wife for Adam. In this way Genesis portrays God's care for man.

If this positive divine stance toward humanity was unusual in ancient theologies, so too was the stern moralism that comes through the Genesis accounts. Whereas according to Mesopotamian tradition the flood was prompted by the noise of the human race, according to Genesis it was man's sin: "The LORD saw that the wickedness of humankind was great in the earth . . . and it grieved him to the heart" (6:5-6). Whereas the Babylonians ascribed the flood to divine caprice, the Hebrews put it down to God's anger at human violence. Adam and Eve were expelled from the garden merely for eating a fruit, and Cain was sentenced to perpetual nomadism for fratricide. After the flood Ham's descendants are cursed for his lack of filial respect. Genesis 3–11 portray what von Rad has called "an avalanche of sin," as one generation's sins are ever more serious than the preceding, triggering off first the catastrophe of the flood and then later the confusion of languages and the dispersion of the nations. By contrast the Sumerian Flood Story "believes in progress. Things were not nearly as good to begin with as they have become since . . ." (Jacobsen 1981: 29).

Running through these opening chapters of Genesis is a persistent critique of the Mesopotamian theology of world origins. While Genesis shares a similar view of the sequence of primeval history to that of neighboring peoples, it may read as a definite polemic against the religious interpretation of them found in their myths. By affirming monotheism Genesis denies polytheism and its concomitant beliefs, such as theogony, divine ignorance, weakness, and caprice. Whereas the Babylonians looked on the creation of man as an afterthought for the gods' benefit, Genesis affirms the centrality of man in the divine purpose and God's concern for human welfare. But whereas other cultures were relatively sanguine about the likely progress of humanity both materially and spiritually, Genesis is emphatic that man's natural tendency is toward waywardness and depravity, which invite divine retribution. The account of the "sons" of God marrying the daughters of men is probably another critique of a much-valued practice in the ancient Near East, sacred prostitution; but whereas many orientals supposed this ensured the fertility of the land and the womb, Genesis declares it was the last straw as far as the LORD was concerned and prompted the flood (6:1-8). The ridiculing of Babylonian pretensions is even more apparent in the tower of Babel story (11:1-9). Far from its vaunted temple tower touching heaven and the name Babel (Babylon) meaning "gate of the god," the LORD had to come down from heaven to see the skyscraper — so far short of his dwelling did it reach; and its name means "confusion" or "folly."

In recasting these ancient tales Genesis is doing more than dismissing the misunderstandings of its ancient contemporaries; it is setting forth a vision of God which is fundamental to biblical theology throughout the Bible. There is one omnipotent, omniscient creator God responsible for all that exists. He is profoundly concerned for the welfare of his supreme creation man, but at the same time he cannot overlook human sin and folly. This prompts him to intervene, first as judge and then as savior, offering the human race new starts after sin has ruined the Creator's plans.

Bibliography. Hess, R. S., and D. T. Tsumura. 1994, *"I Studied Inscriptions from before the Flood": Ancient Near Eastern, Literary, and Linguistic Approaches to Genesis 1–11,* Winona Lake: Eisenbrauns, is a collection of relevant essays by many writers on these chapters, including Jacobsen, T. 1981, "The Eridu Genesis."

COMMENTARY

Seven Days of Divine Activity (P) (1:1–2:3)

The first regular section of the book begins with 2:4, "These are the generations of the heavens and the earth" (cf. above, "Arrangement"). Preceding this, 1:1–2:3 constitutes the prologue to Genesis, or, in Westermann's phrase, a "festive overture" written in an elevated prose style that sometimes is almost poetic. It describes six days of divine activity culminating in the creation of man, followed by a seventh day in which God rested from his work. There are parallels between the first three days and the second three days:

Day 1: Creation of light	Day 4: Creation of "lights," that is, sun, moon, and stars
Day 2: Creation of sea and sky	Day 5: Creation of fish in the sea and birds in the sky
Day 3: Creation of dry land and plants	Day 6: Creation of animals and man; plants given for food

The schematization of these parallels is clear, as is the repetitive use of various formulae, such as "And it was so," "God saw that it was good," and "There was evening and there was morning," which occur a precise number of times. Also evident in this account is the focus on those realms that have most impact on human existence: as the days elapse, the description of God's activity becomes fuller, because the things made later in the week tend to be the most vital for man. The fullness of the description of the sixth day with the doubling of various formulae and especially the last comment, "God saw everything that . . . it was very good," highlight the place of man in the divine program. The creation of mankind is the climax of creation.

The goal of creation, however, is the seventh day of rest (2:1-3). The isolation of the seventh day, which has no other day coupled with it, shows that it is unique. The implication is patent: if God the Creator rested on the seventh day, so should his creature man made in the divine image. Thus this opening chapter is more than a prologue to the book, or even just an aetiology for the sabbath; it gives the sabbath a premier place in the divine blueprint for human life.

1:1-5 The interpretation of these verses is difficult. The NRSV conflicts with the RSV and the majority of modern commentators. Traditionally v. 1, "In the beginning God created the heavens and the earth," has been understood to refer to the very first act of creation, when God produced all the matter of the universe, "heavens and earth," out of nothing. V. 2 then describes the disorganized state of the earth before God started arranging it in the subsequent six days. Many modern commentators accept this traditional translation of v. 1, but see it as a heading to the rest of the story in 1:2–2:3. In other words, what is meant by God's creating the heavens and the earth is explained in the following verses, and since v. 2 presupposes the existence of matter before any of God's creative activity, Genesis 1 does not teach creation *ex nihilo.* A minority of recent commentators still prefer the older view. But very few would support the NRSV, which makes v. 1 a clause subordinate to v. 2. Theologically this has similar implications to the view that makes v. 1 the title of the whole chapter; to construe v. 1 as a subordinate clause, however, is unlikely grammar.

1:2 "[F]ormless void" translates two words; cf. RSV, "without form and void." Etymology and parallel passages (cf. Jer 4:23) suggest (Tsumura 1989: 34-43) that "unproductive and uninhabited" might be the best translation. This contrasts with God's acts on days 3 and 6, when vegetation, animals, and man were created. The before-and-after contrast is continued in "darkness covered the face of the deep." In other words, the whole globe was dark until God said, "Let there be light" (day 1), and covered in water until he separated the seas and the dry land on day 3. "A wind from God swept" implies a primeval storm, which is probably reading too much into "swept": "moving" (RSV) or "hovering" (cf. Deut 32:11, NIV) is preferable.

1:3-5 With the creation of light and time the week of divine activity begins. Light is not divine, as in some Egyptian theologies, but it is often associated with the presence of God (e.g., Exod 10:23) and its creation sets limits to the previously prevalent darkness (1:2). It also makes possible the alternation of light and darkness, day and night, and then the cycle of the week.

1:6-8 The sky is pictured as a dome suspended over the earth, which prevents the waters above the earth falling on it, unless the windows in the dome are opened (cf. Gen 7:11). Once again the narrative is insisting that the sky is not to be identified with God, or even with the corpse of a dead god, as in *Enuma Elish* (4.138; *ANET,* p. 67).

1:9-13 The account of creation reaches a minor peak with the acts of separation and creation on the third day. Note how many of the formulae, for example, "It was so," and "And God saw . . . ," are repeated. Both the land and vegetation are created on this day, and both are vital to human existence; hence the fuller description of these divine acts.

1:14-19 For the regulation of human life, however, the heavenly bodies are also indispensable; so once again their creation is recounted in some detail. They are to "be for signs and for seasons and for days and years." However, there is probably another polemical touch here. Neighboring cultures often regarded the sun, moon, and stars as gods; but Genesis explicitly says that they were made by God, and even avoids calling them sun *(shemesh)* and moon *(yareah),* speaking instead of the greater and lesser lights, to avoid the suggestion that these were the sun god Shamash or the moon god Yarih (cf. Hasel 1974).

1:20-23 In the sphere of action (sky and sea) day 5 matches day 2, just as 4 matches 1 and 6 matches 3, but in other ways the creatures of air and sea created on day 5 anticipate the creation of the animals and man on day 6. Both are described as "living creatures." Both are said to be created *(bara').* Both are blessed *(barek)* and commanded to be fruitful and multiply and fill the earth. These verbal links set the animate creation apart from the inanimate. In a special way God's life is manifested in the animate creation, allowing it to reproduce itself so long as it is sustained by divine blessing. "Blessing" is a key concept in Genesis, occurring more frequently in this book than in any other part of the OT. God's blessing is shown in long life, peace, fertility, and material and spiritual success. It is at the heart of the promises to the patriarchs (cf. 12:1-3). Here Genesis suggests that God originally intended to bless the whole of creation — fish, birds, animals, and of course mankind.

1:24-31 With the creation of the animals and man on the sixth day the creation story reaches its peak. Note the repetition of many of the formulae (e.g., "God said/ saw"), the much fuller account of this one day, and the climactic divine observation: "God saw everything that he had made, and indeed, it was very good" (1:31). Far from man's being an afterthought in the divine plan as in the Atrahasis epic, Genesis declares he is the summit of God's creation. Only man is created in God's image and given dominion over the other living creatures. Furthermore, mankind was not created to provide food for the gods, as Babylonians believed, but God supplied him with food.

It is not just the fullness of this part of the creation story and its contrasts with older accounts, however, but the terminology used to describe the creation of human beings and their role that set it apart. The act of creation is preceded by the exhortation, "Let *us* make humankind in *our* image." What prompts God to speak in the plural here? The most likely explanation is that God is inviting the angels to watch man, the master stroke of creation, being produced. This is preferable to supposing it is a plural of self-encouragement. Understanding "us" as an address to the angels does not exclude later Christian, or fuller, readings, which see in it a trinitarian reference to the work of Christ in creation, but that cannot have been the understanding of the writer of Genesis.

Commentators and theologians have offered all sorts of explanations of the image of God as they have tried to identify those characteristics common to God and man. It is now known that it was widely held in the ancient orient that kings were the image of God, that is, that they were the god's representative on earth and governed the earth on his behalf. This is clearly the idea here, with one great change, namely, that every human being, male and female, not just the king, is God's representative who governs the rest of creation on God's behalf. This is not a mandate to exploit the earth but to manage the earth for the benefit of all creation, for kings in the ancient world were supposed to care for their subjects, not exploit them (cf. Psalm 72). And more particularly God is always portrayed as solicitous for the welfare of his creation; so obviously his representative, man, should be too. Though Genesis does not define what constitutes the image of God in man, it implies that it is those human characteristics that enable him to fulfill his duty of ruling the earth and filling it with his own kind.

2:1-3 Though the seventh day stands apart from the other six days, which go in pairs and are very formulaic, it is linked to the opening verses of the chapter by verbal echoes (e.g., 2:3 with 1:1), and thus rounds off the creation story neatly. But it does more. Nonbiblical creation stories often mention the gods resting after their work, but Genesis ties God's rest to the seventh day. It presents a pattern of six days of work followed by a day of rest. While the seventh day is not called the sabbath, perhaps to avoid confusion with the Babylonian *shapattu* day, it is both blessed and hallowed. In the Bible blessing is usually restricted to animate beings, and it is paradoxical that here a day of rest is blessed: inactivity is not usually seen as promoting fruitfulness and success. Yet this is what the blessing of the seventh day implies. Finally, the seventh day is hallowed, the first thing in Scripture to be called holy, that is, set apart for God and therefore sharing in his perfect life.

In other words, the seventh day is not merely an appendage to the week of creation; rather, it is its goal. The implication of its being blessed and hallowed is that it provides the energy for another week of fruitful labor in the service of God. Not that God needs to go on working in the way he did in creation, but man does. Though the text does not make the point explicitly, God's working for six days and resting on the seventh is a pattern for man made in God's image. Thus the whole creation story is a justification of sabbath observance as well as a celebration of the power and wisdom of the Creator.

Bibliography. Hasel, G. F. 1974, "The Polemic Nature of the Genesis Cosmology," *EvQ* 46:81-102 • Hess, R. S., and D. T. Tsumura. 1994, essays by Bird, Lambert, Tsumura • Tsumura, D. T. 1989, *The Earth and the Waters in Genesis 1 and 2*. Sheffield: Sheffield Academic.

Expulsion from Eden (J) (2:4–3:24)

The Garden of Eden story begins the main narrative of Genesis. 2:4 is the title to the first main section (2:4–4:26), which shows the disintegration of the created order established in ch. 1. It answers the question, Why, if God thought what he had made was very good and he had blessed his creatures, is there so much evil around today? The Eden story shows the situation before and after: ch. 2 develops the picture of God's concern for human welfare already intimated in 1:26-31 and portrays an idyllic picture of relations between the sexes and between man and God, whereas ch. 3 shows the breakup of these relationships and the ongoing consequences of human disobedience. Chapter 4 echoes ch. 3 at many points and shows relationships deteriorating further.

Parallels with other oriental origin stories are less obvious in this section than elsewhere in Genesis 1–11. Motifs such as a paradise island, the creation of mankind from clay, and life-giving plants are known in other sources. Closest to the plot of Genesis 2–3 is the myth of Adapa, which tells how on a visit to heaven Adapa was offered the bread and water of life, but loyal to his god Ea he turned them down and lost the chance of immortality. Genesis 2–3 could be a transformation of this story, replacing an obedient Adapa with a disobedient Adam. This would fit in with Genesis's emphasis on human sinfulness (cf. above, p. 37).

2:5-17 The first scene opens with a flashback to the state of the earth before man appeared: uninhabited and uncultivated, it was periodically flooded by the subterranean water, "a stream" (NRSV). The imagery here suggests a Mesopotamian background, where agriculture depends on human irrigation, as does the creation of man from clay and the geography of Eden. Genesis here implies that humans are both material, made from the ground to cultivate the ground (2:15; 3:17) and ultimately to return to the ground (3:19), and spiritual, filled with the breath of life (2:7).

As in ch. 1, divine goodwill toward man is implied in

the narrative. Thoroughout most of this story God is called "the LORD God," a title used rarely elsewhere in the OT and combining God's covenant name Yahweh (the LORD), first revealed to Moses (Exod 6:3), and Elohim (God), the generic word for God used consistently in Genesis 1 of the Creator. This unusual combination suggests that God is both the almighty Creator and mankind's covenant partner. His solicitude for his creature is demonstrated in his providing a garden well stocked with food (2:9; cf. 1:29), the animals as companions (2:19), and eventually a wife (2:22). The sequence of creative acts here (man-plants-animals-woman) clearly differs from that of ch. 1. If these chapters originated in different sources (P and J), this would partially explain the difference. However, if the purpose was to highlight God's benevolence to man and to contrast the human situation before and after the fall, exact chronology may not have mattered to the narrator, so that he juxtaposed chs. 1 and 2 without sensing that they contradicted each other.

Eden may mean "well-watered place" (cf. 13:10; Tsumura 1989: 136) or "delight." With its four great rivers (the Tigris and Euphrates are well known, but the identity of Pishon and Gihon is uncertain) Eden was certainly blessed with abundant water, which is both essential for life and associated with the presence of God (cf. Ezek 47:1-12). Other features of Eden, its pure gold, onyx, and bdellium stones, its trees of life and knowledge, and its east-facing entrance, all prefigure the later tabernacle and temple. In other words, Eden is depicted as an archetypal sanctuary, where God walks (3:8) and Adam acts like a priest (the words of 2:15, "tilling and keeping," are used of the Levites in Num 3:7-8). It is apparently located somewhere near the head of the Persian Gulf, where Sumerian tradition also placed the paradise island of Dilmun.

But what is most important for Genesis is the divine command not to eat of the tree of knowledge. On the analogy of the tree of life (3:22), which gave life to those who ate from it, the tree of knowledge gave its eaters knowledge of good and evil. But what was this knowledge that God wished to withhold from man? Omniscience, sexual awareness, and moral discernment have been suggested. But more plausible is the view that it means moral autonomy, making decisions without reference to God. In Ps 19:7-9 the tree of knowledge is identified with the law; thus to eat of the tree of knowledge means to decide matters without being guided by the law.

2:18-25 The second scene begins with a surprising reflection from the Creator himself about a deficiency in his creation: man is lonely. So woman is created to be a helper "matching or corresponding to him" (better than NRSV, "as his partner"). The idea is that the sexes complement and support each other. The terminology of helping does not imply that man is superior to woman or vice versa, and the phrase "matching him" suggests complementarity, not identity.

However, God first creates animals for the man. He then fulfills the mandate of 1:28 to rule over them by giving them names. That God created all the animals as potential partners for the man is striking and shows that he could have created any number of male or female partners for Adam. But in the event just one Eve is completely satisfactory; in other words, heterosexual monogamy is the Creator's ideal. Furthermore, a wife is as it were part of her husband: "bone of my bones and flesh of my flesh" is a formula often used to describe close relatives (Gen 29:14). Indeed, a husband's first concern should be for his wife. 2:24 does not describe a literal leaving of the man's parents, for in Israel the bride left her parents to live in her husband's extended family. Rather leaving father and mother and clinging to his wife means that a husband puts his wife's welfare above even his obligations to his parents, which until marriage were paramount (Exod 20:12). Within this framework complete intimacy is natural and appropriate: they were "naked, and were not ashamed." Thus in this brief scene the OT ideal of married life is beautifully sketched.

3:1-5 In this scene a snake appears. Though described as crafty, it is also unclean and therefore a fitting anti-God symbol. Its craftiness is evident from its speech with its subtle half-truths and insinuations. Note how he distances himself from the Creator by calling him "God" (3:1-5), not "the LORD God," which expresses God's partnership with man (cf. comment on 2:5-17). He seduces by questioning rather than inciting. His assurances, "You will not die . . . your eyes will be opened and . . . be like God," prove literally true according to 3:7, 22, but at the more profound symbolic level at which the story operates they are completely misleading. Their eyes will be opened, but all they will see is their own nakedness (3:7). Their likeness to God means exclusion from his presence and the fullness of life in the garden (3:22).

3:6-8 In this scene the couple do not merely disobey God: they usurp divine prerogatives by looking (cf. 1:4, 12, etc.), taking (2:21), and making (2:22). The woman's inflated expectations — "good for food," "delight to the eyes," and "make one wise" — are swiftly punctured as they discover their nakedness, frantically sew themselves loincloths out of fig leaves, and then lurk in the bushes. Perhaps overfamiliarity with the story dulls our sense of the ridiculousness of their behavior. But it is a vivid picture of the immediate aftermath of sin. Particularly poignant is the reintroduction of the term "the LORD God" twice in 3:8: they are hiding from the covenant partner of mankind instead of enjoying their accustomed intimacy with him.

3:9-13 Now follows a swift trial. The divine interrogation is not to elicit information but confession, and this discloses further effects of their disobedience. As the man blames the woman, and the woman blames the snake, the extent of the alienation becomes apparent: it is not just between man and God, but between husband and wife, and between the animal and the human world. The serenity of Eden has been lost.

3:14-19 The story now reaches its peak as sentence is pronounced on the snake, the woman, and the man. Each is cursed in the sphere most central to its existence. Furthermore, these curses have an ongoing impact. They explain the nature of life as it is known as opposed to the perfection of ch. 2. Thus the snake is condemned to crawling, eating dust, and constant warfare with man.

The wife will suffer pain in childbirth and subjugation to her husband. And the man's efforts at agriculture will be dogged, by weariness, weeds, and ultimately death. In each case God's original purpose for his creatures is reasserted, but instead of being attended by joy it leads to frustration. Thus the man was appointed to till the garden, but now has to combat thorns and thistles. The woman was created as man's helper and to bear children, but both roles are now blighted. And the snake, though it should have enjoyed a benevolent human rule (1:28; 2:20), now will find itself struck by Eve's descendant.

Traditionally 3:15 has been called the Protoevangelium and understood as the first messianic prophecy. This understanding is as old as the Septuagint (3d cent. BC), but it is usually dismissed by modern commentators. 3:15 simply refers to the struggle between snakes and humans. But this is too facile. In this highly symbolic story exploring the nature of sin and its consequences, the snake is the anti-God figure. Since 3:15 is a curse on the snake, it must surely come out worse in the human-snake war. This seems to be hinted at by the fact that the snake is struck on the head, while the woman's offspring is struck on the heel. In other words, the curse is predicting victory for mankind over the snake, that is, over the anti-God forces. But how exactly this will be achieved is left obscure.

The curse on the woman is also problematic. The pain of childbearing clouds the joy of being fruitful and multiplying, the purpose of creating mankind in two sexes (1:27-28). But how does the curse affect relations between husband and wife? According to Genesis 2 relations ought to be characterized by supportiveness on the wife's part (2:18), commitment to his wife's welfare by the husband (2:24), and intimacy between them (2:25). But 3:16 suggests that relations will often be marred by the wife's desire for independence (in the light of 4:7 the most likely interpretation of "desire"; so Foh), and the husband's arrogance.

As for the curse on the man, Ecclesiastes offers the fullest commentary on the frustrations of all human existence, which ends in death (3:19; cf. Ecclesiastes 6, 9, 12; Rom 5:12-21).

3:22-24 The story closes with the ultimate penalty: expulsion from the garden means loss of the chance of eternal life and the enjoyment of perfect life in the immediate presence of God. Thus in the most significant sense Adam and Eve did die on the day that they ate of the tree (2:17). The human race is excluded from the divine sanctuary which is Eden and prevented from returning by the cherubim and a fiery sword. The cherubim are human-headed lions or bulls, which served as the guardians of Mesopotamian temples and decorated the Israelite ark of the covenant and its sanctuaries.

Genesis 2–3 may also be read as a paradigm of every sin: it describes what happens every time someone disobeys God. The essence of sin is rejecting God's commands, preferring human wisdom to his. The immediate consequence of sin is disruption of relations, introducing alienation between God and man and between man and man. The long-term effects of sin are toil, pain, blighted relationships, and ultimately death.

Bibliography. Hess R. S., and D. T. Tsumura 1994, especially the articles by Speiser, Hauser, and Walsh • Foh, S. T. 1974/75, "What Is the Woman's Desire?" *WTJ* 37:377-83 • Kempf, S. 1993, "Gen 3:14-19: Climax of the Discourse?" *Journal of Translation and Textlinguistics* 6:354-77 • Moberly, R. W. L. 1988, "Did the Serpent Get it Right?" *JTS* 39:1-27.

The Family of Cain (J) (4:1-26)

Genesis 4 concludes the first section of the book (2:4–4:26). As elsewhere in the opening chapters, there are a number of allusions to other oriental accounts of origins, particularly the Sumerian Flood Story in 4:17-26. The first half of the chapter echoes ch. 3 at many points (e.g., 4:9 par. 3:9; 4:10 par. 3:13; 4:11 par. 3:14, 17; 4:15 par. 3:21; 4:16 par. 3:24). These parallels invite us to read the stories together. They point up the parallels between the sins of Adam and Cain, but the differences are just as significant.

Genesis 3 describes how sin disrupts relations between husband and wife and between God and man. Genesis 4 shows it producing hatred between brothers and deeper alienation from God. Cain is portrayed as a more hardened sinner than Adam. He rejects God's plea not to sin, whereas Adam had to be tempted. Cain murders his brother; he does not just eat a fruit. Cain denies knowledge of his sin, but Adam acknowledges it. Adam accepts his sentence, whereas Cain protests. Genesis 4 pictures sin progressively mastering the human race and causing ever greater ills. Cain's son Lamech is an even nastier character than his father. Not only does he go in for bigamy, a practice implicitly criticized in 2:18-24, but he boasts that he is more vicious than his father (4:23-24).

4:1-16 As in the previous story, the climax is found in the divine sentence passed on the sinner (4:10-15), while the opening section explains the background. Typically children are named by the mother to explain some circumstance peculiar to their birth (cf. 29:32–30:24), but Cain is the first human to be born, and he is given a name that is valid for every child: "I have produced a man with the help of the LORD" (4:1). Abel's name means "breath" or "vanity," anticipating his brief life (Ps 144:4). The likeliest explanation for God's rejection of Cain's sacrifice is its poor quality. He only brought "some [not "offering," NRSV] of the fruit of the ground," whereas Abel brought firstlings and their fat portions, that is, their best parts. Sacrifice must be costly and blemish-free to be fit for God (cf. Lev 22:20-22; 2 Sam 24:24).

God's offer of forgiveness to Cain goes unheeded. Instead he slays his brother. When he is interrogated by God, he first lies and then cracks a joke (4:9). Contrast Adam's candor in 3:9-12. The idea that shed human blood pollutes the land and cries out to God for vengeance is a principle that informs OT attitudes to homicide. Unusually, Cain is not himself sentenced to death but to be a nomad (4:12). In the Sumerian Flood Story nomadism was a plight from which the gods saved mankind, not the punishment of the first murderer. Nevertheless even murderers' prayers are heard, for God assures Cain that he will not be executed. Cain is marked — quite how is obscure — in a way that serves both as a reminder of his sin and a promise of protection; cf. the clothing of Adam and Eve (3:21). However, he seems to end up further away from Eden and God than his parents, showing the more severe punishment of his sin.

4:17-22 Sumerian tradition told of sages who rose from the ocean and taught mankind the arts of civilization, such as metal working, city building, and music. By ascribing such arts to the line of Cain and Lamech, Genesis is intimating that for all their glory they are tainted by sin. The savage boast of Lamech of seventy-sevenfold vengeance suggests that even the young and able-bodied "man" / "young man" would be terrorized by villains like Lamech were it not for the protection of the law of talion (Exod 21:25 echoes the terminology of Gen 4:23), which prescribes punishment proportionate to the crime.

4:25-26 The section ends with a glimmer of hope, however, with the birth of Seth, who is the ancestor of the chosen line via Noah and Shem. It is characteristic of Genesis to deal with the non-elect line (here Cain before Shem) before recounting the chosen line. It also a regular feature of Genesis to have a trailer at the end of each major section to lead into the next section; for example, 6:5-8 appears before 6:9–9:29. Here 4:26 anticipates the genealogy of ch. 5. It also notes the first worship of the true God, another ray of hope, after the grim recital of the deeds of Cain and Lamech. "[I]nvoke the name of the LORD" (NRSV) is an overliteral translation: the Hebrew does not imply that worshipers actually used the name Yahweh (first revealed to Moses in Exod 6:3); as elsewhere in Genesis (e.g., 12:8; 13:4), it simply means people worshiped the God who later made himself known to Israel.

Bibliography. Hess, R. S., and D. T. Tsumura. 1994, especially the articles by Jacobsen and Miller.

The Descendants of Adam (5:1–6:8)

The heading "This is the list . . . Adam" marks this as the next main section of Genesis (cf. 2:4; 6:9; 11:27, etc.). It consists of the genealogy of Adam via Seth, already foreshadowed in 4:25-26, a note about the sons of God (6:1-4), and a trailer for the story of the flood (6:5-8).

5:1-32 (P) It is a feature of Genesis that genealogies alternate with major narratives. Later in the book it is non-elect lines such as those of Ishmael (25:12-18) and Esau (36:1-43) whose history is summed up in a genealogy, but here the saved line of Seth is the focus. Scholars have noted that some of the names in this list are similar to the names in the line of Cain (e.g., Methuselah/ Methushael) or even identical (Enoch and Lamech); so they have argued that the genealogies in chs. 4 and 5 are just variants of one original. However, the similarities may be as easily explained as assimilation of two originally divergent lists to each other (Bryan). Clearly the editor regarded them as distinct lines, for in the case of the two men with identical names Enoch and Lamech he includes a modest amount of biographical data in 5:21-24, 28-31 distinguishing them from their predecessors in 4:17, 19-24.

The ages of these antediluvians is problematic. Though they are modest compared with the tens of thousands of years that the comparable figures in the Sumerian King List reigned (see above on the introduction to Genesis 1–11), they can hardly be taken literally. Various suggestions have been offered to explain them, from gematria (assigning numerical values to words) to astronomy (e.g., Enoch's age 365 = days in a year). Most probable is the suggestion of U. Cassuto (commentary) and Young that there must be a connection with Babylonian mathematics given the frequency of numbers related to 60 and its factors (e.g., $930 = 30^2 + 30$), but they have not suggested a plausible symbolism that explains all the individual numbers. At present all that can be said is that they reflect the author's belief that these people were real yet lived a long time ago.

5:1-2 strongly echo the summary of the creation of man in 1:27-28. It leaves out the command to "be fruitful and multiply," but the genealogy itself shows the fulfilment of this mandate (cf. 6:1). Verse 3 makes the point that every descendant of Adam is in his image and by implication in the image of God.

Thereafter each rung of the genealogy is strongly formulaic; only the names and ages vary, except for the seventh, Enoch, and the ninth, Lamech. Enoch "walked with God" (vv. 22, 24). The repetition of this comment underlines his intimacy with God (cf. 6:9; 17:1; Mic 6:8; Mal 2:6), so it may be that his unusually brief life by the standards of this chapter and the mode of his translation to heaven, "he was no more, because God took him" (cf. 2 Kgs 2:1), are seen as a reward for his piety. Interestingly, according to Mesopotamian tradition the seventh sage, Utuabzu, is also said to have ascended to heaven.

5:29 Lamech's naming of Noah also interrupts the tight genealogical formulae. His name expresses the hope that Noah will counteract the curse placed on mankind for Adam's sin. Note the strong echoes of 3:17. "bring us relief" (Heb. *nḥm*) involves a play on Noah's name (Heb. *nḥ*) that occurs again in 6:6-8. Paronomasia like this is common in Genesis, but here it serves to highlight the significance of Noah within the story. He is a second Adam, from whom the whole human race is descended. In his time the world is destroyed and then recreated. The description of his character in 6:8-9 leads the reader to hope with Lamech that his birth will bring in a new age for mankind.

Bibliography. Hess, R. S., and D. T. Tsumura. 1994, especially articles by Borger, Malamat, and Wilson • Bryan, D. T. 1987, "A Reevaluation of Genesis 4 and 5 in the Light of Recent Studies in Genealogical Fluidity," *ZAW* 99:180-88 • Young, D. W. 1988. "On the Application of Numbers from Babylonian Mathematics to Biblical Life Spans and Epochs," *ZAW* 100:331-61.

6:1-4 Who are the sons of God, and whom did they marry? Among the answers offered by commentators throughout the years are kings, the descendants of Seth, or the descendants of Cain. Corresponding to these identifications, their wives have been viewed as members of royal harems, women descended from Cain or from Seth. However, there is a consensus among modern commentators that concurs with the oldest Jewish and Christian interpretation that the sons of God are spirit beings and their consorts are ordinary human women. The OT pictures the one supreme God attended in heaven by a host of spirit beings. Some of them are called "sons of God" (Job 1:6; Pss 29:1; 82:1-6). Near Eastern and classical mythology related unions between the gods and human beings leading to the birth of semi-divine supermen such as Gilgamesh. They seem to be what 6:4 calls "the Nephilim, the heroes . . . of old," mentioned only in Num 13:33 elsewhere in the OT.

Though this episode seems very strange to modern demythologized readers, it is clearly of great moment in Genesis, for it triggers off God's reflections in 6:5-7 to destroy the human race. What was so heinous about the divine-human intercourse, and why is mankind and not the spirit realm punished for it? Though v. 2 has been read as describing the rape of the women, in fact the verbs imply perfectly legitimate marital arrangements, which could be entered into only with the full consent of the girls' fathers. It has been suggested that perhaps the practice of placing girls in temples to perform sacred marriages with the god is being alluded to here. Thereby the fertility of the ground and ordinary wives was supposedly secured. At any rate, only girls designated by their parents could serve as temple prostitutes, and this could explain why the human race was punished. The Creator had blessed procreation at the beginning (1:28), so this attempt to promote fecundity was totally misguided. It also transgresses the clear line that the OT draws between different species (mixed breeding is banned by various laws in Lev 19:19; 20:16; Deut 7:3; 22:9-11) and particularly between God and man (cf. Gen 3:22).

6:3 The limitation of human life to 120 years is gradually implemented in the Pentateuch. After Jacob only Aaron (123) exceeds it.

Bibliography. Gemeren, W. A. van. 1981, "The Sons of God in Gen 6:1-4," *WTJ* 43:320-48.

6:5-8 This brief paragraph is a trailer for the flood story, but it is much more. Generally regarded as the creation of the author of Genesis, it is a key to the book's theology. It paints human sin and God's reaction to it in the darkest colors. Sin infects every human thought (6:5). It is an outrage to God: "grieved to the heart" describes the strongest and bitterest human reactions to terrible deeds (34:7; 1 Sam 20:34; Isa 54:6). So strong is God's reaction that he decides to wipe out all living creatures — not just man but animals and birds as well. *How* is not described yet.

However, even the announcement of destruction is tinged with hope: hidden within the words "sorry" and "blot out" are letters like those in Noah's name. And eventually we are told "Noah found favor"; even the word "favor" (*ḥn*) in Hebrew is Noah spelled backward. In this way the closing paragraph introduces the theme of the next major section (6:9–9:29), the universal judgment in which only Noah and his family will be saved.

Noah and the Flood (J and P) (6:9–9:29)

The story of Noah and the flood has captured the human imagination for thousands of years. This constitutes the third section of Genesis introduced by the title "These are the descendants of" (cf. 2:4; 10:1). On first glance the coda about Noah's drunkenness does not have much to do with what goes before, but it does serve to foreshadow the next section (ch. 10) and has a close parallel with the end of the other tale of universal destruction in Gen 19:30-38.

Older versions of the flood story (Sumerian, Atrahasis, and Gilgamesh) dating in their original forms from the early second millennium BC are known. As already noted above (pp. 36-37), there are remarkable similarities between the Mesopotamian and biblical accounts of the flood, so close in some cases that it has been alleged that the biblical tale is based on the Mesopotamian. On balance direct dependence seems unlikely: more probably both versions are drawing on traditions about the flood that were common in the ancient orient. A comparison of the biblical and nonbiblical accounts highlights the very different theologies of the accounts. We have already mentioned the monotheistic moralism that informs the biblical narrative over against the caprice, self-interest, and weakness of the Mesopotamian gods and goddesses. Whereas they send the flood to curb the population explosion, the God of Genesis encourages mankind to multiply but is appalled by human sin. They cower at the flood they unleash and do not fully understand its consequences, but in Genesis it is totally under the Creator's control. In the Mesopotamian epics Atrahasis (Utnapishtim = Noah) is glorified as a hero as his epic deeds in building and loading the ark are recounted in full, whereas Genesis simply says, "Noah did all that the LORD commanded him." Obedience to God, not human courage, is what Genesis celebrates. Other points of similarity and difference will be pointed out below.

According to the documentary hypothesis, Genesis 6–9 is an example of the intertwining of two independent sources (J and P) to create the present account of the flood. As elsewhere in this commentary, I shall not discuss this here. Westermann and Ska have observed that if the basic analysis is accepted, P appears to be the basic source, which is supplemented by J. It should also be noted that the existing Genesis flood story looks more like the Gilgamesh version than either of the putative earlier versions J and P. It is also only the final version that has a full-scale mirror-image (chiasm, palistrophe) structure, where a feature at the beginning of the story is echoed at a matching point later on. Up to a point this is almost inevitable in telling a flood story: the waters rise and then fall, the animals enter the ark and later come out, and so on. But there are so many examples of this phenomenon in this tale that it can hardly be coincidence; it must be a literary device. For example, the days in the story exhibit this pattern.

7 days	(7:4)
7 days	(7:10)
40 days	(7:17)
150 days	(7:24)
GOD REMEMBERED NOAH	(8:1)
150 days	(8:3)
40 days	(8:6)
7 days	(8:10)
7 days	(8:12)

Thus the shape of the story does not simply mirror the events it relates, but its center, "God remembered Noah," focuses on the two key actors in the story and reminds us that God is in charge of this cosmic catastrophe. Indeed, within Genesis the flood is most important theologically, for it divides world history into two epochs, before and after the flood. The flood serves to undo the work of creation in Genesis 1. The waters are no longer held in check by the firmament as they burst through the dome of the sky, and the dry land is no longer separated from the seas as even the high mountains are covered. Finally, all God's living creatures, from insects to birds, land animals, and man, are wiped out, except for those lucky enough to have embarked on the ark. The flood may therefore be viewed as a great act of de-creation: the frequent echoes of the phraseology of Genesis 1 in chs. 6 and 7 emphasize this.

However, it is followed by an act of re-creation. When God remembers Noah, creation begins to be restored. The waters above the firmament are restrained. Gradually the dry land reappears. Eventually all the creatures in the ark disembark and are recommissioned to be fruitful and multiply and fill the earth (9:1). Noah is a second Adam, the father of the new human race.

Though creation is thus restored, the situation after the flood is not the same as it was before. The flood was prompted by the incorrigibility of the human heart, "every inclination of the thoughts of their hearts was only evil continually" (6:5). But God gives almost the same reason after the flood for never destroying mankind again, "for the inclination of the human heart is evil from youth" (8:21). In context it appears that God's implacable anger against human sin is turned into forgiveness or at least toleration by the sacrifice of Noah (see 8:20). In the long divine speech that follows other differences between the situations before and after the flood are signaled. Originally the plants were assigned as the only food for man and beast (1:29-30); now animals may be eaten, as long as their blood is not consumed. But human life is sacrosanct: murderers must be executed, for man is made in God's image (9:3-6). Homicide also conflicts with the creation mandate to be fruitful and multiply. Finally, the rainbow is designated the sign of the covenant, a guarantee of the preservation of future generations (9:8-17).

6:9-21 The first scene in the flood story is, like the last (8:20–9:17), essentially a divine monologue about the situation and what God proposes to do.

6:9 Noah is portrayed as a model Israelite. He is "righteous," the normal term for a moral person who keeps the law. More than that he is "blameless," that is, above reproach (like Job in Job 12:4; cf. 1:1, 8), and he walked with God, putting him on a par with Enoch (5:22). Throughout the story he does exactly what God tells him (6:22; 7:5, 9, 16). He is also in covenant with God (6:18; 9:9), distinguishes clean and unclean animals, keeps the sabbath (at least he works on a weekly cycle), and offers acceptable sacrifice (7:3; 8:10, 12, 20-21).

6:11-13 By contrast the earth is filled with violence, that is, antisocial behavior often involving force directed against the poor and weak of society. "All flesh," animals and humans, are misbehaving in this way. Therefore, as they are corrupting the earth, so they will be destroyed (lit. "corrupted") by God. This wordplay shows how the punishment fits the crime.

6:14-20 To allow Noah and a selection of animals to escape, he must build an ark. The ark of the Gilgamesh Epic was a perfect cube, 120 cubits each way, whereas Noah's ark is recognizably boat-shaped, each deck of which was the same height as the tabernacle and three times the area of the tabernacle court. This leads Westermann to suggest that the biblical writers saw both tabernacle and ark as serving the preservation of humanity. "To a cubit above" (6:16) either leaves a gap of a cubit (18 in. or 45 cm.) between the roof and the side of the ark, or lets the roof overhang by a cubit.

6:17-20 further explain the building of the ark and why it must be victualed with food.

6:22 (= Scene 2), in contrast to the Gilgamesh Epic, sums up the vast work of building the ark and loading it in one sentence, thus emphasizing Noah's total obedience.

7:1-4 constitutes the third scene, like the first a divine monologue, and focuses on the command to enter the ark and embark the animals. To ensure their survival a male and female of each species was necessary, but this left no spares for sacrifice. Hence extra clean (sacrificial) animals were taken. The Gilgamesh Epic allows only seven days to build the ark and seven days of rain, whereas Genesis stretches the event out much longer.

7:5-16, the fourth scene, colorfully describes how Noah and the animals obeyed the command to embark. The use of repetition, apposition, and expansive phraseology gives the description a special solemnity. Most striking is the precise dating of the different phases of the flood, which is most unusual in the OT. It underlines that the flood marks the end of one epoch and the beginning of another. Possibly the dates themselves have symbolic significance. If Genesis is using the "Jubilees" calendar, the flood began on a Sunday (= the 17th day of the 2d month; 7:11), and it stopped raining on a Friday 40 days later (7:12). Creation began on a Sunday and was completed on Friday according to Genesis 1, so the work of de-creation also ran from Sunday to Friday.

7:16 "The LORD shut him in," whereas according to the Gilgamesh Epic Utnapishtim himself shut the door. Genesis emphasizes that Noah was saved by grace, not by his own wisdom or effort.

7:17-24 In this scene the narrative reaches its peak, with the waters triumphing over the earth and all flesh dying. The lists of dead creatures (vv. 21, 23) hark back to Genesis 1, as does the submerging of the mountains, which leaves the earth covered with water as it was in 1:2. The work of creation has been undone.

8:1-5 "God remembered Noah" marks the turning point (cf. 30:22; 19:29) and ushers in the process of re-creation. The wind blows (cf. 1:2), the rain stops (cf. 1:7), and the land reappears (cf. 1:9). "Ararat" is Urartu, a kingdom north of Assyria, roughly modern Armenia. Gilgamesh (11:140) grounds the ark on Mt. Nisir somewhat further south.

8:6-14 The bird scene, picturesque in itself, slows down the action and allows the reader to sense Noah's impatience to disembark. In the Gilgamesh Epic a dove, a swallow, and a raven are sent out.

8:15-19 At last they are told to leave, and Noah, exact as ever in his obedience, disembarks.

8:20–9:17 The last scene, like the first (6:9-21), is essentially a divine monologue. The first was prompted by God's reflections on human sinfulness, this by the LORD's reflections on Noah's sacrifice. In the first God declares his intention to annihilate the human race; here he promises to preserve it. But this section does more than this: it sets out the terms of the covenant under which God will continue to ensure the continuation of life on earth, modifying in certain respects the mandates originally given at creation.

In Gilgamesh Utnapishtim also offers a sacrifice when he comes out of the ark, and the gods crowd like flies around the sacrifice because they have gone hungry during the flood since the only surviving human beings, their food suppliers, have been cooped up in the ark! Not only does Genesis reject the idea that man feeds the gods (1:29; 9:3), but it sees a quite different role for sacrifice. It creates a "pleasing odor" (better, "soothing aroma"), which appeases God's anger. Usually this phrase appears in connection with sacrifices offered in the tabernacle (e.g., Lev 1:9; 2:2), which atone for the worshiper. Here the second father of the human race offers a sacrifice which secures the survival of all his descendants.

According to the Atrahasis Epic, after the flood the gods decided to put a brake on human population growth by making some women infertile and others to suffer stillbirth. But Genesis rejects this. Not only are the animals encouraged to reproduce (8:17), but three times Noah and his sons are urged to multiply (9:1, 7). Human life is to be protected from assault by man or beast on pain of the death penalty (9:5-6) and from the threat of destruction in another flood (8:22; 9:11). The rainbow in the sky is a sign of God's covenant never to send another flood. Biblical signs usually serve to remind man of God's promises; here most unusually the rainbow reminds God.

Noah's Drunkenness (9:18-29)

After the tranquil and positive conclusion to the flood story, this episode jars. Noah, we have been told, was "blameless in his generation." His obedience has been exemplary, and his sacrifice led to the promise of future security. What is he doing drunk and cursing his grandson? In fact, though the flood story ended optimistically, it did not suggest that the future would be without problems. The human heart remains incorrigibly evil (8:21), and murders may be committed (9:5). Nevertheless, that Noah, the paragon of virtue, should succumb to wine is disappointing. Some commentators think that Genesis is not critical of Noah's conduct, only Ham's. Certainly the OT values wine as one of God's gifts (Ps 104:15) and insists on its use with animal sacrifice (Num 15:5-10). However, priests had to abstain before officiating, and Nazirites were teetotal for the period of their vow, which indicates that drunkenness is incompatible with holiness (Lev 10:9; Num 6:3-4; 1 Sam 1:14). It thus seems likely that Noah's overindulgence in wine is seen as parallel to Adam's mistake in his garden. This is the fall of the second Adam.

However, the offense of the son is much worse than that of the father (cf. Cain and Adam). But what exactly did Ham do wrong? Was it merely looking at his naked father and gossiping about it to his brothers? This has seemed unlikely to Western readers, who have posited Ham committing incest with his mother or something similar. But since Shem and Japheth remedy their brother's mistake simply by covering Noah up without looking at him, it is unnecessary to posit any acts of sexual intercourse by Ham. Rather, this story gives an insight into the Hebrew sense of propriety (cf. Exod 20:26) and filial duty: sons were supposed to cover up their father's follies, not publicize them.

Just how serious Ham's offense is emerges from Noah's curse on his grandson Canaan, Ham's son. He is to be slave to his brothers; in other words, the Canaanites will be subject to the descendants of Shem and Japheth. This is at least a prophecy of the future conquest of Canaan by Israel, a descendant of Shem, but other aspects are obscure. Surely Ham deserved the curse, not Ham's son? It may be that God's blessing of Noah's sons (9:1) precluded him from cursing Ham himself. It may be that the punishment mirrors the offense: Ham was Noah's youngest son, so his youngest son Canaan is cursed. Or it may be that Ham's attitude anticipates that of his descendants, such as the Egyptians and Canaanites, who by OT standards were notorious for sexual impropriety (Lev 18:3).

9:27 "Let Japheth live in the tents of Shem." All sorts of improbable suggestions have been made about what this refers to. There is no obvious situation in which Shemites and Japhethites were in league against Canaan, unless perhaps Genesis 14 is its fulfillment. Elam descended from Shem (10:22) and Goiim ("coastland peoples") from Japheth (10:5), and both conquered a league of Canaanites (14:1-2).

Though the precise referent of Noah's prophecies is obscure, however, they do serve to suggest the future shape of relationships between groups of peoples, the subject of the next chapter.

Bibliography. Hess, R. S., and D. T. Tsumura. 1994, articles by Anderson and Wenham • Ska, J. L. 1994, "El relato del diluvio," *EstBib* 52:37-62 • Wenham, G. J. 1991, "Method in Pentateuchal Source Criticism," *VT* 41:84-109.

From Flood to Folly (J and P) (10:1–11:9)

Like the second section of Genesis (5:1–6:8), this fourth section begins with a heading, "These are the descendants of," and combines a longish genealogical list with a summary of universal judgment. It begins with a mention of the flood (Heb. *mabbul*) and ends with the similar-sounding word Babel (here associated with "confusion" or "folly"); hence the attempted alliteration in my title of this section. As in 5:1–6:8, a positive account of the increase in human population (cf. 9:1, 7) is followed by a tale of man's attempt to bridge the human-divine barrier, this time by building a skyscraper; in 6:1-4 marriage between gods and humans was the approach. This time judgment does not take the form of a flood, but of dispersion of the peoples over the globe and confusion of their languages.

This dispersal is already hinted at in the Table of Nations (10:1-32), which alludes to their spread across the world (10:5, 25, 32). As elsewhere in Genesis, the nonelect groups are treated before the group associated with the chosen line (here Japheth and Ham before Shem, in ch. 4 Cain before Seth, in ch. 25 Ishmael before Isaac, and in chs. 36–37 Esau before Jacob).

Ethnographically, this Table of Nations is without parallel in the ancient world. It is unique in setting out the relationship between Israel's neighbors and its relation to them. To oversimplify the table, we may say that the Japhethite peoples are those on Israel's geographical horizon with whom it had the least to do. The Hamites include Israel's bitterest enemies, from Assyria in the east to the Egyptians in the west and the Canaanites and Philistines in between. From the Shemites Israel traced not only its own descent but also that of friendly nations such as the Arameans and Arabs. The positive evaluation of the Shemites on the one hand and the negative view of the Hamites on the other indicates how this Table of Nations shows the fulfillment of Noah's blessings and curses in 9:25-27.

Linguists often speak of Semitic and Hamitic languages, but it should be noted that language is not the basis for the categorization of peoples in this table. Several of the Hamites speak Semitic languages (e.g., Canaan, Assyria), while at least one of the Shemites (Elam) speaks a non-Semitic language. Theological politics is the basis of these divisions, not linguistics. Many of these people or places cannot be identified with certainty, so degrees of doubt will be indicated in brackets. For further discussion of the identifications larger commentaries must be consulted.

The Table of Nations (10:1-32)

10:2-5 The Japhethites lived to the north and west of Israel. V. 2: Gomer (Cimmerians), Magog (in Anatolia?), Madai (Medes), Javan (Ionian Greeks), Tubal and Meshech (in Anatolia), Tiras (from Asia Minor). V. 3: Ashkenaz (Scythians), Riphat (near the Black Sea?), Togarmah (north of Carchemish). V. 4: Elishah (city in Crete?), Tarshish (Carthage?), Kittim (Cyprus), Rodanim (Rhodes?), but MT reads Dodanim (Dodona in Greece?)

10:6-20 The Hamites include some of Israel's most dangerous enemies, including Assyria, Egypt, and Canaan. The uniting factor is that the descendants of Ham are under the curse of 9:25.

10:6-14 V. 6: Cush (Ethiopia?), Put (Libya?). V. 7: These places may be in Arabia. Vv. 8-9: Nimrod seems to personify the fighting and hunting ideals of Mesopotamian kings. V. 10: Babel (Babylon), Erech (Uruk/Warka), Shinar (Babylonia). V. 11: Rehoboth-ir (suburb of Nineveh?), Calah (Nimrud). V. 12: Resen (Hamam Ali, south of Nineveh??). V. 13: These peoples must have lived in or near Egypt. V. 14: Pathrusim (southern Egyptians), Casluhim (one of the Sea Peoples??), Caphtorim (Cretans).

10:15-20 This is the first definition of the land of Canaan and its inhabitants in the OT. According to Egyptian texts and Numbers 34, the territory of Canaan comprised much of southern Lebanon, southwest Syria, and modern Israel. This seems to be the area envisaged here (Aharoni 1966: 69-70). It runs down the Mediterranean coast from Sidon to Gaza, across to the Dead Sea (Sodom, Gomorrah, Admah, Zeboiim and Lasha). Though not specified, the inclusion of the Zemarites (from Sumur) and Hamathites (Hamath) shows that Canaan included part of Syria. V. 15: Heth: The sons of Heth (Hittites) lived in Hebron (23:2-3). V. 16: Jebusites lived in Jerusalem (2 Sam 5:6). 10:17-18: Arkites, Sinites, Arvadites, Zemarites (inhabitants of Phoenician coastal cities).

10:21-31 Following the convention of Genesis, the family of the chosen line of Shem comes last. The longer genealogy of Shem to Abram (11:10-26) is anticipated too (10:22, 24, 25). Insofar as the names in Shem's line can be identified, they seem to represent peoples well disposed to Israel. For example, Eber is the eponymous ancestor of all the Ibri or Hebrews (10:21).

10:22 Elam (east of Mesopotamia); Asshur, presumably not Assyria (cf. v. 11), but a Sinai tribe of that name (cf. Num 24:22; 2 Sam 2:9; Ps 83:8). Arpachshad (Kirkuk??), Lud (Lydia?). Aram: Israel had close relations with the Arameans who lived in Syria (cf. 25:20; 31:20; Deut 26:5), but their descendants (v. 23) are hard to locate. Vv. 26-29 are mostly names of places or tribes in southern Arabia or the Yemen. V. 30 presumably mentions places in southern Arabia.

Bibliography. Aharoni, Y. 1966, *The Land of the Bible,* London: Burns & Oates • Hess, R. S., and D. T. Tsumura. 1994, articles by Simons, Speiser, and Wiseman.

11:1-9 The conjunction of the tower of Babel and the Table of Nations illustrates again how human progress in populating the earth and building skyscraper-like ziggurats may lead to hubris and judgment. Babel is the scene of the last great universal judgment on mankind in primeval history. The attempt by man to reach up to heaven is thwarted by the divine decree confusing human languages, making cooperation by the human race on godless projects impossible. Throughout the Bible Babylon is viewed as the great anti-God power (cf. Isa 14:13-15; Dan 2:38; Rev 18:4, 20). Here her folly and impotence before the Almighty are strikingly revealed.

No close oriental parallels to the tower of Babel story

are known. As with Genesis 2–3, it is more a case of familiar Mesopotamian motifs being reused in a final rejection of Babylonian religion and its pretensions. For example, Babel literally means "gate of the god," that is, there you were closer to the gods than anywhere else on earth. It was a commonplace of Babylonian mythology that temples had their roots in the underworld and their tops reached up to heaven (cf. 11:4). But Genesis mocks these ideas. Far from the temple tower reaching heaven, the LORD had to come down just to see it (11:5). Babel does not mean "gate of the god" but "confusion" or "folly" (the Hebrew words "let us confuse" [11:7] and "folly" are almost the same).

According to the Sumerian epic "Enmerkar and the Lord of Aratta" there would come a time when all nations would speak one language — Sumerian — proof of the ultimate triumph of that culture and its religion. But as elsewhere, Genesis contradicts this Mesopotamian optimism; indeed, the home of such human arrogance is the place where it was judged. It was at Babel that God confused the one language of humanity, preventing future cooperation on such ventures and leading to the dispersal of races across the earth. Thus the diversity of human languages, like the pain of childbirth and the toil of agriculture, is a reminder of divine judgment on human sin. But Babel, symbol of universal judgment, is the setting for the beginning of the story of salvation, for Ur, the home of Abraham, is not far south of Babylon.

11:2 "Shinar": cf. 10:10.

Bibliography. Hess, R. S., and D. T. Tsumura. 1994, articles by Kramer and Sasson.

11:10-26 (P) The genealogy of Shem is the fifth section in Genesis to be introduced by the formula, "These are the descendants of . . ." (cf. 2:4; 5:1; 6:9; 10:1). Five more follow, introducing each section of the patriarchal history (e.g., 11:27; 37:2). This genealogy is the first of three which preface the patriarchal narratives. This one precedes the story of Abraham (11:27–25:11), 25:12-18 precedes the story of Jacob and Esau (25:19–35:29), and 36:1–37:1 comes before the Joseph story (37:2–50:26).

On the other hand, its form connects it most closely with what precedes, for it closely resembles the genealogy in ch. 5. The formulae of each rung of the genealogy are like those of the earlier one. There are ten generations from Shem to Abram, as there are from Adam to Noah. The penultimate father in each genealogy has three sons — Shem, Ham, and Japheth, and Abram, Nahor, and Haran. Both genealogies are briefly inaugurated in the preceding section (4:25-26; 10:24-25). In other words, the genealogy of Shem acts as a bridge tying the primeval history and the patriarchal together.

When the genealogies in ch. 5 and 11 are compared, they reveal two obvious differences. First, the closing formulae, "Thus all the days of X were . . ." (e.g., 5:8, 11, 14), are missing in ch. 11. Second, the life spans of the later people are noticeably shorter. This contrast between the ante- and postdiluvians is also evident in the Sumerian King List. In Genesis it illustrates the gradual implementation of the threat to reduce the span of human life to 120 years (6:3).

The Abraham Cycle (11:27–25:11)

With the story of Abraham Genesis changes gears. The tales are no longer pan-oriental traditions retold from a monotheistic standpoint, but stories peculiar to Israel tracing the origins of the nation back to the early second millennium. The historicity of these patriarchal traditions has been much discussed, and there is little sign of the emergence of a firm scholarly consensus. In the mid-twentieth century mainline critics and more conservative scholars may have disagreed about the date of Genesis's composition, but they were sure that many of the stories originated in the period in which they are set, namely, the second millennium BC. It was pointed out that the names of the patriarchs were old-fashioned names beloved of the Amorites. Many of the family customs attested in Genesis could be paralleled in legal texts from Babylon, Nuzi, and other early sites. The migrations of the patriarchs were compatible with the political situation of that time too. Thus whether these stories were committed to writing in the time of Moses, the age of Solomon, or much later, we could be confident that the patriarchs were historical figures (e.g., de Vaux, Bright, and Westermann).

However, in the last quarter of the century skepticism about the historicity of the patriarchs became more common. It was pointed out that the arguments for the age of the traditions were at points shaky, especially those based on legal parallels and archeological remains. When these doubts were coupled with a tendency to date the earliest part of Genesis, the J source, to the late sixth century BC, the whole of the book could be regarded as fiction (so Thompson and Van Seters).

Space does not permit a review of these arguments here; it simply allows me to state a position. It may well be that the scholarly pendulum swung too far from excessive historical credulity to an equally unjustified skepticism. The way that Genesis portrays patriarchal religion as different from later Mosaic religion and the conflict between patriarchal practice and later law is hardly likely to have been created by a novelist who believed in the law and worship as prescribed in the Pentateuch. He surely would have wanted the fathers of the nation to conform to later orthodox practice if he were simply inventing them (Moberly).

But whether modern scholars regard these stories as historical or not, there is no doubt that the author of Genesis intended them to be read that way. And generations of readers have supposed them to be about real people, the earliest ancestors of Israel. To grasp the intention of the writers, therefore, we need to read them, at least to start with, this way as well.

Other clues to the writers' standpoint are apparent from a review of the material in Genesis. First, we should note the bulk of the material relating to the patriarchs, especially Jacob, whose life story spans chs. 25 to 50, more than half the book. Whereas Christian readers have often been most interested in the opening chapters of the book with their focus on creation, sin, and the fall and in Abraham as a model of faith, the book itself is most interested in Jacob. His name was later changed to Israel, and he fathered the twelve tribes. This indicates the chief interest of the book, the origins of the nation of Israel and its place in the divine purpose. Chs. 1–11 serve to set the scene for the main plot, the story of the family of Jacob.

Second, the main narrative of the patriarchs is split into three major sections: 11:27–25:11 (the story of Abraham), 25:19–35:29 (the story of Jacob and Esau), and 37:2–50:26 (the story of Jacob's sons). Each begins with the title, "These are the descendants of . . ." (or, better, as in 37:2), "This is the story of the family of. . . ." Though the Hebrew is the same, the NRSV varies the translation. Then, too, each section ends with the death and burial of the major figure by his surviving sons (Isaac and Ishmael bury Abraham, 25:9; Jacob and Esau bury Isaac, 35:29; and Jacob is buried by his sons, ch. 50). Between these major sections we have genealogies of the descendants outside the chosen family, Ishmael (25:12-18) and Esau (Edom) (36:1–37:1). These genealogies have the same title, "These are the descendants of . . . ," as the major sections. This alternation of long narratives and short genealogies is also the pattern of Genesis 2–11 (see above).

Third, within each major section there are similar topics: (A) the heroes leave home (12:1; 28:2; 37:28); (B) they quarrel with their brother(s) (13:7; 27:41; 37:4); (C) they go down to Egypt (12:10; 37:28; 46:6); (D) their wives are barren and quarrel (16:1-6; 29:31–30:8); and (E) the younger son is divinely favored (17:18-19; 25:23; 48:14; 49:8-12, 22-26). There is a similar sequence of topics toward the end of each section, namely: (A) divine promise (22:15-18; 35:9-14; 48:4); (B) journey (22:19; 35:16; 48:5); (C) birth of sons (22:20-24; 35:17-18; 48:5-6); (D) burial of wife (23:1-20; 35:18-20; 48:7); (E) son's marriage (24:1-67; 35:21-22; 48:8-9; cf. 49:3-4); (F) list of descendants (25:1-6; 35:22-26; 49:3-28); and (G) patriarch's death and burial (25:7-10; 35:27-29; 49:29–50:14). Some of these parallels are merely coincidental, but their frequency suggests that the writer was deliberately inviting the reader to compare the experience of one patriarch with that of another. Within chs. 12–25 there is a loose palistrophic structure (cf. flood story); for example, ch. 22 echoes ch. 12, chs. 18–19 echo chs. 13–14, and ch. 17 echoes ch. 15. This type of pattern is even clearer in the stories of Jacob and Esau in chs. 25–35, but it is not apparent in chs. 37–50, the Joseph story (see Rendsburg and Wenham, 1:262-63; 2:169).

Recurrent patterns and parallels highlight the constancy of God's purposes on the one hand and human failings on the other. But a fourth feature of these cycles is the development of plot and characterization from one to another. In Genesis 1–11 God is the chief actor in almost all the stories, but in the patriarchal stories he progressively retreats into the background. He often speaks to Abraham, more rarely to Isaac and Jacob, and to Joseph only indirectly through dreams. This is not to say that God is absent from the Joseph story; indeed, the whole narrative has been termed a story of divine providence. But there is clearly a development in the way God speaks to man from one cycle to the next. At the narrative level the personalities of the patriarchs are more sharply defined from one cycle to the next. In the Abraham story we have a series of snapshots; with the Jacob and Esau stories we can almost construct a biography; but with Joseph and his brothers we have a well-integrated family tale whose personalities come vividly to life.

Finally, each patriarchal cycle begins with a divine revelation which sets out the program for the ensuing narrative: 12:1, "Go to the land"; 25:23, "The elder shall serve the younger"; and 37:5-11, Joseph's dreams, which envisage his family bowing down to him. However, the first passage (12:1-3) is the most important in that it sets out not simply the program of Abraham's career but the theme of the whole Pentateuch, which Clines has aptly defined as the partial fulfillment of the promises to the patriarchs. Here Abraham is promised a new land, descendants to inherit it, divine blessing and protection, and that through him all nations will find blessing. These promises are clarified, amplified, and made even more specific later on (see 12:7; 13:14-17; 15:4-21; 17:1-21; 22:16-18; 26:2-5; 28:13-15; 46:3-4), and all the narratives from Genesis 12 onward need to be read to see how the action in them promotes or hinders the fulfillment of these promises. But they also relate back to the narratives in Genesis 1–11, which show a world in dire need of divine blessing. These chapters tell of two false starts to human history, the first headed by Adam, the second by Noah. The first ends with universal judgment in the flood, the second with universal dispersal at Babel. The call of Abraham represents a third attempt to cure the human condition, but this time success is guaranteed, for "in you all the families of the earth shall be blessed" (12:3). When and how are not stated, but this and the associated promises should be constantly in the back of the reader's mind as he or she tries to make sense of the rest of Genesis.

Bibliography. Clines. 1978 • Hess, R. S., P. E. Satterthwaite, and G. J. Wenham, eds. 1993, *He Swore an Oath: Biblical Themes from Genesis 12–50,* Cambridge: Tyndale House • Moberly 1992a, 1992b • Rendsburg, G. A. 1986, *The Redaction of Genesis,* Winona Lake: Eisenbrauns • Seters, J. Van. 1975, *Abraham in History and Tradition,* New Haven: Yale University • Vaux, R. de. 1978, *The Early History of Israel,* trans. D. Smith, London: Darton, Longman and Todd.

The Call of Abram (J and P) (11:27–12:9)

This key section begins by explaining Abram's family situation, which may be displayed as a family tree

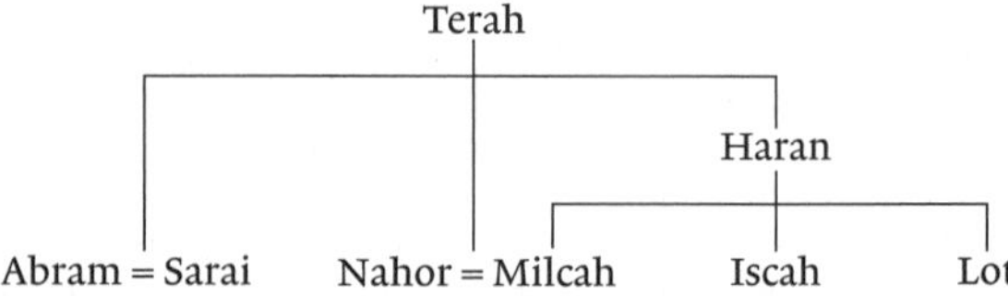

Haran died before Terah and the rest of the family left Ur, so it appears that Lot was adopted by his uncle Abram, or at least joined his entourage. Note that this section is headed "These are the descendants of Terah." Although Abra(ha)m is the central and most active person, he was part of Terah's extended family until Terah died 135 years after the birth of Abram just two years before the death of Sarai (11:26, 32; 23:1). Thus for most of the period covered by Genesis 12–25 Terah was head of the family. Similarly, the titles of 25:19 and 37:2 mention the head of the family, not the leading actors in the subsequent stories. 11:30 mentions Sarai's infertility, another crucial element in the following story. Ur in southern Mesopotamia and Haran in the north were both centers of the moon god Sin, and it may not be coincidence that the names Terah, Sarai, and Milcah were all connected with this religion.

12:1-3 As already mentioned, these verses are not merely programatic for the Abraham stories, but they sum up the theme of the Pentateuch. The hard command to leave his home (12:1) is later echoed in the last divine command to Abraham in 22:2. In both cases there is an initial vagueness about what is required: the "land/mountain that I will show you." But later speeches (e.g., 17:8; cf. 12:5) show that the land being promised was Canaan, a land defined by Egyptian texts as comprising roughly modern Israel, Lebanon, and part of Syria.

The command to go and the promise of land are followed by further promises of numerous descendants (cf. 13:16; 15:5), blessing, and fame, and yet more blessing. Blessing (Heb. *brk*) occurs more frequently in Genesis than in any other book of the Bible. Lists of blessings (e.g., Lev 26:3-13; Deut 28:1-14) show that blessing meant long life, many children, good harvests, peace, and God's presence. Indeed, the name Abraham is almost a pun on blessing, for it contains two of the same consonants. Here he is told that he will be a blessing, that is, people looking at him will say, "May God bless me like Abraham." Further, the LORD says that those who do this will themselves be blessed, and the few (NRSV, "one") who disdain him will be cursed, that is, punished by God. But ultimately all the families (the term refers to quite large groups; 10:5, 18, 20) of the earth will find blessing in him.

12:4-9 records Abram's radical obedience. Uprooting himself and his family, he shortly arrives in Canaan. He is rewarded by a fresh and more specific statement of the promise as "the land I will show you" becomes "this land." Abram himself responds by building altars and invoking the name of the LORD, that is, worships through the offering of prayer and sacrifice (cf. 4:26). Bethel and Ai, usually identified with Beitin and Et-Tell, are about ten miles north of Jerusalem.

Abram in Egypt (J) (12:10-20)

Radical obedience is now followed by craven unbelief. This is the first of three stories where a patriarch describes his wife as his sister and nearly loses her to a foreign king (cf. 20:1-18; 26:1-11). This episode foreshadows the later experience of the nation of Israel in that, when they became aliens in Egypt, the life of their males was endangered, the girls were spared, and they all escaped with the wealth of the Egyptians, though only after plagues had been inflicted on Pharaoh. However, in this case the behavior of Pharaoh is much less blameworthy than that of his successor. Here he sounds genuinely shocked at the way he has been misled (cf. 20:9; 26:10), whereas the Pharaoh of Moses' day persisted in holding Israel despite repeated warnings. Nevertheless, Abram emerges from Egypt relatively unscathed, surely reflecting the divine promise of blessing.

However, this does not justify his behavior in the writer's eyes. Having been promised the land of Canaan in 12:7, he should not have contemplated settling in Egypt as an immigrant, as the Hebrew word *ger* ("alien"; v. 10) implies, nor, given the divine assurance of protection in v. 3, should he have been so worried about his safety, let alone assumed Egyptian immorality (cf. vv. 18-19).

Modern readers are most perplexed at how Sarai could be regarded as so attractive at age 65 (cf. 12:4; 17:17), and why Abram thought describing as his sister would save him from danger. There are no obvious solutions to these problems. Oriental men doubtless preferred well-endowed, matronly figures to slim girls, and it may be that the narrator considers that, if Sarah could give birth at ninety albeit miraculously, she must have still been attractive to men twenty-five years earlier. By describing Sarai as his sister Abram may have hoped to avoid offense by not refusing her hand to a would-be husband but to spin out any negotiations for her marriage for such a long time that nothing would happen. For other examples of such delaying tactics by brothers cf. 24:55; 34:13-17. Unfortunately this plan did not work with Pharaoh, who brooked no delay!

Back to Canaan (J, P) (13:1-18)

Foreshadowing the later exodus from Egypt, Abram leaves with all his family and property and, like his successors, "journeys by stages" through the Sinai wilderness into the dry region of southern Canaan known as the Negeb. He eventually reaches Bethel, where once again he offers sacrifice and worships. His return to this place of promise (cf. 12:7) and his silence after the Pharaonic rebuke in 12:19 suggest that he is intent on making a new start.

His changed attitude emerges more clearly in his generous treatment of his nephew Lot in the dispute about grazing rights. Abram allows Lot to pick the area he would like. Lot chooses the greenest area in the Jordan valley, near Sodom and Gomorrah, because it looked like Eden, "the garden of the LORD," and more ominously like the land of Egypt. If Sodom and Gomorrah were on the east bank of the Dead Sea, at or near Bab ed-Dhra, this means that Lot was moving out of the land of Canaan promised to Abram. That this was an unwise choice is noted by the narrator, who anticipates the cities' later destruction because of their wicked inhabitants (13:10, 13).

Lot's move is followed by a reaffirmation of the divine promises to Abram. They are introduced by the verbs "separate," "raise your eyes," and "look" used earlier of Abram's invitation to Lot in vv. 9-10, implying that the promises are a response to Abram's faith and generosity. But these promises are more than a restatement of what was said earlier; they go well beyond the formulations in

12:1-3, 7, "*all* the land . . . I will give to you and your offspring *forever*." What is more, Abram's offspring will not just be a great nation but uncountable, "like the dust of the earth." Finally, Abram is invited to "walk through the length and breadth of the land," a symbolic gesture for taking possession of it.

The episode closes with Abram settling in Hebron, about twenty miles south of Jerusalem. The traditional location of the oaks of Mamre is two miles north of Hebron. This is the setting of much of the subsequent Abraham story. Here the promises will be further elaborated, and here the patriarchs and their wives will be buried. But as usual Abram makes his campsite a sanctuary by building an altar and, though not said here, offering a sacrifice.

Abram Rescues Lot (pre-J?) (14:1-24)

This chapter is distinctive in its style, in its portrayal of Abraham, and in its historical and geographic detail. It thus poses peculiar problems for historical critics, who sharply disagree about its source and its historicity: some regard it as based on a very early document, while others see it as a late fictional midrash. These issues cannot be discussed fully here, and longer commentaries need to be consulted. Here the focus is on the place of this episode within the present book of Genesis.

This chapter tells of three military campaigns in Canaan by kings of the east. Lot is captured in the second, and this leads to Abraham's intervention in the third. And it is the successful outcome of this campaign that forms the backdrop to the theologically most important scene, Abram's encounter with Melchizedek, king of Salem, and Bera, king of Sodom. Their very different attitudes to Abram, one blessing him and the other disdaining him, presage their contrasting fates (cf. 12:3): Melchizedek represents the first of all the families of the earth who find blessing in Abraham, while the disdainful king of Sodom will experience the curse associated with despisers of Abram in the destruction of his city.

14:1-4 tell of the campaign of four eastern kings against five kings of the Dead Sea valley. The sites of Sodom, Gomorrah, Admah, Zeboiim, and Zoar are uncertain. They have often been supposed to lie beneath the southern shallow part of the Dead Sea, for in this region there is a smell of sulphur (cf. 19:24), and asphalt deposits are most abundant there (cf. 14:10). However, no cities have been found there. More recently five sites on the eastern shore occupied in the third millennium have been discovered; one of them, Bab ed-Dhra, was finally abandoned around 2100 BC. This is rather early for the time of Abraham, but its destruction could be the basis of the story of Sodom.

All sorts of identities have been proposed for the eastern kings and their countries of origin. Amraphel is not Hammurabi, but he does come from Babylonia, or "Shinar" (cf. 10:10). Arioch seems to be a Hurrian name *(Ariwuku),* and Ellasar may be Pontus in Asia Minor. Chedorlaomer sounds like a good Elamite name, and Elam (cf. 10:22) lies east of Mesopotamia in modern Iran. Tidal is probably Hittite *tudhaliya,* but it is uncertain whether Goiim is a designation of the Hittites or a wider grouping of peoples. Unfortunately, though some individuals with these names are known, it is impossible to link them all together at the same time, let alone in the same campaigns, and so locate their campaign chronologically. This does not prove they did not happen, but extrabiblical evidence for this period is too sparse and this account does not allow us to fix the period of Abraham precisely.

14:5-12 The second campaign is described in more detail, partly because Lot was captured in it and partly to show the strength of the forces overcome by Abram. Led by Chedorlaomer, the kings struck southward, defeating a variety of peoples (Rephaim, Zuzim, and Emim) occupying towns on the King's Highway, the main north-south route through Transjordan. When they reached El-Paran, probably Eilat at the head of the Red Sea, they swung westward through the northern Sinai peninsula to Kadesh, probably Ain Hudeirat, a large oasis on the borders of Canaan. They then headed northeast to Hazazon-tamar, which must lie somewhere between Kadesh and the Dead Sea.

The battle with the Dead Sea kings is described briefly, suggesting a rout. It is not clear whether the defeated kings hid in the bitumen pits or whether falling in means that they were trapped and died in the pits. In that the king of Sodom reappears in 14:17, it cannot imply his death. Because Lot now lived in Sodom (he was not in 13:12), he was carried away captive.

14:13-16 From Abram's pursuit it is apparent that the kings were fleeing northward to Dan and then on beyond Damascus. His decisive defeat of them after their series of triumphs over all their other opponents demonstrates that God is on his side. It is striking that Abram could raise 318 fighting men from his group, which would imply that there were at least a thousand people in his clan. However, the quarrel with Lot over grazing rights, his treaty with Abimelech (21:22-34), his title "mighty prince" (23:6), and the mention of his concubines (25:6) all point to his heading a sizable clan.

14:17-24 Abram's reception by Melchizedek and the king of Sodom is the climax of the episode. Its theological significance has already been briefly addressed, but details deserve further comment. Salem is probably Jerusalem (cf. Pss 76:2; 110:2-4). Melchizedek treats Abraham to a royal banquet of bread and wine and then blesses him in the name of El Elyon. El was the high creator God in the Canaanite pantheon, as the epithet "maker of heaven and earth" shows. In response Abram gives Melchizedek a tithe of all his booty. If Melchizedek is viewed as a representative of Jerusalem, this episode bodes well for future relations between that city and later Israel. It may also serve to justify the payment of tithes to the city. If Abram did this, then his descendants should do so too.

By contrast, the king of Sodom, for whom Abram has done much more than he did for Melchizedek, appears ungrateful and grasping. There is no meal offered or blessing pronounced, just a brusque demand. Abram assures him that he is not out to profit from rescuing the people of Sodom; only his warriors will take the regular share of the booty. Given that attitudes to Abram and his offspring are seen in 12:3 as a touchstone of divine benevolence, Sodom's surliness bodes ill for the future.

The Covenant Promise (J/[E]) (15:1-21)

Abram's public triumph over the eastern kings cannot expunge the private tragedy of his childlessness, which was viewed as a disaster in the ancient world. Without children there was no one to carry on the family name, preserve the inheritance, care for you in old age, or carry out the funerary rites for the repose of your soul after death. In Abram's case there was an added poignancy in that he had been promised children by God (12:2, 7; 13:16), yet nothing had happened. It still looks as though Eliezer, one of his household (not necessarily a slave, *pace* NRSV), will inherit from him. In other words, Abram will have to adopt him if he has not done so already.

In response to this the LORD promises Abram a real son and heir fathered by himself. At this point the mother is not specified. Though the reader assumes that Sarah will bear the child, this is not made explicit till 17:16. In ch. 16 we see that Abram and Sarai thought of other possibilities. However, Abram did at least believe he would father a child, and "the LORD reckoned it to him as righteousness" (15:6). Righteousness normally means living a good life and keeping the commands of the law (Ezek 18:5). It is the righteous who are acquitted by God (e.g., Ps 1:6). But here most unusually it is faith in the promise that counts as righteousness, a point to which St. Paul draws attention in Romans 4 and Galatians 3.

This faith prompts a reaffirmation of the land promise (15:7). Again Abram asks for confirmation, and he is asked to produce a number of animals usually used in sacrifice, kill them, cut them in two, and lay them in two lines. Then when darkness fell, Abram heard a prophetic explanation of the Egyptian slavery and subsequent exodus, and saw a smoking fire pot, evidently symbolizing the presence of God, pass between the pieces. Then the extent of the land his descendants will possess is further explained: it will stretch from the Euphrates in the north to the river of Egypt in the south (whether Wadi el-Arish or the Nile is not clear), boundaries that were only achieved by the Davidic empire (vv. 18-21).

The significance of the ceremony of the bisected animals and the fire pot has been much discussed. Most scholars compare the rite to the self-imprecations used in ancient treaty making. Animals were slain, and the partners to the treaty invited the gods to treat them similarly if they were unfaithful to it. In other words, the LORD is invoking a curse on himself should he not fulfill his promise. Another way of reading the ceremony is based on the identification of sacrificial animals with Israelites, a key principle in understanding OT sacrifice. In this case God is passing through the middle of his people in a symbol that anticipates the cloud of fire that appeared at Sinai and accompanied their wilderness wanderings. In other words, the smoking fire pot symbolizes God's presence with the future descendants of Israel as they proceed to the promised land. This interpretation fits in with the message to Abraham about the exodus and conquest in vv. 13-16 and 18-21. According to Lev 11:13-19, "birds of prey" are unclean and therefore represent foreign powers, perhaps in this context Egypt. In other words, it was Abram's faith, displayed in driving off the birds, that preserved his descendants from annihilation in Egypt.

Bibliography. Williamson, P. R. 2000, *Abraham, Israel and the Nations,* Sheffield: Sheffield Academic.

The Birth of Ishmael (J/P) (16:1-16)

Ten years after the promise of descendants had first been made to Abram, there was still no progress, so Sarai decides to take the initiative. The two usual approaches to childlessness in the ancient Near East were to take a second wife (cf. 1 Sam 1:1-2) or surrogate marriage, whereby a slave girl bore a child for her mistress. This had the advantage of avoiding the problems inherent in bigamy, and the child counted as the wife's, not the slave-girl's. But the narrator hints that this is not God's way. He does so, first, by the way Sarai blames God for her predicament, "The LORD has prevented me. . . ." Second, he hints through the way the story echoes Genesis 3, with Sarai taking and giving (cf. 3:6) and Abram listening to her voice (cf. 3:17). Finally, the bitter conflict that ensues between Sarai and Hagar when the latter conceives hardly suggests that the scheme is approved by God.

Hagar is the victim of Sarai's scheming and Abram's acquiescence, and the LORD steps in to rescue her. This is the first appearance of the angel of the LORD in the Bible; it is the human form in which God appears to people, most often in times of crisis (cf. 21:17; 22:11). Often the angel is initially mistaken for a man (18:2; Judg 6:11-22). His demand here that she should return to Sarai sounds harsh, but it is coupled with the first statement of the promises directly to a woman (16:10; cf. 15:5). This is also the first birth oracle, "you have conceived and shall bear a son and shall call his name," a formula that regularly announces the birth of saviors within the Bible (cf. Judg 13:3; Isa 7:14; Luke 1:31). Finally, his name, typical of early Amorite names, means "God [El] has heard." These promises are then rounded off by a prophecy of Ishmael's bedouin lifestyle (cf. 25:18); the wild ass, more like a horse than a donkey, is used elsewhere of a free, unconventional way of life (Jer 2:24).

Hagar gratefully acknowledges God's concern for her by naming him "El-roi," that is, "God, who sees me," for she said, "Truly here I have seen him who looks after me" (so ESV, Booij, and Koenen as opposed to the NRSV). In due course her son was born, but contrary to Sarai's plan, Ishmael did not count as her child, but Hagar's. Three times in two verses the narrator underlines that "*Hagar* bore Abram a son" (16:15-16). God cannot be manipulated.

Bibliography. Booij, T. 1980, "Hagar's Words in Gen 16:13b," *VT* 30:1-7 • Koenen, K. 1988, "Wer sieht wen? Zur Textgeschichte von Gen 16:13," *VT* 38:468-74.

The Covenant of Circumcision (P) (17:1-27)

This chapter represents a high point in the Abraham story. It contains five divine speeches reaffirming and elaborating the promises in the most categorical terms. Abram and Sarai's names are changed to the more familiar Abraham and Sarah. There is little difference in meaning between the old and new names, but the name change marks God's intention that they will both share in the creation of nations. Finally, the rite of circumcision is introduced as a pledge of the eternal covenant between God and Abraham's descendants.

17:1-8 begin with the LORD introducing himself as El Shaddai, God Almighty, the older name of God according to Exod 6:3. Its etymology and meaning are obscure, but wherever it is used in Genesis it is associated with the promise of descendants. And almost immediately the promise of descendants is reaffirmed. On earlier occasions Abraham had been assured that he would become a nation and that his descendants would be too many to count. Now he is assured that he will be the father of many nations and that kings would be descended from him. What is more, the covenant made with him would be everlasting, and as a corollary the land, here designated Canaan for the first time in a speech, is designated as his offspring's perpetual holding.

17:9-14 This statement of the promises, however, requires a response. Abraham must walk before God and be blameless, a high calling rarely attained by OT heroes (cf. 5:22; 6:9; Job 1:1). What is more, he and all his male offspring must submit to the rite of circumcision. Though women are full members of the covenant people and are expected to keep most aspects of the law, male participation in positive religious duties is especially stressed in the OT and later Judaism, and the command to circumcise men alone is of a piece with this attitude.

Circumcision was practiced by other peoples of the ancient orient, including the Egyptians, Canaanites, and Arabs, but not by the Philistines or Hivites (34:2, 14). Only in Israel was it a sign of the covenant, that is, a reminder to them of their obligation to keep the law and love the LORD with all their heart, soul, and strength. So important was the sign that failure to be circumcised could lead to that man being cut off, that is, suffer a premature death sent by God. The episode thus ends with Abraham circumcising himself and all the members of his household "that very day," a phrase that marks the event as a turning point in saving history, comparable to the flood or the exodus from Egypt (7:13; cf. Exod 12:17).

However, before that comes the most astonishing formulation of the promise, this time that the elderly Sarah would bear a child. Abraham had obviously concluded that thirteen-year-old Ishmael was the promised child (17:18). He had given up hope that Sarah would conceive. His very laughter at the idea, however, is an inadvertent confirmation of it, for "and laughed" in Hebrew also spells "and Isaac." Like Jacob and Ishmael, Isaac is a typical early-second-millennium Amorite name. It probably is a shortened form of the phrase "El [God] laughs/smiles," but it could refer to the father's joy — "He laughs" (cf. 21:6). Not only is it now specified that Sarah will be the mother of the promised child, but for the first time his birth date is announced, "at this season next year." Once again the new form of the promise is not a mere repetition of what has been said before but a development making the promise more specific and firm.

Bibliography. McEvenue, S. E. 1971, *The Narrative Style of the Priestly Writer,* Rome: Biblical Institute.

Abraham, Lot, and Sodom (J) (18:1–19:38)

No period of twenty-four hours in Abraham's life is described more fully than this. This suggests the importance of this episode in the plot of the Abraham story; yet on first reading it seems rather a sidetrack. It begins with the renewed promise of a son for Sarah (18:1-15), which seems redundant in the light of ch. 17, continues with Abraham's abortive intercession for Sodom (18:16-33), and describes Lot's last hours in and escape from Sodom (19:1-29) and finally his intercourse with his daughters, leading to the birth of Moab and Ben-Ammi (19:30-38). It is not immediately apparent what all these events have to do with the theme of Genesis, the partial fulfillment of the promises.

This section is not only long, but it is tightly organized. The central section concerning Sodom is a large palistrophe, like the flood story in Genesis 6–8 (see above):

A) Visitors look toward Sodom (18:16)
- B) God's reflections on Abraham and Sodom (18:17-21)
  - C) Abraham pleads for Sodom (18:22-33)
    - D) Angels arrive in Sodom (19:1-3)
      - E) Assault on Lot and visitors (19:4-11)
        - F) Sodom's destruction foretold (19:12-13)
      - E′) Lot's sons-in-law reject appeal (19:14)
    - D′) Departure from Sodom (19:15-16)
  - C′) Lot pleads for Zoar (19:17-22)
- B′) Sodom and Gomorrah destroyed (19:23-26)

A′) Abraham looks toward Sodom (19:27-28)

This mirror-image pattern is further enhanced by the opening section (18:1-15) discussing the birth of a child to Sarah, and the closing section (19:30-38) describing the birth of children to Lot's daughters.

But it is not just the structure of these chapters that recalls the flood story; their topic is similar too. Both are tales of universal judgment from which only one man and his family escape. Furthermore, the terminology of chs. 18–19 echoes the flood story ("destroy," 18:28, 31, etc.; cf. 6:13, 17; "reach out their hands," 19:10; cf. 8:9; "shutting the door," 19:10; cf. 7:16; "find favor with," 19:19; cf. 6:8; "save life," 19:19; cf. 6:19, 20; "preserve offspring," 19:32, 34; cf. 7:3; "rain," 19:24; cf. 7:4). Finally, "God remembered Abraham" recalls "God remembered Noah" (19:29; cf. 8:1). It may also be noted that both stories conclude with a coda in which the righteous hero gets drunk and then is disgracefully abused by his son or daughters (9:20-27; 19:30-38).

So how do these chapters contribute to the theme of Genesis? First, the second announcement of the birth of

Isaac underlines the certainty that Sarah will indeed conceive. As Joseph later explained to Pharaoh, "The doubling of the dream means that the thing is fixed by God, and God will shortly bring it about" (41:32). It must also be noted that this second announcement, though ostensibly directed to Abraham, is really aimed at Sarah, quietly eavesdropping on her husband's conversation from the tent. It is now her turn to express incredulity at the news; nothing is said about Abraham's reaction.

Second, these chapters emphasize Abraham's special status in God's eyes. He asks rhetorically, "Shall I hide from Abraham what I am about to do?" (18:17). Abraham is seen as a prophet (cf. 20:7) who is privy to the secrets of the divine counsel (Jer 23:18), and then he goes on to intercede for Sodom: intercession for sinners is a key prophetic activity (Exodus 32; 1 Sam 12:23; Jer 14:11; 15:1). And the LORD is ready to answer his prayer: if there had been only ten righteous people in Sodom, it would have been spared. Unfortunately, as ch. 19 makes clear, there were not. "All the people to the last man" were involved in attempting to rape the visiting angels. Clearly the wickedness of Sodom typifies that of many of the Canaanite cities that were later to fall to Israel, and explains why not everyone would be blessed in Abraham, however much he interceded for them.

18:1-15 The narrator informs us that "The LORD appeared to Abraham," but to him they seemed to be just men (cf. comments on ch. 16). But later it is apparent that two of them are angels (19:1) and the other is the LORD (18:22). Though Abraham discovers their identity in the course of conversation, his treatment of them certainly befits deity as he prepares a feast of a calf and bread made with choice flour usually reserved for sacrifice (three seahs = six gallons or twenty-four liters). For Mamre (18:1) cf. 13:18.

Like Abraham in 17:17, Sarah is incredulous when she hears the promise of a son, and she laughs, another play on the name Isaac, thereby confirming the promise indirectly. It may seem odd that her disbelief is not more severely reprimanded, but the way she describes herself, "After I am worn out" (ESV), shows that her unbelief is not arrogance but despair after a lifetime of disappointment that had taught her not to clutch at straws.

18:16-33 Abraham's intercession for Sodom is one of the most remarkable in the Bible, not least in that it is for a non-Israelite community; later prophets such as Moses, Amos, and Jeremiah pray for Israel, not for other nations. It is also remarkable in being prompted by the LORD himself. He comments on Abraham's character and then remains standing before him after the angels have left. (This assumes the older reading of 18:22, NRSV footnote.)

Abraham's appeal is based on God's justice, that it would be quite wrong to treat the righteous and wicked exactly alike. V. 25 uses forensic language to stress the inequity of such a judicial sentence. Abraham begins by pleading for Sodom to be spared if it contains fifty righteous, possibly half the adult males of the town, and he then progresses down to forty-five, forty, thirty, twenty, and ten. The intercession proceeds in two cycles of three pleas. In the second cycle Abraham sounds noticeably more diffident and the LORD's replies become increasingly less encouraging, presumably prompting Abraham to ask no more. We are left to wonder whether there are ten righteous in Sodom.

19:1-14 But not for long. Righteous Lot, the only foreigner in Sodom, receives the angelic visitors as hospitably as Abraham had. Though his activities are described more briefly — "he made them a feast" and he insisted that they should stay for the night — he was just as good a host as his uncle. But it is ominous that his visitors were so reluctant to come in and that no Sodomites had welcomed him.

Soon the reason for the angels' anxiety becomes clear as a mob, "all the people" of Sodom, attempt to storm Lot's house, demanding to "know" his visitors. In itself "knowing" is quite an innocent term, but the context here makes it apparent that sexual intercourse is meant (19:8; cf. 4:1). In the ancient Near East outside Israel (cf. Lev 18:22) homosexual acts between consenting adults do not seem to have been banned, but homosexual rape was, except to humiliate prisoners of war. Everywhere it would have been regarded as abhorrent to treat guests this way; rather, there was a sacred duty to look after them. Lot's offer of his daughters shows how seriously he took his responsibility toward his guests. It also suggests little regard for his daughters. However, it is dubious whether this is an example of patriarchal sexism that would have been approved by the author or his earlier readers. Later on Jacob is implicitly censured for not taking the assault on his daughter Dinah more seriously (ch. 34). Rather, Lot's proposal illustrates his desperation: he could not think of any other way of appeasing the mob. Only the intervention of the "men," who thereby disclosed their supernatural identity, saved the situation.

If the assault on Lot's house showed his isolation within the city and that there were no righteous besides him, his sons-in-law's rejection of his appeal to escape the destruction of the city confirms it.

19:15-26 Even Lot himself and his family find it difficult to take the angelic warning seriously. They have to be dragged out of the city, then Lot protests about fleeing to the hills, and eventually he goes to Zoar instead. His wife looks back to Sodom and is turned into a pillar of salt. Though it is often surmised that this is an aetiology for the salt formations around the Dead Sea, in context it is another illustration of the divided loyalty of Lot and his family. Even the most righteous in the city are halfhearted about following divine instruction. Nevertheless, the rescue of Lot is a reminder that Abraham's prayer for the city was not entirely fruitless (19:29).

19:30-38 The final incident is both pathetic and repulsive. It invites comparison with 9:20-27. Lot eventually does settle in the hills, as he had been told (19:17). He had been a rich rancher before settling in Sodom (13:2-13); now, fearful for life itself, he retreats to the abject poverty of a cave dweller. There he is manipulated by his daughters to have intercourse with them. Their excuse (19:31) is patently false, as there were still people living in Zoar nearby. The writer clearly does not approve of their behavior (cf. 9:20-27) and records it simply to mention the origins of some of Israel's nearest neighbors, the Moabites and Ammonites, and to show what can happen to those who walk out of the covenant community and the land of promise (cf. ch. 13).

Bibliography. Wenham. 1991.

Sarah and Abimelech (E or J[?]) (20:1-18)

What an extraordinary sequel to the preceding chapter! After Abraham's intimacy with the Almighty in ch. 18 and his bold intercession for Sodom, it is astonishing to find him behaving with the same fearfulness in Gerar as he had earlier in Egypt (12:10-20). The way ch. 20 is phrased presupposes the reader's knowledge of that earlier episode. It is also noteworthy that the king of Gerar, on the southwestern border of Canaan near Egypt, should be so pious and God-fearing after the Sodomites were so godless. It is also striking that this second royal abduction of Sarah occurs shortly before the birth of Isaac.

The narrative is at pains to point out that although Abimelech had taken Sarah into his harem he never touched her, so there is no question of the parentage of Isaac. The story does imply that she did live in Abimelech's court for some time, for there was time for his wives to stop conceiving (vv. 17-18); indeed, it appears that some illness struck the court which also prevented him approaching Sarah (vv. 6-7).

The episode illustrates the faithfulness of God in keeping his promises to Abraham despite the latter's faults. Abraham and Sarah do escape from this situation physically unscathed; they are financially enriched but also justly rebuked. Abimelech indeed invites him to settle in the land, a reminder of the land promise, and through Abraham's prayers Abimelech and all his household are healed, reflecting the assurance that all the families of the earth should find blessing in Abraham. This episode reemphasizes that it is God's grace, not patriarchal faithfulness, that is the ultimate guarantee of the fulfillment of the promises.

20:1-7 V. 1: Negeb; cf. 13:1; Kadesh; cf. 14:7. V. 4: Note that the sin of the leader may affect his people (cf. 2 Sam 24). V. 7: on Abraham's prophetic intercessory role cf. the commentary on ch. 18.

Bibliography. Alexander, T. D. 1997, *Abraham in the Negev,* Carlisle: Paternoster.

Isaac Displaces Ishmael (J/E/P) (21:1-21)

At last, twenty-five years after the promise of nationhood was first announced, Isaac was born, the first visible fulfillment of the promises. The importance of his birth is underlined by its repeated mention in 21:1-2. It is followed by circumcision, demonstrating Abraham's fidelity to the covenant (17:12). Sarah expresses her own joy by breaking out into poetry with a series of plays on Isaac's name (laugh, laughter).

However, by the time Isaac was weaned at about three years old (2 Macc 7:27) attitudes had changed. Sarah noticed Ishmael Isaacing (lit. "laughing, mocking"; the NRSV's inclusion of "with her son Isaac" is unnecessary). In other words, Ishmael, now about seventeen, was pretending mockingly to be Isaac, Abraham's chosen heir. Doubtless he was displeased at the fuss being made about his baby brother, but his behavior provoked maternal ire. It also showed disregard for the divine plan that the chosen line should pass through Isaac (21:10). That is why in this case, contrary to 16:2, Abraham is told to follow Sarah's advice. Nevertheless, he is very distressed at the prospect of losing Ishmael, his first-born son, whom he had anticipated fulfilling the promises for a long time (17:18). So he shows his affection for them by giving them food and water for the journey.

Despite the NRSV, it is not necessary to suppose that Ishmael rode piggyback on Hagar's shoulders (21:14). Had that been the case, she would have been more likely to have collapsed from thirst than Ishmael, given the difficulty of carrying a skin of water, food, and a child. In fact, except where stressing the bond between parent and child, the story always refers to Ishmael as a "lad" (*na'ar*) (e.g., vv. 12, 17-20), that is, a young man up to the age of forty. This is quite compatible with his being a teenager, as 17:25 implies.

It is striking that God responds to Ishmael's prayer, not his mother's, suggesting that the one responsible for the situation had to acknowledge his responsibility before God would intervene. Though his name is not used in this story, Ishmael means "God will hear" (16:11), and as on the last occasion the angel of God addresses Hagar, making promises about his future nationhood. So just when she was expecting her son to die, she is shown a well and his life is saved. 21:20 describes Ishmael's lifestyle, already anticipated in 16:12. Then, finally, Hagar arranges a marriage for her son from among her own people, a pattern Abraham was later to follow with Isaac (cf. ch 24).

Treaty with Abimelech (E/[J]) (21:22-34)

This quiet interlude describes an incident that happened in the "many days" (v. 34) that Abraham spent in the northern Negeb between Gerar and Beer-sheba, the territory of Abimelech, last mentioned in ch. 20. It begins with Abimelech requesting Abraham to make a treaty with him and his successors because of Abraham's prosperity, evidence, according to Abimelech, that God is with him. Abraham's grudging reply (21:24) indicates that there is something wrong.

Then Abraham explains the cause of the problem, the confiscation of a well his servants had dug. As in 20:9, Abimelech protests his ignorance of the situation. A covenant is agreed upon, and Abraham presents seven lambs to Abimelech in exchange for the use of the well. This explains the meaning of Beer-sheba, "Well of the Seven" or "Well of the Oath." Though this agreement does not appear momentous, it was for Abraham, because it was the first time he had been granted permanent water rights in

Canaan, the first small step to the acquisition of the land itself. So in an act of celebratory thanksgiving he plants a tree and worships (21:33).

"Land of the Philistines" (v. 34) is strictly an anachronism, since the Philistines did not settle in Canaan till the twelfth century. It could reflect the usage of the writer's own time (cf. Dan 14:14, Ur of the Chaldees, 15:7; and the Introduction). Or it may refer to an earlier group of settlers perhaps also from Anatolia, as the name Phicol (21:22) suggests.

The Sacrifice of Isaac (J/E) (22:1-19)

Theologically and dramatically this is one of the most powerful biblical stories. Every reader can identify with the horror Abraham must have felt, though the narrator never mentions his feelings. They are simply hinted at by the frequent echoes of ch. 21, the expulsion of Ishmael, which is said to have greatly distressed Abraham (21:11). If that is how he felt about sending away his elder son, how much worse must he have felt about sacrificing his only surviving younger son, the one through whom all the promises were to be fulfilled. Whereas in ch. 21 Abraham's feelings are recorded, here they are not. Only God's description of Isaac as "your only son, whom you love" (22:2) and Abraham's cryptic comments to Isaac and his servants give any hint of his inner turmoil. Outwardly he simply and promptly obeys God's command.

Sometimes it is suggested that this story is an aetiology explaining why human sacrifice was abandoned in Israel. Such an approach is possible if the account is removed from its present context and remarks conflicting with this interpretation eliminated (e.g., Gen 22:1). Outside Israel human sacrifice was practiced from time to time, so an earlier version of the story could have had a polemical aim. However, throughout the OT human sacrifice is regarded with horror, and that is the reaction expected of the reader of the present story too.

The opening comment, "God tested Abraham" makes the reader wiser than Abraham about the nature of his ordeal. "Testing" usually involves hardship and is designed to discover what a person is really like (cf. Deut 8:2, 16). But nowhere else does God demand the sacrifice of a man's son; indeed, according to Mic 6:7 such a demand was unthinkable. A burnt offering involved the slaying of an animal and its complete incineration on the altar. The OT regards cremation of the dead as horrific (Amos 2:1), so it must have seemed incredible that God was demanding the death of a young man in this fashion. But by echoing his very first command to Abraham, "Go to the land I will show you" (12:1), in 22:2 God reminds Abraham of the nature of faithful obedience.

He does obey promptly, and on the third day he sees the appointed mountain in the distance. He leaves the servant lads behind, and he and Isaac trudge up the mountain alone, giving the climb an added poignancy. The brief dialogue heightens the feeling of uncertainty and desolation. He tells the servants: "we will worship, and then we will come back to you." Why does he say "we" and not "I"? Is this a lie to disguise his intentions, or does it indicate that he does not intend to sacrifice Isaac, or does it express hope that there will be a way out? The ambiguity may well be intentional: Abraham may not yet have decided what to do. Isaac's direct question about the identity of the sacrifice is likewise evaded: "God himself will provide." There is now less doubt that Abraham will go through with a sacrifice, but his response may simply be an attempt to hide from Isaac what he plans but still be an expression of faith, or it could be read as a prayer, "May God provide." Isaac's acceptance of Abraham's answer shows either a degree of naivety or an acceptance of his role as sacrificial victim. In both cases he constitutes the perfect innocent sufferer. "The two of them walked on together" conveys the tension as they approach the summit.

There the narrator slows down describing the preparation for the slaughter. Isaac's willingness to be bound — hence the Jewish title for this episode, the binding (*'akedah*) of Isaac — again shows his readiness to die. But then, just as in 21:17, the angel of the LORD calls from heaven with an urgent double "Abraham," and the sacrifice is called off. Like Hagar, Abraham looks and sees the solution, a ram just caught in a thicket. And like Hagar he hears the promises renewed (22:16-18; cf. 21:18). This is the last point in the Abraham cycle in which the LORD speaks to him, and it would be remarkable to suppose, as some commentators do, that originally there was no reiteration of the promises after Abraham had passed this most grueling test. In fact, they are not merely reaffirmed but developed in a strikingly new way. For the first time the promises are introduced with an oath formula (22:16). The promise of descendants is made more fulsome than before, and the prospect of the conquest of the land sounds closer, "shall possess the gate of their enemies" (v. 17). Finally, the promise of blessing to the nations is restated (v. 18). This transformation of the promises into a guarantee has come about "because you have obeyed my voice."

However, this story also explains the origin of the place name "Moriah," in later times identified with the hilltop in Jerusalem where the temple stood (2 Chr 3:1). That was the place where preeminently God could be "seen," whenever faithful Israelites offered sacrifice there. And it seems likely that this sacrifice of Abraham, of the ram instead of his son, is an archetype of OT sacrifice, where the animal suffers in place of the human worshiper. Certainly this was how the Akedah is interpreted in late Jewish texts. But already in NT times the death of Jesus is compared to the sacrifice of Isaac in passages such as John 3:16; Rom 8:31-32; 1 Pet 1:19-20.

Bibliography. Neef, H.-D. 1998, *Die Prüfung Abrahams,* Stuttgart: Calwer.

The Genealogy of Rebekah (J) (22:20-24)

This brief genealogy of Nahor, Abraham's brother (11:27), gives its purpose away by listing one girl among Nahor's descendants, Rebekah, the future wife of Isaac and mother of Jacob (cf. chs. 24, 25).

Purchase of the Cave of Machpelah (P) (23:1-20)

After Eve, Sarah is the first woman of importance in Genesis. But her life was hardly a happy one. Childless to the age of ninety, twice trapped in a foreign king's harem by her husband's folly, and taunted by her slave-girl and stepson, last but not least she watched her only son taken off to be sacrificed by her husband. Did he really care for her? she must have wondered. But at least after her death, he showed his love by acquiring a large burial ground for her and interring her in style. Indeed, her husband and most of her immediate descendants were buried there too (25:9; 35:29; 49:31; 50:13).

But there is more to this episode than the burial of Sarah and the establishment of an ancestral cemetery. This was the first acquisition of a plot of land in Canaan. In 21:30 Abraham had acquired the right to use a well; now he purchases a large field in which to bury his family. The lengthy negotiations with the Hittite owner are fully described to show that the purchase was fully and publicly agreed upon between the Hittites and Abraham so that he now had an impeccable right to this land in perpetuity. It appears that the Hittites were ready to give the land to Abraham (23:11), but that might not have given Abraham full title to it, so he insists on buying it (v. 13). Despite the high price asked, Abraham pays in full: there is to be no question about future ownership.

23:2-3 Kiriath-arba seems to be the older name for Hebron (cf. 13:18). V. 3: These Hittites do not appear to have any connection with the Hittites of Asia Minor. All OT Hittites have good Semitic names and, where locatable, live in the hills of Canaan.

The Betrothal of Rebekah (J) (24:1-67)

The fullness of description in this episode signals its importance for the narrator. The death of Sarah in the preceding chapter here is followed by Abraham on his deathbed making his last wishes known to his faithful servant. In the typical biblical deathbed scene the dying man summons his sons to him and gives them his blessing (cf. chs. 27 and 49). But here it is the servant, not the son Isaac, who is entrusted with carrying out the patriarch's wishes. But this is characteristic of Isaac throughout Genesis: he is the most passive of the patriarchs and open to manipulation by others.

In this scene Abraham is portrayed as concerned that his son should not marry a Canaanite, only someone from his own clan. He therefore commissions his servant to go and find a suitable wife for Isaac. Arranged marriages were standard practice in OT times, but once again Isaac is surprisingly little involved; usually the man would at least be consulted or tell his parents whom he would like to marry (cf. Judg 14:2).

Promptly the servant sets out for Aram-naharaim, the area in northern Syria between the Euphrates and Habur Rivers. And there by the well he meets the right girl. Here is another example of a biblical type scene: to meet one's fiancé(e) near a well is almost conventional (cf. 29:1-12; Exod 2:15-22). Once again the characters of the actors involved emerge when one example of the scene is compared with the others. Here unusually the groom is absent, but the future bride Rebekah is marked by tremendous energy, volunteering to water ten thirsty camels and running hither and thither in a great display of enthusiasm. Rebekah turns out later to be the most decisive and energetic of all the patriarchal wives.

Having told the story of the encounter at the well in his own words (24:10-27), the narrator then allows the servant to retell the story to Laban and Rebekah's family (vv. 34-49). Superficially this looks like repetition, but a close comparison of the two accounts shows some interesting differences. The servant's retelling is subtly crafted to elicit a positive response from the grasping Laban. Note the stress on Abraham's wealth and the sole heirship of Isaac (vv. 35-36). He also stresses Abraham's desire that Isaac should marry a close relative, not one of the Canaanites (vv. 37-41). Then he presses for a decision. Surely the remarkable answer to his prayer at the well proves that God approves of the match. So Laban and Bethuel approve in principle (vv. 50-51).

However, by the next morning they are stalling for time: "at least ten days" (v. 55) could be translated "a year or so." Eventually Rebekah is asked to resolve the impasse. Her willingness to go and leave her family and homeland marks her out as a female Abraham. Like him her name contains the letters *b* and *r*, also found in *barek,* "to bless." Her obedience, like his, will be the source of blessing to many, as her relatives declare as she leaves (v. 60).

Her reception by Abraham's family is comparatively low key (vv. 62-67). There is in fact no mention of Abraham himself. That the servant now calls Isaac "my master" suggests that Abraham has now died too. Perhaps the mission to find Rebekah took longer than anticipated.

Within the perspective of Genesis this story offers a model and a justification of arranged marriages. Whatever doubts are raised by Rebekah and Laban's subsequent behavior, in the eyes of the author, "The thing comes from the LORD" (v. 50). For the author and his readers this is an example of the intersection of human prayer and divine providence working for the fulfillment of God's promised purpose. Through Abraham's initiative, his servant's obedience, and Rebekah's compliance the mother of Israel left her family and home to become Isaac's wife and so became "thousands of myriads."

Concluding the Life of Abraham (J/P) (25:1-11)

It is unlikely that all the events mentioned in this short epilogue to Abraham's career happened after chs. 23–24. It is probable that 24:65 presupposes the death of Abraham, although it is not formally recorded till 25:7-11, which tells of Isaac and Ishmael reunited to do their filial duty of burying their father (cf. 35:29; 50:4-13). Similarly, it may well be that the narrator envisaged Abraham taking Keturah before Sarah's death (ch. 23). But in order not to lose the track of the story these points have been left to the end.

The main point of mentioning Keturah and her descendants, like the Table of Nations in ch. 10, is to define Israel's relationship with some of the neighboring nomadic peoples, who lived in the deserts nearby or traded with Israel. In modern terms they would be described as Arabs. So far as they can be identified, Keturah's descendants seem to be peoples or tribes, thus fulfilling the promise that Abraham would be the ancestor of a multitude of nations (17:5). The linkage of these peoples with Abraham shows that in the time Genesis was written Israel felt a close affinity with these peoples.

25:2 Zimran may be an Arabian tribe. The Midianites were desert traders (cf. 37:28) and later enemies of Israel (Judges 7–8). Ishbak and Shuah may be located in northern Syria. 25:3: Sheba and Dedan (cf. 10:7) are located in Arabia. The Asshurim were a desert tribe mentioned in Num 24:22, 24 and Ps 83:8. 25:4: Ephah, Epher, Abida, and Eldaah may have Arabian connections.

25:8 "Gathered to his people" refers to being joined with his relatives in the afterlife.

The Family History of Ishmael (P) (25:12-18)

This short family history is one of the ten into which Genesis is arranged. From Genesis 11 onward the long family histories of Terah, Isaac, and Jacob sandwich the short histories of Ishmael and Esau (36:1–37:1). As elsewhere in Genesis, the non-elect line, here Ishmael, is dealt with before the chosen line that follows, that is, Isaac (cf. Cain before Seth in ch. 4, and Esau before Jacob in chs. 36–37).

As the previous section does, this passage shows how Israel viewed her bedouin-like neighbors, the Ishmaelites. It suggests that although they are so closely related, tension between them can be traced right back to the squabbles between Isaac and Ishmael. But it is also a reminder that God made promises to Ishmael, too, that he would live opposite his brothers (NRSV, at odds with all his kin) (16:12), and would father twelve princes and become a great nation (17:20). The fulfillment of the first is mentioned in 25:18 and of the second in 25:13-16. The implication is that, if God fulfilled these rather minor promises, he will surely fulfill his greater promises through his chosen line of Isaac. This bare genealogy should whet the reader's appetite for the next major family history.

The Jacob Story (25:19–35:29)

The story of Jacob, also called Israel, brings us to the heart of Genesis. The book is about the origins of the nation of Israel, whose tribes all traced their descent to one man, Jacob. This section of Genesis tells of Jacob's birth, marriage, how he fathered the ancestors of the twelve tribes, and that after a dramatic struggle with God he had his name changed to Israel. The next major section of Genesis (37:2–50:26), usually called the Joseph story, completes the life story of Jacob, telling how he emigrated to Egypt, settled there, and died there, but was buried in Canaan.

Often it has been held that the Jacob and Joseph stories were originally independent or at least had separate tradition histories, but a closer reading suggests they are intimately connected. In both we have the rivalry between Leah and her sons and Rachel and her sons. In both there are similar motifs, such as deception using a kid. The character of the actors is similar in both. The tensions that develop between family members in the Jacob story are not resolved until the end of the Joseph story. For these reasons it is preferable to regard Genesis 25–50 as constituting essentially one story. The editor has split it into two, sandwiching in between the two parts the genealogy of Esau (Edom) (36:1–37:1), thus making the second half of Genesis match the pattern of the first, with major narratives alternating with genealogies, and each section beginning "These are the descendants of Isaac [Esau, Jacob]" (25:19; 36:1; 37:2).

There are other signs of the editor's hand. Motifs from the Abraham cycle are echoed in the Jacob story (e.g., quarrels between brothers, leaving home, etc.). For other examples see above, p. 48. Even more clearly than the Abraham cycle, the Jacob story is arranged palistrophically.

25:19-34	Jacob and Esau together	A
26:34–28:9	Jacob takes Esau's blessing	B
28:10-22	Jacob meets God at Bethel	C
29:1-14	Jacob arrives at Laban's house	D
29:15-30	Laban tricks Jacob	E
29:31–30:24	Birth of Jacob's sons	F
30:25–31:1	Jacob outwits Laban	E′
31:2-55	Jacob leaves Laban	D′
32:1-2	Jacob meets angels of God	C′
32:3–33:20	Jacob returns Esau's blessing	B′
35:1-29	Jacob and Esau meet again	A′

These are the points that are most obvious in the arrangement, but even sections which do not match so obviously, for example, chs. 26 and 34, may be dealing with the same theme, namely, relations between Israel and the inhabitants of Canaan. The central section of the above palistrophe is the birth of Jacob's sons, the fathers of the twelve tribes, again emphasizing the book's interest in Israel's origins.

Bibliography. Fokkelman, J. P. 1975, *Narrative Art in Genesis,* Amsterdam: van Gorcum • Rendsburg. 1986 • Sternberg, M. 1985, *The Poetics of Biblical Narrative,* Bloomington: Indiana University • Syrén, R. 1993, *The Forsaken Firstborn,* Sheffield: Sheffield Academic.

The First Clashes between Jacob and Esau (J, P, E?) (25:19-34)

Three short sketches from the early life of the twins Jacob and Esau define the temper of their subsequent careers and mutual relationship. First, they are described as smashing each other ("struggling together" understates the violence involved) in their mother's womb. This makes life so painful for Rebekah that she wonders whether life is worth living, foreshadowing the pain their future antagonism will cause her (vv. 21-23).

In her distress she turns to God and through a prophetic oracle is told, "Two nations are in your womb . . . the elder shall serve the younger." This sums up the whole story of relations between Esau and Jacob in Genesis, as the two struggle for supremacy, and Jacob, the younger, regularly betters Esau. It also prefigures the bitter relationship between the nations of Edom and Israel described elsewhere (Num 20:14-21; Obad 10-21; Mal 1:4), and according to Paul the relationship between the elect and the non-elect (Rom 9:10-13).

The same pattern of behavior is evident at their birth (25:24-26), when Jacob emerges after Esau clutching his heel. The names given them at birth sum up their characteristics. Jacob probably is short for *ya'qob-el,* "May El protect," but here it is simply a pun on the word *'aqeb,* "heel," while the red Esau alludes to the territory his descendants inhabited, Edom (= red) or Seir (cf. Esau).

Finally (vv. 29-34), we see Jacob beginning to better Esau by persuading him to sell his birthright, that is, his privileges as firstborn son including extra gifts from his father during his lifetime and from his father's estate. Jacob is pictured as a wily exploiter while his brother is shown to be an uncouth despiser of tradition.

25:20-21, 26 Like Sarah and Rachel, Rebekah suffered a long period of infertility (17:17; 30:1). 25:28 notes the favoritism that is going to be so destructive in ch. 27.

Isaac and the Philistines (26:1-33) (J)

Were Genesis written in strict chronological order, much if not all of this chapter ought to have been placed before the preceding section, for obviously vv. 1-11 relate to a period before the birth of Jacob and Esau: there would have been no doubt about the marital status of Rebekah if she had twin boys! This section consists of a series of flashbacks into an earlier period in Isaac's life to demonstrate the partial fulfillment of the promises made to his father Abraham, blessings that were so evident that even outsiders like Abimelech wanted to be on good terms with Isaac (vv. 28-29). This helps explain why Rebekah was prepared to go such lengths to obtain the blessing for Jacob.

But it is not merely that the promises are partially fulfilled; they are twice reiterated and even enhanced in vv. 2-5 and 24 (note "all these lands," not merely "this land," in v. 3). Furthermore, there are many parallels between this chapter, 12:10–14:20, and chs. 20–21 underlining the similarity between Isaac's life and his father's.

These parallels are clearest in 26:1-11. Once again (cf. 12:10-20; 20:1-18) the patriarch passes off his wife as his sister and infuriates the local king by his deception. As in Abraham's case, we are led to understand that Isaac was not beyond reproach, and his wife's escape owes more to the grace of God than to the merit of the patriarch.

26:12-16 is the only reference in Genesis to a patriarch raising crops. The high yield (cf. Matt 13:8) is proof of divine blessing, as are his large flocks and herds. But as with Abraham before him and Jacob after him, this leads to strife (cf. 13:6-7; 30:25–31:16).

26:17-33 Water rights are vital to survival, so quarrels about wells are matters of life and death. Without access to wells Isaac would have had to leave. These episodes show Isaac handling the disputes with the Philistines in conciliatory fashion (cf. 13:8-9) and being rewarded with a reaffirmation of the promises (cf. 13:14-17), the making of a treaty with their longtime antagonists (cf. 21:25-32), and the digging of yet another well, a foothold in the land promised in 26:3.

The Philistines (26:1, 8, 15, 18), as known from Judges and Samuel, did not arrive in Canaan till the twelfth century, when they settled in the coastal plain. This term is either an anachronistic way of speaking of the earlier inhabitants of this area, or refers to an earlier group of immigrants (cf. Caphtorim; Deut 2:23) from the Aegean area.

Jacob Obtains Esau's Blessing by Deceit (26:34–28:9) (J, P, E?)

The excitement and tension of this story grip every reader. Will Rebekah's ruse succeed or will the aged Isaac uncover Jacob's disguise and curse him instead of blessing him? Will Esau return before Isaac has eaten and pronounced his blessing on Jacob? How will Esau react to his brother's deceit? We wait with baited breath to discover how things will work out. However, the very success of Rebekah and Jacob raises acute moral and theological problems. Does the author really approve of the devices they used to obtain the blessing? Can God's blessing be acquired by such shameful tactics?

Closer reading of the narrative shows that the narrator is not as naive or biased as appears on first sight. The tale of deception is prefaced by a comment on Esau's marriages to his two Hittite wives. This suggests either negligence on Isaac's part, who should have arranged a more suitable match for Esau (cf. 24:1-9), or a disregard for propriety on Esau's part, for he should not have married one Canaanite (on the Hittites see 23:3), let alone two (cf. 4:19). Then when Isaac comes to bestow his parting blessing, he flouts convention again. When a man knew his death was drawing near, he was expected to summon all his sons to hear his last wishes and to receive a final blessing (cf. ch. 49). However, Isaac ignores this custom by summoning only Esau and speciously excuses himself by saying, "I do not know the day of my death." Tradition and principle are rejected because he favors Esau and wants another dish of game.

No wonder Rebekah was incensed by this discrimination against her favorite. But does this mean that the narrator approves of her actions? This is unlikely, for he both mentions Jacob's qualms about the morality and practicality of her plan (27:11-13) and shows with a sympathetic fullness Esau's distress at having being cheated out of his blessing (vv. 34-38). Furthermore, in the ongoing story we see the long-term repercussions of Rebekah's and Jacob's actions. Jacob has to flee for his life, so that Rebekah never sees her favorite son again. Then, staying with his uncle, Jacob is exploited in various ways, most obviously by having to marry Leah before Rachel, for as his uncle cruelly comments, "It is not done in our country — giving the younger before the firstborn"

(29:26). Though Laban justifies his action on a do-as-you-would-be-done-by basis, this forced bigamy was the cause of endless pain and contention in Jacob's family for the rest of his life. Full reconciliation between the sons of Leah and the sons of Rachel is achieved only after his death. As Rebekah mourned the loss of Jacob her favorite son for the rest of her days, so for much of his life Jacob supposed his favorite son Joseph had met an untimely end, for as he had deceived his father with a goat, so his sons misled him by the same means (37:31-35). Finally, Jacob himself acknowledges the injustice of his acquisition of the blessing, for when seeking reconciliation with Esau he says he is returning "my blessing" (ESV; NRSV, "gift") (33:11).

So from a moral point of view Rebekah and Jacob do not get away with their action: they suffer for it for the rest of their days. But theologically speaking it does seem to succeed, for he does obtain the blessing, and this still seems unfair. This is probably the clearest example in Genesis of God's plans not being frustrated by human sin, of God's grace being given to those who do not deserve it, but because it has been promised. Before birth Rebekah was told through a prophetic oracle that the older should serve the younger (25:23), and though she and Jacob acted improperly to secure it, that did not invalidate the promise (cf. 12:10-20; 16:1-14; 20:1-18; 26:1-11). Though such acts of unbelief delay the fulfillment of the promises in the short term, in the longer term the promises are still being fulfilled (cf. Rom 11:1-29).

Jacob at Bethel (28:10-22) (J, E)

Jacob left home under a cloud. Admittedly his parents had put the best gloss on his reasons for leaving to find a wife (28:2), but he knew that it was really fear of Esau's revenge. So his experience at Bethel, some fifty miles north of Beer-sheba, must have been reassuring. His vision of angels going up and down a ladder linking earth and heaven was a promise of God's accompanying protection. In the OT angels are portrayed as patrolling the earth for God and reporting back to him (Job 1:6-12; Zech 1:8-17; 6:1-8). Here they go up to the top of the ladder where the LORD himself stands (NRSV mg., "stood above it," is better than "beside him").

Then for the first time Jacob hears the promises of land, descendants, and blessing that had been made to his father and grandfather reaffirmed and applied to himself (28:13-15). In fact, a new element is added, characteristic of the Jacob story (cf. 28:20; 31:3; 46:4), that God will be with him and bring him back to the land. This could be described as the governing motif of this part of the story: Jacob will be protected and will return to Canaan. The rest of the narrative will show how this happened.

But the experience also explains the name of Bethel, "house of God." Whether it was a holy site before Jacob encountered God there is unknown, but subsequent generations of Israelites who went to the important sanctuary there (1 Kgs 12:29–13:32; Amos 4:4; 7:13) would recall that Jacob had met God there, erected a stone there, and promised to bring his tithes there. The partial fulfillment of this vow is recorded in Genesis 35, but presumably Jacob's deed was supposed to serve as an example to his descendants. Although some see Jacob's vow-prayer in 28:20-22 as redundant in the light of the promises in vv. 13-15, petitionary prayer in the Bible often appeals to divine promises (cf. Exod 32:11-13; Luke 11:5-13).

Jacob Arrives at Laban's House (29:1-14) (J)

The scene is a rerun of the arrival of Abraham's servant at a well near Haran described in 24:10-49, but with some interesting differences which point up the distinctive character of the main actors. There it was Rebekah who ran to and fro, watering ten thirsty camels. Here it is Jacob who heaves away the massive stone single-handedly and waters his cousin's sheep. Then Isaac's servant prays earnestly that his mission will be successful. Now Jacob chats cockily to the other shepherds while he waits for Rachel to arrive, and when she does, he kisses her. In both cases Laban rushes out to meet the newcomer and invites him to stay.

These similarities and differences foreshadow later developments in the narrative. Jacob's tremendous exertion in moving the stone presages the great efforts he will have to make in Laban's household, while kissing his cousin surely looks forward to his falling in love with her. In both situations Laban's rush to greet the visitor is motivated by greed. But whereas Abraham's servant was loaded, Jacob had come empty-handed, yet Laban found a way of exploiting him too.

Jacob Marries Leah and Rachel (29:15-30) (J, P)

The romance hinted at in 29:11 blossoms. But marriage in the ancient Near East did not merely involve the couple but their families. Traditionally betrothal was sealed by a large payment, the bride-price of up to fifty shekels (Exod 22:16-17; Deut 22:29) given by the man's family to the bride's family. But Jacob away from home could not call on his family resources, so he is forced to enter his uncle's service to pay the equivalent of the bride-price. The bride-price usually was equal to a few years' wages, but seven is on the high side, reflecting both Laban's greed and Jacob's love for Rachel (29:20).

At the end of the seven years Jacob has to remind Laban to fulfill his side of the bargain. This was not the last time Jacob would find Laban slow to pay up (cf. 31:41-42). We know little about wedding celebrations in Bible times save what we can infer from this passage, Judges 14, and Matt 25:1-12. A seven-day feast was customary, on the first night of which the bridegroom took his bride to bed for the first time. But morning light showed that it was the wrong woman! Jacob protests that he has been "deceived," thereby echoing what he had done, "came deceitfully" (27:35). But Laban hammers home the point, that Jacob has only been treated as he had treated his brother, by observing: "It is not done in our country to put the younger before the older." Nevertheless, Laban agrees to give Rachel as well, if Jacob will work another seven years for him. As the story goes on to tell, this was the start of a miserable marriage.

29:17 would be better translated, "Leah's eyes were soft [i.e., lacked sparkle], but Rachel had a beautiful figure and a lovely face."

29:24, 29. At marriage it was customary for the bride's father to give her a dowry, which usually consisted of furniture, clothes, and money. Here the wealthy Laban gives his daughters their own slave-girls as part of their dowries.

The Birth of Jacob's Sons (29:31–30:24) (J, E)

The birth of eleven sons to Jacob is the turning point of the story. From this point on, he tries to return home (30:25). For later Israelites this section must have been of special interest in that it relates the origins of most of the tribes and offers explanations of their names, most of which are characteristically second millennium in type. However, this must also count as one of the most poignant sections in the book. Marriage and motherhood were the ultimate goals of pre-modern women (30:1; cf. Psalms 127–128), but here what should have been their greatest joy is turned into a battleground. As they name their children, we glimpse the rivalry, bitterness, and disappointment that blighted their relationships with each other and with Jacob.

Leah's pleasure at motherhood is darkened by Jacob's lack of affection for her. Her sons' names express the hope that their birth will change his attitude to her (see 29:32, 33, 34; 30:18, 20). On the other hand, Rachel's choice of names shows her gloating over her sister (30:6, 8) or pathetically hoping for another child (30:24). It may be noted that those patriarchs who are to play the biggest roles in the Joseph story, Reuben, Simeon, Judah, and Joseph, all have their names explained by reference to the divine name, the LORD *(Yahweh),* whereas the others just have explanations with the generic term for God *(Elohim).* Most of the explanations are not historical etymologies, which would explain what the name meant originally; rather, like most biblical etymologies, they are plays on the word giving the associations of the different names in popular thought.

The episode comes to its bitter climax in 30:14-18, as Leah exchanges her son Reuben's mandrakes, an ancient fertility drug, for a night in her husband's bed. Here we see Leah's desperate desire for her husband's love and Rachel's yearning for children at their most intense. But it was not medicine that solved the problem, but God who opened Rachel's womb (30:22). The tribes owe their origin to the will of God, not human manipulation.

30:21 Dinah may not have been Jacob's only daughter, but she is mentioned because of her role in ch. 34.

Jacob Outwits Laban (30:25–31:1) (J, E)

As soon as Joseph is born, Jacob decides he must return to his country (30:25). He has seen the promises of children and protection fulfilled (28:2-4, 13-16); now he looks for the redemption of the land promise. However, his grasping father-in-law is reluctant to let him go. He puts his objections very suavely (30:27-28), but basically he says he cannot afford to let such an asset as Jacob go. So Jacob offers Laban a deal that will apparently cost Laban nothing.

Sheep are usually white and goats are black: speckled specimens are unusual. So Jacob says that he will just take the speckled sheep and goats: the rest will be Laban's. Laban thinks that this is fine, and leaves Jacob with a flock consisting entirely of white sheep and black goats. However, by putting white-striped rods in front of the goats when they breed and a black goat in front of the sheep when they breed, Jacob succeeds in producing speckled sheep and goats. According to the agreement these belonged to him. What is more, he restricts his selective breeding to the most vigorous sheep and goats, so that his share of the flock turns out to be the most healthy too. It is possible that by restricting his selective breeding to the strongest members of the flock, he chose the hybrids who tended to produce multi-colored offspring. However, the narrator is not interested in the science as much as in the fact that Jacob outwits Laban and thus secures himself a huge flock. Like Abraham before him (12:16) and Joseph after him, Jacob thus secures great wealth for himself in a foreign country.

Note that much of the terminology of this section is quite technical, and more detailed commentaries may need to be consulted to elucidate it. "Learned by divination" (30:27, NRSV) should be "grown rich." V. 40 refers to the black goat put before the sheep when mating.

Jacob Escapes from Laban (31:2–32:2) (E, J, P)

Jacob's success provoked a jealous reaction from Laban's family, but it was a call that echoed the original call to Abraham (12:1-3) that really prompted him to move. However, his wives had to be persuaded to leave home, and he retells the history of his stay in such a way that it will lead them to agree. This apologetic purpose explains the differences between his account and the narrator's version in the preceding chapters. Jacob stresses the duplicity of their father and the evident blessing of God on himself, so Rachel and Leah readily consent to leave.

But their hasty exodus from Paddan-aram, like the later exodus from Egypt, prompts a furious pursuit. The ensuing standoff between Laban and Jacob is tense, particularly the search of Rachel's tent for the teraphim, called gods in 31:31-35. The identity and purpose of the teraphim have been much discussed. Usually they have been supposed to have been images of the family's gods, hence NRSV's "household gods" in v. 19; but van der Toorn thinks that they were images of the ancestors. Why Rachel thought it important to take them with her and Laban was so keen to recover them is unclear. It is possible that possession of the teraphim conveyed inheritance rights, or brought fertility or good luck. The text assumes the reader knows, but we do not.

After the abortive search Jacob takes the offensive and accuses Laban of cheating him. Shepherds in the ancient orient were not expected to bear losses incurred by attacks of wild beasts or in some cases of theft; they were borne by the owner of the flock. But Jacob says that he did bear such losses, and hence he has been underpaid by Laban (see Finkelstein).

At last Laban climbs down and proposes a covenant with ridiculous conditions, insisting Jacob should not invade the territory of Laban from which he was running away or take any extra wives. Although such a clause was frequent in ancient marriage contracts, this was cheek from Laban, who had forced Jacob to marry one more wife than he wanted! But the making of this covenant explains the origin of the place name Gilead, "heap or cairn of witness" (vv. 47-48).

At Mahanaim, perhaps western Tulu edh-Dhahab just north of the Jabbok River, Jacob has another vision of angels. At Bethel he had seen them going up and down a ladder; here they are encamped, perhaps for battle (cf. 2 Kgs 6:17; 7:6). At any rate, as he returns to Canaan he is reminded of God's promise that he would be with him and bring him back to his homeland in peace (28:15, 20-21), an assurance that he most needed at this critical juncture.

31:42, 53 "Fear of Isaac": this unique title of God has prompted much discussion. Though other translations have been offered, the traditional one is appropriate in this context, for it was the fear of God (v. 24) that held Laban back from attacking Jacob.

Bibliography. Toorn, K. van der. 1990, "The Nature of the Biblical Teraphim in the Light of the Cuneiform Evidence," *CBQ* 52:203-22.

Jacob Returns Esau's Blessing (32:3–33:20) (J, E, P).

Would it be out of the frying pan into the fire? Having at last escaped Laban's clutches, Jacob now faces the prospect of a meeting with Esau. His anxiety is palpable. He at once sends messengers seeking Esau's favor with an excessively deferential message. Indeed, the terms "my lord Esau" . . . "your servant Jacob" seem to be the first of several moves by Jacob to undo the effects of his misappropriation of Esau's blessing, whereby Jacob would be Esau's lord and Esau would serve him (27:29, 37).

The messengers return with the news that Esau is on his way with four hundred men, which turns Jacob's anxiety into panic (32:7-8). Preemptive defensive measures are followed by one of the longest prayers in Genesis. This consists in an appeal to God's mercy (v. 11) sandwiched between two reminders of his promises (vv. 9, 12). It was God who had told him to return to Canaan (31:3) and who had promised to make his descendants numerous (28:14; cf. 22:17). For God to allow Esau to exterminate him and his family would be to annul his promises.

But prayer does not make action superfluous. Jacob prepares five flocks of presents totaling 550 animals to "appease" Esau. These references to "presents" *(minḥah),* "appease" *(kipper),* and "accept" *(raṣah)* echo sacrificial terminology (cf. Lev 1:4; 2:1-14), for as Jacob says later, he sees making peace with his brother as making peace with God (33:10; cf. Matt 5:21-26; 1 John 4:12-21).

Then follows one of the most mysterious episodes in the OT, Jacob's struggle with a "man" at the Jabbok. It is mysterious historically, for it is hard to know what really happened. It is also mysterious theologically, in that the "man" somehow represents God, who seems initially intent on harming Jacob but eventually leaves him with a blessing. But there is no doubt about the importance of this encounter, for in it Jacob is renamed Israel, the name of the nation.

Parallels with folktales from Ireland to the Hittites have been drawn to demonstrate the integrity of the story. Many have cited tales of attacks by river demons to explain the origin of the story. Perhaps Jacob's opponent was a Canaanite river god. But Eissfeldt has pointed out that this is not the perspective of the story, which identifies the foe as El, the supreme creator God in the Canaanite pantheon (32:30). This fits in with other dangerous encounters with divine beings in the Pentateuch, where the mysterious opponent turns out to be either the LORD or his angel (Exod 4:24-26; Num 22:22-35), for regularly in Genesis the LORD is equated with El (cf. 16:13).

This makes it the more surprising that the "man" could not prevail against Jacob (32:25), and that he was in a hurry to leave before daybreak (v. 26). The reason for his haste is obscure. Jupiter's demand to leave a city before dawn sounds similar (Plautus *Amphitryo* 532-33). It is probably an attempt to hide his identity, but it may also reflect the notion that no one may see God and live (cf. v. 30; Exod 33:20). These features all enhance the wonder of Jacob's achievement, that he was able to wring concessions from a supernatural being in single combat.

Even with his hip dislocated he is determined to extract a blessing from his opponent. Obtaining a blessing has of course been Jacob's lifelong goal. But in fact he is granted more than a blessing, a name change which announces his new character and destiny just as Abraham and Sarah's change of name did (17:5, 15; cf. Matt 16:18). Israel probably means "God [El] fights, or judges/rules." But as often the OT does not offer a strict etymology, more a play on the name, "you have struggled with God and with men and have overcome" (32:28). The old name Jacob recalled his past underhand dealing (27:36); his new name recalls this triumphant struggle with divine and human foes, and is a pledge to the people, who later were known as Israel, that they too would triumph over all the powers that might assail them. In the immediate context of the story the new name guarantees Jacob a successful meeting with Esau.

Within the Bible this is an extraordinary story. It invites comparison with God's demand to Abraham to sacrifice Isaac, the nighttime attack on Moses, or the testing of Job (Gen 22:1-19; Exod 4:24-26; Job 1–42). In all these situations God appears to be acting abnormally, assaulting those he has promised to care for, indeed called to do his will. This paradox or mystery of divine action was often Israel's experience as a people: the psalms of national lament (e.g., 74; 79; 80; 83) often express the conviction that national disasters are sent by God, yet only God can deliver the nation from them. As Calvin puts it: "he fights *against* us with his *left* hand, and *for* us with his *right* hand." The NT similarly sees Jesus' suffering as the pathway to glory, and one that all his disciples should expect to follow (1 Pet 4:1-2, 13-19).

Bibliography. Coote, R. 1972, "The Meaning of the Name Israel," *HTR* 65:137-46 • Eissfeldt, O. 1966, "Non dimittam te, nisi benedixeris mihi," *KS* 3:412-16.

Jacob's transformation is patent next morning. Instead of following the rest of the party he now steps out in front to meet Esau first. Note, though, his sevenfold obeisance to his brother; he is still trying to reverse the blessing "may your mother's sons bow down to you" (27:29). But as implied in the Peniel experience (32:28), Esau is transformed too. The brother who was last heard of planning to murder Jacob greets him with a warmth and generosity that is astonishing. Though Jacob's comparison of Esau's action with God's sounds too fulsome, it is not inappropriate, for God's mercy is like this according to Scripture (33:4, 10; cf. Luke 15:20). Esau's reluctance to accept Jacob's presents is eventually overcome as Jacob pleads, "Please accept my *blessing*" (ESV; not "gift," NRSV). Jacob for his part is determined to put right his earlier deception.

Esau's forgiveness is reaffirmed as he urges Jacob to come and live with him. It is not clear why Jacob politely declined (vv. 13-14). Was it a lurking distrust or was it obedience to the command to return to Canaan (31:3)? By not clarifying his motives, the narrator allows both possibilities.

33:17 Succoth may be Tell Deir ʿAlla or Tell Ekhas, sites about a mile apart, just north of the Jabbok.

33:18 should be translated, "Jacob came to Salem the city of Shechem. . . ." At last back in Canaan proper, he buys land, builds an altar, and worships, since the promises made at Bethel seem fulfilled (28:13-15).

Dinah's Brothers' Revenge (34:1-31) (J, E/P?)

This episode seems to have little to do with the theme of Genesis, the partial fulfillment of the promises, and its brutality horrifies the modern reader. These issues will be looked at in reverse order, for we cannot understand its thematic relevance without appreciating the ethical stance of the storyteller.

To understand the author's viewpoint, we must realize the stark rejection of sexual intercourse outside marriage in the ancient world. Adultery and rape were punishable by death. Consenting sex before marriage could cost as much as marriage itself, that is, several years' wages (Exod 22:16-17; cf. comments on Gen 29:15-20). Here Jacob's sons make the same point rhetorically, calling the act an "outrage in Israel . . . for such a thing ought not to be done" (34:7). It is treating their sister "like a whore" (v. 31). This is not to say that the author approves of the brothers' revenge, for in fact he holds everyone culpable to various degrees, but he certainly did not view Shechem's deed as venial. Accurately translated, v. 2 reads "Shechem took her, lay with her and humiliated her." The NRSV is quite wrong to imply that Shechem used force. (In rape contexts such as Deut 22:25; 2 Sam 13:11 a different verb is used.) Dinah was humiliated by submitting to sex outside marriage, not by being raped.

She herself was not faultless. For a single girl to "go out," and particularly to visit the local inhabitants, was dubious. But even more shocking was her father's indifference to the news of her liaison. He (cf. David; 2 Sam 13:21) should have been incensed. But whereas David was angry but did nothing, we are not even told that Jacob was angry. Perhaps this was because Dinah was Leah's daughter, and he did not acknowledge her as his wife or her children as his (44:27). This callousness toward their sister spurred her brothers to take the law into their own hands (cf. Absalom; 2 Sam 13:22-29), abuse the covenant rite of circumcision, and perpetrate the horrendous massacre. To mitigate our sense of outrage a little, the narrator points out the duplicity of Hamor and Shechem, who make an agreement with Jacob's sons but then sell a slightly different version to the people of the land (cf. 34:22-23 with vv. 8-17). It also emerges that the brothers negotiated under duress, for Dinah was throughout held in Shechem's house (v. 26).

None of this endeared Jacob's family to the Canaanites, as Jacob lamely points out in an attempt to justify his lack of action (34:30). Nevertheless, despite his fears they were not attacked (35:5). In other words, despite the multiple family failings God's promises of protection to Jacob still held good. Furthermore, this assault on the inhabitants of the land by Ur-Israel foreshadows the later assaults led by Moses and Joshua. In these cases, too, it is the sins of the Canaanites, especially with regard to sex, that justify the conquest, not the righteousness of Israel (Numbers 25; 31:1-31; Deut 7:1-8; 9:4-7)

Bibliography. Parry, R. A. 2003, *Using Genesis 34 in Christian Ethics,* Carlisle: Paternoster • Wenham, G. J. 2000, *Story as Torah,* Edinburgh: T & T Clark, 109-19.

Jacob Returns to Bethel and Mamre (35:1-29) (J, E, P)

This section looks like a miscellany of Jacob traditions randomly lumped together to round off the story of Jacob's homecoming. However, a similar series of topics is found at the end of the Abraham and Joseph stories (e.g., journey, 35:1-8; cf. 22:1-14; 46:2-7; reaffirmation of promises, 35:9-14; 22:15-18; 48:4; birth of sons, 35:17-18; cf. 22:20-24; 48:5-6; death and burial of wife, 35:18-20; cf. 23:1-20; 48:7; son's marriage, 35:21-22; cf. 24:1-67; 48:8ff. (49:3-4); list of descendants, 35:22-26; cf. 25:1-6; 49:3-28; death and burial, 35:27-29; cf. 25:7-10; 49:29–50:14). These parallels indicate an editorial logic. A theological logic is also discernible. Promises were given to Jacob at Bethel, and Jacob made vows there. With the fulfilment of the promises Jacob is duty-bound to return to Bethel to fulfill his vows.

35:1-7 Jacob is portrayed as a model worshiper making a pilgrimage to the great sanctuary of Bethel. The command "go up" (*'alah*) later became a technical term for going on pilgrimage, especially to Jerusalem. Those who went on such pilgrimages had to be of pure hands and heart and particularly forswear idolatry (Ps 24:3-4). So here Jacob's party does these things (35:2, 4). But the command to go to Bethel and build an altar also echoes the end of the Abraham story with the command to go to a mountain and worship.

In Abraham's case that was a difficult thing to do because of the nature of the sacrifice. In Jacob's it was risky because of the massacre of the Shechemites. But both patriarchs obeyed. And both were rewarded by the most powerful statement of the promises in their lifetimes (35:11-13; cf. 22:15-18). In addition, Jacob's name change to Israel is reaffirmed (35:10). This may reflect an alternative source to 32:28, but Genesis regularly uses repetition of key points in the story to underline significant developments (cf. 17:19; 18:10; 37:6-10, etc.). Here the first name change is presupposed, for no explanation of the new name is given (unlike 32:28).

But Bethel was also associated with tragedy. There Deborah, Rebekah's nurse, died. The only other mention of her is in 24:59. Presumably her death is recorded because the oak she was buried under could be visited in later times. Sadder still was the death of Rachel, Jacob's favorite wife, giving birth to her second son. There is a poignant irony in the circumstance of her death in childbirth, for she had said earlier, "Give me children, or I shall die!" and when at last Joseph was born, she prayed, "May the LORD add to me another son!" (30:1, 24).

Though in modern times Rachel's grave is located about a mile north of Bethlehem, that would appear to be based on a misunderstanding of this text. V. 16 probably should be translated, "Then they journeyed from Bethel; and when they were about two hours' distance from Ephrath. . . ." This would place Rachel's tomb somewhere north of Jerusalem, which would fit in with Rachel weeping for her children in Ramah (Jer 31:15). By calling Rachel's son Benjamin, son of the right hand, Jacob was indicating his favored position. The "tower of Eder" (35:20) may be near Bethlehem.

35:22 Reuben's disgraceful behavior requires no comment by the narrator. It is specifically condemned by Jacob in 49:3-4, when he demotes Reuben from his position as firstborn. According to Lev 20:11, this type of incest warrants the death penalty. Reuben's motives are unclear, but it is usually thought to have been an attempt to stop Rachel's maid from taking Rachel's position as Jacob's favorite wife. As the oldest son of Leah Reuben doubtless bitterly resented his father's preference for Rachel.

35:27-28 Eventually Jacob arrives back at his father's house (cf. 28:20), now located at Mamre. And there, as the two brothers, Isaac and Ishmael, had buried their father, so the brothers Jacob and Esau bury theirs (cf. 25:7-9).

The Family History of Esau (36:1–37:1) (P)

This is the last of the short genealogies that alternate with the long cycles of stories about Abraham (chs. 12–25), Jacob (chs. 25–35) and Joseph (chs. 37–50). In each case the genealogy of the non-elect brother (Ishmael and Esau) precedes that of the elect (Isaac and Jacob). The Ishmael genealogy is quite short (25:12-18), whereas this one is much longer. The genealogy of Esau is also distinctive in having a double heading, "These are the descendants of Esau," in vv. 1 and 9. This has led commentators to suppose that originally 36:1-8 and 37:1 stood alone; this would make the genealogies of Ishmael and Esau quite similar. Then later 36:9-43 were added, perhaps after David had conquered Edom and incorporated it into his empire (cf. 36:31). Westermann suggests that this latter material came from the royal archives of Edom.

The origin of this material about Edom remains speculative, but its inclusion reflects the close affinity Israel felt for its near neighbor to the south and east of the Dead Sea. The Edomites were believed to be descended from Esau, Jacob's twin brother. Yet throughout history they were at loggerheads with Israel (Num 20:14-21; 2 Sam 8:13-14; Ps 137:7-9), and this is reflected in Genesis's account of the rivalry between Jacob and Esau. Nevertheless, the note of bitter hatred of Edom found in the later parts of the Bible following Edom's role in the destruction of Jerusalem (e.g., Obadiah, Lam 4:21-22) is noticeably absent from Genesis. The portrait of Esau, while not uncritical, is often quite sympathetic (e.g., chs. 27, 33). This suggests that Genesis reflects early attitudes in Israel.

Read without the later insertion of 36:9-43, 36:1-8 and 37:1 explain how Esau's decision to live in Seir outside Canaan meant that he had excluded himself from the land of promise, which therefore belonged entirely to Jacob and his descendants. It thus implies the partial fulfillment of the promises to Abraham. The insertion of 36:9-43 changes the focus somewhat. It mentions that Esau, too, fathered a nation with kings (vv. 31-39), so that the birth oracle given to Rebekah, "two nations are in your womb," was also fulfilled. The incorporation of Edom into the Davidic empire also demonstrates that "the elder shall serve the younger" (25:23). Implied too, especially by ch. 33, is the hope of reconciliation between Edom and Israel even though they live in different territories. The long list of names contain many familiar Israelite names and thus underline the common roots and heritage of both peoples.

36:2-5, listing Esau's wives and grandsons, do not match 26:34 and 28:9. It seems that the differences stem from different traditions.

36:10-19 fall into two sections in which the names overlap greatly: 10-14 (Esau's sons) and 15-19 (the "chiefs [not "clans," NRSV] of the sons of Esau"). Similarly, vv. 20-30 fall into a list of sons and grandsons of Seir the Horite (20-28) and a list of chiefs (29-30). It seems likely that the Horites were the earlier indigenous inhabitants of Edom, arriving before the descendants of Esau.

36:31-39 The King List reflects a period before the establishment of the Israelite monarchy. But these Edomite kings seem to have been local rulers without any dynastic succession, and the capital city moves with the king. In this respect it is like the situation of Israel portrayed in Judges.

The Joseph Story (37:2–50:26)

The Joseph Story, as the last fourteen chapters of Genesis are usually called, is something of a misnomer. The Hebrew title of this section is "The Story of the Family of Jacob" (37:2), and this is much more apt, for although more space is devoted to Joseph than to the other members of the family, in certain sections there is no mention of him at all (e.g., ch. 38). More exactly these chapters seem to constitute the second half of the biography of Jacob, which began with the account of his birth in 25:21-26 and ends with his death in ch. 50. His sons are viewed as the ultimate ancestors of the twelve tribes, so their deeds are almost as pivotal as their father's. Hence just before the close of the book Jacob gives each of his sons a blessing, which anticipates their future roles and destinies (ch. 49). Longacre has plausibly argued that this represents the peak of Genesis, which gives the reader a glimpse of the embryonic nation of Israel and the glorious future of each of its constituent tribes.

Unlike the Abraham and Jacob stories (chs. 12–25 and 25–35), the Joseph story has no clear palistrophic arrangement. Instead the heart of the Joseph story consists of a pair of three parallel panels, A, B, C, A′, B′, C′.

37:2-36	Joseph sold into Egypt	
38:1-30	Tamar and Judah	
39:1-20	Joseph and Potiphar	A
39:21–40:23	Joseph in Prison	B
41:1-57	Joseph in the Palace	C
42:1-38	First visit of Jacob's family to Egypt	A′
43:1–45:28	Second visit of Jacob's family to Egypt	B′
46:1–47:31	Third visit of Jacob's family to Egypt	C′
48:1–50:26	Last days of Jacob and Joseph	

The Joseph story, like the Abraham and Jacob stories, contributes to the exposition of the theme of the Pentateuch by showing how the promises to Abraham were partially fulfilled. And like the two preceding stories, it begins with a divine intimation of the central figure's future destiny: in two dreams Joseph sees the rest of his family bowing down before him. His brothers' sale of him into Egypt was designed to prevent such an outcome, but inexorably, despite his imprisonment on a false charge, he rises to be vizier over all Egypt. And it is when his brothers come to Egypt that they unwittingly fulfill his early dreams (42:6; 44:14). Some have held that the Joseph story proper ends with his father's move to Egypt, but his brothers fall down before him one last time after Jacob's death (50:18). The key point of the story is expressed in 50:20: "Even though you intended to do harm to me, God intended it for good, in order to preserve a numerous people." It tells of the ultimate reconciliation of the schisms that had rent Jacob's family ever since he had married Leah as well as Rachel, suggesting to later generations that tribal factionalism should also be overcome.

A unique aspect of the Joseph story is its Egyptian setting, which has prompted much reflection by Egyptologists. It is evident, on the one hand, that the author is very familiar with Egyptian customs, but, on the other, he is writing about Egypt in a way that is intelligible to later Israelites. Does this enable us to place the career of Joseph in a definite period of Egyptian history and give any clues as to the period in which the story was written up? Answers differ, but on balance the following conclusions would appear likely.

Many features of the narrative would be at home in Egypt at almost any period, so they cannot be invoked for dating purposes. But Joseph's name, like several other patriarchs', is typical of early-second-millennium Amorite names. Texts show that many Asiatic slaves were brought to Egypt in this era. Joseph's rise to power could well fit the Hyksos period (c. 1650-1540 BC) when Semitic chieftains ruled Egypt; it was also then that the Egyptian capital was in the eastern Nile delta. The names Potiphar, Zaphenath-paneah and Asenath could well have originated then, though the pronunciation seems to reflect the Ramesside era (13th cent.), generally identified with the time of Moses. However, some phrases seem to reflect later Israelite terminology. In 41:23 the good ears of corn are blighted by the *east* wind, as they would be in Canaan, but in Egypt it was the *south* wind that shriveled up the crops. Similarly, Joseph's appointment to be "over my house" (41:40) fits his appointment as Pharaoh's deputy if taken in a Hebrew sense, not an Egyptian one. These data suggest that the traditions about Joseph reach well back into the second millennium, but that they may have received their final form in Israel somewhat later.

Bibliography. Coats, G. W. 1976, *From Egypt to Canaan,* Washington, D.C.: Catholic Biblical Association • Hoffmeier, J. K. 1996, *Israel in Egypt,* Oxford: Oxford University • Humphreys, W. L. 1988, *Joseph and His Family,* Columbia: University of South Carolina • Kitchen, K. A. in Hess, Satterthwaite, and Wenham. 1993, 67-92 • Longacre, R. E. 1989, *Joseph: A Story of Divine Providence,* Winona Lake: Eisenbrauns • Vergote, J. 1959, *Joseph en Egypte,* Louvain: Publications Universitaires.

Joseph Is Sold into Egypt (J, E, P) (37:2-36)

Like the family story of Isaac, Jacob's family story tells of a conflict that will divide the family for some twenty years. Once again it is a conflict between brothers triggered by parental favoritism. Whereas Isaac preferred Esau and Rebekah Jacob, Jacob had always loved Rachel and her sons more than Leah's. (Translators cannot agree whether Jacob marked his favoritism with the gift of a long-sleeved coat or a multi-colored one.) But as before, the children aggravate the problem (cf. 25:25-34; ch. 27) to such an extent that they speak of killing each other. Here Joseph's tactlessness in telling tales on his brothers and then recounting his dreams makes his brothers mad.

However, as already observed the dreams are not Joseph's own imaginings but announcements of God's plans, and the fact that they are paired is an assurance of their eventual fulfilment (cf. 41:32). In the short term, however, they act as a catalyst of family breakdown.

The tension in the story builds as Jacob sends his darling son some fifty miles away from home in Hebron to Shechem in the north into the arms of the brothers who hate him intensely. As they see him approach, some want to kill Joseph, whereas Reuben seeks to stall proceedings by having him dumped in a pit. But evidently while he is away, the other brothers change their plan and decide to make a tidy sum of money (twenty shekels represents two to three years' wages for a hired shepherd) by selling Joseph as a slave.

The identity of the slave traders has long proved a crux for commentators. In 37:25, 28 and 39:1 they are called Ishmaelites, but in 37:28 and 36 they are termed Midianites. Some have supposed that two groups of traders were involved, others that the variation represents the terminology of different sources. However, there is no doubt that the author of Genesis thought Ishmaelites and Midianites were alternative names for the same group of people (cf. 37:36 and 39:1 and Judg 8:24). Why they should sometimes be called Ishmaelites and sometimes Midianites is less clear. It may be that Ishmaelite means "nomadic trader" and Midianite refers to the tribe they belonged to, or Ishmaelites may be the larger tribal grouping of which Midianites were a smaller group.

The last scene with Jacob mourning inconsolably for his dead son Joseph is touching, but the phraseology is doubtless chosen to remind us of how Jacob years before deceived his father using his brother's clothes and a goat (ch. 27). "He recognized it" (37:33) picks up another word from 27:23. In this way the author hints at the inescapability of divine justice. Jacob is being treated by his sons as he treated his father. But, as the story will show, Joseph's sale into Egypt will in the end work out to save many lives, heal the family rift, and forward the fulfillment of the promises.

Tamar and Judah (J) (38:1-30)

On the face of it this episode has very little to do with the surrounding material: the story of Joseph would flow much more smoothly if it were not interrupted by this digression about Tamar and her children. However, as Alter and Humphreys, among others, have noted, this episode offers a significant commentary on the Joseph story and indeed helps to explain the remarkable transformation in Judah's character between chs. 37 and 44.

The most obvious parallel between the Joseph and Tamar stories comes out in 38:25-26. "Take note" or"acknowledge" is the same term as "see now" or "recognize" in 37:32-33. It should also be noted that there is a similarity in the actions of the parties. Jacob deceived his father Isaac, was in turn deceived by his sons led by Judah, who finally was tricked by his daughter-in-law. In all the incidents items of dress and goats play a role.

Another principle emerges in the Joseph story, and this one, let alone elsewhere in Genesis, is God's choice of the younger son in preference to the older (cf. Esau and Jacob, Joseph and his brothers, Manasseh and Ephraim). In this story there is a double statement of this principle. First, Judah's older boys, Er and Onan die, but Shelah survives (38:3-11); then at the end of the story Zerah sticks his hand out first, making him the firstborn, but Perez arrives first, and later proves to be the ancestor of King David (Ruth 4:18-22). This double reinforcement of the principle of God's choice of the younger serves to underline that Joseph's dreams of supremacy will eventually prove justified.

Chapter 37 ended with Jacob inconsolable at the death of one son Joseph, whereas ch. 38 opens with Judah apparently accepting stoically the death of his two sons. This fits in with the hard calculating image of him in 37:26 cold-bloodedly selling his brother into slavery. Yet in 44:18-34 he is seen pleading with great warmth and tenderness for Benjamin's release, so that his father will not have to suffer anymore. The beginnings of this transformation are seen in his confession of guilt in 38:26.

Finally, this episode reinforces some of the key themes of Genesis. Tamar is one of those foreigners (cf. Melchizedek [ch. 14] and Abimelech [chs. 20, 26]) who put the descendants of Abraham to shame by being more concerned with righteousness and the fulfillment of God's purposes than the chosen line. Onan, and by implication Judah, display an indifference to fulfilling the promise by not obeying the command to have children. Tamar, on the other hand, is desperate to have a child, so at the end Judah acknowledges, "She is more in the right than I."

Judah disregards patriarchal principle by marrying a Canaanite (cf. 24:3; 28:1), so it may be that Genesis does not regard his sons' death as entirely unmerited (cf. 38:7). However, according to the customs of the time, it was compulsory for a childless widow to marry the next boy in the family. This rule of Levirate marriage is known among many peoples, including the Assyrians, Hittites, and Canaanites, and is further spelled out in Deut 25:5-10. By the time of Deuteronomy the duty of the Levirate was no longer mandatory, and could be avoided at the cost of public derision. But Judah simply sidestepped the obligation.

However, Tamar makes an even greater laughingstock of Judah than the book of Deuteronomy would have and exposes his callous hypocrisy. Quite how she dressed so that she was taken for a prostitute is not explained, but it worked. And Judah is shown to be more concerned with paying his fee to the prostitute than doing his duty to his daughter-in-law by providing her with a husband. Because Tamar had been promised to be given in marriage to Shelah, though it was never carried out, she was technically guilty of adultery, or at least a capital offense, for having intercourse with a third party (cf. Deut 22:22-24). However, in the later law burning was reserved for particularly shocking offenses (Lev 21:9). Judah's demand for it here again illustrates his brutal callousness. Yet at his moment of self-righteous triumph his daughter-in-law proves her own integrity and his humbug.

Joseph and Potiphar (J) (39:1-20)

The tale of the immoral Israelite male worsted by the upright foreign female Tamar is followed by the story of the immoral foreign female apparently vanquishing the immaculate Joseph. Yet the story begins by insisting that "The LORD was with Joseph" (39:2). The next episode starts similarly (39:21), though it, too, appears to end in disaster for Joseph. These two episodes showing Joseph serving Egyptian overlords for no reward are then complemented and contrasted with a third episode, where he suddenly rises to become Pharaoh's right-hand man, in which it is patently obvious that God is on his side, though the author never says so.

Chapter 39 has often been compared with the thirteenth-century-BC Egyptian "Tale of Two Brothers," and it has been argued that Genesis is dependent on this story. However, there is remarkably little to suggest any connection except that both deal with the issue of a faithful single man who spurns the advances of a married woman, a motif found in many ancient tales. What Genesis stresses is both Joseph's total reliability so that Potiphar made him chief steward over all his estate (vv. 5-6) and also his stunning beauty, perhaps inherited from his mother Rachel, the only other person in the OT described as Joseph is in v. 6 (29:17).

The attempted seduction is described three times. First, accurately by the narrator in vv. 7-12, then by Potiphar's wife to the slaves in vv. 14-15, and finally to her husband in vv. 17-18. In both cases she distorts the events to put Joseph in the worst possible light. In addressing the slaves she identifies with them against Joseph and her husband in v. 14, and when talking to her husband she sides with the Egyptians against foreign slaves in v. 17. Her lies have the required result of infuriating her husband, but maybe they did not entirely convince him. Had he been sure of Joseph's guilt, he might have had him executed: instead Potiphar confines him to the royal prison which he managed. Whereas this looks like further degradation for Joseph, a step worse than slavery, like his sale into slavery years earlier, it actually moves him closer to triumph and the fulfillment of his childhood dreams.

Joseph in Prison (E, J) (39:21–40:23)

This, like the previous episode, begins with the observation that the LORD was with Joseph (39:21; cf. 2) and an account of Joseph's promotion to a position of authority. As before, however, his situation at the end seems more hopeless than at the outset. The chief cupbearer whom Joseph had asked to mention him to Pharaoh forgot and left him there in prison.

As in chs. 37 and 41, two dreams are described: this interest in dreams fits the Egyptian setting of the story, where dreams were seen as the gift of the gods putting one in direct contact with the supernatural world. However, Egyptians also believed that you needed experts to interpret dreams, and they were not readily available in prison. Hence the prisoners' glumness and Joseph's reassurance (40:7-8).

The chief cupbearer's dream compresses three stages of wine production — blossom, ripening, and pressing of grapes — into quick succession, suggesting perhaps the rapid fulfillment of the dream. The cupbearer was probably more than chief wine-taster; he probably acted as adviser to Pharaoh (cf. Nehemiah's similar role in Neh 1:11–2:8). Doubtless the promise of restoration was very welcome to him.

Bakery was a well-developed art in Egypt; so, encouraged by Joseph's interpretation of the other dreams, the chief baker tells his dream. Joseph makes his interpretation of the second dream as much like the first for as long as he can; only with the hanging of the baker does it diverge. The impaling of the corpse on a pole after execution is probably intended. This gruesome and exemplary form of capital punishment was intended to prevent the soul of the criminal from resting in the underworld.

Unfortunately for the baker Joseph's interpretation was fulfilled, but this of course vindicated his claim to have God's help to interpret dreams (cf. 41:16).

Joseph in Pharaoh's Palace (E, J?) (41:1-57)

Chapter 41 concludes the thirteen-year interlude in Joseph's life covered by chs. 39 and 40 (41:46; cf. 37:2). Separated from his family and struggling to make his way in Egypt, Joseph has twice been promoted by high Egyptian officials only later to be cast aside. In ch. 39 he rises to become chief steward in Potiphar's household, but ends up in prison. In ch. 40 he becomes confidant of the royal baker and cupbearer, only to be forgotten when the latter is released. Ch. 41 constitutes the third scene in this great triptych. Compared with the preceding chapters it starts ominously, for it says nothing about the LORD being with Joseph. Yet this time God is more evidently with Joseph than ever before, for he is miraculously brought out of prison, interprets Pharaoh's dreams, and is appointed second man in the kingdom.

The episode begins with two bizarre dreams. But even with access to the royal dream interpreters, Pharaoh cannot interpret them. This jogs the cupbearer's memory, and Joseph is summoned from the prison. The rapidity of Joseph's transformation from forgotten prisoner to royal adviser is accentuated in v. 14. But even to Pharaoh Joseph insists that it is God who enables him to interpret dreams, not his own intelligence. V. 16 should probably read: 'Except for God, who can announce Pharaoh's welfare?" but the drift of the NRSV is much the same.

Pharaoh's retelling of the dream embellishes the first account somewhat (e.g., vv. 19, 21), which helps us to appreciate how disturbed he was by this pair of alarming dreams. Joseph not only interprets them in a fairly natural way and explains the purpose of paired dreams, but he also turns them into a prophetic oracle about the future. The language of v. 29, literally, "Behold, seven years are coming," sounds like prophecy, and the conclusion drawn, "Now therefore let Pharaoh select a man . . . ," is a prophetic call to action. However, "take one-fifth of the produce of the land" (v. 34) is probably too precise at this juncture in the story; it may be translated more simply, "organize the land."

Pharaoh responds promptly and appoints him to the position of second-in-command in the land (vv. 40, 43). As vizier he was the great supervisor of all Egyptian government activities. The title "over my house" would, if it were a literal translation of the Egyptian phrase "master of the palace," indicate an official of lesser authority than the vizier, but it probably has the usual Hebrew sense here. The master of the house in Israel was second to the king, just as the vizier was in Egypt.

The vivid description of Joseph's installation as vizier in vv. 42-43 can be filled out from paintings of similar ceremonies from Egyptian tombs. Indeed, one portrays the appointment of the Semite Tutu as vizier. Various suggestions have been made about the original form and meaning of Joseph's Egyptian name, perhaps "the god has said, 'he will live,'" "the man he knows," or "[Joseph], who is called Ip-ankh." His wife's name Asenath means, "she belongs to the goddess Neit," or "she belongs to her father," or "she belongs to you." Joseph's age at his appointment (v. 46) allows us to calculate how long he had been in Egypt (cf. 37:2).

The explanation of the names of Manasseh and Ephraim (vv. 51-52) is paradoxical. Had he really forgotten his family, Joseph would not have mentioned them here. Besides, his insistence in v. 32 that a doubled dream indicates that fulfillment will be certain and prompt raises questions about his own dreams. Will his family ever see him again? Characteristically of Genesis, the last scene of one episode, here the coming of all the world to buy food from Egypt (vv. 54-57), anticipates the topic of the next section (chs. 42–47), when eventually all the brothers and his father will come and bow before him as the dreams foretold.

First Visit to Egypt by Jacob's Family (E, J) (42:1-38)

This chapter opens a new phase in the family's history. For about twenty years the narratives have focused on Joseph in Egypt: apart from ch. 38 we are told nothing of what was going on with Jacob's family in Canaan. But now three parallel episodes in Joseph's career are followed by three journeys to Egypt by the rest of the family (ch. 42, chs. 43–45, chs. 46–47).

Here Jacob reemerges as a major figure. He may be ageing, but he is still head of the family: it is his decision that leads his sons to go to buy bread in Egypt. But he is still protective of Benjamin, here called Joseph's brother (42:4), as if to remind us of Jacob's special love for the sons of Rachel.

In bowing down to Joseph, his brothers are partially fulfilling his dreams described in 37:6-10. But this of course sharpens Joseph's curiosity: What has happened to his brother Benjamin and his father? The sharp interrogation that follows is partly to elicit this information, but it is also designed to put the brothers into a position similar to that in which they were when they abandoned him. Now he wants to test them (42:15), ostensibly to see if they are telling the truth, but more importantly to see if they will adopt the same heartless attitude to Simeon as they did to him. His brothers clearly sense the parallel between this situation and the earlier one. They feel that divine justice is catching up with them, and they argue about who is most to blame. Interesting details about Joseph's sale, for example, his unheeded pleas for mercy, emerge in their conversation, which ch. 37 did not mention. The narrator alerts us to the fact that Joseph is not as callous as he appears by mentioning his weeping at hearing their confessions of guilt.

It is not clear why he returned their money in their sacks, but their guilty consciences interpret it as another bad omen (42:28). They give Jacob a rather sanitized account of their meeting with Joseph, leaving out some of their more unpleasant experiences, such as their joint imprisonment, describing Simeon's detention in the kindest of ways, and adding a promise Joseph did not make about free trade (vv. 30-34)!

However, the discovery of money in all their sacks alarms them and their father still further. The brothers doubtless saw this as another sign of judgment catching up with them, while Jacob maybe saw it as proof that they had actually sold Simeon into slavery: that is why the money had come back. So the scene ends with another bitter interchange recalling Jacob's distress when the brothers brought back news of Joseph's disappearance. Emotionally this is a rerun of that bitter episode. But the reader is wiser than the actors and can look forward in a more detached fashion to how they will react to the test (cf. 22:1).

Second Visit of Jacob's Family to Egypt (J, E) (43:1–45:28)

The description of this second visit by Joseph's brothers runs in close parallel to the first. (1) Jacob sends his sons to Egypt (42:1-4 par. 43:1-14); (2) arrival in Egypt (42:5 par. 43:15-25); (3) first audience with Joseph (42:6-16 par. 43:26-34); (4) brothers in custody (42:17 par. 44:1-13); (5) second audience with Joseph (42:18-24 par. 44:14–45:15); (6) departure from Egypt (42:25-28 par. 45:16-24); (7) sons report to Jacob (42:29-38 par. 45:25-28). There are many references back to the first visit in this second one. The much greater fullness of the account of this second visit shows that this is the climax of the Joseph story. The narrative tension builds through each scene until following Judah's great confession of guilt and plea for mercy the brothers are reconciled and their father consoled. Here we have Hebrew storytelling at its best, and attention will be drawn to some of its techniques.

43:1-14 As before (cf. 42:1), it is Jacob who takes the initiative and suggests that his sons go down to Egypt to buy grain. But this trip is much more problematic as a result of what happened on the previous outing. Not only is Simeon detained there, but Joseph has demanded that Benjamin be brought to Egypt as well, something Jacob is extremely loath to permit.

So once again the brothers discuss their last visit to Egypt. This time they are forced to stress the seriousness of the warning given to them about the consequences of not bringing Benjamin. And Jacob blames them for letting on that there was a younger brother. Eventually it is Judah's pledge to be responsible for Benjamin's welfare that persuades Jacob to let him go; already Judah's change of heart is beginning to be evident. However, just as he did when going to meet Esau, Jacob does his best to smooth their way by preparing a large present. But he is not sanguine about success, fearing that he will be bereaved again.

43:15-25 The narrative pace slows still further as their arrival in Egypt is fully described (cf. the brevity of 42:5). The tension rises as they are unexpectedly invited to dine with Joseph, who had seemed so hostile last time; only massive reassurances from the steward persuade them that they are not all about to be imprisoned. The restoration of Simeon seems to confirm his promises.

43:26-34 The audience with Joseph seems to go much more smoothly than on previous occasions. Joseph's joy on meeting his full brother Benjamin is mentioned to preclude any misinterpretation of his apparent harshness in the next encounter. But yet again the other brothers are alarmed by the seating plan, which seems to them like a spooky coincidence. But good food and drink help them forget their fears and enjoy themselves.

44:1-13 Modern readers, all too conscious of miscarriages of justice as a result of frame-ups, react uneasily to this account of Joseph's entrapment of his brothers. But this is to overlook the purpose of his actions; he is trying to re-create a parallel situation to the day they delivered him to the Ishmaelites despite the agony it caused their father. He is trying to discover whether they are ready to treat Benjamin in the same way.

His brothers, knowing their own innocence, try to demonstrate it by pointing out their honesty in returning the money found on the first trip. Then they rashly offer that if anyone is found to have stolen Joseph's cup he shall die, and all the others be enslaved. By this offer they are in a sense replicating Joseph's experience: he was enslaved, though his father believed him dead. But Joseph wants to test the bonds between Leah's sons and Rachel's, so his steward insists that only the guilty party must suffer.

The speed with which they submit to a search demonstrates their own conviction of innocence. But the tension rises as the search ends with the youngest and the cup is found. The episode invites comparison with Laban's pursuit of Jacob and his sons and the search for the teraphim. Then Jacob pronounced a death sentence on the guilty, not realizing that his favorite wife was to blame. On that occasion she escaped. But this time the only known surviving son of Rachel has been condemned by his brothers. How will they react to his arrest?

44:14–45:15 In this climactic scene the full extent of the brothers' transformation becomes apparent. They all tear their clothes and return to the city, showing their solidarity with Benjamin. And there Judah, who earlier had appeared to be one of the most hard-hearted and callous of them, makes a "speech of singular pathos and beauty" (Driver) in which he shows an amazing empathy with his father. It includes various details from the past that are already well known to the reader about Jacob's affection for Benjamin and his consequent reluctance to let him visit Egypt, but there are also fresh points. He accepts Jacob's blatant favoritism as a matter of course: "my wife bore me two sons" (44:27) implies that Jacob regarded Rachel as his only wife and only her two sons as his own. Yet Judah does not hold his own delegitimation by his father against him; rather, he cites it as an argument for sparing Benjamin. Then he mentions Jacob's reaction on seeing Joseph's garment, "Surely he has been torn to pieces." Finally, Judah offers, indeed insists, that he, the rejected son, should be taken as slave in place of Benjamin, whose detention would cause the death of his father.

Given this comprehensive change of heart by his brothers, it is little wonder that Joseph breaks down. Nor is it surprising that his brothers are struck dumb by his self-revelation. Joseph does not simply reassure his brothers in a psychological way, though; he argues theologically. "It was not you who sent me here, but God . . . to preserve life" (45:8, 5) sums up the theological message of the Joseph story and ties it in with the theme of the Pentateuch. The sale of Joseph ensured the preservation of Abraham's descendants and of many others as well, so that through him the families of the earth started to find blessing.

Joseph also mentions his special relationship to Pharaoh: "father to Pharaoh" means adviser to him. And whereas Joseph merely offered them the land of Goshen, somewhere in the East Nile Delta, Pharaoh is even more expansive, offering "the best of the land of Egypt" (vv. 18, 20). He not only gives them food and new sets of clothes, but he also supplies wagons (to judge from contemporary paintings, two-wheeled oxcarts) to transport the young and the elderly down to Egypt.

45:25-28 The closing scene offers a marvelous contrast to the last two mentioned returns of the brothers to Jacob. On both of those he declared that he would go down in mourning to Sheol, the abode of the dead (37:33, 35; 42:36, 38). Now he triumphantly declares, "Enough! My son Joseph is still alive. I must go and see him before I die." For other dramatic exit lines anticipating the next section of the story cf. 27:45; 29:14; 30:24; 37:35; 42:38.

Third Visit of Jacob's Family to Egypt (P, E, J) (46:1–47:31)

The third visit of Jacob's family to Egypt differs from the first two in lasting much longer; indeed, it looks like permanent immigration. But as God stresses in the opening vision to Jacob, it will be temporary. And before he dies, he insists that he must be buried in Canaan, the land of promise, with his ancestors. That is the people's true home. Within the total time span of the Pentateuch the Israelite sojourn in Egypt is just a blip in the progress toward settlement in Canaan (cf. 15:13-16).

However, for Jacob, who often anticipated his own death long before it occurred, it was a momentous step moving to Egypt. As he neared the border of Canaan near Beer-sheba, which was often regarded as the practical southern limit of the promised land, he offered sacrifices. There in a night vision he heard the traditional promises of nationhood, protection, and land reiterated for the last time in Genesis (cf. 12:1-3), as well as the unique assurance that Joseph would close his eyes in death. It may also be noted that this is the last statement of the promises to the patriarchs; not until the era of Moses will the LORD reaffirm them and bring their fulfillment much closer.

On the face of it these chapters seem to be a rather unconnected collection of diverse materials. Besides the obviously relevant account of the journey to Egypt and the meeting with Pharaoh, there is a list of Jacob's descendants (46:8-27), a description of Joseph's famine relief measures (47:13-26), and a deathbed oath (47:29-31). But on further reflection these elements are all closely connected to the theme of the Pentateuch.

The list of Jacob's descendants names seventy people who went down to Egypt with him. Seventy is also the total number of nations listed as descendants of Noah in ch. 10, so seventy had some symbolic significance in Bible times. This is confirmed by a careful reading of 46:8-27, which shows the author's keenness to make the total come to seventy. It looks as though he had a list of seventy descendants of Jacob, but then he realized that not all of them entered Egypt (e.g., Er and Onan; v. 12), or that some were born in Egypt (e.g., Manasseh and Ephraim; v. 20). Strictly speaking, just sixty-six descendants went down with Jacob, but if Dinah is added as well as Joseph and his sons, the total reaches seventy (vv. 26-27). Sarna (317) has suggested that seventy represents totality: it expresses the idea that all Israel went down to Egypt. It also shows how the promise of a multitude of descendants, first made to Abraham (12:2), is progressing toward fulfillment. The first readers of Genesis would have recognized these names, not simply as the names of their ancestors but as names of tribes and clans, so to them the fulfillment of the promise would have been even more apparent.

After the pause to list Jacob's descendants the story of the move to Egypt continues. Though the meeting of Jacob and Joseph is described briefly, it is pregnant with emotion. The superfluous remark about Joseph making ready his chariot suggests his excitement at the prospective reunion. Then the author suggests the impact Joseph's coming made on his father. Translated literally, the text says, "he appeared to him" (NRSV, "presented himself to him"). This terminology is reserved elsewhere in the OT for God's appearance to human beings; here it expresses the power and grandeur of Joseph in his chariot, accompanied by all his servants. But it is Jacob's words, "I can die now . . . [for] you are still alive," that are the most evocative for their sweet contrast with his previous comments on his death (37:33, 35; 42:36, 38; 45:28).

46:31-34 For his part Joseph is concerned that his brothers should not put their foot in Goshen until they meet Pharaoh. He will make it clear to Pharaoh that they have brought their flocks with them, so that they will not be sponging off the state. For their part they must describe themselves as "keepers of livestock," not "shepherds," because the Egyptians hate shepherds. Egyptian literature does not disclose a particular dislike of shepherds; it seems likely, though, that Joseph is pointing to the widespread distrust of nomadic peoples (e.g., gypsies) by settled urban people.

47:1-6 But in the pomp of the audience with Pharaoh the brothers forgot Joseph's advice and duly describe themselves as shepherds! Such is the benevolence of Pharaoh toward Joseph's family, however, that it does not matter. Indeed, in stilted official language he gives them permission to settle in Goshen as they had requested and offers them jobs as royal stockmen. Texts from the time of Rameses III show that foreigners were often employed in this role.

Jacob's meeting with Pharaoh is much less formal. The aged Jacob has to be brought into court and is then stood up (NRSV, "presented," fails to bring out the fact that Jacob had to be helped to stand, as the Hebrew implies). Then rather than Pharaoh granting favors to Jacob, it is Jacob who blesses Pharaoh (vv. 7, 10). All Pharaoh does is to inquire respectfully as to his age. Jacob's reply alludes to the many sorrows that have dogged his career (his flight from home, Rachel's death, the ravishment of Dinah, Joseph's disappearance). Then through Joseph Pharaoh grants the family permanent settlement rights in Egypt, "a holding in the land of Egypt," which gave them more rights than the typical immigrant. "The land of Rameses" (v. 11) appears to be a later name for the area of Goshen.

"I will bless those who bless you." Pharaoh's treatment of Jacob and his family certainly put him in the category of those who may expect to be blessed. As far as Genesis is concerned, this blessing extends not simply to Pharaoh but to his land, and this is illustrated by Joseph's handling of the famine. To modern readers this looks like exploitation, but this is not the perspective of the ancient Israelites or according to the story of the Egyptians either. They express their gratitude to Joseph for saving their lives (v. 25).

The OT approach to destitution is set out in Exod 21:2-11, Leviticus 25, and Deut 15:1-18. Free landholding peasants were liable to fall into debt whenever drought led to crop failure. In the absence of a welfare state richer relatives or neighbors were expected to help them out first by buying the debtor's children as slaves, then by giving a mortgage on the debtor's land, and finally, if the worst came to the worst, taking on the debtor as a slave himself. Two points should be noted about these apparently harsh arrangements. To be a slave, as the OT envisages it, was more like being an employee in modern society, whereas being free was like being self-employed. The OT therefore envisages that many slaves may decide to turn down their right to freedom at the end of six years; they may prefer the security of being a slave of a good employer to the risks of being free and self-employed (Exod 21:5-6; Deut 15:16-17). Secondly, when land was mortgaged or a landowner sold himself into slavery, he or it was automatically released without payment in the Year of Jubilee, which occurred every fifty years (Leviticus 25).

The arrangements Joseph made are not exactly those envisaged in the law. Whereas in Israel it was the wealthy relative or neighbor who was expected to bail out the bankrupt, in Egypt it was Pharaoh. Four stages of increasing destitution are described. First, when their own crops have failed, the Egyptians bought grain for money from Joseph. Then they mortgaged their animals; it would seem unlikely that they actually sold them. Then they mortgaged their land, or, more exactly, sold it and leased it back in exchange for grain. Finally, they sold themselves as slaves (47:21). As a result of these deals, they saw Joseph as having saved their lives (v. 25). Though the date of Joseph's career cannot be established on the basis of this story, it certainly reflects accurately the tenancy arrangements in Egypt, where all the land was held by the crown or the temples and private land-ownership hardly existed.

If Joseph's saving Egypt from starvation reflects the partial fulfillment of the promise that "in you all the families of the earth shall be blessed," the episode closes with other clear allusions to the promises, namely, the multiplication of Jacob's descendants and his wish to be buried with his ancestors in Canaan (vv. 27, 30). As often in Genesis, the last scene of one episode anticipates the topic of the next one, here Jacob's deathbed testament.

Last Days of Jacob and Joseph (J, E, P) (48:1–50:26)

The most important figure of Genesis is Jacob, the father of the nation of Israel, and for this reason the narrative gives ample space to describing his death and burial. Indeed, it has been argued that the last words of Jacob, the blessing of Jacob in ch. 49, constitute the book's peak with its vision of the twelve future tribes of Israel each occupying their allocated portion of the promised land.

Initially this section of the book looks somewhat disorganized, and various attempts have been made to explain the diversity of the material in terms of different sources being drawn upon. But as pointed out in the commentary on ch. 35, there is a similar arrangement of topics and material at the end of the previous main sections of the book, that is, 22:15–25:10 and 35:9-29, which suggests that the same author or redactor is responsible for these passages. Running through this whole section is a strong affirmation of the promises and their fulfillment. Jacob's last recorded words, like those of his grandfather before him and his own father Isaac, are all concerned with the promises made by God and the progress toward their fulfillment. Each expresses both his own faith in God's power to fulfill them and the need of his children to exercise a similar faith and work toward their fulfillment.

Jacob begins (48:3-4) by reminiscing about the past, bringing together promises made to him at Bethel (35:11-12), the last words of his father Isaac (28:3), and elements of the promises made to Abraham (17:8). He then proceeds to adopt Joseph's sons, Ephraim and Manasseh, as his own, thereby putting them on a par with his own sons, such as Reuben and Simeon. This explains why the traditional twelve tribes include Ephraim and Manasseh but not Joseph. Adoptions within a family are well known in the ancient orient: a text from Ugarit mentions a grandfather adopting his grandson as his heir.

But in adopting Manasseh and Ephraim Jacob reverses their seniority, putting the younger Ephraim before the older Manasseh by placing his right hand on the younger boy. This so annoys Joseph that he grasps (NRSV, "took," is too gentle) Jacob's right hand to put it on Manasseh's head and addresses his father rather brusquely. But Jacob, despite his blindness, knows what he is doing and insists on the new order. Manasseh will become a people, but Ephraim a multitude of nations, perhaps echoing the promise to Abraham (17:4-6). This recollection of the descendants prompts Jacob to reassert the importance of the land promise: his descendants will return to Canaan and take possession especially of the portion he had conquered by the sword. It is not clear which part of the land he means, but the area where Shechem lived seems most probable (cf. ch. 34).

This incident is full of echoes of Isaac's blessing of his sons Jacob and Esau. It is a deathbed blessing. Both patriarchs are blind or nearly so (cf. 48:8, 10). In both the natural order of seniority is reversed, once involuntarily and once deliberately. In both there is a strong request to maintain the birth order, which is rejected by the patriarch. If Isaac's unintended reversal of seniority is unalterable, how much more is Jacob's deliberate change. But this reversal is not peculiar to chs. 27 and 48; it is also the case with Cain and Abel, and Perez and Zerah (4:1-8; 38:27-30), making it almost a general principle in Genesis.

After adopting his grandsons and blessing them Jacob finally addresses his sons in a long poem that is usually called "the blessing of Jacob" (49:2-27). Much discussion has taken place about the origin and transmission of this poem. It is universally acknowledged to be one of the oldest parts of the Hebrew Bible. It may indeed go back in some original form to Jacob himself, but its present form is later than the patriarchal age. For the most part it pictures the situation of the tribes in the judges era, so it may date from then. But when it portrays the future of Judah, the rise of the Davidic monarchy is clearly in mind, so some would date it then.

It has sometimes been suggested that the blessing of Jacob is really a conglomerate of originally independent sayings, but this seems unlikely because about two-thirds of the poem reflects on the major actors in the rest of Genesis, Judah, Joseph, Reuben, Simeon, Levi, and Benjamin, whereas the others mentioned only in lists have about one verse each. It is hard to see these individual verses ever circulating on their own, or the curses on Reuben, Simeon, and Levi being preserved separately by the tribes themselves. For this reason it seems best to take the poem as a unit and try to understand the individual sayings within the context of the whole.

Like Noah (9:25), Jacob begins by cursing the sons guilty of unfilial behavior. The oldest by right had various privileges and was believed to inherit his father's dynamism (v. 3), but Reuben had forfeited his rights by misbehavior, sleeping with his father's concubine (35:22). Jacob had said nothing about it then, but now on his deathbed he speaks his mind (cf. 1 Kgs 2:5-6) and demotes his eldest from being head of the family.

Simeon and Levi were the next in age, but their behavior in slaughtering the sons of Hamor after the Dinah affair had annoyed Jacob (34:30), and now he more outspokenly condemns their acts. Some of Jacob's imagery is obscure. It is clear that he is referring to their revenge in general, but not what their hamstringing of oxen refers to. Genesis 34 speaks of them capturing oxen, not hamstringing them. It therefore seems likely that the oxen are figurative, referring either to the leaders of the Canaanites who were massacred, or to Jacob himself, whose plans for peaceful coexistence with the Canaanites were ruined by his sons' action. Jacob therefore sentences the descendants of Simeon and Levi to dispersal in Israel. The tribe of Simeon was gradually absorbed by the surrounding tribe of Judah, while the Levites were assigned forty-eight cities throughout the land when it was allocated by Joshua. Thus both tribes could be said to have been divided and scattered.

Judah, next in age, therefore inherits the family headship. The sayings about him are the longest and the first that could be termed blessings. He is pictured as the acknowledged leader of his brothers (49:8), and like a lion that seizes its prey, returns to its den, and dares anyone to challenge it (v. 9). This image foreshadows the military triumphs of David and gave rise to the messianic title "The Lion of Judah."

49:10 continues this picture of Judah as national leader, and declares that it will be permanently his: "the scepter shall not depart." What is more, a permanent Judean dynasty will ensure "ruler's staff . . . feet." Finally, all nations will pay tribute to him. The first part of "until tribute comes to him" has been discussed at great length. The NRSV margin gives some other possible translations, but has put the most likely in the main text. Many psalms mention that the Davidic king was appointed to rule the nations, and this seems to be the allusion in Genesis too (e.g., Ps 72:8-11).

Finally, this age when this king appears will be one of astonishing plenty. The territory of Judah is famed for its grapes, but in this era there will be such a grape harvest that it will not matter if the tethered royal donkey eats them and people wash their clothes in wine. 49:12 either takes this picture of abundance further or is a description of the king's beauty.

The saying about Zebulun (49:13) is problematic, for though they settled in the north near Sidon, they lived inland some way from the coast (Josh 19:10-16). Maybe some Zebulunites worked for the Phoenicians, or the tribe settled by the sea for a short while.

Issachar (49:14-15) will settle in a fertile part of the country and there become a slave to its neighbors. De Vaux (1978: 664) has linked this prophecy with an El-Amarna letter which mentions slave-labor gangs in the area of Issachar's settlement, the eastern Jezreel valley, but this is uncertain.

A pun on Dan's name (= he judged; cf. 30:6) is followed by a comparison with a horned viper, suggesting the tribe will be small but deadly to its enemies. There may be an allusion here to the exploits of Samson, a Danite (Judges 13–16). The prayer in 49:18 may reflect the precarious position of the tribe of Dan in the judges period (they were forced to emigrate northward; Judges 17–18), or indeed of the whole nation. The father of the nation thus prays for his descendants in their future predicament.

A multiple pun on Gad's name (49:19) — four of the six words in this verse contain the consonants *gd* — reflects the tribe's frequent involvement in border wars.

Asher (v. 20) occupied a fertile strip of coastland running north from Mt. Carmel and may have exported its produce to foreign courts.

As translated in the NRSV, the saying about Naphtali (v. 21) sounds like a compliment, but it could be taken as a mild rebuke. The historical allusion is quite unclear.

Though the general drift of the blessing on Joseph is clear, many details of its interpretation are not. As the NRSV translates v. 22, Joseph is compared to a flourishing tree, a frequent OT image for the righteous (e.g., Ps 1:3). But it may be better, as with the other tribal blessings, to find animal imagery here. 49:22 could be translated "Joseph is a wild ass, a wild ass beside a spring, his wild colts beside the wall." The archers in v. 23 may refer to the many opponents that Joseph had to overcome in his career. This image carries over into v. 24, which probably refers to his opponents' bows losing their suppleness. In other words, all the attacks on Joseph proved fruitless in the long run thanks to the strength "of the Mighty One of Jacob," an ancient title for God. The blessing then seems to move into the future, reflecting on the tremendous riches that the tribes of Ephraim and Manasseh will enjoy as the largest tribes dwelling in fertile land.

The picture of Benjamin (v. 27) as a ravenous wolf does not match the picture of him in the rest of Genesis, but it certainly became a militant tribe in the judges period (Judg 3:15-30; 5:14; chs. 19–21). Interestingly, there is no allusion to Saul the first king, an indication of the age of this saying.

Having predicted the glorious future of the tribes in the land of promise, Jacob reiterates his wish to be buried there (49:29-33). In fact, he is given a grand state funeral in Egyptian style. First he is mummified, a lengthy process (also done to Joseph; 50:26), before the huge funeral cortege set out for Canaan. Just before entering the land the Egyptians stopped at the threshing floor of Atad. Traditionally this has been located near Jericho in the Jordan valley (cf. 50:10), but a more modern suggestion is that it is at Tell el Ajjul, four miles southwest of Gaza. At any rate, the Egyptians turned back there, and let the family proceed to Machpelah for a private interment.

The book of Genesis ends with two short codas. First, Joseph's brothers, fearing that his kindness was prompted by love for his father rather than by love for them, plead for mercy and forgiveness. This is the first time they have asked him to forgive them, and so it is by no means redundant. However, it does provide yet another opportunity to stress God's overruling purpose in all the events recorded: "Even though you intended to do harm to me, God intended it for good, in order to preserve a numerous people."

Finally, like Abraham, Isaac, and Jacob on their deathbeds, Joseph's last concern was that the promises should be fulfilled. So he insists that when the family eventually leaves Egypt, they should carry up his bones and bury him in Canaan. In this way the promises that constitute the theme of Genesis are linked to the exodus, which will be the focus of the next book.

Exodus

William D. Johnstone

INTRODUCTION

Perspectives for Understanding Exodus

"There is no earlier or later in the Torah," say the rabbis: timelessness, or applicability to all time, is characteristic of the law of Moses. Such a saying can appear particularly puzzling to the reader when confronted with a book like Exodus. For Exodus gives every appearance of being an account of events, and events by their nature occur but once in the past. It is that concern with the past as past that has motivated much research on Exodus: if only we can re-create precisely the period, conditions, and events to which it refers, we shall be in a better position to understand what it says.

But if the rabbinic saying is correct, that attempt is foredoomed to failure. However related the narrative of Exodus must be to historical events, these events are not recorded for their own sake but as expressive of enduring truths of the human condition. The saying has an echo in Psalms, precisely in connection with an incident recorded in Exodus: "O that today you would listen to his voice! Do not harden not your hearts, as at Meribah . . ." (Ps 95:7-8; cf. Exod 17:7). It is the readers' response in their "today" that is the point of the narrative. Part of the mechanism for securing that response is that the narrative in Exodus is related at every point to religious institutions: the events that happened long ago to somebody else can be appropriated through the observance of religious practices and so made real in every generation. This is true above all of the Passover (ch. 12), still observed annually by the Jewish community as a memorial and as a basis for expectation ("next year in Jerusalem"). But it is true of the other institutions as well: circumcision, the festival of Unleavened Bread, the offering of firstlings, the revelation of Torah, the covenant, and the sanctuary, all of which bulk more or less large in Exodus.

It is likely, thus, that Exodus is not so much about Israel's escape from Egypt, the imperial power of the last half of the second millennium BC, however that is to be reconstructed historically, as about using the undoubted historical facts of Israel's deliverance as a signal example of enduring truths of Israel's existence. A strong case can be made for the composition of a first draft of Exodus during the Babylonian exile of the sixth century BC. It is that moment of national catastrophe, when every agency supporting national life has been destroyed — temple, monarchy, political independence through possession of land — which has precipitated the reappraisal of all the earlier traditions and practices and the attempt to produce a new synthesis. Superimposed upon that first draft is the final edition of the work, which is a response to the actual attempts to re-create national life in the postexilic period. Hopes for the future, which only God can bring about, are here expressed through an idealized portrait of Israel's origins; this is what the journey through the wilderness must be like if Israel is successfully to enter the promised land.

The presentation of Exodus in the following pages as a combination of two major editions may come as a surprise to some readers. To those schooled in the academic tradition of the past hundred years and more it has come to be accepted that the Pentateuch represents the combination of four "sources." The view taken here is that there is no doubt that, behind the older of the two versions identified below, lie preexilic traditions; but it is doubtful whether earlier written accounts of these traditions, which were preserved after all in a vast reservoir of living religious practice, can be recovered by the analysis of the extant literary account. The "older version" of the exilic period is a free literary composition and digest of preexilic traditions, not (or not only) the elaboration of inherited written "kernels." Equally, for some, it may appear disturbing that we should argue that the biblical revelation is not unitary but represents a dialogue between two contrasting presentations. In answer to that it must be pointed out that this dialogue corresponds to the way in which the history of Israel is presented in two contrasting presentations later in the Bible (compare Samuel-Kings on the one hand and Chronicles on the other). It also corresponds to Jewish tradition of the dual Torah revealed at Sinai (the written form accompanied by continuous oral discussion) and to the requirement that any student of the Torah should get a fellow student. It is in debate between wholly acceptable contrasting positions about inherited tradition that further insight is gained. That debate is already present in the form and structure of the biblical record.

COMMENTARY

Linking the Book of Exodus with the Destiny of God's People (1:1-7)

The book of Exodus is a link in a chain of developments, not just a book on its own. It can be understood only against the background of what has gone before, as told in Genesis, just as at the end of the book there is a link through the construction of the tabernacle with the rest of the Pentateuch and beyond.

The link with the past is made in the most succinct way possible — through a family tree. "The sons of Israel" are here portrayed in full individuality as Jacob's eleven sons, who with their entire households come to join Joseph, the remaining son, in Egypt. The drama of how Joseph had been sold as a slave into Egypt by his brothers and had then risen to a position of power at court second only to Pharaoh himself as told in Genesis 37–50 is presupposed. In the reunion of this small family resident as foreigners in Egypt the fate of all Israel is at stake (cf. Gen 45:7).

The sons of Jacob coming down to settle with Joseph are here grouped by mother in order of birth: the six sons of Jacob's first wife, Leah; the son of his second wife, Rachel; the two sons by Bilhah, Rachel's maid; and the two sons by Zilpah, Leah's maid (the story of the birth of all twelve is told in Gen 29:31–30:24; 35:16-18; cf. the summary, following the same sequence as here, in Gen 35:22-26). The sequence of these names changes in later lists in the Hebrew Bible (HB) when the historic significance of the tribes in relation to one another is established (e.g., in 1 Chr 2:3–8:40). The "seventy" members of the family of Jacob are listed in Gen 46:8-27.

But this family does not merely stand in historical continuity with the past. It also inherits the promises made by God in that past. The statement that "they were fruitful and prolific; they multiplied" (1:7) echoes the command to humankind at creation, "be fruitful and multiply and fill the earth" (Gen 1:28, here in the fuller form of the post-flood renewal of the command, Gen 9:7; the Hebrew for "land" in 1:7 is the same as that for "earth" in Genesis 1). But they become not only numerous but also powerful (cf. v. 20), and therein the fateful seeds of tension with the host country are sown. Vv. 1-7 thus look forward to the persecution and deliverance of the following chapters and the means of the fulfillment of the promises to the ancestors.

Persecution of the Hebrews in Egypt (1:8–2:22)

At the end of Genesis, Egypt has become the haven from famine for the family of Jacob. Through a reversal of fortunes, worked by God himself, the deadly schemes of Joseph's brothers have been turned into the means of preserving life. Now Israel as a whole finds itself in a far greater danger; yet God is, once more, about to be its deliverer. The whole of Exod 1:8–15:21 is designed to show how it is God alone who, "by signs and wonders, by a mighty hand and an outstretched arm" (Deut 4:34), saves his people.

Paradoxically, God's blessing of Israel provokes persecution. A "new king" has arisen over Egypt who is entirely ignorant of the blessings bestowed on his country by Joseph's administration. Israel's increase in numbers and power provokes a nationalist reaction on the part of the Egyptians; fear precipitates measures of the utmost barbarity to reassert their control (the vocabulary of blessing in 1:7, "multiplied and grew . . . strong," is picked up in the same or parallel vocabulary in Pharaoh's speech in v. 9 and provides the reason for the persecution about to be detailed throughout the rest of ch. 1).

The historical context is sketched with the utmost brevity. The story is told from the point of view of Israel and is deliberately generalized to serve as pattern to encourage faith. The entire narrative, indeed, is about to be related to religious institutions such as circumcision and sabbath and, especially, the two annual festivals of Passover and Weeks/Pentecost, as the means of perpetual participation in the experience of God's deliverance. Thus Pharaoh is identified only as the "new king . . . who did not know Joseph." The subsequent note of the name of one of the places, Rameses (1:11, usually located in the northeast delta), where the Israelites are to work as slave laborers, is, astonishingly enough, the only positive indication of the historical period envisaged in the entire book; it relates to the famous "Ramesside" period, the nineteenth and twentieth Egyptian dynasties (c. 1320-1085 BC).

The particular fear of the Egyptians is that the Israelites as an alien group will multiply to such an extent that they will become a threat to the security of the state (cf. the prodigious growth of the warriors to 600,000 within three generations, 12:37); especially in case of war they might join forces with the enemy and thus "gain control of the land" (as the meaning of the phrase at the end of v. 10 may be in the immediate context, as in the JPSV). Pharaoh thus looks for measures to reduce the number of Israelites and to keep them in submission. He successively attempts three measures.

The first (1:11-14) is to grind the Israelites down by forcing them to become slave laborers in Pharaoh's building projects. The word translated "forced labor" (v. 11) connotes the manhandling of building materials and well suggests the arduous toil. But the policy has precisely the opposite effect: the more oppressive the regime, the more Israel "multiplies" (against the NRSV, the same verb is deliberately repeated in vv. 10 and 12). The Egyptians become "sick with terror" (v. 12) at the unchecked growth of Israel and now subject them to the most crushing of menial tasks in the pitiless conditions of the delta: brick making, building, and laboring in the fields.

1:13-14 introduce the thematic term which is to dominate this narrative and much of the HB beyond it: "slavery" (the root *'bd,* in its noun and verb forms, occurs five times in these verses and some sixty-two times in Exodus 1–13). The fundamental point to be made is that release from slavery to a human master can only be achieved by God himself, who must in turn be served with no less devotion. To the Israelites the word for "slavery" is the same as that for the "worship" of God (*'abodah,* 12:25-26; 13:5).

We should observe the role of this passage within the widest framework of the exilic version of Israel's history which concludes at 2 Kings 25. It is likely that there is a cross reference between the description of Pharaoh's oppression in 1:11 and the portrayal of the tyrannical acts of Solomon in the last years of his rule. No fewer than three relatively infrequent terms used in v. 11 ("forced labor" [included by the NRSV in "*task*masters"]; "burden"

[NRSV, "forced labor"]; and "supply cities") recur in the 1 Kings narrative on Solomon (e.g., 1 Kgs 4:6; 11:28; and 9:19 respectively; a similar interplay will be noted later between Exodus 32 and 1 Kings 12). By his violation of the law on monarchy in Deut 17:15-17 (cf. the account of his later years in 1 Kings 9–11), Solomon in a sense forced his people "to return to Egypt." The final years of Solomon threaten a rerun of the tyranny of Pharaoh; in the end, the monarchy that had promised the realization of Israel's destiny becomes instead, through its failure, the instrument of its deportation to Babylon. Egyptian enslavement is understood typologically in the time of the Babylonian exile as an ever present threatening possibility of Jewish life. The full pain and horror of it can be felt only in looking back from the ideal of a free people, dwelling undisturbed in its land, each family in the rural model of self-sufficiency living "under its vine and fig tree" (1 Kgs 4:25), which was realized in the early years of Solomon and lost once again — and in a sense forever — under the Babylonians.

Pharaoh now tries his second measure: to turn the Israelite midwives into infanticides among their own people. They are instructed to put to death every Hebrew male child at birth (1:15-21). The words "put to death" (v. 16) are used in the HB of an officially sanctioned death penalty. But the midwives acknowledge a higher authority than Pharaoh: God himself. The term "God-fearer," given here (vv. 17, 21), has already been used of Abraham, the founding father and role model of every community of faith, in Gen 22:12; it implies awe before God's revelation of himself and unconditional obedience to his commandments (cf. Exod 20:18, 20). The commandment in this case — in advance of the revelation of the Decalogue in Exodus 20 — can only be the law on the sanctity of human life made binding on Noah, the second father of humanity, and his sons in Gen 9:5-7 (where, significantly, it is related to the terms "be fruitful, teem, multiply" just used of Israel in Exod 1:7; cf. vv. 12 and 20). But the potential absence of such "fear of God," demanded though it is of all humanity, has already been anticipated among non-Israelites, the Philistines in Gen 20:11 and the Egyptians themselves in Gen 42:18.

Pharaoh's plan is foiled by the resourcefulness of these midwives. Their significance in the narrative is heightened by their being named: in contrast to the unnamed Pharaoh (and all the other anonymous Egyptians in the later narrative), they are given names, "Beauty" and "Maiden." The fact that the growing population of Hebrews can be served by only two midwives, who between them would have to attend every birth in order to carry out Pharaoh's command, lends credibility to their tale of the "vigor" of the Hebrew mothers. Through these God-fearing midwives not a male child is harmed, and so God "gave them families." The reference is probably to families for Israel, not merely for the midwives: the personal pronoun "them" is plural masculine and resumes the end of 1:20; vv. 20b and 21b are parallel; the second plan to limit the Hebrew population founders just as the first had done (v. 12).

A third plan has to be put into effect (1:22): if the midwives will not do the deed, the whole populace of Egypt must be recruited. The MT heightens the irrational and indiscriminate nature of Pharaoh's decree by apparently including the Egyptian boys as well in the drowning.

At this climactic moment of persecution and powerlessness the birth of Moses takes place, Moses who is destined to become the agent of deliverance of his people. The whole of the next subparagraph, 2:1-22, is devoted to his birth, upbringing, and early manhood. It is a story of high drama — and that is precisely the point. The most important observation to make is the absence, for the only time in the book, of direct action by God, however much the reader may sense that events are being controlled "behind the scenes." This apparent absence of God, expressed not least through the flounderings of much of the human action, prepares the way for the next section, 2:23–4:17, where God himself will be portrayed as the one who directly intervenes as the true deliverer of Israel.

The whole narrative in 2:1-22 can thus be read as a drama entirely on the human plane. The inhumanity of Pharaoh is contrasted with the natural humanity of the Hebrew family, who, again with great resourcefulness, seek to preserve the life of their infant son (vv. 1-4), and with the humanity of his own daughter, who is moved by common pity to rescue the doomed, alien child from the Nile (vv. 5-10).

There are satisfying ironical twists in the tale. Pharaoh's omnipotence is undermined by the power of those regarded as weakest in society. The Hebrew midwives introduce a series of women who despite their lack of status prepare the way for Israel's deliverance: the slave woman Jochebed, the mother of Moses, the deliverer to be; his sister Miriam; Pharaoh's own daughter and her attendants; and, finally, the daughters of the priest of Midian, one of whom is to become Moses' wife. All of them, by their fear of God or by their commitment to such basic human values as preservation of life, compassion, or hospitality, provide the first links in the chain of events which lead eventually to Israel's freedom.

The ironies multiply: the Hebrew mother who was to be robbed of her child now becomes his wet nurse and is paid to boot. The objective of Pharaoh to limit the power of the Hebrews is undermined by his own daughter and her ladies-in-waiting: the one who is to become most powerful Hebrew leader and the agent of the destruction of the later Pharaoh and his host in the Red Sea (chs. 14–15) is adopted by Pharaoh's daughter and brought up in his own court. The name "Moses," "the one who draws out," is imparted by Pharaoh's daughter (v. 10). She applies it to her own action in drawing Moses out of the Nile; it might then have been more appropriate for it to have been in the form of the passive participle, "Mashuy," "the one drawn out." The irony is that in naming her adopted son with the masculine active participle, "Mosheh," Pharaoh's own daughter is signaling that he is the one who is destined to achieve precisely what Pharaoh feared and his policy was designed to prevent: to "draw" the Israelites out of the land. It is tempting to see yet another significance in the name: given the Ramesside context, is it possible that "Moses" is a play on the name "Ra-meses" borne by eleven Pharaohs of the period, meaning "Ra [the sun god] has given birth"? That would be especially appropriate given a later theme in Exodus, that God will execute judgment on the gods of Egypt (6:6; 7:4; 12:12).

There is, however, a fitness to later circumstances in the unfolding of events. This fitness is focused in the question of the Hebrew to Moses in 2:14: "Who made you a commander and judge over us?" At this stage the answer to that rhetorical question must be, "No one." Moses is as yet the impulsive human being, moved by raw emotion against injustice against, or even among, the people with whom he knows he is kin (2:11-13; v. 11 picks up 1:11). He takes the law into his own hand to vindicate a Hebrew who is suffering ("fatally" is implied by the Hebrew) at the hands of an Egyptian and another at the hands of a fellow Hebrew. Yet everything in his background and training is preparing him for the day in which God, now concealed in the background, will appoint him precisely as leader and lawgiver of his people. It is then that the purity of his descent from the tribe of Levi (2:1) will become significant, for it is to be from Levi that the teachers of the law and the priests at the altar are to be derived (ch. 28). It is then that Moses' innate gifts of physical strength (cf. 2:2), energy, and moral outrage, here shown in action (cf. v. 17), will be harnessed and brought to fulfillment.

There is thus also pathos in the story in the reversal of roles that Moses has to undergo (2:15-22). He who is to realize the identity of his people is here mistaken for an Egyptian; he who is to be the champion of his people is the victim; he who is to lead his people out at the exodus "with a high hand" into the wilderness toward the promised land is forced to flee in a dead-end exodus into the desert as a fugitive; he who bears the exclusive name of Levi marries the daughter of a foreign priest ("Reuel," however, means "friend of God"). The low point of his fortunes is marked by the name he gives to the first son of that union, "Gershom," meaning "an alien there" (a pun may also be intended on the verb *geresh,* "drive out," used in v. 17). The section ends as it began — with the birth of a son (2:2, 22). But, whatever hopes had been aroused by the amazing deliverance of the infant Moses, they have been dashed, and the deliverance of the people seems farther away than ever.

Moses Commissioned (2:23–4:17)

This section is introduced with a brief passage establishing the link between the external events of history and the unseen workings of God (2:23-25). The death of the king who had driven Moses from Egypt marks a new opportunity. But in the meantime the persecution continues. No fewer than four words for "crying, groaning" (2:23-24) convey the intensity of Israel's suffering. But these are matched by an equal number of verbs for "taking note" on the part of God, arranged in climactic sequence: "he heard . . . remembered his covenant . . . saw . . . and knew" (2:24-25). The covenant which God remembers is that made first with Abraham in Genesis 15. The link with the next two generations of Israel's forefathers, Isaac and Jacob, as in Gen. 50:24, relates that covenant specifically to the promise of land. Israel's hope is not just for deliverance from slavery in Egypt but for the realization of its national destiny by entry into the promised land, where the privileges and responsibilities of deliverance can be lived out (cf. 3:8).

The course of God's plan embedded in the unfolding events is now disclosed (3:1-9). It is appropriate that the nature of the divine act in the realm of the mundane should become clear to Moses in the course of his ordinary duties as a shepherd in the wilderness for his father-in-law. The wilderness pasturage turns out, wittingly or unwittingly, to be located at "the mountain of God"; there a natural object, a bush, becomes invested with supernatural significance: "the bush burned but was not consumed" (3:2). The MT is not completely unambiguous about the nature of the divine apparition: whether the angel of the Lord appeared *in,* or *as,* the flame of fire. For the latter sense, it may be noted that elsewhere in the HB fire is used as symbol of the divine presence (e.g., Exod 19:18); in that case the stress here would be on the communication by God to Moses (cf. 3:4). But why, then, does God speak from the tree and not from the mountain itself (as in ch. 19)? The better interpretation — which is, in any case, the more natural grammatically in the Hebrew — may, therefore, be the former: the Lord appeared *in* the flame of fire. There is here fuller symbolism: the tree stands for Israel, the fire for persecution in Egypt, and the burning without being consumed for the fact that, despite persecution, Israel is not destroyed. It is because God is present in the midst of the affliction of his people that he is able to deliver them and lead them to the promised land (3:7-9). The conventional description of that land as "flowing with milk and honey," introduced now for the first time in the HB (3:8), expresses an ideal of paradisal prosperity based on God's provision: as the first man had to tend the garden of Eden (Gen 2:15), so human cooperation is required to harvest the bounty of the land. But its abundant yield of natural products requires no backbreaking toil such as Israel is now enduring in Egypt.

It is one thing to hear the gracious promises of God, but it is quite another to be commissioned to be the agent by whom these promises are to be carried out (3:10). There now follows an extended dialogue between Moses and God (3:10–4:17) in which Moses objects five times to his being chosen as agent; in response, God provides further clarification of his being and action.

(1) Moses' natural first reaction is modesty, a due sense of personal inadequacy at the overwhelming magnitude of the task (3:11): to confront the world emperor, Pharaoh, to convince his own people, and then to defeat the indigenous inhabitants of the land (in 3:8, 17, the MT lists six of the traditional seven ethnic groups [Deut 7:1]). Moses' expression of inadequacy precipitates the assurance by God of his enabling presence against which no adversary can prevail.

This assurance is coupled with the first "sign." The word is used here and in 4:1-9, where three more signs are given, demonstrations of the invincible power of God in favor of Israel ("wonders" is used of the demonstration of God's power against the Egyptians, especially in the "plagues"; cf. 4:21). This first sign, unlike the three in ch. 4, is not designed as confirmation in advance of Moses' status as leader in the exodus; rather, the success of the exodus will itself be the sign confirming the claims of God. This first sign, "serving God at the mountain," thus links together the whole of the narrative in the Pentateuch from Exodus up to Numbers 10: it is precisely at the Mountain of God that the covenant will be made which will formalize the relationship between God and God's people and the revelation of the law will take place by which God's people can remain in relationship with him.

(2) Moses' second objection turns from "Who am I?" to "Who are You?" (3:13-22). How can he convince his own people unless he has a new revelation of who God is? God has hitherto based his claims on the covenant he made in the past with the patriarchs. That promise is now activated in terms of an exposition of his name, "Yahweh." Given that a name in Hebrew may be held to contain a definition of the character of the person who bears that name (1 Sam 25:25 is a clear example), it is likely that this name of God is meant to be enigmatic: no human being, not even Moses, can fully know the nature of God. The word "Yahweh" by itself is a third-person masculine singular of the verb "to be" in the future tense, "he will be" (or, possibly, "he will cause to be"). Both subject and predicate are left undefined: who God is and what he will be are not indicated. The enigmatic character of the name is still further heightened: not only is it then expounded in first-person common terms, "I shall be," but, above all, a relative clause is added in which the same elusive verb is repeated. A possible translation of the entire phrase, "I shall be who I shall be," fully safeguards the mystery of the divine being and the freedom of his action. Only a God who is of such transcendent nature and power is worth affirming.

Yet the name conveys certain constants: God's nature is not arbitrary or inconsistent. He is the one who can be affirmed as the living God. His own exposition in first-person terms expresses the absoluteness of the divine initiative in all circumstances. The "I" is relational: it presupposes the "you" of his people. Thus he who is inexpressible in his transcendence is, nonetheless, the eternal one who commits himself to constant relationship with his people. He is not just the God of Abraham, Isaac, and Jacob: the promise in the past is continually renewed and moves forward through God's personal action to its fulfillment.

It is with that assurance that God commissions Moses to go to his people and to Pharaoh (3:15-22). The ideal response of the people is portrayed: in the light of this reaffirmation of the covenant to the forefathers in terms of deliverance from their present affliction, they will believe in Moses without hesitation. But it will be different with Pharaoh; only demonstrations of divine power will force him to let Israel go.

This section is closely integrated into the following chapters by a series of thematic terms and concepts and even by the chronology of events envisaged. The motif of "spoiling the Egyptians" here announced (3:21-22) recurs in the context of the final plague, the culminating demonstration of the strength of the LORD's hand, in 11:1-3; 12:29-36. At first sight, the spoiling of the Egyptians by the Israelites may appear mercenary, deceitful, and vindictive. The true significance of the action can be appreciated only in the light of the legislation on the release of Hebrew slaves in Deut 15:12-18. There in the same language it is laid down that when slaves are given their liberty they are not to be sent away "empty-handed": they are entitled to the value of the work which they have supplied; they need resources to set themselves up in their new life of freedom so that they do not revert to the dependency of slavery. (A further instance of the verb "despoil" will be found in 33:6, where, because of its own "enslavement" at the golden calf incident, Israel is "self-despoiled" and forfeits the tokens of its liberty.)

In two further respects, the context of that legislation on the release of slaves in Deuteronomy is still more suggestive. It immediately passes from the release of slaves to the offering of the firstborn (Deut 15:19-23), which is the very point of the final plague in Exodus (11:1–12:36). As the LORD's firstborn son (Exod 4:22), Israel is to be dedicated to the LORD. If Egypt will not free Israel to realize its status as the LORD's firstborn, it will suffer the loss of its own first-born.

The legislation in Deuteronomy then turns to the Passover (Deut 16:1-8), the one-night-plus-seven-days celebration which is distinctive of Deuteronomy. There are grounds for interpreting the whole of the earlier version of the exodus narrative from Exod 2:23–24:8 as commemorated in the chronology of that Deuteronomic Passover: the one night is the night of the escape from Egypt, as recounted in Exodus 12; this is followed by a pilgrimage of three days to the Mountain of God as already envisaged in this chapter (Exod 3:12, 18, a motif to recur in 5:3; 8:27; cf. 15:22, where the alternative chronology of the final version takes over); on the third day after the arrival at the Mountain the Decalogue is revealed to the people (Exod 19:10-11, 16; 20:1-21); on the following, final day the covenant is sealed between God and Israel (Exod 24:3-8).

All of these themes — release of Hebrew slaves, dedication of the first-born, and celebration of the Passover — are being prepared for in Exod 3:15-22.

(3) Moses' third objection is that his own people will not believe him (4:1-9; the motif recurs in 4:31; 14:31; 19:9). There might indeed be many reasons in Moses' early history for such rejection, principally his earlier ignominious flight (2:15). But Moses expresses his fear of rejection in theological terms: the people will object that, no matter who this new Yahweh may be, he has not appeared to Moses. Specifically in response (4:5, 8-9), Moses is now empowered to work "signs": the staff turned into a snake and back again; the hand turned leprous then healed; Nile water turned to blood. It may be that the first two are meant to mirror the career of Moses to date: the staff of authority thrown down, and flight when it is turned against him (2:15); the enforced dwelling apart from the community as though he were a leper (2:22; cf. Lev 13:46). These signs thus express the reintegration of Moses into the community and his restored,

and now soundly based, authority within it. The third sign is an authentication of Moses' power within the land of Egypt itself; it is still directed at the Israelite community, though it anticipates the action of God against Egypt in the series of plagues which begins precisely with the turning of the Nile into blood (7:14-25).

(4) Moses now (4:10-12) gives as an excuse his poor performance as a public speaker ("heavy of mouth and heavy of tongue," v. 10). God seeks to counter this objection by appealing to his power as the creator of human speech. The reassurance of God's presence (as in 3:12) is repeated: the "I will be" (4:12) must now clearly be understood in the light of the "I will be" of 3:14. That promise is now translated in terms of "teaching" (from the root of "Torah," or law) the words to be uttered.

(5) Yet once more Moses seeks to evade the responsibility (4:13). But modesty can be false modesty, a mask for disinclination, and both can be disloyalty to God, who reveals himself as present with power. It is therefore in exasperation that God, having thus made himself known in his being and action as focused in his name "Yahweh" revealed to Moses himself, does indeed find a "mouth" and a "tongue" for Moses by appointing his brother Aaron as his spokesman. The message, however, remains unchanged; it is still the same "I will be" who will be with both (v. 15); the message will come through the authenticated mediator, Moses, and Aaron will but speak what he has heard. Again the verb "teach," from the root of "Torah," is used.

The Redeemer Redeemed (4:18-26)

Exod 4:18-26 contains one of the most puzzling incidents in the HB: God's encounter with Moses and attempt to kill him (vv. 24-26). It seems extraordinary that no sooner has Moses been appointed as the agent of Israel's escape, despite all the resistance on his part described in 3:11–4:17, than God seeks to destroy him, the very human through whom that escape will be brought about. The point being made must once again be that beyond all human effort, even on the part of a Moses, it is God alone who is the deliverer of his people (cf. ch. 2). Through the dispensability of the human agent the primacy of the divine action is declared. Within the wider context of the Pentateuch, there is a suggestive parallel with Genesis 22: God's promise of progeny to Abraham can be fulfilled only through Isaac; but that promise is threatened by the demand for the sacrifice of Isaac to God.

But other points are being made in the incident. The view presented below is that the decisive clue to understanding lies in the fact that the MT presents 4:18-26 as a single section (contrast the three paragraphs into which it is subdivided in the NRSV). The fundamental point at issue is the status of Israel: the astonishing metaphor used is that Israel is not just God's son but his firstborn son (v. 22). The penalty for denying that status is about to be paid by Egypt in terms of "like for like" (cf. the law code embedded in Exod 21:22-25): if they maltreat God's firstborn son, they will forfeit their own firstborn (v. 23). But, equally, God lays responsibilities on Israel. In recognition of their status, they must offer to God their firstborn. Of none is this more true than of their leader, Moses (vv. 25-26).

The narrative proceeds on two levels: the external events and the continuing unfolding of how God's purpose of rescuing his people takes place. The external course of events is sketched with the utmost economy (4:18, 20a, 24a): Moses asks Jethro's permission to leave; the permission is granted; he and his family reach a stopping place for the night. The omission of many circumstantial links in that chain of events shows where the true interest lies: the actions of God.

Moses continues to appear in a somewhat ambiguous light. There is a discrepancy between the reason he gives to Jethro for his departure and the actual reason: "let me go to see whether my kindred in Egypt are still alive" (4:18) sounds like a family visit taken on his own initiative, whereas in truth it is under divine compulsion that he is being sent to save his entire people. It may just be deliberate understatement — in advance of the successful completion of his mission why should he be any more forthcoming to Jethro? But the reticence about his mission may be a continuation of his reluctance in the previous section. Moses' passivity, at least, is notable; whereas he appears to be a headstrong figure in ch. 2, here he first needs an assurance from God of his personal security before he will act (the narrative sequence in 4:18-19 shows that, though he has declared his intention to Jethro to go, he has still delayed: it is back in Midian that God gives him the instruction to return). The two actions of Moses, "and he took" (v. 20), are thus enfolded in two directives from the LORD (vv. 19, 21). When he takes his wife and family (the passage of time since 2:22 is indicated by the plural "sons"; cf. 18:5), he also takes the staff, which, with its proven wonder-working power, is now termed "the staff of God." What had been the "staff in your hand" (4:2) now becomes empowerment to work "portents" before Pharaoh (cf. the matching "in your hand" in v. 21). Though they will be worked through Moses, they are essentially acts of God; therefore, Moses, as their agent, is in a sense a spectator who will "see" them, not just do them (cf. Israel as participants yet spectators at the Red Sea, 14:31).

The word "portents" introduces a thematic term for the demonstrations of the LORD's power before the Egyptians (7:3, 9; 11:9, 10; as opposed to the "signs" in 3:12, etc., worked for Israel's benefit). These are to be termed, fundamentally, the "wonderful deeds" of the LORD (3:20; cf. 15:11), not merely, as in popular parlance, "the plagues of Egypt" (terms for "plagues" are used quite sparingly in the following narrative: *deber*, "plague," appears only in 5:3; 9:15 and as the term for one of the specific plagues themselves in 9:3; cf. the other roots "strike," *nkh*, 7:17, 20; 8:17; 9:25 [2x]; 12:29; *pgʿ*, 5:3; *ngp*, 8:2; 9:14; 12:13, 23 [2x], 27; *ngʿ*, 11:1; "judgments," *shepaṭim*, 6:6; 12:12). They are a cumulative series of disasters which are portents of disorders of a much deeper character (nothing less than the collapse of Egyptian imperial power) and of divine action of still more far-reaching significance (the deliverance and establishment of his people Israel).

It would not be surprising if Pharaoh misses the point of the series of portents as each one occurs. What is surprising is that it is God himself who makes him miss the point (4:21b). The series of portents is a deliberate device to make it clear that the deliverance is the result of no human decision or action but of God himself (the motif recurs in 9:12; 10:20, 27; 11:10; and, in different vocabulary, 7:3, 14; 8:15, 32; 9:7, 34; 10:1; cf. 7:13, 22; 8:19; 9:35, where the same verb is used of Pharaoh's own "heart"). Pharaoh is locked into the consequences of the now ineradicable evil for which he has been responsible from the first. The series of seven (in the underlying version) or ten (in the final edition) punitive acts of God about to be recounted in 7:14–12:36 corresponds to traditional numbers of punishments sent by God (e.g., Lev 26:15-41).

At the end of 4:21 and in v. 22 key terms are introduced from the legislation in Deut 15:12–16:8, which, as suggested above (see on 3:15-22), provides the master pattern for the events described in the earlier version of Exodus up to Exod 24:8: the release of Israel as slaves, its status as the LORD's firstborn son, and the celebration of that status in the festival of Passover. The verb in v. 21, not just "let go," or even "expel," is the technical term for the release of a slave. This verb is now going to appear as a thematic term in the following chapters (some thirty-nine times in all to the end of ch. 13).

In 4:22 Moses is commissioned with the words he is to speak to Pharaoh. These amount to a digest of all the encounters which Moses is to have with Pharaoh throughout chs. 5–11. They are expressed in the two-part form of "messenger speech" so characteristic of the later prophets (cf. the definition of Moses as the prophet par excellence in Deut 18:18; 34:10). Those commissioned by God speak not on their own account but in the name of him who sends them; they thus introduce their words with an authentication of their message: "This is what the LORD has said. . . ."

The first part of Moses' message speaks of Israel's status among all the peoples of the world, including by implication in this context even the imperial power of Egypt. This is expressed in the highest and most intimate terms conceivable: "Israel is my son — not only so, my firstborn son." The term "firstborn," now introduced for the first time, binds the whole narrative of the ten "marvelous deeds of God" together, reappearing (apart from, significantly, the genealogical material in 6:14) as the focus of the tenth, climactic, "marvelous deed" in 11:1–12:36, and then links these marvelous deeds with the legislation on the dedication of the firstborn in ch. 13.

4:23a is unexpected: the second part of the classic prophetic speech — instruction about the appropriate action to take in the light of the situation indicated — would now naturally follow: "Therefore, I command you, release my son." The turning of that command into a report of the past, "I commanded . . . but you refused," presupposes all the events now to follow in chs. 5–10 and prepares for the climactic "marvelous deed" in chs. 11–12.

The second part of Moses' message in 4:23b thus, in effect, announces the impending action of God: because of Pharaoh's refusal to set free the LORD's firstborn, the LORD is going to slaughter Pharaoh's son, indeed, his firstborn (the construction at the end of v. 23 matches the construction at the end of v. 22).

But if Moses is safe from the Egyptians (4:19), he is not safe from God, as the following incident indicates (vv. 24-26). He is saved only by the speedy act of his wife Zipporah in circumcising their son Gershom (presumably) and touching Moses' genitals ("feet" may be a euphemism as in, e.g., Isa 7:20) with the severed foreskin.

As suggested above, this strange incident should be understood within its immediate context. In acknowledgment of its status as the LORD's firstborn, Israel owes to him the offering of its firstborn, both human and animal (as the legislation in 13:1, 11-16 makes clear, the human firstborn are themselves to be redeemed — in the fully developed system by the vicarious dedication of the Levites, Num 3:12-13). In the rite of dedication of the firstborn, there is a threat both to the firstborn and to those who neglect the rite. In this case, Gershom of the levitical family of Moses is protected by the rite of circumcision, as Moses is by the vicarious circumcision of his son. The designated redeemer of the people, whose redemption is to be marked by the dedication of their firstborn vicariously redeemed by the Levites, must himself be redeemed vicariously by his own firstborn. Moses himself is not above duty to God; he who is to be the later mediator of the law is bound by the requirements of what will be enshrined in the law.

The equally enigmatic term for her husband, "a bridegroom of blood," used by Zipporah, is explained in the context in terms of the blood of the circumcision. Zipporah perceives the deadly threat to her son and to her husband that Moses' new status brings; the blood of circumcision indicates the dedication to a new life; that new life may bring with it implications of change in relationship with her. That a separation from his wife took place at this point is stated by the later narrative (Exod 18:2; as I will argue below, there are grounds to hold that that passage stood before Num 10:29 in the original version, i.e., after the revelation of the law at the Mountain of God). By this act, the status of the once unwilling and unresponsive Moses has been irreversibly changed.

The First Encounter with Pharaoh (4:27–6:9)

Once again the MT paragraphing highlights the major point of this section: Moses' — and Aaron's — disastrous first encounter with Pharaoh provokes not only outright rejection of their request to go to the Mountain of God but intensified persecution, and yet leads to a renewed promise by God.

The section functions to establish still more clearly the culpability of Pharaoh. Everything that has been promised and forewarned by God in section 2:23–4:17 turns out to be true. Aaron, and the elders and people, without hesitation respond positively to Moses' commission. But Pharaoh's reaction is even more repressive than predicted; it is only when at Pharaoh's decree conditions become still worse that in despair and recrimination the people turn against Moses.

As promised in 4:14-16, Aaron, designated as Moses'

spokesman to the people, comes to meet him at the Mountain of God (the verb "to meet," v. 27, is the same as that in v. 24, the only times in these chapters that the verb is used: threat has become reassurance). Aaron's acceptance of Moses' commission and the accompanying signs (cf. 3:10–4:9) is so taken for granted that it is not even recorded (4:28). In v. 29 they precisely fulfill the instructions of 3:16: to gather the elders ("all" is now added for emphasis) of the people, to whom Aaron duly acts as spokesman (4:30; it is not clear who "performed the signs"; the syntax suggests Aaron). Again as predicted, the people, too, immediately respond (v. 31; cf. 3:18) with belief that God has indeed "visited" (3:16) them and "seen their affliction" (3:7, 17). The last phrase of 4:31 expresses the unconditionality of their acceptance and submission (cf. 12:27; 34:8).

Strengthened with this complete fulfillment of every promise, Moses, Aaron, and the elders confront Pharaoh (5:1). Their speech echoes Moses' prophetic speech of 4:22-23. The "messenger formula," "Thus says the LORD," remains to authenticate their words, with the necessary identification of the LORD as "the God of Israel"; the accusation is omitted, though the enslavement of Israel is implied by the imperative, "Let my people go free"; "my son" is replaced by "my people"; "to serve me" is explained as "to hold a pilgrimage festival in my honor in the wilderness." Pharaoh's rejection of the word of the LORD triggers the series of "wonderful deeds."

The narrator does not pause to consider how those who to Pharaoh's eyes must have seemed like self-styled leaders of a band of convicts could have been granted audience with the world emperor. He goes straight to the theological point: Pharaoh cannot possibly be impressed by the word of an unknown God, least of all the God of his Hebrew slaves. His fateful words, "I do not know the LORD" (5:2) are to become the point of the whole ensuing narrative, that Pharaoh will, through the "marvelous deeds," precisely come to know and acknowledge the LORD (7:5, 17; 8:10, 22; 9:14, 29).

The identification of the rite in the wilderness as a "pilgrimage festival" (5:1) is an important piece of evidence for recovering the underlying version related to Deuteronomy. Only in Deut 16:1-8 is the Passover identified as a pilgrimage festival to the sanctuary (see above on 3:18, 76). Further Deuteronomic influence is to be observed in 5:3, where the rite is described in terms of the cultus of the central sanctuary as a "sacrifice" (contrast the legislation on the Passover in the final edition in Exodus 12, where the rite is domestic and the formal cultic term for sacrifice is avoided). A fundamental aspect of the Passover as the spring rite of shepherds observed to ward off danger at the time of change of pasture from the wilderness to the agricultural area shines through at the end of v. 3; "pestilence and sword," along with famine (and wild beasts), are regarded as standard instruments of God's punishment, especially in Jeremiah and Ezekiel.

Pharaoh turns from theology to practicalities — and, in so doing, misses the significant factor in the situation, just as he takes truth to be lies (5:9). These religious observances, he judges, are just excuses of a lazy people for a holiday (5:4, 8, 17; there may well be intended in Hebrew puns on "distract," *tapri'u,* v. 4, and "Pharaoh," *par'oh;* cf. 32:25). His response is to intensify the labor which was his first plan for the control of Israel's growing numbers (5:5; cf. 1:9, 11). In Pharaoh's eyes they are just ordinary people, "the people of the land" (cf., e.g., Gen 42:6), to be exploited; in God's eyes they are "my people" (e.g., 3:7). Israelite foremen accountable to Egyptian supervisors (presumably those earlier identified as "taskmasters" in 1:11) are appointed over the workforce (5:14). On pain of death (cf. 5:21) they have to force their own people to comply with Pharaoh's demands.

The new intensification of the labor is to require the same output of bricks but without providing any longer the straw as the necessary binding material (5:6-8). The Israelites have to forage on their own. It is striking that the message of Pharaoh in 5:10-11 is formulated in the same way as the word of God in v. 1: the "messenger formula" for authentication, followed by the message in two parts, the first describing the situation (v. 10b) and the second laying down the appropriate action (v. 11a; the only formal difference is the addition of an explanatory clause at the end of the second part, v. 11b). The doomed Pharaoh tries his own line of destruction.

An ironical touch is introduced in 5:13, 19: the demand by the Egyptian taskmasters that the Israelite slaves perform their appointed tasks each in full, day by day, echoes the cultic requirement on Israel in its service to God (e.g., Lev 23:37; the key term "service," *'abodah,* recurs in 5:9; cf. 1:14).

The refusal of the Israelite foremen to blame God even in their extremity is impressive. Initially they do not turn on Moses but on Pharaoh as the cause of all their troubles (5:15); only when their pleas to Pharaoh are unavailing do they confront Moses and Aaron (5:20). Even then, they do not reject the reality of their experience, only the disastrous outcome of their message. And they consign the issue to God's justice: may he apply the same vigilance to them that he applied over the injustice suffered by his people ("may the LORD look upon you," 5:21, uses the same verb as in "and God took note," 2:25).

By contrast, though all had happened as he had been forewarned, Moses' words to God are direct (5:22-23; for such directness cf. the "why" of the psalms of lamentation, e.g., Psalm 22): "You have brought this disaster on the people . . . you have not delivered them" (the same verb as in the promise in 3:8). The mission to which he has been committed with such reluctance has turned out to be worse than a complete failure: it is precisely speaking in the LORD's name that has brought intensification of the disaster. In reply (6:1) the LORD picks up the forewarnings and promises of 3:19-20; 4:21 ("do, perform" is the linking term): it is only under the duress of the "wonderful deeds" of the LORD that Pharaoh will permit their departure, indeed, "will drive them out."

At this critical juncture the narratives diverge. The older version proceeds directly to 7:14 and the first "wonderful deed." The final edition brings in a long addition (6:2–7:13) with two main purposes: to confirm belief in the nature and purpose of the LORD now put under such strain during the first encounter with Pharaoh, 6:2-9, which provides a new ending to this section; and in five completely new sections to deal once again with Moses' lack of self-confidence by the appointment of Aaron to act as his spokesman (6:10–7:13). Aaron is now to be the spokesman for Moses not only to Israel (as in 4:14-16) but also to Pharaoh and to be a wonder-worker in his own right (6:10-13, 28–7:13). If the final edition comes from the postexilic period, a motive for thus extending the authority of Aaron and, by implication, of the priesthood that stems from him is evident: they are the custodians and exponents of the Mosaic tradition. The remaining verses (6:14-27) thus give a partial list of Israelites, which demonstrates in genealogical terms the status and role of the Levites, in particular the descendants of Aaron, within Israel.

In the final edition, the section ends with a speech by God reaffirming his nature and purpose (6:2-9). The speech begins and ends with the phrase, "I am the LORD" (vv. 2, 8, as also the speech to be reported to the Israelites begins in v. 6; cf. v. 7): everything that God is and does is expressed in the meaning of that name (cf. 3:12-15). As in 2:24, the patriarchs are recalled to provide the basis and continuity of belief; but the knowledge they had of God expressed in the name "God Almighty," overwhelming yet restricted in sense though it was, is now complemented by "the LORD," boundless in its possibility. (That this final edition seems to view the history of revelation differently from many passages in Genesis where God is in fact known as "the LORD" by many of the patriarchs, e.g., Gen 12:8, has been very influential in the source criticism of the Pentateuch.) Again as in 2:24, the specific point in the recollection of the patriarchs is the covenant made with them to give them the land of Canaan (the vocabulary in this passage may be compared particularly with the covenant with Abraham in Gen 17:1-7; e.g., the opening "I am," "establish my covenant," "the land of Canaan, the land of their sojourning"). That unbreakable promise must give Moses and the people the confidence to trust that God is indeed at work to effect his purpose despite every evidence to the contrary: as to Abraham the promise was of uncountable descendants, so now at the time of the cry of these descendants of Abraham for help God will indeed release them from slavery.

Some distinctive vocabulary appears in God's speech in 6:6b. "I will redeem you" uses a theological term familiar elsewhere in the HB (e.g., Isa 41:14) which is borrowed from the realm of property rights: it is the next of kin who has the responsibility of buying back the occupancy rights to land of one who has fallen into slavery through debt. Within the context of the covenant with the patriarchs, this term provides an appropriate and powerful metaphor of God as Israel's next of kin, freeing his people from slavery and vindicating their rights to possession of the land of Canaan.

The last phrase of 6:6, "with an outstretched arm and mighty acts of judgment," is a variant on the phrase characteristic of the earlier version "with a strong hand and an outstretched arm," where the first of the pair seems to refer to the ten "wonderful deeds" and the second to the defeat of Egypt at the Red Sea. In this final edition, the "outstretched arm" and the "judgment" may refer quite generally to both "wonderful deeds" and the defeat at the Sea (cf. 7:4; 12:12).

But the matter is not left with mere recollection and reaffirmation of a covenant made with ancestors. The divine speech climaxes (6:7) in a variation of the covenant formula, "I will be your God, and you will be my people" (cf., e.g., Lev 26:12; Deut 29:13). Here there is the additional element of election, "I will take you . . ." (cf. Deut 4:20; 2 Sam 7:8; Amos 7:15). The entire salvific relationship made known in the past is also fully effective for the present generation. 6:8 brings these promises to past and present generations together.

6:7b introduces a rather different note about the response of the people. Whereas in the older version "a mighty hand and an outstretched arm" are, in general, designed to force the recognition of the LORD by the Egyptians (though contrast 10:2), here they are for Israel's benefit, to bring them to acknowledge the saving acts of the LORD. Their implied present disbelief is confirmed in 6:9. This contrasts with the noble refusal of the Israelite foremen to question God himself, noted above at 5:21. In general, Israel in the older version is (until the first crisis in ch. 32) a people responsive to God and eager for freedom. If, as is probable, that version was penned during the exile, it in turn would be appropriate to the conditions prevailing at the time — a message of encouragement to those enduring the new slavery of subjection to Babylon.

Aaron's Status (6:10–7:13)

Five sections are now introduced to explain the high status of Aaron. It is appropriate to take them together since they have been so linked by the editor himself. Not only do they share a common topic; they are also closely associated by some external indications. The short section 1 (6:10-12), on Moses's disqualification as a speaker, is directly resumed by the still shorter section 3 (6:29-30; some two-thirds of the words are identical). The reason for this repetition is to enfold section 2 (6:13-28), on the pedigree of Aaron and the subsequent Aaronic priesthood, which anticipates how, in section 4 (7:1-6), Aaron is commissioned as Moses' spokesman and, in section 5 (7:7-13), as a wonder-worker. The division between sections 2 and 3 breaks across the syntax of 6:28-29. It is striking that each of these five sections begins in similar fashion: nos. 1-3, "Then the LORD spoke to Moses"; nos. 4-5, "Then the LORD said to Moses."

(1) Section 1 reopens the question of Moses' incapacity as a speaker. God has long since commissioned Moses to go to Pharaoh to demand the release of Israel (3:10). Moses has already proffered his five excuses (3:11–4:17), including the objections, made again here, that the people will not believe him (4:1-9) and that he is a poor speaker (4:10).

A new formulation of Moses' incapacity as a speaker is introduced (v. 12); whereas in 4:10 he had described himself as "heavy of mouth and heavy of tongue," he now terms himself "uncircumcised of lips." This figure may mean no more than "unable, incapable" as in the figure of the inability of "uncircumcised" ears to hear in Jer 6:10

(cf. the metaphor of "uncircumcised" hearts, Lev 26:41; Deut 10:16; Jer 4:4; and the sense of "unfit, unready" in connection with immature fruit trees in Lev 19:23). However, the sacral associations of the term "uncircumcised" are perhaps relevant and are astonishing in connection with the mediator of Israel's law and covenant. Elsewhere in the HB the uncircumcised are synonymous with aliens as threatening (e.g., the Philistines, 1 Sam 14:6; the foreign nations, Ezek 31:18; 32:19-32). Perhaps still more to the point is that uncircumcision is equated with ritual uncleanness (Isa 52:1). This may open up ritual and editorial dynamics in the text: the later, fully developed system of the relation between the priest and the Levite is here prefigured. As the Levites, though teachers of the law and monitors of Israel's practice of it, had to be subservient to the Aaronic priesthood as practitioners of the laws of holiness and purity, so here already Moses, though the original mediator of the law, is enabled by Aaron to be only its practitioner.

(2) Section 2 (6:13-28) opens with a brief subsection (v. 13) which states the whole point of these editorial developments of the text: both Moses and Aaron are commissioned to go to both the people and Pharaoh to secure the release of Israel.

Now follows a subsection (6:14-28) which demonstrates the status of Aaron genealogically. Syntactically, this subsection falls outside the narrative sequence (cf. the broken syntax with which it ends, v. 28); it introduces the circumstances of descent and time presupposed by the narrative. The opening, "these are the heads of their households" (v. 14a), creates the expectation that an update of the complete listing of the Israelites will now be given, matching 1:1-4. In the event, the list covers only Reuben, Simeon, and Levi, the first three sons of Israel as listed in Gen 29:32-34. The reason for this shortened list is now clear. Reuben, it is stressed, is "the firstborn of Israel" (6:14b); but it is to be the function of the Levites to be the tribe of Israel that is dedicated to the LORD by way of redemption of the firstborn of the remaining tribes of Israel (Num 3:12-13). Thus the fundamental function of the Levites is here stated: they do not merely provide the teachers of Israel and the officiants at the altar; they are the tribe who vicariously redeem the firstborn of Israel. Once again the fully developed system of the dedication of the firstborn is anticipated, the rationale for which is being provided by the narrative of the deliverance of Israel as a whole from Egypt at the cost of the Egyptian firstborn (cf. 4:22-23): Israel is "bought for a price"; so, too, are the Levites.

The four sons of Reuben are listed, as are the six sons of Simeon (both as in Gen 46:9-10), in order to indicate the full spread of these tribes, their constituent "clans" (6:14-15, including, incidentally, under the last, their intermarriage with the native population).

The descendants of Levi are listed at much greater length (6:16-25), as befits their function, as vicariously dedicated to God, and the range of their duties within Israel (cf. the slightly different introduction, "according to their generations," which may imply "their hereditary offices"). Thus the three great levitical families are listed, Gershon, Kohath, and Merari (as in Gen 46:11).

But before expounding their relative status genealogically, the book of Exodus supplies some chronological data (6:16b; cf. other such data at vv. 18, 20): the length of Levi's life as 137 years. This note belongs to a series of chronological notes in Genesis, the essential feature of which for the production of an overall chronology is the age of the father at the begetting of the son in question. This series is intact in Genesis 5; 11:10-26 from Adam to Abraham gives a total of 1,976 years. The age of Abraham at the begetting of Isaac (100) is given in Gen 21:5, and of Isaac at the begetting of Jacob (60) in Gen 25:26. The only gap in the chain is the age of Jacob at the begetting of Levi. This can be roughly calculated from the data (assuming that they all share the same conceptual framework) that Jacob was 130 years old when he arrived in Egypt (Gen 47:9) in the second year of the famine (Gen 45:6), by which time Joseph was about 38 (cf. the date of his appointment by Pharaoh at the age of 30 in the first of the seven years of plenty, Gen 41:46); in other words, Jacob begat Joseph at about the age of 92 (cf. Gen 35:28, which states that Isaac died at the age of 180 but was already an old man when Jacob had to flee to Laban and find his wives, Genesis 27). Since, like all his brothers except Benjamin, Joseph was born in the last thirteen years of the twenty-year period of Jacob's employment with Laban (Gen 31:38, 41), Levi as an older brother must have been born at the earliest in Jacob's tenth year with Laban; that is, Jacob must have been about 90, or a year or two less, when he begat Levi. All these figures from creation to the death of Levi would add up to some 2,363 years. The obvious artificiality of these figures from a historical point of view should not obscure the theological point the writer wishes to make: it has been suggested that the final editor is an eschatological writer who is looking forward to the end of a 4,000-year era, in which the revelation to Israel, and in particular the erection of the tabernacle in the year 2666, or two-thirds through this era, as the center of Israel's life, has the key part to play (creation to the descent of Jacob = 2,266 years; sojourn in Egypt = 400 years [Gen 15:13]). The writer is now preparing for that event.

It is from the central family, Kohath, that the priesthood is derived. Part of its family tree is therefore elaborated for four further generations (6:18, 23-25) in order to show the descent of Aaron, the first high priest, who is to be succeeded in office by his son Eleazar (for whose later prominence see, e.g., Num 3:32; Josh 14:1), and in turn by his grandson Phinehas (for whom cf., e.g., Num 25:7-13; Josh 22:30-32).

A number of significant incidents in the history of the priestly Levites is alluded to in this list of names. The marriage of Aaron's father to his aunt (6:20, confirmed in Num 26:59, where she is called "daughter of Levi") would be condemned in the legislation to come (Lev 18:12-14; 20:20); she, oddly enough, bears a name compounded with the divine element *Yo-*, translated into English as "the LORD," thus anticipating the revelation to Moses in 3:14. An intriguing note is the marriage of Aaron to the sister of Nahshon, son of Amminadab (6:23). While an Amminadab is listed in 1 Chr 6:22 as a son of Kohath (cf. the legislation of Lev

21:14 on the marriage of the Aaronic high priest), the only Nahshon, son of Amminadab, known in the HB is the leader of the "host" of the leading tribe, Judah (cf., e.g., Num 1:7; 2:3; 7:12-17; 10:14), who also appears in the genealogy of King David (Ruth 4:19). He is the chief executive in the military realm, the leader of the "host" of Israel, the physical armies on earth which are the sacramental expression of the unseen, cosmic forces of the "LORD of hosts" (cf. the term for Israel as the LORD's hosts in v. 26; 7:4). Intermarriage between the high-priestly family and the royal family is evidenced in the marriage of Jehoiada, high priest at the time of King Joash, to a princess of the royal house of Judah (2 Chr 22:11; her name Jehoshabeath, incidentally, is a variant of Aaron's wife's name, Elisheba).

The names of Aaron's four sons are faithfully recorded (6:23b), but the first two are soon to be destroyed for unorthodox practice at the altar (Lev 10:1; Num 3:4; 26:61; in Exod 24:1, 9 they play a positive role). Of the two remaining, it is the branch of Eleazar which is to be dominant, producing not only the high priest but sixteen of the twenty-four teams of priests (1 Chr 24:1-6).

The maintenance of the exclusive status of the priesthood despite the claims of possible rivals is stressed by the recording of the name of Aaron's cousin Korah (6:21), who is later to lead a revolt (Numbers 16–17). The destruction of Korah, but not of his family, does not prevent his descendants from discharging important roles as non-priestly Levites in the music of the later temple liturgy (cf. the headings of Psalms 42–49, 84, 85, 87, and 88; cf. 1 Chr 9:19).

The non-priestly Levites of all three branches are, on the whole, listed only to the second generation; again it suffices to indicate their chief families. Some of these names recur rarely (e.g., Mishael and Elzaphan in 6:22 reappear only in the important passage in Lev 10:4) or not at all (e.g., Putiel, v. 25) in the HB.

The section ends with the resumption of the main theme (6:26): the status of Aaron in the exodus. Here for the only time in Exodus (and the HB except in family trees or their equivalents, where the fact that Aaron is three years Moses' senior is acknowledged by his being listed first; cf. 7:7) Aaron precedes Moses. The standard order is resumed in v. 27.

(3) Section 3 (6:29-30) resumes Section 1 after the long account of the circumstances of Aaron's birth and status in Section 2, which explains the fitness of Aaron to act as Moses' spokesman and agent.

(4) Section 4 (7:1-7) provides Aaron with his warrant as spokesman for Moses to Pharaoh. He is to speak nothing but what Moses communicates to him from God, so that, in a vivid phrase (v. 1), he is Moses' prophet, his mouthpiece, while Moses is God to Pharaoh. The same unsuccessful outcome to their mission is foretold as in 4:21: guilty Pharaoh is locked into the consequences of his guilt by God's "hardening of his heart" (7:3). The "signs and wonders" will be used to demonstrate the power of God and force acknowledgment by the Egyptians (v. 5; for the key term "know" cf. 5:2; whereas in the earlier version "signs and wonders" were distinguished as "signs" to Israel and "wonders" to Egypt, here the words are used indiscriminately and are termed "judgments" [7:4], as in 6:6).

(5) Section 5 (7:8-13) provides Aaron with his warrant as agent for Moses to Pharaoh. Just as Moses is armed with the "sign"-working staff in 4:1-5, which turns into a snake, so now Aaron is similarly equipped as he goes to confront Pharaoh. The word for "snake" now used is different from that in ch. 4; elsewhere it can mean "sea monster" (though it is parallel to "python" in Deut 32:33), an appropriate reference given the portrayal of Egypt as a sea monster lurking in the Nile in Ps 74:13; Isa 27:1; 51:9-11. That cosmic conflict is intended by the imagery is suggested by the fact that Pharaoh's magicians, too, could turn their staffs into "sea monsters"; nonetheless, the sea monster produced by Aaron swallows them up as a portent of the victorious crossing of the Sea by the LORD's hosts (12:17, 41, 51) at the exodus to come. But again Pharaoh is blind to the portent.

The First Nine "Wonderful Deeds" of the LORD (7:14–10:29)

The series of ten so-called "plagues of Egypt," culminating in 12:36 in Israel's release into freedom, now begins. They should be more accurately termed the "wonderful deeds" of the LORD (3:20). In the older version, 7:14, which introduces the first of these "wonderful deeds," would link directly with 6:1: this is the beginning of the LORD's response by word and act to the despair of his people. The all-too-clear forewarning of Pharaoh's refusal to set Israel free in 3:18-20; 4:21-23 and the all-too-completely-fulfilled experience of that refusal on first encounter in ch. 5 are now to be repeatedly borne out (much of the vocabulary of these earlier chapters is used over and over again in these new encounters; cf., e.g., 7:16). But these demonstrations of the LORD's power will culminate in the release of Israel.

The first nine "wonderful deeds" are related, though here in intensified form and cumulative effect, to regular patterns of devastation for which Egypt is notorious. The cracking of the veneer of order in the natural world demonstrates the fragility of even the most pretentious and tyrannical human power structure. The climactic tenth "wonderful deed," the slaughter of every firstborn male in Egypt, whether human or domestic animal (11:5), is, by contrast, by its very nature an entirely unprecedented event. It is appropriate, therefore, to take the first nine "wonderful deeds" in 7:14–10:29 together and then to treat the exceptional tenth in 11:1–12:36 separately. There are, indeed, a number of recurrent elements in the accounts of the first nine "wonderful deeds" which lend cumulative force to the whole and can best be appreciated in this way (the eight major — and four minor — paragraph markers subdividing 7:14–10:29 in the MT do not all coincide with the nine plagues: plagues 2–4, e.g., are linked together; the narratives of plagues 7 and 8 are both divided into two).

There is reason to believe that, like much of the rest of the book of Exodus, the series of plagues has been developed in two major phases. It is likely that plagues 3, 6, and 9 belong to the final edition and have been added to the original version of seven plagues (including plague 10). They link with the commissioning of Aaron in 6:2–7:13, which, it has just been argued, belongs to the final edition of the work; they are much briefer than almost all the other plague narratives; and they differ from the remainder in structure in that they plunge straight into the action that Moses (and, usually, Aaron) has to perform. The addition of these three plagues to an earlier series of seven would explain some anomalies in the text; for example, in plague 7 (9:15) the reference is to plague 5, not to plague 6; the prohibition on seeing Pharaoh again in 10:28-29 at the end of plague 9 contradicts what happens in 11:1-8. In the process, the narrative of plagues 1, 2, 4, 5, 7, and 8 (and 10, as will be argued below) has itself been added to and adapted. In plague 1, for example, there are adjustments in 7:19-22: Aaron and the Egyptian magicians are introduced (the staff referred to initially in v. 15 is Moses' staff of 4:2-4, not Aaron's of 7:9-12, as the word used for "snake" makes clear); "the water in the Nile" has been extended to "water, even in vessels, throughout all the land of Egypt." There are similar additions to later narratives, for example, to plague 2 in 8:5-7 and to plague 8 in 10:1-3.

The original version of plagues 1-9 presents, in terms suitable to conditions prevailing in Egypt, a coherent set of variations on the themes of famine and pestilence, two of the stock instruments in the HB of divine warning of final punishment to come (cf., e.g., Amos 4:6-13). They are "portents": however unprecedented their coincidence and catastrophic their proportions (9:18, 24; 10:6, 14), they remain events of recurrent possibility in the natural world; but they indicate a deeper meaning. Thus, annually from about the middle of June the Nile floods over, full of the suspended alluvium brought down from its upper reaches (which in fact guarantees the continuing fertility of the soil); at this time it can indeed become undrinkable and be described as "turned into blood" (plague 1). The only uncertainty of that flood is the variability of the height to which it will rise (cf. the Nilometer at Aswan). The spread of repulsive frogs across the surface of the land with those floodwaters, plague 2, is thus equally explainable (cf. the "naturalistic" depiction in 8:3, as opposed to the miraculous element in 8:5-6), as is their death when the flood waters recede. Swarms of flies from the heaps of dead frogs (plague 4) are then inevitable, with the hazards to the health of livestock that they pose (plague 5). The two further natural disasters, hail (plague 7) and locusts (plague 8), are unconnected with the preceding in the normal course of events; that they should strike now with such universal destructive force and complete the devastation is the compelling factor. For those with eyes to see, these events are "portents" of deeper disturbance: the dislocation of the natural order is a summons to look below the surface at the structures of the community, a warning that the apparently securely based institutions of the state are equally conditioned, equally susceptible to attack and overthrow, equally open to impending doom. For those with dulled sensitivity, these disasters are merely interruptions, after which life can go on as before. The obtuse Pharaoh, whose moral sense is already atrophied, as demonstrated by his insensitivity to the suffering of generations of his slaves, is impervious to such transient inconveniences, let alone to any deeper significance they might symbolize (cf. the variations on the phrase "hardening of the heart" throughout the plague narratives, already signaled in 4:21).

The casual cynicism and obduracy of Pharaoh are heightened in plagues 2, 4, 7, and 8 by the motif of the intercession of Moses (a role of the prophet which recurs in the later HB, especially in the Deuteronomistic parts of Jeremiah, e.g., Jer 32:16). Repeatedly opportunities are given to Pharaoh to "know" (another recurrent theme; cf., e.g., 8:10), to acknowledge the incomparability of the LORD (9:14; 10:2) as demonstrated in the control and precise time-tabling of the crises; but, apart from brief moments of expediency or offers of minimal concessions (e.g., 8:25), he refuses to recognize the significance of the "portents." The dawning acknowledgment among the ordinary Egyptians (9:20; 10:7; cf. 11:3) focuses all the responsibility on Pharaoh himself.

The moral lesson to be derived from these portents is portrayed in terms of the sparing from disaster of the area settled by Israel (explicitly noted in plagues 4, 5, and 7; cf. 9:23; 11:7). That sparing could be naturalistically explained in terms of the location of the land of Goshen, outside the Nile valley (cf. Josh 10:41), where Israel was settled (Gen 45:10). But part of the character of these events as "portents" is not just the suffering of the tyrant and his people who are implicated in his guilt, but the sparing of the oppressed slave population whose rights need to be vindicated.

The main reason for the additions and adjustments by the final edition to the older version is to lend a cosmic dimension to the confrontation between God and Pharaoh. A titanic struggle has now begun, the collision between two rival and incompatible belief systems. This is chiefly signaled by the introduction of Aaron and his wonder-working staff, which had been turned into the "sea monster" (7:9-10). Aaron, priest-to-be of the tabernacle, the representation in miniature of the cosmos (chs. 25–31; 35–40), the rites of which are, above all, to maintain that cosmos in being, is in direct competition with the Egyptian magicians and their magic arts (cf. 7:11-12). Initially, the magicians are able to work the same marvels (additions to plagues 1 and 2); but soon they are exposed as charlatans (plague 3) and are driven from the field in humiliation, smitten by the plague they cannot cause, let alone cure (plague 6).

The Tenth "Wonderful Deed" of the LORD (11:1–12:36)

The narrative of the climactic tenth plague which finally forces Pharaoh's hand to release Israel is now set forth. But the true climax of chs. 1–15, the definitive elimination of Egypt as a threat to Israel's freedom, which warns against taking the so-called "plague narrative" as a self-contained unit from 7:14 to, say, 11:10 or 12:36, is not reached until 14:31. It is only at that point that the LORD's outrage at the enslavement of his people, already announced in 2:23-25, is resolved and his intervention to secure their release complete. But the tenth plague marks the end of the first decisive stage in that process: Israel escapes but is yet to be assured of enduring liberty.

As the structure of the narrative of the tenth plague in 11:1–12:36 makes rather clear, there is once again a significant interplay between the older version and the final edition. The narrative of the final plague is contained within the opening and closing subsections, 11:1-3, 4-8; 12:29-36. There are grounds for believing that these subsections, in fact, constitute the entire content of the original version of the tenth plague. 12:29-36 stands in chiastic correspondence to 11:1-8; 12:29-34, the depiction of the sequence of events, the death of the Egyptian firstborn leading to the expulsion of Israel, relate to Moses' ultimatum to Pharaoh in 11:4-8; 12:35-36 pick up the instructions to Moses "to spoil the Egyptians" in 11:2-3. As in the earlier cycle of plagues 1-2, 4-5, and 7-8, so now in plague 10 a confrontation with Pharaoh begins with an accusation of Israel's wrongful enslavement, continues with Pharaoh's peremptory rejection of the request to leave, and ends directly in an act of God, from which Israel is, once again, shielded (11:7; cf. 8:22; 9:4). The crucial difference in this final encounter is that Pharaoh is forced by the overwhelming nature of the catastrophe, the death of all Egyptian firstborn, both human and animal, to propel the Israelites out of the country in fear lest the destruction of the entire population of Egypt should follow. The sequel of commemorating such a hasty expulsion, when there was no time to wait even for the bread to rise, by the rite of eating unleavened bread for seven days is then entirely appropriate (12:34; 13:3-10).

But to place the "plagues" narrative of 7:14–12:36 even within the wider framework of the outrage of God and his intervention to right the wrong in 2:23–14:31 is still not adequate. As has been noted above (on 4:21-23), the sequence of events in Exodus 1–24 exactly matches the order of the legislation in Deut 15:12–16:8 on the release of the Hebrew slaves, the offering of the first-born, and the celebration of the Passover. In order to gain the fullest expression of the action of God, of participation in that action, and of the implications of participating in that action, the "plague cycle" must be related to the celebration of the Passover. The narrative of the tenth plague thus naturally climaxes in the narrative of the Passover. There are grounds to hold that in the original edition the institution of the Passover is first outlined in 13:3-10; but its full exposition then extends to 24:8, including also the theophany and covenant at the Mountain of God as part of the Deuteronomic model of the Passover as a one-night-plus-seven-day observance (Deut 16:1-8). But, even then, the Passover as a commemoration and celebration of the action of God in rescuing Israel his firstborn must be complemented by an expression of thanksgiving on the part of Israel in the offering of their firstborn: the Passover ordinance in 13:3-10 is thus enfolded in the legislation for Israel's offering of their firstborn in 13:1-2, 11-16.

The final edition of Exodus views the relationship of the "plague cycle" to its context very differently. Three new subsections have been introduced between 11:9 and 12:28. The first of these, 11:9-10, is a summary of the plague cycle, which is thus now separated from its natural sequel in the death of the Egyptian firstborn (12:29-36) and the legislation on the offering of the Israelite first-born (13:1-2, 11-16). Instead, the plague cycle now issues in the Passover as redefined in non-Deuteronomic terms in 12:1-13; indeed, a further section on the Passover is introduced in 12:43-50, which is concluded with a yet further summary of events in 12:51. The legislation on the offering of the firstborn in ch. 13 is thus now disconnected from the tenth plague and left in some isolation. Further, the Passover is rigidly understood as a one-night observance, as the new — or newly edited — material in 12:1-13, 21-28, 43-50 makes clear; it is now carefully distinguished from the pilgrimage festival of Unleavened Bread (12:14-20).

These changes in the layout of the material have been caused by fundamental changes in conception. The plague cycle is no longer merely the demonstration of the LORD's redeeming power in the eyes of the Egyptians; part of its purpose is to convince Israel itself of the reality of the LORD's intervention on its behalf (cf. 10:2). Indeed, the tenth plague is now equally threatening to Israel: it is only by the observance of the Passover as a rite of protection even for Israel itself that the firstborn of Israel are spared (12:21-28). The Passover as a one-night domestic observance is separated from the "octave" of the ensuing pilgrimage festival at the Mountain of God, about to be described in the original version of 15:22–24:8. In the process, the covenant is separated from deliverance from Egypt (the primary covenant is that with the patriarchs, as the final edition has already stated in 6:5) and is now overlaid as a revelation of law. Israel as eager covenant partner has become Israel the recalcitrant and disobedient, in need of the sacrificial cultus and its rites of atonement to maintain its relationship with God. Thus two sharply different — though still complementary — portrayals of Israel are presented in the one text. The older version is a message of reassurance for an Israel "in exile" that God's unwavering purpose of bringing freedom to his people through his covenant endures. The later edition is a message of discipline aimed at an Israel "in return from exile." The vast task of building the community in which God's central claims on the loyalty and obedience of his people are fully met is far from complete. The traditional theological terms, "justification" for the older version and "sanctification" for the final edition, themselves equally complementary, congenially fit these two contrasting portrayals.

The first scene (11:1-3) announces the final plague (the term "blow" is used, v. 1, for the first and only time). As foretold in 6:1 and fulfilled in 12:39, Egypt in the end will be only too eager to "drive out" Israel (11:1). The sequence of thought in these verses can only be appreciated from the legislation on freeing a Hebrew from slavery in Deut 15:12-18 (the verb "let go" in 11:1 recurs four times in Deut 15:12, 13, 18). In recognition of the value of the service provided, the erstwhile slave owner is required to "festoon" the freed slave with produce; hence Israel has every right to demand of its Egyptian oppressors objects of silver and gold in recompense for its years of toil (the key term "not empty-handed" in Deut 15:13 has already been used in Exod 3:21-22 in anticipation of this passage and its fulfillment in 12:35, 36). The dignity of the people and the authority of Moses inspire a favorable response on the part of the ordinary Egyptians.

The scene now shifts (11:4-8) to the final confrontation between Moses and Pharaoh (the fact that the addressee is seemingly suppressed in v. 4 and the location of the encounter is not made clear until v. 8 is a reflection of the view of the final editor, who has already been responsible for the addition of plague 9; contrast 10:28-29). It is matched by its direct continuation in 12:29-36. There is a close correspondence within acceptable variations of language between the forewarning of Moses and the outcome; for example, the "great cry" at the unprecedented calamity of the bereaved Egyptians foretold by Moses in 11:6 (which picks up and counterpoises the "cry" of the Israelites to the LORD in 3:7) is bitterly fulfilled in 12:30 and leads directly to the expulsion of Israel laden with valuables. The whole purpose of the narrative has been achieved: Israel is released into the service of God (12:31), as Egypt is compelled to acknowledge (11:7; cf. 5:2).

After his new summary in 11:9-10, which somewhat draws a line in the present text under the "plague cycle," the final editor introduces a revised statement on the Passover in 12:1-28. The importance of this material is indicated by the fact that it is in two matching sections, the first containing the instructions from God to Moses and Aaron (12:1-20) and the second, the communication of these instructions, with some further specifications, to the people (12:21-28; there are already some switches from third to second person in the first section in anticipation; contrast the previous account of the plagues where an equivalent of one or the other of these sections has occurred, at least in plagues 1, 2, 4, 5, 7, 8, and 10, but never both).

The first section, 12:1-20, puts forward a highly distinctive view of the festivals of the Passover and Unleavened Bread, which contrasts with the practice of the older version found in its full form in Deut 16:1-8 and in heavily edited form in Exod 13:3-10 (phrases from Deuteronomy 16 and Exodus 13 are here picked up in Exodus 12 and qualified in a new context; e.g., for v. 12 cf. 13:15; for vv. 15, 19 cf. 13:6; Deut 16:3-4; for v. 25 cf. 13:5).

Both accounts begin with a reference to the calendar. For the final edition in Exod 12:2, the Passover marks the fifteenth of "the first month," reckoned according to the "Babylonian" calendar, which begins in the spring; in the older version in Exod 13:4 it falls in "Abib," the seventh month of the "Canaanite" calendar, which begins in the autumn (cf. Exod 23:14-19). The rites themselves are sharply distinguished in the two accounts. In Deuteronomy the one-night rite of the Passover has entirely engulfed the following seven days of Unleavened Bread, the agricultural festival of the barley harvest; here the two are clearly demarcated in 12:3-13 and 14-20 respectively (for the standard formulae in v. 14 cf. Lev 23:41; Num 29:12). In Deuteronomy the festivals of the Passover and Unleavened Bread are regarded as parts of the one pilgrimage festival to the sanctuary. As a result, the Passover victim is treated like other sacrificial offerings in the sanctuary: it may be selected from cattle as well as from sheep or goats; and it is boiled (incidentally, there is no definition of the age of the victim or of the numbers of victims). By contrast, in Exodus 12 the Passover is a lay domestic rite which is thus necessarily entirely distinct from the specialized priestly rites of the sanctuary: the victim is "slaughtered," not "sacrificed" (though an echo of the vocabulary of the older version remains in v. 27); it is spit-roasted whole (cultic boiling, as in 1 Sam 2:13, is specifically forbidden, v. 9), and any parts not consumed are burned. Provision is sufficient for the company. It is notable that in v. 5 the victim is specified as a yearling ram, not as a firstling; the connection with the firstborn, which has been the whole point of the earlier version of the plague cycle, is thus broken. The specification as a yearling ram does, however, have echoes of ritual practice; cf. Lev 1:10 for acceptable offerings; Lev 9:3 at the dedication of the sanctuary; and, especially, the stated sacrifice at the offering of first fruits at the feast of Weeks in Lev 23:18, which may in fact conceal elements of historical practice in connection with the offering of firstlings, as suggested by Deut 15:19-20.

A feature which both accounts share is that the Passover meal is to be completed that night. But again there is a difference: in Exodus 12 the instructions are, somewhat improbably, that Israel itself on that very night of its expulsion is to eat this very meal (v. 28). It is only by staying indoors until the morning in houses whose doorposts and lintels have been marked by the blood of the victim (v. 22), which has itself been set aside in readiness for the past four days (v. 3), that Israel will be safe from the destruction. The point then of "eating in haste" is somewhat lost (v. 11; as is the eating of the wild "bitter herbs" of the wilderness *before* the departure from Egypt, v. 8).

The older version is more consistent: the rite is to be observed only when Israel is settled in the promised land (13:5; cf. the echo preserved in 12:25). It is a rite not of warding off the threat of destruction (a demonstration of the power of the LORD to deliver as opposed to the powerlessness of the Egyptian gods to protect their people, v. 12), but of commemoration of deliverance. The sign of haste is the eating of unleavened bread, again in commemoration that it was actually during that night that the Israelites were forced out of the country, with no time to let their bread dough prove.

The Passover has now been presented in a twofold fashion: as a memorial in the older version and as a means of deliverance in the final edition. The release of Israel from slavery is now accomplished, but entirely on God's terms, into the service of God, which has been the dominant theme since the beginning of the book (cf. 1:13-14).

The Beginning of the Journey (12:37-42)

This brief section opens up the topic of the route the Israelites follow through the wilderness from Egypt to the Mountain of God before then setting out on the long trek into the promised land. Once again, there are two views on this question in the Pentateuch: the final edition is summarized in Numbers 33, and the earlier version is reflected in Deuteronomy. Once again, both of these, with their associated theological outlooks, are represented in the present combined text in Exodus.

The route Israel follows in the final edition of Exodus 12–19 begins in Rameses, one of the places where Israel toiled as slave laborers (cf. 1:11); thence Israel sets out to Succoth (12:37), then on to Etham (13:20), Pi-hahiroth (14:2), Marah (15:23), Elim (15:27), the wilderness of Sin (16:1), Rephidim (17:1), and, finally, the wilderness of Sinai (19:2). This route matches, with some omissions, and one significant addition in 17:1-7, the summary in Numbers 33.

Corresponding to that route is a distinctive timetable of events: Israel leaves Rameses on the fifteenth day of the first month, the day after the celebration of the Passover; it arrives at the wilderness of Sin on the fifteenth day of the second month (16:1) and at the wilderness of Sinai on the first day (?) of the third month (19:1). This timetable is part of a much wider chronological framework in the final edition of the Pentateuch: in Exod 40:17 the tabernacle is set up on the first day of the first month of the second year; in Num 10:11 on the twentieth day of the second month of the second year Israel departs from Sinai initially to Kibroth-hattaavah and Hazeroth (Numbers 11; cf. Num 33:15-17); eventually Israel reaches Kadesh on the first day (?) of the first month of the fortieth year (Num 20:1; 33:36-38).

Deuteronomy has an entirely different view of the route and its associated chronology, which Israel follows from Egypt to Kadesh. So far from Kadesh being reached only in the fortieth year, the journey from Egypt via the Mountain of God to Kadesh is all accomplished within the first year of the exodus (Deuteronomy 1; 2:14). In particular, no incident is recorded on the journey from the Red Sea to the Mountain of God; it is apparently swift and uneventful. There are materials in Exodus corresponding to such a conception of the journey, for example, the motif of the "three days' pilgrimage" into the wilderness to the Mountain of God, introduced in Exod 3:18, and the bearing of Israel on swift and irresistible "eagles' wings" in Exod 19:4. It would seem that yet once again, now in the matter of itinerary and its associated chronology, a version matching the presentation in Deuteronomy has been overlaid by a final edition corresponding to the summary in Numbers 33.

These contrasting views of route and timetable also introduce contrasting views of the location of God's miraculous deliverance of Israel at the Sea. In Num 33:7-8 the crossing takes place at Pi-hahiroth, the fourth station in the wilderness wandering. From the associated place names Baal-zephon and Migdol, and from the probable meaning of the name Pi-hahiroth ("the mouth of the channels"), it is clear that the location envisaged is the easternmost arm of the delta of the Nile as it flows into the Mediterranean. By contrast, in Deut 11:4 and elsewhere in Exodus (13:18) the miraculous deliverance takes place at the Red Sea (contrast Num 33:10, where the arrival at the Red Sea is at station 7; a matching note has seemingly been suppressed for harmonizing purposes in Exod 16:1).

The reason for the difference of views about the location of the miraculous deliverance of Israel is clear. For the older version, the point of view is geographical: by this act of God, Egypt's empire has been destroyed and with it its power to enslave subject peoples (cf. 12:38, "the mixed multitude" who "went up" with Israel); the frontier of Egypt has been definitively set at the Red Sea. For the final edition the matter is also cosmic. Just as the final editor has introduced Aaron with his wonder-working staff that turned into a sea monster (7:9-10) in order to confront the power of Pharaoh and controvert his magicians, so now Egypt perishes in its own Nile. The deified Nile, whose flooding waters bring life to the country, is now turned into an instrument of destruction (cf. Ezekiel 29–32); by this act, in the words of the final editor, the LORD does indeed work "judgments on the gods of Egypt" (12:12). And these judgments are wrought in favor of the "hosts" of Israel (12:51): the sacramental representation on earth of the hosts in the cosmic realm which "the LORD of hosts" has at his disposal (12:41).

The date of the exodus may equally have cosmological significance: understood in the terms of Gen 15:13, it falls 2,666 years after creation, or two-thirds through an era of 4,000 years (see Exod 6:14-28 above).

The Passover, an Israelite Household Rite (12:43-51)

The subsection on the law of the Passover in 12:43-50 is uniform with legislation already given in 12:1-13 (the Passover is a domestic rite, v. 46; again law is narrated as part of the action of the night of the first Passover and the following day, vv. 50-51, though the situation implied is that of a community settled in the land, v. 48). The structure of the section underlines its significance: it begins and ends with words for "law" (vv. 43a, 49); most clauses begin emphatically with an itemized case and end with the appropriate action (e.g., v. 43b: "no foreigner shall eat of it"). The list has a certain chiastic structure: it begins and ends with those excluded, foreigners and uncircumcised (vv. 43b and 48b); vv. 44 and 48a deal with outsiders who have undergone circumcision. The heart of the matter — Israel's observance of the rite — stands at the heart of the section in vv. 46-47.

In the conception of the final edition, observance of the Passover is the means of protection and deliverance of Israel. The section thus answers in particular the question of who may participate in the Passover: only Israel, understood as those who belong to the community of the primary covenant with Abraham, the sign of which is circumcision. Therefore, no foreigner or temporary resident, no uncircumcised male, may share. The only exceptions are those who have been incorporated permanently into the community, the slave and the resident alien.

Points already made in 12:1-13 are now developed. Since the rite protects each household by the sign of the blood on its lintel and doorposts on the night when the LORD "passes over," it is to be observed within the home. In contrast to the sacrifices offered in the sanctuary, the animal must be roasted whole; there is no cutting up of the carcass to lay it on the altar (v. 46).

The Commemoration of the Exodus (13:1-22)

By contrast, in the earlier version, preserved in edited form in ch. 13:1-16, there is no ceremony on the original night of the tenth plague, the slaying of the firstborn of Egypt: Israel does not need to be protected from the means of its own deliverance. Rather, when Israel is brought into the promised land (vv. 5, 11) two rites of commemoration of Israel's deliverance will be observed (for the stress on commemoration, cf. "remember" [v. 3], "reminder" [v. 9], and its alternate, "emblem" [v. 16]).

The first rite, the dedication of Israel's firstborn, both human and animal (13:1-2, 11-16), relates directly to the tenth plague, the death of the Egyptian firstborn, both human and animal (12:29), and is the appropriate commemoration of the means, and cost, of Israel's redemption. Appropriately, then, it enfolds the second rite (vv. 3-10), here described in terms of "unleavened bread" (v. 6) in deference to the final editor's account of the Passover just given in ch. 12. The unevennesses in the present text of vv. 3-7 (e.g., the abrupt switches in thought in vv. 3-4; the repetitions between vv. 3, 6, and 7) suggest the intervention of the later editor. In the smoother parallel text in Deut 16:1-8 this one-night-plus-seven-day pilgrimage festival is termed "Passover," and so it was, in all probability, in the underlying version here.

It now becomes clear how integrally these two institutions — dedication of firstlings and Passover — are related in providing the framework for the rest of the earlier version of Exodus. The legislation cited here in connection with both institutions is codified in 34:18-20. The link between the two passages is highly significant. I have already argued (on 4:21-23) that not only is the sequence of the legislation on the offering of firstlings and on the Passover in Deut 15:19–16:8 reflected in the earlier version of Exodus 1–24; the legislation on the Passover itself in Deuteronomy 16 provides the chronology of a seven-day pilgrimage festival to the Mountain of God which culminates on the seventh day in the covenant of Exod 24:3-8. Integral to that covenant is the "book of the covenant" (24:7), the content of which has been revealed to Moses on the previous night (20:22–23:33). It is that Book of the Covenant which, I will argue, along with the Decalogue forms the basis for the remaking of the covenant in ch. 34, the final chapter of the original version of Exodus. Strikingly, the clause on the dedication of the firstborn in that repeated version of the Book of the Covenant in 34:19-20 is cited here in vv. 2, 12, and 15. Equally, the clause on the eating of unleavened bread in 34:18 (cf. 23:15) is cited here in vv. 4 and 6. Exod 13:1-16 thus anticipate the original festal "octave" of the one-night-plus-seven-days of the journey to, and presence at, the Mountain of God commemorated by the Deuteronomy version of the Passover, which culminates in the making of the covenant (ch. 24) and the remaking of that covenant on identical terms (ch. 34).

The integral connection between the rites of firstlings and Passover — and their structural function within the narrative, linking earlier and later parts of the book — is made clear by the use of a number of other recurrent themes in both: "bringing out of Egypt with a strong hand" (13:3, 9 and 14, 16); "leading into the land promised to the forefathers," with the itemization of the indigenous population of the land (vv. 5 and 11); the instruction of the son (vv. 8 and 14); and the "sign on the hand and between the eyes" (vv. 9 and 16).

13:17-22 continues the itinerary of the older version (see on 12:37-42): it picks up the language of expulsion of 12:33; Israel passes directly to the Red Sea where the miraculous deliverance of Israel from the pursuing Egyptians is about to take place (contrast the Red Sea as station 7 in the summary of the later edition in Num 33:10; there is a snatch of that later itinerary in v. 20 to prepare for the joint account of the deliverance at the Sea in ch. 14).

The itinerary is directly linked to the question of how Israel should respond to God's action. To achieve God's purpose for their conquest of the promised land, Israel has to be fully participant in God's action. Therefore, the people go up "in battle formation" (13:18). But Israel is not yet ready for the conquest; it is not led into direct confrontation with the nearest inhabitants of the land (v. 17). The battle must await God's timing (v. 18) — the same vocabulary is eventually to be used of Joshua's invasion of the land in Josh 1:14; 4:12. Meantime, Israel is en route through the deliverance at the Sea to the covenant at the Mountain, where the quality of their commitment will be disclosed and tested. Covenant implies an act of deliberate decision on Israel's part, a set of responsibilities assumed. Reliance on God thus means not passivity or inaction but total readiness, as defined by the covenant, for participation in the coming act of God.

The journey thus marks the wide span of God's purpose from promise to fulfillment. That purpose is further symbolized by the bones of Joseph (13:19). In Gen 50:25 Joseph makes the Israelites promise, in the vocabulary reused here, that when they have been "visited" graciously by God in Egypt, they will take up his bones for burial in the promised land. That promise is to find its eventual fulfillment under the conquest of Joshua (Josh 24:32). Moses' action now enables the fulfillment of God's promise as symbolized by Israel's promise to its ancestor.

But there is a direct token of God's unwavering purpose: "the pillar of cloud by day and of fire by night" guiding — and soon protecting (14:19, 20) — the people (vv. 21-22). One may assume that this pillar is the same as the one in 33:9-10, where some of the same vocabulary recurs. The "going before" is then symbolized by the ark and the tent of meeting, which lead the people from camping ground to camping ground. The language may be entirely figurative (cf. cloud and fire as accompaniments to the self-disclosure of God in 19:9, 16) or may apply to the burning of incense (cf. Lev 16:13; "cloud" is not used elsewhere of the smoke from the altar of burnt offerings).

The Crossing of the Sea (14:1-31)

In the discussion of the first stages of Israel's route from Egypt in 12:37-42 I noted that there are two conceptions of the location of the deliverance at the Sea: the earlier version places it at the Red Sea, the later edition at the easternmost branch of the Nile. Each has its corresponding purpose: the earlier is geographical, the later cosmic. In the narrative in ch. 14 these two views are developed and combined.

In the final form of the text the drama is presented in three acts: 14:1-14, 15-25, and 26-31. Each is introduced with the phrase, "Then the LORD spoke/said to Moses"; the action is in every case initiated by the LORD: the hardening of Pharaoh's heart to pursue the fleeing Israelites; the hardening of the Egyptians' hearts to pursue Israel onto the dried-up bed of the Sea; and the drowning of the Egyptian host in the returning waters of the Sea.

The earlier narrative is, broadly, contained in 14:5-6, 10-15, 19-21a, 24, 25b-27a, 28, and 30-31. It carries on directly from the statement of 13:21-22 that the LORD goes before his people in the pillar of cloud by day and of fire by night. That same pillar, here identified with "the angel of God" (v. 19; cf. 3:2; 23:20-23; 33:2), now protects Israel by switching from their vanguard to their rear guard to stand between the fugitive Israelites and the pursuing Egyptian army. It is from that same fiery pillar that panic is spread among the Egyptians (v. 24). The conception of how the sea is dried up is distinctive: it is driven back by "a strong east wind" (v. 21a); the waters recede only to flood back at the end of the narrative (vv. 26-28).

This version resumes central themes of the work: the "cry" of Israel, which the LORD hears (14:10, 15; cf. 3:9); the despair of the people (vv. 11-12; cf. 5:21); the fundamental point that the battle is the LORD's (vv. 14, 25b; cf. on 13:18); the confirmation of faith in the LORD and in Moses (v. 31; cf. 4:1-9, 31; 19:9); and the proper fear (vv. 10, 13, 31).

The chronology of this account is consistent with other parts of the older version. It is now clear how the "three days" (cf. 3:18) of the journey from Egypt to the Mountain are filled. It is toward the end of, presumably, the first day after the Passover that the pursuing Egyptians catch up with Israel. The strong east wind which brings deliverance blows the entire ensuing night (v. 21). It is in the third and last watch of that night that the LORD creates panic in the camp of the Egyptians (v. 24); at dawn (v. 27; thus on the second day) the waters rush back and trap the Egyptians. On the following day, on that version, Israel will reach the Mountain of God.

The vocabulary in this version has notable coincidences with that used in the narrative of the crossing of the Jordan in the "Deuteronomistic History" in Joshua 3–4: "dry land" (14:21a; cf. Josh 3:17; 4:18; the later edition has a different word, translated "dry ground"), "the waters returning" (vv. 26-28; cf. Josh 4:18).

The purpose of the narrative in the older version is to make clear that the liberation of Israel from the tyrant by itself is not enough; all possibility of the tyrant ever again imposing his servitude has to be eliminated (cf. the view of Deut 11:4). The Red Sea is the limit at which the power of Egypt is definitively destroyed.

The second edition amplifies this version with complementary conceptions. The clearest modifications are those which concern the route that Israel is following (14:1-4, 9). The Sea is now envisaged as the easternmost arm of the Nile. A cosmic dimension is implied (see on 12:37-42). The violent language, that the Sea is "split" (14:16, 21b, and therefore that Israel passes through a channel with the waters heaped up as a "wall to their right and left/south and north," vv. 22, 29), matches the mythological language used in encounters with rival belief systems, as in Ps 74:12-15. The encounter with the Egyptian host is provoked by the LORD's hardening of their hearts (14:4, 8, 17, 18). Thus one of the outcomes of Israel's deliverance is the acknowledgment of the LORD's triumph by the world, not least by the Egyptians (vv. 4, 18; cf. 7:5). For the splitting of the Sea Moses' wonder-working staff is reintroduced (cf. 4:1-5; in the older version Moses' hand suffices).

Israel's Hymn of Celebration (15:1-21)

This section provides an excellent example of the principle stated at the beginning of this commentary on Exodus: in the Torah there is no earlier or later (see "Perspectives for Understanding Exodus," 72 above). Thus, when Moses and the men of Israel (for the women, cf. v. 20) raise a hymn in response to the LORD's display of sovereignty over Egypt at the Sea — and, by extension, over any power on earth or in heaven that might challenge his sovereignty — it is not merely the destruction of the Egyptian host which they celebrate. The whole story of God's saving acts on behalf of his people in time, and true for all time, is included in the hymn.

Thus, though the initial reference is to the drowning of the Egyptians in the Sea (15:1, 4, 5, 9, and 10), and to the deliverance of Israel (v. 8), these are but the immediate demonstrations of what is eternally true of God. The specific experience in relation to Egypt is generalized to hold in all circumstances. The LORD is "salvation" (v. 2), a "man of war" (v. 3a), whose mighty right hand shatters his enemies (v. 6); everything he does is in accord with his nature as revealed in his name, "the LORD" (v. 3b; cf. on 3:14-15). The hymn therefore appropriately goes on to celebrate God's subsequent acts: his guidance of his people through the wilderness (vv. 13-15; the rebellion of Korah in Num 16:31-34 may be alluded to in v. 12); the conquest under Joshua (v. 16; cf. Exod 23:27; Josh 2:9 for the "dread" which will fall on the indigenous population); and the climax of the choice of Jerusalem at the time of David (vv. 13, 17).

It is thus appropriate that many of the themes of the Jerusalem tradition of theology, as expressed in the prophets of Jerusalem, particularly Isaiah, and in the liturgy of the Jerusalem temple as reflected in the Psalms, are utilized in this hymn.

Indeed, this poem would be perfectly at home in the book of Psalms. Its title, "a song" (15:1), is one of the commonest in the psalter; the term translated "splendor" in v. 11 is literally "hymns," one of the two main categories of psalm (the other is "prayers"). In structure it has many parallels in the book of Psalms. It begins with an exhortation of the psalmist to himself in the collective first person, "Let me . . ." (cf., e.g., Ps 101:1). It switches from hymnic celebration of the LORD, who is spoken of in the third person in vv. 1-5 and in the conclusion in v. 18, to direct address of God in the second person in the thanksgiving of vv. 6-17 (cf. the structure of, e.g., Psalm 48). From beginning to end there are many other coincidences with the language of the psalter; for example, v. 2a is the same as Ps 118:14; for v. 2b and v. 18 cf. Ps 145:1-2.

The reflection of the language of the Jerusalem prophet Isaiah is equally striking. For example, the same exhortation in the first person as in 15:1 is used in Isa 5:1; v. 2a is also found in Isa 12:2b; and "majesty" (v. 7) is a term for God in Isa 2:10, 19, and 21.

These coincidences in form and language with expressions of the Jerusalem tradition of theology cannot be accidental. This theology is the "Melchizedek" tradition (cf. Gen 14:18-20; Ps 110:4) of the priest-kings of God Most High of pre-Israelite Jerusalem, which was polemically adopted by David and the Davidic house after their conquest of Jerusalem and provided the theological basis of their rule: David is the priest-king of God Most High now equated with the LORD.

The adoption of this Jerusalemite tradition of theology provided massive resources for the development of a creative apologetic response to the challenge and threat of the rival theological systems of the indigenous Canaanites. Language echoing the mythologies of ancient Canaan sounds through the Song: the conflict between Baal and Sea, for instance, and the recognition of the kingship of the victorious God through the exposure of the powerlessness of his rivals. It is through the appropriation of such language and concepts that the themes of the universal sovereignty of the LORD (15:5, 8b), the incomparability of the LORD among the gods (v. 11), and the eternal reign of the LORD (v. 18) are here developed. The power of God to control the forces of creation is equally in evidence in imposing order among the nations. It is thus entirely appropriate that this vocabulary is used here in the context of another challenge and threat: the encounter of Israel and her God with Egypt and her gods.

It is equally appropriate that this Song was, in all likelihood, already present in the older version, for this older, Deuteronomistic version was composed in all probability during the unparalleled crisis of the Babylonian exile, the time of gathering of traditions and the reconstruction of religious life in encounter with yet another rival theological system. The end of 15:1 reflects the view of Deut 11:4; the term "Red Sea" is used for the location of the crossing in v. 4 (cf. the discussion of the route of the exodus in 12:37-42); there is further use of the vocabulary of the crossing of the Jordan in the Deuteronomistic History in Joshua 3–4 in v. 8 (the "heap" in which the waters of the Sea stood up echoes Josh 3:13, 16; cf. 14:21, 26).

But that version is now placed within a framework supplied by the later edition: v. 19 as a summary ties the song into its context by picking up the vocabulary of ch. 14 (for v. 19b cf. 14:22, 29). Thus traditional ideas of the cosmic reign of God exploited in the older version are developed wholly congenially in the final edition.

In a subsection (15:20-21) the traditional role of women as those who greet the returning victorious army with tambourines, dancing, and song (cf. 1 Sam 18:6) is recalled. Miriam, identified here as Aaron's sister (not Moses', perhaps because of their similar public functions; cf. their collusion against Moses in Num 12:1), is called a "prophetess" for the only time, somewhat as in 1 Chr 25:1 the musicians in the temple are said "to prophesy." This "prophecy" is no longer the prediction of the impending act of God, as among the "classical prophets" of the HB, but the celebration in hymn of eternally valid theological truth. The first line of Moses' and Israel's song is cited, but with one modification: as sung by leaders of public praise, the first word is now turned into an imperative, "Sing to the LORD."

Israel's Journey to the Mountain of God (15:22–18:27)

In this section (which the MT divides into no fewer than ten subsections) on the route which Israel follows from the Sea to the Mountain, the final edition has performed one of the most radical reinterpretations in the whole book (see already on 12:37-42). The names of the main stopping places in this section (Marah, Elim, Sin, and Rephidim) correspond to the summary of the route through the wilderness in the final edition of the Pentateuch in Num 33:8-14. None of these names occurs in the reminiscence in Deuteronomy and, therefore, in all probability in the underlying version in Exodus which that reminiscence presupposes. The striking exception is Massah-Meribah in 17:1-7; it, by contrast, is not listed in Numbers 33 but does appear in Deuteronomy (esp. 9:22). But, highly significantly, in Deuteronomy Massah-Meribah features in the journey *after* the departure from the Mountain, not, as here, *before* the arrival at it. The explanation for this occurrence in Exodus of a place name peculiar to Deuteronomy but misplaced according to Deuteronomy can only be that the final editor has incorporated the Massah-Meribah narrative from the older version but has for his own reasons transposed it into a new setting.

The timescales in the older version and in the final edition are equally distinctive. Whereas for the older version Israel departs immediately after the deliverance at the Red Sea for the Mountain of God to arrive there on the third day (cf. Exod 3:18) within the "octave" of the Passover, in the later edition the journey from the Sea to the Mountain is to last at least six weeks (cf. 19:1), thus bringing the arrival at the Mountain and the associated revelation of the law within the ambit of the feast of Weeks (Pentecost). Appropriately, then, the festival of Weeks becomes in later Judaism (and perhaps already in the mind of the final editor here) the occasion for the celebration of the revelation of the law.

Thus, apart from the opening of 15:22, the entire narrative down to 19:2a is, on grounds of route and time scale, the work of the final editor. But that does not mean that he has not made use of materials in the older version. Chief among these reused passages is the incident at Massah-Meribah, just mentioned, in 17:1-7 (others will be noted below). In the light of the evidence of Deut 9:22, that incident occurred originally in the older version between the corresponding narratives of events at the other two places mentioned in that text, Taberah and Kibroth-hattaavah, that is, between Num 11:1-3 and Num 11:4-35.

The final editor has transposed this Massah-Meribah narrative to its present position for a number of reasons. As has been noted, for the final editor the primary covenant is that with the patriarchs (see on 6:4). The events at Sinai (his term for the Mountain, as opposed to "Horeb" in the older version) thus concern, above all, the revelation of Torah. It is this view of the centrality of the Torah that leads him to construct the vast narrative of the revelation of the law at Sinai, with its distinctive chronology, in Exod 19:1–Num 10:28, which, apart from materials in Exod 19–24 and 31:18–34:29, incorporated from the older version, to be noted below, belongs wholly to him. This centrality of the law is matched by symmetry in the narrative. Thus incidents appear to be repeated on each side of this huge Sinai narrative: the gift of manna and quails (Exodus 16, repeated in Num 11:4-34), the striking of water from the rock at Meribah (Exod 17:1-7, repeated in Num 20:7-13), and the deliverance from the Amalekites (Exod 17:8-16, repeated in Num 21:1-3).

The transposition of the Massah-Meribah material is part of this construction. Its particular function is to show how, right from the start of the wilderness wandering, Israel, despite God's promises in the covenant with the patriarchs, has been a rebellious people (contrast the older version where the first open rebellion is the golden calf incident in ch. 32, as in the reminiscence of Moses in Deut 9:7–10:11). As a rebellious people, Israel is, thus, from the beginning in constant need of law for control and discipline, and of appropriate officers of the law. A hierarchy of leadership becomes pronounced: no longer is it Moses the mediator on the one side and Aaron and the people on the other, as in the older version; now the figures of Hur (17:10; 24:14) and the seventy elders (cf. 24:1, 9), who are appointed to act as judges and marshals of the people (18:21), make their appearance alongside Aaron.

The reason for the sequence of events in 15:22–18:27, in the form in which the narrative has left the hand of the final editor, now becomes clear. Despite the unwavering zeal of God (symbolized in this section above all by the "glory" of God in the cloud, 16:10) to fulfill the terms of his covenant with the patriarchs, Israel constantly threatens to fall away in revolt against the arduous route on which it is being led. There is a recurrent pattern of adversity encountered, complaint and rebellion by Israel, and gracious provision by God, not just of the outward necessities of life but also of the most basic necessity of all, the Torah.

This pattern is set in the first incident (15:22b-26): the "three days' journey" brings Israel not on a pilgrimage festival to the Mountain of God (as projected in the older version) but to Marah ("bitterness"). There the people "complain," and God "tests" them. The bitter waters of Marah, themselves turned sweet, are then followed by the sweet waters of the oasis at Elim ("big trees"; 15:27).

The journey to the Wilderness of Sin continues the pattern (ch. 16; "Sin" is a geographical location of uncertain meaning, cf. Ezek 30:15-16; the intervening stage of the Red Sea of Num 33:10 is here omitted in deference to the older version's handling of that already in 13:18; 15:4, 22). It immediately provokes another crisis of complaint, this time about food, and another "testing" of the people. The theological factor is pointed up by the date (16:1); this is the day after the Second Passover, legislated for in Num 9:9-14. Even the gift of manna is met by disobedience (it is as beside the point to attempt a materialistic identification of this miraculous "food of angels," which according to ch. 16 melts in the heat of the sun yet can be baked, boiled, stored, and breed maggots, with, for example, the honey dew of the tamarisk, as it is to attempt rationalistic historical and geographical reconstructions of Israel's exodus and route through the wilderness).

The arrival at Rephidim (17:1-7) heralds yet another bout of strife: this time it is the people who put the LORD to the test (the integration of material from the older version is indicated by the all-too-appropriate alternative names: Rephidim, "food stores," becomes Massah, "testing," and Meribah, "strife").

That God is trustworthy not only in the provision of food and drink but also in the defense of his people from their enemies is demonstrated in the following incident, Israel's victory over the nomads of the Negev, the Amalekites (17:8-16; again there is incorporation of older materials; this incident is in part the narrative counterpart of the legislation in Deut 25:17-19; cf. 1 Sam 15:2).

But the fundamental element in this cycle of narratives in the final edition is the place of the law. The complaint at Marah is met by a promulgation of "statute and ordinance" (15:25) — that combination of capital offenses and civil law which makes up the standard Israelite law code. In contrast to the lightning march of the older version (cf. 19:4), the laborious trek through the wilderness of the final edition requires a framework of law, even in advance of the definitive promulgation of the law to come at Sinai (the pronounced Deuteronomic language of 15:25b-26 suggests that the final editor may, indeed, have developed the episode on the basis of material originally located at Horeb). A similar stress on Torah, this time in connection with the law of the sabbath in anticipation of the Decalogue in 20:8-11, appears in 16:4-5, 22-30.

The need for Torah-based order within the community has, finally, prompted the transposition of the Jethro material in ch. 18, which includes the advice that Moses should appoint judges (18:13-27). According to the version of these events in Deut 1:6-18, the appointment of judges did not take place on the eve of arrival at the Mountain of God, as in the present text of Exodus, but on the eve of departure from the Mountain. The narrative matching Deut 1:6-18 is now contained in Num 11:11-17, 24-30. In the light of that evidence it is likely that the final editor has, once again, transposed a text which in the earlier version stood after the Mountain to before the Mountain (in the older version the story of the arrival of

Jethro now in Exod 18:1-12 was probably thus in immediate connection with the note on Jethro's son Hobab in Num 10:29). The reason for the transposition is clear: during Moses' protracted absence on the Mountain to receive the revelation of the tabernacle (chs. 25–31), it is essential that there should be available authorized personnel to arbitrate in all disputes (cf. 24:14 with reference to the judges now appointed in 18:13-27).

God's Revelation of Himself at the Mountain (19:1-25; 20:18-21)

The "Ten Commandments" — better "Ten Words" or "Decalogue," as I will argue below — constitute the central revelation at the Mountain of God (20:1-17). That revelation is framed by a narrative with matching elements: 20:18-21 reflect the vocabulary and correspond to the presentation of 19:16, 17, 19. It is appropriate, therefore, to consider this narrative framework before looking at the Decalogue itself.

Two conceptions of how events at the Mountain of God are to be understood have already been foreshadowed in the story of the journey to the Mountain in 15:22–18:27. These views are combined in the narrative of events at the Mountain itself.

In the final edition, Sinai, the Mountain of God, marks the twelfth stage of the journey through the wilderness (Num 33:1-15). Arrival at Sinai falls within the ambit of the feast of Weeks (NT "Pentecost"; this passage is central to the understanding of Acts 2), six weeks and more after the exodus (19:1-2a). The rebellious attitude of the people during the march is now matched by the threat of disruptive behavior at the Mountain: Sinai, on which God descends in theophanic fire (19:18), has to be fenced around lest, inquisitive and unconsecrated, the people break through into the realm of the holy to their destruction (19:12-13, 20-25). There is a strict hierarchy of personnel: Moses at the apex of the Mountain, with Aaron in attendance (the status of the priesthood as a whole is recognized in 19:22; cf. ch. 29), while the people have to be rigorously excluded at the base of the mountain. The elders interposing as representatives of the people (19:7; cf. 18:13-27) may belong to the same scenario.

In this final edition, the focus of interest is the revelation of the law, first and foremost the Decalogue seemingly revealed to Moses on the mountaintop and thence relayed by him to the people (there is an awkward transition in the text as it stands between the newer edition in 19:25 and the older version in 20:1; the text now runs: "Moses went down to the people and said to them, 'God has spoken all these words . . .'").

In the older version events unfold as in Deuteronomy (cf. Deut 4:9-40; 5:2-33). The arrival at the Mountain, named Horeb in 17:6, takes place within the ambit of a one-night-plus-seven-day feast of Passover (cf. Deut 16:1-8). After the night of the exodus, a direct journey of three days (reflected here in the metaphor of the speed and power of eagles' flight, Exod 19:4; cf. Deut 32:11) has brought Israel to the Mountain. Three further days of consecration (Exod 19:10, 15, 16) culminate in the revelation of the Decalogue on the sixth day. This revelation is directly in the sight and hearing of the people (Exod 19:19; 20:18). Overwhelmed by the awe-inspiring theophany, the people retreat in terror and ask Moses to continue alone as the mediator of the terms of the covenant (Exod 20:19). The following night Moses receives the "book of the covenant" (Exod 20:22–23:33), in which the terms of the covenant focused in the Decalogue are to be spelled out, and on the basis of which the covenant is to be concluded on the morning of the seventh day (Exod 24:4). For the older version the focus of the narrative is, thus, the sealing of the covenant (Exod 19:5), which is to be brought to its conclusion in Exod 24:3-8.

The sounding of the trumpet (19:16, 19; 20:18) is a significant detail in this older presentation: according to Joel 2:15, the blowing of the trumpet is a summons to a "solemn assembly," a rare term similar to that used for the seventh day of Passover in Deut 16:8.

The divine speech in 19:4-6 provides a summary of the covenant: the relationship it presupposes, its terms, and its desired result. All is based on the prior action of God as deliverer and initiator of the relationship (v. 4). The consequences ("Now therefore," v. 5) for Israel are obedience and observance of the terms of the covenant (in essence, the Decalogue, about to be revealed in 20:1-17, which is itself termed "the covenant" in Deut 4:13). If these conditions are fulfilled, then Israel will receive special status: out of all the nations of the world they will be chosen as God's "treasured possession" (the word recurs in Eccl 2:8; 1 Chr 29:3 of royal treasures), "a kingdom." The special qualities of that kingdom are indicated by the epithet "priestly" and the parallel phrase "a holy nation." There is no stress on hierarchy within Israel; Israel as such is chosen and consecrated to enjoy access to God and to discharge a priestly function on behalf of the nations of the world. It is not the relationship with God that is conditional (he has already "brought them to himself"; he is bound to them as a father to his firstborn, just as God is bound to the rest of the human race in Adam, as the same writer, in all probability, is saying in Genesis 2–3); it is their ability to enjoy their status and to discharge the function for which they have been elected that is conditional on their obedience to the terms of the covenant.

The response of the people to God's opening overture about the covenant is readiness and willingness (19:8), as it has been consistently in the older version (despite moments of despair, 5:21; 14:11-12). This willing response is matched by the terror with which they appropriately react to the experience of the overwhelming self-manifestation of God (19:16, 17). As the sequel to the older version in 20:18-21 makes clear, so far from being tempted to break through to gaze upon God, the people recoil in fear. Their positive response is motivated and maintained by the direct, personal experience of God's self-disclosure. It is their own encounter with the awesome majesty of God, which can never be erased from their memory, that is designed to ensure that they will never fall away (20:20).

The fundamental significance of the Decalogue in the covenant relationship between God and his people is thus demonstrated by the fact that it alone of all the terms of the covenant is communicated to Moses in the hearing of the people (19:9; for the motif of the consequent confirmation of belief in Moses cf. 4:1-9; 14:31).

The Decalogue (20:1-17)

"Decalogue" is the better translation of the phrase "the ten words," which Deuteronomy (e.g., Deut 4:13) and the literature related to it customarily use, than the conventional "Ten Commandments." It also guards against a serious distortion: the equally conventional view is that the Decalogue is a list of "Thou shalt nots" (and there have been scholarly attempts to "recover" such a stereotyped pattern throughout the ten), a series of prohibitions defining basic human duty. But it must be emphasized, in line with the summary of the covenant in 19:4-6, that the first "word" (v. 2, which in Jewish tradition is included within the first "commandment") begins with a statement about the being and action of God, not about human duty. "The indicative of grace precedes the imperative of law" (cf. Barth, *CD*, IV/1, 424).

Much scholarly effort has been expended in the endeavor to date the Decalogue. Comparisons have been made, for instance, with the form of vassal treaties current in the ancient Near East. On the basis of the internal evidence of the addressee in the kind of society envisaged — the male head of the household of the middle generation who has both elderly parents to care for and sons and daughters to bring up, and who is a well-set-up farmer with ox and donkey and even slaves and can provide hospitality for strangers — it is argued that a post-conquest date must be sought. Given that there is no mention of a king or of temple worship, it may be assumed to have arisen in premonarchical times. These arguments are not without validity.

The view taken here, however, as throughout this commentary on Exodus, is that more certain results can be obtained by asking when and how the text functioned than when and how it arose. The text of the Decalogue, as of the remainder of Exodus, is a laminate made up of an older version still preserved in Deut 5:6-21 and a re-edited final edition. As both an "exilic" and "postexilic" text, then, it presents an ideal of Israelite society in terms of an idyllic past of rural self-sufficiency. There are no poor, for instance, to support (cf. Deut 15:4), for according to this ideal everyone has a place in the community within the family, whether relative or dependent, and each family has the necessary land to ensure its support. There is here both pathos and eschatological hope: the irony that the "ten words" achieve currency in an exilic context of dispossession, and the hope that one day the ideal, with whatever transmutations, will become real.

I do not deny that each of these "words" may — must — have had a long prehistory (there is evidence of analogous collections in, e.g., Hos 4:1-2, 12). But I suggest that they are indeed intended to be the essential digest of Israel's belief (cf. their distinctive character as those directly revealed in the hearing of the people, 19:9; their special status as written "by the finger of God," 31:18, as opposed to the following "book of the covenant," mediated and written by Moses, 24:4). As such they are a selection of much wider available materials, deliberately generalized, and worn so smooth by use that it is impossible to get a hold of their date of origin.

Everything depends on the LORD's Name, his revealed nature as in 3:14-15. The opening clauses of the Decalogue outline the LORD's prerogatives by virtue of who he is and what he has done, as expounded in the whole narrative of Exodus up to this point: the recognition that he alone is God; his jealous zeal for his people that can brook no rival or alternative system, portrayal or concept; his claim on the exclusive worship of his people; and the absolute demand that this Name not be misused for any purpose, whether in blasphemy against himself or in perjury or curse against a fellow member of the community.

The major difference (there are more than a score) between the older version of the Decalogue still extant in Deuteronomy and the later edition of it in Exodus concerns the reason for observing the weekly sabbath. In Deuteronomy it is the celebration of liberation from slavery in Egypt and an anticipatory sharing in ultimate liberation from all slavery. In the final edition of Exodus, in line with the cosmic dimension already noted in connection with Aaron's confrontation with the Egyptian magicians (7:9-12) and the drowning of the Egyptians in the Nile (14:30), it refers to the creation narrative in Gen 1:1–2:4a. It is a celebration of God's work as creator and invites participation in the beauty and order of his finished creative work. Here, too, there is an eschatological dimension.

There are, indeed, some puzzling features in the Decalogue; for example, God himself is the speaker only for vv. 2-6; where is the division between the two tables (a question which in part motivates the search for ten short prohibitions): does duty to parents (v. 12, the "fifth commandment," and the second following the two positively formulated commands which lay down absolute obligations) fall in the first section, among the duties toward God, or in the second, among those toward humanity?

In particular, what is the purpose of the "eighth commandment," "You shall not steal," if in the "tenth" even the underlying motivation to steal is forbidden? The suggestion that "steal" has here the sense of "kidnap," as in 21:16, has much to commend it. In that case, the last five clauses have to do with the (ideal) protection of the life (but "kill" is restricted here to "murder" and does not include killing as an inevitable consequence of war [cf. 30:11-16] or the death penalty; cf. the capital offenses in the Book of the Covenant), marriage, freedom, justice, and property of the fellow Israelite. These are all the gifts of the freeborn individual, which have, indeed, been provided by God by his action in liberating his people from slavery. An alternative suggestion is that the "tenth commandment" is aimed at those who would misuse the legal system to misappropriate the possessions of others, a particularly lively issue during the exile (cf. Ezek 11:15; 33:24); in other words, the "eighth commandment" simply deals with the isolated offense (cf. the similar overlap between the "seventh commandment" on adultery and the "tenth"). Perhaps these alternative possibilities simply underline the fact that the Decalogue expresses principles applicable in a great variety of circumstances.

The Book of the Covenant (20:22–23:33)

The Decalogue is the statement of the fundamental duties which the responsible householder owes toward God, family, and community. But as it stands in the present combined text of Exodus, which dates from periods of profound social dislocation, it looks forward to the realization of hopes for the future that are expressed in terms of the recreation of the idealized, self-sufficient rural communities of the past.

Within this context the Book of the Covenant ("B"; 20:22–23:33) happily finds its place. At its heart lies a law code. As a digest of Israel's civil and criminal law, dating back no doubt to the origins of the community, it reflects a long history of ancient Near Eastern law, as studies comparing and contrasting it with the practice of ancient Israel's neighbors demonstrate. This ancient practice, reflecting much the same rural society as the Decalogue, provides Israel with a stock of ideas and vocabulary to express its expectations for the future.

The name "Book of the Covenant" derives from Exod 24:7: it is the document, received by Moses alone overnight after the Decalogue had been revealed in the sight and hearing of the whole community, on the basis of which the covenant between the LORD and Israel was made.

The structure of the work reflects its purpose. Its core (21:1–22:20) is made up of two varieties of law set forth in four blocks in alternating sequence. This core is set within a covenantal framework, 20:22-26; 22:21–23:19. The whole is rounded off with an exhortation, 23:20-33.

The core contains "statutes" and "ordinances." The "ordinances" are set forth in the two blocks 21:1-11; 21:18–22:17. Their title, "ordinances," is supplied by 21:1. The word implies "usual practice" (e.g., in Jer 30:18 it is used in concrete terms of the "customary location" on which fortresses will be rebuilt); that is, it is case law based on precedent. The "customary way" of dealing with a wide variety of issues is listed: slavery for debt; compensation for injuries inflicted on freeman, slave, and pregnant woman, issuing in the principle of "like for like" ("an eye for an eye," etc., interpreted in Jewish tradition as commutable into monetary payment); damages for injuries caused by a goring ox or an open cistern; penalties for theft, destruction of crops by grazing or fire, stolen or damaged deposits, and fornication. The arbitration of the court, presumably "the elders in the gate," is alluded to in 21:22 (cf. the assessment of damages implied in 21:30, 34, 36).

A different variety of law is to be found in two blocks of material relating to capital offenses (21:12-17; 22:18-20). It may be assumed that the term "statutes" applies to these laws (cf. the Hebrew for "law code," "statute and ordinance," as in 15:25). The cases dealt with cover murder (carefully distinguished from homicide), injury to parents, kidnapping, cursing of parents, sorcery, bestiality, and sacrificing to any god other than the LORD.

This combined law code of "statutes and ordinances" is, however, set within the framework of a covenant document. There are essential differences in form and content between a law code and the code of a covenant between God and Israel. In form the outer framework is cast into second-person address, "You shall . . . ," as opposed to the law code in 21:1–22:20, which is almost uniformly expressed in the objective third person, "when someone . . . ," or "anyone who. . . ." The exceptions in the law code to this form of address in 20:2 and 21:18, where the second person "you" is used, make the point: these verses at the outer edges of the law code show how the law code as a whole has been taken up into the covenant code with consequent changes in its formulation into second-person address.

There is also a striking difference in content: in the law code, especially in the "ordinances," God, if he figures at all, appears only as a sanction to enforce observance ("God" in 21:6; 22:8-9 should probably be translated "judges," as in Jewish tradition, e.g., *m. 'Aboth* 3:6; cf. the plural verb at the end of 22:9). The only explicit reference to the LORD in the "statutes" is in 22:20, precisely at the point of transition to the second-person covenantal framework. The law code is the immemorial practice of the community and governs human relations within it (cf. the "second table" of the Decalogue, where God is not mentioned). By contrast, in the framework God addresses Israel (through Moses as his spokesman). It begins and ends with the obligations of Israel in their personal relationship with the LORD as worshipers (cf., in both form and content, the opening of the "first table" of the Decalogue, where God is speaker). Thus the instructions for the building of the altar for sacrifice at the beginning in 20:22-26 are matched by instructions for worship in 23:10-19.

But, once again, at the edges of the material there is a merging of form and content. The closing framework element (22:21–23:19) is laid out in four blocks arranged by content, again in alternating sequence, and has to do with obligations to fellow Israelites (22:21-27, the care of the vulnerable within society, the sojourner, widow, orphan, debtor, and borrower; 23:1-9, the practice of justice, enfolding humanitarian concern for the animals owned even by an enemy; 23:9, virtually repeating 22:21, forms a bracket around this material) and to God (22:28-30, suitable to the theme of the whole book including the obligation to offer firstfruits and firstlings; 23:10-19, the observance of sabbatical year, sabbath, exclusive worship, and festivals). The obligations to the LORD are thus integrated with the obligations to fellow members of the community which he has created. In form these "commands" represent the casting into second-person address of the third-person legal "statute" (e.g., 22:21-23) and "ordinance" (e.g., 22:25-26).

A striking feature of this framework is the addition of reasons for carrying out these obligations, typically appealing to the theme of the whole book, the exodus from Egypt (22:21; 23:9, 15; others are given a humanitarian as well as a theological motive, 22:27; 23:7; and still others are more general, 20:25; 23:8; contrast the body of the law code where only once is such a reason given, and that a purely rational one, 21:21).

It is notable that the code at the heart of Deuteronomy (Deuteronomy 12–26) is the other main collection of "statutes and ordinances" in the HB (Deut 12:1), where third-person law is cast in the form of second-person covenantal address, and where the reason given for observing individual stipulations typically has to do with God's saving acts on behalf of his people, not least their deliverance from Egypt (e.g., Deut 15:15). The law code in Exodus is thus cast by its framework into the same kind of covenant code as is to be found in Deuteronomy. Once again, then, the coincidence of material in Exodus with that in Deuteronomy is striking and justifies the conclusion that the older version of Exodus included B and can appropriately be called "Deuteronomic."

The relation between B in its present form and the Deuteronomistic History (Joshua–2 Kings) is made even clearer in the peroration to B in 23:20-33. At the end of other codes, promises of blessing and threats of curse appear as inducements and sanctions to encourage observance of the terms of the code; this is notably the case in Deut 27:11–28:68 and Lev 26:3-45. In the conclusion of B, the blessing constitutes by far the greater proportion (cf. the presentation of Israel in the older version of Exodus as still responsive to God's action); warnings appear only in vv. 21, 24, 32, and 33. The promise in particular is of an "angel" (cf. 3:2; 33:2) to go before Israel to guide it on the way to the promised land and to lead it in its conquest. This angelic figure must relate to the "pillar of cloud by day and of fire by night" which leads them on the way in 13:21 and which in turn is associated with the tent of meeting and the ark of the covenant (33:7-11; Num 10:33-36; cf. the association here with the name of the LORD, v. 22; cf. 3:15). The condition put upon this promise of blessing is that Israel will be obedient to the guidance of this angel (for what that obedience means compare v. 24 with the Decalogue, 20:5). It is significant that this same angelic figure reappears in Judg 2:1-5 at the end of the narrative of the conquest of the promised land, thus providing a further link between the older version of Exodus and the Deuteronomistic History (cf. the link between Exod 1:11 and the portrayal of Solomon in 1 Kgs 9:19, the burial of the bones of Joseph linking Exod 13:19 with Josh 24:32, and the golden calf incident in ch. 32 which anticipates 1 Kgs 12:28; the "hornet" in v. 28 here links with both Deut 7:20 [the NRSV renders "pestilence" in these two cases] and Josh 24:12; the account of the gradual conquest in vv. 29-30 relates to Deut 7:22; for the "Red Sea" [v. 31] cf. 13:18; for the "snare" in v. 33 cf. Deut 7:16). By the time of the stage indicated in Judg 2:1-5, Israel lies under the curse of the covenant that is to befall the people because of their disobedience, not under the blessing. Israel is to enter the promised land not in triumph but in tears.

The Making of the Covenant (24:1-11)

This section well demonstrates the combination of the two versions of events running through Exodus. At its heart (24:3-8) lies the older, Deuteronomistic version: on this day, as commemorated in the "solemn assembly" on the last day of the Deuteronomic Passover (Deut 16:8), the covenant is made at the Mountain of God. The terms are spelled out in the "book of the covenant" (v. 7), comprising "statutes and ordinances" of the old Israelite law code, set within a covenantal framework, which is laid out in 20:22–23:33. As the Deuteronomic Passover is a "communion sacrifice," so this covenant is now concluded by means of "whole burnt offerings and communion sacrifices."

The whole burnt offering, as its name implies, involves the burning of, essentially, the whole animal on the altar as an expression of total devotion to the LORD (for the method of offering this sacrifice, according, at least, to the later edition, see esp. Lev 1:2-13). The "communion sacrifice" fitly expresses the double bond implied in the covenant (for the method of offering this sacrifice, see Leviticus 3). On the one hand, it acknowledges the bond between God and his people. God himself has given his people their lives and everything which they possess, including the domestic animals from which the sacrificial victims are selected; the vital parts of the animal, especially the blood as its life force, are, therefore, returned in acknowledgment to God as the giver at the altar. As domestic animals, the victims belong, too, to the support system on which the people's lives depend; the gracious acceptance by God of this offering is thus an expression of his favor toward them in every respect. On the other hand, the "communion sacrifice" also involves the sharing of the remainder of the animal in a meal with family and neighbor; it is thus an expression of solidarity within the community and a recognition of the reciprocal responsibilities of each for the others. The responsibilities toward God and humanity, focused in their essentials in the Decalogue and expounded at length in the Book of the Covenant, are thus sacramentally expressed in this sacrificial rite of the Passover.

An additional sacramental act follows (24:8). In a rite unique in the HB, half of the blood of the sacrificial animals is sprinkled over the altar, which Moses constructs, and half over twelve stone pillars (the phrase "blood of the covenant" is equally unique). As the twelve pillars explicitly represent the twelve tribes of Israel, so, it may be presumed, the altar, the place and means whereby the physical offering is raised by the column of smoke into the heavens through the gift of fire upon the altar from God himself (cf. 1 Kgs 18:24), represents the gracious presence and response of God. Altar and pillars alike stand evermore as memorials and witnesses to the commitment of God and his people to each other.

This version is complemented by the later edition (24:1-2, 9-11; cf. the counterpointing of "young men," v. 5, and "elders," vv. 1, 9). The hierarchy, so in evidence in 19:7, 21-25, reappears. Moses is accompanied by Aaron, the head-to-be of the family of priests (cf. 28:1–29:27), who is therefore now accompanied by his two older sons (6:23; cf. Num 3:2; in the Samaritan Version all four sons are included, perhaps correctly; the two mentioned here in the MT are soon to be removed for cultic malpractice, Lev 10:1). The people, immediately responsive and involved in 24:3-8 (cf. 24:3b, 7b with 19:8), are now, as in ch.

19, rigorously excluded from the proceedings; even their representative elders occupy a subordinate position.

There is now no mention of concluding a covenant; for the later edition, the covenant above all is that with the patriarchs (cf. 6:4). Rather, the experience is of the awesome transcendence of God which precisely requires the hierarchy of priest and elder in those who would approach him. It can hardly be God himself whom they see (24:10a); as the clarification in v. 10b makes clear, they can sense his presence only through the translucent blue vault of the heavens (for the description, cf. Ezek 1:26; 10:1). Nonetheless, the relationship God has with his people and the commitment God shows to them are expressed through the fact that these "chief men" of the community (the rather rare word *'atsilim* can hardly be separated from the verb from the same root of the "taking" of the spirit which attended the appointment of the seventy elders in Num 11:17) not only remain unscathed but share a meal (v. 11). The question in the forefront of these verses is the authority of those who will have to maintain good order within the community during the impending absence of Moses on the mountaintop to receive the laws in 25:1–31:17.

The Breaking and Remaking of the Covenant (24:12-18; 31:18–34:35)

In the remaining chapters of Exodus the final editor incorporates two very large additional passages (amounting to more than one third of the total book): specifications for the tabernacle (25:1–31:17) and its construction according to these specifications (chs. 35–40). When these large blocks are for the moment set aside, the remainder as defined in the title of this section bears a strong resemblance to the "reminiscence" in Moses' speech in Deut 9:8–10:11. What the earlier version in Exodus at this point must have looked like can still be seen from a comparison of the present text with that passage in Deuteronomy. From that comparison the stress on covenant in the older version and the sometimes quite radical reconstructions of that version in the final edition, in its concern with the transcendence of God, the revelation of Torah, and the hierarchy within the community, can be all the more appreciated.

The first part of this material, 24:12-18, sets the scene. The verses of the framework, vv. 12 and 18b, are virtually identical with Deut 9:9: the ascent of the Mountain by Moses to receive the stone tablets on which the Decalogue is to be inscribed by the finger of God (as stated in the immediate sequel in the original, 31:18 par. Deut 9:10) and his stay there for forty days and nights. It may be assumed that the version in Exodus would be slightly fuller than the reminiscence in Deuteronomy; thus v. 13, with its note that Moses is accompanied by Joshua (not Aaron!), though it has no parallel in Deut 9:9, must belong to the older version in view of the positive role of Joshua in the sequel (and the negative role of Aaron in ch. 32).

But the remainder of the passage has all the hallmarks of the later editor. True to his view that the fundamental covenant is that with the patriarchs (Exod 6:4), the note in Deut 9:9 that the tablets are "the tablets of the covenant" is suppressed in 24:12. Instead, in line with his view that the Mountain is the place of the revelation of law, he reads "the tablets of stone, and the Torah and the commandment," all of which God now writes "to instruct them" (the verb "instruct" being from the same root as "Torah"). Equally, the preparations for the maintenance of good order within the community made in 18:13-27 are now put into effect during Moses' absence (24:14; for Hur cf. 17:10).

Also characteristic of the final editor is the stress on the transcendence of God, termed here, as typically, "glory" (24:16, 17; cf. 16:7). This "glory," now seen on top of Sinai (the final editor's name for the Mountain), will hereafter fill the tabernacle (40:34). The term thus binds together the whole of this last part of the final edition of Exodus. Accordingly, in the final edition, after a time of preparation double that for the revelation of the Decalogue (24:16; cf. 19:10), the revelation of the specification of the tabernacle now follows in 25:1–31:17.

Meanwhile, as the reminiscence in Deut 9:10 indicates, the older version continues in 31:18. Once again the narrative in the older version is fuller than that provided in the reminiscence: the story of the golden calf, merely presupposed by Deut 9:12, is told in detail in 32:1-6 (its Deuteronomistic character is confirmed by the cross reference between v. 4b and 1 Kgs 12:28).

It is now for the first time in that older narrative that Israel rebels. The direct experience of the awesome self-manifestation of God they have had in chs. 19–20 and the commitment they have given to the covenant in ch. 24 now count for nothing. On the disappearance of Moses on the Mountain, they appeal to Aaron to provide them with alternative gods. Their request, "make gods for us" (32:1), amounts to a comprehensive incrimination of themselves. It is a direct infringement of the opening terms of their covenant with the LORD as expressed in both the Decalogue (20:3) and the Book of the Covenant (20:23). In their identification of Moses as the one "who brought us up out of the land of Egypt," they deny the action of the LORD as expressed in the first "Word" of the Decalogue (20:2; the verb is the one used in 3:8). Their request for someone to lead them is a rejection of the promise of the guidance of the LORD's angel in 23:20. It is thus grimly ironical that the verb in the phrase "they gathered around Aaron" in 32:1 comes from the same root as the word for "sacral assembly," *qahal* (e.g., Deut 5:22; 10:4).

Their self-incrimination is compounded by the action of Aaron, who now, without the slightest demur despite his status as Moses' spokesman to the community (4:16), becomes accessory to the revolt (32:2): the golden earrings melted down by Aaron could have been gained by these former slaves from the Egyptians only as part of their reparation for slavery, demanded precisely by the women and placed on their sons and daughters (3:22). They are the symbols, worn in every household, of the effectiveness of the "strong hand" of the LORD (3:19) by which he restored their independence.

The golden calf which Aaron makes (32:4) is no doubt meant to be a compromise on his part. To the people these are new gods; the plural is used deliberately to echo

Jeroboam I's "golden calves" in 1 Kgs 12:28. But Aaron attempts to integrate the calf into the worship of the LORD, as probably Jeroboam also tries to do with equally disastrous results. Whole burnt offerings once brought in utter devotion to the LORD and communion sacrifices once celebrated as an expression of solidarity between the LORD and his people (24:5) are now made to these vacuous "gods" of the people's own invention. The bacchanalian revels implied by 32:6b reflect the licentious celebrations of the grape harvest at the New Year festival of the indigenous population of Canaan, as the parallel with 1 Kgs 12:32 suggests.

The close parallels with the reminiscence in Deuteronomy resume in 32:7-10 (par. Deut 9:12-14). The LORD himself now takes up the charge of ineffectualness against Moses: it is Moses' people whom Moses has brought up who have quickly turned aside from the way of life marked by the LORD's commandments. Let the LORD destroy them and make of Moses a new and greater people.

But thereafter the final editor intervenes with large-scale rearrangements of the older text as attested by Deuteronomy. The sequence of events in Deuteronomy from this point on (though its text has its own anticipations, resumptions, and editorial history) is coherent and logical. Moses now descends to see the full horror of the people's apostasy (Deut 9:15-16). He breaks the tablets of the covenant he has received from the LORD (9:17). Nonetheless, he returns to the LORD for a second forty-day-and-forty-night period to make intercession for the people (9:18-19, resumed in 9:25-29 and 10:10) and for Aaron (9:20), after grinding the golden calf to powder and casting its dust onto the stream flowing away from the Mountain. During this second period, Moses receives a copy of the tablets, makes an ark for them (10:1-4), and is bidden to arrange the departure from the Mountain (10:11). Accordingly, at the end of the period, Moses descends from the Mountain, deposits the tablets in the ark (10:5, doubtless in the tent of meeting), appoints the Levites as bearers of the ark (10:8-9), and, presumably, organizes the departure.

A text echoing this sequence of events, with typical Deuteronomistic amplifications, is discernible in Exodus. Moses descends from the Mountain with the tablets of the Decalogue in his hands (32:15-16). When he sees the full enormity of what the people are doing, he breaks the tablets (32:17-19). He grinds the golden calf to powder (32:20) and confronts Aaron with his complicity (32:21-24). He returns to the Mountain for a second forty-day-and-forty-night period for intercession for the people (32:30-31). God relents; new tablets are prepared (34:1, 4). Some Deuteronomistic additions follow. After a declaration by God of his Name and nature in terms reminiscent of the opening of the Decalogue (34:5-8), the covenant is remade (34:10). The exclusiveness of the covenant is underlined by the command to avoid any covenant with the indigenous population of the land of Canaan, particularly through marriage, since the marriage contract would involve recognition of the gods of Canaan (34:11-16). The fact that the covenant is being remade on the same terms as before is indicated not simply by the allusion to the Decalogue in 34:5-8, and again in v. 17, but also by the virtual repetition of the closing words of the covenant framework of the Book of the Covenant (34:18-26; cf. 23:12-19; the addition of legislation on the offering of the firstborn, 34:19-20, is particularly significant in view of the overall argument of the book of Exodus; cf. 4:22). As Moses wrote the original Book of the Covenant (24:4), so now he writes the Book of the Remade Covenant (34:27). After the delivery of the rewritten tablets of the Decalogue (34:28; written by God himself, as the parallel with Deut 10:4 makes clear), Moses descends to lead the people away from the Mountain (34:29). The departure from the Mountain toward the promised land would be the climax of the older version of Exodus.

But that clear Deuteronomic/Deuteronomistic text embedded in 31:18–34:29 has, as in 24:12-18 and earlier parts of the book, been closely edited, and in places radically rearranged, by the final editor for his own theological purposes. Given his starting point that the fundamental covenant is that with the patriarchs (6:4) and that Sinai — his term for the Mountain — is, therefore, primarily the place of the revelation of Torah, the tablets of the Decalogue are no longer called by the older version's name, "tablets of the covenant," but "tablets of the testimony" (31:18 par. Deut 9:10-11; so again 32:15 par. Deut 9:15; cf. 34:29 par. Deut 10:5). The tablets are now the objective attestation of the requirements of the LORD for his people; the covenant relationship itself has been established since Abraham. The final editor is concerned with the people's process of "sanctification"; the miracle that they have been "justified," brought into being by an act of free grace as God's people, is taken for granted.

The final editor intervenes again in the golden calf incident, specifically in connection with Moses' intercession. The substance of Moses' prayer, as in Deut 9:25-29, which takes place at the beginning of the second period of forty days and nights, is now transposed to the end of the first period in Exod 32:11-14. This permits a quite new outcome to the beginning of the second period in 32:30-35: not that a greater people will be made out of the descendants of Moses but that a calamitous act of punishment will come upon the guilty people (32:35; words from the root "sent a plague on" have hitherto been used only of the LORD's act against the Egyptians, 8:2; 9:14; 12:13).

It is likely that the immediate act of punishment of the people by the Levites in 32:25-29 also arises from the work of the final editor. In Deut 10:8-9, and thus presumably in the older version in Exodus, the Levites are not appointed to office until the moment of departure from the Mountain, and then as bearers of the newly constructed ark and as officiants "before the LORD," which can only mean in a sanctuary, that is, in the equally new tent of meeting. Here a quite different context is given for the "ordination" of the Levites (the technical expression "fill the hand" is used in 32:29): the bloody punishment they unleash on the Israelites for their sin in constructing the golden calf. In the light of Deut 33:8-11 it is likely that this incident originally took place at Massah-Meribah (cf. v. 29 with Deut 33:9), that is, in the context of the incident which, I have argued, the later editor transposed into Exod 17:1-7 from its original context between Num 11:3 and 4 (cf. the acts of punishment of the people at the two other places mentioned in Numbers 11).

The view that punishment immediately follows a crime is much in evidence in Chronicles, a work probably close in time and authorship to the final edition of Exodus.

Strikingly, the final editor has changed the significance of grinding the ashes of the golden calf to powder (Exod 32:20) from purification (as in Deut 9:21; cf. Deut 21:1-9) to incrimination (cf. Num 5:11-31).

In the light of the reminiscence of Deut 10:1-11, it seems clear that the final editor has also transposed the material on the departure from the Mountain, already beginning in 32:34 and continued in 33:1-6, as well as Moses' habitual practice of pitching the tent of meeting for the ark (33:7-11; obliquely referred to as "for it" [not overtly translated in the NRSV] in 33:7). In the Deuteronomic view all these actions can take place only after the renewal of the broken covenant and the remaking of the tablets of the Decalogue in 34:1-29. The reason for the final editor's transposition of this material is surely clear. Given that he is about to introduce some forty-two new chapters on the construction of the tabernacle and on further revelations at Sinai (Exodus 35–Num 10:28), all within a new and quite extended chronology (Exod 40:17; Num 10:11), it is inappropriate that that material should be left in its original position between Exod 34:29 and its natural continuation in Num 10:29 (including also, as already argued, Exod 18:1-12).

A major difference, reflected in these radical transpositions, between the older version and the newer edition concerns the nature and purpose of the sanctuary. The tent of meeting of the older version, spoken of in 33:7-11, conforms to the Deuteronomic picture of the sanctuary, served by Joshua and the Levites, which goes ahead of Israel and functions as a guide through the wilderness (cf. Deut 31:14-15). It is related to the promise of the presence of God, as the guiding angel and the pillar of cloud by day and of fire by night (cf. 13:21-22). The name "tent of meeting" indicates that it is there that the LORD meets with Moses and "speaks to him face to face, as one speaks to a friend" (33:11; cf. Deut 5:4; 34:10). As we shall see in the final section on the tabernacle, the final editor has a quite different view of the institution. It is given the name "the tabernacle" (lit. "the dwelling place"). While the final editor relates the name "tent of meeting" to "tabernacle" (e.g., 27:21) and thus integrates the two structures, he locates it not in the van of the camp of Israel but at its center. Its function is, above all, to be the place of continuing revelation of Torah and of the altar of the sacrificial cult (cf., e.g., Lev 1:1).

Because of these different views, two questions call for clarification in the final edition in 33:12-23: the nature of the presence of God, and the nature of Moses' encounter with God. 33:12-19 anticipates and qualifies the vocabulary of 34:6, 9. The passage makes it unambiguously plain that it is "the presence" of God himself who accompanies his people (33:14), soon to be termed his "glory" (33:18) or his "goodness" (33:19). But, in qualification of 33:11, the nature of Moses' encounter with God is not that he speaks with him "face to face," for no man can bear to see the full "glory" of the LORD (33:21-22). Rather, even Moses must be shielded and, at most, can only see "God's back" (33:22-23).

These transpositions and qualifications caused by the different point of view of the final editor are matched by two adjustments in ch. 34. In 34:1-4, as the comparison with Deut 10:1-3 shows, he edits out the mention of the ark made by Moses in the second period of forty days and nights on the Mountain. The reason for this change is also clear: as we will again see in the final section, he has already introduced the specifications for the ark (now termed, from his viewpoint, "the ark of the testimony"; cf. 31:18; 32:15) in 25:10-22 and is about to record its construction in 37:1-9. It is therefore inappropriate to speak of it in this context. Instead, he replaces it with material on the transcendence of God and the sacredness of Sinai (34:2-3; cf. 19:12-13, 20-25).

In 34:29-35 the status of Moses as a recipient of revelation is further discussed in line with 33:18-23. Moses does not descend, as in Deut 10:11, to lead Israel away from the Mountain; rather, this descent from Sinai is but the epitome of continual "comings out" from the presence of God (34:34). Even if Moses is not permitted to see the "face of God," his full "glory," yet the modified encounter with the presence of God is enough to make Moses' own face shine with a splendor that the Israelites cannot bear to look upon. Thus, after imparting the teaching to them with this reflection of divine authority physically imprinted on his face, Moses is obliged to cover this supernatural brightness with a veil.

The Construction of the Tabernacle (25:1–31:17; 35:1–40:38)

The surpassing climax of the final edition, as the sheer volume of material makes clear, is the construction of the tabernacle. The presentation is in two roughly matching parts: the revelation of the heavenly blueprint in 25:1–31:17; and the account of the construction of the tabernacle in accordance with this blueprint, and its dedication, in chs. 35–40. The purpose of Moses' stay on the Mountain for forty days and nights is now to receive not just the written Decalogue, as in 24:18; 31:18, the verses from the older version immediately framing the first of these two sections (though that is still part of the reason, 25:16), but also the revelation of the mode in which God will reside with his people (the verb "dwell" occurs already in the first section in 25:8 and in the last section in 40:35 — and at 29:45-46; "tabernacle" itself [*mishkan*], which is named first in 25:9 and fifty-six times in Exodus thereafter, has the same root as the verb "to dwell").

The complementary interests of the two versions of Exodus are, once again, expressed, now through their respective concepts of the sanctuary. The older version (33:7-11) has spoken of the "tent of meeting," the movable structure pitched outside the camp where God descends in the pillar of cloud to give Moses guidance through the wilderness. There the two "tablets of the covenant" are lodged in the "ark of the covenant." In the final edition, the sanctuary is termed the "tabernacle." It is still a movable structure, but it is now pitched in the middle of the camp and is to be the place which the "glory" of God is to fill. In its most holy inner sanctuary it still houses the "ark" with the tablets; but that ark is now called "the ark of the testimony" (e.g., 26:33), and the tablets are "the tablets of the testimony" (cf. the final editor's adjustment of 31:18; 32:15). The covenantal relationship between God and his people is taken as given (6:4); what is now required is the sanctification of the people through obedience to the terms of the law, the objective "testimony" of the LORD's will to Israel, so that God may continue to dwell in their midst. The ark now has the added significance of being the "mercy seat" (e.g., 25:17), the covering of the ark where annually the rites of the Day of Atonement are to be observed (Leviticus 16) and where, uniquely, revelation is to continue to Moses (25:22; the verb "I shall meet [with you]" is from the same root as the noun "meeting" in "tent of meeting").

The complementary character of these two views of the nature and purpose of the sanctuary is indicated by the integration of these two structures and their names in the final edition (e.g., 39:32). The "tent of meeting" is incorporated within the "tabernacle" (the whole structure of shrine plus surrounding court is termed the "tabernacle"; cf., e.g., 27:9; 40:33); sometimes that term is used for the shrine proper (e.g., 26:1), and sometimes the shrine proper is called by the old name, "tent of meeting" (e.g., 27:21; the secondary covering of the shrine, also called "tent," e.g., 26:7; 40:19, is not to be confused with the tent of meeting). The "corporate identity" of the shrine as the "tent of meeting" is retained; but the physical structure, with a whole new range of significance, is now the "tabernacle" (e.g., 40:22). The older version's "cloud" of theophany and the final edition's "glory" of God's indwelling presence are equally combined at the climax of the book (40:34-38).

The tabernacle is not the end in itself; it is the means to the end. As such, it must be entirely appropriate for its purpose. For this reason the heavenly origin of the blueprint ("pattern," 25:9[twice], 40) and the carrying out of that revelation in precise terms are stressed by means of the large-scale "repetition" between the two sections, especially as regards specifications of the structure and its furnishings. There must be an absolute correspondence between the heavenly and the earthly. The tabernacle is, so to speak, a "sacramental" structure: it is the "outward and visible sign" in the physical world of transcendental realities; it is "the means of grace" by which access to these realities is enabled and participation in them granted to God's people.

A table is perhaps the most convenient way of giving a bird's-eye view of these complicated materials and of the relationship between specification and execution.

The specifications of the tabernacle are laid out in the MT in 25:1–31:17 in ten main sections, which are used as the baseline here; the parallels in the account of the execution in 35:1–40:38 are noted alongside (these show at times a quite different order, to be commented on below):

- the ark of acacia wood overlaid with gold surmounted by a lid with two facing cherubim (25:10-22 par. 37:1-9; for the associations of the cherubim, cf., e.g., 1 Sam 4:4; Ezekiel 10);
- the table of acacia wood overlaid with gold for the twelve loaves of the "bread of the presence" representing the tribes of Israel, with its implements of gold (25:23-30 par. 37:10-16);
- the lampstand of gold, with its implements of gold (25:31-40 par. 37:17-24);
- the ten linen curtains over the shrine (26:1-6 par. 36:8-13);
- the eleven goat's-hair curtains to cover the shrine, with skins and leather (26:7-14 par. 36:14-19);
- further structural details and equipment: the paneled walls of the tabernacle, of acacia wood overlaid with gold set in silver sockets with rings of gold and tie bars of acacia overlaid with gold (26:15-30 par. 36:20-34); the veil separating the most holy inner sanctuary set on four acacia pillars overlaid with gold on silver sockets, and the screen at the entrance on five acacia pillars overlaid with gold in bronze sockets (26:31-37 par. 36:35-38); the altar of burnt offerings, of acacia wood overlaid with bronze with its bronze implements (27:1-8 par. 38:1-7); the courtyard (27:9-19 par. 38:9-20); the oil for the lamp (27:20-21; listed among the offerings brought by the people in 35:8, 28); the priestly garments for Aaron and his sons (28:1-5; cf. 39:1);
- the setting apart of the priesthood: the garments for Aaron as chief priest — the "ephod" (28:6-12 par. 39:2-7), an outer garment with settings on its shoulder straps for two stones engraved with the names of the tribes (28:13-14; not explicitly paralleled); the "breastpiece of judgment" for the sacred lots (28:15-30 par. 39:8-21); the "robe of the ephod" (28:31-35 par. 39:22-26); the rosette on the turban, the tunic, turban, and sash; the garments for Aaron's sons — tunics, sashes, and headdresses; undergarments for Aaron and his sons (28:36-43 par. 39:27-31; rearranged in two subdivisions); the dedication of Aaron and his sons (29:1-37; this is not paralleled until Leviticus 8); the specification of the daily offerings (29:38-46; again not executed till later; cf. Num 28:3-8);
- the incense altar of acacia overlaid with gold (30:1-10 par. 37:25-28);
- the rites of maintenance of atonement (30:11-16; cf. 38:21-23 for responsibility for the supervision and construction, and 38:24-31 for, among other things, the per capita payment);
- the bronze basin and stand (30:17-21 par. 38:8), with great variation;
- the ingredients of the oil for anointing the tent of meeting, its furnishings, and personnel (30:22-33; noted only in 37:29*aa*); the ingredients of the incense (30:34-38; noted only in 37:29*ab*); the appointment of Bezalel as chief craftsman and his assistants (31:1-11 par. 35:30–36:7).

A striking feature of the above table is the difference in the sequence of the materials in the "specification" and the parallel "execution" sections. It can hardly be disputed that, as an account of construction, the sequence in the "execution" section (chs. 35–40) is the more logical (cf. the logical order of Moses' construction in 40:18-33). After the appeal to Israel to bring the materials required and the appointment of the chief craftsman and his assistants (ch. 35, in round figures), it begins with the construction of the structure of the sanctuary itself (ch. 36), then its furnishings (ch. 37), bringing the incense altar, which stands in isolation in the "specification" section in ch. 30, into direct association with the other furnishings of the sanctuary, the table for the bread of the presence and the lampstand. It then proceeds to the courtyard of the tabernacle and its furnishings (ch. 38). Finally, the officiating garments for the priesthood are made (ch. 39). But in the "specification" section this logical sequence is, in part, broken up and rearranged — 37:1-24; 36:8-38; 38:1-7, 9-20; 39:1-31; 37:25-28; 38:21-31; 38:8; 37:29; 35:30–36:7.

The main factor in this radical change of sequence in the "specification" section is the introduction of the figure of Aaron (in raw statistics Aaron appears forty times in the "specification" section and only four times in the immediate parallel in 35:1–39:31). In line with the interest of the final editor in Aaron (cf. 6:10–7:13), the high priest and his family are now brought into center stage: he is introduced in the last verse of ch. 27, and that leads directly into chs. 28–29, which are wholly devoted to the priesthood, their vestments, and their consecration (ch. 29 has no parallel in chs. 35–39, thus confirming the dominating position of Aaron in this section). The climax of the "specification" section is reached at the end of ch. 29 in God's promises that he "will meet with the Israelites . . . will dwell among the Israelites, and become their God . . ." (29:43-46, where verbs related to both "tent of meeting" and "tabernacle" are used), but the fulfillment of these promises is dependent on the system of the Aaronic priesthood being maintained. The symmetry of the other chapters of "specifications" relating to the ordination of the priesthood (chs. 25–27; 30–31) is thus striking. But considerations beyond symmetry are involved, for chs. 30–31 lead on into the central roles of the priesthood: rites at the altar of incense, especially annually on the Day of Atonement (30:10); other rites designed to maintain atonement (30:11-16); the lustration required of the priesthood (30:17-21); the anointing ceremonies for sanctuary and priesthood; and the recipe for the incense (30:22-38). Equally, the opening chapters, where the furnishings (ch. 25) are listed before the related structure (chs. 26–27), place the functions which the priests will discharge before the context within which they will discharge them.

By contrast, in the "execution" section the figure of Bezalel, the master craftsman, predominates (he is the grandson of Hur, 17:12; 24:14). But, since he is merely the artificer, executing an itemized list to order, the logic of construction is used rather than the logic of function. It is not Bezalel's place to consider how Moses will integrate each item into the whole or the role of the priesthood within the finished system (thus, e.g., there is no parallel to 25:21-22 after 37:9). Consequently, a long appendix in 39:33–40:33 records how all the elements of the structure and the vestments are finally brought to Moses, a triumphant list of how work for the highest purpose according to the highest standard has been successfully completed, and how his is the final responsibility of bringing the whole institution into being and of setting it in operation. In advance of the inauguration of the priesthood, Moses in this passage fulfills all the functions that later became those of the priests and of the high priest — above all, blessing the people (39:43) and officiating at the altar (40:29). Nonetheless, where Aaron is mentioned in the "execution" section, it is always in a climactic position: in 35:19 in Moses' summons to the people to bring their free will offerings, in 38:21 in connection with atonement rites, and in 39:1, 27 in connection with priestly garments.

Other features call for comment. For example, the account of the priestly vestments underscores the awesome role which Aaron has to discharge as representative of his people in the presence of God himself (cf. the warning bells on the hem of the ephod, 28:35): he bears before God the names of his people (28:12, 21), the lots that guarantee good order within the community (28:29-30), and the symbol of the acceptability of all their offerings (28:38).

The proportions of the tabernacle match those of the later temple, though on half the scale (cf. 1 Kgs 6:2). The most holy inner sanctuary is seemingly a perfect cube, measuring ten cubits in each dimension. The metals used, gold, silver and bronze, descend in value the further from the ark and inner sanctuary, thus matching the descending degrees of holiness of those admitted to the respective areas of the tabernacle.

Already in early Jewish interpretation the structural details of the tabernacle were held to possess cosmic significance, thus bringing the account of creation in Genesis 1 into correspondence with Israel's sanctuary as its focus and climax. Josephus interprets the symbolism as follows:

> When Moses distinguished the tabernacle into three parts, and allowed two of them to the priests, as a place accessible and common, he denoted the land and the sea, these being of general access to all; but he set apart the third division for God, because heaven is inaccessible to men. The veils, too, which were composed of four things, declared the four elements; for the fine linen was proper to signify the earth, because the flax grows out of the earth; the purple signified the sea, because that color is dyed by the blood of the sea shell-fish; the blue is fit to signify the air; and the scarlet will naturally be an indication of fire. (*Ant.* 3.7.7)

> . . . the seven lamps signified the seven planets; for so many there were springing out of the candlestick . . . the twelve loaves that were upon the table signified the circle of the zodiac and the year; but the altar of incense, by its thirteen kinds of sweet-smelling spices with which the sea replenishes it, signified that God is the possessor of all things that are both in the uninhabitable and habitable parts of the earth, and that they are all to be dedicated to his use. (*J.W.* 5.5.5)

The long list of requirements for the construction — the costliest of metals and the most gorgeous of cloths, prepared animal skins and hides, the finest wood and precious stones to be donated by escaped slaves no matter how compensated by their ex-masters — and questions of availability (e.g., of olive oil in the wilderness, 27:20), of compatibility of the free will offerings in kind presented, of the labor and tools involved in metal casting, joinery work, and sewing, of the weight in transportation (approximately two tons of gold, seven of silver, and six of bronze; cf. 38:24-31), all prompt the comment that this is no less visionary — and no less significant — a sanctuary than, say, the temple in Ezekiel 40–48. The point is not one of feasibility but of the ideal participation of the whole people to the utmost of their God-given capacities in materials and skill.

The end which the tabernacle is designed to serve is, above all, the sanctification of the people (e.g., 28:38), so that with no disqualifying factor the glory of the divine presence can take up residence in the tabernacle among them. The sheer mass and complexity of the material on the construction of the tabernacle should not be allowed to obscure three points in this regard which the arrangement of the material already makes clear.

(1) The account begins with the note that it is constructed with the free will offerings of the people (25:1-9; to stress the point, the execution section, 35:4-29, including a summary list of all the items to be contributed and made, is, unusually, much longer than the specification one). Though they do not have access to the tabernacle, its construction is enabled by the dedication of the laity and it is built on their behalf for use by their representatives. The purpose is plain: "that they may make [this root "make" is used some 246 times in this section] a holy place for me, so that I may dwell among them" (25:8).

(2) The final editor links the two parts of his presentation of the tabernacle together with what, at first sight, seems to have little to do with it — the observance of the sabbath (31:12-17, at the very end of the specification section matched by 35:1-3 at the beginning of the execution section). For ordinary Israelites who do not possess the required degree of holiness to gain access to the holy place of the tabernacle (cf. the insistence on hierarchy already in 19:20-25), the climactic seventh day of each week is itself "holy" (31:14; 35:2), the sacred space and time available to all, reserved for sharing in the "rest" of God, which marks the completion of creation and its maintenance in equilibrium ever since (cf. the reason for observing the sabbath in the final form of the Decalogue in 20:8-11). The sabbath is the "sign" (31:13, 17) of the most fundamental covenant of all between God and his people (31:16; cf. Lev 24:8). It is the sacramental means whereby human life is infused with that wholeness which God imparted at creation. Those who do not observe it as a celebration of life are necessarily dead (31:14-15). Within the present context, not even work on the construction of the tabernacle can take precedence over this absolute observance.

(3) Another issue apparently equally tangential to the question of the construction of the tabernacle is broached in 30:11-16: the maintenance of the holiness of the people by a rite of atonement. When the people are mustered for action as the LORD's host, as in the advance through the wilderness, they must be duly prepared for battle. Because of the risk of taking human life in warfare, Israel as the LORD's host must pay an indemnity in advance. Unlike rites of atonement involving sacrifice at the altar (e.g., Leviticus 1–7), which are intended to repair retrospectively the relationship between God and people accidentally breached by impurities of any kind, this legislation presupposes that the relationship is intact and is intended prospectively to maintain that unity. As a result a fixed payment for every male within Israel, irrespective of personal wealth, is to be applied to the construction and maintenance of the sanctuary (cf. the note on the fulfillment of this requirement in 38:24–39:1). Once again, the sanctuary is "sacramental": since it is the outward sign of the indwelling presence of God, its maintenance is equally the symbol of Israel's dedication to maintain the realm of the holy within which that presence may fitly dwell.

Appropriately, therefore, the book closes with the account of Moses' construction and consecration of the tabernacle on the first day of the second year after the exodus (again the account is in two matching parts, the divine instruction followed by Moses' obedience to the letter, 40:1-16, 17-33, each sub-section in the MT, except the last, ending insistently with the phrase, "As the LORD had commanded Moses"; the chronology is that of the final editor, cf. 12:37-42). In gracious response, the cloud associated with the tent of meeting descends to veil the glory of God which now "resides" in the tabernacle (40:34-35). The means whereby Israel, delivered from slavery to the world empire, can live a life of total oneness with God has been established. But the final word (40:36-38) echoes that of the earlier version (33:7-11): the tabernacle is not a structure fixed at one place forever; it is a movable shrine from which God dictates how his people will continue their march through the desert, stopping at various places en route to the promised land.

Bibliography. Several times I have made statements in the commentary above to the effect that "a good case can be made for the view that the present book Exodus represents the thorough re-editing, from a distinctive theological perspective, of an older version recoverable from the reminiscences still available in the book of Deuteronomy." More detailed argumentation to make this case than there is room for in the commentary will be found in the following publications, in which opportunity is also taken to engage critically with the work of other scholars: Johnstone, W. 1990 and repr. 2000, *Exodus,* Sheffield: JSOT Press = pt. 3 of Moberly, R. W. L., W. Johnstone, and J. Rogerson. 2001, *Genesis and Exodus,* Sheffield: Sheffield Academic • Johnstone, W. 2002, "The Use of the Reminiscences in Deuteronomy in Recovering the Two Main Literary Phases in the Production of the Pentateuch," pp. 247-72 in J. C. Gertz, K. Schmid, and M. Witte, eds., *Abschied vom Jahwisten: Die Komposition des Hexateuch in der jüngsten Diskussion,* BZAW 315, Berlin: de Gruyter • Johnstone, W. 2003, "The Revision of Festivals in Exodus 1–24 in the Persian Period and the Preservation of Jewish Identity in the Diaspora," pp. 99-114 in R. Albertz, and B. Becking, eds., *Yahwism after the Exile: Perspectives on Israelite Religion in the Persian Era,* Studies in Theology and Religion 5, Assen: Van Gorcum, 2003 • Johnstone, W. 2003, "Recounting the Tetrateuch," in A. D. H. Mayes, and R. B. Salters, eds., *Covenant as Context,* Festschrift for Ernest Nicholson, Oxford: Oxford University.

Leviticus

Walter J. Houston

INTRODUCTION

In traditional Jewish communities children begin their study of the Hebrew Bible with Leviticus. Among Christians, on the other hand, it may well be the least read of OT books. Leviticus is the heart of the law, which defines traditional Jews as a people and defines many Christians in terms of what they suppose they are against: legal religion and "empty ritual." But if Christians desire any meeting of the mind with Jews, they must try to understand this book.

The main subject matter of Leviticus is ritual, and even those parts of the book that are concerned with morality and social order impose a ritual image on moral requirements. It thus raises two types of question. First, what is ritual and how can we explain it? Second, how has such a book come to exist; what is its purpose; and what meaning can we attach to it?

Ritual

If we are to understand Leviticus, we have to cast off the mind-set which automatically attaches the label "empty" to the word "ritual." The book itself is sparing in its explanation of the rituals it prescribes, but the work of social anthropologists on ritual in a wide range of human societies gives us some clues to finding meaning in these (e.g., Douglas 1966; Turner 1969).

Ritual may be defined as any group of symbolic practices by which a community expresses its understanding of the world and regulates and renews its own life (Gorman 1990: 13-38). Ritual has both *meaning* (cf. Leach 1976) and *function* — it achieves certain ends in society, which the participants are not necessarily aware of.

The meaning and function of various major aspects of ritual in Leviticus are discussed in the comments on the appropriate sections, as follows.

Discussion of:	*in comment on:*
Sacrifice	chs. 1–7
Atonement	4:1–6:7; ch. 16
Priesthood	chs. 8–9
Rites of passage	chs. 8–9
"Uncleanness"	chs. 11–15
Festivals	ch. 23

Underlying these various aspects of ritual in Leviticus is a consistent ritual structure, expressed in the sanctuary which God commands Moses to make in Exodus 25–31 (see comment there). This is the main theater of the rituals in Leviticus, so every reader of the book needs to be aware of it. Its structure is concentric. The presence of the LORD fills the inner sanctum (16:2), and the tabernacle as a whole is made intensely holy by it (Exod 40:34). Hardly less holy is the altar, but the court surrounding them is holy to a lesser degree. Surrounding the court is the camp, where the people live. This is not holy, but it is clean — that is, it is fit for holy things. The area outside the camp, or the wilderness, is considered unclean. A reader in biblical times would apply what is said about the tabernacle to the temple, while the camp stood for the walled city.

To the classification of space corresponds a classification of personnel: only the high priest may enter the inner sanctum (16:2), and only priests may enter the tabernacle or ascend the altar; only persons in a clean state may enter the court (12:4), and the most severely unclean must leave the camp (13:46; cf. Num 5:2-4). For what is unclean can never become holy, and it is dangerous for the two to come into contact (cf. 6:8–7:36; 10:10). The holy is in the sphere of God; what is unclean represents what is opposed to God, which can never co-exist with the holy and constantly threatens it. The holy and the unclean are seen as states or influences that objectively exist, not as mere symbols. Thus the sanctuary is a microcosm: in a small space it presents the cosmic opposition of God and evil.

The idea of a unique place of divine presence, guarded rigorously by successive boundaries, is typically priestly. Priests were the professional guardians and functionaries of a temple, and temples had always been understood as the dwelling place of a god; it was natural for them to understand the place they guarded as the one important channel of communication between God and the people — not to speak of the advantages in wealth and power that accrued to them as a result.

All societies have rituals of some sort, but various societies differ in how far they are shaped by and express themselves in ritual. Modern Western society stands almost at the opposite pole from Leviticus in this respect, and that is why we tend to find the book alien to us. Mary Douglas (1970) shows how the richness of ritual in a group tends to vary in a consistent way with the social structure. Leviticus gives clues as to the kind of society it assumes or prefers: a solid patriarchal family structure (ch. 18), the inheritance of prescribed roles such as the cultivation of the land (ch. 25) or priesthood (chs. 8–10), and the need to define boundaries against outsiders (20:24-26). When a society is concerned to maintain a strong traditional order, and when people experience roles as given rather than achieved (Eilberg-Schwartz 1990: 195-216), they tend to find ritual self-evident and effective because the strict rules of the rite are reinforced by their daily experience and their need for a shape to life. For them the structures of sanctuary and cosmos echo and are echoed by the structure of society.

But the society which Leviticus presupposes was not necessarily the same as the society it was written in. It projects an ideal for society: a priestly ideal, shaped by the priests' experience of life and their primary concern for ritual order (for a contrary view, see Gerstenberger 1996). We cannot tell how far it corresponded to reality, though it has contributed to the shaping of Judaism ever since.

Leviticus as a Book

We will now try to understand the book itself. But *is* Leviticus a book as a coherent whole, or is it simply an arbitrary slice of the Torah (see Sawyer 1996: 22-64)? Leviticus is clearly marked out within the Sinai episode by its opening verse, in which Yahweh is said to "call" to Moses (the only other place where this happens is in Exod 19:3), and by the (doubled) summary at 26:46; 27:34. At the end of Exodus the tabernacle has been set up for the first time, and Yahweh's glory has filled it. In Leviticus Yahweh gives ("from the tent of meeting") all the basic instructions for the conduct of worship at the tabernacle and for the conduct of the people who live around it. Numbers then proceeds with instructions for the journey.

The book is part of the foundation story of Israel. It is held together by a thin thread of narrative: all the commands are given by Yahweh to Moses and/or Aaron in thirty-five separate speeches. Whatever its actual origin, all the teaching in Leviticus becomes the command of Yahweh: this is its basic claim to authority. At a few places the thread broadens to show how instructions were obeyed (chs. 8–9) or to tell a short story as background to instructions (ch. 10; 16:1; 24:10-12). The main divisions of the book are marked by these expanded narratives.

The structure of the book is easy to explain (cf. Douglas 1993). The sacrificial rubrics in chs. 1–7 are followed by the initiation of the sacrificial cult in chs. 8–10; ch. 16, ordaining the purification of the sanctuary and the people, stands between chs. 11–15 on "uncleannesses" and chs. 17–22 requiring both ritual (17; 21–22) and moral holiness (18–20). Chs. 23–25 are linked by the theme of sacred times. Ch. 26 spells out the consequences of obedience and disobedience, and the final chapter, as often happens, brings us back to the start with the subject of dedication to God.

The Writing of Leviticus

Most of the passages of ritual instruction in Leviticus (chs. 1–7; 11–15; 16; 27) are written, with some short exceptions, in a characteristically dry legal style, without direct appeal to the reader or any explanation of the commandments. It is an impersonal style, always referring to God in the third person and generally referring to the person carrying out the rite in the third person (this is often obscured in the NRSV, which changes it to the second person to avoid the masculine pronoun; in fact, usually only Moses is addressed directly). The same style characterizes the narrative in chs. 8–10. All these passages use a precise technical vocabulary; this cannot be detailed here (see Milgrom 1991: 35-42). This is generally recognized as the style of the Priestly code (P).

A distinctly different style prevails in chs. 17–26. Here we find Yahweh speaking directly and personally to his people, using "I" and "you" frequently, especially in the constant refrain "I am the LORD your God." Series of simple commands are framed by sermonlike material calling for obedience. Many of the same ideas and much of the same vocabulary are used as in chs. 1–16, but often in a different, looser way (see Milgrom 1991: 35-42 and Knohl 1995), besides other distinctive expressions. There are also some traces of this style in chs. 1–16 (see 11:44-45; 16:29-34; and below). The leading ideas in the sermonic material are obedience, holiness, the exodus, and separation from the nations. See the major discussions on "I am the LORD" in the comment on ch. 18 and on "holiness" in that on ch. 19.

Most scholars see in these different styles the work of two related schools of writers (see Knohl 1995; against Crüsemann 1996: 277-80). All the texts belong to the priestly writings, but within them chs. 17–26 form a block often called the Holiness code (H), from the overwhelming use of "holy" in chs. 19–22. In the following paragraphs, the symbol P is used for the non-H materials only.

The two groups of material, although they have differences, cohere closely. Although Yahweh speaks in a personal way only in the H material, he also delivers the impersonal instructions; all the material without distinction constitutes the commands of Yahweh. Chs. 17–26 make repeated allusion to the matters dealt with in the earlier chapters. Most significantly, H employs a number of ritual terms such as holiness and defilement, but broadens their meaning from technical terms of ritual to the theological and moral realm. Its ideal of morality and society is shaped by a concern for traditional order which coheres symbolically with the importance of order in the ritual structure. So the ritual structure becomes a model for the relationship of Israel to Yahweh. As the tabernacle is made holy by the divine presence and is kept separate from uncleanness, so Yahweh will dwell among Israel (26:11), whom he separated from other peoples (20:24-26) when he brought them out of Egypt. Thus he also commands them to be holy (19:2) in their daily lives.

Now we can begin to answer the question why Leviticus exists. The ritual instructions seem to have grown out of the practice of priests giving oral instruction and answering questions on ritual matters (see Hag 2:10-13). But it would be a mistake to regard them as a procedural manual. They are concerned not so much with *how* things are to be done as with *what* is to be done (Knierim 1992) and which elements of procedure are essential: how the types of sacrifice are to be differentiated or what a menstruating woman should guard against. They do not aim at instructing the novice, who would have elders to give guidance; rather, their concern is standardizing practice, perhaps at a time when this was in flux or uncertainty.

H, on the other hand, can be seen as the preaching of zealous reformers, concerned to shape Israel's life as a strictly monotheistic community. It aims to persuade and to create obedience rather than simply to instruct. It projects a picture of the ideal Israel, devoted to Yahweh alone, excluding anything which smacks of polytheism or is unworthy of a "holy people" and maintaining social justice and conservative standards of family life. In these ways, it is similar to Deuteronomy (cf. Cholewinski 1976). However, H's origin is in a priestly circle: for H Israel is a community gathered around the sanctuary of Yahweh, and their lives are to be structured on the model of ritual. There is no real distinction between the treatment of morality and of ritual; the prohibition of eating blood (7:26-27; 17:10-14) is handled with the same moral seriousness as the prohibition of incest (ch. 18). But see the next section.

Scholars differ a great deal on dating (for contrasting views see Milgrom 1991: 13-35 and Gerstenberger 1996: 6-10). The Holiness code used to be regarded as an originally separate document later incorporated into P. But such a code would have no obvious coherence on its own. It seems better to think of the H writers as editors who worked with P and other material, developing the priestly themes in new directions (Knohl 1995; see also Milgrom 1991: 13-42) and actually producing the book of Leviticus as we now have it. This more easily accounts for the presence of H traits outside the Holiness code. Knohl (1995: 105) identifies the following passages in Leviticus 1–16 as H: 1:1; 3:17; 6:17-18; 7:19b, 22-36; 9:16b; 10:6-11; 11:43-45 (I would add vv. 41-42); 14:34; 15:31; 16:29-34.

The most probable date for the final editing of Leviticus is in or after the exile (Crüsemann 1996: 282-90). It contains prohibitions of practices which are taken for granted by good Yahwists down to the exile (see the comments on 19:27-28, 26:1), and there are obvious close links between H and Ezekiel. A time of profound disruption, followed by the tentative reestablishment of a small community around Jerusalem, is the most appropriate context for an effort to shape society's life anew in dependence on the sanctuary. However, Knohl may be right in seeing the beginnings of the Holiness movement at the time of Hezekiah, with the collapse of the Northern Kingdom (Knohl 1995: 199-224).

Reading Leviticus

The commands of Leviticus are attributed to God and addressed to Israel. If readers identify themselves to any extent with this Israel, they must decide how far they can accept that God is addressing them literally. For other readers this will be a less pressing issue. Christians are in an ambiguous situation. They have always regarded most of the commandments as of no practical significance for them; but Christians do read the book, and they take some of its commandments with great seriousness: 19:18 is an obvious example, and 18:22 is creating bitter division among Christians at the present time.

Although ritual dominates Leviticus, attention to the book's rhetoric alters the perspective: far more of the effort to persuade is concentrated on its moral and social teaching. It is going too far to say (with Douglas 1993) that the ritual instructions are there as symbolic backing for the moral teaching, though that is *one* way in which they may taken (cf. D. P. Wright 1991). Ritual and moral teaching are integrated into a conception of ideal, holy, obedient Israel. Ritual is also a field in which Israel must express obedience to Yahweh. But the idea that Leviticus teaches that God desires sacrifice rather than mercy is, I suggest, a misreading.

How, then, may the moral teaching of Leviticus be read in the context of the book as a whole? The rhetorical effect of the book is to place ritual and moral demands in parallel: moral and ritual demands are equally aspects of holiness, equally words of the Lord, and equally absolute. Two opposite effects can be observed in readers of the book. Traditional Jews, who observe the ritual laws as a matter of daily routine, tend to interpret their meaning in moral terms (e.g., Milgrom 1991: 704-42 asserts that the dietary laws teach restraint and respect for life). Others appear to derive from Leviticus (or find in it support for) rigidity in moral teaching, especially concerning sex, which is characteristic of ritual. It is perhaps easier to appreciate the value of the moral teaching of some parts of Leviticus without succumbing to this rigidity if one understands the book as a call by a nation's leaders, at a particular point in history, to reshape its life under God rather than as the very words of the God in whose mouth the call is placed.

COMMENTARY

Sacrifices (Leviticus 1–7)

Sacrifice is an essential part of traditional religions in every part of the world, yet it is absent (in the literal sense) from the practice of religion in the modern West. Animal sacrifice in particular is deeply alien to us. What is sacrifice? Why did people offer sacrifice? What does it mean?

Gift

It seems likely that every sacrifice was understood as a gift to God; this is expressed in much of the vocabulary used. However, not all gifts to God were sacrifices (see ch. 27 or Numbers 7). Sacrifice involves further ideas as well.

Consecration

The offering of a sacrifice transfers the victim from the secular realm to the sacred by being brought to the altar (see 105). In the case of offerings that are eaten, this applies to the whole of the offering, not just the portion burned on the altar, for it can be eaten only in conditions of ritual purity, whether it is the priests or the lay worshipers who eat it (6:16-18, 25-27; 7:19-21). And because the victim is in some sense identified with the offerer, its transfer to the sacred realm and mediation with the deity enable the offerer *either* to share this consecration in some way (e.g., when by sacrifice and the application of the blood of sacrifice Aaron and his sons are ordained as priests [ch. 8]) *or* to be released from supernatural danger (as with the sacrifices for unwitting sin in ch. 4).

Expiation

Many sacrifices, therefore, function to atone for sin or to purify ritual uncleanness; they are *expiatory*. The sacrifices in 4:1–6:7 are prescribed for that reason. But 1:4 also gives this function to burnt offerings (see the comments on ch. 1). The simplest, and very likely the popular, view of expiation is that the sacrifice as a gift is intended to gain favor from God; but the priestly prescriptions for expiation do not support this idea: they have various distinct rationales and are much better seen as occasions for God to offer expiation by a prescribed procedure (see the comments on 4:1–6:7; 4:1–5:13; 5:14–6:7; 16).

Meal

The ritual of sacrifice most obviously resembles the preparation and eating of a meal. The offering of ch. 3 became a meal shared by the participants; but the simplest understanding of the divine portion (or burnt offering) is that it also symbolizes a meal taken by the deity. The biblical writers did not believe that God needed feeding (see Ps 50:12-13); but the rites they prescribe and the vocabulary they use suggest a meal nevertheless. Of all secular activities, a meal is what a sacrifice resembles most. Even if no one understood it literally (which we cannot show), that is the character of the symbolism.

Communion

Sacrifice also establishes communion with God through the sharing of a common meal. This obviously cannot apply to the whole offering of ch. 1, where the participants receive nothing, but it may apply to the shared offering of ch. 3, where they eat the flesh of a victim which in principle has been consecrated to God.

This is by no means a comprehensive view of the proposals which have been made for how people understood what was going on in sacrifice, but it covers the major ideas. It is clear that no one idea "explains" sacrifice; all of them are needed to understand a rich and many-faceted institution.

Why did people engage in sacrifice? The most basic reason was in order to approach God and set up communication with him, whether to seek his aid or to rejoice in his goodness. Ancient peoples would not think of approaching a king or official without bringing a present; how much less when approaching God (cf. Exod 23:15)? Social life was governed by a network of mutual favors and marked by occasions of hospitality which created obligations to be discharged when they were needed. It is natural that their religious life should be patterned in a similar fashion. By offering their God the first share of the increase of their produce they acknowledged that blessing came from him, and that he was their benevolent Lord. Occasions of sacrifice were also of importance in binding the community together on a social level.

In Leviticus, however, sacrifice is the most significant means by which the ritual order is maintained and kept in repair (see esp. 4:1–6:7 and ch. 16, and the references to sacrifice in chs. 12, 14, and 15). Against the constant encroachment of "uncleanness" upon the holy, the consecration of sacrificial victims, and especially the shedding of their blood (17:11), acts to preserve people from the disastrous effects of the desecration of the sanctuary and of the ordered world.

All the types of sacrifice here, especially the animal sacrifices, follow the same general pattern. Their key elements are as follows:

a. The offerer. Moses is told to speak to the Israelites, and in 1:2 the potential offerers seem to be restricted to Israelites. However, non-Israelites living among them could offer sacrifice according to 22:18. Moreover, offering sacrifice is not restricted to males (1:2; 12:6).

b. The object for sacrifice (technically the *victim*). Animal victims are confined to cattle, sheep, and goats, that is, those species of animals commonly herded by the Israelites, and doves or pigeons, and in general they come from the offerer's own stock, though it was also possible to buy victims. Animals had to be unblemished (see 22:17-25 and comment). The basis of all the grain offerings is wheatmeal (see on ch. 2), which was the more expensive and highly regarded of the two staple crops of the land, barley and wheat. Thus all the offerings permitted represent the basic produce of the land, on which the people's lives depended.

c. The place. The victim has to be brought "to the entrance of the tent of meeting" (1:3; 4:4). Sacrifice cannot take place anywhere else than at the sanctuary indwelt by Yahweh's glory (cf. 17:3-9 and comment). The phrase means inside the court in front of the tent proper (Exod 27:9-19).

d. The priest. Everything requiring contact with the altar and the tent, the most holy areas, is the exclusive province of the priest; therefore, it is the priest who has to catch and manipulate the blood and burn the victim on the altar.

e. The hand-leaning. In the case of beasts, the offerer presses his or her hand firmly on the beast's head (the NRSV is wrong in translating simply "lay your hand"). The meaning of this act is disputed. It may be to identify the victim with its offerer; but the most widely accepted theory is that it is simply a sign that the beast belonged to the offerer. It is therefore not required in the case of birds and grain offerings, which are carried in the hands (Milgrom 1991: 151-53). But this does not explain why the hand has to be pressed firmly on the head rather than simply touching it. The gesture may be rather "an act by which the animal is officially surrendered to its sacrificial death" (Knierim 1992: 38; cf. 24:14).

f. The victim, if a beast, is slaughtered by the offerer, though at some stage this work was mostly taken over by the Levites. Bird victims are killed by the priest (1:15; 5:8) because the blood has to be applied to the altar at the same time. The blood is caught in a bowl by the priest. Blood belongs to God and may not be used for human consumption (3:17; 17:10-14; and comment on ch. 17). It can be manipulated to express various meanings (see on 4:1–5:13).

g. In all sacrifices, whether animal or vegetable, part at least of the victim is formally brought to the altar. This is essential to its consecration. The blood is dashed against the altar, thus entering God's particular sphere (differently in the case of the sin offering). Solid parts are presented at the altar and then burned on it as God's peculiar portion; in each case the climax of the text comes at this point. It always says that the priest shall "turn into smoke" what he has placed on the altar fire. The idea is probably that the material ascends to heaven as smoke to reach God. It was an *ishsheh* to Yahweh (except for the sin offering in ch. 4), a word found only in ritual connections which probably means "gift" (NRSV, "offering by fire"). It was "of a pleasing odor" or "of appeasing odor."

The Structure of the Text

The text can be grouped into two main divisions. 1:1–6:7 are addressed to the lay community and lay down procedures for various categories of sacrifice. 6:8–7:36 are principally addressed to the priests and give supplementary regulations about the same categories of sacrifice, largely but not entirely in the same order. 7:37-38 is a summarizing note.

1:1–6:7

1:1–6:7 falls into two parts. A single speech occupies chs. 1–3 and deals with the three types of sacrifice that one may voluntarily undertake to offer; then the three speeches in 4:1–6:8 deal with sacrifices that the individual (in one case the community) is required to offer in specified situations.

Chs. 1–3

1:1 introduces not just the speech in chs. 1–3, but probably the whole book (see Introduction, 102).

1:2 introduces not only 1:3-13 but also ch. 3, on the shared offering. 1:14-17 and ch. 2 were probably added afterward.

The Burnt Offering (1:3-17)

Most aspects of this text are dealt with above, in the section on chs. 1–7.

The burnt offering or whole offering comes first since it had the highest status; it also formed the regular daily offering of the community (Exod 29:38-42). It is wholly burned on the altar, apart from its skin (7:8). The victim has to be a male (if a beast [v. 3]). Male animals had greater prestige. Female animals could be offered as sacrifices of well-being and sin offerings, but in being restricted to male victims the burnt offering probably exemplifies ancient practice most exactly.

1:4, dealing with hand-pressing, says that the offering will thereby be looked on with favor "to atone for him." The offering has an expiatory function, but unlike the sin offering and guilt offering it does not have the circumstances for its offering specified. The assumption may be that since human beings always stand as sinners before God, this standard sacrifice will always be graciously accepted by him for atonement. But in view of the great variety of occasions on which it was offered, this cannot be its sole function. As the offering was pure gift, without any material benefit in the way of a feast accruing, it was suitable for solemn occasions and for pleading for God's help in a variety of ways; at big celebrations one burnt offering might precede several offerings of well-being.

The Grain Offering (Ch. 2)

Most flesh offerings were accompanied by grain offerings (Num 15:1-8). But this chapter deals with independent grain offerings. It seems likely to be a later insertion into the context introduced by 1:2 to make clear that it was possible for someone who could not even afford a bird for a burnt offering to bring a grain offering. The offering is "most holy" (2:3, 10), which means that the lay offerer may not eat of it. It is consumed by the priests (vv. 3, 10), with the exception of the "token portion" which is burned on the altar.

All the altar offerings (except for first fruits, 2:14-16) consisted of *solet,* a type of wheat flour (NRSV, "choice flour"). It appears to mean semolina or grits (Milgrom 1991: 179), a coarser meal than bread flour but nevertheless more highly valued. Olive oil was the main fruit product of the country and indispensable in cooking. The distinctions between the different offerings are only in the manner of cooking. Raw flour (vv. 1-3) had to be offered with frankincense, a costly spice. The cooked offerings, however, would be within the reach of the poor.

The prohibition of leavened bread and honey (2:11-12) as altar offerings has not been satisfactorily explained. It is not because fermentation in itself was thought incompatible with holiness, for wine was acceptable (Num 15:5). "Honey" may well have been fruit syrup rather than bees' honey. Salt (2:13) was essential to the offering as it was in cooking; it was also a symbol of hospitality and so of agreement between two parties; thus the salt of sacrifice becomes a symbol of the covenant between Yahweh and Israel.

The Sacrifice of Well-being (Ch. 3)

This chapter resumes the prescriptions for animal sacrifices begun in ch. 1. Many aspects of the text have been dealt with above, in the comments on chs. 1–7. It gives standard regulations for the various types of sacrifice (some listed at 7:12, 16) eaten by the worshipers. They are grouped under the name of *zebaḥ shelamim;* NRSV, "sacrifice of well-being" (3:1). This translation is untrustworthy. *Zebaḥ* is the most usual word for a sacrifice eaten by the worshipers, but *shelamim* is a word of uncertain derivation and meaning ("gift of greeting," according to Levine 1974: 3-52).

Apart from regulations applying to all animal sacrifices, some of which are repeated from ch. 1, the chapter is concerned to define which parts of the animal were

Yahweh's portion and not to be eaten by the worshipers. This text is not concerned with the meal following the sacrifice; there are regulations about this in ch. 7.

3:16b-17 raise instruction to the status of commandment with the characteristic (H) phrase "a perpetual statute throughout your generations." This underlines the importance of a divine law, perhaps particularly one that was in danger of being ignored (Tomes 1988). Why the fat was Yahweh's portion is not clear. But it would not be a sacrifice unless he had his due. For the blood, see above on chs. 1–7, point f, and ch. 17.

Expiatory Offerings (4:1–6:7)

This section deals with two main types of offerings that are mandatory in particular situations. The situation envisaged here is generally one where the offerer has committed an unintentional or unconscious offense (4:2, 13, 22, 27; 5:14, 17); but 5:1-4 and 6:1-3 appear to be exceptions (see below). The first divine speech, 4:1–5:13, deals with the "sin offering"; the other two, 5:14-19 and 6:1-7, with the "guilt offering." These two offerings are quite different in their ritual and functions, but they have one thing in common: in both cases the priest is said to "make atonement" (Heb. *kipper*), and the result of the ritual is that the offender was forgiven. So before we go on to deal with the two offerings separately, we will discuss (a) the rationale of sacrifice for unintentional "sin," and (b) the meaning of *kipper* and its relationship to forgiveness.

We may feel that an unintentional sin is not a sin at all. Why should sacrifice be required for it? First, according to Num 15:30-31, a deliberate, brazen sin cannot be dealt with by sacrifice; although the rites of the Day of Atonement (ch. 16) release the community from responsibility for an individual's sin, the offender has to suffer God's punishment. In that light the requirement to bring a sacrifice for unintentional sin (or negligent or repented sin?; see comment on 5:1-13 and 6:1-7) is an important concession: it recognizes that intention does make a difference in relation to responsibility. Secondly, our own legal and moral systems do not regard unintentional harm as nothing. When we have caused damage or harm, we recognize our responsibility to put things right or pay compensation even when we did not act on purpose. The view reflected in Leviticus is that there is an objective divine order in the world which is reflected in the social and religious order, and any breach of this order brings dangerous consequences both to the world in general and to the offender in particular, regardless of intention. The object of the expiatory sacrifices was to heal the breach and deal with the consequences. If there was harm to fellow human beings, it is not dealt with by these sacrifices. In some cases it may be dealt with by civil law.

The conclusion to each separate case (except the first; see the note on 4:10) states that the priest is to make atonement for the offender, and the offender will be forgiven (4:20, 26, 31, 35; 5:[6], 10, 13, 16, 18; 6:7). These two actions are not the same: atonement is an act carried out by the priest, but forgiveness is an act of God. Forgiveness does not mean exemption from punishment, for the rule in 5:16 is clearly penal. It means that the offender is reconciled to God, restored to his grace. It seems at first as if in these rituals God's forgiveness follows inevitably from the priest's action. But atonement is seen as made possible in the first place by God, the priest acting as his representative in the rite and the offender responding to the opportunity offered to obtain forgiveness (Janowski 1982: 358-59).

The verb *kipper,* "expiate," "make atonement," is used much more widely than in these rituals for unintentional sin. It describes the ritual of the sin offering wherever it is used (see the next section), and that includes a number of occasions in chs. 12–15 in which the problem is not sin but ritual impurity. The original meaning of *kipper* is literally to "rub, wipe," and in connection with the sin offering to "wipe off" or "purge" the sanctuary of impurity engendered in it by either sin or human impurity (Milgrom 1991: 1079-84; see 16:16, 19). But it has acquired the broader connotation of removing or "dealing with" sin, or the effects of sin, as well as impurity, by means of a ritual ("to perform rites of expiation," Levine 1974: 64; cf. Kiuchi 1987: 87-109). The rituals and the effects they deal with must be discussed separately for the two different offerings.

17:11 adds a complication. The verse offers a theological explanation for the prohibition of eating blood: that God has reserved it for another purpose. But the phrase translated "making atonement for your lives" in the NRSV regularly means "ransom you" (Levine 1974: 67-68). Although the verb in Hebrew has the same form as the one discussed above, it probably has a different origin and meaning. The writer is deliberately playing on this ambiguity. Because blood was used in the sin offering to *kipper,* "purify of sin," the blood, which represents life, functioned to *kipper,* "ransom," you from the threat of death. Hence the verse offers a substitutionary theory of atonement (Schwartz 1991: 45-61), but this is a theological interpretation which is not supported in the extensive ritual texts on expiatory sacrifices (Janowski 1982 disagrees).

Wherever in this section the NRSV uses the phrase "incur guilt" or "be guilty," the true meaning is probably "realize guilt" (Kiuchi 1987: 31-34; cf. Milgrom 1991: 342-45), except in 5:17, where "feel guilty" is better. The same Hebrew word is used in 5:5 and 6:4, where the NRSV translates "realize your guilt"; nothing else would make sense. In 4:22-23, 27-28 being told about your sin by someone else is an *alternative* (there ought to be an "or" between the two verses in each case). In each case in ch. 4 it is a question of an unintentional offense which one either realizes oneself or has pointed out to one. In 5:17 it is an unconscious offense: you don't know what you have done wrong, but you suspect you have done something (Milgrom 1991: 331-33).

The Sin Offering (4:1–5:13)

Hebrew *ḥaṭṭā't,* which is a homonym of one word for "sin," has traditionally, as in the NRSV, been translated "sin offering." But the REB, following Milgrom (1983: 67-69), gives "purification offering," deriving it from *ḥiṭṭēʾ*, "to purify." As we shall see, this fits better.

This sacrifice is to be offered when a prohibition has been unintentionally broken, not on the failure to observe a positive command. This is because only a positive act is seen as having a dangerous power which has to be specially dealt with. Myths (like the story of Eden, or the Orpheus story) often make the breaking of a prohibition the source of disaster. (The apparent gap is filled in Num 15:22-29.)

But this is not the only kind of situation in which this offering was required. On the Day of Atonement (ch. 16) it is offered for *all* the sins of Israel, deliberate or not (16:16). It is also to be offered by people purifying themselves of ritual uncleanness, which is not a sin at all (see chs. 11–15 and comments); and on various public occasions.

There are just two distinct variations of ritual among the prescriptions in ch. 4 (there are other variations in chs. 8, 9, and esp. 16). In both, the blood is sprinkled or daubed on sacred objects, and what is left over is poured out at the base of the altar, not dashed against its sides as with normal offerings (1:5; 3:2). In the first type, prescribed for the sin of the high priest (4:3-12) or the whole community (4:13-21), the blood is taken into the shrine proper, sprinkled in the direction of the inner sanctum, and daubed on the incense altar. After the fat pieces have been placed on the altar, as for the offering of well-being, the rest of the animal is taken out of the camp and burned.

In the other type, prescribed for a clan chief (chs. 22–26) or an ordinary person (chs. 27–35), the blood stays in the court and is daubed on the altar, on its four horns, which were projections at each corner. The other difference is that the meat is not burned; according to 6:26, it is eaten by the officiating priest. There is also a gradation of the victims according to rank.

How are these rituals to be interpreted? (See Levine 1974: 55-114; Kiuchi 1987; Milgrom 1991: 226-92.) The sprinkling or daubing of blood must signify the purification of the objects which were daubed or sprinkled. The blood represents the life of the victim (cf. 17:11), and the victim has been made holy by the act of sacrifice; so its blood is seen as having the power to wipe out or absorb the opposing power which has made the objects impure. 16:16, 19 suggest that the holy objects were thought to be polluted by the sins and impurities of the Israelites, and 15:31 suggests that that is why their impurities were dangerous to them, unless they were purified.

The whole idea sounds like magic. But is this idea still active in the priestly texts about the sin offering? One would expect that the victim whose blood was used to wipe away such lethal pollution would be gravely polluted itself, and that is what seems to be suggested by the burning of the victim in 4:11-12, 21; 16:27: it is a way of finally getting rid of the dangerous power. But in that case why are the priests able to eat the flesh of the victim in the second type of sin offering, which, so far from being polluted, is "most holy" (6:26-29)?

One view (Kiuchi 1987: 46-52, 130-41) is that the priest himself bears the guilt (10:17), and the offering does not become infected with pollution. Only when the priest himself is involved in the sin which was being expiated is this impossible — certainly he cannot be allowed to benefit from his own sin — and then the offering is burned. But if this is indeed the view expressed in Leviticus, it means that the simple magical idea of a substance which wipes the sanctuary free of its taint is no longer operative. And this is what one might expect. Rites are more durable than the ideas they express.

A. Marx (1989) points out that the occasions on which the sin offering is called for tended to be times of transition in the life of the individual or the community, such as after childbirth (12:6), or when the cleansed "leper" rejoins normal society (14:31). In many cultures such times are seen as times of danger, and special rituals, known as rites of passage by anthropologists, are often observed (see the comments on chs. 8–9). In these cases the sin offering serves as part of a rite of passage rather than strictly as a purification.

But since the time of transition is generally seen as dangerous, it is natural for the priestly mind to conceive the danger as one of pollution threatening the temple, and so the rite takes the form of a sin offering. For the priest, all life is centered on the temple. Society, the cosmos, and the temple symbolize and echo each other. God is at the center of them all, and dangers that threaten society at times of transition also threaten the temple; conversely, to purify the temple is to remove the threat to society, to expiate sin, or to purify impurity.

One may suggest that the origin of the ritual is the rite of 16:14-19, carried out either once a year or from time to time to rid the entire sanctuary of dangerous pollution and ending in the burning of the victim away from the sacred area (16:27). The rite of 4:3-21 is then a slightly attenuated form of this: entering the inner sanctum was avoided except on the Day of Atonement. One of the causes of pollution might be a mistake by the priest, and so the rite could be adapted to deal with unintentional transgressions by others as well, and also with their points of transition. The blood did not need to be sprinkled inside the shrine because laypeople could not enter it. The idea of the victim picking up a physical taint of pollution from the use made of its blood was fading, and the priests were in need of support, so the adapted offering became a perquisite of the officiant; the fading of the original idea also made it possible to declare a grain offering from the very poor, without any blood rite at all, an acceptable expiation (note the specific declaration at the end of 5:12: "it is a sin offering"). The symbolism seems to be gradually moving toward the idea of a gift to the priests which serves to right the offense.

Whenever Christians speak of "the blood of Christ," they are using language derived from the sin offering. Crucifixion is not a bloody death; to speak of blood in connection with it is to image Christ's death as a sacrifice, and since it is just in the sin offering that blood is used to expiate sin, it is this specific offering that has given rise to the language.

4:10. Why is the prescription of the offering for the anointed priest not concluded like all the others with the statement that "he shall make atonement for him, and he shall be forgiven"? The best suggestion (Milgrom 1991: 241) is that the first two paragraphs form a single case (this explains "the first bull" in v. 21); as the high priest's error brought guilt on the people (v. 3), so the people needed to bring an offering. When the high priest has carried out this rite as well, his forgiveness is doubtless included in the forgiveness of the people (v. 20).

5:1-13. While each case in ch. 4 is introduced in the most general way, four quite specific cases are cited in 5:1-4. The most likely explanation is that these are borderline cases, cited to make clear that that kind of case was in fact included. These cases are all probably examples of offenses committed in negligence rather than by mistake, and are intended to stand for any number of similar cases. Although they are only doubtfully unintentional, they may all be expiated with a sin offering. But because of their doubtful character, confession is required (v. 5; cf. 6).

In v. 1 the "adjuration" is actually a "curse," and it is probably directed at the unknown offender (see Judg 17:2), not, as the NRSV suggests, at possible witnesses. But anyone with information has a moral duty to supply it. Failure to do so is a sin, but it may be due to negligence rather than malice. In vv. 2-3, someone has knowingly become "unclean" (not an offense in itself) and has then forgotten it, so that he or she has failed to take the simple purification measures required (see 11:24-28; 15). The extension of the time makes it a more serious matter. V. 4: failing to fulfill a promise on oath could be just carelessness, but it is certainly more than an accident.

As a further concession the poor may bring doves instead of a goat or lamb, or even wheatmeal. 5:7: when doves are brought for a sin offering, there are always two, one for a burnt offering, perhaps simply to make more of a show on the altar (Milgrom 1991: 304).

The Guilt Offering (5:14–6:7)

The Heb. *'asham* (lit. "guilt") is translated "reparation offering" in the REB, following Milgrom 1976. Its use is much more restricted than the sin offering, and it is never offered in regular public worship. The main case in 5:15-16 concerns sacrilege, when someone inadvertently appropriates what technically belongs to God. According to Milgrom (1991: 320-26), this includes all holy things. But in 22:14 it seems not to include eating from offerings of the lowest degree of holiness (Marx 1988: 184; see the next section). The object of the offering is obviously to compensate God for his loss, or, from another point of view, to compensate the priests who would enjoy the use of the property. The provision that the ram should be valued implies that the offering may be commuted to money; in addition, the offerer has to repay the value of the misappropriation with a 20 percent penalty on top.

Two cases do not quite fit the rubric in 5:15. The first, in vv. 17-19, looks at first sight like one of the cases in ch. 4. But the translation is imprecise. The difference here is that the offerer never realizes what the offense is but only suspects it (Milgrom 1991: 331-34). One of the bugbears of the ancient world was the idea that one might have committed some serious offense against the gods without knowing it; part of the book of Job is spent repudiating this idea, which Job rejects. Since the offense was not known and might be the dreaded offense of sacrilege, the troubled conscience had to offer a ram for reparation rather than the less valuable goat or lamb for a sin offering.

But in 6:1-7 there is no doubt that the offense is deliberate and very serious: profaning Yahweh's name by making a false statement on oath to conceal a property offense (see Exod 22:11). How is it that a deliberate offense can be expiated by sacrifice contrary to Num 15:30-31? Only, it would seem (Milgrom 1976), because the offender voluntarily repents and confesses (since there is no evidence, no one else knows). The offender is no longer sinning "with a high hand," and if he properly restores what he has stolen or embezzled and offers reparation to God for his profanation of God's name, he may be forgiven. Since the penalty for swearing falsely in God's name was death at God's own hands, this provision was a strong inducement to confess. Thus the ritual system, if its rules were judiciously bent, worked to reinforce the criminal justice system.

Regulations for Disposal (6:8–7:38)

This passage is primarily concerned with how the material of sacrifices is to be dealt with after the formal ritual has been completed. The section is primarily addressed to the priests (6:9, 24) because they had the responsibility of disposing of most sacrifices. The exception is the sacrifice of well-being, which is therefore left to the last, and in fact from 7:11 on the text is mainly concerned to regulate the layperson's conduct. Supplements on related topics have been added in the editorial process: these are 6:19-23, 7:8-10, and 7:22-27.

Although the eating or other disposal regulated here is not part of the ritual, the offering remains holy, and care has to be taken not to infringe that holiness. Most of the regulations can be understood if we have in our minds the priestly picture of the world (see Introduction, 101). In this section we may see four grades in the "spectrum of holiness" (Jenson 1992): things may be "most holy" (lit. "holy of holies"), holy, clean (i.e., neither holy nor unclean), or unclean. The basic principle applied throughout the section is that material may not come into contact with people or places more than one grade lower in the scale.

All sacrifices other than sacrifices of well-being are "most holy." They can only be eaten by priests and only inside the sanctuary. Burnt offerings, of course, cannot be eaten; but 6:8-13 ensures that the ashes, which were themselves holy, are safely disposed of. Other sacrifices are eaten by the priests; the raw grain offering is shared equally among the whole corps (6:16; 7:10; see above on 2:3, 10), while the baked grain offering (7:9, but contrast 2:10), sin offering, and guilt offering (6:26; 7:7) are the officiating priest's reward for his work. One priest could hardly eat a whole ram or goat, but the regulations allow him to share it with his priestly brethren; only males of priestly familes could be priests, so only they might eat (6:29; 7:6).

The offering of well-being is holy, not "most holy," so it may be eaten by anyone who is ritually clean (7:19-21), and in any place not contaminated by ritual impurity (cf. 10:14). However, specified portions are priestly perquisites (7:28-36). As these portions are only "holy," not "most holy"; they may be eaten by any (clean) member of a priest's household, not only males (22:10-13). For "elevation offering" (7:30, 34) see the comments on 23:9-20.

The penalty of being "cut off from one's kin" in 7:20, 21, 27 probably refers to divine punishment. See further on ch. 17.

6:9, 12-13. Many peoples have the tradition of an eternal altar fire. It serves a practical purpose: it was difficult to relight a fire before matches were invented; but it is also associated with the myth that the altar fire has an ultimate divine origin (9:24; cf. 1 Kgs 18:38).

7:15-18. A "votive offering" is one offered in fulfillment of a previous vow to do so if God did something for the worshiper (see, e.g., Gen 28:20-22). The difference in the time allowed is difficult to explain. But possibly the thanksgiving offering had to be eaten in the sanctuary, although it was only "holy" (Milgrom 1991: 419). This was the normal practice in older times for all sacrifices (1 Sam 2:13-14). For the limit of two days for other shared offerings see on 19:5-8.

The Consecration and Inauguration of the Priesthood and the Sanctuary (Chs. 8–9)

The narrative flow resumes from Exodus 40. The new sanctuary has been constructed, and God has shown his approval by indwelling it with his glory (Exod 40:34). Leviticus 1–7 has prescribed the sacrifices which will be offered there. Now the ritual for which the sanctuary is designed must be inaugurated, beginning with the consecration of the priests who are to serve there. The account in ch. 8 follows fairly closely the instructions given in Exod 29:1-37, with some influence from Exod 40:9-15.

Priesthood

There are many accounts in the Bible of sacrifices being offered by laypeople, but this would not normally be possible at a temple, where priests officiated. At Jerusalem the status was hereditary in a clan: all males claiming descent in the male line from Aaron were priests of the Jerusalem temple, and traditionally of the tabernacle. Their functions were primarily ritual, to present sacrifices on the altar and, in the case of the high priest (represented by Aaron in this account), to serve God inside the shrine (Exod 30:7-8, 10; Lev 4:3-21; 16; 24:3-4, 8; Haran 1978). His position was not simply the headship of the priests but one of special sanctity (21:10-15).

All this is associated with the concentric holiness of the sanctuary (see Introduction, 101). Wherever there is sacred space, sacred personnel are required to cross the perilous boundaries. Since many roles were hereditary in ancient Israel, this way of choosing them would be taken for granted. Conversely, the doctrine of sacred space was of convenience in reserving privileges.

According to Exod 29:9; 40:15 the ordination of Aaron's sons as priests was of permanent validity; their male descendants after them were born priests and did not require further ordination (Milgrom 1991: 555). But each new high priest, though he was already a priest, would have to be ordained to his role.

This account can be looked at from two points of view. On the one hand, it is the myth of the foundation of Israel's cult and priestly order. Like other parts of the Pentateuch, it is a story in its own right, and the tragic sequel in ch. 10 is motivated by the plot of the story, not by ritual. On the other, it would to some extent be a mirror of the consecration rituals carried out in the author's own time.

The complex of inaugural rites (chs. 8–9) falls into three parts: the rites of purification and consecration in 8:6-30 are separated by a period of seven days (8:33-35), during which Aaron and his sons must remain on the holy premises, from their inauguration on the eighth day (ch. 9). Only then does Yahweh show his approval (9:23-24).

This three-part pattern is one which anthropologists have observed in rites of passage, especially initiation rites, throughout the world (Van Gennep 1909, esp. 148-60; Leach 1976: 77-79). The initiates are separated from normal society in "rites of separation" and reintegrated into society in their new role in "rites of aggregation"; but in between there is very often a time in which they are "on the margin," neither one thing nor the other, segregated from the rest of society in a special place and under special rules. This is known as the "liminal" (threshold) period. When the initiation is to a professional role, the rite of aggregation often consists in their carrying out their new duties for the first time. All these points are clearly illustrated in this account. During the seven days the ordinands are not yet recognized as priests, and yet they are no longer part of lay society.

The rituals in ch. 8 are easily interpreted as rites of separation. Their more precise symbolism tends to fall into one of three categories: (a) purification, moving from the unclean to the clean category; (b) consecration, or separation from secular life altogether, moving from the clean to the holy; and (c) the bestowal of authority. But the distinction between these is uncertain; for example, anointing with oil (vv. 10-12, 30) generally marks the giving of authority — Israelite kings were anointed; but in both places here the text says that it is a sign of sanctification.

The ordinands offer three sacrifices: for the types see the comments on 4:1–5:13, ch. 1, and ch. 3 respectively. The "ram of ordination" (vv. 22-29) is a type of sacrifice of well-being; the unusual feature is the use of the blood to daub the extremities of the offerers as a symbol of purification and/or consecration. The extremities stand for the whole person (likewise for the cleansed leper in 14:25); this follows the same principle as the daubing of the altar horns in the sin offering (ch. 4), or of the lintels and doorposts in the Passover of Egypt (Exod 12:22-23). All these are rites of purification or of protection against danger.

The rites of ch. 9, which inaugurate Aaron's and his sons' service as priests, are a complete festival service. The sin offerings come first in each pair because the whole proceedings are a rite of passage in which Aaron and his sons pass to a higher, more sanctified walk of life and must run greater risks and pose greater threats to the sanctuary; as for the people, this is the first time they have been allowed to present any gifts at the altar, and their sin offering guards against the threats that they may pose.

The theme and climax of the day is the appearance of Yahweh's glory to the assembled people (9:4, 6, 23). In theory, all rites at the sanctuary are carried out "before Yahweh." His visible appearance (not as a form, but as cloud-wrapped brightness) can be told only in story, but it justifies and confirms everything that is done there. His appearance confirms Aaron's blessing. The appearance of the glory is often repeated in P's story of the wilderness wandering, frequently as the prelude to judgment — and we have to wait only three verses for this theme to appear here.

The Death of Nadab and Abihu (Ch. 10)

This chapter concludes the account of the inauguration in two ways. A narrative about the tragedy of the newly ordained priests (10:1-7, 16-20) frames two groups of instructions to them: the first (vv. 8-11) gives basic guidance on the work they must do, while the second instructs them about the disposal of the sacrifices. This leads back to the narrative.

The narrative deserves to be evaluated as literature. If we view it from Aaron's perspective, it is tragic in the strict sense (Houston 2000). He is at the pinnacle of his career and has just received the visible approval of Yahweh when at once his two elder sons (Exod 6:23) in their arrogance are struck down. The theme of sons disgracing a powerful father is common in the Hebrew Bible. Aaron cannot disown his sons, but neither can he defend them; hence his silence at Moses' rebuke. His responsibility for the family tragedy may be more personal than that. He had been deeply implicated in the sin of the golden calf (Exodus 32).

Aaron's agony is increased. Moses, who a moment before had shared his glory, now acts like an enemy, expressing no sympathy, forbidding any expression of grief, and finding fault with the surviving brothers for a technical ritual error. Aaron's dignified and eloquent response receives Moses' approval, thus resolving the tension.

Commentators have detected various coded messages in the story: a struggle between priestly factions (Gerstenberger 1996: 116-22) or a polemic against private incense offering outside the temple (Milgrom 1991: 628-33), with the danger of the invocation of other gods.

The chapter raises a number of further questions. In v. 3 Moses appears to quote a previous saying of Yahweh; but it is not found anywhere else.

Why Moses does not ask Eleazar and Ithamar to remove their brothers' bodies is explained in 10:6-7. They were not allowed because of their sacred ritual status either to defile themselves with dead bodies or to leave the sanctuary (cf. 21:10-12).

The prohibition of alcohol to priests on duty (10:9) is explained in practical terms: priesthood was a calling requiring discernment. They had to be able to make the basic ritual distinctions (v. 10), exemplified in the previous (chs. 1–7) and subsequent (chs. 11–15) groups of prescriptions, and to teach Yahweh's decrees to the people. The understanding of the priest as a teacher would originally have referred to ritual law, but it takes on a broader significance here.

The instructions in vv. 12-15 are explained in the comments on 6:8–7:38.

10:16-19. The offering referred to is the people's sin offering in 9:15. The rule broken by the new priests is in 6:26 (compare 6:30). Given the general belief that substances used for purification were filled with dangerous power, Moses perhaps fears that the burning of the offering may suggest that Eleazar and Ithamar are still ruled by this superstition (Milgrom 1991: 639).

Aaron's answer could mean that the death of his sons in the court of the tabernacle had recontaminated the sin offering, making it unfit to eat, but his mention of the other offerings seems rather to imply that the whole process of consecration had been thrown into doubt by the day's happenings (Gerstenberger 1996: 120).

At all events, the story leaves a ritual loose end: the sanctuary has been severely contaminated by the sin and still more by the dead bodies of Nadab and Abihu. How is it to be restored to purity? When the narrative thread is resumed in 16:1, this very question is taken up.

Impurities (Chs. 11–15)

Most readers will find it alien to regard bodily processes, dead animals, and dead human bodies (Numbers 19) as dangers, not in the hygienic sense but religiously, as hindrances to full participation in worship and in the extreme to the very presence of God with his people. But all peoples, including ourselves, regard certain things or processes as "dirty" and have rules about the "proper place" for certain objects or activities; whether they explain this in hygienic or religious terms, or refer to evil spirits, it is basically the same phenomenon. It is very likely that the ancient Israelites had a wide range of impurity beliefs and avoidance customs (see Deut 23:10-14 and Ezek 4:12-15), and that only some of these have been selected by the priestly writers to be given religious significance.

The system has an internal logic. Over against the holiness of the Tent of Meeting, a source of blessing for the people of Israel, a number of kinds of impurity stand as threats to the holiness of the sanctuary and thereby to the presence of God and the blessing which flows from it. Some have argued that defining these as "unclean" is simply arbitrary and that the internal logic of the ritual system corresponds to nothing in the real world. However, it is more common to explain ritual impurity as symbolically related to the realities of society in one way or another (see Douglas 1966). Ideas of impurity are related to the general structure of ideas in a particular society, and this reflects the structure of society itself. Impurity arises from things which are seen as unacceptable or ambiguous in relation to boundary or structural lines, and it is seen as powerful only where such lines are clearly defined.

Most "impurity" is created by things which pass into or out of the body; in Leviticus many impurities are focused on the passage of blood (see 12:5, 7; 15:19, 25). It may quite naturally be that the sense of uncanniness or of danger in the bleeding of a human body, of the threat of formlessness and destruction, creates the potential for impurity beliefs. The same may be true of the deformation of the appearance of a "leper" (ch. 13). But it is unlikely that this potential would be realized unless this threat to the integrity of the body could be seen as in some way symbolizing a threat to the integrity of society.

Concern about the integrity of Israel as a whole is certainly present in the repeated formula "you shall be holy," and in 20:24-26 this is quite specifically expressed as a concern for the separateness of Israel from all other nations. But this concern exists at the editorial level of the book and does not have a strong influence on the purity system as such, though it is applied as an interpretation to the distinction of clean and unclean animals.

Possibly of greater importance in relation to bodily impurity is concern for structures and lines of distinction within Israel: between men and women, or protecting liminal states (see on chs. 8–9). Very many peoples treat menstruating women as unclean (cf. 15:19-23), and this is generally related to a patriarchal social structure in which women are subordinate. In Leviticus this is balanced by the impurity attributed to male seminal emission and morbid flux (15:1-18). But Douglas (1966: 140-53) notes that where women are under strict physical control there is no menstrual uncleanness; it is the ambiguity of a position which treats women as commodities exchangeable between families but at the same time as persons with freedom to play men off against each other that is signaled by the impurity of their blood flow. Sex is "dangerous" where it creates conflict between different objectives in society.

Childbirth (ch. 12) is ambiguous in a slightly different way. It is a source of new life, of increase for the social group; but at the same time it is dangerous to the life of the woman herself, as suggested by the flow of blood. This has led to its being treated as a liminal state in many societies (Van Gennep 1909: 57-70): the new mother must be separated from general society for a certain period, and this is expressed in Leviticus by a purity prescription.

Another important function of impurity ideas is to back up morality where moral beliefs and social controls are too weak (Douglas 1966: 129-39). This is not operative in Leviticus 11–15, which deals mainly (except for 11:1-23, 41-45) with impurities which are involuntary or unavoidable; but in ch. 18 every type of sexual immorality is warned against on the grounds that it "defiles" both those involved and the holy land.

In comparing impurity in Leviticus with pollution beliefs in societies studied by anthropologists, it needs to be borne in mind that Leviticus does not tell us what popular customs were followed or beliefs held in respect to any of the conditions mentioned. Belief in impurity means a belief in danger: impurity is dangerous, either to people in general or to particular groups, and ethnographic literature is full of the unpleasant consequences which are held to ensue from touching a menstruant, having an adulterous wife, and the like. Milgrom (1991: 948-53) shows that such popular fears were also found among ancient Jews; but none of this appears in Leviticus. The concern of Leviticus has a thoroughgoing religious orientation; the danger feared is in 15:31: if impurities are not purified, the sanctuary, which is the sign of God's presence among the people, will be defiled and the result will be death for the Israelites. According to Milgrom (1983: 75-84), grave impurities (those cleansed by sacrifice) affect the sanctuary without direct contact. This follows from the fact that the "sin offering" is designed to purify the sanctuary. However, the function of the "sin offering" may have evolved (see on 4:1–5:13). Others believe the concern is that an unpurified person might actually enter it. However made, the contact is fatal — not to God's presence but to the people themselves. But because it inevitably happens, there has to be a way of dealing with it; hence ch. 16.

An important effect of these chapters in their context in Leviticus is to bring impurity and sin close together. Although impurity is not sin in itself, neglecting to purify it may be (15:31; cf. 5:2-3), and sin can be thought of as impurity (18:24-30). They are *structurally* identical. Both have the same effect of defiling the sanctuary and ultimately of threatening the existence of the people (see ch. 26). Both are dealt with by the same rites in ch. 16. The repeated call to holiness has both alike in mind. "Purity of heart" is a metaphor for moral blamelessness. But Leviticus is interested in purity of body as well as of heart: its symbols are more than metaphors; they are active, material, everyday reminders of the call to holiness (D. P. Wright 1991).

Clean and Unclean Animals (Ch. 11)

For this whole chapter see Houston 1993 or 2002. The arrangement of this chapter is as follows:

- Vv. 1-2a: Introduction
- Vv. 2b-23: Animals that may and may not be eaten.
- Vv. 24-40: Impurity caused by the bodies of dead animals. This section is not concerned with animals as food, except for v. 40 in passing.
- Vv. 41-45: Crawling animals forbidden as food, moving into the sermonic conclusion relating the prohibition to the holiness of the people.
- Vv. 46-47: Summary.

It is not clear why we leave the subject of food in v. 24 and then come back to it in v. 41. Probably vv. 41-42 were written by the (H) author of vv. 43-45, who realized that vv. 2b-23 had not covered one group of animals (see the comments on vv. 2b-23, 41-45; Houston 1993: 27, 54-55, 250).

The greater part of this chapter is different from the rest of chs. 11–15, including 11:24-40, in that, instead of telling what to do in cases of unavoidable uncleanness, it consists of prohibitions. Eating "unclean" or "detestable" food is forbidden because the people of Israel are to be holy. It may be that the prohibitions in the chapter were originally developed for the ritual situation, but vv. 43-45 apply them to the whole life of Israel: keeping these rules is an everyday way of showing their loyalty to Yahweh. This is typical of the H editors (cf., e.g., 19:2; 20:22-26, and see the Introduction, 102). Another version of the instructions in vv. 2b-20 is included in Deuteronomy (14:3-20), in a similar context.

Rules Restricting the Use of Animals for Food (11:2b-23, 41-42)

All peoples have food taboos, though not all articulate them expressly. For example, English people would be horrified if asked to eat dog meat, and for a good reason: dogs are pets, our "best friends"; or for another, rather contradictory reason: dogs are "dirty." In either case, eating dogs would violate boundaries of social significance.

The ancient Israelites and their neighbors ate a relatively restricted range of animals: mostly the cattle, sheep, and goats that they kept, with some game, mostly deer and gazelle, and birds such as partridge, which were trapped. Many people also ate locusts when they were available. Pigs were kept and eaten by many peoples of the area, especially in earlier times. They were probably fed garbage and were hardly ever brought for sacrifice, which suggests that quite apart from any rules people were consciously or unconsciously applying a symbolic grid to the animal world. They made the basic distinction between tame, vegetarian domestic creatures and wild creatures which ate blood and rejected human rule. Pigs and dogs, even if not wild, fell on the wrong side of the line because they were scavengers. Donkeys were not eatable for a different reason: because they were kept only to share human labor. On the other hand, among wild animals an exception could be made for deer and gazelles, which resembled cattle, sheep, and goats in appearance and habits. A number of East African cattle-raising peoples also restrict their eating of game to animals closely resembling cattle. (See Houston 1993: 124-217 for the whole paragraph.)

So this chapter develops common custom and makes a rule out of it. 11:2-23 fall into three sections corresponding to the three spheres of life: the land, the water, and the air. However, in many other places animals are divided into four groups, not three (see Gen. 6:20; 7:8; etc.), and this is true in this chapter taken as a whole. 11:2b-8 deal with the larger land animals (REB; NRSV in v. 2 is inaccurate), and vv. 41-45 with "creeping things."

No beast is to be eaten which belongs to a type not acceptable for sacrifice (Firmage 1990). The acceptable animals can be identified by three criteria (v. 3): they must have hooves (NRSV here translates incorrectly), their hooves must be divided in two, and they must chew the cud. These tests are not arbitrary: they isolate that family of animals, the ruminants, to which those actually used for sacrifice belonged; it includes cattle, sheep, goats, deer, and gazelles. They also exclude three common domestic animals: dogs (no hooves), donkeys (hooves not divided), and pigs (they do not chew the cud).

11:4-8 deal with borderline cases, which seem to have one or two of the criteria but not all three, and make it clear that to be acceptable beasts have to have all three. Camels do have cloven hooves, but there is a pad under their feet, so that the split does not extend all the way down. The rock badger or coney and the hare do not actually chew the cud, but they may give the impression of doing so. All these beasts are described as "unclean," which implies that their corpses convey ritual impurity as well as being forbidden for food. This applies to all the forbidden beasts (see vv. 24-28). V. 8 is difficult since if it applied to all the forbidden kinds it would be impractical. It may apply only to times when ritual purity was required, that is, when visiting the sanctuary.

Seafood was not important, and only fish (with fins and scales) in dried form are likely to have been widely sold at the markets. So the rule in vv. 9-12 may be based on custom.

The chapter does not have a criterion to offer for birds acceptable for food but only a list of unacceptable ones (11:13-19). The identification of many of them is not at all certain, and the translations are little better than guesses. But there is good evidence that nearly all of them are birds of prey or carrion eaters, consumers of blood. Since locusts were eaten, ways of identifying acceptable insects had to be found. As in vv. 3 and 9, a test is developed on the basis of custom (v. 21); however, to make sure, the edible kinds of locust are also listed — again, the translations are guesses.

All the great variety of "swarming" animals ("moving about on the ground," NIV), including those as large as a mouse (11:29), are prohibited (vv. 41-42); probably, to begin with, they were not even thought of as possible food.

Impurity from Animal Carcasses (11:24-40)

There would be many situations in life in which it was necessary to handle the dead bodies of unclean animals: to bury a donkey, for example. In 11:24-38 this is seen as passing on a minor degree of impurity. This serves to emphasize the prohibition of their flesh. The rule applies only to land animals, and not to all of them. Vv. 24-28 cover all the larger land animals not permitted as food in v. 3. Vv. 29-38 select eight kinds of "swarming" animal; again the meaning of many of the names is uncertain, but the context suggests that they are all small animals which might be found in houses or cooking areas. Their dead bodies pass on impurity not only to people but also to objects.

11:39-40 deal with animals permitted for food which die a natural death. V. 40 agrees with 17:15, but v. 39 clashes with 7:24.

Childbirth (Ch. 12)

See the comments above on chs. 11–15. Probably the ancient custom was to isolate a woman who had just given birth in fear of the dangers associated with that time of transition. But the effect of these prescriptions is less comprehensive. The impurity of the woman is connected with the vaginal discharge which continues for some weeks, at first bloody like the menstrual discharge, later losing its color. Probably for this reason the impurity is seen as a two-stage process. In the initial period of seven to fourteen days, her impurity is of the same degree as if she were menstruating. This refers forward to 15:19-24; see that passage (and comments) for details. Afterward, until the end of forty or eighty days since the birth, she suffers a lesser degree of impurity which does not affect her ordinary activities (though many Jews in ancient times forbade marital intercourse during this time; Milgrom 1991: 748).

Why the period of impurity is longer after the birth of a girl than of a boy is uncertain. A common view is that it is longer because of the lower status of women in ancient Jewish society. But this is unlikely: note that a dead pig (Lev 11:24-26) is *less* polluting than a human corpse (Num 19:11-16), not more. A possible explanation (Magonet 1996) is that vaginal discharge is a not uncommon phenomenon in newborn girls. Magonet suggests that the mother is made to bear the potential impurity of the baby. But the more central role of men is indeed reflected by the circumcision of a baby boy (v. 3) as the formal rite of admission to the covenant community (see the comments on Genesis 17); there is nothing comparable for girls. This is not connected with the impurity of the mother, but is referred to as an essential part of the ritual activities surrounding childbirth.

The significance of childbirth is marked by a formal rite of passage (12:6-8). There are two sacrifices, as is customary in cases of impurity. One is the so-called "sin offering," which has nothing to do with sin but serves the technical purpose of purification (see commentary on 4:1–5:13). The other is a burnt offering, which simply honors God (see also the comments on 5:7-10). After this rite the mother is "clean" in the sense that she can fully rejoin society.

Unclean Skin Disease and Similar Conditions (Chs. 13–14)

The so-called "leprous disease" which is the main subject of these chapters is not what is now called leprosy (Hansen's disease). The descriptions recall such conditions as psoriasis, but they could cover a number of medically recognized conditions.

Beliefs about the supernatural origin of disfiguring disease were and are widespread. In ancient Israel "leprosy" was believed to be the result of offenses against God. (See 2 Chr 26:6-20; Numbers 12.) It seems to have been normal to isolate sufferers (2 Kgs 15:5), and in these chapters this custom is systematized. There is no explicit suggestion that sufferers are sinners, but the fact that they have to bring a guilt offering on readmission to the community (14:12; see on 5:14–6:7) implies that they may have committed sacrilege. Skin afflictions can be the result of psychological conditions, and a feeling of guilt might combine with the knowledge that such a condition was regarded as divine punishment to give rise to one (Lloyd Davies 1988).

Unlike the cases of the menstruant and the new mother, where the authors are not interested in the traditional custom of isolation and may be trying to repress it, isolation is prescribed for the sufferer of skin disease at two different points: a period of quarantine for unconfirmed cases (13:4, 5, 21, etc.), and living "outside the camp," that is, away from the community, for a confirmed sufferer (13:45-46). Affected persons must make sure that everyone who does come near is aware of their condition, and must also behave like mourners (13:45). The purpose is not hygienic but ritual. The skin disease is seen as a particularly potent form of "uncleanness," as potent as a corpse (Numbers 19). The risk is that another person might be unknowingly contaminated and then touch sacred food (Milgrom 1991: 805). Hence the need for exclusion. Symbolically, the condition is seen to be a kind of death in life.

The series of rites prescribed in ch. 14 for the "cleansed" sufferer is a complete example of a rite of passage. It is very much like the ordination ritual in chs. 8–9 (see the comments). The person proceeds from one state of life to another through a liminal stage of seven days marked at either end by a ritual. Here the initial rite of separation includes a traditional rite (vv. 4-7) which is rather like the scapegoat ritual in ch. 16. One bird is killed and its blood is used symbolically to purify the sufferer, while the other is set free, probably seen to be carrying the uncleanness away with it.

After this the sufferer is no longer excluded but not yet fully "reaggregated" to the community (14:8b). The sanctuary ritual in vv. 10-32 fully readmits the sufferer. It includes a ceremony of purification (vv. 25-29) very similar to the rite of ordination in 8:23-24. This marks the movement of the person from a state of impurity to one of purity and perhaps protects the person in this dangerous time.

Alongside the main subject, the text picks out some kinds of mold on fabrics (13:47-59) and rot in buildings (14:34-53) as analogous conditions, and applies some of the same regulations to them. There are Mesopotamian parallels for this.

Genital Discharges (Ch. 15)

For general considerations on ritual uncleanness, see the comments above on chs. 11–15. The final section of these laws is set forth as follows. Note the symmetrical arrangement of the rules.

Verses	
1-15	morbid male discharges, presumably gonorrhea
16-17	normal male emissions
18	sexual intercourse
19-24	normal menstruation
25-30	abnormal female discharges of blood
31	general comment
32-33	summary of 15:1-30

The chapter brings to light an aspect of ritual thinking that has not been apparent in the previous four chapters: that "uncleanness" could be transmitted at a second remove, from a person to an object and then to anyone touching the object.

The first subsection includes more detail than the others, and it is not easy to decide which of the details are meant to apply in the other cases and which are unique to the man with the discharge. Certainly only persons healed of *abnormal* discharges need to bring sacrifices (see the comments on ch. 12 for 15:14-15, 29-30), while bathing is required after all uncleannesses (15:13, 16, 18, but also, though unmentioned, for the women in 19-24, 28-30). It is also clear that the emission of semen is less severely polluting than either menstrual blood or morbid discharges. But do those who touch a menstruant have to bathe and wash their clothes (contrasting vv. 7 and 19); does her spittle convey impurity (cf. v. 8); should she wash her hands before touching anyone (cf. v. 11)?

Now the popular custom among the ancient Jews, as with many other peoples, was to isolate menstruants in the belief that their condition was dangerous to others. Among some groups they would not even be able to live at home (Milgrom 1991: 948-53). (We should remember that fertile women had periods much less often than now; they were married at puberty and spent the rest of their lives either pregnant or nursing — few survived to the time of menopause.)

But in this chapter we do not find such a horror at menstruation. It does not imply that the menstruant can harm others by simply being in the same room or passing by. And the rules make it clear that the uncleanness is concentrated in the menstrual blood or other discharge itself. The only objects which can pass on impurity to people are those which have been underneath the person and so may actually have absorbed the fluid. A man touches his genitals when urinating, hence his hands may become unclean. The same does not apply to a woman; therefore, washing her hands is not mentioned (Milgrom 1991: 911). The conclusion must be that a menstruating woman could safely touch anyone or anything, and could live at home.

The Israelite priests have often been accused of contempt for women and subjecting them to degrading rules. The truth may rather be, once one looks carefully at the surrounding culture, that they tried to lighten the burdens which custom imposed on them. However, it seems that people were generally unwilling to accept their more relaxed approach: so the woman with a discharge in Mark 5:25-34 tries to touch Jesus without his noticing.

15:18: it is a very widespread idea that if one has not cleansed oneself after sex one is not fit for sacred things. Sex and the sacred are seen as belonging to opposed worlds.

For 15:31 see above on chs. 11–15; it applies to the whole section.

The Great Rite of Expiation (Ch. 16)

This chapter is pivotal to the book. It picks up the narrative thread from the end of ch. 10 and looks back to the teachings on sacrifice and on uncleannesses; it also looks forward to the teaching about how Israel is to be a holy people by referring for the first time to their deliberate sins (16:16, 21; the word translated "transgressions" in the NRSV occurs only here in Leviticus). The rite frees only the people collectively from their responsibility; individuals continue to suffer punishment for their own deliberate sins (Num 15:30-31).

From the narrative point of view expiation is now necessary in view of Nadab and Abihu's arrogant sin and the defilement of the tabernacle by their corpses. From the ritual point of view expiation will always be necessary, either in emergencies like the present or regularly every year as v. 33 ordains. Only thus can Yahweh's continuing presence with his people be assured. The chapter ordains the ritual which is to be used each year on the Day of Atonement (v. 29; see also the comments on 23:26-32).

The Day of Atonement involves three main types of ritual.

a. The sin offering, or ritual to purify the sanctuary, for which see the comments above on 4:1–5:13. Here the blood is brought right into the inner sanctum, in this chapter called simply "the holy place" or "inside the curtain," and the rite is explicitly given its original purpose (16:16, 19): to purify the entire sanctuary of accumulated impurity. Aaron offers sin offerings not only on behalf of the people but also on behalf of the priests themselves ("himself and his house," vv. 6, 11), who naturally bear the greatest responsibility

b. A special ritual in which the sins of the people are symbolically laden on the head of a goat, which is then driven away into the wilderness (16:20-22). This is the famous "scapegoat" (from the KJV's translation of "Azazel" [vv. 8 etc.]). The only thing similar in Leviticus is the initial cleansing rite for the so-called "leper" (14:2-7). In each rite there are two similar animals: one is slaughtered and its blood used for purification, while the other is let go to carry the evil far away. The sacrificed goat, along with the bull, cleanses the sanctuary, while the live goat removes the danger from the people in the camp.

c. Thirdly, the public fast or ritual of penitence and humiliation (16:29-31), such as was often called on occasions of public emergency (see Joel 1:13-14; Jonah 3:5-9). Aaron's confession of the people's sin over the scapegoat would be pointless unless the people themselves expressed their sense of penitence before God. The kind of activities involved are vividly rendered in Isa 58:3-5. This part of the rite continues to be solemnly observed by Jews after the temple and its ceremonies have vanished.

The divine speech (16:2b-34a) is structured like this. Vv. 2b-28 give instructions to be passed to Aaron. Vv. 2b-5 explain how he is to prepare. V. 6 begins the instructions for the ritual; but in vv. 7-9 the text digresses to ensure that the two goats are distinguished and prepared for their fates before Aaron begins the sacrificial ceremony. In this way we get an overview of the ceremony. V. 11 then takes us back to where we left off, repeating v. 6, and the prescriptions move straight forward to v. 25; vv. 26 and 27-28 clear up details of disposal, not necessarily in chronological order. Vv. 29-34a switch abruptly into address to the people (characteristic of H), telling them of their own part in the rites. These verses for the first time mention that the rite is to be carried out once a year, and give the date.

The rite is impressive in the weight and range of its symbolism. The priestly system draws sharp boundaries: between clean and unclean, holy and profane, tabernacle, camp, and wilderness, God, priests, and people. But real life is not like that. In reality the boundaries are fuzzy; and sin and impurity continually make them more fuzzy. The rites of atonement restore the confused categories (Davies 1977: 395).

Davies shows how a whole series of symbols reinforces this message. To begin with, everything earthly, including the high priest and the holy of holies, is seen as impure and therefore at the farthest pole from God. The people fast and humble themselves. Aaron wears simple white vestments (16:4) in place of his gorgeous regal robes (Exodus 28; Lev 8:7-9), and puts these on again only after the main ritual is complete (16:24). The blood of the sin offerings represents life (Lev 17:11; Davies 1977: 395), and it is brought into the holiest place to restore God's lively presence. The scapegoat goes out in the opposite direction, out from the holy place into the place of uncleanness, to take Israel's sins away with it. All the symbols work together to suggest that the proper categories and relationships are being restored. The sanctuary and its priests become pure and holy once more, and the people are cleansed of their sins (v. 30).

A few details require explanation.

The words "atone" and "atonement" render Heb. *kipper*. See the comments on 4:1–6:7. This translation is often awkward here, and in places it would be better to translate it "purify" or "remove sin."

The "mercy seat" in 16:2, 13-15 is the golden cover over the ark (Exod 25:17-22). The name in Hebrew, *kapporet*, gives the impression of being connected with *kipper*, "to make atonement"; hence the NRSV translation (from the KJV): the place where atonement is made.

Who or what is "Azazel" in vv. 8, 10, and 26? It is likely to be the name of a demon. It is a surprising thing to find in the strictly monotheistic priestly text, and shows that the scapegoat rite goes back to an earlier stage in Israel's religion. However, if at one time the idea was that the goat was presented to Azazel as a way of diverting his unwelcome attentions from the people, that is not so in this text, where the name simply survives as a way of denoting the destination of the goat.

Which altar is referred to in 16:18: the altar in the court or the incense altar in the tabernacle? Probably the former, but there are some who think that it is the latter, because of Exod 30:10. However, probably the words "so he shall do for the tent of meeting" in 16:16 refer to the purification of the altar of incense (cf. 4:6-7).

In the NT the rites of the Day of Atonement are taken as the (imperfect) model of Christ's sacrifice, particularly by the Letter to the Hebrews (Heb 9:6-14, 23-28; 10:1-20; 13:11-12). Today we are accustomed to the idea of a "scapegoat" as a human victim who is identified as an easy target on which to discharge the accumulated hatreds of a community, or responsibility for a crime, thus reinforcing the bounds and categories of society by the unbridled expression of violence. The rites of the Day of Atonement achieved this, with violence, certainly, but in a strictly controlled and symbolic way. If there must be a victim, which is preferable: two goats or six million men, women, and children?

Shedding the Blood of Animals (Ch. 17)

This chapter is principally concerned with the slaughter of animals for food, and above all with the way in which the blood should be dealt with. It contains five distinct laws: 17:3-7, 8, 10-12, 13-14, and 15-16; the NRSV is misleading in making a break between vv. 13 and 14. All are drafted in such a way as to bring the issue of "blood" to the fore (Schwartz 1991).

For the Israelites, as for many other peoples, the shedding of an animal's blood was a focus of symbolism and ritual. Blood was considered to be impregnated with power, the power of "life" (v. 11), which had to be handled with great care. Consumption of blood, even as part of the meat, was and is scrupulously avoided, and the main object of this chapter is to reinforce this ancient taboo, possibly when it was threatened at a time of traumatic social change.

People normally slaughtered their own animals; slaughtering and butchery were not specialized trades. The method of slaughter is still used by the Jewish slaughterer *(shoḥet)*: a sharp knife is drawn across the throat, and the blood spurts from the carotid arteries as the heart is still beating. Except among the wealthy, the eating of meat was a relatively rare event nearly always associated with a celebration, and in early times it is likely that the slaughter of domestic animals was always a religious ceremony, a sacrifice.

The first law, in 17:3-7, confirms this but demands that the Israelites use only one official altar. It is unclear how it is related to the law which permits secular slaughter in Deut 12:15-16, 20-25 and which regulates Jewish practice today. The best explanation may be this (for a different view see, e.g., Knohl 1995: 218-20; Milgrom 2001: 1503-14). In Deuteronomy 12 the normal ancient practice is specifically challenged and secular slaughter encouraged as part of the attempt to eliminate all altars but one. Probably this attempted transformation of popular culture was not successful. Slaughter would have continued to be surrounded with a religious aura. If it could not be carried out at an official shrine of Yahweh, it might be directed toward some other god (v. 7). This law tries to deal with this danger by requiring all domestic animals for slaughter to be brought to the temple (for which the "tent of meeting" stands in the wilderness setting of the text) for sacrifice to Yahweh. But this remained a dead letter. Vv. 8-9 then reinforce the law of Deut 12:8-14.

17:4 it says that anyone who slaughters an animal away from the sanctuary is "guilty of bloodshed." Normally this phrase refers to the killing of a human being. This language may be used to underline that blood has been let loose in an uncontrolled and dangerous manner, as in manslaughter. There appears to be an implied criticism of Deut 12:16.

For 17:5-6 see the comments on chs. 1–7.

17:11 offers a theological justification for the ancient rule; for detailed comment see above on 4:1–6:7.

17:15 belongs here because an animal that has died of itself or been killed by wild beasts will not have had the blood drained. However, compared with Exod 22:31 or Deut 14:22 this law is not rigorous (cf. 11:40). H imposes a higher standard on priests (22:8) but is concerned for the poor (Milgrom 2001: 1487).

Most of the laws here are binding on the alien as well as the Israelite. This is a characteristic of H and its concern with the holiness of the land they share (18:25).

All the laws have the same sanction attached: that offenders will be "cut off from [their] people." It is uncertain what this means. The death penalty has its own vocabulary (e.g., 20:2); therefore, this phrase seems to refer to divine punishment. It is possible that it refers not to the sudden death of offenders but to their failure to establish a line of descendants or to be gathered to their ancestors in the underworld after death.

Leviticus 18–20 form a small block of teaching on being the Lord's people in the secular realm. Ch. 20 refers back to ch. 18 repeatedly, and this highlights ch. 19 as the central part of the teaching.

Sexual Prohibitions (Ch. 18)

This speech consists of a general sermonic exhortation addressed to the nation as a whole (18:2b-5, 24-30), framing two series of prohibitions addressed to the individual, always the man.

The sermonic framework (18:2b-5, 24-30) is developed around certain key themes and phrases. The moral standards demanded are Yahweh's commands (vv. 4, 5, 26, 30), and correspondingly the reminder "I am the Lord (your God)" frames the entire discourse and is frequently repeated (within the series of prohibitions also at vv. 6, 21). We shall come across this formula repeatedly in the next eight chapters; it is one of the hallmarks of H. It is clearly a seal of authority, reminding the hearers from whom the commandments come; but in origin it is Yahweh's self-introduction (see Exod 6:2); the commandments expand their knowledge of who Yahweh is (Zimmerli 1982:12). But more than that it reminds them, in its longer form, of the basis of Yahweh's authority in that they belong to him and he to them (cf. 25:55; 26:12-13, 42-45); and expansions of the formula (e.g., 19:36; 22:32-33; 26:13) root this in his rescue of them from Egypt.

Second, the standards are seen as setting Israel off against the nations, particularly the Egyptians and the Canaanites. Later passages (e.g., 20:22-26) see the exodus as an act of God dividing Israel from the nations (see Crüsemann 1996: 301-3). Here a sense of national distinctiveness is encouraged by projecting immorality on others. We should not take it at face value and assume that 18:24 is simple historical truth. All the peoples of the area had very similar moral standards, especially when it came to incest.

Third, the sins in question are described as "defiling" both the people and the land. That is, they are comparable to the kind of ritual uncleanness dealt with in chs. 11–15; see the comments there and the Introduction. In vv. 17, 20, 22, and 23, the idea that certain sexual conduct is wrong is based not on its objectively damaging character but on the notion that it is "unclean" or "abominable." This idea is found in many cultures, perhaps arising from the symbolic function of these prohibitions in reinforcing social structure. For a man to take the role of a woman in the sexual act, or for the fundamental boundary between humans and animals to be blurred, symbolically threatens the foundations of society. This is a ritual function: we cannot draw a hard-and-fast line between morals and ritual in Leviticus. (See 103.)

There appears to be a shift in time between 18:3 and 24, where Yahweh is about to cast out the inhabitants of the land, and vv. 25 and 27-28, where they have already gone, contrary to the setting of these speeches. This is a natural rhetorical shift.

Although the difference between the two series is quite clear, the point where one ends and the other begins is not. 18:7-16 prohibit intercourse with close relatives, and the prohibitions are all set in the same style (v. 6 is an introduction, addressed in the plural). Vv. 19-23 prohibit various types of conduct considered outrageous and are more varied in style. Vv. 17 and 18 are similar to vv. 7-16 but are concerned with marriage rather than with sex in general; and v. 17 concludes with the kind of moral assessment found in vv. 20-23, whereas the rationales found in vv. 7-16 appeal to family sentiment. Probably vv. 7-16 (plus 17?) are an old group of instructions for family members taken over by the editor.

The prohibitions are closely related to a particular order of society, and, as far as v. 22 is concerned, the Bible as a whole does not take into account variations in sexual orientation. These facts should be borne in mind whenever it is suggested that texts from this chapter should determine sexual ethics in the present day.

All human societies have incest taboos since society is based on clear lines of structure in the family, but they vary somewhat. 18:7-16 (17) give a restricted list compared with that of many societies; Israelite society was broadly endogamous, preferring marriage within the clan (see, e.g., Gen. 24:3-4, 15). The prohibitions are not based on any one principle. Three types of relationship are prohibited (Bigger 1979): ones with wives of members of the group of related males (vv. 7, 8, 14-16); these women's sexuality is explicitly identified with their husbands'; ones with female members of the male descent group (vv. 9-12); and in v. 13 one relative in the female line. Bigger believes that prohibitions of the first type would lapse on the husband's death (so that v. 16 would not clash with Deut 25:5-6). But this is doubtful in view of 20:21.

The main problems presented by the list are the absence of the daughter — incest with a daughter is the commonest type in our society — and the overlap of vv. 9 and 11. In ancient Israel a man's daughter was directly under his own control. It may therefore have been thought improper to interfere with his rights. However, virginity was a normal requirement for marriage, and if a man abused his daughter he would lose the bride-price he could otherwise expect for her.

It seems possible (Elliger 1966: 231-32) that 18:9 was originally intended to cover one's full sister and v. 11 one's half-sister, but both verses have been expanded in a way which makes them overlap.

In the second series 18:19 deals with what was always considered a major sin (Ezek 18:6 links it with adultery alone) because of the "impurity" (15:19-24) of the woman's periods. V. 20 deals with adultery; the NRSV's use of "kinsman" is misleading — the word means "fellow citizen." V. 21 may be found here because it is also concerned with family relationships; for comments see 20:2-5. Why lesbianism is not mentioned is uncertain; perhaps the men who compiled the chapter simply had no knowledge of it.

Holiness in All Things (Ch. 19)

The central speech in chs. 18–20 differs from the other two, and all other speeches in the book, in that it brings together a variety of instruction on different topics. It does, however, have a detectable structure. 19:2b at the beginning: "You shall be holy, for I the LORD your God am holy," and v. 37 at the end are a theological framework. Everything in between is both a command of Yahweh (v. 37) and a way of being "holy" (v. 2), and most of the groups of commands are linked with this theological framework by the refrain "I am the LORD" (see the comments on ch. 18). The commands fall into three large groups (Magonet 1983): vv. 3-18, 19-29, and 30-36; at the beginning of each is the command to "keep" God's sabbaths or statutes, and the third group echoes and develops the first in several ways. There is a clear climax at v. 18, and this is echoed in v. 34, near the end of the third group. Where there are small groups of commands, they are generally related to each other (e.g., vv. 11-12).

Holiness

The first appearance of the theme of "holiness" in the so-called Holiness code is in v. 2; it is developed through chs. 19–22, and the sermonic material in chs. 18, 25, and 26 is related; see also 11:44-45. What does it mean to call God holy, and what does it mean for the people to be holy? God's holiness is that numinous, awesome, at times terrifying power which we see in Isaiah 6, proclaimed by the seraphim, or in this book in the story of Nadab and Abihu (10:1-3); no sinner can approach it and live.

But in that case how can the people also be asked to be holy? It sounds as if they are being asked to imitate God, but this is not really so. In ritual, people may be holy in that they are dedicated to God and as a result must observe certain taboos: examples are the priests in 21:1-15 and the nazirite in Num 6:1-21. And when laypeople prepared to meet God in his sanctuary they had to be ritually pure (e.g., Exod 19:14-15), and this is called "sanctification," making oneself holy, literally, in the same sense as the priests. But they should also be *morally* pure (Psalm 15; 24:3-6).

Now H uses this ritual idea to apply to the whole of life. Because the Israelites belong to Yahweh, not just when they are in the temple but all the time, they must all the time be "holy" in the sense that they are faithful to him, obey his commands, make the proper distinctions (which we might see as ritual or moral), and live rightly with one another. And Yahweh has "sanctified" (22:32), "separated" (20:24) them (by the exodus) precisely for this purpose. Although in P only some Israelites are holy, H is not in disagreement: it is using the word in a new, expanded sense.

The speech does not aim to be comprehensive but to give examples. It shows connections with the Decalogue (Exod 20:2-17; Deut 5:6-21) and with the Deuteronomic code (Deuteronomy 12–26). But the parallels are haphazard in order and varied in wording. The codes are the work of reformers active around the same period, but they did not necessarily copy each other's work.

19:3-18 are a basic religious and moral code for life in a small but unequal community. Most of the contacts with the Decalogue are in this section.

19:3-4. The opening commands lay down the authority structure of the community; the individual is subject to parental authority, and the community as a whole is subject to Yahweh and no other god; his "sabbaths" (again in v. 30) are a symbol of this. This opening echoes four of the first five of the Ten Commandments (see Exod 20:2-12).

19:5-8 repeat the command of 7:15-18, without the distinction of thanksgiving offerings made there; but see 22:29-30. The code selects one sacrificial regulation which the laity was responsible for keeping. The reason for it has nothing to do with hygiene. The holiness of the offering is profaned, perhaps because time exposed the eaters to the greater danger of uncleanness — for example, a woman might start her period — or of carelessness.

19:9-18 turn to relationships in the community. Vv. 9-10 (see also Deut 24:19-22) seems to offer very meager assistance. However, the practice may be an ancient one, originally for the benefit of the spirits of the field. The monotheistic teachers turn this superstition to the benefit of the community. It is only a minimal demand, and personal generosity may (may!) make it more adequate.

19:11-18 is a series of basic requirements for harmonious community living arranged in four almost equal groups of brief commands. Vv. 11-12 deal with deceitful practices among equals, while vv. 13-14 forbid taking advantage of those weaker than oneself. "Defraud" and "steal" in v. 13 are translated incorrectly in the NRSV; "exploit" and "rob" would be more accurate; both verbs refer to exploitation of the poor. The context of vv. 15-16 is the lawcourt. The phrase translated "profit by the blood" in v. 16 is very uncertain: "place someone's life in jeopardy," "conspire against," and "stand aside when someone's life is in danger" have all been suggested. Both judges and (potential) witnesses have a duty to see that justice is done.

19:17-18, finally, root relationships in basic attitudes and day-to-day conduct. The behavior condemned is the feuds so characteristic of life in small communities. "Anyone of your kin" in v. 17 is misleading: literally it is "brother," but it refers to any member of the community. V. 17b is uncertain. It is not clear whether "reprove" means to act privately (cf. Matt 18:15-17) or to begin a legal action (to prevent grudges from festering), and "or you will incur guilt yourself" might rather be "do not expose *your neighbor* to the guilt" of pursuing the feud. "Love" (v. 18) means to act practically for the neighbor's benefit just as you would act for your own (another interpretation is found in the REB).

The second section, 19:19-29, contains commands placing limits on the use of God's gifts as an expression of holiness. Most of them have close parallels in Deuteronomy, which is also concerned with the holiness of Israel (Deut 14:1).

19:19 (cf. Deut 22:9-11) perhaps shows that these mixtures of species were seen as transgressing boundaries in the same way as bestiality (18:23) and consequently symbolically threatening society. However, it may be that the wool-linen mixture (see Deut 22:11) was reserved for sacred use (see Exod 26:1, etc.; Haran 1978: 160).

19:20-22 are a legal conundrum with a ritual solution. Adultery in this tradition is subject to the death penalty (20:10), and this applies as soon as the woman is betrothed (Deut 22:23-24). But violating a slave is only a trespass against property (cf. Exod 21:20-21). A sin has been committed, but it is not legally punishable. The solution is the guilt offering, which in 6:1-7 may be used in cases of deliberate fraud to supplement an inadequate legal system.

19:23-25 give religious reasons for a sound practice. No fruit may be enjoyed from a tree before God has been given his due. Why is the fruit of the immature tree described as "uncircumcised" (see NRSV footnotes)? Probably because circumcision was originally practiced on boys at puberty to prepare them for marriage, and not in infancy (12:3). There is a symbolic connection between circumcision and fertility and between fruit and the genitals (Eilberg-Schwartz 1990: 146-54).

19:26-28 prohibit ritual practices seen as damaging to Israel's holiness. For v. 26a see on ch. 17 (cf. Deut 12:23-25); for v. 26b (cf. Deut 18:10) see on v. 31. The practices in vv. 27-28 (cf. Deut 14:1) are all mourning rites taken for granted in earlier writings (e.g., Isa 22:12; Jer 16:6). But for H self-mutilation identifies the living with the dead too closely (that is its object), and therefore again (cf. v. 19) blurs boundaries important to society (Schmidt 1994: 178).

19:29 (cf. Deut 23:17) arises, once more, from a standard of decency governed by a concern for proper boundaries. A man might be strongly tempted by poverty to prostitute his daughter; but prostitutes were slaves and foreigners, not free Israelites.

19:30 introduces the final section of the speech, which picks up issues from the first section and supplements them.

19:31 picks up v. 4. It condemns the practice of obtaining oracles from the dead through mediums (cf. Deut 18:11 and see 1 Samuel 28). The NRSV translation is probably incorrect: the Hebrew words refer to the ghosts themselves, not the mediums. All means of attempting to foretell the future are condemned which do not acknowledge Yahweh's authority (cf. v. 26).

19:32 extends the shaping of family authority seen in v. 3 into the community.

19:33-34. People who did not belong to the community and had no landed stake in it were especially vulnerable to exploitation (cf. vv. 9-10, 12-13). Equality in responsibility (17:12; 20:2; 24:22) must imply equality in protection. The command in Exod 22:21; 23:9 is repeated, with the language of v. 18, so that it becomes clear that the command to love one's neighbor is not limited to Israelites. The message of the Good Samaritan (Luke 10:29-37) is not original!

19:35-36 begin with the same command as v. 15 (this is obscured in the NRSV) but goes on to develop v. 12 in its application to the commercial world. There were no publicly ordained standards of measurement in antiquity, which left the door open to sharp practice. The "ephah" was a dry, and the "hin" a liquid, measure of capacity.

Punishment (Ch. 20)

This speech prescribes punishments (mostly capital) for a range of serious offences. All the offenses are ones which have been denounced in the previous two chapters, mostly in ch. 18 but also in 19:3 (implicitly, 20:9) and 19:31 (20:6, 27). The core is 20:9-16, probably an old code prescribing the death penalty for a series of family offenses; the editors have framed this with penalties for offenses they were especially concerned about, and with exhortation. Those in vv. 17-21 are all sexual offenses denounced in ch. 18, and it looks as though the object was to include all significant crimes from that chapter which had not already been dealt with.

Could this chapter be described as a criminal code? Many of the laws (20:6, 17-21) do not prescribe the death penalty but simply say that God will punish (for "cut off" in vv. 3, 5, 6, 17, and 18 see on ch. 17). Why this particular choice of offenses? Can one imagine the chapter being of use to a court of law?

Although we know of many early "codes" of law from the ancient Near East, it seems that they did not directly govern the decisions of courts. A criminal code would include those crimes that by custom were normally punished, without necessarily being binding on courts. Vv. 9-16 is such a code; it includes those offenses felt to be the greatest threat to family and social structure. But the editors' concern is not so much with legal consequences as to warn their audience of those offenses against God's dignity and against decency which most gravely threatened their status as God's holy people. There was no precedent for a humanly executed death penalty for the offenses in vv. 6 and 17-21, so none is given, but the text is confident that God would punish them. In any case, though adultery (v. 10) was by far the commonest of these offenses, we know of no occasion when the death penalty was ever actually enforced (McKeating 1979), though some precedent must have existed (see also Deut 22:22). So even in vv. 9-16 the law may be theoretical rather than practical.

The reason why the death penalty is appropriate is expressed in v. 14, combined with v. 7: that kind of offense has to be rooted out so that the people may be holy to Yahweh. Vv. 2 and 27 speak of stoning. The probable reason for this mode of execution is that the whole community was involved. In case of any dispute over the verdict or penalty, no one person can have the finger pointed at them as the executioner. To make doubly sure, in most cases the phrase "their blood is upon them" is added. This relieves those who carry out the penalty of the guilt of bloodshed.

The subject matter of the offenses has been dealt with in the comments on ch. 18 or 19, except for the first, in 20:2-5. This probably deals with a ritual in which a child of the worshiper was sacrificed (18:21) to a god, here called "Molech," and burned (2 Kgs 23:10); other texts (e.g., Deut 18:10; 2 Kgs 16:3) refer to "passing one's child through fire" without mentioning Molech. "Molech" is probably derived from the divine title *melek,* "king," with the vowels (added by the scribes) of *boshet,* "shame." The god in question may have been a god of the underworld (Heider 1985). But there are many uncertainties. The original "king" may have been Yahweh himself (Jer 7:31; Ezek 20:25-26 might suggest this). This would explain why it "defiles my sanctuary" (v. 3). But if so, the author was passing on a tradition which he did not understand.

In 20:24-26 a new theme appears in the exhortation. Being holy to Yahweh involves being "separated" from other peoples, in order to be granted the land. The dietary laws (ch. 11) are brought in here as a symbol of this "separation." The same verb is used in Ezra 9:1 when Ezra demands that the Jews should put away foreign wives. This understanding of the symbolism of the dietary laws remained influential, and the refusal to share Gentiles' tables expressed it in practice. Acts 10 uses it in order to reverse the demand for separation.

Rules of Holiness for the Priests (21:1–22:16)

It is clearly the ritual functions of the priesthood (see above on chs. 8–9) that determine the presentation here (see 21:6, 8, 12, 17, and 21): it gives ritual taboos and disqualifications and is silent on moral or spiritual qualifications. Because the priests are active in holy places and handle holy things, they must observe rules of ritual holiness which are more stringent than those applying to laypeople. The first group, 21:1-15, gives prohibitions relating to two areas of life: death and sex; and here the high priest (vv. 10-15) is subject to more stringent rules even than ordinary priests. The second, 21:16-23, disqualifies priests with physical deformities from performing priestly functions. The third, 22:1-16, is devoted mainly to prescribing the conditions under which priestly food may be eaten.

21:1-15. See Numbers 19 and comments. Laypeople are expected to bury the dead and comfort mourners, and then be purified from the uncleanness involved. But the priests' degree of holiness demands that this defilement should be avoided in any case. The high priest (vv. 10-11) is absolutely forbidden to go anywhere near a dead body, or even to show any of the customary outward signs of mourning. A concession is made to the ordinary priest: he may bury his close relatives (vv. 2-3). It seems as if this does not include his wife (his sons would see to that), though the translation of v. 4 is uncertain. In Ezek 24:15-24 the specific signs of mourning Ezekiel is forbidden to show (as a prophetic sign) are not forbidden to ordinary priests. V. 5 forbids only what is forbidden to all Israelites in 19:27-28.

It is typical of the patriarchal culture promoted by Leviticus that the threat of uncontrolled sex to priestly holiness is focused on women, as marriage partners (vv. 7, 13-15) or as daughters (v. 9; cf. 19:29), rather than on the conduct of the priests themselves. The requirement that the high priest may marry only a virgin, and one who herself belongs to the priestly clan (v. 14), may be intended to protect the purity of the descent line; but all priests are required to avoid marrying a woman who might be suspected of unchastity.

21:16-23. Just as sacrificial animals must be unblemished (22:17-25), so must the priest who offers them. This is not a matter of ritual purity, for a disabled or deformed priest may eat offerings for which ritual purity is required (21:22; cf. 22:3). Rather, it is a question of what is fitting in the presence of God. (Is this why the healing of deformities is a frequent accompaniment of preaching the kingdom of God in the Gospels?) Many of the items in the list in vv. 18-20 are of uncertain meaning. There are twelve, as there are twelve disqualifying blemishes in victims (22:22-24), and many of the same words are used; this underlines the correspondence between the things and the personnel in each degree of holiness.

22:1-16. Priests were maintained by gifts that were technically gifts to God: portions of sacrifices (see 6:8–7:38 and comments), first fruits, tithes, firstborn of cattle. They are subject to the same restrictions as laypeople (7:19-21) in eating them (21:3-7). For the impurities mentioned in vv. 4-5, see chs. 11–15. 21:8 gives a rule on a related subject; like the rules in 21:1-15 it imposes a more stringent standard than for laity (17:15). Vv. 10-13 make clear who may eat holy gifts (not most holy, which may be eaten only by actual priests [6:16-18, 29; 7:6]): those who are regular members of a priest's household but not temporary bondservants (cf. 25:40). For 21:14-16 cf. 5:15-16.

Rules for Sacrificial Offerings (22:17-33)

The passage on holiness is completed by returning from rules for the priests to address all Israel once more. The rationale for the demand in 22:17-25, which elaborates the words "without blemish" in 1:3 etc., is clearly expressed in Mal 1:8. To offer substandard sacrifices to God is no more acceptable than offering substandard gifts to an earthly ruler, and to allow it would rapidly lead to a situation in which it would be acceptable to get rid of unhealthy animals by way of the altar. For the sacrificial terms see the comments on chs. 1–7, especially 7:11-18.

The two rules in 21:27-28 are probably not due to humanitarian concern. There is once again a concern with symbolic boundaries: birth and death are kept apart. Eilberg-Schwartz (1990: 123-25, 128-34) suggests that, as with the rules on blemishes, rules about animals metaphorically echo rules about human beings: v. 27 echoes the eighth-day circumcision rule for human male children (12:3), and v. 28 echoes the incest rules, particularly 18:17 and 20:14.

22:29-30 repeat the rule in 7:15 (see comment there).

22:31-32. Through chs. 19–22 the idea of holiness has been developed, and it is finally stated here in a more subtle form than in 19:2. Like the priests, the whole people are "sanctified," or called to holiness, by Yahweh himself. Their obedience is required in order to retain their holiness; and though Yahweh is in himself holy in a way that nothing external can affect, he has a "name," a reputation that depends on the obedience of his people, so that his holiness can even be said to depend in a sense on his people. This becomes a constant theme in Ezekiel (e.g., 36:20).

A Calendar of Festivals (Ch. 23)

Two main theological ideas, which in practice are in some tension with one another, have come together to structure this chapter.

The first is the idea of sacred time. Just as there are holy places and people, so there are holy days, times when the normal business of life is suspended and the community is devoted solely to God. In this way the whole of time is claimed as under God's authority. This idea requires that the times should be precisely fixed; so in this chapter there are several dates; and a calendar is presupposed according to which these dates are fixed (see below). Besides the weekly rhythm of sabbaths (23:3), there are seven major holy days in the year, when there is "a holy convocation" (better, "a holy occasion" [JPSV]; lit. "a holy proclamation") and no work is to be done (vv. 7, 8, 21 [but this one not precisely dated!], 24-25, 27-28, 35, 36).

The other idea is that at appropriate times of the cycle of the agricultural year God should be praised for his goodness and his blessing sought for the future. The tension arises in that the harvest does not begin or end on fixed dates every year, or on the same dates everywhere. Probably (Knohl 1995: 8-45) a calendar of sacred time like Numbers 28–29 has been edited to develop the aspect of agricultural rejoicing and seeking of blessing.

This accounts for the missing dates. The firstfruits ceremonies in 23:9-14 and 15-20 depended on the harvest; so "the day after the sabbath" (v. 11) is not a proper date; Jewish authorities later tried to fix it in connection with the feast of Unleavened Bread; for their various interpretations see Hartley 1992: 385-86 and Milgrom 2001: 2056-63. Then the offering of the loaves (vv. 15-21) is dated seven weeks after the raising of the sheaf (cf. Deut 16:9) and not according to the calendar like the other holy days.

The calendar used here begins in the spring (cf. Exod 12:2). The first month (23:5) is roughly March-April, and the seventh month (vv. 23-36) roughly September-October (see *ABD*, 1:814-20). The first day of the "seventh" month (vv. 23-25) is now the Jewish New Year's Day. This name is not used in the Bible; yet 25:9 and Exod 23:16 suggest an autumn new year. The year could have started at different times for different purposes. So the official calendar of sacred time begins in the spring, but the natural turn of the agricultural year is in the early autumn, and that is when we find ceremonies suggesting a new start.

For the sabbath (23:3), see the comments on Exod 20:8-11. In vv. 5-8 no details are given about the Passover and unleavened bread; these have already been given in Exodus 12–13.

The ceremonies in 23:9-21 are firstfruits ceremonies, offering the harvest to God before humans partake of it: v. 14 (the same principle as in 19:23-25). This is complemented by v. 22, a shorter version of 19:9-10; not only God but also the poor have a prior claim on the produce of the comfortable. The "raising" or "elevation" of various offerings in vv. 9-21 is a ceremony in which the offering is swung up and down and from side to side as a formal dedication to God of material which actually goes to the priests (see 7:30). Presumably the offerings of grain are to come from every farmer, while the animal sacrifices will be public offerings. For the terms used for animal sacrifices, see the comments on chs. 1–7. The "raising" of the sheaf in 23:9-14 marks the beginning of the barley harvest in about April, and the ceremony of the loaves seven weeks later (vv. 15-17) marks the wheat harvest. This festival is elsewhere called Weeks (Exod 34:22; Num 28:26; Deut 16:10) or Pentecost (= "fiftieth day") in the NT.

The ceremonies of the seventh month form a complex. The festival of Booths (23:33-36, 39-43) was the chief festival of the year, held after all the produce had been gathered in, and before the first rains; therefore, it was a time both for thanskgiving and for seeking blessing for the coming year; it is prepared for by the blowing of trumpets on the first day of the month (vv. 23-25) and by the day of penitence and atonement on the tenth (vv. 26-32, mostly repeating 16:29-34). The festival of dwelling in booths (vv. 42-43) arose because pilgrims to Jerusalem built themselves shelters for the week; here it is given a meaning as a memorial of Israel's history and God's grace — surprisingly the only such reference in the chapter.

Provision for the Service of God in the Tabernacle (24:1-9)

The material here might seem more at home in Exodus 25–31; 24:2-3 repeat Exod 27:20-21 almost word for word, and vv. 5-9 expand on the brief instruction in Exod 25:30. The reason they are here is probably that v. 2 requires the people to provide the oil for the lamp, and probably they are to supply the flour for the bread as well. V. 8 says that Aaron in setting out the bread fulfills a responsibility of the people, "a covenant [better "an obligation"] forever." So, as in most of the Holiness code, the focus is on the people's responsibilities.

These rituals belong to a class of rituals in ancient temples which symbolically provide the god with his daily needs, such as food and light (Haran 1978: 205-29). The OT authors do not take this literally and openly instruct the priests to eat the bread. Thus the symbolism is reversed, and God is seen as the source of light and bread for his people.

Exod 25:31-40 has a seven-branched lampstand, but

24:2-3 seem to have only one lamp in mind; v. 4 makes it clear that the seven-branched lampstand is meant.

The ephah (24:5) may have been as small as ten liters (*ABD*, 6:903-4), but even so the flat, round loaves would be too big to be set out in rows on the little table of Exod 25:23-30; the tradition was that they were placed in two piles. The burning of the frankincense (v. 7) converts them into a genuine sacrifice: for "offering by fire" see the comments on chs. 1–7.

A Legal Case (24:10-23)

The narrative raises a legal problem which is solved by taking it to God. God's word then gives the rule to be followed in similar cases. A similar teaching technique is used in Num 9:6-14; 15:32-36; 27:1-11. The details of the story are very bare, and it was probably made up for the purpose. For general comments on criminal law, see ch. 20.

What is the problem which leads to the appeal to God? Is it how blasphemy is to be punished or the question whether the law (Exod 20:7; 22:28) applies to an alien? Perhaps both: so far there has been no statement on the punishment for blasphemy. But H insists elsewhere that laws concerning the holiness of the community apply equally to citizen and alien (16:29; ch. 17 and comments; 18:26; 20:2).

Blasphemy in this text involves the explicit pronunciation of the name Yahweh in a context of cursing; otherwise it is deliberately vague about the crime. This is why Jews came to refrain from pronouncing the name at all, even when reading the Scriptures. Death for blasphemy (cf. 20:9) is inevitable in the context of Leviticus: one who explicitly abuses the community's supreme authority must be rooted out. For the use of stoning, see the comments on ch. 20. The witnesses lean their hands on the offender's head (24:14), as the sacrificer does on the victim's (1:4, etc.), and maybe for the same reasons: to dispatch the criminal to his doom and, at the same time, as with the use of stoning, to share the responsibility among them all.

The passage of legal teaching which follows (24:15-22) has broader concerns than blasphemy. One of these is the issue of equality before the law. The other is that of equal restitution, or "talion" as it is called. The passage is arranged as a ring structure in which vv. 15-16a correspond to v. 23, 16b to 22, 17 to 21b, 18 to 21a, 19 to 20b, leaving 20a, the formula "fracture for fracture, eye for eye, tooth for tooth," in the center as the basic principle. It is a common principle in the law of the ancient Near East and appears in the OT also at Exod 21:24-25 and Deut 19:21. We should not think that courts took it literally: Num 35:31-32 suggest that it was normal to accept monetary compensation in all cases but murder. Rather, it sets up a norm by which compensation may be measured.

Sabbath Year and Jubilee (Ch. 25)

The climax of the book of Leviticus is a single very long speech (25:2–26:45). Its central concern is the land which Yahweh is about to give the people of Israel. On what conditions will they retain it?

Chapter 25 can be seen as an attempt to resolve a clash between irreconcilable attitudes to the land in Israelite-Jewish society. The old tribal attitude was like Naboth's (1 Kgs 21:3): land was a trust which family heads held on behalf of their kin group and could not deal with as they chose. It is possible that in the earliest period the land of a village was communally owned and periodically redistributed. At all events a family's use of a recognized portion of land was fundamental to society: it supported not merely their livelihood but their standing in the community.

On the other hand, with the rise of cities and a money economy the idea spread that land was a private possession. When peasants, who always lived close to the margin, needed a loan, they were often compelled to mortgage or sell the land they cultivated. In doing this, of course, they were implicitly accepting the idea that they "owned" their land. Wealthy people took advantage of this to build up large estates (Isa 5:8; Mic 2:1-2), and peasants became slaves or day laborers. Even earlier it was common for people to mortgage or sell their children or themselves (cf. 25:39-55). We have a picture of the process in Neh 5:1-5.

This chapter reaffirms in principle the old idea that land is inalienable, and that Israelite families should be helped to retain their traditional position as landholders. This is part of the wider project of Leviticus to maintain an ordered society in an ordered cosmos (Fager 1993). But the chapter also takes the money economy for granted and realistically accepts that land (and indeed people) will be bought and sold. It affirms that this should not be permanent, so that the "sale" of land becomes in effect its lease until the jubilee (vv. 14-17), and the "sale" of Israelite people is not into slavery but into a kind of indentured service (vv. 39-43, 53-54). But, more fundamentally, it affirms that Yahweh is the Lord of the land and of the people; it does so at the outset in 25:2b-7, and this, for the writers, is the basic reason why neither of them can be sold outright (vv. 23, 42).

Were these laws meant to be observed or are they "utopian"? There are no sanctions for nonobservance; the law relies on the goodwill (25:17!) of the well-to-do, who would be disadvantaged by it. It is possible that selfish interests are involved: the law would give legitimacy to the demand of the exiles for land on their return from Babylon; but the idea of social and divine justice here is bigger than those interests. We know from Josephus and other sources (Milgrom 2001: 2246) that the sabbath year *was* observed in the Second Temple period, but there is no evidence that the jubilee was. As with many other laws, literal observance may not have been the aim, but it is not utopian in the sense of projecting an ideal polity in a nonexistent world; it takes the real world seriously, and sketches an approximation to justice in that world (Fager 1993: 122; but see Houston 2001).

The chapter seems to have grown through successive additions. The following analysis may clarify the text. Some of the paragraph divisions in the NRSV are unhelpful.

Basic text:	2b-19
the sabbath year	2b-7
the jubilee	8-13
consequence of the jubilee for sale of land	14-17
closing admonitions	18-19
Appendix: a problem	20-22
Subsidiary regulations:	
redemption of property before the jubilee	23-28
exemption: walled cities	29-34
responsibility to impoverished fellow citizens	35-38
sale of a person to an Israelite	39-46
sale of a person to an alien.	47-55

Each subsidiary regulation is a variation on the case: "If anyone of your kin [better, "any of your fellow citizens"; lit. "your brother"] falls into difficulty. . . ."

The Sabbath Year (25:1-7)

25:1-7 reaffirm the old practice of the fallow year found in Exod 23:10-11. A rotating fallow is normal; but here the whole land is to lie fallow at once. In v. 4 the religious motivation is stated in words typical of H. A complete rest from human exploitation gives the land a year for God, just as the weekly sabbath devotes a day completely to God. How was it possible for peasants on tight margins to give up cultivation for a year? Fertility could be maintained only if fields were left fallow not just every seven years but every other year. A farmer might divide his holding into two parts, one part lying fallow each year. If he was going to let his whole holding lie fallow in the seventh year, he would cultivate both parts in the sixth year and suffer very little loss of production (Hopkins 1985: 194-201).

25:5-6, 11-12. They may eat from the land but not harvest it. What is the difference? The point is that the produce is open for anyone to pick; it is not for the landholder to gather it in in the normal way.

Why do 25:21-22 say that the sixth year's crops cover three years rather than two? This may be because the official calendar does not coincide with the agricultural year (see the comments on ch. 23). Sowing is forbidden in year 7; this would mean no harvest in year 8, reckoning by the spring calendar; so year 6's crops (actually harvested in the spring of year 7) have to last until year 9. But see Milgrom 2001: 2181-83.

The Jubilee (25:8-13)

The jubilee, like the sabbath year, is an old tradition; the original meaning of "jubilee" (Heb. *yobel*) is lost. But it is not possible to recover the original way in which it was observed. Ancient rulers made occasional decrees remitting debts and taxes, releasing slaves, and providing for the return of people to their land (Weinfeld 1995; see Jer 34:8). But the regularly recurring jubilee is either a new idea or has a different background, possibly in Israel's tribal society, where it may have been connected with the redistribution of communal land (Weinfeld 1995: 177-78). The essence of the jubilee here is that people are to return to their original landholdings, being released from slavery if necessary (25:10, 28, 33, 41, and 54).

Is the jubilee the forty-ninth (25:8) or the fiftieth year (vv. 10 and 11)? The simplest explanation is that it is the seventh sabbath year, that is, the forty-ninth, and that fiftieth is inclusive reckoning (as when Jesus is said to have risen "on the third day"). But see Milgrom 2001: 2250.

Redemption (25:25-34)

Another old tradition in the chapter is the redemption of land or slaves by a relative (25:25-34, 47-55; cf. Ruth 4:1-6). It arises out of the family solidarity of rural society. However, it is not referred to in vv. 39-43: an Israelite who is sold to another Israelite is not to be treated as a slave; therefore, it seems, redemption is not required. The case in vv. 47-55, where the master is an alien, is treated differently. However, Exod 21:2-6, a much older law, and Deut 15:12-18 require a debt-slave to be released after only six years: Is our text a compromise? One problem is whether redeemed land (25:25) is returned to the original holder or kept by the redeemer. The point may be that land is a family rather than an individual holding, so that once the redeemer has acquired it, the law's intention is achieved.

In 25:29-34 city property is exempted from the laws. It was not bound up with people's livelihood and status in the same way as agricultural land. But this was the only stake for the Levites (see Num 35:2-5) in the land.

25:36-37 take up a constant theme (Exod 22:25; Deut 23:19-20). The NRSV's addition of "in advance" is ill-judged: any form of interest is forbidden.

25:45-46 are a plain contradiction of the spirit of 19:33-34. The chapter is concerned with maintaining the connection between Israelite families and their land. One can understand that resident aliens did not have that connection to start with; but a proper working out of the implications of 19:34 would surely have led to second thoughts.

Reward and Punishment (Ch. 26)

This sermon is the rhetorical conclusion to the book, driving home its message, especially that of the last eight chapters with their call to holiness. It is concerned with *communal* obedience and disobedience; the ritual and civil measures in chs. 16 and 20 and the warnings of divine punishment ("cutting off") throughout protect the community from the effects of individual wrongdoing. The original audience, if this was after the exile, could well find the rhetoric recalling their experience and being reinforced by it.

There is, however, a special tie with ch. 25. The land is Yahweh's supreme blessing on Israel; ch. 26 offers them its blessings if they are obedient and threatens them with its loss (v. 33) in case of disobedience. It is therefore appropriate to pair it with ch. 25, in which the land is the symbol of Yahweh's claim on them (C. J. H. Wright 1990: 150). So the loss of the land is an ironic fulfillment of the sabbath year law (vv. 34-35, 43; cf. 25:2-7). V. 13 also picks up 25:42, 55.

Prefixed, however (vv. 1-2), is a reminder of the most fundamental of all Yahweh's requirements: to be faithful to him, negatively (v. 1) and positively (v. 2). V. 2 repeats 19:30 word for word; v. 1 recalls 19:4 (as well as Exod 20:2-6) but expands it. The "pillars" are free-standing undecorated stones which as late as the seventh century BC had been accepted symbols of Yahweh's presence. It is perhaps to avoid even the suspicion of idolatry that they are forbidden (cf. Deut 16:22).

As the conclusion to a law code, Leviticus 26 is similar to Deuteronomy 28, which pronounces blessings and curses on Israel for obedience and disobedience. Both of them follow a tradition which is seen throughout the ancient Near East in law codes and treaties. Yahweh's "covenant" with Israel is therefore a major theme (vv. 9, 15, 25 [?], 42, and 44-45). Heb. *berit* means "treaty" as well as "covenant," so that the idea is appropriate to the literary form. But here there are no blessings and curses, but rather statements by God of his personal intentions. And the punishments are not presented as final vengeance, but rather as a graduated series of disciplinary actions intended to make Israel come to its senses (like Amos 4:6-12), which are expected to be eventually successful (v. 40). Yahweh in fact will never abandon Israel, but will "remember his covenant."

The covenant is seen primarily as Yahweh's promise (Genesis 17). There are conditions which Israel can break (v. 15, perhaps referring to Exodus 24), but this does not wipe the covenant out. The phrase "vengeance for the covenant" in v. 25 is unique and might better be translated "covenant vengeance" or "treaty vengeance," referring not so much to *the* covenant as to treaties in general, with their pronouncement of vengeance on the violator. So in spite of the long series of fearsome warnings, the impression the chapter leaves in the end is of God's irresistible grace and faithfulness to his people.

26:5: threshing, vintage, and sowing occur in that order in the summer and autumn. The meaning is that the harvest will be so fruitful that farmers will not have time to complete one process before the next has begun.

26:29: cannibalism would be resorted to only in the desperate situation of a prolonged siege (cf. 2 Kgs 6:25-29).

26:30: the reference is again to worship which the reformers had censured. The "high places" are the country places of worship, frequently censured in Kings, and the word translated "incense altars" (but of uncertain meaning; see Levine 1989: 188) has the same associations.

Gifts to the Sanctuary (Ch. 27)

By our notions of composition, it is an anticlimax to follow a dramatic conclusion like ch. 26 with some technical priestly regulations. And since the summary in 26:46 is repeated in 27:34, it seems that ch. 27 is in fact an addition to the book. But it ensures that it does not end with the sad picture of Israel in exile, and the last section of the book recalls the first (chs. 1–7), both dealing with dedications to God.

Officially the dedications are made "to the Lord," in practice they are to the sanctuary or to the priests (v. 21), who may have wanted some way to exert control over the popular practice of making vows. The main issue is under what conditions these gifts, which in theory are invariably in kind, may be commuted for a money payment. All such gifts are valued, and if they are to be commuted a premium of 20 percent is added in most cases, perhaps as a disincentive. All the money values are expressed as shekels of silver, and the standard is given in v. 25: a shekel would probably be about twelve grams.

The body of the chapter (27:2-25) concerns objects dedicated to God voluntarily by individuals. Persons and animals (vv. 2-13) may be dedicated by vow (v. 2). It is clear from vv. 2-8 that the vow of a person (oneself or a family member or slave) was always commuted since human sacrifice was not acceptable (cf. Exod 13:13). The passage gives the scale on which this was done. Most likely the prices reflect the economic value of the persons and may be related to the slave market (Wenham 1979: 338).

Animals which could be sacrificed had to be (27:9-10); those which could not (vv. 11-13) — for example, a donkey or a camel; cf. 11:3-7 — could be redeemed. (In some editions of the NRSV the word "redeemed" has been accidentally omitted in v. 13.)

In relation to real estate (27:14-24) the word "vow" is replaced by "consecrate," presumably because it was not customary to vow houses or land, but these might be gifted in some other way. Vv. 16-24 concern land which comes under the jubilee law (ch. 25). The value of the land (vv. 16-18) is assessed according to the rule in 25:15-16; yet if it is not redeemed it passes permanently (unlike other land) into priestly hands (v. 21), provided that the donor was its original holder (vv. 22-24). Redemption was therefore much cheaper, and possibly was the usual course. In v. 20 "sold to someone else" refers to being sold *before* being dedicated by the original holder (this was the holder's right as the legally permanent possessor).

27:25-33 deal with things and persons which legally belong to Yahweh in any case.

The law on the firstborn of animals (27:26-27) parallels that on vows, except that this not a voluntary gift (cf. Exod 13:2). On unclean animals, the law in Exod 13:13 is different; the present law suggests a later period in which more cash was circulating.

27:28-29 are obscure since the practice of "devotion to destruction" (Heb. *ḥerem*) belongs normally to warfare (Deut 7:2; Josh 6:21), except for Exod 22:20, which may explain v. 29. Placing one's own property under such a ban (v. 18) may be a type of oath: "If I do not do so-and-so, may such-and-such be devoted to destruction" (Levine 1989: 199).

The use of tithes (vv. 30-33) is dealt with in Num 18:21-32. But a tithe of livestock is not mentioned elsewhere.

Bibliography. Commentaries. Budd, P. J. 1996, *Leviticus,* NCBC, Grand Rapids: Eerdmans/London: Marshall Pickering • Elliger, K. 1966, *Leviticus,* HAT 1/4, Tübingen: Mohr • Gerstenberger, E. S. 1996, *Leviticus: A Commentary,* OTL, Louisville, Ky.: Westminster/John Knox (ET of *Das dritte Buch Mose: Leviticus,* ATD 6, Göttingen: Vandenhoeck & Ruprecht, 1993) • Hartley, J. E. 1992, *Leviticus,* WBC 4, Dallas: Word • Hoffmann, D. 1905-6, *Das Buch Leviticus,* Berlin: Poppelauer • Levine, B. A. 1989, *The JPS Torah Commentary: Leviticus,* Philadelphia: Jewish Publication Society • Milgrom, J. 1991, *Leviticus*

1–16, AB 3, New York: Doubleday • Milgrom, J. 2001, *Leviticus 17–22,* AB 3A and *Leviticus 23–27,* AB 3B, New York: Doubleday (vols. 3, 3A, and 3B are continuously paginated) • Sherwood, S. K. 2002, *Leviticus, Numbers, Deuteronomy,* Berit Olam, Collegeville, Minn.: Liturgical • Wenham, G. J. 1979, *The Book of Leviticus,* NICOT, Grand Rapids: Eerdmans/Exeter: Paternoster.

Other Works. Bigger, S. F. 1979, "The Family Laws of Leviticus 18 in Their Setting," *JBL* 98:187-203 • Bourdillon, M. F. C., and M. Fortes, ed. 1980, *Sacrifice,* London: Academic • Cholewinski, A. 1976, *Heiligkeitsgesetz und Deuteronomium: Eine vergleichende Studie,* AnBib 66, Rome: Pontifical Biblical Institute • Crüsemann, F. 1996, *The Torah: Theology and Social History of Old Testament Law,* Edinburgh: T. & T. Clark and Minneapolis: Augsburg Fortress • Davies, D. 1977, "An Interpretation of Sacrifice in Leviticus," *ZAW* 89:387-98 • Douglas, M. 1966, *Purity and Danger,* London: Routledge • Douglas, M. 1970, *Natural Symbols: Explorations in Cosmology,* New York: Barrie & Rockcliffe • Douglas, M. 1975, *Implicit Meanings: Essays in Anthropology,* London: Routledge, 249-318 • Douglas, M. 1993, "The Forbidden Animals in Leviticus," *JSOT* 59:3-23 • Douglas, M. 1999, *Leviticus as Literature,* Oxford: Oxford University • Eilberg-Schwartz, H. 1990, *The Savage in Judaism,* Bloomington: Ind.: Indiana University • Fager, J. A. 1993, *Land Tenure and the Biblical Jubilee,* JSOTSup 155, Sheffield: Sheffield Academic • Firmage, E. B. 1990, "The Biblical Dietary Laws and the Concept of Holiness," in J. A. Emerton, ed., *Studies in the Pentateuch,* VTSup 41, Leiden: Brill, 177-208 • Gorman, F. H. 1990, *The Ideology of Ritual: Space, Time and Status in the Priestly Theology,* Sheffield: Sheffield Academic • Grabbe, L. L. 1993, *Leviticus,* Old Testament Guides, Sheffield: Sheffield Academic • Gray, G. B. 1925, *Sacrifice in the Old Testament: Its Theory and Practice,* Oxford: Clarendon • Gruber, M. I. 1987, "Women in the Cult according to the Priestly Code," in J. Neusner et al., eds., *Judaic Perspectives on Ancient Israel,* Philadelphia: Fortress, 35-48 • Haran, M. 1978, *Temples and Temple Service in Ancient Israel,* Oxford: Clarendon • Heider, G. C. 1985, *The Cult of Molek: A Reassessment,* JSOTSup 43, Sheffield: Sheffield Academic • Hopkins, D. C. 1985, *The Highlands of Canaan: Agricultural Life in the Early Iron Age,* Sheffield: Sheffield Academic • Houston, W. J. 1993, *Purity and Monotheism: Clean and Unclean Animals in Biblical Law,* JSOTSup 140, Sheffield: Sheffield Academic • Houston, W. J. 2000, "Tragedy in the Courts of the Lord: A Socio-Literary Reading of the Death of Nadab and Abihu," *JSOT* 90:31-39 • Houston, W. J. 2001, "'What's Just about the Jubilee?' Ideological and Ethical Reflections on Leviticus 25," *Studies in Christian Ethics* 14:34-47 • Houston, W. J. 2002, "Foods, Clean and Unclean," in D. Baker and T. Desmond Alexander, eds., *Dictionary of the Old Testament: Pentateuch,* Downers Grove, Ill.: Inter-Varsity • Janowski, B. 1982, *Sühne als Heilsgeschehen,* WMANT 55, Neukirchen-Vluyn: Neukirchener • Jenson, P. P. 1992, *Graded Holiness: A Key to the Priestly Conception of the World,* JSOTSup 106, Sheffield: Sheffield Academic • Joosten, J. 1996, *The People and Land in the Holiness Code,* Leiden: Brill • Kiuchi, N. 1987, *The Purification Offering in the Priestly Literature,* Sheffield: Sheffield Academic • Knierim, R. P. 1992, *Text and Concept in Leviticus 1:1-9,* FAT 2, Tübingen: Mohr • Knohl, I. 1995, *The Sanctuary of Silence: The Priestly Torah and the Holiness School,* Minneapolis: Fortress • Leach, E. 1976, *Culture and Communication: The Logic by Which Symbols Are Connected,* Cambridge: Cambridge University • Levine, B. A. 1974, *In the Presence of the Lord,* Leiden: Brill • Lloyd Davies, M. 1988, "Levitical Leprosy: Uncleanness and the Psyche," *EvT* 99:136-39 • Magonet, J. 1983, "The Structure and Meaning of Leviticus 19," *HAR* 7:151-67 • Magonet, J. 1996, "'But If It Is a Girl, She Is Unclean for Twice Seven Days . . .': The Riddle of Leviticus 12.5," in J. F. A. Sawyer, ed., *Reading Leviticus: A Conversation with Mary Douglas,* JSOTSup 227, Sheffield: Sheffield Academic, 144-52 • Marx, A. 1988, "Sacrifice de réparation et rites de levée de sanction," *ZAW* 100:183-98 • Marx, A. 1989, "Sacrifice pour les péchés ou rite de passage? Quelques réflexions sur la fonction du ḥaṭṭa't," *RB* 96:27-48 • McKeating, H. 1979, "Sanctions against Adultery in Ancient Israelite Society . . . ," *JSOT* 11:57-72 • Milgrom, J. 1976, *Cult and Conscience: The ASHAM and the Priestly Doctrine of Repentance,* Leiden: Brill • Milgrom, J. 1983, "Israel's Sanctuary: The Priestly 'Picture of Dorian Gray,'" in *Studies in Cultic Theology and Terminology,* Leiden: Brill, 75-84 • Nelson, R. D. 1993, *Raising Up a Faithful Priest: Community and Priesthood in Biblical Theology,* Louisville, Ky.: Westminster/John Knox • Rendtorff, R., and R. A. Kugler, eds. 2003, *The Book of Leviticus: Composition and Reception,* Leiden: Brill • Sawyer, J. F. A., ed., 1996, *Reading Leviticus: A Conversation with Mary Douglas,* JSOTSup 227, Sheffield: Sheffield Academic • Schmidt, B. B. 1994, *Israel's Beneficent Dead,* FAT 11, Tübingen: Mohr • Schwartz, B. J. 1991, "The Prohibitions concerning the 'Eating' of Blood in Leviticus 17," in G. A. Anderson and S. M. Olyan, eds., *Priesthood and Cult in Ancient Israel,* Sheffield: Sheffield Academic, 34-66 • Tomes, R. 1988, "'A perpetual statute throughout your generations,'" in B. Lindars, ed., *Law and Religion: Essays on the Place of the Law in Israel and Early Christianity,* Cambridge: James Clarke, 20-33 • Turner, V. W. 1969, *The Ritual Process,* Ithaca, N.Y.: Cornell University • Van Gennep, A. 1909, *Les Rites de Passage,* Paris: Nourry • Weinfeld, M. 1995, *Social Justice in Ancient Israel and in the Ancient Near East,* Jerusalem: Magnes/Minneapolis: Fortress • Wright, C. J. H. 1990, *God's People in God's Land: Family, Land and Property in the Old Testament,* Grand Rapids: Eerdmans • Wright, D. P. 1991, "The Spectrum of Priestly Impurity," in G. A. Anderson and S. M. Olyan, eds., *Priesthood and Cult in Ancient Israel,* JSOTSup 125, Sheffield: Sheffield Academic, 150-82 • Zimmerli, W. 1982, "I Am Yahweh," in *I Am Yahweh,* Atlanta: John Knox, 1-28.

Numbers

Philip J. Budd

INTRODUCTION

The book of Numbers has some of the characteristics of a travel diary. It tells the story of Israel's journey from the wilderness of Sinai (1:1) to the plains of Moab, close to Jericho and the borders of the land (36:13).

Topographical information is regularly provided at appropriate points, and the journey as a whole (including the story told in Exodus) is tracked in detail toward the end of the book in 33:1-49.

Meticulous attention is also given to the timing of key events — the census (1:1), the Passover command (9:1), the beginning of the journey from the wilderness of Sinai (10:11), and the arrival in the wilderness of Zin (20:1).

It would be a mistake nevertheless to think of Numbers as a diary in the modern sense of the term. It is likely that the story line, represented by the topographical and chronological data, is actually a means of organizing a wide variety of traditional materials which authors and editors were anxious to associate with the Mosaic period prior to the settlement. This observation does not preclude the presence of historical recollection, preserved by groups who eventually became part of Israel in the land, but it is rarely easy to identify such material or assess its extent.

The title "Numbers" comes from the Vg *(Numeri),* which itself translates the title used in the LXX. This draws attention to the numbering of the people with which the book begins (1:1-54), and which is repeated at a later stage in the story (26:1-62). The Hebrew title *In the Wilderness* provides an altogether more comprehensive description of the story line the book embodies.

COMMENTARY

Reading Numbers as a Literary Whole

It is appropriate to maintain that the book has an integrity and distinctiveness of its own. Numbers is not disordered or incoherent. Wenham (1997: 13-25) provides an account of several recent approaches to the structure of the book. Douglas (1993: 98-126), for example, has seen elements which function as commentary on the book of Genesis. Two special contributions to the traditions of the Pentateuch have to do with:

- the Levites as a subordinate clerical order (1:47-54; 3:1–4:49)
- the tent of meeting as a sanctuary located at the *center* of the camp (2:1-34)

In broad terms a threefold structure emerges:

1. Constituting the Community at Sinai (1:1–9:14)
2. The Journey — Setbacks and Success (9:15–25:18)
3. Reconstituting the Community in Moab (26:1–35:34)

Constituting the Community at Sinai (1:1–9:14)

At the outset the dimensions of the community are established (1:1-46) and its character as a priestly theocracy is affirmed (1:47–4:49). Threats to its purity are identified in 5:1-31, and procedures for dealing with them are set forth. The ways in which laypeople can share in higher levels of "consecration" are indicated in the vow of the nazirite (6:1-21), while the priestly blessing brings security and well-being to the community (6:22-27).

An account of exemplary lay commitment to the sanctuary at the community's center, and to the cult which sustains it, is evident in 7:1-88. The roles of Moses as supreme recipient of the divine word, and of the lamps, which perhaps symbolize the light the word brings to the community, are stressed in 7:89–8:4. The consecration of the Levites for their new role within the theocracy is described in 8:5-26. The keeping of the Passover, the community's foundational rite, is recorded in 9:1-14, along with situations connected to Passover observance which may threaten its purity.

In all these ways Israel, as the recipient of the Sinaitic law, is prepared for the journey to the land. The tone is positive, with leadership and people doing what is commanded.

It is important to appreciate the patterns by which the community is structured. These patterns may be depicted hierarchically or in terms of a center with peripheries:

Moses
Priests — the Sons of Aaron
Levites
[Nazirites]
Leaders/Heads of Tribes
Males
Females

Many will regret that women receive little attention in this structuring process. Though largely marginalized, they do have the right, at least in principle, to make a nazirite vow (6:2) (but see also 30:3-15).

The Journey – Setbacks and Success (9:15–25:18)

There are two major themes in the central part of the book — the land as ultimate destination, and the issue of authority within the community now constituted. These themes are dealt with successively in the form of major expressions of divine commitment to the land and to the community on the one hand, and major challenges to the authority of the community's leadership, and ultimately therefore to Yahweh himself, on the other. These challenges represent different forms of faithlessness, ranging from doubts about the practicability of the journey to assaults on the authority of Moses and Aaron.

God's Commitment (9:15–10:36)

That the journey to the land is divinely guided is established at the outset. The cloud signifies God's commitment to the enterprise and his control of its timing (9:15-23). The trumpets signify a derived authority for the priests in assembling the community for action, both on the journey and in the land itself (10:1-10). The departure from Sinai takes place in an ordered way and in accordance with the guidance provided (10:11-36). So far, all is well.

Human Disaffection (11:1–14:35)

There follows a series of incidents in which the feasibility of the journey is called into question and the authority of Moses as its leader seriously challenged. The hardships of the journey are highlighted (11:1-3, 4-35), along with the threat posed by the occupants of the land (13:1–14:45). Those who complain are primarily the people at large (11:1, 4; 14:1-4), and there is no doubt that Moses' leadership and the future of the whole enterprise are at stake (11:10-15; 14:4).

These challenges mean that leadership issues have to be discussed. The role of the elder as sharer of the burdens of leadership is depicted in 11:16-17, and the legitimacy of the prophets as recipients of the spirit and agents of the divine word is affirmed in 11:26-30. In the light of these developments the uniqueness of Mosaic authority remains, despite a direct challenge from Miriam and Aaron (12:1-16).

The ultimate outcome of this faithlessness, particularly the resolve to return to Egypt (14:4), is the death of the current generation in the wilderness (Joshua and Caleb excepted) and a long delay in the occupation of the land (14:26-35).

God's Commitment (15:1-41)

The positioning of the regulations which follow suggests that, despite Israel's faithlessness, Yahweh's commitment to an ordered cultic life in the land remains firm and unwavering. For the most part the material in 15:1-31 reaffirms the laws for the land provided in Leviticus, by means of supplementary detail. The importance of obedience to God's commandments, and of holiness in general, is stressed in 15:32-41, with sabbath observance highlighted.

Human Disaffection (16:1–17:13)

In the second serious phase of faithlessness the basic issue is the legitimacy of the order established when the community was constituted in the wilderness of Sinai (1:1–9:13). This legitimacy is challenged in different ways. There is the truculence of Dathan and Abiram, who reject Moses' right to lead (16:12-14). There is the protestation of the two hundred and fifty leaders that the community as a whole is holy, which therefore calls in question priestly and levitical privilege (16:3), and there is the claim by Korah and his fellow Levites that they, like the sons of Aaron, have the right to offer incense (16:9-11).

The outcome is a decisive confirmation of the order established at Sinai, with the deaths of the rebels and lasting cultic reminders of the legitimacy of that order (16:36-40; 17:1-11). The people are suitably subdued (17:12-13).

God's Commitment (18:1–19:22)

The cultic material which follows again has the effect of reaffirming Yahweh's commitment to the community, to the order established at Sinai, and to the land. Like the material in 15:1-31, much of it supplements prescriptions already provided in Leviticus. There is a clear continuing commitment to the clerical privileges and responsibilities of priests and Levites (18:1-32), while the red heifer rites of 19:1-22 have special relevance at this point, given the many deaths recorded in 16:49.

Human Disaffection (20:1–21:9)

The third failure involves Moses and Aaron themselves (20:12). At Kadesh, in providing water from the rock, they display lack of trust in Yahweh and a failure to honor him.

The consequences are that they, too, are excluded from the land (20:12), and for Aaron death is not long delayed (20:22-29). Further setbacks on the journey are the hostility of the king of Edom (20:14-21) and the continuing discontent of the people in the face of the hardships on the way (21:4-9).

God's Commitment (21:10–24:25)

Yahweh's continuing commitment is already evident in the success at Hormah (21:1-3), but now more substantially in the significant progress through Transjordan (21:10-35) and the frustration of Balak's attempt to halt that progress (22:1–24:5). Balaam's blessings on Israel constitute a potent witness to Yahweh's good purpose for Israel as a people in the land.

Human Disaffection (25:1-18)

The fourth and final phase of faithlessness involves the people at large (25:1-5), and an individual, Zimri, in particular (25:6-15). The issue here is apostasy — the honoring of gods other than Yahweh. Zimri's relationship with the Midianite woman Cozbi is probably to be understood as compromising in the same way. The events are located at Shittim in the plains of Moab, close to the border of the land.

A further twenty-four thousand of the wilderness generation die (25:9). Yahweh's continuing commitment is most evident in the reconstitution of the community in 26:1–36:13, but the affirmation of Phinehas's priesthood (25:10-13) and the call for an aggressive response to the Midianites (25:16-18) mean that Yahweh does not intend to be deflected from his course.

It seems unlikely that these juxtaposed cycles of divine commitment and human failure are accidental. Occupation of the land is integral to the divine purpose, and the ordered community Yahweh has created must be sustained and defended if that purpose is to be realized. Faithlessness in all its forms is disastrous, but Yahweh raises up those who hear "the words of God" (24:4) and whose eye is "clear" (24:15, NRSV), and he is not diverted from his purpose.

Reconstituting the Community in Moab (26:1–35:34)

The temptation to see 26:1–36:13 as miscellaneous appendages to the book should be resisted. A case can certainly be made for seeing 36:1-13 as an appendix, taking up again the issues raised in 27:1-11, but there are good reasons for seeing 26:1–35:34 as integral to the whole.

The disasters which led to the elimination of the wilderness generation and the delay in entering the land are now in the past. Israel is on the plains of Moab, ready to enter, and it is appropriate that the community should be reconstituted, as at Sinai in 1:1–9:14. Deuteronomy, in essence an earlier book than Numbers, had already established this location as a place of Mosaic speeches and lawgiving (Deut 1:1). It is not the intention of the editors simply to repeat the themes of 1:1–9:14, though these are sometimes reflected. The basic structural features of the theocracy are to be assumed, and have been confirmed during the phases of disaffection. The particular concern of the editors is in part to develop some of the themes in 1:1–9:14, but also to stress that this reconstitution of the community should be seen as preparation for entry into the land, the key integrating theme in these chapters.

This process of reconstitution involves reestablishing the dimensions of the community (26:1-65). That the new census will provide a basis for the process by which the land will be divided is indicated by 26:52-56. Issues of inheritance in the land are raised in 27:1-11, and the principle is established that land is to remain within the owning family even if there are no males to inherit (see also 36:1-12). The commissioning of Joshua as leader of the settlement provides an important point of continuity (27:12-23). He and Eleazar are successors to Moses and Aaron, who have both been debarred from entry into the land (27:12-13).

A calendar of daily offerings and key festivals (28:1–29:40), with the appropriate offerings, provides the basis for cultic observance in the land. Its detail supplements information already available in Leviticus. The question of vows, and in particular those made by women, reflects the note in 6:2 that females are entitled to become nazirites (30:1-16). The ramifications of this entitlement in a patriarchal society are dealt with here.

The Midianite war (31:1-54) is important at this point because it indicates a positive response on Israel's part to the divine word in 25:6-18 and because it prepares the way for the invasion of the land. The offerings from the booty (31:25-54) reflect the same measure of commitment to the cultic order which Israel exhibited in 7:1-88. The Transjordanian territory, to be occupied by Gad and Reuben, is the point at issue in 32:1-42. So, too, is the need for the commitment of these tribes to the settlement west of the Jordan. The passage recalls elements from the beginning of the march, as described in 10:11-36.

As the book reaches its climax, the route from Egypt is recalled and painstakingly recorded (33:1-49); attention turns to the land itself, its dangers (33:50-56), and its dimensions (34:1-15). As in 1:5-15 and 2:1-34, leaders are appointed to assist, in this instance in the apportionment of the land. The Levites who were consecrated in 8:5-26 are now provided with cities and land as possessions (35:1-8), an important supplement to their entitlements in 18:21-24, and already presupposed in Lev 25:32-33. Certain cities are also to function as cities of refuge (35:9-34), whereby blood feuds can be checked and space created for a proper consideration of intention in cases of homicide. A key concern in 5:1-31 was that the community be protected from ritual impurity; a similar anxiety is reflected here with regard to the well-being of the land (35:33-34).

Detecting the Processes of Composition

While Numbers may well have been subject to very deliberate and distinct processes of editing, it is also true that it cannot be fully understood apart from its wider literary context within the Pentateuch (and perhaps the book of Joshua too). The story line is obviously dependent on themes introduced in the books of Genesis and Exodus; and, as suggested above, much of the cultic material supplements, and is therefore dependent upon, the book of Leviticus. The conclusion of the book leaves major issues such as the circumstances of Moses' death and the settlement of the land unresolved.

It is commonly held that the Pentateuch, as we know it, is the product of a major revision and supplementation of tradition, undertaken by priestly circles in the late Babylonian and early Persian periods (from about 550 BC to about 400 BC). It is arguable that a similar literary endeavor had already been undertaken at a slightly earlier period (from about 620 BC to 550 BC) in scribal circles, resulting in Deuteronomy and the Deuteronomistic History (Joshua to 2 Kings in the HB). A prominent alternative to this view holds that the priestly work was completed during the preexilic period and that the Deuteronomistic work is later (see, e.g., Milgrom 1991: 3-34).

The precise circumstances under which the priestly work was undertaken are of course unknown, but it may be that much was accomplished between the return (539 BC) and the completion of the Second Temple (516 BC). This major literary achievement would have been most appropriate as a formative program for the new order emerging under Persian auspices. By showing how much that was crucial to faith was revealed by God *outside* the land it served to authenticate a program which had its roots among the exiled priests in Babylon. At the same time it embodied a story line, as we have seen, which envisages the land as the ultimate destination.

This priestly work entailed the editing and supplementation of existing narrative tradition and the incorporation of cultic material (preserved now in Leviticus) from the First Temple. To the extent that Numbers includes cultic material supplementing that in Leviticus and depicted as given at places other than Sinai, it possibly originates within the period of the Second Temple. On the other hand, there is no substantial reason for thinking that Numbers, much as we know it, was not complete by about 500 BC.

To what extent can the pre-priestly earlier traditions in Numbers be identified? Here, too, there are bound to be many uncertainties. There are some signs that the deuteronomists have edited these traditions, but their influence is probably not extensive. A common view, held less widely and with less confidence nowadays, is that the earlier traditions consist very largely of two independent narrative sources — a blending of Yahwistic and Elohistic traditions (titles deriving from the use of the divine name) which derive respectively from the southern and northern kingdoms.

As far as Numbers is concerned, the priestly cultic material (of a legislative nature) is easily identified and very widely recognized by a variety of scholars. Priestly narrative is marked by such indicators as the depiction of Israel as "congregation" or "assembly," of Aaron as high priest, and of the Levites as a subordinate clerical order. It also locates the sanctuary at the center of the camp. The early narrative tradition identifies the community as "the people" or simply as "Israel," Aaron is a leader but not obviously a priest, and the tent of meeting is pitched outside the camp. This third point indicates that the priestly revisers did not wish to eliminate the tradition of a tent outside the camp (they may have thought there were two), but they do wish to stress the tradition of the sanctuary at the center, which they identify as the tent of meeting and which is also a place where oracles are given (Num 7:89). The tradition of two tents may have helped authenticate both Babylon and restored Jerusalem (outside and inside) as places where God's will is made known.

The circumstances under which the early narrative materials came to be written are of course very difficult to establish. It seems likely that the "national epic" they seem to constitute would have begun to take shape during the period of the united monarchy, either under David or Solomon. The Balaam oracles in Numbers 22–24 are of interest in the attempt to track this process. The Yahwistic and Elohistic redactions may be crystallizations of the tradition at crucial points in the histories of the kingdoms of Israel and Judah. If the beginnings of the deuteronomistic movement are to be traced to the reign of Josiah, then the form of the early narrative tradition with which the priestly writers worked, with Yahwistic and Elohistic material combined, may be traced perhaps to the Yahwistic revival associated with Hezekiah, in the late eighth or early seventh centuries BC.

For general purposes of interpretation it is sufficient to note that the early narrative tradition is represented primarily by:

- stories of disaffection and opposition to Moses
- the journey through Transjordan
- the blessing of Israel in Balaam's oracles

The priestly revision supplements the stories of disaffection and of journeying through Transjordan and adds material about:

- the dimensions and ordering of the community
- the distinction between priests and Levites
- cultic observance

Reading Numbers Thematically

While a sequential reading of Numbers, as previously indicated, is entirely appropriate, it is also methodologically sound to address the text on a thematic basis. The final editors of the book, the priests, wished to preserve and incorporate into the community's traditions a number of concerns which can be distinguished and which give the book many of its peculiar characteristics. These themes can be organized as follows:

1. Numbering and Ordering the Community (1:1-47; 2:1-34; 26:1-56, 63-65)
2. Priests and Levites (1:48-54; 3:1–4:49; 6:22-27; 7:89–8:26; 18:1-32; 26:57-62; 35:1-8)
3. Purity and Offering (5:1–6:21; 7:1-88; 9:1-14; 15:1-40; 19:1-22; 28:1–29:40; 31:1-54)
4. The Journey to the Land (9:15–10:36; 20:14–21:3; 21:10-35; 27:12-23; 32:1–34:29)
5. Disaffection (11:1–14:45; 16:1–17:13; 20:1-13; 21:4-9; 25:1-18)
6. The Story of Balaam (22:1–24:25)
7. Community Law (27:1-11; 30:1-16; 35:9–36:13)

1. Numbering and Ordering the Community (1:1-47; 2:1-34; 26:1-56, 63-65)

The Size of the Community (1:1-47; 26:1-56, 63-65)

The priestly writers are responsible for the statistical and organizational detail of these chapters. A good indicator of this is the depiction of Israel as a congregation (1:2, 16, 18; 26:2). So, too, is the stress on a close association between Aaron (and his son Eleazar) and Moses with regard to function (1:3, 17, 44; 26:3) and as joint recipients of the divine word (2:1), and on Aaron (and his son) as priest (26:1, 3). The chronological detail (1:1), linking Numbers with Exod 40:17, is a key part of the editorial adhesive which holds the books together. For the priestly writers the tent and the tabernacle are interchangeable terms (Exod 40:1), and the story of the construction of the shrine is told in Exod 25:1–27:21; 35:4–40:38.

The priestly writers seem to presuppose a systematic organization of Israel's life, but since terminological usage is not always clear, there is some difficulty in describing it. The following is one possibility.

The largest unit is the *tribe*. The concern to present the priestly tribe of Levi as quite distinct from its brothers means that in order to preserve the tradition of twelve tribes (based on the belief that Jacob had twelve sons) the tribe of Joseph in priestly lists is split into two — Ephraim and Manasseh (the two sons of Joseph). Earlier listings preserve the tradition that the twelve (including Levi) were all the immediate sons of Jacob (e.g., Gen 49:1-27; Deut 33:1-29). Justification for treating Levi as distinct rests on the fact that traditionally the tribe of

Levi was landless, depending for its upkeep on its priestly expertise (cf., e.g., Deut 10:9; 33:8-11; Judg 17:7–18:31).

It is widely held that the tribal system reflects the administrative needs of the early monarchy and that the ethnic connections between the various groups which comprise it were far more complicated than the tradition of Jacob's twelve sons would suggest.

Within the tribe were smaller units, identified here as *clans*. It is difficult to say how many clans each tribe might contain, but Num 26:1-51 does identify clans within tribes, in some instances noting descendants (subclans). It is unlikely that this information is simply fictional, but it is difficult to determine to what situation and circumstance it relates. It may be assumed that clans constituted groups of closely related people living in the same or neighboring settlements.

The *ancestral house* is a smaller unit again, within the clan, and approximating perhaps what would now be called the extended family (but see Levine's view [1993: 131-33] that the "ancestral house" is the primary unit). The subclans noted above, and cited in Num 26:1-51, may in effect be ancestral houses. The head of the house (1:4) had a distinct place within the group, and only those with this dignified status might assist Moses with the census. The list of men chosen for the task may be derived from archival sources (it differs from the men chosen to be spies in Num 13:4-16), but what these archives were cannot now be established. In 2:1-34 the same men are designated as leaders of their respective tribes.

The numbers (only men capable of military service) are impossibly large from a purely historical perspective. Once again it is unlikely that such information is simply fictional. The dimensions of each tribe are certainly expressed in round numbers, but they are by no means as round as they could be, and it is appropriate to ask on what basis the differentiations are made, both between individual tribes in the same list and between the two lists as a whole. What was the original point of reference, and what was the significance of the numbers for the priestly writers? A discussion of various attempts to answer these questions is provided by Davies 1995: 14-18.

One suggestion is that "thousand" originally denoted units of some kind (connected perhaps with military needs) within each tribe. On this basis Reuben had 46 such units and a total of 500 men available for military service. This reduces the numbers in 1:1-47 to 5,550. It is puzzling nevertheless that Judah, in comparison with Reuben, and with as many as 74 units, mustered only 600 men.

Another possibility is that the numbers are derived from the quantity of silver that, for some reason, the priests believed had been used in the construction of the tabernacle. According to Exod 38:24-31, this amounted to 100 talents, 1,775 shekels (with 3,000 shekels to the talent), a total of 301,775 shekels. Since the sanctuary tax was half a shekel (Exod 30:13), there must have been 603,550 eligible to pay it. In short, the census return is deduced from the size of the silver offering. This does not explain, of course, how the distribution of the total among the twelve tribes was computed. Perhaps the proportions are related to priestly perceptions of the size of the territory and number of settlements inherited by each of the tribes (Num 26:54).

The importance of the temple tax as a means of providing for the daily offerings (Num 28:1–29:40) is clearly one reason for priestly interest in census taking. Those registered are the ones liable to pay. This raises another possibility — that the lists are based on archival material containing information of this kind. It is conceivable from this point of view that numbers of settlements are the point at issue, with Reuben having 46, including approximately 500 per settlement. If this were the case, then the size of the silver offering in Exod 38:24-31 would be deduced from the census return.

The differences between the two lists are of interest. Despite a slight overall reduction during the wilderness period seven tribes record an increase in population, and five a decrease. Simeon's catastrophic losses might be traced to texts such as Gen 49:7, but Manasseh's large gains are hard to explain on the basis of textual tradition. In Gen 48:8-22; Deut 33:17 it seems to be implied that Ephraim is the dominant of the two.

It is possible that the adjustments in the second list simply reflect assessments of the relative strengths of the tribes in early postexilic times. Given the centrality of Judah within the postexilic community, its preeminence in both lists is understandable.

The Community Encamped (2:1-34)

The ordering of the camp reflects a distinctive priestly understanding of the nature of the community, and of God's presence within it. In diagrammatic terms it can be depicted thus:

	Dan	Asher	Naphtali	
Ephraim		Levites		Judah
Manasseh	Levites	TENT	Priests	Issachar
Benjamin		Levites		Zebulun
	Reuben	Simeon	Gad	

The first-named tribe in each group of three has a certain priority, so that the first of the four major encampments are the camps of Judah, Reuben, Ephraim, and Dan. The groupings, moving from south to east to west to north, follow the order in 1:1-47, but there is a wish here to mention the camp of Judah first, and so the listing moves from east to south to west to north. This also becomes the order of the march — Judah-Reuben-Ephraim-Dan (2:9, 16, 24, 31). Clearly it was important to the priests, as exponents of the traditions of the Southern Kingdom, that the priority of Judah be affirmed. The "priority" of Reuben, Ephraim, and Dan seems to be based only on their position in the list. The position that Gad has (third) in the lists of 1:20-47; 26:1-56 (Levi's place in earlier lists) is unusual; it is not derived from known earlier traditions. It could indicate the use of archival material now lost, but it does keep Judah at the head of a group of three, and therefore, from the point of view of the compilers' methodology, its natural leader.

This ordering of the camp gives perfect expression to the priestly theology of the God who lives among his people (Exod 29:45). The structures which characterize periods of encampment are preserved for the journey (2:17), so that there is a continuing witness to the character of the community and its God.

That this is a patriarchal community is evident in the male authority figures (Moses and Aaron) and in those chosen to help with the census and to lead generally. It is also clear that thoughts about war are present — another reason for the limited nature of a census that excludes women, children, and the elderly (1:3). The priests of the postexilic community are evidently sustaining this order and exerting their influence within the community in their revision of its formative story. That this influence is designed to secure their own place within both story and community is easy to see. The census has connections with the size of the offerings for the sanctuary (Exod 38:24-31); one of its outcomes is "registration" for the temple tax (Exod 30:13).

But such pressures are often ambiguous or more complex, with respect both to motivation and effects. Under Persian rule the priests took advantage of the opportunity to reconnect the community to its roots in the land and to preserve its identity, its purpose, and its sense of self-worth in an environment which in many respects remained unfriendly and difficult. They remained true to the traditions which spoke of liberation from the oppressions of imperial power (Egypt) while downplaying the significance of human militarism in achieving that goal (see also Lohfink's discussion of the Pentateuch and war (1994: 173-226). One underlying effect of the census is to indicate God's grace in causing the community to grow and prosper.

Priests and Levites (1:48-54; 3:1–4:49; 6:22-27; 7:89–8:26; 18:1-32; 26:57-62; 35:1-8)

The sharp distinction between priests (sons of Aaron) and Levites (other males from the tribe of Levi) is one of the most characteristic features of Numbers. In earlier texts Levites are highly valued as priests (e.g., Judg 17:7-13), though it seems to be assumed that others could serve in that role. In such texts the right of Levi as a whole to undertake such duties is affirmed (Deut 33:8-11). Deuteronomy confirms that right, and insists that it is exclusive to Levi (Deut 18:1-7). By contrast, Numbers insists that only the sons of Aaron and their descendants have full priestly rights and responsibilities; the remaining Levites (the majority) have a subordinate role as clerical assistants to the priests but with their own dignity and rights to income. The effect of this development is to give the word "Levite" a functional connotation, in addition to the tribal significance it retained.

It is sometimes held that this development within the priestly office is traceable to the upheavals of the exilic period, and perhaps to adjustments or compromises which had to be made in the light of competing claims to legitimacy among exiled priests and those who continued to serve the cult in Palestine. In any event, the priestly editors and writers of Numbers are responsible for the relevant passages. Israel is identified as a "congregation" (1:53; 31:13, 16, 26, 43), and a preoccupation with the content of the tabernacle is readily apparent (1:50-51; 3:8, 25-26, 31, 36-37; 4:5-16, 24-33; 7:89). Aaron as a joint recipient with Moses of divine words is evident in 4:1; sometimes he even receives commands on his own (18:1, 8). That the general content of the passages is of immediate interest to the priests is obvious throughout.

Priestly Responsibilities

The priests belong to the family of Aaron — Aaron himself and his sons Eleazar and Ithamar serving as such in the wilderness period (3:1-4). The fate of the elder sons is described in Lev 10:1-7. The duties of the priests are:

- to oversee the Levites with respect to their care of the sanctuary and its furniture (3:32; 4:28, 33), and to protect the Kohathites in particular (4:17-20)
- to protect the sanctuary from intrusions by outsiders (3:38)
- to take responsibility for dismantling the inner sanctum and preparing its furniture and utensils for the journey (4:5-16)
- to pronounce the priestly blessing (6:22-27)
- to take responsibility for the positioning of the lampstand (8:1-4)
- to present the Levites as *tenupah* ("elevation offering" — NRSV) (8:10-11), an obscure procedure, which apparently dedicates them as gifts to the priests (8:20-22)
- to carry out sacrificial duties connected with the altar (both the altar for sacrifice and the incense altar) and all functions in the inner sanctum (18:5, 7, 8)

These duties involve supreme care, for the sanctuary and for the community. The divine blessing will be negated by any defilement of the sanctuary, inadvertent or not, and divine wrath in those circumstances would endanger the community.

Priestly Rights and Privileges

The privileges attaching to the priestly office are:

- the priesthood itself, the duties of which are conceived of as a divine gift (18:7)
- to have the Levites as assistants and as a gift (3:9; 8:6, 19; 18:2-3). The point of the *tenupah* (elevation offering) is that it is a priestly source of income (Lev 7:34)
- to receive as income the elevation offerings (18:11), the first fruits (18:12-13), the firstborn of clean animals (18:15), the redemption price for the firstborn of human beings and unclean animals (18:15-19), and a tithe from the resources (the best of them) received by the Levites (18:28-30)

These rights and privileges clearly brought a degree of power and well-being to the priestly families in postexilic times.

Levitical Responsibilities

All Levites belong to one of three levitical families: Gershon, Kohath, and Merari. Gershon has two clans, Kohath four, and Merari two (3:14-20). They begin to serve at the age of twenty five and retire from their duties at the age of fifty (8:23-26).

The main duties of the Levites are:

- to take responsibility under the priests for the tabernacle (1:50) and its furnishings (3:8):
  - Gershon — the tent covering, the hangings, and the screen (3:25-26; 4:24-28)
  - Kohath — the sacred utensils and furniture (3:31; 4:15, 17-20)
  - Merari — the frames of the tabernacle (3:36-37; 4:31-33)
- to assist the priests (3:6) in duties not connected with the altar(s) or inner sanctum (3:7; 18:3-4, 6, 23)

These duties are clearly those of supervised assistants, but in the nature of the case they are deemed vital and honorable (contrast Ezek 44:10-14).

Levitical Rights and Privileges

The privileges attaching to the levitical office are:

- receipt of the tithes as income (18:21, 24, 30-32).
- receipt of forty-eight cities with their pastureland (35:1-8). The priestly writers take the view that Levites *do* have a right to landed property (cf. Lev 25:32 and contrast Deut 10:9).

The effect of these rights and privileges is to provide a degree of economic independence and security within the community (contrast the impression given of their status in Deut 14:29).

The Significance of the Priestly Hierarchy

The priestly writers stress the distinctiveness of the priestly tribe by insisting that the Levites are numbered separately (1:49). That this has to do with proximity to holy things is confirmed by 4:1-4. The total (22,300, not 22,000 [3:39]) makes Levi the smallest tribe; the males counted here include those from one month old and upward (3:22; contrast 1:3). As with the census in 1:1-47, we can only speculate about how the figures were calculated; the breakdown among the three families may have been influenced by estimates as to what their respective tasks required.

A second levitical census (4:1-4, 21-23, 29-30) identifies those between thirty years of age and fifty, that is, the men who are required to do the work in connection with the sanctuary.

When the next generation is counted on the plains of Moab, the Levites have increased slightly — 23,000 males from the age of one month upward (26:62).

The pattern of encampment further enhances the distinctiveness of the Levites. They, together with Moses and the priests, camp closest to the tabernacle and encircle it (1:53). The picture is as follows:

	Merari (3:35)	
Gershon (3:23)	TENT	Moses/Aaron/Priests (3:38)
	Kohath (3:29)	

This proximity to the holy place is a mark of the higher holiness which the Levites and the priests embodied. Moses, Aaron, and the priests are the ultimate expression of this sanctity and thus are positioned on the east side close to the entrance of the tent.

A further function of this proximity to the tabernacle is protection and social stability. Dangers threaten from two directions. Outsiders must be prevented from defiling the holiness of the sanctuary, and the community must be protected from divine wrath, the reaction of holiness to any undermining of the sacred order (1:51, 53; 18:4, 22). The Levites themselves are subject to restraints, and the Kohathites in particular are at risk (4:15, 20); they must not cross the sharp boundary between priest and Levite. A common form that "wrath" could take would be plague (8:19; 16:46). It is clear that "atonement" is significant in this context (8:19), and that the presence of the Levites, keeping laypeople at a distance, has an "atoning" effect. The word has a complex set of possible meanings. In priestly literature it is often best understood as "purification" or "riddance"; the presence of the Levites "eliminates" any sin threatening the sanctuary and "absorbs" any wrath which threatens the congregation (for discussion see Milgrom 1991: 1079-1084).

Another prominent feature of the hierarchical arrangements is the idea that the Levites function as substitutes for the firstborn (3:11-13; 8:16-18), an idea the priestly writers connect with the deaths of the Egyptian firstborn (Exod 12:29). In 3:41 even the livestock of the Levites are substituted for the firstborn of animals generally. That the firstborn belong to Yahweh (in pre-Israelite times this may have entailed sacrifice) is affirmed in 3:13. Early Israelite laws envisage, not sacrifice, but redemption (Exod 13:2; 22:29; 34:20). The priestly innovation regarding the Levites necessitates another count, which yields 22,273 firstborn among the lay tribes (3:43). This means that, using the figure for the Levites given in 3:39 (22,000), there is an excess of firstborn, totaling 273. These must be redeemed at the price of five shekels a head, and the money handed over to the priests (3:44-51). This reestablishes the principle of redemption and may have been a practice the postexilic priests wished to confirm in the circumstances of their time. Once again, a concern to provide for the priests is uppermost.

This priestly view of order, and of the dangers which ensue if boundaries are crossed and confusion introduced, is clearly also a view of the basis for social stability. That this order in some way privileges both priests and Levites within the social order, and also provides them with comfortable means of support, needs to be recognized. Their income, as envisaged in Numbers, looks a good deal more ample than that provided in Deut 14:28-29; 18:1-5. This social order is also decisively patriarchal; only the males are counted, only the males can function in the various clerical spheres, and only the male firstborn need to be considered as belonging to Yahweh.

On the other hand, this stress on a community identity, with a sharply defined social structure, enabled the resettled community to overcome the dislocations and alienation of uprootedness and exile. A sense of communal dignity and purpose was important under conditions which did not allow complete political independence. The priestly blessing (6:24-26) has attained wide recognition as a classic expression of religious aspiration and feeling at its best. Versions of it, dating perhaps to the seventh or sixth centuries BC, have been found in the

Hinnom valley at Jerusalem on silver amulets or plaques (Levine 1993: 236-44). It expresses the community's aspirations for security, well-being, and a peace which embraces all its members. The explanation (v. 27) "put my name"may refer to the priestly gesture of the hand which accompanies the blessing (Davies 1995: 69).

Purity and Offering (5:1–6:21; 7:1-88; 9:1-14; 15:1-40; 19:1-22; 28:1–29:40; 31:1-54)

All the material on these topics is priestly, and the roots of its thought are in Leviticus. A key text is Lev 10:10, which distinguishes between two realms — the "holy" (the space occupied by the sanctuary) and the "common" (the space outside — including the rest of the camp and space beyond). A further distinction is made there between "unclean" and "clean." Though this distinction can be applied to space, it denotes primarily various conditions which attach to objects or people at particular times. If they are "unclean," such people or objects are problematic; safeguards must be observed and steps of a ritual nature must be taken to restore the situation.

Offerings are also part of this worldview. They are sometimes necessary to rectify situations created by uncleanness (the expiation sacrifices [Lev 4:1–6:7]), or they honor God and seek his help, in the process creating bridges between holy and common (the pleasing odor sacrifices [Lev 1:1–3:17]). As events that take place on boundaries (in time or space), they often mark transitions from one state or situation to another.

The priestly writing as a whole is a worldview which constructs a cosmic system of order and stability, and within which the security and well-being of the community are perceived. While the system certainly privileges the priests with respect both to their resources and their influence, it also provides the community with a sense of identity within the scheme of things and a shared meaning system in situations of disruption and dislocation. Douglas (1993: 41, 158-59) has also suggested that it is a "benign" "non-discriminatory" system; she notes that purification is relatively easy and open to all, with good intention as the prime condition.

There remains of course the much discussed question of why purity systems take the forms they do. Historically their growth is probably complex, and ultimate origins are hard to locate. "Incongruity" and "associations with death" provide some of the likely formative influences.

Skin Conditions (5:1-4)

The demand that people with "leprous" conditions be excluded from the camp is found in Lev 13:46. The stipulations here offer a clarification and an expansion.

The expansion requires that exclusion be extended to those with a "discharge" or who have been in contact with a corpse. Leviticus discusses discharges in 15:1-33 and contact with death in a variety of contexts (11:39-40; 17:14-16; 21:1-4), but it makes no explicit reference to exclusion.

The clarification offered here in 5:1-4 is that females are also subject to the exclusion order. The succession of masculine pronouns in Lev 13:45-46 must therefore be interpreted inclusively, though the clarification might also be prompted by the fact that there are distinct female discharges (Lev 15:19-30).

The theological justification for exclusion lies in the claim that Yahweh's indwelling presence at the heart of the camp requires it (5:8). His holiness is such that uncleanness in all its forms has to be set at a distance from him.

Restitution (5:5-10)

This law supplements the material in Lev 6:1-7. It deals with those occasions when compensation both to one's neighbor and to God (in the form of a guilt offering) is required. The supplementary material here in Numbers again specifies that the law is applicable to women as well as to men (5:6).

It also presupposes the role of "next of kin" (or "redeemer") (cf. Lev 25:25; Num 35:12), and indicates that where there is no such person to receive restitution, the compensation (8:10-11), in the event of the injured party's death, is paid to the sanctuary, and specifically to the priest (v. 8). The priests are therefore in receipt of both the guilt offering and the financial restitution. This is another aspect of the tendency, already observed in Numbers, whereby the priests strengthen their access to the community's resources, though it is reasonable to suppose that a situation such as this would be comparatively rare. The insistence on restitution and compensation undermines any supposition that priests were concerned merely with ritual and priestly dues; they also sought to foster practical social responsibility, an essential, in their eyes, if the fabric of the social order was to be restored.

There is the final insistence that every "sacred donation" (a reasonable rendering of *terumah*) is a priestly entitlement. The principle had already been established in Lev 7:14, in connection with a very specific offering. Here all offerings which may be so designated are declared to be priestly property.

The Adultery Ordeal (5:11-31)

The old ordeal rites concerning a woman suspected of adultery can also be deemed supplementary to provisions in Leviticus. In Lev 20:10 there is the very clear stipulation that guilty parties must be put to death. There is also an anxiety about hidden sin and the need to take appropriate precautions (Lev 5:17-19). Here a rite is prescribed which is intended to make known what is hidden, thereby insuring that perceived threats to the well-being and stability of the community can be dealt with.

There is no comparable procedure in biblical law, though the oath taking in Exod 22:10-13 (which may also be implied in the phrase "before God" in Exod 22:8 and 9) appears to anticipate some divine intervention which will resolve difficult cases.

The contrasting experiences of the man and the woman are striking features of the rite. The man's psychological needs (his "spirit of jealousy" [5:14]) are catered for by the rite itself. The woman's anxieties, of whatever kind, are ignored. She must simply await the outcome of procedures over which she has no control and within which she has no influence. Moreover, she is subject to humiliation at the hands of the priest (vv. 18 and 27), who for his part benefits from the grain offering (v. 15) (see Lev 2:10). The disheveling of her hair (v. 18) seems to cast her in a dubious light; such a state would impugn the holiness of the priests themselves (Lev 10:6).

A miscarriage is apparently expected should the woman be guilty (5:22). In the light of what she is required to drink (vv. 23-24) it may be supposed that any such eventuality would be improbable, but the psychological strains to which she is subjected should not be underestimated, and the risk of a serious miscarriage of justice is real. In v. 28, for example, there is at least a possibility that infertility will be interpreted as an indication of guilt, and the concluding comment (v. 31), wryly cited by Arabella in Hardy's *Jude the Obscure* (pt. 5, ch. 8), is a reminder of the exploitation and disadvantage to which women have often been exposed.

Nazirites (6:1-21)

The vow of the nazirite is the means by which laypeople, male or female, can embody something of the holiness which is intrinsic to priestly ministry, though the assumption seems to be that it will be for a limited period only (6:13-20). There are allusions to nazirites in earlier texts (Judg 13:5; 1 Sam 1:11; Amos 2:11-12); there the defining characteristics are abstinence from alcohol and uncut hair. The circumstances prompting such a vow in Judg 13:5; 1 Sam 1:11 are those of grateful parents offering their children to God. Amos 2:11 is also inclined to suggest the dedication of young people. That being a nazirite was a lifelong commitment is clearly indicated in Judg 13:7; 1 Sam 1:11.

It is arguable perhaps that priestly legislators thought such vows threatened the status of the priests, and that they must therefore be subject to controls. The traditional characteristics of the vow are retained (6:1-5), but it seems to be assumed that it will be made by responsible adults on their own accounts and only for limited periods of time.

As is customary, there are various points at which the legislation connects with Leviticus. Abstinence from alcohol places the same demand on the nazirite as on the priest who enters the tent (Lev 10:9). It is perhaps the fermentation process, with its transformative power, changing substances from one thing to another, that underlies its unacceptability in a "holy" context. Hair, like other substances, seems to embody a divine power which those taking the vow must respect.

The concern about a nazirite's inadvertent proximity to a corpse (6:9-12) also connects with legislation in Leviticus, and with the duties and responsibilities of the priest depicted there. The priest is permitted contact with the dead in very limited circumstances (Lev 21:1-4), and any inadvertent indirect contact would require washing (Lev 22:4-6). The risks for a nazirite, circulating more widely in the community, are greater, and here an offering of two birds (burnt and sin offerings) and a male lamb (guilt offering) is stipulated. This is relatively modest in size, being the requirement for a sufferer from leprous disease who is being restored (Lev 14:21-32). The shaving of the head (6:9) indicates being done with the past and starting anew (v. 12).

The transitional character of offerings is also evident in the rites which mark the end of the vow (6:13-20). The person, by means of the offerings made, returns to his or her customary station in life. The burning of the hair (v. 18) may signify the return of divine power and life to God (as in the burnt offering); it also clearly marks the end symbolically of the period of the vow. The elevation offering *(tenupah)* (v. 20) is perhaps a specific ritual action (rendered "wave offering" in older translations such as the KJV and RV), which marks the flesh and the grain as belonging to the priest (Lev 7:28-36).

Offerings for the Tabernacle (7:1-88)

This section draws on elements previously discussed in the priestly writing, in both Exodus and Leviticus. In Exodus 25–31 and 35–40 details about the construction and completion of the tabernacle are provided. In Leviticus 8–9 its priests and its cult are ordained and inaugurated. The construction of the tabernacle had from the outset been a product of the people's resources and skills (Exod 35:4–39:43). The insistence is that it was voluntary (Exod 35:21) and that the response was far in excess of what was needed (Exod 36:5).

The offering brought by the laypeople on the day that the tabernacle was erected (i.e., on the first day of the first month of the second year — Exod 40:17) is here specified as six wagons and twelve oxen. This gift enables the Gershonite and Merarite priests to transport those parts of the tabernacle for which they are responsible; the Kohathites who carry the holiest items (4:5-15) are not entitled to such assistance (7:9).

The process of altar dedication takes twelve days, and offerings by a leader representing each of the tribes are made on each of these sacred days.

The leaders who make the offerings are the same as those who assist with the census in 1:5-15, but there is a distinct order of offering. In 1:5-15 the sons of Leah are listed first (Reuben, Simeon, Judah, Issachar, and Zebulun) and then the sons of Rachel (Joseph [Ephraim and Manasseh] and Benjamin). The remaining four were born to maids of the matriarchs (Dan, Asher, Gad, and Naphtali), but the arrangement does not follow the birth order suggested by Gen 30:1-13 (Dan, Naphtali, Gad, and Asher). Here in 7:1-88 the order of offering is influenced by the order of encampment given in 2:1-34.

The content of each daily offering is the same. Here, too, the legislators are assuming familiarity with earlier texts — the grain offering (Lev 2:1-16), the preparation of incense (Exod 30:34-38), the burnt offering (Lev 1:1-17), the sin offering (Lev 4:1–5:13), and the well-being offering (Lev 3:1-17). These offerings serve to illustrate the importance the priests attached to the involvement of the community at large in the life of the tabernacle and the ministry of the altar at its center.

Passover Law (9:1-14)

This law presupposes the narrative and legislation in Exod 12:1–13:10, where the feast was first instituted. Its basic principles, and an account of its observance, are recorded in 9:1-5. The main purpose of the text, however, is to develop the legislative tradition and to create a framework within which existing law can be interpreted for new and specific problematic situations. Two such situations are addressed here:

- uncleanness through contact with a corpse
- journeys at Passover time

A Passover observance on the fourteenth day of the *second* month (instead of the first) is permitted in these circumstances (9:11). It is to be assumed that these are exceptional and unavoidable situations; the law is not intended to relax the norms (v. 13).

Laws incorporating resident aliens into the life of the people of God are a feature of priestly legislation (9:14) (cf., e.g., Lev 16:29; 17:13; 19:34; 22:18; 25:47-55). Here the participation of aliens in the Passover appears to be voluntary, but, if accepted, the responsibilities and privileges of native and alien are the same.

The supplementary character of much of the legislation in Numbers is also evident in 15:1-31.

Accompaniments to Animal Offerings (15:1-16)

These laws envisage the possibility that burnt offerings (Lev 1:1-16) and well-being offerings (Lev 3:1-17) may be accompanied by grain and wine. The circumstances in which this would be appropriate are when the sacrifice is in fulfillment of a vow, or when freely offered, or on a major festival (15:3). In point of fact, it is hard to envisage a situation in which an individual would offer sacrifices which could *not* be categorized in one of these three ways. The distinction between the votive and the freewill offering has already been made in Lev 7:16, but the concern there is only with the well-being offering and its disposal. The effect of the legislation here in Num 15:1-16 is to make grain and wine offerings a normal accompaniment of both burnt and well-being offerings. The quantities of flour and wine required depend on the size of the animal offered (vv. 5-10). As in 9:1-14, the resident alien is entitled to engage in the cultic life of the community (vv. 14-16; cf. also v. 26).

First Fruits (15:17-21)

The Holiness code (Lev 17:1–26:46) had already legislated for the offering of first fruits (Lev 23:9-14). The first cutting of the harvest must be offered to Yahweh, in addition to burnt, grain, and wine offerings. The distinctive feature here in Num 15:17-21 is that there must also be a *terumah* offering ("donation" — NRSV) of a loaf of bread from the harvest. Such offerings were the special possession of the priests, and were possibly subject to distinct ritual procedures (hence the old translation "heave offering"). This is further indication of a strengthening of the rights and privileges of the priests in those parts of the priestly legislation which occur in Numbers (cf. 18:1-32).

Sin Offerings (15:22-31)

This material can be interpreted as supplementary to that on this topic in Leviticus. A fundamental purpose of the sin offering is to cleanse and protect the sanctuary from ritual defilement. Where the sins of the priests or the community at large are the cause, disposal of the carcass is by burning outside the camp (Lev 4:12, 21). Where the cause is some other source, such as the situations listed in Lev 4:22–5:13, and not involving the priests, there the flesh is a priestly entitlement (Lev 6:26, 29-30; cf. 10:16-20). The sins in question must always be inadvertent, and the impression given in Lev 4:13, 27; 5:2-4 is that sins of *commission* are at issue (contrast Lev 5:1, which seems to envisage a sin of *omission*).

The focus here in Num 15:22-26 is on the sin of the whole community (cf. Lev 4:13-21). There is a hint in 15:22 that this relates to sins of omission (contrast the explicit stress on commission in Lev 4:13). The requirement here is that the bull should be a burnt offering (not a sin offering, as in Lev 4:14). The sin offering consists rather of a male goat (15:24). The "atonement" which the offering accomplishes is purification for the sanctuary and forgiveness (a restored relationship with Yahweh) for the community.

The point of the supplement regarding sin offerings for individuals (15:27-31) is, as elsewhere, to make clear that resident aliens share fully in the community's cultic life (v. 29) and to insist that sin offerings are only efficacious for inadvertent sins. Deliberate high-handed infringements incur the penalty "cut off from among the people" (vv. 30-31). This may have entailed a form of excommunication, or more probably the expectation that God himself would take some kind of direct action against the offender.

Sabbath (15:32-36)

The sabbath principle, along with the penalty for its infringement, has already been strongly affirmed in the priestly legislation (Exod 31:12-17; Lev 19:3; 23:3). It is clear nevertheless that answers to the question of what precisely constitutes sabbath work are necessary. A previous stipulation insists that kindling fire is an infringement of the sabbath (Exod 35:3). The narrative in 15:32-36 reveals the emergence of further answers. Using stories for legislative purposes clearly had its attractions (Lev 24:11-23; Num 9:6-8; 27:1-11; 36:1-12). In this instance the answer is established by a divine word; gathering sticks is sabbath work, and the offender must be stoned to death. While the earlier absence of a ruling on the matter may engender a certain sympathy for the man in his predicament, the supposition of the priestly writers was that he should have been far more cautious about engaging in such activity. This is particularly so since the kindling of fire has already been firmly prohibited (Exod 35:3).

Fringes (15:37-41)

It is appropriate that this section on "tassels" or "fringes" should conclude this body of laws (Num 15:1-36). Whatever the original significance of these blue fringes, they are interpreted by the priests as aids to the memory. Worn on clothes, they constitute a daily reminder of the obligation to follow Yahweh's laws rather than personal predilection. Just as the sabbath story in 15:32-36 has affinities with the Holiness code in Leviticus, so, too, do the concluding verses of this chapter with their reminders that the people must be holy and that Yahweh brought them out of Egypt (cf., e.g., Lev 19:2; 22:31-33).

Purification from Contact with Death (19:1-22)

From the perspectives of the purity system, contact with death was a source of uncleanness which could not be ignored. The matter had already been addressed in Leviticus, in relation to contact with dead animals (Lev 11:24-38), and in the Holiness code as it affected the priests and their dead relatives (Lev 21:1-15). The laws in Num 19:1-22 make it clear that impurity ensues and cleansing is necessary, whenever people (clerical, lay Israelite, or alien) come into contact with a human corpse. The period of uncleanness lasts for seven days (v. 11), and purification is accomplished through washings on the third and seventh days (v. 12). The legislators are particularly alert to the consequences of laxity in these matters — the uncleanness will persist (v. 12b) and the person will be "cut off" (excluded or liable to divine punishment) (v. 13). The tabernacle itself will suffer defilement (v. 13), and the well-being of the whole community thereby put at risk.

The water used for the cleansing process must be specially prepared (vv. 1-10); it comes from water kept at the sanctuary which contains the ashes of a red heifer. There are various obscurities here. Why add ashes to the water? Why a red heifer? Why is it killed and burned outside the camp? Why the burning of the cedarwood, the hyssop, and the crimson material? There are no easy answers to these questions. It may be that the red heifer rite originally served some other cultic purpose and that it has been adapted by the priests to serve this new purpose — for cleansing after contact with a corpse. This might explain why the purposes of some facets of the rite are difficult to identify.

It appears that the ashes insure the holiness of the water. They are gathered by someone clean and deposited in a clean place (v. 9). Perhaps contact with death requires this extra precaution. The heifer is of course an animal suitable for sacrifice and therefore suitable, through its ashes, to be a purifying agent. The slaughter outside the camp makes it clear that this is *not* a sacrificial offering in the customary sense; the ashes remain outside the camp for the use of the people at large. Some of the blood, however, which, as always, is Yahweh's, is sprinkled in the direction of the tent of meeting. This acknowledges the uniqueness of the blood and protects the sanctuary from any inadvertent defilements. Perhaps for this reason the procedures can be called a purification (sin) offering (v. 9). The wood, the plant, and the fabric figure in the cleansing ceremonials for skin diseases in Lev 14:4. It is usually assumed that these had traditional cultic uses and functions now lost to us.

The last part of the chapter (19:14-22) makes it clear that the contaminations of death extend beyond the person(s) who necessarily handle the body. Those who enter the tent, or are present at the point of death, are unclean; so, too, is the tent itself and any open vessels inside it. Contact with death in the open air is also contaminating, whether through bodies, bones, or graves. The procedures and warnings (vv. 17-22) are essentially the same as those in vv. 11-13.

The Daily Offerings (28:1–29:40)

These two chapters contain lists of offerings to be made at different points in the cultic calendar. As with so much of the priestly legislation in Numbers, there is information which supplements issues raised in Leviticus. This appears to be the fullest and final form of the Pentateuchal calendar. Earlier calendrical information can be found in texts such as Exod 23:14-17; 34:18-24. The Holiness code offers an approximation to the calendar here in Numbers and cites all of the occasions except the daily offering and the new month celebration (Lev 23:1-44). Among its particular concerns are to identify "holy convocations" and to insist that they are occasions of abstinence from work.

The information supplied here in Num 28:1–29:40 specifies the daily temple sacrifices which must be offered. They are therefore distinct from the private offerings which individuals might make, whether freely, or as an act of thanksgiving, or in fulfillment of a vow. The daily morning and evening sacrifice is "regular"; in other words, it is offered in addition to the special sacrifices which mark major festivals. Though the quantities and calendar may have been different in preexilic times, it seems likely that the king was responsible for providing the animals for these "public" occasions (cf. Ezek 46:1-8). In postexilic times the temple tax, levied on all registered males, provided the necessary income (Exod 30:13; Neh 10:32-33).

The cult, and the priests who administered it, were demanding by way of animal sacrifice (Coote and Ord 1991: 57-66, 105-15). The special festivals obviously call for more in the way of offerings. Unleavened Bread and Booths were weeklong events; hence the markedly larger requirements. The decreasing quantities at Booths (29:12-38) suggest that the importance of the festival days decreases, but why this should be so is hard to explain. A sin offering on the special occasions helps to protect the sanctuary from any defilements which threaten it on such public occasions and thereby also, from the priestly perspective, preserves the stability and well-being of the community.

The lambs, bulls, and goats were accompanied by grain offerings mixed with oil and by wine offerings. The oil measures for bulls and rams were probably in proportion to the additional quantities of flour required. These quantities of flour, oil, and wine were substantial; an ephah was probably about a kilogram and the hin about a liter (see GNB translation).

The War against Midian (31:1-54)

This account is exclusively priestly in content and is a reminder that "holy war" is not entirely absent from priestly thought. This particular conflict arises out of the priestly accretions to the Baal of Peor story in 25:1-18, which identify Midian (not Moab) as the major devious and destructive influence in that event (31:16-18). Balaam too, despite his prophecies in Israel's favor, is killed (v 8). The priestly hostility to Midian is not easy to explain. There was, of course, a fierce rejection of intermarriage in postexilic times (cf., e.g., Ezra 10:1-44), and the priestly scribes may have thought it vital to make clear that the old tradition which has Moses related by marriage to Jethro, priest of Midian (Exod 18:1), was not applicable as a model for the present. The story of the war in 31:1-54 carries through Moses' command in 25:16.

Despite priestly adherence to the concept of holy war, there is much that is stylized and unrealistic about this conflict. A round figure of 1,000 from each of the twelve tribes provides the army (31:4 and 5), which is accompanied, not by the ark, but by sanctuary vessels (v. 6). The victory is total and all-embracing (vv. 9-12). The quantities of booty captured are enormous (vv. 25-54), and all of this apparently without a single casualty on Israel's side (v. 49).

The truth is that the priestly writer is less interested in the war as such than in purity and in the use and distribution of resources — hence the relevance of the "war" at this point in the discussion. The distinctive features of the priestly attitude to war are discussed by both Lohfink (1994: 195-224) and Niditch (1993: 78-89).

The interest in *purity* becomes apparent immediately when the army has returned to the plains of Moab. Moses is angered by an apparent breach of purity principles. All the captive women have been preserved, along with their offspring (31:15-17). As Moses perceives it, only the female virgins pose no threat to the purity of the camp, and only they can therefore be allowed to live (v. 18). It seems that the young Midianite males embody something fundamentally alien and dangerous, which the females who have engaged in sexual relations now share. The situation is exacerbated by the events at Peor, in which these females are said to have been implicated (v. 16).

The difficulties which purity systems pose are all too evident here; it is not simply the exclusion of that which is felt to be different and threatening, but its extinction. Purity systems help us understand our world and our experience, and their prevalence in human societies (and perhaps necessity) needs to be acknowledged. But they are deeply ambiguous and should always be open to criticism.

It is easy to see how ancient patriarchal societies, frequently endangered and threatened perhaps with extinction, would value the procreative power of virgin female captives. It is interesting to note, too, that the priests do not exclude them from the holy community. The problem for the priests has nothing to do with modern fantasies about racial purity. It is not Midianite blood (the virgins who survive are born and bred Midianites), but Midianite maleness, and the womenfolk these men have made theirs through sexual relations, which threaten defilement and the supposed danger to tabernacle and community.

The war has also brought defilements on the army through killing and contact with death, and appropriate purity rites must therefore be observed (31:19-20, 24) (cf. 19:1-22). Miriam suffered a week's exclusion for leprosy in 12:14, while the purification procedures (v. 19) would be those of 19:12. Garments and other items could also become contaminated, and for them, too, water would be necessary (Lev 11:32).

Metal items, primarily weapons, need, in addition to water purification, the purging influence of fire (vv. 21-23) (cf. Isa 6:6-7). Here, too, it is apparent that the priests are interested in war, not as a means to political ends but as a threat to the purity system which sustains the community.

In 31:25-47 attention turns to *the distribution of the booty.* The items captured (humans and animals) are divided equally between soldiers and congregation (v. 27). From the share of the soldiers one item in every five hundred is Yahweh's and goes to the priests (vv. 28-29), while from the share of the congregation one item in every fifty is Yahweh's and goes to the Levites (v. 30). The association of priests with soldiers highlights the sanctity of the war and the way in which such activity is brought within the all-encompassing embrace of the priestly vision.

A key concern is to insist clearly that a fixed quantity of the resources accruing from the war belong to Yahweh, and that these items become the property of the temple clergy, the priests, and the Levites. It is appropriate to ask what interest would be served by such attention to detail in the circumstances of the Second Temple since the prospects for real war and real booty were negligible under Persian rule. The priestly writers were of course working with traditional themes about Yahweh's war, and in telling the story about Israel's past it was natural that they would wish to bring those themes within the compass of the priestly system. At one level this chapter serves to confirm the point that *all* resources, in all circumstances of life, are subject to levies which sustain and in some measure enrich the priestly classes. Evidence that the priests were seeking to establish and extend their power within the community are easy to find in Numbers. Yet this same process, which affirms Yahweh's rights and power within the community, was one which served, in times of inescapable subordination to a foreign power, to provide social identity, cohesion, dignity, and durability.

The concluding element in the chapter (31:48-54) deals with the use and distribution of other items taken in the war. Here the same concerns are paramount — to strengthen the position of the priests and the distinctive identity of the community. The items in question are valuable ornaments and pieces of jewelry (v. 50), and *all* of these are brought as an offering to Yahweh. This contrasts with the deviousness of Achan in Josh 7:6-26. The offering is voluntarily made by the army officers, and in making the offering they seek "atonement" (31:50). It is interesting to note that the word can be used in a situation which does *not* involve the blood of animals. It seems to signify purification from any ritual defilement and protection from any consequences which defilement might bring. The valuables amount to 16,750 shekels of gold, and they are used in some unspecified way to enrich the tent of meeting (v. 54). In this way they function as a "memorial" (NRSV), a continuing witness to the success which God gave, and to the faithfulness and devotion of the participants in the war.

The Journey to the Land (9:15–10:36; 20:14–21:3; 21:10-35; 27:12-23; 32:1–34:29)

These parts of Numbers constitute the travel story at the book's core. Most of the material comes from the priestly writers, but there are clear and reasonably substantial traces of the earlier narrative traditions which they employed. An indicator of earlier tradition is the presence of ancient poetic fragments — for example, 10:35, 36; 21:14-15, 17-18; 21:27-30. In one instance the Book of the Wars of Yahweh is cited (21:14) as the source. These poetic pieces were probably already embedded within the earlier tradition when taken over by the priestly scribes. Texts which lack the characteristic description of Israel as a "congregation" or which fail to depict Aaron in priestly guise are probably early. Texts which betray overall editorial interests can be attributed to later levels of priestly tradition.

On this basis we can reasonably attribute the main outline of the wilderness journey to the early narrative tradition. Israel is traveling (10:35-36) and seeks, with some success, to enter the land from the south, close to Arad (21:1-3). But this fragmentary tradition is dominated by the stronger insistence that Israel took a Transjordanian route which avoided Edom (20:14-21) but which led to successful settlement further north (21:10-35). These territories become the possession of Gad, Reuben, and half of Manasseh, who agree to join an invasion of Canaan from the east (32:6-27, 33-42). It is clear that there are different levels of tradition within the story, which may perhaps be differentiated as follows:

- the old poetic fragments
- traditions of settlement from the south and in Transjordan
- the final form which envisages a journey *through* Transjordan to Canaan.

The priestly writers do not modify the journey outline in any significant way. Their first concern is to show that it was conducted in priestly fashion (9:15-23; 10:11-28). They are also interested in authority and leadership issues — in the death of Aaron and the investiture of Eleazar as his successor (20:22-29), in the appointment of Joshua as eventual successor to Moses (27:12-23), and in Eleazar's involvement in decisions about the invasion (32:1-5, 28-32). Their overall editorial interests are evident in the comprehensive account of the itinerary and settlement preparations (33:1-56) and in the account of the land's dimensions (34:1-29).

Study Bibles generally contain relevant maps of the southern deserts and the Transjordanian region, with an indication of the sites which can be identified with some confidence.

The Order of the March (9:15–10:36)

The priestly writers begin their account of the journey from Sinai with reminders about the means by which Yahweh guides and guards his people. The "pillar," apparently cloud by day and fire by night, is present in the early narratives (Exod 14:19-20, 24). The priestly writers accept this and associate with it the notion of Yahweh's "glory," which signifies his awe-inspiring but protective presence (Exod 40:34-38).

The stress here at the beginning of the journey is on the guidance God gives through these agents of his presence (9:15-23). The way in which the points about guidance and obedience are insisted on at length is characteristic of the attention to detail in priestly thought. It was clearly important to the priests to indicate divine care and control *before* beginning the account of the journey itself (10:11). The "trumpets" cited in 10:2 are not the same as that in Lev 25:9, nor are they actually mentioned by name in the festival texts of the Holiness code (Lev 23:24; cf. Num 29:1). They are essentially for assembly. Use of one trumpet indicates that only leaders need assemble; use of both indicates that all must come. Distinct from the call to assembly are the "alarms" which these trumpets sound. The use of this word suggests a background in time of war (made explicit in 10:9). The primary interest at this point in the story is to indicate that the alarm is a command to set forth on the journey (10:5-6). For the priestly writers in Numbers these "trumpets" are indeed the festal musical instruments and can be used on a wider range of occasions than the festival texts themselves might suggest (10:10). Their use on these other occasions — war and cult (which for priestly writers are closely related) — serves to bring Israel to God's mind (10:9 and 10).

The march begins nineteen days after the census (10:11; 1:1). The order of the march corresponds with the order of encampment in 2:1-34. Placing the Levites in central positions helps to preserve the sense that God is at the center, among his people, as the symbolism of 2:1-34 makes clear. Giving a distinct position to the Kohathites helps to emphasize their uniquely weighty responsibilities, as indicated in 4:4-20. The tribal leaders on the march are those who assist Moses and Aaron with the census (1:5-15).

This highly stylized and schematic picture of the way the journey begins is built on a shorter and possibly fragmentary account from the early narrative tradition (10:29-36). Moses' father-in-law is here remembered as Hobab (contrast Jethro in Exod 3:1; 4:18; 18:1). These variants are probably indicative of diversity in the tradition. Hobab apparently belongs to the Kenites (Judg 4:11), early allies of Israel (Judg 5:24). The brief story here (10:29-32), in which Hobab is seemingly persuaded to continue the journey, helps to explain this close association. The tent-dwelling Kenites have an expertise which Moses values (v. 31). That Hobab should act as advisor about places to encamp contrasts with the priestly stress on divine advice (9:15-23).

The position of the ark at the head of the Israelite column (10:33) is another point of contrast. The cloud in this story is over Israel (v. 34). The ark was a sacred box which, in deuteronomistic thought, contained the law tablets. The account of the construction of the ark in the early narrative has been supplanted by the priestly version in Exod 25:10-22. A number of features in this early story make the people look like an army on the march. Earliest tradition saw the ark as signifying Yahweh's presence in time of war, and it might well be carried into battle (cf., e.g., 1 Sam 4:5-9). Both the poetic fragments (vv. 35 and 36) have associations with war. The first appears to envisage Yahweh as enthroned upon or above the ark and is a prayer for his enemies to be vanquished. The second is obscure, but in the word rendered "thousand" there is probably reference, not to families but to Yahweh's armies (Davies 1995: 98).

The Journey through Transjordan (20:14–21:35)

The account of the detour around Edom and through Transjordan depends primarily on traditions from the early narrative (20:14-21; 21:10-35), but it incorporates an isolated account of victory over the king of the southern city Arad (21:1-3). The priestly writer is content simply to insert an account of the death of Aaron and the investiture of Eleazar as his successor (20:22-29).

Moses addresses the king of Edom as "brother" (20:14) because of the ancestor traditions in Genesis which identify Esau (Jacob's twin brother) as father of the Edomites. Though the stories celebrate the supremacy of Jacob/Israel the younger twin, as foretold in the birth oracle (Gen 25:23), there is an ultimate reconciliation (Gen 33:1-17). Moses has no wish to antagonize or in any way threaten a "brother" (cf. Deut 23:7-8).

Moses assumes that Edom will know of Israel's experiences (20:14-16). The tradition of angelic leadership out of Egypt, which he cites in v. 16, is preserved in parts of the early narrative (Exod 14:19; 23:23). The conviction that the exodus was an escape from oppression is attested here (20:15), a central element in both narrative (e.g., Exod 5:1–6:1) and legal sources (e.g., Exod 22:21; 23:9). The King's Highway was the main north-south route through Transjordan, and Moses promises to use it merely as a means of passage through Edomite territory.

The request seems reasonable, and the reader may be surprised that Edom is suspicious, hostile, and unyielding (20:18-21). As the oracles of Balaam will make clear (Numbers 22–24), Israel is widely feared as a potentially powerful people. Moses acquiesces because of the brotherly ties which bind Israel and Edom and because Edomite territory, unlike other Transjordanian areas to the north, is not part of Israel's settled land.

The location of Mt. Hor (20:22) is unknown, but the priestly writer, in accordance with the story of rebellion in vv. 1-13, must give an account of the death of Aaron. It must take place before Israelite land is reached; hence this site somewhere on the borders of Edom.

Eleazar, the third son of Aaron, had not been implicated in the sin of Nadab and Abihu (Lev 10:1-7), so he is the appropriate successor. The priestly writer does not wish to exonerate Aaron for the sins associated with him in tradition (Exod 32:1-6), and the rebellion which leads to his exclusion from the land is frankly acknowledged (Num 20:1-13). In some ways the priestly account mirrors the experience of exiled priests in the sixth century BC. The writer acknowledges the justice of their exile but affirms very strongly the authenticity of the religion they represent through his stress on the Aaronic order instituted by God at Sinai.

The short account of a victory at Hormah (21:1-3) belongs to the early narrative but stands in some tension with its dominant story line. It suggests perhaps a successful incursion from the south, and in remembering Hormah as a place of victory it deviates from the main plot in which Hormah was a place of defeat which leads to the need for a detour through Transjordan (14:39-45). Arad was an important city on the southern boundaries of the land, and "the way of Atharim" is presumably to be located in that region.

The itinerary (21:10-20) comes from the early narrative. The water courses Zered and Arnon can easily be identified, but the place names with less certainty. The intention is clear, however — to indicate a route which takes Israel well to the south of the Dead Sea (avoiding Edom) and then northward through Transjordan to Pisgah, which must clearly be located to the north of the Dead Sea, opposite Jericho. In addition to avoiding the Edomites, the Israelites keep clear of Moabite territory, the writer identifying the Arnon as Moab's northern boundary (v. 13). The inclusion of poetic fragments is characteristic of the early narrative.

The first of these (21:14) is said to come from "the Book of the Wars of Yahweh." There are various difficulties for translators here, and the text is too slight to judge with certainty of what kind it is. Is it simply indicating boundaries or is it a celebratory song? "The Book of the Wars of Yahweh" appears to contain material of the latter type. If v. 14 contains such a song, it may commemorate victories in the region to the north of Moab. Ar was clearly a Moabite town of some importance (v. 28), but its capture or defeat is not necessarily implied.

"The Song of the Well" (21:17-18) is another ancient fragment. It evidently reflects the experience of peoples living on the margins of the desert. It may celebrate the successful discovery of water, or be a text for use in the search for this vital resource. Reference to the scepter may indicate royal rites as part of procedures and observances at potential or discovered water sources.

The early narrators go on to record victories and settlement in the territory to the north of Moab and to the east of the Jordan River (21:21-35). Sihon is the monarch of a small Amorite kingdom. Amorites could be found elsewhere, and the word can sometimes be used of Canaanites in general. Moses' request (v. 22), like that made to the king of Edom (20:14-19), asks for passage and promises to keep to the King's Highway, avoiding any expense to Sihon and his people. Sihon's refusal, unlike that of the Edomites, leads to a battle, near Jahaz, and a comprehensive victory which secures for Israel all the territory between the Arnon and the Jabbok rivers. The main prize is Heshbon, which Sihon, according to the story, had previously captured from Moab (v. 26).

A more substantial poem is incorporated at this point (21:27-30). Like many such pieces, it is not fully intelligible (for detailed discussion see Davies (1995: 231-34). The allusions to Heshbon clearly explain its inclusion by the narrators. The song calls for the rebuilding of the city and recalls a successful campaign conducted by Sihon its king against Moabite territory, and particularly against Ar, one of its major cities. Moab is evidently the target of the singer's mockery (such texts are sometimes called taunt songs), and the song highlights the destruction, slavery, and diminution suffered.

If it is correct to see taunts and mockery in the song (and in other such biblical texts), then the apparent delight in human suffering and the effects of war is distasteful, to say the least. The songs were themselves a product of precisely such suffering, often at the hands of those whose downfall is now celebrated. The texts are a reminder of the vicious cycles of violence and revenge that greed, oppression, and war generate.

A further episode of military engagement, victory, and settlement occurs in 21:33-35. Bashan must have been still further to the north, somewhere to the east of the Sea of Galilee and in territory subsequently occupied (according to the story) by the Gadites (one of the Israelite tribes). For the narrators this was always part of the land, and so Moses makes no request to pass through. Og, the king of Bashan, is remembered by the deuteronomists as the possessor of an unusually large bed (Deut 3:11). The victories over Sihon and Og became a familiar motif in Israelite hymnody (Pss 135:11; 136:19-20).

The historicity of this journey through Transjordanian territory is very hard to assess. The story presupposes a united Israel under single leadership at a stage when strong historical evidence, inside and outside the Bible, points to much more complex processes of migration and settlement. Israel, in the sense in which the story understands it, probably did not exist prior to the monarchy. The ancient poetic fragments give the historian little to work with, and their content suggests that the early narrators were in the same predicament. The story they told may have various functions. It certainly affirms the legitimacy of settlement and royal rule in parts of Transjordan. The story may also be a means of uniting southern traditions associated with Kadesh and eastern tribal tradition. The effect is to produce a single national epic, a natural and necessary interest from the point of view of kings and their courts.

The Commissioning of Joshua (27:12-23)

The priestly writers add to the story an account of the commissioning of Joshua as the successor to Moses. It is worth considering why they do so at this particular point. The early narrators had brought Israel to the place in Transjordan where Moses was to die, but the Deuteronomists do not set forth the account of his death and the mysterious circumstances of his burial until Deut 34:1-12. Perhaps the priestly writer thought it important that the event should not be far removed from the circumstances that gave rise to it (Num 20:1-13) and that assurances about the succession were available to the reader.

Joshua was already established in early tradition as an assistant (Exod 33:11) and a man of prophetic inspiration (Num 11:18). He is also identified here as a man endowed with "spirit" (divine insight and power) (27:18). The main concerns of the priestly writer, however, here in vv. 12-23, are to stress once again the reason for Moses' exclusion from the land (vv. 12-14) (cf. the account of Aaron's death in 20:22-29) and to bring the Mosaic succession within the orbit of priestly order (27:15-23).

The reason for God's refusal to allow Moses to cross the Jordan is found in the story of Num 20:1-13. As in the case of Aaron, the failure of Moses was not an embarrassment for the priests of the exile. It helped to show that those who had been excluded from the land, as they themselves had, could still be recipients and agents of an authentic religious order.

Joshua's task as leader is depicted with the help of images from pastoral husbandry. The Deuteronomistic stress on Joshua as an aggressive man of war is here modulated into a picture of him as a shepherd, offering guidance and protection (v. 17). This corresponds well with the circumstances of the Jewish community under Persian rule in postexilic times. The Jewish priestly leadership has no ambition to lead or encourage a war of liberation or conquest. Their task is to care for the community through observance of the cult.

Eleazar, as chief representative of the priestly order, is drawn into the rites of commissioning (27:19). It is important to stress that Joshua's shepherding is undertaken under the direction of Eleazar's sacred oracle (the Urim) (v. 21). It seems likely that eventually the Urim (and Thummim) had little more than symbolic significance. In Exod 28:30 they are decorative elements in the high-priestly vestments, though we should not assume that a functional role had ceased altogether in early postexilic times (Ezra 2:63). In earlier tradition they are clearly means (perhaps stones for throwing) by which consultations with God can be made (Deut 33:8; 1 Sam 14:41-42).

The laying on of hands in this passage (27:18, 23) evidently confers Mosaic authority on Joshua as the man commissioned to take Moses' place (v. 20).

Settlements in Transjordan (32:1-42)

The literary evidence suggests that an early story of this event has been overlaid with minor priestly accretions. The priestly elements are notes to the effect that Eleazar is consulted along with Moses (vv. 2, 28), and that Israel is structured as a congregation with tribal leaders (vv. 2, 4). They also reflect a knowledge of the priestly account of the spies and the forty years of wandering (vv. 12, 13).

The land of Jazer and Gilead (32:1) is situated to the east of the Jordan and consists of the land captured in the battles of 21:21-35. Its suitability as grazing ground for cattle impresses Gad and Reuben, and they note nine places of settlement in particular which attract them (v. 3). Most of these names reappear in what appears to be an independent and larger list of Transjordanian settlements, incorporated by the early narrative in vv. 33-42. If Sebam and Sibmah are identical, then only Nimrah and Beon (v. 3) are absent from the larger list. Evidence from the book of Joshua suggests that Gad's territory lay to the north of the region (Josh 13:24-28) (i.e., to the north of Heshbon). Reuben's area was to the south, from Heshbon down to the Arnon (Josh 13:15-23).

The larger list of settlements (32:33-42) records Transjordanian activity by elements from Manasseh who occupy parts of Og's territory, well to the north and bordering on the Golan to the east of Galilee (Josh 17:1-3). It would appear that while this information was available to the early narrators, they chose not to incorporate it into the texture of the story in 32:1-32. This may reflect the administrative arrangements which obtained when they wrote and under which Manasseh was situated to the west of the Jordan.

Israel's hold on land to the east of the Jordan was variable during the period of the monarchy and at its most extensive during the reigns of David and Solomon. The settlements envisaged here are more modest. They nevertheless affirm a significant presence there.

At the same time, the fact that Moses himself does not order the settlement and needs to be persuaded by Gad and Reuben is a peculiarity that deserves explanation. If it is correct, as currently held by some, that Israel's historical origins lie in the hill country to the west of the Jordan and were a result to a significant degree of migration from the lowlands, then the Transjordanian settlements probably represent a subsequent expansion eastward. The dominant motif in the early narrative epic, a story of a united Israel on the march through Transjordan and entering the land from the east, reverses the historical flow and establishes the Transjordanian tribes as the first settlers. The historical realities about Transjordan (later settlement and harder to hold) might be reflected in the need to persuade Moses.

The Itinerary (33:1-56)

This section reviews the whole journey thus far, from Egypt to the east of the Jordan, opposite Jericho. It includes data from both the early and priestly traditions and is probably to be traced to the priestly editors who gave the book its present form. The journey is perceived as a march, in formation (v. 1), presupposing the priestly processional order in 10:11-28. A number of the place names have not previously occurred, but the editors presumably had enough locations within the traditions to enable them to reconstruct their view of the route. The journey had three main components:

- from Egypt to Sinai (vv. 5-15)
- from Sinai to Kadesh (vv. 16-36)
- from Kadesh to the Jordan (vv. 37-49)

The text notes that Moses wrote down the itinerary (33:2); the view that Moses engaged in literary work and was ultimately the author of the Pentateuch emerged strongly in postexilic times. Aaron's age at the time of his death (v. 39) is also additional information (cf. 20:22-29).

A review of progress thus far comes appropriately at this point in the story. The priestly writers were of course well aware of Israel's disaffection in the desert and at some points developed it, as in the story of the manna in Exod 16:1-36, but they retained the sense that the exodus was a triumph of God's grace and power (Exod 14:17) and saw the journey and its route as the successful outcome of God's purpose.

The concluding verses of the chapter (33:50-56) issue a command to expel the inhabitants of Canaan and severe warnings about the religions they practice. There may be an early base to these verses, but the theme is more characteristically Deuteronomistic in its allusions to the exclusion of alien practices and to the stones and images of Canaanite religion (v. 52). Priests of the exilic and postexilic periods shared such concerns (cf., e.g., Lev 26:1). The concept of apportionment of the land by lot (v. 54) is one which might be attributed to the Deuteronomists but which can as readily be associated with the "ideal" perceptions held by the priests (cf. Josh 18:6-7). The word "ancestral" (v. 54, NRSV) is reminiscent of priestly usage in 1:2.

The biblical hostility to religions deemed alien has sometimes been used as a justification for intolerance and cruelty and, on the face of it, sits uneasily with pluralistic worldviews. It is certainly arguable that this hostility has its roots in a resistance to the oppressive power of prevailing religious ideologies and their exploitation by kings and others who wield that power. But if that is the case, the texts ought to function as a stimulus, not to authoritarianism and the abuse of power but to an informed critique of both power and religion, a critique from which faith itself might benefit.

The Boundaries of the Land (34:1-29)

An extensive tract of land is envisaged, stretching from the Egyptian border (34:5) to Lebo-hamath (v. 8), well to the north of Damascus. David's campaign in the north is described in 2 Sam 8:3-8 and his friendly relations with the king of Hamath in 2 Sam 8:9-12. This "ideal" appears to be Deuteronomistic in origin (1 Kgs 8:65), but it raised no problems for the priestly editors.

The western boundary is the Mediterranean coast (34:6). The eastern boundary appears to lie somewhere to the east of the Sea of Galilee and then becomes the Jordan and the Dead Sea (vv. 10-12). There are large areas to the north and east here which Israel rarely, if ever, controlled. Since the terms of the story assume that the Transjordanian tribes are already settled, the allotment of land will effectively occur only in land to the west of the Jordan (vv. 13-15). The narrator locates himself to the west of Jericho (v. 15) and therefore perhaps at the royal court in Jerusalem.

Another list of tribal leaders is required to assist Joshua and Eleazar in conducting the apportioning of the land. It is obvious that of those who conducted the reconnaissance of the land (13:1-16) only Caleb (representing Judah) will have survived to assist, and he is cited first. The ordering of the rest, with Gad, Reuben, and Levi (the priestly tribe) excluded, follows a new listing pattern. The southernmost tribes (Judah, Simeon, and Benjamin) come first, followed by Dan in the far north, then those in the central hill country (Ephraim and Manasseh), and finally the Galilean tribes (vv. 16-29).

The struggle for land continues to be a problematic, and sometimes deeply divisive, issue. There are biblical "ideals" about the extent of the land, sometimes expressed with a degree of precision, as in this chapter. It has to be said that rarely, if ever, were these ideals realized in biblical times, while a major theme of the Deuteronomistic history is that land can be lost as well as gained. Insofar as biblical land signifies access to vital resources and human well-being (a land "flowing with milk and honey"), it represents a vital and legitimate human aspiration (for substantial discussion see Brueggemann 1977). Insofar as it becomes associated too strongly with sovereignty, power, and exclusion of others, its symbolism remains deeply problematic.

Disaffection Stories (11:1–14:45; 16:1–17:13; 20:1-13; 21:4-9; 25:1-18)

The tradition of Israel's disaffection during the journey is well established in both early narrative and priestly traditions. It is also present in the earlier phases of the journey recorded in the book of Exodus (e.g., Exod 14:11-12; 15:24; 16:2-3; 17:2-3; 32:1). The early elements can usually be identified by their depiction of Israel as "the people" or simply "Israel"; the priestly writers invariably deploy the word "congregation."

The early narratives of this kind have a variety of functions. Some exhibit etiological interests, providing explanations for place names on the journey (11:3, 35). This follows a pattern already established in the story in Exod 15:23; 17:7. It seems likely that these explanations are secondary, presupposing the disaffection motif; they are sophisticated and literary, and the place names could as well lend themselves to other interpretations. The interest in disaffection as apostasy (25:1-5) is reminiscent of Exod 32:1-35, but it is too occasional to be the traditional core of the motif.

An issue more central to the stories is the legitimacy of the journey itself. Elements among the people look back regretfully to the comforts and securities of Egypt (11:4-6; 21:5) and even plan to return there (14:4). The leadership provided by Moses is thus a matter of serious concern (16:13-14). Not surprisingly, this prompts questions about the demands of the project (11:10-15), which in turn provide a basis for stories dealing with issues of a more general nature — the validity of prophecy (11:24-30) and the uniqueness of Mosaic authority (12:1-16).

There are biblical traditions which view the wilderness experience in positive terms (Hos 2:14; Jer 2:2), while Psalm 105 focuses on the period entirely as one of gracious provision. What prompted the belief that it was also a period of rebellion (reflected in Psalms 78; 106) is debatable. The motif certainly provides a means of explaining Israel's long detour and entry into the land from the east. But there is still the question — why explain the detour in terms of disaffection? There must have been other less negative ways of accounting for the route taken. The critique of Israel embodied in the motif probably reflects the work of the prophets, Israel's earliest and greatest critics. If we can indeed attribute the latest elements in the early narrative to the time of Hezekiah, the collapse of the Northern Kingdom and its incorporation into the Assyrian Empire (721 BC) may have contributed to the picture of Israel as persistently rebellious. The specific interest in returning to Egypt in the handling of the motif may mirror criticism of pro-Egyptian policy in Judah (cf., e.g., Isa 30:1-7; 31:1-3), a further example, as some might have seen it, of the same rebellious tendency.

Priestly interest in the motif tends to consist of accretions to the existing tradition. The story of water from the rock (20:1-13) reworks the early tradition now found in Exod 17:1-17. The priestly writers wish to stress failure to enter the land as the fruit of faithlessness (14:26-38; 20:12). They also employ "opposition to Moses" in earlier tradition as a means for legitimating priestly order (16:1–17:13; 25:10-13). It proved useful as a tool for pressing their essential distinction between priests, the sons of Aaron, and the rest of the Levites.

Fire at Taberah (11:1-3)

The story of complaints at Taberah reveals very clearly the simple structure of the disaffection stories in the early narrative as they appear in Numbers. Disaffection, hostile divine intervention, intercession, and divine restraint are the four essential elements. The stories in Numbers are less sympathetic to the people insofar as there is no preliminary account of their predicament (contrast Exod 15:22-23; 17:1) and in that Yahweh's hostility is more immediate and destructive. The divine fire at the camp's perimeters is reminiscent of the divine fire in the prophetic stories associated with Elisha (2 Kgs 1:10, 12, 14). The etiology (11:3) is a scholarly note appended by the narrators. The place name does not generate the story. Taberah could have been understood as a place where fire consumed Israel's enemies. It is the existence of the disaffection motif which prompts the thought that Taberah must have been a place where a tragic outcome of disaffection was experienced.

Quails (11:4-35)

This story is complex. The familiar elements of desert disaffection stories are present, but particular features of that tradition are much expanded in the interests of new motifs which are of special concern to the early narrative. A basic story can be detected in 11:4-6, 31-35. It tells of complaints about the monotonies of wilderness food and of a divine response which turns out to be an act of judgment. There is also the familiar scholarly note which interprets the place name Kibroth-hattaavah in terms of disaffection. It would appear from Ps 105:40 that desert quails, at least in cultic circles, were not always thought of negatively (though they are in Ps 78:30-31). The power of the disaffection motif to transform a tradition is thus very evident. For the priestly writer, whose account of desert provision dominates in Exod 16:1-36, quails, along with the manna, are an earlier gracious response to need. The quails and manna constitute respectively the "meat" and the "bread" which Yahweh supplies (Exod 16:12 and 13).

The story also contains a scholarly note about the appearance of manna and the ways in which it was collected and used (11:7-9) (cf. similar notes in Exod 16:14, 31). Manna is usually associated with insect excretions found on the tamarisk tree. The quails tradition also reflects a familiarity with a food which might occasionally become available in desert places.

The complexity of the story arises, however, from the use of the basic tradition of wilderness disaffection in the interests of an exploration of the question of leadership in the community. Whereas Moses might have been expected to intercede with Yahweh (as in 11:2), he here delivers an extended protestation about the difficulties of leadership (vv. 10-15). The themes resemble an issue already addressed in Exod 18:13-27, where the problem is the weight of judicial decision making which burdens Moses. The solution there is the appointment of able, God-fearing men to assist. Here the problem is of a more general kind — the pressure of leading and providing for a disaffected people, who appear to have lost faith in the journey and its goal. At the heart of Moses' complaint is the fact that Yahweh, not he, has conceived and given birth to this people; the burden of motherly provision, a notable metaphor, should therefore be with Yahweh (11:12-13).

The protest is accepted, with Yahweh indicating that he will indeed provide — albeit in a way which will make the people regret their discontent (11:18-23). The phrase "consecrate yourselves" (v. 18) (cf. Exod 19:10) suggests that the quail giving is as solemn an act of divine intervention as God's revelation of himself at Sinai. The pressures of leadership in general are to be shared with seventy elders (11:16). Leadership is clearly characterized by spirit endowments (v. 17) which enable the recipients to function as prophets (vv. 24-25).

A further episode involving Eldad and Medad (11:26-30) authenticates prophecy at large, and not simply the authorized prophecy of temple and court. In point of fact Eldad and Medad are among the seventy ("registered" [v. 26]), but for some unspecified reason they are not present with the rest at the external tent of meeting (cf. Exod 33:7-11). The authenticity of prophecies in places other than temple and court is thereby affirmed. The aspiration of Moses that all should be prophets (v. 29) goes further still; the freedom of the divine spirit means that prophets are not necessarily "registered" or officially authorized.

It is of interest to speculate why it was felt important to engage in this particular discussion. As court writers from Jerusalem the early narrators would naturally associate spirit endowment with the charisma of kings, and particularly with that of the Davidic dynasty. It may be the case that traditions of this kind legitimize the involvement of the prophets in affairs of state. If we can trace the early narrative to the time of Hezekiah, it is reasonable to associate this interest with a much increased respect for northern prophetic tradition in the wake of the fall of Samaria (721 BC). The prophecies of Hosea, the stories about Elijah and Elisha, and perhaps the Elohistic parts of the Pentateuch are all testimony to a southern seal of approval for northern Yahwism at about this period.

The text's critique of the craving for meat is also of interest. In a context in which frequent meat consumption was familiar only in courts, temples, and the homes of the wealthy generally (see, e.g., Coote and Ord 1991: 57-66), the description of the instigators of this particular example of disaffection as the "rabble" (11:4, NRSV) is inherently ambiguous. Is the narrator critical of envy and unrest among the poor or of the indulgence of the rich? If his work can be tracked to a period of social reform such as the reign of Hezekiah appears to have been, then the rich may have been the objects of his attack. His sympathy in this episode for the stance of the prophets, even of those not authorized, is suggestive in the same way.

Miriam and Aaron (12:1-16)

The story of Miriam's "leprosy" is another vehicle for the consideration of questions concerning authority and leadership. That this is also part of the early narrative is suggested by the absence of any priestly characteristics for Aaron and by a tent of meeting located outside the camp (12:4). There are some indications that here, as in 11:4-35, older tradition has been developed in the interests of these questions about authority and leadership. A curious feature of the story is that although Aaron is implicated in the criticism of Moses and is said to be one of the objects of Yahweh's anger (12:1-9), he escapes any unpleasant consequences and is depicted as intercessor on Miriam's behalf (vv. 10-12). We may therefore suspect an older tradition in which Miriam alone was the critic and in which the point at issue was Moses' choice of a Cushite wife (v. 1). The expansion of the tradition implicated Aaron and focused on the question of the uniqueness of Moses as divine spokesman (v. 2).

Miriam's place in ancient Israelite history cannot now be determined, but her importance as an ancient leader, comparable to Deborah (Judg 5:1), is suggested by the old tradition preserved in Exod 15:19-21. Cushites were customarily people from Egypt, and since the name Moses is itself Egyptian in form, there may well be ancient and accurate tradition here about his origins and marriage. The hostility of Miriam may also have historical roots.

The main interest of the narrators, however, is the question of the uniqueness of Moses as a divine spokesman. Aaron is drawn in as critic in order to dramatize the absolute authority attaching to the words of Moses. It must be understood that although seventy elders are endowed with Mosaic spirit (11:25) and although Moses wishes that all the Israelites were prophets (11:29), his own status as one with privileged access to Yahweh and his will is unique and not to be challenged. It may be that in their day the early narrators thought of the king as embodying Mosaic authority, but late in preexilic Judah, and under the influence of the Deuteronomists, Mosaic authority came to be located independently, in written laws and reform programs. The work of the scribes who produced the early narrative here may well have fostered that process. Moses, after all, was a humble man who did not seek dignity or homage (12:3).

The pillar of cloud which marks the divine appearance (12:5) recalls the protective divine presence at the Sea of Reeds (Exod 14:19). The reference to it here clearly heightens a sense of the importance of the occasion and of the revelations which are to come. These are the divine words in 12:6-8. Their main aim is to draw a clear distinction between the inspiration of the prophets and the authority of Moses. Prophetic words, like other forms of divine speech, are *mediated.* They may appear more spontaneous than, for example, the priestly oracle, but in reality they are communicated through "visions" and "dreams." Nor are they wholly unambiguous. There may be something obscure or elusive in the words of prophets (hence the "riddles" in v. 8). Moses, by contrast, enjoys *immediate,* "face-to-face" access to the presence of Yahweh, which clearly gives a priority to the words he speaks. A prophetic inspiration which challenges or contradicts his words must be deemed suspect.

The belief that God is visible to human eyes is affirmed elsewhere in the early narrative (Exod 24:10). For Jacob this is a "face-to-face encounter" (Gen 32:30), but not apparently for Moses in Exod 33:20-23. Here, however, Moses shares the privilege of Jacob (v. 8). The encounter "face-to-face" is a metaphor for the clarity and finality of God's message to Moses.

It is important to note the terms in which Moses is described. He is "my servant," and also "entrusted with all my house" (12:7). Both phrases aptly describe the status and role of the king as understood in preexilic Judah. The probability is that the concern here is not so much to legitimize the king — that would need to be more explicit — but to establish Mosaic tradition as the final and decisive authority in the life of the people, a task effectively carried through by the Deuteronomists. Moses is the ultimate "servant," whose authority and message insure the well-being of the community.

The "leprous" condition which afflicts Miriam (12:10) could be one of a variety of skin complaints. Laws about these conditions are preserved in Lev 13:1–14:57. Aaron's plea for mercy, followed by the intercession of Moses, calls forth a curious divine response (12:14). To spit in someone's face is clearly an expression of utmost contempt. It is endured, along with removal of the sandal, by the man who refuses to marry his dead brother's wife (Deut 25:9), in accordance with custom. The circumstances under which a father might treat a daughter in this way, and exclude her, can only be guessed at. Yahweh's reference to such a practice could be read in different ways. Perhaps his intention is to stress the gravity of the offense; she is the object of contempt and suffers withdrawal of family privilege and protection for a period. Perhaps the response is to be understood as gracious. A disowned daughter would suffer only seven days' exclusion; Yahweh will demand no more.

It may reasonably be assumed that with her return to the camp Miriam is healed of the condition. Certainly the priestly editors of Numbers would have made that assumption. While the history of the tradition (as previously suggested) may offer some explanation for Aaron's escape from the consequences of his offense, this aspect of the story remains unsatisfactory. Later traditionists do not seem to see the problem, let alone offer answers. In Mic 6:4 Moses, Aaron, and Miriam stand together as founders of Israelite faith. Pentateuchal tradition, for its part, finds fault with all three (cf. also Exod 32:1-6; Num 20:1-13). Moses nevertheless becomes the great lawgiver, and Aaron the founding father of a privileged priesthood. Only Miriam remains in relative obscurity and without a major impact on the tradition.

Reconnaissance of the Land (13:1–14:45)

This long and much amplified tradition is difficult to analyze in detail, but there appears to be:

- part of the early narrative telling of a report by the spies in which only Caleb speaks favorably, which provokes disaffection, a change of plan, and ultimately an abortive attack from the south (13:17-20, 22-24, 27-30, 33; 14:3-4, 25, 39-45)
- some expansion (14:13-24), possibly Deuteronomistic, which stresses the role of Moses as effective intercessor (cf. Exod 32:7-14)
- a major priestly revision which lists the spies, includes Joshua along with Caleb as a faithful spy, develops the disaffection, depicts Moses and Aaron as pleading with the rebellious, and makes it clear that the faithless spies and the whole of the rebellious generation will not enter the land (13:1-16, 21, 25-26, 31-32; 14:1-2, 5-12, 26-38)

The intentions of the early narrative are influenced by a need to account for the failure to invade from the south (the obvious direction) and to affirm a tradition of conquest across the Jordan from the east. The Deuteronomists had a particular interest in Moses as the great intercessor and mediator between God and the people (cf., e.g., Deut 4:9-24; 9:8-21). The priestly interest in lists of tribal representatives is familiar (cf., e.g., 1:5-16; 26:5-51), and there is a particular concern to establish this incident as the great watershed between one generation and the next. It may be that the priests of the early postexilic period saw parallels between this rebellion at Kadesh and the circumstances of the exile. In both instances access to the land was at stake, and they, like the new generation in the wilderness, were the nucleus of God's future.

The leaders listed as spies in 13:4-15 are not the same as those who undertake the census in 1:5-16. The background and origins of the names are as difficult to establish as in the other priestly lists. The order in which the tribes are listed is again distinct. Like other priestly lists, it ignores Levi and instead of Joseph uses the names of his sons Ephraim and Manasseh, thereby creating twelve tribes. A principle of ordering is suggested by the fact that the sons born to Jacob's wives Leah and Rachel are listed first, and then the four born to the slaves Bilhah and Zilpah. It seems likely that the name "Hoshea son of Nun" attracted the attention of the priestly scribes and led them to the identification with Joshua (13:16).

The mission the spies are to undertake, as conceived in the early narrative, covers the southern desert (the Negeb) and unspecified parts of the hill country further north (13:17). The nature of the land and the strength of its occupants are the key elements in the brief (vv. 18-20). The arrival at Hebron (v. 22), and the fruit gathering nearby at Wadi Eshcol constitute a fulfillment of the task, at least with respect to the Negeb. The majority report carries a mixed message. The land is fruitful and eminently desirable (13:27), but the towns are large and heavily fortified, and defended by the physically intimidating Anakites (13:28). Caleb's minority view is that these are not insuperable objections (13:30) and that an invasion should begin immediately. In tradition Hebron becomes the location which Caleb inherits (Josh 14:6-15).

This part of the story has been amplified with various scholarly notes about the building of Hebron (13:22), the inhabitants of the land (v. 29), and the connection between Anak and the legendary Nephilim (v. 33; cf. Gen 6:1-4). Priestly amplifications suggest that the mission of the spies covered the whole land (13:21) — Lebo-hamath is in the far north — and remind the reader about the location of the congregation at Kadesh in the wilderness of Paran (vv. 25-26). The amplifications also accentuate the faithlessness of most of the spies; they appear to change their view of the land, which has now become "one that devours its inhabitants" (vv. 31-32).

The account of the community's complaint is typical of the disaffection stories at large. The priestly writers make it clear that this is a cry of the congregation against both Moses and Aaron (14:1-2). The validity of the whole enterprise is called into question (v. 2). The anxiety about death by the sword (v. 3) reflects the majority report, and is probably an early element in the story, along with the discontented talk about a return to Egypt (v. 4).

The further attempt on the part of Caleb and Joshua to bring the community to its senses (14:5-12) is essentially priestly. Since the faithless generation will not enter the land, Joshua, as one of the spies, must have aligned himself with Caleb's view. The prostration of Moses and Aaron at such crises of discontent (v. 5) is suggestive of desperate intercession, as indicated in Num 16:22. Appearances of divine glory (14:10) are also a feature of such times (Exod 16:10; Num 16:19; 20:6). This shining light, indicative of splendor and royal power, is essentially the means by which the invisible God can be discerned and his presence known.

The protestations of Caleb and Joshua are directed in the first instance at disparagements of the land (14:7 as in 13:32). In their judgment it embodies the best, since it "flows with milk and honey." This turn of phrase is rooted in the older traditions (e.g., Exod 3:8; Num 16:13). It is reminiscent of the "curds and honey" of which Isaiah speaks (Isa 7:15), and which may carry similar overtones of well-being. The phraseology of 14:9 is unusual, but the vulnerability of the inhabitants, of which it speaks, is clear to see.

Yahweh's plan to disinherit the people is first made clear in 14:12. Much of what follows in 14:13-19 carries echoes of the discussion which ensued from a previous act of apostasy — the affair of the calf image (Exod 32:7-14). Common motifs are the divine proposal to make a new nation from the descendants of Moses and the fears, voiced by Moses, that Yahweh's reputation among the Egyptians will be fatally compromised. The celebration of Yahweh as a God of patience and forgiveness (14:18) reiterates themes from Exod 34:6-7. It also took root in liturgical sources (e.g., Ps 103:8-14). The sense that divine judgment against the guilty extends to several generations reflects a theme in the Decalogue (Exod 20:5; Deut 5:9). That the divine love is stronger and more extensive in its scope should not be forgotten (Exod 20:6; Deut 5:10)

It is customary to think of Moses as the divine leader and mouthpiece, but his role on Israel's behalf, as powerful intercessor and savior of the people, is of comparable significance. It culminates in the Deuteronomistic view that his exclusion from the land was vicarious, something endured on Israel's behalf, and that it was connected with this occasion at Kadesh (Deut 1:37; cf. Deut 3:26; 4:21).

Yahweh does relent to the extent that faithful Caleb will enter the land and that disinheritance will be confined to the rebellious generation (14:20-24). The prospect of ongoing judgment to a fourth generation, or of a new beginning excluding all but the descendants of Moses, is averted. The motif of the whole earth filled with divine glory seems to have a cultic background; it is strongly reminiscent of the song of the heavenly beings in Isa 6:3, which sets the scene for the prophet's call in the temple.

To enable the emergence of a new generation a return to the wilderness is necessary, and a much prolonged journey. This is apparently the point of 14:25 (cf. Deut 1:40), an important link with the traditions of a conquest from the east. It is curious, therefore, that the reason given relates to the presence of Amalekites and Canaanites in the valleys. It is reasonable to assume that these are the valleys of the hill country where Amalekites and Canaanites reside (14:43, 45). Perhaps the linking of traditions of advance from south and east had been established before disaffection was identified as the major cause.

The priestly writers offer their own account of Yahweh's judgment upon the faithless generation (14:26-35). It stresses the poetic justice of all that will ensue; faithlessness reaps the fruit of what is feared (v. 28). A connection with the census (Num 1:1-47) is established (1:29), and forty years are affirmed as the period of divine displeasure. The faithless spies receive their just deserts at once (14:36-38). It seems likely that priestly thought would have seen parallels between the forty years in the wilderness and the exilic experience in Babylon.

The early narrative records an attempt on the part of the people to evade the prospect of disinheritance (14:39-45). Confident of their ability to effect an invasion from the south into some unspecified part of the hill country, they defy Moses and ignore the absence of the ark but are driven back by the Amalekites and Canaanites. Hormah must be located somewhere near Arad (Num 21:1-3), which implies a total failure to reach even Hebron, let alone the hill country further north. The tradition assumes disaffection — "we have sinned" (14:40) — and looks to be an intensification of the motif.

These two chapters constitute the critical central event in the story of Israel as told in the book of Numbers. Taking all the traditions together, the ordered, unhindered march from the wilderness of Sinai (chs. 1–10), which begins to founder in chs. 11–12, is decisively and disappointingly halted here in the southern desert. Yet failure is never the last word, and the rest of the book recounts the slow and sometimes difficult process of reconstruction and renewed purpose and vision. There is a realism about the larger sweep of the biblical narrative which resists triumphalism on the one hand and despair on the other.

Korah, Dathan, and Abiram (16:1–17:13)

The faithlessness of the people after the exploratory reconnaissance and the misguided attempt to enter the land from the south (Num 13:1–14:45) are not the only disasters which occur at Kadesh. Further rebellions, led by Korah, Dathan, and Abiram, bring about deaths which begin the process of insuring that the wilderness generation, with the exception of Joshua and Caleb, will fail to enter the land.

The story contains an early narrative core (found essentially in 16:12-15, 25-34) which told of the rebellion of the Reubenites, Dathan, and Abiram and of the opening of the earth to swallow them, their families, and their tents. This is the tradition recorded in Deut 11:6.

It has been greatly expanded by substantial priestly accretions, within which at least two levels are discernible. Both extend the scope of the rebellion. The first adds 250 leaders (presumably from different tribes) as rebels. Their protest is about the right to offer incense and is based on the holiness of the whole community (essentially 16:2-7). A test proves their claim to be false and leads to their deaths by fire (16:16-18, 35).

A further level builds in a rebellion of Korah and some Levites who are seeking full priestly rights alongside Aaron and his family (16:8-11). They seem to secure the support of the whole congregation (v. 19). Intercession by Moses and Aaron insures that only the instigators of rebellion die (vv. 20-24), so that the Levites perish along with Dathan and Abiram (v. 32).

The remaining material probably assumes both levels of priestly tradition. The censers of the 250 are to be used as a covering for the altar, but it is clear that the point at issue is that only Aaron and his descendants can offer incense (16:36-40). The story which follows (16:41-50) is a dramatic demonstration of the atoning power of incense, used by the right person (Aaron). The concluding tradition about the twelve staffs (17:1-11) could conceivably belong to the first level. The point at issue seems to reflect, not disputes within the house of Levi, but between Levi and the other tribes, as seemingly is the case with the rebellion of the 250 leaders. But the story can be read as summing up the overall stance of the priestly writers. The staff which blossoms is emphatically Aaron's. It is a vivid reminder that priestly privilege is indeed confined to Levi, but also specifically to Aaron and his descendants, and it constitutes a potent warning to all rebels (17:10).

Speculation about the motivations of the writers might suggest that the early narrators had an interest in explanations for the decline of Reuben, as attested in early poetic texts (cf. Gen 49:3-4; Deut 33:6). The refusal of Dan and Reuben to answer the summons of Moses (16:12) also accentuates the circumstances that necessitated the long, circuitous journey and the death of the wilderness generation. Obedience to authorized leadership (the Davidic king for Hezekiah's scribes) recalls the authority issues raised in Num 11:1–12:16).

The priests had their own agenda in elaborating and developing the tradition. It was important to them to insist that Deuteronomy's belief in the holiness of the whole community did not imply that priestly duties, such as the offering of incense, were open to all. The Deuteronomists, in the context of exile under the Babylonians, had offered a radical view of the future which undermined aspects of priestly privilege. The priests, enjoying the support of the Persians who wished to reestablish local cults, were able to reassert priestly power and prerogative. The insistence on the right to offer incense is part of that program. A subsequent struggle within the priesthood, between Aaronides and other Levites, completed the development of the tradition. This may perhaps be dated to the later years of the sixth century, when the Second Temple had been successfully established under Persian auspices and when there was scope and opportunity for rivalries within the priesthood.

These tensions regarding power and privilege within communities of faith have persisted through the centuries. The notion of a priestly community (Exod 19:6) or its modern variant, the "priesthood of all believers," is an attractively "democratic" perspective, which has frequently come into conflict with pragmatic and/or self-interested concerns about leadership and authority. The tendency to accept without question the view that authorization for specific functions is also the only route to power and influence is a factor which arguably sustains these tensions.

Moses and Aaron (20:1-13)

There is one further act of rebellion at Kadesh before the journey to the land resumes. This is the incident in which Moses and Aaron are found to be seriously at fault, and which culminates in their exclusion from the land. The story is a variant of the tradition preserved by the early narrative in Exod 17:1-7, and emanates essentially from the priestly authors. The "congregation" or the "assembly" defines Israel (20:1, 2, 4, 6, 8, 10, 11, and 12), and the two leaders, as is commonly the case in the priestly narratives of the journey, prostrate themselves as they witness the divine glory (v. 6; cf., e.g., Num 14:5, 10; 16:19, 20, 42, 45). It remains likely nevertheless that elements of the story are variants of the old account in Exod 17:1-7. The tradition of Kadesh as the place of Miriam's death and burial (20:1), elements in v. 3 which speak of the "people" and of a quarrel against Moses alone, and the etiological link with Meribah (v. 13) are the most likely traditional features.

The structural outline of the story is common enough in the disaffection tradition. A situation of deprivation (20:2) leads to complaints (vv. 2-5), which in turn are followed by intercessory prostration and a theophany (v. 6). Divine instructions (vv. 7-8) bring relief (v. 11) but at the cost of the future leadership of Moses and Aaron (vv. 9-12).

The complaints are a typical and familiar challenge to the policy which has brought Israel to Kadesh, a place without grain or fruits — in short, a policy which has failed to deliver in every respect. There are no unfavorable contrasts with the nostalgic and unrealistic memories of life in Egypt (Num 11:5), but there is little doubt that the leadership is deemed to have reneged on its promises.

The most difficult problem with the passage is to determine precisely what the sin of Moses and Aaron is, and some deliberate vagueness or suppression of tradition (considered by Davies 1995: 204-6) is not to be excluded. It seems unlikely that the striking of the rock is wrong. Moses is certainly required to address the rock (20:8), but the command to take the staff and the legitimacy of striking in the earlier tradition (Exod 17:6) make it improbable that blows are the issue. The double blow (20:11) is noted, but had this been problem, it would be reasonable to expect attached critical comment. That the consequences for Moses and Aaron are so severe (v. 12) is an indication of the seriousness of what they have done. The explanation (v. 12) is the best starting point in the search for answers. The sin is a failure of trust and a failure to demonstrate Yahweh's holiness to the congregation.

It is feasible that the speech of Moses in 20:10 implies

that it is his own and Aaron's power, not God's, which will provide the water. But it is also noteworthy that earlier priestly disaffection tradition emphasizes Moses' insistence that the rebellion is not against him (or Aaron), but against God (Exod 16:8). Perhaps it is this which Moses should have pressed in his address. His description of the people as "rebels" (20:10) (i.e., against *his* leadership) rather than murmurers or complainers against *God* may lie at the heart of his failure of faith and of witness to divine holiness.

Priestly explanation for the exclusion of Moses and Aaron from the land has a new dimension. Whereas Deuteronomy is inclined to attribute blame to the people (3:23-29), the priestly writers are content to find fault with the leadership. This may have been prompted by circumstances in their situation. The tradition for which they stood had been preserved among the Babylonian exiles, who had been driven from the land and excluded for sins which were recognized and acknowledged (the sin of Moses and Aaron was a generalized description of the sin of their priestly ancestors). This exclusion did not, however, compromise the authenticity and authority of their program, which is precisely that of Moses and Aaron, whose experience is thereby mirrored in their own.

Fiery Snakes (21:4-9)

This disaffection story has many of the familiar structural characteristics of the tradition — complaints about the hardships of the journey (21:4-5), a divine punishment in the form of poisonous snakes (v. 6), intercession (v. 7), and gracious divine provision to alleviate the situation (vv. 8-9). There is every reason to associate it with the early narrative tradition, there being no clear signs of priestly influence and some affinities with the story of the rebellion of Miriam and Aaron in 12:1-16 (e.g., the verb "spoke against" (21:5; cf. 12:1).

At the heart of the story is an explanation for the origins of Nehushtan, a bronze serpent which apparently stood in the Jerusalem temple (2 Kgs 18:4) and which was probably an important focus for pilgrims seeking healing and health. Its ultimate Canaanite origins are quite likely. The scribe, working perhaps during Hezekiah's reign, is anxious that its Mosaic origins should be acknowledged. Only so could its continuing presence in the temple be justified. The deuteronomistic historian also affirms its Mosaic origins, but he believes that it attracted alien forms of devotion and attributes its removal to Hezekiah.

The story interests the narrator for two reasons. It provides one further example of the rebelliousness which necessitated the protracted journey and a delayed entry into the land. It also gives an interpretation of Nehushtan's origins and a justification for its existence as a cult object.

Baal of Peor (25:1-18)

A further serious act of disaffection takes place in Moabite territory at Shittim, close to the Jordan and within sight of Jericho. The story has received major supplementation from priestly sources (25:6-18) and addresses the question of apostasy, the honoring of deities other than Yahweh. The story of the golden calf (Exod 32:1-35) is the only earlier incident among the wilderness narratives, but the tradition of serious apostasy at this period became well established (Ezek 20:16).

The older tradition, embedded in 25:1-5, is probably from the early narrative. There may be independent elements within it, one witnessing to relations with Moabite women and the service of Moabite gods (vv. 1-2) and the other to a more specific commitment to the Canaanite deity Baal, as worshiped at Peor (vv. 3-5).

The Moabite apostasy arises out of the sexual opportunities which these new contacts provide (cult prostitution does not have to be assumed) and from the attraction of the cultic meals which were integral to the Moabite rites. In the context of the story it can be supposed that these meals provided richer and more varied fare than the Israelites had become accustomed to during the hardships of the journey.

The "yoking" of which the Baal of Peor material speaks suggests some kind of covenantal agreement with the deity. According to Ps 106:28, ancestor cults were an aspect of the apostasy. That Israel should begin to look for support from a fertility god on the borders of the land is at a certain level understandable, but the storyteller clearly sees it as a crass example of faithlessness. The belief that Yahweh himself was a god of rain and storm, essential for fertility, is clearly attested in an ancient text such as Judg 5:4. That the "yoking" was institutional, organized by leaders in the name of the community, is suggested by the killing of the chiefs. Impaling is the fate which overtakes descendants of Saul (2 Sam 21:6, 9). It is for the treatment of the corpse in these circumstances that Deuteronomy legislates in Deut 21:22-23. There is clearly an assumption that such actions appease the wrath of Yahweh, who has been excluded and offended by this new relationship with Baal. Further action is to be taken by the judges against others who are known to have entered into the agreement with Baal (25:5). According to other texts (Deut 4:3; Ps 106:29), and implied perhaps by 25:8-9, a damaging plague ensues.

It is reasonable to expect a new sensitivity to the perils of apostasy in late eighth-century Judah. The compilers of the early narrative were aware of the fall of the Northern Kingdom in 721 BC, and probably also of the construction which prophets such as Hosea had put upon it. The testimony of the historian in 2 Kgs 18:4-6, to the effect that Hezekiah was a religious reformer seeking to establish the exclusive worship of Yahweh, is further evidence that these issues were on the agenda. It was appropriate, therefore, that when the history was compiled, readers would be reminded of how deeply rooted the dangers were, and how serious the consequences.

The hostility of elements in the biblical witness to other religious beliefs and insights continues to be problematic. To those who find a "pluralistic" sensitivity essential, they will be particularly so. How can we be so arrogant as to assume that all religious truth is to be found where we happen to be? Is not such an assumption the antithesis of a proper religious sense of sin and limitedness? For those, on the other hand, who find religious pluralism problematic there is the question of the coercion to which other perspectives are subjected and the savagery which sometimes accompanies it. How can killing be morally justified as a resolution to a religious dispute?

To the extent that Israel experienced the oppressiveness of both Egyptian and Canaanite power, in politics, society, and religion, the desire for a "clean break" and a "new order" is intelligible and a cause for sympathy. There are signs that this desire is deeply rooted in Israel's history, however we construct the details of its circumstances. How such desire can be translated into action, legitimately and morally, remains unresolved and is a question rarely addressed in the texts themselves. It is for this reason that the canonical process, whereby testimony and texts become sacred, needs to be treated with critical caution, even if a commitment to the Scriptures is finally deemed appropriate. Problems of this kind are common to both Testaments.

The priestly supplementation (25:6-18) introduces yet another crisis of apostasy into the tradition, involving in this instance an Israelite and a Midianite woman. The hitherto friendly relations between the two peoples — Jethro, the father-in-law of Moses, was priest of Midian (Exod 18:1) — here begin to turn sour, by way of preparation perhaps for the destructive war of Num 31:1-54. Intermarriage is the issue, and the event is set in the context of a devastating plague which eliminates a further twenty-four thousand of the wilderness generation (25:8-9).

The story serves two main purposes for the priestly writers. The need to draw boundaries around the people of God and to prevent intermarriage was a matter of prime concern to the exiled priests, and Ezra's subsequent policies reflect their point of view (Ezra 10:1-44). Nehemiah apparently shared this exclusive attitude (Neh 13:23-31), and its prevalence in other texts relating to the early postexilic period raises the possibility that this was in part a matter of Persian policy (Ezra 4:3; Neh 13:3). There may have been advantage in supporting religious attitudes which created social stability.

For many readers the exclusivity inherent in this and other such texts will be distasteful and deeply problematic. At one level communities need boundaries in order to discover and define their identities, and this is all the more the case in situations of humiliation, oppression, and alienation, as experienced by exiled peoples. The very survival of such communities may depend upon the boundaries they are able to locate or construct. It is easy to see, on the other hand, that such boundaries can begin to stifle interaction and communication, to engender isolation, and even to foster oppression and cruelty toward others.

The other priestly interest the story serves is to establish that the high-priestly succession is to be traced through Phinehas and his descendants. This was not in itself remarkable since the two elder sons of Aaron had died offering unholy incense (Lev 10:2), and Eleazar the father of Phinehas (Exod 6:23, 25) replaced them as third in line. With the death of Aaron (20:22-29) Eleazar clearly began to function in the same way that his father had done (e.g., 26:1; 27:2; 31:13, 21, 26, 31). The effect of the story in 25:6-13, therefore, is to confirm Phinehas in his priestly role; his zeal is potent evidence of his qualifications for the job, and his reward is a "covenant of peace" with Yahweh (v. 12). This distinctive phrase suggests a permanent divine commitment to the priestly order Phinehas represents and a position of privilege and well-being for the priest and his descendants.

The action of Phinehas is reminiscent, in its effects, of the atoning intervention of Aaron in 16:41-50. There, too, a rampant plague called for decisive priestly action. The weeping of the people (25:6) is to be understood presumably as a response to the deaths recorded in vv. 4-5. It is conceivable that "the tent" (v. 8), an unusual word ("inner room" — RSV), was a part of, or attached to, the tent of meeting, and that the action of the offenders had cultic connotations. In any event, the zeal of Phinehas averts a worse disaster and comes to be widely remembered in later tradition.

It is interesting to note that a variant and probably earlier tradition makes reference only to a plague, which itself was apparently the outcome of the Baal of Peor apostasies recorded here in 25:3-5. If this tradition, preserved in Ps 106:28-29, is assumed to lie behind the story in 25:1-18, the extent of the plague's effects in v. 9 is easier to understand. It is also remarkable that in Ps 106:30 the saving intervention of Phinehas seems to be an act of intercession. In short, the Midianite motif, with the killing of the couple, may be a reinterpretation of the nature of the event.

An additional note identifies the offenders (25:14-15); such notes look to be scholarly accretions to the tradition, but it is difficult to identify the techniques by which the information they contain has been established.

The priestly writers find in these sad events a basis for continuing hostility toward the Midianites and for their subsequent defeat in 31:1-54. They are blamed in 25:16-18, not only for the activities of Zimri and Cozbi but also for the apostasy at Peor, which, according to v. 18, was provoked by Midianite deceit. There is no hint of this in vv. 1-5 themselves, nor in other texts which refer to Baal of Peor, and one can only assume that this development of the tradition was initiated by the priestly writers themselves in pursuit of their interest in the Midianite war (31:1-54) and the issues which emerge from it.

The Story of Balaam (22:1–24:25)

The three chapters containing the story of Balaam are in many ways a unique feature of the Pentateuchal books. They are a largely self-contained piece of tradition, embodying narratives and ancient poems and celebrating Israel's place in the purposes of Yahweh.

The self-contained character of the tradition suggests that it has been drawn in from some other source or setting by a biblical author and used to give further substance to the Transjordanian journey. The author in question would probably be one of the early narrators since traces of priestly influence are entirely lacking and, characteristically, Israel is depicted as "the people" (e.g., 22:3, 41). Substantial parts of the tradition are Elohistic and the deity identified as "God," and this might assist in identifying earlier elements. The priestly writers make no contribution to the tradition except to identify Balaam as one of the casualties in the Midianite war (31:8) (but note the suggestion of Douglas 1993: 216-34 that the story is political satire for early postexilic times). Inclusion of the story here (after 21:35) is appropriate because Balak the hostile king is a Moabite and Israel has now reached the plains of Moab (22:1).

The general aims of the narrators in taking over this older story and deploying it here seem to be to renew faith in Yahweh's commitment to Israel and in his good purpose for the people. The faithlessness exhibited at Kadesh by spies and people alike (Numbers 13–14), and the rebellions and deaths associated with Dathan and Abiram (Numbers 16) and the snakes (Num 21:4-9), belong to the past and have not affected Yahweh's determination to support and sustain his people against enemies. The success achieved against King Og (21:33-35) is confirmed by the frustration of Moabite attempts to undermine Israel and defeat the march toward the land.

It is difficult to know with certainty what ensues in the early narrative. Some have thought the story ends here, but others would see it continuing into the book of Joshua or even as far as the story of David. If we are correct to see the story as a product of court scribes at Jerusalem, whatever earlier elements may be embedded in it, some account of the processes of settlement in the land is likely. Otherwise the story fails to provide a full enough account of present experience. Joshua's farewell address (Josh 23:1-16) and the covenant making at Shechem (Josh 24:1-33) would appropriately round off a work completed during Hezekiah's reign. The bearers of Shechem's traditions came south after the collapse of the Northern Kingdom (721 BC) and were accepted there, as is clear from the elements preserved in Deut 27:1-26. The conclusion of the early narrative may mark this acceptance, though Joshua 23–24 in their present form have clearly been influenced by Deuteronomistic editing.

The Narrative

The introductory material in the Balaam story (22:1-6) sets the scene, indicating clearly the basis of Balak's fear (vv. 2-4) and the plan to involve a diviner capable of invoking a powerful curse on Israel (vv. 5-6). The civilizations of the East were well known for their skills in these arts (cf. Isa 2:6, where some such expertise seems implied). Nonbiblical evidence about Balaam the seer has been found in the Deir 'Alla texts (for a discussion of their importance see Davies 1995: 281-84). Balak has unbounded confidence in the power of Balaam to weaken Israel and to remove the threat that it poses (22:6).

The initial request for assistance is rebuffed (22:7-14). The story affirms that Balaam, though a non-Israelite resident in a distant land, is genuinely in touch with God and has no initial intention of disobeying God's will.

The story is skillfully developed by means of a second embassy, more numerous, more distinguished, and offering bigger rewards (22:15-21). Balaam's resistance to these blandishments remains firm, but he is prepared to consult God again, and on this occasion he is encouraged to go with Balak's officials, on condition that he adheres strictly to God's instructions.

The fable about Balaam's donkey and the angel of Yahweh (22:22-35) may well be an intrusion, introduced perhaps by the early narrators themselves, since "Yahweh" predominates as the divine name. Such an assumption makes it easier to understand why the divine anger, somewhat inconsistently in the light of v. 20, is stirred against Balaam. Nevertheless the tension at this point in the story still needs to be interpreted. Why should the narrators have voluntarily introduced material which they must have known generated a logical unevenness? The answer perhaps is that the episode allows them to insist again on the essential hostility of God to the whole enterprise and to reaffirm that Balaam is allowed to engage in it only on strict conditions, and under strict control. So it is that God's anger is renewed (v. 22) and the controls reaffirmed (v. 35).

The fable of the talking donkey brings ridicule on the head of a foreign diviner. This supposed "expert" in discerning the mind and will of the gods is outperformed in spiritual insight by his donkey! His cruel treatment of the animal, in contrast to its own reasoned response, only accentuates his blindness and folly. The essential elements of the story might have an earlier point of reference which has been applied by the early narrative to the story of Balaam.

The "angel of Yahweh" also appears to Hagar (Gen 16:7), and it is clear here, as there, that the words this messenger utters are Yahweh's. The insistence that Balaam should speak only what he is told to speak (22:35) is reminiscent of the control on Balaam's actions in v. 20. These points are stressed yet again in the conversation between Balaam and Balak when they finally meet (vv. 36-38). The sacrifice of oxen and sheep (v. 40) and the shared meal that presumably ensues are acts of welcome on Balak's part.

The rest of the story consists of the four oracles Balaam eventually delivers (23:7-10; 23:18-24; 24:3-9; 24:15-24); these are connected by repetitive narrative indicating the persistence and increasing frustration experienced by the king.

The narrative moves from Bamoth-baal (22:41), to Pisgah (23:14), and finally to Peor (23:28). These are all high places from which Israel, at least in part, is visible to the two men. The final oracle is delivered, not at Balak's instigation or wish but in a spirit of prophecy about the damage Israel will do to Balak's people. On the three high places altars are built and substantial sacrifices offered (23:1, 17, 29). The intention presumably is to attract God's attention.

Balaam for his part removes himself some distance on the first two occasions, in the hope of meeting Yahweh (23:3, 15). His intentions apparently are to seek some kind of omen (24:1). This would presumably have been the result of divinatory actions or observation. Even then what comes to him is not a mediated sign but a prophetic oracle, the very words of God himself. On the third occasion Balaam abandons omen seeking, looks toward the wilderness, and is seized by the spirit of Yahweh (24:1-2). The point seems to be that he has now learned where to look for and expect the voice of God. He is to be found in the wilderness among his people. Given the unpromising content of Balaam's oracles, it is scarcely surprising that Balak's irritation increases and his anger finally explodes (23:11, 24; 24:10-11). Balaam, for his part, continues to insist on the story's overarching theme — that he can speak only what God commands him to speak (23:3, 12, 26; 24:12-13).

Balaam's performance in this part of the narrative thread is without fault, and it is therefore surprising to see his emergence in subsequent tradition as evil, along with the likes of Cain and Korah (Jude 11; Rev 2:14). The view seems to have developed that he was motivated by financial gain, or that he instigated the eating of food offered to idols in Israel, through his influence over Balak. His blindness in 22:22-35 scarcely warrants this demonization of a figure whose words speak only well of Israel and who obeys God unflinchingly. The tradition may have arisen through associations and assumptions. Balaam was associated with Peor. It was one of the places where sacrifices were offered (23:28), and a place shortly to become a scene of serious apostasy (25:3, 5, 18) on Israel's part. Questionable associations very easily lead to false assumptions.

The Oracles

These texts are fascinating, albeit difficult to interpret. There are indications that they are ancient, though the "scepter" and "rule" of the monarchy seem to be presupposed (24:7, 17, 19). A celebration of David's achievements is quite plausible by way of setting. Most of the difficulties lie in the detail; the overall picture is reasonably clear. A pattern of developing and increasingly precise insight into Israel's place is discernible in each of the oracles.

In the first (23:7-10) Israel is at present isolated, and peripheral in international affairs (v. 9), yet her potential is huge and her destiny desirable (v. 10).

In the second (23:18-24) Yahweh is identified as Israel's king (v. 21), having led the people out of Egypt with irresistible strength (v. 22). The "misfortune" and "trouble" of v. 21 might be read as "iniquity" and "mischief" (REB), or "guilt" and "perversity" (NJB), though the NRSV is probably preferable (Davies 1995: 262); in either event God and his people are united in a common endeavor. Divination against Israel will not succeed (v. 23) (or there is no divination in Israel — REB). Among the nations the people will emerge as a powerful and fearsome predator (v. 24).

In the third (24:3-9) Israel's resources are recognized as plentiful (vv. 5-7a), and the human king who leads will be a man of renown (v. 7b). The predatorial image (vv. 8-9a) is given substance in terms of the fulfillment of the promise to Abram (Gen 12:3) (v. 9b).

In the fourth (24:15-24) the king to come is likened to a star (REB also has comet [for "scepter"]); he will crush the territories and kingdoms to the east of the Jordan (vv. 17-19). In the history of interpretation the "star" (v. 17) has often been read messianically (Davies 1995: 273).

In addition to these main themes there are also revealing points of textual detail. The repeated phrase "uttered his oracle" (23:7, 18; 24:3, 15; NJB, "declaimed his poem") seems to stress the distinctive nature of Balaam's inspiration over against the various divinatory techniques which called for the manipulation of objects and/or the reading of signs. The inspiration of Balaam is not mediated; it is a divine word (the noun is often "proverb") placed directly in Balaam's mouth (23:5, 16) through the agency of the divine spirit (24:2).

The third and fourth oracles seem to stress the uniqueness of this access to God in other ways. Some such concern is intended by the obscure phrase "whose eye is clear" (24:3, 15, NRSV) (or "far-seeing" — NJB; see Davies 1995: 267 for further discussion). Balaam is one who hears divine words, encounters God in visions (24:4, 16), and is endowed with special knowledge (24:16). The encounter is with Shaddai ("Almighty," 24:4, 16) and Elyon ("Most High,"24:16), ancient names for God or manifestations of his being and presence (cf. Gen 14:19, 20; 49:25).

A vital connecting thread in the first two oracles, and throughout the narrative parts of the story, is the stress on the immutability and irresistibility of God's good purpose for his people (23:8, 19-20).

The three concluding oracles (24:20-24) appear to have been added subsequently, but they pose many problems for translators and interpreters (see Davies 1995: 276-81). Following the NRSV, the first (v. 20) predicts or celebrates the fall of Amalek from a position of eminence among the nations to final dissolution and destruction. The second (v. 21) reflects upon the experience of the Kenites, an ancient and enduring people, but one due to suffer dispersion without evident end at the hands of Assyria. The third (vv. 23-24) foresees a check on Assyrian expansionism (Asshur and Eber) at the hands of a fleet and forces to the west. Assyria's ultimate end is also affirmed. If these identifications are correct, the oracles apparently reflect, at least in part, some experience of the Assyrian Empire and may have been worked in by the early narrators from sources known to them.

The militantly aggressive elements in some of the oracles raise pressing questions about the ease with which religion legitimates land acquisition, along with militarism and the cruelties of war. It must be remembered, of course, that access to resources may well be a struggle for those on the margins; slave refugees from Egypt would clearly belong to such groups. It is also true that the historical emergence of Israel in the land of Canaan was probably much less of a military campaign than many of the traditions suggest, with infiltrations into thinly populated areas and with many of its first members already settled. On the other hand, the content of the predatorial images remains and is best confronted and challenged rather than explained away. A sensitivity to processes of religious legitimation is one safeguard; so, too, is a critical (though not necessarily unsympathetic) attitude to the processes by which texts become sacred in communities of faith.

A bigger theme in the story is the prevailing critique of the culture of divination. This is one aspect of a tendency in the Hebrew scriptures, sometimes noted by sociologists, toward the desacralization of religious belief and practice. Some (e.g., Berger 1967: 113-21, supported by Bruce 1996: 9-10) have seen in this tendency a contributing factor to the secularization of the modern Western world. The point at issue in the Balaam texts is not so much the *exclusion* of God from areas of human interest and activity (a working definition of secularization) as *competing claims* to influence within a world which remains pervasively religious. It is true nevertheless that the critical, combative spirit of much biblical religion may have contributed to the questioning, testing frame of mind which has always marked the search for truth and meaning, especially since the Enlightenment. There is nothing necessarily irreligious about such an attitude. It is because the believer affirms dimensions to the divine which lie well beyond human understanding that a critical attitude to religious claims and authority is always appropriate, and a suspicion about the workings of religious legitimation desirable.

Community Law (27:1-11; 30:1-16; 35:9–36:13)

The later sections of the book of Numbers contain a miscellany of laws on such matters as property (27:1-11; 36:1-13), vows (30:1-16), and asylum (35:9-34). The priestly character of the legislation is evident in references to Eleazar and/or the congregation (27:2; 35:24, 25, 26), in the way in which the Korah tradition is assumed (27:3), and in presuppositions about the high priest (35:25, 32) and the jubilee (36:4; cf. Lev 25:1-55). There is also the familiar tendency of Numbers legislation to build on or develop issues already raised in the book of Leviticus. Property law has been addressed in Lev 25:8-55 and again in connection with vows in Lev 27:1-34. Earlier asylum law can be found in Exod 21:13-14 and was also an issue for legislators in Deuteronomy (Deut 19:1-13; cf. Deut 4:41-43). The material on property and vows also provides important insights into the status of women in ancient Israelite society.

Property (27:1-11; 36:1-13)

The tradition that property belonged to a family in perpetuity was ancient, though it was apparently threatened by the power of kings (1 Kgs 21:1-29) and probably also by the commercialization of land and agriculture during the period of the kings. That males would be the inheritors was taken for granted, and this continues to be assumed in the restoration (or perhaps creation) of the jubilee laws (Lev 25:1-55), whereby land sold would return to its original owners in the jubilee year, that is, every fiftieth year. As part of the Holiness code this legislation in its present forms is perhaps exilic.

It is in Num 27:1-11 that the possibility of female inheritance is raised for the first time. The five daughters of Zelophehad, a deceased member of the tribe of Manasseh, have no close male relative to inherit their father's property. Having observed that Zelophehad was not implicated in Korah's conspiracy (v. 3) and that there is therefore no reason why his family should be disadvantaged, they press their case. This is based not so much on new perceptions about the rights of women but on a concern for their father's ancestral name and the well-being of his clan (v. 4). In this respect their case assumes and affirms patriarchal norms, and the solution they seek — to have "a possession" among their father's brothers (v. 4) — might be interpreted simply as a request that they and their land become part of their uncles' families and possessions.

The legitimacy of the case is recognized in Yahweh's response to Moses, and it goes on to make clear that in certain circumstances there would be inheritance by women *in their own right*. The only thing to prevent such inheritance would be the presence of brothers (27:8). A father's name can therefore be vested and preserved in the daughter(s). Inheritance passes to the dead man's brothers only if there are no daughters (v. 9). More remote possibilities are addressed in vv. 10-11, with the "nearest kinsman" (NRSV) as the final recipient.

The conclusion of the book returns to the theme (36:1-13), addressing the wider problem of tribal, as opposed to family, identity. There is anxiety among the heads of the tribe of Manasseh, one of the two Joseph tribes, that the previous ruling in favor of daughters will threaten tribal possessions should the daughters marry into other tribes, taking their inheritance with them. The assumption here is that independent property rights granted to women in the previous judgment are vested in the husband's family when marriage takes place.

Once again Yahweh accepts the validity of the concern (27:5), and a restriction is placed on intermarriage between the various tribes where property complications of this kind are involved. In short, the daughters must marry within the tribe of Manasseh. The aim is to preserve the identity, integrity, and wealth of each distinct tribe. This apparently poses no problems for the women, and they marry cousins (vv. 10-12). This kept their property within the tribe, while Zelophehad's name lives on among his brothers.

It would appear that problems of this kind exercised the priestly writers, and that definitive rulings were required. The serious dislocations, the loss of land and identity, which must have accompanied the exilic experience called for a legislative framework within which social structures could be reestablished and community recreated.

Vows (30:1-16)

A good illustration of what might be entailed in a vow is provided by the story of Jacob at Bethel (Gen 28:18-22). The seriousness of such commitments is reflected in Jephthah's vow (Judg 11:30-31) and its terrible consequence (Judg 11:34-40). The usual content of a vow would probably have been the promise of an offering to God in return for guidance, success of some kind, or answered prayers.

The insistence that vows must be kept under all circumstances was already well established in legal forms. The legislators in Deut 23:21-23 had stressed the importance of a prompt fulfillment of what had been promised, though they also give the impression that the making of vows is not necessary and certainly not obligatory. The priestly writers had already worked on the subject in Lev 27:1-34, dealing in the main with the circumstances under which vows involving persons, animals, or property might be redeemed by money equivalents.

The issue here in Num 30:1-15 is the status of vows made by women. Existing views are reaffirmed in the case of men (vv. 1-2), but vows made by women are affected by their marital status. In two situations a vow can be disallowed by the appropriate male — in the case of an unmarried woman still resident in her father's house (vv. 3-5) and in that of a married woman living with her husband (vv. 6-14). The father or husband must reject the vow at the point when he hears it (vv. 5, 8). In these situations the woman's vow is evidently subject to male approval.

The vows of widowed and divorced women, however, must stand (30:9), and there is the further insistence that if a husband wishes to disallow his wife's vow he must do so at once (vv. 10-15). Failure to disallow at once means that the vows stand and that he must accept ultimate responsibility for them (v 15). It is reasonable to suppose, in view of the stress on "the time that he hears it" in v. 5, that the same applies to a father in relation to vows made by an unmarried daughter.

The concern of the priestly legislators in all this is evidently to protect and preserve the patriarchal social order. Religious commitment and devotion on the part of women can be exercised only within the constraints of that order. From a practical point of view it is true enough that the father and husband were financially responsible in an ultimate sense, and to that extent they needed controls over the activities of their womenfolk. But this is the sort of argument which leaves women in a "no win" situation. It is the legitimacy of patriarchy itself which is at stake. The modern world, whatever its faults, has created some opportunity for women to discover and express their own forms of faith and spirituality.

This legislative material on property and vows provides useful insight into the position of women in the ancient world. Their subordinate status within the prevailing social order is apparent throughout, and must be confronted. At the same time there is an emerging public profile for women in the legislation, which in theory raises the thought of other possibilities, even if these are not as yet appreciated or implemented. As 30:9 makes clear, a woman who has a life outside the prevailing order — though this can rarely have been of much material advantage or benefit to her — is recognized as on a par with a man in respect to her religious commitments.

Asylum (35:9-34)

These regulations (35:9-34) are part of the processes whereby the administration of justice passed from family and tribe to the institutions of the state.

Ancient custom saw murder as an offense against the victim's family and placed responsibility for effecting justice (by the killing of the offender) in the hands of the nearest relative. It is easy to see how such practice would tend to overlook considerations about the wilfullness or otherwise of the deed and generate lasting and destructive blood feuds. Early legislation sought to intervene in such vicious circles by establishing the principle of asylum (Exod 21:13). Initially local sanctuaries functioned in this way (cf. 1 Kgs 1:50), giving space for inquiry, probably under the auspices of priests, as to whether the death was willfully caused or not. If it was found to be deliberate, responsibility for the killing of the murderer would presumably remain with the victim's nearest relative.

The emergence of the monarchy brought with it an interest in "law and order" on a wider scale. Without a "rule of law" within the king's domain the stability of his position and the security of his dynasty were at risk. This must have strengthened the principle of asylum and the necessity of distinguishing between deliberate and unintentional killings. Kings came to see themselves as responsible for righting wrongs in relation to murder and bloodguilt (cf., e.g., 2 Sam 4:11).

The idea that there should be cities as places of asylum is best traced to the centralization of worship under King Josiah and the elimination of local sanctuaries. An alternative, as a place of refuge for those killing unintentionally, was clearly required. The laws in Deuteronomy identified three cities to the east of the Jordan for this purpose (Bezer, Ramoth, and Golan — 4:43), and insisted that three more should be found to the west (19:3). According to Josh 20:7, the cities selected were Kedesh in Galilee, Shechem, and Hebron.

Here in the priestly laws of Num 35:9-34 the question of intent is clearly the starting point (v. 11), and the need for six cities, distributed on both sides of the Jordan (vv. 13-15), is affirmed. Situations which constitute murder are those in which the killer "strikes" (vv. 16, 17, and 18), with whatever weapon or implement. The verb presumably embodies the notion of deliberate assault. In accordance with ancient custom "the avenger of blood" (v. 19, NRSV) (i.e., the nearest relative of the dead person) carries out the sentence of death. Any kind of malicious or premeditated assault is interpreted as deliberate (vv. 21-22) and is therefore to be treated as murder.

Situations which must be reckoned as unintentional are those which are not premeditated or prompted by malice (35:22-23), an example being the flying ax head of Deut 19:5. In these instances the priestly laws insist that the congregation must act as judge and protect the person suspected from the "avenger of blood" (v. 24). In Deut 19:12 "elders" are responsible for surrendering a killer to the avenger of blood, where appropriate, and would presumably be expected to act as representatives of the congregation here in Num 35:24-25.

The new element in the priestly laws is the place given to the office and person of the high priest in the arrangements affecting the slayer and the avenger of blood (35:25b-28). The stipulation effectively "frees" the slayer from confinement in the city of refuge when the high priest dies. It is conceivable that the principle itself is not a priestly innovation; it might once have applied to the rule of kings. It may also have been informed by the sacrificial system, where death in some way "atones" for sin. The holiness of the high priest brings protection against the consequences of defilement caused by the shedding of blood, but only within the confines of the city of refuge. The stipulation is also an element in the process whereby high-priestly theocracy was established as the social and political norm. The rule of the high priest touches all aspects of life, including the administration of justice.

The chapter concludes with the insistence that murder — premeditated, malicious, and intentional killing — can be resolved only by the death of the murderer (35:30-34). The recognition that there must be witnesses (more than one) (v. 30) is a requirement which is also attested in Deut 19:15. Whereas the laws in Deuteronomy go on to deal with the possibility that some witness may be motivated by malice, the priestly laws here proceed to address specifically priestly interests. The possibility of redemption was something to which priestly legislators were alert (cf., e.g., Lev 27:1-33; Num 3:44-51) — after all, it brought resources to the sanctuary — but the seriousness of murder is such that redemption cannot be entertained (35:31). The priests were informed in this attitude by their fundamental belief that the shedding of blood brought defilements to the land which could not be resolved by monetary means (v. 33), but only by further bloodshed, the death of the offender (v. 33). That belief also entailed a theology of the divine presence (v. 34). Since blood above all else signifies the life of God, the shedding of blood is the ultimate insult to his very being.

It has to be acknowledged that the priestly insistence on what would today be called "capital punishment" cannot properly be separated from the whole system of thought which priests taught, on holiness, defilement, blood, sacrifice, and related matters. The origins of animal sacrifice in human history are clouded in obscurity, but if there is any sense at all in which "execution" in the ancient world was a form of "sacrifice" — a recompense to God for a kind of acted blasphemy — then current discussion of penal issues in relation to murder cannot seriously be expected to engage with such material. Other considerations must inform the discussion. The biblical literature in the main is moving beyond such perspectives — the recognition that killing may be unintentional is an illustration of this — but its antiquity as human literature continues to be evident at many points. There is no reason why aspects of the priestly system may not be found informative and helpful, but the selectivity and thinking entailed in such processes of discovery are in significant measure what we as interpreters contribute. To attempt to treat the literature as determinative of belief and action demands a consistency which takes the whole on its own terms.

The recognition that intention is a significant consideration in assessing the morality and culpability of actions is an important indicator of the trajectories which biblical literature sometimes exhibits. There is no overt consideration of negligence as a complicating factor in cases of accidental death, either here in Numbers or in Deuteronomy, but it is addressed in an older law in Exod 21:29-32 (cf. also 21:33-36; 22:5-6). It would appear that death or a fine might be imposed in such circumstances, and certainly the latter in the case of a dead slave.

Concluding Observations

It is important to remember that the themes of the book are elements which constitute a story, and one volume in a much larger story contained in the books which surround it. A key motif in that larger story, and one which has informed various trends in modern theology, is "liberation." Israel's escape from slavery in Egypt (as told in the book of Exodus) has become a crucial paradigm, among others, whereby God's will for his people, and for humanity at large, has been identified and interpreted. The book of Numbers is a reminder that "liberation from" is only one aspect of the story, and that "liberation for or to what?" is an equally important consideration. It tells of the difficulties and setbacks which the journey from slavery to freedom entailed, and it gives insight into the ways in which the community sought to organize its "liberated" life through its laws. To put it another way, the first experience of liberation (from Egypt) was one thing; the challenge to create and sustain a just and participatory community is quite another. Whether the "mixed success" (triumph and disaster) of which the book of Numbers speaks is always to be the human "story" is very much in human hands.

Bibliography. Berger, P. L. 1967, *The Social Reality of Religion,* London: Faber and Faber • Budd, P. J. 1984, *Numbers,* WBC, Waco: Word • Bruce, S. 1996, *Religion in the Modern World: From Cathedrals to Cults,* Oxford: Oxford University • Brueggemann, W. 1977, *The Land: Place as Gift, Promise, and Challenge in Biblical Faith,* London: SPCK • Coats, G. W. 1968, *Rebellion in the Wilderness,* Nashville: Abingdon • Cody, A. 1969, *A History of Old Testament Priesthood,* AnBib 35, Rome: Pontifical Biblical Institute • Coote, R. B. and D. R. Ord. 1991, *In the Beginning: Creation and the Priestly History,* Minneapolis: Fortress • Davies, E. W. 1995, *Numbers,* NCB, London: Marshall Pickering • Douglas, M. 1993, *In the Wilderness: The Doctrine of Defilement in the Book of Numbers,* JSOTSup 158, Sheffield: Sheffield Academic • Jenson, P. P. 1992, *Graded Holiness: A Key to the Priestly Conception of the World,* JSOTSup 106, Sheffield: Sheffield Academic • Levine, B. A. 1993, *Numbers 1–20,* AB, New York: Doubleday • Lohfink, N. 1994, *Theology of the Pentateuch: Themes of the Priestly Narrative and Deuteronomy,* Edinburgh: T&T Clark • Milgrom, J. 1991, *Leviticus 1–16,* AB, New York: Doubleday • Niditch, S. 1993, *War in the Hebrew Bible: A Study in the Ethics of Violence,* Oxford: Oxford University • Sakenfeld, K. D. 1992, "Numbers," in *The Women's Bible Commentary,* London: SPCK , 45-51 • Wenham, G. J. 1997, *Numbers,* Old Testament Guides, Sheffield: Sheffield Academic.

Deuteronomy

John W. Rogerson

INTRODUCTION

Deuteronomy is a speech delivered by Moses to the Israelites in an area north of the Dead Sea and east of the River Jordan, on the eve of the people's crossing of the Jordan to take possession of the land of Canaan. In his speech Moses reviews Israel's recent history as one of disobedience to God's commandments, and he warns the people of what will be required of them when they settle in Canaan. It will be necessary for them to avoid religious contact with the inhabitants of Canaan, they must set up a sanctuary only in the place which God commands and chooses, and they must observe the laws which God commands. These laws occupy chs. 12 to 26 of Deuteronomy, although they are preceded by a statement and exposition of the Ten Commandments in chs. 5 to 11. In ch. 27 Moses and the elders order a ceremony to be held on Mt. Gerizim and Mt. Ebal at which curses are uttered against anyone who breaks any of twelve commandments. Ch. 28 lists the consequences of observing or ignoring God's commandments in terms of blessings and disasters, and in chs. 29 to 30 Moses sets before the assembled people two alternatives: either to obey the commandments, which is to choose life and prosperity, or to ignore them, which is to choose death and disaster. Ch. 31 records the appointment of Joshua to succeed Moses, and the final chapter (34) records Moses' death and burial. This is preceded in chs. 32 and 33 by two long poems entitled the "Song of Moses" and the "Blessing of Moses" (on the individual tribes).

Deuteronomy is thus an elaborate and extended farewell speech by Moses which sets out a blueprint for how Israel is to live as the people of God in the promised land, and it serves as an introduction to the books of Joshua to 2 Kings which relate what happened to the people after the promised land had been occupied.

For some seventeen hundred years Jewish and Christian interpretation of Deuteronomy took for granted that it was indeed a speech of Moses delivered on the eve of the occupation of Canaan. If critical comment was needed, it dealt with apparent contradictions between the laws in Exodus and those in Deuteronomy. For example, the instructions about observing the Passover in Exod 12:1-27 imply that the Passover lamb will be killed locally by heads of families and that the lamb must be roasted. Deut 16:1-8 requires that the Passover be eaten "at the place which the LORD will choose as a dwelling for his name" so that the lambs can be killed at the central sanctuary. In addition, the lamb is to be boiled (NRSV, "cook," at 16:7 obscures this). Traditional Jewish interpretation dealt with these apparent contradictions by distinguishing the "Passover of Egypt" (described in Exodus 12) from the "Passover of the Land" (described in Deuteronomy 16) and maintained that the Hebrew word for "boil" at Deut 16:7 was a general term for any kind of cooking. Another passage in Deuteronomy that called for comment was its version of the Ten Commandments in Deut 5:6-21 as compared with the version in Exod 20:2-17.

The suggestion made in 1805 by W. M. L. de Wette that the lawbook discovered in the temple in 622 BC in the reign of Josiah (see 2 Kgs 22:8) was Deuteronomy or part of it radically changed the interpretation of Deuteronomy. This suggestion was based on the similarity between the insistence in Deuteronomy that sacrifice to God should be offered only at a central sanctuary chosen by God, and Josiah's reform, as described in 2 Kings 22–23, which involved closing down all the sanctuaries in Judah except that in Jerusalem. Josiah also ordered that the Passover be celebrated in Jerusalem (2 Kgs 23:21-23; cf. Deut 16:1-8). It would be possible, of course, to link Deuteronomy with Josiah's reform and also to maintain that it was a speech delivered by the historical Moses. In this scenario Deuteronomy would have been concealed in the temple and would have been long forgotten, only to be discovered during repairs to the temple in the seventh century and then used as the basis for Josiah's reform. However, fundamental to de Wette's argument was the fact that if Moses commanded that there should be only one legitimate sanctuary where sacrifice could be offered to God, no one was aware of this before the time of Josiah. Samuel, for example, offered sacrifices at Mizpah (1 Sam 7:5-9), at a city in the land of Zuph (1 Sam 9:5-15), and at Gilgal (1 Sam. 11:12-15), while Elijah complained that the people had destroyed God's altars while he himself repaired an altar on Mt. Carmel to offer a sacrifice there (1 Kgs 18:30; 19:10).

Research subsequent to de Wette has concluded that Deuteronomy probably began to be composed in the seventh century BC albeit using older material, and that it did not reach its final form until after the exile (i.e., late sixth to early fifth century BC). It has noted that Deuteronomy is dependent on, or implies knowledge of, material elsewhere in the opening books of the Bible. Thus, the résumé of Israel's progress from Mt. Sinai to the River Jordan in Deuteronomy 1–3 implies familiarity with stories in Exodus and Numbers. Some of the laws in chs. 12 to 16 seem to be adaptations of laws found in Exodus 21–23 and 34.

A broad consensus has emerged that describes the origin and growth of Deuteronomy in the following general terms. After the destruction of the Northern Kingdom, Israel, in 722/721 by the Assyrians, refugees came south and settled in Jerusalem and Judah. The need to absorb them into the social and economic systems of Judah gave rise to social problems, including greatly adding to the class of "strangers," that is, Israelites living in towns and villages who were refugees and thus not members of the established families in those places. However, the refugees also brought with them laws and theological traditions, including a prophetically inspired loyalty to Yahweh as the only God who should be served. Their outlook influenced certain circles in Judah, especially "the people of the land" (independent landowners) and the leading families that provided the administrative elite in Jerusalem. When, on the death of King Manasseh in 640 BC, his son Amon was murdered by court officials (2 Kgs 21:23), "the people of the land put the assassins to death" and placed on the throne the eight-year-old Josiah. The motives of those who murdered Amon are unknown, but their action gave "the people of the land" the opportunity to take over the government of Jerusalem and to implement social and religious policies formulated in the laws of Deuteronomy 5–26. The authors of this material will have been scribes in the Jerusalem administration in sympathy with the objectives of "the people of the land."

Judah at this time (640-622) was still technically a vassal of Assyria, but as Assyrian power declined, a desire for independence in Judah expressed in terms of loyalty to Yahweh grew. By the eighteenth year of Josiah (622 BC) independence could be overtly pursued, and a full-scale reform of the cult was undertaken based on an early form of Deuteronomy 5–26. It may well be that these chapters formulated a treaty between Yahweh and Judah which was meant to replace the vassal treaty that Judah had been forced to make with Assyria. This covenant was formulated in terms of an address by Moses to the Israelites when they were assembled together (Deut 5:1).

The next stage in the growth of Deuteronomy occurred during the exile. The trauma of the destruction of Jerusalem by the Babylonians in 587 BC led to much theological reflection on the meaning of this tragedy, and the history of Israel and Judah was seen as one of disobedience to God's commandments, the end result being the destruction of Jerusalem as a divine punishment. This story was told in the books of Joshua to 2 Kings. On the eve of the return of some of the exiles to Jerusalem after 540 BC Deuteronomy was made the introduction to Joshua to 2 Kings, and chs. 1–4 and 29–30 were added. These latter chapters presuppose that Israel is in exile and promise that God will restore the people to the promised land if they return to God and obey him (Deut 30:1-5). The opening chapters of Deuteronomy picture the Israelites as about to enter the promised land. The analogy is easy to see. The reality of a people about to *return* to the promised land is addressed by a narrative about a people *initially* entering the promised land.

The final stage in the growth of Deuteronomy was the addition of material such as ch. 27, expansions to the legal sections of Deuteronomy 19–25 to meet new situations that had arisen after the return, and of the addition of chs. 31–34.

This conjectural outline of the origin and growth of Deuteronomy raises difficulties for commentators and readers. The book can obviously be read in several different ways. Taken on its own terms, it is a unified farewell speech by a single speaker; and this is how Jewish and Christian interpreters understood it for some seventeen hundred years. If it alludes to a situation of exile in chs. 29 and 30, it can be argued that these prophecies were later fulfilled. On the other hand, there is undoubtedly much to gain from trying to understand the laws in chs. 12 to 26 in terms of what can be conjectured about social conditions in Judah in the seventh and sixth centuries. These laws then cease to be timeless instructions about life in Canaan issued before the people had actually arrived there. Instead, they arise out of real situations of crisis and are instances of contextual and applied theology — the work of leaders trying to apply religious principles to social problems in order to solve them compassionately and in a way that reflects God's graciousness to his people.

Probably no one strategy will solve the problems faced by readers and commentators on Deuteronomy; being aware of these problems, however, will to some extent alleviate them. In what follows, references to passages from Exodus and Numbers which are thought to underlie Deuteronomy will be made only when absolutely necessary. Where the social situation implied in the laws is crucial for understanding them, this social background will be invoked.

The Literary Units of Deuteronomy

The book divides neatly into several sections, which are marked by literary introductions.

1. 1:1–4:43
2. 4:44–11:32
3. 12:1–28:68
4. 29:1 (Heb. 28:69)–30:20
5. 31:1-29
6. 31:30–32:52
7. 33:1-29
8. 34:1-12

COMMENTARY

Deuteronomy 1:1–4:43

The introductory verses, 1:1-5, set the scene for Moses' speech and are in the third person singular. The perspective of the writer is that of someone who is in Israel, for he describes the setting as being beyond the Jordan, that is, on the eastern side. While the places named in 1:1 cannot be identified, the general area is the broad plain immediately to the north of the Dead Sea and east of the River Jordan. The area is further specified in terms of its journeying distance from Mt. Horeb, Deuteronomy's name for Mt. Sinai. The fortieth year (1:3) is reckoned from the exodus, and no doubt a certain irony is intended in the fact that an eleven-day journey has taken forty years. Why a comparatively short journey should take so long is explained in 1:46 and 2:14. The Israelites spent thirty-eight years between leaving Kadesh-barnea and crossing the brook Zered (probably the modern Wadi El Hesa at the southern end of the Dead Sea), when the unbelieving generation that refused to go up and possess the land had died out. In the irony of the eleven-day journey taking forty years, one of the main themes of the opening four chapters, the persistent refusal of the Israelites to trust in God's promises, is introduced.

The speech of Moses in the first-person singular begins at 1:6 and continues to 4:40. **Ch. 1** describes the circumstances that led to the prolonged stay at Kadesh-barnea. Whereas this oasis in the Negev desert should have been the base from which the Israelites entered Canaan from the south, it became instead the scene of the first major rebellion recorded in Deuteronomy.

That the people had become numerous is indicated by 1:9-18 (cf. Exod 18:25-26; Num 11:10-25). Moses had had to appoint helpers to assist him in dealing with disputes that arose among the people. Yet this populous nation was not prepared to advance to the promised land. In spite of God's promise that an advance into Canaan, described here as the "hill country of the Amorites" (1:7, 19; Amorite is a general term for the pre-Israelite occupants of Canaan), will be successful, the people refuse to advance. They have been frightened by the reports of the men sent to spy out the land (1:28) and ascribe their situation to God's malevolent will: "because the LORD hated us he has brought us forth out of the land of Egypt, to give us into the hand of the Amorites" (1:27). When God decides to let only Joshua and Caleb enter the promised land out of all the people gathered at Kadesh-barnea, the people decide, against God's counsel through Moses, to fight after all (1:41-46). The inevitable defeat endorses the point that without God the people are powerless.

Chapters 2–3 indicate that the lesson was learned, at least by the second generation of the men of war. Moses' résumé charts the journey from the brook Zered to the plains of Moab, avoiding battle with the Ammonites (2:19) just as Israel had avoided battle with Edom and Moab prior to crossing the brook Zered (2:4-9). However, no mercy was shown to Sihon, king of Heshbon, and Og, king of Bashan (2:26–3:11; cf. Num 21:21-35). Their cities were captured and their inhabitants were killed, including women and children (2:34; 3:6).

The accounts of Israel's success in warfare raise for the first time in Deuteronomy a matter that is problematic for modern readers: the wholesale killing of inhabitants of defeated cities. Rules of warfare are given later, in Deut 20:1-20, and they are less harsh than in chs. 2–3. They require the killing of males only, and give cities the option of surrendering, in which case the inhabitants are put to forced labor. These rules will be commented on later. However, even they will be offensive to modern readers.

Various attempts have been made to soften the impression created by this material. Attention has been drawn to one of the likely sources of Deuteronomy, Exod 34:10-28, with its uncompromising insistence that the Israelites have no dealings with the inhabitants of Canaan and its promise that God will cast out the nations that dwell in Canaan (Exod 34:24). But even if Deuteronomy 2–3 is an interpretation or misinterpretation of this source, this hardly ameliorates the sentiments expressed in Deuteronomy. Again, it has been argued that the language of Deuteronomy merely employs the rhetoric of conquest typical of the ancient Near East, a rhetoric that is not meant to be taken literally. For example, in the so-called Moabite Stone (c. 850), Mesha, king of Moab, claims to have killed seven thousand Israelite men, boys, women, girls, and maidservants in Nebo on the instructions of the god Chemosh (*ANET,* 320).

An older view, that language about wholesale destruction of inhabitants is a survival of ancient practice in Israel, is no longer tenable. The actual Israelite occupation of Canaan was a gradual and mostly peaceful one, and it is later literature that portrays it in such violent and destructive terms. The most likely explanation is that these descriptions were written at a time when Judah was under the control of powerful empires such as Assyria and Babylon. By looking back to a supposed time when God had driven other nations before them, they gained encouragement for their own future. If they obeyed God, he would free them from the yoke of foreigners. Readers must judge for themselves whether this helps them come to terms with chs. 2–3. Two further points can be added. If the OT represents God as driving out nations before the Israelites, it also insists that God uses other nations to punish Israel (e.g., Isa 10:5-11). Second, the justified moral indignation that readers feel when they read about the indiscriminate slaughter of men, women, and children must be tempered by the recognition that the slaughter of human beings was carried out on an unprecedented scale in the world wars of the twentieth century. This does not in any way justify it, but it does qualify our right to judge other times and places. The real problem of Deuteronomy 2–3 remains that it is God who is presented as requiring and bringing about the slaughter, and readers are entitled to ask, with Abraham in Gen 18:25, "Shall not the Judge of all the earth do what is just?"

Chapter 3 ends with an account of the settlement of the tribes of Reuben and Gad in Transjordan and of the acquisition by part of the tribe of Manasseh of territory east of the Jordan (3:14-15). The decision to bar Moses from entering the promised land is confirmed (3:23-30). It seems paradoxical and ironical that Moses should be both the great deliverer and lawgiver of his people, and yet the one who shares the fate of the redeemed yet disobedient generation that is denied entry to the promised land. Yet this harsh judgment on Moses is in line with what is found elsewhere in the OT, that human leaders are just that (cf. the treatment of David's adultery and murder in 2 Samuel 11–12), and that those who heed the call of God find themselves drawn into suffering and possible rejection.

Chapter 4:1-40 switches from the narrative about Israel's progress from Mt. Horeb to the threshold of Canaan and becomes a passionate exhortation to Israel to observe God's statutes and ordinances. It alludes to past events: to Israel's apostasy at Baal-peor (knowledge of

Num 25:1-18 is assumed by 4:3-4), to the giving of the Ten Commandments on Mt. Horeb (4:9-14), and to the exodus from Egypt (4:34-38). It also hints, prophetically from Moses' point of view, at the Babylonian exile, when Israel will be scattered among the nations and subject to peoples that serve gods made by human hands (4:25-28).

The purpose of the exhortation is not simply to advise the Israelites of what is in their best interests. The exhortation is driven by the belief that there is no God in heaven and earth other than the God of Israel (4:39), and his commandments are the most just ordinances that could be devised (4:8). By observing them, Israel will be seen by the world to be a great, wise, and discerning people (4:6). The special relationship between God and Israel is also indicated, as well as the privilege and responsibility that this entails. "Has any god ever attempted to go and take a nation for himself from the midst of another nation?" (4:34).

The exhortation takes the general form of a collection of laws, such as that of Hammurabi, with an introduction (4:1-8), a setting forth of the law (4:9-31), and an epilogue (4:32-40). Further, vv. 9-31 have been compared with vassal treaties, with vv. 10-14 being a prologue, vv. 15-19 and vv. 23-44 demanding the complete loyalty of the people, and vv. 25-31 containing blessings and curses. Vv. 15-20 are an exposition of the commandments in the Decalogue that forbid the making of any human, animal, or natural representation of God and the worship of the sun, moon, or stars. This anticipates the later general patterning of the laws of Deuteronomy around the Ten Commandments.

4:41-43 switches to third person narrative and describes how Moses designated three cities of refuge in Transjordan to protect anyone who had accidentally killed another person. Once in a city of refuge, the killer would be protected from a member of the deceased's family taking revenge for the killing. The passage presupposes Num 35:9-34, where the operation of the cities of refuge is explained in detail and the designation of the cities is described as a task to be carried out *after* the crossing of the Jordan into Canaan (cf. Josh 20:1-9, where this is done). Within the context of Deuteronomy, 4:41-43 is best seen as an anticipation of 19:1-13, where the operation of cities of refuge is commanded but no cities are designated. The compiler has placed these verses immediately before one of the other rare pieces of narrative in Deuteronomy so as not to intrude third person narrative into material in the first person or imperative command forms. The three cities designated are located in the three main regions of Transjordan northward from the top of the Dead Sea. Whether there were Jews living in this area when Deuteronomy reached its final form (6th-5th cents. BC) is uncertain, and the purpose of this regulation may simply be to claim Israelite possession of these areas of Transjordan.

Deuteronomy 4:44–11:32

4:44-49 introduce the laws and statutes that Moses is to set before the people, whereas 1:1, "These are the words . . . ," introduces a historical résumé. Commentators have seen in the apparent duplication of material in vv. 44 and 45, "This is the law that Moses set . . . ," and "These are the decrees . . . that Moses spoke . . . ," evidence of compositional processes. Certainly, vv. 45-49 could be a summary of chs. 1–3 (or are these chapters an expansion of 4:45-49?), leaving v. 44 as an "original" introduction to Deuteronomy before 1:1–4:40 was added as a preface. These compositional matters do not fundamentally affect the interpretation of the verses.

In **5:1-5** another introduction, "Moses convened all Israel, and said . . ." (5:1), prefaces Deuteronomy's version of the Ten Commandments in ***5:6-21***. The emphasis is on the immediacy of the divine revelation. "Not with our ancestors did the LORD make this covenant, but with us, who are all of us here alive today" (v. 3). It is reasonable to suppose that in the context of late seventh-century Judah, the people were assembled to hear the laws contained in Deuteronomy read to them, with the implication that they should think of themselves as representing the generation addressed by Moses.

The Ten Commandments are most familiar in their form in Exod 20:2-17. The Exodus version, supplemented for Lutherans and Catholics by Deut 5:21, has been used in church liturgies and catechisms for centuries. The major difference between the two versions is the reason why Israel must observe (5:12; Exod 20:8 has "remember") the sabbath day. In Exod 20:11 the commandment is grounded in an appeal to the creation story, with God resting on the seventh day. In Deut 5:15 the commandment is connected with the exodus and with Israel's deliverance from slavery. Appeal to the exodus deliverance as the ground for observing the commandment is characteristic of Deuteronomy.

The other main difference concerns the final commandment. Whereas Exod 20:17 reads "You shall not covet your neighbor's house; you shall not covet your neighbor's wife," Deut 5:21 puts the neighbor's wife at the head of the prohibition. This is not a way of saying that a man's wife is his most important possession, a formulation that would rightly offend modern readers. Deuteronomy is sensitive to the position of women, and the Deuteronomic reformulation of Exod 20:17 removes the wife from a subordinate position among other goods and chattels to be the prime subject of a separate commandment. For commentary on the details of the other commandments see the commentary on Exod 20:1-7.

5:22-33. In Exodus 19–20 the description of the divine presence on the mountain in all its awe and wonder precedes the Ten Commandments. Here it follows as part of Moses' narrative. While Moses is designated as the intermediary through whom God spoke, this passage emphasizes that God was speaking to the whole people and not just to Moses (cf. 5:4-5). The role of Moses as intermediary is necessary because the leaders of the people fear that they will be destroyed by the fire with which the mountain burns (cf. Exod 19:12-24, where it is God who warns the people not to approach the mountain). This mark of respect is acknowledged by God (5:28) and used as an object lesson for the presumed hearers/readers of Deuteronomy. Anyone who fears the destructive fire of the holy mountain should take seriously the commands of God.

6:1-25. A new section is introduced by the words "Now this is the commandment . . . ," but the emphasis moves from an address to the generation that stood at Mt. Horeb (5:4) to instruction to children and children's children. If the generations are obedient, they will multiply greatly in the promised land (6:3). V. 4 begins the opening section of the most famous prayer of Judaism, the Shema, so named because of the Hebrew imperative *shema'*, meaning "hear!" The whole prayer consists of Deut 6:4-8; 11:13-22 and Num 15:37-42 and is recited twice daily by observant Jews. The translation and interpretation of the opening words are problematic, as indicated by the various alternative renderings provided as footnotes in the NRSV. The Hebrew is literally, "Yahweh our God, Yahweh one," with the NRSV representing Yahweh as "LORD." On the basis of usage elsewhere in Deuteronomy, it is unlikely that "Yahweh our God" should be rendered "Yahweh is our God," against the NRSV text; it is more likely that "is" should be added between "Yahweh" and "one." This yields the translation "the LORD our God, the LORD is one." It is then necessary to explain what is meant by "one." This most likely refers to Yahweh's uniqueness. He alone is God, and he needs no other gods to assist him. However, this unique and incomparable God is also, for Israel, *our* God, not because of what Israel deserves or merits but because of God's graciousness (cf. 7:7). The uniqueness of God leads to a unique claim upon Israel: the Israelites must love God with heart, soul, and might (6:5). "Love" in this context includes an emotional element, as indicated in 7:7-8 where it is said that God set his heart on Israel (Heb. *hashaq*, meaning "to love" or "become attached to") and chose and loved them. But it also entails loving obedience to God's commandments.

The phrase "with all your heart and with all your soul" is a trademark of Deuteronomy and of books influenced by it, and it occurs for the first time at 4:29. The metaphors do not mean the same as in English. The "heart" is the seat of the intellectual faculty of a person, while the "soul" (Heb. *nephesh*) is the seat of emotional and spiritual faculties. *Nephesh* can also mean "person." Heart and soul taken together thus mean a person's total life, physical, mental, and spiritual. In 6:5 "might" is added, probably referring to a person's material possessions. The injunction to recite "these words" when a person lies down and rises up and that they should be placed on their hands, foreheads, and doorposts has given rise in Judaism to the recitation of the Shema prayer evening and morning, to the wearing of phylacteries at times of prayer, and to the placing of *mezuzot* on doorways. These practices continue to this day. Phylacteries contain Deut 6:4-9, 11:13-21, and Exod 13:1-10, 11-16, while *mezuzot* contain Deut 6:4-9 and 11:13-21. In the original context of 6:6-8 "these words" refers to all that is to be commanded, and the injunctions about why the words should be recited and where they should be placed are powerful rhetoric stressing the abiding importance of what is enjoined. It may also be based, however, on the fact that, in the ancient Near East, people wore amulets to give them protection, and that doorposts inscribed with sacred words have been found in Egypt (see Weinfeld 1991: 341-43 for further details).

6:10-19 set the demand for loyalty to God alone in the context of the fact that in Canaan the Israelites will benefit from things that they have not themselves produced: large cities, well-stocked houses, hewn cisterns for collecting water, and vineyards and olive orchards. They imply that this prosperity will lead them to forget the God who freed them from slavery and tempt them to serve other gods. This brings two warnings: God's zealous anger will be kindled against his people if they act thus. The people are also reminded of the Massah incident (Exod 17:1-7) when they complained about the lack of water and questioned whether God was with them. They are not to repeat this testing of God.

In **6:20-25** the reason for obeying God's commandments, that they are Israel's response to God's graciousness in freeing them slavery in Egypt, is emphasized by way of an answer to questions from future generations. To the question "What do these things mean that God has commanded?" the reply is given in terms of a rehearsal of the exodus deliverance. The implication is that what was true for those who were delivered from slavery is true for all subsequent generations, including that to which Deuteronomy is addressed.

7:1-6. The Israelites are commanded to make no covenant with the inhabitants of Canaan nor to intermarry with them. These injunctions in vv. 1-4b are in the second person *singular* imperative. The command to destroy their altars and other sacred objects in v. 5 is in the second person *plural* imperative and widely regarded as the work of a later editor. The narrow exclusivism demanded will not be attractive to modern readers; but what is being expressed is the conviction that the standards of justice and compassion demanded by God for his people will not be found among the occupants of Canaan and that mixing with these peoples will compromise those standards. The reference to the "sacred poles" (Heb. *'asherim*) in v. 5 is interesting in the light of recent archeological discoveries, which raise the question whether, in some forms of popular Israelite religion, the God of Israel had a female consort, Asherah. This possibility cannot be ruled out and would make sense of the command here to destroy such objects.

The seven nations named in 7:1 represent the Deuteronomic version of a tradition that elsewhere speaks of six nations that occupied Canaan prior to the Israelites (Exod 23:23). These "nations," that is, groups who occupied particular cities (e.g., the Jebusites in Jerusalem, the name of which was also Jebus; see Judg 19:11) or who could be identified in some other way, had long since ceased to exist when Deuteronomy was composed, and now symbolized human forces that could not have been defeated by Israel unaided by God.

7:7-11. Amid the warnings to Israel of the consequences of turning away from God occur sublime verses that emphasize his compassion and mercy. The redemption from slavery in Egypt, which is the basis of God's claim on Israel, was accomplished not because Israel was a numerous people but because it was the fewest of all peoples. A contrast with the seven mightier and more numerous nations of v. 1 is implied. God's action in Egypt was motivated by his love for Israel and his loyalty to his promise to the ancestors, Abraham, Isaac, and Jacob. God not only demands loyalty from his people: he is faithful and loyal to the covenant that he makes.

7:12-26 enumerate and emphasize the advantages that will accrue from loyalty to God. They include fruitfulness of the womb, the land, and domesticated animals, and freedom from illness. These blessings presuppose the possession of Canaan. This latter task, impossible from a human standpoint, will be achieved with the help of God, who defeated Pharaoh and Egypt at the exodus. However, once Canaan has been occupied, the idols and images of the people there must be destroyed so that they do not become a snare to the Israelites. The "abhorrent thing" in v. 26 is probably the idol of a false god.

Two lifestyles are contrasted in **8:1-20:** a prosperous one that will accrue from living in the land with flowing springs, abundant trees, and minerals such as iron and copper; and the lifestyle of the wilderness in which the Israelites depended not on the natural resources of the land but on God's special provision, as in the giving of the manna (cf. Exodus 16). The Israelites are warned not to suppose that the prosperity that they will enjoy in Canaan is the result of their own efforts, for then they will forget God.

The rhetoric of the chapter relies on a certain amount of idealization. Life for subsistence farmers in the hill country of Judah and of Samaria was not easy, and famines are mentioned in the stories of Abraham, Jacob, and Ruth as well as in prophetic warnings. On the other hand, groups that inhabited the wilderness lived largely off the natural vegetation and other resources of the area, and they did not have to construct terraces, organize plowing, sowing, and harvesting, or arrange for fields to lie fallow more frequently than once every seven years. On the face of it, Deuteronomy 8 has reversed what was actually the case, namely, that settled life needed much more organization and application than the mobile life of the wilderness.

We may detect in the rhetoric something of an antagonism that was widespread in the ancient Near East between the wilderness and settled ways of life. The simplicity of the wilderness, its closeness to nature, and the virtues of independence, courage, and hospitality that it engendered were prized above what was seen to be the idle luxury, corruption, and injustice of life in cities (cf. Isa 3:16; 4:1; Amos 4:1; 6:4-7). The God of Israel was a God who had come from the wilderness (Ps 68:7-8) and who had revealed his law in the wilderness. The problem addressed in Deuteronomy 8 is therefore how the Israelites could maintain honesty, simplicity, and justice in reliance on God in an environment which bred and had bred in Israel's history a disregard for God, and which produced in its turn a disregard for fellow Israelites.

9:1–11:31. Chapter 9 begins a long section which contains a résumé of Israel's history of rebellion against God during the wilderness wanderings, with particular reference to the incident of the golden calf (Exodus 32). It is structured as follows:

1. **9:1-7.** A summons to Israel to remember that they are a stubborn people and that their forthcoming success in occupying Canaan will depend on God's grace to them in spite of their stubbornness. Also, their conquest will be God's way of punishing the wickedness of the nations that occupy Canaan.
2. **9:8–10:11.** A résumé of the golden calf incident: how Moses smashed the two tablets of the commandments, how he interceded for Aaron and the whole people, and how he made an ark to contain the new tablets on which God wrote the Ten Commandments (a literal translation is "Ten Words"). There are two digressions in this block: 9:22-24 and 10:6-9. The first alludes to other occasions when Israel provoked God's anger: at Taberah (Num 11:1-3), Massah (Exod 17:1-7), Kibroth-hattaavah (Num 11:31-34), and Kadesh-barnea (cf. Deut 1:19-33). The second refers to the death of Aaron, the succession of his son Eleazar as priest, and the designation of the tribe of Levi as bearers of the ark of the covenant. The place names in 10:6-7 are evidently taken from Num 33:31-33, although this latter passage is a small part of a much fuller itinerary. Beeroth-bene-jaakan means the wells of the "bene" (sons of) Jaakan, a tribal group in the wilderness west of the central rift valley. Gudgodah contains the same Hebrew consonants as Hor-haggidgad at Num 33:32. In contradiction of Num 33:38 where Aaron dies on Mt. Hor, 10:6 places Aaron's death at Mosarah, which may involve a pun on the Heb. *musar* — "reproof." The two digressions are generally seen as later additions to Deuteronomy, although not necessarily from the same hand because the first retains the first person address to Israel while the second is in the narrative third person. The purpose of the second digression would appear to be to legitimate the priestly functions of the descendants of Aaron and the tribe of Levi.
3. **10:12–11:12.** This section demands Israel's loyalty, with "all their heart and all their soul" (10:12). It reiterates the contrast between God's greatness as God of gods and Lord of lords and his choosing of one particular people. It contains a noble account of God's ways, who takes no bribes and who cares especially for orphans, widows, and strangers. Also repeated are the themes of God's power manifested in the exodus deliverance and the promised land as one well provided for in terms of fertility.
4. **11:13-31.** The blessings that will accrue from obedience to God's commandments are again rehearsed, as is the command to bind these words on the hand and the forehead, to affix them to gates and doorposts, and to teach them to one's children. The alternatives of blessing and curse are set before the Israelites, and a ceremony of blessing and curse on Mt. Ebal and Mt. Gerizim is commanded once the Israelites have occupied Canaan. This latter command is carried out at Josh 8:30-35; there is an amplified version of the injunction in Deuteronomy 27.

Deuteronomy 12:1–28:68

12:1-14. The words "These are the statutes and ordinances" in v. 1 are generally held to introduce the central legal section of Deuteronomy, which continues to the end of ch. 26. Earlier (7:5, 25) the Israelites have been instructed to destroy the cult objects of the inhabitants of Canaan: altars, idols, and sacred poles. This command is repeated here (v. 4) with the addition that the sacred *places* of the Canaanites are to be destroyed also. This latter command is the prelude to the injunction that God must be worshiped only in the place that he will choose (vv. 4-7, 11-12, 13-14).

The designation of the *single* sanctuary, which is never actually identified with a specific place in Deuteronomy, is generally held to be an innovation in Israelite religion and is attributed either to Hezekiah (2 Kgs 18:4; 2 Chr 31:1-2) or to Josiah (2 Kgs 23:4-20). In the books of Samuel and Kings characters such as Samuel and Elijah are portrayed as sacrificing at *various* shrines, and they seem to be unaware of the command to use only a *single* sanctuary (see the Introduction, 153). The crucial question, which cannot be answered with complete certainty, is whether Deut 12:4ff. reflects something that was carried out in the eighth or seventh centuries or whether it accords with the situation in postexilic Judah in which Judah was a comparatively small community centered in the temple in Jerusalem.

Those who favor the connection with Josiah point out that, apparently, the altars in the frontier towns of Arad and Beersheba were dismantled in the seventh century. Also, seals of officials in Jerusalem and a frontier town have been discovered that are aniconic, that is, they bear nothing but the name of the official. Earlier seals bear religious symbols. These details would support the account of Josiah's cultic reforms in 2 Kgs 23:4-20, although they cannot prove that this is what Deut 12:4ff. is implying or reflecting.

It is necessary to distinguish two separate things: the destruction of pagan altars, and the command to sacrifice only at a single sanctuary. The first does not entail the second, for it would be possible to destroy all pagan places of worship and to have several legitimate sanctuaries dedicated to the God of Israel. The command to have a single sanctuary is a practical way of expressing the need of Israel to pledge exclusive loyalty to one God.

The command, however, has serious practical implications. If offerings to God can be made only at a single sanctuary (12:5-7) and if whole households are expected to gather at it, how was this to be organized? Later practice did, indeed, involve long journeys to Jerusalem at Passover time (see Luke 2:41-51); but how often could this have been done without disrupting normal life to the point of breakdown? Another implication is considered in vv. 15-27. For the moment we should note that the apparent impracticalities of any *regular* (several times a year or more) assembly of whole households at a single sanctuary are an argument in favor of linking the commandment to the small, postexilic community centered in Jerusalem.

12:15-27. These verses raise two issues: "secular" slaughter (vv. 15-16, 20-25) and the economic implications of the single sanctuary (vv. 17-19, 26-27). It is often claimed that, prior to the law of Deut 12:15-16 and the like, all slaughter of animals for the purpose of human consumption was considered to be a sacred act and was carried out at a local sanctuary. The only exception was if game was hunted and killed in the chase (see 12:15). On this view, Deut 12:15-16 and similar passages introduce "secular" slaughter, that is, slaughter purely for the purpose of human consumption as opposed to killing an animal in sacrifice to God. The reason is that the single sanctuary now makes it impractical to carry out *any* killing for food there. This may be correct; but we have no evidence that *all* Israelites regarded *any* killing of an animal for food as a sacred act to be performed only at a sanctuary, and the injunction could just as well be an attempt to clarify an already existing distinction between killing to eat and killing to sacrifice to God, given the impracticalities introduced by the single sanctuary. The command not to eat the blood but to pour it onto the ground (12:23-24) safeguards the sacred quality of blood. It represents the life force of a person (its loss brings about death), and it is used in sacrifice as a substance with great symbolic cleansing power.

The economic implications of eating tithes of grain, wine, oil, the firstlings of herbs and flocks, and other freewill offerings and donations not locally but at the single sanctuary (12:17-19) would be considerable, and involve a massive transfer of resources away from local towns and sanctuaries to the single sanctuary and its town. Presumably, the tithes and other goods would not be entirely consumed by the household that produced them. Dues would be rendered to the sanctuary. Because of the massive transfer of resources implied by these verses, it has been argued that they reflect the circumstances of the postexilic, temple-based community centered in Jerusalem; or if the reign of Josiah is envisaged, they have been seen as part of fiscal reorganization that benefited Jerusalem and the ruling classes at the expense of peasant farmers and their local towns and villages.

12:29-32 (Heb. 12:29–13:1). The demand for absolute loyalty to the God of Israel is strengthened by claiming that the inhabitants of Canaan offer even their sons and daughters to God in sacrifice.

13:1-18 (Heb. 13:2-18). With this section we meet for the first time in Deuteronomy a form of law that is generally known as casuistic. This is case law and argues from specific instances. It is usually opposed to apodictic law, which lays down a categorical commandment applicable regardless of circumstances.

Three examples are given of how the people might be tempted to follow other gods. They might be induced by a prophet (13:1-5), by a member of their own family (vv. 6-11), or by the example of a whole town (vv. 12-18). No mercy is to be shown to any of these. In the case of the town the notion of collective responsibility required the destruction of all its inhabitants. The questionings of Abraham about the morality of destroying the innocent with the guilty (see Gen 18:22-32) may be implied by the injunction that a thorough investigation be made, and the destruction can be carried out only if the charge of apostasy is established. Included with all the inhabitants are the town's livestock and its "spoil" (Heb. *shalal,* the term for what is taken by an invading army). The implication is that an apostate city has become, in effect, a Canaanite city and is to be dealt with as such (see Deut 20:16-18).

Comparisons have been made between this injunction and the clauses in vassal treaties, in which a vassal is threatened with the destruction of his cities if he breaks faith with his overlord. This way of expressing vassalship may well be presupposed in Deuteronomy 13; but it is given a religious dimension in that the apostasy of an Israelite town is not merely disloyalty to God but an embodiment of uncleanness and of temptation to others, and must be eradicated without trace.

There is also, however, a social dimension to the need to execute the prophet or member of one's family who tries to lead people away from the God of Israel. In both instances the Israelites are reminded that God redeemed them from Egypt, from the house of slavery (13:5, 10). This gives God a claim on the Israelites' loyalty; but it also has social implications in that God expects Israel to organize itself in such a way as to express in social relationships the graciousness that God has shown to it in delivering the people from slavery. This latter point, not stated explicitly in ch. 13, assumes great importance, especially in ch. 15. Apostasy from God is therefore not merely a matter of what people *believe;* it profoundly affects their understanding of justice and how society is *organized.*

At this stage in Deuteronomy, there is no attempt to distinguish true from false prophets (see on 18:22). The sense of 13:3 is that God is using a prophet who advocates apostasy to test the loyalty of Israel. Nevertheless, such a prophet is to be put to death and is by implication a false prophet.

14:1-2 prohibit two practices associated with mourning rites: gashing one's skin and shaving the hair of the forehead. Jer 16:6 mentions these signs of mourning, along with others, without any indication that they were other than normal practice, and this raises the question why they are prohibited here (at Lev 21:5 they are restricted to priests, and at Lev 19:28 used with reference to gashing only). The prohibition may, of course, be an ideal: an attempt to get Israelites to abandon mourning practices that they shared with other peoples. The commentaries mention similar practices among peoples ancient and modern. Some also suggest that there is an allusion to fertility rites and to mourning carried out in connection with the "death" of a fertility god. What is clear is that Israel's special relationship to God as his children (14:1) and as a holy people and treasured possession (v. 2) must be marked by behavior different from that of other peoples.

14:3-21. The theme that being God's special people entails special behavior is continued in the prescriptions about which animals are clean and may be eaten and which are unclean and forbidden. The animals are divided into land animals (vv. 3-8), sea creatures (vv. 9-10), and birds and insects (vv. 11-20). Similar prescriptions are found in Leviticus 11 except that there only general regulations are given for classifying unclean animals, whereas Deut 14:3-8 provides a list of names. Lev 11:20-23 deals more extensively with insects than the single verse in Deut 14:20.

Various attempts to account for the classifications and prohibitions have been made, none of which is entirely satisfactory but some of which probably contain elements of truth. Thus, some of the prohibited species may have been believed to be animated by evil forces, or they may have been used in heathen rites, or their flesh may have been unhealthy or had a foul taste. The birds may have been prohibited because some of them were birds of prey that ate the corpses of animals. There may also have been economic reasons behind the ban. It has been argued that pigs were prohibited because they competed with humans for scarce resources of grain. A recent suggestion is that the prohibited species were anomalies that did not precisely fit into the classificatory schemes used by the Israelites to distinguish animals. It is likely that a mixture of superstition, custom, practical economics, and observation combined to produce the lists and that attempts to justify them rationally, for example, by allowing animals that divided the hoof and chewed the cud (v. 6), were retrospective justifications rather than considered first principles. Whether or not ordinary Israelites observed these injunctions is unknown. The injunctions in v. 21a not to eat anything that dies of itself is best understood in terms of the command not to eat blood with the flesh (see 12:23). 14:21b has excited much comment. It occurs also at Exod 23:19 and 34:26, in both cases in contexts regulating the presentation of first fruits. Explanations such as that the killing of an ewe that is suckling its young is prohibited ignore the actual content of the injunction, which is that a kid should not be boiled in its *own* mother's milk. It has been claimed on the basis of a fragmentary text from Ugarit that this was a Canaanite practice, although even on the most generous reading the Ugaritic text does not allude to a kid being boiled in its *own* mother's milk. An older suggestion (Driver 1902: 166) that the practice was a method of preparing milk that would make fields and orchards more productive is a warning against supposing that attention should be focused on the kid rather than the milk. Labuschagne (1990: 71) links the practice to first fruits, suggesting that the initial milk of the ewe might contain blood and that the regulation was designed to avoid eating blood which had contaminated the milk in which the kid was boiled. This suggestion has the virtue of linking the half verse with the rest of the verse and its implied prohibition of eating blood. However, no interpretation is entirely satisfactory.

14:22-29. A tithe was a tenth of the produce of the land, whether grain, wine, or oil. This quantity, depending upon time and place in the ancient world, could be required by a king, a sanctuary, or a local ruler as a tax to support central or local administration or the functioning of the religious cult. In 1 Sam 8:15-17 the Israelites are warned that if they have a king he will take from them a tenth of the produce of their land and of their flocks.

In Deut 14:22-29 the tithe law is reformulated as a consequence of the centralization of the cult. If it was the case that, prior to centralization, the peasants offered their tithes to local sanctuaries to support, among other things, the priest(s) there, the abolition of local sanctuaries would make a number of priests destitute and create a surplus of produce no longer needed to support local sanctuaries. What would happen to the destitute priests and surplus produce? The answer is that the produce is to be brought to the single sanctuary either as produce, or in its monetary equivalent if the peasant lives too far from the single sanctuary. There the produce, or what its monetary equivalent can buy, is to be consumed by the household that produced it, not forgetting the destitute priests (i.e., the Levites). As with the centralization law of ch. 12, this raises questions about the practicality of whole households (see v. 26) traveling to the central sanctuary for this purpose. Presumably, somebody had to remain at home to do the milking and protect the property! Crüsemann (1997: 252-56) argues that the regulations abolished tithes as a form of taxation since they are not to be paid to anyone but to be enjoyed by the producers. For him this proves that the "people of the land" — the landholders — were the authors of or the inspiration behind the Deuteronomic legislation, since this regulation is very much in their interest.

If 14:22-27 raise practical problems, the same is not true of vv. 28-29. Here a third-year tithe is enjoined which is not to be brought to the central sanctuary but to be stored locally and to be used to feed the Levites, as well as orphans, widows, and resident aliens (Israelites living apart from their kin groups). This has been seen as part of the attempt in Deuteronomy to legislate for the support of the underprivileged, legislation that is continued in ch. 15.

15:1-6. A seventh year in which the land was to lie fallow and its produce was to be left for the poor and for wild animals is commanded in Exod 23:10-11. Research (Hopkins 1985: 194-95) indicates that actual practice in the highlands of ancient Israel required fields to lie fallow every other year. The regulation in Exod 23:10-11 may well be an ideal rather than a necessity made into a theological virtue. Deuteronomy contains no law about a seventh, fallow year. Instead, 15:1-16 commands a remission of all debts in the seventh year, in obedience to "the LORD's remission" (v. 2). The remission applies only to Israelites and not to foreigners (v. 3); and if this is offensive to modern readers, the rule can be explained (but not necessarily justified) as follows. God wants his people to be a community of brothers (the NRSV renders the Hebrew word for "brother" as "member of the community" in vv. 2-3 to avoid gender-specific language), in which case it is inappropriate that it should contain people whose relationship is determined by long-term indebtedness. Foreigners are not members of the people of God and are therefore excluded from the provision.

15:4-5 can be understood in several ways. The first problem is whether v. 4 states that there will be no one in need (NRSV), or whether it enjoins that there *ought not* to be anyone in need (NJB, "must not"; NIV, "should not"). The second problem is how to connect this statement or command to what follows. The REB and the GNB rearrange the translation so that the absence of the poor is dependent on obeying God by diligently observing his commandments. There will be no poor if the Israelites remit loans, as commanded. The NRSV implies that there will be no poor because God will bless the Israelites if they obey him. However the verses are rendered, they seem to be contradicted by v. 11, which states that there will always be someone in need; unless, taking the two passages together, the sense is that situations of need will always arise but will not lead to permanent poverty if loans are remitted. V. 6, which envisages Israel lending to nations and ruling over them, need not be read in a sinister way. A people to whom God has been gracious ought to be gracious to other nations.

This passage received particular attention in the "Jubilee 2000" campaign to persuade rich nations to cancel the debts owed to them by poor nations. The biblical Jubilee (Leviticus 25) says nothing about the cancellation of debts or interest, and if biblical support is sought for the campaign, it has to depend on Deut 15:1-6. This in turn raises the question whether this passage is concerned with the remission of *interest* or the remission of *debts*. Judaism at the beginning of the common era (see Danby 1933: 50-51) certainly understood it to enjoin the remission of *debts;* it had to find a way around the fact that nobody would be willing to make a loan shortly before the seventh-year cancellation of loans! The seven-year periods were fixed periods in later Judaism rather than periods that began to be counted only from the date of granting of any particular loan.

15:7-11 articulate a view of social responsibility in which the powerful kin term "brother" is applied to any Israelite in need. The NRSV, avoiding gender-specific language, obscures this, and the RSV is a better indicator of the force of the Hebrew. An Israelite could be afflicted by need in several ways, especially if he was a subsistence farmer. Illness or an accident could affect his ability to work, there might be a failure of the rains, or crops could be affected by blight or insects. Tax demands from a ruler or invader in the form of produce could leave a farmer below subsistence level for himself and his family. It is also possible that refugees are in mind: Israelites driven from their own lands by an invader and sheltering among fellow Israelites. The loans mentioned here could be of produce, animals, or their monetary equivalent; and the imminence of the seventh year of remission of debts must not deter an Israelite from lending to his brother Israelite (see above on the problem in later Judaism). Failure to be generous is a wrongdoing in the sight of God (v. 9b).

15:12-18. The laws governing the slavery of Hebrews are probably dependent on those in Exod 21:3-11, with the difference that in Deut 15:12 women slaves are given the same right of release as men slaves. Strictly speaking, these laws would not be necessary if there were no poor (v. 4) and if loans cancelled at the seventh year were made to Israelites in need. However, there are many variables in human relationships and organization. The important points about these verses are their inclusion of women in the law of release (there is no similar provision in Exodus 21) and their appeal to the exodus deliverance from slavery as a reason for acting generously toward released slaves, who will have to establish some form of economic independence (15:14-15). God did not free his people from slavery so that they could enslave each other. Further, the slave is described as a "brother" (v. 12; NRSV, "member of your community"). The public ceremony to be undergone by a slave who wishes to remain as such after six years is taken from Exod 21:5-6, with women being included (v. 17b).

15:18 adds to the theologically driven reasons for releasing slaves the practical economic one, that a master has enjoyed free of charge services for which he would have had to employ hired laborers.

15:19-23. Laws about firstborn domestic animals are found at Exod 13:2, 11-16; 22:29-30; 34:19-20 and at Num 18:15-18. The formulation in Deuteronomy is distinctive in that it presupposes the single sanctuary and therefore commands that firstborn animals be consumed there annually, whereas Exod 22:30 requires that they be offered on the eight day after birth. Further, the animals will be enjoyed by the household of the producer (cf. 14:22-26). Combined with the injunction is the regulation that only perfect animals are to be offered to God (cf. 13:1). Therefore, any firstborn animal with a defect is eaten locally and not at the central sanctuary.

16:1-8. Ch. 16 contains Deuteronomy's cultic calendar, detailing three festivals: Passover (vv. 1-8), Weeks (vv. 9-12), and Booths (vv. 13-18). Vv. 16-17 enjoin three festivals (Heb. *hag*) which are named as Unleavened Bread, Weeks, and Booths (cf. Exod 34:18, 22-23). However, in 16:1-15 only two festivals are named (vv. 10, 13), and Unleavened Bread has become the Passover sacrifice during which no leaven must be seen for seven days. Vv. 16-17 undoubtedly reflect earlier practice, because a festival *(hag)* is a pilgrim celebration in which the Israelites are expected to appear at the sanctuary (v. 16). Evidently Passover was originally observed as a local festival. The requirement that there should be a single sanctuary made Passover a centralized observance, entailing its combination with the festival of Unleavened Bread.

Compared with the regulations concerning the Passover in Exod 12:1-13, those in Deut 16:1-8 are noteworthy in several ways. First, the mention of flocks and herds (v. 2) implies that another animal instead of a lamb may be offered (cf. NEB, "you shall slaughter a lamb, a kid or a calf"). Second, no mention is made of the blood of the Passover sacrifice. The explanation for observing the Passover is connected with the unleavened bread and the haste with which the Israelites left Egypt (v. 3). The unleavened bread is also called "the bread of affliction" (v. 3 — only here in the OT, perhaps recalling Exod 3:7, "the affliction [NRSV, "misery"] of my people"). No doubt the lack of reference to sprinkling the blood on the doorposts so that the angel could *pass over* is occasioned by the practicalities of killing the Passover sacrifice at the central sanctuary. Nevertheless, a wholesale reinterpretation as well as transformation of the ceremony as implied in Exodus 12 is envisaged.

16:9-12. Unleavened Bread/Passover was celebrated at the time of the barley harvest (late March/April). The festival of Weeks was named after the seven weeks that were to be counted from the time that the wheat began to be harvested. This would vary slightly from region to region. Later Judaism, basing itself on Lev 23:1-21, developed a strict timetable which linked Weeks to Passover by beginning to count the fifty days (Lev 23:16 — Pentecost) from the second day of Passover, when, it was reckoned, the sheaf offering was to be made (see Lev 23:15, taking sabbath to mean Passover). No such strict timetable is envisaged here. The Deuteronomy version of the festival requires the presence of entire households including male and female slaves, strangers, orphans, and widows at the central sanctuary, presumably to share in consuming the offering set aside from the harvest.

16:13-15. No precise date for the festival of Booths or Tabernacles is given except that it follows the ingathering from the winepress. Nor are details given about how the festival is to be observed or what the significance of the booths is. Presumably this was common knowledge. See Lev 23:33-43 for further details about the festival and its meaning. Again, the presence of entire households at the central sanctuary is required.

16:18–18:22. There is broad agreement among commentators that 16:18–18:22 is a distinct block of material dealing with four kinds of office: judges (16:18–17:13), the king (17:14-20), priests (18:1-8), and prophets (18:9-22). However, this convenient division should be regarded more as a general guide to reading the passages than as a satisfactory way of interpreting the details. To take one example only, 16:18–17:13 deals explicitly with judges only at 16:18-20 and 17:8-13; and this latter section is concerned with cases that are too complicated for the local judges. Such cases must be referred to the levitical priests and the judge *(sic)* who is in office at the central sanctuary. 16:21–17:1 deals with worship and sacrifice. It may be possible to explain these diversities in terms of the processes by which the material has been edited into its present form; but this presupposes that readers were and are very sophisticated users of the material. In what follows the diversity of the material will not be suppressed in favour of a neat general classification, however attractive the latter may be.

16:18-20. This provision, that judges and officials are to be appointed in all the towns and that they must administer justice impartially, may be compared with 1:9-18. In this passage, Moses describes how he appointed leaders to administer justice in the wilderness, reserving for himself the function of dealing with the most difficult cases. In ch. 16 there is the difference that the judges and officials are to be appointed by the people themselves. This may reflect the fact that Deuteronomy is being written long after Moses' death; and it cannot be supposed that the appointments were made democratically (in the modern sense) by procedures that disregarded traditional structures of leadership such as the headship of the most powerful families. However, it may be significant that the first reference in Deuteronomy to the exercise of power is not in terms of hereditary priests or of monarchy but in terms of local decision making. Although the local exercise of power is not necessarily less corrupt than the central exercise of power, it may be more amenable to accountability.

16:21–17:1. These three verses are often identified as belonging to older material that was included in Deuteronomy, the reason being that 16:21-22 seem to prohibit certain practices at *any* altar dedicated to Yahweh. In the context of Deuteronomy they can only refer to the central sanctuary; and the mention of the sacred pole (Heb. *'asherah)* is relevant to the time of Josiah's reform.

Whether Asherah was a goddess or a fertility pole is not clear, but such poles were destroyed by Josiah (2 Kgs 23:6), having been introduced into the temple by his grandfather Manasseh (2 Kgs 21:3, 7). The stone pillar (Heb. *maṣebah*) is harder to interpret. The twelve pillars set up by Moses alongside an altar (Exod 24:4) are described by the same Hebrew word. A stone pillar as such was not objectionable, but some usage associated with it, whose precise nature we do not know. The prohibition against sacrificing a defective animal (17:1) repeats 15:21.

17:2-7. Judges having been appointed (16:18-20), there follow rules governing evidence; but the illustrative case is a religious rather than a civil one and concerns a man or woman who serves other gods. The passage thus continues the cultic theme of the preceding verses. The possibility that people could be falsely accused and wrongly punished (cf. 1 Kings 21, the story of Naboth's vineyard) is addressed at 19:18-19. Here the judges (although they are not mentioned explicitly) must "make a thorough inquiry." Two or three (independent) witnesses are required for a successful proof of guilt. An apostate member of the people is as much an abomination (17:4) as a pagan cult object or defective sacrificial animal. However, this indicates a widening of the notion of ritual offense to include religious allegiance as well as ritual practice.

17:8-13. It is not clear from the Hebrew whether the cases that are to be referred to the central sanctuary are exclusive (i.e., only these cases and no others) or illustrative (NRSV, "any such matters of dispute"). The translations vary. Further, modern translations (e.g., the RSV, NRSV, NIV, and NJB), following much older Christian exegesis, spell out the cryptic Hebrew ("between blood and blood, between plea and plea, and between stroke and stroke") in a way that differs from traditional Jewish understanding of the passage. For the latter (Rashi 1946: 89) "blood" refers to that of the menstruous woman, while "stroke" is understood as a plague that may be clean or unclean. Modern translations and commentaries are well represented by the NRSV, "between one kind of bloodshed and another," for example, murder or manslaughter (Exod 21:12-14); "one kind of legal right and another," for example, theft or embezzlement; or "one kind of assault or another," for example, some kind of personal injury (Exod 21:18-27). The difference between traditional Jewish and modern critical interpretation is not trivial because the mention of the levitical priests in v. 9 could indicate that the cases referred to were technical ritual cases rather than civil ones. If the modern critical interpretation is correct, the role of the priesthood as envisaged in Deuteronomy is not confined to ritual matters. The levitical priests are to act as interpreters of a civil body of laws.

17:14-20. Several important features of the law regarding the king should be noted. First, a king is not essential for the people of God as envisaged by Deuteronomy. If they wish, the people may choose a king, the implication being that they do not have to. Second, such a king is as much subject to God's commandments as any other Israelite, and he even has the obligation to possess and regularly study a copy of the law. No doubt this section presupposes the kind of evaluation of kings that is found in the books of Kings. There the view is maintained that disobedient kings were primarily responsible for the division of the kingdom at the death of Solomon (1 Kgs 11:29-33), the destruction of the Northern Kingdom, Israel (2 Kgs 17:21-23), and the fall of Judah (2 Kgs 23:26-27). The Deuteronomic law is designed to prevent any repeat of this in the future and hints strongly that Solomon was a bad example in 17:17. If there is any truth in the view that the whole section 16:18–18:22 deals with offices in Israel, it is significant that rules about the king are preceded by rules about provincial judges and the priests and judges at the central sanctuary. The king is not at the top of the tree.

18:1-8. This is perhaps the most difficult section in the whole of Deuteronomy. Little is known for certain about the meaning or derivation of the name "Levite" or about the history of the Levites. The tantalizing glimpses that we get in stories about Levites (Judg 18:1-31) or in sayings regarding them (see esp. Deut 33:8-11) do not provide sufficient information to construct any sort of "history." Further, our lack of knowledge of the exact nature and history of ancient Israelite social organization makes any attempted theorizing about the Levites highly speculative. Deuteronomy clearly states that any Levite is entitled to exercise priestly functions at the central sanctuary (18:7). In the books of Chronicles (1 Chr 23:2-32) the Levites are assigned less important duties in the sanctuary in support of the sons of Aaron, who alone carry out the priestly tasks. The same division is implied in Num 18:21-32. What history or struggles for power by differing groups lie behind these different pictures is not known.

The present section of Deuteronomy presupposes two situations in which Levites who are priests find themselves. Those already at the central sanctuary (their location is not explicitly stated) are entitled to the shoulder, the two cheeks, and the stomach of an ox or sheep brought for sacrifice as well as the first fruits of grain, wine, oil, and sheep skins (18:4) Different parts of the sacrificial animal are allocated to the priests as their due at Lev 7:32-34. These offerings support the Levites and their families economically. The other class of Levite is not at the central sanctuary but living in the towns (18:6). The law gives such Levites the right to come to the central sanctuary and to receive the same privileges and dues as those Levites already there. This may be an ideal that could not be put into practice — the resources of the central sanctuary were not limitless — and the common theory may be correct that sees the later distinction between Aaronic priests and Levites as the result of Josiah's reformation. The closure of local sanctuaries would mean the loss of economic support for their priests, and if they were Levites and prevented from coming to the central sanctuary, whatever the law might say (cf. 2 Kgs 23:9), they would become an underclass, dependent on the charity and goodwill of the local communities they had once served (see Deut 14:27). But all this can only be conjecture.

18:9-22. The section on prophets begins with a prohibition of child sacrifice, and then condemns various types of occult divination. Taken together with the concluding verses, which define true and false prophets in terms of the accuracy of their forecasts, the prophecies are understood as divinely given as opposed to human or occult methods of ascertaining the future. Embedded in the passage, and giving a different view of the function of a prophet, is the famous promise of God that he will raise up a prophet like Moses for the people of Israel: not a prophet who forecasts the future but a prophet who conveys God's laws to the people; this is recognized in v. 19, where God requires that the prophet's words (i.e., laws spoken in God's name) be obeyed. The promise is therefore of one who will mediate God's commandments, not of one who will be an exceptional forecaster. The NT, following Jewish exegesis of this passage, indicates that hope in the fulfillment of the promise was strong in the first century AD (cf. John 1:21).

Chapters 19–25. These chapters constitute the third block of legal material within the collection 12–26.

19:1-13. In 4:41-43 three named cities in Transjordan are designated as "cities of refuge," without specifying how they are to function. Here their functioning is described, but the three required cities are not designated. The Hebrew of v. 3, "You shall prepare the road (or route, or way)," leads to renderings such as "build roads" (NIV) to "you shall calculate the distances" (NRSV). Rashi (96) charmingly suggests that at each crossroad was to be a notice inscribed "refuge" pointing to the nearest such city. Although the NRSV rendering is free, it is probably closest to the realities of the situation in ancient Israel. The regulations about the cities of refuge are straightforward and provide protection from blood revenge for anyone who accidentally kills another person with whom he has not been at enmity. Noteworthy are the considerations of the nature of the relationship between victim and agent, and the view that the killing of someone guilty of an accidental death would itself be a crime. In 19:11-13 the elders (mentioned for the first time in Deuteronomy in a judicial capacity) are given the duty of handing over to the avenger of blood (a relative of the victim) anyone who has reached a city of refuge but is guilty of murder.

19:14. Today one can commonly see orderly piles of stones marking the division of fields or property in the Middle East. Inscribed boundary stones containing curses against anyone who moves them are known from the ancient world. Clearly, in a world in which there were no maps as we know them, the division of land depended on tradition and goodwill, and could easily be abused.

19:15-20. What was touched upon in 17:16-17 regarding witnesses is spelled out in greater detail here, in a passage which is evidently older than the composition of Deuteronomy since v. 17 implies that there will be priests in office in places other than the central sanctuary. The principle is stated that a convicted false witness must suffer the punishment that the accused would have suffered if he (or she) had been found guilty on the basis of the false evidence. This principle leads to an alternative interpretation of the law of talion (an eye for an eye, etc.) from that in Exod 21:23. There it is applied to physical damage inflicted on a person. Here it is connected with the law of evidence.

20:1-20. The rules of warfare in Deuteronomy have no parallel elsewhere in the OT, and modern readers might well regret their presence here. At the same time it can be argued that, in presenting these rules, the writers of Deuteronomy have tried to suffuse some compassion into them. War is an inescapable, if highly regrettable, feature of human existence, and even in the twenty-first century international bodies have both recognized the right of nations to defend themselves by force of arms if attacked, and tried to ameliorate the effects of warfare on prisoners and civilians.

The extent to which Deuteronomy 20 reflects or includes actual procedures in warfare in ancient Israel is hard to determine. The priestly exhortation to the Israelite army to be unafraid when confronted by superior armies because God would go before them to give them victory (vv. 2-4) must surely express a pious hope rather than describe the real world, as well as arguably introducing the concept of a God who exists for the benefit of Israel and not vice versa. The OT contains abundant evidence that Israelite armies were not invincible. In fact, the verses express the typical themes of passages that elsewhere describe "holy war" (cf. Exod 14:10-18). It is easier to accept such material as a literary creation than to see it as a reflection of actual practice.

The section that provides for exemptions from fighting for those who have just built but not dedicated a house (20:15), those who have planted but not enjoyed the fruit of their vineyards (v. 16), those who have betrothed but not yet married a wife, and those who are afraid are hard to reconcile with the real world, and imply, in the case of those frightened, that the priestly assurance of divine assistance had not produced the desired effect! The justifications for exemption in the first three cases are compassionate, if not utopian, and can be compared with Isa 65:21-22, where the divine creation of a new heaven and earth will create the situation in which

> They shall build houses and inhabit them;
> they shall plant vineyards and eat their fruit.
> They shall not build and another inhabit;
> they shall not plant and another eat.

The present passage can thus be read as an attempt to put into practice utopian ideals in the most brutal of human situations.

The same cannot be said of the next section, which commands the complete extermination of the non-Israelite population of the cities of Canaan which the Israelites will capture. Cities outside of Canaan are to be treated differently, with only the males slaughtered if there is fighting, and with all the people put to forced labor if the city capitulates without fighting. Distasteful though this material is, it belongs to rhetoric rather than reality. As pointed out earlier (7:1-5), the Israelite occupation of Canaan was gradual and peaceful, and the purpose of the material about conquest and destruction is to stress the need for the people to maintain absolute loyalty to God.

The attempt to breathe at least a small element of humanity into rules of warfare concludes with the provision that the fruit trees of a besieged city must not be cut down in order to make siege works. The aspect of the real world that comes to the fore here is the knowledge that fruit trees take some years to mature and produce fruit, whereas war can destroy them in a very short time. Such insights have not, alas, been of any interest to those who waged "total war" in the past century.

21:1-9. This interesting section, embedded in the rules about warfare (which continue at 21:10-14), probably owes its position here to the fact that war was one of the ways in which the body of a slain (lit. "pierced" — e.g., with sword or arrow) person could be found in open country. However, the regulation is not restricted to someone killed in war. Unavenged bloodshed — it was normally the duty of a person's family to execute a murderer (cf. Deut. 19:4-13) — was held to be an offense in God's eyes and to pollute the whole land. In the laws of Hammurabi (paras. 23-24; *ANET,* 167) a city or territory in whose governance a crime has been committed, including murder, has the responsibility of compensating the victims. The regulation in Deuteronomy is a detailed ritual with many "primitive" features.

The chief agents are the elders and judges (the reference to the levitical priest in 21:5 is clearly a Deuteronomic gloss, for the Levites take no part in the ceremony), and their actions are paralleled elsewhere in the OT only in the ritual for cleansing a "leper" in Leviticus 14. The feature common to the two procedures is the killing of a bird (Lev 14:5) or heifer (Deut 21:4) over running water and the symbolic removal of guilt or uncleanness. The point of using a heifer that has not been used for work is that it is a young animal not yet used for secular purposes whose first use can be for a sacred ritual. A perpetual stream in a valley neither plowed nor sown is a tall order! Not only were there comparatively few perpetual streams in the land; they were precisely where the land was likely to be worked because of the irrigation that they provided. The provision may, as with specifying the unworked heifer, be a way of indicating sacredness within a natural environment. Perhaps less likely, the perpetual stream would carry any blood from the heifer away from the spot, and there would be no danger of it ending up on human produce if the valley was untilled and not sown (although the text neither mentions any blood nor tells exactly how the heifer's neck is to be broken — see Rashi [105] for the view that a hatchet was used). How the ceremony was symbolically to remove the guilt belongs to the strangeness of the prescription for modern readers; in its present version it is accompanied by a prayer (21:8). Taken as a whole the passage indicates the sacredness of human life in God's sight and the need for the community to take this seriously.

21:10-14. The attempt to make rules of war compassionate continues with the regulation about the treatment of foreign female captives. The shaving of the head and the paring of the nails, together with the month's mourning for her parents, are a kind of rite of passage that disconnects her from her past. She can now be married to her captor, but if she is subsequently divorced she may not be sold. Uncongenial though these provisions may be for modern readers, they display a higher morality and respect for gender and ethnic differences than those which informed the armies of supposedly civilized nations in the past century, some of whose soldiers regarded the rape of enemy women as one of the rewards of victory.

21:15-17. The theme of compassion to women is continued in the law requiring a man to leave the major portion of his inheritance to his firstborn son. A polygamous family is presupposed in which it is likely that a second, and younger, wife has been taken by a man after his first wife became less attractive. The regulation preserves the rights of the son of the elder wife (who is most likely to have borne the first son) to his inheritance, and thus to her support if she survives her husband. The right of the firstborn, which is common in the ancient world, is a sensible and practical arrangement for providing for the family on the death of its head. That it caused contention is indicated by stories such as that of Jacob and Esau (Gen 25:29-34).

21:18-21. The power of a father over his children in the ancient world was, in theory, absolute and could extend to power over life and death. What is interesting in these verses is that the mother is included with the father in the judicial process and that there is public accountability. The conclusion is ambiguous. The evil purged from Israel is no doubt the son whose rebelliousness is not only a social inconvenience but a refusal to obey God's ways as taught by his parents. But the indiscriminate, publicly unaccountable killing of a son could also be part of the evil.

21:22-23. The final section of the chapter continues the theme of not defiling the land, by ordering that the bodies of executed criminals should be displayed (hung on a tree) for no more than a day. Presumably, the purpose of such a display was to act as a warning against wrongdoing; but it was also the exhibition of a person and deed that had violated divine law, and as such its open display needed to be limited. Although the verses do not refer to crucifixion, Paul in Gal 3:13 associated them with this form of Roman execution.

22:1-4. Ch. 22 begins a miscellany of regulations. The first is an enlargement of Exod 23:4-5 which specifies help in restoring to a person's enemy his lost ox or ass, or helping his ass if it is lying under its load. In Deuteronomy the enemy has become the brother, and Otto (1995: 193) has argued especially that in the particular circumstances of Deuteronomy the obligations normally met within the family group have become the responsibility of the whole people. Every Israelite is a brother, to whom kin obligations apply. The NRSV's "neighbor" (the literal translation is "brother") obscures this point. The regulation here not only expands Exod 23:4-5 (and has sheep instead of ass) but also enlarges the scope of the provision to include a garment or any other possession. The command to help the ass is extended to include an ox, and the plight of these animals is broadened to "fallen down by the way."

22:5. Most commentators regard this verse as a prohibition of pagan religious practice in which gender roles were reversed. The word "abomination" usually refers to religious abuses. However, the words rendered "man's apparel" are literally "baggage" or "equipment of a man," and this may support the view that it is female participation in warfare and male avoidance of warfare by disguise as a woman that is prohibited.

22:6-7. Permission to benefit from the eggs of a bird is tempered by a ban on killing the mother bird. This is prudent management; but it also embodies respect for the species as such.

22:8. The protection of a roof, which could be slept on or otherwise used, by a parapet is common sense. Here it becomes a way of stressing the sanctity of human lives and the blood guilt that is incurred if life is wantonly lost.

22:9-11. The prohibition against sowing with two kinds of seed may derive from the practical observation that one type of seed can hinder the germination of another (Borowski 1987: 150). Plowing with an ox and an ass yoked together will put unbearable strains upon the ass. Again, prudent management expresses concern for the weaker of the two animals. The prohibition of wearing a garment of mixed stuff may be meant to rule out garments associated with magic.

22:12. One has to look to traditional Jewish scholarship (Rashi: 110) for an explanation (whether convincing or not) of why the law about tassels occurs at this particular point in Deuteronomy. According to this interpretation the occurrence of the word for "tassels," which is at the beginning of the sentence in the Hebrew, shows that while garments may not be made of mingled stuff, tassels may be so made. A fuller and more theological reason for the tassels is given at Num 15:37-41. Some experts have drawn attention to the tassels shown on garments worn by *shasu* nomads (groups mentioned and pictured in Egyptian sources) and have made a link between the *shasu* and proto-Israelites who may have migrated from Egypt to Canaan.

22:13-21. The space devoted to regulating marriage in the OT laws is meager in comparison with the more than fifty paragraphs in the laws of Hammurabi (out of the total of 282 paragraphs). There are no explicit instructions in the OT laws about betrothal, marriage contracts, or divorce procedures (see 24:1-4). Yet the material preserved in Deuteronomy 22 is weighted heavily toward the protection of married women.

The first seven verses are designed to protect a married woman from being divorced on the grounds that she was not a virgin when she married. She is to preserve the garment (22:17) in which she slept on the occasion of her first intercourse with her husband as evidence to be produced in case she is accused of not having been a virgin. The fact that the father takes the initiative in his daughter's defense may indicate that he was to retain the garment. If the elders of the city are satisfied that the charge is groundless, the husband is whipped, required to pay a fine to the girl's father, and excluded from any further attempt to divorce his wife. The value of the fine, a hundred shekels of silver, is not easy to determine, but by way of comparison, Jeremiah (Jer 32:9) is reported to have paid seventeen shekels of silver in order to purchase a piece of land. Perhaps the fine prescribed was sufficiently large to deter husbands from making frivolous charges against their wives. If the proofs of virginity cannot be produced, the girl is to be stoned to death at the door of her father's house by the men of the city. The blatant unfairness that regards the female as a source of evil to be purged from Israel (v. 21) but not the male who despoiled her prior to her marriage is partly, but not entirely, mitigated in what follows.

22:22-29. Betrothal was the first stage of marriage in ancient Israel, so that a betrothed woman was regarded in these regulations as a wife. There is a measure of equality in vv. 22-24 in that both the man and the woman caught in adultery are to be stoned to death. Vv. 25-27 and 28-29 tilt the laws in favor of the woman. A betrothed virgin who has intercourse with a man in the open country is given the benefit of the doubt that she has been raped because her cries for help would not be able to be heard. The man is condemned to die. If an unbetrothed virgin is presumed to have been raped, the man is fined (for the value of the fine, fifty shekels of silver, see above on v. 19) and must marry her without the possibility of divorce. However, even this attempt to protect the woman raises questions for modern readers such as whether she would want to marry the man and how he would treat her in marriage. Unfortunately, the quality of relationships is not something that can be legislated, and modern readers should be given at least some credit to the attempt in these laws to do something to protect the legal standing of women.

22:30 is the beginning of ch. 23 in the Hebrew numbering, but goes most naturally with ch. 22. The prohibition against a man's taking (i.e., having intercourse with) his father's wife or wives could apply to two situations. Absalom is said to have gone into David's concubines when he forced David to flee from Jerusalem (2 Sam 16:21-22), thus indicating his usurping of power. The other situation would arise on the death of a man and the assumption of power by his son. The *motive* for the regulation is not stated. It could be an expression of repulsion at incest, or it could further extend protection to vulnerable women. The second part of the verse is usually taken to mean that the private sexual life of a man is not to be invaded by a son (cf. Gen 9:22-23, where Noah's "nakedness," that is, the fact of his having intercourse with his wife, is treated with respect by two of his sons).

23:1-8. This is one of the most difficult sections in Deuteronomy. We do not know what the nature or function of the assembly was, and it is not certain whether a *mamzer* was a person born of a union such as that forbidden in Leviticus 18 and 20. Furthermore, two different justifications for excluding males from the assembly are given. Those with defective male sexual organs and those born of incest (if this is what being a *mamzer* refers to) are defective human beings on analogy with the requirement to offer in sacrifice to God only perfect animals (15:21). The reasons given for excluding Ammonites and Moabites (23:3-6) and including Edomites and Egyptians are based on the traditions of interaction between these peoples and Israel. It is likely that two different kinds of material have been put together here. Plausible reasons for the exclusions and the linking of the material can be given. It has been argued that v. 1 refers to men who had deliberately destroyed their ability to procreate, as part of a pagan rite. They are therefore excluded because they serve a foreign deity. The *mamzer* of v. 2 has been linked to the Ammonites and Moabites with reference to the story of Lot's incest with his daughters in Gen 19:30-38, which resulted in the birth of the ancestors of the Ammonites and Moabites. Again, historical reasons can be given for the passage. The book of Nehemiah explicitly refers to a regulation "in the book of Moses" excluding Ammonites and Moabites from the assembly of God (Neh 13:1) and records hostility toward Nehemiah by the Ammonites (Neh 4:7). The passage may therefore reflect a situation in which the Jewish community was being threatened from Transjordan (Ammon) but was being supported by the Edomites and Egyptians to the immediate south; but this is only speculation. It is probably impossible to be certain about the significance of the section within the book as a whole; for modern interpreters its redeeming feature is that it is not totally exclusive.

23:9-14. These verses, strangely to modern readers, equate sanitary with ritual purity. That soldiers on active duty avoided sexual intercourse is indicated in narratives such as 1 Sam 21:4-5, so that it may not be illogical that masturbation (23:10) in camp was regarded as an act from which a man needed to be purified (v. 11 and cf. Lev 15:16-18). That the passing of feces was thought to contaminate the camp (23:12-14) is harder to understand, although there were obviously good hygienic reasons for making soldiers bury their excrement outside the camp.

23:15-16. The rule forbidding an escaped slave to be returned to his master is apparently unique among the laws of the ancient Near East, and, if exploited to any great extent by slaves, would have put that institution under some pressure. Traditional Jewish interpretation (Rashi: 115) took the slave to be a non-Israelite. If the regulation was meant to apply to Israelites also, it is an indication that slavery was tolerated because the social mechanisms required for its abolition were not in place (and did not come into being until the eighteenth century in Europe, and even later in America!). However, the toleration of slavery violated the notion that God's people should not be enslaved, and this regulation undermined the institution to some extent.

23:17-18. That sacred prostitution existed in ancient Israel, including in the Jerusalem temple, is indicated by passages such as 1 Kgs 14:24 and 2 Kgs 23:7. It may have served several functions, from being a symbolic act imitating and therefore stimulating fertility of crops or animals, to being a regulated form of prostitution that provided revenues to support a sanctuary. The mention of male prostitutes, referred to in v. 18 as dogs, may indicate that homosexual acts were performed. The vows referred to in v. 18 were presumably vows made by prostitutes. The prohibition of sacred prostitution served to make Israel distinct from its neighbors; but it may also have had a humanitarian effect if not aim. Temple prostitutes were the product of social conditions that the Deuteronomic laws aimed to abolish — in theory, at any rate.

23:19-20. The prohibition against charging interest to a fellow Israelite must be understood in the first instance in its historical and social setting. If people needed loans, whether of money or produce, it was not in order to invest but to survive. It is entirely in keeping with Deuteronomy that the need of an Israelite to survive should be the occasion for assistance, not of taking advantage. The same attitude does not extend to a non-Israelite, however, although it is not known to what extent the latter would have needed assistance from Israelites in the postexilic community. Christian tradition for over a millennium and Muslim tradition to this day took this and other passages (Exod 22:25 and, especially for Christian tradition, Luke 6:35) to teach a ban on charging interest.

23:21-23. The need for vows to God to be taken with the utmost seriousness needs no elaboration.

23:24-25. These two regulations permitting anyone to eat a neighbor's grapes from his vineyard and to pluck ears of corn from his grain, provided that neither a container nor a sickle was used, could have been abused and have been disastrous to landowners. They are best seen as a humanitarian provision for the poor and hungry in extreme need.

24:1-4. This is the only passage in the Bible that describes the method of divorce in ancient Israel (the "certificate of divorce" is alluded to at Isa 50:1), and yet this is not the section's primary purpose, which is to forbid a man from remarrying a wife whom he divorced and who married another man before becoming available for remarriage by divorce or widowhood. Such an act is declared to be abhorrent (Heb. *to'ebah* — usually indicating a ritual offense against God). This is more likely to be an old taboo than theological justification for the humanitarian attempt to prevent the first husband from getting a second payment of "bride wealth" (cf. Jer 3:1). Because of the passage's unique content on divorce it became the center of discussion in early Judaism, with the followers of Hillel and Shammai differing in their interpretation of the difficult Hebrew phrase translated as "something objectionable." The latter took the phrase to mean "unchastity"; the former broadened it to include almost anything displeasing. It must be emphasized that this discussion was about the interpretation of a difficult piece of Hebrew; divorce practice was weighted in order to make it difficult. Something of that stringency is indicated here. Although nothing is said about the nature or content of the divorce document, the stipulation (twice) that it must be put in the wife's hand suggests a properly witnessed public procedure. Divorce would have dire economic and social consequences for a woman and her family, and it is interesting here that an old taboo against remarriage outweighs the social advantages that remarriage would bring for the woman.

24:5-22. This section contains a set of miscellaneous laws with a strong humanitarian bias. Much of the material can be paralleled elsewhere, but there are interesting differences in some cases. The tendency in Deuteronomy to equate what we would regard as civil and ritual offenses is used to make kidnapping and forcible enslaving ritual abuses (v. 7; cf. Exod 21:16), while the Exodus prohibition against taking a male neighbor's cloak in pawn (Exod 22:26-27) appears in 24:17 as a prohibition against taking a widow's garment in pledge. The Exodus version of the law presupposes that a day laborer was required to give a kind of deposit that could be withheld if he did not do sufficient work; how this might affect a widow is unclear. Vv. 10-15 contain the strongest regulations anywhere in the OT in support of day laborers or those needing a loan. Creditors may not forcibly enter a debtor's house; wages must be paid daily before sunset. To act fairly in these matters will earn God's favor (v. 13); to ignore them will be to incur guilt (v. 15).

24:16, preventing parents from being put to death for their children's offenses and vice versa, is meant to operate within human affairs. Divine action could entail corporate responsibility and corporate punishment (Deut 5:9). Whether individual responsibility was first "discovered" in Israel at the exile (cf. Ezekiel 18) is to be doubted. Without a notion of individual responsibility there can be no sustainable ethical, legal, or ritual practice; yet this has to be held alongside the easily observable fact that the decisions of those in power affect the lives of the powerless, often to their disadvantage. What was seen as the punishment of a king was bound to affect the king's subjects also.

The humanitarian provision about allowing aliens, orphans, and widows to benefit from the wheat and grape harvests (24:19-21; cf. Exod 23:10-11; Lev 19:10) is justified here by reminding the Israelites that they were once slaves in Egypt.

25:1-3. Judicial flogging as a penalty for crime is well attested in the laws of the ancient Near East (see *ANET,* 175). Strangely, there are no indications in the OT laws of which offenses were to be punished in this way, while instances of people being beaten (e.g., Jeremiah by Pashhur, Jer 20:2) do not precisely fit the law that is enunciated here. The rabbis (*m. Mak.* 3:1-15 in Danby 1993: 405-8) did specify which offenders were punishable by flogging, for example, those guilty of the illicit sexual liaisons prohibited in Lev 20:17-21. The purpose of the law here is twofold: to insure that flogging was a publicly witnessed process, and to restrict the punishment to what was appropriate in the opinion of judges so that the guilty person was not humiliated. Significantly, the guilty person is described as the innocent person's brother (in the wider sense of a member of the same community; NRSV, "neighbor").

25:4. The reason why an ox might be muzzled while pulling a threshing sledge over the newly harvested ears of barley or wheat was to prevent it from eating the separated grain. Such muzzling is prohibited. A domesticated animal is to be treated compassionately (cf. Exod 23:12). Paul was wrong if, in quoting this passage, he implied that God did not care for oxen (1 Cor 9:9).

25:5-10. Levirate marriage, the marriage of a childless widow with one of her late husband's brothers (Lat. *levir,* "brother-in-law") so that any children inherit the deceased's name and property, is attested in many societies (*Notes and Queries on Anthropology:* 117-18). Only here is it found among OT laws, although it is implied in the stories of Tamar and Judah (Genesis 38) and Ruth (Ruth 3:1–4:14), where it is a secondary marriage and not strictly a levirate marriage). To what extent it was regularly practiced is not known, but that the Deuteronomic legislation regarded it as a fundamental way of protecting and providing for childless widows and their deceased husbands, quite apart from their property, is indicated by the ignominy to be suffered by any brother-in-law who refused this obligation.

25:11-12. This is the only passage in the OT laws that specifies mutilation as a punishment for an offense, although it is implied in the law of talion ("eye for eye," etc.; Exod 21:22-25; Deut 19:21). Jewish interpretation took the passage to be referring to a monetary fine (Rashi: 123). A similar Middle Assyrian law (*ANET,* 181, law 8) assumes that a woman has damaged a man's testicle in a brawl with him, in which case she is to lose a finger. A male's sexual potency, both for his own self-esteem and for preventing his family from dying out (this is the possible link with the preceding law), was regarded as sufficiently important in the Deuteronomic legislation to want to deter a woman from even attempting to catch hold of a man's testicles in defense of her husband.

25:13-16. This is another instance (cf. 24:7) in which a civil offense is described in terms of a ritual offense (Heb. *to'ebah,* "abomination"). That dishonest trading is so fiercely condemned is typical of Deuteronomy's extension of responsible behavior in God's eyes to the practicalities of everyday life.

25:17-19, which recall Israel's encounter with the Amalekites during the wilderness wanderings (Exod 17:8-16), is linked, via the word "rest" (25:19), with 12:9-12. They form, together with the material in ch. 12, a narrative framework for the laws of chs. 12–25.

26:1-11. Following the conclusion of the main body of laws, a number of ceremonies are enjoined, of which two occur in this chapter. The first, that of first fruits, incorporating the "small historical creed" of vv. 5-9, has been the center of much discussion since G. von Rad's monograph *The Form-Critical Problem of the Hexateuch,* published in German in 1938. Von Rad saw in this summary an ancient, basic "creed" which had been the core of the narrative traditions as developed in Genesis to Joshua. The lack of reference to Sinai and the giving of the law led him to suppose that the latter traditions were associated with a covenant festival at Shechem (see further on Deuteronomy 27), while the "creed" of 26:5-9 was associated with a *Landnahmefest* (festival of occupying the land) at Gilgal near Jericho (Josh 4:19). The general view now seems to be that, far from being ancient, 26:5b-9 were composed by exilic or postexilic Deuteronomists, expanding older material, traces of which can be found in vv. 2a, 5a, and 10a. On this view, Israelites were accustomed annually to taking their first (or best) fruits to a local sanctuary where they recalled that their ancestor (Jacob; but some would include Abraham) was a wandering (or on the point of perishing) Aramean, whereas the offerer was now settled and able to produce and present a harvest. The passage reached its present form, it is held, by locating the ceremony at the central sanctuary (v. 2b), giving the priest a role in the ceremony (contrast v. 4, where the priest sets the basket down before God, and v. 10, where the worshiper does this) and perhaps a share in the produce. The reference to the wandering ancestor was expanded to include a summary of the story of the oppression in Egypt, the exodus, and the occupation of the land. The final form of the text, in its context in Deuteronomy, prescribes a striking ceremony that serves to remind the Israelites of the divine graciousness to which they owe their security and prosperity (v. 11).

26:12-15. The third-year tithe is first introduced in Deuteronomy at 14:28. Its inclusion in a ceremony (at the central sanctuary? 26:13) again combines the social and the ritual in a manner unfamiliar to modern readers. The purpose of the third-year tithe was to provide for the Levites, aliens, orphans, and widows (v. 12), yet the prayer to be said by the Israelite who has paid the tithe refers to it as a sacred portion (i.e., one dedicated to God so as to be set apart from secular use). Further, the confession of innocence in v. 14 not only declares that the tithe has not been used by the offerer but that it has not been used while he was ritually unclean. The latter declaration about being ritually unclean is not strictly necessary and gives some plausibility to the view that it comes from a declaration that the worshiper has not taken part in any pagan religious activities. What is clear is that the passage strongly links the performance of this humanitarian action with God's promise to bless the land with abundant harvests (v. 15).

26:16-19. The two ceremonies are followed by a passage which resumes the address of Moses and therefore rounds off the "sermon" in which the laws and ceremonies have been included. The verses refer to the preceding "statutes, commandments and ordinances" which constitute the agreement between God and his special people. They will be holy to God — a concept in Deuteronomy which combines humanitarian concern and action with ritual purity.

27:1-26. This is an intriguing chapter in several ways. First, it appears to interrupt the speech of Moses begun in 26:16-19 and continued in 28:1ff. Second, 27:2-8 seem to combine two traditions: that the Israelites are to set up twelve stones as soon as they have crossed the Jordan (v. 2, "on the day that you cross"; cf. Josh 4:1-9) and that they are to set up the stones as well as an altar on Mt. Ebal (if this is the correct reading), which could certainly not be reached on foot from the River Jordan in one day by a large group of people traveling with their possessions. Third, in 27:11-26 the tribes are divided into two groups on Mt. Ebal and Mt. Gerizim — the former to curse, the latter to bless the people. Yet only curses are uttered, and by the Levites, although Levi is one of six tribes on Gerizim whose function is to bless! It is clear from these unevennesses that different types of material have been combined together, some of which may be older than the composition of Deuteronomy.

The so-called Shechemite Dodecalogue (twelve commandments delivered at or near Shechem, which was flanked by Mt. Ebal and Mt. Gerizim), is unparalleled as a collection in the OT although its individual prescriptions can be paralleled from Exodus 20 and 22 and Leviticus 18, 19, and 20. Its form ("Cursed be . . .") is also unique for a set of laws in the OT although the curse formula is found, for example, at Gen 3:14. However, the curses in Deuteronomy 27 (and 28) differ from that in Gen 3:14 in that a sentence is pronounced there upon the serpent; here no sentence is indicated. In ancient Near Eastern treaties curselike formulae are found and directed against those who break treaties. The present passage, if it is to be read in treaty terms, understands disloyalty to God in terms of offenses against other people.

The collection is typical of Deuteronomy in the sense that ritual and social offenses occur together. Four of the twelve "commandments" (27:20-23) concern illicit sexual relationships, while six (27:16-19, 24-25) are humanitarian. Only one is specifically "religious" (v. 15, concerning the setting up of an idol or the casting of an image), while the final curse is directed against anyone who does not observe "this law." It has been noted that a number of the curses refer to private or secret actions such as setting up an idol in secret (v. 15), deliberately misdirecting a blind man (v. 18), and secretly striking down a neighbor (v. 24). As such, and whatever the origin of the Dodecalogue (it is probably a late Deuteronomic composition combining some earlier material), it adds a dimension to the moral responsibility that God is believed to require from his people.

27:11-14 probably reflect a different ceremony from that implied in vv. 15-26, a more familiar covenant-ratification ceremony in which blessings and curses are uttered (see further on ch. 28).

27:9-10 may be an introduction to 28:1 and a continuation of 26:19. The participation of Moses and the levitical priests (27:9) contrasts with 27:1, where Moses and the elders address the people (unless one emends the text to read "Moses charged the elders"). Some commentators maintain that the Samaritan Pentateuch is correct in reading Mt. Gerizim instead of Mt. Ebal in v. 4, and that anti-Samaritan sentiment was responsible for the present text. The German *Einheitsübersetzung* (United Translation) actually has Mt. Gerizim in its main text. For vv. 5-7 cf. Exod 20:25. 27:7 contains the only reference in Deuteronomy to peace or well-being offerings. Burnt offerings (v. 6) are mentioned elsewhere in the book only in 12:6, 11-13, 27.

Chapter 28 sets before the Israelites the choice of blessings that will follow obedience and punishments that will follow disobedience. For modern readers this may sound immoral. Is the service of God that is undertaken in order to enjoy blessings and avoid disasters really worth the name? This question will be tackled at the end of the section, where it will receive sharpened focus in the light of the grizzly nature of some of the threatened punishments.

The first striking thing about the chapter is that the threatened punishments far exceed the promised blessings. The latter occupy 28:3-14 and are followed by curses in vv. 16-19 that parallel exactly the blessings of vv. 3-6. At this point the similarities end. The seven verses (7-13) that describe blessings are overbalanced by forty-nine (20-68) that detail disasters. However, vv. 20-68 can be divided into three sections: 20-44, 45-57, and 58-68, with vv. 45 and 58 clearly introducing new sections.

A striking feature of 28:20-44 is their similarity at some points with the vassal treaties of the Assyrian king Esarhaddon (681-669; *ANET,* 534-41). Particularly interesting is the similarity between paras. 63-64 and vv. 23-24.

Esarhaddon	Deuteronomy
May all the gods . . . reduce your soil in size to be as narrow as a brick, turn your soil into iron, so that no one may cut a furrow in it.	The sky over your head shall be bronze, and the earth under you iron.
Just as rain does not fall from a copper sky, so may there come neither rain nor dew upon your fields and meadows, but let it rain burning coals in your land instead of dew.	The LORD will change the rain of your land into powder, and only dust shall come down upon you from the sky. . . .

Whether these, and some more general, thematic similarities prove that the writer of Deut 28:20-44 actually used a version of the Assyrian vassal treaties is a matter of opinion (see Steymans 1995 for an attempt to prove the case). However, at the least they indicate that Deuteronomy 28 is to be seen as a Hebrew version of a type of literature well known in the ancient Near East at one time. A plausible case can be made for the view that during the seventh century the kings of Judah had been required to agree to an Assyrian vassal treaty similar to that known from the vassal treaties of Esarhaddon, and that a similar form was employed in Deuteronomy in order to articulate Israel's need for exclusive loyalty to God. On the basis of comparisons with the Assyrian treaties it has been proposed that the core of ch. 28 is vv. 20-44 (the vassal treaties contain only threats against disloyalty), that the bulk of vv. 3-19 was composed before the exile, and that vv. 47-57 (which vividly describe war and siege) and vv. 58-68 (which presuppose the exile and scattering of the people "from one end of the earth to the other" [v. 64]) were appended after the exile. Within vv. 20-44, vv. 36-37 also presuppose exile and may be a latter addition.

The subject matter of the chapter needs little comment. The real problem of the material is its apparent attempt to coerce Israel's obedience by the threat of dire punishment. No entirely satisfactory answer can be given to this problem for modern readers, but several points can be made.

1. The use of the treaty formula inevitably highlights the coercion factor.
2. Within the context of Deuteronomy, with its stress on the humanitarian treatment of others, particularly the poor and disadvantaged, the coercion takes on a different significance. God, as opposed to an Assyrian overlord, does not desire blind loyalty as much as humane and sensitive dealings with fellow Israelites. God's threats of punishment are directed against a nation that ignores social justice.
3. Other parts of the OT (e.g., Psalm 73 and the book of Job) make it clear that there cannot be a simple correlation between obedience and blessing, and disloyalty and disaster. The OT at its most realistic knows that the righteous may suffer and the wicked may prosper. Faith and obedience then become things done for their own sake; yet they need the confidence that the universe is ultimately a moral universe, and this is certainly what the Deuteronomic scheme of blessings and curses is meant to uphold.

Deuteronomy 29:1 (Heb. 28:69)–30:20

This section contains, according to 29:1 (Heb. 28:69), a covenant made between God and the Israelites in the land of Moab, additional to that made at Mt. Horeb (i.e., Mt. Sinai). Many commentators have detected a covenant form known from extrabiblical texts within the section: (a) historical introduction (29:2-9), (b) statement of the covenant bond (vv. 10-15), (c) a sermon warning of the consequences of disobedience (vv. 16-21), (d) a description of the consequences of disobedience and their causes (vv. 22-29), (e) a sermon giving hope and promising blessing (30:1-10), (f) and a final address promising blessings and threatening disaster, and urging obedience. Whether or not a dependence upon covenant forms can be demonstrated, the analysis gives a useful breakdown of the material.

This section contains many allusions to other parts of the OT. 29:10-15 echoes Deut 5:1-5 but also has reminiscences of Josh 9:3-26. In that passage a covenant is made with the Gibeonites, who become hewers of wood and drawers of water. The same phrase occurs in 29:11. Another passage that has been cited is the incident in Josh 7:1, 16-26 in which Achan wrongly and secretly kept some of the spoil of Jericho. 29:18 warns against individuals who may secretly turn away from God, trusting that the general loyalty of the people will keep them safe. These allusions (they are not exact parallels) may indicate that the material of chs. 29–30 has its origin in "preaching" that was undertaken in the postexilic community, including the use and interpretation of written or oral stories. Thus, there is a reference to the story of the destruction of Sodom and Gomorrah in 29:23. The implied context of 30:1-5 is the exile, with its promise that God will gather and bring back to the promised land those "who are exiled to the ends of the world" (v. 4). This does not mean, however, that these words were composed during the exile. Among the postexilic community was the knowledge that many Israelites remained in exile.

The chapters contain one problematic and several memorable passages. The NRSV translates 29:19 "thus bringing disaster on moist and dry alike," with a note that the meaning of the Hebrew is uncertain. The Hebrew (29:18) has the sense of something (a severe storm?) sweeping away the fertile land together with the parched land. The phrase appears to be a way of indicating total disaster.

30:11-14 is a noble, almost poetic, passage about the availability and accessibility of the commandment. The rendering of v. 14, "the word is very near to you," raises the question as to what is meant by "the word." Does it simply mean the commandment of v. 11? The NEB understandably has the rendering "it is a thing very near to you." Heb. *dabar* can mean "word" and "thing"; yet the following phrase, "it is in your mouth," points in the direction of "word" rather than "thing" despite the fact that its exact meaning is not clear. It is quite likely that

vv. 12-14 once existed independently and have been used here for a different purpose from that of their original context. We are given no clue as to why it should be objected that the word was too high in heaven or too far across the sea to be available. At the same time the enigmatic and poetic nature of the verses has made them attract the attention of later interpreters. In Bar 3:29-30 the verses are quoted in a hymn to Wisdom which uses them to argue for the inaccessibility of Wisdom. In Rom 10:6-8 Paul quotes them in order to maintain that the word of faith which he preaches is close to his readers.

Chapter 30 ends with the call to choose life, which is defined as loving God and holding fast to him. This helps to put into perspective the difficult language of chs. 28–29, which appears to attempt to coerce faithfulness with threats. Ultimately, the appeal to love God is based on his promises to the ancestors, not on the consequences of disloyalty.

Deuteronomy 31:1-29

It is easy to recognize that several different types of material have been combined in this chapter. At the level of general content, the theme of the appointment of Joshua to succeed Moses begins in vv. 2-8 and is continued in vv. 14-15 and 23. The account is interrupted, first by vv. 9-13 where Moses commands that the law be read every seventh year at the festival of Booths. It is further interrupted by vv. 16-22 in which God commands Moses to write down a song and teach it to the Israelites so that it will be a witness against them when they serve other gods and are punished by God. The theme of the septennial reading of the law appears to be resumed in vv. 24-29, while v. 30 serves as the introduction to the Song of Moses in ch. 31 and can therefore be seen as resuming vv. 16-22. The results so far can be represented as follows:

Moses and Joshua (vv. 2-8, 14-15 and 23)
Moses and the reading of the law (vv. 9-13 and 24-29)
Moses and his song (vv. 16-22, 30).

However, it is necessary to look deeper and to note that the first theme, at least, may combine material from different traditions. In 31:2-8 Moses himself introduces the matter of his succession by Joshua, in language that echoes earlier passages in Deuteronomy (cf. the reference to Sihon and Og in v. 4 with Deut 2:26–3:7). V. 14, however, indicates that it is God who intimates to Moses that his end is near and that he and Joshua must go to the tent of meeting — a location mentioned nowhere else in Deuteronomy but familiar from Exodus, Leviticus, and Numbers. Further, there is already an account of Joshua's installation as Moses' successor at Num 27:12-23. These duplications (within Deuteronomy 31 and between Deuteronomy and Numbers) no doubt reflect various stages and processes in the growth of the material to its present form. It has also been pointed out that vv. 16-22, dealing with Moses' song, contain many phrases not otherwise found in Deuteronomy.

The origin of the "song" will be discussed in connection with ch. 32; but its appearance is anticipated in ch. 31 in language that is not characteristic of Deuteronomy but which has been embedded within the chapter and not merely appended. It should also be noted that the phrase "be strong and bold" is found at v. 7 and v. 23, in literature that is Deuteronomic (Josh 1:6). The chapter has therefore combined Deuteronomic and non-Deuteronomic material in order to introduce Joshua (who will feature in the continuation of the story in Joshua), the song of Moses, and the important periodic readings of the law. Gatherings to hear the law read are mentioned, elsewhere, in Neh 8:1-8. As throughout Deuteronomy, God's faithfulness to his people (v. 8) is contrasted with the people's potential disloyalty (vv. 16-22). Yet, as mentioned before, God does not require obedience only for his own sake but for the sake of the people, especially the weak and vulnerable, whose protection and support are enjoined in the law. It is no accident that the occasion of the septennial reading of the law is one in which, according to 15:1-11, debts are to be remitted (cf. 31:10, "the scheduled year of remission").

Deuteronomy 31:30–32:51

Chapter 32 divides into three sections: the song (vv. 1-43), an account of Moses' words following the song (vv. 44-47), and God's command to Moses to ascend Mt. Nebo, where he will die.

The song is a noble poetic composition that echoes other parts of the OT while remaining unique. From the point of view of the Hebrew several verses are difficult (vv. 5a, 13b, 15a, 19, 26a, 31b, 43), while in vv. 6 and 7 there are awkward switches between the second person singular and plural. The literary figure of Moses is the speaker in vv. 1-19, 28-33, 36-38, and 43, while God is the speaker in vv. 20-27 (with the introduction "he said"), 34-35, and 39-42 (with no introduction). While these alternations, certainly from v. 28 onward, may be the result of later interpolations, the poem in its final state is not disjointed.

The purpose of the song, according to 31:19-22, was to confront the Israelites when they turned to other gods in the promised land. Whether it can be said with confidence that this was not the purpose of the author of the song (so Luyten in Lohfink 1985: 347) is debatable. What may seem to modern readers to be the purpose of a text cannot be assumed to be the view of ancient readers. Leaving aside speculations about the author's purpose, the following general observations can be made.

The poem begins as though it were the speech for the prosecution in a lawsuit (cf. Isa 1:2ff.) but soon becomes a résumé of Israel's history reminiscent of Psalms 78, 105, and 106 (and cf. the similar opening of Psalm 78). Yet the review of the past makes no mention of the ancestors Abraham, Isaac, and Jacob (Jacob in vv. 9 and 15 is a name for Israel as a whole) nor of the exodus from Egypt. Instead (vv. 10-14), the emphasis is on how God discovered a people in the wilderness that needed to be sustained, and how he met that need. The material has echoes, at the level of theme, of Ezekiel 16 and its parable of the foundling, and it is tempting to see the popular story of an abandoned boy behind these verses. There is no hint here, as against the traditions of the wilderness wanderings in Exodus, Numbers, and the opening chapters of Deuteronomy, that the wilderness was a place where the newly freed Israel constantly put God to the test. The language expressing how God cared for the people in the wilderness is vividly poetic.

This section is preceded by another remarkable one (32:4-6) which deals with creation not from the point of view of the origin of the material universe, but of a system of divine oversight of the peoples of the world. Here the text of the Hebrew at v. 8 is crucial. The traditional Hebrew text, followed by the AV and the RV (and still by the NIV) has, "according to the number of the children of Israel." Several of the ancient versions together with a manuscript from Qumran have "gods" or "God" for Israel, and most modern translations follow this. The idea (cf. Psalm 82) is that God had appointed divine beings to care for the nations of the earth, reserving for himself the care of Israel. This takes the idea of God's election of Israel back to creation. The traditional Hebrew text is probably an alteration to remove the reference to other gods. Jewish interpretation refers the verse to the scattering of the nations after the destruction of the tower of Babel and reckons the number of the children of Israel at seventy (Exod 1:5).

In the passages that tell of Israel's turning from God and their punishment (32:15-27) it is not possible to identify for certain the exact occasions of apostasy or of punishment. The threat to make Israel jealous with what is "no people" (v. 21) is too vague to be identified, although attempts have been made to link "no people" with the Assyrians or the Samaritans. There does not appear to be any explicit reference to the Babylonian exile, and the bulk of the poem may therefore predate the exile. Vv. 39-42 have strong resonances with Isa 41:4; 45:6-7; 48:12; and 63:3-6.

A notable feature in the poem is the space given to sentiments of compassion, especially for the future (32:36-42). This may help to give a rough idea of the date of the poem in its final form. If the first part echoes sentiments such as those found in Hosea 11 and Ezekiel 16 and the latter part sentiments of encouragement as found especially in Isaiah 40–55, the guess could be hazarded that the poem was composed any time in the decades prior to the Babylonian exile and that it was completed when hopes were high that the Babylonians would be defeated. The date of the poem is, however, less important than its unusual and powerful presentation of important theological themes.

32:44-47. Perhaps as though to emphasize that Joshua has already succeeded Moses, v. 44 attributes the song to Moses *and* Joshua (whose name is given in Hebrew as Hoshea; cf. Num 13:8). The immediately following verse, however, implies that only Moses has recited the song.

32:48-52. The "very day" on which God commanded Moses to ascend Mt. Nebo (v. 48) may be referred back to 1:3 (the first day of the eleventh month of the fortieth year), the implication being that Moses addresses the people on that day and then dies on the mountain. The reason given for not allowing Moses to enter the promised land is referred back to the incident at Kadesh (Num 20:2-13), although the narrative in Numbers 20 does not make clear what Moses' offense actually was.

Deuteronomy 33:1-29

The Blessing of Moses. The idea that the leader or ancestor should give a blessing at the end of his life is found in Gen 27:27-29, 39-40 (the blessing of Isaac) and Genesis 49 (the blessing of Jacob). Valedictory speeches are also attributed to Joshua (Joshua 24) and Samuel (1 Samuel 12). However, despite the similarities between Deuteronomy 33 and Genesis 49 in that both passages contain sayings that relate to individual tribes, Deuteronomy 33 sets the sayings within a hymnal framework (vv. 1-5, 26-29).

As the footnotes of modern translations indicate, there are many textual difficulties and variations between the Hebrew and the ancient versions. The present commentary is not the place to discuss these in detail, except as they touch on the matter of the date of the chapter. The difficulty of the text and its variants has been used as an argument for the antiquity of the passage. These phenomena can also be explained by the importance of the text within the literature (the blessing of *Moses*) and the fact that it has led to enlargements and interpretations within the versions themselves. Beyerle (1997: 272-73) argues that the various ancient versions should be regarded as editions in themselves and should not be used to try to reconstruct an original text. The only textual comment that needs to be made is that readers familiar with older translations will search in vain in the main text of the NRSV for the words "The eternal God is your dwelling place, and underneath are the everlasting arms" (33:27, RSV).

Three broad issues affect the interpretation of the chapter: (a) whether the hymnic framework was independent of the sayings concerning the tribes, (b) how the sayings relate to those in Genesis 49 and whether they provide material for reconstructing ancient Israel's history, and (c) what the chapter conveys in its key position at the close of Deuteronomy.

(a) A widely held view is that the hymnic framework (33:2-5, 26-29) is independent of the sayings. Further, the similarities between v. 2, describing God's coming from Sinai and Seir, and Judg 5:4-5, Ps 68:8, 17, and Hab 3:3 have led to the argument that the framework derives from an ancient theophany tradition (a tradition about God's "appearing," perhaps as part of traditions about holy war). However, the argument about the antiquity of the framework has to regard the reference to Moses in v. 4 as a later addition as well as adopting similar tactics in relation to Psalm 68 (the reference to the temple in Jerusalem [v. 29]) and Habakkuk 3 (taking it to be the addition of an ancient poem to the rest of the book, which dates from the late seventh century). It can just as plausibly be argued that the framework of Deuteronomy 33 is postexilic or that it is not to be separated from other material in the book. The rare designation for Israel, "Jeshurun" (vv. 5, 26), occurs elsewhere only in Deut 32:15 and Isa 44:2 (an exilic text).

(b) It has been usual to read the sayings about the tribes in conjunction with Genesis 49, drawing historical conclusions from the differences. Thus Simeon (Gen 49:5) is absent from Deuteronomy 33, Levi is a secular tribe in Genesis 49 but a priestly one in Deut 33:8-11, while Reuben (Gen 49:3-4) gets only the briefest of references in Deut 33:6. These differences led to the view that in the period between the composition of Genesis 49 (in the 11th cent. BC) and Deuteronomy 33 (the 8th cent. BC) Simeon had disappeared, Levi had ceased to be a secular tribe, and Reuben had almost died out. The arguments presupposed the existence of a tribal confederacy in the premonarchic period, a view that is little supported today. More recent studies (e.g., Schorn 1997) have argued that the twelve-tribe concept is a late literary and theological creation and that ancient tribal history cannot be extracted from Genesis 49 and Deuteronomy 33.

Whatever the truth of the latter opinions, two observations are necessary. First, it is northern tribes that are to the fore in Deuteronomy 33. The house of Joseph (i.e., the tribes of Ephraim and Manasseh which occupied the heartland of the Northern Kingdom, Israel, vv. 13-17) receives the longest treatment, while Judah gets only one verse (v. 7). Further, there are sayings about tribes that occupied areas north of the Jezreel valley as far as Dan, and possibly Transjordan (vv. 20-21). The whole of the Northern Kingdom was lost to the Assyrians in 722/721, which is why it has been argued that the sayings must date from before that loss. On the other hand, the opening chapters of 1 Chronicles (usually dated 400-350 BC) contain genealogies of the northern tribes including Simeon and Reuben, indicating that interest in these groups or areas existed long after they had ceased to be part of Israel.

The second point to be noted is that material in the sayings about tribes can be paralleled elsewhere in the OT. The material concerning Levi (33:8-11) can be paralleled in Exod 32:26-29, while the Joseph saying (33:13-17) has correspondences with Gen 49:25-26. The sayings can, in some, perhaps most, instances be regarded as literary compositions rather than fragments of ancient history preserved by word of mouth.

(c) The function of Deuteronomy 33 in its present context is twofold. It gives to Moses the status of someone entitled to give a blessing to the people. Up to this point in Deuteronomy Moses has almost entirely been a mouthpiece for God. Now he speaks in his own name, expressing hopes for the tribes that carry the authority of God's spokesman. Moses is shown to be in full command of his powers at death (cf. 34:7), speaking with the authority of age and the vigor of one whose powers have not declined.

Second, the Blessing of Moses enables the book to end on the theme of blessing. In some cases (chs. 27–28) threats have outweighed promises. At the end, there are only promises, based on the conviction of the incomparability of the God of Israel, who is his people's hope and salvation (33:26-29).

Deuteronomy 34:1-12

What ch. 33 implies of Moses in poetry, ch. 34 sets forth in prose. Moses dies with unimpaired sight and undiminished vigor, having glimpsed the promised land from Mt. Nebo. Although his grave is said to be unknown (v. 6), his epitaph is unsurpassed in the Bible: "Never since has there arisen a prophet in Israel like Moses, whom the LORD knew face to face. He was unequaled for all the signs and wonders that the LORD sent him to perform . . ." (vv. 10-11).

Bibliography. Beyerle, S. 1997, *Der Mosesegen im Deuteronomium: Eine text-, kompositions- und formkritische Studie zu Deuteronomium 33,* BZAW 250, Berlin: Walter de Gruyter • Borowski, O. 1987, *Agriculture in Iron Age Israel,* Winona Lake: Eisenbrauns • Braulik, G. 1 (1986) and 2 (1992), *Deuteronomium,* Kommentar zum Alten Testament mit der Einheitsübersetzung, Würzburg: Echter • Crüsemann, F. 1997, *Die Tora: Theologie und Sozialgeschichte des alttestamentlichen Gesetzes,* Gütersloh: Kaiser • Danby, H. 1993, *The Mishnah, Translated from the Hebrew with Introduction and Brief Explanatory Notes,* Oxford: Oxford University • Driver, S. R. 3d ed. 1902, *A Critical and Exegetical Commentary on Deuteronomy,* ICC, Edinburgh: T. & T. Clark • Hopkins, D. C. 1985, *The Highlands of Canaan: Agricultural Life in the Early Iron Age,* The Social World of Biblical Antiquity Series 3, Sheffield: Almond • Labuschagne, C. 1a (1987), 1b (1987), 2 (1990), *Deuteronomium,* De prediking van het Oude Testament, Nijkerk: Uitgeverij G. G. Callenbach • Labuschagne, C. 1993, *Deuteronomium,* Belichting van het Bijbelboek, 's-Hertogenbosch: Katholieke Bijbelstichting and Brugge: Uitgeverij Tabor • Lohfink, N., ed. 1985, *Das Deuteronomium: Entstehung, Gestalt und Botschaft,* BETL 68, Leuven: University Press & Peeters • Mayes, A. D. H. 1979, *Deuteronomy,* NCB, London: Oliphants • Nielsen, E. 1995, *Deuteronomium,* HAT 1/6, Tübingen: J. C. B. Mohr • Committee of the Royal Anthropological Institution of Great Britain and Ireland. 6th ed. 1951, *Notes and Queries on Anthropology,* London: Routledge & Kegan Paul • Otto, E. 1994, *Theologische Ethik des Alten Testaments,* Stuttgart: Kohlhammer • Otto, E. 2000, *Das Deuteronomium im Pentateuch und Hexateuch,* Tübingen: Mohr Siebeck • Pritchard, J. B. 3d ed. 1969, *Ancient Near Eastern Texts Relating to the Old Testament,* Princeton: Princeton University • Rashi. 1946, *Pentateuch with Targum Onkelos, Haphtoroth and Prayers for Sabbath and Rashi's Commentary,* ed. M. Rosenbaum and A. M. Silberman, London: Shapiro, Vallentine & Co. • Schorn, U. 1997, *Ruben und das System der zwölf Stämme Israels: Redaktionsgeschichtliche untersuchungen zur Bedeutung des Erstgeborenen Jakobs,* BZAW 248, Berlin: Walter de Gruyter • Steymans, H. U. 1995, *Deuteronomium 28 und die adê zur Thronfolgeregelung Asarhaddons: Segen und Fluch im Alten Orient und in Israel,* OBO 145, Freiburg: Universitätsverlag and Göttingen: Vandenhoeck & Ruprecht • von Rad, G. 1964, *Das fünfte Buch Mose: Deuteronomium,* ATD 8, Göttingen: Vandenhoeck & Ruprecht • Weinfeld, M. 1991, *Deuteronomy 1–11,* AB 5, New York: Doubleday.

Joshua

K. Lawson Younger Jr.

INTRODUCTION

The book is named after Joshua (Heb. *yehoshuaʿ*), the young apprentice and successor to Moses, who was the military commander in the "conquest" of Canaan and the administrator of that land's allotments to the tribes. Moses renamed Hoshea (Heb. *hosheaʿ*, "salvation") Joshua (Heb. *yehoshuaʿ*, "Yahweh saves"), introducing the Yahwistic theophoric element (Num 13:16).

The authorship of the book of Joshua is anonymous, and its final date of composition is unknown (although some recent studies possibly point to the period of Josiah). The book is commonly understood by scholars to be part of a large historical work, the Deuteronomistic history, stretching from Deuteronomy through 2 Kings.

The book's canonical narration imposes a number of forms on the presentation. First, the law (Torah) plays a normative role in the book. This can be seen from the very outset. Joshua's (and Israel's) relationship to Yahweh is based on the law and is crucial for Israel's success. Obedience or disobedience to the law determines success or failure.

Second, the book consistently develops the typology of Joshua as parallel to Moses. This can be seen in the following (by no means an exhaustive list!):

Moses	**Joshua**
1. Leads the Israelites *out of* Egypt	1. Leads the Israelites *into* Canaan
2. Sends out spies (Numbers 13)	2. Sends out spies (Joshua 2)
3. Crossing of a body of water (Red Sea) (Exodus 14)	3. Crossing of a body of water (Jordan) (Josh 4:23)
4. Circumcision (Exod 4:24-26; 12:48); Passover (Exodus 12)	4. Circumcision (Josh 5:2-9); Passover (Josh 5:10-12)
5. Theophany: the burning bush (Exod 3:1)	5. Theophany: the commander of Yahweh's army (Josh 5:13)
6. Allotted land to the 2½ Transjordanian tribes (Josh 13:8-33)	6. Allotted land to the 9½ Cisjordanian tribes (Josh 14:1–19:51)
7. Made provisions for the cities of refuge (Num 35:6-34) and levitical towns (Num 35:1-5)	7. Made provisions for the cities of refuge (Joshua 20) and levitical towns (Joshua 21)

Third, the book follows a general, logical sequence: A (preparation for the conquest), B (the conquest's campaigns), B′ (the allotment of the conquered land), A′ (the conclusion to the conquest).

1. The Conquest (1:1–12:24)
   - A Preparation for Conquest (Inclusion of Transjordanians, Crossing of the Jordan, Rituals, the Law among the Leaders and People, Commitment to Yahweh) (1:1–5:12)
   - B Conquest of the Land (the Central, Southern, and Northern Campaigns, and Summary) (5:13–12:24)
2. The Allotment of Conquered Land (13:1–24:33)
   - B′ Division of the Land (Land Remaining, Transjordanian Tribal Allotment, Cisjordanian Tribal Allotment, Allotments to Persons of Marginal Status, Ironic Conclusion) (13:1–21:45)
   - A′ Conclusion of Conquest (Inclusion of Transjordanians, Crossing of the Jordan, Rituals, the Law among the Leaders and People, Commitment to Yahweh) (22:1–24:33)

Fourth, the book's presentation is arranged along geographic lines. An east-to-west crossing into Canaan (chs. 2–5) is followed by military campaigns directed at the center (6–8), south (9–10), and north (11), concluded by a summary list (12). The division of the land first covers the Transjordanian tribes (13), next the central tribes (14–17), then the peripheral and nongeographic tribes (18–21) (Nelson 1997: 1).

Finally, land and territory dominate the book of Joshua, which contains 358 place names out of the biblical total of 746. Of these, 198 occur only in Joshua (Aḥituv 1995). The book utilizes a number of different "land" ideologies (whether anchored in concrete reality, or purely idealistic or a mixture) (Nelson 1997: 2). These "mental maps" conceptualize the land-producing tensions within the narration and set the stage for irony. The dominant land ideology is the territory of the twelve tribes (both west and east of the Jordan) who completely "fill up" the land (Joshua 15–19; cf. Deut 4:45-49). In this view, the twenty-two Transjordanian tribes are an integral and vital part of "all Israel." A contrasting ideology restricts the true land of inheritance to the territory west of the Jordan (Cisjordan, the land of Canaan) (cf. Deut 12:10). It is this image of the land that lies behind the belief that crossing the Jordan was a step of exceptional significance (Joshua 3–4). This view also creates the ironic tensions in Josh 22:10-34.

In addition, two other, more expansive maps are present. The first is the "land that remains" (13:2-6), which consists of claimed but unconquered territory in Philistia and Phoenicia. This ideology recognizes the limits of Israelite territory in Cisjordan and corresponds to the remainder of the ancient Egyptian province of Canaan. The second is the expansionistic aspiration of Josh 1:4, the dream of "Euphratic Israel," which claims the distant Euphrates as the northern boundary of Israel's promised land (cf. Gen 15:18; Deut 1:7; 11:24). These last two utopian notions of the "land that remains" and "Euphratic Israel" instill the book of Joshua with the flavor of unredeemed promise and again set the stage for ironic tensions. The text develops two understandings of Israel's unfulfilled expectations. On the one hand, the incomplete conquest is viewed as the result of Israel's disobedience or military inability (15:63; 16:10; 17:12-13; 19:47) and thus serves as the basis for future threats to Israel's well-being (7:12; 23:12-13). Yet, on the other hand, these two expansionistic land ideologies are put forth as hopeful indications of greater future land blessings to Israel (13:6b; 17:18; 23:5).

A concept that plays an important role in the book of Joshua is the *ḥerem.* The noun form is usually translated "devoted thing," and the verbal forms "totally destroy." Roughly 85 percent of its occurrences are in the context of warfare and destruction. It is clear that the *ḥerem*-narratives are connected with the notion of obedience/disobedience to Yahweh (i.e., the execution/non-execution of the *ḥerem*) (Schäfer-Lichtenberger 1994).

The essential delineation of the law of the *ḥerem* is found in Deuteronomy 7. The prescriptive phrases (7:1-5, 11, 16, 25) and promises (7:20-22) echo the covenantal terms of Exod 23:20-33. The implications of the *ḥerem* are clear: no covenant (treaty) with the inhabitants, no mercy, and no intermarriage. Its purpose, according to Deuteronomy 7, was to "drive out" or "dispossess" *(yarash)* the Canaanites. The apparent reasons seem to be threefold: judgment of the Canaanites (but cf. Gen 15:16), protection of the Israelites from Canaanite religious influence, and fulfillment of the patriarchal promises concerning the land. In Deut 20:17, the *ḥerem* is defined by the clause "you shall not leave alive anything that breathes" (referring to humans in particular).

This kind of warfare does not originate in a theology of "holy war" peculiar to OT theology but is a political ideology that Israel shared with other nations in the ancient Near East (Younger 1990: 235-36). In that context, all wars waged by a nation were "holy wars," dedicated to the glorification of its deity and the extension of the deity's land and reign. Thus the use of the phrase "holy war" is an inadequate description often given to the *ḥerem.*

COMMENTARY

The Conquest (1:1–12:24)

Joshua 1:1-18 and 11:16–12:24 serve as a type of prologue and epilogue to the conquest narration. The stories of 2:1–11:15 are bound together by story pairings (Rahab–Jericho; Jordan crossing–Jericho; Jericho–Achan; Achan–Ai; Rahab–Gibeon; south coalition–north coalition).

In addition, chs. 2–11 are bound together by the theme of the Canaanites "hearing" and "fearing," which occurs five times throughout the narration: 2:9-10a; 5:1; 9:1-3; 10:1-2; and 11:1-2 (Nelson 1997: 13).

Preparation for Conquest (1:1–5:12)

This first major section has four parts: the commission (1:1-18), the spies/Rahab story (2:1-24), the crossing of the Jordan (3:1–4:24), and the story of cultic rituals at Gilgal (5:1-12).

The Commission (1:1-18)

The book begins and ends with interpretive speech (Joshua 1 and 23–24) in which the transitions of leadership from Moses to Joshua and from Joshua to the succeeding generations is recounted. After an initial statement providing the setting (1:1), the commission (1:2-18) contains four speeches arranged in chiastic form (Hawk 1991: 58): A: Yahweh's speech (1:2-9), B: Joshua's speech to the officers (1:10-11), B′: Joshua's speech to the Transjordanian tribes (1:12-15), and A′: the Transjordanian tribes' speech to Joshua (1:16-18). Yahweh's speech confirms Joshua's election to succeed Moses and points programmatically toward the goal of total military success through his assurance of victory (1:2-5a). At the same time Israel's success according to Yahweh will come through the nation's obedience to the law (1:5b-9). Yahweh's speech foreshadows the main themes of the book: the *crossing* of the Jordan (1:1–5:12), the *conquest* (5:13–12:24), the *distribution* of the land (13:1–22:34), and the emphasis on *obedience to the law* (23:1–24:33) (Hess 1996a: 68-74; Nelson 1997: 30). The success of Joshua (and Israel) in obeying the law will be derived from the law's internalization, spoken of in 1:8 in terms of meditation. This suggests that what follows is the beginning of the implementation of the Deuteronomic program (cf. Deut 11:24-25 and Deut 31:7-8). The instruction of God to Moses is recapitulated in its presentation to Joshua (Polzin 1980: 32).

Joshua's obedience is immediately highlighted in his speeches to the officers (1:10-11) and to the Transjordanian tribes (1:12-15). In the fourth speech (1:16-18), the Transjordanian tribes affirm Joshua's leadership, echoing Yahweh's assurances of 1:1-9 above (cf. Deuteronomy 9–10).

The Spies/Rahab Story (2:1-24)

The sending out and the return of the spies (2:1; 2:23-24) frame three dialogues: Rahab's dialogues with the king's contingent at her door (2:3-5), her negotiations with the spies on her roof (2:8-14), and her negotiations with them at her window (2:16-21). Although ch. 2 interrupts the narration of the expected movement from ch. 1 (command to cross) to ch. 3 (actual crossing), it functions as a type of parenthesis that introduces important items that will form the background to the stories of the crossing of the Jordan and the conquest of Jericho.

Joshua commissions two spies (who remain nameless) to go and investigate the land, that is, Jericho (cf. Numbers 13; Deut 1:21-23; Josh 7:2-3). The spies go, but surprisingly they enter the house of a prostitute *(zonah).* While the text does not explicitly state that there was a sexual liaison between the spies and their hostess (Hess 1996a: 83), it provides an undercurrent of ambiguous sexual innuendo (Nelson 1997: 43). The place from which the spies were sent, Shittim, is the infamous place where the men of Israel "began to have sexual relations with the women of Moab" (Num 25:1). And now these two spies enter a prostitute's house. The occurrence of the words "Shittim" and "prostitute" in the same verse cannot be fortuitous. From the lofty expressions in Joshua 1, the reader's expectations are suddenly dashed.

If the Israelite spies were indeed trying to gain information in the least likely place to be noticed (Boling and Wright 1982: 145), they did not have much luck. For almost as soon as they arrived, their whereabouts and intentions were known to the king of Jericho. Fortunately for the spies, Rahab hid and protected them. In her conversation with the royal contingent, she immediately agreed with their assertion — yes, the Israelites had been there. But she deflected the guards with the statement that the men had left.

Thus it is Rahab, and not the ill-fated spies, who is at the center of the narrative. She is the only character with a name, and without her the spies would have had no success. In fact, even after the deflection of the guards, the spies were still in great trouble since "as soon as the pursuers had gone out, the gate was shut" (2:7). Why was Rahab kindly disposed toward the spies? Self-interest alone cannot explain her commitment since the risk of siding with an unknown enemy against one's own people is too great to ascribe solely to that motive. Either faith or discernment, or perhaps both, is required to explain such loyalty (*ḥesed*). This is demonstrated in Rahab's confession, which forms a chiasm (Hess 1996a: 90):

- A Rahab's confession: "I know that Yahweh has given this land to you" (2:9a)
  - B Military information: "all are melting in fear" (2:9b)
    - C Summary of Yahweh's mighty deeds: the Red Sea and Transjordanian kings (2:10)
  - B′ Military information: "all are melting in fear" (2:11a)
- A′ Rahab's confession: "for Yahweh your God is God in heaven above and on the earth below" (2:11b). Cf. Deut 4:39.

Rahab's confession is anticipatory on two counts. First, the disposition of the enemy — "melting in fear of the Israelites" — is anticipatory of the "hearing and fearing" expressed in 5:1; 6:1; 9:1-3; 10:1-2; 11:1-5. This theme ties the "conquest" section of the book together. Second, Yahweh's power over "heaven and earth" is anticipatory of the Divine Warrior's mighty actions: once at the Jordan, once at Jericho, and twice in the skies over Gibeon. Yahweh's action in the latter case is climactic of his involvement in the conquest.

Moreover, the narrative contains covenant/treaty aspects: preamble (2:11b); prologue (2:9-11a); stipulations (2:12-13); sanctions (2:18-20); oath (2:14, 17); and sign (2:18-21). Thus through her confession with its covenantal overtones, Rahab negotiates and secures the deliverance of herself and her family (cf. Josh 9:1-27 and contrast Deut 7:2).

Finally, Rahab easily solves the problem of the closed gates through the use of her window. Even when the spies are outside (2:16), Rahab remains very much in charge, giving these inept secret agents detailed instructions on how to avoid capture, dictating the route and schedule. But when the spies are safely out, they modify their oath, hedging it with conditions in order to absolve themselves from keeping the covenant to which they had just sworn loyalty (*ḥesed*). They put three stipulations on her in order for her to guarantee the protection of herself and her family: the scarlet cord must be tied to the window, all her family must be in her house, and she must not do anything that compromises the spies' safety. Interestingly, Rahab, the Canaanite prostitute, shows unconditional loyalty toward the spies, risking everything; but the spies show conditioned loyalty to Rahab, minimizing their risks. Who really *knows* Yahweh?

The scarlet cord (*tiqwah*) is the sign that Rahab must use for the spies. Its use here may add a touch of humor as well as being a wordplay with another sort of *tiqwah*, "expectation, hope" (Hawk 1991: 70; Nelson 1997: 52).

The report of the spies to Joshua is a repetition of Rahab's words to them. Without Rahab these men would not have returned, nor would they have been able to tell Joshua anything about the Canaanite disposition. They give Joshua a report entirely based on Rahab's words and interpret the situation with a faith statement also derived from her.

The story of Rahab is one of irony. Mighty men of God are ultimately found to be much less than expected, while a whore, whom we expect to be in the depths of sin, is the one who truly knows Yahweh and is obedient to him.

The Crossing the Jordan (3:1–4:24)

The narrative about the crossing of the Jordan is difficult with its digressions and reiterations. At times it seems to be convoluted. Usually these difficulties have been explained either by understanding the text as a combination of two self-contained narratives or by proposing multiple redactions.

Some recent scholars, however, have proposed a structural unity. They understand the irregularities as shifts in temporal perspectives or points of view, as the presentation of simultaneous actions in a sequential form, and as the development of instructions in ever greater detail as they are repeated (Polzin 1980: 94-99; Winther-Nielsen 1995: 169-90). The use of anticipatory statements and resumptive repetitions provides a means of narrating these simultaneous events (e.g., the anticipatory statement in 3:12 is tied to the resumptive repetition in 4:1). In addition, chs. 3 and 4 are linked together by speech/action bonds: 3:7 to 4:14; 3:11 to 4:11; 3:12 to 4:1-2; and 4:6-7 back to 3:16 (Nelson 1997: 58). These speeches initiate actions by means of command and prediction, and also explain the significance of what happens.

The repetitions and the miracle at the center of the story emphasize the crucial, transitional event of crossing the Jordan and entering the land. The crossing symbolizes the importance of all boundaries in the book, particularly those of the allotments (chs. 13–21), and of the tribal dispute of ch. 22 (Hess 1996a: 98). Thus while the Jordan is a military factor, it is more importantly a cultic and ideological symbol. It represents the boundary between landlessness and settled peoplehood. The fact that the procession of Josh 3:1–4:24 begins and ends at an early Israelite cult center ([Abel]-Shittim and Gilgal) reinforces this cultic significance.

The story has five episodes: 3:1-17; 4:1-10; 4:11-14; 4:15-18; and 4:19-24. The first three episodes are related from a spatial vantage point outside the land (i.e., east of the Jordan), whereas the last two episodes are oriented from a spatial vantage point inside the land (i.e., west of the Jordan) (Polzin 1980: 32). Episodes one, three, and four report the basic story of the crossing. Episodes two and five describe the story of the setting up of the memorial stones.

Episode one (3:1-17) narrates the preparational commands, explanations, and predictions as well as the actual miraclous stoppage of the water and crossing. It subdivides into 3:1-13 and 3:14-17. The initial subunit is composed of five commands given by the officers, Joshua, and Yahweh. These are accompanied by explanations and predictions: first command with explanation (3:3-4); second command with prediction (3:5); third command (3:6); fourth command with prediction (3:7-8); and fifth command with explanation and prediction (3:9-13).

After traveling from Shittim to the river, the officers pass through the camp a second time, commanding the people to follow the ark since the way is not known (i.e., this is the first time that they have crossed the Jordan). The distance that the people are to keep from the ark, two thousand cubits, is roughly nine hundred meters or a thousand yards. This separation takes place because of the presence of God represented by the ark. Joshua commands the people to sanctify themselves (reminiscent of Exod 19:10-25) because the LORD will do wonders (cf. 2:9-11).

Joshua commands the priests to lift the ark and go in front of the people. Yahweh predicts Joshua's exaltation among the Israelites just like Moses', and then he commands the priests through Joshua: they are to stand still in the Jordan. Joshua explains to the people that the Lord himself is crossing *before* them (a concept that has military overtones to it; see Younger 1990: 262-63). This event will confirm that the living God (i.e., the God who is active) will defeat and drive out the peoples listed in stereotyped fashion in 3:10.

3:12 is anticipatory of 4:2. It introduces a new element to the story that will transpire simultaneously with the crossing of the people. Thus it creates suspense. 3:13 contains a prediction: the water will stop (lit. "cut off" and "stand still").

The second subunit of episode one (3:14-17) records the actual miraculous stoppage of the water and crossing. The "wonders" promised in 3:5 are first anticipated in 3:13, then reported in 3:14-16, then summarized in 3:17. There is a chiasm between 3:13 and 3:16: A ("cut off"), B ("stand still"), B′ ("stood still"), and A′ ("was cut off") (Nelson 1997: 61). The two verbs describe a single image: the waters were cut off because they stood still. There is also a wordplay between the water that "stands" and the ark carriers who also "stand" (3:8, 17; 4:10). Moreover, there is a very clear link between this miracle and another later in the book: "and the waters stood still" (Josh 3:16) and "and the sun stood still" (Josh 10:13e). The miracle's magnitude is increased in two ways: the Jordan is at springtime flood, and the gap in the river is as far away as Adam, about eighteen miles north of Jericho. Thus the miracle was practical, providing a quick and effective crossing. Importantly, 3:17 stresses the continued presence of the priests with the ark in the midst of the dry riverbed. Thus the story is not finished. The verse is anticipatory of 4:10. Time is frozen while 4:1-14 explores in more detail the crossing and the matter of the memorial stones. It is unfrozen in 4:15, with the command for the priests to come up out of the Jordan. This literary technique of freezing time and shifting perspective is cinematic.

Episode two (4:1-10) explains the erecting of the twelve-stone memorials. This story is simultaneous with the conclusion of the people's crossing and the stationary position of the ark in the riverbed. V. 9 refers to a second set of stones. Once these commands are all fulfilled and the people have hastened across, the ark also moves across. This action is stated in a general way in 4:11. Vv. 15-18 describe it fully, but only after a "flashback" which provides further information on the crossing (4:12-13) and a comment on its significance (4:14). The narrative which began with 3:15-16 is finally completed in 4:18. V. 19 then fixes the time and place of the crossing and introduces Gilgal. The purpose of the memorial is to glorify Yahweh who did this mighty deed.

Episode three (4:11-14) recounts the crossing over of the ark and the Transjordanian tribes, along with Joshua's exaltation. A flashback (4:12-13) reports that the eastern tribes have done what Moses commanded and Joshua reiterated (1:14; Deut 3:18). Resumptive repetition in v. 14 stresses again the fulfillment of Yahweh's exaltation of Joshua, as with Moses.

Episode four (4:15-18) narrates the coming up out of the Jordan of the priests and the ark with the unstopping of the water. 4:15-17 represent the command phase, and v. 18 the action phase. Joshua commands the priests to come up out of the Jordan. V. 18 reports an item-by-item reversal of what happened in 3:15-16. In fact, the verse backtracks to "the middle of the Jordan" before reporting that the priests actually leave the water.

Episode five (4:19-24) describes the instructional value of the memorial through comparison with the Red Sea crossing. V. 19 returns the focus to the people instead of the priests, and provides a chronological and geographic marker. In fact, Gilgal will be the center for numerous Israelite activities in the conquest of the land and the initial allotments (9:6; 10:6-7; and 14:6). Resumptively the stones are mentioned (4:20). The erecting of stones has covenantal significance (cf. Exod 24:4 [twelve stones] and Josh 24:26). 4:24 elevates the purpose of the crossing to a universal level.

Final Preparatory Events at Gilgal (5:1-12)

Hearing of the drying up of the waters of the Jordan and Israel's crossing, the Cisjordanian kings' hearts "melt" with fear (5:1). While the verse is resumptive of 2:9-11, it is also anticipatory of all the campaigns in the land (9:1;

10:1; 11:1), especially Jericho. Three events (two of them cultic rituals) are recounted: circumcision (5:2-9), the Passover (5:10), and the first consumption of the produce of the land at Gilgal (5:11-12). As Polzin notes, "together with Joshua 2, this chapter deals primarily with the theme of God's mercy and forgiveness in allowing Israel to occupy the land" (Polzin 1980: 110).

In the first event (5:2-9), the text contrasts the disobedience of the older generation (those of the first circumcision who came out of Egypt and died in the wilderness) and the obedience of the new generation (who now participate in a second circumcision, 5:2). Thus Israel's disobedience at Mt. Sinai and Kadesh-barnea and God's threat to destroy them (Deut 1:19-35; 9:12-23) are recalled and contrasted with the faith of the generation that Joshua circumcises. The exposure/trust motif in this ritual also emphasizes the Israelites' faith, since a circumcision performed in safety on the other side of the Jordan would not require faith in God's protection. Gilgal's very close proximity to Jericho heightens this exposure/trust motif (cf. Genesis 34). The description, "a land flowing with milk and honey" (5:6), anticipates the consumption of the land's produce (5:10-12) and reinforces the graciousness of Yahweh toward Israel.

In fact, Yahweh declares that he has "rolled" (hence the name Gilgal) away the reproach of Egypt from Israel (Josh 5:9). This refers specifically to Deut 9:28 and demonstrates that the crossing and the circumcision are God's graciousness toward Israel in spite of Israel's lack of faithfulness in the wilderness. The covenant people must be in proper covenant relationship with Yahweh in order for him to fight on their behalf. Hence the very sign of that covenant must be in place. Importantly, too, circumcision is a prerequisite for celebrating the Passover (Exod 12:48).

In the second event (5:10), the narrative compares the older generation (participants in the first Passover in Egypt) with the new generation (participants in a second Passover). Like the first event, this cultic ritual act reinforces the portrayal of Joshua as parallel to Moses. Like the first, this Passover is a national Passover rather than a familial celebration.

The third event is the first consumption of the produce of the land (5:11-12). This event also emphasizes God's graciousness to undeserving Israel (cf. Deut 26:1-3). Unleavened bread and roasted grain are foods of disordered circumstances and time pressures since they involve uncomplicated preparations. While roasted grain is a typical "first fruit" (Lev 2:14; 23:14), it is also connected to the Passover and First Fruits (Lev 23:5-8, 9-14). The link and emphasis on first fruits is anticipatory of and has special implications for the first conquest in the land: Jericho.

Thus the land claim of the book of Joshua, usually presented as a matter of conquests (Joshua 6–12) and geographic lists (Joshua 13–21), is set forth in terms of cultic events and diet. The change from manna to produce of the land signifies Israel's relocation from wilderness to land. Israel does not have to wait for the completion of the conquest, for the gifts of the land are already available from the plundered fields (Nelson 1997: 80).

Conquest of the Land (5:13–12:24)

Central campaign (5:13–8:35)

The central campaign divides into three sections: the capture of Jericho (5:13–6:27), Achan and Ai (7:1–8:29), and covenant renewal at Shechem (8:30-35).

Jericho (5:13–6:27)

The story of Jericho's fall is comprised of two parts: the numinous appearance of the commander of Yahweh's army (5:13–6:5) and Jericho's capture (6:6-27). Jericho's capture is important because it is the first implementation of the *ḥerem* by the Israelites in the conquest.

The confrontation found in the numinous appearance of the commander of Yahweh's army (5:13–6:5) is reminiscent of the confrontation between Moses and the LORD at the burning bush (Exod 3:1–4:17; cf. also Gen 32:22-32) (Schäfer-Lichtenberger 1995: 210). But Joshua's acceptance of the figure's authority rather than objection is a major difference. The motif of a divine being with brandished sword is known from the literary and iconographic traditions of the ancient Near East. Usually these figures promote confidence-building oracles of victory. On the surface the figure's reply to Joshua's question appears enigmatic. But the commander is neither Israelite nor Canaanite. He is not part of a human army, but rather the commander of the heavenly forces. The commander's words (5:15) duplicate those of Yahweh to Moses at the burning bush (Exod 3:5): "remove your sandals because the place is holy." In a positive sense, the place is holy because it is where God is. It may also be holy in the negative sense: analogous to the state of *ḥerem*. The metal objects of Jericho will be proclaimed both *ḥerem* and holy (6:19). Thus Jericho as a "shoes off place" is off-limits to ordinary human usage, in accord with the curse of Josh 6:26 (Nelson 1997: 82-83).

Some interpreters see no connection between 5:13-15 and 6:1-5, understanding 6:1 to be an abrupt ending to a very enigmatic and perhaps fragmentary appearance of the commander of Yahweh's army (Hawk 1991; Nelson 1997). But it is also possible to understand 6:1 as a type of parenthetical statement and 6:2-5 as a continuation of the scene of 5:13-15. The passage deliberately parallels Joshua to Moses: both have theophanic calls with instructions. Thus, as in Moses' call, the divine word introduces the mission with an explanation of the problem that the mission will resolve (cf. Exod 3:7). Josh 6:1 introduces the obstacle to Israel's possession of the land (Hess 1996a: 128). With the stress on Jericho's impregnability, the writer heightens the contrast by giving Yahweh's oracle of assurance in v. 2. Yahweh gives the instructions for the city's capture in vv. 3-5. These emphasize his role in the city's capture.

The capture of Jericho is narrated in 6:6-27. Yahweh's instructions are followed. Ritual plays an important symbolic function: seven priests, seven trumpets, seven days, seven encirclements on the seventh day, and a seventh-day climactic victory. Thus ritual ceremony overcomes the walls of Jericho. But it is not simple ritual ceremony alone that accomplishes this. The Israelites' trust in Yahweh's plan is fundamentally tied into the ritual actions of the seven days. The preponderance of "sevens" in the narrative recalls the seven days of creation and seems to imply that this is the creation of a new order in the land. Consequently, it continues the land claim by ritual narrated in the previous section (5:2-12, esp. 11-12). Hence the description of the destruction of Jericho portrays the city as a sacrifice to God, a "first fruit" of the conquest.

In addition, the city's fall is important in the larger context as the first implementation of the *ḥerem*. Jericho (the first Canaanite town) is put under the *ḥerem*. Ironically, Rahab, a Canaanite prostitute along with her family, is not put under the *ḥerem*. Hence Jericho's importance is connected to the thematic thread regarding the *ḥerem* (Jericho/Rahab : Achan : Ai).

Thus the fall of Jericho is really more ritually symbolic than military in its significance. Its importance is connected not to its size but to its didactic purposes. The narrative functions to reinforce the Israelites' claim to the land and to instruct Israel concerning important issues related to the *ḥerem* (6:17-19, 21-25). The text's concern to emphasize the victory of Joshua and Israel under God's direction may have led readers to confuse the stress on the miraclous victory that God brought about with an emphasis on the size of the obstacle to that victory.

The repetition concerning the "devoted things" (*ḥerem*) in 6:19 and 24 functions to indicate Israel's faithfulness in the implementation of the *ḥerem;* and yet, on the other hand, to contrast this with Achan's unfaithfulness regarding the *ḥerem,* anticipating his climactic admission (7:20-21). The more stern implementation of the *ḥerem* (putting all non-living booty under the *ḥerem;* cf. Deut 7:25-26; 13:15-18) seems appropriate because Jericho's conquest was so completely the work of Yahweh that all of its booty should have been his possession. It may also be that Jericho represents a paradigm for the entire enterprise of conquest (8:2; 10:1; 24:11).

The curse of Joshua on Jericho (6:26) may also emphasize the complete dedication of the city to Yahweh since cursing (like salting, cf. Judg 9:45) was sometimes an act of consecration to a deity. The climactic conclusion (v. 27) states that Yahweh was with Joshua and that his fame was in all the land.

Achan and Ai (7:1–8:29)

First battle of Ai — Achan's sin (7:1-5) Immediately the text narrates a contrast to the climactic conclusion of the Jericho story: "but the Israelites broke faith in regard to the devoted things: Achan . . . took some of the devoted things." Just as the narration of Jericho's capture received great attention because of being the first victory in the land, so the narration of Achan's sin occupies a large amount of space because it documents the first breach of Israel's purity before God.

No other character has been introduced in the book with such familial detail — four generations are listed for Achan. In contrast to the nameless spies of ch. 2, Achan's genealogy is profuse.

Although only one person is unfaithful, all Israel is held liable. This is understandable in the light of Israel's ritual context, as well as in the context of corporate personality. According to 6:18-19, the booty from Jericho is thought of as both "holy" *(qadosh)* and "devoted" *(ḥerem)* because it belongs to Yahweh. Because the state of being devoted *(ḥerem)* is contagious, the booty would contaminate Israel's camp and put it into a state of "devotion" *(ḥerem),* bringing trouble *(ʿakar)* on it (i.e., "making the camp taboo"; cf. 7:12, 25).

The description of the first battle of Ai has numerous similarities to the description of Israel's failure to the enter the land in Numbers 13–14. Joshua's instructions to the spies sent to Ai resemble those given by Moses to the spies in Num 13:17-20. The spies' explanation, that they do not wish to "weary" the other Israelites, evinces their lack of faith in Yahweh. In Numbers 13–14, the Israelites lacked faith because they did not believe they were strong enough and feared the Canaanites; but here the Israelites lack faith because they believe that Israel is too strong to worry about such a small fortress (Hess 1996a: 146). Overconfidence spells a lack of dependence on Yahweh. Finally, the men of Ai thoroughly repulsed the Israelite contingent, just as the Israelite contingent was repulsed in Num 14:42-45, resulting in "the heart of the people melting" and "becoming like water" (7:5; cf. Josh 2:11; 5:1).

Interestingly, when Yahweh is consulted, there is victory (Jericho, second battle of Ai). When there is no consultation, there is defeat (first battle of Ai, Gibeonite ruse).

Second application of ḥerem — Achan's execution (7:6-26) Joshua and the Israelite elders (mentioned here for the first time) respond to the defeat with humiliation and repentance. While Joshua's complaint in Josh 7:7-9 resembles those of the people found in Num 14:2-4 and 20:3-5, questioning God's guidance, there is a difference. Joshua concludes his complaint with a concern for God's honor, a concern that Moses had expressed in his prayers (Exodus 33; Num 14:13-19). However, although Joshua and Israel thought that they were obeying God, they were ignorant of Achan's hidden transgression of the *ḥerem*.

Thus God answers Joshua with a rebuke (7:10). Rather than question God's guidance and faithfulness, Joshua and the elders need to understand that there has been a covenant violation. Since the devoted things *(ḥerem)* belonged to God, to take God's property is theft. The denial of the theft is deceit. As long as Israel possesses the devoted things, God will consider them as devoted things! Therefore, Joshua and the Israelites need to sanctify themselves *(qadash)* and remove the devoted things *(ḥerem)*.

This will require the offender's identification. As Hess notes, the verb "take" (Heb. *lakad,* vv. 14ff.) normally describes the capture of an enemy (cf. 6:20). The selection ceremony symbolizes God's act of warfare against the nation in which God captures the person who stole his property. Moreover, the process of selection only heightens Achan's guilt and recalcitant attitude. He hopes that with each selection another tribe, clan, or family will be taken, and he will get away with his theft. At each point, he could have come forward and confessed his guilt. But instead, he is willing to let another innocent person — thirty-six already have — suffer his punishment so that he will escape.

The actual *ḥerem* objects are listed in Achan's admission (7:20-21): a beautiful mantle from Shinar (i.e., Babylon), two hundred shekels (about 2.7 kg. or 6 lb.) of silver, and a fifty-shekel bar (about 560 gm. or 1.25 lb.) of gold. Obviously, the entire horde could be transported and hidden with ease (especially if there were familial support).

The return of the goods and their display before Yahweh symbolize the return by Israel of these items to God's rightful possession. The act called upon God to bear witness that Israel held back nothing that belonged to him. It also ritually removed the *ḥerem* things from among the Israelites, rescinding the Israelites from being "taboo" (*ʿakar*). This may explain the mention of the valley of Achor (from the same root as *ʿakar*), emphasizing the concern to remove the impurity from Israel's midst. 7:25 refers back to 6:18, Yahweh's explicit command concerning the *ḥerem* booty of Jericho.

The execution of Achan and his family (outside the camp) implies that God would not only take Achan's own life but also demand his name, here a reference to all future generations (cf. Lev 24:10-23; Num 15:32-36; Acts 5:1-11). They would all be given back to God as part of the devoted things. Ironically, the deliverance of Rahab and her family preserves her name within the very tribe (Judah) from which Achan's is removed. Furthermore, it is not Achan's name that is preserved in the valley where he died, but rather a name, Achor, derived from a wordplay on his final state of "taboo, trouble, disaster" (*ʿakar*).

Second battle of Ai — third application of ḥerem — Ai's destruction (8:1-29) Yahweh gives assurance and instructions (8:1-2); Joshua relates these instructions to the Israelites (8:3-8); and Ai is captured and put under the *ḥerem* (8:9-29). Yahweh's instructions give clear indication that Achan's sin has been removed so that God can once again give Israel the land. Not only are the instructions filled with reassurances of divine guidance, but they also include a provision concerning the booty of Ai: they may have the plunder of Ai.

In this battle, in contrast to the first, *all* of the Israelite warriors participate in a stratagem initiated by Yahweh. The thirty thousand (8:3) is better understood as thirty units. What Yahweh commanded, Joshua and the Israelites did. The repetitions are used by the writer to build suspense (Boling and Wright 1982: 240). The mention of Bethel (v. 17) may indicate that Ai was simply an outpost for that city. (For the archeology of Ai, see Hess 1996a: 157-58.)

The description of Joshua's actions (8:18-29) portray him in a similar way to Moses' actions in Exodus 14, although Moses uses a staff and Joshua a sickle sword (not NIV, "javelin"). The Israelites fulfill Yahweh's instructions concerning the king, people, and city of Ai. Ai's burning is described in terms of a burnt offering. The hanging of the king of Ai and his stone memorial in the gate of the destroyed city are not only common actions in ancient Near Eastern warfare but are anticipatory of the five kings of the south in Joshua 10.

This central campaign can be summed up in relation to the implementations of the *ḥerem:*

- The first implementation is the Canaanite city of Jericho, which serves as a type of first fruits of the Israelite conquest. Ironically, Rahab, a Canaanite prostitute, and her family are not put under the *ḥerem.* But Achan, an Israelite, takes plunder that is under the *ḥerem.* His sin places Israel under the *ḥerem* and causes its defeat at the first battle of Ai.
- The second implementation is Achan and his family. Thus ironically an Israelite and his family are put under the *ḥerem* while a Canaanite prostitute and her family survive within the same very tribe. The removal of Achan's sin causes the victory at the second battle of Ai.
- The third implementation is the Canaanite city of Ai. God graciously allows the Israelites to take some of the plunder that is under the *ḥerem.* Since God no longer was providing the manna for the Israelites as he had done in the wilderness, he provides specifically for the physical needs of his people through the plunder. Ironically this serves as a lesson to trust or wait on Yahweh. If Achan had trusted in, waited on, and obeyed Yahweh's word, he may have received some of the booty that he sought. Thus God's goodness and fairness were at issue with Achan. He did not believe that God was being fair to him in Jericho's *ḥerem* and seized what belonged to God. Faith in God would have brought different results.

Covenant Renewal as Land Grant: Shechem (8:30-35)

The central campaign's conclusion takes a geographic (and chronological?) leap from Ai to the Shechem area (specifically Mt. Ebal and Mt. Gerizim). In contrast to raising a heap of stones over the deceased king of Ai (8:29), Joshua erects an altar to Yahweh on Mt. Ebal (8:30). (For the archeological context, see Mazar 1990: 251.) Having introduced covenantal concerns with the implementations of the *ḥerem* in Joshua 6–8, and having just described the burning of Jericho and Ai in terms of sacrifice, this ceremony readdresses Israel's relationship with God through sacrifice and covenant renewal.

Moreover, Josh 8:30-35 seems to evince elements of a divine covenantal land grant ceremony, similar to royal land grant ceremonies in Mesopotamia. Thus, just as *kudurru*-stones were used in Mesopotamia in connection with land grants, Moses directed the erection of a stone on which the words of the covenantal land grant were to be written: "When you pass over to enter the land which the LORD your God gives you" (Deut 27:2-8).

Joshua plays the central role: erecting the altar, writing a copy of the law on stones, reading the words of the law, and fulfilling all the words of Moses (Josh 8:30-32 is presented as a direct fulfillment of Deut 27:2-13). All societal categories are represented, including women, children, and aliens. The mention of aliens may allude to those who by faith in Yahweh had joined with Israel (like Rahab and her family).

With the covenantal issues resolved through the covenant renewal with its land grant implications, the text can relate the southern and northern campaigns in more abbreviated fashion. The motifs of ruse (8:2-29) and alien presence in Israel (8:30-35) will be joined together in the story of the Gibeonites in Joshua 9.

The Southern and Northern Campaigns (9:1–11:15)

The conquests of southern and northern Canaan share the same historiographic aims and ideology. The same geographic pattern is used in both: center → periphery. Furthermore, both narrations use stereotyped components in such a way as to produce a high-redundance message that, in turn, supports the imperialistic ideology of the text.

***Conquest of Southern Canaan* (Josh 9:3–10:43)**	***Conquest of Northern Canaan* (Josh 11:1-15)**
Expositional setting: the Gibeonite deception and treaty	
Introductory setting: organization of an opposing Amorite alliance (Adonizedek, king of Jerusalem)	Introductory setting: organization of an opposing Canaanite coalition (Jabin, king of Hazor)
Oracle of assurance to Joshua from Yahweh	Oracle of assurance to Joshua from Yahweh
Victory in one decisive open-field battle: Gibeon	Victory in one decisive open-field battle: Waters of Merom
Pursuit of the retreating enemy to the southernmost boundary of the tribal inheritances	Pursuit of the retreating enemy to the northernmost boundary of the tribal inheritances
Capture of the leading cities	Capture of the leading city of Hazor
Summary of the campaign	Summary of the campaign

The southern campaign is a much more developed narrative than the northern campaign. This augmentation is observable in the basic components of Josh 10:1-43 and 11:1-15. Thus the region that became Judah's tribal allotment receives the greater emphasis (a pattern also noticed in Joshua 13–19 and Judges 1).

In the first instance, Joshua 10 contains an expositional setting in which the Gibeonite deception and treaty are narrated. Joshua 11 does not have an expositional setting. Second, the introductory setting in ch. 10 contains both the content of what the organizing leader "heard" and the content of his message to the other kings. Ch. 11 lacks both of these items. Third, in the oracle of assurance in ch. 10, there is the further assurance that none of the enemy would "stand" (*'amad,* which has special significance in Joshua 10) before Joshua. In ch. 11, however, Yahweh gives special instructions concerning the Canaanite horses and chariots. Fourth, the open-field battle in Joshua 10 includes significant narration of Yahweh's divine interventions (i.e., the miracles of the hailstones and the "sun standing still"); in the open-field battle in Joshua 11 the particulars of the divine intervention are not narrated. Fifth, in Joshua 10 the pursuit of the enemy is further developed in the story of the capture and execution of the fleeing kings (Josh 10:16-27); the pursuit of the enemy in Joshua 11 contains only a very general statement of capture and execution of the Canaanite kings (only the king of Hazor is specifically mentioned). Finally, the account of the capture of the leading cities is fully developed in Joshua 10; in Joshua 11 only the capture and destruction of Hazor are mentioned.

Introductory Statement (9:1-2)

While the statement of Josh 9:1-2 is similar to those previously given in 2:10 and 5:1 insofar as it mentions the Canaanite kings "hearing," it is also very different in the reaction to this "hearing." In the previous instances, the reaction was fear. In this passage (as well as in 10:1 and 11:1), the reaction is aggressive hostility (only the Gibeonite reaction in 9:3 is different). Likely the impact of Achan's sin in the defeat at the first battle of Ai is intended to be in view (Hess 1996a: 175-76).

Southern Campaign (9:3–10:43)

Gibeon (9:3-27) Ironically, Israel has just defeated Ai by means of a ruse; now Israel is defeated by means of a ruse. The Israelites do not turn to God to discern the Gibeonite strategy. As in the case of the first battle of Ai, the Israelites' overconfidence in their ability to discern the situation leads them to a lack of dependence on Yahweh.

The Gibeonites are apparently Hivites who assert that they are from a distant land (hence the Israelites are permitted to make an alliance with them). The detailed manner in which they provision themselves is meant to undergird this claim. They want a treaty with the Israelites and are prepared to be in vassal relationship to Israel (for similar appeals in the ancient context, see Younger 1990: 200-204). While 9:14 blames specifically "the men of Israel" for not consulting Yahweh, Joshua is apparently included (Butler 1983: 103). None of Israel's leadership was exempt from blame.

After the Israelites discover the Gibeonites' true origin, the text twice narrates the subservience of the Gibeonites as hewers of wood and drawers of water in parallel: the leaders of the people save them and conclude their slave status, as does Joshua (9:18-21 and 9:22-27).

The Defeat of the Amorite Alliance (10:1-43) Joshua 10:1-43 contains two scenes (10:1-15; 10:16-43) both of which end with identical statements (vv. 15, 43). Both scenes utilize temporal panels that employ the compositional technique of backtrack and overlap (Nelson 1997: 138-39; Hess 1996a: 186-87). Each of these panels takes a part of the previous panel and develops it further. The movement throughout the chapter is from the general to the particular. After the initial panel, the second and third panels of scene one are devoted to recounting God's role in the battle. The two panels of scene two are devoted to recounting Israel's role.

Scene one (10:1-15) contains three panels. The first panel relates the circumstances and initial issues of the battle (10:1-10). This panel is comprised of two parts: the formation of the Amorite alliance headed by Adoni-zedek of Jerusalem (10:1-5), and the initial open-field battle between the Israelites and the Amorite alliance with the slaughter and pursuit to Azekah (10:6-10). Jerusalem, an important Amarna period city-state, is the driving force in the alliance. Ironically, Adoni-zedek's appeal to the Amorite kings to "come up" (*'alah*) and "help" (*'azar*) him in v. 4 is undone by Israel "coming up" (*'alah*) and "helping" (*'azar*) Gibeon in v. 6. An impressive night march by Joshua and the Israelite army leads to the surprise attack and rout of the enemy. The pursuit from Gibeon to Azekah makes perfect geographic sense (Nelson 1997: 141) and is well within the distance that an ancient army could cover in a day's battle (approximately 30 km.). V. 10, with its mention of Azekah and Makkedah, anticipates the second panel of scene one as well as the first panel of scene two.

The second panel of scene one (10:11) backtracks and overlaps the first panel describing the enemy flight again to Azekah with the further development of the divine intervention with deadly hailstones (lit. "large stones from heaven"). Divine interventions are common motifs in ancient war accounts (see Younger 1990: 208-11). Such an intervention here may have had a debunking purpose: to undermine the Canaanite storm-god, Baal. These hailstones anticipate the large stones (same words in the Hebrew) that seal the kings in the caves (10:18-27).

The third panel of scene one (10:12-15) also backtracks and overlaps, describing Joshua's request to Yahweh at the beginning of the battle with the further development of the "miracle" concerning the sun and moon. The interpretation of this divine intervention is complicated by the facts that the request is poetic (a quote from the book of Jashar — a poetic book celebrating Israel's wars) and that this is, in turn, embedded in the prose of 10:12-14. It is impossible to enter into a full discussion of this tremendous crux (for the most recent discussions see Nelson 1997: 142-45 and Hess 1996a: 196-99). Whatever the case, the emphasis is on Yahweh, who listened to Joshua's request and directed the cosmic entities (which the Canaanites understood as deities) in his fight against this Amorite alliance on Israel's behalf. The third panel of scene one concludes with Joshua and Israel returning to Gilgal (10:15). This verse is a compositional technique and should not be pressed literally.

Scene two (10:16-43) contains two panels and a summary. The first panel (10:16-27) backtracks and overlaps the pursuit, developing the capture and execution of the Amorite kings. The mention of Makkedah in v. 16 is resumptive (cf. 10:10 above). Ironically, the cave that the kings choose as their hiding place becomes their prison, and then their tomb. The kings are ceremonially executed (the placing of feet upon the neck was an image of defeat in biblical and ancient Near Eastern war accounts) and hanged on trees (also a common image in these ancient accounts). The passage also emphasizes the obedience of Israel to Joshua and Joshua's obedience to the Deuteronomic legislation (cf. Deut 21:22-23).

The second panel (10:28-39) also backtracks to the pursuit and develops the capture and *ḥerem* of the cities in a stereotyped and redundant manner (Younger 1995). As a typical ancient Near Eastern war account, it uses hyperbole — overstating the outcomes of the campaign — in order to persuasively emphasize the success of the Israelite army. The mention of the king of Gezer at the center of the seven short episodes emphasizes that city's importance. While the city is not captured, the defeat of its king and army in open battle crowns the southern campaign.

Joshua 10:40-42 gives a concluding summary of the southern campaign. Again, overstatement emphasizes the greatness of the Israelite victory. Scene two concludes (like scene one above) with Joshua and Israel returning to Gilgal (10:43).

Northern Campaign (11:1-15)

Defeat of the Canaanite coalition (11:1-11) 11:1-15 is a literary mirror of 10:1-43 both in general structure and in vocabulary (Nelson 1997: 151; Hess 1996a: 207), though less developed. A large and powerful Canaanite coalition is organized and headed by Jabin, the king of Hazor. This enemy is superior to the Israelite army, both numerically ("as innumerable as the sand of the seashore") and technologically (they have dreaded horses and chariots). Furthermore, this coalition is not like the southern one, comprised only of Amorites. It contains many diverse, imposing groups (11:3). This coalition presents the most significant threat to Israel's success in conquering the land.

Yahweh's oracle of assurance precedes the victory (cf. 8:1; 10:8). His command to hamstring the horses (i.e., cutting a tendon of a rear leg) and burn the chariots is not divine guidance on battle tactics as it is sometimes understood, but a type of *ḥerem* that makes the animals and military equipment (cf. Ps 46:9 [Heb. 10]) useless for military purposes in any future engagement by either the Canaanites or the Israelites (Nelson 1997: 153). In the case of the latter, this would guarantee trust in Yahweh rather than in military technology (cf. Deut 17:16).

Israel's "sudden" attack at the waters of Merom (11:7) implies that Yahweh provided victory in the shape of an unreported panic as in 10:10 (Nelson 1997: 153). Pursuing the enemy in a clockwise fashion, the Israelites come full circle almost back to the initial battlefield, which puts them in position to capture Hazor, the most important northern city. Hazor is totally destroyed by burning, just as Jericho and Ai were (cf. 6:24; 8:8, 19). Thus Jericho and Hazor frame the conquest of the land of Canaan.

Summary of northern campaign (11:12-15) 11:12-15 summarize the Israelite conquest in the north. An *inclusio* showing Joshua's complete obedience to the commandments of Yahweh and Moses (vv. 12, 15) frames the narration. Even so, it is qualified (vv. 13-14): Israel did not burn any of the captured towns (except Hazor) but appropriated them (realizing the principle of Deut 6:10-11 and Josh 24:13).

Summary of Total Conquest (11:16-23)

The summary of the entire conquest of the land follows (vv. 16-23). Again there is an *inclusio* in which Joshua is credited with taking the entire land (vv. 16-17, 23). And again this is qualified, in this case, twice.

The first qualification on Israel's success makes it

clear that the swift threefold campaign as described in the book of Joshua was only part of a prolonged conflict. The book does not begin to narrate all of the battles of this period. But Yahweh used even this protracted war to accomplish his purposes. Thus Yahweh hardened the Canaanites' hearts so that Israel could exterminate them (11:20; cf. the hardening of Pharaoh's heart in Exodus).

The second qualification (11:21-22) dampens the success in another way. The defeat of the Anakim/Anakites is predicted in Deut 9:1-3. These peoples — loosely connected with the Nephilim (Num 13:33) and Rephaim (Deut 2:11) — were apparently mighty warriors of renowned height. Although driven from Hebron, Debir, and Anab, the Anakim/Anakites continue to live in Gaza, Gath, and Ashdod.

After the final framing statement that Joshua took the entire land (11:23a-c) comes the declaration that "the land had rest from war" (11:23d). This declaration will recur (14:15c), forming a link between the defeat of the Anakim/Anakites by Joshua (ch. 11) and the defeat of them by Caleb (ch. 14).

A Selective List of Conquered Cities (12:1-24)

Joshua 12 elucidates the vanquished kings of Transjordan and Cisjordan. It is clear that the kings of the named towns were defeated, not necessarily that every town was captured and destroyed. In fact, a number of these cities were not captured by the Israelites until the time of the monarchy. While the sites mentioned cover many parts of the land, it is evident that some regions are not mentioned. Thus the list is a natural link to the description of the land not yet conquered at the beginning of ch. 13.

The Allotment of the Land (13:1–24:33)

Having completed the conquest, Joshua turns his attention to his second task (1:6): "put the people in possession of the land" (*naḥal* hiphil; cf. Deut 4:21; 15:4; 19:10). The noun *naḥalah* forms an important link for the section (13:6; 14:3, 13; 17:4, 6, 14; 19:49).

Division of the Land (13:1–21:45)

The tribal boundaries serve to minimize intertribal strife and maximize cooperation. These foster an ideology of land claim and tribal solidarity. The land is split into two parts: the land remaining and the tribal allotments.

This entire section (Joshua 13–21) is a type of covenantal land grant (Weinfeld 1993; Hess 1996b; 2000). Yahweh, as king, is issuing to the tribes their land as a covenantal grant. The cities of refuge and levitical cities are attached at the end of the section since it is necessary for the tribes to receive their inheritance before they can allocate parts of it to others.

There are four types of materials in this section: boundary descriptions (Type A), town lists integrated into boundary descriptions (Type B), town lists (Type C), and short narratives (Hess 1996b). Boundary descriptions (Type A) delineate the tribal borders through place names separated by prepositions and verbs. Town lists integrated into boundary descriptions (Type B) are lists of place names that occur within or are appended directly to the boundary descriptions. Town lists (Type C) are those lists of towns distinct from the tribal boundary descriptions. These are longer and appear separable from their present literary context. The short narratives are vignettes that relate incidents of importance within the allotments providing didactic significance to the division of the land.

The subtle message of Joshua 13–19 is one of decreasing tribal success in occupying the allotments. The description of Israel's lands in Canaan begins with the general success of Judah and concludes with the failure of Dan. The entire corpus manifests the steady unraveling of coherence (Hawk 1991: 112-13). A comparison of the amount of textual space devoted to each tribe in Joshua 13–19 strengthens this pattern of declivity (cf. Judges 1).

Land Remaining (13:1-7)

The land remaining is defined by those towns and regions inside the borders of Canaan (cf. Num 34:1-12) which are not under Israelite control. Two areas are particularly singled out: the land of the Philistines (along the seacoast, in the southwestern corner of Canaan), and the land of the Geshurites (east of the sea of Galilee).

The land remaining is conveyed in a speech by God to Joshua. This foreshadows other speeches and passages in Joshua 13–21 that document Israel's failure to capture all of the land, or in which foreigners live among the Israelites. These contrast with the idealistic reports given in the context in such a way as to produce irony (cf. 15:63; 16:10; 17:11-13; 18:2; and 19:47).

Introduction (General)			(12:1a) (12:1b)	"These are the kings of the land whom the Israelites smote *(hikkah)*" "and whose territory they possessed *(yarash)* east of the Jordan"
Transjordanian	A	List	(12:2-5)	List of defeated kings and specifying of regions
	B	Moses	(12:6a) (12:6b)	"Moses and the Israelites smote *(hikkah)* them" "Moses gave *(natan)* their inheritance"
Cisjordanian	B′	Joshua	(12:7a) (12:7b-8)	"Joshua and the Israelites smote *(hikkah)* these kings" "Joshua gave *(natan)* their lands as an inheritance"
	A′	List	(12:9-24)	Specifying of regions and list of defeated kings

Transjordanian Tribal Allotment (13:8-33)

Before the allotments of Cisjordan can be described, the Transjordanian allotments that Moses made must be recounted. The passage has a clear A:B:A′:B′ structure in which the general description of the extent of the Transjordanian lands is given (A, 13:8-13), followed by a declaration that the Levites received no inheritance (B, 13:14). This is followed by a specific description of the Transjordanian territories (A′, 13:15-32), followed by a declaration that the Levites received no inheritance (B′, 13:33). The specific description (A′) contains:

Reuben (13:15-21)	Boundary Description — Type A
Reuben (13:17-23)	Town List Integrated into Boundary Description — Type B
Gad (13:24-27)	Boundary Description — Type A
Gad (13:27-28)	Town List Integrated into Boundary Description — Type B
Manasseh (13:29-32)	Town List — Type C

Joshua 13:13 expresses the first of a number of mitigations against Israelite success in possessing the land: "Yet the Israelites did not drive out the people of Geshur or the people of Maacath; but Geshur and Maacath live among the Israelites to this day." This statement foreshadows the lack of success among the other tribes in the book in possessing their allotments.

Cisjordanian Tribal Allotment (14:1–19:51)

The story of the Cisjordanian allotments is framed by an introduction (14:1-5) and a summary (19:51). The main text is divided into two major sections: the Judah and Joseph allotments (14:6–17:18) and the seven other tribal allotments (18:1–19:51).

Introduction to the Process of Allotment (14:1-5)

This section may have taken place at Gilgal (according to 14:6; though this may be referring only to the Caleb narrative). Eleazar (the high priest), Joshua, and the heads of the tribal families are involved in this allotment, which is performed by lot.

Judah and Joseph Allotments (14:6–17:18)

The section divides into two parts: Judah (14:6–15:63) and Joseph (Ephraim and Half-Manasseh) (16:1–17:18). The two parts are chiastically parallel (cf. Hawk 1991: 102-10).

Judah (14:6–15:63)

- A Narrative Frame: Judah's Success: Caleb (14:6-15)
  - B Judah Boundary Description — Type A (15:1-12)
    - C Narrative: Vignettes (15:13-19)
      - Men: Caleb and Othniel (15:13-17)
      - Women: Achsah (15:18-19)
  - B′ Judah Town List — Type C (15:20-62)
- A′ Narrative Frame: Postscript: Judah's Failure (15:63)

Joseph (Ephraim and Half-Manasseh) (16:1–17:18)

- A Narrative Frame: General Summary of Joseph (16:1-4)
  - B Ephraim Boundary Description — Type A (16:5-10)
    - C Narrative: Vignettes (17:1-6)
      - Men: Machir, Town List — Type C (17:1-2)
      - Women: Daughters of Zelophehad (17:3-6)
  - B′ Manasseh Boundary Description — Type A (17:7-13)
- A′ Narrative Frame: People of Joseph (17:14-18)

Judah (14:6–15:63) In the initial narrative frame (A), the success of Judah is specifically illustrated by Caleb's conquest of Hebron (14:6-15). Caleb was one of the original twelve spies sent into the land of Canaan (Num 13:30; 14:24). Only he and Joshua supported the immediate invasion of the land, while the other spies testified in fear concerning the Canaanites' strength. Accordingly, Caleb, who was promised by Moses at that time the territory around Hebron (in the allotment to Judah), is now seeking this allotment from Joshua. With Joshua's endorsement, Caleb and his clan conquer Hebron, which the text notes was originally called Kiriath-arba since Arba was the greatest man among the Anakim/Anakites. The resumptive repetition of the statement in v. 15, "and the land had rest from war," obviously connects this story to 11:21-23. The mention of the Anakim/Anakites is ironic since it was the fear of these very Anakim/Anakites that caused Israel's disobedience and failure at Kadesh-barnea (Num 13:28; Deut 1:28).

Thus Caleb is presented as the paragon of honesty and fidelity to Yahweh. Caleb's monologue represents the response that Israel as a whole has been expected to offer. He is an eager partner with Yahweh in dispossessing giants and conquering fortified cities (Hawk 1991: 103). There is even some evidence that Caleb's name, "dog," would have suggested fidelity and self-abasement to one's god or overlord. Ironically, this prime example of Judahite success is accomplished by a non-Israelite: Caleb is a Kenizzite (14:6, 14)!

The next section (B, Josh 15:1-12) gives Judah's boundary description in a five-piece, counterclockwise arrangement: south (15:2-4), east (15:5), north (15:6-11), and west (15:12a; cf. Josh 11:21-22; 15:63; Judg 1:18-19), with a concluding boundary description (15:12b).

Section C is a narrative that contains short vignettes concerning Judah's heroes (15:13-19; cf. Judg 1:9-15). It subdivides into two parts: a description of heroic men: Caleb and Othniel (15:13-17), and a description of a heroic woman: Achsah (15:18-19). In the first, Caleb (already mentioned, 14:6-15) conquers Hebron and then attacks the city of Debir. After the recording of Caleb's challenge and offer of his daughter, Othniel steps forward as the conquering hero of Debir (Kiriath-sepher).

In the second part, although Achsah is introduced as the object traded for the city in the previous vignette, here she takes the initiative. Her father has given her to Othniel in fulfillment of the deal, but Achsah now urges her husband to ask for a field. But this is only preliminary to a further direct request. At her dismounting (cf. Gen 24:61-67; 1 Sam 25:23), Caleb inquires immediately what the problem is. While Caleb has given her land, it lacks sufficient water. Her request to her father is now for springs or pools *(gullot)* of water, since land without water is land without life. She seeks a sufficient blessing of God in the land. The response is powerful: "and Caleb gave her the upper springs and the lower springs" — a double portion! In taking the initiative to obtain more of the blessings of God (represented by the land and springs), Achsah parallels the daughters of Zelophehad (see below). Ironically, all three of Judah's heroes are non-Israelites (Kenizzites).

The fourth section (B′, 15:20-62) is a list of Judah's towns (Type C). It, like section B above, is comprised of five parts (with additional subunits):

1. Introduction (15:20)
2. Southern District (i.e., the Negev) (15:21-32) parallels Simeon (in part) (Josh 19:2-8)
3. Western Districts (15:33-47)
4. Hill Country Districts (15:48-60)
5. Desert Districts (15:61-62)

The final section (A′, 15:63) is a narrative frame, a postscript, which notes Judah's failure in conquering Jerusalem (15:63). This tribal failure contrasts with Caleb's individual success in the initial narrative frame for the section (14:6-15).

Joseph (Ephraim and Half-Manasseh) (16:1–17:18) The first section of the Joseph allotment (A, 16:1-4) is a narrative frame that gives the general outline of the southern borders of the Joseph tribes (i.e., the southern boundary of Ephraim). There is ambiguity concerning the people of Joseph from the beginning. They receive one allotment (16:1), as if they constitute one tribe, yet they are recognized as two distinct tribal units (Manasseh and Ephraim; 14:4a). This ambiguity is bolstered by the narrative framework, which puts data concerning "Joseph" at either end of the section (A, 16:1-4; A′, 17:14-18) and recounts the portions to Ephraim and Manasseh in the main text (B, 16:5-10; B′, 17:7-13). In addition, one of the tribes, Manasseh, is further divided. Part of the tribe has already received an allotment in Transjordan, while the remainder receives its allotment in Cisjordan.

The second section (B, 16:5-10) delineates Ephraim's boundaries. It is a boundary description — Type A. The section begins with a continuation of the southern boundary (16:5-6a). It then sketches the eastern and northern borders (which equates to the border between Ephraim and Manasseh) (16:6b-8a). Finally, it concludes its description for Ephraim (16:8b-10). The final verse documents the Ephraimites' failure to dispossess the Canaanites, although putting them under forced labor (16:10).

The third section (C, 17:1-6) corresponds to Judah's third section: reports of heroes. First, there is the description of the allotment of the mighty warrior (somewhat corresponding to Caleb and Othniel above): Machir, Manasseh's firstborn (see Hawk 1991: 106). Yet the allotment for the "rest" of the clans of Manasseh is given in the form of a town list (Type C, 17:1-2) without any connection to the ancestral hero. This is followed by a description of the allotment to the tribes' heroic women (corresponding to Achsah above): the daughters of Zelophehad (17:3-6). Ironically, the daughters of Zelophehad (Num 27:1-11; 36:1-12) and Machir (Num 32:39-40) are technically Transjordanians, not Cisjordanians.

The fourth section (B′, 17:7-13) is Manasseh's boundary description (Type A). It also includes a list of towns that the tribe had within the tribal allotments of Issachar and Asher (17:11). However, as in the case of Ephraim above, the Canaanites were not driven out but were put to forced labor — a mitigating statement, to say the least (17:12-13).

Although the descriptions of the territories of Ephraim and Manasseh correspond to the accounts of Judah's territory in 15:1-12 and 15:20-62, there are, nevertheless, major differences. While the description of Judah's borders is related with precision and detail, those of Ephraim and Manasseh are fragmentary, take up much less textual space, and present numerous topographical difficulties. The integrity of Judah's territory is thus contrasted with the broken borders of the Joseph tribes (Hawk 1991: 106). Moreover, the towns of Judah are organized into districts, whereas the towns of Ephraim and Manasseh are mixed together and Manasseh commingles with Issachar and Asher. Thus confusion rather than territorial integrity predominates.

The final section (A′, 17:14-18) is a narrative frame in which the people of Joseph demand and receive a double portion. This final story serves as an ironic counterbalance to the story of Caleb's quest for land (14:6-15), and perhaps also of Achsah (15:18-19). While Caleb is courageous, faithful, loyal, and zealous, fearing neither giants nor fortified cities, the Josephites convey trepidation, contentiousness, and failure (Hawk 1991: 109). Caleb's request for land is a confession of faith, whereas the people of Joseph's is a whiny complaint. They are discontented with their territory and insist that they should receive more than one allotment since they are so numerous. The contrast is particularly noticeable as they press for a place that will be easy to settle (Caleb had asked for a difficult place to conquer). Caleb had dispossessed giants in fortified cities. The people of Joseph face giants (the Rephaim; cf. Deut 3:11) and fortified cities, but respond very differently (17:15-16). When Joshua responds to their petition by instructing them to clear the forest region of the Perizzites and Rephaim, they complain further (contrast Caleb's confident declarations). They pick up and distort Joshua's reference to the narrow Mt. Ephraim highlands *(har 'eprayim)* to assert that the entire hill country *(hahar)* of their allotment is inadequate. In addition, the Canaanites' technological advantage, namely, their iron chariots, is cited as the reason for their inability to exploit their allotment. But Joshua reasserts that they can clear the forests to their edges (the hill country in its widest sense [*har* and not just *har 'eprayim*]) and that they will overcome and dispossess the Canaanites. But the outcome remains uncertain.

Seven Other Tribal Allotments (18:1–19:51)

The allotments of the remaining seven Cisjordanian tribes is narrated in 18:1–19:51. There are short frame narratives on both ends: the assembly of Shiloh (18:1-10) and the final allotment to Joshua (19:49-50). Except for Simeon (19:1-9), the allotment order is the reverse of the patronymic birth order.

Assembly of Shiloh (18:1-10) Through the national assembly at Shiloh (Joshua 18–19), Joshua (and Eleazar and leaders; cf. Josh 19:51) supervises the lottery, which includes a survey of the territorial lands. Thus the seven tribes' allotments are approximately the same size. The story asserts that the geographical shape of Israel in the land was not the result of human will or historical contingency, but of Yahweh's will and of Israel's obedience (Nelson 1997: 209).

First Lot: Benjamin (18:11-28) As in the case of Judah, a counterclockwise boundary description (type A) is first given for Benjamin (18:12-20), after which its town list (type C) (18:21-28) follows. The town list is held together by the brackets of vv. 21 and 28. Two districts of towns (vv. 21-24 and 25-28) are presented in the same format as those for Judah (many scholars assume from the same source).

Second Lot: Simeon (19:1-9) The allotment for Simeon comes next because of its integral relationship with Judah (cf. Judg 1:3, 17). 19:1 introduces Simeon's situation, and v. 8b concludes it. The allotment is described purely in terms of a town list (type C) (cf. also 1 Chr 4:28-33). Simeon concludes the town list with a gloss explaining why these do not follow a boundary description (19:9).

Third Lot: Zebulun (19:10-16) The third lot went to Zebulun. Enclosed by a formulaic envelope (19:10a, 16), the allotment is described in terms of a boundary description (type A) (19:10b-14) and a town list integrated into the boundary description (type B) (19:15).

Fourth Lot: Issachar (19:17-23) The fourth lot belonged to Issachar. It is composed from a town list (type C) (19:18-21) and a boundary fragment (19:22), with v. 17 providing a formulaic introduction. Issachar was the designation of Solomon's tenth district (1 Kgs 4:17). Consequently, there may be some relationship between this datum and that adminstrative unit (Kallai 1986: 315-18).

Fifth Lot: Asher (19:24-31) The allotment to Asher is composed of a boundary description (type A) (19:26-30) and a town list integrated into the boundary description (type B) (19:25-26, 28, 30).

Sixth Lot: Naphtali (19:32-39) Naphtali's allotment is delineated through a boundary description (type A) (19:33-34) and a town list (type C) (19:35-38). Vv. 32 and 39 provide the framework. The allotment seems to be missing a northern border (Na'aman 1986: 46).

Seventh Lot: Dan (19:40-48) The allotment for Dan is given only in the form of a town list (type C) (19:41-47), with vv. 40 and 48 providing a formulaic framework. The town list for Dan, like the one for Simeon, concludes with a gloss that explains why the tribe could not occupy its allotment and had to settle elsewhere (cf. Judg 1:34; 18:1-31).

Final Lot: Joshua (19:49-50) Joshua's individual allotment (19:49-50) concludes the division of the land, just as Caleb's individual allotment began it (14:6-15). However, Joshua comes off poorly by comparison (Hawk 1991: 113). Caleb requests the hill country of Judah where the Anakim/Anakites, the giants, lived in fortified cities (14:12). Caleb's success and vigor in capturing Hebron is contrasted to the exploits of Joshua, who requests a city in the Ephraimite hill country which he builds up for himself.

The city's name is preserved here and in Josh 24:30 as Timnath-serah ("portion of excess"). In Judg 2:9 it is preserved as Timnath-heres ("portion of the sun"). The difference is not easily resolved. Some scholars argue that Timnath-serah is correct: a scribe reversed the consonants. Others argue that Timnath-heres is the original: a scribe changed the spelling to Timnath-serah for polemically religious reasons. Whatever the case, neither name is very flattering to Joshua, who appears to prefer the sparsely settled hills to the fortified cities of the giants.

Summary of Process of the Allotment (19:51)

19:51 notes that Eleazar and the leaders of the families were involved in the allotment to these tribes. This points back to 14:1 and thus provides part of a concluding bracket to the whole process of Cisjordanian land distribution. In other words, v. 51 does double duty as a closing bracket for the structural segments of 14:1–19:51 (nine and a half tribes) and 18:1–19:51 (seven tribes).

Allotments to Persons of Marginal Status (20:1–21:42)

This section delineates the final, secondary-type allotments that also form a transition to the practical concerns of how life is to be lived in the land. The manslayers maintain a marginal status, perhaps in the service of the priesthood, until the guilt incurred by the accidental taking of human life is expiated by the high priest's death. The Levites also represent a marginal class. They do not receive an allotment but are nonetheless given towns "to live in" along with surrounding pasturelands for their livestock (Hawk 1991: 114). Neither group is bounded by the tribal borders just enumerated in Joshua 13–19. The establishments of both the cities of refuge and the levitical cities were on the basis of Mosaic commandments. Both are supplemental land grants (Hess 1996b: 166). As God had allotted the land of Canaan to the Israelites, so the Israelites granted land to these marginal peoples. Yet the cities of refuge and especially the levitical cities also function to unify the twelve tribes under Yahweh's authority.

Cities of Refuge (20:1-9)

The towns of asylum (lit. "towns of the admittance or inclusion") are a land grant in which the towns are given as a refuge to a particular class of person, those who commit accidental homicide. In the case of a wrongful death, a blood avenger (lit. "kinsman redeemer of the blood"), the victim's nearest male relative, would revenge the the killing of a clan relative in order to restore clan or familial wholeness (Num 35:12, 19-27; Deut 19:6, 12; Josh 20:2-

3, 5, 9). The right of asylum helped to limit the social damage of unrestrained blood vengeance or feuding. This would be especially important in a tribal society like early Israel.

The description of the towns is given in the form of a town list (type C) starting with three Cisjordanian towns listed in a north-to-south pattern and then listing the three Transjordanian towns in a south-to-north sequence. In Joshua, all six are appointed at once. These six are also listed as levitical cities (21:1, 11, 27, 32, 36, and 38).

Levitical Cities (21:1-42)

The levitical cities' list is a land grant that supplements the larger grant of Joshua 13–19. It is given in the form of a town list (type C). The list explains how the priests and Levites fit into Israel's settlement in the land. While they technically have no inheritance (Josh 13:14, 33, 18:7; Deut 10:8-9) and have their own special role and status, they are nevertheless integrated into the unity of Israel (cf. 1 Chronicles 6).

Moses had commanded the Israelites to allot cities to the Levites in order they might have *some* provision (Num 35:1-8). However, even with the surrounding pasturelands for the cattle, the total area assigned to the Levites came to fifteen square miles, or about 0.1 percent of the land. In a society where farmland was wealth, this minute fraction of land meant that the Levites would still be dependent on the generosity of the secular tribes among whom they lived. Thus the statement that the Levites had "no inheritance in the land" (Num. 18:20-32) is certainly true when their allotment is compared to that of the other tribes. While the list may have some roots in historical reality, there is, as in the delineation of the tribal boundaries above, a touch of idealization.

While the total number of levitical cities (forty-eight) is very likely symbolic (being a multiple of twelve), the towns are not equally divided among the tribes. They are allotted to the three clans of the Levites, the Kohathites, Gershonites, and Merarites, with only the Kohathites being distributed among the major Cisjordanian tribes. However, each levitical clan receives two cities of refuge. The division according to clan looks like this:

	Kohathites		Gershonites		Merarites
	Towns		*Towns*		*Towns*
13*	Judah Simeon Benjamin	13	Issachar Asher Naphtali ½ Manasseh (Transjordan)	12	Reuben Gad Zebulun
10	Ephraim Dan ½ Manasseh (Cisjordan)				

*Aaronic

Ironic Conclusion (21:43-45)

The overstated claims of unmitigated success in these verses seem incongruent with the subtle statements given throughout 13:1–20:42, which assert that there were nonsuccesses among the tribes — some quite significant — as each one attempted to secure its allotment. Thus the short passage offers an ironic conclusion to the conquest and allotment sections of the book (Gunn 1987: 107-10; see also Polzin 1980: 127-32 and Hawk 1991: 115-16).

Conclusion of Conquest (22:1–24:33)

As in the first part of the book (1:1–5:12), issues concerning inclusion of Transjordanians, crossing of the Jordan, rituals, the law among the leaders and people, and commitment to Yahweh recur.

Misunderstanding with the Transjordanian Tribes (22:1-34)

The passage breaks down into two parts: the departure of the Transjordanians (22:1-9) and the debate over the altar (22:10-34). In many ways the first part is the counterpart to Josh 1:12-18, where, after Joshua challenged the Transjordanians to fulfill their responsibilities in helping to conquer the land of Canaan, they declare their willingness and loyalty to Yahweh and Joshua. Josh 22:1-9 also has links with Numbers 32, where Moses gave the initial command that the Transjordanians should help their brother tribes conquer Canaan. In this way, the passage continues the motif of Joshua parallel to Moses.

In the second part, the debate over the altar (22:10-34), the faithfulness of the Transjordanians is developed further. Jobling has demonstrated the chiastic structure (Jobling 1986):

- a Transjordanians build the altar (v. 10)
  - b Cisjordanians threaten war (vv. 11-12)
    - c Cisjordanians send an embassy (vv. 13-15a)
      - d Accusatory speech by the embassy (vv. 15b-20)
        - e Transjordanians reply (vv. 21-29)
          - e1 invocations and oaths expressing innocence (vv. 22-23)
            - e2 explanation of the altar (vv. 24-27a)
            - e2′ explanation of the altar (vv. 27b-28)
          - e1′ invocations and oaths expressing innocence (v. 29)
      - d′ Accepting speech by the embassy (vv. 30-31)
    - c′ Return of the embassy to Cisjordan (v. 32)
  - b′ Withdrawal of the Cisjordanian threat of war (v. 33)
- a′ Transjordanians name the altar (v. 34)

Upon their departure the Transjordanians build "an altar of great size" (i.e., it was obvious, not hidden). Assuming it to be a sacrificial altar, the Cisjordanians construe the altar as an act of disloyalty to Yahweh and muster for war (cf. Deut 12:13-14). Appointing Phinehas, the son of Eleazar, as head of an embassy, the Cisjordanians confront the Transjordanians.

Their speech reflects their biases. They describe the Transjordanian action as "rebellion" (*marad*). Although this term is used most frequently in the HB in this chapter of Joshua, it is clear from other contexts that it has international political nuances referring to disloyalty to a covenant (e.g., 2 Kgs 18:7; 24:1, 20). Thus in this context it refers to a broken covenant relationship and disloyalty to Yahweh. Ironically, not only has the text just affirmed the Transjordanians' loyalty to Yahweh (22:1-9), but the Transjordanians' own words (1:18) declared that death should come to whoever rebelled *(marah)* against Joshua's orders. The Cisjordanians also liken the Transjordanians' action to the sin of Peor. Such a reference would be especially *penetrating* in light of the action of Phinehas in that incident (cf. Num 25:1-18)! Furthermore, their statement (22:19) is especially provocative: if *your* land is *unclean* (implication: ours is not), cross over into *Yahweh's land* (implication: your land is not his), where Yahweh's tabernacle now stands (implication: it used to be over here, but now it is on *our* side of the Jordan). Finally, the Cisjordanians admonish the Transjordanians not to be like Achan, who brought wrath on the whole congregation, with judgment coming on him and his family!

Surprisingly, war did not break out after such a speech. But the Transjordanians' reaction is godly. They lament that their motive may have been misinterpreted (22:22-23). Their motive was honorable — namely, they built the altar as a witness to their loyalty to Yahweh (22:24-25). They feared that in the future the Cisjordanians might discriminate against the Transjordanians — a fear well founded in light of this story. Thus the Transjordanians come out looking better in this passage than the Cisjordanians.

Concluding Charges (23:1–24:33)

There are a number of similarities between Joshua's speech to the leaders and his charge to the people (Koopmans 1990: 396-99). Both resemble the deathbed testaments of prior Israelite leaders: Jacob (Genesis 48–49), Joseph (Gen 50:22-26), and especially Moses (Deuteronomy 32–33). And both have framing links with Joshua 1.

However, Joshua 23 has a narrower focus than Joshua 24. It elaborates a demand for obedience to the law *(torah)* showing that such obedience would expedite the inheritance of the land. Joshua 24, on the other hand, stresses the issue of sole allegiance to Yahweh rather than other gods (expressed through the repetition of the term "serve").

Joshua Charges the Leaders (23:1-16)

Joshua's address to the leaders consists almost entirely of reflection from the law (especially Deuteronomy). The passage divides into three parts: God's past mighty acts of conquest (23:1-5); an exhortation to remain faithful to Yahweh and his covenant so that the remaining land can be conquered (23:6-11); and warnings of judgments if Israel is unfaithful to God's covenant, going after foreign gods (23:12-16).

The initial verses of the passage have similarities with Joshua 13. In both, "Joshua is old and advanced in years." Both contain descriptions of the land that remains to be conquered. One of the key themes in the first part is found in the phrase "it is the LORD your God who has fought for you" (v. 3). Another key theme is found in the phrase "those nations that remain" (vv. 4, 7, and 12). Thus, as in many ancient Near Eastern covenants, past benefactions are the basis for trust in the sovereign's actions in the future on behalf of his vassals.

The second part (23:6-11) emphasizes the need to "be careful," suggesting that this is the key to victory. This care includes issues of precise obedience, the avoidance of the worship of other gods, and love of Yahweh alone.

The law plays a vital role in this process. The "book of the law of Moses" was mentioned in Josh 8:31, and the book of the law is mentioned in 1:7-8. Both seem to refer to the Book of the Covenant (Exodus 20–24). A comparison of Josh 23:6 and Josh 1:7 demonstrates the necessity of this law in the process of land occupation (see the Introduction above, 174).

The command against idolatry (Exod 20:3-6; Deut 5:7-10) seems to be the main test of obedience to the covenant stipulations. "To love the LORD your God" described a covenantal commitment to God and his word (cf. Deut 6:4-9).

The third part (23:12-16) discusses the curses for unfaithfulness to Yahweh's covenant. Such violations of the covenant (and their consequences) include association and intermarriage with the inhabitants in the land (vv. 12-13) — a clear violation of Deut 7:3, the certainty of God's judgment (23:14-15), and idolatry (v. 16).

That this final part is parallel to the second can be seen through a comparison of 23:8 and 12. V. 8 envisions that Israel would hold fast *(dabaq)* to Yahweh, while v. 12 describes the Israelites who turn away and ally *(dabaq)* themselves with the Canaanite survivors. Thus there is an intended contrast (by the use of the same verb) between those who remain faithful and their reward (vv. 8-11) and those who are unfaithful and their punishment (vv. 12-16).

Joshua Charges the People (24:1-28)

Joshua's final meeting with the people takes place at Shechem, as did an earlier meeting (cf. 8:30-35). Both gatherings evince overtones of covenant ritual ceremonies. In Josh 24:1-28, the text is framed by the setting (24:1) and concluding covenant ritual ceremony (24:25-28). The main text (24:2-13) is comprised of two parts: a historical summary that is analogous to the prologues of ancient Near Eastern suzerainty treaties, and a dialogue between Joshua and the people (24:14-24) in which the issue of serving Yahweh, not other gods, is weighed.

The setting (24:1) ties the ceremony to the previous one in ch. 23 through the listing of the same four groups of Israelite leaders. It also ties the ceremony to Shechem.

The historical summary (24:2-13) divides into three subdivisions: the patriarchal period (vv. 2-4), the Egyptian period (vv. 5-7), and the conquest period (vv. 8-13). The patriarchal promises of posterity, divine-human relationship, and land are thematically present in each respectively. God's mighty acts on behalf of Israel throughout its history are emphasized as the basis for Israel's dedication and service to Yahweh.

The dialogue between Joshua and the people (24:14-24) formalizes the Israelites' commitment to the covenant with Yahweh. This dialogue consists of four exchanges between Joshua and the people. In the first, Joshua's exhortation to serve Yahweh — which climaxes with his own "house's" commitment to serve Yahweh (vv. 14-15) — is followed by the people's response (vv. 16-18). In the second exchange, Joshua challenges the people's response. Yahweh is a holy and jealous God who will not accept mere confession of commitment and will judge Israel when they abandon him and serve other gods (vv. 19-20). The people's response reaffirms their commitment (v. 21).

The third exchange in 24:22 records both Joshua's and the people's declaration of legal witness. The fourth exchange contains Joshua's final admonition: "put away the strange gods which are in your midst and incline your hearts to Yahweh" (v. 23). This obviously implies that, while the people have declared their allegiance to Yahweh, reality attests to the contrary — the people still have foreign gods/idols among them. But the people give their final assertion of service to Yahweh (v. 24).

With this dialogue finished, Joshua can perform the concluding covenant ceremony (24:25-28). Writing the words of the covenant in a book, he raises a large stone in the open-air sanctuary of Yahweh. This stone would serve as a witness to Yahweh's words and Israel's commitment to them. At the end of the ceremony Joshua dismisses the people.

Appendices (24:29-33)

The final verses provide three short notices. The first describes the death and burial of Joshua, including a comment concerning Israel's faithfulness to Yahweh (24:29-31; cf. Judg 2:6-9). The second is a notice about the reburial of the bones of Joseph in Shechem in the patriarchal plot (v. 32). And the third is a notice of the priest Eleazar's death and burial (v. 33).

Bibliography. Aḥituv, S. 1995, *Joshua: Introduction and Commentary,* Mikra le-Yisra'el/A Bible Commentary for Israel, Tel Aviv: Am Oved and Jerusalem: Magnes/Hebrew University (Hebrew) • Boling, R. G., and E. G. Wright. 1982, *Joshua: A New Translation with Introduction and Commentary,* AB 6, Garden City, N.Y.: Doubleday • Butler, T. 1983, *Joshua,* WBC 7, Waco: Word • Fleming, D. E. 1999, "The Seven-Day Siege of Jericho in Holy War," pp. 211-28 in R. Chazan, W. W. Hallo, and L. H. Schiffman, eds., *Ki Baruch Hu: Ancient Near Eastern, Biblical and Judaic Studies in Honor of Baruch A. Levine,* Winona Lake, Ind.: Eisenbrauns • Fritz, V. 1994, *Das Buch Josua,* HAT 1/7, Tübingen: J. C. B. Mohr (Paul Siebeck) • Gunn, D. M. 1987, "Joshua and Judges," pp. 102-21 in R. Alter and F. Kermode, eds., *The Literary Guide to the Bible,* Cambridge, Mass.: Belknap/Harvard • Hawk, L. D. 1991, *Every Promise Fulfilled: Contesting Plots in Joshua,* Literary Currents in Biblical Interpretation, Louisville: Westminster/John Knox • Hawk, L. 2000, *Joshua,* Berit Olam, Collegeville, Minn.: Liturgical • Hess, R. S. 1996a, *Joshua, An Introduction and Commentary,* TOTC, Leicester: Inter-Varsity Press • Hess, R. 1996b, "A Typology of West Semitic Place Name Lists with Special Reference to Joshua 13–21," *BA* 59/3:160-70 • Hess, R. 2002, "The Book of Joshua as a Land Grant," *Bib* 83:493-506 • Howard, D. M. 1998, *Joshua,* New American Commentary, Nashville: Broadman & Holman • Jobling, D. 1986, "The Jordan a Boundary: Transjordan in Israel's Ideological Geography," pp. 88-134 in *The Sense of Biblical Narrative: Structural Analyses in the Hebrew Bible II,* JSOTSup 39, Sheffield: JSOT • Kallai, Z. 1986, *Historical Geography of the Bible: The Tribal Territories of Israel,* Jerusalem: Magnes and Leiden: E. J. Brill • Kitz, A. M. 2000, "Undivided Inheritance and Lot Casting in the Book of Joshua," *JBL* 119:601-18 • Koopmans, W. T. 1990, *Joshua 24 as Poetic Narrative,* JSOTSup 93, Sheffield: Sheffield Academic • Mazar, A. 1990, *Archaeology and the Land of the Bible: 10,000-586 BCE,* ABRL, Garden City, N.Y.: Doubleday • Na'aman, N. 1986, *Borders and Districts in Biblical Historiography,* Jerusalem Biblical Studies 4, Jerusalem: Simor • Nelson, R. D. 1997, *Joshua: A Commentary,* OTL, Louisville: Westminster/John Knox • Polzin, R. M. 1980, *Moses and the Deuteronomist: A Literary Study of the Deuteronomic History, Part One: Deuteronomy, Joshua, Judges,* New York: Seabury • Pressler, C. 2002, *Joshua, Judges, and Ruth,* Westminster Bible Companion, Louisville: Westminster John Knox • Schäfer-Lichtenberger, C. 1994, "Bedeutung und Funktion von *Ḥerem* in biblisch-hebräischen Texten," *BZ* 38:270-75 • Schäfer-Lichtenberger, C. 1995, *Josua und Salomo. Eine Studie zu Autorität und Legitimität des Nachfolgers im Alten Testament,* VTSup 58, Leiden: E. J. Brill • Weinfeld, M. 1993, "The Covenantal Aspect of the Promise of the Land to Israel," pp. 222-64 in *The Promise of the Land: The Inheritance of the Land of Canaan by the Israelites,* Berkeley: University of California • Winther-Nielsen, N. 1995, *A Functional Discourse Grammar of Joshua: A Computer-Assisted Rhetorical Structure Analysis,* ConBOT 40, Stockholm: Almqvist & Wiksell • Younger, K. L., Jr. 1990, *Ancient Conquest Accounts: A Study in Ancient Near Eastern and Biblical History Writing,* JSOTSup 98, Sheffield: Sheffield Academic • Younger, K. L., Jr. 1995, "The 'Conquest' of the South (Jos 10,28-39)," *BZ* 39:255-64.

Judges

P. Deryn Guest

INTRODUCTION

The book of Judges introduces some of the most well-known characters of the Bible — Deborah, Gideon, Samson, and Delilah, for example. Its tales, full of dynamic action and suspense, have inevitably left a lasting impression on readers. Certainly, scholarly interest in the book has never been lacking and has branched into several areas of interest. There have been studies which attempt to reconstruct the lives of the various judges in the context of early Iron Age Canaan as well as studies which attempt to uncover the history of the text's formation. More recently, some scholars have concentrated on the text as it now exists, noting the careful literary structure of the book, while other areas of interest have included the rhetoric of the text, the interplay of ironic perspectives, the role women are given, and the encoded gender ideologies implicit in the text.

These diverse spheres of interest call for varying methods of analysis. As we move into the twenty-first century, the trend is not to privilege any one methodology, but to allow a plurality of approaches which may each contribute to our understanding of this fascinating text. The historical-critical school of thought continues to play a leading role with its philological and historical interest. Approaches which study the ideologies present in the text helpfully shed light on the implied author and his agenda for his own generation. Those which study the text's literary structure readjust our sight to recognize narratives full of delightful intricacies of detail, purposeful repetition, artful allusion, puns, satire, subtle rhetoric, and so forth.

Judges studies have certainly not stood still, and although many aspects of last century's scholarship hold good, these welcome developments provide a richer understanding of a text which has much more to offer the reader than a straightforward presentation of a particular period within the life of ancient Israel. Indeed, these developments are most significant given some scholars' doubts that the text of Judges offers any such straightforward presentation of life in ancient Israel. Although Judges scholarship of the twentieth century exerted much effort in identifying the earliest sources of the text in an attempt to reach back to the origins of each story, the extent to which the book reflects real events which happened to tribal leaders of "ancient Israel" in the early Iron Age has come under rigorous scrutiny within the broader "quest for ancient Israel" debate of recent years (see, e.g., P. R. Davies 1992). Consequently, the following discussion makes no attempt to reconstruct a "period of the judges," but rather concentrates on the story world of the text, noting how the narratives provide judgments on characters and events and thereby encourage the reader to follow a given perspective.

The book of Judges is most easily divided into three major sections: a double prologue (1:1–3:6), a main body (3:7–16:31), and a double epilogue (chs. 17–21). Although commentaries conventionally begin with ch. 1, v. 1, I will commence with the section contained in 3:7–16:31. The prologue will be considered later, together with the epilogue, since they act rather like bookends bracketing the main body in an aesthetically pleasing, informative manner. It will also be helpful to identify some major themes and interests of the main body of stories before attempting to illustrate how these are both introduced and concluded in the prologue and epilogue.

COMMENTARY

Main Body (3:7–16:31)

This section is widely thought to be built around a basic collection of savior stories. The careful reader will soon detect that these stories share common features: Israel does evil in the eyes of Yahweh; is subsequently given over to the hands of enemies; cries to Yahweh; Yahweh raises up a leader to resolve the crisis; the spirit of Yahweh comes upon the leader; the enemy is defeated; peace is regained. This stereotypical formula is clearly set out in the prologue at 2:11-19, and I will refer to it as the cyclic pattern of Judges. As the stories progress this cyclic pattern will recur, but in modified and disintegrating forms. It will be seen that these modifications are significant and provide keys to interpretation. By the time we reach the final judge, Samson, the cyclic pattern will have broken down considerably, the fabric of the text thus mirroring the social and religious breakdown in the story world.

The fact that the stories of judges have been presented within this cyclic pattern indicates a deliberate molding of each narrative. W. Richter's pivotal study of 1964 argued that the cyclic pattern's stereotypical form was not likely to have been original, for if these stories had been told among different tribes, at different locations and times, as many supposed, then it would be rather unusual for them all to have the same format. He therefore argued that the stories had a prior existence in tribal folklore before they were incorporated into a "Book of Saviors," whose editor pressed them into this stereotypical literary form. The essence of Richter's theory has gained wide currency in Judges scholarship, though, as we shall see, it is one that may be challenged.

Othniel (3:7-11)

The account of Othniel provides a key for reading all the subsequent stories from Ehud to Samson. Notice how there is virtually no story or plot attached to the account; it is constructed entirely on the stereotypical aspects of the cyclic pattern. Othniel's story thus operates as a prototype, and he acts as an ideal paradigm judge figure. Accordingly, many concur that we have here a literary rather than a historical figure, created by the writer in order to provide a key to understanding how the judges stories can be expected to run. So despite attempts to locate him within the early Iron Age of the ancient Near East, his significance may lie less in any historical setting than in his representative value.

As a representative figure Othniel appears as the ideal judge who unambiguously wins the day for Israel. Note Othniel's excellent credentials — seen in his kinship to Caleb. Caleb was one of Moses' spies who, despite his fellow Israelites' fears, did not reckon the size and number of the Canaanites to be an obstacle for the people of Yahweh and advocated an immediate attack (Num 13:30). Such qualities are prized in the story world of Judges, where reluctance to fight (seen in Barak and Gideon) is portrayed as weakness. Moreover, Caleb is the one whom Yahweh declares has "followed me wholeheartedly" (Num 14:24), which is another quality esteemed in Judges. Othniel likewise goes out unquestioningly to war, endowed with the spirit of Yahweh, and delivers Israel.

As for his enemy, here too is an archetypal character. Hebrew names have literal meanings, and the Hebrew reader would pick up on their significance more easily than English-speaking readers. Cushan-rishathaim has been translated in differing ways, but perhaps the translation which is most entertaining and captures his paradigmatic value is "Superblack Double-Villain" (Y. T. Radday and A. Brenner, 1990: 63). Moves to locate this enemy in ancient Egyptian texts or to remove the rhyming structure of his name and place of origin (Cushan-rishathaim of Aram-naharaim) in an attempt to make historical sense of the narrative (R. G. Boling 1975: 81-82) are probably misguided ventures.

The Othniel narrative thus provides the reader with a set piece — ideal judge versus archetypal rogue. The account provides an optimistic opening to the series of judges. If this bright start could be maintained, all would be well. But what we will see developing is a degenerative decline that culminates in Samson the anti-judge.

Ehud (3:12-30)

This story, like many of the following, is a tale of the unexpected. We are introduced to a man of Benjamin — that is, a man of the right hand — only to be immediately advised that he is *left-handed.* This incongruity may be designed to cast a shadow over Ehud since the Hebrew adjective *'iṭṭer* belongs to a type of word which denotes physical defects. Some have therefore translated "crippled in the right arm" rather than merely "left-handed." Certainly the writer makes a negative comment regarding his right hand rather than a positive comment about his left, thereby raising questions about this character's ability to win a military victory given his handicap. Moreover, since he is a "son of the right hand," his disability is immediately suggestive of ambivalence, of things not being as they should be, which is entirely consistent with the narrative as a whole where his words are full of double entendre and his actions of double-dealing.

Once again names are significant: Ehud's enemy is Eglon, a name that bears phonetic similarity to the noun *'egel,* meaning "calf." Combining this with the information that Eglon was fat results in a confrontation between an Israelite hero and a fatted calf — the outcome is inevitable.

Throughout the narrative, Ehud playfully uses double entendre, which is lost on the lumbering leader of the Moabites. It is seen in 3:19, where, having returned to the king alone, he declares that he has a secret *dabar* for the king. What the Hebrew reader knows is that *dabar* means both "word" ("message") and "thing" and that Ehud certainly does have a "thing" from God, of which Eglon is most unsuspecting! Eglon, taking the other meaning, dismisses his soldiery and even rises to "receive" the "word" of God.

The manner in which Ehud addresses this king of Moab contributes further to the mockery. His "I have a secret message for you, O king" (v. 19) dispenses with any formalities of etiquette. There is no courtesy title, no "my lord," no "King of Moab," not even his name, merely — "O king." As Webb (1987: 129) notes, the king has already been given his full title — Eglon, king of Moab — four times (vv. 12, 14, 15, 17), which makes Ehud's address all the more burlesque. There were more favorable forms of address that could have been used (consider 1 Sam 24:8; 26:17; 2 Sam 4:8). This lack of any courtesy title emphasizes the separate spheres of these two men — Ehud the Israelite is dealing with a foreign king; there is accordingly nothing that would blur that distinction, and there is no deferment to the king, whose politically superior position receives no submissiveness from the confident Ehud.

In this satirization of Eglon we see a theme developing whereby foreign kingship is exposed as an unworthy institution. Eglon is satirized in a number of ways. Most obvious is his fatness, which is certainly overstressed — he is so fat that the sword is swallowed, hilt and all (3:22). Not only is Eglon's physical obesity the subject of derision, however, for fatness operates as a cipher for other qualities as well.

First, fatness might indicate gullibility — evidenced by the way he takes Ehud at face value. His servants' gullibility is similarly exposed in their belief that the king is relieving himself — assumed, of course, from their king's prolonged stay in the roof chamber and the odor that wafts through the locked room. Note that these servants, too, are described in 3:29 as "strong, able-bodied" (in Hebrew, "fat") men.

Second, fatness might indicate greediness not only in the context of physical eating but in acquiring material goods. Obesity here is suggestive of an uncontrolled hunger that is never satisfied — precisely the attack Samuel makes on kingship in 1 Sam 8:18-19. Foreign kingship is thus depicted as an institution that is gullible, acquires more than it should, and grows slovenly on its gains.

Third, Eglon's fatness feminizes his person. Certainly, sexual innuendoes have been detected in the story's vocabulary. While the two men are alone in the roof chamber, Ehud "came to" Eglon (3:20). This verb *bo'* can be used simply to indicate movement into a place, but it also has connotations of sexual "entry." Given the alternatives that could have been selected, a deliberate innuendo should not be ruled out. Then there are the references to Ehud closing doors and locking them in v. 23 (emphasized again in vv. 24-25). These verbs are used in Cant 5:2 and 4:12 with sexual implications. The short and double-edged sword plunged into Eglon's body is thought by some (R. Alter 1981: 39; M. Z. Brettler 1995: 82) to represent deliberately a phallic image, and 3:30 refers specifically to Israel subduing Moab under their "hand" — a word which can also be used euphemistically for the penis. This sexual imagery is compounded by the fact that it refers to the actions of two men. The fatness feminizes this Moabite king, and the story can be read as a male rape scene which, in that political context, would have exacerbated the mockery of this Moabite monarch.

Given these literary features, it is understandable that the genre of this story has been identified not as "history" but as political satire whereby foreign kingship in general, and the Moabites in particular, are mocked. A recollection of some ancient skirmish with the Moabites may be in view, but as M. Z. Brettler (1995: 88) has noted, it is more likely that we have here a story composed for political purposes, which may merely be *set* in the past. For Brettler, the story contains "history" only in the sense that a historical enmity between Israel and Moab existed. This is quite a move away from interpretations which concentrated on finding the historical nucleus of the account, often seeing Ehud as a guerilla-type leader winning a memorable local battle against the odds, whose story has been preserved through tribal tradition.

While the escapades of Ehud no doubt entertained the Hebrew reader at the expense of Eglon and the Moabites, there are also features of the account which emit messages to the audience about themselves.

First of all, the story introduces a theme of *idolatry.* In 3:19 we are told Ehud turned back at the sculptured stones, and in 3:26 that he passed beyond them. They seem innocent enough remarks, but the sculptured stones are *pesilim* — a Hebrew term which refers to idols. Moreover, the verb "to turn back" often refers to repentance, and the verb "to pass over" indicates "transgressing." These are not throwaway statements. On the contrary, they are heavily loaded phrases, and the fact that Ehud's victory takes place within these framing remarks is telling. This has been perceived by R. M. Polzin (1980: 160), who believes that these two references provide an ideological frame for Ehud's deliverance. Ehud is successful because he "turned back" from the idols at Gilgal and "passed beyond" the idols and fled to Seirah, just as one "turns away" from the evil way (as in 1 Kgs 13:33; 2 Kgs 17:13) and "returns" to Yahweh (as in Deut 30:10). The Ehud story, like the subsequent stories, is thus a vehicle for a writer's religious ideology and agenda, and, for the writer of Judges, victory lies in turning away from idolatrous images.

R. H. O'Connell (1996) contrarily commends Ehud for acting quickly and defeating an enemy, but sees the continued presence of the *pesilim* as troubling. These symbols should have been destroyed, but they are left standing, and here begins a theme of cultic irregularity that develops throughout the book. This may be the first sign of another theme that pervades the book — that of the *flawed judge.*

Finally, the story highlights *Yahweh's sovereign freedom.* Although Yahweh is not always a prominent character within the stories, he is always hovering in the background, working to bring matters to his own ends, often through unlikely means. This is a theological interest that pervades the book of Judges and is demonstrated in a variety of ways, notably here in his choice of unlikely characters. This Ehud character is immensely enjoyable, but his story also exhibits some dubious qualities — deception, gore, and a macabre relish for the assassination. While some argue that these features should not unduly trouble us, his actions can be discomforting. Yet Yahweh uses this ambivalent man despite, or maybe *through,* those very flaws, manifesting his sovereign freedom.

If the Ehud story is a narrative vehicle for theological and ideological conversation, the question of which particular audience the writer had in mind when compiling this text becomes an intriguing issue. It would not be appropriate at this stage to delve into this question since there are other stories and themes to be discussed. However, some possibilities will be raised in due course.

Deborah — Barak — Jael (4:1–5:31)

As we move into the next story, various connecting features can be noted which form a kind of literary bridge between the two. In 3:27 Ehud blew the trumpet in the highlands of *Ephraim* — a detail that connects with 4:5, where we are told Deborah sits in the highlands of Ephraim. In 3:20 we read of Ehud's dagger *thrust* into the belly of Eglon. 4:21 speaks of Jael *driving* the tent peg into Sisera's temple — and the same Hebrew verb *(taqa')* is used. In 3:31 there is a brief note about the days of Shamgar, son of Anath, and they are pointedly recalled in 5:6. There is also a scenic link. At the close of both stories there is a dead foreign oppressor and people who draw mistaken conclusions about the delay of their leaders (Eglon's men presume that he is taking a long time at his toilet, while the Canaanite ladies of 5:30 presume that Sisera is engaged in raping his female victims). B. G. Webb (1987: 177) refers to these linking devices as short-range connections — bridges between adjacent stories which create a carefully woven tapestry.

Such connections do suggest that there is a careful hand at work in Judges and does raise the possibility that the stories integrate so well because the Judges writer supplied his own "source" material, together with the connections. However, it has been more commonly thought that these integrative elements are the work of a Judges editor who has worked them into received source material.

Among the sources posited for Judges, ch. 5 has long been hailed as one of the oldest pieces of Hebrew poetry in the Bible. Accordingly, scholars of the previous century spent much time reconstructing its historical background, and it was widely accepted that Deborah's judgeship could be dated c. 1125 BC on the basis of the archeological evidence for the destruction of Taanach and Megiddo at this time. However, such certainty has been tempered in recent decades. G. W. Ahlström (1993: 57-58), for instance, says that it is impossible to determine the derivation of any sources within Judges, or indeed whether the narratives were inspired by a fictitious tradition. He claims that the Deborah tradition has no factual basis known to us. Contrary to earlier scholarship which has emphasized the importance of the Song as an early witness to an infamous battle, he claims that the poetic form of the victory does not necessarily offer reliable ancient details since "a poet's celebrations are usually not reliable historical sources" (1993: 379). Dating the battle on the basis of the Taanach and Megiddo destructions is said to be a poor argument. These cities may have been included only to place the action within some recognizable geographic locale — their destruction not necessarily being inferred or even known.

It is now thought that the Song is not necessarily a separate, older, independent tradition to the prose account of the preceding chapter. Rather, literary analyses (see A. Brenner 1990) have demonstrated the complementary nature of these narratives. Whatever nucleus of historical data may or may not lie behind them, the writer of Judges now uses both prose and poetic accounts as vehicles for his own agenda.

Immediately the reader is confronted with one of the writer's major themes — *the sovereign freedom of Yahweh.* The Deborah story, like that of Ehud, is a tale of the unexpected. This is immediately evident in the opening verses of ch. 4, where the anticipated raising of the deliverer is conspicuously absent from the cyclic pattern. We have already noted that the cyclic pattern has been provided as a hermeneutical key, with any deviations being significant for interpretation. Assuming then that this feature is deliberately withheld, we need to ask what purpose is served by the omission. For Y. Amit (1987), this purpose lies in a deliberate attempt to disorient the reader concerning who exactly does bring deliverance to Israel.

The first impression is that Deborah is the new judge — she is certainly referred to at the appropriate juncture and is said to be "judging" Israel. But there is no expected formula, and she is not linked with any military activities; on the contrary, she *sits* beneath a palm and is a *woman.* The writer goes out of his way to emphasize her gender by including the female pronoun where not strictly necessary. As R. Alter indicates, conventional English translations have smoothed over "a certain purposeful awkwardness" or "stylistic bumpiness" in the Hebrew which he suggests is "intended precisely to bump our sensibility as an audience" (1981: 41). If her gender was not sufficient to preclude her fulfilling our expected role, the possibility of Deborah being the judge is finally undone by her appointing of Barak as the leader of the attack. Barak thus becomes our second possibility. But his reluctance to go alone leads to a prophecy that Sisera will die by a woman's hand, perhaps reinforcing the Deborah option.

Finally, the third possibility arises as a completely unexpected assassin appears in Jael. The reader has been lulled into a false sense of security regarding Jael since 4:17 has informed us of the peace between the house of Heber and King Jabin (Heber's name even means "ally"). As such, the murder comes as a complete shock. Just as Ehud the left-handed man of double entendre was an unlikely judge, Jael is another unorthodox candidate — a tent-dwelling woman who alone, using her words cunningly and with an unlikely improvised weapon, outwits a superior military force.

Amit's conclusion is that the human participants act almost as "red herrings" in a story which deliberately drives the reader to recognize the *divine* deliverer. She proposes that the purpose is precisely "to convince the reader that the happenings in the human world constitute a revelation of God's power — an expression of his will" (1987: 89). Yahweh, in sovereign freedom, uses highly unorthodox agents and means to accomplish his designs, outfoxing the foreign oppressors and even his own people (notice how Barak is also outwitted in the process).

The *satirization of the foreign king* continues. The reference to Jabin as "king of Canaan" has always produced extensive footnotes in traditional commentaries because Canaan was never united under one king at this purported time in history. Few commentators have looked to the literary value of the name and its possible representative usage. The name Jabin has its root in the verb *bin,* meaning "to have perception, discernment, knowledge." Given the play on knowledge evident in this story, and in the book as a whole, the name is probably not insignificant. This mighty king who can amass an army of considerable proportions (nine hundred chariots of iron) is routed by a people who, in his *perception,* must have been unlikely victors. His general is assassinated by one who, in his *perception,* was an unlikely murderess. The ironic lack of perception on the "Canaanite side" is made further apparent in the conversation between the *wise* ladies of 5:28-30 who await their glorious victors with the spoils. Their sense of self-assurance and comfortable security is utterly misplaced. Far from their belief that their victorious men are finding a womb or two for every man, the great general Sisera has met his end sinking and dying between the legs of a woman (5:27). The sexual imagery is thus reversed, as noted by S. Niditch (1989). The name Jabin is thus of ironic value to a writer who increasingly demonstrates the hollow nature of human "perception." Jabin trusts in a false security, and, as with Eglon, a foreign king heading an oppressive regime comes to nothing. The implicit claim is that this kind of regime can be dislodged by the people of Yahweh when properly mobilized under his appointments.

However, the theme of the *flawed agent* also develops. In Barak a deterioration emerges as an elected man challenges his nomination. Despite being given the imperative "Go!" by Deborah, his timorous response, as translated by R. Alter, is, "If you will go with me I will go, and if you won't go with me I won't go" (1992: 42). This half-heartedness of Barak contrasts starkly with the zeal of Deborah and Jael, which in the social word of the ancient Near East would undoubtedly have been a humiliating comparison. Even Barak's name ("flash" or "lightning") is ironical since he is hardly a prime example of incisive, effective, dramatic action. On the contrary, Barak is presented as a comic slow-coach. His bout of hesitation leads to all manner of unfortunate knock-on effects. Notice how Barak and his ten thousand men are apparently left standing around surveying the scene while Yahweh wreaks havoc in the Sisera camp. Then, as Sisera alights from his chariot and flees on foot, Barak pursues not Sisera, but the empty chariot (the NRSV plural assumes the generic "chariotry") together with the final remnants of the army. Sarcasm is thus directed at the hapless Barak who spends his time on this wild goose chase, apparently unaware that Sisera — the object of the entire exercise — has been delivered into a woman's hands. Only when Jael has dispatched the sleeping Sisera does "lightning" make his tardy arrival.

Barak is not the only Israelite who is depicted in a poor light. In 5:15-17 Deborah rebukes those tribes who did not rally to her side, and here emerges another feature of the book as a whole — a focus on the *disintegration of Israelite communal life.* From this point on, an insidious disunity seeps in which will resurface in the Gideon story when the Ephraimites upbraid him for not calling them out.

Gideon (6:1–8:35)

As we move into the Gideon account, short-range connections with the Deborah account can be identified. Gideon's story opens with the sending of a prophet in 6:8, which recalls Deborah's prophetess status in 4:5. In 6:11 a messenger goes to Ophrah and sits beneath the oak, which is reminiscent of Deborah's sitting beneath the palm in 4:5. The verb *taqa'* makes another appearance. It has already occurred in the story of Ehud and Jael, who *taqa'* (thrust) their unusual weapons into their unsuspecting male victims. The verb is now used at 6:34; 7:18-20 in its other sense, to describe the *blowing* on the trumpets. These connections weave the stories together.

The stories are also interconnected through the shared cyclic pattern, and again there is a telling divergence in the elaborated detail given for the Midianite oppression. It is only after prolonged subjugation that the people eventually cry to Yahweh. We may deduce from this that sustained oppression is needed to jolt Israel out of an emerging complacency and that this is a first step toward a more prolonged abandonment of that relationship and a life lived according to human terms (what is right in their own eyes) rather than those of Yahweh.

The lengthened introduction also documents a delayed response to their tardy pleas. Israel's cry is greeted not by the immediate rise of a deliverer but by the appearance of a prophet, who rebukes the Israelites rather than granting help.

This ominous opening is telling. It foreshadows a sharp decline in the story of the judges as a whole, and particularly a sharp decline in the nature of the judge eventually appointed — Gideon. For while on a surface level Gideon appears to be a victorious judge, modest about his origins and capabilities, honoring Yahweh with the creation of an ephod following success, the narrator subtly provides a critique of this character which undermines that apparently positive portrayal. This tension is most evident in the comparison of Gideon with Moses. While depicting Gideon in Mosaic terms may appear to give Gideon great credentials, the way in which the comparison is drawn actually discredits him.

Both men receive divine visitations — Moses in Exod 3:2 and Gideon in Judg 6:11 — but their differing reactions to those visitors provides a telling commentary. Moses seeks to shield himself from the Deity in reverence, but Gideon makes no such respectful response. On the contrary, he is abrupt and somewhat sarcastic with his visitor, asking, without any respectful etiquette, where all these wonders of the LORD are, given the present situation.

Moses receives a commission to liberate his people from the Egyptians (Exod 3:10) and, having made excuses, finally accedes to the divine command. Gideon receives his commission to liberate his people from the Midianites and likewise puts obstacles in the way of the divine imperative. Gideon's excuses, however, are belabored, with a double fleece test being carried out before Gideon is prepared to take on Midian. Even on the battlefield, Gideon needs further comfort (7:9-15). He is no modest hero, providing the kind of pious objection typified in the Moses tradition. His hesitation should be seen negatively as human reluctance and a preference to yield to human securities (a preference seen further in his amassing an army well in excess of twenty thousand men).

Both men are granted signs of proof. The difference is that Moses is granted his signs — the leprous hand and the rod which turns into a snake — freely, on God's own initiative. Gideon, on the contrary, *requests* proof, and his tests are *self*-devised. He wishes to be in control of the situation and dictates his own experiments.

Finally, the creation of a cultic object features in both men's lives. In Exodus 32 the people sin by making an idolatrous golden calf, and Moses's reaction is one of grave displeasure. Gideon *himself* makes an ephod — an act described in terms which smack strongly of the golden calf incident, with earrings being used on both occasions to create the offending object.

There are, however, other connections, and there may also be an anticipation here of King Jeroboam's creation of two bull images in 1 Kgs 12:25-33. The purposeful link between Jeroboam's actions and the story of the golden calf has long been noted, but all three narratives — those of Moses, Gideon, and Jeroboam — are linked. Both Gideon and Jeroboam are described as mighty men of valor

(Judg 6:12 and 1 Kgs 11:28). An apostate altar is torn down in both stories (Judg 6:25-27 and 1 Kgs 13:5). Both men's lives are sought at the beginning of their careers due to their activities (Judg 6:30; 1 Kgs 11:40). Both men are approached to be rulers over Israel (Judg 8:22; 1 Kgs 12:20). In both stories one of their sons rules after them, but the heir and house is destined for elimination. Even the names Jerubbaal and Jeroboam invite comparison. And of course both men create cultic objects that lead to apostasy in the eyes of the writer. Taken cumulatively, these parallels appear sufficient to warrant a comparison, and would indicate that Gideon is portrayed in a negative light as a successor of Aaron, who allowed the creation of the golden calf, and as a forerunner of King Jeroboam, who also created idolatrous images. As such, Gideon's ephod should be seen as an idolatrous thing that, as the text comments, becomes a snare for Israel.

In the story of Gideon, a number of themes already introduced are developed — that of *idolatry,* that of the *flawed judge,* and the *satirization of kingship.* Notwithstanding, Gideon has usually been presented as a hero in commentaries. Can he not at least be acclaimed for his courageous battle in which, despite initial reluctance, he does subsequently rout the Midianites (though, as with Barak, it is Yahweh who is active in the Midianite camp, turning the soldiers against themselves (7:22), before Gideon and his army have done anything more than broken a few jars and blown their trumpets)? Gideon then pursues the fleeing Midianites with a vigor and zeal that are quite the reverse of his previous cautiousness and timidity. On the surface these activities commend Gideon, who goes extra lengths to ensure the utter defeat of Midian and, with a mere three hundred fatigued and hungry men, in single-minded determination takes on fifteen thousand men and routs the entire, unsuspecting army. He is unresting (despite his men's exhaustion noted in 8:4) until the two foreign kings, Zebah and Zalmunna, are in his grasp. The transformation in Gideon is truly remarkable; now he acts with immediacy, fearlessness, and defiance in the face of the enemy. Why, then, am I suggesting that Gideon is actually portrayed in a negative light?

The answer to this lies in Gideon's motivations, which the narrator does not reveal until 8:19 — Gideon has all this time been pursuing the killers of his brothers. So the chase has not been undertaken to exalt the name of Yahweh but to seek personal satisfaction in a blood feud. M. Sternberg has rightly commented that once Gideon's true colors are exposed, the reader is impelled to review the previous events, and "Gideon's personality emerges as more complex and less admirable than before" (1985: 312).

Gideon's capture of Zebah and Zalmunna is certainly described in ruthless terms. While his own son shrinks from acting as a cold-blooded executioner, Gideon himself has no such foibles. What we do not recognize easily in our English translations is that Zebah ("sacrifice") and Zalmunna ("no protection") bear names entirely suitable for those about to be executed. This heightens the harsh portrayal of Gideon, whose callous, implacable execution of "Sacrifice" and "No Protection" appears harder and more merciless given the pathetic names of his victims.

Gideon's transformed character is matched by his transformed name. Alternations between the names Gideon and Jerubbaal have generally been explained by saying that two sources have been combined. This is possible, of course, but such preoccupations leave little or no room for seeing an ideological usage behind the switch. Gideon means "The Hacker" — an appropriate name for the one who will hack down the altar of Baal, albeit in a hesitant and seemingly reluctant way. The name Jerubbaal has the sense of "Contender" — a name that becomes ever more apt as we move from his early characterization to that of ruthless pursuer of his enemies. The Baal element is also indicative of foreign deities, which is consistent with the apostasy that begins before he dies.

As soon as Gideon moves away from the divine initiative into personal operations (revenge for the death of his brothers), three significant things happen in the narrative: (1) Gideon becomes ever more royal; (2) Yahweh disappears from the narrative; (3) Gideon's community fall into apostasy. These are not an unrelated set of affairs.

First of all, Gideon appears most like a foreign oppressive king when carrying out revenge. When Gideon has the two Midianite kings in his power facing imminent death, they significantly tell him that he "resembled the sons of a king" (8:18). This action is immediately followed by the request from his compatriots that he does indeed become king (v. 22). Additional information provided in 8:30-31 draws attention to his many wives, whose presence is strongly reminiscent of the royal harem. The final incriminating factor lies in the name of one of his seventy sons — Abimelech, "My father is king." Thus, for all Gideon's emphatic disavowal of kingship in 8:22-24, implicit commentary from v. 18 on undermines his words. For all his denial of human kingship and advocacy of divine rule, Gideon is depicted as one who bears traits typical of a king, and this is not portrayed as a good development for Israel.

It is significant that as Gideon becomes ever more regal, Yahweh accordingly withdraws from the action (point b). From 8:34 only the name Elohim, "God," is used, and as the plot moves into the story of Abimelech — who certainly behaves like a foreign monarch — only references to Elohim are found. If these name switches are intentional, Yahweh is clearly removed from any association with monarchic tendencies. It would appear that such monarchy rule belongs to "others" and not to Yahweh's people.

Finally, Gideon's community becomes ensnared by the ephod (point c). This is an ominous development, for apostasy now begins before the death of the deliverer, and the idolatry is not a foreign temptation but something instigated by the judge. In this decline the Israelites grow further away from any trust and commitment to Yahweh toward a trust in and commitment to their own cultic strategies. The ephod represents something tangible and, like the golden calf, satisfies the desire for concrete security. By the close of the Gideon story we end up back at Ophrah, with all Israel committing apostasy at an ephod of Gideon's making. The irony is telling. As

B. G. Webb notes, "Gideon, champion of Yahweh against Baal, presides over the national apostasy" (1987: 153).

Abimelech (9:1-57)

Abimelech's story is a continuation of the Gideon plot which now takes a new turn, issuing in a story of exact retribution in which he who dispatches his seventy brothers on *one stone* has his own skull crushed by a woman dropping *a stone* on his head.

As noted above, Yahweh does not appear in this narrative. It is the spirit of Elohim who comes between Abimelech and the Shechem leaders. Why Elohim? If the appearances of Elohim in Judges are considered part of a consistent and deliberate ideological ploy rather than the result of conjoining differing tribal traditions, one possible answer soon presents itself. Elohim is a generic term for deity and is used predominantly by foreigners in the book of Judges. Thus, in 1:7 Adoni-bezek declares the rightful retributive action of Elohim. In 3:20 Ehud uses Elohim when speaking to Eglon of Moab, and in 7:14 a Midianite soldier uses Elohim. It is interesting, then, that in the case of Abimelech, it is not Yahweh but Elohim who appears in the narrative; this might suggest that Abimelech functions as the foreigner within Israel's own ranks and becomes an oppressor of Israel.

Indeed, the fate suffered by Abimelech — a humiliating end at the hands of a woman — is one that has befallen a previous foreign oppressor. And again we have an unlikely female heroine with an equally unlikely weapon which damages the head of the victim. By portraying such an end for Abimelech the writer undercuts at one blow the view that hard-lined, rigorous, single-minded, strong leadership can be beneficial — so much for all this when such an ignominious death befalls the man who would rule as king.

Abimelech's story is a study in the consequences of unworthy, humanly appointed leadership, with the parable of Jotham (9:8-15) providing the theological key to its meaning. The bramble's acceptance of the proposition that a king be appointed over the trees and its subsequent suggestion that the other lofty trees come and partake of its shade are obviously portrayed as absurd. Kingship is clearly not for Israel since only the most unsuitable candidate, unworthy and unable to fulfill the responsibilities of the task, would accept the role. The loftier, superior person would have the good sense to deny the offer and continue with his more useful natural role. Israel has already been shown a suitable mode of leadership. The pursuit of kingship is both unnecessary and dangerous, and Abimelech is the bramble who amply demonstrates this danger.

That the book of Judges has an interest in leadership politics has long been recognized. D. Jobling (1986) takes an approach which is sensitive to the way in which the narrative of Judges and the first twelve chapters of 1 Samuel are structured, and has discerned a careful pattern which reflects an interest in two major systems of leadership — judgeship and kingship.

Judgeship is given an early nod of approval in the exemplary career of Othniel; but as this system of leadership is further explored through the careers of subsequent judges, flaws emerge. Similarly, the kingship option is advantageous in some ways — chs. 17–21 appear to demonstrate how the absence of a monarch leads to civil war — yet in Abimelech we see all the negative aspects of this: brutality, oppression, despotic behavior, and an ignominious end.

For Jobling, the ultimate problem lies in the tension between the desire for guaranteed continuity and security, and the simultaneous desire to preserve the free initiative of Yahweh. With the arrangement of monarchy, continuity is assured through dynastic succession — but where is Yahweh's freedom in this? With the system of judges, Yahweh's initiative is well preserved, but there is no guarantee that Yahweh's elect will prove worthy and they have to wait, with faith, for Yahweh to act — where is the security in this? Jobling believes that the editors had no clear and easily definable opinion and concludes that they had views which could not be resolved simply.

R. H. O'Connell (1996) also stresses the political rhetoric at work within Judges. In his view, however, there is not so much a contradiction between *systems* of government as a debate regarding *parties* of government. For O'Connell, as with Brettler (1989), Judges endorses a divinely elected Judahite king and attempts to sway the reader away from any sympathies/loyalties to the Saulide dynasty. The rhetoric is subtle, and analogies between Judges texts and later narratives, particularly in the books of Samuel, do much to achieve this purpose.

Jephthah (10:6–12:7)

Divergences from the ever-disintegrating cyclic pattern continue in the Jephthah story. The marked difference on this occasion is that the Israelites' cry to Yahweh for deliverance is detailed, so that the reader hears their negotiation tactics. This emphasis on bargaining indeed proves to be the very essence of the Jephthah story, whose name aptly means "he opens" (i.e., his mouth).

Previously, crying out to Yahweh has stimulated the desired effective action on their behalf, though the prophet's words of ch. 6 gave an early warning against any presumption that crying to the LORD would necessarily or automatically provide deliverance. The Israelites have their part of the bargain to keep, and the ominous words of the prophet hinted that their repeated apostasy might well jeopardize any deliverance by Yahweh. The threat turns into reality here. Yahweh's interjection (10:11-14) demonstrates that a crude self-serving crying out, even when accompanied by "repentance," will not act as a mechanistic guarantee of his favorable response — Yahweh refuses to be used in this way.

After they have suffered this rejection of their plea, the ambivalent nature of their professed repentance is exposed as they counter Yahweh's rebuke with an almost indifferent acknowledgment of guilt, "we have sinned; do to us whatever seems good to you," followed by the repeated request, "but deliver us this day" (10:15). This rather nonchalantly proposed deal is described by R. M. Polzin as the "smug confidence of a spoiled child" (1989: 73). Its temporary status is made evident by the following narratives of Judges where, significantly, Israel does not bother to cry out to Yahweh again.

The only positive thing in their favor is that they "put away the foreign gods from among them and worshipped the LORD" (10:16). And it is in response to this activity that we appear to see a change of heart in Yahweh, who, according to the NRSV, "could no longer bear to see Israel suffer." However, "could no longer bear" may be a tame translation of a Hebrew verb which refers to the "shortening" of patience or endurance. The RSV, for instance, had "and he became indignant over the misery of Israel." This raises an important question. Is Yahweh short of patience given the hostilities raised against Israel (i.e., sympathetic to their misery and unable to tolerate their cries any longer?), or is he short-tempered, exasperated, and indignant with Israel's profession of misery given their calculated "repentance"?

The latter option seems the most likely. His ambiguous activity in the remainder of the narrative can be seen as being borne out of this exasperated anger, for this tale teaches Israel a lesson in divine independence and the dangerous folly of attempting to control God, as we shall see.

A second negotiation scene between Jephthah and the elders of Gilead (11:6-11) exhibits Jephthah's opportunism, turning an initial offer of leadership into an offer of headship. But this opening does not bode well for Israel — Jephthah is clearly a man motivated by promises of leadership, and as such he reminds the reader of Jotham's bramble, the only tree willing to accept the offer of kingship. Here is a judge who is eager to grasp leadership and careful to obtain a guarantee of the offer from the elders of Gilead before returning to fight Ammon.

The next negotiations are between Jephthah and the king of Ammon (11:12-28). There are two major views on this. Some see his lengthy speech as evidence of his skills of disputation, which cannot be answered by the king of Ammon (for a full defense of this view see R. H. O'Connell 1996: 196-200). Others see it as a mocking presentation of a botched attempt to negotiate. The issue hinges on whether Jephthah's reference to the *Moabite* deity Chemosh as the god of *Ammon* is understandable in the historical context, or simply an error on his part.

For the first view to work the reader has to assume that the king of Ammon legitimately controls land of Moab south of the Arnon, having expanded into that territory. As a controller of Moabite lands, he could then legitimately be said to have been given the land by Chemosh. But the reader has to supply this information, and there has been no attempt by subsequent editors to provide an explanation for later readers.

If, however, Jephthah simply has his facts wrong and has confused the deity of Moab with that of Ammon, then the laconic response of the king to Jephthah's long and elaborate speech is perfectly understandable, and Jephthah is exposed as an inept negotiator. When considered in this light, Jephthah's entire speech becomes suspect. J. C. Exum (1992: 62) has shown how his speech could actually work against him. For example, his claim to land via divine grant works both ways — if Yahweh can give land to his people, then, equally, Ammon can be granted disputed territory by a deity. As for the claim that the Ammonites have let the issue lie dormant for three hundred years, Exum rightly points out that the time is about ripe for renewed discussion!

If we take this view we will be motivated to ask why Jephthah should have been given such an ignominious portrayal, and L. R. Klein (1988) has advocated a persuasive solution to this question. For her, the matter goes back to his origins and Jephthah's impure line of descent. His mother, we are told, was a harlot, and his father is said to be "Gilead" — a none too subtle comment upon his mother's sexual laxity. For Klein, the serious implications are that he would not have the benefit of Israel's traditions being passed down to him by a "sound" mother. Jephthah's negotiations certainly do indicate that he has insufficient understanding of his past and the ways of Yahweh. For example, Chemosh's existence and rights are spoken of in terms comparable to those of Yahweh — implicitly acknowledging a polytheism in which the two gods are on a par, which could hardly be viewed as a favorable point.

His ignorance of the ways of Yahweh may be seen in his subsequent negotiation with Yahweh in 11:30. Here again we see Jephthah's desire to secure a deal before going to battle. His vow is an attempt to guarantee the favorable regard of Yahweh — an insurance ploy. Only when he is confident that he has ensured success does Jephthah venture out against the Ammonites. Again the tendency to trust in his own self-made contingency plan is evident. Yet the story illustrates how such a vow imprisons the vow maker within his own ideology. When his only daughter comes out to meet him, Jephthah despairs that he has opened his mouth to Yahweh. Thus the one who has tried to manipulate Yahweh to his own ends, pinning the Deity down by the oath, is taught a severe lesson. The perception that certain human initiatives can procure a favorable divine response is not wisdom but folly. Vow making of this ilk is permitted to achieve the end sought (victory over the Ammonites), but the cost to Jephthah is such that its negative portrayal is clear. The dangers of improper negotiation with Yahweh are thus an evident concern of the story. But it is not its only concern.

Undergirding the Jephthah account is a strong message concerning purity. Just as Gideon's relationship with the Shechemite concubine issued in the birth of Abimelech, Jephthah's upbringing has dangerous consequences. The implicit ideology of the text, as Klein argues, is that the Israelites should contain their sexual desires, for "whether with foreign women (Gideon's case) or not (the harlot-mother of Jephthah), non-familial Israelite proliferation is shown as potentially destructive" (1988: 99).

However, if Jephthah's mother was an example of what dangers can emerge from improper sexual activity, his daughter's submission to the patriarchal system is a perfect model for purity, with her virginity clearly stressed. This undoubtedly adds to the pathos of the story, but, more significantly, as a virgin she is seen as one of the noblest of young woman — pure, untainted. She is praised for her courageous and dignified acceptance of her duty, rewarded by a record of her death, and has a custom initiated in remembrance of her.

Feminist scholars note the rhetoric inherent in this portrayal. The virginal daughter appears in this light because the male writer is providing an idealized portrait of womanly behavior under dire circumstances. Note the exceptional nature of her reactions — no questioning of the father, no outburst of indignation, no tears, just utter submission and perfect obedience. Exum (1992: 66) states that this lack of protest indicates how her portrayal serves a patriarchal agenda, and she invites female readers to resist the encoded message of the text.

In his final scene Jephthah undertakes one last negotiation strategy, this time with the Ephraimites who are resentful that they had not been summoned to battle against Ammon. This is reminiscent of their quarrel with Gideon in 8:1-3, and provides a short-range connection between the two stories. In this case, however, the situation has worsened and the Ephraimites threaten Jephthah's life. Jephthah does not share the diplomatic, conciliatory attitude displayed by Gideon. On the contrary, diplomacy is the last thing on Jephthah's mind, and he reacts with a vehemence out of all proportion, murdering forty-two thousand Ephraimites at the fords of the Jordan. This, of course, contrasts glaringly with Ehud's rallying of the Ephraimites at the fords of the Jordan, where the Moabites (i.e., the *foreign* enemy) were defeated. Disunity is spiraling and will reach its nadir in the civil war against Benjamin in chs. 19–21.

Yet for all the damning features of his story, there is something to be said for sympathizing with Jephthah. Jephthah seems to be in the power of a deity that has held sway over him ever since he uttered his devastating vow under the influence of Yahweh's spirit — thereby rendering Yahweh's spirit an ambiguous power indeed.

Certainly Jephthah is another *flawed judge* whose desire for power and attempts to control outcomes through his own skills of negotiation have pedagogical value. But again Yahweh's ability to achieve his will despite, or through, these flaws is evident, and the writer of Judges is able to teach his contemporary generation a lesson in divine *sovereign freedom* and the foolishness of the notion that one may control God.

The Minor Judges (10:1-5; 12:8-15)

The story of Jephthah is framed by details of five characters who are conventionally referred to as "minor" judges. These details have long been seen as a separate literary strand interwoven into Judges during its formation, derived from a record compiled during the period of the monarchy. This was thought to be evidenced in the format of their details, which contrasts markedly with the stereotyped framework that embraces the major narratives of the book. The new format includes the name of the judge and his place of origin, details of family offspring in some cases, length of office, record of death, and burial site. The dry, chronicle-like descriptions hardly match the previous entertaining plots.

Once the deduction was made that this was a separate literary strand which partially preserved an ancient chronicle, it was a natural move to investigate the function of these individuals. It became widely thought that these figures were tribal elders with administrative, judicial, and governing functions — perhaps transitional figures between elders and kingship. A sociological analogy has pointed to the roles of similar individuals in African segmentary societies who act as mediators between the two community modes. A. D. H. Mayes (1985) claims that figures like these would have a useful part to play when a premonarchic society was faced with an emergent monarchical mode of government. Whatever the plausibility of such reconstructions, the way in which these details are now interwoven into the book of Judges evidences significant literary strategies at work that merit closer inspection.

First of all, the tactical placing of these figures is informative. The first listing occurs after the turmoil of the extended Gideon-Abimelech cycle, and the brief, unemotive listing provides welcome relief from the turbulence and involvement of the previous stories. It has thus been suggested that these details supply an intentional "breather" in the book, offering relief after the rapidity and sheer brutality of recent events (so Webb 1987: 160; Boling 1975: 189).

The notices of Jair and Ibzan may also have been tactically placed around the Jephthah narrative. Jair, listed immediately prior to Jephthah, has Gileadite connections, and this provides a short-range connection with Jephthah the Gileadite. The judgeship of Ibzan, which follows the Jephthah narrative, offers a conspicuous contrast. For, after reading of Jephthah's loss of his only daughter, Ibzan, in stark distinction, has no less than thirty daughters and thirty daughters-in-law. This juxtaposition does appear to be cruelly deliberate, particularly when it is considered that none of the other minor judges is credited with a prestigious female line of descendants (so Hamlin 1990: 122).

Secondly, these figures may be intended to indicate how judgeship is always teetering on the brink of kingship. The form in which their details are recorded is reminiscent of king notices, and perhaps this is a deliberate indicator for interpretation. Notice how their successive reigns follow immediately after one another with no period of interregnum. This suggests periods of continuous successive leadership (typical of the king pattern). Indeed, if Shamgar (3:31) is included as one of these figures, as some scholars suggest, then the sequence of minor judges follows an ever-enlarging pattern — 1 (Shamgar), 1-2 (Tola and Jair), 1-2-3 (Ibzan, Elon, Abdon) — itself perhaps indicative of kingship with its dynastic tendencies. Then the notices regarding family size, livestock, and cities are suggestive of the king's tendency to accumulate wealth, prestige, and status.

If these features are indicative of would-be kings, it is interesting to note that Yahweh is never mentioned in conjunction with their reigns, especially since we have conspicuously moved away from acknowledging the victories of *Yahweh,* to a record of the personal acquisitions, prestige, and status of humans. It may be that the description of their acquisitions (cities and asses) is not so much an ancient reminiscence as a negative comment from a writer who thereby subtly satirizes these characters.

However useful or appropriate the attempt to retrieve a suitable matrix and role for these minor judges in early Israel may be, more recent literary commentaries and essays indicate that their value for the writer now lies in their representative function. The details about the minor judges are strategically positioned so as to provide a peaceful interlude in a turbulent story, and draw a stark contrast between a previously bereaved judge and the abundant female offspring of the next. Perhaps more significantly, they provide an introduction to monarchic rule, perhaps illustrating the trend it will follow if left to its own devices.

These considerations indicate that while the listings of the minor judges are *reminiscent* of an annalistic source, such affinities do not necessitate the assumption that we are actually dealing here with genuine archive material. It may be that their names and details derive from a source now lost to us, but it is equally possible that their details do not derive from the separate literary strand commonly posited. It is conceivable that a writer would utilize different literary strategies in order to achieve certain effects, and the annalistic form may simply have been appropriate for his purpose. We may at least consider the possibility that these figures may be the free creations of the writer, playing their part in a well-crafted story. Nothing here is "provable." We cannot insist that they are literary inventions; but then there is no adequate basis for confidently claiming that they are the "early federal administrators" of Boling (1975: 215).

Samson (13:1–16:31)

The last judge of the book may well be the most notorious. If not exactly an endearing figure Samson is certainly an enduring one, continually occupying the popular imagination and stimulating musical, artistic, poetic, and film compositions, especially in relation to his amorous adventures with Delilah. The three chapters that deal with his life have spawned an abundance of scholarly material. In the past century, the solar imagery contained within his story has been discussed (his name means "little sun"; the location *Beth-shemesh* means "house/temple of the sun"; he is associated with fiery activities — burning the Philistine woman and her house, tying torches in the tails of foxes; and some have seen his final blinding at the hands of his captors as an image of a solar eclipse). Other areas of interest have included the apparent parallels between Samson's adventures and those of Heracles; the aesthetics of a text which abounds in rhetorical devices such as double entendre, assonance, pun, bawdy humor, hyperbole, plot retardation, and the role of women in the story.

Just as the characters within Samson's story have endured in the popular imagination, possessing cultural afterlives in art, music, and film, they have also long been thought to have enjoyed a prior existence to that of their Judges setting. The Samson stories are widely thought to have been popular saga material circulating in oral tradition before finding fixed form in the book of Judges. Several studies have accordingly been made of these stories quite independently of their placing within the text of Judges.

The fact that Samson's story does not appear to follow the format typical of the preceding judge stories has indicated to some that we are dealing with material formulated in different and independent circumstances. The pristine cyclic pattern is hardly to be found in these chapters, having disintegrated into a few isolated elements placed here and there. The opening statement that Israel did evil in the sight of the LORD is clearly represented, as is the spirit possessing Samson and victory over the oppressor. The elements are there, but in a less identifiable format — for example, while Israel does not cry out to the LORD, Samson does (15:18; 16:28). On the other hand, the disintegration of the cyclic pattern may be intentional. J. C. Exum (1990: 412) suggests that the disintegration may serve as a deliberate literary device whereby the literary fabric of the text matches the content to a striking degree. Thus the social, political, and moral instability that has developed in Judges is reflected in a textual instability.

Whatever the case, chs. 13–16, as they now stand within Judges, provide a most fitting conclusion to the preceding stories in a variety of ways. First, the geographical journey undertaken in the book of Judges as a whole reaches its northernmost point. It is notable that as we have steadily moved in a south-north direction there has been a corresponding decline in the standards of judgeship and a deterioration within the Israelite community generally. The tribe of Dan is inevitably tarnished by this factor. Just as Samson will ignore his Nazirite status and pursue foreign women, Dan becomes a cultic site that will eventually rival the elect status of Jerusalem, where worship will be deemed apostate and adulterous against Yahweh.

These chapters also provide a point of culmination for various themes and motifs that have been running through all the previous narratives. Certain word motifs make their final appearance here:

The verb *taqaʿ* appears at 16:14, where Delilah is said to fasten *(taqaʿ)* the hair of Samson with a pin *(yated).* This is a most striking reminder of Jael's thrust *(taqaʿ)* of the tent peg *(yated)* into Sisera's head. Moreover, on both occasions the victims are sleeping unsuspecting and are betrayed with cold ruthlessness. The noun *lappid* ("flame" or "torch") appears again in 15:4-5 when Samson ties three hundred torches into the tails of foxes. Previously in 7:16, 20 reference was made to the torches that Gideon's army (significantly *three hundred* strong) held within their jars. There was also the description of Deborah as a woman of *Lappidoth* in 4:4, which may well not be referring to the name of her husband, as commonly thought, but rather that she was a woman *of flames* or a "fiery woman" — a fitting appellation for such a significant woman and consistent with the text's penchant for strong, effective women. The reference to bees in 14:8 also throws the reader back to Deborah, whose name means "honey bee."

These examples highlight a few of the connecting words within Judges and demonstrate the cohesive forces that are present. Such interconnections suggest an artistic, guiding hand that has successfully and subtly linked narratives together, weaving a rich tapestry of terms and motifs.

Not only do the narratives connect on this "narrative texture" basis, but D. W. Gooding (1982) believes there is a deliberate symmetrical system operating within the book whereby the last judge is the antithesis of the first and his antics are a reversal of all the good provided by that first judge. Thus whereas Othniel participates in a good marriage, Samson enters into a foreign marriage with a Philistine. Othniel's wife provides the incentive to drive Gentiles out, whereas Samson's wife leads to living among the Philistines. Othniel's wife obtains further benefits (better water conditions), while Delilah's liaisons with Samson are to his detriment (obtaining secrets leading to his downfall). Essentially, Othniel delivers Israel from the foreigner, whereas Samson is handed over to the foreigner by his own people and only delivers through his suicide.

Thematic interests noted in previous stories are also carried forward to the Samson account: the *satirization of foreign kingship* continues in the comic depiction of the Philistines, who are mocked to such an extent that R. H. O'Connell (1996: 227) wonders if this could originally have been the main point of the narratives. The theme of *cultic irregularity* continues as Samson flouts his nazirite status. Samson is another *flawed judge* through whom Yahweh works and exercises *sovereign freedom.* These themes can be examined further in a general discussion of the chapters themselves.

We begin with ch. 13, which opens on a familiar biblical note — the barren wife promised a child by divine initiative. This raises hopes, for it is a common biblical device which sets the stage for a great figure who will fulfill a particular destiny. At last it seems that the decline is about to be reversed, for here is one who has all the credentials one might expect of a Yahweh-elect figure — a nazirite, holy to Yahweh. However, as the chapter progresses we are treated to a comical display of human struggles to contain the divine word.

We are first introduced to Manoah, whose name means "rest" or "repose." This turns out to be an ironic name given his distinct lack of repose in the ensuing narrative where his restless mind will relentlessly question and challenge his wife and the divine messenger. In Manoah we see a man who looks for clarity, for certainties; one who strives to achieve some measure of control in this unnerving situation. This is seen most strongly in his inquiry for the name of the messenger. Although Manoah declares his desire is to honor his visitor, knowledge of the name would grant Manoah some sense of power or control over this situation.

Manoah *is* given an answer, but it is an enigmatic response: "Why do you ask my name? It is too 'wonderful.'" This adjective "wonderful" occurs again in this form only in Ps 139:6 — a psalm which deals with the inscrutability of Yahweh and the omniscient nature of his knowledge. It says, "Such knowledge is too wonderful for me; it is so high that I cannot attain it." Clearly the adjective "wonderful" has connotations of incomprehensibility and the unfathomable nature of divine knowledge. The name, however, is crassly misunderstood by Manoah, who immediately makes an offering to Yahweh, the "wonder-worker."

When the messenger finally ascends in the flames of the offering and abstains from any further visits, Manoah "knew that he was the angel of the LORD" (13:21). But even here, his new-found vision is shown to be inadequate as he simultaneously declares that he and his wife will die — a dogmatic statement of mechanic consequences. Only the woman — left unnamed — seems to have some measure of understanding as she effectively tells Manoah not to be so stupid. The woman, in fact, is the one who is content to hear and accept the message without needing to inquire further, test, or secure the identity or origins of the messenger. She willingly accepts the words of the messenger without question, and can see past dogmatic principles (such as "he who sees God shall die") to another plane where deities may act in unforeseen and independent ways.

In the opening verses of ch. 14 all our hopes for Samson, raised by the glowing introduction, are dashed as he turns out to be a boorish prankster — another flawed judge. As each judge has been paraded before the reader, their self-serving attitudes have been exposed. Samson's ready capitulation to his own needs and desires are such that commentators have regularly described him as a self-gratifying brute of a man. His greatest weakness is for foreign women. But again Samson's very flaw — his weakness for Philistine women — is used by the Deity as a means to an end — indeed, we are told that Samson's desire for Philistine women has been planted by the Deity himself. It would seem that Samson's flagrant breaches of his nazirite status are all somehow within the will of Yahweh, who uses his "fatal attractions" to give the Philistines (and Israel) instruction. Once more, then, Yahweh's choice of agents is shown to be beyond human comprehension, as our expectations are once again utterly overturned as Samson is used despite his flagrant misuse of nazirite status.

Samson's attractions to Philistine women, particularly Delilah in ch. 16, raises another thematic interest of Judges — the *danger of assimilation.* The book of Judges as a whole contains many warnings against assimilation, but we see in the story of Samson and Delilah that the dangers of assimilation facing Israel are not posed solely by "other peoples" on a large scale, but there is also a smaller category of foreigners singled out for attention who present a more subtle but equally dangerous threat to purity — that of foreign women. We have already noted how Gideon's victory for Israel was undermined by his co-habitation with a Shechemite concubine, and how Jephthah's tainted line of descent plays a part in his reckless understanding of Yahwism and his people's history. Now, in the disastrous unions of Samson, we see how his attraction to Philistine women leads directly to his eventual capture and death. There seems to be a concern here with "socially correct motherhood." Men must be careful whom they choose as partners — otherwise their choice could spell disaster in terms of the impure offspring. The anti-assimilation message is clear.

The Samson and Delilah encounter is thus full of tension and of forbidden desire, and the tension is evident from the beginning in their very names. Delilah's name has obvious associations with *dallah,* a noun which means "hair" — which is certainly appropriate for this story. But it is also reminiscent of Heb. *laylah,* meaning darkness. Will Samson ("little sun") be overcome by "darkness"?

Delilah's place of origins also stands in tension with Samson's nazirite status. She is said to hail from *naḥal soreq.* Klein (1988: 120; 1993: 55) suggests that *naḥal* carries suggestions of torrential waters passing through the cleft of the wadi — these perhaps being symbolic of the torrents of passion. Torrents bring to mind qualities of fertility, freshness, and vigor, as well as rashness and uncontrollable movement. *Soreq* has the basic meaning of redness (a scarlet woman?), and *soreqah* refers to choice vines. The choice grapes remind the reader of nazirite abstention from strong drink. The tension is obvious — one of them must give way.

Delilah is a doubly dangerous woman given her apparent independence. It is interesting to note that she is not identified by a male relationship — not the daughter, or wife, or sister, of anyone. She appears in her own right and undertakes contractual arrangements with the Philistine lords. As an unattached, quite literally "loose woman," she poses the danger of the "forbidden other" for Samson and has often been represented as a *femme fatale* in subsequent interpretation, whether that be in biblical, artistic, musical, or screen representation.

However, as Exum has pointed out, her popular image as Philistine prostitute figure is, to some extent, the result of readerly imaging since the text never makes this clear. The text informs us that Samson is attracted to Philistine women, that Delilah is in association with Philistine rulers, and that she colludes with them to betray Samson. But against these textual indicators it should also be noted that Delilah bears a Hebrew name and that Sorek lies between Philistine and Israelite land. Our negative view of Delilah as a bad character is one that is possible (and has been reinforced in subsequent portrayals of her character), but there are several "gaps" in the narrative that might mitigate against this, such as the lack of motive and the lack of closure — was Delilah content with her work, was she forced into the betrayal, did she feel remorse? Exum's feminist reading notes how the encoded ideology of the text is that the bad, sexually independent, foreign woman is a snare to good Hebrew men. The narrator does not directly need to state these things, for "he can simply assume and build on the prejudices against Philistines and foreign women that he expects his audience to hold" (1996: 188). The gap filling that takes place is easily done and occurs automatically. For a female reader, however, the story serves only to reinforce a stereotyped image, and Exum offers a reading strategy which offsets this naturalized reading which has privileged a male point of view.

The rhetoric against the foreigner in Judges serves to draw a strong contrast between Israel and its neighbors. On the one hand, Israel is upheld as an alternative community that should maintain its purity in a sea of hostile and infiltrating forces. Yet, on the other hand, Judges demonstrates how this ideal is easily lost by a people who continually "forgot" their one major distinguishing feature — Yahwism — and turned instead to the religion of their neighbors. In so doing, Israel assimilated the norms and values of the "other," simultaneously losing their Yahwistic norms and values.

What is the pedagogical value of this anti-assimilation theme? Perhaps to educate an audience as to how successful existence in the land had been won and lost. The rhetoric inculcates a specific group identity, teaches the importance of developing proper community relations, advocates loyal adherence to Yahwism, and constantly reminds readers of the unique identity of Israel and potential ruin brought about by dangerous liaisons.

After Samson's dismal performance, the reader is prepared for the final downward spiral as events move toward their degenerative climax in chs. 17–21.

The Double Prologue and Epilogue (1:1–3:6; chs. 17–21)

The prologue to Judges consists of two parts — 1:1–2:5 and 2:6–3:6. The first section reads like a list of conquests and failures as the Israelites attempt to consolidate their settlement in the land. One of the accepted teachings of the twentieth century was that this unit preserves some ancient traditions which, given its confession of failures, provide a more reliable conquest account than the book of Joshua. According to this view, it had been inserted between Joshua and Judges for the sake of preservation. Notice, for instance, the repetition of Josh 24:28-30 at Judg 2:6. The intervening material interrupts the natural flow of the story. One of the consequences of this view was that 1:1–2:5 was not seen to be an integral part of the book of Judges but rather a collection of old fragments of tradition tacked on to the beginning of Judges since it was deemed an appropriate place within the larger story.

Judg 2:6–3:6 is commonly thought to be a purposefully composed introduction to the book. It sets the tone and provides an interpretive key for readers' judgments. The style and tone of this language are those often attributed to the Deuteronomist.

The epilogue is also divided into two parts. Chs. 17–18 deal with the migration of the tribe of Dan and explain the origin of their cult site, while chs. 19–21 deal with the Benjaminite civil war. G. F. Moore's commentary of 1895 suggested that this civil war story may well go back to a tenth-century source, and various subsequent "Histories of Israel" imply that these chapters record a significant Iron Age event.

Thus the double epilogue was thought to be constituted of independent literary strands, held together by the repeated refrain that these activities took place when there was "no king in Israel" (17:6; 18:1; 19:1; 21:25). They were preserved here since they provide examples of the declining fortunes of Israel in this period before the onset of the monarchy.

These views on the opening and closing chapters of Judges inevitably conspired to detach the prologue and epilogue from the main body of the book, with each literary strand being studied independently as a tradition in its own right. However, during the latter decades of the twentieth century literary studies paid greater attention to the final form of the book, noting the substantial literary connections between the prologue and the epilogue, and how the main body connects strongly with these chapters.

In 1975 R. G. Boling had already made significant steps in seeing the prologue and epilogue as a tragic-comic framework around the main body of the text, included by an exilic reviser to provide a coherent framework. In 1982 D. W. Gooding noted how each "half" of the double prologue is carefully balanced by the converse halves of the double epilogue. Thus, the first part of the prologue (1:1–2:5) is balanced by the *second* part of the epilogue (chs. 19–21). For example, the opening inquiry of the LORD by all the tribes as to who would fight the Canaanites (1:1) is paralleled by the inquiry in 19:1, though the fighting this time is against one of their own tribes. In 1:13-15 Othniel gains a new wife, Achsah, by a commendable battle against a foreign group. In 21:8-24 the Benjaminites snatch wives against their will in unbefitting circumstances.

The second part of the introduction (2:6–3:6), which details the religious decline of the post-Joshua generation (forsaking Yahweh, worshiping the Baals and Asherahs), is balanced by the first part of the epilogue (chs. 17–18), where this apostasy comes full circle. Here Micah creates idolatrous images, a legionnaire Levite operates at the shrine, and the Danites commit apostasy at a self-created shrine. Gooding thereby also shows how "each part of the epilogue presents a serious decline in, or a worse example of, the state of Israel's affairs as presented in the corresponding part of the introduction" (1982: 76).

The double prologue and epilogue thus frame the main body of Judges in an instructive manner. If the material that makes up these chapters does derive from source material of various provenance and date, then the compiler of Judges has substantially reworked it to create the contrastive design. As Gooding says, the "most natural and economical theory" to account for this arrangement is one that sees the book of Judges as the work of one creative mind who "carefully selected and positioned each piece of source material so that the symmetrical structure of the whole would make those trends apparent to the reader" (1982: 77).

Having noted how the double prologue and epilogue share contrasting features between them, we should now note how they introduce and conclude themes and interests for the main body of the text. A more detailed consideration of the stories in these chapters is required to demonstrate this point.

The Prologue (1:1–3:6)

We have already noted how Josh 24:28-30 is repeated at Judg 2:6-9. Such repetition has been recognized as a Hebrew literary device known as ring composition. Among other effects, ring composition can be used for analeptical purposes — an analepsis being something that brings the natural sequence of the story to a halt while the narrator provides character detail, background information, and any data that enhance the reader's understanding of why characters behave in the way they do when the main narrative picks up again.

Judges 1, although ostensibly set in the period following the death of Joshua, is analeptical. Time comes to a halt while we pause for the narrator to provide a retrospective update for the reader in which the settlement which had been concluded in Joshua appears to happen all over again. This update supplies several snippets of informative detail which explain developments in the main body of Judges:

1. It explains why the Israelites find themselves in the midst of other peoples who will oppress Israel.
2. The presence of other peoples explains the presence of other deities, thus providing the conditions for the apostasy we meet in Judg 2:6. Had we moved directly into this verse, omitting the intervening material, the lapse into apostasy would be very abrupt.
3. It prepares us for future northern failure among the judges, since all northern tribes experience setbacks in their attempts to settle in the land.
4. 2:1-5 forcibly recalls the terms of the covenant, which sets the scene for high tension as the reader recalls the negative side to the covenant should Israel not keep her side of the bargain. It thus prepares for the subsequent indignant action of Yahweh, who hands them over to oppressors and finally detaches himself from their pleas.
5. The south-north geography of the opening chapter, which correlates with initial success and later failures, is entirely consistent with the south-north/success-failure move within the main body.

If the essential function of analepsis is to convey explanatory antecedents, then Judges 1, when read as an analepsis, certainly seems to serve its purpose well. The unit recapitulates the situation the tribes find themselves in at the end of Joshua's leadership (using material already stated in that book) and then uses that material to set the scene for what is to follow in the new epoch.

The prologue also contains three cameo sketches — those of Adoni-bezek, Achsah, and the man of Bethel, each of which provides a first sounding of motifs that will recur in the main body of Judges. Thus, the Adoni-bezek story acquaints the reader with a theme of brutality and savagery. This initial forceful introduction to blood, mutilation, and death offers a brusque and grim first meeting with what will prove to be a feature of the book. The Achsah incident introduces a motif of female opportunism, shrewdness, and manipulation of men. She thus acts as a prototype for the qualities exhibited by later effective women — Deborah, Jael, Jephthah's daughter, Delilah, and the "certain woman" who throws the millstone on the head of Abimelech. The Bethel story introduces the motif of treachery, which will reecho in the stories of Ehud, Jael, Gideon, Abimelech, and Samson. These three cameo sketches thus offer the first sounding of themes whose echoes will resound throughout the work as a whole. B. G. Webb describes this opening section as an "overture" sounding the key notes and musical motifs that the attentive ear will pick up in the succeeding portions of the work.

This is very different from the older view, which thought of the opening material as "foreign" elements tacked on to the book of Judges to preserve them from obscurity. Far from being an alternative conquest account containing a conglomeration of old reliable traditions, Judges 1 can now be seen to operate as a deliberately contrived opening to a new book and a new "era." It cannot be unequivocally stated that it has always been part and parcel of the book. It could have been added at a later stage, as an introduction to the book as a whole, by editors.

However, if ring composition was a common device of narrative prose, the repeated phrases could be seen as an inherent literary device rather than a typical "scissors and paste" technique of inserting source material. This allows the prologue to be treated far more generously as an intentional introduction to the book which *need* not have been added later at all. The prologue is well rooted in its surrounding material, and it would be simpler to see the unit as an integral feature of Judges, possibly composed at the same stage, and by the same hand, as the book itself.

The Epilogue (chs. 17–21)

Chapters 17–18 provide a low point for a number of themes that have been developing in the main body, such as the tendency to rely upon human strategies to secure the favorable regard of the Deity and the disintegration of tribal unity. The chapters are loaded with satire, now no longer directed at foreigners but at the Israelites themselves, and there are several damning features to note.

First of all, the images Micah makes are created from stolen money that had originally been consecrated to Yahweh, and only two hundred of the eleven hundred pieces are sent to the silversmith. Secondly, the images made are a *pesel, masseka, 'ephod,* and *teraphim.* The *'ephod* reminds the reader of Gideon's creation, which became a snare for all Israel. The *teraphim* also has bad connotations — in 2 Kgs 23:24 Josiah removes them from the temple, in Hos 3:4 we are told that Israel should live without them, and in 1 Sam 15:23 the word is translated as idolatry. The *pesel* and the *masseka* are also idolatrous images. It seems that every word for idol that the writer could think of has been brought into play. Supreme irony thus lies in the name of this character. Although the Hebrew text refers to him mostly as Micah, the first mention of his name is spelled *Micayehu,* which means, "Who is like Yahweh?" This question would most appropriately be answered, "None" — there is none like Yahweh, and this is the point. Yahweh is a Deity aloof and independent. He alone is God. But we find "Who is like Yahweh" immediately engaged in the production of idolatrous images which indicate that there was something else that could indeed be "like Yahweh" or even stand in the place of Yahweh.

Thirdly, there is the Levite whose services Micah secures and thereby believes he has gained Yahweh's favor (17:13). But it transpires that this Levite has definite mercenary traits, willing to offer his services to the highest bidder. Both the priest and the idols are lost to the marauding Danites, who themselves become objects of scorn. Their "conquest" of Laish is a parody of the conquest stories. Note how the town they so overwhelmingly "conquer" is remote, defenseless, and unsuspecting — nothing like the great Canaanite cities of the conquest stories. This is a rather pathetic little victory, and sympathies go not to the tribe of Dan but to the people of Laish.

These negative features reveal a strong polemic against the shrine of the Danite tribe that has been founded in such dubious circumstances, and a none too subtle treatise on those who would attempt to make God work for them. In Micah and his mother we have characters who believe they can control the Deity. Note how both make free use of Yahweh's name in these narratives. Ironically, it is highly unlikely that Yahweh will bless any of these goings on, but he is invoked with an alarming display of casualness. This is not without its humor, of course, but a serious point is being made. Chs. 17–18 above all demonstrate the chasm between human and divine perspectives, and the contest for control of events. While Yahweh himself is notably silent in this section, the characters are all busy organizing the Deity to suit their own ends. But the text merely demonstrates their precise inability to do this and underscores the folly of human wisdom and perception. Over against their preference for human insurance and their feeble attempts to guarantee divine insurance lurks a Deity who alone possesses knowledge and acts in sovereign freedom, one free of any human control. One way that the writer makes this evident is in having Yahweh act contrary to human expectations. For this we need to switch our attention to chs. 19–21.

Judges 19 is, without doubt, a horrific text. It is also one which operates on a number of levels. At surface level, the atrocity committed against the Levite's concubine becomes the catalyst for all subsequent atrocities. The irony is that the attempts to recompense the original offense result in worse acts committed against other hapless female victims. By the close of the book the rape of one woman has been compounded rather than avenged as hundreds of other women are taken against their will by opportunist males. On this level, ch. 19 serves to initiate a string of related events, bringing the book of Judges to a close on a grimly ironical note.

On another level, chs. 19–21 have an important foreshadowing function. There are several features which connect with the subsequent story of Saul's rise. The Levite's donkeys and his servant will be brought to mind when Saul has to go and look for the lost asses and takes a servant with him. The emphasis on the place name Gibeah in 19:12-16 (mentioned in every verse) is significant, for this will be the hometown of Saul. We have a butchered concubine who foreshadows Saul's butchering of the oxen and posting of its parts to the tribes of Israel. The Benjaminites figure prominently, and Saul himself is a Benjaminite. In 21:8 Jabesh-gilead is singled out as the tribe that did not turn out, and Jabesh-gilead also figures in the Saul stories.

Whatever tradition may or may not lie behind chs. 19–21, it is clear that they serve to discredit the Saulide dynasty. In 1885 Wellhausen had suggested that the whole account was an artificial construct — in fact a late imitation of the Lot story, written to condemn Gibeah and Benjamin, the hometown and tribe of Saul. M. Z. Brettler (1989) believes that there was a continuing presence of pro-Saul factions long after the house of Saul was overcome by David and that the polemic of Judges 19–21 was aimed at potential advocates of the Saulide dynasty in the postexilic period.

On still another level, the fate of the woman in ch. 19 continues the polemic against sexually free women. Judges 19 provides a telling replay of Genesis 19, but here no angels intervene as in the story of Lot, and the Levite and his host save male honor by throwing out the woman to be gang-raped all night. This story thereby emits a powerful message about the dangers of female sexual freedom. Here is a female character who acts in an independent manner and is punished accordingly.

This independence is seen in the opening verse of ch. 19, where the concubine takes leave of her husband. There is a textual difficulty regarding v. 2, and English Bibles vary in translation. The NRSV translation is based on the LXX and the Old Latin (OL) texts. Yet the Hebrew and Syriac texts say that she "played the harlot" against him. This puts rather a different complexion on the matter, the significance being that if she behaved like a harlot, our sympathy for the woman in her subsequent death is somehow minimized. However, whichever translation is adopted, the fact remains that she went away to her father's house. All agree upon this, and this is the crucial act. In leaving the Levite, the woman makes a statement of independence, of sexual autonomy — an act which could not be tolerated. The message that repeatedly comes across in this story is that the woman is safe when she is in her proper space and sphere, and is of the proper pure category — either a virgin and the property of the father, or a married woman. Notice how she is just able to reach the doorway of the house — the threshold of the safety zone, and her hands are clinging to it where she falls. But she remains, crucially, *outside* the home. As Exum notes, she "puts herself beyond male protection, and for this she must be punished. The men who ordinarily would be expected to protect her — her husband and their host — participate in the punishment because her act is an offense against the social order; that is, against the patriarchal system itself. . . . As narrative punishment for her sexual 'misconduct', her sexual 'freedom', she is sexually abused, after which her sexuality is symbolically mutilated" (1993: 179-80).

Exum argues that what we have here is not a conscious misogyny but a subtext. The male fear of female sexuality lurks beneath the surface of the text. Thus, while the foreground of the text deals with the question of tribal disunity, the near loss of the Benjaminite tribe, and subsequent moves toward monarchy, the background of the text is encoded with a gender polemic.

Chapter 19 is what P. Trible (1984) would call a "text of terror." It reinforces male domination and oppression of women, and it has a deeply encoded subtext concerning the punishment of women's sexuality and the place of women in society. It is a story that requires deconstruction given the considerable status the story has as part of a sacred and authoritative collection of texts. Not to do so is to conspire with the ethics of the text.

Moving on now to chs. 20–21, we noted above that Yahweh preserves his freedom by acting contrary to human expectations, and we saw this happen in the unfolding drama. Yahweh sends the Israelites to battle against the Benjaminites twice, and twice they are defeated. The Israelites clearly are bemused by Yahweh's activity and undertake further consultation, but note how they ask a slightly modified form of the question. On the second consultation (20:23) they mention our *brother* Benjamin, and on the third occasion (20:28) they ask whether they should go *or not*. It is only at the point when they acknowledge Yahweh's choice in the matter that Yahweh's word proves faithful. Then there is an utter massacre of Benjamin, killing men, women, children, and cattle. This account is very reminiscent of the infamous conquest battles of Joshua such as the battle for Ai recorded in Joshua 8, but ironically the great conquest is here delivered with great success against their own people!

Despite the fact that divine ambiguity or unreliability seems to have been pointedly avoided by scholars of the early and mid-twentieth century, quite clearly Yahweh is involved in this slaughter. For the writer of Judges, the ambiguous behavior of Yahweh is the didactic means by which he may demonstrate his independent freedom, supplying a valuable lesson in divine consultation. Yahweh will not simply do what you want him to — no cultic symbols necessarily ensure his favor — images, priests, sacred vows, and consultations are no guarantees of divine pleasure, for Yahweh, it seems, will not be confined or constrained to act mechanically. In short, to try to "get God to work for you" is a folly that is well exposed throughout the entire book of Judges. The God in this book is above all cajoling, all manipulation, all human control. We readers have been placed in a superior position, ideally placed to see the workings of Yahweh and, simultaneously, the ignorance of some of the characters; to appreciate the ironic humor which permeates their activities; and to feel the tragedy of their end.

Conclusion

The book of Judges invites its readers to learn the lessons of the carefully contrived "past" that has been laid before them. The most significant lessons appear to be how Israel is best led, how Israel can live successfully in the land, and how Israel may easily lose her distinct identity.

To this end, the judges that are exhibited for the reader appear to be vehicles for a writer's thoughts, serving as representative figures in order to facilitate a discussion of certain issues.

First, Judges shows that the leadership of the community rightly lies in the hands of Yahweh, who can use the most unlikely of characters to achieve his ends. The concept of human leadership which can of itself provide security and success is mocked and shown to be a false notion. Even when leaders do walk deliberately in their own ways, seemingly ignorant or contemptuous of the ways of Yahweh, he can move events to suit his own purpose. If there is an appropriate mode of government, then it is one that bows to Yahweh's supreme lordship, recognizing that any human leadership is but an extension of his arm.

Secondly, the text exhibits a concern for Israel's relation to foreigners. This is most evident in the representative ethnic names utilized in the text. In 3:5 the writer includes a standard list which includes Canaanites, Hittites, Amorites, Perizzites, Hivites, and Jebusites — all terms which clearly define nations who are "other" to Israel. J. Van Seters affirms the ideological purpose that lies behind usage of such ancient names; these are people who represent "the primeval wicked nations whom God displaced in order to give Israel its land" (1972: 78). On one level, the ancient names were necessary because of the retrospective viewpoint of the construct — archaic terminology was required for nations who might have lived in the land before Israel arrived. But on another level, castigating contemporary peoples with these labels also serves to present them clearly and strongly as "other" — the primordial archetypes of the non-Israelite.

Social theory indicates that when groups are in tension with each other, then the closer the relationship, the more vehement the polemic. It is possible that the writer includes this standard list of nations to describe surrounding peoples, not because they derive from any ancient source, or layer of tradition, but because it serves ideologically to separate Israel clearly from surrounding peoples, who may actually have been much more closely related to the author and his community. Employing these conventional ethnic terms helps the writer create an "us and them" mentality, distancing his community from the actual surrounding peoples.

In the ensuing narratives of Judges, told on a smaller and more localized scale, the enemies met are not drawn from this standard list, but are the Moabites, Midianites, Ammonites, and Philistines — enemies scaled down from the mighty primordial ethnic units to more localized hostile powers who the writer probably believed would "fit" into the world of his construct. They serve as "boundary peoples" who highlight the distinctive place of Israel in the land and provide the means of chastising Israel for apostasy. Their representative value is made evident from the outset in the sample story of Othniel, who rises against the symbolic foreign power "Superblack Double Villain." In a story world which tells of the steady Canaanization of Israel, we have a pedagogy which affirms the ideal Israel as an alternative community that should maintain its purity in a sea of hostile and infiltrating forces. A text such as this serves to reinforce group identity. Holding out such a world to his readers, with its strongly defined ethnic labels, helps to maintain and perhaps intensify the boundaries between the community he presents as Israel and all other groups.

Thirdly, any physical coexistence which threatens social assimilation to the other's way of life has religious ramifications. The major problem ensuing from living among the Canaanites is the threat this poses to Yahwism. The two aspects — social and religious assimilation — go hand in hand. In turning to the Baals and Ashteroth, the Israelites turn also to the characteristics and values that are satirized and implicitly deplored as belonging to "the other." By the closing chapters the reversal is complete, as an idolatrous cult site is set up within Israel replete with forbidden images and a mercenary priest, at a site whose conquest has been satirically portrayed as a parody of the conquest narratives.

Within these three interests there is one overriding concern — the issue of identity. It is seen in the question of leadership which shuns the monarchical rule of the "other" and seeks to define for Israel something distinctly Yahwistic. It is seen in the anti-assimilation stance which seeks to uphold Israel as a pure enclave in the midst of heathen peoples. And it is seen in the concern for a pure cult since the identity of Israel should lie in their awareness of their Deity's scheme of things.

As part of this concern with identity is a call for unity. A major aspect of the degeneration that takes place in Judges is the disintegration of Israelite communal life. At each step along the way we can detect disunity seeping in. It is seen in the Deborah poem when certain tribes are chastised for not entering into the coalition (5:15-17). It resurfaces in the Gideon story as the Ephraimites upbraid him for not calling them out sooner (8:1-3). It is also present when Gideon punishes the men of Penuel and Succoth (8:13-17). It becomes even more apparent in the story of Abimelech, who commits fratricide and sets city against city (9:5, 22-49). In the case of Jephthah, we read that he has already experienced life as an outcast (11:1). The nadir of disunity comes in the closing chapters with the civil war undertaken against one of Israel's own tribes — an action which ironically brings Israel back to a discredited unity. The ground won by the Joshua generation is thus slowly eroded by a generation who can achieve unity only at a tremendous cost to their own distinct heritage. By overtly exhibiting the chaotic mayhem that proceeds from lack of Israelite unity, the writer encourages his audience to find common bonds and inculcates a "united we stand, divided we fall" mentality. In the unity of a common front, there is strength and identity.

With that call for unity comes an appeal for ethnic and marital purity. This is seen in the polemic against foreign women and the clearly drawn lines between Israel and its neighbors, who are depicted in archetypal terms as eternal enemies. The prologue outlines the reasons for Israel's subsequent failures in terms of its loss of purity — they have not rooted foreigners from among them, but have intermarried with them and taken their gods as their own (3:5-6). With the purity of the Israelite heritage lost, the Israelites fall into a syncretized existence and become increasingly "Canaanized" as the book proceeds.

Whom, then, does this book address? Who is the "Israel" that the writer has in mind, where are they located, and in what age? These very interesting questions have no tried and tested answer. The idea that Judges, as part of the Deuteronomistic history as a whole, was written in order to explain or interpret the defeat by Babylon and subsequent exile is common and has appeared plausible. Indeed, dating the Deuteronomistic history any later than the mid-sixth-century BC is deemed problematic since 2 Kings closes without any apparent cognizance of the Cyrus edict or mention of a return to Palestine by some of the exiles. This leads D. N. Freedman to argue that the date cannot be later than c. 550 BC. He speaks of this history as a legacy whereby "the serious student could read sobering lessons for himself and his people" (1962: 713).

But it has to be questioned why those who had suffered the apparent humiliation of defeat and deportation would wish to write in a context of deportation, loss of land, and identity. What is the point of recounting a story of God's covenantal promise once it had ended? As P. R. Davies (1992: 42) has pointed out, deportation was a policy intended to *break* national links, not to form them anew. One would imagine that the immediate decades following the 587 defeat would have been marked by grief, bitterness, and confusion — hardly a spirit that would set about the construction of a national history.

But it is not only a question of whether the exiles would have possessed the motivation to write, but also of the *utilities* available to create such a history? Where would they be based to undertake writing on this scale, with what financial support, and with what material? As Davies (1992: 80) claims, the picture of chained prisoners trudging across miles of country with scrolls and writing materials beneath the arm is a little fanciful. Such factors necessarily lead to a consideration of the possibility that Judges (as part of a wider history) was written in a later, more prosperous age, in which a rebuilt temple complex and supported scribal class would provide the facilities for writing of this caliber. The Persian period was a time of repatriation, a period which witnessed the restoration of the temple and possibly the codification of new constitutional laws. From among these constitution makers perhaps we find appropriate motivation, agenda, and context for the concerns detected in Judges.

Writing of this kind also requires readers. To whom would the pedagogy of Judges be pertinent? A group of despairing exiles, having lost their homeland and all sense of hope, is hardly an appropriate audience to receive this teaching. In the more hopeful context of the post–sixth century, possibly a later Persian period, the pedagogy would be relevant and useful. In the indigenous people of the Yehud province perhaps we find the biblical "Canaanites" with whom the Israelites (the returning "sons of the exile") must not mingle. Here perhaps is an audience to whom the pedagogy would not only be relevant but imperative if a new constitution was to be realized. In this context, the concerns for identity, unity, and purity make good sense. David Janzen (2002) indicates how the expulsion of foreign women can be seen as a scapegoating measure at a time when the social order was perceived to be in danger of crumbling. The question of appropriate leadership in the newly emergent community, the anti-assimilation stance that separates this community from the "other," thereby instilling their own distinct identity, and the emphasis on national Yahwism, all find a pertinent audience in this later age.

As it now stands, the book of Judges occupies its position within a wider story, the net effect of which creates a "period of the judges" within a constructed history of Israel. It carries the story of an early Israel from its conquest and entry into the land to the time of the monarchy. But the narratives of Judges, while presenting themselves as "history," have a kind of parabolic function, or, as I have suggested above, a representative value. The characters and their activities act in some cases as foreshadowers of things to come, but simultaneously they act as vehicles for the writer's ideology and concerns for his day. The story is told so that such things may never happen "again." By portraying an Israel hopelessly losing its way, and simultaneously its own distinct identity, the present generation is shown how *not* to progress. The rather desperate story line is offset by the humorous touches and enjoyable aesthetic qualities. However, these entertaining features of the text never detract totally from the weighty didactic element, as messages are pushed home time and time again.

Bibliography. Ahlström, G. W. 1993, *The History of Ancient Palestine from the Palaeolithic Period to Alexander's Conquest,* Sheffield: Sheffield Academic • Alter, R. 1981, *The Art of Biblical Narrative,* New York: Basic • Alter, R. 1992, *The World of Biblical Literature,* London: SPCK • Amit, Y. 1987, "Judges 4: Its Content and Form," *JSOT* 39:89-111 • Boling, R. G. 1975, *Judges: Introduction, Translation, and Commentary,* New York: Doubleday • Brenner, A. 1990, "A Triangle and a Rhombus in Narrative Structure: A Proposed Integrative Reading of Judges iv and v," *VT* 40:129-38 • Brettler, M. Z. 1989, "The Book of Judges: Literature as Politics," *JBL* 108:395-418 • Brettler, M. Z. 1995, *The Creation of History in Ancient Israel,* London: Routledge • Davies, P. R. 1992, *In Search of 'Ancient Israel',* Sheffield: Sheffield Academic • Exum, J. C. 1990, "The Centre Cannot Hold: Thematic and Textual Instabilities in Judges," *CBQ* 52:410-31 • Exum, J. C. 1992, *Tragedy in Biblical Narrative: Arrows of the Almighty,* Cambridge: Cambridge University • Exum, J. C. 1993, *Fragmented Women: Feminist (Sub)versions of Biblical Narratives,* Sheffield: Sheffield Academic • Exum, J. C. 1996, *Plotted, Shot, and Painted Cultural Representations of Biblical Women,* Sheffield: Sheffield Academic • Freedman, D. N. 1962, "Pentateuch," in G. A. Buttrick, ed., *The Interpreter's Dictionary of the Bible,* New York: Abingdon, 3:712-26 • Gooding, D. W. 1982, "The Composition of the Book of Judges," *ErIsr* 16:70-79 • Hamlin, E. J. 1990, *At Risk in the Promised Land: A Commentary on the Book of Judges,* Grand Rapids: Eerdmans • Janzen, D. 2002, *Witch-Hunts, Purity and Social Boundaries: The Expulsion of the Foreign Women in Ezra 9–10,* Sheffield: Sheffield Academic • Jobling, D. 1986, *The Sense of Biblical Narrative: Structural Analyses in the Hebrew Bible,* 2, Sheffield: Sheffield Academic • Klein, L. R. 1988, *The Triumph of Irony in the Book of Judges,* Sheffield: Almond • Klein, L. R. 1993, "The Book of Judges: Paradigm and Deviation in Images of Women," in A. Brenner, ed., *The Feminist Companion to Judges,* Sheffield: Sheffield Academic, 55-71 • Mayes, A. D. H. 1985, *Judges,* Sheffield: Sheffield Academic • Moore, G. F. 1895, *A Critical and Exegetical Commentary on Judges,* Edinburgh: T&T Clark • Mullen, E. T. 1982, "'The "Minor Judges': Some Literary and Historical Considerations," *CBQ* 44:185-201 • Niditch, S. 1989, "Eroticism and Death in the Tale of Jael," pp. 109-24 in P. L. Day, *Gender and Difference in Ancient Israel,* Minneapolis: Fortress • O'Connell, R. H.1996, *The Rhetoric of the Book of Judges,* Leiden: Brill • Polzin, R. M. 1980, *Moses and the Deuteronomist: A Literary Study of the Deuteronomic History,* New York: Seabury • Polzin, R. M. 1989, *Samuel and the Deuteronomist: A Literary Study of the Deuteronomic History,* New York: Seabury • Radday, Y. T., and A. Brenner. 1990, *On Humour and the Comic in the Hebrew Bible,* Sheffield: Almond • Richter, W. 1964, *Die Bearbeitungen des 'Retterbuches' in der deuteronomischen Epoche,* BBB 21, Bonn: Peter Hanstein • Sternberg, M. 1985, *The Poetics of Biblical Narrative,* Bloomington: Indiana University • Trible, P. 1984, *Texts of Terror: Literary-Feminist Readings of Biblical Narrative,* Philadelphia: Fortress • Van Seters, J. 1972, "The Terms 'Amorite' and 'Hittite' in the Old Testament," *VT* 22:64-82 • Webb, B. G. 1987, *The Book of Judges: An Integrated Reading,* Sheffield: Sheffield Academic • Wellhausen, J. 1885, *Prolegomena to the History of Israel,* Edinburgh: Adam & Charles Black.

Ruth

Gerald West

INTRODUCTION

Ruth is a remarkable book, offering a range of different interpretations. Some readers insist that the meaning and significance of the book of Ruth depend on correctly determining its date of composition. The traditional Jewish view, as recorded in the Babylonian Talmud (*B. Bat.* 14b-15a), states that Ruth was written by the prophet Samuel. That Samuel wrote Ruth is rather unlikely, however, given the internal evidence of the Bible itself, which is that Samuel died sometime before David, who is referred to in the genealogies in 4:17, 18-22 (Larkin 1996: 18).

Scholarly opinion on the dating of Ruth ranges from the reign of David to the mid-second century BC, with most scholars falling into two broad groups: those who date the book before the exile, and those who date the book after the exile. The internal evidence (including subject matter and language) and the external evidence (including sociohistorical, literary, and theological context) are not conclusive, and so scholars reach different conclusions from the same evidence (Larkin 1996: 18-19). Some scholars posit both an early and a later authorship by suggesting that it is quite possible that an early oral version of the story was later edited and elaborated in written form (Laffey 1989: 554).

Those who date the book of Ruth before the exile, in the time of the monarchy, tend to argue that the primary purpose of the book is to establish David's lineage and commend the Davidic dynasty. Read within this historical and ideological context the book of Ruth deals with David's known Moabite ancestry by Judaizing his Moabite great-grandmother. In so doing it "encourages popular acceptance of the Davidic dynasty by appealing to the continuity of Yahweh's guidance in the lives of Israel's ancestors and in particular of David's own ancestors" (Larkin 1996: 54). Such a purpose would also explain the prominence given in the book to the practice of levirate marriage, which made possible the perpetuation of a patriarchal line in those families where the husband died before his wife had conceived any offspring (Laffey 1989: 554). A secondary, but related, concern of the book of Ruth in this sociohistorical context could be the consolidation and legitimation of the Davidic dynasty; the book of Ruth demonstrates the ease with which neighboring peoples are incorporated into the political kingdom of Israel. And, significantly, when the birth of Ruth's son is celebrated (4:14), the women ask that his name may be renowned in Israel as well as in Judah (Larkin 1996: 54 and Hubbard 1988: 39-46).

Those who date the book of Ruth after the exile, and this is the majority view in recent times, tend to see the story as standing in the same trajectory as Deutero-Isaiah and Jonah and its purpose as countering the theological positions of Ezra and Nehemiah, which prohibited mixed marriages (and even enforced divorce within existing mixed marriages). The ease with which Ruth embraces Yahweh as her God and Israel as her people and the absence of any resentment toward her provide a very positive picture of the potential of inter-ethnic relationships. Some scholars emphasize the subversive nature of the story — "a brilliant polemical performance under the guise of an antique and innocuous tale" — in the context of postexilic politics where the Jerusalem hierocrats were attempting to cling to power on the basis of an ideology of chosenness (LaCocque 1990: 84-85). Others focus more on the theological dimensions of the story in the postexilic context in which the story serves to strengthen the theological position that other ethnic groups, provided they were faithful to Yahweh, were acceptable to Yahweh and so ought to be acceptable to the Jews; for, after all, a Moabite woman was the great-grandmother of David (Laffey 1989: 551).

Questions of date have not been the only concerns, however, of biblical scholarship. Literary studies have drawn attention to the narrative itself, focusing on questions of structure, setting, plot, characterization, rhetorical effect, and theme (Berlin 1983, Sasson 1989, and Fewell and Gunn 1990). Such close readings of the text show that Ruth is a carefully wrought literary work with a range of possible meanings.

Feminist and other liberationist perspectives have also made an important contribution to reading Ruth. Studies such as these have brought the experiences and questions of marginalized communities into dialogue with the book of Ruth, and in so doing have recovered neglected aspects of the story (Trible 1978, Weems 1988, Brenner 1993, and Exum 1996).

There seems to have been no difficulty over the acceptance of Ruth into the canon, though there is some disagreement about its appropriate location in the canon. In the Hebrew Bible (HB) Ruth is placed in the Writings, whereas in the Septuagint (LXX) it is placed in the Prophets. It is not clear which of these locations should be regarded as the original, though the most likely scenario is that Ruth belonged originally to the Writings, where it is the first book, but that it was later placed between Judges and Samuel, probably because it begins with a reference to the period of the judges (1:1) and ends with a reference to David (4:17, 22), and so this location appeared to be logical (Larkin 1996: 33-34).

The book of Ruth may be divided into four episodes

or acts, each corresponding to a chapter, with the following subdivisions (Larkin 1996: 42):

Act 1
Setting the Scene (1:1-5)
Naomi Returns Home (1:6-18)
Arrival of Naomi and Ruth in Bethlehem (1:19-22)

Act 2
Ruth in the Field of Boaz (2:1-17)
Ruth Reports to Naomi (2:18-23)

Act 3
Naomi's Plan (3:1-5)
Ruth at the Threshing Floor of Boaz (3:6-15)
Ruth Reports to Naomi (3:16-18)

Act 4
Boaz with the Men at the Gate (4:1-12)
A Son Is Born to Naomi (4:13-17)
Genealogical Appendix (4:18-22)

COMMENTARY

Act 1

Setting the Scene (1:1-5)

The opening sentence of the book of Ruth sets the scene for the story that is to unfold. Although the first sentence has a historical feel about it, referring to a particular time ("when the judges ruled"), a particular event ("a famine in the land"), particular places ("Bethlehem in Judah" and "Moab"), and particular people ("a certain man . . . and his wife and two sons"), it is more narrative than historical. The initial sentence provides the reader with important details of the narrative setting, and determines to a significant extent how we interpret the story that follows.

The story is set in the time of the judges. While it is difficult to determine the force this setting would have had for its original readers or hearers, setting the story in this period foregrounds the family rather than the nation. This is primarily a story about an ordinary family: a man and his wife and two sons. The first sentence also provides the impetus for the action of the story, which is a famine in the land. An ordinary family must migrate if they are to find food in a time of famine. Clearly, the struggle for survival is at the center of the story. Finally, the struggle for survival knows no boundaries; the family moves from Bethlehem (ironically, "house of bread") in Judah to the neighboring country of Moab. An ordinary family must find food where it can, irrespective of ethnic and national boundaries.

The specific reference to Moab raises a number of questions, mainly because of the negative connotations associated with Moab in other Israelite literature. Moab is associated with hostility (Numbers 22–24; Judg 3:12-30), sexual perversity (Gen 19:30-38), and idolatry (Num 25:1-5), and Deut 23:3-6 explicitly excludes Moabites (and Ammonites) from "the assembly of the LORD." That Moab and Moabites are never a problem in Ruth may indicate that Ruth reflects an early period of Israel's history when the Moabites were merely Israel's neighbors; the negative attitude toward the Moabites in the texts cited above thus represents a later period when there were problems with the Moabites, and such attitudes have been legitimized by linking them with Israel's past and their entrance to the land (Laffey 1989: 555). Alternatively, the portrayal of mutual acceptance between Moabites and Israelites in Ruth may indicate a tradition in Israelite literature that rejects the kind of ethnic slander found in the texts cited above and many others (Ezra 9:1; Neh 13:1; Zeph 2:9). From this latter perspective Ruth may be seen either as a form of political parable addressing national questions in postexilic politics (LaCocque 1990: 84-116) or as a more localized tale of the strategies marginalized communities use in order to survive socio-economically.

In 1:2 the names given to the characters introduced in v. 1 are significant and are a further indication that we are most likely dealing with fiction rather than history. The husband and father is named Elimelech ("my God is king"), the wife and mother is named Naomi ("pleasing"), and their two sons are named Mahlon (perhaps meaning "sickness") and Kilion (perhaps meaning "wasting"). The names have a narrative function. Elimelech's name foreshadows Ruth's future commitment to Yahweh (1:16), and Naomi's name contrasts with the name she later gives herself in her despair (1:20). The names of the two sons are probably symbolic, providing a strong sense of foreboding in the introductory scene. It is also possible that the name Elimelech echoes and alludes to texts like 1 Sam 8:7 where the people reject Yahweh as king and Zeph 3:15 where Yahweh is again proclaimed king of Israel (Laffey 1989: 555).

By the end of the introductory scene only three widows remain; all the male characters have died. What looked like a story about "a certain man" and his family has now become a story about women. The focus has gradually shifted from Elimelech to Naomi. In 1:1-2 all the characters are described in relation to Elimelech; in 1:3-5 all the characters are described in relation to Naomi.

Naomi Returns Home (1:6-18)

Naomi now becomes the main actor, initiating and controlling the action for the remainder of the story. Once again the impetus for the action is the search for food (1:6). However, it appears that as Naomi sets out *to return* to her country with her daughters-in-law she reconsiders, realizing perhaps that this may not be the most strategic survival option for her daughters-in-law (1:8). So she tells them each *to return* to "your mother's house" (1:8). There is a play on the word "return" throughout this and the next scene, with the same Hebrew word being variously translated as "to return," "to go back," "to turn back," and "to bring back." Naomi's reference to their home as "your mother's house" is unusual, as the usual practice in the OT is for a house to be designated as one's father's. Such a reference, however, emphasizes the absence of men and the interconnectedness of women's lives in matters of survival.

Naomi utters the first of many blessings in the book of Ruth when she blesses her daughters-in-law (1:9; see

2:4, 12, 20; 3:10; 4:11-12, 14). Naomi knows their vulnerability as widowed women, and so her blessing is that Yahweh may grant them security (1:9). When Orpah and Ruth insist on returning with her, Naomi explains to them in blunt terms that their best chance of survival is to find a husband, and that since she cannot provide them with husbands (as she had previously), they must turn back (1:11-13). The narrator makes no judgment as he/she tells us that Orpah decides to follow Naomi's advice and to seek a husband (and her security — 1:9) among her own people (1:14). Orpah adopts a sensible strategy in order to survive (Weems 1988: 27). When Ruth refuses to accept this obvious option, Naomi pushes her further, reminding her that in following her she not only gives up having a husband but also her people and her gods (1:15). Ruth's impassioned response silences Naomi (1:16-18). Ruth's choice is to find her security (1:9) with another woman, and in so doing she is willing to take on another people and another god. The women make different choices in order to survive; the narrative now follows the woman who has taken the route with the most risk.

Arrival of Naomi and Ruth in Bethlehem (1:19-22)

The people in Bethlehem are perhaps surprised that Naomi has survived, given that she returns without the male members of the family (1:19). Naomi's response echoes her earlier despair (1:13); in taking the males of her family God has made survival difficult; her fullness has become emptiness, and God is responsible (1:20-21). But bitterness, Naomi's new name, does not have the last word in this act. Future possibilities for survival are foreshadowed by the reminder of the narrator that Naomi is not alone but has Ruth with her, and that they have returned when the barley harvest is beginning (1:22).

That there is no apparent reason in terms of the plot as to why Ruth is described here (1:22) as "the Moabite" "from the country of Moab" has lent support to those who claim that the story is dealing with ethnic issues (LaCocque 1990: 85).

Act 2

Ruth in the Field of Boaz (2:1-17)

Just as the end of Act 1 foreshadowed possibilities for future survival, so the beginning of Act 2 offers another possibility for survival: Naomi has a male relative who is prominent and rich (2:1). But it is not Naomi who acts. Naomi is "empty." So Ruth acts, having consulted first with Naomi and being unaware, it seems (2:3b), of what the narrator has told the reader concerning Boaz.

In asking to whom Ruth belongs (2:5) Boaz demonstrates the prevailing patriarchal perspective. In the cautious reply of the servant Boaz learns that Ruth does not belong to a man, but that she "came back with Naomi" (2:6). The reader learns that not only does Ruth not belong to a man, but she does not belong to Naomi either; in this story women do not belong to each other but they are "with" each other.

Ruth acts within the provisions Israelite law makes for the poor and vulnerable (Lev 19:9-10), but she is fortunate to encounter the spirit of that law in the generous response of Boaz (2:8-17). The exaggerated expression of thanks and servile behavior of Ruth in encountering Boaz (2:10) are typical of the strategies the poor and marginalized use in order to survive (Scott 1990). The foreignness of Ruth is never a factor, although it is overtly acknowledged (2:10-12); rather, her own generosity (*ḥesed*) and care for her mother-in-law are brought to the fore.

Ruth Reports to Naomi (2:18-23)

Ruth's will to survive and the news of God's (and Boaz's) kindness revive and energize Naomi, who takes control of the action once again. It seems strange that Naomi had not remembered her rich relative Boaz before this (2:20), but perhaps this is a sign of the depths of her despair.

As Ruth and Naomi talk together (2:19-22) the focus remains on their immediate prospects of finding food, though there are also hints of longer-term prospects in Naomi's reference to Boaz as "one of our nearest kin" (*go'el*) (2:20), one who had the right to redeem all the possessions of Elimelech, including land and women (Lev 25:25-55).

But even as Ruth and Naomi contemplate a measure of security, like Boaz (2:8), Naomi is acutely aware of the dangers facing a woman working in a field. Fortunately, by working with Boaz's young women Ruth minimizes the risk of being "bothered" (2:22).

By the end of Act 2 Ruth has begun to occupy the place in Naomi's heart once filled by a husband and sons. Together they have found healing and empowerment, each one reaching out to the other as she is able. They are mother-in-law and daughter-in-law, a relationship often fraught with tension and manipulation, but they have become friends (Weems 1988: 31).

Act 3

Naomi's Plan (3:1-5)

With the barley harvest ending (2:23), Naomi initiates a strategy to ensure their future survival — to provide them, particularly Ruth, with "security" (3:1). The plan is overtly sexual. Ruth is instructed to go to the threshing floor (a place associated with extramarital sexual activity; see Hos 9:1), to wait until Boaz has finished eating and drinking (alluding perhaps to the incestuous sex between the drunken Lot and his daughters in Gen 19:30-38), and to lie at his uncovered "feet" (a euphemism for genitals). Is this typical male typecasting of what women do (Levine 1992: 82), or is it a realistic strategy of poor women attempting to survive in a patriarchal world?

Ruth at the Threshing Floor of Boaz (3:6-15)

Naomi imagines that Boaz will take control of the situation once it is initiated by Ruth, but she is wrong; Ruth maintains the momentum throughout, even going as far as to inform Boaz that he is "next-of-kin" (*go'el*) (3:9). Technically, by serving as *go'el* Boaz will be protecting the future of Naomi and her property, yet Naomi is not mentioned in the exchanges between Ruth and Boaz. Instead,

Boaz speaks of his willingness to act "as next-of-kin for you" (3:13). But there is a complication, for another male is more closely related to Naomi than Boaz and his right to redeem must be waived before Boaz can act as *go'el* (3:12-13).

The complication is not insignificant in that Ruth clearly feels safe with Boaz. In this encounter with him she abandons the servile demeanor that characterized their first meeting. Boaz no longer asks "whose" she is (2:5), but rather "who" she is (3:9). He treats her as a person, not as property, and so there are prospects of ruptures in the patriarchal system in their relationship. They recognize and draw out the *ḥesed* in each other (3:10). Another male may not be as caring.

Ruth Reports to Naomi (3:16-18)

The women wait to see what the men will do in response to their action. Boaz's concern that Ruth not return to her mother-in-law "empty-handed" offers a sign of hope for the future — Naomi's emptiness (1:21) may yet be filled.

Act 4

Boaz with the Men at the Gate (4:1-12)

As the women wait, the men, in typical patriarchal fashion, ignore them and concentrate on the dead man Elimelech's land (4:3-4). The next-of-kin agrees to redeem the land until he realizes that Ruth is also a part of Elimelech's property and that he would therefore be responsible for providing an heir, through Ruth, to whom the land would ultimately belong (Laffey 1989: 557; LaCocque 1990: 96-98). The next-of-kin therefore relinquishes his right, and Boaz, as next-in-line, takes it up (4:6).

The narrator then explains a practice that the readers/hearers would not recognize since it comes from an earlier time (4:7). As the text indicates, the gesture of removing a sandal is more than merely the sealing of a contract; it is a ritual apparently associated with many aspects of next-of-kin redemption (Deuteronomy 25; LaCocque 1990: 103).

The people (probably mainly men) and the elders at the gate recognize Boaz's "acquisition" (male language) of Elimelech's property, including Ruth (4:9-10). They pronounce a blessing on Ruth and Boaz, making explicit reference to Rachel and Leah and to Tamar. The reference in each case is, ostensibly, to Ruth's fertility. However, there are other connections between Ruth's story and the stories of Rachel and Leah (Gen 29:21-30) and of Tamar (Genesis 38), and so there may be allusions to other aspects of these stories as well (Levine 1992: 82-84; La Cocque 1992: 105-7).

A Son Is Born to Naomi (4:13-17)

The story concludes by returning to the women. Boaz (and the other men) recedes into the background. In a patriarchal world they are necessary for survival, but they are not the focus of this story. The focus is on women, particularly Naomi. She who was empty (1:21) because she had no husband or sons has had her life "restored," not through men, but through her daughter-in-law who loves her and who is more to her than seven sons (4:15). Just as Naomi and Ruth shared the struggle for survival, so now they share the fruits of their security, of which *their* son is a sign (4:16-17).

Although Ruth is honored and praised (4:15), she remains on the periphery in the final scene. The narrator announces the birth of her son, her mother-in-law nurses him, and the women of the neighborhood name him and proclaim him Naomi's son. Is this an indication that in the end Ruth's Moabite identity is problematic (Levine 1992: 84)? Or does the story end appropriately with Naomi taking central stage, celebrating the survival and fullness of one of society's most vulnerable?

Genealogical Appendix (4:18-22)

Most scholars believe these verses to be a postexilic priestly addition (Campbell 1975). Although the genealogies add nothing to the plot and actually detract from the story, they are carefully crafted and function to link Ruth to the narrative that runs from Genesis to Kings. They are repeated in Matt 1:3-6 and are also found in 1 Chr 2:10-17 (LaCocque 1990: 112-13).

Conclusion

Ruth and Naomi are determined to survive in a world where the search for food and security is the fundamental reality. Resistance for poor women can be construed only within the framework of survival. To survive is, in fact, the ultimate act of resistance for poor women. In a patriarchal world survival is possible only by engaging, strategically, with men; but while men are necessary, and while a few men like Boaz are caring and kind, what really enables women to survive is the solidarity and strength they find in God and in each other.

Bibliography. Berlin, A. 1983, "Poetics in the Book of Ruth," in *Poetics and the Interpretation of Biblical Narrative,* Sheffield: Almond • Berquist, Jon L. 1993, "Role Dedifferentiation in the Book of Ruth," *JSOT* 57:23-37 • Brenner, A. 1993, *A Feminist Companion to Ruth,* Sheffield: Sheffield Academic • Campbell, E. F. 1975, *Ruth,* AB, Garden City, N.Y.: Doubleday • Exum, C. 1996, *Plotted, Shot, and Painted: Cultural Representations of Biblical Women,* Sheffield: Sheffield Academic • Fewell, D. N., and D. M. Gunn. 1990, *Compromising Redemption: Relating Characters in the Book of Ruth,* Louisville: Westminster/John Knox • Hubbard, R. L. 1988, *The Book of Ruth,* Grand Rapids: Eerdmans • LaCocque, A. 1990, *The Feminine Unconventional: Four Subversive Figures in Israel's Tradition,* Minneapolis: Fortress • Laffey, A. L. 1989, "Ruth," in R. E. Brown, J. A. Fitzmyer, and R. E. Murphy, eds., *The New Jerome Biblical Commentary,* London: Chapman, 553-57 • Larkin, K. J. A. 1996, *Ruth and Esther,* Sheffield: Sheffield Academic • Levine, A.-J. 1992, "Ruth," in C. A. Newsom and S. H. Ringe, eds., *The Women's Bible Commentary,* London: SPCK and Louisville: Westminster/John Knox, 78-84 • Nadar, Sarojini. 2002, "A South African Indian Womanist Reading of the Character of Ruth," in M. Dube, ed., *Other Ways of Reading: African Women* *and the Bible,* Atlanta: Society of Biblical Literature and Geneva: WCC Publications, 159-75 • Sasson, J. M. 1989, *Ruth: A New Translation with a Philological Commentary and Formalist-Folklorist Interpretation,* Sheffield: JSOT • Scott, J. 1990, *Domination and the Arts of Resistance: Hidden Transcripts,* New Haven and London: Yale University • Trible, P. 1978, "A Human Comedy," in *God and the Rhetoric of Sexuality,* Philadelphia: Fortress, 166-99 • Weems, R. J. 1988, *Just a Sister Away: A Womanist Vision of Women's Relationships in the Bible,* San Diego: Luramedia.

1 and 2 Samuel

Graeme Auld

INTRODUCTION

There are two common types of strategy for reading the books of Samuel. They are related to each other, but they must also be distinguished. Literary approaches focus on the text. Since the text is an ancient text, we will need some historical background to help us set it in its time and read it better. However, our main concern is how best to respond to the text's invitation to enter its own world as created by its author or authors. Historical approaches do require literary awareness but have different interests. They may use the book as evidence for the period in which it was written or completed. If major sources or separable elements can be detected, these may be studied for traces of that earlier time in which they were written. And, of course, they may use the book as evidence for the still earlier period on which it reports. If I come on a twentieth-century textbook which claims to offer a representative selection of eighteenth-century studies of the fifteenth century, I will be interested not only in the twentieth-century choice made and commentary offered but also in the eighteenth-century views of the fifteenth century and what may or may not be learned about the fifteenth century itself.

In the Hebrew Bible (HB), as in most English Bibles, these books are called the two books of Samuel. However, in the Septuagint (LXX) and some other ancient traditions, they are but the first two of four books called Kingdoms; that is, Samuel and Kings are clearly recognized as a connected story. And it is the overlapping fates of the first two kings which dominate these first two books. Though in the Hebrew tradition they bear the name of Samuel, it is David's story which is the biggest — the biggest in Samuel or Kings — stretching from 1 Samuel 16 to 1 Kings 2. And Saul's story bulks almost as large and is further spread out: introduced in 1 Samuel 9, he dies in 1 Samuel 31; but his shadow and the shadow of his house remain over the story of David till 2 Samuel 21, or even 1 Kings 2. It is not these two kings, however, but rather Samuel who anointed them, who is remembered in the Hebrew title.

And that title is at home in the wider context of our books, for the HB calls Joshua, Judges, Samuel, and Kings the Former Prophets. Just as Elijah and Elisha, not Solomon and his successors, are the heroes of the books of Kings, so Samuel may be said to edge both Saul and David off center stage even in their own play. Prophecy is an important theme of the books of Samuel. Not only do Nathan and Gad play an important role after Samuel is gone, but a number of significant relationships are probed in scene after scene: of prophet and medium; of prophet and seer; of prophet and prophets; and of prophecy and kingship.

Another important theme of the book is Yahweh's "people." The meaning of "Israel" is flexible, now including and now excluding Judah. Sometimes, in fact, "the people" refers to David's own foreign guards and not to Israelites of any description. Tensions between north and south, which are more obvious from the rift between Jeroboam and Rehoboam after the death of Solomon (1 Kings 12 onward), are already anticipated both in the rivalry between northern Saul and southern David and in Absalom's appeal to the north in his rebellion against his father.

The reading of the books of Samuel that follows invites readers to keep track of all of these issues: literary and historical approaches, kingship and prophecy and the people of God — and all from a novel perspective. I have become persuaded that we can still reconstruct from the largely parallel biblical accounts of the monarchy in the biblical books of Samuel-Kings and of Chronicles the source that both share — simply by identifying as their major source the accounts that both tell.

This source, which I call "The Book of Two Houses" (the house of Yahweh and the house of David), began with the death of Saul and ended with the removal to Babylon of the last descendant of David who would rule in Jerusalem. Near its start was the story of David's arrival in Jerusalem and the transfer of the ark to that city soon afterward. And at its finish the fall of the city some four hundred years later, and the despoiling of its temple, were reported. It is this shared source material which we find much expanded but still recognizable in Samuel-Kings and in Chronicles. However, it begins only where 1 Samuel ends, with the death of Saul (ch. 31); the Book of Two Houses bulks larger in Kings than in Samuel.

Much of Samuel, on this account, was composed as a greatly enlarged introduction to the story of the houses of David and Yahweh, anticipating its main themes. That means in turn that, to read properly 1 Samuel especially, we already have to know how the later story develops, which tells of Israel's and Judah's kings and prophets.

1 Samuel

COMMENTARY

Hannah, Eli, and Samuel (1 Samuel 1–3)

There is no richer material in the book than in its opening chapters. They resonate with many other passages, in Samuel and elsewhere in the Bible. They anticipate key themes of Samuel, and of Kings as well. The story starts with Samuel's birth to long-barren Hannah. The aged priest Eli first misunderstands her, then blesses her after her prayer. Eli's scoundrel sons offer a sad contrast to his new attendant dedicated by his mother: Samuel grows up in Yahweh's presence; Hophni and Phinehas slight the Deity. The divine summons to Samuel is first misunderstood by Eli as well as the lad; but once Samuel hears, it is an oracle against Eli that he receives. The third chapter ends with a note on Samuel's maturity and Yahweh's support of him — especially relating to the efficacy of his word.

Yet that account of the story line gives little indication of its riches. Two principal strategies assist a more adequate reading. Many elements of the story are readily compared or contrasted with episodes elsewhere in Samuel or biblical narrative: if we read side by side the birth of the two nazirites Samson and Samuel, or the vows of Jephthah and of Hannah, this helps detect the specific flavor of each. Then there is much wordplay — and that has to be recovered from the Hebrew text.

If we are told about the special circumstances of a character's birth, as in ch. 1, we are led to expect that he will be prominent in the story as it develops. In the story of Eli and his sons (ch. 2), we are reminded before the royal story ever begins

- that a dynasty can lose divine favor, as will the house of Saul and every royal house in northern Israel; and what about the house of David?
- that a father can be blamed for the excesses of his sons, like David(?)
- that a servant in the house can become the new leader, like David; but also like Jeroboam and like Jehu.

In the story of the divine call to Samuel (ch. 3), we encounter a more dense concentration of significant words relating to prophecy than anywhere else in the Bible.

Ch. 1 Hannah's name is related to and evokes the common word *ḥen,* or "favor." Yet not only is she not favored with children of her own, but her rival wife Peninnah taunts her regularly with her lack of them, and especially at the time of feasting. Her husband loves her, and his name means "creator god"; yet even the marriage of "creator god" and "favor" does not result in children. Naomi's neighbors showed good sense and good taste in rating daughter-in-law Ruth better than seven sons (Ruth 4:15). Elkanah betrays his lack of both when he claims to be better than ten (1:8). Hannah must have thought that, like her, he too was ill named.

We have not yet been told that Eli is old (2:22) or not able to see well (3:2). However, when we first meet him (1:14) we find that he lacks insight, and he misinterprets Hannah's behavior after the feast from his official seat at the temple. Hannah is so desperate for success in having a son that she is prepared to vow a male child back to God. The word "nazirite" is not said, but it is suggested by the similar Hebrew word for "vow" and by the promise that no razor will be used on his head. The priest has added to the hurt, taking her distress and prayer for the drunken babbling of someone who has feasted too well. But strong drink would have been as inappropriate for her as for the wife of Manoah (Judg 13:7). The full import of her spirited retort is lost on us till the next mention of Eli's sons (2:12); they are "Sons of No Use," but she denies being a "Daughter of No Use." Eli now responds (1:17) as a priest should to a suppliant at his temple, with an assurance of a divine answer to her prayer. And Hannah responds — is it to Eli or to the god whose representative he is? — with the hope that her situation may at last reflect her name: "May your servant find *ḥen* in your eyes."

They go home after formal worship the next day. The common Hebrew euphemism for sexual union — "Elkanah *knew* Hannah his wife" — is all the more striking when we read it in 1:19 for two reasons. The one is the suggestion we have already noted in 1:5 and 8 that Elkanah's love for Hannah was deficient in understanding. And the other is that, while her husband "creator god" (Elkanah) "knows" Hannah, the deity Yahweh "remembers" her. Yet the child is not called Zechariah ("Yahweh remembers"), as we might have expected. Several natural expectations of an experienced Bible reader are disappointed when he is given the name "Samuel."

This name has left commentators over the ages puzzling even more because it does not fit straightforwardly the explanation Hannah offers. The problem is less that the second part of Samu-el is "El," or God, rather than the Yahweh of whom Hannah has asked him (1:20). More surprising is that "Saul," not "Samuel," is the meaning of the Hebrew for "asked." Samuel most naturally means "God is his name"; however, it has also been claimed to mean "he who is of God," or "heard of God," or even to be a contraction of "asked of God." But Hannah's clear hint at Saul's name will be no accident, even if it comes as a surprise. Just as the story of Eli and his family alerts us to the fate of royal dynasties which will come and go in the story to follow, so Hannah's account of Samuel's name reminds us that the fates of Samuel and Saul were desperately commingled, and that Saul, too, was asked for and desperately wanted by his people, who badgered their god for a king.

Hannah absents herself from the next annual pilgrimage and in fact stays at home with Samuel till he is weaned, perhaps aged two or three. Elkanah does make the journey as usual; but what is reported of his purpose is puzzlingly brief: "to sacrifice the regular sacrifice and his vow." These last words can be read as meaning that the annual sacrifice was the result of a vow by Elkanah; and yet we suppose that such a sacrifice was obligatory on all householders. Another interpretation assumes that two actions are meant although only one verb is used. "His vow," offered at Shiloh, may then be shorthand for his endorsement of his wife's vow; and this would be in line with Numbers 30, which makes a father or husband responsible for his daughter's or his wife's vows or pledges. When Hannah does come again to Shiloh, she approaches Eli deferentially, reminds him of their earlier meeting, and demonstrates the answer to her prayer. As Eli then had spoken for Yahweh, so now he takes custody of the lad left to minister to Yahweh (1:27-28; 2:11).

Ch. 2 We might have supposed that it was with her husband that Hannah came to bring Samuel to the shrine, but Elkanah is not specifically mentioned till "he" goes home (2:11). It is she who addresses Eli, and it is she who "prays to" Yahweh (2:1-10). The Song of Hannah is the first of four poems which play an important role within the two books of Samuel. The Song of Hannah, David's lament over Saul and Jonathan (2 Sam 1:19-27), and the last words of David (2 Sam 23:1-7) are of similar length. The Song of David (2 Sam 22:2-51), which is also Psalm 18, is a very much longer piece.

Hannah's words are introduced as her prayer, and yet Yahweh is mostly spoken of in the third person and is explicitly addressed only in 2:1-2. Indeed, it is others (whether human or divine, "you" is left unspecified) that are spoken to in v. 3. Yahweh's stability and support are prominent at the beginning and end of the song. At the center, a series of contrasts is the theme: these verses (4-8) appear to have most immediate relevance to the Hannah we read of in the opening chapter.

The lack of a close fit between the poem and its immediate literary context can be differently evaluated. At the local level, the first ten verses of this chapter might not be missed if they were not there. And talk at the end about a king and an anointed one ("messiah" in Hebrew) introduces a theme which will not be developed till several more chapters have elapsed. Yet Hannah's son will become chief "judge" of Israel and will anoint Israel's first two kings, and these two kings will be depicted in a whole series of contrasts. However, it is not till we read the Song of David, almost as close to the end of the books of Samuel as Hannah's song is to their opening, that we more fully appreciate the strategy of our storyteller: several of the themes introduced briefly here are more generously developed there. Looking more widely afield, Mary's song in Luke 1:46-55 (the Magnificat) resumes many of Hannah's themes.

Samuel ministering to Yahweh (2:11), Samuel the son of "Favor" who is no daughter of "No Use," immediately puts our storyteller in mind of two veritable "Sons of No Use" (v. 12). This fairly common Hebrew phrase for types we would call scoundrels or wastrels is doubly suitable for Hophni and Phinehas, for the letters that spell the Hebrew for "use" are the same three letters that spell Eli, but in a different order. The narrator is either hinting that they are no proper sons of Eli, or in fact that Eli himself is No Use. Again, and in immediate contrast to the young lad Samuel ministering before Yahweh, it was through their servant lads that they oppressed the people at sacrifice: demanding more than the due priestly share of the meat. So angry is our storyteller at the behavior of his characters that he begins to write with the exaggeration of those who must have complained at them: "Give the priest meat for him to roast. He will not take boiled meat from you, but raw."

After a further brief reminder of Samuel's acceptability before Yahweh and of Eli's blessing of Elkanah and Hannah (2:18-21), we are returned to Eli and his sons. Despite his great age, Eli heard of their behavior and remonstrated with them — yet, if the text is in order, his scolding was barely coherent: the stuttering Hebrew is hard to translate but may suggest enfeebled age or impotent rage or both. Yet, if so, we should note that he returns to neatly balanced speech in a pithy warning (v. 25a). What he says, however, seems oracular to the point of obscurity. Yet three comments should be made. (1) His warning may be specifically directed to these renegade priests. If one person sins against another, there can be a divine appeal — after all, part of the business of priests was to manage such appeals. But when it is against Yahweh himself that a priest sins, what then? (2) Even if this is the primary issue, the more general point is at least suggested as well: humans in dispute can appeal to (a) god; but if you fall foul of Yahweh, to whom do you turn? (3) This is the first mention of the theme of sin among humans and between humans and the Deity; it is repeated and varied throughout the books of Samuel, and it comes to a climax at the very end in the report of David's sin over counting his people.

These few verses (2:22-25) are capped by an even shorter note (v. 26) that Samuel was growing physically and in the respect of both Yahweh and humans. Chs. 1 to 3 end with much more extended developments of these two themes. First, an unnamed "man of God" comes to Eli and in Yahweh's name utters a comprehensive threat against him and his house (2:27-36). He is reminded that his tribe was chosen at the time of the exodus from Egypt as sacrificial priests and of the grant to them of the burnt offerings. He is also accused of honoring his sons more than Yahweh, and not stopping them from taking the best parts of the meat that were Yahweh's own due. The remnant of his family are to watch a new faithful and enduring priestly house take their place. Much of the significant language is drawn from the promises to David's house; and the story deftly anticipates two themes from 2 Samuel: the remnants of Saul's family watching the establishment of David, and the older priestly families giving way to Jerusalem's Zadokites. No response from Eli is reported, and nothing else is said.

Ch. 3 The story of young Samuel's call appears at first to show no knowledge of the visit of the man of God. The unusualness of visions or the receipt of Yahweh's word is emphasized (v. 1). Does this underscore the significance of what has just been said to Eli? Or does it help explain what is so important — and so unexpected — about Samuel's strange experience? It is a remarkably finely crafted chapter. Several rare words are set together, illuminating each other and reflecting flashes of light from more distant parts of the biblical collection. To change the image from jewelry to theater, the stage set is very carefully explored with much slower deliberation (vv. 1-3) than is common in biblical narrative, which is often more active and economical. Nothing happens till the LORD calls (v. 4).

Yet even when we pay close attention to the detail, we cannot be confident that we know what is being said, or how many things are being suggested. Young Samuel was attending to Yahweh "before Eli": Was he serving Yahweh in preference to Eli? better than Eli served? under Eli's supervising eye? Yahweh's word was "precious": because held in high esteem? or because virtually nonexistent? And does the unique verbal form, used to describe what vision was not, mean "diffused" or "broken through"? Was it not widespread, or had it not begun? And, whatever the answer to that last question, should we hear in this unique form an echo of the very similar and no less unique verb rendered "is let loose" in Prov 29:18, which is also immediately preceded by the identical Hebrew for "absence of vision"? Eli is in the right place (even if inactive?), but what first appears to describe the enfeeblement of age also suggests an inactive inner eye, the absence of second sight. The divine lamp not yet extinguished, and the haunting reminder that it could be, catches a reflection of the horror of David's champions at the other end of the book of Samuel that his death would extinguish the lamp of Israel (2 Sam 21:17). (And even if *nr* ["lamp"] is not just an alternative spelling of *nyr,* that latter word important in the divine promise relating to the house of David is also suggested.)

The divine call that begins the action (3:4) develops hints from the setting (1). "Called" *(wyqr')* is a word that sounds like "precious" *(yqr),* and it is addressed to Samuel, not to Eli. Yet it is Eli who first discerns what is going on (v. 8) — and we in turn are helped to discern the implicit recognition offered to Eli in this wording, when we remember the proverb that calls the man of discernment "precious in spirit" (Prov 17:27). We are told for the first time, when Samuel is sent back for the third time, that he, like Eli (3:2), is lying in his "place" (v. 9) — we learned earlier (v. 3) that he lay in Yahweh's shrine, where the divine ark was.

What follows is a quite remarkable statement for the Bible to make: Yahweh came and "took his stand," or position. It is a commonplace in the Bible for humans (or even divine beings, as in Job 1) to "take their stand" before Yahweh, but not the other way around. The nearest parallel is the case where Yahweh's agent takes his stand in the road to block Balaam's passage (Num 22:22). The uniqueness of the statement adds to the significance of the summons. Yet the third call itself is said to have been like the former ones. Was it from a closer position? Or was the closeness of the divine approach only fully declared this third time?

The magnitude of the threat is suggested by the reaction of those who will hear of it (3:11). The wording anticipates warnings against Davidic Jerusalem by Jeremiah (19:3) and "his servants the prophets" (2 Kgs 21:12). The hint at the later royal house is reinforced by talk of Eli's "house" (3:12). Vv. 12b and 13 revisit wording from v. 2. Eli's eyes had begun to "weaken." Yahweh's response to Eli's whole house will both begin and finish because the father did not "weaken" his sons. The idea already introduced (2:25) that guilt may be too great for a remedy in terms of sacrifice is restated in fresh terms (3:14). The triangle of relationships, whose essential ambiguity was caught in the opening words, is now further explored (vv. 15, 16). Yahweh would declare his verdict on Eli (v. 13). Samuel opens doors, but also fears to declare "what he had seen" (an alternative term for "vision" of v. 1). And the real Eli now calls Samuel, who answers as he always had to the supposed Eli. Only under threatened curse does Samuel report every last word of the divine message (vv. 17, 18).

To the repeated mention of Samuel's growth (3:19a — cf. 2:21, 26), the narrator adds that Yahweh let none of Samuel's words fall to the ground. That Yahweh was "with him" and that he was "established" as a prophet of Yahweh echo the presentation of David, as did the lamp. The poetic "last words of David" (2 Sam 23:1-7) include, "Yes, my house is established with God; he has made an everlasting covenant with me." Samuel's prophetic status is described in royal terms ("God with me" — remember also Isa 7:14). Samuel is to Eli as David will be to Saul. Dan to Beer-sheba defines the extent of Israel in the report of David's census (2 Samuel 24). And the massing in this chapter of almost all of the Bible's terms for prophecy in the widest sense of that term, along with the insistence in the final verse that revelation and vision continued through Samuel by the divine word, suggest that Samuel and prophecy are to be remembered as prior to David and kingship — not just in time but also in importance.

The Ark Lost and Returned (1 Samuel 4–6)

The first three chapters focused on Israel from within and on the [in]adequacy of her leadership. Attention now turns to that aspect of the external context which will be most apparent in the books of Samuel: conflict with Philistia — but, more importantly, where real power and autonomous action belong.

Ch. 4 In a first engagement, Israel is worsted. However, to see how the book of Samuel understands what it is reporting, it is vital in this case to translate the Hebrew literally: "Israel was beaten [perhaps better: smitten] before the Philistines" (v. 2). The narrator chooses a verb that can suggest a divinely inflicted blow or plague. Throughout the Bible Yahweh is almost always the subject of this verb in the active, and in the passive, too, he is the assumed agent. What happens happens in front of the other human party, but it is not done by them. The elders are less reticent, and name Yahweh (v. 3a). Their diagnosis cannot be faulted; and modern translators should not alter the text.

But the elders were less successful in their prescription for a cure (4:3b). The ark plays only an occasional role in the Bible's stories of Israel's early past. It appears mostly as one of the elements present at Israel's principal shrine. In Num 10:33-36, it is the principal symbol of Yahweh's presence with his people in the wilderness. In the stories of Joshua, it is prominent at the crossing of the Jordan and the taking of Jericho (3–4; 6). Israel's elders hope that its presence will mean Yahweh's presence with them and his support. So it is summoned from Shiloh with Eli's two sons and greeted with a massive shout.

"When they learned" (4:6) is an interpretation of the Hebrew "and they knew," which I prefer to translate literally. The Philistines were first confused by the din, and then came to understand what it was about. When they realized it was the ark that had arrived, they knew enough of Israel's early traditions to be afraid. But their version of their opponents' history was rather mixed up (v. 8): they said that a god had come, and they knew that this was unusual (v. 7), but they went on to worry about mighty gods (in the plural — they speak like wicked Jeroboam in 1 Kgs 12:28) who had caused much trouble for the Egyptians in the desert (an odd way of telling that story too!). The story pauses with the ark taken and Eli's sons dead (4:11). The Philistines presented themselves again for battle, the Israelites were "smitten" even more heavily (v. 10), the ark was taken, and its priests were killed (v. 11). And the heavy defeat is described with a term (v. 10) that the Philistines have just rightly cited in their bowdlerized version of the exodus (v. 8).

Eli was sitting fearful near the road. But presumably the messenger entered Shiloh by another way. It is Eli's ears that tell him that something is happening in town (4:14); and we are reminded that he is poor-sighted. Eli was the next after the Philistines to have to interpret din from a distance. The Benjaminite came to him from the town, but he was slow to come to the point in his report and had to be helped by the old man. There are four parts to the short report: Israel in flight, a great blow or smiting, the two priests dead, and the divine ark taken — and at the final climactic point Eli falls over and dies. "Taken" — this is a remarkably rare passive in the Hebrew Bible (half of its ten occurrences are in this chapter — 11, 17, 19, 21, and 22); and as with "smitten" the unspoken agent is the Deity. The same passive is used of Elijah being "taken" into heaven (2 Kgs 2:10). To get the true flavor of the story, we have to pay exact attention to what it says, and not adjust what it says to our understanding of what must really have happened. The Philistines neither defeat Israel nor capture the ark; Yahweh smites Israel and lets the ark be taken.

Phinehas's pregnant wife immediately went into labor, and died while giving birth. Being told she had a son was no help. But she was able to name him. That in itself, taken together with the fact that the name she gave is explained twice by the storyteller (in his own words and then quoting hers), throws unusually great emphasis on the name — literally "No Glory" or "Inglorious." Perhaps her shorter explanation with no mention of Eli or her husband corrects his: she, like Eli, was concerned only for the ark. "Glory" was an alternative designation of the ark (compare Ps 78:61). It is related to the Hebrew word for "heavy" (also "honored" — like "great" or "substantial" in English it conveys either size or distinction). In these chapters they pun and play on each other (in v. 18, was Eli old and "heavy," or old and "honored"?).

Ch. 5 When the Philistines themselves do become the active subjects of the verb "take" (vv. 1, 2, 3), things go wrong for them. They "take" the ark and bring it to Ashdod; they "take" it and bring it into the temple of Dagon, the grain god whom we know better by the Latin name Ceres; when they find Dagon fallen before it, they "take" him back to his place. But the next time he has a worse fall. After noting the failure of their "taking," this chapter moves on to spotlight the word from the previous chapter related to "glory" and "honor": the hand of Yahweh was "heavy" (vv. 6, 7) — they had Yahweh's glory *(kbwd)* among them, and at the same time his hand was heavy *(kbd)* on them. If they attempted to control the one, they got the other. They were afflicted by tumors; later tradition identified the swellings as hemorrhoids. Moving the ark to another of their cities was of no help; it should return to its own "place" (v. 11) — a frequent alternative in Hebrew for "sanctuary" or "shrine" (see above on 3:2, 9).

Ch. 6 It was seven months before the Philistines took expert advice about their troublesome religious booty. Our narrator pairs "diviners" with "priests." "Diviner" is always pejorative when used of practitioners in Israel. The Philistines had "diviners"; they could not be expected to have had "seers" or "prophets"! The query they put to their experts is quite limited: they are already decided to send the ark to its "place," and they know that they should send something with it. But what? The experts agree that if it is being sent (and they make no comment on that — perhaps they are peeved at not being consulted on that prior question), then it cannot go "empty-handed." A "guilt offering" should accompany it, and that will bring healing and . . . — ancient traditions divide over whether the "healing" will be accompanied by "ransom" or "knowledge."

The offering should be in the form of one golden "tumor" for each of their five cities — and some traditions surprisingly add five golden "mice" as well, although such creatures have played no part in the story. The expert wordplay in 6:5 is rich: their people should give "glory" to the God of Israel. Obviously this means that they should honor Yahweh. But the Hebrew phrase is also sometimes used for "give someone a present," and they are doing that too. However, they are also returning the "glory" (i.e., the ark) to its place; and, for good measure, when they hope that he will "lighten" his hand, they remind us of the related wordplay in his "heavy hand" (5:6, 7).

Though the experts were asked quite limited and straightforward questions, their advice once begun develops its own momentum. They are concerned not just with a safe return and with healing for the Philistines, but also with proof that it was in fact Yahweh who had caused all the trouble. Like their colleagues in the battlefield (4:7-8), they have some knowledge of Israel's early traditions (6:6): the Philistines should not replicate Pharaoh's mistakes. Their test for whether Yahweh is in fact intimately associated with the ark is ingenious. If milking cattle, just separated from their calves, drag the cart without guidance (and away from their young) toward Israelite territory, then it is Yahweh who caused the Philistine troubles (vv. 7-9). The alternative is equally interesting: if not Yahweh, then "chance" — or perhaps we should call it "fate," for in the books of Samuel, it always seems to be malign.

The cattle do head straight for Beth-shemesh, where the ark is greeted by the harvesters. The "large stone" on which the ark is laid (vv. 14, 18) may be a euphemism for an earlier altar or standing stone. The dutiful cows become a burnt offering — the Israelite population of the town do not share David's later scruples (2 Sam 24:24) about not using for an offering what he had not paid for. But there were casualties among the people because of divine displeasure. The ancient texts give quite different reasons: either one clan did not join in the celebrations (LXX), or some people looked into the ark (MT). The upshot is that the Israelite people of Beth-shemesh, not unlike the Philistines of Ashdod and Gath, want to be rid of it. After severe losses they pose the double question: "Who can stand before Yahweh?" and "To whom will he go from here?" Their emissaries are sufficiently economical with the truth that their neighbors in Kiriath-jearim come and relieve them of their holy burden. Its new host consecrates his son as its priest. The ark is not mentioned again till 2 Samuel 6.

Within these opening chapters which cast a long shadow, Yahweh letting the ark be taken may be a foretaste of Yahweh letting his temple, or "house," in Jerusalem be taken by the Babylonians. If so, then its return to Israel unaided should remind Israel of the source of valid initiatives in response to that later collapse. And yet, if we are to see particular significance in the loss of the ark immediately after the call of Samuel, it may be that once prophecy was established, the ark was dispensable. Certainly, the book of Jeremiah (3:14-18) invites its readers not to expect a postexilic ark.

Samuel as "Judge" (1 Samuel 7)

The opening two verses of 1 Samuel 7 belong more with what has gone before: v. 1 completes the previous story, and v. 2 is transitional to this new chapter. Israel's lamentation (v. 2) elicits a double response from Samuel. Vv. 3-4 occasion some surprise. This is partly because of their position and partly because of their content. Vv. 5-11 would make a good continuation from 7:2, and I suspect they did once follow it immediately. Samuel's offer to "pray for" Israel to Yahweh (v. 5) may provide the clue to the relationship of these passages. His offer appears to encourage the people's admission (v. 6) that they have "sinned." And that verbal link reminds us of Eli's warning question (2:25) whether there is anyone who can pray for the one who has sinned against Yahweh. Samuel now claims to be such a one. "Praying to" Yahweh toward the central sanctuary is also part of the appropriate response to "sin" according to Solomon's prayer (1 Kgs 8:46-49). However, when the leaders of his later community approach Jeremiah with the request to "pray for" them to Yahweh (Jer 37:3; 42:2), they have a different sort of prayer in mind: they are seeking Yahweh's guidance rather than his forgivenness. Vv. 3-4 appear to understand "pray for" in that latter sense, and offer the guidance before it is mentioned: they anticipate the alternative meaning of the verb Samuel is about to use.

There is much discussion among scholars of how "Deuteronomistic" the books of Samuel are. Even on the most minimal account of that matter, 1 Sam 7:3-4 are generally held to betray "Deuteronomistic" influence. Yet "setting the heart," though used in Ps 10:18, is an expression known elsewhere only in Chronicles (1 Chr 29:18; 2 Chr 12:14; 19:3; 20:33; 30:19). Ashtoreth, or Ashtaroth, are warned against in Judg 2:13; 10:6; 1 Sam 7:3, 4; 12:10; (31:10); 1 Kgs 11:5, 33; 2 Kgs 23:13. "Removing foreign gods" is also a theme of Gen 35:2, 4; Josh 24:23; Judg 10:16; and 2 Chr 33:15. "Return with your whole heart" is commended in Joel 2:12 — Deuteronomy never uses "with all your heart" without adding "and with all your soul." Good connections with the language of Deuteronomy are hard to find in those supplementary verses.

Ebenezer, which already figured under that name in the stories of the ark (4:1; 5:1), is only now reported as being so named (7:12) because of a stone erected by Samuel in memory of Yahweh's aid against the Philistines. Among other roles, the now adult Samuel is presented as judge of Israel (vv. 6, 15-17), in terms similar to those for Samson (Judg 15:20; 16:31) and Eli (4:18), but perhaps most similar to those for Deborah (Judg 4:4-5). The pairing of Bethel and Gilgal is most reminiscent of Amos 4:4-5; 5:4-6. Describing them with Mizpah as "places" underscores their cultic associations (a sense we meet first in Gen 12:6, of "the place" at Shechem by the sacred oak, and often thereafter).

A King like Those of Other Nations (1 Samuel 8–12)

Neither the special circumstances of his birth nor of his call save the old ways of government from popular criticism. Samuel must unwillingly preside over the appointment of a king. Saul's election, too, is attended by special features, including initial military success. Samuel takes his (first) leave with a long warning.

Ch. 8 Samuel's sons prove no better than Eli's — and that reinforces the warning from ch. 2 against the hereditary principle. What is said of their perversion of justice (8:3) reminds us of the critique by Amos. When Samuel "prayed to" Yahweh (v. 6), he was seeking divine direction. It is the demands of a royal court on a people which are at issue in the remainder of this chapter. Nothing is said about the king's sons or who will succeed him. The focus is solely on the burden of a growing establishment. Once all these individuals detailed in vv. 11b-17a are in the king's service, the people as a whole are too (v. 17b)! However, kingship is exactly what Israel wants (vv. 19-20); and Yahweh has already assured Samuel that he, not Samuel, is the king being rejected in favor of a (human) king. Whether in his final order that the people should disperse (v. 22b) Samuel is really obeying the Deity or only seeking to forestall his will is an open question.

Ch. 9 The father of Saul is introduced (v. 1) in terms very similar to those of the father of Samuel (1:1), and this is just the first of several comparisons and contrasts the text very economically suggests we should make. Saul's name means "asked for," and of course Samuel was asked for by his mother. Like Samuel, too (2:26), he is described as "good." The Hebrew word rendered "young man" can also mean "choice," of high quality, and that reminds us awkwardly that the house of now rejected Eli was once "chosen" by Yahweh (2:28). More immediately, it recalls Samuel's warning (8:18) that the people would have cause to complain of the king they had "chosen" for themselves.

The search for lost asses brings Saul to seek advice of Samuel, variously described as a "man of God," "seer," and "prophet." The latter two terms are introduced only to be immediately questioned: Samuel claims the term "seer" (9:19), though the text has already made plain that it is the Deity who does the significant "seeing" (v. 16). And the etymological and narrative play on prophet/profit (Heb. *nby'* means both "prophet" and "we shall bring") does the reputation of the man of God no good. As for the silver quarter-shekel, which Saul's servant produces as appropriate payment, it almost certainly fixes the date of the story in the Persian or Hellenistic period.

Ch. 10 The promised "divine word" (9:27) comes in action and speech: anointing on behalf of the Deity, a kiss of approval from Samuel, and the divine commission. Imparted in confidence, it is the culmination of words and actions the previous day (Saul as Israel's "pleasure," the top place at the feast). And it does not stop with 10:1. A multiplication of signs is to follow: two men (v. 2), three men (vv. 3-4), a whole band of prophets (vv. 5-6); not to speak of two further words — of advice (v. 7) and instruction (v. 8). The NRSV has disguised significant variety in the Hebrew by repeating "meet" throughout these verses — the Hebrew has "you will find" (v. 2), "will find you" (v. 3), "you will encounter" (v. 5), and "when these signs come about for you" (v. 7). "Find" is particularly appropriate in the first sign: Saul's purpose had been to find his father's donkeys; what he will now find is that they are already found. "Encounter" or "bump into" is good for the exotic group of prophets. And "come [about]" is the right word for the actual happening of predictions or promised signs. When the signs come about, Samuel says, Saul should do "what comes to hand" because God is with him — is he giving him real freedom, or is it a test? Whatever our answer to that question, he must then go to Gilgal and wait for further instructions. Taking the two verses together, we can suggest that the new king was given responsibility, but within limits set by Samuel.

The "coming" of all three signs is noted (10:9), but only the third reported (vv. 10-13). Is this simply a typical example of the economy in much biblical storytelling (one narrated fulfillment doing duty for three), or is a summary noting of fulfillment enough to guarantee Samuel's reliability? The episode with the band of prophets does not release its secrets easily. Their ecstatic frenzy was accompanied by or induced by music and rhythm; the divine spirit empowered Saul to join them; those who had known him were surprised; what they said became a saying; and someone from there puzzlingly responded, "And who is their [or his?] father?" "His father" (preserved in the ancient Greek and Syriac translations) is the easier and perhaps less likely text; it would mean that we would have expected better or differently from Kish's son. "Their father" (in the standard Hebrew text) would refer to the prophets' leader or patron. But does the question imply that people do not know who is in control, or does it hint that Samuel (or God) is their patron — and so now Saul's as well?

Prophets in groups are most often disapproved of in the Bible. However, we need not remain with such a general remark, for two stories may be compared quite closely with this one. Later in this book (19:18-24), David takes refuge with Samuel from Saul. When Saul's messengers arrive, they find a prophetic band in ecstasy with Samuel in charge — as they approach, the same happens to them, and again to Saul himself, as to Saul in our story. Possibly more instructive is the story told in Numbers about Yahweh coming down to talk with Moses and seventy elders, and to put on the seventy some of the spirit that was already on Moses (11:16-17). When this happened, the elders "prophesied" (11:24-25) — this Hebrew translates the same verb as is rendered "fell into a prophetic frenzy" in 1 Sam 10:10. If Samuel was patron to the group, then his patronage was being extended to Saul.

When Yahweh consented to the demand for a king, Samuel sent the people home (8:22). He now summons them back to Mizpah, the scene of ch. 7, and scolds them for rejecting the God who had rescued them from Egypt and all other oppressors in favor of a king (10:17-19). This is an ironic anticipation of the scene at Mizpah after the fall of Jerusalem in which a group of Judeans decide to go to Egypt for fear of the Chaldeans (2 Kgs 25:22-26 — the story is told at greater length in Jeremiah 40–44). Saul, already privately anointed and commissioned (he did not enlighten his uncle — 10:16), is now publicly selected from the entire nation by divine lot — what should we make of the fact that the same procedure is used to identify Achan in Joshua 7 and Jonathan in 1 Samuel 14 *as culprits*? We are given no indication whether Saul hiding himself demonstrates commendable modesty or a flaw in character. Samuel concludes the proceedings by explaining to the people the "norms" of the new kingship. The expression used is very similar to "ways of the king" (8:9, 11). There, in the context of a warning, Samuel sketched how any king might act. Here he lays down, and records in writing, how kingship should be.

Ch. 11 The Ammonite aggressor's name could be suggestive of three Hebrew words; but if we could choose among bronze, diviner, and snake, the last might be the most appropriate hint at the significance of "Nahash." His northern Transjordanian neighbors are at first prepared to subject themselves to him. His proposal of universal mutilation as a condition is explicitly intended as a challenge to Israel. When the messengers from Jabesh-gilead reached Gibeah of Saul, "the people" wept, a remarkably rare expression in the Bible. In 10:5, Gibeah was called "Gibeah of God" — not only was Saul to meet "prophets" there, but it was also a Philistine garrison. Is it relevant to recall David's self-protective (feigned) madness in the presence of the Philistine king (21:12-15)?

Saul hears the news only after it has so affected his people. God's spirit empowers him — note another God-Saul transfer — and he is angry, thus sharing a frequent divine response to molestation of his people when helpless: if all the people of Jabesh stand to lose their right eye, all defaulters in the rest of Israel stand to lose their oxen. It is dread of the Deity that brings out all Israel as one man — yet, interestingly, they are immediately counted separately as Israel and Judah, in the ratio ten to one. When the action comes, they are a body that moves with three "heads." The repeated interest in numbers culminates in the observation that whereas Israel mustered as one, Ammon's survivors are to be found only in ones (11:11).

The doubters of 10:27 have received their answer but escape their come-uppance. If the weeping reminded us of Judg 2:4; 20:23, 26; 21:2, and the divine spirit recalled Jephthah and Samson in the same book, the escape of those of "No Use" contrasts with the treatment Gideon meted out to the leaders of Succoth and Penuel who fearfully refused to help him. The doubters had questioned his kingship; he ascribed the victory to Yahweh. The result was a formal and united fresh start to his kingship — and, at the end of ch. 11, Israel's unity is no longer marred by discontented mutterers. And yet we may note with a wry smile that the people take this complaint to the very one who had been most doubtful about kingship at all!

Ch. 12 Samuel has apparently taken the initiative at the end of chs. 10 and 11. But his farewell speech opens by crediting (or is it blaming?) the people. The people are in a position to judge. Saul now, like Samuel before him, has "moved about" (not "led," as in the NRSV) in front of them, and his sons have been among them. They had enjoyed no special status. In fact, it was because his sons did not walk in Samuel's ways when made judges that the people had asked for a king instead (8:1-6). Yahweh had attempted to reassure him (8:7) that it was not Samuel but Yahweh himself whom the people had rejected. Samuel here seeks formal reassurance from the people (12:3-5) of his reliability.

His own worth attested, he now turns the argument on his people by having them admit Yahweh's reliability, too, in support of them, from the time of the oppression of Jacob's family in Egypt to more recent troubles up to his own time — and he lists himself as one of the judge-deliverers (12:11). More surprising is the novel "spin" he provides to the story. Moses and Aaron it was who settled their fathers "in this place"; Joshua receives not a mention. Even if Barak (of the old Greek and Syriac translations) is more original than the unknown "Bedan" of the Hebrew text, the order of the book of Judges is not followed. And, strangest of all, he reframes the account we have just read of the Nahash episode: Israel had not followed Saul's spontaneous lead (as the previous chapter told the story) — it had requested a king (12:12)! Obedience to Yahweh by both king and people is enjoined — and, to cover any gaps in the argument (shout when the argument is weak?), Samuel's and Yahweh's status are each confirmed by the display of power in a late thunderstorm.

The speech ends by probing further into the meaning of rejecting Yahweh. When the people acknowledge that choosing a king had been a further example of sin, and that sin merits death, Samuel moves to a new conclusion in line with a main concern of Deuteronomy. It had been suggested earlier that to choose a king was to reject Yahweh. However, the bottom line is that to choose other gods — even if other gods are only empty and useless (12:21) — is the ultimate rejection of Yahweh. He will not reject them for choosing a king. It would be a sin for Samuel to stop praying for his people (v. 23), yet such prayer may not be effective. If they choose other gods, thus acting only badly (v. 25), they and their king will be swept away. Samuel renews the warning of Moses (e.g., Deut 29:25-28), but his fresh anticipation of the end of the monarchy, uttered just as kingship begins, is all the more poignant.

Saul: Early a Disappointment (1 Samuel 13–15)

Although he is king of Israel until his death, reported at the very end of 1 Samuel, Saul loses the confidence of Samuel and of his God at a very early stage. The second half of 1 Samuel (chs. 16–31) depicts the outworking of a tragic, ineluctable fate. These three chapters open the account of how it is so.

Ch. 13 Only after Samuel's warnings at the renewal of the kingdom do we read the formal notice of the beginning of Saul's reign (v. 1); and these few words have long puzzled scholars. The Hebrew text begins the regular age formula but supplies no number; then the two years it does offer for the length of Saul's rule seem impossibly short, though powerfully suggestive of impermanence.

Of the three hundred and thirty "thousands" who had mustered against Nahash, only three are retained in Benjaminite territory under command of Saul and his son. But they are enough to dispose of a Philistine garrison and throw down the gauntlet to Israel's powerful neighbors by the coast. Israel is summoned to Gilgal, where Saul's kingdom had been renewed (13:4); but the majority response is to go into hiding (vv. 6-7). The foot soldiers that accompany the substantial Philistine cavalry are innumerable as the sand of the seacoast — an expression used in the Bible either in promises to Israel or to underscore the odds against her (as in Josh 11:4; Judg 7:12). Saul held his ground at Gilgal, and "all Israel trembled after him." After Israel in hiding and their enemy as the sand by the sea, talk of the people trembling confirms the connections between the telling of this story and the tale of Gideon/Jerubbaal and the Midianites (Judg 6:2, 5; 7:1, 12).

Saul waits at Gilgal for Samuel seven days, but not long enough for Samuel. Once he has begun to sacrifice, his forces slipping away from him, Samuel does arrive and blames him for not keeping a command that had emanated from Yahweh. In another anticipation of the final story in 2 Samuel (see below on 2 Sam 24:10), he chides Saul for acting "foolishly" (1 Sam 13:13). We readers cannot check Samuel's version — the instruction from Samuel has not previously been reported. But we note how he uses the charge of Saul's noncompliance to explain Yahweh's rejection of what would have been Saul's perpetual kingship over Israel — an alternative "prince" has already been looked for and given orders (v. 14). The impression that the "two years" of the opening verse suggested instability is somewhat confirmed. Samuel leaves Gilgal for Gibeah of Benjamin (13:2, 15) — is this the same or a different Gibeah from Gibeah of God (10:5) and Gibeah of Saul (11:4)?

Saul and his forces also return to the hill country of Benjamin — one of many elements in this story not stated in so many words. It is an unstable situation: they now occupy Geba (13:16), where the Philistine garrison had been defeated (v. 3); and the Philistines are now in Michmash, where Saul had started (v. 2). "The destroyer" comes out of the Philistine camp with three "heads" (like Saul against Ammon in 11:11), but what these achieve is left to our imagination. However, we are told that the battle was uneven in terms of equipment. The Philistines controlled iron smithing; among the Israelites only Saul and Jonathan had a sword or a spear.

Ch. 14 Jonathan and his armor bearer put their weapons to such good use (vv. 1-15) that trembling now afflicts the Philistines, including their "destroyer" commando. When Saul detects the neighboring hubbub and finds that his son must be involved, he first calls for the ark, which now (regularly?) accompanies Israel, and seeks a consultation with the Deity. But, as the tumult increases, he no longer fears for his son but commits all around him to the fight, cursing any who pause to eat before evening. Jonathan, who was not there to hear, refreshes himself with wild honey.

In their faintness, Saul's people slaughter and eat plundered livestock as they find it, without pouring out blood appropriately. Saul devises an impromptu altar to save them from further sin and then proposes pursuit and plunder till morning. Though the people agree, the priest asks that God be consulted. When no answer comes, a further consultation is required to detect whose sin has blocked communication. When the sacred lot identifies Jonathan, working on the same system as identified Saul as king (10:20-21), Saul is prepared to put the "guilty" party, however unwitting, to death. This long narrative describes a decisive, but far from final, victory over the Philistines. The Philistines are not pursued further that day, but are among his enemies for the rest of Saul's life. Toward the end (vv. 47-48), his success is described in language used of the judges (Judg 2:14, 16).

Saul's rash curse in the absence of Jonathan reminds us of Jephthah's vow, thoughtless of his daughter. Whether because Jonathan was a son or already a hero, his forfeit life is ransomed — financial compensation is an important principle of biblical and Jewish law. The story is also concerned to urge that meat, even when slaughtered in haste by famished warriors, should not be eaten with its blood.

Ch. 15 Saul himself is the butt of the next object lesson in the book. Although he has been warned by Samuel that his kingdom will not continue (13:14), he is still Yahweh's anointed and that status enjoins obedience to the Deity. Amalek should finally pay for the trouble they caused Israel after the exodus from Egypt. The story of that bitter conflict (Exod 17:8-16) ends in all-too-typical angry inconsistencies: it is to be solemnly recorded in writing that Amalek is to be utterly erased (15:14), and war is to continue with Amalek from generation to generation (v. 16)! Yet Samuel's statement of the divine commission this time is completely clear: the precise meaning of one of the four verbs in v. 3 may have to be discussed below; yet the surrounding words, even without its contribution, already add up to annihilation and obliteration: "strike down . . . all . . . do not spare . . . put to death . . . ."

Saul musters a large force (15:4). It is not quite as large as his force against Nahash (11:8), but again we note that Judah is given separate mention. Telaim may be the same place (in Judah) that is called Telem in Josh 15:24; but spelled this way it suggests "lambs," whether gathered in a shepherd's arms (Isa 40:11) or offered in sacrifice (1 Sam 7:9). The Kenite "smiths" maintained relations with different peoples of the area. Saul appears to associate them with the Midianites, whom Exodus (2–4; 18) reports had helped Moses and Israel, and are now warned to get out of the conflict zone. Shur belongs to the wilderness area south of Judah and east of Egypt, associated especially with Abraham and Ishmael in Gen 16:7; 20:1; 25:18 — and the third of these passages associates Shur with Havilah in exactly the terms we find here.

15:7-9 carefully document a partial response to the precise terms of the commission in v. 3: Saul did strike down Amalek and did "utterly destroy" all his people; but he kept King Agag alive and spared the best of the Amalekite animals. And we note that the [in]actions in v. 9 are attributed to the people as well as to Saul. Yahweh informs Samuel that he regrets making Saul king because he has not performed his words. Now that his God tells Samuel what Samuel himself has already told Saul, Samuel appears to show sympathy with Saul — or is he simply concerned with his own reputation since he was intimately concerned with the choice of Saul? There are two places called Carmel in the southern part of Judah. However, if the Carmel on which Saul celebrates his victory is the third and most famous one, then celebrations of a victory in the south that extend to Carmel near the northern coast and Gilgal near the Jordan imply control of most of historic Israel.

The Hebrew word *ḥerem* is as prominent in this chapter as in Joshua 6–7 and 10–11. It often, or even mostly, appears to be used as a mere metaphor for eliminating or "finishing off" an enemy (1 Kgs 9:21 uses the verb from *ḥerem* where the parallel 2 Chr 8:8 uses the literal "finish off"). But sometimes, as in this story, the literal meaning of the word may be closer to the surface of the narrative. *Ḥerem* is what is fully and finally given over to the deity in a vow so solemn that it cannot be redeemed (Lev 27:28-29). Everything living which becomes *ḥerem* is killed, and everything combustible is burned; only metal, which can pass through fire unscathed, is given over to the sacred treasury. It is, therefore, a sort of offering or sacrifice. That was the fate prescribed for some Canaanite cities at the taking of the land, and now for Amalek.

Saul greets Samuel with the report that he has performed Yahweh's word. Yet again at Gilgal, where his kingdom had been recognized by Samuel and the people after his first victory, Saul is upbraided by Samuel: the last time he should have waited to sacrifice (13:11-13); this time there should have been nothing to sacrifice on an altar. As Saul begins to note that the people had chosen to retain the best of the animals for sacrifice to Samuel's own God, Samuel cuts him short. What is introduced as a message from Yahweh does not normally require the permission of the recipient; but King Saul, though interrupted, graciously or truculently says, "Speak on."

Samuel starts boldly, calling Saul small in his own eyes. Is he referring straightforwardly to his reluctance to become king (9:21; 10:22), or is he ironically showing knowledge of Saul's monument at Carmel (15:12). Saul claims compliance with the divine mission: Agag is in his hands; his people are wholly destroyed; the best of their livestock are due for sacrifice at Gilgal — he could be implying that, even if not yet dead, all soon will be. Yet, when he does again say that it was the people who preserved the beasts (even if for sacrifice), Samuel again interrupts — and this time (vv. 22-23) in the formal, balanced, poetic lines most suitable for solemn communications from the Deity. He repeats the prophetic commonplace that Yahweh prefers obedience to sacrifice, and reinforces it by aligning disobedience with false religion. Saul's rejection of Yahweh will be matched by Yahweh's of Saul.

Saul no longer protests compliance. And when, on his third mention of the people's role, he lets slip that he had feared them (15:24), he tacitly recognizes his unfitness to rule. Though he now admits his sin, he asks for it to be removed. Samuel does not answer directly, but he refuses to accompany him to worship and confirms his rejection as king. When Saul grabs Samuel's garment and it tears, Samuel underscores what he has said by presenting Saul's action as a parable of Yahweh tearing the kingdom from Saul — anticipating the story in 1 Kgs 11:29-31 about Jeroboam and a later prophet and Solomon's kingdom. Once it is plain that Saul requires only to save face with humans, Samuel does accompany him to worship (15:30-31). Effective ruler again, Samuel, who had described himself as old when Saul took power (12:2), must now complete the physical destruction of Amalek (15:32-33), famously hacking Agag to pieces. He never again sees Saul.

David, the New Divine Choice: From Saul's Champion to His Rival (1 Samuel 16–18)

As soon as the divine regret over Saul is expressed, moves toward the succession are undertaken. In as short a narrative space as it took for Saul to fail, David is anointed, becomes a hero, an army chief, and Saul's son-in-law, and falls out of royal favor.

Ch. 16 At first sight, the last words of ch. 15 suggest convergence between Samuel and his divine master in their regret over their failure with Saul. But the opening words of the next chapter distance master and servant. In fact, though the Deity is often said in the Bible to regret or repent of some of his actions or decisions, he is never said to lament or grieve over them — to be emotionally involved with them. Yahweh is ready to begin the story of David; Samuel is well aware of the continuing power of Saul (16:2). And that uneasy situation dominates the second half of 1 Samuel.

Yahweh reminds Samuel that organizing sacrifice is a convenient expedient to explain his presence anywhere. Saul, too, was quietly anointed after a similar civic function (1 Samuel 9–10). When the reason is given why David's eldest brother Eliab is rejected, we remember the description of Saul as head and shoulders above the people. The rejection of Abinadab calls to mind two rejected pairs of similarly named sons: Aaron's Nadab and Abihu, and Jeroboam's Abijah and Nadab. Jesse's remaining sons are listed as a group until the absent David, the junior minding the beasts. Despite the earlier warning about appearances, David's looks are reported favorably (but see 17:42). Then, unlike Saul, whose servant was asked to withdraw, David is (semi-)openly anointed amid his brothers.

The gift of the divine spirit, next noted (16:13b), associates David with both Samson and Saul but also distinguishes him from both. Reports of the spirit empowering or taking over Samson and Saul appear as short-term responses to a particular stimulus, whether of danger (Judg 14:6, 19; 15:14), anger (1 Sam 11:6), or contagious behavior (1 Sam 10:6, 10). Here the divine spirit accompanies the anointing and continues with David "from that day forward." The consequence for Saul is carefully stated in the next verse: the spirit of Yahweh leaves him (it cannot be divided?), and an evil spirit from Yahweh afflicts him.

The change is immediately manifest to his staff, who recommend music therapy. Saul agrees that they should seek out a good player, and one of them nominates a member of Jesse's family, yet with a recommendation so far beyond what would normally suffice even a royal musician (16:18) that we are surprised that Saul makes no adverse comment. If he still had any wits about him, he would prefer that such a potential rival be kept under his eye. Faced with what he might fairly have suspected to be a dangerous invitation, Jesse responds generously. Saul is immediately impressed, and David's military qualifications are as quickly utilized as his musical skills.

Ch. 17 The story of David and Goliath is one of the best known from the Hebrew Bible (HB). People know it who know little or nothing of its biblical context. Two or three points are immediately remarkable about it. The story is a longer version of an exploit attributed to another Bethlehemite, Elhanan, and reported very briefly in 2 Sam 21:19. Then, while one version of this extended tale is known to us from its ancient Greek translation (the LXX), the version in the HB is almost twice as long. The Greek and Hebrew versions of the book, though different throughout Samuel, are never as divergent as here. And many scholars add, but on a surface reading of one of the Hebrew supplements (17:55-58), that David is introduced to Saul as if they had never met, let alone been intimately connected. In short, and for all these reasons, even within 1 Samuel it stands alone and somewhat distinctive.

Much biblical narrative is quite briefly told. This one lingers on: the size of the enemy giant and the specification of his equipment; the challenge repeated over forty days; David coming backward and forward between his father and his sheep in Bethlehem and his brothers in the line; David is scolded by his big brother and his offer disputed by the king till he is persuaded by stories of lions and bears dispatched; shepherds' weapons, chosen in preference to proper armor, defeating a gigantic hero in proper array; Goliath's head cut off with his own sword.

Some of the language in which the story is told is very distinctive within Samuel, allowing interesting links to be noted with other parts of the book but also with (other) late biblical texts. David's appearance as seen by Goliath is described in exactly the same terms as when he was presented to Samuel (16:12), and the Philistine despises what he sees (17:42) as just the good looks that belong to youth. Goliath is insulted at David's approach with a stave, but no proper weapon; David portrays the imbalance differently — one man's fine weapons against a God who controls "hosts." When the Philistine giant does turn to fight the agent of this God, he ends by falling on his face to the ground (v. 49) just as Dagon, his own people's god, fell before Yahweh's ark (5:3, 4).

The climax to David's challenge notes what "all this assembly" will learn (17:47). The word "assembly" itself is very rare in Samuel and the other Former Prophets — qualified by "all," the expression is at home only in Chronicles, Ezra, and Nehemiah (with another isolated example in Exod 16:3). Then the Hebrew verb and noun translated "draw up" and "ranks" are forms of the same word. This, too, is used most frequently used in "priestly" texts of the Pentateuch and in Chronicles; but it is also found in two other Philistine contexts in 1 Samuel (4:2, 16 and 23:3). Yahweh seldom bears the fuller title "of hosts" in the Former Prophets (Joshua-Kings). "Yahweh of hosts" (17:45) is much commoner throughout the Latter Prophets and in some psalms; but we will also find it anchored in the traditions of David as new king in 2 Sam 5:10 and 7:8, 26, 27. Whatever the precise sense of Yahweh's "hosts" elsewhere in the Bible, it will hardly be chance that this use of the title within 1 Samuel comes right beside "the God of Israel's ranks," each rare expression acting to illumine the other.

So far I have commented almost exclusively on the shorter form of the story known also from the ancient Greek translation. The two substantial additions in the Hebrew version of 1 Samuel 17 are vv. 12-31 and vv. 55-58. Among other things, the first of these helps integrate the story with the account of David and his older brothers in the previous chapter. But one verse deserves more extended mention. What is the social or political setting of the offer to make the victor's father's house "free in Israel"?

In many traditional tales, the hero or savior is offered "my daughter's hand and whatever you want up to half of all I own." Here it is not Saul who offers; yet the people know the familiar formula (v. 25). When David questions the going rate, the people reaffirm it (vv. 26-27). Most often in the Bible, freedom is what comes after the due number of years to the "Hebrew slave" (Exodus 21; Deuteronomy 15; Jeremiah 34), though Job 3:19 and Ps 88:5 suspect more bleakly that it is (only?) in death that a slave achieves freedom from his owner. David as victor did in a sense free his family and all others in Israel from being "Hebrew slaves" to the Philistines. Yet the introduction to his anointing suggested that Jesse was already one of the property-owning elders of Bethlehem. The people actually echo Goliath's contemptuous contrast between himself, "a Philistine," and these "servants of Saul" (17:8), and the "royal offer" they mouth functions ironically to confirm his condemnation of King Saul as their slave owner.

It is the shorter addition at the end of the chapter that provides the bigger puzzle: Why does Saul no longer recognize David? Yet several of the added elements serve to compare and contrast David with the figure of Saul as described in chs. 9–10. The answer may be that David after his great exploit, like Saul after his encounter with the prophets, has "turned into another man" (10:6); and onlookers have to inquire after the parentage of both.

Ch. 18 The implications of David's heroic success for the kingship are immediately noted. Saul's son "adopts" David and hands over to him the insignia of the crown prince. David becomes Saul's military leader, and the popular response credits him with ten times greater success than his master. Saul knows that nothing less than the kingdom is at stake and "eyes" David from then on (vv. 8-9), but Yahweh's spirit is blamed (vv. 10-11) for the evil impulse to pin David to the wall. Yahweh himself, as distinct from his (evil) spirit, is now with the successful David, of whom Saul (when in his right mind?) stands in awe (v. 15). The offer of Saul's daughters in marriage is not part of a belated prize (17:25), but is explicitly conditional on David's continuing campaigns against the Philistines, in which sooner or later he should perish. David learned all too well from his royal master; in ironic turn, as we shall see, he was to wait for the Philistines to dispatch Saul and Jonathan and open his way to the kingship.

The negotiations over Michal are rather more explicit — in fact, the shorter Greek version knows nothing of the earlier offer of Merab (18:17-19). David's polite answer to the king's overture says neither yes nor no. His mention of poverty is taken literally; no marriage present will be required except for one that is in his power to provide. The one hundred gruesome tokens would identify the victims as Philistine males; for only they in the region did not practice circumcision. Like Samson in Judges, David is delighted to comply over Philistine-bashing, and in double measure (vv. 26-27); and his successful "cooperation" effectively sealed perpetual enmity with Saul (v. 29).

Jonathan and Michal between Saul and David (1 Samuel 19–20)

Saul's son and daughter, Jonathan and Michal, repeatedly foil their father's attempts on David without themselves being dispossessed.

Ch. 19 Having failed to lure David into death at enemy hands, Saul now discusses his elimination with his council. Jonathan persuades his father not to incur blood guilt, and secures from the king a solemn oath (vv. 5-6). David's next success elicits a further divine impulse to pin him to the wall, and, when he escapes home, to ambush him in the morning. This time Saul's daughter intervenes, covering David's absence in an age-old ploy. Within the Bible, it is reminiscent of Rachel's mischief on behalf of her husband Jacob, involving the teraphim of Laban her father (Gen 31:25-35).

In flight from Saul, David now seeks out Samuel in his home territory of Ramah, and comes under his protection there. Repeated sets of messengers sent by Saul to take David are caught up in the contagious behavior of a group of "prophets." The scene is reminiscent of what happened to Saul at nearby Gibeah, on his departure from Samuel after his own anointing (10:9-13). However, this time Samuel is actually at the head of the ecstatics. Saul must finally come too, and is himself caught up — to the extent that he strips and lies naked before Samuel a day and a night. The question of the relationship between Saul and the "prophets" (10:11-12) is repeated (19:24), and leaves us readers wondering whether it has the same significance now as earlier. Prophets command both positive and negative evaluations in the Bible. Apart from the behavior that overpowers Saul, the role of Samuel is common to the two stories: in the first, he knows what will happen; in the second, he is at the head of the group. This scene is in some tension with the statement at the end of the Amalek episode that Samuel never saw Saul again (15:35), yet the divine spirit here did hinder and frustrate Saul's approach to David (and Samuel).

Ch. 20 From ch. 19 onward the theme of David in flight from Saul keeps reappearing. The two men never meet again, except for a couple of chance encounters when David has the advantage over a sleeping Saul (chs. 24 and 26). The nature of the relationship between them is explored in episodes involving third parties. Jonathan had achieved one reconciliation (19:1-7), which quickly proved fragile (19:8-10). It is to him that David now turns. Jonathan had declared to his father that David had not sinned against him (19:4). David now asks Jonathan whether any of his deeds constitutes guilt or sin: only in this way would he be in danger of his life. Jonathan seeks to reassure him and claims confidence that he is privy to his father's intentions, but David sees grounds to doubt this (20:3). They hatch a plot to test and report on Saul's intentions at the beginning of the month (a regular holy period) when David would be expected to feast with Saul and his entourage.

In the older story on which Samuel and Kings are based, the words "guilt" and "sin" are used very sparingly and therefore tellingly — and of David only in the story of his census (2 Samuel 24). Their importance for the books of Samuel is underscored by Eli's warning (already discussed at 2:25 above). David admits to "sin" over his adultery with Bathsheba, but he repeatedly disputes (both David himself and Jonathan on his behalf) that he can be held to have sinned against Saul.

Saul notes but does not remark on David's absence on the first day of the feast. He calls on Jonathan the next day to explain David's continued absence. When he offers the rehearsed excuse, Saul comes quickly and coarsely to the point: Jonathan does not deserve to be called his son, he is fitting offspring to his perverse and rebellious mother, and his dealings with David will cost him the kingdom. When Jonathan puts David's question to Saul, Saul answers with the spear he has twice thrown at David (20:32-33) — the more realistic David had warned Jonathan to expect a hard response (v. 10). As Jonathan angrily leaves the table, we wonder whether the disgrace mentioned in the last words of v. 34 is David's or — in the light of what his father has publicly said and done to him — Jonathan's own.

One question which remains with us through the chapter is: Which is the wiser response to David's rise, Saul's or his son's? Saul sees and says that David threatens Jonathan's succession to the throne (v. 31). And he is right. He also seeks to eliminate the threat to his family. But Jonathan has already tacitly accepted the same analysis in his words to David (vv. 13-16): may Yahweh be with David as he has been with Saul. May Jonathan not die, may his name not be cut off, when Yahweh takes vengeance on the enemies of David. May the relationship between them, reiterated when they meet again (v. 42), survive what must come. Saul still wants the kingdom for his son, but Jonathan will settle for the continuance of his family.

David in Flight from Saul (1 Samuel 21–23)

That could well be the heading for the remainder of 1 Samuel. David's bandit-like period begins on the southern and western margins of Judah's hill country, between Israel and the Philistine heartlands.

Ch. 21 Ahimelech responds to the arrival of the lone David as the elders of Bethlehem did earlier to Samuel (16:4-5); both are afraid and suspect that something is up. In fact, the distances involved in the story are small; and we may suppose that the priest already knew that his visitor was out of favor with his king. A master of the boldest ruse, or just plain devious, David claims to this priest (whose name means "my brother is king"!) that he is on top-secret king's business: a word that cannot be spoken. He does have men "somewhere or other." Though he claims a mission and supporters, he needs something the priest has: bread is mentioned, yet we suspect that the "or whatever" (21:3) may have been of more interest to David, though not to the much later Gospel writer (see below).

Ahimelech first takes up the safer subject of the bread. The bread in his charge is holy. Part of the business of a priest was to know about, and rule on, the distinction between sacred and secular, holy and profane. I suspect that by the normal rules the priest's clarification that there was only holy bread there should have put an end to the matter. However, in awe of David, Ahimelech backtracks and cites another ruling within his priestly competence: to participate at all in sacral business, David's men would have had to have been abstaining from women. David claims — and the reader is free to arbitrate — that his men's "implements" are always holy when on an expedition, and all the more so "today" (when he is on king's business? when he is visiting a priest?). The Hebrew word I have rendered "implements" is useful and nonspecific: when used with the sacred bread and the table of the "presence" it would normally refer to vessels, and in connection with soldiers it would indicate weapons and armor — and some have suspected that the men's "members" may really be the "implements" hinted at here. Accepting David's assurance at face value, Ahimelech parts with the bread.

The Gospels have understood this story differently. They suppose a motive of which the book of Samuel gives no hint: that David and his men were hungry. Jesus was defending his disciples against the charge of breaking the holy sabbath by "harvesting" heads of grain as they walked through a field. Satisfying human needs, he argued, comes before attention to normal rules of what is holy (Luke 6:1-5).

Mention of Doeg, one of Saul's staff, detained at the sanctuary both impedes our approach to the next and more intriguing part of the story and adds its own menace to the mix. Is not David right to remember the presence of a weapon in the sanctuary? Goliath's is the only one, the priest responds, but David can take it if he wants! And, when David responds that there is none like it, he will be thinking less of its size and more of its double symbolism: for a refugee fleeing to Goliath's own city, and for a rival who outshone his master in battles against the Philistines.

When he arrives in Gath, his past is too well known and he is embarrassed to be hailed as "king of the land." Saul had become another man by contagion with the ecstatics (chs. 10 and 19 above). David now feigns madness — he tries to assure King Achish that he is no threat; he is not the man he was. However, the king of Gath is not prepared to entertain another madman; and David has to escape into hiding.

Ch. 22 David takes refuge first in a cave in the lower hills between the heights of Judah and the Philistine coast, and he is joined by his family and various discontents. He then moves east of the Dead Sea to a stronghold in Moab. When he commits his family to the protection of Moab's king, we are reminded of the tradition in Ruth that there was Moabite blood in their veins.

Saul apparently hears from a source outside his immediate circle at Gibeah that David has been discovered in a forest of Judah; he berates them for their disloyalty in not providing him with intelligence. Doeg volunteers the story of David's visit to Nob. Ahimelech, summoned to answer for his doings, might have been better advised to organize his defense differently. He might have pleaded first that for David to approach him was neither new nor remarkable. Leaping to David's defense was bound to antagonize the king and show up his own lack of awareness. Saul does not dispute with him; he merely passes sentence and orders the guards to carry it out.

When they refuse to lay hands on the priests, Saul turns to an alien hatchet man. Doeg is a suitable name for a useful "go-for" and man of business; it means "worrier," and as a normal verb it described the concern of Saul's father about his lost donkeys, and then his long-absent son (10:2). The bloody "cleansing" of the priestly settlement at Nob might encourage a Hebrew reader of Samuel to remember our introduction to Doeg (21:7) and detect a menacing hint in his being "detained" or "restrained" at the sanctuary: the verb so translated normally has "plague" as its subject. David had been aware when he noted the presence of Doeg at Nob that he was putting Ahimelech at risk. It is said, though it is not always true, that my enemy's enemy is my friend. Abiathar, the sole surviving member of the priestly clan, is persuaded to commit his security to David (22:23).

Ch. 23 David is told that the Philistines are "plundering" the threshing floors of a nearby town in Judah. The verb is not very common: in the Former Prophets it is used more often in editorial comment (Judg 2:14, 16; 1 Sam 14:48; 2 Kgs 17:20), and it is part of the Goliath story (1 Sam 17:53). David's men, already in flight from Saul, are understandably reluctant to engage with a second major foe; and so David has to check with the divine oracle a second time. They duly have success (23:1-5). It appears that 22:20-23 and 23:1-5 are not in chronological order, for it is only when David controls Keilah that Abiathar joins him (v. 6). Abiathar and his ephod are now the means by which David asks the Deity whether he can trust the townsfolk he has just saved from the Philistines, supposing Saul comes against him at Keilah. David moves south into more open, uninhabited country, with Saul in daily pursuit.

Jonathan is able to meet David. He assures him that his father will not be able to catch him. Do his next words spell out what is already his understanding with David, though we readers have not yet been told? Or does Jonathan here make a new bid, not just to preserve his family but to become David's second in command? Or possibly to preserve his family by becoming the new king's designated lieutenant? Whether or not the bid surprised him, David accepted its terms (23:18). It was convenient for a fugitive from Saul to know that the whole royal house was not against him.

The people of Ziph in southern Judah, like the people of Keilah, were content to supply vital intelligence to Saul. But, just as Saul was closing in, David was saved by the (chance?) intervention of an unspecified Philistine attack "on the land" which Saul had to break off and deal with. David took himself further east, to the west coast of the Dead Sea, and the neighborhood of "Goat Spring," one of the most prominent of the few freshwater sources in the area. There are many natural clifftop fortresses there, Masada (its name just the common word for stronghold used here) being the largest and most famous now.

David's Waiting Wisdom (1 Samuel 24–26)

Two incidents in which Saul comes into David's power bracket the story of Nabal and Abigail. David refuses to move against "the LORD's anointed" (24:6), but in each case he lets Saul know what might have been. The long and sensible waiting game he plays with Saul is thrust into relief by his hotheaded response to Nabal's senseless lack of generosity — he has to be saved from his own folly by Abigail, who quickly becomes his wife.

Ch. 24 Having chased the Philistines, Saul returns to pursue David in the precipitous haunts of the ibex. Near sheepfolds where more domesticated beasts could be penned in, Saul uses the front of a cave to answer a call of nature. Had he but known it, David and his men were gathered in his grasp. David's men tell him the obvious: he could do with Saul whatever he wanted. More puzzlingly, they preface that remark by telling him that the day had now come on which Yahweh had promised to give David's enemy into his hand. We readers have never been told of this promise; David has never spoken of Saul as his enemy. Encouraged into action by their words, he cuts off part of Saul's cloak without his knowledge; but he immediately counters the implication of both parts of what they had said. Saul was Yahweh's anointed (and could not be his enemy); what David wanted was not to harm Saul but to demonstrate his own loyalty.

He follows Saul out of the cave, and makes a most public display (24:8). Prostration, other than before Yahweh, is little mentioned in the books of Samuel. But David now does obeisance to Saul, as he had (three times) before Jonathan when the king's son warned him to get away from Saul's presence (20:41-42). He adopts his men's words — Yahweh had given Saul into his hands — but distances himself from their meaning. Some of them had wanted him to kill Saul, but he would not. The proof of what had happened in the cave is in his hands for all to see. But his pleading is so intense that Saul himself could not only see with his eyes but know in his heart that there was no proper cause of any sort to hunt him down: no wrong, no treason, no sin (24:11).

David now takes his case to a higher court of appeal (24:12, 15). Yahweh may decide for David, but, even so, his hand will not be on Saul. It is proverbial that you expect wrong from those who are wrong; but his hand will not be on Saul. Does that mean that, even should Yahweh decide him guilty, he will not move against Saul? One ancient proverb (v. 13) seems to lead to another (v. 14). David scorns Saul's perception of the threat he poses him: Saul should see him as no worse a problem than a dead dog or a single flea!

In words that echo Judah's to his wronged daughter-in-law Tamar (Gen 38:26), Saul concedes (24:17) that David is more in the right than he — and in so doing, he confirms that *rasha'* in v. 13 should be understood in its forensic sense of "guilty," and not just "wicked." He admits that David could not have regarded him as an enemy (v. 19): an enemy is never allowed to go free. Most significantly, and taking up David's appeal not just to see but to know (v. 11), Saul declares that he now knows that David will become the established king of Israel. He leaves his own personal fate unspoken, but appeals to David as Jonathan had for the continuance of his family (20:13-16). David does so swear; but when they part, only Saul goes home — David stays in his desert stronghold. But he stays there knowing that he has been anointed by Samuel; that he has now been "recognized" by the present king as his successor; and that he has kept his hands publicly clean.

Ch. 25 Samuel had anointed first Saul and then David in the name of Yahweh. With Saul now accepting Yahweh's will, Samuel dies. "All Israel," represented in the previous chapter in Saul's select force against David (24:2), now gathers to mourn and bury him at his home. No more is said. It is not even clear whether David was there: Was it from the funeral that he went down to Paran, or from his stronghold?

Both Nabal and Abigail offer interesting comparisons and contrasts to Saul's treatment of David. Nabal is like Saul before his most recent encounter with David. His people have had unsolicited, but beneficial, "protection" from David and his men; yet David receives no benefit. To turn David away from the great shearers' feast is both socially churlish and diplomatically foolish: the response (25:13) is that of a mafia capo defending his "honor." The day is saved when one of Nabal's staff alerts his wife.

She responds generously with such alacrity that we must suppose it is with (a good part of) the food for the feast that she seeks to head off David's wrath. As they approach, we have spelled out for us the extent of David's threat (25:21-22). "One male" comes well short of a Hebrew expression which invites us to make a pair of connections. "Any that piss on the wall" is the more colorful Hebrew. David anticipates words which Yahweh or one of his prophets will use four times in Kings of the wholesale destruction of a royal family of northern Israel. When we recall Saul's business in the cave, we are powerfully reminded what might have been his and his family's fate at David's (or Yahweh's?) hands had he not been Yahweh's anointed, and had David not loved his son.

Abigail's diplomacy is disarming. She starts by prostrating herself, admitting guilt over what has happened and begging that she be held responsible. David has quoted an ancient proverb to Saul: we expect guilty behavior from guilty people (24:13). Abigail now asks, What other behavior do you expect from someone called Nabal? There are two aspects to the Hebrew word *nabal*, and I used them both above: churlish and foolish. Isaiah might have been reflecting on this scene when he said that you would never expect to be able to call a *nabal* "generous/honorable/free-spirited" (32:5). Is Abigail also playing on what, from our perspective at least, is the other sense of the word and suggesting that he is too "foolish" to bear blame for his ungenerous conduct: that that role must fall on her? She herself did not see the men David first sent (25:25), and she should have (?).

Though it is she who is interrupting his raid on Nabal, she invites him to consider that it is Yahweh who is restraining him. May all his enemies be like Nabal: let Yahweh decide their fate (25:26). Before she says any more to David, she undemonstratively presents the provisions as a "blessing" for his men (v. 27). The second stage of her argument resumes the theme of herself as a mere servant (v. 28, like vv. 24-25) and of the blame she bears, but this time she asks that he forgive it. No sooner has this request been slipped in than she plies him with good wishes and good advice as Yahweh's next prince over Israel. Using a neat contrast between two sorts of everyday folded container, she assures him that Yahweh will protect his life against opponents in his wallet or bag of valuables; the lives of his enemies, however, will be placed in a sling and thrown far away. There is an immediate meeting of minds. David accepts that Yahweh has sent her and blesses him for his gift (v. 32). But in the same breath he praises her for exhibiting the opposite of folly and keeping him from avenging with his own hand (v. 33). He tells her the full gravity of what he had intended; only then does he accept both her gift and her petition.

Abigail had not left home with all the supplies for the party. When she returned, she found Nabal hosting a feast on a royal scale — though not generous, he was no stranger to conspicuous consumption. "Drunk as a lord," he was beyond being spoken to. We use the expression "stone cold sober." Nabal may have been hardly as sober as that implies by morning, but Abigail was able to brief him on the day before. Her account of what was done and said causes heart death and "petrifies" him; we might describe this as "puts him in shock." Death comes from Yahweh, and follows ten days later (vv. 36-38).

David blesses Yahweh a second time, this time for avenging him on Nabal and making the churl responsible for his own churlishness. David has been kept from evil, and Abigail's move to take on herself responsibility for the folly is ignored. After admiring the skill of her plea to David, we might just wonder whether her unrecorded report to Nabal was a deliberate contribution to her husband's demise. Be that as it may, David and Abigail are quickly wed. She may describe herself as "servant of the servants of her lord," which reminds us of a papal title, and she is appropriately not without style, in the number of her own servants as well as in her words.

The chapter ends as it had begun, with a brief paragraph. This one offers an update on David's marital situation. The fruitfulness of Abigail and Ahinoam is suggested by their places of origin: the one from "orchard," the other from "God sows." Two gained, but one lost: as with Samson before him (Judg 14:20–15:2), his first wife Michal had been given by his father-in-law to another man.

Ch. 26 Our first reaction to this story may be of some impatience. It is so much like the encounter in the cave. It may just be an alternative version. Its inclusion slows down the progress of the larger narrative. We meet many similar issues as we read Genesis and the first part of Exodus. Here as there, it may help if we concentrate on two sets of issues: What is different about this story, and with which other stories does this one have links?

The people of Ziph are again Saul's informants (23:19-24), and again Saul takes three thousand choice men of Israel. But this time it is David who wants to satisfy himself ("see and know," 26:4-5) precisely where Saul is. With just two associates, he takes the initiative at night. As in the cave, he has Saul in his power, but he again refuses the urging of a comrade to let him dispatch him (this time with Saul's own spear). One could not both kill Yahweh's anointed and be in the clear: as Yahweh's anointed himself, that was an important lesson to inculcate among his troops.

At their previous encounter David called on Yahweh to avenge him on Saul. Since then he has seen Yahweh avenge him on Nabal. He is now more explicit about wanting Saul dead, one way or another — but not by his hand (26:10-11). Again David and his men take proof of their having been in Saul's presence (another link with the story of Judah and Tamar). But this time we learn that David did not just profit, as from a lucky meeting in the darkness of a cave: Yahweh had caused a specially deep sleep to fall on Saul and his men.

David wakens Saul's camp from a safe distance and teases Abner for not guarding his master. Saul again asks whether it is really David's voice he is hearing. David launches into a complaint against his ostracism. Who has instigated Saul's mistaken move? If it is Yahweh, let him take pleasure in the odor of an offering — let Yahweh, in fact, be as sensible as David had been with Abigail. If humans, let them be under Yahweh's curse. From David's recognition of the convergent responsibility of Yahweh and Abigail in restraining him from vengeance (25:32-34), we have already learned that he did not suppose it was a matter of choosing one answer rather than the other.

David protests that the result of driving him out is that he cannot "attach himself to the heritage of Yahweh." Both parts of this expression are rare. The "heritage" of Yahweh or God is a phrase special to the books of Samuel (1 Sam 10:1; 26:19; 2 Sam 14:16; 20:19; 21:3); it refers to the land Yahweh gives his people as their heritage. (Ps 127:3 provides the only other instance in the Bible; there "sons" are said to be the heritage Yahweh provides.) The fear of being unattached resonates with one further threat in Samuel: where the unnamed man of God (1 Sam 2:36) warns Eli that the remnants of his house will seek attachment to another of the hereditary priesthoods. Being unattached to Yahweh's heritage also implied serving other gods: Yahweh the High God, who allotted lands to peoples, also allotted each their god (Deut 32:8-9).

David's former alternative, that Yahweh had prompted Saul's actions, is just one of several indications that this story is yet another deliberate anticipation of the fateful and climactic account of David's census (2 Sam 24:1). Confirmation comes when Saul makes his admission (26:21) in the very language David will use then: he has sinned and acted very foolishly (24:10), words paired nowhere else in the Hebrew Bible. It is interesting that Saul is now prepared to admit, toward the close of his career, what Samuel had charged him with at his first mistake as king (13:13): "folly." The Hebrew word used here is not *nabal,* but the parallel between David's two opponents, Saul and Nabal, is there for all to see.

Yahweh had incited Saul, and Saul had been foolish. The same Yahweh had also given Saul into David's hands, yet David had not acted wrongly against his anointed. Again concerned as much for his own fate as for Saul's, he asks that Yahweh will deliver him as he delivered Saul (26:23-24). Saul responds by blessing him (again a theme shared with ch. 25 rather than with ch. 24) and recognizing him in quite unspecific terms as a future high achiever. There are many links between this second story of Saul in David's power and not only neighboring chapters but also wider themes of Samuel. This suggests that it is not just an alternative version of the story preserved for completeness, but a deliberately crafted reworking of the theme.

Saul's End and David's Alibi (1 Samuel 27–31)

David becomes so well trusted by Achish of Gath that he enrolls him in the Philistine muster against Israel. Saul adopts means that he himself had outlawed to secure divine guidance in a national crisis when he finds his God silent — but he succeeds only in hearing his fate confirmed. David is rejected as a fellow combatant by the other Philistine leaders. He has to go south to avenge an Amalekite attack on his base at exactly the time of Saul's defeat and death in the north.

Ch. 27 "May Yahweh deliver me out of all tribulation" (26:24) does not mean that David should do nothing about it himself: exile among the Philistines would offer greater security than being a fugitive at the margins of Israel. So David goes again to Achish of Gath (see above, on 21:10-15) — this time with his men and his household. On the earlier occasion David feigned madness. This time he affects to be harrying the southern margins of Judah. But the booty he is showing to Achish, and doubtless sharing with him, comes in fact from further afield toward Egypt. No prisoners survive to become slaves and tell tales in this grim transaction; apparently neither the animals nor the clothing betrays its real origins to Achish. He is confident in the belief that a fratricidal David will be bound to his service forever.

Ch. 28 It is time for another showdown between the Israelites and the Philistines. On the one side, Achish is so trusting of David that he and his men are to serve alongside the Philistines, and David is even made his bodyguard. On the other side, Saul, afraid of the enemy force, is worried at receiving no divine omens. We are reminded that the great Samuel is dead and buried (25:1), and we are told that Saul had earlier banned all illicit intermediaries. None of the normal legitimate means is producing an answer from Yahweh: not dreams, not the sacred lot, not prophets. We know from the earlier story concerning Jonathan (1 Sam 14:36-42) that he should have tried to identify the problem that was causing this blockage in divine communication. We must suppose that he either overlooked this or already knew the answer only too well. As we learn his remedy, we understand why the storyteller has bracketed Samuel's death with Saul's removal of mediums.

The two sorts of intermediary specified here are almost always paired; and the second is never found apart from the first. Manasseh, the most reviled king of later Judah, is blamed for association with them and for other forms of divination. I suspect that his is the bad example warned against in the Mosaic books (Lev 19:31; 20:6, 27 and Deut 18:11), as well as anticipated here to discredit Saul. The second is the masculine term, as well as the more transparent: the Hebrew word is related to the common verb to "know," as "wizard" in English is to "wit" and "wise." The word itself does not betray by what arts the knowledge is acquired.

The term that concerns us here is more opaque. It seems to refer properly to one of the diviner's tools. Saul's command is for his staff to find a woman who "possesses" or "is mistress of" whatever-it-is. The implement itself may have been a "bottle" made of skin or a belly or a bladder — at least the word is identical to the one Elihu uses when he is bursting to speak, like a new bottle ready to spill its wine (Job 32:19). In disguise Saul asks her to use her "bottle" to "divine" for him — and the last time we met that word in Samuel was when the Philistines needed advice about how to handle Yahweh's ark (6:2). Saul is desperately using Philistine means to cope with his Philistine foe.

The woman is cautious. Wiser than she yet knows, she says to Saul: "You yourself know what Saul has done"! While the narrator simply told us that he had "removed" the intermediaries from the land (28:3), she tells us that they had been cut off: this present entrapment could cost her life (v. 9). Saul swears immunity to her by Yahweh (with whom he had lost communication!). As she calls up Samuel, something alerts her immediately to Saul's deception. She now knows that she is dealing with Saul; Saul, however, has yet to be persuaded that he is dealing with Samuel. To his "What do you see?" she replies puzzlingly: "Gods I saw, coming up from the earth." Suspecting that she was prevaricating, he asks, "What did he look like?" "An old man wrapped in a robe." This garment seems to have been Samuel's hallmark: when first in Eli's service his mother used to make and bring him a little one (2:19); and when he last encountered Saul, the king tore the one he was then wearing (15:27). Saul prostrates himself before Samuel.

Nathan is later to say to David in Yahweh's name that he would plant his people Israel that they might dwell in their own place and be disturbed no more (2 Sam 7:10). Samuel complains to Saul that he has "disturbed" him by bringing him up — he should have been left to his shadowy rest in the underworld. He brushes aside the explanation that Saul could get no divine answer any other way: if not by any other means, then not by him either — disobedience was the problem. Samuel's explanation now is exactly what it had been after the Amalek fiasco (1 Samuel 15), but he adds for grim good measure that Saul and his sons would join him on the morrow. Fear and lack of food lead to Saul's total collapse. The specialist medium reverts to the no-nonsense hostess: "I've listened to you — now you just listen to me"! With the help of his two servants, she gets a meal into him before they leave while it is still night.

Ch. 29 As the Philistine commanders review their troops, they notice the "Hebrews" with David. Achish's explanation that he has found no fault in David since his "fall" (v. 3) is not good enough for them. More worldly wise than Achish, they fear that a man who has turned once could turn again — and what better way to rejoin his first master than with their heads! They remind Achish of the earlier Israelite victory song, leaving him to supply the memory that the thousands and myriads of slain had been Philistines. Achish breaks the news gently to David. He says that he has found (devious) David straight. He would be happy to fight alongside him but has been overruled. When David protests, he asks him to go quietly as soon as possible, while flattering him as being "blameless as an angel of God." If David has "fallen," as the Hebrew says, then he has also "fallen on his feet," as we say in English. Not only does he not have to fight against his own people, but he has a Philistine good conduct medal as well.

Ch. 30 David may have succeeded on the national and even international stage, but matters were not at all well at home. Amalekite raiders from the southern desert had plundered his own town. They had not copied the brutal methods he had been using on their own people and their neighbors (27:8, 11), but added their human captives to the spoil, including David's own wives. His men blamed him, and thought to stone him. The opening paragraph closes with the unique expression, "David took strength in Yahweh his God" (30:6). It is a puzzle to know what that means, unless it is explained in the first part of the next paragraph (vv. 7-8): David consulted Yahweh with Abiathar's help, and received a response beyond the terms of his question: he would certainly overtake the raiders if he pursued them, but he would also effect a rescue.

All of his men set off with him (six hundred, as in 27:2). But after the first stage a third of them had to be left behind, dead-tired (the expression, found only here and in v. 21, is related to the common noun for a corpse). Vital intelligence now comes from paying attention to the needs of a sick and famished Egyptian slave, left to die. He leads them to his former master, the rout is complete, and everyone and everything is recovered. They also plunder the Amalekite cattle, and his men designate that bonus "David's spoil."

We knew from the beginning that there were rough diamonds among David's men — their first base (22:1-2) has become proverbial for a band of desperadoes — a veritable "Cave of Adullam." When those who were too dead to complete the rescue come to meet David and he asks after their welfare, those who were "of no use" move to exclude them from sharing the spoil: they allow that families should be reunited, but no more. David generously (re)interprets what had happened: the two hundred had had a valid job to do; they had stayed to mind the baggage. And he reminds his men that the victory had been their God's. David's ruling on that occasion was to endure as a solemn principle: base troops and frontline troops share and share alike. Just as he used to send spoil from his raids to Achish (27:9), so now at this crucial point he sends gifts to the elders of several towns in Judah.

So far so good: the story makes perfect sense on its own. Yet, alerted to the wider context by the presents sent at the end, we do well to look further about us as we reread the chapter. The David who was in the front line against the Amalekites was the same David who had been sent out of the Philistine battle line against Israel. He stood to benefit from the death of Saul. There was quite as much self-interest as noble generosity in David's rule that those who stayed behind could benefit with those who fought. What is more, Saul's kingship, too, had started with that king-to-be hiding among the baggage (10:22-23).

Ch. 31 This short chapter is the first shared by Samuel and Chronicles (1 Chronicles 10), and I suspect that it was also the beginning of what I call the "Book of Two Houses," the material that I find to have been the main source of the biblical books of Samuel-Kings and of Chronicles. Critics ask how the story of David could have begun so baldly — with an account of the demise of Saul and his sons, but no preceding account of his life. One answer is that the story of Samuel with which we began started quite as suddenly with the demise of the previous regime, of Eli and his sons. A strong case has been made that the shorter version preserved in 1 Chronicles 10 is also the more original of the two: not just in its greater brevity but also in its wording where that differs from 1 Samuel 31. The additions and alterations in Samuel will help us focus on what was important to the author of that book.

As far as the (shared) report goes, the battle is over as soon as it has begun. The Israelites fled before the Philistines, but only to be hacked down and lie slain (31:1). The storyteller is more interested in the fate of Saul and his house (vv. 2-6). Three sons were named at the end of the first report on his kingship (14:49). The eldest had already appeared with his father in chs. 13 and 14, and only Jonathan features in the stories that link Saul and David throughout the second half of 1 Samuel. His two brothers are named for the second time only in death; and one of them now bears a different name: no longer Ishvi but Abinadab. Each son's name can be read as a significant claim for his father: Jonathan means "Yahweh has gifted"; Malchishua, "the king is deliverance"; and Abinadab, "my father is noble or generous" (*nadab* is the opposite of *nabal*). We noted above (on 16:8) some resonances with another Abinadab. It is interesting that Samuel reports both Saul and Jesse as naming a son similarly to the ill-fated sons of both Aaron (Num 3:1-4) and Jeroboam (1 Kgs 14:1, 20).

"Found" by the archers, or at least by their arrows, Saul asks his armor bearer for a swift death. He expects humiliation at the hands of his enemies; and the fact that he scorns them as "the uncircumcised" adds to the suspicion that it is sexual mishandling he fears. His present armor bearer is no more willing than his predecessor (16:21) to lay hands on his master and run him through, yet he does not lack courage to follow his example. The Israelites nearby view the grim scene and evacuate their cities. The dead Saul loses his head and his armor as trophies, the armor dedicated to a temple, like Goliath's sword in Nob (21:9). Representatives from Jabesh, across the Jordan in Gilead, collect the royal bodies and bury them.

The Samuel version expands the territory lost by Israel to the Philistines, and only Samuel mentions Beth-shan in the Jordan valley as now controlled by the enemy. Chronicles has the royal bones buried under an oak, which has many suitable connections in stories of the OT. Samuel has changed the tree to a tamarisk, perhaps to link the burial of David's adversary to the scene at Gibeah where Saul had sought information against David (22:6). The author of Samuel has also spoiled the noble action of the men of Jabesh, who owed their right eyes to Saul (1 Samuel 11), by adding that they burned the royal bones before burial — not cremation but desecration (compare 1 Kgs 13:2; 2 Kgs 23:20; Amos 2:1).

2 Samuel

COMMENTARY

King David of Judah and the House of Saul (2 Samuel 1–4)

David does kill the messenger, an Amalekite who announces the death of Saul; then he leads lamentation for Saul and Jonathan. David is anointed king of Judah at Hebron. More members of Saul's family and entourage are killed, sometimes at the hands of David's men but never at his instigation.

Ch. 1 2 Samuel begins with the same formula as the books of Joshua and Judges, found elsewhere only in Gen 25:11. We are quickly reminded how distant David had been from the tragedy at Gilboa, and how preoccupied at the very time with activity proper to an Israelite leader — slaughtering Amalekites. His alibi is stressed: he had been at Ziklag (1:1-2) all the time it took to travel there from Gilboa (1 Sam 30:1). The messenger is described in exactly the same terms as his counterpart in 1 Sam 4:12 and as Hushai in 15:32. As with the report to Eli, which is very similarly structured, the most important news — here the deaths of Saul and Jonathan — is left till the end.

It is just possible to combine into one interlocking account the reports of Saul's death provided by the storyteller in 1 Samuel 31 and by the self-confessed Amalekite here, but it is probably not wise. I suspect that we readers should understand what David cannot know: that the messenger is offering him a self-serving fiction, or at best an embroidered version of the truth. However, at the least he was able to prove that he had immediate access to the body; for he was bearing to David Saul's royal insignia (1:10). There is immediate public lamentation among David's men, who mourn and fast till evening. Now Saul and Jonathan are mentioned first, before the unique pairing of the "people of Yahweh" and the "house of Israel."

David asks the messenger about his origins. Had his attention been distracted from the continuing story (1:8) after the report of the royal deaths (vv. 4-5)? Or was he simply cross-checking an important detail? After all, he himself had just returned from a raid on the Amalekites, and one of Saul's important campaigns had been against the same ancient foe (1 Samuel 15). As soon as he admits his race and his action, he loses the protection that belonged to a resident alien. His death is a further example of David propagating the doctrine that Yahweh's anointed must remain inviolate (24:6, 10; 26:9, 11, 16, 23). The Amalekite may or may not have done what he claimed, and all he claimed was to have administered the coup de grâce. But, for David's purposes, he had done what David had twice refrained from doing (1:16). And we know well that one person's mercy killing is another's murder.

Some elements of David's elegy have entered independently into our language. The repeated "How are the mighty fallen!" (1:19, 25, 27) contributes powerfully to the dirge, not least the way the final repetition follows so soon after the second, and itself leads so quickly to silence. "Tell it not in Gath" (v. 20): it adds to the grief and pain over loss and defeat to know that others will be celebrating as soon as they hear; and the song of the Philistine women will be very different from the erstwhile "Saul has killed his thousands" of the women of Israel. No wonder Gath was the first Philistine city in David's mind, given its associations with Goliath and Achish.

The word for "slain" or "pierced through" in this poem is not common in the many war stories of Samuel — in fact, it is common only in Ezekiel. But it has just been used in the story of Saul's death (1 Sam 31:1, 8), and it was the word for "run through" Philistines falling dead after Goliath's collapse (1 Sam 17:52). It is not easy to understand the development of 1 Sam 1:21. The hills where the tragedy happened are cursed for allowing it. Should they have provided a better shield? What is the link between the fruitful moisture they should no longer enjoy and the anointing oil? One ancient tradition offers the less surprising "the shield of Saul anointed with oil" at the end of the verse.

Son and father (1:22), father and son (v. 23): undivided in life or death — and yet, as soon as he sings these words, David does divide them. Saul will be lamented by Israel's women whom his successes have enriched and adorned. But Jonathan's is the loss David especially mourns. He lies pierced on the heights (v. 25): was he especially Israel's "glory" (v. 19)? Saul had been the boast of Israel's women, but there was something deeper in what held David and Jonathan together (v. 26). And what do the last words of v. 27 convey — that, with Saul and Jonathan gone, there can no longer be any pleasure or glory or security in arms? The lament was to be taught to the people of Judah; and it was inscribed in the book of the "straight" or "upright" (v. 18). The traditional Hebrew text, but not the ancient Greek translation, adds puzzlingly that the people of Judah were to be taught the bow (or Bow?). This was Jonathan's weapon: Was it also the name of the tune, or David's name for his song?

Ch. 2 "Inquired of Yahweh" is a formula used several other times of David consulting the Deity (1 Sam 23:2; 30:8; 2 Sam 5:19, 23), and always securing an answer — the only time that it is used of Saul (1 Sam 14:37) there is no communication. Usually in such questions "Shall I go up?" refers to a proposed attack, but here the intention seems more pacific. David's headquarters now move to Hebron from Ziklag (note the identical and almost unique phraseology in 1 Sam 27:3), and the men of Judah — remember how he had distributed Amalekite spoil as presents quite widely (1 Sam 30:26-31) — anoint him king. He immediately makes pointed overtures to that free Israelite city in northern Transjordan which had buried Saul.

East of the Jordan was also the area where the remnants of Saul's people were regrouping. 1 Samuel 31 had spoken only of Saul having three sons, now all dead. But there were others, and one of these was "made king" over several territories amounting to "all Israel" by Abner, Saul's relative and commander — "made king" (2 Sam 2:9), not "anointed king" (vv. 4, 7). At quite a late stage in the development of the text, the Hebrew text has distorted his name from Ishbaal (which the Greek preserves) to Ish-bosheth ("man of shame").

The forces of the two new kings meet at Gibeon, by a great pool (now excavated), near a great sanctuary (1 Kgs 3:1-15), close to the border between Benjamin (and so Israel) and Judah. The terms of Abner's challenge are tragically ironic given the bloody outcome. Was it really as "play" that the dozen youths from each side were to meet: for jousting or martial arts? If so, it went horribly wrong, with all twenty-four in interlocked death. A much bigger battle was set loose, and the forces of the challenger badly worsted.

Yet Abner did have two successes, against the flow of the battle. The first was in felling one of Joab's brothers. Seeing gazelle-swift Asahel dead stopped everyone else involved in their tracks, except for his brothers; they pursued Abner till he fell in with a crowd of Benjaminites who closed ranks around him. Then it was Abner's plea, "Shall the sword devour forever . . . ?" that brought an end to the internecine strife. His poignant words had their desired effect, yet Joab's reply (2:27) is far from clear. Does he mean: Had you not spoken now, we should have pursued you through the night till morning? Or: Had you not spoken the way you did this morning, none of this would have happened? David may have lost twelve of his youths and a few others, including a brother of Joab; but the losses to Saul's house were almost twenty times greater. As Abner was a relative of Saul, so Joab and family belonged to David's town of Bethlehem (v. 32).

Ch. 3 Abner may have brought to an end the fighting that day, but not to the war. And the progress of the larger struggle, like the fighting that broke out at Gibeon, was in David's favor. There is a significant little grammatical detail at the end of v. 1 which does not show up in English translation: while David on the stronger side is obviously singular, the Hebrew treats the weakening "house of Saul" as a plural, perhaps hinting at its disunity. David as a single force was being strengthened, not just in military victory but also at home with added wives and new sons. Strengthened — at least for the moment; it will be no accident that the first mention of Absalom among David's sons (v. 3) is immediately followed (vv. 6-11) by charges relating to a royal harem (see below on 2 Samuel 16). Note the claims made by David in some of their names: Amnon comes from the word used in a "sure" or "established" house; Absalom (ironically?) links "father" and "peace"; Adonijah and Shephatiah acknowledge Yahweh as "lord" and "judge."

The larger pattern of a strengthening house of David and weakening house of Saul is itself composed of smaller patterns. David had appealed to the people of Jabesh across in Gilead to show themselves strong after their king's death and, as we would say, "do the right thing" (2:7). Saul's chief lieutenant was himself becoming stronger. His new king makes a sexual complaint against him about the accuracy of which we are not informed. Scornfully, Abner neither accepts nor rejects the charge. Instead he insists that it is quite irrelevant, given his continuing loyalty to the wider house of Saul — loyalty albeit defined negatively, as not handing Ishbaal and Saul's house over to David. Now he swears by "God" to be the agent who brings about what Yahweh had sworn to David: kingship over Israel and Judah from north to south. Ishbaal is silenced.

Abner's embassy to the court at Hebron brings David a puzzling opening, "To whom does land belong?" — "land," not "the land" as often translated. What follows is the straightforward offer that in return for sworn terms by David he will deliver all Israel to him. Covenanted terms would be offered only if Abner brought with him to Hebron David's first wife. Abner of all people, just charged with unfaithful relations with a woman in Saul's harem, would understand the meaning of restoring Saul's daughter to David: establishing his legitimacy in and with Saul's family. David reminds the general how many mutilated Philistines the dynastic marriage had cost him. We might have supposed that the details of Abner's dealings with David, despite his sworn declaration, would remain unknown to Ishbaal. But it is the king who issues the demand that Paltiel return David's wife to him; Abner's involvement is restricted to sending the grieving man home.

We normally think of Judah and Israel as the two constituent bodies. However, Abner's discussions are first with the elders of (the rest of) Israel and then with Benjamin, Saul's own immediate people. At their conclusion, he is able to report to David that Israel and (or including) all of Benjamin recognize David as the agent of Yahweh in defending them from Philistine and all other foes. Able now to bring Michal and that news to David, Abner joins the Israelite visitors to Hebron and is received at a royal banquet (3:20): he does "see David's face" (v. 13). Abner's choice of words (v. 18) is interesting: he reports a divine promise which is spoken of nowhere else in these books. David may have been told by Yahweh to go and "save" Keilah from the Philistines (1 Sam 23:1-6), and Yahweh was to "save" David whenever he went against his enemies (8:6, 14). But what comes closest to what Abner says here is the divine commission to Samuel to anoint Saul (1 Sam 9:16). David would bring that to fulfillment.

News that Abner has been in his king's power and that David has let him "go in peace" is too much for Joab. Joab's absence from Hebron will have been convenient for the negotiations. But he has returned from action, his blood up, brimming with confidence. He tricks Abner into returning to Hebron and avenges his younger brother Asahel. David had not known what had happened (3:26); now he fears guilt by association (v. 28). He utters a comprehensive oath against the house of his commander, and presides at Abner's funeral in Hebron. His short elegy eulogizes Abner, but it does not praise him as his royal kinsmen had been praised (1:19-27): he had fallen as a fool *(nabal),* as a fool who did not look out for himself against the wicked. Yet his words and his public fast till evening assured his people that he had no complicity in the death. It was only privately that he praised Abner, admitted he could not cope with Joab and clan, and again cursed him.

Ch. 4 The house of Saul staggers on from tragedy to tragedy. Ishbaal, and indeed the rest of Israel, cannot have found it as easy as David's people to believe in David's innocence or that he had insufficient control of Joab. Our storyteller is very effective in putting similar but different situations or characters side by side and leaving us to consider the implications. With Abner gone, he now introduces two commanders of raiding bands (vv. 2-3), and we remember that Joab, while David's commander as Abner had been Saul's, had just come back from raiding when he dispatched Abner. The story pauses (v. 4) to tell us of one more descendant of Saul, a son of Jonathan, who had been saved but also maimed when taken into hiding.

The two fellow Benjaminite freebooters murder their lord, and take his head by night to Hebron by the much longer but less conspicuous Dead Sea coastal route. They present it to David using David's own language in the cave about Yahweh avenging him on Saul (1 Sam 24:12). But David will not accept them as Yahweh's agents, and he has them executed as common murderers. Was their own mutilation to pay for the removal of their king's head? The comparison implied in 2 Sam 4:11 is again instructive. Joab, though his deed had been wicked, had struck down the killer of his brother when fully conscious and in a public place: his fate was God's business (3:39). These scoundrels had assassinated an innocent man, not only in his own house but asleep on his bed: they were assuredly guilty.

The previous four chapters have developed the twin themes of the end of 1 Samuel. Fatally weakened by the death of the king and his three sons on Mt. Gilboa, the house of Saul disintegrates mortally through unequal strife between Abner and Judah and the deaths of Ishbaal and Abner. And David, though beneficiary of this collapse, remains untainted by it. He could not have been near Gilboa when Saul died. He was not witness to the fatal "play" between Joab's and Abner's lads. He led public mourning for Saul, Jonathan, and Abner; solemnly buried Ishbaal's head; and executed all those — except Joab — who proudly claimed responsibility for their deaths. This section marks the end of Saul and the innocence of David.

David, King of All Israel (2 Samuel 5–8)

Israel now anoints David at Hebron; he takes Jerusalem, and there is a campaign against the Philistines. The ark is brought to Jerusalem. Nathan assures David of divine support for two "houses": David's royal line and a temple in Jerusalem. David demonstrates his military preeminence over neighbors on all sides.

Ch. 5 The older form of the story, which we see expanded in Samuel, moved straight from the death and burial of Saul (1 Samuel 31) to Israel's invitation to David to be their next king (5:1-3). We still read that immediate connection in the alternative biblical elaboration of the Book of Two Houses (1 Chronicles 10–11). In that older, shorter story, which tells nothing of David at Hebron before the royal covenant, "Israel" was quite clearly the whole of Israel, including Judah. Many hearers of the old story had needed persuasion that David was uninvolved in the collapse of Saul's house. 2 Samuel 1–4 has provided that.

The Israelites present themselves to David as his "bone and flesh" (5:1). Just because that is a familiar part of our idiom too, it is worth pondering exactly what they are meaning. Are they simply protesting their interrelatedness before going on to note that David had been their commander when Saul was king (v. 2)? David, significantly, will quote these words of approach as he seeks restoration to his kingship after Absalom's death (19:13, 14). Laban uses them (Gen 29:14) in recognition of his nephew Jacob. And Abimelech employs them to bolster his approach to the people of Shechem (Judg 9:2).

Here I suspect the people are not making an approach on the basis of easy familiarity. They do not say "you are our bone and flesh," but "we are your bone and flesh" — and the unspoken implication is that they recognize David as the life of this corporate entity of Israel. This can be tested in the second discussion about Job between Satan and Yahweh. Yahweh observes that Job remains blameless after the loss of all his family. The tester retorts, "Touch his bone and his flesh . . ." — that is, after the loss of all his metaphorical bone and flesh, afflict also his own literal bone and flesh. Yahweh allows him so to touch Job, but insists that he "spare his life" (Job 2:3-6). The complete Job, and so too the complete Israel, is a composite of bone, flesh, and life.

David's first move as newly anointed king of Israel is against Jerusalem, only five miles north of his own town of Bethlehem, and occupied by the Jebusites. The old Book of Two Houses, if we may judge from what we still read in 1 Chr 11:4-9, dealt with the capture, occupation, and repair of the city in as few words as possible. Like Samuel, it implies that taking Jerusalem must have posed quite a challenge: whoever got there first would become his commander. Samuel will have omitted this detail about Joab because 2 Samuel 2–3 have already portrayed him as David's right hand. The details added in Samuel's longer version have fascinated and puzzled interpreters and historians.

One of these additions, a word usually understood here to mean "water shaft" (5:8), appears in just one other verse in the Bible (Ps 42:7), in a context speaking of the watery deeps. Commentators and archeologists have been encouraged to suppose that David's men entered Zion by means of one of the partly natural clefts through the karst rock which gave access to the spring below. But the detail Samuel is most concerned to add, it adds three times in 5:6 and 8 — "the blind and the lame." It is they who are to be specifically attacked, and they will not "enter the house." Which house? If our clues to this riddle should come from the books of Samuel themselves, then the allusions may be to the one blind person, Eli of the fallen priestly house (1 Sam 3:2; 4:15), and to the one lame person, Mephibosheth of the fallen royal house (2 Sam 4:4), of whom they tell. The future story of Jerusalem, in whichever of its two houses, will not belong to the families of Eli or of Saul.

David goes from strength to strength: the narrator says so (5:10), Hiram of Tyre reacts accordingly (v. 11), and David realizes it himself and attributes his success to Yahweh (v. 12). He expands his household (v. 13), yet we note that none of the eleven new sons has a name that celebrates Yahweh (as did two of the six born in Hebron, 3:2-5). The first military challenge to the new king comes from the Philistines. Good omens are received from Yahweh (5:19, 23), and the old enemy is comprehensively defeated (vv. 17-25). These are the last such consultations of the Deity reported in Samuel — and the first and last such in Chronicles (1 Chr 14:10, 14).

Ch. 6 This chapter of 2 Samuel reports, one immediately after the other (vv. 1-11 and 12-19), the two stages by which David brought the ark up to Jerusalem from the foothills to the west. The two parts of the journey were three months apart, and 1 Chronicles offers other information which we have already met in 2 Sam 5:11-12, 17-25, between its two expanded reports (13:1-14 and 15:1–16:3). It is not easy to reconstruct how the Book of Two Houses had ordered this information; but we can note that a house for David himself (5:11-12) and warfare come earlier in Samuel, whereas in Chronicles the ark of God has begun its journey toward Jerusalem before David accepts Tyrian help with his own residence. The anti-Philistine campaign, from Geba (or Gibeon) to Gezer, and the route of the ark belong to the same part of the country.

As we view the complete books of Samuel, we may be forgiven a little surprise that we read of David collecting the ark from Kiriath-jearim without a backward glance at what had gone before: no Eli, no Shiloh, no Philistines, no Dagon, no golden presentation tumors. Thirty chapters separate 1 Samuel 6 from 2 Samuel 6, but we are not helped to make the connection. Many scholars have been persuaded that 1 Samuel 4–6 and 2 Samuel 6 originally had a life of their own: together they constituted "The Ark Narrative." Others have cautioned, quite apart from the lack of backward links just noted, that 2 Samuel 6 breathes a rather different spirit from the earlier story. I would suggest paradoxically that 2 Samuel 6 is the earlier story, and that 1 Samuel 4–6 is a new preface to it — that is why our chapter has no knowledge of what went before.

Some features of the designation of the ark in these verses are worth mentioning. It is never called here "the ark of the covenant," although often elsewhere in the Bible, including some verses the Chronicler adds to the alternative version of this story (1 Chr 15:25-29; 16:6). The opening verses of the story (in both versions) call it "the ark of God" (6:2, 3, 6, 7). Only Samuel, but not Chronicles, calls it "the ark of Yahweh" (vv. 9, 10, 11). And the information that this divine ark bears the name of Yahweh who is seated over the cherubim (v. 2) seems to have been added rather clumsily to both versions. Where Yahweh is specifically rooted in the story is as the source of the anger that erupts fatally on Uzzah (is it because he simply touches the sacred ark? or because he faithlessly offers it human support?). The incident made David angry as well (v. 8), and then afraid to continue the project (v. 9).

The place name (6:8) that commemorates the worrying incident has an interesting double resonance. The Perez part of Perez-uzzah refers to the same sort of eruption or breakthrough that was celebrated in the previous chapter at Baal-perazim, where the Deity broke through the enemy like a flood (5:20). And the Uzzah part reminds us of the Hebrew word for might. The same word is used to describe the enthusiasm or strength of David's dancing (v. 14). This word *'oz* is often associated with Yahweh, and memorably with his ark in the psalm which celebrates David's efforts to find a dwelling place for the Almighty: "Arise, O Yahweh, and go to thy resting place, thou and the ark of thy might" (Ps 132:8). Baal-perazim is translated "Lord of breakthroughs." Perez-uzzah is ambiguous: it could, in the spirit of the psalm, suggest "Breakthrough of Might"; but it is understood in our story as "Breakthrough on Uzzah." The versions we read in Samuel and Chronicles were not the only biblical recollections of the arrival of the ark.

When David learned that the presence of the ark could mean blessing for Obed-edom as well as death for Uzzah, he returned to join it as it completed the journey to Jerusalem, with similar accompaniment of music and dancing (6:5, 14-15). Michal, Saul's daughter, despises David's dancing as she watches him enter the city. The ceremonies over which David presides in Jerusalem offer a foretaste of Solomon's at the completion of the temple: sacrifice, a blessing of the assembled people, and a feast. Only Samuel goes on to record the personal confrontation between Michal and David on his return home. To her jibe that his energetic dancing had in fact been shameless self-exposure before the servant women, he explains that he had been — and would go on — dancing for Yahweh. As for the servants, he will give them as much ground for pleasure as he will give her for contempt — and, when the story ends with the note that she remained childless, we can guess the nature of his boast.

Ch. 7 David approaches Nathan in embarrassment that he now has a house, but the ark only a tent. Nathan tells him to get on with what he had in mind, and assures him of divine support (vv. 1-3). Samuel has added to the older story the note that David now had rest from his enemies (v. 1b). Given what is to follow in 2 Samuel, the next campaign no later than the very next chapter, the addition is a little odd. Yet it is true that David has many more campaigns behind him in Samuel than in Chronicles or their shared source. Two features do link this opening with some of the other "rare" (both few and very important — cf. above on 1 Sam 3:1) prophetic narratives in the Book of Two Houses: particularly Micaiah summoned before Kings Ahab and Jehoshaphat, and Huldah consulted by representatives of King Josiah. The first is that each of these kings seeks advice from a prophet; in many other biblical stories, the prophet challenges a king. And the second shared feature is that each prophet gives his own opinion first, and this is then followed by a message from the Deity which they duly report.

The "word of Yahweh" comes to Nathan "by night"

(7:4) in a "vision" (v. 17). Yahweh has never done other than accompany moving Israel in a tent; he has never requested a house of any of the authorities before David. He has dealt with David's enemies in the past (v. 9), and will do so in the future (v. 11). He in fact will make for David a house (v. 11): a royal house in the sense of a royal family. His son and successor in that house will build a house for Yahweh (v. 13): a temple. However, after that quick mention, Yahweh returns (vv. 13b-16) to promises of the sure and everlasting establishment of David's house; there may be punishment, where appropriate, but the promise will never be revoked as happened with David's predecessor. It is of course from this early chapter in the Book of Two Houses that I have drawn my title for the source used so differently by Samuel-Kings and Chronicles. And it is typical of a speech of a great and generous royal or feudal master that much more is said about what he will do for you than of what you may be able to do for him.

David responds to the divine promises by going in and sitting before Yahweh, presumably entering the tent and placing himself before the ark. He is duly grateful: he praises his God, who is like no other (7:22), and recognizes the incomparability of his people Israel (vv. 23-24). He then dwells on what most concerns him, the promise to him of a (royal) house (vv. 25-29). Of the house that should be built for Yahweh, of the project with which this whole episode began, not another word is spoken. Yahweh said little about his own house (v. 13a), but for him that was appropriate. From David's self-centered response we may deduce that he had not even registered these few divine words.

Of course David's prayer has to be read at another level as well. It does not exist in and for itself as a report of the past. It is also part, and a very early part, of the whole Book of Two Houses. That book, like the books of Samuel-Kings and of Chronicles after it, told the intertwined stories of the houses of David and Yahweh in Jerusalem until both were destroyed by Babylon more than four hundred years later. Written and read after that collapse, the concentration in the prayer on whether David's house was really "confirmed — established — blessed — forever" represents a much more anguished searching of the divine heart than first appears.

Ch. 8 Just as "have cut off all your enemies" (7:9) could have corresponded to the Philistine campaign of 2 Sam 5:17-25, so it may be that in this chapter we find the correlate of the promise in Nathan's vision to give David rest from all his enemies (7:11). The Philistines are briefly mentioned again (8:1) as defeated; then the Moabites, equally briefly (v. 2); then the Syrians, or "Arameans," of different cities (vv. 3-8). Plunder was taken, and tribute was brought by some who had heard of his reputation (vv. 9-12). On his return south, David reduced Edom (vv. 13-14). All the victories are attributed to Yahweh, and the more precious metal objects from the spoil and tribute, the gold and silver, are dedicated to him. One of the functions of sanctuaries in the ancient world was to serve as banks or safe deposits: because of the aura of the place, no one would dare. . . . It is on the peoples, or armies, of Moab and Edom — those more closely related to Israel — that his enormities are practiced. How would David's behavior have been judged by Amos (see 1:3–2:3)? The reported massacre of two thirds of the Moabites (8:2 — but not mentioned in 1 Chr 18:2) comes as a particular surprise after what we read earlier about David sending his family there for safekeeping during his struggle with Saul (1 Sam 22:3-4).

This portion of the book ends (8:15-18) with the briefest of summaries of his rule at home. In Israel, whatever he did abroad, he "administered justice and equity." And he did so with the support of a few named officials. This report and the version in 1 Chr 18:14-17 are virtually identical, till they reach David's sons at the end. Samuel tells us that they were priests — surprisingly because both Zadok and Abiathar have already been listed in that role. For the Chronicler they were, literally, "first at the king's hand" (we might call such "the king's righthand men"); but that phrase is found only in the latest books of the Hebrew Bible. What wording had the Book of Two Houses used?

David in Public and Private (2 Samuel 9–12)

David is publicly solicitous, first for Jonathan's surviving son, then for a new king of Ammon. Hanun's misbehavior, however, leads to new campaigns east of the Jordan. David does not take the field for the final battle, but instead commits adultery at home in Jerusalem ("justice and equity"!) with the wife of one of his officers whom he then has killed at the front. Nathan voices the divine rebuke.

Ch. 9 Samuel here leaves the script in the Book of Two Houses (it will return in ch. 10) to pick up the theme of David and the (remnants of the) house of Saul. David is bound by his mutual undertakings with Jonathan. He had begged Jonathan's loyalty to their relationship when he thought it wise to absent himself from Saul's table (1 Sam 20:8). And Jonathan in turn obtained David's assurances for himself or his house (20:14, 15). We have already been informed (4:4) of one survivor, Mephibosheth, snatched to safety by his nurse, though also dropped and maimed in her haste. Saul's steward is summoned, and tells David that Jonathan's own son is a refugee in the area that might equally be called northeastern Israel or southern Syria. David has him brought to Jerusalem, and "makes him an offer he cannot refuse." He will restore to him all Saul's land — his private estates, not the land of Israel! And — or is it "but"? — he will be entertained at the king's table in Jerusalem. Restoration and/or house arrest? Unlike David, who was due to eat with Saul only on "high days and holidays," Mephibosheth would be his guest continually.

When Mephibosheth arrives, he prostrates himself before David. Such obeisance before another human is not often reported in these books — and, in fact, the only instance in the Book of Two Houses is that of Araunah the Jebusite before David (2 Sam 24:20). The echoes between the few relevant stories are all the more interesting. David had done obeisance, three times, to Mephibosheth's father before taking leave of Jonathan

(1 Sam 20:41); and then to his grandfather in the cave (24:8). On that occasion he had protested to Saul that he was an opponent unworthy of the king's attention: a dog already dead, or a flea alive but on its own. Mephibosheth repays the double family compliment: he abases himself again, and calls himself a dead dog (9:8). David can hear his own words returned to him as he chooses: Is Mephibosheth unworthy of the king's entertainment, or does he pose no threat?

Ziba is very well paid for doing the king's bidding. All Saul's lands are formally restored to his grandson. However, Ziba and his household will manage them to produce income for the owner — which he will not need. Ziba and his whole household become officially retainers of Mephibosheth. But one could equally say that Saul's estates are being milked to finance Ziba's clan's loyalty to David. The narrator ends (9:13b) as Ziba began (v. 3b), with a reference to the disability of Jonathan's son. Yet the storyteller does not simply repeat Ziba's expression; he replaces it with the word used three times in the account of David's takeover of Jerusalem. It was said there that David's very being hated the blind and the lame (5:8). David makes correct and solicitous arrangements for Mephibosheth; but any warmth in his feelings may be of an ugly sort.

Ch. 10 After 1 Samuel 11 (and 12:12), it is rather surprising to find David in apparently friendly relations with the house of Nahash. Of course the shorter source, like the Chronicler still, does not cause us to face such a problem. We may not have been certain when reading that earlier chapter in Samuel whether Nahash signified "snake," but there is no doubt that Hanun means — however ironic or inappropriate in this story — "gracious." David "does the right thing" in sending an embassy to "Ammon" on the death of a neighboring king. The new king's advisers interpret the visit as hostile; they may have been good David watchers. But their master makes the mistake of humiliating David's envoys. The Ammonites hire Syrian help, but the first joint force of Syrians and Ammonites is defeated by Joab and his brother. When the Syrians regroup in larger numbers, David takes to the field himself and forces them to an unequal peace.

There is no good single English translation of the Heb. *ḥesed* which David displays in 2 Samuel 9 and 10. It is not very common in the narrative books, and is most at home in the Psalms. Modern versions tend to oscillate between "loyalty" and "kindness." My "does the right thing" in the previous paragraph, though rather colloquial, tries to catch the sense of acting in a manner which will be seen as appropriate to the given relationship. In the Book of Two Houses, it is used three times of Yahweh (twice of his support of the house of David) and just once of a human (of David here to "Gracious"). It is a rich word, more readily used of divine than of human behavior. And it is this aspect of the word which is caught in both 1 Sam 20:14 and 2 Sam 9:3 — they talk of showing "the loyal love of Yahweh" or "the kindness of God" to the house of Saul.

Ch. 11 The story of David and Bathsheba and Uriah and Nathan is set within the report of a campaign against Ammon, which brings the previous episode to a close. If 2 Samuel 10 started with David sending an embassy of consolation to Rabbah of Ammon, this chapter starts with him sending Joab and an army. The military report begun in 11:1 is brought to a conclusion in 12:26-31. This same report is given, from start to finish, with a little less detail, in 1 Chr 20:1-3. Our Samuel storyteller has taken the opportunity of the army's absence while David remained in Jerusalem to tell a shameful tale of the king's adultery with the wife of one of his absent men and some of its consequences.

It was far from unusual for Joab to take the field himself. Although David's revenge on Ammon had to wait for "the turn of the year," when it was time for kings to wage war on each other, that did not in itself imply that David was shirking his responsibilities. The LXX of Samuel still preserves the original text of this opening verse, as does the Chronicler. But a Hebrew scribe has made a delicious pun on the Hebrew words for "kings" and "messengers," which are written and sound almost alike, so that the traditional Jewish text now reads, "At the time of the turn of the year, when messengers go out to battle, David sent Joab. . . ." That deliberate "mistake" alerts us to trouble coming.

Like many who add a story to an existing context, our narrator has used words from that context to build the new tale. The not-very-common temporal marker "at the time of [the turn of the year]" (11:1) is repeated in "at the time of [the evening]" (v. 2). And the word which dominates the whole new story is drawn from the old v. 1. No other chapter of the HB, however long, uses "send" more than seven times. This story uses it eleven times: it is a story about (the misuse of) authority.

David viewing Bathsheba is a scene that has fascinated — and been exploited by — storytellers, painters, film makers, and commentators. The text is brief and thus leaves many gaps to be filled by voyeuristic imagination. And even what it does say is no longer obvious to us. The beautiful woman the king saw from his roof was "bathing" (11:2): not necessarily taking a bath, not necessarily substantially naked, only certainly washing herself. It is a little later (v. 4) that we are told she had just had her monthly period, but the text does not explicitly link these two details. Some readers have supposed, but the story does not say, that the bathing was part of her ritual cleansing. The purpose of the king's first "sending" (v. 3) is ambiguous in Hebrew: it could mean either "and asked about the woman," or "and asked for the woman." Then, since no other subject is mentioned, I expect that it is David who says, "Is this not Bathsheba . . . ?" He is checking his own identification of a woman half-seen as darkness falls.

If the first sending was to check, the next one (11:4) is to take. The Hebrew "and she came to him" has suggested to some readers willing cooperation, while others see whatever she did as controlled by the taking. The LXX reads, "and he came to her," a familiar biblical euphemism for initiating intercourse. The following note about her menstrual uncleanness is puzzling, in part because the verb used of Bathsheba is always used elsewhere in the Bible of "consecration" for a duty or a sacred festival; and other verbs are used for ridding oneself of an impure state. "Consecrating herself from her uncleanness" is then a unique and odd expression. That apart, are we to suppose that she was not yet completely free of her ritual impurity? If so, David will have defiled himself ritually in addition to his criminal adulterous behavior.

Bathsheba does the next sending (11:5). Three sendings in the next short verse underscore that we are dealing with curt military orders obeyed without question. And that was no less true of Bathsheba's message: as a beautiful woman, she was sent for; pregnant with the king's child, she now had authority. David's questions to Uriah (v. 7) suggest that it is he who has been entrusted with the daily bulletin to the capital: no interest is expressed in his own welfare, only in the welfare of the commander, the army, and the course of the campaign. The Hebrew expression for the last of these gives one a jolt: translated literally, David asks, "And what is the peace of the war?"

No more explicit sending is done till 11:14. However, David makes every effort in the intervening verses to induce Uriah, sober or drunk, to visit his home and wife during his few days' leave in the city. Many readers have supposed that Uriah knew well, or at least may have strongly suspected, what David had done to his wife and was seeking to do to him. His eloquent retort (v. 11) may represent the code of a proud soldier, or the passion of a husband wronged by a man he cannot oppose. Either way, it is hard not to hear in his words some criticism of a king lying in his own house with wives, whether his own or others', while his commander and army are in the field. Uriah perhaps held that it was the season for kings literally to be themselves in the field.

Though never "sent" home, he is now sent back to Joab bearing his effective death certificate. Joab duly placed him in the most dangerous sector of the front, then schooled another messenger in a code that David would understand — indeed, which would pacify David if he complained about losses. David's last word back to Joab's messenger is to encourage or "strengthen" his commander. This is not a common word in these narrative books, but it is probably adapted from the closely related words "strong" and "good courage" in the previous chapter (10:11-12). Uriah's wife mourned her husband. When the due period was over, David sent for her again. This time we are told, not that he "took" her, but that he "gathered her to his house." The last gathering David did in Samuel was of all Israel for battle (10:17), and there was doubtless little choice about that. But the closest parallel may be in 1 Sam 14:52: "When Saul saw any mighty man, or any valiant man, he gathered him to himself." Bathsheba was added to a collection. And Yahweh was displeased.

Ch. 12 It has often been observed how little Yahweh is mentioned in 2 Samuel 9–20. The intervention here is all the more powerful. And it opens with the keyword of the previous chapter: Yahweh also has authority; he also "sends." But it is an unusual sending. Nathan does not first speak in Yahweh's name; that follows only in 12:7b. Nor, as in the case of many parables, does he use his own story to explore a problem already identified (many of Jesus' parables start: "Well, it is like this"). Instead he starts by entrapping the king through bringing to him a legal case for his opinion. His tale is all too believable. The king is rightly appalled.

Two points about David's angry judgment deserve comment. Translated literally, his opening comment runs: "As Yahweh lives, surely a son of death [death?] is the man who does this." There is plenty evidence that the biblical expressions "he is a son of death" or "man of death" correspond closely to our "he is a dead man." But the proximity in Nathan's words of "Yahweh's life" and "son of death" also urges tellingly that the behavior in question is the polar opposite of Yahweh's interests. What appears to be an oath is already implicitly a divine judgment. The second issue can be stated more briefly. We have already met in Samuel (2 Sam 3:39) an example of the common biblical (or simply human?) belief that punishment should be proportionate: "Yahweh requite the evildoer according to his evil." David holds that restoration should in this bad case be fourfold. Nathan's trap is sprung: David is the culprit.

Before David makes any response, Nathan changes into familiar prophetic gear (12:7) and speaks as Yahweh's messenger. Yahweh reviews what he has given David and done for him; he could have provided more, but David should not have done the taking. The correspondences between the story and the story-within-the-story are close, though not exact: the bosom in v. 3 is the poor man's, and in v. 8 the rich king's. David's crimes and punishments are interrelated, and as in his own judgment they will be manifold. *One* Uriah was eliminated; the sword will *never* leave David's house. *One* wife was taken; David's *many* wives will be taken forcibly by another. David acted *secretly;* he will be acted against *openly.* David now confesses that it was not only "sin" but sin "against Yahweh" (v. 13), a recurrent theme of these books. And Nathan promptly responds that Yahweh has removed the sin — but there will be punishment: the death of the expected child.

We are told nothing of the child other than that it became sick. David fasted prostrate for the seven days till it died. On its death he bathed and ate. As we have read on earlier occasions in Samuel, it was customary to fast when mourning. When his staff remark on his behavior, he explains the fasting and the weeping as supplication that Yahweh might be "gracious" to him (the same word as the name of Hanun, king of Ammon — 10:1). Fasting now will not bring the child back. They can be reunited, but only by David's going to join him. One reminiscence of ch. 10 is followed immediately by another: David comforting (this time his new wife) after a bereavement. Their next child is a son whom David names Solomon. Yahweh exercises authority for a second time in the story. David's actions with Bathsheba and Uriah had displeased Yahweh, so he sent Nathan. Their second child he loved, so he sent Nathan with instructions for a name — a name which not only means "beloved of Yahweh" but may also play on the name of David himself.

Joab did take encouragement (11:25), did renew his campaign against the Ammonites, and took the royal (quarter of the) capitol. Again he "sent" to David with a summons to the front, for David to complete the campaign himself. Perhaps Joab was wary about being deemed part of the "evil" that Yahweh was to raise against David out of his own house (12:11). David duly took command, was able himself to strip the king of his heavy gold crown, and spoiled and enslaved Rabbah and Ammon's other cities.

The Problem at the Heart of David's House (2 Samuel 13–18)

Absalom's sister Tamar is raped by their elder half-brother, who is then killed on Absalom's orders. Absalom goes into exile. David allows him back to court, but he foments rebellion and leads a march on Jerusalem from Hebron. David vacates his capital, crosses the Jordan out of his heartlands, but finally triumphs.

Ch. 13 The realization of Nathan's threat to David's house began to be unfolded immediately. David's eldest son became infatuated with the sister of his third son, but knew that to achieve anything would be a "marvel": something wonderful but impossible for anyone but God. Yet he was friendly with one of David's nephews who bore the name "Yahweh is noble [or generous]" and who had a reputation for "wisdom," a word which in Hebrew includes the meaning of (practical) skill. Jonadab recommended that he capitalize on his haggard appearance and request of the king a sick visit from his half-sister: she would have to spend some time with him preparing food. Jonadab cannot be accused of telling Amnon (how) to drink; but he certainly shows him the way to the fountain.

As the story develops complications, we recall that Tamar shares her name with Judah's wronged daughter-in-law in Genesis 38, married in turn to three of his sons (and there is only one other Tamar in the Bible, Absalom's daughter — 14:27). When Amnon grabs hold of her, and she replies in language used only in two nearby stories in Genesis both of which tell of mischief within families relating to women — "it is not done so in Israel" (34:7) or "in our place" (29:26) — we become more confident of the connection. But when a significant part of the action takes place as in the other Tamar story in connection with a sheep-shearing party away from home, coincidence has to be excluded. We can be sure that stories at the heart of the book of Genesis have provided key building blocks for this narrative. Readers or hearers of this tale would have been conscious of added menace as they noted these and other links with tragic stories from their past.

As with much of the dialogue in biblical narrative, as indeed in everyday conversation, we find Tamar's response to Amnon's move ambiguous. "Speak to the king; he will not withhold me from you" (13:13). Does she fully consent, but only provided Amnon's approach is regularized? Is she playing for time, expecting her father will refuse? Does she at least grudgingly consent, knowing that she is dealing with the king's eldest son? Be that as it may, she uses still more language with richly relevant associations. He should not do "churlish folly" — she charges him with behavior worthy of Nabal (1 Samuel 25) and spoken of in the remarkably similar story of Dinah (Gen 34:7): the very opposite of what should have been recommended by someone called Jo*nadab*. Where would she bring her "disgrace" — a rare word in biblical prose, but used also in Gen 30:23; 34:14 and in the story of Nabal (1 Sam 25:39).

Snatched love turned immediately to hatred for Amnon, and he ejected Tamar, protesting that this was an even greater wrong. With ashes on her head and her long robe torn, she made her wrong public. Ordered by her brother to keep silent, she stayed in his house "devastated." He himself ignored Amnon. Her father heard and was "very angry," but did nothing; perhaps he was mute in face of Nathan's threat. David begged off the shearing party (13:24-25) — earlier in his career, he, too, had begged an invitation (to Nabal's) and been refused (1 Sam 25:4-13). "Could Amnon come [in his place]?" David was rightly surprised at that approach. No, no — Absalom intended Amnon and all his other brothers!

News of a disaster within the royal family arrived in Jerusalem more quickly than any of the royal brothers themselves on their mules. But it was grossly exaggerated. However, even before their arrival could prove the rumor wrong, "wise" Jonadab had already briefed his king on what had happened and why. With a grim satisfaction that only he and we readers appreciate, he adds ambiguously that everything has worked out as he said (to Absalom, no less than to David). Absalom also fled, but in another direction: into exile among his mother's family in Syria (3:3). The very end of the chapter holds its own puzzles. Absalom's flight to Geshur is noted in both 13:37a and 38. And two points are made about David: that he mourned daily for his son (v. 37b) and that he missed Absalom, being comforted that Amnon was dead (v. 39). Are they another case of repetition? Which lost son was he mourning daily?

Ch. 14 Whatever the answer to that question, mourning provides the transition to the next narrative. And this new story resumes key elements from the openings to the previous two chapters. Just as Amnon's real sickness over his desire for Tamar becomes his feigned sickness in a plot suggested to him, so now David's real mourning becomes the woman's feigned mourning in a ruse put to her by Joab. Like Jonadab, the woman from Tekoa was "wise," though she was prepared to speak lines which were not her own. And like Nathan, who had also been given his words (in his case by Yahweh — 12:1, 7), she engaged the king's attention by appealing to him on a matter of justice. Her surviving son — like Cain, the Bible's first fratricide — should be protected, not executed: to take the life of the killer was to continue, and not to break, the vicious circle of blood guilt.

The king's first response is opaque: he will give orders (14:8). The woman persists: whatever he decides, let her take the blame. May he, God's representative on earth, remember Yahweh his God and prevent the avenger of blood from indulging in "destruction" (v. 11). This strong word appears just twice elsewhere in 2 Samuel: in David's charge against the Amalekite (1:14) of destroying the anointed of Yahweh, and in Yahweh's messenger moving to destroy Jerusalem (24:16). If something as awful as either of these is what is at stake, David is prepared to guarantee her son's well-being. Her response, "In speaking this way, the king is as if guilty," is more wordy than Nathan's "You are the man." Yet, though more deferentially expressed, the point is the same. Joab's trap is now sprung. And the courtly politeness continues, with the king compared to a divine messenger.

The king proves her point, discerning Joab's hand in her approach, and receives renewed compliments (14:18-20). Joab is given permission to summon Absalom, and seeks to interpret this as himself having secured royal favor (vv. 21-22). David passes over that in silence, but makes clear that Absalom's return to court in Jerusalem is physical only: he will live in his house, but he will not "see the king's face." The short paragraph (vv. 25-27) about his looks and his children, who include a second beautiful Tamar, makes us sure that that is not an end to the story. And, after two years, Absalom forces Joab into seeking an audience with the king which will in fact amount to a judicial appeal: better to be killed if found guilty. However, nothing is reported of anything said. Absalom does obeisance (in his means of approach, he does not presume to "see the king's face") and is kissed by his father. Actions like these may be natural and far from remarkable in themselves (Exod 18:7). However, the fact that the only precedent within Samuel for such an exchange of greetings is the ill-fated bond between David and Jonathan (1 Sam 20:41) does not bode well.

Ch. 15 The first part of this chapter offers glimpses of greater and lesser independence of Absalom from his father. There is no question in the text of his having to seek permission to have a chariot and horses and a few dozen attendants or bodyguards. And, perhaps even more surprising, no one stopped him from greeting suppliants making their way to a hoped-for audience with the king (vv. 1-6). Like many a usurper, he practiced or at least affected familiarity: like his father to him, he kissed the suppliants after stopping them from doing obeisance (v. 5). But two clues suggest to me that the narrator is offering a warning of trouble to come that we can easily fail to hear. In English, "stole the heart" (v. 6) is, I suspect, morally neutral. Yet the nearest parallel in the Hebrew of the Bible is in Gen 31:20, 26, where it is used of Jacob "cheating" Laban. Again there is only one parallel to Absalom's "your words are good and direct." This comes at the end of a short poem in Prov 24:23-26 that warns against partiality in judgment, and that poem itself immediately follows a warning against disobeying either God or the king. We have seen already that our storyteller expected readers to know the Jacob stories — perhaps also the Proverbs.

However, the next episode (15:7-12) suggests that Absalom did need permission to leave the Jerusalem district to go to Hebron. That would correspond to his having to clear with the court the invitation to Amnon and his brothers to attend his shearing feast, especially when David himself was not intending to come (13:23-27). We already noted that Mephibosheth was summoned to eat at the king's table "like one of the king's sons" (9:11) so that an eye could be kept on him — as it was on them. Only three other biblical contexts link the three words "pay," "vow" (15:7), and "sacrifices" (v. 12). And 1 Sam 1:21 and Jonah 1:16, like this passage, may all be drawing on the remaining one: the great thanksgiving psalm, Psalm 116 (especially vv. 17-18). Quite an entourage accompanied Absalom, from Jerusalem (15:11) and elsewhere. These "invited guests" are also part of a pattern. The term is used only in 1 Sam 9:13, 22; 1 Kgs 1:41, 49; and here — and, in the singular, in Esth 5:12. In Samuel and Kings, all three celebrations are associated with the designation of a king who will not last: Saul, Absalom, and Adonijah. The point is made explicit here (15:11), but it seems true of the other two parties also, that the invitees are simple "extras," unaware of what is to happen.

As far as space in the text is concerned, David capitulates remarkably quickly (15:13-14) on the news of popular support for Absalom, and vacates Jerusalem to spare it destruction. David may have known well that he had lost the favor of his people. Absalom's two hundred guests from Jerusalem must have accounted for most of its citizens of any substance. And the review over which David presides at the last house in Jerusalem, just short of the Kidron crossing, is significant: those of his military servants who are identified are all non-Israelite.

The Cherethites and Pelethites appear already in the Book of Two Houses (8:18, resumed in 20:23); they apparently constituted his bodyguard. In the David narratives, they are always paired (see also 2 Sam 20:7; 1 Kgs 1:38, 44). But we meet the Cherethites in three further biblical passages. The Egyptian ex-slave to an Amalekite reported to David that his erstwhile masters had raided the Cherethite Negeb (1 Sam 30:14), apparently not far from Ziklag (which David had been gifted by the Philistines). The only other mentions of Cherethites are in two pieces of prophetic poetry (Ezek 25:16; Zeph 2:5) which explicitly link them with Philistines; thus it is not unlikely that *Plty* (Pelethite) was simply an alternative spelling of *Plšty* (Philistine). Non-Israeli Palestinians in the intimate entourage of King David! Tell it not in Gath! Except that Gath was precisely where another element of the force loyal to him hailed from (15:19-22).

If his mercenary troops had a close link with David, so, too, did the ark (vv. 24-29). Borne by Levites and attended by the senior priests, the ark was also near the Kidron as all David's "people" passed by and over. The associations of that description are less with the recent arrival of the ark in Jerusalem in 2 Samuel 6, and more with Israel's arrival in the promised land in Joshua 3–4 — especially 4:11. That encourages us to view David's exit now as a formal quitting of the city of promise. If the "fords of the wilderness" (15:28) are in fact the Jordan fords, then the symbolism of this narrative is all the more powerful. But David would not have the ark leave the city: he hoped to return, and the priests' sons could be his spies. The end of the chapter introduces us to the other main agent he would leave behind, who slipped into the city just as the upstart was also entering. Hushai was destined to outclass David's former adviser. David's comment on the defection of Ahitophel may play on his name, "my brother is *tophel*." Hebrew words very similar to *tophel* mean "tasteless" and "whitewash"; both of these are effective symbols for ineffective folly.

Ch. 16 As he left Jerusalem to the northeast, moving into Benjaminite territory, it was hardly surprising that David's first encounters were with members of the house of Saul. Ziba's provisions (v. 1) are remarkably similar to those brought by Abigail (1 Sam 25:18). Like her, he is seeking favor from a David now again at bay. However, while she at least overtly was seeking to undo her husband's damage, he was set on causing damage to his master. David was not in any position to dispute the claim that revolt within his house might return the kingdom to the house of Saul, and duly rewarded Ziba for his "loyalty" (16:4). While Ziba used generosity to plant a lie, one of the relatives of his "master" abused David with stones and an uncivil version of the truth (vv. 5-8).

Abigail continues to hover in the background of the unfolding story: where she had praised David precisely for refraining from blood (1 Sam 25:26), Shimei reviles him as a man of blood — we will find a similar charge of blood guilt against the house of Saul itself in 21:1. Alongside "blood," the other currency used in the rival accounts of the two houses is a Hebrew word variously rendered "evil" or "ruin." David in the cave seeks to refute those who tell Saul, "David seeks your ruin" (1 Sam 24:9). David on the death of Abner expects Yahweh to "requite the evildoer according to his evil" (3:39). Shimei now gloats, seeing David "in his evil/ruin," suffering from the very principle he had himself stated. But Solomon, prompted by his dying father, has the last word (1 Kgs 2:8, 44).

A third element in the exchanges between the two houses — "Who is the dead dog?" — now has its third and final outing. What started as a soothing, self-deprecating remark by David (1 Sam 24:15), and was courteously repaid by Mephibosheth (9:8), is now turned into a taunt by Joab's hotheaded brother: the "dead dog" should suffer the further indignity of losing its head (16:9)! David turns Abishai's threat by proposing that the cursing may have been instigated by Yahweh.

The refreshment enjoyed by David at the Jordan is noted in a rare verb (16:14). This might be more literally rendered "took breath" or "received life," and is used just twice elsewhere in the Bible, both times of the recreation enjoyed on the sabbath — whether by one's household staff or by God himself (Exod 23:12; 31:17).

David's friend Hushai comes successfully through his first questioning by Absalom. His answers (16:18-19) are so much those of a smooth courtier that they might have excited suspicion. However, like many who are new to power, Absalom may have been only too pleased to hear the right answers. He was more concerned to have Ahithophel's counsel. The ten women left by David to look after his house would be taken to a tent pitched on its roof. No sooner said than done: Absalom was as one with his father in valuing Ahithophel's advice as highly as a consultation of the divine word. The drama enacted on the royal roof had demonstrated his potency and constituted Absalom's claim to mastery of the whole household. But Ahithophel's explanation is given in other terms, which we have met twice already; literally, "you have become smelly to your father." Israel insulted the Philistines by defeating one of their garrisons in Benjamin (1 Sam 13:4); Hanun, king of Ammon, insulted David and Israel by abusing ambassadors (10:6); and now Absalom mistreats his father's womenfolk. In each case the humiliating action is deliberate, the unpleasant result planned: a gauntlet thrown down.

Ch. 17 The sage counselor, after his first success with Absalom, does not just wait to be consulted but next offers to lead a force in immediate pursuit of an exhausted David (vv. 1-3). To Absalom and the elders this "seems right" (v. 4) — an expression used both in Samuel-Kings and in Chronicles, but only in portions additional to the Book of Two Houses. However, further advice is taken, this time from Hushai, and the story develops some resemblance to the account in the Book of Two Houses in which Ahab and Jehoshaphat are also planning a campaign in Transjordan (1 Kings 22 par. 2 Chronicles 18) — with court favorite Ahithophel in place of the four hundred court prophets ministering the word of Yahweh, and Hushai in place of critical Micaiah.

Hushai comes straight to the point: on this occasion the great man's advice has been faulty — David is too much the old campaigner to be so easily caught. Hushai nicely clashes the normally positive image of the mighty hero with the normally negative one of discontent or bitterness of spirit, illustrated by a she-bear deprived of her cubs, to produce the equivalent of our proverbial image of danger from an angry or wounded lion (17:8). In fact, even a lion-hearted hero will quail (v. 10). Nothing less than complete mobilization of all Israel will suffice. He wins the argument, and alerts his real master: David crosses the Jordan by night (v. 22). Hushai's rival has lost face, rides to his hometown, sends orders to his house, and hangs himself (v. 23). David bases himself in Mahanaim (vv. 24, 27), exactly where the remnants of the house of Saul had made their home after Saul's death and David's anointing at Hebron over Judah (2:8, 12, 29). More striking, he is sent provisions by three contributors who include his own erstwhile enemy in Rabbath Ammon (chs. 10–12) and Mephibosheth's erstwhile host in Lo-debar (9:4-5). Absalom, having replaced Joab as commander-in-chief by one of his relatives, camps nearby in Gilead.

Ch. 18 Perhaps David's insistence that he join the battle ("Go out with you I too most certainly will," v. 2) would have been more convincing had he taken personal command of one section of his forces. His troops appear to persuade him easily that they are more expendable than he, and that he will be of more help to them in the city than in the field (vv. 3-4). The commander joining his army in person has been stated in much more formal terms in 17:11, where Hushai counsels Absalom, "Your face will enter the battle." David had allowed Absalom to return to Jerusalem, but not to "see his face" (14:24); and he had warned Abner that without Michal he would not "see his face" (3:13). Hushai wanted Absalom to be hazarded, and so he persuaded him to enter the field by using the diplomatic speak for "you must be seen to lead *in person*."

Apart from his appointment of three commanders, David's only reported order-of-the-day concerned Absalom, who should be treated gently. David's men are often called "the people" in Hebrew, largely foreign mercenaries though they may have been. This makes 18:6 read rather strangely: "And the people went out into the field against Israel." The wording becomes even more curious if we are right to suppose that "the people," of whom "the forest consumed more than the sword" (v. 8), were Absalom's forces, not David's. Certainly the loss of Absalom himself to a tree was the most notable casualty. Absalom may have "chanced" to meet David's men (v. 9); however, it is no accident that the last case of "chance" we encountered was in 2 Sam 1:6, where one of his men "happened on" Saul just before his death.

The fellow who reported Absalom's plight to Joab speaks clearly over the centuries for so many in junior positions who are criticized by their seniors for not taking decisive action — and especially action against official "company policy": he would have been wrong whatever he did, and would have been held responsible (18:12-13). Joab himself has no such compunction, and with his bodyguards finishes off the upstart king. With Absalom dead, Joab called off the pursuit, so compounding his inversion of the gentle treatment commanded by David. The treatment of the corpse could, conveniently, be variously interpreted. On the one hand, it was flung unceremoniously into a great pit. On the other, Absalom had prepared himself a monument in Jerusalem, and he now did have the honor of a great cairn — in the depths of the forest.

David's eyes and ears (15:36-37) were also there. Ahimaaz wanted to be the first to bear the news to David, but Joab put him off with what seems like a lame excuse. The fact that it was the day the king's son died did not stop Joab from enlisting "the Cushite" for the same task. We are given no further information about this Ethiopian. After another excuse greeted his second attempt, Ahimaaz was lucky the third time — and then outran the Ethiopian. Seemingly Joab had no reason to doubt the youngster's discretion, for he avoids a straight answer to David's question about Absalom's fate. The Cushite, while diplomatic, says enough for David to understand, and to stagger into mourning.

David Restored to Jerusalem (2 Samuel 19–20)

David's return west of the Jordan highlights continuing sensitivity over Saul's remaining grandson, together with other difficulties between Judah and Israel, also focused on Benjamin.

Ch. 19 David's grief leads to one of the more poignant scenes in the book: his victorious men slinking about as if their victory, their defense of their king, should cause them shame (v. 3). David is caught between private grief (although all too publicly displayed) and public responsibility. Joab's scolding speech (vv. 5-7) is powerful; at its climax, tellingly, it is an appeal to David's self-interest. Attitudes throughout Israel were varied, but they included a movement to restore David (vv. 9-10). David apparently capitalizes on this, cleverly overstating "the talk of all Israel" in his appeal to Judah not to be backward in bringing him home. He also promises them a change of army commander; and that is enough to achieve unanimity in Judah, who issue a welcome not only to David but explicitly to all his (foreign) servants. In tune with the symbolism we detected in his departure (15:23-25), the appointed Jordan crossing place for David's return is at Gilgal. And those Benjaminites who first met him as he left Jerusalem hurry to join Judah's representatives to welcome his return west of the Jordan.

Shimei, the cursing stone thrower, is the first "northerner," or, more strictly, the first from the central highlands, to welcome the king home — after all, he has pardon to seek. He knows that he has sinned (19:20), but he pleads not to have to bear his guilt (v. 19). The David of the Book of Two Houses had already made an identical approach to Yahweh (we shall read it in 24:10). Abishai, who had failed to secure permission to remove Shimei's head when he was cursing, is again refused by David. At the time of his first request (16:10), the curses might have been Yahweh-inspired. Though events since have shown that unlikely, now is a time of celebration not to be spoiled (19:22). David gave Shimei not only his word, but even an oath (v. 23) — yet, on his deathbed, he was to demonstrate his real attitude to the curser and to make plain his belief that his oath was valid only till his death (1 Kgs 2:8-9).

As for Ziba, he has every reason to demonstrate gratitude. The narrator seems to take pleasure (19:17) in reminding us of the size of his (parasitic) household (9:12b). But this time Mephibosheth comes to meet David too (19:24-30), his very appearance evidence that he has been in mourning for the absent king. Though slandered by his steward, he has no further call on David's generosity — he must simply appeal to the divine scope of the king's wisdom. Apparently impatiently, David rules that Saul's property be divided between him and Ziba. Mephibosheth, having won the argument and not requiring personal income, has the last — and grandest — word (v. 30): "Your return is enough for me; let Ziba take all."

Barzillai had been David's principal host and supplier in Mahanaim (17:27-28). His business at the Jordan crossing was not to "build bridges" by greeting him but to escort him safely to the home side (19:31-40). David offers, not to have him "eat at his table," but — more generously — to provide for him in Jerusalem. The eighty-year-old protests that he is too old to enjoy the lifestyle of the palace, and requests the peace of his own home and family tomb. We suppose that Chimham, whom he recommends to David in his place, is his son.

It is far from easy to pinpoint exactly what groups are referred to in the last verses of this chapter (19:39-43). That of course is part of the essence of a civil war situation. As we noted when commenting on vv. 9-15, David himself seems to have been responsible for the tensions between Judah and Israel, bouncing his own kindred in Judah into not being left at the back of a movement which had in fact hardly started. That there is conflict between the claims of the majority (Israel in v. 43) and those of the activists (Judah) is too familiar in the politics of all peoples and all times to need explanation. But the differences in numbers have interesting resonances. Jeroboam is promised ten "tribes" of Israel at the end of Solomon's reign, as against one only for the house of David (1 Kgs 11:31-32 — see above on 1 Sam 11:8; 15:4).

Ch. 20 We know nothing of Bichri except for his son Sheba. They are not said to be related to Saul, but they are also from Benjamin. Sheba is the third character in 2 Samuel whose "happening" on a situation led quickly to his death. And yet the fate of each is no surprise: the first is an Amalekite (1:6, 8) and the second a royal rebel (18:9), while Sheba is identified at the outset as a scoundrel (20:1). Sheba sounds the trumpet as a rallying call, or at least to call for attention; he shouts out a version of what all Israel say to Rehoboam, according to the Book of Two Houses, when the negotiations at Shechem fail (1 Kgs 12:16 par. 2 Chr 10:16). All Israel do follow him, but the people of Judah "stick by" their king. David's only reported act on gaining Jerusalem and before dealing with Sheba is to provide for his ten concubines defiled by Absalom in the previous revolt. They are to be in "house arrest" till their death, but apparently comfortable — the same word, "provide," is used of the hospitality exchanged between David and Barzillai. There are not many "tens" in the story. Are these women a symbol of the Israelite majority (temporarily) alienated from the house of David? Is their confined "widowhood" till their death an image which anticipates the view from a Davidic perspective of northern Israel after Solomon: spoiled and fruitless till it existed no more?

The recently appointed army commander (19:12-13) is summoned, but, for some unexplained reason, he delays too long (20:4-5). David entrusts the pursuit of Sheba to Joab's brother, who takes Joab's and David's men. Joab was certainly one of the party: he personally assassinated Amasa at Gibeon, just north of Jerusalem. The precise location is given as "the great stone," which is probably a euphemism, or rather bland description, of a (once) sacred standing stone or altar associated with the "great high place" for which Gibeon was once famous (1 Kgs 3:4 — compare also Josh 24:26; 1 Sam 6:14-15; 14:33-35).

Abel, where Sheba was finally besieged, was one of Israel's northern border cities. Strong efforts were being made to reduce the city (20:15) when Joab was summoned to speak to a wise woman on the walls (vv. 16-17). Abel used to be a place where matters were brought to a conclusion by consultation — she does not say whether consultation of the Deity, or of wise people like herself. She is among the associates of the faithful in Israel (her terminology here is quite unique in the Bible), but he wants to destroy and swallow up. What she says he wants to destroy is ambiguous: either "city and mother in Israel," or "a city — and [one that is] a mother — in Israel" (an Israelite "metropolis").

But what is he to swallow up? We met the "heritage of God" in 2 Sam 14:16 in the mouth of another wise woman, that time from Tekoa. She told of her concern for the life of her son in a family feud — and her words had been put in her mouth by Joab (14:3). Another wise woman is now returning to Joab his own words. The other two contexts in Samuel suggest that the nation's land is "what Yahweh gives as a heritage" (1 Sam 26:19; 2 Sam 21:3). But from the mouth of a woman and mother we may expect instead, or as well, to hear an echo of Psalm 127. It speaks, in between mention of guarding the city (v. 1) and speaking with one's enemies in the gate (v. 5), of sons as "indeed a heritage from Yahweh" (v. 3). She reproaches Joab with his will to destroy mothers and children among his people.

When he explains that he wants only rebel Sheba, she promises his head, confident that she can negotiate that in the city (20:21-22a). The head duly thrown to Joab, he now sounds the trumpet (compare v. 1). Mention of Joab's return to the king in Jerusalem (v. 22b) leads naturally to a repetition, with some changes (vv. 23-26), of the information transcribed in 8:16-18 from the Book of Two Houses (v. 23 corresponds to 8:16a, 18a; the mention in v. 24a of Adoram in charge of the forced labor is new; v. 24b corresponds to 8:16b; v. 25 to 8:17, but reordered; and Ira as priest of David replaces David's sons as priests in 8:18b.

Supplication for the Land (2 Samuel 21–24)

Two powerful and mysterious stories bracket the closing chapters: Gibeon's revenge against the house of Saul, and David's tragic mistake in counting Israel. Next to them are miscellaneous notes about David's fighting men. And at the heart of these well-structured chapters are two poems which articulate the royal ideology.

Ch. 21 The wise, peace-seeking words of the woman in Abel ill prepare us for the chilling, tragic episode that follows. A three-year famine sets the scene; and famine was always interpreted as a divine punishment. David "sought Yahweh's face": a rare expression, unique here within Samuel — the best parallel being 1 Kgs 10:24, which talks of the whole earth paying court to Solomon to learn of his (divine) wisdom. Saul's putting the Gibeonites to death is not part of the Saul story we have been told in 1 Samuel, and so that omission is put right in v. 2 — Joshua 9 does tell the part of the story relating to Israel's oath to spare the people of Gibeon. Saul's attempt to finish them off is attributed to his zeal for Israel ("and Judah" is oddly added).

Expiation or appeasement — the same Hebrew word is translated both ways. The term is very rare in the narrative books of the Bible: the two occurrences in the books of Samuel put an interesting bracket around this extended preface to the story of Israel's kings. The bald message is given in 1 Sam 3:14 that the guilt of the house of Eli simply cannot be expiated. But David here puts a question that expects a positive answer, and takes responsibility for achieving it. He is seeking blessing for the "heritage of Yahweh" — in a famine, it little matters whether that means the land or its people. If expiation and appeasement translate one Hebrew word, so too zeal and jealousy another. The idea that Yahweh's "jealousy" can lead to punishment of an extended family over a few generations, for a crime as serious as idolatry, is familiar from the Ten Commandments. Saul's "zeal" (21:2) for Israel and against the Gibeon enclave was similarly uncompromising — and also their riposte.

The Gibeonites give a riddle as a response, which in a few words (21:4) is both diplomatic and firm. The first element is ambiguous and might have meant that there are no financial obligations between "us." But when they go on to say that they do not have the power to put to death in Israel, we realize that they meant that the problem between them could not be solved financially. David wants them to put their request clearly. They resume the seriousness of their complaint against Saul before asking that seven of his male descendants be put to death by some form of exposure — at Gibeon for, or before, Yahweh (vv. 5-6). Joshua 9 explains how the Gibeonites become Israel's temple servants, and 1 Kings 3 notes Gibeon as the great "high place" before Solomon built the Jerusalem temple, offered vast sacrifices, and received a night vision there. Given these associations, we might fairly suppose that it was also at Gibeon that David had sought divine wisdom (21:1). David had no question about handing them over — for him to lose further members of the house of Saul was hardly inconvenient. But Mephibosheth was exempt because of his oath to Jonathan.

Rizpah was the mother of two of the victims, all of them guilty only by (family) association. Her vigil over the many hot months from harvest to the first rains, protecting the corpses from dismemberment by carrion day and night, recalls Antigone's vigil over her dead brother immortalized by the Athenian tragedian Sophocles. Her piety came to David's attention and brought to his mind the hazardous care shown by men from Jabesh in Gilead for the corpses of Saul and Jonathan (1 Sam 31:11-13), exposed by the Philistines though for different reasons. He had them duly (re-)buried in the family tomb. The Hebrew puts "after that" at the very end of 21:14. The suggestion is that Yahweh was moved as much by the due burial of Saul and his family as by the awful price exacted by Gibeon.

The remainder of the chapter returns, in two short episodes, to military struggles between David's men and the Philistines — and particularly with vast individual opponents who were said to be descended from giants of an earlier age. Abishai had on one occasion to come to the aid of an exhausted David (21:16-17), and after that his men dared him to join them in battle. If he died, he would thereby "quench the lamp of Israel." The main interest in vv. 18-22 to readers of Samuel is not the unnamed giant with six digits on hands and feet — some of the (royal) Stuart family had a similar distinction — but rather that Goliath of Gath, killed by David in 1 Samuel 17, reappears among these giants. Here he is again killed by a Bethlehemite, this time called Elhanan. This second episode is also reported in 1 Chr 20:4-8, immediately after that book's version of the Ammonite campaign. It will have been drawn from the Book of Two Houses. A note in that source about one of several personal victories over Philistine giants will have been reattributed to David as his legend developed, with the end result in the famous story we earlier read. But the source was not simply deleted. And this will be testimony to the high regard in which the traditions of the Book of Two Houses were held.

Ch. 22 The Song of David is the first and longer of two poems close to the end of the books of Samuel. It has to be read as a poem in its own right, as well as part of the whole work. And realizing each of these aims is more interesting than we might at first expect — or more problematic, if one's taste is more anxious. As poetry it is distinctive in its context; it has to be read in its own right, as in a sense discontinuous with the prose context. And yet what is "its own right"? It is only one version of the poem — another, very similar, version can be found as Psalm 18. Then, in what sense is it part of Samuel? How far is it like the shorter songs we have already discussed, the Song of Hannah and the lament of David over Saul and Jonathan, which seem more immediately tied to their context? There are other long poems positioned just before the end of Genesis and of Deuteronomy. In what sense do Genesis 49, Deuteronomy 32–33, and 2 Samuel 22 and 23:1-7 belong to the individual books, and how far do they represent wider structures in the biblical canon? Of all these poems near the end of books, only our chapter is preserved in the book of Psalms.

2 Samuel 22 and Psalm 18 share the same prose introduction to this praise for victory. It is hardly insignificant that only Saul is named here out of all David's many enemies: for the books of Samuel, he was the principal foe. Twenty chapters have passed since David lamented Saul's death and that of his eldest son. But he has only just buried Saul and Jonathan, only just given his permission for the elimination of most of the survivors of his house. In the Book of Two Houses, in this case faithfully preserved in 1 Chronicles 10, Saul, like Elhanan and Goliath, had simply a walk-on part: he was killed, "and his three sons, and his whole house together" (10:6). But the authors of Samuel first build him into a major tragic character and then prolong the death agonies of his house. Many other psalms have a heading which ties the poem to a particular point in David's career. A group of four (52; 54; 57; and 59) introduce (what purport to be) cries of David for divine help when under pressure from Saul. Psalm 18 is in a different mode: it celebrates the stage at which David recognized that he had been given victory over all his enemies, not least Saul.

The song opens with repeated talk of God as a rock, refuge, and stronghold — and of the singer as delivered or saved (22:2-4). It was death that had threatened to entrammel the singer (vv. 5-6). The distress call was quickly answered — note how briefly that point is made (v. 7). Yahweh's display is in the form of a terrifying storm of thunder and lightning (vv. 8-16). He acts to deliver, because of his delight in the singer (vv. 17-20). The delight is explained in terms of the singer's activity (vv. 21-25) and of God's nature (vv. 26-31). Some of the language of the opening section reappears in vv. 32-43, which make plain that the form of defense used was attack. The opponents also cried to Yahweh, but they were not helped (v. 42). Explicit mention of the response of foreign nations (vv. 44-46) makes it possible, even likely, that the psalmist's enemies of the long previous section were from within. The final verses (vv. 47-51) return to language used at the beginning; but they now specify that, just as deliverance was provided from foes that included outsiders, so too praise for this rocklike God will be offered among the nations.

We have to wait till the very last words of the song to have the beneficiaries of the divine love identified as "David and his descendants forever." Historically speaking, the language of the song is very general. Indeed, on internal evidence, the only safe conclusion would be that it was composed for the use of a member or members of the Davidic house at some stage in its long history. Only the prose heading ties it to David himself, and it specifies the (principal) internal enemy as Saul. The book of Psalms as a whole, like the Book of Two Houses, is unconcerned with Saul: Saul in the headings of Psalms is in fact like Saul in the books of Samuel — a secondary narrative development.

The poem is readily comprehensible as an official hymn for use by or in the royal household on an occasion of special thanksgiving for deliverance. It is a feature of the royal ideology to portray the deity and his royal representative as sharing similar or overlapping characteristics. Some of the correspondences have become masked in translation. It is the same Hebrew word that is rendered "blameless" in vv. 24 and 26 and "perfect" in v. 31, but is lost in the rendering of the difficult v. 33. I would prefer "perfect" in each case. Indeed, the link between vv. 31 and 33 is closer in Hebrew, which uses the same word for "way/path."

That is a straightforward matter of report. But it is not easy to square the claims of the central sections (22:21-31) with the David about whom we have been reading in much of Samuel. "I was perfect before him, and I kept myself from guilt" (v. 24) reads strangely after David's confession of sin before Nathan (12:13). Did Yahweh's immediate removal of the sin restore David's perfection, or is there a tension here? There are other interesting connections and echoes. Yahweh as the psalmist's "lamp" (22:29) corresponds to David as "the lamp of Israel" (21:17). On the other hand, the synonymy of 22:26-27 contrasts with Joab's complaint against his king — "for love of those who hate you and for hatred of those who love you" (19:6).

Ch. 23 The second and much shorter "concluding" poem (vv. 1-7) also encapsulates the official royal ideology, but it is much more unusual. The surprise is not that the narrative introduction presents it briefly as "David's last words," while there is still a major episode to follow in ch. 24 — the situation of the blessings in Genesis 49 and Deuteronomy 33 is similar. The strangeness consists more in the formal poetic introduction (23:1b), which can be matched only in two oracles of the seer Balaam, reported in Num 24:3-9, 15-19. The first of these utters a rich blessing on Jacob/Israel; the second foresees in the distance a star/scepter rising from Jacob/Israel which will dominate the various peoples of Transjordan. In this third and far separated oracle, David claims by the authority of the God of Jacob/Israel to be that long foreseen king. This poem is the only point in the books of Samuel at which there is talk of a divine "covenant" with David (v. 5).

It is this biblical oracle which establishes the important postbiblical tradition of David's status as prophet, whereby many of the psalms became understood as prophetic oracles. And its suggestion at the end of 2 Samuel of a prophetic role for David corresponds in an interesting way to the presentation of Samuel the prophet as something of a royal figure in the early chapters of 1 Samuel.

The remainder of this chapter offers a list of David's principal military men. Most of this material in Samuel is found also in 1 Chronicles 11, just after the report in that book of David's takeover of Jerusalem. The Chronicler's list is some 60 percent longer and is immediately followed by a long account, not represented at all in Samuel, of support David received in men and supplies from each of the tribes while he was still in Ziklag. Although here and there 1 Chr 11:11-41 may have preserved a name better than Samuel, we do well to prefer the shorter version here in Samuel. It is sometimes hard to keep track of the arithmetic, but the text broadly maintains a distinction between three superheroes, of whom some exploits are mentioned (23:8-12), and thirty heroes who are simply listed (vv. 24-39). Yet exploits are also reported of Abishai and Benaiah, who, though leaders of the thirty, did not attain the level of the three (vv. 19, 23). We should note that the Samuel list ends with Uriah the Hittite; as with Goliath and Saul, his is a name we already know far better from the much fuller story we have earlier read.

The most famous and poignant story in this section is set immediately after the three superheroes have been introduced (23:13-17). Yet it is attributed to three heroes of the thirty. Since these remain unnamed, the matter of their relationship to the surrounding lists cannot be settled. In any case, the action is more striking than the actors. David is in the Cave of Adullam — this mention of the cave in a story drawn from the Book of Two Houses may be the source on which 1 Sam 22:1-2 draws — but prevented by a Philistine garrison from entering Bethlehem, not many miles above. Like many an exile, he longs for nothing more than the familiar water of home, but he is incautious enough to say so in the presence of daring and devoted heroes. When his dream actually materialized, he would not even drink the water but poured it out as a solemn libation. It was not for drinking, for it was men's blood — and all blood had to be poured on the soil (Deut 12:16, 23-25). Water that is men's blood is powerfully suggestive of bread that is a man's body and wine that is his blood. However, in the context of the Christian eucharistic communion, the command is to eat and to drink remembering the cost — not to abstain and treat as too holy.

Ch. 24 The books of Samuel close with a chapter that is enigmatic and at the same time very rich in its biblical associations. The parallel account in 1 Chronicles 21 of David's census of the people and its aftermath is both shorter and longer at several points. I find it best to suppose that the original report in the Book of Two Houses was shorter, and was differently expanded and developed in Samuel and Chronicles.

Our problems as readers begin at the beginning: "Again Yahweh's anger was kindled against Israel." This expression has been used only once before in Samuel — of Yahweh bursting out on the wretched Uzzah (6:7). Is Samuel deliberately linking these rather distant episodes? And, if so, why the anger now? If we should look beyond the precise wording, this renewal of anger may resume the more recently reported divine displeasure manifested in the three-year famine (21:1). Israel, for some reason, is in the divine "sights," and the incitement of David to conduct a census is the means of realizing it. The Chronicler starts the story differently: "Satan/the accuser stood up against Israel. . . ." In both versions, there is a small cluster of neighboring and uncommon words that share the first two consonants of *s-t-n,* and that persuades me that the Chronicler is following the original here and that the divine "anger" we meet in Samuel has suppressed a partly independent divine figure.

It is Joab rather than David who questions the initiative: the king's interest in numbers is proper, but there is still something wrong about his instructions. Joab distances himself somewhat from Yahweh, calling him David's God, and hopes ominously that, if there is an increase in population, David will be able to see it. Solomon in his vision more circumspectly states that he is among a people who cannot be counted or numbered (1 Kgs 3:8). We have never met Joab so hesitant in the face of action. However, he is under orders, and the count goes ahead throughout the whole land. We (modern) readers learn only at the end what David and Joab had known at the outset, that the count was of men of military age (24:9).

Presumably David had understood Joab's reservations when he overruled him, but it was only after the census was complete that he took his error to heart (v. 10). He confessed to sin and folly, and asked Yahweh to take away his guilt. We have found the terms of this confession, drawn here from the Book of Two Houses, anticipated by the authors of Samuel in the confessions of Saul to David (1 Sam 26:21) and David to Nathan (2 Sam 12:13). The divine answer comes in the morning via Gad, his seer. There is no explicit divine response to the terms of his confession, simply a choice between famine, war, and plague as punishment. David opts for the first or third — "better the 'devil' you know" — hoping desperately for greater mercy from God than from a human foe.

Pestilence is Yahweh's choice, and it claims some 5 percent of those counted. When the messenger of death reaches Jerusalem, Yahweh for his part relents and calls a halt; and David on his side asks that the (innocent) people be spared and only he (the guilty party) bear the guilt. The divine response, again implicit, comes through Gad: erect an altar on Araunah's threshing floor. Both the place and the means for sacrifice are offered free, but the offers are refused: sacrifice should cost. Yahweh responds, and the plague is averted, not just halted.

There are many interesting echoes of this narrative in other biblical stories. It shares a whole cluster of rare Hebrew words with the prose prologue to Job (1–2), not just the common theme of the testing of the hero. But the resonances in the books of Kings and Chronicles, and so originally in the Book of Two Houses, may be more significant. The divine plague, as in the revolt of Israel on the death of Solomon and as with the Assyrian army in the time of Hezekiah, stopped short of Jerusalem. Divine incitement to disastrous behavior is mirrored in the story of Ahab and Jehoshaphat and their campaign in Transjordan.

The Chronicler makes explicit (22:1) what many readers of Samuel-Kings find implicit in this story and its wider context: that Araunah's threshing floor is the site of the temple and altar Solomon constructed. In addition to occupying the city for Israel, David is credited with two vital religious preparations: moving the ark to Jerusalem, and acquiring the site of the (future) temple where it would be lodged. The first of these resulted in the dread death of Uzzah, while the second was associated with a terrible plague. We should not be surprised that the Samuel version of the census may have alluded to the earlier story when it warned us at the outset that we would find in 2 Samuel 24 a second kindling of divine anger.

But what was wrong with counting? Why was it sin and folly for a leader to know how large a force could be mustered? Why did David fall for a proposal which Joab found immediately problematic? Does divine entrapment simply blind one to normal reason? Several campaign stories in the Bible make plain that the armies of Israel were simply human "extras" to a divine fighting force. Their number did not matter; indeed, the story of Gideon and the Midianites suggests "the fewer the better" (Judges 7). Additional material (in 1 Chronicles 27) develops the issue after a listing of monthly divisions of labor, with an odd reversal of roles: "David did not count those below twenty years of age, for Yahweh had promised to make Israel as numerous as the stars of heaven. Joab . . . began to count them, but did not finish; yet wrath came upon Israel for this" (27:23-24). To count Israel was to lack trust in the divine promises.

Afterword

David's actions, and Saul's too, are described at greater length and in greater detail than those of any other character in the HB. The Moses books, Exodus-Deuteronomy, may take up more space, but through much of them Moses simply receives the divine will and transmits it to his people. His standing is all the higher, but our knowledge of him is less. With David and Saul, their families, and their lieutenants, we are dealing with all-too-recognizable characters of flesh and blood. Familiar as flesh and blood they may be, but that also means as difficult to fathom and comprehend as complex humans are.

Reading literature like this is not unlike reading life and society: making sense of it is a matter of picking up the appropriate clues. I hope to develop the approach I have sketched above in a larger commentary in the future. The A-B-C-C-B-A structure of the last four chapters (see the introduction above to 2 Samuel 21–24) is a particularly obvious example of patterning. If we have not noted others like it before, it should encourage us to reread the books of Samuel to check what we have missed at a first reading. At several points I have detected hints left by the author, such as rare wording, which suggest that we should ponder two or three passages together. Mostly these were other passages within Samuel, even if quite widely separated in the text. However, some of the significant links are with other biblical books; I have noted interesting connections with Genesis (the two

Tamars, most obviously), Psalms (such as 127 and 132), Proverbs, as well as the surrounding narrative books.

My suggestions for reading Samuel should be tested by the interested reader against the text of Samuel, of course, but also against other currently available English studies. A selection of these is listed below. Among the commentaries, mention is made of four further studies. My own *Kings without Privilege* explains why I prefer to interpret the obvious relatedness of Samuel-Kings and Chronicles in terms of a source common to both; and my *Samuel at the Threshold* develops a number of the suggestions made in this commentary about the interpretation of that book. The two volumes by Robert Polzin and the massive four-volume study by Jan Fokkelman demonstrate impressively (but differently) what can be achieved by much more minute attention to possible clues within the books of Samuel as how to read them. And the historical/biographical reconstructions of King David by Baruch Halpern and Steven McKenzie nicely demonstrate how different presentations are possible of the king about whom the Bible tells us most.

I have said little about the theological significance of the books of Samuel. They contain very little explicit probing of the Deity. Perhaps the least ambiguous comments are offered in the poems at the beginning and the end: the Songs of Hannah and of David, and David's "Last Words"; yet we noted just above (on the end of 2 Samuel 22 and the beginning of 2 Samuel 23) how these poems stand in some tension with the prose narratives in which they are now embedded. As we saw, the question of how Yahweh will respond to "sin," "guilt," and "folly" directed against himself is asked but not answered; and we are left pondering whether David's final folly was the ultimate cause of his family's demise. The return of the ark from Philistine hands without human aid may hint where hope should be focused after the collapse of both of Jerusalem's houses at the hands of Babylon.

But there are deeper and darker themes. Samuel may start the story, seek out and anoint both Saul and David, and (at least in Hebrew tradition) give his name to the book; but he plays an ambiguous role, and his divine master no less. And so, without reservation, my first commendation for further reading is Cheryl Exum's haunting and compelling account of Saul, Jephthah (in the book of Judges), the house of Saul, and David in terms of tragedy, both ancient and modern.

Bibliography. Ackroyd, P. R. 1971 and 1977, *1 Samuel* and *2 Samuel,* CBC on the NEB, Cambridge: Cambridge University • Anderson, A. A. 1989, *2 Samuel,* WBC, Waco, Tex.: Word • Auld, A. G. 1994, *Kings without Privilege,* Edinburgh: T&T Clark • Auld, A. G. 2003, *Samuel at the Threshold: Collected Essays,* Aldershot: Ashgate • Brueggemann, W. 1990, *First and Second Samuel,* Interpretation, Atlanta: John Knox • Exum, J. C. 1992, *Tragedy and Biblical Narrative,* Cambridge: Cambridge University • Fokkelman, J. P. 1981, 1986, 1990, and 1993, *Narrative Art and Poetry in the Books of Samuel,* 4 vols., Assen: Van Gorcum • Gordon, R. P. 1986, *1 and 2 Samuel,* Exeter, U.K.: Paternoster • Gordon, R. P. 1984, *1-2 Samuel,* Old Testament Guides, Sheffield: Sheffield Academic • Halpern, B. 2001, *David's Secret Demons: Messiah, Murderer, Traitor, King,* Grand Rapids: Eerdmans • Jobling, D. 1998, *1 Samuel,* Berit Olam, Collegeville, Minn.: Liturgical Press • Klein, R. W. 1983, *1 Samuel,* WBC, Waco, Tex.: Word • McCarter, P. K. 1980, *1 Samuel* and *2 Samuel,* AB, Garden City, N.Y.: Doubleday • McKenzie, S. L. 2000, *King David: A Biography,* Oxford and New York: Oxford University • Polzin, R. 1989 and 1993, *Samuel and the Deuteronomist* and *David and the Deuteronomist,* New York: Harper & Row and Bloomington: Indiana University.

1 and 2 Kings

Roger Tomes

INTRODUCTION

1 and 2 Kings and the Former Prophets. Although in the Septuagint (LXX) 1 and 2 Kings formed two books (under the titles 3 and 4 Kingdoms), in the Hebrew Bible (HB) they originally formed a single book, the fourth of the Former Prophets (Joshua, Judges, Samuel, and Kings). It was composed according to a common plan, an account of the reigns of each of the kings of Israel and Judah. It may not originally have been intended as a continuation of the other Former Prophets, but it has at least been edited and read as such. There are frequent references back to the reign of David, including the promises made to him (2 Sam 7:1-17; cf. 1 Kgs 8:14-26) and "the matter of Uriah the Hittite" (2 Samuel 11; cf. 1 Kgs 15:5). The fulfillment of the sentence on the house of Eli is noted (1 Sam 2:27-36; 3:11-14; cf. 1 Kgs 2:27); and the circumstances of the rebuilding of Jericho are treated as a fulfillment of a prediction by Joshua (Josh 6:26; cf. 1 Kgs 16:34). In the Lucianic recension of the LXX, 3 Kingdoms (= 1 Kings) begins at what we know as 2:12: this is probably not evidence that any Hebrew mss. divided Samuel from Kings at this point, but a recognition by readers that 1 Kgs 1:1–2:11 is as much a conclusion to the story told in Samuel as a beginning to the story told in Kings.

The Text: Hebrew and Greek. The text translated in the English versions is the Masoretic Hebrew text. The LXX has some significant departures from the MT. After 1 Kgs 2:35 and 46 scattered pieces of information are brought together to illustrate the theme of Solomon's wisdom; the account of Solomon's building projects in 1 Kgs 6:1–7:51 is rearranged so that the account of the building of the temple is not interrupted by the description of other buildings; the account of the division of the kingdom in 1 Kgs 11:26–12:24 is followed by an alternative version; and 1 Kings 20 and 21 are transposed. These variations are probably in the main editorial; it is unlikely that they represent a superior Hebrew original. (There are few fragments from Qumran, and none that supports the LXX against the MT.)

A Deuteronomistic Compilation. The story of how 1 and 2 Kings were compiled is a matter of conjecture, but certain reasonable deductions can be made from the text itself. The fundamental structure is a summary account of the reign of each king: when he began to reign; sometimes how old he was at his accession; how long he reigned; in the case of the kings of Judah who his mother was; a verdict on his reign; where further information could be found; how he met his death and where he was buried; and who succeeded him. The verdict on each reign is always confined to the king's religious policy. If he encouraged the worship of foreign gods or even tolerated any cultic activities outside Jerusalem, he is judged to have "done evil in the sight of Yahweh." Only if he carried out religious reforms is he judged to have "done what was right in the sight of Yahweh." This focus on religious practice, and in particular on the unacceptability of worship outside Jerusalem, suggests the standpoint of Deuteronomy's law of one sanctuary (Deut 12:1-14), and hence the compilation of 1 and 2 Kings is attributed to a member or members of the Deuteronomistic school. This supposition is supported by the prominence given to the discovery of "the book of the law" in Josiah's reign and the congruity of his reforms with the injunctions of Deuteronomy (2 Kgs 22:1–23:25); by the Deuteronomistic language of some programmatic passages (1 Kgs 9:1-9; 2 Kgs 17:7-18); and by some more or less direct quotations from Deuteronomy (1 Kgs 11:2; 2 Kgs 14:6).

A Variety of Sources. This framework is filled out from a variety of sources. Three are mentioned: "the book of the acts of Solomon" (1 Kgs 11:41), "the book of the annals of the kings of Israel" (1 Kgs 14:19, etc.), and "the book of the annals of the kings of Judah" (1 Kgs 14:29, etc.). Many of the details of Solomon's reign and the briefer notices of events in other reigns are probably taken from these sources. But it is likely that other sources have been used as well, particularly for the longer accounts. 2 Kgs 18:17–20:19, for example, since it is almost identical with Isaiah 36–39, could well be taken from the book of Isaiah at some stage in its development, or from some earlier collection of Isaiah legends. The stories of Elijah and Elisha are unlikely to have come from official royal records: the kings are sometimes anonymous (2 Kgs 5:5; 6:9, 26) and the stories often critical of them (1 Kgs 21:1-16; 2 Kgs 1:3; 3:13).

A Variety of Material. Whatever the nature of the sources used, the material is very varied in character: lists of officials (1 Kgs 4:1-19), popular legends (1 Kgs 3:16-28; 10:1-13), detailed description of the temple (1 Kgs 6:1–7:51), a prayer at the dedication of the temple (1 Kgs 8:22-53), long narratives relating significant political events (1 Kgs 1; 12:1-20; 2 Kgs 9:1–10:27), and reflection on political events (2 Kgs 17:7-23).

Date of Compilation. The books of Kings must of course have been completed after the last event recorded in them: the release from prison of Jehoiachin in the thirty-seventh year of his exile, that is, 560 BC. However the process of compilation may have begun earlier: one view is that a "first edition" was produced in the time of Josiah, making the discovery of the lawbook and the subsequent reforms the climax of the story, and that it was later supplemented with the account of the events leading up to the fall of Jerusalem and the fall of the city itself. Much depends on the interpretation of passages which seem to betray no knowledge of those events: the ark and its poles are said to be "there [in the temple] to this day" (1 Kgs 8:8); Solomon's prayer, while it envisages the possibility of exile (1 Kgs 8:46-53), assumes that the temple will still be standing (v. 48); the promise that David would always have descendants on the throne of Judah (2 Sam 7:12-16) is periodically repeated, sometimes indeed conditionally (1 Kgs 9:1-9; 2 Kgs 21:7-8) but sometimes without any indication that there were conditions attached or that events had put it in doubt (1 Kgs 11:36; 2 Kgs 8:19). It may be that the final compilers decided to leave their sources and the earlier stages of compilation as they found them, believing that there was some value in keeping even the misplaced hopes of earlier generations on record, and relying on their own occasional commentary (e.g., 1 Kgs 9:1-9; 2 Kgs 17:7-23; 21:10-15) to put them in perspective in the light of subsequent events. Some compilation of material from northern Israel probably took place before the fall of Samaria: 2 Kgs 13:23; 14:27 do not seem to know that this would happen.

1 and 2 Kings as History. The overall category into which the books of Kings fall is undoubtedly that of history. They represent a considerable achievement. That they have produced a reasonably accurate chronicle of the reigns of the kings of Israel and Judah over nearly four centuries has never been seriously challenged, and one cannot fail to admire the skill with which for much of that period the histories of the two kingdoms have been intertwined. This is not to say that the chronology they provide is completely accurate: some adjustment is needed both to make the figures self-consistent and to relate them to the dates which sources outside the Bible provide. But there is no comparable continuous account over such a long period from anywhere else in the ancient world. No doubt the material used is not all of equal value or reliability as history. For example, modern readers will always have problems with stories (such as that of Elijah on Carmel) which rely heavily on miracle; one story about Solomon (1 Kgs 3:16-28) not only has a more realistic counterpart later in Kings (2 Kgs 6:26-31) but also has parallels in other literatures; there is no archeological confirmation of Israel's legendary prosperity in the time of Solomon.

Comparison with 2 Chronicles. As with all historical writing, it is necessary to allow for the historians' bias. Ideally one should be in a position to compare 1 and 2 Kings with other accounts of the same events, but this is rarely possible. There is of course a parallel history in 2 Chronicles, but this has generally been supposed to be dependent on 1 and 2 Kings for its outline. The comparison favors Kings. Not only does the Chronicler ignore the history of the Northern Kingdom almost entirely, but it is difficult to avoid the impression that he is often rewriting history as he would have liked it to be, for example, in giving David a major role in the plan to build the temple, in ascribing far-reaching reforms to the time of Hezekiah, and in postulating repentance on the part of Manasseh to account for his long reign. Only occasionally does the Chronicler appear to preserve important material not available to the compilers of Kings (e.g., the account of Uzziah/Azariah in 2 Chr 26:1-15).

Other Sources for the Period. Nonbiblical sources offer material for the period which is useful in a number of ways. Some events related in Kings, such as the fall of Samaria (2 Kgs 17:1-6; 18:9-12) and Sennacherib's invasion of Judah (2 Kgs 18:13–19:37), are also related in the annals and inscriptions of the Assyrian kings. We know of other events in which Israelite kings were involved, such as Ahab's participation in the battle of Qarqar and Jehu's submission to Shalmaneser III, only from Assyrian sources. (See the commentary on 1 Kgs 16:15-34 and 2 Kings 9–10.) The accounts of relations between Israel and Moab (2 Kgs 1:1; 3:4-27) can be compared with the inscription of Mesha, king of Moab. The discovery of the Lachish letters gives some insight into the situation in Judah outside Jerusalem in 587 BC.

Not a Social History. The extrabiblical evidence does not give grounds for any radical distrust of the history in 1 and 2 Kings. We may regret, however, that it is a history of the kings and not a social history of the whole people. To some extent this deficiency can be made up through a study of settlement patterns (e.g., Jamieson-Drake 1991); through information gleaned from the Samarian ostraca (see the commentary on 2 Kings 14); above all, perhaps, from the allusions the prophets make to social, economic, and religious conditions in their time. Even in 1 and 2 Kings some of the stories about Elijah and Elisha are informative about social conditions.

Political Factors Underplayed. Another reservation we may have about the historical value of the history in 1 and 2 Kings is that it explains events in theological terms, ignoring political factors. "In those days Yahweh began to send King Rezin of Aram and Pekah son of Remaliah against Judah" (2 Kgs 15:37). But what were their conscious motives? Most commentators say that they wanted to force Judah into an alliance against Assyria, but we are not told that. In the biblical period there was nothing unusual about theological explanations of events: Mesha king of Moab explained his country's subjection to Israel by saying, "Chemosh was angry with his land"; the Assyrian kings attributed their victories to the help of their gods.

Religious Policy Overstressed. A more serious criticism is that the offenses with which the kings are charged nearly always concern their religious policy rather than their treatment of their subjects. The rare exceptions are Rehoboam's refusal to reduce the burden of forced labor, Ahab's acquiescence in the murder of Naboth (both probably deriving from the source material), and Manasseh's shedding of innocent blood. We know from Jer 22:13-17 that Jehoiakim was accused of oppression and violence and contrasted with Josiah, who "judged the cause of the poor and needy," yet in Kings Jehoiakim is not blamed for the one course nor Josiah praised for the other.

Worship of the Right God. It would be a mistake, however, to assume that religious policy was a matter of indifference to everyone but the Deuteronomists. Everything from the anointing of kings to the survival of the poorest family was ultimately a religious matter. The fortunes of the nation depended on the worship of the right god in the right way. There was general agreement that deities could be appealed to for guidance, protection, and deliverance from dangerous and desperate situations. There was less agreement about which deity might be appealed to. A common assumption was that each people had its own deity to look after its interests: Astarte for the Sidonians, Chemosh for the Moabites, and Milcom for the Ammonites. But what should happen when people from neighboring countries settled in Jerusalem? Should they be allowed to have their own places of worship (1 Kgs 11:1-8)? Should a king introduce chapels for foreign deities into the temple to reflect the pluralism of his kingdom (2 Kgs 21:4-5, 7)? And what should the foreigner do, when convinced that "there is no God in all the earth except in Israel," on his return home (2 Kgs 5:15-18)? The books of Kings provide evidence that the worship of a plurality of deities was at different times and in different circles tolerated, stamped out with fanatical zeal, and disapproved of rather helplessly.

Worship in the Right Way. There was disagreement, too, about the way in which Israel's God, Yahweh, should be worshiped. Could the God who had brought Israel up out of the land of Egypt be legitimately represented by golden bull images (1 Kgs 12:28-30)? Could he be worshiped at local shrines or only in the temple in Jerusalem? Were stone pillars and wooden poles the conventional cult objects of any shrine (2 Kgs 17:10; 18:4; 23:14) or the symbols of Baal and Asherah respectively (1 Kgs 16:33; 2 Kgs 13:6; 21:3; 23:15)? God might be expected to communicate his intentions and the outcome of critical situations through prophets, and perhaps also through dreams (1 Kgs 3:5-15), but other forms of divination had a more ambiguous status (2 Kgs 17:17; 21:6). That God welcomed sacrifice was taken for granted, but was the relatively rare practice of human sacrifice really regarded as service to a god Molech (2 Kgs 23:10)? If so, why were prophets at such pains to insist that Yahweh had not commanded it (Mic 6:6-8; Jer 32:35) or so anxious to explain why he had (Ezek 20:25)?

Yahweh's Character. Although the Deuteronomists at first sight appear to have theological beliefs as definite as any in the Bible, the portrayal of Yahweh's character in Kings is not as straightforward as might be expected. Certain ideas can of course be ruled out: that he is a god of the hills but not of the valleys (1 Kgs 20:23, 28) or that he is the god of the land, who can be worshiped alongside others (2 Kgs 17:24-33). Israelites (1 Kgs 8:23, 60; 18:39) and foreigners (2 Kgs 5:15) alike confess that he is the only God. But his relationship to his people is problematical. It is not clear whether he has promised not to "blot out the name of Israel from under heaven" (2 Kgs 14:27; cf. 13:23) or whether a stage may be reached when he has to "remove them out of his sight" (2 Kgs 17:18, 20, 23; 24:3). Similarly, it is not clear whether the promise to David that his dynasty will endure forever is conditional (1 Kgs 2:1-4; 9:1-5) or unconditional (1 Kgs 11:36; 2 Kgs 8:19). Yahweh has commanded that children shall not be put to death for the sins of their parents (2 Kgs 14:6), yet he himself can punish the sins of some of the northern kings by blotting out their whole families (1 Kgs 14:10-11; 15:29; 16:3-4, 11-12; 21:21-22, 24; 2 Kgs 9:8-9; 10:10-11). Yahweh's prophets are expected to tell the truth (1 Kgs 22:16), yet he can apparently countenance deception (1 Kgs 13:18) and actually use it to lure a king to his doom (1 Kgs 22:19-23). Through his prophets he calls both for compassion toward enemy prisoners (2 Kgs 6:21-22) and for their destruction (1 Kgs 20:31-34, 42). These conflicts arise partly from the variety of source material employed, but also from unresolved tensions in the minds of the Deuteronomists themselves. Yahweh's compassion and forgiveness are by no means to be taken for granted, but are still the object of hope and prayer in the most desperate situations (1 Kgs 8:27-53).

Influence of 1 and 2 Kings. The books of Kings have been influential in the history of Europe in seeming to provide models for the good and bad behavior of rulers and their subjects. Monarchs have wanted to be thought as wise as Solomon and have not lacked courtiers willing to make the comparison. The division of the kingdom after Solomon's death was at the time of the Reformation taken as both condemning and justifying the schism in the church. That kings could dedicate temples, inaugurate festivals, and appoint and dismiss priests and were held responsible for religious practice seemed to justify monarchs like Henry VIII breaking with Rome and imposing their own religious settlements. Jehu's revolt seemed to some to legitimize atrocities committed in the name of religion and to others to be a dangerous incitement to fanaticism; to some it appeared to support the view that subjects might rebel against their rulers and to others to be an exceptional case which made a bad rule. These instances provide a warning against accepting as God's actual verdicts what are presented as such in the Bible while discounting the human factors which lay behind the writing of the history.

1 Kings

COMMENTARY

1 Kings 1:1–2:46

Beginning or Ending? Although these chapters recount the accession of Solomon and his early steps to secure the throne, they form the conclusion of the reign of David rather than the introduction to Solomon's reign. None of the actors in these chapters (apart from Solomon) plays any significant part in the subsequent account of Solomon's reign, whereas several of them had a leading role in the story of David.

Rival Bids for the Throne. In 2 Sam 3:2-5 Adonijah is listed as David's fourth son. Since Amnon (2 Samuel 13) and Absalom (2 Samuel 15–18) (and presumably Chileab) are dead, Adonijah might have been expected to succeed David, and he won the support of Joab, who had been very loyal to David but given to taking matters into his own hands (2 Sam 2:12-32; 3:17-39; 11:1-25; 14:1-33; 18:1-17; 19:1-8, 13; 20:4-22; 24:1-9), and Abiathar, the sole survivor of the priests Saul had massacred (1 Sam 22:20-23). But his bid to make himself king before David's death alarmed another party at court who supported Solomon and feared that his life and that of his mother Bathsheba would be in danger if Adonijah's bid succeeded. They therefore persuaded David to declare Solomon king, and the news of his anointing brought about the collapse of Adonijah's rival bid.

Solomon Removes His Rivals. Solomon first put Adonijah on probation (1:50-53) and then had him murdered, interpreting his wish to marry David's last concubine, Abishag, as a renewed bid for the throne (2:13-25). Of his supporters, Abiathar was dismissed but allowed to live privately (2:26-27), but Joab was killed, officially for implicating David's family in guilt for the murder of Abner and Amasa (2:28-35). Solomon is represented as carrying out David's wishes in this and in the execution of Shimei, whose life David had spared despite the way he had cursed the king during Absalom's revolt (2:36-46; cf. 2 Sam 16:5-13; 19:16-23). The dismissal of Abiathar from the priesthood is justified as the fulfillment of the doom pronounced years before on the family of Eli (1 Sam 2:27-36; 3:11-14).

For or against Solomon? We do not know when or by whom these chapters were written. It is possible that the story was told by Solomon's supporters early in his reign to justify his accession to the throne and the actions he took to dispose of the opposition. It could also be that it was told by opponents (or a later historian) to reveal the hypocrisy and cold-bloodedness which underlay Solomon's reputation for wisdom (2:6, 9). Some scholars think that an originally anti-Solomonic narrative has been revised in a pro-Solomonic direction. Others again, who are primarily interested in the artistry of the narrative rather than the supposed political context, think that one author has deliberately kept us guessing about where his sympathies lie and what the truth of the matter was. For example, did David really promise Bathsheba that Solomon should be king (1:13, 17)? Was Bathsheba naive or calculating when she passed on Adonijah's request to Solomon (2:13-25)?

A Deuteronomistic Comment. 2:1-4, which represents David as urging Solomon to keep Yahweh's commandments as the condition for the survival of the dynasty, stands out from the rest of the narrative and is generally recognized as one of a number of additions by a Deuteronomistic editor who wants to explain both why the dynasty lasted so long and why it did not survive the exile of 587 BC. The farewell speech is a favorite device of the Deuteronomists to express the conviction that every generation in Israel has been reminded of the necessity of keeping Yahweh's commandments (cf. Deut 29:1–31:6; Joshua 23; 1 Sam 12:1-25). Later, many of the writings of the intertestamental period were cast in the form of "testaments," predictions and warnings by revered figures of Israel's past (*OTP,* 1:773-995).

No Summing Up of David's Reign. 2:10-12 is the first of the notices which will record the end of each king's reign and the accession of his successor throughout 1 and 2 Kings. But we might have expected some appreciation of David's character and achievements. For that we have to wait until 1 Kgs 15:4-5. Preachers in the eighteenth century who wanted to hold David's reign up as the ideal turned to 1 Chr 29:28: "He died in a good old age, full of days, riches, and honor." Not everyone has thought David's reign was ideal, however. Pierre Bayle, who included a famous article on David in his historical and biographical dictionary of 1695-97, asked about his dealings with Shimei "whether, strictly speaking, a man who promises his enemy his life keeps his promise when he orders him to be put to death in his will."

Influence of the Story. The chapters contribute to our knowledge of how kings were installed in Israel (1:38-40; cf. 2 Kgs 11:12) and of the practice of seeking asylum at a sanctuary (1:50-53; 2:28-34). They have influenced the British coronation service, which includes anointing and acclamation. Handel used the words of 1:39 in his anthems for the coronation of George II: Zadok and Nathan would have been surprised to hear their hurried ceremony perpetuated in such magnificent music!

1 Kings 3:1-15

Solomon's Exemplary Piety. This section presents a very different picture of Solomon from that in the previous chapter. Instead of the calculating and ruthless politician we have a king exemplary for his piety. Invited by God to ask for one gift, he chooses wisdom to rule rather than long life, riches, or the life of his enemies. (The Solomon of ch. 2 was only too anxious to take the life of his enemies.)

An Ideal for Future Kings? This could have been a contemporary public relations exercise. Other ancient Near

Eastern kings published accounts of how the deity appeared to them in a dream and commissioned them for their task. One often quoted is the Sphinx Stele of Thutmose IV of Egypt (*ANET,* 449). There is no obvious ideological reason for locating the dream at Gibeon. Since worship at the "high places," sanctuaries outside Jerusalem, is going to be consistently condemned in Kings, it is rather an embarrassment and has to be explained (1 Kgs 3:2-3; cf. 2 Chr 1:3-6, where it is justified by supposing that the tent which preceded the temple as Israel's sole legitimate sanctuary was there). This may suggest that the historian is using an ancient tradition. On the other hand, the correctness of Solomon's request, the idealization of David, and the condition attached to the promise of long life may indicate that the story has been written, or rewritten, as an ideal for later kings to live up to. It is noteworthy that Solomon is the only king said to have been addressed by God directly (cf. 6:11-13; 9:3-9; 11:11-13); this claim is not made even for David.

A Typical Prayer. Solomon's prayer shares some features with other biblical prayers. Self-deprecation ("I am only a little child," etc.), description of one's plight ("Who can govern this your great people?"), and recollection of God's past mercies ("You have shown great and steadfast love to your servant David my father") are all familiar elements in appeals for God's help. The idea that Solomon was young and inexperienced is taken up literally in Chronicles (1 Chr 22:5; 29:1).

The Significance of Dreams. Dreams were one of the expected ways in which God would declare his purpose. A person might seek such guidance by sleeping at a sanctuary. Dreams are often regarded as symbolic, requiring interpretation (Gen 37:5-10; 40; 41:1-36; Daniel 2; 4:4-27; Acts 10:9-16), but sometimes, as here, as direct revelation (Gen 28:11-17; Matt 1:20-21; 2:13, 19-20; Acts 18:9-10; 27:23-24). "Then Solomon awoke; it had been a dream" (v. 15) should not be read as if it meant "'it had *only* been a dream."

The Wisdom of Solomon. The wisdom Solomon asks for is the wisdom to govern his people. The story which follows (3:16-28) suggests that this was particularly needed in the settlement of hard cases which were brought before him personally. But Solomon is regarded as the type of other kinds of wisdom as well: knowing how to pursue his political ends (2:6, 9), the ability to coin wise sayings and compose songs (4:32), knowledge of the natural world (4:33), the ability to answer all kinds of questions (4:34; 10:2-3), and the enterprise to undertake the building of the temple (5:7). See further on 1 Kgs 4:29-34.

Relations with Egypt. This section is introduced by mention of Solomon's marriage to an Egyptian princess. She is mentioned again in 7:8 and 9:24. Solomon is neither praised nor criticized for this: there is no suggestion that she, unlike the other foreign wives he married, led him into idolatry (11:1-8). This connection with Egypt has, however, encouraged scholars to look for Egyptian influences on Solomon's style of kingship: his court (4:1-6) may have been modeled on the Egyptian court; the tradition of Solomon's wisdom (4:30) may be an indication that Israel became receptive to the extensive wisdom writings of Egypt.

1 Kings 3:16-28

Judicial Wisdom. As the concluding words of this passage show, the story is intended to illustrate the wisdom in administering justice for which Solomon had asked.

A Story with Many Parallels. There are many parallels to this story in which a deity or a ruler or a judge solves a dispute when there is nothing but the claims of the opposing parties to go on. The closest is the Indian story of the woman who left her child on the bank of a pool while she bathed. It was carried off by a female demon. The resulting dispute was brought before a goddess, who ordered the two to pull the child apart and awarded it to the one who balked at the test. In other stories the dispute over the child is between two wives of the same man. No doubt this kind of story "traveled" from one culture to another, but it is impossible to say where it originated. It is interesting that Solomon is not named as the king in the story; this may mean that in Israel the story was once told about "a king" and not specifically about Solomon.

The King's Judicial Role. In this context the story implies that deciding difficult cases was a recognized function of the king of Israel (cf. 2 Sam 14:1-20; 15:2-4; 1 Kgs 20:35-43; 2 Kgs 6:26-31; 8:1-6) and that ordinary citizens, even prostitutes, could have direct access to the king. There is no hint here that the case might have been decided by consulting an oracle (Exod 22:7-9) or by requiring the defendant to swear an oath (Exod 22:10-11). The intention of the story is more to illustrate shrewdness and insight than to instruct us about regular judicial procedure.

A Detective Story? Meir Sternberg (Sternberg 1985) has suggested that the story operates with the conventions of the detective story. We are given the same data as Solomon and invited to match our wits with his. It might be added that, like the detective story, it caters to the wish that justice should be done, however unorthodox the method; and that, as in the detective story, the outcome is contrived: What would have happened if both women had protested against the king's barbarous solution? The similar story in 2 Kgs 6:26-31 is more realistic.

The Attitude to Women. Feminists interrogate the story regarding its attitude to women. In Phyllis Bird's view (Bird 1989) the introduction of prostitutes would immediately have suggested that here are women whose testimony cannot be trusted. But the king sees beyond the stereotype and appeals to their motherly instincts.

Other Wisdom Stories. The story, in its focus on the way the king makes the women give themselves away, has some affinities with those in which prophets and others trap the king into passing judgment on his own actions (2 Sam 12:1-14; 14:1-13; 1 Kgs 20:35-43). We may also compare the stories in the Gospels in which Jesus is faced with a trick question and gives a reply which silences the opposition and wins the admiration of bystanders (e.g., Mark 12:13-17; John 8:2-11). Recognition of this could underlie the comparison of Jesus with Solomon in Matt 12:42 = Luke 11:31.

1 Kings 4:1-19, 27-28 (Heb. 4:1-19; 5:7-8)

Two Lists. Here we have two lists: that of Solomon's chief officers of state (4:1-6), and that of the governors of the twelve regions into which the kingdom was divided (4:7-19).

Solomon's Officers of State. The first list is similar to the lists of David's chief officers (2 Sam 8:15-18; 20:23-26). There is some continuity: Jehoshaphat is still recorder; Zadok and Abiathar are still priests; Adoniram (Adoram) was already in charge of the forced labor in David's time. There are changes, some no doubt due to the passage of time and one at least (Benaiah for Joab in charge of the army) a result of the events recorded in 1 Kings 2. There are also some new offices: Azariah supervises the work of the officers to be listed in 4:7-19; Ahishar is in charge of the palace. It is possible that some of the offices were modeled on those at other ancient Near Eastern courts (Mettinger 1971; De Vaux 1961: 127-32; Fox 2000).

Regional Government. The division of the kingdom into twelve regions seems to cover only what after Solomon's death became the Northern Kingdom. (There is no warrant in the Hebrew text for the mention of Judah in 4:19; the RSV and NRSV translation is based on the LXX.) Various solutions have been proposed: (a) Judah had already been dealt with in the time of David; (b) the LXX text is justified because v. 19a duplicates v. 13; (c) Judah had a favored position, which explains why they remained loyal to the Davidic dynasty after the death of Solomon.

The division into twelve regions has more to do with the months of the year (4:7, 27-28) than with the tradition of the twelve tribes of Israel. The seven regions from v. 13 follow the tribal boundaries described in Joshua 13; 18–19, but the first five split up the traditional territory of Ephraim and Manasseh. It has been suggested that Solomon wanted to reduce the power of these the largest tribes, or that he needed to integrate the Canaanite cities into his kingdom. Of course, he may simply have wanted to create regions of roughly comparable population and productivity.

Some of the regional officers are introduced only by their patronymics (Ben-hur, Ben-deker, etc.). This way of naming people was not common in Israel; it may mean that the officers were Canaanites. Two of the officers were sons-in-law of Solomon, including one (Ben-abinadab) from the group just mentioned. Solomon seems to have chosen men on whose loyalty he could rely rather than tribal leaders.

A Heavy Yoke. The purpose of the division into regions is clearly stated in 4:7 and elaborated in 4:27-28. The levy of forced labor for Solomon's building work may have been organized separately (5:13-18) and may not have involved free Israelites (9:15-23). But events after Solomon's death showed that the northern tribes at least found this taxation in kind burdensome (12:1-5). It is possible that Samuel's vivid picture of an oppressive monarchy in 1 Sam 8:10-18 is drawn from the experience of Solomon's reign.

Contemporary Lists? Lists of officials are not given for any subsequent reign. We hear of officials only incidentally (e.g., 2 Kgs 18:18; 22:3-13). Since it is unlikely that such lists would have been invented at a much later date, we may assume that the account of Solomon's reign is based at least in part on records kept at the time.

1 Kings 4:20-26 (Heb. 4:20; 5:1-6)

A Golden Age. Solomon's reign is presented as a kind of "golden age" in Israel's history. The nation was populous (4:20), contented (v. 20), and at peace at home and abroad (vv. 24 and 25). All the kings west of the Euphrates were his vassals and paid tribute (vv. 21 and 24). Solomon maintained a large court in lavish style (vv. 22-23) and a large chariot force (v. 26). The picture of all Judah and Israel living safely "under their vines and fig trees" (4:25) is also used to portray the ideal future (Mic 4:4; Zech 3:10) — and the advantages of submitting to an invading army (2 Kgs 18:31 = Isa 36:16)! The early British-American colonists used this metaphor to express their goal of achieving independence and security through the acquisition of property.

An Idealized Picture. These descriptions were probably written much later than Solomon's time and contain an element of idealization and exaggeration. It has been estimated that from the beginning of the monarchy to the end of Solomon's reign the population of Judah had increased by 25 percent (Jamieson-Drake 1991: 72), but there were much bigger population increases to come. The fact that the kingdom is described as "Judah and Israel" (4:20 and 25) warns us of the tensions which would split it on Solomon's death. Relations between Solomon and Hiram of Tyre (one of "the kings west of the Euphrates"), as described in 1 Kings 5, suggest an alliance of equals rather than a relationship between suzerain and vassal. And there is little in the way of archeological evidence to show that the period of Solomon was more prosperous than later periods.

Horses, Not Horsemen. It is generally agreed that the word *parashim* in 4:26 and 10:26, which can mean either "horses" or "horsemen," means "horses." There were no cavalry in Solomon's time, and 12,000 horses for 4,000 chariots (if that is the intended number; 10:26 according to some mss. of the LXX) would be about right (Mowinckel 1962; Ap-Thomas 1970).

1 Kings 4:29-34 (Heb. 5:9-14)

An International Reputation. The theme of Solomon's wisdom is resumed here. He was wiser than the sages of Israel and of the surrounding countries, and he had an international reputation. This will be illustrated later by the story of the visit of the Queen of Sheba (10:1-10, 13; cf. 10:23-25).

The Tradition of Solomon's Wisdom. But what did Solomon's wisdom consist of? There is no mention here, as there is in 1 Kings 3, of wise judicial decisions. He is credited with the coining of proverbs and the composition of songs, and with knowledge of the natural world. It is true that most of the wisdom literature of the OT (Proverbs, Ecclesiastes, and in the LXX the Wisdom of Solomon), the Song of Songs, and, again in the LXX, the *Psalms* and *Odes of Solomon* are attributed to Solomon. (In later tradition the differences between them were explained by saying that the Song of Songs was the work of his youth, Proverbs that of his middle age, and Ecclesiastes that of his old age.) But these works can hardly have been in mind when this passage was written.

There are, for example, nothing like 3,000 proverbs in the biblical Proverbs, and very few of them concern the natural world. What we have in this passage is a popular conception of Solomon as a wise king without very much content. This was developed on the one hand in later Jewish and Muslim stories which attributed to Solomon knowledge of the language of birds and animals and power over demons and skill in healing (e.g., Josephus *Ant.* 8 §45), and on the other in the expansion of the scope of intellectual wisdom in Wis. 7:17-22 (embracing cosmogony, astronomy, the calendar, the nature of animals, human nature, and the varieties of plants and their uses). In the *Testament of Solomon* (*OTP* 1: 935-59; fourth century AD?) and other writings Solomon is associated with the lore and practice of magic (Torijano 2002).

Wisdom from Egypt? It has been suggested (Noth 1955; Heaton 1974) that behind this popular conception may lie a less personal cultural contribution. Solomon's contacts with Egypt could have meant that Israel became aware of the extensive wisdom literature of Egypt and began to imitate it. (There are close connections between the Egyptian Wisdom of Amenemope and Prov 22:17–24:22.) However, others think that the period of Hezekiah, when there were also contacts with Egypt and the prophet Isaiah was using wisdom forms, was a more likely time for this cultural movement to have been encouraged (cf. Prov 25:1; Scott 1955: 262-79).

A Mirror for Princes. James VI and I of Scotland and England provides an illustration of the influence of this tradition of Solomon's wisdom (Huntley 1981: 48-56). There is evidence that he deliberately modeled himself on Solomon in his writings, his decision making, and his foreign policy. Writers evoked the memory of Solomon in dedicating their works to James; a courtier put on a masque on the theme of "King Solomon's Temple"; preachers frequently made the comparison in their sermons; Rubens' painting on the ceiling of the Whitehall banqueting house depicts James as Solomon uniting England and Scotland through two women struggling over a male child (Charles, the heir to the throne)!

1 Kings 5:1-12 (Heb. 5:15-26)

A Relationship Resumed. Solomon enlists the help of Hiram, king of Tyre, in the building of the temple. The account presupposes what has been related in the earlier history: Hiram had provided materials and craftsmen for David's palace (2 Sam 5:11); David had intended to build a temple but had been prevented (2 Sam 7:1-7; the reason given there is different from that given here, and 1 Chr 22:8; 28:3 give a different reason again); God had promised David that his son and successor would build the temple (2 Sam 7:13; 1 Kgs 8:18-19). Hiram also pays tribute to Solomon's wisdom, recognizing it as God's gift (cf. 1 Kgs 3:12; 4:29; 5:12). He is one of a number of foreigners in the Bible who praise or acknowledge Israel's God (5:7; cf. Exod 18:10-11; 1 Kgs 10:9; 2 Kgs 5:15-19).

Hiram of Tyre. The theme of Solomon's relations with Hiram is taken up again later (9:10-14, 26-28; 10:11, 22). Our other knowledge of Hiram comes at third hand, from extracts Josephus (*Ag. Ap.* 1 §§112-20; *Ant.* 8 §§144-49; first century AD) gives from Menander of Ephesus (date unknown), who is said to have translated the Tyrian records into Greek, and Dius (date unknown), who was believed "to have written the Phoenician history after an accurate manner." From these extracts it appears that Hiram was himself a keen temple builder who made extensive use of timber from Lebanon. (Both writers also say that Hiram and Solomon exchanged problems and paid each other fines if they could not solve them.) Josephus also rewrites the exchange between Solomon and Hiram in the form of letters (*Ant.* 8 §§50-56), saying that copies were still preserved at Tyre, but he makes no claim to have inspected them.

Relations with Phoenicia. There is, however, plenty of evidence for Phoenician maritime enterprise in general and for the use of the Lebanon as a source of timber by the Assyrians and the Egyptians (Ezekiel 27–28; *ANET,* 227; Ap-Thomas 1973: 264-65, 274-78). Israel (and later Judah) continued to export agricultural produce to Tyre (Ezek 27:17).

Other Ancient Temple Building Accounts. The account of the building of the temple has been compared with the building inscriptions of Sumerian, Assyrian, and Babylonian kings (Hurowitz 1992). These generally recall the background to the project (cf. 5:3), announce the decision to build (cf. v. 5), and declare that the project has received divine approval (cf. v. 5). The similarities do not necessarily mean that the biblical account is, like the ancient Near Eastern inscriptions, a contemporary document designed to advertise the king's achievements. Deuteronomistic phraseology in vv. 3-5 ("a house for the name of Yahweh," "rest on every side") suggests that it may have been written much later for a different reason, namely, as a reminder of what Israel stood to lose if the temple was destroyed (Tomes 1996).

1 Kings 5:13-18 (Heb. 5:27-32)

Conscript Labor. In order to carry out his building projects Solomon had to use conscript labor. Some worked regular shifts in the Lebanon (cf. 5:6), presumably helping to fell timber; others worked in the central hill country of Israel itself, quarrying and dressing stone.

Different Traditions. There is another account of Solomon's use of conscript labor in 9:15-23, which differs from this passage in some respects: (a) the labor was used for many more projects than the temple; (b) the labor force was made up of non-Israelites; (c) the conscripts had the status of slaves rather than people who would return home between spells of "national service"; and (d) the number of officials is different (550 against 3,300). There is no point in trying to reconcile the two accounts. They represent independent traditions. But whereas 5:13-18 helps to explain and justify the resentment which led to the revolt of the northern tribes after Solomon's death (Adoniram is killed during the revolt [1 Kgs 12:18]), 9:15-23 seems to suggest that the revolt was unjustified.

Phoenician Influence on the Temple. Mention of Hiram's builders and "the Giblites" (= people from Byblos, on the Phoenician coast north of Tyre and Sidon) among those who dressed the stones and cut the timber suggests that there may have been Phoenician influence on the design of the temple.

1 Kings 6:1-10

The Building of the Temple Begins. The only events in Solomon's reign which are dated to the year and the month are the laying of the foundation of the temple and its completion (6:1, 37-38). (The month in which the temple was dedicated is given, but not the year [8:2].) The months which marked the stages in the fall of Jerusalem will be given at the end of 2 Kings (25:1, 3, 8, 25). One reason for mentioning the month is that such events were commemorated annually (cf. Zech 7:5; 8:19).

The Temple and the Exodus. But the beginning of the building of the temple is also dated from the exodus from Egypt. This may mean that in the eyes of the Deuteronomistic historians and possibly in earlier tradition it was with the building of the temple that the goal of the exodus was finally achieved. (Note that the Song of Moses in Exod 15:1-18 commemorates both the exodus and the building of the temple.)

The Dimensions of the Temple. The temple was not very big: 90 feet long, 30 feet wide, and 45 feet high (taking a cubit to be 18 inches). Westminster Abbey is 513 feet long, its nave 75 feet wide and 102 feet high. Of course, unlike Westminster Abbey, the temple was not built to house a choir and congregation. It is not unreasonable that Solomon's other buildings in Jerusalem should have been larger and have taken longer to build (cf. 6:37–7:12). For Jewish commentators the fact that Solomon took less time to build the temple was evidence of his zeal (*Ant.* 8 §§130-31; *b. Sanh.* 104b).

Description of the Exterior. The outside of the temple is described first: the vestibule at the front (6:3), the windows (v. 4; the phrase "with recessed frames" reflects the way the ancient versions understood two technical terms whose meaning is uncertain), the wooden roof (v. 9), and the side chambers (vv. 5-6, 8, 10; arranged in three stories on three sides of the building). The observation that these stories rested on ledges built outward from the wall, alongside the note that the stones were dressed before they were brought to the site (v. 7), may suggest that these measures were taken to preserve the holiness of the building. On the other hand, the intention may simply be to draw attention to impressive architectural features. The Assyrian kings also had statues fashioned elsewhere brought to their buildings (Hurowitz 1992: 216-17).

1 Kings 6:11-13

A Conditional Promise. Both the language and the position of this passage, interrupting the description of the temple, mark it out as an insertion into the original account. The language is more characteristic of Priestly than of Deuteronomistic writers: "walk in my statutes" (cf. Lev 26:3), "obey my ordinances" (cf. Lev 18:4), "I will dwell among the children of Israel" (cf. Exod 25:8; 29:45; Lev 26:11-12). If it was written after the destruction of the temple it was probably intended to justify God's nonintervention: he had never made an unconditional promise to David.

1 Kings 6:14-36

Description of the Interior. The interior of the temple was lined throughout with cedarwood (6:15, 18), decorated with carvings (vv. 18, 29), and overlaid (in places) with gold. It consisted of two rooms, a larger outer one (v. 17) and a smaller inner one, cubic in form (vv. 16, 20). The function of the inner room was to house the ark (v. 19), which was overshadowed by two olivewood cherubim (vv. 23-28). There were decorated doors separating the inner room from the outer room (vv. 31-32) and the outer room from the vestibule (vv. 33-35).

The Ark. It is assumed that readers will know what the ark was and what cherubim looked like. The ark had an independent existence before the temple was built (1 Sam 4:1–7:2; 2 Samuel 6). Tradition had it that it accompanied the Israelites in the wilderness (Num 10:33-36). It was the visible symbol of God's presence. In Priestly tradition it was made to serve as the focal point of the tabernacle, the place from which God would issue his commandments to Israel (Exod 25:10-22; Lev 16:2; Num 7:89). The Deuteronomists, on the other hand, regarded it simply as the box in which the stone tablets on which God had written the Ten Commandments were kept (Deut 10:1-5; 1 Kgs 8:9). It is this conception which is implied here by calling it "the ark of the covenant of Yahweh."

The Cherubim. It is doubtful whether cherubim had a place in Israelite tradition before this time. By the time of Josephus what they looked like had been forgotten (*Ant.* 8 §73). But they are almost certainly to be identified with the winged sphinxes (lions with human heads) which figure prominently in the iconography of the ancient Near East. They guarded the entrances to palaces and temples; they flanked the thrones of monarchs. They are represented as guarding magical trees (6:29; cf. Gen 3:24). They could also be imagined, perhaps in the form of clouds, as carrying the deity or the deity's throne in flight (2 Sam 22:11 = Ps 18:10; Ezekiel 10). In the temple they were probably regarded as guardians of the ark as Yahweh's throne (1 Sam 4:4; 2 Sam 6:2; Ps 80:1). But the author of the account is interested in their size and symmetry rather than their symbolism.

A Notable Building Technique. The way the wall of the "inner court" was constructed is considered worthy of comment (6:36). The wall of the "'great court" and that of the vestibule were constructed in a similar way (7:12). The technique was well known in the ancient Near East (cf. Ezra 6:4): the course of timber may have been intended as protection against earthquake aftershocks (Thompson 1960).

1 Kings 6:37–7:12

Other Buildings in Jerusalem. These are briefly described. The House of the Forest of Lebanon was apparently used as an armory (10:16-17; Isa 22:8). It no doubt took its name from the rows of cedarwood pillars (rather than internal walls) used to support the roof. The Hall of the Throne is listed here, but the throne itself is not described until 10:18-20. All these buildings may have been within the "great court"; the story in 2 Kings 11 presupposes that the temple and the palace were close together. Later writers were not happy with the idea that Pharaoh's daughter's house or indeed any secular building should be within the sacred precincts (2 Chr 8:11; Ezek 42:20). The emphasis of this writer is once again on the size and costliness of the materials used in all these buildings.

1 Kings 7:13-51

Description of the Fittings. The temple fittings and utensils are now described. They are all cast in bronze and are the work of a craftsman from Tyre, called Hiram like the king of Tyre.

The Pillars. The two bronze pillars had no architectural function but were freestanding. It has been suggested that the names of the pillars are the opening words of inscriptions written on them: "*He will establish (yakin)* the throne of David, and his kingdom, to his seed forever"; "*In the strength (bo'az)* of Yahweh shall the king rejoice" (Scott 1939). In Mesopotamia it was common to give the gates of cities and the doors of palaces names which are wishes for the king (Hurowitz 1992: 257n.). The symbolic significance of the pillars is not indicated here.

The "sea." The function or significance of the bronze "sea," placed in the temple court to the southeast of the building itself (7:39), is equally mysterious. According to 2 Chr 4:6 it was for the priests to wash in, but this would hardly explain the great quantity of water it is said to have held (v. 26; about 10,000 gallons). It is now generally held that it was meant to represent the cosmic sea and Yahweh's control over it (cf. Ps 89:9). The "sea of glass" in front of God's throne in Rev 4:6; 15:2, which should probably be visualized in similar terms to the bronze sea in the temple, certainly has this kind of symbolic significance. But the author of the account is more interested in its size and decoration than in its symbolism.

The Basins. The ten basins on ten movable stands appear to have been placed along the sides of the outer room of the temple (7:39). Their function is said in 2 Chr 4:6 to have been to rinse what was used for the burnt offering. Again, their true function is uncertain. Why ten of them? Why movable? Why did they hold so much water (200 gallons each)? The author is still much more impressed by their ingenious workmanship and elaborate decoration than with any symbolic significance they may have had.

Traditional Objects. By contrast, the other items of temple furniture and implements are passed over summarily, even though they were made of (or overlaid with) gold (7:48-50). They include more traditional objects, said to have figured in the tabernacle: the golden (incense) altar (cf. Exod 30:1-10; 37:25-28), the golden table for the Bread of the Presence (cf. Exod 25:23-30; 37:10-16), the ten lampstands (cf. Exod 25:31-39; 37:17-24: a single lampstand with seven branches). The bronze altar on which sacrifices were offered, which stood immediately in front of the temple (2 Kgs 16:14), is not even listed here, though it does receive passing mention in 8:54, 64. The interest here in Kings is not in these traditional objects, which were no doubt modest in size, but in the massive novelties which distinguished this temple from other sanctuaries. The fate of these monuments will be followed in the subsequent history (2 Kgs 16:17; 25:13-17; cf. Jer 27:19; 52:17-23), but the fate of the ark will be completely passed over.

Christian Exegesis. For Christian exegetes the question has been: Why should such a detailed description of the temple (as, in Exodus, of the tabernacle) be part of Scripture? The answer given has been that the description as a whole and each individual feature must be symbolic of spiritual reality. The Venerable Bede (c. 673-735) was the first to produce detailed exegesis of tabernacle and temple along these lines (Connolly 1995). John Bunyan (1628-88), in *Solomon's Temple Spiritualised,* saw in each feature a hint of some aspect of Puritan theology or spirituality (Midgley 1989: 1-115).

Masonic Interpretation. The whole structure of Freemasonry is built upon a version of the building of the temple. The three "degrees" to which masons are admitted are based on the three-storied side chambers (6:5-6, 8-10), to which the masons who worked on the temple are supposed to have gone to collect their wages, giving passwords as they moved from story to story. The Hiram who cast the bronze fixtures, known as Hiram Abiff, was in masonic tradition killed by fellow craftsmen for refusing to divulge the secrets of the Third Degree and thus is the exemplar of the loyal freemason who likewise keeps what goes on in the lodge secret (e.g., Hannah 1963).

1 Kings 8:1-11

The Ark Is Brought to the Temple. The story of the ark, last heard of when David brought it to Jerusalem (2 Samuel 6) and housed it in a tent (2 Sam 7:2), is now resumed. At festival time, already established and still celebrated at the time of writing, when all the traditional leaders of Israel had gathered, it was brought from the old city, Zion, which David had captured (2 Sam 5:7), to the new complex which Solomon was building. (Jewish tradition locates Zion on Jerusalem's western hill, but it is now recognized that "the City of David," the original Jebusite city, was on the spur to the south of the present Old City.)

Priestly Revision. There are indications that this passage has at least been revised by the Priestly school: the mention of "the tent of meeting" (8:4), the distinction between priests and Levites (v. 4), the references to the inner sanctuary and the outer room as "the most holy place" and "the holy place" respectively (vv. 6, 8, and 10), the mention of the poles of the ark (vv. 7-8), and the conception of Yahweh's glory as a bright cloud (vv. 10-11). These revisions represent an adaptation of the description of the temple to that of the tabernacle in Exodus 25–27; 36–40. On the other hand, the cherubim, which were separate from the ark (8:6), must be those described in 1 Kgs 6:23-28 since the cherubim described in Exod 25:18-20; 37:7-9 were made of gold and attached to the cover of the ark. The note, "they are there to this day," suggests that the passage is based on an account written before the exile, while the temple was still standing.

1 Kings 8:12-13

An Ancient Poem. This would seem to be a citation from an ancient collection of poems. The LXX, which places the poem after 8:53, at the end of Solomon's prayer, adds: "Is this not written in the book of the song?" The Hebrew for "song" *(shir)* differs from *yashar,* "upright," by the transposition of only one letter, and other poems are said to have been taken from a "Book of Jashar" (Josh 10:13; 2 Sam 1:18).

An Apologia for the Temple. The LXX also has an extra line at the beginning of the poem, which probably represents an original "Yahweh has set the sun in the heavens." The poem would then represent an apologia for the building of the temple. Yahweh is not to be identified with the sun, which is his creation; he prefers to make his home in a dark room. While the temple, with its monuments and decoration, suggests his majesty, the windowless room, removed from the common gaze, suggests his mystery.

1 Kings 8:14-26

The Fulfillment of a Promise. Solomon puts the building of the temple in context (8:14-21). It is the provision of something that has been lacking ever since Yahweh brought Israel out of Egypt — a place where his name will be honored and the ark, the symbol of the covenant, will be housed — and more immediately the fulfillment of Yahweh's promise to David that a son of his would accomplish this.

Deuteronomistic Theology. The passage clearly looks back to 2 Sam 7:12-13 and 1 Kgs 5:3-5. All three passages avoid saying that the temple is for Yahweh to *live* in. They go no further than saying that "his *name* will be there." This emphasis, together with the implication that the temple has been built in Jerusalem because that is the place Yahweh has *chosen* (8:16), marks them out as Deuteronomistic (cf. Deut 12:11, 21; 14:23; 16:6, 11; 26:2). The theology will be elaborated further in vv. 27-30.

Prayer for the Dynasty. But the promise that his son would build the temple was only half of the promise to David. Yahweh also promised to build David a "house," that is, a dynasty, which would endure forever (2 Sam 7:11b-16). David had been succeeded by one of his own sons (Saul was not); this was an encouraging start (cf. 1 Kgs 1:48). The consolidation of Solomon's rule was further encouragement (1 Kgs 2:12, 46b; 5:4). But "forever" is a long time, and so Solomon prays, as David did, for the continuation of the dynasty (8:22-26; cf. 2 Sam 7:18-29), relying on Yahweh's fidelity but not forgetting the condition of loyalty to Yahweh on the part of the kings.

The Ideal and the Reality. This tradition, that Yahweh had promised David a dynasty which would endure forever, did not originate with the Deuteronomists. Deut 17:14-20, while it stresses that Israel's kings should be people of Yahweh's choosing and holds out the hope of dynasties which will earn stability through fidelity to the law, does not hint at a promise to any particular dynasty. On the other hand, the promise to David figures in writings which are not Deuteronomistic (Pss 89:19-37; 132:11-12). The subsequent history will witness to the long continuance of the Davidic dynasty as a fact, but hardly as a realization of the ideal envisaged in the covenant with David. The dynasty continues, but it rules over only a small part of David's kingdom. It does so not because of the fidelity of the later kings but "for David's sake."

1 Kings 8:27-53

God is Asked to Hear Prayer. There was no doubt a spectrum of beliefs in Israel about God's relation to the temple. For some it was indeed the spot on earth in which he had chosen to make his home (1 Kgs 8:12-13; Exod 15:17; Ps 132:13-14; Hab 2:20); for others it was the footstool before his heavenly throne (1 Chr 28:2; Ps 99:5; Lam 2:1; cf. Isa 6:1); for still others it was unthinkable that his presence could be localized on earth (Isa 66:1; cf. Acts 7:48-50; and v. 27 here). Solomon's prayer draws out the consequences of this last stance. Although God is not in residence, as it were, he is implored to hear and answer every prayer which is addressed toward the temple. (The idea of the temple as a place of prayer is not confined to this passage; cf. Isa 56:7.)

The Occasions for Prayer. There follows a catalogue of the occasions on which Israel and individual Israelites might be expected to pray. They are all prayers which the petitioners make on their own behalf — there is no mention of intercession for others in this context — and they are all related to crisis situations. The catalogue reflects the content of the appeals made by the nation and individuals which constitute much of the Psalter, and in one case at least has been used to suggest a possible *Sitz im Leben* for some of them.

The Person Falsely Accused. 8:31-32 instances the case of a person faced with an accusation which, in the absence of witnesses, can only be met by swearing that he is innocent. The vindication or punishment is then left in the hands of God (cf. Exod 22:7-11 [Heb. 6-10]). It has been suggested that some of the protestations of innocence in the Psalms (Pss 7:3-5; 17:1-5; 35; cf. Job 31) are the prayers of people so falsely accused.

National Crises. Then follow such occasions as the beginning of a military campaign (8:44-45), defeat in battle (vv. 33-34), drought (vv. 35-36), and famine or epidemics caused by crop failure or siege warfare (vv. 37-40). God is urged to hear the prayers of foreigners (vv. 41-43). Finally, the prayers of those who have been taken into exile are commended to God at length (vv. 46-53).

The Temple Is Still Standing. This last section of the prayer has often been taken as evidence that the prayer (and the history as a whole) was compiled after the fall of Jerusalem in 587 BC, perhaps by those who were themselves in exile. But it should be noted that the prayer everywhere presupposes that the temple is standing (8:31, 33, 38, 42, 44, 48). A case can therefore be made that the prayer — and indeed the description of the temple as a whole — was compiled between 597 and 587, when Judeans were in exile but the temple had not yet been destroyed (Tomes 1996).

The Grounds of Appeal. Why should Yahweh attend to these prayers? Not on the ground of Israel's deserts. There is a strong sense that the crises will be the outcome of Israel's sins and that they will need to repent (8:30, 34, 35-36, 39, 47-50). Rather, the appeal is to God's justice (v. 32), his knowledge of the human heart (v. 39), his concern for his own reputation (vv. 40, 43), his regard for his own interests (vv. 51, 53), and his promises to Israel's ancestors (v. 53).

Concern for the Nation and for God. The space devoted to this prayer indicates that the historians are no detached chroniclers of events nor ideologues presenting one party in a favorable light, but people deeply concerned about the fate of their nation and the reputation of their God.

1 Kings 8:54-66

More Deuteronomistic Ideas. In the blessing at the end of the prayer Solomon has in mind, not the fulfillment of God's promises to David, but the fulfillment of his promises to Israel's ancestors; not the stability of his own rule (as in 5:4) but the settled conditions Israel at last enjoys in the land. The language is that of Josh 21:43-45; 23:1, 14. The plea that God will not leave or abandon Israel similarly is reminiscent of Deut 31:6, 8; Josh 1:5. These passages, like the present one, stress the importance of keeping the law (Josh 1:7-8; 23:6-8), and perhaps we should recognize them as the work of a particular Deuteronomistic editor. On the other hand, the idea of Yahweh's maintaining Israel's cause and acting so that the peoples of the earth may recognize that he is God has already been introduced in 8:43 and 45. A Deuteronomist author may be capable of more variety of expression than is often thought.

A Place for Sacrifice as well as Prayer. The dedication of the temple was carried out with sacrifice as well as with prayer. So many sacrifices were offered that the bronze altar, normally used for a quite limited number of sacrifices (2 Kgs 16:15), proved too small. Nevertheless, the number of sacrifices said to have been offered is quite incredible: 10,142 animals slaughtered each day if the festival lasted fourteen days, 17,750 if it lasted eight days. (The MT of 8:65 is at variance with the LXX and the MT of v. 66.) The question is: Why should the author want to exaggerate? One possibility is that he is trying to compensate for such a summary treatment of sacrifice in comparison with the eloquent and extended treatment of prayer. (Solomon's prayer makes no mention of sacrifice: Josephus thought it proper to insert one [*Ant.* 8 §108].) Prayer is what the author believes in, but fidelity to the facts compels him to acknowledge that the temple was designed as a place of sacrifice.

1 Kings 9:1-9

A Deuteronomistic Warning. Solomon receives Yahweh's response, as in 3:5-15, in a direct revelation, though this time it is not said to have been in a dream. The language is so thoroughly Deuteronomistic that the attribution to a divine revelation is probably no more than a literary convention. Yahweh declares that he has adopted the temple as his own, "putting his name there"; the (conditional) promise to David is reaffirmed; and a typical Deuteronomistic warning of the consequences of not obeying the commandments, in particular of serving other gods, is issued (for the form of the warning cf. Deut 29:16-28; Jer 5:18-19; 16:10-13; 22:8-9). The stress on keeping the law has suggested that this passage comes from a particular Deuteronomistic editor, and the fact that the destruction of the temple is contemplated (as it is not in Solomon's prayer) suggests that it was written during the exile, after 587 BC.

1 Kings 9:10-25

Earlier Themes Resumed. Now that the account of the building of the temple and its dedication is complete, some of the themes of the earlier chapters are resumed: Solomon's relations with Hiram, king of Tyre (from 5:1-12); the measures Solomon adopted to raise a labor force (from 5:13-18); and the housing of Pharaoh's daughter (from 3:1; also mentioned in 7:8).

Hiram's Displeasure. Relations with Hiram were apparently not idyllic. Solomon had to cede towns in Galilee to him in return for supplies of timber and gold, in addition to paying the wages of Hiram's workmen (5:6) and supplying wheat and oil (5:11). The tradition of Hiram's displeasure could be derived from the name of the territory rather than vice versa.

Building outside Jerusalem. Solomon's building activities extended beyond the temple/palace complex. The Millo ("filling") was possibly a building up of the gap between the old City of David (3:1; 8:1) and the new temple/palace complex. Hazor, Megiddo, and Gezer have all been extensively excavated, and all have the same distinctive type of gateway built into a casemate wall from the Solomonic period (Iron Age IA). It was once thought that stables from the time of Solomon had been discovered at Megiddo, showing that it was a garrison town for the cavalry and chariot force (9:19), but it was later concluded that the buildings in question were neither stables nor as early as Solomon. (On the question of the conscripted labor Solomon used see on 5:13-18 above.)

The Role of the King in the Cultus. Solomon continued to offer sacrifice on the altar three times a year, presumably at the three festivals prescribed in the law codes (Exod 23:14-17; 34:18, 22-23; Deut 16:1-17; 2 Chr 8:13). There was no bar to the king's offering sacrifice in person (cf. 2 Kgs 16:12-13); indeed, the king was regarded as a priest in his own right, a role he may have inherited from the Canaanite priest-kings of Jerusalem (Gen 14:18; Ps 110:4). What the king was not allowed to do, at least in postexilic tradition, was to enter the temple building itself and offer incense (2 Chr 26:16-20).

1 Kings 9:26–10:29

Trade Prospers. This section is mainly devoted to the development of trade during Solomon's reign. Hitherto the references to trade have been confined to that with Tyre related to the building of the temple/palace complex (5:1-12; 9:10-14). The theme of Solomon's dealings with Hiram is resumed (9:26-28), but now they concern trading expeditions by sea: Solomon provided the port (on the present Gulf of Eilat) and the ships, Hiram the experienced crew. ("Ships of Tarshish" was probably the name given to ships capable of long voyages such as that to Tarshish far away to the west.) The main object seems to have been to import gold for ceremonial and decorative items (10:16-21): the estimates are of the value of the metal rather than of trade as a whole (9:28; 10:10, 14-15). But there were other exotic luxury imports as well (10:2, 11-12, 22, 25), and a flourishing trade in the import and export of chariots and horses (10:26-29).

Lack of Archeological Evidence. "Solomon in all his glory" became proverbial. (His "great ivory throne" [10:18-20; cf. 7:7] provided the image for God's "great white throne" at the Last Judgment [Rev 20:11].) There is, however, no archeological evidence that this was a particularly prosperous era in Israel. There are no especially impressive buildings, and no gold or ivory objects. Such marks of prosperity did not appear until the ninth century and later. Evidence of copper mining in the Timna valley north of the Gulf of Aqaba and of copper smelting at Ezion-geber at its head, although neither is mentioned in the Bible, was once claimed as evidence of the prosperity of the period, but the mines appear not to have been worked after the twelfth century and the "smelter" is now thought to have been a storehouse. The lack of corroborative evidence may be partially explained by later rebuilding in Jerusalem, removing the traces of Solomon's time, and the depredations which accompanied invasion (e.g., 1 Kgs 14:26; 2 Kgs 12:17-18). But the possibility that the prosperity of later times has been read back into the Solomonic era must also be considered.

The Visit of the Queen of Sheba. This story is placed after the mention of Solomon's trading voyages to Ophir probably because Ophir and Sheba were thought to lie in the same general direction, in Somalia and Yemen respectively. Excavations have been carried out in the capital of Sheba, Marib, in east Yemen, though not to a depth sufficient to reach tenth-century levels. There is abundant evidence of prosperous trade from the seventh century onward (cf. Job 6:19; Ps 72:10, 15; Isa 45:14; Ezek 27:22-23; 38:13), principally in frankincense and myrrh (Isa 60:6; Jer 6:20). The story possibly reflects a trade mission (Kitchen 1997: 126-53).

Jewish and Muslim Legend. If Solomon's wealth became proverbial, the visit of the Queen of Sheba became legendary (Pritchard 1974). In Jewish and Islamic tradition the Queen of Sheba (Bilkis in Arabian tradition) is summoned by Solomon, under threat of annihilation. When she arrives, thinking that she has to cross water to approach Solomon, she lifts her skirts and discloses that her legs are hairy. In Jewish legend, therefore, she is sometimes identified with Lilith, queen of the demons. The legends also purport to preserve some of the riddles she put to Solomon. The outcome of the visit in the Qur'an is that she is converted from worshiping the sun to worshiping God (Sura 27:15-44).

Ethiopian Tradition. Sheba is generally identified with present-day Yemen. But Josephus describes her as "queen of Egypt and Ethiopia" (*Ant.* 8 §165), and in Ethiopian tradition her name was Makeda and she lived in Axum. She and Solomon had a son, Menelik, who became the ancestor of the Ethiopian monarchs and removed the ark of the covenant from Jerusalem to Axum. (See also commentary on 2 Kgs 24:18–25:30.)

Christian Tradition. The story of the Queen of Sheba is one of a number in which a prominent foreigner praises Yahweh for what he has done (10:9; cf. Exod 18:10-11; 1 Kgs 5:7). In Western Christian tradition, therefore, the Queen of Sheba becomes a type of Gentiles who accept Christianity and a prophetic witness to the Last Judgment (cf. Matt 12:42 = Luke 11:31; and the "Sabean" gifts of the wise men in Matt 2:11).

1 Kings 11:1-13

Solomon's Foreign Wives and Their Religions. The following chapter will relate the breakup of the kingdom which David and Solomon ruled. This passage explains why God allowed this to happen. It was principally because Solomon actively promoted the worship of the gods of the neighboring peoples, which was in turn the result of his marriages with women from those countries. Objections to such marriages in themselves elsewhere are postexilic (Ezra 9:2; Neh 13:25); the earlier feeling was against intermarriage with the original Canaanite inhabitants of the land (Exod 34:16; Deut 7:3). The attitude to the neighboring peoples varied: at one period Edomites and Egyptians were looked upon more favorably than were Moabites and Ammonites (Deut 23:3-8); at other times relations with Moab were good (1 Sam 22:3-4; Ruth) and relations with Edom very bitter (Ps 137:7; Lam 4:21-22; Ezekiel 35). The passage must represent a standpoint much later than the time of Solomon: his marriage with an Egyptian princess has been mentioned without praise or blame in earlier chapters; the number of his foreign wives must surely be exaggerated; different reasons for the breakup of the kingdom will become apparent in the next chapter. The real offense for the Deuteronomists was setting up altars to foreign gods east of Jerusalem. These were later to be among the objects of Josiah's reforming zeal (2 Kgs 23:13).

Yahweh's Regard for David and Jerusalem. The kingdom will be "torn" from Solomon and given to another. (A symbolic action underlies the metaphor; see 1 Sam 15:27-28; 1 Kgs 11:29-31.) But the historian has to explain why the division of the kingdom did not take place in Solomon's lifetime and why his son would retain a small part of it, including the all-important Jerusalem. It is because of the continuing regard Yahweh has for David and for Jerusalem, which must not be allowed to fall into the wrong hands.

Solomon's Tarnished Image. Although Solomon was portrayed earlier as a model of piety, it is David and not Solomon who will provide the standard by which later kings of Judah are judged (e.g., 1 Kgs 15:3, 11). Solomon will figure only as a bad example (2 Kgs 23:13).

1 Kings 11:14-43

Disturbers of the Peace. The impression that Solomon's reign was a peaceful one (4:25; 5:4) is now qualified. We learn that Hadad of Edom, a survivor of Joab's ruthless treatment of the Edomites (cf. 2 Sam 8:13-14), and Rezon of Damascus, who had taken advantage of David's defeat of Hadad-ezer (cf. 2 Sam 8:3-8), caused trouble for Solomon throughout his reign. Hadad married into the Egyptian royal family before Solomon did.

Jeroboam's Rebellion. The Egyptian pharaoh Shishak also gave asylum to Jeroboam, one of the superintendents of the conscripted labor force, who rebelled against the king. Why did he do so? The text is at the point of telling us (11:27a) when it breaks off to relate an oracle delivered to Jeroboam by the prophet Ahijah (vv. 29-39) which predicts events after Solomon's death, to be related in the following chapter. Jeroboam's rebellion against Solomon himself and his flight to Egypt (v. 40) remain unexplained. The alternative account of the rebellion in the LXX between 12:24 and 25 may give some idea of what has been omitted. It says that Jeroboam (whose mother was a harlot rather than a widow) built a town called Sarira in Ephraim and fortified the city of David (the latter is attributed to Solomon himself in 11:27b), that he had three hundred chariots, and that he aspired to the kingdom.

Ahijah's Arithmetic. Ahijah's oracle elaborates on the sentence passed on Solomon in 11:11-13. The reasons given for the breakup of the kingdom, its postponement, and the retention of one tribe by Solomon's son are the same. The new elements are the symbolic action by Ahijah, tearing his new coat into twelve pieces and telling Jeroboam to take ten, and the conditional promise to Jeroboam. The question is: What has happened to the twelfth tribe? The answer seems to be that the status of the tribe of Benjamin was ambivalent. At first it sided with Judah (12:21-24; cf. 2 Chr 11:1-4); but the northern and southern kings both tried to establish fortified cities in its territory (15:17, 21-22; cf. 2 Chr 11:5-12).

1 Kings 12

Solomon's Kingdom Is Divided. The story of Solomon began with a narrative of swiftly moving events; it ends with an equally compelling narrative. In 1 Kings 1 Solomon gains his throne through smart diplomatic moves by his counselors; in this chapter his son loses most of his kingdom through ignoring the advice of his father's trusted advisers in favor of the rash advice of a younger generation.

Deep-Seated Causes. There are, however, indications that the causes of the division of the kingdom were more deep-seated. Solomon had been less successful in putting down opposition toward the end of his reign than he had been at the beginning (11:14-28, 40). His policy of taxation (4:7, 22-23, 27-28) and conscripted labor (5:13-18; 9:15-22) had been deeply unpopular. Adoram (Adoniram in 4:6) was quite the wrong person to send to win back the rebels. Prophetic opposition to the appearance of foreign cults in Jerusalem (11:33) may not have been entirely after the event. Even in David's time the northern tribes seem to have felt that the king was not one of them (12:16; cf. 2 Sam 19:9-15, 41-43; 20:1-2). But the narrator's final verdict, as in 1 Kgs 2:15, is that it was "a turn of affairs brought about by Yahweh" (12:15), already justified in the oracle Ahijah had addressed to Jeroboam, and reinforced by Shemaiah when he dissuaded Rehoboam from trying to restore his rule by force.

Jeroboam's Capital. Jeroboam had problems of his own, however. Where should his capital be? The fact that first Shechem (cf. Judg 9:45) and then Penuel (cf. Judg 8:17) needed to be rebuilt is a reminder that the northern tribes had not always lived peacefully together. They were both in the territory of Manasseh: Jeroboam's residence in those towns and in Tirzah (14:17) may have been a tactful decision on his part since he came from Ephraim (11:26).

Two National Shrines. One of Solomon's undoubted successes had been the building of the temple in Jerusalem and its establishment as the national shrine. To counteract its appeal Jeroboam enhanced the status of two established sanctuaries, Bethel in the territory of Ephraim in the south (cf. Gen 28:10-22; 35:1-15) and Dan in the north (cf. Judg 18:27-31), by commissioning two golden calves.

The "Sin" of Jeroboam. The narrative explicitly calls the worship at Bethel and Dan, involving the use of these images, a "sin." This reflects the standpoint of the Decalogue (Exod 20:4-6; Deut 5:8-10). People make images to worship them; since Yahweh has forbidden the making of any image, worship involving the use of an image must be the worship of an alien god. The story of the golden calf in Exodus 32 dramatizes this standpoint and contains a barely veiled judgment on Jeroboam's action. Such images should be ground to powder and their worshipers put to the sword.

Not Necessarily Idolatry. However, we do not know when the Decalogue became the standard for Israel's faith and life or how widely it was accepted. A less hostile account of the golden calves could be given. The narrative itself is honest enough to admit that the images were made in honor of the God who brought Israel out of Egypt (12:28; cf. Exod 32:4). There is no suggestion that the calves were representations of a god who had more to do with fertility than with interventions in history on behalf of his people. It has been suggested that, as Baal was depicted as standing on the back of a bull, so the calves were regarded as pedestals on which the invisible Yahweh stood, serving the same function as the ark in the Jerusalem temple.

Celebration at the Wrong Time by the Wrong People. The Deuteronomic standpoint, that worship should be conducted only at the one place in the land that Yahweh had chosen (Deut 12:1-14), is not emphasized here. However, Jeroboam compounds his sin (a) by appointing priests who are not Levites and (b) by instituting a festival in the eighth month instead of the seventh. Deuteronomy takes for granted that all priests with a claim to officiate in Jerusalem will be Levites (Deut 18:1-8), but it sets no fixed time for the autumn festival (Deut 16:13-15).

1 Kings 13

Hostility to Bethel. This chapter is linked to the preceding one by its hostile attitude to the cult at Bethel. 12:33 has related that Jeroboam went to Bethel at the festival he had inaugurated to offer incense at the altar. 13:1-6 relates how an unnamed prophet predicts the altar's desecration by a named king, Josiah (some three centuries later). The prediction is reinforced by immediate damage to the altar and the withering of the king's hand when he orders the prophet's arrest.

Josiah's Reforms Anticipated. However, the hostility here is directed to the very existence of the altar rather than to the particular cult practiced at it. There is no mention of the calf images. Even at the end of the chapter (13:33-34) Jeroboam's sin is the appointment of priests for the "high places" rather than the making of the images. In its present form the chapter reflects the policy behind Josiah's reforms, which was particularly severe toward the sanctuary at Bethel (2 Kgs 23:15-20). (The sacred object Josiah destroyed was the Asherah, the sacred pole, not a golden calf.) Why Bethel should have been singled out in this way is impossible to say. Even Deuteronomy takes a more understanding attitude to the multiplicity of sanctuaries in its call to sacrifice only at the one Yahweh has chosen (Deut 12:8-28).

A Reminiscence of Amos? From the time of Wellhausen readers have been reminded of another prophet who came from Judah and uttered oracles of judgment at Bethel (Amos 7:10-17). He, too, criticized the cult there (4:4-5; 5:4-5) without any mention of the calf image. The story here could be a popular reminiscence of what Amos did, transposed from the time of Jeroboam II to that of Jeroboam I. The tomb Josiah spared at Bethel (2 Kgs 23:16-18) could have been that of Amos. We do not know whether Amos got home safely!

The Moral of the Story. The "man of God" (the prophet from Judah is consistently referred to by this term here and in 2 Kgs 23:16-18) did not get home safely. Although he resisted the king's invitation to delay his return, he believed the "old prophet" who claimed divine authorization for his invitation. It is difficult to know what moral to draw from the story. It might be a cautionary tale told in the "schools of the prophets," making the point that they should trust to their own inspiration rather than to (supposedly) divine instructions mediated by others. Or it might be a warning to the general public that a claim to divine inspiration is not sufficient guarantee that a prophet is speaking the truth and that other tests must be devised. It seems to be suggesting that deceit (13:18) can be a legitimate tactic in testing someone's fidelity (a similar consideration will arise at 2 Kgs 10:19).

"Men of God." The use of the term "man of God" may suggest that in the popular imagination an aura of mystery surrounded the prophets. They could predict the future; they had signs at their command to reinforce their predictions; even animals showed respect for a prophet's corpse (13:24, 28; contrast the fate of Ahab [1 Kgs 22:38], Jehoram [2 Kgs 9:25-26], and Jezebel [2 Kgs 9:30-37]).

1 Kings 14:1-20

Condemnation of Jeroboam's Dynasty. This passage contains the rest of what the historian has to tell us about the reign of Jeroboam I in Israel. It begins with Jeroboam sending his wife to the prophet Ahijah about their son's illness. Ahijah tells her that the child will die, and so he does. But Ahijah uses the occasion to announce Yahweh's judgment on Jeroboam and his whole family (14:7-11), in terms which will be repeated in verdicts on subsequent dynasties (16:1-4; 21:20-24; 2 Kgs 9:6-10). Some scholars see in these announcements and the accounts of their fulfillment (15:29-30; 16:11-13; 2 Kgs 9:36-37; 10:10, 17) additions to the original history offering a rationale for the violent changes of dynasty in the Northern Kingdom and the role of prophets in instigating them. Here, however, the condemnation of the dynasty and the answer to Jeroboam's inquiry about his son are woven together: his death from natural causes, escaping the terrible fate which awaits the rest of the family, should be seen as a mark of Yahweh's favor.

Rationale of Later Events. A further prophecy of the events of 722 BC, when the independence of the Northern Kingdom, the greater part of "Israel," was brought to an end by the Assyrians, is also put into Ahijah's mouth (14:15-16). This anticipates the explanation of those events in 2 Kgs 17:7-18. There we are told that Yahweh had repeatedly warned Israel through the prophets to repent (vv. 13-15), but we hear nothing of any warning Ahijah gave to Jeroboam beyond the conditional promise in 1 Kgs 11:38. No mention is made of any sins other than cultic offenses (vv. 9, 15), in contrast to the emphasis on social wrongs in the eighth-century prophets. The historians are more concerned to give a rationale of later events from their own standpoint than to present a realistic picture of the work of prophets.

The Popular View of Prophets. However, the story in which these grim prophecies are inserted gives us a glimpse of what prophets were expected to do. They were consulted in times of illness, sometimes in the hope of a cure (cf. 1 Kgs 17:17-24; 2 Kgs 4:18-37) but sometimes, as here, only for a prognosis (cf. 2 Kgs 1:2-4; 8:7-10; 20:1-11). People expected to pay them for their services (14:3; 1 Sam 9:6-8) or reward them if the outcome was favorable (2 Kgs 5:15-16). They were believed to have "second sight" and to be able to see through disguise (14:2, 5-6). They could predict an event to the very moment (vv. 12, 17).

Further Information. The historians tell us (14:19-20) that there was much more about Jeroboam's policies and actions in their source. We have no independent evidence that careful records of each reign were kept.

1 Kings 14:21-31

Arrangement of the History. The history of the now divided kingdom is skillfully arranged, accounts of the reigns of the kings of Israel alternating with accounts of the reigns of the kings of Judah.

Rehoboam (Judah 922-915). There is theological tension here: Rehoboam reigns in Jerusalem, the city which Yahweh has a vested interest in preserving (v. 21); but cultic practices on the face of it more reprehensible and less Israelite in spirit than Jeroboam's innovations in the north are tolerated in Judah (14:22-24). The pillars and sacred poles (*'asherim*) were stylized symbols of a male and a female deity respectively. Sometimes more explicit images were made (cf. 1 Kgs 15:13; 16:33; 2 Kgs 13:6; 21:7; 23:6).

Shishak's Invasion. The chief event in the reign was the invasion by Shishak of Egypt. This is the first point in the biblical history at which its account of a specific event can be compared with extrabiblical evidence. Shishak was Shoshenq (or Sheshonq) I, founder of the Twenty-second Dynasty in Egypt. In the temple of Amun at Karnak there is a list of the Palestinian and Syrian towns he conquered in this campaign (conveniently in Rohl 1995: 124, although Rohl rejects the identification of Shishak with Shoshenq). A fragment of a monumental stone bearing Shoshenq's name has also been found at Megiddo, one of the towns listed. Oddly, while the biblical account mentions the invasion only in relation to Judah, Shoshenq's list includes several towns in the Northern Kingdom but none in Judah. The discrepancy could be explained by supposing that Rehoboam bought off the invader (cf. 2 Kgs 18:13-16), but that is not what the biblical text says.

Loss of Temple Treasures. The historians here do not interpret Shishak's invasion explicitly as God's judgment on Judah for its cultic transgressions, as does the Chronicler (2 Chr 12:1-2). The emphasis is rather on the loss of some of the treasures of the temple and palace. This is a theme which will recur at intervals (cf. 1 Kgs 15:18-19; 2 Kgs 12:17-18; 14:11-14; 16:8; 18:13-16).

The King's Mother. We are twice told the name of Rehoboam's mother (14:21, 31), and this information will be given for all but two of the kings of Judah (the exceptions are Jehoram in 2 Kgs 8:16 and Ahaz in 2 Kgs 16:1). The significance of this will be discussed in the next section (1 Kgs 15:1-24).

The Two Kingdoms at War. No details are given of the "continual" wars between Rehoboam and Jeroboam. 2 Chr 11:5-12 describes measures Rehoboam took to fortify towns in Judah.

1 Kings 15:1-24

Abijam (Judah 915-913). This reign was marked by continuation of warfare between Israel and Judah. (A rather idealized version of this is given in 2 Chronicles 13.) There was apparently no attempt at reform of the cultus, and so the historians try to explain why Yahweh allowed the dynasty to continue. David's faithfulness outweighed the disloyalty of his successors. The stability of the dynasty and Jerusalem was a kind of "lamp" to David's memory.

Asa (Judah 913-873). Abijam's son was, in contrast, the first of a number of reforming kings of Judah. Although the country sanctuaries were allowed to continue, images were destroyed and male prostitutes removed. Asa also replenished the temple treasures.

Asherah. Asherah (Athirat) was a Canaanite deity, sometimes represented by a wooden pole, sometimes by a carved image. In the Ugaritic myths she is the consort of El, particularly associated with the coastal Phoenician cities. In 1 Kgs 16:32-33; 18:19 she is associated with Baal. Where she is mentioned on her own, the implication may be that she was considered the consort of Yahweh. Stones discovered at Kuntillet Ajrud, northwest of Eilat, have inscribed on them "I bless you by Yahweh of Teiman and his Asherah" and "I bless you by Yahweh of Samaria and his Asherah"; and the wall of a burial chamber at Khirbet el-Qom near Hebron has the inscription "Blessed be Uriyah by Yahweh . . . (and) his Asherah" (Cogan and Tadmor 1988: 268; discussed, e.g., by Emerton 1982; Olyan 1988).

The "Great Lady." Particular interest attaches to Asa's removal of Maacah from being "queen mother" (*gebirah,* lit. "great lady"). The fact that Maacah is said to be mother of both Abijam and his son Asa suggests that we are being given the name of the holder of an office, usually but not always the king's actual mother. This would explain why we were told who the king's mother was rather than who his wife was. There is too little evidence to say what the *gebirah*'s role was: Maacah's removal for making an image of the Canaanite goddess Asherah may indicate that she had some official responsibility for the cultus (De Vaux 1961: 117-19).

The Two Kingdoms Continue at War. The war between Judah and Israel continued in the reigns of Asa and Baasha (Jeroboam's successor but one). Baasha's fortification of Ramah, in the territory of Benjamin, only five miles north of Jerusalem, was a sufficient threat to make Asa call in aid from the Aramean king Benhadad, who invaded Israel from the north and occupied what would later become Galilee. (Ahaz will later make a similar appeal to the Assyrian king Tiglath-pileser [2 Kgs 16:7].) The alliance was bought at a price, but it made Baasha move to Tirzah, where he could more effectively deal with threats from the north, and allowed Asa to dismantle the fortifications of Ramah. The Chronicler disapproved of the alliance nonetheless and for once presents a rather less attractive picture of a Judean king (2 Chr 16:7-10).

Length of Asa's Reign. Asa reigned a long time and suffered some of the disadvantages of old age (15:23). Again the Chronicler criticizes him for relying on doctors instead of on Yahweh (2 Chr 16:12).

Dating the Reigns. The reigns of the kings of Judah are from this point onward until the fall of the Northern Kingdom synchronized with those of the kings of Israel. The total of the reigns of the kings of Israel is not an exact match with that of the reigns of the kings of Judah, and there have been various attempts to reconcile the figures (e.g., by postulating that the reigns of some kings overlapped in so-called "co-regencies"). Absolute dating at least of events in some reigns becomes possible when they are recorded in Assyrian inscriptions as well, because the Assyrians kept lists of years and significant events which took place in them, and one of those events was an eclipse which can be dated to the year 763 BC. Several different dating schemes have been arrived at by scholars (Hayes and Miller 1977: 678-83); the one used here is that of Albright (1945), adopted in Bright (1959, etc.). It should be taken as a rough guide only.

1 Kings 15:25–16:14

Assassination of Two Kings. Two royal families in Israel come to a violent end, and these events are interpreted by the Deuteronomists as the fulfillment of prophetic sentences on them for persisting in the cultus which Jeroboam had introduced. Baasha's assassination of *Nadab (Israel, 901-900)* is regarded as the fulfillment of Ahijah's prophecy of doom on Jeroboam's family (14:7-11), and Zimri's assassination of *Elah (Israel, 877-876)* is regarded as the fulfillment of a similar prophecy by Jehu son of Hanani (16:1-4). Note, however, that Baasha's assassination of Nadab is not condoned: his death is partly punishment for that crime (16:7b). Zimri's assassination of Elah is also remembered as a treacherous crime (2 Kgs 9:31).

Few Achievements. We are not told very much about what the kings did during their reigns. Nadab was killed during the siege of a Philistine city (15:27); the war between *Baasha (Israel, 900-877)* and Asa of Judah has already been described (15:32; cf. 15:16-22). The fact that Elah was murdered while drunk (16:9-10) suggests that Zimri had lost patience with an incompetent ruler. There is a similar hint that drunkenness leads to complacency and bad decisions in 1 Kgs 20:12, 16.

Tirzah. Baasha made Tirzah his capital (15:21, 33). Tell

el-Far'ah, seven miles northeast of Nablus, has been identified as the site of Tirzah (De Vaux 1967: 379-82). Although no royal palace has been found in the ninth-century stratum, de Vaux found evidence of unfinished building, followed by signs of depopulation, which would fit in with the removal of the capital to Samaria in the reign of Omri (16:23-24). The attraction of Tirzah (if this identification is correct) was that it had good communications north and south and a plentiful supply of water (De Vaux 1967: 371).

1 Kings 16:15-34

Zimri (Israel, 876) was not supported in his seizure of the throne by the army, which was still besieging the Philistine town of Gibbethon (16:15; cf. 15:27). Within the week Tirzah had been taken by the army under its commander, Omri, and Zimri had committed suicide. The standard formulas are applied to him (16:19-20), despite the fact that seven days did not give him time to do much evil or indeed much at all. Even killing all of Baasha's family (16:11) was a tall order in seven days.

The Role of Mercenaries. Even Omri did not have universal support, and he had to defeat the followers of Tibni before he could establish himself as king. Zimri, Omri, and Tibni are not typical Israelite names, and only Tibni's parentage is mentioned. This has led to speculation that all three were foreign mercenaries in Israel's army.

Omri (Israel, 876-869). The account of his reign is relatively brief, but it is noted that he was a powerful king (16:27). Extrabiblical evidence confirms this: he was well known on the international scene. The inscription of Mesha, king of Moab, relates that Omri "oppressed Moab" and occupied "the land of Medeba" in the north of the country (*ANET,* 320; *DOTT,* 196). From the ninth century to the seventh Israel was known to the Assyrians as "the house (land) of Omri" (*ANET,* 281, 284, 285; *DOTT,* 51-52, 55, 60); and Jehu, the king who brought Omri's dynasty to an end (2 Kings 9–10), is nevertheless described as the "son of Omri" (*ANET,* 280, 281; *DOTT,* 48).

Samaria. The one achievement which is recorded here is Omri's purchase and fortification of a new capital, Samaria. The hill on which it was built rises about three hundred feet above the surrounding valley, lies in a fertile area, and has good communications to the west, north, and east. Excavations have revealed both the palace and the fortifications (Ackroyd 1967: 343-45).

Ahab (Israel, 869-850). Omri was able to pass on the succession to his son. The historians' judgment on Ahab is very severe (16:30, 33b; cf. 21:25-26). Of course he perpetuates the cultus established by Jeroboam. But his chief offense is to marry Jezebel, daughter of Ethbaal king of Sidon, and to introduce the worship of the Tyrian Baal (and his consort Asherah [16:33a]) into Israel. This involved building a temple in Samaria. The conflict this engendered will be the theme of subsequent narratives (1 Kings 18–19; 2 Kgs 10:18-27), but the now familiar judgment on the dynasty by the prophets will apparently be for a quite different offense (1 Kgs 21:20-24). There are other stories, too, which suggest yet further reasons why Ahab incurred the hostility of the prophets (20:35-43; 22:5-28).

The International Scene. Ahab figures as Omri's son in the Mesha inscription (*ANET,* 320; *DOTT,* 196), and under his own name in the annals of the Assyrian king Shalmaneser III, when he claimed to have defeated a coalition of twelve kings, from Damascus, Hamath, Cilicia, Israel, and the like, at Qarqar on the Orontes (north of Hamath and south of Aleppo; *ANET,* 278-79; *DOTT,* 47). Ahab is credited with having two hundred chariots and 10,000 soldiers.

Building and Decoration. Ahab was remembered for building an "ivory house" and other cities in Israel (1 Kgs 22:39). Excavations at Samaria have yielded many items of ivory decoration (Ackroyd 1967: 345-46; they are not all necessarily from the reign of Ahab since Samaria was renowned for its ivories in the next century as well [Amos 3:15]), and many of the buildings and fortifications at Megiddo once attributed to Solomon are now thought to come from the time of Ahab (Yadin 1960).

Jericho Rebuilt. The reference to the rebuilding of Jericho by Hiel of Bethel (16:34) takes up the tradition, recorded earlier in the Deuteronomistic history, that Joshua laid a curse on anyone who tried to restore it (Josh 6:26). The sacrifice of his two sons was presumably intended to ward off any ill fortune, but we cannot really know whether it was done in conscious fulfillment of a prediction.

1 Kings 17

Ahab and Elijah. Within the chronicle-like account of the reign of Ahab (16:29-34; 22:39-40) historians have incorporated a number of narratives, generally of some length, and very varied in character. The king appears in most of them, but often the chief figure is Elijah, the man of God (17:18) and prophet of Yahweh (18:22; 19:16).

Theme and Variations. Chs. 17–19 can be read as a continuous story, the account of Elijah's lone struggle against the Baal cultus which Ahab had introduced into Israel (16:31-33). But it incorporates other stories about Elijah not directly related to the main theme, particularly in ch. 17.

The Drought. Elijah announces that there will be a prolonged drought. His authority for doing this is that he stands in Yahweh's presence (an idea which is elaborated in 22:19-23). He has also been given the authority to announce, or even to order, the end of the drought. It is clearly under the control of Yahweh or his representative. No one questions the announcement. But since it is not suggested that it is a punishment, no indication is given to Ahab that he can do anything to avert it or bring it to a speedy end. Confirmation that the drought was remembered as particularly severe may be provided by Josephus, who cites his Tyrian source Menander as mentioning a drought in the reign of Ithobaal (= Ethbaal [1 Kgs 16:31]), Ahab's Phoenician contemporary, which was brought to an end as a result of the king's prayers (*Ant.* 8 §324).

Elijah Provided For. The consequences for Ahab and the nation as a whole must wait until the next chapter. Meanwhile Elijah is as liable to suffer from the drought as anyone, and Yahweh has to see that he is provided for. The provision is a mixture of the natural, the human, and the miraculous. He is directed to one of the last wadis to dry up, and then to a widow in Sidon on the Phoenician coast who takes the risk of sharing what she expects to be her and her son's last meal with the man of God. But at the Wadi Cherith Elijah is also fed by ravens (the temptation to rationalize the miracle and read *'orebim* as "Arabs" rather than "ravens" is to be resisted), and the widow's jar of meal and jug of oil are miraculously replenished until the end of the drought. In Luke 4:25-26 the story is cited as an illustration of the fact that prophets are rarely welcome in their own country.

The Widow's Son. The story of the widow's son is not strictly relevant to the account of Elijah's survival. Its function here is to heighten the impression of the prophet's standing with Yahweh and to create the expectation that more momentous deeds are to follow. A similar story is told of Elisha (2 Kgs 4:8-37). Comparison of the two reveals that this story is more conventionally religious — the widow believes that her son's illness is a punishment for some long-forgotten sin of hers (17:18); Elijah protests to Yahweh and prays for the boy's revival (vv. 20-21); the widow is moved to a confession of faith (v. 24) — and somewhat less concerned with ordinary human reactions (Rofé 1970: 433-35). In both, however, prayer is accompanied by what looks like sympathetic magic (1 Kgs 17:21; 2 Kgs 4:29-31, 34-35).

1 Kings 18

A Trial of Strength. 1 Kings 18 is one of the great stories of the Hebrew Bible (HB). It continues the story of the drought, begun in the previous chapter, but interweaves with it an account of a trial of strength between Yahweh and Baal, necessitated by the account of Ahab's religious policy in 16:31-33.

Prophets in Danger. Just as the announcement of the coming of the drought had to be made to Ahab in person, so the announcement of its ending has to be delivered directly. This is a dangerous errand, for two reasons. The effect of the drought on the country has been severe, and Ahab has been searching for Elijah, the person he holds responsible, for some time. It has also been a hard time for Yahweh's prophets generally: Jezebel has killed many of them, while many others have had to go into hiding. These dangers are skillfully sketched in Elijah's encounter with Ahab's minister, Obadiah, who is helping Ahab cope with the consequences of the drought, secretly giving asylum to Yahweh's prophets, and fearful for his own position.

Who Is Bringing Trouble on Israel? Elijah does not at once announce the end of the drought. When Ahab accuses Elijah of bringing trouble to Israel (the drought), Elijah counters by accusing Ahab of doing so (by forsaking Yahweh and worshiping Baal). No direct link, however, is made between Baal worship and the drought, and the latter is temporarily forgotten (18:33-35) while a test of the rival gods' ability to answer prayer is carried out.

The Prophets of Baal begin with all the advantages. Elijah's straightforward appeal to the people to decide which god to follow wins no response (18:21). They have superiority in numbers and by implication the support of authority (v. 22). They are allowed to choose their bull (vv. 23, 25), and they are given all day to bring down fire from heaven (vv. 26, 29). All this serves only to emphasize the lengths to which they have to go (vv. 26, 28-29), and the futility of their efforts. The word translated "limped" in v. 26 probably refers to a ritual dance, but in the context it echoes the "limping" of the people who are afraid to commit themselves in v. 21. The word translated "raved" in v. 29 on the other hand, is the usual term used in the Bible to describe the "ecstatic" behavior common to prophets in Israel and elsewhere (cf. 1 Sam 10:5-6, 10-13; 19:20-24; and the account given by the Egyptian traveler Wen-Amon of such behavior at Byblos c. 1100 BC [*ANET*, 26]).

Foreign Gods Ridiculed. The whole episode dramatizes one dominant attitude of Israel's prophets and psalmists to foreign gods. They and their worshipers are only fit to be ridiculed (Pss 115:4-8; 135:15-18; Isa 40:18-20; 44:9-20; 46:1-7). The other attitude is, of course, to denounce Israel's worship of foreign gods as disloyalty (Jeremiah 2–3; Hos 2:2-13). The anthropomorphic picture of Baal which Elijah draws (18:27) goes beyond the human characteristics used in envisaging Yahweh (the word the NRSV translates "has wandered away" is in Jewish tradition taken to mean "is relieving himself"), but the thought that Yahweh may be only an occasional visitor or asleep is not entirely absent from biblical prayers (Ps 44:23; Jer 14:8-9).

Self-Mutilation a Religious Custom. There is no reason to doubt that 18:28 reflects actual custom in non-Yahwistic religion. Cutting oneself is forbidden in Lev 19:28 and Deut 14:1, though the reference there is to mourning customs.

Elijah's Confidence in Yahweh. If the initial advantages of the prophets of Baal are emphasized, Elijah's disadvantages are made light of. The task of rebuilding the altar is methodically undertaken (18:30-32; the rebuilding of the altar on Mt. Carmel by so devoted a Yahwist as Elijah shows that the author of this story did not share the strict Deuteronomic and Deuteronomistic standpoint that there should be only one sanctuary in the land). The fact that he leaves the test until late in the day (vv. 29, 36) is a sign both of confidence and respect for the appointed time for sacrifice. Pouring water over the sacrifice is an extravagant demonstration of the belief that nothing is too hard for Yahweh. (This point is completely destroyed by those who suppose that he must have used naphtha instead of water!)

God of Abraham, Isaac, and Israel. The tradition to which Elijah appeals in his dignified prayer is not the exodus tradition (cf. 1 Kgs 8:51, 53; 12:28) but that of the patriarchs, particularly Jacob/Israel (18:31, 36). References to Yahweh as "the God of Abraham, Isaac, and Jacob" are rare outside the passages in the Pentateuch where the identification is made (Exod 3:15; 6:3). The use of the title here may be due to a local tradition that the sanctuary on Carmel had been founded by one or other of the patriarchs; or it may be an indication that the story was composed at a time when the patriarchal and the exodus traditions had long been fused. This particular variant, "Abraham, Isaac, and *Israel*," is found in the late post-exilic books of Chronicles (1 Chr 29:18; 2 Chr 30:6).

No Mercy for the Losers. The fire from heaven convinces the people that Yahweh is Israel's true God. It is sad, however, that the victory had to be sealed with the slaughter of the prophets of Baal, thus establishing a biblical precedent for the burning of heretics, particularly in the sixteenth century. The author of the story recognizes that Elijah's action will have repercussions for him (19:1-3), but he seems to regard it as an acceptable expression of "zeal" for Yahweh (19:10, 14).

History or Drama? Did such a decisive confrontation really take place? The major difficulty lies in believing that a miracle of this kind could have occurred. But there is also the problem that a generation later Baal worship had to be eradicated from Israel all over again, in a much more down-to-earth way (2 Kgs 10:15-27). Perhaps we should regard the story as a dramatization of beliefs and hopes about the relationship between Yahweh and other gods rather than as verifiable history.

Elijah's Superhuman Powers. After the contest, the end of the drought can be announced. Elijah's credentials as a prophet are confirmed by his performance of sympathetic magic (?) (18:42) and by a feat of superhuman strength (v. 46).

1 Kings 19

Elijah Travels Again. Like ch. 17, this chapter relates how a crisis led Elijah to travel to escape danger. But whereas the first time this was at God's command, this time it is out of human fear. Whereas the first time the concern was for his physical survival, now the focus is on a spiritual crisis. There is supernatural provision for his bodily needs in both cases, but whereas the first journey culminated in affirmation of his role as a "man of God" (17:24), this second journey culminates in arrangements for him to relinquish that role and hand it on to a successor.

A Realistic Sequel. The story comes as a surprise after the triumph of ch. 18. We expect something more like the story endings in 2 Kgs 6:23b or 10:28. But perhaps the intention is to be realistic about the prophetic experience: success can be short-lived, and the most confident of prophets can end up feeling abandoned and a failure. The story may also be intended to explain how it was that the eradication of Baal worship was achieved only through the bloody events of the next generation.

Fanatical Devotion. Elijah describes himself as having been "zealous" for Yahweh (19:10, 14). The word is the same as that used in the Decalogue to describe Yahweh as a "jealous" God, ready to go to extremes not to admit any rival (Exod 20:5; Deut 5:9; cf. Exod 34:14; Deut 4:24; 6:15; Josh 24:19; Nah 1:2). It is possible that this fanatical streak of devotion to Yahweh originated with Elijah and other ninth-century prophets.

Yahweh's Altars. Elijah complains that the people of Israel have thrown down Yahweh's altars. Once again we note that the story does not take the Deuteronomic standpoint that there was only one legitimate sanctuary at which Yahweh could be worshiped.

The Theophany at Horeb. It is difficult to determine the significance of the account of the theophany (19:11-13). The traditions of the original theophany at Horeb (or Sinai) emphasize dramatic phenomena, such as thunder and lightning, fire, and an earthquake (Exod 19:16-19; 24:17), and this story has often been taken as repudiating the idea that God is to be known through such phenomena. Cf. the hymn "Dear Lord and Father of Mankind." This would run counter to a number of passages which portray God's intervention in storm imagery (Judg 5:4-5; Pss 18:7-15 [Heb. 8-16]; 29; 68:7-8 [Heb. 8-9]; Hab 3:3-12). But is God known here *in* the silence or *after* it? The significance of the theophany is not drawn out, and it seems unrelated to the rest of the chapter. The repetition of Elijah's answer to the question "What are you doing here?" (19:9b-10, 13b-14) may mean that the narrative originally lacked vv. 11-14.

Elijah's Commission. The commission Elijah receives in 19:15-18 anticipates later parts of the history; for Hazael see 2 Kgs 8:7-15; 10:32-33; 13:3-7, 22-25; for Jehu 2 Kings 9–10; for Elisha 2 Kgs 2:1–9:1; 13:14-21. But in the later narratives there is no mention of Elijah anointing any of the three. This is a further indication that the historians have made use of varied traditions about the principal actors in the history.

A Righteous Remnant. 19:18 is partly responsible for the idea that the prophets believed that God would always ensure that, however far Israel as a whole strayed from their allegiance to him, there was a "righteous remnant" which remained loyal (cf. Isa 10:20-21; Ezek 9:4-8; Zeph 3:12-13). However, it is not at all certain that this was a fixed belief. In some of the passages cited, the prophets seem to be saying that *only* a remnant will survive invasion, without implying that they would be the righteous (Isa 1:9; 6:9-13a; 10:22-23; see also the commentary on 2 Kings 18–19).

Elijah and Elisha. The account of how Elisha became associated with Elijah must be an independent tradition since it does not involve the anointing anticipated in 19:16. There is another tradition of how Elisha acquired Elijah's mantle in 2 Kgs 2:12b-14. It is possible that the story has influenced the accounts in the Gospels of how people became Jesus' disciples, both positively (Matt 9:9; Mark 1:16-20; Luke 5:27-28) and negatively (Luke 9:57-62).

1 Kings 20

Israel and Aram. This story of warfare between Israel and Aram must originate in a quite different source from that of the Elijah narratives. While Benhadad of Aram is named throughout, the king of Israel is usually referred to as such, and only occasionally identified as Ahab (20:2, 13, 14). The story may therefore have been told originally of an anonymous Israelite king. Various prophets figure in the story, but they are all anonymous. Two of them encourage the king of Israel with favorable oracles and guidance about military tactics (vv. 13-14, 22, 28); the one who condemns the king does so on grounds quite different from those of Elijah (v. 42; cf. 18:17-18; 21:17-24). The charge — that the king has spared an enemy "devoted to destruction" (*ḥerem*) — is reminiscent of the holy war tradition in which God enables Israel to overcome vastly superior numbers (vv. 13, 28). The intention is to testify to Yahweh's reality and power, in the valleys as well as in the hills, but he is not necessarily contending with the gods of the Arameans, as he was with Baal in ch. 18.

The Narrative as a Story. The story is a mixture of the stylized and the realistic. The account of the two battles is lacking in any realistic detail. We hear of the events leading up to the battles but are given no indication of how the Israelites were able to inflict such heavy casualties on the Arameans. On the other hand, the account of the negotiations between Benhadad and the king of Israel (20:30b-34) and the prophet's ruse to make the king pass judgment on his own actions (vv. 35-43; cf. 2 Sam 12:1-7a; 14:1-20) have much greater narrative interest. The former, while giving us a glimpse of the way trade was carried on between the two nations (20:34), wins our approval for the king of Israel's clemency (it is a good thing to be "merciful" or, rather, a person of one's word [v. 31]). The latter keeps us guessing (why this none-too-obvious role play?), and the point, that to a strict Yahwist the king's action is disloyalty, is something of a shock when it comes.

A Proverbial Saying. 20:11 contains one of the few biblical proverbs which are purely figurative sayings (cf. Isa 10:15; Jer 13:23; Jer 31:29 = Ezek 18:2). The most likely translation is that of the NRSV; the NEB, "The lame must not think himself a match for the nimble," preferred to follow the LXX. The REB (and the GNB) follow *Tg. Neb.* in explaining rather than reproducing the proverb: "The time for boasting is after the battle."

1 Kings 21

A Story about Human Rights. In their judgments on the kings of Israel the Deuteronomistic historians normally confine themselves to their actions with regard to the cult. Up to this point Ahab has been no exception, and in 21:20-26 the charge of idolatry is resumed. But in the story of Naboth's vineyard Ahab is condemned for using his position to murder one of his subjects and steal his possessions.

Comparison with an Earlier Story. The closest parallel is the story of David and Bathsheba in 2 Samuel 11–12. In both stories the king wants something the subject possesses; the subject refuses to go along with the king's plans, appealing to a fundamental principle of the Israelite way of life; a ruse is employed to conceal the reason for the subject's death; others are implicated in the murder; the king's guilt is exposed by a prophet; and the king's repentance brings about a mitigation of the punishment.

The Principles at Stake. The principle to which Naboth appeals is that the land an Israelite inherits should not be alienated from the family (Lev 25:23; Num 36:7). The temptation to which the king was exposed was not unique to Ahab (1 Sam 8:14; Ezek 46:18). Nor was that to which the elders of Jezreel succumbed, of obeying Jezebel's transparently unjust orders (cf. 2 Kgs 10:1-9). Although they are not explicitly blamed, comparison with the story of Saul's servants refusing to kill the priests of Nob shows that in the view of biblical narrators the elders had a choice (1 Sam 22:17).

General Condemnation of Ahab. 21:20-26 should probably be read as an editorial addition to the story. The charges against Ahab (vv. 20, 22) are general and concern idolatry rather than injustice toward his subjects, and the threatened punishment is phrased in terms similar to that against Jeroboam and Baasha (1 Kgs 14:7-11; 16:1-4). The specific threat to Ahab (21:19) may, however, have been part of the original story since it was transmitted in more than one version (cf. 2 Kgs 9:26) and two contexts were suggested for its fulfillment (1 Kgs 22:38; 2 Kgs 9:25-26). The threat to Jezebel, on the other hand, is possibly a reading back of her eventual fate (2 Kgs 9:30-37).

1 Kings 22:1-40

Israel and Aram Again. This chapter has more in common with ch. 20 than with ch. 21. (In the LXX it follows ch. 20 directly.) Once again it concerns relations between Israel and Aram. Prophets offer assurance of the success of a military campaign. The king of Israel is only once identified as Ahab (22:20), whereas the king of Judah is named as Jehoshaphat throughout, two of the prophets are named (vv. 8, 11), as are the governor of Samaria and the king's son (v. 26).

An Alliance between Israel and Judah. The object of the campaign is to recapture Ramoth-gilead in Transjordan from the Arameans. This campaign was not successful (22:36), though Ramoth-gilead appears subsequently to have fallen into Israelite hands (2 Kgs 9:14). It was notable, however, for the willingness of Jehoshaphat to join the campaign. In the reign of Jehoshaphat's predecessor, Judah had persuaded Aram to invade Israel (1 Kgs 15:16-20). This new alliance between Israel and Judah lasted throughout the Omride dynasty (2 Kgs 3:7; 8:28) and was strengthened by the marriage of Jehoram of Judah to Athaliah the daughter of Ahab (2 Kgs 8:18). Relations deteriorated again during the Jehu dynasty, however (2 Kgs 14:8-14).

Attitude to the Prophets. A major difference between this story and that in ch. 20 is that the assurances of the prophets do not go unquestioned. Jehoshaphat at once expresses misgiving at the easy promises of success (22:5-7). The king of Israel admits that they do not always give unanimous advice: Micaiah has a reputation for prophesying disaster (v. 8). Neither the symbolic action Zedekiah is inspired to take (v. 11) nor Micaiah's initial confirmation of the predictions of success (vv. 15-16) is regarded as conclusive. The king of Israel both does and does not want to hear the truth: while he urges Micaiah not to spare him (v. 16), what he hears makes him order the prophet to be taken into custody (vv. 26-28). (For a similar incident, featuring a clash between two named prophets and a symbolic action, see Jeremiah 28.)

The Prophets' Inspiration. Micaiah's justification of his dissent from the predictions of the other prophets (22:19-23) may indicate how other prophets thought of their inspiration, and what they meant when they spoke of standing before Yahweh (1 Kgs 17:1; 18:15) or in his council (Jer 23:18, 22; cf. Amos 3:7). However, the appeal to inspiration does not settle the question which prophet is giving the right advice. Zedekiah does not give up his own claim to inspiration (v. 24); only time will tell whether he is wrong (vv. 25, 28; cf. Deut 18:21-22). For the idea that God deliberately deceives some prophets so that they give bad advice see Ezek 14:9; 2 Thess 2:11. This is not always the explanation given: they act from mercenary motives (Mic 3:5), they give their own opinions without any mandate from God (Jer 23:16; Ezek 13:6-7), and they copy each other (Jer 23:30).

The King as Shepherd. The image of the ruler as shepherd of his people (22:17) is one that was widely used in the ancient Near East. Despite the evident hostility between the king and Micaiah •, the intention here is not to characterize Ahab as a bad ruler (as in Ezek 34:1-6), but to predict the loss of firm government when he is killed in battle.

The Hand of Fate. An odd sort of battle it is, too. The king of Israel tries to avert his threatened fate by disguising himself. But it seems rather ungenerous of him to tell Jehoshaphat to wear his robes and thus lay himself open to being mistaken for the king of Israel. (Royal robes seem to have an unusual fascination for this writer; cf. 22:10.) The king of Aram at first appears to be cast as the instrument of fate through his plan to eliminate the king of Israel. How can thirty-two charioteers fail? (The idea that they could conduct the battle without fighting anyone else seems rather unrealistic, however.) But just at the point when the plan looks like being frustrated fate reasserts itself and the king of Israel is killed (cf. Josephus *Ant.* 8 §419).

How Did Ahab Die? It is doubtful whether we have here an authentic account of the death of Ahab. The anonymity of "the king of Israel" and the unrealistic features of the battle suggest that this is a traditional story about the impossibility of avoiding one's fate, loosely attached to a narrative illustrating the problem of true and false prophecy. It is noteworthy that no mention is made of the death of the king fulfilling the prediction of Micaiah, but only of the approximate fulfillment (v. 38) of Elijah's prediction in 21:19. No doubt Ahab was killed in battle, but not necessarily in the circumstances described in vv. 29-36.

1 Kings 22:41-53

The Chronicle Resumed. The historians return to the summary accounts of the reigns of the kings of Judah and Israel.

Jehoshaphat (Judah, 873-849) receives qualified praise for his religious policy. He continued his father's drive to remove the male temple prostitutes (cf. 1 Kgs 14:24; 15:12) but did not shut down the sanctuaries outside Jerusalem. The healing of the hostility with Israel (illustrated in 1 Kgs 22:1-40 and in 2 Kings 3) is noted, though the trust did not extend to mounting a joint expedition by sea. It is not clear whether the failure of Jehoshaphat's expedition was due to natural hazards or incompetence, but this is certainly not the golden age of Solomon (cf. 1 Kgs 9:26-28; 10:22).

Judah's Judicial System. In 2 Chr 19:5-11 Jehoshaphat is credited with establishing a judicial system in Judah. The lack of any mention of it in Kings may be due to a lack of interest in the matter on the part of the Deuteronomistic historians (but cf. Deut 16:18-20) or to the desire of the Chronicler to locate in a particular reign the inauguration of a system whose origin was actually unknown.

Ahaziah (Israel, 850-849; not to be confused with Ahaziah of Judah [2 Kgs 8:25-29; 9]) continued the religious policy of Ahab. A story about him will follow in 2 Kings 1.

2 Kings

COMMENTARY

2 Kings 1

Rebellion of Moab. The opening sentence of the chapter has no relation to the rest of its contents. It is, however, repeated at 3:5, where it makes a fitting introduction to the account of the joint campaign of Israel and Judah against Moab. It is therefore possible that chs. 1–2 were inserted in the history at a relatively late stage.

An Independent Elijah Story. Although the story concerns Elijah, it is probably independent of the cycle in 1 Kings 17–19. Elijah is the champion of Yahweh against a foreign god, but Baal-zebub is the god of Ekron rather than the Tyrian Baal. He calls down fire from heaven, but to burn up the king's messengers rather than as a sacrifice, and to prove that he is a man of God rather than to prove that Yahweh is the true God of Israel.

The Story in the New Testament. Although the story is less momentous than those in 1 Kings 18 and 21, it has been remembered just as much. The description of John the Baptist (Matt 3:4; Mark 1:6) is modeled on that of Elijah here (1:8). The readiness of James and John to call down fire on a Samaritan village was recognized by early copyists as a reminiscence of the story (Luke 9:54 mg.). Baal-zebub becomes the prince of the demons (Mark 3:22 and pars.).

2 Kings 2:1-18

Elisha Succeeds Elijah. Although Elijah figures in this story, it really belongs to the Elisha cycle (Rofé 1970: 436-37; 1988: 44-45). Elsewhere "the company of prophets" (lit. "the sons of the prophets") figures only in the Elisha stories, and the title "the chariots of Israel and its horsemen" is more appropriately applied to Elisha, who rescued Israel in battle (cf. 2 Kgs 6:8-23; 13:14-19), than to Elijah, who did not. The theme of the narrative is the confirmation that Elisha is Elijah's successor. The ascension of Elijah is not dwelt on, except that Elisha's witnessing of it is proof that he is to inherit a double share of Elijah's spirit (twice as much as anybody else, not twice as much as Elijah had; cf. Deut 21:17).

Elisha's Insight and Powers. Elijah does not at first disclose to Elisha what is about to happen, but the prophets at Bethel and Jericho know, and so does Elisha (2:3, 5). Elijah's mantle ceases to be simply an article of clothing (1 Kgs 19:13; 2 Kgs 1:8) and becomes the means of performing a miracle which convinces the bystanders that the spirit of Elijah rests on Elisha (2:8, 14-15). There may be an intention here to evoke continuity with Moses and Joshua (Exod 14:21-22; Josh 3:14-17), though this is not made explicit. The prophets' search for Elijah (2:16-18) may be intended to reinforce the supernatural character of Elijah's departure since he had a reputation for sudden disappearances (cf. 1 Kgs 18:12), or to demonstrate that, although the sons of the prophets had knowledge of coming events, Elisha's judgment was superior to theirs.

Elijah in Tradition. The circumstances of Elijah's departure gave rise to the tradition that he would return to prepare Israel for "the day of Yahweh" (Mal 4:5-6 [Heb. 3:23-24]) and, in the NT, for the coming of the Messiah (Mark 9:11-13; Luke 1:17). A glass of wine is poured for Elijah at the Passover Seder, and a chair is put out for him at the circumcision ceremony.

2 Kings 2:19-25

Elisha's Reputation with the Poor. The first story here (2:19-22) is one of several short accounts of minor miracles which Elisha performs (cf. 4:1-7, 38-41, 42-44; 6:1-7; 13:20-21; Rofé 1970: 430-33; 1988: 13-18). They relieve the needs of poor people, usually using magical means. The man of God sometimes accompanies the miracle with a divine promise (2:21; 4:43), but not always. This story and its promise are reminiscent of the story of Moses making the waters of Marah drinkable (Exod 15:23-26). The concern for people's everyday lives suggests that the stories were popular in origin, probably passed on orally (cf. 8:4). They offer a valuable glimpse into the social history of Israel in the ninth century.

Veneration for the Man of God. The second story (2:23-25) illustrates the awe in which the man of God was held and the efficacy of a curse uttered in the name of Yahweh. Attempts have been made to excuse the curse and its disastrous outcome, but the punishment will always seem disproportionate to the crime. Forty-two small boys are expendable when the veneration due to a man of God is at stake.

Elisha's Journeys. No explanation is given for Elisha's journeys from place to place (2:23, 25; 4:8, 38; 8:7). There is no suggestion that he exercised judicial functions as Samuel did (1 Sam 7:15-17); the stories which imply that he exercised oversight over "the company of the prophets" (4:1-7, 38-41, 42-44; 6:1-7) generally lack reference to journeys. Probably various places had their stories about Elisha, and the journeys figure as links between them (cf. the patriarchal stories in Genesis).

2 Kings 3

Jehoram (or Joram) *(Israel, 849-842).* This chapter contains the only substantial narrative in which this king, the son of Ahab, figures, apart from the account of his assassination by Jehu (2 Kings 9). (He is not to be confused with his contemporary, also Jehoram, son of Jehoshaphat, in Judah [2 Kgs 8:16-24].) An unnamed king of Israel figures in other Elisha stories (2 Kgs 5:1-7; 6:8-23; 6:24–7:20; 8:1-6), but he is not necessarily to be identified with Jehoram. Jehoram is credited here with beginning to dismantle Baal worship in Israel, which is surprising in view of the severe judgments passed on the dynasty and the measures still needed to eradicate Baal worship in the narrative of Jehu's revolt (2 Kings 9–10).

The Campaign against Moab. The story of this campaign is told in much the same way as the campaigns against Aram in 1 Kings 20 and particularly in 1 Kings 22. Once again it is a joint venture by the kings of Israel and Judah, though this time they are joined by the king of Edom, whose territory lay to the south of Moab; the king of Israel again takes the initiative; Jehoshaphat is always named, but Jehoram is sometimes just "the king of Israel"; it is Jehoshaphat who wants to consult Yahweh about the success of the expedition; the prophet expresses reluctance to comply with the wishes of the king of Israel. Nevertheless, the oracle is entirely favorable. Not only is a miraculous supply of water promised, but complete conquest of Moab as well. Both predictions are fulfilled except that, when the king of Moab in desperation offers his son as a burnt offering, Israel experiences "great wrath" (in what form is not specified) and withdraws. It is characteristic of a number of accounts of military campaigns in the Bible that they end in withdrawal without an adequate military explanation (cf. 2 Kgs 7:6-7; 19:7-9a, 35-37). Josephus, following the LXX's "great regret came upon Israel," says that the armies withdrew out of compassion for the Moabite king (*Ant.* 9 §43).

The Inscription of Mesha. Light has been shed on the story by the discovery in 1868 of an inscription of the king of Moab, Mesha (*ANET,* 320-21; *DOTT,* 195-98; Beyerlin 1978: 237-40). It confirms the occupation of much of Moab during the time of Omri and Ahab, and records several campaigns in which Mesha recaptured lost territory. He claimed to have overcome the dynasty and was confident that Israel had perished forever.

Elisha's Role. This is interesting: he is known as Elijah's former assistant (cf. 1 Kgs 19:21b) rather than as a well-known prophet in his own right. In other stories he delivers Yahweh's oracles directly; here he is dependent on music to bring on prophetic inspiration. His oracle encourages a ruthless policy to deprive the Moabites of home and livelihood. It contravenes the spirit, if not the letter, of Deut 20:19. (Mesha also practiced the *ḥerem,* the slaughter of the entire population of captured towns, as an offering to the Moabite god Chemosh.)

2 Kings 4

The Miracles of Elisha and Jesus. This chapter contains three of the popular stories about Elisha as a miracle-working man of God, meeting the needs of poor people: the widow of a son of the prophets in debt (4:1-7), the prophets at Gilgal threatened with food poisoning (vv. 38-41), and a hundred people fed with twenty loaves (vv. 42-44). Divine promise is invoked only once (v. 43). The feeding of the hundred people inevitably recalls the story of the feeding of the five thousand in the Gospels (Mark 6:30-44 and pars.). Indeed, the miracle stories in the Synoptic Gospels generally resemble these Elisha stories closely in form and present Jesus in a very similar light: as a prophet more concerned with the welfare of ordinary people than with political issues or religious reform.

Debt Slavery. Although the Book of the Covenant mentions only punishment for theft as a reason for an Israelite being sold into slavery (Exod 22:3 [Heb. 2]), it is clear from this passage (4:1) and Lev 25:39; Neh 5:5 that debt must have been the principal reason. Various measures were proposed to prevent this from happening at all (Exod 22:25 [Heb. 24]; Lev 25:35-37; Deut 15:1-6; 23:19-20) or from becoming a permanent state (Exod 21:2-6; Deut 15:12-18), but it is likely that enforcement was only rarely achieved (Jer 34:8-10; Neh 5:7-13).

Elisha and the Shunammite. The other story in the chapter (4:8-37) is told at much greater length, and consists of three episodes in the relationship of Elisha with a wealthy Shunammite woman and her family. Giving him an occasional meal develops into giving him a *pied-à-terre.* (Roof chambers seem to have been relatively rare in houses of the Iron Age II period, and there is too little archeological evidence to say anything confident about their construction.) Elisha wants to repay her, but she is not conscious of any pressing need except for what her social position cannot give her, a son. This episode is reminiscent of the story of Abraham and Sarah (Gen 18:1-15; 21:1-2). In each case the husband is old, and the son is born "at the appointed time." But, as in the Abraham and Sarah story, it looks as if the child so unexpectedly given will be cruelly taken away. The final episode is told with great insight and sympathy: the mother takes decisive action without telling her husband exactly why; the prophet's concern for her distress is mingled with injured *amour propre* that Yahweh has not given him advance warning of it; the mother already feels the injustice of having a gift she did not ask for taken away; the servant cannot revive the child, and even the man of God cannot do so instantaneously.

The Story's Artistry. The story is obviously a literary elaboration of the popular miracle story (Rofé 1970: 433-35; 1988: 27-31). The situation which calls for each miracle is fully developed, and the characters of the protagonists are well brought out. Even the husband has a role in both furthering (4:9-10, 18-19) and hindering (vv. 22-23) the plot, and Gehazi is by turns insightful (v. 14), obtuse (v. 27) and ineffective (v. 31).

Echoes in the Gospels. Again there are echoes in the Gospel stories: the person who tries to dissuade someone in distress from seeking assistance (Mark 5:35); the zealous disciples who try to turn a suppliant away (Mark 10:13); the disciples who fail to effect a cure (Mark 9:18); and the cure which takes place in stages (Mark 8:22-26).

New Moon and Sabbath. Why does the Shunammite's husband suggest that it is only appropriate to consult a man of God at new moon or on the sabbath? Perhaps these were regarded as particularly auspicious days. This would be the converse of the Babylonian belief that certain days in the month were inauspicious days for undertaking any activity. It does not sound as if the sabbath was yet regarded as a day on which no journey should be undertaken.

2 Kings 5

No God but Israel's God. The story in 2 Kgs 4:8-37 does not set out to prove anything but simply invites us to follow a human story sympathetically. Gratitude to God and awe at the powers of the man of God are implicit rather than directly expressed. 2 Kings 5, in contrast, is unashamedly out to teach (Rofé 1974: 145-48; 1988: 125-31): to demonstrate that there is no God but Israel's God (v. 15), that the prophet speaks and acts with that God's authority (vv. 8, 14), and that the transgressor cannot hope to deceive him (v. 26). The story may be said to fulfill a similar role in the Elisha cycle to that of the Carmel story in the Elijah cycle: in both the prophet is the champion of Yahweh when others are undecided (1 Kgs 18:21) or fainthearted (2 Kgs 5:7), and when the rival gods are impotent. The fact that Elisha sanctions Naaman's continued nominal recognition of Rimmon, whereas Elijah had the prophets of Baal put to death, reflects the different attitudes taken to the worship of their own gods by foreigners and the worship of other gods by the Israelites rather than an attempt to depict Elisha as a milder character than Elijah. The scene in which he confronts and punishes Gehazi recalls God's dealings with Adam and Eve (Gen 3:8-19) and with Cain (Gen 4:9-16) and Samuel's confrontation with Saul (1 Samuel 15). All the offenders try to conceal their guilt, and all are dealt with very severely.

Irony and Suspense. Even a didactic story may be skillfully told. It opens with the irony that the fate of a great man should depend on a young girl he had captured. The progress of the cure has to negotiate the obstacles of the king of Aram's failure to get the message right, the king of Israel's alarm and mistrust, and Naaman's own pride. The overcoming of the last obstacle again depends on the intervention of servants. The Gehazi episode awakens our interest by making us wonder what story he will tell to get something from Naaman and whether he will get away with it. (We should know better: this is a didactic story!)

Leprosy. It is generally agreed that the Hebrew word *ṣara'at* must refer to a variety of skin diseases (in Leviticus 13 it also covers mold and fungi in clothes and buildings) and that true leprosy (Hansen's disease) is unknown in the Bible. Hence the GNB and NJB refer to "a dreaded [or virulent] skin disease," and some other translations (NRSV, JPSV, and NIV) have notes to this effect.

The Attitude to Other Religions. Perhaps the chief interest of the story today is the light it sheds on Israel's attitude to other religions. The aim is a positive one: to affirm the reality and power of Israel's God rather than to attack another faith. There is no polemic against the worship of Rimmon (another name for the storm god Hadad), and no mockery of it. We are not told that Naaman had prayed to Rimmon for a cure without avail. Although his bowing down in the house of Rimmon will henceforward be a mere formality, it will not do him any harm. (Of course it would be a different matter for an Israelite to do such an act of nominal reverence; cf. 1 Kgs

19:18; Dan 3:18.) While he himself will be a worshiper of Yahweh, he is not given a commission to convert his king or his nation. The belief that each *land* (rather than each people) has its own deity is expressed in Naaman's request for some of the soil of Israel; without it he would not be able to offer sacrifice to Yahweh.

2 Kings 6:1-7

Elisha and the Company of the Prophets. This is yet another of the popular stories in which Elisha comes to the aid of a person in distress (6:1-7; cf. 2:19-22; 4:1-7, 38-41, 42-44). In these stories it is assumed that there is only one "company of the prophets" (contrast the different groups at Bethel and Jericho in 2:3, 5), and here Elisha is acknowledged as their head. It would be a mistake to look for a rational explanation of the miracle: we are probably intended to understand that the new stick (cf. the new bowl in 2:20) had magical properties which made the ax head float.

2 Kings 6:8-23

Elisha and the Nation in Crisis. This story (6:8-23) reintroduces the kings of Israel and Aram. They are anonymous, and this suggests that the main focus in the story is not on the episode as a historical event. Elisha figures once again as "the prophet in Israel" (5:8; 6:12) who can be counted on in a national crisis. This time the situation is one of war, and the prophet's ability to warn the king of Israel of the Arameans' movements puts him in personal danger. He is represented as a model of faith (in contrast with his servant, vv. 15-17), of piety (he prays for deliverance, v. 18), and of mercy (in contrast with the king of Israel, vv. 21-22; the theme is developed further in 2 Chr 28:8-15). This does not preclude a certain duplicity (v. 19). It is taken for granted that God will answer his prayer: there is no sustained, anxious appeal as in Elijah's prayer on Mt. Carmel (1 Kgs 18:36-37). The idea that God has horses and chariots of fire at his command (cf. 2:11) is one possible explanation of the divine title "Yahweh of hosts." These normally unseen forces reassure Elisha's servant but play no further part in the action of the story (Rofé 1988: 62-63).

2 Kings 6:24–7:20

Elisha No Longer Revered. The independence of this story from the one before is indicated by the fact that 6:23 does not lead us to expect further stories about conflict between Aram and Israel. Note also that the king of Aram is named even if the king of Israel is not, and that Elisha is no longer the revered "prophet in Israel." The king of Israel threatens to kill him (6:31), and one of his officers expresses skepticism about Elisha's favorable oracle (7:2).

Famine in Samaria. Samaria is under siege, and this has gone on long enough to cause famine. The most unlikely sources of food are bringing very high prices (6:25). It is difficult to translate prices into present-day terms (a shekel of silver would be worth over £1 [$1.50] today), but we might note that in normal times thirty shekels was the price of a slave (Exod 21:32) and that David could buy a threshing floor and some oxen for fifty shekels (2 Sam 24:24). Presumably normal prices are given in 7:1.

No Clever Solution. The famine has also led to cannibalism (6:26-29). The king of Israel is confronted with a situation similar to the one Solomon dealt with (1 Kgs 3:16-28), but he has no clever solution to offer. The king is as distressed and helpless as his people. Not only was he wearing sackcloth, but the people could *see* that he was (6:30).

Siege Warfare. Walled towns could hold out for a considerable time against an enemy. Samaria held out against the Assyrians for three years (2 Kgs 17:5), and Jerusalem against the Babylonians for six months (2 Kgs 25:1-12) and against the Romans for seven months (Josephus *J.W.* 5-6). Resistance was broken down more by famine than by direct assault (cf. 2 Kgs 25:3; Jdt 7:19-22; Josephus *J.W.* 5 §§424-38; 6 §§193-213).

Samaria Delivered. The deliverance of Samaria is brought about by God, causing the Arameans to think that they are going to be overwhelmed by foreign allies of Israel (7:6; cf. 2 Kgs 19:7). But the realization that the siege has been lifted is dependent on the decision of the lepers, first to desert to the Aramean camp (7:3-4) and then not to keep the news to themselves (v. 9). The king suspects a trap (cf. 5:7) and has to be persuaded by one of his servants to take a risk (cf. 5:13).

Skepticism Punished. The fate of the skeptical officer is explained with unusual explicitness (7:17-20). The intention, as in v. 16, is partly to stress how exactly Elisha's predictions had been fulfilled. But it is possible to detect some uneasiness that the officer should be punished so severely for his understandable reluctance to build up apparently unwarranted hope.

2 Kings 8:1-6

Elisha's Deeds Recounted. This story presupposes that of the wealthy Shunammite woman (4:8-37) and provides a sequel to it. The account of her move to Philistia in time of famine and subsequent return also presupposes the other popular miracle stories (see on 2:19-25) and hints that they were at first handed on orally (8:4-5). It shows the same concern for the welfare of ordinary people as the other stories, though this time the need is met by the king's ruling rather than by a miracle performed by or through the prophet. The narratives of chs. 5–7 do not seem to be presupposed: they show no awareness of a seven-year famine; Gehazi is Elisha's faithful servant of 4:8-37 rather than the greedy one afflicted with a skin disease of ch. 5; there is no indication that the king has had the personal dealings with Elisha recounted in chs. 5–7.

2 Kings 8:7-15

Elisha Consulted in Aram. There is more continuity with chs. 5–7 here. This story concerns relations between Israel and Aram, at present peaceful but always potentially hostile. As in ch. 5, a leading Aramean figure consults Elisha about his illness, sending a substantial present. (In 2 Kings 1 an Israelite king consults a foreign god; here a foreigner consults a prophet of Israel's God. The irony is probably not intentional.) But the story makes a more direct contribution to political history than does that of chs. 5–7. The king of Aram is no longer anonymous but named as Benhadad, and his emissary, Hazael, is not, like Naaman, a man who disappears as soon as the story is told, but one whose career has already been foreshadowed (1 Kgs 19:15-17) and who will figure again in the history (2 Kgs 8:28-29; 10:32-33; 13:3-7, 22-25). The story is also a kind of curtain raiser for the story of Jehu's revolt in ch. 9. In the commission given to Elijah Hazael and Jehu both figure, and although that commission was not literally fulfilled it created the expectation that a prophet of Yahweh would be concerned in some way in the coming political upheavals.

Incitement to Treachery? It is not quite as certain as it sounds from the English translations of 8:10 that Elisha told Hazael to lie. The *written* Hebrew text reads "Go and say, 'You shall certainly *not (lō)* recover,'" though in the margin the Masoretes indicate that they believed it should have read "Go, say *to him (lō)*, 'You shall certainly recover.'" Presumably at some point a scribe altered the text to try to absolve the prophet from deceit. In this instance, however, Elisha does not actually commission or sanction the assassination of Benhadad, and whether or not he advised Hazael to dissemble, his predictions about Hazael's future career must be construed as incitement. The narrator's feelings are ambivalent. He makes Elisha weep at the thought of what Hazael is going to make Israel suffer; but he half believes that Israel deserved it (13:3), and it is important to him that it should happen with Yahweh's foreknowledge and consent.

Hazael in Assyrian Records. Hazael may have been the scourge of Israel, but he had his troubles too. In 841 BC Shalmaneser III, on one of his many campaigns in the west, inflicted a heavy defeat on Hazael's army and devastated much of his country. An inscription on a statue of Shalmaneser III may record an alternative version both of this event and of the circumstances in which Hazael became king. It says that Hazael, "son of nobody," seized the throne in Damascus after the previous king, Hadadezer, had been defeated and killed in battle with the Assyrians. Hazael was also defeated and had to leave Damascus to save his life. Three years later Shalmaneser invaded Aram again, but this time claimed only to have taken four of his towns (*ANET*, 280; *DOTT*, 48).

2 Kings 8:16-29

Jehoram (Judah, 849-842; not to be confused with his contemporary, Jehoram of Israel). The summaries of the reigns of the kings of Judah is resumed (the last one, that of Jehoshaphat, appeared in 1 Kgs 22:41-50). Jehoram is said to have behaved like the kings of Israel. This was understandable since he had married a daughter of Ahab (not yet named as Athaliah, but see v. 26), but it created a problem: Why was Judah not destroyed as Israel was? (The eventual fall of the Northern Kingdom rather than of the Omride dynasty must be in mind.) The answer is once again Yahweh's promise to David that he would always have a (memorial) "lamp" in Jerusalem, here as in 2 Sam 7:12-16; 1 Kgs 11:36; 15:4 regarded as unconditional (contrast the conditional promises in 1 Kgs 2:1-4; 6:11-13; 8:25; 9:1-9; Ps 132:11-12). In Jehoram's time Judah suffers the relatively minor setbacks of the revolt of Edom, which had been subject to Judah since David's time (2 Sam 8:13-14; 1 Kgs 22:47; though 2 Kgs 3:9 seems to imply that Edom was independent earlier), to the southeast, and Libnah to the west.

Ahaziah (Judah, 842). The connection of this king with the house of Ahab is rather misleadingly described. If he was the son of Jehoram, and Jehoram had married a daughter of Ahab, then Ahaziah's mother was not the daughter of Omri (so MT; LXX) but his granddaughter (as the English versions assume), and it was his father who was the son-in-law of Ahab (unless *ḥatan* means simply "related by marriage," as English versions other than the NRSV translate). The notice in 8:25-29 anticipates both the fate of Joram of Israel and Ahaziah of Judah (ch. 9) and the events in which Athaliah features (ch. 11).

2 Kings 9–10

Divine Retribution. The story of Jehu's revolt and his subsequent removal of the Baal cult from Israel is told at considerable length. It is skillfully told, with changes of scene and perspective (from Ramoth-gilead to Jezreel, 9:17; from Jerusalem to Jezreel, 9:30; from Jezreel to Samaria, 10:1) to maintain momentum and suspense. There are a few editorial additions to link it with the larger history. (i) The language in which the young prophet declares Yahweh's commission (9:7-10a) is very similar to that used in the sentences passed earlier on Jeroboam and Baasha (1 Kgs 14:10-14; 16:4). (ii) 9:36-37 makes Jehu recall a prediction of the fate of Jezebel, in part reproducing the language of 1 Kgs 21:23 and 2 Kgs 9:10. (iii) 10:10 makes Jehu claim that the fate of the house of Ahab is the fulfillment of prophecy by Elijah. (iv) In 10:17 the historian makes a similar claim. (v) 10:28-31 gives summary verdicts on Jehu's revolt and subsequent reign. All these additions are designed to present the downfall of the house of Ahab as divine retribution and to justify Jehu's actions as in line with God's intentions.

Jehu as a Religious Zealot. If, however, we read the story without these passages, the standpoint of the narrative is less clear. There are certainly features in the story which make the foregoing interpretation plausible. The anointing by Elisha's messenger strongly suggests that Jehu is the chosen instrument of judgment on the house of Ahab. There is no indication that Jehu previously entertained the idea of seizing the throne; he seems to be taken completely by surprise and begins to act only when his fellow officers proclaim him king. The description of Jehu's driving, "like a maniac" (*beshigga'on*, 9:20), may be intended to suggest that he has caught the contagion of prophetic inspiration from the young prophet, "this madman" (*hammeshugga' hazzeh*, v. 11). In the exchange between Joram and Jehu (v. 22) there is probably an allusion to the foreign religious practices Jezebel has introduced into Israel, an indication of a religious motivation for the revolt. Jehu's recall of the oracle denouncing Ahab for the death of Naboth (vv. 25-26) is another sign that he believed he was executing God's vengeance. And the meeting with Jehonadab (10:15-16) represents Jehu even more clearly as acting from religious motives. He is portrayed as a religious zealot, even a fanatic.

Jehu Calculating and Cruel. On the other hand, there are features in the story which cast doubt upon Jehu's motives. He did "conspire" against Joram (9:14, 23, 31 [like Zimri he was a trusted officer of the king; cf. 1 Kgs 16:8-10]; 10:9). Why did he not wait for God's good time, as David did? Why was he not afraid to lift his hand against God's anointed (1 Sam 24:6, 10; 26:9, 11, 23; 2 Sam 1:14)? The murder of Ahaziah (9:27-28) and of his relatives (10:12-14) was entirely gratuitous and no part of his commission. In demanding that Jezebel should be thrown down from her window (9:32-33) and that the rulers of Samaria should send him the heads of Ahab's sons (10:1-9) he made no reference to his divine commission but only to his own bid for the throne. His treatment of Jezebel was unnecessarily savage and callous (9:30-35). His second letter to the authorities in Samaria is unpleasantly reminiscent of David's letter to Joab ordering the liquidation of Uriah (2 Sam 11:14-15) and Jezebel's letter to the authorities in Jezreel telling them to bring a trumped up charge against Naboth (1 Kgs 21:8-10). The way he trapped the worshipers of Baal (10:18-27) also arouses misgivings. Was such duplicity permissible? Why didn't he give them the chance to change their minds, as Elijah did? Even the Deuteronomistic historians do not include this massacre either in the commission Jehu received (9:7-10a) or in the praise he is accorded in the summing up of the narrative (10:30).

Responses to the Story. The ambiguity of the story has been reflected in later responses to it. When the Deuteronomistic interpretation has been taken as authoritative, it has been used to justify the removal of kings by force and atrocities committed in the name of religion. But there has also been unease about the encouragement the story gives to religious fanaticism and the implication that the end justifies the means. It is to the credit of the historians that, while making their own convictions clear, they have not disguised the brutality, duplicity, and fanaticism of Jehu's actions (Tomes 2000).

Jehu (Israel, 842-815). The historian has little more to tell about Jehu's reign. The territory east of the Jordan, in whose defense against the Arameans at Ramoth-gilead Jehu was engaged at the time of his revolt (2 Kgs 8:28–9:15), was all lost to Hazael during his reign (10:32-33). This hardly conveys the impression of his "power" (10:34). Perhaps a glimpse of it is provided by the Black Obelisk of Assyrian king Shalmaneser III, who claims to have inflicted a heavy defeat on Hazael in 841 but only to have received tribute from the people of Tyre and Sidon and of "Jehu son of Omri" (*ANET*, 280-81; *DOTT*, 48). It is possible that Shalmaneser hesitated to take on Jehu and his army; he certainly regarded Jehu as significant enough to name.

2 Kings 11

Athaliah (Judah, 842-837). Since Jehu had killed Ahaziah of Judah as well as Joram of Israel, his revolt had repercussions in Judah as well as in Israel. Athaliah, Ahaziah's mother and daughter of Ahab and Jezebel (2 Kgs 8:18, 26), seized the throne, thus becoming the only queen in either Judah or Israel. She was as ruthless as Jehu in killing all the members of the royal family (though Jehu had already lightened her task, 10:12-14). But whereas Jehu had acted to remove Baal worship, Athaliah at least continued to tolerate it (11:18). The seventeenth-century French writer Racine, in his play *Athalie,* makes Athaliah a devotee of Baal and an opponent of Yahwism, but there is no firm basis for this in the Kings account. (2 Chr 22:3 probably implies this.) The temple was not appropriated for Baal worship, and its normal routine was not interrupted. The name Athaliah, meaning something like "Yahweh is great, exalted," indicates that her parents at least intended her to be a worshiper of Yahweh. Opposition to her rule may have been based on the fact that she was a usurper and not a descendant of David, and therefore lacked divine legitimation.

Joash Survives. However, Joash, a very young son of Ahaziah, survived, brought up secretly in the temple by his aunt Jehosheba. (2 Chr 22:11 makes her the wife of the priest Jehoiada. In any event, Jehoiada must have been in on the secret.) When he was seven years old (11:21 [Heb. 12:1]), Jehoiada secured the cooperation of the army in having him declared king.

Installation of the King. The story incidentally tells us how the temple and palace in Jerusalem were guarded. It is strange that the priest had to issue the soldiers weapons; perhaps the association of these weapons with David helped to emphasize the legitimacy of Joash's succession. The installation of the king is described in some detail, and it is possible that this was the ceremonial customary at every king's accession (cf. "according to custom," 11:14). The pillar (v. 14) was presumably one of the bronze pillars in front of the temple (1 Kgs 7:15-22). It has been suggested that the "covenant" or "testimony" (11:12) was similar to the Egyptian protocol, a document legitimating the pharaoh's claim to the throne (De Vaux 1961: 103). There is, however, no mention of anointing (cf. 1 Kgs 1:39). Perhaps custom varied over the centuries.

Execution of Athaliah. Athaliah, like Joram in Israel, realizes too late that she is the victim of a conspiracy (11:14; cf. 2 Kgs 9:23). Jehoiada's only scruple is that she should not be killed in the temple precinct.

The Covenant Renewed. It should not be assumed that covenants such as those described in 11:17 were made at the beginning of every reign. The covenant that Judah should be "Yahweh's people" should be seen as the equivalent of the decision made in Israel on Mt. Carmel (1 Kgs 18:17-40): by allowing a Baal temple in Jerusalem Judah had been wavering between two allegiances. The covenant between the king and the people was required because Joash's accession was the result of a coup and needed popular assent.

The People of the Land. Mention is made several times in 11:18-20 of "the people of the land" (*'am ha'areṣ*). Here the term refers to the people of Judah generally (cf. 2 Kgs 14:21 with 21:24; 23:30). In the postexilic texts of Ezra and Nehemiah, however, "the people [or peoples] of the land" are the non-Jewish inhabitants of Palestine as opposed to the returned exiles. They hinder the rebuilding of the temple (Ezra 3:3; 4:4) and the observance of the sabbath (Neh 10:31), and marriages with them are frowned upon (Ezra 9:1-2; Neh 10:30). In rabbinic times the meaning changed yet again: "the people of the land" are those who are ignorant of the law or do not practice it (De Vaux 1961: 70-72).

Jehoiada and Jehu. The story invites comparison with the story of Jehu's revolt. Since here the rightful claimant to the throne is being restored, there is less need to justify Jehoiada's actions. Hence there is no attempt to invoke prophetic legitimation or to see Athaliah's fate as prophecy fulfilled. Athaliah is not made into a Jezebel; on the other hand, sympathy for her is not aroused. That will be left to Racine.

2 Kings 12

Jehoash (or Joash; Judah, 837-800). The chief item of information about the reign of Jehoash concerns repairs made to the temple. The responsibility was at first that of the priests, who had to finance necessary repairs out of their own income from the statutory and voluntary payments made to the temple. But in the first half of Jehoash's long reign they failed to carry out any repairs. And so a new system was introduced. Contributions to the temple were to be placed in a secure chest and paid out directly to the workmen doing the repairs by the king's secretary and the high priest. The only revenue the priests retained was that from guilt offerings and sin offerings.

Payments to the Temple. What were these payments made to the temple? The legal codes offer various possibilities. At some period there was a poll tax levied on all adult males (Exod 30:11-16; cf. 2 Chr 24:9). Other obligatory payments were supposed to be made in kind, but money payments could be substituted, for example, for the firstborn (Exod 13:11-16; Lev 27:26-27; Num 18:15-16) or for tithes (Lev 27:30-33). Voluntary contributions again were in the first place thought of in terms of agricultural produce (Lev 1–3; 7:11-18), which could be replaced by money payments 20 percent greater in value (Lev 27:1-25). The codes are generally believed to have come from widely separated periods and in themselves give no indication when their regulations were in force. This account may therefore be a valuable indication that during the monarchy money payments had become standard.

The Income of the Priests. The priests were left with income from guilt offerings (REB, "reparation offerings") and sin offerings (REB, "purification offerings"). When these were in the form of animal sacrifices, they were the perquisites of the priests (Lev 6:24–7:10 [Heb. 6:17–7:10]; Num 18:9). Presumably they, too, could be commuted to money payments, though the legal codes make no mention of this. They were also entitled to at least some of the following (the entitlements probably varied at different periods): parts of the sacrifices of well-being (earlier versions, "peace offerings"; REB, "shared offerings"; Lev 7:28-36; Num 18:11, 18; Deut 18:3); the firstborn of animals (Num 18:17-18); first fruits (Num 18:12-13; Deut 18:4); and a tithe of the tithe (Num 18:25-32). It is not clear from this account what happened to these entitlements.

Jehoiada's Political Influence. Jehoiada continued his influence over Jehoash, at least for a great part of his reign. It is the only instance in the story of a priest being said to exercise political power. According to the account in 2 Chr 24:17-27, the regime ceased to be loyal to Yahweh after his death, and the reason for the assassination of Jehoash was that he had Jehoiada's son Zechariah murdered for his outspokenness (cf. Matt 23:35; Luke 11:51).

Hazael Threatens Judah. Hazael was a thorn in the flesh to Judah as well as to Israel. He advanced down the coast, took the Philistine town of Gath, and threatened Jerusalem. Jehoash got rid of him at a price: another episode in the depredations of the temple (see the notes on 1 Kgs 14:21-31).

2 Kings 13

Jehoahaz (Israel, 815-801). The historian twice attributes Israel's weakened state in the reign of Jehoahaz to its continuing in the religious tradition established by Jeroboam. There is no mention of Baal worship: Jehu's actions had so far proved effective. However, the existence of an *'asherah* in Samaria is singled out (13:6), an image of the goddess Asherah. The fact that the worship of Asherah could persist when the worship of Baal had been stamped out may suggest that Asherah was not necessarily always thought of as the consort of Baal. She could have been regarded as the consort of whichever male deity was ascendant at a particular time. (See the commentary on 1 Kgs 15:1-24.)

Aramean Inroads into Israel. The Aramean kings Hazael and his son Benhadad made further inroads into Israel, reducing the army's effectiveness (13:7). Although the numbers of infantry were the same as those Shalmaneser III attributed to Ahab, the two hundred chariots had been reduced to ten. However, for at least part of the reign the Aramean threat receded (v. 5). The historian attributes this to Jehoahaz's prayers, in response to which Yahweh gave Israel a "savior." Whether this was the king (as in 2 Kgs 14:27) or someone else we are not told. One possibility is that the Aramean threat was removed as a result of defeats inflicted by other states to the north of Damascus, perhaps with the support of the Assyrians. In an inscription on the base of an image found in 1907 near Aleppo, Zakir, king of Hamath and Lu'ash, claims to have defeated Bar-hadad, son of Hazael and his allies (*ANET*³, p. 501; *DOTT,* 242-50). Zakir also claims that his victory was an answer to his prayer to Baal-shemayn.

Joash (or Jehoash; Israel, 801-786). The account of this king's reign is summarized twice, in 13:10-13 and in 14:15-16. Thus several stories or pieces of information about his reign follow the (first) announcement of his death. From Assyrian sources we learn that he, along with the Aramean king of Tyre and Sidon, had to pay tribute to Adad-nirari III (the Tell al-Rimah stele: Cogan and Tadmor 1988: 335).

Death of Elisha. The story of his visit to Elisha (13:14-19) also gives the historian the opportunity to round off the life of the prophet and to relate a final, posthumous miracle (vv. 20-21). Both stories reflect a belief in magic. In the first, the prophet and king engage in an act of sympathetic magic, the one consciously, the other unconsciously. The king unwittingly determines the limits of his own military success. The second story is an early example of belief in the miraculous power of relics.

End of the Aramean Menace. With the death of Hazael the Aramean danger disappears from the history. As promised (13:19), Joash wins three battles against his son and recovers the towns Hazael had taken east of the Jordan (vv. 24-25; cf. 10:32-33). The Arameans will reappear only as allies of Israel against Judah (2 Kgs 15:37; 16:5), as a result of which the Assyrians will capture Damascus and deport its population (2 Kgs 16:9). The historian attributes this deliverance to Yahweh's respect for his covenant with Abraham, Isaac, and Jacob as well as to his compassion on the present generation (13:23). Reference to the patriarchal tradition is rare in Kings (cf. 1 Kgs 18:36). The statement that Yahweh has not "banished them from his presence until now" either implies that the passage was written before the fall of Samaria or that despite that event Yahweh had not forgotten his deported people.

2 Kings 14

Amaziah (Judah, 796-767) receives qualified praise from the historian. His religious policy was the same as that of his father Joash: the worship of Yahweh was the established religion, but there was no attempt to remove the country sanctuaries.

The Sins of the Parents. Amaziah had those who had killed his father put to death; unlike Jehu and Athaliah, however, he did not put their families to death. This is hailed as responding to a principle embodied in Deuteronomy (24:16). But it is not easy to forget that (another?) Deuteronomistic contributor to the history has recently portrayed Yahweh as threatening to wipe out whole royal families for the misdemeanors of particular kings (1 Kgs 14:10-11; 16:3-4; 21:21, 24; 2 Kgs 9:8) and even deferring punishment to the next generation (1 Kgs 21:29). That Yahweh would act in this way seems to have the backing of the Decalogue (Exod 20:5; Deut 5:9). But if human beings are not to punish children for their parents' sins, how much less should Yahweh! That this is the principle Yahweh upholds is passionately argued by Ezekiel (Ezek 18:19-20; cf. Jer 31:29-30). The problem is squaring the principle with what actually happens. Yahweh does not seem to *ensure* that children are not punished for their parents' sins. And so, when Yahweh's representatives threaten and carry out reprisals on whole families, they persuade themselves and others, too, that Yahweh himself has commanded them to do so.

Defeat by Israel. Amaziah had military pretensions. The account of his campaign against the Edomites presupposes that the latter invaded Judah (the Valley of Salt is thought to be in the vicinity of Beersheba) and that Amaziah retaliated by taking Sela, a fortress deep in Edomite territory (near the later Petra). (In 2 Chr 25:12, however, *selaʿ* is taken to mean "a rock" from which thousands of Edomite soldiers were hurled to their deaths.) This victory seems to have prompted a rash challenge to Jehoash of Israel which ended in defeat at Beth-shemesh, west of Jerusalem; Amaziah's capture; destruction of part of the north wall of Jerusalem; and removal of hostages and some of the treasures of the temple and palace.

The Thornbush Trampled. Jehoash used what must have been a popular fable (14:9; cf. Judg 9:7-15) to try to dissuade Amaziah from risking battle. Israel was the more populous and prosperous kingdom, and presumably had recovered from the weakness to which Hazael had reduced it (13:7).

Amaziah Assassinated. Amaziah, like his father, was eventually the victim of a conspiracy. But once again the conspirators did not abandon the dynasty and were content that Amaziah's son should succeed him (cf. 12:20-21).

Jeroboam II (Israel, 793-753). Despite the fact that Jeroboam did not abolish the religious institutions his namesake had introduced, the historian has to recognize that he was a successful king, who captured most of the Aramean kingdom and the territory east of Jordan. This is seen as an expression of Yahweh's concern for Israel's previously weakened state. Jeroboam had the support of a prophet named Jonah, son of Amittai. The book of Jonah purports to tell the story of this prophet, but since it was written much later with didactic motives it should not be taken as a source for the historical career of the prophet who encouraged Jeroboam.

Amos. The prophet Amos was also contemporary with Jeroboam (Amos 1:1) and was anything but encouraging (Amos 7:10-17). His prophecies are, however, a valuable source for the social and religious history of Jeroboam's reign. The country was prosperous, but at the expense of a widening gap between the rich and the poor and a corruption of the judicial system. There is little or no evidence of the worship of gods other than Yahweh, but Amos is concerned that enthusiastic support of the cult centers is not matched by a concern for social justice.

The Samarian Ostraca. During excavations at Samaria a large number of documents written on broken pottery were discovered (*ANET,* 321; *DOTT,* 204-8). They are invoices accompanying deliveries of oil and wine to the palace, and probably date from the time of Jeroboam II. Some of the names mentioned in them are compounded with the divine name Baal and some with Yahweh, reflecting a period when the worship of both went on side by side in Israel.

2 Kings 15:1-7, 32-38

Azariah (Judah, 783-742) and *Jotham (Judah, 750-735).* The chapter opens and closes with summaries of the reigns of these two kings. Because Azariah was ill for part of his reign, he had to hand over responsibility to his son (though the text simply says that Jotham was "in charge of the palace," that is, that he occupied one of the offices of state). It is assumed in reconstructions of the chronology of the period that those overlapping years are counted in the length of each king's reign.

Azariah/Uzziah and Jotham in Chronicles. This history gives hardly any information about the long reign of Azariah. (His rebuilding of Elath on the Gulf of Aqaba, following his father's victories over the Edomites [2 Kgs 14:7], has already been mentioned in 14:22.) However, in 2 Chr 26:1-15 (where Azariah is called Uzziah; cf. Isa 1:1; 6:1; Hos 1:1; Amos 1:1) he is presented as a successful and prosperous ruler, who set up settlements in Philistine territory, improved the fortification of Jerusalem, equipped his army with new weapons, and cultivated hitherto barren tracts of Judah. Although Chronicles often seems to idealize events in Judah, there seems no reason to doubt that reliable records or traditions have been used here. In Kings Jotham is credited with providing the temple with a new gate; according to 2 Chronicles 27 he did more building in Jerusalem and elsewhere and forced the Ammonites to pay tribute to him for three years.

Azriau of Yaudi. Azariah may also figure in Assyrian records. In 742 BC Tiglath-pileser III, on an expedition in Syria, received tribute from "Azriau of Yaudi" (*ANET,* 282; *DOTT,* 54, 56). Many scholars think that this must be a reference to the king of an otherwise unknown state in northern Syria, but others believe that it is possible that Azariah (Uzziah) of Judah is meant.

Azariah's Illness. This history attributes Azariah's illness to Yahweh but without offering any reason for it. In 2 Chr 26:16-23 it is explained as punishment for impiously offering incense in the temple, which is assumed to be the prerogative of the Aaronic priesthood. In later tradition the earthquake referred to in Amos 1:1 and Zech 14:4-5 is envisaged as happening at the precise moment when the offense was committed (Josephus *Ant.* 9 §225; *Tg. Isa* 28:21). The reticence of Kings is to be preferred. According to 2 Chr 26:23 the king was buried, not in the city of David, but "in the burial field which belonged to the kings," thus presumably outside the city. A first-century-BC plaque discovered in Jerusalem ("Here were brought the bones of Uzziah king of Judah. Do not open!") at least supports this tradition.

2 Kings 15:8-31

The Last Kings of Israel. Between the accounts of Azariah and Jotham we have the sorry tale of the last kings of (northern) Israel. The last representative of the dynasty of Jehu, *Zechariah (746-745),* reigns a mere six months before he is assassinated. The assassin, *Shallum (745),* lasts only a month before he is killed by Menahem in a campaign marked by extreme brutality (15:16).

Menahem (745-738) had to deal with another campaign of Tiglath-pileser (15:19; "Pul(u)" is the name by which Tiglath-pileser is known in the Babylonian king list; *ANET,* 272) and was forced to buy him off to secure his own position. To raise 1,000 talents of silver at 50 shekels a head Menahem would have had to levy the tribute on some 50,000 of his more prosperous subjects. Tiglath-pileser mentions Menahem's submission and says that he "returned him to his place," receiving tribute of "gold, silver, linen garments with multicoloured trimmings" (*ANET,* 283-84; cf. the Iran stele: Cogan and Tadmor 1988: 172, 335).

Menahem was succeeded by his son *Pekahiah (738-737),* but he was assassinated by an army officer, Pekah, with support from men from east of Jordan. *Pekah (737-732;* he cannot have reigned for twenty years) made common cause with Rezin of Aram in attacking Judah (2 Kgs 15:37; 16:5; Isa 7:1-9). Tiglath-pileser was conducting another campaign in the region, and as a result of an appeal by Ahaz of Judah he overran Aram and annexed three areas of Israel: the coastal plain, Galilee, and Gilead (east of Jordan), deporting the population to Assyria (15:29; 16:7-9). As a result of these events Pekah was assassinated by *Hoshea (732-722),* who became Israel's last king.

The Assyrian Account. Tiglath-pileser records the deportation of many of the inhabitants of Israel (which he calls *Bit Humri,* "the land of Omri"). He says that the Israelites overthrew Pekah and that he made Hoshea king over them, after exacting tribute again (*ANET,* 284).

No Reference to Prophets. The theme of prophecy and fulfillment is not pursued through this chronicle of assassinations and usurpations. It is noted that the promise to Jehu that his dynasty would survive for four generations was fulfilled (15:12; cf. 2 Kgs 10:30), but nothing is said about Shallum, Menahem, Pekah, or Hoshea acting at the instigation of prophets, as was the case with Jehu.

Hosea. Some at least of the prophecies of Hosea probably belong to this period and allow us to picture it much more vividly. Although there is a compassionate and hopeful strain in Hosea, it does not cancel out a strong sense of foreboding about the course Israel was following. Hosea was troubled about the general lawlessness (Hos 4:1-3) and the return of Baal worship (2:2-13 [Heb. 4-15]), as well as the idolatrous element in the official cultus (8:4b-6; 10:5-6; 13:2). He was scathing about the dissolute character of life at court and the perpetual climate of intrigue (7:3-7). He did not believe that the usurpations had divine approval (8:4a); indeed, Yahweh was taking away the whole institution of kingship (13:9-11). He believed that looking now to Assyria, now to Egypt, for support was futile (5:13; 7:11; 8:8-9). The death of Zechariah was the long-delayed punishment of Jehu's dynasty for the blood shed in the revolt, but merely heralded the end of the kingdom of Israel (1:4-5), which is pictured in a number of ways (9:3, 17; 10:13-15; 13:15-16 [Heb. 13:14–14:1]). The conviction that the kingdom of Israel was responsible for its own downfall was not merely the verdict of hindsight (see 2 Kings 17).

The Reign of Jotham. Despite the troubles the Northern Kingdom was going through and the beginning of aggression against Judah by Aram and Israel (15:37; why should it be said that Yahweh was instigating this? Isaiah did not think so [Isa 7:3-9]), Jotham's reign was relatively uneventful. He was even able to provide the temple precincts with a new gate (15:35b). A seal found at Elath, bearing the inscription *lytm* ("belonging to Jotham") above the figure of a horned ram, may possibly have belonged to him.

2 Kings 16

Ahaz (Judah, 735-715). The judgment on the religious policy of Ahaz is as severe as that on any king of Judah hitherto. Not only does he actively encourage worship at the high places, the country sanctuaries outside Jerusalem, but he is said to have "made his son pass through fire." The same charge is leveled at his grandson Manasseh (2 Kgs 21:6). It is probably a euphemism for "burning" one's child as a sacrifice, which seems to have been a practice in which others besides the two kings shared. It is described elsewhere as "an offering to Molech" (2 Kgs 23:10; Lev 18:21; 20:2-5; Jer 32:35; or to Baal: Jer 19:5) and was carried out at "the Topheth" (= "fireplace"?) in the Hinnom valley, below the southern walls of Jerusalem (2 Kgs 23:10; Jer 19:1-6). It is regarded as a Canaanite custom (16:3). The chief evidence for the practice of child sacrifice on any scale comes from Carthage in North Africa, originally a Phoenician colony (Day 1989).

Arameans or Edomites? The loss of Elath, temporarily

won back by Azariah/Uzziah (2 Kgs 14:22), is mentioned. The MT says that "King Rezin of Aram recovered it for Aram," and the *written* text goes on to say, "and the Arameans came to Elath and have lived there to this day." However, the Masoretes indicate in the margin that they thought the correct reading was "Edomites" (only one consonant is different), and most translations (but not the NIV and JPSV) assume that the reference is to Edom throughout.

The Syro-Ephraimite War. But the main political event in Ahaz's reign was the invasion of Judah by Aram and Israel (the Syro-Ephraimite War), probably in 734 BC. It is often asserted that Aram and Israel were trying to force Judah to join an alliance against Assyria since Tiglath-pileser was conducting another campaign in the west in that year. But no biblical text says so, the Assyrian sources make no mention of a coalition, and invading a neighboring country seems a strange way of making it into an ally. It is possible that the quarrel with Ahaz had more local causes, but ultimately we have to admit that we do not know the reason for the war (Tomes 1993).

The Assyrian View. However, the Assyrian sources confirm that Ahaz (Jehoahaz) paid tribute to Tiglath-pileser at a time when Pekah and Rezin did not (*DOTT,* 56; *ANET,* 282), and record the downfall of Rezin (*ANET,* 283) and the deposition of Pekah (*DOTT,* 55; *ANET,* 284). This does not directly confirm the account of Ahaz's appeal to Tiglath-pileser (16:7-9), but it at least makes it plausible.

Isaiah and Hosea. These events are certainly reflected in Isaiah, and possibly in Hosea. According to Isa 7:1-17, Isaiah encouraged Ahaz to believe that the crisis would be resolved without any action on his part because God had decreed that the attempt to conquer Judah and replace its king would fail. It is implied that an appeal to Assyria would bring more troubles than it would remove. If Hos 5:8-15 relates to these events, it suggests that the Israelite prophet regarded Judah as the aggressor v. 10). Hosea is as wary as Isaiah of appealing to Assyria for help (v. 13).

Changes in the Temple. The historian is just as interested in the changes Ahaz carried out in the temple. He had a larger altar constructed, in imitation of one he had seen at Damascus, and had the older bronze altar moved. The account is interesting as indicating (a) the sacrifices the king was in the habit of offering (16:13); (b) the sacrifices which were offered daily (v. 15); and (c) the use of an altar in divination (v. 15). The necessity of paying tribute to the Assyrian king meant that the temple and palace lost not only their movable treasures (v. 8) but also the semiprecious metals used in some of the fixtures (vv. 17-18). Tiglath-pileser lists "gold, silver, tin, iron, antimony, embroidered linen garments, purple woollen garments . . . everything precious . . . the desirable things of their countries" as the tribute he received from Ahaz and others (*DOTT,* 56; *ANET,* 282).

2 Kings 17

The Fall of Samaria. This chapter records and explains the fall of Samaria and the end of the Northern Kingdom. *Hoshea (732-722)* rules over what is left of the Israelite kingdom (2 Kgs 15:29) but only as an Assyrian vassal. He in his turn is deposed and imprisoned by Shalmaneser V when he shows signs of independence. Then Shalmaneser begins the long siege of Samaria. According to Assyrian inscriptions the city was actually captured by Sargon II at the beginning of his reign. These inscriptions confirm that the Assyrian action was provoked by rebellion but state that this was incited by Ilubi'di of Hamath, that various states besides Israel took part, and that Sib'e, the Egyptian commander-in-chief, supported it with his army. Sargon claimed to have deported 27,290 people from Israel (still "House of Omri"), conscripting some of them for his own chariot force (*DOTT,* 59-61; *ANET,* 284-85).

Replacement of the Deported. Assyrian policy was not only to deport populations which caused trouble but also to settle others in their territory, and both the Bible and the Assyrian inscriptions testify that this happened in this case (17:24; *DOTT,* 59-60; *ANET,* 284).

Theological Explanation. So much for the political explanation of events. 17:7-20, however, insist that all this happened because Israel had not been loyal to Yahweh. But whereas the history has emphasized the setting up and perpetuation of the golden calves at Bethel and Dan and the introduction of Baal worship by Ahab as the chief examples of this disloyalty, the concern here is with the continuance of Canaanite customs (v. 8), the multiplicity of sanctuaries (v. 9), and the customary cult objects, the stone pillars and the wooden poles (v. 10). The golden calves are not mentioned until v. 16, and then along with worshiping the host of heaven (not mentioned until 2 Kgs 21:3 in the history), making sons and daughters pass through the fire (mentioned only in connection with Judah, 16:3; 21:6; 23:10), and practicing divination (again mentioned only in connection with Judah, 21:6). Israel has also ignored the warnings of the prophets, whereas the prophets who have figured in the history of the Northern Kingdom have not called Israel and its kings to repentance but have simply pronounced their doom. The passage reflects the general standpoint of Deuteronomy (e.g., other gods: Deuteronomy 13; high places and cultic objects: Deut 12:2-3; host of heaven: Deut 4:19; child sacrifice: Deut 18:10; divination: Deut 18:10-11) rather than the actual course of the history which has been related.

The Original Charge. 17:21-23, on the other hand, does summarize the charge against Israel which has been maintained throughout. It may be that this was the original comment of the historian and that vv. 7-20 have been inserted by a later commentator, writing at a time when Judah had suffered a similar fate (vv. 19-20). If it was a comment on the religious life of the whole nation, the inclusion of practices prevalent only in Judah would be more understandable.

An Unacceptable Syncretism. The people the Assyrians settled in Samaria naturally brought their own gods and their own religious customs and personnel (17:29-34a). But they also felt under some obligation to meet the requirements of "the god of the land," if only for superstitious reasons (vv. 24-28). The Deuteronomistic commentator is at pains to point out that this was not worship which satisfied Yahweh's demands for exclusive and wholehearted allegiance (vv. 34b-40).

No "Postexilic Period." At the time of writing, possibly in the postexilic period, this kind of syncretism still obtained (17:41). There was no "postexilic period" inspired by returning exiles for the northern tribes. The relationship of the settlers to the later Samaritans is, however, less than clear since the latter were (and are) monotheists, rejecting images, observing the sabbath, and practicing circumcision (Coggins 1975). Josephus regards the Samaritans as the descendants of the settlers but recognizes that they worshiped "the Most High God" zealously, attributing this to an early conversion (*Ant.* 9 §§288-91).

2 Kings 18–19

Hezekiah (715-687). For the first time the historian has unqualified praise for a king of Judah (18:1-8). The allegiance of Hezekiah to Yahweh was unswerving, and he both destroyed the country sanctuaries and their cult objects and removed the venerated bronze serpent from the temple. His military campaigns against the Philistines prospered, and his rebellion against Assyria is related with approval. Assyrian sources indicate that the two were connected: the citizens of the Philistine city of Ekron overthrew their pro-Assyrian king Padi and handed him over to Hezekiah. This brought Sennacherib to Palestine. He defeated the Egyptians, to whom Ekron had appealed for help, recaptured Ekron, reinstated Padi, and invaded Judah (*ANET*, 287-88; *DOTT*, 66-67).

Hezekiah's Reform. Hezekiah's reform is described at greater length in 2 Chronicles 29–31, but it is doubtful whether that account should be used to supplement the briefer one in Kings (in the way that 2 Chr 26:1-15 fills out the picture of the reign of Azariah/Uzziah). It assumes that the temple was actually closed by the end of Ahaz's reign and had to be reopened, and that Passover had been discontinued and had to be reinstated. It also says that Hezekiah summoned members of the northern tribes to the Passover in Jerusalem, with very limited success, but completely ignores the drastic change in the political situation in the north.

A Chronological Problem. 18:9-12 records the fall of Samaria once again, and dates it in Hezekiah's sixth year. There is, however, a serious discrepancy in the chronology of his reign since Sennacherib's invasion of Judah is said in v. 13 to have taken place in Hezekiah's fourteenth year. The invasion can certainly be dated to 701 BC, which would make Hezekiah's accession take place in 715, some seven years *after* the fall of Samaria.

Sennacherib's Account. 18:13-16 relates that Sennacherib captured all the fortified cities of Judah except Jerusalem, and that Hezekiah capitulated and paid the tribute the Assyrian king demanded. This agrees with Sennacherib's account. He claimed to have systematically besieged and taken forty-six walled towns, and he seems to have been particularly proud of his conquest of Lachish, for he had two reliefs made for his palace at Nineveh, one showing the town under siege and the other showing the inhabitants submitting to him as prisoners (*ANEP*, 371-73). He claimed to have taken 200,000 prisoners in all. Then he shut up Hezekiah in Jerusalem "like a caged bird," forcing him to pay tribute: 30 talents of gold and 800 talents of silver (*ANET*, 287-88; *DOTT*, 67-70).

An Account in Common with Isaiah. 18:17–19:37 is also concerned with the events of 701. It agrees that Sennacherib did not besiege Jerusalem, but it gives a very different account of what happened. This passage appears almost word for word in Isaiah 36–37. It is introduced with the equivalent of 2 Kgs 18:13, but there is no equivalent of vv. 14-16. It is impossible to say whether it was taken over into 2 Kings from Isaiah, or into Isaiah from 2 Kings, or whether both incorporated it independently from their source. The common material is not integral to either book. It appears to contradict the account of the invasion given in 18:14-16 and therefore is unlikely to have been in 2 Kings from the beginning. It is also quite unlike the other biographical material in Isaiah.

Two Versions Combined. The story it tells seems to be told twice. The Assyrian king sends an embassy to Jerusalem to tell Hezekiah and the inhabitants of Jerusalem that it is useless to resist (18:17-37). Hezekiah sends to Isaiah and receives a reassuring message (19:1-7). Then the Assyrian king sends a further embassy with a letter; Hezekiah takes it into the temple and asks God to deliver them (vv. 9b-19). Isaiah sends to Hezekiah with a series of reassurances (vv. 20-34). Since the course of events is roughly the same each time, it is likely that two further traditions about the events have been combined. It looks as if the first version was intended to end with Sennacherib hearing news that persuaded him to end the invasion, only to be assassinated at home (19:7-9a plus 19:36-37), while the second hints at more direct divine intervention (19:28b, 34), which takes the form of the mysterious death of many of the Assyrian troops (v. 36). The fact that Tirhakah (v. 9) did not become king until 690 BC and that Sennacherib was not killed (v. 37) until 688 or later has led to the suggestion that the differences between 18:14-16 and the accounts which follow are to be explained by assuming that Sennacherib invaded Judah twice. But there is no Assyrian evidence to support this. The multiplication of traditions over a period of time would not be strange, especially if they enabled Judah to remember the events as less humiliating than they actually were. The important thing is that the Assyrians did not besiege Jerusalem.

The Assyrian Officials. The titles of the officials the Assyrian king sent to Jerusalem (18:17) are attested in Assyrian sources. The Tartan (*turtanu*) was the highest official after the king; the Rab-saris was the "chief eunuch"; and the Rab-shakeh was the "chief cupbearer."

Jerusalem's Water Supply. The Assyrian officials met the officials from the Judean court at a site which cannot now be identified (18:17; cf. Isa 7:3). That they could get so near to Jerusalem's water supply suggests that this would be a major worry in the defense of the city. Water from the Gihon spring was apparently carried by a channel running outside the city to a reservoir within it. We are told elsewhere that Hezekiah dammed up this outside source (2 Chr 32:2-4) and diverted its waters to a new reservoir on the west side of the city (2 Kgs 20:20; 2 Chr 32:30; cf. Isa 22:9, 11). These measures have long been associated with the tunnel through the rock beneath the city and the inscription describing how it was constructed (*DOTT*, 209-11; *ANET*, 321), though doubts about this identification have recently been expressed (Rogerson and Davies 1996; Norin 1998).

Shebna. Two of the Judean officials (18:18) are mentioned elsewhere. Shebna was once "in charge of the palace" but is threatened with removal and replacement by Eliakim in Isa 22:15-25 (a passage which gives some idea of the importance of the office). His offense was to have an ostentatious tomb carved out for himself, and such a tomb has been discovered in the modern village of Silwan (the biblical Siloam). The inscription says that the tomb belonged to the official "in charge of the palace," though most of the name is missing (Auld and Steiner 1996: 80).

Language. The Judean officials ask the Assyrian delegation not to use "the language of Judah" (i.e., Hebrew) but Aramaic. Although the language of the Assyrian inscriptions is Akkadian, written in cuneiform, Aramaic, a language closer to Hebrew, written alphabetically, was used in the western territories of the Assyrian Empire.

A Mocking Song. Part of Isaiah's reassurance to Hezekiah takes the form of a poem taunting or mocking Assyria (19:21-28). It is in a meter generally known as the *qinah,* in which a half line of three beats is followed by a half line of two.

Isaianic Themes. Some of the themes of the Rabshakeh's speeches echo themes in the prophecies of Isaiah: the judgment that Egypt is "a broken reed" (18:21, 24; cf. Isa 30:1-7; 31:1-3); the idea that the Assyrians were Yahweh's instruments to punish Judah (18:25; cf. Isa 10:5-11); the boast that the gods of the nations have not been able to prevent the Assyrian conquests (18:33-35; 19:11-13; cf. Isa 10:7-11). The oracle in which God condemns Sennacherib for his arrogance (19:20-28) is reminiscent of Isa 10:12-19. Isaiah's confidence that the city would not be taken (19:6-7, 32-34) recalls his repeated exhortations to Judah and its kings to put their trust in Yahweh alone in times of crisis (Isa 7:3-9; 28:16; 30:15; 31:4-5).

Assurance for the Future. A "sign" (19:29) is generally the immediate (often miraculous) fulfillment of a minor prediction which is taken to guarantee the later fulfillment of a major prediction (e.g., Judg 6:36-40; 2 Kgs 20:8-11). But here, as elsewhere in Isaiah, the sign seems to be the fulfillment of a promised deliverance at a set time or in an orderly sequence (cf. Isa 7:10-16; 8:1-4), by which it can be recognized that Yahweh is in control. The "zeal" of Yahweh (19:31b; cf. Isa 9:7b) probably means his "jealous" concern for his reputation. The promise here is that over the next three years those who have survived the invasion will be able to restore normal life. (References to a "remnant" are sometimes merely to the survivors of a disaster, without any implication that they were more faithful than those who perished, e.g., 2 Kgs 19:4; Isa 11:11; Jer 40:11; 42:2; 43:5.)

Miracle or Natural Event? It is possible that a natural event underlies the tradition that 185,000 Assyrians were struck down in a single night. Herodotus was told by the Egyptians that Sennacherib had to withdraw from Pelusium, on the border of Egypt, because mice had gnawed through all the army's equipment (Herodotus *Hist.* 2.141; cited by Josephus *Ant.* 10 §§18-19). Rats are carriers of bubonic plague, and this has led to the speculation that an epidemic had a part to play in the Assyrians' withdrawal.

2 Kings 20

Hezekiah's Illness. This chapter also includes material found in Isaiah (Isaiah 38–39). The account of Hezekiah's illness and recovery (20:1-11) is told in a more orderly way than in Isaiah, where Hezekiah's request for a sign (Isa 38:21-22) comes after the account of the sign itself (Isa 38:7-8). On the other hand, the Isaiah text includes a psalm of thanksgiving attributed to Hezekiah after his recovery (Isa 38:9-20).

Hezekiah's Prayer Answered. There have been other stories in which a prophet has to announce to a king that he or a child of his will not recover (2 Sam 12:14; 1 Kgs 14:1-18; 2 Kgs 1:2-17; 8:7-15). Sometimes, but not always, this is regarded as a punishment for the king's sins. Here, however, Hezekiah protests his loyalty to Yahweh. (It is noteworthy that in the individual laments in the Psalter such protestations are more frequent than confessions of sin.) Isaiah returns to announce that Hezekiah's prayer has been heard. Such an announcement by a prophet must have been one of the ways in which a worshiper became certain that a prayer had been answered: a favorable dream or a casting of lots would be other possibilities (1 Sam 28:6). Hezekiah is promised recovery within three days, and according to the MT, followed by most translations, a popular remedy is applied and he recovers (20:7). It is strange, therefore, that Hezekiah still asks for a sign — in the sense of the immediate fulfillment of a minor prediction — that Yahweh will do what he has promised. (The RSV and the NRSV try to overcome this difficulty by reading the whole of v. 7 as Isaiah's instructions.) The sun's shadow is made to go ten "steps" in the wrong direction on some form of sundial; the use of the word *ma'alot,* "steps," has suggested that a staircase to a roof chamber was used as a sundial. (Isa 38:8 in the LXX and in 1QIsa[a] mentions a roof chamber; 2 Kgs 23:12 suggests that worship of astral deities was carried on there.) Curing Hezekiah's illness might seem the easier miracle, but there is no point in trying to find a rational explanation for the sign.

Hezekiah as "Prince." It is interesting that Hezekiah is called *nagid* ["prince"] of my people" rather than "king" (v. 5). Such a phrase has been used of Saul (1 Sam 9:16; 10:1), David (1 Sam 13:14; 25:30; 2 Sam 5:2; 6:21; 7:8), Jeroboam (1 Kgs 14:7), and Baasha (1 Kgs 16:2). It should not be taken to imply a position less than that of king; the emphasis is on Yahweh's appointment of the king in question to a position of responsibility for Israel, Yahweh's people.

A Promise of Peace and Security. Yahweh's promise to defend the city against the Assyrians (20:6b) forms a link with the previous story (19:34) and contributes to Hezekiah's assurance that the remaining fifteen years of his life will be a time of peace and security (20:19).

The Babylonian Embassy. The account of the embassy of Merodach-baladan (Marduk-apla-iddina), king of Babylon, stands in Isaiah immediately before the chapters in the book (Isaiah 40–55) which come from the period of the exile of the Jews in Babylon. But it also foreshadows subsequent events in Kings. Judah's downfall will come, not at the hands of Assyria, which has seemed so threatening in Hezekiah's time, but at those of Babylon, which at the moment seems friendly (20:12) and far away (v. 14). Once again Judah's calamity is described in terms of the loss of the temple treasures (cf. 1 Kgs 14:25-27; 15:18-19; 2 Kgs 16:8). It is not clear whether we are intended to infer that Hezekiah caused or contributed to the eventual fate of Judah by his readiness to show the embassy all that he possessed. If we are, it would not be on the practical ground that the Babylonians would be able to weigh up Judah's strength and weakness, but on the superstitious ground that it was unlucky to be so open with strangers or on the religious ground that Hezekiah was placing his reliance on wealth and weapons rather than on Yahweh. Marduk-apla-iddina was king of Babylon in 722-710 and again briefly in 704-703.

2 Kings 21

Manasseh (687-642). The Deuteronomistic historian regards the religious practices encouraged in the reign of Manasseh as worse than anything the pre-Israelite inhabitants of Canaan did (21:9, 11). Not only were the country sanctuaries restored, but Baal worship was reintroduced (v. 3; "Asherah" here means an image of the goddess, as in 1 Kgs 15:13, rather than a stylized sacred pole; cf. v. 7), and the "host of heaven" (probably Assyrian deities since most of them were associated with the sun, the moon, planets, etc.) were worshiped (v. 3b). To make matters worse, altars for these deities were provided in the temple courts (v. 5), and the image of Asherah was placed in the temple itself (v. 7). Like Ahaz, he "made his son pass through fire" (see the commentary on 2 Kings 16) and practiced divination in ways other than those traditionally regarded as acceptable (21:6; cf. Deut 18:9-14; 1 Samuel 28). The fact that he shed "much innocent blood" (v. 16) is almost an afterthought here, though given a more prominent place in the charges against Manasseh later (2 Kgs 24:3-4). Later tradition maintained that Isaiah was martyred by being sawed in two during Manasseh's reign (*b. Sanh.* 103a; *Mart. Isa.* 1–5; *APOT,* 2:159-62; *OTP,* 2:156-64; Sparks 1984: 784-94).

The Last Straw. For the historian, reflecting on subsequent events, Manasseh's reign was the last straw, forcing Yahweh to decide to let Judah suffer the fate of the Northern Kingdom, in effect to abandon his people to the depredations of their enemies (21:10-15; 23:26-27; 24:1-4). When Jerusalem fell, this was by no means the only explanation put forward — others were that Zedekiah had broken his oath to the Babylonians (2 Kgs 24:20b; Ezek 17:1-21), that Judah had made the mistake of abandoning worship of the "queen of heaven" (Jer 44:15-19), and that Yahweh was forgetful of the covenant (Psalms 44; 74; 79) — but there is an indication that it may have been widely held in the proverb criticized in both Jeremiah (31:29-30) and Ezekiel (18:1-4).

Manasseh in Chronicles. The Chronicler did not share the Deuteronomists' view, believing that the final point was reached in the reign of the last king, Zedekiah (2 Chr 36:15-16). Manasseh was punished for his sins by being taken in chains by the Assyrians to Babylon, where he repented. He was then allowed to return to Jerusalem, where he carried out some of the reforms attributed in Kings to his grandson Josiah (2 Chr 33:10-13, 15-16). This account is generally regarded as history as it should have been; it was unthinkable that Manasseh should have been allowed to reign so long if he had persisted in his idolatrous ways. Although Manasseh is mentioned several times in the inscriptions of the Assyrian kings Esarhaddon and Ashurbanipal as a vassal king who provided them with labor and troops (*ANET,* 290, 291, 294; *DOTT,* 73), there is no independent corroboration of his being taken captive by the Assyrians, and it is unlikely that they would have taken him to Babylon. However, the Chronicles account does preserve a notice about his building an outer wall for Jerusalem, probably on the eastern side of the city (2 Chr 33:14).

Amon (642-640). The only significant event recorded for the reign of Amon is his assassination. If that had threatened the end of the Davidic dynasty, the threat was averted since the assassins were killed in their turn, by "the people of the land" (see the commentary on 2 Kgs 11:18-20), and Amon's son Josiah was made king despite his extreme youth.

The Royal Burial Ground. Both Manasseh and Amon were buried "in the garden of Uzza." This may suggest that their tombs could still be identified at the time of writing.

2 Kings 22:1–23:30

Josiah (640-609). The account of the reign of Josiah is almost entirely taken up with the story of the discovery of "the book of the law" in the temple and the carrying out of a series of reforms to the cultus. It begins (22:3-7) with preparations for repairs to the temple similar to those described in 2 Kgs 12:4-16. But the account of the repairs is never finished; the discovery of the book is much more important. In the last resort Judaism could survive without the temple but not without the law.

The "Book of the Law." It has long been assumed that the book in question was a version of Deuteronomy because the reforms conform to the requirements of Deuteronomy as they do to no other code in the Pentateuch. There are moves to centralize worship in Jerusalem (23:5a, 8a, 15, 19; cf. Deut 12:13-14). Foreign cults are removed (23:4, 5b, 6, 11-14; cf. Deut 7:5, 25; 12:2-3; 17:3). The practice of child sacrifice is ended (23:10; cf. Deut 12:31; 18:10). Untraditional methods of divination are repudiated (23:24; cf. Deut 18:10-11). Cult prostitution is proscribed (23:7; cf. Deut 23:17). The Passover is celebrated in Jerusalem (23:21-23; cf. Deut 16:5-6). The intended provision for the displaced priests of the country sanctuaries is either not implemented or not taken up (23:9; cf. Deut 18:6-8).

Deuteronomy and the Reform. On the basis of these correspondences it was concluded that Deuteronomy in some form was in existence at least by 621 BC and this dating was made the basis for the relative dating of the different strands of the Pentateuch. There would be less consensus about these conclusions now, and further reflection on these chapters is partly responsible (Barrick 2002). The account of Josiah's reform has been written by Deuteronomists, and they would have a vested interest in making it conform with Deuteronomy even if Deuteronomy were a later compilation. For various reasons relating to its style and content Deuteronomy cannot have been an ancient book. It is preferable to think that the account of the reform has been colored by *subsequent* knowledge of Deuteronomy than that Deuteronomy was written as a program for reform and planted in the temple in order to make it appear much older than it really was. In any case, the connection of the reforms with Deuteronomy is not very explicit. Only in connection with the Passover celebration and the divinatory practices is it said that the requirements of the book are being carried out (23:21, 24); and that part of the reform which brings it most closely into line with Deuteronomy — the ending of priestly service at the country sanctuaries (23:8a, 9) — interrupts the series of reforms in and around Jerusalem and may be a later insertion in the account. Perhaps the identity of "the book of the law" was meant to be left vague.

The Reform and the Earlier History. Many of the reforms could equally well be explained as the removal of abuses which have been mentioned at various points in the history hitherto. The cult objects for Baal and Asherah and the astral deities were introduced into the temple by Manasseh (23:4, 5b; 2 Kgs 21:3b-5, 7). There had been earlier attempts to remove male cult prostitutes from Judah (23:7; 1 Kgs 15:12; 22:46). Ahaz and Manasseh made their sons pass through fire (23:10; 2 Kgs 16:3; 21:6). There are direct references to the altars for astral deities Manasseh had constructed in the temple courts (23:12; 2 Kgs 21:5) as well as to those Solomon had provided east of Jerusalem for the deities of the surrounding peoples (23:13; 1 Kgs 11:7; the "Mount of Destruction," *har hammashḥit* [NRSV], is a contemptuous term for the Mount of Olives, *har hammishḥah* [REB, GNB, NJB]). 23:15-18 is an extended allusion to the story of the prophet who denounced Jeroboam's altar at Bethel (1 Kgs 13:1-32). Thus the catalogue of reforms takes up the earlier history much more directly than it does the text of Deuteronomy.

The Reform in Chronicles. The account in Kings presents the reform as entirely a response to the discovery of the book of the law. But 2 Chr 34:3-7 asserts that the reform began ten years before that discovery. Since these early measures included the destruction of sanctuaries in what had been the Northern Kingdom, it has been widely supposed that the reform was originally inspired by political motives and that Josiah was taking advantage of Assyria's decline to assert Judah's independence and to reclaim the northern territories for a united Israel. The removal of Assyrian cults and the measures taken at Bethel in the Kings account would be further evidence for this political dimension to the reform. We should, however, be cautious about accepting the Chronicles account as reliable. On the one hand, the Chronicler completely ignores the Assyrian conquest of northern Israel and assumes that Hezekiah as well as Josiah was able to exercise some kind of control over the religious life of the northern territories (2 Chr 30:1-12; 31:1); on the other, his account of Manasseh's repentance has meant a considerably modified record of Josiah's reform.

Dramatis personae. Some of the people who figure in the account of the discovery also figure in the narratives in Jeremiah: Ahikam directly (Jer 26:24; cf. 39:14; 40:5) and Achbor, Hilkiah, and Shaphan indirectly (Jer 26:22; 29:3; 36:10-12). This fact and the details given about the prophetess Huldah suggest that there is genuine reminiscence behind the story.

Huldah's Oracles. Nothing is known about Huldah apart from this story. (Rabbinic commentators wondered why she was consulted rather than her better-known contemporaries, Jeremiah and Zephaniah.) She delivers two oracles, one announcing that the threats the book contains will indeed be carried out because of Judah's unfaithfulness to Yahweh (22:15-17) and the other promising Josiah that the disaster will not come in his time (vv. 18-20). The fact that the latter oracle seems to assume that Josiah will die peacefully and to have no knowledge of his death in battle has been taken as evidence that a first edition of Kings (or the Deuteronomistic History as a whole) was produced in Josiah's reign. But the oracle is not concerned with *how* Josiah will die but *when* he will die in relation to the disaster that will befall Judah. And even if the oracle is ignorant of events which would be known to the final compilers of the book, it would be only one of several such passages in the history (cf. 1 Kgs 8:8; 9:21; 2 Kgs 13:23; 14:27).

The Making of a Covenant. The account of the making of the covenant (23:1-3) is again reminiscent of the account of the reign of Joash/Jehoash (2 Kgs 11:17). Once again the king stands by the "pillar" (23:3; cf. 2 Kgs 11:14).

Particular Cult Practices. The detailed account of the reforms provides some information about practices not attested elsewhere or only obliquely: the weaving of vestments for the image of Asherah (23:7; cf. Ezek 16:16-18 and the cult of the queen of heaven, Jer 44:15-19); the horses and chariots dedicated to the sun (23:11; cf. the worship of the sun, Ezek 8:16); the roof altars on which incense was burned to astral deities (23:12; cf. Jer 19:13; 32:29; Zeph 1:5). The offensive cult objects were burned or dumped in the Kidron valley east of Jerusalem (23:4, 6, 12), and their remains and sites were treated with contempt (vv. 6, 14).

Bethel. The sanctuary at Bethel was treated with, if possible, even greater disrespect (23:15-20). Graves were desecrated in order to defile the altar; only the grave of the prophet who had predicted the sanctuary's fate was spared (cf. 1 Kgs 13:29-32). The ruthless slaughter of the priests who had officiated at the northern sanctuaries completed this fanatical purification of the cultus.

The Passover. The account of the Passover (23:21-23) is clearly written with Deuteronomy in mind and probably intends us to understand that this was the first time it had been celebrated as a pilgrimage festival in Jerusalem. Neither the instructions for the Passover in Exod 12:1-28 nor the brief reference in Exod 34:25b indicates that it is to be observed centrally, whereas Deut 16:5-6 reads as an attempt to reform existing practice.

Still Not Enough. Josiah receives high praise for the reforms he carried out (23:24-25). But it was not enough to avert the threatened disaster; in the eyes of the historians God had made up his mind during Manasseh's reign and would not change it (23:26-27). The fall of Judah, like the fall of Samaria, is to be explained entirely in theological terms.

Precedent for Iconoclasm. Josiah's reform involved the violent destruction of images (23:4, 6, 11, 14, 15). In sixteenth-century England this was regarded as sanction for the destruction of images in churches. Edward VI, who, like Josiah, became king when he was a boy, was looked upon as "a second Josiah" (Aston 1988: 246-49).

Josiah's Death. The only glimpse we are given of other events in Josiah's reign is the account of his fatal encounter with Pharaoh Necho at Megiddo. The NRSV does not make it clear whether the pharaoh was going to fight the Assyrians or to help them: in 2 Kgs 17:3 the phrase employed (*'alah 'al*) clearly means "went up against." Those translations which say or imply that Necho was going to *help* the Assyrians depend on the evidence of the Babylonian Chronicle, which says that the Babylonians captured Harran on the Euphrates in 610 and that the Assyrians and the Egyptians failed to recapture it in 609 (*DOTT,* 77-78; *ANET,* 305). The fact that Josiah opposed the Egyptians shows that he was pursuing an anti-Assyrian policy. Later tradition tried to explain Josiah's untimely death theologically: Necho warned him that he would be resisting God, but he would not listen (2 Chr 35:21-22); he would not listen to Jeremiah (1 Esdr 1:28); destiny led him on to his destruction (Josephus *Ant.* 10 §76). However, the Deuteronomists' favorable verdict on him (22:2) is echoed by Jeremiah (Jer 22:15-16). His loss was lamented long after his death (2 Chr 35:25; 1 Esdr 1:32).

The End of Assyria. The Assyrians now disappear from the history. Their capital, Nineveh, had fallen to the Babylonians in 612, and they were finally defeated at the battle of Carchemish in 605.

2 Kings 23:31–24:16

Jehoahaz II (609). The judgment that Jehoahaz did what was evil in the sight of Yahweh seems an unnecessarily harsh way of saying that he did not carry out any reforms. He hardly had the opportunity, being deposed after only three months and taken first to Riblah (a fortified town in the Lebanon which Nebuchadnezzar later made his headquarters during his campaigns in the west; 2 Kgs 25:6, 20-21) and then to Egypt. More sympathy for his fate is expressed in Jeremiah (Jer 22:10-12, where he is called Shallum).

Jehoiakim (609-598). The similar judgment on Jehoiakim receives more support from Jeremiah, where he is charged with building a new palace with forced labor and shedding innocent blood (Jer 22:13-19), having the prophet Uriah brought back from Egypt and murdered (Jer 26:20-23), and burning the scroll on which Jeremiah's prophetic oracles were written (Jeremiah 36). Nevertheless his political position deserves some sympathy: put on the throne by the pharaoh, committed to raising a large sum in tribute money, contending with raids from the neighboring countries, and then becoming a reluctant vassal of the Babylonian king Nebuchadnezzar for the last three years of his reign. (After a decisive battle at Carchemish in 605 Nebuchadnezzar had driven the Egyptians out of Syria-Palestine; *DOTT,* 78-80.) Perhaps some recognition of his difficulties is reflected in the view that it was the sins of Manasseh rather than his sins which had deserved them. (It is not easy to see what significance changing his name from Eliakim to Jehoiakim would have; it is not as if he was expected to take a name which honored another god, as with Daniel being given the name Belteshazzar, Dan 1:7.)

Jehoiachin (598; also known as Coniah in Jer 22:24, 28; 37:1 and as Jeconiah in Jer 24:1; 28:4). Jehoiakim left his son Jehoiachin the legacy of unsuccessful rebellion against Babylon. Jehoiachin's surrender is again lamented in Jeremiah (Jer 13:18-19; 22:24-30), and the Babylonian Chronicle records the siege (which lasted three months), the capture of the king, the appointment of a king of Nebuchadnezzar's own choice, and the imposition of a heavy tribute (*DOTT,* 80-81). Once again the historians stress the depredation of the temple and the royal treasures, mentioning it before the exile of "the elite of the land." It is not clear precisely what prophecy is in mind in 24:13b; the nearest approach to it in Kings is in 2 Kgs 20:17 (cf. Jer 20:5). According to the account in Jeremiah 27–28, there was as much concern in Jerusalem about the return of the temple vessels (Jer 27:16; 28:3) as there was about the return of the exiles (Jer 28:4).

Various Estimates. The numbers exiled in 597 are variously estimated: 10,000 (24:14), 8,000 (24:16), and 3,023 (Jer 52:28).

2 Kings 24:18–25:30

Zedekiah (598-587). Historians tell us little about the reign of Zedekiah apart from his appointment by Nebuchadnezzar (cf. Jer 37:1) and his change of name (the significance of which is again elusive), his rebellion against Babylon, his flight from the besieged city, his capture, and his removal to Babylon in tragic and humiliating circumstances (cf. Jer 39:4-7).

Zedekiah in Jeremiah. We are not told why it was his reign that made Yahweh decide finally to expel Judah from his presence (24:20). The verdict against him (24:19) needs to be balanced by the more sympathetic impression given in Jeremiah of an optimistic king who was prepared to consult Jeremiah and ask him to pray for the nation (Jer 21:1-2; 37:3), even if he was afraid to do so openly (Jer 37:16-17; 38:14-16, 24-27); a king who felt insecure (Jer 38:19-22, 24-26) and by turns imprisoned Jeremiah (Jer 32:1-5) or gave in to others who wanted him imprisoned (Jer 38:4-6) and tried to protect him (37:18-21; 38:7-13). Jeremiah did not think he deserved the terrible fate which actually befell him (Jer 34:2-5).

Zedekiah in Ezekiel. In Ezekiel it is Zedekiah's rebellion against Babylon which is unforgivable (2 Kgs 24:20b; Ezek 17:11-21). There seems to have been some attempt to unite the nations of Syria-Palestine in rebellion (Jer 27:3) and to enlist the aid of Egypt (Ezek 17:15). Indeed, Egyptian intervention led to a temporary raising of the siege (Jer 34:21-22; 37:5).

The Lachish Letters. Nothing is said about the Babylonian campaign in the rest of Judah. Jer 34:7 informs us that Lachish and Azekah, west of Jerusalem, also held out against them. Ostraca (pieces of broken pottery used to write messages on) discovered on the site of Lachish contain messages to the commander of the troops in the city from the officer in charge of an outpost between Lachish and Azekah. He reports that he "cannot see Azekah," which may mean that the city had fallen and was no longer sending signals (*DOTT*, 216-17; *ANET*, 322).

The Siege and the Fast Days. The stages in the siege and the fall of the city are dated to the month and the day of the month (25:1, 3, 8). We know from the prophecies of Zechariah that fast days were held during the exile in the months that were singled out (Zech 7:1-5; 8:18-19), and therefore it is probable that these fast days recalled the beginning of the siege, the breach in the city wall and the capture of the king, the destruction of the temple, and possibly also the murder of Gedaliah (25:25).

The Siege in Deuteronomy. It is possible that the description of famine during a siege in Deut 28:47-57 is drawn from the actual experience of those who lived through the siege of Jerusalem (25:3).

Zedekiah's Attempted Escape. The king intended to escape to the south, beyond the Dead Sea to the Arabah, the valley leading down to the Gulf of Aqaba. But he went only as far as Jericho, north of the Dead Sea, and was taken to the king's headquarters at Riblah in Syria, well beyond Damascus (25:4-7).

Those Left Behind. Nebuzaradan took "all the rest of the population" into exile, leaving only some of the poorest to cultivate the land (25:11-12). This may be a considerable exaggeration. Jer 52:29 says that only 832 people were exiled at this time, with a further 745 five years later, and Ezek 33:24 reports those left behind as saying, "We are many." That passage and Jer 39:10 hint that these poor people were not averse to owning some land for the first time. Jer 40:11-12 adds that the Jews who had fled to the neighboring countries also returned to harvest the now ownerless crops. The fact that the Babylonians, in contrast to the Assyrians, did not replace the exiles with colonists from other parts of the empire made it easier for some at least of the exiles to return later.

Loss of the Temple Fittings. The historians are much more precise about the loss of the bronze pillars, the bronze sea, and the implements and decoration of the temple (25:13-17). Jeremiah is said to have predicted that they would be taken (Jer 27:19-22). The impression given is that their loss was regretted more for its material value and its architectural interest than for any symbolic significance the temple furnishings may have had (see the commentary on 1 Kgs 7:13-51). It is strange that nothing is said of the fate of the ark or the cherubim. There were later traditions either that Jeremiah retrieved the tent, the ark, and the altar of incense and hid them for the time of restoration in a cave on Mt. Nebo (2 Macc 2:4-8; cf. *2 Apoc. Bar.* 6:7-10) or that Josiah, foreseeing the destruction of Jerusalem, removed the ark from its place and hid it in a secret tunnel beneath the foundations (*b. Yoma* 52b; *b. Hor.* 12a; *b. Ker.* 5b; interpreting 2 Chr 35:3). The Ethiopian tradition that Menelik, the son of Solomon and the Queen of Sheba, removed the ark to Axum is based in part on the Bible's silence about it after the time of Solomon.

Chaldeans. The Babylonians are called "Chaldeans" here as in Jeremiah, although the Chaldeans were originally a Semitic tribe who settled in Babylonia alongside its city dwellers. In the book of Daniel the Chaldeans have become a professional caste of fortune-tellers (Dan 2:2; 4:7; 5:7).

Assassination of Gedaliah. To ensure that the people left in Judah remained submissive, their potential leaders were taken to the king at Riblah and executed (25:18-21). A governor, Gedaliah, was appointed, with his headquarters at Mizpah, northwest of Jerusalem. He was a member of a family already mentioned in the history (2 Kgs 22:3, 12; cf. Jer 26:24), and may have been in royal service himself. A seal impression of the late seventh century from Lachish bears the inscription "Belonging to Gedaliah, who is over the household" (*DOTT*, 223-24). However, he and his staff and the Babylonian garrison at Mizpah were assassinated by Ishmael, a member of the royal family, according to Jer 40:14 at the instigation of the Ammonite king. Fear of reprisals led to a mass exodus to Egypt (25:22-26). A fuller account of these events is given in Jeremiah 40–44.

Jehoiachin's Exile. Meanwhile Jehoiachin lived on in exile in Babylon. In about 560, when he was 55, his status changed from that of a prisoner to that of a pensioner at the court of Amel-marduk, the son and successor of Nebuchadnezzar. Even before that, in 592, he and other royal captives were receiving rations of oil and grain, according to tablets found in Babylon (*DOTT*, 84-86; *ANET*, 308).

Hope Centered on the Exiles. The book may end in this way because Jehoiachin was still considered to be the Judean king. Jeremiah shared with others the belief that hope for the future lay with Jehoiachin and his fellow exiles rather than with Zedekiah and those who remained in Judah, even though they disagreed about how long it would be before those hopes would be fulfilled (Jeremiah 24; 27–28; 29). Whether we are indebted to those exiles or later ones or those who remained in Judah for the history in the books of Kings we shall never know.

Bibliography. Ackroyd, P. R. 1967, *Archaeology and Old Testament Study*, ed. D. W. Thomas, Oxford: Clarendon • Albright, W. F. 1945, "The Chronology of the Divided Monarchy of Israel," *BASOR* 100:16-22 • Ap-Thomas, D. R. 1970, "All the King's Horses," in J. R. Durham and J. R. Porter, eds., *Proclamation and Presence*, London: SCM • Ap-Thomas, D. R. 1973, *Peoples of Old Testament Times*, ed. D. J. Wiseman, Oxford: Clarendon • Aston, M. 1988, *England's Iconoclasts I: Laws against Images*, Oxford: Clarendon • Auld, A. G. 1986, *Kings*, Daily Study Bible, Edinburgh: Saint Andrew • Auld, A. G., and M. Steiner. 1996, *Jerusalem I: From the Bronze Age to the Maccabees*, Cambridge: Lutterworth • Barrick, W. B. 2002, "The King and the Cemeteries: Towards a New Understanding of Josiah's Reform," VTSup 88, Leiden: Brill • Beyerlin, W. 1978, *Near Eastern Religious Texts Relating to the Old Testament*, London: SCM • Bird, P. A. 1989. "The Harlot as Heroine," *Semeia* 46:119-39 • Bright, J. 1959, *A History of Israel*, London: SCM • Cogan, M., and H. Tadmor. 1988, *II Kings*, AB 11, New York: Doubleday • Coggins, R. J. 1975, *Samaritans and Jews*, Oxford: Blackwell • Connolly, S. 1995, *Bede: On the Temple*, Liverpool: Liverpool University • Day, J. 1989, *Molech: A God of Human Sacrifice in the Old Testament*, Cambridge: Cambridge University • De Vaux, R. 1961, *Ancient Israel: Its Life and Institutions*, London: Darton,

Longman and Todd • De Vaux, R. 1967, *Archaeology and Old Testament Study,* ed. D. W. Thomas, Oxford: Clarendon • DeVries, S. J. 1985, *1 Kings,* WBC 12, Waco: Word • Emerton, J. A. 1982, "New Light on Israelite Religion," *ZAW* 94:2-20 • Fox, N. S. 2000, *In the Service of the King: Officialdom in Ancient Israel and Judah,* Monographs of the Hebrew Union College 23, Cincinnati: Hebrew Union College • Hannah, W. 1963, *Darkness Visible,* Chulmleigh, Devon: Augustine • Hayes, J. H., and J. M. Miller. 1977, *Israelite and Judaean History,* London: SCM • Heaton, E. W. 1974, *Solomon's New Men,* London: Thames & Hudson • Hobbs, T. R. 1985, *2 Kings,* WBC 13, Waco: Word • Huntley, F. L. 1981, *Essays in Persuasion: On Seventeenth-Century English Literature,* Chicago: University of Chicago • Hurowitz, V. 1992, *I Have Built You an Exalted House,* JSOTSup 115, Sheffield: JSOT • Jamieson-Drake, D. W. 1991, *Scribes and Schools in Monarchic Judah,* Sheffield: Almond • Jones, G. H. 1984, *1 and 2 Kings,* NCBC, Grand Rapids: Eerdmans and Basingstoke: Marshall, Morgan & Scott • Kitchen, K. A. 1997, in L. K. Handy, ed., *The Age of Solomon: Scholarship at the Turn of the Millennium,* Studies in the History and Culture of the Ancient Near East 11, Leiden: Brill • Knoppers, G. N. 1994, *Two Nations under God: The Deuteronomistic History of Solomon and the Dual Monarchies,* 1: *The Reign of Solomon and the Rise of Jeroboam;* 2. *The Reign of Jeroboam, the Fall of Israel, and the Reign of Hosiah,* HSM 52-53, Atlanta: Scholars • Mettinger, T. N. D. 1971, *Solomon's State Officials,* ConBOT 5, Lund: Gleerup • Midgley, G. 1989, *The Miscellaneous Works of John Bunyan,* VII, Oxford: Clarendon • Mowinckel, S. 1962, "Drive and/or Ride in the Old Testament," *VT* 12:278-99 • Nelson, R. D. 1981, *The Double Redaction of the Deuteronomistic History,* JSOTSup 18, Sheffield: JSOT • Nelson, R. D. 1987, *First and Second Kings,* Interpretation, Louisville: John Knox • Norin, S. 1998, "The Age of the Siloam Inscription and Hezekiah's Tunnel," *VT* 48:37-48 • Noth, M. 1955, "Die Bewährung von Salomos 'Göttliche Weisheit,'" in M. Noth and D. W. Thomas, eds., *Wisdom in Israel and the Ancient Near East,* VTSup 3, Leiden: Brill • Noth, M. 2d ed. 1991, *The Deuteronomistic History,* JSOTSup 15, Sheffield: JSOT • Olyan, S. M. 1988, *Asherah and the Cult of Yahweh in Israel,* SBLMS 34, Atlanta: Scholars • Pritchard, J. B. 1974, ed., *Solomon and Sheba,* London: Phaidon • Provan, I. W. 1995, *1 and 2 Kings,* NIBC, Peabody, Mass.: Hendrickson and Carlisle: Paternoster • Provan, I. W. 1997, *1 and 2 Kings,* Old Testament Guides, Sheffield: Sheffield Academic • Rofé, A. 1970, "The Classification of the Prophetical Stories," *JBL* 89:427-40 • Rofé, A. 1974, "Classes in the Prophetical Stories," *Studies in Prophecy,* VTSup 26, Leiden: Brill • Rofé, A. 1988, *The Prophetical Stories,* Jerusalem: Magnes • Rogerson, J., and P. R. Davies. 1996, "Was the Siloam Tunnel Built by Hezekiah?" *BA* 59:138-49 • Rohl, D. M. 1995, *A Test of Time,* London: Century • Scott, R. B. Y. 1939, "The Pillars Jachin and Boaz," *JBL* 58:143-47 • Scott, R. B. Y. 1955, "Solomon and the Beginnings of Wisdom in Israel," in M. Noth and D. W. Thomas, eds., *Wisdom in Israel and the Ancient Near East,* VTSup 3, Leiden: Brill • Sparks, H. F. D. 1984, *The Apocryphal Old Testament,* Oxford: Clarendon • Sternberg, M. 1985, *The Poetics of Biblical Narrative,* Bloomington: Indiana University • Thompson, H. C. 1960, "A Row of Cedar Beams," *PEQ* 92:57-63 • Tomes, R. 1993, "The Reason for the Syro-Ephraimite War," *JSOT* 59:55-71 • Tomes, R. 1996, "'Our Holy and Beautiful House,'" *JSOT* 70:33-50 • Tomes, R. 2000. "'Come and See My Zeal for the Lord': Reading the Jehu Story," in G. J. Brooke and J.-D. Kaestli, eds., *Narrativity in Biblical and Related Texts,* BETL 149, Leuven: Leuven University • Torijano, P. A. 2002, *Solomon the Esoteric King: From King to Magus, the Development of a Tradition,* JSJSup 73, Leiden: Brill • Van Seters, J. 1983, *In Search of History: Historiography in the Ancient World and the Origins of Biblical History,* New Haven: Yale University • Yadin, Y. 1960, "New Light on Solomon's Megiddo," *BA* 23:62-68 • Yerushalmi, S. 1994, *The Book of I Kings;* 1997, *The Book of 2 Kings,* trans. and adapted by N. Bushwick, New York: Moznaim (an anthology of traditional Jewish interpretation).

1 and 2 Chronicles

Richard J. Coggins

INTRODUCTION

The Contents of Chronicles

1 and 2 Chronicles are consecutive works like 1 and 2 Samuel and 1 and 2 Kings; they are not like 1 and 2 Maccabees, where parallel accounts of the same period are offered. An immediate implication of this is that the introduction to the present commentary is concerned with both 1 and 2 Chronicles.

1 Chronicles begins at the very beginning, with Adam, and the story is taken forward in chs. 1–9 almost entirely by means of genealogical lists. These lists reach to the beginning of the Israelite monarchy, the time of Saul and David, though, as we shall see, they also refer to a number of figures from a later period. Saul is quickly disposed of, and the remainder of 1 Chronicles (chs. 10–29) is concerned with the reign of David. 2 Chronicles begins with the accession of David's son Solomon, and chs. 1–9 are devoted to an account of his rule. Then the remainder of the work (2 Chronicles 10–36) is concerned with the Judahite monarchy, with occasional references to its northern neighbor, Israel. In the last chapter the Babylonians under Nebuchadnezzar overrun Judah and destroy Jerusalem; the people are taken into exile. Only in the last two verses does a more hopeful note emerge with the arrival on the scene of Cyrus of Persia, who authorizes the restoration of the temple and, apparently, a return of the exiles to Jerusalem.

Who Was the Chronicler?

Before we try to answer this question we need to remember that we do not know the "author" of any book of the OT. Even the prophetic books, the most obvious apparent exceptions to that statement, have reached their present form by means of developments and editing of the words of the prophets after whom the books are named. So it is most unlikely that we should ever be able to identify the Chronicler in the sense of putting a name and a date to him. (And "him" is used advisedly; we shall see that one of the central concerns of the Chronicler is the Jerusalem temple and the worship that took place there. There were very severe limitations on the role that women could play in that temple, and so it is wildly unlikely that a feminine hand could be detected in the writings of the Chronicler. Whether we are to think of one author or of a group is less clear; it is only for convenience that we shall use the singular here: "him" and "his.")

We have already noted one thing about the Chronicler: his concern with the Jerusalem temple. In the books of Samuel and Kings, which offer a parallel with the greater part of Chronicles, concern for a temple is deferred until the reign of Solomon, the son of David. 2 Samuel 7 makes clear that the building of a physical "house" is to be undertaken not by David but by his son (v. 13); and by a play on the meaning of the word "house," which is possible in both Hebrew and English, David's house is to consist of the line of his successors. In Chronicles, by contrast, though Solomon is still the builder of the temple, far more attention is paid to the work of preparation envisaged as taking place during David's lifetime. Indeed, 1 Chronicles 21–29 are largely devoted to spelling out the preparations for temple building.

It is likely that concern with the temple is revealed even earlier. Possibly some of the genealogies of 1 Chronicles 1–9 represent free compositions by the Chronicler, but insofar as they are dependent on earlier sources, as is likely in many cases, those sources will have been found within the temple complex. There were no public libraries or record offices in ancient Israel to which those seeking information about their forefathers could have recourse.

We may suppose, then, that the Chronicler was closely connected with the Jerusalem temple. That temple will have been what is often called the "Second Temple," built or rebuilt late in the sixth century BC, when the community was under Persian rule. The very end of 2 Chronicles refers to the rise of Cyrus, effectively the first Persian emperor and certainly the first of whom the Jewish community shows any knowledge, and it is clear that the Chronicler was anxious to stress the continuity between the First Temple, promised to David and built under Solomon, and the Second Temple of his own day. We shall see numerous examples of this concern as we work through the two books of Chronicles.

Is it possible to be still more specific in identifying the Chronicler? It would be helpful if an approximate date could be suggested, but there are no certain clues to this. Persian rule over the Jerusalem community came to an end with the conquests of Alexander the Great c. 333 BC, and there are no clear signs in Chronicles of the influence of Hellenism which followed Alexander's conquests. Some scholars have suggested a date early in the Persian period for the work of the Chronicler, but if there are close links with Ezra and Nehemiah (see below), that becomes unlikely. A date in the fourth century BC seems probable, but it is impossible to be more specific, and we need to recognize that we know virtually nothing of the history of the Jerusalem community during that period.

The other proposal which has been made in the attempt to be more specific about the identity of the Chronicler is to note the frequent favorable references to the Levites scattered through the two books and to suggest that this may imply Levite authorship. The history of the Levites is far from clear; in Deuteronomy (e.g., Deut 18:1) it looks as if all Levites were to be regarded as priests. Perhaps that claim was made, but if so, it was ultimately unsuccessful, and in the Second Temple the Levites had come to be regarded as a lower rank within the structure of the clergy, confined to more menial tasks than the sacrificial rites which were performed by those who were accorded full priesthood. It is certainly noteworthy that Levites are often commended, whereas the priests come in for their share of criticism (e.g., 2 Chr 29:34). Whether that means that Chronicles should in some sense be regarded as an "apology" on behalf of the Levites is an open question. We know that the question of priesthood and who might legitimately exercise it was a sensitive issue (see the various claims and counterclaims to true priesthood at the time of the Hasmonean rising, c. 170 BC, as detailed in 1 Maccabees), and it may be that part of the purpose of Chronicles was to ensure that the role of the Levites in the Jerusalem temple was not sidelined.

What Material Did the Chronicler Use?

Much of the content of 1 and 2 Chronicles can be found elsewhere in the Hebrew Bible (HB), and so it has usually been supposed that the Chronicler made use of other biblical material as his sources. Indeed, in the Greek Bible, the Septuagint (LXX), the books of Chronicles are given the title *ta paralipomena,* "the things left out." That is to say, it seems as if Chronicles was regarded as a kind of supplement to other books. Duplications could then be explained as due to the concern that nothing of the people's traditions should be omitted; better to include it twice than not at all. And so the usual scholarly view has been that the Chronicler had access to Genesis and to Samuel-Kings in something like their present form, and that these supplied the material for the greater part of his work.

It may be so. But it is worth noting that various developments in the study of the HB make it more difficult to sustain this view than was once the case. At one time it was assumed that the Pentateuch, and Genesis in particular, had reached their final form well before any likely date for the Chronicler. A number of recent studies have, however, postulated a very late date for at least some parts of Genesis, and it would now be much less widely held that Genesis was available to the Chronicler in something like the form in which we know it. The possibility must at least be held open that some of the material common to both Genesis and Chronicles was used independently by the two final authors rather than one being simply dependent on the other.

A very similar view has been proposed in another study (Auld 1994) regarding the relation of Samuel-Kings to Chronicles. The usual understanding has been that the Samuel-Kings account of the monarchical period was available to the Chronicler, and that part at least of his purpose was to act as a kind of commentary upon the earlier work, resolving difficulties both historical and theological. (Classic examples would be the issues of who killed Goliath [see 1 Chronicles 20] and why David's census was so unacceptable [see 1 Chronicles 21].) But again the date when Samuel-Kings reached their final form has been put later than was once customary, and Auld's view is that Samuel-Kings and Chronicles should be seen as parallel works rather than as the latter being dependent upon the former.

These recent scholarly developments should certainly be borne in mind, but not necessarily followed. As we shall see as we work through the books of Chronicles, there are many places, more particularly in 2 Chronicles, where the most plausible explanation of the text before us is that it is based on a known existing text which, if not yet formally regarded as "Scripture," was certainly coming to be esteemed as an important repository of the community's traditions. In this setting it has been very widely argued that Chronicles should be seen as a rereading (a "relecture," in the French term often used of this process) of the books of Samuel and Kings, regarded as primary sources of Chronicles.

The possibility of tracing sources within the Chronicler's work other than the biblical parallels has been much discussed, and nothing approaching agreement has been reached. At least two issues are at stake here. First, did the Chronicler have access to sources other than the biblical material? If so, and particularly if it could be established that such sources were ancient, it would be possible to claim a greater degree of historical reliability for the work than has been usual in critical circles. An example would be 2 Chronicles 17–20, where the account of Jehoshaphat's reign is much fuller than that found in Kings. Secondly, is it possible to trace redactional levels within the final form of the books? This would imply that "the Chronicler" was not an individual or a single group, but is a way of speaking of those active over an extended period. An example here would be the way in which 1 Chronicles 23–27 appear to interrupt the buildup toward Solomon's accession and the construction of the temple.

It is not possible in a commentary of this size to examine these questions in detail, but it should be noted that there is a strong tendency in much modern scholarship to be concerned with the books in the shape in which they have come down to us rather than to speculate on questions concerning sources and redactions which must in the end be unanswerable.

It will be apparent from what has been said that the Greek title *ta paralipomena,* "things left out," is not a satisfactory description of Chronicles. But for better or worse it has had important implications for most modern commentaries, including this one. Where the Chronicler shares common material with Samuel-Kings (and, in the case of 1 Chronicles 16, with the Psalms), it has become customary to refer the reader to commentaries on those other books for a more detailed discussion. Space limitations make it necessary to follow that practice here.

The Extent of the Chronicler's Work

Again we find here a widely held view which has recently been challenged. It has been customary to regard the books of Chronicles as the first and most substantial part of a composite work which found its completion in Ezra and Nehemiah. There are a number of reasons for such an understanding. First, the last two verses of Chronicles (2 Chr 36:22-23) form the beginning of Ezra (Ezra 1:1-3a). This has traditionally been explained by the suggestion that Ezra-Nehemiah, which have little parallel material elsewhere in the HB, came to be regarded as sacred earlier than Chronicles. Later 1-2 Chronicles, which follow Ezra-Nehemiah in the Hebrew order of scrolls, also came to be part of the collection of Scripture, and the link between them was emphasized by the repetition of these verses. The apocryphal book 1 Esdras draws on material from both 2 Chronicles and Ezra as if they formed a coherent whole.

Less specifically, but in a more wide-ranging way, scholars have drawn attention to similarities of vocabulary between Chronicles and Ezra-Nehemiah, as well as to a broadly similar theological stance, with its base very firmly set in the conviction of God's presence with his worshipers in the Jerusalem temple. It seemed as if the unity of Chronicles-Ezra-Nehemiah could properly be regarded as "an assured result of scholarship."

If one thing is certain in biblical studies, it is that the supposedly "assured results of scholarship" will sooner or later be challenged. And so it has been here. Two scholars in particular, Japhet and Williamson, have drawn attention in a series of studies to features which suggest to them that the two collections come from diverse origins. Japhet (in her 1968 article in particular) has shown that the alleged linguistic links between Chronicles and Ezra-Nehemiah are much less secure than had previously been supposed; Williamson's emphasis has been upon the much more open attitude to other groups, especially the northern tribes, in Chronicles as compared with Ezra-Nehemiah. Those books also show little interest in the family of David, which is so central to the concerns of Chronicles (Williamson 1977).

It would be misleading, however, to suppose that the earlier consensus was simply wrong. The question of linguistic similarities and differences continues to be disputed and can hardly be discussed in detail in a commentary of this kind. In due course we may hope that computer-based analysis will provide a more secure answer. What is clear is that both Chronicles and Ezra-Nehemiah are closely bound to the Jerusalem temple. Some scholars see that as an important common element; others regard the temple as so central to the life of the community that reverence for it proves little. We also need to remember that the actual mechanics of authorship in the ancient world are largely unknown to us, so that a measure of uncertainty on this issue is inevitable.

A Historical Work?

At first glance it might seem obvious that Chronicles is a work of history, covering as it does the period from Adam (1 Chr 1:1) to the time of Cyrus of Persia, who ruled from 550-529 BC (2 Chr 36:22-23). But it does not require much detailed study of Chronicles to reach the conclusion that, if the Chronicler was a historian, he was in important respects a very poor one. Wellhausen, more than a century ago, was scathing about the way in which the Chronicler had transformed the figure of King David from a mighty warrior to one who spent his time arguing about ecclesiastical niceties. In addition, there are many other places where the accounts in Samuel and Kings, regarded as historically more reliable, have been transformed by the Chronicler in a historically very implausible way. The account of King Manasseh's repentance (2 Chr 33:11-16), unsupported by other evidence, looks more like an attempt to account for the length of his reign, with its implications of divine favor, than like a means of access to fresh historical information.

Increasingly in recent years, however, the Chronicler's reputation has been restored, not because his historical reliability has been upheld (some attempts in that direction have been made but have not gained much support), but because of the realization that modern canons of historical accuracy may not be the appropriate tools to use. First, greater attention has been paid to the literary skills of the work, and some of these will be briefly noticed in the commentary that follows. Secondly, alternative purposes, other than the strictly historical, have been proposed as the Chronicler's underlying intention. It has been suggested, for example, that he wished to act as an interpreter of older traditions, explaining them and making them relevant to the circumstances of his own time. Recently there has been much interest in the way in which the later parts of the HB were consciously concerned with interpreting earlier material, and in that process the Chronicler had an important role. Thirdly, there has been a changing perception of the role of genealogies. Traditionally these were treated literally, as pieces of historical information, and much time was spent in trying to reconcile incompatibilities, real or apparent, within the various lists. Comparative studies by social anthropologists in recent years, however, have shown that genealogies are often social constructs designed to spell out more precisely the identity of a particular group or society, and in this context inconsistencies can be tolerated. This will be important to remember as we look at the opening chapters of 1 Chronicles.

1 Chronicles

COMMENTARY

1 Chronicles 1

The modern custom is to regard a book as something to be read, and we expect the opening pages to engage our interest, to invite us to explore further. By such criteria 1 Chronicles would fail miserably. Nearly the whole of chs. 1–9 consists of lists of names. But these are not just any names; "their aim is to paint a portrait of the people of God in its ideal extent as a symbol both of the particularity of his election and the breadth of his grace" (Williamson 1982: 39). Bearing in mind the social function of genealogies that we have just noted, we can see that the lists are structured in such a way as to bring out two crucial points. First, they establish the principle of continuity. The community of the Chronicler's day could see in itself the heirs of a tradition which went right back to the creation of the world and Adam. Secondly, these genealogies are highly selective; they are not a random listing of names, but focus in particular on the lines of Judah (3:1–4:23) and of Levi (ch. 6), whose role was to be so decisive in the story that the Chronicler was going to tell. We should also recall that the practice of starting a story of good news in this way is not peculiar to the Chronicler; the Gospel of Matthew also begins with a highly selective list of names (Matt 1:1-17) intended to set the context for the story which is to follow.

It is customary to say that the beginning of this genealogy has its source in Genesis, but it is not Genesis as we know it. There the best-known sons of Adam are Cain and Abel (Genesis 4); here, by contrast, the list found in Genesis 5 forms the basis of the names in 1:1-4. It is then rather unexpected to find in vv. 5-23 a detailed listing of the descendants of the "other" sons of Noah. The chosen line is envisaged as that through Shem, which is taken up in v. 24; we have a brief treatment of the Japhethites (vv. 5-7), a more extended list of those descended from Ham (vv. 8-16), and an alternative listing of the Shemites (vv. 17-23) before we return to the main story. This section has sometimes been seen as secondary, but it is difficult to see why a later editor should have introduced this material (Johnson 1969: 73). These verses are closely linked to the genealogies in Genesis 10, and like them they share some variations in spelling (see, e.g., Diphath and Rodanim at vv. 6/7, names whose initial letters are reversed in the Hebrew text of Genesis 10). Most of the names are those of peoples rather than of individuals; this is obvious in such cases as "Egypt" and "Canaan," and is indicated in 1:11-12 by the use of plural names (the ending *-im* is the Hebrew plural). The inclusion of these varied groups fulfills an important function in providing a setting. The Israelites knew well enough that they were not the only people in the world, and these verses bring out the common humanity of the different peoples of that world.

Abram is reached at 1:27, and the better-known form of his name, Abraham, is given. In the remainder of the chapter the genealogies take on a different form. In the Second Temple period, Abraham (who is hardly mentioned in earlier parts of the HB outside Genesis) became increasingly important as a founder figure of the community; the NT amply illustrates this. From this point on, instead of covering many generations by normally making reference to only one member of each generation (Noah's sons, Shem, Ham, and Japheth, are an exception to that custom), attention focuses on the descendants of Abraham and Isaac, with extensive details about those not in what would be regarded as the "chosen" line. As in Genesis, particular attention is paid to those who traced their descent to Jacob's brother Esau, regarded as the ancestor of the Edomites. There were close and often bitter relations between Judah and Edom at different periods. Here the emphasis is on their common ancestry, with the names for the most part those also found in Genesis 36. Nothing is known of the individuals listed or of the source of the information.

1 Chronicles 2

The opening verses of this chapter mark an important watershed; from here on attention will be devoted almost entirely to those who claimed Israelite ancestry; Jacob is here, as regularly in Chronicles, given his other name "Israel." His twelve sons are listed in 2:1-2, in a curious order: first those by Leah (Reuben-Zebulun), then the first of Rachel's handmaid Bilhah (Dan), then Rachel's own children (Joseph and Benjamin), and finally the remaining "handmaid" tribes, Naphtali (whose mother was Bilhah) and Gad and Asher (the children of Leah's maid Zilpah). No satisfactory explanation of this curious order has been offered, the usual solution being the despairing one of "scribal error." If Genesis 29–30 were the source here, they have been used very creatively.

The genealogies of the different tribes follow. We should note, however, that of those here listed Dan and Zebulun appear to be missing, whereas Ephraim and Manasseh, the sons of Joseph, are listed separately. Nor is the order of 2:1-2 adhered to in the lists; the line of Judah is given attention first, even though tradition held that he was only the fourth of Jacob's sons. The people of the Chronicler's time used the name "Judah" of their own community, and so the line of Judah was of paramount importance to them. We do not know the exact sources available to the Chronicler or the principles on which he ordered his material.

The Judah names are introduced (2:3-4) with a reference to Judah's escapades in Genesis 38, including the fact that he was said to have had children by his own daughter-in-law, Tamar. The less important descendants of Judah are mentioned first. The names in v. 6 appear to be taken over from a completely different context in

1 Kgs 4:31, where they are apparently not Israelites at all. Then follows a reference to "Achar" (v. 7), which alludes to Joshua 7. There he is called "Achan," but the change reflects a wordplay on the verb "to trouble" (*ʿakar*), a point already made in Joshua.

But the center of the Chronicler's interest is in the line through Hezron and Ram (2:9). ("Chelubai" is a variant spelling of "Caleb," who has a prominent place further on in the chapter.) We reach Jesse, with no reference to Ruth his grandmother, whose story is told in the book of that name (another indication of androcentricity?). Then the single line of descent gives way to a spelling out of Jesse's sons, culminating in David, the eighth of his sons according to 1 Sam 16:10-11, but here given the prestigious position of the seventh son (2:15). Zeruiah and Abigail are here identified as David's sisters. Opinions will differ whether the Chronicler's creative imagination was here at work, or whether he had access to otherwise unknown sources. They are probably mentioned because of the significant role in the narrative about David's times played by their sons.

Having introduced David, the Chronicler mentions various other Judahite traditions, using principles which are not always clear to us. Thus parts of 2:18-22 are found again in variant form in vv. 50-52. Caleb plays a prominent part, suggesting that many of the Judahites of the Chronicler's time claimed descent from Caleb. In vv. 42-49 in particular we see how various localities (Hebron, Maon, and others) are treated as if they were individuals and given a place in the Calebite genealogy. Though David and his family are the center of interest, it was important for a wider range of the people of Judah to establish their identity through family trees. Thus in v. 55 we have reference to both Kenites and Rechabites, who, unlike most foreign groups, were regarded as acceptable within Israel.

1 Chronicles 3

Interest returns to David, who is in effect the central human character in 1 Chronicles. Most of the sons of David listed in 3:1-9 are known to us from 2 Samuel. "Daniel" here replaces "Chileab" of 2 Sam 3:3; nothing more is known about either of them. Whereas some less attractive features of David's life and conduct are passed over in silence in Chronicles, his polygamy seems not to have been regarded as a problem. "Bathshua" is found at 3:5 instead of the better-known form "Bathsheba." There may have been a deliberate linkage with Judah's wife of the same name (2:3). It is curious that Solomon is listed as the fourth of her children; certainly 2 Sam 12:24 implies, without specifically stating, that Solomon was her first surviving child.

3:10-14 set out the kings of Judah from Solomon to Josiah; then, with Josiah, a different form of listing is found, mentioning all Josiah's sons, including the otherwise unknown Johanan. When we meet these characters again in 2 Chronicles, they are sometimes given different names. Thus "Shallum" here is Jehoahaz in 2 Chr 36:1-4, and "Jeconiah" (3:16) is Jehoiachin in 2 Chr 36:5-10. His brother Zedekiah may be a confusion with the Zedekiah who succeeded him (2 Chr 36:10), who is variously described as his uncle (2 Kgs 24:17) or his brother (2 Chr 36:10). This uncertainty as to precise relationships continues at v. 19, where Zerubbabel, well known from Haggai and there called the "son of Shealtiel," is here the son of Pedaiah.

Zerubbabel lived around 520 BC, that is, later than the story in 2 Chronicles takes us. The remaining verses of this chapter give us one of our few indications of the members of the Davidic family during the Persian period. But they are no more than names. The tradition does not always seem reliable (cf. the reference to "six" sons of Shemaiah in 3:22 when only five are listed). Nor is it clear whether vv. 21-22 are to be emended, as by the NRSV, to read "son" rather than "sons." If the emendation is accepted, we have a text which takes the story far later than Zerubbabel, the latest otherwise-known character. If the Hebrew text is followed, we simply have a listing of families which cannot be dated. Despite the prominence of David himself, no special role seems here to be envisaged for any of his descendants. There are no links here with the list of those following Zerubbabel in the Davidic line of Jesus in Matt 1:13-16.

1 Chronicles 4:1-23

We return to the nonroyal descendants of Judah. The five names of 4:1 are not brothers but successive members of one family. A rather miscellaneous collection of notes follows, which are linked to the end of ch. 2. The footnotes in the NRSV indicate the uncertainty of some of these lists, since "father" in the Hebrew text appears as "sons" in the Greek version, which attempts to make the list more coherent. Also, the reference to a sister, and still more her improbable name "Hazzelelponi" (v. 3), is unexpected. (Later rabbinic tradition identified her with the unnamed mother of Samson, who received an angelic vision in Judges 13.) Since most of the names and the incidents referred to are otherwise quite unknown to us, it is impossible to place this material within our overall picture of ancient Israel. It is unlikely that 4:17 (v. 18 in the Hebrew text) is to be understood literally, so that Bithiah was actually the daughter of the Egyptian pharaoh. She bears an Israelite name, and the text is in considerable confusion at this point. It seems as if a variety of fragmentary information has been assembled here as part of the larger intention of showing the significance of the whole community.

1 Chronicles 4:24-43

Simeon, though theoretically a northern tribe in the stylized accounts of the division of the kingdom, in fact occupied the southernmost area of the land and was subordinate to Judah, a point expressed in terms of size at 4:27. Here, as elsewhere in these lists, there are links with other lists, particularly those in Numbers 26 and Joshua 19. It is from Joshua 19 that we discover that "Baal" of 4:33, very unusual as a place name, is actually "Baalath-Beer." "And they kept a genealogical record" may be a claim to the reliability of this information despite the fact that it came from the well-nigh extinct Simeonite group. The section closes with a reference to the long-standing hostility between Israel and the Amalekites (cf. Exodus 17, esp. v. 18).

1 Chronicles 5:1-10

Reuben is named the firstborn son of Jacob in Gen 29:31, but, as often in Genesis, the firstborn does not receive the birthright. In Reuben's case the reason was his incest with Bilhah (Gen 35:22). What is without parallel elsewhere is the assertion that Joseph received the birthright (5:2), a remarkable point in that the Joseph tribes came from northern Israel, over against Judah. "Tilgath-pilneser" is the form regularly found in Chronicles for the Assyrian ruler called "Tiglath-pileser" in Kings. Since both forms are renderings of another language, it is pointless to ask which is "correct." Sometimes the HB gives "wrong" forms of names for insulting or polemical purposes, but that scarcely seems to be the case here.

1 Chronicles 5:11-17

The area occupied by the Reubenites was in trans-Jordan, and this was also the home of Gad. These verses appear to have no parallels in other lists.

1 Chronicles 5:18-22

This brief section interrupts the genealogies and introduces a theme which will be prominent later in Chronicles, a kind of theology of warfare (5:20). Those who cry to the LORD are assured of success because of their trust in him. Here as elsewhere this explanation of success is accompanied by vastly exaggerated numbers. The Chronicler may indeed have been quite peace-loving, but, as with many Christian hymn writers in more recent centuries, the description of the role of the religious community in terms of warfare came readily to him.

1 Chronicles 5:23-26

More military material follows, relating to the trans-Jordanian element of Manasseh. When they ceased to trust in God they were defeated in war — this time by "Pul" of Assyria, who was actually identical with "Tilgath-pilneser." The NRSV's way of arranging the material implies this, but the Hebrew is more naturally understood as if the Chronicler thought they were separate rulers.

1 Chronicles 6

After the relatively brief material relating to Simeon, Reuben, Gad, and Manasseh, that dealing with Levi is second in length only to that on Judah and reflects the Chronicler's concern with the priestly groups. There is much repetition in this chapter, and many scholars claim to detect secondary additions here. This may be so, though criteria for such decisions are not easy to reach. We should also notice that these genealogies are not intended as an exact record, as might be assumed in the modern world for those, say, wishing to establish the right to an inheritance. There are contradictions both within this chapter and in comparison with other parts of Chronicles, and these need not be ascribed to carelessness — the author is concerned with the overall picture rather than exactitude of historical detail. Thus Levi's first son is sometimes named Gershon (6:1) and sometimes Gershom (v. 16) in the Hebrew text; the NRSV has tidied up the usage.

Moses is listed without comment in the names of the first four generations following Levi, and in general Chronicles shows no interest in him as an individual, though he was important as the mediator of the divine Torah. 6:4-15 gives a list of "high priests" (the title may be anachronistic) down to the exile. It is quite artificial; variants of the same list occur elsewhere in Chronicles (cf. 1 Chron 9:11) and in Ezra 7. It may be based on deliberate listings of twelve generations (Williamson 1982); cf. the listing of Jesus' ancestors in groups of fourteen in Matthew 1.

6:16-30 offer another list of Levi's descendants. The striking name here is that of Samuel (v. 28), who is elsewhere given Ephraimite parentage (1 Sam 1:1). Strictly speaking he is not brought into the genealogy here (though he is at 6:33), but it seems clear that to the Chronicler anyone who had legitimately exercised priestly functions, as Samuel had, must have been of Levite stock.

Somewhat confusingly, in 6:31-48 the main genealogy goes upward, from son to father. The theme is the temple music, an important concern throughout the books of Chronicles. The "house of the LORD" is described as if it already existed in David's time. This list ends with a reference to the duties of the Levites (v. 48). The following verses emphasize that the tasks which could only be carried out by the priests themselves were performed by the family of Aaron, another brief list of whom is appended. For the proper appreciation of material of this kind it is important to remember that there was often bitter rivalry between different groups claiming priestly rights.

The chapter ends (6:54-81) with a detailed description of the levitical dwelling places. The theory was that the tribe of Levi did not receive a territorial allotment, and so specific places had to be set apart. This list closely resembles that in Joshua 21, with differences in order and other details, and has usually been held to be dependent on the Joshua list, though this has been challenged by Auld (1978).

1 Chronicles 7

In this chapter several other tribal genealogies are set forth much more briefly. Issachar (7:1-5) was a northern group and may well have seemed quite remote to the Chronicler; the details here are scanty. Benjamin (vv. 6-12) is unexpectedly introduced here, since fuller details will be offered in ch. 8 and the surrounding material relates to northern groups. The names of Bela's sons given here are quite different from those at 8:3. But these names are mostly those known from other Benjaminite lists, and the suggestion that this list originally referred to Zebulun (which has no list) can be no more than speculation. Many commentators (e.g., Japhet 1993), followed by the NEB/REB, have found in 7:12 a brief reference to Dan, another tribe without a list, but the emendations required are speculative and rather drastic, and the NRSV prefers to see that verse as listing Benjaminite names. The Manassite list that follows is usually thought to have undergone serious textual corruption; see the larger commentaries for details. In the Ephraimite list (vv. 20-27) the main interest lies in setting forth the family of another hero of the people's early days: Joshua. The list is broken by fragments of tribal lore and a characteristic wordplay linking the name Beriah with disaster (*bera'ah*). Various place names follow; many versions (NEB/REB) include "Gaza" as one of them, but the NRSV is probably right to retain the otherwise unknown "Ayyah." Details of the last northern group, Asher, round off the chapter (vv. 30-40).

1 Chronicles 8

Whatever the origin of 7:6-12 this material seems clearly to relate to Benjamin, with more details offered than for any other group except Judah and Levi. Its territory bordered on Jerusalem (8:28), and this will have increased its importance for the Chronicler. Though there are a few links with Genesis 46 and Numbers 26, it is only with the last part of the chapter that otherwise well-known names emerge. This is the section beginning at 8:33, where the family of Saul is listed. Since Saul plays so insignificant a role in Chronicles, it is surprising that his family should be listed twice, here and again with minor variations at 9:35-44. The reason for the NRSV's footnote "or Shaul" is not obvious; the name is spelled identically here as in the well-known stories in 1 Samuel. His immediate ancestors listed here are, however, different from those of 1 Sam 9:1. The names "Esh-baal" and "Merib-baal" for Saul's son and grandson are striking since in 2 Samuel they are called "Ishbosheth" and "Mephibosheth" respectively. The forms given here are more likely to be original; perhaps the Chronicler was less embarrassed by names compounded with the divine name "-Baal" than was the author of Samuel, or perhaps he did not wish to express the antagonism to Saul's house implied in the "-bosheth" suffix. The word means "shame." Another difference is in the extent of the Saulide genealogy, which in Samuel stops with Micah (2 Sam 9:12); here it is extended, apparently for nine generations, an interesting contrast to the emphasis in 10:6 that all of Saul's house died in the one battle (cf. also 2 Sam 2:1-9).

1 Chronicles 9:1

This verse serves as a summary of what has preceded, emphasizing the wholeness of Israel. Whether there was an actual "Book of the Kings of Israel" is uncertain; this is not likely to be a reference to the biblical books of Kings. Though the main story is to begin with an account of David, we first have a "fastforward," here to the exile and then to the restoration which followed. This is an important way in which the Chronicler emphasizes the continuity between the ancestors whom he has listed so far and the community of his own day.

1 Chronicles 9:2-34

We are not yet done with lists of names. Those found in this section bear close similarities (though they are far from identical) with Nehemiah 11. In historical terms it is not easy to envisage a large-scale "return from exile," but it is important for the Chronicler to emphasize that at the earliest opportunity the community, and especially those concerned with the temple, returned to the holy land. Though Judah was of central importance, they were Israelites (9:2) and included some from the northern tribes Ephraim and Manasseh (v. 3). They were welcome, though they must of course base themselves in Jerusalem. In the lists of temple officials which follow we may note the prominence given to the "gatekeepers" (vv. 17-27). Access to the temple was strictly limited to those properly qualified. We have noted already that it was anachronistic to attribute the temple arrangements to David; in v. 22 the anachronism is extended by linking with them "the seer Samuel," who according to 1 Sam 25:1 died before David even captured Jerusalem. Precise historical reconstruction is not the Chronicler's main concern. 9:34 rounds off the section and shows a close similarity with 8:28.

1 Chronicles 9:35-44

The Saulide genealogy of 8:29-38 is repeated almost verbatim. Now it functions as a direct introduction to the main narrative which begins in ch. 10.

1 Chronicles 10

The assumption is made from the outset that the story to be told will already be familiar. Thus no attempt is made to explain who the Philistines were, even though to the Second Temple community they will have been figures from a distant past. The chapter not only serves to set off the splendor of the account of David's reign; it is also a model of the disaster of the exile, with David's reign comparable to the restoration that followed. Israel is defeated, its king killed; the old order has come to an end (notice the stress on "death" in 10:5-7). In vv. 13-14 we have a summary conclusion unparalleled elsewhere, in which the Chronicler brings out a characteristic emphasis on the way in which unfaithfulness brings its inevitable results. Though at one level the Philistines or the armor bearer might be thought to be the instruments of Saul's death, fundamentally it was Yahweh who "put him to death" and inaugurated David's reign, which will be pictured as a complete contrast to that of Saul. This whole section seems to assume knowledge of the account of Saul in 1 Samuel.

1 Chronicles 11:1-9

This chapter stresses immediately that David is king of "all Israel." In Samuel, Hebron, south of Jerusalem, had been David's power base while he acted as a freedom fighter (or terrorist, according to the point of view); here this is a religious gathering, sealed by a covenant (11:3), and followed by a procession to Jerusalem. There is no thought here of the seven-year period of rule at Hebron mentioned in 2 Sam 5:5. "Jebus," given here as the name of Jerusalem, is probably derived from the inhabitants, "Jebusites." Extrabiblical texts seem to imply that the city had long been known as Jerusalem, but the Chronicler perhaps deliberately implies that Jerusalem was a distinctively Israelite name. The actual account of the capture is much simpler and more straightforward here than in 2 Samuel 5, but it is impossible to be certain whether this is a deliberate simplification of a difficult original or whether it offers a reliable alternative. The Millo, "filling," may refer to the elaborate terracing of the steep eastern slope of the city.

1 Chronicles 11:10-47

The reference to David's "general" Joab in 11:6 and 8 provided the occasion for more lists, this time of the warrior chiefs, who seem to have formed a kind of guerrilla force. The basic material as far as v. 41 is also found at 2 Sam 23:8-39, with a fresh introduction here stressing divine approval of David's kingship. There were apparently two groups, known as "the three" and "the thirty"; textual evidence relating to them is not clear (see the NRSV footnotes), and it is also not certain whether each group actually had three or thirty members (cf. the "centuries" of the Roman army, which did not necessarily have a hundred members). The best-known episode in this section is found in vv. 17-19, where the apparent folly of needless risks is overridden by the way in which the devotion to David of the warriors is brought out.

The last few verses of the chapter (11:41b-47) have no parallel in 2 Samuel 23. The last name there is "Uriah the Hittite," the unfortunate husband of Bathsheba, and it has been suggested that the author of Samuel deliberately curtailed the list for dramatic effect. But Williamson (1982: 103-4) and others have noted that these last verses do not form a natural continuation of what has preceded, and so they probably have a different origin. It is noteworthy that the immediately following material, in ch. 12, is also without parallel in Samuel, but is clearly intended as part of a larger unity in the Chronicler's work.

1 Chronicles 12

As we have just noted, this chapter should be seen as part of a unity with ch. 11; notice in particular the conclusion (12:38), emphasizing the way in which all Israel joined in recognizing David's kingship at Hebron (cf. 11:1). The lists are given a sketchy narrative setting with their references to the enmity between David and Saul (12:1; the way it is expressed there would hardly lead one to think that Saul had actually been king at the time!) and to those from Transjordan (Gad and Manasseh, vv. 8 and 19) who had joined David in unknown circumstances. Some of the themes here mentioned are found elsewhere, such as the military expertise of the Benjaminites, even as left-handers (v. 2; cf. Judg 3:15ff.), but details of the names are unknown.

The particular purpose of this chapter seems to be twofold. First, it again emphasizes the "all Israel" nature of David's kingship, already introduced at 11:1; even the northern tribes rallied to his support. In addition to those from Gad and Manasseh, representatives of all the other tribes are listed in 12:23-37. Some kind of military register may underlie this list, but the numbers are frankly incredible. Either "thousand" should be understood as representing some smaller unit, or this is simply an example of exaggeration on the Chronicler's part.

Secondly, this chapter emphasizes the "help" given to David, not only by his subjects but also by God himself. Here the poetic fragment in 12:18 is notable. It forms a (perhaps deliberate) balance and contrast with 2 Chr 10:16. There some had deserted David's house; here the stress is on the widespread loyalty which David evoked. The chapter ends with David proclaimed as "king over all Israel" and gladly accepted as such even by those from the far north — "Issachar and Zebulun and Naphtali."

1 Chronicles 13

The next major theme, dominating chs. 13–16, is the ark. The usual view is that the ark was destroyed along with the First Temple in 587 BC, so that for the Chronicler's readers this story will have been of only historical interest. But it is an important part of the community's story, and its role must be clarified; in particular the setting provided by vv. 1-2, of a religious gathering for the whole community, would be highly relevant to the Chronicler's audience. Saul's neglect of the ark (cf. 10:13-14, where Saul had sought guidance from a medium rather than via the ark) may provide a clue for the unhappy conclusion of this chapter. The extent of "all Israel" in 13:5, from the Egyptian border (exact site unknown) to the far north (Lebo-hamath, probably Lebweh in modern Syria), went far beyond the usual "Dan to Beersheba," and is an idealization of the extent of David's rule, and possibly represents a longing in the Second Temple community for an extension of their constricted territory.

The detail of the story implies knowledge of 2 Samuel 6, on which this account is closely based. The divine title in 13:6 is new, but the Hebrew text is obscure and its original form much disputed. The Chronicler simply records without additional comment or explanation the feature of the story which will most disturb modern readers: the death of Uzzah, attributed to divine displeasure against what is at most a very trivial offense. Various proposals have been made concerning the earlier significance of this story, but for the Chronicler there was clearly an important and potentially dangerous unpredictability about God.

1 Chronicles 14

The sojourn of the ark in the household of Obed-edom (13:14) offers a kind of space, which is filled by this material relating to the increasing prosperity of David. Parallels can be found in 2 Sam 5:11-25, which shows how the Chronicler has modified the order of events in 2 Samuel. Hiram of Tyre is mentioned in all the varied accounts of temple building, but his offering is here simply noted. Then God's blessing on David through the gift of children is emphasized by the repetition of the account already found in 3:5-8, with some variations in the spelling of the names. One difference is more than variant spelling; Eliada of 3:8 is here Beeliada. If this reflects a reliable ancient tradition, it shows that David, like Saul, felt no compunction in giving his child a Baal-compounded name.

Just as the gift of children to David is set over against the death of Saul and his sons, so David's success in battle against the Philistines (14:8-17) offers a striking contrast to Saul's failure. Though the substance of these victories is found also in 2 Samuel 5, v. 17 is an important addition, turning a local skirmish into victories which resounded through all lands and nations.

1 Chronicles 15

We return to the story of the ark. It is essential that Levites carry the ark (15:2), for failure to honor this requirement had led to the death of Uzzah (v. 13); the bringing up of the ark is, however, the responsibility of "all Israel" (v. 3). It is characteristic of the Chronicler to add verisimilitude to his story by appending lists of the names of those involved, and so vv. 4-10 and 17-24 set these out, with several names already familiar from the Levite genealogy in ch. 6. The name "Obed-edom" is a potential source of confusion; in addition to the Gittite at whose house the ark had stayed (13:13), there appear to be two or three more with the same name here (15:18, 21, and 24). There is a clear tension here, not least because the name seems more likely to be Edomite or Philistine ("Gittite" means "from Gath," a Philistine city) than Israelite; perhaps a family of that name was prominent in the Chronicler's own time and was given a special role in his lists. There follows an account of the bringing of the ark to its place, closely paralleling 2 Sam 6:12-19. But whereas there David was so scantily clad as to expose himself and earn Michal's scorn, here he wears the clothes appropriate for a religious procession ("a robe of fine linen," 15:27). Michal's despising David here (v. 29) is simply a further example of the estrangement between Saul's family and that of David.

1 Chronicles 16

Here more clearly than anywhere else we can see how the account of David's establishment of the ark in Jerusalem reflects the worship of the Chronicler's own time. Whereas 16:1-3 are substantially in line with the account in 2 Samuel 6, what follows has no parallel there. First, the important role of the Levites is spelled out and their names given. It is unexpected to find that those who blew trumpets were priests (v. 6) since elsewhere this was a levitical function. There follows an extensive psalm quotation. This is introduced by a reference to "Asaph and his kindred": Psalms 50 and 73–83 are attributed to Asaph, and probably the Asaphites were a guild of Second Temple musicians.

16:8-22 are based on Ps 105:1-15 and 16:23-33 on Psalm 96, while 16:34-36 may reflect particular psalms (e.g., Ps 106:1 and 47-48) or may simply be an instance of the use of psalm-type language without a specific reference. There are minor but unimportant differences in detail between the text of the psalms and that found here. It is striking that the section of Psalm 105 quoted is confined to that concerned with the patriarchs, who like the Second Temple community were "few in number, of little account, and strangers in the land." The mighty deliverance of Israel by God at the exodus is, perhaps deliberately, not mentioned; the Chronicler's community were not to expect that kind of transformation of their condition. Psalm 96 is a hymn in praise of Yahweh as king, which is quoted almost verbatim, though "place" (16:27) may be a deliberate modification of "sanctuary" (Ps 96:6) since the Jerusalem sanctuary was not yet built in David's time.

The psalm quotations are rounded off by one of the first recorded instances of the congregational use of "Amen" ("So be it") to register the commonality of the worship. Once again the ubiquitous Obed-edom appears; there are two such people according to the NRSV, whereas the NEB/REB understands both references as being to the same person. The mention of Gibeon is somewhat unexpected, and many have seen it as a deliberate fabrication to provide an acceptable explanation for Solomon's conduct (2 Chr 1:3), although Williamson (1982: 131) has argued that ancient traditions may underlie this reference.

1 Chronicles 17:1-15

Both in Samuel and here this section is of considerable importance, but it functions in somewhat different ways in its two contexts. In 2 Samuel 7 its special concern is with the promise to David of a house, that is, a series of successors, with God's promise to "establish the throne of his kingdom forever" (2 Sam 7:13). Here that promise is again found (though without the expression "of his kingdom"), but the emphasis is on the building of a house in the sense of a temple. For the Chronicler and his audience that was of central significance. (Here as elsewhere the assumption being followed is that Chronicles is dependent on, and has knowledge of, Samuel; as we have already noted, that assumption has been challenged, most recently by Auld 1994.)

We see therefore that the Hebrew word *bet,* regularly translated "house," can have the sense of either a building or a dynasty, and that double meaning is basic here; cf. 17:3-6 with vv. 10b-12. But there is also an implicit contrast between the house of David, which receives the divine favor, and the rejected house of Saul.

The wording of this section follows 2 Samuel 7 closely, though with some interesting modifications. Thus 2 Sam 7:6 refers to God bringing the people from Egypt; for the Chronicler the exodus experience of deliverance from Egypt is no longer the paradigm event of God's mighty power and so the reference is omitted, though the verb "brought out" might still seem most naturally to refer to the exodus. Again, our text omits the reference to the expected sin of Solomon found in 2 Sam 7:14. The Chronicler brackets David and Solomon very closely together and does not envisage the likelihood of their falling away. This much seems clear; much more disputed is the question whether it is legitimate to read into this section anything that can be called a "messianic" hope. Did the Chronicler look for a revival of the Davidic line? A future revival of the Davidic house is not excluded, but it cannot be said to play a major part in the Chronicler's theology. Those commentators who do see messianic expectations here (e.g., Braun 1986) tend to do so in disturbingly supersessionist terms, as if those expectations could only legitimately be understood in a Christian context.

1 Chronicles 17:16-27

The appropriate response to the blessings promised is prayer, and so David's prayer is recorded in words closely modeled on 2 Samuel 7. The prayer is essentially a thanksgiving; unfortunately David's self-description in 17:17 is very unclear, and different English versions have translated it very differently. V. 21 contains one of the few explicit references to the exodus (see on v. 5 above), and even here it is essentially regarded as a model for the redemption of his people carried out in the restoration after exile and as a preliminary to the act of salvation which God is pictured as bringing about through David. The strongly religious concerns emphasized here alert us to the fact that, if there were "messianic" expectations, they were not of a political kind.

1 Chronicles 18

The next three chapters turn from David's preparations for the temple and its worship to his success in war. He has been assured of divine support and can embark with confidence on military activity. War was a fact of life in the ancient world and is treated as such in both the OT and the NT; God himself could be regarded as a warrior (Exod 15:3). But even successful wars involved bloodshed and were thus not regarded as an unmixed blessing, and it was David's involvement in wars that provided the Chronicler's explanation why it was not David himself who built the temple (1 Chr 22:8; 28:3). The reason for inserting these military accounts at this point may be to explain why David's preparation for a temple did not culminate in his actually having one built.

The account of David's victories (and for the Chronicler all his wars were victorious) closely parallels 2 Samuel 8. This is one of the texts which is held to lend support to the argument that the Chronicler is not simply dependent upon Samuel in its usual HB form. In 18:4, for example, the numbers of those captured greatly exceed those in 2 Samuel, and this has commonly been held to be an example of the Chronicler's tendency to exaggeration. But the Greek text of Samuel, and, less certainly, a Dead Sea Scroll fragment from Qumran, agree with the Chronicler's figure of captured cavalry (7,000 as against the 1,700 of the Hebrew text of 1 Samuel); this is probably one of a number of places where the Chronicler had access to a different source (McKenzie 1985: 53). There are a number of other minor discrepancies with the Samuel text which cannot be discussed in detail here.

The chapter ends with an account of David's officials. At 18:16 the NRSV has changed "Abimelech" to "Ahimelech" (without any explanatory footnote), but it has not followed another widely proposed emendation, accepted by the NEB/REB, to "Zadok and Abiathar son of Ahimelech, son of Ahitub, were priests." The point is more than a mere curiosity because the emendation would support the widely held view that Zadok was a Jebusite, without an Israelite ancestry, who was, so to speak, "adopted" (as in the unemended text here) when David took Jerusalem. The final phrase of the chapter, speaking of David's sons attending upon the king, should be compared with 2 Sam 8:18, where "David's sons were priests." Critical scholars have mostly taken this as a deliberate modification by the Chronicler, for whom non-levitical priests were not acceptable, and this still seems to be the most probable explanation.

1 Chronicles 19:1–20:3

The account of David's wars against the Ammonites closely parallels 2 Samuel 10, but quite a different impression is created when the two accounts are read in their immediate context. In 2 Samuel the absence of the army provides the opportunity for David's adultery with Bathsheba, as part of the long "Court History" so vividly told in 2 Samuel 9–20 and 1 Kings 1–2. Here, by contrast, the context is the successful warfare of David described throughout chs. 18–20. We need not suppose a deliberate attempt to "hush up" the Bathsheba episode, but the Chronicler certainly did not wish to highlight this aspect of David's character. There are other differences from 2 Samuel, particularly in the numbers listed in 19:6-7, but as we have already seen, various explanations of this kind of inconsistency are possible. The "omission" of the Bathsheba episode is most obvious in 20:1-3 because those verses correspond to 2 Sam 11:1 and 12:26-31, the intervening part of 2 Samuel being devoted to David's encounter with Bathsheba, the death of her husband Uriah, Nathan's rebuke of David, the death of Bathsheba's first child, and the birth of Solomon.

1 Chronicles 20:4-8

This brief episode, whose parallel is in quite a different part of 2 Samuel (21:18-22) is mainly noteworthy for what appears to be an attempt to bring together two different traditions concerning the death of the famous Philistine giant Goliath, either through bringing order to a corrupt text or through harmonizing to resolve a historical difficulty. In the famous story in 1 Samuel 17 the giant killed by David is mostly anonymous; only in two verses (4 and 23) is he named as Goliath. In 2 Sam 21:19 Elhanan is said to have killed Goliath, so David's victim may originally have been anonymous. But the Chronicler was aware of a tension within the tradition, and his solution was to credit Elhanan with the killing of Goliath's (otherwise unknown) brother "Lahmi" (a name itself suspect, as probably originally an element of the place name Beth-lehem). We see here a good example of one of the Chronicler's purposes: to be an exegete commenting upon and clarifying older traditions which he felt to need resolution.

1 Chronicles 21:1-17

This section is commonly regarded as an exception to the usual rule, that the Chronicler avoids giving any negative picture of David. Here, it seems, he is openly criticized for following the incitement of Satan. The inclusion of the story would then be justified because of its portrayal of David as a repentant sinner (21:8, 17) and because the story reaches a climax in the purchase of the site for the future temple. Wright (1993) has argued, however, that this understanding of the episode is dependent on our reading it with 2 Samuel 24 in mind. If we take the story as it stands, it is Joab's objections and his failure to complete the census that are condemned; David takes on the responsibility for his general's failure and is eventually vindicated by the reward of the temple site. Such an understanding certainly removes one problem, why a census should be regarded as an evil when, to take but one example, 1 Chr 9:1 specifically states with apparent approval that "all Israel was enrolled."

The use of "Satan" in 21:1 is remarkable, given that the parallel account in 2 Samuel 24 has "the LORD." It is widely held that Satan here has come to be regarded as a personal name, and many have understood this passage in almost dualistic terms, with Satan the embodiment of evil, just as he came to be regarded in later Judaism and the NT (cf. Rev 12:9). A pointer in that direction may be the fact that "Satan" here is not preceded by the definite article, but it may still be better to see this passage in the light of other places in the HB where "the Satan" is a member of the divine court, but one charged with the duty of laying accusations against those whose reputation he suspected. Is it too fanciful to see a parallel between David and Job, also overzealously accused by the Satan (Job 1:9-11)?

The reason for Joab's hostility to the idea of a census is not stated, nor is his failure to complete it explained. Levi may be omitted because that tribe received no territorial allotment, but that does not account for Benjamin also being left out. In Wright's view this was the cause of the divine anger in 21:7, the reason for which is not specified in the text. The three possible punishments closely parallel those listed in 2 Samuel, but the thrust of v. 13 is not clear. It could mean either that David leaves to God's decision what the punishment shall be, or that he deliberately (and hopefully: "for his mercy is very great"!) chooses divine rather than human agency.

The conclusion of this section finds God changing his mind, as he is liable to do in the HB, and it again stresses David's repentance. But an important new development is found: the change of mind comes when the destroying angel has reached the "threshing floor of Ornan the Jebusite." This character is named "Araunah" in 2 Samuel, but there seems to be no special significance in the variation of names. In any case, his threshing floor was to be the site of the temple; this was the place where God's anger with his people might be turned away. The picture, with the king accompanied by the elders, is reminiscent of a regular service of penitence. The whole account differs markedly from the biblical text of 2 Samuel, but here as elsewhere fragmentary texts of 2 Samuel from Qumran seem to be much closer to the Chronicler's version.

1 Chronicles 21:18–22:1

As the climax of this story is reached, the links with 2 Samuel 24 become looser, and links with other texts can be detected. Thus in 21:20 the theme of threshing wheat in the presence of the angel recalls Gideon in Judges 6; even more clearly 21:22-24 are modeled on Abraham's purchase of the cave of Machpelah as a burial place in Genesis 23, with its emphasis on the payment of the full price — twelve times increased (is the multiplier significant?) from the fifty shekels of 2 Samuel. David, though not himself a priest, is allowed to offer "burnt offerings and offerings of well-being," and he receives the favorable response of "fire from heaven," reminiscent of Elijah's sacrifice on Mt. Carmel (1 Kings 18). The story is rounded off in 22:1 (rightly set by the NRSV with what precedes) with the assertion that this is to be the site of the temple. Gibeon had been only a temporary and inadequate resting place.

1 Chronicles 22:2-19

The remainder of 1 Chronicles is devoted to David's preparations for the temple and is without close parallel elsewhere in the HB. It is striking that resident aliens play an important part, whereas their equivalents were regarded with much greater suspicion at the building of the Second Temple in Ezra 4. But it is not only the materials that must be prepared; Solomon himself is as yet "young and inexperienced," for he has not received the divine wisdom (2 Chronicles 1), and the blood shed in David's wars excludes him as an appropriate builder. Solomon, by contrast, will be, as his name *(shelomoh)* implies, a man of peace *(shalom)*. The exclusion of David is reminiscent of Moses' exclusion from the holy land, and the commands to Solomon are closely reminiscent of, and surely based on, Moses' commands to his successor Joshua (Deut 31:5-8). The chapter ends with an appeal to the "leaders of Israel" to be loyal to Solomon and presumably his successors; the later disloyalty to the Davidic line manifested by much of Israel is surely in mind here.

1 Chronicles 23

23:1 can be regarded as anticipatory of what will be described in fuller detail in ch. 29, while 23:2 anticipates (and is largely repeated in) 28:1. Older commentaries took this as an indication that the intervening section (23:3–27:34) was a later and secondary addition, but the more usual modern tendency is to doubt such large-scale modifications of an existing text. The repetitions can be seen as a deliberate literary device, though opinions will differ whether such contradictions as the enrollment age for Levites (30 in v. 2, 20 in vv. 24 and 27) can be explained satisfactorily in this way. Perhaps amendments were made according to the usage of different periods, and other minor changes to the basic text may well have been introduced. In any case, there is clearly no objection, divine or human, to counting here; cf. ch. 21. 23:4-5 give a clear indication of the functions of the Levites, presumably in the Second Temple of the Chronicler's own day. This will be elaborated and made more specific in the closing verses of the chapter.

23:7-23 apparently consist of lists of the names of those enrolled, but even a glance will show that as they stand they cannot plausibly be dated either to the Chronicler's own time or to that of David. Thus vv. 13-14 stress the priestly (rather than the more generally levitical) functions of those who claimed descent from Aaron and give a slightly more extended reference to Moses than is usual elsewhere in Chronicles. He is "the man of God" (cf. Deut 33:1) and in some sense above normal human considerations. The remaining names show links, but are by no means identical, with the genealogies of Levi in ch. 6. (For detailed analysis see Williamson 1979.)

The chapter concludes (23:28-32) with a more precise setting forth of the duties of the Levites, taking care to make a clear differentiation from the "descendants of Aaron" (vv. 28, 32), to whom specifically priestly roles are reserved.

1 Chronicles 24

It is natural to follow the setting forth of the Levites' role at the end of ch. 23 with more detailed attention to the priests, though the arrangement here is at odds with the classification at 23:6. In looking at these lists we need to recall what has already been said about the social rather than historical basis of genealogies. 24:1-2 give some indication of the rivalry between different groups claiming descent from Aaron. Those who might have claimed descent from Nadab and Abihu failed to establish their claim and were, so to speak, written out of the script (cf. Lev 10:1-2). Those of Ithamar were more successful, but only to the extent of achieving a minor role. The main priestly line consisted of those who could establish a genealogy going back to Eleazar. (It is interesting to note that the Samaritans, at a slightly later period, rejected the priestly claims of Ithamar and claimed an exclusively Eleazarite priesthood.)

An explanation is then given of the established Second Temple practice whereby the priesthood was divided into twenty-four "courses." Nothing else is known of the "officers of the sanctuary" and "officers of God" mentioned in 24:5; they may have been two separate groups, or the two phrases may stand in apposition to each other. Most of the individuals mentioned are no more than names, but Judas Maccabeus and his brothers were of the Joarib family (1 Macc 2:1), and that is almost certainly another spelling of Jehoiarib (24:7). In the NT John the Baptist's father Zechariah was a member of the order of Abijah (Luke 1:5), mentioned here in eighth position. Josephus also alludes to the arrangement of twenty-four priestly courses, which no doubt continued until the destruction of the Second Temple in AD 70.

The chapter ends somewhat unexpectedly by listing "the rest of the sons of Levi," introduced in this context because of their duty of casting lots (24:31). There are several overlaps with the names in ch. 23, but the lists are far from identical and speculation about the reason for the differences can only be guesswork.

1 Chronicles 25

We know few details about music in ancient Israel, but this chapter makes clear what has already been hinted at (e.g., 6:31-32): that the proper performance of the temple music was a matter of major concern to the Chronicler. Those in charge of the music are those listed in 6:31-49, with the variant form "Jeduthun" here replacing "Ethan" in the earlier list. All are listed in the titles to various psalms: Asaph in Psalms 50 and 73–83, Heman in Psalm 88, Ethan in Psalm 89, and Jeduthun (though only as part of a larger title) in Psalms 39, 62, and 77. No doubt both the Chronicler's lists and the psalm titles reflect Second Temple usage. Heman is described as "the king's seer," a title previously given to Gad (21:9), but the roles associated with the two men are very different.

The reference to prophecy in 25:1 has been understood in different ways by different translations. The NEB/REB understand it as prophecy being accompanied by musical instruments; the NRSV takes the playing of the instruments as itself prophecy. This is perhaps more probable in view of the references to prophesying in vv. 2 and 3. Another respect in which translations differ is found at v. 4, where the NEB/REB suggest in a footnote that the names from Hananiah to Mahazioth are proper names made up from the words of a prayer. There is no reference to this in the NRSV, and certainly the final compiler understood them as proper names, for in the allocation to courses, which concludes this chapter, they are treated as individuals. One possibility (Myers 1965: 173) is that these curious names originated as the opening words from a catalogue of hymns.

The remainder of the chapter consists of the allocation by lot of the different musicians to the twenty-four priestly courses. The similarity of the order here to the way in which the names were introduced in 25:1-6 has suggested to many commentators that the lot was not entirely random.

1 Chronicles 26:1-19

We have noted already (9:17-27) that the function of the gatekeepers, who are regularly listed after the musicians, was an important one. They will have had important financial responsibilities; in Jesus' time, in addition to the widow with her "two mites," "many rich people put large sums" into the treasury (Mark 12:41-42), and no doubt this will have been true in the Chronicler's time as well, though coins were then something of a novelty; we may note the references to "treasuries" in vv. 24-26 of this chapter. It will also have been important that the gatekeepers ensured that no one went further into the different parts of the temple complex than was proper for their status allowed. At the turn of the eras the death penalty could be imposed on those who broke this rule, though it is uncertain whether it was ever caried out.

Many of the names listed here are found already in ch. 9. An exception is the ubiquitous Obed-edom (26:4), who is given no genealogy and who appears to be so well known that his presence can be taken for granted (cf. chs. 13 and 15).

Lots are then cast for the allocation of duties, as is commonly asserted in Chronicles. This appears here as elsewhere simply to be a way of claiming divine approval for the way matters were arranged. Some of the names listed in 26:12-19 are those already mentioned earlier, but new names (e.g., Shuppim, v. 16) are also introduced without explanation. Curious also in a list of names is the description of Zechariah as "a prudent counselor"; it is not clear whether this refers to some aspect of his gatekeeping duties or to his general reputation.

1 Chronicles 26:20-32

The listing of the levitical duties is concluded with references to other temple tasks (26:20-28) and to their role as judges (vv. 29-32). "Ahijah," the first named in v. 20, is not known elsewhere, and many commentators and the NEB/REB have made a small emendation, reading "fellow Levites." Most of the following names have already occurred in 23:7-19. The idea of "holy war" is supported by the note that "booty won in battles" was dedicated to God and laid up in the temple; whether successful soldiers were in practice quite so ready to part with their gains is another matter. But the names of those listed in 26:28 as dedicating their gifts are a curious mixture. Samuel is described here simply as a seer, with no hint of the priestly status accorded him in 6:28, and Saul's successes are never elsewhere alluded to in Chronicles.

There are also curiosities in 26:29-32, where the Levites are described as judges. This is one of the few places in which Levites are given "outside duties" (the NEB/REB offers a good paraphrase: "secular affairs"). The reference to their work in Transjordan (v. 32) is no doubt intended to offer a plausible setting in the time of David, but the important position of the Levites was in fact a development from well on in the Second Temple period. Striking also is the reference in v. 31 to David's fortieth year; the Chronicler does not elsewhere spell out the chronology of his reign and omits such references when they are found in 2 Samuel (cf. 11:1-9 above).

1 Chronicles 27

We move, perhaps unexpectedly, from the specifically religious duties outlined in chs. 23–26 to a broader picture of David's kingdom. In fact, the links with David are very limited; we have virtually no reliable indication as to the origin of these lists. If those "who served the king" (27:1) is reliable, they will have originated in the monarchical period, but such reliability will be widely questioned. The frequent references to "twenty-four thousand" suggest a deliberate linkage with the twenty-four priestly courses, but the names found in vv. 2-15 have already featured in quite a different way in ch. 11. In 27:4 it is unexpected to find the chief officer named; the RSV, along with many commentators, emended the text so as to omit the reference to "Mikloth." Vv. 16-24 provide tribal lists in accordance with the "all Israel" stress which was an important theme of the Chronicler. There are several distinctive features of these lists: Aaron appears as if it is a separate tribe, distinct from Levi, and Zadok is mentioned as its representative. He is given no genealogy, though that is in itself a slender basis for the argument that he was not an Israelite at all. Elsewhere in Chronicles he is given a genealogy (cf. 18:16), though it has often been regarded as suspect. No brother of David named Elihu is known; either this is a variant of "Eliab" (2:13), or "brother" simply means "kinsman" (thus the NEB/REB). With Aaron counted as a tribe and both halves of Manasseh included, the numbers would go beyond the standard twelve, and so both Asher and Gad are omitted with no explanation. This section ends with a note somewhat at odds with ch. 21, stressing that David took no census of those below 20 years of age. Here, as in one reading of that chapter (see the commentary above), Joab is blamed for his action.

Further royal officers, pictured as stewards of the royal property, are listed in 27:25-31. Not all would share Williamson's judgement that "there is no reason to doubt the essential historicity of the list" (1982: 177); far too little is known of David's time and administrative arrangements for that to be the case. Then, following these otherwise unknown names, we return to more familiar figures, with references to Jonathan, Ahitophel, and others known from 1-2 Samuel in vv. 32-34. Actually the identity of this Jonathan is not known; it may be an unusual way of describing the well-known Jonathan, Saul's son and David's companion, or a reference to an otherwise unknown figure: the NEB/REB calls him David's "favourite nephew," an unlikely translation.

1 Chronicles 28:1-10

Whether or not we speak of distinct "sources," chs. 23–27 have functioned to heighten tension as the audience looks forward to the climax of David's reign and the building of the temple under Solomon. Thus 28:1 here is a repetition and elaboration of 23:2; this is probably a deliberate stylistic device of the kind known as "repetitive resumption." Other links with ch. 22 are provided by the prohibition of David from building the temple because of the blood he had shed in his wars, and by the theme of the commissioning of Solomon in a manner reminiscent of Moses' commissioning of Joshua.

28:5 stresses that David had many sons, and in 2 Samuel and 1 Kings 1 attention focuses on the bitter and often bloody struggle between them as they aimed for the inheritance of the aging David. Here, by contrast, David is in full control of his faculties, and Solomon is the one whom the LORD "has chosen." Three times in these verses (5, 6, and 10) and again in 29:1 this theme, God's choice of Solomon, is stressed. It is found in no other biblical writer (Japhet 1989: 449-52). God's choice of a temple (itself at odds with the tradition recorded in 2 Samuel 7) and of Solomon as the approved ruler of his people are set out together and strongly stressed. The section ends with David's sermonlike address to the community being followed by words of encouragement and warning to Solomon himself.

1 Chronicles 28:11-21

Responsibility for the actual building of the temple was clearly ascribed in the tradition to Solomon. For the Chronicler, however, there was a real sense in which it was "David's temple," just as some of the psalms ascribed to David seem to imply the existence of a temple. In these verses great stress is laid on the detailed provision made by David for the appropriate construction of the buildings, the proper ordering of the sacred ministers, and the necessary furnishings for the services. This was done by David as the LORD "made clear to me — the plan of all the works" (28:19). Whether the writing was envisaged as being done by God himself (so the NEB/REB) or at divine dictation (the NRSV) is not entirely clear. The chapter ends with a further exhortation to Solomon, with the added assurance that he will be able to rely upon much willing help.

1 Chronicles 29:1-19

Solomon is described as "young and inexperienced," but this seems to be a dramatic way of bringing out his dependence on divine guidance; perhaps we may compare the Gospel injunction to childlikeness as being especially acceptable to God (Matt 18:3). Certainly Solomon's behavior on accession is not that of one who is "young and inexperienced," and there is no reliable record of his actual age. The temple is here (29:1 and 10) uniquely described as a "fortress" (NRSV mg.). The word used *(birah)* seems to be a word taken into Hebrew only at a later stage and is something of an anachronism here, just as is the reference to "darics" in v. 7. These were Persian coins, named for Darius, and certainly not earlier than the late sixth century BC. The theme of vv. 1-9 is the importance of adequate provision for the temple, and as part of this the generosity both of David himself and of the community is stressed. It is not fanciful to see here an encouragement to comparable generosity in the community of the Chronicler's own time.

This leads into a prayer of thanksgiving from David, expressed in the form of a blessing. Human beings (and not only priests) could bless God, just as God blesses them. Whereas large parts of the work of the Chronicler seem very alien to modern readers, this prayer is one with which religious people will readily identify, and words based on it are widely used in Christian worship, especially in connection with the offering of money or gifts in church. Praise and thanksgiving predominate in 29:10-17. Many of the themes have already been noted in 1 Chronicles, and this prayer probably reflected the usual language of prayer in the Second Temple period. The prayer is completed with a petition (vv. 18-19), in which we may note the stress on the ancestors, Abraham, Isaac, and Israel (v. 18), rather than, for example, Moses, as the role models, and the provision of an appropriate context by introducing Solomon at the very end.

1 Chronicles 29:20-30

The ceremony reaches its climax with the anointing of Solomon, set in a context of overwhelming and spontaneous religious ceremonies. This is very different from the atmosphere of plotting and intrigue found in the account of Solomon's accession in 1 Kings 1–2, though the Chronicler stresses here that "all the sons of King David pledged their allegiance" (29:24). Despite the difference, a number of phrases have been taken over from 1 Kings, and it has been argued that the curious reference to a "second time" in v. 22 envisages the clandestine ceremony in 1 Kings 1 as the first time (Williamson 1982: 187). This may be overly subtle, and the reference is more likely to be to 23:1. Religious language frequently goes beyond literal accuracy, and that can be seen in the reference to "any king before him in Israel" (29:25): in the Chronicler's reading there had only been one predecessor, and that was David, himself the subject of similar extravagant praise.

1 Chronicles ends by recording David's death, "in a good old age, full of days" — an expression virtually identical with that used of Abraham (Gen 25:8). Nothing corresponding to the "records of Samuel . . . Nathan . . . and Gad" is known from other sources, and it may well be that that this is the Chronicler's way of referring to the books of Samuel and Kings, in whatever version was available to him. Part of the Chronicler's understanding of the role of seers was that they were responsible for recording the chief events of their time.

2 Chronicles

As I indicated in the introduction to 1 Chronicles, the two books of Chronicles are continuous works, and so many of the characteristic features which have already been noted in 1 Chronicles will be found again here. Nevertheless, the two books are importantly different in character. After the genealogies of 1 Chronicles 1–9, the rest of the book was set within a reconstruction of the lifetime of David. At first it seems as if the same stately rate of temporal progress will characterize 2 Chronicles, for nine chapters are devoted to the reign of Solomon, with continuing emphasis on the temple. But from then on chronological coverage is much more rapid; the remainder of the book touches on something approaching four hundred years, from Solomon's death, which may have taken place in the 920s BC, to the rise of Cyrus in the 540s.

Much of this material may also be found in 1-2 Kings, and to appreciate the significance of this we must keep in mind what has been said above about the Chronicler as an interpreter of earlier material. Sometimes, old and presumably familiar stories are retold with some particular aspect emphasized or reshaped, enabling the Chronicler to bring out for his audience their contemporary significance; sometimes new material is added. Opinions will differ as to the historical value of such additions, but since we can never attain certainty on that score, it is more useful to ask why such additions were made. What purpose did they serve within the Chronicler's overall plan?

COMMENTARY

2 Chronicles 1

The theme of this chapter is Solomon's establishment as king, though whether "established himself" (1:1) gives the right nuance may be questioned; it was the LORD who established Solomon (de Vries 1989: 234). Any embarrassment caused by Solomon's visit to Gibeon is removed by making it into a solemn religious procession of "all the leaders of all Israel" to the tent of meeting. This gives the impression that God's appearance to Solomon was something sought through inquiry rather than a spontaneous divine visitation in a dream. Though messages received through dreams continued to be highly regarded in some Jewish contexts (cf. Matt 1:20; 2:19; and even 27:19), it was also recognised that they were liable to abuse (Jer 23:25-32), and that may account for the Chronicler's omission of any reference to Solomon's encounter as a dream.

Solomon's reputation for wisdom is given its appropriate origin in 1:7-12, but it is also noteworthy that the first example of that wisdom offered by 1 Kings, the story of the two prostitutes and their children, is not recorded. This was not the kind of Solomonic wisdom which the Chronicler wished to emphasize.

The remainder of the chapter (1:14-17) offers an account of Solomon's wealth which closely follows 1 Kgs 10:26-29. These verses are closely repeated in 9:25-28, which might imply a secondary insertion but can also be taken as a deliberate device by the Chronicler, finishing his account of Solomon's reign in the same way as he had begun it. The clash with the law of Deut 17:16, which warns the king not to acquire many horses, especially from Egypt, seems not to have been a cause of concern to the Chronicler.

2 Chronicles 2

The NRSV translation "Solomon decided" may be acceptable as a rendering of the Hebrew, but it gives quite the wrong nuance here. It suggests a new idea, whereas for the Chronicler Solomon is fulfilling his part in a long-established plan. Historically the temple complex may well have been just a substantial part of the royal palace, but the "secular" structures get no more than passing references in Chronicles (7:11; 8:1). In the Chronicler's day there was no king to have a palace, and his concern is with the continuity of the temple from Solomon's day to his own.

The chapter as a whole is a good example of what I called "relecture" in the Introduction (283). Much of its material is parallel to 1 Kings 5, but by modest omissions and additions and by placing the story in the context of his own work, the Chronicler uses this tradition to develop his own theme. Thus, in 1 Kgs 5:1, Hiram (as he is there called; the Chronicler's form "Huram" seems simply to be a spelling variant) could be seen as taking the initiative, so that verse is omitted, and Solomon initiates the correspondence.

The letter itself as presented here is very curious, for the brief request of 1 Kgs 5:3-6 has given way to a theological disquisition. It is as if Huram was familiar with the Pentateuch and could observe how faithfully Solomon was intending to follow its ritual requirements. Even the request for an artisan (2:7) has a basis in the Pentateuch, for the skills he is required to display are strikingly similar to those of Bezalel, the artificer of the tabernacle (Exod 35:30), and mentioned by the Chronicler in the previous chapter (1:5). Another minor variant from Kings occurs in the name of the timber, here called "algum," but "almug" in Kings. On literary grounds the Kings form is to be preferred, but the identity of the tree remains as unknown to us as it probably was to the Chronicler.

In 2:12 Huram of Tyre writes as if he were himself a worshiper of the LORD. This could be diplomacy, but it is more likely that for the Chronicler anyone engaged in the preparation for the temple must give due honor to its God. The artisan whom he sends is somewhat confusingly called Huram-abi. The suffix "abi," literally "my father," is interpreted by the REB ("my expert Huram") as referring to his skill in craftsmanship. The suffix may be intended to make a comparison with Bezalel's colleague Oholiab (Exod 35:34), who was a Danite; it is noteworthy that Hiram (again the spelling variant) was from Naphtali on his mother's side according to 1 Kgs 7:14, whereas here Huram-abi's mother is a Danite woman. It seems unlikely to have been mere coincidence that the king of Tyre and his artisan shared the same name, but no satisfactory explanation has been put forward.

The Chronicler often employed the literary device of *inclusio,* rounding off a section by a clear reference back to its beginning, and that is found here, with 2:18 largely repeating v. 2. Those required for forced labor on the temple were aliens; no native Israelite could be employed in such a way according to the Chronicler, though Kings gives a different picture (1 Kgs 5:13-14 — one of the Chronicler's significant omissions).

2 Chronicles 3

Given the great interest in the temple shown throughout the Chronicler's work, it is perhaps a little surprising that his story of its building is much shorter than that in 1 Kings. Probably the Kings account was taken for granted as a known, and presumably accessible, source; the Chronicler is content to draw attention to what he regarded as especially important features.

The particular concerns of the Chronicler are well illustrated in 3:1, which is without parallel in Kings. Moriah is known elsewhere in the HB only from Genesis 22, the story of the sacrifice of Isaac. Despite the hesitations of some scholars (cf. *ABD* under "Moriah"), it still seems probable that we have here a deliberate linkage to Gen 22:2 ("one of the mountains" there now being identified as the temple mount) and 14, with its emphasis on the "mount of the LORD." This identification is still widely accepted in traditional Judaism and Islam, and provides one of the reasons for the sensitivity of contemporary political debate concerning Jerusalem. The remainder of the verse maintains the Chronicler's well-established esteem for David, with the reminder that the site is that of the LORD's appearance to him (1 Chr 21:16).

Most of the features of the building in the following verses are based on 1 Kings 6. The Chronicler's penchant for exaggerating numbers has not extended to the description of the measurements of the temple. "Sixty cubits" (3:3) will have been something like thirty meters; the proportions are those of a small village church rather than those of a great cathedral, if modern Christian parallels are found helpful. Some details of the measurements seem very implausible, for example, the height as "120 cubits" — twice the length. The account does contain a few peculiar features. One such is "Parvaim" in v. 6; presumably an otherwise unknown geographical designation, it later became the subject of rabbinic speculation as a distant and exotic land of gold. The quantity of gold said to have been used is enormous (600 talents = approximately 23 tons), but in the Chronicler's view it was more than adequately provided for by David (1 Chr 22:14).

We need not suppose that Solomon himself took part in the building works, but the text is very emphatic in ascribing everything to his activity; "and he made" recurs repeatedly throughout this and the next chapter, down to 5:1, where the verb translated "did" is the same as that translated "made" elsewhere. This was very emphatically Solomon's temple.

The cherubim provide a good example of a word which has changed its meaning very significantly, and this change was already under way in the Chronicler's time. They seem to have originated as half-human, half-winged creatures, frequently found in temples in the ancient world. Here they have been thoroughly "Israelitized," as an acceptable feature of temple ornamentation. (They are still a long way from the "cherubs" of Renaissance and later paintings.) In a similar way the two probably free-standing pillars, whose original significance is unknown but which were again characteristic of ancient temples, have been reduced to mere architectural ornaments.

2 Chronicles 4:1–5:1

The repetition of "he made" at the beginning of each paragraph within this unit shows it to be a continuation of what has preceded, with the emphasis now on the furnishings of the temple rather than the actual construction of the building. The basis of the Chronicler's account can be found in 1 Kings 7; some of the details there were probably already obscure to the Chronicler himself and are in general abbreviated here. It is also possible that the Chronicler has deliberately modified or added to the earlier account. Thus the "sea" (4:6) may once have had mythological associations, linked with the idea of the primeval deep; now it has become purely utilitarian, a place for the priests to wash.

4:11 differs from what has preceded by ascribing the work to Huram. The section that follows corresponds very closely to 1 Kgs 7:40-51, whereas the earlier verses showed only a general linkage. For more detailed discussion of the temple furnishings, see the commentary on 1 Kings.

The section is rounded off in 5:1 by a conclusion which closely follows 1 Kgs 7:51, but it actually fits into its context better here than in Kings and may offer support for the view that Kings and Chronicles should be seen as parallel narratives rather than that Chronicles is dependent on Kings. Perhaps the second half of the verse, which speaks of "the house of God" rather than "the house of the LORD," should go with what follows (de Vries).

2 Chronicles 5:2-14

The next three chapters of the work are concerned with the dedication of the newly built temple, in an account much of which has parallels in 1 Kings 8. The first concern is with the ark. The ceremony takes place "at the festival that is in the seventh month," that is, the autumn feast of Tabernacles or Booths. The Levites carried the ark, in accordance with the Chronicler's liturgical rules (cf. 1 Chr 15:2); in 1 Kgs 8:3 the priests performed this function. A compromise is necessary in the following verses since only the priests could enter the inner sanctuary of the house.

An unexpected feature of the description of the temple which follows is the comment in 5:9, "they are there to this day," since Solomon's temple was destroyed long before the Chronicler's time. Regarded by some as an addition (*BHS*) or a corruption (Japhet), they may well be seen as the Chronicler's concern for continuity outweighing the details of history. "To this day" implies perpetuity.

5:11-13 are without parallel in Kings, but may be seen as a characteristic development by the Chronicler, introducing several of his special concerns: the priestly divisions, the singers and their instruments, and the allusion back to 1 Chr 16:34 in the psalmlike passage in 5:13. The section ends with the triumphant assertion that the divine presence has "filled the house." The sentiment is the same as that of Ezekiel, where "the glory of the LORD filled the temple" (Ezek 43:10).

2 Chronicles 6:1-11

The opening verses correspond to 1 Kgs 8:12-13 (printed there by the NRSV as poetry, with "dwell" as against "reside" here; the reason for these changes is not clear. The more extensive correction proposed by the RSV in the Kings text has not been followed by the NRSV). In Solomon's subsequent blessing he is both bringing out the significance of the events which have just taken place and anticipating the prayer which is to follow. The remainder of these verses follow closely the text of 1 Kings 8: the apparent addition by the Chronicler of parts of 6:5-6 probably means nothing more than that he had access to a different text of Kings than the one which has come down to us. It is striking that the section ends without the reference to the deliverance from Egypt found in 1 Kgs 8:21. The deliverance from Egypt is certainly not ignored (cf. 6:5), but it is less prominent than in Kings. For the Chronicler the promise to David and the commitment of the people of his own time to the covenant obligations are the key concerns.

2 Chronicles 6:12-42

Solomon's great prayer "follows 1 Kings 8:22-53 remarkably closely" (Williamson). We are so apt to think of the temple as the place of sacrifice that we are liable to forget its important function as a "house of prayer" (Isa 56:7), and this was probably especially the case with the Second Temple of the Chronicler's day. 6:13 has no parallel in the present text of Kings (though some have supposed it to have been there at an earlier stage) and may well express the Chronicler's wish to project back the liturgical practices of his own time to an alleged origin with Solomon. The prayer of intercession follows. In v. 16 the more general language of 1 Kgs 8:25, "before me," is replaced with "in my law [Heb. *torah*]," an indication of the important place of the law in the life of the community. It is too early to speak of "Scripture," in any formal sense, but clearly some bodies of writing were coming to be regarded as in a special sense authoritative.

The series of conditions in the remainder of the prayer may well have had resonances for the Chronicler's own audience in the circumstances of the life of their community, but it is perilous to try to use them for reconstructing those circumstances. The prayer was almost certainly based on the text of 1 Kings rather than being a reflection of contemporary experience. Indeed, foreigners are not simply a dangerous threat; 6:32-33 display a remarkably open attitude with a genuinely universalistic hope ("that all the peoples of the earth may know your name"). The prayer concludes, not as in 1 Kings 8 with a reference to the exodus as the model of divine deliverance, but with a poetic passage (6:41-42) closely based on Psalm 132. As the Chronicler's presentation thus far has made clear, it was the work of deliverance through David which was the paradigm of God's saving power.

2 Chronicles 7:1-11

God's response to the prayer is immediate. Just as David's prayer when he purchased the site of the temple was answered by fire (1 Chr 21:26), so Solomon at its completion received this vivid sign of divine favor. There may also be a reminiscence of God receiving Elijah's prayer in 1 Kgs 18:38, an episode in the account of the Northern Kingdom not recounted in Chronicles. The "glory of the LORD" is pictured, here as elsewhere (5:14), as a physical object filling the temple, to which the only possible response is praise, expressed in terms already familiar from the Psalms and 5:13. Sacrifices and feasting follow. It may not be much comfort to animal lovers to be told that the number of animals killed is probably exaggerated, as is often the case with numbers in Chronicles; the killing of animals as a means of offering to God was a fact of life in ancient Israel. Throughout this section there runs the twin stress on the successful completion of the God-decreed task and the linkage between what Solomon was doing and the inaugural inspiration of his father David.

2 Chronicles 7:12-22

God has already in one sense "answered" Solomon's prayer through the manifestations described in the last section, but now a further answer is expressed. This section closely follows 1 Kgs 9:2-9, though without any reference here to Gibeon; for the Chronicler any supposed encounters with God away from Jerusalem were at best an irrelevance. 7:13-15 are largely without parallel in Kings, and Williamson 1982 regards v. 14 as "vital for the Chronicler's theology." It emphasizes the way in which God commits himself to respond to the people's prayer. If they "humble themselves, pray, seek my face, and turn from their wicked ways" they can be sure of God's favorable response. Williamson is surely right in seeing this as addressed to the community of the Chronicler's own day, and a great deal of the remainder of 2 Chronicles will illustrate this basic theological principle. Indeed, its applicability is already made apparent at v. 21, where the Hebrew text is somewhat obscure but clearly refers to the destruction of Solomon's temple and the exile of many of the people. The continuing relevance and validity of God's promises to a "post-exilic" community is thus stressed.

2 Chronicles 8

Whereas the account of David's rule described his "secular" activity and then moved on to the preparations for the temple as a kind of climax, with Solomon the order is reversed. The temple comes first; then a much briefer account of his other achievements is offered, and even this is interspersed with references to the temple. This chapter for the most part follows 1 Kings 9, though with some significant differences.

The first of these differences occurs in 8:1-2, which appear to contradict 1 Kgs 9:11-13 directly. There Solomon had ceded twenty cities; here it appears as if it was Huram who had given cities to Solomon. Textual corruption has been suggested as the cause of this reversal, but it seems more likely that the Chronicler found it impossible to envisage that Solomon should voluntarily have ceded part of the promised land and supposed that the transaction must have been in the opposite direction, especially since Huram is pictured very much as Solomon's subordinate.

The latter part of 8:3-6 closely parallels 1 Kings 9, but vv. 3-4 have no close links and picture Solomon's military exploits on an improbably large scale. Hamath was the northern boundary of the ideal land (cf. 7:8), but "Hamath-zobah" is unknown apart from this reference. Again, "Tadmor in the wilderness" was the great oasis city better known as Palmyra, far out in the Syrian desert. The thought of Solomon's influence reaching thus far owes more to the Chronicler's creative imagination than to historical likelihood. The remainder of the section is set in a much more domestic context and closely follows 1 Kings 9. This includes the important ideological assertion that no Israelites were enslaved for Solomon's work. To the Chronicler the native-born Israelites must have been free; whether the economic necessities of extensive building projects respected this view is another matter.

The Chronicler has made no previous reference to Solomon having married a daughter of the Egyptian pharaoh (cf. 1 Kgs 3:1), but it was part of the tradition that he accepted. (Historically, the likelihood of such a match must be questioned; there was a tradition dating back at least as far as the Amarna period, c. 1400 BC, that members of the Egyptian royal families did not marry foreigners.) The androcentric nature of his writing is well illustrated by the automatic assumption that the holiness of the temple would be fatally endangered by the presence of a woman.

8:12-15 set together two themes which have sometimes seemed to be in tension. Solomon was loyal both to "the commandment of Moses" (here particularly as set out in the book of Numbers) and to "the ordinances of his father David." The two were regarded as complementing each other. The chapter ends with a brief reference to an expedition to Ezion-geber in the Gulf of Aqaba. Solomon is said to have gone there himself; historically this is perhaps an improbable detail, but it is less difficult to envisage than the logistical problems involved in Huram's ships getting from Tyre, on the Mediterranean, to Ezion-geber. There was no Suez Canal at that time!

2 Chronicles 9

The story of the visit of the Queen of Sheba (9:1-12) has been taken over from 1 Kings 10 with only minor modifications. It has generated a considerable literature, which must be consulted (along with the commentary on 1 Kings) for issues ranging from the whereabouts of

Sheba (perhaps in modern Yemen) to the later developments of the legend, especially in the Ethiopian tradition, which take their origin from Solomon granting the queen her "every desire" in 9:12. At v. 7 the NRSV's concern to avoid sexist language stands it in good stead. Earlier versions hesitated between "men" (so the Hebrew text) and "wives" (followed by the RSV and the NEB); "people" here leaves both options open. It may be that the Chronicler deliberately avoided reference to Solomon's wives, considering it an unworthy weakness on the part of one of his heroes.

9:13-24 build up the picture of Solomon's wealth; here the parallel is with 1 Kgs 10:14-25, the commentary on which must again be consulted. There are a few changes; at 9:18 the Hebrew text of Kings (followed by the RSV and the NEB, though not by the NRSV) has a reference to "a calf's head," omitted by Chronicles as inappropriate for the Jerusalem temple; and at v. 21 "Tarshish," originally descriptive of a kind of ship, has become a place name, somewhere in the western Mediterranean. The Chronicler has thus deliberately or inadvertently transferred Solomon's fleet from the Red Sea to the Mediterranean.

As was noted earlier, 9:25-28 are substantially identical with 1:14-17. While some form of textual corruption cannot be excluded, it may be that this manner of beginning and ending the account of Solomon's reign in almost identical language is a deliberate literary device. Following these verses, the story of Solomon comes to an abrupt conclusion, with no reference to the negative verdict passed in 1 Kings 11. It is probably pointless to try to allot praise or blame to Solomon. More usefully, we can see something of the different motives of the authors of Kings and of Chronicles. Kings was written at a time when Jerusalem and its temple were in ruins, and some measure of blame for that was to be attributed to Solomon and his failings which had led to the division of the kingdoms. Chronicles was written when the Second Temple was established, and it was an important part of its purpose to stress the centrality of the temple in the divine plan and to show that the temple of his day maintained unbroken the pattern of worship first established by David and Solomon.

As with David's reign (cf. 1 Chr 29:29) the account of Solomon is, as it were, validated by reference to various "sources." It is most unlikely that these included material independent of the books of Kings which had somehow survived and was available to the Chronicler. Rather, this is a different way of referring to the Kings tradition; Nathan and Ahijah play a prominent part there; Iddo is not mentioned in Kings, but it is possible that the unnamed prophet of 1 Kings 13 had already been given this name, as he certainly was later by Josephus. The references to the "prophecy" (lit. "words") of Nathan and Ahijah and the "visions" of Iddo may well be based on the headings of prophetic books, which often take this form. They are thereby given an authoritative status (Schniedewind 1995: 218).

2 Chronicles 10

The attentive reader of the account of Solomon's reign in 1 Kings will have foreseen imminent trouble, for the account of Ahijah the Shilonite in 1 Kings 11 focussed on the inevitability of the division of the kingdom. That is mentioned here at 10:15, as if the Chronicler's audience knew all about it, but it is not included in the account of Solomon's reign. Indeed, in Chronicles the hints of impending division are much more oblique, being confined essentially to the reference to Ahijah's prophecy at 9:30. The result is that while much of this chapter is taken from 1 Kings 12, the different context means that quite a different impression is given. We follow Rehoboam to Shechem with no intimation of the trouble that that visit would engender.

Shechem was later the religious center of the Samaritans, but it is treated quite neutrally here — a warning against the probably anachronistic attempts made by some scholars to call Chronicles "anti-Samaritan." "All Israel" gathered there, the term here taking in southerners as well as the northern tribes referred to in 1 Kings 12. The account of Jeroboam's role differs markedly in the Hebrew and Greek forms of 1 Kings; in Chronicles he is here introduced for the first time apart from the allusion in 9:29, and in what follows he is made to bear the responsibility for the division of the kingdom (cf. 13:4-6).

The well-known story of the advice given to Rehoboam by different groups follows 1 Kings very closely. At 10:14 the best Hebrew mss. make no reference to "my father"; it is as if Rehoboam himself is made to carry all the responsibility. (The variant reading is noted by the NEB/REB, but not by the RSV/NRSV.) The poetic fragment at v. 16 is taken over from 1 Kings 12:16 but is also reminiscent of 1 Chr 12:18. There loyalty to David was the work of the spirit; here disloyalty is envisaged, though the blame for that disloyalty has not yet been apportioned. Rehoboam's hurried return to Jerusalem and the curious statement that Israel was in rebellion against the house of David "to this day," written at a time when the former Northern Kingdom had long since come to an end, bring the chapter to an end. Though it would be wrong to identify the northerners of the Chronicler's day with the later Samaritans, there may have been groups hostile to Jerusalem's claims in the northern area, such as those loyal to Sanballat in Nehemiah's time, against whom this is aimed. There is no mention of Jeroboam's establishment as king over Israel; from now on the Chronicler will have little to say about the Northern Kingdom except when its affairs impinged directly on those of the south.

2 Chronicles 11:1-12

The use of "Israel" is somewhat confusing, for in 11:1 it is used of the Northern Kingdom, whereas in v. 3 "all Israel in Judah and Benjamin" must refer to the south. The former usage corresponds to that in 1 Kgs 12:23; the latter is without parallel there, and may thus be seen as reflecting the Chronicler's own usage. Some have supposed that for the Chronicler the south was now the only true Israel (Myers 1965b: 65), but Williamson (1977: 98-110) has shown that in the Chronicler's usage either kingdom could legitimately be described as Israel. Shemaiah, "the man of God," offers a rare example of a southern prophet being named; designating him as a "man of God" hints at his importance, and he will play a leading part in ch. 12.

The list of fortified cities in 11:6-10 is without parallel in Kings, but it is usually thought to be based on an otherwise unknown source available to the Chronicler. Whether in fact it reflects the time of Rehoboam or that of some later king is less certain. In any case building is a frequent sign of divine blessing and prosperity in Chronicles.

2 Chronicles 11:13-23

For the moment at least all goes well for Rehoboam. "Israel" in 11:13 and 16, as the context makes clear, refers to the Northern Kingdom, though the "LORD God of Israel" is to be found at Jerusalem. A vivid contrast is drawn between the true worship at Jerusalem, maintained by the priests and especially the Levites, and the abominable practices sponsored by Jeroboam in the north. It is doubtful whether the Chronicler had reliable information as to what those practices were; "goat-demons" were condemned in Lev 17:7, and Jeroboam is pictured as in breach of the Torah. But the reference to "three years" of security in v. 17 strikes an ominous note, for we know that Rehoboam's reign was much longer than that.

Rehoboam's marital arrangements are next described. Most of the names are otherwise unknown; where there are apparent references to those known elsewhere, this only generates confusion (e.g., "Maacah daughter of Absalom": historically this can hardly be the only other known Absalom, David's son; in 13:2 she is named "Micaiah" and given a different parentage). Eighteen wives and sixty concubines would not be legally, still less politically, correct today, but here there is no indication that this was unacceptable. Rather, it seems to be presented as a sign of favor so that Rehoboam's wise dealings included the provision of many wives for his sons. On the other hand, the Hebrew text is uncertain and could be slightly emended (as by Jerusalem Bible) to mean "he consulted the many gods of his wives." Whether or not the changed view of Rehoboam begins at the end of this chapter, the favorable presentation of him is at an end.

2 Chronicles 12:1-12

Overconfidence now leads Rehoboam to the basic wrongdoing: abandoning the Torah. The Chronicler presents the attack by Pharaoh Shishak (probably Sheshonq I, c. 931-910 BC) as a direct consequence of Rehoboam's falling away. Just as God had once delivered the Israelites and punished an Egyptian pharaoh who trusted in his own strength, so now an Israelite king is punished by an Egyptian pharaoh for presumption. The brief reference to Shishak in 1 Kgs 14:25 is much elaborated by the Chronicler.

But all is not lost. Shemaiah reappears and shows who is to blame for the disaster; repentance follows, and the LORD allows "some deliverance," because the king and his officers humbled themselves. This is a classic example of the Chronicler's theology of divine retribution and response to prayer. Several of the phrases used in this episode will recur again in 2 Chronicles. And so, despite the depredations of Shishak, we are told that "conditions were good in Judah." Williamson (1982: 248) brings out the right nuance with his rendering, "There were still some good things in Judah."

2 Chronicles 12:13-16

The details of Rehoboam's reign, used to introduce it at 1 Kgs 14:21, are here made into a concluding summary. His age on accession contrasts oddly with the description of him as "young and irresolute" at 13:7; the latter may be a theological judgment rather than a statement about age. Here, too, the final verdict on him is negative. Of the sources noted for the reign, we have already met "the seer Iddo" (9:29), and Shemaiah is the prophet whose words have twice been recorded. The meaning of "recorded by genealogy" is unknown. Rehoboam is succeeded by the son first mentioned in 11:20 and consistently called "Abijah" in Chronicles. In 1 Kings 14 and 15 he is called "Abijam." The Chronicler may have had access to a more accurate tradition, but it is also possible that the form Abi-jam contains a reference to the Canaanite sea god Yam, and that the name has been "corrected" here.

2 Chronicles 13:1-12

The names both of the king (see the previous note) and of his mother are uncertain. "Micaiah" is normally a male name, and in 11:20 and at 1 Kgs 15:2 the mother is called "Maacah" (so the NEB/REB here), though she has a different parentage. We are reminded of the uncertain basis of our knowledge of details of this kind.

The main feature of this section is the speech of Abijah, one of the most characteristic of the "addresses" in Chronicles (analyzed by Mason 1990). Its delivery on the otherwise unknown "Mount Zemaraim" has led to its being called the Chronicler's "sermon on the Mount." It is addressed to "Jeroboam and all Israel," but is clearly meant to be "heard" by the Chronicler's own audience, to offer them an explanation of their place in God's plans. The legitimacy of the Davidic kingship and of the priesthood of the Jerusalem temple is stressed. The circumstances of the division of the kingdom were wholly exceptional, brought about by "certain worthless scoundrels" (who these were is not more clearly defined, but that may be unimportant); now the northerners should see the error of their ways and realize that their cause was hopeless.

2 Chronicles 13:13–14:1a

What follows this speech is a battle quite unlike normal human warfare. It has already been stressed that the northern army was twice the size of the southern (13:3). Jeroboam indeed pursued correct tactics in setting an ambush to entrap the forces of Judah. But when they appeal to God, divine intervention brings the battle to a swift and bloody conclusion. It is clearly quite inappropriate to ask historical questions of an account such as this; this is a special kind of "holy war" in which God fights on behalf of those who put all their trust in him. Thus, there is no other evidence to support the statement in vv. 18-19 that northern Israel was "subdued" before Judah, though some have argued that temporary successes in the continual skirmishing between the two countries have provided the basis for the generalization here.

It is possible to interpret Abijah's "strength" in 13:21 as an indication of too great confidence in human power, and thus a move toward the very negative verdict on him found in 1 Kings 15, but there is no other hint of this — the extended family is not a cause for condemnation in the Chronicler's eyes — and the reference may simply be to the successes against the north already mentioned. Abijah's death is recorded in 13:23 of the Hebrew text but in 14:1 in the English versions.

We may note that these events are described in "the story of the prophet Iddo." The word here translated "story" is *midrash,* a term which will occur again at 24:27 (there translated "commentary"). The word came to have an important significance in later Jewish interpretation, denoting an elaborate retelling of earlier material. Whether this meaning is already present, or the plain sense "story" is more appropriate, is much disputed. There is a sense in which, if Kings be accepted as a source for Chronicles, Chronicles can itself be described as a *midrash* on the earlier material.

2 Chronicles 14:2-15

The account of Asa's reign and that of his son Jehoshaphat is much more extensive in Chronicles (chs. 14–20) than in Kings. These two rulers attracted much attention among preachers in England at the time of the Civil War; how kings could be pleasing and displeasing to God was a major concern in a very biblical culture. (See the index of Hill 1993 under "Asa" and "Jehoshaphat" for illustrations.)

Some have supposed that the Chronicler had additional sources available, but it is more likely that these two rulers are chosen as examples to illustrate some of the basic theological concerns of the author.

It is certainly very difficult to regard the story of Zerah the Ethiopian as serious history. It is preceded by an account of Asa having carried out the appropriate religious reforms; in at least one instance, the removal of "the high places" (14:3), the Chronicler flatly contradicts 1 Kgs 15:14, and he indeed seems to modify his source at 15:17. It is very unlikely that the various religious objects referred to were live concerns in the Chronicler's own day; this is conventional language describing what must have been done by a ruler faithful to God's commands, particularly as laid down in Deuteronomy. Later he would fall away and his reputation would be tarnished.

The account of the "battle" with Zerah illustrates the Chronicler's conception of holy war. The enemy army is vast beyond human imagining; battle lines are drawn up, but the only real way to repel such forces is to cry to the LORD. This done, God himself defeats the Ethiopians; all that Asa and his army have to do is to pursue them, seize the booty, and so return in triumph to Jerusalem. Meanwhile Zerah and his million soldiers have all been killed. "Million" in Hebrew is actually "a thousand thousands," and some have supposed that a "thousand" can also refer to a small military unit; Dillard 1987: 120 rightly recognizes, however, that any attempt to reduce the numbers of Zerah's army to something more realistic would undercut the very point that the Chronicler wished to make, God's capacity to overthrow any human force, however imposing.

2 Chronicles 15

Asa's success is now linked with prophetic preaching, inspired by the "spirit" of God. This picture of God "breathing" on those chosen to set forth his will, be they prophets, priests, or Levites, is characteristic of Chronicles. The sermon itself is taken by the NRSV and most versions and commentators as referring to the people's past, but some versions (e.g., the JB) and some commentators have understood it as referring to a future danger. If, as seems likely, the reference is to the past, it is too vague to be attributable to some particular historical circumstances; rather, it is a general spelling out of the troubles which confront the community when it is "without the true God, without a teaching priest, and without law." As such, it has also a future reference, warning the Chronicler's own community of the dangers of falling away from their commitment.

The Hebrew text attributes the prophecy, said in 15:1 to be given by Azariah, to Oded in v. 8 (see the NRSV footnote). Then Asa appears to repeat the reforms already set forth in ch. 14. It is possible to set forth a historical explanation of this; much more likely the author is aiming for deliberate literary effect, the repetition emphasizing how loyal Asa was while under prophetic influence (contrast 16:10). The wholeness of Israel is stressed by the reference to Ephraim, Manasseh, and Simeon in 15:9, though it is not clear why these three groups should have been singled out, widely separated as they were geographically. Like the prophecy in the earlier part of the chapter, this account is applicable to the current community; note particularly its reference to a covenant, a theme of great importance in Second Temple Judaism. The threat of the death penalty in v. 13 is likely to be poetic license.

The last verses of the chapter closely follow 1 Kgs 15:13-15. The one important modification is the addition of "out of Israel" in v. 17; we have already been told of the removal of the high places from Judah in 14:5. A further contradiction is removed by the NRSV at 15:19; the word "more" is not in the Hebrew. 1 Kgs 15:16 speaks of continuous wars between Asa and his northern neighbors, and we have already had the wonderful victory over Zerah. Perhaps the NRSV may be allowed as sympathetic to the Chronicler's purpose of showing peace to be the reward of the religious reforms just described.

2 Chronicles 16

This chapter provides a good example of the Chronicler's creative use of his source to illustrate his own theological standpoint. With the exception of the chronology, since "thirty-sixth year" here cannot be reconciled with 1 Kgs 15:33, which implies that Baasha died in Asa's twenty-seventh year, 16:1-6 follow 1 Kgs 15:17-22 very closely. The only significant change is that the Kings reference to the dispatch of "all the silver and the gold" is modified, perhaps to save something of Asa's reputation.

But that reputation is to come under severe criticism from "the seer Hanani." He is otherwise unknown but presumably to be understood as the father of Jehu (19:2), who warned Asa's son Jehosphaphat of the danger of flirting with foreign alliances. We are used to thinking of seers and prophets as speaking of the future; here, as often in Chronicles, their role is to interpret past events. The overall picture is clear; when Asa trusted in the LORD, he was delivered from even so great a threat as that of Zerah (16:8). But when he relied on Aram, he was less successful — the Arameans escaped. But this is very odd since Aram was supposed to be his ally! Some versions (e.g., the NEB/REB) emend "Aram" to "Israel" in line with the sense of 1 Kings and some Greek texts. The NRSV keeps the Hebrew text, and this may imply that had Asa been faithful he would have overcome Aram and not needed to seek its alliance. The close of the section portrays Asa's further fall from grace, with his critic put in the stocks, a detail that would remind the audience of the mistreatment of another prophet critical of the establishment — Jeremiah (20:2).

The closing summary of Asa's reign largely follows 1 Kgs 15:23-24, but it elaborates both on his disease and on the details of his burial. The nature of the disease (the NRSV wisely leaves it unspecific) is unknown; "feet" here may, as often in the HB, be a euphemism for the sexual organs. Physicians were clearly not highly regarded in the Chronicler's context, but the stress is less on their possible engagement in magical practices than on Asa's failure, once again, to turn to God.

2 Chronicles 17

Asa's son and successor Jehoshaphat is only a minor figure in Kings, where the account of his time is dominated by the figure of Elijah and Elijah's confrontation with Ahab and Jezebel in the Northern Kingdom. But four chapters in 2 Chronicles are devoted to his reign, with a complex mixture of praise and blame. To some extent the pattern of loyalty followed by disobedience which characterized the account of Asa is followed, but the story becomes more complicated with the introduction of the theme of repentance leading to renewed favor. Why Jehoshaphat has been given this extended treatment is not certain; there *may* have been additional sources available, but it is perhaps more likely that the meaning of his name, "Yahweh judges," invited a kind of parabolic treatment. The commentary must look at the development of the story, but it is worthwhile for the reader to look at these chapters as a whole.

The opening verses (17:1-6) offer a sketch of the reign in auspicious terms. "Israel" is here clearly the Northern Kingdom, now pictured as the enemy. The NRSV modifies the Hebrew text at v. 2 by omitting "David"; it may be right that the comparison is with Jehoshaphat's physical father Asa, but it is also possible that the comparison is intended to be with David, whose "earlier ways" were followed by something of a falling away. This admittedly is the picture of 2 Samuel rather than Chronicles; here as often elsewhere the question arises how far the Chronicler is making conscious references to other biblical material. Certainly the Chronicler seems to be comparing Jehoshaphat with Solomon; there are strong echoes of 1:1 in this description. As elsewhere in Chronicles (e.g., in the account of Asa) there is a contradiction between the statement here that the high places were removed and that in 20:33 which asserts the contrary. We are warned once again against regarding the Chronicler as a historian in our modern sense of the term.

An otherwise unknown teaching mission is now described. It is to be envisaged as the first and entirely proper act carried out by Jehoshaphat as sole ruler. Interestingly the list of names begins with laypeople, then the Levites, then the priests. Teaching "the law of the LORD" is a universal obligation. If there is any ancient tradition underlying this story, we have no means of knowing what the "book" (better, "scroll") will have been; the Chronicler himself will have pictured it as *the* Torah, the Pentateuch.

17:10 is set out as beginning a new paragraph, but it continues from what has preceded, and we are no doubt meant to understand that the proclamation of the law led to this favorable reaction among the neighboring kingdoms. Even traditional enemies brought tribute to Jehoshaphat. "Arabs" are rarely mentioned outside Chronicles (Isa 13:20 is an exception), and the reference to them may point to the circumstances of the author's own time. We might have supposed that if peace was prevailing and tribute was coming from potential enemies there would be no need for "fortresses" and great works, which will have been city defenses; still less would an army in excess of a million men be needed. (It is doubtful whether the total population of the kingdom of Jehoshaphat will much have exceeded a quarter of a million.) Again we are reminded that the Chronicler's technique is the broad brush, giving a vivid overall impression rather than anything like our modern concern for accuracy of detail.

2 Chronicles 18:1–19:3

This is a long section, but it can only be treated as a unity. It is largely based on 1 Kings 22, which tells of the determination of a king of Israel to capture the border territory of Ramoth-Gilead. The body of court prophets encourages him to go ahead, but he is warned of his likely fate by another prophet, Micaiah, and is killed by a bow "drawn at a venture." In 1 Kings the king in question is unnamed in most of the story, but he has come to be identified as Ahab and is so named at 1 Kgs 22:20. The form of the story in Chronicles leaves no doubt that Ahab is the king referred to, but the Chronicler's interest is much more in Jehoshaphat of Judah (a peripheral figure in the Kings version). This is the first "down" in the curiously up-and-down portrayal of Jehoshaphat to which we have already alluded.

The opening phrase of 18:1 repeats 17:5, but the consequences are different. "Riches and honor" may be a sign of divine favor; but they may also lead their possessor astray, as here with the marriage alliance and his subsequently being "induced" by Ahab into joining his military plans. "We will be with you in the war" (v. 3) is without parallel in Kings and emphasizes Jehoshaphat's responsibility.

The story which follows, one of the most vivid in the OT, particularly in its account of prophetic activity, follows 1 Kings very closely; see the commentary on 1 Kings for more detailed discussion. In both Kings and Chronicles (18:27 here) we find the apparently irrelevant phrase, "Hear, you peoples, all of you," which is actually "borrowed" from the book of Micah (1:2). Micah and Micaiah, who is speaking here, are different forms of the same name, and this is an early example of a tendency to identify people with the same name and a similar role, even if historically they are quite unconnected.

The details of the king of Israel's death are drastically reduced from the version in Kings, but an important pointer to the restoration of Jehoshaphat to favor is given at 18:31; he cried out, and the LORD helped him. The possibility of repentance for an ill-considered venture is still open. But before his full restoration he must face the prophetic verdict, delivered in 19:2-3 by Jehu. The parallel between Asa and Jehoshaphat is further strengthened. Asa had encountered the seer Hanani (16:7). So now Asa's son Jehoshaphat is met by Hanani's son Jehu. The message is a warning against the folly of participating in foreign alliances rather than an outright rejection, and the closing reference to the "sacred poles" shows how overtly religious concerns are introduced into what we might otherwise regard as a strictly political venture.

2 Chronicles 19:4-11

After the dangerous flirting with alien forces described in the previous section, Jehoshaphat's behavior returns to acceptable standards. He "resided at Jerusalem" — no more foolish going down to Samaria (18:2); then he took pains to ensure, by personal visitation, that God's ways were known and followed in the land (a somewhat larger area here than in other descriptions of Judah) for which he was responsible.

There follows, in 19:5-11, an account of a major legal reform, appointing local judges and setting up a centralized structure for the administration of justice in Jerusalem. This has long been recognized as a key section for our understanding of the Chronicler. For some he is essentially a historian, providing information from otherwise unknown sources, which offers valuable supplements to the basic story provided in Kings. Others have seen the Chronicler's concerns quite differently. There is much in these verses which is closely related to Deut 16:18–17:13. 19:7 is a clear allusion to Deut 16:19, and 19:10-11, which envisage a kind of appeal court, to be presided over by the chief priest, show the practical outworking of what is laid down in Deuteronomy 17. So an alternative, and perhaps more likely, reading of this section is to see these verses as scriptural interpretation: this is how the law laid down in Deuteronomy is to be carried out. It is natural to place such an explanation in the reign of Jehoshaphat, whose name, as we have already seen, means "Yahweh judges." It is certainly possible that an additional reason for incorporating this story was the desire of the Chronicler to inculcate loyalty to the central judicial system of his own day by claiming its antiquity, going back to the Torah of Moses.

2 Chronicles 20:1-30

Another long episode needs to be treated as a unity. This time there is no parallel in Kings, and as is usual where this is the case, scholarly opinion is sharply divided whether the Chronicler had access to independent sources of reliable historical information.

Geographical uncertainties arise in the first two verses, where the repetition of "Ammonites" in 20:1 and the reference to "Aram" in v. 2 are emended by the NRSV and most modern versions to "Meunites" (of uncertain location; they are mentioned in 1 Chr 4:41, but where they lived is not known — perhaps near Petra, southeast of Judah) and "Edom." The reference to Hazazon-tamar well illustrates the different understandings of this story; those who see a historical basis think of this as the starting point of a route into Judah from the Dead Sea; others find a deliberate literary linkage to be more plausible, associating this story with the battle described in Gen 14:7, where the LORD protected Abraham.

But the story offers much more detail about the reactions of the king and "all Judah" than about military activity. In the face of this threat Jehoshaphat responds in a wholly admirable way, seeking the LORD, proclaiming a fast, and summoning the assembly to meet in the temple. There follows a prayer (20:6-12), comparable to the communal laments found in the Psalms, though much less ready than are some of them (e.g., Ps 44:9-26) to blame God for the troubles that have come about. Here we find more specific allusions to past history, beginning with Abraham, mentioned in terms reminiscent of Isa 41:8, through the expulsion of the previous inhabitants of the land, down to the building of the temple. This is pictured as in Solomon's prayer of ch. 6, a place in which true prayer could be offered with confidence in God's reply. The prayer is concluded by reference to the present enemies, and their ingratitude for not remembering their immunity from invasion by the Israelites in their wilderness wanderings. (When we recall that those wanderings are supposed to have taken place at least three hundred years earlier, we perhaps should not be surprised at this forgetfulness.)

God responds to this prayer with an oracle of salvation. (It is often thought that such oracles of salvation were also delivered following the Psalms of Lament.) God's spirit guides a Levite. His words begin with the characteristic formula "Do not fear," here given the explicit context of Jehoshaphat's fear in 20:3, and it is developed in ways strikingly similar to the instructions to the Israelites at the Red Sea (Exod 14:13-14) (Mason 1990: 67 sets forth the close similarities of the two addresses in parallel columns.) These more general characteristics are then given their appropriate context by the details in v. 16.

The only proper response to such an oracle is praise, and this is offered. Many psalms and prophetic passages (e.g., Ps 30:5) make reference to God's victory early in the morning, and so the people are ready at that hour. Tekoa is best known as the home of Amos, but that does not seem here to be a deliberate linkage. But there is one more important ceremony to describe before the battle; the assurance of victory is given by Jehoshaphat himself, in the way laid down for the priest in Deut 20:3-4. Jehoshaphat's words are based on Isa 7:9. (The word here translated "established" is that rendered by the NRSV as "stand firm" in Isaiah. It comes from the same root *'-m-n,* which gives us the word "Amen," implying the commitment of those who so respond to the prayer just spoken.) In Isaiah faithless King Ahaz had not stood firm; but here Jehoshaphat and his people are pictured more sympathetically. The command to "believe his prophets" may also be an allusion to Isaiah but is no doubt also addressed to the community of the Chronicler's own day. The liturgical ceremonies (for that, rather than preparation for war, is the only appropriate description) reach their climax with the singing of psalms (cf. 5:13; 7:3).

After all this the battle itself is a mere formality. The enemies are in total confusion, and "they all helped to destroy one another" so that none escaped. All that remains for the people of Judah to do is to gather the booty in vast quantities and assemble once more this time in the appropriately named Valley of Beracah, which means "Blessing." The triumphal procession returns to Jerusalem, and the situation described at the beginning of Jehoshaphat's reign (17:10) is now restored as it approaches its end.

2 Chronicles 20:31-37

But all is not wholly well. We have seen already that the account of Jehoshaphat's reign is a story of ups and downs, and there is one final "down" to report. Here the Chronicler uses his source, 1 Kgs 22:42-43, 45, 48-49, to show how even good rulers could fall from grace. The note about the high places seems directly to contradict 17:6, and shows how the stress on failure overrules the need for consistency. The account ends with an illustration of the king's folly. Despite all that God had done for him he joined in yet another foreign alliance, which predictably ended in disaster, in accordance with the warnings of the otherwise unknown prophet Eliezer. He is the right person to bring the story to an end, for his name means "God is help," and he warns Jehoshaphat against trusting in any other supposed source of help.

2 Chronicles 21

The death of a king is usually recorded at the end of a chapter (e.g., Jehoram at 21:20 here), but all versions, Hebrew and English, have Jehoshaphat's death at v. 1, perhaps because Jehoram, his son and successor, is also mentioned here (Japhet 1993: 785). The NRSV follows the MT in using the longer form "Jehoram"; the NEB/REB has the shorter "Joram." He is to receive a negative verdict, and this provides the rationale for the details of Jehoshaphat's family with which we begin. (Did he have two sons both named Azariah? — perhaps one died early, or one of the names should be modified.) It seems as if he had some say in the succession arrangements (cf. the story of David's succession in 2 Samuel 9–20, 1 Kings 1–2), though the usual custom was for the firstborn to succeed. Having done so, Jehoram is pictured as killing all possible rivals. Is a comparison being drawn with his hated wife Athaliah, "the daughter of Ahab" (21:6), who attempted the same action (22:10; cf. 2 Kgs 11:1)?

In this way an ominous prelude is established for the negative judgment taken over from 2 Kgs 8:17-22. Everything that can go wrong for Jehoram does go wrong. He is defeated in war by the Edomites — nothing is done in this battle to enlist divine favor. He loses territory (21:16) to both the Philistines and the Arabs, though this is "theological geography," for neither of those peoples could be described as "near the Ethiopians."

Still more serious for the author than these material losses is the religious falling away. Rather than high places being taken away, new ones are made. A letter is received from the prophet Elijah, spelling out Jehoram's offenses and warning of their inevitable consequences. To us such a letter must appear somewhat anachronistic, for according to 2 Kings 2 he had been "taken up" before Jehoram's time. Later Jewish tradition used our passage as a basis for its belief in Elijah's future return, but we are more likely to suppose that the letter is the Chronicler's own composition; its concerns are not those of the Elijah pictured in 1-2 Kings, and a written message is much more characteristic of the Chronicler's own day, when such written oracles were regarded as authoritative.

The final disaster to befall Jehoram is incurable disease. The lurid details are present so as to add the final ignominy to a life which in the Chronicler's judgment had gone so disastrously wrong. It is doubtful whether the community of the Chronicler's day had a clear picture of a future life, but it was important to carry out the appropriate rites following death. It was the final negative touch for Jehoram that these were not performed: no fire, no burial in the royal tombs. "He departed with no one's regret"; the precise meaning of this phrase is uncertain, but it replaces the usual reference to other sources. Jehoram is best forgotten, save as an awful example. This is the first, but will not be the last, thoroughly negative verdict on a Davidic king.

2 Chronicles 22

Jehoram is succeeded by his one remaining son, called Jehoahaz in 21:17 but Ahaziah in this chapter. (It is the same name, and both have the divine elements "Jeho" or "iah," derived from the name Yahweh, one at the beginning and the other at the end.) The succession of a youngest son might lead us to think of David, but this is a false analogy; all the wrongs of his father's reign continue under Ahaziah. He is said to have been forty-two years old on his accession, but since his father had just died at forty an error has clearly crept in. We have no way of knowing the origin of the error; the "corrections" of versions and commentaries are guesswork. Also disputed is whether his wife Athaliah was the daughter (so the MT) or granddaughter (so the NRSV, without any footnote, but perhaps on the basis of 2 Chr 21:6) of Omri. Whatever her parentage she was a hate figure for the authors of Kings and Chronicles, as bad as her more notorious sister- (or mother-)in-law Jezebel. Whether either of them deserves her reputation is a matter which regrettably cannot be discussed here, but we may note that a woman in power, especially an alien woman, represents a threat which many males still find difficult to come to terms with.

22:1-6 largely follow 2 Kgs 8:25-29, with the emphasis on wrongdoing heightened (e.g., in 22:3 the reference to the wicked counselors). There follows a drastically reduced version of the story in 2 Kings 9 showing how it was "ordained by God" that his links with the Northern Kingdom were literally fatal. The word translated "downfall" has often been emended, but it should be retained; it stresses the total disaster which befell Ahaziah. It is a disaster so great as to threaten the continuance of the Davidic line, for v. 9 warns that there was no one able to rule the kingdom and v. 10 (inevitably!) puts the blame on Athaliah. She rules, but, presumably all unknown to her, the child Joash survives in hiding. The motif of the one surviving child is characteristic of folk tales, though here curiously domesticated; the search for members of the family to be killed cannot have been very thorough if it was possible to hide Joash in a bedroom. But we should note the introduction of the priest Jehoiada, whose wife hid Joash; Jehoiada has an important part in the story. Meanwhile, however, Davidic rule seems to be over.

2 Chronicles 23

This chapter is dependent on 2 Kings 11, with various points emphasized so as to bring out the Chronicler's distinctive concerns. Its overall theme is the reversal of the danger set forth at the end of the previous chapter: the Davidic line is not at an end but can be restored through the action of a faithful priest. It is certainly possible, though there is no direct evidence for it, that the Chronicler envisaged that the community of his own day might similarly see the restoration of the Davidic line, if priests and community were faithful. A pointer in that direction may be found in the Chronicler's stress, absent from Kings, on the participation of the Levites and all "the heads of families of Israel" (23:2), so that "the whole assembly" covenanted "with the king" as if he were already restored. What in 2 Kings and to some extent in the later part of this chapter seems to be pictured as a secret and surprise uprising has become in these early verses a major public event taking place in the house of God. Athaliah is now presented not only as wicked but also as totally incompetent, if she takes no steps to prevent such a gathering. The conspiracy itself, described in 23:4-11, similarly loses its secret character with the participation of "all the people" in the temple courts. Indeed, according to v. 8 "all Judah" was involved. The ceremony reaches its climax with the coronation of the young king. There has been much discussion as to the significance of the *'edut* (NRSV, "covenant"; REB, "testimony"); the longstanding suggestion that it refers to some kind of decree setting out the royal status and obligations remains the most likely understanding (cf. Ps 2:7-9, though the word there translated "decree" is a different one).

At last Athaliah is alerted to the danger she is in, but her situation is of course hopeless. With what we are intended to regard as fine sensibility Jehoiada has her removed from the temple precincts (in which as a woman she had no business to be) before she can be killed.

The chapter ends with the rededication of the community as the LORD's people; this is done through a covenant (*berit,* the usual word for "covenant"). As is so often the case with religious rededication, it begins with destruction and violence; the "house of Baal" had presumably been set up under the patronage of Athaliah, despite her true Yahwistic name. We do not know whether it was actually part of the temple-palace complex. After that the true priesthood can be restored in accordance with the instructions laid down by David, and the cult renewed as laid down in the Torah, the law of Moses. Joash's reign has made a promising start; will it continue in the same vein?

2 Chronicles 24:1-14

We have seen in the Chronicler's account of Jehoshaphat a series of "ups and downs," as the king's behavior was judged now favorably, now unfavorably. More usual for the Chronicler was a simple twofold division: a time of doing what was right either followed or preceded by a time of disobedience. The reign of Joash follows this pattern; in his early years, described in this section, all goes well. He is under the benign guidance of Jehoiada the priest, and during his days Joash "did what was right." Interestingly, this extends to having two priestly approved wives; it is a drastic reduction from the harems of Solomon, Rehoboam, and Abijah, and is regarded as a sign of divine favor.

The note about Joash's wives is not found in Kings, but most of the rest of this section is based on 2 Kings 12 with significant modifications. One characteristic modification is the introduction of Levites into the repair work; less characteristic is the criticism of the Levites for their dilatoriness in 24:6. This may reflect some otherwise unknown circumstance of the Chonicler's own time. Another point stressed by the Chronicler (vv. 6, 9) and not in Kings is the identification of the tax to be paid with that laid down by "Moses the servant of the LORD/God." Presumably the reference is to the half-shekel tax required by Exod 30:12-16, paid here with more enthusiasm than some modern taxes ("rejoiced," v. 10). As in Exodus 35–36 the response is a generous one, and there is sufficient money available for additional utensils to be made.

The picture in 24:10-11 envisages coins being placed in the chest. This again reflects the time of writing. Coined money was unknown in the time of Joash. But however the payment is pictured, this section reaches a climax with the assurance that the structure and worship of the temple, so direly threatened by Athaliah (v. 7), are now fully restored.

2 Chronicles 24:15-27

Jehoiada's death and burial are described with most unusual detail for a non-royal figure; indeed, his burial among the kings suggests a comparison with royalty, perhaps reflecting the status of the high priest as head of the community in the Chronicler's own day. The remarkable age with which he is credited also points to the veneration in which he was held. In its context, however, the note of his death is also ominous, for we recall (24:2) that Joash did what was "right all the days of Jehoiada." Which way will he now turn?

As in the time of Rehoboam, bad counsel comes from the "officials" of Judah (cf. 12:5, 6, where the same word is translated "officers." The reason for the change is not clear; the RSV has "princes" in both cases). What they said is not recorded in detail, but it leads to the abandonment of the newly restored temple and a lapse into idolatry. Prophetic warnings go unheeded, though these may refer more to the general tendency of the people to ignore the prophets than to any particular "outbreak" of prophetism at this time.

At last Jehoiada's son tries to bring the king back from his folly, with a brief sermon. Though Zechariah is a priest, the form both of the introduction and of the message itself is characteristic of prophets (Mason 1990: 79-83). His word is an epitome of the Chronicler's message, that those who forsake God will be forsaken by him. The sin is compounded by the stoning to death of Zechariah. This is the last such murder of the innocent described in the HB, wherein 2 Chronicles is the last book; hence the reference in Luke 11:51, with its disturbingly anti-Jewish implications, to Jesus' opponents being charged with the responsibility of killing the innocent from Abel to Zechariah.

The Aramean wars are also mentioned in 2 Kings 12, but the account there is very different. Here the invasion is specifically described as judgment upon Joash. When Judah was faithful, God had fought for them and mighty foreign armies had been routed; here only a few foreigners are enough to defeat a "very great army" of Judah because of its apostasy. The NRSV could be read as implying that the army had abandoned the LORD; more probably the reference is to the officials. The members of the army suffered for the sins of others — the fate of the poor infantry in many wars.

The Chronicler concludes his account of Joash by weaving together matters reported separately in Kings. There the domestic conspiracy is not linked with the Aramean wars; here Joash is wounded in the war, and his servants, mindful of the treatment of Zechariah (and others?: Hebrew has "son*s*"), kill him. And — ultimate ignominy — he is not buried in the royal tombs. We note that the conspirators were foreigners; Joash had turned to foreign gods and was murdered by their servants. (On "commentary" [Heb. *midrash*] see the note on 13:22.)

2 Chronicles 25

As with so many of the kings, the reign of Amaziah is seen as a mixture of positive and negative elements. 25:1-4 correspond closely with 2 Kgs 14:1-6, with minor changes, such as the introduction of the phrase "yet not with a true heart," to warn of weaknesses to be revealed. The sparing of the murderers' children in 25:4 accords with the requirements of Deut. 24:16.

The middle section of the chapter, 25:5-16, is without close parallel in Kings, save for the reference to a war against Edom. The gathering of an army is not in itself regarded as wrong — as we have frequently seen, and v. 12 of this chapter will demonstrate in the most appalling way, the Chronicler was no pacifist — but the hiring of mercenaries from the Northern Kingdom of Israel is another matter. An anonymous "man of God," another name for a prophet, is introduced to warn against Israelite involvement. Reliance on God, not on such human allies, is required. Vv. 9-10 offer a curiously modern exchange, with Amaziah concerned about wasted expenditure and the mercenaries furious about the lack of any payout.

The next section should provide us with a forcible reminder that we should not always expect to be on the side of the biblical writers. In the Chronicler's age there were periods of bitter hostility between Judah and Edom, and he is manifestly unable to rise above such hostility; whether or not the massacre here described actually took place, he clearly delights in the thought. Something has gone wrong in 25:13, for Samaria certainly and Beth-horon probably were not cities of Judah; either the place names have been wrongly transcribed or a textual misunderstanding has taken place.

Amaziah's fall from favor continues with his decision to worship the gods of his beaten enemies —an act of folly which will soon be compounded. First, he disregards a prophetic warning by the familiar device of trying to stop the prophet from speaking, though not before the gist of the message has been delivered. Next he threatens to kill the prophet; then he becomes involved once more with the rejected Northern Kingdom, laying down a foolish challenge to the more powerful northern king. This episode restores the links with 2 Kings 14, which refers to Amaziah's defeat of Edom. It may well be that the extended account in 25:11-16 of the war against Edom was a *midrash* (see on 13:22) explaining this reference. The account of the disastrous outcome of the encounter with Israel, involving destruction in Jerusalem and the despoliation of the temple, follows 2 Kings. The addition of fifteen years to Amaziah's life might be seen as a sign of renewed divine favor, but it is only temporary; he is murdered, yet he is allowed the favor of burial among the royal tombs in Jerusalem.

2 Chronicles 26:1-15

The ambiguous verdicts passed by the Chronicler on so many of Judah's kings appear again with Uzziah. As with Joash (ch. 24), there is here a clear twofold division: a period of religious loyalty rewarded by divine favor, described in this section; a time of falling away and consequent punishment, set out in the next section. We may note that Uzziah is so named in this chapter and when he is mentioned in prophetic books (e.g., Isa 1:1; 6:1); in 2 Kings 15 (and in the list in 1 Chr 3:12) he is called Azariah. One of these names may have been a "throne-name," but if so, we have no means of knowing which. The account in 2 Kings 15 is extremely brief; here it is much elaborated, as befits so long a reign, either through free composition or because of the availability of sources otherwise unknown to us.

At first all goes well: "as long as he sought the LORD, God made him prosper" (26:4) is almost a summary of the Chronicler's theology of kingship. We have no knowledge of the Zechariah referred to in the same verse. Illustrations of Uzziah's prosperity follow. He is successful in war to the west (Philistines) and to the east (Ammonites); Jabneh, first mentioned here, and better known in the Greek form Jamnia, became an important center of Judaism in the first century AD. An ambitious program of building work is described, both in Jerusalem and in the surrounding area. Archeological excavations have shown the eighth century BC, the time of Uzziah's reign, to have been a time of considerable building activity, so the account here is historically plausible, though it is certainly not possible to make exact correlations between this account and the archeological discoveries. The account of Uzziah's prosperity ends with a — no doubt exaggerated — account of his army. He "became strong." But that is an ambiguous position; it might lead one to trust in one's own strength.

2 Chronicles 26:16-23

The danger inherent in his strength becomes reality; he becomes proud and tries to take on religious duties regarded by the author as proper only for the priests. The story that follows may most plausibly be regarded as a *midrash* on the bare statement in 2 Kgs 15:5 that "the LORD struck the king so that he was leprous." Its assumptions are those of the latest strands in the Pentateuchal legislation for religious rites, and do not reflect the reality of the monarchical period, when priests are most unlikely to have addressed kings in the manner here envisaged, telling them what they might not do and ordering them to leave the sanctuary! David, Solomon, and other kings seem regularly to have performed major religious rites without criticism. It is noteworthy that the priest is named Azariah, which in other traditions was the name of the king himself; was the name deliberately chosen to show where true authority lay?

The story has a dramatic climax, with Uzziah stricken with "a leprous disease"; this will not have been Hansen's disease but some other skin affliction (cf. the NRSV footnote). The account is given in a way reminiscent of Miriam's punishment, also for claiming improper liturgical status, in Numbers 12. The distinctive point having been made, the Chronicler largely follows 2 Kings 15 for the remainder of his account of Uzziah. The reference to Isaiah is an addition; perhaps the book of Isaiah, with its reference to Uzziah (1:1), was coming to be regarded as a kind of royal chronicle. Uzziah is buried, though apparently not in the usual royal tombs. The consequences of his folly outlasted his life.

2 Chronicles 27

Historically Jotham is an enigmatic figure. The length of his reign is unclear (compare vv. 30 and 33 in 2 Kings 15); and the Chronicler's account seems to imply some kind of co-regency with his father (26:21). By comparison with the detailed judgments passed on his predecessors and successors, his reign is here passed over in a curiously perfunctory way. There are a few details which are not found in 2 Kings 15, but they do not seem to add anything of great significance. He followed the good practice of the first part of Uzziah's reign, without "invading" (the NRSV's odd translation) the temple. He was like Uzziah, too, in successful warfare and in rebuilding works in Jerusalem. And with that the account ends, with 27:8, most unusually, simply repeating information already given in v. 1. This is the merest interlude, preceded and followed by more dramatic events.

2 Chronicles 28:1-15

Several reigns have been described as involving two phases, one of divine favor, one of falling away. Now that division is set forth in different terms, not within the reign of one king but so as to present Ahaz as wholly evil and his son Hezekiah as wholly good. Ahaz is pictured in negative terms in 2 Kings 16; sometimes the Chronicler modifies the negative judgments of his sources, but here they are intensified.

28:1-4 closely follow 2 Kgs 16:2-4; we may note, but cannot resolve, the chronological problem. According to v. 1 Ahaz died at 36, but his son Hezekiah was 25 when he succeeded him (29:1). The "therefore" of 28:5 is interpretative, with no exact equivalent in the Hebrew, but it brings out the Chronicler's sense well: divine punishment follows wrong behavior. Vv. 5-7 offer an account of the conflict between Judah and Israel and the Arameans, often known as the "Syro-Ephraimite war." Whereas in other accounts of that war (2 Kings 16; Isaiah 7) the ineffectiveness of the northern coalition is stressed, here we have them pictured as inflicting vast losses on Judah. This may be historically plausible, but whether the Chronicler had access to an independent source describing the war must remain doubtful.

A particularly striking and attractive elaboration, with no parallels elsewhere, occurs in 28:8-15. The northerners are pictured as acknowledging their sins but as capable of repentance. They have a true prophet among them who, like the southern prophets, is a genuine instrument of God's word. They knew that to enslave fellow Israelites would be to go against the commands of the Torah. They had chiefs (no mention is made of their king) who counseled and practiced generosity. Thus the whole episode ends with the captives fed and clothed, and returned to Judah. The fact that they were returned to Jericho provides an obvious linkage with the story of the "Good Samaritan" (Luke 10:30-37), which is surely based on this account. Whether it was also intended as in some way applicable in the Chronicler's own time is more difficult to decide, but he clearly hoped for the unification of all Israel.

2 Chronicles 28:16-27

Ahaz played no part in the Samaria story, and now that we return to him we immediately discover that there is no improvement in his behavior. He needs help, for he has been punished by Edomites and Philistines. But in seeking such help, he turns not to the LORD but to Assyria. And of course the king of Assyria proves to be not a help but an additional oppressor. "Tilgath-pilneser" is the Chronicler's rendering of the name better known as "Tiglath-pileser"; he initiated the conquests which led to the final overthrow of the Northern Kingdom, and it is possible that knowledge of that leads the Chronicler to describe Ahaz as "king of Israel" (28:19); there was now no other claimant to that title.

The sum of his wrongs has not yet been reached. A note in 2 Kgs 16:10 tells of Ahaz having a copy of the (probably Assyrian) altar at Damascus introduced into the temple; the Chronicler assumes that the altar was Aramean and then has Ahaz cap his previous wickedness with actual apostasy — he worships the gods of Damascus. Everything associated with true worship is destroyed, culminating in the closing of the doors of the temple. Not surprisingly, therefore, Ahaz's burial is not with the tombs of the other kings. The situation seems desperate, but is about to be dramatically reversed with the accession of Hezekiah (whose Yahwistic name we note despite his father's alleged apostasy).

It is not the purpose of this commentary to engage in historical reconstruction, but it should be noted that it would be easy to make a case for Ahaz as an extremely skillful king, who preserved his kingdom in the face of the Assyrian threat when neighboring kingdoms collapsed. But historical evaluations of that kind are a long way from the Chronicler's concerns.

2 Chronicles 29

Hezekiah is regarded favorably by 2 Kings, but that approbation is taken even further here: he is the ideal king, whose reign is treated at greater length than that of any ruler since Solomon. Later Jewish pictures of Hezekiah as the model for the Messiah owe much to the depiction in Chronicles.

For the Chronicler any such ruler must begin with religious reform, and so the brief account in 2 Kings is here greatly elaborated, in a way comparable to the elaboration in 1 Chronicles of the religious features of the reign of David, with whom Hezekiah is immediately compared. His reform starts with no delay ("in the first year . . . in the first month"). Ahaz had "shut up" the doors of the temple (28:24); Hezekiah reopens them, assembles the clergy, and preaches a sermon, setting forth many themes dear to the Chronicler. All that has gone wrong is due to the misuse of the temple; the Levites in particular are to be loyal in carrying out their duty to ensure God's continuing favor. This is a message obviously appropriate for the Chronicler's own day, and the references to the evils experienced make best sense if the exile is in mind. The covenant renewal is perhaps better understood as "a covenant before God" than as a ceremony renewing God's covenant with king and people (Williamson 1982: 354).

The Levites, faithful as ever, respond to the challenge and put right the damage done by Ahaz in terms reminiscent of the account of Josiah's cleansing of the temple in 2 Kings 23. The temple vessels — an important symbol of continuity between the first and second temples (Ackroyd 1987: 56) — were made ready and sanctified.

All of this reaches its climax in a major ceremony of rededication, of sanctuary and people. The general picture is of the rites following what is required in the Torah, for example, Leviticus 1 and 4, but with special emphasis also on the carrying out of the instructions laid down by David. Notice how frequently David and his contemporaries are mentioned in 29:25-30. David had been king of "all Israel"; now the Northern Kingdom had been destroyed (a fact not mentioned but surely taken to be known by the Chronicler), and Hezekiah is once again king of all Israel (v. 24).

The chapter ends with the whole assembly and "all who were of a willing heart" — surely, by implication, everyone — bringing offerings. The Chronicler, like the rest of the biblical tradition, shows no anxiety about animal sacrifice. Unexpectedly, however, one polemic note does cross the account; the priests are overworked, but their real problem is that they were less conscientious than the Levites. This must surely reflect some dispute between different religious groups in the Chronicler's own day. However that may be, all ends happily, with everyone rejoicing over God's gracious and speedy action.

2 Chronicles 30:1-12

One of the strongest reasons for rejecting the commonly held view that Chronicles-Ezra-Nehemiah are one continuous story is found in this section (Williamson 1977: esp. 119-31). Here we find an openness to the inhabitants of the former Northern Kingdom and a willingness to have them join in worship at Jerusalem quite different from the attitude of Ezra 4. Hezekiah is pictured as a second Solomon, ruling over a united kingdom with the holy temple as his base.

From this base Hezekiah addresses "all Israel and Judah." In this context "Israel" once again refers to the former Northern Kingdom, as is made more specific by the reference to the leading tribes, "Ephraim and Manasseh." Passover should properly be kept in the first month (Exod 12:1), but provision was made in Num 9:11 for individuals to observe it in the second month, and that is now extended to the whole community, with an explanation repeating earlier digs at the priests for their slowness. All of Israel, from Beersheba to Dan (the only occasion when the southern- and northernmost boundary points are listed in that order), is to assemble in Jerusalem for Passover. 30:6, like the rest of the section, implies that the Northern Kingdom had fallen to the Assyrians, who are pictured as leaving behind only a "remnant."

"Letters" are sent, but these are no ordinary letters; they are in effect sermons inviting the people to forsake their past wrongdoings which had led to their present plight and to return to the LORD. Such appeals to repentance are also characteristic of the later prophetic collections. But as is often the case with appeals to repentance, not all respond. Most of the northerners mocked the messengers, but a few responded and came to Jerusalem. Judah, by contrast, is pictured as totally loyal. It is very doubtful whether any significance can be discerned in the Chronicler's choice of particular named areas as more responsive than others; his geography does not always inspire confidence.

2 Chronicles 30:13–31:1

Preparations are now complete; the festival can be celebrated. While some scholars have discerned historical traditions underlying this account, it seems more likely to be part of the idealization of Hezekiah, who plays here the role enjoyed by Josiah in 2 Kings. It is unlikely that the feast of Passover/Unleavened Bread was as prominent in the monarchical period as is implied here; it was in the Second Temple period, the Chronicler's own time, that Passover became *the* festival. The preparations described in 30:13-15 had no doubt already taken place. Hebrew does not have a pluperfect tense, so the English verbs could be rendered "had come," or the like. The shame mentioned in v. 15 no doubt refers less to personal shortcomings than to the state into which the temple had fallen under Ahaz. Indeed, ritual shortcomings had not yet been overcome, for not all had cleansed themselves. But it is striking that the Chronicler, for all his supposed absorption with ritual matters, is content for them to participate, with Hezekiah's prayer acting as the inspiration for God to cleanse the people.

At last all can go ahead, and the festival is observed. It is striking that both at the beginning of this section and in the account of the observance itself it is described as "Unleavened Bread"; it has often been thought that Unleavened Bread and Passover were two originally distinct observances which came to be celebrated together. The account of Hezekiah stresses the former, that of Josiah in ch. 35 the latter. In any case, the observance was such a success that a repeat was immediately demanded, in a way reminiscent of Solomon's dedication festival (1 Kgs 8:65; see the NRSV footnote there; the link with 2 Chr 7:8 is less clear). In any case, the comparison with Solomon is made explicit in 30:26. The conclusion of the festival leads to an orgy of destruction inspired by religious fervour, described in a manner more characteristic of the Deuteronomistic historian than the Chronicler. Historically it is scarcely likely that these events will have been feasible in territory occupied by the Assyrians.

2 Chronicles 31:2-21

Hezekiah's concerns continue to be religious — the proper ordering of the temple and its ministry. Before dealing with political matters, our author's intention is to present him as an ideal religious leader and reformer. First of all the proper responsibilities of priests and Levites are laid down; then the king's personal generosity is stressed in a way reminiscent of Solomon (8:12). The inhabitants of Jerusalem are bidden to contribute, but news of this command spreads more widely, and all the people of Israel are pictured as contributing generously to the needs of the temple. In its literary form this is not a sermon, but the story is surely aimed at reminding the people of the Chronicler's day of the generosity of their forebears, with a clear hint that they should follow such an example. This theme of the willingness of the people to contribute all that was needed and more is found frequently in the HB (cf. Exod. 36:2-7).

Such generosity produces a need for storage, and appropriate chambers are prepared. As is often his practice at times he regarded as being of particular significance, the Chronicler then provides a list of the names of those taking part. The origin of such lists is quite unknown; many of the names are known from other levitical lists, but they are no more than names. 31:16 is curious: the first phrase is translated very differently in different versions (NEB/REB, "irrespective of their registration"); and it is odd to find a reference to three-year-old children. The point may be that when young children of priestly families were weaned they were enrolled on some special list (cf. v. 18), which implied that the obligations of priestly status were binding upon them. Whatever the details, the reforms win the wholehearted approval of the Chronicler. So far we have no inkling that the country was under severe political pressure during much of Hezekiah's reign.

2 Chronicles 32:1-23

It is to the political crisis that the author now turns. Sennacherib's invasion of Judah in 701 BC is known to us both from his own annals and from the detailed description in 2 Kings 18–19. Here it is treated as an appendix to the more important religious reforms. 32:2-6 describe Hezekiah's military preparations, regarded here as a praiseworthy supplement to the call for trust in God which will follow and offering a comparison with David (1 Chr 11:7-9). Isa 22:8-11 was much more scathing about the folly of such preparations. For the Chronicler, too, real preparation for war meant trust in God, and Hezekiah is provided with a sermon which is a kind of pastiche of scriptural quotations and gives the necessary encouragement to the people.

As in 2 Kings, Sennacherib sends envoys to Jerusalem mocking the efforts of Hezekiah to save his people and likening the LORD to the useless gods of other nations whom the Assyrians had overthrown. The Chronicler takes pains to point out the blasphemy inherent in such a comparison (32:19).

The prophet Isaiah is now introduced without further explanation as joining with Hezekiah in the only proper response to such profanity: prayer. And of course their prayer is answered. The Assyrians are defeated by means of an angel, and Sennacherib himself is killed when he returns to his own land. The drama of the 2 Kings account, with 185,000 Assyrians killed at the very gates of Jerusalem, is played down. Here the Assyrians are presumably still at Lachish (cf. 32:9), and only their military leaders suffer. Sennacherib's death is also foreshortened; it was in fact twenty years later that he was killed. But these are unimportant details for our author, compared with the fact that the LORD has saved Hezekiah and his people; somewhat improbably he "was exalted in the sight of all nations."

2 Chronicles 32:24-32

Even Hezekiah, however, was not beyond reproach. Illness was regarded by the Chronicler as a test of one's faithfulness (cf. Asa, 16:12), and though Hezekiah prayed and was given a sign, in some unspecified way he became proud. In its present brief presentation it is difficult to see what this means; the story needs to be clarified by reference to 2 Kings 20 and Isaiah 38, which set it forth in fuller detail. But it is no more than a passing glitch; he humbled himself and the wrath of God was postponed. Probably 32:25 is a pointer to the exile, as *the* manifestation of the wrath of God; Hezekiah's humbling himself allows a temporary reprieve.

The last verses sketch the prosperity of Hezekiah in a manner very different from, for example, 2 Kgs 18:14-16. Here, as with Solomon, with whom Hezekiah is surely being compared, material prosperity is a clear sign of divine favor. It has usually been thought that the reference in 32:30 to the redirection of the waters is to be linked with the "Siloam Tunnel," still visible in Jerusalem, though how much of the work goes back to Hezekiah's time is disputed. The reference to Babylonian envoys makes little sense without reference to the fuller account in 2 Kings 20. The long treatment of Hezekiah then concludes by mentioning the proper burial ceremonies and giving a twofold literary reference. The "vision" of Isaiah is probably an allusion to some form of the book of Isaiah (cf. Isa 1:1), whereas the "Book of the Kings" may be our books of Kings.

2 Chronicles 33:1-9

It is appropriate to divide the treatment of Manasseh into two parts because of the extraordinary transformation of his character which is described. In 2 Kgs Manasseh is the paradigm wicked king, the sins of whose reign were so great that no subsequent amendment could prevent divine punishment (2 Kings 23:25-26). There is no hint in that account that Manasseh changed his ways. In Chronicles, however, as we shall see in the next section, a remarkable change took place. It is possible that the great length of Manasseh's reign (55 years) was felt to need explaining, since a long reign normally implied divine favor.

This section can be dealt with very briefly since it follows 2 Kgs 21:1-9 very closely. The religious rites which the biblical authors found so abhorrent may have had their roots in the Assyrian requirement that subject kings (which Manasseh in practice was) should conform to their practices, but the way they are described here is purely conventional — these were the evils against which kings throughout the monarchy should have guarded.

2 Chronicles 33:10-25

The verses here dealing with Manasseh have no parallel in Kings. Instead of directly punishing Manasseh for his refusal to listen to warnings, the LORD (who is, of course, pictured as the real director of Assyrian military operations) has him brought to Babylon. While it is certainly possible that there is a historical foundation for this, perhaps related to various uprisings against the Assyrian king Asshur-bani-pal, it is more likely that it lacks any historical basis. In particular, bringing Manasseh to Babylon can be seen as prefiguring the exile of the whole people (in the Chronicler's view) to Babylon less than a century later. More important, Manasseh repented of his wrongdoing. For this Kings offers no parallel, and it is in any case not easy to pass historical judgments on such a development. The Chronicler pictures Manasseh as fulfilling the model laid down in 7:14 (Williamson 1982: 393-94). Manasseh's repentance is followed by the restoration of Jerusalem (a frequent concomitant of divine favor in Chronicles) and religious reform. It is curious that this account of reform has not led to any modification in the description of the evils confronting Josiah (ch. 35), which according to Kings were directly caused by Manasseh's wickedness. In any case, the basic point, surely intended for the Chronicler's own audience, was that repentance brought a renewal of divine favor.

The concluding summary of Manasseh's reign has been significantly modified from that in Kings because of the dramatic change in Manasseh's behavior. In particular there are two references to his prayer (33:18, 19), and this provided the model for the apocryphal book, the Prayer of Manasseh.

Virtually nothing is known of the brief reign of Amon, though the reference to conspiracy has provided ample opportunity for historical speculation. The Chronicler has simply followed the account in 2 Kings 21, with the modification made necessary by Manasseh's repentance.

2 Chronicles 34:1-7

In 2 Kings Josiah was the one who most fully lived out the ideals of the Davidic line (2 Kgs 22:2; 23:25). For the Chronicler that role has been played by Hezekiah. His evaluation of Josiah is still positive, but his reign lacks the crucial significance which it had for the author of 2 Kings.

After two verses which follow 2 Kings very closely, we find a new development in 34:3-7. In Kings nothing is said of Josiah's reign before the great reform which dominates the account and which began in his eighteenth year. Here an earlier reform, dating from his eighth year, is reported. In fact, the change is less dramatic than it might appear, for much of the religious destruction described here finds a place elsewhere in the Kings account. Therefore, it seems more likely that the Chronicler has rearranged the material there than that he had access to a different source. As in 15:9, Manasseh, Ephraim and Simeon are bracketed together, in defiance of geography; an important theme in the account of Josiah's reign, as with that of Hezekiah, is that the territory of the old Northern Kingdom is once more linked with Jerusalem.

2 Chronicles 34:8-33

This long section follows 2 Kgs 22:3–23:3 very closely, and the commentary on 2 Kings must be consulted for its full significance. The events of the "eighteenth year" of Josiah's reign, so dramatically set forth in Kings, are here treated as no more than part of a series which had already begun in his eighth year. 34:9 and 21 repeat the emphasis we have already noted on the participation of those from the north, supervised, of course, by Levites.

The finding of the "book of the law," the climax of the story in 2 Kings 22, is here reported in a much more matter-of-fact way, as of something chanced upon during the course of repair work. It is widely thought that in 2 Kings the "book" is presented as being all or part of Deuteronomy; here it seems more likely that the Chronicler envisaged the whole Pentateuch. Whereas in Kings it was immediately read twice, here the reference is only to "reading in it" (34:18; the NRSV misrepresents the Hebrew here). In other respects, however, the reaction of the various officials and of the king himself to the implications of the book follows 2 Kings very closely — surprisingly so at times, as when we compare the prediction of Josiah's peaceful death (v. 28) with the account given in 35:22-24. Also to a much greater extent than in Kings, the finding of the book and the reaction to it are presented as preliminary to the account of the Passover celebration.

2 Chronicles 35:1-19

We have seen enough of the Chronicler's concerns to know that the central element in his depiction of any acceptable king is likely to be the keeping of a festival in the temple. And so it is here: Josiah's Passover is the climax of his reign. The much briefer account in 2 Kgs 23:21-23 is used at the beginning and end of this section, but the greater part of it is probably a composition by the Chronicler, reflecting the practice of his own day. Our knowledge of Second Temple liturgical practice is very slight, and this may provide one of our best guides to it, though no doubt in an idealized form. (Was such a slaughter of livestock regular custom?) As is still often the case with religious and other formal occasions, the preparation seems to become more important than the event itself and is described in greater detail (35:2-9 as against vv. 10-15). Very striking once again is the emphasis on the Levites, who are here formally described as those who "taught all Israel" (v. 3), a role often implied but not specifically stated elsewhere. The description ends with a comparison familiar from such occasions. Just as each of the modern Olympic Games is conventionally claimed as the best there has ever been, so this was the finest Passover there had ever been throughout the monarchical period. The reference to Samuel is a little unexpected since he plays no significant part in Chronicles, but he appears to be pictured as the inaugurator of the monarchy in Israel.

2 Chronicles 35:20-27

As we have seen, the Chronicler certainly envisaged that bad kings could repent. Conversely, good kings could go wrong, and that is what has happened here. The account reads as if the death of Josiah immediately followed the celebration of Passover; in fact there was a gap of twelve years, but this was not an issue which would have concerned the Chronicler (cf. the death of Sennacherib in 32:21). That Josiah's death, cut off in his prime when he seemed to have done everything right, was a problem in Kings is clear enough; the Chronicler has begun to develop a theological explanation of it.

It is possible to reconstruct something of the political situation at the time, with Pharaoh Neco attempting to prop up the declining Assyrian power against Babylonian inroads and Josiah hoping to establish a stronger position beyond the narrow confines of Judah and going as far as Megiddo in the former Northern Kingdom. But these are not the Chronicler's concerns. For him Neco, somewhat unexpectedly, is pictured as a prophet of God (the divine name is of course not used), warning Josiah to desist from his warlike ambitions. But Josiah does not listen to this prophetic warning; instead he acts in the same wicked and foolish way as had Ahab of Israel (18:29), disguising himself (Coggins 1991: 59). Like Ahab he was wounded and had to be carried in his chariot away from the battlefield to die (18:33-34). Thus we see part of the Chronicler's explanation of Josiah's unhappy end; the comparison with the fate of the house of Ahab, begun in 2 Kings with reference to Manasseh (2 Kgs 21:13), is carried a stage further. Josiah had imitated that wicked ruler and earned the same fate.

But there is more to be said about Josiah. He was not simply a bad ruler who had received his deserts. His falling away was a real cause of lament. Jeremiah was known to have spoken favorably of Josiah (Jer 22:15-16), so it was appropriate to picture that prophet, now regarded as a prominent figure in the last days of Judah, as lamenting the fate of Josiah. It is much more likely that this was what Jeremiah "must" have done than that the Chronicler had knowledge of an actual lament; and it is also unlikely that the "Laments" referred to are our book of Lamentations; the name is different and there is nothing in Lamentations which could be taken to refer to Josiah. The final verdict on the king, despite his lapse, is a favorable one.

2 Chronicles 36:1-21

The run down to exile is now described with remarkable brevity; perhaps the story was well enough known not to need setting out again. It is told in more detail both in 2 Kings and in Jeremiah, which had probably reached its final form by the time of the Chronicler. So even the usual death notices for the different kings are omitted as we are taken through the unhappy story. Only in 36:6-7 are there significant departures from the more extended account in 2 Kings. At v. 6 it is said that Jehoiakim was bound and taken to Babylon. Historically, though not impossible, this is unlikely; it may have given rise to the legend in Dan 1:1 of a siege of Jerusalem at this time. In 36:7, along with v. 10, we note the Chronicler's renewed interest in the temple vessels. Their removal to the royal palace in Babylon provides the motif for the story of Belshazzar's feast (Daniel 5) as well as for the return of the vessels in Ezra 1. Jehoiachin's age at accession is given here as "eight," but nearly all commentators agree that this is likely to be a scribal error for "eighteen," as in 2 Kgs 24:8. An objective historian would be likely to regard the fall of Jerusalem under Jehoiachin, probably in 597 BC, as the real end of the kingdom of Judah, but for the Chronicler the destruction of the temple was the real horror, and so the story continues without stressing the events of that year.

Zedekiah was in practice no more than Nebuchadnezzar's nominee as ruler, but he is treated by the Chronicler as another in the succession of evil kings. His reign is, however, treated in slightly greater detail because of the terrible events which brought it to an end. So Jeremiah (already mentioned in 35:25 as a lamenter) is now pictured as the last in the series of prophets and other messengers referred to in 36:15-16 warning the kings of the folly of their behavior. He features again at the end of this section in a third capacity: as a predicter of future events, in the sense that "prophet" has come to have in popular usage.

The Chronicler probably wished the community of his own day to be loyal to their rulers (at that time probably the Persians; cf. 36:22-23) so that they could pursue their religious duties undisturbed. So both Josiah (35:22), and still more Zedekiah here, are condemned for their failure to obey the proper foreign ruler. But his is not the only fault; priests and people (though, interestingly, not the Levites) are condemned for faithlessness, in particular against the temple. This, rather than the sin of Manasseh in particular, as in 2 Kings, is seen as the cause of the exile.

So the story ends with the destruction of Jerusalem.

The death of many people was bad enough; still worse for the Chronicler, it would appear, was the removal of the remaining vessels and — ultimate horror — the destruction of the house of God itself. This is a much briefer account than that found in 2 Kings 25, but it brings out the Chronicler's characteristic concerns. In his view all survivors were carried into exile. Historically this is most unlikely, and Jer 52:28-30 gives a very different picture. But it is an important theological concern of the Chronicler that the entire true community should have gone through the experience of exile as an essential preliminary to being restored to enjoy God's favor in his land and city. For the Chronicler "exile" was more than physical translocation; a spiritual element was involved (Coggins 1989: 165-66).

Even the land itself is pictured as undergoing a period of special observance. The Chronicler develops the picture of a land keeping sabbath sketched in Lev 26:34-35; it owes more to religious idealism than to any consideration of the social and economic probabilities of the case. It is not helpful to speculate on what actual period of "seventy years" was in mind; the point is the fulfilling of various references in Jeremiah to such a length of time (Jer 25:11; 29:10). A whole human lifetime may well be envisaged. In any case, the vital impact of 36:20-21 is to stress that beyond the disaster lies hope, and that hope is associated with the rise of Persia.

2 Chronicles 36:22-23

Those who suppose that Chronicles and Ezra-Nehemiah were originally separate regard these two verses as a later borrowing from Ezra 1 to show how the implicit hopes of 36:20-21 were actually fulfilled. If Chronicles-Ezra-Nehemiah were originally one work, then the events described in these two verses can be seen as so important an element in the ongoing story as to warrant repetition. They form the vital beginning of Ezra (see the commentary on Ezra for fuller discussion); they provide a hopeful conclusion to the story of Chronicles.

Bibliography. Ackroyd, P. R. 1973, *I and II Chronicles, Ezra, Nehemiah,* Torch Bible Commentaries, London: SCM • Ackroyd, P. R. 1987, "The Temple Vessels: A Continuity Theme," in his *Studies in the Religious Tradition of the Old Testament,* London: SCM, 46-60 • Auld, A. G. 1978, "Cities of Refuge in Israelite Tradition," *JSOT* 10:26-40 • Auld, A. G. 1994, *Kings without Privilege: David and Moses in the Story of the Bible's Kings,* Edinburgh: T. & T. Clark • Braun, R. L. 1986, *1 Chronicles,* WBC 14, Waco: Word • Coggins, R. J. 1976, *The First and Second Books of the Chronicles,* CBC, Cambridge: Cambridge University • Coggins, R. J. 1989, "The Origins of the Jewish Diaspora," in R. E. Clements, ed., *The World of Ancient Israel,* Cambridge: Cambridge University • Coggins, R. J. 1991, "On Kings and Disguises," *JSOT* 50:55-62 • de Vries, S. J. 1989, *1 and 2 Chronicles,* FOTL 11, Grand Rapids: Eerdmans • Dillard, R. B. 1984, "The Literary Structure of the Chronicler's Solomon Narrative," *JSOT* 30:85-93 • Dillard, R. B. 1987, *2 Chronicles,* WBC 15, Waco: Word • Graham, M. P., K. G. Hoglund, and S. L. McKenzie, eds. 1997, *The Chronicler as Historian,* Sheffield: Sheffield Academic • Hill, C. 1993, *The English Bible and the Seventeenth-Century Revolution,* London: Allen Lane • Japhet, S. 1968, "The Supposed Common Authorship of Chronicles and Ezra-Nehemiah Investigated Anew," *VT* 18: 330-71 • Japhet, S. 1989, *The Ideology of the Book of Chronicles and Its Place in Biblical Thought,* Beiträge zur Erforschung des Alten Testaments und des Antiken Judentums 9, Frankfurt am Main: Peter Lang • Japhet, S. 1993, *I and II Chronicles: A Commentary,* OTL, London: SCM • Johnson, M. D. 1968, *The Purpose of the Biblical Genealogies with Special Reference to the Setting of the Genealogies of Jesus,* SNTSMS 8, Cambridge: Cambridge University • Jones, G. H. 1993, *1 and 2 Chronicles,* Old Testament Guides, Sheffield: Sheffield Academic • McKenzie, S. L. 1985, *The Chronicler's Use of the Deuteronomic History,* HSM, Atlanta: Scholars • Mason, R. A. 1990, *Preaching the Tradition,* Cambridge: Cambridge University • Myers, J. M. 1965a, *1 Chronicles,* AB 12, Garden City, N.Y.: Doubleday • Myers, J. M. 1965b, *2 Chronicles,* AB 13, Garden City, N.Y.: Doubleday • Schniedewind, W. M. 1995, *The Word of God in Transition: From Prophet to Exegete in the Second Temple Period,* JSOTSup 197, Sheffield: Sheffield Academic • Williamson, H. G. M. 1977, *Israel in the Books of Chronicles,* Cambridge: Cambridge University • Williamson, H. G. M. 1979, "The Origins of the Twenty-Four Priestly Courses: A Study of 1 Chronicles xxiii–xxvii," in J. A. Emerton, ed., *Studies in the Historical Books of the Old Testament,* VTSup 30, Leiden: Brill, 251-68 • Williamson, H. G. M. 1982, *1 and 2 Chronicles,* NCBC, London: Marshall, Morgan and Scott • Wright, J. W. 1993, "The Innocence of David in 1 Chronicles 21," *JSOT* 60:87-105.

Ezra

Lester L. Grabbe

INTRODUCTION

Literary Structure of Ezra-Nehemiah

In the Hebrew Bible (HB) Ezra and Nehemiah have been treated as one book. The Greek version of the two books (usually known as Esdras B) also takes them as one literary unit. As we will discuss ("Introduction" to Nehemiah, 320), the Ezra and Nehemiah traditions seem to have developed independently but were brought together by an editor in these two books. The book of Ezra is actually made up of two separate stories. There is the account of the initial return and rebuilding of the temple (Ezra 1–6), and then there is the story of Ezra himself (Ezra 7–10). The book of Nehemiah is essentially one story, but it has a number of chapters which interrupt the narrative flow to some extent and look like a set of miscellaneous lists and the like (Nehemiah 7–12).

A number of parallel elements link the first and second parts of Ezra as well as the two books in their present form. The list of those who supposedly returned originally is given twice (Ezra 2 par. Nehemiah 7). The reading of the law by Ezra would naturally follow Ezra 10 but is now found as part of the book of Nehemiah (Nehemiah 8). The question of marriage with the "peoples of the land" is addressed by both Ezra (Ezra 9–10) and Nehemiah (Nehemiah 9–10). Joshua and Zerubbabel rebuild the temple despite opposition from the surrounding peoples (Ezra 3–6); Nehemiah rebuilds the wall, also in adverse circumstances (Nehemiah 3–6). A return of exiles takes place under Joshua and Zerubbabel (Ezra 1) and under Ezra (Ezra 7–8).

As they presently stand, the two books supply a more or less coherent sequence of events. Ezra ends on a rather gloomy note if it is expected to stand on its own, but this is no problem if Nehemiah 1 immediately follows. Reading from Ezra 1 to Nehemiah 13, one sees the providence of God in bringing "Israel" back to the land rebuilding the temple, and rebuilding Jerusalem. Running alongside God's solicitude for his people is the continual threat from the "foreigners" in the land, who oppose the building of the temple (though they initially offer to help with it) and the repair of Jerusalem's walls. They pose the threat of intermarriage, assimilation, and religious apostasy for the returnees. The narrative ends with Nehemiah driving out the son of the high priest, who has married the daughter of Sanballat.

Sources and Historicity

The author of Ezra drew on a variety of sources. Ezra 1 is difficult and may have had more than one source. Ezra 2 is some sort of preexisting list. It has been argued that the basis of Ezra 3–6 is solely the books of Haggai and Zechariah and some alleged Persian documents (Williamson 1983; 1985: xxiv). It has long been assumed that an "Ezra memoir" was the basis of Ezra 7–10. This is possible, but, if so, it has been submerged under a great deal of editing and reinterpretation. The historical Ezra is very difficult to get at through the weight of tradition (Grabbe 1994). For this reason, the idea of an Ezra memoir as a source is rather unhelpful.

At a number of points, allegedly official Persian decrees and documents are quoted. All but 1:2-4 are in Aramaic, the administrative language of the Persians. The authenticity of these documents has been debated intensely at different times over the past century. Many scholars accept them as authentic and proceed from there, but others have doubted whether they are genuine. Through my own study I have found that some of the documents exhibit an earlier stage of the language, whereas others are a mixture of earlier and later forms. The Aramaic narrative in which they are set generally has the later forms. This suggests that original documents may have been the basis of what we find in Ezra in a number of cases, but the original text has been reworked to fit the outlook and purposes of the writer. Further information can be found in discussions on the individual documents at 1:2-4, 4:11-22, and 5:6-17.

These problems with sources affect the question of the book's historicity. Its theological message can be appreciated regardless of whether the events took place as described. But if one wants to know whether, for example, Ezra really came with the authority of the Persian king, as Ezra 7 says, we have to ask questions about sources and credibility. The commentary will take up such questions in a number of passages. For further information, see also Grabbe 1991; 1992: 136-38; 1998.

Time and Place of Writing

Determining when and where Ezra was written is very difficult. The story itself is set in the Persian period. Various Persian kings are named, such as Cyrus, Darius, and Artaxerxes. But there were three kings by the name of Darius and three by the name of Artaxerxes. The Aramaic of the narrative fits best in what is conventionally called Middle Aramaic (c. 300 BC to AD 200), though some parts of the documents show an earlier form of Aramaic with Achaemenid features (see above under "Sources and Historicity," 313). Apart from the Aramaic linguistic features there are no specific indications of the Greek period, but neither is there anything to require a date earlier than the Greek period. The author of Sirach (Ecclesiasticus) (writing a little after 200 BC) does not seem to know the unified composition of Ezra and Nehemiah. Although the unified book of Ezra and Nehemiah may well be earlier than Sirach, it had apparently not been around long enough to become authoritative (Ezra is completely ignored, which would be impossible if the unified composition was known and authoritative for Sirach). This suggests a composition sometime during the Ptolemaic period. Everything is written from the perspective of Judah, which is the most likely place of writing.

COMMENTARY

Cyrus's Decree and the Initial Return of Exiles to Judah (Ezra 1)

The first chapter sets the scene for the entire section chs. 1–6: the decree allowing the return to Jerusalem, the initial return led by Sheshbazzar, and the restoration of the sacred temple vessels. This chapter marks the transition from the books of Chronicles, which ended in the destruction of Jerusalem. Ezra 1 reverses the misfortunes recorded in the last part of Chronicles and sets the stage for the complete restoration of the Jewish community in Judah. (At some point the first few verses of Ezra were also added to the end of 2 Chronicles, but that only reinforces the argument here.)

The decree of Cyrus is essential. The Jews did not just wander back or slip away from Babylon in the middle of the night. On the contrary, God caused the very ruler of the new Persian Empire to give official permission for the Jewish people to return to their land — and immediately, in Cyrus's very first year of rule. Furthermore, this was not just an accident or a whim of Cyrus himself: it was a specific fulfillment of the seventy-years prophecy of Jeremiah (Jer 25:11-14; 29:10-14), though one might also think of the prophecy about Cyrus in Deutero-Isaiah (Isa 45:13). This ties in very well with the return of the temple vessels. Their removal was part of the desecration of the temple; therefore, their return was an important indication of its restoration and reconsecration. The one who brings them back, along with a contingent of settlers, is Sheshbazzar. His title and function are not mentioned, and many questions are left open, such as his relationship to Joshua and Zerubbabel. This raises questions about the structure of the book and matters of historicity (see on 5:6-17).

1:2-4 Cyrus's decree is not just verbal but is also put in writing (1:1). It is given in Hebrew, contrary to the other alleged Persian documents, which are all in Aramaic, and, indeed, to normal Achaemenid bureaucratic practice. This and the blatant Jewish religious language are two of the reasons why many scholars have concluded that this decree cannot be genuine.

1:7-8 The return of the temple vessels is a key theme here at the beginning. Despite the fact that they would probably have been melted down by the Babylonians after the capture of Jersualem, as indeed 2 Kgs 24:13 and 25:13-17 imply, the story not only asserts their continued existence but even enumerates their exact number as 5,400. The writer clearly wants us to understand that the vessels were miraculously preserved and sets the scene for their use as a vital link between the destroyed "temple of Solomon" and the new temple to be built under Zerubbabel.

The Genealogy and List of Those Who Returned (Ezra 2)

The writer has shown the importance of exact detail in getting his point across with the vessels in ch. 1. It is not enough that the people are said to return to the land: they are listed by genealogy, family, and place of habitation. Who could doubt the veracity of the author with such detailed data at his fingertips? This chapter does more than affirm the reality of the return, however; it also provides an important witness to the preeminence of certain families, the right of some to serve in the temple, and the certification of ownership of the land. Recent studies have shown that genealogies may have a variety of functions and not just show blood descent as viewed from a modern perspective. Genealogies in traditional societies often show social and power relationships rather than biological relationships.

The genealogies in this chapter seem to function as authenticators of who has a right to be classified as an "Israelite"; for this reason, the *assertion* (whether true or not) of physical descent is important because those who could not prove their genealogy were excluded (2:59-63). This is especially true of temple personnel because service in the temple was purely by birth. But the mixed nature of the list is indicated in vv. 20-35, which represent place of settlement rather than ancestral line.

Rebuilding of the Temple Begins (Ezra 3)

The people gather for their first religious observance, the feast of Tabernacles or Booths (Heb. *sukkot*) in the seventh month (September/October). The chief protagonists in Ezra 1–6 are Zerubbabel and Joshua the high priest, yet they appear for the first time in Ezra 3. Just as interesting is the fact that Zerubbabel's office is never named in Ezra. He must have been an important figure, but only in Hag 1:1, 14; 2:2 do we learn that he is "governor of Judah" *(paḥat Yehudah)*. Similarly, Joshua is not specifically said to be the high priest here, but we know this from other passages (Hag 1:1, 12, 14; 2:2; Zech 3:1). Why does not Ezra so identify him? One reason seems to be to place greater emphasis on the actions of the community and its leaders as a whole and not just those of the two main leaders: this is especially evident in 3:8; 4:2-3; 5:2, 5. Also, in 3:2 it is "Zerubbabel and his brothers" and "Jeshua and his brothers the priests." See further at 6:7 and the articles by S. Japhet.

The festival is observed "as prescribed in the law of Moses" (3:2) with the appropriate sacrifices. The sacrifices are not enumerated, but they are said to be offered as they are supposed to be. This includes the twice daily or *tamid* sacrifice (Exod 29:38-42; Lev 6:12-16; Num 28:3-8). The performance of this sacrifice was extremely important, and when it ceased, it had cosmic implications (Dan 8:11-14). According to Num 29:12-39, a different sequence of sacrifices is offered on each day of the feast of Tabernacles, and the text evidently alludes to something like this (though we cannot be sure that the "law of Moses" referred to here is precisely the same as our present Pentateuch). The important point is that the law was followed precisely, even though the temple itself had not been rebuilt but only the altar set up again.

3:6 The people began to offer sacrifices from the first day of the seventh month. This is a significant figure since in some periods the new year began with the seventh month. Possibly the only more appropriate time for beginning would be the first day of the first month.

3:7-13 This section describes the laying of the foundations of the new temple to replace the destroyed "Solomonic" temple. It emphasizes the prominent place of the priests and Levites in the work. They supervise it (3:8-9) and have an integral part in the ceremony of dedication. In the books of Chronicles the Levites are responsible for singing and music in the temple (1 Chr 23:5; 25; 2 Chr 5:12; 7:6). There is a delay of several months between the first offering of sacrifices and the laying of the foundations (from the seventh month to the second month of the next year; since the solar-lunar calendar could have thirteen months, the difference could be either seven or eight months).

3:12-13 Not surprisingly, the temple of Zerubbabel is persistently represented as inferior to the temple of Solomon in early Jewish literature (*1 Enoch* 89:73; Tob 14:5).

Adversaries Get the Rebuilding Stopped (Ezra 4)

In a story one cannot expect everything to go smoothly. We can anticipate a threat to the protagonists which creates a necessary tension to keep up the readers' interest. Ch. 4 introduces the "adversaries of Judah and Benjamin," who seem to have no other motive than to harm the new state. Real life is much more complex, of course, but a black-and-white picture of the "good guys" and the "bad guys" is frequently found in such stories. This is not to suggest that the story has no basis in reality, but it has been assimilated to a literary pattern, a fact which we must keep in mind in evaluating its historicity. A point continually made about such people is they are "foreign," that is, outside the new community being established by the returnees. The fact is that in many cases these were descendants of the Israelites and Jews who had not been taken captive. A central assumption of the book seems to be that only those who returned from captivity were genuine Israelites, and they returned to an empty land. This "empty land" was in fact filled with the descendants of those who had not been taken captive but had been left on the land by the Babylonians. This "myth of the empty land" explains a number of the actions taken in the book (cf. Barstad 1996).

4:2 The "adversaries" are identified with people who had been brought in by King Esarhaddon of Assyria (680-669 BC). There is no reference to such transporting of peoples into the area of Samaria in either the Bible or any of the known ancient Near Eastern literature. The Assyrians began a policy of deporting rebellious peoples to Assyria and transplanting other settlers in their place, a practice which was continued by the Babylonians and Persians. 2 Kings 17 describes how "all Israel" was taken captive to Assyria, and peoples from Mesopotamia were settled in their place. The statement that "all Israel" was taken captive is a blatant exaggeration since only a portion of the population was taken away (as we know from the inscriptions of Sargon II, who carried out the deportation). This is partially acknowledged in the case of the Babylonian captivity in the statement that "the poorest in the land" were allowed to stay (2 Kgs 25:12). Although it is possible that some of the people in the region of Samaria were part of a settlement under Esarhaddon, the bias of the writer against "the adversaries" means that this could be a purely literary device to brand these people as "foreigners." It should be noted that these opponents are worshipers of Yahweh, the God of Israel (4:2).

4:4 The "people of the land" is used a number of times in Ezra and Nehemiah to mean people who were not part of the new Jewish community. The implication is that they were non-Israelites and "foreign," which was probably false (see above). The term "peoples of the land" was used later in rabbinic literature to designate those ordinary Jews who were not careful to apply strict rabbinic laws of purity; however, the term is otherwise used of Jews rather than Gentiles, as here.

4:4-7 This attempt to subvert the community of returnees is said to last from the time of Cyrus (died 530 BC) to the reign of Darius, presumably Darius I (522-486 BC), but it then goes on to mention Ahasuerus (probably Xerxes [486-465 BC]), and finally settles on Artaxerxes (465-424 BC). As a result of accusations, a decree of Artaxerxes (4:17-22) stops the building of the temple "until the second year of the reign of King Darius of Persia" (v. 24). This is all very puzzling because a decree of Artaxerxes, who lived long after Cyrus and Darius, stops a project in the reign of Cyrus and keeps it suspended until the reign of Darius, while the reign of Cambyses (530-522) is completely ignored. Despite some attempts to defend the account here, there is clearly a good deal of confusion. Whatever the ultimate cause of the confusion (e.g., misplaced documents), the final author/editor was not very clear about the sequence of Persian kings or of Persian history and chronology.

4:8-10 The text changes from Hebrew to Aramaic at this point (the Aramaic begins with v. 8). It is not surprising that the alleged Persian documents are in Aramaic since the normal administrative language of the Persian Empire was Aramaic, but the narrative around the documents is also Aramaic. (See under "Sources and Historicity" in the Introduction, 313.)

4:9-10 The "adversaries" here include Persian officials, evidently, though for good measure a miscellaneous listing of "judges, envoys, officials, Persians," and the like, down to "the rest of the nations" is given. These "nations" were supposed to have been brought in by Osnappar as settlers in the old kingdom of Israel. There is no king "Osnapper" of Assyria, though many think this is corrupt for Ashurbanipal (668-627 BC). If so, we have people brought into Samaria not only by Esarhaddon but also by his son Ashurbanipal. Again, whatever the historical truth of this statement, here is another attempt to picture those who oppose the protagonists with being foreign.

4:11-22 There are several puzzling things about these two writings, said to be a letter sent by local Persian officials to the king and the king's reply. The contents do not fit their context at several points. It is the building of the temple which is of concern in Ezra 4, yet the letters say nothing about the temple; however, they talk about the rebuilding of the *city* and the *walls*. Also, the alleged senders of the letter in v. 7 are not the same as those in vv. 8, 9, 17, and 23. The reply by Artaxerxes refers to the kings of Israel who ruled over the whole province of Beyond-the-River, that is, the whole region to the west of the Euphrates. This is puzzling because no Israelite king ever ruled over this entire region. The statement that Jerusalem is known in the records to be particularly rebellious is also dubious since Jerusalem was no more rebellious than any other city. We have no evidence that under Persian rule Jerusalem was at all rebellious, so where did Artaxerxes find evidence for Jerusalem's supposed past history of sedition? From a linguistic point of view, the letters contain mainly later grammatical forms, suggesting that the letters have been thoroughly worked over, whatever historical documents might have originally existed. Finally, as already noted, a letter from the time of Artaxerxes is used to stop a project under Cyrus, who reigned almost three-quarters of a century earlier.

The Rebuilding Is Resumed, and Persian Officials Investigate (Ezra 5)

This chapter continues the story begun in ch. 4. Having allowed the work to lapse for a number of years, the Jews are stirred by the two prophets Haggai and Zechariah to resume the rebuilding of the temple. These prophets have books in their names, though it is not clear whether the author of Ezra takes the information here from the books themselves (as some scholars believe) or whether he has another source of information. This time the Persian administration serves as the benefactor of the Jews, investigating the charges in a fair way; however, the Jewish leaders do not let up with their building even while their situation is being taken before the king (v. 5).

5:6-17 The letter said to be from Tattenai has some differences from the documents elsewhere in Ezra. We know that there actually was such an official known from Persian sources (Olmstead 1944). Also, this letter mentions data not found elsewhere in the book. It emphasizes Sheshbazzar, whose role is briefly mentioned in Ezra 1 but then forgotten. Sheshbazzar is said to have "laid the foundations of the house of God," even though in Ezra 3 this work is ascribed to Zerubbabel and Joshua; Sheshbazzar is additionally said to be "governor," showing that he was an important individual and further drawing attention to how the rest of the book slights him and his activities. The Aramaic grammatical features of the letter tend to be the earlier ones, also arguing that this version is more likely to be authentic than some of the other documents.

The Temple Completed with the Persian King's Blessing (Ezra 6)

Ezra 1–6 reaches its climax in this chapter, and the story is brought to a successful conclusion. Not only does the faithfulness of the Jews triumph but they receive the official support of the Persian government. Their enemies are officially rebuked and completely routed; even the officials themselves seem to be addressed rather abruptly, as if being rebuked for doing their job (6:6). The cost of rebuilding is taken on by the state itself (vv. 8-10) — what greater authentication could the Jews have for their endeavors!

6:2-5 The "memorandum" seems to be an authentic form of document used in Persian administration; nevertheless, there are problems with this particular one. The temple described has only two dimensions, height and breadth but no length, and the height in proportion to the width is rather peculiar. It is approximately 90 feet high (or about 27 meters) but also 90 feet wide and an unknown length. Thus, to explain the difficulty as purely a textual corruption (i.e., that the length of the building has been accidentally left out at some point) is insufficient because the building is an unlikely height.

6:7, 8, 14, 16 In chs. 3-5 the leaders are Zerubbabel and Joshua, even though they share their work with other leaders of the community and the people (3:2, 8; 4:2-3; 5:2, 5). In ch. 6 these two leaders are not mentioned; instead, the focus is on the "elders of the Jews" (vv. 8, 14) and "the people of Israel, the priests and the Levites, and the rest of the returned exiles" (v. 16). The text definitely wishes the reader to see collective responsibility and leadership, not just a focus on Joshua and Zerubbabel.

6:13-15 This section stresses that the Israelite God used the Persian administration and even famous kings such as Cyrus, Darius, and Artaxerxes to carry out his purpose (cf. also v. 22). The date of finishing (the sixth year of Darius, or about 516 BC) is often taken as trustworthy. It may be, but this is not at all certain. The writer does not seem to be aware that there was more than one Darius and more than one Artaxerxes, and the confusions in Ezra 4 suggest that the writer did not have very good information about Persian history.

6:16-22 The ultimate interest of the writer is in religious matters, including those relating to the cult. Ezra 1–6 is primarily a story about the rebuilding of the temple under difficult circumstances. This passage rounds off these chapters by emphasizing how the work of the temple, the priesthood, and the cult have been properly established and are now functioning. Yet once again, the returnees are contrasted with the "nations of the land" with their "pollutions" (v. 21). The author never lets up in condemning the native peoples, who were themselves Jews in most cases.

The Activities of Ezra the Scribe and Priest (Ezra 7–10)

These chapters form a new episode in the history of the postexilic Jewish community, though it has been well integrated with the events in Ezra 1–6. The community so hopefully established in Ezra 1–6 is now threatened by a new crisis but is delivered by a man raised up by God to do the task. Moreover, this individual is not just anyone but a man of stature and in great favor with the Persian regime. Ch. 7 tells us who Ezra was and then devotes a lot of space to the decree which gave him great powers by official Persian sanction. Ch. 8 ends by describing how Ezra made the perilous journey to Jerusalem, under God's protection alone. Chs. 9–10 then describe the "problem" and its solution.

In addition to being a continuation of Ezra 1–6, chs. 7–10 are in some ways parallel to them. Just as the altar and cult, and finally the temple, were reestablished under Joshua and Zerubbabel along with the priests, so Ezra brings priests and Levites and gifts for the temple. It is almost as if he is establishing the divine service for the first time. In fact, it seems strange that he brings a law with him which was already being observed, if the cult was functioning. One wonders whether there were once two separate traditions about the renovation of the temple worship, one featuring Joshua and Zerubbabel and the other headed by Ezra. Then these separate traditions were fused by an editor into a single writing with two episodes rather than two versions of the same thing.

Ezra's Commission (Ezra 7)

Ezra's ancestry and profession are summarized. He is a "scribe skilled in the law of Moses" (7:6), but he is also a priest descended from Phinehas and Zadok. Could anyone be more suitable to sort out the Jerusalem community? He and others made the journey to Jerusalem "in the seventh year of King Artaxerxes" (vv. 7-8). A great debate has gone on for decades as to whether this was Artaxerxes I or Artaxerxes II; in other words, did Ezra make his journey in 458 BC or 398 BC? However, this may also be a symbolic date without any direct relation to historical reality. It should be noted that the temple was finished in the "sixth year" of Darius (6:15). Ezra now makes his journey in the "seventh year" of Artaxerxes. The two dates may function to link together the two chapters — and thus the two sections of the book (1–6 and 7–10) — rather than serve as accurate chronological data. The author shows no awareness of a long span of time between the events of the previous chapter and this chapter.

7:11-26 This document or "rescript" has often been taken as evidence of Ezra's mission. If authentic, it would be an extremely important historical document. As it is, it seems to be a *theological* document. It has a mixture of earlier and later grammatical forms, perhaps suggesting that an original document has been taken over and reworked to fit the message of the writer. More importantly, it has the Persian authorities give unbelievable powers and concessions to Ezra. The Persian king himself and his seven counselors authorize Ezra to take gifts from themselves, plus "all the silver and gold that you shall find in the whole province of Babylonia" (7:16), plus the freewill offerings from the people. If this is not sufficient, it can be supplemented by up to one hundred talents of silver from the royal treasury. Furthermore, none of the temple personnel was subject to Persian taxes. Ezra himself is allowed to appoint magistrates and judges over all the people in the province of Beyond-the-River, and anyone who does not obey the law of God will be punished.

If the details of this decree are accepted, Ezra has practically unlimited power over a major section of the Persian Empire. He has control of enormous gifts from the king and from the people, and if this is not enough, he has another hundred talents of silver (about 300 kilograms or 650 pounds [$975]) for supplementary expenses. One might expect that he had been appointed governor of this large province, yet no such statement is made, and it seems unlikely. Ezra in fact seems to exercise very little power when all is said and done (see below on 8:21-30; 9:3-15).

Thus, if we look at this decree as historians, we find a number of problems. But as a theological statement it fits the main thread of the book very well: once again God's providence is exercised on behalf of his people so that even the might of the Persian Empire is harnessed to bring the divine law to Jerusalem. Furthermore, Ezra was not just an insignificant leader of an insignificant people but had the favor of the Great King himself.

Ezra's Journey to Jerusalem (Ezra 8)

The theme begun in Ezra 7 is developed in more detail in this chapter. Despite the great powers conferred on Ezra in ch. 7, he seems to make no use of them; instead he relies on God to bring him and those with him safely to Jerusalem. This group includes a large contingent of priests and Levites and an enormous treasure for the temple. The author's theological message could not be clearer: God was truly with Ezra.

8:1-14 One of the parallels with chs. 1–6 is the inclusion here of a genealogy of those returning to Judah, similar to that in ch. 2. The initial group of returnees includes priests and ordinary Israelites. Only the males are listed by family and numbered, but presumably they were accompanied in many cases by wives and children.

8:15-20 Realizing that there are no Levites among those with him, Ezra sends an embassy to Casiphia to request some Levites to accompany them. This was evidently a settlement of Levites and "temple servants." The text is ambiguous as to whether the temple servants are separate from the Levites. Some OT passages seem to make the temple servants a branch of the Levites (cf. Nehemiah 12), whereas others seem to make them separate (Ezra 2:40-58 par. Neh 7:43-60).

8:21-30 This is an extremely curious passage when we consider its context just after Ezra 7. Ezra has been given extraordinary authority, not to mention the blessing and favor of the entire Persian Empire. Yet in this passage Ezra is ashamed to ask the king for a guard to protect his group of returnees. Surely he could have given a simple command! Surely he could have afforded to hire one! After all, he has seven and a half *tons* of gold and silver. But, more astonishingly, the Persian government allows him to transport this huge treasure of precious metal hundreds of miles to the west without military protection. Is Ezra ashamed to ask for a guard? The king would have insisted on it! After all, the king himself had contributed a considerable amount of his own treasure to this large fund for the Jewish temple.

The point of the passage is God's providence — that he gives his protection and blessing once again to his servants and those willing to trust him. Ezra does not call on military might; he does not ask for soldiers and cavalry. Rather, he fasts and prays. He does not entrust his seven and a half tons of silver and gold — the equivalent of several years' tribute from the entire Persian province of Beyond-the-River, taking up the entire territory between the Euphrates and the Mediterranean — truly a king's ransom — to a column of heavily armed troops. No, he turns it over to twelve priests. This is faith!

8:21 In the earlier books of the OT fasting is generally the accompaniment of periods of trial or disaster. It was a way of humbling oneself before God (2 Sam 12:15-23; Ps 35:13; Joel 1:13-14; 2:15-17) and calling for his help. Gradually, it became a way of calling on God at other times and an act of piety (Jdt 8:4-6). This passage represents a partial development toward the later theological concept. Ezra is concerned about the forthcoming journey and seeks to gain God's attention by this act of self-denial.

8:31-35 The journey itself is not described, showing that it is not of much interest, though the passage indicates that God had answered their prayers. More important is what happens when Ezra and his company arrive: they turn over the huge quantity of donations exactly — to the penny, as it were. They give it to the priest Meremoth (the high priest?), accompanied by three Levites, fulfilling the obligation of the bearers. The treasure has gone from priests/Levites to priests/Levites. They then offer a very costly sacrifice, considering the value of the animals listed.

There is a certain surreal quality to the scene. It is almost as if Ezra is coming into a vacuum. He has priests with him from the start and makes an effort to bring Levites as well. He is bringing a law which tells how to conduct the cult. When the returned exiles arrive, they offer a special lot of costly sacrifices, almost as if it were a consecration ceremony. Yet it is also clear that priests and Levites already function in Jerusalem and the cult is in complete operation. There is no evidence that they need more priests or Levites or that they need to be told how to carry out their cultic duties by a written law. This paradox is not addressed in the text.

8:36 The sweeping powers granted to Ezra have not been forgotten. He hands over his authorization to the governors and satraps (plural, though there was only one satrap in this region). Yet this is drawn to our attention despite the fact that Ezra has not used these powers so far, nor does he use them in the following chapters either. This is extremely puzzling, though the clue may lie in the theology of the book. On the one hand, the granting of great powers to Ezra is a means of symbolizing how God uses the great Persian Empire as an instrument to aid the Jews. On the other hand, for Ezra to have used these powers would in some sense have diminished his dependence on God.

The Problem with Intermarriage (Ezra 9–10)

Just as the new polity was threatened by outsiders (those trying to stop the building of the temple) in Ezra 1–6, so the community at the time of Ezra is threatened by outsiders, the "foreign" wives whom many had married. The entire people was guilty; the entire community was jeopardized. One would have thought that Ezra would have used his great powers as delegated by the Persian government to resolve the problem. After all, he could set up and depose judges and magistrates, and he had the right to enforce "the law of your God and the law of the king," including imprisonment, banishment, confiscation of goods, and even execution of the death penalty in the entire satrapy of Beyond-the-River (7:26). Yet he makes no use of this power. This encourages us to read the decree of Ezra 7 not as a historical Persian enactment but as a Jewish theological writing (even if perhaps based on a genuine decree) whose aim is to stress the favor granted to the Jews. On the other hand, to have used the alleged powers would have been to detract from the providence of God; instead, the problem is resolved by prayer.

9:1-2 When 9:1-2 states that "the officials" told Ezra about the problem of intermarriage, this is a bit puzzling because the leaders as well as the people have engaged in this "sin." Presumably, only a part had done so, but no qualification is given. It is "the people, the priests, and the Levites"; indeed, the "officials and leaders" had led the way. If so, who are those who expose the problem? It must be a part of the very same leadership, perhaps a very specific part. Ezra 9:4 mentions those who "tremble" at the words of God, an expression also found in Ezra 10:3 and Isa 66:2, 5. It has been suggested that this is the Ezra support group who take a particular view of the law (Blenkinsopp 1990).

9:3-15 Ezra's reaction to the crisis is extremely interesting and not a little baffling. The decree of Artaxerxes has granted him great authority over the whole province of Beyond-the-River. Little seems to be withheld from his jurisdiction if he chooses to exercise it. He had just delivered the king's commission to the leaders in Jerusalem (8:36). All he had to do was issue a few orders and, presto, the crisis would have been over. Instead, he tears his clothes and hair and sits appalled all day (in the street?). Then he prays.

The prayer here is a standard confession of guilt:

shame at the sin of his ancestors, shame at the people's lack of gratitude for what God had done in restoring them after captivity, guilt for present sin. The sin is intermarrying with the inhabitants of the land who commit great abominations, for which the evidence is a reference to the ideas known from such passages as Deut 7:1-5; 18:9; Lev 18:24-30. As so often in a homiletic context, what these abominations and pollutions are is unspecified.

10:1-8 Apart from Ezra's prayer and public mourning, the actions seem to lie in the hands of others. A multitude assembles in sorrow, confessing their sin. Strangely, this assembly includes women and children — apparently the very women and children who were to be expelled from their homes (10:3). It is a man by the name of Shecaniah who tells Ezra what to do. Then, apart from administering an oath at this point, Ezra again does nothing but fast. It is rather others who call together all the people of Judah.

10:9-17 According to this passage, almost everyone seems to accept Ezra's judgment that they have sinned by their marriages; but because the situation cannot be dealt with quickly, a mechanism has to be established to take care of the matter. 10:15 may indicate that some refused to cooperate; at least, that is how some understand the passage. However, the Hebrew is ambiguous, and others take it to mean that the named individuals simply assist in the process.

10:18-44 The book ends rather abruptly with a list of those who sent away their "foreign" wives and children. If this list is complete, it contradicts the impression given in the rest of the chapter that this was a widespread problem. Only seventeen priests, six Levites, one temple singer, three gatekeepers, and sixty-six ordinary "Israelites" divorced their spouses. Although we do not know the precise number in Judah at this time, this list could be only a small portion of it. The story of Ezra seems to be primarily a cautionary tale — to warn future generations of the dangers of intermarriage to the community.

Surprisingly, nothing is said about what happened to the women and children sent away. It was customary for a divorced wife to return to her father's house, but this was hardly an option for all of them. What Ezra required here seems very cruel and heartless to the innocent women and children. No doubt from the author's point of view, carrying out the divine command despite the pain and suffering caused was a mark of the piety and repentance of those involved. It is difficult for most people today to see it from that point of view. The book thus ends on a very somber note. It is only the fact that it is now continued by Nehemiah that this bleakness is relieved.

N.B. My interpretation of Ezra and Nehemiah in the light of Jewish history in the Persian period, with extensive bibliography, is given in ch. 2 of Grabbe 1992 and also in Grabbe 1998. Only a basic bibliography is given here.

Bibliography. Barstad, H. M. 1996, *The Myth of the Empty Land: A Study in the History and Archaeology of Judah during the "Exilic" Period,* SO 28, Oslo/Cambridge, Mass.: Scandinavian University • Blenkinsopp, J. 1989, *Ezra-Nehemiah,* OTL, London: SCM • Blenkinsopp, J. 1990, "A Jewish Sect of the Persian Period," *CBQ* 52:5-20 • Clines, D. J. A. 1984, *Ezra, Nehemiah, Esther,* NCBC, London: Marshall, Morgan & Scott; Grand Rapids: Eerdmans • Grabbe, L. 1987, "Josephus and the Reconstruction of the Judaean Restoration," *JBL* 106:231-46 • Grabbe, L. 1991, "Reconstructing History from the Book of Ezra," in P. R. Davies, ed., *Second Temple Studies: The Persian Period,* JSOTSup 117, Sheffield: JSOT, 98-107 • Grabbe, L. 1992, *Judaism from Cyrus to Hadrian:* Vol. 1: *Persian and Greek Periods;* Vol. 2: *Roman Period,* Minneapolis: Fortress, 1994; British ed. in one-volume paperback, London: SCM • Grabbe, L. 1994, "What Was Ezra's Mission?" in T. C. Eskenazi and K. H. Richards, eds., *Second Temple Studies,* Vol. 2: *Temple Community in the Persian Period,* JSOTSup 175, Sheffield: JSOT, 286-99 • Grabbe, L. 1998, *Ezra and Nehemiah,* Readings, London: Routledge • Gunneweg, A. H. J. 1985, *Esra,* KAT 19.1, Gütersloh: Mohn • Gunneweg, A. H. J. 1987, *Nehemiah,* KAT 19.2, Gütersloh: Mohn • Japhet, S. 1982, "Sheshbazzar and Zerubbabel — Against the Background of the Historical and Religious Tendencies of Ezra-Nehemiah," *ZAW* 94:66-98; 95:218-30 • Olmstead, A. T. 1944, "Tattenai, Governor of 'Across the River,'" *JNES* 3:46 • Williamson, H. G. M. 1983, "The Composition of Ezra i–vi," *JTS* 34:1-30 • Williamson, H. G. M. 1985, *Ezra, Nehemiah,* WBC 16, Waco: Word • Williamson, H. G. M. 1987, *Ezra and Nehemiah,* Society for Old Testament Study Old Testament Guides, Sheffield: JSOT.

Nehemiah

Lester L. Grabbe

INTRODUCTION

Relationship to the Book of Ezra

The book of Nehemiah can be read in one of two ways, on its own or as a single unit with Ezra. If we read it with Ezra, it forms a single story beginning with the initial return under Cyrus and leading on to a time about a century later when the new community is threatened in various ways. In their present state, the books have a small but significant overlap in Nehemiah 8–9, where Ezra takes part in reading the law (especially 8:1-12), and in Nehemiah 12, where Ezra leads a procession (12:36). This makes Ezra come in the seventh year of Artaxerxes I (465-424 BC), with Nehemiah following along thirteen years later in the twentieth year of Artaxerxes.

One possible connection with Ezra has to do with the sad state of Jerusalem as reported to Nehemiah at the beginning of the book. We are never told how the city came to be that way when the rebuilding had begun almost a century earlier and Ezra had brought large amounts of silver and gold more than a decade before and had the promise of further cash if needed. We may imagine several possible situations: (1) something had happened between Artaxerxes's seventh year when Ezra came and the twentieth year when Nehemiah heard the news; (2) restoration of the cult and temple worship had been carried out under Joshua and Zerubbabel, but no further repairs to the city had taken place; (3) Nehemiah is an independent tradition and originally had nothing to do with Ezra; an editor has only secondarily brought them together (see the next section).

Another way to read the book is to see it as independent of Ezra. If we accept the widespread view among scholars that Neh 8:9 had "Nehemiah" put in as a secondary insertion and Neh 12:36 seems to have "Ezra" inserted, there is then no formal connection between the two stories: Ezra and Nehemiah can be read independently as two separate books, though Nehemiah 8–9 would be removed to go with the Ezra tradition. Some also argue that the Artaxerxes of Ezra is Artaxerxes II (404-359 BC), a different king from Artaxerxes I (465-424) of Nehemiah. That would mean that Nehemiah came to Jerusalem about 445 BC but that Ezra did not come until 398. In that case, the two men had nothing to do with each other. This draws our attention to another important topic for consideration: the original independence of the Ezra and Nehemiah traditions. The next section will consider this fact.

The Ezra and the Nehemiah Traditions

As noted earlier ("Introduction" to Ezra, 313), the books of Ezra and Nehemiah presently form a literary unity. This unity has been achieved editorially, however; that is, two separate traditions have been skillfully edited together to create a coherent narrative and integrated literary unit. There are strong indications that the traditions about Ezra and those about Nehemiah developed independently and continued to exist independently even after the final editor of Ezra/Nehemiah had brought them together into a single book. This is important to be aware of because one may have the impression that the Ezra and Nehemiah stories were always connected simply because they occur together in the best-known version, which is the Hebrew version of Ezra/Nehemiah.

For example, the book of 1 Esdras has only the Ezra traditions, including the one about the reading of the law presently found in Neh 8:1-12. Nehemiah is completely absent. On the other hand, there is a Nehemiah tradition in 2 Macc 1:18–2:15 which not only ignores Ezra but also makes Nehemiah responsible for rebuilding the temple. Sirach (Ecclesiasticus) knows of Nehemiah but says nothing of Ezra (49:13). Josephus uses the book of 1 Esdras to describe the initial return and activities of Ezra. He then goes on to give a version of the Nehemiah story, but it is not clear that he has used the current book of Nehemiah; he may have made use of another Nehemiah tradition (*Ant.* 11.5.6-8 §§159-83). 4 Ezra (2 Esdras) places Ezra very close to the fall of Jerusalem (4 Ezra 3:1); it also has a story in which the law is lost and Ezra redictates it under divine inspiration (4 Ezra 14).

Sources

There is widespread agreement among scholars that an actual autobiographical account by Nehemiah himself lies behind part of the book. The reason why this narrative was written is not entirely clear, and the account is called different things, depending on the proposed reason for writing. It is sometimes called the "Nehemiah Memoir," which suggests that it was written to pass on information to others, perhaps the Persian government. Others call it the "Nehemiah Memorial" on the analogy of other Near Eastern writings which were intended as an address to the gods. If this was its function, Nehemiah is mainly concerned to "set the record straight" with God, not his fellow humans, though it could have the latter as a secondary purpose.

The exact reason for writing is of less importance

than the fact of a contemporary account. A writing from Nehemiah's own hand is a valuable source. It is not only written by someone who lived when the events took place, but it is even an "eyewitness" account of some of them. Even if we accept that Nehemiah left behind his own account, however, there are still two problems: (1) that account has still been edited into the present book of Nehemiah, with some dispute over its boundaries, and (2) the account is given from a very personal perspective. It reflects Nehemiah's own views and prejudices and does not tell us the other side of the story. We still have to consider how the same events might have been seen and interpreted by Sanballat, Tobiah, Noadiah, the elders of Jerusalem, and others who interacted with Nehemiah.

Time and Place of Writing

The place to start the discussion is with the "Nehemiah Memorial," which is so widely accepted as the core of the book of Nehemiah (see the previous section). Nehemiah comes to Jerusalem in the twentieth year of Artaxerxes (1:1; 2:1). It is widely (if not universally) accepted that this is Artaxerxes I, which gives the date of his coming as 445-444 BC. Nehemiah's mission continued until at least Artaxerxes' thirty-second year (13:6), or 433-432 BC. Nehemiah would have written his "Memorial" sometime after this. Yet Nehemiah's own writing has clearly been edited and supplemented in its present form. The list of high priests in 12:10-11, 22-23 mentions "Darius the Persian," who is probably Darius II (424-404 BC), though possibly Darius III (336-331 BC). The book is thus no earlier than about 400 BC but is likely to be rather later than this, especially if the "Darius the Persian" is Darius III. The book could have been essentially in its present form before it was combined with the Ezra tradition. If so, a date in the late Persian period or early Greek period would be most likely. However, as noted above ("Introduction" to Ezra, 313-14) the present combined book of Ezra/Nehemiah was probably produced in the Ptolemaic period.

COMMENTARY

How Nehemiah Came to Jerusalem (Neh 1:1–2:10)

The focus of the book is already indicated from the first verses. No background is given other than a brief sentence identifying these words as those of Nehemiah. Immediately the problem of the book is introduced: the sad state of Jerusalem. How to remedy this situation and restore Jerusalem to its proper physical and spiritual condition is the theme which will occupy the rest of the narrative. The entire contents of the book relate in some way to the threat to the Jerusalem community and how that threat might be countered or eliminated.

Nehemiah holds an important post in the service of the Persian king Artaxerxes, usually identified as Artaxerxes I (465-424 BC). If so, the story begins in the year 445 BC. Nehemiah's position is that of cupbearer (1:11). This was not the high office of "royal cupbearer," which seems to have been reserved for Persian nobility. Rather, Nehemiah appears to have been one of the many serving as waiter at the king's table. Nevertheless, this meant that he was regularly in the king's presence and thus had the opportunity to be noticed by him. How Nehemiah obtained such a position in the Persian administration is never explained, any more than it is explained how Ezra obtained his favor with the king. Nehemiah's stature in relation to the Persian government is, of course, a key element within the story.

The setting is Susa, one of the important cities of Persia, and the king would be expected to spend some of his time there. Susa was also the setting of the book of Esther, which may be significant. For example, 2:6 mentions that the queen is sitting next to the king when Nehemiah makes his request to go to Jerusalem. This is one of those unexplained and intriguing details (like the dog in Tob 6:1; 11:4) whose presence in the narrative seems irrelevant. However, anyone familiar with the story of Esther may well wonder whether this woman is Esther herself. Never mind that Esther was married to Ahasuerus, who is usually identified as Xerxes I (486-465 BC), the father of Artaxerxes. Possibly "queen" in this passage could be taken to mean "queen mother"; on the other hand, the Greek version of Esther makes her marry *Artaxerxes.* The author of Nehemiah could possibly have had access to this tradition rather than the one in the current Hebrew Esther with its "Ahasuerus."

1:4-11 Nehemiah's piety is demonstrated from the beginning. When he hears of the troubles in Jerusalem, he immediately goes to God in prayer. The first part of this prayer, with its confession of the sins of Israel past and present, is parallel to Ezra's prayer (Ezra 9:6-15), but the context is somewhat different. Ezra's prayer is primarily one of asking forgiveness, whereas Nehemiah's is a prelude to asking for God's help in approaching the king (Neh 1:11).

2:1-8 Surprisingly, Nehemiah does not put his petition to the king until several months after hearing about Jerusalem. He hears the news in Kislev (November/December), but it is not until Nisan (March/April) that he is able to tell the king. However, Nehemiah's petition is successful. We might wonder whether an actual king would have given up a trusted advisor so readily, but we should expect success in a story like this. After all, Nehemiah has enlisted God's help.

2:7-10 Unlike Ezra, who seems to have been given authority over the entire satrapy of Beyond-the-River, Nehemiah needs documents for his passage. He also has an escort of officers and cavalry, unlike Ezra, who transported large sums of gold and silver with only priests and Levities. Despite Nehemiah's official authorization, resistance from Sanballat and Tobiah is contemplated from the beginning. Or perhaps it is *because of* Nehemiah's official status that they are concerned, since, as a figure with considerable political power, he would be a potential rival to them.

The Rebuilding of the Wall Begins (Neh 2:11–3:32)

As one might expect, Nehemiah's first act after arriving is to survey the damage to the city. Surprisingly, though, he does not ask the leaders in Jerusalem to take him around; instead, he makes a reconnaissance inspection in secret at night. This shows a basic distrust of the Jewish leadership in the city. Although his account does not condemn them, at the very least he is afraid that they cannot keep his intent to themselves. This fundamental lack of trust between Nehemiah and many in the Jerusalem community is a consistent theme throughout the book.

Despite this rather conspicuous failure of Nehemiah to take them into his confidence, the priests, nobles, and other leaders seem to be wholeheartedly behind the project of rebuilding the walls of Jerusalem, at least for the most part. From the description given, the walls are in a bad state. Nehemiah 3 is given over to describing who worked on each section of the wall. Modern readers may find this a bit dull, but it was obviously important to the original writer and presumably to the readers. The most obvious explanation is that the question of which families worked on the wall was significant information to pass down to later generations. This list may have been a way of legitimating certain families or supporting other sorts of claims made by them.

Several features of this list can be noted. One is the extent to which work was done by priests and Levites and by important officials. In one case, a man's daughters are mentioned as aiding him (3:12). Another notable feature is that people often repaired the portion of the wall nearest to their own dwellings, which would have been a natural incentive to do the work. But many of those who worked seem to have lived in regions outside Jerusalem. All was not completely harmonious in this setting, however. We already have intimations of opposition from Sanballat and his colleagues (2:19-20). And some did refuse to take part, the nobles of the Tekoites being specifically singled out (3:5).

Opposition from Sanballat and His Colleagues (Nehemiah 4 [Heb. 3:33–4:17])

In Ezra 1–6 it was the "enemies of Judah and Benjamin," "the peoples of the land," and various officials who hindered and even stopped the building of the temple. Here it is a set of individuals whose position is not identified. Sanballat is simply called a Horonite (2:19). Tobiah is an "Ammonite slave" (2:19); Geshem is an Arab. Associated with them are the Arabs, the Ammonites, and the Ashdodites (4:7 [Heb. 4:1]). Readers would be left with a definite sense that these are foreigners and probably men of low stature. They could be dismissed as stereotypical "bad guys" whose sole function was to be evil.

Other information, both in the book of Nehemiah itself and from external sources, gives a rather different picture, however. Sanballat was the official Persian governor of Samaria, as we know from contemporary documents (Cowley 1923: ##30, 31). Tobiah was himself Jewish, apparently from an ancient family whose ancestral territory was across the Jordan in the old area of Ammon (hence his designation "Ammonite"). He was probably also a Persian official, the title *'ebed* being "slave, servant" but also "(royal) servant," though one has the impression that Nehemiah uses the title contemptuously (cf. Mazar 1957). We know of a Geshem king of the Arabs from inscriptions, and he is plausibly to be identified with the Geshem of Nehemiah.

Thus, the opposition to Nehemiah was not a gang of low-born foreigners and outlaws but an important group of leaders and Persian officials in the area. Why they opposed Nehemiah is never made clear. It may have been simply a matter of power politics. It has been argued that until the time of Nehemiah, Judah was under the control (and governed as a part) of the province of Samaria. The matter is disputed, but Sanballat and his circle may have had a legitimate interest in what was going on in Jerusalem; in any case, Nehemiah wanted no interference with what he was doing. He heard rumors of an impending attack and prepared for it. It did not come, so they went back to work. To what extent Nehemiah's fears were real and to what extent he was irrational about Sanballat and the others is difficult to know from our extant sources. They may well have been a bit of both. That is, the threat may have been real but not nearly as formidable as Nehemiah had made out in his own mind. There is no doubt that an external threat — real or imagined — was an excellent way of uniting the Jews behind his project.

The Plight of the Poor (Nehemiah 5)

This chapter breaks the flow of the story, which resumes in ch. 6, but is an important element in expressing Nehemiah's character and leadership ability. The charge is that members of the Jewish community were exploiting their own people. Some had borrowed money for food in time of famine or to pay the royal taxes. They were paying interest on these loans, contrary to regulations in the Pentateuch (see below). More shockingly, some of the sons and daughters of indebted families were being sold into slavery to pay off the debt.

Nehemiah's solution is a cunning one. He calls an assembly and charges the nobles and officials with misconduct. He holds up his own example of helping the people with loans and gifts; in addition, he has bought back some of those sold into slavery outside Judah. Naturally, those accused have no answer in such a situation, and they agree to his demands. Nehemiah's actions here have been compared to those of Solon, who set up certain reforms in Athens shortly after 600 BC. The actions are certainly parallel, though whether we are to see any direct connection between them is a moot point.

5:1-13 In the Near Eastern societies of the time, the debtor could pay off debts by selling himself and/or his family into slavery. The law of Moses regulates this practice (Exod 21:2-11; Lev 25:39-55; Deut 15:12-18). Israelites were not to enslave their fellows permanently, nor, during their period of servitude, were they to treat them as alien slaves. They were to be freed in the sabbatical year (Deuteronomy) or the jubilee (Leviticus). They were certainly not to be sold to Gentiles. Also, loans were to be made without interest and as a kindness to the debtor, not for purposes of enriching the one making the loan (Exod 22:24-26; Lev 25:35-38; Deut 15:7-11).

Whether these laws were actually in effect and practiced in Israelite society or whether they were only theoretical concepts of the pentateuchal literary writer(s) is a moot point. However, in many cases the substance of the law seems to have been traditional in society long before the Persian period; furthermore, the text of Nehemiah appears to have such laws or something similar in mind.

5:14-19 Nehemiah makes the point that he governed for twelve years, yet during that time he did not avail himself of his rights as governor to provide maintenance for his office (including the many officials and others who ate at his table) from taxes on the people. This is a noble example, no doubt, if we take it at face value. Many of the Jews were not well off, and any relief from taxes and imposts would have been welcomed. Thus far Nehemiah's self-defense is justified.

But we need to go beyond the surface since, after all, we have only Nehemiah's version of the situation. The question is, If he was not taking the taxes he was entitled to as governor, where did his financial support come from? He must have had an income from somewhere, either a private income or an allowance from the central Persian administration. It is good to hold oneself up as an example of not taking from the people when one can afford to live without their support. What about those governors who did not have the benefit of his other income? If they were to do their job, they had to be maintained by someone. We all know that government has a price; it has to be paid for. It is rather self-serving of Nehemiah to proclaim his goodness without explaining how he managed to feed 150 people a day without any sort of income. The money did not fall from heaven. Somebody somewhere was paying for it.

The Wall Is Finished, Despite Attempts to Intimidate Nehemiah (Nehemiah 6)

The story interrupted by Nehemiah 5 now resumes in ch. 6. The threatened attack feared in Nehemiah 4 did not take place. Nevertheless, Sanballat, Tobiah, and Geshem harass Nehemiah, this time trying to get him to meet them in out-of-the-way places. When this does not work, they resort to the old but effective stratagem of accusing him of disloyalty to their Persian overlords. This is similar to the charge made by "the adversaries of Judah and Benjamin" in Ezra 4. Because of Nehemiah's strong personality, they can accuse him of seeking to become king, a charge which may also have been leveled at Zerubbabel (with truth, some think).

Nehemiah's enemies are not confined to those on the outside. An individual called Shemaiah suggests that they meet in secret for fear of assassination. What reason he gave for wanting to meet is not stated, but he is identified as a prophet (6:12). Nehemiah suspects him of being hired by Sanballat, but we do not have Shemaiah's side of the story. He may have had what seemed to him good reasons for arranging this meeting with Nehemiah in this way. Similarly, Noadiah the prophetess and other prophets were supposedly against him. Was this real opposition? Or was Nehemiah simply so neurotic that he read major significance into simple acts and words? If the former, it is interesting that this opposition comes from prophetic figures. The accusation against Nehemiah by his enemies, quoted in v. 7, suggests that there were prophets who supported Nehemiah. Apparently, Nehemiah had prophets both for and against him.

6:17-19 This passage suggests another interpretation: that the opposition to Nehemiah was mainly in his own mind. According to Nehemiah 3 and 4, the rebuilding program had been widely supported, yet there were many nobles who maintained good relations with Tobiah, who was, after all, Jewish. Nehemiah sees this, along with the letters which Tobiah wrote to him, as evidence of ill will. Is it possible that the nobles supported the building of the wall but saw no reason not to have good relations with Tobiah? In other words, they saw part of Nehemiah's program as good but part of it as extreme, especially the desire to cut off the Jewish community from outsiders. If so, the nobles — and even Tobiah — were not against Nehemiah as such, but they did not agree with some of Nehemiah's measures. On this view, Nehemiah was an extremist who refused to accept that Tobiah was also acting in good faith. This interpretation is in part guesswork, but it takes into account the fact that the story of the rebuilding of the wall is given from Nehemiah's perspective alone and represents his own bias and interpretation.

The Genealogical Register of the Settlers (Nehemiah 7)

Most of this chapter is an almost word-for-word repetition of Ezra 2 (Neh 7:6-73 par. Ezra 2:1-70). Why this should all be repeated is an interesting question. The genealogy in Ezra was important for establishing who had first settled there after the captivity because it legitimated any claims they had. The genealogy here could be a way of reaffirming those claims. The slight differences might suggest that the one was not just copied from the other, but most commentators feel that one chapter originated as a copy of the other. If so, which one is more original is difficult to establish. The repetition serves to unite the two books; the common list of settlers serves to link the two traditions, which probably originally developed separately (see "Introduction," 320).

7:1-5 Even when the wall is finished, Nehemiah still suspects foul play. It is interesting that the inhabitants of Jerusalem do not appear to have been threatened before the wall was repaired, yet suddenly a careful guard has to be kept. Again, one must ask whether the danger was mainly in Nehemiah's mind.

7:4 This is a very curious verse and further hints that the Nehemiah tradition was once independent of the material in the book of Ezra. It states that "no houses had been built" in Jerusalem. This is an extremely strange statement to make when some builders build a section of the wall which is opposite their own houses (e.g., 3:10, 21, 23, 24). Furthermore, it is scarcely credible that people would have been living in Jerusalem for almost a century without building houses. The book of Ezra gives no hint that Jerusalem was not inhabited as one might expect of the major city in Judah. However, the verse makes perfect sense if the Nehemiah tradition once made Nehemiah the restorer of Jerusalem instead of Joshua and Zerubbabel (cf. 2 Macc 1:18-36).

7:70-72 This section has some of the few main differences compared with Ezra 2. In Ezra the contributions are listed as a sum total of 61,000 darics (a Persian coin) of gold, 5,000 minas of silver, and 100 priestly garments. Nehemiah breaks it down as follows:

	darics	*minas*	*basins*	*robes*
Governor	1,000		50	530
Heads of houses	20,000	2,200		
Rest of people	20,000	2,000		67
Total	41,000	4,200	50	597

The totals are different in each case, but not completely unrelated: The number of darics differs by 20,000 exactly, while the number of minas is fairly close. The number of robes is quite different, and Ezra does not even mention the basins. The resemblance of the two lists might suggest that Ezra gave only round figures. The difference in the number of darics could then be explained as a case of textual corruption. However, this still gives no explanation for the rather different figure for priestly robes. It is possible, therefore, that rather than describing the contributions made in the time of Ezra and Zerubbabel, the list in the book of Nehemiah is referring to donations at another time, perhaps in Nehemiah's own time.

A Fragment of the Ezra Tradition (Nehemiah 8–9)

Apart from one verse, which is suspect, Nehemiah is not mentioned in these two chapters. Rather, the focus is on Ezra alone. A text almost the same as Neh 8:1-12 is also part of the book of 1 Esdras (9:37-55), further suggesting that these chapters are part of the Ezra tradition rather than the Nehemiah story (see the "Introduction," 320).

Ezra's Reading of the Law (Nehemiah 8)

Apart from the genealogy (Ezra 2 par. Nehemiah 7), this chapter makes one of the few direct connections between the two books of Ezra and Nehemiah since Ezra appears only here and in chs. 9 and 12 of the book of Nehemiah. On the other hand, the only mention of Nehemiah (8:9) is problematic textually and is often thought to be a later insertion. This suggests that the Ezra and Nehemiah traditions grew up separately and were brought together only at a late time (see below on Neh 12:36).

This chapter has become extremely important in discussions about the writing of the Pentateuch, the public reading of the law, and the development of synagogues. In many cases, however, the weight of evidence placed on it is unjustified. The assembly and reading of the law here are in no way comparable to what we know of synagogue services. In any case, our knowledge of synagogues indicates that they developed much later, and not in Jerusalem but in Egypt. Our first indications of synagogues in the Palestinian region are in the Roman period. Some have thought that the Hebrew text is being translated into the vernacular Aramaic in this passage (8:8), but the text does not clearly say that. In fact, there is no evidence that Hebrew had been forgotten at this time; it continued to be used and to develop as a living language over the next several centuries. The first attestation of translation from the Hebrew text into Aramaic occurs in the Mishnah, after the fall of Jerusalem in AD 70. Those who find evidence for synagogue services in this chapter are reading later practice into the text. For a further discussion, see Grabbe 1988; Levine 1996.

8:1-8 The reading takes place in the seventh month. According to Deut 31:10-13, the law was to be read completely every seven years at the festival of Booths. This passage is not a a parallel, however, because it takes place on the first day of the seventh month, whereas the feast of Booths was 15-22 of the seventh month.

8:9-12 According to pentateuchal legislation, the first day of the seventh month was the Day of Trumpets, a holy day. In later Judaism it also became the start of the new year, and many scholars think this was already the case in ancient Israel. Others have argued that the beginning of the new year was in the spring, Nisan or the first month (cf. Exod 12:2). The annual holy days have a long history in Israel and originated in ancient harvest festivals. On the other hand, the relationship with such pentateuchal passages as Leviticus 23 and Deuteronomy 16, which describe the holy days and festivals in detail, is unclear and their dating is controversial. As noted below, some important celebrations mentioned in the Pentateuch seem to be ignored by Ezra and Nehemiah.

8:13-18 This section describes the celebration of the feast of Booths or Tabernacles (*Sukkot* in Hebrew), which is usually thought to have originated in the ancient celebration of the grape harvest and wine making. The temporary booths or shelters were built in the fields for workers to sleep in at night, both to guard the harvest and to save time in getting on with the task of gathering the grapes. This passage suggests this was a celebration which had been "forgotten," a strange state of affairs if Ezra had brought the law to them thirteen years earlier.

Confession of Sin (Nehemiah 9)

No sooner had they finished celebrating the feast of Booths, the main religious festival of the year, than they called a day of fasting and repantence. This makes one ask what they did on the Day of Atonement (tenth day of the seventh month), but this important religious observance is nowhere mentioned in Ezra or Nehemiah.

Again, it is Ezra who is the main figure in the chapter; Nehemiah is not mentioned (see on Nehemiah 8 above).

9:1-5 The precise reason for calling the day of repentance is not given; it seems to cover a number of sins not only on the part of the people but even of their ancestors. One of the acts of repentance is that they "separated themselves from all foreigners" (9:2). This sounds very much like the situation in Ezra 9–10 and, as we see in Nehemiah 10, is an important theme in Nehemiah as well as in Ezra. Yet this is rather puzzling since Ezra had supposedly sorted out this problem thirteen years earlier. However, if this is part of the Ezra tradition, it might belong with Ezra 9–10 or perhaps even be a variant tradition of those two chapters.

9:6-35 This long prayer of Ezra rehearses the history of Israel, which is seen as a period of continual falling away. It has many of the overtones of Deuteronomy and the Deuteronomistic History (Joshua to 2 Kings), which are the product of what many scholars call the "Deuteronomic School." This literary circle is thought to have edited not only the book of Deuteronomy but also the traditions of the judges and kings and even a number of the prophetic writings. The perspective of this Deuteronomic School is that Israel had its religion revealed in the beginning but kept falling into disobedience. God would punish them for their sins, and they would come back to right worship for a period of time but would then fall away again.

One of the main causes of this falling away was the "foreigners" whose ways corrupted them. These foreigners are identified as the traditional Canaanite tribes, but these groups had probably long since ceased to exist. So who were these foreigners? The people living on the land when the exiled Jews returned are usually seen as foreigners, yet they were descendants of those who were left in the land and were thus Jews themselves. As noted in our discussion of Ezra 3, the new community created by the returnees seems to have attempted to exclude any of those who had not gone into captivity. This means that those labeled "foreigners" were fellow Jews in many cases.

9:36-37 The books of Ezra and Nehemiah are generally favorable toward the Persian Empire. Yet this passage shows a widespread frustration that the Jews were little more than slaves, however well they were treated by the Persians. The editors of Ezra and Nehemiah at least did not want to alienate the Persian authorities, but occasional passages such as this one betray the underlying feelings of many individuals.

9:38 (Heb. 10:1) This forms the first verse of Nehemiah 10 in the Hebrew text, which makes more sense since it introduces the list of individuals who signed the pledge.

Pledge to Separate from "Foreigners" (Nehemiah 10)

This chapter suggests that the main reason for the day of repentance was intermarriage with foreigners. It may well be that this interpretation was created only when the editor put the Ezra material at this point in the book. In other words, the position of the tradition in Nehemiah 9 may originally have been one of general repentance. However, once it is put before Nehemiah 10, the latter chapter interprets Nehemiah 9 as mainly repentance from marriage to foreigners.

10:1-27 (Heb. 10:2-28) This is a signed document and reminds one of the similar pledge in Ezra 10:20-43. Is one only a variant tradition of the other? While a similar situation could have arisen again, with a similar result, it seems strange that this would have happened so quickly (only a little more than a decade) after Ezra had sorted it out. Some have explained it by dating Ezra to the time of Artaxerxes II (i.e., 398 BC), thus many decades after Nehemiah. That is one way of solving the problem, but is it a historical problem or a redactional one? Is one tradition just a variant of the other rather than a "historical record" of two separate events? This is definitely a Nehemiah tradition, however, because "Nehemiah the governor" heads the list (v. 1) and Ezra is not even mentioned.

10:28-31 (Heb. 10:29-32) The focus in 10:28-31 is on the prohibition of intermarrying with the "peoples of the land," but the rest of the chapter goes on to promise other observances, especially taking on the support of the priesthood by paying the various priestly dues. If the priesthood was to do its duty, it had to be maintained. Otherwise the priests had to take up agriculture to make a living (cf. 13:10).

10:31 (Heb. 10:32) One of the ways of remaining separate from "foreigners" was by not buying or selling on the sabbath day. The seventh day of the week as a day of rest or as in some way special may have had a long history in Israel, though many scholars have pointed to passages such as this one to argue that the sabbath as a major religious observance did not develop until the postexilic period. Although the command to keep the seventh day of the week holy is found in the Ten Commandments (Exod 20:1-4; Deut 5:6-18), sabbath breaking is not usually one of the sins preached against by the prophets or condemned in the Deuteronomistic History (Joshua to 2 Kings).

According to Exod 23:10-11 and Lev 25:1-7, the land was not to be worked but allowed to rest every seventh year. This was also tied up with a time of remission of debts and freeing of Israelite slaves (Deut 15:1-18). Although the weekly sabbath was not emphasized, failure to observe the sabbatical year is said to be one of the main reasons why Israel was taken captive (Lev 26:34-35, 43; 2 Chr 36:21): this allowed the land to have the rest it should have been given if this law were properly observed. According to extrabiblical sources, the seventh year was observed during the Second Temple period. The Torah is not consistent on the matter, however, since Leviticus 25 seems to presuppose a jubilee cycle. According to it, the year when property returned to its owner, debts were cancelled, and slaves were released was the jubilee year (usually interpreted as the fiftieth year). Although the sabbatical year cycle could be fitted into it (i.e., a jubilee equals seven sabbatical cycles), there is no evidence that the jubilee was ever observed, unlike the sabbatical year. (For further information on this subject, see Grabbe 1993: 94-97.)

10:32-33 (Heb. 10:33-34) This requirement to pay one-third of a shekel per year for each member of a Jewish family is first mentioned here; Exod 30:11-16 states that a half shekel is to be paid for all entered into the records at a census, but it does not state that this census is to be taken yearly. In later Jewish sources, this "temple tax" is said to be half a shekel, interpreted as the equivalent of two Greek drachmas (cf. Josephus *Ant.* 3.8.2 §§194-96). Whereas the agricultural tithes were paid only in the Palestinian region, the half-shekel payment seems to have been considered obligatory on all Jews. We have evidence in later sources that it was collected in the diaspora and provided a great deal of wealth for the temple (e.g., Josephus *Ant.* 18.9.1 §§312-13; cf. *J.W.* 7.6.6 §218).

10:34 (Heb. 10:35) The requirement of a wood offering is not mentioned in the Pentateuch. It is referred to (along with the festivals of new wine and new oil) as an annual celebration in the *Temple Scroll* (19-25) and by Josephus (*J.W.* 2.17.6 §425). Thus, the book of Nehemiah shows that there were laws to be observed which were not necessarily found in the Torah (the five books ascribed to Moses).

10:35-39 (Heb. 10:36-40) This passage and 12:44-47 give a valuable description of the organization of the priestly dues. No one likes taxes, whether religious or secular, yet we all recognize that government is necessary and has to be financed. Similarly, the temple and its cult could function only if supported by dues of some sort. The point of them all is that they were remuneration to the priests for their work in the temple. Otherwise, they would have nothing to live on and would "neglect the house of our God" (10:39 [Heb. 10:40]). The Pentateuch lays down rules about what gifts and payments were to be made to the priests and Levites: dough (Num 15:17-21), portions of each sacrifice (Lev 7:29-32), firstlings (Exod 13:11-15; 34:19-20; Lev 27:26-27; Num. 18:15-18), first fruits (Lev 2:14-16; Num 18:12-14; Deut 18:4; 26:1-11), and tithes (Num 18:21-32). Some of those rules, or something very similar, are presupposed here and in Neh 12:44-47. Neh 12:47 states that gifts went first to the Levites, who then themselves contributed to the priests. A similar system relating to the tithes, in which the people tithe to the Levites and the Levites tithe to the priests, is laid down in Num 18:21-32. What is new here is the emphasis on singers and gatekeepers who do not figure in any of the pentateuchal legislation. Although these singers are said to go back to David, they are really emphasized only in late books such as 1 and 2 Chronicles and Ezra and Nehemiah.

Those Who Lived in Jerusalem (Nehemiah 11)

This chapter links back with, and is a natural continuation of, the completion of building the wall which was last discussed in 7:4. This is a further demonstration that chs. 7–10 are likely an insertion into a narrative which already existed. That narrative gave the story about the building of the wall, apparently ending with the repopulation of Jerusalem and the dedication of the wall (chs. 11–12). The list in ch. 7 was then (supposedly) an enrollment of those in the province according to the list of those who had returned at the beginning of the Persian period, followed by chs. 8–10, which describe a ceremony of the people's dedicating themselves to God that might have taken place once the wall was complete. Thus, the editor apparently felt this was a good place to put the account in chs. 7–10 even though it breaks up the original narrative.

The list here in Nehemiah 11 may also tell us something about the organization of the temple at this time. Included in it are priests and Levites but also "sons of Solomon's servants" (v. 3). However, these are not found in the detailed list later on; instead we have "gatekeepers," "temple servants," and "singers." The singers are evidently seen as part of the Levites, and, interestingly, they apparently had their duties assigned by royal decree (11:22-23).

11:1-3 Neh 7:4 had made the point that Jerusalem was underpopulated, a judgment apparently made with regard to its vulnerability to attack. We are now told what was done about the problem: the governor required that 10 percent of the people in the province of Judah must live in Jerusalem. Also, the leaders had to live in Jerusalem, which is what one might expect. Even though the property of the individuals might have been outside Jerusalem, the leaders and a tenth of the population had to live in Jerusalem. Presumably they had to make arrangements to have the agricultural land worked by someone else. The total number of settlers comes to about three thousand. This is probably a reasonable number for the population of Jerusalem at this time. Ancient cities were not necessarily very big by modern standards.

Dedication of the Wall (Nehemiah 12)

We come back to the main concern of the book, the wall. The event of its building is now celebrated in an ostentatious ceremony. This might seem to be a case of unnecessary pomp; after all, it was only a matter of repairing breaches in the wall. However, if there are overtones of a first restoration of Jerusalem, as has been hinted at in various passages, then one would expect a significant ceremony of dedication. This chapter creates a tension with chs. 8–9, however. Nehemiah 8–9 describes a period of reading the law, celebrating the festivals of the seventh month, and expressing repentance — all of which seem to follow the completion of the wall. We would have expected the dedication of the wall to be part of these activities. Yet Nehemiah 12 appears to know nothing of all those celebrations but describes the natural follow-up to the work of building the wall, a dedication ceremony. This is further evidence for the development of the tradition.

12:1-26 The dedication ceremony is preceded by a further genealogical list, this time specifically of the priests and Levites. The priests and Levites are supposedly those who came in the time of Joshua and Zerubbabel, but the genealogy is carried down to a later time in the Persian period. The exact cutoff point is unclear. According to 12:26, the list comes down to the time of Ezra and Nehemiah, but this looks somewhat artificial. One or both of these names is likely to have been added to the text. Neh 12:22 mentions the rule of "Darius the Persian," who is unlikely to be Darius I (522-486 BC). Darius II (424-404 BC) and Darius III (338-331 BC) are also candidates. The book of Nehemiah does not appear to know of more than one Artaxerxes and only two kings by the name of Darius. This suggests that the Darius of v. 22 was Darius II.

12:10-11 The names in this list look like a roll of the high priests over a period of a number of generations. One influential theory assumes that this list covers the entire Persian period (in which case the Darius of v. 22 would have to be Darius III). The trouble is that the list of names does not seem sufficient to cover a period of two centuries. To overcome the problem, this theory assumes that certain gaps were created by scribal omissions caused by several identical names in the list, created when a grandson was named for a grandfather. The list as it stands does not have duplicate names, however, and their existence has been inferred from coins and from Josephus. If we do not assume that the list must stretch for two hundred years, there is no need to assume scribal omissions. There may have been some scribal corruption, of course, as suggested by v. 26, which is slightly different from vv. 10-11, but the names are sufficient to reach to the time of Darius II. (All this discussion naturally assumes that these names are genuine historical data. Another view would be that they are an invention of the writer and not to be taken as a genuine list.) For further information, see Grabbe 1987.

12:31-43 This section is in the first person, as if part of the Nehemiah Memorial. This is the only other passage (apart from Neh 8:9) where Ezra and Nehemiah come together in this book. However, the name of Ezra looks like a later addition. If the formation of the two groups of the procession are compared, they form a symmetrical parallel, but only if Ezra's name is omitted. Also, Ezra is said to lead one group (12:36), but his name comes only at the end of the list, not at the beginning as we would expect. If this section indeed derives from Nehemiah's own writing, it has probably been edited by later redactors.

12:44-47 See further at 10:35-39.

Nehemiah Addresses Himself to Problems Arising in His Absence (Nehemiah 13)

This chapter is made up of a series of problems to which Nehemiah has to address himself. It mentions that he had to return to report to the king and was thus away for a period of time. Whether we are to deduce that all the problems arose as a result of that absence is not clear, but if not, we are left with the impression that Nehemiah was not in control; having to solve problems which had already been solved or which his leadership should have nipped in the bud does not reflect well on him. That is why the reference to his absence is probably intended as a key to interpreting the chapter. Although many think that this chapter is based on the Nehemiah Memorial, it has been argued that much of it is by a later writer imitating Nehemiah's style. Several of the issues here are developments — or even repetitions — of issues found earlier in the book. For example, the question of mixing with the local peoples comes up twice (13:1-3, 23-28).

13:4-9 Tobiah is allowed a room in the temple court by Eliezer the priest (high priest?) (13:4-9), just as Jerusalem nobles kept good relations with Tobiah earlier (6:17-19). Nehemiah is naturally incensed.

13:10-14 The Levites and singers have left their temple duties because their contributions have been stopped (13:10-14), a possibility which was anticipated in 10:35-39 (Heb. 10:36-40). Nothing is said about the priests. This makes one wonder whether the problem was that the tithes and other dues were being paid directly to the priests, leaving the Levites completely out.

13:15-22 See further at 10:31.

13:23-31 This passage addresses an issue similar to that in Ezra 9–10 and Neh 10:29-31, which is marriage outside the community. The people of Ashdod lived on the coast to the west, and those of Ammon and Moab across the Jordan to the east. In all cases, they were neighbors of Judah. Why Ashdod is singled out is a bit puzzling, though Ashdod was probably under Phoenician control at this time. Pehaps it was a case of Jewish traders going into adjacent regions or, more likely, traders from those areas lodging in Judah. Unlike the "peoples of the land" in Ezra, who were likely to be the descendants of Jews not taken captive by the Babylonians, the Phoenicians, Moabites, and Ammonites were "foreigners," even if not distant foreigners; however, they usually worshiped deities other than Yahweh (e.g., Baal, Asherat, and Chemosh). Nehemiah's objections seem to have a different basis from those in Ezra 9–10, even if the language used is not so different. On the other hand, 13:28 represents a rather different case: Sanballat worshiped Yahweh, not a pagan deity. Nehemiah could hardly accuse him of leading the high priest's son into pagan worship. In this case, though, Nehemiah regarded Sanballat as his enemy and the marriage, therefore, as a betrayal. There is also the question of whether this son was heir to the high-priestly office. The context does not suggest that he was the eldest son, which may mean that he was only a more remote heir, though this was still likely to be seen as a problem by Nehemiah. Once again, the divisions within the Jewish community at this time are highlighted.

N.B. Only a few items cited in the commentary are given here. The bibliography for Ezra also has items relating to Nehemiah. For a much more extensive bibliography on both books and on the history and scholarship of the period, see ch. 2 of my *Judaism from Cyrus to Hadrian* and my *Ezra-Nehemiah* commentary.

Bibliography. Cowley, A. 1923, repr. 1967, *Aramaic Papyri of the Fifth Century B.C.*, Osnabruck: Otto Zeller • Grabbe, L. L. 1987,

"Josephus and the Reconstruction of the Judaean Restoration," *JBL* 106:231-46 • Grabbe, L. L. 1993, *Leviticus,* Society for Old Testament Study, Old Testament Guides, Sheffield: JSOT • Grabbe, L. L. 1988, "Synagogues in Pre-70 Palestine: A Re-assessment," *JTS* 39:401-10; repr. 1995 in D. Urman and P. V. M. Flesher, eds., *Ancient Synagogues: Historical Analysis and Archaeological Discovery,* SPB 47.1, Leiden: Brill, 1:17-26 • Levine, L. I. 1995, "The Nature and Origin of the Palestinian Synagogue Reconsidered," *JBL* 115:425-48 • Mazar, B. 1957, "The Tobiads," *IEJ* 7:137-45, 229-38.

Esther

Sidnie White Crawford

INTRODUCTION

The book of Esther, part of the Writings in the Hebrew Bible (HB), is an exciting story about the deliverance of the Jews of the Persian Empire from threatened genocide by two Jews living in the Persian court, Queen Esther and her cousin Mordecai. Esther purports to be recounting real events, but it is historicized fiction; a quick check of the historical record indicates that it is very unlikely that the story of Esther actually happened. The story is set in the reign of the emperor Xerxes (486-465 BC) in the capital city of Susa. The actual date of composition for Esther is most likely the late fourth or early third centuries BC, the period of the demise of the Persian Empire and the establishment of the Hellenistic kingdoms. The author demonstrates some knowledge of Persian geography and administration, and uses several Persian loanwords (esp. in ch. 1). It is unlikely that Esther was written later than the third century BC since the book lacks any Hellenistic vocabulary or coloring and generally displays a much more positive attitude toward Gentiles and Gentile rule than later works such as Judith or 3 Maccabees. The provenance of Esther is the eastern diaspora; the plot centers there, and the author shows no interest in Judea or its institutions. The assumption of the book seems to be that the Jews live in the diaspora and expect to remain there. In fact, Esther's lack of interest in Judea or Judaism, including the temple and the law, is most striking. The most remarked-upon characteristic of the book of Esther is its failure to mention God even once; this lack of overt religiosity caused the book to have difficulty obtaining canonical status in Christianity (Moore 1971: xxx-xxxi). This characteristic has also led some modern critics to condemn the book as irredeemably secular (Paton 1908: 96-97), but this judgment is probably too harsh. The theology of Esther appears to be that there is a divine providence which works to protect the Jews; however, this divine providence works behind the scenes and through human agency, not by direct intervention in events, and the working out of the divine plan is never transparent to its human participants (see esp. ch. 4). Nevertheless, for those seeking conventional piety Esther will be a disappointment; the book contains no prayers or hymns, and the heroine Queen Esther is married to a Gentile, does not observe the dietary laws, and to all appearances leads a completely secular life. Judaism in Esther is a matter of ethnic identity, not of observance.

As the book now stands, it serves as an etiology for the festival of Purim, the annual festival commemorating the deliverance of the Persian Jews from the threat of destruction. The origins of Purim are cloudy; it first appears in the postexilic period, but its antecedents may lie in a pagan festival, either a Persian or Babylonian spring festival. This hypothetical pagan origin may explain the secular nature of the festival and why Purim, and the book of Esther itself, had difficulty winning acceptance among some communities of Jews (Moore 1971: xxi-xxv).

Purim quickly became a popular Jewish holiday, as it is today, a happy celebration emphasizing feasting and hilarity along with charitable giving. The only rabbinic command associated with Purim is that the scroll *(megillah)* of Esther be read in its entirety on the fourteenth of Adar (*Meg.* 3b). Purim parties for children are common, with the participants dressing up as Esther, Mordecai, Vashti, Ahasuerus, and Haman.

The genre of the book of Esther is the novella or short story; it is related to the tale of the royal courtier (e.g., Daniel 2–6) and uses some of the themes of wisdom literature. As a literary composition, it is meant to be read; as such the author employs a variety of literary devices. It is meant to be entertaining; to achieve this, the author maintains a tone of comic irony or even satire throughout. The ironic tone, however, hides a very serious subject: the aversion of a threat of genocide. For the Jewish audience, Mordecai and especially Esther become role models for living successful lives in the sometimes inexplicable and dangerous Gentile world in which they find themselves. The theme of reversal (peripety) is important as well; throughout the book the expected outcome is reversed, and people's status and character undergo sudden changes. As Levenson notes, this theme is summed up in 9:1 by the Hebrew phrase *nahapok hu'*, "the reverse occurred" (Levenson 1997: 8).

The theme of power, who has it, who gets its, who loses it, and how it is used, is likewise important. Esther, the least powerful character in the book by virtue of being both female and Jewish, becomes the most successful character by the end of the book, gaining the most real power by means of her wisdom and skill. She is a type for the Jew living in diaspora, whose goal is to lead a successful life in an alien environment. Ahasuerus's power, his by birth, is shown to be no power at all as he is manipulated by a series of clever courtiers (among them Esther). Haman gains much power, only to lose it all by his unethical and foolish behavior; while Mordecai, who has little individual power, receives Haman's power and shares Esther's as a result of his righteous conduct. Power, according to the book of Esther, is ephemeral; although it can be obtained by those who are wise, it may also fall into the hands of the foolish or wicked. Those who have power, whether by merit or accident of birth, should use it for good, not selfish reasons.

Banquets, which recur throughout the narrative, are important structuring devices. They signal important events, indicate closure, and provide settings to move the action forward (Berg 1979: 31-57). This "banquet structure" can be illustrated as follows (Fox 1991: 157):

1. Xerxes' banquet for the nobility (1:2-4)
2. Xerxes' banquet for all the men in Susa (1:5-8)
3. Vashti's banquet for the women (1:9)
4. Esther's enthronement banquet (2:18)
5. Haman and Xerxes' banquet (3:15)
6. Esther's first banquet (5:4-8)
7. Esther's second banquet (7:1-9)
8. The Jews' feasting in celebration of Mordecai's glory and the counter decree (8:17)
9. The first feast of Purim: Adar 14 (9:17, 19)
10. The second feast of Purim: Adar 15 (9:18)

As can be seen in the chart, banquets often occur in pairs, as do other elements in the story: the main characters appear in three pairs of men and women: Ahasuerus and Vashti, Esther and Mordecai, and Haman and Zeresh. There are two groups of seven servants or noblemen (1:10, 14; the names of the two groups are suspiciously similar); two helpful eunuchs (2:8-9; 7:9), two meetings of Haman and Zeresh (5:10-14; 6:13); two decrees (3:12-14; 8:9-14), and a two-day celebration of Purim (9:21).

The book of Esther differs from other books of the HB in that it exists in three separate versions. The Hebrew version is the Masoretic Text (MT), canonical for Jews and Protestants (the version treated by this commentary). There are also two Greek versions: the first, the Septuagint (LXX), is a translation of the MT but with six additional large blocks of text and numerous internal changes. This version is canonical in the Orthodox and Roman Catholic churches. The second Greek version, the Alpha Text (AT), survives in only four manuscripts. It is a translation of a Hebrew original similar but not identical to the MT. The AT was later revised to bring it into closer conformity with the LXX. Both the LXX and the AT mention God at appropriate moments in the text and portray the Jewish characters performing religious acts.

The existence of three distinct versions of the book of Esther indicates that there were probably sources behind it. Scholars have posited separate Esther and Mordecai sources (Cazelles 1961) or separate Esther, Mordecai, and Vashti sources (Bardtke 1963). Neither argument is entirely convincing. Further, among the Qumran documents an Aramaic manuscript has recently come to light which narrates the adventures of Jews living in the Persian court. J. T. Milik has argued that this manuscript (4Q550 or 4Q*Tales of the Persian Court*) was the Semitic source for the book of Esther (Milik 1992). There are indeed several striking parallels between Esther and 4Q550, but there are also many discrepancies, which indicates that the two works are at best only distantly related (Crawford 1996). The search for Esther's sources is unresolved.

COMMENTARY

The Deposition of Queen Vashti (1:1-22)

Chapter 1 provides the background and framework for the story of Esther. The story is set in Susa, one of the four capitals of the Persian Empire. King Ahasuerus is to be identified with Xerxes (486-465 BC), whose kingdom extended from India to Ethiopia. The figure of 127 provinces is historically inaccurate; this is an instance of the author's ironic hyperbole. The entire description of the banqueting scene, which contains several *hapax legomena* and Persian loanwords, is hyperbolic; the author wishes to impress the reader with the luxury and opulence of the Persian court.

The banquets hosted by Ahasuerus for his officials and the citizens of Susa introduce the important banquet motif. These banquets have a certain unrealistic quality. The first, given for all the officials of the empire, lasts for six months; it is difficult to believe the king would allow official business to grind to a halt for the sake of a party. The second banquet introduces another major theme in Esther, that of the law (Heb. *dat*). As will be seen, everything in the Persian court is done according to the law; however, at this banquet the drinking is *not* governed by the law but according to free will. In other words, under normal circumstances at the Persian court even the drinking of wine proceeded according to law, a notion both humorous and ironic.

Vashti the queen is introduced in 1:9. She is unidentified in extrabiblical sources; Xerxes' queen throughout his entire reign was Amestris (Herodotus *Persian Wars* 7.61; 9.109-13). It is unusual for Vashti to be giving a banquet for women only; Persian men and women could eat together, although women left when the drinking began. The separation is a plot device.

The final verses are fraught with comic irony. The king's actions reveal his character and foreshadow his responses throughout the story. He is sensuous, prone to emotional outbursts, and incapable of acting without the advice of others. His characterization reflects the author's bemused attitude toward Gentiles, especially Gentile rulers. Vashti's refusal to answer her husband's summons is unexplained; the rabbis speculated that the king wished her to appear naked before the assembly *(Meg., Tg. Esth I, II)!* The reaction of Ahasuerus and his advisors turns a domestic dispute into a national crisis. Vashti, who refused to appear before the king, is now forbidden to appear before the king. Next, an inane decree is promulgated; every man is to rule in his own house and speak his own language. The author is careful to explain that the law *(dat)* of the Medes and the Persians is unalterable, an important theme that will recur.

Esther Becomes Queen (2:1-18)

This section introduces the two protagonists Esther and Mordecai. The sexual contest proposed by Ahasuerus' servants demonstrates the power of the king; all eligible young women are to become his concubines, and their obedience is presumed. This obedience extends to Esther and Mordecai. Mordecai is a royal courtier, a Jew descended from Kish, presumably the Kish who is the father of Saul (1 Sam 9:1; 14:51). Esther (who also has a Hebrew name, Hadassah, like Daniel in Dan 1:7) is an orphan adopted by Mordecai; her only evident characteristics are youth and beauty. Esther enters the king's harem without protest; this seeming willingness to obey an immoral command troubled the rabbis and later commentators (Paton 1908: 96), but it should be recalled that Esther, as the king's subject, really has no choice. Once in the harem, Esther begins to display the "political" skills which will serve her well throughout the story; by winning the favor of Hegai she positions herself for a favorable reception by the king.

The author emphasizes that Esther, following Mordecai's command, did not reveal that she was Jewish. This may indicate that Jews were not fully accepted in the Persian court, in spite of the fact that Mordecai was a courtier. Esther plays her role well; unlike Daniel, she eats non-kosher food, and her ostensible goal is sexual intercourse with the Gentile king. It is likely that strict observance was not important to the original audience of the book.

Esther (now given a proper genealogy and her relation to Mordecai explained) is completely successful in her first test of courtly strategy; she wins the king's heart and becomes queen. The scene closes with a banquet; as Vashti fell at a banquet, Esther's rise is completed at a banquet.

Mordecai Discovers the Eunuchs' Plot (2:19-23)

The "second gathering" of the virgins is unexplained and probably reflects a textual problem in the Hebrew (Clines 1984: 209 et al.). Palace intrigues were common in the Persian court; Xerxes himself was murdered in a harem coup. Mordecai's discovery of the plot, which goes unrewarded, puts the king in his debt. The text emphasizes that although Esther is married, her primary loyalty still lies with Mordecai. By their actions they both prove themselves to be loyal subjects of the Persian king, an important notion for the diaspora audience.

Haman's Plot to Destroy the Jews (3:1-15)

Haman, the chief antagonist, is introduced as an Agagite. Agag was the Amalekite king who was the cause of Saul's downfall (1 Sam 15:8-33). Further, the Amalekites were hereditary enemies of Israel (Exod 17:8-16; Num 24:20). Thus Haman and Mordecai (a Jew and a kinsman of Saul) are natural antagonists. Haman's promotion does not bode well for the Jews.

The practice of prostration before superiors is familiar both in the Persian court and the HB (Gen 42:6), so Mordecai's refusal to bow to Haman is puzzling. He cannot be making a general refusal since then he would be unable to function in the court; he must be refusing to bow to Haman specifically. The final clause of 3:4, "for he had told them that he was a Jew," at least explains why the other courtiers report his insubordination to Haman, and may also be meant as an explanation for his refusal to bow; however, the actual reason for his refusal is not stated. The LXX and Josephus claim that Haman demanded *divine* honors, which Mordecai as a Jew could not pay. The targums state that Haman wore an idol pinned to his breast, which would make bowing by Mordecai idolatry. The fact that Haman is an Agagite is probably the best explanation; Mordecai will not bow to his hereditary enemy. This may also explain why the other courtiers report Mordecai's behavior to Haman; they see this as a power struggle between Mordecai the Jew and Haman the Agagite. Although Mordecai is portrayed as a wise courtier, his point-blank and unexplained refusal is similar to Vashti's. Her refusal had devastating personal consequences; Mordecai's refusal will have even graver repercussions.

Haman, like Ahasuerus, overreacts to the insubordination. He decides not only to punish Mordecai but also to wipe out all Jews, thus reversing the Holy War command against the Amalekites in 1 Sam 15:3 (Dommershausen 1968: 62). 3:7 presents the etymology for the festival of Purim, the ostensible reason for the writing of the book of Esther. The casting of lots to determine an auspicious day was common in the ancient world (see the use of Urim and Thummim by the high priest in Exod 28:30 and Num 27:21). The fact that Haman casts the *pur* in Nisan is an oblique, ironic reference to the exodus; the Jews now seem headed for destruction rather than salvation!

Haman's charges against the Jews are a tissue of truths, half-truths, and outright lies (Fox 1991: 47-48). The Jews are "scattered" throughout the empire (truth); they do have their own law (the Torah), but they also observe the laws of whatever country they are in (thus a half-truth). Finally, it is a lie that they do not keep the king's law, as witnessed by the previous behavior of Esther and Mordecai. Haman offers no proof, nor does Ahasuerus ask for any; he does not even inquire concerning the people's identity. The bribe Haman offers is enormous, probably the equivalent of 375 tons of silver. It is not clear in this passage whether Ahasuerus accepts the bribe, but in 4:7 and 7:4 Mordecai and Esther imply that he does. Haman is the active enemy of the Jews; but Ahasuerus, although only passive and thoughtless, is just as dangerous.

In 3:12-15 Haman sets the wheels of the Persian bureaucracy in motion to carry out his genocidal plot. The decree *(dat)*, written in the name of Ahasuerus and sealed with his ring, is irrevocable. The language of the decree is both a foreshadowing of events to come and a reminiscence of the events of the exodus and conquest; now, however, the roles appear to be reversed. Haman assumes that there are people in the empire who would be willing, even eager, to destroy the Jews. The reaction of the citizens of Susa in v. 15, however, hints at a better reaction from the Gentiles; while Haman and Ahasuerus sit down to a banquet (signaling the close of an episode), the city is thrown into confusion. It is Haman the Agagite who is the Jews' enemy, not Gentiles in general.

Mordecai Turns to Esther (4:1-17)

Mordecai's immediate response to the news of Haman's edict is to enact the typical gestures of mourning: sackcloth, ashes, and lamentation (Gen 37:34; 2 Sam 13:19; 18:33). The Jews also mourn ritually; it is striking that God is not mentioned as the object of these gestures, even at this moment of great peril. The omission is almost certainly deliberate in a book written by a Jewish author for a Jewish audience, but the motivation for it is not transparent.

In fact, Mordecai turns not to God but to Esther, who would presumably have great influence with the king. Her sheltered life in the harem is apparent from the fact that she has no knowledge of Haman's decree and that her dialogue with Mordecai is conducted entirely through a third party, Hathach. Mordecai's demand that Esther go to the king to avert the disaster is simple, and he expects to be obeyed; the last indication the author gave concerning Esther was that she continued to obey her cousin (2:20). Her refusal, then, is unexpected. Unlike Vashti's and Mordecai's earlier refusals, however, Esther's is reasonable: she risks death by appearing unsummoned before the king. Further, she has not been summoned by her husband for thirty days, implying that her influence is at a low ebb. The historical accuracy of her claim is doubtful; Josephus claims it applies only to the royal family (*Ant.* 11.204), while Herodotus knows of a Median tradition that made unannounced entry before the king unlawful but allowed a petitioner to request an audience in advance (*Persian Wars* 1.99; 3.72, 77, 84, 118, 140). Whatever the historical validity of Esther's claim, it serves the author's purpose to emphasize the precariousness of her position, even after five years on the throne. Esther's position as a woman in a male court mirrors that of the Jews in a Gentile world, with the threat of danger ever present below the seemingly calm surface.

Mordecai will not accept Esther's refusal. The ensuing dialogue reveals at least in part the author's theology. First, Esther cannot escape the danger because of her position. In spite of the fact that her identity is hidden, she remains a Jew, and that ethnic identity is her primary one. Second, in 4:14 Mordecai makes the claim that if she does not act the Jews will still be delivered, but she and her family will perish. This statement appears to assume the existence of a providential order, but it is again striking that God is not mentioned by name. Some of the versions understood the word "quarter" (Heb. *maqom*) as a circumlocution for God (Josephus, *Tg. Esth I, II;* see Moore 1971: 50), but it may simply refer to another unknown human helper (Fox 1991: 63). Mordecai is certain that Esther, in spite of the ambiguity of her situation, must act, for it is possible ("Who knows?") that this is the very reason that she became queen. This again implies belief in divine providence, but in order for the divine plan to work, humans must respond and act. The author's theology is profoundly contemporary in its acknowledgment of human uncertainty concerning the divine purpose in the face of ambiguous circumstances (see also Levenson 1997: 81).

Esther's response in 4:16 reveals an astonishing change in her character. From being a pliant and obedient beauty queen, she becomes a figure of royal authority, an active risk taker. She devises a plan, delivers a command to Mordecai, and expects to be obeyed. The fast she orders is the only overtly religious action in the book, but even here God is not mentioned as the object (*contra* the AT and the LXX). Esther is fully aware of the risk she is taking ("if I perish, I perish"), but her primary focus of loyalty has shifted from herself to her people. Esther has become the leader of the Jews, and Mordecai hurries to obey her.

Esther Goes to the King (5:1-8)

The report of Esther's unsummoned appearance before the king is almost anti-climactic; the MT's report is so brief that the redactor of the LXX added two long sections (Additions C and D) to his text. These Additions drastically heighten the dramatic quality and religious tone of the scene.

Esther's act of donning "royalty" (Heb. *malkut*) emphasizes her status as queen and contrasts her with Vashti, who refused to wear the royal crown. Esther is relying on the qualities that gained the king's favor in the first place: her beauty and agreeableness. Although this may be distasteful to contemporary feminists, Esther should be admired; she is using the tools available to her within the male power structure (White 1989: 173). In this case, the end clearly justifies the means. After dressing appropriately, Esther sets out for the throne room, evidently at some distance from her own apartments. The narrator gives no insight into Esther's inner state; she simply walks to the throne room (cf. LXX Addition D and Josephus).

Esther is immediately successful in her approach; the extended scepter is a sign of Ahasuerus's clemency. Her title, "Queen," is emphasized several times in this section, suggesting her elevated and favored position. However, it also suggests her reliance on the king's favor and its inherent uncertainty.

Ahasuerus realizes the urgency behind her appearance, for he immediately asks for her request and promises to grant it. The author deliberately begins to build narrative suspense here. Esther's first request is not, as expected, to avert the edict of genocide, but an invitation to a dinner party! Esther now reveals her skills as a courtier. The king's consent to a dinner party, on its surface a simple and foolish request, gives Esther several advantages. In the play of courtesies, it puts the king under obligation to her, making it more likely he will grant her real request. Further, it places both Ahasuerus and Haman in the harem, Esther's own territory, rather than in the male-dominated public court. Esther is portrayed as a skillful and wise courtier.

The banquet scene, as a recurring motif, signals that something important is about to happen. Now both Ahasuerus and the reader expect Esther to make her real petition. Instead she invites him to a second banquet! Her reply forms an ellipsis: "And Esther replied, and she said, 'My request and my petition . . .'" (5:7). Does this imply hesitation? The language of her reply, culminating in the invitation to the second banquet, is a masterpiece of strategic rhetoric. She begins by presuming on the king's favor, then on his good judgment; finally, she boldly asks the king to prove his favor by coming to her second banquet, where she will make her real petition. If the king comes to the second banquet, he has thereby promised to do whatever she wants (Clines 1984: 305). Esther has backed her husband into a corner, and he has allowed it. The silent Haman has become the pawn of the clever queen.

Haman Builds a Gallows (5:9-14)

This pericope is a reminder that Haman, although Esther's dupe, is still a dangerous force. Haman is portrayed as the stereotypical fool; unlike the wise Esther, who successfully conceals her emotions and motives, Haman's are fully revealed (see Prov 29:11). Hurrying home, he is "good of heart," only to encounter the still truculent Mordecai, who makes him "full of wrath." Mordecai has returned to his usual court position; his continued defiance of Haman is enigmatic. Whatever the original reason for his refusal to bow to Haman, it still holds in spite of the fact that his action has placed the Jews in mortal danger.

Haman's reaction is out of all proportion to the crime, in keeping with the reactions of the other male Gentiles throughout the story. Although extraordinarily well off by the usual wisdom standards (wealth, sons, and good standing with the ruler), Haman the fool can only focus on the personal slight by Mordecai. However, he is also stymied by Mordecai's continued recalcitrance.

Zeresh, Haman's wife, suggests the obvious solution. Zeresh is the third strong female character in the book of Esther; her introduction suggests a deliberate contrast between pairs of stronger females and weaker males: Vashti/Ahasuerus, Esther/Mordecai, Esther/Ahasuerus, and Zeresh/Haman. The males in the story all ultimately rely on female strength to achieve their goals. Zeresh's suggestion that Haman build a gallows for impaling Mordecai is a practical solution to Haman's original problem which Haman's grandiose plan of Jewish genocide did not solve. Haman accepts the plan, leaving the reader aware that the danger to the Jews is still present.

Haman's Humiliation (6:1-13)

The author of Esther gives his sense of comic irony full rein in this scene. There are several coincidences that may be more than coincidences, and "multiple silences" (Dommershausen 1968: 86; Fox 1991: 78) that propel the action forward. The first coincidence is the king's sleeplessness (compare Dan 6:18; 2 Esdr 3:1). The AT, the LXX, and Josephus find this so uncoincidental that they simply give the credit to God. Second, when the royal annals are opened, it is the passage concerning Mordecai's unrewarded service that is read. Third, Haman happens to be standing in the court when the king, as is his wont, seeks an advisor.

The "multiple silences" begin in 6:6. The king does not say who is to be honored; Haman does not know it is Mordecai; the king does not know that Haman and Mordecai are enemies; and Haman does not tell the king the real situation. Add to this Esther's silence concerning her Jewishness and her relationship to Mordecai, and Haman is caught in a trap of his own making. The author takes great delight in Haman's egocentricity and subsequent humiliation; the reader is called upon to sit back and chuckle with him. The king, in his question to Haman, uses the phrase "the man whom the king delights to honor" (v. 6). This phrase, an ironic foreshadowing for both Haman and Mordecai, will be lovingly repeated by Haman four times in his reply. Haman's eloquence in vv. 8-9 is extraordinary, for what he is requesting is no less than royal honors for himself. The honors that Haman requests are modeled on those given to Joseph in Gen 41:42-43; Joseph receives linen garments, rides in the second royal chariot, and is hailed wherever he goes. However, the contrast is significant: Joseph's honor is deserved while Haman's imagined honor is not. The royal clothing reflects status and could only be worn by those entitled to it; Esther puts on "royalty" when she goes unsummoned to the king (5:1). The royal horse could only be ridden by the king. The crown on the horse has given trouble to commentators (some have assumed that a crown that the *king* has worn must be meant), but the problem may be solved by Assyrian reliefs showing horses wearing tall, pointed headdresses (Moore 1971: 65). The "man whom the king delights to honor" is to be robed and set on the horse by one of the "princes of the king, the nobles" (6:9), a member of the seven noble Persian families. Finally, this noble is to proclaim to the entire city the honor given to the man by the king. This is an unusually high honor that Haman has concocted!

As we have seen before, the king immediately and without reflection accepts the advice. The author now gives the theme of ironic reversal full play: it is Mordecai who is to be honored, not Haman. What is more, the king calls him Mordecai the *Jew,* heaping humiliation upon Haman. This also indicates that the king does not connect the edict of destruction he so blithely approved with the Jews, another example of the "multiple silences" of the text.

Haman obeys the king; in 6:11 the report of his action mirrors what Haman says in vv. 8-9, but very laconically; and we do not get any insight into Haman's emotions or Mordecai's reaction to this extraordinary event (cf. the Greek versions). The rabbis add the colorful, if apocryphal, note that Haman's daughter, seeing Haman and Mordecai from her roof and supposing that Haman was riding and Mordecai leading him, emptied her chamberpot on Haman's head. When she discovered what she had done, she killed herself by jumping from the roof (*Meg.* 16a).

Finally, 6:12-13 articulate the great turning point of the story. According to the wise Zeresh, Haman will surely fall, indeed has already begun to fall, before Mordecai *the Jew.* The reason is unstated, but the reader can presume it: the Jews are divinely protected, and Haman the Agagite is the hereditary enemy of the Jews. Therefore he must fall. As Levenson puts it: "Actions seem to come out of nowhere in this tale, but they gradually link together to form an immensely positive and meaningful pattern of Jewish deliverance: if the term 'theology' means anything in reference to the book of Esther, that is its theology" (Levenson 1997: 95).

Esther's Second Banquet (6:14–8:2)

As the scene opens, the emphasis again switches to Esther. The reader should recall that Esther knows nothing of Mordecai's honor and Haman's humiliation; further, Haman is still the second-in-command and the edict against the Jews still stands. As far as Esther is concerned, the situation is as dangerous as ever.

The dialogue between Esther and the king brings to a climax the suspense of the previous scenes. When Ahasuerus asks for the third time for Esther's "petition" and "request," Esther is prepared with her reply. She begins with the proper courtly phrases, then goes on to match the words of the king's offer. The parallelism of "petition" and "my life" and "request" and "my people" indicate that Esther has now fully identified herself with the still unidentified Jews. 7:4 is difficult to translate; Esther declares that she and her people have been "sold," implying that Ahasuerus accepted the bribe offered by Haman, and she repeats the verbs of the decree in 3:13, "destroyed," "killed," and "annihilated." The last clause, however, is unclear. A literal translation would be "for there is not distress equivalent [cf. 3:8] in injury *(hapax legomenon)* to the king." Esther seems to mean that she would not have protested if the Jews had only been sold into slavery, for that would not be worth the king's concern. It is their potential annihilation (which includes her, his queen) that forces her to bring it to his attention.

Ahasuerus's response is one of complete bewilderment; he does not connect her petition with the edict of destruction, which he approved in ch. 3. He has been malleable and lazy; the consequence is shame brought about by his failure to protect his wife (Klein 1995: 153-56).

The scene is brought to a climax by Esther's ringing accusation in 7:6. The wording of the verse links Ahasuerus and Esther (the king and queen) against Haman, and foreshadows the outcome. The emotional Ahasuerus is once again "full of wrath" (cf. 1:12) and his exit to the garden (to cool off?) sets the stage for a scene of black comedy. Haman, understandably terrified for his life, proceeds to plead with the queen for mercy. Haman the Agagite, proud annihilator of the Jews, must now beg Esther the Jew for his life. The king, spotting Haman prostrate before the queen, sees not a plea for mercy but an attempted rape! The accusation, ridiculous on its face, allows the king to take action against Haman: he cannot punish Haman for a plan that he himself approved, but he can punish him for the attempted rape of his wife. In a final ironic twist, Haman is impaled on the very gallows he intended for Mordecai.

Some commentators have taken Esther to task for not showing mercy to her enemy: "her character would have been more attractive if she had shown pity toward a fallen foe" (Paton 1908: 264). However, the criticism reveals a gender bias against strong women; it is unlikely that such pity would have been demanded of Mordecai in the same situation. Esther is locked in a life-and-death struggle on behalf of the Jews; Haman is not an innocent victim, nor does he exhibit remorse. His continued presence would leave the fate of the Jews unresolved. The parallel with Saul is likewise instructive (1 Sam 15:1-9): Saul spared Agag and lost the kingship and eventually his life; Esther will not make the same mistake!

8:1-2 brings to an end the "multiple silences" of the story. Haman the Agagite is revealed as the enemy of the Jews. Queen Esther is identified as a Jew; and Mordecai, the benefactor of the king, is introduced as Esther's cousin. The most significant reversal of the story has occurred: Esther/Mordecai and Haman have switched places. Only Ahasuerus remains the same; he gives his new favorite, Mordecai, his signet ring (just confiscated from his old favorite, Haman). Only one loose end remains: the irrevocable decree against the Jews still stands.

The Undoing of Haman's Plot (8:3-17)

Without the convention of the MT version that the law of the Medes and the Persians "cannot be changed," Esther and Mordecai could simply annul Haman's decree (as they do in the AT). This would render the battle scenes superfluous, and the story's connection to the festival of Purim would be made more tentative. Given the MT's convention, however, Esther and Mordecai now have to find a way to neutralize Haman's edict. Esther must first, by her charms, obtain the king's permission to circumvent the decree. Her appeal is based on her personal favor with the king, not on the ethics of mass murder; Ahasuerus has already shown himself indifferent to the affairs of his wider realm, but quick to act when he is personally affected. Esther's ploy works; Ahasuerus gives her carte blanche although he once again eludes responsibility by placing the matter entirely in her hands. For the Jews, the general situation of the Persian court has not changed; the basic indifference of the Gentile ruler to their fate continues; their hope lies in the power of their leaders.

Mordecai's decree is an obvious contrast to Haman's, but also contrasts with the decree against Vashti that opened the book. Scribes are gathered together (cf. 3:12), their writing is according to *Mordecai's* command (cf. 3:12), and it is written to the satraps, the governors, and the princes (cf. 3:12) of the provinces from India to Ethiopia, 127 provinces (cf. 1:1). The decree is written in every group's writing and language (cf. 1:22; 3:12), in the name of Ahasuerus and sealed with his ring (cf. 3:12), and it is sent by the official Persian postal system (cf. 1:22; 3:13). The narrator is emphasizing that this is an official decree, the same as Haman's; it becomes part of the law of the Medes and the Persians and is therefore irrevocable. The Jews receive permission to "destroy, kill, and annihilate" (cf. 3:13; see also 7:4) any ethnic or provincial force, any adversaries, including(?) women and children (cf. 3:13), and take their booty (cf. 3:13). The major difference lies in the fact that Mordecai also writes to the Jews, no longer innocent victims. The decree gives the Jews permission to defend themselves; that right may seem self-evident to modern readers, but in the world of the Persian court in Esther, where everything is done according to the law (1:8), even self-defense must be legislated. The parallelism with the previous decrees emphasizes the wisdom doctrine of retributive justice, but Mordecai's inclusion of women and children in his counter decree has made him vulnerable to the charge of "bloodthirstiness" (Paton 1908: 274; Moore 1971: 80, 83). Robert Gordis, in an attempt to solve the moral dilemma, proposes that the last phrase of Mordecai's decree is a "citation" of Haman's decree, so that "women and children" refer to *Jewish* women and children who might be attacked according to the terms of Haman's decree. Mordecai's decree thus simply allows the (male) Jews to defend themselves and their women and children (Gordis 1976: 49-53). The Hebrew, however, does not clearly identify to which ethnic group the women and children belong; therefore, Gordis's solution is not certain. A more likely solution is that the author viewed these battles as the equivalent of a holy war; therefore, all the enemies fell under the ban (Heb. *ḥerem;* Deut 20:16-17).

In 8:15-17 Mordecai's ascension to the pinnacle of (nonroyal) power is completed. There are parallels in the description of his appearance both to previous scenes in Esther and to the Joseph story (1:6, 11; 5:1; 6:8; Genesis 41). In this scene Mordecai gains exactly what Haman wanted in ch. 6. Esther's absence is noteworthy; the author is slipping back into his androcentric world, and she is once more sequestered in the harem.

The Jews, as we would expect, celebrate the reprieve. The reaction of the Gentiles is informative. The city of Susa, thrown into confusion in 3:15, shouts and rejoices. There is no hint of anti-Semitism here; it is Haman who was the enemy, not Gentiles in general. Finally, in the provinces many Gentiles "professed to be Jews" (8:17; Heb. *mityahadim*) out of fear. This is enigmatic; the Hebrew word may indicate actual conversion (the LXX states that they were circumcised). But the meaning of conversion in the nonobservant atmosphere of the story is uncertain. It is clear that some Gentiles identified themselves with the Jews in some way, and that this was acceptable to the author.

The Battles (9:1-19)

The endings of the MT, the AT, and the LXX diverge radically at this point, leading to the conclusion that the original tale of Esther and Mordecai (proto-Esther, now lost) did not include an extended battle report or an etiology of Purim, but rather ended with the triumph of Esther and Mordecai over Haman. Thus proto-Esther would have had more of the character of the tale of a royal courtier, such as Daniel 2–6 or 4Q*Tales of the Persian Court* (4Q550), which never depart from their court setting (Wills 1990: 153). The MT as it now stands, however, forms a unified literary whole, with the two banquets of Purim in 9:17 and 9:18 forming an envelope construction with the king's banquets in 1:3 and 1:5 (Berg 1979: 31-47).

9:1-5, set in the provinces on the thirteenth of Adar, bring the themes of ironic reversal and power to a climax. The Jews, who were to have been destroyed, instead destroy their enemies. The Gentiles now fear the Jews instead of being feared by them since Mordecai the Jew rather than Haman the Agagite is now the emperor's second-in-command. The Jews overcome their enemies easily. The text suggests aggressive rather than defensive action; compare Josh 8:21-22; 10:28; 11:10, all examples of holy war which use the same verb *nkh,* "to smite." Likewise in Esther, all the enemies are slaughtered, but the author makes the point three times in these verses (9:10, 15, 16) that the Jews took no plunder (cf. Abraham in Gen 14:22-24). These are not battles for human gain, but aggressive actions in the cause of self-defense. They are thus morally permissible.

The Jews of Susa, the seat of Haman's power, kill five hundred in the citadel alone, along with the ten sons of Haman, thus finally fulfilling the command of Deut 25:17-19 to "blot out the remembrance of Amalek from under heaven." The fact that the fighting takes place in the citadel (Heb. *birah*) rather than the city of Susa is strange; it seems unlikely that the king would allow fighting in the palace itself (Moore 1971: 87)!

Esther reappears in this chapter in a somewhat bloodthirsty guise. The necessity for a second day of slaughter in Susa is unclear. Gerleman is probably correct when he claims that 9:11-15 owe their existence only to the need to explain the historical fact of the two-day festival; Susan (or urban) Jews celebrated on the fifteenth of Adar because they were still fighting on the fourteenth (Gerleman 1982: 308-49). The impaling of the corpses of Haman's sons illustrates the principle of intergenerational retribution (Deut 5:9); as Haman is punished, so are his sons.

The celebrations that follow the fighting celebrate the respite from danger, not the slaughter itself. The number of enemies killed (75,000) is hyperbolic; the LXX reduces the figure to 15,000 and the AT to 10,107 (a mysteriously exact number). The festival originates in the provinces, where it is celebrated on the fourteenth; urban celebrations follow on the fifteenth. The festival, in keeping with the tone of the rest of the book, is essentially secular; no prayers or sacrifices are mentioned. Rather, the actions of the celebrations imitate or oppose earlier actions in Esther. The feasts mirror the king's banquets in ch. 1; the rejoicing contrasts with the mourning in 4:3; and the portions of food (Heb. *manot*) that the Jews send each other recall the *manot* that Esther received from Hegai in 2:9, arguably the one incident that began Esther and Mordecai's ascendancy.

The Letters of Purim (9:20-32)

The purpose of these letters is to give official sanction to the non-Mosaic festival of Purim. Purim, an essentially secular festival originating in the diaspora that may originally have been a Jewish version of a Babylonian or Persian holiday, may have had trouble winning acceptance in Judea. It evidently was not celebrated at Qumran, for example. The author thus attempts to establish royal sanction for the festival through the letters of Mordecai and Esther. None of this, however, has any actual historical basis.

Mordecai's letter is not a royal decree but rather a request of the Jews that they confirm the yearly celebration of a festival already begun. The celebration is a two-day feast for all Jews, whether provincial or urban, thus reflecting later historical reality. The days chosen indicate again that the celebration is for respite from danger rather than victory; if victory were to be celebrated, the thirteenth and fourteenth of Adar would be more apt. The manner of celebration echoes that of 9:19, with the addition of gifts to the poor; the festival remains secular in nature.

9:24-26 give a synopsis of the events of the book, severely telescoped, and in some cases in disagreement with the main plot (cf. 9:25 [where the Hebrew does not contain Esther's name] with 8:9-14, 9:7-10), possibly indicating a secondary redactor. In spite of the author's best efforts, the connection of the name Purim with the *pur* that Haman casts remains murky; it is especially unclear why the festival is named after an action of the enemy Haman!

The Jews confirm the holiday in 9:27-28, which probably are meant to convince those not celebrating the festival in the time of the redactor that it is an established Jewish holiday. The royal authority by which it was established is provided by Esther's letter.

The mention of Mordecai in 9:29 is probably an interpolation; what follows is an official letter from Esther the queen giving Purim royal sanction. The irony of the establishment of a Jewish festival by the Persian (albeit Jewish) queen should not be missed; but compare the establishment of the Torah as the official law of the Jews by the Persian king Artaxerxes (Ezra 7:11-25). The referent of the "second" letter is unclear since only Mordecai's letter has been sent; it is probably a later gloss meant to refer to Esther's letter. The official nature of the letter is emphasized by the fact that it is sent to the 127 provinces (1:1; 8:9). The addition of *the Jew* Mordecai in v. 31, and the statement that the Jews had established Purim for themselves, may be meant to soften the idea that a foreign queen had established Purim. However, it is clearly Esther's authority as queen that establishes the festival of Purim. The reference to "fasts and lamentations" is unclear; it may refer to other non-Mosaic observances the Jews had taken upon themselves in the postexilic period (see the mention of the Day of Nicanor in 2 Macc 15:36, followed by Mordecai's Day, possibly a reference to Purim). In later Jewish tradition, the minor "Fast of Esther" is observed on Adar 13.

Appendix concerning Mordecai (10:1-3)

These verses, together with 8:1-2, form an envelope for the battles and letters in ch. 9. The *mas* or tax mentioned in 10:1 may be a corvée of labor (1 Kgs 5:13) or a straight tax. This may be the same tax that Ahasuerus lifted in honor of Esther's crowning (2:18); it is now reimposed.

The last two verses, which concern the greatness of Ahasuerus and Mordecai, are notable for the disappearance of Esther. Although she has been the heroine of the book, saving the Jews through her bravery and political skill, obtaining high office for her cousin Mordecai, and establishing the festival of Purim, in the last passage the author reverts to the androcentric world of the postexilic period and closes by extolling, not Esther, but Ahasuerus and Mordecai.

Mordecai's rule is declared to be beneficial to the Jews, but, like Joseph's, his policies benefit the entire empire as well (Gen 47:13-26), and no one suffers because he is Jewish. For the author, the ideal situation has obtained; the Jew Mordecai serves the Gentile Ahasuerus, and the Jews throughout the Persian Empire live in peace and harmony with the Gentiles.

Bibliography. Bardtke, H. 1963. *Das Buch Esther,* Gütersloh: G. Mohn • Berg, S. B. 1979, *The Book of Esther: Motifs, Themes, and Structure,* Missoula, Mont.: Scholars • Berlin, A. 2001, *The JPS Commentary: Esther,* Philadelphia: Jewish Publication Society • Cazelles, H. 1961, "Note sur la composition du rouleau d'Esther," in *Lex tua veritas: Festschrift für Hubert Junker,* Trier: Paulinus • Clines, D. J. A. 1984, *The Esther Scroll: The Story of the Story,* Sheffield: JSOT • Crawford, S. W. 1999, "Esther," in *New Interpreter's Bible,* Nashville: Abingdon • Crawford, S. W. 1998 [1992], "Esther," in *The Women's Bible Commentary,* Louisville: Westminster/John Knox • Crawford, S. W. 1996, "Has Esther Been Found at Qumran? 4Qproto-Esther and the Esther Corpus," *RevQ* 17:307-25 • Dommershausen, W. 1968, *Die Estherrolle,* Stuttgart: Katholisches Bibelwerk • Fox, M. V. 1991, *Character and Ideology in the Book of Esther,* Columbia: University of South Carolina • Gerleman, G. 1982, "Studien zu Esther: Stoff — Struktur — Stil — Sinn," in *Studies in the Book of Esther,* New York: Ktav • Gordis, R. 1976, "Studies in the Esther Narrative," *JBL* 95:49-53 • Klein, L. R. 1995, "Honor and Shame in Esther," in *A Feminist Companion to Esther, Judith and Susanna,* Sheffield: Sheffield Academic • Laniak, T. S. 1998, *Shame and Honor in the Book of Esther,* Atlanta: Scholars • Levenson, J. D. 1997, *Esther: A Commentary,* Louisville: Westminster/John Knox • Milik, J. T. 1992, "Les Modèles Araméens du Livre d'Esther dans la Grotte 4 de Qumrân," *RevQ* 15:321-99 • Moore, C. A. 1971, *Esther,* Garden City, N.Y.: Doubleday • Paton, L. B. 1908, *A Critical and Exegetical Commentary on the Book of Esther,* Edinburgh: T&T Clark • White, S. A. 1989, "Esther: A Feminine Model for Jewish Diaspora," in *Gender and Difference in Ancient Israel,* Philadelphia: Fortress • Wills, L. M. 1990, *The Jew in the Court of the Foreign King,* Minneapolis: Fortress.

Job

Katharine J. Dell

INTRODUCTION

The book of Job is, on the face of it, a simple tale of a man of good works and religious faith who finds himself struck down by misfortune and illness in the prime of life. He seeks to understand the reasons for his suffering and to work through his relationship with God after what has happened. Friends come to comfort him and he has an impassioned debate with them, but when finally he has a visitation from God himself, he feels in some way justified or answered. The book ends with his restoration to good fortune, to a new set of children, and to twice as many sheep and cattle as he had before. However, when we start to dig deeper than the surface story we find hidden undercurrents, contradictions, and complex themes that have made the book of Job a source of great interest in the scholarly community and have led to its being regarded generally as a masterpiece of world literature. When we start to look at the way the book might have been put together, its context and audience, its theological themes and its reception over the centuries, a picture starts to emerge of a book that not only comforts but frustrates; one that raises questions without providing clear answers and yet addresses some of the issues closest to the hearts of human beings seeking to put their faith in God. The book has a contemporary feel to it — humanity wrestles with God in an existential vein, the issue of innocent suffering rings down the centuries into our own, and questions of faith in the face of injustice and even persecution are as fresh today as they were when the book was written.

The book of Job is generally dated between the sixth and the fourth century BC. This was the period of Israel's history after the exile in which a people had been taken from their homeland. A generation had suffered the injustice of captivity in a foreign land, and the prophets had spoken of punishment for wrongdoing as the reason for this exile and aired the theme of the suffering of the innocent. A new generation was now back in Israel, rebuilding their temple and their lives and seeking new answers to their questions. The idea that all suffering was punishment for wrongdoing began to be questioned, certainly on an individual level. We have many varied writings from this period, and Job is just one of a whole range of material dealing with many different issues that were of concern to the postexilic community. The book is usually seen as belonging to the wisdom literature of the OT, literature which dealt with questions of an individualistic and universal character from a human starting point, very different in style from much of the prophetic, legal, and narrative material of the OT. This would explain the fact that a non-Israelite character is used as the hero of the tale — Job from the land of Uz, which is usually identified with Edom, an area south of Israel — since the wisdom literature links up with a more international genre of wisdom known to us from surrounding nations.

One might be surprised at this suggestion of a postexilic dating since the book has a much older feel to it. Job is described in terms reminiscent of Abraham or Isaac, a man whose wealth was measured by the number of flocks he had. We find this portrayal in the first two chapters of the book and in the last. But one perceives a problem, for the issues raised in the main body of the book do not belong to this early period; rather, they fit into the early post-exilic period. This has led to the suggestion that the book is to be regarded as made up of two separate parts. The chapters that surround the dialogue also differ from the rest in that they are in prose rather than in poetry, and their style is therefore very different. The likelihood is therefore that these prose chapters may be the vestiges of an older story which may have circulated down the centuries in an oral tradition and then been written down in a fresh context for a later age by the main author of the book of Job. Another suggestion is that the "frame story," as it is often called, was composed by the author in a deliberately older style to give the impression of antiquity to the tale. However, the question is raised whether, if the work is a unity, an author would have sat down to compose the book in this very disjointed way. A third suggestion is that the frame story was added later than the fourth century. But how credible is it that a dialogue was in circulation without a story around it, unless of course it was simply assumed that people knew the story and so nobody took the trouble to add it until later? These are the kinds of problems that start to emerge when we dig deeper into the construction and setting of the book.

The issue of the relationship of the frame tale to the dialogue is not the only literary-critical problem raised in connection with the book. Once we start to look for disjointedness and inconsistency, we find them in many places in the book. We read at the end of the Prologue that Job's friends sat in silence with him, but then when we turn the next few pages we find Eliphaz, Bildad, and Zophar speaking to Job at some length. We also see a very different Job in ch. 3 than we did in the Prologue. The patient response of "Shall we receive good at the hands of God, and not receive evil?" (2:10) has been replaced by words that curse the day of his birth and the night of his conception, and the stance of protest is in the air. Later in the book we find that the speeches of Job and the friends become confused — people start to say the wrong things, and the reader is confused as to who is arguing what. This is usually explained as a dislocation of the third cycle of speeches, scribal error perhaps, or confusion in transmission of the text. Then we have the hymn to wisdom in ch. 28, which some see as belonging to the speeches but many others regard as having a separate provenance — maybe a hymn from a liturgical context, or a piece composed by the author himself, or a later addition by editors or redactors of the book. This is followed by the speeches of Elihu, and again the feeling is one of disjointedness. This is not one of the three friends introduced in the Prologue; rather, Elihu comes along unannounced, says his piece, and then is seemingly ignored by the others. Further, he repeats much that has already been said in the dialogue and anticipates some of what God is about to say, and so the presence of his speeches rather spoils the climax that is to come. Again, this has been widely regarded as a later addition, although some regard these speeches as an integral part of the work. The speeches of God then form the climax to the book, but once again the reader is jarred into the realization that God is coming from a very different starting point from that of Job and that there is a disjointedness between the concerns of Job and those of God. Is God simply a bombastic, powerful creator who puts Job down in these chapters or is there more profundity in the portrayal than that? How far does God answer Job's questions? Or does he simply create a set of new ones that are in the end unanswerable? Job repents, and so it seems that he has found some kind of answer — is it an answer inspired simply by the presence of the godhead, a kind of religious conversion, or is it one that satisfies Job intellectually as well as emotionally? Then, finally, the ending — is it credible after the debate that has just ensued concerning the insufficiency of the idea that suffering is simply a result of wrongdoing, that Job should simply be restored according to the old principle that, once proved worthy, material rewards flow thick and fast? All these seemingly intractable questions are raised by the structure of the book and its varied content, providing puzzles that have exercised scholars of the book since the rise of historical criticism in the late eighteenth century.

A primary question that is raised by all readers of the book of Job is whether we are dealing here with a historical person. We have already aired the possibility that an older tale, circulating in an oral tradition, may have been used as a vehicle for the dialogue section. Was Job a well-known figure from the distant past and thus as historical as Abraham, Isaac and Jacob, whose existence may well have been historical but to whom stories may well have been attributed as traditions about them grew? Or is Job more of a paradigm, a kind of everyman, used to give a storylike feel to what is essentially an abstract debate? Are we to believe in the patriarchal setting, which, although accurate in its details — for example, in this period individuals were able to sacrifice to God without the constraints of later temple regulations — seems wrong for a man from the land of Uz and hence a non-Israelite? Furthermore, the description of this setting has a folktale character. So, for example, the numbers of children and cattle are all round ones (interestingly, Solomon had seven hundred princesses and three hundred concubines among his wives in 1 Kgs 11:3), and the exact doubling of the numbers of animals at the end of the tale suggests that this is a stylized piece rather than a real story. The insight into heavenly happenings also lends an unreal quality to the story. Furthermore, the dialogue in the Prologue is terse and formulaic, in the manner of a folktale in which one is told just enough to keep the plot moving but no detail is given. Even the characters are caricatures rather than real people — Job and his wife in particular representing piety and its opposite.

However the claim to historicity of the character of Job is strengthened by reference to him in another part of the OT, the book of Ezekiel, and this also sheds light on the relationship of the frame story to the rest of the book. Ezek 14:14, 20 mentions Job as an exemplar of piety alongside Noah and Daniel, both known to be historical figures — the sentiment here is that even if these pious men were there, they would not be able to save others from their sin; in other words, there is no overflow of piety from one generation to another. This is part of Ezekiel's argument regarding responsibility for one's own actions. This suggests that some knowledge of a person called Job was widespread enough to be part of Israelite tradition and culture and would thus support the idea of an earlier oral tradition with roots in history and yet remembered chiefly for its theological import. That import would have been the remembrance of Job as a pious and righteous person in the face of calamity. The dialogue section is probably based on the real experiences of an actual sufferer who saw the opportunity for airing the suffering theme in the context of this story of a popular figure.

It is interesting to note changes in the scholarly climate and varied approaches to these problems. The tendency in scholarship of the early part of this century was to carve the book of Job up into original material and later additions so that succeeding versions of the book were posited (e.g., Driver and Gray, Snaith). In more recent years there has been a certain frustration with these attempts to reconstruct the development of the book, largely in the light of the sheer number of possible reconstructions and very varied suggestions as to the dating and provenance of the material and the context of the author(s). This has led to a reaction in the opposite direction, which is an interest in reading the text as a whole and assuming that, as far as possible, the book is the work of one author (e.g., Habel). This has largely been inspired by an interest in genre and in the possibility that the tensions in the book can be explained by recourse to categories of plot development and irony in the mind of the author. It is further argued that, whatever the original makeup of the different parts of the book, that information is lost to us and so the best approach is to take the work as a whole, thus letting it impact upon us in the same way that it would have done people of the past. However, there are scholars such as myself who feel that a middle way between these two positions is of more value in interpreting the book. There is still a place for literary criticism, but one that takes on board the question of the book of Job as a piece of literature with an author for whom literary technique was an important tool. There is clearly a place for reading the book as a whole, but that reading is enhanced by the recognition of different sections, notably of a distinction being made between the frame story and the dialogue where the most obvious change in genre and style occurs.

A sociological and literary context is generally found for the book of Job, and so too for its author, in the wisdom literature of the OT. The definition of what wisdom includes is itself a vexed question; on a narrow definition, one might well see Job as breaking outside its boundaries, in its overturning of the wisdom model, found in the book of Proverbs, of exact reward and retribution for deeds. Many regard Job as wisdom in revolt, part of a critique from within wisdom of its own presuppositions, although it can also be seen as on the edges of the mainline development of the wisdom material. The kinds of issue raised in Job regarding innocent suffering and how to understand it and with relationship with God in the face of terrible happenings clearly have a universal character that fits in well with what we know of other wisdom literature, especially from outside the OT. The quest for comparative material has led to some interesting parallels from the ancient Near East — the Babylonian Job and the Babylonian theodicy, for example — and has also led to some fascinating parallels with Greek tragedy. It seems that the kinds of sentiments expressed in situations of extreme suffering are similar whether you are Job sitting on his ash heap, or Prometheus bound in chains to a rock. It is difficult to know whether there was any interdependence of such literature or whether reflection on the human condition in different ages led to the production of material of a similar nature. Some scholars have made a great deal of such parallels, while others prefer to see Job mainly in the context of the OT and its homegrown wisdom. On the latter model, we might come to view Job as linked more closely theologically to other books from the same culture than to an international wisdom tradition. The question of theodicy, for example, was not new to Israel — it was raised by Abraham, by Moses, by Jonah, as well as by the prophets of the exile and by the psalmists who felt that God had hidden his face from them during their time of need.

What really gives the book of Job its profundity and lasting relevance are the theological themes aired in the book. These have been variously evaluated, scholars liking to find one theme that is the "key" to unlocking the book. Thus disinterested righteousness was seen to be the key by those who put their emphasis on the frame tale. After all, was not the whole context of Job's suffering to be seen in the light of the wager between God and Satan on the issue of whether Job was being pious and upright just because he wanted to receive the rewards brought by that kind of behavior? Did Job really love God? This was what needed to be tested, that Job's religiosity was not simply self-motivated but sprang from real faith. Thus the whole debate that takes place in the book about suffering and reward and Job's relationship with God needs to be seen in this context. On this reading the Epilogue is the inevitable ending — once Job has passed the test with flying colors, the time is ripe for the rewards to flow.

For some this reading was too limited. They preferred to put the emphasis on the dialogue between Job and the friends, which, after all, makes up the bulk of the book. There the argument is on this wisdom concern of whether the pious always get rewarded and the wicked are always punished. Job's argument is that he is pious and so does not deserve the punishment he is receiving. The friends, on the contrary, argue that Job is wrong in his belief in his innocence and that it is impossible that he should suffer so and not have done wrong. This debate is then worked through by Elihu, who takes broadly the same line as the friends. God himself then places fresh emphasis on being unable to know his ways, which are beyond human comprehension. His answer seems to justify neither Job nor the friends in their debate, serving rather to expose the limited nature of their discussion. It is only in 42:7 that Job appears to be vindicated by God over his friends, who are chastised for "not having spoken of me what is right as my servant Job has." However, the Epilogue then grates on the reader, for having just decided that the friends were wrong, we now find that, although they were wrong about Job having sinned, they were right about the doctrine of retribution. Job is proved innocent; so he is rewarded and harmony is restored.

A third approach is to see the book through the eyes of Job and God. The human-divine relationship is at the center of concern on this reading. Job is concerned that his old way of relating to God has proved inadequate, a faith that probably resembled that of the friends. He is thrown back on himself and his pain and grief, and so questions the very foundations of the relationship. He sees God as having proved cruel and victimized him, and he finds no way of receiving a fair trial before such a godhead. God's response can on these terms be seen as cutting Job down to size in reminding him of the power and wonder of creation and the many questions that remain unanswered when viewing the ways of the natural world and the behavior of animals. However, it can also be seen as a response which confirms the presence of a relationship in which both parties are defending their position. Job's repentance is sometimes seen as disappointing — it spoils the portrayal of the tragic figure standing up against his God to defend his position at all costs. Rather, Job capitulates to God's superior power and wisdom, and repents of his words. Then comes the real twist in the tale, that God vindicates Job over the friends and with this action suggests that it is better to question the relationship in the angry manner in which Job does than simply to accept stock answers as the friends have done. The Epilogue, on this reading, is then rather tongue in cheek. Job's restoration is achieved in order to fit in with common perceptions of reward and retribution, but Job knows, as do we, that his relationship with God is deeper than this and that for those who go through the fire of tribulation and come out with a deeper understanding, things can never be the same again.

Thus, when assessing the theological themes of the book of Job, we need to bear all these different readings in mind and to a certain extent hold them together. The different emphases have often emerged from preferring a certain section of the book to the others, which demonstrates that interpretations vary depending on where you happen to be standing and what concerns and emphases you bring to the text. This phenomenon of interpretive stance has come to be increasingly recognized in recent biblical study. So we find feminist, liberationist, and even vegetarian readings of the book of Job, readings that begin with a particular set of concerns and bring those to the text. Interest has also been aroused in precritical interpretations of texts and in what presuppositions earlier readers, both Jewish and Christian, brought to the text. And even earlier than that, what kinds of concerns led to the canonization of the book of Job, which never seems to have raised any questions about inclusion in Holy Scripture, despite some of its more unorthodox sentiments? These questions are now being asked, and they have added a rich dimension to the study of what has always been and continues to be a tantalizing tale.

COMMENTARY

The Prologue and Epilogue (Job 1–2 and 42:7ff.)

A primary reason for treating the Prologue and Epilogue together as a unit is that they display a consistent style which differs from the poetry of the dialogue and that they contain the only real narrative in the book. They have often been regarded as having a separate, probably earlier, provenance to the dialogue section. However, the problem is that there are inconsistencies between the two halves of the prose story which suggest that there must have been a stage at which the material was presented differently. The inconsistencies include the fact that in the Prologue the friends do not speak, and yet in the Epilogue they are chastised for not having spoken rightly of God. This fact suggests that some kind of dialogue may once have had a place in this section. Another inconsistency is that there is no mention of Job's illness in the Epilogue — there is concern with Job's property but not a word about the healing of his disease. In the Prologue the infliction of the disease is attributed to Satan. Interestingly, there are no corresponding heavenly scenes in the Epilogue in which Satan might have appeared, which has suggested to some scholars, including me, that the Satan passages in the Prologue are to be regarded as secondary in literary terms. This has the effect of making God the main heavenly player, which is fully consistent with Job's attitude in the dialogue — he never blames Satan for his misfortune — and explains Satan's absence in the Epilogue. I have divided the Prologue and Epilogue into scenes that take place on earth and scenes that take place in heaven to show that the story makes sense without the Satan passages, although it becomes a slightly different story. Without the wager section, the Prologue serves to show the attitude of a patient man in the face of calamity from God — God is presented as squarely to blame for natural disasters. This is the point from which the debate departs.

A second reason for treating the Prologue and Epilogue as a unit is that centuries of interpretation of the book have also done so. Interpretation of Job in art and music has all focused on the "story" of Job (e.g., Vaughan Williams's "'Job,' a masque for dancing," and Brueghel's "Job, visited by his wife"). Furthermore, in early interpretive circles the book of Job was read through the eyes of the frame story. So we find in the Epistle of James reference to "the patience of Job," a phrase with which most of us are no doubt familiar, referring to Job's paradigmatic responses to calamity and to his wife. We find a Job tradition running through the Middle Ages of a patient saintly man, a paradigm of morality, even the patron saint of music. So it is Job the patient, the Job of the prose, that has been received through the centuries, and it is only with the rise of biblical criticism that the less savory aspects of his wrangle with God have been fully appreciated.

Scenes That Take Place on Earth (Job 1:1-5, 13-22; 2:8-13; 42:7-17)

Job 1:1-5

The book of Job opens with an introduction to the character of Job. In the very first verse we are told that he is "blameless and upright, one who feared God and turned away from evil." The pair of words "blameless and upright" is familiar from both proverbial wisdom and from the psalms, for example, Prov 2:21; 28:10; Ps 37:37. "Fearing God and turning away from evil" is also found in other wisdom literature (Job 28:28; Prov 3:7). Clearly these words are used to locate Job as a man who represents the wisdom ideal. This is the essential starting point for the problem that will be raised by the book — that of how to understand the suffering of an innocent person. We are told of his location in Uz, generally thought to be Edom. (In Lam 4:21 "the daughter of Edom" is said to dwell in the land of Uz, but in Jer 25:20 the land of Uz is mentioned separately from Edom but alongside the Philistines, which would also suggest the south. The name "Uz" is found also in two genealogies in Genesis, but the evidence is contradictory.) More importantly we are told of his family situation and social standing. We are thus immediately shown that, as a result of his loyal behavior, he is a man of material wealth according to the pattern of retribution known from the book of Proverbs, the airing of which will be a main issue of the book. We are also straightway given two examples of his piety — his ritual purification of his children after feasts and his getting up early to offer burnt sacrifices on behalf of his children in case they might have sinned. The latter action is almost excessively pious and serves to confirm Job's innocence, which will later be called into question.

Job 1:13-22

The stage is set for calamity to strike, and this happens in the next earthly scene. After presenting a picture of harmony in which the sons and daughters were feasting at the house of their eldest brother, the narrative tells of Job being informed by four messengers of calamities to his property and family of increasing magnitude, ending with the death of his children by a hurricane. The first calamity is an invasion of Sabeans, who take his oxen and donkeys and kill his servants. The Sabeans may be the inhabitants of Sheba in southwest Arabia, although these inhabitants are nowhere else referred to as plunderers. They may have come from a closer region, they may have been nomadic, or they may be folktale enemies rather than any real group. The second calamity is "fire from heaven," which probably refers to lightning and which burns his sheep and servants. The third is another group of attackers, this time Chaldeans, probably northern nomads, who raid his camels and kill his servants. The final hurricane that strikes the house of Job's eldest son and causes it to fall on all his children could well be an exaggerated folktale wind, but such winds were known to come in from the south and east across the desert. Job's reaction is to fall to the ground in self-abasement, tearing his garments in a common rite of mourning (cf. Gen 37:29), and to bless God, an exemplary reaction by any standard. The narrator confirms this response by his comment (1:22) that Job did not sin or blame God in any way after these calamities struck.

Job 2:8-13

The next time we encounter Job is when he is scratching his sores, the result of a skin disease, the exact nature of which has occasioned much debate, as he sits among the ashes and his wife questions his perseverance. Job's disease may be leprous, which would fit in with his sitting on a heap of ashes. These ashes may well have been located outside the city wall and be the burnt remains of dung, since lepers had to stay outside the city walls. Other possibilities are elephantiasis, a disease producing swollen limbs and blackened skin, chronic eczema, smallpox, ulcerous boils, syphilis, scurvy, or vitamin deficiency. Sitting among ashes may be a ritual expression of mourning — we know that ashes were put on the head or rolled in as a sign of mourning, and sitting is often a posture of weeping. Job's wife suggests that he curse God rather than bless him, but Job chastises her as a foolish woman, again accepting good and bad from the hand of God. Her role in the book is very minor (unlike that in the LXX, where her role is expanded and she utters a long speech expressing concern for Job, and she does not reappear in the Epilogue section). No attention is given to the fact that she presumably suffers as much as Job does in the loss of property and family, a factor noted by feminist scholars in recent work (Brenner, Van Wolde). The scene ends with Job's friends, whose names also suggest Edomite connections, coming to comfort him, not recognizing him at first, and then sitting on the ground with him in mourning and empathy but without saying a word.

Job 42:7-17

In the Epilogue God speaks out against his friends for not having spoken of him what was right, and Job is instructed to intercede on their behalf. God then accepts Job's prayer as atonement for them all, another ritual act that balances the ones we saw Job undertaking in the Prologue. The tale ends with the restoration of Job and his provision with twice as much as he had before. He is once again integrated into what remains of his family and into society, and he is given animals in abundance. A new set of children is mentioned consisting of seven sons and three daughters. The daughters are named and said to be very beautiful, both curious details seemingly extraneous to the plot. The detail is also mentioned that they are to be given an inheritance as well as their brothers, a breach of usual convention. Job is then blessed with longevity, a traditional Hebrew sign of blessing, and with knowing his grandchildren and great-grandchildren, many offspring being another traditional sign of blessing.

Scenes That Take Place in Heaven (Job 1:6-12; 2:1-7)

Job 1:6-12

The earthly scenes are interspersed with heavenly ones — that of God and his heavenly council, with Satan posing the question of Job's integrity to God and God defending his servant Job's motives. The motif of a heavenly council is found in 1 Kgs 22:19 and in a number of psalms, where we also find as here mention of the "sons of god" over whom God presides in the manner of a royal council. "The Satan," or "the Adversary," is clearly among them, although it is not clear whether he belongs to the group or is an outsider. He would appear to be one of a number of messengers sent by God to survey life on earth. Satan accuses God of having placed a protective hedge around Job. He suggests that if calamity strikes, Job will soon be exposed as one whose faith is motivated only by self-interest, and so God, in order to prove him wrong, gives him permission to carry out the test. The four disasters then strike, from all different directions, two natural and two human (cf. the four plagues that attack humans in Ezek 14:12-23).

Job 2:1-7

When Job remains steadfast in his response to calamity, a second heavenly scene, of a repetitive nature to the first, presents God gloating over Job's predicted response and reveals the intention of Satan to inflict Job's body with a loathsome disease. This will be the decisive factor that will deflect Job from his piety, Satan argues, and so God allows Satan to inflict disease on Job, with the only proviso that he spare his life. This is the end of the insight into scenes in heaven until we come to the theophany of God. There is no corresponding scene where Satan is seen to capitulate in the Epilogue. Here God is in control of all the action, restoring Job to his fortunes. Satan is forgotten.

If we omit these Satan passages from the original form of the story as used by the author, we need to ask, Does the story that is left make sense? I believe that it does. According to this suggestion, the Prologue then starts with the folktale introduction to Job and his possessions and stresses his piety (cf. Ezek 14:14, 20). After 1:6-12 are omitted, the story continues with an account of the afflictions that are sent upon Job's animals, household, and family. These are said to come from God (as, of course, does the restoration of these things to Job in the

Epilogue). Job then speaks, responding as a patient man would respond to suffering — he is a model believer. Following this, 2:1-8 are removed, and the plot continues with the words of Job's wife, "Curse God, and die," and Job's reply. Next, the three friends appear but cannot speak to him, such is their shock at his condition. Turning to the epilogue in 42:7-8, God then condemns the friends for not having spoken words of comfort to Job and tells them to make a sacrifice, Job acting as intercessor on their behalf. Finally, the fortunes of Job are doubled, and a happy ending closes the book. On this reading Job is no longer seen as the victim of a bet which suggests that God is simply playing with Job to prove a point in a debate with Satan. Rather, the central concern shifts to the relationship between God and humanity (as aired later in the book), and the Prologue depicts the attitude of a patient man in the face of calamity sent by God. The central moves from the question of Job's motives for trusting God to his actions and attitude of patience in the face of calamity. God is no longer exonerated from actually inflicting the disasters; rather, he is squarely to blame for them, and this is the point from which the debate departs.

Why would anyone have added the Satan sections? Possibly this addition was made by someone concerned to make a separate contribution to the problem of God's infliction of suffering on Job, for it was unthinkable to the orthodox that God should be seen as inflicting this kind of misery on humans — it must be the work of the Satan. The idea of "Satan" is unlikely to be pre-Persian and so may date from the fourth to third centuries BC, the probable time of such secondary redactions.

Job's Opening Soliloquy (Job 3)

This section of the book is one of two soliloquies or monologues which, if they are addressed to anyone, are addressed to God but which function as the means by which Job's sentiments and situation are explored. The combination of curse and lament is distinctive here and marks it off from the debate which follows in which elements of both reappear but in the context of dialogue with others. The division into three is made on the basis of genre, and between the two laments by the stylistic marker "Why?" in 3:11 and 20. There is also clear thematic development between the different parts, although the imagery of light and dark provides unity to the chapter.

An important aspect of this chapter, notably the first section, is its closeness to Jer 20:14-18 in sentiment, imagery, and theme. Jeremiah 20 forms one of Jeremiah's confessions, which are stylized laments expressing the anguish of the prophet at the burden of his prophetic task. He, like Job, wishes that he had not been born so that he could not have undertaken this responsibility, and he curses the day his mother bore him. He also curses the man who brought the glad tidings of his birth to his father — a slight variation on the Job sentiments, almost amounting to a curse on first his mother and then his father (which would break the fifth commandment). The sentiment is also found that dying in the womb would have been a better fate than being born, "so my mother would have been my grave, and her womb forever great" (20:17b). The context is different but the sentiments are similar, and both curses are equally futile in that they are concerned with the past. Job's curse is more vivid and powerful in the way that it calls for creation's reversal — Jeremiah's curse focuses on the more human aspect of the process of childbirth.

Job 3:1-10

The dialogue opens with a curse by Job on the day of his birth — a stark contrast to the words he had previously uttered in the Prologue. We are now in the different world of the dialogue, in which a fresh picture of Job emerges as one who is longing to understand his plight, who is angry with God, who wishes for death, and who even makes recourse to legal arguments to try to pin God down. This is the first of two soliloquies, the second being Job's closing soliloquy at the end of the dialogue in ch. 27. It consists of a type of curse and a lament, such as we might find in the psalms, but it soon becomes apparent that the sentiments expressed are somewhat different from their psalmic counterparts. The cursing by Job here forms an interesting counterpoint to the advice of Job's wife at the end of ch. 2. Scholars (e.g., Clines) are generally concerned to make the point that Job does not curse God directly here, but rather curses day and night instead, which is arguably not so blasphemous. Furthermore, the question is raised whether it is legitimate to curse the past since nothing can change what has happened. The power of the curse is usually to change things in the present or immediate future. Thus Job's whole complaint here is rather futile. Maybe what we have here is a kind of parody of a curse rather than a curse proper. The whole chapter can be regarded as a death wish — the idea of cursing one's day of birth is a plea for nonexistence. In these first ten verses we find an expansion on this theme of the day and the night, both of which are personified as entities in themselves, and the desire is for a reversal of creation itself in order to obliterate them from memory. The formulation "Let that day be darkness!" (3:4) echoes the words of Gen 1:3, "Let there be light."

The idea of cursing the day of one's birth probably consists of wishing that day out of the calendar. Job sees that day as the source of his misery in that he began to exist from that moment, and each time his birthday comes around he is reminded of this fact. Then he goes on to consider the time even before birth, the moment of conception, when he was first an entity. The night is personified here, and to it is ascribed knowledge of the sex of the child to be conceived. In 3:3 we are back to the day of birth, which Job hopes will be one of darkness so that the light of God's creative power will not seek it out. There is an image here of God seeking out each day as it comes along as a day on which to effect certain purposes. Job's wish is that darkness will obliterate the day and take possession of it, in the manner of an eclipse or storm. In v. 6 we have the explicit wish that this particular day should lose its place among the others in the calendar, and not only among days but among months too. In v. 7 we return to the night, which Job curses with the hope that never again will such a conception occur during its hours, with the inference that if no one is born during that night again they might be spared his misery. There is almost an astrological influence here — the idea that there is a link between fortune and time of birth may have influenced the author's thought.

In 3:8 we find the reading "Let those curse it who curse the Sea." This reference to the sea *(yam)* is an emendation of the Hebrew, which reads "day" *(yom)*. Clearly the emendation to "sea" fits in better with the second part of the verse, which refers to Leviathan, the mythical, serpent-like sea monster (cf. Ps. 104:26). Thus the verse could be calling on those who have the ability to utter powerful curses, such as would rouse Leviathan, to do so for this night. A coherent meaning can, however, also be yielded by keeping "day," suggesting that those who can most effectively curse the day following the night in question are those "skilled to rouse up Leviathan." Eclipses were often thought to be caused by the swallowing up of the sun or moon by this monster (see discussion in Gaster), and so the reference could be a continuation of the desire for darkening and obliteration of the day.

3:9 mentions "the stars of its dawn," referring to the night stars which gradually fade as dawn approaches, personified here as looking out for the day, hoping for light. The wish here is that the process may not happen and that dawn — personified in the reference to eyelids, an image of the early morning sleepiness of the day — may not break on the day after the night of conception (not to be confused with the day of birth). This is then another cursed day, that is, the day that follows the night in which Job's mother's womb conceived him. The expression "shutting the doors" of a womb is a figurative way of describing the preventing of conception (cf. 1 Sam 1:6). This is seen as the beginning of Job's existence and so of his suffering. The more prosperous part of his life seems to have been forgotten in the shadow of his present misery.

Job 3:11-19

In this section we have what is ostensibly a lament but actually turns out to be a parody of the lament form. Use of the question "Why?" and a description of the distress caused to the sufferer are characteristic of a lament. However, they usually focus on a particular situation and an appeal to God to change it. Here again the reference is to the past — nothing about the situation of Job's birth can be changed by an appeal to God, and so the lament is futile. Again, we have the death wish which parodies passages in the psalms where death is undesirable (e.g., Ps 88:4-5). The lament opens with the wish that he had died at birth, the next stage on from lamenting that there had even been a day of birth. The moment of birth is recalled in the reference to the womb in 3:11 and the knees and breasts in v. 12. Some (e.g., Duhm, Peake) have seen the knees as a reference to the father's knees — his acknowledging the child as his — but the mother's knees are more likely. The thought is then that, having died at birth, Job would now be resting in Sheol with all those who have died before him. Here we have the first airing of the idea that Sheol, the land of darkness, might be a preferable fate to the life Job is now forced to live. The sentiment is expressed in v. 13 that death would simply be quiet, rather like sleep. The references to kings and princes demonstrate the transience and futility of life and may contain overtones of the status Job once enjoyed. The palaces they built are now ruined — if Job had died, his own achievements would be forgotten by now. The reference to princes filling their houses with silver may well be a recalling of the wealth which he also enjoyed.

Job then goes on to the idea that he might have been better off being stillborn or buried as if he were stillborn, which presumably means killed at birth. Again there is reference to the light and the desire for darkness — powerful imagery that runs through this section. The picture of Sheol is then expanded — there is rest there for prisoners or captives, freed from their taskmaster. Could this have overtones of his perception of his new relationship with God? Death is the great leveler. The sentences here have a hymnic character and yet they are used in this context as reproaches. Many of the sentiments in this section recall the book of Ecclesiastes, where we find reflections on the meaninglessness of life and of the unimportance of status in the light of the common fate — death — that awaits us all (Eccl 9:2, 10).

Job 3:20-27

This section can be seen either as a continuation of the same lament or as a second lament characterized by the opening "Why?" which parallels 3:11. There is some development of ideas here and more of an address to God, although in this section the lament, rather than being to God, is about God. Further, rather than calling God into question, Job is still calling his own existence into question. The lament begins with reference to the light — rather than rejoicing in the light that makes life possible, he once again longs for darkness. Light cannot be enjoyed by the tormented person, and life is not desired by such a one as he, and yet he is given both. His complaint here is that he receives the opposite of what he desires. He longs for death with an active eagerness. The image of digging for death is used to express his fervor — the words are reminiscent of digging for precious gems (cf. ch. 28, where wisdom is described as more inaccessible than hidden treasure). The pleasure those who dig for treasure receive when they actually find it is compared to the gladness of those who wish to die when they find the grave. Job feels lost in his path, and yet God gives him the light he requires but does not know how to use and does not want. Normally it would be a source of praise that light is given, but not for Job. He feels fenced in by God — a sentiment that reappears later in the speeches and is reminiscent of Satan's accusation to God that he had fenced Job in with a protective hedge (Job 1:10). God's presence is a burden to him, not something to be praised. In 3:24 we move on to a description of Job's pain. He sighs so often that it is like eating, and his loud groans are like drink. His fears are drawn out here; they are being magnified by his thoughts of what might happen to him. This is a crucial point — his anger is a foil for an underlying fear. He longs for death and rest because that is the one thing that is denied him as his fear overtakes him. God is no longer the anchor of his life, and he feels exposed and forsaken.

I have begun to draw attention to the technique of parody at work in the dialogue section of Job. Traditional ways of expressing sentiments — such as the curse and lament — are taken and by subtle changes in content and context adapted to a fresh purpose, that of undermining the very genre that it imitates. So the curse here is not really a curse in the usual sense because it refers to the past and is not directed specifically at God. Similarly, the lament forms are filled with unusual sentiments such as the desire for death, the longing to escape God, and the feeling of being hedged in by God. Normally the lament contains a longing for God and a recognition of the benefits that he can bestow. Job, on the other hand, longs for death and endless darkness when he is offered the gifts of light and life.

Eliphaz the Temanite: The First Speaker in the Three Rounds of Speeches in the Dialogue (4:1–5:21; 15:1-35; 22:1-30)

We might begin with the question of who Eliphaz the Temanite might have been. Is he likely to have been a historical person or is he being used here as a literary foil to Job? Do he and the other friends hold substantially the same point of view or are there subtle differences that lead us to characterize them differently? The answer to the question of historicity remains open and uncertain. Teman is an Edomite region, which may lend an air of historicity to the claim of an Edomite setting for the book. However, the keynote is what is said by this character rather than by who he is. That having been said, there is a certain blandness in the characterization of all three friends of Job. They are not as fully developed as characters as Job is. Yet one gets the impression from the speeches of Eliphaz that here is someone who is desperately trying to use all the arguments at his disposal, including appeals that are not entirely reasonable, as with his vision of God's presence and voice. We will have to look at the speeches of the other friends before we can pass judgment on the question of individual characterization. However, there is little character development from one of Eliphaz's speeches to another — basically similar points are repeated by Eliphaz, and the same structures of questioning, argument, and admonition are found throughout. He is a little more sympathetic toward Job in the first speech, but as the speeches progress he makes less attempt to veil his accusations and he becomes more heated in his arguments. He is the most sympathetic of the three friends, as we shall go on to see when we look at the speeches of the other two.

Eliphaz is a representative of the long-standing wisdom tradition to which he frequently makes appeal. This tradition is found in the book of Proverbs and involves a just accounting of the deeds of the righteous and the wicked by God, manifested in material rewards. We find long descriptions of the ultimate punishment of the wicked and of the perversity of foolish behavior. It is a black-and-white view of the world that is under attack by Job, and through him the author, who nevertheless is presenting both sides of the debate in the manner of a disputation.

Eliphaz's First Speech (Job 4:1–5:27)

Eliphaz begins his speech with a question to Job: Will he be offended if spoken to? Up to this point the friends have been silent with Job, exercising the kind of restraint commended by the wisdom tradition (cf. Prov 10:19). Now Eliphaz feels compelled to speak out, probably in response to Job's lament in ch. 3. The theme of the power of words runs through the first few verses of Eliphaz's speech — in happier times Job's own words of encouragement supported others. Eliphaz recalls what a strength Job was to others in distress when he himself was prosperous and compares this to now when Job is unable to retain his previous confidence in God. He indirectly confirms what God had said about Job in the Prologue — that he was God-fearing and did good works. He urges Job to have confidence in God and in his own integrity as he had in the past rather than to give up as easily as Job appears to have done. Eliphaz's mood here is relatively sympathetic, although, as the speech goes on, the element of chastisement which will characterize his later speeches begins to emerge.

In 4:7 he moves into his main argument, namely, that those innocent of sin are not normally those who have died a premature death. The inference here is that Job, although suffering, has not yet perished, and so there is still hope for him. He then launches in traditional wisdom mode into a statement of the punishment to be expected by the wicked in traditional wisdom mode. He appeals to personal experience — "As I have seen. . . ." He stresses the power of God in his punishment of the wicked, using the imagery of the hot wind of the desert rising up and destroying the harvest in an instant and the breaking of even the king of the forest — the lion — by God in his anger. The image of the sirocco wind recalls the fate that came to Job's children in 1:19, and one wonders whether this is not a deliberate overtone, hinting that they were sinful, and hence a veiled attack on Job in that he atoned for them on a regular basis (1:15). Although Eliphaz does not criticize Job directly here, his emphasis on the fate of the wicked rather than on that of the righteous could be seen as a thinly disguised inference that Job has in fact sinned.

In 4:12-16 we find a description by Eliphaz of a vision he received in the night that made him fearful. He describes the physical presence of a spirit and form and then a voice, presumably a description of the presence of God. In wisdom style, the content of the vision is described as a "word" spoken to him, although such revelatory experiences are not normal in wisdom, belonging rather to prophecy. This may be a ploy to lend credence to his words as having divine authority. It is also an indication that Eliphaz is trying to go beyond traditional wisdom ideas. He hears the voice asking what kind of righteousness human beings think they have in comparison with God. The suggestion here is that only God is truly righteous and so all humans are less than perfect and hence must expect some suffering, designated for all the unrighteous. This is not the traditional line, which stresses rewards for the righteous and punishment for the wicked. Instead Eliphaz stresses here that all fall short of God, even his angels. Eliphaz thus sees Job's suffering as part of the human condition — he will not allow Job's argument that he is blameless and thus deserves nothing but favor from God. Reflection on the transience and futility of human life in comparison with that of God leads Eliphaz on to a more traditional wisdom emphasis on the difference between the fates of the wise man and the fool. The suggestion here, however, is that all humans are devoid of wisdom and so born to foolish behavior. The idea that human beings can never attain complete wisdom is a common theme in Proverbs (e.g., 20:24); God alone holds the key. The fragility and mortality of humanity are emphasized in the sentiment that people die with such regularity that it is scarcely noticed, and, worse, they die without wisdom.

Eliphaz now ventures to offer his advice to Job. He argues that resentment against God only leads to disastrous consequences. Fools bring suffering upon themselves by their vexation and jealousy. Sin is a human thing — trouble does not sprout from the ground. He tells Job to commit himself to God the Creator, who displays his power in the natural world and lifts up those humans who trust in him, but who punishes the wicked and champions the underdog. In hymnic style, Eliphaz pictures God as one who provides for the earth and reverses the fortunes of those who are lowly. However, in addition to being on the side of the poor and needy, God acts in justice to bring the wicked to a swift end (there are two sides to God's character): "For he wounds, but he binds up; he strikes, but his hands heal" (5:18). He tells Job to accept the chastening that he is receiving from God for his misdeeds and to trust in the deliverance that God will effect. He sees suffering here as a positive act of chastening and not just as the consequence of human sin — also a wisdom theme (cf. Prov 3:11-12). In 5:19 we find a wisdom form known as numerical heightening: "He will deliver you from six troubles; in seven no harm shall touch you." This leads him to enumerate the blessings Job will receive. Eliphaz is certain of the power of God to redeem those who trust in him both in the negative forces encountered in life and in longevity, offspring, and descendants, signs of real blessing. The picture of security and harmony painted here contrasts strongly with Job's chaos and despair but ironically anticipates the Epilogue, when Job receives these blessings. Eliphaz speaks as a representative of wisdom — of those who have learned these things of God through experience. He now calls on Job to own this wisdom for himself.

Eliphaz's Second Speech (Job 15:1-35)

This speech follows a similar pattern to the first in its beginning with a question, not this time a personal one but a general comment on wise behavior: "Should the wise answer with windy knowledge, and fill themselves with the east wind?" (15:2). In fact, this is a veiled criticism of Job, suggesting that his words are as violent as the sirocco wind — not the usual recommendation for the words of the wise. We are back to the theme of the importance of words again, and there are overtones in the mention of wind of the fate that met Job's children. Thus, after a short reflection on the futility of the wise engaging in "unprofitable talk," Eliphaz becomes more open and accuses Job of forgetting the fear of God, hindering meditation (presumably by his verbosity) and condemning himself by his own words. Eliphaz's tone in this speech is harsher than before and more critical, moving toward open sarcasm in what follows.

Eliphaz goes on to accuse Job of immense arrogance in the face of God and the representatives of wisdom, notably himself and the other friends. He appeals to a longstanding tradition of wisdom of which he is a part. There are overtones in 15:7 of the myth of a primal man and of the primeval figure of wisdom in Proverbs 8. Eliphaz sarcastically asks Job if he was there at the beginning to know all wisdom — a sentiment reminiscent of God's words later in the book (Job 38:1-3). He asks Job why he has the arrogance to think that he knows more than those older and wiser than he. All attempts at consoling and gentle talk have failed. He sees Job as falling away from the straight and narrow by his angry questioning. He reiterates the need for righteousness as the only thing that gives life purpose. Again he uses the argument that God can trust no one fully, not even his angels, but even less one who is wicked. All humans are imperfect and so have no cause to complain at their suffering.

In the final part of his second speech, Eliphaz appeals once again to experience — to the wisdom of the sages handed down from ancient times regarding the fate of the wicked. We find in 15:20-35 a long description of the miserable life destined for the wicked who have forsaken God. There is no accusation of Job here, although the emphasis on the fate of the wicked can hardly be seen as coincidental. The picture of the wicked is one of endless pain, despair, and death. Even in times of prosperity, there is constant fear of the sword of doom descending at any time. The reason for this punishment is that "they stretched out their hands against God, and bid defiance to the Almighty" (v. 25) — this begins to sound remarkably akin to Job's own behavior. The prosperity of the wicked is seen as short-lived — their wealth is transient and their offspring will be annihilated. Again Job has also suffered this ultimate punishment, so does that not suggest that he, too, is a sinner?

Eliphaz's Third Speech (Job 22:1-30)

Each of the speeches becomes progressively shorter. In this final speech Eliphaz does not openly chastise Job, although he accuses him of sinful behavior which has led to his suffering. Rather, he offers advice and experience in the manner of the previous speeches. He asks why God should want to punish Job if indeed he is blameless. He once again stresses the great divide between God and human beings and so sees it as futile for God to punish one who has not sinned since humans are of little use to him anyway. He accuses Job of having done wicked deeds — likely to be the kind of sins he might have committed rather than ones that he has actually committed. Interestingly, in ch. 31 Job constructs a similar list of sins with the purpose of denying that he ever did them. The four sins mentioned here by Eliphaz are all mentioned by Job in ch. 31, notably, exploitation of the destitute (22:6), inhumanity toward the needy (v. 7), misappropriation of another's land (v. 8), and disregard of the defenseless (v. 9). From v. 12 Eliphaz launches into praise of God as creator and questions those who think God is hiding his face or unable to see and judge what is happening. Job cannot expect to be safe from punishment because God is so far away. From v. 15 on he is back on his old tack of describing the wicked — this time in the language of a dialogue between God and the wicked in which they are exposed as foolish and the righteous win the day. In the last section of the speech Eliphaz offers his final advice and admonishment to Job — listen to God, he says, and your peace of mind will be restored; repent of unrighteousness, and you will be delivered and restored to a right relationship of prayer and devotion. This will result in renewed prosperity, and "light will shine on your ways," an interesting recalling of the light and darkness theme found throughout the book but particularly in ch. 3. He stresses the deliverance that God purposes for the righteous and even for those who are not righteous on behalf of those who are. He maintains that the righteous can intercede for sinners — an ironic anticipation of 42:7-10, when Job intercedes on behalf of the friends but not in the way that Eliphaz would have anticipated!

Bildad the Shuhite: The Second Speaker in the Three Rounds of Speeches in the Dialogue (8:1-22; 18:1-21; 25:1-6; 26:5-12)

Bildad the Shuhite is also thought to be a character with Edomite connections. The name Shuah is not a place name. One of Abraham's sons by Keturah was called Shuah, and he lived in the "east country" (Gen 25:1-6). Another option is that this is a reference to a country named Suhu on the Euphrates River, but this is generally felt to be less likely. The name Bildad is not found elsewhere in the OT. It may mean "son of Hadad," but it is unclear what connections this would have had for a Hebrew audience. It is probably safer to say that the three friends are foreigners, possibly wise men, from distant lands and that their names are meant to be exotic.

The speeches of Bildad are often seen to be somewhat unrelated to each other. However, he is pursuing his own line of argument, and two presuppositions of his thought stand out. The first is that God is just and in charge of an unchanging world order. This comes through in all his speeches, particularly in the third if we include the section in 26:5-14, which I suggest we do. The second is that God metes out this justice according to the principle of just retribution. The first two speeches contain lengthy descriptions of the fate of the wicked, which seems to be Bildad's focus here, but the fate of the righteous is not ignored. There is no hint of the idea, introduced in the Prologue, that suffering is a test by God. There are overtones of Eliphaz's ideas in the third speech, on the littleness of humanity in comparison with God, but generally his appeal to personal experience is ignored. Bildad is more directive to Job than is Eliphaz — in the first speech in particular he is giving Job advice, and in both the first and second there are thinly disguised inferences that Job is guilty of wickedness; otherwise why have these calamities, such as fall on the wicked generally, descended? The rather stylized nature of some of the material suggests that Bildad's speech is drawing on traditional wisdom ideas — in keeping with his appeal to the wisdom of the ancients rather than to personal experience. He and Job are poles apart in their approach, and this lack of understanding and interaction is conveyed by the increased hostility between the two as the speeches progress.

Bildad's First Speech (Job 8:1-22)

Bildad does not mince words when he criticizes Job of speaking falsehood. There is no acknowledgment of Job's exemplary character, as Eliphaz outlined at the beginning of his first speech. Rather, the opening words are critical and suggest that Bildad already suspects that Job is guilty. Bildad picks up Job's own phrase "How long?" (cf. 7:9) to mock Job perhaps, or at least to show that he has been listening. He describes Job's words as "a great wind," both empty and violent. He asks a rhetorical question in v. 3 to which the answer "No" is clearly expected. He thus maintains the justice of God; the idea of his not being just is not even an option. His view of the world is even more black-and-white and narrow in scope than that of Eliphaz. He firmly upholds the doctrine of retribution — that God rewards good behavior and punishes wickedness — as found in the book of Proverbs in the idea of two paths along which a person can decide to walk, that of righteousness or that of wickedness.

In 8:4-6 we encounter a number of clauses beginning with "if," suggesting a series of hypothetical cases. However, the hypothetical comes dangerously close to the truth when Bildad suggests that if "your children" sinned they would have been punished. This is usually seen as a reference to 1:5 in the Prologue, which mentions that Job's children were killed. Bildad then, by using a veiled accusation, makes known to Job that he assumes Job's children to have sinned against God and so to have met their just fate. This is to scorn Job's repeated efforts, as described in the Prologue, to make supplication to God on behalf of his children in case they may have sinned (Job 1:5). The next "if" is to tell Job to seek God, who will restore him to even more than he had before "if," again, he finds evidence of Job's uprightness. There is again a mocking here of Job's former state — the Prologue made clear that Job's devoutness and blameless life were not open to question. Bildad is then telling Job to be how he, Job, in fact was! And yet he tells Job to seek God afresh, with the inference that, by his words, Job has already fallen away from uprightness. Bildad suggests that God will "rouse himself" to activity when he realizes Job's uprightness — ironic since Job has complained that God is too active (7:12, 16-19). In 8:7 there is further irony — an ironic prophecy by Bildad of what will in fact happen in the Epilogue — Job's latter days will be greater than the former. The irony is that this most conventional of Job's friends is predicting the necessary outcome of Job's innocence according to the strict principles of the doctrine of retribution while Job is in fact challenging this principle on the basis of his contrary experience. There is an assumption here that misfortune must mean wicked behavior and that good behavior must elicit a favorable response from God — God's actions are thus limited to a strict moral principle which allows him no freedom. Job's claim that God is being unjust to him and his consequent questioning of any underlying principles of justice carry no weight with Bildad, who sees God as the guarantor of order.

There follows an appeal to the wisdom of the past, but this time not in reference to personal experience but to accumulated intelligence. This is made in the context of an emphasis on the fleeting nature of each individual life; hence the need to rely on the cumulative wisdom of many generations. There are ironic overtones of Job's complaints on the brevity of life. Bildad seems to forget here that the past, too, is made up of many individuals. It is a rather thin argument to allow him to call for adherence to traditional wisdom, to learn from truths passed down rather than to rely on personal experience. It is thus an argument against the kind of approach Job is taking.

From 8:11 on we find the common wisdom technique of asking questions to which the answers are known to be impossible (cf. Amos 3:3-8). We also find the use of images from the natural world in true wisdom style. Of course plants cannot grow without water, and papyrus is known to dry up more quickly than any other grass if it has no water to sustain it. This is used as an illustration of those who neglect God — of course they will not survive. Their demise and destruction are inevitable. There is a note of warning to Job contained in the illustrations in this section. Two other images are used, first that of a "spider's house," a symbol of the false confidence of the wicked — when they lean against their house, it collapses. The second is again from the plant world; this time a well-nourished and prospering plant is described that seems to be gaining an irreversible hold. There is the suggestion here that sometimes there is a time delay — the wicked seem to prosper. However, this plant will be destroyed to such an extent that it will not even be remembered. It will be replaced by others and so lost to memory completely.

The converse of this is that God will not mistreat those who are innocent; thus Bildad ends his speech on a note of hope. He begins with the general principle that God metes out good as well as bad, and he mentions the "blameless," which we already know is a description of Job. He then turns to Job's case. Job will again be joyful when God acknowledges his blamelessness and his enemies are put to shame. Bildad's speech ends with a reference to being "no more," just as Job's previous speech had ended with his suggestion of nonbeing, that is, imminent death if God would not restore him. This may be a deliberate overtone — Bildad maintaining that nonexistence is proof of wickedness while Job is afraid that he will die before being vindicated by God.

Bildad's Second Speech (Job 18:1-21)

In this second speech Bildad's frustration with Job is more apparent. He dislikes not only what he is saying but the way he treats the friends, acting as if their opinion is worthless. There is a suggestion that Job is speaking words without due consideration, linking up with the "windy words" of his previous speech and reminiscent of the warnings against verbosity in the wisdom tradition (Prov 15:1-7). There can be dialogue only with one who has considered his opinions. The comparison of the friends to animals is a reference to the way Job downgrades them. Bildad sees Job as overstepping the mark in his anger and in his complaints — they are not as earth shattering as Job would have us believe. Picking up on Job's own words that God has "torn me" (16:9), Bildad suggests that it is Job who tears himself. The fault is not God's but Job's, and hence his suffering is regarded as self-inflicted. The reference to the earth and the rock implies that God's order will not be disturbed simply because Job feels sorry for himself — the suggestion would be ridiculous. There is more than a hint of irony in Bildad's words as well as a clinging to his previous position regarding the permanence of God's order.

From 18:5 on Bildad launches into a description of the punishment of the wicked, using the imagery of light and darkness. This is to revisit the second argument in his first speech — that the doctrine of retribution is alive and well. This speech does not explicitly identify Job with the wicked, but contains some uncomfortable parallels to his plight in vv. 11, 13, 15, and 19. It appears to be a veiled accusation, as before, and at the very least is designed to frighten Job into submission. This poem about the fate of the wicked could well have had another context as it is quite stylized. It is full of powerful images. The darkness of death is described; the stumbling steps of the wicked could refer to old age but are more likely to contain overtones of the rough path along which the wicked choose to walk, one paved with thorns, as described in Proverbs (e.g., Prov 2:12-22). In vv. 8-10 various traps are described, but v. 8 makes clear that the wicked fall into their own trap; it is a matter of their own choices, as in the previous verse, where their own schemes throw them down. The description of snares for birds contains overtones of Prov 1:17, where the same fate meets the wicked. Terrors are all around, and there is constant danger in unforeseen places. Hunger and disease are ready to pounce as soon as the wicked stumble. The description of their disease demonstrates how illness was seen as the forerunner of death. The "firstborn of Death" consumes their limbs — possibly a reference to death itself or his emissary. There may be a mythological background lying behind this description — in Ugaritic mythology the god of death Mot has gaping jaws ready to swallow people up. In v. 14 the description moves to the process of death, whereby a person is pried from the security of his or her home and sent to the underworld. All is then destroyed of what remained of their home so that no memory remains of them. Sulphur was used as a powerful disinfectant and renders land infertile. The reference in v. 16 to roots drying up could be a reference either to the wicked themselves or to their offspring;

the foundations laid by the wicked — the roots and branches put out by them — all wither away. There is total annihilation of the memory of them and no descendants — the worst fate possible in Hebrew thought. In v. 20 the effect of their fate on onlookers is described — people far and wide are appalled and horrified. One's reputation is in tatters. Bildad summarizes this frightening description with the conclusion that this surely is the fate of those who have insufficient piety. There is no upbeat ending for Job this time.

Bildad's Third Speech (Job 25:1-6 [26:5-14?])

Bildad's third speech break into almost hymnic praise of God and asks the question of human righteousness before God, using Eliphaz's words in 4:17 and 5:14-16. If not even God's creation is perfect, how much less humanity, who are like maggots and worms. This speech stresses the majesty of God and the terror of God's rule. His heavenly armies are mentioned to stress his power — how lowly human beings are by comparison. How dare a human being set up his own righteousness in the face of the majesty of God? It is impossible for a human being to be pure before God, for not even the stars and moon are perfect. This section emphasizes God's power over the heavenly bodies.

Many scholars attribute parts of chapter 26 to Bildad, notably vv. 5-14, which describes God's power as creator. Such a description would follow naturally from the sentiments of 25:1-6, and yet nowhere else does Bildad describe God's work in such terms. In fact, such thoughts are more common in the thought of Job in ch. 9, although they do not relate to the opening or close of Job's speeches in chs. 26–27. The theme of God's power is continued, first over the subterranean regions (26:5-6), then over the natural order (26:7-9), and finally over creation itself in the beginning (26:10-13). There is thus some thematic consistency. This idea also forms a main theme of the Yahweh speeches.

In 26:5-6 we have a reference to Sheol, the region of the dead and of shadows. The earth was seen to be placed over the sea, and so the inhabitants of the waters are the fish. God's eye sees all that goes on. He is the sole cause of creation. In v. 7 it is not clear what Zaphon or the North refers to. Possibly it is an allusion to the northern reaches of the vault of heaven; Zaphon was a mountain in the north, and so it could also refer to the propping up of heaven by the mountains. Following Isa 14:13, it could be a reference to the hidden place where the gods were said to dwell in ancient Near Eastern mythology. The earth is described as suspended in space. The clouds were regarded as waterskins holding in the rain; miraculously they did not split. God's action extends to eclipses. The earth is described as a flat disk encircled by waters, and the boundary between light and darkness is a reference to the horizon, thought by the Hebrews to be fixed. The pillars of heaven in v. 11 are the mountains supporting heaven. In v. 12 we move on to a recounting of God's deeds in creation. God's breath or wind clears the clouds and brightens the sky after a storm. God's ways are so marvelous that creation is but a whisper compared to the thunder of the power of God's deeds.

Zophar the Naamathite: The Third Speaker in the Three Rounds of Speeches in the Dialogue (11:1-29; 20:1-29; 27:13-23)

Zophar the Naamathite has less obvious Edomite connections since Naamah is a town in Judah. The name "Zophar" has some link to the genealogy of Esau, which itself has Edomite roots. Genesis 36 mentions a Zopho, grandson of Esau, son of Eliphaz, and brother of Teman. The LXX here and in 1 Chronicles 1 mentions a Sophar.

Of the three friends Zophar seems to be the most outspoken; he makes no secret of the fact that he perceives Job to be guilty. He is lucky that he is not suffering more, and he needs to make a fresh start — repent and get on with his life. The descriptions of the fate of the wicked in the speeches of Zophar are the most terrifying of those of the three friends and are designed to frighten Job into practical action to change his situation. The problems of reconstructing the third speech mean that we are unable to find any development of his thought, although between the first and second speech he becomes more openly accusatory and his aim to frighten Job with the threat of the terrible fate awaiting him if he fails to repent is more pronounced.

Zophar's First Speech (Job 11:1-20)

Zophar also begins by complaining of Job's many windy words. He is using a frequent wisdom motif about the importance of right words and the destructiveness of babbling talk (e.g., Prov 13:3; 29:20). He questions that it is right that Job's talk silences others, and sees it as wrong that the friends are being mocked. He has quite an aggressive tone. He picks up Job's argument that he is pure but accuses him of shortsightedness. If he knew God's superior wisdom, he would know that he was not being punished enough for his wickedness. Job is mocking God by his insistence on being in the right. In 11:5, Zophar wishes that God would speak and reveal to Job his greatness. There is irony in that God does in fact appear later in the book, although clearly here Zophar does not expect this to happen. There is a fresh argument here in the thought of the friends — the idea that Job is fortunate that he is not being punished more. God is thus seen as being merciful to Job in withholding punishment. Zophar openly acknowledges that he thinks that Job has sinned and is being punished in part but not in full.

This leads Zophar into a description of God's knowledge, a foretaste of what is to come in the God speeches. The message is that God's wisdom is greater than ours. His purposes, too, are not open to question — they are unfailingly just. His argument differs from God's in that the appeal to greatness is a reason for God's being able to do what he likes without constraint, while here it is a witness to his fairness in matters of right and wrong. Zophar thus limits God in terms of retribution, although Zophar sees Job as limited in his understanding of God because of his useless attack on God's providence. Using traditional language, Zophar describes how God's knowledge is higher than heaven and deeper than Sheol; longer than the earth and deeper than the sea. The inference is that since humans have no such power, who are they to question God's actions? God is able to see all that happens in the world and acts in judgment on his people so that even if a cause for punishment cannot be found by humans, God will have his reasons. Zophar stresses the impossibility of a stupid person to receive understanding, using a well-known wisdom technique of stating two impossibilities alongside one another. Just as a wild ass's colt could never be born human, so a stupid person will never understand. This could be a dig at Job, although the next verses suggest that Job is not so stupid.

In the last section of the speech, Zophar turns to offering Job practical advice. He admonishes Job to repent and be restored and thus regain his equilibrium and peace of mind. He needs to sort out his thoughts, pray to God, and acknowledge his sins. Then he will be cleansed, his darkness will turn to light, and his confidence, hope, security, and honor will return. The speech ends on a downbeat note of warning — there is no hope for the wicked. Job has been warned!

Zophar's Second Speech (Job 20:1-29)

Zophar's frustration and distress come across at the beginning of this speech; he is mortified and insulted by Job's words and makes claim to a will to speak coming from a spirit outside him — rather similar to Eliphaz's technique in ch. 4 and done to enhance the divine authority of his words. Again we hear the appeal to reason, to long experience of knowing of the fate of the wicked, being used here to counter Job's claim to knowledge from personal experience. Despite the apparent prosperity of the wicked, it will be short-lived, they will be brought low, and none will remember them. A picture is drawn of an arrogant, gluttonous person reaching for the sky but ending up in the dirt. There is an overtone here of the sin of Adam and Eve in overreaching themselves and trying to be like God; similarly of the Tower of Babel story. Although the wicked person appears tall and solidly built, the next verses make it clear that his existence is like the characters in a dream — they seem very real at the time but turns out to be a phantom. The wicked person will be ignored — he will not be seen any more by others, either literally or metaphorically. According to 20:10, the children of the wicked person will be poor and will need to beg. The second part of the verse does not follow from the thought of the first, so maybe the answer is to invert the two halves so that the first has reference to the wicked person whose hands will give back his wealth, that is, he will be forced to return all he has taken from others, even to the extent that there is nothing left for his children and they have to beg. Finally, the wicked person will age before his time and come to a premature death.

In the next verses the message is that sweet things will turn sour — all will become pointless in the light of the behavior of the wicked. Sin is tasty and is savoured by the wicked, but tasty food turns sour in the stomach and becomes snake poison that will kill him. The wicked person eats to his fill — probably at the expense of others — but then vomits the food up (perhaps a reference to overeating). God is seen as the cause of the vomiting. The wicked person has in fact been swallowing poison all along without realizing it, and this poison will kill him. Wholesome food will forever be denied him, and he will never enjoy the gains of his toil. He is wicked because he has exploited others — that exploitation will rebound against him. Greed self-destructs. The message of 20:20-23 is that the wicked person eats so heartily that his appetite becomes insatiable — riches lead to dissatisfaction. In the moment of greed and apparent prosperity, he will become miserable; distress and misery will be his daily bread. Again God is described as sending anger to fill his belly, a reversal of the usual idea of God feeding his people, as with manna in the wilderness. Here God is force-feeding the wicked man and leading him to an inescapable end.

The final section of the speech describes the end of the wicked. God's arrows are fired at the wicked person. As he removes the arrow from his body and his insides fall out of his stomach, he will be filled with terror as he realizes that he is at the point of death. Again we have images of utter darkness and the fire of total annihilation — the eater will be consumed by fire. God's judgment is the cause of this fate, and heaven and earth are the legal witnesses to his misdeeds. All his possessions are taken away, and the divine order is restored. Zophar's purpose is not to accuse Job directly, although we have seen from his previous speech that he considers Job to have sinned. Rather, he uses this description to frighten Job and try to persuade him of the falsity of his line of reasoning. He needs to acknowledge his sin or his fate will be as described above.

Zophar's Third Speech? (27:13-23)

There is no designated third speech for Zophar, but scholars have traditionally reconstructed it from words attributed to Job but felt to be out of place in his mouth. Various verses and small sections of verses have been considered to be part of Zophar's third speech, including 27:8-12 or sometimes 27:8-10 only, 24:18-20 and sometimes 24:22-25 as well, or at least v. 24. However there is such scholarly disagreement and uncertainty over the reconstruction of Zophar's third speech that I have decided to take the only section that seems to be almost universally agreed to be Zophar's third speech, namely, 27:13-23.

This section treats the portion of the wicked and is very reminiscent of what Zophar has already maintained in ch. 20. It is clearly not a full speech since there are not the usual jibes at the beginning or summary at the end. The section may be a fairly stylized, traditional description of the wicked, as in ch. 20. The start of this section makes clear that God is behind this ordering. While the wicked may seem to prosper with numerous offspring, this will not last. The children will either be killed by the sword, starve, or be struck down by famine. 27:15a seems to belong with v. 14 and refer to the fate of the children, but then there is a reference to "their widows" who do not mourn their death. This could refer to the widows of older, married children, or it could be a reference to the widows of the wicked (who die later in the passage) or to the widows of the wicked who mourn over their children. There is some question as to whether "their widows" means that each person had more than one wife or whether the sense is the wife of each of them. According to this verse, a person who has died of disease is not buried, and so there is no proper funeral at which the widows can mourn in the usual way (cf. Jer 22:10, 19). 27:16-17 refer to the wealth and possessions stored up by the wicked — ultimately it will pass to the righteous. In vv. 18 and 19 the houses of the wicked are not solid; rather, they are "like nests" or "like booths," likely to be swept away. According to v. 19, the wicked person will go to bed rich for the last time. On waking up in the morning , all will be gone. Some have seen this as a reference to dying in the morning; however, it would be more of a punishment for the wicked to lose their wealth one day and then have to go on living without it. It seems that the death of the wicked person is to come in the next verses. Vv. 20-22 describe the terrors of the Almighty — natural phenomena such as flood and whirlwinds will sweep the wicked away. There could be an overtone here of the fate that met Job's children, just as earlier in the reference to disease causing death there could have been a veiled reference to Job's state. God's anger manifests itself in such ways. The clapping and hissing in v. 23 could be a reference to thunder and wind, although it can be taken to refer to the clapping of hands by mourners as a sign of grief, whether genuine or not, and to hissing in contempt and scorn.

Job in Dialogue (6–7; 9–10; 12–14; 16–17; 19; 21; 23–24; 26–27)

The First Round of Speeches

We discover in this first cycle the whole range of Job's arguments. He mainly directs his complaints at God, but he is also aware of the critique offered by the friends, and he responds in like vein. He swings from criticism of their words (6:6-7) to criticism of their attitude toward him (6:14, 24-27). In 12:1-2 he accuses his friends of thinking that they have special access to wisdom, and in 13:7-12 he tries to frighten them with accusing words, suggesting that they may have sinned in what they have said. By ch. 14 Job's attention is more fully on God. He is obsessed with assessing God's character in the light of his bitter experience. God is no longer to be trusted, and his might is not to be praised but feared as arbitrary and lacking moral foundation. He uses legal motifs in an attempt to pin God down, and parodies sentiments from the Psalms in particular to overturn traditional sentiments about God and show that bitter experience teaches otherwise.

Job 6:1–7:21

The beginning of Job's period in dialogue with his three friends bears little resemblance to a dialogue at all. He appears not to have heard Eliphaz and instead addresses his words to God. Only in the second part of ch. 6 does he launch into criticism of his friends. The speech begins with a cry of anguish — his vexation weighs heavily on him. God is his enemy — God's poisoned arrows pierce him. In traditional wisdom style he asks a few rhetorical questions. The message here is that if you give animals what they are expecting, that is, grass for the wild ass, they will not complain. Job, on the other hand, is not receiving his reward for righteousness. He speaks of tasteless food — this is what he is now experiencing from God. In 6:8-10 we find an affirmation of loyalty to God in the form of a death wish. This is a parody of lament forms that long for safety (e.g., Ps 55:6-8). Job, on the other hand, longs for personal destruction by God. He feels weak in the face of all the suffering he is bearing; he has neither physical strength nor internal strength, and so he simply wishes that death will come quickly — he does not even have the strength to be patient in waiting for it.

In the second part of ch. 6 Job curses his friends, parodying passages in the Psalms which would be used to curse one's enemies (e.g., Pss 31:11-12; 38:11; 41:9). He accuses them of not providing the support he needs. The speech begins with a proverbial sentence suggesting that the friends are not following the traditional line in their treatment of him. He lashes out at them, comparing their loyalty to that of a wadi in the desert which seems to be full of water but dries up when the hot summer comes. When thirsty travelers come to drink they are disappointed, in the same way that Job was expecting more from the friends. In 6:22-23 Job states that he has never asked anything of his friends — no money or favors. The inference is that they thus have no basis for grievance against him; he has never impinged on their friendship, and so he deserves better treatment. He wishes to learn from them what his errors might be, not receive insults. There is a reflection here, in wisdom style, of the validity of words — words of honesty; but wrong words of reproof are worthless. Not listening to the words of others and treating them as mere babbling, as they have done with his words, is inexcusable and shows a lack of sympathy. In the final verses of the chapter Job begs for attention and asks his friends to have faith in his integrity and trustworthiness.

In ch. 7 Job is back to lamenting to God, first bewailing the human lot, which consists of hard labor, striving for money, and constant longing for the respite following hard work, and then likening it to his own situation. His life is empty — he does not even have rest or money to look forward to — and his nights are full of terror so that he cannot rest. There is reference to his disease — probably some form of leprosy, which is characterized by hardening scabs which then break out afresh with pus. They seem to heal, but then they reappear and his hope is gone. His nights are long, and correspondingly his days are short and seem to be running out. He is not concerned here about the brevity of life per se but about the hopelessness of his situation. He sees himself as on an inevitable path to death. Rather, as the friends spoke of the importance of cumulative human experience because the life span of an individual is so short, so Job expresses the brevity of his own life in the overall scheme of things. He calls on God to "Remember," not in a mood of appeal, as is usual in lament psalms, but in a mood of reproach. The fragility of human life comes across here with its comparison to a breath. He will never again experience good things, and people will no longer see him when he dies. Once dead, there is no return and they are soon forgotten. Then in v. 11 his mood suddenly swings, this time into an expression of anger, and we find him openly charging God with being his tormentor. God's constant attention is seen as oppressive. God guards him like the sea monster (7:12) and scares him with terrifying visions (vv. 13-14). He wishes not for healing, as might be usual for one suffering in this way, but to die and, failing that, to be left alone. In a parody of Ps 8:4, he asks, "What are human beings, that you make so much of them, and that you set your mind on them?" (7:17). God's constant attention is usually to be praised, but Job wants to be rid of this attention — can't he even swallow his spittle in peace? He asks why God should mind if he sins, questioning the traditional teaching that sin offends God because he is concerned for humanity. He accuses God of doing his target practice on him, a reference back to the poisoned arrows perhaps. He asks, "Why me?" At the end of the speech Job seems to acknowledge his sin — he must mean here the sin that God is charging him with, of which he in fact is not guilty. At this stage he is desperate to be relieved of the burden of suffering before he dies. After death he will not be able to continue his conversation with God — a realization which later makes him feel ambivalent about his previous desire for death.

Job 9:1–10:22

In his second speech in chs. 9 and 10 Job discusses the doctrine of retribution. Job's desire for vindication leads him to speak of contending with God. He argues that even if one wished to do so one could not answer him — God would overwhelm humans by posing unanswerable questions (this is an ironic anticipation of what God in fact does later in the book). In a manner reminiscent of the arguments of the friends, Job upholds the wisdom and might of God in hymnic style but gives it a negative application — God's work in creation is about power and he always comes off best. God can do what he likes; he can pass by unnoticed, and he can snatch away as he pleases. No one will call him to account. No one can restrain his anger. There is parody here in the note of reproach against the unassailable God whose actions are unpredictable. Normally hymns praise the unknowability of God and the marvels of creation (e.g., Psalm 104). Job then moves into a more legal mode. He argues that humans have no power to appeal against God, who is both enemy and judge. His power is such that mere mortals can do nothing — they will probably not even be heard. Job argues that God sets the standard of justice, but there is no higher court to which appeal can be made against his decisions. It is an unequal relationship in which God is the powerful one who can crush humans both physically and mentally. His experience of God as an oppressive presence comes through again here. Job would be so overcome by God that he would be unable to state his case anyway.

In the next section Job goes on to question God's moral government of the world. The righteous and the wicked are both destroyed, and God mocks the innocent, allowing the wicked to dominate. Covering the eyes of judges is probably a reference to bribery and refers to social injustice condoned by God and to be ranked alongside the natural disasters sent by him. God has turned cruel. From 9:25 on Job goes back to his own situation and the sentiment that the days of his life go by all too swiftly. When he tries to forget his plight he becomes afraid because he knows that God is against him. Job 9:25-28 is another example of parody — Job complains that he is troubled when he tries to forget his suffering, a sentiment which parodies Jer 20:7-9 where Jeremiah says that trouble comes when he tries to forget God. Job can never be clean while God covers him with the dirt of guilt. Job then returns to the thought of the impossibility of meeting God on equal terms before a fair court. There would be no equality and no umpire who would be able to take both parties under his authority and protection, and so Job is at a disadvantage because he is suffering under God's power and so terrified that he is unable to speak. If these burdens were taken away, then Job feels that he could speak confidently of his innocence.

In ch. 10 Job is still bewailing his lot. He pleads with God not to condemn him and to tell him the reason for this hostility. He asks God whether he enjoys oppressing people. He also asks God if he sees things the way humans do — is his conception of right and wrong the same? He is so convinced that he has not sinned that there must be another reason for his punishment; perhaps this is it. Maybe God is acting in a shortsighted human way, rushing to condemn Job before time runs out, even though he knows Job is not really guilty. However, v. 7 could be taken separately from what precedes it to mean that Job is simply asserting that God knows that he is not guilty. This implies that God does have the same standards regarding just rewards, but that because he is able to, he has trapped Job in his power. The problem to which Job again and again returns is that there is no one to justify Job against God since God himself is the only judge who has control of him. In vv. 8 and 9 he states that God has created him and then destroyed him. Job 10:2-12 contains a parody of passages which praise God's watch over human beings as found in psalms such as 139. This passage in Job, by contrast, contains a request to be delivered from God, whose care is oppressive.

There follows a wonderful description of God's creation of Job in the womb in which God's care is underlined. But from 10:13 it is clear to Job that there is a hidden agenda, that of accusing Job of wrongdoing and using him for target practice. In v. 14, God his protector has become his warden. There is deliberate irony in the choice of the words "work wonders" in v. 16 — God's wonderful works in the creation of Job are now matched by his wonders in tormenting him. In parody of psalms which ask God for punishment where it is deserved (e.g., Psalm 7), Job 13–17 suggest that God punishes even when it is not deserved, so that there is no evidence of Job's innocence. From 10:20 on Job returns to his sentiments of ch. 3, wishing he had died at birth. He then goes into the brevity-of-life theme and renews his request to be left alone so as to enjoy a little respite before the journey to Sheol, the land of the dead.

Job 12:1–14:22

In response to the speeches of the friends, Job makes a sarcastic comment on their claim to wisdom — they are such profound representatives of wisdom that it will no doubt die with them. He states his position again: he will not be put down. He points out that he was the epitome of the wise man himself and has now become a laughingstock. Only the wicked seem to have security. The inference here is that through his experience and observation Job has reached a more profound wisdom than the friends. The next section from vv. 7 to 12 seem misplaced since Job is uttering a hymn of praise to God and often appears to agree with the friends but then reveals a profound disagreement. So while here Job states in the manner of positive praise to God that God's created things bear witness that God's hand is always at work, later this is reversed and God is to blame for the evil happenings in his dealings with nature since he is all-powerful. The contrast is thus highlighted by the different sentiments, and we should therefore be cautious about excising verses. There is parody in 12:7-9 since nature usually proclaims God's glory, as in Psalm 98, whereas here nature bears witness to God's actions. This could mean his good actions, but it could equally well refer back to his bad actions, for example, in making Job a laughingstock (v. 4) or in the bad actions to come in vv. 13-25. Vv. 11-12 are often seen to be traditional wisdom sayings, but they are relativized by this statement about God's power. Life and death are in God's hands — this can be seen as praiseworthy and yet terrifying if God has become the enemy. In v. 11 there is a sentiment that resembles one expressed by Elihu, the fourth friend — just as a person discriminates about what he or she wants to hear or eat using the senses, so in v. 12 wisdom is a matter of discernment, not simply the preserve of a few aged men. Elihu in his speeches uses this argument to explain why he held back from speaking; he now speaks because he has decided that wisdom is a matter of personal discernment rather than maturity. In v. 13, then, Job goes on to assert that wisdom is with God alone, and in that sense it is a redundant exercise for human beings. God knows how to cope with every situation, and there is no opposition to his will.

The problem that is made clear in 12:13-25 is that God often acts capriciously and arbitrarily in nature. He reverses human fortunes, and humans are helpless to do anything about it. This recalls his earlier sentiments on the frailty of human beings. His actions toward humans are inextricably linked to his actions in nature; just as he can shut a person in, so he can withhold waters. From v. 17 on God is seen to mock those who rise to positions of human authority. In v. 23 the rise and fall of nations does not appear to be governed by any moral principle and provides another example of God's arbitrary use of his power. Thus, against the friends' assertion that God's wisdom can be understood according to certain rules, Job stresses God's arbitrariness. Job 12:13-25 is thus a hymnic description of God's wisdom and power, but it is a negative one. It is a parody of the friends' descriptions of God's beneficent power as well as a parody of positive praise of God and his moral actions such as is found in Psalm 107, of which there are a number of overtones in this section. In Ps 107:39-41 the princes who have oppressed God's people are punished, whereas here (12:21) no reason is given for the humiliation of princes. Because the moral justification is absent, this becomes just another example of God's destructive power. God's power here flaunts strict moral principles and is a danger to humankind, working against them rather than helping them. God mocks the mighty — leaders grope around in the dark and stagger like drunkards.

In ch. 13 Job pleads with God for an opportunity to state his case; he is tired of the conversation with the friends. He wishes they would be quiet. He accuses them of false talk of God and threatens them with the thought that God may one day seek them out for their false words. There is a new mood of confidence here that his own reasoning is right and that that of the friends is wrong. He also issues a confident challenge to God. He has nothing to lose now, and so he issues his challenge to God to defend himself. We are back to the legal language of a previous speech. We find the same sentiments: that Job feels hampered in stating his case because of the power of God's hand upon him and because of fear of him; he now asks that these may be withdrawn. He thus wants freedom from God, a sentiment that parodies passages such as Ps 27:4 that ask to see the face of God because it is a joyous thing. He also calls on God to tell him what his sins are, if indeed he has sinned. He wants to know why God has turned nasty, and he expresses once again feelings of being trapped by God.

In ch. 14 Job returns to the theme of God's oppressive watch over humankind, but in a more general sense rather than focusing entirely on his own position. Job asks why God takes such trouble over frail humanity. V. 4 suggests that human beings are inherently sinful; so why does God take so much trouble? God has already determined the length of people's lives, a boundary which they cannot pass. Why does God not leave human beings alone to enjoy their lives! Job 14:1-12 closely resembles 7:11-21 in subject matter and, like 7:11-21, also parodies Psalm 8. Job describes the human condition in the first three verses and then makes a plea to God to leave humans alone. While Psalm 8 praises humanity as God's highest creation, Job describes humans as "born of a woman," and rather than seeing them as a "little lower than the angels" pictures them as "full of trouble." In 14:7-12 he contrasts humans with a tree stump which, although seemingly dead, will sprout again given the right conditions. Humans, on the other hand, die and are gone forever. In v. 13 Job pleads with God to hide him away in Sheol until his anger has passed but then to recognize him afresh after his sojourn there. This passage has overtones of Ps 55:6-7, where the psalmist also wishes to flee, but from his enemies rather than from God. However, Job does not want to die and be forgotten. Here he begins to see that there is another side to longing for death; it means being cut off from God altogether. While he wishes for this when God is angry and he is suffering, here he realizes that he will lose his chance of vindication if he dies — he wants to be in favor again after the wrath has passed.

If Job knew that there was some restoration of his old relationship with God to look forward to, he says that he would wait forever. He has a moment of longing in 14:15 for the old relationship in which God would long for him too. In v. 16 the NRSV inserts "not" — that is, "you would not number my steps." Numbering the steps can, however, be seen as a positive sentiment of care from God, so that Job's wish could be that God would once again keep watch over him; hence the "not" would not be necessary. On the other hand, it is perhaps more in keeping with Job's sentiments that God's constant attention is oppressive, and so on balance the sentence makes more sense with the "not" retained.

In the last part of the speech Job expresses the idea that humans cannot escape destruction, just as nature, too, is eventually destroyed. Here he views God as hostile again. Because of death humans do not see the success of their children, and if they suffer there is no parent to comfort them. God thus destroys hope. This section of the speech parodies hopeful passages in the psalms which express confidence that God will rescue his people and deliver them from their enemies (e.g., Ps 28:6-8). Psalm 31 contains complaints closely akin to Job's, but in the end the psalmist trusts and hopes in God: "But I trust in you, O Lord; I say, 'You are my God.' My times are in your hand; deliver me from the hand of my enemies and persecutors" (vv. 14-15). It is this note of trust and hope that Job lacks, and his contender is God himself, not human enemies.

B. The Second Cycle of Speeches

The speeches of Job in this cycle are largely repetitive of what has gone before, although the personal element comes across more strongly. He fluctuates between moments of weakness and despair and moments of confidence. He both derides the friends and begs for sympathy. He longs for justification from God and clings to the hope of vindication before death, a hope which is looking increasingly unlikely given his condition. The legal motifs are less pronounced, and there are more passages of lament. The parodying continues unabated in this section, serving to highlight the untraditional nature of Job's sentiments.

Job 16–17

In this speech Job returns to criticizing, calling his friends "miserable comforters" and using their own words in 8:2 and 15:2 against them. Once again the theme of the importance of communication is raised — words can be used either to good effect or to bad. Job calls their words "windy," that is, empty and lacking comfort. He states that he could have adopted their stance and offered shallow comfort but he could also have given more encouragement, which they have chosen not to do. If Job speaks to himself, his pain is still there; but if he is silent, it is there too. This attack really disguises Job's true complaint, which is against God. There is some mixing of third person and second person address here (all changed to third person in the NRSV), which suggests that Job is fluctuating between talking about God and addressing him directly. God has taken everything from him — his energy, his household, and his health. God is compared to a wild beast in 16:9, parodying psalms which compare the enemies of Israel to wild beasts, while God is a safe haven by comparison, giving humans the will to live and meaning to life (e.g., Psalm 94). In Job 16:10 other human beings are ranged against him, presumably as a result of God's attack. God has cast him into the hands of the wicked and broken him. In v. 12 Job emphasizes the unexpectedness and violence of God's onslaught. The picture of God as a warrior emerges here and is followed by the image of God as an archer, with which we are already familiar from Job's speeches. In v. 14 we have overtones of the military act of breaching the walls, the final moment in a campaign. Job is the one under attack, and so he is overwhelmed by God's might. He describes God as having sewed sackcloth onto his skin. This clearly denotes that the sackcloth has become such an integral part of his body that it is inseparable from him. It may refer to the open sores to which sackcloth may have stuck so that it becomes a part of his flesh. His strength is gone, and weeping has made his face sore and his eyes heavy. Yet Job maintains his innocence, and there is a pathetic tone to his words.

In 16:18 Job breaks into a plea that he should not die without vindication, using language of blood vengeance to introduce the idea that if he were to die he would want his innocent blood to cry out from the ground. Despite God's treatment of him, he is his only witness and to him Job must appeal. He calls for just treatment and begs that his rights be recognized. These verses can be read as containing a call on Job's part for a mediator with God (cf. Job 19:23-29), but in my view there is no mediation, and that is the problem. Job is determined to maintain his rights before God and begs that these be maintained — the mediator idea is a source of hope but an empty one. In 9:33 he had lamented that there was none to whom he might appeal to stand between him and God. God is the only one who can take up Job's case, and Job begs for this before it is too late and is in the snares of death. In 16:20 Job reiterates that his friends scorn him and have become his accusers, but he later accuses God of making the friends not understand (in 17:4).

In ch. 17 Job feels that he is on the verge of death. Even now, at his weakest point, he is mocked by those around him. No one will take his part, and he argues that one day their children will suffer for their callousness. Then God comes under attack once more — it is his fault that he is rejected, that he suffers such grief, and that his body is shriveled up. In vv. 8-10 he asserts that the upright are appalled at this treatment of a righteous man. Presumably they then assume Job's guilt and, as expected, range themselves against the wicked, among whose number Job is counted. Yet the righteous, including the friends here, have such a black-and-white view of the world that they cannot see Job's innocence (v. 10). In the final verses of the chapter Job is preoccupied with death. He realizes that if he embraces death, that will be the end. His hope of vindication will be gone. Here then Job, longing for death as a release on the one hand, realizes its negative aspect on the other. This is the same tension we have encountered before in his thought.

Job 19

In Job's second speech in this cycle, there is some repetition of the sentiments we found in the first. Once again the friends are addressed and rebuked by Job for their cruel words, and he accuses them of humiliating him beyond what he deserves. In 19:4, Job is not admitting sin, but he is merely saying that even if he had sinned, God's punishment is disproportionate to the sin committed. Further, if Job has sinned, why should the friends take it upon themselves to preach self-righteously at him. He then turns his attention to God, who is the cause of this treatment since he appears to be guilty when he is not. In v. 6 we find imagery of God as a hunter — God has trapped Job as a hunter traps animals. He cries out but is not answered. He feels shut in by God. The idea of life as a path comes in here — a traditional wisdom motif. Here Job says that his path is blocked so that he cannot proceed and in darkness so that he cannot see where he is going. God has stripped Job of the honorable reputation he once enjoyed. He is broken down, uprooted like a plant, and the enemy in warfare — Job uses all these different images to convey the basic point that God has turned against him and caused his innocent suffering. He begs for sympathy — he is alone without family, friends, or household, he is physically repulsive to his wife, and he is ill, and it is all God's fault. Things could not get much worse. In v. 20 Job is concerned about his illness and reverses the normal image of flesh hanging on bones and therefore giving shape to the body. Here his bones are so weak and decayed that they cling to his flesh, presumably making him shapeless. The skin of my teeth is a curious phrase for Job to use since the teeth is the one place where there is no skin, so to have escaped by the skin of the teeth is a way of saying that one has barely escaped. This fits in with Job's sentiments here. In v. 21 he calls for pity from the friends, but he then realizes in v. 22 that the friends pursue him just as much as God does — a traditional attack by enemies has become one by friends.

In 19:23-29 Job wishes his avowal of innocence were inscribed in a book or in rock forever so that they are not forgotten. There are overtones here of the blood vengeance called for in his last speech. He wants something to outlast him so that he knows he will be vindicated. He expresses the desire, even certainty, that one day God will vindicate him. One day he will see God on his side, even if it is after his death (or, anyway, after his skin has been destroyed, which either could be a reference to his illness or could mean that he would then be dead). "In my flesh I shall see God" (v. 26) suggests that Job will be aware of his own vindication, presumably while he is still alive (the translation "outside my flesh" has been suggested, which would suggest after death, but this rendering would be less consistent with his overall thought). At this hopeful idea Job's heart faints within him; he is overcome by the thought, which seems too wonderful to be possible. This section (vv. 25-27) has been seen as evidence of a belief in an afterlife, and clearly the boundary line for Job between life and death is thin here. However, up to this point Job has been calling for vindication before death and has been anxious that he should not die before such vindication. Although he is grasping here for a way that his words could outlast him, he knows that this is an impossibility, that God is the only one who can vindicate him, and that it must be now before he is gripped by death and unable to continue the conversation with God. There is no separate mediator figure here — God has been the one throughout to whom Job has called for vindication. This is a moment of hope that God will restore him before it is too late. The closing verses of the chapter are addressed to the friends, warning them that if they torment him and are proved wrong judgment will be right around the corner. There is a mood of confidence here that contrasts strongly with Job's pitiful words earlier in the speech — the vision of hope in his redemption by God has given him renewed energy to have a dig at the friends. However, it does seem curious that Job seems to be upholding the doctrine of retribution here, as the friends have usually done. Maybe this shows his confusion of mind, or expresses a hope that after vindication things will return to their normal pattern (which of course they eventually do).

Job 21

Chapter 21 is a traditional diatribe about the wicked, except that they are seen to prosper instead of being punished. The chapter opens with an appeal for a hearing. The suggestion in v. 4 is that Job's complaint is not addressed to mortals but to God, which, he thinks, gives him the right to be impatient with the response he is getting. V. 5a — "Look at me, and be appalled"— could refer either to Job's physical condition at which the friends are appalled or to the words he is about to say. He suggests that they keep quiet by laying their hands on their mouths. Job goes on to refute the friends' arguments about the certain punishment and short triumph of the wicked. In vv. 7-16 he asks why they prosper and live long, become powerful, and have a peaceful end. They see their children become prosperous too. They have no fear but dwell in safety, and even their animals are no problem to them. They sing and dance, and even die in peace. They choose to reject God, seeing no advantage in serving him, seeing that their prosperity was won by their own achievements. This section parodies passages in the psalms which discuss the prosperity of the righteous by using the same language reserved for them to describe the wicked. This description can also be compared with passages in which the prosperity of the wicked is described (e.g., Pss 10:5-6 and 73:3-9) in that their prosperity is generally seen to be short-lived, whereas in Job it is more far-reaching and enduring.

In 21:17-22 Job asks how often the godless suffer, with the inference that the answer is not very often. In vv. 17-18 commonplaces about the fate of the wicked are thus made into questions expecting the answer "No." In v. 19 Job anticipates an objection which the friends might offer at this point, namely, that even if the wicked should escape punishment, their children will have to suffer it. In 20:10 the friends had spoken of the inheritance of suffering that the wicked leave to their children, as well as heaping disaster on themselves. Job here protests that it would be no justice for a person to sin and his or her children to suffer; rather, the sinner is the one who should be disciplined. Job questions whether anyone would take an interest in the affairs of his family once he is dead. V. 22 could be a reproach to his friends for imposing their own rigid doctrine on God himself. It could, however, refer to God, who, since he is judge, needs to realize that the wicked do not care for what comes after them. This could imply a limitation on God's knowledge of humanity and would be a much more radical statement. In 21:23-26, death levels all — the wicked person dies at ease and in prosperity and the good person dies in bitterness, but the same fate is meted out to both — and in the grave the bodies of both rot away. In 21:23-26, a contrast is set up between two types of people — one type has prospered in life and the other has suffered — and the same fate awaits them all. This contrasts with traditional ideas about the reward of the good and the punishment of the wicked (e.g., Ps 1:6). In 21:27 Job accuses the friends of schemes to wrong him, possibly referring to Job's realization that when his friends, Zophar in particular, spoke of the fate of the wicked they really meant himself. Job anticipates that they will declare that the wicked leave no memory among those left behind. However, in fact the wicked are spared and no one requites them. There is no reparation for what they have done. Rather, they are honored even after death. 21:32-33 is a parody of passages which speak of the honorable fate of the pious man; here it is transferred to the wicked.

The Third Cycle of Speeches (23:1–24:25; 26:1–27:12)

The element of dialogue is further removed in this section, and this is partly exacerbated by a dislocation of speeches, which may be a deliberate fragmentation to show the dialogue breaking down and both sides tired of arguing. Job's thought has also been seen to fluctuate greatly during the course of his speeches, and so it is entirely in keeping that he might in one mood uphold the traditional line and in another make a searing attack on his usual beliefs. After all, he did once share the worldview of the friends, and at times, when he speaks of the fate of the wicked, he seems to lapse into old beliefs. He may even be deliberately suspending judgment in his different portrayals of their fate — from envying their prosperity to describing their end. If this is the case, we may not need to excise verses in ch. 24 or ch. 27 as scholars have been tempted to do. The dialogue clearly ends in a stalemate in that neither side is listening to the other and criticism is replacing any attempt at discussion. The starting points of Job and the friends are different, and Job finds no comfort in his friends' stance. The progressively shorter speeches of his friends suggest that their arguments are becoming less effective. Job, on the other hand, despite a low point in the middle of the second cycle, appears to grow in strength and determination as the cycle reaches its end. His most unorthodox words have been about God, whom Job always blames for his condition. His experience of God as his enemy has led him to be skeptical of all the traditional answers to his suffering and to the usual assertions about God's justice. In the next section we shall see how this challenge to God is uppermost in his thoughts.

Job 23:1–24:25

In this third cycle God is clearly the real object of Job's concern. God is the cause of his suffering. He expresses the desire to find God in order to lay his case before him in person and learn the content of God's complaint against him. He would expect to be given a fair trial, not overwhelmed with power — a certain irony is here given to what is to come in the God speeches. He has looked for God but cannot find him — this is another injustice because God knows every step he is taking. Here Job complains about God's absence in contrast to psalms where God's presence leads a person through life (e.g., Psalm 23). This complaint also parodies passages in the Psalms which imagine that there is no way to escape God (e.g., Ps 139:7-12). These sentiments contrast with earlier sentiments from Job of feeling trapped by God. Now God is hiding and cannot be found anywhere. He even sees his punishment as a test in v. 10, a new idea for Job anticipating the speeches of Elihu. He speaks here of certain vindication. The idea of life as a path continues here with the sentiment from Job that he has walked in God's way and hence does not deserve this suffering. But what he has come to realize through this experience is that God does what he wants to do. He has his own reasons for treating Job as he does. When Job thinks of God's inscrutability, he is frightened and wishes he could disappear too, as God has done.

In ch. 24 we begin to move into the area of dislocation of the third cycle of speeches. Part of the chapter does not fit in the mouth of Job; thus either he is quoting his friends or some set piece of wisdom on the fate of the wicked, or we have to see the section from vv. 18-25 (possibly minus v. 21) as part of the speech of one of the friends. Alternatively this could be a separate fragment, somewhat like ch. 28. There is no problem with the first half of the chapter. Here Job wonders why God does not have set times of judgment and mete it out on set days — the question here is really why God does not let the righteous see that he is punishing wickedness. He argues that God is seemingly inactive in the face of human suffering at the hands of the wicked. The wicked have time to get away with removing landmarks — a serious trespass in the entire ancient Near East — and stealing from the poor, the orphan, and the widow, or those at the lower end of society. This exploitation by the wicked leaves the poor in a terrible state, scavenging for food and working as slaves, without clothing or shelter. In 24:9 Job describes the way the wicked snatch the children of the poor — a verse that seems out of place here and should perhaps be moved to later in the chapter. Then he is back to his description of the poor, who are naked, hungry, and working hard. God pays no attention to any of them despite their prayers. From v. 13 on there are descriptions of the wicked, the murderer, and the adulterer, who work at night and shun the day. They are thus associated with the darkness of Sheol and described as friends of the "terrors of deep darkness." From v. 18 on we have the reversal mentioned above. These verses are obscure but clearly refer to the fate that awaits the wicked people just described. Here we have a gruesome picture of the destruction of evildoers, a sharp contrast to Job's description of the prosperity of the wicked in the last cycle. Of course this is what should happen to them. They will have to flee quickly when doom descends, when their land is no longer fertile and their vineyards are empty of grapes and in no need of grape treaders. Just as water is very rapidly dried up by heat, so they will be snatched away by death. Even their mother's womb will forget them. As it devours the body of the wicked person, the worm will find it sweet. Their memory is gone, and wickedness will be no more. V. 21 could belong with vv. 9-18 since it describes another action toward the weak — this time women — by the wicked. However, it can also be seen to provide the reason for v. 20 — "the womb forgets them." This is retribution for the fact that they have harmed childless women and so insulted the childbearing role of their own mother. V. 22 suggests that the wicked may survive for a time but they will receive their just punishment in the end, the same argument used by Eliphaz in 15:20-22. Some have placed 24:22-23 in Job's mouth, but then v. 24 does not fit. It is probably best not to carve up the text too much but to regard the whole of this second section of the chapter as displaced. Having said this, Job's rebuttal at the end in v. 25 could well be original to him and yet clearly misplaced. One aspect of these two chapters is that they do not continue the usual diatribe against the friends; this is the only hint of what might have originally been a longer section.

Job 26:1–27:12

In ch. 26 we are definitely back to Job's own words. He is back to his usual diatribe against the friends, referring sarcastically to their assistance and advice and how helpful it has been. He questions the source of this false wisdom of theirs and then goes on to describe Sheol — a deliberate juxtaposition of two ideas perhaps. Job 26:5-14 is a hymn in praise of God's power and could belong in the mouth of Job or of his friends. It might have been an existing hymn reused by the author, and some scholars excise the section from Job's speech. However, my own inclination is to leave it in, partly on the ground that it does contain a slightly unorthodox note which we have seen to be characteristic of Job's speeches in the dialogue. Vv. 5-6 tell of God's dominion over the underworld, but vv. 7-14 of his power reflected in his creative activity. The unorthodox note here is that God's power in creation is seen as frightening, whereas usually in the psalms and in the prophets it is to be praised (in Isa 40:9-11, e.g., God's greatness in creation is extolled and is a source of comfort for humanity).

In ch. 27 Job repeats that it is God who has taken his rights away from him and left him in this state, and yet he swears an oath by this God that he will never concede guilt. He is determined to hold fast to his innocence despite the evidence to the contrary seemingly found by God. Two conceptions of God are found in Job's thought — on the one hand, a picture of the God who has wronged him and, on the other, the recognition that this is the God whom he had previously trusted and with whom he longs to be in communion once again. Here we find some of the fervor of his earlier sentiments about his innocence. He has no guilty conscience and no regrets. From v. 7 on Job launches an attack on his enemies, presumably the friends, wishing on them the fate that should come to the wicked and criticizing their vanity. Some have wanted to excise vv. 8-10 from Job's speech and put them in the mouth of his friends, but in my opinion there is no inconsistency in Job's quotation of the usual fate of the wicked at this point.

The Hymn to Wisdom (Job 28)

The hymn to wisdom in ch. 28 is presented as a continuation of Job's speech, but it makes no sense as coming from Job since it actually provides Job with a fresh perspective, rather in the manner of the God speeches. Nor does it belong in the mouths of his friends since it lacks their disputational style and does not place an emphasis on retributive justice as their speeches do. It is widely thought to be a separate poem, either by the hand of the same author or by another hand. It is well placed in the fragmented third cycle as offering another perspective — it is hard to know where else in the book it might have fitted in.

Scholarly evaluations of this hymn have varied enormously. Some have seen it as a real centerpiece to the book, providing the ultimate answer to Job that he will never understand his suffering in the light of the power and majesty of God the Creator, in much the same manner as is done in the God speeches (see discussion in Rowley). Others have regarded it as a later addition, largely because of the anticipation of what is yet to come in the God speeches and because of its awkward position. It could have been added by someone wanting to stress the wisdom theme in the book and the inaccessibility of God's wisdom. It may have been a kind of first attempt by the author to answer the problems raised in the dialogue, followed by further reflections in the God speeches. Or it may have been added by the same author later on as a kind of finishing touch. It may have had a separate context — maybe a liturgical one — before it was placed in this context. The description of mining suggests an intimate knowledge of that area of life, and the poem, or at least that part of it, may have originated in such circles. The options are many and varied. There is rich imagery here, a distinct genre and a self-contained feel to the hymn that lead one to see it as a separate section, but its origin and place in the book probably have to remain open questions. The hymn-to-wisdom form is known to us from other parts of wisdom literature and was clearly a standard form of expression among the wise, especially in postexilic circles. The hymn may have been added to the book of Job, maybe as an attempt to make it more orthodox as a wisdom book.

Job 28:1-11

The first part of the poem uses the imagery of digging for silver, gold, iron, and copper. Human beings use all their ingenuity in the quest for precious metal. It is seemingly hidden and therefore needs to be sought out, mined, and then refined or smelted. The life of miners is described — they put an end to darkness by the use of lamps, and they discover hidden things down in the bowels of the earth. They dig down in remote areas and, because they are underground and people aboveground, forget about their existence. People above are plowing the fields and making bread while underneath heavy mining work is going on to which they are oblivious. There are hidden delights down in this place of darkness — sapphires and gold are their reward. The ways into the mines are not even known by the birds known for seeking out their prey, such as the falcon. Even "proud beasts" do not walk that way. The miners see the hidden stones and cut them out of the rock, also finding underground rivers. They bring them all to light. This section of the hymn seems to be praising human ingenuity and wisdom rather than putting it in its place as the rest of the hymn does. Of course, the final message is that, despite all this, God's wisdom is greater than human attempts to understand. However, this section of the hymn does praise the technological achievements of humans — even in dark, remote, and inaccessible places, humans are able to discover hidden treasures and precious gems.

Job 28:12-22

In the second part of the hymn we move on to the inaccessibility of wisdom. Despite all the digging in the depths of the earth, humans cannot find wisdom. There are limits to knowledge in every generation. It is not to be found on earth, the land of the living, nor in the sea. It cannot be bought or valued in terms of precious stones. It is incomparable to these precious jewels, and its price is much higher. Even the birds do not know where to find it. Only death has heard a rumor of it. The gold of Ophir mentioned in 28:16 is the most highly prized gold of the time. Onyx was similarly valued, a gem used for engraving. The next verse mentions glass, which was highly prized in antiquity. And in v. 19 we find reference to the chrysolite of Ethiopia, probably yellow rock-crystal, a kind of topaz. It is interesting that the powers of death, Abaddon or Sheol and Death, are described as having no knowledge of wisdom and having heard only a rumor of it. Death is personified here as having ears. The rumor may be a reference to the idea that on the threshold of death, humans enjoy deeper wisdom than they had during their lifetimes.

Job 28:23-27

Now we come to the answer — only God in his omniscience as creator knows where wisdom is. This section picks up an idea expressed by Zophar, that nothing escapes God's eye (Job 11:11). He used it to persuade Job to confess his sin; here the reference is simply in praise of God as creator. He is so great that all is in his vision. He ordered all creation, giving the wind a maximum of force or weight when it blew to ensure that it did not exceed its boundaries. He gave the sea its limits so that the land was not washed away by it. This forms an interesting contrast to descriptions of God's anger in which he lets natural forces run away in tornados or floods (e.g., Job's sentiments in 9:1-12 and 12:13-25). God also determined the laws of rainfall and the habits of thunderbolts. God therefore fixed the order. He surveyed it, set it up, and thoroughly explored it. There are overtones here of Prov 8:22-23, which describe God's setting up of the created order through Wisdom. There is a more overt personification of wisdom in Proverbs 8 than here. One difference between this poem and Proverbs 8 is that there this wisdom is also accessible to human beings, if only they will follow the path of the wise. Here it is the preserve of God alone, until we come to the final verse of the hymn.

Job 28:28

This verse serves as a crucial bridge between God and humanity and should not be excised, as some older scholars suggested. Here God says to humankind that the fear of the Lord is wisdom and to depart from evil is understanding. The inference here is that human beings in their inability to understand all that the Creator understands are best advised to fear God and keep the moral law. There is a strong overtone of the conclusions of the author of Ecclesiastes, who, after surveying all possible paths to happiness, concludes, "Fear God and keep his commandments; for this is the whole duty of everyone." The wisdom that is accessible to human beings, then, is more limited here than it is in Proverbs 8 — there are even overtones of the friends' arguments in the mention of retributive justice. Job has questioned the point of fearing evil if in fact you suffer anyway, while the friends, in contrast, have maintained the principle throughout. The suggestion here is that it is best to do just this because a deeper understanding of the cosmic order is denied to humans. This hymn lacks the optimism of Proverbs that wisdom is on offer to those who embrace her ways. The ultimate answer is that, despite human attempts to discover the ways of the universe, such knowledge is not to be found. Divine wisdom is related to human wisdom, but the two are also rather different.

Job's Closing Soliloquy (Job 29–31)

These three chapters represent three stages of Job's final plea to God: the first looks back on the good relationship Job once had with God, the second examines his present situation, and the third is an attempt to force God to appear to him to justify his actions by stating an oath of innocence. This threefold structure recalls psalms of lament which look back to the past, view the present, and then look forward to a better relationship with God in the future.

This self-contained section is distinct from the speeches of Job in the dialogue in that it has a different character and contains a movement from enumeration of past actions to present distress, and then to a statement of innocence that would stand up in a court of law. In the manner of a psalmic lament, the whole section is addressed to God, and here we find Job trying to define the limits of the relationship. He looks back to the past relationship he enjoyed with God when he knew the rules. He looks at his present anguish when all the rules seem to be broken and he is suffering public humiliation and private distress. He then presents his case to God, stating his innocence and calling down punishment if indeed he has deserved it. This is another attempt to recall the previous rules and call God to account.

Job 29

This chapter offers Job an opportunity to remember his good relationship with God before calamity struck. He felt looked after by God, he walked in the light enjoyed by the righteous (in contrast to the darkness of evil and death), and he felt God to be a friend and even part of his family life. He could do no wrong. He commanded respect, even from the higher members of society — everyone was in awe of him because of his good deeds. He helped the poor, the orphan, the wretched, and the widow. Righteousness and justice were so much a part of his actions that they were like his clothes. He helped disabled people, and he showed care to those in need and hospitality to strangers. He even frightened the wicked away. He thought that longevity and prosperity were his inheritance, and he looked forward to a peaceful future. There is an echo here of the legend of the phoenix, an early folktale that spoke of an immortal or long-lived bird. People waited on his words, and in a leadership role he gave them a confidence they could not engender within themselves. This is a very idealistic picture, totally unlike anything Job has spoken before. It has been suggested that it was a hymn about the glory of the righteous, adapted by the author of Job to refer to Job's past prosperity. The chapter is designed to form a contrast to what has gone before and what is to come in the next chapters. The main focus is the respect that he gained from the public — he was treated almost like a king; there is also reflection on his flawless ethical conduct and on God's constant favor to him. Job's relationship with God seemed so easy, and yet it has now become so complex.

Job 30

Chapter 30 provides a complete contrast. Job's situation has now changed dramatically, and he is held in contempt by all in society, including those younger than he or lower on the social scale. He would once have treated the fathers of these youngsters as on the level of dogs, that is, at the bottom of the pile. Dogs were seen as vicious and dirty, and so the word was applied as an insult. He is left to associate with the starving and the outcasts of society. They have no strength to offer, presumably to enable them to labor, because their hunger has dried up their strength. They live on leaves and other inferior food. They are treated badly by others, thrown out of towns, and forced to live in the desert, among rocks and bushes. Job is mocked, avoided, or spat at. God is seen to have punished Job for wrongdoing, and so people have also cut him off. Loosing the bowstring refers to untying a cord, the opposite of girding the loins, which is a sign of strength. He feels a rabble of people rising up against him, rushing at him, and building roads (cf. the military rampart of Job's earlier speeches) to block his way. The image of life as a path is found here; now society is breaking up his path, not allowing him even to walk along it. There is also storm imagery in 30:14 — Job feels chased by the power of his enemies, and his former honor and prosperity are blown away in a gust of wind. Society has become his unhindered enemy just as God has. This public acknowledgment of his lowered status, coupled with his physical suffering, leads him to despair.

Job goes on to the afflictions that he feels, not just in his body but as dealt out to him by God. He feels spent and weak from all the grief that he has poured out. God is seen to have seized his garments of righteousness and cast him into a pit of mud. God does not answer his cries; he just looks on. He feels tossed about by God as in a storm — a return to the storm imagery — and expects death at any time. Job cannot understand this reversal. He himself never turned against anyone who was suffering; rather, he took their burdens on himself. Yet when he expected a reward for his good actions, all he received was darkness rather than light. Job is racked with troubles and in darkness. His cry for help is unheard. His company is jackals and ostriches; in other words, he cries and wails like a jackal in the desert, an outcast from society. The ostrich, too, lives in desolate regions and hides its face in the sand — appropriate metaphorical companions for Job. His skin is black and falling off, and his music is no longer glad; instead it is that of mourning and pain, mingling with the laments of the women who will come and weep when he is dead.

The basic theme here is Job's agony, both mental and physical — mental in being so despised by those who respected him before and physical in the ongoing suffering of his body. And at the center of both types of pain is God, who has rejected him and caused his suffering. It has sometimes been noted that at the beginning of this chapter Job seems to be looking down on the outcasts he was once so keen to help. This betrays Job's upper-class background — philanthropy is an admirable thing, but being ranged among the lowest classes oneself quite another matter. The author is revealing an interesting insight into human nature here. This is not, however, a reason for condemning Job or for excising vv. 1-8 to exonerate him, as has been occasionally suggested.

Job 31

In the final chapter Job lays his case before God in a statement of his integrity that parallels Egyptian mortuary texts in which the deceased affirms his virtue before Osiris and the gods with a list of offenses of which he has not been guilty. This is probably a set-piece formula, being used here by the author of Job in a legal-type context. Job as defendant needs to state his case. This style of confession parodies passages elsewhere where God is the defendant, for example, Mic 6:3-5 in which God wishes to know what he has done to his people. The point here is that Job has definitely not done these things and yet he is being punished as if he had. He thus has to form his own defense, since God will not do so. In 31:2-4 he asks three questions indicating the punishments to be expected in the light of traditional theology if he had gone wrong; then he makes oaths relative to various matters, for example, falsehood (vv. 5-6) and upright conduct (vv. 7-8).

This chapter contains the strongest declaration of his

innocence. Its formulation in terms of an oath strengthens it even more. Normally in oaths, a conditional curse section is evaded and the part containing the naming of the dire consequences if the oath taker commits perjury is avoided. In each section here, however, Job states that if he has done anything wrong, then appropriate calamity may come upon him (e.g., vv. 5-8 and vv. 9-10). In not being afraid to be evasive over the possible consequences of unrighteous deeds, the author of Job is creating a dramatic effect. Job is unafraid to suffer all the consequences of unrighteous actions — in many ways he already has. He has nothing to lose. Fourteen sins that Job might have committed are on the list in ch. 31 — lust (v. 1), lying and deceiving (vv. 5-6), taking the belongings of others (vv. 7-8), adultery (vv. 9-10), unfair treatment of slaves (v. 13), uncaring treatment of the poor, widows, and orphans (vv. 16-17), lack of pity for the homeless without clothing (v. 19), perversion of claims of the orphan (v. 21), confidence in wealth (vv. 24-25), sun and moon worship (vv. 26-27), joy in the face of the calamity of enemies (v. 29), failure to offer hospitality (v. 32), concealing sins because of fear of public opinion (vv. 33-34), and appropriation of land belonging to others (vv. 38-39). Interestingly, only one of these sins is a cultic sin (sun and moon worship); the rest concern ethical and charitable actions beyond the strict call of duty. The list does not include more heinous crimes such as murder — there is no suggestion that Job's sin was ever that great. The inference is that Job has definitely not done all these things, as witnessed by his exemplary character in chapter 29; therefore, he does not deserve the punishment he is receiving. In fact, the hypothetical "If I have done this . . ." nature of the piece is broken down in places where Job says that he has in fact done this or that (e.g., vv. 16-18). The punishments Job invokes vary in degree depending on the crime, from a mere others reaping what he has sown if he has cheated anybody, to allowing his wife to be with another man if he has committed adultery (v. 10), to even losing an arm if he has not put out the hand of friendship to the orphan (v. 22). In vv. 35-37 we have what might be the original ending of the piece, which is then supplemented in vv. 38-40 and may suggest that some rearrangement would be sensible. In these summarizing verses, instead of finding the usual lament to God at the end of an oath of innocence, we discover Job wishing God would answer him and longing to pin God down with a legal document. The idea of writing something down to give it more force is prominent here, as is the idea of carrying something about with one all the time so that it becomes part of one. If vindicated by God, Job would never let his indictment leave his body, such would be his pride in his vindication.

Elihu (Job 32–37)

Elihu, son of Barachel the Buzite, of the family of Ram, has long been regarded as rather an embarrassment in the context of the book of Job. This new character appears at ch. 32 after Job's final speech and before God's reply. He has not been introduced in the Prologue, where only three friends are mentioned, and we are not aware that anyone else is listening to the debate between Job and the friends. Elihu has a few small points to add, but essentially his words are a repetition of those of the friends and an anticipation in the final chapters of the sentiments to come in the God speeches. In dramatic terms the plot of the book is somewhat spoiled by this intrusion. Job is poised at the limits of his anguish, ready for God's response. Likewise, God's response would more effectively have been placed at this juncture. This has led many scholars to regard the Elihu speeches as a later addition, either by the author himself at a later stage or by an inferior author or redactor. As with ch. 28, more orthodox wisdom circles may have added the speeches with the aim of putting traditional views more strongly and in a better light.

Scholars have evaluated these speeches very differently, some seeing them as representing the central message of the book (e.g., Marshall) — that suffering is a discipline and that God's ultimate ways are unknowable — and others seeing them as adding little new thought to the book and spoiling the plot (e.g., Driver and Gray). It is true that the material is largely repetitive of what has been and what is to come. Elihu's character, too, is unattractive — he is self-important, dogmatic, and somewhat naive despite his claim to God's wisdom. The speech is not acknowledged by Job or the friends, which increases the suspicion that it is an addition. Nor do the Yahweh speeches or Epilogue refer to Elihu's solution. The style is long-winded and may betray a slightly inferior editorial hand. The mention of angelic intermediaries might suggest a Persian influence on the thought here, the product perhaps of the same redactor who added the Satan speeches in the Prologue.

Job 32:1-5

The section begins with a narrative introduction justifying Elihu's appearance. He is an angry young man who attacks both sides in the debate and sees himself as needing to provide the answer that the friends have not managed to do — he disagrees that suffering is always the result of sin — and to put Job right by countering his claim that God is unjust. The reason for his previous reticence is said to be his youth, but anger compels him to speak out. The giving of Elihu's family credentials may have been intended to show that although he is young he comes from a good family. He is of the family of Ram, who was a descendant of David. Elihu gives four speeches, into which we shall divide the material.

Job 32:6–33:33

At the beginning of his speech, Elihu reiterates the reason for his reticence, uttering the usual wisdom opinion that with age comes wisdom. There are overtones of Zophar's appeal to the weight of experience here. However, listening to the debate has made him think otherwise. He now argues that understanding is God-given at whatever age; it is not the preserve of the old. The reference to a spirit of understanding suggests that God decides to whom to give his gift of wisdom on an individual level. It is a claim to authority rather like that of

Eliphaz in his personal vision in ch. 5. In vv. 11-12 it is clear that Elihu is addressing the friends, and he accuses them of not providing Job with an adequate answer. He also argues that they have given up on Job in thinking that only God can answer him now. Elihu presumably thinks he can do better. He sees the silence of Job's friends at this juncture as his opportunity to speak. He describes himself as being "full of words" — he is bursting to speak and compares his compulsion to speak with wineskins full to overflowing. He claims to be impartial and incapable of flattery — he certainly has a high opinion of himself!

In ch. 33 he turns to address Job. He calls on God-given authority through his spirit. He wants Job to answer him and stresses his likeness to him as a human being so that Job need have no fear. No wonder he is often regarded as self-righteous! He cites Job's argument that he is innocent and that God has put him in the wrong, and he attempts to counter it. He states that God answers humans in two ways, first in a dream or vision (cf. Eliphaz) and second by using suffering as a discipline (cf. Zophar). The dream functions as a warning — presumably a reference to nightmares. Humans suffer illness and come close to death, but there can be a reprieve if a mediator declares a person upright before God. The reference to a mediator or guardian angel is interesting here, for Job has called for that in the speeches, although in a legal context. Once the mediator has spoken, there is a return to youthful vigor, and prayer leads to forgiveness. The emphasis on the mediator figure here may suggest a later hand since this idea became more popular during the Persian period and after under the influence of Persian dualism. There is an expression of the need for repentance too — in v. 27 the redeemed person tells others that they sinned but that they did not receive the full punishment of death, but have been saved at the last minute. This is Elihu's reading of Job's suffering and yet his explanation, too, of the fact that Job is still alive. He tells Job to pay heed to his wisdom in no uncertain terms.

Job 34:2-33

In ch. 34 Elihu turns his attention back to Job's friends. He appears to cite their own arguments back at them in the claim that Job is wrong to claim innocence in asserting that God is always right and cannot do wrong, and in stating that God is in charge of the world and all-powerful and his judgments are infallible. Here he is in support of the friends' depiction of God's just meting out of punishment. But there is also a further sense here that God can do what he likes — he can choose to punish immediately or he can choose to delay punishment, allowing the opportunity for repentance. The meaning of the Hebrew of vv. 29-33 is very uncertain, but there seems to be a reference in v. 29 to the inaction of God, his hiding of his face, which is taken negatively by some but fits into Elihu's theory of delayed punishment. In vv. 31-32 the possibility of repentance and a corresponding humility before God seem to be held out, while v. 33 stresses the choices available to Job. The speech ends with an accusation of Job — the longer he holds out, the more he is adding to the amount of his sin in God's eyes.

Job 35:2-16

Elihu now addresses Job. He argues that neither human virtues nor sins can affect God, but they do affect the people themselves and others around them. He goes on to state that oppressed people who cry to God are not necessarily answered; God decides in his own time which cries are genuine and which not. This is perhaps to be seen as an acknowledgment of the problem of the oppression of innocent people under the hands of tyrants, or it might simply suggest that their cries are false. Elihu stresses God's greatness and power manifest in creation and through wisdom. He accuses Job of wasting his time in asking for God to appear to him and of babbling like a fool.

Job 36:2–37:24

In his final speech, Elihu is still speaking to Job "on God's behalf." His argument that suffering is a discipline emerges here. He speaks of God's wisdom in meting out retributive justice. He warns Job that he should stop aligning himself with the wicked in questioning God's ways, but instead acknowledge God's discipline, as manifest in the suffering sent upon him. He ends ch. 36 with a hymn to God's greatness and might, as shown in his creative acts and his performance in the lightning and thunder of the natural world. Thunder is a reflection of God's anger and even causes Elihu to tremble with fear. Ch. 37 continues this theme of the ways of God in nature, but stresses even more its mysteriousness and God's consequent inscrutablity. In v. 13, God's motive for his actions is seen to be unknown. In the final part of ch. 37 we have the full anticipation of the God speeches in Elihu's call to Job to consider whether he understands the ways of God in creation and nature. They emphasize God's greatness and majesty. There is the sentiment that God is so entirely other that human beings can say nothing to him.

God (Job 38–41)

The climax of the book is reached when God appears to Job in a whirlwind. There are two speeches from God, the first of which is usually seen as original, and the second about which there is more doubt. Job's wish seems to be granted. God appears to him as requested; however, the content of the speeches is very different from his expectations in that God makes no attempt to answer his specific charges. Rather, God's reply consists of a series of rhetorical questions, a display of his power, and a taunting of Job for his limited view of the world. In my view, the appearance of God is Job's answer — at least he is not hiding his face or continuing the stony silence that Job found so unbearable. The content of what he says, however, does not provide satisfactory answers to Job; rather, it merely confirms his lack of knowledge, including his lack of answers about why he has suffered. It is curious that after these chapters Job repents. His trust in God seems to have been restored. This might suggest that there is more in the content of God's speeches to restore Job's confidence.

However, my contention is that it is the appearance of God that restores his trust (see also Rowley). In fact, God goes on to do exactly what Job was afraid he would do in ch. 9, and that is to overwhelm him with a catalogue of his workings in the world which underlines that he can do what he likes. God actually confirms what Job had feared, that it is impossible to hold God within human boundaries of justice. God is saying that there is an order in nature and the world, but it is beyond human comprehension to understand. He is thus stressing the limitations of human wisdom by posing questions that are impossible to answer. The positive message here is that God does things in the world that are there for us to wonder at; the negative is that human beings will never understand the reasons for all of God's actions. The picture of God here is not one of tyranny; it is simply one of power. And Job's response is what God is calling for — the need to trust in God despite not having all the answers. The theophany, then, is a two-edged sword — on the one hand, it brings God and Job together and restores some kind of relationship in the appearance of God and the response contained in that. On the other hand, it distances Job from God because he does not receive the answer he desires but instead has to live with the fact that he must trust in a God who does do things that are outside human comprehension and norms of justice and whose concerns are wider than just human ones.

In these speeches God makes a rare appearance in order to justify his ways. They present a view of God as creator and orderer of the universe, with no mention of his redemptive acts in history as one might expect in other parts of the biblical literature. The speeches put Job in his place in no uncertain terms and yet engender a kind of awe and reverence at the same time. They make the boundaries of the God/human relationship clear — human beings have to learn to trust in God and look in awe at the world around them. They will never have all the answers. God's power is such and his purposes such that no amount of narrowing them down to human patterns of justice will work. The speeches use rich imagery. They work in many ways, against the wisdom quest; they emphasize the unknowability of the order of the world and the lesser place of humans within that order.

Job 38:1–40:2

God appears to Job in a whirlwind, a common context for a theophany experience. His first words accuse Job in a way that sounds remarkably like the sentiments of one of the friends, namely, that Job is full of words but without understanding. God tells Job to gird up his loins, suggesting that Job needs to muster some strength. There is a suggestion here that Job needs to take his destiny into his own hands instead of blaming God for his misfortune. God declares that he will question Job and expect some response, although in fact all his questions turn out to be unanswerable and Job has little to say. There is a parody here of passages in which human beings praise God as creator, asking questions out of wonder (e.g., Isa 40:12-26). Here the tables are turned, and God is asking the questions. God speaks of his task of creation and inquires whether Job was there so that he would know the order contained within it. How can Job hope to understand the order in the world if he had no part in the task? This section describes the wonders of the natural world. The greatness of God's deeds are highlighted by his creative actions in restraining the sea in 38:8-11. There is some mention of the wicked in God's listing of his deeds (vv. 13 and 15), but it is almost incidental given the greatness of the actions being described. This part places strong emphasis on the sheer expanse of the earth — God has walked the ocean shore and been to the gates of death. He asks Job if he knows the way to such places. He also inquires whether Job knows where the storehouses of snow or hail are kept or the way to the source of light and wind. He mocks the idea of the path of wisdom down which a person may walk, confident of the answers. God has done everything in his own time to benefit the earth, bringing rain in a desert where there is no human life. His sphere of action is far greater than just providing for human needs or creating an order and system of justice to satisfy human desires. God is the originator of all, the one who gave birth to ice and frost, the one who controls the stars and the heavens, the one who causes floods and storms. This is a real attack on human wisdom — given by God in the first place, we are reminded, and yet by its nature limited. When it comes to the real questions about order and creation, humans are left behind.

God now moves on to a catalogue of living creatures and their ways at the end of ch. 38 and in ch. 39. Can Job hunt as a lion does to satisfy its young? Does he know the time when the mountain goat gives birth? This sentiment recalls the book of Ecclesiastes and its doctrine of the proper time (Ecclesiastes 3). There is a time for things to happen and order in the universe, but only God knows them; human beings are unable to know. The times of activities in the world of nature, that is, of wild animals, are unknown to humans (39:1-4). Animals do things that humans cannot comprehend — they are outside the bounds of human wisdom. God has provided for these animals who refuse to be domesticated. God laughs at human attempts to tame such animals: "Is the wild ox willing to serve you?" The description of the ostrich suggests that animals may do things that human beings feel to be immoral — it leaves its eggs and deals cruelly with its young. Yet this is the way God has ordained it, and the ostrich is happy with that; it does not question God's ways as Job has done. God asks Job whether he has made horses mighty, beautiful, and strong or whether it is because of his command that the hawk and eagle soar high. God cares for all his creatures, not just human beings, and their ways are beyond human comprehension just as God's ways are. At the beginning of ch. 40 God taunts Job to respond to him, in terms reminiscent of Job's taunt to him. This elicits Job's first response. The basic message here is that the universe is a mystery; it was not created just for human use, and so neither it nor its creator can be judged solely by human standards. The natural world reveals God's order; its pattern and meaning are discernible although its secrets are with God. There are strong overtones in this sentiment of ch. 28 — humans search the depths of the earth but never find wisdom.

Job 40:6–41:34

In his second speech God makes clear to Job that he should not have put God in the wrong. Again Job is told to gird up his loins, to summon his strength, and to channel his anger against the wicked. Here God cites Behemoth as an example of great strength; have the strength of Behemoth, he taunts. Behemoth is a hippopotamus, seen here as a primeval creature that only God can overcome. It is not beautiful by human standards, and yet God takes delight in it. Again the power and majesty of God emerge from this description of the creatures in his world — no one except God can harness the power of these creatures for his own purposes. Likewise Leviathan is a crocodile, but here seen as the enemy of God in creation whom God alone has tamed. There is a certain amount of boasting here on God's part. The power of the beasts is such that only God can tame them. Job is thus shown that human beings are not the only orbit of God's concern and that his power is beyond human comprehension. Within the wider perspective of God's work in the universe from the beginning until now, Job's anguish is reduced to nothing.

Many scholars (e.g., Driver and Gray, Rowley) are of the opinion that the second speech of God is to be regarded as secondary because it adds little to the argument of the first, and the long descriptions of primeval animals overcome by God at creation are out of keeping with the praise of real animals in the first speech. However, it is not as if the second speech adds nothing, even though they both emphasize the same point about God's power over creation. The second speech adds that if God spares the wicked it is not because he lacks the power to overthrow them, while the first emphasizes that the suffering of the just enters into the scheme of divine providence as do all the phenomena of nature, and thus that human beings have to accept that God's motives are his own affair. The long descriptions of Behemoth and Leviathan may have been added by an orthodox editor who wished to reinforce the point about God being all-powerful, but in general it would seem safer to treat the speeches as a unit and to avoid carving up the text too much.

Job's Responses and God's Vindication (Job 40, 42)

Job's responses are crucial for an understanding of the book. There appears to be an incongruity in Job's repentance in the face of the divine tirade that has just occurred, and yet on the profound level of meeting with God, Job is satisfied. His relationship is restored, and he has learned to realize God's otherness and the breadth of God's concerns outside simply the human sphere. There are some problems with Job's repentance — some think it spoils the story. Job has been depicted as a hero of tragic proportions, holding on to his essential grandeur in the face of a hostile deity. But then he spoils it all by repenting for no good reason other than that he is overwhelmed by God (see Raphael in the context of a discussion of Job's links with Greek tragedy). However, these problems are negated by the recognition that Job does receive his answer in the communion with God that he experiences. The restored relationship turns his thoughts around. His story can be compared with that of Psalm 73, where the author is worried about the prosperity of the wicked. But then, we are told, he went into the sanctuary and saw that everything would work out as expected after all. Job of course does not believe that, but he does have an experience of God on a profound level that turns his world around and makes him realize the futility of arguing with God. Then the final irony appears in 42:7. Here he is told that he was right all along — presumably not right in all he said, although many of his sentiments do ring true in the light of God's words, but right to question rather than to be locked into a limited and narrow view of God's justice.

Job 40:3-5

The first response of Job is not one of repentance; it is rather one of acknowledgment of his weakness. He realizes that he cannot answer God, and he lays his hand to his mouth, meaning that words fail him. It is perhaps ironic that he lays his hand on his mouth since he has not been given a direct answer and in the light of all the "windy words" spoken in the dialogue, but here the author is probably enjoying a little irony. In 40:5 Job recalls that he has already spoken and so has nothing more to say. The technique of numerical heightening is used here — once, twice — suggesting many times. Some have suggested that this first response is an addition or that it should be put together with the second. It is odd that having said that he would not speak in this response, Job then goes on to give a second response. Also, this one does not add to the plot in the way that the second response does, with Job actually repenting (see discussion in Gordis). Some have suggested that this is a standard ritual response of prayer in the face of God and that he does not mean what he is saying. However, this is probably to read too much into Job's words. They are probably simply designed to convey that Job is completely overwhelmed by his experience of God.

Job 42:1-6

The second response has Job acknowledging God's power and then citing God's opening words in 38:2. In 42:4 Job again cites God's words from 40:7. V. 5 is the crucial one — Job claims that he had only heard of God by hearsay, but now he sees God. This suggests that it is the experience of meeting God face-to-face that has led him to a response, rather than the actual content of the speeches. His deep longing for communion has been granted. Then in v. 6 Job repents, despising himself for what he has said. He has, however, been vindicated in that God has pointed out that his justice is on a different level from human justice. Thus Job's contention that all human bounds of justice have been broken because of his experience is proved correct. He does not have a reason for his suffering, but maybe he is coming to understand that there is no reason why that he will ever comprehend. This is not what matters any more; it is his relationship with God that is, and always has been, at the center of the debate. Some (e.g., Williams) have suggested that this is a kind of tongue-in-cheek repentance, a recognition that God has his limitations and that there is no justice in the world after all. This, however, is too cynical an interpretation of what seems to be genuine obeisance in the face of an all-powerful and overwhelming Deity whose justice is on another plane than ours.

Job 42:7

This verse is usually seen as part of the Epilogue, and it does form part of the narrative section. Yet it is pivotal for the entire book. Up to this point Job is in the wrong. Even God's words have suggested that he should have trusted in God, marveled at the created world, and stood up against wickedness whenever he saw it. Job's repentance, too, suggests that he needed to repent and that he is recognizing in this act that he was wrong to question God's ways. This verse, however, changes the whole message because here Job is vindicated by God over against his friends. God here tells to Eliphaz that he has not "spoken of me what is right as my servant Job has." Clearly Job's friends were left behind in the speeches of Job in his closing response, and they were not mentioned in the God speeches. The surprising element here is not that his friends are perceived as wrong but that Job has spoken what is right. This perhaps suggests that it is right to question God's ways and put God in the wrong as Job did rather than utter platitudes as his friends did. Job has at least learned something from his experience of suffering — he has grown as a person, while his friends were locked in their stock positions.

But then the irony deepens as we realize that we are now in the realm of the Epilogue, and Job is about to be rewarded according to the strict doctrine of retribution. He is once again an innocent man rewarded by God with twice as much as he had before. So, in a sense, his friends are proved right! Yet in the speeches God has shown that his justice is on another plane, and presumably that means that while human ideas of justice do prevail at times, at other times they do not. Job was right to question the strict enforcement of such principles, and his friends were wrong to think that suffering always meant that one had sinned. Job was right to protest rather than thinking that he knew all the answers as his friends did. So in the end Job is vindicated by God and is asked to intercede on behalf of his friends, thus preparing us for the happy ending in view. The idea of Job interceding for his friends is ironic in the light of Eliphaz's words that he could intercede for sinners, implying Job (22:26-30).

This is therefore a profound and important verse and could in many ways have formed the ending to the book — a surprise ending indeed after such torment and soul searching on the part of Job and after an oblique reply from God. It has been suggested that this verse does indeed form part of the prose tale and so refers to Job's words in the Prologue rather than justifying his words in the dialogue. The problem with this view is that Job's friends have said nothing in the Prologue and so cannot be said not to have spoken what is right. This then leads to ideas of an original version of the story in which there was a much shorter dialogue. However, with this we are in the realms of fantasy, and it is better to deal with the text as we have it. It is more likely that the author joined the dialogue and Epilogue, using this verse as a deliberate juxtaposition of the two parts and as part of the ironic effect he was trying to create. We have found the book of Job to be made up of intriguing juxtapositions of different sections, throwing up tensions and providing different and sometimes contradictory answers. This is in my view a characteristic of the author, who wished to raise questions about traditional approaches to the relationship between God and humanity and the problems of innocent suffering. Using parody and a disjointed juxtaposition of different sections of the book, the author displayed a skeptical attitude intended to undermine the easy answers of the early wisdom enterprise. The editors of his work tried to make the book more orthodox, and thus we have a rich variety of additions from their hands. But in the process none of the protest of the original is lost; rather, the book as a unity has gone on to inspire generations seeking to understand their own relationship with God in all its complexity.

Bibliography. Brenner, A. 1989, "Job the Pious? The Characterization of Job in the Narrative Framework of the Book," *JSOT* 43:37-52 • Clines, D. J. A. 1989, *Job 1-20*, WBC 17, Waco: Word • Dell, K. J. 1991, *The Book of Job as Sceptical Literature*, BZAW 197, Berlin and New York: Walter de Gruyter • Driver, S. R., and G. B. Gray. 1921, *A Critical and Exegetical Commentary on the Book of Job together with a New Translation*, ICC, Edinburgh: T&T Clark • Duhm, B. 1897, *Das Buch Hiob*, Kurzer Handkommentar zum Alten Testament, Freiburg: Mohr • Gaster, T. H. 1969, *Myth, Legend and Custom in the Old Testament*, New York: Harper and Row • Gordis, R. 1965, *The Book of God and Man: A Study of Job*, Chicago: University of Chicago • Habel, N. C. 1985, *The Book of Job*, OTL, London: SCM • Marshall, J. T. 1905, *Job and His Comforters: Studies in the Theology of the Book of Job*, London • Peake, A. S. 1904, *Job*, Century Bible, London: T. C. and E. C. Jack • Raphael, D. D. 1960, "Tragedy and Religion," in *The Paradox of Tragedy*, Bloomington: Indiana University, 37-51; reprinted 1968 in P. S. Sanders, ed., *Twentieth-Century Interpretations of the Book of Job: A Collection of Critical Essays*, Englewood Cliffs, N. J.: Prentice-Hall, 46-55 • Rowley, H. 1970, *Job*. NCB, London: Thomas Nelson and Sons • Snaith, N. H. 1968, *The Book of Job: Its Origin and Purpose*, SBT 2/11, London: SCM • Van Wolde, E. 1997, *Mr and Mrs Job*, London: SCM • Williams, J. G. 1971, "You have not spoken truth of me": Mystery and Irony in Job," *ZAW* 83:231-54.

The Psalms

Willem S. Prinsloo

INTRODUCTION

The psalter is undoubtedly the book of the Bible which has played the biggest part in the liturgy of OT times as well as in the Jewish and Christian church. Furthermore, the Psalms have played a very significant role in the personal lives of people because people's deepest emotions are verbalized in the psalms: these include joy and thanksgiving but also sorrow and the anxiety caused by critical situations. Some of the psalms express exuberant praise to the LORD, but others are complaints against him. There are psalms that speak of the beauty of life and of good relations with fellow humans; there are psalms that speak of broken relationships — even of revenge against enemies; there are psalms which are prayers to God but also psalms in which the ungodly are cursed. The psalms wrestle with the unanswered questions of life, such as why the righteous have to suffer while the wicked live in apparent prosperity. These are all topics which help to make the book of Psalms one with which we can identify — in good times and times of adversity. The psalter remains relevant for all times because it is so human.

In the past century research on the Psalms has been dominated by a few methods. First of all, H. Gunkel's (1862-1932) form-critical approach had a major influence. The point of departure of this method is that the psalms can be classified into certain *Gattungen,* genres or literary types in terms of the presence of common forms and elements of content which together point to a common setting. This approach led to the classification of the psalms into various types, such as individual and collective laments, collective and individual psalms of praise, collective and individual psalms of thanksgiving, wisdom psalms, psalms of revenge or imprecation, psalms expressing trust in the LORD, and royal psalms — to mention the most important types. The positive contribution of the form-critical method to a better understanding of the psalms can never be overestimated. In this commentary I have drawn freely from the results of the form-critical method. The individual laments, which make up almost a quarter of the psalter, are not discussed individually here but as a group (cf. the discussion under "Individual Laments," 366-73). If one were to express a criticism of the form-critical method, however, it would be that it does not always do justice to the distinctive individuality of specific psalms. It must always be remembered that *Gattungen* are theoretical constructions since practically no instances of a pure *Gattung* exist. In other words, *Gattungen* are not ready-made schemes into which psalms should be forced.

A second important approach is to study the psalms from a cultic perspective and to reconstruct the original cultic context. S. Mowinckel (1884-1965), a student of Gunkel, is a leading figure here. He proceeds from the hypothesis that an enthronement festival at which the LORD was annually proclaimed king is the cultic context of numerous psalms. Although it is important to try to reconstruct the cultic context, the danger is that psalms may inappropriately be forced into particular cultic contexts. It is also possible that a psalm which did not originally arise in a cultic context may later have functioned in a cultic context or even in more than one cultic context. To determine the original cultic situation and dating of each psalm accurately is therefore no easy matter. Even the titles of the psalms, which were probably mostly later additions, give no real information on the original historical or cultic situation.

The approach followed here may be described as text-immanent. Although it is important to try to reconstruct the original historical and cultic context and the redaction history of a psalm and the psalter as a whole, we have to deal with the psalter in its present form as a poetic text. A text-immanent approach does not mean, however, that the psalms should be read ahistorically or that no attention should be paid to the historical and cultic context. What it does mean is that we shall be concentrating on the content, function, poetic strategies, and meaning of each psalm. The final text is therefore the point of departure. Wherever the text permits or yields information, however, the cultic and historical aspects will also be examined.

In current research on the psalms increasing attention is being given to the fact that the psalter should be read not only as individual psalms but also as a book. There is a growing interest in understanding the psalter as a literary whole. Increasingly, scholars are emphasizing the purposeful placement and arrangement of psalms within the collection, and attention is being drawn to links between individual psalms and groups of psalms. A great deal of research has yet to be done on this approach. Even those who agree that a systematic arrangement is evident in the psalter do not agree on the nature of the arrangement or how it might have arisen. On the other hand, some scholars deny that the psalms show evidence of having been placed in a deliberate order.

Traditionally the psalter is divided into five books (cf. the NRSV), namely, Book I: Psalms 1–41; Book II: Psalms 42–72; Book III: Psalms 73–89; Book IV: Psalms 90–106; and Book V: Psalms 107–150. Each of the collections ends with a doxology (cf. Pss 41:13; 72:18-19; 89:52; 106:48; and 150:6). There are also smaller collections to which attention will be drawn in the course of this commentary. Psalms 1 and 2 should be seen as the introduction to the entire psalter.

COMMENTARY

Psalm 1

Psalm 1 can be described as a wisdom psalm. One of the features of wisdom literature is that it makes use of contrasts. This is precisely what is done in Psalm 1, where the righteous are contrasted with the wicked. The contrast is also reflected in the structure of the psalm: the righteous are described in 1:1-3 and the wicked in vv. 4-5. The psalm is summarized and culminates in v. 6, in which the righteous and wicked are once again contrasted.

The righteous (1:1-3) are described as being "happy." This happiness is first explained negatively in v. 1, then positively in v. 2, and eventually by means of a simile in v. 3. V. 1 states how the righteous should not act, namely, they should not "follow the advice of the wicked, or take the path that sinners tread, or sit in the seat of scoffers." Although these three phrases are sometimes interpreted to mean that the wicked get progressively more sinful, the manner in which the phrases are constructed suggests that they should rather be understood as synonymous expressions. By repeating the same idea three times, the psalmist emphasizes that the behavior of the righteous should be totally different from that of the wicked. V. 2 describes the righteous positively. Although the phrase "law of the LORD" can be interpreted as the Ten Commandments, the Pentateuch, or even the whole OT, it has a more general meaning in this context, namely, the guidelines which God gives for human life. The righteous are described as those who "meditate day and night" on the law. This means that they have a close and permanent relationship with the LORD which encompasses their entire life. This idea is further explicated by means of a simile in v. 3. The simile of a tree planted by streams of water portrays the life of the righteous as being fruitful, permanent, and continuous.

"The wicked" (1:4-5) are exactly the opposite of the righteous. Again a simile is used, this time to describe the life of the wicked as being meaningless and worthless. The simile of winnowing is used in which threshed corn is tossed up for the "chaff" to be blown away, leaving only the grain behind. This idea is elaborated in v. 5: the wicked will not withstand the judgment of the LORD, and there will be no place for them among his people.

In 1:6 the psalm reaches its culmination by again contrasting the righteous and the wicked. The righteous can be sure of the LORD's loving care. It is he who secures their stability. The wicked, on the other hand, have no future and will perish.

Psalm 1 has a didactic function. By contrasting the two ways of life and by describing the righteous in an extremely positive manner, the psalm aims to persuade the reader to make the right choice, namely, to lead a righteous life and to walk the right path. The compiler presumably placed this psalm at the beginning of the psalter in order to call the reader to obedience to the LORD's will.

Psalm 2

This psalm deals with the position of the Judean king and his relationship with the LORD. It is sometimes classified as a royal psalm or even designated as a coronation psalm. The psalm can be divided into four strophes of equal length, namely, vv. 1-3, 4-6, 7-9, and 10-12.

The first strophe (2:1-3), introduced by a rhetorical question, immediately brings the theme of the psalm to the fore, namely, the futile rebellion of foreign peoples and their kings against the LORD and his anointed, the Judean king. By using the direct form of speech, the arrogance and rebellion of the kings against the LORD and his anointed are brought to a climax: "Let us burst . . . and cast their cords . . ." (v. 3). Psalm 2 provides no direct information to reconstruct the original historical background of the psalm. The psalm may refer to the reign of Solomon, to Hezekiah's accession to the throne (c. 720 BC), or to the time of King Josiah (c. 621 BC). An exilic or even a postexilic date is sometimes suggested as a possible historical context. Whatever the historical context may be, the point made is that rebellion against Judah's king would be rebellion against the LORD's rule, because the king is explicitly identified as the anointed of the LORD.

The second strophe (2:4-6) is in direct contrast to the first. The focus shifts from the powerless kings to the LORD as the Almighty King, sitting on his throne high above the turmoil and plotting of the nations, laughing at them and scorning them in his majesty. The first strophe ends with the defiant words of the rebellious kings. The second strophe ends with the words of the LORD — a direct form of speech in which the LORD emphatically states that he himself has consecrated his king on Zion.

The king himself features in the third strophe (2:7-9). As in the case of the two preceding strophes, the direct form of speech is used to describe the main characters, in this instance the king: "I will tell of the decree of the LORD: He said to me: 'You are my son . . .'" (v. 7). These words of the king, which quote the words of the LORD, must be understood against the background of the anointing and installation of the king on the day of his enthronement and against the context of the David covenant and the commitment made to the dynasty of David (cf. 2 Samuel 7, esp. vv. 13-14). These words of Psalm 2 confirm the authority of the king. Unlike some other ancient Near Eastern civilizations where the king was deified and sometimes even regarded as a physical son of the god, the Israelites considered their king to be a human being. He is adopted as the son of the LORD on the day (v. 7) of his enthronement. The words "I have begotten you" are a metaphor to underline the authority of the king and the intimate relationship that exists between the LORD and the king. As the son of the LORD, the king is entitled to certain privileges. At the king's request the LORD will give him nations and "the ends of the earth" as his inheritance (v. 8). The king will also have the power to break his enemies into pieces. V. 8 should be read in the light of the first strophe and is a hyperbolic way of emphasizing the universal supremacy and power of the LORD as embodied by the king as his representative. This strophe, in which the authority and power of the king are brought to the fore, is an elaboration of the preceding one (vv. 4-6) and contrasts with and replies to the first strophe (vv. 1-3), where the futile rebellion of the nations is portrayed.

The psalm is brought to a climax in the fourth strophe (2:10-12), where the rebellious rulers of the earth are exhorted to act wisely by submitting to the LORD and his king. Failure to do so will result in the wrath of God devastating them. On the other hand, those who submit to, obey, and take refuge in the LORD will be "happy" and secure.

The structure and content of the psalm can be summarized as follows:

1. The rebellion of the kings of the earth against the LORD and his anointed is futile (vv. 1-3).
2. The LORD is the almighty king (vv. 4-6).
3. The earthly king is installed and authorized by the LORD as his powerful representative (vv. 7-9).
4. The rebels are exhorted to serve and submit to the LORD (vv. 10-12).

The function of the psalm is to reject rebellion or hubris against the LORD totally and to exhort service to him.

Psalm 2 is one of the passages of the OT that is most frequently "quoted" and reinterpreted from a christological perspective in the NT. For example, in Acts 13:33, 2:7b is linked to the resurrection of Jesus Christ; in Heb 1:5 it is used to illustrate the supremacy of Jesus Christ to the angels. In Heb 5:5, Ps 2:7 is used in connection with Jesus Christ's glorification as High Priest. It is clear from these examples that the NT is not consistent in the way it deals with Psalm 2. The NT writers approach the OT in terms of the exegetic methods of their own time, read the OT through christological spectacles, and use the OT to create a new text for their own situation. The interpretation of the OT by the NT cannot be used as a criterion for our interpretation of the OT. The OT — and therefore also Psalm 2 — should be interpreted primarily in its own literary, historical, and theological context.

Psalms 3–41 are the first big collection in the psalter and are known as Book I. These psalms are called the Davidic collection because with a single exception (Psalm 33) the name of David occurs in all the superscriptions. But, as I shall explain, the Davidic superscriptions are not an indication that David was the author of these psalms. Another characteristic of this group of psalms is that the divine epithet "Yahweh" (LORD) is used throughout.

Psalms 3, 4, 5, 6, and 7 (*see* Individual Laments, 356-63)

The Individual Laments

The use of *Gattungen* or literary types remains a helpful way to divide the psalms into categories because there are certain common features, such as literary form, structure, content, themes, mood, intent, and function, that justify the grouping of psalms.

One of the most prominent literary types in the psalter is the individual lament. For the purpose of this commentary it is justifiable to deal with the individual laments as a group. Yet, despite many decades of research, there is still no clarity on the terms "complaint" and "lament." Sometimes scholars distinguish between these terms by stating that "lament" refers to an irreparable, hopeless catastrophe, while "complaint" refers to a situation in which there are still hope and time to argue a case before God.

Even the terms "individual" and "I" are not clearly distinguishable, and the dividing line between "individual" and "collective" psalms remains vague. Was the recurring "I" an individual or a corporate person? It is also true that in a number of lament psalms, the poem swings from the congregation to the individual or vice versa (cf., e.g., Psalms 14, 25, 51, 66, and 130). This is an indication that the distinction between individual and collective is overemphasized. In some psalms the "I" may represent the community with which the speaker identifies himself. It may also be that a psalm that was originally intended to be an individual psalm was later reinterpreted and used as a collective psalm (cf., e.g., Psalm 30, which is, strictly speaking, an individual lament to which a collective superscript was later added).

The question may be asked whether "lament" is an appropriate term because a "lament" is always addressed to God and is therefore a prayer in the strict sense of the word. These psalms are actually cries to God. Although it may be the most important element, the "lament" remains only one of a number of elements of the psalm. It should also be borne in mind that the "lament" is not simply a description of suffering; its purpose is rather to obtain an end to the suffering and to move closer to God.

As a prayer the "lament" consists of two basic elements, namely, a plea or petition and praise. One of the main characteristics of the "laments" is that they do not merely lament. At the end of a "lament" there is normally a section that deals with praise. The lament does not end on a "negative note," but something changes in the course of the psalm so that it often ends in praise after the "I" has been assured of being heard by the LORD.

A "lament" expresses a person's deepest needs. It is essentially a prayer addressed to God by a person afflicted by some calamity or by someone who is in a disastrous situation, expressing sorrow about the situation and appealing to God for deliverance.

The "laments" reflect the totality of life and describe life as it really is. Psalms of "lament" acknowledge that life does not consist of prosperity only, but that it also has pain, grief, darkness, and evil. The laments illustrate that it is not wrong or an act of unbelief to complain to God about misfortune and to even hold him responsible for it. The psalms in general, and the "laments" in particular, are timeless and universal in that they ask the same questions, refer to the same things, and experience the same problems and disasters that humankind has experienced throughout the ages. These psalms should not be interpreted solely as historical prayers, but they should rather be seen as examples that can serve as models for the modern reader.

Another feature of "laments" is that although God and the petitioner form the focus, the enemies of the petitioner also play an important part in many of them. Many of these psalms reflect a dynamic triangular relationship, namely, petitioner-enemy-God.

The main function of a "lament" is to persuade. On the one hand, its purpose is to persuade God to change his attitude toward the suppliant and to act decisively. On the other hand, it has the function of persuading the petitioner to trust the LORD despite a seemingly hopeless situation. To accomplish these goals, the laments often use hyperbolic and exaggerated language.

All the elements do not appear in each psalm. The elements occur in different combinations, and the order may vary from one psalm to the next. The boundaries between the various elements are not fixed, and one element often flows into another. Some of the elements described here as features of the individual lament may also appear in other psalms that are not normally classified among the laments.

Although there is a lack of agreement regarding detail and the inclusion or exclusion of specific psalms, the following psalms are classified as individual laments: 3, 4, 5, 6, 7, 13, 17, 22, 25, 26, 27, 28, 31, 35, 38, 39, 41, 42, 43, 51, 54, 55, 56, 57, 59, 61, 63, 64, 69, 70, 71, 77, 86, 88, 102, 109, 120, 130, 140, 141, 142, and 143. These psalms represent more than a quarter of the psalter.

Following this introduction, a commentary is given on the "individual laments" on the basis of their main features. It is not a verse-by-verse or a detailed commentary. Rather, it is an effort to give the modern reader some general principles with which to come to grips with these psalms as a whole and to shed light on some problems.

The Main Features of the Individual Lament

1. An *invocation* of the LORD, usually including an appeal and an initial *petition:* "Give ear to my words, O LORD . . ." (Ps 5:1). These invocations can frequently be found at the beginning of a psalm (cf., e.g., Pss 7:1; 25:2; 28:1; 102:1), but they can also appear at a later stage or even be repeated in the same psalm (Pss 17:6; 86:6; 140:6). The invocation reflects the personal relationship that exists between the petitioner and God. Expressions such as "my God" (Pss 3:7; 22:1, 2; 38:21; 40:17), "O LORD, my God" (Pss 7:1, 3; 13:3; 30:12; 35:24; 109:26), "O God, my God" (Ps 43:4), and "O God, you are my God" (Ps 63:1) illustrate this relationship. The invocation often includes adoration of the LORD and confidence and trust in him as the only refuge in times of distress:

> Incline your ear to me. . . .
> Be a rock or refuge for me. . . .
> (Ps 31:1-2; cf. also, e.g., Pss 28:1; 140:7)

The functions of the petition are to reestablish contact between the petitioner and the LORD, to accentuate the seriousness of the situation, and to ensure that he hears the appeal.

2. The actual *complaint* or description of the crisis, that is, the *real problem* of the petitioner, is one of the most important elements of the lament. In the attempts to emphasize how desperate the situation is, to evoke the LORD to act, and to remind him of his responsibility, the metaphors, descriptions, and expressions that are used are mostly somewhat exaggerated and hyperbolic. The complaint is described in a provocative way. The situation is portrayed as if everything is on a knife edge in order to persuade the LORD that he should intervene before it is too late: "They track me down; now they surround me . . ." (cf., e.g., Pss 17:11-12; 54:4). In a reproachful way, the petitioner holds the LORD responsible for the crisis which he is experiencing: "for it is you who have done it. . . . I am worn down by the blows of your hand" (Ps 39:9b-10; see also Ps 88:6-7). He accuses God of shooting arrows at him like an archer and of wounding him (Ps 38:2).

The petitioner accuses the LORD by way of rhetorical questions that he has forgotten him (Ps 42:9), forsaken him (Ps 22:1), cast him off (Ps 43:2), and is hiding his face from him (Ps 88:14). He accuses God of being a passive onlooker and of not helping him (Ps 35:17; cf. also Ps 6:3). He thus blames God for the situation that has ostensibly arisen because of God's inattentiveness. Ps 13:1-2 offers a textbook example of these reproachful rhetorical questions. The impatience of the speaker as well as his misery is emphasized by repeating the question "How long . . . ?" four times. The suppliant experiences the crisis on three levels: he has the impression that God has forgotten about him and has turned his face away from him; he experiences grief on a very personal level; and he senses that his enemies have the upper hand. It is typical of the individual laments that the disastrous situation is presented in terms of a triangular relationship, namely, that of petitioner-God-enemies. These questions reflect the uncertainty and stress that the petitioner experiences with regard to his relationship with God and his enemies.

Instead of leveling an accusation, the complaint is sometimes put indirectly: "I had said in my alarm, 'I am driven far from your sight'" (Ps 31:22). The complaint is often molded in the form of a "negative prayer": "Do not hide your face from me . . ." (Ps 27:9). Several more examples can be given: "do not hide yourself from my supplication" (Ps 55:1; cf. also, e.g., Pss 6:1; 22:11; 28:1; 35:22; 38:21; 51:11; 69:17; 71:12; 102:2; 109:1; 143:2, 7). These prayers reflect the feeling of uncertainty that the petitioner experiences during times of distress and emphasize that without the help of the LORD there can be no real solution to the problem. There is no one but God to whom the petitioner can turn. It is also obvious that the petitioner often uses as a ground for his petition the fact that he is a servant of the LORD.

One of the main characteristics of these psalms is that the petitioner is complaining about or lamenting his *personal situation*. This is sometimes done in general terms: "for I am poor and needy" (Ps 86:1; cf. also Ps 109:22) or by way of metaphors and similes: "I sink in deep mire, where there is no foothold . . ." (Ps 69:2; cf. also Pss 102:7, 11; 109:23).

The situation may be depicted in terms of illness: "my pain is ever with me" (Ps 38:17; cf. also vv. 3, 5, 7, 8); "my mouth is dried up like a potsherd . . ." (Ps 22:15); "I can count all my bones" (Ps 22:17); and the emotional effects of illness: "My heart throbs . . ." (Ps 38:10; cf. also Ps 6:3). It should be stressed that in the OT in general and in the book of Psalms in particular "illness" and related words do not necessarily have a strictly medical meaning. These words may also refer to someone experiencing misfortune, a crisis, sorrow, or disaster of one kind or another. It may also be a metaphorical way to describe the dire straits in which someone finds him- or herself.

The crisis is sometimes sketched in terms of the nearness of death and the anxiety caused by death: "For my soul is full of troubles, and my life draws near to Sheol" (Ps 88:3-5; cf. also Ps 6:5). The sorrow and grief experienced is described in a moving manner: "I drench my couch with my weeping . . ." (Ps 6:6-7; cf. also Pss 31:9; 42:3a). The suppliant is isolated, and scorned and mocked by others: "But I am a worm . . . despised by the people" (Ps 22:6-7; cf. also Pss 31:11-12; 35:16; 41:9; 109:25). He is portrayed as somebody who is disheartened and depressed: "my spirit faints within me; my heart within me is appalled" (Ps 143:4). He is the laughingstock and the subject of gossip of the whole community (Ps 69:10).

He is forsaken not only by his enemies but also by those closest to him. Instead of supporting and comforting him in his sorrow, his friends are abandoning him. He has become a horror to his neighbors, and his acquaintances flee from him when they see him in the street (Ps 38:11). One can almost feel his bitterness when he complains that he has been betrayed, even by a close friend (Ps 55:12-13; cf. also Ps 41:9). Above all, he has become a stranger to his closest relatives (Ps 69:8). The implication of Ps 27:10 is that he is even forsaken by his father and mother. The words of Ps 142:4 give a good description of the utter despair of the petitioner: "no one cares for me."

Although the description of the situation of the petitioner forms an important element of the complaint, it is never presented in such a way that it dominates the psalm. The suffering and sorrow of the petitioner should be seen as part of the complaint, which has the function of persuading the LORD to intervene.

The description of the *enemies* occurs in nearly forty of these psalms and therefore forms a very important part of the lament. The enemies are part of the crisis experienced by the petitioner as he is persecuted and threatened by them. It is impossible to identify the enemies as specific individuals or groups within the community or as a foreign power or to reconstruct the precise situation of each psalm with regard to the enemies concerned in it. The psalms describe the enemies in such general and conventional terms and metaphors that the question may indeed be asked whether it is the intention of these descriptions to identify the enemies as specific persons or groups. Without denying the possibility that these psalms could originally have emanated from actual conflicts between the petitioner and an enemy or enemies and that they could therefore have been the product of concrete situations, the descriptions serve a specific purpose. The purpose is to highlight the contrast between the righteous petitioner and the ungodly enemy and to strengthen the plight of the petitioner before the LORD. Although enemies play a very important role in these psalms, it should always be borne in mind that enemies are but one of the elements of the individual psalms of lament. The enemies should be viewed in relation to the petitioner and his suffering on account of them, which occurs in relation to God and in the light of the purpose. It would therefore be contrary to the purpose of the laments to use the portrayal of enemies to reconstruct specific situations or to link them to particular people. These enemies reflect and are symptomatic of a community in which the relationships between individuals as well as their relationship with God have been violated so that the rights of the individual are no longer honored.

By using the first person singular suffix "my" in "my enemy" (cf., e.g., Ps 13:2, 4) or "my enemies" (cf. Pss 3:7; 25:2) no fewer than seventy-two times in this regard, the psalmist accentuates that the petitioner stands against his adversaries and that he is alone in his sorrow.

The enemies are described with numerous words, for example, "my pursuers" (Ps 7:1), "my persecutors" (Ps 31:15), "those who fight against me" (Ps 35:1), "my accusers" (Ps 71:13), "those who seek to hurt me" (Ps 71:13), "who devise evil" (Ps 35:4), "those who deride me" (Ps 102:8), "the bloodthirsty" (Ps 59:2), "evildoers" (Pss 27:2; 140:1), "workers of evil" (Ps 6:8), "those who treacherously plot evil" (Ps 59:5), "the wicked" (Ps 55:2), "the mighty" (Ps 59:3), "the insolent" (Ps 86:14), "the arrogant" (Ps 140:5), "the ruthless" (Ps 54:3b), "the unjust and cruel" (Ps 71:4), "false witnesses" (Ps 27:12), "those that are violent" (Ps 140:1), "those who are deceitful" (Ps 43:1), and "ungodly people" (Ps 43:1).

One of the features of these psalms is that the actions of the enemies are frequently portrayed by the use of *metaphors*. These metaphors mainly emphazise the threatening onslaught of the ungodly. The military metaphor is one of the predominant ones used: the enemies are arrayed in battle against the petitioner (Ps 55:18); he proposes peace, but they are for war (Ps 120:7); the enemies are shooting from ambushes at the blameless (Ps 64:4); the wicked draw their swords and bend their bows to bring down the poor and needy (Ps 37:14).

The hunting metaphor is also employed to describe the activities of the enemies: "For without cause they hid their net for me . . ." (Ps 35:7). Pss 57:6 and 140:5 express the same idea, namely, that the enemies have set snares for the psalmist and have hidden a trap for him. This metaphor primarily underlines the treacherous conduct of the wicked toward the righteous. The enemies are sometimes (cf., e.g., Pss 56:6; 59:3) described as robbers. The metaphor of wild beasts is also used to portray the aggression and assault of the ungodly against the meek: they gnash their teeth at him (Pss 35:16; 37:12); they devour his flesh (Ps 27:2); "they are like a lion eager to tear . . ." (Ps 17:12; cf. also Pss 7:2; 22:13); they are like strong bulls encircling him (Ps 22:12) and like dogs all around him (Ps 22:16). The metaphor in Ps 69:21 ("They gave me poison for food . . .") illustrates that they are doing exactly the opposite of what is expected of them.

Besides the metaphors by means of which the enemies are portrayed, there are other descriptions of their deeds and words: they hate him with "violent hatred" (Ps 25:19) and "are breathing out violence" (Ps 27:12). They rise as false witnesses against him (Pss 27:12; 35:11) and accuse him falsely (Ps 69:4). Their right hands are full of bribes (Ps 26:10), and they meditate treachery all day long (Ps 38:12); they bring trouble upon him and cherish enmity against him (Ps 55:2); they desire his hurt (Ps 40:14), taunt him (Ps 102:8), scheme together against him, and plot to take his life (Ps 31:13). They boast against him when his foot slips (Ps 38:16), and they rejoice at his calamity (Ps 35:24, 26). Even with peace-loving people they do not speak peace, but conceive deceitful words (Ps 35:20). Sometimes they pretend to be upright by speaking peace with their neighbors, but in reality they are evildoers with malice in their hearts (see Ps 28:3). The sole intention of the enemies can be put in a nutshell in the words of Ps 140:4, namely, they have planned the downfall of the petitioner.

Ps 5:9 gives a good account of the true nature of the enemy: "there is no truth in their mouths." They have only one thing in mind, and that is to destroy the petitioner, but they conceal their true intention with false friendliness. They bless with their mouths, but inwardly they curse. They are hypocrites because their speech is smoother than butter, but their hearts are set on war (Ps 55:21).

One of the main purposes of these descriptions is to underline the contrast between the enemies and the petitioner: they repay him evil for good, whereas he wore sackcloth when they were sick (Ps 35:13). They are his adversaries because he follows after good. They are treacherous and aggressive, but he is righteous and meek. This contrast comes to the fore on another level, too. While the situation of the petitioner is lamentable and his life filled with sorrow, the wicked are seemingly prosperous, rich, and powerful (cf., e.g., Pss 10:5; 73:3-5, 7).

In some instances, the enemies are exposed by means of direct speech: "'Commit your cause to the LORD; . . . let him rescue the one in whom he delights!'" (Ps 22:8). Ps 35:21 provides another excellent example of the arrogance of the enemies: "They open wide their mouths against me; they say, 'Aha, Aha, our eyes have seen it.'" (see also Ps 40:15). The purpose of these sarcastic, taunting words of the ungodly is to anger God and to cause him to act on behalf of the petitioner.

The most serious transgression of the enemies is that they rebel against God (Ps 5:10) and "do not regard the works of the LORD" (Ps 28:5). God means nothing to them (Pss 54:3; 86:14). They do not fear God (Ps 55:19), or love and respect him. They are ungodly in the true sense of the word. This is illustrated by their mocking questions and daring statements: "'Where is your God?'" (Ps 42:3, 10; cf also Ps 3:2). They deny his omnipotence by boasting: "'Who can see us?'" and "'Who can search our crimes?'" (Ps 64:5-6). They are questioning God's ability to deliver the petitioner (Ps 71:11). The heart of the matter is that they do not acknowledge him as God. Ps 14:1 summarizes their position succinctly in their own words: "'There is no God.'"

3. The *appeal for help* is often regarded as the most important element and the very heart of the complaint psalm. This element occurs in almost all the psalms in this category. In fact, all the other elements play a supportive role in preparing the ground for the prayer or the appeal for help. The appeal is usually in the form of an imperative, although it may also be a wish expressed in the form of a jussive.

The imperative is often of a general nature, calling to God for his attention; for example: "LORD, hear my voice!" (Ps 130:2). An even better example appears in Ps 102:1-2, where the imperatives are strung together: "Hear my prayer, O LORD; . . . Incline your ear to me; answer me . . ." (cf. also, e.g., Pss 17:6; 27:7; 64:1; 86:6). These examples illustrate that a wide spectrum of formulations are used, but all with the same purpose, namely, to bring the seriousness of the situation to the LORD's attention and to persuade him to heed the petitioner.

Another important element is the plea for compassion and mercy: "be gracious to me and answer me!" (Ps 27:7b; cf. also Ps 86:16). The petitioner uses the "steadfast love" and mercy of God and the fact that he is a servant of God as pleading ground for mercy (Ps 86:15-16). The urgency of the matter is often emphasized by bidding God to rise up and awake (Ps 7:6; cf. also Pss 35:2; 59:5). It is as if the petitioner becomes impatient and insists that God should deliver him (Pss 17:13; 40:17b). He demands that God should not be far away and that he should come quickly to his aid (cf. Pss 22:19; 38:22; 40:13; 71:12).

These commands prepare the way for the actual plea for help. This plea is often formulated in general terms such as: "Deliver me" (cf., e.g., Pss 3:7; 6:4; 22:20), "save me" (Pss 31:16; 69:1), "Rescue me" (Ps 35:17), "Help me" (Ps 109:26), and "Preserve my life" (Ps 86:2). These general pleas are sometimes specified, in which case they reflect the disastrous situation which led to the cause of the complaint. For example, the petitioner pleads to the LORD for healing (Pss 6:2; 41:3) and to give light to his eyes (Ps 13:3). These pleas illustrate that the petitioner is dependent on the LORD's help for the fulfillment of his basic needs.

We have seen that the petitioner's enemies often form an important part of his crisis because he is persecuted and threatened by them. Where this is the case, he prays to the LORD to deliver him from his enemies (Ps 31:15). In Ps 17:13, a military metaphor is implemented to express the idea: "By your sword deliver my life. . . ." The metaphor of wild beasts is also employed in the plea for help against the enemies: "Rescue me from their ravages . . ." (Ps 35:17). Some of these prayers could even be described as curses against enemies. In a very harsh, merciless and seemingly unbelieving manner, the LORD is requested to pour out his indignation upon them and to let his burning anger overtake them (cf. Ps 69:24). Ps 143:12 formulates this sentiment in an even more drastic manner: "cut off my enemies. . . ." These words can easily be misunderstood as being revengeful and cruel if they are not interpreted within the context of their purpose and genre. To reiterate, this element of the plea for help also has as its purpose the enhancement of the difference between the righteous and the ungodly. Thus it is not that the petitioner has a personal vendetta against someone, but in the language of Ps 143:11, the righteousness of God is at stake, and being the servant of the LORD, the petitioner has the right to speak out against the ungodly. For the sake of his honor, the LORD has to intervene on behalf of his servant. This element should also be understood against the background of all the terrible things that were done to the petitioner by his enemies. It should be taken into account that, as persuasive texts, these psalms implement hyperbolic and exaggerated terminology and that they cannot be interpreted literally.

To underline the contrast between himself and his enemies and to strengthen his case before God, the suppliant prays: "Teach me your way, O LORD . . ." (Ps 27:11). Sometimes the prayer of the petitioner is a plea for justice; then it is cast in the form of a metaphor of God as a judge (Ps 43:1; cf. also Pss 7:9; 35:23). He insists on his rights because he is certain of his own integrity before God (Ps 26:1). The plea for help in Ps 17:8, "Guard me as the apple of the eye; . . . ," expresses affection for God as well as the certainty that God will protect the psalmist from his enemies.

The contents of the plea, as well as a description of the circumstances in which the plea is being uttered, are sometimes given. Psalm 88 says that the petitioner prays "at night" (Ps 88:1), "every day" (Ps 88:9), and "in the morning" (Ps 88:13). These phrases stress that the petitioner is in continuous prayer before the LORD. The spirit in which the prayer is brought before God is fittingly pictured in Ps 142:2: "I pour out my complaint before him. . . ." The prayer is, among other things, designated as a just cause (Ps 17:1) and a loud cry to God (Ps 77:1). The petitioner cries "out of the depths" (Ps 130:1), that is, in anger and distress, to the LORD. His relationship with God and his yearning for God are described by way of a moving simile: "As a deer longs for flowing streams, so my soul longs for you, O God" (Ps 42:1). He desires that his prayer should be counted as incense, in other words, that it should be acceptable to God (Ps 141:2).

One of the most important elements of the plea is the prayer that begs for forgiveness and restoration; for example: "pardon my guilt, for it is great . . ." (Ps 25:11b, 18b). In Ps 41:4b an appeal is made to the LORD as the great physician to "heal" the petitioner because he has sinned against him. In unparalleled manner, Psalm 51 concentrates mainly on prayers for forgiveness and on confession of sin: "Have mercy on me . . . blot out my transgressions . . . and cleanse me from my sin" (vv. 1-2); "Purge me with hyssop . . . wash me, and I shall be whiter than snow" (v. 7); "Create in me a clean heart, O God" (vv. 9b-10a). Repentance and confession of sin usually go hand in hand with the prayers for forgiveness. Once again Psalm 51 provides a good example: "For I know my transgressions. . . . Indeed, I was born guilty, a sinner when my mother conceived me" (vv. 3, 5; cf. also Pss 38:18; 69:5). These psalms illustrate that sin is one of the greatest human crises and that God alone is in a position to forgive and restore him.

Related to the prayers for forgiveness are those prayers in which the speaker beseeches God to prevent him from sinning, for example: "Set a guard over my mouth, O LORD . . ." (Ps 141:3), and requests God to teach him to do his will (Ps 143:10; cf. also Pss 5:8; 25:4; 86:11). These prayers accentuate human weakness and inclination toward sin as well as the fact that only God can show people the right way.

The obverse of the prayers for forgiveness are the prayers wherein the innocence of the petitioner is asserted: "Prove me, O LORD, and try me . . ." (Ps 26:2a, 4a). So assured is the petitioner of his innocence that he insists on his rights: "judge me, O LORD, according to my righteousness . . ." (Ps 7:8). These assertions of innocence support the plea for help, especially for help against his enemies. They highlight the difference between the petitioner and his enemies to the extent that he has the confidence to demand of God: "Do not sweep me away with sinners . . ." (Ps 26:9; cf. also Ps 28:3). The petitioner claims that he is innocent and therefore entitled to God's help.

The appeals for help normally occur in the form of imperatives. These appeals do, however, also appear in the form of a *wish* or in the *jussive* form. It is mainly the elements that were discussed above in connection with the appeals in the imperative form that again appear in connection with the wishes: prayers calling to God for his attention: "Let my prayer be counted as incense before you" (cf. Ps 141:2:); prayers asking God for protection against the wicked, for example: "Do not let the foot of the arrogant tread on me" (Ps 36:11:); pleas for justice: "From you let my vindication come . . ." (Ps 17:2); prayers expressing the wish to live near to God: "Let me abide in your tent forever . . ." (Ps 61:4). Sometimes the jussive form is implemented in the third person so that God is not addressed directly. An example is Ps 57:3, in which the petitioner prays that God should rescue him in a miraculous manner. An element that does not occur in the imperative prayers, but only in the jussives, is the prayers for fellow believers, for example, Ps 5:11-12: "But let all who take refuge in you rejoice . . ." (cf. also Pss 40:16; 69:6).

Imprecations against enemies are also expressed in the form of wishes or jussives. These wishes are even harsher and articulated in more severe terms than the prayers (i.e., imperatives) against the enemies. Often the suppliant wishes that his enemies would be put to shame, be confused, and suffer dishonor (cf., e.g., Pss 31:17; 35:26; 40:15; 109:29). The petitioner's basic request is that God should act decisively against his enemies. In the words of Ps 69:24, God should pour out his indignation upon them and let his burning anger overtake them. The suppliant prays in no uncertain terms for the extinction of his enemies. This is done in several ways: "Let burning coals fall on them!" (Ps 140:10). The destruction of enemies is also portrayed in metaphorical language: "they shall be prey for jackals" (Ps 63:10). The latter metaphor describes the bodies of the enemies as unburied and as carrion for jackals — the most dreadful misfortune. It is even explicitly stated that the suppliant's enemies should die: "let them go dumbfounded to Sheol" (Ps 31:17b; cf. also Ps 55:15). In Ps 69:28, the petitioner prays that they should be "blotted out of the book of the living," that is, blotted out or removed from those who are kept alive by the grace of God. Ps 35:5 implements the same simile as Ps 1:4 to describe the doom of the ungodly: "Let them be like chaff before the wind." Ps. 56:9 summarizes the whole issue, namely, that the petitioner has the assurance that he is righteous before God and that God is on his side to punish the wicked.

4. One of the purposes of the laments is to persuade God to act. All the elements fulfill a supportive role in this regard. An element that has not yet been discussed in this context is the *reasons* for divine intervention. The suppliant is in a desperate situation, and it is of paramount importance for him to make an impact on the LORD by advancing the reasons why God should act on his behalf. These reasons are an essential part of the prayer and cannot function separately.

Often the petitioner uses God's nature, his characteristics, such as his "righteousness" (Pss 5:8; 35:24; 71:2), "steadfast love" (cf. Pss 6:4; 51:1), "power to redeem" (Ps 130:7), and "mercy" (Ps 25:6), as a reason to beg for deliverance. The psalmist in Ps 102:25-28 advances the LORD's everlasting years as creator and his eternal presence as the grounds why he should act on behalf of his children. In Ps 109:21 the suppliant expects God to act as he has done in the past. Over and above the "steadfast love" or the lovingkindness of God, Ps 109:21 (cf. also Pss 31:3; 143:11) also uses God's "name" as a reason. An appeal is therefore made to God's own reputation. If God is unable to help his servant, his power will be questioned and his own reputation shattered.

The position of enemies also has a role in the reasons advanced. In Ps 13:3-4 the petitioner says that if God does not rescue him, his enemy will boast, "'I have prevailed'"; and his foes will rejoice because he is shaken. Ps 35:25 expresses the same thought: "Do not let them say, 'We have swallowed you up.'" If the enemy gets the upper hand over the righteous, it will be to his as well as to God's shame. Since his enemy is too strong for him, God must save him from that enemy (Ps 142:6b).

The petitioner often uses his own miserable situation as a reason for God to intervene. In Ps 86:1 he prays to God to answer him, "for I am poor and needy." In v. 2 he supplies a second reason, "for I am devoted to you." Ps 17:3-5 presents a detailed description of the righteousness and devotion of the petitioner as a reason for God to act. To persuade God to act, the psalmist in Ps 143:12 uses the argument that he is the "servant" of God. Ps 22:11b beseeches God's help, for there is no one else to help. However, the impression is often gained that the speaker is bargaining with the LORD. An example of this approach is the petitioner's request that God should rescue him from death because there is no profit in death and because nobody will be able to praise the LORD and to remember his faithfulness in Sheol, the place of the dead (cf. also Pss 6:5; 30:9; 88:11-12). Ps 142:7 argues along the same lines, that the petitioner asks God to bring him out of prison so that he can give thanks to his name.

5. Interpreters often regard the *expression of trust* as the primary motive of the plea for help. The plea presupposes faith in God and a close relationship between the petitioner and God. It is an expression of the fact that the suppliant trusts that God will intercede on his behalf. Expressions of trust and pleas are often alternated. An example is found in Ps 31:2, in which the petitioner prays, "Be a rock of refuge for me"; the next verse contains an expression of trust using virtually the same words: "You are indeed my rock and my fortress." These verses illustrate the close interrelationship between plea and expression of trust: on the one hand, trust in the LORD makes it possible to plead before him; on the other hand, the plea in itself is a demonstration of trust. The importance of the expression of trust is underlined by the fact that it appears in almost every individual psalm of lament and that its occurrence is not restricted to a specific part of a psalm. Even psalms that apparently consist only of complaints and petitions have trust in the LORD as their basis. Psalm 143, for example, speaks of the "faithfulness" (Ps 143:1) and "steadfast love" (Ps 143:8, 12) of the LORD.

Trust is expressed in various forms. First, there are explicit expressions directed to the LORD in person and formulated in the first person singular: "O my God, in you I trust" (Ps 25:2). The expression of trust is sometimes shaped into an antithetical clause such as in Ps 13:5a: "But I trusted in your steadfast love" (cf. also, e.g., Pss 31:14; 38:15; 141:8). The purpose of these antithetical clauses is mostly to indicate a transition from lament to trust or to underline the great difference between the righteous petitioner and his wicked enemy.

Over and above the verb "trust" itself, other verbs such as "take refuge" (e.g., Ps 57:1), "wait for" (Ps 130:5), and "hope" (Ps 130:5) are used to express trust. Trust in the LORD is sometimes described metaphorically, for example, in Ps 3:3: "But you, O LORD, are a shield around me." This metaphor expresses faith that the LORD will certainly protect the speaker and come to his aid. The expression of trust in Ps 3:3 contrasts sharply with the arrogant remark made by the enemy in the preceding verse: "'There is no help for you in God.'"

Trust in the LORD is also brought to the fore by the use of epithets of God, such as "my King" (Ps 5:2), "my salvation" (Ps 27:1), "my helper" (Ps 54:4), "my refuge" (Ps 142:5), "my strong refuge" (Ps 71:7), "my strong deliverer" (Ps 140:7), "my rock" (Pss 28:1; 42:9), and "my strength" (Ps 59:9). The first person singular pronoun is frequently used in this regard. It emphasizes the personal relationship between the petitioner and God as a prerequisite for and basis of the expression of trust. Trust in God is highlighted in Ps 31:14: "But I trust in you, O LORD; I say, 'You are my God.'" Even a text such as Ps 22:1, "My God, my God, why have you forsaken me?" which reveals great anxiety, nevertheless portrays a solid basis of trust in God by means of first person pronouns.

Texts such as that of Pss 25:15a, "My eyes are ever toward the LORD," and 38:15, "But it is for you, O LORD, that I wait," reflect the expectation that the LORD will listen to the suppliant and come to his deliverance. Psalm 55:19, "God, who is enthroned from of old, will hear . . . ," expresses trust in the eternal God who, unlike unfaithful friends, will remain faithful (cf. Ps 55:13-14).

The petitioner in Ps 22:4-5 looks back into history and becomes aware of the fact that his ancestors also believed in God. This fact gives the petitioner reason to believe that God will help him in his present miserable situation because he has also trusted God since his youth — he has leaned upon God from the time of his birth (Ps 71:5-6).

The earnestness of trust in God is sometimes pictured in hyperbolic terms: "I am not afraid of ten thousands of people . . ." (Ps 3:6). Rhetorical questions such as those posed in Ps 27:1, "The LORD is my light and my salvation; . . . of whom shall I be afraid?" are used to describe the faith of suppliants. In this particular instance, the psalm emphasizes that the righteous person need not be afraid of anything because the LORD is with him.

6. An element which is closely related to the expression of trust and often follows it is the *assurance of being heard* by God. This element reflects a change from lament to certainty — a conviction that the LORD will respond positively, or that he has already responded. There is a close association between this element and the element of praise to which attention is given in the following section. Some interpreters even consider the assurance of being heard as part of the praise element. It cannot be denied that with the statement of assurance of being heard — as in the case of praise — a change takes place in the psalm. The desperate situation of the petitioner changes to certainty, well-being, and gratitude. The expressions of trust as well as the assurances of being heard should be considered preparations for the praise element.

The statements of certainty of being heard usually appear in the imperfect form. For example, the speaker in Ps 130:8 is convinced that God will intervene on his people's behalf. In Ps 27:4 the petitioner asks God to permit him to "live in the house of God" all the days of his life and is certain that God will indeed conceal him "under the cover of his tent" (Ps 27:6). He has the assurance that God has heard his prayer and has a firm belief that he will experience the "goodness of the LORD in the land of the living" (Ps 27:13). He knows that God is on his side (Ps 56:9) and that God defends the cause of the needy and ensures justice for the poor (Ps 140:12). Considering God's deeds in the past, the petitioner is assured that his children and even their offspring shall live in certainty (cf. Ps 102:25-28). In all these cases, the petitioner is certain that the deliverance of God is imminent.

Some of the statements of certainty of being heard appear in the perfect form in the Hebrew Bible (HB). This emphasizes the element of certainty to a greater extent. The prophetic perfect can indeed be described as a perfect of certainty because, even though the LORD has not yet reacted to the plea, this form is implemented as if he has already done so. Ps 3:7 is a good example of a statement of being heard: "For you strike all my enemies on the cheek. . . ." It is this conviction of being heard by the LORD that enables the petitioner to say that he is not afraid of his enemies, however powerful and numerous they may be (cf. Ps 3:6).

Psalm 6 contains a good example of the change from a lament to a statement of certainty of being heard. In the first part of Psalm 6 the speaker is lamenting: "My soul also is struck with terror . . ." (cf. vv. 3-7). Then suddenly the psalm changes to a mood of certainty of being heard by God: "The LORD has heard the sound of my weeping . . ." (vv. 8-9). In reading Psalm 13, an unmistakable change from v. 3, "Give light to my eyes, or I will sleep the sleep of death," to v. 6, "I will sing to the LORD . . . ," is discernible. The question is, What happens between these verses? Should a change in mood be ascribed to a radical change in the real circumstances of the petitioner? Or is it an inward, emotional change on the part of the suppliant? Since it is impossible to reconstruct the situation of the petitioner precisely, it is my opinion that the present text of Psalm 6 has a rhetorical function. By juxtaposing the lament and the assurance of being heard, the psalmist emphasizes that only the LORD can bring about change in a desperate situation. The function of the text is therefore to persuade the reader to trust only in the LORD, however critical his situation may be.

7. The *vow of praise* and *payment of vows* are important elements of the lamentation psalms. This element normally follows the assurance of being heard and can usually be found at the end of the petition. The vow reflects the changed situation and is an illustration of the faithfulness of the petitioner in remembering that the LORD has come for his deliverance. The petitioner realizes that the matter has not been concluded when he has prayed and God has heard him. Something must follow, and he still owes something to God. However, the vow is not a means of manipulating God; rather, it enhances the importance of the petition and reflects the intimate relationship that exists between God and the petitioner. The vow forms a transition between petition and praise. The vows of praise give expression to an overwhelming feeling of gratitude toward the LORD (Ps 31:7).

Psalm 61:8 provides a good example of such a vow of praise: "So I will always sing praises to your name, as I pay my vows day after day." The vow of praise often appears as a vow to bring an offer of praise or thanksgiving (Ps 27:6; cf. also Pss 43:4; 54:6; 56:12). Ps 69:30-31, also a vow of praise, emphasizes another aspect, namely, that to praise the LORD with a song will be more pleasing to him than the offering of "an ox or a bull with horns and hoofs." Ps 51:15b-17 is not a rejection of an offering as such. These verses say that the merciful reaction of God will not be received on the basis of sacrifice alone. God despises superficial offerings which attempt to manipulate him. Only offerings given in the right attitude, namely, with a crushed and broken heart, will be acceptable to God.

The circumstances under which the praise should be given are also described in these psalms: the psalmist is so grateful toward the LORD that he vows to express his praise and thanks in a manner that will be heard by all. He promises to praise the LORD not only among his fellow believers (Ps 22:22; cf. also Pss 26:12; 35:18) but also "among the peoples and among the nations" (Ps 57:9). He will praise the LORD "all day long" (Ps 35:28; cf. also Ps 71:8), and he will pay his vows day after day (Ps 61:8). He will sing aloud (Ps 59:16) and give thanks with his whole heart (Ps 86:12; cf. also Ps 109:30). These descriptions all underline great gratitude toward the LORD and signify the change that has taken place from complaint to praise.

8. The lamentation psalms not only contain vows of praise, but some of them also contain elements of praise and thanks. Ps 22:23 is an example of such an individual lament that changes into an imperative to praise the LORD: "You who fear the LORD, praise him! . . ." Ps 69:34 employs the jussive form: "Let heaven and earth praise him. . . ." These praises not only comprise calls to praise and thank God but sometimes also contain a description of the greatness of God (Ps 22:28) and the reasons why the LORD should be praised: "Blessed be the LORD, for he has wondrously shown his steadfast love to me" (Ps 31:21; cf. also Ps 28:6). Although these psalms are called individual laments, it is evident from the above-mentioned examples that to praise the LORD is not a private or individual matter because the whole universe is called upon to share in the praise (Ps 69:34).

In conclusion, the individual laments are not laments in the strict sense of the word. They are not merely petitions — they are answered prayers. They are not merely complaints, but change into praises. One of the main features of these psalms is the polarity between complaint and praise. This polarity reflects real-life situations. Therefore the element of praise does not necessarily imply that a miracle has occurred and that the concrete situation of the petitioner has changed. What it does mean, however, is that he is convinced that God has heard him and that he can trust God. In this sense, these psalms do not represent an unrealistic or a pie-in-the-sky religion, but can be used by believers of all times and will remain relevant.

Psalm 8

Psalm 8 is a hymn or a song of praise. It is both introduced and concluded with the hymnic phrase "O LORD, our Sovereign, how majestic is your name in all the earth!" This phrase provides the keynote to the reading of the entire psalm. It is the central theme and a summary of what the psalm conveys, namely, that the LORD must be acknowledged and praised as the majestic sovereign.

Apart from the framework (8:1a, 9), the psalm can be divided into the following strophes: vv. 1b-2, 3-4, and 5-8. Although every strophe reflects a particular perspective, each of them has the same purpose, namely to convince the reader that the LORD is praiseworthy.

The content of the "hymnic framework" (8:1a, 9) can be summarized as follows: by means of an exclamation ("how . . ."), two aspects are brought to the fore. First, the majesty and sovereign power of the LORD embrace the whole world and all spheres of life, and, second, God has a close relationship with his people. He is not a distant God but "our Sovereign." This theme is elaborated in the remainder of the psalm.

In the first strophe (8:1b-2) the elaboration is done by contrasting the "infants" and the "enemy." Although the text is obscure and problematic, it can be illustrated by means of the following diagram:

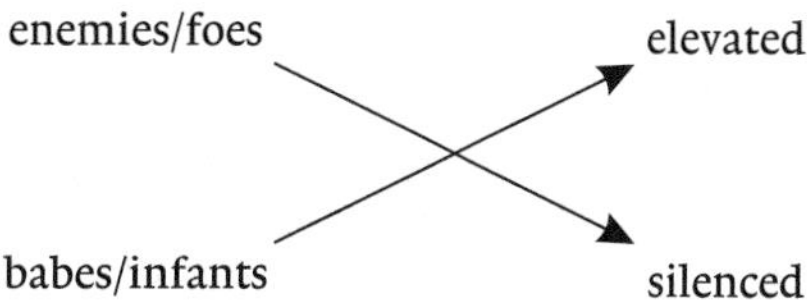

On the one hand, the "infants," that is, the weak and humble ones who proclaim the glory of the LORD, are elevated. On the other hand, the "enemy," that is, the arrogant and mighty ones, are humiliated and silenced. The glory and greatness of God are therefore proclaimed by small and insignificant people.

The second strophe (8:3-4) underlines the greatness of the LORD by contrasting the size of creation with the insignificance of "human beings." So great is God that he created the immense firmament and all the heavenly bodies effortlessly, merely by using his "fingers." In comparison to God, "human beings" or "mortals" are nothing. By using the same Hebrew word with regard to human beings ("what . . . ?" v. 4) that was used earlier with regard to God ("how," v. 1a) and by stating it as a rhetorical question, human insignificance is accentuated. The lovingkindness of the LORD is demonstrated by his mindfulness of humans in spite of their insignificance.

The poet prefers the use of contrasts to make his point. This preference occurs again in the third strophe (8:5-8), which contrasts with the preceding one. Whereas the weakness of humans is emphasized in the second strophe, in the third strophe their dignity as representatives of the LORD is placed in the foreground. The LORD is the subject of all the verbs in vv. 5-6. Humans have no authority or dignity in themselves; rather, they receive all their power from God. A striking metaphor, that of a king, is used to describe their responsibility. The LORD has crowned human beings with "glory and honor," God's own attributes of royalty. Since they are image bearers of God, the LORD has made humans a little less than his divine being. In language reminiscent of Genesis 1, their dominion is described in detail in vv. 7-8. Human beings rule over domestic animals, wild creatures, the birds of the air, the fish of the sea, and all the other creatures of the ocean.

The psalm concludes (8:9) with the same hymnic verse with which it began (v. 1a). The first and the last thought is about the glory of God. In this way the psalm demonstrates that everything points to God and that without doxology there can be no human dignity. Only when human beings are aware of their own insignificance can they recognize the greatness of God and will they be able to represent the LORD in the right way on earth.

It is not possible to date Psalm 8 or to determine its cultic origin with any degree of certainty. Even its title is of little help because it is probably a later editorial addition. The meaning of "The Gittith" is even more obscure. It could refer to a musical instrument, a tune, or a cultic ceremony of some kind.

Psalms 9 and 10

There are several reasons why these two psalms should be read as a unit:

1. Although these psalms, and particularly the beginning of Psalm 10, are somewhat disordered and fragmentary, there is an acrostic or alphabetical scheme embracing them. The scheme arises from pairs of verses which commence with successive letters of the Hebrew alphabet, a device that unites the two psalms.

2. The absence of a title for Psalm 10, which is rather exceptional in the first part of the psalter, may be an indication that it was originally part of a unit together with Psalm 9.

3. The LXX and some of the other ancient translations treat Psalms 9 and 10 as a single poem.

4. The two psalms display a conspicuous similarity with regard to the words and expressions they contain. The following are examples: "in times of trouble" (Pss 9:9 and 10:1); "the oppressed" (Pss 9:9 and 10:18; cf. also 10:12); "Rise up, O LORD" (Pss 9:19 and 10:12); "the nations" (Pss 9:5, 15, 17, 19, 20 and 10:16); "forget/forgotten" (Pss 9:12, 17, 18 and 10:12); "the wicked" (Pss 9:5, 16, 17 and 10:2, 3, 4, 13, 15); and "the LORD sits enthroned forever/ The LORD is king forever and ever" (cf. Pss 9:7 and 10:16). These repetitions of phrases and words confirm the unity of and reflect the most dominant themes in these two psalms.

It is undeniable, however, that there is also a difference between these psalms. In general terms, Psalm 9 can be labeled a thanksgiving psalm, while Psalm 10 is reminiscent of a lament (see "Individual Laments" above). In my opinion this order is used to accomplish a specific effect. It can be explained as follows: like many other psalms, Psalms 9 and 10 reflect a triangular relationship, namely, righteous-wicked-God. In Psalms 9 and 10, the psalmist identifies himself with the righteous, who are also termed the oppressed, the poor, and the like. These terms bring the problematic situation in the psalm to the fore, namely, that the petitioner has the impression that God is indifferent to the persecution of the righteous by the wicked. The wicked act as if God does not exist.

If the two psalms are read as a unit, the solution to the above-mentioned problem is given at the very beginning of Psalm 9, where the LORD is thanked in advance for everything that he will do. Is it possible that by using this technique the author wants to convince the reader that, whatever the situation, the LORD is in control? These two psalms do not necessarily reflect a historic situation and their content is not presented on the basis of chronology or logic. Rather, the two psalms, as they appear at present, serve a rhetorical purpose. The purpose could be to highlight the contrast between the righteous and the wicked and to stress that the LORD will certainly hear the prayer of the petitioner.

Against this background, by implementing the dynamic triangular God-wicked-righteous relationship and taking into account the interaction between the agents, the following observations can be made about Psalms 9 and 10:

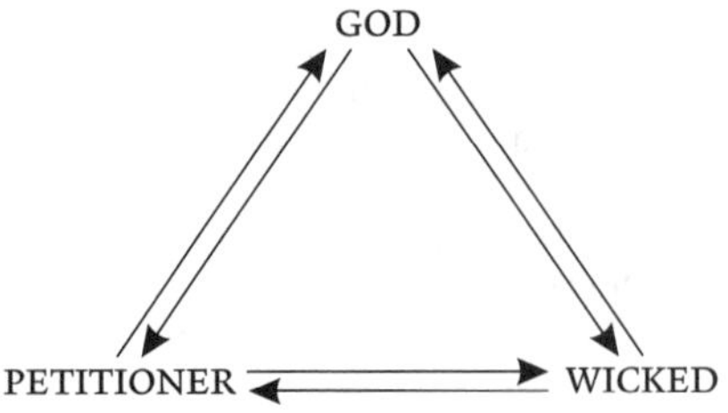

God

In two instances the LORD is the object of praise and thanksgiving (Ps 9:1-2 and 11-12). The reason for the thanksgiving is to be found in his conduct toward the wicked and the righteous. He has destroyed the wicked, and he did not forget the cry of the afflicted. Or, to put it in the words of Ps 9:8a, "He judges the world with righteousness." The metaphor of the LORD as a judge, sitting on his throne and administering judgment, is used throughout the two psalms (cf., e.g., Pss 9:4, 7-8, 16, and 19 and 10:18). Tension is created, on the one hand, by blaming the LORD for being distant and hiding himself in times of trouble (Ps 10:1-2) and, on the other, by praising him because he does see, notes trouble and grief (Ps 10:14), and does not forget the cry of the afflicted (Ps 9:12). The close relationship between the petitioner and the LORD is reflected in the fact that the LORD is the object of prayers and petitions directed to him (cf., e.g., "Be gracious to me, O LORD," Ps 9:13; and "Rise up, O LORD," Pss 9:19 and 10:12). This description of the LORD can be summarized as follows in the words of Ps 10:16, which is the theological core of these two psalms: "The LORD is king forever and ever."

The Wicked

The wicked are pictured as arrogant people who do not care for the LORD and do not recognize him as God. Violence, oppression, and lies are the rules by which they live. The poor and the helpless are the victims of their might. However, the obverse is also presented in Psalms 9 and 10, namely, that their deeds will be avenged (cf. Ps 9:15). Their destination is "Sheol," the place of death, where there is no hope and no communication with the LORD.

The Righteous

The situation of the righteous is directly opposite that of the wicked. They are the oppressed, and they are described, among other things, as "the poor, the afflicted, the needy, the helpless, the meek," and "the orphan." In spite of all their trials the significant difference between them and the wicked is that they are in constant contact with the LORD. He is their stronghold in times of trouble (Ps 9:9). Consequently, in contrast to the wicked, they have hope (Ps 9:18) and the assurance that the LORD will hear them and do them justice.

The meaning of the title "according to Muth-labben" is uncertain. It could refer to the tune in accordance with which the psalms were to be sung or accompanied. Translated literally, it could mean "death/die for the son." Neither the date nor the authorship of the two psalms can be determined with any measure of certainty.

Psalm 11

Psalm 11 is a psalm of trust. The structure of the psalm can be shown as follows:

A: The LORD is a refuge (v. 1)
  B: The actions of the wicked (vv. 2-3).
  C: The actions of the LORD (vv. 4-6).
A: The LORD is righteous (v. 7).

The psalm forms a frame in that it commences and concludes with an utterance about the LORD. In the middle section the actions of the wicked are contrasted with those of the LORD. By means of this *inclusio* and sharp contrast the poet attempts to persuade the reader to trust in the LORD and to identify with the petitioner, who is described as being righteous.

To attain this goal the author employs several poetic devices, of which the metaphor is the most important. With a rhetorical question, in which a negative answer is presupposed, the thought to "flee like a bird to the mountains" is rejected (11:1b). The implication is that the LORD should be one's only refuge.

By means of a hunting metaphor ("they have fitted their arrow . . ."), which carries the simile of the bird a step further, the actions of the wicked against the "upright" and the latter's consequential crisis are described in 11:2. By using an ironical question, "If the foundations are destroyed, what can the righteous do?" the crisis of the righteous is brought to a climax. If the very foundations of the community are broken down, the righteous are powerless to do anything.

11:4 and the verses that follow it contrast starkly with the preceding section. The emphasis in these verses is on security and stability. The LORD is pictured as the ruler and judge of heaven and earth. He is in total control, and he scrutinizes everything and everybody. Like one who tests the purity of metals, the LORD "tests the righteous and the wicked" (v. 5). The LORD's judgment of the wicked is described in harsh terms: he "hates" them. In reaction to their violence, he will destroy them as he did Sodom and Gomorrah (cf. also Gen 19:24). The metaphor of the burning desert wind, which destroys promising crops, is combined with the apparently peaceful metaphor of a drink during mealtime (v. 6). This brings God's judgment of the wicked to a climax.

The expression of trust (11:7) forms a striking contrast with the preceding section. By means of an obvious wordplay — the wicked loves violence (v. 5), but the LORD "loves righteous deeds" (v. 7) — the contrast between the wicked and God is further accentuated. While the wicked will be destroyed, the righteous have the prospect of enjoying the permanent presence of the LORD: "the upright shall behold his face."

The function of this psalm is to evoke trust in the LORD. By contrasting the fate of the wicked and of the righteous, Psalm 11 seeks to convince the reader to put his faith in the LORD only and to lead a righteous life. It is impossible to reconstruct the original historic or cultic situation. Even the title of the psalm, which is not necessarily an indication of its authorship, does not assist in this regard.

Psalm 12

Psalm 12 is the prayer of a righteous person who trusts the LORD unconditionally. The psalm has a concentric structure which can be represented as follows:

A[1] Prayer to the LORD in the *second person* (vv. 1-2).
  B[1] Wish expressed to the LORD in the *third person* (vv. 3-4).
    C Oracle (answer of the LORD) (v. 5).
  B[2] Hymnic words on the LORD in the *third person* (v. 6).
A[2] Prayer to the LORD in the *second person* (vv. 7-8).

The oracle (12:5) is the focal point of the psalm. The psalm is framed by the word "humankind" (lit. "sons of man"), which appears at the beginning (v. 1b) and at the end (v. 8).

The first strophe (A[1]) is an earnest cry to the LORD for help, the reason being that fidelity has vanished from the community. The infidelity that prevails is specified in the second part of the strophe as being deceitful and hypocritical speech.

The second strophe (B[1]) is a wish expressed to the LORD for the destruction of the ungodly. By means of word repetition — also from the previous strophe (cf. "[flattering] lips," 12:2, 3, 4; "tongue[s]," vv. 3, 4) — and by the use of a metaphor ("cut off . . ."), the destruction of the speech organs with which the transgression was committed is described. The hubris of the wicked is further exposed by the use of direct speech (v. 4): they boast that their strength lies in their tongues and that no one can call them to account. By way of an ironic question implying a negative answer ("Who is our master?"), their arrogance is brought to a climax. They do not acknowledge God. They are their own masters.

The concentric structure places the emphasis entirely on the third strophe, the middle section (C, 12:5). The words of the LORD contrast sharply with those of the wicked (cf. v. 4). The LORD says, "I will now rise up." This can be either a military or a judicial metaphor, and it indicates God's active intervention on behalf of his people. The reason for the LORD's intervention is given prominence by placing it in the first part of the verse: it is on behalf of the "poor" and the "needy" that he will act. He will liberate the underdogs of society who have no real political power or social status and who are exploited and oppressed by the powerful. The words "place them in the safety" (v. 5b) are a repetition of the stem in the Hebrew text that is used in v. 1 ("Help . . ."). This indicates that the earnest cry to the LORD is being heard.

The fourth strophe (12:6) is a hymn on the reliability of the word of God (cf. v. 5). The metaphor of the purification of silver by means of a melting process is used to underline this fact. The word of God contrasts sharply with the impure and hypocritical words of the wicked.

The fifth strophe (12:7-8) balances with the first (cf. vv. 1-2) in that it is also a prayer to the LORD. Yet a progression can be noted from the first strophe to the fifth in that the prayer in the first strophe focuses on the hopeless human situation while the prayer in the fifth strophe expresses firm belief that the LORD will protect his people against the wicked.

It is impossible to determine the date of Psalm 12. The language is of a general nature, and the psalm could have originated in any era.

Psalm 13 (*see* Individual Laments, 366-73)

Psalm 14

With the exception of a few variations, Psalm 14 recurs in Psalm 53. The basic difference is that Psalm 14 employs the divine name "LORD" (Heb. *Yahweh*), while Psalm 53 uses the name "God" (Heb. *'elohim*). There are also textual variations between these two psalms (compare Ps 14:5-7 to Ps 53:5-6). The variations indicate different transmission processes and different traditions, which have resulted in the two psalms being included in different collections of the psalter.

Although other elements, for example, prophetic elements (cf. v. 4), can also be detected in Psalm 14, I would classify this psalm as wisdom literature, particularly because it contains a striking contrast between "fools" and the "wise."

Psalm 14 accentuates two aspects of "fools," namely, their words and their deeds. These are summarized in v. 1: "Fools say in their hearts, 'There is no God'" and "They are corrupt, they do abominable deeds. . . ." In other words, v. 1 concentrates on their religion and their ethics. Their "religion," which boils down to practical atheism, has an influence on how they act and how they treat their fellow humans. Wherever the LORD is not acknowledged and honored, corruption and perversion occur. These deeds of fools are underlined by the repetition of a hyperbolic expression, "there is no one who does good" (cf. vv. 1, 3), and by amplifying it with the phrase "no, not one" (v. 3). The acts of "evildoers" toward their fellow countrymen are also described in v. 4.

This is, however, only one side of the coin. The psalm also stresses that the LORD still rules. The metaphor of the LORD as king, looking down from heaven, is again used to emphasize that he is in control of everything and everyone. The contrast between evildoers and the righteous is highlighted by stating that the former will be struck by fear, while the LORD takes the side of the latter (14:5). The abominable plan of evildoers to destroy the people of God is frustrated by the LORD: "the LORD is their refuge" (v. 6). Ps 14:7 places this idea in an even wider context. This verse is probably a redactional addition dating from the exilic/postexilic period because the phrase "the LORD restores the fortunes of his people" actually means "bring back the captivity." It therefore expresses a wish for the restoration of the land. It is the LORD who does it all, and his people are therefore called upon to rejoice in him.

The meaning and function of Psalm 14 can be summarized as follows: on the one hand, fools and evildoers, that is, those who do not acknowledge the LORD, are reprimanded. On the other hand, Psalm 14 emphasizes that the LORD rules and that he is a refuge for his people. As in other wisdom literature, this contrast is used to convince the reader not to be foolish but to be wise — in other words, to seek the LORD and to take refuge in him.

Psalm 15

Apart from the title, Psalm 15 can be divided into three strophes, namely, (1) question (v. 1); (2) answer to the question (vv. 2-5a); and (3) conclusion/summary (v. 5b). Psalm 15 should be considered a wisdom psalm. To be more precise, I prefer to call it a didactic psalm in the sense that its function is to teach the reader that there is an indissoluble link between religion and ethics, between humans' relationship with the LORD and their relationship with their fellow humans. Psalm 15 teaches that religion should embrace one's entire life and that it has everything to do with everyday life. Psalm 15 communicates that there should be a clear-cut difference between the behavior of those who say that they "fear the LORD" and that of the "wicked."

The Question (15:1)

The psalm commences with a double question in the form of a synonymous parallelism: "O LORD, who may abide in your tent? . . ." This verse should not necessarily be associated with a real cultic situation or with an entrance liturgy in which a pilgrim puts a question to the priest. Rather, it is a metaphorical way of asking who may dare to enter into the presence of the LORD. The main part of the psalm is used to answer this question.

The Answer to the Question (15:2-5a)

The answer to the question in 15:1 is that only the righteous may enter the presence of the LORD. V. 2 gives a general description of righteous conduct by means of three parallel phrases:

> Those who walk blamelessly,
> and do what is right,
> and speak the truth. . . .

No cultic prescriptions are given in this context, but the focus is on ethical qualifications. The righteous person, that is, the one who may enter into the presence of the LORD, is described in what could be called hyperbolic terms, namely, blameless in word and deed. The participles that are used to describe the righteous person stress that righteousness ought to be a permanent and not merely a temporary way of life. The general description of the righteous person is specified in v. 2, and concrete examples of such a person are given in vv. 3-5a. In v. 3 three negative phrases describe what righteous persons should not do:

> who do not slander . . .
> and do no evil . . .
> nor take up a reproach. . . .

All three phrases have to do with the proper relationship of the righteous with his or her neighbor. 15:4 uses an antithetical parallelism to emphasize the vast difference between "those who fear the LORD" and the "wicked." The integrity of the righteous and the fact that he or she honors an oath are in the foreground. V. 5 repeats the negative formulation of v. 3 by using a parallelism:

> who do not lend money at interest,
> and do not take a bribe. . . .

This verse does not mean that the principle of lending money at interest is wrong, but in the light of the Israelite laws on interest (cf., e.g., Deut 23:19-20) it is a pronouncement against exploitation of fellow citizens. It conveys the idea that honesty should govern a person's conduct in the economic sphere.

Conclusion (15:5b)

The phrase "Those who do these things shall never be moved" (lit. ". . . shall never stumble") summarizes the psalm and goes even further than the opening question. These words cannot be interpreted as a promise of prosperity and that nothing will ever go wrong with those who fear the LORD. The reality of life demonstrates that the righteous person is indeed often in distress. This verse must be understood within its context as an example of didactic wisdom literature which seeks to convince the reader to be wise, that is, to lead a God-fearing life, and that to experience the presence of the LORD is the fulfillment of life.

Psalm 15 bears many resemblances to Ps 24:3-6 and Isa 33:14-15. It is virtually impossible to determine which of these texts is the oldest and which is dependent on the others. However, it can be said that Psalm 15's dependence on wisdom literature and its acquaintance with other OT texts (cf., e.g., Exod 22:25; 23:8; Lev 25:17; Deut 27:25; Isa 1:23; Ezek 18:8; 22:12) compel one to conclude that it originated in the postexilic period.

Psalm 16

The text of Psalm 16 is so uncertain, particularly vv. 3 and 4, that it complicates its interpretation and translation.

Psalm 16 shares the title "Miktam" with five other psalms, namely, Psalms 56–60. The meaning of "Miktam" is obscure. There are many suggestions as to how it should be translated. The following are examples: (i) the LXX translates it as "inscription." (ii) The translation "golden Psalm" is sometimes suggested with reference to the "precious" contents of the psalm. (iii) The word "Miktam" is also understood as a characteristic of David and rendered as "humble" or "blameless." The psalm can be divided into the following strophes, namely, vv. 1-2, 3-4, 5-6, 7-8, and 9-11.

The first strophe (16:1-2) has to do with the psalmist's relationship with the LORD and is the key to understanding the psalm. It consists of a prayer for protection, "Protect me . . ." (v. 1); secondly, the petitioner acknowledges the LORD as the one and only God ("'You are my Lord . . . ,'" v. 2) and his only fortune.

The meaning of the Hebrew text of the second strophe (16:3-4) is uncertain and ambiguous and presents problems in respect to interpretation and translation. To mention but one example: the word for "holy ones" (Heb. v. 3), if seen as an ironic expression, is sometimes translated as "pagan deities." In other words, it is given exactly the opposite meaning as in, for example, the NRSV. I have, however, opted for the translation "holy ones." Seen in this light, this strophe spells out the consequences of the petitioner's relationship with the LORD (cf. the previous strophe). The fact that he acknowledges the LORD as his God also has an influence on his relationship with other people. This is the main point emphasized in this strophe. On the one hand, the psalmist associates himself with "the holy ones in the land" and states that his "delight" is in them. On the other hand, he dissociates himself from those who worship other gods. His loyalty to the LORD prevents him from participating in any of their religious practices, such as worshiping false gods. It is important to draw attention to the contrast between this strophe and the previous one. In this strophe the psalmist refuses to utter the names of the pagan gods (cf. v. 4), while in the first strophe (cf. vv. 1, 2) he praises the name of God.

The third strophe (16:5-6) restates and expands on what is stated at the end of the first strophe: "I have no good apart from you." In an exuberant way and by using metaphorical language, the poet describes what the protection and salvation of the LORD mean. Two metaphors are used. The words "chosen portion," "my lot," "boundary lines," and "heritage" suggest that the metaphor of the allotment of the land to the tribes is used in this context to describe the benevolence of the LORD. The expression "my cup" points either to a festive or to a sacrificial meal. In both instances the function of the metaphor would be to illustrate the joy and abundance of his heritage.

The fourth strophe (16:7-8) describes the mutual relationship that exists between the petitioner and the LORD as well as the permanent presence of the LORD of which the petitioner is aware and which makes him thank the LORD. The petitioner is always guided by the advice of the LORD and by his own "heart" (lit. "kidneys" or "reins"). In this context, "heart" denotes the innermost being and can probably be interpreted as the petitioner's conscience.

The fifth strophe (16:9-11) describes the outcome of the relationship between the petitioner and the LORD. The emphasis is on outward security and inward joy. The words "my heart," "my soul," and "my body" (v. 9) are synonymous and an indication of the whole person. The two lines of v. 10 are parallel: "For you do not give me up to Sheol. . . ." "Sheol," from an OT perspective, is the realm of the dead, the subterranean place where all who die go, where they live a shadowy, gloomy, joyless existence, and where a relationship with the LORD is impossible. The petitioner rejoices in the fact that the LORD has not given him "up to Sheol," in other words, death. Acts 2:25-28 reinterprets Ps 16:8-11, and particularly v. 10, as referring to the death and resurrection of Jesus Christ. These verses should, however, not be interpreted christologically or eschatologically in the NT sense of the word, simply because that is not the original intention of Psalm 16. V. 10 should be read as a contrast to v. 11. In the latter verse, the focus is on the presence and immediate deliverance of the LORD (cf. v. 11b-c) or, to summarize it in the words of the first part of v. 11, on the "path of life." This expression does not refer to life after death but to the abundance of day-to-day life in the presence of the LORD. The psalmist is convinced of the active presence of the LORD in his life and that the LORD will not surrender him to sudden or untimely death.

Although there is no direct indication of the date of Psalm 16, the emphasis on devoutness and certain elements of wisdom literature (e.g., "no good apart from you," 16:2; "path of life," v. 11) and the resemblance to Deutero- and Trito-Isaiah (cf., e.g., vv. 3-4 with Isa 57:5ff. and 66:3) are indicative of the postexilic period.

Psalm 17 (*see* Individual Laments, 366-73)

Psalm 18

The first important fact to be noted in respect to Psalm 18 is that it has a parallel in 2 Samuel 22. Except for minor differences, these two texts are virtually the same. It is, however, extremely difficult, if not impossible, to determine the exact relationship between Psalm 18 and 2 Samuel 22. It is not certain which is the older or authentic text. The fact is that each text has a unique function and meaning within its present context. Each text must therefore be treated according to its own merits. Consequently I will give attention only to Psalm 18 and not to 2 Samuel 22 in the discussion that follows.

It is uncertain whether the title of Psalm 18 ("To the leader. A Psalm of David, . . . He said:") formed an original part of the psalm and whether David was the author of the psalm. Like many other psalms, this title could also be a later addition ascribed to David. It should be remembered, however, that Psalm 18 is not primarily a historical document in the strict sense of the word. In the first instance, it is a theological reinterpretation expressed in poetry. This having been said, it would be quite possible for later generations to link this psalm, which is essentially a hymn on the LORD who intervenes and comes to the aid of the petitioner, to the name of David.

Although this psalm may be the result of a long and complex redactional process, in its present shape it nevertheless forms a logical and coherent whole. The psalm can be divided into two sections, namely, 18:1-29 and vv. 32-49. Vv. 30-31 function as a bridge or transition between the two sections.

One of the features of Psalm 18 is that the psalm as a whole and even some of the subsections or strophes are framed by similar phrases. A double *inclusio* is discernible at the beginning and end of the psalm:

- A: Title of the psalm: "Historical" information. A reference to David.
  - B: Hymnic section. The LORD is referred to as "my rock" and "my shield" (vv. 1-3).
  - B: Hymnic section. The LORD is referred to as "my rock" (vv. 46-49).
- A: Epilogue: "Historical" information. A reference to David (v. 50).

18:30-31, which I regard as the theological core of the psalm, the part which combines the two sections, again takes up the epithets (shield, rock) that are used in respect to the LORD in the hymnic sections at the beginning (v. 2) and in the last part (vv. 35, 46) of the psalm.

18:30 and 31 summarize the entire psalm: The LORD is the only God, and no other god can be compared to him. The rhetorical question ("For who . . . ?") has the polemic function of emphasizing that the LORD is superior to all other gods. God is blameless and reliable and a shelter for all who take refuge in him.

The historical framework (the title and 18:50) associates the psalm with David (he is described as, among other things, the "servant of the LORD" [cf. also Psalm 36] and as "his king" and "his anointed") and with his deliverance from his enemies by the LORD.

The hymnic section (18:1-3) is introduced by the phrase "I love you," which dominates the psalm and gives expression to the intimate relationship that exists between the petitioner and the LORD. In an unparalleled manner, and using metaphorical language, the poet lists epithets of the LORD: "my rock" (twice); "my fortress"; "my deliverer"; "my shield"; "horn of my salvation"; and "my stronghold." These metaphors are mainly derived from the military sphere and from a country abounding in caves and cliffs. They all convey the idea of safety, protection, and deliverance and are a summary of everything that is mentioned about the LORD in the remainder of the psalm. All the above-mentioned function as reasons for the hymn and show that the LORD is "worthy to be praised." The second hymnic section (vv. 46-49) links up with the first by using similar words and expressions (e.g., "rock," "my salvation," "enemies"), but it concentrates to a greater extent on the deeds of the LORD, especially the deliverance of the petitioner from his enemies.

18:4-6, which form a separate strophe, are reminiscent of an individual lament. This section displays several of the features of the individual lament, for example, the invocation of the LORD and the cry for help (v. 6), as well as the complaint and the description of the crisis (vv. 4-6). The metaphor of death and "Sheol" (cf. Ps 16:9-10) is implemented to describe the utter despair of the psalmist. Like many other individual laments, these verses contain an assurance of being heard.

The author of this psalm favors *inclusios*. This device is also used to demarcate the next strophe of the psalm (18:7-15). This strophe, which could be described as a theophany, is introduced and concluded with similar words and expressions:

foundations . . . of the mountains (v. 7)
Smoke . . . from his nostrils (v. 8)

foundations of the world (v. 15b)
breath of your nostrils (v. 15c).

Theophany — the term "epiphany" is also used by some authors — is a technical term to denote the genre in which divine appearance and intervention and the effect thereof on nature are described (cf. also, e.g., Exod 19:18ff.; Judg 5:4-5; Ps 97:2ff.; Hab 3:3ff.). It would be a mistake to read this strophe as a literal or factual report on a specific historical or cultic incident. Rather, this strophe is a poetic, and specifically a metaphorical, way of describing the power and awesome presence of the LORD. In language reminiscent of ancient Near Eastern mythology, and using metaphors from several spheres of life, a hyperbolic style, and anthropomorphism, the psalmist focuses on the LORD. The archaic and mythological terminology is reinterpreted and cast in a new form with the intention of describing the power of the LORD and convincing the reader/hearer thereof. God's wrath (cf. 18:7-8 and 15) is described in an anthropomorphic way and in terms of a volcanic eruption which resembles the Sinai event (cf. Exod 19:16-18). The metaphor of a violent storm, combined with military terminology (v. 14), is employed to describe God's approach (cf. vv. 11ff.). It is of prime importance for the poet to emphasize the LORD's overpowering might in the context of the psalm as a whole. The main function of the theophanic description in vv. 7-15 is to indicate that the LORD has the power to rescue.

The next strophe (18:16-19) links up with the previous section by describing in cosmic terminology ("mighty waters") the LORD's deliverance of the petitioner from his enemy. This strophe probably has a polemic function, namely, to emphasize again the power of the LORD over the gods.

The next strophe (18:20-24) is once again demarcated by the use of an *inclusio:*

> 20 The LORD rewarded me according to my righteousness;
> according to the cleanness of my hands he recompensed me.
>
> 24 . . . the LORD has recompensed me according to my righteousness,
> according to the cleanness of my hands in his sight.

The reasons for deliverance by the LORD are described in terms of the integrity of the petitioner, using legal or covenantal ("his ordinances" and "his statutes") and cultic terminology ("cleanness of hands" and "blameless"). Although the first impression may be that human virtues are overemphasized within the context of the entire psalm, it is in fact the righteousness and graciousness of the LORD that are emphasized. The description of the petitioner as a virtuous person should also be seen in its contrast to the description of the enemies.

18:25-27 link up with the preceding verses by describing what the righteousness of God really means. The LORD's dealings with humankind are described in terms of principles which are based on the tenet that the LORD's attitude toward human beings is determined by their attitude toward him. Vv. 28-29, which are written in the first person singular, concretize the foregoing general principles. By using metaphors the psalmist describes the intervention of the LORD on behalf of the petitioner in a more personal manner: first, the "lamp" and "light" metaphor, which symbolizes life and prosperity as opposed to the danger of "darkness," and, secondly, a military metaphor — "troop" and "leap over a wall" — which expresses deliverance from enemies.

18:30-31, the theological core of the psalm, flow over into the second part of the psalm (vv. 32-50), which can be described as a victory song. It was this facet of the psalm that enabled later generations to link it to David. This second major part of the psalm can furthermore be roughly subdivided into two parts, namely, vv. 32-45 and 46-49.

In the first section (18:32-45), which abounds with military terminology (cf., e.g., "girded me with strength," vv. 32, 39; "war," v. 34; "bow of bronze," v. 34; "shield," v. 35; "enemies/assailants," vv. 37, 39, 40; "struck them down," v. 38; "under my feet," v. 38; and "strongholds," v. 45), the emphasis is placed on the fact that the petitioner is trained as a warrior by the LORD himself and that he is also strengthened and made victorious over his enemies by the LORD.

The psalm is concluded with a song of praise and thanksgiving (18:46-49). This section is introduced by a declaration of faith, namely, "The LORD lives!" This expression may have a polemic function in that the LORD is contrasted with the other gods who are dead. It is precisely because the LORD is alive that deliverance is possible. V. 46 contains another epithet for the LORD, namely, "my rock." This expression links this latter part of the psalm to the beginning of the psalm (cf. v. 2). The rest of the section describes what is really meant by the fact that the LORD lives and that he is "my rock"; the focus is on the LORD and his actions. He is the "God of my salvation" (v. 46); "the God who gave me vengeance" (v. 47); he "subdued peoples"; "he delivered" (v. 48 [twice]), and he "exalted" (v. 48). In contrast to the above, the enemies are described as "violent" (v. 48). It is because the LORD has delivered the petitioner from these enemies and because he has "exalted" him (cf. v. 48) that the petitioner exalts the LORD (v. 46) and sings "praises" (v. 49) to his name.

The last verse (18:50), which can be ascribed to a later editor, harks back to the title of the psalm by identifying "his king" and "his anointed" with David. It emphasizes that the LORD's "steadfast love" is not limited to David, but that it is also extended to all his descendants. In this sense the psalm can be termed a messianic psalm; it is probably an allusion to 2 Sam 7:12-16, in which promises are made to David. This last verse is an application to the life of David of what the steadfast love of God, as described in the rest of the psalm, really means.

Psalm 19

Notwithstanding the fact that most commentators consider vv. 1-6 and 7-14 of Psalm 19 originally to have been two independent psalms, at present the psalm is viewed as forming a cohesive and meaningful unit.

The following are the reasons why the psalm is considered to be two separate entities. First, two different names are used for God. In 19:1-6 *'el* ("God") is used as a divine name, while "Yahweh" ("LORD") is used in the second part. Secondly, the difference with regard to content and genre can be stated as follows: the first part (vv. 1-6) is a hymn that testifies to the glory or majesty of God in nature; the second part (vv. 7-14) is a poem in praise of the law or Torah. When one reads Psalm 19 in Hebrew, it becomes apparent that the metric pattern of the first part differs from that of the second.

I would nevertheless suggest the following strophic division: (1) nature praising God (vv. 1-6); (2) the "law of the LORD" is perfect (vv. 7-10); and (3) the petitioner as "servant" of the LORD (vv. 11-14). The contents of the psalm can also be depicted in the form of concentric circles, the last part being the pivot or central point of the psalm. The psalm commences with a cosmic view but works up to a personal relationship between the petitioner and the LORD.

The first strophe can be divided into two sections, namely, 19:1-4b and 4c-6. In the first section (vv. 1-4b), nature is personified to proclaim the glory of God. By using terms and expressions such as "telling" (v. 1); "proclaims" (v. 1); "pours forth speech" (v. 2); "declares" (v. 2); "speech" (v. 3); "words" (vv. 3, 4b); and "voice" (vv. 3, 4), the psalmist emphasizes "telling" the glory of God. The "witnesses" who proclaim the "glory" of God are named: the "heavens" and the "firmament," which are synonymous here, are cited first. By mentioning "day" and "night" as witnesses, he stresses that the praise of God continues uninterruptedly. The paradox is that while this "speech" is not audible and not expressed in normal human words, it is nevertheless universal and reaches the "end of the world."

In the second section (vv. 4b-6) of the first strophe, emphasis is placed on the function of the sun as a creation of God. This function is described by using terms such as "comes out," "runs" (v. 5), "rising," and "circuit" (v. 6), and by implementing two similes (the bridegroom and the military hero) in v. 5. The description of sunrise and sunset, the circuit of the sun and the importance of its heat and light for the whole of creation, is reminiscent of mythological hymns of the ancient Near East where the sun is deified and praised as a god. However, Psalm 19 differs entirely from the aforementioned in that it personifies and pictures the sun as a creation of God which receives its mission from him. The sun is not God, but, like the "firmament," "day," and "night," is subject to the one true God.

The second strophe (19:7-10), which uses wisdom terms, is a hymn on the "law" of the LORD. The law is described by means of six adjectives: "perfect" and "sure" (v. 7); "right" and "clear" (v. 8); "pure" and "true" (v. 9). In the second part of each of these six lines, which have the same basic structure, the beneficial effect of the law on humans is described: "reviving the soul" and "making wise the simple" (v. 7); "rejoicing the heart" and "enlightening the eyes" (v. 8); and "enduring forever" and "righteous altogether" (v. 9). The law must glorify the LORD who stands behind it and from whom it derives its value and authority. The positive terms in which the law is described stress that it is the source of a rich life, and that the LORD expects humans to conduct themselves in a morally correct manner. Finally, the law is compared to fine gold and sweet honey because it is precious and delightful. The law is deemed to have a higher value than all earthly objects and pleasures.

The psalm reaches a climax in the third strophe (19:11-14). It commences with the macrocosm (vv. 1-6), moves on to the preciousness of the "law" for humans (vv. 7-10), and reaches a very personal level in the last strophe where the petitioner twice calls himself "your servant" and addresses the LORD as "my rock" and "my redeemer." The importance of the law is applied to the personal life of the petitioner and his intimate relationship with the LORD. The negative and positive functions of the law (cf. v. 11) are brought to the fore. The petitioner is fully aware of his own weakness, sinfulness, and unworthiness. He humbly beseeches the LORD to remove his hidden faults and to preserve him from pride so that he can be innocent of grave sins. The concluding verse is a prayer of the psalmist that his speech and his thoughts may be acceptable to the LORD. Just as nature tells of the glory of God (cf. the first strophe), so the psalmist speaks with his "mouth" about his "rock" and his "redeemer." The juxtaposition of praise by nature and by the "law" enables the poet to conclude the psalm with a personal testimony to the LORD. This is the ultimate goal to which the psalm wants to lead the reader or listener.

Despite the title of the psalm ("A Psalm of David"), which should not be interpreted as an indication of authorship, there are no direct indications in the psalm of its date of origin or of its original cultic setting. The wisdom character of the psalm may, however, reflect an exilic or postexilic date.

Psalm 20

Psalm 20 can be divided into two strophes, namely, (1) a prayer (vv. 1-5), and (2) the assurance of being heard (vv. 6-9).

The psalm forms an *inclusio* in that it is introduced by the expression "answer . . . in the day of trouble" (20:1) and is concluded by echoing virtually the same expression, "answer . . . when [lit. "in the day when"] we call" (v. 9). When we consider that the keyword "answer" is also used at the beginning of the second strophe (v. 6), it becomes clear that everything in the psalm hinges on the prayer to the LORD and the answer expected of him. What is pleaded for is "deliverance" (in Hebrew the same word is used three times; in vv. 5 and 9 the NRSV translates it as "victory" and in v. 6 as "help"). It is also important to note that "deliverance" is used twice in combination with "answer."

The first strophe (20:1-5) is an intercessory prayer of the congregation (v. 5) on behalf of somebody who is designated no fewer than eleven times by the personal pronoun "you/your." However, the phrasing of v. 6 ("his anointed") and v. 9 ("the king") makes it apparent that in this context "you" refers to the king. The military terminology in the psalm (cf. "banners," v. 5; "right hand," v. 6; and "chariots" and "horses," v. 7) indicates that the word "trouble" (v. 1) refers to a military threat. The description is presented in such general terms that it is impossible to determine the particular historical circumstances. The cultic terminology (v. 6) gives further reason to suspect that the psalm could have been written for use by the congregation on an occasion when Israel's king was in special need of divine help. The aspect of prayer is stressed by the use of nine jussive forms in the first strophe. Although the king is a prominent figure in the first strophe, the power of the LORD as the only one who is able to bring about deliverance is also emphasized by designating him as the subject of the following verbs: "answer" and "protect" (v. 1); "send help" and "give support" (v. 2); "remember" and "regard with favor" (v. 3); "grant . . . desire and fulfill . . . plans" (v. 4); and "fulfill . . . petitions" (v. 5).

This pattern of thought is even more prominent in the first part of the second strophe where an individual (20:6) is assured that the LORD "will help" — the Hebrew actually reads "has helped" — "his anointed." The power of the LORD is accentuated in v. 7 by juxtaposing the "name of the LORD" (cf. also vv. 1, 5) and "chariots and horses." In this context, "chariots and horses" represent military power as well as human arrogance and might. Vv. 7 and 8 state that those who rely solely on human strength and military strategy will be ashamed and subjugated. In contrast, those who trust in the LORD will triumph. The psalm reaches its climax in the last verse (v. 9), which repeats the word "answer" of v. 1 and in this way expresses confidence that the LORD has answered the prayer of the congregation.

The overarching function of the psalm is to convince the reader/hearer that military strength, and even the presence of such a powerful person as the king, is of no avail if there is no trust in the LORD. He is the only answer in the day of trouble.

Psalm 21

Psalm 21 resembles Psalm 20 in many respects: the king plays a prominent part in both; there are striking word repetitions (cf., e.g., "heart's desire," Pss 20:4; 21:2; the Hebrew stem *yš'*, which is translated as "victory" and "help" occurs many times, Pss 20:5, 6, 9; 21:1, 5; "right hand," Pss 20:6; and 21:8); in both psalms the LORD is addressed as "you" several times; both psalms end with an imperative: "Give victory" (Ps 20:9) and "Be exalted" (Ps 21:13), and both psalms end on a collective note: "we" (Pss 20:9 and 21:13).

The main theme of the psalm is the relationship between the LORD and the king and everything that the LORD bestows upon the king. The structure of the psalm can be summarized as follows:

- A^1 The king rejoices in the LORD (v. 1)
  - B^1 The LORD blesses the king (second person "you" dominates, vv. 2-6)
    - C The king trusts in the LORD (v. 7)
  - B^2 The victories of the LORD (or: victories of the king) (second person "you" dominates, vv. 8-12)
- A^2 "We" rejoice in the LORD (v. 13).

The psalm is framed (see A^1 and A^2) by the expression "O LORD, in your strength." This phrase is to a great extent a summary of the content of the entire psalm. This is confirmed by v. 7 (C), the theological core of the psalm, in which the relationship between the king and the LORD is expressed by words such as "trust" and "steadfast love" and the might of the LORD is emphasized by referring to him as "the Most High." It is also important to note that v. 1 (A^1) and v. 7 (C) are the only places in the psalm where the king is the subject of a verb. In both instances a hymnic undertone can be detected. The "help" (i.e., "deliverance"), "strength," and "steadfast love" of the LORD are given as reasons for praise. V. 13, which, as indicated, forms an *inclusio* with v. 1, correlates with everything that is said in vv. 1 and 7 with one exception, namely, that in v. 13 the congregation participates in the praise. These three verses (vv. 1, 7, 13) constitute the essence of the psalm.

21:2-6 (B^1) stress the LORD's "blessings" (cf. vv. 3, 6) on the king. These "blessings" are detailed in the remainder of this strophe: the LORD "set a crown of fine gold on his head." The king receives his power and authority from the LORD. He is king by the grace of God, and he represents God. The LORD also gives him "life" and "length of days forever and ever." This does not imply immortality or life after death in the NT sense of the word, but refers to a long, fruitful life or even more likely to a continuous, stable dynasty. The LORD also bestows "glory," "splendor," and "majesty" on the king. All these attributes are normally applied to God in the OT. In this psalm it is an indication of the special position of the king as the LORD's representative among the people.

21:8-12 (B^2) are ambiguous in the sense that it is not clear to whom the personal pronoun "you/your" refers. It can refer either to the LORD or to the king. In all probability it is meant to be ambiguous in order to illustrate that the king's enemies are also the LORD's enemies. The total destruction of the enemies is described using the hyperbolic and typical military terminology of the ancient Near East. Once again the "strength" of the LORD is illustrated in vivid descriptions.

The last verse (21:13, A^2), a prayer and praise of the congregation, returns to the idea contained in v. 1 and brings the psalm to a climax by praising the power of the LORD, who has given victory to the king.

It is impossible to reconstruct the exact cultic (e.g., a coronation ceremony) or historical context (e.g., a victory feast after a war) from its contents. This psalm reflects the close relationship that exists between the LORD and the king and the fact that the king's authority and the future of God's people are totally dependent on the strength and lovingkindness of the LORD.

Psalm 22 (*see* Individual Laments, 366-73)

Psalm 23

Psalm 23 is one of the most loved and well-known passages in the Bible. Apparently a simple text to understand, it nevertheless presents many problems in respect to interpretation, due particularly to its wealth of imagery or metaphoric language. One of the questions is how many and which metaphors are used in this psalm. Most exegetes prefer to perceive only the shepherd metaphor in vv. 1-4 and the host metaphor in vv. 5-6. Other exegetes identify a third one, that of the guide in v. 4. Another question is whether the speaker in Psalm 23 is an individual or a collective subject.

In spite of the above-mentioned uncertainties, there is no doubt about the main thrust of Psalm 23. It is a psalm of trust or confidence which has as its central theme that, in the midst of all problems encountered in life, one can be assured of lasting security, intimate communion, abundance, and happiness in the presence of the LORD. In order to communicate this message the poet employs, among other things, the metaphors of the shepherd and of the host. Psalm 23 does not, however, sketch an idyllic, carefree picture of green pastures in the European sense of the word, but speaks of "evil," darkness (v. 4), and "enemies" (v. 5).

The strophic division of Psalm 23 can be summarized as follows:

Vv. 1-4a (shepherd metaphor: "The LORD/me")
V. 4b (shepherd metaphor: "You/me"; hinging verse)
V. 5 (host metaphor: "You/me")
V. 6 (host metaphor: "The LORD/me").

The reasons for this division are as follows: the name of the LORD (Heb. *Yahweh*) occurs only twice in the psalm, namely, in the first verse and in the last (v. 6). In this way a framework is created which places the emphasis on the LORD. Characteristic of the first strophe (vv. 1-4a) are the shepherd metaphor, the verbs in the third person singular with the "shepherd" as subject and "me" as object ("He makes me lie down . . . ; he leads me . . . ; he restores . . . ," and "He leads me").

23:4b ("your rod and staff — they comfort me") functions as a hinge between the foregoing strophe and the next strophe in that it continues the shepherd metaphor of the previous section; but it is also similar to the next section in that it is direct speech to the "shepherd" in the second person. V. 5 forms the third strophe in that it employs a new metaphor, that is, that of the host, although it continues the direct form of speech. V. 6 continues the host metaphor, but it introduces a new strophe as it reverts to the third person ("the LORD" instead of "you").

The first words of the first strophe, "The LORD is my shepherd," are in essence a summary of the contents of the psalm. The second part of v. 1 spells out the implication of the shepherd metaphor: "I shall not want." The rest of the strophe, elaborating on the shepherd metaphor, concretizes what the "sheep" "shall not want," namely, food ("green pastures"), vitality ("he restores my soul"), guidance ("He leads me . . ."), and security and safety ("I fear no evil").

The hinging verse (23:4b) is the climax of the psalm. The tone of the psalm turns to a prayer. The LORD is addressed directly and a confession of faith follows: "you are with me." The presence of the LORD amid dangers and enemies is the central theme of the psalm. The "rod and staff," an expression which extends the shepherd metaphor, are concrete manifestations of the LORD's protecting presence.

23:5, the host metaphor, conveys the same ideas as that of the shepherd metaphor, namely, hospitality and provision ("You prepare a table before me"), protection ("in the presence of my enemies"), and abundance ("my head with oil"; ". . . my cup overflows"). As in the first strophe, the reality and presence of "evil" (cf. v. 4a), dangers ("the darkest valley"; cf. v. 4a), and "enemies" are not ignored, but the LORD's presence and provision are there and are stronger than those of the enemies.

The line of thought of the previous strophe is continued in the last one (23:6). "Goodness and mercy" are personified and act as the LORD's agents to give permanent protection ("all the days of my life") to the petitioner as a concrete sign of the LORD's love. The petitioner is no longer pursued by enemies, but by "goodness and mercy." The expression "I shall dwell in the house of the LORD," that is, in the temple, should not be understood in such a way that the poet of Psalm 23 was a priest or a Levite, but it is a continuation of the host metaphor and describes the lasting relationship that exists between the petitioner and the LORD and the protection that the petitioner receives from the LORD.

Most modern readers would apply Psalm 23 to their own personal relationship with the LORD. I agree, however, with those commentators who are of the opinion that in a subtle, metaphorical way the psalm recalls the LORD's provision for and guidance of his people, especially during the exodus from Egypt and their travels and sojourn in the wilderness. Traditionally David has been closely associated with Psalm 23 (cf. also the superscript). However, the reference to the temple in v. 6 makes it impossible for David to have been the author since the temple was built by his son Solomon after his time.

The psalm intends to bring home one central idea, namely, that in the midst of dangers and threats one can rely on the protective presence, abundant love, guidance, and care of the LORD. The psalm is therefore not concerned with a problem-free or an idyllic existence. On the contrary, it concerns the expression of trust by a believer(s) in the active presence of the LORD in the midst of life's problems and tensions.

Psalm 24

Psalm 24 consists of three parts (vv. 1-2, 3-6, and 7-10) which are so diverse in style and content that some commentators have questioned its original unity. Vv. 1-2 are basically hymnic, praising the LORD as creator. Vv. 3-6 have similarities with Psalm 15 and describe the conditions for entrance into the presence of the LORD. Vv. 7-10 are liturgic in form and describe the entrance of the LORD as "King of glory" into the sanctuary. Some exegetes defend the unity of the psalm by relating it to a specific cultic situation. As it is virtually impossible to reconstruct the so-called original cultic setting, I will rather endeavor to illustrate that in its present form Psalm 24 constitutes a logical whole.

In the first strophe (24:1-2) the LORD is described as owner and creator of the whole earth and all its creatures. Using a building metaphor and terminology which is akin to the creation myths of the ancient Near East, the psalmist describes the LORD as the creator and sustainer of the cosmos.

In the second strophe (24:3-6) the dominion of the LORD over the whole world (cf. the preceding strophe) is associated with admission into the presence of the LORD. The LORD, who is master of the whole world, obviously also holds the key to the temple on Zion. This strophe comprises a double entrance question in the form of a parallelism: "Who shall ascend . . . and who shall stand . . . ?" (v. 3); an answer to the question (v. 4); a blessing (v. 5); and an affirmation (v. 6). This strophe resembles Psalm 15 in describing the one who may enter into the presence of the LORD. The NRSV refers to "Those" (v. 4) and "They" (v. 5), but the Hebrew actually reads "He." As in Psalm 15, it is striking that no cultic prescriptions are given in Psalm 24, but that the focus is rather on moral qualifications: he is innocent in deed ("clean hands") as well as in thought ("pure hearts"). The "blessing" and "vindication" are not earned, but are gifts from the LORD that exceed all the foregoing good deeds. V. 6 is a confirmation that the blessings of the preceding verse are not to be understood individually but collectively. The blessings include those who "seek" the LORD, in other words, those people (NRSV states "company," but the word could also be translated "people" or "generation") who have a lasting relationship with the LORD.

The kingship of the LORD is the main theme of the third strophe (24:7-10). The expression "King of glory" appears five times in this section. The LORD is described as a victorious king returning home after a war (cf. the military terms "strong and mighty"; "mighty in battle"; and "LORD of hosts"). The gates of the city are personified and commanded to "lift up" their heads so that the great king can enter. Although this can be a reference to a specific situation, for instance, when the ark was brought to Jerusalem, I prefer the interpretation in which these verses are a metaphorical description of the greatness of the LORD. The strophe is organized in a parallel manner using refrains:

A^1 "Lift up your heads . . ." (v. 7)
B^1 "Who is the King of glory? . . ." (v. 8)
A^2 "Lift up your heads . . ." (v. 9)
B^2 "Who is the King of glory? . . ." (v. 10).

This structure as well as the rhetorical questions (24:8, 10), which presuppose that the LORD is the "King of glory," emphasize his glory as the victorious king. A^1 (v. 7) is an exact duplicate of A^2 (v. 9). However, B^2 differs slightly from B^1 since God is termed "the LORD of hosts." Although this expression can refer to celestial bodies or even to celestial beings, within this context it has a military meaning, referring to the LORD as the victorious commander.

There are obvious similarities between the second and the third strophes (24:3-6 and vv. 7-10). Both sections concern an entrance, the first being the entrance of the righteous into the presence of the LORD and the second being the victorious entrance of the LORD. As indicated, rhetorical questions fulfill an important role in both sections (cf. vv. 3, 8, and 10). In Hebrew the same verb stem is used for "lift up" (v. 4) and "receive" (v. 5) in the second strophe and "lift up" (vv. 7 and 9) in the third strophe. These similarities and word repetitions bring about a close connection between the two strophes.

Although it cannot be ruled out that the three strophes have divergent origins, the psalm in its present composition forms a coherent and meaningful whole. The function of the psalm could be to stress the kingship, the glory, and the power of the LORD (24:1-2 and 7-10) and to spell out the consequences thereof for the people of the LORD.

Psalms 25, 26, 27, and 28 (*see* Individual Laments, 366-73)

Psalm 29

The main question regarding Psalm 29 is to what degree it is dependent on or influenced by Canaanite poetry and mythology. Some commentators even state that Psalm 29 is an adaption of an older Canaanite hymn in which Baal is praised as the weather god (cf. esp. Ps 29:3-9). It has also been said that the terminology used in v. 1 (cf. "heavenly beings," lit. "sons of gods") is reminiscent of the way in which the Canaanite god El was worshiped and that characteristics of El are applied to the LORD. The similarities between Psalm 29 and Ugaritic texts cannot be denied. It is impossible to say what the exact relationship between Psalm 29 and the Ugaritic legacy is. What can be said, however, is that in its present form the psalm places all the focus on the LORD by using his name Yahweh no fewer than eighteen times and by describing his majesty and overwhelming power in a picturesque way. It may even be that the poet purposely used mythological terminology in such a polemical way to convince his readers/hearers that the LORD is superior to and stronger than the gods, especially Baal the weather god.

Psalm 29 can be divided into three strophes: vv. 1-2 comprise the introduction and a summons to praise the LORD; vv. 3-9a focus on the "voice of the LORD" as a great power; vv. 9b-11, which are hymnic, describe the LORD as the eternal and victorious king.

In the first strophe (29:1-2), in which the metaphor of the heavenly council is used, the "sons of gods" are deliberately degraded as servants and called upon to pay homage to the LORD. In order to emphasize the power and glory of the LORD, the imperative to pay tribute to the LORD is repeated three times and brought to a climax by a fourth imperative, "worship the LORD." The word "glory" is used twice in this strophe to emphasize the greatness of the LORD.

In the second strophe (29:3-9a), thunder is portrayed as the voice of the LORD and as an expression of his majesty and overwhelming power. The effect of the "voice of the LORD" on nature is described. However, the spotlight is not on natural phenomena as such but on the might and glory of the LORD. All the emphasis is placed on the "voice of the LORD" by repeating it seven times (cf. vv. 3, 4 [twice], 5, 7, 8, and 9a), seven being considered the perfect number, expressing totality. The effect of the "voice of the LORD" on the sea (v. 3), on the mountains (v. 6), on the trees (vv. 5, 9a), and on the wilderness (v. 8) is described in this strophe. A part of the strophe (vv. 5-9a) has a symmetrical pattern with regard to the effects on nature:

A: Trees ("breaks the cedars," v. 5)
  B: Earthquake ("Lebanon skip like a calf," v. 6)
    C: Thunder and lightning ("voice . . . flashes forth"; and "flames of fire," v. 7)
  B: Earthquake ("shakes the wilderness," v. 8)
A: Trees ("oaks to whirl"; and "strips the forest," v. 9a).

The devastating power of the LORD affects the whole land from north ("Lebanon" and "Sirion," v. 6) to south ("Kadesh," v. 8). The massive and seemingly everlasting mountains, symbols of stability and the dwelling place of the gods, become unstable, "skipping like a calf" or "a young wild ox" in the presence of the LORD. The colossal trees of Lebanon, symbols of strength and durability, are shattered. The shortest verse in the psalm, v. 7, positioned in the center of the structure (see C), sketches the most dangerous and frightening aspect of the "voice of the LORD," namely, thunder and lightning. The function of the entire strophe is to emphasize that nothing can be compared to the strength of the LORD.

The third strophe (29:9b-11) refers to the beginning of the psalm by describing the LORD, who is in full control of everything: he reigns as king over the "flood," the symbol of chaotic powers. The phrase "glory and strength," which occurs at the beginning of the psalm (vv. 1, 2), is taken up again (cf. vv. 9b, 11) and creates an *inclusio* within which the whole psalm should be read. The entire psalm evolves around the "glory and strength" of the LORD. To enhance this idea, the word "LORD" is used in each of the last four lines of the strophe. The psalm is brought to a climax when it is stated that the same mighty God who controls all powers also reaches out to bless his people with "strength" and with "peace." This must have been a reassuring and comforting thought for the original readers of the psalm, who probably lived among peoples who proclaimed that their gods were powerful.

Psalm 30

Psalm 30 is an *individual praise* and *thanksgiving* psalm. The key theme of the psalm is praise because it begins and ends with thanksgiving and praise:

I will extol you. . . . (v. 1)
O LORD my God, I will give thanks to you forever. (v. 12b)

The elements of praise and thanksgiving appear throughout the psalm (vv. 4, 9). Two other elements also play an important role. They are (a) an account of the trouble, danger, or *disastrous situation* in which the petitioner finds himself; and (b) an account of the *deliverance* of the LORD. The latter element obviously provides the reasons for the praise and thanksgiving.

(a) The crisis or *disastrous situation* is depicted by means of the metaphor of sickness and death ("you have healed me," v. 2; "you brought up my soul from Sheol, . . ." [for "Sheol," cf. also Pss 9:15, 17; 16:10], v. 3; cf. also v. 9). It is virtually impossible to tell whether these expressions refer to a specific situation and a concrete illness or whether they are used metaphorically to express the utter despair of the psalmist.

(b) It is the LORD himself who has delivered the petitioner and who has transformed everything: "You have turned my mourning into dancing" (30:11). The emphasis throughout is on the intervening actions of the LORD (cf. vv. 1, 3, 11). The LORD is the faithful and gracious one who, due to the petitioner's prayer, has come to his deliverance. All this is possible because an intimate relationship exists between the petitioner and the LORD (cf. "O LORD my God," vv. 2, 12; and "my helper," v. 10).

The intervention of the LORD on behalf of the petitioner is the reason for thanking and praising him. The petitioner even invites the congregation to participate in the praise and thanksgiving and to acknowledge the LORD (30:4).

When we consider the superscript of the psalm (". . . A Song at the dedication of the temple. Of David"), it becomes clear that this title cannot refer to the original context of the psalm, but represents a later liturgical phase when it was used to commemorate the dedication of the Second Temple (cf. Ezra 6:16-18; and Neh 12:27-43). In other words, the manner in which an individual originally experienced the intervening action of the LORD was extended and made relevant for a later community.

Psalm 31 (*see* Individual Laments, 366-73)

Psalm 32

This psalm cannot be classified in terms of the usual literary types. It is unique in the sense that it is a combination of several elements, for example, penitential (v. 5), thanksgiving (v. 7), hymnic (v. 11), and wisdom (cf. the beatitudes, "Happy . . . ," vv. 1-2; exhortations, vv. 6, 9; simile, v. 9; proverb, v. 10; instructional terminology, v. 8; contrast between the "wicked" and "those who trust," v. 10; all of which indicate sapiental influence).

It is not easy to demarcate the psalm into clear-cut strophes since some of the sections flow into each other. It could nevertheless be divided into two encompassing strophes, namely, vv. 1-5 and vv. 6-10, as well as a conclusion, namely, v. 11.

The first strophe (32:1-5) can be subdivided into two sections, namely, vv. 1-2 and vv. 3-5. Three synonymous words are used in vv. 1-2 and repeated in v. 5:

"transgression" (v. 1a)	"sin" (v. 5a)
"sin" (v. 1b)	"iniquity" (v. 5b)
"iniquity" (v. 2a)	"transgressions" (v. 5c).

The word "forgiven/forgave" is also used in both sections (v. 1a, v. 5c), and in Hebrew the same stem is used for "covered" (v. 1b) and "hide" (v. 5). These word repetitions call for a comparison of the two sections. Vv. 1-2 have an introductory function and are a general statement: to be forgiven by the LORD is true happiness. In v. 5, on the other hand, sin and iniquity are acknowledged and confessed to the LORD.

For the purpose of emphasis the expression "Happy are those . . ." is repeated at the beginning of a line (32:1, 2). The three synonymous terms stress the totality of human sin ("transgression," v. 1a; "sin," v. 1b; and "iniquity," v. 2). The passive forms ("is forgiven" and "is covered," v. 1) and the expression "to whom the LORD imputes no iniquity" (it can also be translated as "accuses of no guilt") indicate that happiness is brought about by the LORD and that he is the only one who can remove guilt completely.

The next section of this strophe (32:3-5) changes to the first person form, and the LORD is addressed directly. Vv. 3-4 describe the negative and v. 5 the positive side of the coin. In vv. 3-4 silence and unwillingness to confess are reported, while v. 5 represents willingness and openness to confess. The description in vv. 3-4 should not be understood as an indication of actual illness but as a metaphor expressing a hopeless situation, inner struggle, distress, and conflict due to guilt. In v. 5 it becomes clear that there is no escape from God and that the only solution — already stated in vv. 1-2 — lies in acknowledging iniquities to the LORD. The confession in v. 5 is also made using three synonymous verbs ("acknowledged"; "did not hide"; "confess") to indicate the sincerity and completeness of the confession which results in being forgiven by the LORD.

On account of his experience of the LORD's deliverance the petitioner exhorts (cf. v. 6) those who believe in the LORD to turn to the LORD when they are in trouble. V. 7 returns to the second person by again addressing the LORD directly and comprises a testimony by the petitioner that he is safe and secure in the hands of the LORD. In v. 7 the poet again implements the device of using three successive synonymous expressions to emphasize his testimony:

> You are a hiding place for me;
> You preserve me from trouble;
> You surround me with glad cries. . . .

This device underlines the all-embracing protection and presence of the LORD.

32:8 is ambiguous in the sense that it can be understood either as an oracle — a response of the LORD — or as sapiental instruction. In the light of the immediately preceding verse and the rest of the psalm in which the second person refers to the LORD, it is likely that the second person in v. 8 also refers to the LORD. In the typical style of this poet the instruction is also presented by means of a triad:

> I will instruct you
> and teach you. . . .
> I will counsel you. . . .

Continuing the wisdom language, 32:9 uses the simile of a "horse" and a "mule" to admonish righteous people not to be stubborn like an unreasonable animal which can be controlled only by force and which is incapable of understanding an instruction. V. 10 continues the wisdom language by contrasting the fate of the "wicked" with the fate of "those who trust in the LORD."

The purpose of the wisdom section in particular and of the psalm in general is to convince the reader/hearer to act wisely, that is, to be righteous. In the context of this psalm, to be wise is to confess transgressions and to acknowledge that only the LORD can bring about real happiness by forgiving sins.

The psalm ends on a hymnic note, calling all "righteous" people to rejoice in the LORD and thus to participate in the joy of those whose sins have been forgiven by the LORD.

The precise meaning and function of the superscript "A Maskil" (cf. Psalms 42, 44–45, 52–55, 74, 78, 88, 89, and 142, where it also occurs) is uncertain. Translations that have been suggested are, among others, "skillful psalm" and "didactic psalm."

Psalm 33

It is apparent that whereas Psalm 33 lacks a superscript, it bears a strong resemblance to the last verse of Psalm 32. Psalm 32 ends as follows:

> Be glad in the LORD . . . O righteous,
> and shout for joy, all you upright in heart,

while Psalm 33 commences with:

> Rejoice in the LORD, O you righteous.
> Praise befits the upright.

Ps 33:1 repeats the call to praise with which Psalm 32 ends. The rest of Psalm 33 gives the reasons why the LORD should be praised.

Psalm 33 is a typical communal hymn. The psalm has the following structure:

Vv. 1-3, a call to praise the LORD.
Vv. 4-19 are the main body of the psalm and give reasons for the call to praise.
Vv. 20-22 are a confession of trust and hope. The first person form is used for the first time in the psalm, and in v. 22 the LORD is addressed personally for the first time as "you[r]."

Psalm 33 consists of twenty-two lines, precisely as many letters as there are in the Hebrew alphabet. This device creates the impression of completeness and purposefulness in the psalm. Deliberate word repetition also enhances cohesion in the psalm.

The first strophe (33:1-3) summons the believing community by using five imperatives to praise the LORD. The "new song" (cf. also Pss 40:3; 96:1; 98:1; 144:9; 149:1) that has to be sung bears the meaning of creating something new, but also of renewing and reactualizing the past.

The second strophe (33:4-19) consists of several sections. The *word* and *work* of the Lord, which form the basis of the summons to praise, are summarized in vv. 4-5 with four words, namely, "upright," "faithfulness," "righteousness," and "justice." The rest of the psalm gives an exposition of the word and deeds of the LORD. A deliberate connection is made between the praising congregation and the praised LORD by describing both with the same words, namely, "righteous" (cf. vv. 1, 5) and "upright" (cf. vv. 1, 4).

The first reason for praising the LORD is found in 33:6-9. In this section the LORD is hailed as creator. The emphasis is on the creative "word" of the LORD, already mentioned in v. 4. In fact, this section (vv. 6-9) begins and ends with creation by divine word:

> By the word . . . the heavens were made. (v. 6)
> For he spoke . . . and it stood firm. (v. 9)

This description of creation reflects the threefold worldview of the ancient Near East: "heavens" (v. 6), "waters of the sea" (v. 7), and "earth" (v. 8). This description is particularly reminiscent of Genesis 1 (cf., e.g., Gen 1:3, 9-10). 33:7-8 are also reminiscent of Exod 15:1-18 (cf., e.g., v. 7 with Exod 15:8; and 33:8 with Exod 15:14-15), a victory song that celebrates the deliverance from Egypt. By combining creation terminology with that of salvation history, the poet stresses both the LORD's power to create and his omnipotence.

In 33:10-12 the scene changes from creation to human history. The LORD controls everything. The "counsel of the LORD" is contrasted with the "counsel of the nations." His plan endures forever, while theirs is brought to nothing. The counsel of the LORD reaches its culmination in the election of Israel as his own possession (v. 12).

The metaphor of the LORD as king and judge who scrutinizes everybody is used in 33:13-19 to underline once more the fact that he is in control of everything. The LORD comforts those who fear (i.e., respect and love) him because he sees their need and comes to their assistance (vv. 18-19). By using a military metaphor (cf. vv. 16, 17) the psalmist emphasizes that those who trust in human power hope in vain. He thus condemns trust in human strength. It is only the LORD in whom humans can trust for deliverance.

The psalm reaches its climax in the last strophe (33:20-22) in which the congregation applies the preceding section (cf. vv. 6-19) to themselves (cf. "our soul," etc.). By using a military metaphor once again, the psalmist hails the LORD as their only help, protection, and hope. The psalm ends with a prayer: "Let your steadfast love, O LORD, be upon us. . . ." In this sense this last strophe is an answer to the summons of the first strophe (cf. vv. 1-3). The expression "the steadfast love of the LORD," with which the second strophe begins (cf. vv. 4-5), is resumed (v. 22). The entire psalm is a hymn on the "steadfast love of the LORD," which the community experienced in creation and in salvation history. The "steadfast love of the LORD" is actually a summary of all the LORD's words and works (vv. 4-5). The function of the psalm is to convince the congregation that the LORD is praiseworthy and trustworthy.

Psalm 34

The superscript links the psalm to "David, when he feigned madness before Abimelech, so that he drove him out, and he went away." This is probably a reference to the incident described in 1 Sam 21:10-15 where David feigned madness before Achish — not Abimelech, as in Psalm 34 — the Philistine king. The difference between 1 Samuel 21 and Psalm 34 can be due to a scribal error or it can be that Abimelech is a general name for Philistine kings just as Pharaoh is for Egyptian kings. It is probable that this title was also a later addition and ascribed to David, especially since there is no explicit resemblance between the psalm itself and the incident in 1 Samuel 21. A later editor probably tried to associate the several miraculous escapes of David described in 1 Samuel 21–23 with Psalm 34, in which the LORD is praised as the good one who answers and rescues the humble and brokenhearted.

Psalm 34 is an acrostic or alphabetical poem in that its verses begin with the successive letters of the Hebrew alphabet. The psalm lacks a verse beginning with the sixth Hebrew letter *(waw)* and has an additional verse at the end of the psalm that begins with the letter *pe*. In this respect, Psalm 34 is similar to Psalm 25. A further item of correspondence is that in the HB four verses of both psalms commence in a similar way (cf. Ps 25:12 to Ps 34:12; Ps 25:15 to Ps 34:15; Ps 25:16 to Ps 34:16; and Ps 25:22 to Ps 34:22). Another characteristic of Psalm 34 is the word repetition that occurs throughout (cf. "hear/listen," vv. 2, 6, 11, 17; "deliver/rescue," vv. 4, 17, 19; "fear," vv. 7, 9a, 9b, 11; "good," vv. 8, 10, 12, 14; "evil[doers]," vv. 13, 14, 16 ["afflictions" in v. 19 is from the same Hebrew stem], 21; "righteous," vv. 17, 19, 21; "sought/seek," vv. 4, 10). These repetitions, together with the acrostic nature of the psalm, create cohesion and the impression of completeness. Psalm 34 is also connected to the preceding psalm (cf. vv. 1 and 15 to Ps 33:1 and 15 respectively) and the following psalm (cf. 34:7 to Ps 35:5-6) with word and phrase repetitions.

The psalm can be divided into two strophes, namely, 34:1-10 and vv. 11-22. Vv. 1-10 consist mainly of elements of an individual thanksgiving, while vv. 11-22 can be classified as wisdom literature.

The first strophe (34:1-10) comprises the following sections: vv. 1-3 are a self-exhortation to thank and praise the LORD. They conclude by inviting the congregation to join the thanksgiving and praise. The emphasis is placed entirely on praise and thanksgiving by the use of words such as "bless," "praise," "boast in the LORD," "be glad," "magnify the LORD" and "exalt his name." The entire life of the petitioner is supposed to be one of thanksgiving, and the whole community must also share in it. The glory of the LORD is accentuated by the fact that it is the humble ones, the "low" ones, that should "exalt" and "magnify" the LORD. The theme of the humble and poor ones fulfills a central role in the psalm (cf., e.g., vv. 2, 6, and 18).

The next section, 34:4-10, is a testimony from the petitioner's personal experience, giving the reasons for praise. V. 4 is an excellent summary of the section: "I sought the LORD, and he answered me. . . ." Several verbs are used, especially in vv. 4-6, to describe the deliverance of the LORD ("answered" and "delivered," v. 4; "heard" and "saved," v. 6). The figure of the "angel" (lit. "messenger") of the LORD, who is a representation of the LORD as well as a protector ("encamps around those . . . ," v. 7), is used to depict further the deliverance and the protection of those who "fear" the LORD. Vv. 8-10 form an *inclusio* as they commence and are concluded with the word "good," while the word "fear" is repeated strategically:

. . . that the LORD is good (v. 8)
fear (v. 9a)
fear (v. 9b)
. . . lack no good thing (v. 10).

The function of this entire section is to underline the goodness of the LORD to those who "fear" him. Although the wisdom part of the psalm commences in v. 11, this section also displays wisdom influence. The expressions "good," "fear," and "happy are those . . ." and the lion metaphor are clear indications thereof. The function of the lion metaphor is to indicate that the powerful and those who think that they are self-sufficient will go empty and hungry, while those who depend upon the LORD will "have no want."

The second strophe (34:11-22) is introduced in a didactic tone which is typical of wisdom literature: "Come, O children, listen to me" (cf. also Prov 4:1; 5:7; 7:24; 8:32). The main feature of this section is the contrast which is created between the "righteous" and "evildoers." The LORD is on the side of the "righteous": his "eyes" are on them; his ears are open to their cry; he hears, rescues, and saves them; he is near to them, redeems their life, and so on. In contrast to his attitude to the "righteous," the LORD is opposed to "evildoers": he will destroy them and condemn them; they are doomed to death. The "righteous" are expected to act wisely. Vv. 13-14 in particular contain a summons to a wise life. To be wise means to act righteously in speech and in action, both in a positive ("do good") and in a negative sense ("depart from evil").

The last part of Psalm 34 — and for that matter the psalm as a whole — has a didactic function. By contrasting the "righteous" and "evildoers" and by describing the fate of the righteous in a very positive way, the poet aims to persuade the reader to make the right choice, namely, to "fear" the LORD, to acknowledge him as God, and to praise him constantly for his deliverance.

Psalm 35 (*see* Individual Laments, 366-73)

Psalm 36

The first and the last verses are the key to understanding the psalm: the beginning and the end of the psalm form a striking contrast. The psalm commences by describing the arrogance of the "wicked": ". . . there is no fear of God before their eyes," and it ends: "There the evildoers lie prostate; they are unable to rise." The function of the contrast is to indicate that evildoers are struck down, never to rise again, while the "steadfast love" of the LORD lasts forever. This expression occurs no fewer than three times in the psalm (vv. 5, 7, and 10).

Psalm 36 can be divided into three strophes:

A The world of the "wicked" (vv. 1-4)
B The world of the "LORD" (vv. 5-9)
AB The world of the "wicked" plunges into misery, but the world of the "LORD" continues forever (vv. 10-12).

The title of the psalm resembles the first part of the title of Psalm 18. Like the titles of many other psalms, this one could also be a later addition, and it is not clear precisely why David is referred to in this psalm as "the servant of the LORD."

The first strophe (36:1-4) is a description of the wicked. "Transgression" is personified, and the strophe reflects the arrogance, "mischief," and "iniquity" of the wicked. The psalmist states in ironic terms that the wicked flatter themselves "in their own eyes." This description of the world of the wicked boils down to practical atheism.

The second strophe (36:5-9) is a hymn. The LORD is addressed directly in the second person. The second person pronoun "your" is used ten times to maintain emphasis on the LORD. Vv. 5-6b list four attributes of the LORD that are more or less synonymous: "your steadfast love," "your faithfulness," "your righteousness," and "your judgments. . . ." V. 6c explains these attributes of the LORD by saying that he saves "humans and animals alike." The expressions "to the heavens," "to the clouds," "like the mighty mountains," and "the great deep" emphasize the comprehensive range of the "steadfast love" of the LORD. It is universal, inexhaustible, and immeasurable. In fact, it embraces both humans and animals. V. 6c is elaborated in vv. 7-9. First, the preciousness of the steadfast love of the LORD is again emphasized. Five metaphors are used to define precisely what the steadfast love of the LORD means: ". . . refuge in the shadow of your wings," ". . . the abundance of your house," ". . . drink from the river of your delights," ". . . the fountain of life," and ". . . in your light we see light." These metaphors bring to the fore the protective care of the LORD. He is the bountiful host. He is the source of life and joy. Only with the LORD are protection, security, and abundance to be found. The second strophe contrasts sharply with the first.

The third strophe (36:10-12) is a prayer which concerns the three parties in the psalm, namely, the LORD, the petitioner, and evildoers: (a) the petitioner beseeches the Lord to continue his "steadfast love"; (b) he prays that the wicked may not get the upper hand over him; and (c) he prays that evildoers may be struck down so that they are unable to rise again.

With this prayer the psalm has come full circle. The arrogance of the wicked is futile. What counts is the steadfast love of the LORD.

Psalm 37

Psalm 37 is a classic example of a wisdom poem. It also has an alphabetical structure in that the opening letters of alternate verses are arranged in accordance with the Hebrew alphabet. As a wisdom psalm, Psalm 37 has a didactic character. The poet assumes the role of a teacher. He speaks from personal experience, imparting his wisdom to the ignorant.

The most important function of the psalm is to convince the righteous to trust in God and to obey him in spite of the behavior of the wicked. The righteous can be tempted to envy by the prosperity of the wicked and to fall into unbelief. The psalm teaches, however, that the success of the wicked is temporary, but the reward of the righteous is permanent and sure. The statement that the righteous "shall inherit the land" is used time and again to express this idea (cf. vv. 3, 9, 11, 18, 22, 27, and 34). Psalm 37 says that eventually all will be well for the righteous.

However, the reality of life illustrates that Psalm 37 offers only a partial solution to life's problems. Life is not a bed of roses for the righteous since he is indeed often in distress. Psalm 37 should therefore be read in the light of the whole of the OT, especially in the light of the book of Job and the individual laments. The psalm cannot be interpreted literally as a promise of prosperity — that nothing will ever go wrong for the righteous. Psalm 37 must be interpreted within the context of didactic wisdom literature. The idea of retribution and recompense — the connection between deed and consequence — which figures prominently must also be understood in the light of the didactic purpose of the psalm: in order to convince the reader to act wisely, that is, to be righteous and to trust in the LORD, the poet portrays the righteous and the wicked in sharply contrasting colors. The righteous are of course portrayed positively and the wicked negatively.

In order to achieve his goal the poet uses many poetic devices, for example, antithetical parallelism:

> For the wicked shall be cut off,
> but those who wait for the LORD shall inherit the land. (v. 9)

In order to describe the destruction of the wicked the psalmist uses military metaphors expressing irony: though the wicked draw the sword to kill the righteous, their plans will boomerang and "their sword shall enter their own heart . . ." (v. 15). A simile is used to illustrate that the success of the wicked is temporary and to convince the righteous not to "fret" because of them: "they will soon fade *like* grass . . ." (v. 2; cf also v. 20). Psalm 37 concentrates on everyday life. Although it emphasizes the salvation of the LORD (cf. esp. vv. 39-40) it also sets forth human responsibility.

Because of its alphabetical structure the psalm has no clearly demarcated strophes. Only a broad division can be made: 37:1-11 abound with imperatives. The righteous are admonished to trust in the LORD alone in spite of the irritation caused by the wicked. Vv. 12-26 are more descriptive and are mainly made up of declarative sentences. The contrast between the wicked and the righteous is accentuated. In vv. 27-38 imperatives again dominate (cf. vv. 27, 34, 37), and the psalm concludes by stressing the deliverance of the LORD (vv. 39-40).

In a nutshell, Psalm 37 is a wisdom psalm whose main function is to convince the reader to trust in the LORD.

Psalms 38 and 39 (*see* Individual Laments, 366-73)

Psalm 40

The question of unity is the most important problem in respect to the interpretation of Psalm 40. Most commentators regard it as a composite psalm consisting of two originally independent psalms, namely, vv. 1-10 and vv. 11-17 (some commentators take the position that the division should be between vv. 1-11 and vv. 12-17). The first part is classified as an individual thanksgiving, while the second part is considered to be an individual lament. One of the arguments of those who say that Psalm 40 is a composite psalm is that the thanksgiving and lament occur in reverse order. They argue that there is tension between the first part, the thanksgiving for deliverance (vv. 1-10), and the lament (vv. 11-17), in which the suppliant prays for deliverance. Another argument in favor of two originally separate psalms is that vv. 13-17 are a duplicate, with small variations, of Psalm 70. Without denying the composite character of Psalm 40, the psalm in its present state nevertheless forms a cohesive and meaningful unity. Moreover, it is almost impossible to reconstruct the redactional process by means of which the psalm came into being, or the original cultic situation of the psalm.

The psalm is introduced with the expression "I waited patiently for the LORD" and is concluded with the prayer "do not delay, O my God." The intention of the psalm is reflected in the relationship between "I waited" and "do not delay," in other words, the tension between the possession of faith (40:1ff.) and the striving for faith and deliverance (v. 17). This tension, which describes the living relationship between the petitioner and the LORD, is the cohesive element in the psalm. The repetition of words and phrases, which occurs throughout the psalm, also creates unity. In v. 9 the psalmist says he has "not restrained" his lips from praising the LORD; in v. 11 he begs the LORD not to "withhold" (the Hebrew uses the same stem) his mercy from him. The same word in Hebrew is used to express the "delight" (v. 8) of the petitioner in the LORD and the LORD's willingness ("Be pleased, O LORD . . ."; cf. v. 13) to deliver the petitioner. The psalmist says that evils "without number" have encompassed him and that his iniquities "are more than" the hairs on his head (cf. v. 12). This is contrasted with the wondrous deeds of the LORD, which are said to be "more than can be counted" (v. 5). In v. 10 the psalmist explicitly says that he has spoken of the "steadfast love" and "faithfulness" of the LORD. He is bold enough to beseech the LORD not to withhold his "steadfast love" and "faithfulness" from him. The personal relationship between the petitioner and the LORD is expressed throughout the psalm by direct address and invocations (cf., e.g., "O LORD my God," v. 5; cf. also vv. 8, 9, 11, 13, and 17).

In 40:1-3a the LORD's intervention on behalf of the petitioner is emphasized by the use of five verbs with the LORD as subject ("he inclined to me," "heard my cry," "drew me up . . . ," "set my feet . . . ," and "put a new song . . ."). A metaphor of contrast ("from the desolate pit, out of the miry bog" par. "upon a rock"), depicting respectively utter desolation and the security of the LORD's presence, is used to further underline the deliverance of the LORD. This is followed in v. 3b by a song of praise, and in v. 4 with the contents of the "new song" (cf. v. 3). The keyword in vv. 3b-4 is "trust" in the LORD.

The praise and the contents of the "new song" are continued in v. 5, but a new element appears, namely, the LORD is addressed directly in the second person. Furthermore, deliverance is no longer seen to concern the individual only, but is described as "your wondrous deeds . . . toward us." The phrase "wondrous deeds" is probably a reference to the exodus from Egypt.

40:6-8 are not a rejection of sacrifices as such, but state that the attitude in which the offering is presented is more important than the offering itself. Vv. 9-10 are framed by the expression "in/from the great congregation." Praise is not only a private matter; the LORD should also be praised in public. Vv. 11-12, which can be considered part of the lament section, repeat words and phrases from the praise section: the petitioner begs the LORD not to withhold his "steadfast love" and "faithfulness" (cf. v. 11 to vv. 9 and 10; also v. 12 to v. 5). Two kinds of reasons are given in the petition for deliverance, and they are presented in a parallel manner:

> For evils . . . without number have encompassed me;
> my iniquities . . . are more than the hairs of my head.

The petitioner is "intimidated" externally (by his enemies) and internally (by his own "iniquities").

In a style typical of the individual lament, 40:13-15 are an urgent petition for help against enemies. V. 16 contrasts with the preceding verses in that it is a prayer of blessing for God-fearing people. It reflects both praise and confidence ("'Great is the LORD!'") in the LORD. The contrast between enemies and God-fearing people is highlighted by using the same word for both of them:

> Those . . . who seek to snatch away my life (v. 14)
> . . . may all who seek you. . . . (v. 16)

The psalm is concluded by a personal prayer (v. 17). The psalmist reverts to his own personal circumstances. It is the LORD in whom he trusts in his deepest need. The last verse is an expression of true faith. It is, however, a faith which is not without tension and problems. In the words of Psalm 40, faith is both waiting patiently for the LORD and praying to him not to delay his help.

Psalm 41 (*see* Individual Laments, 366-73)

Psalms 42–72

Psalms 42–72 are known as Book II of the psalter. These psalms are usually known as the Elohistic collection because the divine epithet "Yahweh" (LORD) is replaced in virtually all instances by the more common epithet "God" (Heb. *'elohim*). The Elohistic collection consists of two small compilations, namely the Korah psalms (Psalms 42–49) and a Davidic compilation (Psalms 51–72). This collection also includes one Asaph psalm, namely, Psalm 50. The other Asaph psalms (Psalms 73–83) occur in Book III.

It appears probable that the Korah collection (Psalms 42–49; cf. also Psalms 84–85 and 87–88) originated with the Korahites. As temple singers, the Korahites played an important part in the Jerusalem temple cult, especially during the Second Temple period (cf. 1 Chr 9:19; 2 Chr 20:19). It is striking that Jerusalem, the city in which the LORD dwells, plays an important part in the Korah psalms. In these psalms the dwelling place of God is interpreted in a wider sense than just the temple because the temple mount, Zion, and the city of Jerusalem are included.

Psalms 42 and 43
(*see* Individual Laments, 366-73)

Psalm 44

The main issue regarding Psalm 44 is the sharp contrast — some would even call it a contradiction — between vv. 1-8 and vv. 9-16. This issue can be illustrated by the following examples: "you with your own hand drove out the nations" (v. 2) and ". . . you have saved us from our foes . . ." (v. 7), which seem to contradict: ". . . you have rejected us and abased us" (v. 9). On the one hand God is credited for his saving actions toward his people, and on the other he is reproached for casting them off and humiliating them.

The psalm can be divided into the following four strophes:

1. Recollection of salvation history and utterances of trust in God (vv. 1-8)
2. Blaming God for the present disaster and for rejecting his people (vv. 9-16)
3. A declaration of their innocence (vv. 17-22)
4. A plea for help (vv. 23-26).

The first part (44:1-3) of the first strophe recalls God's saving acts toward Israel. The present generation reinterprets and relives the past and makes it its own. The dispossession of the Canaanites and their (i.e., the Israelites') possession of the land was not a consequence of their own achievements or the strength of their armies, but a result of God's direct intervention. It was by God's "hand," by his mighty strength, that Israel was "planted" in Canaan. The second part (vv. 4-8) continues in the same vein. The saving acts of the past give them confidence for the present. The present generation affirms their faith in God. The psalmist confesses that God is "my King and my God" (v. 4). This forms the keynote of the whole section and of the entire psalm. Everything that was said of God in the past is true. It is God alone who can give victory; therefore, he deserves the continuous praise and gratitude of his people.

The second strophe (44:9-16) is in direct contrast to the first part of the psalm. The recollection of the glorious past and trust in God are replaced by the reproach of God and total disillusionment with the present situation. The complaint against God can be summarized in the words of v. 9: "Yet you have rejected us. . . ." By using in succession ten verbs in which God is the subject, all the blame is placed squarely on him (cf. vv. 9-14).

44:9-11 describe how God has "rejected" his people, and vv. 12-14 show how he has abased and humiliated them. God in whom they have placed their trust has abandoned them. Because he has "not gone out with" their armies, they have suffered a devastating defeat: his people have been slaughtered, their possessions plundered, and some of them sold as slaves in a humiliating way to the enemy. To crown it all, they have been scorned and mocked by the enemy. The blame is brought to a climax in v. 15 in which an individual voices the following reproach: "All day long my disgrace is before me. . . ." Although there is no precise information in the psalm to link it to a particular historical situation or military defeat, it appears that the most appropriate era is the exilic period.

The third strophe (44:17-22) states even more starkly that God's actions toward his people are beyond comprehension and mysterious: if they were unfaithful to God the present disasters would be a just penalty, but the fact of the matter is that they were loyal to God in every aspect. They respected the covenant and obeyed the most important commandment, namely, to worship God only. They have not forgotten God, but he has forgotten them. They expected him to protect them and to be with them, but he has crushed them. Why does God act in such a way? This is the enigma of Psalm 44.

Although the perplexing problem is not solved, the psalm nevertheless concludes with a petition for help. God remains their final hope. The fourth strophe (44:23-26) is characterized by imperatives addressed to God and by "Why" questions. By implementing mainly military terminology and by using four imperatives God is beseeched to intervene on behalf of his people: "Rouse yourself . . . "; "Awake . . . "; "Rise up . . . "; "Redeem us. . . ." The questions addressed to God express the existential need of the people and are an additional appeal to God to come to their help: "Why do you sleep . . . ?" "Why do you hide . . . ?" "Why do you forget . . . ?" The last word in the psalm is the "steadfast love" of God. Even though the mystery of God's inactivity is not answered, the covenant community's faith in God prevails. The "steadfast love" remains the only ground for their existence.

Psalm 45

In the case of Psalm 45 a distinction has to be made between the original meaning of the psalm and the history of its interpretation, especially in the Jewish and the Christian traditions.

Psalm 45 is unique in being a "profane" royal wedding song. It is also in this context that part of the superscript ("A love song"; the expression "according to Lilies" is probably an indication of the melody to which the psalm was sung) should be interpreted. However, in the Jewish and Christian traditions the psalm was read allegorically and interpreted in a messianic way. In Heb 1:8-9 the psalm is applied directly to Jesus Christ: "But of the Son he says, 'Your throne, O God, is forever and ever. . . .'" The ancient Christian church considered the relationship portrayed between the king and his bride in Psalm 45 as a reflection of the relationship that exists between Christ and his church. However, the psalm itself does not provide any indication of such an allegorical meaning.

The structure of the psalm can be summarized in the following manner:

A personal opening word by the poet (v. 1)
Praise of the king (vv. 2-9)
Praise of the king's bride (vv. 10-15)
A final word by the poet directed to the king (vv. 16-17).

The psalm forms an *inclusio* in that it is introduced ("I address . . . ," v. 1) and concluded ("I will . . . ", v. 17) by the poet in the first person. A double *inclusio* can be detected because the expression "therefore God has blessed you forever," which occurs in v. 2, recurs in a different form in v. 17: "therefore the peoples will praise you forever and ever."

45:1 is a *self-presentation* in which the poet introduces himself ("my tongue is like the pen of a ready scribe") as well as the theme of his song ("a goodly theme"). Vv. 2-9 deal with the *praise of the king.* Vv. 2-7 in particular concentrate on the king, while vv. 8-9 function as a transition to the next section, which deals with the royal bride. The poet gives an idealized picture of the king, concentrating on his personal beauty (v. 2), his enduring kingship, his military power, and his judicial role, especially as defender of justice. This eulogy may even give the impression that the king is deified. In v. 6 the king is actually addressed as *'elohim* ("god") and ascribed divine attributes ("glory and majesty," v. 3). This entire section should, however, be interpreted within the broad theological context of the Davidic kingship. There is no proof in this text, or in any other OT text, of the deification of the Israelite or Judean monarch as is the case in some ancient Near Eastern civilizations, for example, Egypt, where the king was deified. The Judean king was seen as the representative of God, and there was an intimate relationship between God and the king. He was even seen as the adopted son of God (cf. Ps 2:7), but there was no question of deification. This fact is also brought to the fore in Psalm 45, where the praise section is framed by the expressions:

therefore God has blessed you . . . (v. 2)
Therefore God . . . has anointed you. (v. 7)

These phrases state explicitly that the king is divinely approved and that the LORD is his God. In this sense the psalm and the royal wedding, which is celebrated in song in the psalm, are not "profane" but have a theological basis.

45:8-9 describe the scene of the marriage. The focus is on the splendor of the royal court, the bridegroom dressed in costly clothes, and, as a climax, the royal bride who receives all the attention in the next strophe.

Using typical wisdom language (45:10-15), the poet urges the bride to give up her own land, adapt to her new home and new love, and take up her position as queen. He also advises her to pay homage to the king since "he is your lord." As in the case of the bridegroom, the bride is also described as she appears in the splendor of her bridal clothes and accompanied by her bridal procession.

The last strophe (45:16-17) is again directed to the king. It is in essence a blessing for the king and posterity for a universal monarchy. By mentioning the king's ancestors and sons, the psalmist emphasizes the continuation of the dynasty.

A royal marriage was an important occasion for both the people and the monarchy. Because in OT times the king was regarded as the representative of the LORD and because he was also the instrument through which the people were blessed, the well-being and continuation of the monarchy were important. In this context a royal marriage was an important occasion that had political and religious consequences. Psalm 45 gives a glimpse of such an occasion. In this sense it is not a "profane" song, but it does say that God is totally involved in marriage, human love, and posterity.

Psalm 46

The central theme of Psalm 46 is unconditional trust in God no matter what should happen. This theme is aptly summarized in v. 1 ("God is our refuge . . .") and by the refrain: "The LORD of hosts is with us; the God of Jacob is our refuge" (cf. vv. 7, 11). On the grounds of both the term "Selah" and the refrain, this psalm can be divided into three strophes, namely, vv. 1-3, 4-7, and 8-11. In each of the three strophes the same theme emerges, namely, trust in God when faced with danger and menace.

In the first strophe (46:1-3) the dangers are described as chaotic forces, in other words, cosmic disorder. This strophe states that even if the impossible should happen, namely, that the earth and the mountains — symbols of permanence and security — should crumble and fall, even then God would stand firm. Even if order should change to disorder, the faithful can still place their trust in the LORD. He is an unshakable refuge for his people and has been proved faithful. This trust is expressed as a personal testimony ("we will not fear," v. 2). Three nouns are used in v. 1 to describe God's faithfulness, namely, "refuge," "strength," and "help in trouble."

The second strophe (46:4-7) makes the same statement but looks at it from a different angle. The menace is not portrayed as cosmic forces, however, but as a political disorder: "The nations are in uproar . . ." (v. 6). It is significant that the Hebrew uses the same verbs to describe both the cosmic disorder ("mountains shake" and "waters roar") and the political disorder. In contrast to the raging waters at the end of strophe 1 (v. 3), at the beginning of the second strophe (v. 4) we have the calm waters of the city of God. The paradise motif is used here in combination with the Zion tradition to express the calm, peace, joy, and stability of the city of God. However, this does not refer to the strength or invincibility of the city as such, but rather to the presence of God in the city (v. 5), as also emerges in the refrain. As in the previous strophe, God is described as a helper (cf. vv. 1, 5). To summarize: amid the most terrible menace and danger, safety and security are to be found in God.

In the third strophe (46:8-11) the psalm reaches a climax. This strophe differs from the previous ones in that it is written in direct speech. This strophe is a general appeal, expressed in imperatives, to honor the deeds of the LORD and to confess that he is God ("Come, behold the works of the LORD," v. 8; and "know that I am God!" v. 10). The mighty deeds of the LORD that are described in general terms in v. 8 are specified as warrior's deeds in v. 9. The warrior metaphor is used to describe the LORD. He conducts the war, while his people are just observers. Here, however, an extra dimension is added to the holy war tradition, namely, that the LORD is not a warrior who conducts war but one who brings war to an end. In this sense he is the peacemaker (v. 9). Since the LORD is victor and conqueror, he has the right to determine the conditions of peace: he must be recognized and praised as God to the end of the world (v. 10). In the refrain verse this strophe also spontaneously bears witness to the LORD's omnipotence and the fact that the only security is to be found in him.

Many scholars regard the year 701 BC as the historical context for this psalm, when in a wondrous manner the LORD delivered Jerusalem from the Assyrians' siege during the rule of King Hezekiah (cf. 2 Kgs 18:13–19:36). However, the psalm was probably also used in the postexilic period, when the people of God were suffering, to encourage them and restore their faith in the LORD.

However, the psalm was not a guarantee for the people of God that faith in the LORD gives automatic protection from danger and catastrophes. The context of the psalm alludes to menacing dangers. The people of God experienced danger and suffering throughout their history — particularly during the exilic period when Jerusalem and Zion, the symbols of their security and the presence of the LORD, were destroyed.

Psalm 47

Psalm 47 is a hymn whose central theme is that God is the universal king. The psalm falls into two strophes, namely, vv. 1-5 and 6-9, which are parallel in form:

A^1: Summons to praise God ("Clap your hands . . . ," v. 1)
B^1: Reasons for praising God ("For . . . ," vv. 2-5)

and:

A^2: Summons to praise God ("Sing praise . . . ," v. 6)
B^2: Reasons for praising God ("For . . . ," vv. 7-9).

The psalm is characterized by striking word repetitions. These repetitions enhance the unity of the psalm and highlight the most important themes. The kingship of God plays a central role in the psalm. The psalmist repeats three times that he is "a great king over all the earth" (47:2; cf. also vv. 7, 8). The exalted position and glory of God are further emphasized by using the Hebrew stem *'lh* ("high") three times: "the Most High" (v. 2); "God has gone up" (v. 5); and "he is highly exalted" (v. 9). The themes "nations" (vv. 3, 8), "[all] peoples"/"people of God" (vv. 1, 3, 9), and "all the earth" (vv. 2, 7) fulfill an important role in the psalm. Imperatives praising God occur in vv. 1, 6, and 7. When one considers word repetitions, the theme of Psalm 47 could be stated as follows: God is praised as the great king in his relationship to his own people and all the nations.

The psalm can be divided into two strophes (47:1-5 and 6-9). The first part (A^1, v. 1) of the first strophe uses a parallelism ("Clap your hands . . ."; and "shout to God") and is a universal summons to praise God. In the second part (B^1, vv. 2-5) two reasons are given for the praise. The first (v. 2) is the universal rule of God. The second concerns the election of Israel and is presented as a reflection on the past history of Israel (vv. 3-4). Using military terminology, the psalmist presents the conquest and possession of the land as a sign that the LORD is king. This part of the strophe reaches a climax with the ascendance of God to his throne (v. 5). This part also forms an *inclusio* in that it is introduced by the loftiness of God ("the Most High," v. 2) and concluded with it ("God has gone up," v. 5).

The second strophe (47:6-9) is a mirror image of the first strophe. The first part of the second strophe (A^2, v. 6) is a summons to praise God. The imperative "sing praises" is repeated five times. The reason for the praise is again the universal kingship of God (cf. vv. 7, 8). Israel and all the people acknowledge and praise God as the exalted king.

Much has been written on the possible cultic and historic setting of Psalm 47 and the other so-called enthronement psalms (Psalms 93, 96–99). One of the most popular hypotheses is that Psalm 47 is related to a New Year festival in which the LORD was acclaimed king in a way akin to that in which the Babylonian god Marduk was enthroned each year during the autumn festival. Another approach is to interpret the psalm eschatologically, describing God's future rule. Still other scholars propose a variety of specific historic situations during which Israel achieved military victories as settings for Psalm 47.

However, all these hypotheses and proposals are far from convincing, and there are no direct indications in the psalm itself about its historic or cultic setting. If I were to speculate about its setting, I would opt for the exilic/postexilic period. It was during that time that the people of God were disillusioned by their kings and monarchy and acclaimed the LORD as the universal and eternal king.

Psalm 48

Psalm 48 has a hymnic character, praising God's greatness and the glory of his city (Jerusalem and Mt. Zion) in the same breath. It praises God in Jerusalem and Zion, for they are symbols of his presence and protection. Their strength and glory are due to his presence. V. 1 summarizes the contents of the psalm: "Great is the LORD . . . in the city of our God." The first strophe (48:1-3) focuses on God as the great king and on the impregnability of the city of God. Zion is described in a hyperbolic way as the center of the earth.

The second strophe (vv. 4-8) describes two contrasting reactions to the greatness of God and the impregnability of Zion. On the one hand the hostile kings who were aligned against Zion saw it and were panic-stricken and horrified. Two similes are used to describe this reaction in greater detail, namely, that of a "woman in labor" (v. 6) and that of a devastating storm (v. 7). On the other hand, "we" — referring to the worshipers of the LORD — also saw (v. 8) the city, but seeing it through the eyes of their faith they interpret and recognize it as the stronghold and symbol of God's presence. This contrast further highlights the greatness of God and contributes to his praiseworthiness.

In the third strophe (48:9-11) God is addressed directly for the first time. Using second person suffixes superfluously, the psalmist lists the "attributes" of God: "your steadfast love," "your temple," "your praise," "your right hand," and "your judgments." This description emphasizes the reliability, the power, and the protective presence of God and serves as the basis for the summons to praise contained in v. 11. This praise is not confined to the surrounding towns, but states that God should receive worldwide recognition.

The fourth strophe (48:12-14) is a summons to view the city and to scrutinize it: "Walk about Zion. . . ." The purpose is to keep the tradition alive by telling it to the next generation and by confessing that the LORD is God and that he has proved himself to be a guide and a protector of his people forever and ever.

Psalms 46, 47, and 48 form a trilogy. The theme of Psalm 46 is that God is a true refuge whatever may happen. The city of God is a symbol of his protection and presence. Psalm 47 is a hymn whose central theme is that the LORD is the universal king. Psalm 48 combines the themes of the preceding two psalms and carries them to a climax by praising God as the great king who provides refuge for his people by means of his stronghold, Jerusalem. A king, albeit a human king, is also the central character in Psalm 45. One of the keynotes of Psalm 44 is that God is confessed as king. These examples indicate that the various psalms do not appear in a random sequence but that the final editors had a definite purpose in mind when they arranged the psalms.

Psalm 49

Psalm 49 is a wisdom psalm and, like Psalm 37, addresses the problems and issues of life. In fact, the psalm attempts to give answers to the questions of life and guidelines for everyday living (cf. vv. 1-4). It is a didactic psalm in the sense that it aims to convey a certain general truth of life.

The psalm deals with the question of the value of

wealth. The psalmist apparently lives in a society where wealth is highly respected and in which the perception exists that wealth can give one permanence, security, and power. One might also deduce from the psalm that there was tension between the rich and the poor.

The truth that the psalm attempts to convey is that death is the great equalizer. People cannot take their wealth with them to the grave. They must leave it behind for others. However, Psalm 49 is not a rejection of wealth as such, but rather a rejection of those who place all their trust in wealth (v. 6) and who believe that they can put everything right with wealth. For those, a great surprise is in store. Their destination is the grave, and they cannot ransom their wealth from death.

The refrain verses (cf. 49:12, 20) put this in a nutshell: those who put their trust in wealth are like animals whose path leads only to the grave.

Typically of wisdom literature, Psalm 49 is characterized by contrasts. The greatest contrast exists between those who trust in wealth and those who put their faith in God. The contrast can be most clearly seen when one looks at the use of the word "ransom" in the psalm:

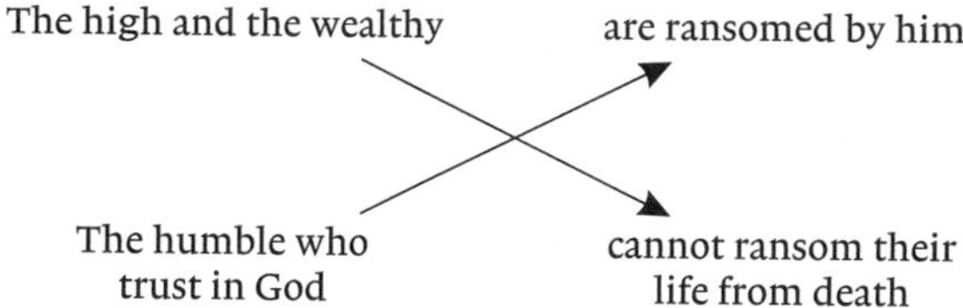
The high and the wealthy
are ransomed by him
The humble who trust in God
cannot ransom their life from death

Here is a chiasm showing an exchange of power. 49:15 is the verse where the contrast emerges most clearly and the only verse where God is the subject: "But God will ransom my soul from the power of Sheol. . . ." The purpose of the contrast is to say that God is mightier than wealth and prosperity. What wealth cannot do, God can do.

Psalm 49 has the function of persuading. By contrasting the futility of wealth with the power of God, the psalmist hopes to convince the reader/listener not to trust in wealth but in God. The psalm also has a pastoral, comforting function. It probably was intended to encourage people who had suffered financially and socially. It could possibly have been situated in the postexilic period when people did experience this type of hardship. Psalm 49 is a relevant psalm — for both the wealthy and the underdogs of society.

Psalm 50

Psalm 50 is one of the psalms which bears the title "A Psalm of Asaph" (cf. Psalms 73–83, where the same title appears). According to Chronicles (cf. 1 Chr 15:17, 19; 2 Chr 29:30), Asaph was an important temple singer in the time of David. We do not know much more about Asaph, and the titles are not an indication of authorship, nor are they of any assistance in dating the psalm.

The psalm can be divided into the following strophes:

1. Introduction, vv. 1-6: God, in his capacity as judge, is the speaker.
2. God's words to the righteous, vv. 7-15: the emphasis falls on the correct way of making sacrifices.
3. God's words to the "wicked," vv. 16-22: they are rebuked for their wrongdoing.
4. Summary, v. 23: the words of God regarding the right attitude when sacrificing.

Throughout the psalm the emphasis falls on the utterances of God. This is evident in the first strophe (50:1-6), where there is a climactic choice of verbs (". . . speaks and summons," v. 1; "He calls," v. 4) to express God's actions as a mighty "judge" (vv. 4, 6). The psalm uses theophanic language (cf. Psalm 18) in v. 3 to describe God's awe-inspiring coming as a judge: "before him is a devouring fire. . . ."

Heaven and earth (50:4) are summoned to bear witness to God's judgment. The first strophe sets the scene for God's judgment, to which the remainder of the psalm is devoted.

The second strophe (50:7-15) contains the first judgment of God and is directed to the righteous. Sacrifices are the main theme of this strophe. What this passage conveys is that God cannot be manipulated by the sacrifices of his people and is not dependent on them because all the beasts of the field belong to him in any case. The strophe reaches a climax in vv. 14 and 15: God wants his people to recognize his "glory" and serve him, and to express this by making the "sacrifice of thanksgiving" in the right spirit. Such people are at liberty to call upon God in their time of need.

The third strophe (50:16-22) contains God's second judgment and is directed at the "wicked." God's judgment is on them because they are merely paying lip service by outwardly accepting the "covenant," which does not find expression in their actions and their daily life. On the contrary, they break all the commandments (cf. vv. 17-20). This strophe concludes with a warning — which one might even call a threat — that God will tear such people to pieces like a lion and that they will have no one to turn to. The last part of this strophe is in striking contrast to the previous one, where God promises salvation to those who serve him in the right way.

The fourth strophe (50:23) is directed to both the righteous and the wicked and sums up the contents of the entire psalm. It also emphasizes "thanksgiving" (strophe 2) and the "right way" (strophe 3).

Sacrifice and the service of one's fellow humans are two sides of the same coin. Because God is the mighty ruler, it is not permissible to try to manipulate him through sacrifices. Those who are in a covenant relationship with God are also expected to obey the second table of the Ten Commandments: service of God includes service of one's neighbor as well.

Certain exegetes have linked Psalm 50 to some specific liturgical occasion, such as the festival of the renewal of the covenant. However, the psalm contains no direct reference to any specific situation or date.

Psalm 51 (*see* Individual Laments, 366-73)

Psalm 52

It is impossible to place Psalm 52 in any of the traditional genres. For this reason the psalm should be approached from another angle. The following aspects should be taken into account: First, the triangular relationship — "God"–"the righteous"–"the evildoer" — plays a dominant part in this psalm (cf. also, e.g., Psalms 9–10). Secondly, the contrast motif has an important function here. By looking at the psalm from these two perspectives, we can gain a greater awareness of all its most important aspects.

1. The "evildoer" is described mainly in 52:1-4. He is represented as a "mighty one," as arrogant. These verses are a direct reproach to the "mighty one," who is depicted as a vilifier, as someone who perpetrates violent deeds with his slanderous and deceitful tongue.

2. "God's" reaction is reflected in v. 5 in the form of a judgment pronounced on the "evildoer." The total destruction of the ungodly is described in four successive verbs of which God is the subject: "God will break you down. . . ." The oppressor will be utterly destroyed, and his tongue will be silenced forever.

3. To emphasize the judgment on sinners even more strongly, the mockery of the "righteous" is described in v. 6.

In the closing verses the contrast motif is again prominent. The "righteous" are sharply contrasted with "evildoers." While "evildoers" face destruction, the "righteous" will be like "a green olive tree in the house of God." The comparison with the olive tree introduces the idea of fertility, abundance, and stability. While the "evildoer" trusts in his wealth to provide security (v. 7), the righteous trusts in the "steadfast love of God." The "evildoer's" attempts to create his own security lead to destruction, but there is a secure future for the "righteous."

The poet uses the device of contrast with a dual purpose in mind: first, as a warning against arrogance, vilification, and the idea that one can obtain security through possessions, and secondly to persuade the reader to trust in God alone.

The title ("when Doeg the Edomite came to Saul") links the psalm to 1 Samuel 22, which contains an account of how Doeg betrayed David. It is by no means certain that this title was originally part of the psalm. It is more likely that the content of Psalm 52 (esp. vv. 1-4, which deal with slander and vilification) gave a later editor the opportunity to link the psalm with the name of Doeg, who was known as an archtraitor (for the expression "Maskil" cf. Psalm 32).

Psalm 53

Psalm 53 is identical, with a few exceptions, to Psalm 14 (cf. the discussion of Ps 14). In this discussion we merely point out the most striking difference between the two psalms, namely, that between Ps 14:5-6 and Ps 53:5:

> There they shall be in great terror,
> for God is with the company of the righteous.
> You would confound the plans of the poor,
> but the LORD is their refuge. (Ps 14:5-6)

> There they shall be in great terror,
> in terror such as has not been.
> For God will scatter the bones of the ungodly;
> they will be put to shame, for God has rejected them. (Ps 53:5)

Although the Hebrew text of Ps 53:5 contains numerous problems and is therefore difficult to interpret, it is nevertheless possible to define the difference between the two psalms as follows: Ps 14:5-6 concentrates on God's relationship with the "righteous." God is the protector of the poor. But in Ps 53:5 there is greater emphasis on God's wrath toward the "ungodly." Strong terms are used to describe God's acts of destruction: "For God will scatter the bones of the ungodly . . ." (v. 5b).

Although Psalms 14 and 53 are virtually identical, there is a cardinal difference in the manner in which God is described. The difference is so great that the existence of two separate psalms is justified. There is a possibility that one of the psalms originally formed part of a smaller collection and was subsequently incorporated into the larger collection of psalms. Each psalm probably had its own unique function within its original context.

The title of Psalm 53 is longer and different from that of Psalm 14. There is no certainty about the meaning of the word "Mahalath." For the term "Maskil," see Psalm 32.

Psalms 54, 55, 56, and 57 (*see* Individual Laments, 366-73)

Psalm 58

The central theme of this psalm is that those who wield judicial power and who might be expected to conduct themselves justly may be the very ones whose actions are unjust and who commit acts of violence.

The psalm forms a closed unit in that it is introduced by a question: "Do you judge people fairly?" (v. 1) and is concluded by a succinct profession of belief: "surely there is a God who judges on earth" (v. 11), which may be regarded as an answer to the question in v. 1. These two verses are intentionally contrasted (cf. the verb "judge," which occurs in both vv. 1 and 11, and the expression "on earth," which occurs in both vv. 2 and 11). V. 1 deals with earthly rulers (the word "gods" in v. 1 refers to earthly rulers) who act unjustly and who do not fulfill their responsibilities as "judges." V. 11, on the other hand, expresses confidence in God as the only righteous "judge."

In the first strophe (58:1-5) there is a description of the "mighty lords," who are said to be "wicked." Their unjust and violent actions are first described in general terms, after which their treachery and venomousness are brought into sharper focus by similes:

> . . . like the venom of a serpent,
> like the deaf adder . . . (v. 4).

The second strophe (58:6-9) is a direct prayer to God to destroy the "wicked." The violent nature of the "wicked" is highlighted by the use of the metaphor of a lion ("young lions," v. 6). Four similes are used to describe God's judgment of the "wicked":

Let them vanish like water . . .
    like grass let them be trodden . . .
Let them be like the snail that dissolves . . .
    like the untimely birth. . . .

These similes emphasize the ephemeral and transient nature and the weakness of the "wicked." They form a sharp contrast with the similes in v. 4, where the dangerous nature of the wicked is stressed. Instead of being venomous serpents, they will be like water that flows away. The "wicked" will therefore be destroyed by God's actions.

The "righteous" are mentioned directly for the first time in the third strophe (58:10-11). Through the use of judicial terms, especially terms relating to retribution, the "righteous" and the "wicked" are contrasted. The "righteous" will emerge from the struggle as joyous victors because God will reward them (v. 11). In contrast, the blood of the "wicked" will flow. This is the answer to the problem posed in v. 1: When those who are supposed to administer the law fail in their responsibility, God intervenes as a judge, taking revenge on those who are mighty but godless.

The psalm is a strong condemnation of violence and the abuse of power by those who are supposed to wield power justly.

The meaning of the expression "Do not destroy" (cf. the title) is not obvious. For an explanation of the word "Miktam" (cf. the title), see Psalm 16.

Psalm 59 (*see* Individual Laments, 366-73)

Psalm 60

The main theme of the psalm is expressed by the words in 60:1: "O God, you have rejected us. . . ." The psalm ends (cf. v. 10) with almost the same expression: "Have you not rejected us, O God?" We are dealing here with a communal complaint in which God is accused and reproached for rejecting his people and tearing the land apart. The following strophal division suggests itself:

- A^1 First strophe: lament and supplications for help (vv. 1-5).
- B Second strophe: an oracle which emphasizes the proprietary rights of God over Israel (vv. 6-8).
- A^2 Third strophe: lament and supplications for help (vv. 9-12).

The psalm forms an ABA symmetry, with the oracle in the middle. There is an internal tension in the psalm, caused by the contrast between the disaster which has overtaken the people and the land and which is interpreted as rejection (A^1, vv. 1-5; A^2, vv. 9-12), and the proprietary rights (B, vv. 6-8) of God over the land. How can God reject his own country and his own people? In this respect Psalm 60 has a lot in common with Psalm 44.

In the first strophe (A^1, vv. 1-5), in which the catastrophe is described in cosmic terms and by means of metaphors (cf. "the land to quake," v. 2; "wine to drink . . . ", v. 3), and in the third strophe (A^2, vv. 9-12), the laments and prayers are directed to God. The complaint against God is that he allowed his own people to suffer (cf. v. 3) and that he did not go out with their armies (v. 10), with the result that the enemy vanquished them. The supplications addressed to God are that he should restore the land and the people (v. 1; cf. also v. 2), and that he should answer his people's prayers by giving them the victory over their enemies (cf. vv. 5, 11).

The second strophe (B, 60:6-8) is cast in the form of direct speech. The strophe is written as a song of victory by a military commander. God is portrayed as the victorious commander to whom the whole land of Israel — on both sides of the River Jordan — belongs. He even controls the neighboring countries ("Moab," "Edom," "Philistia"). Whereas the first and the third strophes speak of the devastated and divided country and of a God who has rejected his people, this second strophe paints a picture of the country as a coherent whole in which God is in control. The purpose of this oracle is probably to show that in the midst of this desperate situation God is in control and can be trusted.

The motif of trust in God is, however, also expressed in 60:12, which is part of the third strophe: "it is he who will tread down our foes." The psalm therefore begins with an expression of no confidence in God (v. 1) and ends with an expression of complete confidence in him (v. 12).

This psalm creates the impression of a poem written after a defeat suffered by the people. It is impossible, however, to determine the exact historical context of the psalm. The final editors of the psalter, who gave this psalm a title (cf. the title "A Miktam of David . . . in the Valley of Salt"), linked the place names and nations mentioned in this psalm (cf. esp. vv. 6-8) with David's victories as described in 2 Samuel 8. The part of the title that reads "according to the Lily of the Covenant" is probably an indication of the melody to which the psalm was sung and is found in variant forms in Psalms 45, 69, and 80. Ps 60:5-12 is repeated in Ps 108:6-13. However, the verses have unique functions within the two psalms and should be interpreted within the context of the psalms in which they occur.

Psalm 61 (*see* Individual Laments, 366-73)

Psalm 62

Psalm 62 is a psalm of confidence. In the midst of dangers, threats, and false accusations the poet continues to trust in God. He finds true rest and security in God, and he exhorts others to trust in God as well.

In 62:1-2 the main theme of the psalm is put very succinctly:

For God alone my soul waits in silence;
from him comes my salvation.
He alone is my rock and my salvation,
my fortress; I shall not be shaken.

The importance of these two verses is evident from the fact that they occur in almost exactly the same form as a refrain in vv. 5-6.

The psalm can be divided into five strophes:

1. In vv. 1-2 confidence is expressed in God. One can trust God because salvation and safety are to be found in him.
2. In vv. 3-4 the suppliant complains about his enemies. They are violent, they plan to overthrow other people, and they delight in lies.
3. Verses 5-8 are another expression of confidence and are virtually identical to vv. 1-2.
4. Verses 9-10 contain a wisdom saying which reflects human transience and unreliability. It is also a warning not to trust in earthly possessions.
5. The psalm ends in vv. 11-12 with an expression of confidence: God alone has power and he will repay all according to their work.

The function of the psalm is to persuade the reader to trust in God in all circumstances. The poet uses contrasts to achieve this purpose. People can trust God because he is powerful and is the source of salvation. Human beings cannot be trusted because they are insignificant, ephemeral, and unreliable. There is a striking contrast between the way in which God and people — probably the enemies of the suppliant — are described in the psalm:

GOD	HUMANS
my salvation (62:1, 2, 6)	falsehood (v. 4)
my (mighty) rock (vv. 2, 6, 7)	a breath (v. 9)
my fortress (vv. 2, 6)	lighter than a breath (v. 9)
(my) refuge (vv. 7, 8)	delusion (v. 9)
power (v. 11)	

The Hebrew word *'ak* (only/alone) is prominent in this psalm, occurring no fewer than six times. When this word is used with reference to God, it emphasizes that we can trust God alone ("For God alone . . . ," vv. 1, 5; "He alone," vv. 2, 6). When it is used of people, however, the emphasis falls on their deceit ("their only plan is to bring down a person of prominence," v. 4) and their ephemeral nature ("Those of low estate are but [= "only"] a breath," v. 9).

In the last strophe (62:11-12) God is addressed directly for the first time (cf. v. 12). It becomes apparent that faith and trust in God is a personal matter to the suppliant. This should culminate in a personal profession of faith.

The function of the psalm is to persuade the reader to trust in God alone and at all times. 62:8 sums up the purpose of the psalm: "Trust in him at all times, O people. . . ."

The proper name "Jeduthun," which occurs in the title (cf. also Pss 39:1; 77:1), refers to one of David's chief musicians (cf. 1 Chr 16:41). This liturgical title is, however, of little use in helping to determine the original historical situation of the psalm.

Psalms 63 and 64
(*see* Individual Laments, 366-73)

Psalm 65

Psalm 65 is a hymn in praise of God. The psalm can be divided into the following three strophes:

1. The praiseworthy God in Zion (vv. 1-4).
2. The Savior God in control of the entire cosmos: history of salvation, and creation (vv. 5-8).
3. God takes care of the earth and makes it fruitful (vv. 9-13).

The first strophe (65:1-4) concentrates on God's presence in Zion. The strophe forms an *inclusio* in the sense that it begins with "Zion" (v. 1) and ends with "your holy temple" (v. 4). The temple therefore fulfills an important function in this strophe (cf. also "your courts," v. 4a; and "your house," v. 4b). Another characteristic of this strophe is the expression "to you," which is repeated no fewer than three times. This repetition emphasizes that God should be praised, that he hears prayers, and that he forgives sin when it is confessed to him. The content of this strophe can be summed up in the words "the goodness of your house" (v. 4). The subject of this strophe is therefore the congregation who find themselves in the presence of God, who is worthy of praise.

The second strophe (65:5-8) is a hymnic description of God's mighty deeds as redeemer and creator of the entire cosmos. This section also forms an *inclusio* in that it is introduced and concluded by similarly worded expressions: "you are the hope of all the ends of the earth" (v. 5); and "Those who live at the earth's farthest bounds . . ." (v. 8). These expressions emphasize the universality of God's salvation and creative power. The expression "you answer us" in v. 5 is reminiscent of the previous strophe ("O you who answer prayer!" v. 2), and God's presence in the temple is linked to his acts of salvation toward his people. In this strophe the emphasis falls chiefly on the creative power of God, who created order by subduing the forces of chaos: "You silence the roaring of the seas. . . ." The effect of God's creative power is to make the whole of the earth — from east to west — burst forth in a song of rejoicing.

In the third strophe (65:9-13) the poet uses rich imagery and hyperbolic terms to describe how God cares for nature, the plants, people, and the animals. In v. 9 this idea is expressed in general terms; then it is worked out in detail in vv. 10-14: God drenches the earth with rain. He supplies the people with wheat. He is the source of fertility and abundance. Even the wilderness is luxuriantly green, and the livestock are fat. Like the second strophe, this strophe ends with "joy" (v. 13). All of nature bursts into song in praise of God, who crowns "the year . . . with bounty" (v. 11).

It is difficult to determine the exact historical and cultic situation of the psalm. The last strophe in particular (65:9-13) may well refer to a good rainy season and harvest. Psalm 65 is a stirring hymn of praise in which God — the God whose presence is so strongly felt in the temple — is praised for his forgiveness, his awe-inspiring deeds of salvation toward his people, his creative power, and his loving and abundant care for nature, his people, and the animals.

Psalm 66

The psalm consists of two major sections, namely, 66:1-12, a collective hymn, and vv. 13-20, an individual song of thanksgiving. Although some exegetes read these two parts as originally two separate psalms, the collective praise in vv. 1-12 does provide an effective context for the individual song of thanksgiving in vv. 13-20. God's mighty deeds of salvation toward his people give the individual believer a reason for thanksgiving. This psalm indicates that the faith of the community and that of the individual cannot be separated; instead their voices should be raised in unison to the glory of God.

Although the psalm can be divided into two major parts, further minor strophic divisions are possible. The first strophe (66:1-4) is characterized by four successive imperatives to praise: "Make a joyful noise. . . ." The reasons why God should be praised are couched in general terms, in references to "your deeds" and "your great power" (cf. v. 3). The use of the expression "all the earth" as a frame for the strophe (cf. vv. 1, 4) indicates that this is an all-embracing invocation to praise and that everyone should participate.

The second strophe (66:5-7) also begins with an imperative. While the first strophe speaks in general terms of the deeds of God, God's deeds of salvation are more closely defined here as the passage through the Sea of Reeds (v. 6) and the passage through the Jordan (v. 6). The exodus from Egypt (cf. also Exodus 14–15) and the entry into the land (cf. Joshua 3) are seen as God's supreme deeds of deliverance. In consequence of God's deeds of salvation his own people should rejoice in his power, and the nations should subject themselves to him.

The third strophe (66:8-12) is also introduced by an imperative in which the nations are called upon to praise God. The reasons for the invocation are given in v. 9 and in v. 12: God is praised for preserving his people and giving them a place to live. These reasons frame vv. 10-12a, in which various trials which have befallen the people are described in metaphorical language:

> For you, O God, have tested us;
> you have tried us as silver is tried.
> You brought us into the net;
> you laid burdens on our backs;
> you let people ride over our backs;
> we went through fire and through water; . . .

These trials did not come about by chance but were sent by God and are witnesses to his "great power" (cf. also v. 3). Despite the powerful imagery of this description, it is so ambiguous that it is difficult to link it to a specific historical situation. It could refer to the exodus, the journey through the wilderness, the passage through the Jordan, or the occupation of the land, but it could also refer to a specific situation at the time of the writing of the psalm.

In the fourth strophe (66:13-15) there is a deviation from the previously used first person plural forms, and this strophe is characterized by the use of four verbs in the first person singular. The poet wants to make sacrifices to God as a personal expression of gratitude to him. This aspect is strongly emphasized by the abundance of cultic terminology and the words "I will . . . ," which are repeated four times.

The fifth strophe (66:16-19) is also introduced by a double imperative ("Come and hear . . ."; cf. also v. 5). The poet is still speaking in the first person, but in these verses he is telling his fellow believers that God has heard him. He is sharing a personal experience of faith with fellow believers.

The psalm is concluded with a sixth strophe (66:20) in which it is carried to a climax with a blessing in which God is praised by the poet for having heard his prayers and shown him "steadfast love."

In this psalm, therefore, the faith of the community and that of the individual complement each other. Psalm 66 indicates that faith cannot be practiced except within the context provided by a community of faith and that it needs to be expressed in the individual's personal relationship with God.

Psalm 67

The most important problem of interpretation revolves around the question whether the psalm refers to the past or the future. This problem is especially pertinent in 67:6. If we translate v. 6 as "May the earth yield its harvest," we could regard the psalm as a prayer for the future. My view, however, is that Psalm 67 is a song of thanksgiving for what God has already done and that v. 6 should therefore be translated (as in the NRSV), "The earth has yielded its increase."

The psalm can be divided into three strophes, namely, vv. 1-2, vv. 3-5, and vv. 6-7. The psalm is characterized by a symmetrical structure. The symmetry consists in the striking similarities between the first (vv. 1-2) and the third strophes (vv. 6-7), with the middle strophe (vv. 3-5) also showing a symmetrical structure in the form of the refrain (cf. vv. 3, 5):

A May God be gracious to us and bless us (v. 1)
B Let the peoples praise you, O God; . . . (v. 3)
B Let the peoples praise you, O God; . . . (v. 5)
A May God continue to bless us. . . . (v. 7)

Another characteristic of the psalm, which is related to the symmetry and the refrain, is the striking word repetitions. The word repetitions clearly reflect the most important themes of the psalm: The verb "bless" occurs three times (67:1, 6, 7) — once in the first strophe and twice in the third; the word "earth" occurs in each of the strophes — once in the first two strophes (vv. 2, 4) and twice in the last strophe (vv. 6, 7); the words "nations" and "peoples" occur numerous times (vv. 2, 3, 4, 5); and the word "all," which conveys God's all-embracing salvation and the idea of universality, recurs frequently throughout the psalm (cf. vv. 2, 3, 5, 7).

Psalm 67 is a persuasive text. First of all, this text tries to persuade the hearer or reader to thank and praise God for his presence, which is described as conferring salvation and blessing. In the first strophe (vv. 1-2) God's deeds of salvation are described in general terms. In the second strophe (vv. 3-5) there is a prominent use of judicial terminology to describe God's just dealings with the "nations." The third strophe (vv. 6-7) is chiefly concerned with the fact that it is God's blessing that causes the earth to yield a good harvest.

God's blessings and his deeds of salvation are not, however, restricted to his own people. His power extends to other people as well. They should also be brought to acknowledge God's deeds of salvation: "Let the peoples praise you, O God. . . ." God also blesses the earth on which the people live. Without God's blessing the earth cannot yield a harvest.

Psalm 67 tells us that this God, whose deeds of salvation are so comprehensive that they embrace his own people, all the nations, and even the earth, commands our praise and gratitude.

Psalm 68

Psalm 68 is considered to be one of the most problematic psalms, if not the most difficult psalm in the whole psalter. The main reason for the interpretative problems is that there is thought to be a lack of cohesion and unity in the psalm. Corruptions in the text are a further complication, and consequently Psalm 68 presents many problems relating to textual criticism. The psalm also contains numerous unfamiliar terms, which are not found elsewhere in the OT. In addition, there are widely divergent opinions about the dating of the psalm and its exact place and function in the cult.

The underlying theme of the psalm could be formulated as follows: God is described as a mighty warrior and king marching triumphantly through history to occupy his sanctuary on Zion in Jerusalem:

> . . . the Lord came from Sinai into the holy place.
> You ascended the high mount. . . . (vv. 17-18)

God's presence in the temple therefore plays a central part in the psalm (cf. vv. 16, 17, 24, 29, and 35).

As a warrior, God is a destroyer of his foes (68:21) but at the same time a savior to his own people (v. 20). The psalm reaches a climax with the statement that God gives his people "power and strength" (v. 35). Like a benevolent earthly monarch, God, the great king, takes care of the marginalized figures in society. He serves as the "father of orphans and protector of widows" (v. 5). He gives the "desolate" shelter and shows charity to the "prisoners" (v. 6).

The psalm also emphasizes God's past deeds of deliverance (cf. 68:7-18). Salvation history is described as a journey from Sinai to Zion. The deliverance which spanned centuries is sketched with a few strokes of the pen. The psalm refers to the journey through the wilderness and God's revelation on Sinai (vv. 7-8), the occupation of the land and the conquest of the nations (vv. 11-14), and the time when God took up his abode in the sanctuary in Jerusalem (vv. 15-18) where the kings of the nations came to honor him as the great king (v. 29).

The purpose of this description is to emphasize the greatness and almighty power of God. It is self-evident that the psalm has a hymnic function. The hymnic aspect finds expression chiefly in the invocations to praise and thanksgiving which are a recurrent theme in the psalm (cf., e.g., vv. 4, 19, 26). The psalm is concluded by three successive imperatives (cf. vv. 32, 34) to praise and reaches a climax with the exclamation "Blessed be God" (v. 35). The power of God is further underlined by a theophanic description (cf. also Psalm 18) which emphasizes God's awe-inspiring presence: "the earth quaked, the heavens poured down the rain . . ." (cf. v. 8). Mythological terminology which is probably of Canaanite origin and in which God is described as the God of storms (v. 4; cf. also v. 33) is employed to describe God's greatness.

Although it is impossible to establish the original historical and cultic context of the psalm and although there is a wealth of interpretative problems attached to this psalm, its gist can nevertheless be summed up in the words of 68:34, in which God is described as follows:

> God . . . whose majesty is over Israel;
> and whose power is in the skies.

This is the God who is praiseworthy and in whom his people can find shelter. Psalm 68 therefore aims to persuade its readers of the almighty power and greatness of God.

Psalms 69, 70, and 71
(*see* Individual Laments, 366-73)

Psalm 72

Psalm 72 corresponds to Psalms 2, 45, and 110 in that the king is the principal figure in each. In this respect Psalm 72 can be regarded as a royal psalm; it may be more closely defined as a prayer for the king. This emerges clearly in the very first verse of the psalm, in which a prayer is directed to God on behalf of the king: "Give the king your justice, O God. . . ." The remainder of the psalm consists chiefly of jussives in which intercession is made for the performance of the king's official duties. The concluding verses of the psalm (vv. 18-20) consist of an exhortation to praise God.

The title, "Of Solomon," does not necessarily indicate that Solomon was the author or that the psalm dates from Solomon's time. On the contrary, linguistic evidence seems to indicate that the psalm was written long after Solomon's time. The question that arises is: Why is the psalm linked with Solomon — probably by a later editor who added the name of Solomon in the superscript? The first point to note is that Psalm 72 is not a realistic description of a specific king but a delineation of the characteristics of the ideal king. The terms used to describe the king in this psalm verge on hyperbole (e.g., "May he live . . . as long as the moon," v. 5). Since Solomon was traditionally regarded as the most prosperous king of Israel, a later editor would readily have linked Solomon's name with this psalm. Secondly, there are points of correspondence between Solomonic history and Psalm 72 (cf. v. 8 with 1 Kgs 4:21 and 24; v. 10 with 1 Kgs 10:1 and 22; and v. 15 with 1 Kgs 10:22).

For a thorough understanding of Psalm 72 it is necessary to know that there was a special relationship between God and the king of Israel. The king was regarded as God's surrogate on earth. He acted as the intermediary between God and the people and ruled on behalf of God. The kingship of the king was a commission from God. Although the king of Israel was not deified as were the kings of some of the peoples of the ancient Near East, he was nevertheless regarded as the adopted son of the LORD (cf. Psalm 2). Unlike Psalm 2, however, Psalm 72 does not deal with the relationship between God and the king. In Psalm 72 the emphasis falls on the way in which the king carries out his basic task and the consequences of his reign.

In 72:2-4 and 12-14 the essential task of the king emerges clearly, namely, to defend the cause of the poor. It is his duty to serve as the redeemer and the helper of the needy, the poor, and the weak. It is the king who must ensure that "righteousness" prevails and that "oppression" and "violence" are countered. The role played by the king mirrors the kingship of God because God is frequently described as the protector of underdogs (cf., e.g., Ps 68:5).

The supplications in Psalm 72 serve to emphasize the immutability and permanence of the king and his reign: "May his name endure forever . . ." (v. 17; cf. also vv. 5-7). Psalm 72 also contains supplications regarding the scale of the king's dominion and the subordination of other peoples: "May he have dominion from sea to sea . . ." (v. 8; cf. also v. 11). Then, too, Psalm 72 emphasizes the benefits of kingship for the country, all its peoples, and even other nations: "May there be abundance of grain in the land . . ." (v. 16) and "May all nations be blessed in him . . ." (v. 17). As an intermediary between God and his people and as the representative of God, the king is the source of abundant "peace" (v. 7).

Psalm 72 is not the realistic description of an actual king, but an idealization of Israelite kingship. It is probable that this idealization was created during a period when the king was failing to fulfill his basic responsibilities. The psalm could even have been written after the monarchy had ceased to exist. In this sense the psalm is a desperate appeal by the people to God and reflects the expectation that God, the true king, will come to their aid.

It is scarcely surprising that Psalm 72 ends with an exhortation in praise of God (v. 18; cf. also v. 19). This exhortation to praise diverts attention from the king and focuses it on God. The reader is reminded that it is the LORD alone who does "wondrous things." The glory of the LORD by far surpasses that of the king.

72:19 ends with the expression "Amen and Amen." This expression, which is generally used to validate an important matter, also occurs at the ends of Book I (Ps 41:14) and Book III (Ps 89:52) of the psalter. Like Psalms 41 and 89, Psalm 72, the last psalm of Book II, ends with the "Amen" blessing and an exhortation to praise.

72:20 reads: "The prayers of David . . . are ended." This subscript indicates that v. 20 probably originally concluded a collection of Davidic psalms. That this is no longer the case in the psalter in its current form is evident from the fact that Psalm 72 is headed "Of Solomon."

Psalm 73

This is the first psalm of Book III, which comprises Psalms 73–89. Psalm 73 is also the first of eleven successive psalms (73–83) which include the word "Asaph" as part of the superscript (for "Asaph" cf. Psalm 50). This title indicates that Psalms 73–83 made up a smaller collection within the greater unit. Despite numerous attempts to determine the nature of the link between the Asaph psalms, this remains an unresolved question. There have been attempts to link the psalms to the same cultic or historical situation. Some scholars have referred to a common theme (e.g., the covenant) or to word repetitions which occur frequently in this group of psalms.

Psalm 73 deals with the problem of the "prosperity of the wicked" and the adversity suffered by the righteous. The problem confronting the poet of Psalm 73 is: Why do the eyes of the wicked swell out with fatness while the upright suffer adversity? Psalm 73 ponders the same problems as Psalms 37 and 49 and Job, for example. As one might expect of a wisdom psalm, Psalm 73 is an exploration of the meaning of life.

The three principal themes of the psalm are aptly summarized in vv. 1-3:

A: "God is good . . ." (v. 1)
B: The adversity/vexation of the faithful (v. 2)
C: The "prosperity of the wicked" (v. 3)

These three themes are then presented in converse order so that the psalm as a whole takes the form of a mirror image, an ABCcba structure, as follows:

c: Description of the "wicked" (vv. 4-12)
b: Description of the situation of the faithful (vv. 13-16)
a: God is good (vv. 17-28)

The psalm forms an *inclusio* in the sense that it is introduced by the word "good" (v. 1) and concludes with the same word (v. 28).

Although cogent arguments can be advanced for translating the end of the first part of 73:1 as "to the upright" (cf., e.g., NRSV), for example, this would fit in better with the context, there is no convincing textual evidence for such a translation, and the translation "Israel" is to be preferred. The poet is therefore speaking as a member of the people of Israel and expressing a universal truth, namely, that "God is good to Israel."

The wicked are described in greater detail in 73:4-12 (element c). Three aspects in particular emerge: first of all, the wicked are prosperous in every respect and their lives are free from problems. Secondly, they are proud and arrogant and do not submit to God. Thirdly, they are violent. They oppress others and amass riches by dint of robbery. To crown it all, other people find no fault with their actions. On the contrary, the wicked receive praise from others (v. 10). One striking feature of the description of the wicked is that it is made up of physical metaphors ("their bodies," v. 4; "their eyes," "their hearts," v. 7; "their mouths," "their tongues," v. 9). This serves to emphasize the wickedness of their manner of thinking and living.

The lamentable situation of the poet is described in 73:13-16 (element b). His situation forms a striking contrast to the prosperity of the wicked and is also contrary to the universal truth which forms the introduction to the psalm, namely, that "God is good . . . to those who are pure in heart." This is the problem with which the poet is confronted. His attitude to life ("my heart," v. 13) and his way of life ("my hands," v. 13) are pure and blameless. But his upright way of life has not benefited him, as one might have expected on the basis of the adage in v. 1. All has been in vain. In fact, he is continually plagued and chastised. He finds it incomprehensible that he, being innocent, should suffer so much while the wicked flourish.

73:17 is the turning point of the psalm. The situation remains incomprehensible to the poet "until I went into the sanctuary of God." The encounter with God and the presence of God are responsible for his change of heart. He came to realize that the prosperity of the wicked was to be short-lived and that there was no future for them. Whereas destruction is the destiny of the wicked (cf. vv. 18-20), the poet enjoys the permanent protection and presence of God (vv. 23-24). The poet realizes that he has been "stupid and ignorant" (v. 22) to doubt the goodness of God. Although the poet is weak and fragile (v. 26), God is his rock, his source of strength, and his refuge. The realization of the permanent closeness of God is the solution to the psalmist's problem. The psalm therefore ends on a high note:

> Indeed, those who are far from you will perish; . . .
> But for me it is good to be near God;
> I have made the Lord GOD my refuge. . . .
> (vv. 27-28)

This psalm, which begins in doubt and a lack of confidence in God, ends triumphantly.

Psalm 74

For the word "Maskil" in the title, cf. Ps 32:1. For "Asaph," cf. Psalms 73 and 50.

Psalm 74 is a communal lament in which God is entreated to save his people — the people with whom he has a long-standing covenant — from their desperate situation following the destruction of the temple by the Babylonians in 587 BC. It is a theological reflection on the destruction of the temple and the exile.

As is characteristic of laments, *accusatory questions* play an important part in Psalm 74: "O God, why do you cast us off forever?" (v. 1; cf. also vv. 10, 11). It is evident from these questions that the people are reproaching God for their distress. Not only has he withheld his hand but he has continued to cast them off. Their complaint against God is that he is responsible for the destruction of Jerusalem and the exile. They feel that this is aggravated by the fact that he has forsaken the "sheep of his pasture" and the "tribe of his heritage."

Closely related to these accusatory questions is the description of the disaster (cf. 74:4-8). Not only has the sanctuary of God in Jerusalem been totally destroyed and desecrated by the enemy, but "all the meeting places of God in the land" have been burned down. What makes the disaster worse is that communication with God has been disrupted because there is no prophet left to preach God's message in difficult times. The result of all this is that God's honor has been tarnished and his name called in question. The function of both the complaints against God and the description of the disaster is to persuade God to intervene to save them.

74:12-17 form a *hymnic passage* the subject of which is God's mighty deeds of the past. V. 12 provides a summary, and the following verses expand on it:

> Yet my King is from of old,
> working salvation in the earth.

Two aspects of God's past deeds are highlighted here, namely, his acts of salvation and his acts of creation. Great emphasis is placed on God's deeds by placing the personal pronoun "You" — referring to God — at the beginning of a clause in a number of sentences (vv. 13-17). God's acts of salvation and creation are so closely intertwined that they cannot really be separated. God's acts of creation are described here as an ordering of the primal chaos. The images used here are taken from the Caananite creation myths (cf., e.g., "you broke the heads of the dragons in the waters"). This is a polemic description which demonstrates that it is God who is powerful, and not the other gods. The aim of this description was to encourage the people, who were in a desperate situation and were doubting the role of God, while knowing that God is in control of all things. This hymnic description also forms the basis for the prayers for help which follow in vv. 18-23.

74:18-23 form a continuous "prayer," consisting of eight petitions, to God. Some of these prayers are positively formulated (cf., e.g., v. 20, "Have regard for your covenant"), while others are negatively formulated, asking God to prevent something (cf., e.g., v. 19, "do not forget the life of your poor . . .").

The psalm forms an *inclusio* in that it begins and ends with a petition for help:

> Remember your congregation . . . (v. 2)
> remember how the impious scoff at you . . . (v. 22).

The word "remember" sums up the theme of the whole psalm: God is being entreated not to forget his own people during their dire exile, and to prevent the "adversaries" from defiling his name.

Psalm 75

The substance of this psalm is summed up in the last verse (75:10). This verse implies a reversal of power. The "horns" — the symbol of power — of the "wicked" will be destroyed. The "wicked" will be humiliated. The "righteous," on the other hand, will be exalted. It is God who brings about the reversal of power. He does this as judge. The psalm makes it clear that it is God who executes judgment (v. 7; also v. 2). It is because God is the almighty creator that he can also act as judge. While the earth totters (v. 3) and the wicked perish (v. 10), God, the creator of the universe, keeps "its pillars steady" (v. 3b).

Psalm 75 is a condemnation of self-glorification, pride, and arrogance. It is a warning not to be guilty of boasting. This aspect is emphasized by placing three warnings in succession: "'Do not boast . . .'" (cf. vv. 4, 5). The Hebrew word which is rendered "lift up" or "exalt" occurs five times in the psalm (cf. vv. 4, 5, 6, 7, and 10). The striking incidence of this word underlines the theme of human self-aggrandizement and humiliation by God which plays a central role in the psalm: people who try to exalt themselves or each other should realize that it is only God who can do this. Self-exaltation leads to humiliation by God. A familiar metaphor is used to describe judgment on self-exaltation, namely, that of the cup of wine poured out by God, which the wicked shall "drink down to the dregs" (cf. v. 8).

God's actions as judge are also a source of joy and thanksgiving as the people talk about his mighty deeds (cf. 75:1), and the element of thanksgiving and praise occurs again at the end of the psalm (cf. v. 9). There is no consensus regarding the meaning and translation of the expression "Do Not Destroy" (cf. also Psalms 57, 58, and 59) which occurs in the title. These may well be the opening words of a well-known song, possibly referring to the tune to which the psalm should be sung.

Psalm 76

Psalm 76 is an expression of the awesome power of God. The element of praise occurs right at the beginning — ". . . his name is great in Israel" (v. 1) — and also concludes the psalm: "Make vows to the LORD . . ." (v. 11).

The metaphor of God as a warrior is used to underline his praiseworthiness and power. God inflicts a crushing defeat on enemies: "he broke the flashing arrows . . ." (v. 3; cf. also vv. 5 and 6).

There is a contrast between God and the enemies. Whereas God is "awesome and glorious" and "more majestic than the everlasting mountains" (v. 4), the enemies are "not able to lift a hand" (v. 5). God is the king "who has his dwelling place in Zion." In contrast, the enemies have been "stripped of their spoil." As in Psalm 75, the judgment of God plays an important part in this psalm. On the one hand, God's judgment inspires fear in the "kings of the earth." They cannot remain upright in the face of God's wrath. On the other hand, one consequence of God's judgment is that the "oppressed of the earth" are saved. Although God is seated high in the heavens, he descends to earth in order to help the oppressed.

The manner in which God's victory over the enemies is described is so universal that it is virtually impossible to link it to a particular historical situation.

Psalm 77 (*see* Individual Laments, 366-73)

Psalm 78

Psalm 78 is a "historical" psalm in that the greater part of the psalm is devoted to the history of Israel (cf. also Psalms 105 and 106). What we have is not, however, an objective, exact account of historical events. The poet does not present events in historical sequence; in fact, he deviates from the familiar order of events. The poet deals with history selectively, using only those parts of it that are relevant for his purpose. The poet reinterprets the history of God's chosen people in a unique and free manner for his own purposes, so that "history" in Psalm 78 becomes "his story."

The purpose of the psalm could be described as didactic. The poet is using history as a means of bringing an important truth home to his audience. This is why the poet begins like a typical wisdom teacher with an invocation to his audience/readers to listen to him and heed his words: "Give ear, O my people, to my teaching . . ." (v. 1; cf. also vv. 2, 3, 4). The purpose of the teaching is to impress upon the people the "glorious deeds of the LORD, and his might" (v. 4). They cannot be allowed to forget "the works of God," and they should always keep his "commandments" (v. 7). The story of God's deeds of salvation must be handed down from one generation to the next so that all future generations will know about them (cf. vv. 4-6). An important purpose of the narration of history in Psalm 78 is to warn the present generation. They are cautioned not to be as "stubborn and rebellious" as their ancestors (cf., e.g., v. 8).

The poet allows the history of the people of Israel from the exodus to the ascent of the throne by David to unfold before the eyes of his people like a film. As in a good film, however, the events do not take place in strict chronological order. The focus is on specific historical episodes. Certain sections of history are repeated for the sake of emphasis.

To gain a better understanding of the historical perspective of the poet of Psalm 78, we really need to know the historical situation of the poet himself. Unfortunately the psalm itself does not provide us with any very distinct guidelines. However, one could make the deduction from the psalm that the exile of the Northern Kingdom must already have taken place (cf. vv. 62-64, 67) but that the Judean monarchy still existed, and the exile of the Southern Kingdom therefore still lay in the future (cf. vv. 68-70). Psalm 78 should probably be dated at some point between the exile of the Northern Kingdom (721 BC) and that of the Southern Kingdom (586 BC). If this dating is accepted, the psalm could be regarded as a commentary on the exile of the Northern Kingdom and a warning to the people of the Southern Kingdom.

In his account of history the poet concentrates mainly on the exodus from Egypt and the wanderings of the people in the desert. The entry into the promised land (78:54-55) and the selection of "Zion" (v. 68) and of David (cf. v. 70) are, however, also mentioned.

There is a discernible pattern in the development of

certain themes in the psalm. After the introductory section (cf. esp. 78:1-8), the following elements are repeated several times: (i) God's mighty deeds of salvation; (ii) the disobedience and rebelliousness of God's people; (iii) God's punitive wrath on account of his people's disobedience; (iv) the people's repentance, and God's merciful forgiveness of their sin.

In his account of the "exodus" (78:12-13, 42-52) the poet places emphasis on the power of God. God's glorious deeds during the exodus are described as "miracles" (vv. 11, 43). The plagues of Egypt (only seven plagues are mentioned instead of the usual ten; cf. vv. 43-51) are depicted as a manifestation of God's power.

The description of the "journey through the wilderness" (78:14-41 and 52-53) emphasizes the all-embracing guidance of God and the fact that he protected his people: "In the daytime he led . . . and all night long . . ." (78:14; cf also v. 52). The poet also emphasizes the abundant care of God for his people during the journey through the wilderness: "He . . . gave them drink abundantly . . ." (v. 15; cf. also vv. 24, 25, 27, and 29). God meets all his people's needs, but in response they show a lack of faith. Two of the main themes of the psalm are the rebelliousness and unfaithfulness of the people. V. 32 sums this up very well: "In spite of all this they still sinned. . . ." The psalmist asserts that the people were stubborn and rebelled against God (cf., e.g., vv. 8, 17, 40, 56); that they were not faithful to God (cf., e.g., vv. 8, 22, 57); that they were unfaithful to his covenant (cf. vv. 10, 37); and that they tested God time and again and provoked him to anger (cf., e.g., vv. 18, 41, 56, 58). The poet uses this perspective on history to persuade the people of his own time to remain faithful to God.

It was to be expected that God would react sharply to this disobedience, and indeed the "wrath" of God is one of the main themes of the psalm: "When God heard, he was full of wrath . . ." (78:59; cf. also vv. 21, 31). The sins of the people caused the wrath of God to descend on them with destructive force. This reaction on the part of God is described in vv. 62-64, where he is said to act as a warrior against his own people. This description is probably a reference to the exile of the Northern Kingdom and a warning to the Southern Kingdom, the realm of King David. The contrast between "Ephraim" (i.e., the Northern Kingdom) and "Judah" (the Southern Kingdom) is striking. While God rejected "Ephraim" he chose "Judah" (vv. 67-68). David, the most famous of the kings of Judah, is described in positive terms (vv. 70-72). He is the shepherd of his people, and he led his people with a "skillful hand." One can deduce from this description that this psalm originated in Judah and that the intention was to legitimize the dynasty of David and the Southern Kingdom above that of the Northern Kingdom.

There is no such thing as objective historiography. All historiography, even that of the OT, is to some extent subjective. Psalm 78 provides evidence that even in poetry history can be used to bring home an important message to people. This didactic psalm uses the history of Israel to warn the people on the one hand but also to comfort and reassure them that God is in control of history.

For the title "Maskil," see Psalm 32.

Psalm 79

Psalm 79 is a communal lament and is closely related to Psalms 44 and 74. Conditions during the destruction of Jerusalem and the Babylonian exile in 587 BC comply best with the description found in Psalm 79. The two principal motifs in the psalm are the prayers that God should help his own people and that he should punish the nations.

The psalm can be divided into the following strophes:

The lament (vv. 1-4)
The supplication (vv. 5-12)
Trust and praise (v. 13).

The first strophe (79:1-4), and therefore also the psalm as a whole, is introduced by the name of God. In the lament the appeal is directed to God. The reason for the lament, namely, that the nations have invaded the land, is given in vv. 1-3. Five verbs are used to describe the devastating invasion. Not only did God's enemies invade his territory, his country, but they also injured his honor by defiling his holy temple and laying waste Jerusalem. Worst of all, they bitterly humiliated the people of God by refusing to bury the bodies of the fallen. The descriptions in vv. 1-3 culminate in the actual lament in v. 4, namely, that they have become a laughingstock in the eyes of their neighbors.

The second strophe (79:5-12) consists chiefly of supplications in the form of jussives and imperatives. However, even the supplications are introduced by a reproachful question: "How long, O LORD? Will you be angry forever?" It is apparent from this that the people were reproaching God for the dreadful disaster which had befallen them. Worst of all, it appeared to them that there would be no end to their ills. Their reproaches culminate in the question in v. 10: "Why should the nations say, 'Where is their God?'" It was because God was not there, because he was conspicuous by his absence, that they had been overtaken by all these misfortunes. Furthermore, they had to suffer the humiliation of having the nations rubbing it in that their God was not with them.

The second strophe is dominated by supplications directed to God. Their two main prayers to God are for vindication against the nations and for help and salvation for themselves. Just as the nations have poured out blood all around Jerusalem (79:3), God should pour out his anger on the nations (v. 6) in order to avenge the blood of his servants (v. 12). The taunts of the nations should be avenged sevenfold, that is, in full. The help which they entreat God to give them centers around two matters. First of all, they entreat God to forgive their sins (v. 9; cf. also v. 8). These prayers for the forgiveness of sins are an indication of progression in the psalm: where initially the people blamed God for their desperate situation, they now accept responsibility themselves. Secondly, they entreat God to help them. God's intervention is not to be for his people's sake, however, but for the glory of his name (v. 9).

The psalm reaches a climax in the third strophe (79:13). This strophe expresses trust and culminates in grateful praise. The trust is evident in the image of the shepherd and his sheep.

Psalm 79 reflects the dilemma of a disoriented society. The people accuse God, but they turn to him again in their need. He is the only source of salvation.

For the title "A Psalm of Asaph," cf. Psalm 50.

Psalm 80

Psalm 80 is a communal prayer in which God is entreated for help after a disaster has overtaken his people. The psalm can be divided into three parts, namely, vv. 1-3, vv. 4-7, and vv. 8-19, on the basis of the refrain (cf. vv. 3, 7, 19), which is placed at the end of every strophe. The refrain also epitomizes the theme and function of the psalm:

> Restore us, O God [O God of hosts/O LORD God
> of hosts];
> let your face shine, that we may be saved.
> (vv. 3, 7, 19)

The crisis referred to in Psalm 80 would probably have been the destruction of the country by the Assyrians (cf., e.g., vv. 12, 14). The use of "Joseph" as a synonym for Israel (v. 1) and the references to the tribes "Ephraim," "Benjamin," and "Manasseh" (v. 2) support the supposition that the psalm should be read against the background of the destruction of the Northern Kingdom by the Assyrians during the years 732-722 BC. It is significant that the LXX added the expression "concerning the Assyrians" to the title of Psalm 80.

The first strophe (80:1-3) is a prayer for deliverance and is characterized by a series of appeals to God: "Give ear . . ." (v. 1); "Stir up your might . . ." (v. 2; cf. also the refrain in v. 3). God is addressed directly in the second person throughout. This strongly emphasizes the personal relationship between God and his people. Two metaphors, which serve to provide grounds for supplication, are used to describe God. First of all, the shepherd metaphor (v. 1) is used to bring home the realization that the LORD leads, protects, and cares for his people. Psalm 79 (v. 17) is concluded with the shepherd metaphor. This creates a close tie between Psalm 79 and Psalm 80. The second metaphor is that of God "enthroned upon the cherubim" (cf. also 1 Sam 4:4 and 2 Sam 6:2). According to Exod 25:19-22, the "cherubim" were depicted on the cover of the ark of the covenant. The ark was the symbol of God's presence and especially of the fact that he protected and led his people and gave them victory in war. The "cherubim" metaphor, like the shepherd metaphor, is therefore the symbol of the LORD's protective presence.

The second strophe (80:4-7) deals with the anger of God. The strophe begins with a reproachful question in which the LORD is called to account by his own people: "How long, O LORD? Will you be angry forever?" Israel has become the laughingstock of its neighbors, and it is holding the LORD responsible for its misery.

The third strophe (80:8-19) is characterized by the vine allegory, which is used to describe the way God has dealt with his people throughout history. The vine is frequently used in the OT to describe the relationship between God and his people (cf., e.g., Isa 5:1-7; Ezek 17:5-10; Hos 10:1). The allegory is used here to describe the salvation history of Israel from the exodus from Egypt (80:8), the occupation (v. 8b), and the settlement in the land (v. 9) up to the time of the monarchy when the borders of the country were at their most expansive (v. 11). The vine allegory refers to the exile ("Why then have you broken down its walls . . . ?"; v. 12; cf. also v. 16). Salvation history is here used in support of the complaint in the previous strophe. God is reminded of the past, when he still supported and succored his people, but he is reproached for the fact that he has now abandoned them. Nevertheless, the LORD remains their only hope of deliverance, and they therefore pray to him for help (v. 14; cf. also v. 18).

In the time of crisis the people of Israel perceive God as being far removed from them. Now, however, God must help them and he must cause those who destroyed the vine to perish (v. 16).

The Hebrew word which literally means "turn around" occurs no less than four times in the psalm: three times in the refrain ("Restore . . ."; 80:3, 7, 19), and once in v. 14 ("Turn again . . ."). The content of the psalm is epitomized by this one word: God is being entreated to turn back to his people, to return to them. The psalmist pleads with God to reverse the situation.

The meaning of the title of this psalm is not obvious. For "on Lilies, a Covenant," cf. Psalm 60; for "Asaph," cf. Psalm 50.

Psalm 81

The psalm can be divided into two strophes, namely, vv. 1-5a and vv. 5b-16. The first strophe (vv. 1-5b) is in hymnic style and is a summons to praise God and to celebrate a festival. The second strophe (vv. 5b-16) is an oracle in which God addresses his people in the first person.

The main theme running through the two parts of the psalm is that religious celebration and cultic observance are not in themselves sufficient: the community of faith needs to listen to God as well. In terms of Psalm 81 "listen" means to serve God alone and to walk in his ways (v. 13). The implication of Psalm 81 is therefore that religious celebration can degenerate into superficiality if it is not accompanied by obedience to God.

Although Psalm 81 has a patent association with the cult (cf. v. 3) and is sometimes linked to a specific cultic occasion, such as the autumn feast of Tabernacles or the Passover feast, it is impossible to reconstruct the specific cultic context of the psalm. The date of origin of Psalm 81 is just as difficult to establish.

The first strophe (81:1-5a) is a hymnic exhortation to praise God and to participate in the cult. It is characteristic of the strophe that imperatives are strung together. This is a summons to all-inclusive praise. Both the voice (v. 1) and various musical instruments — percussion instruments (v. 2), stringed instruments (v. 2), and wind instruments (v. 2) — are to be combined in praise. The festival has been appointed by God, the same God who is described here as "the God of Jacob" (cf. vv. 1, 4) and as "God our strength" (v. 1). The motivation for the summons to praise and the celebrations lies in salvation history, namely, the exodus from Egypt (v. 5a). At this cultic festival salvation history is commemorated and brought alive.

The second strophe (81:5b-16) is an oracle in which God speaks to his people in the first person. The strophe begins (v. 5b) in typical prophetic style as if a prophet had introduced the oracle that follows: "I hear a voice I had not known." The main part of this strophe can be summed up in the words of v. 8a: "Hear, O my people, while I admonish you" (cf. also v. 13).

The oracle begins where the hymn is concluded, namely, with the exodus. God reminds his people of salvation history with the object of persuading them to listen to him. But his people have not listened to him (cf. 81:8b, 11), and God has been disillusioned by his own people. The liberation from Egypt was the supreme moment in salvation history (v. 10; cf. also vv. 6-7). However, the LORD also reminds his people of the events at Sinai (v. 7b) and of the journey through the desert (v. 7c). Everything culminates in the admonition that: "there shall be no strange god among you . . ." (v. 9). These words epitomize the content of the First Commandment — in fact, of the entire Ten Commandments. God gives his people a choice. If they will listen to him — that is, do his will — he is prepared to make a new beginning with them. They receive the promise that God will bring their enemies low, but bless his own people abundantly (v. 16). Disobedience to God, however, will lead to disaster (v. 15).

Although Psalm 81 is unique in the sense that religious celebration is combined with a warning to obey God, the psalm nevertheless shows similarities with Psalms 50 and 95 (cf. the discussion of the two psalms).

For the words "The Gittith" in the title of the psalm, cf. Psalm 8.

Psalm 82

The major interpretative problem which has engaged the attention of researchers for many years and which has not been resolved with any certainty is the question what the word *'elohim* in 82:1b and 6 refers to. While one group of scholars is of the opinion that the word refers to people, in particular to human judges, another group contends that the reference here is to gods. The view expressed here supports the latter belief, namely, that the poet is referring to gods. Through the use of metaphorical and mythological language the poet is attempting to persuade his readers of the greatness of God. In contrast to this, the gods are portrayed as insignificant and impotent beings. To this end the poet uses the judge metaphor.

There is a notable *inclusio* in the psalm in that it is introduced by key concepts such as "God" and "judgment/judge" (cf. 82:1) and concluded by the same concepts (cf. v. 8). We can deduce from this that the principal theme of the psalm is the representation of God as a "judge." V. 1 may be regarded as the introduction to the psalm since in this verse God is represented in anthropomorphic terms as judge in the midst of the divine council, an image which is frequently used in the OT (cf., e.g., Ps 29:1). God's acts as judge are spelled out in greater detail in vv. 2-4. God accuses the judges of failing to fulfill their responsibilities (cf. v. 2) because they favor the wicked. In vv. 3-4 God admonishes the gods in four successive imperatives to exercise their judicial function faithfully. The first two imperatives are purely judicial terms, whereas the last two have more to do with the concrete rendering of assistance. The people to whom assistance should be rendered are the marginal figures of society; those who have no support base and who are usually exploited: "the weak," "the orphan," "the lowly," "the needy," "the destitute."

82:5 states emphatically that the gods have no insight, and that in consequence they cannot be judges. Instead of allowing justice to prevail, they behave in such a way that there is total chaos. Any remaining doubt as to who is under discussion here is removed by v. 7, where the gods are designated as mortal. In contrast to this is v. 8, which harks back to v. 1 and forms the climax of the whole psalm: because the *'elohim* are powerless and incompetent to act as judges, the only true *'elohim* (God) is now performing this function. In contrast to the gods who have fallen, God is called upon to rise up as judge. God is both ruler and judge. He alone is mighty.

The psalm was probably written at a time when the people were suffering distress of one kind or another, when the poet had to deliver an apology of some sort to convince his readers that the LORD was the only true God. Thus, the psalm must have had a comforting effect on the people of God.

For the title "Asaph," cf. the note to Psalm 50.

Psalm 83

This psalm is a communal lament. It reflects a crisis situation during which Israel's survival was being threatened by hostile nations.

The first strophe (83:1) is a plea for help and consists of a threefold prayer to God in which he is requested not to be passive but to intervene and help his people. This threefold repetition emphasizes the seriousness of the situation and the urgency of the people's prayer.

The second strophe (83:2-8) is a description of the crisis which gave rise to Israel's lament. The first part of the strophe (vv. 2-5) describes the enemies, and in the second part of the strophe (vv. 6-8) these enemies are expressly identified by name. The enemies conspire with a single purpose in view, namely, to destroy Israel as a nation. The survival of Israel as the chosen people is threatened. To emphasize the extent of the danger and to persuade God to intervene, the names of no fewer than ten states are mentioned. This list contains the names of smaller states that were more or less contiguous to Israel. It concludes with the name of Assyria, the superpower of the time, which had carried the Israelites away into exile. This list should be regarded as a summary of Israel's traditional enemies and not as an exact historical list on which an exact dating could be based. The impossibility of dating the psalm on the basis of this list is apparent from the fact that attempts to date the psalm have yielded dates varying from the ninth century BC to the Maccabean period during the second century BC. There is a strong possibility that the psalm could date from the time when Assyria posed a threat to Israel, particularly during the eighth century BC.

The third strophe (83:9-18) is a prayer to God for assistance, specifically a prayer for the downfall of the enemies. The first part of the strophe (vv. 9-12) harks back to salvation history and contains an appeal to God to intervene as in the past to save his people. This strophe recalls two episodes from the period of the judges (cf. Judges 4–8) in which God as a warrior defeated the Canaanites and the Midianites in order to gain the victory for his people. The second part of this strophe (vv. 13-15) begins on a very personal note ("O my God . . .") and is a supplication for the destruction of the enemies. The poet uses a number of similes and metaphors drawn mainly from nature (cf. the comparison with the whirling wind, the chaff in the wind, and a bush destroyed by fire) to depict the intensity and scale of the destruction. The arrogance of the enemies (vv. 2-5) rebounds on them. Shame and disgrace are their lot (v. 17). The purpose of the destruction of the enemies is not random revenge or the self-preservation of Israel, but rather to preserve the honor of the LORD's name (cf. v. 18). Everything that happens should be conducive to the admission by the LORD's enemies that the LORD rules over the entire earth.

Psalm 83 is the last of the psalms of "Asaph" (Psalms 50, 73–83) and also the last of what is known as the Elohistic collection (Psalms 42–83) in which the divine name *'elohim* is mainly used.

Psalm 84

Psalm 84 is a striking expression of the poet's longing for the house of the LORD, and especially for the presence of the LORD. One of the characteristics of the psalm is that it is both introduced (cf. v. 1) and concluded (cf. v. 12) with the divine epithet "LORD of hosts" (cf. also vv. 3, 8). The repeated use of this divine epithet allows the emphasis to fall on the almighty power of God. Emphasis is also placed on the temple or the house of the LORD through the use of various terms, such as "your dwelling place" (v. 1), "courts of the LORD/your courts" (vv. 2, 10), "your altars" (v. 3), and "your house/the house of God" (vv. 4, 10).

There is no conclusive evidence for the exact dating of the psalm, which could possibly belong to either the preexilic or the postexilic period. There is no certainty about the original cultic situation either since some exegetes are of the opinion that this is a pilgrim song whereas others contend that the psalm concerns exiles longing for the restoration of the temple.

The first strophe (84:1-3) begins with an exhortation which places the emphasis on the temple: "How lovely is your dwelling place. . . ." It appears, however, that the poet is referring not only to a yearning for the temple but also, and especially, to focusing on the "living God." The poet gives even greater emphasis to his longing for the temple by using the parallel of birds that nest in the temple. While the poet is still pining for the temple, the birds have already made their home there.

The first part of the second strophe (84:4-7) is characterized by the expression "Happy are those . . . ," which occurs twice (cf. vv. 4, 5). To dwell in the presence of the LORD and to trust in him are sources of joy, or pinnacles of contentment. The second part of v. 5 poses interpretative problems and is translated in the NRSV as "in whose heart are the highways to Zion." It would be preferable to translate this line as "in whose hearts are songs of praise," which would fit in better with the immediate context (cf. vv. 4b, 5a). V. 6, and especially the expression "through the valley of Baca," is another source of interpretative problems. Without going into detail, one could say that the first part of v. 6 evidently refers to a drought and the second part to water. The two metaphors are used to develop the central idea, namely, yearning for the presence of the LORD: to see God (v. 7) is supreme happiness. It is like traversing a dry valley before finally reaching a spring.

In the third strophe (84:8-10) the LORD is addressed directly in the second person. There are two important elements in this strophe: first, an appeal is made to the LORD to hear the suppliant's prayer and grant it. Second, there is a return to the central theme of the psalm, namely, that to be allowed to dwell in the presence of the LORD is the most important thing of all. The idea is expressed in one of the best-known verses in the entire psalter: "For a day in your courts is better than a thousand elsewhere . . ." (v. 10). In view of the fact that "shield" in v. 11 refers to the LORD, v. 9 should probably be translated as a vocative ("O God, our shield, look with favor on your anointed one") so that "shield" here would also refer to the LORD. It would appear that the expression used here ("your anointed") refers to the poet himself.

In the fourth strophe (84:11) the poet speaks of God in the third person again. The strophe is an endorsement of the preceding one and makes one point, namely, that God is almighty and that we are safe in his presence. The sun and shield metaphors should be regarded as royal attributes of God and serve to underline his almighty power.

The fifth strophe (84:12) carries the psalm to a climax. The LORD is again addressed directly in the second person, and trust in almighty God is seen as the pinnacle of happiness.

The main function of Psalm 84 is to express the poet's longing for the temple and especially for the presence of the LORD.

For the title, "according to The Gittith," cf. Psalm 8. Psalm 84 shares the title "Of the Korahites" with Psalms 42–49, 85, 87, and 88. For a discussion of the title, cf. Psalm 42.

Psalm 85

Psalm 85 is a communal prayer written in a time of need. In it the LORD is entreated to lay aside his wrath toward his people. They interpret the crisis they are going through as a sign of the LORD's anger.

85:1-3 form the first strophe. These verses look at the past and recall the acts of salvation performed by the LORD for his people. They single out two acts of salvation, namely, that the LORD restored his land and forgave the sins of his people. This retrospective view probably reflects the situation shortly after the return from the Babylonian exile in the sixth century BC, when the people experienced the LORD's salvation in a very special way. The content of this strophe largely corresponds to the message of the book of Deutero-Isaiah (Isaiah 40–55), which dates from this period. The acts of salvation from the past form the basis for the prayers found in 85:4-7.

While the first strophe takes a retrospective look at history, the second strophe (85:4-7) is a prayer which relates to the crisis situation of the present. This situation should probably be related to the period of the book of Trito-Isaiah (Isaiah 56–66), when the promises of salvation of Deutero-Isaiah did not materialise in the way the people expected. This strophe forms an *inclusio* in that it is introduced and concluded by the word "salvation." And this is what the strophe is all about — a prayer for the LORD's salvation. This salvation should consist in the LORD's forgiving their sins, restoring them, and putting an end to the present situation. It is time for the salvation of the past to make way for new salvation.

The third strophe (85:8-13) is a prophetic oracle carrying a message of hope and salvation to those who remained faithful to the LORD. This salvation is described in metaphorical language, and the LORD's gifts are listed (cf. vv. 10-11 in particular) and personified in that they are portrayed as people acting on behalf of the LORD. They "meet" (v. 10), "kiss each other" (v. 10), "spring up" (v. 11), and "look down . . ." (v. 11). Although different terms are used to describe God's salvation — "steadfast love" (v. 10), "faithfulness" (vv. 10, 11), "righteousness" (vv. 10, 11, 13), "peace" (vv. 8, 10) — the words are all almost synonymous in this context and refer to God's personal presence and unfailing love toward "those who fear him." In this sense v. 12 forms the climax of the psalm and sums up everything that has been said so far: "The LORD will give what is good. . . ."

This psalm reflects the postexilic Judaic community's faith and hope that God's loving presence could make a difference in their desperate situation. Prayers to God and faith in his "steadfast love" make it possible for them to survive the crisis.

For the title "Of the Korahites," cf. Psalm 42.

Psalm 86 (*see* Individual Laments, 366-73)

Psalm 87

In the first strophe (87:1-3) the holy city of Zion forms the central motif. Although there is strong emphasis on the glory of Zion, God, and not Zion, is the primary subject. This is expressed in the emphatic statements that the LORD founded Zion and that Zion is "the city of God." The psalm even asserts that God loves Zion more than all the other holy shrines in Israel. If this psalm was written during the postexilic period, as most exegetes rightly suppose, this means that even the destruction of the temple in 587 BC by the Babylonians and the reconstruction of a far more modest temple after the return from exile (around 520 BC) did not detract anything from Zion's glory and the love of the LORD for Zion. The psalm may well have been written in that troubled period to persuade the people of God that he still loved Zion and that despite the exile he was still present with them. The basic principle of the Zion tradition is that God chose Zion as his dwelling place and founded the city. Zion becomes a symbol of the presence of the LORD and a source of strength and security.

While the first strophe is more particularistic and concentrates on Zion, the second strophe (87:4-7) deals with the universal dominion of the LORD and his relationship with alien peoples. The alien peoples who recognized the LORD as God are mentioned here: "Rahab" (a poetic name for Egypt; cf. Isa 30:7); "Babylon," the cruel people who destroyed Jerusalem and Judah; "Philistia," a traditional enemy of Israel; "Tyre," the rich and powerful trading city; and "Ethiopia," the most remote corner of the ancient world as it was known then. When it is said of the peoples, "'This one was born there'" (i.e., in Zion), this should not be interpreted literally but taken as a poetic, hyperbolic manner of saying that these peoples are citizens of Zion and that they therefore also belong to the LORD. It is, however, important to point out that the same expression is also used of Zion in v. 5. The fact that other peoples belong to the Lord does not mean that he has rejected Zion. Zion still belongs to the LORD, so that in Psalm 87 particularism and universalism are not mutually exclusive. The nations even praise Zion as the source of their joy (v. 7).

To sum up: The LORD chose Zion and made the city his dwelling. This does not mean, however, that he is restricted to Zion or that he is a local god. The nations also fall under the LORD's command. As the chosen sanctuary Zion enjoys international status.

For the meaning of "Of the Korahites," a part of the title, cf. Psalm 42.

Psalm 88 (*see* Individual Laments, 366-73)

Psalm 89

If one is to understand this long and intricate psalm, the best place to begin is with the last section. 89:49 provides a pithy summary of the problem dealt with in the psalm:

> Lord, where is your steadfast love of old,
> which by your faithfulness you swore to David?

Although the psalm consists of various elements, it is the last section of the psalm, which deals with the destruction of the dynasty of David and the accompanying humiliation, which determines its nature. One does gain the impression that the psalm deals with the Babylonian exile, which resulted in the destruction of Jerusalem and the termination of the Davidic dynasty. The problem which emerges in this psalm is the contradiction between the LORD's "steadfast love" and his early promises (cf. 89:1-4), and, on the other hand, the historical fact that the Davidic kingdom had been destroyed. The poet says that the LORD had promised that David's kingdom would endure forever, whereas in fact that kingdom no longer existed and the king had been defeated and humiliated by his enemies. The poet does not suggest any instant solutions; he merely voices his complaint to the LORD. The "How long . . . ?" questions (vv. 46-47) do, however, hold out a slender hope that God's wrath is not the last word and that there is still hope.

The psalm consists of three long stanzas (vv. 1-18, 19-37, and 38-51, and then v. 52, which concludes Book III of the psalter). These stanzas are each made up of a number of strophes. Although this psalm has undergone a growth process, in its present form it nevertheless has a coherent structure with a flowing line of thought. The coherence is affirmed by the striking repetition of keywords which are distributed through all three parts of the psalm. The most important word repetitions include "steadfast love" (vv. 1, 2, 14, 24, 28, 33, 49), "faithfulness/faithful" (vv. 1, 2, 5, 8, 14, 19, 24, 33, 49), "my servant David/David/servant" (vv. 3, 20, 35, 39, 49, 50), "throne" (vv. 4, 14, 29, 36, 44), "anointed" (20, 38, 51), "covenant" (vv. 3, 28, 34, 39), "forever/for all generations/always" (vv. 1, 2, 4, 21, 28, 29, 36), and "enemies/enemy" (vv. 10, 22, 42, 51). These repetitions reveal the most important themes of the psalm.

The first stanza (89:1-18) is a hymn. The introductory strophe (vv. 1-4) lauds the "steadfast love and faithfulness" of the LORD. The covenant with David and the promise that David's throne would endure "for all generations" are cited as the chief examples of the LORD's "steadfast love" and "faithfulness." The actual hymn is to be found in the next strophe. In the first section (vv. 5-8) the metaphor of the heavenly counsel (cf. also Psalm 29) is used to praise the LORD, who, surrounded by divine beings, is the incomparable God and ruler over the entire universe. The LORD's creative power is advanced as another reason why he should be praised (cf. 89:9-14). This section draws on Canaanite mythology and describes the LORD as the conqueror of hostile and chaotic forces. He is the mighty God to whom everything belongs and whose throne is firmly established. The qualities of "steadfast love" and "faithfulness" are personified and described as God's helpers with whose aid he rules. The last strophe (vv. 15-18) of this stanza takes us back to the human world since its subject is the congregation of God's people, who pay due tribute to the LORD.

In the second stanza (89:19-37) the poet amplifies the subject he touched on in vv. 3-4, namely, the election of David. This section is written in the form of an oracle with the LORD speaking in the first person, and there are many correspondences with Nathan's oracle to David (cf. 2 Sam 7:14). The LORD speaks of "my servant David," and all David's privileges are described. David's reign becomes a reflection of that of the LORD. The LORD chose David from among the people, anointed him, and clothed him with authority. David was given a promise that his enemies would never conquer him and was assured that his dynasty would last forever. He was the most important king on earth. The LORD also promised his "steadfast love" to David's descendants. Even if David's descendants fell into sinful ways, the LORD would not be entitled to revoke his covenant with David.

The third stanza (89:38-51) is a contrast to the previous section and could be described as a lament. While the rest of the psalm describes a past rich in promises, this section deals with the reality of the present. The expression "But now . . ." refers to the reversal which has taken place. In this stanza God is no longer speaking in the first person; instead he is held directly responsible for everything that has gone wrong. God's wonderful promises have not materialized. Jerusalem's king has suffered a humiliating defeat, and the country has been plunged into misery. To make matters worse, the LORD is accused of having brought about the enemies' victory. The stanza is concluded with a prayer (vv. 46-51) in which the poet demands accusingly of God how long he will keep his distance and how long his wrath will endure. God is reminded of his own promises of long ago — promises which he did not keep.

Psalm 89 describes the experience of a disoriented community, a community which sees a paradox between what God originally promised them and the harsh reality of their present circumstances.

The psalm ends with a doxology (89:52) which does not form part of the psalm itself but indicates the end of Book III (Psalms 73–89) of the psalter. It is characteristic of the psalter that such doxologies are placed at the end of smaller or larger collections of psalms (cf., e.g., Pss 41:13; 72:19-20; 106:48).

Psalm 90

Psalm 90 is the first of the series of psalms (90–106) which are known as Book IV of the psalter. It is impossible to establish whether this group of psalms originally formed a book on its own or whether it was part of the psalter from the beginning. Another question is whether the psalms in this group are interrelated in any way and, if so, what the nature of the relationship is. Some scholars are of the opinion that the composition of this book follows a liturgical pattern, such as that of the feast of Tabernacles. Another view is that a deliberate and precise structure and arrangement are discernible in this collection. There are a number of recurring themes in Book IV. Some of the most important themes are: the kingship of the LORD; the LORD's victory over the forces of chaos; the LORD is the universal creator who established the world; the LORD's judgment of the foreign nations and the wicked; and a retrospective account of the salvation history of Israel. Another characteristic of this collection is that it contains a number of untitled psalms (see Psalms 91, 93, 94, 95, 96, 99, 104, 105, and 106). This contributes to a sense of unity in that there are no strict divisions between the psalms since one psalm appears to flow into the next.

Psalm 90 itself is a communal prayer. The problem dealt with in the psalm is the nature of man: we are dust, we are mortal, and our nature is ephemeral. The psalm reminds us that our life span is limited. Time is an important theme throughout the psalm (cf., e.g., "our days," vv. 9, 12, 14; "our years," vv. 9-10).

Although a national catastrophe through which the people might have been passing could have given rise to this poem, Psalm 90 can rather be said to deal with a more general human problem. The congregation are speaking in this psalm, but they speak as individuals. The psalm reflects humility, and the tone is personal: on the one hand there is a realization of the greatness of God, but on the other there is a recognition of the ephemeral nature of human beings. The psalm forms an *inclusio* in that it is both introduced and concluded by the divine name *'adonay* ("Lord"; cf. vv. 1, 17). The function of this is to emphasize the role played by God, even though the psalm deals with the passing nature of human beings.

The aim of the psalm could be summed up in the words of v. 12: "So teach us to count our days that we may gain a wise heart." This verse is a wisdom saying which tells us that in the midst of the problem of human mortality there is still hope for humankind. The most important challenges humans have to face are to act wisely, to know what to do, and to master the art of living.

The first strophe (90:1-2) is hymnic in nature. Confidence is expressed in God as "our dwelling place," in other words, the one with whom his people have always been able to find shelter and security. God is praised as the eternal, universal creator who has been God from all eternity and will be forever. The two things which are said about God here, namely, that he is the protector of his people and the universal creator, are relevant to and form the basis for everything else discussed in the psalm.

The second strophe (90:3-6) is a lament on the transience of human beings. While God is everlasting, people are mortal beings who return to the dust. Human beings are likened to a passing dream. They are like the grass which is green in the morning but wilts in the evening after the heat of the day.

The third strophe (90:7-12) has the same subject matter as the previous one although there is evidence of progression. By the repetition of the expression "your anger/your wrath" (vv. 7, 9, 11), a link is forged between the anger of the LORD and the transience of humans. It is as a result of human sin that God's wrath brings misery upon humankind. Even if one enjoys long life, it is filled with "toil and trouble."

The fourth strophe (90:13-17) continues with the "we-you" form of address. Whereas the previous strophe was a lament, what we have here are petitions for the LORD's compassion. V. 13 is literally a turning point in the psalm ("Turn, O LORD . . .") in that the people of the LORD (cf. vv. 13, 16) here appeal to the steadfast love of the Lord. It is not, however, a prayer for an escape from the mortality of human beings or their sinful nature, but a prayer for quality of life. Life and "the works of our hands" gain meaning only when we become aware of the LORD's glorious power. This is the answer of Psalm 90 to the problem of the mortality and the transience of humankind. In this sense Psalm 90 is instructive and edifying but also offers pastoral comfort, especially to people wrestling with this problem of life.

The title "A Prayer of Moses, the man of God" is not an indication of authorship. The psalm is probably attributed to Moses because of the similarities between Psalm 90 and Genesis 1–3 (Genesis is also known as "the First Book of Moses"), which also contains references to the creation and the ephemeral nature of human beings. Moses was known as a "man of God" (cf. Deut 33:1; Josh 14:6), and the fervor of his belief would correspond to the fervor of belief reflected in the psalm.

Psalm 91

Psalm 91 is a promise that the LORD will offer protection to his people, who trust in him and seek refuge in him. Metaphors depicting the protection afforded by the LORD (cf., e.g., "my/your/refuge" [vv. 2, 4, 9]) occur frequently in the psalm. Psalm 91 shows strong similarities to sapiential texts such as Job 5:17-26 and Prov 3:21-26, where the motif of the complete protection afforded to the righteous by the LORD also occurs. The contention that God affords complete protection does not, however, accord with the realities of life, for those who trust in the LORD are sometimes far worse off than the ungodly (cf., e.g., Psalm 73, where this problem is raised). Psalm 91 should therefore not be interpreted as a literal and unconditional promise that nothing will ever go wrong for those who trust in the LORD. The psalm should rather be seen as a didactic wisdom text which aims to persuade the reader to trust in the LORD in all circumstances.

The psalm can be divided into two stanzas, namely, vv. 1-13 and vv. 14-16. The first stanza can be further subdivided into four strophes (vv. 1-2, 3-6, 7-8, and 9-13). The first strophe (91:1-2) is a general testimony (the "You who live" of the NRSV should preferably be translated "He who lives"), namely, that those who trust in the LORD will find safety in him. Four divine epithets, namely, "the Most High" *('elyon)*, "the Almighty" *(shadday)*, "the LORD" *(Yahweh)*, and "my God" *('elohay)*, are used in these two verses. Four metaphors, namely, "shelter," "shadow," "refuge," and "fortress," are used to depict the security to be found with God. The second strophe (vv. 3-6) again uses metaphors to describe affliction and perils (e.g., "snare," "deadly pestilence," and "arrow") but also deliverance from peril and the protection afforded by God (e.g., "wings" and "shield and buckler"). The third strophe (91:7-8) is introduced by the well-known verse, "A thousand may fall at your side . . . ," in which the contrast emerges between the one who trusts in the LORD and the wicked, who will be punished. The fourth and last strophe (vv. 9-13) proceeds from the previous ones and says that in the midst of great peril and menaces those who seek shelter in the LORD will be completely safe and unassailable. This strophe also uses ornate and metaphorical language. The metaphors and images transcend earthly life (cf. "angels," v. 11) and evoke associations with mythological aspects (cf., e.g., "serpent" in the NRSV, which could better be translated as "dragon"; cf. also Ps 74:13).

The second stanza (91:14-16) differs from the first in that its subject is not promises made to "you"; this stanza is a divine oracle in which the LORD speaks in the first person and in which the preceding promises of the LORD's protection are confirmed: the LORD saves and protects those who love him and gives them a long and blessed life.

This psalm does not promise that believers will have a carefree existence. The function of Psalm 91 is rather to appeal to people and persuade them to have complete trust in God. In view of the sapiential characteristics of this psalm it probably dates from the postexilic period.

Psalm 92

The psalm contains elements of a thanksgiving psalm as well as hymnic passages. Further, contrasts, which are so typical of wisdom literature, also play a decisive part in the psalm. All these elements have one purpose in view, and that is to praise the LORD as the "Most High" (92:1) and as the one who is "on high forever" (v. 8). The thanks and praise expressed to the LORD in this psalm do not, however, as in most other psalms, relate to the LORD's mighty deeds in creation and in history. Here the focus is on the LORD's dealings with people at a personal level — specifically, his dealings with the "wicked" and the "righteous."

It is apparent from the psalm that the imposed duty of thanking and praising the LORD is not a burdensome one but rather a good and enjoyable practice which should continue unceasingly. Praise should not be confined to words of thanks, but the "steadfast love" and "faithfulness" of the LORD should be exuberantly praised in song and with the aid of musical instruments (92:3).

The praiseworthiness of the LORD is illustrated chiefly by means of contrasts. The wicked flourish for a short while, for they are like green grass which soon becomes parched (92:7; cf. also Ps 90:5) and is doomed to certain destruction. In contrast, the righteous flourish as a palm tree does (v. 12). This image suggests continuity, stability, abundance, and lasting welfare. The wicked are portrayed as stupid and foolish because they are unable to recognize the greatness of God (v. 6). The righteous, on the other hand, rejoice in and celebrate the works of the LORD and see and hear about the destruction of evildoers (v. 11). While the "downfall of the enemies" is described, the psalmist says of himself, "you have exalted my horn . . ." (v. 10). These images highlight the aspects of might and joy. There is also a contrast between the wicked and the LORD. While the wicked are "doomed to destruction forever," the LORD is "high forever."

The expression of confidence in 92:15 is the highlight of the psalm and forms an *inclusio* with the beginning of the psalm, not only because the psalm begins and ends with the name of the LORD but because the same Hebrew verb *(ngd)* is used for "showing" (v. 15) and "declare" (v. 2). To proclaim that the LORD is upright is regarded as the chief purpose of the righteous. By describing the LORD as "my rock," the poet identifies closely with the personal character of the rest of the psalm and emphasizes even more strongly the safety to be found with God.

The title "A Song for the Sabbath Day" is found only here in the psalter. This title is probably an indication that the psalm was used in the sabbath liturgy. We do not know why this title, which was probably not originally part of the psalm, was added to the psalm. Although there are no direct clues in the psalm by which to date it, on the basis of the wisdom characteristics most exegetes rightly ascribe it to the postexilic period.

Psalm 93

Psalm 93 is part of a group of psalms (93, 96–99; cf. also Psalm 47) in which the expression "The LORD is king" occurs. The question regarding these psalms is whether the verb should be translated as a durative ("The LORD is king"/"the LORD reigns") or an ingressive ("The LORD has become king"). Without rehashing the long and complicated debate on this question, it may be said that Mowinckel was one of the main proponents of the *ingressive meaning*. His hypothesis is that a New Year festival took place in Israel in autumn and that the LORD's enthronement as king was celebrated annually at that time. According to Mowinckel, this festival was celebrated by analogy with the Babylonian festival honoring the ascension to the throne of the god Marduk. This group of psalms is sometimes also given an *eschatological* interpretation in that it is said to be concerned with the establishment of the LORD's kingship at the end of the world. *Historical interpretation* of these psalms is another possibility: some exegetes have tried to link individual psalms with specific historical contexts.

The point of view adopted here is that the expression "The LORD is king" should be given a durative interpretation. It should, however, not be treated as a static theological concept but as an expression of the belief of God's people that he is always in control. It would appear that the expression "The LORD is king" was used most frequently in the postexilic period when the Judean monarchy no longer existed and there was therefore no longer an earthly king on the throne. It was in this period that the Judean community fell back on the LORD as the only king in whom they could trust.

Psalm 93 is a persuasive text the function of which is to convince the reader/listener that the LORD is king, that his kingship is stable, that he is powerful, and that he is everlasting and reliable.

The metaphor of the LORD as king dominates the first strophe (93:1-2), and the emphasis falls on the LORD as the subject. The LORD is described as the victorious military king who is girded with "strength and majesty" and whose throne is "from of old," which is to say that it was there before creation. The description takes on cosmic dimensions when it is said of the LORD: "He has established the world." Because the creation motif and the kingship motif occur at the same time here, the implication is that the stability of the world is based on the permanence of the kingship of the LORD. Psalm 93 tells us that it is because God is king that there is stability in the world.

The second strophe (93:3-4) forms a contrast to the first and contains allusions to the creation myths of the ancient Near East, according to which the creator god had to begin by defeating the forces of chaos. The "floods" represent the primeval chaos here. The stylistic device of staircase parallelism is employed when the expression "the floods have lifted up" is repeated three times in succession in order to emphasize the threat posed by the forces of chaos and carry the strophe to a climax. By using the same adjective — "majestic" — for both the LORD and the floods, the poet emphasizes that the LORD is "more majestic" than the "mighty waters." Psalm 93 is not a creation myth, but terminology from the creation myths has been taken over to demonstrate that the kingship of the LORD is unassailable and unconquerable and that he is mightier than the gods.

The third strophe (93:5) carries the psalm to a climax. The purpose of this strophe is to concretize the mighty, almost transcendental God of the previous strophes in the human world. The "house" and the "decrees" of the LORD make it possible to experience God in a tangible form. Just as the earth, which the LORD created, is firm and just as God's throne is firmly established, so are his decrees and his house "very sure." The theme of stability plays an important part in this psalm. In perilous and insecure times such as the exile, this psalm would have offered the worshipers of the LORD comfort and security.

Psalm 94

This psalm forms a balanced entity in the sense that it is introduced by a prayer that the LORD should punish the wicked: "LORD, you God of vengeance . . ." (94:1) and concluded by a statement that this punishment will come about: ". . . the LORD our God will wipe them out" (v. 23).

This balance clearly expresses the theme of the psalm: Psalm 94 is an appeal to the LORD to restore justice in society by punishing wrongdoing. The key message of Psalm 94 is that the LORD will not let the righteous down. Where people are living in a society in which right is distorted and violence committed, this psalm could serve to give comfort and strengthen their faith. The psalm has elements of different genres such as the communal lament, wisdom literature, and individual prayer. All these different elements help to emphasize the comforting nature of the psalm.

The first strophe (94:1-2) is an appeal to God to "judge the wicked." The expression "you God of vengeance," which is repeated twice, is not intended as a negative description of the LORD as an arbitrary and cruel God but as judicial terminology describing the LORD's task of ensuring that justice and order prevail.

The second strophe (94:3-7) is a lament (cf. the "How long?" questions in v. 3, which are characteristic of a lament) in which the wickedness and arrogance of the evildoers are described. The conduct of the evildoers is described in hard, hyperbolic terms ("crush," "afflict," "kill," and "murder") to emphasize further the severity of their offense. The offense of the wicked is that they exploit and crush defenseless people ("the widow," "the orphan," "the stranger"), who are the very ones who deserve protection. By exploiting the defenseless people in society, evildoers are really violating God's property, and God's honor is called in question. For this reason the "God of vengeance" is called upon to execute judgment.

The third strophe (94:8-15) is wisdom literature. The first part of the strophe (vv. 8-11) is a rebuke to the wicked because they are so foolish that they do not see that God the Creator is greater than his creatures and can call on them to answer for their actions. This is an appeal to the good sense of the wicked. The second part of the strophe (vv. 12-15) is an antithesis to the first part and is a blessing ("Happy are those . . .") for the "upright in heart." These people are given the assurance that "the LORD will not forsake his people." As is typical of wisdom literature, this psalm sketches a contrast between the wicked and the righteous. Vengeance is contrasted with blessing.

The fourth strophe (94:16-19) is characterized by first person singular forms. It is a personal confession, expressed within the context of the community of faith but based on the experience of an individual that the LORD has always been faithful.

The fifth strophe (94:20-23) is closely related to the previous one and is also a confession, this time of the belief that where God is the judge the wicked will not escape punishment. In fact, they will be wiped out. The just and those who have been innocently oppressed will find security with the LORD. This is the solution to the problem sketched at the beginning of the psalm (cf. vv. 1-2). The psalm displays a neatly rounded off sequence of ideas. Psalm 94 should not be interpreted as an unqualified promise that things will always go well for the righteous (cf. also Psalm 91 in this regard). The function of the psalm is to comfort righteous people who have been wronged and support them in facing their difficulties.

Psalm 95

Psalm 95 is an exhortation. The function of the psalm could be summed up in the words of v. 7b: "O that today you would listen to his voice!" The psalm consists of two stanzas (vv. 1-7a and 7b-11) both of which contribute to the admonitory character of the psalm.

The first stanza (95:1-7a) consists of two strophes (vv. 1-5 and vv. 6-7a) which have a parallel construction in the sense that they both contain hymnic invocations followed by the advancement of reasons why the LORD should be praised:

> O come, let us sing. (v. 1)
> O come, let us worship. (v. 6)
>
> For the LORD is a great God. (v. 3)
> For he is our God. (v. 7a).

Verses 1-2 of the first strophe (95:1-5) are a hymnic invocation in the form of an imperative and four cohortatives in the first person plural enjoining the people to praise the LORD exuberantly. The reasons for the invocations to praise are given in vv. 3-5. The first reason why the LORD should be praised is that he is a "great

God" and a "great King above all gods." The latter expression most probably comes from a polytheistic background and is used to indicate the powerlessness of the gods. The second reason why the LORD should be praised is that he is the Creator (vv. 4-5). Where v. 4 embodies a vertical view of the world ("depths of the earth . . . heights of the mountains"), v. 5 reflects a horizontal view ("sea . . . dry land"). This polarity emphasizes the all-encompassing sovereignty of the Creator God, who has made everything with "his hands." By repeating the word "great" twice, the poet further emphasizes the praiseworthiness of the LORD.

The second strophe (95:6-7a) follows the same pattern as the first. The creation tradition is advanced as the reason why the LORD should be thanked. The substantiation is, however, taken further, and the shepherd metaphor is used as a further reason for praise. God the Creator (v. 6) is also the God of the covenant (v. 7). Universalism (the LORD's creative power) and particularism (the LORD's close relationship with his people) are considered to be equally important reasons for praising the LORD. These hymnic passages form the basis for the exhortative and condemnatory words in the final stanza.

The second stanza (95:7b-11) is introduced by a prophetic admonition: "O that today you would listen to his voice!" V. 7b is a warning to the present generation, but the following verses (vv. 8-11) hark back to the past and then become an oracle in which the LORD admonishes his people directly. Vv. 8-11 have to do with the wilderness tradition as the reason for the LORD's wrath. Through the use of the words "Meribah" and "Massah" (cf. Exod 17:1-7 and Num 20:1-13) the entire wilderness period is encompassed. History is reinterpreted and brought alive, the object being to admonish the people of the day. This could be called a didactic use of history. The LORD's dissatisfaction with his people is expressed in various ways. In addition to using the words "I loathed," the psalmist accentuates the extent of this discontent by the expression "forty years" and the neutral term "that generation." God's disgust with his people culminates in the oath he takes (v. 11) that they will not enter his "rest" (this word refers primarily to entry into and dwelling in the promised land).

The last stanza stands in an antithetic relation to the first one: in contrast to all the praiseworthy things the LORD has done (stanza 1), the behavior of the LORD's people has been contemptible (stanza 2). The function of the contrast and consequently of the whole of the psalm is to warn the readers/listeners that their association with the LORD should not be taken for granted. This is achieved by contrasting the LORD's praiseworthiness and greatness and the people's history of failure.

Psalm 96

Psalm 96 is a hymn to the LORD, the universal creator, king, and judge. The universalistic trend is a characteristic of the psalm. Another characteristic of Psalm 96 is that it contains correspondences or references to numerous other passages in the OT. The principal resemblances are to other psalms and to Deutero-Isaiah; vv. 7-9 show a marked similarity to the beginning of Psalm 29, for example; Psalm 96 occurs in the same form in 1 Chr 16:23-33. This anthological character of Psalm 96 gives rise to the supposition that it is a more recent text drawing on older texts.

The first strophe (96:1-6) is an invocation to praise containing a succession of six imperatives: the expression "sing to the LORD" is repeated three times and followed by three more imperatives ("bless . . . tell . . . declare . . ."). It is a universal invocation — "all the earth" is to praise the LORD. The LORD's people are, however, specifically instructed to proclaim his glory and marvelous works continually among the nations. Israel and all the earth should therefore with one voice sing a "new song" on God's salvation. This is probably a reference to the LORD's act of salvation when he delivered his people from exile. Two reasons are supplied for this universal injunction to praise: first, the LORD is great by reason of his creative power. He even created the heavens, the dwelling of the gods. The gods are nonentities in comparison with the LORD. Secondly, the transcendent God is present in strength and glory in his sanctuary.

The second strophe (96:7-10) is likewise a universal invocation to praise and displays parallels with the first strophe. Like the first strophe, it is introduced by an imperative which is repeated three times ("Ascribe to the LORD") and then followed by four more imperatives. All nations are enjoined to acknowledge his glory and strength and to worship him. The strophe is carried to a climax when Israel is called upon to proclaim to the nations that "'The LORD is king!'" (cf. also Psalm 93). The fact that the LORD is king means that both the cosmic ("the world is firmly established") and the social order ("He will judge the peoples with equity") are stable and secure.

The psalm sweeps to a climax in the third strophe (96:11-13) with a personification: the entire creation is urged to break into an expression of exuberant joy since the LORD is coming to judge the earth. The verb "judge," which is used twice, does not refer to a negative, destructive action on the part of the LORD. It also has nothing to do with the last judgment; in the context of this psalm it is part of the LORD's royal task and an expression of his ability to ensure justice and stability.

Psalm 96 is a hymn in which the LORD as the universal king and creator is praised by his own people, all the nations, and the entire creation. The psalm would fit in well with the difficult postexilic period when it must have been important for the people to hear that the LORD reigns, that he is more powerful than the gods, and that Israel has a responsibility toward the nations.

Psalm 97

Psalm 97:1 ("The LORD is king! Let the earth rejoice") cogently sums up the content of this psalm, the subject of which is the universal call to rejoicing because the LORD is king (for a discussion of this expression, cf. Psalm 93). We find an *inclusio* here in that the word "rejoice" occurs both at the beginning (cf. v. 1) and the end (cf. v. 12) of the psalm. The importance of this theme is further underlined by the occurrence of "rejoice" in the middle of the psalm as well (v. 8; cf. also "glad" in vv. 1 and 8).

The theme that God is the universal king who reigns in majesty is expressed largely through the use of contrasts: while the adversaries of the LORD are easily defeated (v. 3), the lives of his faithful ones are protected. While the righteous are called upon to rejoice (v. 12), the worshipers of images are put to shame. The coming of the LORD and his presence as king are awe-inspiring events, the effects of which are felt throughout the cosmos. Vv. 2-5 are a theophany (cf. Pss 18:8-16 and 50:3) and a dramatic description of the effect of the LORD's reign. In contrast, idols are worthless nonentities and frauds. The LORD is exalted on high (v. 9), and the gods have to bow low before him (v. 7). The LORD is seen almost in transcendent terms, but is nevertheless personally present with the righteous in the sense that he loves, protects, and saves them (v. 10). On the one hand the LORD's kingship is universal (cf. vv. 5, 9), but on the other it is particularistic, in that Zion and the towns of Judah serve the LORD (v. 8).

One of the most important reasons why the kingship of the LORD is a source of joy lies in the fact that "righteousness and justice" are the foundations of his throne (97:2; cf. also v. 6). This means that the kingship of the LORD has to do not only with dramatic and extraordinary things but also and especially with ordinary matters like human behavior and an orderly society.

Psalm 97 contains a polemic against idolaters and idols. Furthermore, we cannot exclude the possibility that an indirect contrast is implied between the kingship of the LORD and the failed preexilic Judean monarchy. In the post-exilic period, when the monarchy no longer existed, Psalm 97 functioned as a consolatory text for the faithful by persuading them that the LORD is stronger than the gods and that he is the only king his people can rely on.

Psalm 98

Psalm 98 shows numerous similarities to Psalm 96 (cf., e.g., the conclusion of both psalms) and to Deutero-Isaiah (cf., e.g., Isa 55:12-13). The similarity to Deutero-Isaiah and the anthological character of Psalm 98 (cf. Psalm 96 for this as well) indicate that the "victory" of which Psalm 98 speaks probably has to do with liberation from the Babylonian exile. The content of Psalm 98, which may be classified as a hymn, can be summed up as follows: God has proved himself to be king by liberating Israel before the eyes of the world. For this reason the whole world has a duty to praise the LORD, who will come to judge the world with righteousness. The psalm can be divided into three strophes, namely, vv. 1-3, 4-6, and 7-9.

The first strophe (98:1-3) is an injunction to sing to the LORD "a new song" because he has done "marvelous things." These "marvelous things" are more closely defined as a "victory" (the word is repeated three times in the strophe). Military terminology is used to indicate that the LORD did everything in his own strength. The LORD has worked salvation for his own people, but he has done this in such a way that it should be known to "the ends of the earth." Particularism (Israel) and universalism (the nations) are mentioned in the same breath, and the poet gives God full credit for the act of salvation.

The second strophe (98:4-6) forms an *inclusio* in that it is both introduced and concluded by the expression "make a joyful noise." The object of this strophe is to call upon everyone to praise God with all their heart. This is expressed by a succession of six imperatives (cf. esp. v. 4). In v. 4 we are told *who* should praise the LORD, namely, "all the earth." V. 5 *by what means* the LORD should be praised and the musical instruments to be used for praise (cf. vv. 5 and 6). All the elements of this strophe combine to express the exuberance and the universality of the praise of the LORD, who is also described as the "King."

The third strophe (98:7-9) forms an *inclusio,* like the previous one, because the word "world" occurs in the first and the last verses (vv. 7, 9). The imperatives of the second strophe are replaced by jussives. Natural elements ("the sea," "the floods," "the world," and "the hills") are personified and enjoined to praise God. V. 7 especially ("the sea roar") and v. 8 ("the floods . . .") contain terminology that was probably related originally to the primeval chaos. Here this original terminology is stripped of its mythological meaning and used in a hymnic context to praise the LORD. The reason for the cosmic praise is given in v. 9, namely, that the LORD "is coming to judge the earth." This expression does not refer to the distant eschatological end of the world; it means that the LORD is bringing about a just dispensation and order on earth.

The injunction to praise in Psalm 98 follows an ascendent line. At first the psalmist speaks only of singing, then of rejoicing and shouting for joy. Next the stringed instruments and the more powerful wind instruments are raised in praise. Finally, the whole of creation combines to form a mighty choir singing praises to the LORD, the king. Furthermore, the membership of the group bringing praise to the LORD comes from an ever-widening circle: first, only the people of God, then all countries, and finally the entire creation are called upon to give praise.

Psalm 99

Psalm 99 is a hymn and the last of the "The LORD is king" psalms. Characteristic of Psalm 99 is the refrain which occurs in vv. 5 and 9:

> Extol the LORD our God;
> worship at his footstool (v. 5)/at his holy
> mountain (v. 9).
> Holy is he! (v. 5)/for the LORD our God
> is holy (v. 9).

The refrain divides the poem into two strophes (vv. 1-5 and vv. 6-9); it also indicates the main theme of the psalm: the LORD our God is a holy and exalted king. Israel must obey and worship the LORD, and the whole world must pay homage to him. The word "holy" occurs twice in the refrain and is used a third time in v. 3. This also applies to the expression "the LORD our God," which occurs in the refrain and for a third time in v. 8.

In the first strophe (99:1-5) the emphasis falls on the LORD as the great and exalted king whose seat is in Zion. From the central point of Zion the kingship of the LORD radiates outward in all directions. His kingship has international and even cosmic consequences. Elsewhere in the OT the expression "He sits enthroned upon the cherubim" is usually related to the ark of the covenant (cf. Ps 80:1; cf. also 1 Sam 4:4; 2 Sam 6:2; 1 Chr 13:6). In Psalm 99 it should rather be interpreted in the light of the royal metaphor, so that "He sits enthroned among the cherubim" should be taken to mean that the LORD reigns over the entire earth. The LORD is described in the strophe as the ideal king who ensures that justice and equity prevail (cf. "justice," which occurs twice in v. 4). What the poet has to say about God culminates in the refrain (v. 5), namely, that the LORD should be extolled by bowing low before him, the holy king.

The second strophe (99:6-9) differs from the first in that it has a nationalist-particularist character as a result of the reference to Moses, Aaron, and Samuel. The psalmist is referring back to salvation history — especially to the journey through the wilderness and the Sinai tradition — as an illustration of the kingship of the LORD. The general statements about God's kingship in the first strophe are illustrated and explained by means of examples from history. Moses, Aaron, and Samuel are mentioned as heroes of the faith with whom God had a special relationship. The emphasis lies on the fact that throughout history the LORD has been a king who hearkened to his people's need and conducted a dialogue with them. Because God is a good and forgiving king, this does not mean, however, that he will simply overlook his people's sins. The fact that he is holy means that of necessity he is an avenger of wrongs.

Like most of the "The LORD is king" psalms, Psalm 99 probably also dates from the postexilic period. At this time, when the monarchy was no longer in existence, it would have been important for the people to hear that the LORD is the exalted and holy king before whom the whole world ought to bow in worship but that he is also their God who cares about them. In this sense Psalm 99 would have had a consolatory effect.

Psalm 100

Psalm 100 is a hymn consisting of invocations to praise followed by reasons for praise. The title of the psalm (". . . thanksgiving") should therefore be understood in the broader sense of praise. The psalm consists of two strophes (vv. 1-3 and vv. 4-5) which have a parallel construction and in which both of the above elements, namely, invocations to praise and reasons for the praise, occur.

The first strophe (100:1-3) is introduced by four successive imperatives. The emphasis falls on the all-embracing praise which is due to God. The first three imperatives chiefly concern the cult, where praise should be given in the presence of the LORD with exuberant joy and gladness. The fourth imperative ("Know that") carries the previous imperatives to a climax and emphasizes the fact that worship should incorporate the acknowledgment that the LORD is the only true God.

The last part of v. 3 gives two reasons for praising the LORD, and the profound relationship between God and his people plays an important part in both: the psalmist first employs the creation motif, saying that the LORD made his people and they belong to him. Secondly, the shepherd metaphor is used to express the close relationship between God and his people.

The second strophe (100:4-5) parallels the first. Its content is the same as that of the first strophe, but it develops the theme. After the imperatives ("Enter . . . "; "give thanks . . ." ; "bless . . .") the reason given is that the LORD is good. The expression "the LORD is good" probably refers to historical instances of the LORD's deliverance. These acts are expressions of his "steadfast love." God's love is not restricted to a particular time, however, but is constant and permanent. Israel can therefore rely on the LORD and should serve him with praise.

Psalm 101

Psalm 101 is regarded by most exegetes as a royal psalm, and more specifically as a code of conduct for the ideal king. This point of view cannot, however, be substantiated on the grounds of the content of the psalm, since nowhere in the psalm is a king directly mentioned. Instead the psalm should be regarded as a wisdom text. Numerous examples of wisdom terminology are found in Psalm 101: "walk with integrity of heart"/"in the way that is blameless," vv. 2, 6 (cf., e.g., Prov 10:9; 20:7); "perverseness of heart," v. 4; a "haughty look and an arrogant heart" (v. 5; cf., e.g., also Ps 131:1; Prov 6:16-17; 21:4; 30:13) are well-known wisdom terms for describing hubris; the theme of slandering a neighbor (v. 7) is also found frequently in wisdom literature (cf., e.g., Prov 10:8); polarity, and especially the contrast between the righteous and evildoers which plays a part in Psalm 101, is typical of wisdom psalms (cf., e.g., Psalm 1). Psalm 101 is a persuasive wisdom text in which the poet presents the reader/listener with a choice — largely through the contrasts he uses — and tries to persuade him to choose God and a righteous way of life. The psalm is therefore a code of conduct to be followed not only by kings but by everyone who reads or hears it. Expressions such as "I will destroy all the wicked in the land . . ." (v. 8) should not be interpreted literally but should rather be seen as hyperbolic language in which the function of the psalm, which is to persuade the reader, is clearly seen.

The first strophe (101:1-2) contains the poet's injunction to himself to praise the LORD and expresses his desire to live a blameless life. The second strophe (vv. 3-5) forms a contrast to the first: while the first strophe is a positive description of the poet's actions, the negative description in the second strophe presents the other side of the coin ("I will not set before my eyes . . . ," v. 3; "I will know nothing . . . ", v. 4; "I will not tolerate . . . ", v. 5). In order to demonstrate his loyalty to God, the poet emphatically states that he is distancing himself completely from evildoers and their actions. The third strophe (vv. 6-7) is a combination of the positive and negative elements of the previous two strophes: v. 6 makes the positive statement that only the faithful will be admitted to the poet's household, and v. 7 sets forth the negative side of the picture ("no one who utters lies shall continue in my presence"). The intention of the strophe is also to underline the contrast between the evildoer and the righteous. This contrast is carried to a climax in the fourth strophe (v. 8), which contains the hyperbolic and exaggerated statement that the wicked will be cut off from the city of God.

The purpose of Psalm 101 is to persuade readers/listeners to trust in the LORD and to live upright lives; the psalm warns them against a godless lifestyle. On the basis of its wisdom characteristics, the psalm should probably be ascribed to the postexilic period.

Psalm 102 (*see* Individual Laments, 366-73)

Psalm 103

The hymnic invocation, "Bless the LORD, O my soul," with which the psalm is introduced (v. 1) and concluded (v. 22) creates the framework within which the psalm should be read. The invocation in v. 1 is followed by an identical invocation in v. 2. The invocation in v. 22 is preceded by three hymnic invocations in the plural. The remainder of the psalm is substantiation for the hymnic invocations. Psalm 103 concentrates on the "steadfast love" (cf. vv. 4, 8, 11, 17), the "mercy" and "compassion" (vv. 4, 8, 13), and the forgiving nature of the LORD as reasons why he should be praised.

In the first strophe (103:3-5) God's benevolent deeds are testified to from the perspective of an individual. This could be described as a mini-biography containing a testimony to the love of God. Not only is the LORD the merciful God who forgives sins; he is also the physician who heals and ransoms us when we are threatened with death. The LORD gives the ransomed the status of kings and crowns them with "steadfast love and mercy." It is God who overwhelms us with abundance and renews our strength.

In the next major division (103:6-18) the reason the poet gives for praising the LORD has to do with the history of Israel. After a general observation on the LORD's aid to his oppressed people in the past (v. 6), his acts of salvation are more closely described in terms of the Sinai tradition. Moses is held up as the instrument through which God's law was revealed (v. 7), and God's attributes are strung together in a hymnic succession (v. 8). In vv. 9-10 the long-suffering nature of God is examined: even if God were fully justified in punishing his people for their sins forever, it is evidence of his mercy that he does not punish them as they deserve.

The incomparable nature of the LORD's love is portrayed in 103:11-13 in three similes. The first simile concerns the "height" of God's love. Higher than the very heavens, so great and immeasurable is his love. The east and the west, symbolic of total remoteness and endless distance, are used as similes to indicate how far the LORD removes "our transgressions." The LORD is also like a loving father who forgives his disobedient children time and again.

God has sympathy with human beings because he is aware that they are fragile and ephemeral, akin to dust, and he made them himself (103:14-16). Humans are like the grass which, in the parched Palestinian climate, grows for a brief period in winter and spring, only to dry up in the hot summer. Our lives are as brief as that of a spring flower. In contrast to insignificant, transitory humans, God's love is "from everlasting to everlasting" (vv. 17-18) and is not bestowed at random, but reserved for those "who fear him" (cf. also vv. 11 and 13).

The psalm ends (vv. 19-22) in the same way in which it began, namely, with a call to praise the LORD. But whereas at the beginning of the psalm an individual was called upon to praise the LORD, the psalm ends with an injunction to the entire cosmos to praise God. The metaphor used is that of the LORD as king and head of his heavenly council (cf. also Ps 29:1); all his creatures are called upon to praise him and acknowledge his kingship.

Psalm 103 may be summed up as follows: the invocation to praise begins on a personal, individual note (vv. 1-5); it then moves to a national level (Israel, vv. 6-18), and eventually takes on a cosmic-universal dimension (vv. 19-22a) before reverting to a personal note at the end (v. 22b).

If the Aramaisms in Psalm 103 are taken into account (cf., e.g., the suffix forms in the Hebrew text of vv. 3-5), in addition to the fact that the psalm shows certain similarities to Deutero-Isaiah (Isaiah 40–55) (cf., e.g., 103:11 with Isa 55:9 and 103:15-16 with Isa 40:6-7), it appears likely that the psalm was written during the postexilic period. In this psalm therefore, as in the case of numerous others, the title "Of David" cannot be taken as an indication of authorship. The fact that despite the exile God continued to show his steadfast love, mercy, and compassion to his people and did not forget them should have been a source of renewed courage to them and an inducement to praise the LORD.

Psalm 104

Psalm 104 is a song of praise to God as the creator who made all things in his wisdom, who sustains the entire creation, and who supplies every creature's needs. Psalm 104 is often called the pearl of the psalter. The best way to appreciate the greatness of this poem and take in its message is simply to sit down and read it.

Numerous exegetes have pointed out the similarities between Psalm 104 and other biblical (esp. Genesis 1) and extrabiblical texts (esp. creation hymns from Egypt and Mesopotamia). It is impossible to determine the exact relationship between Psalm 104 and these texts. What can be said, however, is that the poet of Psalm 104 created a new poem to portray the greatness of God as the creator and the harmony between him and his creation. The psalm offers a comprehensive perspective on the entire cosmos as a meaningful and ordered whole. The literary form and the theological message of the psalm complement one another because the perspective of both is that creation and the LORD's relationship with his creation form a coherent whole.

The injunction to praise with which the psalm begins and ends (cf. 104:1a, 35b) forms the framework within which the whole psalm should be read. The function of the rest of the psalm is to support these invocations to praise. Although Psalm 104 concentrates chiefly on the creation, it is not merely a description of the creation but primarily a laudation of the creator. It is not only a depiction of nature but also a confession of faith by a poet who contends that the LORD is the Creator who sustains the whole world and is the only true God.

Theophanic language (cf. Ps 18:7-15) is used in the first strophe (104:1b-4) to describe God as the omnipotent and illustrious king and triumphant warrior. In the second strophe (vv. 5-9) the emphasis falls on the creative power of the LORD and on the origin of the habitable world. In line with the worldview of the time, the LORD's creative acts are seen in terms of the partition, ordering, and establishment of the earth. The terminology used here is reminiscent of the chaos struggle of Canaanite mythology, and it is intended to signify that the LORD is the victor over the chaotic forces (cf. also Pss 89:9-12 and 93:3-4).

It becomes clear from the third strophe (104:10-18) that not only is the LORD the Creator but that he also supplies the needs of his creatures. The water subdued by him now becomes a source of life. The LORD provides water, food, and shelter. He makes provision for the whole realm of nature — plants, animals, and people — and is concerned about all living things.

In the fourth strophe (104:19-23) the subject is the rhythm of life. God is in command of the day and the night. He has the seasons in his charge. He is in command of all life. The sun and moon, which are deified by some other nations, were made by the LORD to indicate time. Human working rhythms and rhythms of life have been laid down by God.

In the fifth strophe (104:24-26) the poet expresses his amazement about the variety to be found in creation. God has created everything in his wisdom and given everything a place. The LORD is in control of the entire creation, and everything is a sign of his wisdom. The sixth strophe (vv. 27-30) emphasizes that the entire creation is dependent on God. It is God who feeds all creatures and is in control of life and death. The creation and all creatures depend on the LORD for survival and venerate his providence.

In the seventh strophe (104:31-35) the psalm ends in the same way in which it began, namely, with an injunction to praise. The entire poem is characterized by praise to God for his benevolent act of creation, and this is enhanced by the theophanic description (cf. v. 32 and vv. 2-3). The poet of Psalm 104 does, however, show signs of being aware of the realities of life and of the fact that the harmony expressed in the remainder of the psalm is not always the norm: sinners (v. 35) are a discordant note in the LORD's creation and should therefore be removed. This curse, which is couched in strongly hyperbolic language, is intended as a warning to all who are out of step with the harmony of creation.

The greatness and perfection of the creation inspired the poet of Psalm 104 to write a song of praise to the LORD. All people should react in the same way and should be inspired, furthermore, to maintain the natural order in God's creation.

Psalm 105

In common with Psalms 78 and 106, Psalm 105 offers a review of the history of Israel. Psalm 78 draws on history to serve as a warning to the present generation. This admonitory tone is wholly absent in Psalm 105, however. This psalm is a song of praise to God who, faithful to his promise to the patriarchs, has protected his people throughout history, liberated them, and finally brought them to the promised land. In addition to being an invocation to praise, Psalm 105 has another function, as is evident from v. 45, namely: "that they might keep his statutes and observe his laws." Historical events are therefore recounted to serve as an injunction to obedience to God.

Psalms 105 and 106 were deliberately placed next to each other. The two psalms complement each other. While Psalm 105 is dominated by praise and thanksgiving for God's faithfulness, Psalm 106 emphasizes the unfaithfulness of Israel despite the LORD's deeds of salvation for them. Whereas Psalm 105 is an invocation to praise, Psalm 106 is an invocation to repentance.

Although it is difficult to determine the precise original cultic context and time of origin of Psalm 105, most exegetes rightly agree on dating it to the postexilic period: the similarities between Psalm 105 and Deutero-Isaiah are indicative of this (cf., e.g., v. 43 with Isa 55:12). Psalm 105:11-15 resembles 1 Chr 16:18-22, one of the latest books in the OT; terms such as "servants" and "his chosen ones" (cf. vv. 6, 25, 43), which are applied to Israel, also indicate that Psalm 105 is a postexilic text. It therefore appears possible that during this period, when the people of God had experienced his salvation in a special way in that he had led them out of exile and back to their own country, the poet intended to refresh his people's memories by taking them back through history and showing them that God had always been true to his promises. Psalm 105 is not an exact, objective account of history. The poet reinterprets history in order to achieve a specific purpose.

The psalm forms an *inclusio* in that it is introduced by invocations to praise in the first strophe (105:1-6; cf. the nine imperatives strung together) and concluded by an invocation to praise in the last verse (cf. v. 45b). The rest of the psalm gives reasons for the need to thank and praise the Lord. In fact the psalm contains a double *inclusio* in that the expression "his servant Abraham"/ "Abraham, his servant" occurs both at the end of the introduction (v. 6) and at the beginning of the last strophe (v. 42; cf. also v. 9). This conveys the principal theme of the psalm, namely, that the LORD entered into a covenant with Abraham and the patriarchs, that he promised them the land, and that he was true to his promise (v. 44; cf. the numerous occurrences of the words "land," "country," "ground," "earth," and "inheritance" in vv. 7, 11, 16, 27, 28, 30, 31, 32, 33, 35, 36, and 44).

Although the psalm does not show a strict strophal division, it could be divided into sections according to the history of Israel: after the invocation to praise (vv. 1-6), vv. 7-11 deal with the covenant with the patriarchs and the promise of their own land. Vv. 12-15 tell of the wanderings of the patriarchs under God's protection. The story of Joseph is recounted in vv. 16-22, and we are told how the LORD used Joseph's suffering and imprisonment to bring about salvation for his people. Vv. 23-28 deal with the sojourn in Egypt and the eventual deliverance and exodus. The plagues that afflicted Egypt are dealt with in detail, and the emphasis falls on the LORD's actions, so that it is clear that it was he who defeated the powerful Egyptians to bring salvation to his people. Vv. 39-44 sketch the wilderness wanderings in which God led his people and provided for all their needs. This section concludes with the occupation of the land, which was seen as a gift from the LORD and as the climax of his deeds of salvation.

The poet uses this review of history as an illustration of the LORD's faithfulness to his covenant with Abraham, while also giving the postexilic community a reason why it is still incumbent upon them to praise God and obey his laws.

Psalm 106

Psalms 105 and 106 both review the history of Israel, but from entirely different perspectives. The two psalms recount the two sides to Israel's history and should be read together. Psalm 105 deals with God's faithfulness and mighty deeds, and its function is to call upon the people to praise the LORD. Psalm 106 deals with Israel's sin despite God's acts of salvation. Psalm 105 tells how the LORD brought his people to the promised land, and Psalm 106 says that Israel eventually lost the land on account of the sins of its people. Psalm 106 is basically a confession of sin, and its content is tellingly summed up by v. 6: "Both we and our ancestors have sinned. . . ." This confession of sin affects not only the ancestors, however, but also the present generation so that the past and the present converge here and past history is used to address the present generation. We can deduce from v. 46 (". . . by all who held them captive") and v. 47 (". . . gather us from the nations"; cf. also v. 27) that the exile must already have taken place. If this is the case, the recounting of the history in Psalm 106 was an attempt to supply an explanation for the exile: the exile happened because the people had disobeyed God throughout history. Psalm 106 is not an objective view of history; rather, it is history used to express judgment on Israel.

Although Psalm 106 is a confession of sin, it is notable that it is both introduced and concluded by the hallelujah invocation (vv. 1, 48). Praise of the LORD's mighty deeds forms the basis for the confession of sin. Psalm 106 deals not only with a confession of sin but also with the people's appeal to God for help; in vv. 44-45 we read that the LORD "showed compassion according to the abundance of his steadfast love." Even after God's wrath there is still hope of forgiveness. This fact must have given new hope to the postexilic community, who were so aware of their history of failure.

The history recounted in Psalm 106 stretches from the sojourn in Egypt to the entry into Canaan and the years spent there. The whole history reflects the impatience, ingratitude, rebelliousness, and lack of faith which characterized the Israelites' relationship with God. Psalm 106 reports these events as follows: vv. 7-12 recount the miraculous deliverance at the Sea of Reeds and show that Israel did not appreciate this. Psalm 106 concentrates mainly on the wilderness period (vv. 13-33) as the pinnacle of Israel's disobedience. The psalm tells how the LORD met all the people's needs in the desert but that they turned their backs on him (vv. 13-15); Dathan and Abiram rebelled against Moses and Aaron (vv. 16-18); the people worshiped the golden calf (vv. 19-23); they refused to enter the promised land from the south and as a punishment had to wander in the desert (vv. 24-27; cf. also Numbers 13–14); they "attached themselves" to Baal of Peor (vv. 28-31; cf. also Numbers 25); they angered the LORD at Meribah so that even Moses became embittered (vv. 32-33; cf. also Num 20:2-13); and in Canaan they did not subdue the foreign nations but instead adopted their idolatrous practices (vv. 34-39). This history of disobedience and rebellion caused God's wrath to flare up against them (vv. 40-44). The LORD again showed compassion when the people called upon him for help, so that the confession of sin was transformed into thanks and praise (vv. 43-47).

The psalm, and the section of the psalter known as Book IV, is concluded with a doxology (cf. 106:48; cf. also Pss 41:13; 72:19-20; 89:52; 150:1-6).

Psalm 107

Psalm 107 is the first of the series of psalms (107–150) which is generally known as Book V of the psalter. Smaller divisions can be distinguished in this collection: Psalms 108–110 have "Of David" as part of their title; Psalms 111–118 are known as the Hallelujah psalms (cf. also Psalm 135) because the hallelujah invocation occurs in all of them; Psalms 120–134 are the "Songs of Ascent"; Psalms 138–145 also have the title "Of David," and Psalms 146–150 are also Hallelujah psalms. There is a great deal of uncertainty about the organization of Book V and about the way individual psalms are related to one another; indeed, it has been questioned whether the book has a coherent structure at all. What can be said, however, is that Book V has a strong hymnic undertone. Over and above the hallelujah invocations to which we have already referred, the Hebrew verbs *hll* (praise) and *ydh* (praise, give thanks) occur in all except a few of these psalms (cf. Psalms 110, 119, 134, 137, 143, and 144). Whereas in Book IV (Psalms 90–106) the kingship of the LORD is emphasized, Book V appears to concentrate on the Davidic aspect of the kingship. Another general characteristic of Book V is that it is suffused with Zion theology and motifs from temple theology and that it has a strong cultic character.

Although Psalm 107 introduces a new book, it is nevertheless striking that a link is created with Psalm 106 by the similarity between the first verses of the psalms: "O give thanks to the LORD . . ." (cf. Pss 106:1 and 107:1). Psalm 107 is essentially a song of praise for the "steadfast love" of the LORD.

107:1-3 are an introductory call to thanksgiving and praise in which reasons are given why the LORD should be thanked and praised. By repeating the word "redeemed" twice, the psalmist makes clear that God is to be praised because he has ransomed his people (Heb. *g'l*) and gathered them from all four points of the compass (v. 3). The expression "gathered in from the lands" (v. 3) and the similarities between Psalm 106 and Deutero-Isaiah indicate that the deliverance from exile is the reason for praising the LORD.

107:4-32 form a congruent whole and deal with people experiencing various forms of distress. The psalm speaks of four such situations: the hunger and wanderings of those lost in a desert (vv. 4-9); the suffering of people in prison (vv. 10-16); people mortally ill due to sin (vv. 17-22); and seafarers caught in a violent storm (vv. 23-32). These four sections show a fixed pattern. First of all, the situation of distress is described; then follow the prayer for help and the deliverance from distress, expressed in the form of four refrains (cf. vv. 6, 13, 19, 28); thirdly, the deliverance is more closely defined, followed by a call to give thanks, which also takes the form of a refrain (cf. vv. 8, 15, 21, 31); in conclusion, the invocation is taken further (e.g., "Let them extol him . . . ," v. 32) or substantiated (e.g., "For he satisfies the thirsty . . . ," v. 9). The description in vv. 4-32 should not be taken literally as a description of specific situations. It should rather be seen as an ambiguous passage in the sense of a subtle allusion to Israel's history (vv. 4-9 could refer to the wilderness period or to the exile). The four groups of people in the distress situations should be seen as representative of extremes of human need and show a correlation with the four points of the compass from which the LORD redeemed people (v. 3). This section, therefore, deals with comprehensive need, but it also speaks of comprehensive salvation.

The last section (107:33-43) differs from the preceding in that there is a movement from the particular to the more general. This section shows unmistakable wisdom characteristics, and the poet makes use of striking contrasts. The LORD radically changes existing situations: "He turns rivers into a desert . . ." (v. 33). He punishes sinners and aids the hungry. He humiliates the proud and uplifts the humble and those in distress.

As is typical of a wisdom text, this section ends with a warning: "Let those who are wise give heed to these things . . ." (v. 43). The function of this piece of wisdom literature is to persuade the reader/listener to make a choice for the LORD and against wickedness. To be wise means to recognize the "steadfast love" of the LORD. The psalm displays an *inclusio* in that it begins with "steadfast love" (v. 1) and ends with it as well (v. 43), thereby confirming that Psalm 107 is a song of thanks and praise for the "steadfast love" of the LORD.

Psalm 108

Psalm 108 is composed of extracts from two other psalms, namely, Ps 57:7-11 [= Ps 108:1-5] and Ps 60:6-12 [= Ps 108:6-13]. Barring a few minor variations, Psalm 108 is identical to these two texts. Psalm 57 is an individual lament, and Psalm 60 is a national lament. The poet uses the individual praise section from Psalm 57 and the oracle and utterance of confidence in Psalm 60 to create an entirely new text. In response to a new situation the poet had to use older texts to bring a new message to his people. The poet was probably living in the uncertain postexilic period; thus the intention of Psalm 108 was to comfort the people and give them new courage. The psalm shows unmistakable confidence that God will defeat the enemies of his people.

The first part of the psalm is an individual song of praise which expresses the feelings of the community and which was intended to be sung among the nations to carry the message to them. The psalmist praises the LORD as the exalted God and prays that he will demonstrate his "glory" over all the earth by bringing about victory for his people.

The second part (108:6-9) is an oracle (cf. Ps 60:6-8) which is written as a song of victory by a military commander to show that in the midst of a desperate situation God is still in control and can be trusted. The third strophe (108:10-13) is a collective prayer for God's help in making the foregoing oracle come true. The crisis of the exile is also expressed in the lament, however (cf. v. 11, "Have you not rejected us, O God . . ."). The intention of the psalm is clearly expressed in the last verse (v. 13, "With God we shall do valiantly . . ."), which reflects firm confidence in God.

Psalm 109 (*see* Individual Laments, 366-73)

Psalm 110

Although Psalm 110 is a royal psalm and probably owed its origin to the ascension to the throne of one of the Davidic kings, the psalm focuses chiefly on the LORD's kingship, so that we can say that the psalm reflects a theocracy. Psalm 110 is divided into two strophes (vv. 1-3 and 4-7) each beginning with a well-known prophetic formula ("The LORD says . . . ," v. 1; "The LORD has sworn . . . ," v. 4).

In the first strophe (110:1-3) the poet speaks with the authority of a prophet who has received a message from the LORD ("The LORD says . . .") to convey to the king ("to my lord"). The content of this strophe is that the king does not rule on his own but that he is the authorized representative of God. The king's authority and power depend on those of the LORD. He occupies this position of honor ("at my right hand") because the LORD has appointed him to it. Military terminology is used to describe how God will extend the king's sphere of power and influence. V. 3 contains so many text-critical problems that it poses virtually insurmountable interpretative problems. There are two possible interpretations. The first is a militaristic interpretation, as in the NRSV (cf. the translation of v. 3); it takes v. 3 to mean that the king's military forces, especially his young fighting men, are prepared to wage war for him. The other possibility is to translate v. 3 as the JB does: "Royal dignity was yours from the day you were born . . . royal from the womb, from the dawn of your earliest days." The latter translation refers mainly to the descent of the king and to the fact that the LORD adopted him as a son when he ascended the throne.

The second strophe (110:4-7) is also introduced by a prophetic formula. In addition to having received his authority as a ruler and his military powers from the LORD, the king also receives his priesthood from God (v. 4). Just as the priesthood and kingship were united in the person of Melchizedek, king of Salem (= Jerusalem; cf. Gen 14:17-24), so the present king of Jerusalem would also be both priest and king. The ideal situation of the theocracy is sketched here. In v. 5 there is a return to military terminology. The repetition of the words "at my right hand" (v. 1) in v. 5 ("at your right hand") brings about a reversal of the roles. In v. 1 this expression refers to the king's position of honor. In v. 5 the LORD is at the king's right hand and the expression refers to God's aid in a military situation. In v. 6 the LORD is portrayed as the universal judge who is also victorious in war. In v. 7 the military metaphor is continued, but the king is now the subject of the military action. He is described as pursuing his enemies. Although tired, he pauses only for a moment to drink water so that he "will lift up his head," that is, will triumph over his enemies.

Psalm 110 sketches the ideal Davidic monarchy. The sovereignty of the LORD takes on concrete form in the person of the king. The king is the personification of the sovereignty of the LORD because the altar (priestly functions) and the throne (regal power) are combined in the king. This text could be used at the coronation ceremony of any new king.

In the NT the psalm takes on a totally new meaning in that it receives a direct christological interpretation and is made applicable to Jesus Christ in various ways (cf., e.g., Matt 22:44; Acts 2:34-35; 7:55; Rom 8:34; 1 Cor 15:25; Eph 1:20; Heb 1:13; 5:6; 7:11-25; 10:13). It is, however, apparent from the above discussion that the psalm did not originally have a christological meaning.

Psalms 111 and 112

Psalms 111 and 112 have frequently been called twin psalms. Apart from the fact that they are both acrostic poems (for the term cf. Psalms 9–10), there are numerous similarities between the two psalms: both psalms are introduced by the invocation "Praise the LORD," and there are numerous repetitions of words and phrases (cf. Pss 111:3 with 112:3 and 9; 111:5a and 10a with 112:1a; 111:2b with 112:1b; 111:1b with 112:2 and 4; 111:4b with 112:4b; 111:7 with 112:5; 111:1b with 112:7 and 8). Both psalms show characteristics of wisdom literature. For example, Psalm 111 ends with a wisdom saying ("The fear of the LORD is the beginning of wisdom . . . ," v. 10), and Psalm 112 begins with a well-known wisdom saying ("Happy are those who fear the LORD . . . ," v. 1). Psalm 112 cannot be read separately from Psalm 111 since the latter supplies the theological framework within which the ethical statements of Psalm 112 are to be interpreted. Where Psalm 111 praises the great works and the righteousness of the LORD, Psalm 112 tells us how "those who fear the LORD" — the righteous — should live and conduct themselves. It appears from these repetitions that the righteous in Psalm 112 are described in a manner analogous to the way in which the LORD is described in Psalm 111. It is said of the LORD in Ps 111:4: "the LORD is gracious and merciful." Of the righteous it is said in Psalm 112:4: "they are gracious, merciful and righteous." Psalm 112 is thus saying that the righteous should serve as the image of the LORD.

Psalm 111 is a hymn, as may be deduced from the fact that it is introduced by "Praise the LORD" (v. 1) and concluded by "His praise endures forever" (v. 10). Vv. 2-9 give reasons for the call to praise and contain general and cryptic references to the "wonderful deeds" of the LORD (cf. vv. 2, 3, 6, 7). There are two references to the covenant of the LORD (vv. 5, 9), which serve to emphasize that the LORD has remained true to his promises throughout history. The praiseworthiness of the LORD is further enhanced by listing his attributes: his "righteousness" and "power," and the fact that he is "gracious," "merciful," "faithful," "just," "holy," and "awesome."

The wisdom character of the psalm emerges strongly in v. 10: "The fear of the LORD is the beginning of wisdom." Only those who fear the LORD, that is, who have a living relationship with him and love him, are able to praise him.

Psalm 112 begins where Psalm 111 left off, namely, with a wisdom saying: "Happy are those who fear the LORD." Only those who love the LORD are truly happy and have attained the pinnacle of joy. The rest of the psalm describes the lifestyle of those who are called "happy" in v. 1.

In 112:2-3 the subject is the blessing that will befall the descendants and households of the righteous. The people of the OT regarded descendants as very important. They believed that they would achieve immortality through the lives of their descendants. The righteous received a double blessing (vv. 2-3). Not only were they promised innumerable progeny, but their progeny would also be rich and influential.

112:4-5 say that the wish to be the image of the LORD should be expressed in practical ways. It is the task of the righteous to defeat darkness, to behave in a just and equitable manner toward their neighbors, and to maintain a right relationship with them. The righteous are concerned about others, help those who are in trouble, and are unselfish in their actions. V. 6 confirms the above: the lives of the righteous are characterized by stability and security. A righteous person makes a lasting impression on his contemporaries and is remembered by them.

112:7-8 examine the lives of the righteous from another angle. A righteous person is not immune to the problems of life. He goes through bad times. He is also subjected to the onslaught of enemies. Because of his faith in the LORD, however, he is not afraid. His faith gives him peace and security. In v. 9 the theme of vv. 4-6 is taken up again. As the LORD dispenses blessings to those who fear him (Ps 111:5), so the righteous should also be generous to the poor.

The psalm is carried to a climax in 112:9c-10. The righteous are honored and have influence and authority. The wicked see this and become so vexed that they are consumed with impotent rage, melt away, and gnash their teeth! (v. 10). The righteous have a future, but the future of the ungodly is uncertain.

The aim of this contrast and the purpose of the wisdom psalm is to persuade the reader/listener to make a choice against wickedness and for a life of righteousness. When Psalm 112 is read in the light of Psalm 111, it is clear that this lifestyle is possible only if one sees and recognizes the "wonderful deeds" of the LORD. Only then can one try to live in the image of God in the sense intended in Psalm 112.

Psalm 113

In Judaism Psalm 113 is known as the first of the Hallel psalms (113–118), which are sung at the three main annual festivals and play an important part, especially in the Passover liturgy. Psalm 113 is a typical hymn and forms an *inclusio* in that it is both introduced (v. 1a) and concluded (v. 9b) by the hallelujah invocation. The psalm can be divided into three strophes. The first strophe (vv. 1b-3) is a call to praise. In the second strophe (vv. 4-6) the reason for praise is given, namely, that the LORD is "above the nations." The third strophe (vv. 7-9a) expands on this by spelling out the results of the LORD's exalted nature.

The first strophe (113:1b-3) is a call to praise and forms an *inclusio* in that it is introduced (v. 1b) and concluded (v. 3) with *praise/d*. The emphasis falls on the "name of the LORD" (this phrase occurs three times; cf. vv. 1, 2, 3), which is to be praised. The "name of the LORD" is used to indicate the LORD's personal presence, especially his presence in the assembled congregation. The psalmist is referring to all-embracing praise, for he says that the name of the LORD must be praised at all times and in all places.

The second strophe (113:4-6) gives the reason why the LORD should be praised. This strophe is also characterized by an *inclusio* in that the word "heavens" occurs in the first (v. 4) and the last (v. 6) verses of the strophe. The use of the word "heavens" indicates that the psalmist is referring to God's exalted nature. Heaven does not refer to a specific place but should be seen as a metaphor for the LORD's royal dignity. Psalm 113 tells us that the LORD has not withdrawn to heaven but plays an active part in events on earth. For this reason the LORD is incomparable, unlike all other gods, and therefore even more praiseworthy.

The third strophe (113:7-9) tells us that the LORD's magnitude and exaltedness may be seen in his merciful dealings with powerless people and those of low social standing ("the poor," "the needy," "the barren woman") and in the way he brings about a radical change in their situation. These are typical terms to describe the critical situation of the people in exile as well as to portray the height of suffering and the LORD's identification with his people.

Psalm 113 shows us that the LORD is both transcendent and immanent; he is the exalted God but also the God who intervenes in times of need. For this reason he is to be praised by his servants at all times and in all places.

Psalm 114

Psalm 114 is a poetic reinterpretation and actualization of the salvation history of Israel. The poet does not allow himself to become bogged down by detail and gives no chronological account of history. Rather, he gives theological meaning to this concise account of salvation history and reduces the geographical map of the routes out of and into the land to a few well-defined strokes of the pen.

In the first strophe (114:1-2) the exodus is described as the cradle of Israel, the beginning of the road which ultimately led to Israel's becoming the chosen nation. The exodus also represents the theological end of salvation history as Israel is made the sanctuary and kingdom of the LORD. Psalm 114 thus reflects the tension between Israel who is enslaved by Egypt and Israel who is governed by the LORD.

In the second strophe (114:3-4) the exodus and the entry into the land are presented dramatically as the reaction of personified elements of nature ("the sea," "the Jordan," "the mountains") to salvation history. To heighten the tension, the name of the LORD is not mentioned. Instead, the presence of the LORD and his deeds of salvation are subtly implied in the anxious reaction of the elements to the LORD's awesome intervention. The greatness of the LORD is underscored by dramatizing salvation history.

Although the third strophe (114:5-6) is virtually a refrain (cf. vv. 3-4), a new element is introduced as well, namely, a rhetorical question ("Why is it, O sea . . ."), to which the strophe itself supplies the answer, namely, that this unparalleled reaction of nature is occasioned by nature's perception of the LORD's awe-inspiring intervention in history. The ironical tone of the question again emphasizes both the LORD's omnipotence and the helpless subordination of nature.

The denouement occurs in the fourth strophe (114:7-8). The tension is discharged, and what the sea observed, why the Jordan flowed back upon itself, and why the mountains skipped become clear: the matter at issue is the presence of almighty God, for whose sake the earth, which stands for the whole universe, is exhorted to tremble. By reverting to salvation history once more — this time to the wilderness tradition — the psalmist indicates that the LORD can accomplish the impossible, such as turning the impenetrable rock into a fountain.

By reinterpreting the history of Israel the poem seeks to focus attention on one idea, that God is in complete control of history and that he can accomplish that which seems impossible to human beings. Psalm 114 could have been used in times of hardship, such as the exile, but can also be used at any time to encourage and console God's people when their faith is shaken.

Psalm 115

Psalm 115 is a polemic against the idols of the nations. The mocking question ("'Where is their God?'" v. 2) and the prayer (cf. v. 1) that the LORD should maintain his "glory" imply that the people of God found themselves in a hostile environment. A likely setting would have been the postexilic period, when the defeated people of God must have doubted the almighty power of God when they had to face powerful empires with apparently mighty gods and endure the mockery of the nations. The polemic is intended for the assembled congregation of the LORD, and its function is to persuade them to trust in the LORD and give them new courage to face their difficult circumstances.

115:4-8 are a sarcastic mockery of idols (see Ps 135:15-18, which is virtually identical; cf. also Isa 44:9-20 and Jer 10:1-10). Despite the fact that idols are made of the most precious materials and are perfectly formed, they remain the products of "human hands" and are lifeless, powerless, and useless objects. The people who fashioned the idols and trust in them are as powerless as the idols themselves.

Characteristically, the LORD is contrasted with idols. The LORD is not bound to the earth as the idols are, but is exalted in the heavens (cf. 115:16) and free to do whatever pleases him (v. 3). The LORD was not made by humans; no, he made heaven and earth and is in control of all things. Unlike the impotent idols in which people cannot trust, the LORD is the powerful and reliable God with whom those who believe in him can take shelter. The poet emphasizes this idea by repeating it three times as a refrain: "He is their help . . ." (cf. vv. 9, 10, and 11). It is for this reason that Israel should trust in the LORD. The poet again uses a threefold refrain to emphasize the appeal to trust in the LORD (cf. vv. 9, 10, and 11).

The poet calls upon the whole congregation by using three names for them ("Israel," "the house of Aaron," and those "who fear the LORD"; cf. 115:9, 10, and 11). The poet's predilection for the refrain is further revealed by his repetition of these three designations in vv. 12-13. They are used here within the context of the promise that the LORD will "bless" his people. The poet emphasizes the matter by using the word "bless" five times in vv. 12-15. The meaning of this verb is to bring about contentment and to confer peace and salvation.

Psalm 115 is concluded by a hymn (vv. 16-18). The praiseworthiness of the LORD is emphasized by the poet's use of a contrast: the "dead" do not praise the LORD, "but we," that is the faithful people of the LORD, have no other choice than to praise him continually.

Psalm 115 is intended to persuade the people of God who are in need that the LORD is mightier than the idols of the nations.

Psalm 116

Psalm 116 is an individual thanksgiving from someone who experienced the wonderful salvation of God in a special way in his personal life. A characteristic of the psalm is that it begins with an emphatic foregrounded personal confession of the poet's love and trust in the LORD after his supplication had been heard. The psalm ends with an invocation to praise. Another characteristic of the psalm is that the first person singular plays a dominant role throughout. The psalm deals with an individual's need, faith, and relationship with God.

There is no obvious strophal division in the psalm. Some exegetes have contended that there is little evidence of coherence in it. The LXX even divides Psalm 116 into two separate psalms, namely, vv. 1-9 and 10-19. However, coherence is to be found at a thematic level and is effected by the use of the first person singular throughout the psalm. The following themes occur repeatedly: the poet's need; the poet's prayer to God for aid; the fact that the Lord helped the poet and heard his prayer; thanksgiving and praise toward the LORD.

The situation of distress is not clearly spelled out. The description should be regarded as metaphorical language in which the pinnacles of human need, such as death (cf. 116:3, 8, 15), false accusations by people (cf. v. 11), and captivity (cf. v. 16), are depicted.

The poet's only refuge in distress is to call upon the LORD for help. This is emphasized by the triple repetition of the expression "I call/ed on the name of the LORD" (cf. 116:4, 13, 17; cf. also v. 2) and by the appeal for help (v. 4b).

The fact that the LORD "saved and heard" the poet plays an important part. 116:6 sums this up very well: "when I was brought low, he saved me" (cf. also vv. 5, 7, 8, 12, 16). The only proper response to the salvation of the Lord is to thank and praise him. The climax is the invocation to praise in the last verse. The refrain strongly emphasizes the theme of thanksgiving and praise. "I will pay my vows to the LORD . . ." (cf. vv. 14, 18). As the servant of the LORD (cf. v. 16, where the expression "I am your servant" is repeated twice), the poet may not keep his experience of the LORD's salvation to himself; it is necessary for him to bear witness before the whole community of faith.

Because of the numerous Aramaisms that occur in the psalm (cf., e.g., the suffixes in the HB in 116:7, 12, 19), it is likely that the psalm originated during the postexilic period. The individual who expressed his or her deepest experience of the LORD's salvation may have done so on behalf of the delivered post-exilic community.

Psalm 117

Although Psalm 117 is the shortest psalm in the psalter, it is nevertheless a classic example of a hymn in that it contains the basic elements, namely, invocations to praise and reasons why the LORD should be praised. In addition to the imperatives to praise with which the psalm is introduced and concluded ("Praise the LORD!" vv. 1a, 2b), forming an *inclusio,* there is a third invocation to praise, namely, "Extol him" (v. 1b). A surprising aspect is that the invocation to praise is not directed to Israel but to foreign nations. Although Psalm 117 is a short psalm, its range is universal. The nations are enjoined to praise the LORD because he has shown his steadfast love to the despised little nation of Israel. This universalistic tone of Psalm 117 corresponds to the message of the book of Deutero-Isaiah (Isaiah 40–55), which makes it probable that Psalm 117 also dates from the exile.

Psalm 118

When one reads the commentaries on Psalm 118, the same question arises time and again: Which genre does this psalm belong to? Is it an individual or collective song of thanksgiving? Although the cultic character of the psalm is generally accepted (cf., e.g., v. 27), there is no certainty as to exactly which cultic occasion or festival the psalm refers to. There is also a difference of opinion on whom the first person singular in the psalm refers to. Does it refer to a specific individual or should it be understood collectively? Other points on which scholars differ are the strophal division of the psalm and the question whether the psalm was originally written by one person or whether the history of its origin was complex. Most of these questions can be said to have been imposed on the psalm; the text itself does not answer them.

The first matter which strikes the reader is that the psalm is introduced and concluded by the same refrain: "O give thanks to the LORD, for he is good . . ." (cf. 118:1, 29). The refrain creates the framework within which the entire poem should be read and indicates that the subject of the psalm is the thanks due to the LORD for his goodness and faithful love. The rest of the psalm is an explication of the meaning of "for he is good" and "his steadfast love endures forever." The remainder of the first strophe (i.e., vv. 2-4) is a continuation of v. 1 and contains three jussives in which the entire community is called upon to acknowledge that the LORD's "steadfast love endures forever." The latter expression is repeated three times as a refrain. The refrain occurs repeatedly in the remainder of the psalm. Another characteristic is the number of brief confessions that occur: "The LORD is on my side . . ." (v. 7; cf. also v. 6); "The LORD is my strength and my might" (v. 14); "The LORD is God" (v. 27).

118:5-21 form a unit in which the first person singular occurs frequently. The "I/me" in vv. 5-21 should be interpreted collectively in the sense that it refers to someone speaking on behalf of the people. Vv. 5-21 can be divided into smaller sections. In vv. 5-9 the central idea is that with the LORD as ally there is nothing to fear. This idea is underlined by two refrains, namely, "The LORD is on my side" (vv. 6, 7) and "It is better to take refuge in the LORD than to put confidence in mortals" (vv. 8-9). In vv. 10-14 we are told that it is only the power of the LORD that made it possible to repulse the fierce onslaughts of the enemies. The verb "surrounded" is used four times to describe the onslaught of the enemies, but the refrain "in the name of the LORD I cut them off!" is used three times. This theme is carried further in vv. 15-16, which are a short, triumphal song of the righteous. By again repeating a refrain three times (cf. vv. 15b, 16), the psalmist gives all the praise for the victory to the LORD: "'The right hand of the LORD does valiantly.'" In the next section (vv. 17-21) the poet again refers to the critical situation, using a contrast: "I shall not die, but I shall live." The "punishment" meted out by the LORD was a temporary chastisement, and now that it is over the LORD is to be praised for it in his temple (cf. vv. 19-20). Vv. 5-21 form an *inclusio* in that they are introduced by "the LORD answered me" (v. 5) and concluded by "I thank you that you have answered me" (v. 21). This is further evidence that Psalm 118 deals with thanksgiving to the LORD for hearing his people in their time of need.

In 118:22-27 the first person singular is replaced by the first person plural. A metaphor from the building trade ("The stone that the builders rejected . . .") emphasizes that it is the LORD who has done this marvelous thing. A hint of the crisis is again seen in the use of a refrain (v. 25).

Because the LORD has wrought salvation, the congregation are to praise him "in festal procession" (v. 27). Those who come to the house of the LORD in this spirit may entreat his blessing (v. 26). V. 28 returns to first person singular forms with exuberant praise, which is expressed in the refrain "you are my God." The psalm concludes in the same way in which it began, namely, with thanksgiving to the LORD.

It seems likely that the broad historical context of the psalm is the exile. The description of this critical situation, but also the words of gratitude toward the LORD and confidence in him because he has saved his people are placed in the mouth of an individual.

Psalm 118 is one of the psalms quoted most frequently in the NT (cf., e.g., vv. 22-23 with Matt 21:42; Mark 12:10-11; Luke 20:17; Acts 4:11; 1 Pet 2:7; and v. 6 with Heb 13:6). Space does not permit me to examine the above NT texts in detail or to comment on the way in which the NT "quotes" the OT.

Psalm 119

Psalm 119 is the longest psalm in the psalter. On a superficial reading it might appear tedious on account of the numerous apparently unnecessary repetitions. Psalm 119 is also an acrostic psalm. An acrostic psalm is a poem in which each successive line begins with the following letter of the alphabet (cf. also, e.g., Psalms 9–10, 25, 34, 37). Psalm 119 is, however, unique in the sense that it consists of twenty-two stanzas of eight lines each, that is, 176 lines. The first eight lines, that is, the first stanza, begin with the first letter of the Hebrew alphabet *(aleph),* the second stanza with the second letter, and so on, until eventually all twenty-two letters of the Hebrew alphabet have been worked through.

The central theme of Psalm 119 is the *torah* (NRSV = "law") of the LORD. In all, eight synonyms for "law" are used in the psalm, namely, *torah, dabar* ("word"), *mishpaṭim* ("ordinances"), *'edut* ("decrees"), *piqqudim* ("precepts"), *ḥuqqim* ("statutes"), *miṣwah* ("commandments"), and *'imrah* ("promise"). With two exceptions (vv. 90 and 122), each of the 176 lines contains one of the synonyms for "law." The acrostic structure of the psalm and the facts that eight synonyms are used and that eight lines are devoted to each letter of the alphabet make for a sense of completeness. Psalm 119 deals with dedication to the *torah* and the role the *torah* plays in the life of a believer. The psalm explores this theme thoroughly and from various points of view.

However, no logical structure or progressive development can be seen in the psalm. The unity and coherence of the psalm lie in the central theme, which is repeated again and again from various perspectives.

Exegetes are virtually unanimous in their belief that Psalm 119 dates from the postexilic period. The wisdom character of the psalm, the emphasis placed on the law, and the use of other books of the OT such as Deuteronomy, Proverbs, Job, Jeremiah, Ezekiel, and Isaiah 40–55 would seem to indicate a post-exilic date for Psalm 119. In the preexilic period the temple and the monarchy were the symbols of the LORD's presence with the people. When these symbols were destroyed during the exile, new symbols for God's presence had to be created. In the postexilic period the *torah* became the supreme symbol of God's presence.

Although the emphasis in Psalm 119 falls on the law, the psalm does not fall into legalism. The poet does not use the umbrella term "law" as representing a rigid code of regulations. For the poet of Psalm 119 the *torah* is the good news of the LORD's intervention. It promises the healing of broken relationships and provides a guideline for human conduct. The *torah* is the instrument through which God interacts with humans and humans are permitted to approach God. The *torah* is a call to obedience and dedication to God and serves as the norm for distinguishing the righteous from the wicked. In Psalm 119 it is always linked to God by means of a pronominal suffix ("your laws," "your decrees," "your commandments," etc.). This signifies that the *torah* is not regarded as of the same magnitude as the LORD or placed on the same level. The *torah* belongs to the LORD. Furthermore, the relationship of the righteous with the *torah* cannot be detached from his/her relationship with God, as v. 63 shows: "I am a companion . . . of those who keep your precepts." This is the *torah* the poet loves. The *torah* is his promised land ("my portion," v. 57), his "delight" (vv. 24, 77, 92, 143, 174), the joy of his heart (v. 111), his riches (v. 72), and a light to his path (v. 105).

Although the eight words used for law are largely synonymous, it should be remembered that there is no such thing as a true synonym. For convenience' sake these eight words may be divided into at least two semantic categories: the words *'imrah* ("promise"), *dabar* ("word"), and *mishpaṭim* ("ordinances") have to do with the LORD's promise or assurance to humans and his deeds of salvation. These terms, therefore, supply a norm for the LORD's actions. The other five words — *torah* ("law"), *'edut* ("decrees"), *piqqudim* ("precepts"), *ḥuqqim* ("statutes"), and *miṣwah* ("commandments") — have to do with God's instructions to humankind and can be regarded as a norm for our actions.

There are three characters or groups of characters in Psalm 119: the "righteous," who speaks about himself and his experiences and associates with other believers; the "enemies" of the righteous, that is, the wicked, who mock and taunt the righteous in various ways; and the "LORD," who has a personal relationship with the righteous and is called upon to help him by punishing his enemies. These three characters form a triangle of relationships which can be represented as follows:

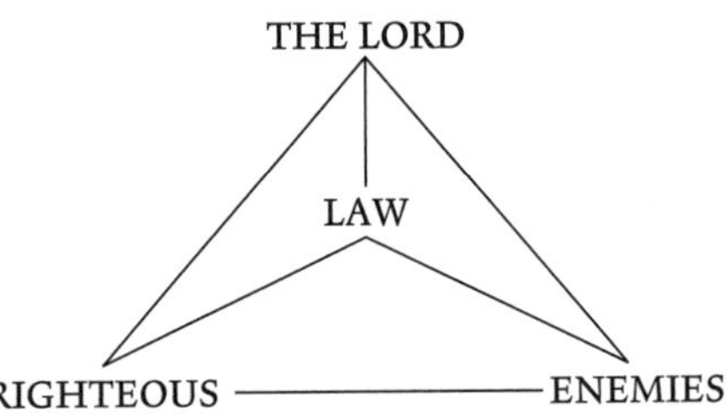

The law plays a primary role in this triangular relationship. It serves as a kind of buffer between the LORD and the just man and the LORD and the enemies. In his love for the LORD the just man focuses on the law. The LORD uses the law as an intermediary in his relationship with believers, and the law serves as an instrument of judgment and punishment for the enemies of the believer. This representation of the triangular relationship indicates that the LORD's relationship with people — divided here into the righteous and the wicked — is another important theme of Psalm 119.

Any attempt to describe the contents of Psalm 119 must take account of the fact that the psalm is written in the first person, in other words, from the perspective of an individual. In terms of the triangular relationship in which the *torah* plays such an important part, the poet's attitude toward life and his relationship with the other characters may be described as follows:

The poet describes his own circumstances as a situation of *need.* In these sections the poet chiefly uses the genre of the individual lament. The poet experiences the world as hostile and strange; he is like a traveler in a strange land (v. 19). Worry, anxiety, and distress embitter his life (vv. 28, 120, 143). He is not respected by other people but mocked by them (vv. 22, 39, 141). His condition is miserable (vv. 50, 92, 136, 153). Nevertheless he expects to be *saved* from his distress (vv. 17, 77, 116-117). He says that he will not be put to shame (vv. 6, 46, 80). He therefore still has reason to praise the LORD (v. 62) and is even thankful for his adversity (v. 71). He is innocent (v. 161) and has found security (v. 152).

The poet expresses his feelings about his *enemies* in

strong language. He hates all those who do not obey the *torah* (vv. 104, 113, 128, 163). He becomes angry with the wicked (v. 53) and regards their actions with loathing (v. 158). For this reason he distances himself from them (v. 115) and avoids them (v. 101). He describes them as callous (v. 70), arrogant (v. 78), deceitful (v. 118), faithless (v. 158), and dross (v. 119). The wicked are characterized chiefly by their contempt for and disobedience of the *torah* (vv. 21, 53, 85, 118, 126, 136, 150, 155, 158). The adversaries are continually and actively engaged in injuring the righteous; they plot against him (v. 23), deride him (v. 51), and lay snares for him and dig pitfalls for him (vv. 61, 85, 95, 110); they pretend that he is a liar (v. 69) and persecute him without cause (v. 161). The enemies are defined in terms of their attitude toward the *torah;* all who do not serve the LORD in this way are defined as his adversaries. In contrast, the poet is a friend of all who serve the LORD (v. 63).

His personal relationship with *God* is very important to the poet. He wishes to praise the LORD, even seven times a day (vv. 7, 62, 108, 164, 171, 175), and he even thinks of him at night (v. 55); he seeks the LORD with his whole heart (v. 10); he honors the LORD (vv. 38, 120); he knows that he belongs to God (v. 94) and calls upon him for help (v. 145); he experiences God as righteous, merciful (vv. 41, 64, 65, 68, 76, 77, 124, 137, 142, 149, 156, 159), and faithful (v. 90). The LORD made him (v. 73), and the LORD is his refuge (v. 114). For this reason he prays unceasingly that the LORD will save him (vv. 37, 40, 77, 94) and teach him the *torah* (vv. 12, 26, 33, 108).

The poet loves the *torah* (cf., e.g., vv. 47, 97, 127, 163); he is also in awe of the *torah* (vv. 120, 161), trusts in it (vv. 42, 66), and longs for it (cf., e.g., vv. 31, 45, 81, 131). He will never forget the *torah* (cf., e.g., vv. 14, 24, 47, 54, 70, 103), and he meditates faithfully on it (cf., e.g., vv. 15, 23, 48, 78, 148).

When Psalm 119 is read in its entirety, it is striking that phrases and expressions from the remainder of the psalter, Deuteronomy, Proverbs, and the prophetic writings have been taken up and used to create a new text. The poet also combines a variety of genres — especially the individual lament and wisdom literature — to create a unique text which we could call a prayer of dedication. Psalm 119 expresses dedication to the *torah* and therefore also to God, the giver of the *torah.* The poet uses the length of this psalm, its comprehensiveness, and its numerous repetitions to persuade the reader/listener to dedicate himself or herself fully to the LORD.

Psalms 120–134

Psalms 120–134 form a collection in the sense that all these psalms (with a small variation in the case of Ps 121:1) have "A Song of Ascents" (Heb. *shir hamma'alot)* as the title. One of the unanswered questions regarding the "Song of Ascents" is whether there is a relationship between these psalms, and, if so, what the nature of that relationship might be. Another related question concerns the meaning of the title *hamma'alot.*

On the one hand, some exegetes are of the opinion that the collection originally formed a unit and may even have been written by a single author. On the other hand, there are people who feel that the collection owes its origin to an editorial process and did not originally form a single unit.

There is no certainty as to the meaning of the title "Song of Ascents": a *cultic* meaning would be one possibility. One of the most popular explanations of the significance of the title is that these psalms were sung by the Levites on the fifteen steps (whence the fifteen psalms) of the temple during religious festivals. The most usual cultic explanation is that the title refers to three of the principal festivals, namely, the feast of Tabernacles, the Passover, and the feast of Weeks. These psalms would then have been sung by pilgrims on their way to the temple in Jerusalem, whence the name "Songs of Ascents" or "Pilgrim Songs." Some exegetes give a *historical* explanation based on the supposition that the title is a reference to the return of the Judean exiles from Babylon to Jerusalem. Other scholars give a *literary* explanation for the title because a stylistic figure recurs throughout the book in which the last words of a line are repeated at the beginning of the next line. An example of this is to be found in Psalm 121:7 and 8:

> . . . he will keep your life (v. 7b)
> The LORD will keep your going . . . (v. 8a).

There is a stepwise development of ideas, and the title *shir hamma'alot* is translated "step songs."

Although Psalms 120–134 form a unit in their present form, it is by no means easy to supply definite answers to the above questions. Furthermore, a variety of genres are discernible among these psalms. The arrangement of the psalms shows no logical succession or dramatic development. The title is the product of a later editorial addition or a cultic situation. The psalms must have had something in common, however, to make this reinterpretation possible. When the psalms are read in the Hebrew, one is struck by the fact that each individual psalm shows evidence of sophisticated artistry on the part of the poet. It is notable that the same poetic techniques are used throughout the collection and that there is a striking network of word repetitions. Themes such as the enemies, idolatrous forces, personal and domestic life, Zion/Jerusalem/the temple, the Davidic monarchy, the cult, and the blessing of the LORD recur frequently. The theme of trust is like a golden thread running through these psalms. The high frequency of songs of trust is related to this theme. The LORD is described as the almighty creator, merciful savior, and the God who bestows abundant blessings, who can be trusted unconditionally, and in whom shelter can be sought. The LORD's care is all-embracing and everlasting. Not only does he care for the righteous, but he also punishes and destroys the ungodly. The recurring theme of trust would have made a highly suitable message of encouragement in the desolate postexilic situation. This collection would probably have been used both inside and outside the cult as a consolation. It is doubtful whether it was originally intended as a cultic-liturgical manual.

Leaving aside all the questions about the origin of

this collection and the degree of unity it displays, each of the psalms needs to be read and discussed on its own merits.

Psalm 120 (*see also* Individual Laments, 366-73)

Psalm 120 consists of two sections, namely, vv. 1-4 and vv. 5-7. The LORD has come to the suppliant's aid in the past (v. 1), and he prays that the LORD will deliver him now from those with "lying lips" and "deceitful tongues." The enemies' punishment is described in military terminology (vv. 3-4). Although the suppliant strives for peace, he finds himself among those who hate peace (vv. 5-7). We do not know to what or to whom the names "Meshech" and "Kedar" refer. It would be best not to interpret the names literally but to regard them as general names representative of hostile nations (cf. also Ezek 38:2 and Isa 21:13-17).

Psalm 121

Psalm 121 may be classified as a psalm of trust or confidence. The poet casts the psalm in a deliberately planned form that will enable him to arrive at this expression of confidence. The psalm could be represented as an inverse triangle:

Question: ". . . from where will my help come?" (v. 1)

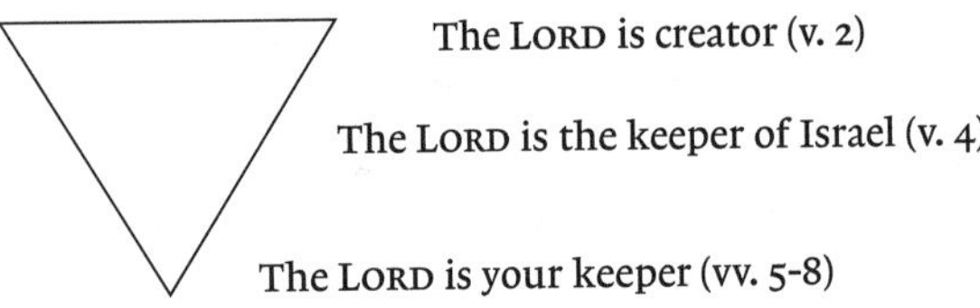
The LORD is creator (v. 2)
The LORD is the keeper of Israel (v. 4)
The LORD is your keeper (vv. 5-8)

The psalm begins with a question which reflects anxiety and uncertainty. It was not originally written as a pilgrim song. The hills spoken of in 121:1 are not the hills which the pilgrims had to cross on their journey to Jerusalem. In view of the polemic qualities that are evident in the rest of the psalm, hills should also be interpreted in a polemic sense, namely, as the dwelling place of the gods. Consequently, v. 1b is a rhetorical question which expects a negative answer, namely, that one's help does not come from the hills, that is, from the gods. The remainder of the psalm answers the question in a positive manner by stating that the source of help is God alone.

121:2 says that all help comes from the LORD. The poet rejects the mysterious force of the hills and draws on the creation tradition by saying that the LORD has made "heaven and earth." He is in control of all things and is able to help his people.

Where 121:2 begins with general, indeed universal concepts — the creation — in vv. 3-4 the circle is narrowed. Salvation history is given as the reason why we can expect help from the LORD. The LORD is described as "He who keeps Israel." It is striking that the LORD's deeds are described in negative terms (". . . not let your foot be moved . . . not slumber . . . nor sleep"). Vv. 3 and 4 also contain strong polemic elements. Whereas the fertility gods are subject to the cycle of nature, die annually, and then come to life again, the LORD is always active. He is alive, he is not asleep, and he is always capable of coming to his people's assistance.

The psalm reaches a climax in vv. 5-8, and the question posed in v. 1 is answered in full. The answer to this question begins with the statement that the LORD is the creator (v. 2). This is taken further with the statement that the LORD is the keeper of Israel. Vv. 5-8 conclude on a personal note, namely, "The LORD is your keeper." The LORD is not only the powerful creator of heaven and earth. Nor is he only the God who has worked salvation in the history of his people. But he is also personally involved with individuals. V. 5 describes the helping, sheltering presence of the LORD. V. 6 should also be interpreted in polemic terms: the sun and moon, heavenly bodies which are often worshiped and credited with divine powers in some other religions, are demythologized and stripped of their powers. The LORD rules over these forces as well, and will protect his people against them. In vv. 7-8 the LORD's protection is described in greater detail. The LORD protects our lives against all evil. He protects his people throughout their life, and his protection is everlasting. The description of the total, permanent, all-embracing protection of the LORD is carried to a climax in these verses.

The psalm begins with doubt and uncertainty but ends as a triumphal song of confidence. Psalm 121 may not be taken as a guarantee that all believers will enjoy a life free from care. The function of the psalm is rather to persuade believers that they can trust in the LORD in all circumstances. During the exile and during the post-exilic period the people of the LORD must have found it a great source of comfort and renewed confidence.

Psalm 122

Psalm 122 is a song of praise to Jerusalem. Although Jerusalem occupies a central place in the psalm (cf. vv. 2, 3, 6) and is honored and personified in the psalm, the psalmist is not concerned with Jerusalem for its own sake but with Jerusalem as the dwelling place of the LORD. The expression "the house of the LORD" is placed in the first and last verses, forming an *inclusio* and a thematic frame for the psalm.

Psalm 122 is the only one of the "Songs of Ascents" in which there is specific mention of a pilgrimage to Jerusalem (vv. 1-2). Jerusalem is lauded as the unifying factor and central meeting place for fellow believers and countrymen. Jerusalem is the religious center because this is where God is worshiped. It is also the judicial and political capital because it is the seat of the Davidic monarchy (v. 5).

The word "peace" (Heb. *shalom*) plays a central part in vv. 6-8, where it occurs three times. It has to do with the peace and prosperity of Jerusalem. Jerusalem's fate is her citizens' fate as well. If the city prospers, the inhabitants prosper too. The citizens of Jerusalem should therefore strive for peace as well as petition the LORD for peace. Jerusalem is not only a symbol of the LORD's presence but also a symbol of the people's welfare. The psalm ends as it began, namely, with the concept of Jerusalem as "the house of the LORD." The main theme of Psalm 122 is that Jerusalem is where God is.

If this psalm also had a function during the postexilic period — when the monarchy and the illustrious temple no longer existed — then what we are dealing with is an idealization of preexilic Jerusalem. This idealization would also have brought the people comfort and renewed courage when the temple had to be rebuilt.

Psalm 123

Psalm 123 consists of two strophes, namely, vv. 1-2 and 3-4. The first strophe (vv. 1-2) is an affirmation of faith in and reliance on the LORD. The second strophe (vv. 3-4) is a petition for mercy.

The key word in the first strophe (123:1-2) is "eyes." The poet uses the word "eyes" to develop the theme of trust in and reliance on God. This strophe shows a distinct chiastic structure:

A^1 To you I lift up my eyes . . . (v. 1)
B^1 As the eyes of the servants . . . their master (v. 2a)
B^2 as the eyes of a maid . . . her mistress (v. 2b)
A^2 so our eyes look to the LORD our God . . . (v. 2c).

A^1 and A^2 deal with the relationship between the worshiper(s) and the LORD. He is the one to whom they turn for help and on whom they depend. While A^1 speaks of the LORD as the remote, exalted God "who is enthroned in the heavens," A^2 speaks of him as "the LORD our God." This underlines the psalmist's intimate relationship with and dependence on the LORD. In B^1 and B^2 this dependence on the LORD is further illustrated by a double simile. Just as a servant and maid in an Israelite household were totally dependent on their master and mistress to meet their needs, so the people of God are totally dependent on him. What they chiefly need is the "mercy" of the LORD.

The second strophe (123:3-4), a supplication for mercy, has a thematic link with the end of the previous strophe in the form of a double imperative:

Have mercy upon us, O LORD, have mercy upon us. . . .
a b a

This aba pattern — the repetition of "mercy" with "O LORD" in the center of the sentence construction — places renewed emphasis on the total dependence of the people on the LORD. The reason for the prayer for mercy is also given here, namely, that they have had to put up with too much mockery and contempt from proud enemies. Their intolerable situation is emphasized by a repetition ("had more than enough," v. 3; "has had more," v. 4) and by the description of the attitude of the enemies in two words ("scorn," "contempt").

Most exegetes date Psalm 123 to the postexilic period and relate the psalm to the oppression endured by the people of God under Persian rule. But here there is no direct evidence which permits exact dating. As in most of the other "Songs of Ascents," trust in God plays an important part here.

Psalm 124

Psalm 124 is a communal song of thanksgiving. It is, however, not clear to which specific historical event the psalm owes its origin.

The first strophe (124:1-5), which consists of an extended conditional sentence, describes what would have happened if the LORD had not come to his people's rescue. The conditional statement consists of a protasis — "If it had not been the LORD who was on our side" (vv. 1, 2) — and a fourfold apodosis — "then they would have swallowed us . . ." (vv. 3, 4a, 4b, 5). This extended conditional sentence, together with the use of metaphors (wild animals; a devouring fire; raging waters), emphasizes on the one hand the threat and danger to which the people were subjected and on the other the intervention of the LORD and his deliverance. The metaphors evoke associations with the mythological forces of chaos. The LORD is able to protect his people against all these forces. Deliverance was possible only because God was on their side.

The second strophe (124:6-7) is a thanksgiving. Two metaphors, namely, escape from the jaws of a wild animal and the escape of a bird from a snare, are used to illustrate how the people escaped from danger by a hair's breadth, thanks to the LORD.

The psalm is carried to a climax with a confession of faith in God as the almighty creator of heaven and earth (124:8). It is for the very reason that God created everything and is in complete control that he is able to save his imperiled people.

Psalm 125

The beginning and end of Psalm 125 form a contrast: v. 1 says that those who trust in the LORD will endure forever. On the other hand, v. 5 tells us that evildoers will be punished by the LORD. The psalm abounds in the kind of contrasts that are typical of wisdom literature (cf. Psalm 1), such as:

Zion/Jerusalem	scepter of wickedness
the righteous	evildoers
those . . . upright	those . . . crooked ways
the LORD . . . surrounds	the LORD . . . lead away
to do wrong	Do good

The poet is deliberately using these contrasts to persuade his readers/listeners to trust in the LORD and lead upright lives.

The first strophe (125:1-3) is an affirmation of faith in the LORD. He has the power to protect all those who trust in him. Two similes, both of which have to do with mountains, are used to describe those who trust in God and to illustrate the enduring and reliable protection offered by God: as stable as Mt. Zion, the symbol of security and strength, are those who trust in God. Just as the eternal and immutable mountains surround the city of Jerusalem, so the LORD's protection permanently surrounds his people. By contrasting "wickedness" with the "righteous" the poet conveys God's assurance to his people that the hostile forces of evil will not prevail over them. The LORD will also ensure that the righteous are not tempted to sin.

The second strophe (125:4-5) contains another contrast between "those who are upright" and "evildoers." The LORD is entreated to do good to the upright, but evildoers must be punished. The psalm is concluded with a benediction.

This psalm, with its distinctive wisdom characteristics, probably reflects the struggle of the postexilic Judean community to survive but also shows their faith in God as the only source of help and protection.

Psalm 126

Psalm 126 is a prayer that the LORD will intervene and ameliorate the lot of his people. The psalm is probably related to the reconstruction of the postexilic Judean community. The perfect tenses of the first few verses (e.g., "restored," "has done great things") do not refer to the past but should be seen as prophetic perfects constituting a prayer for the future.

The first strophe (126:1-4) has a symmetrical structure:

A Restoration (v. 1)
B Joy (v. 2a)
C The LORD has done great things (v. 2b)
C The LORD has done great things (v. 3a)
B Joy (v. 3b)
A Restoration (v. 4).

It is apparent from the first strophe (126:1-4) that there was an expectation among the community of faith, who had their center in Jerusalem (Zion), that the LORD would alter their lot. They were so sure of God's intervention that they experienced it in advance as a reality. These "great things" to be done by the LORD had two consequences: first of all, they held the promise of great joy for the people (cf. vv. 2a, 3b; cf. also vv. 5, 6 in the second strophe where the element of joy is strongly emphasized). Secondly, the LORD's acts of salvation were such that the other nations were obliged to take note of them (v. 2b). God's acts of salvation have an international dimension. The expression "restore the fortunes" places the emphasis on the LORD's power to change the situation radically through a miraculous intervention. Just as the dry watercourses of the Negev (the arid southern part of Judah) could suddenly change into torrents during the winter rainfall season, so the LORD could change the hopeless situation of the Judean community, filling them with new hope and vitality (v. 4). This would be almost too good to be true — it would be like having a pleasant dream (v. 1).

The second strophe (126:5-6), in which the metaphor of sowing seed is prominent, says the same thing as the rest of the psalm and is the key to interpreting the psalm as a whole: the metaphor expresses the expectation that the situation of distress will be changed into good fortune by the LORD. Tears will turn into joy. Tension is created by the contrast between the sowing of the seed and the ultimate harvest. Sowing is a laborious task and an act of faith. The metaphor used here serves as a promise to the community that the present distress and suffering is not the end of the road. It is the means by which the LORD will bring about salvation. In this way the suffering acquires a meaning for the believers and their tears are not in vain.

Psalm 127

Psalm 127 is a wisdom psalm with a didactic-persuasive function. The basic insight of the psalm is that without the LORD's active presence and involvement all human endeavor and activities are in vain.

In the first strophe (127:1-2) three human activities are mentioned that would be undertaken in vain unless they were accompanied by the LORD's blessing. This idea is emphasized by the threefold repetition of the expression "in vain": (1) the building of a house — this could be extended to mean the building of a household or family — is one of the basic necessities; without it people cannot live decently. However, if the LORD is not involved the work of the builders is in vain. (2) One of the basic needs in the cities of the ancient Near East was for security. This was the reason for the high, reinforced walls built around the cities and the guards positioned at strategic lookout points along the walls to sound the alarm in the event of danger or enemy attack. However, human attempts to create security count for nothing unless the LORD's sheltering presence also plays a part. (3) Further, hard work and toil will not bear fruit if God is left out of account and if labor is not performed in dependence on him. The expression "he gives sleep to his beloved" forms a contrast to the preceding section. Whereas some people work day and night in vain, the "beloved" of the LORD — in other words, those who maintain a right relationship with God — can sleep peacefully because they trust in God. All human activities — including the building of a house, the fortification of a city, and labor — are in vain without the LORD's involvement.

The second strophe (127:3-5) focuses on the family. Children are regarded as a blessing from the LORD and a source of joy and security. A term from the tradition of the promised land, namely, "heritage," is used to convey that children are a gift from God. Just as the land of Canaan did not belong to Israel but was a gift from God, so children are a heritage from the hand of the LORD. The blessing which children bring is illustrated by the simile in v. 4. Sons are like arrows in the hands of a soldier. This means that children are a powerful defense against attack and a source of security against danger. Another perspective is added (cf. v. 4b), namely, that children born while their parents are still young are a weapon against the miseries of old age. According to v. 5, such parents are happy. They are like someone whose quiver is full. They have great reserves of strength with which to ward off blows. Anyone with children is assured of help and assistance even when, for example, he has to contend with enemies at the city gate. Children are a source of blessing, joy, assistance, and security to their parents. They are a gift from God.

The psalm forms an *inclusio* in that it begins and ends with the family (cf. 127:1, 5). The psalmist views the family as the most important institution in life and emphasizes that without the LORD's involvement all human activities and institutions are in vain. The title "Of Solomon" is neither an indication of authorship nor a clue to the original historical situation. The reason why the psalm is ascribed to Solomon is probably that Solomon was often associated with wisdom. Furthermore, Solomon was also known as Jedidiah, which means "beloved of the LORD" (cf. v. 2 with 2 Sam 12:25).

Psalm 128

128:1a, "Happy is everyone who fears the LORD," both indicates its main theme and places the psalm in the category of wisdom literature. The first strophe (128:1-4) forms an *inclusio* in that it is both introduced (v. 1) and concluded (v. 4) with the expression "who fears the LORD." The verb "fear" is not intended to indicate anxiety in the presence of the LORD but is qualified in v. 1 by "who walks in his ways." To fear the LORD therefore means to acknowledge and obey him. Anyone who does so will be "happy" and "blessed." To be happy is more closely defined as to have a happy and blessed working (v. 2a) and family life (v. 3). The comparison of a wife and children with a "fruitful vine" and "olive shoots around your table" (v. 3) is a common OT usage in which people are compared with trees (cf., e.g., Gen 49:22; Ps 92:12-14; Jer 11:16). These plants are stock images for fertility and abundance and are used to indicate a happy and blessed household.

Whereas the first strophe deals with the blessing of the individual, the second strophe (128:5-6) is a supplication in which the narrow family context is transcended and expanded to include the entire nation. The psalmist is concerned with the prosperity of Jerusalem and with the well-being of all Israel and even of future generations. By drawing a parallel between the family and the nation and integrating the one with the other, Psalm 128 shows us how these two social institutions may influence one another for good. If the family is healthy, so is society as a whole, and vice versa.

Psalms 127 and 128 could be regarded as twin psalms and were probably deliberately placed alongside each other. Besides the fact that they are both wisdom psalms and they both contain the expression "Happy is . . ." (cf. Pss 127:5 and 128:1), there is also great similarity regarding themes: the family, children, and descendants; work and the city are common themes. Nevertheless, the psalms elucidate the same matters from different perspectives. Where Psalm 127 says that all human activities are meaningless without the presence of the LORD, Psalm 128 emphasizes human initiative and entrepreneurial spirit, which is blessed and rewarded by God. In the terms of Psalm 128, human beings and God cooperate to create a successful life. While people have to fulfill their responsibilities, it is the LORD who blesses human endeavor.

Psalm 129

Psalm 129 can be divided into two strophes, namely, vv. 1-4, a retrospective look at the past, and vv. 5-8, a prayer for divine judgment.

The first strophe (129:1-4) is presented as the words of an individual speaking on behalf of the people. By repeating the expression "'Often have they attacked me from my youth'" (vv. 1, 2), the psalmist emphasizes Israel's traumatic history from the period in Egypt throughout salvation history. In v. 3 a metaphor is used to describe enemy attacks on Israel: "The plowers plowed on my back; they made their furrows long." Two images are combined here to describe the cruelty of the hostile onslaught, namely, the ripping of a plow and the image of a slave's back torn and furrowed by a lash. This retrospective look at history is not intended to emphasize Israel's humiliation but rather the fact that the LORD has always come to his people's rescue. The first strophe culminates in the statement that the LORD is righteous. The plow metaphor is continued when the psalmist says that the plower's harness has been broken so that the plowing, namely, the destruction of Israel, can no longer continue. The purpose of recounting this part of the history of Israel is to show that enemies did not prevail over Israel because the LORD aided his people.

The second strophe (129:5-8) is a prayer for divine judgment or that those who hate the LORD's people will be brought to shame. The agricultural metaphor is continued, but it is loaded with irony. The labor of the plowers (v. 3) produces no harvest (v. 7) because they plowed on shallow ground. The work of the tillers receives no blessing. The implication is clear: the enemies of Israel have not achieved their purpose. Israel is saved, but its enemies perish.

This retrospective look at history is intended to instill hope for the future. The psalm probably dates from the postexilic period when the people had little hope for the future. The intention of the psalm is to tell the people of God that if they put their trust in him there is always hope.

Psalm 130
(*see also* Individual Laments, 366-73)

Although most exegetes rightly place Psalm 130 among the "Individual Laments," it does show great similarities with the other "Songs of Ascents." The psalm moves from desolation (v. 1) to confession of sin (vv. 3-4), to hopeful waiting for the LORD's saving intervention (vv. 5-6), to a climax in which Israel is assured of God's salvation and forgiveness. The poet holds up his own experience as an example to the community of faith. The purpose of the psalm was to encourage the congregation in troubled times and to persuade them to trust in God under all circumstances.

Psalm 131

Psalm 131 is a condemnation of hubris or self-aggrandizement. It is the prayer of someone who has found peace in the LORD in such measure that he desires nothing more than to do the will of God. As a wisdom text with a didactic function, the psalm aims to teach people that the practice of self-aggrandizement should be abandoned.

In 131:1 the central theme is approached from a *negative* perspective. The poet tells us what characteristics he does not have and repeats this three times:

> my heart is not lifted up . . .
> my eyes are not raised . . .
> I do not occupy myself. . . .

In the first two lines, where the heart and eyes are used to represent the whole person, the poet uses the double negative to indicate that he rejects with his whole being any self-exaltation over his fellow human beings. The third line is a rejection of self-exaltation toward God, for if the poet were to occupy himself with great and marvelous things he would be trespassing on God's territory.

Where 131:1 illuminates the theme from a negative perspective, v. 2 does so from a *positive* one. The statement made in v. 2a ("I have calmed and quieted my soul . . .") is illustrated with a beautiful simile in v. 2b: the child who is with his mother creates an image of security, tranquility, and satisfaction. Similarly, the poet is not at odds with himself. He has made peace with God and with himself. He is not torn in two but instead has found inner peace.

In 131:3 the poet breaks away from his personal life and the psalm is transformed into a parenetic invocation to Israel. The people of God are enjoined to live in total dependence on the LORD and to continue to hope in him. This should not be a passing phase but a permanent way of life.

The wisdom character of the psalm and its position in this collection point to the postexilic period. The message of Psalm 131 would have been eminently suited to this time of crisis.

Psalm 132

The dynasty of David and Zion as the dwelling place of the LORD are the two central themes of Psalm 132. There are four references to David in the psalm (cf. vv. 1, 10, 11, 17) and a variety of terms are used to describe the temple ("place," v. 5; "dwelling place," vv. 5, 7; "resting place," vv. 8, 14; "his habitation," v. 13). The poet combines the two matters that were so important for the survival and the religion of the chosen people in a single poem. Psalm 132 gives a poetic account of part of the history, which is recorded in 2 Samuel. The psalm consists of two stanzas, namely, vv. 1-10 and 11-18.

The first strophe (132:1-10) forms an *inclusio* in the sense that it is both introduced and concluded with a prayer for David ("remember . . . David," v. 1; "For . . . David's sake do not turn away . . . ," v. 10). The reason why the LORD should not forget David is that David has labored hard and sworn an oath to build a dwelling place for the LORD. By applying the term "the Mighty One of Jacob" twice to the LORD (vv. 2, 5), the poet demonstrates that the God of the patriarchs and the God of whom he is speaking now are the same. In vv. 6-8 the poet gives an account of the events that took place when David brought the ark from the Philistine city of Kiriath-jearim (= "fields of Jaar," v. 6) to Jerusalem (cf. 1 Sam 7:1-2 and 2 Sam 6:1-19). This part of the psalm advances a further reason why the LORD should not turn his face away from his "anointed one" (= David; cf. vv. 10, 17).

While the first strophe (132:1-10) focuses on the oath David swore to the LORD, the second strophe (vv. 11-18) tells us of the oath God swore to David. The first aspect of the LORD's oath concerns the promise to David that his dynasty would endure forever (vv. 11, 12; cf. also 2 Samuel 7). The second assurance given by God is that he has chosen Zion as his "resting place forever." This election of Zion brings blessings in its wake, namely, that the LORD will supply food for the poor (v. 15), that he will clothe her priests with joy (v. 16), that he will ensure that the dynasty of David endures forever (v. 17), and that the enemies of his people will be humiliated (v. 18). The poet uses this oath sworn by God to combine the two important themes of the psalm so that it reaches a climax.

The Davidic monarchy and the temple were symbols that served to reinforce the faith of God's people. They were the visible signs of the LORD's presence and love. However, the exile meant the end of the monarchy and the temple. This naturally plunged the people into a crisis of faith. Although Psalm 132 contains old, preexilic traditions, the intention of the poet in taking this retrospective look at the story of David and the temple was to give the despondent postexilic congregation new hope for the future.

Psalm 133

The central theme of Psalm 133, a wisdom text, is that where "kindred" live together in unity and solidarity the LORD bestows his blessing. By "kindred" the psalmist means not the narrow family circle but God's people as a whole. Both political and religious unity are included. If the psalm dates from the postexilic period, as most of the "Songs of Ascents" do, this psalm may well have been an appeal to the divided postexilic congregation to unite and stand together.

Two similes (cf. 132:2, 3) are used to describe the blessing of such unity. Oil, and here in particular the fragrant oil with which the high priest Aaron was anointed, is used to represent the abundance of the blessing. Because the high priest is representative of the whole nation, the psalmist is conveying by means of this simile that the whole nation will share in the blessing. The second simile is closely related: dew is an image that stands for refreshment and divine blessing. In a hyperbolic simile the poet tells us that unity is as if the dew and cool moisture of snow-covered Mt. Hermon in the north had fallen on Zion in the arid south. The north/south theme also emphasizes the idea of unity. In the Hebrew the verb *yrd* (lit. "descend") is used three times ("running down," twice in v. 2; "which falls," v. 3) to indicate that the LORD's blessing descends on his people.

The point the poet wishes to emphasize is that unity in Zion would have a life-giving, fruitful, and wholesome effect on the entire nation.

Psalm 134

The "Songs of Ascents" end on a high note with this hymn in which "all servants of the LORD" are enjoined in three imperatives (vv. 1, 2) to praise the LORD. "All servants of the LORD" probably refers to the cultic staff of the temple, that is, to the priests and the Levites. The expression "by night in the house of the LORD" seems to imply a nocturnal cultic occasion. The first and most important reason why the LORD should be praised is that he made heaven and earth and is therefore in control of everything (v. 3). This psalm also makes it clear that worship is an interactive process. The worshipers go to the temple with the purpose of praising the LORD (Heb. *brk,* v. 1), but they also go there to be blessed by him (*brk,* v. 3). In this sense Psalm 134 forms an *inclusio* and conclusion to the "Songs of Ascents," and one of the main themes of that book, namely the blessing of the LORD, is given prominence again.

Psalm 135

Psalm 135 is a hymn consisting of two basic elements, namely, imperatives to praise and reasons why the LORD should be praised. The imperatives form a frame around the rest of the psalm, and the first strophe (vv. 1-4) and the last strophe (vv. 19-21) together contain ten of them (cf. the verbs "praise" and "bless," which occur repeatedly). The priests and the whole nation are exhorted to praise the LORD (vv. 2, 19-20). Those who praise the LORD are more closely defined as "servants of the LORD" (v. 1) and as "You who fear the LORD" (v. 20), which signifies those who love the LORD.

The reason why the Lord should be praised is summed up in the clauses "for the LORD is good . . . for he is gracious" (v. 3). The rest of the psalm gives a description of what "good" and "gracious" involve.

The first reason why the LORD should be praised is that he chose Israel as his personal "possession" (135:4). Furthermore, the LORD demonstrated his love to Israel throughout history. He delivered them from slavery in Egypt (vv. 8-9). As a military commander he conquered Palestine, defeated the hostile nations, and gave the land to his people as their heritage (vv. 10-12).

Another reason why the LORD should be praised is that he is "great." His greatness finds expression in the fact that he is "above all gods" (135:5). While these idols are made of precious materials, they are nevertheless the product of human hands and are therefore impotent and lifeless (vv. 15-17). Those who fashion the idols and trust in them are just as impotent as their handiwork (v. 18). In contrast with the gods, the LORD is the almighty One who is in full control of the entire cosmos (v. 6). He is also in control of nature because it is not the gods but the LORD who brings rain to the earth (v. 7). Unlike the gods, which are ephemeral and mortal, the LORD endures forever and has proved himself throughout the ages. The ultimate expression of the greatness of God is that he has "compassion for his servants."

Psalm 136

Psalm 136 is identified as a song of thanksgiving by the imperative "give thanks," which occurs at the beginning (three times in vv. 1-3) and the end (v. 26), thus forming an *inclusio.* The most striking characteristic of the psalm is the refrain ("for his steadfast love endures forever"), which forms the second half of every verse of the psalm. Although the refrain — which was probably sung by the full congregation or by a chorus — at first sight appears to be unnecessarily repetitive, the function of the repetition is to convey to us that God's love is endless. The refrain repeatedly reminds the congregation of God's past deeds so that these deeds become a living reality to them. The psalm is a description of the steadfast love of the LORD throughout history.

In the first strophe (136:1-3), which shows polemic characteristics in its use of "God of gods" and "Lord of lords," we are told that the LORD is the only and the undisputed God. The second strophe (vv. 4-9) deals with the creation. Polemic elements are also to be found in this part of the psalm. It was God alone — without help and unopposed — who created the world. God made everything — heaven and earth — and he spread out the earth upon the waters. The heaven-earth-waters combination is a reference to the tripartite worldview of the time (cf. Psalm 33). God also made the sun, the moon, and the stars — heavenly bodies which were deified in some of the religions of the ancient Near East — and assigned to them their places and functions. This section on the creation emphasizes the almighty power and greatness of the LORD.

The third strophe (136:10-22) deals with salvation history, with the emphasis on the almighty power of the LORD and his nurturing love for his people. The LORD defeated both mighty pharaoh and the mighty Egyptian gods on their home territory (vv. 10-15) in order to deliver his people. The LORD also accompanied his people during the journey through the desert (v. 16). It was the LORD who conquered the mighty kings of the Transjordanian region to carve open a path to the promised land for his own people. Because the LORD had taken the land as a warrior, it was his property, and his people received it from him as a heritage (vv. 21-22).

Salvation history forms the basis for the confession in the fourth strophe (136:23-25): "It is he who remembered us in our low estate. . . ." Through these words the people identify with the LORD's past deeds of salvation and apply them to their own situation of distress. The dire situation and the foes mentioned here probably refer to the exile. The creation tradition and salvation history are summed up in v. 25: the LORD "gives food to all flesh." He provides the basic necessities of life. He is not only Israel's God but also the God who cares for all living creatures.

The psalm is concluded (v. 26) with the same call to thanksgiving with which it began. The divine epithet ("God of heaven") used here emphasizes the exalted nature of the LORD.

The purpose of the psalm is to show the people of the LORD, through a review of creation and their history, that "his steadfast love endures forever." This fact compels their gratitude but also gives them courage to face their own dire circumstances with faith in the LORD.

Psalm 137

It has been said of Psalm 137 that because of the "bloodthirsty" statement in v. 9 ("Happy shall they be who take your little ones and dash them against the rock!") it does not belong in the Bible — and especially not in the Christian canon. When interpreting the psalm, however, we should take into account that the poet combines various genres in the psalm to create specific effects — including a sharply ironical effect. Like any other text, Psalm 137 — including the apparently problematical v. 9 — should be read within its own literary and historical context.

The first strophe (137:1-4) is a communal lament. It is clear from the past tenses (e.g., "there we wept") that we are dealing with a retrospective look at the situation of the Judean exiles during their sojourn in Babylon. The poet transports his readers to the situation of the exiles by putting the words of the lament in their mouths in the first person plural. The emphasis is on the wretchedness and longing of the exiles. They yearn for Zion, the center of their religious practice and the source of their joy. But Zion has been destroyed and deserted, and their harps, instruments for expressing praise and joy, have been hung up on the willows. The sorrow of the exiles is aggravated by the fact that their captors force them to sing a song of joy when they have no reason to rejoice. The exiles refuse to sing a song of Zion when ordered to do so by their captors because this would mean mocking and making a caricature of the LORD.

Although the second strophe (137:5-6) appears at first glance to be an individual hymn, its contents really constitute an individual lament. This gives the strophe an ironical tone. What the poet wants to say is: I refuse to sing as my captors tell me to sing. It is nevertheless impossible for me to forget Jerusalem. I can do no other than sing about Jerusalem, the pinnacle of my joy. The irony in this strophe contributes to the bitterness and self-imprecation of the poet, but it also emphasizes his wholehearted loyalty toward Jerusalem and toward God.

In the third strophe (137:7-8), which is an imprecation, God is addressed ("Remember, O LORD, . . . the Edomites"). After the events of 587 BC when Jerusalem had already been destroyed by the Babylonians, the Edomites, the brother nation of Israel, continued to plunder the city and even killed the fugitives (cf. Ezek 25:12-14; Obad 10-16). This is why the LORD is asked to execute his judgment on Edom (137:7). The judgment on Edom is, however, merely the prelude to the actual judgment on Babylon (vv. 8-9). Babylon, the mighty world power that destroyed all the other nations, has itself been destroyed. Even Babylon's hope for the future ("your little ones") has been destroyed. The poet uses the military terminology characteristic of the OT (cf., e.g., 2 Kgs 8:12; Isa 13:16; Hos 10:14; Nah 3:10) to describe the destruction of Babylon. Babylon will suffer the same fate as it inflicted on other nations. In this description of the destruction of Babylon the motive is not unbridled cruelty but a concern that justice should be done and the LORD's honor maintained. This strophe is given an ironical tone by the use of a blessing. This blessing does not, as one might expect, herald prosperity and happiness; ironically, it introduces a terrible curse. The psalm begins with Babylon (137:1) and ends with Babylon as well (v. 8). In v. 1 Babylon was still the mighty conqueror, but in v. 8 Babylon itself has been destroyed. The roles have been reversed.

Psalm 137 is a retrospective look at and a reinterpretation of the exile of 587 BC: the LORD, the God of Israel, did not cease to exist with the exile. He still reigns. Babylon, the mighty world power, has to submit to his judgment. This thought must have held a comforting message for the despondent Judean community in the postexilic period.

Psalm 138

Psalm 138 is a thanksgiving psalm because it contains the most important characteristics of this genre such as the expression of thanksgiving, the reasons for this thanksgiving, an invocation to praise, and an expression of confidence in the LORD. Owing to similarities to Deutero-Isaiah (Isaiah 40–55), the psalm can be regarded as an expression of thanksgiving and confidence in the LORD after the return from exile.

In the first strophe (138:1-3) the thanksgiving is placed in the mouth of an individual. The comprehensive and intense nature of the thanksgiving and worship is emphasized by the use of four verbs (cf. vv. 1, 2) and by the expression "with my whole heart." Because Israel is confronted by the gods of heathen peoples, the poet expresses his thanks to the LORD "before the gods." The reason for the thanksgiving to the LORD is said to be "your steadfast love and your faithfulness." The psalm also ends with a reference to "steadfast love" (v. 8). Thus the psalm is framed by this concept. The "steadfast love" is concretized by the statement that the LORD answered when the poet called on him and renewed his strength. The third strophe (vv. 7-8), which is closely related to the first in that it is written in the first person, is an expression of confidence in the LORD. God's "steadfast love" and "faithfulness" are again described in terms of his actions, namely, "you preserve me . . ."; "you stretch out your hand . . . and deliver me." The poet's faith and trust in the LORD are apparent from the fact that his "trouble" and the enemy threat are not yet things of the past. Nevertheless he has so much confidence in the steadfast love of the LORD that he is thanking him in advance.

The greatness and glory of the LORD are further highlighted by the invocation of "all the kings of the earth" to thanksgiving in the second strophe (138:4-6). Not only Israel but the entire world should take note of the greatness of God, one manifestation of which is that, exalted as he is, God still pays attention to the "lowly."

Both this psalm and the following seven psalms (139–145) bear the title "Of David." This is not intended, however, as an indication of authorship; in fact, there is no certainty as to the reason for this title.

Psalm 139

When the psalm is read as a whole, the most striking characteristic is the *inclusio* which is formed by the repetition at the end of the psalm of the three words that occur at the beginning ("search," vv. 1, 23; "know," vv. 1, 23; and "way," vv. 3, 24). This *inclusio* highlights the central theme of the psalm, namely: the LORD knows me through and through as well as whether I am on the right road.

The first strophe (139:1-6) concentrates on the LORD's omniscience. The LORD knows all the details of the poet's actions and inner thoughts. There is no way of hiding anything from God. He surrounds the poet completely so that he is continually conscious of the LORD's presence. The reality of God's omniscience is so overwhelming that it is too vast for the psalmist's understanding. The intention of this strophe is not, however, to present the LORD's omniscience in a negative light but rather to underline the LORD's positive involvement.

In the second strophe (139:7-12) the focus shifts to the LORD's omnipresence. It is impossible to escape from the presence of God. Even if the poet were to go to what the ancient worldview envisaged as the ends of the earth ("heaven" and "Sheol"; for Sheol cf. Ps 9:17), even if he were to go to the farthest corners of the east ("wings of the morning") or the west ("farthest limits of the sea"), he would still be in the presence of God. In the improbable event of darkness suddenly descending on the poet by day it would make no difference to the presence of God. The poet is overawed by the greatness of the LORD's protection.

The third strophe (139:13-18) deals with God's involvement in the origin of human life. It is God who is responsible for the inception of life in the womb, and it is God who completes the process of creating a new life. In a wonderful way the LORD skillfully forms the unborned life in the womb. When the poet thinks of the LORD's works of creation, he can do no other than raise his voice in praise. The poet responds with wonder to the realization of God's involvement with his entire life, from beginning to end.

The fourth strophe (139:19-22) hardly seems to belong in this context since it does not mention the LORD's omniscience or omnipresence. These verses are a prayer for the extermination of the wicked. Although this passage was probably a later editorial addition, it does nevertheless have a significant function in its present context. This strophe tells us that despite God's presence there are still discordant notes in the creation. The presence of the wicked disrupts the harmony between God and humankind, whence the poet's urgent prayer that the wicked should be destroyed. The poet's concern is not, however, personal vengeance or the arbitrary extermination of enemies, but the restoration of God's honor. The poet is ranging himself on God's side. God's enemies are also his enemies and should therefore be punished.

The fifth strophe (139:23-24) is related to the first and is a prayer that the LORD will involve himself actively in the psalmist's life and will restrain him from going astray. This prayer tells us that the poet has placed his trust wholly in God.

This psalm contains elements of different genres, such as a hymn, an individual lament, thanksgiving, and wisdom literature. It is difficult, therefore, to place the psalm in any particular genre. The intention and function of the psalm are quite clear, however: the poet wishes to praise the omnipresent God and promises to be loyal to him. The psalm itself contains no direct clues as to its date of origin. On the basis of its Aramaisms the psalm is usually ascribed to the postexilic period.

Psalms 140, 141, 142, 143 (*see* Individual Laments, 366-73)

Psalm 144

One of the characteristics of Psalm 144 is that vv. 1-11 show major similarities with Psalm 18 (cf. v. 1 with 18:2, 34; v. 2 with 18:2, 31, 46; v. 5 with 18:9; v. 6 with 18:14; v. 7 with 18:16, 44, 45). 144:1-11 also show similarities with other psalms (cf., e.g., v. 3 with 8:4; v. 9 with 33:2, 3). A second characteristic of Psalm 144 is that vv. 12-15 differ completely from the preceding vv. 1-11 in respect to grammar and style: vv. 1-11 are written in the first person singular, whereas vv. 12-15 are written in the first person plural. Vv. 12-15 also contain a number of obscure expressions which occur only in Psalm 144. As a result of all this, some exegetes regard vv. 1-11 and 12-15 as two separate psalms.

The psalm is a unit in its present form, however, and should be interpreted as such. It is impossible to reconstruct the origin and growth of the psalm in detail. What does emerge clearly is that the poet of Psalm 144 deliberately borrowed from Psalm 18 and other psalms in order to create a new and independent text. Vv. 12-15 may have been an original creation of the poet, or he could have borrowed it from another source and then added vv. 1-11 in order to round it off. The main theme of Psalm 144 is summed up in the refrain (vv. 7b-8, 11): "Rescue me from . . . the hand of aliens, whose mouths speak lies. . . ." The anthological character of the psalm, that is, the fact that it has borrowed a great deal from other psalms, and the expression "rescue me from the hand of aliens" indicate that it probably dates from the postexilic period. Furthermore, there is a reference to the exile in v. 14. The title "Of David" and the reference to David in v. 10 should therefore not be interpreted as indications of authorship. By ascribing the psalm to David and putting the content in David's mouth, the poet is petitioning the LORD to save his people from their enemies during the difficult postexilic period just as he saved "his servant David" from his enemies long ago. The psalm may be divided into two stanzas, namely, vv. 1-11 and vv. 12-15. The first stanza can be subdivided into a few strophes, namely, vv. 1-2, 3-4, 5-8, and 9-11.

In the first stanza (144:1-11) the poet is speaking in the first person singular. In the first strophe (vv. 1-2) the poet praises the LORD as the one who taught him skill in battle and helped him to gain a military victory. A large number of metaphors (including "my rock," "my fortress," "my stronghold," and "my shield") are used to indicate that the LORD is the mighty God with whom safety and security are to be found. The second strophe (vv. 3-4) forms a contrast to the first strophe in that the poet expresses his wonder at the fact that Almighty God is so intimately concerned with the lot of insignificant mortal beings. The third strophe (vv. 5-8) is a prayer that the LORD will use military force to intervene and save the poet "from the hand of aliens." The urgency of this prayer is evident from the fact that seven imperatives are used ("Bow," "touch," "make," "send out," "stretch out," "set free," and "rescue"). The LORD's awe-inspiring coming is described in theophanic terms (cf. Ps 18:7-15) which remind us of his appearance at Sinai (cf. Exodus 19). The fourth strophe (144:9-11) is a vow of thanksgiving for the victory which the poet is certain the LORD will give him. The strophe ends with a renewed prayer for deliverance (v. 11) which functions as a refrain for vv. 7b-8.

In the second stanza (144:12-15) we no longer have an individual speaking, but a congregation. In a prayer which shows distinct wisdom characteristics (cf. v. 15), the poet implores God's blessing so that there will be peace and prosperity for the nation and no sorrow will again come upon them — probably a reference to the exile.

Psalm 144 is wrestling with the crisis brought about by the exile. The poet of Psalm 144 is trying to give his people renewed courage for the future by referring to familiar examples from the past. He does this by giving existing texts new meaning and harking back to David, one of the great figures of the OT.

Psalm 145

Psalm 145 is a hymn to the greatness of God. The most striking characteristic of Psalm 145 is that it is an acrostic or alphabetical poem (for an explanation, cf. Psalm 9; the Hebrew letter *nun* is absent from Psalm 145, however). Another characteristic of the psalm is that it forms an *inclusio* in that it is both introduced and concluded by the word "praise" (vv. 1, 21). The *inclusio* is further reinforced by the verb "bless" and the expression "your name"/"his holy name," which occur both at the beginning and at the end of the psalm (vv. 1, 2, 21). This *inclusio* creates the framework within which the psalm should be read, namely, that, in the words of v. 1, the object is to extol "my God and King."

A characteristic of some acrostics (cf., e.g., Psalm 37) is that they exhibit no distinct strophal divisions. This is the case with Psalm 145 as well. This does not mean, however, that we are dealing with a disjointed poem. On the contrary, Psalm 145 consists of a network of associations, created by the repetition of words and phrases, from which distinct themes emerge. The psalm consists of the two classical ingredients of a hymn, namely, first, injunctions to praise the LORD and, secondly, reasons why we should praise God.

Regarding the first element, it is striking how many words that fall into the semantic category equivalent to announce/tell/praise occur in the psalm: "bless," vv. 1, 2, 10, 21; "laud," v. 4; "declare," v. 4; "meditate" (= I will tell myself), v. 5; "speak"/"tell"/"proclaim," vv. 6, 11, 21; "celebrate"/"sing aloud," v. 7; "make known," v. 12. The use of these terms makes it clear that the praise of the LORD is one of the principal elements of the psalm. The psalm is dominated by the poet's desire to praise the LORD at all times and in all places.

The second element of which the psalm consists has to do with the reasons why the LORD should be praised. Special emphasis is placed on the following aspects: the unsearchable greatness of the LORD (vv. 3, 6); the mighty acts and wondrous works of the LORD (vv. 4, 5, 6, 9, 10, 17); the everlasting kingdom of the LORD which is emphasized in vv. 11-13, as in v. 1; the LORD's steadfast love, compassion, mercy, kindness, and graciousness are also important reasons why he should be praised (cf., e.g., vv. 8, 9, 13b); the love of the LORD is clearly evinced by his tenderness toward and assistance to those who are in need and who are dependent on him (cf. esp. vv. 14-19). Although the psalm emphasizes that God shows love to and cares for those who are in need, his love is not unconditional. He does preserve those who love him, but he will destroy the wicked. These themes are not detached from one another; indeed, they are interwoven and interact in various ways. In this passage the greatness and power of God are related to his love; his goodness and mercy are not in conflict with his wrath but are the obverse side of the same coin; the kingship of the LORD is mentioned in the same breath as his condescending love toward those who are in need.

Psalm 145 is literally a song of praise from A to Z in honor of the greatness, kingship, and love of the LORD. Because the poet of Psalm 145 shows familiarity with and draws on numerous other psalms, it is probable that the psalm dates from the late postexilic period.

Psalm 146

Psalm 146 can be divided into the following strophes:

vv. 1-2:	Hymnic invocation
vv. 3-4:	Do not put your trust in mortals plus reasons
vv. 5-10a:	Trust in the LORD plus reasons
v. 10b:	Hymnic invocation.

The five psalms with which the psalter ends (Psalms 146–150) all begin and end with the same hymnic invocation "Praise the LORD!" and are known as the Hallel. Naturally all five of these psalms are hymns. In Psalm 146 the "Praise the LORD" invocations (vv. 1a, 10b) are the key to its interpretation. The hymnic element is carried further in the remainder of the first strophe (vv. 1b-2). The praise of the LORD pervades the poet's existence and extends to the end of his life.

The second strophe (146:3-4) is an admonition containing a warning against false confidence in human power. One cannot put unqualified trust in people, however powerful they may be, because they are impotent, mortal beings. The "princes" mentioned in v. 3 could refer either to the failed preexilic monarchy about which the poet expresses his disillusionment or foreign potentates in the postexilic period.

The third strophe (146:5-10a) forms a contrast to the previous strophe in that it tells us in whom we can put our trust, namely, in God alone. A number of reasons are given why we can trust in God. First, there is an appeal to the patriarchal tradition in which the LORD is described as the "God of Jacob." The LORD can be trusted because he has proved himself to be trustworthy throughout history, from the time of the patriarchs. The second reason why we can trust in God is that he created the heavens, the earth, and the sea — that is, the entire cosmos and everything in it — and is therefore in full control. The third reason is spelled out in vv. 6b-10a: the LORD is not only the great God of history and the creation but he also concerns himself with humble and insignificant people — the *personae miserae,* those who are despised and rejected by society: the oppressed, the hungry, prisoners, the blind, those who are bowed down, strangers, the orphan, and the widow. The LORD is aware of these people's need, and he assists them. He does not take the part of the underdogs unconditionally, however. He loves the righteous but does not accept ungodliness, whether it is found in the privileged or the underprivileged. The LORD differs radically from earthly rulers. They cannot be trusted (cf. vv. 3-4 again) because they are ephemeral. In contrast, God will reign forever and can always be trusted (v. 10a).

Psalm 146 probably reflects the disillusionment of the postexilic Judean congregation with the preexilic monarchy, which let them down and brought them misery. For this reason they are reaching out to the LORD, the only king in whom they can trust. Consequently the LORD is worthy of all their praise.

Psalm 147

Psalm 147 forms part of the group of psalms (146–150) which are introduced and concluded by the hymnic invocation "Praise the LORD!" Psalm 147 consists of three strophes, namely, vv. 1-6, 7-11, and 12-20. Each of the strophes is introduced by an imperative to praise the LORD: "Praise the LORD!" (v. 1); "Sing to the LORD . . ." (v. 7); "Praise the LORD . . ." (v. 12). All three strophes end with contrasts: in v. 6 the LORD uplifts the helpless but humiliates the wicked; in vv. 10-11 the psalmist tells us that the LORD takes no pleasure in those who trust in military might but his delight is in those who serve him; in vv. 19-20 we are told that the LORD gave his ordinances to Israel only and to no other people. These contrasts enhance the hymnic character of the psalm.

After the imperative to praise and after the statement that it is good and fitting to praise the LORD (147:1), the remainder of the first strophe (vv. 2-6) advances reasons why the LORD should be praised. In vv. 2-3 the psalmist refers to salvation history, and specifically to the Babylonian exile. Not only did the LORD rebuild the ruins of Jerusalem but he allowed the exiles to return to their own land. V. 2 probably refers to the time of Nehemiah, that is, after about 445 BC, when the walls of Jerusalem were rebuilt (cf. Neh 4:7). V. 3 uses the metaphor of a physician to describe the LORD's loving treatment of his wounded people during the exile. Vv. 4-5 describe the power of the LORD at the time of creation. He determined the number of the stars and gave them names. The stars, which the Babylonians in particular regarded as powers capable of determining the fate of human beings, are spoken of here as creations of the LORD. To determine the numbers of the stars is a feat beyond human capacity, but the LORD does it because he made the stars. This knowledge brings his people to a confession, namely, that he is great and powerful and that his knowledge is unbounded. The first strophe is concluded (v. 6) by another reference to humankind: because the LORD is so powerful he also settles disputes among people by acting as a judge. The pious, who subject themselves to the LORD in humility, are assisted by him. On the other hand, the ungodly, who live their lives in opposition to the LORD, are humbled by him.

The second strophe (147:7-11) is introduced by a double imperative and gives reasons why the LORD should be praised. In vv. 8-9 the emphasis falls on the LORD's care for nature. He is the source of rain and fertility. He ensures that the bare mountain slopes are covered with grass. In this way he ensures that the animals have enough food. He even gives heed to the irritating cawing of the young ravens, which some consider simply a nuisance but which the LORD feeds when they call. In vv. 10-11 the psalmist returns to the subject of humans. Human powerlessness is revealed. Things that impress people, namely, the strength of a horse or the strong body of a man, do not impress the LORD. Military force is really weakness since it does not last. What does endure and what the LORD delights in is the love and trust of his faithful servants.

The third strophe (147:12-20) is also introduced by a double imperative. This time the invocation is specifically to "Jerusalem"/"Zion." The reason advanced for the praise is that the LORD gave Jerusalem security by reinforcing the gates of the city. He also assured the future of Jerusalem by blessing her children. Not only the city but the entire country was blessed with prosperity and ample harvests. In vv. 16-17 the psalmist says that the LORD not only brings natural phenomena like snow, frost, and hail to the earth but by his power also causes them to melt and dissipate. Just as the LORD uses his word as a dynamic agent to get nature stirring, so he sends his word out among his people. The psalm reaches a climax with the statement that the LORD will make his ordinances known to no other nation but Israel.

Psalm 148

Like the other Hallel psalms (146–150), this psalm is introduced (v. 1) and concluded (v. 14) by the imperative "Praise the LORD!" As a hymn this psalm functions therefore to persuade its hearers or readers to praise the LORD. To this end the poet introduces two "choirs" — one to praise the LORD "from the heavens" (vv. 1-6) and the other to praise him "from the earth" (vv. 7-14). The message the poet is conveying is that the entire cosmos must praise the LORD.

The first strophe (148:1-6) — praising the LORD "from the heavens" — comprises a call to praise (vv. 1-4) and the grounds (vv. 5-6) for praising the LORD. The dominant feature of vv. 1-4 is the seven imperatives. V. 1 tells us that the mighty chorale which the created world must sing to its creator must echo from the highest place in creation — the heavens. In v. 2 a metaphor is used to depict the celestial court in which the sovereign LORD rules, surrounded by his servants. In v. 3 the heavenly bodies are personified. They are seen as the LORD's servants and called upon to praise him. In the ancient Near East the sun, moon, and stars were often deified; here they are explicitly presented as the LORD's handiwork and called upon to praise him. V. 4 concludes the imperatives and is a partial echo of v. 1 (cf. "heavens," v. 1, with "heavens" and "highest heavens," v. 4). In vv. 5-6 grounds are given for the preceding imperatives to praise the LORD. The first reason adduced for praising the LORD is that he created the universe by a mighty word or command. Psalm 148 describes the creation in the same way that Genesis 1 does. The LORD not only created the world but also sustains it and protects it from the powers of chaos. In contrast to other creation stories of the ancient Near East, where creation is said to be accomplished in the midst of conflict, in the biblical story the LORD creates by a mighty word.

The second strophe (148:7-14) is the second choir in this great recital, this time echoing "from the earth." This strophe is parallel to the first one in that the imperatives to praise the LORD (vv. 7-12) are followed by grounds for praising him (vv. 13-14). In contrast to the first strophe, where the highest regions of the cosmos were summoned to praise the LORD, this one starts with the depths of the earth. The first to be summoned are the "sea monsters," which in the creation myths of the ancient Near East had the connotation of being hostile monsters of chaos (cf. Pss 74:12-14; 89:10). Here they are demythologized, for these majestic monsters are the LORD's handiwork and are called upon to praise the Creator. The habitat of the monsters ("deeps") is personified and called upon to praise. These "deeps" or primordial floods also have mythological connotations and are related to powers of chaos (cf. Tiamat in the Babylonian creation myth). The point is that the LORD is not at war with the primeval waters, but that they, too, are summoned to praise him. The natural phenomena of the skies are also called upon to praise the LORD (v. 8): "fire and hail," "snow and frost," and "stormy wind." These dangerous natural forces against which humans are powerless are subject to the LORD and praise him. *Terra firma* ("the solid earth") — represented by the voices of the mountains and hills — is likewise enjoined to praise him (v. 9). The vegetable kingdom, the animal realm, and humankind are summoned in ascending order to voice their praise. Starting with the leaders ("kings," "princes," "rulers"), the whole of human society — male and female, old and young — is exhorted to praise. Although the summons to praise reaches a climax in the address to humans, it should be noted that human beings are not set apart. They are summoned on a par with the rest of creation to sing in a choir of praise to the LORD. The reasons for the praise are found in vv. 13-14. The grounds advanced for praise are that "his name alone is exalted." As in the previous strophe, there is a polemical element. The LORD alone is exalted — no other gods can aspire to this. The same universal element is apparent as in the previous strophe: the LORD's glory extends above heaven and earth, that is to say, everywhere. The expression "above earth and heaven" (v. 13) in a sense fuses the two strophes (cf. "from the heavens," v. 1, and "from the earth," v. 7) into one. V. 14 advances another reason for praising the LORD: "He has raised up a horn for his people." The horn symbolizes power (cf. Ps 89:17), and here it probably refers to a specific historical act by the LORD. Most exegetes rightly believe this to be a reference to the deliverance from the exile. Thus the psalm reaches its climax in the invocation of salvation history as grounds for the imperatives to praise the LORD.

Because the LORD has proved himself to be the one and only God — both in creation and in history — universal praise is due to him.

Psalm 149

As is the case with the other Hallel psalms (146–150), Psalm 149 must be read within the framework of the hymnic invocation, "Praise the LORD!" (vv. 1a, 9b). The fact that a "vengeance" motif is to be found in this hymn (cf. vv. 7-9) is a problem to many exegetes. Some interpreters are repelled by the warlike tone of vv. 6-9 and say that the vengeance motif is quite unexpected in a hymn and that consequently Psalm 149 forms a harsh contrast to the rest of the Hallel psalms.

The argument put forward here is that praise and vengeance are two sides of the same coin. The psalm can be divided into two strophes, namely, vv. 1-5 and 7-9. Vv. 1-5 contain the element of praise, and vv. 7-9 the vengeance and warlike motif. V. 6 is the nexus or cardinal verse between the two strophes in that the element of praise occurs in v. 6a and the warlike motif in v. 6b:

> Let the high praises of God be in their throats (v. 6a)
> and two-edged swords in their hands. (v. 6b)

The two apparently diverse elements are found side by side in v. 6, which can be regarded as a summary of the psalm.

The psalm's second strophe forms a mirror image of the first strophe in terms of the words "praise," "faithful," and "king":

A Praise the LORD (v. 1a)
B the faithful (v. 1b)
C their king (v. 2)
c their kings (v. 8)
b his faithful (v. 9a)
a Praise the LORD! (v. 9b).

This structure is evidence both of the coherence of the psalm and of the fact that praise and vengeance complement each other.

The first strophe (149:1-5) concentrates on the praise which should be rendered to the LORD. This praise should be expressed in a "new song" (cf., e.g., Ps 96:1). We are told *where* the praise should be rendered: "in the assembly of the faithful" (149:1) — that is, in public — and "on their couches" (v. 5) — that is, in private. The psalmist also tells us *to whom* the praise should be rendered, namely, to the LORD as "Maker" and as "King" (v. 2). We are told *who* should render praise (cf. the different names used for the congregation, such as "the children of Zion," and "his faithful ones"). We are told *how* the praise should take place ("with dancing," "with tambourine and lyre") and *why* the LORD should be praised (cf. v. 4).

In the second strophe the vengeance of the LORD on the nations is described in a dramatic and hyperbolic manner in the terminology of the Holy War tradition. A sharp contrast between the LORD and the nations is evident. The contrasts both reveal the nations to be powerless and emphasize the praiseworthiness of the LORD. While the LORD is to be praised as king and creator (v. 2), the kings of the nations are to be bound with iron fetters (v. 8); the kings of the nations are ironically described as "their nobles" (lit. their "heavyweights"), whereas in fact they are impotent lightweights. The irony is that it is the humble people (v. 4) who have to take the sword in their hand and execute judgment. The faithful praise the LORD and carry out sentences on the nations in the name of the LORD. What this psalm is referring to, therefore, is not personal or random revenge but the righteous punishment of the LORD.

The key to the interpretation of the psalm lies in v. 6, namely, that the vengeance element is not foreign to the psalm but combines with the praise element to form an integral part of the psalm. The praise on the lips and the sword in the hand complement each other.

Psalm 150

The Hallel psalms (146–150), Book V of the psalter (Psalms 107–150), and the entire psalter reach a climax in this doxology. Just as the other collections in the psalter end in a doxology (cf. Pss 41:13; 72:18-19; 89:52; 106:48), so Book V ends in a doxology. Psalm 150 forms a doxology in its entirety and builds up to a powerful, exultant final chord which allows the psalter to culminate in a Hallelujah. When the hymnic frame (vv. 1, 6b) is taken into account, it appears that no fewer than twelve imperatives and one jussive (v. 6) are used here to praise the LORD. The contents of the psalm can therefore be summed up in the words of v. 6: "Let everything that breathes praise the LORD!"

The psalm consists of only one strophe since the numerous imperatives give it a uniform character. In 150:1 the psalmist tells us *who should be praised,* namely, the LORD. The LORD is described here in terms of his dwelling place. Although the words "in his sanctuary" may be a reference to the earthly temple in Jerusalem, the expression "in his mighty firmament," which balances the first expression, refers to the LORD's heavenly dwelling. Heaven, in terms of the poet's worldview, would have been the highest point in the cosmos. The metaphor of the LORD as the heavenly king is used to emphasize his exaltedness and praiseworthiness.

In 150:2 we are told *why* the LORD should be praised. His "mighty deeds" and "surpassing greatness" are given as reasons for praise. These words are intended to refer not only to the LORD's deeds of creation but also to his deeds of deliverance throughout history.

The major portion of the psalm (150:3-5) is used to indicate *how* the LORD should be praised. By listing all the possible musical instruments — stringed, wind, and percussion — the poet emphasizes that the LORD should be praised in every possible manner, with exuberance and abundant joy.

The psalm concludes by saying *who* should praise the LORD, namely, "everything that breathes." Everything and everyone created by the LORD, all who received breath and life from him, should recognize that he is the Creator by praising him. To praise the LORD is the first and most important duty of all creatures. This is the conclusion reached by the psalm and the entire psalter. Just as the hymnic framework, "Praise the Lord!" indicates the beginning and end of the psalm, so our lives should be framed and regulated by the praise we owe to our savior and creator.

Select Bibliography. Aejmelaeus, A. 1986, *The Traditional Prayer in the Psalms,* Berlin: de Gruyter • Allen, L. C. 1983, *Psalms 101–150,* Waco: Word • Anderson, A. A. 1981, *The Book of Psalms,* vols. 1 and 2, Grand Rapids: Eerdmans • Booij, T. 1994, *Psalmen III,* Nijkerk: Callenbach • Botha, P. J. 1986, "Die teologiese funksie van die Torah-woordveld in die driehoeksverhouding Jahwe-vrome-vyand in Psalm 119," Unpubl. D.D. diss., University of Pretoria • Briggs, C. A., and E. G. Briggs. 1925, *The Book of Psalms,* vol. 2, 3d impr., Edinburgh: Clark • Briggs, C. A., and E. G. Briggs. 1927, *The Book of Psalms,* vol. 1, 4th impr., Edinburgh: Clark • Brueggemann, W. 1984, *The Message of the Psalms,* Minneapolis: Augsburg • Buttenwieser, M. 1938, *The Psalms,* Chicago: University of Chicago • Craigie, P. C. 1983, *Psalms 1–50,* Waco: Word • Croft, S. J. L. 1987, *The Identity of the Individual in the Psalms,* Sheffield: Sheffield Academic • Crüsemann, F. 1969, *Studien zur Formgeschichte von Hymnus und Danklied in Israel,* Neukirchen: Neukirchener • Day, J. 1990, *Psalms,* Sheffield: Sheffield Academic • Duhm, B. 1922, *Die Psalmen,* 2. Aufl., Tübingen: Mohr • Ferris, P. W. 1992, *The Genre of Communal Lament in the Bible and the Ancient Near East,* Atlanta: Scholars • Gerstenberger, E. S. 1988, *Psalms: Part I with an Introduction to Cultic Poetry,*

Grand Rapids: Eerdmans • Gunkel, H., and J. Begrich. 1933, *Einleitung in die Psalmen. Die Gattungen der religiösen Lyrik Israels,* Göttingen: Vandenhoeck & Ruprecht • Gunkel, H., and J. Begrich. 1986, *Die Psalmen,* 6. Aufl., Göttingen: Vandenhoeck & Ruprecht • Hossfeld, F.-L., and E. Zenger. 1993, *Die Psalmen I,* Würzburg: Echter • Kirkpatrick, A. F. 1957, *The Book of Psalms,* 12th repr., Cambridge: Cambridge University • Kraus, H.-J. 1978, *Psalmen. 1. und 2. Teilband,* 5. Aufl., Neukirchen-Vluyn: Neukirchener • Kraus, H.-J. 1979, *Theologie der Psalmen,* Neukirchen: Neukirchener • Lamparter, H. 1961, *Das Buch der Psalmen I,* 2. Aufl., Stuttgart: Calwer • Lamparter, H. 1965, *Das Buch der Psalmen II,* 2. Aufl., Stuttgart: Calwer • Mays, J. L. 1994, *Psalms,* Louisville: John Knox • McCann, J. C., ed. 1993, *The Shape and Shaping of the Psalter,* Sheffield: Sheffield Academic • Miller, P. D. 1986, *Interpreting the Psalms,* Philadelphia: Fortress • Mowinckel, S. 1961, *Psalmenstudien I-IV,* Amsterdam: Schippers • Mowinckel, S. 1962, *The Psalms in Israel's Worship,* vols. 1 and 2, Oxford: Blackwell • Prinsloo, W. S. 1984, *'n Eksegetiese erkenning van enkele psalms,* Pretoria: Nederlandse Gereformeerde Kerkboekhandel • Prinsloo, W. S. 1991, *Die Psalms leef!* Halfway House: Nederlandse Gereformeerde Kerkboekhandel • Ridderbos, N. H. 1972, *Die Psalmen: Stilistische Verfahren und Aufbau mit besonderer Berücksichtigung von Ps 1–41,* Berlin: de Gruyter • Rogerson, J. W., and J. W. McKay. 1977, *Psalms I–III,* Cambridge: Cambridge University • Schmidt, H. 1934, *Die Psalmen,* Tübingen: Mohr • Seybold, K. 1986, *Die Psalmen: Eine Einführung,* Stuttgart: Kohlhammer • Seybold, K. 1996, *Die Psalmen,* Tübingen: Mohr • Seybold, K., and E. Zenger, eds., 1994, *Neue Wege der Psalmenforschung,* Freiburg: Herder • Spieckermann, H. 1989, *Heilsgegenwart: Eine Theologie der Psalmen,* Göttingen: Vandenhoeck & Ruprecht • Tate, M. E. 1990, *Psalms 51–100,* Waco: Word • Van der Lugt, P. 1980, *Strofische structuren in de Bijbels-Hebreeuwse poëzie,* Kampen: Kok • Van der Ploeg, J. P. M. 1973, *Psalmen I,* Roermond: Romen • Van der Ploeg, J. P. M. 1974, *Psalmen II,* Roermond: Romen • Van Uchelen, N. A. 1971, *Psalmen I,* Nijkerk: Callenbach • Van Uchelen, N. A. 1977, *Psalmen II,* Nijkerk: Callenbach • Watson, W. G. E. 1984, *Classical Hebrew Poetry: A Guide to Its Techniques,* 2d ed., Sheffield: JSOT • Weiser, A. 1955, *Die Psalmen. I und II. Teil,* 4. Aufl., Göttingen: Vandenhoeck & Ruprecht • Whybray, R. N. 1996, *Reading the Psalms as a Book,* Sheffield: Sheffield Academic.

Proverbs

Ronald E. Clements

INTRODUCTION

Among the OT writings the book of Proverbs is classified as a book of wisdom. Indeed, more than any other book, it reflects the style, themes, and general characteristics of the Israelite wisdom tradition. Related books are Job and Ecclesiastes and, among the OT Apocrypha, Ecclesiasticus (Sirach) and the Wisdom of Solomon. To characterize what such a tradition implied, we may say that it was an intellectual tradition which aimed at recognizing and apprehending the realities of life as they were actually experienced. Wisdom, therefore, set itself the task of mastering the art of living. In doing this it focused primarily on establishing practical, matter-of-fact rules for conduct, giving it a strongly ethical flavor. At the same time it ventured upon speculative attempts to trace the fundamental order of the created world, to perceive the rules which governed its operation, and so to establish reasons for human success and failure.

Other characteristics of the biblical wisdom tradition are its concern with artistic expression, or striving to find apt metaphors and similes by which to understand human actions; it also explored motives for conduct, stressing the importance of attitudes and established lifestyles. So it frequently contrasted the behavior of the righteous with that of the wicked, the fool with the wise person, the lazy with the industrious, and the God-fearing with the malicious and arrogant troublemaker. Particularly relevant to the book of Proverbs is its concern to construct short, epigrammatic sayings of the kind which predominate in Proverbs 10–29. Metaphors and similes provide opportunity for humor, most frequently by drawing exaggerated parallels. Practicality predominates over cleverness, and the collections of proverbial instructions provide a basis for a general education. There is a desire to encourage thoughtful, restrained conduct, to emphasize obedience toward parents, and to cultivate polite speech.

The authors of collections of proverbial instuctions are for the most part unknown, but the worldview they adopt, the goals they strive for, and assumptions they make about the demands of everyday living point to a modestly secure, middle-class agricultural commmunity. On account of its intellectual goals wisdom had links with politics and statecraft; it called for respect for those who governed the nation and controlled its affairs, seeing them as pillars of the community. It recognized the powerful effects of distinctions created by wealth and poverty and called for care and charity toward the latter. Toward the former it displays an ambivalent attitude, regarding wealth, honestly worked for, as a God-given reward but also recognizing the temptations which surrounded those who would get rich quickly.

For the law and its administrators it showed respect, seeing it as the most vital and necessary of the social orders, over which the king presided as head. Such laws rightly threatened wrongdoers and brigands; at the same time the wise viewed with concern the ease with which legal processes were corrupted so that their competence to deal with many of the most pressing problems of daily life were undermined. Wisdom touches on matters of health and religion, calling for a deep and unwavering loyalty to God and trust in the divine rule over all things, without being a form of medical or priestly learning. It is not secular in any sense of discounting the importance of religious activities, but neither is it inclined to appeal to religious ideals of holiness and a sacrally structured universe. It stands within, rather than against, the demands of a sacral world order.

Overall, the moral concerns of wisdom relate to individual and personal well-being and happiness. It notes the psychological factors which may govern this and the behavior patterns which threaten it. Along with this it is alert to the broader social context in which life is lived and affirms the necessity of establishing positive, trusting relationships within this. It is world-affirming and concerned with a secure and stable social order. In its earliest period it appears to have had links with officials who administered state affairs. In line with their anxiety to discourage antisocial and criminal behavior the wise looked to the roots of the social and moral order at the deepest level — in a divinely created world order. Just as the Babylonian king Hammurabi's celebrated law code portrayed the king as the recipient of a divine gift of justice, which he then administered, so wisdom saw its task as fulfilling a similar role, not through a system of law but rather through a process of education which began in the home in a child's earliest days. However, it shows no very clear connection with the setting up of formal schools, although it seems probable that such eventually came into being. It appears at an early period to have formed connections with scribal skills and to have developed an interest in rhetoric and poetic artistry.

The origins of proverbial sayings are to be found in popular oral culture. They display artistic skill by making unexpected comparisons and promoting careful observation of life and human behavior. Persuasion, rather than authoritarian admonition, often colored by humor and exaggeration, formed part of their technique. They frequently gave new meanings to old images and ideas, such as "the tree of life" (cf. 3:18) and "the fountain of life" (10:11; 13:14; 14:27; 16:22). Writing made possible sophisticated forms of verbal artistry, developing similes into complex allegories. Some wisdom compositions perhaps emanated from a stage of semiliteracy when tightly formulated sayings and allegories could be expanded upon orally and moralized.

Considerable critical debate has arisen over two particular aspects of the Israelite wisdom tradition. First is the undoubted connection with a closely similar type of instruction which flourished in Egypt from the second millennium BC. The strikingly close parallels between Prov 22:17–23:19 and the Egyptian *Wisdom of Amenemope* (*ANET*: 421-24) show that there existed at one period a considerable level of mutual interaction between Egyptian didactic literature and Israelite wisdom (Bryce 1979; Würthwein 1976: 113-33). Almost certainly the predominant direction of influence was from Egypt to Israel. Other contacts with aspects of Egyptian instructions appear in Proverbs 1–9 (Whybray 1965).

An issue that is related to this concerns the extent to which Israelite wisdom displayed a disinterest in religious and cultic affairs in its earliest period, only grafting such a concern into its teaching at a late stage (cf. McKane 1965: 65-93). In spite of the broad claim now evident in the book that the teaching of wisdom rests on "the fear of the LORD" (1:7, etc.), this is at a surface rather than at a foundational level. The careful reader cannot overlook the degree of distance between many of the emphases of wisdom and those of the cult. Most especially the cultic concern with protection of the sphere of holiness is almost entirely lacking.

From the several informative headings contained in the book, as well as from the varying literary forms and styles of presentation within it, it is apparent that the book of Proverbs is a "collection of collections." On account of their greater literary sophistication and complexity the sayings contained in Proverbs 1–9 appear to be of later origin than those of chs. 10–29. However, the differences are more in matters of form than of content. It is in any case impossible to offer precise dates for the origin of sayings which relate to a pattern of life which lasted for more than a millennium.

Throughout Proverbs the readers who are addressed are evidently assumed to be relatively young (reflected in the frequent address to "my child" [NRSV; lit. "my son"]) and predominantly male. They are assumed to be tolerably secure economically, looking with charitable concern on those who are poorer than themselves but also aware that those who are rich often behave oppressively toward them. They are frequently expected to manage, own, and farm small estates which provide the livelihood for the household's members. Children are urged to show high deference to their parents and elders and to think highly of the king as the supreme ruler. This latter point may reflect that, at some period in its development, wisdom was promoted among circles of scribes in the royal court. In spite of some instructions which relate directly to behavior in a courtly setting (e.g., Prov 23:1-9), the great majority of sayings reflect a setting that is more rural than courtly and more related to farming than to state administration. Nevertheless, Proverbs looks upon the king as enthroned at the top of a pyramid of human society which reflects an order ordained at creation by God.

COMMENTARY

The Meaning of Wisdom (Prov 1:1–9:18)

The Preface to the Book (Prov 1:1-7)

1:1-7 presents the reader with an introduction explaining the character and purpose of wisdom and setting forth its primary goals. The opening ascription of authorship to Solomon appears as a relatively late assignment of the book to the king, whose fame for wisdom elevated him to become its chief patron. It is based on the fame which Solomon enjoyed and which is affirmed in 1 Kgs 4:29-34 and 10:23-25. Differing explanations have arisen concerning how such a broadly based claim for the tradition of Solomon's wisdom arose. It undoubtedly relates directly to the importance of royal wisdom in the ancient Near East (cf. Porteous 1967: 77-91) and may also bear some connections with Solomon's undoubted trade and cultural ties with Egypt. That it related closely to the setting up of a Solomonic system of state administration, requiring educated officials and scribes to control it (Heaton 1974), is less probable. Chapter headings in Prov 30:1 and 31:1 point to other, imperfectly known, sources of proverbial collections. From the content of the sayings themselves and the implicit indications of the kind of readership envisaged for the book, it is apparent that wisdom had a widely popular origin and was largely based on everyday experience.

The description of wisdom's purpose in 1:2-6 shows that Proverbs was addressed to all who were willing to learn, irrespective of social standing or wealth. The book gives certain features particular prominence: wisdom declared itself to have a paramount ethical interest, promoting righteousness and equity in social affairs; it taught shrewdness and discernment in listening to, and assessing, the speech of others. It aimed to foster prudence in decision making and to promote good relationships and prosperity through commercial integrity. It strove to nurture good character as the foundation for good conduct, and interesting, thoughtful speech, using a variety of artistic and rhetorical speech forms. The picture of the typical wise person is that of a careful, slightly taciturn, and hard-working citizen, diligent in building up his small farm to support a family and generous toward less fortunate neighbors.

Much of this is epitomized in the summarizing affirmation of 1:7, which is repeated with slight variation in 9:10 and 15:33 (cf. also Job 28:28 and Ecclus 1:14). As it stands here, it affirms that the fear of the LORD (Yahweh) is the first step toward attaining a knowledge of wisdom and practicing the lifestyle which wisdom upholds. The phrase "the fear of the LORD" implies not anxiety and dread but rather unwavering devotion to the God of Israel, whom the proverbial tradition consistently prefers to identify by the ancient name YHWH. That such a title carried a positively monotheistic significance throughout the book is certain, but this would not have precluded that sayings emanating from a very early period of Israel's life have been included in the collection. The claim that the earliest forms of the Israelite wisdom tradition showed an indifference to religious affairs and practice is scarcely sustainable. Nevertheless, it does seem highly likely that, as the canonical wisdom tradition was developed in Judaism, a stronger concern to harmonize the teaching of wisdom with that of the Mosaic Torah arose. In time the process of literary collection brought about a stronger theological direction by harmonizing differing streams of tradition — cultic, legal, and educational.

Wisdom was essentially pragmatic, claiming to be based on actual experience and not primarily aimed at either supporting or countering the claims of cultic life and the protection of Israel's holiness. Yet it could also be dogmatic, and even optimistically theoretical, in its insistence that good and bad actions brought, respectively, good and bad consequences for the doer.

It seems certain that, from initially offering critical observations on a variety of actions, wisdom developed the aim of providing a more comprehensive portrayal of the ways of the world as they were experienced and the shaping of human character that was most desirable to cope with these. It affirmed that such summarizing teaching was in accord with the designed order of life created at the beginning by God, and it assumed, if it did not demonstrate, that such teaching was in conformity with the laws of God revealed through Moses and the prophets. This viewpoint is beautifully expressed in Job 28:28. Such an understanding permeates the different sections of the book of Proverbs, establishing connections between social, individual, and political activities and even relating these to phenomena in the natural world. For the teaching of wisdom to carry conviction it was necessary to believe that all life has intelligent purpose and meaning and that by careful observation one can see the interrelationships of the various spheres of human activity.

A First Hindrance to Wisdom – Evil Companions (Prov 1:8-19)

The opening address concerning the central importance of wisdom to virtue and happiness draws attention to various hindrances and barriers which could dissuade the intended reader from its pursuit. First among these it places the enticements of evil companions. The message is set forth in the form of an admonition which commences by urging adherence to the teaching given in childhood by one's father and mother within the home (1:8). The inclusion of the mother may be regarded as surprising (but cf. 31:1) in view of the fact that the order of life which wisdom recognized as normative is strongly patriarchal in its structure. The inclusion of the mother's role as teacher may partly reflect the realities of a conventional Israelite household, but, in any case, it was necessary at this juncture to draw attention to the family-oriented set of values which protected the household and its estate. The teacher viewed the enticements of evildoers as contrary to these values and as promoting disruption and disorder in the close bond within each household and to economic stability in the community.

Undoubtedly many recurrent themes of wisdom instruction point to the home as constituting its primary setting. Even at a stage when a class of professional teachers emerged, it is apparent that these would have been primarily employed as private tutors to relatively well-to-do families. Throughout Proverbs the protection of the houshold as a unit, including all its dependent members, remains a primary concern. Actions and attitudes which threatened this, either through disruptive behavior within it (e.g., quarrelsomeness, sexual irresponsibility, or laziness) or challenges to its security through criminal behavior, were all repeatedly and vigorously opposed. Wisdom presumed a family-based household as the primary unit of society, which was also assumed normally to represent an independent and self-contained economic unit.

The inducements proffered by wrongdoers to join their company, set forth in 1:11-14, point to behavior embracing physical violence, muggings ("lying in wait for blood"), theft, and general disruptive conduct, ridiculing social conformity and honesty. The instructor's argument is that those who choose such ways of violence eventually come to a violent end (vv. 18-19). The advice presumes an inbuilt momentum to the ways of violence which eventually overtake and overwhelm the perpetrators of such actions. Those who choose such as a way of life are doomed. This appears as the intended inference of the imagery used of the bird trap presented in v. 17. Violence itself is the baited net which eventually entraps its victim.

The Call of Wisdom (Prov 1:20-33)

Proverbs commends the importance of acquiring wisdom in order to be successful in life by portraying wisdom as a beautiful woman calling in the streets and offering the benefits of her teaching to all who are willing to accept it. Some persons are assumed to respond negatively to such attractive inducements and to refuse her guidance because it entails reproof, discipline, and self-restraint. The portrayal of wisdom in personal form and feminine gender has occasioned extensive discussion (cf. Camp 1985: 23-68). Much of this centers on whether it is to be understood primarily as a literary device aimed at showing the attractiveness of wisdom as a code for living or whether some deliberate counterpart is intended to the temptations of sexual promiscuity offered by adulterers and street women. The latter offer short-term excitement and pleasure but at the price of eventual ruination and death.

Opinions have differed greatly as to the extent that ancient traditions of a mother-goddess, especially a goddess of wisdom whose favors comprised both sexual knowledge and understanding of "life," have been channeled into the Hebrew wisdom figure (Camp 198: 272-91). Such developments cannot be directly linked with wisdom, although it is a marked characteristic of the teaching of Proverbs that it focuses attention on disorderly sexual relationships as a major evil to be opposed. To this extent it is possible to view the wisdom tradition as one which drew to itself a wide range of imagery and mythology in which divine-human relationships, including those carrying sexual overtones, were involved.

Proverbs describes those who refuse the appeal of wisdom variously as fools, simple ones, and scoffers. The latter term particularly points to arrogance and blustering behavior. The terms for foolishness point to different attitudes, sometimes those of simple naivete and at others those of willful and obstinate refusal to accept unpalatable discipline.

It is also a major theme of Proverbs that the path of folly leads ultimately to disaster (cf. 1:24-32). The strong confidence that the refusal to listen to wisdom carries its own destructive consequences and leads to ruin is a repeated theme. At times it is no more than a sense of poetic justice — the violent get what they deserve — while at other times the doctrine goes deeper than this, insisting that God ensures that wrongdoing does not go unpunished. Proverbs claims that it lies in the very nature of the created order that evil unleashes evil, which eventually and inevitably comes back on the head of the evildoer. Whether God takes punitive action, whether the community are urged to take such action, or whether it lies simply within the nature of evil that it acts as an uncontrollable destructive force, the end results are claimed to be similar. Wisdom uncovers the rules and "laws" of life, insisting that good must ultimately triumph over evil and that virtue and happiness are inseparably connected. It became a fruitful exploration of the validity of this doctrine of retribution that wisdom sought to test its universality in the light of actual human experience (so especially in Job and Ecclesiastes).

The Path of Temptation (Prov 2:1-22)

This unusual chapter consists of a single complex sentence in the original Hebrew text. It sets forth the stark moral choices which the reader, addressed at the beginning as "my child," faces in life and for which wisdom claims to provide an essential path of guidance. It establishes a condition — "If you accept . . ." (2:1, 3, 4), "then you will understand . . ." (vv. 5, 9). It sums up the entire situation with a firm declaration in v. 20 — ". . . therefore walk in the way of the good. . . ."

In spite of this cohesive structure there are clear indications of variation since in the opening verse the message is based on the authority of the teacher. This is subsequently identified with the authority of wisdom's insights and understanding of the nature of life. In turn this is held to derive from God (2:6). So an assimilation of the path of wisdom to that of piety is seen to be seamless and complete. Acceptance of wisdom's precepts is knowledge of God and therefore knowledge of the world as it is.

The chapter shows repetition to a marked degree which has been contrived, at least in part, for rhetorical effect. However, it appears certain that the original central report has later been expanded. Many of wisdom's favorite themes are given prominence, among them that it shows the path to all virtue. Thus righteousness, justice, integrity of purpose ("walking blamelessly," 2:7), and "every good path" (v. 9) are included in it. It should be the chosen path of those who are "faithful to God" (v. 8). Opposed to this we find the choices of wrongdoing, involving evil speaking, deviousness, and sexual immorality (vv. 14-15).

The passage introduces us to the distinctive theme of temptation to sexual immorality (2:16-19), which subsequently appears as a dominant theme in Proverbs 1–9. The portrayal of wisdom as a desirable woman contrasts with the temptations offered by "the loose woman" (v. 16). The precise meaning of the Hebrew term has aroused considerable discussion since at one level it appears to suggest "foreignness." More convincingly, however, it refers to a woman, not necessarily of non-Israelite origin, who stands outside the established structure of family and social life. She is hence an "outsider," either because she betrays her marital vows as an adulteress or because she has renounced all direct kinship ties as wife, daughter, mother, or sister within the male-dominated order of a patriarchal kin group.

The assertion that sexual promiscuousness "leads down to death" follows the contention that wisdom offers a way that leads to life. Factors relating to health (Clements 1982: 65-93), social harmony, and general well-being are thereby seen to contribute to "life," understood broadly and positively, against which violence, family disloyalty, and commercial ruin all constitute a way to "death." The point is significant for understanding the way in which wisdom moralizes broad concepts. It highlights a formative feature of wisdom's revaluation of ideas, otherwise common in the realm of formal worship. A conflict between the powers (usually separate deities) of life and death at one time formed a major feature of ancient Near Eastern cultic ritual and mythology. To some extent wisdom either refutes altogether, or moralizes, a wide range of mystical notions of powers of life and death. In doing so, however, it still retains much of the dualistic tendency inherent in popular belief and experience.

The concluding assurance of 2:20-22, with the promise that those who heed the teaching of wisdom will "abide in the land," serves as an appendix. It aims to show that the benefits of life and prosperity are to be enjoyed in a specific realm. OT historical and prophetic literature presents living in the land promised by God to Israel's ancestors as an ultimate goal, to be enjoyed to the full in an undefined future age. To be denied that privilege was to forfeit a central aspect of the biblical hope. The passage is striking in view of the fact that the teaching of Proverbs is largely universalistic in its outlook, for the most part standing aside from the political and geographical concerns that belong to the traditions about the acquisition and loss of the land promised to Abraham's descendants.

Wisdom and Piety (Prov 3:1-12)

The preceding chapter has asserted that wisdom is inseparable from piety and that the teachings of wisdom are wholly in agreement with the demands of the fear of the LORD. Deeper than this, however, lies the insistence that without reverence for the LORD as God there can be no recognition of the claims of wisdom (1:7; 2:5-6). This focuses on the point that there is a potential, if not explicitly acknowledged, tension between wisdom's pragmatic concern to show the path to human well-being and happiness and the sometimes unfathomable demands of

God. The section 3:1-12 has evidently been carefully introduced at this point to show that an essential agreement exists between the teaching of wisdom and the demands of worship and piety. Scholars have noted the close connections between this section and the overall content of the book of Deuteronomy, especially Deuteronomy 5–9. The teaching of wisdom is identified as deriving from the "commandments" of the teacher, assuming an authority comparable to that of Moses in Deuteronomy. The imagery of Prov 3:3 compares closely with the language of Deut 6:6-8. The most convincing explanation of these similarities is that the authors of Proverbs 1–9 have striven to assert a basic conformity between the instructions of wisdom and the teaching of the Torah. This development marks a major step in the growth of the biblical canon. At the same time it is not to be denied that the book of Deuteronomy shows a substantial level of connection with the Israelite wisdom tradition (cf. M. Weinfeld 1972: 244-319), most probably because of its links with an official body of governmental scribes.

Wisdom offered guidance to a way of life that promised health, long life, and success. This is implied in the promise that God will "make straight" (i.e., successful) the paths of those who follow its dictates. This assurance is then reinforced by the promise that to honor God by fulfilling the worship requirements of offering tithes and first fruits would itself bring material reward (3:7). Clearly, with all the risks and uncertainties of life, this did not always happen. So vv. 11-12 present what is undoubtedly the most important feature of the section. When things go wrong, and illness and misfortune blight the lives of righteous and pious persons, such eventualities must be accepted as God's discipline. In later wisdom writings, particularly Job and Ecclesiastes, the wisdom tradition explored such ideas further. Here the fundamental conviction of traditional wisdom instruction is upheld — that God rewards the righteous with material blessings. Nevertheless, it is modified to take account of the reality of undeserved misfortune. Such painful experience is to be regarded as a mark of divine discipline and reproof, akin to the discipline which a loving parent imposes on a child (Prov 19:18; 23:13).

In Praise of Wisdom (Prov 3:13-20)

Prov 3:13-18 contain a hymn in praise of wisdom which has all the markings of being a poetic composition, modeled on the style of similar hymns in praise of a particular deity. The aim is evidently to employ a well-established poetic form to show the desirability of acquiring wisdom. Much of the impact of the passage lies in its use of conventional imagery to affirm that wisdom is "more precious than jewels" (cf. Job 28:15-19) and "a tree of life" to those who find her. The hymn thereby aims to assert the superlative value of wisdom and the importance of adhering to her teachings. Nothing is to be compared to her. In this praise of wisdom she is presented as a distinct personal being. There is, however, no reason to suppose that this is more than a feature of poetic imagery. It does not therefore prove that, at one period, Israel worshiped a goddess of wisdom. Nevertheless, it is possible that the teachers of wisdom hoped to establish the recognition that all aspects of the feminine associated with the divine world were expressed through wisdom. In this way any associations with ritual actions carrying unwanted sexual connotations could be eliminated. Prov 8:1-36 carries forward the imagery of wisdom as a feminine semidivine figure with yet more detailed elaboration.

The possibility that wisdom might be misunderstood as a deity alongside, and even on a level with, the LORD God of Israel is further precluded by the addition in 3:19-20 of the hymnic assertion of the supreme sovereignty of the LORD God as the Creator of the world. Wisdom was present with God at creation, so that all the intricate workings of the natural order are to be seen as fashioned in accordance with her principles. Nevertheless, the LORD alone is the Creator, wisdom being merely the instrument of construction and design by which the world was fashioned. In this way the connection between God and wisdom is shown to exist, but with the latter in a wholly subordinate position. The validity of the connection between wisdom and piety is thereby shown to belong to the basic structure of the world's order.

Wisdom and the Good Neighbor (Prov 3:21-35)

The teacher of wisdom here develops two very important central themes which characterize the moral and sociological assumptions around which the entire structure of wisdom teaching is built. The first focuses on the "neighbor" (3:28, 29) as the person to whom obligation is especially due (Clements 1993: 209-28). The second looks to the "house," or more comprehensively "household," as the foundational institution of social and economic order. So the person beside whom one lives, or with whom one works, is a fellow human being who feels and acts like oneself and who is to be treated accordingly. The advice given in vv. 27-29 at first appears rather obvious, until its full range is appreciated. Ancient societies almost universally made sharp discriminatory distinctions between persons on the grounds of their family and tribal affiliation. Ties of kinship and family connection — even relatively remote ones — governed relationships and determined the level of good or ill will toward fellow human beings. Wisdom was deeply concerned to introduce a changed emphasis by affirming that simple contact and geographical proximity establish a relationship calling for trust and compassion. It then defines this relationship in terms of friendship and good neighborliness. Most English versions reflect this emphasis by translating Heb. *re'* (= companion, neighbor) as "friend." So the admonitions to respect the existence of such a relationship and the obligations it entailed were to be observed constantly. The significance of the concept lay in its insistence that good and responsible behavior could not be limited to those who stood within certain narrowly defined tribal or family groups. The lasting importance of the idea is seen in that its basic contention, supported by a quotation from Lev 19:18, was taken up in the NT to constitute the second of the two Great Commandments (Mark 12:31, 33; Luke 10:27; Rom 13:9; Gal 5:14; Jas 2:8).

The warning against quarrelsomeness in 3:30 and the

repetition of earlier warnings against violent and perverse conduct (vv. 31-32) reflect wisdom's wholehearted concern to uphold and protect the integrity and wellbeing of each household. The household was seen as the primary unit on which society was built. It was accordingly to be used as a school of education for its younger members. At the same time it was to be a place of peace and contentment which avoided stressful actions and attitudes. Throughout Proverbs it is regarded as a self-contained and independent entity, represented by its paternal head, in which the prosperity of all its members was a shared responsibility. Even with its strongly paternalistic structure each of its members, both male and female and even slaves, was looked upon as a contributing worker and beneficiary. Actions could therefore be judged by their usefulness to this small and closely knit unit.

3:34-35 show the extent to which the teachers of wisdom focus their attention on the nurturing of positive attitudes and the building up of strong, positive characters, even more than on the goodness or badness of particular actions. The latter were largely to be seen as the result of success or failure in achieving the former. Those members of society who pursued foolishness and despised wisdom did so because their attitude was based on arrogance and scorn. Conversely, a receptive attitude toward the instructions of wisdom called for humility and a willingness to abandon mere selfish opinion — "being wise in one's own eyes." The less experienced could learn from those who were older and wiser than they.

The Commendation of Wisdom (Prov 4:1-27)

Chapter 4 consists of three separate instructions, each of which affirms, with the aid of particular collections of word imagery, the highest possible value of wisdom. The three word pictures of vv. 1-9, 10-19, and 20-27 probably once existed separately and have been assembled into a larger composition. Each takes the form of an introductory recommendation for the acceptance of wisdom. The first two conclude with an assurance of the success, happiness, and wellbeing which the pursuit of wisdom will bring to those who adhere to its doctrines (vv. 8-9, 18-19). The third of them sets forth such an assurance as the center of its commendations.

Taken as a combined unit, the instruction and commendation offer nothing in the way of detailed information concerning the content of wisdom's teaching; nor is there any further development of the claim that the teachings of wisdom and those of religious commitment are essentially in agreement. Wisdom is shown to exist as a body of instruction based on parental teaching (4:1, 10, 20), but the artistry of the presentation assumes that the authority of wisdom lies within its own essential nature, backed up by its power to bring success, long life, and happiness. It therefore needs no further reinforcement from any claim to a unique divine origin. It is enough that it accords with the true nature of the created world. Its authority is drawn from the experience of life itself rather than from any unique event or person who can guarantee its special claims. This appears prominently in v. 7, where the recognition of humanity's need for wisdom provides it with reason enough to support its claims.

The overal commendation of wisdom is strengthened by drawing attention again to its opposite (4:14-17, 19 — most commentators have suggested that the order of vv. 18-19 should be reversed). The word imagery by which the instructor affirms the desirability of wisdom gives only broad promises concerning the benefits that its acquisition will bring (v. 9 — a beautiful crown; v. 22 — healing to all the flesh; v. 18 — a path which becomes brighter like dawn breaking). By implication the instructor contends that the acceptance and employment of wisdom's precepts will bring happiness. Wisdom knows the path to virtue, and virtue brings happiness!

The Foolishness of Sexual Infidelity (Prov 5:1-23)

A major threat to the security and well-being offered by adherence to the teachings of wisdom is seen to be presented to a young man by the seductive allure of sexual temptation. Besides the extensive treatment here, the subject has already been mentioned in 2:16-19 and appears again in 6:24-25 and 7:5, 24-27. Its dangers are highlighted here in a threefold sequence: 5:1-6 identifies the loose woman as the subject of temptation; vv. 7-14 point to the public shame and ruination which will befall the man who falls for the woman's wiles; vv. 15-21 declare the satisfaction and contentment to be found in marital fidelity. The section ends with a warning that all human conduct, even that carried out in secret, is seen and judged by God, thereby acknowledging the secretive nature of sexual promiscuity. A concluding admonition in vv. 22-23, which seems to be an afterthought, enlarges on this point. It reiterates the strong conviction of the wisdom teachers that the way of foolishness and self-indulgence leads to inevitable disaster. Wickedness carries its own destructive power within itself and is to be resisted by a self-imposed discipline and attention to the precepts of wisdom.

Throughout this teaching on the seductive temptations presented by the loose woman the subject is consistently dealt with from a male perspective. The woman is viewed as the primary source of temptation, and male sexual desire is catered to in marriage and fidelity to its obligations (5:15-19). The question of the correct translation of the phrase rendered "loose woman" in the NRSV (NIV and REB, "adulteress"; GNB, "another man's wife") has occasioned extensive discussion. It becomes evident from 6:24-26 that the phrase included a woman already married, hence "adulteress." However, the term likely applied to women who either had no immediate family ties or who were disloyal to them.

The apportioning of blame to the woman for behaving as a temptress (5:3) is strongly made. Less clear is the description offered of the shame and ruination which consorting with her brings to the male reader addressed (vv. 9-11, 14). The inference appears to be that retribution would come from the woman's husband or family. The dissipation of the wayward man's wealth implies a kind of "Rake's Progress," and there is an implied warning that such conduct could imperil a person's health (v. 11). Overall, such sexual misconduct is held to be socially disruptive and a cause of shame in the public assembly (v. 14). The community as a whole would learn of such bad behavior and condemn it, holding the man as well as the woman responsible for acting dishonorably. The social standing of the culprit would then be undermined. Such warnings seem to indicate that it was improbable that the death penalty which the law imposed on adulterers would be imposed (Deut 22:22-29; cf. John 8:1-11). The portrait in 5:18 of the reader's own wife as herself beautiful draws upon imagery familiar to romantic poetry (cf. Cant 2:7; 3:5). It aims at emphasizing still further the pointless folly of wayward sexual behavior. The teachers of wisdom express a strong concern for the preservation of the integrity, vitality, and harmony of the household. They observe that sexual misdemeanors have wide-ranging consequences for the wrongdoer's own family.

Warnings concerning Personal Responsibility (Prov 6:1-19)

Four moral issues are dealt with in this section, each of which is couched in a form of instruction employing the varied techniques of the teachers of wisdom. The reason for their placement in the order of topics at this point is not obvious. They do neverthless illustrate well the subjects and didactic literary techniques which give wisdom its special character. The first theme in 6:1-5 concerns the foolishness of seeking to help a neighbor by giving a pledge for a financial liability undertaken by him. The teacher is wholly opposed to such an action — a theme which recurs in several short proverbial instructions. It is looked upon as a well-meant deed that is wholly undesirable, putting at risk the would-be helper's own financial position. It left a person at the mercy of others over whom he would have no real control — the debtor as well as the creditor. Moreover, slavery to debt was a real threat for the unfortunate and the unwary, and to jeopardize one's own position and family unnecessarily was seen to be utter folly. The powerful word pictures employed to serve as a deterrent from such action (vv. 4-5) reflect the urgency with which the matter was regarded. They may be taken to imply that it was a situation which had happened with sufficient frequency to warrant special mention. More particularly, in view of the many admonitions which appear in Proverbs to display a spirit of good neighborliness, it was one in which good intentions could prove ruinous.

The second issue is a warning against laziness (6:6-11). It shows an awareness that such warnings often fall on deaf ears. To counter this, the industry of the seemingly unimposing ant (vv. 6-8) and the ironic chiding of a sharp-tongued bystander (vv. 9-11) give force to the warning.

The third theme (6:12-15) warns against the damage inflicted by a willful mischief maker, using the wiles of crafty speech and guileful gesture to cause discontent and needless trouble. The technique here is that of straightforward description showing how the trouble can be created and the crafty ways that the mischief maker employs to achieve damaging ends. No specific wisdom language is employed, and it is left to the broader recognition that the teacher was emphatically concerned with upholding good behavior in society in general.

The fourth theme (6:16-19) employs the rhetorical device of listing a number of examples of bad behavior to which attention is especially drawn. This technique of using a numerical saying for rhetorical effect is employed more extensively in Proverbs 30. Opinions among scholars have differed whether all the examples are intended to share equal condemnation or whether the technique employed is intended to point out that the final instance — in this case, some discord in a family — is being made the subject of special attention. What may have been passed over as a lesser evil is pinpointed as equally bad as the others.

Further Condemnation of Sexual Misconduct (Prov 6:20-35)

This section returns to the theme of the great importance of avoiding adultery. In the perspective of literary forms it is noteworthy for the similarity of its opening admonitions to expressions in Deuteronomy (Deut 6:7; 11:19). How this similarity is to be explained has been variously judged since, even though some literary influence appears certain, it is unclear which passage is older. For the rest the passage is a further warning against adultery, once again firmly addressed to a male reader. The basic discussion of 6:20-25 is backed up by the use of highly meaningful metaphors and examples aimed at showing how serious and inevitable the destructive consequences of such action will prove to be. Problems arise because no biblical law requires sevenfold compensation for theft (v. 31), and we can only assume that the figure is purely rhetorical. Nor is the reasoning behind v. 30 very clear. It is best taken to suggest that, just as a thief will be punished even when his action could claim to be the consequence of some human necessity, how much more serious would be the fate of an adulterer who had no such mitigating excuse. Vv. 34-35 strongly hint that the death penalty was unlikely to be imposed on an adulterer. Both pentateuchal law and the emphatic teaching in Proverbs reflect the difficulty experienced in antiquity in obtaining satisfactory proof that adultery by consenting adults had taken place.

Further Warnings concerning Sexual Temptation (Prov 7:1-27)

Following the fervent warnings against sexual misconduct that have already be given, it appears more than a little repetitive to find an additional admonition to the same effect here. The style and technique, however, are varied greatly, and it would appear to be the author's desire to use the artistic color and appeal of the poem of 7:6-23 to influence the presentation. This poem, which bears all the marks of having been an independent composition, uses the emotional appeal of the story of an encounter between a young man and a prostitute to maintain interest. It has been given a general wisdom introduction in vv. 1-5 which is of special interest because of its identification of the teacher-parent's wisdom as "commandments" (cf. 2:1; 6:20). This close association with God's commandments is further enhanced by the advice to "bind them on your fingers," which compares closely with Deut 6:8; 11:8. All the indications are that it marks a further concern to bring together the content of wisdom instruction and the commandments of God's covenant law in the Pentateuch. It marks the assimilation of wisdom into a canonical tradition of scriptural "law."

The portrayal of the seductive allure of the prostitute, her spurious pretension to piety to allay the young man's fears (7:14), and her clever talking (v. 14) lead to a declaration of her ultimately destructive power (v. 23). As earlier (5:5), a summarizing epilogue (v. 27) asserts that the final end of those who consort with such a woman is death (v. 27).

Together the subtle artistry of the encounter described here, the repeated warnings given more extensively, and the disastrous nature of the declared end of those who pursue promiscuous sexual relationships indicate that the wisdom teachers felt promiscuity to be a major source of social dislocation. The extent of the treatment of the subject in Proverbs 1–9 suggests that the harsh rulings of the Pentateuchal legislation concerning adultery could not confidently be imposed. Sexual promiscuity in biblical times, as so often since, was revealing itself as a problem which the legislative authority of the law could not easily control and on which the educational persuasiveness of wisdom was seen to provide a much needed support.

Wisdom in All Her Beauty (Prov 8:1-36)

Both from a literary and a theological perspective this chapter is the most complex of those contained in the book of Proverbs. It has, accordingly, been extensively discussed, and its possible connections with ancient traditions of a goddess of wisdom have been variously evaluated. It presents wisdom in the guise of an attractive young woman — a rhetorical device already well evidenced in the wisdom instructions (cf. Prov 1:20-21) — standing in the streets of a city and addressing its young men. Her bold and forthright appeal reflects not a little of the brash enticements offered by the loose women who are condemned. However, her gifts and promises are not those of the women described in 5:1-14 and 7:6-27. Instead they are positive, virtuous, and not at all deceitful. Whereas the street woman points to a path which leads to ruin and death (5:11; 7:27), wisdom offers a way to life and happiness (8:31).

The figure is clearly a literary personification, but its origins and associations are undoubtedly more than simply artistic and imaginative. The portrait draws heavily on traditional features of a goddess of wisdom who stands beside the highest deity as a consort and adviser. So most scholars have recognized in 8:22-31 the core of an older poem, or at least major elements of popular religious themes. These concern a member of the divine court of the kind that is portrayed in all the major polytheistic traditions of Egypt and Mesopotamia. Even the form of self-introduction and self-praise which characterizes the style of the poem emulates a feature of such religious poetry. Such a figure, however, is here transformed and shorn of its earlier polytheistic connections. Wisdom becomes not a divine consort but instead the first creation of the one LORD God of Israel (v. 22). The very title first, or chief, of the LORD's creations both magnifies and limits her position.

Her gifts and insights are then used as a kind of model, or guide, through which the universe was fashioned. Wisdom is not herself either a goddess, or even a divine Architect, but rather the perfect prototype of the created order. This order is uniquely held to be the work of the LORD God of Israel, and Lady Wisdom's role is that of a pure and perfect onlooker. Her attributes inform and enrich the created world without herself becoming a second deity. The point appears deliberately made that she is a creature fashioned by God (8:22), not a companion divine figure.

Since there are abundant indications that religion itself frequently played a part in many of the immoral rituals and conventions of the ancient world generally, from which ancient Israel was certainly not exempt, the development of this figure of Lady Wisdom appears certainly to have been targeted at them.

The poem falls into four parts (8:1-11, 12-21, 22-31, and 32-36). The section comprised of vv. 22-31 constitutes the most distinctive unit on account of its powerful assertions concerning the antiquity and universal efficacy of wisdom. Yet these assertions underlie and serve to explain the important attributes of wisdom that are outlined in the other three units. They therefore provide a kind of core theological description of the nature and role of wisdom in the world, with the consequence of this universal efficacy being commended in the other sections.

In the first part (8:1-11) the scene is set. As in 1:2-31, wisdom steps forth into a busy city street, taking a central position in the city's life and activities. In the very place where commerce was conducted, lawsuits heard and decided, and intellectual discussion eagerly pursued, there the insights of wisdom were most called for. Wisdom understood the science of "life" in all its personal, social, and commercial aspects.

Significant in the manner in which wisdom commends herself is the assumption that the major issues of life were determined by whether wisdom was received eagerly or rejected. To receive her was to gain access to the values and truths of justice, prosperity, and contentment. To reject her was to forfeit the opportunity of obtaining the richest treasures of life (8:10-11).

In the second part (8:12-21) the reasons why the reception and acquisition of wisdom were so important are set forth. V. 13 would appear to be an addition made to reaffirm conformity between the precepts of wisdom and reverence for the LORD as God. It tends to disrupt the flow of ideas. Wisdom provides the insight and knowledge which govern the political realm (vv. 15-16); she rewards with prosperity those who follow her teachings (vv. 17-21). The combination of intuitive insight into the springs of human conduct with the virtues of right dealing and justice ensure that those who adhere to the way of wisdom attain a position of respect, honor, and leadership in the community.

Why wisdom is so central and fundamental to making a success of life is then detailed in the disquisition on her role in creation (8:22-31). We have already noted that this appears to make extensive use of widely known and popular imagery concerning wisdom, on the one hand, as a goddess-like figure who intercedes for human beings, and, on the other, as a divine architect and adviser among the heavenly host when the world was created. All the polytheistic features have been eliminated from Proverbs 8. Similarly, the idea that the LORD God needed an assistant at creation has been removed. Instead, wisdom is present at creation (v. 30), observing its symmetry and rejoicing in the divine accomplishment. The aim is to demonstrate that wisdom observes the order of the universe and that this displays a coherent and harmonious wholeness. Wisdom is timeless, universal, and all-embracing, affirming in poetic imagery that knowledge of her is built on critical observation of "the way things are." She holds together the physical, moral, and social realms of experience. Wisdom, then, represents a class of preeminent knowledge because she belongs to a primordial supernatural realm.

The concluding section (8:32-36) returns to the situation of the pupil and the teacher, urging yet again the importance of what wisdom has to teach and stressing further the ultimate issues that are at stake. They are fundamentally issues of life and death since to ignore wisdom or to forsake her injunctions is to cut oneself off from the source of virtue, happiness, and well-being (vv. 35-36). The claims of wisdom are immense but are no less than appropriate to a body of teaching which brought together practical usefulness and wonder at the majesty of the universe.

Life's Choices – Wisdom or Folly (Prov 9:1-18)

The poem which now reasserts the choices which Wisdom offers marks a fitting conclusion to the whole of the instructions and admonitions of Proverbs 1–9. It presents Wisdom in the guise of a generous hostess who has built her house and invites her guests to celebrate at a great feast (9:1-6). At the same time Lady Foolishness also makes an appeal. She sends out her invitations and seeks to entice the unwary into her house (vv. 13-18). In spite of the superficial attraction of the delights she has to offer, those who succumb to her enticements find themselves feasting with the dead. They realize too late that they have slipped down into the realm of the departed in Sheol (v. 18). The contrasting pictures are beautifully presented and show how the imagery which has been employed earlier in Proverbs 1–8 could be yet further developed. The portrait of the two different hostesses, each eager to attract her guests, reaffirms the benefits and gains to be won from paying attention to wisdom's teaching. Together they show the vital importance of the choices that have to be made and the ultimate consequences that they carry.

The social position and reason for the generous hospitality of Lady Wisdom in 9:1-6 begin with the enigmatic assertion that she has built her house with seven pillars. Architecturally these pillars must have presented a formal portico, showing the house to be one of style and imposing dignity. It implies that the teaching that wisdom offers will bring honor and status to the ardent listener. In contrast, the stolen water with which Lady Foolishness entertains her guests (v. 17) quickly turns to bitterness once the true nature of the other partygoers and the location where they are celebrating are recognized.

The verses which separate the contrasted figures (9:7-12) constitute a series of short, epigrammatic statements concerning the impossibility of teaching wisdom to the unreceptive. There are no benefits for one who does not listen. Through their insistence that attempts to teach an insolent scoffer are doomed to failure, the pupil is warned against indifference or inattention. The purpose of v. 7 is plain, even though the precise meaning of the verb (whether it means "gets hurt" or "gets nowhere") is uncertain. In drawing attention in v. 8 to the need for a responsive attitude to the teacher, v. 10 carries this idea further by its reassertion that such must begin with reverent regard for the LORD God. This supplies the formal note of religious devotion which is otherwise lacking in the main poem.

The resumption in 9:11 of wisdom's speech declaring the benefits she has to offer gives further content to the artistic portrayal of Lady Wisdom and Lady Foolishness. The meaning of v. 12 is not wholly clear since it sets forth an uncharacteristic note of strong individualism. This may, nevertheless, be an intentional feature showing that the outcome of the choice between the two ways is ultimately a personal and individual one. Overall, though these verses break up the basic poetic form, they add a note of practicality to the value of what wisdom teaches. They point to the contrasting lifestyles and consequent destinies as originating deep within different attitudes of responsiveness. It remains a consistent feature of Proverbs that it shows concern for listening and responsiveness. Attitudes which encourage a positive response (humility, fear of God, respect for parents, or concern about society) are repeatedly praised and encouraged. Conversely, those which block such a response (arrogance, empty-headedness, or listening to hot-headed rebels) are condemned. This sensitivity to what in the modern world would be described as "the psychology of moral education" stands out as a prominent feature of the book.

Overall, the poetic impact of the major parts of the poem in 9:1-6 and 9:13-18 is clear. The comments in vv. 7-12 serve as a kind of application and commentary, possibly indicating that this would have been commonplace in the formal teaching of wisdom. An artistic poem which has the one main point of commending the value of wisdom is reinforced by providing unmistakable admonitions as to its implications. Such a procedure illustrates well the two fundamental characteristics of the proverbial teaching of wisdom. In the forefront striving for interesting artistic and rhetorical effect leads to widespread use of metaphors and often complex word imagery. Alongside this, and intertwined with it, is an urgent moral appeal to build up good character, exercise firm discipline, and live a socially responsible lifestyle. Wherever possible the two aims are held together, presenting clear-cut moral admonitions and advice wrapped up in interesting and memorable wordplays and visual imagery.

The Proverbs of Solomon (Prov 10:1–15:33)

In Prov 10:1 we encounter a new series of wisdom sayings carrying the title "proverbs," rather more obviously than the contents of Proverbs 1–9. This is because they are in the form of short, epigrammatic sayings expressing a fundamental truth, or two contrasted truths. A noticeable change of form is to be found commencing at 10:1, which continues, with only minor variations, until 29:27. The sayings are characterized by their brevity and educational value. Usually they consist of two short lines, and they are frequently antithetical in structure. They contrast a form of good and desirable behavior with its counterpart.

Most often the sayings make basic assertions concerning human behavior. Thus they constitute a form of sentence instruction, obviously intending that the good behavior provide a model to be emulated.

In some instances the sayings are couched in a synthetic form associating one type of conduct with another related to it. In many instances the connection between the two subjects is based on similes and metaphors, some of which carry a surprising and unexpected character. The intention throughout is evidently to draw attention to particular types of conduct or the adoption of specific attitudes, through commendation or reproof. There is an underlying concern to recognize and categorize the fundamental "rules" and "orders" of life (cf. von Rad 1972: 30).

Overall, the subject matter displays features that have been noted earlier in chs. 1–9, although the balance of emphasis is markedly different. The sayings exploit the possibilities of imaginative artistry, sometimes humorous and heavily exaggerated, in order to make a point. At the same time the broad aim is ethical in its thrust, instilling a number of basic moral values and encouraging the nurture of a particular kind of personal character. These values relate especially to the preservation of the nuclear family or household, to the necessity for hard work, and to the careful accumulation and use of wealth. Along with this, the wisdom sayings emphasize the avoidance of needless conflict and stress and of arrogant and violent conduct, and urge careful and restrained use of speech.

The form of such teaching further divides between sayings presented as statements of fact — "sentence instruction" — and those set forth in the form of admonitions. In neither case is direct appeal made to the authority of the teacher in order to validate the point being made. Proverbs assumes that reality itself gives the saying authority. It aims to point out "the way things are." A broad assumption is implicit in the style of address that the recipient of the teaching will be young and male and will one day carry responsibility for the wealth and reputation of the household to which he belongs. The instruction promotes a positive work ethic, with the general inference that a household's wealth will largely depend on agriculture carried out on land belonging to it as a form of inherited patrimony. It presumes that money is in use as a means of exchange, with noted contrasts between the poor and rich in society. It reckons with modest commercial ventures, but it sees debt as a major social hazard which can be avoided only by diligence and restraint from taking undue risks.

The origin of these sayings, assuming that they were originally composed as independent units, is never clearly evident. They have been brought together, written down from a presumably oral original form, and set out in longer collections with little by way of obvious structural or thematic connectedness. Who their original authors were, even in broad terms, cannot be defined with precise detail and confidence. Their broad applicability and rural, agricultural ambiance point to a simple folk origin. However, the predominantly respectful attitude toward the king, together with a number of references to the circle of court officials, points to a link, at some stage in the chain of their preservation, with the royal court.

The sayings seek to preserve and distill useful and necessary instruction about coping with life and its demands in a manner which will prove useful to a wide readership. However, the presence of a more sophisticated side to many of the sayings in their polished and refined artistry leads us to look to a well-educated, often professionally literate, circle of men. The references to the king, who is never assumed to be other than a native Israelite, as supreme arbiter of justice and the social order indicates a settled, politically conformist circle of people. Violence, brigandage, and rebellion are all regarded as disruptions of God's intended order; warfare, although several times referred to in illustrations of conduct and success, is presented as a remote and distant activity, which, nevertheless, implements the just order of God. The suggestion that the sayings may themselves have originated in the royal court appears improbable in view of the strongly rural setting in which wealth is accumulated and preserved. A "middle class" atmosphere pervades the instructions, whose authors clearly did not regard themselves as among the rich. A property-owning body of free citizens, eager for a secure and happy life and respectful of the order which they saw around them, must make up the circles who composed and valued such a form of teaching. They focused on the basic virtues of industry and respect for one's neighbor; they encouraged shrewdness, commercial caution, and careful speech, regarding religious devotion as a mark of wise humility and respect for a divinely created world of order.

Since this proverbial wisdom teaching points directly to experience and the practical facts of life, the interspersing among the sayings of some which urge reverence for the LORD as God appears to be a relatively marginal feature. It has, consequently, been suggested that such positive religious references represent a kind of overlay to a form of instruction that originally stood largely apart from all such formal religious demands and assumptions. Yet clearly Israel's wisdom teaching was never secular in the modern sense, nor yet antireligious in any explicit manner. It assumed religion to be a necessary and routine aspect of life. It is noticeable, however, from the all-embracing nature of some of the religious claims for wisdom's role in creation, that in the final shaping of the book of Proverbs a conscious effort has been made to show the importance of "the fear of the LORD." However, at no stage in wisdom's development in Israel can religious themes have been very far away. Life brought many incalculable risks and uncertainties. Thus a recognition of the ultimate finality of the divine will made submission to it a cause for respect and submissiveness.

In essence such proverbial sayings as are found in Proverbs 10–29 are essentially timeless and anonymous. They reflect a particular level of human social, economic, and educational development, but they are not related to specific events or persons. The identity of the various authors involved in their composition is not known, nor would it make any difference to understanding the sayings if it were otherwise. The sentence instructions encapsulate useful images and ideas, presenting guidelines by which situations can be assessed, dangers identified, and undesirable attitudes rejected. They both guide the youthful and hesitant and warn the headstrong against impetuous and foolhardy actions.

An initial collection of sayings appears to have stopped at 15:33, where a reaffirmation of the essential religious foundation of wisdom's teaching is made. A fresh, and closely similar, collection follows from 16:1 and extends as far as 22:16. Thereafter further shorter collections appear to have been put together.

After 10:1 Proverbs is evidently a "collection of collections" in which it is for the most part left unclear what principles have governed the ordering of particular sayings. Sometimes a major theme appears to have been responsible for bringing sayings together; in a few instances contrasting, and apparently contradictory, sayings have been put side by side; at other times contrasting sayings have been conjoined. As an overall guide, each saying is complete in itself. It represents a truth about life, not necessarily universal but certainly widely applicable, so that it could be remembered, reflected on, and used to shape actual human behavior when relevant situations arose. An underlying substructure of ideas looks toward building up set attitudes and lifestyles which can be defined as representing a virtuous character.

Wisdom as the Key to Virtue (Prov 10:1-32)

The opening sayings of 10:1-5 set a thematic tone to the larger collection by pointing to the home and family as the setting where education begins and where fundamental attitudes are inculcated. The summing up of evil and misfortune as constituting "death" (v. 2) reveals how closely wisdom regarded the order of right and wrong as a reality that permeated all aspects of life. Furthermore, right conduct was the only valid way to achieve prosperity (v. 3), and an industrious "work ethic" was essential to security (vv. 4-5). The threat of shame (v. 5) as a sanction against laziness points to far more than mere public disdain and reproof and points rather to a powerful level of public rejection and exclusion. Shame was not far short of total failure.

We find consistently that the sharp antithetical affirmations of the majority of the sayings imply that the reader faces a vitally important element of personal choice which will determine his or her ultimate success or failure. On the one hand, the reader is assumed to be confronted with the possibility of listening carefully to, and acting upon, the instructions given by the teacher of wisdom. Alternatively, the possibility exists of rejecting such teachings, with the serious consequences this will entail. Much of the force of the individual sayings, which seek to be memorable and are often artistically phrased, lies in the starkness of the affirmations made about the consequences of the lifestyle that is to be chosen. Rather surprisingly for such powerfully asserted claims for morality and a sense of social responsibility is the fact that there is little precise definition of the actions and deeds that are called for. Instead the contrasted lifestyles that are described, with their declared inevitable consequences, are usually portrayed only broadly — either "righteous" (vv. 6, 7, 11, 16, etc.) or "wicked" (vv. 6, 11, 16, etc.). The teacher takes for granted that the reader will recognize the specific opportunities and temptations for wickedness as they arise. By bringing together the descriptions of the various behavior patterns associated with the two contrasted patterns of conduct, the reader can see how a primary goal of shaping personal character was striven for. The righteous are those who heed instructions (v. 8), are respectful of their parents (v. 1), are hard-working, and are straightforward in what they say (v. 10) Over against this the wicked are unduly talkative (vv. 8, 14, 19) and prone to deceitfulness and furtive gestures (vv. 10, 18). Consequently they invariably stir up ill-feeling and strife (vv. 12, 18).

In dramatizing and emphasizing the ultimately disastrous consequences of bad behavior (10:7, 8, 9, 14, 21, etc.), the teacher points out the threat of punishment and eventual ruin that bad choices will bring. The technique is one of persuasion, but persuasiveness appealing to an ultimate level of reasoned self-interest. The fundamental assumption that pervades all this teaching is that the world, including its human social environment, is created in such a way that evil consequences ensue upon evil actions, which are themselves the result of ill-nurtured attitudes. In the final analysis there is an all-embracing claim that eventual retribution awaits the person who develops evil habits and a bad character. How such retribution will take effect is usually left undefined, or assumed to be an inevitable result of the inner, divinely governed forces at work in the moral order of the world.

Sometimes the instruction appears to imply that evil is impelled by an inner momentum toward destruction which eventually overwhelms the wrongdoer (10:24, 25). At other times it argues that the wrongdoer's fellow citizens act in their own interest to bring punishment (vv. 9, 13). More frequently it claims some form of divine retributive action, although how it will take effect is not made clear (vv. 3, 29). The issue is not made into a formal theological proposition. Rather, it is taken for granted that retribution represents an established and recognizable feature of the real world. Whereas good actions promote health, long life, and happiness (v. 22), bad ones lead to indignant opposition, punishment, and eventual ruin and death. The ways in which such retribution for wrongdoing takes effect are therefore many and various, sometimes requiring human action to enforce it but at others leaving the punitive result to come from providential action on the part of God.

The Righteous and the Wicked (Prov 11:1-31)

The sayings of this chapter are, with the exception of v. 7 which displays a synthetic coupling, all couched in an antithetic form contrasting a good with a bad mode of conduct. A contrast is consistently made between the behavior, and consequent fate, of the righteous and the wicked. A number of the instructions make virtually the same point with only slight variation of subject matter. The setting of the path of wisdom over against that of folly is left in the background, although it is prominent in 11:14; in vv. 14-15 the assertions deal with civic and public behavior. The return in v. 16 to contrasts which lie in the mainstream of wisdom's concern with types of conduct is complicated by difficulties of translation. The central theme that pervades most of the sayings concerns the difference between the righteous and the wicked. This commences with a denunciation of cheating in the marketplace by employing false weights. The sense of outrage, combined with the recognition that in spite of careful legislation it was a form of cheating that was difficult to eliminate, is expressed by affirming that God also feels outrage at such activities. We may also compare v. 20 and the extensive use of the idea of outrage — a feeling that some thing or action is "an abomination" — in the book of Proverbs as a whole to express strong disapproval (Clements 1996: 211-26).

It is a marked feature of the type of character which Proverbs seeks to encourage that it should be "humble" (11:2), by which it envisages a cautious, unaggressive, and thoughtful mode of conduct. Over against this it condemns an arrogant, assertive, and scornful manner. Such is regarded as leading to reckless, impetuous, and ill-tempered violence. It is not difficult overall to construct a portrait from Proverbs of what was considered to represent an "ideal type" of character, with recognizable behavioral patterns. At the same time the authors of the sayings were sufficiently familiar with real-life persons not to expect their pupils to fit into a single mold. There is in general a consistent emphasis on character formation as the primary basis of education, although more detailed technical knowledge of husbandry and commerce is widely presupposed.

In close conformity with such a striving for a humble disposition was a strong antipathy to abusive, self-praising, and garrulous talk (11:9, 11, 12, 13). Still worse were malicious slanders and gossiping which betrayed the confidences of neighbors and family (vv. 4, 13) and promoted deep social division. The privacy of close personal relationships was to be respected and upheld. Even more destructive were deliberate lies and accusations aimed at discomforting and humiliating others (vv. 9, 11, 12).

Another major wisdom theme which appears in these sentence instructions concerns the marked difference between the respective situations of the rich and the poor. Wealth and poverty were seen to create great distinctions, not only of health and happiness but also in forming attitudes and shaping conduct. In spite of the strong emphasis placed by the teachers of wisdom on hard work, frugality, and cautious use of wealth and property (10:4), the sayings display a prominent assumption that "the rich" were closely allied to "the wicked" (Whybray 1990: 35-44). Wealth is often assumed to have been acquired by oppressive means, and even when this was not the case, it is taken as normal that the rich would be strongly inclined to exploit the power which their wealth brought them. They would be tempted to trust in its power and to regard it as a security against life's uncertainties (v. 28).

Nevertheless, the book generally accepts the fact that whether a person was rich or poor marked a major, if sometimes inexplicable, distinguishing feature of society. A real measure of tension exists between the guarded, and sometimes openly hostile, references to wealthier citizens, whose wealth is regarded as endangering their moral and spiritual well-being, and the repeated assurances that the path of wisdom was the way to success and prosperity. The differences between the rich and the poor are seen to be the result of God's inscrutable will, but they must not be allowed to overrule recognition that a common destiny is shared by both. Even the poorest citizen is a creation of God who must be respected. So the rich had a responsibility to act generously toward those who were not so fortunate (11:24-25); they were not to exploit the power afforded by their riches (v. 26) and certainly not to put their trust in their riches as a security against misfortune (vv. 28-29). Aggressive and exploitative behavior could lead to the better off themselves coming to grief.

The authors view riches as a temptation and a hazard as well as the result of God's blessing. To risk the wealth of one's own household unnecessarily by ill-judged and unsecured loans for the benefit of others was to be studiously avoided (11:15). Overall, the contrasts between wealth and poverty are seen to have far-reaching social consequences. While the facts of such social divisions are taken as the expression of a social world in which mysterious forces are at play which could not always be understood or thwarted, the victims of poverty were always to be treated with compassion. Evidently the authors of these instructions regarded themselves as standing on a kind of middle ground, certainly not aligning themselves with the rich, who are usually portrayed in negative terms. Yet neither did the authors of the sayings see themselves as belonging to the poorer underclass of society, who were to be pitied and helped whenever possible.

11:16 reflects the importance attached to marriage and the value of a virtuous woman — a theme which fits in with the concern of wisdom to contrast the good and the bad aspects of male-female relationships. V. 22 expresses this contrast by warning against being deceived by feminine beauty and charm where discretion is lacking. The two sayings, like virtually all the instructions of Proverbs, reflect the consistently male viewpoint of the authors and indicate a corresponding expectation of a predominantly male readership. The perspective adopted is that of "women observed" and points to a situation in which the major decisions affecting households and their security were in the hands of its male members (cf. 12:4). Even the celebrated portrait in praise of a virtuous wife and mother (31:10-22) does not essentially depart from this perspective. The result is that whereas a reasonably clear and generally commendable portrait is offered of the ideal type of male character, that of the good woman is largely colorless and utilitarian.

The Foundations of Character (Prov 12:1-28)

The general pattern of contrasting the righteous and the wicked continues as the teachers note the different destinies which are likely to befall them. The predominant literary form is that of antithetical sentences. These define the actions and characters of good and bad persons, pointing out, sometimes with dramatic emphasis and exaggeration, the sharply contrasted consequences of their behavior. Exceptions to this form are in 12:9, which establishes a relative scale of values by the use of the formula "It is better to be . . . than . . . ," and in v. 14. In this verse two characteristics, both of which are good, are praised and set alongside each other. A thoughtful disposition combined with hard work and industriousness is commended. The message appears at first to be unduly obvious, but the aim is to affirm and commend aspects of character and conduct which may at first appear relatively unimportant but which are potentially very serious in their longer-term consequences. This is achieved by setting them alongside more obviously major features of conduct.

The extended sequence of sayings in 12:14-25 all deal with matters of speech. It represents a prominent feature of wisdom instruction that the springs of all human action lie hidden in the inner recesses of the human mind, or "heart." A further step is reached when these hidden intentions take outward form in speech. This public disclosure of a person's thoughts reveals the character of a person. It mattered greatly to the teachers of wisdom that this progression from thought to speech should be straightforward and consistent. The inner intention and the outward expression of it should be in conformity. Deliberate deception, or the unrestrained disclosure of ill-considered thoughts and aims, was regarded as a sign of at best foolishness and at worst malicious wickedness. It was therefore important that there should be time for reflection and cautious self-examination before revealing one's inner intentions to the public at large.

The sayings of 12:1-13 begin with a general statement concerning the value of what wisdom has to teach (v. 1) and the major consequences which follow from doing so (v. 2). As with a majority of the sentence instructions, there is little precise definition of actual courses of action but a broad insistence on conformity to the aims of the family household, and of society's interests more generally. The instructions again emphasize the importance of the careful choice of a suitable wife (v. 4) since her support and cooperation would prove vital to the stability, peace, and economic viability of every household. Such careful choice of a marriage partner was felt to be one of the biggest, and genuinely risk-laden, steps in life. The need to marry a woman from outside the most immediate family circle involved bringing in a person with a different background from that of the known family grouping, and often from another kin group altogether. Since a wide range of social and economic values were enshrined in the strongly felt ties of family and kinship, this was a risk-laden proceeding. So the taking in marriage of a relative outsider was recognized to involve uncertainties which needed careful weighing. Alongside this call for care in choosing a partner there existed a need for substantial financial arrangements in order to support the newly formed household. In a strongly patriarchal society it was evidently possible for a woman, even though married, to find her position marginalized.

The general concern with speech in 12:14-25 recognizes that it impinges directly on the contrast between wisdom and foolishness (vv. 14, 15, 23), since lack of sense, coupled with a talkative disposition, could quickly reveal itself. Most of these sayings, however, are concerned with deceit and lies (vv. 17, 19, 20, 22), which served evil purposes. Anger and sharp retaliation for an insult (vv. 16, 18) could also provoke bitter relationships, whereas encouragement at a time of personal stress (v. 25) could serve to build up positive ones.

The allusion in 12:27 is not entirely clear, although the broad implication is that success in life will depend on hard work and effort. The contrasting saying of v. 28 then summarizes the general conviction that good behavior makes for a successful life.

The Happiness of the Righteous (Prov 13:1-25)

Direct references to God are completely lacking in this chapter, but the general conviction that a beneficent and just providential order governs the world pervades all the sayings. The major theme is that, as a guide to life, blessings reward the righteous person who works hard and who refrains from evil conduct. The opening sentence appears as a general restatement of the oft-repeated principle which urged children to adhere to parental instruction. The wider range of subjects covered in other of the sayings points to a more adult readership. No overall structure is evident in the makeup of the chapter, and the major themes dealt with are closely similar to those that have already dominated the collection.

The theme of resisting laziness and of the necessity for hard work is given a new direction in the assertion of 13:4 (also v. 25) that both the lazy person and the diligent experience hunger at some time or other. For the industrious it is a spur to work, while the lazy goes hungry. Wealth and poverty further provide broad categories by which human conduct is judged. The teachers constantly note the very considerable social consequences of the possession of wealth, or the lack of it, giving special attention to the way in which conduct is affected by it. In spite of the wisdom teachers' emphasis upon the rewards that come to the hard-working and the general need for frugality in personal demands, Proverbs offers a broadly negative portrayal of rich persons. The sayings of vv. 7-8 and 11 view the effects of the sharp distinctions which wealth and poverty entail. For some the claim to wealth and prosperity is simply a pose, while others who are well off may publicly deny it. The intention that lies behind v. 8 is not clear. The most plausible interpretation is that it is asserting that the rich are vulnerable to major threats on account of their possession of wealth, whereas the poor suffer no such threats. However, such a willingness to comfort the poor in their lack of security and the other benefits that money brings runs counter to the general tenor of wisdom teaching. V. 23 points out that, even when for a time the poor appear to prosper, injustice on their part will swiftly deprive them of its benefits. However, the rich are inclined to arrogance and show themselves eager to take advantage of those less fortunate than they.

There is a general consensus in the wisdom sayings that wealth is desirable and a mark of divine blessing, but it must be gained honestly through hard work (so 13:11). Risky commercial ventures in expectation of gaining rapid wealth are to be strongly distrusted and resisted. Even more reprehensible are persons who lend money at exorbitant rates of interest or those who take advantage of hard times in order to increase their gains to the misfortune of others (cf. 12:26).

Overall, the picture of commercial and economic activity presented in Proverbs is of a relatively advanced and complex world. The primary form of wealth is regarded as deriving from the productive farming of a modest agricultural estate; the need for loans, guarantees, and honest trading practices is recognized as a paramount concern for economic welfare and social harmony. Where earlier sayings have emphasized strongly the contrasting lifestyles of righteous and wicked people, a further comparison between the virtues of wisdom and the inevitable ruin that faces those who are foolhardy is repeated. Accordingly, the willingness to seek and accept advice (13:10) shows itself as a major facet of good character. Conversely, garrulous talk (v. 3), the spurning of advice (vv. 10, 13, 18), and consorting with fools (v. 20) lead only to disaster. The goal is clearly to commend careful listening to advice (v. 14) and to enjoy the company of the wise in order to become wise oneself.

The House Built by Wisdom (Prov 14:1-35)

Many of the themes which have already shown themselves to be high on the scale of priorities of the wisdom teachers reappear here. So we find a concern with truthful and honest speech, especially where the character and well-being of other persons are at issue (14:5, 25). Repeatedly the teachers set forth the value of wisdom as contrasted with foolishness (vv. 1, 3, 6, 8, 16, 18, 24, 33). Several new emphases appear which open up fresh insights into the problems and concerns of the typical citizen of ancient Israel. Notable among such fresh emphases are a concern to demonstrate that the teachings of the wise are at one with the demands of piety and veneration of the LORD as God (vv. 2, 26, 27). The claim that loyalty to God and adherence to the divine commandments are essentially in conformity with the perceptions of wisdom is couched in very general terms. The traditions and assumptions that motivated and shaped the formal worship of God are to be respected and observed. It is accordingly regarded as a characteristic of fools that they mock the guilt offering by which their own, and the community's, sins are forgiven (v. 9). Even the wisest of persons could not claim to be altogether guiltless.

More striking, and more intriguing in their insights, are the several psychological reflections on the inner workings of the mind. Already such observations are implicit in the contention that the adoption of a hostile attitude of mind could prevent a person from benefiting from the teaching of wisdom. Accordingly, it would be in vain for arrogant persons to seek wisdom since they would not appreciate its value (14:6). More remarkable is the insight concerning the intensely private and personal nature of experiences of grief and joy (v. 10). There is an inner world of the mind where intense feelings may lodge which can never be shared with others. This also appears to be the meaning intended in v. 13, which need not be understood to imply a fundamentally pessimistic viewpoint regarding the inevitability of sorrow. Rather, it draws attention to the great depths of human thoughts and feelings, which may lie "too deep for tears."

The wisdom teachers rejected quick-temperedness and impatient haste in making decisions. They recognized rushing into important decisions (v. 12), believing everything that one is told without due care in sifting its content (v. 15), and giving way to anger without self-restraint (vv. 17, 29) as characteristics of a person who has not taken to heart the lessons of wisdom. In much the same direction lies the observation that a calm and controlled disposition is a vital step toward good health and happiness (v. 30). So, just as the source of good speech lies in right thinking (v. 3), so the basis for healthy living takes its origin in the cultivation of a thoughtful and disciplined mind.

In 14:28 we encounter the first of a number of affirmations concerning the role of the king within the nation. There is uncertainty and doubt as to the intention that underlies it. Its purport would appear to be to draw attention to the point that every person has some place in the divine scheme of social order. Such are even the poor, who are creatures of the divine Creator. They are entitled to respect and compassion. Correspondingly, however high and exalted the person of the king may be, it is the multitude of ordinary people who confer his greatness upon him. No person is so mean and worthless that he, or she, has no proper place in the purposes of God.

The Eyes of the LORD Are in Every Place (Prov 15:1-33)

The general themes of the sentence instruction that have been dealt with in earlier chapters continue here, but two discernible developments become evident. Foremost among these is the greatly increased number of references to the LORD God (nine instances). Moreover, these references have evidently been intended to show that the demands of piety and allegiance to wisdom's precepts are wholly in agreement with each other. The pursuit of wisdom and adherence to the commandments and worship of the LORD as God are at one. The second feature that now becomes more demonstrable is a process of grouping sayings together which deal with related themes. They then form a little compendium of guidance on a specific topic. Among such units 15:8-11 deal with the ability of God to see into human hearts and so to be able to judge the intentions that underlie human actions. The theme of poverty provides a common feature of vv. 15-17, with their affirmation that wealth and riches do not represent the most important goals of life. The claim of wisdom is that other facets of behavior affect more directly the sum of human happiness. Even a house filled with plenty may be marred by strife and ceaseless quarreling. In vv. 20-23 the theme that wisdom's guidance provides the only sure key to achieving success in life links the verses together. Good relationships, right conduct, and thoughtful and timely speech all contribute toward insuring that human endeavor and insight serve to build up households and communities into happy and flourishing entities.

The concluding unit (15:25-33) sums up most of the major themes that have occupied the sentence instruction and reaffirms the fundamental contention that the demands of religious loyalty underlie all that wisdom has to offer. The pursuit of wisdom is based on the loyal and faithful service of God. The concluding v. 33 sums up the comprehensive claim of 12:7 that all wisdom's teaching presupposes as its first requirement a pious and unfeigned reverence for the LORD as God.

It is in this deepened emphasis on bringing together the demands of wisdom instruction with those of religious devotion that a number of the most memorable and distinctive ideas emerge. Prominent among these is that, because God is able to see in every place (15:3) and to look into the deepest thoughts and feelings of the heart (v. 11), so all worship and prayer are subject to divine scrutiny (vv. 8, 29). The sacrifice of the wicked can draw no favors from God since true worship requires that right actions go hand in hand with even the most costly tokens of submission to God. Similarly, the prayers of the wicked will go unanswered. The ethical insights and claims of wisdom are at one with the demands of piety so that to attend to the one without the other is worthless.

Prominent in the chapter is increased attention to the psychological aspects of behavior and their far-reaching consequences for happiness. Inner contentment quickly shows itself in outward appearance (15:13). Even in bad times and impoverishment it is possible to keep a cheerful disposition (v. 14). Provocative and quarrelsome conduct can ruin even the most sumptuous of feasts (v. 17). So the teaching of wisdom probes deeply into the attitudes and feelings which govern life. The truly wise person is willing to learn from a rebuke (v. 12) and shows a keenness to explore the potential for mastering life which wisdom offers (v. 14). To ignore instruction could amount, if pursued relentlessly, to contempt for oneself since such conduct misses the opportunity for improvement. All such probing and seeking of self-knowledge draw great attention to the far-reaching consequences of the life choices posed by the contrasting ways of wisdom and folly.

Men and women can outwardly observe and judge the actions of their fellow human beings, but they cannot delve into the hidden reasons and motives which prompted them. Even when the body language of winks and gestures indicates a gap between thought and speech, one cannot fully disclose the inner processes of thought, for they remain hidden. When pressed to the extreme, even the person speaking the word or committing the deed might not be fully aware of the motives that prompted it! Only God can know that! So wisdom points to the existence of a secret inner world of the mind (lit. "heart"), into which only God can see. Nevertheless, it is this inner world which holds the key to understanding the ultimate behavior of human beings and the reasons which shape their choices in the life-or-death issues of human destiny (v. 10).

Further Proverbs of Solomon (Prov 16:1–22:19)

A significant break separates the instructions of chs. 10–15 and 16–22, which is marked by a change in the form of presentation. Those presented hitherto have almost all been couched in antithetical form contrasting one type of conduct with another which serves as its counterpart. Those which now follow in 16:1–22:19 are largely synthetic in form. The second line of the two-part instruction adds to, or otherwise significantly modifies, the statement made in the first line. There is, moreover, a significant change of content, with a number of new themes being introduced from 16:1 onward. They develop and enlarge on the basic themes already dealt with but extend their range further by giving greater attention to social concerns, notably those relating to politics and social justice. Overall, the theological interests appear to have been more fully integrated into the wisdom context. Since we cannot identify the precise status of the authors, or their situation in society, we are left to infer from the sentences themselves the general background. This is that of a property-owning middle class who had come to view their existence as bounded by a mysterious frontier established by an inscrutable divine will.

The LORD Weighs the Spirit (Prov 16:1-33)

This chapter is immediately striking on account of the large number of sayings which affirm the sovereign reality of God and God's providential will in the world. So, with the exception of 16:8, vv. 1-9 all refer to the LORD as the ultimate Ruler and Controller of human destiny. In spite of the evident formal break between chs. 15 and 16, the author/editor appears to have exerted considered effort to integrate the contents of the separate units. So 15:33 establishes a summarizing conclusion to the six preceding chapters and prepares for the broad emphasis on the boundaries which circumscribe human action. Furthermore, the assertion of 16:1 both takes up and extends the import of 15:11. The LORD God not only sees into human hearts but alone is able to put the right words into the mouths of those who are faithful in their devotion. A person may be confident of having sought and striven to pursue what is right but may, nevertheless, fail to understand the unseen complexities of thought and motives (16:2).

There is a frontier of understanding which God's superior knowledge alone can cross and which will prove to be far greater than human understanding. The truly wise will therefore recognize this, will accept it with humility, and will commit all their work and plans to God (v. 3). A faithful expression of wisdom is to recognize that human understanding is so much more limited than God's. Complacency, overconfidence, and the refusal to listen to good counsel are all therefore the mark of arrogant persons, who will pay a price for their folly (16:4-5). All of this is summed up in a considered reflection on the limits of human understanding and the necessity for humble submission to the overriding will of God (v. 9).

The reflection of 16:8 appears rather out of place since it repeats the basic thought expressed in 15:16-17.

The theme of a "higher wisdom" of God introduces a series of reflections concerning the role of the king as the pillar of society (16:10-15). That the supreme earthly ruler is merely the agent of God's heavenly rule underlies the thought of 16:10. The king, as the Guardian and Patron of humanly administered justice, is guided and inspired by God in passing judgement (cf. Solomon's judicial wisdom in 1 Kgs 3:3-15). Although the claim assumes that the king possesses a prophetlike insight into human affairs, the assertion is essentially a commendation of royal responsibility for the administration of a just juridical order. This conviction underlies the affirmation of vv. 12-15 and is also presupposed in v. 11, which deals with the just administration of weights and measures. These and other references to the king cannot be held to prove an origin of the sayings in the royal court. Even in the postexilic age when Judah was governed by foreign rulers, the idea of kingship portrayed in the sayings is evidently a matter of political theology rather than one based on direct personal experience of royal administrative affairs.

The sayings of 16:21-24, 27-29 return to the theme of pleasant and persuasive speech. In content the ideas extend beyond the more basic insistence of the wisdom teachers concerning restraint in speech to the need to refrain from angry words. They point to the necessity of learning to say things "at the right time," of learning to be judicious, persuasive, and to a modest degree entertaining, in speech (vv. 23-24). This calls for artistry as well as honesty. At the same time all instances of guile (v. 30), unprincipled incitement (v. 29), and malicious slander (v. 28) are condemned as manifestations of wickedness.

The concluding declaration of 16:33 is rather ambiguous in its implications. It has acquired its present location since it illustrates the basic contention of vv. 2 and 9 that no human counsel or plan can prevail against God. The sacred lot, by which the priest could adjudicate difficult legal cases (cf. Deut 17:8-13), expressed the decision of God. So it could be used as an example of the superiority of divine to human wisdom. It accepts the validity of the process by which difficult decisions were determined by the sacred priestly lot, but uses this as an illustration of a deeper principle. Human wisdom is so much more limited than God's. The instruction could, alternatively, be taken to imply that even when the seemingly most definitive means had been employed to reach a decision (concerning future action), the final outcome of events must be left in the hands of God. If this is the meaning, then it implies a measure of divine inscrutability. Such an understanding has the advantage that it would provide a lead to several of the following assertions which point out the limitations that life imposes on all human plans.

Fools and Their Folly (Prov 17:1-28)

The affirmation of 16:33 points to a feature relating to the limitations which surround all human plans and intentions. Even when careful thought has been given and good advice sought, certain incalculable factors affect the outcome of life's fortunes. Modest wealth and prosperity could not insure happiness since ill temper and quarrelsomeness could ruin a sumptuous feast (17:1). Even with a good and loyal wife as a helper and companion, it nevertheless remained impossible to ensure that children grew up into adulthood to take on their full family responsibilities. A lazy youth could refuse to work so as to secure the maintenance of the family's inheritance (v. 2). As a result a conscientious and loyal slave who acted wisely might one day supplant a willful and wanton son. So the values of loyalty and hard work could outstrip those of kinship and parenthood in the race of life. All such observations show that there are hidden and unforseeable factors relating to personal motivation and integrity which may ultimately outweigh all the rest of life's advantages — a conclusion which show why such values were in the forefront of wisdom's claims. God tests the very inner springs of the human mind (v. 3).

It is salutary to reflect how repeatedly the teachers of wisdom place only relative importance on the values of kinship and the support of the extended family — features which extensively colored the thinking and actions of most ancient (as well as many modern) societies. They preferred instead to lay emphasis on the virtue of good neighborliness, industriousness in work, and honesty and trustworthiness in dealing with other people. These, they contend, are the virtues which ultimately prevail in life. Kinship and family ties could lead to nepotism, undue reliance on accumulated wealth, and a temptation to laziness. More insidiously it could lead to attempts to subvert the implementation of justice through the exercise of family influence (cf. 15:26).

The theme that dominates Proverbs 17 is that of fools and their folly. No less than ten examples of folly are held up for scrutiny and condemnation (vv. 2, 7, 10, 12, 16, 18, 21, 24, 25, and 28). The catalogue of foolish modes of behavior repeats many of the situation-based features that have already shown themselves to be central to the concerns of wisdom instruction. The new feature that now emerges is partly built up from a portrayal of the cumulative effect of such conduct with its inevitable end in disaster and partly focused on the contention that the consequences of folly are unforeseeable and irremediable. Why people should choose to act foolishly and to resist accepting wise instruction remained a mystery. Once the fool had embraced the ways of folly, there appeared to be no hope and no way out from the inevitability of eventual ruin. Fine speech and persuasive words would not change a warped character (v. 7); nor would repeated rebukes, no matter how sharp and forthright, penetrate the mind of a fool (v. 10). Fools paid no attention to matters close at hand, which might teach them important lessons, but instead looked everywhere else (v. 24).

For all these truths, the fool might nevertheless be well aware of the absurdity of his conduct since the roots of folly lay hidden in the deep recesses of the human mind which only God could test (17:3). Worthy parents might find themselves burdened with an unworthy child (vv. 21, 25). Even money to pay a tutor to provide instruction would be of no avail to a scorner or a dullard (v. 16). The only ameliorating reflection is presented at the end: that the best thing a fool could do was to stay silent (v. 28) in order to hide his inability to talk sense.

Woven into these pessimistic reflections on the way of fools and their folly are a number of admonitory comments regarding dangerously destructive forms of antisocial conduct. To pervert the course of justice for whatever reason struck at the very heart of social order (17:15, 26). To attempt to do so by bribery was thoroughly reprehensible (v. 23). The related comment in v. 8 is sometimes taken to be neutral in its evaluation of giving gifts to gain favors. This would, however, be at variance with the goals of the whole legal tradition which developed in the ancient Near East. Friendship, neighborliness, and a forgiving spirit were regarded as the bedrock on which society rested (vv. 6, 9, 17).

The Words of the Mouth (Prov 18:1-24)

The sayings of ch. 18 continue in the predominantly synthetic sentences made up of two loosely parallel lines. The subjects dealt with cover general matters of social behavior (vv. 1, 24), with a strong emphasis on speech (vv. 4, 6-8, 13, 20, and 21). The instructions gave close attention to the importance of learning to think carefully before venturing to speak, of guarding one's tongue from ill-tempered or hasty answers, and of learning to discriminate in listening to the speech of others. The emphasis upon using speech as a guide to a person's character and intentions is brought out in v. 21, where the ultimate issues of life and death are held to lie in the power of the tongue. Clearly there is an element of hyperbole in this, although it evidently did not exclude an awareness that evil talk could literally lead to death. This is true in such cases as appear as the immediate context of the sayings of vv. 16-18. Malicious accusations, the poor administration of specific cases (v. 17; cf. v. 13 and 1 Kgs 21:1-19), and the prevalent resort to bribery (v. 16) were all potential hazards to justice. Repeatedly the wisdom instructions probe into the psychology that governs and underlies all social action.

Complacency and overconfidence induced by wealth (18:11, 23) and the adoption of a haughty and contemptuous attitude toward others (v. 12) were forms of antisocial behavior which could foment trouble and undermine the basic concepts of justice on which a healthy social order rested.

Probing into the inner world of thought and feeling motivates the contention of 18:14 that there is an inner principle of selfhood which can be broken. What precisely is meant by "a broken spirit" is not entirely clear, but the statement points to the fact that the will as the center of personality could undergo total collapse. The importance of the concept of "the good neighbor" is excellently expressed in v. 24, where the favorable comparison between the support and value of a friendly neighbor and that of a person's nearest kin relative highlights the concept of "good neighborliness." In a society where traditional loyalties of kinship were strongly felt, and often expressed to the detriment of those who stood outside such supportive kin groups, wisdom sought a more unprejudiced ethic. Wisdom's concern for building up friendship across social and kinship barriers recognized the central role played by interactive relationships in a healthy society. Where the hazards of life often reduced many to the margins of a community on account of gender, family, or economic antipathies and restraints, wisdom endeavored to bridge such hurtful divisions.

Wealth, Poverty, and the Quality of Life (Prov 19:1-29)

A special interest of Proverbs 19 lies in its increased attention to questions of wealth and poverty as issues which especially affected the quality of life for most individual families. In the six sayings which concern wealth or poverty (vv. 1, 4, 6, 7, 10, and 17) special focus is placed on the effect such contrasts have on personal relationships. Thus, v. 4 points to the effect that wealth had on gaining friends and attention from others, while the poor were often left friendless, thereby adding to a situation of hopelessness. V. 6 brings out part of the reason for this inevitable pattern of social behavior by pointing to the popular expectation of generosity on the part of a person of substantial means. V. 7 then makes a further comment on the social consequences of poverty. As a matter of formal grouping it may well be that there is a broad intention to deal with a number of issues concerning social relationships in extended comment on the instruction of 18:24. This compares family relationships with those based on neighborliness and friendship. In a community where kin relationships provided the most fundamental cement of social order, the way in which wealth could disrupt such ordering deserved close observation and comment. It remains unclear whether any particular prescriptive, or admonitory, intention lies behind such comments. In general the situation of the author and potential reader of such sentences appears that of someone standing on a middle ground to which neither of the extremes of wealth or poverty strictly applies. An explicit and relatively compassionate attitude toward the poor is then expressed in v. 17, where poverty is understood as a dire misfortune to which no special blame attaches. The statement of v. 10 concerning the inappropriateness of the situation in which a fool lives in luxury tends to undermine the general conviction of the authors of Proverbs that, in the end, people get what they deserve. It is, however, a significant feature of Proverbs that, even with its strong attention to the inescapability of the moral ordering of life, it maintains a frank and open recognition that such an order functions only as an approximation and that ultimately all retribution lies in the power of God.

Just as poverty could lead to the distortion or even ignoring of kinship ties, so marriage to an unsuitable wife could lead to disharmony and eventual ruination in a household. Accordingly, 18:22 raises the question of marriage and the major part played by a loyal and capable wife in a very forthright manner. The question is dealt with again in vv. 13 and 14, which tend to modify the point of 18:22. Not every household was blessed in the way envisaged since a woman's quarrelsomeness (19:13) or imprudent behavior (v. 14) could undermine an entire household. The firm discipline of a headstrong and rebellious child (v. 18) was therefore advocated. The general level of strictness, with resort to physical punishment as a necessary sanction, points to a deep level of social anxiety regarding the protection and upholding of a household as an independent family unit (cf. vv. 13, 26). The presumption is that such a household was usually a small farm estate in which consistent hard work was essential for survival (vv. 15, 24; cf. also 20:4, 13). Even so, cautious and humble submissiveness to the (ultimately unknowable) will of God was necessary (v. 21).

The appeal to the manner and conduct of a king in 19:12 should be taken to mark a traditional and stereotypical portrayal of this supreme office of the state. The king stood as an "ideal" figure — distant and largely unknown — but eulogized in a strongly favorable manner. If v. 12 is taken as a carefully placed comment on the general human need for curbing a hasty temper (v. 11; cf. also v. 19), it must be taken to imply that only kings could afford to display their deepest feelings. Lesser persons needed to display strong self-control and circumspection.

The King upon His Throne (Prov 20:1-30)

Two themes dominate this chapter. The first is that of justice in society, over which the king presided as head and supreme judge. The justice that he administers, however, is ultimately and ideally a divine order of justice. The second theme is a psychological one, concerning the difficulty of discerning human motives, including an awareness that human beings may ultimately not even be truly aware of their own motives (esp. v. 9).

The fact that kingship is used as an example of human conduct in a significant number of proverbs has been one of the factors that has given rise to the suggestion that the work of shaping the collection as a whole, and perhaps also the composition of many of the proverbs, took place in the royal court. This could appear all the more possible since in such sayings the king is presented as the model example of just administration. It is certainly understandable that the cultivation of writing and the promotion of limited literacy went hand in hand with the need for administrative skills in a palace context.

However, in view of the consistent, middle-class agricultural setting of a majority of the proverbial instructions, this professional court context appears unlikely to explain more than a few. More probably the focus on the kingship as the highest office of state uses this high office to portray the image of an ideal figurehead whose role embodied that of the state itself. In a sense the king was the state, and it is this political message that is implied in the proverbial sayings which refer to him.

Predominantly Proverbs portrays the king in a rather distant and artificial manner as the judge who presides over all human justice. He is the supreme arbiter of conduct so that royal anger (20:2) is regarded as an expression of righteous anger against wrong, not the sign of an irascible temperament. The king is viewed as possessing absolute authority, and his royal throne is said to be established on a foundation of righteousness. Even so, behind the justice of the king lies the absolute justice of God. Even kings could fail to embody the true ideal.

In this regard there is a relevant linkage between divine outrage at human cheating and deceit (20:10, 23), which constitute an "abomination" to God, and the administration of justice, for which the king was directly responsible (v. 28).

From the perspective of the religious associations of wisdom kingship marked a significant point of connection between God and the world. The teachers of wisdom sought to observe and reinforce by their instructions the patterns of order which structured the experienced world. In the social and political spheres the king stood at the top of a pyramid of orders. Justice flowed down from the divine throne, at least in theory, because a divine gift of insight into the nature of justice was given to him. It is in this direction that we should compare the claim set forth in 20:8 that the king could see into the innermost parts of the human mind (v. 8) — he "winnows all evil with his eyes" and "winnows the wicked" (v. 26) — sifting the outward pretensions and claims of human beings and uncovering their hidden inward intentions.

It is possible that the appearance together of several instructions concerned with kingship and its responsibilities for upholding justice, along with other sayings relating to human psychology, has been carefully planned. A paramount problem for the administration of justice in antiquity (and since) has lain in the difficulty of ensuring the reliability of accusers and witnesses in the giving of evidence. The potential for malicious accusations and perjury could all too easily undermine the course of justice. The relatively rudimentary rules for assessing the admissibility of evidence in the OT legislative collections shows this (cf. Deut 19:15), as do the warnings against abuse in the psalter (cf. Ps 15:3). The supreme human judge in the person of the king therefore needed the aid and guidance of the divine Judge in order to exercise his duties effectively.

But why were the workings of human thinking and acting so difficult to discern? Wisdom's teachers perceived the answer to this to lie in the richly complex nature of the human mind (20:5). Its purposes and intentions were "like deep water." Even children had to be judged by their actions rather than by their thoughts and words (v. 11). The instruments of human discernment — "the hearing ear and the seeing eye" — (v. 12) were the creation of God and needed to be employed to their fullest capacity. There was a constant need to look and listen beyond the protestations of goodwill that men and women made (v. 6). Even in simple commercial transactions it was essential to recognize the personal interest of everyone concerned, whether buyer or seller, since such personal engagement would determine whether what was said was valid or not (v. 14). So all human speech needed to be tested as to its veracity, and all advice carefully weighed (v. 18). In similar fashion, when a person was an outsider or foreigner, his or her word was not to be trusted at all. Where no bonds of family or community obligation imposed a demand for honest dealing, no such trustworthiness could be presumed. Only a fool would risk possessions on the word of such a stranger (v. 16).

All the above instructions allude to situations — commercial transactions, taking a pledge on loans, and waging war — which indicate that these sayings have been devised in order to illustrate typical situations which brought to light wider principles of conduct and trust. Such wider principles show that all human speech and knowledge are shaped by personal interest, which the truly wise person will recognize. It was significant for the teachers of wisdom that truth, integrity, and righteousness were absolute values which could not easily be translated into specific human actions. Only God and the king expressed such absolute qualities of righteousness in all their deeds. In a similar vein, even a person's feelings could change quickly so that what had been acquired by deceit might bring pleasure for a time, only to lead later to a sense of self-recrimination and guilt (v. 17). For ordinary human beings the goals of true wisdom and righteousness were ideals to be striven for (v. 7).

The Fate of the Wicked (Prov 21:1-31)

Proverbs 21 gives evidence of a significant change of mood from what has preceded it, with a noticeably large number of the instructional sayings being devoted to the subject of the ultimate fate of the wicked. In line with this fact a number of them return to the antithetical structure in which an approved and beneficial line of conduct is contrasted with its opposite. Overall, the theme that dominates the chapter is that of the fate of the wicked. This is contrasted with the happier fortune that awaits the righteous. The assurance that the wicked will ultimately encounter a bad end is found in the conviction that all life is controlled by God so that all human destiny is made subject to the divine will. The firmness with which such a doctrine is presented clearly indicates the currency of observations that sometimes the wicked prospered, at least for a time, while the righteous waited in vain for the reward for their righteousness. The concluding two assertions of vv. 30 and 31 reassert the traditional doctrine with a renewed note of certainty, possibly out of a desire on the part of the teachers to reassure themselves. Just as victory in battle ultimately derives from God, so no human schemes or plotting can avert the final implementation of God's will.

The four sayings of 21:1-4 connect closely with the preceding chapter, using the theme of divine control over the king as an illustration of God's ultimate control over all human destiny. Certainly the imagery of 21:1, with its background in the practice of irrigation, implies that the royal administration of justice is essentially part of the divine order of the world. So God's role as judge over human actions is even more fair and just than that of the mind of the doer (v. 2). The picture that unfolds of the ways of the wicked is a multicolored one. The idea expressed in v. 4, that proud and arrogant looks are "the lamp of the wicked," implies that such a manner of conduct is a mark by which they show themselves for what they are (cf. v. 24). Very much the same idea appears to underlie the statement of v. 29 that the wicked maintain a tough, brazen attitude, whereas the truly upright person is more modest and circumspect in behavior. Impatience (v. 5) and the use of a lying tongue to gain wealth (v. 6) are hallmarks of wickedness which will, in the end, sweep away the wicked themselves (v. 7). The rapaciousness of the wicked arises because they actually "desire" evil (v. 10).

Proverbs 21 sets forth various characteristic traits of wickedness, including a lack of compassion for the poor (v. 13) and a failure to hide the expression of dismay when justice is done (v. 15). Similarly, undue love of pleasure, wine, and sumptuous living (v. 17) are all trademarks of wickedness showing that a person has embarked on the road to ruin. Two sayings take up a theme that has already appeared (15:8). This is that right conduct is of greater importance to God than are the acts of formal worship (vv. 3, 27). A fundamental concern is the insistence that, since God weighs and tests all behavior, the wicked cannot hide behind a mask of piety. It is not altogether clear what is implied by the phrase "with evil intent" in v. 27. The most straightforward understanding is that the act of worship is purposely carried out to disguise the worshiper's wicked deeds. The assertions of vv. 27-29 are especially concerned with acts of dissimulation and deceit as particular features of gross wickedness in the eyes of the teachers of wisdom. In the case of a wicked person's offering of sacrifice such a public show of loyalty to God contradicts the reality of worship itself. Although there is some obscurity as to the exact contrast implied in v. 29, it would appear to be that of the brazenness of the hard-faced wicked person over against the courtesy and modesty of the righteous. In the end, however, God sees through all human pretense and judges people accordingly.

Reputation and Reward (Prov 22:1-16)

This section brings to a conclusion the series of sentence instuctions which commenced at 16:1. There appears to be some editorial structuring and a concern to present a comprehensive and rounded picture of life. It begins in v. 1 with a broad affirmation of the goal of wisdom, which is to insure the building up and retention of a good reputation (name). A trusted and respected place in the community is of far greater worth than the amassing of wealth and riches. Wisdom's claims remain consistent, and the teacher draws a sharp line between the destinies of the righteous and the wicked (vv. 4, 8, 12). As he perceives it, the shaping of life's fortunes begins in the minds of young persons, assumed consistently to be male; thus he gives a great deal of attention to the task of education. This task is assumed to constitute a duty in the home, with openly physical punishment when necessary (vv. 6, 15) and reverent respect toward parents. The teacher considers the religious dimension to be essential, an inner recognition that a divine order of justice and right ultimately prevails in the world. He regards this order as self-adjusting, although ultimately he appeals to the direct and personal action of God (v. 12). The acquisition of wisdom is seen to lie predominantly in recognizing the long-term consequences of character and its formed attitudes. These demand the curbing of violence, quick temper, and quarrelsome speech. Wisdom also encourages a careful scrutinizing of the motives and intentions of others. Speech is a key to discerning a person's character, so that the cultivation of thoughtful, restrained, and artistically expressed words is the mark of the wise person. So he regards education as primarily for life in society, with its moral restraints, but also as training for good husbandry and cautious commercial dealings. He also shuns the "get rich quick" mentality as a dangerous illusion.

At the borders of a well-prepared and well-managed life, however, were a number of unforseeable hazards. Foremost among these was the strange unknowability of what lay deep in the mind. A person may not even be openly aware of the secret inner desires and intentions that motivate action. To all life there were boundaries, which meant that the final outcome of all human plans and designs could never be fully known. They remained in the hands of an all-powerful God, whose ways were just and right.

The assertions of 22:1-16 repeat themes already dealt with, especially those relating to the contrasted lifestyles of the rich and poor. While retaining the belief that piety, integrity, and hard work would ultimately be rewarded by God with modest riches (22:4), the teacher considered it essential that the poor person should not be despised. Even the poorest was a creation of God who deserved respect and compassion according to need (22:2; cf. 14:31; 17:5; 29:13). An inalienable dignity was everyone's birthright.

That riches brought power and the consequent temptation to exploit this power by abusing the poor lies behind the instruction of 22:7. The same idea appears to lie behind v. 16, where, however, difficulties of translation render the meaning uncertain. Possibly the present text is a conflation of two separate sayings where lines have been lost. Generosity was the mark of the truly educated person (v. 9). Laziness would prove ruinous (v. 13), where humor serves to soften the tedium of repeated warnings. The warning against the "loose [i.e., unattached] woman" in v. 14 stands out strikingly in Prov 10:1–22:16. It is, however, covered more prominently in chs. 1–9.

Further Words of the Wise (Prov 22:17–24:22)

The section that now commences is distinctive in form and content from the sayings that precede it. The short, two-line couplets of the sentence instructions of 10:1–22:16 are now dropped in favor of longer, discursive admonitions in which the teacher gives instruction in separate commands. The evaluation of the distinctiveness of the section has been rendered more, rather than less, difficult by the discovery, translation, and publication of the ancient Egyptian papyrus text of *The Teaching of Amenemope* (Lichtheim 1976: 146-63). The latter was a high government official in the Egyptian royal administration, proffering advice and reflection on life and human behavior. The precise date of its writing is not certain, although Lichtheim ascribes it to the Ramesside period of the second millennium BC (Lichtheim 1976: 147). The "thirty sayings" referred to in 22:16 (which require a slight emendation of the text) have been connected with the thirty "sections" or "chapters" of the Egyptian text. Some relationship between the two texts appears probable but not unquestionably demonstrable. Differences are also evident, and the Egyptian text is not without its own textual difficulties. While it is certain that the "Words of the Wise" of Prov 22:17–24:22 show a close similarity to Egyptian educational instruction, it is possible that both Amenemope and Proverbs represent the developments of a common tradition. Perhaps the Hebrew text is a free adaptation and translation of the Amenemope text.

The status of the teacher in this section of the book of Proverbs appears to be decidedly that of a high-ranking and authoritative official. The sayings presume that a comparable status is at least potentially true of the reader of the teaching although the precise nature of the relationship is not clear.

23:1-2 gives specific advice concerning conduct at an official banquet. The atmosphere throughout is of a high level of administrative responsibility. This would be commensurate with the status of the Amenemope text. The urging of caution and extreme circumspection covers matters of etiquette but probably also extends to more serious issues such as those in which drunkenness might lead to serious diplomatic difficulties. The allegation that the host's delicacies were "deceptive food" may indicate either the insincerity of the hospitality offered or even its unpalatable nature (cf. Ecclus 31:12).

The Words of the Wise (Prov 22:17-29)

The introduction in 22:17-21 adopts a markedly rhetorical style of address, designed to commend the teaching given, although the reference to "thirty sayings" in v. 20 strongly suggests written transmission of the material. Although the emendation is widely adopted, it is not wholly certain and lacks any word for "sayings."

The ethical teaching includes strong injunctions not to oppress the poor (vv. 22-23), not to consort with an ill-tempered person (vv. 24-25), and not to act as surety (bail) for others (vv. 26-27). The command not to remove an ancient landmark, when taken literally (v. 28), illustrates a deep-rooted social problem of antiquity which reappears in legal contexts (Deut 19:14; 27:17; cf. also Prov 23:10-11). Possibly it is included here as an admonition to respect the inherited customs and traditions of the past more generally. The remark of 22:29 concerning the prospect of advancement and prestigious promotion may incorporate an element of rhetorical exaggeration, although it accords with the presumed high standing of both the teacher and the pupil. Comparable Egyptian texts refer to promotion as a scribe, whereas this passage envisages a variety of professions and skills.

Reflections on Life at a Royal Court (*Prov 23:1-35*)

The series of injunctions set forth in 23:1-21 reveals a number of connections between themes: for example, dining with rulers (23:1-3) leads to the folly of striving to be rich (vv. 4-5). This, in turn, leads to the temptations attendant upon eating a formal meal with a mean or, more probably, "craftily disposed" person (lit. "of evil eye"; i.e., miserly, jealous, or ill-intentioned). The inference is that obligations might be incurred which could later lead to trouble and recriminations. The several references to eating and drinking in these sayings reflect the high level of importance and commitment attached to mealtime hospitality. Since such guidelines for royal banqueting can have applied only to a very narrow circle of readers, we must conclude that they have been introduced for their intrinsic interest. They have probably also been retained because they illustrate principles of behavior which apply more widely. Concern with behavior at formal banquets then moves on into an extended, and intentionally humorous, disquisition on the dangers of wine and drunkenness in 23:29-35. It is noteworthy that the reason given for the reproof of overfondness for wine is that it leads to laziness and subsequent poverty (vv. 20-21).

Fresh commands concerning the necessity of instructing the young then appear between these admonitions against forms of social excess. The teacher expresses an overall concern with actions and a lifestyle which could bring about the loss of honor and wealth. The forms of address employed shift between urging parents to be strict (23:13-14) and urging the young to listen attentively so as to obey the instructions given (vv. 15-28).

The use of colorful and ear-catching warnings against the dangers of too much wine reflects the teacher's use of poetic artistry to inculcate a message which might otherwise be so unwelcome as to be passed over and ignored. The attractions of wealth and high living to a community where extreme poverty and hunger were more commonplace required a special word of caution. If sumptuous eating and drinking appeared to present an unclouded delight, it was essential that its dangers be recognized. 24:30-34 later gives a comparable use of poetic color and skill to impress an unwelcome message in a warning against laziness.

The Superiority of Wisdom (*Prov 24:1-22*)

The question of the ultimate fate of the wicked provides a repeated and consistent theme for the wisdom instructions to deal with. The instructor vigorously condemns bad conduct of various kinds which could disrupt the family, lead to financial ruin, and generally provoke friction and enmity in society. He repeatedly presents the justification for such condemnation in the form of bold assurance that those who pursue such behavior will come to a bad end. Yet quite evidently the actual experience of many in ancient society was that this did not always happen. The doctrine was more confident and assured than actual experience justified, even when a relatively long-term view was taken. Prov 24:1-2 clearly recognizes the truth of this perception by insisting that those who practice evil are not to be envied. There is a hint that evil is self-destroying. 24:8-9 reasserts essentially the same truth. All reasonable people find the wicked to be an abomination. Between these two reaffirmations of the traditional doctrine there is a fresh commendation of the virtues and value of wisdom (vv. 3-7). It echoes sayings given earlier in 9:1; 14:1 (cf. further 3:19-20) which assert that wisdom is a positive, home-building, world-building acquisition which is to be sought eagerly. The importance of wisdom in the conduct of war, leading to clever strategies and tactics which could bring about the overthrow of a physically stronger enemy, is adduced as an instance of its value in life more generally (vv. 5-6). The reference to "in the gate" (v. 7) may refer to the hearing of legal cases in this part of a town where most business was done. The reference may, however, be to a wider range of activities than those concerned with legal practice.

The description of an implicit obligation on the part of a student of wisdom to rescue "those taken away to death" (24:11) cannot reasonably be a reference to persons sentenced to death for crimes committed. Taken literally, it must then refer to all victims of brigandage and violence. It is possible that, in making such an allusion, the teacher intends the injunction to be taken metaphorically to refer to delivering people from the results of their own folly by teaching them a wiser path. By teaching wisdom the teacher would be rescuing them from death.

The sharp contrasts between the respective fates of the righteous and the wicked is further reiterated in 24:13-16, with a measured awareness that the inevitability of such good and bad destinies may often appear to be unfulfilled, or at best delayed. Vv. 19-20 then state with renewed conviction the assurance that an evil fate would certainly overtake the wicked. Before this restated insistence, however, vv. 17-18 set forth a disconcertingly conflicting admonition. It is an important feature of wisdom's teaching that the exaction of vengeance upon an enemy was to be left to God, and not to be a matter of a private vendetta. The moral well-being of ancient society was often seriously threatened by family feuds and the belief that family honor required the exacting of vengeance. That proper human compassion could take no pleasure in the downfall of an enemy established a safeguard against vindictiveness and selfish rejoicing at the misfortunes of others. However, the self-regarding motive given for such restraint in v. 18 is wholly at variance with the more general urging of compassion that colors proverbial wisdom instruction. The two verses can best be understood as an expansive comment introduced with a view to reconciling the need for compassion at any person's downfall with the traditional insistence of wisdom that disaster is God's way of punishing the wicked.

Uncertainty as to its intention obscures the significance of the admonition concerning the authority and judgmental powers of God and the king in 24:21-22.

There obviously existed a fundamental rightness in summoning the student of wisdom to be conscious that God and the king served as the twin pillars of judicial authority. Judgment was the prerogative of God, but since the king served as the representative human power through which divine judgment was mediated to human society, the royal administration of justice required obedience and submission. The reminder was apparently necessary to make plain that leaving judgmental decisions to God (as through the priestly lot) did not preclude the exercise of judicial power through duly authorized officials. Rather, such justice presupposed it. Where legitimate juridical authority was vested in the king, this authority had to be obeyed.

Further Sayings of the Wise (Prov 24:23-34)

The brief collection of instructions set forth at the conclusion of ch. 24 constitutes a short epilogue to what has gone before. The collection is located differently in the ancient Greek (LXX), coming after 30:14, where its reading of the text differs substantially from that of the Hebrew. The impression is left that we now have only a part of what was originally a much longer collection. The primary subject dealt with is again that of the administration of justice, with further advice to the farmer, particularly urging industriousness. 24:21-22 affirm the administration of justice through the courts, supported by the safeguards of a tradition of law and legal principle. Yet it is apparent, both from the preserved laws themselves and from a number of wisdom admonitions, that such justice was relatively undeveloped and not difficult for unscrupulous persons to pervert. The possibility of this is recognized in the unusual one-line assertion of v. 23b that impartiality in the administration of justice was a primary necessity. Examples of failure to achieve this are given in vv. 24-25 where, in the latter verse, the phrase "rebuke the wicked" must imply a formal legal condemnation. In a similar fashion, malicious, or careless, witnesses (v. 28) meant that even the best-ordered system of justice could be abused to convict the innocent, as the story of Naboth's vineyard demonstrates (1 Kgs 21:1-16). 24:29 also probably relates to the administration of justice since private vengeance-taking became an inevitable resort of those deprived of justice through proper legal action. Such actions could then lead to long-running feuds.

Throughout the teaching of Proverbs the perspective offered regarding the efficacy of human laws and legal administration is instructive. Proverbs fully defends and upholds the divine authority of such laws for the punishment of the wicked. At the same time the compilers of the proverbial sentence instructions show themselves to have been well aware of the imperfections of such systems in practice. Their response was not to deny the rightness of such necessary activities, in spite of their vulnerability to corruption. Rather, it was to affirm their limitations and to warn against expecting too much from them. Their importance was upheld in a determined effort to outlaw private vengeance-taking and feuding while recognizing that the final judgment of the wicked must be left in the hands of God.

The warnings against self-indulgence (24:27) and laziness (24:30-34) illustrate how narrow was the margin between success and failure which regularly faced the ancient Israelite farmer. Climate, political insecurity, and punitive financial constraints in the event of commercial failure all combined to make the choices of life urgent and the threat of hardship and ruin real. In v. 27 the phrase "build your house" may refer literally to the setting up of a dwelling but also to marriage and the raising of a family. The concern behind the admonition reveals the urgency the people felt regarding the provision of food for survival.

Supplements to the Teaching of Wisdom (Prov 25:1–29:27)

25:1 sets forth a fresh heading marking the first of a series of what are effectively appendices to the main sections of the book. Most of the themes dealt with have already been covered in the sentence instructions, but there is a noticeable change of style. There is more consistent use of similes and metaphors, indicating a striving after artistic forms of presentation, and there are indications that many of the sections once formed independent units characterized by consistency of style or attempts to provide particular compendia dealing with certain major ethical themes. Such a conclusion is further supported by the inclusion of several separate headings introducing the sections (so esp. 25:1, but cf. also 30:1 and 31:1).

The Throne of Justice (Prov 25:1-28)

The introductory note of 25:1 defines the collection which follows as "proverbs of Solomon which the officials of King Hezekiah of Judah copied." It marks the ensuing verses as an appendix to the sayings that have preceded them. It seems likely that the group of sayings in 25:2-27 once constituted a self-contained, independent collection. This is comprised of an introduction in vv. 1-5, two main sections in vv. 6-15; 16-26, and a conclusion in v. 27.

The sayings are distinctive in form, employing a large number of similes comparing human characteristics to aspects of the natural world. The reference in 25:1 to "the men of Hezekiah" may be of historical importance in showing how this king's reign marked an attempted revival of the power and glory of Solomon's reign and of the role played by official court scribes in the compilation of the proverbs collection.

The sayings of 25:2-7 concerning the king serve as a further elaboration on basic perspectives set forth in 24:21-22 concerning the royal administration of justice. The formal claim of 25:2 reasserts the belief in royal authority over a nationwide administration of justice in a rather paradoxical fashion. It is the glory of God to conceal things (i.e., by creating a richly diverse and mystery-laden world), whereas kings are to search out and bring to trial those who offend against God's order. The primary emphasis is on the unique responsibility of the king to apprehend felons and criminals. Though lacking the absolute nature of God's knowledge, the king is nevertheless authorized to administer justice. Accordingly, "the mind of kings is unsearchable" because they are endowed with divine assistance for their formidable task (cf. Solomon's prayer in 1 Kgs 3:1-15).

This endowment of the king with judicial insight did not necessarily extend to royal courtiers and officials, who must evidently be the persons referred to in 25:4-5. These could, and almost certainly often did, include "some of the wicked among their number." The sequence of sayings thereby sets forth an idealized concept of kingship. Nevertheless, such a king could be served by officials who fell short of this righteous ideal. We obtain from such sayings, which must have originated from the period when Israel was ruled by a native monarch, a rather mixed portrayal of the institution of the king and of life at the royal court. Almost certainly the king was often a distant, little seen figure, but responsible for the juridical and commercial well-being of his kingdom.

The saying in 25:6-7 concerning humility and circumspection in matters of palace protocol finds an echo in the NT in Luke 14:7-11. The saying is aimed generally at avoiding personal humiliation in public ceremonies. At the same time it illustrates the power of a social order over which the king stood as head and final arbiter. The question of justice further pervades the sayings of vv. 7c-10. Their import is strongly to discourage the reader and pupil from acting as a witness in a court of law or of actively bringing a case against a neighbor. Several commentators have suggested emending the phrase "into court" (v. 7c) to "to the multitude," implying a warning against spreading privileged, and potentially harmful, information to a wider audience. It urges extreme discretion in public matters rather than serving to discourage legitimate resort to law.

The inference appears to be that such action, when hastily done, could lead to personal shame and ignominy (25:10), although this is never clearly explained. The general context seems to warn that ill-timed or ill-considered talk could lead to the forfeiting of a person's "good name." If the context is more narrowly legal, it urges being sure of all the facts before acting as a witness.

25:11-15 provide a sequence of sayings concerning the good effects of thoughtful and appropriate speech. Encouragement (v. 11), reproof (v. 12), truthfulness, and the avoidance of boastful claims and showing off are all commended. Even a ruler might be subject to persuasion if the right words were chosen (v. 15). Throughout the sayings the primary emphasis is on the functioning of speech in building up and maintaining good and healthy relationships. Even the weak can influence the powerful when they employ the right words. The authors of Proverbs consistently show a strong awareness that speech functions primarily as an instrument in shaping relationships, either positively or negatively. Surprisingly, they view even the need to impart instruction and information largely in relation to this larger awareness of speech as a mode of interpersonal activity. So good and bad talking determine good and bad relationships.

The theme of 25:16-19 can be summed up as urging moderation and caution in all social habits. The simile of finding honey and of not eating too much of it (v. 16) provides a metaphor for wider aspects of handling the good things of life. Pleasure is approved, but overindulgence in it may turn even legitimate enjoyment into a threat. Neighborliness is highly approved in general, but busybodying can make it offensive (v. 17). So the sayings explore the notion of subtlety and discernment as a feature of keeping control of life. Words and actions which are good in themselves must be governed by a sense of "the right time." Vv. 18-20 list three further instances of bad-neighborly conduct. The offense of perjury (v. 18) is dealt with in the Ten Commandments (Exod 20:16; Deut 5:20). Unfortunately, the text of v. 20 is seriously disturbed, and the NRSV's translation follows that of the ancient Greek, which is by no means assured. Overall, and in spite of the difficulties, the message appears to be that unseasonal and thoughtless words can do much harm.

25:21-22 deal with the treatment of enemies, advocating a measure of generosity toward them. The injunction falls short of a call to love one's enemies, but it nevertheless urges a positive and creative attitude toward them so as to disarm their enmity. Uncertainty clouds the significance of the assurance that such actions will "heap coals of fire" on their heads. Opinions differ whether this is a reference to a form of torture, a form of ritual humiliation (cf. the Christian use of ashes at the beginning of the season of Lent), or a metaphor for feeling shame.

A similar obscurity lessens the force of the simile of 25:23 since, in the climate of the biblical lands, the north wind did not usually bring rain. However, the point of this admonition and the following one in v. 24 are both reasonably clear: ill-tempered speech can readily turn into provocation to anger, thereby creating a lasting rift in personal relationships. By contrast the bringing of good news can be a source of joy and refreshment (v. 25).

25:26-28 set forth the roles played by honor, resolution, and integrity as marks of a virtuous individual. To yield to the impositions and bluster of the wicked is wrong (v. 26) and points to an insistence that "peace at any price" is not to be sought. Honor, too, is a mark of the dignity and respect for social order and right living. Yet such honor, if sought inordinately for its own sake, may become a snare and a cause of eventual shame (v. 27), undermining the very virtues to which it points. A person who lacks self-control, for whatever cause and no matter what the provocation, always loses the battle to uphold goodness (v. 28).

Folly, Laziness, and Evil Speaking – Three Enemies of the Good Life (Prov 26:1-28)

The collection of sentence instructions in this chapter has a number of distinctive features which evidence the editorial grouping of specific themes. The topics covered in the instructions are threefold: the hopelessness of the fool (26:1-12), laziness (vv. 13-16), and the threat to social order posed by malicious speech and deceit (vv. 17-28). None of the sayings makes overt reference to the LORD as God, but there is throughout an implied knowledge of a divine order which governs all human conduct. All of the topics have been frequently covered in earlier instructions. There is an extensive use of similes and metaphors, with the repetition of a number of keywords and phrases which may have contributed toward bringing these particular sayings together.

The idea of honor as a fundamental quality which marks out the worthy and virtuous members of a community was of great importance to ancient Israelite society. It represented more than simply a psychological attitude of respect since it was expected to accord with qualities of authority, leadership, and the possession of wealth. So in the well-ordered society honor would belong to those who exercised these qualities. Yet sometimes they did not, so that to show respect and accord authority to a person who behaved foolishly was wholly out of place (26:1). Accordingly, the notion of what "is not fitting" was an important category of reproof denoting forms of conduct to be avoided. Just as the idea of "outrage, abomination" gave strong reproof to certain attitudes and actions, so the concept of "not fitting" denoted attitudes and acts which disrupted good order in life.

The bringing together of two, apparently contradictory proverbial instructions in 26:4-5 aims clearly at drawing attention to teachings that belong to specific circumstances. The disagreement is superficial rather than fundamental and illustrates that proverbs did not intend to lay down absolute rules of conduct. The discerning person would need to decide which action was appropriate in a particular situation. In this case the circumstance is that of the mentality of the fool. The error of "being wise in one's own eyes" (vv. 5, 12) was subject to particular reproof because it closed off the possibility of accepting rebuke and correction. Not to answer such persons could lead to the assumption that their attitude was acceptable.

The sharply drawn similes of 26:6 and 7 are evidently aimed at ridiculing conduct to which the unwary might be tempted. The point of v. 8 is that binding the slingshot into the sling ensures that it will not function as a missile! At first reading the instruction of v. 12 appears to fall outside the overarching theme of types of folly. However, pointing to the particular character trait of complacency as being worse than outright stupidity adds emphasis to the point to round off the series.

Earlier instructions have sharply condemned laziness, which is repudiated as a fault that leads to poverty and ruination. The incongruous similes used in vv. 13-16 are aimed at heaping ridicule on lazy people and their habit of making weak excuses for their behavior. This section is then concluded by the heavy exaggeration with which their bogus self-esteem is condemned in v. 16.

The instructions of 26:17-28 firmly condemn the dangers of malicious whispering, quarrelsomeness, and deceitful speech. Following on from this, even well-intended attempts to sort out other people's quarrels are rejected as futile and dangerous. So also is the conduct of a person who deceives a neighbor and then tries to pass it off as a joke (vv. 18-19). Gossipmongers and argumentative neighbors may wreak great havoc in a community by their words, yet their activities prove almost impossible to control. So, too, deceit and dissembling mean that persons are not to be judged by their outward demeanor and blandishments. Throughout Proverbs the teachers of wisdom insist that truthfulness and straightforward dealing are vital to maintaining the well-being of the community.

The assertion of 26:27, which, in its metaphorical dress, insists that whoever behaves badly will in due time suffer as a result returns to the basic doctrine of retribution. Evil actions set forces in motion which cannot be controlled until they eventually return to the evildoer. It is an inevitable law of life which mixes a rather idealistic sense of "poetic justice" with the idea that evil is itself a quasi-physical force which must be brought to rest by returning to its initiator. Such teaching was obviously a basic axiom for the teachers of wisdom, although it leaves open any firm conclusion as to how the evil is punished. Evil is seen as a self-destructive force. Often it is only in the longer term that evildoers suffer the consequences of their actions. The very rigidity of many of the wisdom teachers' assertions on the subject betrays an awareness that real life did not always, and perhaps not often, bear out their claims. The author of Qoheleth, who clearly recognized the limitations of such a doctrine, raises the whole issue very thoughtfully.

The section 27:1-7 concerns the building up of a right attitude with a view to establishing good personal relationships. V. 1 urges modesty and caution regarding divulging one's plans and intentions since life brings many unforeseen hazards. This point is emphasized still further in Qoheleth 9:11 with the awareness that time reveals the unpredictable nature of events, since all are subject to chance. Self-praise and provocative behavior are condemned in vv. 2-3, and harboring jealous thoughts and attitudes is sharply opposed in v. 4 with the assertion that such are more dangerous than anger.

27:5-6 urge the acceptance of well-intended rebukes, even though they may be painful when first received. A similar concern is expressed in v. 7, where note is taken of the fact that even bitter food may seem good to the hungry. Conversely, honey may lose its attraction if there is too much of it (cf. Prov 16:2ff.; 24:13; 25:16, 27). This suggests that the point of the contrast is: "Do not overdo it; too many rebukes will lose their effect!"

27:8 condemns the wanderer, one who fails to maintain a secure and stable role in the home. The following verse (9) has proved difficult to interpret, and the NRSV follows a reconstruction based on the ancient Greek text. The point then made, however, is so obvious that it appears unlikely to represent the correct original text. The Hebrew states that "the sweetness of a friend is better than one's own counsel" (cf. NRSV mg.). The point would then be that sharing the making of difficult decisions with a trusted friend is preferable to doing so alone. The general theme of friendship or neighborliness is very important for the teachers of wisdom and is found again in v. 10. The neighbor who becomes a trusted friend can be of greater help in times of difficulty than members of one's own immediate kin group, who may, in any event, live at too great a distance to offer immediate assistance.

27:11 apparently marks the beginning of a new short collection of sayings dealing with the general theme of education for the demands of life. It begins by repeating the well-established injunction to pay attention to the teaching of the wise. There is an implied inference that such instruction will first be given by parents to their children. Practical moral education for the acceptance of responsibility in the larger world is seen as a primary necessity so that the maturing child can begin to learn early to face the demands of life. So v. 12 follows out the point by noting that there are many hidden pitfalls and dangers which wisdom can anticipate and warn against. The ignorant and empty-headed person, who has no such forewarning, will inevitably come eventually to grief.

27:13 gives one such instance of danger for the unwary with the repetition of the warning not to accept financial obligations as surety for outsiders. It applies the latter term not only to foreigners in the ethnic sense but to any person who stood outside the established community circle. The Hebrew text, which refers to "a foreign woman" (cf. NRSV mg.), must certainly be a later assimilation of the warning to the separate issue of engaging in promiscuous sexual relationships with unattached women.

The conduct admonished in 27:14 is not particularly clear since the phrase "rising early in the morning" can hardly be intended literally as a warning not to disturb a neighbor's sleep. It must rather mean "overzealously." Such overdone praises would then end up by conveying the wrong message, as flatterers quickly discover.

27:15-16 return to the theme of the troublesome wife whose bickering and arguing create a stressful home background, destroying its security and peace. The goal of a secure and peaceful home, as the foundation of all effective social life, forms a central platform of wisdom's idea of a virtuous and flourishing society. The comment that is added in v. 16, that it could sometimes prove impossible to curtail the troublesome behavior of a difficult wife, lends force to the contention made elsewhere that the careful selection of a life partner was an important issue for the teachers of wisdom (cf. Prov 12:4). It is noteworthy that, although Proverbs conveys a rather negative and unsatisfactory picture of women and their place in society, it does recognize the complexities brought about by marriage and the importance of ensuring as a priority the general welfare of the home and family. There is a frank recognition that marriage may raise problems in that it brings together in the most intimate way members of two separate kin groups. The need, therefore, was to insure that the incoming partner in a marriage was integrated into the larger kin circle as smoothly as possible.

The didactic assertions of 27:17-22 relate to a number of general issues regarding the value of wisdom as a basis for education. The simile of v. 17 regards the interplay of skilled conversationalists and the presentation of instructive and persuasive argument as processes of sharpening the mind. It bore similarities to the craft of the smith at his forge. V. 19 makes a somewhat deeper reflection on the importance of open and constructive relationships where the reflection of a human face in water is compared to the recognition that only when one personality is reflected (i.e., responded to) in that of another person is the true "self" uncovered. The optimistic assurance of v. 18 that the dutiful and trustworthy servant will find honor and reward in the appreciation shown by the master finds a suitable comparison in the simile of tending a fig tree. The care for delicate and delicious fruits provides a telling picture of the extent to which the wisdom tradition assumes that the master-servant relationship forms a fundamental feature of the order of life.

The purpose that underlies the assertion of 27:20 that, just as Sheol and Abaddon — the all-consuming and insatiable realms to which the dead are taken — are never satisfied, so human desires never achieve full satisfaction. The saying intrudes an ethical note if it is understood as a warning against greed and covetousness. These were enemies of the search for true contentment and peace because they undermined the acceptance of one's position in life. Vv. 21 and 22 appear to have been drawn together because they find moral "lessons" in the basic forms of technology. As precious metals can be produced only by a process of refining, so praise is regarded as providing such a test. The idea already expressed in vv. 1-2, which warn against self-praise, is carried further here. Genuine praise from another may serve as an encouragement, in which case it becomes a spur to higher attainments. Contrastingly, if it leads to complacency it will be a damaging experience undermining further effort. The imagery of crushing grain with a pestle and mortar (v. 22) suggests to the teacher that some people prove to be hopelessly unteachable, frustrating even the best efforts of the wise.

The "Instructions for the Diligent Farmer" in 27:23-27 are unusual in offering an extended series of images which are clearly intended to deal with wider issues of life than those which apply to one occupation. The admonitions in v. 24 against trusting in riches or a crown raise the possibility that the saying is addressed to rulers and those who serve directly under them. Yet this is too narrow an interpretation to be plausible for the likely readership intended. The inclusion of the verse almost certainly provides the best clue to understanding the purpose of the whole sequence of farming imagery. Just as the successful farmer is faced with a wide variety of tasks if his work as a whole is to succeed, so everyone who aspires to becoming head of a household will be faced with a multiplicity of responsibilities. "Be prepared to face and honor them all" is the advice given. The extreme case that is referred to of wearing a ruler's crown provides the lesson that even this is never so secure that it may not be lost. The warning, therefore, is that the truly wise person must be prepared for all of life's unforeseen eventualities. Nothing is so certain in life that it may not be lost or bring trouble. Qoheleth develops the point further in setting forth a doctrine of "chance" (Eccl 9:11-12).

The Fates of the Righteous and the Wicked (Prov 28:1-28)

Proverbs 28 returns to the type of antithetical sentence instruction which appears most prominently in chs. 10–22. In a few of the sayings there is also a return to an affirmation of the role of the LORD God as the Supreme Ruler of the world whose moral will determines the ultimate destiny of everybody.

A high proportion of the sayings contrast the different fates of the righteous and the wicked, the major emphasis being upon the latter. Such assertions contain an implict warning against forms of behavior which have disastrous consequences and so should be shunned. By contrast those persons who nurture good attitudes and who repudiate paths of wrongdoing will ultimately prosper and be rewarded for their actions. A distinctively new feature is the pointing to the law *(torah)* of God as the way by which the wise person can find the right path. Elsewhere in Proverbs this term refers to "law" or "instruction" as the teaching given by parents or teachers to children and youths. However, in this chapter it clearly indicates the existence of a written body of divine rules and guidance (cf. probably also Prov 6:23). What precisely was covered by this written law, whether it included all the five books of Moses (Genesis–Deuteronomy) or only a single book such as Deuteronomy, cannot be determined.

The usage is significant in showing how, in the gradual formation of a written corpus of Scripture, a central core was recognized which served as a key by which a far wider range of writings was to be interpreted. Such canonical growth brought about a steady assimilation of the ideas and teachings of wisdom, originating with parents and teachers, to a larger, more overtly religious corpus of instruction.

Most of the themes set forth in 28:1-28 have already been dealt with in earlier sayings, with a few having very close parallels among them. V. 1 sets the vulnerable and fear-laden state of the wicked over against the confident (rather than "bold") attitude of the righteous. Where there is no guilt there is nothing to fear. The claim that firm and established government stood as the foundation of a just society is reflected in the instruction of v. 2. Vv. 15-16 express a closely related idea concerning the evil consequences of wicked rulers. At the heart of a well-ordered community there had to be firm and effective government to prevent brigands and criminals from exercising their power. The idea is that rebellion in a land leads to anarchy and the transfer of power to irresponsible rebel rulers who serve only their own interests. Defense against such misrule lay in the imposition of discipline and justice by a strong ruler. Proverbs consistently upholds the perspective that at the head of a just society sat the king, regarded rather idealistically as a just and noble figure, enthroned as the upholder of the good order which God willed for all human society. The authors of Proverbs regarded justice and politics as inseparably interwoven threads which held society together. So the primary responsibility of a ruler lay in the administration of justice and the suppression of brigands and rebels. The NRSV translation of v. 3 makes this verse an almost exact counterpart of the one that precedes, declaring an oppressive ruler to be a destructive influence over a land. The Hebrew text, however, reads "when a poor person oppresses the poor" (cf. NRSV mg.), which has been set aside as an unlikely original text. In spite of its unexpectedness, the assertion makes excellent sense and has every claim to being correct. It points out the destructive effect that the poor have upon those as unfortunate as themselves, showing no compassion in spite of being in the same condition. This agrees well with the simile of heavy rain which, in bringing necessary fertility to the fields, nevertheless beats the crops down and ruins them.

28:4 regards the written law of God as a compendium of guidance which enables justice and prosperity to flourish. Consequently it readily distinguishes between good and evil persons. Much the same idea appears in v. 5, reflecting a strong awareness, which colors the entire book of Proverbs, that justice in the narrow legal sense must ultimately rest on the conviction that God has decreed that justice and righteousness should form the foundations of the universe (cf. Ps 72:1-4).

The teaching of Proverbs consistently sticks to the belief that, in the end, the just attain to prosperity and happiness, while the wicked come to ruin, even though they may for a time appear to benefit from their wickedness. The heavy repetition of the theme, insisting that this is the case even when experience seems to belie it, indicates that it increasingly came to be felt as a problem requiring further reflection and explanation. So 28:6 insists that every person seeking the right path in life must set up a scale of personal priorities which recognizes that integrity and honor are of much greater importance than riches.

In 28:7 the keeping of the law of God is seen as the mark of a wise youth, whereas parents are brought to shame when children become wanton (preferable to "glutton" since a whole lifestyle is envisaged). The thought of v. 9 closely parallels that expressed in 15:8 and 15:29: acts of piety are acknowledged by God only when they are performed by persons whose way of life accords with God's laws. So also, if evil behavior is repudiated by God, the punitive consequences for those who entice others to follow in evil ways must be all the more serious (v. 10). Once again, however, the doctrine of retribution that is set forth presents it as a feature of the order of life that evildoers bring about their own downfall. They "fall into pits of their own making" (v. 10).

The foolishness of "being wise in one's own eyes" (28:11) is a recurrent theme of proverbial teaching. To indulge in exaggerated self-esteem or to trust in the possession of wealth (cf. 18:11), was an attitude which closed the mind to true wisdom and was to be rejected. In spite of the insistence that good and bad conduct inevitably brought about correspondingly good or bad results, the recognition that in the short-term realities of life the opposite results could occur is reflected in v. 12. In a further reflection on the theme, v. 13 affirms the accepted doctrine of retribution, but, quite uniquely in proverbial teaching, it asserts that forgiveness is possible. When the wrongdoer confesses the wrongful act, then it can be repudiated and forgiven.

The injunction of 28:17 concerning the importance of outlawing the murderer and violent criminal, refusing them any acceptance in a just society, reads more akin to a legal prescription than a typical wisdom sentence. It may have been introduced at this point to add a rider to the preceding two verses about wicked rulers. V. 19 returns to the theme of the necessity of honest work if poverty is to be avoided, and v. 20 gives further reinforcement by insisting that those who seek to obtain riches quickly will come to grief and encounter punishment. The subtle ambiguities of wisdom's attitude to wealth emerge here in asserting that true wealth could only be acquired slowly and as the result of hard work. To seek to gain riches hurriedly, implying the adoption of high-risk commercial ventures or extortion from the poor, was regarded as a mark of a greedy and oppressive person. Those who pursued such goals made wealth a symbol of wickedness, and it is such ill-gotten wealth that the wisdom teachers condemn.

28:21-22 give examples of ways in which a person could seek to obtain wealth dishonorably. In the former the unscrupulous judge, or witness, in a court of law could accept a bribe — even a modest one — in order to manipulate justice. The miser of v. 22 (lit. a person of "evil eye") is portrayed as so greedy for profit that it disorients his entire lifestyle, thereby bringing ruin.

28:23-27 outline and contrast different types of bad conduct with their opposites. Flattery may appear to be a useful method of obtaining support and friendship, but in the end it will fail to achieve its goals (v. 23). To rob one's own parents is akin to the most contemptible forms of violent conduct (v. 24). Greed, complacent self-esteem, and miserliness toward the poor are all reprehensible actions which mark off evil behavior from good. To note these attitudes and to cultivate those habits which develop into a positive lifestyle are the marks of the pupil who heeds the teaching of parents and the law of God.

Lifestyles of the Righteous and the Wicked (Prov 29:1-27)

The theme of the contrasting lifestyles of the righteous and the wicked continues in ch. 29. It largely consists of further antithetical sayings dealing with broad moral themes, all of which have appeared earlier. V. 17 offers the sole admonition in the chapter, but vv. 3 and 15 also contain its theme, namely, the need for discipline in the education of children. Otherwise the most prominent subjects dealt with are those of the authority of kings and the unhappy lot of the poor. A broad emphasis on the central importance of the moral framework of society, as exemplified in the power exercised by those set in authority, is a noteworthy feature. In this regard there is less direct insistence on the moral choices that face each individual and a recognition that the conduct of persons who wield power and influence deeply affects the quality of life that each individual may enjoy. The individual is not isolated and is inevitably subject to the way people behave in the wider sphere. The chapter does not indicate what exactly the individual can do to remove the wicked from power.

29:1 gives a new direction to the observation that the fool may remain obstinate in the path of folly. The instruction makes the observation that frequent reproof may lead to a point where all openness to further reproof is foreclosed. The practical psychological point would appear to be that overzealous attempts at correcting an obstinate person will prove useless. Such persistence will then bring about a negative response in which further guidance will be refused altogether. However, the point that a person's spirit may be "broken beyond healing" indicates a state of mind in which all self-esteem is lost, with the most serious personal consequences.

The insistence that when the wicked achieve power and authority the entire community will suffer as a result (v. 2) is a recurrent one. Such an instruction is a variant of the more central theme of this section that even kings may behave wickedly. They may do so through failing to insure that justice is properly administered (v. 14), or by imposing extortionate taxes on the people (v. 4), or by listening to the lies and false accusations of their officials (v. 12). Since the role of the king is usually presented in a strongly positive light, especially in ch. 15, the shift of emphasis is noteworthy. In 25:1-7 the king is portrayed in a favorable manner as the upholder of public justice, with only a small concession to the reality of palace corruption (25:5). The wider, and undoubtedly more realistic, picture of ch. 29 may indicate a more considered phase of development, perhaps from a relatively late postexilic period. The broader principle concerning the evil consequences of wicked rulers raises larger, unexplored issues concerning how the righteous are to counter this. The underlying assumptions, adopted by the wisdom teachers, that all creation, including the structure of society, is pervaded by a providential order ordained by God (cf. Rom 13:1-7) clearly had certain outer limits which could not be ignored. The renewed assurance that ultimately the wicked will experience downfall (29:16) and that their own conduct may help to bring this about (29:6) indicates an unresolved dilemma.

The need to discipline children is dealt with in three instructions (29:3, 15, 17). The related problem of the need to maintain firm authority over slaves is the subject of vv. 19 and 21. Mention of the "mother" in v. 15 is significant as a reflection of the concern to demonstrate the involvement of both parents in their children's education (cf. 1:8; 31:1).

Concern for the poor is another recurrent theme that appears. The general assertion that it is the mark of the righteous person to show concern for the poor is set forth in 29:7. The phrase "know the rights of the poor" should be understood as "caring for the needs of the poor" rather than as an indication of belief in a set of basic human rights to which everyone was entitled. There is no doubt, however, that the Israelite understanding of justice contained a genuine note of compassionate concern to assist and protect the weaker members of society. A more difficult problem exists over the interpretation of v. 18. The close parallel between "prophecy" and "keeping the law" in the two lines seems to point to a rather weak sense of "prophecy" as meaning little more than "an authoritative statement" (REB reads "with no one in authority . . .").

Besides the hopelessness and unteachability of the fool in 29:1, the general reproof of foolish conduct is carried further in v. 20, where "someone who is hasty in speech" (i.e., "eager to talk") is singled out as an extreme kind of fool. Self-control (v. 22) and humility (v. 23) are especially commended. The general suspicion that resort to the processes of law was likely to prove unsatisfactory is further reflected on in v. 9, where the behavior of fools in defending themselves is held up to ridicule. The actions are so grotesque as to nullify the whole legal process. The particular offense singled out in v. 24 of aiding and abetting a thief also appears, if the indications of the second line are taken to refer to behavior in a lawsuit. The phrase concerning "hearing the victim's curse" is best understood as a refusal to divulge incriminating information when put under oath (cf. REB's "put on oath but divulges nothing").

Sayings of Agur (Prov 30:1-14)

With ch. 30 a distinct change in style and character in the sayings takes place in Proverbs with what are effectively four short literary appendices (30:1-14; 30:15-33; 31:1-9; 31:10-31). Two of these are given separate headings (30:1 and 31:1), although the significance of these is of only limited assistance in classifying the content. In the ancient Greek (Septuagint) translation 30:1-14 is placed immediately after 24:22 and 30:15-33, followed by 31:1-9, which in turn follows after 24:34. This variant text tradition confirms the recognition that several short collections have been brought together and incorporated into the book after 22:16.

From the point of view of style and content the most notable feature of 30:1-14 is the transition to longer poems, with the primary emphasis upon the rhetorical artistry and originality of the saying rather than close attention to a specific aspect of behavior or attitude. However, 30:10 presents an admonition, and the four types of unacceptable conduct set forth in vv. 11-14 prepare the way for the more formal number sayings of vv. 15-31. Rhetoric and artistic interest rather than moral earnestness are to the fore, although the characteristic wisdom concern to brand certain lines of conduct as reprehensible still remains evident. To some extent the artistry remains a dress for urgent moral instruction, with the added touch in the subsequent number sayings that the unexpectedness of the connections lends humor and interest.

It is not clear how much of what follows 30:1 is intended to be covered by the heading. The word rendered "oracle" may be taken as an indication of a local tribal affiliation (Massa is a northwest Arabian tribe in Gen 25:14). The poetic use of the self-abasement formula of vv. 1-3 establishes a question, How can anyone, however wise or foolish, know anything of the mystery of the world and its Creator? The answer in v. 4 is then spoken by God, or by an anonymous speaker on God's behalf. The rhetorical questions (cf. God's answer to Job in Job 38–39) clearly point to God as the Creator of all things, who alone possesses understanding of the world's marvels and mysteries. Even a little wisdom is only a fractionally small insight into the truth about life. The celebration of God's truth and power in vv. 5-6 displays close echoes of other biblical texts (cf. Deut 4:2; 12:32; Job 13:10).

The speaker of 30:7-9 resumes the theme of self-effacing humility begun in vv. 1-3 by praying to God for the gifts of truth and adequacy for the demands of daily life. Either riches or poverty would bring extremes which would lead either to complacency in the case of the former, or dishonesty and theft in that of the latter (v. 9). The intrusion of the admonition in v. 10 against speaking ill of a servant is directed primarily against abuse of a position of authority, taking advantage of a situation in which the victim cannot reply. Its presence is unexplained although it serves well to introduce the four types of objectionable personal conduct of vv. 11-14. Those who curse their own parents violate the fundamental order of family life and integrity (v. 11). Similarly, the complacent fail to see the extent of their own wrongdoing (v. 12). The two further types of unacceptable person listed in vv. 13-14 — the arrogant and the greedily oppressive — then serve to interpret the first two examples.

By making a list of four types of bad character in 30:11-14, the teacher prepares the way for the more formal and overt lists of "four related things" which follow in 30:15-31.

Numerical Sayings (Prov 30:15-33)

The rhetorical and artistic interest of wisdom led to the bringing together of several number sayings in which the formula x, x+1, is used (cf. the earlier comments on 6:16-19, where the sequence "six, yes seven" is used; cf. Roth 1965). The feature is primarily for rhetorical effect. There is no consistent indication that the formula was aimed at bringing unlikely, or formally connected, realities into a list. At most the last of the examples listed may evidence some element of surprise, so as to express a moralistic point. Already the four examples of unpleasant person catalogued in 29:11-14 prepare for the lists of four examples. In the six number sayings of 30:15-31 there is an intermixing of animal and human behavior patterns which may point to some attempt to present a picture of a moral order that pervades all living creatures, both human and animal.

The theme of insatiability which pervades the number saying of 30:15b-16 is anticipated by the example of the leech given in v. 15a. There appears to be an implicit admonition against greed which is common to both sayings; some persons are as greedy as leeches! The inclusion of the "barren woman" among the list of v. 16 may have been intended as a warning against consorting with such a person. The strong opprobrium of disrespect for parents given in v. 17 disrupts the order of the number sayings but highlights a strongly felt aspect of the "family values" of the wisdom teachers.

30:18-19 list four surprising activities: bird flight, the locomotion of snakes, the passage of a ship through the seas, and the unseen force of sexual attraction. It is an oversubtle interpretation which sees in all these actions forms of activity that leave no trace; however, this understanding of sexual attraction leading to misconduct has likely led to the inclusion of the further warning against the adulterous woman in v. 20.

The list of four classes of person in the saying of 30:21-23 displays a touch of humor in view of their improbability. If a degree of admonitory interest is present, it must lie in the warning against contravening the natural order of society and its educational expectations. In a similar vein the "four things" of vv. 24-28 contain an implicit commendation of wisdom. It is a variation on the theme "small is beautiful," highlighting instances where wisdom proves greater than physical strength. No very obvious moralistic, or admonitory, significance can be discovered in vv. 29-31 with its list of four proud creatures. The inclusion of the king is surprising in view of the general reproof given in wisdom against pride and haughty demeanor. The significance, however, may be that it marks conduct that is right only in its appropriate place. The saying which rounds off the section in vv. 32-33 provides a general admonition against pride, deviousness, and bad temper — all themes which have occupied many of the character-forming instructions of the wise.

The Words of King Lemuel (Prov 31:1-9)

Since a new section portraying the role of the "ideal wife" is set forth in 31:10-31, the title identifying vv. 1-9 as the words of King Lemuel must apply to these verses alone and should not be regarded as relevant to the whole chapter. The title identifies the sayings as conforming to the class of royal instructions — a form known from Egypt and Babylon. The added note that it represents instruction given to the king by his mother makes it unique and would indicate parental responsibility for the education of a royal prince. However, it is noteworthy that the king is addressed in v. 4, and it cannot be ruled out in view of the conventional topics relating to royal responsibilities that the form is essentially a rhetorical device reaffirming basic royal duties. It may then have been composed for a state occasion or even for the enthronement of a prince. The country of the king's origin is not disclosed, but it is likely that of a northern Arabian tribe (cf. the comments on 30:1).

The three subjects dealt with are those of maintaining authority over the women of the royal court (30:2-3), avoiding overindulgence in wine (vv. 4-5), and showing concern for the poor and disadvantaged. The injunction to "give strong drink to them" (vv. 6-7) appears to offer a cynical recommendation to give such drink to them in order that they may forget their many cares. However, it can be better regarded as a rhetorical transition from the preceding warning against self-indulgence, urging that the gift of wine should be given not for selfish excess but for the pleasure of those who would not otherwise enjoy such satisfaction. This more honorable concern for the welfare of the weaker members of society comes to the fore in vv. 8-9.

The Role of the Virtuous Woman (Prov 31:10-31)

Most of the references to women and their role in society that have appeared earlier in Proverbs have been of a markedly negative character. Predominantly in chs. 1–9 the threat to young men posed by the "unattached," or "loose," woman is given prominence. She is there perceived as a temptation and sexual threat whose activities undermine marriage and the integrity of the family. Even in 10:1–22:16 the role of women in the household is presented with considerable caution, warning that a wife can be troublesome and disruptive of the peace of the home. So a wife must be chosen with great care. Yet marriage was an important feature of life and essential to the small family unit which formed the social and commercial basis of community life. Thus the teacher commends marriage and motherhood and notes the role of the mother in giving instruction to her children. She is a pillar of the household and deserves respect at all times.

The poem is in the form of an acrostic, with each of its twenty-two verses commencing with a different letter of the Hebrew alphabet. With this formal structure, and no doubt partly as a consequence of it, there is little by way of internal development of thought. Basic central themes reappear at more than one point within it. Throughout the poem the virtues of the woman are seen in her relationships to other members of the household unit — husband, children, and servants. Moreover, her very life's mission and purpose are to reside within this household, to which she contributes but over which she cannot be head.

It is this latter concern to uphold the formative role of a wife and mother in the family household, and through this in society more generally, that the poem obtains its vigor and appeal. Its fulsome praise of her value here is no doubt strengthened by the need to avoid allowing such a compendium of wisdom instruction as Proverbs represents leaving an unwarrantably negative portrayal of womanhood. So 31:10-31 presents a eulogy of praise for women and their role in the household. C. V. Camp regards the need to offer a focus on the negative and positive aspects of a woman's place in the social order as constituting a framework for the book in its completed shape (Camp 1985: 255-61).

Wisdom's concern with the place of women may be set alongside wisdom's attention to the "neighbor" or "friend" as fulfilling a vital function in a normal healthy community. In a society where the inherited social values drew heavily upon the patriarchal structure of the extended family, a review of the role of women, like those of "the good neighbor," pointed toward important modifications of outlook. In this measure the overall social perspective of the wisdom teachers reveals a significant shift away from the rigidity of the older traditional patriarchal, kinship-based order of life. Women are accorded a noticeably larger share in contributing to the welfare of the home. Set closely alongside the figure of the father/husband, a woman finds her role as wife and mother constitutive and worthy of the highest praise. She is no longer simply the childbearer for the patriarchal head, but a primary figure in the whole range of the household's responsibilities.

The language used to praise the "ideal" woman in 31:10-31 is fulsome and unrestrained in its commendation. It celebrates her worth as "far more . . . than jewels" and shows her as unceasingly full of good works. Yet for all this commendation, when one makes a close examination of the contribution of such a person, it is striking how strongly the residual patriarchal outlook and assumptions of ancient Israelite society still emerge. This appears to be the case right at the beginning with the commendation that her husband places his complete confidence in her and the assurance that he has no lack of gain and prosperity from her endeavors (vv. 11-12). The benefits that she brings to him appear to be the foremost concern (v. 12).

Such a woman is portrayed as continually industrious in managing the household's affairs (31:14-16, 22, 24, 27), making its essential furnishings herself, organizing her servants, and caring for the needs of the entire household (v. 27). She has many children, who express affection and gratitude to her for her teaching and wisdom (v. 26) and for the example that she sets of unceasing hard work.

For all this singling out of the woman's virtuous achievements, her personal qualities remain almost entirely hidden and her importance as a companion and person of courage and leadership is left unmentioned. Even her resourcefulness, piety, and courage, as in the biblical portraits of Ruth and Esther, are not taken into the reckoning.

All through the eulogy the author gives the impression of a strongly idealized portrait of womanhood which marked out, from a male and largely patriarchal standpoint, a role for women which was almost completely domestic. Recognition of this strongly stylized portrayal of the ideal woman has given birth to the suggestion that it may have been intended to provide a picture of personified wisdom rather than of a flesh-and-blood person. Yet this appears to be highly unlikely, not least because it runs counter to the characteristic attractions of personified wisdom set forth in Prov 8:1-36. More plausibly the eulogy of the virtuous woman represents wisdom's portrayal of womanhood which was seriously concerned to offset the threatening and largely negative features of gender differentiation which characterized the warnings of chs. 1–9.

Bibliography. Bryce, G. E. 1979, *A Legacy of Wisdom: The Egyptian Contribution to the Wisdom of Israel,* Lewisburg: Bucknell University • Camp, C. V. 1985, *Wisdom and the Feminine in the Book of Proverbs,* Bible and Literature Series 11, Sheffield: Sheffield Academic • Clements, R. E. 1992, *Wisdom in Theology,* The Didsbury Lectures, Grand Rapids: Eerdmans • Clements, R. E. 1993, "The Good Neighbour in the Book of Proverbs," in H. A. McKay and D. J. A. Clines, eds., *Of Prophets' Visions and the Wisdom of Sages: Festschrift for R. N. Whybray,* JSOTSup 162:209-28 • Clements, R. E. 1996, "The Concept of Abomination in the Book of Proverbs," in M. V. Fox et al., eds., *Texts, Temples and Traditions: Festschrift for M. Haran,* Winona Lake: Eisenbrauns, 211-26 • Crenshaw, J. L. 1982, *Old Testament Wisdom: An Introduction,* London: SCM • Crenshaw, J. L., ed. 1976, *Studies in Ancient Israelite Wisdom,* New York: Ktav • Fox, M. V. 1996, "The Social Location of the Book of Proverbs," in M. V. Fox et al., eds., *Texts, Temples and Traditions: Festschrift for M. Haran,* Winona Lake: Eisenbrauns, 227-39 • Heaton, E. W. 1974, *Solomon's New Men: The Emergence of Ancient Israel as a National State,* London: Thames and Hudson • Gammie, J. G., and L. G. Perdue. 1990, *The Sage in Israel and the Ancient Near East,* Winona Lake: Eisenbrauns • Lichtheim, M. 1976, *Ancient Egyptian Literature,* vol. 2: *The New Kingdom,* Berkeley and Los Angeles: University of California • McKane, W. 1965, *Prophets and Wise Men,* SBT 44, London: SCM • McKane, W. 1970, *Proverbs: A New Approach,* OTL, London: SCM • Martin, J. D. 1995, *Proverbs,* Old Testament Guides, Sheffield: Sheffield Academic • Murphy, R. E. 1987, "Religious Dimension of Israelite Wisdom," in P. D. Miller, Jr., P. D. Hanson, and S. D. McBride, eds., *Ancient Israelite Religion: Festschrift for F. M. Cross, Jr.,* Philadelphia: Fortress, 449-58 • Perdue, L. G. 1977, *Wisdom and Cult: A Critical Analysis of the Views of Cult in the Wisdom Literatures of Israel and the Ancient Near East,* Missoula, Mont.: Scholars • Perdue, L. G. 1994, *Wisdom in Creation: The Theology of Wisdom Literature,* Nashville: Abingdon • Porteous, N. W. 1967, "Royal Wisdom," in *Living the Mystery: Collected Essays,* Oxford: Basil Blackwell: 77-91 • Roth, W. M. W. 1965, *Numerical Sayings in the Old Testament,* VTSup 13, Leiden: Brill • von Rad, G. 1972, *Wisdom in Israel,* London: SCM • Weinfeld, M. 1972, *Deuteronomy and the Deuteronomic School,* Oxford: Clarendon • Whybray, R. N. 1965, *Wisdom in Proverbs,* SBT 45, London: SCM • Whybray, R. N. 1972, *The Book of Proverbs,* CBC, Cambridge: Cambridge University • Whybray, R. N. 1974, *The Intellectual Tradition in the Old Testament,* BZAW 135, Berlin–New York: de Gruyter • Whybray, R. N. 1989, "The Social World of the Wisdom Writers," in R. E. Clements, ed., *The World of Ancient Israel,* Cambridge: Cambridge University, 227-50 • Whybray, R. N. 1990, *Wealth and Poverty in the Book of Proverbs,* JSOTSup 99, Sheffield: Sheffield Academic • Whybray, R. N. 1994, *Proverbs,* NCBC, London: Marshall Pickering • Würthwein, E. 1976, "Egyptian Wisdom and the Old Testament," in J. L. Crenshaw, ed., *Studies in Ancient Israelite Wisdom,* New York: Ktav, 113-33.

Ecclesiastes

John Jarick

INTRODUCTION

The book of Ecclesiastes is an enigma. Down the centuries its readers have been unable to agree on who has written these "words of the Teacher" (1:1), what that writer is trying to say, and whether those words ought to be said within the Bible. But despite these disagreements, or perhaps partly because of them, many readers find this book to be one of the most intriguing works in the Hebrew scriptures, a fascinating mixture of darkness and light, confidence and doubt, piety and irreverence. Some interpreters have been so unsettled by the shifting patterns of thought expressed in the book that they have postulated the presence of more than one authorial voice here, with perhaps an original pessimistic writer's words having been overlaid with more optimistic sentiments from another hand. But as the following comments will seek to show, it is best to understand the book as substantially the work of one eclectic thinker (with only the epilogue of 12:9-14 representing the opinions of another individual, perhaps an early reader who was both transfixed and troubled by the Teacher's words).

The teachings presented in Ecclesiastes seem to go round and round (something like the wind that is described in 1:6 as going "round and round" and returning "on its circuits"), in the sense of the writer circling around certain ideas and returning again and again to the same places where his thoughts had taken him before. For this reason it will be useful, rather than to offer a verse-by-verse treatment of the book, to gather the various reiterated elements together, and set them out in terms of a thesis, antithesis, and synthesis, the better to unravel and understand the "threefold cord" (4:12) that the author has woven together. But first some comments are in order about that author.

The designation of the personality behind this book as "the Teacher" is the NRSV's attempt to pin down in English the puzzling Hebrew title *qohelet,* which appears seven times in this book (1:1, 2, 12; 7:27; 12:8, 9, 10) but nowhere else in the Bible. The term has some relationship to the word for assembling or gathering *(qahal),* and so may indicate someone who is involved in an assembly of people or who gathers together a collection of some kind, such as a compendium of wise sayings. In other words, our *qohelet* might indeed be a teacher, robustly addressing a gathering of eager listeners, but he might equally be a keen listener to the words of others, avidly noting various contributions to a discussion, and thus perhaps the designation ought to be translated as "the Student" instead. The body of the work does not make clear where the thoughts of this *qohelet* are being presented and where the ideas of others are being put forward, either to be agreed with or to be negated, so it is not surprising that already in the Hebrew title given to the author (and accordingly also to the Hebrew book) there is considerable ambiguity. The early Greek translators thought they had partly cracked the code by rendering it *ekklēsiastēs* (from which the English title of the book is derived), meaning "a member of the assembly" or more specifically "the Speaker/Preacher" at an assembly, but it remains a puzzle, and "the Teacher" is as good a guess as any.

The identity of this "Teacher" is a mystery, despite some tantalizing information at the beginning and end of the book. The introductory verse says that he was a "son of David" and a "king in Jerusalem" (1:1), which seems in keeping with the regal autobiographical touch in the early part of the work (such as at 1:12). On the other hand, the epilogue pictures him as a sage who made his living by teaching and writing (12:9-10), which seems in keeping with various pieces of advice from the perspective of a nonregal person (such as at 8:2-4 and 10:4). Some have read 1:12 as implying that the writer was once a king, but was no longer so at the time of writing. Many, particularly in antiquity, assumed that the writer was Solomon since the legendary wisdom and wealth of that monarch seemed uniquely applicable to the descriptions of those attributes in 1:12–2:11, as well as evidently filling the "son of David" shoes. However, the words of the Teacher are expressed in a kind of Hebrew that did not yet exist at the time of King Solomon (near the beginning of the first millennium BC), but rather in a form of the language which looks decidedly postexilic (i.e., a type of Hebrew that emerged only in the second half of the first millennium BC), which makes Solomonic authorship impossible. The granting of the title "king" to the Teacher is perhaps something of a tease for the reader, inviting respect for what is to be presented but at the same time playfully undermining traditional wisdom.

Various unsuccessful attempts have been made to pin the writing down to a particular time and place. The place is perhaps not so slippery: Jerusalem is mentioned five times in the scene-setting section (1:1, 12, 16; 2:7, 9) and, although the book does not say that the writer is there at the time of writing, it is at least plausible that he was; in any event, no other city is explicitly named in the text, although some readers have proposed various candidates for the proverbial places mentioned in 4:13-16 and 9:13-16. Many more suggestions have been put forward regarding the date of composition, one particular focus being to ascertain the precise period in which certain observations of oppression (4:1), corruption (4:8), and economic turbulence (5:13-14) are to be placed. But most readers in any age will recognize these passages as depicting eternal verities of human society — when has there not been a period in which at least some measure of oppression, corruption, and economic turbulence is to be found? If a proverbial saying carries truth, it will transcend its own time and place. That is why the Teacher chose the sayings that he did, and that is why his little collection retains its ability to stimulate its readers to this day. Whether it was committed to writing around 1,000 BC or closer to the year "dot," it remains abidingly relevant and topical to the third millennium AD.

COMMENTARY

Thesis

The thesis statement of Ecclesiastes is presented at the beginning (1:2) and at the end (12:8). "Vanity of vanities" is an example of the Hebrew way of expressing something to the nth degree, like calling the holiest place "The Holy of Holies" (Exod 26:34) or the greatest song "The Song of Songs" (Cant 1:1). Thus the Teacher is putting forward the most profound sense of vanity imaginable. "Utter vanity" might be another way of saying it in English, but we need to be clear on which sense of the English word "vanity" is applicable here: it is not the phenomenon of overweening pride that is in view, but the nuance of purposelessness or lack of achievement — that is to say, everything is ultimately "in vain," worthless, futile.

The key Hebrew word that translators struggle with here is *hebel,* literally "breath" or "vapor," and evidently in Ecclesiastes carrying a figurative meaning of transience and insubstantiality, or more particularly of emptiness and futility; hence the NRSV's choice of "vanity." It seems to be the Teacher's favorite word since he frequently uses it to label whatever frustrates or irritates him, such as his supposedly grand achievements in life (2:11), the ultimate leveling of all life in death (3:19), the unhappy lot of various people (4:8), the insatiable desires of the human heart (5:10), the inequities of the divine scheme of things (6:2), the laughter of fools (7:6), the injustices to which people are subject (8:14), and so on. This spread of examples illustrates that the word recurs and reverberates throughout the entire treatise. The "all is vanity" of the thesis statement (1:2; 12:8) is reflected in similar statements elsewhere (e.g., 1:14; 2:11; 3:19) and is underpinned by the comment on various matters that "This also is vanity" (e.g., 2:19; 4:8; 5:10). Sometimes the specific idea of transience seems particularly relevant to the Teacher's usage of the word, notably in the sayings concerning a miscarried fetus (6:4) and the fleetingness of youth (11:10), and the expressions regarding "the few days of one's life of vanity" (6:12) and "all the days of your life of vanity" (9:9), but in most cases it seems rather a catchall term for whatever is deemed to be unsatisfactory about human life and experience.

On several occasions the Teacher links his keyword *hebel* with another expression to flesh out the idea. The most frequent collocation is "vanity and a chasing after wind," the latter phrase — which can also be translated as "a feeding on wind" or "a desire for wind" — clearly denoting an aimless and futile striving after something transitory and unattainable, the empty pursuit of the insubstantial. It is applied to all human activity (1:14; 2:17), including all of the author's own accomplishments (2:11), the accumulation of goods which are turned over to someone else (2:26), a person's envy of what other people have (4:4; 6:9), and the succession of initially promising but inevitably disappointing rulers (4:16). The expression "chasing after wind" also occurs without "vanity" in 1:17, where it is applied to a fruitless quest for discernment between wisdom and foolishness, and in 4:6, where it goes hand in hand with a great expenditure of effort when in fact restfulness would have been the better option.

But restfulness is not much in evidence in Ecclesiastes. Another recurring word is "toil," introduced immediately after "vanity" in 1:3, where the Teacher sets up the rhetorical question that he will seek to answer in what follows, repeating the question in similar terms on three later occasions (2:22; 3:9; 5:16). His contention is that there is no ultimate gain or advantage in any human toil, insofar as chance events can undermine a person's accomplishments at any moment and in any case death will eventually and certainly undo everything one has achieved; yet it is the human predicament that we must expend effort to survive and perchance to flourish for a time. This verdict of uselessness is pronounced on his own toil (2:11, 20) and on everyone else's as well (5:15-16), but he foresees no cessation of the sad treadmill in human society (4:8; 6:7), and indeed the suggestively oppressive repetition of noun and verb in the phrase "the toil at which one toils" reiterates the gloomy scene (e.g., 1:3; 2:18, 22), while two verses which depict human restlessness in its most nightmarish clothes are 2:23 and 8:16.

One particularly famous passage of Ecclesiastes, the poem on everything having its season (3:1-8), fits into this theme of ceaseless human activity as well. Although some readers prefer to view this poem in a rosy perspective of all things fitting into their own good time, the Teacher's own comment (in 3:9-10) demonstrates that he sees these times as simply containing "busyness" that keeps everyone busy, but without any gain for those who toil away at the various activities. The style of the poem itself, in which forceful contrasts such as birth and death or construction and destruction are juxtaposed in quick succession, suggests that activities and counteractivities cut across each other in a sequence of constant change. The rhetorical question of 3:9 is thus in effect, "What advantage accrues to the person who has to undergo this incessant routine of planting/plucking/killing/healing/wrecking/building/weeping/laughing/mourning/dancing/scattering/gathering/embracing/refraining/seeking/losing/keeping/discarding/tearing/sewing/hushing/speaking/loving/hating/fighting/pacifying?" and the implied answer is "No permanent advantage or satisfaction can be gained from toiling in a world marked by such maddening ambivalence!"

The world as a whole, and not just the realm of certain human activities, is shot through with signs of restlessness and circularity, according to the Teacher, whose opening poem (1:3-11) depicts ceaseless, goalless cycles in all of creation. The sun is constantly going up and down, the wind is rushing "round and round," and the water cycle is in perpetual motion; all three agents get no rest from their labors — the sun, for example, has to "hurry" back (the Hebrew verb actually means to "gasp" or "pant") to start all over again (1:5) — and they have no appreciable gain for their efforts — the rivers, for example, never achieve their objective of filling the sea (1:7). The processes of nature are so wearisome in their monotony and pointlessness that the matter cannot adequately be put into words (1:8), though the Teacher makes an attempt at it with the pithy saying "there is nothing new under the sun" (1:9).

"Under the sun" is a much-used phrase in this book (e.g., 1:3; 2:11; 4:1), occasionally expressed alternatively as "under heaven" (1:13; 2:3; 3:1). It denotes of course the realm of human experience. The Teacher also refers to another realm, namely, "heaven," where God dwells (5:2), but that is a place beyond human experience and knowledge. The book takes for granted that God exists, but the gulf between the divine and the human is so large that people can know very little about what God is like — does he love us or hate us, for example? (9:1) — or what he is up to in the things that he does — some teachers may claim to know about divine matters, but this Teacher knows that they know nothing (8:17). All we really know about God is that he has set up the subsolar system in which we are caught (1:13; 3:10) and that he has deliberately kept from us any real understanding of the meaning of that system (3:11; 7:14) and any ability to reshape it to meet our own desires or interests (3:14; 7:13). He is simply to be feared (3:14; 5:7; 8:12-13).

That the Teacher focuses his attention on this world "under the sun," remote from God, does not imply that he looks forward to a human afterlife lived with God in heaven. In common with the Hebrew Bible (HB) as a whole, he does not believe in life after death. On the contrary, he is sure that death is the end for all creatures on earth (3:18-19). The breath of life that God grants for a time to each individual creature is eventually withdrawn or taken back by the Creator (12:7), and the creature inevitably returns to the dust from which it had been formed (3:20). There is an evident allusion in these matters to the old creation story in Gen 2:7, but there is also a reference to a newfangled idea that the fate of humans might differ from that of other animals — an idea which the Teacher rejects (3:21) in favor of the traditional notion that there is no life after death (9:5, 10).

Certain other traditional notions, however, are not affirmed in this book. Despite the assertion that the writer held office in Israel (1:12), there are no signs of such standard Israelite concepts as the religious law (apart from a mention of divine commandments in the epilogue at 12:13) or the idea that God has acted powerfully in Israel's past and will do so again in Israel's future. The name of Israel's God, Yahweh (or "the Lord," as NRSV renders it), is absent from Ecclesiastes, almost uniquely in the HB. Esther and the Song of Songs make no explicit mention of God by any name, but all the other books frequently use the personal name of the deity worshiped in Jerusalem, so the avoidance of that name in this particular book — which purports to have been written in Jerusalem — is significant. This Teacher is definitely not a teacher of the law of the Lord, as may be seen from the fact that he comes no closer to upholding the legal traditions of Israel than to say that people should fulfill what they vow (5:4; cf. Deut 23:21), and he actually contradicts the Mosaic law when he advises young people to follow their heart's desires while they have the chance (11:9; cf. Num 15:39). He has no time for the sacrificial system that dominated religious life in Jerusalem (5:1), and he has no faith in the dominant scriptural contention that God rewards the righteous and punishes the wicked (7:15; 8:14).

It is this last observation that lies at the heart of the Teacher's thinking. He had apparently thought at one time in traditional terms of divinely ordained justice for the righteous and the wicked (3:17), but his acute observations of the world had undermined that picture. He saw that wickedness flourished (3:16) and God did not intervene (4:1), that there was no correlation between what people did and what happened to them (9:11-12), and thus that there was no ultimate advantage in being righteous (9:2) — or, to put it another way, that there is no decisive use in attempting to live wisely (2:15; 6:8). He had represented his own quest as a search for wisdom (1:17), and the epilogist acknowledges him as a teacher of wisdom (12:9, 11, in which verses the word "wise" may well denote a professional sage), so his admission that this quest had been fruitless (1:17; 2:15) and his assertion that such a quest can never be anything but fruitless (8:17) are strikes against traditional wisdom by one of its own practitioners. Here is a Teacher steeped in the wisdom traditions of ancient Israel who is saying that, far from helping a person discover answers to the questions of life, wisdom only makes things worse (1:18), insofar as it is attainable at all (7:23-24).

Such, then, is the rather dark and distressing thesis of the book of Ecclesiastes. Its colors are probably painted darkest of all at 9:3, but in a sense everything that is written between 1:2 and 12:8 may be seen as variations on the theme that "all is vanity."

Antithesis

There is another side to the Teacher's coin. Mixed in among the gloomy pronouncements about toil and trouble come some considerably brighter spots, which are all the more noticeable on account of their darker surroundings. It is as though an inner dialogue were going on in the author's mind, since a seemingly opposite point of view is put forward at intervals throughout the book.

From this alternative standpoint, wisdom does not appear to be so ineffectual after all. It is a far greater prize than foolishness (2:13) since it is a more certain guide in life (2:14), both for ordinary folk and for rulers (4:13). It is worthwhile for admonishing those who might be tempted by folly (7:5), for facilitating economic prudence among those who might fritter away their possessions (7:11), and for granting an immeasurably richer life to those who have this one essential possession, namely, wisdom itself (7:12). If people have wisdom, then whatever situation they are in is appreciably improved (7:19; 9:15), since it is a quality far superior to any other supposed strength among humankind, such as having the loudest voice or the biggest gun (9:16-18). The wise are successful in life (10:10, 12) because they have a decided advantage over foolish people (10:2), not least in their ability to know when they are in the right place and the right time for certain courses of action (8:5). Wisdom is in fact so beneficial, and so enlightening, that it makes a person's face glow with confidence and satisfaction (8:1).

It seems that life is not so bad after all. It can be very pleasant indeed (11:7), and there is at least always hope, no matter how humble one's circumstances (9:4). It turns out that we live in a world in which prudent or thoughtful actions do bring rewards (11:1), and comfort can be taken from the traditional religious teaching that God blesses those who deserve to be blessed and curses those who deserve to be cursed (8:12-13). There are solid grounds for banishing anxiety from one's mind and embracing life in all its fullness (11:10).

The key statement of this antithesis in the book of Ecclesiastes is met with in several variations on the theme of "eat, drink, and enjoy yourself." This theme is first introduced in 2:24, at the end of the Teacher's account of his life's quest. It pops up again in 3:12-13, after the poem on the changing times, and is reiterated shortly afterward in an abbreviated form (without mention of eating and drinking) in 3:22, following the discussion of human and animal similarities. It reappears in 5:18, where the Teacher had been pointing to a situation in which people lost the wealth they had amassed; it is placed before the reader once more in 8:15, where he had been considering matters of righteousness and wickedness; and it makes its final appearance at somewhat greater length in 9:7-9, in the context of the lack of guarantees about how life will treat various types of people. It bears the hallmarks of being a conclusion drawn after sundry considerations throughout the book, a matter affirmed and reaffirmed after each twist and turn of the thesis, a counterperspective to respond to the reiterated theme of "vanity."

Three of these passages commending enjoyment phrase the matter in terms of a Hebrew phrase meaning "there is nothing better than . . ." (3:12, 22; 8:15), thus setting forth what the Teacher regards as the best policy in life. More literally, the Hebrew phrase says "there is no good, except . . . ," which shows that this is the answer to the question the Teacher had set himself concerning "what was good" for people to do during their lives (2:3). He confirms this finding with the way he expresses matters in 5:18, where he sets out again what he has "seen to be good," namely, these simple pleasures in life of eating and drinking and enjoying oneself. Yet when he first raises the issue, at 2:24, he appears less sure since he actually says (contrary to the NRSV) that "There is no good for mortals in eating and drinking and finding enjoyment in their toil," which sounds like the pessimism of the thesis rather than the optimism of the antithesis. The NRSV is probably following the right instinct in pretending that the Hebrew equivalent of "except" is in the phrase in 2:24, as it is on the other three occasions itemized above, and thus rendering this instance, too, as "There is nothing better than . . . ," bringing it into line with the teaching expressed elsewhere in the book.

Apart from that slip of the pen, if that is what it is, 2:24 is in agreement with the sentiments expressed on the other occasions, including the important follow-up clause which makes reference to the God-givenness of the situation. The advice that one should take pleasure in eating, drinking, and enjoying oneself is constantly validated by an assurance to the reader that such pleasures come "from the hand of God" (2:24) or that they are "God's gift" to us (3:13), the "lot" or portion that the Creator has given to his creatures (3:22; 5:18; 8:15), or that they represent a joyful attitude to life that the deity has approved (9:7). God is occupied with placing joy in the human heart — and enough of it to last a lifetime (5:20)!

Thus the divinely sanctioned imperative for human beings, the one real commandment that the Teacher places before the reader, is: "Enjoy life!" (9:9). He counsels that life is likely to be most enjoyable if one has a companion with which to share it (9:9 again), since after all companionship and solidarity bring many advantages (4:9-12), and of course having good fortune of various kinds will not go amiss in life either (7:11; 10:19). But worrying and waiting for conditions to be just right are not sensible (11:4). People should rather seize the present, for whatever opportunities come along are there to be grasped (9:10), and it would be foolish to hold back from making the most of them (4:5).

Such, then, is the rather bright and cheerful antithesis of the book of Ecclesiastes. Its colors are probably painted whitest of all at 9:8, but in a sense every subject that is talked about in the book seems to keep ending up in the advice to "eat, drink, and enjoy yourself."

Synthesis

What are we to make of the book of Ecclesiastes after all these repeated twists and turns in the Teacher's presentation? Some readers have made one thing, and others quite another, by focusing either on the thesis or alternatively on the antithesis. Accordingly, there are interpretations of the book that see the dark side as completely dominant, thus representing the Teacher's message as concerning the unremitting meaninglessness of life, and there are interpretations that regard the bright side as the essential element, thus summarizing the message as having to do with an unbridled joyfulness in life.

Neither of those one-sided alternatives is entirely satisfactory in encapsulating the book's teaching. Nor, for that matter, is the early attempt at a kind of summary of the book that is made by the epilogist, who, after expressing his admiration for — and feelings of unease about — this book (12:9-11) and books in general (12:12), has tried to suggest that it should all end in a rather more traditional and pious conclusion (12:13-14) than the one with which it had seemed to end. The Teacher's sayings had culminated in a beautifully evocative but deeply disturbing description of breakdown and cessation in human life (12:1-7) and a restatement of the thesis that "all is vanity" (12:8), making that keyword "vanity" the last one to be heard from the Teacher himself, just as it had been his very first word in 1:2.

But taking "the words of the Teacher" (1:1) as a whole, a thoughtful reader need not think that a choice must be made between the supposedly pessimistic words and the apparently optimistic words, as many interpreters have done down the centuries, in some cases regarding one set of words as those which the Teacher affirms and the other set as the teachings of others with whom he disagrees. In fact, the thesis and antithesis can be readily synthesized, as each is related to the other in the development of an honest and endurable, well-rounded approach to life: on the one hand, the Teacher found no ultimate answers to the Big Questions of life, but, on the other, he did find that the simple pleasures of life can make those questions less relevant. This synthesis is perhaps most clearly expressed at 5:20, which says that enjoying the time that has been allotted to a person is the way one can avoid spending one's time brooding over the brevity and inscrutability of life, and at 8:15, where a simple exclamation says it all: the Teacher shows that he has found the answer to that overwhelming "vanity" of which he is so aware by exclaiming in regard to his commendation of enjoyment that "*this* will go with them!" *this* is the thing that can sustain people through their life of toil under the sun.

This is the point at which the Teacher arrived after his long journey to discover wisdom. It was a journey with highs and lows, and he wanted his readers to see both aspects clearly. Life is complex, and it will not do either to pretend that there is no darkness (7:2) or to imagine that there is no light (10:19). The wisest path is a middle way that recognizes the manifold vanities of life on the one hand and the value of the simple pleasures of life on the other. But for the most forceful and potentially shocking presentation of the Teacher's general advocacy of a middle way through life, the reader must look to 7:15-18, where the advice is given that, just as people should not be too wicked or too foolish for their own good, so too they should not seek to be very righteous or very wise, since they may well receive nothing but ruination for all their efforts. For the best results in life (according to v. 18) — although of course the Teacher offers no guarantees — a person should hold fast to "the one" rule of behavior (the avoidance of extreme righteousness and cleverness) just as surely as not abandoning "the other" rule of behavior (the avoidance of extreme wickedness and foolishness).

It is a striking piece of advice, in the middle of a book of wisdom in the middle of the Bible, that one should no more strive to be highly righteous or wise than one should strive to be highly wicked or foolish (though the NRSV softens matters a little by interpreting one of the parallel expressions as "do not *act* too wise"). But the balancing of thoughts in this manner is typical of the Teacher, who also speaks of "the one" type of good thing that God does for people and "the other" type of bad thing that he does (7:14), and who describes his own enterprise as a consideration of "one thing" as well as "another" in order to see the complete picture (7:27) — though the picture he paints at that point, with a very bleak assessment of his fellow human beings (7:28) and especially of women (7:26), is not an appealing one and does him no credit.

Overall, though, the picture that is presented in Ecclesiastes is that life can be endlessly frustrating and is ultimately inscrutable, but nevertheless the simple joys of life, eating and drinking and companionship, are to be prized as the things which can make it enjoyable. This book sets before the reader the notion of how silly it is to spend your life rushing about restlessly and eagerly in efforts to heap up wealth or acquire honors, forever wanting more and more and never being satisfied, and, by the same token, how silly it is to increase the troubles of life by denying yourself the enjoyment of harmless and indeed recommended pleasures that are a gift from the Creator to his creatures. "Avoid both extremes" is the advice that Ecclesiastes gives. Do not try to make life an unbridled feast or an unmitigated fast. It will have its good times and its bad times, and it is full of uncertainties, but one thing is certain: you will only make it worse for yourself if you do not cultivate an attitude of contentment with those simple joys of life.

Addendum: Two Popular Passages (3:1-15 and 12:1-7)

The best-known sections in the book of Ecclesiastes, two particularly evocative passages which stand out for many readers and which thus merit some additional comments, have to do with the passage of time. The first is the famous "Catalogue of Times" and associated remarks in 3:1-15, and the second is the equally renowned "Allegory of Old Age" in 12:1-7.

The "Catalogue of Times" (3:1-8) and the remarks which the Teacher appends to it (3:9-15) demonstrate well the various themes that have been itemized above. As the comments under the Thesis section made clear, the concept of ceaseless human activity yielding no permanent advantage or satisfaction is writ large in this passage; yet as the comments under the Antithesis section revealed, this is at the same time one of the key passages for the concept of the divinely approved policy of eating, drinking, and enjoying oneself. So too, in the very nature of the cataloguing of activities and counteractivities, the Teacher illustrates his method of considering "one thing" alongside "another," a method outlined in the comments under the Synthesis section.

The sequence of pairs of contrasting times in 3:2-8 is finely crafted. The series begins with birth and death, the parameters of each life and the aspects over which the individual has the least control and comprehension, and it ends with war and peace, the only nouns in the list and in a sense a summation of all the verbs that are used to characterize various activities thoughout the catalogue. On the one side of the ledger stand such things as birth, planting and building, laughing and dancing, seeking and keeping, speaking and loving — in general, it might be said, being at peace with oneself and the world — and on the other side are placed such things as death, uprooting and destroying, weeping and mourning, losing and throwing away, keeping silent and hating — in general, being at war with oneself and the world.

Within these rounds of multifarious activities certain compositional patterns may be detected. In 3:2 the procreation and curtailment of human life is matched with the human activities of facilitating and terminating plant life. Similarly, in v. 3, bringing about a person's death and alternatively healing wounds or other inflictions has a parallel in bringing about a building's destruction and alternatively constructing or rebuilding one. There is an evident relationship between the two lines of v. 4, as also between the two lines of v. 6; so, too, the two halves of v. 8 are obviously related, though in this last case the second line reverses the order of the first, presumably so as to end on the good note of peace. Perhaps less obvious are the affinities in v. 7, but if all four activities there are understood in the light of ancient mourning customs of rending one's garments and observing a period of forbidden speech, and sewing up the rent and speaking again after the mourning period has passed, then these activities, too, may be seen as firmly linked. Only v. 5 remains as something of a puzzle, but if the ancient rabbinic interpretation (recorded in *Midrash Qohelet*) is accepted that "scattering stones" is used symbolically of sexual intercourse and "gathering stones" of abstinence, then the first half of this verse is eminently connectable with the second half concerning "embracing" and "refraining from embracing" and thus is seen to contain the same internal pattern as all the other verses in the catalogue.

While these patterns suggest considerable artistry on the part of the writer, they do not suggest that he sees any grand purpose in the overall scheme of "every matter under heaven" (3:1). The basic pattern remains one of every situation being transformed into its opposite; the only constant is that the times are constantly changing in endlessly repetitive cycles. As the Teacher remarks a few verses later (at v. 15), "That which is, already has been; that which is to be, already is; and God seeks out what is pursued" (NRSV, "what has gone by"). That expression "what is pursued" is a puzzling phrase, but it can be invested with an attractive nuance in the context of the catalogue of times, where each particular time is followed by its opposite number with such a pace (usually there are only two words in each Hebrew phrase) that one can well imagine the latter time in each case chasing the former out of the way, only to be pushed off the scene again by its opposite. Acts and events occur continually, each pursuing the other in a revolving circle: a time of weeping, for example, is nudged out of the way by a time of laughter, until it is itself brought back by God for a time, before being driven away again. Like the sun going down and hurrying to the place where it will rise again (1:5) or the wind returning on its circuits (1:6), the endless cycles will go on and on.

Something of this endlessness is perhaps glimpsed in 3:11, where the Teacher says that God "has put eternity in their hearts" (NRSV, "has put a sense of past and future into their minds"), an expression juxtaposed with the phrase "yet so that they cannot find out the work that God has done from beginning to end," suggesting that the former has much to do with the human desire to achieve the latter. In 7:27-28 the Teacher records that he wanted to find out "the sum" of things, but he could not; and in 8:17 he notes that people seek to find out "all the work of God . . . that is done under the sun," but they cannot. 3:11 makes excellent sense as a kind of parallel to these two verses. Human beings have "eternity" in their hearts: their Creator has made them thinking beings, and so they want to know how everything fits together, to see things in their full context, to pass beyond their fragmentary knowledge and to discern the fuller meaning of the whole pattern. But the Creator will not let the creature be his equal: as surely as he has put "eternity" in the human heart — a consciousness that there is more than the immediate "time" of this or that (vv. 2-8) in which the creature finds itself — he has also put a veil upon the human heart so that the finite human mind is unable to reach beyond the "times" into "eternity" to see as God does. Although this is not the way human beings might like it, God "has made everything beautiful in its time" (NRSV, "suitable for its time") — that is, the Deity has created the whole setup in such a way that nothing happens in the world sooner or later than he wants it to happen (cf. Gen 1:31, "God saw everything that he had made, and it was very good," because it corresponded exactly to what he intended).

That time is not on the side of human beings becomes obvious in that other famous passage in Ecclesiastes, namely, the "Allegory of Old Age" in 12:1-7. Here are described certain forthcoming "days of trouble" (v. 1), and there is general agreement among interpreters, both in ancient and in modern times, that these "days of trouble" are the days of advancing old age and approaching death, depicted by means of various allegorical descriptions of the state of an old person. There is, however, no agreement on the details of the allegory, with some readers claiming that the approach of death is pictured primarily as an advancing storm, others seeing it rather in terms of the fall of night, and yet others identifying the main image as the decay of a wealthy estate. There are also readers who regard the passage as dealing, not with the decline and death of a representative individual human person, but rather with the general propensity of everything we know to break down and decay.

Nevertheless, the most enduring interpretation of the passage is to take the various items as images of the failing of specific organs of the body. This common allegorical reading is well illustrated by the targum to Ecclesiastes, which begins in 12:2 by interpreting the sun as an image of the brightness of the face, the moon as a picture of the cheeks, and the stars as a reference to the pupils of the eye, all of which are affected by the aging process, while "clouds" and "rain" mean the eyelids and tears. In v. 3 the "guards of the house" who now tremble are the old person's knees, the "strong men" who now become bent are the arms, the "grinding women" who become few and cease grinding are the teeth, and "those who look through the windows" are the eyes. The doors being shut in v. 4 is paraphrased by the targumist as having to do with an elderly person being prevented from going into the street, "grinding" is again taken as referring to the chewing of food, and "the daughters of song" who are brought low are said to be the lips which, being aged, are no longer able to sing as they did when they were young. In the case of the enigmatic references in v. 5 to the almond tree, grasshopper, and caperberry (NRSV, "desire"), the targumic interpretation is that "the top of your hipbone will come out from leanness like the almond, the ankles of your feet will be swelled, and you will be hindered from rest." And even more graphic portrayals of bodily deterioration are given as the unpicking of the metaphors in v. 6: "your tongue will become dumb, and the brain in your head will be dashed in pieces, and the gall in your liver will be broken, and your body will hasten into the grave."

Whatever precise interpretations are given to the various images in this passage, there is little doubt that it is a moving — and perhaps even chilling — picture that the Teacher paints here, ending it in v. 7 with a depiction of death as an undoing of the creative act pictured in Genesis (Gen 2:7; 3:19). Little wonder that he presents this as the last thing that he has to say, following it immediately with the short restatement of his thesis in v. 8, and no more (though the book as we have it carries on just a little more with the epilogist's words of 12:9-14). Death is the end of the matter; all has been heard. Enjoy life while you may, for although "eternity" is in your mind (3:11), it is not in your body (12:7).

Bibliography. Barton, G. A. 1908, *The Book of Ecclesiastes,* ICC, Edinburgh: T. & T. Clark • Brown, W. P. 2000, *Ecclesiastes,* Interpretation, Louisville: John Knox • Crenshaw, J. L. 1988, *Ecclesiastes,* OTL, Philadelphia: Westminster; London: SCM • Fox, M. V. 1999, *A Time to Tear Down and a Time to Build Up: A Rereading of Ecclesiastes,* Grand Rapids: Eerdmans • Fredericks, D. C. 1993, *Coping with Transience: Ecclesiastes on Brevity in Life,* Sheffield: JSOT • Gordis, R. 3d ed. 1968, *Koheleth — The Man and His World: A Study of Ecclesiastes,* New York: Schocken • Lohfink, N. 2003, *Qoheleth,* A Continental Commentary, Minneapolis: Fortress • Murphy, R. 1992, *Ecclesiastes,* WBC, Dallas: Word • Ogden, G. S. 1987, *Qoheleth,* Readings: A New Biblical Commentary, Sheffield: JSOT • Plumptre, E. H. 1881, *Ecclesiastes, or The Preacher,* Cambridge: Cambridge University • Seow, C. H. 1997, *Ecclesiastes,* AB, New York: Doubleday • Whybray, R. N. 1989, *Ecclesiastes,* NCBC, Grand Rapids: Eerdmans.

Song of Songs

John W. Rogerson

INTRODUCTION

Why is the Song of Songs (SoS) in the Bible? It contains no reference to God and can be read as a not particularly subtle set of references to sexual liaisons between a man and a woman. The question can be broken down into two questions which are not unrelated: (1) Why was the final product included in a collection of religious texts? (2) How did the final product come to be written/compiled? The answer usually given to the first question is that from the first half of the first century BC Jewish interpreters took the book to be a description of God's dealings with Israel. Yet the allegorical interpretation of SoS was more likely an attempt to justify the fact that it had already been accepted into the collection of sacred texts than the means by which it came to be accepted.

If this reasoning is correct, it becomes necessary to look for a connection between the composition/compilation of the book and its inclusion in the collection of sacred texts. This takes us into an area in which there are gaps in our knowledge and where the evidence is at best circumstantial. Hans-Peter Müller has attempted more explicitly than anyone else to suggest a situation and date for the author/compiler (Müller 1992: 4-5). According to Müller, the circle that produced SoS in its final form was an upper class in third-century-BC Jerusalem that had lost political power, had become indifferent to the official religion, and sought to rejuvenate its aesthetic and spiritual understanding of life by drawing on pagan mythical and magical symbols that were known in "wisdom" circles. Müller does not deny that SoS is about sexual love, but his commentary constantly points out how details in the poems can be seen as allusions to pagan deities and symbols.

Although Müller's approach is illuminating, it contains the difficulty that it is hard to see how his suggested circle could get SoS into the collection of sacred texts if, as he points out (p. 5), the circle was a small group at the edge of and in opposition to the mainstream of tradition in Jerusalem at the time. It is safer to think of a literary, upper-class group or individual with sufficient standing to enable a text whose treatment of sexual love was bound to have a wide appeal to gain acceptance by the religious establishment.

From this standpoint it is possible to inquire into the sources and origins of the poems in SoS. Similarities between SoS and love poems from Sumeria, ancient Egypt, and nineteenth-century-AD Syria/Palestine have been noted, and conclusions have been drawn such as that SoS is to be interpreted as a sacred or secular marriage ritual. However, what these similarities show is that when all allowance has been made for the way in which gender roles are culturally shaped, evidence exists, at any rate in the ancient and modern Near East, that people have deep-seated sexual desires, longings, and frustrations which have been expressed in love poems, which in turn have had a wide and lasting appeal.

At this point it is worth considering some of the distinctions made by modern sociological study of sexuality and love (Giddens 1992). Two are relevant: passionate love and romantic love. According to Giddens (p. 37), passionate love is

> marked by an urgency which sets it apart from the routines of everyday life in which, indeed, it tends to come into conflict. The emotional involvement with the other is pervasive — so strong that it may lead the individual, or both individuals, to ignore their ordinary obligations. Passionate love has a quality of enchantment which can be religious in its fervour. Everything in the world seems suddenly fresh. . . .

These words certainly make sense of two aspects of SoS: the uninhibited exuberance of expression in statements such as "You have ravished my heart, my sister, my bride, you have ravished my heart with a glance of your eyes . . ." (4:9). But there is also a deep sense of conflict in SoS between the demands of love and the institutional constraints and duties laid upon the lovers. In particular, the watchmen of the city (rendered "sentinels" in the NRSV at 3:3; 5:7) represent institutional conventions that frustrate the woman's search for her lover, while at 8:1 the woman wishes that her lover were her brother, in which case she would be able to kiss him in public and take him to her room without any public disapproval.

According to Giddens (40-46), romantic love goes beyond mere sexual ardor and concerns itself with what might loosely be called the spiritual side of mutual relationships, in the sense of being attracted to another because of virtues and sublime traits of character that are perceived in the other. Giddens further observes, from the way in which romantic love was written about in eighteenth- and nineteenth-century Britain, that it was a feminized love: "Ideas about romantic love were plainly allied to women's [*sic*] subordination in the home, and her relative separation from the outside world. But the development of such ideas [of compassionate love] was also an expression of women's [*sic*] power, a contradictory assertion of autonomy in the face of deprivation" (43).

While there are obvious dangers in reading back eighteenth- and nineteenth-century Western attitudes into SoS, two observations can be made. The first is that although there are references to sexual relations in SoS, they are covert, and the material can be read as expressing a wish for companionship as well as a desire for physical love. Keel (1984) has argued that phrases such as "your eyes are doves" (1:15) may refer to inner rather than to outer characteristics. Second, there is an undoubted feminine priority in SoS. The woman is not a passive partner in the relationship, and one of her desires is to bring her lover into *her* sphere of power (3:4; 8:2).

All that has been said above about passionate and romantic love must now be seen in the light of the fact that for probably the majority of men and women in human history these types of love have been available only in the form of fantasy and fiction. The lack of fit between the organization of societies (especially in the way men have controlled women) and the sexual and emotional desires of men and women has given rise to oral and written literature that has become a substitute for unfulfilled wishes of various (including pornographic) kinds.

The view taken in what follows is that SoS is a collection of poems or fragments of poems that express sublime aspects of passionate and romantic love as perceived in ancient Judah, and that they were included in the collection of sacred texts because of their sublime expression of harmony and mutuality between two people — a simplicity and sincerity that was at the same time a criticism of the constraints and corruptions of aspects of human institutions. In this regard, writers such as Trible (1978) are correct in seeing SoS as a countertext to the account of the breakdown of mutual human relationships in Genesis 3.

A matter that has been considerably discussed in the past twenty years is whether SoS is a literary unity; but whereas differing schemes of intended literary organization of the material have been proposed by writers such as Exum (1973), Shea (1980), and Heinevetter (1988), they have not been adjudged to be totally convincing. It cannot be denied that the two similar poems, 3:1-5 and 5:2-7, have a central, and perhaps even structurally balancing, position in the work, and that refrains and repeated material appear at 2:7; 3:5; 5:8; 8:4 ("I adjure you, O daughters of Jerusalem . . ."); 2:6; 8:3 ("O that his left hand were under my head . . ."), and 2:16; 7:10 ("I am my beloved's . . ."). Whether they can be used to demonstrate literary unity is another matter, and the possibility cannot be ruled out that some material has been deliberately excised for theological or other reasons (Müller 1992: 45). In this commentary literary unity will not be assumed.

Another matter that has been discussed, especially following the work of Horst (1935/1961), has been the form-critical study of SoS. Horst's categories, such as poem of wonderment (e.g., 7:7-10), poem of longing (2:14), or poem of description (of the beloved) (4:1-7), are in many cases little more than rather obvious instances of content criticism, and recent work on SoS has been more concerned to look for literary unity than to break the work up into different categories. In the present commentary form-critical matters will not be stressed.

Modern Translations of SoS

Readers who do not have access to Hebrew are disadvantaged when reading SoS because in Hebrew it is clearer than in English whether a man is addressing a woman or vice versa. The RSV and NRSV do little to help readers here. On the other hand, the NEB and REB go too far in dividing the material among a bride, her bridegroom, and companions. The NIV (dividing the material among a lover, his beloved, and friends), NJB (lover, beloved, chorus, and poet), and GNB (man, woman, and women) are more helpful, although some of these words (e.g., lover and beloved) imply for modern readers passive/active, dominant/subordinate frameworks. The NJB and GNB also insert headings which impose on the text their view of where poems/songs begin and end.

COMMENTARY

1:1 *The Editorial Title.* The ascription of the work to Solomon by means of a title is similar to the ascription of many psalms to David, and is probably the work of editors who were involved in the later stages of putting the Bible into the form in which we have it. On the one hand, there are references to Solomon in the poems (e.g., 1:5; 3:7, 9, 11; 8:12), while 1 Kgs 4:32 (Heb., 5:12) credits him with the composition of 1,005 songs, using the same Hebrew word *shir* (meaning "song") as in this verse. The claim to Solomonic authorship was accepted by Jewish and Christian interpreters until the eighteenth century. The view of modern commentators is that the references to Solomon and the king are part of the fantasy world in terms of which the man and woman idealize their relationship.

1:2-4 These verses are probably a soliloquy by the woman in which she longs for the kisses of her lover, whom she then addresses in his absence. The reference in 1:4 to the king has been understood by some to mean that the woman had been taken into the king's harem. The most likely translation (Müller 1992: 12) is "let the king bring me into his chambers," which provides a parallel to "draw me after you." "King" is not to be taken literally but is part of the sensual vocabulary used by the lovers to praise each other's virtues. The first person plural "we will exult" probably refers to the woman and her lover rather than to maidens who accompany her. The woman imagines longingly the intimate and private contact that she might have in her lover's domain.

1:5-6 The woman's soliloquy probably continues as she addresses in her imagination the daughters of Jerusalem. Here and elsewhere they represent conventional attitudes, including here the ideal that beautiful women should be light-skinned. The *Genesis Apocryphon* from Qumran, usually dated to the second century BC, praises the beauty of Sarah with the words "how beautiful all her whiteness" (Vermes 1997: 454). In contrast, the woman justifies the dark complexion that the sun has given her in terms of natural beauty. In the reference to the tents of Kedar (the black tents of desert dwellers) there is a hint of the antagonism between the city, or civilization, and the life of the countryside. The woman's banishment to look after the family vineyards gave her opportunities for making herself ("my own vineyard," v. 6) available to her lover that she would not otherwise have had.

1:7-8 On the face of it, 1:7 is the direct address of the woman to her lover, while v. 8 is his reply. Yet it would be odd if the woman did not know where her lover pastured his flocks unless she had seen him only fleetingly. It is thus possible to see the verses as a continuation (or another instance) of the woman's soliloquy, expressing an imagined conversation. The meaning of "like one who is veiled" is problematic and has been much discussed, especially in view of the NEB/REB, "that I may not be left picking lice." A solution favored by many, and supported by the ancient versions, is to read *to'iyyah,* meaning "like one who wanders," for *'otiyyah,* meaning "veiled." If "veiled" is retained, it might indicate a disguise that could be mistaken for the attire of a prostitute, although it is not clear why the woman would need to be disguised or, indeed, to be veiled.

1:9-17 This passage is either a dialogue between the man (1:9-11, 15) and the woman (vv. 12-14, 16-17) or several fragments (vv. 9-11, 12, 13-14, 15-17; so Müller: 17-20). The NRSV, following the tradition of the AV, obscures the fact that the Hebrew word used by the man to describe the woman in vv. 9 and 15 ("my love" in the NRSV) is different from that used in vv. 13, 14, and 16 by the woman to describe the man ("my beloved" in the NRSV). Other modern translations prefer "darling" (NIV) or "dearest" (REB) for the former term. The Hebrew *(ra'yati)* has the sense of "friend" as in English girl/boy friend and indicates an informal relationship. The word used by the woman (Heb. *dodi*) has a stronger sense, well conveyed by "my beloved."

Modern readers will be struck by the exotic language used in the comparisons, the woman being likened to a royal Egyptian mare (1:9), the man to a cluster of henna blossoms (v. 14). In the former case the rich adornments of the mare may be in mind, while henna blossoms indicate exotic luxury. Also striking is the absence of the comparative particle "like" in the statement "Your eyes are doves" (v. 15). Keel has argued that physical organs can be symbols for inner attitudes (cf. the English use of "heart" as a symbol of the emotions), so that "eyes" here may mean "glances." For the most part, it is possible to accept that conventions are being used which, while strange to modern readers, can be appreciated by outsiders. The male is again described as king (v. 12). In vv. 16c-17 there appears to be a switch in setting from that evoked by vineyards (v. 14) to longed-for, settled luxury (the "switch" may simply indicate that vv. 15-17 are a separate fragment). The house (lit. "houses") is built of the finest materials; the couch (i.e., bed) is luxuriant (NRSV, "green"), a term that may denote abundant sexual productivity.

2:1-3 In these three verses there is a reciprocal dialogue spoken by the woman (2:1, 3) and the man (v. 2). The woman's self-description as an asphodel or narcissus (NRSV, "rose") and a lily is not sufficiently complimentary for the man, who states that she is like a lily among brambles. The woman then takes the idea of the distinctive plant and likens the man to a fruit tree (NRSV, "apple"; NEB, "apricot") in a wood. It provides both shelter (protection) and fruit (sexual pleasure).

2:4-7 The rendering "he brought me" (2:4), which accepts the medieval Hebrew voweling, is followed by all modern translations. However, a good case can be made for following the LXX, which implies the second person masculine plural imperative "bring me," which is also found in v. 5 in "sustain me" and "refresh me." If this path is followed, the second part of v. 4 will mean "let his intention toward me be love" and vv. 4-6 will be a poem of longing. If the translation "He brought me" is preferred, it is best to connect v. 4 with vv. 1-3. The identity of those addressed in the masculine plural ("sustain," "refresh," v. 5) is a problem, but one eased by the fact that the daughters of Jerusalem are addressed (v. 7) using the masculine plural "you" rather than its feminine plural equivalent in Hebrew. It can be assumed that in v. 5 (and v. 4 if the revocalization as an imperative is accepted) the woman is speaking in fact or fantasy to her female companions. She longs to be taken to her lover's wine house (NRSV, "banqueting house"), where she will enjoy physical contact (v. 6) and food and drink that will arouse passions (vv. 4-5).

2:7 recurs elsewhere in SoS (cf. 3:5; 8:4) and provides several problems. The first is that of the identity of the speaker, taken by the NEB and REB, for example, to be the man. The Hebrew does not indicate the gender of the speaker; decisive may be the fact that at 3:5; 8:4 the speaker is most naturally the woman, although the NEB and REB assign these verses to "the bridegroom." The second matter is in the form of the oath. The Hebrew consonants are very close indeed to an oath that would adjure the women "by the God of hosts and God Almighty." They can also be translated "by the spirits and goddesses of the field" (REB). We simply do not know whether an oath referring to God has been altered out of consideration for avoiding the divine name, or whether the translation "by the gazelles or the wild does" is meant to be in harmony with the rustic imagery of SoS. The verse appears to caution against attempts to create passions artificially, for example, by the use of wine or aphrodisiacs.

2:8-14 In spite of the argument that the references to stag and gazelle in 2:9 and 17 form an *inclusio* that shows vv. 8-17 to be a literary unit, only vv. 8-14 will be accepted here as a unit. They form one of the most beautiful poems in the whole Bible and have inspired not only popular and folk songs but also church anthems such as S. S. Wesley's "My Beloved Spake." The poem is probably a soliloquy on the part of the woman, with the speech of the man (vv. 10b-14) being what the woman imagines. The opening verses are full of energy in the Hebrew, with the use of participles (leaping, bounding) and wordplay on *ṣebi,* which means both "gazelle" and "beauty." The woman pictures herself as confined to her (mother's) house and thrills at the thought of her lover coming to seek her. He seems to be barred from admittance, but she hears his voice urging her to leave the house and to come away with him. The portrayal of the season as spring, with its freshness, new colors, and sounds, appeals to the profound impression that nature can make on humans at certain times and in certain situations. Perhaps it is the onset of spring that arouses in the woman a deep longing for freedom and for companionship with a lover, away from the restrictions of her home.

2:15 It is not easy to identify the speaker or the (masculine plural) persons addressed ("catch us"), nor can the verse be convincingly interpreted in relation to the material that precedes and follows it. "Foxes" may refer to young men, and "vineyards" to young women. The background may be mating or similar games (cf. Judg 21:20-23, where the Benjaminites hide in the vineyards and seek wives from among the young women of Shiloh who come out to dance). It is difficult to say more.

2:16-17 These verses contain memorable phrases without conveying any certainty of interpretation. 2:16a, "My beloved is mine . . . ," has been used to express the relationship between God or Christ and believers in hymns, and works such as Bach's church cantatas. The AV of v. 17, "until the day break and the shadows flee away," evokes the coming of morning and the beginning of life (even of the hereafter), even though the words can also be taken to refer to evening rather than morning. The statements about the man pasturing his flock (or feeding himself) among the lilies and the invitation to him to be a young stag on the mountains of Bether (v. 17c; NRSV, "the cleft mountains") are problematic. V. 17 *may* mean something like: when morning comes, leave me and become like a gazelle or young stag (i.e., return to your duties but be ready to return to me); but certainty is impossible.

3:1-5 This is one of two similar and central poems in SoS (cf. 5:2-8) in which the yearning and imagining of the woman reach a sublime high-point. The fact that 3:1 states that the woman sought her lover upon her bed does not entail that these verses describe a dream (although 5:2-8 may well be a dream). Many thoughts pass through people's minds as they lie awake at night, and they may well partly recall things that actually happened. It is not impossible that the woman had roamed the streets seeking her lover (modern readers must remember that Jerusalem covered a comparatively small area), and that she had sought help from the watchmen (3:3; NRSV, "sentinels"). Whether the search was realistic can be left as an open question; sometimes yearnings for a particular person can be partly satisfied by action that we know from the outset will have little chance of success. Whether the woman did indeed find her lover (v. 4) and is now recalling the delicious hours that followed, or whether she is imagining that she did, is left open by the poem. It is noteworthy, however, that she brought him into her own domain, which perhaps argues for imagination rather than reality given the likely conventions that regulated sexual contact between young people. The concluding adjuration to the daughters of Jerusalem (see on 2:7) seems less appropriate in this context than at 2:7, unless the sense there is that even imagining events brings pain and sorrow to the woman as well as pleasure.

3:6-11 Some editors of the Hebrew text and commentators believe that the words "Look, it is the litter of Solomon!" (3:7a) are a later gloss. If these words are removed and particular attention is paid to the Hebrew feminine forms translated "coming" (v. 6a) and "[around] it" (i.e., around her; v. 7b), the passage can be taken as a description of the procession of a woman, perhaps a wedding procession of a woman to her husband's house. However, this leaves unexplained why the woman's procession should be coming from the wilderness (v. 6) and why the daughters of Zion should be invited to observe Solomon (unless v. 11 is a separate fragment).

If the text is taken as we have it, it is best understood as a soliloquy on the part of the woman, as she imagines her lover coming to meet her. Whereas the poem of 2:8-14 pictures him as a gazelle or young stag coming from the hill country, the present poem accords him imaginary royal status, with the corresponding pomp and magnificence. On this reading, the feminine form of "coming" in 3:6a can be taken as a neuter (NRSV, "What is that coming?") and the feminine "it" or "around it" in v. 7 refers to the litter (lit. "bed") of v. 7a, which is feminine in Hebrew. In v. 9 the Hebrew word *'appiryon* (NRSV, "palanquin" — a covered litter) probably means some kind of carriage (carried by human bearers). The phrase "its interior was inlaid with love" (v. 10) does not make particularly good sense, and proposed alternatives include "leather" (NEB, REB, based on an Arabic word) or "ebony" (NJB, involving a slight emendation). It is interesting to observe that the lover as king and beneficiary of the luxury products of culture also needs to be protected by soldiers (vv. 7-8). There may be an implicit criticism here of the city, as opposed to the world of nature.

4:1-7 Repeated Hebrew words in 4:1 and 7 ("beautiful" and "my love") may indicate the beginning and end of the poem. It is a description of the woman by the man drawing on imagery from culture (v. 4) as well as nature and resulting in strange, exotic language for modern readers. In v. 1 the words "behind your veil" may be a later addition as they overload the poetic structure of the line and raise the question of how the woman's hair can be described in v. 1b as veiled! The likening of the hair to "a flock of goats moving down the slopes of Gilead" suggests thick and perhaps curly hair that creates waves when the head is shaken or the wind blows through the hair. A veil is also mentioned in v. 3. Pictorial representations of Israelite women (e.g., in the 8th-cent. Assyrian reliefs of the capture of Lachish) show them wearing a cloaklike garment with a hood. On the reliefs of the capture of Lachish the hoods are probably being worn as a sign of mourning. However, it does not appear that Israelite women covered their heads as a matter of course, and v. 3 may only mean that *when* the woman covers her head, the effect is to emphasize her cheeks. It is also possible to speculate that the insertion of the references to veils (if they are insertions) points to a change in culture, which began to require the veiling of women. Among the images used, it may be noted that it was apparently rare for the ewes domesticated in ancient Syria/Palestine to bear twins (cf. v. 2). V. 4 seems to mean that the woman's neck is long, and the shields and bucklers (small, round shields) presumably refer to the necklaces that she wears. In v. 6 the "mountain of myrrh and the hill of frankincense" may refer to the woman. If this is correct, 2:17 may have a similar meaning, that is, the woman invites the man to enjoy her physical presence.

4:8 This verse appears to be a fragment of a larger poem. Precisely what the man's bride (the Hebrew word for "bride" occurs only here and in 4:9, 10, 11, 12; 5:1 in

SoS, which may be why 4:8 has been placed before the poem of 4:9–5:1) is doing in the Lebanon region among the haunts of wild animals is impossible to say. Murphy (1990: 159-60) suggests that the items in the verse are metaphors for the woman's inaccessibility, which is possible, but hardly concordant with v. 6, which implies accessibility.

4:9-11 There are at least two ways of defining the extent of the poem to which these verses belong. It is possible, on the basis of the occurrence of the words "bride" and "sister" in 4:9–5:1, to regard this as one poem. On the other hand, 4:12–5:1 can be seen as a separate unit marked by the use of the word "garden" as an *inclusio* (vv. 12; 5:1). This is the view taken here.

4:9-11 describe the effect of the woman upon the man, using his words. Her glances (v. 9), her loving gestures (v. 10), and her kisses and conversation (v. 11) have enchanted him, as has the fragrance of her clothes (v. 11b). The words "sister" and "bride" are not to be taken literally, but as terms of endearment.

4:12–5:1 The figure of the garden in this poem is a designation for the woman. Its abundant sources of water and its exotic plants are poetic descriptions of the woman's beauty from the man's perspective, but beneath the surface there are elements of tension. The descriptions of the garden as locked and its fountain as sealed imply inaccessibility — most likely because of conventional and institutional constraints. In 4:16 it is clear only that the words "Let my beloved come . . ." are spoken by the woman. The first half of the verse could be spoken by either. The view taken here, on balance, is that the woman speaks the whole of v. 16. Her appeal to the north and south winds to blow the garden's fragrance abroad is a poetic expression of longing for the constraints to be removed so that her lover can enter the garden (i.e., have contact with her). In 5:1 the man responds (perhaps in the woman's imagination) to her plea. The Hebrew verbs used in his response ("I come," "I gather," "I eat," "I drink") are in the perfect, or completed aspect, conveying the sense of action envisaged as completed. The final words of 5:1, "Eat, drink . . . be drunk" cannot be assigned with any confidence to a particular speaker. They may be spoken by the man in imagination as he invites his friends to the wedding feast, but this is simply a guess.

5:2-8 This is the most dramatic poem in SoS, and it can be read at several levels. On its own admission it is a dream (5:2), and it contains elements that will be familiar to many readers from their own dreams. Thus v. 5 may express the powerlessness to perform an action (in this case, the need to open the door quickly) that is experienced in dreams. Also, the sexual overtones of some of the language (see below) may derive from sexual fantasies that can be experienced in dreams. On the other hand, dreams can contain memories of actual occurrences, and the beating of the woman by the watchmen when she is searching for her lover at night may have happened to her. In addition, the incident of believing that her lover was knocking at the door and finding nobody there may recall actual or fantasized events.

Whatever the origins of the material, 5:2-8 is a poem. It begins vividly with participles (lit. "I am asleep, but my heart is awake; listen — my beloved is knocking!") inviting hearers/readers to imagine the scene. The heart in Hebrew is the seat of the intellectual faculties, while the bowels (NRSV, "inmost being," at v. 4) are the seat of the emotions. The speech of the man is deliberately overloaded with terms of endearment ("sister," "love," "dove," "perfect one"), which makes the initial response of the woman oddly restrained. The NRSV makes v. 3 a statement apparently justifying the difficulty of the woman to respond immediately. It is also possible to take v. 3 as a reply of the woman to her lover: "I have taken off my (under)garment." At all events, the initial reluctance is at odds with the passion that is stirred up in the next verse, and it is here that a sexual rather than a straightforward reading may be indicated. On the face of it the man inserts his hand into (Heb. *min,* usually meaning "from") the hole (NRSV, "opening"), presumably of the door. The use of the preposition *min* in a sense opposite to its normal basic meaning, even if it can be justified from Ugaritic, has led some editors to alter Heb. *shalak,* meaning "send" or "put," to *shalap,* meaning "to withdraw." Whether or not this is correct, the connotations of "hand" as penis and "hole" as vagina are sufficiently well attested to suggest that the woman is stirred to passion and action by the thought of physical intercourse or masturbation.

The exact point of the dripping myrrh on the hands and fingers of the woman and on the bolt is not clear unless there is a covert reference to body fluids. Myrrh is an oily resin which, when dry, is a fragrant spice. Perhaps here the references to dripping and liquid myrrh indicate an inability to grasp the bolt firmly so as to open the door. The intense disappointment at discovering the departure of the lover is expressed in the phrase "my soul failed me," a construction which, when used with the third person in Hebrew, can mean "he died." We are left to speculate on why he had gone. Was it because of the woman's cold reply in 5:3 or her delay in opening the door, or was his presence only a fantasy? The words rendered "when he spoke" should probably be translated "when he turned his back." The incident leads to the woman's fervent search, her unfortunate encounter with the watchmen (NRSV, "sentinels"), and her appeal to the daughters of Jerusalem to assist her in her quest. The watchmen represent here most explicitly the institutional constraints on the woman's natural passions. While the appeal to the daughters of Jerusalem may be an adapted refrain (cf. 2:7; 3:5; 8:4) ending the poem, it may also be an editorial gloss linking 5:1-7 with vv. 9-16.

5:9–6:1 5:9 is probably an editorial verse that links the poem of 5:10-16 to the preceding material by way of the verb "adjure." It is a reply by the daughters of Jerusalem to the woman, and it takes the narrative out of the dream world of the woman's soliloquy into the genre of dialogue. The woman's reply describes her lover beginning with his head (v. 11) and ending with his legs (v. 15), and it has been pointed out that the description draws its imagery from the description of a statue (cf. the description of the statue seen in Nebuchadnezzar's dream in Dan 3:31-33). Interwoven with statue images are figures drawn from nature which repeat or echo material that has already appeared in SoS (note the echoes of the description of the woman in 4:1-7). Whereas culture and nature are often at odds in SoS, they are combined in this poem. The language likening the man to a statue can be seen as a variation of the theme that the woman's lover is like a king (cf. 3:6-11). 6:1 is a further editorial gloss which links the dialogue between the woman and the daughters of Jerusalem back to 5:8.

6:2-3 These verses may also be editorial compositions designed to round off 5:2–6:3 as a unit; but if so, the woman's knowledge of the whereabouts of her lover (6:2) hardly agrees with her fruitless search in 5:6, nor her enlistment of the daughters of Jerusalem in this search (5:8; 6:1). 6:2-3 may therefore be an independent fragment or fragments, which repeat(s) earlier material (cf. 2:16; 4:16).

6:4-12 Some of the material in this poem, in which the man addresses the woman and praises her beauty, can be paralleled almost exactly from 4:1-3. Thus, 6:5b-7 is verbally identical with 4:1b-2, 3b except for two words. In vv. 8-9 the language changes from second person address to third person statement, and the reference to sixty queens and eighty concubines (v. 8) is impossible to integrate into the context. It may therefore be best to see vv. 8-9 as a separate fragment using royal imagery to claim that if a king had sixty queens and eighty concubines, these women would agree that the man's beloved surpassed them all. The opening verse likening the woman to Tirzah (a former capital of the Northern Kingdom, Israel), Jerusalem, and an army with banners fits uneasily with what follows. If the words "terrible as an army with banners" are a gloss taken from v. 10, the shortened v. 4 idealizes the two capital cities as great achievements of human culture and then compares the woman's beauty with these wonders. This still leaves the words "terrible as an army . . ." in need of explanation, together with v. 10. The Hebrew verbal and adjectival forms indicate that the woman is being described. The fact that she is likened to the dawn, the moon, and the sun is remarkable. That these natural objects/occurrences were also used to describe goddesses and gods in the ancient world and that in the OT the heavenly hosts (stars) were also regarded as armies (cf. Judg 5:20) provide a clue to the background to this imagery; it is clearly mythological in origin, although we cannot know to what extent, if any, this would have registered on hearers/readers of SoS. (How aware are English speakers of the mythological background of the names of days of the week?) What the verse appears to express is the inviolable uniqueness of the woman as an Other to the man. In spite of endearing language and the desire of the man and woman for mutual openness, it is vital that the otherness of the woman should be treated as sacred. Only in this way can a relationship flourish and the familiarity be avoided that breeds contempt.

The speaker of 6:11-12 is evidently the woman, although this allocation rests on the virtually untranslatable v. 12, and some versions (e.g., NEB, REB) assign the verses to a male speaker. Two problems face the translator/interpreter: the name Amminadib (or, according to some Hebrew manuscripts and the ancient versions, Amminadab) and the word *markebot,* which is a plural of the Hebrew word for "chariot." The consonants of Amminadib can be read as "my people, a prince" or "with a prince" or "my people are noble." Whereas the older versions (e.g., AV) offered a literal rendering such as "chariots of Amminadib," modern versions tend to take the *nadib* part of the name to mean "prince" or "royal" or "noble." Another strategy is to change the order of the letters of the word for "chariots" to yield a word connected with the stem *barak,* "to bless." Taking vv. 11 and 12 together, there appears to be a play between nature and culture. The speaker visits the place where blossoms in the orchard and vineyard might be expected. There may be covert allusions to sexual maturity here. The speaker's imagination then switches to the realm of the royal, picturing a royal procession with him- or herself riding in a royal chariot.

6:13–7:9 (Heb. 7:1-10) There are two main ways of taking this section. Most modern translations appear to separate 6:13 from what follows, attributing the whole of v. 13 to a chorus (so NJB) or dividing it between a chorus (v. 13a) and the man (v. 13b; so NIV, NEB, REB). The NRSV separates 6:13 from 7:1 by a section heading. Another view is that the Shulammite is a dancer whose costume makes possible an intimate description of various parts of her body. If 7:1-9 is interpreted without reference to 6:13, it becomes an intimate description of the man's lover. If the connection with 6:13 is made, the origins of the poem can be sought in descriptions of dancers on festive occasions.

In 6:13 there are three difficulties: the verb "return," the personal name "Shulammite" and the place name "Mahanaim." "Return" makes little sense in the context since there has been no account in the narrative of the woman departing. Other possibilities are "turn (round)" with the implication that the woman is facing away from the speakers or "turn" (or "twist") within the context of a dance. If the latter interpretation is correct, "looking upon" the woman is not a physical inspection but an appreciation of the dance. The name "Shulammite" is similar to, and probably influenced in form by, the adjective "Shunammite" in 1 Kgs 1:3 and 2 Kgs 4:8-37. Many commentators have noted that "Shulammite" contains the consonants of "Solomon" (this is more apparent in Hebrew than in English) and have argued that the woman is thus being called a female Solomon. The woman appears to reply to her admirers in 6:13b (the NIV, NEB, and REB take the speaker to be the man), asking why they want to see the "dance of Mahanaim." "Mahanaim" was a place east of the river Jordan (2 Sam 17:24), and it also means "two camps." Whether "dance of Mahanaim" was the name of a well-known dance, or whether it was a dance performed between two lines of dancers/spectators cannot be said. NRSV, "two armies," takes "two camps" in a military sense.

The description of the dancer/lover begins with the feet rather than the head (cf. 4:1-5; 5:10-15), combining images taken from culture (jewels, 7:1; ivory tower, v. 4) and nature (fawns, gazelles, v. 3). Some of the descriptions are strange to modern readers (cf. v. 4b, "your nose is like a tower of Lebanon") but are presumably complimentary. The translation of the end of v. 5 is uncertain, and "tresses" is gained more from the context than from demonstrable philology. The Hebrew word rendered "you are stately" (NRSV) at v. 7 occurs elsewhere in connection with "height" (1 Sam 16:7). Evidently, being tall and slender was a physical ideal for Israelite women, as the comparison with a palm tree indicates. This is not surprising since palm trees are also associated with goddesses in the iconography of the ancient Near East. The image of the palm tree then becomes the occasion for sexual allusions as the man longs to climb the tree and lay hold of its branches (v. 8).

7:10-13 (Heb. 7:11-14) There are probably three fragments here. 7:10 is a variation on 2:16, while 7:11-12 recall 6:11. Read as one unit, 7:10-12, spoken by the woman, express the sense of freedom from constraint provided by the countryside as opposed to the city (cf. 8:1-4). There is a symmetry between the anticipations of nature reawakening after the winter (v. 12; cf. 2:10-15) and the stirrings of physical love. V. 13 is probably a separate fragment, the reference to "our doors" hardly fitting the rural setting of the preceding verses. Mandrakes were believed to assist procreation (cf. Gen 30:14-16), and it can be assumed that the "choice fruits" had the same function. The fragment seems to speak of an ideal setting created by the woman in which she and her beloved can enjoy physical love.

8:1-4 This poem of longing, which is perhaps to be confined to 8:1-2 with vv. 3-4 as an expansion taken from 2:6-7, can be compared with 3:1-5 and 5:2-8. In the mind of the editor of SoS the present poem was linked to the others by the concluding reference to the daughters of Jerusalem. The poem expresses the woman's frustration that social convention would prevent her from publicly demonstrating her feelings for her lover were she to meet him in the street. It is true that elsewhere in the OT there are narratives in which people demonstrate their affection publicly (Murphy 1990: 188). But the examples hardly prove that public displays of affection between people not related were approved of. Isaac and Rebekah are husband and wife, although claiming to be brother and sister (Gen 26:8), while Jacob and Rachel are uncle and niece (Gen 29:11). The text makes it clear that affection could be demonstrated in public with a close relative such as a sibling, whereas it would be impossible with someone not a member of the family. However, the poem does not simply deal with public displays of affection. More importantly, the woman could take a brother into her private domain, there to enjoy his company. That is denied to her if the man is her lover. The woman's frustration leads to her longing to be in physical contact with her lover, and her adjuration to the daughters of Jerusalem.

8:5-14 The closing verses of SoS display the greatest lack of coordination anywhere in the book, and may indicate that the editor(s) simply added fragments to the collection. 8:5a is a fragment which recalls 3:6 without being developed in any way. V. 5b has echoes of vv. 1-2. The speaker is the woman, and it is as though she was present at the birth of her beloved, something that gives her an older sister prerogative over her beloved. The connection between the apple tree (NEB, "apricot trees") and the birth can be construed from 7:13 (Heb., 7:14). The birth was not under a tree as such but in a place surrounded by trees or decorated with their fruits. However, a particular tree may have been imprinted on the memory of the woman as the place where love had first blossomed.

8:6-7 affirm the intense power and strength of love. It cannot be put out as water quenches fire; it cannot be purchased (v. 7). The mention of death and the grave (Heb. *Sheol*) in v. 6 and the fact that the Hebrew for "flashes" contains the name of the god *Resheph* (a god of war and sickness) have raised speculation about the mythological background to the poem. As with 6:10, it is difficult to know how far hearers/readers of the poem were aware of the possible mythical allusions. The point of comparing love and passion (NIV, "its jealousy") with death and Sheol is presumably to link them with the awesome power of forces (i.e., death) that humans ultimately must succumb to. The reference to "flashes" well describes the metaphorical heat of passion and leads naturally to the claim that floodwaters cannot quench such fire. The whole set of claims about love's power is introduced, and it is justified by the request of the woman that he should regard her as though she were a seal worn around the neck or on the arm of her beloved (cf. Gen 38:18). Yet this arguably deconstructs what follows. If love is as persistent as is claimed, why are physical tokens and reminders necessary? Is there a hint of recognition that whereas love ideally ought to endure permanently, in practice this is often not so?

8:8-10 The interpretation of these obscure verses is complicated by the fact that many commentators see hidden references to what they call bride price, which they take to involve the selling of the bride. This is to misunderstand the function of bride wealth (a payment by the bridegroom or his family to the bride or her family; see Committee of the Royal Anthropological Institute 1951: 116-22). Bride wealth is often a mechanism designed to work in the woman's favor, especially if it is retained after the woman is divorced and must return to her family. "The bride is never actually purchased as a chattel" (Committee: 116). If v. 9 is a declaration by the woman's brothers that they will do all that they can to guard her chastity, this is not their calculated way of getting the best price for the sale of their sister in a marriage (they might have to return the bride wealth if her behavior was adjudged to be the reason for a marriage's breakdown); it is a way of ensuring that the woman does not become unmarriageable, or liable to immediate divorce (cf. Deut 22:13-19) because she has lost her virginity.

Naturally, the control exercised over the woman by her brothers (cf. Gen 24:50, 55) and the implication of an arranged marriage (if this is what is meant by "when she is spoken for") will emphasize to modern Western readers the difference in culture between SoS and their own world. However, the male control of the woman is not the last word. If these verses are spoken by the woman, with 8:8-9 being her account of what her brothers said, which she then contradicts in v. 10, then the woman has the last word. Other ways of allocating the material include assigning vv. 8-9 to the brothers, or v. 8 to the brothers and v. 9 to the woman's suitors. The words "his eyes" imply that she has a lover and thus her own ideas about whom she will marry, whatever her brothers' plans. This interpretation is another variation on the theme of convention versus the desires of love. The text leaves open whether the woman gets her way.

8:11-12 The speaker of these verses is not obvious, although the NEB and NIV probably rightly allocate them to the woman. She reports what is most likely a popular story about King Solomon. His vineyard at Baal-hamon (an unidentified or imaginary location) was so vast and productive that the keepers to whom it was entrusted were each expected to pay a thousand pieces of silver for this privilege. The woman's own vineyard (her lover) is superior to this legendary one, in which case the vast sums of money mentioned are meaningless.

8:13-14 The Hebrew verbs and possessive markers indicate that the man addresses the woman in 8:13. V. 14 can either be the words of the woman herself (cf. 2:17b), or the man recalling her words, which he longs to hear her utter. In either case, the book ends without an ending. The man and woman are apart, and either each expresses a desire to see and hear the other, or the man alone does so. Love may have unstoppable power (cf. 8:6-7), but it also stirs up deep, and sometimes unfulfilled, longings.

Reading and Using SoS

Texts are produced and used in specific situations, and although the way a text is used is not necessarily conditioned by its milieu of production, modern users of biblical texts are rightly interested in the circumstances in which particular texts were produced. Whatever the origins of the materials found in SoS, the collection as we have it suggests a peaceful, prosperous, urban, and not especially religious milieu as the situation of production. There are no references to poverty or social injustice, or to wars. If the countryside is seen as the place of freedom over against the city as the place of constraints, it is an idealized countryside viewed from a prosperous urban perspective. There is no hint of famine, or of working the soil by the sweat of one's brow. Religiously speaking, there is nothing that is distinctly Israelite in the text. Indeed, the close rapport with the natural world and the linking of the promise of spring with aroused human passion (cf. 2:8-15) are reminiscent of the kind of natural religion so roundly condemned, for example, by Hosea. Yet if there are no references to positive religion, the poems articulate a quest for meaning in expressing desires for human relationships that social conventions do not permit. In this sense, there is a longing for a different and better world.

In this different world there is no domination of the one partner by the other. Indeed, it is striking that the woman so often takes the initiative in the relationship, and that so many poems see things from her point of view.

Why and how might people want to use SoS today? There are not likely to be sermons on it in churches, and theological students will most likely have to study it only for assessment purposes, if at all. In academic biblical studies, SoS is a rich source for those interested in the history of interpretation and in cultural studies. It has also been identified by feminists as providing a picture of the equality of the sexes in opposition to the subordinate role of women in Israelite society. If it does have anything to say to modern users, this may best be approached via the respect shown for each other by the man and the woman. In an age in which pornography, the commercialization of sex, and the constant encouragement to conform to certain role models are ever-present pressures, SoS has a simplicity, straightforwardness, and perhaps even naivete in its desire for a different and better world. Perhaps its message is that this better world will begin to come only when people treat each other as individuals, to be respected, to be treated tenderly, to be allowed to retain their mystery. At all events, the Bible would be a poorer book if SoS were excluded from it.

Select Bibliography. Brenner, A. 1989,*The Song of Songs,* Old Testament Guides, Sheffield: Sheffield Academic • Committee of the Royal Anthropological Institute. 1951, *Notes and Queries in Anthropology,* London: Routledge & Kegan Paul • Exum, J. C. 1973, "A Literary and Structural Analysis of the Song of Songs," *ZAW* 85:47-79 • Falk, M. 1982, *Love Lyrics from the Bible: A Translation and Literary Study of The Song of Songs,* Bible and Literature Series 4, Sheffield: Almond • Giddens, A. 1992, *The Transformation of Intimacy: Sexuality, Love & Eroticism in Modern Societies,* Cambridge: Polity • Heinevetter, H.-J. 1988, *Das Hohelied als programmatische Komposition,* BBB 69, Bonn: Hannstein • Horst, F. 1935/1961, "Die Formen des althebräischen Liebesliedes," in *Festschrift E. Littmann,* Leiden: E. J. Brill, 43-54, repr. in *Gottes Recht: Studien zum Recht im Alten Testament,* Munich: Christian Kaiser • Keel, O. 1984, *Deine Blicke sind Tauben: Zur Metaphorik des Hohen Liedes,* SBS 114-15, Stuttgart: Katholisches Bibelwerk • Keel, O. 1992, "Hohelied," in *Neues Bibel-Lexikon,* 183-90 • Müller, H.-P. 1976, "Die lyrische Reproduktion des Mythischen im Hld," *ZTK* 73:23-41 • Müller, H.-P. 1992, *Das Hohelied,* ATD 16/2 • Murphy, R. E. 1990, *The Song of Songs: A Commentary on the Book of Canticles or The Song of Songs,* Hermeneia, Minneapolis: Fortress • Shea, W. H. 1980, "The Chiastic Structure of the Song of Songs," *ZAW* 92:378-96 • Trible, P. 1978, "Love's Lyrics Redeemed," in *God and the Rhetoric of Sexuality,* OBT, Philadelphia: Fortress, 144-65 • Vermes, G. 1997, *The Complete Dead Sea Scrolls in English,* London: Allen Lane.

Introduction to Prophetic Literature

Paul L. Redditt

Many people think of prophets as *foretellers,* those who predict the future, and many modern studies of prophets find allusions to contemporary events or events someone thinks will occur in the next few years. Since people naturally want to know what the future holds for them, such studies meet a deep need. They might not, however, draw carefully on the prophetic literature of the OT. To be sure, the OT prophets at times foretold the future, but more often they were *forthtellers,* perhaps explaining their own time or the past, and perhaps warning their audiences to repent. Even when they predicted the future, for the most part the future they envisioned was that of their own generation or perhaps the next. Occasionally, their eschatological hopes included the end of evil and a radical new direction for the world (Gowan 1986), but it is impossible to show that the new direction is about to unfold in the twenty-first century. So, if the OT prophets did not draw a blueprint for modern times, what were they about?

What Is a Prophet?

Prophecy in the Ancient Near East

Prophecy was not unique to Israel. Something similar appeared elsewhere in the ancient Near East. Divination was attested from an early age. Texts from the ancient city of Mari testify to the giving of messages and oracles as early as the eighteenth century BC. An eleventh-century text about an Egyptian traveler named Wen-Amon describes the actions of an ecstatic prophet in Phoenicia. The OT itself gives evidence of prophets of Baal in connection with the account of Elijah's triumph over hundreds of them on Mt. Carmel.

If prophecy itself was not unique to Israel, were the prophets of Israel in any way different from their predecessors and contemporaries? The answer seems to be a strong affirmative. The OT prophets distinguished themselves at least in degree by their insistence on moral behavior and by their attention to the hand of Israel's God in political affairs. Indeed, their insistence on morality and social justice at times led them to contemplate God's abandonment if not destruction of Israel, a conclusion from which they (or those who preserved their sayings) always pulled back, none more eloquently than Hosea (cf. 11:8-9).

Terms for "Prophet"

One way prophecy in the OT may be studied is by paying attention to the principal Hebrew terms used of prophets: *ro'eh,* from a verb meaning "to see"; *hozeh,* from a different word meaning "to see"; and *nabi',* the meaning of which is disputed. A *ro'eh* was one who "saw" what was hidden, usually by inquiring for information from God. Today a *rō'eh* might well be called a *diviner,* that is, one who can discover things that are hidden. One classic text for understanding the term is 1 Samuel 9–10, where Saul and his servant seek out Samuel to divine the location of the donkeys of Saul's father. Samuel was so blessed by God as a diviner, however, that prior to Saul's arrival Samuel already knew that the donkeys had returned home, that Saul's father was worried about his son, and that God wanted Saul to become king of Israel!

The term *hozeh* was used in connection with revelations the prophet "saw" (cf. Ezek 13:16, 23). The term denoted visions in many cases, and as in the case of Balaam's oracles (cf. Num 24:4, 16), the visions often included auditions as well. In other cases, for example, the superscriptions of Isaiah, Amos, Micah, and Habakkuk, the term probably referred to the entire revelation the prophet received (Smith 1986: 3:987).

The term *nabi'* appears frequently in the prophets, and the verbal form of the word is used of the action of speaking or delivering a message. That use seems consonant with the idea of the prophets as messengers of God (Westermann 1967: 90-128). Still, sometimes a *nabi'* could turn out to be a false prophet (1 Kgs 22:22), and occasionally God could even be the source of the error in the message (1 Kgs 22:23).

True and False Prophets

The issue of true versus false prophets surfaced on numerous occasions. The book of Deuteronomy (18:20-22) offers two tests for determining who was a true prophet: (1) one must prophesy in the name of Yahweh, and (2) the prophecy must come true. Those two criteria (among others, anyway) seem to have been employed by the scribes who selected the books for the prophetic canon, but they might well have been inconclusive in a real-life situation where people had to decide which of two or more opposing prophets to follow. In a classic confrontation with the prophet Hananiah, Jeremiah prophesied that God would allow King Nebuchadrezzar of Babylon to capture Jerusalem if King Zedekiah did not surrender to him (27:12-15). He even called the prophets counseling resistance liars. Not surprisingly, one of them, Hananiah, repudiated Jeremiah's message (28:1-4). In response, Jeremiah reminded their audience that in the past true prophets had prophesied doom. Only when a prophecy of hope proved true, Jeremiah warned, should the people accept it (28:8-9). Clearly, Jeremiah's response did not establish a third criterion because prophecies of doom are not always correct. Rather, he gave them a rule of thumb that false prophets are more likely to prophesy what people want to hear, whereas true prophets are more likely to tell people bad news they received from God.

Who Were the Prophets of the Old Testament?

Prophets Known by Name

The names of the prophets are numerous. The names of the "writing prophets" are well known. The "major" prophets are Isaiah, Jeremiah, and Ezekiel. The "minor" prophets are Hosea, Joel, Amos, Obadiah, Jonah, Micah, Nahum, Habakkuk, Zephaniah, Haggai, Zechariah, and Malachi. Besides these, a number of other well-known prophets appear earlier in the OT, including Moses, Nathan, Elijah, and Elisha. There are also prophetesses like Miriam (the sister of Moses), Deborah, Huldah, and Noadiah. Consequently, in the Hebrew Bible the books of Joshua, Judges, 1 and 2 Samuel, and 1 and 2 Kings are called the "Former Prophets," and the others the "Latter Prophets." One of the characteristic motifs of 1 and 2 Kings is that a prophet would predict something before it actually happened (cf. Jeroboam's revolt, which was predicted in 1 Kgs 11:26-29 and fulfilled in 1 Kgs 12:20-23; cf. Thompson 1978: 126).

Anonymous Prophets

Modern scholars are convinced, moreover, that countless other anonymous prophets have added their insights to the ones known by name in the Latter Prophets. Consequently, they speak of a Second and Third Isaiah or a Second and (perhaps) Third Zechariah, indicating thereby divisions in those books that seem to point to different authors. Even books as short as Joel, Micah, and Zephaniah, however, probably also include a substantial amount of secondary material with no indication of a change in authorship. The book of Amos, as another example, ends with a prophecy of salvation (9:11-15) that looks back on the fall of the Davidic dynasty in 586, while the prophet flourished in the mid-eighth century. Apparently, the end of the book of Amos as it stands was added by someone from the exilic or post-exilic period, who expected the restoration of the Davidic dynasty.

Central and Peripheral Prophets

People in ancient Israel clearly thought that there was such a thing as an office of prophets alongside the offices of priests and wise men. Jer 18:18 quotes enemies of Jeremiah as saying, "... instruction shall not perish from the priest, nor counsel from the wise, nor the word from the prophet." It does not follow from that statement, however, that the all the "prophets" in the prophetic canon held any such official office. Professional prophets played a significant role in the cultus, particularly the temple in Jerusalem, to promote the welfare of the people. They spoke the word by delivering the message of God to them and by interceding with God on behalf of the people (Johnson 1962: 74). Such official prophets likely included Isaiah, Haggai, and Zachariah, and *may* have included Joel (cf. 1:1–2:18) and Nahum. Their message would have been reinforced by the authority of their temple office, and in the case of Isaiah by ready access to the king (Isaiah 7).

Other prophets were peripheral, having no official relationship with the temple or other sanctuaries, as a few examples will show. Amos denied that he was a professional prophet or even an apprentice to one (Amos 7:14). In addition, he was from Judah, but flourished in Israel, from which he was unceremoniously banished (7:12-13). Jeremiah was from the North (from Anathoth in the tribe of Benjamin), and attempted to work in the South. Further, he was from the priestly family of Abiathar, who was banished from the temple by Solomon (1 Kgs 2:35). Micah was from the tiny town of Moresheth, and railed against the corruption of cities. The post-exilic prophet Malachi was probably a Levite, and thus associated with the Second Temple in Jerusalem (Redditt 1995: 151-52), but at a time when the Levites were losing power to the priests (Boccaccini 2002: 68-72, 87-89). Even Ezekiel, who was a priest from Jerusalem, lived and flourished in exile, deprived of any contact with the Babylonian king or the temple in Jerusalem. Likewise his audience was comprised of exiles in Babylon.

Protest by Prophets

At times a reader can detect a reconstructionist element in the sayings of the OT prophets (Ezekiel 40–48). The questions Knight 2000 (99) advised readers of the HB to keep in mind bear repeating here: "Whose text is it? For whom and why was it important to fashion the stories ... [and] prophetic sayings ... into their present form? Who stood to gain? Who had the power to see to the survival of the text?" This is not to say that prophetic literature should be seen as mere propaganda, but often it should be seen as a "minority report" against the established religion in ancient Israel.

Prophets and Their Audiences

It is clear, therefore, that the recognition of people as prophets implies an audience with its own needs and wishes. One community's prophet could be another community's madman. One biblical prophet might, thus, have a perspective diametrically opposed to that of another. The prophet Nahum, flourishing in the dying days of the cruel and hated Assyrian Empire, could call down God's destruction on the capital city of Nineveh (Nahum 2–3). The *prophet* Jonah seems to concur, but the *author* of the book of Jonah felt quite differently and portrayed God as One moved to compassion by human repentance. Perhaps it was because that author lived centuries later, long after the sting of Assyrian oppression had subsided. Perhaps it was because in his own context the *author* hoped for generous treatment at the hands of foreign rulers. Hence God had to correct the *prophet* with the question with which the book ends: "And should I not be concerned about Nineveh ... ?" The pre-exilic/exilic book of Jeremiah could proclaim the unending demise of Jehoiachin (22:24-27), employing the image of Jehoiachin (called Coniah) as God's signet ring that God would throw away. By contrast, the post-exilic temple prophet Haggai

(2:23) proclaimed that God would make Zerubbabel, grandson (?) of Jehoiachin, his new signet ring. New or different circumstances sometimes called for a new word.

Prophets, Kings, Priests, and Wise Men

How did the prophets relate to the other identifiable officeholders in ancient Israel: kings, priests, and wise men? With respect to kings, it is clear that the careers of many, though by no means all, of the so-called "writing prophets" fell during the period of the divided monarchy, particularly between the mid-eighth and early-sixth centuries, that is, between the time of Amos (c. 760) and the fall of the temple (586). In the Former Prophets of the HB, however, prophets anoint, correct, advise, condemn, and praise the monarchs, beginning with Nathan's remonstrance of David for his sin with Bathsheba (2 Samuel 12). Moreover, King Ahab called Elijah "you troubler of Israel" (1 Kgs 18:17), and complained that Micaiah ben Imlah "never prophesies anything favorable about me, but only disaster" (1 Kgs 22:8, NRSV). The central prophet Isaiah was in a position to criticize Ahaz (Isaiah 7). King Jehoiakim could shred the written oracles of Jeremiah and throw them on a brazier to warm his hands (Jer 36:23), but Jehoiakim's brother, King Zedekiah, was reduced to bringing Jeremiah from prison to the palace to consult with him (Jer 37:16-21). Clearly, the prophets' right of royal review depended on who the king was and whether he cared to face the prophet. Still, a king might be criticized openly by a prophet, even in a sanctuary sponsored by a king, regardless of the king's wishes (Amos 7:11).

Prophecy did not die out after the exile, though it fell into disfavor among some people, as Zech 13:3-6 shows. The priests gained exclusive control of the Second Temple, so that Johnson 1962: 75 surmised that they reduced prophets to the rank of temple singers. Boccaccini 2002: 88 thinks that the post-exilic Zadokites made a prophet out of Moses and used him to legitimize their own takeover of religious life, with Aaron as their real hero. Regardless, the latter prophets were preserved, copied, edited, combined, and canonized by scribes, who passed on a more-or-less fixed set of writings to the rabbis (Davies 1998: 33-35). Presumably they collected — and modified — the sayings of the particular prophets now in the OT because they had turned out to be correct, at least essentially, in their assessment of their own days, and could be "updated" to speak to new days (Gerstenberger 2003: 86-88). Ultimately, behind the prophetic voices is not the issue of monarchy, but the issue of "the political role of Judeans in their [G]od's historical scheme" (Davies 1998: 123). In other words, the scribes saw in the prophets' messages the key to the future. In that sense they were *foretellers* for the scribes.

What Constitutes Old Testament Prophetic Literature?

Former and Latter Prophets

As mentioned above, the HB differs from modern Christian Bibles in terms of which books it reckons as prophetic literature. In the HB, the Former Prophets include Joshua, Judges, 1 and 2 Samuel (taken as one book), and 1 and 2 Kings (also counted as one book). The Latter Prophets also number four: Isaiah, Jeremiah, Ezekiel, and the Book of the Twelve (or "Minor Prophets"). Lamentations and Daniel appear among the "Writings," the third section of the HB. In answering the question "What is prophetic literature?" therefore, one must ask whose canon is under discussion. This discussion emphasizes issues involving the Latter Prophets of the HB, but does not exclude the Former Prophets or Daniel.

Prophetic Genres

The genres of prophetic literature (March 1974: 141-77) include prophecies of doom, prophecies of salvation, admonitions, disputation speeches, and visions. *Prophecies of doom* can take various forms. The most basic is the so-called *prophecy of disaster* (e.g., Amos 1:3-5, 6-8, 9-12, 13-15; 2:1-3, 4-5, 6-16). Various formulae may introduce this genre, but most frequently one finds the phrase "Thus says Yahweh." In its fullest form, the prophecy of disaster will include an indication of the situation current at the time of the prophecy, the transition word "therefore," and a prediction of the disaster to follow. Sometimes one or more components may be missing, if, for example, the punishment makes clear the offense. Also, while the messenger formula is not unique to prophecies of disaster, it is characteristic enough of that genre to stand for it in the call vision of Ezekiel, where God commissions the prophet to say to the people, "Thus says the Lord GOD" (Ezek 2:4; 3:11, 27).

Typically, such prophecies appear unconditional. The book of Jonah, however, offers a study on prophecy and forgiveness. Jonah preaches the fall of Nineveh, knowing quite well that God would forgive the Ninevites if they repented (Jonah 4:2), a possibility the king of Nineveh contemplated (Jonah 3:9).

A similar genre is the *trial speech* (Isa 3:13-15; 41:1-5), in which God summons someone like the nations or something like the mountains or the heavens to be witnesses at a trial. There follows an indictment and the sentencing. Again, not all components are always present. Some trial speeches, furthermore, make explicit appeals to Israel's covenant with God (Hos 4:1-10) and are considered a sub- or even a separate category called a "Covenant Lawsuit."

A third genre of judgment is the so-called *Woe Oracle* (Amos 5:18), named from the first word of the genre *hoy*, translated "woe" in the RSV, but "alas" in the NRSV. It consists of the word "Woe" (proclaiming punishment) followed by a series of participles (listing offenses), thus: "Woe to the ones doing X, to the ones doing Y, to the ones doing Z." What the woe oracle shares with the prophecy of disaster and the trial speech are components that list offenses and punishments.

Prophecies of Salvation

Prophecies of salvation (Hag 1:2-11), by contrast, consist of three basic components: an indication of the bad situation in which the people found themselves, a prediction of salvation or a better tomorrow, and an indication that the present was the time for the situation to improve, perhaps because they were turning to God or perhaps because God was turning to the people. Introductory formulae might include the messenger formula or the phrase "Behold, I. . . ." More specialized genres, or perhaps subtypes of the prophecy of salvation, include the "oracle of salvation" (Isa 41:8-13), introduced by or including the distinctive command "Fear not," and the "proclamation of salvation" (Isa 41:17-20; 42:14-17), with allusions to laments or lament ceremonies.

Admonitions

Admonitions are commands (Isa 1:16-17) or prohibitions (Amos 5:5) given by the prophet to the people in the name of God. Often an admonition was conditional in that it spelled out what would happen if the hearers obeyed (Amos 5:14-15), or ignored (Amos 5:6), the command. Sometimes an admonition was coupled with the possibility that God would withhold deserved punishment if the offenders repented (Isa 1:18-20; Joel 2:12-14). In other examples the prophet simply commanded the people to behave without spelling out consequences. One such admonition is the literarily superb Amos 4:4-5, which utilizes irony or sarcasm. One might expect a cult prophet to urge people to "Come to Bethel and sacrifice," or "come to Gilgal to multiply sacrifices." In the hands of Amos, however, the expectation is inverted by substituting the word "transgress" for "sacrifice." The result is a skillfully wrought warning against false worship at the sanctuaries of Bethel and Gilgal.

Disputation Speeches

At times the prophets engaged people in dialogue. The genre designed to represent such conversations, real or rhetorical, is called the *disputation speech* (Mal 1:2-5, 6-14; 2:10-16, 17; 3:8-12). In it, a prophet reports one or both sides of a discussion, sometimes beginning from a point of agreement and progressing to the point the prophet wanted the people to adopt.

Visions

The last primary category of prophetic genres is *visions,* in which prophets see the action and perhaps even hear the words of God (Amos 7:1-3, 4-6, 7-9) or another divine being (Ezek 1:5-21) or agent (Zech 2:1-5). Clearly, in visions prophets see (and hear) things not discernible by ordinary human perception. The books of Ezekiel, Zechariah (at least chs. 1–6), and Daniel contain a preponderance of visionary material. A subcategory of a vision is the "call vision" of a prophet (Exod 3:1–4:17; Isa 6:1-10; Jer 1:4-10; Ezek 1:4–3:15). Several themes seem characteristic of these visions: the prophet expresses inadequacy and/or sinfulness; the prophet's mouth and/or the word of God plays a prominent role; and God commissions the prophet.

Other Forms

Other narrative forms appear in prophetic literature as well. At times someone narrated a symbolic act by a prophet (Jer 13:1-11; Ezek 4:1-17). Typically, these reports included God's order to perform the act, an indication that the prophet had obeyed, and an explanation of the meaning of the act. 2 Kings collected a number of narratives about Elijah and Elisha that have been termed "prophetic legends," and someone (Baruch?) penned biographical accounts of the prophet Jeremiah (chs. 26–28, 36–45). Sometimes one finds long prose sermons of a prophet (e.g., Ezekiel 16); at other times a reader encounters what appear to be short prose summaries of prophetic messages originally delivered in poetic form (Isa 37:33; Jer 22:11-12). In addition, prophetic books contain isolated examples of other genres of literature, for example, proverbs (Jer 31:29; Ezek 18:2), laments (cf. all or in part the so-called "confessions of Jeremiah": 11:18–12:6; 15:10-21; 17:14-18; 18:18-23; 20:7-13; 20:14-18), hymns (Jonah 2:1-9; Habakkuk 3), doxologies (Isa 6:3; Amos 4:13; 5:8-9; 9:5-6), and allegories (Isa 5:1-7; 27:2-6).

Oral and Written Prophecy

Form critics have long assumed that prophets delivered their messages orally in short speeches and that those speeches were secondarily recorded in writing, joined to one another, edited, and expanded to form the books of the "writing prophets." That general outline may well have been true for many of the books, especially those of the pre-exilic prophets. Even with those prophets, however, the modern reader needs to recognize the possibility of secondary hands. The book of Jonah, however, is simply a narrative, with almost no prophetic message contained in it. Ezekiel, too, is almost entirely prose. It contains a number of dates (something not necessary for oral delivery), and generally reads like a literary production. Thus, it may originally have composed in writing for the purpose of public readings. Further, Zechariah 9–14 and Joel seem so full of literary allusions that some scholars suggest they were written from the beginning. In addition, Isaiah and Jeremiah passed through the hands of tradition bearers who shaped and added significantly to the corpora, and the Book of the Twelve gives signs of being an edited, multi-staged growth, beginning with the books of Hosea, Amos, Micah, and Zephaniah (Redditt 2001).

What Did the Old Testament Prophets Teach?

The prophets whose sayings found a place in the OT, like the rest of its authors, were motivators and reformers, not systematic theologians. Nor, as already noted, did they necessarily agree on all points. Hence it is not possible to write *the* theology of the prophets. Instead, one must be satisfied with finding and articulating a series of themes sounded and re-sounded by the prophets. Not all prophets addressed all these themes, though the books of Isaiah, Jeremiah, and Ezekiel did. What follows, therefore, is a presentation of seven themes selected that seem crucial for the relevance of the prophets for the contemporary church and synagogue.

God's Election of Israel

The prophets inherited a view of God's dealings with Israel, dealings fundamental to the prophets' calling and message. According to von Rad 1962 (1:66-68, 127-28), this view of who Israel was appears in the Deuteronomic credo:

> A wandering Aramean was my ancestor; he went down into Egypt and lived there as an alien, few in number, and there he became a great nation, mighty and populous. When the Egyptians treated us harshly and afflicted us, . . . we cried to the LORD, the God of our ancestors; the LORD heard our voice and saw our affliction, our toil, and our oppression. The LORD brought us out of Egypt with a mighty hand and an outstretched arm, with a terrifying display of power, and with signs and wonders; and he brought us into this place and gave us this land. . . . (Deut 26:5-9)

While this formulation may be later than von Rad thought, it does express the basic conviction that God had chosen Israel and given it the land.

Occasionally the prophets spoke of Abraham, Isaac, and Jacob (cf. Jer 33:19-22, which admittedly is prose written in Deuteronomistic style) or of the time of the exodus (Jer 2:6-8; Ezek 20:6-8; Hos 11:1-4) as foundational. That they did not do so more often is perhaps explicable by the following: the prophets could assume that the people knew their own religious story, and they were more concerned with preventing the people from squandering what God had given them than with repeating the story itself. Even when they predicted disaster, they often foresaw a better day beyond. Hosea, for example, predicted destruction but looked beyond it to a new exodus (11:5, 11). When the anonymous voice behind much of Isaiah 40–55 spoke of the future, he too did so in terms of a new exodus (e.g., Isa 40:3-5; 43:1-2, 19-21; 48:20-22), and the tradition bearers responsible for the book of Jeremiah spoke of a new covenant (Jer 31:31-34).

Monotheism

Monotheism may be defined as "the belief in and worship of one God, combined with the denial of the existence of all others." As such, monotheism does not appear in the Pentateuch or the Former Prophets. To be sure, the Ten Commandments restricted Israelite worship to God alone ("You shall have no other gods before me," Exod 20:3), and Joshua is reported to have laid the same requirement on the Israelites on Mt. Shechem (". . . choose this day whom you will serve, whether the gods your ancestors served in the region beyond the River or the gods of the Amorites in whose land you are living; but as for me and my household, we will serve the LORD," Josh 24:15). Still, neither of these verses expresses the view that the God of Israel was the only God; rather, they taught that out of all the gods Israel was to worship only one.

Scholars often argue that the first OT book to teach monotheism was Second Isaiah, and obviously it did teach that Yahweh was the only god (cf. Isa 40:12-31; 44:6-20; 45:5-8; 46:1-13). The prophet taunted the Babylonians about their so-called gods, who were so helpless they had to be carried about by humans on carts; unlike the God of Israel, they could help no one (Isa 44:9-20; 46:6-11). The prophet may well have been guilty of special pleading here. No doubt people in Babylon understood full well that the images were mere representations of the gods and not the real things. For Second Isaiah, however, the distinction between a nonexistent god and the representation of such a god was not a distinction worth making. Hence he ridiculed them for worshipping decorated sticks.

Still, the honor of being the first prophet to articulate monotheism may well belong to Jeremiah. In an early poetic sermon, he challenged his audience to conduct a search to see if any other people besides Israel had been so foolish as to change its gods. He asked rhetorically (2:11): "Has a nation changed its gods, even though they are no gods?" Since the implied answer was "No," Israel was to worship Yahweh only for the simple reason that there were no other divinities.

Israel's Fidelity to God

Some of the prophets feared that Israel would so break faith with God that they would forfeit not only their land but their raison d'etre as the special possession of God. Hence most of them (Nahum constituting a clear exception) called Israel to fidelity to God alone. Idolatry in the sense of image making was forbidden in the Second Commandment. Obedience to that commandment may have been spotty, but it was far-reaching enough to mark Israel as unique in its resistance to making images (Harrelson 1980: 61-72). A reader can feel the indignation of Ezekiel in his exposé (often by name!) of religious leaders who violated the commandment by worshipping the images of terrestrial and subterrestrial beings (Ezekiel 8).

Israel had met God in the desert, and may have thought of God as a god of fire. In Palestine, however, the Israelites were grain farmers, husbandmen of grapevines, and owners of livestock. They dwelled in an agrarian society, where the Canaanites worshipped Baal as the god of rain and fertility. The prophets railed at Israel's infidelity in worshipping Baal (Hosea 2), presumably through fertility rites, possibly even including ritual prostitution (Amos 2:7b). Or, even worse, the people may have worshipped Yahweh as if Yahweh were a fertility god.

If the temptation to worship the Canaanite deities was strong, so was the temptation to worship the gods of the powerful kingdoms around Israel, kingdoms that exerted strong economic and political pressure. Standing behind the decisions of Judah's kings to build sanctuaries to the deities of those countries, particularly Egypt, Babylon, and Assyria, must have been an insistence by the kings of those lands that loyal subjects worship their gods in addition to local gods. Hence the prophets predicted the overthrow of those nations as much out of religious as of political motivation.

Social Responsibility

Some of the prophets also called their people to observe social responsibility. Peripheral prophets in particular called for social justice. Widows, orphans, resident aliens, and the righteous poor, that is, people without material clout and therefore without political clout, were to receive justice (cf. Amos 2:6-7a; 4:1-3; 5:5, 11-12, 24; Mic 2:1-2; 3:1-4, 9-12; Zeph 1:10-12; 3:1-5). Likewise the central prophet Isaiah reprimanded those who foreclosed on lands and houses when the poor could not pay their bills (Isa 5:8).

Punishment for Sin

Sin in the OT could be unintentional (Lev 5:2, 15-19) or intentional (Exodus 20), spontaneous (Exod 22:18-19) or premeditated (Exod. 22:1), ritual (Exod 34:11-26) or moral (Exod 20:12-17), individual (Exod 21:12, 15-17; Lev 4:27-31) or collective (Lev 4:13-26), active (Lev 6:12) or passive (Lev 5:1). All sin, however, was a violation of the law of God, and the prophets proclaimed or warned of God's punishment for all types of sins. Still, primarily the prophets condemned idolatry, both corporately and privately, and social sins, where one person or one class of persons took advantage of another. The major sins of adultery, murder, and theft of all sorts called forth warnings of God's punishment.

At times they threatened punishments that seem excessive to modern readers. Dempsey 2000 points to passages that depict creation's suffering when there is a breach between God and humans (cf. Isa 1:2-9), that announce God's intention to assert power in such a way that it deals with sin by destruction rather than reconciliation, and even prejudge the poor as incapable of repenting (Jer 5:1-17), and that promise the use of divine power destructively against idolaters (Ezek 6:1-7). She points to feminine-gendered language used to impugn a nation whose leaders were male (Mic 1:2-7).

In the face of such passages, the reader needs to remember that the prophets were not trained ethicists. They were preachers and poets, people caught up at times in personal stress, but whose understanding of God's justice at times needed improvement. Sometimes those images were clearly hyperbolic (Zeph 1:2). Further, more than once (e.g., Amos 7:1-3, 4-6; Ezek 11:13-21; cf. priests in Joel 2:17; Abraham in Gen 18:22-33; and Moses in Exod 32:7-14), the OT portrayed a prophet interceding with God, imploring God not to destroy God's people. These passages may well have the characters reversed. It seems likely that forgiveness lay in the heart of God and vengeance in the hearts of the people. The prophet Ezekiel grapples with the issue of God's potentially destroying Israel, following as it were God's train of thought, and has God pull back (Ezekiel 20).

God's Fidelity to Israel

This topic is central to the prophets and might well have been the first discussed, but God's punishment of Israel for sins seemed at times to call God's fidelity to Israel into question. While the people feared that God had abandoned them (Isa 49:14; cf. Lam 5:20-22), and while the prophets entertained such thoughts too (Joel 2:14), ultimately the people who transmitted those messages saw God's turning to Israel. Even the book of Amos ends with five verses of hope! The exiles in Babylon must also have felt that all was lost and that God was defeated. Second Isaiah would not exonerate them from responsibility for their exile, and could describe it as a divorce (Isa 54:7), but his final word was remarriage (Isa 54:5-6; cf. Hosea 3).

Eschatology

If by the word "eschatology" one has in mind the end of time, the day of judgment, and consignment to eternal life or condemnation, then the OT contains no eschatology. Many prophets hoped for and depicted a day when Israel would repent and be blessed again by God, but there was nothing of an *end,* an *eschaton,* in such preaching. Only the apocalyptic book of Daniel portrays an end with a resurrection (Dan 12:5-13), and even there resurrection probably is not universal. In some of the prophets, however, especially among the exilic prophets Ezekiel and Second Isaiah and the post-exilic prophets Third Isaiah (Isa 56–66), Isaiah 24–27, Joel, and Zechariah, one finds a reasonably consistent expectation of the end of evil. Gowan 1986 argues that their eschatology has a center, the restoration of Zion, and develops three basic themes. The first is the transformation of human society, including restoration to the promised land, a place for the nations, and sometimes the hope for a Messiah. The second theme is the transformation of the human person, brought about by God's forgiveness, and involving a new heart, a new spirit, and a new covenant with God. The final theme is the transformation of nature, including a new ecology.

Prophecy and Apocalyptic Literature

As mentioned above, the book of Daniel is an apocalypse rather than a prophetic book. One can observe several differences immediately. (1) Apocalypses constitute a distinct literary genre (see the next paragraph). (2) Typically they bear the name of an ancient worthy (e.g., Adam, Shem, Enoch, or Abraham) or a scribe (e.g., Baruch, Ezra, or Daniel), but rarely the name of a prophet. (3) They are pessimistic about the course of history and anticipate a divine inbreaking putting an end to it, not simply ending evil.

Definition

Apocalypses reveal the hidden future by narrating the sweep of history or a trip through the cosmos, through which narration they reveal an imminent end-time salvation and/or an otherworldly reality that interpret the readers' present, earthly circumstances in light of the supernatural world and of the future, in order to influence both their understanding and behavior (J. J. Collins 1979: 9; A. Y. Collins 1986: 7). This theology is not limited to apocalypses, however, so any work that exhibits this theology may be termed "apocalyptic."

Characteristics

Apocalypses typically exhibit several literary characteristics: pseudonymity, coded speech, graphic imagery, and exhortation. The subject matter, often seen by a visionary who does not understand, typically requires an otherworldly interpreter and/or guide. Themes characteristic of apocalypses include a periodization of history, in which there emerges a repeated and predictable pattern that will be ended by God's eschatological inbreaking. Much "prediction" in historical apocalypses is "prophecy after the fact," since the narrative begins with the life of the pseudonymous ancient author and comes down to the time of the real author, seen as standing just prior to the eschaton. This end may be accompanied by cosmic upheavals and the reversal of fortunes. God may act on God's own or utilize a Messiah.

Origin

Apocalypses are by no means unique to Israel and the early church; rather, they were common in the ancient Near East before and after the time of Jesus. Hence, earlier scholars sometimes denigrated apocalypticism as a product of foreign influence. Its ties to the OT are too obvious, however, simply to view it as an import. Because apocalypticism draws on themes similar to those of the prophets, it has been termed the "child of prophecy." Other scholars have noted its similarities to the wisdom literature of the OT. That apocalypses draw on both types of literature proves little about their origin. It appears now that they could arise in any kind of group in Israel (or elsewhere) that *perceived itself* as relatively deprived and developed its own program for the future.

Conclusion

No sketch of the messages of the prophets can do justice to their richness and complexity, but these themes highlight the seriousness of the prophetic task in the OT and the abiding relevance of the prophets to those who worship God. Some themes, for example, the concept of the Messiah, might have received more attention than they have here. That theme, however, is relatively minor in the prophetic books in comparison with the prophetic focus on the kings contemporary with the prophets. Its importance for the NT in its quest to explain who Jesus was makes it seem more important to the Christian reader than it was to the OT prophets. The comments on the individual books within the prophetic corpus will give more balance to such themes.

Bibliography. Boccaccini, G. 2002, *Roots of Rabbinic Judaism: An Intellectual History from Ezekiel to Daniel,* Grand Rapids: Eerdmans • Collins, A. Y. 1986, "Introduction: Early Christian Apocalypses," pp. 1-11 in *Early Christian Apocalypticism: Genre and Social Setting,* Semeia 36, Decatur: Scholars Press • Collins, J. J. 1979, "Introduction: Towards the Morphology of a Genre," pp. 1-20 in *Apocalypse: The Morphology of a Genre,* Semeia 14, Missoula: Scholars Press • Davies, P. R. 1998, *Scribes and Schools: The Canonization of Hebrew Scriptures,* Library of Ancient Israel, Louisville: Westminster/John Knox • Dempsey, C. J. 2000, *Hope Amid the Ruins: The Ethics of Israel's Prophets,* St. Louis: Chalice • Gerstenberger, E. S. 2003, "Psalms in the Book of the Twelve: How Misplaced Are They?" pp. 72-89 in *Thematic Threads in the Book of the Twelve,* eds. P. L. Redditt and A. Schart, BZAW 325, Berlin and New York: Walter de Gruyter • Gowan, D. 1986, *Eschatology in the Old Testament,* Philadelphia: Fortress; 2d ed. 2000, Edinburgh: T&T Clark • Harrelson, W. 1980, *The Ten Commandments and Human Rights,* OBT, Philadelphia: Fortress • Johnson, A. R. 1962, *The Cultic Prophet in Ancient Israel;* 2d ed. 1962, Cardiff: University of Wales Press • Knight, D. A. "Whose Agony, Whose Ecstacy? The Politics of Deuteronomic Law," pp. 97-112 in *Shall Not the Judge of All the Earth Do What Is Right? Studies on the Nature of God in Tribute to James L. Crenshaw,* eds. D. Penchansky and P. L. Redditt, Winona Lake, Ind.: Eisenbrauns • March, W. E. 1974, "Prophecy," pp. 141-78 in *Old Testament Form Criticism.* Trinity University Monograph Series in Religion II, ed. J. H. Hayes, San Antonio: Trinity University • von Rad, G. 1962, 1965, *Old Testament Theology,* New York: Harper and Brothers • Redditt, P. L. 1995, *Haggai, Zechariah, Malachi,* NCBC, London: HarperCollins; Grand Rapids: Eerdmans; • Redditt, P. L. 2001, "Recent Research on the Book of the Twelve as One Book," in *CR:BS* 9:47-80 • Smith, J. V. "Prophet," in *ISBE,* rev. ed. 1986, ed. G. W. Bromiley, Grand Rapids: Eerdmans, 3:986-1004 • Thompson, L. L. 1978, *Introducing Biblical Literature: A More Fantastic Country,* Englewood Cliffs: Prentice-Hall, 1978 • Westermann, C. 1967, *Basic Forms of Prophetic Speech.* Philadelphia: Westminster.

Isaiah

Margaret Barker

INTRODUCTION

Reading Isaiah

The book of Isaiah was not written by one person at one time and in one place; rather, it was the product of a long and complex history. Traditionally, we have read the final form of the text and allowed the words to make their own impact. The complex literary history of Isaiah has been unknown to most of its readers, but this has in no way diminished the value of the book or the power of the prophetic word. Nevertheless, the fruits of scholarship can greatly enrich any reading of Isaiah and enable an appreciation of the processes by which the words of the prophets, not just Isaiah, were preserved, transmitted, augmented, and interpreted as part of the living tradition of the faith community.

The ancient view, recorded in the Babylonian Talmud (*b. B. Bat.* 14b; 15a), was that Isaiah's oracles had been collected and preserved by King Hezekiah; but modern study has detected a more complex process. First it was recognized that the book was not a unity. By the end of the eighteenth century, scholars had recognized a division at the end of ch. 39; then in 1892 Bernhard Duhm suggested that the two sections had originally been separate works, joined together after the time of the Chronicler. He also suggested a further division at the end of ch. 55. Chs. 40–55, he said, were the work of a prophet who lived and wrote in Phoenicia during the exile. Many, but not all, scholars adopted this new prophet, "Deutero-Isaiah" but most located him in Babylon as the prophet of the exile. The theory which eventually emerged was that the first section (chs. 1–39) consisted of the oracles of Isaiah in Jerusalem in the period 750-700 BC; the second (chs. 40–55, Deutero-Isaiah) came from an unknown prophet in the exile in Babylon, and the third (chs. 56–66, Trito-Isaiah) was a postexilic work. The date suggested for this final "Isaiah" varied between the late sixth century and the third century BC. Subsequent study suggested that the first section was not the work of one author but rather a collection of material adapted and interpreted over several generations. The same was then said of the third section; it was a collection of prophetic material from many different voices.

The second phase was a study of how the various materials in the book had been assembled and transmitted. It soon became apparent that the words of the prophets had remained a living force in the community and that they were, as a result, used and reused by subsequent generations. These later readers did not simply collect and read the texts; they added their own interpretation, set the older prophecies within new frameworks to show their relevance to a new situation, and so on. This reuse of prophecy may, in some cases, have shifted the emphasis of the original or even altered it. All these stages of change and growth can be detected within the text, and the intention of the "redactors" (or editors) emerges from the texts they had transformed while transmitting and preserving them. One theory is that there was a major reworking of the original Isaiah oracles about a hundred years after the prophet's death, in the time of King Josiah (Barth 1977). Another proposes eight stages in the development of Isaiah 1–35: the original, a seventh-century redaction, two reworkings by Deuteronomists during the exile, a further reinterpretation in the early fifth century by priests returned from Babylon, additions by Torah-oriented Jews who wanted the unfaithful destroyed, a further fourth-century redaction, and some early Hellenistic additions (Vermeylen 1977). The most recent, comprehensive theory is that Isaiah 1–55 is the work of Deutero-Isaiah, who took the earlier prophecies and reworked them for his new situation in the exile as well as adding the oracles formerly attributed to him. The message of "Isaiah" became one of punishment followed by restoration. Thus the elements of chs. 1–39, which resemble those of chs. 40–55, are explained (Williamson 1994).

Some scholars envisage a group of the prophet's disciples (mentioned in Isa 8:16) who wrote down, or perhaps memorized, the original sayings and then handed them on to their own disciples. All the teachings of that "school" would have been attributed to the founder, the original prophet, much as the laws of Israel were attributed to Moses or the psalms to David. The sayings of the rabbis, centuries after the time of Isaiah, were transmitted by their disciples in this way, and a similar process is thought to underlie the Gospels. The sayings of Jesus were originally memorized by disciples and reached their present form only after a period of oral transmission within the Christian communities. The problem with this theory is that there is no real evidence for such schools of disciples in the OT period unless we find links to the bands of prophets who appear in the stories of Saul, playing music and falling into ecstasy (1 Sam 10:5-6). There were groups like this in Jerusalem; in the Chronicler's account of the temple service certain of the sons of Asaph were appointed to prophesy in the temple with lyres, harps, and cymbals (1 Chr 25:1). The story of Elijah's mantle falling on Elisha shows that at least one prophet had a designated successor (2 Kgs 2:9-13), and Jeremiah had a personal scribe named Baruch who wrote down his words (Jer 36:4, 32). The three court officials mentioned in Isaiah 36 may have been responsible for collecting the earlier Isaiah material, the basis for the talmudic tradition of Hezekiah and his retinue.

Closely linked to the problem of material added to the original words of the prophet is the question of pseudepigraphy, writing under a false name. This was not seen as forgery but rather as a close identification with the master in whose name the words were uttered or written. The extraordinary exchange between Jesus and his disciples (Matt 16:13-14 and pars.) shows that even in the first century AD people believed that the prophets could return from the dead, and that Jesus was originally identified as one of them. In John's vision of the heavenly Jesus in Revelation 2–3 he is told to write down the (new) words of Jesus and send them to the seven churches. These were accepted as the words of Jesus, received by his disciple in a state of inspiration. The prophet continued to speak after his death. There were also many writings in the name of Enoch, clearly from different periods yet assembled into collections and preserved by people committed to their characteristic traditions. All are anonymous except insofar as they bear the name of Enoch, presumably received and transmitted by the followers of the ancient sage.

Something similar happened with the oracles of Isaiah; he continued to speak through his disciples, and his name was still being attached to new compositions as late as the first century AD. A complex and possibly composite text known as the *Martyrdom and Ascension of Isaiah* described the martyrdom of the prophet on the orders of the wicked king Manasseh. Incorporated into the story are two visions of Isaiah, both describing the early years of Christianity. The present form of this text is clearly a Christian composition and raises the interesting question: Why should the first Christians in Palestine (which is where the work probably originated) have attributed their own "visions" to Isaiah? It may have been because he was the prophet of the "last things" (Sir 48:24), the particular concern of the first Christians. New material, however, attaching to the name of Isaiah was still appearing in the early Christian period, a fact which must be borne in mind when considering how the book of Isaiah reached its final form. The period between the final additions to the canonical book of Isaiah and the earliest stratum of the *Martyrdom* cannot have been very great.

A more prosaic explanation of the collection and transmission of Isaiah material is that it was the work of scribes. The most extreme version of this theory is that chs. 40–66 were odds and ends added to the original Isaiah scroll to fill up the space since Isaiah was shorter than Ezekiel and Jeremiah. Or, it is suggested, the basic prophetic texts were expanded with all sorts of material not necessarily prophetic in origin. This process, a "rolling corpus," has been compared to a snowball growing in size as it rolls along (McKane 1986: l-lxxxiii). The oracles ascribed to any one prophet were expanded in the light of other texts and traditions known to later scribes, and thus the similarities between, say, Hosea 13–14 and Isaiah 26–27 could be explained.

The most recent phase of Isaiah scholarship has returned to a study of the whole text as it now stands, the final form of the book. This "literary" reading of Isaiah, while being aware that it is not the work of one author, nevertheless accepts the overall unity of the book. Thus canonical criticism adds theological as well as literary reasons for accepting and reading the final form of the text; *this* is the book which the faith communities accepted as Scripture, not any of the hypothetical earlier forms. This is also the form which is used today, and the present context of Isaiah is the faith community which reads it as Scripture.

In addition, it is important for Christian readers to know how Isaiah was understood in the first century AD since it accounts for most of the OT quotations and allusions in the NT. More than half the quotations attributed to Jesus himself are from Isaiah, suggesting that he identified closely with the book and possibly also with the prophet himself. The names "Jesus" and "Isaiah" are similar in form and meaning, and Isaiah's Servant was central to Jesus' self-understanding. The story of the synagogue sermon at Nazareth may be one of Luke's literary creations, but if there is a substratum of accurate recollection, it must be that there was an Isaiah scroll in the synagogue of Jesus' home community. Scrolls were expensive items, and poor communities would have had very few; perhaps only the Law and the Psalms. If Jesus' home community possessed an Isaiah scroll, he would have been very familiar with its contents, and this could account for the extraordinarily prominent place it has in his teaching and in the early church. Jesus identified himself as the prophetic voice of Isaiah 61 at the start of his ministry (Luke 4:18-21), and Matthew presents the ministry as largely the fulfillment of Isaiah's prophecies. This may be one of Matthew's literary fictions, but it could just as easily be an accurate record of what Jesus thought he was doing. The book of Revelation is also steeped in the words and images of Isaiah.

One complete scroll of Isaiah and part of another were found among the Dead Sea Scrolls, so it is reasonably certain what was in an Isaiah scroll in the first century AD. With some significant exceptions, which will be noted when the passages are discussed in detail, the Hebrew text is the one generally used today. But having the words is not the same as knowing how those words were understood, and for this we are dependent on the Targum, a translation of Isaiah into Aramaic. When Hebrew was no longer the everyday language of Palestine, readings in the synagogue were translated, not as a literal, word-for-word rendering but rather as a free translation incorporating a variety of other material, showing how Isaiah was understood at that time. The *Targum of Isaiah (Tg. Isa)* is particularly significant for understanding some of the messianic prophecies used by the first Christians, and these, too, will be noted later.

An Outline of the Book

Ch. 1	Various poems, possibly compiled as an introduction to the final form of the book
Chs. 2–12	Oracles about Judah and Jerusalem reflecting the political crises of the late eighth century BC caused by the westward expansion of Assyria

Chs. 13–23	Oracles against other nations
Chs. 24–27	The Isaiah Apocalypse
Chs. 28–31	More oracles about the Assyrian crisis
Chs. 32–33	Oracles about kingship
Ch. 34	Oracles against Edom
Ch. 35	Oracle of salvation for Israel
Chs. 36–39	Historical material; stories about Isaiah during the Assyrian crisis
Chs. 40–55	The oracles usually attributed to Deutero-Isaiah
Chs. 55–66	Collection of later oracles, usually attributed to Trito-Isaiah

Prophetic Speech

The words of the prophets were not delivered and recorded in the normal day-to-day speech patterns of their time. Investigation has shown that certain forms of speech frequently recur, and these can give some indication of the setting in which the prophets spoke. There are, for example, oracles of judgment, when the prophet warns of impending doom and gives the reasons for it. Some were directed against Judah and Jerusalem, for example, Isaiah 5 among the early material and Isaiah 58 in a later and slightly different form; others were directed against foreign nations (e.g., Isaiah 13–19). There are also oracles of salvation, announcing that help from the LORD was either assured or at hand. Many of these are to be found in Isaiah 41–44, and it has been suggested that oracles of this type in the earlier part of the book are a sign of reworking by Deutero-Isaiah.

Oracles of judgment and salvation probably originated in the temple. In response to Hezekiah's prayer for help against the Assyrians, for example, Isaiah delivered an oracle of judgment against the king of Assyria (Isaiah 37). Presumably this was a typical setting for his pronouncements. How the oracles of the prophets related to the oracles of the priests is a matter for speculation; there is no concrete evidence. They could have been the same; Jeremiah and Ezekiel *were* priests. Deutero-Isaiah, the prophet of the exile, adapted the traditional forms to a new situation. Since he had neither king nor temple, he was responding in recogniszable style to the pleas of his people in exile.

There were also trial scenes which could have been based on the everyday court procedures of the time, but it is possible that these, too, originated in a temple setting. Ps 73:15-20 describes the judgment of the wicked in the sanctuary of the temple, the place of the LORD's throne, and Psalm 82 describes the heavenly court where worthless heavenly beings are judged. When a prophet described how the LORD judged Israel (Isa 3:13-15; Mic 6:1-5), the gods of the nations (e.g., Isa 41:21-24), or even the high priest himself (Zech 3:1-5), it is likely that he was describing the heavenly court and a corresponding temple ritual.

There are hymn forms, and again we are pointed to a temple setting. The style of Deutero-Isaiah in particular (e.g., Isa 42:10-13) was much influenced by the formal hymn style found in the Psalms, and those who argue that the original Isaiah prophecies were reworked by Deutero-Isaiah consider Isaiah 12 as another of his characteristic hymns. It has been suggested that the whole of Isaiah 40–55 was a reworking of traditional liturgical patterns and that the autumn New Year festival from the first temple was the basis of Deutero-Isaiah's message of hope and renewal (Eaton 1979).

The most intriguing questions raised by the forms of prophetic speech are those most often overlooked or taken for granted because they are so familiar. Some of the prophet's words, such as the threat of the Day of Judgment in Isa 2:12-19, described what the LORD was about to do. These pronouncements suggest that a prophet had access to the heavenly court where these matters were decided (Isaiah 6; Amos 3:7). This right was also granted to the high priest (Zech 3:7), and, like Isaiah, he had to have his iniquity taken away before he could enter the presence of God (Zech 3:4; cf. Isa 6:7). This is the setting of the earliest material in *1 Enoch*. The seer described his experience as a sleep in which he saw visions and was summoned into the presence of the Great Holy One to hear his words (*1 Enoch* 14).

On many occasions, however, the prophet spoke not as himself but as the LORD, for example, in Isa 30:1, 12, 15 or 31:4. Isaiah has more divine speech than Jeremiah or Ezekiel; the personality of Isaiah himself is not important (Seitz 1988: 116-23). We simply do not know in what context and with what authority a human being was able to speak and have his speech accepted as that of the divinity. It appears that the prophets went into a trance and believed themselves possessed by the Spirit of the LORD. They became his mouthpiece, as did the king (2 Sam 23:2; Ps 2:7). Something similar was implied of Jesus; the Spirit came upon him and he spoke with authority, not like the scribes (Mark 1:10, 22). He was the LORD.

We can only speculate as to where and on what occasions such possession occurred, but a ritual or temple setting is likely. We have domesticated the prophets, but the originals were probably rather wild and terrifying figures. Saul was overcome by the music of a band of prophets, "the Spirit fell upon him mightily, and he prophesied" (1 Sam 10:10); Elisha fell under the power of the LORD as a minstrel played for him (2 Kgs 3:15); David appointed musicians to "prophesy"in the temple (1 Chr 25:1); Ezekiel "flew" (Ezek 8:3); and Isaiah "saw the LORD" (Isa 6:1).

There has been a tendency, especially among Protestant scholars, to present the prophets as the guardians of Israel's religious purity, opposed to the dubious practices of the temple and priestcraft. The reality was rather different; Ezekiel was himself a priest (Ezek 1:3), Jeremiah was from a priestly family (Jer 1:1), and it is possible that the Levites were the musician-prophets of the first temple; 2 Kgs 23:2 describes a procession of priests and *prophets*, whereas the later reworking of the same passage (2 Chr 34:30) has "priests and *Levites*." One of these Levites' prophecies is recorded; about a century before Isaiah, the Spirit fell upon one Jahaziel while he was in the temple area, and he prophesied success in a forthcoming battle (2 Chr 20:14-17). Priests and prophets are linked as temple personnel (e.g., Jer 6:13; 26:7, 16; Lam 2:20); there may even have been accommodation for them. The "sons" of a man of God had a chamber in the temple (Jer 35:4). *Prophetic speech forms did not "imitate" those of the temple; they were the speech forms of the temple.*

How the oracles were recorded in the first place is a matter for speculation, but the oracles of ancient Greece may shed some light on the process. Plutarch, in his treatise *The Oracles at Delphi* 25, records "the oft-repeated tale" of men who used to wait for the cryptic utterances of the oracle and then turn them into accepted poetic forms for oracular pronouncements. Perhaps the most imaginative way into this strange world of the prophets is William Golding's novel *The Double Tongue,* in which he reconstructs the life of a young woman who became the "oracle" at Delphi, how she read and memorized the library of ancient oracles kept at the shrine, how her pronouncements came when she was in a smoke-induced trance, how she was manipulated by, and in her turn manipulated, the priests, and how together they influenced the politics and trade of their time by their pronouncements.

It is often impossible to establish an "original" meaning for an oracle, let alone the circumstances in which it was first delivered. The reuse of oracles can sometimes be detected from obvious additions to the text, but theories of wholesale reworking are at best precariously based.

Oracular speech in any culture is ambiguous, allusive, and enigmatic. Those who have never experienced living prophecy find the OT oracles opaque, as would a reader of T. S. Eliot who was alien to English culture. His poetry is full of allusions and echoes which communicate far more than the words on the page. Commentaries with detailed notes may help "outsiders," but they do not, in the end, create contact with the poet and his words. How much more must this be true of modern readers of the Hebrew prophets.

Isaiah and *1 Enoch*

Most readers of the prophets today read with the eyes of the Deuteronomists, who gained influence and eventually altered the beliefs and worship of Israel about a hundred years after the time of Isaiah. Known as "Josiah's reform," this movement put in place what we now accept as the preexilic religion of Israel: a belief in one God, who was heard but not seen, with emphasis on Moses, the exodus, and the covenant at Sinai. It had a secular view of kingship, no theology of creation, a hostility to many temple traditions and practices, and no place for the idea of atonement.

The influence of the Deuteronomists on our perception of Israel's religion has been enormous, not least because they wrote or edited most of the "primary" sources. Their influence can seriously distort any reading of First Isaiah.

The greatest of Israel's prophets had seen the LORD, knew nothing of Moses and the exodus, and his covenant was not that of Sinai. *One of the keys to understanding Isaiah is being aware that he spoke of the eternal covenant,* the cosmic covenant which bound together the whole natural and moral order (Murray 1992). The bonds of this covenant were broken by the rebellion of the angels, the sons of God, and by the sin of humans who fell into their power. When this happened both creation and human society began to collapse.

The covenant was restored and renewed by atonement rituals which annually enacted the LORD coming to his people to destroy whatever breached the covenant and threatened the security it offered. He destroyed enemies, removed the destructive consequences of sin, and then healed and restored both creation and human society. Fertility was restored, and people who had been cut off by their sins were brought back into the community. The king "was" the LORD in human form, the son of God, enthroned in the sanctuary of the temple. This pattern of atonement, judgment, healing, and renewal is fundamental throughout Isaiah and suggests a temple context for the oracles. They were setting contemporary events, fears, and hopes within the framework of tradition. Preaching, in fact.

The temple reformers had to adapt these fundamental ideas of covenant and atonement when they declared that the host of heaven was no longer part of Israel's religion (Deut 4:19). The LORD was no longer "the LORD of hosts" (Isa 37:16; cf. 2 Kgs 19:15), the Deuteronomists' version of the same passage. Covenant for them became a "treaty" between Israel and her God, and the king was merely human, one who upheld the law of the LORD (Deut 17:14-20). Once the framework of Isaiah had been thus obscured, the basis for understanding the texts was distorted.

Isaiah believed that he had seen the LORD, he described the king as divine, and he was steeped in the earlier temple tradition. *Isaiah's was the faith and tradition of Jerusalem before the influence of the Deuteronomists.* One aspect of this, the Zion tradition, has been reconstructed from the imagery of the Psalms, especially Psalms 46, 48, and 76. The LORD was believed to defend his city, and all enemies were mysteriously defeated (von Rad 1975: 155-69). The king was his anointed one, his "son," the sign of the LORD's presence with his people (Psalms 2, 89, and 110).

The heirs to Isaiah's faith wrote *1 Enoch,* which describes the work of the Deuteronomists as "the blinding of those in the temple." At that time a man, almost certainly Isaiah, ascended to the divine presence, and then the temple was burned (*1 Enoch* 93:8). There are numerous places where themes in *1 Enoch* illuminate the text of Isaiah. *1 Enoch* could be an elaborate construction which chose to draw on themes from Isaiah, but the opposite seems to be the case, namely, that Isaiah knew the tradition which survived in *1 Enoch.* Nobody can date the material in *1 Enoch,* but many fragments have been found at Qumran, confirming that it was an important pre-Christian text. Beyond that, we can only guess its age.

The earliest stratum of *1 Enoch* describes how some angels (the "sons of God," who appear briefly in Gen 6:2) conspired against the Great Holy One, came to earth, and corrupted the creation with their heavenly knowledge. Their victims cried to heaven for help, and the archangels were sent to imprison the fallen angels and heal the earth. In another section Enoch is transported to heaven, where he sees the Great Holy One on his throne and is told to warn the angels of their fate. The heaven which Enoch enters is recognizable as the temple, and Enoch as a priest is trying to intercede for the fallen angels. Since temple worship after about 600 BC is condemned as impure and its personnel as blind (*1 Enoch* 93), *the similarities between* 1 Enoch *and Isaiah suggest that the Enoch tradition was that of the first temple, the royal cult of Jerusalem. The "blinding" of the priests suggests a division over the issue of changes in the temple.*

The book of Isaiah opens with these rebel sons condemned for lack of knowledge. Isaiah's call vision in the temple is exactly like Enoch's, and like Enoch he has to warn of judgment. The sins he condemns are "pride" (Isa 2:11, 17; 5:15; 9:9, etc.), "rebellion" (Isa 1:23, 28; 24:4-13; 30:8-14, etc.), and "abuse of wisdom" (Isa 2:6; 3:12; 5:21, etc.), exactly those of the fallen angels. Kings who do not trust their Holy One, who rely on the help and counsel of foreign courts, are condemned in terms of the Enoch myth. The punishments envisaged by Isaiah are those of "fire" (Isa 9:18; 10:16; 30:27-28), "desolation" (Isa 3:1-5; 5:5-6; 6:11, etc.), "falling from a great height" (Isa 2:12-16; 14:12, etc.), "imprisonment in a pit" (Isa 5:14; 14:15; 24:22, etc.), and "destruction by alien powers who were agents of the powers of heaven" (Isa 7:20; 10:5-6; etc.). All these are Enochic (*1 Enoch* 10, 21, 56, 69).

The book of Isaiah is crowded with angels, often unnoticed. The prophet receives his call in an assembly of angels, the taunt against Babylon (Isaiah 14) is the clearest example of Enochic mythology in the OT, and the Assyrian army is destroyed by an angel (Isa 37:36). The wicked rulers are judged like the evil angels (Isa 3:14; 43:28; cf. Psalm 82), a heavenly army appears (Isa 13:2-6), and angel figures attack Jerusalem (Isa 22:1-8). There is a whole host of angels in Isaiah 33.

Angels were the basis of Isaiah's political philosophy, just as in *1 Enoch,* where they appear as the seventy shepherds (*1 Enoch* 89:59), given limited powers to punish the people of Israel for their apostasy. The angels were to be judged, however, for any destruction beyond what the LORD had commanded, and their deeds were recorded by the angel scribe. These Enochic histories were probably written down long after the time of Isaiah; just as Isaiah described the Assyrians as agents of the LORD's anger against his people (Isa 10:5) but also warned that they would be punished for their pride and excesses (Isa 10:12-19), so the seventy shepherds who appear in the Enochic histories at exactly this point (*1 Enoch* 89:59) are permitted to rule and punish his people but not to excess. The seventy were the rulers of history who appear in the later gnostic texts as the Archons, the Rulers. The writer of the *Enoch* histories did not use the paradigms of the Deuteronomist or the Chronicler, the interpretations of history which appear in the OT. The Enochic writer used the same pattern as Isaiah did, suggesting that the Enoch tradition goes back to the time of Isaiah, independently of anything now in the OT.

As in the Enoch tradition, Isaiah knows of heavenly books (Isa 4:3; 30:8; 34:16) and a custom of presenting written petitions to the LORD. In a time of crisis, King Hezekiah takes the letter from the Assyrian messengers and "spreads it before the LORD" in the temple (Isa 37:14). Isaiah brings the LORD's reply (Isa 37:21). The fallen angels persuade Enoch to take their written petition into the presence of the LORD, and Enoch brings them the reply (*1 Enoch* 13).

The messianic and royal traditions, so clear in Isaiah, are a major theme in *1 Enoch,* forming the whole of the section known as "The Parables" (which have not been found at Qumran). "The Parables" also describe the cosmic covenant, "the great oath" which maintains the creation (*1 Enoch* 69:16-25). Isaiah's characteristic name for God is the Holy One of Israel; Enoch's is the Great Holy One. Both traditions describe the LORD as the King and as the LORD of hosts ("Spirits" in *Enoch*). Both portray the angels singing "Holy, Holy, Holy" around the heavenly throne.

The persistence of Enochic imagery throughout the entire Isaiah corpus, used and reused by Deutero- and Trito-Isaiah, suggests that all worked within a common framework which was too fundamental to abandon but rather had to be reinterpreted for the new situations. The most significant of these was the growing influence of the Deuteronomists. Trito-Isaiah is overtly critical of their beliefs and practices.

1 Enoch, like Isaiah, was not the work of one prophet but the collected traditions of several centuries. The relationship between them is complex. The oldest material, "The Book of the Watchers" (*1 Enoch* 6–16), was probably known to Isaiah. "The Apocalypse of Weeks" (*1 Enoch* 91, 93) and "The Dream Visions" (*1 Enoch* 83–90) show that Isaiah's interpretation of history was in use in the second century BC. "The Parables" (*1 Enoch* 37–71), which cannot be dated in their final form, are the fullest evidence for the royal ideology of the first temple. Similarities between "The Parables" and Isaiah's Servant are due to the fact that both of them know the royal traditions. It is important to recognize that some of *1 Enoch* is an interpretation of Isaiah's prophecies, but simplistic to say that *1 Enoch* is dependent on Isaiah (Knibb 1996: 228).

The Temple

The temple and its rituals were at the center of Isaiah's world. Time and again he presents contemporary events as the fulfillment of temple rituals and predicts their outcome accordingly. Whether or not he was the first to do this we cannot tell, but ritual becoming history is one of the characteristics of the Isaiah prophecies.

The temple was sacred space in sacred time. The building had been erected by Solomon about two hundred years before the time of Isaiah as the house of the LORD. The interior was divided into two areas: the holy of holies, which represented heaven, and the body of the temple, which represented the garden of Eden. The two were separated by an elaborately woven curtain which represented the material world hiding the LORD from human eyes. Behind the curtain were two huge cherubim which formed the golden chariot throne of the LORD. The best description of this is in 2 Chronicles 3–4, written long after Isaiah's time but incorporating authentic detail. Such monstrous figures were part of a cult which did not prohibit images. The king sat on the throne of the LORD and was worshiped as the LORD (1 Chr 29:20-23).

The main body of the temple was decorated with trees, flowers, and cherub figures (Ezek 41:15-26). It was Eden, the garden of the LORD. A small incense altar stood in front of the curtain, protecting the temple, and thus the world, from the wrath of the LORD, which could break out from the holy of holies at any time. Num 16:45-48 describes this process. Only priests could enter the temple, and only the high priest the holy of holies. When they did, they passed beyond the material world and so beyond time. They became part of the heavenly world with access to the secrets of creation and history as they stood in the presence of the LORD. Those who were cast out from the divine presence became mortal and suffered death, the fate of all mortals (Ps 82:7).

All the decorations of the temple were the earthly counterparts of a heavenly reality; Moses (Exod 25:40) and David (1 Chr 28:19) had both been given heavenly plans to reproduce on earth. In the prophets' visions, the temple came alive and they glimpsed the other world. Thus Isaiah heard the throne creatures speaking and saw the LORD (Isa 6:1-3); Ezekiel saw a fiery man seated on the chariot throne (Ezek 1:26-28), in fact a memory of the king but to him a vision of the LORD.

Many of the psalms were written for festivals in the temple, and it is from them that we can attempt to reconstruct what happened. At the start of his reign the king was transformed into a "son" of the LORD. Ps 89:19-37, read literally, gives an idea of what took place: a vision, an otherworldly experience, when the king was raised up (v. 19), anointed (v. 20), given power over the sea and the rivers (v. 25), and made the firstborn (v. 27). Psalm 110 adds detail: the king was to sit by the heavenly throne (v. 1), rule his enemies with God-given weapons (v. 2), and be a Melchizedek priest (v. 4). The obscure lines which now form v. 3 probably conceal a description of the "birth" of the king: he was born a son of the LORD from the womb of the morning, that is, from the sun goddess (Wyatt 1995: 588; cf. Rev 12:1-5, where the woman clothed with the sun gives birth to the Messiah). Psalm 2 is similar; the LORD and his anointed, his son, triumph over their foes. The king was also responsible for maintaining the created order by means of the justice and righteousness which flowed though him (Psalm 72). He spoke the words of the LORD (2 Sam 23:2) and upheld his law.

One of the great mysteries of the First Temple is the ritual of atonement. In the Second Temple period the annual Day of Atonement ritual was performed by the high priest, but during the monarchy it is likely that the king, the Melchizedek priest, was the key figure. Echoes and fragments in later texts and traditions suggest that the king had symbolically sacrificed himself (using an animal substitute) and used his own lifeblood to renew the creation by cleansing it from the effects of sin. He absorbed into himself all the residue of the people's guilt, and thus it was borne away. All who had been excluded by sin from the sacred community were thus readmitted (Barker 1996: 57-84).

Some of the mythology which accompanied these rites has been preserved. Deut 32:43 describes the LORD coming to avenge the blood of his servants and atone for the land. Hab 2:20–3:6 describes the LORD emerging from his sanctuary to wreak havoc on his enemies. The *Assumption of Moses,* a much later text, has preserved the interesting detail that the one who emerged from his holy place to bring the judgment was an angel priest (*Assumption of Moses* 10). The judgment was envisaged as the triumph of the LORD (in the person of the king) over his enemies. Psalm 58 and especially Psalm 82 afford glimpses of the judgment in Isaiah's time; the "Parables of Enoch" preserves the full picture.

Isaiah, like John on Patmos centuries later, saw the events of the heavenly world being realized in the history of his own time. He spoke to the king as the divine son who was assured of victory over his enemies; he knew that foes which massed against the LORD and his anointed (Ps 2:2) would be destroyed. The role of the royal high priest on the Day of Atonement inspired the Servant poem of Isaiah 53. The festival scenes in Isa 2:2-4, 4:2-6, and 25:6-9 depict the temple, both heaven and earth. Isaiah had stood before the heavenly throne.

Who could have had access to all this temple tradition? It is unlikely that it was common knowledge among the populace of Jerusalem. One possibility that cannot be dismissed is that Isaiah was a priest, as were those whose oracles were added to his to form the final scroll.

A Priestly Book?

Jeremiah was a priest (Jer 1:1), and Ezekiel was a priest (Ezek 1:3). There is much to suggest that the book of Isaiah, the third great body of prophecy, was also the work of priests. First, Isaiah uses the traditions found in *1 Enoch,* whose authors, by implication, identify themselves with the priests in Jerusalem before Josiah's reform. This they described as "the blinding" of those who lived in the temple (*1 Enoch* 93:8); the cult of the Second Temple was apostate (*1 Enoch* 93:9), and its offerings were polluted (*1 Enoch* 89:73; see on Isa 66:3). Second, there is the recurring theme of liturgy fulfilled which is central in Isaiah, explaining the royal oracles and the confidence that Jerusalem will, ultimately, be secure. Third, there are the sanctuary visions: the calls in Isaiah 6 and Isaiah 40 and the revelation of a new history and a new creation (see on Isa 40:12-31). Isaiah fears for the future of the temple (see on Isa 5:1-7). Deutero-Isaiah is concerned for the temple vessels (Isa 52:11). Clearest of all are the concerns of Trito-Isaiah: access to the temple (Isa 56:1-8), the corruption of the temple (Isa 57:7-10), the true meaning of atonement rites (Isa 58:1-10), and the recognition of priesthood (Isa 61:5). He scorns the rebuilt temple (Isa 66:1) and mocks at the hypocrisy of the new purity laws (Isa 66:3-4).

The changes of mood in the book can best be explained as reflecting the changes and divisions within the priesthood as the royal temple cult absorbed and came to terms with the ways of the Deuteronomists. Isaiah says nothing about Hezekiah's "reform," but neither does he condemn Ahaz's sacrifice of his son. The full impact of the Deuteronomists' changes was yet to come.

It is Deutero-Isaiah who testifies to the first impact on temple tradition. There was monotheism; the LORD and El were declared to be one. The vision of the LORD (Isaiah 6), became just the voice of the LORD (Isaiah 40; cf. Deut 4:12). There could be no image of the LORD (Isa 40:25; cf. Deut 4:1; see on Isa 40:1). The worship of the host of heaven was no longer permitted (Isa 40:25-6; cf. Deut 4:19). Wisdom, the Queen of Heaven, the heavenly Mother of the king, was abandoned, becoming a symbol for Jerusalem in Deutero-Isaiah (see on Isa 49:14-26) and being replaced by the law in Deuteronomy (Deut 4:6).

Trito-Isaiah is the voice of the ousted priests, those who kept to the older ways but found themselves excluded by postexilic innovations. Ezra 2:62 par. Neh 7:61-65 records the names of priests who were no longer acceptable, and Nehemiah 13 clearly describes the situation addressed by Trito-Isaiah: priests driven out of Jerusalem along with "the people of the land" who did not meet the stringent new requirements for purity.

The priestly laws in Numbers and Leviticus recognized obligations to all the worshipers of the Lord; the stranger *(ger)* kept the laws and benefited from the rituals (Douglas 1995: 280-92). The status of the stranger in the priestly laws of Numbers and Leviticus is clearly not that recognized in Ezra-Nehemiah, which is based on the requirements of Deuteronomy. Ezra, a priest (Ezra 7:11), implements changes which exclude fellow priests. The priests of the old temple, however, kept the larger vision and included in the LORD's people those who cried out against their Jewish kin (Neh 5:1). Thus the book of Isaiah draws to a close with a prophecy of division: "You shall leave your name to my chosen to use as a curse" (Isa 65:15). This division within the tradition and the priesthood was to shape the history of the Second Temple period.

The Historical Background to the First Section of Isaiah

Isaiah prophesied during the reigns of Uzziah (783-742 BC; also known as Azariah), Jotham (742-735 BC), Ahaz (735-715 BC), and Hezekiah (715-687 BC). These were turbulent years. The first half of the eighth century BC was a period of weakness for Assyria which the kings of Judah and Israel exploited. Jeroboam II in Israel and Uzziah in Judah regained control of neighboring territories, and by the middle of the century their two kingdoms extended almost as far as the empire of Solomon. Increased trade brought about the great prosperity and social change which Amos and Hosea condemned. Jeroboam II's death in 746 BC coincided with the resurgence of Assyria under Tiglath-pileser III and was followed by political anarchy in Israel (Isa 9:18-21). Jeroboam's son Zechariah was assassinated by one Shallum, himself soon murdered by Menahem, who then became king and paid tribute to resurgent Assyria. His son Pekahiah was killed after only a year on the throne and his assassin, Pekah, became the next king (2 Kings 15). He formed a coalition with Rezin of Damascus and some of the Philistine cities to resist the expansion of Assyria.

They tried to persuade Judah to join them, but when Jotham refused the allies prepared to attack him (2 Kgs 15:37). After Jotham's death, the northern allies tried to replace the new king, Ahaz, with a puppet of the coalition, one Ben Tabeel (Isa 7:6). The Edomites, who had been subjects of Judah for half a century, regained their independence at this time and expelled the occupying garrison from Elath (2 Kgs 16:6); it is not clear whether it was Edom or Aram, that is, the coalition, who expelled the troops and took possession of Elath. "Edom" and "Aram" look very similar in Hebrew. The Philistines also invaded and occupied the southern parts of Judah. Ahaz was thus attacked on three sides: from the north, the west, and the south. Isa 7:1–8:18 reflect this situation.

Ahaz practiced the old religion of Judah; he sacrificed and burned incense on high places and under trees. History has condemned him (2 Kgs 16:1-4; 2 Chr 28:1-4), but these may have been the actions of a devout man who was desperate in the face of his enemies. He lived before the Deuteronomists exerted their influence, and the account of his life in 2 Kings bears their hostile imprint. Not all the worshipers of Israel's God accepted the new ways of the Deuteronomists; Jer 44:15-19 records what some were saying after the "reform," when Jerusalem had fallen to the Babylonians. It was neglect of the ancient ways which had brought disaster to Judah; *1 Enoch* says much the same (*1 Enoch* 89:72-74; 93:8-9). Ahaz even "caused his son[s] to pass through fire" (2 Kgs 16:3; 2 Chr 28:3), a practice of which little is known, except that the children were "for the king" or "for Moloch"; the Hebrew can be read either way (2 Kgs 23:10). Since this is one of the few facts recorded about the reign of Ahaz, it must have been very significant to the writers of the Deuteronomic histories *even though Isaiah does not mention it.* Something similar is recorded of the king of Moab (2 Kgs 3:27); when he was besieged by a coalition from Israel, Judah, and Edom and in dire straits, he offered his son as a sacrifice on the city wall, and his enemies withdrew. Perhaps Ahaz initially sought to defend Jerusalem through the sacrifice of his son. Isaiah does not condemn this sacrifice, but it probably prompted the words of Mic 6:7, "Shall I give my firstborn for my transgression?"

Ahaz suffered disastrous defeats at the hands of the Syrians and the Israelites; large numbers of his subjects were taken to Samaria and saved from slavery only by the prophet Oded, who accused their captors of a crime against kinsfolk. The people of Judah were then released and sent home. Finally Ahaz ignored Isaiah and appealed to Assyria for help (2 Chr 28:16); according to the Deuteronomists, he said, "I am your servant and your son. Come up, and rescue me" (2 Kgs 16:7). He had to modify the temple in Jerusalem, presumably in recognition of his new overlord (2 Kgs 16:10-16), and a new altar was installed.

Tiglath-pileser moved westward and destroyed the coalition. The Philistines were subdued (734 BC; Isa 14:29-31), and the coast was secured as far as Egypt to prevent help from that quarter. He then overran Israelite lands in Galilee and Transjordan (2 Kgs 15:29). The Israelite king Pekah was assassinated by Hoshea, who became a vassal king of Assyria and saved a remnant of the Northern Kingdom for a few more years. He soon tried to reassert Israel's independence, hoping in vain for help from Egypt. Assyria attacked again in 724 BC and after a two-year siege Samaria fell in 721 BC to Sargon II, the new ruler of Assyria (Isa 28:1-4). This marked the end of the first phase of Isaiah's activity.

The second phase was the crisis which culminated in the Assyrian threat to Jerusalem in 701 BC. Ahaz remained a vassal of Assyria, but his successor Hezekiah ruled when the region's balance of power was changing. While Assyria was weakened and distracted by problems elsewhere in her empire, Egypt regained her strength under new Ethiopian rulers and decided to foment rebellion among Assyria's vassal states. The Philistine cities were the first to be drawn into revolt. Assyrian records show that Judah, Moab, and Edom were invited to join; Judah was offered support from Egypt (Isaiah 18). Jerusalem was divided; Isaiah warned against trusting Egypt (Isaiah 20; 30:1-5; 31:1-3), but Hezekiah's reaction is not known. When the revolt was crushed by Assyria, Judah was unharmed, and Hezekiah remained a subject king during the reign of Sargon.

Under his less able son Sennacherib, however, Hezekiah formally refused to pay tribute in 705 BC. He improved the defenses of Jerusalem and took steps to protect the city's water supply in case of siege (2 Chr 32:2-4). One account of his reign (2 Chr 29:3) says that he began immediately to purify and restore the temple. He invited the survivors in Israel to come to a great celebration of the Passover in Jerusalem, one month later than usual, so that there was time for the preparations (2 Chr 30:1-2). Some came. Great changes were made to the worship in Judah and Jerusalem, with the people abandoning the high places and pillars and destroying the Asherah and Nehushtan, the bronze serpent in the temple (2 Kgs 18:1-4). Isaiah does not mention this "reform"; one wonders whether he saw it that way or whether he would perhaps have agreed with the envoy of the king of Assyria (Isa 36:7) that Hezekiah could not expect help from the LORD since he had destroyed the holy places. Revolt against the LORD (Isa 1:2), which Isaiah condemned, could have included destruction of the older cult. The punishment for revolt against the LORD was "wrath" in the form of a plague (e.g., Num 16:43-49), and this would have been the most obvious interpretation of the plague which nearly killed Hezekiah (see on Isa 38:1). Isaiah's attitude to the king's plight is distinctly unsympathetic; perhaps he had predicted such a fate. The king recovered, and Isaiah pronounced that the city would also be saved (see on Isaiah 53).

Several other states (Tyre, the Phoenicians, and some Philistines) rebelled at the same time as Hezekiah, but he seems to have been the leader in the south, trying to persuade the remaining Philistines to join the coalition (2 Kgs 18:8). The Assyrians moved to crush the revolt in 701 BC, first taking Tyre (Isa 23:1-12) and then moving south against the Philistine cities. After defeating an Egyptian army which had been sent to help the rebels, the Assyrians began to attack Judah. Their own records tell how they destroyed forty-six cities and left Hezekiah trapped "like a bird in a cage" in Jerusalem (*ANET*: 288). According to the Deuteronomists, Hezekiah was in a desperate position and surrendered. He was forced to pay heavy tribute and cede territory to the conquerors (2 Kgs 18:13-16), an incident of which Isaiah says nothing. The Assyrian records are curiously ambiguous at this point and do not necessarily confirm the account in 2 Kings (see below on Isaiah 36–39).

2 Kgs 18:17–19:37 and the corresponding passage in Isaiah 36–37 are usually read as describing an attack on Jerusalem which ended with miraculous deliverance. The besieging army was devastated by the angel of the LORD, and the remnant returned home. The Assyrian records have nothing about this. Various solutions have been proposed. Perhaps there was a second campaign against Judah. After a period of internal problems when Assyria was again weakened, it is suggested, Hezekiah made another attempt to regain his independence, and the Assyrians returned in about 688 BC (Bright 1960: 282-87). Jerusalem was besieged and miraculously saved. Or perhaps, after Sennacherib had accepted his tribute, something caused him to doubt Hezekiah, and he returned to demand unconditional surrender, resulting in the devastation of his army by the angel of the LORD, a proposed context for Isaiah 33. Or perhaps the army really was devastated, but at Lachish, not Jerusalem (see on Isaiah 36–39). Isaiah, who had originally seen Hezekiah's plague as punishment for destroying the temple tradition, realized that he was the sin bearer for them all, the Servant, and thus the city had been saved. *The rite of atonement had been realized in the events of history.*

Hezekiah died in 687 BC and was succeeded by his son, the apostate Manasseh, who, according to later tradition, had the prophet Isaiah put to death with a saw (*Martyrdom of Isaiah;* cf. Heb 11:37).

COMMENTARY

Isaiah 1

The first verse is the first introduction to the prophecies; a second introduction, found at 2:1, suggests that this chapter may have been added to the completed collection of prophecies at a later date. The name "Isaiah" means "The LORD delivers"; no other person of this name is known in the First Temple period. Amoz, his father, was not the prophet Amos. Little is known about him. He prophesied in the days of four kings: Uzziah, Jotham, Ahaz, and Hezekiah. Some oracles seem to come from the time of Uzziah, even though his call was not until the year of that king's death (see below on 2:10-21). At least one could date from the reign of Manasseh (see below on Isa 19:18-22); a legend in *The Martyrdom and Ascension of Isaiah,* a first-century-AD text, says he was martyred in the time of the apostate Manasseh, being sawn in two (cf. Heb 11:37).

The prophecies are described as "the vision which he saw." It is possible that the word is used loosely here since there is little in the book which is obviously a vision. It could, however, be an indication of the way all the oracles were received, even though no visionary setting is mentioned. Jeremiah recorded how the prophets received oracles; they stood in the council of the LORD to perceive and hear his words. False prophets spoke "the vision of their own minds," not from the mouth of the LORD (Jer 23:16-18).

It is customary to suggest a context for the prophet's oracles: where he stood when he spoke in this way, to whom he spoke, and what situation prompted his words. Another question has to be: *How did the prophet receive these oracles?* Were they his private inspiration, or did he have the mystical experiences implied by the words of Jeremiah and Amos (Amos 3:7)? Standing in the council of the LORD means being present before the throne in heaven. We cannot assume that his call was his only mystical experience nor that he was unique among the prophets. Zechariah says he stood in the presence of the LORD (Zech 3:1-5) and saw the high priest Joshua vested for office. The place of the presence of the LORD was the holy of holies in the temple, and so these experiences were probably part of the temple cult. Habakkuk received his visions standing on a high tower, that is, in the holy of holies (see below on Isa 5:2), and he was told to write down on tablets the vision he saw there (Hab 2:1-2). What follows is a collection of woe oracles like those of Isaiah, and yet the present form of Habakkuk implies that they were the vision he received in the sanctuary. Ps 73:17-19 shows that visions of the judgment were received in the sanctuary of God. Amos saw the LORD standing next to the altar (Amos 9:1), that is, just outside the holy of holies, when he received a vision of the judgment. Zechariah, the father of John the Baptist, saw the angel of LORD standing in exactly the same place (Luke 1:11). It is likely that Isaiah also received his visions in the holy of holies, in the council of the LORD. His call vision alone is proof that he was familiar with this temple tradition; all that he proclaimed as his oracles could have been the words he received, or spoke, when he was in the presence of the LORD.

It is possible that the incense of the sanctuary created the conditions for these experiences, as did the burning leaves in the oracle at Delphi. The sanctuary incense was a special blend, for use only in the holy of holies when meeting the LORD (Exod 30:34-38). Its use elsewhere was absolutely forbidden. We can only guess what lies behind the traditions of Moses speaking with the LORD above the mercy seat (Exod 25:22), but the experience of Isaiah in the holy of holies when "the house was filled with smoke" (Isa 6:4) was clearly similar. *1 Enoch* 14–16 describes in detail what the other accounts assume: the prophet's ascent to the presence of God to learn of his imminent judgment on the fallen angels.

The first chapter is a collection of poems and fragments; vv. 21-26 and v. 28 are in the distinctive style of a lament, and vv. 2-17 may be a single poem with varieties of rhythm, but there is no general agreement about this.

The first poem opens with a clear reference to the fallen angels, *the sons of God:* "Sons have I reared and brought up, but they have rebelled against me." Heaven and earth are summoned to witness (v. 2; cf. Ps 50:4; also Deut 31:28; 32:1). The LXX of v. 2 differs from the MT: "sons have I begotten and exalted," as in Ps 89:19, which gives an even clearer picture of the sons in question. Given the other allusions in this passage, these "sons of God" must be the fallen angels who appear briefly in Gen 6:2 but are fundamental to *1 Enoch,* where they rebel against the Great Holy One, marry human wives, and produce children who corrupt the creation. Thus in v. 4 we meet "the offspring of evildoers, corrupting sons," perhaps originally "sons of the corrupters," who have forsaken the LORD and despised the Holy One. In *1 Enoch* the archangels are sent to punish the wicked and restore the creation. Here in Isaiah the sons, that is, the rulers, rebel, and the land of Judah is made desolate. The close relationship of king and land can be seen clearly in Psalm 72; when the royal son maintains justice and righteousness the whole land prospers. (Sophocles' *Oedipus the King* is a vivid illustration of this widely held belief; the unwitting sin of the king brought devastation to his kingdom.)

The title "the Holy One of Israel" is characteristic of Isaiah and of *1 Enoch.* It occurs twenty-eight times in Isaiah, with variants such as "his Holy One" at Isa 10:17; 49:7 and "your Holy One" at Isa 43:15. Elsewhere the title occurs in Jer 50:29; 51:5, in Pss 71:22; 78:41; 89:18, and as "the Holy One in Israel" in Ezek 39:7. Some scholars suggest that the title originated with Isaiah to describe the sense of awe and holiness which he felt at his call, but more likely is the suggestion, based on comparison with Ugaritic and Phoenician usage, that a "holy one" was one of the sons of God who appeared in radiant (human) form. In Ps 89:5-7 the holy ones are the heavenly court, and in Deut 33:2 the heavenly entourage (Van Selms 1982: 257-69). The title "the Holy One of Israel" describes the LORD as the radiant heavenly being who has special care of Israel, as the greatest of the heavenly court, but nevertheless as one of them (Barker 1992: 70-94). Other nations had their "holy ones"; in the time of First Isaiah, Israel still believed that its God was one among many, and as late as the second century BC history was still described as a struggle between angel princes (Dan 10:13, 20). Mary's royal child of the house of David was to be called a "Holy One, Son of God" (Luke 1:35). These national deities were the sons of God described in Deut 32:8 and *1 Enoch.* Isaiah views the political situation of his time as a battle between the various holy ones; when any one of them becomes too proud he is punished (e.g., Isa 10:15; 37:23 of Assyria; Isa 14:12, now applied to Babylon; cf. Phil 2:5-11 of Jesus).

1 Enoch opens with an extended comparison (*1 Enoch* 2–5), between the natural order which obeys God and the works of godless sinners. Isaiah is similar; 1:3 is a wisdom saying contrasting the folly in Jerusalem and the wisdom of dumb animals. The ox and the ass are familiar from Christmas crib scenes; early Christian tradition explains that the ox and the ass at the manger fulfilled Isaiah's prophecy that Israel would not understand (Justin *1 Apol.* 1.63; Pseudo-Matthew in Hennecke 1991: 1:410).

The devastated land (1:5-9) may reflect the state of Judah in 701 BC when Sennacherib invaded and ravaged the land, forcing Hezekiah to pay a huge tribute (1 Kgs 18:13-16). The personification of the land (1:5-6), wounded and untended, is reminiscent of *1 Enoch* 10:7, where the archangels are sent "to heal the earth which the angels have corrupted."

1:10-17 condemn the *rulers of Jerusalem.* Several details suggest that these rulers were the priests, who were certainly regarded as angels in the Second Temple period (Mal 2:7) ("messenger" and "angel" are the same word in Hebrew). They have betrayed their calling and are compared to the rulers of Sodom and Gomorrah, the evil cities destroyed by the LORD (Gen 19:24). Many scholars think that this story was originally independent and incorporated later into the Abraham saga. It is no coincidence that a story of angels on earth is mentioned in Isaiah; it belongs with the avenging angels of the Enochic tradition. They see the sinful cities for themselves before destroying them, just as the angel of the LORD goes out to destroy the Assyrian army (Isa 37:36).

The evil rulers have brought their sacrifices, but the LORD would not accept them. Since the LXX of 1:11 omits "lambs," some scholars suspect that the word was a later addition. Without it the list could be the Day of Atonement prescriptions in Lev 16:3-5: rams for burnt offerings and the blood of bulls and he-goats for sin offerings. There is no explicit reference to the Day of Atonement in the First Temple period, but this poem alludes to many elements of the later rites. Since there is no way of telling whether this is a late poem or early evidence for later practices, the question must remain open.

The rulers (priests?) appear before the LORD (1:12), offer incense (v. 13), and "stretch out their hands," that is, offer prayers (v. 15), but the LORD will not look on them (v. 15; cf. Num 6:22-26, the high priests' blessing). Their hands are full of blood. 1QIs[a] adds here, "and your fingers with iniquity," as in Isa 59:3. A priest was described as one whose "hands had been filled," that is, with incense (the Hebrew meaning, "fill the hands," is translated "ordain" in, e.g., Exod 28:41; 29:9, 29). Here the prophet uses the wordplay typical of his style (see below on Isaiah 5); instead of approaching the LORD with hands full of incense, they have hands full of blood. Blood and incense were the two offerings taken into the holy of holies, that is, into the presence of the LORD, on the Day of Atonement.

Washing (1:16) was an essential preparation for service in the temple (e.g., Lev 16:4). By the end of the Second Temple period the washings had become very elaborate; no one could enter the temple court unless he had immersed himself, and the high priest had to immerse himself five times and wash (his hands and feet) ten times (*m. Yoma* 3:2). Here the prophet pleads for real purity and echoes the words of Psalm 82, where the "sons of God" (v. 6) are commanded in the heavenly council to maintain justice (vv. 3-4) or face God's judgment. Other prophets spoke of the futility of sacrifice without the practice of justice and humanity (Jer 7:21-26; Hos 6:4-6; Amos 4:4; 5:21-24; Mic 6:6-8).

1:18-20 are the LORD's appeal to the rulers to choose between obedience and its reward or rebellion and its consequences.

In the Second Temple period it was the custom to tie a red thread to the door of the sanctuary when the scapegoat was led into the desert carrying the sins of Israel (Lev 16:21; *m. Yoma* 6:8). When the goat reached the desert, the thread became white (presumably it was replaced by a white thread!) to fulfill 1:18: "Though your sins are like scarlet, they shall be like snow."

1:21-26 are a lament for *the harlot Jerusalem.* The poem divides into two equal halves: vv. 21-23 and 24-26. The theme of Jerusalem the harlot appears in Trito-Isaiah (Isa 57:7-10) and eventually became the symbol of the corrupted temple (Revelation 17) (the great harlot was originally Jerusalem, the city destined to rule the whole earth, but was later reinterpreted of Rome). Jerusalem's infidelity, according to Isaiah, has not been with the Baals, and so a comparison with Hosea's teaching is not really apt. Jerusalem has played the harlot with foreign kings rather than remaining faithful to her own King and Holy One. By Ezekiel's time Jerusalem had shown infidelity with Assyrian and Babylonian rulers (Ezek 23:11-21); in the time of First Isaiah there had been only the Assyrians, but by the time of the book of Revelation her lovers had been "the kings of the earth" (Rev 17:2).

The princes of the city have "rebelled" (1:23), a significant charge against them, and the result is a breakdown of justice, as in Psalm 82. The LORD then arouses himself against these princes who have become his enemies (v. 24) and threatens judgment by fire to smelt away their impurity. Fiery judgment was another facet of the temple tradition (see below on 4:3-4). After the judgment, the LORD would restore good rulers to Jerusalem so that it would again be a place of righteousness (v. 26).

1:27-28, promising redemption and judgment, could be the conclusion of the poem or a separate fragment. Vv. 29-30 are a condemnation of fertility cults; those who follow such ways will be like a tree which dies through lack of water, an apt comment on the trees, which were an important symbol in such cults (cf. 17:10-11).

1:31 is *a cryptic fragment about Azazel.* "The strong ones and their work shall burn together" is the reading of 1QIsa[a]. The MT has singular forms here and is probably the original. The word translated "strong one" occurs nowhere else in the OT even though related words and the LXX confirm the meaning. In *1 Enoch,* the leader of the fallen angels is named Azazel, which means "the strong one." He was to be burned on the Day of Judgment (*1 Enoch* 10:7; cf. Matt 25:41; Rev 20:10). The most likely explanation is that this strange verse refers to the judgment on Azazel, but this would not necessarily indicate a date in the Second Temple period. There was a garden of Uzza, "the strong one," in Jerusalem, where King Manasseh was buried in 642 BC (2 Kgs 21:18).

Isaiah 2–5

Isaiah 2–4 form a unit: 2:2-4 and 4:2-6 describe the future glory of Zion, and the material between them is a vivid picture of a corrupt society and God's judgment on it. Much of it consists of fragments, suggesting a long history, perhaps back to Isaiah himself. The hazard in attempting to date such material is that it becomes a circular argument; the history and traditions of Israel can be reconstructed only from the OT, and that reconstruction is then used to date the material on which it was based.

The first verse is another introduction, perhaps to the original collection of Isaiah oracles. It is Isaiah's *vision,* "the word that he saw."

2:2-4 is almost identical to Mic 4:1-3. Who copied whom, or were both prophets quoting an earlier oracle? There can be no answer to such questions! The relationship between Isaiah and Micah is not easy to establish: they were contemporaries, both active in the reigns of Jotham, Ahaz, and Hezekiah (Isa 1:1; Mic 1:1), with Isaiah also prophesying in the time of Uzziah. About a century later, Jeremiah's contemporaries quoted Micah as the one who warned that Jerusalem would be destroyed (Jer 26:18), suggesting that he, not Isaiah, was remembered as the great prophet in Hezekiah's reign. Nevertheless, a far greater mass of prophetic material came to be associated with Isaiah than with Micah. This we cannot explain.

Isaiah had *a vision of the holy mountain of the LORD,* exalted in the last days. The LXX of both Isaiah and Micah suggests that "house of" was added later; the earlier version probably read, "The mountain of the LORD shall be established. . . ." The mountain in question was not the actual mountain on which the temple was built, but the heavenly mountain it represented. This was a mountain garden, the original Garden of Eden, as can be seen from Ezek 28:13. Ezekiel the priest recorded and preserved one of the ancient beliefs of the Jerusalem temple cult. The holy mountain appears again at Isa 11:9 and 65:25, where it is more obviously the Garden of Eden.

An oracle in Jeremiah suggests that the height of the mountain reflected the status of its deity. He described the destruction of Babylon as the LORD's causing a mountain to roll down and be burned (Jer 51:25). Babylon, or rather its guardian deity, was brought low. *1 Enoch,* which has preserved many temple traditions, describes the punishment of the fallen angels in a similar way: ". . . bound and cast down like great mountains burning with fire . . ." (*1 Enoch* 21:3; in the Gizeh Greek text; cf. *1 Enoch* 18:13; Rev 8:8). When Isaiah saw the mountain of the LORD as the highest mountain, he would have implied that the LORD was supreme over the earth. Again, Enoch has the tradition; in his visions he saw a mountain which reached right up to heaven (*1 Enoch* 18:8; 24:3), whose summit was the throne of the Great Holy One (*1 Enoch* 25:3).

Isaiah had *a vision of many people traveling to Jerusalem,* perhaps a recollection of the crowds who came for the festivals. Although the Passover festival was not centralized in Jerusalem until the reform of Josiah, a century after the time of Isaiah, there were other festivals involving the king which would have attracted large numbers of pilgrims. Just as the mountain on which the temple stood became, in his vision, the heavenly mountain of the LORD, so the pilgrim crowds became all the nations and peoples of the earth. We do not need to look for an occasion when Isaiah might actually have seen such a group of many nationalities and conclude that this must be a postexilic insertion into the text. This is the mind of a visionary, seeing beyond what is actually there.

He had *a vision of the LORD giving his law from Jerusalem.* This, too, would have been based on a temple ceremony in which the king received the law and renewed his vow to uphold it. Scholars have suspected for a long time that there are echoes of royal ceremonies in Exodus; Moses became more kinglike as the stories were handed on. Thus the account of renewing the covenant in Exodus 34 could have been colored by memories of a temple ceremony. Moses ascends the mountain and receives the law again, after the people have sinned through idol worship. The covenant is made with Moses alone, not with the people as a whole, and Moses becomes the mouthpiece through which God continues to speak to his people (Childs 1974: 604-10). Similarly, the king was believed to speak the words of the LORD to his people (2 Sam 23:2; Ps 2:7), and he vowed to uphold God's law (Psalm 101); he was set on the holy mountain (Ps 2:6) and at his coronation was given not only the crown but also the "testimony," exactly what Moses brought down from Sinai (2 Kgs 11:12; cf. Exod 34:29; also Isa 33:8, where "witnesses" is the same word).

Once the LORD had appeared to give his law (2:4), Isaiah saw what we would recognize as the *Last Judgment, establishing the kingdom of God.* He saw it, however, at a much earlier stage of its development. Since this was to happen "in the days to come" (lit. "latter days") (v. 2), it is interesting to speculate whether or not Isaiah believed that these things would happen in the distant future or whether, in his time, "the days to come" meant something else, perhaps a particular time of the year (cf. Deut 11:12). Amos, Isaiah's older contemporary (Amos 1:1), linked the time of harvest to the time of judgment (Amos 8:2-3), as did Joel (Joel 3:13), and it may be that there was an established link between the end of the year and the LORD's judgment. In the Second Temple period this was the season of the Day of Atonement, which dealt with sin, and of the feast of Tabernacles, which celebrated the fertility of the earth and the coming of the Messiah, the Anointed One. It is not hard to imagine an earlier festival at the turn of the year when the king appeared in public to reaffirm the law and his own role as the anointed king. The same pattern appears in Revelation: judgment on sin, harvest imagery (Rev 14:14-20), and the appearance of the Messiah.

Isaiah's picture of the judgment is found elsewhere in the OT, but he has made alterations which are consistent with other aspects of his message. This suggests that the passage was very significant for him whether or not he was its author. Psalm 2 describes a hostile influx of nations coming to attack Zion and being repulsed by the power of Zion's LORD and King; Psalm 46 describes the power of the LORD in the face of raging nations to destroy all weapons of war and establish the security of Zion; Joel 3:9-17 describes the day of the LORD as a time when all will become warriors, turning their plowshares into swords and their pruning hooks into spears, when all nations will be judged. Isaiah has turned these pictures around; the nations come to Zion because they want to learn the law of the LORD, and they destroy their own weapons, putting them to better use. It was to be a cornerstone of Isaiah's message that the security of Zion depended on the presence of its LORD and not on weapons of war.

"The light of the LORD" (2:5) was believed to shine out from the holy of holies in the temple. The Psalms describe the shining face of the one enthroned over the cherubim (Psalm 80), the one who shines forth from Zion (Psalm 50). Ezekiel describes the glory of the LORD returning to the temple from the east and making the earth shine (Ezek 43:1-5). The imagery is clearly that of the sunrise, and it may be that the sun shining directly through the east door of the temple did illuminate the holy of holies at the equinoxes. Ezekiel saw the glory returning at the new year, the autumn equinox (Ezek 40:1), another indication that Isaiah's vision may have been based on an autumn festival in the temple. The coming of the LORD is often compared to that of the dawn (e.g., Isa 9:2; 60:1-3; Luke 1:78-79).

2:6-22 is a separate collection of oracles in a rather poor state of preservation describing a *land corrupted by fallen angels.* There are signs that the originals have been brought together by a later compiler who added his own framework. The themes are "bringing low" (vv. 9, 11, 17), in contrast to the mountain of the LORD being established as the highest place (v. 2), and attacking soothsayers and idol worshipers. Separate units can be seen in vv. 6-9, vv. 10-21, and v. 22. Vv. 6-9 give reasons why the LORD rejects his people. The land is filled with "diviners" (the Hebrew seems to be damaged at this point, and the translation "diviners" is a reconstruction) and "soothsayers" with "wealth," with "weapons," and with "idols." Such a description would have fitted the time of Uzziah (2 Chronicles 26), who amassed wealth and weapons and allowed high places to flourish (2 Kgs 15:4, where Uzziah is called Azariah); or the reign of Jotham, who allowed the people to follow corrupt practices while he himself grew rich on the tribute of subject people (2 Chronicles 27). Ahaz, while surpassing his predecessors in religious practices which the Deuteronomists abhorred, lost much of his wealth in buying protection from the Assyrians (2 Kgs 16:1-9), and a land "full of silver and gold" (v. 7) would not have been his land. "Idols" means literally "worthless things" and occurs ten times in Isaiah (2:8, 18, 20 [twice]; 10:10, 11; 19:1, 3; 31:7). It is used elsewhere in Ps 96:5, duplicated in 1 Chr 16:26, and Ps 97:7, psalms which extol the LORD as king; in Hab 2:18, where idols are contrasted with the LORD about to emerge from his temple, and in Lev 19:4 and 26:1, the Holiness code. This could suggest that it was a technical term from a temple or priestly context even though the explanatory phrase "the work of their hands" is characteristic of the Deuteronomists (e.g., Deut 4:28; 27:15; 31:29). The combination of magic and divination, gold and silver, weapons and armor as signs of a corrupt society may not have been original to Isaiah. *The oldest account in* 1 Enoch *of the secret skills with which the fallen angels corrupted the earth lists these very things: the making of weapons and armor, the smelting of gold and silver, the arts of magic and divination, and the use of cosmetics.* When *1 Enoch* is read in conjunction with Isa 3:16–4:1, Isaiah depicts a society under the rule of evil angels.

The day of the LORD. The details in 2:10-21 could well have been inspired by the earthquake in the reign of Uzziah (Amos 1:1) (Milgrom 1964: 164-82). People were to hide from the terror of the judgment (vv. 10, 19, 21), a theme found also in *1 Enoch* 10, where the archangel Uriel is sent to warn Noah to hide before the destruction of the earth, and in Isaiah's older contemporary Amos, who warns that there will be no hiding place (Amos 9:2-3). For Isaiah the great sin is pride, as it is in *1 Enoch* 5:8, raising oneself up when it is only the LORD who is to be exalted. The imagery of "bringing down" lends itself naturally to the destruction wrought upon high buildings and tall trees by an earthquake. Being cast down from the presence of the LORD is a recurring theme in temple contexts: the mysterious figure in Ezekiel 28 (originally the high priest if his costume [v. 13] is compared to that of Aaron in Exod 28:17-20) was "thrown down" from the mountain garden of God because he was proud (Ezek 28:2, 16); the king of Assyria came in pride against Jerusalem and its Holy One and was turned back (Isa 37:22-29); the king of Babylon attempted to set himself above God Most High and was "thrown" down (Isa 14:12-15), but the Servant Israel would not be cast off (Isa 41:9). The Servant Messiah humbled himself and did not grasp at equality with God (Phil 2:6-8).

"The LORD of hosts" (2:12) is an ancient title for the LORD. The hosts were the heavenly beings who attended the throne of God (1 Kgs 22:19; Pss 103:21; 148:2), but they were also the stars (Ps 33:6). Angels and stars were identical in temple tradition, as is clear in *1 Enoch* 21, where the prophet sees the fallen angels as fallen stars imprisoned for ten thousand years. The worship of the stars, that is, of angels, was forbidden by Deut 4:19; 17:3 and condemned by those who sought to reform temple worship in Jerusalem (2 Kgs 23:4-5). It must, however, have been widely practiced (e.g., Jer 8:2; 19:13), and what is known of it has the mark of authentic temple practice insofar as heavenly archetypes had earthly counterparts. The stars were the angels whose earthly counterparts were kings (Isa 24:21). Psalm 89 shows this is in its cultic context; the LORD was the chief of the heavenly host (vv. 5-8), and his "firstborn," the Davidic king, was therefore the greatest king on earth (v. 27). Amos uses the title (Amos 3:13; 6:14; 9:5), but it occurs most frequently in Isaiah (esp. Isaiah 1–39). The image of the LORD coming to judge the earth at the head of his host of angels is found at Isa 13:4-5; in Habakkuk 3, where the LORD emerges from his temple with his hosts to fight for his anointed (v. 13); in Judg 5:20, where the stars in heaven fight with the LORD against the Canaanites; and in Rev 19:11-16, where the King of kings and LORD of lords rides out on a white horse followed by the armies of heaven. The day of the LORD of hosts was the day of judgment.

The day of the LORD was the day when the LORD appeared and took his place as King to judge the earth. In temple ritual this would have been represented in some way, probably by the king ascending the sanctuary throne of the LORD as his visible counterpart or manifestation on earth. The psalmist describes a procession celebrating the triumphs of the LORD when his "God and King" enters the sanctuary (Ps 68:24). When Solomon was crowned he sat on the throne of the LORD and was worshiped (1 Chr 29:20, 23). The day of the LORD in Isaiah's time was probably a temple festival in the autumn which realized on earth the heavenly reality of the LORD's judgment. It is inappropriate to ask whether Isaiah thought of the day of the LORD as something imminent or in the distant future; it was an aspect of the eternal reality which could break through at any time.

There are many descriptions of the day: the earliest is Amos 5:18, where he warns that the day will be a day of gloom even for Israel, perhaps the first time that they, and not just their enemies, had been threatened with judgment (cf. Amos 2:4-8). The undatable Joel 2 describes the day as the time when the LORD punishes Zion through the action of invading enemies; seventh-century Zephaniah implies a cultic basis for the day (Zeph 1:7), when worshipers of other gods will be punished; Isaiah 34 describes a cosmic catastrophe when the LORD takes action against Edom, the enemy of Zion. Renewal would follow destruction (Isaiah 35), the new year following the judgment on the old. History was both interpreted and predicted in terms of the temple rituals. 2:22 is a prayer that these things should not be, similar to those which follow Amos's visions of judgment (Amos 7:3, 6); twice his prayer averted the threat of judgment.

Isaiah 3 divides into three sections: vv. 1-12 are sayings about the rulers of Jerusalem; vv. 13-15 are the LORD's indictment of the rulers; and 3:14–4:1 condemn the vanity of the women of Jerusalem.

The corrupted ruling classes of Jerusalem (3:1-12). The king and the priests are not listed; Isaiah condemns the military, those who practice magic, and the prophets. Having just condemned a society which trusts in weapons and idols, the military and the magicians are an obvious choice; but why the prophets? The punishment for such corruption, he says, is chaos; all the structures of an ordered society disappear, with young ruling old and the disgraced ruling the honorable. There are similar pictures of social chaos in Prov 30:21-3 and Eccl 10:6-7, 16-17. Sin causes the natural order to collapse (Isa 2:12-21; 24:1-13; 34:4), and it does the same to the social order. For Isaiah, the social and natural order are part of one system. In contrast (3:10-11), the LORD will maintain the balance; the righteous and the wicked will each have their due (Murray 1992: 60-62).

A trial scene (3:13-15). "The LORD has taken his place to argue his case," and he accuses the rulers who have abused their position of trust and exploited the people. There are similar scenes in Psalm 82 and *1 Enoch*. In the psalm, God judges the divine beings in his heavenly council, and the charges are the same: they have failed to uphold justice and are condemned to mortality, to death. The divine rulers are called the "sons" of God Most High. The rulers whom Isaiah condemns are their earthly counterparts, the rebel sons (Isa 1:2). In Psalm 82 the victims beg the LORD to arise in judgment (cf. Pss 58:6; 74:22; 82:8; 94:1-2; 96:13; and 98:9), and Deut 32:43 describes how the LORD appears to bring judgment but also atonement, that is, a judgment scene was part of the Day of Atonement rites. Isaiah's trial scenes were rooted in temple tradition. *1 Enoch* has the same sequence; the earth suffers at the hands of the fallen angels, and "as men perished, their cry went up to heaven" (*1 Enoch* 8:4). The archangels are then sent out by the Great Holy One to judge the wicked and heal, that is, atone the earth.

The vanity of the women of Jerusalem (Isa 3:16–4:1). Amos attacks the women of Samaria (Amos 4:1), not for their vanity but for their selfishness. The attack in Isaiah has a different basis. The rulers are condemned like the fallen angels, and the women are condemned for practicing their arts. There is a long tradition of guessing what the various garments, jewels, and cosmetics might have been; the LXX gives a glimpse of the fashion scene in third-century Alexandria, and the AV, with its "bonnets, wimples, crisping pins, and stomachers," a picture of seventeenth-century English modes. The reason for Isaiah's attack on women's dress is to be found in *1 Enoch* 8, the oldest material in the book, which describes the work of the fallen angels who corrupted the earth. They taught women about jewelry and cosmetics and "beautifying the eyelids" (*1 Enoch* 8:1) such that men were led astray. Isaiah's attack is yet more evidence for Jerusalem being ruled by the fallen angels. The punishment for these women, far from attracting angels, would be hunting for any man they could find and sharing him with several others (Isa 4:1)!

Jerusalem on the day of judgment (Isa 4:2-6). "The Branch of the LORD" (v. 2) was a title for the Anointed One. The *Targum of Isaiah* here has: the "Messiah" of the LORD. The Hebrew word translated "branch" means literally "what springs up," and the LXX understood it as a light shining out, the meaning of a similar Aramaic word. The later Greek translators (Aquila, Symmachus, and Theodotion) gave "the (sun) rising of the LORD," as in Luke 1:78: "the dawn from on high will break upon us." "Branch" is a title used for the Davidic king, the righteous Branch (Jer 23:5; 33:15), as well as for the high priest Joshua (Zech 6:12), but the text is confused here (cf. Zech 3:8, where "my Servant the Branch" could also refer to the high priest). Similar imagery occurs in Isa 11:1. "The Branch of the LORD" (another word for "Branch") shows that the king was regarded not only as the son of his natural father but also as the "son" of the LORD (cf. 2 Sam 7:12-14; Pss 2:7; 89:26). With the royal son in place, the land would prosper, the righteousness of the royal son bringing both justice and fertility to the land (Psalm 72; see above on vv. 10-11).

All the survivors, presumably of the judgment, would be considered "holy," that is, priests or angels (vv. 3-4). The correspondence of heaven and earth in temple tradition meant that the angels in heaven "were" the priests on earth in the temple. Both were known as "holy ones" ("priests," Lev 21:7-8; Num 16:5, 7; "angels," Deut 33:2; Dan 7:25). They had been "recorded for life," their names written in the LORD's book, which is often mentioned or implied elsewhere (Exod 32:32; Pss 69:28; 87:5-6; Dan 12:1; Phil 4:3; Rev 3:5; 13:8; 17:8; 20:12, 15; 21:27). The earthly counterpart of the book of life was probably the priestly genealogy which determined who was permitted to eat the sacred food (Ezra 2:62-63). The LORD washed them (4:4) and "cleansed the bloodstains" (a technical term used of sacrificial offerings, Ezek 40:38; 2 Chr 4:6) by a spirit of judgment and a spirit of burning. Thus the "holy ones" were prepared by means of a threefold purification: washing, then the judging Spirit, then the burning Spirit. This latter, the baptism of fire, was part of the temple tradition: Malachi described the fire which would purify the priests (Mal 3:2-3; cf. Isa 33:14-15); John the Baptist spoke of a future baptism of Spirit and of fire (Matt 3:11; Luke 3:16); and there was an early Christian tradition that Jesus had been baptized with fire in the Jordan (Justin *Dial. Tryph.* 88). The later *Enoch* texts describe angels purifying themselves in a river of fire before they can join the heavenly liturgy (*3 Enoch* 36); those who passed through the fire, that is, survived the judgment, would be called "holy," a holy one, an angel.

The obvious similarity to the cloud by day and smoke and fire by night over the temple mount (4:5-6) is the story of Israel in the desert (Exod 13:21-22), but this could be another example of temple tradition influencing the way the desert stories were told. The smoke and fire of the temple sacrifices would have formed a "cloud" over the temple during daylight and a fiery glow at night. We tend to forget that sacrifices were offered at night (Stern 1976: 10). These fires were recognized as proof of the LORD's presence. A (later) targum describes Abraham approaching the temple mount to sacrifice Isaac and seeing the cloud of the glory of the LORD smoking on the mountaintop even before he had built the altar there (*Tg. Ps.-J.* Genesis 22)! There was to be a canopy over the glory to provide shade and shelter for the holy ones, the protecting presence of the LORD; cf. Isa 22:8, where the "protection" of Judah, a similar word, is taken away. The cloud on the mountaintop and the tabernacle indicates the autumn festival (Riesenfeld 1947). Luke's account of the transfiguration (Luke 9:28-36) is clearly of the same tradition: the bright cloud on the mountaintop, Peter wanting to build tabernacles, and seeing the Messiah in his glory. So, too, is the vision of Rev 7:9-17, the washed robes of those who have passed through the tribulation, the shelter of the divine presence, protection from the sun, and the white robes of those who stand before the throne, as holy ones, as priests (cf. Rev 22:3). It is impossible to date material such as this, and it is false confidence to state that it must be late- or postexilic for whatever reason. The cult of the king who was "son of God" and who enacted this role in the great temple festivals must have developed when there were kings in Jerusalem. What has been described as the later eschatologizing of these beliefs was in fact the survival of one aspect of the original, namely, the belief in the heavenly reality which the temple cult depicted.

Isaiah 5

The Song of the Vineyard (5:1-7) is a warning of judgment with a harvest theme, indicating the autumn festival as its setting (cf. Isa 63:1-6; Amos 8:1; Joel 3:13; Rev 14:14-20). The vineyard was carefully prepared and planted, but it produced only wild fruit, representing the people who had not responded to the care their LORD had shown them. The key to the parable is two pieces of wordplay in v. 7: "justice," *mishpat,* sounds like "bloodshed," *mishpaḥ,* and "righteousness," *sedaqah,* sounds like "cry," *se'aqah.* "Bloodshed" and "cry" appear together in Gen 4:10, where Abel's blood cries from the ground, but perhaps more significantly in *1 Enoch*'s account of the impending judgment; people "cry out," and the angels look down and see "the blood being shed" (*1 Enoch* 8:4–9:1); the earth is filled with "blood," and the victims "cry out" (*1 Enoch* 9:9-10). The cause of the cries and the bloodshed is the evil of the fallen angels, the rebel sons of God. One wonders whether "blood and cry" was a traditional combination which Isaiah developed, or whether he was the source, which the Enochic writer retained.

Once we are alerted to the prophet's style of wordplay, other possibilities appear, and it becomes clear that this parable is also about the destruction of the temple. The vineyard of the beloved on a hilltop is also the temple in the city of David, whose name means "beloved." The tower in the midst is the sanctuary. This was certainly the interpretation of the *Targum of Isaiah* and one interpretation of R. Jose, who taught in the early second century AD (*t. Sukk.* 3:15; the other, in *b. Sukkah,* was that the vine was the temple and the tower was the altar), but there is earlier evidence which suggests that the tower was the temple: Habakkuk received his visions on the tower (Hab 2:1); Enoch was taken into the sanctuary, a high tower, to receive his vision (*1 Enoch* 87:3-4), and throughout the history of Israel as depicted in *1 Enoch* 89, the sanctuary is a tower, distinct from the house; the early Christians described the church as a tower (e.g., *Herm. Sim.* 9:3, 12). Once we have the temple context, other wordplay is evident: the Hebrew word for "hedge" sounds like the words for "covering" (as in Isa 22:8 and Ezek 28:13) and for tabernacle (as in Isa 4:5, "canopy"). This protecting cover will be "burned," another meaning for the word translated "devoured." The word for "prune" is written the same as the word for "making music to praise the LORD," and the word for "hoe" is like the word for "make glorious." There are two pictures here — of a vineyard and of the temple whose tabernacle and walls are to be destroyed, where the music and the glory will be no more.

The vineyard image is used differently in Psalm 80, where the vine is both the people (v. 8), and the king (vv. 15, 17; cf. Exod 15:17; Jer 2:21; 12:10; Hos 10:1). Jesus used Isaiah's parable of the vineyard as the basis for his own (Mark 12:1-9 and pars.). He was in the temple, speaking to the chief priests and scribes (Mark 11:27), and the parable was for them, the custodians of the temple. He prophesied that the priesthood would be destroyed and the temple given to others (Mark 12:9). Temple tradition did become the basis for Christian theology.

Seven oracles of woe (5:8-25), some only in fragments (also 10:1-4, which is another passage in the same style and in its present setting belongs with the sequence 9:8–10:4), depict the bitter fruits of the vineyard. The oracles could have been delivered on different occasions, but the fact that there are seven suggests a set of pronouncements for one occasion associated with a liturgy (cf. the seven seals, the seven angels with trumpets, and the seven bowls of wrath in Revelation). The account of Amos at Bethel (Amos 7:10-13) gives some idea of where they might have been delivered and what their effect might have been. Isaiah probably spoke in a very public place, inspiring fear because the words of a prophet had power (cf. Isa 55:10-11).

The first oracle (5:8-10) condemns *those who accumulate land;* there is no suggestion that the land has been stolen (as in the story of Naboth's vineyard, 1 Kings 21), but even to purchase land in perpetuity was forbidden (Lev 25:23). On the Day of Atonement, which began the year of jubilee, all land returned to its original owner. Perhaps those who broke the law of jubilee were being condemned. Isaiah curses what has been taken: the houses will become deserted and the land barren. The punishment fits the crime.

The prophet has heard this from the LORD (cf. Amos 3:7). We can only speculate about these auditions, but *The Martyrdom and Ascension of Isaiah* (a text which probably reached its present form at the end of the first century AD) describes the prophet's trance as he went into the divine presence. He was shown the door into an alien world (cf. Rev 4:1), he became silent, and his mind was taken up from him, but his breath was still in him, for he was seeing a vision (*Martyrdom and Ascension of Isaiah* 6). Jesus spoke in a similar way (e.g., John 3:11-12).

The second oracle (5:11-14) condemns drunkards. Although the vows of the Rechabites and Nazirites forbade wine (Num 6:1-4; Jer 35:6), it was otherwise considered to be one of the LORD's blessings (Hos 2:8). Popular wisdom warned against excess (Prov 23:29-35), and the prophets condemned it (Amos 6:6; Mic 2:11). Isaiah has strong words for the drunkards of Ephraim (Isa 28:1-8). Again matching the punishment to the crime, the people as a whole are parched with thirst for real knowledge, and Sheol, the shadowy subterranean place for the dead, "swallows" a great multitude.

5:15-17 seem to be misplaced (perhaps from chap. 2). They contrast the haughty who will be brought low and the exaltation of the LORD.

5:18-23 are the remains of four further oracles, naming the evildoers but not their punishments. The prophet condemns *those who mock the plans of the Holy One* (vv. 18-19), not unlike the false gods whom Deutero-Isaiah challenges in 41:21-24. He condemns *those who invert moral values* (5:20) and are wise in their own eyes (v. 21), a possible allusion to the sins of the fallen angels (cf. Ezek 28:2-7; Ps 82:5) and reminders that the fear of the LORD is the beginning of wisdom (Ps 111:10; Prov 9:10). He condemns *those whose strength is in what they drink* (5:22), and *those who promulgate unjust laws* (Isa 10:1-2). A similar situation is described in Amos 2:4; 5:10-11; 6:4-6; 8:4-6; and Mic 2:1-2; 3:1-3; 6:10-12. The first concern of the ideal king would be justice for the poor and the oppressed (Isa 11:3-5).

The chapter continues with a threat of punishment, detached from the preceding oracles but similar in style to Isa 9:8–10:4, each section ending with "For all this his anger has not turned away, and his hand is stretched out still." The prophet warns of a destroying fire (5:24, 25), as does Amos 2:5; 7:4-6, suggesting that the image of the Lord as a destroying fire was well known at the time (cf. Isa 10:16-17; 31:9; Mic 1:4; also Isa 66:15-16). "The mountains quaked" could refer to the earthquake in Uzziah's reign; the punishment had already begun.

5:26-30 and 10:5-11 are similar and will be discussed together below.

Isaiah 6

Isaiah's call to be a prophet is one of the most mysterious and remarkable passages in the OT. Written in the first person, it appears to be his own account of a vision of the LORD.

Uzziah (783-742 BC), also known as Azariah (2 Chr 26:1; cf. 2 Kgs 15:1), came to the throne at the age of sixteen and embarked on an ambitious program of building, economic development, and expansion, taking advantage of the weakened state of Assyria. Uzziah was able to secure his borders by subduing the Philistines, Arabs, and Ammonites, to fortify Jerusalem, to build up his army, and to improve both water supplies and agriculture (2 Chr 26:6-15). His personal prosperity, however, was short-lived, and he died a leper. Only the Chronicler records the circumstances of his affliction. There had been a dispute with the priests over the right to burn incense in the temple; Uzziah had entered the holy place and been punished with leprosy (2 Chr 26:16-21). In the year that Uzziah died Isaiah had his vision of the throne.

Isaiah does not say that he was in the temple when he received his vision, even though the passage is often read in that way. What we have here is an early description of a throne vision in which a prophet or visionary was taken into the presence of God. The temple and its rituals were believed to make visible on earth the reality of heaven; and so the setting of Isaiah's vision was both heaven and the temple. In such visions the temple furnishings come alive as their heavenly archetypes (see the Introduction, 494). Isaiah saw the heavenly throne in the holy of holies (Ps 11:4), the chariot of the two golden cherubim (1 Chr 28:18; 2 Chr 3:10-13). Nobody knows the ultimate origin of such visionary material, but something similar appears in the *Songs of Sabbath Sacrifice,* used by the Qumran community eight centuries after the time of Isaiah: in the *Songs* the figures on the walls of the temple become the heavenly host worshiping God.

There are other throne visions in the OT: the elders on Mt. Sinai saw the God of Israel (Exod 24:10); Micaiah saw the LORD enthroned in the midst of his hosts (1 Kgs 22:19); Ezekiel saw the throne chariot leaving the polluted temple in Jerusalem (Ezek 11:22-23) and appearing to him in Babylon (Ezek 1:26-28); Daniel saw the Ancient of Days sitting on a fiery chariot throne and a human figure approaching him (Dan 7:9-10, 13-14); Jesus told the parable of the sheep and the goats, assembled for judgment before the King on his throne (Matt 25:31-46). *1 Enoch* records many such visions, some in detail, others only in fragments (e.g., *1 Enoch* 14, 40, 46, 61, 71), but the pattern is the same: a temple setting, a human figure approaching the throne or observing another approach, and the threat of judgment. The best known of these visions is recorded in Revelation 4–5, where John observes the Lamb approaching the throne before the judgment begins.

When Isaiah saw the throne, the hem of the LORD's robe filled the temple. Later tradition associated the robe of God with his entourage, the heavenly host, and it may be that the more ambiguous "train" better captures the sense of the vision; "His train," that is, his attendants, "filled the temple." The *Targum of Isaiah* and the LXX say that the temple was filled with his glory; again, later tradition found in Philo (*Conf. Ling.* 171) shows that the visible glory of the LORD was the angels who filled the created order, and since the *hekal* (nave) of the temple represented the created order, we see here that the LXX is quite consistent with what is known of temple imagery in a later period. The cherubim depicted on the walls of the temple (2 Chr 3:7) became the heavenly host. Above the throne Isaiah saw the six-winged seraphs (lit. "the burning ones"), the golden pair which formed the throne in the sanctuary; but in Isaiah's vision they, too, have come alive. They call to each other (although it has been suggested that the Hebrew could mean "called in unison"): "Holy, holy, holy is the LORD of hosts; the whole earth is full of his glory" (6:3); exactly what is implied in v. 1, the temple filled with his robe being the same as the earth filled with his glory. This is also the song of the heavenly host in *1 Enoch* 39:12, where the "LORD of hosts" becomes the "LORD of Spirits," and in Rev 4:8, where the Greek for "LORD God Almighty" renders "LORD of hosts,“ as in the LXX of, for example, Hab 2:13; Hag 2:4. It is still repeated in the liturgy: "Therefore with angels and archangels and with all the company of heaven, we proclaim your great and glorious name, ever more praising you and saying, 'Holy, Holy, Holy, LORD God of power and might. Heaven and earth are full of your glory. . . .'" Origen, a Christian biblical scholar in the first half of the third century AD, said that the two angel figures of the vision were the Son of God and the Holy Spirit, an interpretation which he claimed to have learned from a rabbi (Origen *On First Principles* 1.3.4).

A voice spoke in the temple (6:4), exactly as is recorded of Moses in the tabernacle: ". . . from between the two cherubim. . . . I will deliver to you all my commands . . ." (Exod 25:22), and of St. John, who saw a heavenly figure in the midst of the seven temple lamps (Rev 1:12; the NRSV here has the plural in 6:4: "the voices of those who called," but both the MT and the LXX have the singular). "The house was filled with smoke" (v. 4), probably incense, but compare 1 Kgs 8:10-11, the consecration of Solomon's temple, where the priests were unable to stay in the sanctuary because of the cloud of the glory. Isaiah was overcome with a sense of his own uncleanness, a cultic term, a condition which should have excluded him from the sanctuary. His reaction, "I am lost," becomes "I have kept silent" in Aquila's Greek and in the Vg since the Hebrew words for "be silent" and "be lost" look very similar. Jerome, in his *Commentary on Isaiah,* says that this indicates the prophet's regret either that he did not join in the song of the angels or that he did not rebuke Uzziah's sin in entering the sanctuary (2 Chr 26:16-21).

Isaiah saw the King, the LORD of hosts (6:5). One of the seraphim then picked up a coal from the incense altar and took away the guilt and sin from his lips (v. 7). This small altar inside the temple was used for incense offerings (Exod 30:1-6; 1 Kgs 6:22), and so the heavenly and earthly temples coalesce. The incense altar appears also in Ezekiel's vision, where the man in linen is told to take coals from between the cherubim and set fire to Jerusalem (Ezek 10:6), and in John's vision, where an angel takes coals from the golden altar before the throne and throws them onto the earth (Rev 8:5).

The voice spoke to Isaiah a second time: "Whom shall I send, and who will go for us?" (6:8), and Isaiah responded by accepting the call to be a prophet. Again, the pattern is repeated elsewhere; when Enoch had been taken up on winds and clouds to the heavenly throne, he was at first filled with fear at the sight (*1 Enoch* 14:24), but then the voice summoned him and told him to warn the fallen angels of their imminent judgment. John was filled with fear when he saw the heavenly man figure and was then told to take the seven letters to the churches of Asia Minor (Rev 1:17-19).

Isaiah's commission was strange: he had, apparently, to ensure that the people did not understand his message (6:9) and repent. It is possible that we have here an idiomatic usage, whereby the result of an action is depicted as its purpose, that is, to speak to the people even though they would not listen to him. Such a suggestion is not really satisfactory, however, and it may be that this is one of those enigmatic utterances which later generations tried in vain to understand, just as we do. It has been suggested that some passages in Deutero-Isaiah were intended as a response to it (Isa 42:16, 18-19; 43:8), and that Isa 29:18 and 35:5 are additions to the original Isaiah which envisage a different situation, when people really will understand. Isa 44:18 applies these very words to idol worshipers in their blind folly (Clements 1980: 8; discussion in Williamson 1994: 46-49). This passage was used to explain why Jesus taught in parables (Mark 4:12 par. Matt 13:14-15), and why his signs were not recognized (John 12:39-40), but the NT usage implies that only Jesus' closest disciples were to understand the "secrets" of which he spoke and to see his glory. Perhaps there was something of this in the original; Isa 8:16 does speak of sealing the teaching among his disciples. Or perhaps Jesus identified with the situation of the ancient prophet.

Isaiah saw the LORD, whom he described as the King, the LORD of hosts. This in itself raises several questions and points to two distinct and incompatible beliefs. Isaiah saw the LORD, as did Ezekiel (Ezek 1:26-28), Moses, who spoke with God face-to-face (Exod 33:11), and the elders who ascended Sinai with him (Exod 24:10). *Other texts deny such a vision.* Moses heard only a voice at Mt. Sinai; he saw no form (Deut 4:12), and he was told that he could not see the face of God and live (Exod 33:20). The temple setting of the visions suggests that they originated there, perhaps in the traditions of the Jerusalem priesthood. It was the Deuteronomists, reformers of the temple cult, who were opposed to this aspect of the tradition (see on Isaiah 40).

The King and the LORD of hosts ("LORD God of Sabaoth" in the older versions) were two ancient titles for the LORD, one linking him to the royal dynasty in Jerusalem and the other proclaiming him the ruler of the angel hosts (see above on Isa 2:12). A comparison of Isa 37:16

and 2 Kgs 19:15, the Deuteronomic historian's version of the same passage, shows that the title "LORD of hosts" has been removed by the disciple of the reformers.

The call vision of Isaiah was an important text for the early church. They believed that what the prophet had seen in the temple was an anticipation of the glory of Jesus, the exalted Lord, but Jesus' contemporaries could not believe what they were seeing and hearing (John 12:41).

Isaiah 7

Isaiah encounters Ahaz, who became king of Judah when he was only twenty years old and immediately had to deal with a threat from the north. Rezin, king of Syria, and Pekah, king of Israel, had united to resist the westward expansion of Assyria (7:1-2). They tried to coerce Ahaz into joining the alliance, but when he resisted, they prepared to attack Jerusalem and set up another king, "the son of Tabeel," in his place (v. 6). Isaiah spoke to the young king at this time of crisis. He was told to take his son Shear-jashub with him and meet the king on the road to the Fuller's Field at the end of the conduit to the upper pool. It is usually suggested that the king was inspecting the city's water supply because an attack was imminent, but the Fuller's Field had other significant associations. There was also a Fuller's Spring, "En Rogel" (albeit different Hebrew for "fuller"), which stood at the boundary of Judah and Benjamin (Josh 15:7; 18:16), south of Jerusalem on the road to Bethlehem. En Rogel was the place where Adonijah had offered sacrifice when he made his claim to the throne. There is no account of any coronation; we are simply told that Adonijah had become king after he had sacrificed at En Rogel (1 Kgs 1:9-11). This suggests that En Rogel had special significance for the kings of Jerusalem, a reason, perhaps, for meeting Ahaz there. He had been king for only a few months; Isaiah reminded the king of the LORD's promises to the royal house. Whatever happened at En Rogel was a recent memory.

First there is a salvation oracle: "Take heed, be quiet, do not fear" (7: 4, in classic form cf. Isa 35:4; 40:9; 41:10, 13, 14; 43:1, 5; 44:2; 54:4; also 2 Kgs 6:16; 1 Chr 28:20; 2 Chr 20:15, 17, the Levite's war oracle in the temple; Deut 20:3, the priest's exhortation before battle; and many more). Ahaz is told that the two kings will fail because they have devised evil against him (7:4-9). The oracle concludes with a warning (v. 9b). The wordplay is lost in translation, but the gist is: "If your faith is not firm, your throne will not be firm." There is a similar wordplay in 2 Chr 20:20: "Believe, and you will be established," suggesting that both the beginning and the end of Isaiah's oracle were couched in a traditional form.

Isaiah then offers a sign to establish the salvation oracle, a sign which Ahaz refuses (7:10-12), after which the Immanuel oracle follows, addressed not to Ahaz but to the house of David (v. 13), the dynasty as a whole. This is the first of three royal oracles, the others being Isa 9:2-6 and 11:1-9.

An identical sequence occurs in Luke 2:10-12. First there is the salvation oracle to the shepherds: "Fear not . . ."; this is followed by the sign of the heavenly child, described as the anointed one, "Christ," who is also divine, "the Lord."

The Immanuel prophecy is one of the most difficult passages in the OT. It describes the birth of a child named "God with us." It has to be considered in several ways. First, what might it have meant in its original situation? The prophet was giving a sign of the stability of the Davidic house and the security of Jerusalem threatened by enemies. Psalms 2 and 89 give a context; both describe the king as the divine son, secure in the face of his enemies (Pss 2:7-9; 89:19-29). Since Isaiah promised security in the face of enemies, Immanuel must be sought here, and the most obvious child would be a son of the royal house, guaranteeing its future in the face of threatened attack and deposition. Hezekiah, the heir, was already born (although a comparison of 2 Kgs 16:2 and 2 Kgs 18:2 makes it impossible to calculate when Hezekiah was born; the implication is that Ahaz was only ten years old when his son was born). The Psalms, however, suggest that the one who was Immanuel, God with his people, was the reigning king, declared "son" when he was made king.

The form of the announcement is traditional (cf. Gen 16:11; Luke 1:31), but there is nothing to indicate the time of the birth; it could refer to a conception in the past, the present, or the future, and so it could refer to an eternal truth such as was depicted in the ritual of the temple. Since the king himself is addressed as "Immanuel" in Isa 8:8 (MT; the LXX differs), the oracle was probably a reminder to Ahaz of his recent royal birth as the divine son. The "young woman" would then be not the king's wife, nor the prophet's wife, nor indeed a pregnant young woman standing nearby at the time Isaiah spoke (all of which suggestions have been offered to explain the oracle), but a heavenly figure who was the divine mother in the same way that the LORD was the father of the king. Since Isaiah knew the LORD as "The King, the LORD of hosts," the mother of the Davidic king was probably "The Queen." Isaiah's contemporary, Micah, spoke of such a figure: an unnamed woman expected to give birth to the ruler, the great shepherd of Israel (Mic 5:2-4), in Bethlehem, the ancestral home of the house of David and a short distance from En Rogel.

No female figure is included in the customary accounts of Israel's religion, and yet she is there: Jeremiah, more than a century later, recorded that the Queen of Heaven was worshiped in Jerusalem and in Judah (Jer 44:17-19). He considered such worship an abomination, but he did not deny it. "The Queen of Heaven," also known as "Wisdom," had been banished from Israel's worship by the temple reformers (see p. 495 above). These reforming kings, Hezekiah and Josiah, appear in the biblical records as the heroes of Israel's true religion, but other texts give a different opinion. Embedded in *1 Enoch,* for example, is an ancient summary of Israel's history which says that Wisdom was abandoned before the First Temple was destroyed (*1 Enoch* 93:8), almost certainly a reference to these reformers. Those who restored the temple worship in Jerusalem after the exile did not restore true worship, says Enoch; they were apostates. The point of contention was Wisdom, the Queen of Heaven. The reformers removed her symbols from the temple: the Asherah and the bronze serpent (2 Kgs 18:4) and the horses and chariots of the sun (2 Kgs 23:11). She had been a sun deity, illuminating humankind with her gift of wisdom. Hers had been the sacred tree, represented in the temple by the seven-branched lampstand, and she was the mother of the kings (Wyatt 1995: 588). Archeologists have found female figurines and sun horses dating from this period not far from the temple site (Kenyon 1974: 142). The photographs of 1QIsa[a] 7:11 show clearly "Ask a sign of the mother of the LORD . . ." (Burrows et al. 1950).

The evidence for the Queen of Heaven has all but disappeared from the Hebrew Bible (HB); she was transformed into the Zion figure by Deutero-Isaiah (see on Isa 49:14-26), but she is still recognizable in the Scriptures of Greek-speaking Jews. Wisdom, they said, had been established in the temple like a great tree (Sir 24:8-17); she shared the divine throne (Wis 9:4, 10); she was given to kings and made them immortal (Wis 7:7; 8:13). These later writings, both from the first century BC, have retained memories of ancient Wisdom in their metaphors. In Rev 11:19–12:6 she appears as her true self, the sun deity, divine mother of the Messiah, emerging from the temple to give birth to her son. *Christian tradition honored Mary, the mother of the Messiah, as the Queen of Heaven, the virgin mother.* This was the "young woman" of the Immanuel oracle, the mother of the kings of Israel before she was banished from the temple. Isaiah describes her as *ha'almah,* which means literally "the young woman." There has been endless debate as to whether or not this implies literal virginity, but, as there is insufficient evidence in the Hebrew text to decide the issue, there can be no conclusion. The choice of word, however, may owe something to the prophet's characteristic wordplay since *ha'almah* and the word for "hidden" are identical (Jerome makes this point in his commentary), and the word for "eternity" is very similar. The secret or hidden aspect of wisdom is mentioned in Job 11:6 and 28:21.

More significant, however, is the question: Why did the translators of the LXX choose the word *parthenos* ("virgin") when they had available an exact translation, *veanis* ("young woman")? What did the oracle mean in their time? It may be that, just as their community kept alive the memory of Wisdom, so too they remembered that the woman of the Immanuel oracle had been Wisdom, known in other cultures of the ancient Near East as a virgin mother figure. Thus "virgin" was a more appropriate rendering than "young woman." There is other evidence which suggests that the translators of Isaiah preserved an ancient understanding of the text (see on Isa 9:6). The Greek translators made the birth of the child a future event because by their time the royal traditions of the temple had become a memory transformed into the hope of a future Messiah.

Second, Christians saw the Immanuel oracle as a prophecy of the birth of Jesus (Matt 1:23), but it is simplistic to say that it was not used as a messianic prophecy before this. If it had been used to describe the birth of the anointed kings, then it would have been part of the royal ideology which became the messianic hope after the monarchy had ceased in the time of the Second Temple. *This royal ideology surfaced intact in early Christianity,* showing that it had been preserved throughout the Second Temple period (Barker 1987). Where and by whom is not yet known, but it was there. That the issue of the Immanuel oracle was sensitive can be seen from the post-Christian Jewish Greek versions of Isaiah, which avoid the word "virgin" and opt for the more literal "young woman."

Immanuel was to eat curds and honey, but the meaning of the passage as a whole is not clear. Curds and honey may have been the foods of the gods or no more than the blessings of a fertile land flowing with milk and honey (Josh 5:6). (In Assyrian rituals, butter and honey were offered to the sun deity and were smeared on walls in dedication ceremonies.) If Immanuel was a baby about to be born, then the gist was perhaps that the danger to Jerusalem would have passed before he was old enough to know right from wrong. The infancy may have meant his inexperience as a king. Before he had learned to choose right, that is, to trust in the LORD, the lands of his enemies would be devastated, and then there would be times unlike any since Ephraim departed from Judah. This is ambiguous: it could mean that the danger from the north would have passed and the kingdom would enjoy prosperity; or it could mean that with the Northern Kingdom gone, Judah would be the next to fall, hence the addition "the King of Assyria" (7:17). Isaiah's original message was probably positive: trust in the LORD and all will be well; but a later editor saw the ambiguity and, by adding the ominous note "the King of Assyria," was able to append the series of oracles which follows (vv. 18-25).

7:18-25 are four pieces, each beginning "on that day," which describe the Assyrian devastation.

Ahaz did not trust in the LORD but made himself a vassal of Assyria. Not only was he threatened by the kings of Israel and Syria from the north, but also by the Edomites in the south (2 Kgs 16:5-6). He appealed to Tiglath-pileser, king of Assyria, "I am your servant and your son" (2 Kgs 16:7). As the Davidic king, he was the servant and son of the LORD (Ps 89:20, 26), and such an alliance was apostasy. Ahaz sent tribute from the temple treasury (2 Kgs 16:8) and altered the temple in various ways because of the king of Assyria (2 Kgs 16:18).

Isaiah 8

The third sign of a child, "Maher-shalal-hash-baz," is given in 8:1-4; the others are "Shear-jashub" (7:3) and "Immanuel" (7:14). First the prophet advertised the name of the future child by writing it on a large tablet; we can only guess why he needed witnesses and what he then did with the tablet. Then the son was born. Nobody knows what is meant by "the prophetess" (8:3), the child's mother. She could have been Isaiah's wife or a prophetess in her own right, as was Huldah (2 Kgs 22:14), or both. The child's name means "The spoil speeds, the prey hastens." It is perhaps intentional that the incident recalls the Immanuel oracle; before the child could speak his first words, Damascus and Samaria would be despoiled. The following section (8:5-8a) certainly takes up the earlier theme of the watercourses. The people had rejected the gentle waters of Jerusalem when faced with the threat of the king of Syria, and so as punishment they would be flooded by the mighty river of Assyria.

8:8b-10 are the remains of another poem. The outspread wings which fill the land are the protecting wings of the LORD (cf. Pss 17:8; 36:7; 63:7), temple imagery recalling the winged cherubim of the throne. The people can feel secure because God is with them, "Immanuel" (8:8b, 10b). (The MT of v. 8b suggests that the king is being addressed "O Immanuel," but the LXX has "for God is with us," as in v. 10.)

8:11-15 are not easy to read. There is good reason to believe that the text has been altered over the years. (The LXX differs considerably from the MT here.) Faced with Ahaz's refusal to trust, the prophet felt the LORD's strong hand upon him (v. 11), and he warned his disciples not to join the popular movement in Jerusalem. "Conspiracy" (v. 12) may originally have been "holy"; the Hebrew words are similar, and this would make sense in the context of v. 13. It is likely that these were Isaiah's last words in the time of Ahaz (Isa 14:28-32 implies that he resumed his ministry when the king died). His teaching was entrusted to disciples and sealed away, but his two sons, growing up in the community with their strange names, were a constant reminder of their father's words (8:16-18).

The rest of the chapter is fragments: 8:19 condemns the use of mediums (cf. 1 Sam 28:8-25), and 8:20-22 describe imminent anguish and despair, a time when the people will curse their king and their God (v. 21).

Isaiah 9

The chapter opens with another royal oracle, linked to the previous material by the theme of gloom and darkness. The original described a temple ceremony in which darkness was banished by the appearance of the LORD (Reventlow 1971: 321-25), in the ritual the appearance of the king.

There is no agreement as to the meaning of "birth" in this passage. Some scholars favor the physical birth of a royal son and give examples of the recognition ceremonies at the birth of the pharaoh's heir; this oracle would then have been the public announcement of the birth of a Davidic prince, guaranteeing the future of the dynasty (Mowinckel 1956: 102-10; Wildberger 1991: 399). A comparison with other royal birth texts, however, suggests that the original ritual concerned the presentation of the newly born king (Kaiser 1963: 128 following Alt 1954: 220). The oracle is best understood in the light of Psalm 2 and the LXX of Ps 109:3 (= MT Ps 110:3), which differs from the MT: "A host (or power) is with you on the day of your power, in the glory of the holy ones; from the womb before the dawn I have begotten you." This is the birth of a king, describing how he triumphs over his foes and is then declared "a priest forever according to the order of Melchizedek" (v. 4). Psalm 2 is similar: triumph over foes and then the declaration, "You are my son; today I have begotten you" (v. 7) In Isaiah's oracle there are the same dawning of light, triumph over enemies, and birth of a royal son. The common source has to be temple ritual. When enemies were defeated, it was the light of the LORD which shone forth as a sign of salvation (Pss 4:6; 27:1). Psalm 2 clearly links the defeat of enemies and the recognition of the new ruler, as do Isa 52:14 and *1 Enoch* 46 and 62. The original "walkers in darkness" (Isa 9:2) were the fallen angels awaiting judgment when the LORD appeared (Ps 82:5). (See also Ps 73:17, where the wicked are destroyed in the sanctuary.) This is the theme of *1 Enoch* 1–16; the Holy and Great One comes from his dwelling in the heavens to judge the fallen angels (cf. Deut 32:43 [Qumran text 4QDeut[q]]; Isa 26:21; Mic 1:3; and *1 Enoch* 1:3). Isaiah describes the people rejoicing in the temple "before you" (9:3), and their joy is compared to the joy of harvest time, or the sharing of booty.

There is a similar sequence in Isaiah 33; the LORD arises in the face of his enemies, and those who are worthy will then see the king in his beauty (Isa 33:17); Zion will be secure because the LORD is her king (Isa 33:22).

The new royal son is given to the people who utter the oracle "given to us" (Isa 9:6). One possibility is that they are the nation as a whole, or someone who speaks for them. Another is that they were the priests receiving their new Melchizedek; Ps 110:3 mentions the glory of the holy ones, that is, angels, at the moment of the royal birth. This suggests a priestly setting since the priests were the earthly counterparts of the heavenly host (Mal 2:7). At his call Isaiah was appointed spokesman for the heavenly host (Isa 6:8), and so he it was who announced the royal birth. In Luke 2:8-14 it is the chief of the heavenly host who announces the birth of the royal child, but there it is "to you" (Luke 2:11), not "to us."

Isaiah's oracle, then, was probably based on the kingmaking ceremony of the temple, especially since what follows is very similar to Egyptian practice. The king was given throne names. It was the custom to give the pharaoh five "great names," but here we have only four; perhaps one has been lost, or perhaps the Jerusalem temple gave only four. The names themselves give a fascinating glimpse of what was believed about the Davidic kings, and *the fact that we cannot translate and explain any of them with absolute certainty shows how little we really know about the ancient monarchy.* They describe a god-king. He is "a Wonderful Counselor," but a comparison with Isa 25:1, "You have done wonderful things"; Isa 28:29, "wonderful in counsel"; and Isa 14:24 shows that this was said of the LORD. ("Counselor" as a title for the king can be seen from the contemporary Mic 4:9.) "Planner of wonders" is suggested as a possible understanding (Wildberger 1991: 403), and this fits well with the theme of Deutero-Isaiah, but again it is the LORD who plans and brings about the wonders. "Mighty God" means what it says (cf. Ps 45:6, addressed to the king, which probably reads "Your throne, O God, is forever"; also Ps 68:24 and Mic 2:13, where the king and the LORD appear in parallel, which, given the conventions of Hebrew style, means they are synonymous). "Everlasting Father" is obscure; perhaps the king was the father of his people. Some Greek translations have "Father of the age to come." "Prince of Peace" could be describing the king as the one who keeps his people free from war. It could also indicate his role in maintaining the Covenant of Peace, the harmony of all creation (see on Isa 53:5). "Prince" is used in later texts to describe the angels of the nations (Dan 10:13), but Isaiah's throne name may be an early example of this usage since the LXX paraphrases all the names in an extraordinary way: "His name shall be called the Angel of Great Counsel." This is given instead of the four throne names and suggests that the translator regarded the names as four titles for one angel figure. The LXX continues, "I shall bring peace to the rulers and health to him," which may be a misreading of the Hebrew (a popular solution to such problems!) or a further paraphrase. When the Holy One appears in *1 Enoch,* the fallen angels are punished and the earth is healed (*1 Enoch* 10). The "peace" which comes to the rulers may in fact be requital or punishment. The same Hebrew letters can mean "peace" or "requital and punishment," translated "vindication" in Isa 34:8; "repay" (59:18); also "recompense" (Deut 32:35); and "punishment" (Ps 91:8). The LXX paraphrase here suggests that the translator knew the Enoch tradition and associated it with the throne names of the royal son in Isaiah's oracle. The Prince of Peace was the angel prince of Jerusalem who brought judgment before the earth could be healed.

The newly born king would establish justice and righteousness in his kingdom (9:7). "Justice" and "righteousness" are key aspects of royal ideology; Ps 89:14 has them as the foundations of the throne. Psalm 72 shows how they result in the well-being of both nature and society, resulting in "peace," the harmony of the whole created order (cf. Isa 11:1-5 and 32:16; also 42:4).

Isaiah interpreted contemporary events and predicted their outcome in the light of temple beliefs. Seeing history in terms of temple ritual is a characteristic of the Isaiah prophecies, seen most clearly in chs. 40–55 (Deutero-Isaiah). The ritual darkness here in ch. 9 becomes for him the darkness of despair in the Northern Kingdom after the Assyrian onslaught in 732 BC (Alt 1954: 206-8). His assurance of light after darkness is based with confidence on the temple theophany when the royal child is born and his enemies are defeated. "As on the day of Midian" (9:4) points to the current crisis, since Gideon's rout of the Midianites (Judg 7:9-23) had also been a battle triumph in the north, the land of Naphtali. Burning the loot was the custom of the *ḥerem,* destroying all the booty that belonged to the LORD (Josh 7:22-25; 11:6, 9). The very presence of the king in Jerusalem would ensure the defeat of her enemies. Lam 4:12 shows the depth of this belief; it was impossible for any foe even to enter the gates of Jerusalem.

Isa 9:8–10:4 (together with 5:25) are five sections each ending, "For all this his anger is not turned away, and his hand is stretched out still." There have been various theories about these verses which seem to belong together and yet are displaced. One of the most satisfactory is that the "Isaiah Memoir" (the section from the call in Isa 6:1 to the end of his second royal oracle at 9:7) was inserted into a poem about the chaos of his time. The original order was Isa 9:8–10:4; the next few lines of the poem are missing, and 5:25 is the end of the damaged section. The description of an Assyrian invasion (Isa 5:26-30) is the conclusion of the poem, describing the punishment which Israel's wickedness has brought upon them.

Read in this way, the pattern is fairly clear: Isa 9:8-12 describes the Syrians and Philistines who have already attacked the Northern Kingdom. The people, however, have not recognized this as punishment from the LORD and simply decided to rebuild on a grander scale; 9:13-17 condemn the corrupt rulers who have led the people astray so that all, both "head and tail," are destroyed; 9:18-21 describes the civil war (another element of the angel mythology which was a sign of imminent judgment, *1 Enoch* 10:12) which tore the Northern Kingdom apart after the death of Jeroboam II in 746 BC (2 Kings 15); and Isa 10:1-4 describes the situation of corruption and injustice which Amos and Hosea also addressed. Isa 5:25 is all that remains of a lost passage describing another punishment, the earthquake in the reign of Jeroboam II in Israel and Uzziah in Judah. 5:26-30 is a vivid description of the Assyrian army and the terror it would bring as the LORD's punishment for the sins of the Northern Kingdom.

Isaiah 10

Isaiah's attitude to Assyria is a problem. Whereas 5:26-30 clearly shows that he thought of Assyria as the LORD's judgment on the Northern Kingdom, most of Isaiah 10 describes the LORD's judgment on Assyria. It would appear that the north had to be punished, but Jerusalem not. 10:5-10 describes Assyria, sent by the LORD against a godless nation but then in its own pride claiming the triumphs for itself and setting its sights on Jerusalem. Assyria was the first of the seventy shepherds to whom the LORD handed over his people (see Introduction, p. 493. The places mentioned in v. 9 are progressively nearer to Jerusalem: Carchemish about 360 miles away, then Calno, Arpad, Hamath, Damascus, and finally Samaria, the capital of the Northern Kingdom itself. They mark the menacing expansion of Assyria; Samaria had fallen in 722 BC, and Carchemish in 717 BC, so they are not a chronological progression. Finally, Jerusalem itself is threatened by the arrogance of the conquerors and this is to be their undoing (v. 12). Those who claim to gather cities like birds' eggs (v. 14) will themselves be destroyed.

Isa 10:15-19 probably reflects the events described in Isa 37:36, when the Assyrian army under Sennacherib was destroyed by a plague under the walls of Jerusalem. The compiler of the oracles placed descriptions of the pride of Assyria immediately before the description of its fate. The "wasting sickness" and the "burning" indicate the plague which destroys "in one day" (10:17). The account of the plague in Num 16:41-50 gives a similar picture: the glory of the LORD appeared (Num 16:42), and began to devour the sinful people with a plague. Isaiah describes the burning under the glory (v. 16), which blazes up to devour the Assyrians like a forest fire. Isa

37:36 says that "the Angel of the LORD went forth and slew. . . ."

Isa 10:20-23 resumes Isaiah's theme of the remnant ("Shear-jashub," his son, 7:3) and prophesies that they will no longer put their trust in foreign powers, who then turn against them so that they "no more lean upon him that smote them." Ahaz had paid tribute to Assyria (2 Kgs 16:7-8). Isa 10:24-27 promises an end to the punishment at the hand of Assyria; its burden and yoke will be removed (cf. 9:4).

Isa 10:27b-32 describe the progress of the Assyrian army approaching Jerusalem from the north.

Isa 10:33-34 form a link to the next chapter. In their present context they imply that the trees to be felled are the royal house in Jerusalem, which will be severely lopped but not destroyed.

Isaiah 11

11:1-9 describes the king. In Christian interpretation this passage has been read as a prophecy of the Messiah for the distant future. Scholars (e.g., Eissfeldt 1965: 319) have suggested its original context as the exile or even the postexilic period, when some hoped to restore the monarchy. There is no reason, however, why the poem should not have come from Isaiah, the third of his royal oracles. Nor need it be translated in the future tense; the Jerusalem Bible, for example, uses the present. It could easily be a "happy augury for a Davidic prince" (Murray 1992: 106), drawing on themes from the royal ideology of Jerusalem. Mic 5:2-4 has a similar hope for the Davidic line who come from Bethlehem. Isaiah's ideal king was to be endowed with justice and righteousness (Ps 72:1; Isa 9:7) to restore and maintain the peace of the eternal covenant. These were the very qualities which the LORD had looked for in his vineyard (Isa 5:7).

11:1-3a reveal the source of the king's justice; vv. 3b-5 show it working in society ("justice" and "righteousness" or related words occur five times in these verses); vv. 6-9 describe the effect on the creation as a whole. They employ the tree imagery so common to royal houses in the ancient Near East. The word for branch, *neṣer,* is usually given as the explanation of the mysterious saying in Matt 2:23, "He shall be called a Nazarene," playing on the fact that Nazareth and *neṣer* sound similar. The king was given the sevenfold Spirit of the LORD, the gift of wisdom in all its aspects. The Spirit came upon David when he was anointed (1 Sam 16:13) and enabled him to speak the words of the LORD, to rule justly, and to bring light and fertility to the creation (2 Sam 23:1-4). Solomon asked for wisdom to rule (1 Kgs 3:5-9; cf. Prov 8:15-16), and according to Wis 7:7 and 9:5-6 it was the gift of wisdom which made kings different from ordinary people. Wisdom made humans like heavenly beings (2 Sam 14:20; cf. Gen 3:5), and it was the gift of wisdom imparted with the Spirit that made the king a son of God (Ps 2:7 — "Today I have begotten you"; cf. the alternative reading of Luke 3:22, where Jesus is given the Spirit at his baptism and then hears these words from Ps 2:7). The sevenfold Spirit was probably represented in the temple by the seven-branched lamp, the seven eyes of the LORD (Zech 4:10), which appear in Rev 1:4 as the seven spirits before the throne in heaven and as an ornament of the slain Lamb (Rev 4:6); that is, the Lamb was also endowed with the sevenfold Spirit.

According to 11:3b-5, the king was expected to uphold justice and righteousness (cf. Psalm 72; Jer 23:5-6). The mysterious Servant was to bring forth justice when the Spirit of the LORD came upon him (Isa 42:1, 3, 4). The king's weapons against the wicked were the rod of his mouth and the breath of his lips. Just as the LORD creates by the breath of his mouth and his word (Ps 33:6), so the king's weapons against wickedness were the rod of his mouth and the breath of his lips. Later tradition represented this as the fiery breath of the Messiah (2 Esdr 13:8-11; cf. 2 Thess 2:8) or, more literally, as a sword held in his mouth (Rev 1:16; 19:15). Righteousness the girdle of his waist and faithfulness the girdle of his loins (11:5) may refer to the actual symbolism of royal robes. Later tradition had the high priest vested by angels with the crown of righteousness, the breastplate of understanding, the garment of truth, and the plate (i.e., the golden plate on the turban) of faith (*T. Levi* 8:1-2; cf. Eph 6:13-17).

In 11:6-9 the king restores the wholeness of the creation as in Psalm 72. Since the temple on the holy mountain is a representation of the Garden of Eden (cf. Ezek 28:12-19; 41:15-20), what the king restores is the primal peace of Eden, and the earth is filled with the knowledge of the LORD as the waters cover the sea. Again, one wonders whether the allusion here is to the work of the fallen angels who had destroyed this harmony and caused the animal creation to devour each other (*1 Enoch* 7:5 seems to mean this; there is also a hint of this in Gen 6:4-7, which says that Noah's flood followed the wickedness of the fallen angels, and only after the flood "did Noah begin to eat meat," Gen 9:2-3). The line "The earth will be full of the knowledge of the LORD as the waters cover the sea," which also appears in Hab 2:14, could be an allusion to undoing the work of the fallen angels who had corrupted the earth by their perverted knowledge (*1 Enoch* 8; also Psalm 82, which links their activity to injustice and declares their knowledge worthless). The fallen angels brought the judgment of Noah's flood when the waters covered the earth. Isa 65:25 echoes these verses but adds "dust shall be the serpent's food," confirming the association with Eden. 1QIsa[a] has "the calf and the young lion shall fatten together."

The rest of ch. 11 is almost certainly postexilic. A later writer has joined his own vision of the glorious future onto the royal oracle, which had by that time become a prophecy of a future Davidic king. V. 10 stands alone; all people will seek out the king in his glorious city. Vv. 11-16 comprise four sections: vv. 11-12 list the places from which the dispersed people will return to their homeland from the four corners of the earth. This in itself indicates a postexilic date for the piece. Exiles had gone to Assyria after the fall of Samaria in 721 BC; to Egypt after the fall of Jerusalem in 597/586 BC (Jer 43:7); to Pathros (Upper Egypt) as papyri from a Jewish community were found at Elephantine near Aswan; apparently to Ethiopia, although there is no record of this except local legend, which claims that the ark of the covenant was taken there to escape the destruction in Manasseh's reign; to Elam and Shinar (Babylon) after the fall of Jerusalem in 597/586 BC; to Hamath, a Syrian city on the River Orontes, although there is no record of this; and to the mysterious coastlands of the sea, perhaps the lands of the Phoenicians and the Philistines, or perhaps the Greek islands where the Phoenician and Philistine traders had sold Jews into slavery (Joel 3:6).

11:13 looks forward to a time when there will be no more hostility between Ephraim and Judah, perhaps a reference to the hostility between the returned exiles and the indigenous worshipers of the LORD (implied in Hag 2:10-14 and explicit in Neh 4:1-5), or perhaps a reference to the building of the Samaritan temple on Mt. Gerizim in the fourth century BC.

11:14 looks forward to the power of a reunited people, able to conquer their old enemies as in the days of the undivided kingdom of David and Solomon: Philistines, Edomites, Moabites, and Ammonites.

11:15-16 describe the exiles' routes home; some will come from Egypt, crossing the rivers on dry land (the only reference to the exodus in this first section of Isaiah, and this is a postexilic addition!). Some will come from Assyria on a raised highway through the desert, as described in Isa 40:3.

Isaiah 12

The end of the first section of Isaiah is marked by a psalm of thanksgiving. In its final form, the sequence of chs. 11 and 12 is: the future appearance of the messianic king, the return of the scattered people, and, finally, their thanksgiving to the Holy One. There is considerable debate about the date and author of this little chapter; some think it could have come from Isaiah himself; others believe it was written by Deutero-Isaiah since he has similar hymns; yet others suggest a writer in the Second Temple period.

The hymn echoes lines found elsewhere; v. 2b is the same as Exod 15:2 and Ps 118:14; v. 5b is very similar to Exod 15:1a. This could be conscious or unconscious imitation; perhaps the writer thought the Exodus poem an appropriate model to celebrate the return of the exiles, as Deutero-Isaiah had done (Isa 51:10-11); or perhaps the poem in Exodus 15 and this chapter of Isaiah were drawn from a common source.

Oracles against Foreign Nations (Isaiah 13–23)

The prophets were a considerable force in the politics of their time. Not only had they stood in the presence of the LORD to hear what he was planning; they also gave curses or blessings which were vital to any operation. The stories of Balaam (Numbers 22–24), although set in the time of Moses, were probably written down in their present form during the exile. They show a prophet at work. The storyteller gives no explanations for his hearers; we can only assume that they were familiar with such figures. Balaam the prophet was hired by the king of Moab to weaken his enemies so that he could defeat them (Num 22:6). Balaam, however, could only speak what the LORD had told him and so could not curse the Israelites (Num 23:11). No amount of money could make him alter his words (Num 24:13). Amaziah, the priest at Bethel, begged Amos to prophesy elsewhere; the land could not bear his words (Amos 7:10-13). The kings of Israel and Judah consulted their prophets before going to war (1 Kgs 22:5-7); they even took a second opinion (1 Kgs 22:7-8), and Micaiah ben Imlah then described how he had stood in the heavenly council and seen the LORD planning defeat for Ahab, the king of Israel.

There are several oracles against foreign nations in the book of Isaiah. Some could well have come from Isaiah himself as there is a vivid account of him in action, cursing the Assyrians as they threatened Jerusalem in the time of Hezekiah. Envoys from both sides had met outside the city, and the Assyrians warned Hezekiah's courtiers that they had no hope of victory. They mocked the LORD and Hezekiah's faith in him (Isa 36:4-10). The king had this reported to Isaiah, who sent an oracle of hope: "Fear not . . ." (Isa 37:6). When Hezekiah received a second mocking message from the Assyrians, he took it to the temple and prayed for help (Isa 37:14-20). It was Isaiah who gave the reply to his prayer and reported what the LORD had said about the king of Assyria (Isa 37:21-22). Presumably he had had an experience of standing in the heavenly council and reported what he had heard and seen. There follow an oracle against the king of Assyria and a curse on his pride. Because of his arrogance against the Holy One of Israel, he would be humiliated and turned back (Isa 37:22-29). We have to imagine a similar setting for all the oracles against the nations; there would have been a specific crisis for which they were delivered, perhaps to the king and certainly in a public place.

Originally the words of the prophets were for their own times. Warnings about the consequences of sin or curses against one's enemies had to have immediate effect if they were to be relevant. The proof that a prophecy was genuine, according to Deut 18:22, was that it came true. Most prophecies, however, were kept because they had not been fulfilled, suggesting that there was more than one way of recognizing genuine prophecy. Even as early as Jer 26:18, the elders of Judah quoted as genuine the *unfulfilled* prophecy of Micah that Jerusalem would be destroyed (Mic 3:12). An ancient oracle was being reused in a new situation, implying that Micah had spoken for a future generation and not for his own times. By the Second Temple period, prophecy was regarded as prediction of the distant future: Jeremiah's prophecy of seventy years in exile (Jer 29:10) was reinterpreted as seventy weeks of years (Dan 9:24). The *Habakkuk Commentary* found at Qumran shows how that prophet provided a detailed prediction of contemporary events; the "Chaldeans" of Hab 1:6 became the "Kittim," the Romans.

Many of the oracles against the nations in Isaiah have been reused in a similar way. In their present form some are unlikely to have come from the original Isaiah since they tell of judgment on enemies who were not a threat to Jerusalem in his time. Other oracles were probably composed later and incorporated into the collection. The oracle against Babylon in Isaiah 47 is the only example of the type in Deutero-Isaiah.

Isaiah 13–14

13:1–14:23 are oracles against Babylon and cannot have come from Isaiah. Only the framework, which is reminiscent of Deutero-Isaiah, relates them to Babylon (Isa 13:1; 13:17–14:4; 14:22-23). Isa 14:1-4 describes foreigners helping exiles to return (cf. Isa 49:22-23); the time of hard service will be ended (cf. Isa 40:1-2). It is easy to distinguish earlier oracles.

13:2-16 describe the day of the LORD, the time when he comes to destroy his enemies, that is, the enemies of his people. He musters his host (v. 4) to destroy the whole earth (v. 5), to punish evil and bring down the proud (v. 11). The sun, moon, and stars will be darkened (v. 10), and the whole world shaken (v. 13). There is no way of dating such material: similar imagery occurs in the undatable Joel 1:15; 2:2; 2:10-11; 3:14-15, in Zeph 1:14-18, in Isa 2:12-22, and in Amos. Almost identical words occur throughout Jeremiah's oracles against Babylon (Jeremiah 50–51; Isa 13:2, cf. Jer 51:27; v. 5, cf. Jer 50:25; v. 8, cf. Jer 50:43; v. 14, cf. Jer 50:16, etc.). Similar imagery occurs in 2 Sam 22:8-16 par. Ps 18:7-15.

The host of heaven in the original oracle introduces the day of the LORD; only the interpretation identifies this as the advance of the Medes on Babylon. That the LORD should use the Medes and Persians as his agents is a theme familiar from Deutero-Isaiah (Isa 45:1-3), another indication that it was he who reused the ancient oracle. The host of heaven fighting with the LORD against the enemies of Israel appears both in the Song of Deborah (Judg 5:20; one of the earliest texts in the OT) and in the *War Scroll* (1QM) found at Qumran, which describes preparations for war against Rome in the first century AD (col. 1 describes the defeat of the "Kittim" as the day appointed from ancient times for the defeat of the sons of darkness; col. 12 describes how the hosts of holy ones and angels smite the rebels of the earth). Given that Amos and Isaiah both proclaim that the day of the LORD will include judgment on Israel and Judah and not just on their enemies (Amos 2:4-8; 5:18-20; and Isa 2:6–4:1), the original oracle in Isaiah 13 was probably addressed to Judah and Jerusalem, that is, from the same period as Isa 2:6–4:1.

Day of the LORD imagery also appears in Deut 32:43, which describes how the LORD appears to take vengeance on his enemies and "to atone the land," and in Deut 33:2-3, which describes his coming with a host of ten thousand holy ones on the day he becomes King. *These suggest that the day of the LORD was a tradition of the first temple, enacted annually on the day of Atonement when the king was reaffirmed as the LORD's son and ruler in Jerusalem.* In 1QM 7 it is seven fully vested priests who lead the army to the great battle, blowing their trumpets. An identical tradition in Revelation 8 describes the heavenly aspect of the operation. Seven angels, that is, priests with trumpets, bring the destruction and disasters of the day of the LORD, pouring out wrath (Rev 8:5; cf. Isa 13:9), making the earth a desolation (Rev 8:7-9; cf. Isa 13:9), and darkening the sun, moon, and stars (Rev 8:10; cf. Isa 13:10). The King of kings and Lord of lords rides out from heaven on a white horse to judge the earth (Rev 19:11-16).

Both of these sequences in Revelation include the fall of an evil angel: Rev 8:10 and 9:1 tell of a fallen star, and Rev 20:1-3 describe the imprisonment of Satan. Isaiah 14 also describes a star figure who became proud and was thrown down. In its present form it is an oracle against the king of Babylon, but this, too, could be a reworking of earlier material. Isaiah 13–14 is a glimpse of temple mythology, lost to our way of reading the OT but *not to those early Christians who compiled the book of Revelation.*

The core of this oracle against Babylon is Isa 14:12-20. The Day Star, son of Dawn, *Helel ben Shaḥar* has attempted to become like the Most High, *'Elyon* (v. 14), and sit in the assembly of the gods (v. 13). He has been brought down, killed, and left unburied (vv. 16-20). It is customary to see here a Canaanite myth about a god, depicted as a star, being banished from heaven. Comparisons have also been made with the Greek myth of Phaeton, son of Helios the sun god, who drove off with his father's chariot and nearly set the earth ablaze (Kaiser 1974: 39-40). Neither of these is satisfactory since the Greek myth is no real parallel and there is no evidence yet of any Canaanite myth of a god being thrown from heaven. The closest parallels are in the OT itself and suggest that it was the Hebrews who told of someone being thrown from God's presence because of his pride or sin. There are echoes in the story of Adam and Eve, cast from God's presence because they wanted to be like him (Gen 3:5; cf. Isa 14:14 and Phil 2:6). Ezekiel twice describes someone dressed like a high priest (Ezek 28:13) being thrown from Eden, the Garden of God, because he was proud and thought he was a god (Ezek 28:2, 6, 17). In their present form these oracles condemn the ruler of Tyre, but, like the oracle in Isaiah 14, they were probably being reused (cf. Isa 43:27-28). These were the myths about kings, who were also described as stars (cf. Num 24:17; Isa 24:21). Deutero-Isaiah tells of princes of the sanctuary who have been "profaned" (Isa 43:28), exactly the fate of the proud being in Ezekiel. "Profaned" means being made mortal and subject to death. He also reassures Israel that he is the chosen one, the Servant who is not cast off (Isa 41:9; cf. Ps 16:10, where the psalmist is sure that he will not see Sheol and the Pit).

The royal star being of Isaiah 14 had ambitions to set himself on the mount of assembly (v. 13); Psalm 82 describes this assembly and the judgment on the erring sons of the Most High. They are to fall and die, exactly the fate of Isaiah's proud figure. They are to become mortal, exactly the fate of Adam and Eve when they are driven from the Garden of Eden. The context of this star myth is not the lost mythology of Canaan, although that may have been very similar; it is the lost mythology of Israel and its temple, some of which has survived in the Enochic tradition and a great deal in Christianity (cf. Phil 2:6-11, where the one who did not grasp at equality with

God is exalted, or Matt 2:2, where the King of the Jews has a star, or Acts 2:27/13:35, where Jesus' resurrection is understood in terms of Ps 16:10, albeit differently translated, that the Holy One would not endure the corruption of mortality).

Because he had destroyed his land and killed his own people, his sons were to be slaughtered lest they fill the face of the world with "cities" (Isa 14:20-21). Several unsuccessful attempts have been made to match these details to the deeds of Assyrian and Babylonian kings. They are in fact an element of the underlying myth which appears in *1 Enoch* 10; the fallen angels brought death and destruction to the earth, and their offspring were to be killed. The "cities" should be translated "watchers," a name for the fallen angels; in other words, "lest the face of the earth be filled with fallen angels." The Hebrew is identical.

The oracle was probably used at one time against the king of Assyria; it is similar in tone to that recorded in Isa 37:22-29. In its present form it is against the king of Babylon, another proud ruler who declared himself to be a god. It is used again in 2 Thess 2:4, perhaps of Caligula, who declared himself a god.

14:24-27 are another oracle against Assyria from the time of the invasion in 701 BC.

14:28-32 are two oracles which have been distorted; v. 30 belongs after v. 32, giving the sequence: vv. 29 and 31, an oracle against Philistia, then vv. 32 and 30, a reassurance to Zion. "In the year that King Ahaz died" (v. 28), may be only the work of the editor, but Tiglath-pileser III, who had crushed a Philistine revolt, died in 727 BC and his successor, Shalmaneser V, reigned only five years. There is some dispute as to the date of Ahaz's death (725 BC or 715 BC), but either date could have coincided with a revival of Philistine hopes when they heard of the death of an Assyrian ruler. The messengers (v. 32) are envoys from Philistia trying to persuade Judah to join their revolt; the prophet counsels faith in the LORD, who keeps Zion secure.

Isaiah 15 and 16

These are oracles against Moab. Isa 16:13-14 are obviously a later addition, but beyond that there is little agreement among scholars. The disaster which has befallen Moab could be Jeroboam II's attack from the north in the middle of the eighth century (2 Kgs 14:25), or it could be the invasion of the Nabateans from the south which took place perhaps in the fifth century BC. Little is known about the history of Moab, and so any attempt to date these oracles must be speculation. There is no reason why the original should not have been Isaiah's; he prophesied in the reign of Uzziah, that is, when Jeroboam attacked Moab. Even if the verses were made relevant to a new situation in the postexilic period (Isa 16:13-14 suggest this), the originals were available when the oracles of Jeremiah were compiled since some of the material in these chapters appears with variations and in a different order in Jeremiah 48: Isa 15:2-7 appears in Jer 48:34, 36, 37, 38, and 41 and Isa 16:6-11 in Jer 48:29, 30, 32, 33, and 36. Isa 15:1-6 describe the disaster, a night attack. The next section (15:7–16:5), which tells of refugees seeking protection from the king of Judah, is not in Jeremiah. The suppliants ask the king for justice and refuge; such a throne would be established and secure (15:5).

In their present setting, 16:6-7 contrast the pleading humiliation of the refugees with the prophet's explanation of the disaster; Moab has been destroyed because of pride and arrogance, very Isaianic themes; cf. his older contemporary Amos, who condemned foreign nations for acts of inhumanity but not for pride (Amos 1:2–2:3). The "raisin cakes" (16:7), a well-known food (2 Sam 6:19; Hos 3:1), but perhaps especially associated with this region, appear in the LXX as the "dwellers" of Deseth, and in the very similar verse Jer 48:31 as the men of Kir-heres.

16:8-12 describe the rich vineyards of Moab which have been destroyed; there is the cry of battle instead of the songs of vintage. Prayers at the high places bring no help.

Isaiah 17

17:1-11 is an oracle against Syria (Damascus) and Israel (Ephraim), who had become allies in 736 BC to resist the Assyrian threat; it comes from the same period as Isa 7:1-9. Damascus, the capital of Syria, fell to the Assyrians in 732 BC. Isaiah compares the aftermath of the disaster to the end of the harvest in the valley of Rephaim, a fertile area south of Jerusalem. When grain was harvested, any forgotten sheaf had to be left for the poor. When olives were gathered, the tree could be beaten only once; anything left was for the poor (Deut 24:19-20). The disaster in the north would leave just a few behind, those not gathered at the harvest. The original poem resumes at 17:10 with another image of harvest. Israel had forgotten its God (v. 10) and had apparently joined in the cult of a Syrian nature deity. Isaiah's older contemporary, Hosea, had described such cults in Israel and predicted a similar disaster (e.g., Hosea 10). The allusion in 17:11 may be to a fertility cult practice of taking cuttings and raising them in optimum conditions to induce rapid growth. The one who set the cuttings absorbed the power of their growth. Even though the practice was so successful that they flowered on the day they were planted, warned Isaiah, there would be no harvest from such practices.

17:7-9 are a later comment, emphasizing that the disaster in the north was due to idolatry.

17:12-14 are directed against Assyria; an obvious context would be the disaster before the walls of Jerusalem (Isa 37:33-35), when the army was destroyed overnight (17:14). The image of Assyria as waters flooding Judah also appears in Isa 8:7-8; water was a symbol of chaos and the breakdown of the created order, challenging the kingship of the LORD (see on 19:5). Scholars who deny the authenticity of the disaster story (see on 37:36-38) consider these verses an addition made in the time of Josiah (late seventh century BC), when the overthrow of Assyria was imminent.

Isaiah 18–20

These are oracles against Egypt, which played a significant part in the politics of Judah during the latter part of Isaiah's life. When Hezekiah became king, Egypt had regained its former strength under a new (the twenty-fifth) dynasty of Ethiopian pharaohs, and they fomented revolt among Assyria's vassal states. The Philistines rebelled in 713 BC, and Assyrian records show that Moab, Edom, and Judah were invited to join them. Egypt promised aid.

18:1-6 was prompted by the embassy received from the Ethiopian pharaoh. "Whirring wings" could refer to the insects of Ethiopia or, in the light of a similar Arabic word, it could be read as "winged ships," that is, sailing ships (Driver 1968: 45; as in the NEB). "The Nile" (v. 2) is literally "the sea," but in 19:5 the same word has to mean "Nile." In 19:6, 7, and 8, however, there is another (Egyptian) word for Nile. The embassy, perhaps inviting Hezekiah to join the revolt, has traveled by papyrus boat, inviting speculation that they traveled by sea from the Nile delta and approached Jerusalem from the coast. Isaiah's response is to warn of imminent judgment on Egypt. Swift "angels" (18:2, not "messengers"; the Hebrew can be either) are sent to the land of many rivers; the translation "tall and smooth nation" is not certain, but for Ethiopians it would be appropriate. (Herodotus *Hist.* 3.20, written in the fifth century BC, says that the Ethiopians were held to be the tallest and best-looking people in the world.) The angels (as in *1 Enoch* 10) announce the judgment which the prophet has heard pronounced (18:4). The imagery again is of a harvest, but here a premature harvest, forestalled by savage pruning. What should have borne the harvest will be left as summer food for the birds. 18:7 is probably a later comment.

19:1-15 describe the judgment on Egypt. The LORD rides on a cloud (v. 1; cf. Pss 18:10-12 and 68:4), as he does in Ezekiel's vision of the glory (Ezek 1:4), and comes to Egypt. A cloud was the sign of the LORD's presence (Exod 40:34; 1 Kgs 8:11; Mark 9:7). He brings chaos to Egypt, as part of the judgment on them (19:2), and shows that their idols and magicians have no power to predict what he will do. This is also a theme of Deutero-Isaiah (Isa 41:21-24).

19:5-10 are a vivid description of the disaster when the Nile waters fail; the writer had probably visited Egypt. The translations in the NRSV are based on 1QIsa[a] and are better than those in the older English translations.

The most intriguing aspect of this oracle against Egypt is the imagery used in Isa 19:5. The Nile is described as the sea, "Yam," and the river, "Nahar," the two names of the Canaanite deity who represents the rising forces of chaos in the world. Baal, who rides on a cloud, as does the LORD in v. 1, does battle with him and kills him. After his triumph over chaos, Baal is proclaimed King, Isaiah's characteristic title for the LORD. Isaiah uses imagery also known in the Canaanite texts, but it would be unwise to speak of "borrowing." Israel had its own mythology.

19:11-15 return to the theme of v. 3; the wise men of Egypt know nothing of the plans of the LORD, who has deliberately confused them; cf. the story of the lying spirit which confused the prophets of the king of Israel (1 Kgs 22:20-23).

19:16-25 is a group of five oracles, each beginning "In that day" (vv. 16, 18, 19, 23, 24). All deal with the future condition of Egypt, and there is no reason why some of the material should not be from Isaiah.

The second and third describe a Jewish community in Egypt; "five cities" (19:18) and "an altar and pillar" (v. 19). The questions they raise are: Were they "prophecies after the event," later additions to Isaiah to justify the existence of a Jewish community in Egypt? Or were they predictions that a community about to be founded would flourish? And what community, and when?

There is evidence of a Jewish settlement on an island in the Nile, Elephantine, in the southern part of Egypt near Aswan (Syene in the OT). A collection of Aramaic documents has been found there describing the destruction of a temple in 410 BC but revealing nothing of the origin of the community. Their temple was like Solomon's in Jerusalem: the same size, twenty cubits wide and sixty long (1 Kgs 6:2), and roofed with cedarwood. Sacrifices were offered, showing that the community did not recognize the reform of King Josiah (about 620 BC) which had banned sacrifice except in Jerusalem (2 Kgs 23:8). He closed all local places of worship but invited the priests to Jerusalem. The colony at Elephantine believed that the LORD was dwelling in their temple, and they used the ancient title "LORD of hosts" (details in Porten 1968: 109 and Kraeling 1953: 85). All this implies that the community had settled in the southern part of Egypt before the time of Josiah and had priests with them to perform sacrifices. One obvious time for such an emigration of priests was the reign of Manasseh, when the temple in Jerusalem was desecrated (Porten 1968: 121-22); the ark of the covenant probably disappeared from the temple at this time (Haran 1978: 277-88).

The tradition in the later *Martyrdom and Ascension of Isaiah* is that Isaiah was martyred at this time by Manasseh. Tradition can be a useful source of information. Isaiah with his temple connections knew of the group departing to Egypt (and taking the ark with them? Hancock 1992: 454). Though he was too old himself to escape, these oracles were the blessing he gave to their enterprise. There would be five cities in Egypt speaking the language of Canaan, loyal to the LORD of hosts (19:18), unlike contemporary Jerusalem. There would be an altar in the midst of the land and a pillar at its border. Since the reformers had forbidden such pillars (Deut 7:5), just as they had banned sacrifice other than in Jerusalem, the community envisaged in this oracle was to observe the rules of Isaiah's time. A pillar at the border would well describe Elephantine since the settlement was a frontier garrison on the border with Ethiopia, but for the first twenty years or so of Manasseh's reign Egypt was still ruled by Ethiopian pharaohs; in other words, Elephantine was also in the middle of the empire at that time. The altar and the pillar would be a sign and a witness (cf. Isa 7:11, 14; 8:18). The LORD would "come down" (19:20, as in 1QIsa[a], rather than NRSV, "defend") to that place and deliver them, reveal himself to the people of Egypt, and receive sacrifices there. "Coming down" is an anthropomorphism which later editors would have avoided, hence the change. What is envisaged in vv. 18-21 is the wholesale transferal of temple worship to Egypt.

The letters from the community in southern Egypt cease in 400 BC and we know no more about it, but another temple community was established in the northern part of Egypt in the second century BC. According to Josephus (*J.W.* 7 §§422-32), written toward the end of the first century AD), the community was founded by Onias III, the legitimate high priest in Jerusalem, who had been ousted by his hellenizing brother Jason (2 Macc 4:7-17). This prophecy in Isaiah was claimed by Onias when seeking permission from the rulers of Egypt to build his temple at Leontopolis, according to Josephus (*Ant.* 13 §64); that is, this was the story told in his time.

The name given to one of the cities reflects the history of this passage and illustrates well how information can be gleaned from the various ancient translations of Isaiah in order to piece together something of its history. The LXX, the Greek translation used by the Egyptian Jews, named it "Polis Asedek," obviously a transliteration of the Hebrew for "City of Righteousness," which must have been the original name and the one they knew. It was also the name promised by Isaiah (Isa 1:26) to the city which offered legitimate and pure sacrifices. One of the cities in Egypt would be an Egyptian Jerusalem (Gray 1912: 335). In other words, it would be the home of the priesthood. 1QIsa[a] names it "City of the Sun," not a hostile comment, but identifying it as the Egyptian city of that name, Heliopolis, which became the new home of the priesthood in the second century when Onias built his temple at nearby Leontopolis. "City of the Sun" appears in Symmachus's post-Christian Greek translation and in the Vg and is adopted by the NRSV. Most Hebrew texts, however, have "City of Destruction" ("sun" and "destruction" look very similar in Hebrew). This definitely is a hostile comment on the temple in Egypt.

19:23-25 look forward to the day when Israel will be a world power equal to Egypt and Assyria.

Ch. 20 describes one of Isaiah's acted prophecies. He himself became a sign and a portent by walking around Jerusalem for three years naked, like a captive in war. The sackcloth (v. 2) may have been the traditional garb for a prophet (cf. Matt 3:4). The Egyptians had persuaded the Philistines to revolt against Assyria in 713 BC, and three years later the revolt was crushed (v. 1) and the Philistines taken captive as Isaiah had warned. This was the fate of those who trusted Egypt for help, and before long the Egyptians and Ethiopians would also be led away naked and ashamed.

Isaiah 21

This chapter comprises four oracles: vv. 1-10, 11-12, 13-15, and 16-17. The originals are lost beyond recovery and, with them, any hope of establishing their historical setting.

The first oracle is fragmented and obscure; it may be from Isaiah himself, but the present form is evidence of later reworking in the sixth century. Elements of both versions survive in the present confusion. It is suggested that the original was Isaiah's warning not to put any faith in Babylon, which was at that time attempting to revolt against Assyria. He predicted the destruction of Babylon and her gods (21:9), and he was horrified (v. 3) at the disaster he foresaw for Jerusalem if she put her trust in anyone but the LORD (21:10). Sennacherib did destroy both Babylon and its gods in 689 BC.

The fragments of this oracle enable us to glimpse the eighth-century prophet at work. He is the "watchman who stands on the tower" (21:8, just as in Hab 2:1; thus 1QIsa[a], but older translations use the impossible MT "lion"), and he sees history unfold before him, as does Enoch (*1 Enoch* 87:1-4), Abraham (in the later *Apocalypse of Abraham* 21–29), and Jesus (Luke 4:5: "all the kingdoms of the world in a moment of time"). This is temple tradition, seeing all history from beyond time from the presence of God in the holy of holies (see on Isa 40:12-31).

Several commentators have recognized that the original danger must have been to Jerusalem, threatened from the southwest, "the wilderness of the sea" (21:1), while its rulers were unprepared (v. 5). The "betraying betrayer" and the "destroying destroyer" are moving in like a wind from the desert. The allusion here could be to the desert demons who appear in Ugaritic mythology as the Devourers and in Hebrew tradition as the consuming wrath of the LORD. Habakkuk in his vision sees the LORD advancing from the desert with demonic attendants, plague and pestilence (Hab 3:5), coming to take vengeance on the enemies of his people and his anointed one (Hab 3:13). The opacity and ambiguity of such oracles is due in part to their cultic setting, but it is clear that temple tradition saw evil forces as a constant threat to the whole created order. They could manifest themselves in enemy action or in natural disasters such as locusts or drought, as can be seen in Joel 1:4, 11-12, 17-18; 2:4-9.

The role of the priests was to protect against such disasters and to control the natural and supernatural order by their temple service (Joel 2:17; cf. *m. 'Abot* 1:2). 1QM, another priestly writing of unknown date, is a vivid account of demonic hordes (the "sons of darkness," the "company of Satan") in the form of the Assyrians, the Kittim, and many other enemies attacking the sons of light. The battle is led by the priests, and the rituals in the sanctuary are an important part of the battle plan, as is the participation of the angel host.

In the sixth century, it is suggested (Mackintosh 1980: 113-30), Isa 21:1-10 was used in a new situation and became an (inaccurate) description of the fall of Babylon to the Medes and Persians in 539 BC, inaccurate because Cyrus did not destroy the gods of the conquered city (v. 9), and sympathy for the endangered city (v. 10) would hardly have applied to Babylon (cf. Isa 46:1-2). Later commentators saw the feast in 21:5 as a reference to Belshazzar's feast, described in Daniel 5 as the occasion when Babylon was surprised by the invading Medes and Persians, and captured.

The oracle in 21:11-12 is opaque; it refers to Dumah, translated in the Greek as Idumea, which is consistent with Seir (v. 11), a region of Edom.

The oracle concerning Arabia (21:13-15) probably refers to refugees fleeing from the troubles in Judah, and vv. 16-17 seem to be a later addition, prophesying judgment on Kedar, a region in Arabia. The Jerusalem Talmud (*y. Ta'an.* 4.5) saw vv. 13-15 fulfilled when "80,000 young priests" who had served with Nebuchadnezzar against Jerusalem (cf. Jer 38:19) — presumably the priests of the older faith who had been ousted by Josiah's purges — later settled in Arabia. This would account for the Jewish communities in Arabia in the Second Temple period, and might explain why Paul went to "Arabia" after his conversion (Gal 1:17).

Isaiah 22

22:1-14 are another scene of demonic warfare, but on this occasion the prophet warns that the covering of Judah has been taken away (v. 8). "Covering" is the word used by the priests to describe the sanctuary curtains which marked the entrances to the court, the tent, and the sanctuary, each representing a significant boundary within the created order. The ancient priests envisaged a protective covering around the whole of the natural order, the bond of the eternal covenant, which ensured its stability and security, and this is the covering which Isaiah warns has been taken away. When sin weakened and eventually destroyed the protective covenant bond, the whole fabric of life disintegrated (cf. on Isa 24:4-6). The piece is typical of Isaiah; the city has looked to its defenses, stockpiling weapons, strengthening the walls, and securing the water supply (22:8-10), with no regard for the LORD. There has been feasting and rejoicing (vv. 1, 2, 13) when there should have been penitence (v. 12). The LXX of 22:1 has "Zion" for the Hebrew for "vision," suggesting that this was Isaiah's vision of the day of the LORD against Jerusalem, as in Isaiah 3. The slain (22:2) have suffered the same fate as the heavenly figure in Ezekiel 28 whose city fell when he was thrown from heaven: "defiled," "wounded," and "profaned" in Ezekiel 28 are all translations of the same Hebrew word. This is not just the death of the city rulers; it is the destruction of the corrupted heavenly guardians of the city, as in Ps 82:6-8. Isa 43:28 describes the same situation; the princes of the sanctuary are profaned, and Jacob is given over to destruction. The text of 22:3 is unclear, but a reconstruction from other ancient versions suggests the gist as: "Your rulers fled; they were stubborn and revolted." The *Annals of Sennacherib* (*ANET*: 288) say that Hezekiah's elite troops deserted him in 701 BC, information which could identify this oracle as Isaiah's reaction to the unseemly feasting after the great deliverance from the Assyrian army (see on Isa 37:36).

Kir (22:6) cannot be identified with certainty; Elam lay to the east of Babylon. It is not easy to find a time in Judah's history when Elam would literally have been fighting against Jerusalem. Isaiah's characteristic wordplay probably accounts for his choice of names: the host of Elam and Kir could well conceal a host of heavenly beings known as "gods" and "watching angels" (the Hebrew words are very similar), and their tasks of "bearing the quiver" and "uncovering the shield" are similar to the Hebrew for "taking away exorcists" and "destroying soothsayers," the very people who fill the land (Isa 2:6) and bring the LORD's judgment.

Isa 22:15-25 is probably just a glimpse of palace politics (cf. Rev 3:7).

Isaiah 23

This is an oracle against Tyre. 23:1-12, 14 are poorly preserved. Sennacherib attacked the coastal cities in 705-701 BC, which could have prompted the oracle. The ideas and the language, however, are different from Isaiah's style elsewhere, and this has led to the suggestion that the oracle comes from a later period, perhaps the reign of Esarhaddon (681-669 BC), who also attacked Phoenicia. Sidon was destroyed in 678 BC and, since the words for Tyre and Sidon in Hebrew are similar and easily confused, the original subject may have been Sidon. Sidon was also captured by the Persians in 343 BC, and Tyre was subjected to siege by Alexander the Great in 332 BC. All these have been proposed as occasions for the oracle; doubtless it was used and reused for each of them.

The piece begins and ends with the line "Wail, O ships of Tarshish" (23:1 and 14), a reference to the Phoenicians' power as a sea-trading nation. Tarshish is usually located in southern Spain. There are several places where 1QIsa[a] has a clearer text, which has been adopted by the NRSV, for example, v. 2, "your messengers crossed over the sea"; or v. 9, "to defile the pride of all glory, to shame all the honored of the earth."

23:10 is also obscure; it could also be translated "till your land, daughter of Tarshish, for there is no more harbor."

Tyre had strong links with Cyprus (23:12); her king fled there in 701 BC.

23:15-18 are later additions: first, Tyre is compared to a forgotten harlot who will return to her old ways of trading after seventy years; then there is the hope that all her wealth will be given to those who dwell before the LORD, that is, serve as his priests. This theme was popular at the time of the return from Babylon — that the wealth of the nations would flow to the impoverished new temple state in Jerusalem (cf. Isa 60:11; Hag 2:6-9).

Isaiah 24–27

Much of the material in Isaiah 24–27 resembles the apocalyptic writings which scholars have found so difficult to fit into the generally accepted account of Israel's religion. It is assumed that these writings were composed later than the OT books and that the strange ideas in them were the result of foreign influences. Thus, it is argued, these chapters in Isaiah must be a very late addition to the Isaiah scroll. Much effort has also been expended in trying to find one particular disaster which could have prompted the original prophecy. Dates as late as the second century BC have been proposed (Kaiser 1974), and the chapters have been described as a bridge between the prophetic books of the OT and the later apocalypses (Clements 1980: 196-200).

If, however, the strange material originated in *the traditions of the first temple,* these chapters in Isaiah can be read differently. In the margin of one manuscript of the LXX copied in Egypt (the sixth-century-AD codex Marchalianus), there is one of those tantalizing clues which make a scholar's task both exciting and frustrating. Other copies of the LXX do not include any translation of a few words in Isa 24:16, where the impossible Hebrew is translated "my leanness" (AV), "I pine away" (NRSV), or "Villainy" (NEB). The Egyptian codex has "mystery," understanding the Hebrew as though it were the Aramaic word "mystery," which occurs many times in Daniel (e.g., 2:18) but nowhere in the HB. How this codex came to have a translation for the missing words is not clear, but "mystery" is a very significant translation.

In the light of this one word, Isaiah 24 becomes a revelation of the mystery of judgment. Whatever the actual date of composition, its roots lie deep in the tradition which inspired Isaiah, and in no sense can it be described as a late insertion. What we have is a vision of judgment, that part of temple mythology which was enacted every autumn in the festival of judgment, atonement, and renewal which in the Second Temple period became the festival sequence of New Year, Day of Atonement, and Tabernacles. A similar scenario forms the framework of the earliest material in *1 Enoch* and of several psalms (e.g., 58; 73:15-20; 82). There is no question of one being dependent on the other; all knew a common (probably priestly) tradition.

Chapter 24 describes *the collapse of the created order following the destruction of the cosmic covenant;* the structures of society have gone (v. 2), the land is barren (vv. 3-4, 7-9), and a city (any city but probably here Jerusalem) has become desolate (vv. 10-12). Everything has reverted to the state of chaos which preceded creation, hence the name "the city of chaos" (v. 10). The reason for the disaster is that the earth has become polluted by its inhabitants, who have broken "the everlasting covenant" (v. 5) (Murray 1992: 17-22; see Introduction, 492). The inhabitants here are not simply the people of the land; the word can also mean "rulers," and a comparison with v. 21 shows that this must be the meaning here. The rulers who have broken the eternal covenant are to be punished, along with the host, who, in the Enoch tradition, are their heavenly counterparts. The pollution of the earth (v. 5) was probably by the shedding of blood (Num 35:33) since the apocalypse later describes the LORD coming forth from his holy place to punish the inhabitants of the earth for bloodshed (26:21), as in Deut 32:43, another Day of Atonement text, Mic 1:3, and *1 Enoch* 1:3: "The Great Holy One will come forth from his dwelling."

The judgment is described as a flood; the windows of heaven are opened, as in Noah's flood (Gen 7:11; 8:2), and the foundations of the earth tremble, as in Ps 82:5. *From* 1 Enoch, *Genesis, and the Psalms we can reconstruct the sequence which underlies Isaiah 24.* The rulers of the city have fallen under the influence of the evil angels, who have polluted the land with bloodshed (cf. *1 Enoch* 9:1 and Gen 6:1-12). The "treacherous ones" (24:16), the inhabitants of the earth, are punished with a flood (the punishment of the fallen angels in the Genesis account) and with the collapse of the created order, as in Jer 4:23-26. The "host of heaven" and "the kings of the earth" are to be imprisoned for many days until the time of their final punishment (24:21-22; cf. *1 Enoch* 10:5-6; 21:1-6; or the more detailed later account in *1 Enoch* 90:24-26). After the great judgment, the LORD will reign in glory in Jerusalem, in the presence of his elders. These elders are something of a mystery; they also appear in Exod 24:9, ascending Mt. Sinai to behold the glory of God, and in Rev 5:6. The same sequence is implicit in the longer (and probably original) LXX of Deut 32:43, where the LORD emerges on the Day of Atonement to punish the bloodshed and to atone the land (lit. "soil") from its pollutions. All the angels and sons of God worship him. The same sequence forms the climax to the book of Revelation; after the destruction of the wicked city (Revelation 18), the heavenly warrior figure emerges with his angel army to wage war on the beast and the kings of the earth (Revelation 19). The leader of the evil ones is imprisoned for a thousand years and then, after the great throne of judgment had been set up, is cast into the lake of fire. Finally, there is the vision of the glorious throne with all the servants of the Lord before him (Revelation 22).

Isaiah 24–27 is a sequence based on the old temple mythology. It is not evidence of Second Temple syncretism and the influence of alien ideas, but a glimpse of Isaiah's Jerusalem in the eighth century BC. Like the book of Revelation, another sequence based on the old mythology, the chapters are punctuated by hymns (Isa 24:14-15; 25:1-5; 25:9; 26:1-6; 27:2-6), perhaps in imitation of temple ritual or perhaps drawn directly from it. The temple vision of judgment was the basis for all the oracles against the nations as well as the predictions of judgment on Jerusalem. The sons of God Most High, mentioned in Deut 32:8, were the guardian angels of the nations, known in the mythology of Ugarit as the seventy sons of El and in the Enoch tradition as the seventy shepherds of the nations (*1 Enoch* 89:59), who were given power over Israel and Judah from the eighth century onward but eventually judged for their misdeeds and excesses. Thus Isaiah's oracles regard Assyria as part of the LORD's plan and yet predict judgment for going beyond the divine commands. Isaiah's interpretation of history presupposes the same worldview as the Enoch tradition.

The sequence is interrupted by a hymn (25:1-5), but the link between 24:23 and 25:6 is clear. Once the LORD has been revealed in his glory, there is a great feast, as with the elders on Mt. Sinai in Exod 24:11, and then the climax of the whole vision. The LORD destroys "the shroud and the sheet" (25:7), and then death itself. These verses have often been read as a description of mourning veils, but in fact the reference is to the sanctuary curtain. The first of these words can also mean "mystery" or "secret," and the second indicates the covering of the sanctuary, the veil which represented the material world and veiled the glory of the LORD from human eyes. It was the stuff of mortality, and those who lived on the earthward side of the veil were destined to die. After the great judgment, the veil of mortality would be removed and the glory revealed. The belief is echoed in the more familiar story of Adam being banished from Eden, from the presence of the LORD, and being condemned to dust and mortality. It occurs also in the tearing of the temple curtain when Jesus died (Matt 27:51) and the explanation in Heb 10:19-21, that his death has opened the way into the heavenly sanctuary.

The temple sequence returns in Isa 26:19, where the bodies rise from the dust, freed from the curse of Adam and those like him who have been separated from the glory of God. The word for "body" is related to the word "wither" in Isa 24:4, used twice to describe the condition of the earth when the cosmic covenant has been broken. A dew of light gives life to the dead (26:19), a belief echoed in Ps 110:4, obscure Hebrew, which seems to describe the king being "born" as the divine son and dew playing a part in the ritual. The conclusion of the covenant sequence is what we should expect: the earth restored, the dead raised, and the glory of the LORD revealed. Thus a belief in resurrection is as old as the tradition of the temple, but the hope was probably limited to a priestly and royal elite who were reborn ("born again") as sons of God. *This is the ultimate origin of the Christian belief in resurrection* (Barker 1996: 1-26).

Chapter 26 concludes with a warning of imminent judgment; the LORD is about to emerge from his sanctuary for judgment and the great atonement, as in Deut 32:43. Perhaps the prophet thought that here, too, ritual was about to be fulfilled in history, that the end really was near. An addition in Isa 27:1 gives further detail; on the Day of Judgment the chaos dragon will be destroyed. Since the destruction of such monsters is a creation motif, we see that *the ritual of judgment was also the ritual of renewal and re-creation.* It was not the end of all things but the end of the year, the renewal of all things. In Revelation, too, the judgment on evil and chaos is followed by the vision of a new creation (Rev 21:1).

The remainder of the "apocalypse" reflects these themes and seems to come from many hands and many periods: confidence that the other heavenly powers will be judged (Isa 26:13-14) and the joy of the restored vineyard (27:2-5 in contrast with 5:1-7). The true sign of a land that has been "atoned" will be the removal of foreign altars and signs of alien worship (27:9), a comment from a Deuteronomistic hand. The ingathering for the great festival becomes the ingathering of scattered exiles (27:12-13).

The trumpet (26:13) suggests the year of Jubilee, which occurred after seven weeks of years (Lev 25:8). In this holy year, everyone who had left his property due to debt was allowed to return (Lev 25:13). The exiles in Assyria and Egypt who had lost their land due to their debt of sin would be allowed to return (cf. Isa 40:1-2).

Isaiah 28–31

Most of these oracles were prompted by the Assyrian threat.

28:1-4, however, comes from an earlier period and predicts the destruction of Samaria in 721 BC. The hilltop city of Samaria (a scurrilous report in 1 Kgs 16:24 says that Samaria took its name from the hill of Shemer, which King Omri bought to build his capital; the Samaritans themselves said their name derived from the word "observe" because they were the true observers of the law!) is compared to the garland on the head of a drunkard which will be destroyed by the imminent storm of the LORD's judgment.

28:5-6 are later comments, added here because they are also about a "garland."

28:7-13 and 14-22 both describe Isaiah's reception in Jerusalem. The priests and prophets (v. 7), and the rulers of the city (v. 14), have all refused to listen to him. The priests and teachers of the people, both here and in 29:9, are accused of drunkenness. They no longer give true teaching, and mock Isaiah for his (28:10). He warns that they will learn the LORD's teaching from people who speak a foreign language. The rulers of the city have made a "covenant with death" (v. 15), perhaps a reference to their alliance with Egypt against the Assyrians, but primarily a reference to the countercovenant described in *1 Enoch* 6 in which the rebel angels bind each other by oath in their revolt against the Great Holy One. The oracle which follows is obscure; it cites a foundation stone in Zion in which people can trust and "not panic." Thus the MT as well as the NT citations agree with the LXX: "not be ashamed." There is much debate but no agreement as to the meaning of the original, although the first Christians recognized it as a messianic prophecy (Rom 9:33; 10:11; 1 Pet 2:4-6). It could also have been the inspiration for Jesus's parable of the house on the sand and the house on the rock (Matt 7:24-27).

The crux of the problem lies in 28:21, which refers to two occasions in Israel's history when the LORD acted against their enemies and sent a storm: on Mt. Perazim in the time of King David he attacked the Philistines like a bursting flood (2 Sam 5:17-21), and in the time of Joshua he defeated the Amorites with great hailstones in the valley of Gibeon (Josh 10:6-11). It appears that the LORD is now to attack Jerusalem and not her enemies. The rulers of the city, the scoffers, are compared to those who rise up against the LORD and his anointed. The allusion in v. 22 is to Psalm 2, where hostile rulers take counsel together and plot to burst their bonds, that is, to refuse service to the LORD and the king. They are warned of their fate; they will perish in the wrath of the LORD. This is temple imagery from the coronation of the kings. Read with the *Annals of Sennacherib* (*ANET*: 288), which record that Hezekiah was deserted by his elite troops at the height of the Assyrian threat, a picture emerges of Hezekiah facing rebellion within his own city.

One of the strange facts about Isaiah's oracles in the Assyrian crisis is that no one condemns Hezekiah by name; there are plenty of references to people who advocate alliance with Egypt (Isa 30:1-5; 30:16-17; 31:1-3), but no word that Hezekiah himself was involved (Seitz 1988: 75-81). This would accord with the picture of Hezekiah in Isaiah 36–39, that he trusted in the LORD and accepted Isaiah's oracle. One of the "problems" in the book of Isaiah is the alleged discrepancy between Hezekiah the rebel who relied on Egypt and the ideal king depicted in chs. 36–39, who, it is said, must have been enhanced by later redactors (see on Isaiah 36–39).

28:23-29 are a parable comparing the work of God to the work of a farmer, which varies with each season and each crop.

Chapter 29 begins with an oracle against Jerusalem. "The city where David encamped" must be Jerusalem, but there is no agreement as to what "Ariel" means. The best suggestions are that it means the "altar hearth," as in Ezek 43:16 (thus also the *Targum of Isaiah*), or "mountain of God," as in Ezek 43:15, which is clearly parallel to Ezek 43:16 but spells a similar-sounding word differently, indicating "mountain of God" as the meaning. The great courtyard altar in the temple could well have symbolized a mountain, and so both meanings may be appropriate. A cultic context is confirmed by the second half of the verse: "the feasts going their annual round." "Ariel" appears again in 29:2, perhaps meaning that the whole city will become like a great burning altar; or there may be Isaiah's characteristic wordplay, which is now lost on us. "Ariels" (plural) appear in 33:7 as types of heavenly beings. The oracle envisages the LORD laying siege to Jerusalem (29:3). The MT has: I will encamp against you "round about," but the NRSV uses the LXX "like David," very similar Hebrew. The LXX has probably preserved the original. In the future the people of Jerusalem would speak only as the voices of the dead (v. 4).

29:5-8 are exactly the reverse; the LORD defends Zion against the enemies who mass against her. These verses are sometimes offered as evidence of a redaction of Isaiah's prophecies in the time of Josiah. Here, it is suggested, the events of 701 BC, when the Assyrians withdrew from Jerusalem, have been taken as evidence for a new and ultimately disastrous belief in the inviolability of Zion. Another explanation is equally possible, namely, that the temple cult of Isaiah's time already believed that Zion, the city of the LORD, was under his protection. Foreign powers could be used to punish the city, but only within the limits imposed by the LORD, as seen in the Enochic belief in the seventy angels. The assurance that the LORD would manifest himself to save the city (v. 6) is a traditional description of a theophany, and there is nothing to suggest that was inspired by the events of 701 BC, when thunder, an earthquake, and whirlwind simply did not happen. Isaiah does have descriptions of these momentous events, but they are embedded in Isa 10:16-27, where the disaster is described, accurately, as a wasting sickness and a devouring fire, that is, the wrath of the LORD.

The next three sections, 29:9-12, 13-14 and 15-16, are Isaiah's comments on the leaders of Jerusalem in terms drawn from the angel tradition. The leaders are "blinded" (v. 9), and in a "deep sleep" (v. 10), descriptions which also occur in the enigmatic Enochic histories to describe the changes which took place in Jerusalem at this time. Those who lived in the temple became "blind and forsook wisdom" (*1 Enoch* 93:8), but in the last days some would be "awakened from their sleep," and "wisdom" would be restored to them (*1 Enoch* 91:10). Isaiah looks forward to a time when false wisdom will be removed (29:14) and "the human commandment learned by rote" will be no more (v. 13). The allusion here is unmistakable; Deut 4:5-8 proposed that the law become the wisdom of the chosen people, and *Isaiah here is reacting to the earliest manifestation of the reformers, who were ultimately to destroy the temple cult of Jerusalem.* The Enochic tradition is equally clear; those who lived in the temple became blind, and then the temple was destroyed. The leaders of Jerusalem have rejected the temple vision; the old tradition has become for them a sealed document which they cannot read (29:11). These are the ones who work in darkness (v. 15; cf. Ps 82:5), originally said of the fallen angels. They have tried to turn things upside down (v. 16).

29:17-21 are often said to be postexilic, resembling material found in later apocalypses. Since those apocalypses originated in the traditions of the First Temple, the appearance of "apocalyptic" elements in Isaiah is to be expected. The content of this passage cannot be used to determine its date. The prophet looks forward to a time of renewed fertility (v. 17), the healing of the blind and the deaf, joy for the oppressed, and retribution for the oppressors. These are the customary descriptions of the end time; renewed fertility, judgment on the evil ones, and joy for the chosen ones are an established sequence as early as Deut 32:43 (reading the longer 4QDeut[q]) and the earliest parts of *1 Enoch.* The blind and the deaf, however, are missing, making it likely that these are cryptic references to hostile divinities (see on Isa 33:5-6). The verse should be read in conjunction with 29:24; those who err will eventually come to understand.

29:22-23 may be a later addition. Abraham and Jacob do not belong in Isaiah's Jerusalem. The community at Elephantine (see on 19:18-23) did not use any of these "early" names, which "reappear" in fifth-century Judah.

Chapter 30 reflects the situation in Jerusalem as the crisis of 701 BC approaches. The leaders of the city (Hezekiah is not mentioned) have opted to go to Egypt for help, but Isaiah counsels trust in the LORD. The whole is depicted in terms of the rebel angels of the Enoch tradition.

30:1-5 describe the rebel angels, the sons of God, "rebellious children," who plan to go their own way. They have formed a plan and made an alliance. The Hebrew here can mean "pour out a libation" or "weave a web," but the LXX understood the phrase to mean "make a pact." The angels in *1 Enoch* did exactly this; they bound themselves together in a pact to disobey the LORD.

30:6-7 are a description of the envoys, laden with offerings (v. 6), who pass through a fearful desert on their way to Egypt. Isaiah compares Egypt to its own sphinxes; they look like powerful monsters but in fact sit still and do nothing. Rahab (cf. 51:9, the chaos monster) sits still.

30:8-14 describe the book of judgment. Enoch is the scribe of righteousness who writes down all evil deeds (*Jub.* 4:23), and in the later Enochic histories there is an angel who writes down the deeds of the seventy angels and deposits the book before the LORD in readiness for the judgment (*1 Enoch* 89:71; cf. Isa 62:6-7). Here it is Isaiah who writes a book which is to be a witness forever, clearly the same tradition (cf. 34:16, which also mentions the LORD's book). The book is to record the rebellion of the sons (30:9), who do not heed the true prophets but prefer the false (cf. the contemporary Mic 3:5-8). The sins of these rulers will be like a crack in the wall which protects the city; it will be completely destroyed.

30:15-17 are Isaiah's word to the rulers: return and trust.

The remainder of the chapter describes the great autumn festival, not just the events in Jerusalem but what they represented and celebrated. The LORD hears the cry of his people and answers them (v. 19), but the "answer" takes the form of a "teacher" (v. 20) who has been hiding himself. This mysterious "teacher" has caused many problems; one solution has been to alter the word slightly and read "early rain," as in Joel 2:23, where the early rain is a gift from the LORD. This is not really satisfactory since the next verse refers to hearing his teaching. The *Targum of Isaiah* found the Shekinah here, the presence of the LORD. The hidden teacher is a curious motif which occurs elsewhere: the Servant was hidden (49:2) and a teacher (50:4); Enoch was "hidden" (one possible translation of *1 Enoch* 12:1) until the time came for him to be the messenger of the Great Holy One announcing judgment on the fallen angels; the Messiah was to be "unknown" until Elijah revealed who he was (Justin *Dial. Tryph.* 8; cf. John 1:26; 7:27). "A Righteous Teacher," clearly a priest, was the leader of the community described in the Dead Sea Scrolls, a figure whose appearance was a sign of the last times. God would reveal to him all the mysteries of the words of the prophets (1QpHab 7; cf. Luke 10:24; 1 Pet 1:10-12). It is possible that such a teacher was part of the temple tradition and that he was to be revealed. Jesus went to the temple at the autumn festival (John 7:2, 10), and he taught there. John emphasizes this (John 7:14, 16, 28; 8:20) and says that when Jesus was not well received and "hid himself" (John 8:59). Isa 30:22, probably a later addition, says that when the teacher appears, false worship will be abandoned. The fertility of the land will be restored (vv. 23-25). The great light of the sun and the moon may indicate supernatural signs at the end time, but if we recognize vv. 27-28 as an insertion and read on into v. 29, we recognize that this is a further description of the autumn festival and that the great moon must be the full moon. The music and flute playing at Tabernacles became proverbial, according to the (much later) *m. Sukk.* 5:1, which also describes nocturnal revels in the temple courts by the light of enormous lamps (cf. 30:29). The autumn festival was the time when the LORD would appear to atone the land; atonement meant healing and restoring (v. 26), presumably the wounds caused by sin or inflicted by the LORD as punishment (cf. Isa 1:5-6). He would also come in judgment to destroy his people's enemies (Deut 32:43). Again the pattern of the festival merges with the events of history; perhaps they were still hoping for the destruction of the Assyrians (30:31) at the time of the autumn festival, or perhaps they were recalling the actual events.

The burning place (30:33) was the Valley of Hinnom, to the west of the city, a place of human sacrifice in Isaiah's time (2 Kgs 23:10), but in the mythology of Zion it was also the place of punishment for those who spoke against the LORD. Enoch saw it on his heavenly journey (*1 Enoch* 27). This could even be a recollection of the mass cremation which followed the death of the Assyrian soldiers; the breath of the LORD lit their pyres (30:33). Vv. 27-28 also describe the LORD as a consuming fire.

Isaiah 31

These verses also reflect the divisions in Jerusalem in the closing years of the eighth century BC. Isaiah condemns those who seek military support from Egypt and warns that the LORD will punish not only the evildoers but also those who help them (31:2).

31:4-5 describe *the Lord protecting Jerusalem.* The image of a lion protecting his prey should not be isolated from the rest of the passage and taken to imply that the LORD is hostile to his city. The overall picture is of protection; the LORD comes down onto Mt. Zion to protect it (v. 5). The shepherds who threaten the city are the dominant image, and the LORD as the lion defending his city against the shepherds suggests that those shepherds are more than simple sheep keepers. In passages such as this, shepherds are the rulers, the seventy angels of the nations, the sons of El. They appear by name as the seventy shepherds in the Enochic histories, judged for their evil deeds against Jerusalem and cast into the fiery abyss (*1 Enoch* 89:61; 90:22-5). Here they must be the Assyrians, threatening Zion and being repulsed by its guardian deity. There is a very similar passage in Jer 25:30-8, where the LORD, again as a lion, wreaks havoc on the "lords of the flock." When Jesus described himself as the "good shepherd" (John 10:11), he, too, spoke as more than a simple keeper of sheep; he was claiming to be the LORD, the guardian of Israel.

31:6-9 are sometimes said to be later additions to the oracles; v. 7, with its emphasis on idolatry may be postexilic, although idols are condemned elsewhere, for example, Isa 2:8. V. 6, which in the Hebrew reads "Turn back to him whom they have deeply betrayed . . . ," confirms that the prophet here is addressing a divided city; he appeals to the people as a whole to return to the LORD from whom their leaders have revolted. This again presupposes the angel mythology of Enoch; *the revolt of which Isaiah speaks here and elsewhere is not revolt against Assyria;* he would hardly counsel returning to the Assyrians, for whom he immediately prophesies destruction (v. 8). Rather, he counsels return to the LORD, against whom the leaders of the city have revolted. The first part of v. 9 is obscure; there is probably another meaning for the word we know as "rock." The gist, however, is clear enough.

Isaiah 32

There follows a description of *the cosmic covenant restored.* Just as the rulers of Jerusalem have broken the covenant with all its disastrous consequences of invasion by enemies and devastation of the land (also the theme of the prophet Joel), so now Isaiah depicts the covenant restored. The vision begins with the reign of righteousness and justice (32:1; see on Isaiah 11) and shows how the present disorder will be reversed (see on 2:6-22). A key figure here is "the fool" (vv. 5-7). In Hebrew the words for "being a fool" and "withering" look the same and may well have been related (Murray 1992: 56-58). The fool, then, with his "folly," "iniquity," "ungodliness and error concerning the LORD" (v. 6), was both a sign and a cause of the collapsing natural order so vividly described in ch. 24, where the earth itself withers away (Isa 24:4). There is a similar sequence in both passages: the broken covenant leading to the destruction of vineyards and the desolation of the city (Isa 24:7-9, cf. 32:13; 24:10-13, cf. 32:14). The covenant was upheld by a king who had been given wisdom to establish justice and righteousness.

When the Spirit is poured out (here in v. 15 "on us" but in Isaiah 11 "on the king"), the whole creation is transformed by justice and righteousness (vv. 15-17). The outcome is peace, quietness, and trust (v. 17), exactly what Isaiah promised to the kings of Jerusalem if they would rely on the power of the LORD in times of crisis and not break the cosmic covenant by rebellion against him.

Isaiah 33

Often described as a prophetic liturgy, Isaiah 33 is complex and full of allusions to the practices of the temple in Isaiah's time. The key to understanding is v. 24, which assures that atonement has been made; iniquity is forgiven, literally "carried away." Everything that precedes relates to the great atonement ritual which repaired the bonds of the cosmic covenant, restored the creation, and ensured the security of Zion. When the covenant bonds were fractured, protection was gone and the created order exposed to the wrath. This is vividly illustrated by the account of Aaron making atonement in Num 16:41-48 to stop the wrath of the LORD against his people. The *Targum of Isaiah* remembered this as the original context and meaning for the passage, as can be seen from some of its otherwise inexplicable renderings.

The mysterious "destroyer and traitor" (33:1), was probably Assyria in Isaiah's time. Like the enemy in Isaiah 21, however, it was in fact the current manifestation of wrath and chaos which threatened to destroy the created order. The fallen angels, the angels of the nations, insofar as they had broken the bonds of the covenant, were agents of destruction but destined ultimately to be themselves destroyed.

The first section (33:2-6) summarizes the passage as a whole. The people wait for the LORD to appear, scatter his enemies, and establish his reign of justice and righteousness as in Psalms 46, 48, and 76. The remainder of the chapter repeats and expands the theme.

33:7-9 are very similar to Isa 24:4-8 (Murray 1992: 22-23) and indicate that here, as there, the treaty which has been broken (v. 8) is the cosmic covenant, not a political treaty. The natural order is dying (v. 9). The figures in vv. 7-8 are the heavenly actors in this drama; "the death spirits howl" (this is how Jewish midrash understands them), the "angels" of peace weep bitterly (v. 7). The "oaths" (v. 8), presumably renders 1QIsa[a] "witnesses" (cf. 2 Kgs 11:12, where the king receives whatever this is as part of his regalia). The MT has "guardians," that is, guardian angels (Murray 1992: 184).

With all the heavenly actors in position as the covenant collapses, the LORD "arises," "is lifted up," and "exalted," the description of the LORD on his throne in Isaiah 6, and the enemy is threatened with destruction (33:11-12). Just as Isaiah reacted to the sight of the LORD with a sense of his own impurity, so here the sinners and godless in Zion tremble at the sight of the fire and the everlasting burning of the heavenly throne. Ezek 1:13 and Dan 7:9 in the OT itself and, in more detail, *1 Enoch* 14:15-22 and 71:5-6 all describe the place of fire where humans dare not enter. Isaiah assures us that the righteous one (33:15) has nothing to fear. He will dwell in safety "on the heights" (v. 16) and see "a king in his beauty" (v. 17). The *Targum of Isaiah* has retained the original meaning here; the high place is the sanctuary, and the king in his beauty is the glory of the heavenly throne. *Here is the mystical ascent of the priest-king to stand before the throne and see all history set out before him.* Your (singular) eyes will see. "The land that stretches far away" refers to an experience like that recorded in *1 Enoch* 17–36, where the exalted one, having stood before the throne, is taken on a heavenly journey and sees fiery places of punishment for the evil ones. "You shall see those who go down into the land of Gehenna" is how the *Targum of Isaiah* renders this verse; again, it has retained the original significance of the cryptic words. The exalted one will see his enemies far below him (33:18-19). "Counted" and "weighed" (v. 18) are a common theme in these judgment traditions: the mysterious hand at Belshazzar's feast wrote "numbered," "weighed," and "divided" (Dan 5:25). Enoch stood before the throne and saw how kingdoms were "divided" and actions "weighed" (*1 Enoch* 41:1). The *Targum of Isaiah* understood the curious activity of "counting towers" (33:18) as the "counting of mighty men" ("exalted ones," a possible understanding of the Hebrew), another description of heavenly triumph (cf. Isa 40:26, where the LORD numbers the host of heaven and names them as a sign of his power). The exalted one will also see Jerusalem at peace (33:20), a place of broad rivers and streams. This is temple imagery. The throne in the heavenly sanctuary was the source of a stream which was fire to those who were destined for judgment (Dan 7:10) but the water of life for others (Barker 1995: 32-33). Ezekiel the priest described this river of life (Ezek 47:1-12), as the climax of his temple vision; John did the same (Rev 22:1). The "Parables of Enoch" have an identical sequence: the Righteous One stands before the throne, and then fountains of wisdom are opened for the thirsty and the rulers of the earth are burned up like straw (*1 Enoch* 48). Finally, the LORD is established as judge, ruler, king, and savior (Isa 33:22).

Nobody is to be excluded from the city (33:24). Here we see the real significance of the ancient atonement rituals; they were designed to remove whatever excluded sinners, "sickness," from the bond of the covenant. The paradox of Israel's law was that the purity laws excluded, but the rituals of the temple purified and reintegrated. Ezekiel the priest describes in detail what Isaiah's hearers knew. The covenant has been despised and broken but will be reestablished by the LORD when all is forgiven (Ezek 16:59-63). When the LORD becomes king, he brings his people back into the bond of the covenant, purging out rebels and showing that he is the LORD (Ezek 20:33-38). Thus Isaiah links the LORD as King

(33:22) with the forgiveness which renews the covenant (v. 24).

Isaiah 34

1QIsa[a] has a space between Isaiah 33 and 34. What this indicates we can only guess, but there are grounds for thinking that Isaiah 34 and 35 come from a period after the Babylonian destruction of Jerusalem in 587 BC when the Edomites (descended from Esau) had exploited the disaster and begun to occupy the southern parts of Judah (1 Esdr 4:50). Jer 49:7-22 predicts that Edom will become a horror, a taunt, a waste, and a curse and that all its cities will be permanent wastes (v. 13). Ezek 25:12-14 promises that wrath will come on Edom because of their actions against Judah. The whole of the prophecy of Obadiah warns that there will be no survivor left in the house of Esau because they helped the Babylonians to destroy Jerusalem, rejoiced in the calamity, prevented the escape of refugees, and even handed them over to the enemy (Obad 11-14). It is in this context that the ferocity of Isaiah 34 must be set.

The whole chapter is a description of the day of the LORD and his judgment on the host of heaven (cf. Isa 24:21). The LORD is enraged against all nations and against all their hordes, that is, host of patron angels (34:2), who will lose their immortality and die like mortals. The word "slain" (v. 3) is significant in this context and has many meanings (cf. Isa 43:28). In Ezekiel 28 a heavenly being is also cast out from the heavenly Garden of Eden; all his many punishments are described by this one word, which is to be translated by "pierced," "wounded," "desecrated," "defiled," or "killed." Those who were at home with temple tradition knew these were the same; like the sons of God in Ps 82:6-7, the guardian deities of all nations were to be cast out to mortality and death. The imagery of 34:4 also appears in Rev 6:13-14, when the sixth seal is opened and the Day of Wrath arrives; it also accounts for Mark 13:25 and parallels.

The scene then moves to the earthly counterpart of the destruction of the host; as in Isa 24:21, the host of heaven is punished in heaven and the kings of the earth below. The whole of Edom is to be a great burnt offering (34:6). For "My sword has drunk its fill," 1QIsa[a] has, "My sword has appeared in the heavens." The judgment then comes to earth, to Bozrah the capital city of Edom. "Blood" and "fat" (v. 7), were the most important parts of any offering, and separate instructions were given for dealing with them (e.g., Lev 3:1-4). The day of vengeance would turn Edom into one huge furnace, like Sodom and Gomorrah, which were also destroyed by avenging angels (Gen 19:24-25). Enoch sees similar destruction on his heavenly journey as the rebel angels burn in a blazing abyss (e.g., *1 Enoch* 21; cf. Rev 20:14). The ruins of Bozrah will be marked out for confusion and chaos (34:11); the same words are used to described the state of things before the LORD began to create heaven and earth (Gen 1:2), "formless and void." Wildcats and goat demons (34:14) will inhabit the ruins. All these horrors are written in the book of the LORD, not a reference to earlier prophecies against Edom but to the book in which the heavenly scribe recorded all the evil deeds of the angels of the nations (see on Isa 62:6-7). It was read before the LORD and then sealed in readiness for the Day of Judgment (*1 Enoch* 89:70-71).

Isaiah 35

After the great judgment comes renewal. As in Revelation 21, where the new heavens and the new earth follow upon the great judgment, so too here, centuries earlier, there is the same sequence. Originally it probably marked the renewal of nature with autumn rain after the fiery heat of the summer, but in the liturgy of the temple and the vision of the prophet it has become a picture of the new age after the fiery judgment. The dry land blooms (35:1-2), both literally and spiritually, since the dry land was the curse on Adam when he was cut off from the presence of God and the rivers of Eden (Gen 3:17-19). In the new age the glory of the LORD would be seen again (35:2), coming to strengthen the weak (vv. 3-4).

The disabilities described in 35:5-6 indicate more than a physical condition since the words for "blind," "lame," "deaf," and "dumb" are almost identical to the names of four types of heavenly being. With wordplay characteristic of the Isaianic style, we see here the ending of their power as their victims are released from disability. The words "the blind" and "the lame" appear in 2 Sam 5:6 concealing the guardian deities of old Jerusalem, "the watchers and the threshold guardians"; "the dumb" is a word which looks the same as "the gods" who are judged in Ps 58:1, and "the deaf" is the same word as for "those who practice magic arts" in Isa 3:3. Jesus alludes to this prophecy in his reply to the messengers from John the Baptist (Luke 7:22); that the healings were largely of these four disabilities is no coincidence. They were acted parables, signs (35:6-7), like Ezekiel's river from the temple (Ezek 47:1-12).

A highway appears in the desert to bring the scattered people home (35:8-10; cf. 11:16, the highway from Assyria, and 40:3-5, a way for the LORD to return). This is clearly hope for the future with the exiles returning home, and the book must be a postexilic composition. The underlying pattern, however, also comes from the temple traditions, when those who had been excluded for any reason could return at the great atonement, "the ransomed of the LORD" (35:10), and become part of the LORD's people again.

Isaiah 36–39

This extended historical narrative is similar to the account in 2 Kgs 18:13–20:19, but differs in some important details. 2 Kgs 18:14-16 says that Hezekiah surrendered to Sennacherib at Lachish and paid him tribute, but this is not mentioned in Isaiah. Isaiah includes a psalm of thanksgiving after Hezekiah's recovery from illness (Isa 38:9-20) which does not appear in 2 Kings.

The questions which cannot be answered are: Which

is the original? Did both copy from a third text? Most scholars have adopted the view that these chapters were compiled by the writer of Kings (presumably from an Isaiah source?) and then used by the compilers of the Isaiah corpus to form a link between the first section and the second. A comparison is made with Jeremiah 52, which duplicates 2 Kgs 24:18–25:30 and forms a historical appendix to Jeremiah, but this appendix does not mention the prophet whereas the "historical bridge" between the two parts of Isaiah has stories about him. Further, Isaiah is the only "writing" prophet mentioned in 1 and 2 Kings, which could suggest that the Isaiah traditions were the historian's source at this point, just as the Chronicler refers the reader to the book of Isaiah for further information about Hezekiah (2 Chr 32:32).

If Isaiah 36–39 have been taken from 2 Kings, we have to envisage an editor using the passage to join two blocks of prophetic material, the first dealing with Jerusalem and the second with Babylon. The historical narratives *can* be read in this way. They link the deliverance in the time of Isaiah and the situation in the exile by means of the prophecy to Hezekiah that his house and his treasure will be carried off to Babylon (Isa 39:5-8), and the difficulty of Hezekiah's paying tribute to Sennacherib has simply been removed to make a smoother narrative. The material in Isaiah 35, however, forms a natural preface to Isaiah 40, and there is no convincing reason for an additional bridging narrative.

If, on the other hand, the stories originated in the Isaiah tradition and were *incorporated* into 2 Kings, there has to be a reason for the historian to add the incident about the tribute money and to remove Hezekiah's psalm of lamentation and thanksgiving. These two differences combine to give a less favorable picture of Hezekiah in 2 Kgs 18:4-7, and it may be that the tribute incident was added in order to present not Hezekiah but Josiah as the greatest king of Judah (2 Kgs 23:25; Seitz 1991: 73). It may also be that the Deuteronomic historian needed the story of the tribute money to explain the continuing Assyrian threat despite Hezekiah's piety and the miraculous deliverance of Jerusalem. The Chronicler does not mention tribute money.

A key factor has to be the contemporary record in the *Annals of Sennacherib,* which most scholars, surprisingly, assume to be accurate and more reliable than material in Isaiah and 2 Kings.

> As to Hezekiah the Jew, he did not submit to my yoke. I laid siege to forty-six of his strong cities . . . and conquered them. . . . Himself I made a prisoner in Jerusalem his royal residence, like a bird in a cage. I surrounded him with an earthwork in order to molest those who were leaving the city's gate. . . . Thus I reduced his country, but I still increased the tribute and the katru presents to me as his overlord which I imposed on him beyond the former tribute to be delivered annually. . . . Hezekiah himself . . . did send to me later, to Nineveh, my lordly city (a list of tribute follows). (*ANET:* 288)

The *Annals* do not mention the demise of the army near Jerusalem, nor do they mention a successful siege. They do not mention Hezekiah submitting at Lachish, nor his paying tribute there, and only later does he send tribute to Nineveh (Geyer 1971: 604-6; Seitz 1991: 63-64). Most scholars have treated as accurate the 2 Kgs 18:14-6 account of Hezekiah's submission and tribute but regarded the destruction of the army as fiction; in other words, they have preferred the *Annals* to the OT. (This is reflected in the standard designations for the component parts of the problem; the story of the tribute is "source A," whereas the story of the angel of the LORD is known as "Source B2"; see below). Herodotus's story of an Assyrian army destroyed by mice at this time is also dismissed as unreliable (*Hist.* 2.141).

Those who accept both the submission story and the deliverance have attempted to explain the inconsistencies. Perhaps two Assyrian campaigns were confused: the first in 701 BC when Hezekiah paid tribute, and the second in about 688 BC when Jerusalem was delivered by "the angel of the LORD" (Bright 1960: 282-87). This would explain the otherwise anachronistic reference to Tirhakah of Ethiopia (Isa 37:9 par. 2 Kgs 19:9), who was only a child in 701 BC and the statement that Sennacherib, who died in 681 BC, was murdered when he returned from the campaign (Isa 37:37-38 par. 2 Kgs 19:36-37). It would also fit with Herodotus's tale of the army being destroyed when Sethos was ruler of Egypt.

Another suggestion is that Hezekiah submitted and then, for some unknown reason, Sennacherib changed his mind and proceeded to besiege Jerusalem, where his army was destroyed. Another is that the events have been recorded in the wrong order: Hezekiah submitted and paid tribute after the siege had been successful. This suggestion has no place for the story of the great deliverance. 2 Chr 32:9-23 implies that only an embassy came to Jerusalem; the Assyrian army remained at Lachish, where it was destroyed.

If, however, we consider Isaiah the original account and read carefully both the *Annals* and Herodotus, another possibility presents itself. Jerusalem "was threatened," and the Assyrian army "was destroyed by plague." Only later did Hezekiah send tribute to Nineveh, as the *Annals* record. The *Annals* are clear that Hezekiah did not submit but remained as king in Jerusalem. There is no mention of Jerusalem being sacked. That he later paid tribute may find an echo in the extraordinary story in Isaiah 39 of envoys from Babylon who inspected his treasury.

It has long been recognized that Isaiah 36–37 divides into two sources: 36:1–37:9a; 37:37-38 (B1) and 37:9b-36 (B2). Each can be read as a self-contained account with similar elements. The message from the king of Assyria is delivered (36:4-20, B1; 37:9-14, B2); Hezekiah reacts (37:1-4, B1; 37:14-20, B2). In B1 Isaiah is asked to mediate, but in B2 the king himself goes to the temple to pray. Both accounts describe a message from the LORD through Isaiah (Isa 37:5-7, B1; 37:21-35, B2).

The question is: Why are there two accounts, and how do they relate to each other? B2 seems to be closer to the style of Isaiah, with the prophet more prominent than in B1: the speech to Hezekiah echoes his description of Assyria's boasting in Isa 10:8ff.; Hezekiah goes into the temple himself with the letter and prays to the LORD of hosts, one of Isaiah's characteristic designations for the LORD (2 Kgs 19:15 omits the title; the Deuteronomists did not use it). Isaiah delivers an oracle against the king of Assyria, who has come in pride against Jerusalem. Prophets and their oracles were an important part of ancient warfare; the *Annals* describe how Sargon attacked Gaza as a result of orders from his god Ashur, presumably in the form of an oracle (*ANET*: 285). Isaiah's oracle against the king of Assyria (Isa 37:22-29) resembles the style of Deutero-Isaiah, but this does not mean that it was composed at that time; the later prophet could as easily have been using the style of his predecessor. The oracle to Hezekiah is a sign; after three years the land will have recovered from the effects of the Assyrian invasion and will be a sign of the people's recovery. This was the year his son and heir was born. The third oracle (in B1 at 37:6-7) is assurance that the king of Assyria will be sent home.

B1 has a different style. The speeches of the Assyrian envoys resemble those recorded in the Nimrud letters (Childs 1967: 80-81) and, even allowing for later interpolation, could be an authentic recollection of what happened. Since the key figures in this account are the named palace officials, Eliakim, Shebna, and Joah (Isa 36:3, 11, 22), they probably wrote it. Later tradition said that "Hezekiah and his retinue" had collected the works of Isaiah (*b. B. Bat.* 14b, 15a).

The major problem in these chapters is the account of the destruction of the army (wherever it may have been), the climax of B2. "The angel of the LORD set out and struck down . . ." (Isa 37:36). It has become popular to treat the story as fiction, although that word is not used. Later generations, it is said, perhaps in the time of Josiah, looked to the prophecies that the LORD would overthrow the Assyrians (e.g., Isa 10:16-19; 29:6; 31:5-9) and reflected this hope back into the historical narrative about Sennacherib's siege. Those events inaugurated the defeat of Assyria, which was believed to be imminent. The "legend" developed by historicizing the ancient cult traditions found in, for example, Isa 17:12-14; 29:1-4 and Ps 46, in which the LORD defends his city by destroying the evil hordes that come against it (discussion in Childs 1967: 51-53; Clements 1980: 90-108).

Seeing the liturgy fulfilled in contemporary events, however, was characteristic of Isaiah (see on 9:2-7), and he drew on the lost mythology of Israel (see on 19:5). It is entirely possible that he predicted the deliverance of the city on the basis of temple mythology. The tale, albeit disordered, can be recovered. When the Assyrian army was approaching Jerusalem, Hezekiah was smitten with a plague, the fatal illness mentioned in Isa 38:1. 2 Chr 32:25 describes his illness as "wrath," the traditional description of a plague (Num 16:46). This had been seen as punishment for destroying the ancient shrines, and Isaiah was hostile to the king. Since the life of the king and the well-being of the city were the same, this did not augur well for Jerusalem, and the Assyrian envoys knew this (36:7). After the king's prayer, Isaiah pronounced that both he and the city would be saved (38:6), and he would go up again to the temple (38:22). The king would live for fifteen more years. (Later tradition said that he was childless and that he was granted his reprieve so that he could get an heir. Manasseh, his son, was born three years later [cf. Isa 37:30].)

Isaiah then ordered a fig poultice to be applied to the king's boil, an indication of his illness since the last stage of the plague is marked by boil-like swellings and the ancient treatment for plague sores was a fig poultice.

The sequence of events requires that Isaiah 38 should precede Isaiah 36–37 since the king's recovery coincided with the deliverance of the city, and the army at Lachish was destroyed by the same plague. Josephus, the first-century-AD Jewish historian, knew that the army had been destroyed by a plague (*Ant.* 10 §21). He probably read the story in the light of Hab 3:5, Num 16:46, or 2 Sam 24:15-16, all of which show that when the wrath of the LORD went forth against his enemies, it went like a plague. This is exactly what Herodotus knew (*Hist.* 2.142); he told of an Egyptian army waiting near Pelusium and of an Assyrian army destroyed by mice who ate the quivers, the bowstrings, and the leather of the shields. Mice were known as plague carriers, as can be seen from the golden mice and golden tumors which were returned with the ark after it had brought a plague on the Philistines (1 Sam 6:4). Hezekiah's plight was one inspiration of the fourth Servant Song (see on Isaiah 53), which implies that the explanation of the sufferer's plight changed (Barker 2001).

These chapters originated in the Isaiah tradition. There is evidence of disorder in them, but the original scheme is clear. First, they contrast Hezekiah and Ahaz; the one trusted the LORD in time of crisis, but the other became a vassal of the Assyrian king. Isaiah received his call in the year that Uzziah had died a leper, a punishment from the LORD for his pride in entering the sanctuary (2 Chr 26:16-21); his last prophecies were in the time of Hezekiah, the good king who recovered from the plague, returned to the temple, and lived a further fifteen years.

Deutero-Isaiah: The Prophet of the Exile?

Toward the end of the eighteenth century, scholars began to doubt that the book of Isaiah was the work of one prophet. Eichhorn (1783), followed by Doderlein (1789), thought Isaiah 40–66 were a later addition. Duhm (1892) further divided the book; Isaiah 56–66 were a separate work which he named Trito-Isaiah. This threefold division of the book has been generally, but not universally, accepted.

The name Isaiah does not appear in chs. 40–66; they are anonymous, with no editorial marks or indications of authorship. It has, however, been argued that Deutero-Isaiah reworked into their present form the Isaiah prophecies that existed in his time (Williamson 1994). Second, there is a change of mood in these chapters; Deutero-Isaiah exudes confidence and hope, assured of the demise of the other gods and of a bright future for Israel. On the other hand, both Isaiahs are steeped in temple imagery and see the cultic patterns realized in history. Both rely on wordplay to add impact to their message. Their methods are exactly similar even if their style is not. Their relationship may well have been that of master and disciple, not in the sense that the one knew the other but that the later prophet inherited the traditions of the original Isaiah and used them in a new situation.

Isaiah 40–55, although similar in many respects, separate into two halves, perhaps from two stages in the prophet's life. Isaiah 40–48 deal with the rise of Cyrus, and the style and themes of these chapters (and only these) are similar to those of the Cyrus Cylinder (*ANET*: 315-16). Deutero-Isaiah could have been influenced by the pro-Cyrus propaganda of the disaffected Marduk priests or of Cyrus's own agents who proclaimed that Marduk had chosen Cyrus to liberate Babylon from the disastrous Nabonidus (Smith 1963: 415). Isaiah 49–55 focus on Zion, personified as the wife whom the LORD abandoned and then took back.

The Historical Background to the Second Section of Isaiah

Between the times of Isaiah and Deutero-Isaiah there had been two great crises in the history of the temple in Jerusalem. First, there had been the "reform" in Josiah's reign (640-609 BC). As described in 2 Kings 22–23, it followed the discovery of an old lawbook which was believed to be Deuteronomy, and the changes were to bring temple worship into line with the requirements of Deuteronomy. All traces of Canaanite religion, and a good deal more besides, were banished. The Asherah and the host of heaven (2 Kgs 23:4-5) probably conceal the Queen of Heaven and the angels (cf. Jer 44:16-19), who had been worshiped in Jerusalem for generations. Josiah also removed the horses and chariots dedicated to the sun (see on Isa 7:14). The reformers have found allies in the translators of the Hebrew Bible (HB) and in several archeologists who "interpret" what they find as evidence for alien practices. Josiah *altered* what happened in the temple. Whether this was reform or destruction has to be a matter of interpretation.

The second major crisis was the destruction of the city and temple by the Babylonians. In 597 BC the temple was looted (2 Kgs 24:10-15), and in 586 BC it was pillaged again and then burned (2 Kgs 25:8-17; Jer 52:4-23). The ruling class was deported to Babylonia (3,023 people in 597, 832 in 586, and 745 in 581; Jer 52:28-30). It is widely held that the prophecies of Deutero-Isaiah were given to this small group who went into exile. The prophet seems familiar with life in Babylon (see on Isa 46:1-2), and he was acquainted with the politics of the time. Most of the people, however, remained in their own land, and it is important to remember that only a few experienced exile (Ezek 33:21-29) (Barstad 1946).

Nebuchadnezzar, who had conquered Jerusalem, had been the greatest of the Babylonian kings. After his death in 562 BC there eventually came to the throne in 556 BC Nabonidus, who antagonized the priests of Marduk by encouraging the worship of other deities. He then removed his court from Babylon to Tema in north Arabia, which meant that for several years it was impossible to celebrate the great New Year festival in Babylon (*ANET*: 306) in which the king played a central role. Since the prosperity of the city depended on these rites, the king's absence was regarded as a disaster. In addition, the Medes were already posing a threat in the north. Cyrus, king of Persia, was at first an ally of Nabonidus against the Medes, but when he defeated them and became king of both the Medes and the Persians, Nabonidus had to watch as his power increased. In the west he conquered Lydia and the Greek cities of Asia Minor, while in the east his power stretched almost to the border of China and north into what is now southern Russia.

Nabonidus returned to Babylon to celebrate the New Year festival in 545 BC, but six years later Cyrus conquered Babylon and the neo-Babylonian Empire was ended. Belshazzar's feast (Dan 5:1-30) is the OT account of the fall of Babylon. Belshazzar is described as the son of Nebuchadnezzar when he was in fact the son of Nabonidus, and the conqueror of the city is said to be Darius when it was really Cyrus. Nevertheless, the story shows how deep an impression was made by the fall of the great city. Herodotus *Hist.* 1.190-91 and Xenophon *Cyr.* 7.15-30 describe how the river which protected the city was diverted so that the army could walk across the riverbed and take the city by surprise. A great festival took place at the time, and the people continued to dance and enjoy themselves without realizing what had happened.

In the light of Cyrus's career, the early oracles of Deutero-Isaiah can be dated between 550 BC, when Cyrus defeated the Medes in battle, and 539, when he conquered Babylon. The prophet wrongly predicted that Cyrus would dishonor the gods of Babylon (see on Isa 46:2; also 21:1-10). Chs. 49–55 probably come from a later period, when the return to Jerusalem was a real possibility.

Isaiah 40

Isaiah 40 and Isaiah 6 have a similar setting; both describe a prophet's call. The earlier prophet heard the heavenly voices and saw the LORD on his throne, but Deutero-Isaiah heard only the voices: the voice of God (v. 1), and two unidentified voices in vv. 3 and 6. *Since the time of First Isaiah the Deuteronomists had altered the ancient religion of Jerusalem. The vision of God was no longer described.* Their account of Mt. Sinai makes this quite clear: the LORD spoke out of the fire; there was the sound of words but no visible form (Deut 4:10). Traces of the old temple pattern still remain in the vision of Deutero-Isaiah; there are two voices in the sanctuary, those of the two heavenly beings whom First Isaiah saw beside the throne. The occasion is the autumn festival; iniquity has been pardoned (v. 2), and the LORD himself is about to appear to save his people (v. 10). Since they are to return to their land (Isa 40:9), this suggests the Day of Atonement, which began a year of Jubilee (Lev 25:9-10), when anyone who had left land because of debt (here, debt of sin) would be allowed to return (cf. Isa 27:11). The Jubilee years, however, were 572 BC and 522 BC, neither of which supports the customary dating of these verses.

The prophet then reveals the secrets of the creation and the secrets of history, both of which were granted to those who had entered the sanctuary to stand before the throne. Deutero-Isaiah and the Deuteronomists were part of the great movement which reshaped Israel's religion during the exile; their common concerns are apparent, but much of the tradition they reworked can still be recovered.

Like First Isaiah, *the prophet of the exile sees the myths and liturgies of the temple realized in history.* Isa 40:1-11 is the opening scene; "A voice cries" (v. 3). The MT invites the translation, "A voice cries, 'In the wilderness prepare the way of the LORD,'" but the LXX has, "A voice cries in the wilderness, 'Prepare the way of the LORD. . . .'" This is the form used in the Gospels to preface the story of John the Baptist in the desert (Mark 1:3 and pars.).

In a great procession the LORD appears: Jerusalem/Zion is the herald (feminine) of good tidings to the other cities of Judah (40:9), announcing that the LORD is coming like a shepherd (v. 11) but also to bring judgment (v. 10). The heavenly messengers are told to speak tenderly to Jerusalem (lit. "to her heart") that her penalty is paid (v. 2) (better, "iniquity is pardoned," but see below on 41:8-9), suggesting a Day of Atonement setting. She has received double for all her sins (40:2), a sentiment echoed bitterly in Rev 18:6, where the voice from John's heaven condemns "Babylon," that is, the Jerusalem of his time, to receive double for all her evil deeds.

The desert highway (49:3) was probably a sacred way from the eastern gate of the temple, the Holy Way of Isa 35:8. In former times there had been processions when the God and King of Jerusalem had entered his sanctuary (Ps 68:24), bringing fertility as he passed (Ps 68:7-10; cf. Isa 35). Ezekiel saw the glory of the LORD returning through the eastern gate at the same season (New Year; Ezek 40:1), just as he had seen it leave the polluted city (Ezek 43:1-5; cf. Ezek 10:18-19). Here Deutero-Isaiah is told by a heavenly voice that all people will see the glory returning (40:5). Vv. 6-8 resemble Ps 103:15-18; the prophet may have been drawing on a festival psalm.

The rest of this chapter introduces *one of Deutero-Isaiah's great themes: monotheism.* First Isaiah had lived in a world of many gods: El and his seventy sons with their many offspring who were demons and other minor divinities. Israel had its Holy One, the LORD, who was the chief of these sons of El, to whom Israel had been allotted (Deut 32:8-9). Deutero-Isaiah and the Deuteronomists both proclaimed monotheism. The Deuteronomists had put this into practice with their policy of "one God, one temple," and had destroyed the shrines where the local LORD had been worshiped. Deutero-Isaiah proclaimed the same monotheism within the temple tradition of El ʿElyon and his sons; some climactic statements in the prophecy can be understood only in this way. Thus Isa 43:12-13 actually says that the LORD is El (God), and 45:22 declares, "I am El, and there is no other." The argument of Isaiah 40 reaches a climax in v. 28, "The LORD is the everlasting God" (here *'elohim,* not El), "the Creator of the ends of the earth." The series of questions which precede should be read in the light of this ending.

There is no agreement among scholars as to how or whether 40:12-31 should be divided into smaller units, but such considerations are less important than setting the prophet's confident declarations about creation in their temple context. The easiest way to recover this is by using the Pentateuch, which was, at about this time, retelling the story of Moses in terms of the older royal cult. Moses replaced the king figure after the end of the monarchy. Moses on Mt. Sinai was told to build the tabernacle as an exact copy of what he had seen (Exod 25:9, 40), but the summary account of the tabernacle building in Exod 40:17-32 suggests strongly that what Moses "copied" was not a heavenly temple but a vision of the whole creation which the tabernacle/temple represented. The construction of the tabernacle replicates the account of the creation: first the basic structure was set up (Exod 40:19) on day 1 of creation; then the veil screened the sanctuary (Exod 40:21), the creation of the heavens on day 2; then a table for bread was installed (Exod 40:23), day 3, the creation of vegetation and seeds; then the lampstand was set up (Exod 40:25), day 4, the lights of heaven. It would appear that the "Book of the Origin of Heaven and Earth" (Gen 2:4a, LXX) refers to the preceding account in Genesis 1 and was a record of the vision seen in the sanctuary (in heaven) by those granted the secrets of the creation. The tradition in *Jubilees* is identical; Moses on Mt. Sinai is told to write an account of the six days of creation (*Jub.* 2:1) and then of history until the institution of the Passover. *Creation and history were one process in the temple tradition* as preserved in *Jubilees* 2 (Barker 2001:17-25).

Behind Moses we glimpse an earlier figure, the royal high priest who had witnessed the creation in a sanctuary experience. Later tradition was reticent about these sanctuary experiences; they became the forbidden things of the mystics: the chariot throne, the *maʿaseh merkabah,* and the first day of the creation, the *maʿaseh bereshit.* The two mysteries appear together in Isaiah 40; the voices of the throne and the work of creation. The sanctuary setting appears again in v. 22, where the LORD spreads out the heavens like a curtain, represented in the temple by the veil, and in v. 27, where Jacob-Israel complains that he is hidden from the LORD. The prophet in the sanctuary is reminded of something he learned when he first saw the mysteries of creation (v. 21), namely, that the LORD in heaven brings princes to naught (v. 22), that is, he is also the creator of history, an important theme, for Deutero-Isaiah must have been a priest.

The vision of creation in the sanctuary (see above in 40:12-31) also accounts for the two questions: To whom will you "liken" El (v. 18), or the LORD (v. 25)? The older tradition had required Moses to make the tabernacle in the *likeness* of what he had seen; here the prophet ridicules those who make an idol and believe it to be the *likeness* of a deity (vv. 18-20; also 41:6-7 and in greater detail 44:9-20). Nothing on earth could represent the LORD, a departure from temple tradition in which the king had been the LORD in the temple. The climax comes with the second comparison: Who is *like* the Holy One (Isaiah's characteristic title for the LORD)? No longer the king or indeed any visible form; the prophet's insight here is that only the LORD can be likened to the everlasting God (v. 28). El ʿElyon and his firstborn son, the LORD, are one deity (this is stated more clearly in 43:12-13 and 45:22), and the monotheism is thus established which became characteristic of Judaism.

It is possible that the questions in 40:13-14 compare what Israel believed about its God with the beliefs of contemporary Babylon, which included a heavenly counselor who advised the gods when the world was created (Whybray 1971: 79-84). Such a figure would have had no place in Israel once monotheism had been established, but there are several passages which imply that more than one heavenly being was present at the creation (e.g., Gen 1:2; Job 38:4-7; Prov 8:22-31; and John 1:1-4).

1QIsa[a] suggests a different meaning for 40:13: "Who ever fathomed the mind of the LORD, or what man of his counsel has made it known?" (Brownlee 1964: 220).

Isaiah 41

The speaker in this chapter is the LORD and *the setting is the heavenly court on the holy mountain,* a part of the great autumn festival when the LORD appeared in the temple to judge his enemies and atone for the land (Deut 32:43).

He addresses the "coastlands" (41:1), one of many words in Deutero-Isaiah which seems to have another meaning. "Coastlands" and hyenas haunt ruins (Isa 13:22), "coastlands" and wildcats haunt ruins (Isa 34:14); they are parallel to "gods of the earth" in Zeph 2:11 and to "the adversaries of the LORD" in Isa 59:18. The word translated "coastlands" in Isa 41:1 seems to mean a hostile demon. The "coastlands" in v. 5 tremble at the imminent judgment and are associated with idolatry (Barker 1987: 174-75). These lines in Isaiah were written too long ago for us to be certain exactly what the prophet had in mind; but it was not simply "coastlands." If this cluster of words does conceal hostile heavenly figures, vv. 8-9 has revealed its original context. Israel the Servant, the Chosen One, has been rescued from these creatures (v. 9) and not cast off. This is reminiscent of the Canaanite myth of Baʿal and the Devourers, desert demons who threatened him and the fertility he represented. Rites were performed in the autumn to ensure and to celebrate Baʿal being rescued from such peril (Wyatt 1976: 415-36). This sequence in Deutero-Isaiah suggests a similar setting; the gift of water and fertility in the desert is proof of the triumph over these creatures (vv. 17-20).

The identity of the Servant is one of the major problems in this prophet; here it is a single figure (the verbs are singular), but often he stands for the whole people in exile (see on 42:1-4, where the Servant was originally the royal high priest). In Isa 41:8-10 the Servant is the people, and this passage offers some of the earliest evidence for the democratization of the old royal cult. The promises to Abraham in, for example, Gen 15:18-21 had originally been promises to the house of David, but with the demise of the royal house, the Servant became the whole people. Their enemies would be crushed before them (41:14-16); they had not been cast off. V. 9 mentions exactly the same promises as to the king in Psalm 2, that he would be secure on Zion and triumph over his enemies. This is the myth of the holy mountain; those who sinned were cast down from it. Ezekiel 28 is a thinly disguised description of the royal high priest being expelled from the holy mountain, that is, from the sanctuary; when the heavenly guardian figure was expelled, the downfall of his people was assured. Deutero-Isaiah here assures the people that the Servant is "not cast off," that is, their condition is not beyond hope. True, their rulers had sinned and been driven out of their temple (Isa 43:27-28), but the Servant had not been cast off forever.

The problem with Deutero-Isaiah is that his thought does not move one step at a time; he was truly a prophet and a visionary, making connections, moving forward, leaving the details and the problems to others such as us. He depicts the trial of the lesser gods and their defeat, not as an annual reenactment but as an event in recent history, already in the past. It is possible that the words translated "served her term" in 40:2 should in fact be "her host" (of divine beings) "is no more." In other words, the angel figures who were the basis of First Isaiah's worldview were a thing of the past. This is another aspect of his assertion of monotheism: the LORD and El are One, and the others are nothing. One consequence of this insight is the problem of evil; the new monotheism, with its one Creator, meant that the LORD created evil (Isa 45:7).

The "victor from the east" (41:2), may be a reference to Cyrus (see "The Historical Background to the Second Section of Isaiah," 524). The *Targum of Isaiah* thought the victor was Abraham, not unreasonable in the light of Abraham's prominent new role at this period. A similar figure in v. 25 is also ambiguous, and the texts are confused. The MT has "he called upon my name," as is said of Abraham in Gen 12:8, and 1QIsa[a] has "his name," which gives the NRSV "he was summoned by name."

The phrase "I stirred up" suggests that the figure was Cyrus. "Roused" (v. 2) and "aroused" (45:13) translate the same Hebrew word, which also appears in Isa 13:17 and in Jer 50:9; 51:1, 11. There were several exilic prophecies of the same form, the LORD stirring up a foreign nation against Babylon. This form derived from Israel's oldest tradition; prayer in time of crisis was answered by the oracle "I will stir up . . ." (Westermann 1969: 88).

The gods of the nations are challenged to reveal their knowledge of the future (41:23) but also of "the former things" (v. 22). This phrase occurs frequently in Deutero-Isaiah (Isa 42:8-9; 43:9-13; 46:8-10; 48:3-5; 44:6-8; and 45:20-21 have this theme even though the phrase is not used), but there is no agreement as to its meaning. It could refer to earlier events or to the earlier prophecies of Isaiah (see the survey in Childs 1979: 328). It is best understood as the older angel mythology; First Isaiah had seen the events of the cult realized in historical events; Deutero-Isaiah saw that the fallen angels, the other gods, had themselves been judged and were no more. *The ancient mythology had fulfilled itself.*

41:21 introduces the former things; the other gods are asked to tell of the former things and reveal the future as proof of their power (see on 43:9-13). The overall pattern in these passages is that the power of the LORD has been demonstrated by the former things which actually happened and by the new things which none of them had predicted. The conclusion is that the other gods are a delusion (41:29).

Isaiah 42

Since Duhm's commentary of 1892, four texts (Isa 42:1-4; 49:1-6; 50:4-9; and 52:13–53:12) in Deutero-Isaiah have been grouped together as a literary unit, *the Servant Songs* (Duhm 1892 [1968]: 311). The original proposal was that they were not from Deutero-Isaiah but a later addition, from the time of Trito-Isaiah. Many modern scholars accept that the Songs are a distinct group of texts within the prophecies, but there is no agreement as to their extent, origin, or date. The questions are still open. The main problems are: Did Deutero-Isaiah compose the Songs? Did he incorporate them from an earlier source or were they a later insertion into the prophecies? How does the individual figure in the Songs relate to the figure who clearly represents the whole nation (see on 41:8-9)? And, most important of all, *Who was the original Servant?*

The title "Servant" appears frequently in the OT: Abraham was the LORD's "Servant" (e.g., Gen 26:24); Moses is thus named around forty times, most interestingly in Num 12:7-8, where he is distinguished from the other prophets as the "Servant," the one who "beholds the form of the LORD," to whom the LORD speaks "plainly" and not in "riddles." David was a "Servant" (Ps 89:3, 19-20), exalted, chosen, and anointed, upheld by the hand of the LORD, before whom his enemies would be crushed. The covenant with David the "Servant" was part of the covenant with the day and night, that is, the cosmic covenant (Jer 33:21-6). Psalm 2 describes such a king, secure on the holy hill. In the postexilic prophets, the Servant is the "Branch" (Zech 3:8), the "Chosen One," and the "Seal" (Hag 2:23). All these features appear in the Servant Songs and raise the question: Did all the other OT texts know and use the Servant figure of the Songs, or are they independent evidence for the existence of the figure who inspired the Songs? The former suggests that Isaiah's Servant was a major figure in the tradition of the First Temple period if Moses, David, and the future Messiah acquired his characteristics; the latter, that the Songs were inspired by a major figure in the preexilic tradition who influenced the descriptions of Israel. Either way, we are looking for a key figure.

Many attempts have been made to identify the Servant. The structure of the poems suggests that a comparison is being made; the suffering of an individual and the suffering of the whole people are both described in terms of the Servant. Given that the titles, promises, and expectations of the monarchy were democratized and transferred to the people as a whole during the exile (cf. Isa 41:8; 42:5), the most obvious explanation for the individual-then-corporate Servant would be that the original Servant had been the king, the Melchizedek high priest of the First Temple. Since "the servants of the LORD" were the priests (Pss 134:1; 135:1) and the corresponding verb was used for tabernacle/temple service (e.g., Num 3:7, 8; 8:11, 19, 22), the Servant of the LORD was probably a title of the ancient royal high priest. Several people have been proposed as the historical figure whose suffering was the immediate inspiration for the Songs, especially the fourth (Isa 52:13–53:12): Hezekiah, the king who became fatally ill and then recovered (see on Isaiah 38); First Isaiah, who was martyred by Manasseh; Uzziah, the king who became a leper; Jeremiah; Second Isaiah himself, or perhaps an unknown prophet in the exilic community; Jehoiachin, the last real king of Jerusalem; Zerubbabel his descendant, who led the exiles home to Jerusalem; or Cyrus, the king whose decree allowed the exiles to return. Others have seen in the figure a prophecy of the Messiah (see the survey in North 1956). In passages where the Servant clearly refers to a group of people, they have been identified as the whole nation, as a faithful group, perhaps prophets or priests, or as the ideal of the nation.

In the first Song, Isa 42:1-4 or 42:1-9, the speaker is the LORD, but the hearers are not named. The Servant is introduced as though present, perhaps being confirmed in his role: he is "my servant, my chosen," upheld by the LORD (v. 1; cf. Pss 2:7; 89:3). He has been given the Spirit of the LORD "to bring forth justice to the nations" (cf. Ps 51:10-13; Isa 11:1-9). The passage is modeled on the coronation rites; the king is presented to the people or their representatives (Eaton 1979: 48). In the accounts of Jesus' baptism. "You are my Son, the Beloved, with *you* I am well pleased" (Mark 1:11 and pars.) has long been recognized as a paraphrase of Isa 42:1.

The Servant is described in the imagery of the temple lamp (42:3). The word for a branch of the lamp in Exod 25:32 is "reed," and the Servant here is "a bruised reed who will not be broken" and a "dimly burning wick who will not be extinguished." This is a possible and more satisfactory reading than the traditional "a bruised reed he will not break . . . ," making vv. 3 and 4 parallel:

> v. 3: "A bruised reed he will not be broken, a dimly burning wick he will not be quenched; he will faithfully bring forth justice."
> v. 4: "He will not grow faint, that is, not burn dimly, or be crushed until he has established justice in the earth." (Barker 1987: 229)

The lamp was a symbol of the king (2 Sam 21:17; 1 Kgs 11:36; 2 Kgs 8:19; Pss 18:28; 132:17).

The main theme of this text is the Servant's role in bringing forth justice to the nations. The exact meaning of *mishpat,* "justice," is uncertain, but this and *sedaqah,* usually translated "righteousness," are the characteristics of the ideal king. His qualities influence the balance of the natural order, bringing "justice to the wilderness, and righteousness to the fruitful field," after the Spirit has been poured out (32:15-16). "Bring forth" is a curious phrase; it probably refers to the Servant king emerging from the holy of holies at the autumn festival, representing the LORD on the Day of Atonement and Judgment, as in Deut 32:43 or the *Assumption of Moses* 10.

When the LORD speaks to the Servant (v. 6), he says, "I have called you in righteousness, I have taken you by the hand and *kept* you," words translated in Jer 1:5 as "before I *formed* you in the womb. . . ." Something similar would be appropriate in Isa 42:6, "I formed you and appointed you as a covenant to the people," better "eternal covenant" (see on 49:8-13).

This the only Servant Song in the Cyrus chapters, and it is possible that Deutero-Isaiah has taken one traditional Servant text and applied it to Cyrus. Isa 42:6-7, leading the Servant by the hand and releasing prisoners, is closely paralleled in the Cyrus Cylinder (*ANET*: 315). The imagery of the damaged temple lamp, however, is hardly appropriate to Cyrus.

42:5 illustrates Deutero-Isaiah's new monotheism (see on 40:28). If there was only one God, everything formerly ascribed to El would be ascribed to the LORD. Here we see traditional epithets of El not only transferred but also transformed. El had been "Procreator of heaven and earth" (Gen 14:19), a title known elsewhere in the ancient Near East to belong to El (Habel 1972: 333-37). He had been the father of the angels, the sons of God, and of the creation. Deutero-Isaiah took this title and expanded it: "The LORD who created [not procreated] the heavens . . . and stretched out the earth. . . ." Elsewhere the rejection of the sons of God and El as procreator is even more marked; in Isa 44:24 and 51:13 the title has become, with embellishments: "the LORD, the maker . . . of heaven . . . and earth." The verb has changed, and all idea of procreation has gone. In other words, the idea of a procreator God with sons fell out of favor among those who equated the LORD and El to create monotheism. Those who retained a belief in sons of God, for example, *the later Christians, continued to distinguish between El and the LORD, as the Father and the Son* (Barker, 1995: 1-10). Recognition of this innovation by Deutero-Isaiah is crucial for understanding Christian origins because not everyone accepted the new ideas. *Not all the heirs of Israel's older religion became the new monotheists.*

There follows a hymn (42:10-13), which resembles Psalms 96, 98, and 149; it is a new song to celebrate the LORD as king, or, as here, the heavenly warrior. Vv. 14-17, perhaps the second half of the hymn, describe the warrior emerging, crying out like a woman in labor (v. 14). The heavenly warrior was an ancient description of the LORD (cf. Exod 15:3; Judg 5:23; Ps 24:8). The LORD led the heavenly hosts, hence his title LORD of hosts. Here he transforms the creation and rescues his people.

In 42:18-21 the LORD is the speaker, and he contrasts the Servant with "the blind and deaf," that is, the other gods (cf. Isa 35:5, where the deaf and the blind conceal the names of these discredited gods). Here the defeated heavenly beings are shown the superiority of the Servant; the deaf (plural) are told to hear and the blind to see. The exact meaning of the words translated "blind" and "deaf" is lost, but "blind" probably indicates the guardian gods, and "deaf" those with supernatural powers. As in the triumph scenes of Enoch's "Parables" (e.g., *1 Enoch* 62), also based on the royal rituals of the temple, the defeated powers have to recognize and acknowledge the Servant, here called the Son of Man. The gist of 42:19a is, ". . . there is no guardian god but my Servant, none with supernatural powers except my angel [messenger: the same word] whom I send." The Servant is then named as "Meshullam" (NRSV, "the dedicated one"), but the name probably means "the one who is bound by the covenant of peace," or, better, "the one who makes the covenant of peace." This covenant maker is the angel of the LORD (my angel) and the Servant of the LORD. The Servant here is an ideal heavenly figure, presumably the one whom the human servant figure manifested on earth. This indicates temple symbolism, heavenly archetypes with earthly counterparts.

42:20 is obscure: "You [singular] see many things but do not observe them, with open ears he ["you" makes more sense here] does not hear." V. 21 is probably an insertion, a later comment. Vv. 22-25 show what it was that the unnamed person of v. 20 had failed to see. The robbed and plundered people (v. 22), had explained their misfortune as the triumph of other gods rather than as just punishment from the LORD, against whom they had sinned (v. 24).

Isaiah 43

Oracles of salvation such as First Isaiah had given to the king now become oracles for the ancestor Jacob-Israel who represents the whole people, another example of transforming the older royal cult (cf. 41:8; 42:5). This chapter opens with the traditional form, "Do not fear" (43:1, 5).

The whole of 43:1-7 assumes *the Day of Atonement as its setting;* a "ransom" has been given for the people (v. 3; the word can also be translated "atonement"); as a result those cut off can be gathered in again (vv. 4-7), and the creation can be renewed (cf. the pattern in Leviticus, where the consequence of sin is being "cut off" from the people of God). The sinner bears his own guilt (e.g., Lev 20:17) and is cut off. Those whose guilt is "atoned for" can be reintegrated. The LORD has created and formed Israel (43:1, echoed in v. 7); he is Israel's Holy One, the characteristic title for the LORD in First Isaiah. Egypt, Ethiopia, and Seba (v. 3) could be what was given to Cyrus by the LORD in exchange for the release of his people (cf. Isa 45:14).

Like 41:1-5 and 41:21-9, Isa 43:8-13 (or perhaps vv. 8-15) are a trial scene, challenging the nations to show their power by declaring the former things and bringing their witnesses. The nations have witnesses, and Israel is the LORD's witness and Servant (v. 10). Here we glimpse the old mythology which encompassed both Israel's LORD and the gods of the other nations, the sons of El ʿElyon who appear in Deut 32:43. Just as First Isaiah had interpreted and predicted the history of his times in terms of the temple mythology, so *here Deutero-Isaiah announces that the myth of the autumn festival has been realized in history.* The LORD has emerged from his holy place, and the gods of the nations have been judged, as in Ps 82:6-7, and defeated. They no longer exist. The LORD is the only God (v. 11), and he alone determines the course of history. It is no longer a conflict between the warring sons of El ʿElyon.

In 43:14-21 the LORD, using the old titles of Holy One and King, declares himself the Creator of Israel. In the cult the judgment had been followed by the healing and renewal of the creation, a pattern still discernible in

1 Enoch 10. *Here the pattern becomes the recreation of the nation* (vv. 15, 21).

Having been introduced as the Holy One and King, the LORD is then identified with the God of the exodus, the one who brought Israel from Egypt. He exhorts his people to forget the former things and gives a whole new picture of the LORD. *He has become, for the first time in Isaiah, the God of the exodus.* When scholars first began to analyze the texts of the Pentateuch, they observed that separate blocks of tradition had been seamed together. The story of the exodus, for example, was joined to the saga of the patriarchs by means of Exod 3:13-17, where the LORD of the exodus is identified as the God of the patriarchs. Deutero-Isaiah does something similar; the titles of the Jerusalem cult are joined to the exodus tradition, and the annual recreation in the temple becomes the new exodus in history. Thus the former things, the ways of the old cult, are superseded (43:18), and in the future there are to be new ways.

The next section (43:22-28) also moves forward from the old ways. Implicit is the people's accusation that the LORD had failed them and allowed them to suffer the disaster of defeat and exile. *The response to the accusation is cast in terms drawn from the old atonement ritual.* The text is difficult, and 1QIsa[a] has several different readings in v. 23. The gist, however, is the contrast between v. 23b and v. 24b. "The LORD has not made Israel [singular] serve him with offerings or wearied him with incense" (v. 23b), "but Israel has made the LORD his servant with his sins and wearied him with his iniquities." This is Servant terminology; the LORD was the Servant who bore the sins and was wearied with iniquity, and those who should have borne them, the mediators, the princes of the sanctuary, failed through their own sin (v. 27). They were profaned and driven out, and Israel, as a result, was destroyed. *The LORD himself therefore takes the role of the sin bearer (v. 25) and performs the great atonement* (cf. Ezekiel 34, where the evil shepherds are judged and the LORD himself becomes the shepherd of his people).

In the time of the former things, the high priest, the prince of the sanctuary, had borne the sin of the people. He wore the sacred name on his forehead, and this enabled him to bear (i.e., forgive; the same Hebrew word) the sin of Israel (Exod 28:36-38). But, says the prophet, the "mediators" (NRSV, "interpreters," but this meaning is not appropriate here) themselves rebelled, as did the angels who fell from heaven, and they were profaned. Ezekiel 28 gives a parallel account of the demise of the ancient high priesthood, now in the form of an oracle against Tyre, but originally, as can be seen from the vestments of the heavenly figure, describing the high priest in Jerusalem (v. 13; cf. LXX Exod 28:17-20). The prince or king (vv. 2, 11) was a heavenly figure who walked in the mountain garden of God (v. 13), but his wisdom made him proud, and so he was cast out and became mortal (cf. Isa 14:12-20). All the words used to describe the punishment of the prince-king are translations of the word *hll,* which Isa 43:28 renders "profaned." Ezekiel's prince was "defiled" (Ezek 28:7), "met a violent death" (Ezek 28:8), "was wounded" (Ezek 28:9), "cast out as profane" (Ezek 28:16), and "profaned" (Ezek 28:18). He became mortal. Deutero-Isaiah describes the mediator as the first ancestor, Adam, showing how the two Eden stories in the OT relate to each other. The more familiar version in Genesis 2–3 grew out of an older temple myth about the royal high priest in the heavenly mountain garden, represented in Jerusalem by the temple. Adam, who had walked in the garden of the LORD, was remembered as the sanctuary priest; as he left Eden he offered the special blend of incense which could only be used in the sanctuary (*Jub.* 3:27; cf. Exod 30:34). Here is yet another example of the democratization of the old cult; Adam, formerly the Man figure (the Son of Man) in the heavenly sanctuary who rebelled against God, has become Everyman.

Deutero-Isaiah's "new things" were a cult without such a mediator figure; the LORD himself, who gave his glory to no other (Isa 42:8), would no longer be represented in the temple by the high priest. He himself would perform the great atonement and blot out his people's transgressions (43:25).

Isaiah 44

44:1-5 is another oracle of salvation; like the kings of old, the Servant and Chosen One is told, "Do not fear." The name "Jeshurun" occurs also in Deut 32:15 and Deut 33:5, 26, but the meaning is unknown. "Water on thirsty land" (44:3; cf. Isaiah 35) is reminiscent of the water-pouring ceremony of the (later) feast of Tabernacles; in the First Temple it had probably been part of the autumn festival, bringing the autumn rains. The temple was seen as a source of water (cf. Ezekiel 47; Zech 14:8; Rev 22:1), a symbol of the Spirit (cf. John 7:37-39), but here to be given to all the Servant's descendants (cf. Joel 2:28-29). Each person who receives the Spirit will have the Name written on his or her hand (44:5; reading with the LXX) and perhaps also on the forehead. The high priests wore the Name on their forehead, and the early Christians, who received water and the Spirit at baptism, were marked with a diagonal cross, the old sign for the Name (cf. Rev 14:1). The faithful in Jerusalem were marked as belonging to the Lord by the Hebrew letter *tau* on their foreheads (Ezek 9:4). In Ezekiel's time, the letter *tau* was a diagonal cross. The "Name of Jacob" and the "Name of Israel" probably mean the God of Jacob/Israel. Deutero-Isaiah describes here a universal priesthood (cf. Rev 1:6), a democratization of the old ways.

In 44:6-8, 21-23 the festival pattern continues with the LORD again proclaiming himself King (cf. Zech 14:8-9, where the gift of water precedes the LORD becoming king, the God who alone knows the future, "the First and the Last"; cf. Rev 1:17, where the title is used of the heavenly Jesus). The Servant is told that he has not been forgotten; his transgressions have been taken away, and he can return (44:22).

Inserted here is the longest of Deutero-Isaiah's seven passages deriding idols (cf. 40:19-20; 42:17; 45:16-17; 46:1-2, 5-7); the worshipers of idols are as blind as their images.

The LORD, the Creator (v. 24; adapting the ancient titles of ʿElyon [see above on 42:5]), then re-creates. Just as

Genesis 1 describes creation by the LORD's command (cf. 48:13), so here the LORD commands, and it is done. The deep will be dried up (v. 27) so that Jerusalem can be rebuilt (cf. Ps 24:2 and the tradition in *b. Sukk.* 53b that King David had to subdue the deeps before he could build Jerusalem over them). Jerusalem and the temple were to be rebuilt, and Cyrus, apparently, was to bring this about. Elsewhere, rebuilding the temple was the task of the Servant (Zech 6:12; *Tg. Isa* 53:5); Deutero-Isaiah may here be proclaiming Cyrus as the Servant who will rebuild the temple. Josephus *Ant.* 11:5-6 says that Cyrus read Isaiah's prophecies and desired to make them come true, so he allowed the Jews to return home.

Isaiah 45

The original text describes the work of the anointed king and was probably another Servant poem which Deutero-Isaiah applied to Cyrus. The LORD speaks to him as his anointed (45:1; cf. Pss 2:2, 7; 110:1); he is to subdue nations and rule them (cf. Pss 2:8-9; 110:1, 5); the LORD holds his right hand (cf. Isa 41:13, where he holds the right hand of the Servant). Many phrases resemble those on the Cyrus Cylinder (*ANET*: 315-16). The first Christians read vv. 2-3 as a prophecy of the harrowing of hell (*Barnabas* 11).

The identification of Cyrus as the Servant may have caused the disagreements apparent in the later parts of the prophecy. First Isaiah had seen Assyria as the LORD's agent (Isa 10:5; 13:2-16), and it would be quite consistent for a later disciple to see Cyrus in the same way. To proclaim him as the anointed, however, was for some a step too far. The city which he rebuilt became for them the harlot Babylon as in Rev 17:1-6, and the temple where prayers were offered for the foreign king (Ezra 6:10) was described as the harlot's bed (Isa 57:7-10).

Even in Deutero-Isaiah dissent can be seen; 45:9-13 are clearly addressed to someone who does not like the new ways, and the objection is met by a declaration of the LORD's might. Since there is only one God, the LORD must create both weal and woe (v. 7), and nobody can question his acts. This is exactly the situation of Job, who had suffered unjustly and wanted an answer to the problem of evil. He took up Deutero-Isaiah's unanswered question; thus Isa 45:7, 9-11 can be read as the preface to Job. Without Deutero-Isaiah's terrifying declarations of absolute divine power, there could have been no answer from the whirlwind to Job's question about suffering (Job 38–39). And this was no real answer.

45:14-17 are four individual sayings: v. 17, with its promise of foreign nations bringing tribute, resembles Isaiah 60 and may originally have belonged there; v. 18 reminds us that just as the LORD was hidden in the temple behind the sanctuary veil, so he hides his ways from his people even though their ways are not hidden from him (Isa 40:27).

45:16 and 20-21 are attacks on idol worshipers, those who carry their gods (v. 20), playing on the fact that "carry" and "forgive sin" are the same word in Hebrew. Thus the prophet contrasts the saving forgiveness of the LORD with the inability of wooden idols to save. The defeated and discredited gods and their peoples are not, however, abandoned; they are invited to acknowledge the LORD and be saved (v. 23). A consequence of Deutero-Isaiah's monotheism was that, if there was only one God, that God no longer belonged exclusively to one nation. "To me every knee shall bow" became an important proof-text for the first Christians. It appears in Rom 14:11 and in Phil 2:10 as the final act in the Servant drama; after his sacrificial death the Servant is exalted and receives the homage of all creation.

45:18-19 are obscure: they seem to refer to a creation story we no longer know and offer in contrast, as an indication of the nature and power of the LORD, the familiar Genesis picture of an ordered world established for people to live in.

Isaiah 46

The gods of Babylon are powerless; their images are carried away into captivity (46:2), and they cannot prevent the disaster. Bel, later identified with Marduk, was the god of the city of Babylon. Nebo, the god of Borsippa, was his son, the patron of the royal house. The great kings Nabopolassar, Nebuchadnezzar, and Nabonidus bore his name. He was also the god of wisdom and writing, and at the New Year festival he wrote down what the gods had decreed for the coming year. Such irony, in a prophet who declared that the other gods could not predict the future, must have been intentional.

This chapter was probably a visionary prediction of the fall of Babylon, inspired by a procession in which the images of the gods were carried through the city (see on Isaiah 21), which was reworked at this time as a prophecy of the fall of Babylon. When Babylon did in fact fall to Cyrus in 539 BC, he respected the temples, and their images were neither moved nor harmed. The contrast, as in Isa 45:20, is between the gods who are carried and the LORD who carries and forgives his people, that is, carries their sins, the Hebrew idiom.

The prophet emphasizes that nothing can be like the LORD (46:5), linking the two themes: no image can depict the LORD, and no other god can claim his power to predict and to create (vv. 8-10). Here he summons an unnamed man from a far country to bring deliverance to Zion. Why he should be described as a bird of prey (v. 11) is a mystery.

Isaiah 47

Although there are oracles against foreign nations in Isaiah 13–23, this is the only one in Deutero-Isaiah. In the exile Babylon was the only enemy of any significance, and so the LORD speaks against it through his prophet. Nebuchadnezzar, king of Babylon, had conquered and destroyed Jerusalem in 597 and 586 BC (2 Kings 24–25). There are many oracles against Babylon in this period: Jeremiah 50–51 is the largest collection, but the present form of Isaiah 13–14 is older material reworked to apply to Babylon and Psalm 137 is a curse on the city.

Babylon is personified as a proud mistress of kingdoms (47:5), humiliated because she showed no mercy to the LORD's people (v. 6), who, like Assyria before her (Isa 10:5-6; 13-19), had exceeded the punishment which the LORD intended. Nahum described Nineveh in a similar way, a proud city humiliated despite her charms and sorcery (Nah 3:4-7). Babylon had trusted in her wisdom and knowledge (v. 10) and in her sorcery (v. 12), but these had led her astray. The question of wisdom and knowledge was vexed at this period, and there are echoes here of the fallen angels who had corrupted their wisdom and thus corrupted the earth. Ezekiel described a heavenly figure thrown from heaven because he corrupted his wisdom and understanding (Ezek 28:2-10). Adam and Eve sinned because they coveted wisdom (Gen 3:4-6). Wisdom, however, had not always been considered dangerous; King David was described as being like an angel of God, discerning good and evil (2 Sam 14:17). It was the Deuteronomists who offered the law of Moses as the (new) wisdom for Israel, a wisdom which would be the envy of other nations (Deut 4:6). The old wisdom became suspect and was abandoned (*1 Enoch* 93:8).

The prophet warned that there would come upon Babylon evil which she could not "ward off" (Isa 47:11), a word elsewhere translated "atone." Here we glimpse what atonement must have meant (see on Isa 53:12); it was protection against evil in the same way that the Passover blood was a protection against the Destroyer and his plagues (Exod 12:23). Ezekiel the priest, perhaps a generation earlier than Deutero-Isaiah, regarded the Passover and the Atonement as similar festivals (Ezek 45:21-25).

Isaiah 48

The first section of Deutero-Isaiah concludes with this chapter, and all the characteristic themes make their last appearance: Cyrus (perhaps 48:15), the heavenly trial (vv. 14-16), the former things (v. 3), and the polemic against idols (v. 5).

The LORD speaks to the descendants of Jacob and, significantly, Judah (48:1), perhaps a reference to the Jews (lit. "Judeans"), the new name for the group who returned from exile in Babylon. Josephus (*Ant.* 11.173) says that "Jews" was the name given only to the people who had been in exile and not to those who had remained in the homeland. The text is obscure here; the NRSV, "loins of Judah," is literally "waters of Judah" in the MT; the *Targum of Isaiah* has "seed of Judah." The second half of v. 1, together with vv. 2 and 4, is very harsh, in the style of Trito-Isaiah. The people call on the LORD but without truth or right (v. 1), and they are obstinate (v. 4). Without these additions, vv. 1-8 read smoothly as the final appeal to the former things. This time the challenge is addressed not to the other gods (plural, as in 41:23) but to an individual, almost certainly the Servant, who had seen former history (48:5-6a). V. 6a is better translated, "you have heard; you have seen in a vision . . ." (cf. Amos 3:6-7). He had never seen the new history because it was part of the new creation (48:6b-7). These were the new hidden things, the new secrets of the sanctuary (cf. on Isaiah 40; also Rev 21:3-5). In contrast the law was revealed to all (Deut 29:29).

48:9-11 describe the great atonement. The LORD's anger is deferred so that the person addressed is not cut off, a state of ritual separation resulting from unatoned sin (cf. Lev 20:17; the one who bears his own sin is cut off). He has been tested in the furnace (cf. Mal 3:2-3), a later text but one which testifies to the belief that priests had to be purified in a baptism of fire. Deut 4:20, a text from the time of Deutero-Isaiah, applies the image of the furnace to the whole people, another example of democratizing the ancient cult. Egypt and Babylon were both represented as experiences of fiery purification. Deuteronomy apparently addresses those who have just left Egypt, but in fact it was written for those leaving Babylon.

The rest of Isaiah 48 falls into four sections: vv. 12-13, 14-16, 17-19, and 20-22.

48:12-13 are the words of the LORD to his Servant, the one he called (cf. 42:6; 43:1). He declares his Name, "I am He, the First and the Last" (cf. 41:4; 44:6), and his power as the Creator. The title "The First and the Last" was given to the heavenly Jesus in Revelation and is important for establishing who the first Christians believed Jesus to be (Rev 1:17; 22:13).

48:14-16 seem to be addressed to the other gods. 1QIsa[a] and the LXX differ from the MT: "Let them all assemble and hear" rather than "Assemble, all of you, and hear," as in the NRSV. The meaning is the same. The prophet summons them to learn about an unnamed person whom the LORD loves, appointed for the overthrow of Babylon (v. 14). He is usually assumed to be Cyrus but the *Targum of Isaiah* here says it was Abraham, brought to the land of the LORD's temple (v. 15). Traditions about Abraham said that he, too, had destroyed the idols of the Chaldeans in Ur before setting out to take possession of Canaan. Deutero-Isaiah's words about idols are quoted in the story (*Jub.* 12:1-14). Isa 48:16 is obscure; it seems to mean that the LORD was present at the creation and has never spoken in secret (cf. 45:19). The verse is alluded to by Jesus (John 9:58). The last line of v. 16 is opaque.

It is not clear whether 48:18-19 refer to the past or the future; they can be read either way: "Had Israel listened they would not have been punished and cut off," a reference to the exile and the need for atonement and ingathering; or, "If Israel will listen, they will prosper and not be cut off," cut off being the expression for ritual exclusion from the people. The comparison of descendants and sand is also made in the promise to Abraham (Gen 22:17).

On 48:20-21 cf. Jer 51:6. The exiles are told to leave Babylon and celebrate their redemption. The return from Babylon is described as a new exodus, with the miraculous gift of water in the desert (cf. Num 20:2-11).

Isaiah 49

Isa 49:1-6 are often designated the second Servant Song, but the Servant theme extends through to v. 12. *1 Enoch* 48 is very similar to this Servant Song, but since *1 Enoch* 48:5-6 parallels Isa 49:7, vv. 8-13 must also refer to the Servant

(Knibb 1996: 222). The Servant himself is the speaker, addressing the coastlands and peoples. "Coastlands" probably means a hostile supernatural being (cf. Isa 41:1). The Servant was chosen before his birth and then kept "hidden," a characteristic of the later Messiah; cf. 30:20, the hidden teacher who will be revealed. See also on Isa 50:4; *1 Enoch* 48:6, the hidden chosen one; *1 Enoch* 62:7, the heavenly Man hidden away until the judgment day when the kings of the earth will recognize him and receive their punishment; 2 Esdr 13:25-26, the Man kept for many ages who will deliver the creation; John 1:26-34, the unknown Messiah whom John the Baptist revealed. "The sharp sword of his mouth" is his word of judgment (cf. 11:4; also 2 Esdr 13:27; 2 Thess 2:8; Rev 1:16; 2:16).

The LORD speaks directly to the Servant (49:3; cf. Ps 2:7). "Israel" as the name of the Servant (v. 3) could be an addition (Mowinckel 1956: 462) since vv. 5, 6, and 7 use "Israel" to designate the people, not an individual. It could be a throne name meaning "Ruler" (Eaton 1979: 64) or the "Man who sees God," which is how it was understood by Philo *Conf Ling.* 56, 72 (Barker 1996: 125). Moses the Servant spoke with the LORD "face-to-face" (Num 12:8), and Isaiah's Servant "saw the light" (see on 53:11). The Servant feels he has exhausted himself in vain (49:4; cf. Ps 73:13). 49:4b is obscure; it probably means that the Servant is establishing the LORD's *mishpat,* "right order" (NRSV, "my cause"; cf. 42:3-4, where the same word is translated "justice").

49:5-6, 7, and 8-13 are three oracles to the Servant. He has to bring Israel/Jacob back to the LORD, another example of temple imagery fulfilled in history. *Atonement enabled sinners to be brought back into the covenant people;* cf. Ezek 16:59-63 and 20:33-37, which describe the LORD reestablishing the everlasting covenant when he "atones" (Ezek 16:63; NRSV, "forgives"), becomes king, and "brings them into the bond of the covenant again" (Ezek 20:37). The Servant is to be a "light to the nations" (cf. 42:3-4, the Servant as the lamp, and Luke 2:32).

49:7 presents the recurring Servant theme; even though he is despised (cf. 53:3), the rulers of the world will recognize him (cf. 52:15; also *1 Enoch* 48:8; 62:7 and Mark 14:62). The "slave of rulers" should probably be "Servant Meshullam" (cf. on 42:19 as this links to the next theme, "covenant").

49:8-13 proclaim the Servant as "a covenant to the people" *(librit 'am),* but the original was probably *librit 'olam,* "eternal covenant," renewed by the atonement which restored the land (cf. Deut 32:43, where NRSV, "cleanse the land," is better translated "atone for the land"). All could return through a transformed landscape, even those from the Jewish community in Syene (Elephantine) (v. 12; see on 19:18-23).

49:14-26 introduce a new theme — *Zion,* personified as a woman abandoned by her husband and then reunited with him. Much time has been spent on the Servant, a key figure in the temple cult who was democratized to represent the whole people. Little time has been spent on *Zion, another key figure, democratized to represent the city of Jerusalem.* The title "daughter of Zion" appears in Isa 10:32; 16:1; 52:2; 62:11. In Lam 2:1, a contemporary text, she is put "under a dark cloud" (NRSV, "humiliated") and described as "the splendor of Israel thrown down from heaven." Her fall was the fall of her city (cf. 43:22-28). "Daughter of Zion" was probably yet another name for the female deity of the city, the mother and the spouse of her kings. Micah, a contemporary of First Isaiah, affords a glimpse of her as she leaves her city in agony at the hands of her enemies (Mic 4:10), but she later triumphs over them (Mic 4:13). She appears again in Mic 5:3 as the mother of the Shepherd who will gather in his people (see on Isa 7:14). Also known as Wisdom, the Queen of Heaven, she was removed from the temple cult by the reforming Deuteronomists, who offered the law as a substitute (Deut 4:6). She survived among the Jews of Egypt: the Elephantine community worshiped a deity named Anat-Yahu, perhaps the spouse of Yahu, the LORD, or perhaps a compound deity with male and female aspects (cf. Gen 1:26: "God created humankind in his image . . . male and female"). She also survived in the gnostic texts as Sophia, the consort and mother goddess who fell from grace.

The Servant and the female figure in Isaiah 49 have had similar experiences: a sense of failure (v. 4; cf. v. 14); a feeling of being despised (v. 7; cf. v. 21); and the assurance that kings will acknowledge them (v. 7; cf. v. 23) (Sawyer 1989: 99). In each case the LORD denies that they have been abandoned (41:9; cf. 49:15). *What we have in the Zion poems is another of the prophet's transformations; just as the Servant became the people as a whole, so the Daughter of Zion became the city of Jerusalem.*

49:14-26 is the complaint of an abandoned wife who is assured that she will become a great mother again (vv. 19-23). V. 16 refers to the walls of the ideal city which the LORD sees in heaven even though they are not yet built on earth.

In 50:1-3 the LORD protests that his queen has not been divorced, only put away because of the behavior of her children.

51:17-23 describes a woman drunk with grief for her children, destroyed by the husband who at last takes away the bowl of his wrath (v. 22). Such sentiments show how different were the mores of ancient Israel; few would now agree with Torrey (1928: 403) that this poem shows tenderness insofar as the wife need never again endure her LORD's wrath!

In 52:1-2 Zion is released from captivity and puts on her beautiful clothes.

54:1-2 call on the barren woman to rejoice and enlarge her tent at the prospect of many children. Her past condition is described in many ways: shameful youth and widowhood (v. 4), forsaken by her husband and cast off (v. 6). The LORD admits (v. 8) that he abandoned his city in his anger, a remarkable statement.

52:9-10 affirm that the covenant has been restored. The eternal covenant, the covenant of peace, had guaranteed the stability and perpetuity of the natural order. It had been renewed after the judgment on Noah's generation (Gen 9:16), and now it was to include not only the natural order but Jerusalem herself (cf. Jer 31:35-37).

The city is to be dressed like a queen (54:11-12), and no weapon brought against her will succeed (v. 17). The bejeweled city appears in Rev 21:10-14, where she is the queen consort, the bride of the enthroned Lamb.

62:1-5 is another Zion poem, indicating the origin of the female figure. She will become glorious, no more forsaken but renamed to show her new state. *In temple tradition the virgin goddess had been both mother and consort of the kings;* here we see that Zion's "sons" (thus MT; NRSV, "builder") will marry her as a young man marries a virgin (thus MT; NRSV, "young woman"). She was remembered as the mother of the king (Rev 12:1-5), but also as his bride (Rev 21:9), the bejeweled city (Rev 21:10-14).

The last of the Zion poems is 66:7-14; she is about to give birth to her son, but the image is democratized and becomes the city giving birth to a land and a nation. Jerusalem will nurse her children and prosper.

Isaiah 50

On 50:1-3 see above on Zion.

50:4-6 or 4-9 is the third Servant Song, different from the others insofar as the Servant is not named but assumed to be the speaker. He has been inspired by the LORD to speak, but the word translated "sustain" (v. 4) is obscure and so the purpose of his inspiration is unknown. The LXX has "the word I ought to speak." The reference is probably to the Servant revealed as a teacher from the LORD (cf. 49:2) and the hidden teacher (30:20). The *Targum of Isaiah* has "the tongue of them that teach wisdom to the righteous." The king was inspired to hear and speak the words of the LORD (Ps 2:7 and 2 Sam 23:2).

The suffering (50:6) has been compared to the kingship rites in Mesopotamia, the *akitu* celebrations when the king was dragged by the ears and struck on the face in front of the god Bel before being reinvested with his regalia (*ANET:* 331-34). This followed a temple purification, not unlike the Day of Atonement ritual as described in Leviticus 16, but using the carcass of a ram. Later tradition linked this suffering of the Servant to that of the scapegoat who bore away sin on the Day of Atonement (*m. Yoma* 6:4; *Barnabas* 7). With the LORD to "make him righteous" (NRSV, "helps") he can face his enemies, a trial scene like 41:21-22 and 43:8-10. See also Job 19:25-27.

50:10-11 are obscure. They seem to contrast those who heed the Servant even in his darkest hour and those who kindle fires for light and will find in them their punishment.

Isaiah 51

This chapter is a series of short pieces.

51:1-2 show the growing importance of Abraham at this period; his journey in faith from Mesopotamia to Canaan is offered to the exiles as an example, as is his childless state (v. 2). *The covenant with David became the covenant with Abraham.* The *Targum of Isaiah* finds Abraham in all the passages where modern commentators find Cyrus. This is the only reference to Sarah outside Genesis.

51:3 is a fragment about the transformation of Zion; she will again be like Eden.

51:4-5 and 7-8 could well be the Servant speaking again; teaching and justice go forth from him (v. 4; cf. 42:4); the "coastlands" wait for him (v. 5; cf. 49:1); he is a teacher (v. 7; cf. 50:4). But is the Servant the one who brings salvation and deliverance (v. 6)? If the Servant was originally the royal high priest who "was" the LORD with his people and he sat on the throne of the LORD in the temple (1 Chr 29:20, 23), then the ambiguity of vv. 6-7 is explicable.

51:9-11 recall an ancient creation myth in which the dragon who was the primeval waters was defeated so that order could be created. In the Babylonian New Year festival the story of Marduk's triumph over Tiamat, the Sea, was re-enacted. She was defeated, and her split carcass was used to form heaven and earth. The lesser gods then built Marduk a temple in gratitude. *Here the myth has been fused with the exodus story,* as also in Exod 15:1-18, *the return from Babylon being both a new creation and a new exodus.* 51:11 echoes 35:10.

The text of 51:12-16 is disordered ("you" in v. 12 is first masc. pl., then fem. sing. and in v. 13 masc. sing.), but the sense is clear. Those who know the power of the LORD the Creator (vv. 13, 15, 16) have no need to fear an oppressor. The victims will neither die (the Pit was the shadowy underground dwelling of the dead; see Ezek 32:17-32) nor go hungry, but they can be confident because they are the LORD's people.

On 51:17-23, see above on Zion (49:14-26).

Isaiah 52

On 52:1-2, see above on Zion (49:14-26).

52:3-6 are obscure. The experiences of Egypt and Babylon are compared (v. 4), and the reference in v. 6, "it is I," seems to be cultic. It is Deutero-Isaiah's characteristic name for the LORD (cf. 41:4), but the NRSV does not make this clear. The sense of v. 6 is the LORD's self-proclamation of his Name: "I Am He" is speaking, "behold me"; cf. Exod 34:5, where the LORD stood with Moses and proclaimed his Name, a description probably colored by memories of temple practice. At the climax of the Day of Atonement ritual in the Late Second Temple period, the high priest put the sins of Israel onto the scapegoat and then recited Lev 16:30, uttering the Name itself rather than a substitute, as was the custom at other times (*m. Yoma* 6:2; cf. John 18:6).

52:7-10 return to the procession of 40:3-11. A herald proclaims the "good news" (LXX, "gospel") and announces the kingdom of God. 52:7 was a key text in the *Melchizedek* text from Qumran Cave 11, which described the advent of the heavenly deliverer Melchizedek, the royal high priest. The messenger of v. 7 was understood as the Messiah (who was also Melchizedek), bringing the final Day of Atonement at the end of the tenth jubilee (see on Isa 61:1). Hence Mark 1:15. The prophet sees the return of the LORD to Zion; Deutero-Isaiah must have believed that the LORD had left the city just before it fell to the Babylonians (cf. Ezekiel 8–11) and had been with his people in exile.

52:11-12 is addressed to the temple personnel who will carry back the sacred vessels. Ezra 1:7-11 describes how the temple vessels looted by Nebuchadrezzar were returned. It was the abuse of these sacred vessels which had precipitated the destruction of Babylon (Dan 5:1-30). Just as the LORD had led his people from Egypt and been their rearguard (Exod 14:19-20), so, too, he would guide and guard the return to Jerusalem.

On 52:13-15 see below.

Isaiah 53

52:13–53:12 is *the fourth and last Servant Song, which became, for the first Christians, the most important prophecy of the death and exaltation of Jesus.* The text is far from clear in places, but readings in 1QIsa[a] have thrown valuable light on early Christian usage. This passage gives the fullest description of the Servant and his role, but it also reveals something of the historical figure whose suffering was interpreted as that of the Servant.

52:13. The Servant "becomes wise" (NRSV, "prosper"); "wise" is the more usual meaning for the verb (as in Gen 3:6, the tree "to make one wise"; LXX, "understand"). He is "exalted and lifted up," as was the LORD in Isa 6:1 (cf. Ps 89:20, the king "raised up") and the Son of Man in John's Gospel. The Servant's wisdom is an aspect of his exaltation, not, as in Genesis 3, the occasion of sin. The *Targum of Isaiah* has "my Servant the Messiah," showing that it was not only Christians who read this as a messianic prophecy.

52:14 is obscure. Modern translations all use the MT, but 1QIsa[a] has a significant difference. For MT *msḥt,* "marred" or "disfigured" as in the *Targum of Isaiah* and the NRSV, 1QIsa[a] has *msḥty,* "I have anointed him" (Brownlee 1964: 204-15). The verse then describes not a human being unrecognizable because he has been disfigured, but *one whose appearance has changed because he has been exalted and made wise, and the LORD has anointed him* (cf. Ps 89:19-20, and especially *2 Enoch* 22–24; Michael takes Enoch up to the heavenly throne, where he is anointed and transformed into a shining angel. The LORD then teaches him the secrets of heaven). This explains Luke 24:26; *no other passage in the HB says the anointed one has to suffer to enter his glory.*

The Servant then "startles" many nations (52:15). Thus the NRSV, but the MT has "sprinkles," as does the Vg and the Greek of Aquila and Theodotion. "Sprinkles" is a priestly term (cf. Lev 16:14), suggesting a priestly context for this passage. Kings are astonished at the sight and recognize him, exactly as the kings and the mighty recognize the Chosen One in *1 Enoch* 48 and 62. The royal son is revealed but not immediately recognized. Since "arm" and "seed/son" are similar in Hebrew, 53:1b is better read "to whom has the seed/son of the LORD been revealed?" (cf. LXX Isa 48:14). This makes better sense of MT 53:2a, literally "sucking child" (cf. LXX, "little child"), not "young plant" as in the NRSV (cf. Isa 11:1). The sense is: "To whom has the LORD's son been revealed?" a question answered in 53:10, not "he shall see his offspring" but, with differently pointed Hebrew, "he shall be revealed as the son." The revealing of the Chosen One is a recurring theme in *1 Enoch* (e.g., *1 Enoch* 48:7; 62:7; 69:26).

The Servant has no "majesty" (53:2b). "Suffering and infirmity" (v. 3; LXX, "plague") could describe any human in distress, but "stricken, struck down by God and afflicted" implies that the suffering of a particular figure has been explained in the Deuteronomic manner, as punishment for wrongdoing. This was the first explanation offered for the suffering, but the speakers reject it in favor of the priestly view, that the sufferer was in fact the sin bearer. Here we glimpse the Servant behind Isaiah's suffering figure. He carried "the infirmities" of others (v. 4a); the *Targum of Isaiah,* "the sins" of others. He was pierced (*mhll,* v. 5a), elsewhere translated "defiled, profaned" (see on Isa 43:28). The midpoint of the poem is 53:5b; the MT can mean not only "upon him was the punishment that made us whole, and by his bruises we are healed" but also "the covenant bond of our peace was upon him, and by his joining us together we are healed." The words translated "punishment that made us whole" refer also to "the bonds of the cosmic covenant," as in Ps 2:3; Ezek 20:37; and the usual translation for "bruises" is "joining together," as in Exod 26:4, 10 "joining" the tabernacle curtains. This is characteristic Isaianic wordplay (Barker 1996: 128).

53:6 repeats the reason for the Servant's suffering, but the keyword "laid" is obscure since it appears in another form in v. 12 as "made intercession." The meaning is probably illustrated by the role of Aaron in Wis 18:23, where, as the Servant, the high priest positions himself to "intercept the wrath" in the form of a plague, the result of transgression. Num 16:47 describes the same incident as "making atonement." Isaiah's Servant "intercepts the iniquity" of all the people and thus begins the atonement which is completed in 53:10, when he makes himself the offering for sin. Technical terms for sacrifice are problematic; here the word is *'asham,* a priestly term but used also in 1 Sam 6:3, 4, 8, 17 of the golden images returned by the Philistines with the ark *when they, too, had been smitten with plague, the LORD's wrath.* The *'asham* here seems to mean an atonement offering. When the Servant is the sacrifice (MT, "When you make his soul the *'asham*"), he will be recognized as the royal son (see above on v. 1), and "he will prolong his days" (cf. *1 Enoch* 71:17). "Crush" (v. 10) was read by the LXX as the similar word "cleanse," giving "cleanse him from his plague."

He was "oppressed" (53:7; LXX, "abused"; the *Targum of Isaiah,* "was praying" — all very similar Hebrew words). After his time of trial (v. 11) *he sees light* (thus 1QIsa[a] and the LXX; the MT lacks "light"). The Servant again sees the glory. He finds "satisfaction with knowledge" (thus the NRSV); 1QIsa[a] has "saturated with knowledge." The sense seems to be, "when the Servant sees the glory he is given the heavenly knowledge" (cf. 52:13); he then makes many righteous, that is, restores them to the covenant bond because he has borne/forgiven their iniquities. The *Targum of Isaiah* has retained this original meaning: the Servant brings many "into subjection to the law." The triumph in 53:12 refers to the Servant's role as Judge, clear in later texts, for example, the sequence in *1 Enoch* 47–48: the blood of the Righteous One is taken up into the presence of the LORD and then the books are opened and the judgment begins, clearly part of the older rituals (cf. Isa 9:2-7).

The reference to the Servant's "grave" and "tomb" (v. 9) follows 1QIsa[a]; the MT has "deaths." This implies that he dies and is buried with the wicked, but the LXX and the *Targum of Isaiah* understood the verse differently: the wicked and the rich are punished because the Servant was innocent.

The confused state of the fourth Servant Song in both the MT and the ancient versions makes certainty impossible, but *the original Servant was probably the royal high priest on the Day of Atonement, symbolically offering his own blood to cleanse and heal the land, bringing judgment on his enemies and rescuing his own people* (cf. Deut 32:43). He was the heavenly messenger (cf. Isa 50:14; 61:1; *1 Enoch* 15). Once atonement had been made, those whose sins had cut them off from the covenant bond could return, what Paul was later to call justification. The *Targum of Isaiah* has retained this association with Deut 32:43 in its rendering of the fourth Servant Song; for example, the Servant builds up the polluted and abandoned sanctuary (53:5), judges the wicked and sends them to Gehenna (v. 9), and the purified remnant see the kingdom of the Messiah (v. 10). The clearest expression of these ideas is found in Revelation; the Lamb, triumphant after being sacrificed (Rev 5:6), is enthroned. John's vision describes his judgment in heaven and the renewal of the earth (Rev 21:1).

The ritual suffering and self-offering of the royal high priest inspired someone to interpret the sufferings of a historical figure in this light. Given the poem's prominence in the Isaiah tradition, the original was probably composed by First Isaiah after the near fatal illness of Hezekiah. His suffering had originally been seen as just punishment (53:4b), reflected in Isaiah's harsh judgment on the king (Isa 38:1b). After he had recovered from the plague (cf. LXX Isa 53:3, 10, "plague," a traditional sign of the wrath of the LORD [2 Chr 32:25; see on Isa 38:1-22]), the city was saved from the Assyrians. Hezekiah's illness was then seen in a new light. *He had literally fulfilled the atonement rite and borne in his own suffering the effects of the city's rebellion against the Holy One. He had been the* 'asham *sacrifice.* First Isaiah's confidence that the rituals of the temple would be actualized in history reached its climax in the deliverance from the Assyrians; Hezekiah's recovery from the plague was an aspect of that fulfillment and may even have prompted Isaiah's confidence that the city, far from being punished, would be delivered. As the story is told, the two events are closely linked (Isa 38:6). Later storytellers must have seen Hezekiah in the fourth Servant Song. Josephus (*Ant.* 10.24-27) records that the childless Hezekiah was allowed to live fifteeen years after his illness in order to get an heir, a clear reference to the traditional understanding of Isa 53:10, "he shall see his offspring, and shall prolong his days."

Deutero-Isaiah, along with the others who were reworking the old traditions to accommodate the disaster of the exile, democratized much of the ancient royal cult. The suffering of the Servant became the suffering of the people in exile, and other aspects of the cult were actualized in history. The other gods were finally defeated, both creation and history were renewed, and those cut off from the covenant bond were brought back after the great atonement.

Trito-Isaiah saw himself as the Servant in his time, anointed and clothed with the Spirit (Isa 61:1). There was "a succession in Servanthood" (Beuken 1989: 438-40), and Jesus saw himself as the Servant in his time (Luke 4:17-21). *The Servant sequence of atonement, renewal, and reintegration is fundamental to the NT.* The imagery appears in Phil 2:6-11 (Jeremias 1957: 97), where Jesus the Servant emptied himself, an allusion to the blood pouring from the atonement sacrifice, the blood being the life or soul (Lev 17:11). *Kenotic theology describes the self-giving of the divine life for the renewal of the creation and the reintegration of sinners into the covenant bond.* Paul describes this reintegration as justification in Romans 8, with emphasis on being inseparable from the love of God (Rom 8:39).

The fullest picture of the Servant is found in the "Parables" of *1 Enoch,* which describe him triumphant in heaven, that is, in the sanctuary, after he has effected the great atonement which precedes the judgment. This is described in *1 Enoch* 46–50. He is the "Anointed One" (Isa 52:14; cf. *1 Enoch* 48:10; 52:4); the "Chosen One" (Isa 42:1; cf. *1 Enoch* 40:5; 45:3, 49:2, 51; etc.); "the Righteous One" (Isa 53:11; cf. *1 Enoch* 38:2; 47:4); he has the "Spirit" (Isa 42:1; cf. *1 Enoch* 62:6); he "establishes justice" (Isa 42:4; cf. *1 Enoch* 41:9; 45:3; 49:4; etc.); he is the "light of the peoples" (Isa 42:6; 49:6; cf. *1 Enoch* 48:4); he is "hidden" (Isa 49:2; cf. *1 Enoch* 39:7; 48:6; 62:7); and "kings are amazed and humbled before him" (Isa 49:7; 52:15; cf. *1 Enoch* 48:5-10; 55:4; 62:1-9). So many motifs from Isaiah's Servant are combined in the "Parables" and given a clear context which is not apparent in Isaiah but obviously their original setting. The only realistic explanation for the Servant texts is that they were part of the royal cult, perhaps sanctuary visions or the record of a mystic's experience (Isa 50:4; cf. 2 Sam 23:1-7). Their form in the "Parables" includes material from later periods, but the similarity to the book of Revelation shows that this was a living tradition throughout the Second Temple period.

Isaiah 54

See above on Isa 49:14-26: "Zion."

Isaiah 55

55:1-3b resembles Wisdom's invitation to her table (Prov 9:5); like Wisdom (Prov 9:11), the LORD offers life (55:3b). Vv. 3b-5 promise renewal of the everlasting covenant, formerly made with the royal house but now to be made with the whole people, "you" (plural; v. 3b). Ps 89:39 bewailed the breaking of the royal covenant when Jerusalem was destroyed. *Here Deutero-Isaiah shows clearly what has been implicit in all his teaching: that the eternal covenant with the royal house, with all its mythology, hopes, and traditions, has been transferred to the whole people.*

55:6-11 are the conclusion of the prophecy, in the form of a summons to repentance and worship: "Seek the LORD," "call upon him," "return to him."

55:8-9 refer to the strangeness of Deutero-Isaiah's message; these are new ways, new plans, far beyond anything human beings could have imagined. The word of the LORD through his prophet is a creative word, as it was in Genesis 1, and it will accomplish the LORD's purpose. The words of Deutero-Isaiah in themselves bring about what he has prophesied.

55:12-13 promise that all creation will join in the joy of their return, the renewal of the creation being part of the great atonement and ingathering.

Trito-Isaiah

The date and author of the final chapters of Isaiah are unknown. There is a great variety of material here, threats of judgment contrasting with the vision of a glorious future for Jerusalem. Trito-Isaiah used the oracles of Deutero-Isaiah as the basis for his polemic, either as a critical contemporary (just as Haggai and Zechariah were contemporaries but did not agree) or speaking for a disillusioned later generation. Those for whom he spoke also knew the oracles of Deutero-Isaiah and the teachings of the Deuteronomists. What has to be explained is how the considerable bitterness in these chapters came to be part of the Isaiah scroll.

Trito-Isaiah illuminates the gap between the first return of the exiles under Joshua and Zerubbabel and the subsequent returns under Ezra and Nehemiah. Ezra-Nehemiah is silent about this period, but it must have been a time of deteriorating relationships in Judah. Ezra 4:2-4 says that "the people of the land" offered to help rebuild the temple, but their help was rejected. In contrast, Haggai, a contemporary, implies that it was accepted (Hag 2:4). Ezra 6:21 shows how the returned exiles *separated* themselves from the people of Judah, the worshipers of the LORD who had not been taken to Babylon. Trito-Isaiah says much about the enemies of the LORD, but he does not mention the people of the land. *He was their spokesman, and the enemies of the LORD were the returned exiles.*

The people left in the land had not accepted the Deuteronomic reform, but kept the ancient ways. We have to imagine the impact of the newly returned exiles, with their new form of religion, regarding themselves as the chosen ones, thanks to Jeremiah's vision of the baskets of figs (Jer 24:1-10) and despite their own earlier teaching that possession of the land was a sign of the LORD's favor. They had more stringent laws and emphasized racial purity.

There were also troubles in the priesthood. Zech 3:1-5 declares Joshua, the Jerusalem high priest, to be pure; someone presumably had questioned this! Ezra, the great reformer, is presented as the true high priest in his time (Ezra 7:1-6), but *1 Enoch* 89:73 thought otherwise. Some priests kept to the older, more inclusive view of Israel, but even the high priests found themselves excluded under the new marriage rules. The contemporary Elephantine letters show that the families excluded by Nehemiah (Neh 2:20; 13:28) were worshipers of the LORD, but apparently no longer acceptable (Barker 1987: 184-200).

The situation was exacerbated by economic problems. There had been bad harvests (Hag 1:6), and the people of the land were cheated by the returned exiles (Neh 5:1-5). Most significant of all was the Persian money used to rebuild the temple (Ezra 6:3-5).

In order to understand Trito-Isaiah it is necessary to put aside all attempts to harmonize the evidence from this period. The Jerusalem group made accusations of impurity, and the Enoch group accused them of impurity and apostasy. Those for whom Trito-Isaiah spoke questioned the legitimacy of the new temple, the new priesthood, and the new ways of the reformed religion. Ezra was remembered by the Jews as the founder of their tradition, the first of the men of the Great Synagogue, but he was remembered by the Samaritans as the one who destroyed the old ways. Some reconstructions of the troubles of the restoration conclude that they were over by the time of the Chronicler (Hanson 1975: 269-79). Evidence from the nonbiblical sources, however, shows that the troubles and divisions continued into NT times.

Isaiah 56

Isaiah 56 introduces *the parties in the conflict;* both claim to speak from the LORD, but one group has the power to exclude the other. "Foreigners and eunuchs" (v. 3) have been excluded, yet the prophet assures them that those who keep the sabbath and the covenant will have a place within the city and the temple (vv. 4-5; cf. Wisd 3:13-19). "Foreigners who minister to the LORD" (v. 6), that is, serve in the temple (see on Isa 66:21), will go again to the holy mountain and offer sacrifices (v. 7). They would be part of the great ingathering of Israel (v. 8), and the temple would be for all peoples (cf. Isa 2:2). These were the aspirations of the people for whom Trito-Isaiah spoke. Reading between the lines, one senses that their opponents emphasized the sabbath, separation, and posterity to perpetuate their name. Deut 23:1-3 excludes foreigners and eunuchs from the LORD's assembly, an indication of who the oppressors were, whereas Psalm 15 gives the older view of who could stand on the holy hill. A comparison of Deut 7:1-6 and Ezra 9:1-2 shows how closely *the returned exiles identified with the Deuteronomists' ideal of separation from the people of the land* (see on Isa 59:2). The implication is that the worshipers of the LORD who had not been in exile were treated as though they were Canaanites. 56:7 is quoted by Jesus as the reason for cleansing the temple (Mark 11:17 and pars.).

It has been suggested that 56:9–57:13 is a collection of material denouncing idolatry from the preexilic period, either misplaced here or else reused (Westermann 1969: 325). Given the style of Trito-Isaiah, the latter is more likely.

56:9-12 pictures the enemy, a passage full of Isaianic wordplay. The "wild animals" (v. 9) are similar in Hebrew to "the watchers of a field" (Jer 4:17). Both are in fact the "watchmen of Shaddai," the living creatures of Ezek 1:19. They are summoned, as in Jer 4:17, to punish the city (Barker 1987: 207). The "blind sentinels" are also supernatural creatures, as are the "dumb dogs" (see on Isa 35:5-6). 1QIsa[a] differs slightly; for "dreaming, lying down, loving to slumber" (56:10), it has the very similar "sleeping seers, loving oracles." The dogs and "shepherds" (v. 11; perhaps "seers," a similar word) are the evil rulers. The picture is that of *1 Enoch* 90; the rulers of Jerusalem and the temple are in league with the fallen angels.

Isaiah 57

57:1-2 resemble Ps 12:1 and Mic 7:2, a lament for the plight of those who try to live a good life.

57:3-6 is full of wordplay and shows the prophet at his most bitter.

Those who claim pure descent, the children of the LORD's restored spouse Zion (cf. 54:1-3) are in fact the children of an adulterer and whore (57:3). Their lust to acquire the land is a form of idolatry, as evil as any of the old fertility cults. "Smooth stones," "valley," and "lot" can also be, respectively, "apportion," "inherit," and "stony place." The children of the land are the new sacrificial victims.

57:7-10 introduces *Jerusalem the harlot,* an image which was to persist for centuries in the writings of the dispossessed (e.g., Revelation 17). The new temple was the harlot's bed (v. 8), "bed" and "tabernacle" coming from similar Hebrew words (Hanson 1975: 199). V. 9 is obscure, but it seems to be a comment on what has happened to the worship of the King in Jerusalem. Originally a title for the LORD (Isa 6:5), the new "king" in Jerusalem is the Persian monarch for whom prayers were said (Ezra 6:10). He is described as Molech, a Canaanite deity whose name means "the King."

The harlot city appears also in Proverbs 1–9, where the language used is very similar to that of Trito-Isaiah. Wisdom, the city's ancient guardian, calls to her children and warns them of the harlot's ways: the harlot's envoys go to Sheol (57:9; cf. Prov 2:18; 5:5; 7:27); she is a loose foreign woman (NRSV, "adulteress," Prov 2:16), who has left her husband and her "covenant" (Prov 2:17; see also on Isa 59:1-8) (Barker 1992: 60).

57:11-13 is obscure. Those who make the LORD their refuge will inherit the land (v. 13), in contrast to those who have emphasized their righteousness and their works (v. 12). The promised rewards in the Beatitudes (Matt 5:3-10) reflect the similar aspirations of the descendants of the dispossessed.

57:14 is reminiscent of 40:3, preparing the way for the exiles to return. Here the original oracle has been turned against the exiles themselves; *they must prepare the way for those they have rejected and remove obstacles from their path* (cf. 62:10). The Holy One, Isaiah's characteristic title for the LORD (see on Isa 1:4), is not only in the high holy place, the temple, but also with the humble. These people are still waiting for their healing and their comfort (57:18; cf. Isa 40:1). *For some, the exile was not over, a position maintained in many writings of the Second Temple period* (Knibb 1976: 253-72). Jeremiah's prophecy of seventy years' exile (Jer 29:10-14) was reinterpreted to mean seventy weeks of years (Dan 9:24), after which the anointed one, their Servant, would come bringing the judgment. It was to those who believed themselves still in exile, that is, rejected, that Jesus proclaimed, "The time is fulfilled" (Mark 1:14).

57:20-21. There would then be peace for all (v. 19), except the wicked.

Isaiah 58

In Isaianic manner, Trito-Isaiah makes the autumn festival the framework for his oracles. The trumpet *(shopar)* and the declaration of sin (58:1; cf. Lev 23:24-27) indicate the cultic setting. The Day of Atonement was the only ritual fast (v. 3; cf. Lev 23:27), but the prophet declares the fasting useless (58:5). Their prayers will not be heard, and the LORD will not appear to heal them (v. 8), both atonement motifs. The passage is full of satire and wordplay: "oppress all your workers" (v. 3) is very similar to "draw near to worship idols" (Barker 1987: 210). "Seek," "delight to know," "practice righteousness," and "draw near" (v. 2) are all cultic terms. The mistreatment of the people for whom the prophet speaks is idolatry, a mockery of true worship. What is required is social justice and compassion (vv. 6-7), echoed in Matt 25:35-36. ("Do not hide yourself" [58:7b] quotes Deut 22:1, another indication of who the oppressors are). This will bring the glory of the LORD to their community (58:8; cf. 52:12).

58:11-12 echoes Isaiah 35 and 41:17-20. Jerusalem will again become the garden of the LORD, its temple the source of water (cf. Ezek 47:1). The ruins will be rebuilt. This is the renewal which follows the judgment and atonement.

58:13-14 reflects the situation in Neh 13:15-22. The people of Jerusalem were not keeping the sabbath. When they did, their reward would be to ride on the heights of the earth (58:14), exactly as in Deut 32:13 (the NRSV obscures the similarity), the Song of Moses, which culminates in the great affirmation of judgment and atonement (Deut 32:43).

Isaiah 59

This chapter divides into three sections. The third (59:15b-21), describes the LORD coming to bring judgment, the second (vv. 9-15a) the sad state of his people, and the first, the evil doings of their enemies. 59:1, 16 resemble 50:1-2 and may be a later comment on the hope expressed by Deutero-Isaiah, that Jerusalem had not been abandoned.

59:1-8 addresses people who feel that the LORD neither hears them nor cares for them. Their prayers had not been answered, and the prophet suggests the reason. *Those who have separated themselves from the people of the land,* who made separation from impurity their ideal (Ezra 6:21; 10:11), are told that they, too, *have been separated from God by their iniquity.* There follows a picture of a corrupt society which has failed to make straight the way of the LORD (59:8; cf. 40:3).

The sequence in Prov 6:16-19, doubtless traditional, forms the basis for Isa 59:1-8, and there are other points of contact: Prov 1:16; 2:12-15; and 4:16-19. Trito-Isaiah addresses the same situation as the wise man who calls to Wisdom's erring children, reminding them that the upright and innocent will inherit the land and the wicked and treacherous be rooted out (Prov 2:20-22; see on Isa 57:7-10).

The speakers then consider their own condition (Isa 59:9-15a). They had hoped for a glorious new Jerusalem, with the justice and righteousness of the Davidic kings restored (v. 9; cf. Psalm 72; also Ezek 37:24-28). Instead there had been gloom and darkness, with justice and righteousness far away. The confession (59:12-13) implies that the situation in Jerusalem was punishment for their sins, not the sins of breaking the Ten Commandments, but the sins of the fallen angels: "lying words," "turning from the LORD," and "rebellion." This theme is taken up in 61:1.

The climax of ch. 59 is vv. 15b-21. The LORD appears, appalled that there is no one to "intervene" (v. 16). The same word is used to describe the atoning acts of the Servant (see on Isa 53:6 and 12). Here the LORD appears as a warrior (as in 63:1-6; cf. Exod 15:3), bringing judgment on the "adversaries," "enemies," and "coastlands," hostile supernatural beings (see on Isa 41:1). As in Deut 32:43, the LORD emerges to bring vengeance but also to "atone" (NRSV, "cleanse") the land. This was the other aspect of atonement; destroying evil as well as healing. "A pent-up stream" (v. 19) is an odd expression for the LORD and unique in the OT. Another translation of "stream" could be "radiance," which in the context of a sunrise (v. 19) seems more likely. The LORD comes like a "mighty [NRSV, "pent-up"] flood of light," and the Spirit of the LORD puts to flight his enemies, as in Deut 32:30. 59:21 could be an insertion, but the subject is appropriate here. The LORD speaks of his eternal covenant, "my covenant forever," which was renewed by the great atonement.

Isaiah 60

The prophet speaks to the city of Jerusalem (60:1-9); she is to arise from her dejected state and shine with the glory of the LORD, who rises like the sun and dispels the darkness. The image was traditional and probably part of a night liturgy (cf. Ps 46:5; Isa 9:2b; 33:2). Zion would become a place of pilgrimage, and she would receive great wealth to build the temple (60:7, 13), Trito-Isaiah's priestly concern. The returned exiles were promised such riches (Hag 2:7-9) in contrast to the hardship of their return (Hag 1:5-6).

Then the LORD speaks to the city: kings would be her servants (60:10), and foreigners build her walls. Her children would return, and her gates would be open day and night to receive tribute (v. 11). Once forsaken and deserted (v. 15), the royal lady is restored to her former state. She shall no longer hear of violence and destruction, nor shall she ever know darkness again (vv. 18-19), for the LORD will be to her both sun and moon (cf. Rev 21:22-26, which describes the new heavenly Jerusalem, the bride of the Lamb, in the same way). *What began in the sixth century BC as hope for rebuilt Jerusalem was transformed by the disappointments of history into hope for a heavenly city, the ideal finally realized on earth.*

The aspirations of the prophet's people are seen in 60:21-22: to possess the land and become numerous again.

Isaiah 61

We have here a glimpse of the prophet himself. The LORD has anointed him and given him the Spirit (61:1), as was said of the Servant (42:1 and see on 52:14). This is probably an account of Trito-Isaiah's call (see on Isaiah 53) (Beuken 1989: 438-40). Isaiah had seen the LORD and then been sent as a messenger (6:9), Deutero-Isaiah had heard the voices telling him to comfort Jerusalem (40:1-2), and here Trito-Isaiah describes the experience of becoming a Messiah, an anointed one sent to proclaim good news. *Jesus chose this passage to describe his own experience of baptism,* when he received the anointing of the Spirit (Luke 4:21; Acts 10:38).

Trito-Isaiah was to bring good news to people still oppressed; the restoration of Jerusalem had not been for his people a time of joy. Like the Servant, the prophet was to "release prisoners" (42:6-7; 49:9), to "open blind eyes" (42:7), and to "establish the land" (49:8), but the MT of 61:1 is difficult. "Release to the prisoners" is literally "open the eyes of prisoners" (cf. LXX, "sight to the blind," and "sight to the blind" in Luke 4:18 as well). This would mark the year of the LORD's favor, the day of his vengeance, that is, the time described in Deut 32:43. It would be the great Jubilee: proclaim liberty, *d^e^ror,* is the Jubilee prescription of Lev 25:10.

Imprisonment was not a common punishment in Israel, but linked to blindness it suggests the fallen angels. The history of the Second Temple period is described in *1 Enoch* as a time when the evil angels, the shepherds, ruled over the blind, the apostates in Jerusalem (*1 Enoch* 89:72–90:27). Their blindness was a sin for which they were punished, for they had fallen under the influence of the evil angels (*1 Enoch* 90:26).

The *Melchizedek* text from Qumran Cave 11, of whose ultimate origin and date nothing is known, illuminates these obscure lines in Trito-Isaiah and may hold the key to their original meaning since they are quoted, together with Isa 52:7. During the year of Jubilee (Lev 25:13) all return to their rightful property. Melchizedek, the royal high priest (Ps 110:4), appears to proclaim "liberty to captives and prisoners" (cf. Isa 61:1), releasing them from the power of Satan and his angels and restoring them to the people of the sons of heaven. *Thus two concepts are linked; the rule of evil angels and the loss of the land.* Melchizedek, the anointed one, appears in the Year of his favor (cf. Isa 61:2) for the great Day of Atonement when good news is brought to Zion. Melchizedek was "to comfort" (cf. Isa 61:2) and "to establish the covenant" (cf. Isa 42:6; 49:8), although the text is not certain at these points. The atonement would happen at the end of the tenth Jubilee, after 490 years. Jewish tradition remembered that the 490 years ended in AD 66 or 68, in other words, that the final Jubilee began in AD 17 or 19. Melchizedek would appear in the first "week" (i.e., seven years) of the tenth Jubilee, and this is exactly when Jesus' ministry began. He claimed to be Melchizedek, bringing the great Jubilee, when he announced the fulfillment of Isaiah 61 in the synagogue at Nazareth (Luke 4:21) (Barker 2000).

Thus later tradition read these words of Trito-Isaiah as a description of *the royal high priest restoring the people and their land, bringing judgment on the evil angels.* This was probably the prophet's original meaning too. The anointed one of Isaiah 61 proclaims the imminent judgment, the Day of Atonement and Jubilee when his people regain their rightful property and rebuild their cities. They "rejoice" and are called "oaks of righteousness," but "families of righteousness" in the LXX and "princes of righteousness" in the *Targum of Isaiah.*

61:5-9 is clear evidence of a divided community. The prophet speaks first to the exiles (vv. 5-7a): their city would prosper, and they would be recognized as legitimate priests of the God they all worshiped, "our God" (v. 6). There had been dispute about the priesthood in Jerusalem; someone had declared Joshua unclean (Zech 3:1-7). Second he speaks of his own people. In their land they would "inherit a double portion" (v. 7b) and "everlasting joy." The crux lies in v. 8; they had been "robbed," but the LORD would "recompense" them. He would make with them the "everlasting covenant," which was renewed on the Day of Atonement, another link to the *Melchizedek* text. Then they would be acknowledged as the LORD's people (61:9).

61:10 probably refers to the high priest's vestments, as the *Targum of Isaiah* suggests; they are a symbol of his role in the ritual to bring salvation and righteousness which would spring up like the vegetation of the renewed earth.

Isaiah 62

On 62:1-5, see above on Zion (49:14-26). The prophet longs for the time when Jerusalem will be restored.

62:6-7 afford another glimpse of the Enochic tradition. It was suggested long ago that the text described heavenly figures such as appear in 1 Kgs 22:19 and Zech 1:12, and as the "Watchers" in *1 Enoch* (Duhm 1892 [1968]: 460-61). The "sentinels who remind" is better translated "the watchers and recorders." In the Enochic histories, the LORD hands over his people to the seventy shepherds (see the Introduction, 493) but appoints an angel "to observe and mark "everything the shepherds do (cf. Isa 30:8-14). All their misdeeds are to be recorded and brought up to the LORD (*1 Enoch* 89:61-64). The recording angel "implored" and "besought" the LORD to help his people (*1 Enoch* 89:76). Eventually the LORD came and brought judgment on the fallen angels and their "blinded" followers (*1 Enoch* 90:18-27). A new temple was then erected, and foreigners came in homage to the LORD's people (*1 Enoch* 90:28-30). Trito-Isaiah here recalls the LORD's promise: there are indeed "watching and recording" ones, and he appeals to them to do their duty and arouse the LORD to action. The earliest material in *1 Enoch* describes just such a prayer to the four archangels; people cry out to them, and they speak to the LORD. The LORD then sends them to punish the evil ones and heal the earth (*1 Enoch* 9:1–10:7).

The prophet can then assure his people (62:8-9) that the time of injustice is ended.

62:10-12 is addressed to the people in Jerusalem: "go through the gates." Like his predecessor, the prophet tells the group from Babylon to "prepare the way," not for God (v. 10; cf. 40:3) but for other "exiles." They must have recognized the words of his predecessor. Salvation comes to the Daughter of Zion as her LORD comes to bring the Day of Atonement and judgment (v. 11; cf. 40:9-10). The prophet's people will be brought back into the community "Holy," "Redeemed," and Zion will be recognized as the city which the LORD has "sought out." This is exactly the reconciliation envisaged in 61:5-11.

Isaiah 63

The traditional description of the LORD coming in judgment answers the prophet's prayer of 62:6-7. There is complex wordplay. "From Edom," *m'dwm,* and "from Bozrah," *mbṣrh* (the capital of Edom), are probably evidence of a secondary application of the oracle. The original, as implied by v. 2, was the very similar "reddened," *m'ddm,* and *mbṣr,* "a harvester of grapes," itself a wordplay on *mbsr,* the "herald of good tidings" (cf. 40:9; 41:27; 52:7; 61:1). Treading grapes was a traditional image of judgment (cf. Lam 1:15; Joel 3:13; Rev 14:17-20), and the one emerging from the holy of holies on the Day of Atonement/Judgment would also have had his clothes spattered with blood (cf. Rev 19:13). The messenger was not announcing comfort to Zion, but the day of vengeance and redemption (63:4), which the prophet expected to befall her (cf. Rev 18:1–19:4), the final judgment on the harlot city for the blood of his servants.

63:7-14 is the first part of a complex psalm of lament which ends at 64:12. The poet recalls how the LORD chose his people and cared for them in days of old. "No messenger or angel" suggests a problem with the new monotheism of the exiles. Later rabbinic tradition emphasized, but only in the exodus and Sinai stories (Goldin 1970: 412-24), that it was the LORD himself and not an intermediary who acted for Israel at that time. The new monotheism, with its formless, unseen God (Deut 4:12), meant that anthropomorphisms in the older tradition had to be explained as the appearance of angels, exactly what the *Targum of Isaiah* does here. Trito-Isaiah denies this: it was the LORD, himself the guardian angel of Israel (Barker 1992), who came to save them. The people rebelled (63:10), and then recalled their past. In their current state of despair, where was the God whose servant Moses had brought them through the sea?

63:15-19 appeals to the LORD to look down and see the wrongs done to his ancient people. God is their "Father," a title avoided by the new monotheism (see on 42:5), but Abraham, the figurehead of the group from Babylon (see on 51:1-2), does not recognize them. The prophet's people cannot understand why they are being tested in this way and caused to err and to doubt, so that their faith is weakened (63:17). The LXX of v. 18a has "inherit your holy mountain" for MT, "your holy people took possession." The original probably referred to the destruction of the temple by the Babylonians, but in the present context there are other enemies in possession of the holy place, and they are excluding the LORD's people.

Isaiah 64

The prophet longs for the LORD to appear in judgment. Ps 18:6-15 is similar, and much of the language of Isa 64:1-4 is probably traditional. The prophet's concerns are apparent in v. 9: "we are all your people." They acknowledge their sin, that they had strayed (v. 5); thus the LXX; the MT is opaque. The temple and the cities of Judah are still in ruins (cf. Ps 79:1-13; Lam 5:19-22), indicating an exilic date for this passage.

Isaiah 65

65:1-7 are similar to 57:1-10. The answer to the prophet's question, "Will you keep silent?" (64:12), is given in vv. 1-2. The LORD had been waiting for his rebellious people, who did not want to know him. The accusations of Canaanite practices (worship at high places [v. 3], unclean foods, necromancy, and incubation; the LXX adds "to receive dreams" [v. 4]) are hyperbole since it is unlikely that these would have taken place in the temple itself. "Before my face continually" (v. 3) is the language of the cult (cf. Exod 28:29; Lev 24:3-4). So, too, are the terms used in 65:5, "Keep to yourself" (better, "distance yourself"), "do not come near me," and "I am too holy for you" (perhaps "I shall communicate holiness to you"; cf. Ezek 44:19, a contemporary text) are all key terms to express the sanctity of the priesthood in Ezekiel and the priestly writings (Hanson 1975: 149). There are also echoes of the Deuteronomists here: if they "provoked" the LORD (65:3) with "idol worship," they would not "live long in their land" but be destroyed (Deut 4:25-26). Addressed to people who were committed to the teaching of Deuteronomy, this accusation of idolatry, which would cost them their land, was bitter indeed. But they were warned; everything was recorded before the LORD (see on 62:6-7), and he would "requite" (NRSV, "repay") not only their own iniquities but also those of their ancestors, just as their history writers had said of old Jerusalem (2 Kgs 24:3-4).

65:8-12, addressed to the people in Jerusalem, show how Trito-Isaiah understood the oracle of the remnant (see on 7:3) and the promise to the Davidic house (65:8b; cf. 1 Kgs 11:36). Some would survive to inherit the promises. The Servant and Chosen One have become plural, "servants and chosen ones," and, like the original Servant, they will "stand on the holy mountain" (singular with the LXX; the NRSV has plural) and not be cast off (65:9; see on 41:9, but here, literally, of being allowed into the temple). Those who have sought the LORD will enjoy prosperity in a fertile land (v. 10). Those who forsake the LORD and do not choose his ways (vv. 11-13) are threatened with judgment.

65:13-16 describe what their judgment will be and show clearly how economic factors exacerbated the religious problems. The prophet's people did not have the support of Persian money; they had been exploited by the returned exiles and denied the fair treatment due to fellow Israelites (Neh 5:1-13). In the glorious future, their enemies would suffer economic deprivation (65:13-14; cf. Luke 6:20-26) and their name would become a curse. The prophet's people would have a "new name" (v. 15); and if we knew this name, the history of this period could be written with more confidence! Abraham had been promised that people would bless themselves through his descendants (Gen 12:3; 18:18; 22:18; 26:4), but this the prophet emphatically denies (Isa 65:16).

65:17-25 describe the renewed creation which follows the Day of Atonement and Judgment. *The closest parallel to this text is the Enochic account of renewing the earth after the fallen angels had been judged* (*1 Enoch* 10:17–11:2). This is the oldest material in *1 Enoch,* and since the compiler of Genesis knew of the fallen angels (Gen 6:1-4), it is likely that Trito-Isaiah, his younger contemporary, knew the Enochic description of the renewed creation. 65:25 recalls Isa 11:6-9, with the addition of the snake. The Eden story in Genesis 2–3 was an exilic reworking of the priestly myth of expulsion from the garden on the holy mountain (cf. Ezek 28:12-19; see on Isa 41:9). Trito-Isaiah here comments that the "snake" which caused the disastrous expulsion would indeed be cursed.

Isaiah 66

66:1-4 is a savage attack on the temple cult. Vv. 1-2 comment bitterly on the words of the Deuteronomist's Solomon when he dedicated the temple. He asked how God in the highest heavens could live in the temple he had built and prayed that he would look toward the place to hear the prayers offered there (1 Kgs 8:27-29). Trito-Isaiah deftly turns these words and asks why the temple they are building is necessary if the LORD made everything and is enthroned in heaven. There was no temple in John's heavenly city (Rev 21:22). The LORD did not look "toward the temple," as "Solomon" had prayed, but toward the humble and contrite "who tremble at his word" (cf. 66:5). The returned exiles also described themselves in this way (Ezra 9:4; 10:3).

The people of the land had helped rebuild the temple in Jerusalem (Hag 2:4), but Ezra 4:1-5 tells a different story. The people of the land had offered their help but were rejected, the returned exiles preferring the favor of Cyrus, king of Persia (Barker 1987: 191-94). The new temple in Jerusalem was despised by those it rejected; in *1 Enoch* both "The Apocalypse of Weeks" and "The Dream Visions" describe the rebuilt temple and its cult as impure (*1 Enoch* 89:73; 93:9). It has been suggested that the Samaritan temple was the object of this invective, an illegitimate temple with an impure cult (Duhm 1892 [1968]: 482), but the evidence of *1 Enoch* indicates the Jerusalem temple.

66:3-4 declare the cult of the new temple to be as impure as any pagan rites; legitimate offerings such as lambs, grain, and incense are as bad as dogs, pig's blood, or idolatry. The LXX differs here, combining the first two lines to give "Whoever unlawfully sacrifices to me a young bull is like one who kills a dog. . . ." This indicates an illegitimate priesthood since the bull was the priests' offering (Lev 4:3; 16:3; Ezek 43:19). The Jerusalem group had complained that their prayers were not heard (58:9), but it was *the* LORD *who had called out and received no answer* (v. 4).

66:5 assures the prophet's people that their own kin who hate them (cf. Neh 5:1-5) and "reject" them (the word later became the technical term for banning from the synagogue) for the sake of "the name," another sign of the Deuteronomists (Deut 12:11; 1 Kgs 8:29), would themselves be put to shame.

66:6 is an isolated verse, or perhaps it should be read with vv. 15-16. The prophet hears the voice of the LORD in the temple as he brings judgment on his enemies (cf. Deut 32:43; Isa 26:21; Mic 1:3; *1 Enoch* 1:3). Mal 3:1-4 describes a similar situation; a day of judgment in the temple when the Lord will be like "a refiner's fire" for the corrupted priesthood.

66:7-9 explains the troubles in Jerusalem as the birth pains without which her children cannot be born. The prophet's people were the children, and they hoped to be restored to their mother city.

66:10-14 depict Jerusalem the mother city, feeding her children and receiving the wealth of nations (cf. Isa 60:1-22).

The rest of the chapter is fragments.

66:17 is an isolated piece about pagan worship.

66:18-21 return to the theme of ingathering, but this time it is the ingathering of "all nations" (v. 18), not just the dispersed of Israel. After the judgment (vv. 15-16), the survivors from the nations will bring back the dispersed Jews, "your kindred," like a great grain offering to the temple (v. 20). Some foreigners had formerly served in the temple, namely, the Nethinim, or "temple servants" (1 Chr 9:2). Ezekiel had sought to exclude them (Ezek 44:5-9), but Trito-Isaiah spoke of their right of access to the holy mountain (Isa 56:6).

66:22-23 resemble Jer 31:35-37. What had once been the promise to the Davidic dynasty, that they would endure as long as the created order (Ps 89:28-37), has become a promise to the whole people. All flesh will worship the LORD.

The survivors will see the fate of those who have rebelled against the LORD (66:24). They will burn in Gehenna (see on Isa 30:33; cf. *1 Enoch* 27 and Mark 9:48). "Rebellion" indicates the myth of the fallen angels. It became the custom in the synagogue to read 66:23 again after v. 24, so that the prophecy should not end with a curse.

Bibliography. Alt, A. 1954, "Jesaja 8,23–9,6, Befreiungsnacht und Kronungstag, *Kleine Schriften,* Kleine Schriften 2, Munich; 2:206-25 • Barker, M. 1987, *The Older Testament,* London: SPCK • Barker, M. 1991, *The Gate of Heaven,* London: SPCK • Barker, M. 1992, *The Great Angel,* London: SPCK • Barker, M. 1995, *On Earth As It Is in Heaven,* Edinburgh: T. & T. Clark • Barker, M. 1996, *The Risen Lord,* Edinburgh: T. & T. Clark • Barker, M. 2000, *The Revelation of Jesus Christ,* Edinburgh: T&T Clark • Barker, M. 2000, "The Time Is Fulfilled," *SJT* 53.1:22-32 • Barker, M. 2001, "Hezekiah's Boil," *JSOT* 95:31-42 • Barstad, H. M. 1996, *The Myth of the Empty Land: A Study of the History and Archaeology of Judah during the 'Exilic' Period,* Oslo and Cambridge, Mass.: Oslo University • Barth, H. 1977, "Die Jesaja-Worte in der Josiazeit," WMANT 48, Neukirchen-Vluyn: Neukirchener • Barton, J. 1995, *Isaiah 1–39,* Sheffield: Sheffield Academic • Beuken, W. A. M. 1989, "The Servant and the Herald of Good Tidings," in J. Vermeylen, *The Book of Isaiah,* Leuven: Peeters, 411-40 • Bright, J. 1960, *A History of Israel,* London: SCM • Brownlee, W. H. 1964, *The Meaning of the Qumran Scrolls for the Bible,* New York and Oxford: Oxford University • Burrows, M., J. C. Trever, and W. H. Brownlee. 1950, *The Dead Sea Scrolls of St. Mark's Monastery,* New Haven, Conn.: Yale University • Childs, B. S. 1967, *Isaiah and the Assyrian Crisis,* SBT, 2d ser., London: SCM • Childs, B. S. 1974, *Exodus,* London: SCM • Childs, B. S. 1979, *Introduction to the Old Testament as Scripture,* London: SCM • Clements, R. E. 1980, *Isaiah 1–39,* NCBC, Grand Rapids: Eerdmans and London: Marshall, Morgan and Scott • Douglas, M. 1995, "Demonology in W. R. Smith's Theory of Religious Belief," in W. Johnstone, ed., *William Robertson Smith: Essays in Reassessment,* Sheffield: Sheffield Academic, 274-92 • Driver, G. R. 1968, "Isaiah 1–39: Textual and Linguistic Problems," *JSS* 13:36-57 • Duhm, B. 1892 [1968], *Das Buch Jesaia,* Göttingen: Vandenhoeck & Ruprecht • Eaton, J. 1979, *Festal Drama in Deutero-Isaiah,* London: SPCK • Eissfeldt, O. 1905, *An Old Testament Introduction,* ET Oxford: Oxford University • Geyer, J. 1971, "2 Kings XVIII 14-16 and the Annals of Sennacherib," *VT* 21:604-6 • Goldin, J. 1970, "Not by Means of an Angel and Not by Means of a Messenger," in J. Neusner, ed., *Religions in Antiquity,* Sup to *Numen,* Leiden: Brill, 14:412-24 • Golding, W. 1995, *The Double Tongue,* London: Faber and Faber • Gray, G. B. 1912, *The Book of Isaiah,* ICC, Edinburgh: T. & T. Clark • Habel, N. C. 1972, "Yahweh the Maker of Heaven and Earth: A Study in Tradition Criticism," *JBL* 91:321-37 • Hancock, G. 1992, *The Sign and the Seal,* London: Heinemann • Hanson, P. D. 1975, *The Dawn of Apocalyptic,* Philadelphia: Fortress • Haran, M. 1978, *Temples and Temple Service in Ancient Israel,* Oxford: Clarendon • Hennecke, E. 1991, *New Testament Apocrypha,* vol. 1, rev. W. Schneemelcher, Cambridge: Cambridge University • Kaiser, O. 2d ed. 1963, *Isaiah 1–12,* London: SCM • Kaiser, O. 1974, *Isaiah 13–39,* London: SPCK • Kenyon, K. M. 1974, *Digging Up Jerusalem,* New York: Praeger and London: Benn • Knibb, M. A. 1976, "The Exile in the Literature of the Inter-Testamental Period," *HeyJ* 17:253-72 • Knibb, M. A. 1996, "Isaianic Traditions in the Book of Enoch," in J. Barton, ed., *After the Exile: Essays in Honour of Rex Mason,* Macon, Ga.: Mercer, 217-29 • Kraeling, E. S. 1953, *The Brooklyn Museum Aramaic Papyri,* New Haven and London: Yale University • Mackintosh, A. A. 1980, *Isaiah XXI: A Palimpsest,* Cambridge: Cambridge University • McKane, W., 1986, *Jeremiah,* vol. 1, ICC, Edinburgh T. & T. Clark • Milgrom, J. 1964, "Did Isaiah Prophesy during the Reign of Uzziah?" *VT* 14:164-82 • Mowinckel, S. 1956, *He That Cometh,* Oxford: Oxford University • Murray, R. 1992, *The Cosmic Covenant,* London: Sheed and Ward • North, C. R. 1956, *The Suffering Servant in Deutero-Isaiah,* Oxford: Oxford University • North, C. R. 1964, *The Second Isaiah,* Oxford: Oxford University • Porten, B. 1968, *Archives from Elephantine,* Berkeley: University of California • Pritchard, J. B. 1969, *Ancient Near Eastern Texts Relating to the Old Testament,* Princeton: Princeton University • Reventlow,

H. Graf, 1971, "A Syncretistic Enthronement Hymn in Is 9:1-6," *UF* 3:321-25 • Riesenfeld, H. 1947, *Jesus Transfigured,* Copenhagen: n.p. • Sawyer, J. F. A. 1989, "Daughter of Zion and Servant of the Lord in Isaiah," *JSOT* 44:89-107 • Seitz, C. R. 1988, "Isaiah 1–66: Making Sense of the Whole," in Seitz, ed., *Reading and Preaching the Book of Isaiah,* Philadelphia: Fortress, 112-23 • Seitz, C. R. 1991, *Zion's Final Destiny: The Development of the Book of Isaiah,* Minneapolis: Fortress • Smith, M. 1963, "II Isaiah and the Persians," *JAOS* 83:415-21 • Stenning, J. F. 1949, *The Targum of Isaiah,* Oxford: Oxford University • Stern, M. 1976, *Greek and Latin Authors on Jews and Judaism,* vol. 1, Jerusalem: Israel Academy of Sciences and Humanities • Torrey, C. C. 1928, *The Second Isaiah,* Edinburgh: T. & T. Clark • van Selms, A. 1982, "The Expression 'The Holy One of Israel,'" in W. C. Delsman et al., eds., *Von Kanaan bis Kerala,* AOAT 211:257-69 • Vermeylen, J. 1977, *Du Prophete Isaïe à l'apocalyptique,* Paris: Gabalda • von Rad, G. 1975, *Old Testament Theology,* vol. 2, Edinburgh: Oliver and Boyd • Westermann, C. 1969, *Isaiah 40–66,* London: SPCK • Whybray, R. N. 1971, *The Heavenly Counsellor in Isaiah xl,* Cambridge and New York: Cambridge University • Wildberger, H. 1991, *Isaiah 1–12: A Commentary,* Minneapolis: Fortress • Williamson, H. G. M. 1994, *The Book Called Isaiah,* Oxford: Oxford University • Wyatt, N. 1976, "Atonement Theology in Ugarit and Israel," *UF* 8:415-36 • Wyatt, N. 1995, "The Liturgical Context of Ps 19," *UF* 27:559-94.

Jeremiah

A. R. Pete Diamond

INTRODUCTION

Reading Peculiarities Posed by the Book

Israel's prophetic collections do not make easy reading. Jeremiah provides no exception and, in addition, offers peculiarities of its own.

It starts clearly enough with the third person introduction attributing the contents of the book to one Jeremiah ben Hilkiah — an ancient Judean recipient of divine oracles during Judah's late preexilic period. In short, Jeremiah was an Israelite prophet (1:5).

But for the modern reader the ensuing fifty-two chapters render the attribution increasingly problematic and of little use as a guide to reading — at least on modern Western expectations and experiences of books that collect the "words of . . ." notable personages and religious figures.

For example, chs. 26–46 primarily consist of third person narrative or first person prose speeches. The narratives give us the clearest concrete representations of Jeremiah's activities set within unsuccessful Judean attempts to prevent the successful imperial strategies of the Neo-Babylonian rulers from incorporating Syria-Palestine into its Levantine Empire. Nevertheless, the rest of the Jeremiah collection consists of poetic and prose speeches rarely so concrete and helpful with respect to social occasion and historical context. How is a reader to manage these variant strategies employed in the representation of "Jeremiah's" words?

No chronological or topical scheme seems to govern the structure of the book as we have it. True, the third person narrative clusters around two events occurring in 597/598, and 586/587 — stages in the final siege and destruction of Judah's royal capital, Jerusalem. Nevertheless, the book does not follow a consistent chronologically sequenced narration of the events — episodes appear dischronologized. Use is made of chronologically sequenced material only to violate quickly such temporal evocations. Similarly, the material clusters around common topics or themes — for example, chs. 21–24 offer oracles against national leadership and chs. 46–51 offer oracles against foreign nations — but it does not represent characteristic strategies for presenting "Jeremiah's" words. Nor is it obvious why such groupings occur where they do in the book — for example, chs. 30–31 constitute oracles of hope interrupting the apparent narrative flow of the final capture of the royal capital. Or, for that matter, why are other oracles with related themes still to be found scattered elsewhere in the scroll — for example, two collections of oracles against the nations in ch. 25 and chs. 46–51, and periodic restoration oracles in chs. 2–20 and in chs. 30–31.

Even the ending of the collection is not handled decisively. For no sooner does 51:64 announce a conclusion than 52:1-34 contravenes the notice! This is not the first time the reader will have to face false starts and endings in the present arrangement of the collection (e.g., ch. 25 in relation to chs. 1–24).

Past the puzzlement of the larger structure of the scroll, the reader's travail only increases as his or her familiarity with the details of the book increases. For example, how are we to correlate the third person oblique voice with that of the first person claim as they periodically interchange throughout the collection? Does the prophet shift voice strategy, or do we seek another greater collector of the prophetic reminiscences? Further, what rationale exists for shifting between poetic and prosaic literary speech patterns? Why do some themes appear explicitly only in certain speech representations — for example, the covenant in first person prose speeches — and not others. The biblically literate reader will also notice, amid the interchange of first and third person prose, thematic, stylistic, and ideological associations with the great narrative history of Israel represented by Deuteronomy and Joshua through Kings. How is the reader to make sense of and use this intertextual triangle that exists between Jeremianic poetry and prose and the prose of the Deuteronomistic history? The puzzlement becomes even worse than this!

For it seems clear that the Septuagint (LXX) translation of Jeremiah witnesses to an alternate Hebrew version of Jeremiah with its own literary peculiarities, relocations, and editorial interests. Which Jeremiah should we read?

And why should the Jeremiah scroll offer the modern reader so many inconcinnities?

Unraveling Modern Reading Problems — Some Theoretical Considerations

An author and his or her readers sustain a dynamic, unstable relationship. An author's work enters the slipstream of the cultural processes from which it has emerged. Authority is ceded to the reading community, who must perform the work of constructing its meaning. The author's authority derives from its latent rhetorical presence in the form of the work. The meanings of the work emerge from this conversation between authors and readers through the text.

Both authors and readers come to the work through

expectations shaped both by a tradition of literary (oral or written) performances and a tradition of performed works. The performance of the immediate work by author-reader will proceed from these traditions and act back on them, contributing to the performance tradition. In addition, each specific work will in time attract "classic" performances that surround any subsequent approach to the work by later author-reader generations, materially conditioning expectations and reading strategies. The wider matrices of cultural interests and desires circulate material, psychosocial, and political needs through the work and continually fuel transformations of it in the eyes of the communities of the author and the reader. Transformations occur both as to substance and import — what the work is as well as what it means. Communal focus on the social performance of the work is most intense for works perceived as symbolically pregnant to contemporary cultural interests — in short, where a specific work or collection of works consists of verbal cultural icons.

Thus when the modern reader enters the symbolic space of Jeremiah, both it and we are heavily encumbered. The scroll offers us Jeremiah, a prophet. The scroll presents itself as containing prophecy. From these representations stem our difficulties as modern readers. For what, in fact, is a prophet? And what, in fact, is a prophetic book?

Expectations encumber the evocations of the terms "prophet" and "prophecy." Religious readers from communities who have directly inherited Jeremiah as part of their sacred scriptures (Jews, Christians, or Muslims) will differ in their engagement with this intensely religiously constructed role and rhetoric from religious readers shaped by traditions of teachers who bring enlightenment or shamans or wise elders teaching the ways of the spirits. So, too, will it be for the "secular" reader, and on and on. . . .

Jeremiah has migrated culturally and historically from its originating ancient Near Eastern context to an increasingly diverse set of communities around the globe, each with their own sociocultural needs and desires. It will not be easy to read the scroll of Jeremiah for and in such a context — if it ever was a work for easy reading!

We Read in Pockets

Conscious of Jeremiah's textual migrations, critical biblical scholarship has positioned itself in alignment with a peculiar reading strategy termed "historical critical." It seeks to construct the meaning of biblical texts by reconstructing the "original" cultural arena in the horizon of ancient Israel in which it was produced. The task has had the salutary effect of sharpening our reading objectives — and our difficulties!

For, like it or not, we have no direct access to the historical figure of Jeremiah or his cultural matrix. Our primary witnesses remain heavily interpreted traditions whose cultural projects differed from those of the biblical scholar. Israel's prophetic collections come to us as heavily used literary artifacts. In the form we have received them, they already offer interpretative representations rather than raw cultural transcripts (if any such could actually exist!). We access all the available contemporary comparative sources, from annals to inscriptions to potsherds, but in the last analysis we are thrown back on the primary verbal icon itself in the effort to negotiate our reading quest.

Until very recently, the reading strategies employed by biblical scholarship would have been fairly proscribed with the procedures for framing the interpretative task well rehearsed around Jeremiah. In the context of the old post-Wellhausenian reconstruction of Israelite history and religion, Bernhard Duhm had posed the problem of the quest for the historical prophet and his authentic sayings. Under Duhm's tutelage students of Jeremiah would have analyzed intensively the three macro literary styles in the Jeremianic tradition (poetic oracles, prose speeches, and oblique narratives). A critical scholar would have relied on a familiar repertoire of approaches ranging from form- to tradition- to redaction-critical analysis. The objective would have been the historical reconstruction of the work and words of Jeremiah ben Hilkiah with attendant religious and theological valuations. Whether this portrait was minimalist or maximalist in regard to detail, pessimistic or optimistic in regard to goal, depreciative or appreciative in valuation depended in part on judgments made about the authenticity accorded the Jeremianic scroll. While some scholars might view very little of the book as authentic to the historical prophet (Duhm, e.g., reduced the authentic kernel to 280 verses), others might see most of the book as the product of Jeremiah's own compositional activity and/or that of a close associate such as the scribe Baruch. Assessing the literary relationship to Deuteronomy and the Deuteronomistic history played a large part in distributing the consensus of scholarship along the points in this debate.

This debate has reached an impasse, as the most recent full-scale commentaries exhibit. Often their readings are so radically different that novices might wonder if they were reading the same Jeremiah!

Current Jeremiah research is engaged in a search for routes through the reading impasse generated by its predecessor — that is, the historicist model for interpretation (meaning is discovered through literary archeology). Historicism's literary excavation went behind the current prophetic book to elucidate literary genesis, and even through this literary genesis to the historical realities it was believed constituted the work's subject matter to some degree or another. The interpreter read inside Jeremiah in order to move behind and outside it, so he or she could then turn from that vantage point to construct Jeremiah's meaning.

Along the path of this historicist quest, research has periodically shifted the general answers given to our two fundamental questions: What is a prophet? What is a prophetic book? This has materially affected the kind of historical figure Jeremiah ben Hilkiah might reasonably be expected to have been as well as judgments of probability about the character of prophetic writings. Preoccupation with prophets as oral speakers of inspired utterance — whether as mantics, ecstatics, visionaries, or highly rational/ethical reformers — largely obscured our ability to read the prophetic scroll in its extant form. The goal was deconstruction of the present work into its reconstructed oral speeches. As tradition- and redaction-critical approaches to analysis came more to the fore, however, they made possible a more positive assessment of the literary transformation of prophecy and the "genius" of the tradition bearers — whether of prophetic writers, Jeremianic disciples, or Deuteronomistic schools. Nevertheless, the solution of the problem of the scroll in its final form continued to elude since the textuality of prophecy was still framed largely in historicist categories. Reading Jeremiah properly is a matter of reading it along the path of its literary development. The text before us explicitly and/or implicitly has been judged to be unreadable. While degrees of coherence-incoherence might be debatable, nearly all recent commentary agrees that a clear plan of literary organization and thematic development is not discernible.

Given the continued absence of direct, nontraditional historical data about Jeremiah ben Hilkiah and the paucity of objective control over our hypothetical reconstruction of Jeremiah's compositional history, the present consensual impasse in the historical-critical project for reading Jeremiah should be labeled a stalemate.

Jeremiah — Textuality and Interdisciplinary Discourses

Paradigm shifts are under way for modern biblical studies. Spurred by the limits experienced in traditional historicist models of interpretation and aided by renewed interdisciplinary dialogue, experiments with new interpretative strategies of biblical literature are under way. This commentary on Jeremiah is carried out in the spirit of these explorations and reorientations. A particular debt should be acknowledged to the reformulations and debates in the wider fields of modern literary theory, semiotics, and aesthetics, along with other renewed attempts to trace out social theories of literary symbols labeled vaguely with the rubric of postmodernity.

This commentary takes seriously the task of assessing Jeremiah as a social and literary symbol. Therefore, Jeremiah is viewed as symbolic space invested with the devices and desires of the late Davidic Judean monarchy, the latter's client community, and the diasporan communities laying claim to the material and symbolic inheritance of that old regime in the aftermath of its political destruction. And we ask, What do the performances of Jeremiah — prophetic figure and prophetic scroll — do with and to the myth of Israel and its patron deity, Yahweh? I use the term "myth" in its loosely defined anthropological sense of a culture's sacred narrative.

Internal Setting: Time in the Scroll

As already mentioned, the first three verses of ch. 1 provide a chronological starting point dating the span of Jeremiah ben Hilkiah's mission from the thirteenth year of King Josiah to the eleventh year and fifth month of King Zedekiah, when the royal city fell to its Babylonian assailants. Jeremiah's literary mission spans, then, from c. 627 to 586/587 BC.

The attempt to match this introduction with the contents of the rest of the scroll is instructive. In the next twenty chapters no such clear chronological notices appear at all. The reader must rely on creative ingenuity and elusive allusions to known, datable historical events. If one can be sure that the ambiguous "foe from the north" represents Neo-Babylonian forces, then the oracular materials are already post-Josianic. The lack of Josianic references (except in 3:6) in chs. 2–10 induces some to doubt the accuracy of the beginning date for Jeremiah's mission in the Josianic reign though nothing in the first part requires us to have a complete anthology of Jeremianic oracles from each period of the prophetic mission.

The next clear chronological references occur in the thematic block chs. 21–24, with references variously to Zedekiah (21:1, 588/587), Shallum (22:11, i.e., Jehoahaz, 609), Jehoiakim (22:18, 609-598), Jeconiah (22:24, 597), and back again to Zedekiah (24:8, clearly dated after 598/597). Ch. 25 returns the reader to the fourth year of Jehoiakim (v. 1, April 605–April 604), synchronized to the Babylonian ruler's first regnal year (April 604) in order to summarize the mission of Jeremiah to this point as spanning a period of twenty-three years.

Chronological notices will occur from this point on in the scroll with more frequency, though in dischronologized sequence: chs. 26 (Jehoiakim), 27 (Zedekiah), 30–31 (undated though it assumes that deportation has occurred), 32–33 (10th year of Zedekiah), 34 (Zedekiah, Jerusalem experiencing a temporary halt in the Babylonian attack), 35 (Jehoiakim), 36 (4th year of Jehoiakim), 37–38 (Zedekiah with resumption of the final siege), 39 (11th year, 4th month, 9th day of Zedekiah), 40–44 (Gedalian governorship after the fall of Jerusalem), 45 (4th year of Jehoiakim), 46–51 (largely undated except for 46:2 [the battle of Carchemish, 609], and 51:59 [4th year of Zedekiah]). Ch. 52 summarizes the fall of Jerusalem, providing a chronology for the final siege that was narrated in various parts of chs. 26–39. Three deportations of Judaeans are synchronized with Nebuchadrezzar's regnal years: the seventh (597), the eighteenth (587/586), and the twenty-third (582/581). The third deportation is not narrated. The final verses (31-34) leap ahead to the accession year of Amel-marduk (c. 560), correlated as the thirty-seventh year of the exiled Judean king, Jehoiachin.

While the introduction broadly situates the contents of the book in the last forty years of Judah's existence, substantial portions of it cannot be located more specifically within this period. Chs. 2–20 largely resist concrete chronological and historical specification. Other portions fall outside and postdate this time frame even though they are represented as the words of Jeremiah (chs. 30–31; 40–44; 52:31-34). The expectations of a thorough sampling of Jeremiah ben Hilkiah's words from each portion of this forty-year period are not met.

Dischronologization represents a significant tactic of time management from chs. 21 to 51!

External Setting: The Time of the Scroll

The time of the scroll is not the time in the book! On the principle that the scroll, as we have it, cannot have been written earlier than the last datable event recorded in it, attention returns again to 52:31-34. A voice presents itself here that cannot be dated before 560 BC. Is this narrative voice the same one encountered in 1:1-3, or is it only an appended voice? In the latter case, other parts of the Jeremiah collection could be earlier but need not be. In the case of the former, we still are offered no fixed point for the compositional completion of the scroll.

The reconstruction of Jeremiah's compositional history remains highly contested in contemporary scholarship, with the major proposals at an impasse. Maximalist models take their cue from Jeremiah 36 and recapture the bulk of the scroll's composition in the lifetime of the historical prophet and his scribal associate, Baruch. Minimalists question the authenticity and reliability of the first person and third person prose upon which the maximalists depend, positing instead compositional agency among diverse exilic and/or postexilic editorial elite. Compromises between these two theoretical poles have also been made, viewing the point of origin of the Jeremiah tradition within the historical lifetime of the prophet but extending in literary development far beyond the prophet to diverse and disconnected editorial agents.

Why not take the internal chronological representations and authorial allegations at face value? Authorial practices in the first millennium BC render such an assumption ill advised — an act of literary naïveté. For performance strategies ranging from anonymity to pseudonymity accompany those making explicit "historical" attributions and authorial claims. Further, literary cultural practices in the Near East exhibit the dynamic interchange and intertextual dialogue between performances by cultural elite and those we would today label folkloristic performances of non-elite social locations. Processes of legend and myth formation intermingle with realistic annalistic "histories" and autobiographical fictions. Even a surface survey of the literature of Second Temple Judaism provides ample illustration — Jeremiah ben Hilkiah and Baruch receive significant legendary amplification, symbolic enhancement, and even inversions of role. Put with this the connections of style, theme, and form that exist between Jeremiah and the Deuteronomistic history, along with the issues raised by the alternative Jeremiah represented by the Septuagint, and the impression of numerous nonidentical editorial-authorial hands seems hard to resist, though able critics of such reasoning are represented in the critical debate.

A face-value approach to the authorial representations of Jeremiah commits an error of "commonsense" judgment when it treats the world represented inside the text as a literal, correspondent representation of the world outside the text. The relationship between these two worlds is more complicated, convoluted, and oblique. They may correspond. They need not. Face-value naïveté fails to take seriously enough the problems of textuality.

Recourse to some of the analytical categories current in contemporary literary theory adds precision to the problems of textuality offered by any work. Narratives and narration, whether of prose fiction or other dramatic forms such as lyric or epic poetry, in addition to the dramatic personae (the characters) that populate the plot, utilize other imaginative constructs equally dramatic in function which need have no "real" correspondent to "historical" persons outside the world of the text. I think here of narrators and the audiences whose visage they hint in trace forms "at the margins and between the lines" of the work or of implicit authors and readers "standing" at further remove in the work. The latter figures of representational imagination and projection need not be identical or identifiable with actual "historical" authors, editors, audiences, and readers. And even where overlap can be shown, the vested interests projected into the performance of the work may imaginatively and creatively elaborate the representation of such personae unchecked by the "real," "historical" characters. For example, how are we to discuss carefully, after all, the historicity of the "George Washington" who chopped down the cherry tree!

Working Hypotheses for Jeremianic Agency

In light of the preceding problems, critical debates, and historicist impasse, a reader might wish to hedge all bets and postulate a point of origin for the Jeremianic tradition in the mission of the historical Jeremiah ben Hilkiah with the present form and substance of those traditions the heavily encumbered artifact of symbolic processes reaching into the postexilic period of Second Temple Judaism. In so doing the reader might surmise a number of discreet historical occasions which have left traces of their influence in the tradition, but many others will remain opaque — for example, exilic Deuteronomists, early postexilic restoration groups, and continuing voices represented by the textual precursors to the Septuagint, Masoretic, and Qumran editions of Jeremiah. Such a hedge has the advantage of temporizing faced with a dearth of external data as well as offering an attractive bare courtesy to the internal authorial representations offered by the tradition. For as the critical impasse illustrates, it is very difficult to say with confidence what portions of the tradition actually were produced by the historical figure, Jeremiah ben Hilkiah. True, a discernible common style and theme in the poetry may provide circumstantial evidence of a distinctive authorial voice; nevertheless, it falls far short of independently proving that that voice belongs to the historical Jeremiah. That conclusion hangs on assumption in view of the gap that exists between style and authorial claim.

Why even offer the barest courtesy? The courtesy presumes some "good faith," some measure of reliability on the part of the narrative and editorial framework provided for the tradition. Admittedly, in light of authorial practices in the first millennium, this presumption is a very tenuous one and hardly required by the mere presence of the editorial framework. We have so little "hard evidence" to go on! On the other hand, to postulate a hypothetical historical core and point of origin in a historical figure, Jeremiah ben Hilkiah, provides the modern reader with some chance of explaining why there was all this symbolic interest in the literary figure, Jeremiah prophet of Yahweh. Yet our modern rational and historicist needs may lead us astray here. For the needs of societies create wholesale verbal worlds, figures, and events without a shred of empirical basis in "reality" or literal correspondent causes and agents, as folkloristic field study repeatedly dramatizes, as well as our own processes of fictionalization.

After all, how would visitors from a distant time and culture decide what the historical Tom Sawyer was like, if in fact such a person ever existed in late-nineteenth-century America, based on Mark Twain's book alone. This is precisely our predicament with the book of Jeremiah!

In the last analysis, we have immediate access in Jeremiah only to a literary figure and work — prophet and prophecy. We must read them sensitive to the "textuality of history and the historicity of texts," attentive to all the strategies of representation and their intertwined "intentions" for ideological, rhetorical persuasion. As a result, we may judge better the courtesies we had initially extended to the work. Every reading at last only leads to another.

Textuality and Text Transmission

We have repeatedly mentioned the significant implications for reading Jeremiah offered by the manner of its textual preservation. The basic "fact" is that the book of Jeremiah as represented by the Masoretic Text (MT) is significantly different from the representation offered in the Septuagint (LXX) — a "fact" long recognized in contemporary scholarship but newly addressed in modern Jeremiah commentary.

In short, the LXX offers a much shorter and differently arranged scroll of Jeremiah. The greater brevity ranges from the absence of large blocks (e.g., 39:4-13) to individual terms and titles (the title "prophet" for Jeremiah in chs. 27–28), accounting for the fact that the LXX is about an eighth shorter than the MT. These two features intersect at the center of the book around the oracles against the nations. For the LXX has all of the oracles against the nations gathered here that the MT had separated into two blocks (ch. 25 and chs. 46–51) and in different order. Beyond differences of length and arrangement, the content of the Jeremiah tradition varies within the MT and the LXX. Variant readings range from subtle grammatical shifts to matters of style, word order, and diction culminating in significant alternative presentations of the tradition.

Before the discovery of ancient fragments of Jeremiah in the Qumran materials, progress in the scholarly assessment of this state of textual affairs was hampered. The central issue remained: How many of the LXX differences could be traced back to Hebrew originals (LXXV)? How many reflect idiosyncrasies of the translators? But with the aid of the Qumran material it has been possible to confirm the existence of at least three different Hebrew families of text-types for Jeremiah: one on which the MT is based, one on which the LXX is based (LXXV), and a third that goes its own way. The fragmentary preservation of these manuscript types at Qumran, however, falls far short of providing Jeremiah students with complete alternative versions. Nevertheless, the evidence has moved the debate forward to consider the relative merits of one text-type over against the others, with proposals grouping them into three categories or valuations: the MT is superior, the LXXV is superior, or superiority depends on an eclectic, case-by-case evaluation. At the least, it has meant that scholars can no longer dismiss LXX readings out of hand. For in its differences potentially lie readings which point back to an alternative Hebrew version of equal if not better claim to antiquity than the MT.

The work of Emanuel Tov moved the debate another step forward, for he has been able to show at least an editorial quality for MT pluses (versus LXXV minuses). Thus processes of generative literary composition overlap processes of textual transmission in the Jeremianic textual tradition. In this connection, Tov has proposed a relationship of the LXXV to the MT as that of edition one to edition two.

Tov's model has already proved significant for the debates over the editorial history of the tradition. The recent major commentaries on Jeremiah accept Tov's proposal to some degree. It argues strongly for an extended and complex compositional history for the scroll(s). For up to and through the period of the LXX translators and on into the era of the Qumran community, "Jeremiah" has been circulating and is being performed in alternative forms. Perhaps "Jeremiah" in the MT and the LXXV represent only a small, surviving part of communal writing-reading of the Jeremianic tradition.

In any case, debate over the character of Jeremiah I (LXXV) and Jeremiah II (MT) has been tied up with larger compositional theories about the presence or absence of Deuteronomistic, pre-Deuteronomistic, and post-Deuteronomistic editorial contributions to the tradition. Tov saw in the MT a further editorial layer from the hand of the Deuteronomists. Others are less convinced of its Deuteronomistic character (see Louis Stulman), detecting in the expanded material the voices of postexilic restoration groups not directly or properly labeled Deuteronomistic. The debate remains unresolved.

Literary theoretical, aesthetic, and hermeneutical assessment of the poetics of these recensional differences lags behind, with only beginning probes explored in Jeremiah studies. Where possible and appropriate to the scope of this commentary, I will engage such factors. Potentially the gap opened by the differences between these editions of Jeremiah provides a resource for readdressing the theoretical and practical reading problems offered by the tradition canvassed above.

One must realize the reconstructive methodology involved in the performance of such analysis. First, the LXX Greek of Jeremiah must be retroverted (translated back) into Hebrew. Judgment must be made about the reliability of any retroversion where it poses an alternative Hebrew precursor. In the nature of the case, the ambiguity and tentativeness of the retroversion must be recognized. Then follows evaluation of the literary significance (if there is any) for the alternative reading. The first step, retroversion, produces an alternative scroll of Jeremiah. The second determines the significance for the meaning and performance of the Jeremiah tradition.

The commentator ends up with more than one "biblical" Jeremiah to read. Jeremiah shatters the usual practice of establishing a single, reliable, authoritative canonical text! Our usual strategies for reading Jeremiah MT must also be applied to Jeremiah LXXV. But positing two Jeremiahs also requires the development of strategies to read the two together, the two in light of each other, and the one against the other in an effort to make sense of Jeremiah, the prophet and the prophecy.

Conclusion

The overlap of textual transmission and literary composition in Jeremiah's case suggests the metaphor of a play staged and performed numerous times and, consequently, rewritten in the process. Yet each performance has its own integrity and calls for its own "reading" and critical assessment. One must assess the symbolic and mythic, cultural and ideological, religious and theological significance that attaches to each performance and to all the performances taken together. Commentary on Jeremiah is not yet that mature.

Thus the complexity of reading Jeremiah derives from the texture of its textuality. It is a textuality not unlike that of oral traditional genre even if it cannot be identified with it. The Jeremiah that actually exists is a performed instance of it. In time Jeremiah is anchored nowhere, unhinged as it is from a pristine historical genesis and agency. Yet there is a tradition of performance attached to Jeremiah conditioning how the work will be embodied in each new instance of performance. "Historicity" becomes a matter of constantly refiguring its occasion. The latter is now understood more fluidly and dynamically as the literary, symbolic, psychosocial, and political currents circulating around and into the work. Occasions are projections into the work. Such a performance tradition makes it possible for the community to name Jeremiah outside and in anticipation of its performance. It permits the community to expect Jeremiah to be a certain way — in form, quality, and substance — even as innovations insinuate themselves into it. In short, Jeremiah becomes recognizable apart from any single instance of performance. The varying competencies of writer-readers in accessing this tradition within the arena of symbolic performance materially affects the quality of their engagement anew with Jeremiah even as they extend Jeremiah with their own symbolic devices and desires.

Outlining Jeremianic Performance

According to LXXV	According to MT
Introduction	Introduction
1:1-3	1:1-3
Indictment: The Case against Judah	Judgment from Babylon to Judah
2–20	2–20
21–24	21–24
God's War against the World	Fulfillment in Retrospect and Prospect
25–32 *Oracles against the Nations*	25
	Judgment from Judah to Babylon
Doom: Punishing Judah, Fulfilling Jeremiah	*The Fall of Judah*
33–43	26–36
44–51	37–45
	The Fall of the Nations
	46–51 *Oracles against the Nations*
Historical Summary	Hope's Trace: An Aftermath
52	52

COMMENTARY

Jeremiah 1:1-19

Overview

Anticipations of prophecy at the beginning of the composition entangle the figure of Jeremiah and the traditions attributed to him within the constructive desires and anxieties of the implicit writers and readers. The composition provides a dramatic "historical" setting for the oracular mission of Jeremiah ben Hilkiah from the thirteenth year of Josiah (627 BC) until the eleventh year of Zedekiah (586 BC). The implicit reader is intended to take the present scroll as the collection of Jeremiah's oracular tradition ("words of Jeremiah") revealed to him by Yahweh. Hence the composition mythologizes the Jeremianic scroll, appropriates oracular power to the act of composition, and writes "Jeremiah" under the sign of Moses. An enlarged myth of prophecy — prophet and scroll — animates this performance of "Jeremiah," with the latter figuring its representations.

Dramatic Composition

The first chapter anticipates key thematic interests pursued throughout the entire scroll of Jeremiah. In the process, the composition dramatizes the inception of oracular mission as the product of a visionary encounter between Jeremiah and Yahweh in which Yahweh not only commissions the prophet, authorizing his oracular power, but also reveals in advance the entire tenor and course of the prophetic mission. Hence the prophet and the implied reader know in advance the content of the oracular message as well as the outcome of Jeremiah's prophetic efforts. But not all its surprises!

Historical criticism has no decisive means to establish the reliability of the chronology offered for the inception of Jeremiah's oracular mission. We have no direct nontraditional information about the ancient Israelite oracular speaker, Jeremiah ben Hilkiah. True, the modern historian has access to the thin hints and allegations proffered by archeologically recovered seal impressions and ostraca from the period of the end of the Judean monarchy. And certainly ample evidence exists for the corroboration of the major public events — such as Nebuchadrezzar's capture of Jerusalem in 587/586 BC. But the more the historian focuses on a specific event or detail offered in the traditions of the scroll the more judgments have to weigh in within a profound vacuum of extrinsic corroborating evidence.

The "historical" Jeremiah thus becomes a construct no matter whose is offered. For whatever else we might someday learn or suspect, the "Jeremiah" offered in the scroll is at least the representation of the composition — even where that representation is performed in the first person of "Jeremiah's" oracular voice!

Does this rule out any presence of an "authentic" Jeremiah ben Hilkiah in the scroll? Not necessarily. But by what extrinsic canon can one judge the issue? For the composition has long disconnected the traditions utilized in the writing of the present scroll from whatever originating historical-cultural moments gave them birth. A bigger game is afoot than just transcription and memory! For the composition must use the "Jeremianic" traditions in order to mythologize the historical-political fate of Israel. In the process, the composition will have to rewrite the myth of Yahweh and prophecy on which "Israel" depends.

Jeremiah, Prophet to the Nations (1:4-10)

Older form criticism connected this passage with others narrating the "call" of prophetic and other charismatic figures in ancient Israel — for example, Moses, Samuel, Gideon, Isaiah, Ezekiel. Common motifs occurred suggesting the existence of oral genre as precursors to the written texts that served, especially in the case of prophets, as apologetic oral forms defending the legitimacy and authority of the oracular speaker. Be that as it may, in the present literary context meaning and function outstrip such postulated oral performances. For Jeremiah's remonstrance, "I am not a skilled speaker; I am too young" (1:6), which seeks unsuccessfully to refuse the divine commission, hints at a characterization that is subsequently elaborated in chs. 11–20. There the prophet fails in the face of divine and human violence to escape and defeat his oracular destiny. The composition gains an elaborate psychologization of the myth of prophetic mission even as it ironically founds Jeremiah's "success" as the prophetic destroyer of Judah in his failure to escape oracular destiny.

That characterization begins to intrude in the present context even as Jeremiah's fate is rooted in prenatal divine predestination. Reassurances offered here will reappear again in the more strident conflict between Jeremiah and Yahweh to come (cf. 15:20). Even so, the composition writes Jeremiah under the sign of Moses. For Yahweh's sign-act ("I have put my words in your mouth"; 1:9) plays off Deut 18:18 ("I will put my words in his mouth, and he will proclaim to them whatever I command him"; cf. Jer 1:7, "whatever I command you, you will proclaim") and enrolls Jeremiah in the Mosaic prophetic succession.

Surprising in that regard, however, is Jeremiah's designation as "prophet to the nations" (1:5) — a comprehensive international focus reemphasized in v. 10. The prophet wields oracular power and sets the destiny of nations for woe and weal! What this will mean for Judah is left indeterminate in the present unit, though the terminology of tearing down and uprooting, building and planting (v. 10) will recur as catch phrases throughout the composition. Should the implied reader have not more readily expected a designation focused more narrowly upon Jeremiah's Judean prophetic horizon? It is the burden of the following units to clarify the surprise in Jeremiah's prophetic designation.

Visions of Oracular Power and Doom (1:11-16)

Two visions spell out the tenor of Jeremiah's prophetic mission. The first (1:11-12) stakes out Jeremiah's Yahwistic agency and power. With the almond staff *(maqqel shaqed)* Yahweh puns the myth of oracular power. For the efficaciousness of Jeremiah's oracular mission depends on the attentiveness of the Deity ("I am watching *[shoqed]* over my word . . .") to bring prophetic pronouncements into reality, thus making and unmaking the world(s) heralded in prophetic speech.

The unwary reader might easily miss exposure of the primary anxiety animating the composition's performance. For the threat of God's failure and the failure of prophecy is the great mythic terror haunting the entire symbolic space called "Jeremiah." Hence, at the outset the composition anticipates its later preoccupations with true and false or failed prophecy and its deeper terror at the defeat of Yahweh in the fall of Jerusalem. The need for a theodicy that can rehabilitate the myth of Yahweh is paramount. Thus the vision of the almond rod begins to anticipate the ground for rewriting the mythic fortunes of Yahwistic faith.

The second vision (1:13-16) spells out what Yahweh effects through the oracular speech he has put on the prophet's lips. It is evil or calamity. "From the north" at least has geographical significance for the originating source of the boiling evil, as v. 15 makes clear in its interpretation of the phrase. Yet it may also hint mythological overtones as the abode of the Canaanite deity Baal, the location from which he comes to do battle. If present, the symbolic allusion transfigures imminent political events as threatening a divine storm. The fantastic landscape effected by that storm will become the theme of poetic development in the cycles narrating the invasion of the foe from the north in Jeremiah 4–6. Interestingly, Zion/Jerusalem, too, can be imagined "in the far north," the location from which Yahweh effects his vengeance and suzerainty in the world (Ps 48:3).

Intriguingly, the boiling cauldron of calamity narrows the scope of Jeremiah's oracular appointment to emphasize its destructive pole (cf. 1:10, "tear down and uproot"). At the same time it introduces ambiguity complicating the meaning of Jeremiah's designation as "prophet to the nations." For the victims of this divinely inflamed calamity are "all the inhabitants of the land/earth" (v. 14). Read with the preceding context, a global reference can be understood in "land" equivalent to "earth" (cf. 25:29, 30). The vision then anticipates the global, divine, imperial crusade explicitly adumbrated in Jeremiah 25. Is Israel to be included? No mention of the impact on Israel has yet been explicitly made for Jeremiah's oracular mission.

But the "commentary" which Yahweh supplies (1:15-16) to his visionary metaphor (vv. 13-14) reads it otherwise! The elaboration (note "for," v. 15) focuses on the invasion of Judah and the destruction of Jerusalem, thus equating "land" with the land of Judah. Ironically, the nations over whom Jeremiah has been given oracular power become not the objects of "tearing down and uprooting" but rather the agents of that destructive destiny for Israel! Are the nations thus beneficiaries of an oracular power which "builds up and plants" their suzerainty in the world? An irony deeper than this inhabits the imagery of Yahweh's "commentary."

For the imagery of the nations streaming to Jerusalem, arrayed outside her walls, and laying siege to Yahweh's city and people evokes old tropes in which the nations have risen like some great cosmic storm to overthrow Yahwistic-Davidic suzerainty (e.g., Psalms 2, 46, 48, 76, 110; cf. Ezekiel 38–39; Joel 3, Zech 12:1-9; 14:1-9). In the old tropes, Yahweh intervenes to destroy the chaos-wielding powers arrayed against Zion.

Ambiguity in the present context plays on this tradition only to invert it. Influenced by this traditional trope, "all the inhabitants of the land/earth" could refer to Judah's political enemies and even be read (however briefly) as the objects of divine sentence (v. 16, "I will pass sentence on them" [i.e., the clans of the kingdoms of the north]) as the nearest antecedent in context. Such a "hope" from Jeremiah's oracular mission is quickly effaced since the following verses (16-19) clearly identify Judah/Jerusalem as the subject of defeat. In this inverted imagery, Yahweh inhabits the invading chaos power against his own Zion!

1:16 sets forth in nucleus the heart of the theodicy advocated by the composition even as it exhibits ideological indebtedness to Deuteronomistic themes and perspectives that it will reiterate and elaborate especially in the prose traditions of the scroll. Jerusalem's destruction and colonization by Babylon represents an act of Yahwistic punishment for the community's religious-cultic violations. Thus the implied writers relocate the true cause of Jerusalem's colonization from extrinsic political agency or from the failure of Yahweh to withstand Babylonian "principalities and powers" to Yahwistic wrath. In the process, it constructs a rhetoric of blame in order to expose the shameful evil that has torn Israel apart from the inside out. In the commitment expressed here to *Yahweh-alone* and a cult that embodies such exclusivity, the composition polemicizes the destruction of the old Davidic state even as it anticipates restoration hopes founded on a reinvented myth of Yahweh and Yahweh's purified cult.

Jeremiah, "City" of Jerusalem's Doom (1:17-19)

Yahweh turns now to address the prophet's interior posture in the execution of this oracular mission of national destruction. The exhortation mixes challenge, threat, and assurance. Read in light of the preceding resistance of the prophet (1:6), perhaps the Deity still detects or at least anticipates a continuing undercurrent of Jeremianic denial. In the myth of prophecy at work here, the reader witnesses the commandeering of the life of Jeremiah ben Hilkiah.

Tropes common to oracles of assurance (e.g., 1:19, "I am with you to rescue you"; cf. v. 17, "do not be dismayed because of them lest . . . ," as a parody of the more expected "fear not because of them, for . . ." in v. 8) are combined with threat repeating aspects of vv. 4-10 as well as anticipating later divine-prophetic encounters over oracular mission (15:20-21). The prophet's penalty for giving in to fear in the face of communal enmity and persecution (anticipations of dramatic structures in poetry [chs. 11–20] and narrative [e.g., chs. 37–39]) is divine terrorization and destruction — that is, the prophet defeated by his national enemies. In contrast to Jerusalem, Jeremiah is the true invincible city (1:18, "fortified city," "iron pillar," "bronze wall"). The image curiously repositions the posture of Jeremiah's mission so that it is static, almost passive, as if only his oracular presence is required to effect Yahwistic intentions. Jeremianic mission is prophetic mission under assault.

The prophet's destiny, like Jerusalem's, is to come under siege. Ironically, it is his own countrymen who are his besiegers. They carry the fight to him, not vice versa. Even more ironic is that this is the mechanism of God's punishment of the community. For their attempt to destroy Jeremiah's oracular power will prove the "stone" upon which they destroy themselves. This is grim assurance indeed. For whatever one might have hoped oracular mission to accomplish on behalf of Israel, here it has become inverted as the ground provoking national destruction — Mosaic succession with a vengeance!

Evaluation

As the anticipation of Jeremiah's mission dramatized in the rest of the scroll, ch. 1 emphatically orients Jeremianic oracular power toward Israel's doom. In so doing, the composition creates a world and opens a space called "Jeremiah" where it can control the symbolic crisis of Judah's destruction and enduring subjugation.

From the outset Jeremiah and the implied reader must know that the outcome of his prophetic energies will be the death of the nation. It is a death that must signify the enduring suzerainty of Yahweh amid the nationalist, imperial, polytheistic struggles of the world. At the same time, that death must also gather to itself, into the grave of the old Davidic state, all the blame, shame, and responsibility in order to load it onto the backs of that late Davidic regime and community alone. False worship, not the failure of worship, is the defending trope designed to prevent the failure of God and thus the end of "Israel" as the restoration interests vested in the composition imagine it.

No doubt as the prime "historical fact" around which the composition must weave its anxiety-driven performance, it could not present Israel's fate in the face of Jeremiah's Yahwistic mission any other way. At the same time, however, the composition begins its long embrace of aporia that ever drives its symbolic crisis to deeper levels, threatening the stability of its mythic refigurations, its rewriting of the myth of Yahweh and Israel.

For in ch. 1, Jeremiah's mission is dedicated to the death of "Israel." Worse than that, the mere presence of the Jeremianic mission offers the mechanism of national destruction. For the composition, the myth of oracular power must be elevated above political and historical exigencies.

On the one hand, might not one have expected that the powers of Mosaic succession could have successfully turned the community from its course of religious folly and self-destruction? Or at least could not Jeremiah's intercessory powers, like Moses', have secured more merciful results? The "Jeremiah" heralded here seems eccentric, more like an anti-Moses. The death of the nation implies the failure of prophecy to provide an oracular bulwark for the sake of national security — especially Jeremiah's prophetic mission. Ironically, the old Davidic regime in its drive toward "false worship" successfully defeated the energies of oracular power under the sign of Moses. And the deeper terror in the failure of oracular power is the mythic abyss of the failure of Yahweh.

On the other hand, if doom was inescapable, what value would there be in repeated subsequent dramatizations of Jeremiah interceding for divine mercy, pleading for communal penitence, and offering thin amelioration of the destruction or even elaborate avoidance — all elements of the performance of "Jeremiah" rendered highly ironic by the symbolic framework erected in ch. 1?

And though ch. 1 pushes to the margins that other pole of Jeremianic agency, "to build and to plant," and though it leaves unexplored the full scope of Jeremiah's designation as "prophet to the nations," it is not for lack of desire since subsequent developments of these themes will return. Thus underlying its anxiety over the abyss of Yahwistic failure sits compositional desire for national restoration and greediness for hope at any symbolic price. Consequently, the consolations of oracular power turned toward defeat of national enemies, Israel's vengeance for brutal colonization, or the consolations of oracular power remaking a utopian "Davidic" national existence must be prevented and postponed at all costs until such powers can be symbolically relocated and repossessed for the sake of the colonial elite, the inheritors of the Jeremianic tradition, subservient to their dreams of cultural power revitalized in *Yahweh-alone*.

Thus "Jeremiah" constitutes a symbolic arena in which poetics negotiate performances that mask bids for the acquisition of symbolic power. This will to power proves its creative suppleness and generative alacrity. For while the dissonance of its cultural and mythological crises cannot be overcome, at least it can be postponed. Where there is a will to power, faith apparently can find a way. The futility of Yahwistic symbols to prevent the collapse and colonization of the old Israelite regime can be rehabilitated and rewritten. The composition must enter the arena of Jeremianic space to offer a sleight-of-hand performance. It must delegitimize Yahwistic symbols with respect to the old Israelite regime and any rival faction it seeks to write off under the sign of that old regime. At the same time, it revitalizes their legitimacy in the compositional bid to claim "Israel" and the myth of Yahweh for themselves alone.

Jeremiah 2:1–4:2

Overview

Sexual politics and a marital narrative trope make up the prophet's exposé of Israelite-Judean religious polity. The call narrative's anticipation of inescapable national doom is laconic with respect to the indictment of national sins supplying doom's rationale. With this marital exposé the composition remedies that lack. The composition narrates a root metaphor. It tells the history of a failed marriage as a national religious parable. Husband and wife, a friend of the groom, and the children of the marriage are stand-ins for Yahweh and Israel, the prophet, Jerusalem's citizenry, and exilic survivors. The religious sins of the nation are read under the sign of a tale of sexual morality from the perspective of the cuckolded husband. Historical exile is linked to its metaphorical equivalent, divorce. The failure and shame of "Israel" are subsumed under erotic female dangers, with dreams of restoration the prerogative of male dictates.

Dramatic Composition

A marital metaphor organizes the disparate units, themes, and images of the tradition. Through recourse to a narrative arc, a history of a failed marriage plots and divides individual oracles into two blocks: 2:1–3:5 and 3:6-25; 4:1-2. The first narrates a dispute, an indictment that builds the case against the faithless wife and climaxes in the actual divorce proceedings. The dramatic scenario casts Yahweh as the husband cuckolded by his wife Israel. He remains the principal speaker, haranguing his mute wife before the prophet and the children of the marriage (the citizens of Jerusalem) as dramatic audience and witness of the "husband's" bitter and violent diatribe. The voice of the accused wife appears only as grist, citations in the mouth of the enraged, betrayed divine husband, serving as self-incriminating evidence against the accused.

The second section, 3:6-25; 4:1-2, moves forward in time to the other side of the divorce in order to wrestle with the terms and possibility of any rapprochement that might be effected between the divorced couple. In the process, the population of dramatic characters and voices will be complicated. Jeremiah will be drawn more intimately into the scene as the friend of the husband, the one employed in the machinations of Yahweh to test the readiness of Yahweh's estranged "wives" to return on their husband's terms. All the while Yahweh broods over his wounds, laments lost possibilities in love, and pontificates the conditions of restoration. A history of multiple failed marriages emerges as the implicit reader learns of a prior marriage to the present that also ended in failure. Yahweh's women remain mute and apparently unresponsive to the dictates of reacceptance. Thus husband Yahweh will turn as the father of his children, the fruit of his failed love interests, to plead their (re-)alliance in spite of their mothers' incurable deviance. The narrative arc will close by allowing the children to profess in their own dramatic voice their acceptance of father Yahweh's conditions for the resumption of familial bonds.

Gender-mixing Israel's Unfaithful Passions (2:1-3)

A crucial substructure of this national parable and the performance of the marital metaphor is the mixing of genders in the identity of the dramatic addressees. Hence the introductory unit begins in direct address to wife Israel in 2:2 (2d fm. sg.), only to turn in v. 3 to address male Israel (2d ms. sg.). The narration of the history of the marriage begins by looking back on the idyllic period of the honeymoon, celebrating bride Israel's marital fidelity. The gender shift parses the marital metaphor with reference to national religious history, equating female and male dramatic personae.

As it stands, reference to the wilderness sojourn evokes exodus-election traditions and imagines that earlier period in Israel's existence to be one of idyllic cult fidelity and purity. The relationship between the patron Deity and the national cult is characterized in harmonious terms — the proper Yahwistic devotion on the part of the community enjoying the special protective status of the divine husband/patron. Already the composition creates a world that founds national existence and security — that is, the freedom from "poaching" appropriate to sacral national status ("holy," "[Yahweh's] first fruits") — within a matrix of cultic purity and fidelity.

But the MT has subtly introduced the reference to the wilderness sojourn into its performance of the tradition at the same time that it more explicitly draws in the implicit audience from the margins of the dramatic scene. The LXXV has for 2:2b only "How you followed me, oracle of Yahweh" (MT, "How you followed me in the wilderness, in a land not sown"). And instead of the laconic LXXV in v. 2a, "and he said," the MT expands: "The word of Yahweh came to me, saying, 'Go and announce in the hearing of Jerusalem, saying.'" The MT is clearly intent on parsing the marital metaphor in political terms. It does so in advance of the oracle by concretizing its "historical" occasion and dramatic audience. Within the oracle it does the same by referring a period of the marriage to national myth, allegorizing the marriage and the cult history of the nation as parallel.

The Failure of Yahweh's Love (2:4–3:5)

The idyllic turns sour. The husband rages in his pained harangue. The alternation of genders organizes the following units in which the harangue finally climaxes in irrevocable divorce. The cuckold relives scenes of his wife's lurid sexual escapades like some horrified voyeur. The "male" national addressee is written under the sign of sexual dangers to females. Jeremiah, with the rest of the implied audience, the children of the marriage, is seduced into a rhetoric of sympathy for the cuckold. The rhetoric of shame intends the enabling and legitimization of spousal violence under the sign of punishment deserved for egregious infidelities — a violence of last resort in the face of the bride/wife/mother's willful sexual addictions. "I could do nothing else with her. She drove me to it!" Compositional hope lies in the transfer of this "male" ethic, its affectations, and its embroilment in sexual politics to the political horror of Judah's destruction and Babylonian colonization. One horror writes over another in order to efface the mythological crisis of exile under the sign of punishment for egregious cultic sins even as the composition fabricates the myth of *Yahweh-alone*.

The alternating genders of the addressee subdivide the section into four poems: 2:4-16 (male Israel), vv. 17-25 (female Israel), vv. 26-32 (male), and 2:33–3:5 (female). The divine harangue catalogs the crimes of the two personae (who are actually one) as well as God's failure to turn Israel from its infidelities.

In the poems addressing the male persona, the crimes are explicitly national-political-cultic in nature. At its core, the entire national community is guilty of "idolatry," from the leadership down to individual citizens (2:13, 27, 28). All of Yahweh's efforts to prevent this have been to no avail (v. 30). The two poems (vv. 4-16, 26-32) here project a national history of infidelity and rebellion that has finally climaxed in political defeat and national destruction (vv. 14-16, 26). The great rebellion began early in their history — as soon as the "exodus" generation entered the land — and it has continued unabated into the present (vv. 7, 32). A theodicy of Judean destruction is laid at the feet of cultic impurity — the failure to practice a religion of *Yahweh-alone*.

In a similar fashion, Yahweh rings the charges against his wife Israel (2:17-25, 33-37 and 3:1-5) as the reverse, the undoing of the husband's now dashed boasts (2:2-3). In the rage of his long harangue lies embedded his pain, his mourning, his longing for the lost devotion of his spouse and the exclusive loyalty enjoyed in the early days of their marriage. Except that in the case of the female persona, the accusations are more lurid, the cultic sins parsed in terms of sexual politics. Political-cultic violations of the religion of *Yahweh-alone* are written under the sign of adultery (vv. 20, 23, 24, 33; 3:1-3) — adultery of the most egregious kind! For the sexual appetite of the wife has known no bounds or restraints. She is a madam of whores (v. 33)! Her sexual escapades and addictions operate at the level of uncontrollable animal lusts (vv. 24, 25). As with the male persona, there has been a long history of the husband seeking to do everything in his power to win his wife's exclusive love. But these efforts have proved fruitless, falling on deaf ears (vv. 20-22, 25; 3:3). The theodicy writes over the horror of national destruction. It transfigures the pain and shame of colonization under the sign of a lewd, nymphomaniac wife rejected by her cuckolded husband and exposed to rape and abuse by her former paramours. Her fate is the consequence of her own self-inflicted suffering (2:19, 36, 37). "She was asking for it!"

The divine patron/spouse places self-incriminating citations on the lips of the accused and thus offers a psychology of nation/wife Israel as perceived by the enraged Deity/husband. The male persona has failed to remember their Yahwistic patron heralded in exodus traditions (2:6, 8, "they did not say . . ."). Instead, they profess cultic devotion to stone and tree (v. 27, "they say . . ."). Worse, they have pledged/refused to participate in Yahwistic cult never/ever again (v. 31, "my people say: 'Let us go down; we will never come to you again'").

More attention is lavished on the psychology of the female persona. In addition, compositional obsession with its sexual metaphor plays itself out in the alternative performances offered by the LXXV and the MT. The adulterous wife declares her intention to practice infidelity (2:20, "I will not serve") and yet lives in denial of her guilt (v. 23, "I have not sinned, after the *ba'alim* I have not gone"). Nevertheless, in the grip of her sexual addictions she can only respond to her husband Yahweh's appeals by professing the uselessness of her reform (v. 25, "Useless, no, for I love strangers; after them I must go"). Unstable in her self-awareness, she persists in the presumption of innocence and the forgiving love of her husband: "I am innocent; surely his anger has turned away from me. . . . I have not sinned" (2:35); "My father, the friend of my youth you are; will he keep anger forever, will he retain wrath with no end?" (3:4-5).

While both the LXXV and the MT direct their efforts to parsing the marital in terms of the national application and while both seek to perform the female persona in an effort to ruin her image, to render her as unsympathetically as possible, the details shimmer between the two performances. At 2:16 the MT has adjusted the image to the political ("they have grazed/broken the crown of your head") — a reference to the Israelite monarchy — while the LXXV preserves the sexual imagery ("they have known [sexually] and trifled with you"). In 3:1-5, both the MT and the LXXV are under influence of Deut 24:1-4. But the MT focuses on the pollution and ruin of the land as a result of wife Israel's adultery: "Would not that land be utterly defiled?" (3:1); "the showers have been withheld, and the spring rain has not come" (v. 3). Contrast the LXXV: "Would not that woman be utterly defiled?" (v. 1); v. 3, "your many shepherds have been your snare" (v. 3). In the latter case the LXXV has adjusted the image toward its political application while retaining sexual connotations.

To further characterize wife Israel's egregious character, both the MT and the LXXV will take turns extending her citations. At v. 2:20 the LXXV expands the MT, "I will not serve!" to include, "Indeed, I will go up on every high hill and under every luxuriant tree; there will I spread in my harlotry." At v. 25 the tables turn. The MT extends the LXXV's "Useless," to "Useless, no, for I love strangers; after them I will go." Where the alternative performances cannot ruin the wife's image in direct citation, they alter instead her cosmetic presentation. It is the MT's performance that introduces the images of animal sexual obsessions (vv. 23-24, the she camel and wild ass in heat), replacing the LXXV's "In the evening she cries; she enlarges her ways by the waters in the desert." Perhaps the latter refers to an isolated, uninhabited location of the desert as the place for her adulterous trysts (cf. Cant 8:5 and 3:6). Finally, the MT transforms the faithless wife into a sex expert, a "madam" of whores (2:33): "so that even to wicked women you have taught your ways." Contrast the LXXV: "'Not so!' except you acted wickedly by defiling your way."

In the face of such an egregious character, the last unit ends the harangue in "legal" contemplation of an irrevocable divorce. However wife Israel might seek to take up cohabitation again with her cheated husband, the husband is bound not to for fear of deeper pollution (3:1; cf. Deut 24:1-4). Does the cuckolded Yahweh now perceive such intention on the part of his adulterous wife? Possibly (3:1, ". . . would you return to me?"). Even so, he does not look for an end to her sexual escapades — only a continuation of her delusions and sexual addictions with their accompanying rationalizations (3:2-5). That marriage is over.

Yahwistic Longings in the Aftermath of Divorce (3:6-25; 4:1-2)

The divorce may be final, but the matter apparently is not settled in the mind of the jilted divine husband. He remains obsessed with the affair. The themes of sexual politics and cultic violation continue from the preceding section, but not its structure of alternating units of gendered addressee. The reader is now drawn to the aftermath of the divorce. Multiple addressees appear, some drawn in from the margins of the preceding section to take on more significance here: Jeremiah (3:6-12), female Israel (vv. 12-13), male/female Israel (vv. 19-20), the male children of the marriage (vv. 14-18, 21-22; 4:1-2), and Yahweh (vv. 22-25). Prose mixes with poetry (prose — vv. 6-12a, 15-18, 24-25; poetry — vv. 12b-14, 19-23 and 4:1-2). Interestingly, the prose creates a dramatic "historical" setting within the reign of Josiah (the only attempt to locate any specific section of the Jeremianic tradition within that reign — apart from the generalized rubric at 1:1). Along with the multiplication of addressees — eventually representing a shift from exclusive monologue on the part of the divine patron/husband — it enhances the dramatic construction of generational stratification and displacement for the implied audience of the composition.

The distraught husband turns to Jeremiah (3:6) as if to a confidant to complain of his ill treatment at the hands of his wife only to reveal that this is not his first failure at marriage (vv. 6-7). There was another — a sister to his second (the designation of the two wives as sisters is a feature of the MT performance; the LXXV consistently lacks them [vv. 7, 8, 10]; cf. Ezek 16:46-63; perhaps the latter passage is the source of the MT's narrative elaboration)! She, too, had cuckolded him. The second had learned nothing from his treatment of her sister — that he had indeed been willing to punish the first wife with divorce. In fact, the escapades of the latter render the former an innocent by comparison (3:11)! Neither wife had been willing to turn from her paramours in order to return to him. The twice-burned husband regarded even the second wife's posture of return as mere gesture, deceitful proffers (vv. 8-10). He dismissed them out of hand. Now fresh from renewed marital pain and the loss of his second wife, he implores his friend, Jeremiah, to seek the return of the first on condition that she simply acknowledge her guilt (vv. 12-13). Intriguingly, he will now permit the rhetoric of forgiveness so easily ignored when on the lips of "faithless Judah" (vv. 7, 8, 10, 11; cf. v. 5). Apparently sister "wayward Israel" (vv. 6, 8, 11, 12) is no longer as reprehensible an option for love.

But the reader hears nothing concerning her response. The distraught husband turns instead to the children, the sons of his failed marriages. The wives are lost to the past, though he can still mourn his shattered hopes for the marriage (3:19). Yahweh turns to his surviving children in the present to plead their return (vv. 14-18, 22a). A restoration to harmonious family relations is promised without precondition (vv. 14, 22a).

The composition parses restoration in terms of return from national exile and the creation of transfigured leadership — a leadership (monarchy?) capable of securing national existence and well-being (3:14-15). Restoration takes in Jerusalem's reversal of world fortune, for it becomes the center of Yahweh's worldwide imperial reign, with the nations subject and submissive to Yahwistic rule (v. 17). The colonized will colonize the world! Even the fracturing of the Davidic regime into Judah and Israel will be healed in this diasporan return (v. 18).

Curiously, the restoration utopia promised Yahweh's sons dispenses with an aspect of the older generation's Yahwistic cult — the ark of the covenant of Yahweh is abandoned to the past (3:16). Do the restoration dreams of the composition expose a mythic abyss facing the cult of *Yahweh-alone*? Do they face down a barrier to their restoration of the cult and myth of Yahweh in the "practical" absence of continuity with the accouterments of the old Judean Yahwistic cult? Or do they hint at a newly discerned impropriety in the old generation's cultic practice — that is, an illicit Yahwistic faith? These are all symbolic anxieties exercising the elite performers of the Jeremiah scroll — anxieties they will repeatedly have to face down in their effort to rewrite a myth of *Yahweh-alone*. But while so much of the compositional performance lies ahead, such symbolic aporia rise less apparently to the surface in the present context. Instead, as v. 17 might imply, the old ark, as the throne/footstool of Yahweh, finds displacement in its transfiguration. For the entire city becomes Yahweh's throne over the world.

The section closes, however, with a significant change of speaker. Yahweh's wives remain mute, divorced to the past. But the sons now dramatize their acknowledgment of father Yahweh's lesson in sexual/cultic politics (3:20). They enact the penitence which Yahweh's wives never exhibit (vv. 21-25). A family reunion in play, the father accepts the sons back into the fold on condition of the integrity of their return founded in the practice of a religion of *Yahweh-alone* (4:1-2).

Evaluation

The composition has rhetorical designs upon its implied audience for whom it constructs the outline and hint of an identity within the folds of its symbolic performance. Dramatized both as the citizens of Jerusalem and the children of Yahweh's faithless wives, the implied audience is repeatedly placed and replaced in relation to the narrative arc of the marital metaphor and in relation to the temporal fall of Judah/Jerusalem.

Led through a rehearsal of the father's account of the marriage, the sons are offered a rhetoric of sympathy for husband Yahweh. Playing on "male" sympathies and anxieties, the composition renders female sexual passions the metaphorical scapegoat, justifying the destruction of the old Judean Davidic state. Given the cultural regimes of sexual politics regnant in Israelite old world culture, the gender symbolism can serve the construction of an effective rhetoric of shame. The composition projects an implied reader in need of a theodicy for the destruction of Judah. On the surface the marital metaphor and sexual politics address men about women and cast the reader as male in their exploitation of the gender symbols. The performance of the female persona enhances this effect. Given her unsympathetic presentation and her disfigurement, the children are left no choice but to side with their father's version of the world.

But a theodicy shielding the reader from the failure of God is not enough. To rehabilitate the myth of Yahweh is also to lay the ground for utopian dreams of a restoration of cultural power. Thus the composition also projects a reader as the object/subject of restoration devices and desires. Hence the rhetoric of perennial erotic dangers recasts the reader as female in its performance of the marital narrative. For the narrative arc of the metaphor places the children of Yahweh's faithless wives in a plot development on the other side of the divorce/exile where they are once again subject to a renewed appeal for reconciliation by the father. As such they are offered a rhetoric of erotic danger. As the dramatized objects of restoration, they too are displaced and replaced into the structural location of the female — 2:31 taken as an apostrophe to the implied audience: "You are the generation, acknowledge the oracle of Yahweh" (MT; cf. LXXV, "Hear the word of Yahweh; thus says Yahweh"). The children, the implied audience, relive the crisis of unfaithful female passions. Her passions not only serve to vindicate her violent treatment at the hands of her jilted husband but also threaten to break out again and again within her children (4:1-2). The composition constructs a rhetoric of fear to inflame restoration passions and keep a crisis ethos alive, as well as an ethic attendant to it.

To prevent the death of restoration dreams, the return to cultural power of the colonized elite and their client community, the "heirs" to Israel must suppress the failure of *Yahweh-alone* in the downfall of the old Davidic state. Thus they rewrite the myth of Yahweh advocating the religion of *Yahweh-alone* as the original religion of Israel. They make the latter the strict ground of any national future. Into this rewritten and repristinated myth of Yahweh, they must deeply embed the psychology of sexual politics of marriage in the effort to rationalize the apparent God-forsakenness of enduring Judean colonization. The Jeremiah tradition is not the first to make mythological capital on sexual symbolism in Israel (cf.

Hosea 1–3, upon which Jeremiah depends). But "Jeremiah" rewrites his tradition, rearranges its traditional plot, or omits characteristic features in service to his generational polemic. The wives cannot become the subjects of restoration (contrast Hos 2:18-25). For they represent an old regime (parsing the marital metaphor in political terms) that must be disenfranchised at all costs, scapegoated as the exclusive culprits of Judah's demolition, whose religion of Yahweh represents a corruption of the religion of *Yahweh-alone.* The claim to Israel and the myth of Yahweh belongs to their children alone, the generation of the cultural elite performing Jeremiah for themselves alone.

The rhetorical moves on display in chs. 2–3 (4:2) anticipate subsequent symbolic strategies repeatedly encountered in the rest of the Jeremiah scroll. Increasingly, they will also expose aporia haunting compositional symbolic needs, launch new cycles of mythological anxiety, and threaten to dismantle the rehabilitation of Yahweh so necessitated by their effort to revitalize cultural power.

For the marital metaphor constructs an interior landscape for Yahweh as irrational and unstable as any "male's" — and might one also say equivalent to a whole pantheon of Near Eastern claimants to divinity! This interior landscape of Yahwistic passions "polytheizes" the psychology of *Yahweh-alone.* The high price of *Yahweh-alone* will require many symbolic compensations.

For *Yahweh-alone* has secrets to keep! An alternate account of the "marriage" is hidden in the margins of husband Yahweh's tirade — no matter how appealing the image of a suffering Deity, losing at love, might be. Perhaps the affective volume of the latter and its overwhelming emphasis on monologue are designed to suppress this "other" account. In a story that Yahweh's savaged wives — for Yahweh is twice the loser at love — might tell, true blame for the failure of the marriage might lie at the "feet" of this metaphorical husband — a character whose initial loving attentiveness went the way of profound character dysfunction. In time he degenerated into paranoid fits of jealousy and became increasingly controlling, vindictive, violent, and abusive. Yahweh's women were driven into the arms of other divine paramours as a result of Yahwistic dysfunction and failure. Or perhaps the secret is worse than that. Perhaps old Israel did indeed find sources of power in her other "divine" paramours — patrons alongside Yahweh from the very first. *Yahweh-alone* was insufficient amidst the global polytheistic struggle of nations.

Jeremiah 4:3–6:30

Overview

War. The brutal realities of imperial politics would have been very familiar to the Judean colony of the postexilic period — familiar, for that matter, throughout the entire history of ancient Israelite politics. In 4:3–6:31, the prophetic rhetoric captures those brutal imperial realities to create an imaginary landscape with the Judean state subject to an invading military force from the north. Presumably, the historical prophet had the Babylonian imperial military machine in mind. But nowhere does the poetry seek historical or chronological specificity. No doubt the horror of the inpouring chaos receives heightened effect. In any case, post-598/597 editors and readers of the prophetic tradition would easily have connected the "fantastic" military descriptions in the poetic discourse with the events of 598/597 and subsequently also with those of 587/586, when the armies of Nebuchadrezzar destroyed Jerusalem.

The prophetic rhetoric mythologizes the realities of Judah's historical experience by linking the demise of Judah's political independence with the deeds and desires of Israel's divinity, Yahweh. For the myth of Israel digests these political events as an act of punishment by her national deity, a punishment meted out for Israel's failure to practice cultic exclusivity — to worship *Yahweh-alone.* Never mind that such an interpretation represents an innovation on the part of those traditionalist social elements for which the prophet spoke (both historically and later merely symbolically). This is an anachronistic religious innovation since the polytheistic matrix of late preexilic Judah would not have uniformly understood the demand for cultic exclusivity as part of the necessary configuration for the central nationalist cult. The preexilic perception of Yahwistic "orthodoxy" would have been otherwise. In the prophetic rhetoric we discern the clash of competing Yahwistic visions seeking hegemony in Israel's ideological horizon.

This act of mythologization by the Jeremiah tradition is at home with the traditions of polytheistic hermeneutics in the ancient Near East, at least partially. For the wars for imperial rule represent the statecraft of competing nationalist deities. The irony in Jeremiah's discourse is that Israel's own divine patron has turned against it. On the surface, the prophet's rhetoric represents ideological heresy for his own culture's vested interests. At least this is how it looked to competing Yahwistic voices among Israel's cultural elite.

Dramatic Composition

If, for the moment, a modern reader were to don the strategies of a traditional form critic, he or she would easily discern the presence of the normal tropes, themes, and rhetoric of prophetic judgment speech. Yet the division of the collection into subunits would remain very problematic; discernment of an organizing rationale on form-critical grounds would remain elusive. For on the surface, the form-critical reader encounters a jumble of whole oracles with oracle fragments as well as sporadic prose intrusions. If the oral forms postulated for prophetic speech ever truly existed in ancient Israelite prophetic culture, surely here in the Jeremiah tradition they have been fragmented, malformed, and reformed by some type of editorial strategy whose rationale has constituted the definitive reading problem for modern biblical scholarship. In broad strokes, redaction criticism has proved to be a more successful reading strategy, at least in the sense of discerning a compositional tendency aimed at theodicy. And yet this has not always proved fruitful when it comes to reading the specifics of this compositional block. Granted the presence of the theodicy theme, how are we to account for the present structure of the tradition aimed at service to it?

Clearly the dominant image, the root metaphor of this literary block is that of the invading military force from the north. Unlike the pattern in 2:1–4:2, there appears to be no attempt to narratize this metaphor. There are dramatic scenes of an invading army, portrayals of a siege operation, and portrayals of the predicted outcome, but, nevertheless, no attempt to arrange them in a discernible, coherently structured plot. Echoes of the female imagery are maintained, for often the addressee is dramatized as daughter Zion. Yet full characterization, or at least as full a characterization as in the previous literary block, is not executed.

Indeed, citations multiply the presence of diverse dramatic voices, which in turn complicate point of view. Of particular interest is the increased attention to the dramatization of Jeremiah's role vis-à-vis the community and vis-à- vis the Deity. All these voices cluster around the narration of these "little scenes" of invasion. Here lies the clue to penetrating compositional rationale and its rhetorical, persuasive interests.

Dramatic tone focuses on imminent threat and alarm. It portrays a community under siege. Thematically and rhetorically the "central" dramatic voice seeks to persuade its audience of the necessity, inevitability, and legitimacy of Jerusalem's fall. The destruction of the community is divine punishment. The true enemy of the people is not the external invader; rather, it is the religious corruption of internal leadership accompanied by the general religious infidelity of the whole community. The death of the community is considered a *fait accompli* in essence. In fact, the poet understands his oracular mission as one of "singing" the death of the community into being. For the poet no route forward exists except through this communal death.

Yet a contrary, dissonant voice to the preceding dominant one occurs; it, too, is ranked "above" the other dramatic voices — those, that is, which do not participate in oracular privilege. There are appeals for repentance to fend off the calamity; there are assertions that the destruction will not be total. The correlation of these dissonant voices with each other — for they share equal oracular privilege — constitutes a major challenge for the reader. If the reader is to unravel this problem, he or she will first have to turn to the construction of the various dramatic personae employed.

Ineluctable Yahwistic Terror (4:3-31)

The little scenes of invasion and national devastation (4:5-7, 11-12, 13a, 15-17, 19-22, 23-28, 29) construct a blended addressee imagining the dramatic audience, clearly identified as the citizens of Jerusalem/Judah, as a masculine plural collective (explicit address — vv. 5-6, 8; pronominal reference — vv. 12, 22; and direct citation — vv. 5, 6, 8, 13) and as the feminine singular lady Jerusalem/daughter Zion (explicit address — vv. 7, 11, 14, 17, 18; pronominal reference — vv. 7, 14, 17-18; and direct citation — v. 31).

It is about responses — the response actually made by the addressees versus the one desired by the principal speaker, Yahweh. It is about the responses of Yahweh to the latter. And, finally, it is about the prophet's response to oracular deceptions entailed in Yahweh's war.

Within the narrative scene of the invasion, only one response, mourning (4:8, 13b, 28), is enjoined or occurs. It signals the irrevocable, absolute fate of national defeat and colonization before Yahweh's invading army (v. 6b, "I am bringing calamity from the north . . ."). The community may flee for security to their fortifications (v. 5b, "Gather together! Let us enter the fortified city"; v. 6a, "raise the standard . . . take refuge, do not delay!"). But the outcome is a foregone conclusion given the overwhelming force descending upon the community (vv. 7, 11-12, 13, 16, 20). All that is left is the cry of defeat and the knowledge of divine wrath (v. 8, "Yahweh's burning wrath has not turned away . . ."; v. 13, "woe to us, for we are destroyed"; v. 31, "woe to me, for I faint because of slaughterers").

Yahweh is adamant about the irrevocable, ineluctable, total destruction (4:28, "I have spoken, I have purposed; I will not repent or turn away from it"). The prophet has a vision depicting nothing short of the complete undoing or unmaking of creation (vv. 23-26), which Yahweh quickly interprets and applies to the national fate (v. 27a). The rationale for so terrible a punishment remains laconic. Yahweh relies on clichés and tropes already signaled by the metaphor of sexual politics in chs. 2–3 (cf. 4:18) or, equally opaque, the rhetoric of folly (4:22). Both continue to project Yahweh's perspective that the community is incorrigible. All that is left is his taunting witness chastising his wife for continuing her "sexual" schemes of seduction even in the midst of her imminent demolition, her rape (4:30). It is she who has courted death to the last!

It can come, then, only as a surprise to find the prophet Jeremiah drawn at 4:10 into dispute with Yahweh over oracular power: "Ah, Lord Yahweh, surely you have utterly deceived this people and Jerusalem, saying, 'Peace you will have,' while a sword reaches the throat." Even more surprising are explicit appeals for communal repentance (vv. 3-4, ms. pl. addressee; v. 17, fm. sg. addressee). And most astonishing of all is the presence of divine grief and lamentation (vv. 19-22), even the promise of ameliorated destruction, Yahweh's other expostulations to the contrary (v. 27b, "but a complete end I will not make"; contrast v. 28). On the surface such moves place the theodicy argument at risk.

Too potent to remain in repression, there are aporia the composition feels compelled to embrace in the effort to blunt their power. The pain of God over the destruction of "Israel" is designed to mask the pain over God everywhere driving the performance of the Jeremiah tradition. The divine lament (4:19-22) projects a conflicted interior space in Yahweh. It mythologizes a psychology of patriarchy faced with threats to its social power. It sustains the "innocence" of God, torn over the destruction of the community, his patrimony, yet forced to these extreme measures in the face of egregious cultural folly (v. 22). In so doing, the composition seeks to rehabilitate the myth of Yahweh through a rhetoric of sympathy, the latter rationalizing cultural destruction and colonization under the sign of a Deity left without any other psychological options. The composition also lays the ground in these conflicted divine passions for the reappropriation of hope later in the scroll even as it deeply anchors patriarchal psychology within Yahwistic myth.

Such desires for restoration require additional symbolic exertions even as they risk divine coherence and fracture Yahwistic unity. If Yahweh is so resolved on destruction, why the appeal for repentance? Perhaps the appeal at 4:14 (2d fm. sg. addressee) can be written off given Yahweh's characterization of lady Jerusalem and his pessimism over the possibility of her reformation. As a formal appeal, then, it sustains the appearance of Yahwistic innocence, fidelity until he is left no other recourse but to abandon her to cultural rape.

But the opening appeal at 4:3-4 is addressed to a "male" persona (2d ms. pl. addressee) identified explicitly as the men of Judah and inhabitants of Jerusalem. This renewed call for repentance comes as a transitional move from the prior section (2:1–4:2) on the heels of the contingent familial reunion offered husband Yahweh's returning sons (dramatic constructs of the implicit audience, the generation on the other side of national destruction). If that dramatic persona continues here and the opening summons is taken as an introduction to the fantastic landscape of Yahweh's war against Israel, does it not (along with 4:27b) subvert the hopelessness of the terror streaming into the land from the north? The dramatized war and its theodicy apologetic become transfigured into a morality tale for the implicit audience, the survivors. They are placed again and again into the symbolic crisis of Yahwistic threat "lest the fire of my wrath breaks out . . ." (v. 4b). Elite desires for revitalization write themselves and the client community they seek to enlist under the sign of the myth of exile and return. They anchor the security of "Israel" in communal fulfillment of the Deuteronomic ideal, a utopian self-transformation where they become the true circumcision to *Yahweh-alone* (cf. Deut 10:16; 30:6). And Jeremianic oracular power is made to exploit a theology of repentance in order to tame oracular pessimism and fatalism. The latter, along with the rhetoric of unrelenting annihilation, is rendered oracular hyperbole, thus loading all blame on the religious failure of the old Davidic state. The failure of Yahweh can be masked even as Jeremiah deconstructs Jeremiah.

This, however, embraces another aporia that exercises the entire composition — the failure of oracular power faced with conflicted oracular claims. Thus Jeremiah resists and disputes Yahweh's oracular performance. He can cite a counter-Yahwistic oracular tradition (4:10) — an oracular tradition that the old regime relied upon to their destruction (v. 9)! At this juncture the composition lets stand the irony of Jeremianic oracular power disputing the mission of doom. Jeremiah pits prophecy against prophecy, even Jeremiah against Jeremiah!

Such conflicted space within the myth of oracular power only deepens the cultural abyss encountered in the fall of the old regime. For the specter of Yahwistic deceit threatens the moral blamelessness of God upon which the theodicy apologetic hangs. The composition begins to construct a world in which not all claimants to Yahwistic oracular power are equal. They will also represent a world where oracular themes and traditions are distributed in applicability relative to "party" affiliations. In the process the claims of *Yahweh-alone* are factionalized, and the composition expropriates oracular power from "Jeremiah" to the compositional elite that "wield" him!

And yet Jeremiah protests a form of Yahwistic oracular power that proves an effective opiate as the old regime rushes to its doom. Does Jeremiah assume a myth of prophecy and an oracular mission for himself other than his songs of death indicate? Does he include himself among the prophets dismayed (4:9) by the outcome of events — events that proved capable of defeating the prophetic will to power to the contrary? The composition will increasingly dramatize Jeremianic self-conflict in its effort to suppress aporia present to their myth of oracular power. For whether Jeremiah proclaims irrevocable doom or temporizes national destiny and oracular contingency in the face of a summons to repent — or even absent the Jeremianic mission for his oracular antipole ("you will have peace"), it still comes to the same ineffaceable result. The old Davidic regime falls prey to Babylonian imperial aspirations. How can restoration dreams sustain the myth of oracular control and the efficacy of Yahwistic agency in the face of such a historical abyss?

Unpardonable Yahwistic Failure (5:1-31)

The composition must root out any suggestion of pardonable innocence within the predestruction community. The voice of resistance to the message of doom raised initially on the lips of the prophet (4:10) must be disputed and refuted no matter which of the dramatic or implicit addressees are imagined to give "voice" to it.

The imagery of destruction continues to rely on little narrative depictions of the invading army (5:6a, 10, 15-17) whose power is bestial (v. 6a), overpowering, insurmountable, inescapably all-devouring (vv. 15-17). Israel is the vineyard to be destroyed and burned (v. 10). In contrast to 4:3-31, which was laconic toward the description of national crimes, ch. 5 articulates national corruption at length: the citizenry are more than ignorant of Yahweh's social order. Rather, they are obdurately opposed and insubordinate to God's yoke with rebellions too numerous to number (vv. 5b, 6b). Below such generalized moral rhetoric, little narratives depict the social corruption in action and point to a dysfunctional social order characterized by idolatry (v. 19), sexual license, and adultery (vv. 7-8), a society approving elite victimization of the weak and the perversion of justice (vv. 26-28, using motifs drawn from the characterization of the wicked in the Psalter) with the collusion of religious authorities (vv. 30-31).

The indictment of the community is totalizing. The whole citizenry is implicated without exception. Citations placed in the mouth of the communal voice exemplify their obdurate wickedness at work: possessed by a false sense of security, they deny prophetic warnings of the coming invasion (5:11-13). Constitutionally they have become incapable of taking to heart the God proclaimed in hymnic tradition (vv. 20-25; cf. especially v. 24, "They do not say, 'Let us fear Yahweh . . .'"). Picking up the wisdom motif of wickedness equivalent to folly, the composition develops at length a theme only broached in 4:22. Thus the effort to secure their penitence fails (5:21b, 25; cf. v. 3). Yahweh completely distrusts any communal invocation of his name — the latter only deepens their communal corruption (v. 2). The possibility of any divine clemency is excluded (v. 7; n.b. the only point in ch. 5 at which the female persona, the mother of the corrupt sons, is directly addressed). The absence of the mourning songs and dirges that appeared in ch. 4 underlines the pitilessness of the communal character and destiny.

The compositional argument is repeated three times across the section (5:1-9, 10-19, 20-29), underlining its dogmatic intransigence and insisting on its version of history and religion. The first and third cycle repeat the refrain, "Must I not take vengeance on a nation such as this?" It sounds the note of moral obligation on Yahweh's part to render such a community its due even as it universalizes a divine moral order in which Israel, one nation among many, experiences a fate based on the same standards by which all must be judged. The middle cycle turns from the generation of doom to address the generation of exilic survivors (vv. 18-19). It renders explicit the theodicy apologetic (v. 18, "Why has Yahweh our God done all these things to us?"), driving the compositional defense of Yahweh before the national destruction and colonization of Israel by rationalizing its necessity in the obdurate religious apostasy of the old regime.

Perhaps explicit evocation of the implied audience here in 5:18-19 can clarify the ambiguity in the dramatic addressees elsewhere in ch. 5. This subsection opens with instruction to an unidentified second masculine plural to enact a Diogenes-like search through the community for the presence of at least one righteous person. If such a person could be found, God might pardon the entire nation (v. 1; and therefore shield Judah from Babylonian imperial encroachment?). The report of the search results, however, shifts to an unidentified first masculine singular dramatic speaker, with Yahweh now the addressee (vv. 3-5). It is attractive to identify the latter speaker as the prophet and the unit as a dramatization of his prophetic mission. As such it would be in keeping with the dispute between the prophet and God broached in 4:10 but not developed. The prophet must be persuaded of the justice and legitimacy of unavoidable national destruction.

Who, then, are the referents of the second masculine plural address? A reader could leave them indeterminate, with the prophet the individual who has taken up the collective charge. Or perhaps they are to be connected with the second masculine plural addressed in 5:10, the invaders enjoined to destroy the vineyard. V. 1 would then imagine them charged with the task of communal inspection before they are allowed to begin the work of destruction. In vv. 3-5 the prophet has participated with them and reports the failure to find any basis for pardon. Then, again, they might be the implicit audience invoked at vv. 18-19 as witnesses of the divine justice. On this reading the composition continues to carry forward the dramatization of the "exilic" generation as children of the marriage from 2:1–4:2 into 4:3-31 as the "readers" of a morality tale enjoined to a theology of repentance and now into 5:1-31 as subjects of a theodicy rhetoric that argues the failure of penitence within the old regime.

That such a complicated alteration and blend of dramatic addressee can occur is nothing new for compositional strategy. It appears again in 5:10-17: the invading force (v. 10; 2d ms. pl.), the citation of the community (vv. 12-13; 1st person pl.), the response to the citation (v. 14a, "because you said . . ."; 2d ms. pl.), the prophet (v. 14b, "I place my words in your mouth . . ."; 2d ms. sg.), the community (v. 15, "I bring against you . . ."; 2d ms. pl. and 2d ms. sg. in vv. 15b-17).

The failure of this mission — to surface a basis for pardon — carried out by the prophet as dramatic proxy for the implicit audience transfigures the Jeremianic mission. Jeremiah's oracular power becomes the very mechanism of destruction, the devouring fire (5:14b). Jeremianic oracular power constitutes Yahweh's agency of national destruction parallel to and controlling the invading terror from the north (cf. v. 14b, "Behold, I set my words . . . ," to v. 15, "Behold, I bring against you a nation . . ."). The fire of the prophetic word devours the community just as the invading nation will eat them up like spoil (note the repetitions of the verb "to eat" throughout vv. 14-17). The search to find one righteous person (v. 1, "if you can find . . .") collapses into its opposite (v. 26, "for there is found . . .").

The corrupt leadership and client community are left with a taunt (5:31): "What will you [2d ms. pl.] do at its [3d fm. sg.] end?" Taken by themselves perhaps the referents of the pronominal address can be easily identified with "my people" and the puzzling feminine suffix on "end" (*'aḥariyt*) referred either to "land" (v. 30) or perhaps read more abstractly through present contextual association with the time of divine visitation (*pequdah*, influenced by use of the verb *paqad* in v. 29). If read with land, the emphasis is placed on the devastation of the existing regime and attendant corrupt social order. But if read with visitation, the emphasis falls on the fulfillment of Jeremiah's prophecy of doom so denied by the counter-Yahwistic tradition (vv. 12-13). But by making vv. 30-31 a conclusion to the three cycles of the subsection, the composition may be effecting a duality in the horizon of the addressee — that is, once again replacing and placing the implicit audience of the exilic and colonized generation under rhetorical challenge faced as they are with the realization of the end of "Israel."

The fantastic landscape of destruction is total. But the existence of survivors as implicit audience turned witnesses of divine justice coupled with bald assertions that the destruction was in fact not total (5:10, 18) opens the door to aporia easily unraveling the force of the colonial elite's polemic.

For one righteous soul, God could have forgiven and spared his kingdom! Why not spare the community for Jeremiah's sake and those among the old regime supportive of him? Why the need to qualify the rhetoric of doom, rendering it oracular hyperbole? Why, then, are there survivors? Why did not the complete destruction, which was prophesied, occur (a circumstance convenient to elite restoration dreams)? Worse than that, the poor whose Yahwistic piety is emphatically denied in 5:1-6 reappear as *innocent* victims in vv. 20-29. Could not Yahweh have relented for their sake? A complete absence of faithful Yahwists in the old regime is not credible, though for the composition those "old believers" may have been Yahwists of the wrong kind. One moment the community is said to disbelieve the prophets (v. 13); the next they are in love with oracular activity (v. 31). Even Jeremiah must wrestle with and entertain the possible legitimacy of a Yahwistic oracular tradition that is confident of national security and divine patronage. The oracular argument of pitiless total doom apparently strains credulity even for its own messenger!

Either way it seems that the community is condemned by the "oracular" voice dominating the composition. The rhetoric of sin hardly dips below the level of sloganeering and does not qualify for concrete evidence. The community is homogenized by polemical hyperbole that delegitimizes the old regime writing over the signs of alternative and/or anterior Yahwistic religions.

When God cannot be to blame, at any cost, the community must be made to pay the bill! In this case theological accounts are settled for the exilic generation on the backs of the "criminal" dead no longer able to speak in their own defense. A brutal Deity pontificates his own innocence at the expense of all other perspectives by constructing a fantastic version of his history with Israel. Such psychologically motivated fictions, remaking the past for its own selfjustification, are not uncommon in the history of cultural world making. But then these are the exertions of faith faced with the unraveling of its mythic symbols caught as they repeatedly are in the exigencies and dissonance of history.

The Failure of Jeremiah's Oracular Assay (6:1-30)

The failure of communal repentance continues to receive thematic interest for the composition as it constructs a theodicy around the ineluctable necessity of divine punishment for the old Davidic regime. A failure in Israelite religion foots the bill for national destruction and colonization.

Two brief poems narrate the central event — the inbreaking of Yahweh's terror from the north (6:1-6a, 22-26). As in the previous subsections, the description of the devastation to be wrought is total. The principal addressee once again is female, lady Jerusalem (v. 2, "daughter Zion"; v. 26, "my daughter people"; vv. 3-6 — 3d fm. sg. pronominal reference; vv. 23b, 25, 26 — 2d fm. sg. address). There are also first person plural citations of the populace making their cry of distress in the midst of the invasion (v. 24), coupled with the recurrence of mourning/dirge motifs from ch. 4 that had disappeared in ch. 5 (v. 26). Taken together, the motifs argue the irrevocable, inescapable destiny of national doom.

One or more units dramatizing the failure of the Jeremianic mission to secure national repentance follow each war poem (6:10-21, 27-30). In vv. 10-12 the prophet complains about national antipathy and moral incapacity before his oracular mission — a surprising admission given the presence once again of the counter-oracular mission touting national security (v. 14, "Peace, peace"; cf. 4:10). The community apparently has no difficulty with Yahwistic oracular power per se but only with Jeremiah's version of it! Triangulated between Yahweh and lady Jerusalem, the prophet represents the bursting receptacle of divine wrath, now wearied in the attempt to restrain it (cf. 4:10). Yahweh instructs him to abandon restraint and to pour out the devastation on the entire population — young and old alike (6:11). Yahweh is determined beyond prophetic persuasion to bring his fist down upon the community (v. 12).

Yahweh's accusation (6:13-15) maintains the incorrigible tenor of the social character, the absence of innocence; the perversion of the entire community by violent greed (v. 13) has subverted Yahwistic institutions of priesthood and prophecy (v. 14). Ironically, the latter now prove sufficient to effect the mirror image of their intended function — v. 19b, "my oracles they do not heed; my instruction they reject." He dramatizes the claim with citations of the community refusing (v. 16b, "we will not walk"; v. 17b, "we will not give heed") the Jeremianic appeal to repentance (vv. 16a, 17a). In a final disputational outburst Yahweh rejects any countersuggestion (notice the direct address "why do you [2d ms. sg.] bring me . . . ?") that the sacrificial cult might provide the hedge against divine wrath and national destruction (v. 20). Ironically, Yahweh denounces Yahwistic institutions! Are the latter the stumbling blocks now effecting the mechanism of national destruction (v. 21)? The "ancient paths" (v. 16) refused, they have become perverted through national schemes (v. 19, "fruit of their schemes") which Yahweh employs to block the national path.

The cycle returns. The second war poem (6:22-26) is followed once again by reflection (vv. 27-30) on the failure of the Jeremianic mission to secure the national revitalization and purification which alone could anchor national existence and security. Jeremiah's oracular power is set the task of refining the community, of separating the dross from the pure silver. But the prophetic assay has failed. All that remains is Yahweh's irrevocable rejection (v. 30). The failure of the Jeremianic mission is designed to exculpate the myth of Yahweh from the destruction of the old regime.

Evaluation

The destruction of Jerusalem, mythologized as theodicy, gathers Israel's dramatic presence locked in dispute over its historical fortunes and chances. The little scenes of the invasion populate the composition with voices gathered under the tropes of sexual rhetoric and imperial politics. The tradition projects an audience for whom the destruction of the community posits the problem of divine justice. To admit the failure of God is to permit the unraveling of Israel's mythic inheritance in service of the restoration interests of the colonial elite. Hence it must stake everything on establishing a picture of the Yahwistic bankruptcy of the old Davidic regime — a community without exception mired in social injustice, violence, and religious impurity. That old regime resolutely rejected the Jeremianic mission for alternative prophetic voices, with the latter aiding and abetting the wholesale corruption of the general leadership. All blame and shame are placed squarely on the religious and social failure of the community. For the composition, it was the latter's Yahwistic fidelity, not God's, which was and remains the key issue. The destruction and colonization of "Israel," God's act of punishment, comes as a last resort. The divine hand was forced. Through the Jeremianic oracular mission every effort was made to turn the community back from its chosen path of self-destruction. In that context, their doom became assured.

The composition has had to offer a fantastic landscape that carries within its argument the seeds of its own refutation. This is no doubt a contribution of two factors: first, the writers have had to build their performance of "Jeremiah" out of disparate "oracular" materials all represented as Jeremianic in origin. As a consequence they must repeatedly transfigure these traditional materials disengaged as they are from their "original" occasions but which now come to them as a blend of variant viewpoints and which pose repeated inconcinnities to its reader, who must navigate the sense of the whole. Second and more importantly, the performance deconstructs itself under pressure of the cultural and symbolic anxiety afflicting the tradition as it seeks to assert its religious way conscious of the thin tissue of its rhetoric.

For the composition is unable to suppress the existence of an alternative Yahwistic oracular tradition resistant to Jeremianic oracular posture. Thus it must posit the corruptibility of Yahwistic oracular power itself! Ironically, the composition must represent a myth of revelation that is susceptible to communal interests and desires. The community controls the destiny of oracular power even as the latter asserts its claim to shape communal destiny. Even more surprising in the arena of "Jeremiah" is the inability of the prophet (understood by the composition as the authentic Yahwistic voice) to secure national reform, though he seems quite powerful enough to secure the destruction of the old regime by wielding the foe from the north against any and every countermove on the part of the old regime's will to power!

This inability, of course, brings the representation of the Jeremianic mission under the sign of repentance into collision with the representation of that same mission in ch. 1 as the Yahwistic agent of communal destruction or with the marital metaphor enacted as divorce and violation in chs. 2:1–4:2 or with the tenor of the war poems which map inescapable national doom in 4:3–6. Worse than that, it brings Yahweh into collision with Yahweh. For it is Yahweh himself who enjoins the prophet to both exertions, the latter countermissions of each other. If Yahweh has determined unconditional national woe, why turn this into oracular hyperbole with a mission of repentance. If, on the other hand, Yahweh intends national reform, why weaken the appeal for repentance with overblown calls to alarm. The community indeed appears long nourished in the presumption of divine patronage (4:10) and the reliability of divine compassion and long-suffering (cf. 2:35; 3:4-5 to 5:12; 6:14, 20). The citations project a community that believes it has fulfilled the conditions for retaining divine favor (5:2). And even Yahweh believes in his ability to forgive (cf. 3:12). The summons to repent implies as much. A Jeremianic oracular mission proclaiming irrevocable, complete national rejection and abandonment could appear nothing more than incredible — the very perversion of Yahwistic oracular power! Thus Jeremiah himself must protest his own mission (4:10)! And even Yahweh speaks against the Yahwistic intention of the un-creation of Israel (4:23-27a) — "I will not make a full end" (4:27b)!

Conflicted Yahwistic voices face the composition's readers with choices. Either they can see the rhetoric of doom as hyperbole — a rhetorical shock tactic — designed to provoke terrified compliance with the summons to repent, or they can read the rhetoric of repentance as a pessimistic gesture. Its presence, then, provides apologetic fodder justifying ineluctable doom because the community failed to heed the divine oracular appeal. Or perhaps the reader might suppose a change in the texture of the prophet's message over time faced as he was with resolute rejection — hence the summons to change gives way to proclamation of unconditional doom. Perhaps, too, the emphasis upon the latter represents the exaggeration of the composition wielding Jeremianic oracular traditions on the other side of Judah's collapse and colonization. In the latter case, the reader might as well see the notes of qualified devastation (4:27b) equally as the product of the same fusion of horizons.

Nevertheless, dissonant Yahwistic oracular postures and authority insinuate themselves within the performance of Jeremiah. Which is the reader to privilege over another? And when? The composition may not provide enough guidance to definitively ease a reader's uncertainty, though subsequent compositional negotiations in the scroll will seek to hedge in that uncertainty. But Jeremiah as an arena for the performance of the Jeremianic tradition offers the raw authority of the interpretative community a space which can overcome these aporia in oracular tradition, bending the latter in whatever direction best serves the iconic passions of the moment. Ineluctable aporia are embraced in the effort to reap symbolic compensations in support of ideological factional interests.

Ironically, the oracular tradition deconstructs its bid for authority. Compositional anxiety to the contrary, the oracular tradition cannot fix the future and destiny of the community. For example, does it lie in a predetermined divine decision or does communal penitence radically condition the rhetoric of a settled future? For all the composition's anxiety to anchor the Jeremianic vision as the authoritative one, it cannot prevent a reversal of authority from its myth of oracular power to the receiving community. It projects a world in which the nation lives or dies by the prophetic word. It expects a responsive community to subject itself to this oracular authority. But then the latter shatters on a conflicted Jeremianic mission and the aporia embraced in the dilemma: Is it too late for turning in face of a doom postured as inevitable? A deeper terror presses to the surface — the irrelevance of the myth of Yahweh in the face of "Israel's" historical exigencies.

The symbolic agony of the composition requires the splintering of the myth of Yahweh, and oracular power for it must represent the old Davidic regime's reliance on Yahwistic traditions and institutions as a form of falsehood and communal self-deception in the very act of reasserting the symbolic generative power of those old traditions for restoration interests. In the process it anachronizes new religious moves that rewrite the myth of Yahweh toward cultic exclusivity and *Yahweh-alone* as mediated by the colonial elite who now perform the Jeremianic scroll.

Jeremiah 7:1–10:25

Overview

Death must be managed — it seems at any price — especially when the death of a culture is at issue. Whatever material and symbolic bulwarks were at the disposal of the Judean state elite against the imperial politics of the great powers had proved futile. Now the surviving elite must manage that cultural death for their own sakes and that of their client symbolic communities.

To do so, the composers must enter the arena of surviving traditions and memories to fabricate the fantastic landscape of that old world and, within it, the Jeremianic prophetic mission prior to its collapse. They must perform the Jeremianic tradition to assess the causes of that old world's demise and their prospects in the present as a disenfranchised elite with dreams of a return to cultural power. The historical, cultural defeats and deficiencies of the colonized must have their symbolic compensations. The constitutive imagination of antiquity, as for most human societies, turns to its divinized symbols. Cultural power makes its bid for restoration through recourse to the symbolic battlefield of its cultural gods.

This subsection offers the reader some familiarities based on the compositional strategies employed so far. Disparate tradition elements populate the section with multiple dramatic voices and perspective. The dominant, privileged narrative voice, the voice that appropriates oracular authority, even over the prophet Jeremiah's claims, repeatedly shatters temporal perspective and dramatic distance from the fantastic landscape constructed within the composition. In so doing, the dominant voice constantly puts the reader in relationship to the fantastic death narrated throughout the dramatic scenes. At some points the reader has been placed back into that old dying world, in the very moment of its death. At others, the reader has been removed to the status of a survivor reflecting back on the deceased.

Dramatic Composition

Unlike Jeremiah 2:1–4:2, which pursues a narrative arc (the marital root metaphor) in order to organize the traditional materials into its dramatic scene, chs. 4–6 and 7–10 set little scenes evocative of the invasion at center stage and then multiply voices and reflections around those depictions in interpretative dispute. For chs. 7–10, in contrast to chs. 4–6, it is the funeral song motif that is brought to the fore and around which the apologetic polemics circle. As usual, reading individual pieces in Jeremiah is relatively easier than the attempt to read them all together in the form the tradition has finally taken. Implementation of the military root metaphor without an overarching narrative arc complicates serial reading of the section. Encapsulation of the oracular tradition by prose speech, epexegetical expansions, and liturgical compositions further obfuscates the reading process.

Singing the Death of Jerusalem: Funeral Songs and Mourning Women (8:4-23; 9:1-10, 16-21; 10:17-22)

Funeral songs occupy the center of compositional (or rhetorical) focus (8:18-23; 9:9-10, 16-18, 19-20; 10:19-21). Of course, echoes of invasion scenes so dominant in chs. 4–6 continue (8:14-17; 9:21; 10:17-18, 22). The remainder of the poetic oracles of judgment offer accusations and indictments, the rationale for the former (8:4-7, 8-13; 9:1-5, 6-8).

The surface of the rhetoric is seductively straightforward. The burden of the indictment is to locate all blame for the death of Jerusalem on Jeremiah's generation and their complete failure to acknowledge Yahweh by maintaining the appropriate cultic and social order. Any claims to the contrary are undermined by the vocabulary of deceit and falsehood piled up in the characterization of the community and its leadership. At points the characterization of the community repeats or echoes the vocabulary, motifs, and tropes used to describe the stereotypical "wicked," the "violent" persecutors of the faithful familiar from the Psalter.

This only extends the tenor of the poetic tradition into this subsection; for it repeats the themes of the poetry in chs. 4–6, advancing the death of the community at the hands of the northern foe. Major dramatic addressees in the poetry are professional female mourners now invited to begin in advance the funeral dirge.

Since this is judgment speech, Yahweh through the prophet remains the principal speaker (both as implied agent and as dramatized speakers). Within this framework, however, dramatic voices are multiplied. In so doing, the horror and chaos of the military invasion, the death of the city, are evoked and disputed; the poetry thus offers multiple points of view in this cacophony of voices, lending depth to its characterization of dramatic personae.

The funeral songs work a certain irony into the rhetoric. For the dramatic setting has them as oracles of the prophet uttered to his generation facing imminent invasion. As dirges in advance of the actual event, they dash all hope of fending off the invading host. This is rhetoric designed to undermine the resolve of resistance. Of course, in the context of the present composition, this very dramatic setting for the oracles is fictional.

The sense of irony increases. Dramatic voices multiply. The prophet distinguishes the divine voice alongside the voices of "my daughter people" and "lady Zion" mourning their fate. All are intertwined in the songs. That the community and personified Mother City would sing such songs is no surprise of characterization (9:16-

18, 19-20; 10:19-21). What does surprise is that the dramatized prophet adds his own voice to theirs (8:18-19a, 21-23). Even more astonishing is the divine voice engaged in mourning (9:9), especially since the preceding funeral song (8:18-23) has Yahweh rejecting (v. 19b) the complaint/petition for healing of his "daughter people" in exile (vv. 19a, 20). It is the latter two who are so bent on pressing the indictment of the community and announcing the inescapable necessity of this death in its portrayal of a generation beyond compassion.

The rhetoric of the mourning daughter people/lady Zion places the tropes of the pious petitioners of the Psalter on their/her lips. Lady Zion will even acknowledge the destruction as her legitimate punishment (10:19). For the reader, these yield a very ironic portrayal in light of the surrounding indictments that repeatedly confess the failure of the prophetic mission to procure the repentance of the community. Should the reader use the characterizations there concerning treachery and deceit to now reread a superficial sincerity into the use of such traditional pious language? Is it only now in the midst of the pain of her judgment that the community is ready to make the "turn" so assiduously desired by the Deity and his prophet? Only now it is too late for turning.

Or do we detect in this display of the piety of the Psalms key evidence to deconstruct the summary, comprehensive, absolute denunciations of Judah's religious bankruptcy? In any case, these aporia reveal the simultaneous power and powerlessness of the prophetic mission and word. The mission could not secure the piety it wanted and thus ward off the death; indeed, the prophetic oracles actually sing the death into being, only to elicit the very piety it so strenuously sought in the mission of repentance. And now in the presence of this death the prophet cannot effectively petition divine compassion toward a healing of the community. Yet Yahweh mourns!

Dismantling the Temple: Prophetic Sermons and Ideal Worshipers (7:1–8:3; 9:11-15, 22-25; 10:1-16, 23-25)

To save Yahweh and his prophet from such aporia and fend off the symbolic abyss so generated, the composition intervenes with prose speeches (7:1–8:3), commentary (9:11-15, 22-25), and liturgical proclamation (10:1-16, 23-25). By framing, surrounding, and interrupting the oracular tradition it seeks to mask such aporia, sustain the theodicy apologetic, and render that tradition amenable to its ideological interests. As a result, cultic purity and communal security are brought to intensified thematic attention.

Temples and their cults focus cultural power, gather and bind cultural anxieties. The desire for an unimpeachable theodicy of the state's destruction now turns to the demise of its temple. Symbolic anxiety must mythologize the event to overcome the religious dissonance generated by it. To do so it must pit one mythos of the temple against another rationalized under the sign of the nation's death. The rhetoric of treachery and deception becomes the coinage of the rationalization. The theodicy cannot afford any allowances for alternative myths; all contenders must be subjugated, declassified, and delegitimated as falsehood and idolatry — even when they are representations of alternative Yahwistic regimes. Rhetorical opponents dramatized or implied in the composition are denied a legitimate place and the possession of a common symbolic heritage.

Prophecy's space is in the temple gate (7:1–8:3). Both the prophet miming Yahweh and his dramatic audience share the myth of the temple as the dwelling place of the divine name. The difference of perspective is over the implication of that ideology. For the dramatic audience, flocking to worship, the temple acts as the guarantor of the divine presence and national protection. The reader is allowed to hear only snatches of this ringing hope directly from the lips of citizens (7:4, "temple of Yahweh"; 7:10, "we are delivered"). The prophet, on the other hand, understands the temple as the repository of threat where communal violations of covenant stipulations occur — echoes of the Decalogue provide the points at issue under stereotyped demands for social justice and purity of worship. The temple is the guarantor of nothing unconditionally; only heeding a summons to cultural reform can offer the much-desired historical security on the plane of ancient Near Eastern imperial politics.

The rhetoric, literary forms, and ideology of the Deuteronomistic literature heavily intersect the prose speeches of Jeremiah. 7:1–8:3, as the largest such block encountered so far, exhibits typical features to be encountered in subsequent speeches distributed throughout Jeremiah. Whole pieces of this one will be reused verbatim. And, of course, its stereotyped catch phrases will act as rhetorical code words and platitudes guiding the reader into a regime of reason designed to mask aporia present in the composition. It will mirror, supplement, and transform the themes and representations offered by the poetic tradition.

The familiar tension afflicting the theme of repentance recurs. For as the composition begins, the dramatic scene has the prophet standing before the temple gate and issuing his summons to the entire worshiping citizenry of Jerusalem. Yet all subsequent pieces in the prose sermon immediately assume the failure of that call and the inevitability and irrevocable character of the coming destruction. The aporia, however, is not left standing this time.

The great terror haunting the composition flows from the death of Israel. For the death of Israel implies the failure of Yahweh, Israel's portion. That such an implication must be fended off at any price is the foregone conclusion of the anxiety at work in the tradition. The myth of Israel is at risk! To preserve it, the composition must rewrite it and thus rewrite the story of the preexilic generation.

In this case, it is the preexilic temple cult and the generation attached to it that is rewritten and consequently written off. In the process, a distinct representation of prophecy and divinity is offered, aimed at masking the aporia noted above.

Indeed, for the composition, the failure that has occurred is exclusively the failure of the preexilic community to honor the demand for cultic purity wedded to the preservation of a social order. Stock phrases spell out the specifics and echo Deuteronomistic socioreligious neologisms ("practicing justice" [itemized under oppression of resident aliens, orphans, and widows, shedding of innocent blood, or theft, murder, adultery, false oaths, and offerings to Baal] and "not going after foreign gods" [cf. Deut 5:17-20; 6:14; 8:19; 10:18; 11:28; 13:3; 19:10, 13; 21:8, 9; 27:19, 25; 28:14]). These are the conditions of communal existence and security.

Assumptions about the moral contingency of oracular utterance reread the specter of prophetic failure and impotence by representing the mission of repentance as the initial stage of the prophetic act. Oracular utterance opens in the proclamation of alternatives that give way to inescapable declarations of doom — once, that is to say, refusal to heed the summons to repent proves intransigent. At this point, not even customary expectations of prophetic intercession apply (7:16). The role of "true" prophecy reconstitutes itself to become the very agent of communal destruction. For the composition, this represents the way of all prophecy. Indeed, it mythologizes a history of prophetic succession upon this cyclical pattern of prophetic mission (v. 25).

There has been a failure of the preexilic cult, not a failure of Yahweh or his prophetic agents. Ironically, it is not the failure of the preexilic generation to worship Yahweh that led to national downfall; rather, it is failure to worship correctly — that is, according to Deuteronomistic conceptions. Astonishingly, the rhetoric equates and associates the Jerusalem cult with idolatry and infidelity. An exclusive brand of the Yahwistic cult here castigates another more syncretistic variety. A new Yahweh confronts an older. A history of Yahweh insinuates itself under the name. Conflicting interpretative communities project their own patron deity into the interstices of the textual symbolic battlefield. One party excludes another from ownership of the national deity. The former is clearly more aniconic in its tastes and zealously concerned to expunge those elements from the cult perceived as infiltrating from surrounding non-Israelite cultures (7:16-20, 30-32; 8:1-3). Intra-Yahwistic conflicts are thus dramatized by this polemical rhetoric.

To ensure the hegemony of its particular Yahwistic regime, the composition rewrites part of the Israelite myth of Sinaitic law by denying cultic/sacrificial legislation to the Mosaic Torah (7:21-22). Thus it delegitimizes the Jerusalem cult as a post-Sinaitic innovation and corruption (the language goes far beyond the typical relative prophetic critique of sacrifice versus obedience; contrast the more dialectical 1 Sam 15:22; Ps 51:18-19 [Eng. 16-17]; Isa 1:4-15; Hos 6:6; 5:21-24; Mic 6:6-8). Therefore, the presence of the temple cult is no sign of divine patronage or protection (7:4, 10-15). Deep aporia open up as a result of this polemical claim.

No doubt by risking such aporia the composition can further serve its summary castigation of all the generations after the exodus generation to its day as violators of the divine demand for "obedience" (as understood by the *Yahweh-alone* party). The myth of Israel is rewritten as a history of perpetual disobedience in face of divine forbearance and the long-suffering prophetic mission (7:23-26). Yet in so doing they must sacrifice Sinaitic traditions, even other Deuteronomistic intertexts more accepting of the Davidic temple cult, as well as earlier representations in Jeremiah of the pre-conquest period as a time of religious fidelity (2:1-3, 7). More profoundly, they fragment the myth of Yahweh by pluralizing conceptualizations of it. The irony of this *Yahweh-alone* discourse is that it must "polytheize" the religion of Israel even as it clutches for an authoritarian definition and homogenization of the same. Their rhetoric dismantles itself even as it seeks to dismantle alternative representations of Israelite myth. Apparently, this is not too high a price to pay if it successfully masks the dissonance of divine failure and launches the *Yahweh-alone* voices to cultural hegemony. The colonized here reenact the drama of Near Eastern imperialism, transmuted to the level of mythic compensation, within their dreams of restoration to cultural power.

In common with the prose speech, short pieces of prose commentary reframe the underlying poetic compositions for the implied audience and their instruction as survivor and witness to the dramatic enactment of the preexilic prophetic mission. These pieces more effectively shatter the temporal horizon of the dramatic setting, thus replacing the reader in relationship to it. Reperformance of the prophetic tradition has become a means to wisdom ("who is wise?") — that is, instruction in the way of the Deity in national history. The national destruction is rationalized as divine punishment (9:11-15), and the human carnage of Near Eastern imperial struggles is mythologized as a reflection of Yahweh's struggle to secure a utopian earthly social order ("steadfast love, justice, and righteousness," v. 24). Finally, within this struggle, Israel is displaced from being Yahweh's "insider" to being one among the list of "outsider," "uncircumcised" Syro-Palestinian states (v. 26). Ironically, a Deuteronomistic neologism — "uncircumcised in heart" — engulfs all these nations indiscriminately in Yahweh's imperial struggle.

Appropriate to the theme of cult and worship which the composition polemicizes, pious instruction continues in the offering of two liturgical poems which model religious sentiments expressive of the vested interests of *Yahweh-alone.* The hymn, 10:1-16, celebrates the exclusive Yahwistic claims of the composition by satirizing "alien" religious belief and cultic practice. Of all the strategies of the composition, this hymn best reveals the deep core anxiety focusing the energy of the performance — that is, Yahweh's failure among the Near Eastern pantheons. It projects an implicit audience ideologically besieged and demoralized as a result of its colonization by more powerful cultural forces. The literary interconnections with similar poems in the exilic Isaiah traditions have suggested to many a similar exilic setting and origin for the present poem. The bilingual nature of the poem in v. 11 (Aramaic rather than Hebrew) draws this implicit audience more directly onto the stage of the composition, providing them (notice the 2d ms. pl. addressee) a stock retort, an anti-language, couched in the *lingua franca* of the Persian imperium. This offers performance of the prophetic tradition rhetoric designed to reestablish an "insider" identity for the colonized. Through transmutation of the Jeremianic tradition, the symbolic arena of the colonized, the myth of Yahweh's supremacy provides compensation for the colonized as they dream of restored hegemony in the cultural-political arena.

Jeremiah 7–10 concludes with prayer (compare the tropes familiar from the Psalter: 10:23, confession of trust; 10:24-25, petition). The identity of the speaker is uncertain. Because it occupies the same temporal space as the hymn and the prose commentary, I am inclined to ascribe it to the voice of the implicit audience, finally dramatized explicitly. The harder reading is to see this as the prophet's prayer. As such it would work similarly to the so-called "confessions" in the next compositional section (chs. 11–20). Indeed, the prophet's individuated lament and complaint back in 8:18, 21-23 could lend contextual support for this view. Yet it could also take up and resume the voice of lady Zion in lamentation (10:19-21). If so, it would take its place among the aporia mentioned earlier of a piety learned too late or only from the ashes of national death.

Even more curious is the substance of the confessional motif and its petition. The posture of humble dependence on divine guidance is certainly intelligible within the motifs of the Psalter. But in the present symbolic arena it goes wildly awry, out of tenor as it is with the gravity of the national catastrophe so portrayed. If it confesses moral impotence in the absence of divine aid, how does that suit the tenor elsewhere in the section of moral outrage over the refusal and inability of the community to pay heed to prophetic instruction. Or as divine guidance, why did the prophetic admonitions not prove more effective? If, instead, it should be related to the wisdom/folly motifs and the theme of the inaccessible character of wisdom except for divine help (a more suitable reading perhaps to the compositional strategy), then the voice of the audience abandons itself to divine wisdom and hopes by so doing to avoid divine wrath and prevent a return of the national holocaust. The voice of the colonized postpones and sublimates its anxiety over the failure of God and reestablishes an "insider" identity by dreaming of divine vengeance for its colonization.

The colonized compensate for the failure of God by discovering in the imperial fortunes of Near Eastern states the myth of Yahweh's wrath yearning for utopia. They protect their dreams of restoration from dissonance by abandoning themselves to the divine wisdom which proceeds through this process of human carnage to the new Israelite state of the *Yahweh-alone* party, understood as the reestablishment of divine sovereignty in the world. As allies of the divine imperialism they find hope in the spreading storm as the mechanism of the triumph of *Yahweh-alone* and his party. Ironically, the prayer, like an amulet, serves to usher the faithful through the storm unharmed.

Evaluation

Cultural power is at stake, circulating within the arena of "Jeremiah." Whatever we may be able to establish regarding the authenticity or inauthenticity of the traditions collected within the composition, it remains a representation of the prophetic mission constructed toward rhetorical and polemical ends in service of "Israel's" cultural work. The dramatic portrayal effected in the tradition offers a conceptualization of Israel with theodicy as its burden. This vision of Israel serves the defense of a factionalized Yahwistic faith, the latter's supporters, and the dynamic cultural agenda advocated by them. Thus the myth of Israel at stake in the polemics must also sustain representations of Yahweh and his prophet, Jeremiah, which embody their core anxieties.

The great anxieties of the implicit agents writing-reading-managing the tradition tip their hand in thematic emphases. The construction of a cultural identity, a social ethos, and a pattern of life lies under stress. For the hard historical exigencies of life amid Babylonian imperialism must be meaningfully managed. The identity of the colonized (elite) is at stake. It is only to be expected that symbolic compensation must be sought in national mythic traditions — the very traditions put at risk by the experience of colonization. To the extent that this (implicit, anonymous) elite succeeds in its construction, it hopes to sustain a dream of national restoration, the meaningfulness of "Israel" beyond the cultural catastrophe of colonization. Of course, this includes the continued establishment of the elite in its "place" of cultural inner-Israelite hegemony.

In chs. 7–10, the composition focuses on the national cult as the fulcrum of its symbolic rehabilitation. It must prevent at all costs the obvious conclusion from the national cultural encounter with Babylonian imperialism — the defeat and failure of Yahweh and his national cult.

That the historical crucible afforded by Judah's "political" place amid the endless contests for Near Eastern hegemony would be symbolically productive for the splintering and pluralization of Israelite myth is only to be expected coupled as it was with the diverse, competing sociopolitical interests within the monarchic court — that is, the royal house, Judean nobility, and their client constituencies among the rest of the populace.

To protect *Yahweh-alone,* all other contending "performances" of the myth of Israel must be written off. After the calamity, even "legitimate" forms of Yahweh at play in the royal temple-palace complex must be written over with the sign of idolatry and placed at the same level as "foreign" gods — exemplars of all the impurity afflicting the monarchic cult(s) of Yahweh.

The dominant voice of the composition chronologizes its own authority in the community. Now in charge of the past and in reflection on the Jeremianic tradition, it attempts to practice symbolic hegemony in favor of its own brand of Yahwistic faith. It traces its voice, its presence pre-calamity as a minority voice, ignored by the community to its own hurt and destruction. Of course, the lead representative of their voice is the prophet re-presented in the tradition.

In so doing, the implicit agents at play in Jeremiah bolster their symbolic authority and encode themselves as the true arbiters of community identity and destiny. Thus they rewrite the myth of Israel to serve current colonial interests while fanning the wick of postcolonial dreams subject to their own terms and visions. Presumably, this vision of Israel furthers their continued cultural appropriation of power.

Whether this is done in good faith or bad will be hard to say since we have so little direct access to the historical voices masquerading anonymously behind the implicit presences within the world of the composition. All we can go on from within the tradition is the "face" of the implicit agents projected into the work. There they inhabit Yahweh and Jeremiah, the latter symbols embodying elitist desires.

At one level, it is hard not to miss the sincerity of the passion energizing the rhetoric, posturing as it does within its claimed status as inspired utterance. Nevertheless, the potential for abuse — political, cultural, and religious — lies readily apparent. Provided, of course, that recourse to it becomes the means to a symbolic terrorism — a form of cultural exchange productive of an alienation emptying authenticity out of communal life. The problem is that one person's medicine is another's poison.

What, then, are we to think of the composition's tendency to tear itself apart in its desire for power? That it undermines itself in the process of sublimating cultural anxiety and fear at any price?

For this old world composition, the thinkable, of course, is clear. Yahweh's accounts in relation to the historical casualty of Israel are balanced on the backs of a dead and written-off generation. From the arena of Israel's mythic traditions, Near Eastern imperial politics have become the exigent necessity of God's justice. The landscape of God's interior pain and rage psychologizes as it legitimizes the mechanisms of cultural holocausts. Cultural violence and human carnage have become deeply anchored and integrated into Israel's mythic structures (whether intentionally or unintentionally) and thus insinuated into the core of the divine personality as their motivating center.

But should such metaphysical constructions remain morally thinkable and culturally affordable? If the question bids us write "unthinkable" over the Jeremianic construction of God, it at the same time launches a contemporary quest toward the purification of myth and perhaps human symbolic processes in general. This is choice irony! For immediately we are plunged by this impulse toward purity and utopian mythic endeavor back into the very deep structures driving the performance of the Jeremianic arena! We remain mired in the Jeremianic battlefield. We are returned to the crisis of divine symbols in face of cultural exigencies and anxieties. We recast (place) ourselves in the role of the ancient elite who must rewrite the myth of Israel and reperform divine symbols in their quest for cultural purity and security. Apparently, the mythic space opened in the arena of Jeremiah offers subtle seductions. Symbolic trust or suspicions trace themselves to shared conceits and deceits. Which offers the more affordable symbolic coinage? The myth of Sisyphus comes to mind.

Jeremiah 11:1–20:18

Overview

Oracular power — prophecy — risks the divinity it intermediates amid the cultural crisis of colonization. For if oracular power truly guides, or, better yet, creates the destiny of nations, why could not that social institution have prevented the colonization of Judah in the first place? Anxiety about the failure of prophecy deeply intertwines with the failure of God. A newly elaborated myth of prophecy becomes apologetic fodder for the rehabilitation of a particular Yahwistic myth. In this instance, the figure of Jeremiah within the prophetic mission must be individuated and psychologized. An interior landscape must be constructed for the prophet as well as the Deity and the two then intersected to sustain the regime of reason advocated by the composition. Since Jeremiah has already been represented as a prophet in the Mosaic succession, the composition must now rescue his mission from its failure to fully embody the Mosaic legend. Where the prophets fracture themselves in contradicted missions, oracular power risks its own deconstruction. Hence interest in the figure of Jeremiah as *the* true prophet achieves new levels of intensity in chs. 11–20. Not only does this entail external representation and evaluation of the prophetic mission, but also through the continued use of narratized dialogue it offers an interior landscape of the prophet that intersects with an interior landscape constructed for Yahweh. Thus the myth of God and his oracular agent are rehabilitated, enlivening hope in the restoration dreams of the composition.

Dramatic Composition

Representing the figure of Jeremiah has been important from the outset of the book, as the call narrative illustrated and foreshadowed (ch. 1). Even where that representation has not occupied center stage, it has still been very much part of the dramatic composition. Thus in 2:1–4:2 Jeremiah plays a role in the root metaphor (beyond that of oracular speaker) as confidant of the aggrieved divine husband. In chs. 4–6 the prophetic mission has the function of smelting Judah (6:27-30), thus sealing the death of the nation. In chs. 7–10, the figure of the prophet is intertwined with that of Yahweh mourning that very death.

But now, in chs. 11–20, the figure of Jeremiah takes center stage. Ironically, the prophet Jeremiah as implicit agent (a fictional construct) of the composition not only mimes the Deity but also himself engaged in prophetic mission. A sequence of eight passages (11:18-23; 12:1-6; 15:10-14, 15-21; 17:14-18; 18:18-23; 20:7-13, 14-18), traditionally labeled "confessions," narratize a dialogue between the prophet and Yahweh over the nature of the prophetic mission. Around this dialogical sequence the composition gathers additional tradition in order to construct a number of scenic tableaux of Jeremiah in prophetic engagement with Judah (chs. 11–13, 14–17, and 18–20). Chs. 11–20 thus offer a meditation on the meaning of Jeremiah as the true prophet in service of the larger apologetic interests of the composition.

Between Jeremiah and Yahweh (11:18-23; 12:1-6; 15:10-14, 15-21; 17:14-18; 18:18-23; 20:7-13, 14-18)

With one exception (20:14-18), the so-called confessions adapt a liturgical genre, the complaint psalm, to the concerns of prophetic mission. The first four follow a common pattern of complaint plus divine response. That the last four depart from this pattern, omitting any divine response, and, in the case of 20:14-18, a self-curse, even the use of psalm genre can be correlated to their thematic development and function within the sequence. The MT performs the confessions to sustain construction of a concrete, specific prophetic mission and hence an interior view of Jeremiah. The LXXV performs the passages to evoke a communal voice responding to divine judgment through prophetic intercession. In the latter's case the features of prophetic mission are not completely or consistently effaced; rather, the liturgical associations of the passages are exploited in order to insinuate a communal, representational reading, thus bringing these passages more into line with the conventional piety of traditional liturgical genre. The dramatized interior psychology of Jeremianic oracular power is lent paradigmatic potency for the implicit reader.

11:18-23

11:18-23 revolves around a conspiracy to kill the prophet by his own town. It is important to notice that the tone of the petition (vv. 18-20) hovers between confidence and complaint (blending motifs of thanksgiving and complaint psalms). The divine response constitutes an oracle of doom upon the conspirators. After all, it was Yahweh who had alerted the prophet to his danger. Prophet and Deity are in solidarity with each other.

The LXXV alters v. 18 from "And Yahweh made known to me, and I knew" (MT) to the more usual introductory address and petition of cultic lament: "Yahweh, make me know, and I shall know. . . ."

12:1-6

With 12:1-6 the latter is turned on its head. Rather than the prophet being persecuted, delayed fulfillment of the prophet's message of judgment forms the core issue of the complaint (vv. 1b-2, 4). Rhetoric protesting the prosperity of the wicked (cf. the wisdom motifs in the Psalter and Job) is here appropriated with reference to the whole nation. Yahweh constitutes the problem. Failure to fulfill the prophet's prediction of judgment threatens the prophet with exposure as a false prophet (v. 4, "they say, 'he does not see our end'"). The tone is similar to Joban complaints and ironic, for Yahweh is both judge and defendant (v. 1). For the prophet, the continued existence of the nation represents the failure of God!

The LXXV alters the prophet's complaint in 12:1 to reduce the virulence of its ironic accusation: "Righteous are you, O Yahweh, so that I will defend myself before you; albeit matters for judgment will I speak with you" (cf. MT, "Innocent are you, Yahweh, if I lodge a complaint before you. Yet sentence must I pass on you!").

This time the divine response rebukes and challenges the prophet (12:5-6). The relationship between the two parts of the response is not easy to discern. V. 5 formulated metaphorically attempts to shame the prophet. In effect, it views the prophet's present discomfiture as a sign of weakness and evaluates current challenges to the mission as minor compared to those to be encountered in the future. V. 6 concretizes that future challenge, predicting Jeremiah's betrayal by his own family members. The vocabulary and imagery link back to Jeremiah's description of the wicked nation ("practicing treachery," "near are you in their mouths but far from their inmost being"). Thus the Deity's response creates a parallelism between the prophet and God indicating a destiny for the prophet that mirrors Yahweh's conflict with Israel.

15:10-14 and 15-21 take this developing crisis between Jeremiah and Yahweh deeper.

15:10-14

15:10 pronounces a cry of self-woe. The prophet mourns his role as combatant of the nation. The divine response comprises vv. 11-14; it bristles with textual difficulties. The solution taken here sees a blend of rebuke and encouragement, subtle shift of addressees, and a fragment of judgment speech readdressed to function as assurance for the prophet.

The prophet protests the destiny laid out for him in the previous divine response (12:6). Yahweh counters by reasserting the prophet's role as enemy of the nation (translating v. 11, "Surely, I have inflicted you in time of trouble and in time of distress with the enemy"). The LXXV reperforms this as a normal profession of innocence rather than a divine oracle: "Verily, Yahweh, though they condemn, did I not stand before you in the time of their evil and in the time of their tribulation for good against the enemy?" Then God likens the prophet to unbreakable iron, assuring the prophet of his invincibility (v. 12). Vv. 13-14 readdress a judgment oracle (cf. 17:3-4). Here it functions as further assurance to the prophet that his enemy — that is, his own nation — will go into exile in defeat. Shifts of addressee occur within it, constituting most of the oracle as an apostrophe to the prophet's opponents. "For a fire burns in my wrath, against you [2d person pl.] it is kindled" provides the obvious signal of the shifts. V. 13, though articulated in second person singular address, makes more sense if the community is understood as a collective singular. V. 14a interrupts the apostrophized address to the nation by turning to address the prophet directly with the promise of his opponents' exile ("I will cause your enemies to pass over, into a land you do not know").

When the prophet reinterprets his prophetic vocation as a mistaken life, he implicitly rejects prophetic destiny and opens a crisis between himself and Yahweh. Yahweh's response rejects the prophet's interpretation. More than engendering enmity and opposition as a mere adjunct, Jeremiah's prophetic role embodies at its center the enmity of God toward the community. Ironically, Jeremiah's presence dooms the nation. The victory and salvation of the prophet spell the despoliation and exile of the community.

15:15-21

Brushing aside the divine response (15:15, "you know," an addition of the MT), the prophet steps up his attack on God (vv. 15-19). Qualities of Yahweh normally a cause for celebration and confidence (cf. the liturgical poetry in the Psalter) fall prey to the prophet's biting parody (which the LXXV in its performance attempts to blunt).

Divine "forbearance" (v. 15) toward prophetic opponents leaves the prophet under life threat regardless of God's protestations to the contrary. The prophetic mission subjects Jeremiah to unending suffering, contravening the prophet's expectations as a loyal member of the covenant community (vv. 16-17). The MT performs those expectations with reference to oracular power (v. 16, "Your words were found, and I ate them; your word was to me . . ."; v. 17, ". . . because of your hand [i.e., oracular power] I sat alone"), while the LXXV performs them in terms of general piety toward divine instruction (vv. 15-16, "know that I receive on your behalf reproach from those who set aside your words"; v. 17, ". . . but I behaved reverently before your hand. Alone I sat because I am filled with bitterness"). In light of those expectations, the prophetic mission represents a divine curse and pestilence (v. 18a). The realities of the Jeremianic prophetic mission reveal the failure of Yahweh! Yahweh is false, unreliable water (v. 18b; contrast the LXXV, "Surely it [my wound] has become to me like false water, unreliable"). The prophet reduces God to the level of the "foreign deities" (contrast "fountain of living water" to "broken cisterns" in 2:13)! This is a prophet attempting to abandon his mission. He must deconstruct his Deity in the process.

Realizing the nature of the attack, Yahweh responds with a summons to repent (15:19). If he is to continue as Yahweh's prophet, he must abandon his bitter opposition to the way of the mission that God has laid out for him. He must not be terrorized into solidarity with the community. Oracular power must not come to Israel's aid. The deliverance so longed for by Jeremiah can be acquired, ironically, only through recommitment to the terms of his original prophetic call (cf. vv. 20-21 to 1:18-19).

The conflict between Jeremiah and Yahweh has reached its climax in the confessional sequence.

17:14-18

17:14-18 creates a transition between the preceding confessions and those that remain. With it the prophet complies with the summons to repent (15:19). Jeremiah abandons his "misinterpretation" of his prophetic mission. The LXXV incorporates 17:12-13 more smoothly into the passage, performing it as normal introductory address, petition, and expression of confidence: "O endurance of Israel, Yahweh, all who forsake you, let them be ashamed; those who revolt in the land, let them be inscribed, for they have forsaken the source of life, Yahweh." In the process it effaces a characteristic Jeremianic polemical idiom, "fountain of living water" (cf. 2:13).

The preceding sequence had begun with opposition to the prophetic mission as the core issue. Yahweh and Jeremiah are depicted over against the nation. The issue shifted through complaint and divine response, repositioning the prophet over against God, with the core problem the very nature of the prophetic mission. For not only must the prophet in the course of his mission mirror the betrayal of Yahweh by Israel but he must also mirror the betrayal of Israel to the enmity of Yahweh. The prophet becomes the iron pillar, the proof-stone on which the community founders and meets its death. Rather than perpetuate his attempt to abandon the mission, the prophet repents and returns to the original issue of opposition to prophetic mission.

The delayed fulfillment of the promised national destruction opens the prophet to charges of false prophecy (17:15). The plea for healing and deliverance means nothing other than the demise of the nation. The prophet resumes his alignment with Yahweh against the community. He pleads his integrity denying both the attempt to abandon his prophetic calling (the LXXV reperforms and effaces the prophetic reference: "I did not grow weary following after you . . ."; contrast the MT, ". . . I did not hurry away from being a shepherd after you . . .") and any personally motivated desire for communal destruction (v. 16). The manner of the Jeremianic mission represents the determination and desire of God. The negatively formulated petition (vv. 17-18) seeks to avoid the penalty for betraying his prophetic call (cf. the threats of "shame" and "shatter" to the threats in 1:17). Ironically, Jeremiah's healing and restoration means the breaking of the nation.

18:18-23

The crisis highlighted in the initial development of the confessional sequence — a crisis over the nature of the prophetic mission — resolves into a crisis over the fate of the prophetic word. Citations of Jeremiah's opponents develop the theme (17:15; 18:18, 20a; 20:10). In 17:15 the citation challenges the legitimacy of Jeremiah's prophetic claim. In 18:18 denial of prophetic legitimacy to Jeremiah leads to a plot ("Come, let us smite him with the tongue . . .") to destroy him. Presumably, this will be done through legal means. For, after all, false prophecy is a capital crime. Ironically, it is Jeremiah's message of judgment that reveals him to be a false prophet in the perspective of his opponents (reading v. 20a as a citation of the opponents: "Will he reward with calamity instead of good?" Note that v. 19b introduces the citation, "Listen to the voice of my adversaries"). They assume a different function for the exercise of oracular power — that is, it should achieve the "good" of the state by securing beneficent oracles through prophetic intercession on the state's behalf. Jeremiah returns the unthinkable — oracles of "calamity." Ironically, Jeremiah pleads his innocence in terms congruent with their assumptions. In fact, he has sought to secure the type of oracles they expect (v. 20b). Except that those attempts failed. Consequently, he imprecates his opponents with rhetoric reminiscent of judgment oracles elsewhere in the Jeremianic tradition (even in earlier confessions, e.g., 11:18-23).

20:7-13

20:7-13 concludes and recapitulates the thematic progression in the confessions. The prophet's complaint resolves the fate and fortunes of Yahweh's prophetic word in the face of any and all opposition within figures of invincibility, power, and domination. Ironically, opposition has come from two sources: first, Jeremiah, *the* prophet, has attempted to hold back its power by aborting his prophetic mission (20:9; cf. the first half of the confessional sequence, 11:18–15:21). The LXXV redirects the references away from oracular inspiration, using "I will not name the name of Yahweh, I will not speak again in reference to his name" for MT's "I will not mention him, or speak anymore in his name." The more he has fought against it, the more violated and dominated by it he has become (note the vocabulary of violence and power in vv. 7-9: forced [seduced or enticed], violence, destruction, overpowered, prevail, uncontainable burning fire). Second, Jeremiah's futile attempt to escape prophetic vocation has been motivated by his rejection and consequent persecution by the community (v. 7b; cf. the second half of the confessional sequence, 17:14–18:23). Jeremiah has been "martyred" because of the prophetic word. Even now opposition against him crescendos. Just as Yahweh forced (seduced/incited) prophecy upon Jeremiah, so now his compatriots seek to incite him to treasonable behavior (20:10b) so that they can inform against him (v. 10a), securing his execution and their revenge. The LXXV at v. 10 reperforms a characteristic Jeremianic oracular idiom for the predicted judgment, "terror on every side" (6:25; 20:3; 46:5; 49:29): "For I heard the censure of many gathering together from all around . . ."; contrast the MT's "For I have heard the whisperings of many, 'Terror on every side!'"

Ironically, Jeremiah's hope in their defeat lies in his very possession and domination by the violent God, Yahweh, the dread warrior (20:11; cf. the adjective with its prior use in 15:21 describing the wicked). If Yahweh's prophetic word has had to face two oppositions, so also the prophet — victim of both divine and communal violence. Ironically, it is the victory of his divine "enemy" over him that spells the doom of his human enemies. The invincibility of oracular power resolves the threats to the prophetic mission by dominating the prophet in the manner of its execution and thus overwhelming the nation with destruction. The prophet's plea (v. 12) for vengeance resolves into anticipatory praise for the victory of the ruthless God, his deliverer (v. 13).

The invincibility of the divine word restores the three "subjects" (I, Thou, They) of Jeremiah's complaints concerning their initial relationship: Jeremiah and Yahweh against Israel. Explicit dialogue and confrontation between the prophet and God (11:18–15:21) shift to the silence of Yahweh before Jeremiah's petitions (17:14–20:13) — a sign not of rejection, but of Jeremiah's failure to overpower his own prophetic vocation. The gap between prediction and fulfillment had opened this space for vocational crisis. Similarly, it opened space for a crisis of authority in the Jeremianic mission to the community. Ironically, rehabilitation of Jeremiah's prophetic authority requires the doom of Israel. His petitions shatter the prophetic icons of communal expectation. Those expectations are mirrored in the citations of the enemy (17:14–20:13). His mission of personal vengeance against his persecutors mirrors the mission of Yahweh to destroy the nation through Jeremianic agency. The pain of God seeks realization in the pain of Jeremiah and its relief in the death of the nation.

20:14-18

All that remains at the end of the confessional sequence is lamentation (20:14-18). Jeremiah's self-curse (cf. Job 3) mourns his prophetic destiny as harbinger of national destruction (cf. the motif of reaction to bad news in Jer 6:22-26; 49:23; Isa 13:6-8; and self-lamentation associated with messages of divine judgment in 4 Ezra 5:35; 1 Macc 2:7, and especially Jer 45:3). Given his prophetic destiny, Jeremiah reaches back to his birth, echoing the imagery of his call. His emergence from the womb (20:18) signals Israel's end (1:5). Jeremiah's pain is the provocation of Israel to national self-destruction. A Joban prophet here mourns his controverted expectations.

Between Jeremiah and Israel (chs. 11–13, 14–17, 18–20)

The composition distributes the confessional sequence across chs. 11–20 to effect stylized scenes of the prophetic mission complementary to the thematic progression within the confessions.

Chs. 11–13

The first two confessions (11:18-23; 12:1-6) create a parallelism between Yahweh and Jeremiah. That parallelism gathers the tradition in chs. 11–13 to itself to effect the first scene. The prose sermon (11:1-17) mimics a covenant ratification liturgy in order to dismantle Israel's reliance on the covenant bond to Yahweh as an unconditional guarantee of national security. The blessings of covenant are contingent on Israel's fidelity to covenant stipulations. The Deuteronomistic rhetoric focuses the demand for obedience on the exclusive worship of Yahweh. The import of the sermon is to set Israel under the sign of the covenant curse for its unending practice of idolatry. But the figure of Jeremiah appears as more than that of the "preacher" of the terms of the covenant. He also appears as the sole ratifier of it (v. 5, "Amen, Lord"; cf. Deuteronomy 27). For the rest, God exposes a conspiracy of infidelity perpetrated against himself (11:9), just as, we might add, the prophet was to experience in the execution of his own mission (v. 18; cf. vv. 15-17). Both the prophet and God are innocent victims of national wickedness. The nation's doom is inescapable. Consequently, the prophet must not intercede on their behalf (v. 14).

Just as Jeremiah's discovery of the plots, both national and familial, to destroy him launches his complaints and petitions, his lamentations over betrayal, and his crisis of vocational mission, so, too, Yahweh laments. Betrayed by "wife and lover" Israel, he launches his own cry of mourning. The pain of God runs deep. The hate and rage of a betrayed husband issue in Israel's doom (11:7-13).

Opposition to the prophet's mission mirrors the nation's enmity and infidelity to Yahweh. The rejection of the prophet vindicates God's accusation and justifies national destruction. Yahweh and Jeremiah are alike: they share a common psychology and a common experience. The reappearance of the female figure for Israel (11:15-17; 12:7-13) draws the national, political, covenant rhetoric of the prose into the sphere of the familial, complementing Jeremiah's own betrayal by his next of kin.

The prose cooperates with the dramatic figuration of the confessional series, extends it, and develops it, thus interpreting it in directions amenable to its interest in theodicy and cult purification. Though the prose rhetoric is full of its own slogans, repeatedly replayed from sermon to sermon, from its perspective as "reader" of the oracular tradition it concretizes a cultural critique left more opaque by the poetic oracular tradition alone with its construction of the prophetic tableaux.

The materials in ch. 13 cooperate further with the dramatic scene, keeping interests in theodicy paramount. Within ch. 13 prose and poetry combine around the themes of pride-glory/ruined-shamed. The poetic oracles (vv. 15–27) echo earlier sections in chs. 2–10: the theme of the invader from the north (v. 20), futile appeals for repentance (v. 16), the incurable nature of national impurity (vv. 23, 27), the theme of wife-harlotry (note especially the fm. sg. addressee in vv. 20-27), and the prophet's mourning of communal corruption and doom (v. 17). Resolution of theodicy concerns is explicit: "Why have these things befallen me?" wife Israel asks (v. 22).

The prose narrates a symbolic prophetic action (13:1-14) and a prophetic parable (vv. 12-14). The prophet's symbolic actions continue to mirror the intentions and experience of God with Israel in the manner of the prophetic act, sustaining the tableaux under construction in chs. 11–13. Like the prophet's ruined loincloth, so is God's experience of Israel — they have become "good for nothing" (vv. 7, 10). Incorrigible as they are, like wine jars they are "good" only for holding wine. Ironically, the only vintage they will contain is the divine wrath. It will induce a mad drunkenness shattering national existence (vv. 13-14).

The terror at the heart of the composition issues from the pain of God. The demise of the nation represents God's personal, pitiless violence. It is spousal rape and abuse (13:26) *legitimated* by national cultic impurity/covenant infidelity made egregiously concrete in the violence she/Israel perpetrates against the Jeremianic mission.

Chs. 14–17

To mirror God's intention to irrevocably destroy the nation, the prophet in the previous scene had been prohibited from interceding on the nation's behalf (11:14). Jeremiah now violates that command. The violation complements the crisis that erupts in the prophetic mission exemplified in the next two confessions (15:10-21).

14:1–15:9 portray that violation in a cycle of national laments with divine responses (14:1-10; 14:17–15:4). Each petition (14:7-9, 19-22) seeks the mercy of God in the midst of the gathering doom. Traditional cultic genre and rhetoric drawn from the sphere of the national temple cult provide the mechanism of appeal. From the perspective of this appeal, which does acknowledge national sins (vv. 7, 20), whatever national faults may exist, none of them warrants total annihilation. In fact, the national perspective views the prospect of such devastation as Yahweh's violation of covenant fidelity (vv. 8-9, 21-22). In each case the petition is rejected (14:10; 15:1-4). Yahweh's rebuff places the community beyond redemption. Even more astonishing is that these rejections make clear that Jeremiah is the one *interceding* for the nation (14:1, 17). After the first cycle, God must repeat his prohibition to Jeremiah (v. 11). Jeremiah disputes the injunction (v. 13)! He relies on an alternative oracular perspective: ". . . true peace I will give you in this place." The countermessage of other prophets motivates disputation with his own — that is, the message of merciless destruction. Yahweh must give Jeremiah, the true prophet, an oracle exposing the other prophets as false (vv. 14-16). Their countermessage of peace represents another form of opposition to the Jeremianic mission.

Once again Jeremiah launches into intercession! The futility of this attempt is more emphatically stated: not even Moses or Samuel (legendary intercessors) could successfully shield the nation from divine wrath (15:1-4). The prophet like Moses is unable to exercise Mosaic power! Jeremiah meets defeat in the attempt to procure the peace his prophetic opponents announce. The compositional strategy complements and motivates the crisis that erupts over the nature of the prophetic mission in the following confessional sequence (vv. 10-21). For in it the prophet seeks to subvert or, if not, at least to escape the manner of that mission. Oracular efficacy on their behalf is denied him (v. 19). He is the proofstone that provokes national self-destruction (vv. 11-14, 20-21). To underline the fact, the prose sermon of ch. 16 aggravates the impact of symbolic action on Jeremianic existence. He may not marry, bear children, or mourn (cf. the complaint in 14:17). Jeremiah must fully embody divine wrath over Israel. He is set contrary to national desire and normal cultural life.

The prophetic tableaux construct theodicy as the paramount anxiety: "Who will have pity on you . . . ?" (15:5), ". . . because of what King Manasseh did . . ." (15:4), "Why has Yahweh pronounced all this great evil against us?" (16:10), ". . . I am going to teach them my power and my might, and they shall know that my name is Yahweh" (16:21).

As argued earlier, 17:14-18 constitutes a transitional point in the confessional sequence. It represents the prophet's compliance with Yahweh's demand that he abandon his struggle against the prophetic mission. In the rest of ch. 17 the composition cooperates with that function by taking a new tack in the construction of the tableaux. A dispute is still effected in the scene, but it no longer involves the prophet over against God. These two are allied once again and contrasted with the nation. This time wisdom motifs are used (instead of national lament genre) clustered around themes of righteous/wicked, wise/foolish, and blessing/curse. Disparate materials provide the building blocks: fragments of judgment oracles (vv. 1-4, 12-13), proverbial and other wisdom genre (vv. 5-11), and a prose sermon (vv. 19-27).

The proverblike motifs in 17:5-8 provide the interpretive structure for the tableaux. Using traditional descriptions which contrast the fate of the wicked and the righteous, the blessing/curse formulary links onto the theme of Israel's corrupted heart (vv. 1-4) to assign the nation, by implication, to the ranks and destiny of the wicked (v. 5, "whose heart is turned away from Yahweh").

17:9 and 10 interject disputation and effect a dialogue between the nation and God. In v. 9, the nation skeptically challenges wisdom's claim. The heart is so deceptive that true moral assessment is impossible. But God counters in v. 10 by asserting his power and ability to mete out accurate judgment on the human heart and, hence, the nation's collective heart. The proverb in v. 11 signals the ephemeral character of unjustly acquired prosperity which on the surface contradicts wisdom's predictions (that the wicked could never prosper), correlating by implication the impending despoliation of Israel (vv. 1-4) with it. The fragment of judgment speech continues the dispute. It begins by citing the cultic, hymnic cry of the nation (vv. 12-13a) with its confidence in the temple and the hope it constitutes. Pious Israel rejects its categorization among the wicked with the latter's commensurate destiny. God counters (v. 13b, reading 1st person sg. pronoun, "those who turn from me"). They will be assigned to the Netherworld precisely for the reasons that the cultic cry implicitly denied (note the echo of 2:13, "fountain of living water").

Throughout the dispute, Israel is aligned with the wicked, with folly, and with the curse. By contrast, Jeremiah's confession (17:14-18) marks him off as Yahweh's righteous suppliant. In the confessional sequence he is turning from the folly that the crisis with prophetic mission had engendered. He effects a penitence seeking restoration. His petition stresses his innocence over against the nation which rejects his prophetic word (v. 15, "Where is Yahweh's word? Let it be fulfilled!"). Correlated with the wisdom motifs, the prophet enrolls under the sign of the righteous the wise and deserving recipient of blessing appropriate to his fidelity to the prophetic mission.

In this tableaux the figure of Jeremiah achieves exemplary status, which may account for the conclusion of this section with the sermon on sabbath keeping. In its alternative structure (17:24-27), the prophet sets forth "the two ways," wisdom and folly, sabbath keeping or sabbath breaking, upon which national security hinges. Once again Deuteronomistic rhetoric concretizes the opaque poetic traditions, thus highlighting its peculiar cultic concerns. The prophet appears as the righteous sage counseling the nation in the way of wisdom and life. The tenor of the dialogue across the current tableaux indicates that his instruction has fallen on deaf ears (note v. 23, "to receive instruction"; it is an idiom deeply rooted in wisdom literature and the mission of the sages). The irrevocable doom of Israel receives rationalization under the sign of wisdom as the deserved fate of the wicked and the national folly of cultic impurity leading to it.

Chs. 18–20

With this last subsection, the narrative impulse leading the composition to construct its prophetic tableaux takes a literal turn. Foreshadowing literary styles and plot structures predominant in the second half of the book, the composition correlates the confessions not only with symbolic action and prose sermon but also third person oblique narrative with explicitly named agents (cf. chs. 26–29, 36, 37–43).

The confession (18:18-21) enhances the thematic shift of the sequence (begun with 17:14-18) to the fate of the prophetic word. Recall that the citations (18:18, 20a) indicate national denial of Jeremiah's message of judgment and launch a plot to silence him. This dispute has been set within a larger dispute between God and Israel. The symbolic action of the potter's house (vv. 1-11) climaxed with a summons to repent (v. 11). It is immediately followed in v. 12 by a change of speaker (3d person pl. citation). The nation summoned to repentance rejects the appeal ("It is no use!"). Consequent to this refusal (v. 13, "therefore"), Yahweh responds with an oracle of judgment because of national apostasy and idolatry. The nation (3d person pl.) responds, yet again, with its denial and plots against the prophet (v. 18).

The strategy of the composition is by now familiar. Jeremiah and Yahweh are paralleled and locked into a dispute with the nation over the message of judgment. The egregious apostasy of the community is demonstrated by their persecution of Yahweh's messenger. The dramatic scene demonstrates the necessity and legitimacy of national destruction. The dialogue offers a disputational tableau, making concrete the rationalization of divine behavior signaled in the symbolic action. The divine posture toward a nation and its destiny is morally contingent on that nation's responsiveness to Yahweh (18:7-10). Its failure to repent lays the blame for national destruction squarely at Israel's feet.

Yet Jeremiah's petition for national destruction (18:21-23) — that is, the fulfillment of his message of judgment — still hangs unresolved. 19:1-13 (note that it reuses the Topheth material from ch. 7) represents the divine response to the petition ("Thus says Yahweh"), initiating the next phase of the dramatic scene. When Jeremiah shatters the pot (19:10; Yahweh's instruction), he signals Israel's irrevocable end (v. 11, ". . . so that it can never be mended"). The divine potter practices fidelity, not infidelity, when he does this: "because they have stiffened their necks, refusing to hear my words" (v. 15).

The narrative structure shifts the scenic setting of the prophet's mission from the Topheth valley to the temple court (19:14-15). In keeping with the theme of opposition to the Jeremianic mission, Pashhur, a high-ranking priest, responds to Jeremiah's proclamation with an attempt to silence the prophet. To silence and bind Jeremiah is to prevent the efficacy of his prophetic word (20:1-2). But God vindicates Jeremiah from the stocks with an oracle (vv. 3-6) promising to sweep Pashhur away in the coming doom of the nation. More than that, Pashhur's opposition actually guarantees and hastens the coming storm. He is a sign of the "terror on every side" (v. 3). For his attempt to silence Jeremiah represents false prophecy (v. 6). The remaining confessional units follow (20:7-18). Not only do they rehearse, vindicate, and mourn God's whole way with the prophet, but in the context of the dramatic scene they offer Jeremiah's interior response to and reflection on the Pashhur incident. The way of Jeremiah's mission is defended and vindicated. Through its incorrigible opposition the nation draws its destruction ever more ineluctably to itself. The proofstone succeeds.

Yet Is There No Hope for Israel? (12:14-17; 16:14-15, 19-21)

Readers of the Jeremianic tradition were led by the call narrative to expect restoration oracles and themes at some point in the composition (1:10, "to build and to plant"). Even if the composition seeks to anticipate and foreshadow the major collection of restoration tradition in chs. 30–33, why these brief passages here and now? Especially since the way of the prophet figured in the dramatic scenes of chs. 11–20 strives to destroy all hope of avoiding colonization by Babylon. Ironically, not even Jeremiah, the prophet like Moses, can prevent the calamity, even when extorted into the attempt by external persecution and internal terrorism! The defense of God has created a fantastic landscape of total devastation and depopulation for the land in the name of God's pain. The interior landscape of divine and prophetic psychology renders its production inescapable.

Taken singly, the point of each oracle is clear. Their role within the current literary context is not.

12:14-17

Addressed to the neighboring Syro-Palestinian states, the oracle sweeps them up into the storm taking Judah. Their predations on (12:14) and subversions of Judah (v. 16, ". . . they taught my people to swear by Baal") offer the specific rationale for Yahweh's actions. Yet this judgment contains the backhanded promise of hope. For they all will be restored to their indigenous territories on condition that they learn to "swear by Yahweh" (v. 16). In effect, they are to be incorporated into the broader covenant orbit of Israel (v. 16, "they shall be built up in the midst of my people"). Otherwise only complete national oblivion remains (v. 17).

The prose oracle erodes the distinction between insider and outsider nation, Israel and its political neighbors. It sets the scope of God's way in the Jeremianic mission on a world stage. The composition fulfills its promise in the call narrative that Jeremiah constitutes a "prophet to the nations" (1:5; note that the verbs in 12:14, 16, 17 — "pluck up, destroy, build" — echo the prophet's tasks toward the nations in 1:10). God's judgment purifies not only Judah but also the world. The stain of the world is its idolatry. The destiny of nations plays out according to a common Deuteronomistic schema. God's annihilation of the Syro-Palestinian commonweal seeks the production of a community realizing the ideal of the "true" Israel projected by the covenant oath (11:1-5). Their restoration depends on willing recolonization to Yahwistic rule. The present scenario of irrevocable national destruction is maintained and universalized. The concept of hope metamorphoses, rationalized within a larger myth of Yahweh's war for imperial hegemony. One regime of hope replaces another. A misplaced false hope gives way to another.

16:14-15, 19-21

The prose oracle (16:14-15, repeated in 23:7-8) interrupts the flow of the sermon. It promises a restoration of Judah's exiles. That restoration will be the new defining national moment akin to the exodus from Egypt while it also replaces it. Curiously, the introductory conjunction (v. 14, "therefore") marks the oracle as a conclusion responsive to the preceding context. The prose sermon finds in Jeremiah's singleness, childlessness, and nonparticipation in expected funerary rites symbols of inescapable national doom. As v. 13 concludes, "I will hurl you out of this land. . . ."

Similar to 12:14-17, the composition displaces restoration to the future, maintaining the necessity of exile and colonization for the present. Only from those national ashes does hope become conceivable, and only for the dispersed, but "first" (v. 18; note that vv. 16-18 resume the announcement of judgment) must there be double recompense for Israel's defilement with idolatry. Unlike its use in 12:14-17, the rhetoric of restoration here is not explicitly conditional. It presumes that the restoration is as inevitable as the present national destruction. Perhaps, for the composition, the punishment constitutes atonement.

16:19-20 (poetry) return to the sense of world stage constructed by 12:14-17. There the condition of restoration for all the "outsider" nations was abandonment of idolatry. Here the nations dramatically confess and renounce their idolatry in fulfillment of those intentions (vv. 19b-20; should we read in the speaker of v. 19a the same dramatic voice that doxologizes in 10:23-25? Recall in context there the long hymn in parody of idolatry). Perhaps, within the current tableaux (chs. 14–17), the nations offer a negative foil to Judah, for as witnesses of Judah's demise they practice the piety and cultic purity Judah cannot in her continued opposition to the Jeremianic mission.

These brief restoration tropes connect the stylized scenes of prophetic mission to larger structural and thematic interests at work across the larger arc of the whole literary arrangement of Jeremiah. Yahweh's domination of the manner of the Jeremianic mission furthers the divine imperial struggle in the world. God's way with Israel is becoming Yahweh's way for the world — his struggle for universal imperial supremacy and recognition (16:21). Ironically, the failure of Israel propels Yahwistic hegemony in the world rather than defeat. The mechanism of Israel's cultic purification is Yahweh's paradigm for history. The elite composition rationalizes its place among the colonized through recourse to a larger myth of Yahwistic history that presages an ultimate reversal of fortunes. Israel's doom is the harbinger of the world's.

Evaluation

The colonized must find their symbolic compensation, and thus their consolation, by rediscovering the myth of Israel writ large.

The Neo-Babylonian destruction of the old Davidic state remains an undeniable, unforgettable fact. Equally undeniable for the myth of Israel and the voices of the surviving cultural elite (whose implicit authorial voices everywhere permeate the composition) is their enduring colonization by Babylonian then Persian powers. To surmount the historical defeat of Israel's nationalist myth and the cultural demoralization it engenders, Yahweh must be rescued on the back of an elaborated Jeremianic legend.

And yet the tradition is profoundly aware, anxious about the existence of counter-Yahwistic myth and prophetic legend. The hints and allegations of these signal the failure of Yahweh as well as of Jeremiah's prophetic authority. Left unanswered, they subvert the symbolic hegemony so coveted by the compositional voice. Hence the dramatic tableaux of Jeremiah in prophetic mission painted by chs. 11–20.

Thus, intertwined with the theodicy impulse is the

reconceptualization of prophecy over the true and the false. The symbolic crisis the composition discovers in prophecy is that it can be subverted and perverted so that prophetic claims and phenomenology do not a prophet make! For Jeremiah had prophetic opponents. Whoever one was inclined to accept as legitimate, "false" prophecy is still in the mix — in fact, a counterprophecy effectively subverting Yahwistic purity. The figure of Jeremiah is made to live out that struggle, not only in his combat with the community but also within his interior landscape. Thus the composition resolves its crisis in the refuge of an enlarged conceptualization of the myth of oracular power. The true divine word proves invincible in face of any and all attempts to subvert it — whether Jeremiah's or someone else's. Exigent escape from mythological dissonance baptizes historical hindsight as the measure of inspiration's presence! Admitting the dissonance can be postponed for another day.

The baptism of the Jeremianic figure under the sign of Moses carried risks at the same time it sought transfer of symbolic authority from one to the other. Evocations of the Mosaic legend raise expectations of national deliverance, the hope that Moses-like intercessory power could propitiate divine wrath and thus prevent Israel's end. Idiosyncratic Jeremiah violates the Mosaic icon. The dramatic tableaux legitimate the iconoclastic figure while retaining the authority of Mosaic succession for him. Ironically, later prophetic legend will focus precisely on Jeremiah as an efficacious intercessory figure holding divine wrath away from Israel (cf. 2 Macc 15:12-16; *Lives of the Prophets* 2:1-4).

Iconoclastic motives run deeply in the composition, for they must deconstruct alternative Yahwistic faiths — how else secure hegemony for their brand of Yahwistic purity! Hence the strenuous effort to render those "faiths" broken cisterns, reduced to empty icons indeed. Legitimate, orthodox, Yahwistic traditions of the old Davidic court must be displaced. For Zion-temple ideology guaranteed Jerusalem's inviolability and Yahweh's fidelity. It exposes the Jeremianic announcement of the end of Israel, its loss of special status as Yahweh's chosen, and motivates the counteroffensive to destroy or subvert the Jeremianic mission. The tableaux reevaluate these popular, "orthodox" expectations, misplaced as they are. For they gravely mask a profoundly compromised Yahwistic purity of cult with a superficial nationalistic piety. At a deeper structural level, however, the voice of Yahwistic exclusivity has not in the last analysis simply abandoned that older orthodoxy. For it passionately longs to preserve and realize its promise. Historical exigencies and the mythological dissonance springing from them force, inexorably, a reconfiguration upon those voices. The myth of Yahweh will change, though it continues under the name. Religious innovation will establish itself under the sign of its own repristination.

Finally, this new "orthodoxy" of the colonial elite seeks to school its reader in a piety commensurate with the myth. For the Jeremianic tableaux achieve a legendary status (in the proper sense of martyrology or exemplary saints' tale) for the prophet. Jeremiah has become the Joban prophet, the suffering, obedient servant. Construction of an interior landscape for Jeremiah from the palette of typical psalm genre, motifs, and themes aids this intent. The prophet appears as the righteous, innocent suppliant of Yahweh in need of deliverance from the wicked. The internalized vocational crisis of the prophet resolves in Yahweh's victorious domination of Jeremiah's interior landscape. Jeremiah becomes the exemplary pious-righteous man who in the face of undeserved hardship and suffering preserves loyalty to Yahweh's service, weep though he may, accepting the struggle as a divine test (20:12a) and expectant of ultimate vindication (v. 13). The Jeremianic legend offers parenesis and encouragement for those enduring the hardships of service to Yahwistic exclusivity.

The presentation of the MT keeps the individuated figure of the prophet concrete to serve this design. But the LXXV offers an alternative performance of the tableaux. While it does not fully obscure the prophet's voice in the confessions, it does reperform them to enhance a national voice present and interpenetrating them. The implicit reader in the mix of the composition is placed and replaced within the tableaux in order to be schooled in the piety proper to Yahwistic purity.

The elaborated Jeremianic legend serves the rehabilitation and reformulation of a Yahwistic myth that sets "Israel's" colonial exigencies within the arch symbols of exile and return. The hope is in the revitalization of Israelite myth, its defense before the lassitude and demoralization attendant upon historical cultural defeat and the postponement of faith's dissonance to future historical fortunes and contradictions. In the process, the composition elevates the cruelties of Levantine imperialism and the tide of human suffering left in its wake to mythic proportions. Imperial devices and desires are deeply anchored in the divine character. The violence attending nation building and cultural purification represent God's war in the world to realize dreams of Yahwistic hegemony. A ready mechanism is offered future historical exigencies where the dissonance of divine failure is met. Renewed blood letting can mask the symbolic defeats of Yahweh since it is always possible to discern new conspiracies and threats toward Yahwistic purity from within the community.

But then what choice was left to the surviving colonial elite? Total abandonment of cultural heritage and identity must have seemed unthinkable especially for those dreaming of a return to cultural power and dignity. It seems that the imperial impulses and ideological interests toward nationalist survival of the old Davidic monarchy and its client elite, so excoriated and pilloried by the Jeremianic tableaux, have not been superseded. There has been a dislocation in order to reinscribe them with greater, more inexorable, symbolic power. The countermyth lives in its successor.

Jeremiah 21:1–24:10

Overview

For the colonized elite, the Davidic kingship was profoundly implicated in the myth of Yahweh and the theodicy designed to mask the failure of God. The chronological attention to specific named kings should not seduce. There is explicit dischronologization (coupled with a dehistoricization of the tradition) in the effort to dispense with the failure of specific Davidic monarchs while at the same time sustaining the ideology of Davidic kingship. Common to Old World mythologies of the Levant (and wider for that matter), the ideology of kingship constitutes a necessary ingredient in the rehabilitation of the myth of Israel.

Chapters 2–20 have spared no expense in asserting the total corruption of the community from top to bottom (e.g., 5:1-5). The present excoriation, however, of the entire elite in the old Judean monarchy (including prophets and priests), and the attempt to load special blame for the sins of the nation on them should come as no surprise. Such a turn has been repeatedly anticipated (1:18; 2:8, 26; 4:9; 5:31; 6:13, 14; 8:1-3, 8, 10, 11; 10:21; 13:18, 19; 14:13-16; 15:4; 17:20; 19:3; 20:1-6). What is distinctive is that for the first time (cf. 3:11-18) compositional interests splinter "Israel." Different royal claimants and their client communities are apportioned variant histories under that name. Succession to the name "Israel" depends on membership in the right client community. Restoration interests must be made to serve only Yahwistic exclusivism. Ironically, some Israelites will be denied legitimate access to the benefits of the royal-temple-Zion cult only to have that symbolic efficacy transferred to others. Hence we witness in this critique of the old Davidic monarchy not the rejection of the institution per se, but appropriation of its ideological power by the wrong parties.

Dramatic Composition

Two prose sermons (21:1-10; 24:1-10) are used to encapsulate marked collections, against the Davidic house (21:11–23:8) and against the prophets (23:9-40). Compositional strategy makes a new departure with its use of chronologically specific materials (21:1; 24:1) and specifically named Judean monarchs (cf. 1:1-3; 3:6; 15:4). The construction of stylized dialogues/disputes (whether around narratized root metaphors such as the marriage metaphor in chs. 2–3 or the invasion from the north in chs. 4–10 or tableaux of the prophetic mission in chs. 11–20) to organize the disparate Jeremianic traditions does not continue. Echoes of them do, however, appear within individual units (e.g., 21:13-14 and 22:20-23, wife/harlot, female addressee; 21:1-10, Jeremianic prophetic intercession; 23:9, the mourning prophet). Rather, the two prose sermons provide the governing interpretative frame.

Between Zedekiah and Jeconiah: Claiming David's Throne (21:1-10; 24:1-10)

The composition negotiates the fate of "Israel" between these two framing pieces and between two claimants not merely to David's throne but to cultural identity under the sign of "Israel." Linear chronological arrangement is not the concern. For 21:1-10 postdates 24:1-10. The former, set toward the *end of the reign* of Zedekiah, takes place during the final siege of Jerusalem by Nebuchadrezzar in 587/586 BC. 24:1-10 takes place at the *beginning* of Zedekiah's rule after the exile of his royal predecessor. Zedekiah was Jeconiah's uncle and the latter's successor to the throne after Jeconiah's deportation to Babylon along with the royal court in 598/597. As is so often the case in Jeremiah, the point of individual units is clear. It is their editorial association with others that complicates meaningful reading.

21:1-10

With Jerusalem under siege by Babylonian forces, Zedekiah's "embassy" to Jeremiah seeks prophetic intercession on the beleaguered city's behalf. Formally it is a request for an oracle with the expectation that Jeremiah will return an oracle announcing miraculous deliverance of the city by Yahweh (21:2). Duplicates of this narrative incident exist and construct a convoluted relationship between Jeremiah and the last sitting king of Judah (cf. 32:1-5; 34:1-22; and 37:1–38:28). The composition manages the tensions and contradictions between the variant narratives by utilizing them in separate subsections in dischronologized fashion.

The king's expectation of a miracle is presumably motivated by allusion to an earlier miracle of deliverance of Jerusalem from besieging Assyrian forces in the reign of Hezekiah. In that earlier time, the prophet Isaiah secured an oracle proclaiming Zion's inviolability in response to Hezekiah's prayer (Isaiah 36–37). The surprise in Jeremiah's response is threefold: he announces Zedekiah's military defeat and Jerusalem's destruction (vv. 3-7); he encourages Jerusalem's general populace to surrender to the Babylonians (vv. 8-10); and thus Jeremiah appears as an "anti-Isaiah" aiding and abetting the enemy rather than his own community!

Jeremiah's ironic rhetoric ("with outstretched hand and mighty arm," 21:5) reverses exodus and conquest traditions where the expectation of Yahweh is his fighting for, not against, the community (v. 5; cf. Exod 6:6; Deut 4:34; 5:15; 7:19; 9:29; 11:2; 26:8; 2 Kgs 17:36; Ps 136:12). Notice that the oracle is unconditional and promises *inescapable death for king* and populace (21:7), that the city will be burned down (v. 10), and that only traitors who give up defense of the city and go over to the Babylonian side can expect to live (vv. 8-9). Zedekiah's hope and any hope in Zedekiah's rule and, therefore, his "Israel," are crushed.

24:1-10

Ironically, one might have interpreted matters differently. For the original circumstances of Zedekiah's rise to the throne had cost the community only the loss of young King Jeconiah and his royal court at the hands of Babylonian forces — a punitive action in response to Jehoiakim's (Jeconiah's father) disloyal vassalage and insurrection toward Babylonian suzerainty. On the surface, those under the sign of "exile" might be viewed as the delegitimated and judged; those left behind might be viewed the purged remnant ready to carry the burden and promise of "Israel." The symbolic vision of the good and the rotten figs prevents that reading and more.

It evaluates the divided political community of Judah just the opposite. The claim to "Israel" has passed to the Jeconiah group exiled in Babylon. They are the good figs!

They are the heirs of restoration. Notice that the promise is return to the land and reestablishment of national life (24:7; cf. Jeremiah's prophetic mission [1:10]). The restored Jeconiah group will realize the ideal "Israel" projected by covenant formulary (24:7, "They shall be my people and I will be their God"). While the mission to turn the community back to Yahwistic purity failed with respect to the community still in the land, it will succeed with this *one* group of exiles (notice that the Egyptian diaspora is explicitly excluded [v. 8]). For Yahweh will miraculously transfigure the Jeconiah group so that they can fulfill the conditions on which restoration hangs (v. 7, "I will give them a heart . . ."; ". . . they shall return to me with their whole heart"). Notice that the promise of restoration is unmotivated and unconditionally worded, rooted solely in God's act.

Equally unconditional and absolute is the consignment of the Zedekiah group and his "remnant of Jerusalem" (24:8; quite a rhetorical demotion of the literally more populous!) to total destruction as the rotten figs. Their loss of life, destiny, and rights in the land is complete (v. 10).

The composition redefines the rights to "Israel." It writes off all claimants except for the Jeconiah group in Babylon. No explanation is given for the assigned valuation of that group as good figs and therefore of their entitlement to Yahwistic restoration. Mere physical exile from the land is not sufficient (*contra* Egyptian diaspora claims!). Only that group in Babylon receives the title "exile of Judah," by implication an exclusionary label. More than that, the composition begins the process of symbolically depopulating the land — freeing it, therefore, for repossession in the restoration — by announcing the total annihilation of the Zedekian remnant (and all others). Hence the emphasis on the imminent death of Zedekiah, here and in the opening frame piece (21:1-10). The only group left able to claim the heritage of "Israel" is with Jeconiah in Babylon! For the first time, the ideological vested interests of the colonized elite appear more clearly on the surface of the composition in their bid to achieve symbolic and literal hegemony over the restoration of Israel, its tenor and identity, and the revitalization of Yahwistic myth.

Against the Judean Monarchy (21:11–23:8)

The composition must justify the claim of its frame piece by encapsulating a catalogue of indictments against Josiah's dynastic successors for failure to realize the ideals of Davidic kingship in the royal temple cult. In the process they sow seeds for the deconstruction of their ideological interests.

Royal ideology informs the tradition. The units weave between poetry and prose. The majority is addressed to the royal house in general (21:11-12; 22:1-5, 6-9; 23:1-4, 5-6, 7-8). Mostly indictments, three predict restoration (23:1-4, 5-6, 7-8). Two (21:13-14; 22:20-23) are addressed to Jerusalem in her role as female persona (cf. chs. 2–3). Three indictments are addressed to named kings: Jehoahaz (22:10-12), Jehoiakim (22:13-19), and Jehoiachin (22:24-30).

The royal ideology at work in the indictments assumes a special relationship between the king, an ideal social order, and national security. National security, cultural existence, and the preservation of special status before Yahweh are contingent on royal administration and the preservation of a just social order. The special crimes singled out in the indictments epitomize a social order protecting the rights and preventing the oppression of the weakest members of the community (orphans, widows, and the poor). The crimes (21:12; 22:3, 13-17) take in literal violence and the legalized violence of judiciary processes defrauding citizens, especially the least powerful, of their rights. Deeply anchored in the old, royal Zion-temple cult are the types of the king, specially commissioned and divinely gifted for the administration of justice (cf. Psalm 72).

Lady Jerusalem's confidence in her impregnability (21:13; 22:23) is forfeit because of the complete failure of Josiah's scions to realize the royal ideal. While the generalized announcements work like rationalized reflection on the role and conditions of monarchic institutions (especially 22:1-5), the royal oracles to named kings apply those reflections to the doomed, thus justifying the rejection of all three from royal succession and *restoration aspirations.*

22:10-12

Jehoahaz (Shallum's throne name) briefly succeeded his father Josiah, but he was deposed by Pharaoh Necho and taken into captivity to Egypt. There is no return for him; he is to die in captivity.

22:13-19

Jehoiakim, client and appointee of the Egyptian pharaoh, succeeded Jehoahaz (his brother). Exile or captivity is not bad enough for him; his death is to be particularly violent and ignominious.

22:24-30

Similarly, Coniah's (Jeconiah/Jehoiachin) exile and imprisonment in Babylon are irrevocable! Both the prose (v. 27) and poetry (v. 30) are emphatic in their denial of prospects of restoration for Coniah or *any* of his offspring. That there will be a restoration, a new defining moment for Israel, inclusive of a Davidic heir is equally emphatic in the composition (23:1-8). Neither of these three, however, will be around to lay claim to the title "Yahweh is our Righteousness" (23:6).

The contrast with 24:1-10 could not be greater. Redaction-critical speculations postulate multiple historical agency, a reflex of Judean party conflicts, to account for the existence of such inconcinnity. A core of the poetic oracle (vv. 28-30) might even be attributable to the historical prophet. But why should prose articulated in the common Jeremianic style also exhibit ideological inconsistency? Clearly it offers support for a nonunified Deuteronomistic redaction, among others. But the problem remains for the implied reader of the final form — how does one valuate conflicted oracular tradition under the one sign, "Jeremiah"? Colonial vested interests risk Jeremianic prophetic authority in their manipulation and representation of the prophetic figure!

Against the Prophets (23:9-40)

So perhaps there is additional motivation for the excoriation of prophecy itself, along with the monarchy, under the sign of the true and the false. An uneasy conscience manifests further anxiety over oracular traditions not easily mastered in the composition or made subservient to the preeminent interests of the framing pieces (21:1-10; 24:1-10).

Prophets, along with kings, are to blame for the corruption and therefore the destruction of the community. We meet oracular traditions decrying the perversion and subversion of prophecy, the abuse of oracular power. These antiprophetic oracles blend poetic (23:9-12, 13-15, 18-22) and prosaic (vv. 16-17[?], 23-32[mixed], 33-40) traditions. A myth of revelation, coupled with acerbic moral rhetoric, forms the backbone of their indictment. The inability of Israelite mythic traditions to resolve the crisis of authority occasioned by prophetic conflict fuels an abiding symbolic anxiety.

The promotion, procurement, and preservation of a Yahwistic moral order legitimate prophecy (23:32). These "false" prophets have done just the opposite by aiding, abetting, and producing a social reality akin to the notorious Sodom and Gomorrah (v. 14). Accusations of their moral defilement range from global, nonspecific terms (vv. 10, 11, "evil"; vv. 11, 15, "pollution"; v. 13, "unseemliness"; v. 14, "a horrible thing") to egregious adultery (vv. 10, 14). How seriously we are to take the vocabulary of impurity is hard to say. It often masks the revulsion of the speaker in face of generalized cultic impurity and apostasy (cf. Jeremiah 2–3; Hosea 1–3) as much as it refers to specific literal moral depravity. And the falsification of Yahwistic cult purity is explicitly highlighted. Moral rhetoric gives way to the accusation of corrupt misappropriation of oracular power (v. 13, "prophecy by Baal," "lead astray"; v. 16, "they delude you," "vision of their mind"; v. 27, "to make my people forget my name," "forgot my name for Baal").

The contours of cult and society are at stake in this flurry of party polemics, negotiated in conflicted prophetic mouthpieces. The composition is attracted to two opposed oracular postures. One, convinced of the inviolable security of the community (23:17), undermines the power of the other toward repentance (v. 14, "so that no one turns from his wickedness"), sure as the latter is of impending national doom (vv. 19-20). For the composition and its implicit reader, the message of doom has proved true (v. 20, "In the latter days you will clearly understand it"). Undeniably so! The colonization of Jerusalem persists. The perfidy of the "false" prophets is exposed. Given, however, the myth of oracular power contained in the composition, it is ironic that the "false" proved so effective a counterforce in blocking the mission of purification. Pseudo-prophets succeeded where the legitimate could not! And, ironically again, the success of the pseudo-prophets vindicates the prophecy of doom.

Deep aporia emerge. For in the myth of oracular power represented here, true inspiration originates only by divine initiative (23:18, 21, 22). Only privileged Yahwistic intimacy constitutes true inspiration (whether one interprets "council" in generalized terms or as a specific allusion to a mythic heavenly divine deliberative court; cf. 1 Kgs 22:19-23; Job 1; Isa 6:1-9). Authentic oracular speech, Yahweh's utterance, distinguishes itself qualitatively in its effective power (23:28, 29). Precisely the point of anxiety for the composition! Analogies to the ineluctable destructive powers of fire and a rock-smashing hammer within the prose commentary (v. 29) cooperate with poetic images of the land-devouring curse (v. 10) and devastating storm (v. 19) to make that point. And yet they do not mask the additional claim made for oracular power emergent from Yahwistic council — namely, that it should effectively secure the restoration of the community in their conversion from "wickedness" (v. 22). Couple that claim with the accusation of v. 14 ("so that no one turns from his wickedness"), and the specter rises of a pseudo-prophecy capable of preventing that very mission! But if that mission can be defeated or counterprophesied, then either it did not issue from the Yahwistic council in the first place or Yahweh's word can fail. Ironically, the authority of the Jeremianic mission is deconstructed by the very myth designed to sustain it! The composition energizes the anxiety it seeks to repress and will need to mask it subsequently with further symbolic operations.

Perhaps taking the imperfect verbs in the apodosis (23:22) in a modal sense could moderate the aporia: ". . . they would have tried to turn them from their evil way. . . ." But the composition has associated this claim with the comparable accusation in v. 14. It would be forced, though possible, to reread that result clause as purpose (in this case "purpose" is a polemical representation of a result as if it were the intended design; cf. Jer 7:8, "in order" not to benefit; see further BDB, p. 116) instead: ". . . in order that no one turns from his wickedness." The surrounding cola in v. 14, however, indicate conditions that have been effected by the pseudo-prophets, not just their intentions. The compositional collocation argues for the harder reading of v. 22. But, for the sake of argument, grant the softer modal interpretation. The aporia only relocates from the surface to deeper levels of the myth of the divine word since the *intention* (contrast v. 20) of Yahweh's word has proved ineffective!

Prophecy and prophetic mechanisms have become tainted symbols at the same time that the composition is sure that authentic prophecy exists and is epitomized in the Jeremianic mission. The institution must be rehabilitated as it is reasserted.

23:23-32

Oneiromancy falls into disgrace along with the reuse ("theft") of Yahwistic oracles ("my words," 23:30) from one prophet to the next and along with the employment of stylized oracular formulae, ". . . they uttered as an utterance" (v. 31; i.e., in a prophetic manner as an oracle of Yahweh). The basis for this opprobrium is not clear. Why, for that matter, shift attention to prophetic mechanisms commonly employed in Yahwistic prophecy? For the "inspired" dreamers dream their revelations in Yahweh's name (v. 25)! Puzzlement only deepens from recognition that this hostile discourse represents itself with God as its dramatic speaker (as is the case throughout this collection of antioracular material).

Perhaps the core issue is the false practitioners, not the practices (v. 25, "prophesy in my name *falsely*"; v. 32, "prophesiers of *false* dreams"). They are the uncommissioned practitioners of oracular techniques who lead astray (v. 32) and who intend apostasy from Yahweh (v. 27). In the context of the composition, mantic practices would then be downgraded through association with the "false" prophecy of peace. But the implied reader's awareness of the long-standing use of mantic technique in Israel among honored prophetic figures complicates interpretation. Even "Jeremiah" announces a future peace/restoration in the present section (23:1-8; 24:6-7)! Elsewhere, there is even the implication of Jeremiah "dreaming" his message of peace (31:26, "Thereupon I awoke and looked, and my sleep was pleasant to me").

Mere denigration of mechanisms for oracle acquisition seems too trivial a reading given our present contextual thematic interests. Simple polarization of peace over against doom seems equally inadequate. Both open aporia destructive of Jeremianic authority as much as that of his opponents. Perhaps, then, the issue is the misapplication of oracular assurance within a community that has forfeited presumption of divine support through violation of the Yahwistic moral order. This has been the burden of the earlier indictments (23:14, 17). The wrong *group* or *community* is given the promise of peace. Events have validated the application of doom, not peace (v. 20, "In the latter days . . ."). In the eyes of this prose commentary, misapplication has tainted and disgraced external phenomena and mechanisms attendant to oracular performance. On this view, the categorical distinctions drawn between the charlatanism of those performances and speaking "my words in truth" (v. 28) seem analogous to the displacements experienced by other symbols. Older cultural practices become tainted. They possess a newly perceived hostility in the perspective of Yahwistic exclusivism (cf. Hos 2:16-17, "... no longer will you call me Baal"). The calumniation of these "prophetic" opponents includes the denigration and parody of their oracular performances.

The composition risks its authority in the aporia opened by such tactics and by the hypocrisy, in relation to its symbolic opponents, of denying oracular power to modes of prophesying still permitted expression by the "true" prophet, Jeremiah. And so it is that encapsulating the antioracular traditions within 21:1-10 and 24:1-10 may help in the deflection of such inconcinnity. The symbolic division of the community between Zedekiah and Jeconiah rationalizes thematic dissonance in Jeremianic tradition and the inconcinnities of Jeremiah's oracular performance. Yahwistic cultic-moral valuation of the "Zedekian" versus the "Jeconian" community elicits oracular performance suited to their just deserts and consequently discovers all counterprophecy (vis-à-vis Jeremiah) to be an act of charlatanism.

23:33-40

The final prose piece continues in a similar vein. The force of the parody lies in a pun on "burden" = "oracle" (*massa'* can mean either). Oracular formulae are displaced (23:36, ". . . you shall mention no more . . ."). The traditional trope of performance sought a *"massa'"* in oracular inquiry (v. 33). That old language has become a tainted symbol (v. 36) and must be replaced by other phrases: "What has Yahweh answered (*'anah*)?" or "What has Yahweh spoken (*dibber*)?" (vv. 35, 37). Continued use of the old trope constitutes grounds for individual and national destruction (vv. 34, 38-40).

Given its present context the initial addressee of the instruction is Jeremiah (23:33, 2d ms. sg. verb and pronoun). His instruction is then delivered to "this people," "prophet or priest," "each one to another, each to his brother." The tone of the initial citation, the request for an oracle ("What is the oracle of Yahweh?"), is ambiguous. The responses to this tainted symbol are not: "You are the *burden (massa')*, and I will abandon you" (v. 33; or read "What *oracle?* I will abandon you"); "I will utterly forget you (*nashiyti nasho'*) and abandon you" (v. 39; or read "I will utterly lift you — that is, the burden — up [*nasa'ti naso'*] and abandon you"). The responses play on the homonym *massa'* in its senses of burden or oracle.

But is the initial request for an oracle sincere? If it is not, then those who request it also play on *massa'*. "What is the *burden* of Yahweh?" is directed in a satirical sense against Jeremiah as a doom-sayer (note the frequent labeling of judgment oracles as *massa'* against foreign enemies in Isa 13:1; 15:1; 17:1; 19:1; 21:1, 11, etc., and against Israel in Hab 1:1, etc.). Then the harshness of the response makes sense. Their request discounts Jeremianic authenticity. On the other hand, if "What is the oracle of Yahweh?" is sincere, perhaps they "load" *massa'* with its connection to oracles against Israelite enemies, and thus imply Israel's deliverance and restoration (cf. Zech 9:1; 12:1). Again, as a request for an oracle of assurance in the face of the enemy (cf. 21:2), it fits the quest for security that the pseudoprophets wrongly aid and abet in context. The acerbic rejection still makes sense. Either reading would clarify the attraction of this unit to 23:9-40 and its encapsulation by 21:1-10 and 24:1-10.

Evaluation

"Jeremiah" is a symbolic arena for the performance of cultural interests and symbolic needs. With chs. 21–24 the composition manages the heir to "Israel." Restoration interests are more clearly to the fore. A theodicy of Judah's colonization is still offered. Focus on a critique of monarchic and prophetic institutions puts that historical and symbolic calamity to the accounts of the failed leadership. They have concertedly effected a subversion of Yahwistic ideals ("... pollution has spread throughout the land") and taken the whole community (". . . scattered my flock . . .") into the vortex of cultural disintegration.

The advantage of this particular emphasis in chs. 21–24 lies in its symbolic deauthorization of ideological opponents under the sign of the "Zedekian" remnant. "Israel" is reconfigured, rewritten in relation to the restoration and placed under the sign of the "Jeconian" group in Babylon. The critique of Davidic monarchs and prophets legitimates this displacement and elevates the symbolic claims and cultural power of the implicit agents projected into the "Jeconian" sign.

Compositional performance in the symbolic arena maintains strict anonymity. It projects its interests into the Jeremianic traditions already present — adding to, expanding, rewriting, rearranging, rereading, creating fresh material — attempting to bring symbolic shape to the tradition, a landscape in the end serviceable to their cultural needs. Compensation must be found for the collapse of the old Davidic state, the ideal of "Israel" held out by it, in a manner that can enliven restoration dreams while empowering elite interests which pour themselves into the sign of "Jeremiah."

The process of compositional performance, the projection of implicit agents and their needs into the arena, has increasingly dehistoricized the traditions, rendering historical specificity of the tradition and of the setting of the performance more and more opaque. Modern redaction-critical theory may speculate, with good reason, about editorial deposits of competing party interests and their historical occasions. Depending on judgments about authenticity, candidates in the late monarchy, the exile, and the Second Temple period have their attractiveness and plausibility as nodes of compositional intensity. But the dehistoricizing impulse has increasingly knocked the edges of concrete historical agency away. Anonymity has been intensified, frustrating historical definitiveness for any of the proposed redaction-critical models. Agency has remained hidden under the signs, the figures and voices populating the world inside the arena. This in turn has produced an increasingly stylized, symbolic, representational imaginative landscape — "Jeremiah." At the same time this landscape has gradually acquired a structure of trajectories or performances in the service of colonial elite restoration interests. Yet it has also acquired a fictive life of its own under the arch symbols exile and return. Thus the fictive arena "Jeremiah" has gradually acquired its own power of agency (even if only in limited symbolic ways) over every "performer" entering that "space." There is a legend of Jeremiah that must be served in order to rehabilitate Yahweh and keep the myth of Israel alive.

But the traditions in chs. 21–24 have proved more challenging, more anxiety-laden for the composition. Aporia deeply situated all along in the strategies of the composition bubble easily to the surface in chs. 21–24, undermining persuasive power and ideological control. The symbolic arena is also a symbolic battlefield. Its own weapons turn against it.

The contradictory negotiations over Jeconiah cascade into the problem of false prophecy for the figure of Jeremiah. He fulfills the conditions of self-deceit so excoriated in the section against the prophets. This cascades deeply into the very construction of Yahweh. For the restoration themes are unmotivated, consequent solely upon divine determination. Contrast the explicit moralistic and cult purity rationalizations motivating the theodicy for Israel's exile and colonization, the antithesis of presumed security! Does the promise of restoration constitute raw grace? Or is exile itself a sufficient punishment enabling restoration to those who have borne their deserved punishment? If the latter, why then is restoration just for the Jeconiah group? Others also experienced the common, desired precondition — namely, dispersion. If in order to effect the restoration Yahweh is going to *create* repentance, why not make the prophetic mission successful on this score in the first place? Why not miraculously birth the ideal "Israel" for which he so agonizingly longs prior to the bloodshed and suffering of colonization?

Once again the failure of God that so agonizes the composition in its dreams of restoration continues to haunt the very constructions designed to surmount the symbolic crisis. It reasserts itself in the very act of its denial, deconstructing the myth of Yahweh they so long to prop up.

Are they blind to the aporia so created? Perhaps so where they reach more deeply into the construction of God. It's harder to say where the aporia sit easily at the surface. What was a reader to do with the final deposit? To whose voice among the layers should one attend? The last layer or some other? Did ancient readers not see these aporia? Some of the exegetical processes recovered by modern scholarship suggest that in fact they did. They appear to have seen that expansion, addition, alteration, and the like were designed to postpone, delay, mask, or resolve such deconstructive potential in the composition.

Once it is committed to the denial of God's failure and determined to overcome the dissonance of their mythic demoralization at any price, the composition clutches at any stratagem (ruse) to sustain its dreams of cultural revitalization. Thus they hope to smother their mythic anxiety to postpone admitting the death of Israelite myth. Their symbolic success means the metamorphosis of the "realities" under the names.

The composition tears itself apart. It deconstructs its own symbolic mechanisms, schemes, and desires. It could not succeed in solving the crisis for Israelite myth without at the same time more deeply incorporating that very crisis permanently into its rehabilitated myth and thus perennially insuring its deconstructive potential.

How could "Jeremiah" fail at such a deep level when, ironically, on another it succeeds ("plays its part") in the preservation of "Israel" as well as old world communities willing to live historically under that name. Do we say that the arch symbols of exile and return (given expression in the performances of "Jeremiah") prove supple mechanisms for the perennial postponement of such mythic dissonance even as they contain, launch, and sustain within the symbolic battlefield of "Jeremiah" their own deconstructive potentials?

Jeremiah 25:1-38

Overview

Specific date formulae may appear to anchor the tradition to concrete "events," but it is a myth of Yahweh that is under construction by means of the mythologization of history. The theodicy of Jerusalem's destruction is now integrated into the larger myth of God's war with the world. Israel's experience of the prophet to the nations,

Jeremiah, and of oracular power becomes rationalized under assumptions about the destiny-shaping power of oracular utterance, schemata of prediction-fulfillment, and periodization. Judah's brutal experience of Babylonian imperialism has become a sign of Yahweh's imperial aspirations for the world. Israel's subjugation is the harbinger of the world's doom. God's way with Israel is the sign of his way with the world of nations. "Israel," "prophecy," and "Yahweh" survive the collapse and colonization of the old Davidic state through an enlargement of symbolic stature — compensation for Israel's historical shame and crisis of symbols.

Dramatic Composition

Chapter 25 offers a major juncture, a pivot point, in the structure of the book. It constructs a reading map both retrospective and prospective. It looks back over the preceding twenty-four chapters to summarize compositional interests, to pick up neglected or underdeveloped themes signaled in the initial call narrative. These it projects forward into compositional interest and development with the remaining traditions in chs. 26–51. In the process it offers a narrative arc for the entire scroll of Jeremiah: God's war from Babylon to Judah (chs. 2–24), God's war from Judah to Babylon (chs. 26–51). Ch. 1 then supplies the introduction, and ch. 52 a summary conclusion.

The composition has achieved this effect through extensive reperformance of Jeremianic tradition, as the complicated and major divergences between the LXXV edition and the MT edition of Jeremiah indicate. For extensive collections of oracles addressed to foreign nations have been dislocated by the MT to chs. 46–51 in contrast to the LXXV, which has them located at the center of the tradition in 25:14–31:44. In the process, anti-Babylonian oracles have been moved from third (LXXV) to last place in the sequence (MT).

Beneath these overarching structural differences lie numerous puzzlements and challenges. The prose sermon's list of foreign nations (MT 25:17-26 [LXXV 32:1-12]) does not match those addressed in chs. 46–51 no matter whose version is used. At the same time the list in the MT differs from that in the LXXV principally through the *absence* of Babylon in the LXXV.

In addition, the representation of the prophet in the second half of the book is complicated by simultaneous pro- and anti-Babylonian oracles explicitly set within the same historical occasions — Jerusalem's imminent fall in the assurance of Babylonian invincibility. In Jeremiah 25, the MT only enhances the problem by simultaneously expanding the prose to label Nebuchadrezzar Yahweh's servant (v. 9), and the one destined to drink last of all from the cup of wrath (v. 26).

To discern how the MT as a "reader" of the tradition gains in this performance of restructuring enables subsequent readers to negotiate the dissonance in the Jeremianic tradition that both have had to face.

Inscribing Jerusalem's Destiny of Lost Chances (25:1-14)

The date formula sets the prose sermon in 605 BC, Jehoiakim's fourth year, synchronized to Nebuchadrezzar's first (if an accession-year system for the calculation of regnal tenure is not employed, then there is a one-year chronological discrepancy — a discrepancy consistent throughout the Jeremianic tradition; contrast 2 Kgs 24:12; 25:8 with Jer 52:28-29, and the latter with 52:12 and 32:1!). If the narrative is cast as Jeremiah's reminiscence over the preceding twenty-three years, he indicts the nation (25:3-7) for their rejection of the prophetic mission. The objective of that mission had been to turn the community back from general unspecified wickedness (the stereotypical rhetoric of Jeremianic prose) and more specifically to induce cultic purification (Yahwistic exclusivity). Had the appeal succeeded, continued national existence would have been secured (v. 5). The predicted punishment comprises destruction, colonization, and depopulation by Babylonian imperial power for a set period of seventy years (vv. 11, 12). The vocabulary of destruction projects and exaggerates a fantastic landscape of horror inspiring ruin and devastation (vv. 9-10).

The alternative edition is instructive for compositional interests in the MT. All mention of the Babylonians and Nebuchadrezzar is absent. Instead the LXXV speaks only of an unspecified nation from the north. In this case it is probably understood as a generalized collective (LXXV 5:9, "Behold, I will send and take a *family* from the north, and I will bring *them* against this land. . . ."; v. 12, "And when the seventy years are complete, I will exact vengeance on *that nation,* and I will make *them* into a lasting destruction"). Rather than predict a seventy-year Babylonian hegemony, the alternative performance projects a time frame for a *general dispersion* and servitude (LXXV v. 11, ". . . they will *serve among the nations* seventy years"). Further, the MT heightens the presence of Jeremiah's prophetic figure since it transforms representation of the sermon's speaker from consistent divine first person speech (in the LXXV) into prophetic reminiscence (the MT adds "Jeremiah the prophet" in v. 2 and "the word of Yahweh which came to me" in v. 3. It rewords some first person pronominal references to Yahweh into third person — for example, v. 3, "I spoke to you . . ."; v. 4, "and Yahweh sent his servants the prophets . . ."), thus effectively intertwining Jeremiah and Yahweh's voice. The prophet narrates a history of God's speaking.

The composition performs a web of symbolic enhancements. This identification of the "foe from the north" with Babylon does more than state the obvious. It inextricably binds Yahweh, Jeremiah, and Nebuchadrezzar into a nexus of mythic agency and causality. Enhanced insinuation of the prophetic persona into the history of the divine word underscores Jeremiah's representation as the fulcrum around which the nation decides its fate. Nebuchadrezzar becomes God's royal servant (25:9) and thus the "messianic" (anointed) agent of fulfillment. Babylonian imperialism authenticates Jeremianic oracular power at the same time it is wielded by it! Narrowing the seventy-year period of servitude specifically to the period of Babylonian hegemony further underscores the splintering of "Israel" begun in chs. 21–24. The wider diaspora is effaced (LXXV v. 11, ". . . they will serve among the nations"). "Israel" is the community specifically under Nebuchadrezzar's rule — "indentured" for seventy years (MT v. 11, "... they will serve the king of Babylon").

Finally, the periodization of Babylonian rule rationalizes the dissonance of Nebuchadrezzar, simultaneously designated by Jeremiah as both divine servant (25:9) and object of divine vengeance (vv. 13-14). Pro- and anti-Babylonian oracles can be temporally distributed. Oracular fulfillment becomes rationalized within the enlarged myth of a predetermined divine plan for history. And the figure of the prophet acquires symbolic power as the one who knows the mysteries of time.

Administering the Cup of Yahwistic Imperial Wrath (25:15-29)

Recall that the edition of Jeremiah upon which the LXXV is based postpones this unit (LXXV 32:1-15) and the next (MT 25:30-38 [LXXV 32:16-24]) and thus encapsulates the large collection of oracles against the nations (MT 46–51 [LXXV 25:14–31:44]). The edition upon which the MT is based reperforms the tradition in pursuit of a narrative arc that periodizes oracular fulfillment for the Jeremianic tradition. So it moves the oracles against the nations to chs. 46–51 and immediately connects the symbolic action to the preceding prose sermon.

The implications of the seventy-year period for Babylonian hegemony are carried forward and dramatized by the addition (absent in the LXXV) of the king of Sheshach (Babylon) to the end of the list (25:26; he will drink "after them") of the nations (vv. 18-26) who are destined to drink from the cup of God's wrath (v. 15). Their judgment is as irrevocable as was Jerusalem's. Vv. 27-29 stylize a dialogue (cf. the earlier symbolic actions in 13:1-14 and especially 18:1-12, which incorporate disputation from the dramatic addressees). The nations might attempt to avoid God's opiate. But they will fare no better than Jerusalem did with her stratagems to discount and fend off threats of national destruction (cf. the dialogical patterns of chs. 2–20). 25:29 states the rationale. God's war against Israel is subsumed within a larger war against the entire earth. Indeed, it is only the beginning of the greater Yahwistic imperial campaign. In fact, Israel's colonization constitutes both the harbinger and the guarantee of the world's destiny. Notice that in v. 18 the MT expands to "as it is this day," referring to Israel's predicted doom. The implicit reader is displaced temporally. It at least dislocates and relocates the reader somewhere between the beginning of Yahweh's Great War and its denouement. The composition will process its reader in the Jeremianic tradition that remains to that denouement (from Judah to Babylon).

Yahweh, the Tyrant King, Comes (25:30-38)

The poetic unit inaugurates the journey. While the LXXV uses this unit as the closing piece to its section of oracles against the nations, the MT has, through its dislocations of the tradition, lent it an anticipatory and transitional function. The announced divine war spreading from nation to nation with its sense of geographical movement receives dramatization in the second half of the book. For the latter narrates the completion of the war against Judah (chs. 26–45), spreading out to the rest of the nations (chs. 46–49) until it climaxes in Babylon's fall (chs. 50–51).

The preceding prose units of this chapter have emphasized prophetic and Babylonian agency in their portrayal of Yahweh's war. This poetic unit collapses that sense of agency, immediately and profoundly intertwining Yahweh directly with the destructive powers unleashed against the earth. The blend of military, zoological, and meteorological images that makes up this portrait of the divine going to war has a long heritage in Israelite tradition as well as in the mythopoesis of other ancient Near Eastern gods and goddesses. Like Marduk, Ishtar, Baal, or Anat, Yahweh engages the battle with true zest (25:30; his shout of exultation). He is the lion fully committed to the hunt and to destruction (vv. 30, 38). The flocks of the rulers of the nations (notice that the LXXV consistently preserves the shepherd/sheep imagery, labeling them "rams" instead of "lords of the flock") are his prey (vv. 34-36). He is the bereaver and destroyer (v. 36). His anger is the anger of the oppressor (v. 38; notice "wrath of the oppressor" paralleled to "his wrath"; the LXXV omits the latter and reads "great sword" for the former; cf. v. 37, where the MT reads "wrath of Yahweh" for LXXV's "my wrath"). The world of nations now faces the terrible tyrant who comes from the "extremities of the earth" (v. 32; cf. the dwelling places of the Canaanite deities El or Baal).

The motivation for such devastation remains laconic — the wickedness of all flesh (25:31). The prose insertion at v. 33, however, echoes earlier rhetoric (8:2; 16:4, 6) describing Judah's punishment and thus implies here that the rest of the world shares Judah's fate. It also ties the unit to the preceding scheme summarized in v. 29 — a common destiny of judgment begins with Jerusalem. And like Judah, the rest of the world will utter their mourning songs (vv. 34, 36).

Evaluation

Symbolic compensation for the enduring colonization of "Israel" is found in a myth of future Yahwistic imperial supremacy achieved by a divine military conquest that works its way in and through the imperial quests and clashes of the nations. Existing colonial conditions are rationalized under the sign of that Yahwistic imperial quest. The collapse of the old Davidic state, rather than indicating the failure of divine patronage, signals the presence of the warrior God-King achieving world suzerainty. By reperforming the Jeremianic tradition the composition enlarges the myth of Yahweh out of the building blocks of the very royal ideology embarrassed by Babylonian victory and hegemony. It periodizes the oracular tradition with respect to fulfillment and the abovementioned historical schema. In the process, ch. 25 acts as a reading map laying out an overview of the historical plan and the literary arrangement of the Jeremiah scroll.

At the same time the figure of the prophet grows in symbolic stature. For the prophet has the mysteries of the divine plan open before him. The prophetic collection transcends the specifics of the prophet's immediate (dramatic) audience. Oracular dissonance is sublimated.

The implied audience is invited to place itself at the appropriate period of oracular effect associated with the voice of Yahwistic exclusivity. The way is prepared for the revitalization dreams of the colonial elite. The early stages of the transformation and rewriting of prophecy into apocalyptic begins.

The price of rehabilitating the myth of "Israel" lies in the disenfranchisement of competing communities whose claim to Yahwistic legitimacy is denied — whether of the "wrong" generation or cultural pedigree or group location. Ironically, the victims of imperial power construct a myth of Yahweh in the image of the imperial powers they serve. The suffering of Israel is the suffering that will envelop the world. Human life will be shed as fodder in Yahweh's imperial project. The violence and brutality of human history are inscribed deeply into divine aspirations achievable apparently only by such ruthless means. For such a myth the existence of innocent suffering must be written off under the sign of the *wickedness of all flesh* except as it appears in martyrdom to the cause (hence the figure of the suffering prophet). It is a brutal myth rising from the harsh exigencies of Israelite colonization. How else were the colonial elite to resurrect hope in face of their profound cultural demoralization?

Jeremiah 26:1–29:32

Overview

Prophecy is the arsenal of social power. But the prophets compete as reflexes of conflicted party interests. In the presence of prophetic conflict lies the deconstruction of the myth of oracular power. Therein lies a deep anxiety for the composition since prophecy is made the bearer of revitalization dreams.

The composition cannot admit the failure of its myth. To do so would mean the abandonment of their aspirations for "Israel" and the myth of Yahweh. The vortex of their cultural demoralization could never be escaped. It also cannot yet take the step in its conceptualization of oracular periodization of announcing the cessation of prophecy as some voices will do within Second Temple Judaism. Instead the Jeremianic prophetic mission must be lionized. Rather than succumb to cultural despair, they reperform the Jeremianic traditions and project new meanings under the old symbols through a metonymic process. New conceptualizations are substituted under the names. An illusion of continuity is maintained at the same time that their rehabilitation represents a repristination of religious innovation under the signs of the old regime.

Dramatic Composition

Up to this point the composition has employed third person oblique prose only on a limited basis (only 19:14–20:6 if one excludes the narratives of symbolic action [13:1-14; 16:1-9; 18:1-12; 19:1-13] and the vision reports [1:11-13; 24:1-10]). Prose has meant prose speech/sermon/discourse used in combination with the poetic traditions to construct stylized scenes, dialogues, and disputes. In the second half of the scroll, however, it becomes a dominating mode for representing the figure of Jeremiah and vested compositional interests.

In chs. 26–29 three different scenes/episodes of the prophetic mission are narrated yet with a common underlying plot structure. However it is executed specifically, the plot of each episode is built up out of three action types: Jeremiah delivers an oracle, the people reject or oppose Jeremiah's proclamation, and Jeremiah is vindicated. Apologetic motives are apparent, for the authenticity of the Jeremianic mission must be maintained.

Seducing Oracular Power (26:1-24)

The composition backtracks to the beginning of Jehoiakim's reign. Jeremiah is put on trial for false prophecy. The prophet's seditious oracle (26:2-6) is the occasion for the charges. The narrator represents the *private* motives and rhetoric of the prophetic mission for the reader (not Jeremiah's dramatic audience) as a mission of repentance (v. 3). The prophecy of doom is reconfigured as a conditional threat. Doom is the penalty for rejecting divine instruction and the prophetic appeal (v. 4). It is a last-chance appeal that assumes a history of rejection (v. 5, ". . . but you have not listened"). Jeremiah's *public* rhetoric threatening destruction of the temple and the city, however, is calculated to offend the dramatic audience populating the temple court (v. 2). It announces the violation of the inviolable. The prophet's blasphemy strikes at the heart of national confidence by appealing to the destruction of an earlier cult site at Shiloh (v. 6; cf. 7:12, 14). Jeremiah alludes to historical precedent by demonstrating that Yahweh is not above destroying his own temple. Calculating prophetic rhetoric grates against elite and popular assumptions about the security of Zion, anchored as it is in the presence of Yahweh's temple in Jerusalem.

Mob outrage and riot ensue and lead directly to a legal inquiry (26:7-15) designed to engineer Jeremiah's execution. The narrator preserves the anonymity of the prophet's opponents: "the priests," "the prophets," and "all the people" (v. 7). Their characterization is complex, for motives and intentions must be inferred from narrative gaps and the interplay of speech — all of which the composition poses as interpretative puzzlement.

While the posture of "the priests" and "the prophets" remains one of constant opposition toward Jeremiah (they seek the death penalty for him, 26:11), "all the people" are constantly repositioned throughout the episode. Not only are they part of the dramatic audience who hear the initial oracle but they are also joined with "the prophets" and "the priests" as those who seize Jeremiah for execution (vv. 8-9a). V. 9b, however, has them assemble subsequently "against/around (?)" the arrested prophet.

The Judean court officials take up their position to hear the accusations against the prophet (26:10). But it is specifically "the priests" and "the prophets" who level the charges to a dramatic audience consisting now of "the princes" and "all the people" (v. 11). And there they remain, enumerated with "the princes" — who decide to acquit Jeremiah — in opposition to the intentions of "the priests" and "the prophets" (vv. 12, 16). Does the narrator imply by these shifts a vacillating mob under the whim of competing party interests? Or is the reader to project a complicated layering of "all the people" — that is, an initial group outraged and incited against the prophet (vv. 8-9a), joined by additional members of the populace who take their place with "the princes" and are persuaded by Jeremiah's self-defense (vv. 9b, 12, 16). It is hard to say.

The composition does not help when it consistently represents "all the people" as those who have heard the prophet's inflammatory oracle (26:7, 8a, 11b, 12b, 15b). But "the princes," who physically have just arrived, are also included in the same category.

For the latter group there is also complexity of composition. 26:17-19 introduce another set of participants, "from among the elders of the land," who speak in defense of Jeremiah. And if the complexion of the assembly was not confusing enough, v. 24 introduces the Shaphanid Ahikam as the key defender and savior of Jeremiah from the "hand of the people"! Recognition of this character relies on the reader's intertextual knowledge of the Deuteronomistic literature where Ahikam appears among the Josianic officials in pursuit of cult purification and revitalization (2 Kgs 22:12, 14). The Shaphanid family weaves a vital web of support for the Jeremianic mission in subsequent narratives. If the composition, then, singles out by name one of "the princes," is the reader to understand the "elders of the land" in similar fashion as additional constituents of that group? Perhaps so, since the narrator introduces them with "they stood" — that is, from among those sitting to hear the charges (cf. v. 10).

The logic of the elders' role in the plot is puzzling. Since, as it usually is assumed, 26:16 represents the resolution of the judicial process, "all the people" and "the princes" agree that the prophet should not receive the death penalty. Why continue the argument? Does the "assembly of the people" still need to be persuaded of the legitimacy of this verdict (v. 17b)? Unless vv. 17-19, 24 represent a flashback to v. 16's conclusion, a reader might resolve the problem by layering the citizenry present in narrative imagination. For if "all the people" voice Jeremiah's acquittal in v. 16, why the need for Ahikam (v. 24) to deliver Jeremiah from the "hand of the people"? Clearly, vv. 17-19, 20-23, and 24 repeatedly suspend the conclusion to this episode. Vv. 20-23 even fall outside the plot as narrative comment filling in background to the level of risk the prophet endures. This might imply that the narrator does not understand the "trial" as a trial in a formal sense. Rather, all the way through it represents only pretrial debate (including v. 16), as it were, an inquiry which in this case does not proceed to a capital case (cf. McKane 1986: 676-81, "a fact-finding enquiry"; but the expression in v. 11, "sentence of death," as a legal idiom forming the verdict and conclusion of a case, though possible [McKane: 678, "tried on a capital charge"], is hard to evade [Deut 19:6; 21:22; cf. 22:26, "offense punishable by death"]).

Speech is just as perilous as the plotted characterizations. None of the flashback citations offered in the swirl of accusation and debate matches the original prophetic oracle, not even Jeremiah's! The prophet's initial speech is framed as a negative protasis (26:4-5a) whose condition *has been met* (v. 5b). Therefore the promised threat of the apodosis will be actualized (v. 6). In his defense, Jeremiah reformulates. His oracle has become a positive plea for repentance whose motive, known heretofore in the episode only by God, the prophet, and the reader (v. 3; addressed only to the prophet in the dramatic scene!), is the *prevention* of divine punishment (v. 13).

Jeremiah's accusers, however, represent the oracle with the rhetoric of unconditional doom (26:9). Perhaps they are justified in this representation since, after all, the prophet claimed, ". . . but you have not listened" (v. 5b). Their reformulation "reads" seditious motives and draws the appropriate point even though they depart from the wording of the original apodosis (v. 6, "... I will make this city a curse to all the nations of the earth"; contrast v. 9, "... this city will be desolate without inhabitant"). Even their rewording of the latter may only reflect their understanding of the cause or mechanism (desolation) of the promised effect (a sign of curse). (For the nearest formulations elsewhere in the rhetoric of the prophet see 44:8, "a curse and reproach throughout all the nations of the earth"; 44:22, "a curse without inhabitant"; 33:10, 12, "desolate with no one.") They take his point, which Jeremiah now denies!

Interestingly, the remainder of Jeremiah's defense makes his treatment at their hands a new condition and threat to communal security. If they execute him, they shed innocent blood (cf. 7:6)! Hence the facile conclusion of "the princes" and "all the people" (26:16, "in the name of Yahweh our God he has spoken to us") and the pertinence of the testimony of the "elders of the land" (vv. 17-19). For the former accentuate Jeremiah's assurances that he is authentically commissioned by Yahweh to speak as a prophet (vv. 12, 15b) — ironically denied by the accusers, "Why have you prophesied in Yahweh's name?" (v. 9). And the latter cut to the quick of the issue by appealing to the Micah tradition.

In keeping with the perspective of Jeremiah's opponents, Micah's earlier oracle (Mic 3:12) is formulated as an unconditional prediction of doom — and thus is apt for layered argumentation in the mouths of the elders. On the surface, of course, it establishes thematic congruity between Jeremiah's oracle and earlier *accepted* prophetic tradition. In addition, the model piety of King Hezekiah and the community in response to Micah counters the deadly intentions of Jeremiah's opponents in the present (26:19a). For, most importantly, the Hezekian community accepted the authenticity of the prophetic message, repented, and interceded for themselves, successfully turning divine wrath from the community. The elders read into the rhetoric of absolute doom an assumption of oracular contingency. Fulfillment and non-fulfillment of oracular tradition become negotiable in the moral nexus of communal response. The prophecy of doom is interpreted as a threat in service to the prophetic mission of repentance. Jeremiah's defense receives corroboration while he is personally exonerated of seditious motives. For the elders, Jeremiah's presence as a prophet of doom punctuates a moral nexus for the community in which they risk their very survival (v. 19b).

Intertexts abound for this narrator in the weaving of the episode. They intersect multiple textual surfaces. First, of course, are the echoes of the earlier prose sermon in ch. 7. Its literary relationship to the latter lends irony to the present episode. Ch. 7 negotiated the aporia around the possibility of repentance (and therefore avoidance of the calamity) by chronologically negotiating the tenor of prophetic mission in face of national intransigence. The initial plea for repentance gives way to inescapable doom, a historic cycle for prophecy down the generations — a myth of prophecy specifically recited in Jer 26:3, 5.

But to the extent that ch. 26 reproduces the earlier speech it profoundly truncates it and distributes what remains along the developing plot. So ironically Jeremiah does not explicitly *begin* his oracle with an appeal to repent. His rhetoric already assumes the negative alternative (v. 5b, "... but you have not listened")! Why hide divine intention (v. 3)? He only discloses it, now redressed as his purpose all along, under lethal threat (v. 13)! Does Jeremiah barter for his life with oracular power? In any case, the redistribution of fragments of the prose sermon (Jeremiah 7) to different portions of the plot permits Jeremiah 26 to measure rhetorical nuance and anxiety-laden aporia against the shifting moral nexus of the developing community response. Both the composition and the dramatic character engage in ironic behavior under the sign of the divine injunction — "do not *hold back/take away* a single word" (v. 2b; cf. Deut 4:2; 13:1[Eng. 12:32])!

Jeremiah, bargaining for his life, has opened once again the possibility of repentance. That offer finds its positive support in the voices of "the princes," "all the people," and "the elders" and apparently wins the day through the intervention of Ahikam. For surely the refusal to kill the prophet, not to shed innocent blood, represents good faith on the way to the required larger amendment of life. Is there yet hope of preventing the calamity opened up by this episode's outcome? Ironically, Jeremiah's vindication risks the need of the composition to write off the prophet's generation, populace and ruling elite together!

And so the composition exploits a second major intertextual intersection, between Micah and Jeremiah, by incorporating it into a third. Not only has the elders' evocation of Micah proved apt for the representation of the narrator's understanding of prophecy but also the reference to Hezekiah contains a relevant narrative analogy and counterfoil which the composition is quick to develop. The narrator's aside to the reader (26:20-23) evokes a more recent precedent to the elders'. Ironically, King Jehoiakim's physical absence from the plot constitutes a potent threat, potentially capable of nullifying any beneficent national result to be had from Jeremiah's vindication in the present episode. For, after all, the episode is set within Jehoiakim's first year. The imitation of Hezekiah's community at least among some of those gathered at the temple does not reach to the highest level of the land.

The MT performance of the tradition over against the LXXV's illuminates compositional interest. The MT heightens the individual agency of King Jehoiakim in the murder of the prophet Uriah, a Jeremianic-like prophet in message and tone (26:20b). While both versions have the king and his entire court hear Uriah's preaching, the MT assigns the desire to kill him only to the king (v. 21 MT, "the king sought to kill him ..."; contrast the LXXV's "... they sought to kill him"); the royal officials represent royal instruments only (v. 22). The MT also heightens the ignominious quality of Uriah's death and the king's contempt for him by altering the circumstances of Uriah's burial (v. 23 MT, "he threw his corpse in a common grave"; contrast LXXV's "he threw him into his family grave"). King Jehoiakim's visage, already negative, takes on enhanced brutality and impiety! The narrator temporizes toward any resolution of the threat to Jeremiah and consequently the threat to the nation that cascades from harming a prophet. The resolution of this plot tension is left hanging.

Thus the narrator also anticipates wider development of the Hezekiah/Jehoiakim narrative analogy (counterfoil) in ch. 36, while the latter frames the subsection chs. 26–36 and echoes by ironic inversion the plot of the present episode (see further on ch. 36).

At the same time, a layering of political power, intrigue, and intention in the royal court is effected. For what did the princes intend anyway when they came from the royal palace to investigate Jeremiah in the temple gate? Are they not the king's officials? What commission do they act under, if any? Does Jehoiakim remain unaware of the uproar that Jeremiah causes in the temple? Why does this leadership seem divided among itself in the present episode on the question of how to dispose of Jeremiah (Ahikam; "the princes" versus "the priests" and "the prophets")? Certainly the narrator's precedent indicates no compunction on the part of the king's princes of handing up a prophet for execution. The MT performs an interesting increase of detail here by specifically naming as the leader of those charged with capturing Uriah (contrast 26:22 LXXV, "the king dispatched men to Egypt"), Elnathan ben Achbor (in the Deuteronomistic literature he is identified as Jehoiakim's father-in-law! [2 Kgs 24:8]). The reader will encounter him again only in ch. 36 in a very surprising role — defending the prophetic scroll (36:25)! This layered representation of unstable loyalties and shifting coalitions serves the compositional interest ultimately of writing off Jeremiah's generation. In the present episode, it hints at the ephemeral quality of the "hearing" accorded Jeremiah's prophetic mission as well as the eventual cause of its public disgrace.

Falsifying the Yoke of Oracular Power (27:1–28:17)

The performance of Jeremianic tradition achieves the transformation of Jeremiah (prophet and prophecy) and intends the symbolic defeat and disenfranchisement of pre-calamity Israel. In 27:1-22 the composition concentrates on a symbolic prophetic act and its interpretation for a layered dramatic and implicit audience. Ch. 28 narrates prophetic conflict and opposition to Jeremiah's symbolic act resolved into the vindication of Jeremiah's prophetic authority. Themes heralded in ch. 25 — that is, calculation of the duration of Babylonian suzerainty and therefore the time of "Israel's" restoration — are insinuated into the play of this episode.

While the pattern of this episode is clear, its temporal setting is not. The date formulae are confusing and apparently corrupt (27:1; 28:1) as presently constituted in the MT. Internal to the plot of the episode, temporal allusions set the action in the reign of Zedekiah (27:3, 12) between the deportation of 598/597 and of 587/586 (28:3, 4). But 27:1 in the MT dates the first part of the episode to the beginning of Jehoiakim's reign. The LXXV lacks any superscription here, and MT 28:1 offers the conflation of two dating schemes. One places the conflict with Hananiah in the same year as the preceding, marked as the beginning of Zedekiah's reign (i.e., ch. 27). The other dates the conflict to Zedekiah's fourth year and fifth month. The LXXV at 28:1 has a simpler formula: "In the fourth year of Zedekiah, king of Judah, in the fifth month. . . ." The easiest solution is to assume a mistake in 27:1 occasioned by attraction to 26:1. The remaining permutations of the MT would then cascade out from there. Those mss. that substitute Zedekiah for Jehoiakim at 27:1 correct based on the internal plot of the episode. 28:1 is then corrected to match it, resulting in a conflated formula (adding, "In the same year, at the beginning of the reign . . ."). The resultant MT at 28:1 equates "beginning of the reign" with the "fourth year."

Alternatively, the pattern of major expansions in the MT throughout the episode reasserts central themes out of ch. 25. Perhaps the addition of the Jehoiakim date formula at 27:1 deliberately harks back to that earlier prophecy and recasts the episode (at least for ch. 27) as addressed to Zedekiah's time from an earlier temporal standpoint. This would be in keeping with the expanding figure of the prophet as one who sees the course of future events in the divine plan and who exercises power to address oracles directly to audiences within the successive epochs. The MT would then be fusing temporal markers ("beginning" versus "fourth") which it otherwise appears to keep distinct (cf. 26:1 and 36:1). 28:1 ("In the same year . . .") would have to be understood as *in the same year* in which the earlier Jeremianic predictions were coming true — that is, the period of oracular fulfillment.

27:1-22

Jeremiah addresses (27:2, "to me," lacking in the LXXV; Jeremiah does not become the explicit narrator of the episode until v. 12, according to the LXXV) the interpretation of his symbolic act (wearing the yoke) to three audiences: foreign envoys of surrounding Syro-Palestinian states (vv. 4-11), King Zedekiah (vv. 12-15), and "the priests" and "all the people" (vv. 16-22). The alternative is offered to each, either to submit to Babylonian rule and live, or to rebel and perish as a nation. To the envoys the prophet begins with the negative alternative (v. 8), with Zedekiah, "the priests," and "all the people" the positive (vv. 12, 17). Motivational tropes set the three oracles apart and attract attention in performance and reperformance of the tradition.

The alternatives to the foreign envoys are anchored in Yahweh's decision, by right of creation, to apportion imperial sovereignty over the earth (27:5). The latter is Yahweh's gift, which at present he has bestowed on Nebuchadrezzar (vv. 6-7). Hence submission to the Babylonian king represents submission to Yahweh. Response to Babylonian hegemony determines national destiny before God. So far the LXXV and the MT agree. But the latter engages in major expansion and reformulation of the theme.

With the fortunes of Yahweh's rule already intertwined with Babylonian hegemony, the composition makes every effort to deepen the inextricable (for a time) agency of God and Nebuchadrezzar. The MT expands the oracle with 27:7 (absent in the LXXV) to chronologize the alliance between the two to three generations of Babylonian rule, thus offering an interpretation of the earlier seventy-year figure in ch. 25. The gift of the Creator, "all these nations" (v. 6; cf. LXXV, "the earth"), marks the favor of Yahweh to Nebuchadrezzar, "my servant" (v. 6; cf. LXXV, "to serve him"). The epithet makes an honest Yahwist of him — much more than the brute, unwitting rod that Assyrian Yahwistic agency entailed (Isaiah 10)! All that Yahweh has created, from person to animal (v. 5, MT addition), is deeded over to Nebuchadrezzar, included now in the Babylonian imperium (v. 6). The MT represents Yahweh as the emphatic actor in Nebuchadrezzar's destiny in the world. For the MT rereads the tradition to insinuate Yahweh's immediate agency on behalf of Nebuchadrezzar: v. 5 adds a first person pronoun ("I have made . . ."; cf. LXXV, "for" [only a conjunction]); v. 8, "until I completely destroy them" (cf. LXXV, "until they are destroyed . . ."); v. 10, "and I will drive you out, and you will perish" (cf. LXXV lacking). Yahweh directly sanctions Babylonian imperial rule and brings sanctions to bear against any nation that rebels in the face of that rule.

The prophet projects the subversion and rejection of his appeal under the sign of prophetic conflict (27:9-10). Counterprophetic figures and a united counterprophecy exist that predict, "'You shall not serve the king of Babylon.'" The oracular competition is summarily dismissed, "they prophesy falsely . . . ," though Jeremiah does not say how he knows this (he is in a divine speech mode, however, and so technically it is Yahweh speaking through Jeremiah at this point).

The possibility of delusion and subversion of oracular power rises to the surface of Jeremiah's speech. In fact, the problem shapes the representation of the alternatives as the prophet turns to address Zedekiah.

For the LXXV that address is very clipped: ". . . bring your neck in and serve the king of Babylon. . . ." A straightforward injunction without the repetition of the preceding positive and negative alternatives allows the focus to rest on the motivational clauses: "they prophesy falsehood. . . ." Zedekiah's own prophets are lumped in this respect with outsiders, foreign prophets — listening to them will mean the end of the nation. Otherwise they are distinguished from the alien prophets. These Judean prophets are pretenders to Yahwistic oracular power (27:15, "I did not send them . . . ," the sine qua non of oracular authenticity). It goes without saying that the alien prophets lack Yahwistic inspiration.

In the economy of the LXXV, the gap of the positive alternative for heeding the prophet presumably has to be inferred by the reader from the preceding oracle to the foreign envoys, worded as it is as a general principle of God's agency revealed in Babylonian hegemony.

Right on cue, the MT "reader" fills the gap in the narrative economy and gains greater explicitness (MT adds 27:13-14a: ". . . into the yoke of the king of Babylon, serve him and his people and live. Why will you die, you and your people, by sword, famine, and pestilence as Yahweh prophesied concerning any nation who will not serve the king of Babylon? Do not listen to the words of the prophets who speak to you, saying, 'You will not . . .'"). The alternative preaching in the preceding oracle is pulled forward. The Zedekiah community is offered a "chance" for continued national existence.

The MT gains from the shift to alternative preaching because it leaves the king responsible for the calamity. He could have preserved the nation by heeding Jeremiah's injunction. The sense of determinism pervading the episode is masked without, however, being given up. The national collapse happened. It, along with the restoration, will occur according to the times set forth by Yahweh (themes present only in the MT). Nevertheless, the crisis is the fault of the king and his followers, who refused the "chance" held out by the prophet.

The MT nuances Jeremiah's rhetorical point of view. The prophet as actor in the scene apparently perceives the king's imminent intention to lie with those counseling rebellion — at least that is Jeremiah's fear (MT, "Why will you die. . . ?"). The realization of that fear has become the presumption by the time the MT is through reperforming the tradition. Ironically, the only legitimate claimant to Yahwistic oracular power proves unpersuasive. The delusion of counterprophecy has proved more effective!

The laconic narrative economy of the LXXV had provided the reader no citation from Jeremiah's Judean prophetic opponents. The MT remedies that circumstance by an astonishing act of oracular transubstantiation: what once represented Jeremiah's authentic oracular speech (LXXV 27:14b, ". . . serve the king of Babylon . . .") has now become false prophecy in the mouths of his opponents (MT, ". . . You will not serve the king of Babylon . . .")!

The MT is even more creative in the oracle addressed to the priests and all the people. Both performances, the LXXV and the MT, focus oracular attention and dispute on cultic artifacts of the temple cult which survived the earlier deportation of the Jehoiachin faction in 598/597. Possession of them, it seems, remains nine tenths of the law where the continuity and legitimacy of the claim to be "Israel" is a matter of dispute. Jeremiah must persuade the dramatic audience not to listen to his prophetic opponents who proclaim, according to the LXXV, ". . . the temple vessels will soon be returned from Babylon" (27:16). In the perspective of this counterprophecy, not only is the community to expect a speedy return to normalcy in the wake of the 598/597 deportation but even what has gone into exile will shortly be repatriated — fulfillment of revitalization dreams are on their doorstep.

For the LXXV, there is no alternative preaching here either. All of that was set forth at the beginning of the episode with the programmatic themes to the foreign envoys. The assumptions and hopes housed in the counterprophecy are explicitly contradicted (LXXV 17:19-21, "For thus says Yahweh, the rest of the [temple] vessels, which the king of Babylon did not take when he took Jehoiachin into exile, from Jerusalem to Babylon will be made to go — oracle of Yahweh"). An unconditional announcement of doom is pronounced on the existing Judean survivors — even what is left of the cult will be carried off into exile to Babylon. And by implication so will the rest of this "false" Israel, possessed as they are by prophetically inspired false hopes.

The LXXV is oriented to the disenfranchisement of the Zedekiah community. By the time the reader comes to the oracle to the people, the appeal of the positive alternative has proved unpersuasive. In any case, there is an unreality about the positive alternative throughout, marked as the speeches are by the knowledge of the "calamity" as a *fait accompli* for the composition. The unreality of Jeremiah's appeal will only increase under the influence of the MT additions since they explicitly periodize oracular fulfillment and thus "Israel's" historical destiny, including in the scheme a climactic future that holds return and revitalization of national existence for "Israel."

And yet the MT reforms the oracle into alternative preaching (27:17; absent in LXXV)! To the promise of immediate restoration (MT v. 16, ". . . now, quickly . . .") the MT opposes an expanded taunt from Jeremiah (LXXV v. 18, "If they are prophets and possess Yahweh's oracular power, let them intercede with me [divine speaker]") spelling out the content of their intercession: ". . . that the vessels remaining in Yahweh's temple, in the king's palace and in Jerusalem might not be taken to Babylon" (for the itemized list in the MT version cf. 2 Kgs 24:11-17; 25:13-17; 2 Chr 36:7-18; Jer 52:17-23). The MT evacuates this appeal of any sincerity when it also adds within 27:19-22 (absent from the LXXV) that not only will this "remnant" of sacral objects join those already in Babylon but "There they will remain until the day I attend to them; then I will bring them up and restore them to this place." Presumably the temporal frame is under the sign of the three-generation world hegemony for Babylonian suzerainty announced above (only in the MT version). In the present, however, the national destruction is a foregone conclusion.

28:1-17

If the preceding chapter represented Jeremiah's action, this one represents a counteraction of Jeremiah's opponent resolved to vindicate Jeremiah's prophetic authenticity. On the surface, the plot seems straightforward. The composition saves its puzzles for the reader at the level of perspective and motive for its characters, Jeremiah and Hananiah. Shifts in the representation of direct speech between the LXXV and the MT attract attention precisely to these narrative aporia.

Another prophet, Hananiah, proclaims an oracle that contradicts and supersedes the preceding Jeremianic symbolic act and its accompanying interpretation (27:1-22): "I will break the yoke of the king of Babylon. Within two years . . ." (28:2-4). Jeremiah's speech in response (vv. 5-9) is fraught with ambiguities, which we will attend in more detail momentarily. Whatever its tenor, Hananiah follows it with action. He breaks the "yoke" Jeremiah wears as a counter (magical?) symbolic act and further dramatization of his basic oracular claim: ". . . thus will I break the yoke of the king of Babylon . . ." (vv. 10-11). The oddity of Jeremiah's behavior in this episode deepens for in response he "simply" walks away (v. 11b). Subsequently, Yahweh commissions Jeremiah to return to Hananiah with a counteroracle of his own (vv. 12-16). It essentially reasserts Jeremiah's original symbolic act — the nations will wear Babylon's yoke — though the grip of the Babylonian imperium becomes more implacable (an iron yoke replaces the weaker wooden ones, vv. 12-14). And it also announces Hananiah's imminent death (vv. 15-16, ". . . this year . . ."), surely an ironic touch given Hananiah's own oracular penchant for setting the "times" for oracular fulfillment (vv. 3, 11 [MT]). The episode concludes with the laconic and convenient report of Hananiah's death on schedule and in vindicatory fulfillment of Jeremiah's prediction (v. 17).

Without that simple outcome to the episode the reader remains entangled in a crisis of authenticity for oracular power. The play in the narrative between the LXXV and the MT apparently heightens that dissonance for the reader by shifting narrative loyalty between the two protagonists, thus prolonging the tension at work in the plot and in the horizon of the narrative's implicit audience.

Now the narrator's perspective is never in doubt. Jeremiah is the true prophet; Hananiah is false. The larger historical horizon, the reality of Babylonian hegemony, and Jerusalem's colonization are settled realities. The overarching validation of Jeremiah's prophecy of doom remains inescapable. But in the play of the episode the narrator withholds the reader's knowledge of these certainties as well as the certainties of his characters until the conclusion.

On the level of external portrayal, both prophetic opponents appear on equal footing. They are indistinguishable in the exercise of the claim to oracular power. Hananiah, like Jeremiah, speaks and acts in the name of Yahweh with all the usual rhetorical and symbolic strategies available to any Yahwistic prophet. The MT repeatedly emphasizes this fact by expanding the narrative to include the title "the prophet" for both men (the LXXV uses this title for Hananiah only in 28:1; contrast its treatment of Jeremiah, who is never so labeled; the MT adds the title for Hananiah in vv. 5, 10, 12, 15, and 17; it adds the title for Jeremiah in vv. 5, 6, 10, 11, 12, and 15).

The MT is meticulous in its preservation of Hananiah's claim to oracular power, filling out the latter's speech with explicit oracular tropes (MT adds "oracle of Yahweh," 28:4), ensuring that the substance of Hananiah's oracles repeats and echoes Jeremiah's earlier oracles in ch. 27 (MT expands vv. 2-4 to include, ". . . which Nebuchadnezzar king of Babylon took from this place and took to Babylon," ". . . son of Jehoiakim king of Judah . . . who went to Babylon I will return to this place . . ."). Hananiah is consistently "the prophet" in word and act — contrary, of course, to the ultimate perspective of the narrative.

The characterization of Jeremiah is more complicated, for the narrator risks Jeremiah's prophetic stature and oracular power. The MT demotes Jeremiah's first response from oracular status (28:6-7): "Jeremiah said, 'Amen! May Yahweh bring your words to pass which you prophesied — namely, by returning the temple vessels and all the exiles from Babylon to this place. Nevertheless, *listen to this word* [emphasis mine] which I say. . . .'" Apparently the reader is to view Jeremiah's reply as normal speech, though the construction is ambiguous. The LXXV leaves no doubt as to its oracular tenor, introducing v. 7 with "Listen to the word of Yahweh. . . ." True, the MT uses the introductory phrase again in Jeremiah's final oracle to Hananiah (MT v. 15, "Listen, Hananiah," absent from the LXXV) so that it could be taken as an oracular trope here too — thus translated "Listen to this oracle." But Jeremiah's speech in vv. 12-16 wraps the MT phrase in oracular tropes, leaving no doubt how it is to be construed (v. 12, "the word of Yahweh came to Jeremiah"; v. 13, ". . . go say to Hananiah"; v. 14, "for thus says Yahweh"; v. 16, "Therefore, thus says Yahweh"). No such supporting tropes occur in vv. 5-9. Jeremiah the prophet speaks here nonprophetically!

The tone of Jeremiah's asservation must be inferred from narrative gaps, thus deepening the ambiguity of Jeremiah's position and perspective at this juncture in the episode. If Jeremiah is sincere, then ironically he sides with his prophetic opponent, even if with reservations (28:8-9).

On what grounds? For the reader it would not be the first time that he has hoped for nullification of his message of doom, as the dramatic scenes in chs. 11–20 testify. But in the latter effort the prophet was decisively defeated (cf. 20:7-13). Does he now reveal a latent hope that the tenor of oracular intent might still be altered? Though possible, it works oddly in the context of his present symbolic proclamation in ch. 27. Perhaps a better inference would project an assumption of oracular contingency into Jeremiah's understanding of prophecy (an assumption already on display in ch. 26). Thus any prophet's exercise of oracular power remains open to supersession in subsequent oracular exchanges. A thread of uncertainty, indeterminacy, and weakness attends any "prophet's" exercise of oracular power running crosswise to the other constituent of the myth of inspiration, that prophetic speech effectually, even magically, shapes historical-cultural destiny. Thus Jeremiah must admit (hope in?) the oracular legitimacy of Hananiah's representation.

On the other hand, if Jeremiah speaks sarcastically, then he speaks ironically — an inference that works easily in the context, if unsurprisingly. The prophet taunts Hananiah in a way similar to the taunt in 27:18, which Jeremiah offers his other oracular opponents. This would also be in keeping with Jeremiah's emphatic remonstrations in ch. 27 negating any possibility of an imminent restoration of the exiles or that Babylonian suzerainty could be successfully overturned. But then why temporize that perspective now in the face of Hananiah with his weak "nevertheless" (28:8-9)?

Consequently, the reader must assess the cogency of Jeremiah's representation of prophetic tradition. Does he polemicize the difference between them by rewriting the history of prophetic tradition? Apparently. He cites a tradition of war prophecy so long-standing that it has the presumption of authenticity (cf. the appeal of the elders to the Micah tradition in ch. 26). In contrast, prophecy of peace hangs in the balance waiting for fulfillment for its vindication. In so doing, the composition has Jeremiah write off and out of the picture alternative memories of prophetic tradition which do acknowledge authentic prophecy of peace (cf. Isaiah 36–37) of equal lineage.

Jeremiah's polemic is two-edged. Hananiah might as well use Jeremiah's attempt to his own benefit, thus destabilizing Jeremiah's oracular pretensions. Indeed, Hananiah is for war. His oracle aids and abets rebellion against Babylon, promising the defeat of this "great kingdom." It is Jeremiah who works for peace, the peace of Nebuchadrezzar! Who really innovates in his use of oracular power? Jeremiah inverts the flow of the tradition (one thinks here of the long-standing prophetic support for the extant Davidic monarchy exemplified in the Deuteronomistic and Isaian traditions) and rewrites his Deuteronomistic intertexts, for the test of fulfillment (Deut 18:20-22) is the burden of any claim to Yahwistic oracular power, and yet fulfillment brings no absolute certainty of Yahwistic agency (Deut 13:1-6 [Eng. 1-5]).

No wonder Hananiah remains undeterred in his oracular course (28:10-11)! And Jeremiah has access to no privileged tradition that can extricate him from deconstructing before his audience in the temple, leaving oracular power helpless in the context of prophetic conflict. By undermining Jeremiah's oracular claims, the composition deepens the crisis of prophecy for its implicit audience and thus risks the myth of prophetic inspiration it so desperately needs to prosecute its revitalization of "Israel."

Jeremiah's silence and withdrawal from the contest with Hananiah only exacerbate that crisis. Oracular power does not privilege him; he can do no more than walk away (28:11b)! Unless his motive is otherwise. His departure may not imply an admission of defeat but rather his intention to follow the admonition in v. 9 — that is, to wait and see if Hananiah's oracle comes to pass. Jeremiah's prophetic representations hover between weakness and power.

At this point the composition redeploys its narrative loyalty. No longer bereft of oracular support (note the explicit recurrence of revelation formulae in 28:12-16), Jeremiah returns to reassert his original oracle, adding to it the prediction of Hananiah's imminent demise (too bad Hananiah did not reciprocate in kind!). Hananiah's magic is over. His symbolic act will not stand. The Jeremianic tradition prevails (notice that the MT fills out this oracle with phrases that reference or repeat ch. 27: ". . . all *these* nations . . ." for LXXV, "all the nations"; ". . . to serve *Nebuchadnezzar* king of Babylon . . ." for LXXV, "to serve the king of Babylon"; MT adds, ". . . they will serve him, and even the beasts of the field I have given him"). Ironically, Hananiah's act redounds to strengthen Jeremiah's original oracle, propelling its fulfillment forward ineluctably. The MT heightens the sense of Hananiah as the ironic agent of Judah's iron yoke (LXXV v. 13, "I [Yahweh] will make in their place . . ."; MT, "You [Hananiah] have made in their place . . ."; note also MT's emphatic addition of the personal pronoun in v. 15, "*You* made this people trust . . .") and his death as the required execution for religious rebellion (MT v. 16 adds, ". . . for you preached rebellion against Yahweh"; cf. Deut 13:6 [Eng. 5]). In addition, the latter intertextual transfer allows the composition thereby to reclassify "Yahwistic" opponents of the Jeremianic tradition, reducing them in effect to prophets advocating worship of foreign deities (Deut 13:1-6 [Eng. 1-5]) — contrary though this might be to their self-representation.

Only now is the composition willing to resolve the ambiguity raging in this conflict between prophets. The MT is emphatic about the fulfillment of Jeremiah's prophecy now tied as equally as Hananiah's had been to a temporal horizon when it adds, ". . . in that very year . . ." (LXXV v. 17, "He died in the seventh month"). Jeremiah, as prophet, now approaches the numinous power exhibited by only a few. Moses, Samuel, Elijah, and Elisha come to mind! Apparently nothing short of a miracle can rescue Jeremianic authority.

Dispatching Oracular Power (29:1-32)

Everyone is reading prophecy, it seems. Apparently, Jeremiah's other prophetic contenders are not dropping dead as conveniently as Hananiah. With only a hint of narration, the composition reports the flurry of correspondence passing between the two "Israels," the Judean survivors and the Babylonian exiles. Three thematic interests continue: the vindication of Jeremiah's prophetic authenticity, the problem of prophetic conflict, and the question of restoration's timetable. In the process, claims to prophecy and prophetic status will be manufactured in the perspectives of the characters and the implicit reader.

After the narrator's introduction (29:1-3; are we to see here in the mention of the elders an allusion to survivors from among the earlier group in 26:17?) the episode divides into two sections both dealing with correspondence between Jeremiah and the Babylonian exiles (vv. 4-23 and 24-32). An underlying sequence of action is only minimally described (though it preserves in outline the plot structure employed repeatedly across chs. 26–28: the action of Jeremiah, the counteraction of Jeremiah's opponents, and the vindication of Jeremiah), while temporal sequence must be inferred from allusions in the speeches of the actors.

Jeremiah has sent a letter (29:4-23). It is prophecy written. At first we are not told why. As it is presently configured in the MT, it has four parts. The first and third parts return Jeremiah to explicit restoration themes (vv. 4-7, 10-14). The second and fourth focus on the problems of "false" prophets and prophecy among the Babylonian exiles (vv. 8-9, 15-23).

Apparently, the latter are the motivation for Jeremiah's letter-oracle. The content of his prophetic opponents' oracles is never explicitly cited. 29:8-9 reiterate only the clichés of Jeremiah's denials: "do not let them deceive you . . . they prophesy falsely . . . I did not send them, oracle of Yahweh." Vv. 15-23 single out Ahab and Zedekiah specifically by name. Yet they cite as their crime only that they "prophesy in my name falsely" (v. 21) and "speak oracles falsely in my name which I did not command you" (v. 23), adding for good measure aspersions on their moral integrity (". . . they committed adultery with their neighbors' wives . . ." [v. 23; cf. Jer 23:10, 14]).

But as counterfoils eliciting Jeremiah's oracular condemnation, perhaps they veil the "false" oracles projected from the content of Jeremiah's restoration promises. The promise of a return from exile in seventy years (29:10-14), coupled with the admonition (vv. 4-7) to settle into a normal life in Babylon, suggests that Jeremiah's prophetic opponents have been agitating for an imminent return akin to similar themes heralded already in chs. 27–28 by Jeremiah's opponents. The point of prophetic dispute is the timetable for restoration, which importantly carries implications for legitimate claim to "Israel" and the fate of the currently splintered reality of the community in Judah and in Babylon.

Jeremiah wields hope to destroy it. The composition wields hope to enliven it, and in the process the MT rewrites Jeremiah's letter, altering the substance of his restoration horizon.

Now this is not the first time that Jeremiah has announced a return for the Babylonian Golah (cf. 24:4-7), nor the note of the seventy-year time period for Babylonian imperial rule (cf. 25:11-12). But it is left to the exchanges in chs. 27–29 to explicitly tie the two together in an effort to prevent the hope of an imminent fulfillment of Jeremiah's vision in 24:1-10 (27:7 [three generations]; 29:10). No wonder, ironically, that survivors in Babylon or in Jerusalem might have seen no contradiction between Jeremiah's vision (24:4-7) and the announcements of a foreshortened timetable by Jeremiah's prophetic opponents! Jeremiah had not yet offered his own timetable for the return. There is nothing intrinsic in the seventy-year timetable for Babylonian rule that would exclude a return of the Babylonian Golah even within its horizon!

Aware of the ambiguity, the MT draws the earlier prophecy into the present dispute. It expands Jeremiah's letter, with 29:14, 16-19 (all lacking in the LXXV) explicitly invoking the vision of the good and bad figs (24:1-10). Thus it hedges Jeremiah's oracular tradition to prevent its exploitation by those from whom the composition would prevent access to oracular power. Thus the composition defends its role to the implied reader of arbiter, mediator, and interpreter of the Jeremianic tradition, appropriating Jeremiah's oracular power for itself and its own interests.

Ironically, the composition deconstructs Jeremiah's oracular power in the process! For it rewrites his prophecy in light of Deut 30:1-5 (Deuteronomic and Deuteronomistic echoes pervade Jeremiah's oracle; cf. Deut 4:29 to Jer 29:13) and thus writes contradiction into the body of the Jeremianic tradition. The problem of prophetic conflict for the authenticity of Jeremiah's oracular claims leaps to a deeper level — Jeremiah is now opposed to himself! In 24:1-10 only the Babylonian exiles gathered around the Jeconiah group are the objects of the promise of restoration. Not only the Zedekian community in Jerusalem but also other diasporan groups are written out of the picture of restoration (24:8-9). The MT had engaged in a similar restriction at 25:11, rewriting LXXV's "they will serve among the nations" to "they will serve the king of Babylon" (see the previous discussion on ch. 25). But in 29:14 it reverses the restriction: ". . . I will restore your fortunes and gather you from *all* the nations and from *all* the places I scattered you" (cf. Deut 30:1-5).

No doubt the implied reader is drawn into the dramatic composition at the same time that the dramatic situation and its addressees are temporarily displaced. The composition serves its restoration desires at the same time that it must shield against its misappropriations. It is generous of the composition that it now configures its reader as among the "diaspora" and object, therefore, of restoration though nonetheless subject to its Deuteronomistically inspired vision of "Israel." For it is quite willing to write off exiles within the "Jeconian" group who rebel against its vision of Jeremianic "orthodoxy," and the specter of the Zedekian community's fate remains suspended over any who might follow its path — even in exile — of rejecting the true prophetic mission. Note that in 29:19 the odd shift from third to second person plural address (". . . *they* did not listen . . ."; "but *you* did not listen . . .") may, in context, offer a further example of blended addressees, the dramatic recipients of Jeremiah's letter and the implicit reader, in a fashion similar to that of v. 14. The composition layers its sense of readership symbolically, placing all who engage its "writing" of Jeremiah in the time between exile and return and thus faced with the moral nexus occasioned by the exercise of oracular power. It cannot do this, however, without profoundly deepening the crisis for Jeremiah's oracular authority!

Thus Shemaiah is no madman, but he knows that Jeremiah is (29:24-32)! We are to understand that Jeremiah sends a second letter to Babylon. In the interim between the previous letter and this one, Shemaiah, a prophetic opponent among the Babylonian exiles, had sent his own letter to the Jerusalem priesthood agitating for Jeremiah's arrest and punishment. The citation of Shemaiah's letter becomes the substance of Jeremiah's accusation in this renewed correspondence (vv. 26-27).

According to the LXXV, Shemaiah's message is addressed only to an officer-priest, Zephaniah, in the temple charged with maintaining order (MT 29:25 expands his recipients to include "all the people . . . all the priests") — no madman or ranter should be allowed free rein to impersonate oracular power (v. 26). Jeremiah should be locked up and silenced! Jeremiah's madness is known from the content of his previous letter-oracle. Shemaiah makes a summary citation of vv. 4-7, placing emphasis on Jeremiah's primary assertion, "It will be a long time . . ." (v. 28). Ironic force lies in Shemaiah's accusation that Jeremiah prophesied (v. 27), for the verb *mitnabbe'* (*Hithpael* participle of *nabah;* cf. 1 Sam 18:10) can also have the sense of "rave." This, of course, is precisely what Shemaiah implies when he reminds Zephaniah of his duties (LXXV 29:26, "anyone who raves [*mitnabbe'*] and any madman" [Pual participle *meshugga'*]).

Interestingly, neither speaker, Jeremiah or the cited Shemaiah, employs oracular tropes in the other's words, further underlining the intent of each to delegitimize the other. It will be left for the MT to rush to Jeremiah's aid by adding such tropes while still leaving Shemaiah's pretensions exposed (MT 29:25 rewords LXXV, "I did not send you in my name [divine speaker]," to "thus says Yahweh . . . because you sent a letter in your name . . ."). The MT transforms Jeremiah's letter from a simple repudiation of Shemaiah's oracular pretensions to an oracular utterance framed as the accusation element of a judgment oracle! The actual prediction of doom hangs in suspension.

The narration briefly resumes. The priest reads Shemaiah's letter to Jeremiah (29:29; should we detect here support akin to that already witnessed in ch. 26 with Ahikam?). Then follows a complete and proper judgment oracle against Shemaiah with all its oracular tropes in place (vv. 30-32). It is addressed, however, not to Shemaiah directly but rather to the latter's constituency in Babylon. Jeremiah's usual clichés of prophetic denunciation occur ("I did not send him . . . he made you [2d person pl.] trust a lie"). Neither Shemaiah nor his progeny will live to participate in the planned restoration (v. 32). Set within the seventy-year timetable in context, of course, none of Jeremiah's dramatic audience will live either to see this oracle or any other restoration oracle fulfilled. Thus does Jeremiah seek to preserve his own oracular power with "Israel" in exile! The composition's representation of Jeremiah speaks beyond his dramatic addressees to the implicit audience longing for restoration while locked still in the complex crisis that enduring colonization affords.

Importantly, the MT expands Jeremiah's oracle to conclude with "for rebellion he uttered against Yahweh" just as it did in the previous episode with Hananiah (28:16; cf. Deut 13:6 [Eng. 5]). Jeremiah has become the benchmark of "true" Deuteronomistic prophecy. Utilization of oracular power in opposition to his prophetic mission renders even other "Israelite" prophets agitators for apostasy from *Yahweh-alone* (Deut 13:1-6 [Eng. 1-5])!

Evaluation

The periodization of fulfillment rescues oracular power in the long run from dissonance in the present, at the same time that prophecy in the short run must remain contingent and open to communal response. The composition must turn the weakness and failure of Jeremiah — entangled in political intrigue and prophetic conflict — into the coinage of this enlarged myth of prophecy.

The presence of oracular weakness has issued in its own crisis for the myth of oracular inspiration. Upon the latter much hangs. For the composition must postpone the collapse of the myth of Yahweh and thus launch hope in its revitalization dreams.

But to render the myth of Yahweh in a way that meaningfully preserves Yahweh's imperium in the face of Israel's experience of Babylonian suzerainty, the composition must prevent any suggestion that Israel's exigent historical crisis falls outside of Yahwistic power — especially oracular power. And so pre-exilic Israel's dismantling before Jeremiah's prophetic mission is a foregone, ineluctable outcome. But the composition can ill afford Yahweh's moral failure as well. Divine power exercised in Israelite destruction must be felt as a consequence of human moral failure, delusion, and egregious headlong self-destruction. Hence oracular power must be exercised under the sign of contingency — ever open to the play of human agency and response.

Thus, too, the profound subversion of oracular power before prophetic conflict can be transformed coinage preserving divine power and fidelity within the nexus of communal freedom and moral response, Deuteronomistically interpreted.

The consequence for "Jeremiah" is manifold. For in writing "Jeremiah" the composition supersedes (while it affirms) the Jeremiah of flesh for the Jeremiah of the letter, and the latter transfers oracular power to the arbiters of the Jeremianic tradition where the risk to prophecy can be fended off by a "Jeremiah" who calculates restoration's timetable and rehabilitates hope from the corpse of its misappropriations. Jeremiah gains in this exchange of power with the enhancement of legend. Writing prophecy, it seems, carries its own rewards where the myth of Yahweh has become contested rhetoric necessitating reconquest!

Jeremiah 30:1–33:26

Overview

Utopian aspirations provide the lifeline out of cultural demoralization, fueling, as they may, revitalization energies. The colonial elite must re-scribe "Jeremiah." Not only must they confront a profound hostility toward hope within the Jeremianic tradition but they must also sustain hope's symbolic generative power, faced as it is with the dissonance of enduring delay. Ironically, hope must construct itself from the very rhetoric of doom that elsewhere in the Jeremianic tradition had been designed to displace hope! The latter hope, a hope *against* divine violence, is now replaced by a hope *for* Yahweh's violence!

For hope is despair's sister, with both utilizing a third — war — to realize their dreams of Yahweh's imperium. Yahweh's ineluctable war has come to Israel. It has constituted her great crisis. Israel's enduring colonization risks its complete demoralization, its oblivion. For in the teeth of cultural dismantling, Israel confronts Yahweh's failure.

Ironically, Israel's death, the crisis of foreign domination and colonization, now becomes the mechanism of its transfiguration, so that Israel's hope is in Yahweh's war — the very war that administered its death! Israel rises out of the ashes of God's imperial success.

Dramatic Composition

Heretofore in the composition restoration oracles have represented a minor key even if they have always hinted at the composition's prime subtext (3:15-18; 12:14-17; 16:14-15, 19-21; 23:1-8; 24:4-7). With the theme of prophetic conflict in dispute over restoration's timetable, chs. 26–29 have anticipated the inversion offered by chs. 30–33 — that is, the re-elevation and reorientation of hope's place. The composition exploits traditions about the Jeremianic prophetic mission between the deportations and within a splintered "Israel" as the place to anchor hope for its restoration subtext.

Use of explicit date formulae has been avoided in chs. 1–24, and with few exceptions the same has been true of allusions (direct or indirect) to concrete, datable *political* settings (cf. 3:6; 21:1-2; 22:11, 18; 24:1-3). The oracular traditions of the first half of Jeremiah sustain a profound temporal indeterminacy even if they orient to the great destructive event of 587/586 BC as their mythological topos. All of that changes from ch. 25 forward. The tradition is replete with date formulae. Concentration on narrative genre for the representation of the Jeremianic mission is meticulous in its effort to correlate the prose oracular tradition to concrete reigns of Judah's last monarchs and the procession of Jerusalem's last days.

Ironically, it has done this in a dischronologized fashion. Temporal setting and linear sequencing are constantly violated! Ch. 25 places the reader in the fourth year of Jehoiakim only to revert to the beginning of Jehoiakim's reign in ch. 26. However the problem of the date formulae are to be solved (in 27:1; 28:1), chs. 27–29 move the reader once again beyond Jehoiakim to the early days of Zedekiah, before the final siege of Jerusalem has begun. Chs. 32–33 are set in Zedekiah's tenth year; Jerusalem is under siege; Jeremiah has been imprisoned (cf. chs. 37–38). Ch. 34 appears to offer an earlier stage of the siege when the Babylonian forces had temporarily broken off the attack (34:22; cf. 37:4, 5). With ch. 35, the reader is returned once again to an unspecified point in Jehoiakim's reign, though 35:11 suggests that the Babylonian predation of Judah has begun which could direct the reader toward the end of his reign (cf. 2 Kgs 24:1-2; tradition about Jehoiakim's fate and the transition to Jehoiachin's rule are conflicted; cf. 2 Kgs 24:6-8; 2 Chr 36:5-6; Dan 1:1-2); 36:1 turns full circle to the temporal setting of ch. 25 (Jehoiakim's 4th year; note that by 36:9 it is the 5th year).

Chs. 30–31 are the exception in this compositional block (chs. 26–36). No temporal setting or date formulae are offered. And yet by theme they comprise with chs. 32–33 the most extended block of Jeremianic tradition devoted to restoration promises. It is attractive to discern a concentric temporal arrangement from ch. 25 to ch. 36, which then provides a frame for chs. 30–33 (chs. 30–31). The restoration traditions are placed at the center. A daring vision of hope is constructed within the darkest circumstances for both the prophet and the Zedekian community. Prophecy abandons immediate existential relevancy to guide a distant utopian future. For whom does the prophet "write" (30:2)?

Consolation for the Disconsolate (30:1–31:40)

Poetic oracular form returns, and more than that! The rhetoric of doom is reused, revoked and redeployed. Its tropes are pulled from all over the Jeremiah scroll. Rhetoric and imagery used to describe Israel as Yahweh's dissolute wife (cf. 2:1–4:2), to depict the war that destroys her (cf. 4:3–6:30), and to utter lamentation and mourning song over her (cf. 7:1–10:25) reappear. The root metaphor of the female persona, virgin Israel, reemerges as the dramatic addressee. Alternation with a masculine singular/plural addressee provides one of the structuring devices for the whole (masculine — 30:5-11, feminine — 30:12-17, masculine — 30:18–31:1, feminine — 31:2-6, masculine — 31:7-14, feminine/masculine/feminine — 31:15-22). A prose introduction and conclusion frame the poetic collection (30:1-4; 31:23-40). At two points the composition explicitly reuses oracular material (30:10-11 [absent from the LXXV] relocates 46:27-28; 30:23-24 relocates 23:19-20). In the majority of their prior contexts, these tropes and doublets served the message of irrevocable doom for the preexilic community. They are now reversed and turned into the language of hope. Where these tropes and doublets connect to the oracles against the nations, they have the effect of endorsement, punctuating the death of Israel's enemies as the mechanism of its national resurrection.

The units addressed to the male persona, Jacob-Israel, accomplish more than a depiction and promise of Zion's utopian restoration (30:5-11, 18–31:1, 7-14, 18-20). They also figure in its familial metaphor a rationalization of the nation's historical fortunes that introjects a patriarchal psychology deep into the myth of Yahweh. For Jacob-Israel is Yahweh's firstborn (31:9), and the politics of Israel's historical fortunes represent the play and dynamics of a family politic torn by internal psychological strife between father and son (31:20).

We are allowed only a little direct metaphorical insight into the son's psychology. Interestingly, his characterization is not accusation but identification of need! He is in the midst of the "time of Jacob's distress" (30:5-7b; notice the 1st person pl. citation in v. 5a). The pain and terror of God's enduring war is upon him. The citation in 31:18-19 depicts Jacob mourning under the disciplinary hand of divine punishment. Exile and national destruction are presupposed. This is the chastised son, locked in remorse, acknowledging his wrong, pleading for restoration into the graces of his father.

The son's reaction to his current condition is answered by the father's strenuous promise of future parental largess. In the process, the "father" defends his harsh treatment of his son as his just, required chastisement (30:11, "I chastise you justly; I surely do not leave you unpunished"; cf. 31:18, "You chastised me, and I was corrected"). Further, he roots the return of kinder feelings for his son in his fatherly bond (31:20, "precious son . . . child of my delight"). God's imperial war, which sweeps total destruction on the nations (30:11), succeeds in the transformation, return, and restoration of his estranged son. Israel's cultural collapse does not represent divine abandonment; rather, it indicates the yearning rage of the clan father to have the son of his dreams. Yahweh's war is reinterpreted as Jacob's deliverance rather than his death.

The captivity of the son is to be reversed (30:10), the oppressor's yoke permanently broken (v. 8; prose), divine and Davidic suzerainty restored (v. 9; prose; cf. v. 21). Jacob's restored fortunes mean the rebuilding of city life (v. 18), repopulation (v. 20), and an idyllic celebratory communal existence (v. 19). The old exodus and wilderness trek will be repeated and miraculously surpassed. The crippled remnant of Israel will make a festival procession from the north to take up their place in the land as the chief of nations (31:7-9). Zion will become a permanent paradise (v. 12, "like a watered garden") satiated with prosperity and celebration (vv. 10-14).

The oracles addressed to lady Israel tilt in the same direction and yet exhibit a harsher disputational tone. Apparently, her resistance to hope is more intransigent! Although it is Yahweh who narrates her distress, her enduring wound, indirectly this echoes and mediates the woman's own voiced complaints (30:15a, "Why do you cry out . . . ?"). The rhetoric of disease, ill health, and medicinal remedy are drawn from earlier lament and mourning songs (3:22; 8:15, 22; 10:19; 14:17, 19; 15:18; 17:4). Yahweh acknowledges his agency in her pain only to rationalize it in the magnitude of her sinfulness (30:14b, 15b). The latter has justified his cruelty (30:14b, "I struck you with an enemy's blow . . . cruel discipline"). Interestingly, he makes no effort in this context to spell out the details of her criminality (contrast the emphasis earlier on her prurient sexual obsessions in chs. 2–3). Instead, he pleads his love and pledges her healing (30:17; 31:2-6).

Yahweh's motivation is obscure. In 30:12-17, the depth of her pain, the degradation of her enduring suffering is sufficient. Notice the odd use of "therefore" at v. 16. The predation and mockery at the hands of her oppressors require his act of healing (vv. 16-17). Apparently it is no longer her infidelities that create the barrier to their reunion, but her bitterness at her suffering. "Therefore" he must remove the agents of her pain as a demonstration of his enduring love — no matter that these agents of suffering came at his behest. This afflicted and embittered virgin must be re-wooed! Yahweh seeks to remind her of their past experience of love by appeal to the old exodus-wilderness trek (31:2-3, taking "from long ago" temporally rather than spatially, "from far away"; cf. 2:2). In spite of all that has passed between them, his original love for her remains and constitutes motive enough for her restoration (31:4-6).

Yet virgin Israel resists! In spite of Yahweh's pledge and the invitation to make the journey back now (31:21). She is still the "faithless" daughter dithering in her response to Yahweh's love (v. 22, "How long will you waver, O faithless daughter?" cf. 3:15). She is "Rachel" inconsolable over her loss (31:15).

Yahweh intends to persuade and console her in her bereavement. Her childlessness is not permanent (31:16-17). Even as they dispute love, Yahweh points to the lamentation of a humbled, chastised son, still alive, ready for return and for whom he still has a mother's love (vv. 18-20). Yahweh's consolations climax in his promise of new creation — "the female will encircle the man" (v. 22).

Specific interpretation of the obscure climactic statement remains elusive. Suggestions abound, but it is hard to achieve clarity without at the same time undermining the force of the "new thing" that God will create (cf. Gen 1:1). Is this an inversion of the feminized warriors in 30:6 (females surrounding men with protection)? Or is it a larger inversion of male and female roles (not a very intelligible option in the broader picture of the utopian restoration, which though idyllic nonetheless portrays a restoration of normal gender relationships; cf. 31:4, 13)? Is it double entendre for a return to sexual responsiveness? Or, more simply, is it a reference to women encircling men in festal celebration (taking the verb *sabab* more loosely — i.e., go round → march round → dance)? The last two options at least have the merit of answering the issue at stake in Yahweh's plea to lady Israel. Note the assonant wordplay. The new creation is that she will encircle *(tesobeb)* the [divine?] warrior *(geber)* over against virgin Israel's present epithet, "faithless" *(hashshobebah).*

For the resistance to hope constitutes the composition's anxiety. If this resistance succeeds, then the failure of Yahweh is complete. Ironically, while the polarization and estrangement, the dispute between God and Israel, continue, their relative positions have shifted in emotional and psychological tenor! They have displaced each other and take up each other's former postures. Yahweh must now fight for hope where previously in the scroll he faced, in his view, intransigent, misplaced hope in communal security. And lady Israel is now convinced of her hopelessness — her victimization and bitterness being effective barriers to divine protestations of love! Ironically, on the surface, her son Ephraim appears more pliant to Yahweh's parental longings (31:18-20; cf. the similar familial dynamic in chs. 2–3 where it is the sons of the future who prove more responsive to divine appeal), though Yahweh appears confident that ultimately she, too, will come around through his creative act. For out of the ashes of his imperial war, he will create the "son" of his dreams and the "beatific virgin" of his fantasy!

The anxiety over whether hope will prove persuasive motivates further shoring up in the concluding block of prose (31:23-40). It offers a string of assurances and reinserts the persona of the prophet, who apparently dreams these visions of the coming days (31:26; contrast Jeremiah's earlier repudiation of oneiromancy in 23:25-32!). The old ritual blessing of Israel will become meaningfully sanctioned (31:23-25). The turn from destruction to restoration has always been constituent to Jeremiah's mission, with the certainty of the former the guarantee of the latter (31:27-28; cf. 1:10-12). The regime of generational fatalism will be displaced (31:29-30, "the fathers have eaten sour grapes, but the children's teeth are set on edge"). The past will be evaded, for Yahweh will create a new covenantal regime impervious to the violation so often sustained by the old (31:31-34). For the stipulations formerly written on stone will now be internalized within communal hearts effective finally in producing the fidelity so often yearned for in Jeremiah's oracles of doom (e.g., 4:4, "circumcise the foreskin of your hearts"). The stability of the cosmic order is Israel's guarantee of nationhood in relationship to Yahweh (31:35-36; but earlier Jeremiah's oracular power had in fact unmade the cosmos; see 4:23-26). The immeasurability of that created order is a sign of the impossibility of divine rejection (31:37; but this is precisely the claim of Jeremiah's doom; see 6:30, 7:29). Already the boundaries of the new Jerusalem represent an expansion of the holy habitation — the latter never susceptible again to destruction (31:38-40, an ironic return to the disputed theology of Zion's inviolability; see 7:1-15).

Purchasing Hope (32:1–33:26)

Not even the prophet can easily believe his utopian visions! Assurances are required.

It is King Zedekiah's tenth year. The final siege of Jerusalem is under way. Jeremiah is under palace arrest for oracular sedition (32:1-3). Zedekiah retaliates against the prophet's announcement of imminent defeat at the hands of the Babylonians. Interestingly, within the announcement of defeat, Jeremiah has temporized on the severity of the king's fate. Jeremiah predicts the king's personal survival, Babylonian exile, and *restoration* (MT 32:4-5, ". . . until I visit him." The LXXV lacks the phrase. Cf. 27:22, ". . . until the day I visit them [temple vessels in exile]"). Heretofore, oracular tradition set in the same temporal context or even earlier at the beginning of Zedekiah's reign had been emphatic about his *personal* destruction (21:7; cf. 24:8-10; 27:12-15)! No explicit motive is offered for the prophet's oracular shift. His rhetoric is deliciously equivocal. The verb "to visit" *(paqad)* peppers Jeremiah's judgment speech elsewhere in its negative meaning — that is, visit with punishment rather than visit with care (5:9, 29; 6:6, 15; 9:8, 24; 11:22; 14:10; 15:3; 21:14; 23:34; 25:12; 27:8). Does Jeremiah play with the king, hoping to bargain away royal wrath in exchange for "minor" concessions in oracular posture? Zedekiah may just as well hear in the prophet's equivocation only the continuation of Jeremiah's usual rhetoric of doom — that is, the king will be "visited" indeed in Babylon with his execution! This is only the beginning of vacillation and verbal sparring in which both Jeremiah and Zedekiah will engage under the stresses of Jerusalem's last days. The prophet seeks to preserve his life (see further on chs. 37–38). The king seeks oracular hope and deliverance for his beleaguered kingdom. Both use oracular power as the coinage of exchange!

Ironically, the prophet does proclaim a restoration hope completely useless to the current Judean regime! Imprisoned, Jeremiah commits an act of hope so eccentric that even he is left incredulous (32:6-15). His act of patrimonial land redemption (cf. Lev 25:25-28) takes place under oracular sanction and thus becomes transformed into a prophetic sign act (cf. earlier sign acts in 13:1-14; 16:1-9; 18:1-11, and later 51:59-64). Clan obligations present themselves under curious circumstances! Had Jeremiah not been alerted in advance through oracular means, how would he have regarded this action from Hanamel (32:8, ". . . then I knew, it was an oracle of Yahweh"; note that the phrase earlier in the verse, "according to the word of Yahweh," is a MT addition)? The reader must negotiate earlier representation of familial conflict for the prophet. Jeremiah had complained vociferously of familial ostracism and persecution (11:20-23; 15:10). Without divine assurance, the attempt on Hanamel's part to secure liquid assets in face of the national crisis is surely suspect. Who profits whom here? Apparently oracular capital is to be had, for Jeremiah formally contracts his own patrimonial possession at the same time that he symbolically predicts the future return and restoration of a normal existence in the land — normal enough for the usual flow of economic processes to resume. Normal enough so that in time surviving land contracts from the present will be redeemable (32:14, ". . . that they may last for a long time"). Jeremiah's temporal frame ("many days") is tantalizingly vague, especially in light of his strenuous struggle in chs. 27–29 to establish a long, seventy-year period until the restoration. For in the present context is not the implication in Jeremiah's meticulous documentation that he expects to collect on his deed of ownership on the other side of his imprisonment? Some will at least interpret Jeremiah's actions in light of his pro-Babylonian oracular posture as Jeremianic machination to profit from the misfortunes of the present communal elite once the current Zedekian regime has been swept away (cf. 37:11-15) — the restoration as the land-grab opportunity of a lifetime for those shrewd enough to survive the present national crisis!

The folly of his oracular gamble is apparent even to himself. Jeremiah prays (32:16-25).

The setting of the present narrative episode shifts between private and public scenes (private — 32:7, 16-44; public — vv. 8-15). The entire episode offers Jeremiah as its primary narrator. The bulk of attention is on the prophet's prayer (vv. 16-25) and the divine response (vv. 26-44). Though on the surface the interchange takes place in private (no explicit report of oracular delivery is made), so that Jeremiah along with Yahweh remains the dramatic speaker and addressee, appeals are also made to an implicit audience. The temporal setting is shattered to draw "exilic" readers into the dramatic scene in direct address. 32:23b-24 already presuppose Jerusalem's destruction, ". . . you [Yahweh] caused all this calamity to befall them" and ". . . what you [Yahweh] predicted has happened as you now see." Yahweh cites and disputes claims of despair and hopelessness, which are made by second person plural addressees (32:36, 43; note that the LXXV preserves the temporal setting by leaving these citations as statements of Jeremiah — i.e., 2d ms. sg. address!). Cf. 33:10, ". . . of which you say [2d ms. pl.]," and 30:24, "In the latter days you [2d ms. pl.] will understand it [the prophecy]," which also address the reader, thus drawing in an audience on the other side of Jerusalem's fall. Jeremiah's scroll of hopeful oracles "writes" prophecy in a new key, for it is sealed up to the present. No longer accessible in Jeremiah's day, its mystery will "open" only to audiences and days beyond Jeremiah's temporal horizon. The initial stages of Jeremiah's transformation into an occult, mantic mystagogue — a transformation reaching full development in later apocalyptic and pseudepigraphical literature — begins.

32:25 carries the central protest of Jeremiah's prayer. He disputes the folly of his oracular instruction to purchase the patrimonial plot since the "city is handed over to the Chaldeans." All that precedes acts as a mask, a mantle of Deuteronomistic theologoumena and piety (cf. other prayers of the Persian period in Ezra 9:6-15; Neh 9:6-37; Dan 9:3-19), covering prophetic incredulity faced with the eccentricity of hope — in this time of ineluctable doom. This entails irony for both the prophet and the reader. The prophet had had to be cruelly defeated in his attempt to prevent his own mission of wielding oracular doom (20:7-9 in the context of chs. 11–20). Now in the clutch of that mission's fulfillment and his vindication as the true prophet, he must be persuaded, forced once again to take up hope! Ironically, his pious dispute this time is a far cry from the earlier, virulent, blasphemous struggle (15:18, "You [Yahweh] are a deceitful brook"; cf. 4:10, ". . . you [Yahweh] have utterly deceived this people . . . , promising, 'You [2d ms. pl.] will have peace'").

For the creation terminology in 32:17 see Jer 27:5; cf. Gen 18:14; Deut 9:26; 17:8; 2 Kgs 14:36. For the epithets in the revelation of the divine name in 32:18-19 see Exod 20:5-6; Deut 5:9-10; 7:10; 10:17; Neh 9:32; Jer 16:17; 17:10. Cf. these formulations to the analogous Exod 34:6-7; Num 14:18-19; Neh 9:17. For the exodus-conquest terminology in 32:20-22 see Deut 26:8-9; Pss 78:43; 105:27. For the terminology of disobedience in 33:23 see Deut 31:29; Jer 9:12(Eng. 13); 11:8; 26:4; 44:10, 23.

Given the profession of trust in divine power and virtue and given the rehearsal of the fulfilled prophecy of doom, the prophet's protest and doubt are non sequitur (32:25). Are the theologoumena that the composition has placed in Jeremiah's mouth mere formal clichés — clichés that Jeremiah does not believe or does not find fully persuasive in this dramatic moment?

The divine response is swift and to the point (32:26-44): "I am Yahweh, the God of all flesh; is anything too difficult for me?" (v. 26). He throws back at Jeremiah a key theologoumenon from the prophet's very own profession of trust (v. 17, "Nothing is too difficult for you")! All the rest is commentary. Only vv. 43-44, God's peroration, specifically allude to details of Jeremiah's sign-act (v. 43, "Fields will be purchased in the land . . ."; v. 44, "Fields will be sold . . . deeds written, sealed, witnessed . . ."). The judgment speech (vv. 28-35) rehearses national crimes in clichés familiar to the prose speeches in Jeremiah (the history of disobedience, idolatry, and the failure of the prophetic mission of repentance; cf. 7:1-34; 19:1-15). Interestingly, the history of infidelity is extended back to the earliest days (v. 30, "from their youth"; contrast 2:2, "the loyal love of your youth") of their existence from the inception of the Davidic city (v. 31, ". . . from the day they built it . . ."). Why this part of the divine response is relevant is not immediately clear, though it rationalizes the legitimacy of Israel's destruction nonetheless as deserved divine punishment.

Restoration writes over judgment! The restoration oracle (32:36-44) anchors the certainty of restoration in the fulfillment of the prophecy of doom (v. 42). Citations of despair before the devastation of Jerusalem (vv. 36, 43) are ironically overturned. For Yahweh, the doom of Jerusalem provides the assurance of his good purpose (not its demise) to restore their fortunes and return the exiled to their patrimony. The rhetoric of that restoration is calculated to overcome the history of disobedience and doom by envisioning a transfiguration of the community which effectively prevents their religious failure from occurring again (v. 39, ". . . one heart and one way to revere me. . . ." Cf. Ezek 11:19; Jer 32:40, ". . . an everlasting covenant that I will not turn away . . . fear of me . . . in their heart that they will not turn from me." Cf. Jer 50:5; Ezek 16:60; 37:26).

The divine response is doubled for the imprisoned prophet (33:1-26; see v. 1, "a second time"). It offers Jeremiah occult knowledge of the future (33:3). The oracles in this second speech leap over the immediate narrative scene linking back to restoration themes and tropes in chs. 30–31, anchoring by implication the latter in the same setting (33:6, "I will raise up healing . . ."; cf. 30:17). Creation remonstrations (33:2) undergird redemption promises. The composition reasserts the abiding validity of old Israel's creation and election traditions to render its restoration dreams credible.

The first three oracles address broad portraits of Israel's future (33:4-9, 10-11, 12-13). The rebuilt (v. 7) and forgiven (v. 8) community will finally realize the Deuteronomic covenantal ideal to Yahweh's fame before the watching nations (v. 9; cf. Deut 26:19; Jer 13:11; Zeph 3:19, 20). Despair's citation (33:10, ". . . you [2d ms. pl.] say . . .") is swept aside. Festal celebration writes over the rhetoric of doom (v. 11; cf. 7:34; 16:9; 25:10). The life of flocks (the part for the whole) will resume in Israel's territories (vv. 12-13; cf. 32:44).

The second block of three (absent from the LXXV; the MT develops themes from 30:9, 21; 31:14) narrows the focus to monarchic and levitical themes (33:14-18, 19-22, 23-26). Just as 31:35-37 argued the certainty of "Israel's" election from the stability and immeasurability of Yahweh's created order, these units infer the same assurances for the Davidic monarchy (vv. 15-16; cf. 23:5-6) and the levitical priesthood. The composition links the restoration of "Israel" to the enduring validity of these institutions in old Israel — however contingent and brutal the rhetoric of judgment and the accidents of history have been toward them (e.g., chs. 21–24). And in its creation myth it discerns a stability in the pattern of Yahweh's relationship to "Israel." The promise of a return cannot fail (33:14, "I will give effect to my good promise . . .")!

Despair's conclusion (33:24) faced with Israel's historical devastation assumes the end of Israel's national-religious aspirations — not an unreasonable conclusion given the prophetic tradition in Jeremiah 2–20! Notice that the wording of the citation splinters and stratifies the community. "This people says" is usually a reference to Israel in Jeremiah. Yet Yahweh says about them, "they despise my people from being a nation again before them" — a sentiment more comprehensible on the lips of non-Israelites (cf. 30:16-17, ". . . scattered they call her . . ."). The polemics around implicit audiences suggest themselves. For the immediate dramatic addressees in the narrative hardly agree with such despair — whether one thinks of the Zedekian court who still oppose Jeremiah's message of doom or the Jehoiachin remnant from ch. 29 who resist the promise of a lengthy exile before restoration occurs — while these speakers in 33:24 accept doom's fulfillment as a settled permanent reality. The polemic writes out of the community an unspecified audience resistant to revitalization aspirations and thus complicates the symbolic complexion of its "reading" audience. Not every reader as "exile" is assumed to be a "friend" of elite revitalization hopes and thus an outsider, "not "Israel." Against them, the composition discerns in the stability of divine loyalty to the cosmic order the assurance of the enduring validity of patriarchal election tradition (v. 25) and thus the necessity of "Israel" and "David's" return.

Evaluation

Ironically, this very reliance on the old election traditions had rendered the Judean community impervious to Jeremiah's mission of doom (understood by the composition as a mission of repentance). These traditions had spelled Jeremiah's defeat and furthered the oracular realization, the fulfillment of national destruction. Now on the other side of Jerusalem's collapse revitalization interests repossess these disenfranchised traditions. With it the *Yahweh-alone* elite can secure their own aspirations for cultural power, prevent the admission of divine failure, and localize Jeremiah's oracular destabilization of these traditions to the "generation of wrath." Ironically, the tradition wielded so effectively by Jeremiah's opponents (as the composition represents them, whether in poetic or prosaic material) now in the composition of Jeremiah's restoration scroll supersedes Jeremiah once again! This is a stunning vindication of Jeremiah's oracular opponents. One "Jeremiah" defeats another. A history of "Jeremiah" is written under the one name! At the same time, the myth of Israel under the sign of exile and return can be rationalized and the cycle between these two modes of Israel's existence made credible within the one figure, "Jeremiah." Thus the composition believes it can safely and securely take up these old election traditions as well as the myth of Yahweh once again. For in their utopian revision of these traditions there should never be occasion again for the services of a destabilizing prophetic figure — never again (31:40)!

There are consequences for the myth of Yahweh. For mythic refigurations require their symbolic compensations. Hope has sought its assurance in appeal to Yahweh's creative power and the stability of divine virtue. Yet it also seeks to psychologize divine motives through appeal to the familial root metaphors. The poetic tradition constructs an interior life for Yahweh drawn from the dynamics of patriarchal family politics. Just as the composition deeply introjects the empire into divine purposes, it also introjects the emotional complexity and self-interest of a *paterfamilias* into the divine character. Thus it is that husband/father Yahweh now takes up the ebullient hope in love that had once been his intransigent wife's, lady Israel — to her self-destruction — while she now mirrors his old despair. His passion for her and her children leads through violence to their re-creation into the family his love so passionately desires.

But the passion of this divine patriarch is neither univocal nor constant as the tradition of Jeremiah's mission of doom portrays. Divine passions come freighted with psychological complexity, irrationality, and variability. The divine is destabilized! Ironically, exclusivistic Yahwism asserts *"Yahweh-alone"* only to "polytheize" the divine interior life! His passion had proved fruitless in the face of his wife's infidelities — hence, as he claims, the rationale for his violent brutalization of her. And if now as a great act of those same passions Yahweh will miraculously create the family he requires, why the necessity for the violent family tragedy in the first place! Apparently, there are limits to the level of denial that the composition can practice and still compel credence and generative power for its rewritten myth of Yahweh. Jerusalem's fall remains an undeniable mythological topos. Its enduring crisis and cultural pain generate the titanic mythological struggle posed to the constitutive imagination of the colonial elite. While this psychology of divine passions renders the divine motive comprehensible and the divine character sympathetic within the cultural horizon of Israel's colonized elite, it also deconstructs the reliability of divine power and virtue. For it renders divine instability an ever-present possibility in the vagaries of national existence. To mask and prevent that instability the composition must also make recourse to intensified, reelevated creation and election traditions which universalize divine power in the world in *Yahweh-alone.* Imperial sovereignty returns! But then old "Israel" had grasped such utopian desire before only to prove their discomfiture in the face of Babylonian exigency and the winds of divine passion. To take up Jeremiah's metaphorical grammar of doom for the sake of hope remains an equivocal, anxiety-ridden rhetorical act ever open to its symbolic inversion. Such acts of symbolic consolation come with a high rate of exchange. For hope in divine violence ever again opens the end of "Israel" that the composition so longs to surmount.

Jeremiah 34:1–36:32

Overview

Torah obedience within covenantal fidelity is the canon of national security. Prophecy is its advocate, with responsiveness to the prophetic mission the sign of covenantal fidelity. The conditionality of the old regime is its hedge against divine failure and the mechanism of its moral force. The composition exploits Deuteronomistic ideology to write off the mythological threat from its past at the same time that it longs for a future new covenant that has transcended the old vulnerability. And the Jeremianic mission is written under the sign of Moses, with the prophetic scroll a "second" book of the law. Whoever wields these books attracts oracular power and charts the fate of national existence.

Dramatic Composition

The next three chapters complete the concentric frame around Jeremiah's book of hope by reversing the temporal setting from the tenth year of Zedekiah during the final siege of Jerusalem back to the fourth year of Jehoiakim (25:1). The first two minimize narrative for the sake of prose speech. The third returns to the preeminence of narration. All three dramatize the failure of the preexilic community to practice covenantal fidelity or to exhibit the repentance before the prophetic mission that alone would have saved them from destruction. In each case "texts" as Torah are the fulcrum of that demonstration. The prophet Jeremiah appears as the inspired mediator of that Torah.

Jerusalem's Sabbatical Release (34:1-22)

The general temporal setting of chs. 32–33, the tenth year of Zedekiah, continues. The description of the siege, however, suggests a phase of it earlier than that indicated by 32:2. For 34:7 indicates a stage of the invasion (notice LXXV 34:1, "all the lands of his rule"; the MT is considerably more elaborate in intensifying the overwhelming size of the invading military force, "all the kingdoms of the earth," "all the peoples") when other fortresses besides Jerusalem have yet to fall (LXXV, "against the cities of Judah, against Lachish and against Azeqah, for they remained, among Judah's cities, fortress cities"; MT, "against all the cities of Judah which remained, against Lachish . . ."), and the allusion in vv. 21-22 indicates a further stage when a temporary break in the siege of Jerusalem (cf. 37:5) has occurred (34:22 LXXV, "I will bring them back to this land"; cf. MT, ". . . to this city"). There is also no notice of Jeremiah's palace arrest. Jeremiah is free to initiate oracular contact with the king (v. 2, "go and say . . .").

Revelation formulae divide the material in two (34:1-7, 8-22). In the first part, Jeremiah offers an oracle repeating his earlier prediction (in literary, not temporal sequence) from 32:3-5. His prediction of Jerusalem's defeat repeats yet alters the previous oracle, emphasizing the burning of the city rather than its capture (32:3; cf. 21:10; 32:29, but LXXV, ". . . he will capture it and burn it with fire"). More energy is displayed in altering the rhetorical stance of the earlier oracle about Zedekiah's personal fate (32:4-5). The prophet pitches the king's capture more emphatically from Zedekiah's perspective. Captured (34:3 dramatizes the detail of a foiled escape [cf. 39:4-7]: "you will not escape . . . you will surely be captured . . . into his hand you will be given"; cf. 32:4, which offers less, ". . . you will not escape . . . you will surely be given into the hand . . ."), subjected to a face-to-face meeting with Nebuchadrezzar (the MT expands as it alters "his mouth to *your* mouth will speak"; the LXXV lacks the phrase) where he is to have his sentence passed (34:4 emphasizes ". . . your eye . . . your mouth" [i.e., Zedekiah], while 32:4 had only ". . . his eye . . . his mouth [i.e., Nebuchadrezzar]), "to Babylon you will go" (34:3; cf. 32:5, "to Babylon he will bring Zedekiah").

More importantly, the prophet removes his earlier (in literary, not temporal sequence) oracular equivocation, expanding "until I visit him" (32:5) explicitly to predict the king's personal safety, a peaceful death (34:4b-5a; the MT elaborates by adding the phrase, absent in the LXXV, "you will not die by the sword") with traditional burial rites! It is not easy to square this promise with the preceding oracle, which predicts the king's exile (v. 3, "to Babylon you will go"). Mention of the burial rites and mourning rituals implies a "usual" death for a king still in the land. Had v. 3 not predicted exile, Zedekiah might have viewed the oracle as his exception (v. 4, "yet") from the general fate of the populace once the siege succeeded. Does Jeremiah expect the king, does the composition expect its reader, to see no insurmountable stretch between the two oracles — that is, a usual royal death in exile, an ameliorated imprisonment (cf. Jehoiachin in 52:31-34; contrast Jehoiakim in 22:18-19)? On the other hand, the prophet could be offering alternative visions (negative and positive) which depend on the king's response for actualization (an assumption of oracular contingency may be the composition's ideological rationale for integrating variant and contradictory oracles in the Jeremianic tradition — even in the same context), though Jeremiah's rhetoric is not very explicit — much hangs on that adverb "yet"! He could have been clearer, as he will be later (see further 38:17-18). The prophet has traded one equivocation for another of a deeper order! Oracular power hangs suspended, apparently, in a morass of hidden intentions and moral contingencies. Jeremiah resolutely abandons the city to its oracular fate, but why offer such thin hope to the king? Does he wish to further sap Zedekiah's resolve to resist the invaders? Does the prophet self-consciously utilize his oracular power with seditious motives, as it were, as an agent of Babylonian interests?

No explicit reaction of Zedekiah is relayed. The reader is left to infer from the next section that the king's focus remains on securing the safety of the entire community. In the face of the prophet's suspicious oracular equivocations, the king's unresponsiveness is no surprise. Ironically, Zedekiah commits an act of religious rededication and revitalization! He seeks refuge from Babylon and the prophet's threats in covenant traditions!

34:8-22 supplies a thin narrative thread for the prose speech. As an effort to "bargain" a miraculous deliverance on behalf of the community, Zedekiah had successfully instituted a general manumission of Israelite slaves (vv. 8-10). In so doing, the community and its leadership demonstrate their covenantal obedience. But the latter had proved fleeting, for the community had subsequently re-enslaved those temporarily liberated (v. 11, their covenantal oath had stipulated otherwise; v. 10, "that they never again enslave them"), apparently, once the Babylonian troops had actually lifted the siege (v. 21; cf. 37:5). An odd reaction to a miracle indeed!

The oracular response (34:13-14) interprets Zedekiah's general manumission in light of a specific legal tradition. The composition represents Jeremiah as a legal exegete, and prophecy has become a "halakhic" exercise! The details of the legal tradition all depend on a cyclical factor. In the case of the principal legal intertext, Deut 15:12-18, manumission of Hebrew slaves is tied to a sabbatical cycle (cf. Exod 21:2-11). Jeremiah's exegesis extrapolates Zedekiah's extraordinary manumission (where no explicit sabbatical reference has been made) as an extension of sabbatical legislation. The composition discerns in the terminology of 34:9 and 10, *shelaḥ ḥopshi*/"to set free," and v. 8, *qero' deror*/"to proclaim release," the connection to Deut 15:12 (cf. Lev 25:10, *qero' deror,* which, however, has restructured the cycle to the fifty-year jubilee), reading the latter in light of Deut 15:1, the proclamation of debt remission (*qero' shemitah*/"to proclaim remission"). Hence MT Jer 34:14 (LXXV, "six years," with Deut 15:12) sets the temporal factor at the "end of seven years" (Deut 15:1). In the process of making this application, the prophet makes rhetorical gains. For he can catch up Zedekiah's community under the sign of infidelity to the Sinai covenant, with the latter interpreted in Deuteronomistic terms. Thus Zedekiah engaged in superficial covenant reform can appear as an anti-Josiah (cf. 2 Kings 22–23, and see the discussion at Jeremiah 36 and 37 for further compositional use of narrative analogy). The eccentric Jeremiah can appear assimilated to Moses' shadow, mediating Torah to the community.

Jeremiah's oracular speech represents an ironic rereading of the Torah tradition (cf. similar preaching on prior Torah texts such as the Decalogue in 7:6, 9, the sabbath in 17:19-27, and the law of the king in 22:3). Castigating them for such superficial repentance and egregious disloyalty, which joins the present community (34:16) in continuity with the long history of covenant violation (from the inception of the Sinaitic law in v. 13, ". . . on the day I brought your ancestors from Egypt . . . ," and in v. 14, ". . . but they did not obey"), Yahweh proclaims a "release" for them too, their liberation day — to destruction (v. 17)! Notice that the elite officials of ch. 26 appear here as those especially singled out for this "sabbatical" of destruction (v. 19). The violators of the covenant oath experience its curse (v. 18, the reference to the slaughtered calf reflects ritual custom in covenant ceremony, representing the solemnization of the covenant pledge in blood — i.e., the threatened sanctions for violation; cf. Gen 15:9; see Dennis McCarthy, *Treaty and Covenant,* 94).

Rechabite Loyalty as Jerusalem's Counterfoil (35:1-19)

Under the hand of the composition, people and events are transformed into signs and symbols from which mythological and ideological needs can be mined. The tradition of Jeremiah's prophetic sign-acts has been elaborated into a much larger narrative strategy. That strategy is used to construct evaluative analogies between the "historical" figures that populate the narratives, thus serving the rhetorical interests of the composition.

The temporal setting of the episode returns the implicit audience (reader) back to the reign of Jehoiakim, presumably toward its end since the Babylonian incursion has already begun (35:11; cf. 2 Kgs 24:2). The prophet under divine inspiration carries out instructions regarding the obscure community of the Rechabites (about whom we hear only here in the Bible; for the ancestor Jonadab ben Rechab as a participant in Jehu's bloody purge of the Baal cult [if the same person], see 2 Kgs 10:15, 23). 35:1-11 is structured in first person narrative style, with Jeremiah as the speaker. The incident proves symbolically significant and provides the "text" for Jeremiah's ensuing oracular speeches in vv. 12-19. The "prophet" interprets this "text," the significance of the incident, to both his dramatic (Judah/Jerusalem's citizenry) and implied (reader) audience.

Jeremiah is to take the members of the Rechabite community to the temple and give them wine to drink. When he complies with the divine commission, the community refuses out of loyalty to the ancestral obligations that give the Rechabites their distinctive identity. For their ancestor, Jonadab ben Rechab, had enjoined them to live a pastoral way of life — no wine, no houses, no agriculture, the adjuncts of settled urbanized culture; rather, they are to live as resident aliens in tents (35:6-7). Pleading their unbroken loyalty (vv. 8-10) to their Rechabite tradition, ironically, they must now excuse the break in that obedience since they have taken up residence in Jerusalem. It is the exception forced upon them by the extenuating military emergency of the Babylonian auxiliary's incursions (Chaldeans and Arameans, v. 11; cf. 2 Kgs 24:2). That they have come to Jerusalem for safety makes narrative sense inside the episode, but in the context of the composition their act surely acquires even more irony since Jerusalem has become the last place where safety is to be had!

Still, the Rechabites keep steadfast to what little of their tradition remains possible given the exigencies of their circumstances. They drink no wine. The prophet makes this the focus of his oracular address (35:12-19). Rechabite fidelity becomes the foil, the contrastive analogy, to highlight "Israel's" enduring infidelity to the covenant tradition enjoined on it by Yahweh. The terms of the latter are summarized in the clichés typical of Deuteronomistic prose speeches in Jeremiah — obedience and worship of *Yahweh-alone.* Proof of Israel's infidelity lies manifest in their rejection of the prophetic mission to secure national repentance.

The narrative analogy interprets Rechabite tradition within the framework of Israel's national covenant tradition, projecting the terminology of the latter into the former and thus strengthening the force of the analogy. Compare Jonadab's promise (35:7) of long life in the land with Deut 4:26, 40; 5:16, 33; 6:2; 11:9, 21; 17:20; 22:7; 25:15; 30:18; 32:47. For the expression "heed the voice of," cf. Deut 4:30; 8:20; 9:23; 13:19; 15:5; 26:14, 17, etc. with Jer 3:25; 7:23, 28; 9:12; 11:4, 7, etc., and for "do according to all that he commanded" cf. Deut 1:3, 19, 41; 2:37; 4:5, 13, 23; 5:12, 16, 32, 33, etc. and Jer 1:7; 7:23; 11:4, 8; 13:5, 6; 17:22, etc. Yet the substance of the Rechabite "covenant" produces a pastoral existence contrary to Deuteronomistic interests in a nonpastoral community in possession of the land. The Rechabites as ideal exemplars of "covenant" fidelity achieve the inverse of Israel in the land! As "resident aliens" (v. 7) the Rechabites parody Deuteronomistic Israel.

The prediction of doom to Jerusalem turns on the contrast: ". . . they upheld the commands of their father . . . but this people do not obey me" (35:16). Consequently, Judah/Jerusalem will see the fulfillment of Jeremiah's prophecy of doom (v. 17, ". . . all the calamity I promised . . ."). The Rechabites, on the other hand, are promised reward for their "covenant" fidelity. The MT represents v. 18 as direct address: "To the Rechabites Jeremiah said: 'Thus says Yahweh of hosts, God of Israel, because you [2d ms. sg.] obeyed the commandments of Jehonadab your [2d ms. sg.] father and kept all his commandments and acted according to everything he commanded you [2d ms. sg.].'" Contrast the LXXV, which structures the oracle as the prophet's continued address to Judah begun at vv. 13, 17: "Thus says Yahweh: 'because the sons of Jonadab ben Rechab obeyed the command of their father, acting just as their father commanded them.'" More than just surviving (v. 19), their enduring descendants "will always stand before me [Yahweh]" — an expression suggesting a more formal relationship as some type of official functionary, that is, "become the servant of" (used of prophets in 1 Kgs 17:1; 18:15; 2 Kgs 3:14; 5:16; Jer 15:19; used of priests and Levites in Num 16:9; Deut 10:8; Judg 20:28; 2 Chr 29:11; Ezek 44:11, 15); cf. royal attendants (1 Sam 16:22; 1 Kgs 1:2). The formulation parallels Jeremiah's restoration oracles to the Davidic house and the levitical priests (33:17, 18). In this connection, contrast the LXXV, which reads ". . . all the days of the earth," to the MT, "continually."

Ironically, the Rechabites refuse the prophet's instruction to drink wine and for this "disobedience" secure their future! Jerusalem's refusal of Jeremiah does not prove so productive of national safety. And in the Rechabites the composition finds a sign allegorical of ideal covenant fidelity even in the face of exigent circumstances.

Scribing Jeremiah (36:1-32)

The prophet under divine instruction creates a prophetic text. Baruch serves as a scribe to "Jeremiah" and wields oracular tradition on the prophet's behalf. And the figure of Jehoiakim, heretofore only an ominous absence as an actor in the narrative plot (cf. ch. 26), appears center stage as an anti-Josiah, sealing Judah's doom.

From the end of Jehoiakim's reign, the reader is returned full circle to the temporal setting of 25:1, Jehoiakim's fourth year. Temporal congruence, the concentric temporal structure (chs. 25–36), and the summary of the scope and content of Jeremiah's scroll (36:2; cf. 25:3, 13, ". . . everything written in this book") — ". . . all the words . . . against Israel and against Judah and against all the nations . . . from the time of Josiah to the present" — parallel chs. 25 and 36 analogous to the relationship between chs. 7 (speech) and 26 (narrative of the speech). Jeremiah 36 focuses on narrative, nowhere actually permitting the reader to hear the contents of the prophetic scroll as it is read (v. 29 cites only the king's summary of the contents). The parallel with ch. 25 permits the reader to fill that gap appropriately. At the same time the narrative tableau in ch. 36 practices inversion of the tableau in ch. 26 — here it is the prophet who provides ominous absence to a king's active agency in the intrigue between temple and palace.

Explicit motivation for a Jeremianic scroll pleads the "chance" for national repentance (36:3; cf. 26:3). Curiously, the prophet must secure the services of Baruch, the scribe, to carry out the divine commission even to the extent of commissioning Baruch to become the publisher/proclaimer of the prophetic text (v. 6). Jeremiah pleads his disbarment from the temple as the mechanism of Baruch's scribal elevation (v. 5). The reader is not told how this prohibition has come about. Perhaps the composition expects the gap to be filled by assuming the imposition of official interdiction on Jeremiah in consequence of the episode in Jeremiah 26 (temporally prior to chs. 25 and 36, the beginning of Jehoiakim's reign). If so, however, access is inexplicably restored in ch. 35 (temporally after chs. 25 and 36)!

Baruch reads "Jeremiah" at the temple as instructed (36:8). The middle section of the episode (vv. 9-26) actually narrates three readings temporally posterior to the setting for Jeremiah's original commission to write (v. 1) — that is, in the fifth year and ninth month of Jehoiakim! This complicates the relationship to the preceding. Do the verses narrate additional readings on Baruch's part beyond the statement in v. 8 that the scribe did as instructed in the fourth year, or is v. 8 a summary verse, proleptic of Baruch's actual fulfillment of his task, the latter not actually carried out until late in the next year? In the latter case why wait? This would have hardly been the earliest available national fast day (as the prophet instructed Baruch in v. 6)! The LXXV only exacerbates the temporal gap, reading Jehoiakim's eighth year and ninth month!

The alternative suggested by the temporal gap enlarges Baruch's mission and envisions iterative appearances of Baruch in the temple to publish the scroll "on fast days" (note that 36:6, "day of fast," is indefinite). Baruch then understands Jeremiah's request to imply an open, iterative component while the prophet remains prohibited from appearing in the temple (nothing in the 2d ms. sg. verbs, neither the *waw*-consecutive perfects ["you shall go . . . and read"] nor the Qal imperfect of instruction [". . . you shall read them"] of v. 6 prohibits such a nuance). Vv. 9-26 focus, on this view, on one of these repeated occasions — either late in the next year (so the MT) or four years later (so the LXXV) — which the composition lends climactic significance due to the intrigue by the royal palace to foil the prophetic doom contained in the scroll.

It is not a question of choosing between the MT and the LXXV in their chronological difference but rather assessing the narrative consequences of their alternative representations of the episode. In this case, the LXXV gives more room to Baruch's scribal displacement of Jeremiah, even to the point of giving Baruch the scribe the initiative to rewrite the scroll of "Jeremiah" destroyed by the king (LXXV 36:32, "and Baruch took another scroll and wrote on it at Jeremiah's dictation all the words of the book which Jehoiakim had burned, and still more words like these were added"). The inversion of role appears again at 43:3, where Jeremiah's opponents attribute his oracular inspiration to the seditious motives of Baruch! These symbolic inversions will continue in the additional legendary development of the two figures, Jeremiah and Baruch (see, e.g., the apocryphal work Bar 1:1). In the case of the MT Baruch's subordination to Jeremiah is preserved (MT 36:32, "Now Jeremiah took another scroll and gave it to Baruch . . ."). And for both representations Baruch wields a prophetic text and attracts oracular power.

Baruch's "prophetic" act unfolds in three stages. The first (36:10) is in public in the temple on a national fast day. No response of the populace or officials present is narrated, though there is the delicious detail that Baruch took up position for his performance in a room off an upper courtyard at the opening of the new gate of the temple. It was at this gate that Jeremiah had earlier faced capital charges (26:10)! Micaiah, a Shaphanid, reports (informs?) on Baruch's act to the royal officials who are in the king's palace (36:11-13). Summoned to the palace by the royal officials, Baruch reads the scroll a second time in private audience with them (vv. 14-19).

Their response is complex. The officials react with mutual terror and declare that they must inform the king about the scroll (36:16). Then they confirm agency for the scroll — that is, Baruch has come upon it through Jeremianic dictation. But they advise Baruch in advance to hide himself and Jeremiah, presumably for their protection (v. 19). Further, when the officials proceed to report to the king, they first deposit (for safekeeping?) the scroll of "Jeremiah" in the scribal room belonging to Elishama, one of the officials present for Baruch's second recitation (v. 20).

With Baruch and Jeremiah gone, the king has one of his officials, Jehudi, fetch and read the scroll a third time (36:21-25). Jehoiakim's response is uncomplicated! He cuts up and burns the scroll as it is read! The narrator intones that neither he nor his officials were afraid (contrast the response at the second recitation, v. 16) or tore their clothes in response to the scroll. The MT singles out three exceptions, Elnathan (cf. 26:22), Delaiah, and Gemariah. These seek yet fail to persuade the king not to destroy the scroll (v. 25). The LXXV is contrary (in its oldest witnesses LXX[BS]; Ziegler, however, chooses to follow LXX[A] against his usual practice), omitting the negative: ". . . they entreated the king *to burn* the scroll" (also lacking is the phrase, "he did not listen to them")." The MT layers the complexity of political factions and motivations in their responses to the prophetic scroll. The MT gains by deepening the king's egregious culpability. The representation of the courtiers by the MT is in keeping with their "piety" displayed earlier in private audience with Baruch (LXXV v. 16 reads otherwise, "they took counsel"). The LXXV closes the possibility of continued support for "Jeremiah" among the royal court as well as sustaining characterization of the royal henchmen from 26:22. And both nuance dramatic scenes with a mimesis of shifting loyalties and political factions.

According to the MT, in the remonstrations of some of his courtiers, Jehoiakim receives but refuses a last-ditch chance to turn from his opposition to Jeremiah's prophetic word and mission. Instead, the king seeks to put to a complete end not only the oracular scroll but also its scribe and its prophet (36:26; cf. 26:20-23). The MT miraculously saves one and all (v. 26): ". . . Yahweh hid them [Jeremiah and Baruch]." (The LXXV, ". . . they hid themselves.")

Yahweh has the prophet with Baruch resurrect the burned scroll in expanded edition (36:28, 32).

The MT is emphatic that the "original" scroll is recovered: ". . . all the previous words . . . on the first scroll . . ." (the LXXV lacks "previous"/"first"). Presumably, part of this expansion includes the judgment oracle against the king and nation following the divine commission to rescribe "Jeremiah" (36:29-31). Lacking v. 29a ("to Jehoiakim, king of Judah"), the LXXV makes this clearer: v. 28, "again take another scroll and write . . ."; "and you shall say . . ." (v. 29). By burning the original scroll, Jehoiakim, rather than preventing "Jeremiah," has ironically unleashed the threatened doom upon himself and the nation as their ineluctable fate!

Ideological interest and narrative shape for this episode are supplied to the implied reader from both the plot and character in 2 Kings 22–23. Jehoiakim and his generation are evaluated in contrast to King Josiah, his piety, and his posture of reform. For both narratives focus on scrolls authoritative for national destiny, yet contingent on royal responsiveness. In Jeremiah 36, the prophetic scroll is the analog to the "book of the law" rediscovered in the temple in Josiah's day (2 Kgs 22:8). Josiah's response (2 Kgs 22:11, ". . . he tore his clothes"; v. 13, he repents and seeks oracular instruction; contrast Jer 36:24, ". . . they did not tear . . .") saves him and his generation (2 Kgs 22:19, 20; contrast the violent end predicted for Jehoiakim, Jer 36:30) from the divine curses for covenant violation (2 Kgs 22:13, ". . . for great is Yahweh's wrath . . ."; cf. Jer 36:7). The figure of Josiah constitutes the critique of Jehoiakim as his antitype.

The two editions of Jeremiah (LXXV and MT) consciously perform the episode in connection with its narrative intertext in 2 Kings, explicitly duplicating vocabulary or creating echoes of it: MT 36:6, ". . . the scroll on which you wrote at my dictation the words of Yahweh" (LXXV, "this scroll"); cf. 2 Kgs 22:11, 13, 16; 23:2, 3, 24; LXXV 36:7, "great is the anger and the wrath of Yahweh" (MT, "anger and wrath"); cf. 2 Kgs 22:13; MT v. 16, ". . . they were filled with dread" (LXXV, "they took counsel"); cf. 2 Kgs 22:11, 19; LXXV v. 24 (according to its oldest witnesses, LXX[BS] *zēteō;* LXX[A] *ekzēteō;* Ziegler follows a later emendation, *existēmi*), "they did not seek [i.e., inquire for an oracle]" (MT, "they were not filled with dread"); cf. 2 Kgs 22:13, 18.

Evaluation

The composition constructs a narrative world for prophecy. The textuality of oracular power looms large at the same time that it is covenantalized in Deuteronomistic terms. The scroll of "Jeremiah" becomes the stand-in for the prophet, capable of perpetuating the Jeremianic mission beyond the absence of Jeremiah as it also becomes symbolic compensation for so many other absences the colonial elite seek to surmount. For the prophetic scroll offers a place, an arena where the underlying ideological commitments of dreams of revitalization receive their validation and the myth of Yahweh need not admit its failure.

For the composition mimes its own engagement with oracular texts in its representation of Jeremiah's prophetic mission. The eccentricities of the latter are domesticated and transformed as Jeremiah is assimilated to the regime of Moses, Deuteronomistically understood. In so doing, Jeremianic authority is elevated at the same time that it is made derivative of the "Mosaic" covenant and the latter's advocate. Indeed, prophecy becomes mediator, enforcer, and revivalist of Torah. In fact, prophecy has become a scribal act, writing an interpretative performance wielding and establishing oracular power.

For narrative management of the disparate Jeremianic tradition rewrites the prophet, mining his oracular inconcinnity in service to a myth of prophecy. The tenor of oracular utterance is contingent on the shifting moral tenor of its audience. Thus oracles become obsolete or superseded rather than fail should their recipient manifest or not manifest the piety appropriate to the regime of *Yahweh-alone.* In this narrative world, no Jeremianic (true) prophecy fails, for the dissonance of unrealized oracular traditions can also be postponed, as is the case of restoration oracles to the time of their oracular relevance. For ironically, with historical hindsight, the doom of Israel anchors and guarantees hope's realization. Judah's collapse mortgages the present "exile" in a law of averages that masks over the inconveniences of Jeremiah's predictive oracular indelicacy between the already and the not yet!

Jeremiah's assimilation to the "Mosaic" regime matches a deeper assimilation and rationalization of Yahwistic psychology. For the narrative world with its "inspired" prose Yahwistic perorations attempts a routinization and domestication of divine character in contrast to the unstable "polytheistic" passions offered in the root metaphors of the poetic oracular traditions of "Jeremiah." The narrative intervenes in the space called "Jeremiah" to render a deity predictable to the canons of Deuteronomistic assumptions — an ironic displacement of divine suzerainty by the rule of Torah indeed! One Yahweh attempts the supersession of another, deeply introjecting a polytheistic impulse into a myth of Yahweh that so longs for a religion of *Yahweh-alone.* All the while, the composition covets the "polytheistic" passions within the metaphorical grammar of the oracular poetry, hoping to possess them still for its persuasive needs.

Writing Jeremiah offers its symbolic compensations. The composition enters a textual arena, a metaphorical space, where it may repossess its land, rebuild its national identity, and reread its historical exigencies as the triumph of Yahwistic myth.

Jeremiah 37:1–45:5

Overview

In fulfillment of Jeremiah's prophecy of doom, Yahweh's imperial war liberates and depopulates the land. In the symbolic arena of "Jeremiah" no one is left to complicate claims to "Israel" other than those rightfully embodying revitalization dreams. To that end the figure of Jeremiah weaves in and out of this narrative of Jerusalem's final days. The prophet will employ oracular power seditiously to defeat the old Judean regime's efforts to resist Yahweh and his agent, Nebuchadrezzar. In so doing, the prophet fulfills his destiny to be the stumbling block on which the nation founders — an inverted "Mosaic" mission indeed! From Judah the arc of God's war with the world spreads.

Dramatic Composition

The plot development, with two exceptions, now proceeds in linear temporal order. Chs. 37–38, set within the final siege, focuses action on the oracular intrigue between Jeremiah and Zedekiah. 39:1-14 narrate the success of the Babylonian siege in fulfillment of Jeremiah's prophecy of doom. 40:1–44:30 narrate the fate of the survivors left behind under the leadership of Gedaliah, the gubernatorial appointee of Nebuchadrezzar. Punctuating this narrative arc, two passages, 39:15-18 and 45:1-5, offer salvation oracles to individual supporters of the prophetic mission. The first, addressed to Ebed-melech, flashes back to Jeremiah's imprisonment by Zedekiah during the final siege. The second, addressed to Baruch, flashes back to the temporal setting of ch. 36. Each individual is assured personal survival amid the collapse of the Judean state as a reward for his support. The composition lifts these two figures up as models of the piety that alone can secure national revitalization.

Intriguing Zedekiah (37:1–38:28)

Within the final siege, oracular power is the commodity of exchange for security for all the parties in the plot, even Jeremiah. On that and the destiny-shaping power of oracular utterance all agree. The rest is debate and conflict, with the prophet devising and revising his oracles among shifting political motivations and different conceptualizations of "true" prophetic mission.

Alternative representation of the episodes between the LXXV and the MT focus special attention on the characterization and motive of the two principal actors — Jeremiah and Zedekiah. At the same time exploitation of the intertextual relationship to 2 Kings 18–19 effects a narrative analogy with the siege of Jerusalem during the reign of Hezekiah. All these narrative strategies are played out in support of the editorial summation in 37:2, which writes off the entire old Zedekian regime. For the composition, the regime floundered and self-destructed through its opposition to and rejection of the Jeremianic mission. Interestingly, the narrative art risks this estimation of the old regime through its portrayal of a prophet wielding oracular power in service to self-interest and the success of Babylonian imperial designs.

The first scene (37:3-16) is set in a critical moment of the siege. A chance hope for deliverance has occurred. News of allied Egyptian troops approaching for Judah's aid has forced the Babylonian army to lift the siege and withdraw (v. 5). In that context, the king commissions a royal embassy to Jeremiah (v. 3). At this time, Jeremiah remains free to carry out his activities (v. 4). The present story will narrate the mechanism of his imprisonment already encountered at 32:2.

The royal mission seeks prophetic intercession (37:3, ". . . pray on our behalf to Yahweh"), understanding the function of true prophecy to include special intercessory power for the acquisition of beneficial oracles (the intercessory power of "prophetic" individuals to avert divine wrath or deliver from distress is a well-attested tradition;

cf. Gen 20:7; Num 21:7; Deut 9:20; 1 Sam 7:5, 8; 12:19, 23; 1 Kgs 13:6; Job 42:10; Ps 72:15; in Jeremiah see 7:17; 11:17; 14:11; 42:2, 4, 20).

Jeremiah understands their request to be for an oracle (37:7, "to inquire [an oracle] of me"). He knows the hopeful interpretation (Egyptian success, permanent Babylonian withdrawal) of present events that they seek but moves to crush all hope, offering instead an oracle categorical in its pronouncement of doom (vv. 8-10). The Egyptians will turn back, and so, too, the Babylonians to the siege of Jerusalem! The victory of the latter is assured (vv. 7-8). If any miraculous deliverance is to be expected, the Babylonians will be the beneficiaries — even the mortally wounded casualties of defeated Babylonians would rise up to invest the city and its citizenry! Any hope read out of the present "respite" is deception (vv. 9-10).

The prophet adds fuel to the fire of his eccentricity. With the hiatus of the Babylonian siege still in effect, the prophet attempts to leave (desert) the city (37:12). Jeremiah's motives are shrouded in ambiguity and suspicion, with multiple explanations offered in the narrative. The narrator manipulates perspective and point of view. To the implied reader the prophet appears exonerated immediately. The prophet only seeks to take up possession of patrimonial property (v. 12; cf. 32:6-8). For the dramatic characters, the prophet must be interpreted in light of the timing of his action (37:11) as well as the tenor of his pro-Babylonian oracle. Apprehended by an official at the Benjamin gate, "reasonably" accused of desertion to the Babylonians, and remanded to the furious custody of the royal courtiers, with no one accepting Jeremiah's protestations of innocence, beaten, the prophet ends up imprisoned (whose location is termed "the house of Jehonathan the scribe," "into the cistern house and into the cells") for "many days" (vv. 13-16).

Whose privileged knowledge of the prophet should the reader accept? The identity of the prophet's accuser (37:13) complicates the too easy decision of the reader in favor of the privileged knowledge offered by the narrator in v. 12. For Irijah, the officer of the guard present in the MT, is displaced in the LXXV by Saruya, a close associate of the prophet with whom the latter has been lodging ("and there a man, with whom he was lodging, Saruya ben Shelemyah ben Hananyah"). For the reader, the opinion of an official under the judgment of v. 2 can quickly be dismissed. It is a different matter for a close associate of Jeremiah. Does he betray and falsely accuse? Or does he know hidden motives derivative of his close association that the reader has not seen? For either identity of the accuser, it is no wonder the princes remain unconvinced of the prophet's innocence. But if it is Saruya, the composition performs the episode and risks the estimation of Jeremiah's motives even to its reader. The issue of the prophet's eccentricity and integrity as "prophet" receives no closure in the episode. A frustrated quest for state security has now led to a threat to the prophet's safety.

The scene shifts to private machinations between the prophet and the king (37:17-21). From issues of state security, interest shifts to the personal safety of the two characters. After "many days" Zedekiah seeks another oracle. The vaunted reputation of the king as a weak, belated supporter of the prophet is not unequivocally present in the performance of his character, as the LXXV and the prophet apparently perceive him. For the prophet discerns a Machiavellian prince scheming for personal safety. The king under the prior threat of Jeremiah's prophecy of disaster has threatened the prophet with the mechanisms of state and hopes for a change in Jeremiah's oracular posture (v. 17).

The prophet perceives the king's desire and shifts the focus of his oracular response to Zedekiah's personal destiny. Jeremiah, however, does not appear willing to alter the tenor of his prior oracle — "into the hand of the Babylonian king you will be given" (37:17). Ironically, the prophet follows his oracular threat with a plea for his own safety (vv. 18-20). Tinged with the tropes of legal process, Jeremiah's speech pleads the illegality of his imprisonment, raises the issue of prophetic conflict, and infers the validity of his oracular claims in the presence of the besieging troops. In the process, the LXXV has the prophet lay bare a sinister Zedekiah who is ultimately responsible for the prophet's imprisonment, the immediate threat to Jeremiah's safety masked behind the foil of the royal courtiers (v. 18, "you [2d ms. sg.] put me in prison"; contrast the MT, 2d ms. pl.). Further, Jeremiah perceives the imminent failure of his legal appeal with the continued royal stratagem to secure a more palatable oracle through further incarceration: LXXV v. 20, "Why do you intend to return me to the house of Jonathan the scribe. . . ?" (contrast the MT, "do not return me to the house . . ."). Jeremiah remains defiant, counter-challenging the king: LXXV v. 20, ". . . I will not die there" (contrast the MT, ". . . lest I die there"). He clings to the rhetoric of disaster.

Now the prophet uses the mechanisms of prophecy to threaten the king. When Jeremiah in 37:19 raises the taunt about the false prophets of peace — rendered false by the arrival of the Babylonian troops their oracles had proved ineffectual to prevent — he also invokes the tradition of oracular prediction/fulfillment, intensifying his own claim to wield authentic oracular power and thus heightening the threat to royal safety held out in his defiant prediction of royal disaster! For aspects of Jeremiah's earlier predictions have begun their materialization even as the two of them negotiate personal safety. The law of averages for Jeremiah's predictive accuracy tilts to his favor!

Both assume the efficacy of oracular power. But interestingly, the king does not attach connotations of fatalistic determinism to that power. He believes that the power of prediction lies with the prophet and thus that it is politically negotiable — hence his effort at harsh persuasion and intimidation. On the surface, this flies in the face of the categorical, absolute rhetorical form that Jeremiah chooses to use before the king. Unless the reader is to take that form at face value, Jeremiah's perspective on this score remains opaque. The king, for his part, commits an ambiguous act. He reimprisons the prophet, changing only the location of his incarceration with appropriate provisions for Jeremiah's daily rations — 37:21, "the court of the guard." Does he hope that further jail time will render Jeremiah more pliable? Then why ameliorate its conditions? The oldest witnesses for the LXXV (BSA) have the king return the prophet to the very same location ("house of imprisonment"; cf. vv. 4, 15, 18, "house of imprisonment," which labels the function for the "house of Jonathan" in vv. 15, 20). Perform Zedekiah this way, and his character as a ruthless Machiavellian comes to the fore! But the reading so clashes with the formulaic refrain elsewhere in the narrative (37:21b; 38:13, 28) that the LXXV is usually emended (so Ziegler 1976: 404) — without, we should add, any supporting textual witnesses for the conjecture.

Jeremiah's continued "public" oracular activity, from prison, launches the action of the following scene (38:1-13). His "sedition" becomes explicit at the same time that he now alters his prior oracle. There is irony here. Jeremiah preaches surrender or desertion to the Babylonians as the mechanism for anyone seeking safety — precisely what he had been imprisoned for in the first place (v. 2; cf. 37:13). For the rest who refuse this "out" there is only the prospect of the doom already prophesied (though he quietly drops mention of the city's conflagration (v. 3; cf. 37:8, "they will capture it *and burn it with fire*"). Does the prophet open space for a thin hope as a response to Zedekiah's amelioration of his arrest (as per MT 37:21), or does the prophet "bargain" under the continued duress of it (as per LXXV 37:21)? Can this oracular offer be trusted? In either case, the prophet cleverly continues his mission of doom, weakening the old regime's resolve from the inside out.

For the infuriated courtiers (38:1, 4), the prophet's motive is unequivocal. They detect no material alteration in the tenor of his oracles. He works as an active agent of Jerusalem's downfall. His use of oracular power is criminal, the inverse of their expectation. Rather than come to their oracular aid, Jeremiah twists oracular power to their harm (v. 4; note the expression "seek [inquire an oracle] for peace/calamity"). They propose the death penalty (v. 4; cf. 26:11).

The narrator's reticence forces irony on the implicit reader's attribution of motive. For the courtiers apparently discern Jeremiah's seditious intent accurately. He acts here consistent with his prior defiant oracular opposition in private with the king. But overall narrative pressure argues Jeremiah's status as a true prophet of Yahweh (37:2) and reasserts itself subsequently in the present scene with the advocacy of Ebed-melech on Jeremiah's behalf (38:7-18). The charge of criminal exploitation of oracular power is undermined.

The risk to the prophet's safety escalates. Zedekiah hands the prophet over to the courtiers. Jeremiah, cast into Malchiah's cistern (in the court of the guard), sinks into the mud at its bottom (38:6). Does Zedekiah cleverly use his courtiers against the prophet as his cat's paw? The MT has the king plead a comprehensive powerlessness: "he is in your hands, for the king is powerless against you in anything." On the surface, the MT offers the reader a vacillating king, a secret, belated supporter of the prophet, yet unable to maintain control within the political factions of the royal court. The LXXV is more reticent, preserving the public visage of a more ruthless monarch. The narrator, not the king — for the king's voice there is only the command, "he is in your hands" — tells the implied reader only, "for the king did not prevail against them." In either case this royal "powerlessness" will be easily and immediately replaced when the king licenses and takes charge of Ebed-melech's rescue mission (vv. 10-13).

Ebed-melech, however, punches through the king's obfuscation (38:9). According to the LXXV, he holds the king directly responsible for the "criminal" act perpetrated on Jeremiah: "'you [2d ms. sg.] have done wrong in that you [2d ms. sg.] have put this man to death because of the famine,' for there was no longer food in the city." Contrast the MT, which has Ebed-melech accuse only the courtiers: "My lord king, these men have done wrong in what they have done to Jeremiah, the prophet, by casting him into the pit so that he may die, for there is no longer food in the city." Interestingly, Ebed-melech cites the famine, not the seditious, thin hope of the oracular offer, as the basis for Jeremiah's sentence of death. His words remind the king of the negative alternative in the oracle (v. 2) and suggest a ploy to invoke the prediction/fulfillment scheme. The king must recognize in the current famine legitimization of Jeremiah's prophetic claims and thus the illegality of the current sentence.

Irony around the meaning of prophecy deepens for the reader in this play of perspectives. The prophet corroborates Zedekiah's expectation that Jeremiah could modify his oracles if desired. Jeremiah's "sedition," however, creates a double-edged test for the community. Ironically, he opens the possibility of ameliorating the gravity of national defeat. Yet Jeremiah does this in terms compatible with his prior message of doom, designed to further undermine the national anti-Babylonian resolve. Apparently the prophet's criteria for oracular revision differ from the king's! In the process, Ebed-melech vindicates Jeremiah's prophetic integrity. And the narrator invites the reader to discern a moral nexus as the setting of oracular power. When the leadership opposes the prophetic mission, they reveal the depth of national religious decay and their inability to accept the positive alternative offered them. Thus Jeremiah works the doom of the nation with oracular power contingent on audience response. His oracles effect a moral test and a communal crisis. They provoke national self-destruction should the community prove resistant or hostile to the prophetic mission. Oracular power becomes a flexible weapon in the hands of the prophet to defeat his opponents. In so doing, the narrator creates a narrative world for prophecy where the latter is invulnerable to national exploitation and manipulation.

The conflict over prophecy and the polarity of interests around national and personal safety are not finished (38:14-28a). Returned to the court of the guard (v. 13), Jeremiah and the king are free to continue their war of nerves for personal safety. Out in the open, yet in private negotiation (vv. 14-15 at the third gate of the temple), Jeremiah finally secures his guarantee of royal protection (v. 16). That established, he modifies his earlier oracle offering the king an escape (vv. 17-18). Jeremiah individualizes his seditious oracle from 38:2. Zedekiah's oath succeeds where threat and abuse failed! The LXXV portrays a process of character decay. The king capitulates in the war of nerves with Jeremiah only to become too weak to capitalize on Jeremiah's oracular bargain (v. 19).

The prophet strikingly alters his earlier categorical predictions. He offers the king not only personal safety but also that the city itself will be spared ("the city will not be burned with fire") and the entire royal house will be spared ("you and your house"). Could the prophet not have offered these alternatives from the outset? Has the king's persecution of the prophet successfully subverted the integrity of Jeremiah's oracular utterance? Oracular contingency within a nexus of moral circumstances is the narrator's defense of Jeremiah from the charge of exploiting oracular power to secure personal safety. When the king initially promises Jeremiah's safety — now a sign of his responsiveness to the prophetic word — the prophet may revise his prior oracles. Moral circumstances have changed even if external historical and political ones continue the same.

Subsequently, should/when the king fails to access the new alternative (in 38:21 Jeremiah anticipates this royal intention), the prophet's prior categorical predictions of disaster are reasserted (vv. 20-23). The king shatters, ironically, on prophetic cooperation. The latter constituted a double-edged moral crisis. Blame for Jerusalem's destruction is placed squarely on the moral failure of the king rather than on Jeremiah's dereliction of oracular duty.

That moral failure is intensified by the LXXV since the king coerces the prophet with a death threat to conspire against the royal courtiers by keeping their "negotiation" secret. The king matches the prophet's threat (38:18, "and *you* will not escape") with one of his own (v. 24), "and *you* will not die." I suggest that the parallel wording of the threats indicates that the king, not the courtiers, is the source of danger to Jeremiah. Contrast the MT, which has the king express concern for Jeremiah's safety: ". . . lest you die [at the courtiers' hands]" (cf. their hypothetical death threat in v. 25 as the king represents it, "lest we kill you"). Zedekiah is interested in shielding himself alone from incriminating exposure (v. 25): "What did the king say to you?" (contrast the MT, which adds, "What did you say to the king?"). The king concludes their "arrangement" by altering his earlier oath (according to the LXXV). He will honor it only if Jeremiah will conspire against the courtiers for Zedekiah's safety.

As for the prophet's safety, it is accomplished, ironically, through cooperation with, rather than defiance of, Zedekiah's quest for personal safety (38:27). In turn, Jeremiah's opponents, ironically, fail to "hear" the prophet's "negotiated" oracle, foiling their scheme to silence the prophet (LXXV v. 27, "for they did not hear the oracle of Yahweh"; contrast the MT, "for they did not hear the conversation"). Interestingly, in their interrogation of Jeremiah no explicit death threat is made!

Narrative evaluation of the king and his courtiers has been managed alternatively between the LXXV and MT portrayals, though both are equally negative. In the former, Zedekiah, the scheming Machiavellian, eventually shatters on his own stratagems. In the latter, he appears a pathetic, vacillating figure from the outset, caught up in the intrigues and options of the surrounding court. For example, recall that in 37:18 the threat to Jeremiah shifts from the king to the whole community (2d ms. pl.); at 37:20 the prophet no longer perceives sinister royal intentions (from LXXV, "why do you intend to return me?" to MT, "do not return me"); in 38:5 Zedekiah pleads his own powerlessness (MT, "the king is powerless against you in everything"); consequently, in 38:9 blame for the crime against Jeremiah shifts from the king to "these men" (MT); finally, in 38:24 the king does not rescind his initial protection oath to Jeremiah (see above on v. 25). Zedekiah becomes a belated, yet weak, secret supporter. He cannot publicly back Jeremiah, but he does collude in secret conspiracy on the prophet's behalf. In the end, Zedekiah lacks the courage to act on prophetic advice.

Performing Jeremiah also draws narrative attention from the LXXV and the MT. For the latter works to intensify the figure of the prophet as an innocent victim subject to comprehensive mortal threats from the entire community. Suspicious prophetic motives are clarified: "to make a purchase among the people" (37:12) is changed to "receive a portion [of his patrimonial redemption]" (cf. 32:6-44). For the reader, the privileged interpretation of the prophet by his fellow lodger is suppressed for the suspect accusation of a military officer (37:13). The gravity of the threat increases at 38:6, where the prophet no longer is "in the mud" (LXXV) but rather "sinks" (MT) into it (cf. 38:22, where the MT parallels the king's fate to Jeremiah's: "your feet are sunk into the mud" instead of LXXV's "they made your feet rest on slippery places"). Again, in 38:9, Ebed-melech fears the prophet's starvation (MT, "he will die . . . from the famine," rather than LXXV, "to execute him on account of the famine").

This play around principal characters and narrative details serves a deeper narrative analogy present to compositional design. In earlier contexts, the pious figure of Hezekiah has been invoked in contrast to the present Judean monarchs (26:18-19; the king respects the sanctity and authority of prophets). Now the composition evokes 2 Kings 18–19, the narrative of the Assyrian siege of Jerusalem during Hezekiah's reign. Under siege, this pious, "reforming" king seeks the intercessions of the prophet Isaiah on the city's behalf, shows himself responsive to prophetic mission, and thus wins a miraculous deliverance for the community against the invading forces. A repetition of that deliverance lies behind the hope in Jer 37:5, 9 clustered around the withdrawal of Babylonian forces. The earlier prose speech that doubles the tradition, 21:1-10, goes beyond evocation to explicit expression (21:2): "Perhaps Yahweh will act in accordance with all his wonders so that they break the siege."

Zedekiah is the antithesis of the Hezekian symbol! He persecutes the prophet, hopes to coerce intercession, and proves ultimately unresponsive to the prophetic mission. When the MT reconfigures Zedekiah, producing a more craven, weak, pathetic figure, it deepens the analogical contrast with Hezekiah. That contrast between the "then" of Hezekiah and Zedekiah's "now" offers further ideological justification for Jerusalem's destruction. Aware of its intertextual analogy, the MT at 37:10 alters the reference to the dead/wounded Babylonians on the battlefield (LXXV, "each in his place [where he fell]") to the dead/wounded "in their tents." The allusion to the Assyrian forces miraculously slaughtered in their camp becomes more explicit (cf. 2 Kgs 19:35).

Jeremiah's characterization is also caught up in the network of these intertextual analogies. The composition has already been at pains to set the prophet under the sign of Moses (see Jeremiah 1; 15:1; 34–36). Hence in the present episode the narrative interest on Jeremiah as intercessor and prophet is vindicated by the fulfillment of his predictions (cf. Deut 18:15-22). When the composition invokes the 2 Kings analogy, though, it inserts a deep irony into Jeremiah's presentation. Given the analogy, the expected link between Jeremiah and its intertext would be with Isaiah. The surprise is in the discontinuity. For where Isaiah successfully intercedes for Jerusalem's safety, Jeremiah does not.

It is worse than this! As Jerusalem's seditionist, Jeremiah takes up the role of an Assyrian character in 2 Kings, the Rabshakeh. The latter sought to undermine the resistance of the city in Hezekiah's day with his seditious speeches. Analogies between these propaganda messages and Jeremiah's oracles are numerous. Both denounce hope in an Egyptian relief force (2 Kgs 18:21; cf. Jer 37:7). Both argue the deception of hope in miraculous divine aid (2 Kgs 18:29; 19:10; cf. Jer 37:9). Both seek to undermine royal control with direct appeals to the populace to surrender, guaranteeing their well-being in exchange (2 Kgs 18:31-32; cf. Jer 38:2), an alternative which Jeremiah will subsequently extend to Zedekiah personally (38:17, 21). The Assyrian official promises any deserters that they will "eat, each one from his own vine and fig, and each one drink the water of his own well" (2 Kgs 18:31). Thus Jeremiah's ambiguous attempt to leave the city becomes more suspicious (Jer 37:12): LXXV, "to make a purchase there among the people." Jeremiah's oracles are the antithesis of Isaiah's while at the same time echoing their wording. Jeremiah taunts the king, citing as false prophecy "he will not enter this city" (37:19), in contrast to Isaiah who promised "he will not enter this city" (2 Kgs 19:32, 33). Isaiah promised Hezekiah an Assyrian withdrawal, "I will put a spirit in him, so he will hear a rumor and return to his land" (2 Kgs 19:7). But Jeremiah counters to his king, "Pharaoh's army will return to the land of Egypt; and the Chaldeans will return . . . against this city" (Jer 37:7, 8; cf. v. 5, "the Chaldeans heard a report/rumor").

The narrator risks Jeremiah as an agent of the enemy king, the blaspheming Rabshakeh (cf. 2 Kgs 19:4). But the utilization of an achronic narrative arrangement fights this difficulty. With Jeremiah 36 the prelude to the present episode, the composition effects another analogy and assimilates Zedekiah under the sign of Jehoiakim's egregious impiety (cf. Jer 52:2). The contrast with Hezekiah's circumstances is emphasized all the more. Jeremiah's anti-Isaian posture is vindicated. Rather than be a derelict of prophetic duty, he has had to be the prophet the community required in its religious decay. When the MT works to enhance the prophet's innocence as well as the gravity of his near martyrdom, Jeremiah's protection from the Rabshakeh analogy only deepens. The realities of the Jeremianic prophetic mission can still be integrated and subordinated to Deuteronomistic ideological conceptions of prophecy.

Fulfilling Jerusalem's Exile (39:1-14)

Following on the heels of the last reported encounter between Jeremiah and Zedekiah, the composition (according to the MT) narrates the success of the Babylonian attack and thus the fulfillment of Jeremiah's message of Jerusalem's doom. But the LXXV diverges significantly. Representing only 39:1-3, 14, the narrative throws all of its focus on the rescue of Jeremiah from his imprisonment in the court of the guard (38:28). The MT has duplicated material from 2 Kgs 25:1-12, which it also shares with Jer 52:1-16, resulting in a triplication of the tradition. Accidental scribal omission of the verses in Jeremiah 39 is a possible (much favored) explanation of the LXXV's brevity, but the triplicate nature of the material in question renders this less likely.

Date formulae are also at variance. The MT sets the siege in Zedekiah's ninth year, tenth month (cf. 2 Kgs 25:1; Jer 52:4 — ninth year, tenth month, tenth day). The LXXV lacks any reference to the year, citing only the ninth month (so LXX^{BS} against LXX^{A}, which has "year"; see Ziegler 1976: 411, who follows LXX^{A} against his usual preference for LXX^{BS}). Temporal variance and confusion abound in the triplicate tradition. For example, compare Jer 39:2 (some mss., however, have the fifth month) and 52:5, 6, which date the breach of the city to Zedekiah's eleventh year, fourth month, ninth day to 2 Kgs 25:2, 3, which cites only the eleventh year, ninth day (BHS emends based on Jeremiah 52). Or compare Jer 52:12, which has the fifth month, tenth day for the date of the investment of city structures to 2 Kgs 25:8, tenth month, seventh day.

The MT gains as it complicates the compositional picture by reusing this material in the present context. No longer focusing on Jeremiah's release from prison alone, the composition now emphasizes and dramatizes the fulfillment of Jeremiah's judgment oracles against Zedekiah and Jerusalem. The pathetic flight, pursuit, capture, and sentencing of the king and execution of the royal sons with the royal court realize Jeremiah's oracular threats with a vengeance! All the moments of thin hope proffered by the prophet in oracular barter with the king and the community are now superseded.

Ironically, those swept into exile with the blinded king include those very Judeans who had deserted to the Babylonian forces during the siege (39:9) — testimony to the effectiveness of Jeremiah's earlier seditious campaign (38:2)! By adopting this material into its present context the MT introduces a cruel twist to the prophet's earlier promise consequent to desertion — "who deserts to the Babylonians will live and have their life *as a living spoil of war.*" Might those accepting the prophet's earlier thin hope not have expected in these words a better result for their capitulation and national "treason"? Surely as promised, they escape personal slaughter in the midst of the siege and its aftermath of political executions — only to become literal human spoil and booty deported into captivity! Oracular subterfuge? Or is this fulfillment and vindication of Jeremiah's predictive reliability from a peculiar point of view?

Indeed, the composition risks Jeremiah's oracular integrity to create a narrative world emphasizing the depopulation of Palestine, leaving it open for repossession by the legitimate heirs of restoration among the colonized elite (an issue to be noted comprehensively between the LXXV and MT representation of the tradition). The entire Zedekian elite (39:6, "all the Judean nobility") or anyone who might possibly have been seen as a legitimate continuator of "Judah" (v. 9, "the rest of the people who remained") is either executed or removed by deportation. In contrast, some non-elite poor remain in a setting of urban destruction and disorganization, yet as beneficiaries of Babylonian largess and grants of land for agricultural purposes (v. 10).

Such narrative representation works oddly against the detail that apparently the temple still stands, and already there exists indigenous leadership under the governorship of Gedaliah, the Babylonian appointee (39:11-14). The MT works its duplication of the tradition without any notice of the burning of the temple (contrast 2 Kgs 25:9 and Jer 52:13). 39:8 is where this notice should have occurred, but there only an obscure "house of the people" (unless this actually represents a rare reference to the temple; the phrase does not occur elsewhere in the Bible) is mentioned with the palace as subject to burning. Further, for the LXXV v. 14, "they brought him out, and he [Jeremiah] remained amidst the people," the MT has "they entrusted him . . . to bring him out for/to the home/house." Home/house could refer to Jeremiah's repatriation, picking up the theme of his patrimonial inheritance (32:6; 37:12), or it could be taken as an abbreviated reference to the temple (cf. Isa 15:2, which is also textually problematic in light of Jer 48:18, 22; see BDB, p. 110). The composition will have to displace these breaks in narrative logic through other means (see further the discussion for chs. 40–44).

Be that as it may, the composition achieves a contrast between the fate of Jeremiah and that of Zedekiah. Nebuchadrezzar "personally" attends to both! In contrast to Zedekiah (39:7), Nebuchadrezzar (consistent with his Yahwistic title in 25:9, "my servant") ensures the prophet's absolute safety (vv. 11-12). Apparently, Jeremiah's pro-Babylonian oracular effort is not without its reward! Notice that this plot element does not occur in the duplicate narratives (2 Kings 25 or Jeremiah 52). Within the larger representation of Jeremiah's struggle, certainly this fulfills Yahweh's own promises to the prophet that his enemies would shatter themselves on "besieged" Jeremiah (1:18; 15:20), while he, on the other hand, would survive unscathed (1:8, 19; 15:21; 20:11-13). 40:1-6 offer a countervariant to this tradition (see further below).

For the LXXV, the emphasis has focused on Jeremiah's rescue by Nebuchadrezzar's officials. It does not explicitly illuminate Nebuchadrezzar's own disposition toward the act. The advantage of this portrayal lies in the contrast with the "majority" of Zedekiah's court, who were determined to imprison and murder Jeremiah in chs. 37–38.

Rewarding Ebed-melech (39:15-18)

There was an exception, however, in Ebed-melech. Motivation for the achronic placement of the salvation oracle to this other benefactor of the prophet becomes clearer in the context of the briefer LXXV form of "Jeremiah's" performance.

The fate of individuals and factions is gathered and negotiated around the person of Jeremiah. Advocacy for the latter's safety and well-being is taken as a token of a piety responsive to the prophetic oracular mission and thus a sign of the desired loyalty to *Yahweh-alone*.

The salvation oracle is set apparently in the period prior to Jeremiah's release from prison and presumably prior to the fall of the city. The MT is responsible for clarification of this temporal setting when it adds in 39:15, "while he was locked up," and in v. 16, "they [my words] will come true before you on that day." The presence of the phrase "in the court of the guard" makes such clarifications natural and intelligible. But the LXXV lacks these temporal markers. Coupled with the instruction to the prophet, that is, "go and say," does the LXXV deemphasize the prophet's arrest and suggest a less forceful chronological dislocation?

The more limited scope of the narrative (39:1-3, 14, 15-18) makes the connection to the preceding episodes in ch. 38 more immediate. Not only does the fate of Jeremiah receive quick resolution, but so, too, does the fate of his "supporter." The pattern in chs. 37–38 of the prophet's changing conditions of arrest and threat, resolved into rescue from its most lethal variant, receive their mirror here and now with the promised rescue of the prophet's rescuer. Presumably the reader is to take the oracular promise as a stand-in for the narration of its fulfillment! Ebed-melech will not be heard of or seen in narrative act again.

The substance of his salvation oracle is couched in terms of Jeremiah's earlier seditious oracular alternative to the community and king (38:2; cf. 38:17, 20): ". . . your life will be yours as a spoil of war" (39:18). Once the MT has inserted its notice of the deported defectors (v. 9) as prisoners and spoils of war, this promise to the Ethiopian official acquires delicious sinister irony. Hopefully the additional oracular elaboration within which this promise sits proved a sufficient hedge against such ironic dismantling as well as Ebed-melech's literal spoliation! In any event, the oracular elaboration appropriates vocabulary from oracles addressed to the prophet (15:21, "I will deliver you"), Baruch (45:5, "I grant you your life as a spoil of war . . ."), kings (22:25, ". . . given . . . into the hand of those you fear . . ."; 32:4; 34:3; 38:18, 23, "you will not escape"), and the community (19:7; 20:4; 44:12, "fall by the sword").

For both performances (LXXV and MT), his "reward" interprets the network of compared and contrasted figures in the narrative world and renders their respective fates rationalized under the sign of obedience to *Yahweh-alone*.

Loosing (Losing) Jeremiah (40:1-6)

This duplicate narrative of Jeremiah's release in the aftermath of Jerusalem's fall bristles with difficulty no matter which version of these narratives (LXXV or MT) one has recourse to. Already in 39:14 (present in the LXXV) the prophet had been released from his incarceration in the Judean royal palace *and remanded to Gedaliah's care.* Now the reader finds him in Ramah, in chains, stockaded with those of the populace destined for deportation, only to be released *again* (cf. MT 39:11-13) by Nebuzaradan. Then Jeremiah promptly joins up with Gedaliah in Mizpah (40:6). The MT will not help the matter very much when it expands the traditions drawn from 2 Kings 25 to include 39:11-13. It anticipates in Nebuchadrezzar's instruction the choices Jeremiah will be offered in 40:4-5 by Nebuzaradan: ". . . look after him . . . whatever he tells you to do with him, do" (39:12). Notice that according to the LXXV Nebuzaradan does not appear until 40:1-6. If the MT seeks thus to overcome the break in narrative logic offered by 39:14 and 40:1-6, it is not clear that it succeeds. Simply striking out the reference to Gedaliah in 39:14 would have solved much.

Had notice of Jeremiah's relocation with Gedaliah not occurred in 39:14, then those proposals which assume that through some mechanism (provided by the imagination of the commentator) the prophet had been rearrested, thus requiring his re-release, would be more persuasive. But the problem offered by 39:14 renders such an assumption implausible.

Perhaps the ideological gains to be had by incorporating both versions of Jeremiah's fate warranted turning a compositional blind eye to its own narrative dysfunction.

For the episode offers a transition to the following account of the brief yet tragic fate of the Gedalian restoration in Palestine. It places Jeremiah in that context. But to what end? Very striking, indeed, is the stunning silence of the prophet throughout chs. 39–41! Jeremiah's voice — including his active oracular presence — is backgrounded without so much as one nonoracular peep.

Into this prophetic silence, 40:1 inserts its own problem, for it creates expectation of a Jeremianic prophetic oracle. No such oracle appears to break the prophet's silence. Instead, the reader is treated to a Yahwistic speech of the Babylonian official (vv. 2-5a)! The first part of that speech repeats themes and vocabulary characteristic of Jeremiah's prose perorations elsewhere in the book. Nebuzaradan rings the changes on the fulfillment of Jeremiah's prophecy of doom, offering the oft-repeated justification for it — "because you [2d ms. pl.] sinned against Yahweh and you [2d ms. pl.] did not obey his voice" (v. 3). A Babylonian interprets the ways of Yahweh to "Yahweh's people"! The MT drives the fulfillment of Jeremiah's predictions home by adding the phrases, "just as he promised" and "this word happened to you [2d ms. pl.]."

With the rubric of 40:1, the composition creates the impression that Nebuzaradan speaks with oracular authority, even takes up the burden of the prophet's earlier proclamations! Such compositional transfiguration is no more irregular than Nebuchadrezzar's Yahwistic appellative or his positive orientation to the Jeremianic prophetic mission. Notice that the official's rhetoric mimics the prophet's penchant for preaching positive and negative alternatives. The MT has both options in v. 4, while the LXXV lacks the second, "if it is not agreeable to you to return with me. . . ." For the LXXV the second option is provided by v. 5: "and if not, go return to Gedaliah . . ." (the MT represents the initial part as narrative comment, "and he still had not replied, [so Nebuzaradan said] 'return to . . .'" [McKane 1986: 1001]).

In the prophet's rhetoric, the issue of repentance was the fulcrum of alternative structuring speech. Here it has become a matter of where Jeremiah will throw his lot in the aftermath of national collapse. He offers Jeremiah security and patronage under his favor back in Babylon (a fitting choice for the Babylonian prophetic agent!), or he can go wherever he wants — even throw his lot in with the Gedalian gubernatorial regime (40:4-5a). Jeremiah's choice is to remain in the land with Gedaliah — an interesting choice since the prophet had earlier proved his oracular hostility to any survival of a meaningful "Israel" in the land (except of course in the distant future)! Contrast his oracular posture with that of the Zedekian "remnant" coupled with his restoration promise to the Jehoiachin "remnant" in chs. 24 and 29. Might the reader not expect the prophet to throw his lot in with the community from which restoration will issue in the future? Does Jeremiah's linkage with Gedaliah raise the prospect of a restoration of "Israel" with non-deported Judeans on Palestinian soil on the near horizon? The MT has its ideological work cut out for it given its desire to portray the depopulation of the land (39:9)!

Failing Gedaliah's Chances (40:7–41:18)

The narrative of the Gedalian community's utopian failure is deceptively simple. Yet Gedaliah must play the Jeremianic surrogate, and Jeremiah's physical "alliance" with the Judean "remnant" in Palestine proves no boon to communal security. All this in the face yet of communal obedience to Jeremiah's pro-Babylonian oracular tradition! A simple, not so secret, assassination plot proves all too sufficient to sweep away the Gedalian utopian hope in that oracular tradition.

Gedaliah must compensate for Jeremiah's oracular absence. The governor's speech must woo the loyalty of surviving military officers and their troops that we now learn (to the reader's surprise in light of 39:6, 9, 10) still remain in the land. Gedaliah's oath assumes that they have been busy as survivors of Judah's collapse, scooping up vacated land and cities (40:10, ". . . live in your cities you have seized"). Gedaliah hopes for communal security in servitude to the Babylonian imperium, thus echoing Jeremiah's prior oracular assurances (27:7, 8, 9, 11-13, 17). And why not place confidence in Jeremianic oracular tradition faced as they are with the vindicating fulfillment of Jeremiah's predicted Babylonian success. Notice that the MT has shifted the issue of communal fear to willing Babylonian servitude (MT v. 9, ". . . do not be afraid of serving the Chaldeans") from the LXXV representation of the fear of the occupying Chaldean forces (LXXV v. 9,

". . . do not fear the servants of the Chaldeans" [or does Gedaliah here refer to his own regime?]), thus effecting the echo of prior Jeremianic oracular tradition.

The MT further elevates the scenery of hope by insinuating an escalation of returnees gathering around the Gedalian governorship. In 40:7 it adds the notice of the poorest of the land to the Gedalian constituency, linking the initial conditions of the community to 39:10. In 40:12 it expands the scope of the returning diaspora to include "all the Judeans from all the places where they had been scattered" (the LXXV lacks both of these notices). The addition echoes the wording of Jeremianic restoration prophecy (cf. 23:3) and thus raises the stakes for the success or failure of the Gedalian community even as it elevates its prospects under the sign of restoration, Babylonian patronage, and divine favor. Waves of exiles return to constitute a "remnant of Judah" experiencing, in accordance with Gedaliah's oath (40:9), enough security and time to taste the promised prosperity (v. 12, ". . . they gathered wine and summer fruit in great abundance"). Subsequent judgment speech will capitalize on the broad scope of this swelling remnant to efface their claims to "Israel" and remove any and all diasporan competitors to Babylonian diasporan interests. To that end, the MT continues its insinuations and exaggerations of an escalated remnant throughout: MT 41:10, "all the remnant of the people in Mizpah," for LXXV, "the people left in Mizpah"; MT 42:15 adds, "remnant of Judah"; MT 43:5 adds, "from all the nations where they had been scattered"; MT 44:7, "remnant," for LXXV, "no one"; MT 44:11 adds, "all Judah"; MT 44:12 adds, "remnant of Judah," for LXXV's "to destroy all the remnant in Egypt"; MT 44:24 adds, "all Judah who are in the land of Egypt"; MT 44:28 adds "all" for LXXV's "remnant of Judah." The LXXV also appears to engage in this at 41:16 and 43:6 with its reading of "remnant" against MT's "children."

All the more puzzling, then, are Gedaliah's perspective and Jeremiah's silences as Ishmael's assassination plot plays out (40:13–41:10). Why does the governor refuse to believe Johanan's military intelligence about the assassination plot (40:14)? And why suspect Johanan's motives over those of Ishmael (v. 16)? The latter's motives are obvious to the privileged narrator. For Ishmael's royal lineage suggests political jealousy over Gedaliah's Babylonian appointment (41:1, 2). But Gedaliah apparently does not or will not see this. At least why does he not consult with Jeremiah in the midst of these intrigues? The narrative is evasive with its implied reader on this score.

Gedaliah's beliefs are his undoing — perhaps more deeply than the narrative itself would like to probe. For, on the one hand, the reader might well surmise that it is Gedaliah's reliance on Jeremianic oracular tradition that has left him open to discomfiture. The governor pursues (on the MT narrative representation) a utopian restoration policy inspired by trust in Jeremianic oracular power. Perhaps it is just that trust which renders him unwilling to countenance the possibility of effective threat or failure. Is this hubris? Does the governor seek to wield Jeremianic tradition inappropriately? His restoration bid does on the surface rush the seventy-year time frame set elsewhere for restoration's timetable (cf. chs. 25, 29). The implicit reader, on the other hand, might prefer these latter suppositions faced with the great risk to oracular power encompassed in the narrative evasions. Still no Jeremiah speaks up to voice his prophetic disapproval!

Jeremiah's silent presence in the Gedalian community compounds these narrative evasions even as it is the narrator along with Gedaliah who invokes Jeremianic tradition around Gedalian policy. That Gedaliah fails while trusting his fate to Jeremianic oracular tradition carries with it the failure of Jeremiah. Suspicion grows that the prophet's silence proved a snare for Gedaliah. And contrary to compositional practice, the narrative stunningly evades any explicit evaluation of Gedaliah's leadership! The composition finally has a Judean leader aggressively willing to pursue Jeremianic oracular intent. Should not the reader expect Gedaliah's commendation in terms at least commensurate with other Jeremianic supports — e.g., Ebed-melech and Baruch? At the least, the Jeremianically inspired Gedaliah ought to escape defeat and realize his utopian promise — or at least have his life as a spoil of war!

It is left to Johanan ben Kareah and the rescued survivors of Ishmael's putsch, on their way to Egyptian sanctuary (41:17), to summon Jeremiah forth from silence (an ironic contrast to the efforts of Zedekiah's court to produce Jeremianic silence!).

Eliminating Egyptian Diasporan Claims (42:1–44:30)

Having already laid bare the intention of the survivors to seek refuge in Egypt, the narrative charges their extended exchange with Jeremiah with a high degree of irony. And the prophet will more than make up for his stunning silence, masking his abandonment of Gedaliah with the loquacious performance of Deuteronomistic clichés so familiar from the prophet's prior prose perorations.

When the refugees seek oracular guidance (42:1-6), narrator's privilege has already undermined the sincerity of their oath for the reader. They project an openness in the course of their actions rather than an already determined purpose (42:3), unless the reader is supposed to infer hidden communal conflict over the intention exposed at 41:17. To the prophet, however, they promise unflinching obedience to whatever oracular response Jeremiah returns (42:5-6). The prophet, for his part, must wait ten days to discover their perfidy, not to mention oracular illumination (42:7, "at the end of ten days").

But one wonders why Jeremiah must wait so long only to receive an oracular alternative filled with such stock themes and standard rhetorical tropes (42:7-22). The narrative world created by the prose traditions in Jeremiah constructs prophetic power not immediately in the control of the prophet. Jeremiah represents a prophet subjugated by oracular power, yet whose oracular content by this point in the scroll of "Jeremiah" is so predictable that the very need of a prophetic figure is obviated. No doubt mythic anxieties over oracular authenticity and integrity lie behind such narrative figurations since the composition must repeatedly mime its moral-religious vision within "Jeremiah's" oracular performances, thus appropriating oracular power to its symbolic regime.

The prophet's positive alternative (42:9-12) reasserts Babylonian clemency and patronage, divine favor (MT v. 12 intertwines Yahwistic and Babylonian agency when it transforms LXXV's 1st sg. verbs: from "I will show mercy" to "he will show mercy"; from "I will return you" to "he will return you"), and communal security in the present to these very refugees only if they choose to remain a remnant in the land (contrast 24:6 with 29:10-11). The rhetoric explicitly recites Jeremianic restoration themes (42:10; cf. 1:10; 24:6; 31:28; contrast 29:10-11, ". . . only when Babylon's seventy years . . ."). This is the Gedalian utopian promise now back directly on Jeremiah's oracular lips — a belated vindication of the now murdered governor's own remonstrations, indeed!

The negative alternative offers the reverse image of restoration promises (42:13-17) so expanded (vv. 18-22) by its close that it transforms the negative possibility into settled prediction. In advance of communal response the prophet deconstructs their stated intention and oath (v. 21), ". . . you have not obeyed . . . in anything that he sent me to tell you. . . ." The restoration promise proves chimerical (v. 22): ". . . you shall die . . . in the place where you desire to go and settle."

Well they might agree with Jeremiah, and indeed they do when he accuses them of erring in their attempt to secure oracular instruction (42:20, "for you erred fatally . . ."). But, ironically, it will not be as Jeremiah sees it because of their perfidy; rather, they will detect in Jeremiah's "Gedalian assurances" an insidious effort on Baruch's part to ruin them (43:3; cf. Jeremiah 36 and Baruch's displacement of Jeremiah there)! Their suspicions are understandable (in spite of narrative confidence in Jeremiah's authenticity — 43:4, 7, ". . . they did not obey the voice of the LORD"), gathered as Jeremiah's silences are around Gedaliah's failure — consequent as the latter was on the very assurances just re-offered the remnant once again. Thus when he speaks now, protestations to the contrary, he speaks only as co-conspirator and enemy of the Judean remnant. Their courage and wisdom (MT v. 2, however, exposes alternative motives when it adds "insolent" to their characterization, i.e., the LXXV lacks the adjective) is to extricate themselves from the snare of false prophecy and Jeremianic, pro-Babylonian sedition (43:2, ". . . falsehood you speak; Yahweh, our God, did not send you . . ."). Ironically, when they flee to Egypt (43:5-7), they will, all the same, take Jeremiah and Baruch with them! So that trusted or reviled, speaking or silent, Jeremiah serves only to doom the remnant — in fulfillment both of the narrator's assertion of Jeremianic oracular authenticity and the Judean remnant's denial of it!

Two judgment speeches (43:8-13; 44:1-30) offer the final tableaux of the Jeremianic mission to the diasporan Egyptian community. When Jeremiah commits his symbolic act before the Judean diaspora in Tahpanhes (43:9, "Let the Judeans see you do it . . ."), he marks the spot of Nebuchadrezzar's triumph over Pharaoh (v. 9) and especially the Egyptian pantheon (vv. 12-13). Curiously, the judgment oracle puts its emphasis on the latter, though it is still true that the state and the people are to be decimated (v. 11). Presumably the witnessing Judeans are to infer their own decimation along with the decimation of their chosen refuge and sanctuary. But why introduce this judgment on Egyptian religion? Up to this point in Jeremiah's oracular counsel it was the mere fact of fleeing to Egypt that warranted destruction. Now a subtle shift begins to make implicit idolaters of this refugee Judean community — a charge that 44:1-30 will make explicit when it totalizes idolatrous practice among all the Egyptian diasporan locales. Here the oracle only suggests the true problem (on the composition's view) for the relocation to Egypt — to seek sanctuary there from the predations of the Babylonian Yahwistic servant (MT 43:10, "my servant," lacking in the LXXV) Nebuchadrezzar is to seek the patronage of Egyptian deities. The implied accusation is ironic for the composition since it does not draw the same conclusion from its pro-Babylonian oracular posture. For in the latter it is Yahweh who is at work, not the Babylonian pantheon with its high king, Marduk!

The extensive prose peroration of 44:1-30 offers only a thin tissue of plot, though it does mirror the oracular "intrigue" Jeremiah already experienced at the hands of the Gedalian remnant in 43:1-7. The tableau dramatizes a dispute between the prophet and an assemblage of the Egyptian diaspora (44:1; cf. 15, "a great assembly"). The purpose of the (literary) gathering must be inferred from the substance of the debate. The diaspora seeks the meaning of its past and present historical experience of a Judean national collapse and colonization, along with prognostications for its destiny as "diaspora." Jeremiah joins those interests, with their concomitant of cultural pain, by offering a review of Judean religious practice (vv. 2-6). The prophet places their cultural pain under the sign of a punishment deserved, a consequence of a history of religious disobedience termed idolatry. Jeremiah's review of Judea's "tradition" of idolatry is only a prelude to the resumed accusation of the Egyptian diaspora for the very same crime (vv. 7-10). As the mouthpiece for the composition's symbolic regime, Jeremiah constructs his speech from familiar Deuteronomistic clichés (cf. Jeremiah 7). His picture of Jerusalem and Judea's destruction and depopulation is totalizing (44:2, 6). The latter's destiny of national collapse as divine punishment is the only future offered to the diaspora as well (vv. 11-14).

While, according to the prophet, the "remnant" in chs. 42–43 countenanced its destruction from the mere fact of seeking sanctuary in Egypt, the present assembly, "the remnant of Judah" (44:11), destroys itself in egregious "fidelity" to "false" religion. The lesson of the worship of *Yahweh-alone* has not yet been learned. What does the prophet intend by this castigation? Do his rhetorical questions sincerely seek to persuade the community, in fact, to learn the lesson, reform their practice, and thus preserve their well-being in Egypt (v. 7, "Why are you. . . ?"; v. 8, "Why do you. . . ?"; v. 8, "Will you be. . . ?"; v. 9, "Have you forgotten . . . ?")? Would their sincere reform successfully dismantle Jeremianic hostility to the mere fact of an Egyptian diaspora?

Fortunately, the prophet need not face this aporia, for

his dramatic audience will not accept his mythologization of their cultural (mis)fortunes (44:15-19). Unfortunately, the grasp of Jeremiah's symbolic regime does not hold. The diaspora can offer an alternative myth. Ironically, it, too, posits a history of cultic abuses as the rationalization of their cultural pain. It, too, is anchored in their sense of a long-standing cultic tradition, hallowed by experience (v. 17), but unfortunately violated and abandoned (v. 18). Their breach of faith lies in their abandonment of the Queen of Heaven (presumably Ishtar/Isis/Astarte), as well as the security of their future with restoration of her worship. The prophet opines the *addition* of illicit divinities, but the diaspora discerns an illicit *subtraction*. For the prophet, Yahweh can brook no partners. For the diaspora, he can ill afford to do without. They have vows to keep!

Alternative Yahwistic myths clash! Jeremiah's reading of Israelite history proves no more cogent than theirs does in offering a coherent and plausible mythologization of their cultural experience. A deep indeterminacy afflicts Yahwistic myth as much as the institution of its prophets. There is an analogy with Jeremiah's conflict with Hananiah (Jeremiah 28). For Yahweh can no more unmask the "pretensions" of the Queen of Heaven than Jeremiah proved capable of decisively unmasking Hananiah's prophetic tropes (28:11, "At this the prophet Jeremiah went his way"). Judah's historical experience remains radically equivocal — susceptible, as it is, to explanation from competing myths of Israel. Anxious on this score in ch. 28, the composition had recourse to a foreshortened prediction-fulfillment scheme — able, as it was, to avail itself of narrative succor in the report of Hananiah's swift demise (28:17). But no such easy out can present itself for Jeremiah before the Egyptian diaspora. For by now Jeremiah's prophetic legitimacy has been opened up to a deeper indeterminacy. Though the composition seeks to use the success of Babylonian imperial designs, along with its concomitant Jeremianic oracular predictions, to commend its mythic regime of *Yahweh-alone,* nevertheless the Egyptian diaspora has also had to witness the failure of the Jeremiah-inspired, Gedalian restoration bid. The benefits of *Yahweh-alone* remain compromised — as the husband-approved devotees of the Queen of Heaven are quick to argue (44:19).

Thus the composition can do no more than have Jeremiah more stridently repeat the terms of his judgment oracle (44:24-30). The prophet cannot directly refute the diasporan apology for their goddess. And though he views it as a sign of corruption, Jeremiah must even accept their claim about the long-standing presence of the goddess consort within Judean myth and cult (vv. 21-23; notice the nonoracular status of these statements; they fall outside Jeremiah's oracular tropes). The prediction-fulfillment schema is once again the composition's only recourse (v. 28, ". . . whose words will stand, mine or theirs?") in its effort to trump these competing Yahwistic claims! Pharaoh Hophra's demise must play the sign and pledge of Jeremiah's Yahwistic vision (vv. 29-30).

It is not easy to know for whose benefit the invocation of Hophra is. Within the dramatic scene of the composition a narrative world that validates Jeremianic oracular power must be offered. For the dramatic audience only time will serve the prophet's predictions for good or ill of an Egypt decimated by Nebuchadrezzar's troops, of Egypt's divine patrons overthrown and its populations dead or exiled. How another prediction, this time of Pharaoh Hophra's fate within this same framework of Yahwistic punishment, could effectively provide a pledge of Jeremiah's predictive reliability and thus prove sufficient to persuade the Egyptian diaspora of his *Yahweh-alone* vision of the myth of Israel remains unclear. The "sign" is tautological for the current audience. This "proof" of Yahwistic ire and Jeremiah's oracular verity amounts to the argument that you will know it is true when it comes true! But then it will be too late for Jeremiah's current dramatic addressees. For the composition's implied readers, however, the aporia are deeper.

Jeremiah's oracles were an empty wind! Nebuchadrezzar never decimated Egypt. An Egyptian diaspora persisted throughout the Second Temple period. The restoration interests of the colonized elite must refuse such admissions. Thus evocation of Hophra's "oracular" demise intends to mask such Jeremianic failures. Indeed, the sign of Hophra happened as it was foretold (assuming "historical" awareness of the coup engineered by one of his generals, Amasis) — as long as one trades on opacity of referent for Hophra's enemies (v. 30, "his enemies," "those who seek his life"), disengaging their natural linkage in context with Nebuchadrezzar! Oracular duplicity can sustain the sign of Hophra as a pledge of the Yahwistic rejection of Egyptian diaspora claims and countermyths of Israel even as it postpones anxiety over Jeremiah's oracular failure to the future.

Rewarding Baruch (45:1-5)

This brief passage makes a gesture toward ending the scroll of Jeremiah. It does so by reaching back. As with Ebed-melech, so, too, Baruch receives a "salvation" oracle. Its temporal setting ruptures the linear plot development used in chs. 37–44, as with the Ebed-melech oracle. The date formula returns the reader to the fourth year of Jehoiakim, linking this oracle to chs. 25 and 36. Baruch's amanuensis to Jeremiah's oracular power links the oracle more narrowly to the plot in ch. 36. While it is Ebed-melech's act of support on behalf of the prophet that calls forth a "salvation" oracle, here it is Baruch's language and utterance of suffering (45:3). Baruch's rhetoric of pain and protest reaches back to the tropes of lamentation, mourning, and complaint so much a part of chs. 2–20, whether on the lips of the prophet or lady Israel or even the divine (see the analysis for chs. 7–10). In this case, Baruch apparently merits a rebuke as well as a promise (cf. the divine responses to the prophet's complaints in 12:5, 6; 15:19-20), with the latter a partial reiteration of Ebed-melech's — "I will grant you your life as spoil of war wherever you go" (45:5; cf. 39:18). Notice that the threads of commendation so much a part of this promise to Ebed-melech have all been stripped away here for Baruch.

Yahweh's oracular reaction is revelatory in ironic ways. He is determined on violence: ". . . what I build, I tear down, and what I plant, I uproot . . ." (45:4). These are the verbs of Yahweh's imperial rule. Their reiteration at the end of the scroll reaches back to the programmatic announcement at 1:10, as well as its repeated reuse throughout the Jeremianic traditions (e.g., 12:15, 17; 18:7, 9; 24:6; 29:5, 28; 31:28, 38, 40; 42:10). They encapsulate the moments toward weal and woe in Yahweh's theopolitical action. Only here in the present dramatic context, Jehoiakim's fourth year, has the weal countenanced by 1:10 been emphatically overcome by Yahweh's determination for woe — a fitting compliment to Baruch's complaint, "all my moments are woe" (to paraphrase)! Yahweh's imperial reign must fend off Baruch's subversive protest couched as it is in the language of the righteous sufferer. Were he to truly heed that cry, his present imperial purpose would forfeit. The inner necessities of his imperial character lead him to deconstruct motives hidden in Baruch's complaint: v. 5, ". . . are you seeking for yourself greatness [lit. "great things"]?" But the reader with "Baruch" might hear distorted echoes of an alternative intent, now marginalized in the divine rhetoric — that is, the "great things" hinted at in Baruch's complaint refer to a miraculous act of divine rescue (BDB 153 #9; cf. Deut 10:21; Job 5:9; 9:10; 37:6; Pss 71:19; 106:21). Ironically, the source of Jeremiah's oracular power whom Baruch "serves" detects a conspiracy of motive in Baruch — just as the Gedalian refugees suspected Baruchan intrigues for Babylonian self-aggrandizement (43:3)!

Modern commentary has always found the dischronologized placement a problem. But achronic strategies are so much a feature of chs. 25–45 that by now the reader must surely impute motives other than ill-advised linear lapses or chronological missteps. The Ebed-melech oracular "dislocation" is instructive. For at 39:15-18, achronic placement aids punctuation of the prediction-fulfillment scheme as well as offers characterization contrasts with those who had refused to heed Jeremiah's prophetic authority at the very point in the "linear" narrative where Jeremiah's proclaimed fate for Jerusalem finds realization. With the present achronic ploy the composition gains in similar and additional ways.

In lieu of a narrative of fulfillment of the prophet's oracles against the Egyptian diaspora, it can associate this oracle to Baruch with the indications of Baruch's survival in Egypt, thus masking one failed (unrealized) prediction with another of more fortunate outcome. Additionally, the passage as a thematic echo of so much of the preceding can offer a sense of closure for the entire scroll of Jeremiah, with the note of fulfillment strongly sounded in the arc of God's imperial war against every "Israel" falsely laying claim to that title, whether in Judah or Egypt or any other diaspora — except Babylon! Content with underlining that point, the LXXV appends ch. 52 and ends the scroll of Jeremiah. MT has relocated all the oracles against the nations (chs. 46-51), thus capitalizing on the Baruch oracle's transitional potential.

For the achronic redeployment of 45:1-5 allows inherent ambiguities in the divine speech to be exploited. Focused internally, the introductory phrase "all these words" appropriately refers to the oracular composition narrated previously in the temporal setting of ch. 36. Relocated here, it can hint at a larger concluding summary function as well as a larger compositional role for "Baruch." When Yahweh declares his intention to tear down and uproot, the scope of the phrase, ". . . that is, the whole land [MT v. 4; the LXXV lacks this phrase]," can be expanded to anticipate the spread of Yahweh's imperial crusade beyond the boundaries of "Israel" — that is (retranslating), "the whole earth" (cf. v. 5, "I am bringing disaster on all flesh," with 25:31). 45:1-5 bring closure to God's war with Israel and anticipate its spread to the nations in chs. 46–51 in completion of Jeremiah's prediction of the "times" in ch. 25. Notice that the form of the introductory formula (v. 1) used occurs again only at 46:18 and 50:1.

Evaluation

Using "Jeremiah" risks the mythic regime so much at stake for restoration compositional interests. Faced with the cultural abyss of colonization for the myth of Yahweh and Israel, proponents of these interests must construct a symbolic space out of multiple, variant, frequently contradictory traditions inhabiting the Jeremianic arena. They embrace these symbolic risks from Jeremianic traditions, in part, for they discern in them coherence and utility toward the satisfaction of their theopolitical desires vested in *Yahweh-alone*.

Thus "Jeremiah" must be exonerated and vindicated at the same time that tension between Jeremianic tradition and Deuteronomistic conceptions of the myth of prophecy must be negotiated. Ironically, tensions within Deuteronomistic mythic topoi will be exploited to mask and/or suppress "Jeremiah's" eccentricities, failures, and acts of oracular legerdemain — all in support of the myth of "Mosaic" succession.

In chs. 37–39, Yahweh's war against the old Zedekian regime comes to fruition aided by the failure of "Jeremiah," an anti-Moses, to intercede for communal security. On the surface, the prophet exploits oracular power to sap the resolve of the leadership and defenders of the city at the same time that he jockeys with the king over personal safety. "Jeremiah" exercises the rhetorical power of prophecy under the specter of abetting Babylonian imperial interests in return for grants of imperial safety and patronage.

The compositional interests must rehabilitate this anti-Isaiah, this prophetic "Rabshakeh." Thus the narrator allows multiple perspectives and assumptions regarding prophetic mission to intermix through his characters. Jeremiah's dramatic opponents anchor prophetic legitimacy in effective intercession, while Jeremiah, Ebed-melech, and the narrator rely on prediction-fulfillment schemata. The narrator through his characters sets in tension and exploits different aspects of the Deuteronomistic myth of prophecy: intercession and prophecy of disaster. A narrative world is constructed that pits these aspects against each other and at the same time subordinates them to the moral tenor of the community in which oracular power operates. Personal safety versus the persecution of the prophet has become emblematic of the moral texture of the community and thus determinant of communal claim on intercession or liability to the prophecy of disaster. At the same time alternative oracular possibilities and suspensions (failed predictions) can be rendered harmless through a sequence of oracular invalidation within a framework of moral contingencies. The Deuteronomistic criterion of prediction-fulfillment is rendered more flexible, more supple in the face of oracular dissonance. Thus symbolic risks in the Jeremianic traditions can be embraced in an illusion of fairness and narrative honesty that in fact realigns the implicit reader to the Jeremianic mission as the true model of prophecy. A heterodox "Jeremiah" is rendered comprehensible to the Deuteronomistic myth of prophecy, preserving Jeremiah's prophetic authority at the same time that the old regime is left responsible for its own destruction.

But in chs. 40–41 Jeremiah plays the antitype to his normal vociferous oracular self! The narrator hides the prophet — physically present at Mizpah — from Gedaliah and his implicit reader in oracular silence.

Jeremiah's presence, which is really an oracular absence, renders Gedaliah's defeat a deceptive convenience for the composition, for it contains within it a deeper aporia toward compositional anxieties. True, with Gedaliah's defeat a potential threat to the symbolic claims of the Babylonian diaspora fades away, and especially so when the MT elevates the content of "remnant of Judah" so that there are no other diaspora left anywhere except the poor band of refugees who will flee to their demise in Egypt. True as well, had Gedaliah's restoration bid actually succeeded, further threat to Jeremiah's oracular power would have opened up given Jeremiah's vociferous opposition to a speedy return "before the time." So, ironically, the composition capitalizes on Gedaliah's failure only to embrace a deeper aporia — a Jeremianic supportive leader fails! The composition has embraced Jeremianic tradition profoundly problematic for its vaunted sanctuary of moral contingency in the face of oracular dissonance! The failure of Jeremianic prophecy and its divine sponsor which the composition so earnestly seeks to refuse is now deeply embedded within that very mythic structure. A threat to that very symbolic edifice remains perennially incorporate to "Jeremiah."

Jeremiah's silence in the face of Gedaliah's assassination is akin to the narrative silence over the death of Josiah in 2 Kings. Both leaders pursuing the approved *Yahweh-alone* policy (Deuteronomistic and Jeremianic, respectively) fail and fall prematurely, with restoration dreams slipping from their grasp. Mythopoesis turns its back here to sidestep the discomfiture of its mythic commitment to Yahweh. What mythologization cannot accomplish by direct reimagination, apparently it must ignore. Ironically, it encapsulates the seeds of its own ideological collapse. What it seeks to prevent — the failure of Yahweh — and what it cannot afford to admit — the weakness of its mythopoetic grip — has been drawn into the very heart of its symbolic arena. For on their own terms, should we not have predicted through "Jeremiah" Gedaliah's Deuteronomistically sanctioned success? He submits to Babylon. Should he not then live and preserve "Israel"? Instead Gedaliah, perforce, must be his own (Jeremianic) prophet. Jeremiah will offer no oracular proclamation of Gedaliah's utopian prospects. Not even Jeremiah's symbolic players can refuse some events — neither the demise of Jerusalem nor the failure of Gedaliah! For the latter what theodicy suffices?

Thus the composition must distract and redirect its implicit reader. Summoning the prophet from his terrible silence, the composition must deconstruct the apparent integrity of the Gedalian community and its survivors in chs. 42–44. By exposing the flight to Egypt as an ill-advised failure of nerve before the requirement of continued reliance on Jeremianic instruction, the composition has recourse once again to its apologetic of moral contingency for oracular power in the face of prediction-fulfillment aporia. By exposing the "unreformed" worship of the diasporan community in Egypt, the composition further displaces and sublimates renewed symbolic anxiety over the abyss of Gedaliah's restoration failure. Thus the composition exploits its own aporia to solve the problem posed by the splintering of "Israel" into diasporan guises. They hope to write out of the picture rival claims to land entitlements as well as symbolic rights to the sign, "Israel."

A history of utopian failures must be exploited to serve elite restoration interests and at the same time fend off symbolic threats intrinsic to their own utopian desires occasioned by the failure of God. In so doing, they create a narrative world where the myths of Yahweh and Israel lie perennially open to utopian disappointment, living as they must under the shadow of symbolic crisis where all "Israel's" dreams collapse for the generation(s), the faction which will not heed the Yahwistic voice heralded by the "re-possessors" of Jeremianic textual space.

For those who resist such world making (even successfully), there is the sign of Hophra. For those who will submit to their symbolic regime there is the promise of Baruch. Caught between the two, the implicit reader must hope in *Yahweh-alone,* whose struggle to displace all rivals structures distributed cycles of the one divine imperial project in which tearing down and uprooting can turn into their opposites once again in fulfillment of colonial restoration desires and in which the "failure" of the myth of Yahweh can become the mechanism of its symbolic success. Israel's cultural abyss has proved generative for the myth of Yahweh. The latter's rehabilitation has necessitated the practice of ideological distortion in the effort to create an imaginary landscape called "Jeremiah" in service to anguished utopian desires.

But this newcomer, *Yahweh-alone,* must be added alongside the claims of the Queen of Heaven! The composition seeks to suppress the goddess as a constituent of Yahwistic religion. The presence of the Queen of Heaven lays bare the innovation and pretense of *Yahweh-alone.* In her negative invocation, the composition opens a filtered window on alternative understandings of the myth of Yahweh and the Israelite cult present in the old regime. Performing *Yahweh-alone,* the composition embraces deep aporia around what it seeks to prevent. Thus they testify to the fabrication of their posture as traditionalists advocating only a purification and return to an "ancient" Israelite faith. Indeed, they seek the death of a rival form of Yahwistic myth and cult — one whose pedigree they cannot completely refute. Rather, they must reinterpret its claim to the "traditional" by reducing it to a traditional apostasy. The colonial elite voices reveal themselves as the true innovators under the sign of *Yahweh-alone.* They are "modern" apostates to an older Israelite faith; nevertheless, they must repristinate their mythic claims in a play for rhetorical power.

Jeremiah 46:1–51:64

Overview

Devastated "Israel's" hope lies in the escalation and spread of the Yahwistic reign of terror that has already engulfed Jerusalem. The glory of Yahweh lies in a cultural genocide of the world of nations. The colonized elite of Judah refuse the failure of Yahweh in the demise of the Davidic state by writing a myth of Yahwistic imperial desire whose fantastic landscape posits the defeat of national deities and their client peoples. The myth of exile and return has become the way of Yahweh with the world, where the war of God constitutes the promise of Israel to be the pinnacle and paradigm of Yahwistic rule over the nations. These death songs and war poems legitimate Israel's cultural holocaust through the deep embrace of Yahwistic violence. For Israel will rise from the ashes of the world.

Dramatic Composition

The location of the oracles against the nations at the end of the Jeremiah scroll is a feature of the MT representation of the tradition (as noted already in the discussion of Jeremiah 25). In that relocation, the MT also resequences: Egypt (46:1-28), Philistia (47:1-7), Moab (48:1-47), Ammon (49:1-6), Edom (49:7-22), Damascus (49:23-27), Kedar (49:28-33), Elam (49:34-39), Babylon (50:1–50:64). Contrast the LXXV: Elam (25:14-19), Egypt (26:1-28), Babylon (27:1–28:64), Philistia (29:1-7), Edom (29:8-23), Ammon (30:1-5), Kedar (30:6-11), Damascus (30:12-16), and Moab (31:1-44). The MT gains in this rewriting of Jeremiah, for it not only effects its picture of a divine war that spreads out over the world from Israel, but it also thematically divides the oracles against the nations into chs. 46–49 and 50–51. In the former, Babylonian imperial predation still furthers Yahweh's own imperial designs. In the latter, the Babylonian beast falls from Yahwistic instrumentality and goes to the ground as its Yahwistic master treats it to the same fate as the rest of the world. The MT refocuses the tradition on hope and recalculates ("the appointed time/year of punishment," 46:21; 48:44; 50:27; 51:18; cf. 8:12; 10:15; 11:23; 23:12) the progress of the war of God toward the restoration of Israel.

Discerning a rationale for the internal arrangement within each oracle against the nations, however, is much harder to work out. And the term "pastiche" has often been used to describe the texture of the tradition.

Babylon, the Yahwistic Beast, Fells the World (Chs. 46–49)

Significant interplay with the war poetry and funeral songs in Jeremiah 4–10 is effected. Thus the familiar dramatizations of battle and invasion in chs. 4–6 reoccur: 46:3-9, 11-12, 14-19, 20-24; 47:2-5; 48:2, 6, 8, 15, 18, 40; 49:2, 14, 8, 28-29, 30-31, 35, 37; 50:3, 9, 14-16, 21-22, 25-27, 29-30, 35-38, 41-43; 51:1-4, 11-14, 20-23, 27-33, 54-56. Depictions of the devastating outcome of the war occur in 46:10, 25-26; 48:7-13, 16, 21-27, 41-44, 47; 49:4-6, 10-13, 15-22, 26-27, 32-33, 36, 38-39; 50:3, 10, 11-12, 28, 31-32, 39-40, 44-46; 51:24-26, 36-40, 52-53, 57-58. The funeral songs in chs. 7–10 reappear: 46:6, 24; 47:5-6; 48:1, 4-5, 17-20, 28-39, 45-46; 49:3, 23-25; 50:2, 23-37; 51:7-9, 41-44. The female addressee of chs. 2–3 appears, though in very underdeveloped manner (Egypt — 46:11-12, 19, 22, 23-26; Moab — 48:1-2, 4, 7, 9, 18-20, 32; Ammon — 49:4-5; Edom — 49:17; Damascus — 49:24, 26; Babylon — 50:2, 3, 9-11, 13-15, 24, 26, 29, 30, 37, 38, 42; 51:2-4, 6, 8, 11, 13, 14, 27, 28, 30, 33, 36, 41-43, 45, 47, 48, 52, 25, 56-58; Lady Zion — 51:35, 36). Connections range from the use of common vocabulary and imagery up to and including explicit reduplication and reutilization of oracular fragments from earlier sections (e.g., 46:16; cf. 50:16; 46:27-28 = 30:10-11; 49:18 = 50:40; 49:19-21 = 50:44-46; 50:41-43 = 6:22-24; 51:15-19 = 10:12-16). Thus a line of continuity is created between the two blocks of war oracles so that whether directed against Judah or her national neighbors the act of Yahwistic conquest represents only one extended war, tended by Jeremiah's oracular power and launched against Judah as its first victim.

But no regular pattern in the sequencing of battles or dirges, whether in narrative plot or temporal order, is consistently pursued. The reader quickly moves back and forth between war poem and dirge, from the beginning of a military engagement to its completion and back again. In some oracles against the nations, depiction of the battle predominates (e.g., Egypt, Philistia, Kedar). In others it is the dirge that is in the foreground (e.g., Moab, Damascus; but absent entirely for Edom, Kedar, and Elam). Still others focus on describing the outcome of the war (e.g., Ammon, Edom, Damascus, and Elam), and the long oracles against Moab and Babylon blend dirge and depiction of outcome in equal measure. The reader is offered a montage of images. Is this haphazard composition or an attempt to evoke the chaos unleashed on the nations within the larger structural arc of chs. 46–51?

Importantly, the little scenes of war no longer gather around them the dramatized multiplicity of voices in dispute and reaction to the landscape of Yahwistic violence (contrast chs. 4–10). Of dramatic citations that do occur most serve only to characterize a particular nation's hubris (46:8; 48:14; 49:4), or the intentions and actions of invading or defending forces (46:16; 48:2; 50:15; 51:32), or the reaction to suffering (48:17, 19). Only once is a dramatic voice raised to protest the divine violence done to the nations, but it is quickly brushed aside (47:6-7). Elsewhere suffering is lamented or protested when it is Israel's that is in question (50:7; 51:34, 51). As a result, Israel now appears as the one already punished and therefore pardoned for past sins (46:28), or the one destined to be purified of them (50:5, 20), or even more surprising as the one truly innocent victim within God's global holocaust (49:12)! No doubt the symbolic needs of Israelite vengeance hover in the background (50:28). Apparently no need for a theodicy of the destruction of the world commensurate with Israel's is felt. The use of accusation and indictment remains extremely laconic (contrast chs. 4–10). Yahweh unleashes the Babylonian beast on the world and turns against that beast in turn because of its hubris (46:8, 17; 48:14, 26, 29-30, 42; 49:4, 16), vengeance (48:27; 49:1-2), idolatry (46:25; 48:4, 13, 35, 46; 49:3), and the need to effect Israel's restoration (46:27-28). When it is Babylon's turn the same motifs return: hubris (50:24, 31-32), vengeance (50:11, 15, 28, 29; 51:6, 11, 24, 49, 51, 56), idolatry (50:2, 38; 51:17-19, 44, 47, 52), and the need to effect Israel's restoration (50:4-10, 17-20, 33-34; 51:5, 6, 9, 10, 34-37, 45-49, 50-53).

The latter motif also exposes the sustained connection of the oracles against the nations to the collection of restoration oracles in chs. 30–33, even to the point of reusing 46:27-28 (present also in the LXXV, 26:27-28) in 30:11-12 (with modifications; though absent in the LXXV, 37:1-9, 12-24). And in the application of the phrase "restore the fortunes" (30:3, 18; 31:23; 32:44; 33:7, 11, 26) to three of the oracles against the nations (Moab, 48:47, Ammon, 49:6; Elam, 49:39). In so doing it looks beyond the current Yahwistic war to its ultimate aim of establishing the reign of Yahweh's "peace." Notice that the applications to Moab and Ammon are expansions by the MT (LXXV lacks these promises) and that different terminology hinting at a restoration even for Egypt occurs in 46:26. But why this move toward universalizing the myth of exile and return is not consistently extended to all the oracles against the nations is not clear. A reader might suspect the egregious reign of imperial terror as the reason for beast Babylon's destiny of permanent national oblivion (50:39). Still other oracular tradition outside the Jeremianic can be found that will even take the step of promising a future in the Israelite utopia for so cruel a Yahwistic agent as Assyria (Isa 19:23-25). But why not expect restoration notices for all the remaining nations — especially if Egypt is to be promised a restoration?

That the nations might rise with Israel in its restoration is not a theme alien to compositional interests. For Jerusalem is designated to become the "throne of the world" (3:17) on the other side of destruction. Yahweh's "evil neighbors" are subject to exile and return on a broad scale on condition that they foreswear their idolatry and take up the ways of *Yahweh-alone* (12:14-17). Such a "conversion" to Yahwistic exclusivity and piety is even dramatized in a citation placed on the lips of the nations as Yahweh finally succeeds in the vindication of his sole suzerainty over the world of nations (16:19-21). And the composition has wanted to assert a universal, exclusive status for the exercise of Yahwistic power in the world (10:1-16; 18:7-10). This universalized Yahwistic "grace" represents the reversal of Israelite fortunes. The latter recovers imperial glory while the world takes its colonized place at the foot of Yahweh's throne, Jerusalem.

More can perhaps be inferred from the panoply of metaphors used to shape the representation of Yahweh's great war beyond the military tropes. Yahweh's war harvests the nations (48:32; 49:9, 10) or deforests them (46:23). They are ripe for plunder in their supposed security, so he decants them like aged wine (48:11-12). Wielding the powers of creation, he submerges the nations in diluvian disaster (47:2) or winnows them with elemental windstorms (49:36). The nations contract incurable wounds (46:11). An irresistible predator, Yahweh devours the world (48:40; 49:19, 22). Simply and terribly put, the violence of God against the world is violence taken out on his enemies (46:10a). The war is Yahweh's great day on which he makes the world his communal sacrificial feast (46:10b). At this banquet, the nations drink the cup of the wine of destruction (48:26; 49:12-13; cf. 25:15, 17, 27-28).

The Yahwistic Beast, Babylon, Falls (Chs. 50–51)

In chs. 46–49, Babylon is everywhere assumed (explicitly named at 46:2, 13, 26; 49:28, 30; note that the MT has added specificity by supplying the proper name of Nebuchadrezzar at 46:13 and 49:30, along with the entire verse at 46:26; the LXXV lacks them) to be Yahweh's agent in the prosecution of the war. But at times this concrete agency is backgrounded to portray Yahweh unleashing a personified sword on the world (47:6; less explicitly in 46:10, 14, 16; 48:2, 10; 49:37). And when it is finally beast Babylon's turn (chs. 50–51), the metaphorical texture of Yahweh's war is simply applied to it: harvest (50:26-27; 51:33), incurable wound (50:13; 51:8-9), cosmic powers (50:42a; 51:1, 42), hunt/predation (50:24, 44-46; 51:14, 40), cup of the wine of divine wrath (51:7, 39, 57), and sword (50:16, 35-38).

There is, however, an explicit symbolic elevation associated with the recoil of God's war on Babylon's head. Allusions to a mythopoetic creation-chaos struggle familiar in ancient Near Eastern mythic traditions increase in strength (cf. Marduk's battle with Tiamat in Enuma Elish or Baal's battle with Yamm and Mot in the Ugaritic mythological texts). For beast Babylon is the political personification of a dragon in the sea (51:34-36; cf. Job 7:12; Isa 27:1; 51:9; Ezek 29:3; 32:2) whose primordial waters (51:13; cf. Pss 29:3; 93:3-4; 144:7; Ezek 26:19; 27:26; 31:15; Hab 3:15) must be dried up (50:38; 51:36) and who must be forced to disgorge all that she has swallowed (51:44). As with Baal, Yahweh has wielded Babylon as a great war club (50:23; 51:20-24; Babylon as the sword of Yahweh in 47:6 is now turned against itself in 50:35-38) in his savage struggle for cosmic supremacy against the threatening chaos powers of the nations. But now, ironically, the waters of chaos come upon Babylon (50:42; 51:42, 55) from "the north" (50:3, 9, 41; 51:48; for "the north" as the mythic abode of Baal appropriated to Yahweh's dwelling in Jerusalem see Ps 48:3) as once Babylon had flooded Judah and the nations in chs. 46–49 (e.g., 47:2; cf. 1:13-15; 3:12, 18; 4:6; 6:1, 22; 10:22; 13:20; 16:15; 23:8; 25:9, 26; 31:8). The developed presence of the motif in chs. 50–51 suggests its inchoate presence in chs. 46–49, with Babylon the chaos monster wielded by Yahweh's hand. Yet it must be judged very underplayed when chs. 46–49 are read in isolation from their present association with chs. 50–51.

In the slaughter of Babylon as well as of the rest of the nations in chs. 46–49, Yahweh is able to display the futility of the world's imperial intentions (51:58 = Hab 2:13, "labor for vanity, wearied for fire"). And as an oracular

Jeremianic scroll laid Judah waste (ch. 36), so Seraiah, at Jeremiah's commission, can presage Babylon's fall by reading (cf. ch. 36) and then sinking an oracular scroll into the Euphrates as a symbolic act signaling Babylon's oracular destiny (51:59-64). Jeremiah fulfills his commission as a prophet to the nations (1:5).

Evaluation

Yahweh becomes a horror to the world. The Creator wields chaos against his creation, for he discerns roiling in the sea of nations, a rebellion against his kingship. No ancient Near Eastern deity equal to the claim could brook such a challenge to its suzerainty. Thus Yahweh proves adequate to the tyranny inherent in ancient Near Eastern theistic ontology by launching the genocide of the world. In the flux of nation-culture-world making, Yahweh detects the seething heart of chaos. He moves to defeat chaos by chaos. As his royal boasts (49:19 = 50:44; cf. the epithet "the king, whose name is Yahweh," at 46:18; 48:15; 51:57) and self-laudatory creation hymn (50:15-19; cf. 10:1-16) indicate, Yahwistic suzerainty is the burden of the oracles against the nations.

Yahweh's kingship provides the vindication for Yahweh's pitiless savagery (even the use of a funeral song has become completely ironic) since the created order hangs on it, as does Israel's good. The "peace" of the world depends on the violent tyranny of Yahweh's imperial desire. The colonization of Israel, her punishment for religious guilt, has become the snare by which Yahweh entraps the nations, subjugates them, and secures his throne (50:24).

The kingship of Yahweh demands the bloodshed of the world. Theopolitical desires have generated a history of cruelty. The justification of the war lies in the vindication of Yahwistic pride. Yahweh's way with Israel, "exile," has become the paradigm for his way with the world — for his sake and Judah's restoration! History withers the nations under Yahwistic wrath. The carnage of human geopolitical cruelty is mythologized as a sacrifice placating Yahwistic rage, restoring Yahwistic honor. The death of the world constitutes the enthronement of Yahweh and the national resurrection of Israel.

The symbolic embrace of Yahwistic violence by the vested aspirations of the colonial elite, the implicit performers of the tradition, represents not the supersession of human suffering but suffering's divination! Apparently, Yahweh can find no solution for the world (even Israel) except through blood and more blood.

The implication of Judah's fall and her enduring colonization — that is, the failure of *Yahweh-alone* — has been refused and masked over in the oracles against the nations by postulating just such a failure for the pantheon of national deities and their client peoples. For in the fantastic landscape of the oracles against the nations, Yahwistic survivors and dreamers can find symbolic compensation. Faced with a world where the throne of the empire belongs everywhere but in Jerusalem, where the latter's "children" continue subjugated to the powers — in short, within political-cultural realities where exile/dispersion is the preeminent condition, and/or where the "return" fails to live up to its utopian promise — recourse can be had to a world in the oracles against the nations where Marduk, Milcom, Chemosh, and the rest of theistic mockery go down to defeat along with their patrons before the onslaught of *Yahweh-alone.* The myth of exile and return can temporize even the failure of "Jeremianic" predictions about the absolute demise of Israel's political predators (e.g., 46:28, "I will make an end . . ."). For exile and return is the pattern of Yahweh's way with the nations. The latter's national persistence hinges on a future Yahwistic pacification, annexation, and conversion to *Yahweh-alone* (46:26; 48:47; 49:6, 39 read in connection with 3:17; 12:14-17; 16:19-21).

Thus, in its bid to rewrite the myth of Yahweh and Israel by elevating *Yahweh-alone* the composition has succeeded in refiguring or reappropriating what it so desperately seeks to refuse. *Yahweh-alone* cannot escape his polytheistic ontology. Internalizing the royal psychology and motives of the divine "contenders" in ancient Near Eastern pantheons, he rises only to the level of victorious tyrant. No doubt a stubborn cultural resistance and restoration quest can be founded on such a myth.

Jeremiah 52:1-34

Overview

Thus far "Jeremiah" (MT 50:64, lacking in the LXXV). The composition brings the Jeremiah scroll to a conclusion by returning from its vision of the destruction of beast Babylon and the release of captive Israel to what at first glance appears to be a historical appendix. The chronological displacement returns the implicit reader to a present where Jerusalem lies fallen. That event has provided the mythic topos driving the symbolic anxiety over the failure of God embedded in the performance of "Jeremiah." But by now it has been transfigured into the vindication of the myth of *Yahweh-alone* and his prophet Jeremiah. The end of "Israel," however, in the myth of exile implies its return. Already there is a suggestion of Israel's revitalization in the preservation of a Davidic scion and in the preservation of temple vessels in Babylon — all hints of a continuation to come.

Dramatic Composition

The composition duplicates material drawn from 2 Kgs 24:18–25:30 and links the Jeremianic tradition with that of the Deuteronomistic history. In the LXXV, Jeremiah 52 follows immediately after the salvation oracle offered to Baruch (MT 45; LXXV 51:31-35). The LXXV performance of the tradition narrates for the first time the details of the success of the Babylonian siege, the capture of the city and the king, the investment of structures, and the deportation of the population. The overall effect on the macro structure of the scroll is to retain the focus for the LXXV upon the destruction of the old Judean state and the fulfillment of the Jeremianic message of doom. Here the rescue of the myth of Yahweh from the death of Israel still bears the ideological weight. With the oracles against the nations still occupying their place at the center of the scroll inserted within the framework of 25:1-14, 15-38, the mythological construct of a divine war prosecuted against the world (including "Israel") for the sake of Yahweh's imperium and Israel's restoration is still offered. But no effort is made to dramatize so emphatically progress toward that utopian aim — beyond its initiation as doom in the life of the old Davidic community.

The MT has relocated the oracles against the nations after ch. 45 while retaining ch. 52 in its final position. Hence the sense of ending offered by ch. 52 is also tinged with the sense of a new beginning. Judah has felt the full weight of the divine war; the latter has begun its (dramatized) spread (chs. 46–51) out into the world of Judah's colonial captivity. Left in the wake of Yahweh's imperial campaign, a scion of the old Davidic monarchy waits in elevated captivity in Babylon for the realization of "Israel's" reversal of colonial fortune. The MT has moved much further in its rewriting of the Jeremianic tradition toward the dramatized contemplation of restoration aspirations and the opening of that hope already (but not yet!) within the life of the colonized in Babylon.

The narration of Jerusalem's capture and the disposition of Zedekiah and other survivors (52:1-16) represents a triplication of the MT, for it has already presented this material at 39:4-10. With the addition of 52:2-3 (lacking in the LXXV), in agreement with 2 Kgs 24:19, 20, the MT intensifies the contrast between Zedekiah and Jehoiachin already present in the chapter. At the same time, it reasserts the Deuteronomistic royal evaluation formula, reads Zedekiah under the sign of Jehoiakim, and flattens the complicated characterization of the Zedekiah offered in chs. 37–38. The MT further depopulates the land by splintering even the fate of the poor (cf. 39:9). Some of these, too, now join those deported (52:15, lacking in the LXXV). And in v. 16 "the rest of the people" (LXXV) have become "from the poorest of the land" (MT), the latter left behind for agricultural purposes.

The MT continues to sweep clean the remnants of the old Judean state under Zedekiah, leaving the claim to "Israel" to others. Perhaps here, too, the catalogue of deported temple vessels has its role to play (52:17-23; cf. 2 Kgs 25:13-17), along with the decimation and execution of the officials of Jerusalem's royal-temple establishment (52:24-27; cf. 2 Kgs 25:18-21). Not only has the temple as the center of Yahwistic worship been snatched from the possession of the Zedekian community, but the cultic vessels have joined the exiles in Babylon. Zedekiah and the state gathered with him around Yahwistic worship are disenfranchised from the claim of "Israel."

But the location of the temple vessels may have a symbolic role to play beyond signaling the fulfillment of earlier Jeremianic predictions (27:16-22; recall that there the catalogue of vessels and the promise of their return specifically from Babylon are features of the MT, not the LXXV). They have shifted from Jerusalem to Babylon! Notice that the tally of deportees (MT 52:28-30, lacking in the LXXV) locates the exile of Judah exclusively in Babylon. In subsequent, Second Temple literature and legend the place and occlusion of the temple vessels will become an important trope. For in the restoration they must be revealed, recovered, and returned to the restored temple in Jerusalem (cf. 2 Chr 36:18; Ezra 1:7; Dan 1:2; 5:2-4; 2 Macc 2:1-8; *Lives of the Prophets* 2:11-19; *2 Bar.* 6:1-9; *4 Bar.* 3:6-20). Perhaps there is the bare hint of a beginning for that development here with MT 52:28-30.

The seeds of the restored temple and community reside together in and wait from Babylon. These are the 4,600 (numerical and chronological discrepancies between the triplicate traditions are notorious and probably best left inharmonious; cf. 2 Kgs 24:14, 16 and see further discussion at 39:1-18), along with the temple vessels and Jehoiachin, who matter in anticipation of restoration dreams. Hence the MT draws the summary statement in 52:27b (lacking in the LXXV): "So Judah went into exile out of its land" (cf. 2 Kgs 25:21). And it completely passes over repeating (in contrast to the repeat of 39:4-10) mention of the Gedalian gubernatorial regime (contrast 2 Kgs 25:22-26). The latter, too, is of no interest or import for the future of "Israel" having passed into oblivion — assimilated to the fate of the Zedekian community before it as well as to the fate of the "so-called" diaspora in Egypt.

In the context of such a reperformance of the triplicate tradition, the laconic notice of King Jehoiachin's elevation (52:31-34) in Babylon becomes pregnant with the hint of hope.

Evaluation

To snatch the myth of Yahweh from the jaws of cultural defeat has required a deep irony anchored in profound symbolic inversions. The composition must embrace its cultural defeat in colonization as the act of their patron deity in punishment for religious-cultic corruption. The specter of a burned and despoliated temple and the decimation of the "Yahwistic" community (factions?) gathered around it must be counterread against the obvious. For any ancient Near Eastern society would have taken the point of the symbolic deportation — that is, Yahweh led captive to the Babylonian patron deity, Marduk. But the composition has reinterpreted this specter not only as a sign of punishment but also as a pledge toward the future even as it writes off, and scapegoats, an entire generation under the sign of divine wrath (MT 52:2-3). In the process, the colonized elite can reappropriate for themselves what they deny their symbolic opponents and claim a continuation of God and temple, king and land with themselves as inheritors even as they reinvent Yahweh and Israel under the old signs. Revitalization desires practice a poetics in service to dreams of reelevated cultural power. Thus even the myth of Jeremianic oracular power can be risked countermanding with historical narrative and oracular prediction one "Jeremiah" with another (contrast 22:30 to 24:1-10 and 52:31-34). A level of domestication has been practiced on this old Judean oracular speaker which would have been the envy of any of his royal opponents in the days prior to Jerusalem's fall! Ironically, the oracular "pillar" promoting and provoking the destruction of "Israel" proves serviceable to building "Israel" up again even as the composition is able to perform the prophet in service to their will to power. Apparently, the myth of prophecy can be defeated even as those who wield it yield to its embrace. And Yahweh becomes the epitome, the embodiment of cultural projections and desires erected over an abyss of historical pain.

Performing Jeremiah: Poetics and Power in an Israelite Oracular Tradition

It would be facile to understand my evaluative reading of the symbolic and ideological processes at play in Jeremiah as simply some form of theological reductionism, as a mask for some mode of postmodern nihilism. I mean to be more troublesome than that! It is true that as a reader I am deeply formed by the debates between modern and postmodern sensibilities. Rather than rehearse those intractable debates, I have sought in the commentary to elucidate a shadow cast in the creation of a generative symbol, Jeremiah, in its preservation, domestication, and revitalization. For Jeremiah did not escape circulation within cultural matrices of social construction, power, and desire. Writing and reading Jeremiah performs oracular power. To perform oracular power enacts a myth of Yahweh.

Indeed, it may turn out that the debate over "reductionism" is a question about truth as reference. But, in fact, this may not be the most interesting question or set of problems to tackle or pose toward Jeremiah. For it masks excruciating problems surrounding all human efforts when it comes to making a world — whether that world refers or not! For I argue that the will to power that makes human cultural worlds projects itself out of an abyss of ontological, ethical, moral, and spiritual dissonance, the abyss launching generative mythological processes.

Jeremiah is the literary artifact of such cultural processes. Cultural elite voices of a conquered, annexed, colonized, imperial client community supply historical agency and cultural interests that form and mediate the Jeremianic tradition to us, even if those agents have chosen the strategy of anonymity and pseudonymity in their performance of Jeremiah. But whether one allows for glimpses of authentic Jeremianic tradition or not, it still remains true that the sociopolitical stage generating the symbol Jeremiah, the scroll and the figure, testifies everywhere to ancient Israel's long encounter with imperial aspiration and shifting balances of imperial power. The religious imagination expressed within the arena of Jeremiah cannot be viewed as floating free of the imperial-colonial matrix conditioning the aspirations of the elite voices surviving the collapse of the old Davidic regime. The latter have enacted a world in Jeremiah drawing on the available symbolic resources of the Near East. After all, "Israel" was an ancient Near Eastern people.

Jeremiah yearns for "Israel's" restoration to cultural power in the utopian dream of an imperial Yahwistic theocracy. The latter entails mediations inescapable. For the colonial elite project themselves into the role of theocratic stewards. Oracular power is always performed through such mediation with all its currents of cultural power and desire.

When theology has wanted to posit the sign of Jeremiah as a safe, ideologically free zone, it has served only to accept the role cast by the rhetoric of Jeremiah for its implicit reader — that is, to submit to its ideological, rhetorical design. There is a reward for such service no doubt in the posture of ally to the sign of Jeremiah! But theology as the ally of Jeremiah must evade and somehow resist recognition that the Jeremianic oracular tradition offers a symbolic arena, a battlefield for the ideologically embattled, Israelite cultural elite seeking power to revitalize and to repossess "Israel." The latter apparently cannot be achieved apart from the rehabilitation of the myth of Yahweh on the other side of Jerusalem's imperial collapse. This is theological conceit attempting to cover its constructive tracks and escape cultural relativism.

In light of such considerations, I have not wanted to enter the space of Jeremiah as a simple ally. For my desire has been to dramatize the symbolic problems attending the interstices of myth and religion, poetics and power. So I have portrayed a reader who neither abandons his or her freedom of vision to the rhetorical representations of Jeremiah nor rigidly opposes the constructive desires and passions privileged by the sign of Jeremiah. This no doubt offends the portrait of the ideological reader, the ally, for whom the Jeremianic Yahweh lusts. For my offense I can only plead the plurality of passions and interests fragmenting postmodern sensibilities along the conflicted spaces of gender, class, ethnicity, and national identity. I do not leave those behind anymore than contemporary theological "allies" of Jeremiah when we all enter Jeremianic oracular space.

To dance with the god, one must also learn to dance with devils. Monotheism apparently offers no secure refuge in this regard. For Yahweh brings his own internalized symbolic and social demons.

This, of course, invokes the problem of Israelite myth, the process of mythologization, and its mirror, demythologization. Such invocation may seem out of place in a commentary on biblical literature. Modern readers have long been schooled on the absence of myth or the presence of antimyth in biblical literature — in other words, the belief that while ancient Israel forged its religious identity within a matrix of polytheistic myths, it rejected such myth outright or at least profoundly transformed its symbolic dependencies. As communities of faith are accustomed to say, "All the rest have myth, but ancient Israel the truth"! Whether that view is valid or not, a mythologization of Yahweh still occurs. For biblical literature projects a grand epic, a sacred narrative, a myth of creation and exodus, exile and return, within which "Israel" takes on meaning. Yahweh may appear a fully embodied, narrated character on the same plane as other human actors, only in fragmentary or partially realized modes. No doubt this has aided the impression of the marginalization of myth in contrast to sacred narratives of surrounding cultures. Nevertheless, this mode of narrating and imagining the divine, the construction of an exterior landscape in which God appears, has only been repositioned as Israel continues to represent communal existence and experience as the will and intervention of divine agency. In Jeremiah the composition exerts itself toward the interiorization of myth by constructing a psychology of Yahweh rendering meaningful Israel's existence within the epic frame of exile and return. The composition has mythologized the colonization of Judah within the psychology, the passions, of Yahweh's interior landscape.

Everywhere Yahweh is the central fictive dramatic speaker in the rhetoric of Jeremiah. He projects a layered, conflicted interior space, a psychology as variegated and plural as that of any human character, fictive or real, that we might choose to acknowledge in the contemporary world. Yahweh brings the beast — better, becomes the beast — to Judah. Nebuchadrezzar is Yahweh's shadow. It is the panoply of patriarchal and imperial images and tropes that rationalize the interior motives of the divine for the terrorism of conquest and colonization of the old regime. Yahweh, overcome by the fury of his own betrayal, now overcomes Jerusalem, the intractable epitome of religious dysfunction. The myth of the painful deity, the agony of God in the face of evil, is a sympathetic portrait. Yet we know psychologically that such unrelieved interior pain produces its own pathologies — in this case, the frenzied impulse toward violent cultural cleansing. The Babylonian imperial power represents the externalization of the psychic torment of God by his own interior beasts no longer capable of successful suppression (or, if you prefer, testimony to successful divine repression now manifested in dysfunctional divine violence). The cultural agony of the colonized has sought healing and compensation through symbolic displacement and projection onto the mythic plane.

There is a deep, world-dismantling passion enacted in the performance of Jeremiah. Yet there is also a hope that from the rhetorical ashes of this world-destroying imagination a new vitality can spring. Indeed, the voices of the implicit colonial elite projected into the Jeremianic arena represent the fact that a Yahwistic vitality already coheres in the cultural program and constitutive imagination of those allied to the privileged oracular sign, Jeremiah.

Their symbolic regime, Jeremiah, exercises utopian passions, however, at a high price. For it can imagine restoration only on imperial terms and through imperial means. Hence the blood of the world is required for "Israel's" revitalization — indeed, even more blood than this since all forms of "Israel" other than that which imagines *Yahweh-alone* must be conquered, colonized, and exiled into symbolic and social oblivion! The colonial elite perform Jeremiah by writing large the face of imperial power which they experience. They project that face deep into the icon, *Yahweh-alone*. Yahweh's utopian imperial will enacts a world holocaust in the poetic dreams of the colonized toward a return of Israelite power.

With such dreams of theological brutality the human spirit is well acquainted. Visions of future utopias all too often spawn present deeds of terror and blood. The promise of individual chances and communal life in the present is consigned to ashes. For theocracy given poetic wings must be implemented by human deeds exerted toward acquisitions of cultural power. Thus Jeremiah's bright poems inspire, enable, and legitimate dark deeds of cultural terror. *Yahweh-alone* does not live above or beyond Jeremiah's textual representation and both circulate always within poetics and power alone. Some modern readers will see in this mythic celebration of Yahweh's imperial war an ideology too terrible in its writing off of human souls to blood. And thus they might well join their voices with Job to sing "maxims of ashes, defenses of clay" (Job 13:12) over the scroll of Jeremiah. And yet. . . .

Cultural power abhors its abyss! Symbolic homecomings engage many indirections. For a deeper terror anchored in the interstices drives the symbolic terrorism practiced by Jeremiah. Exiled to the symbolic margins of the performance is another world making that represents a far worse dismantling of cherished symbols to the colonial elite. It is nothing less than the unmaking of culturally imagined Israel, the ultimate demythologization of themselves, the abandonment to colonial assimilation — in short, the dissolution of the myth of Israel. It represents the final cultural demoralization. What people can afford for long to be so unstoried, rather restoried, to the ash heap? To prevent that end, the constitutive imagination will grasp every iconic means at its disposal. Otherwise, there is only acquiescence to cultural madness, the abnegation of cultural identity. Piety does not easily succumb to historical dissonance and mythological exigencies. The constitutive imagination remakes its world. It repristinates its new world by projection metonymically into the arena of its old myth, conscious all the while of nothing more than a return to the ancient ways.

The cry of the human in the third millennium constitutes a matrix that renders the symbolic arena of Jeremiah a difficult one to enter. Jeremiah grasps an interpretation of ancient Israel's holocaust at which we blanch — reading it as we do after so many programs of cultural genocide, ethnic cleansing, struggles for national and religious "purification," and back-street vendettas. How does theology dare to put all this into writing as the continued war of an outraged Deity turning the rampage of history over human dreams into a living hell of retribution? Can cherished Deity be preserved only at the high price of rendering conscionable such extreme historical brutality and violence? Jeremiah embraces theodicy at the expense of the innocent and the humane. So much innocent life, its aspirations to rise just to the level of dignity, longing to reclaim its vocation to the human denied by so many others sacrificed and written over with the rhetoric of religion! The haunting shadows of our imperialist ancestors are too much with our postcolonial dreams and dreamers. In the rampaging fury of Israel's mythic divine patriarch, we hear all too well now our own domestic terrors and dysfunction. Broken humans at the margins of cultural, economic, gender, and symbolic privilege cry that surely we deserve a world and a deity less destructive.

It is not easy to contemplate the continued reification of Jeremiah's Yahweh. But then, I suppose, he has long ago passed into symbolic oblivion. For moral and theological offense with the myth of Yahweh and Israel is nothing new. Time and shifts of cultural imagination all do their work only too well. Iconic inheritors enter the symbolic battlefield of Jeremiah with new sensibilities. Whether with quiet subtlety or furious fanfare they insinuate Yahweh's metonym, a Deity with ways more suited to the devices and desires of the age.

The sign of Jeremiah is domesticated to a new age,

though the formal contours of the work remain. And yet . . . and yet at what subtle price and threat does all this occur? Jeremiah, the iconic symbol, so ethically and ontologically slippery, might be prepared to donate new regressions to its contemporary performers. The iconic presence of that more ancient constitutive vision might offer reprieve to the old gods once again. Then might we quake again to the terrors and comforts of Yahweh of hosts! Some may not judge such an outcome hostile if they believe we can wield Jeremiah in beneficial service to our own will to cultural power. But then again, maybe we should. Many a cultural and personal holocaust has had its oracular (biblical) legitimization. If there will be a homecoming for Jeremiah in this millennium, it will be discovered only by performing Jeremiah attuned to the intersections between poetics and power.

Bibliography. Commentaries. Brueggemann, W. 1988, *To Pluck Up, To Tear Down: Jeremiah 1–25,* ITC, Grand Rapids: Eerdmans • Brueggemann, W. 1991, *To Build, To Plant: Jeremiah 26–52,* ITC, Grand Rapids: Eerdmans • Carroll, R. P. 1986, *Jeremiah,* OTL, London: SCM • Clements, R. E. 1988, *Jeremiah,* Interpretation: A Bible Commentary for Teaching and Preaching, Atlanta: John Knox • Craigie, P. C., P. H. Kelley, and J. F. Drinkard, Jr. 1991, *Jeremiah 1–25,* WBC 26, Dallas: Word • Duhm, B. D. 1901, *Das Buch Jeremia,* Kurzer Hand-Commentar zum Alten Testament, Tübingen: J. C. B. Mohr (Paul Siebeck) • Fretheim, T. 2002, *Jeremiah,* Macon, Ga.: Smyth and Helwys • Holladay, W. L. 1986, *Jeremiah 1,* Hermeneia, Philadelphia: Fortress • Holladay, W. L. 1989, *Jeremiah 2,* Hermeneia, Philadelphia: Fortress • Keown, G. L., P. J. Scalise, and T. G. Smothers. 1995, *Jeremiah 26–52,* WBC 27, Dallas: Word • Lundbom, J. R. 1999, *Jeremiah 1–20,* AB, New York: Doubleday • McKane, W. 1986, *Jeremiah,* vols. 1 and 2, ICC, Edinburgh: T. & T. Clark • O'Connor, K. M. 1992, "Jeremiah," in C. A. Newsom and S. H. Ringe, eds., *The Women's Bible Commentary,* Louisville: Westminster/John Knox, 169-77 • O'Connor, K. M. 2001, "Jeremiah," in J. Barton and R. Muddiman, eds., *The Oxford Bible Commentary,* Oxford: Oxford University Press • Overholt, T. W. 1988, "Jeremiah," in J. L. Mays, ed., *Harper's Bible Commentary,* San Francisco: HarperCollins, 597-645.

Bibliography. Monographs. Bauer, A. M. 1999, *Gender in the Book of Jeremiah: A Feminist-Literary Reading,* New York: Peter Lang • Biddle, M. E. 1996, *Polyphony and Symphony in Prophetic Literature: Rereading Jeremiah 7–20,* Studies in Old Testament Interpretation 2, Macon, Ga.: Mercer University • Carroll, R. P. 1989, *Jeremiah,* Old Testament Guides, Sheffield: Sheffield Academic • Clements, R. E. 1996, *Old Testament Prophecy: From Oracles to Canon,* Louisville: Westminster/John Knox • Davies, P. R., ed. 1996, *The Prophets: A Sheffield Reader,* The Biblical Seminar 42, Sheffield: Sheffield Academic • Diamond, A. R. P., K. M. O'Connor, and L. Stulman, eds. 1999, *Troubling Jeremiah,* JSOTSup 260, Sheffield: Sheffield Academic • Diamond, A. R. P. 1987, *The Confessions of Jeremiah in Context: Scenes of Prophetic Drama,* JSOTSup 46, Sheffield: Sheffield Academic • Hill, J. 1999, *Friend or Foe? The Figure of Babylon in the Book of Jeremiah MT,* Leiden and Boston: Brill Academic Publishers • McCarthy, D. 1963, *Treaty and Covenant,* Rome: Pontifical Biblical Institute • McConville, J. G. 1993, *Judgment and Promise: An Interpretation of the Book of Jeremiah,* Winona Lake, Ind.: Eisenbrauns • Perdue, L. G., and B. W. Kovacs, eds. 1984, *A Prophet to the Nations: Essays in Jeremiah Studies,* Winona Lake, Ind.: Eisenbrauns • Stulman, L. 1998, *Order amid Chaos: Jeremiah as Symbolic Tapestry,* The Biblical Seminar 57, Sheffield: Sheffield Academic • Stulman, L. 1986, *The Prose Sermons of the Book of Jeremiah: A Redescription of the Correspondences with the Deuteronomistic Literature in the Light of Recent Text-critical Research,* SBLDS 83, Atlanta: Scholars • Ziegler, J. 1976, *Jeremias Baruch Threni Epistula Jeremiae, Septuaginta Vetus Testamentum Graecum Auctoritate Academiae Scientiarum Gottingensis editum,* vol. 15, 2d ed., Göttingen: Vandenhoeck & Ruprecht.

Lamentations

David J. A. Clines

INTRODUCTION

What Is Lamentations?

The book of Lamentations has been badly served by the title it carries in our English versions. For it is not a collection of breast-beating, self-pitying poems, a mere lamenting of the sorry state of Jerusalem and its inhabitants. It is rather the record of a Hebrew poet's coping with crisis, a deeply reflected proposal for the handling of grief.

Its theological position is quite subtle: it does not take just one perspective, and it does not recommend a single solution. It begins with the reality of disaster, and it concludes neither with cheap grace nor with easy hope but with the bitter possibility that the people of God may now have become the ex-people of God, that this time God may indeed have finally rejected Israel (5:22). And yet, despite its unwillingness to affirm blandly that everything will be well, at its end it does not leave its readers at the same point of despair with which it opened; for at its very midpoint (3:22-33) it has expressed the confidence that the mercies of Yahweh never come to an end — they are new every morning.

The Five Poems

The book of Lamentations consists of five distinct poems corresponding to the five chapters of the book. Each of the five poems may be called an alphabetical poem, the first four being acrostic poems. Chs. 1, 2, and 4 each have 22 verses, the first verse beginning with *aleph,* the second with *beth,* and so on through the 22 letters of the Hebrew alphabet. In ch. 3 there are 66 verses, three to each of the letters in turn. In ch. 5 there is no planned sequence to the initial letters of the verses, but there are just 22 verses in the poem all the same, so that it too may rightly be called an alphabetical poem.

Such parameters impose a severe and apparently artificial restriction on the poet, but not a greater one than many poets in other literatures have willingly adopted (e.g., the sonnet form), with no attenuation of the artistic quality or integrity of their work. It might even be suggested that this very self-restriction represents a kind of containment of the grief it depicts, as if without the closure required by the poetic form the grief might be in danger of becoming limitless and all-pervasive.

The Historical Setting

The historical situation supposed by the poems is the fall of Jerusalem to the Babylonians in 587 BC and the subsequent destruction of the city, the deportation of its leading inhabitants, and the abject condition of those who were left behind. But the poet is not a reporter, and the poetry intends us to reconstruct not the historical actuality but, in imagination, the psychological state of those who were experiencing disaster. It would be wrong to read the poems as a transcript of reality: the poem would then, for example, be asserting both that the city had been deserted by its inhabitants (1:3) and that its citizens still remained (1:11); it might be called in evidence for cannibalism (2:20; 4:10), murders by priests and prophets (4:13), the necessity for payment for drinking water (5:40), and the total absence of music in Jerusalem (5:14).

Assuming that the historical setting of the poem is after the final fall of the city in 587 BC (some scholars think ch. 1 has the situation of 597 in mind), one important historical fact attested by the poem is that despite the destruction of the temple, the royal and other palaces, and the city wall by the Babylonians, and despite the exile of leading citizens (as reported in 2 Kgs 24:14, but cf. 25:11), the city remained inhabited throughout the period of the exile and sustained many of the normal functions of a regional center as a Babylonian dependency.

Authorship

Though the realities of life in a conquered city are graphically described, there is no reason to think that the poet was necessarily a member of the Jerusalem community of that time and was not, for example, a poet of a much later age imaginatively reconstructing the situation of exilic Jerusalem as a vehicle for theological reflection.

The authorship of Lamentations has traditionally been ascribed to Jeremiah, probably on the ground of the reference in 2 Chr 35:25 to a lament on the death of King Josiah spoken by Jeremiah. But there is no reference in Lamentations to Josiah, and no reason therefore to connect the book with Jeremiah. In English Bibles it is placed after the prophecy of Jeremiah, but in Hebrew Bibles with the Writings.

Lamentations as a Theological Resource

Lamentations may properly be regarded as a work of art, whose quality and force do not depend on the rightness of its ideas. One need not be a religious believer to find its pathos realistic and affecting. And yet, set within the context of the scriptural canon as it is, it is inevitable that many of its readers will find its principal value in its theological ideas, which are indeed very rich and creative. In the following ways at least, the book of Lamentations may serve as a theological resource:

1. These poems are a resource for times of crisis. They legitimate grief that is intricately reflected and self-regarding, and they do not encourage sufferers to a hasty confidence in the goodness of God. Nor do they urge that the horror of disaster should be experienced only shallowly.

2. The poet is not shy of holding God accountable for the disaster. Even when it is obvious that Jerusalem has been overwhelmed by an army of Babylonians, the poet regards God as the first cause of the disaster. And even though he acknowledges that his people have deserved what has happened to them, God has still had some choice over whether he would act at this time and in this way.

3. The moment of hope arises from a recollection of the past experience of God's goodness, not from the misery of the present or from the cry of despair of the moment. The cry to God for deliverance may be a motive for God to act, but it offers no kind of guarantee that he will.

4. Repentance is not seen as a way to persuade God to be gracious since God is free to be gracious or not as he chooses. Repentance is understood to be a proper accompaniment of thanksgiving for restoration.

5. In the end, the possibility must be reckoned with that God has come to the end of the road with his people, and may not again deliver them. Otherwise, if God has no freedom, if God is utterly predictable, God is a tool of humans.

COMMENTARY

Poem 1: The Widowed Jerusalem (Lamentations 1)

The scene depicted here is Jerusalem after its fall to the Babylonians in 587 BC.

In this first of the five distinct poems in the book of Lamentations, there are two different speakers. In 1:1-11, it is the poet who speaks, as an external observer of the plight of the sacked city of Jerusalem. The poet pictures Jerusalem as a widowed and abused woman. In the second half of the poem (vv. 12-22), it is Jerusalem itself that speaks, as this sorrowful and comfortless women. The change from one speaker to the other is not just a change of perspective but a dynamic movement, which invites the reader first to observe the city's distress externally and then to experience it at a deeper level, from within the feelings of distress.

The overt purpose of this affecting and sensitively realized text is apparently to urge God to bring upon the conquerors of Jerusalem the same fate as it itself has suffered ("deal with them as you have dealt with me," 1:22). The purpose of the text cannot, however, be wholly expressed in terms of the overt; from the point of view of its readers or hearers, its purpose is to persuade its readers of certain ideas, or to reinforce in their minds ideas they already believe. It is an ideological text. Its key ideas are these: (1) The destruction of the city is essentially the doing of Yahweh (v. 5). (2) Jerusalem's destruction is deserved: it has disobeyed Yahweh and is being punished for its "rebellion" (v. 18). (3) Although the Babylonians have acted at the bidding of Yahweh in destroying Jerusalem, they are themselves also wicked and should be punished just as Jerusalem has been.

The rhetoric and the feeling of the poem persuade readers to accept such ideas, but readers should also ask (1) how the destruction of the city can be Yahweh's doing when it is plainly the work of the Babylonians, (2) whether it is right to think of God as destroying people because they have done wrong, and (3) whether there is any ethical problem in God's punishing the Babylonians for carrying out his will.

The Widowed Jerusalem (1:1-11)

There is no introduction or scene setting; we are immediately presented with a visual image of a bereaved and mourning woman, who is the city of Jerusalem. The language is that of the dirge or mourning poem such as we find in Amos 5:2 and Ezek 26:17-18; the opening word "how" expresses the enormity of the tragedy (as in 2:1; 4:1; 2 Sam 1:19; Isa 1:21; Jer 4:17). This widow was once a powerful princess surrounded by friends and allies (1:1-2), but is now bereft of her husband, which is to say, her people, and vulnerable like any woman in a patriarchal society deprived of male protection.

In more prosaic language, the people of Judah have been forcibly ("by oppression") taken into exile (1:3), and the city of Jerusalem is deserted, without pilgrims for the festivals. Perhaps the city is not entirely empty since there still seem to be priests in it, and young women, who often play a role at festivals (e.g., Judg 21:19-21; Ps 68:25[26]; Jer 31:13) (1:4). But the city has indeed been conquered (v. 5) and its citizens deported (v. 3).

This sorrowful state is not, however, just an unfortunate tragedy. It is a punishment visited upon Jerusalem by God for the sins of the people: it is for its transgressions that its citizens ("children") have been exiled (1:5); it is for Jerusalem's sins that it has become despised and ashamed (v. 8). And what Jerusalem has suffered in the loss of its "precious things" (vv. 7, 10; perhaps the temple treasures plundered by the Babylonians according to 2 Kgs 23:13-17) and in its dishonoring is depicted in the gross language of a woman whom men have humiliated by exposing her nakedness in her menstrual period. Women, who had little honor in the male world of the Bible, could be easily dishonored, and their natural bodily functions, which rendered them "unclean" or "filthy," were evidently an object of disgust to males.

Perhaps continuing the metaphor of the sexually assaulted woman, the poet now envisages the enemies of the city as women "stretching out their hands over her precious things" and "invading her sanctuary" (1:10), with an allusion to the prohibition of foreigners from entering the Jerusalem temple (cf. Ezek 44:9). Its citizens are compelled to trade what is precious to them, perhaps their children (as the same word in Hos 9:16 signifies), for food (1:12). As at the end of v. 9, the pathos is heightened in v. 11 as the poet's voice is interrupted by the city as a woman crying out to God for his attention; the implication is that the suffering is so severe that it needs a mere look from God for him to feel compelled to act.

Jerusalem's Appeal (1:12-22)

Now readers are invited to experience the disaster from the inside. Jerusalem feels its tragedy and dishonor as searing pain ("fire in the bones"), menstrual cramps and weakness (v. 13; cf. also Lev 15:33), and emotional turmoil (1:20). Its eyes flow with tears (v. 16); it groans (v. 21) and is in distress (v. 20). It feels that there cannot be "any sorrow like unto my sorrow" (v. 12, KJV). Travelers who pass by devastated cities typically hiss and shake their heads or their fists as an apotropaic rite (e.g., 2:15; 1 Kgs 9:8; Jer 49:17); the destruction of Jerusalem will be the most appalling sight they will ever see.

The poet is clear that the Babylonians are the originators of the disaster, but what Jerusalem experiences is not their assault but that of God. Yahweh's anger is the cause; it is he who has inflicted Jerusalem's sorrow upon it (1:12), sending the fire of pain from on high like a lightning bolt, tripping it up in a net (v. 13), imposing a yoke upon its neck (v. 14), summoning a festival assembly not for celebration but for assault, treading it down like grapes in a wine press (v. 15). Some of the metaphors are traditional, being found in the psalms of appeal and prophetic texts modeled on them (e.g., Ps 35:7-8; Jer 20:9).

Yahweh's anger is not groundless: though the focus is definitely on the pain of its experience, Jerusalem does not fail to acknowledge that Yahweh is in the right because it has rebelled against his word (1:18) and that it has received the just reward for its transgressions (v. 22). Interestingly, there is no word of repentance. It is enough at this moment to acknowledge guilt; there is no future in view in which amendment of life may be possible.

Another emotion supervenes upon Jerusalem's grief: that of revenge. May Yahweh's day of judgment (the "day of the LORD" in prophetic language) come upon Jerusalem's enemies; may they suffer the same fate as Jerusalem (vv. 21-22). In the end, the focus of the poem seems a little confused; is it upon the realities of Jerusalem's sorry state, upon its emotions in reaction, upon its acknowledgment of guilt, or upon its desire for revenge on its enemies? Perhaps the literary confusion is expressive of the city's confusion in its suffering, and the point to which the whole poem resiles is the dominant note: "my groans are many and my heart is faint" (v. 22).

Poem 2: Yahweh's Anger and the Impossibility of Comfort (Lamentations 2)

In this second poem, the poet speaks not as a detached observer of the fate of Jerusalem and its inhabitants, but as a sympathetic participant in their grief. The poet is personally in distress, with eyes blinded by tears (2:11); the poetic imagination is unable to summon up any comparable tragedy that could perhaps serve as a comfort to the citizens (v. 13).

The dynamic of the poem comes to the surface in the changes that occur in 2:11 and 18. Up to v. 10 the poet speaks in the same voice as in 1:1-11, objectively, if also passionately, about the punishments of Jerusalem at the hand of Yahweh. But at that point the poet begins to speak in a voice of personal grief, addressing the city as "you" and bewailing incapacity for giving any comfort to the suffering people. The tone changes again at v. 18, where, with a sequence of imperative verbs, the poet encourages the citizens to begin a movement toward healing. They should not simply be lamenting their unhappy lot but actively crying out to Yahweh to spare their lives and the lives of their children from the famine that is following the destruction of the city (vv. 18-19).

The theme that binds this poem together is that all that has happened to Jerusalem is Yahweh's doing. He has been a pitiless warrior, attacking the buildings and the leaders and the people. Whether he has been justified in behaving like this is beside the point; the fact is that he has acted in anger, turning himself into Israel's enemy and disowning his own sanctuary, according to his long-established design (2:17). There is not a word in this poem of Jerusalem deserving what has happened to it, for the poet is experiencing the people's grief, not sitting in judgment over them.

Yahweh's Anger against Jerusalem (2:1-10)

Much more strongly than in ch. 1, the poet emphasizes that it is Yahweh's *anger* that is responsible for the fall of Jerusalem. In six outbursts of anger he has taken these actions: he has set Jerusalem under a cloud, forgotten that it is his seat of government (2:1), broken down its strongholds (v. 2), cut down its "horn" or might (v. 2), poured out his fury like fire (v. 4), and spurned its king and priests (v. 6). He has been pitiless in his destruction of Judah's pastures (as the word translated "habitations" in v. 2 should read), he has attacked Jerusalem like an invader (vv. 4-5), betrayed the city to its enemies (v. 7), consumed it like a fire (v. 3), dishonored the city, scorned his own altar, disowned his sanctuary (v. 7), and brought to an end sacred rituals (v. 6) and the practice of law and prophecy (v. 9). Above all, he has brought this destruction into being according to a deliberate plan he has long harbored, measuring the city out by line for demolition, in a bitter reversal of a program of building works (v. 8).

Here the poet's vision is very focused: there is no word of how justified Yahweh has been in all of this destruction, for in this, the *Guernica* of the OT, the overwhelming divine anger fills the whole canvas.

The Poet's Incapacity to Comfort (2:11-17)

For the first time, the poet speaks in a personal voice: "My eyes are spent with weeping; my soul is in tumult" (2:11); in 1:20 this was the language of the stricken city, but here it is that of the observer of its suffering. Though the poet is obviously drawing on conventional rhetorical language for describing the hearing of bad news (cf., e.g., Jer 49:23; Ezek 21:7), the drama of the poem is unmistakably heightened once the purely descriptive mood has given way to the more emotional, and the reader is implicitly invited to adopt the subject position of the poet.

Foremost in the poet's vision is the fate of the children in the conquered city, dying of starvation in their mothers' arms (2:11-12; it is strange, however, that they are crying out for bread *and wine*). There are other elements too: (1) the miserable contrast between the present and the former state of the city as "the perfection of beauty, the joy of all the earth" (v. 15), (2) the allegation that the fall of the city is due in some measure to the prophets, who have either misled the people with false optimism about the future or have not adequately demanded its repentance (v. 14), and (3) the conviction that the destruction has long ago been determined upon by Yahweh (v. 17) — and therefore could not have been averted (which conflicts somewhat with the responsibility of the prophets).

Cry Out for God's Mercy on the Children! (2:18-22)

The poet does not advise acquiescence, even though the state of affairs is the will of God. Even the ruthless destroyer of his people may perhaps be prevailed upon to spare the children, who are in danger of being eaten by their starving mothers (2:20). The poet proffers words to the city that it might use in its appeal to its angry God (v. 22): "Look, O Lord, and see! . . . Those whom I dandled and reared my enemy destroyed" (vv. 20-22). Not so affecting, perhaps, is the sight of priest and prophet slain in the temple (v. 20), since priest and prophet alike bear a share of the responsibility for what has happened to Jerusalem (cf. v. 14; 4:13).

Poem 3: When the Mood Changes (Lamentations 3)

In this third and central poem, three times the length of the others, the poet becomes so totally identified with the experience of the nation that the suffering citizens of Jerusalem disappear from sight altogether and we are confronted solely with the image of a man assailed by God: "I am a man who has seen affliction under the rod of God's wrath" (3:1). So caught up in the inner experience of suffering is the poet that we find virtually no reference either to the nation or to the external realities of the catastrophe; we see only the inner emotions of the poet who speaks on behalf of the people, we hear only how it feels to be suffering at God's hands.

A Man Who Has Seen Affliction under the Rod of God's Wrath (3:1-21)

The speaker is now not the city of Jerusalem depicted as a woman, but the poet represented as one of its citizens, encapsulating in his own experience that of the whole city and its inhabitants. In a hail of metaphor the speaker expresses the sense that God has misled him, destroyed his health, besieged him like a city, thrown him away like a corpse, blocked his way, savaged him like a wild animal, made him his target for shooting practice (many of these images are found also in Job 16:7-14). The question of whether perhaps the suffering is deserved is not being raised; the issue here is the feeling itself, and that cannot be brushed to one side by the more intellectual problem of whether the feeling may be deserved.

Yet Yahweh's Mercies Never Cease (3:22-33)

Just as in the book of Job, it is when the lamenter decides that the issue is not his own guilt but the fact that God is responsible for what is happening that the mood begins to change. There has been no hope at all in chs. 1 and 2, but here, once the poet has focused his mind on God's part in the suffering, he becomes able to hope. For God is not only an avenging God who can punish cruelly (3:32), but he is also a God of enduring love whose mercies are never spent (v. 22). And therefore the word "good," which has not been spoken before in this book, can begin each of the three verses 25-27: Yahweh is good, and if one is patient one will see his salvation. There is no denying that God causes grief, but it is "not from his heart" (RSV, NEB, "willingly") that he afflicts humankind (v. 33). Justice is his strange work, but mercy his darling attribute.

A more judgmental reader might be inclined to say that the people of Jerusalem deserved everything that happened to them, and that instead of blaming God and appealing to his mercy they should have been repenting of their wickedness. To the poet of Lamentations that would be to miss the point; a truly religious view of suffering may more properly be said to be one that does not seek to cast blame. It is one that sees God as the cause and the cure for suffering.

What of Repentance? (3:34-66)

The poem now takes a strange path, reiterating several conventional moral principles such as "to trample underfoot any prisoner in the land . . . the Lord does not approve" (3:34-36). It is perhaps being suggested that such are the sins for which the city of Jerusalem is now being judged, with punishments against which no one can reasonably complain (v. 39). But it may be better to read these principles as the ideals by which God himself lives, the moral standards against which he himself will not offend. That is to say, once Jerusalem's inhabitants have become like prisoners or oppressed people pleading for deliverance, it is against the grain for God to take no notice, to stand back while deserved punishment runs its inexorable course.

A watershed has been passed in the hopeful thoughts of 3:22-33. Now the lamenter begins to speak no longer in his own voice alone, but as a member, a representative, and a leader of his people. And now, once he has gained confidence in God by reflecting on God's mercies that are ever fresh, is the moment for the theme of repentance to be raised. Of great consequence is the fact that repentance is not viewed here as a human initiative that persuades God to take pity; rather, repentance is a response to the assurance of God's forgiveness (vv. 40-42).

In addition, repentance is a quite marginal element in the movement from despair to deliverance. No one is denying that Jerusalem deserves its suffering, but the emphasis in 3:46-66 is very firmly on its sorry state and the surprising salvation of the Lord. Now when the poet reverts to "I"-language (v. 48), he is no longer speaking of himself and his own emotions alone, but offering his fellow citizens words of address to God. He composes for them a psalm in the style of the songs of thanksgiving (e.g., Psalm 18). Out of unceasing tears, hunted like a bird, crying from the depths of a pit, the lamenting people now have the words in their mouth that will be fit for praising God: "you pled my cause, you ransomed my life" (3:58). No matter that the deliverance has not yet happened; if they do not already know the words for gratitude and rejoicing, how will they know when the moment for the words has arrived, how will they know how to speak to the moment? Even the violent curses against their enemies (vv. 64-66) can be seen, in this connection, as a sign of returning confidence in God rather than as simple vindictiveness.

Poem 4: Casting the Blame (Lamentations 4)

It cannot be accidental that in this fourth poem the tone reverts to that of the first two. In a remarkable reversion from ch. 3, there is no hope here, no expectation of God's deliverance, but simply a report of the catastrophe. The poet speaks with pathos, indeed, but with a certain distance from the events; only in 4:17-20 does the speaker even identify himself with the people of the city. The point must be that even the most "blessed assurance," such as stood at the central point of the book (3:22-33), can be put out of mind by the insistent realities confronting poet and people. All that remains of the confident spirit of ch. 3 is the conviction that Jerusalem's enemies, such as the Edomites, who are today gloating over its downfall, will find the cup of God's anger passing to them too (v. 21). It is small comfort that Jerusalem will never again be carried into exile (v. 22, NEB; not "keep you in exile no longer," RSV) since that can only mean that those who remain in the city are not worth anyone's trouble to plunder or exile.

In this poem, the ideological stance is that there are two causes for the calamity. One is the anger of Yahweh, giving full vent to his wrath (4:11). The other is the sins of religious leaders, prophets and priests; by disregarding justice they have "shed the blood of the righteous" (v. 13), a sin of omission rather than commission, one supposes. And what is the relation between these two causes? The logic must be that it is the sin of Jerusalem's leaders that has inflamed the anger of Yahweh. But the speaker is not very interested in saying that; his concern is rather with laying blame — for he is suffering and wants to hit out in whatever direction blame may lie, whether it is God or the national leaders. Perhaps he is right not to lay all the blame on his countrymen. Though their sin may be the ultimate cause, does not God also have some responsibility? Did he have no choice at all about whether to respond to human sin with anger, about whether he should be angry in this way, a way that destroyed so much of what was precious to him?

Most distinctive about this poem is the way it depicts the effect of the fall of Jerusalem upon various classes of Jerusalem society: there are first the children starving to death (4:2-4; cf. 2:19-20), then the previously well-fed wealthy people and nobles wasting away from lack of nourishment (4:5, 7-8), the priests and the elders rejected from their positions of authority (v. 16), and the king, the anointed of the LORD, taken into exile (v. 20). From the children, at the bottom of the social pyramid, to the king at its apex, no group has escaped. The dynamic of this poem is its movement through the classes in turn.

Jerusalem's Inhabitants (4:1-11)

The visual impact in this part of the poem is created by a series of contrasts between then and now: the citizens of Jerusalem, once worth their weight in gold, are now on the level of earthen pots (4:2), those brought up in purple and used to luxury now "embrace" ash heaps, living on the margins of society (v. 5), and the young nobles with fair complexions from delicate indoor living are now sunburned and wasted from hard work in the open air (v. 8). Those who were killed in battles for the city are better off than those who survived the fighting, but they have gradually become weaker and weaker from lack of food (v. 9).

The underlying contrast is between the former belief of the inhabitants of Jerusalem that their city was inviolable and the simple reality that it has now been conquered. It is a belief that is here attributed to the kings of the earth, but it is much more likely that this was the governing certitude of the citizens of Jerusalem, that no enemy could enter the gates of their city (4:12).

Jerusalem's Priests and Prophets (4:12-16)

The priests and prophets of the people are its religious leadership, who bear the blame for much of the sin of Jerusalem. By not upholding the law and ensuring that justice was properly dispensed, they effectively "shed the blood of the righteous" (4:13). That blood defiled their clothes and made them into moral lepers shunned by society (vv. 14-15).

Jerusalem's King (4:17-20)

The metaphor here (at least in 4:18-20) is of the hunt, in which the whole people are pursued for blood sport, with the king being the main target of the chase. The outcome has been that the king, Yahweh's anointed one, who is regarded as vital for the life of the nation, has been captured in pits such as are set for wild animals (cf. Ps 57:6 [7]).

Jerusalem's Enemies (4:21-22)

The only enemies of Jerusalem mentioned in the book are, curiously enough, the Edomites. Their involvement in the downfall of Jerusalem is not attested in any historical source in the OT, but it is frequently alluded to in prophetic texts (e.g., Jer 49:7-22; Ezekiel 35; Obadiah; cf. Ps 137:7-9). There can be little doubt that it was the Babylonians who were chiefly responsible for the destruction of the city, but perhaps the Edomites are especially referred to because of their historical kinship with Israel, which should have made of them allies rather than enemies.

The invitation to them to rejoice must be ironic since the poet envisages them drinking from the cup of God's wrath (cf. Ps 75:8 [9]). Though the RSV has it that "the punishment of your iniquity, O daughter of Zion, is accomplished" (4:22), it seems unlikely that Jerusalem is here being promised release from exile; at best, the poet may be saying that whereas the punishment of Jerusalem may someday come to an end, all that Edom has to look forward to is devastation (v. 22).

Poem 5: Expectations of God (Lamentations 5)

This final poem differs from the others in being addressed to God, in the name of the people. It is cast in the form of one of the psalms of Appeals of the Community (e.g., Psalms 44, 60), but unlike the examples in the book of Psalms, this one has comparatively little appeal to God and comparatively much description of the disaster. So in that respect it resembles the other poems of this book.

The previous addresses to God have been brief and embedded in poems of description (1:9, 20-22; 2:20-22; 3:19, 42-45, 55-56). It can only be deliberate that the poet has chosen to complete his book of "Appeals" or "Lamentations" with a full-fledged prayer to God. But what precisely does he ask for? In 5:1 he asks only in a very general way that God should "remember" the community, which means that he should pay attention to them, or not ignore them (as in v. 20). It is only in v. 21 that he says at all exactly what he desires: "Turn us back to thyself, O LORD, and we will come back." Does that mean "cause us to repent," as the verb "to make return" so often does in Jeremiah (e.g., 31:18)? Or does it mean "restore our city and return our exiles to us," which it could equally well mean? Considering the rather minor role that repentance plays in this book, that can hardly be the one thing the poet desires. Yet he wants more than a simple return to the land; what is important to him is a unitedness between God and people, a turning of God to people and of people to God. Perhaps it is untrue to the poet's spirit to seek in his words a more explicit request than this longing for divine-human reciprocity.

With pathos and a tender delicacy the poet resists any attempt to force God's hand or to revert at the close of his poem to the confidence of ch. 3. In the end, God will be God and no appeal will change his mind, no human expressions of confidence in him will make him do other than what he has determined. The last sentence is a refusal to predict what God's mind may be; perhaps, indeed, God has now utterly rejected his people. The poet presumes nothing, but accepts that he and his people are shut up to the divine will, whether for mercy or for anger.

Bibliography. Albrektson, B. 1963, *Studies in the Text and Theology of the Book of Lamentations,* Studia theologica Lundensia 21, Lund: C. W. K. Gleerup • Gottwald, N. K. rev. ed. 1962, *Studies in the Book of Lamentations,* SBT 14, London: SCM • Hillers, D. R. 1972, *Lamentations: Introduction, Translation and Notes,* AB 7A, Garden City, N.Y.: Doubleday • Joyce, P. 1993, "Lamentations and the Grief Process: A Psychological Reading," *Biblical Interpretation* 1:304-20 • Kračovec, J. 1992, "The Source of Hope in the Book of Lamentations," *VT* 42: 223-33 • Landy, F. 1994, "Lamentations," in R. Alter and F. Kermode, eds., *The Literary Guide to the Bible,* Cambridge, Mass.: The Belknap Press of Harvard University, 329-34 • O'Connor, K. M. 1992, "Lamentations," in C. A. Newsom and S. H. Ringe, eds., *The Women's Bible Commentary,* London: SPCK, 178-82 • Provan, I. W. 1991, *Lamentations,* NCB, London: Marshall Pickering • Salters, R. B. 1994, *Jonah and Lamentations,* Old Testament Guides, Sheffield: JSOT • Westermann, C. 1994, *Lamentations: Issues and Interpretation,* trans. C. Muenchow, Minneapolis: Fortress.

Ezekiel

John A. Goldingay

INTRODUCTION

Ezekiel the son of Buzi (1:3) was an Israelite priest in the deportee Israelite community in Babylonia. Dates in the book imply that he was born in Judah in 622 BC, just before Josiah's reform, and thus lived through much of Jeremiah's ministry there. He was married (24:18), was thirty years old when he began his ministry in 592 BC (1:1), and continued his ministry until at least 571 BC (29:17).

Nothing is known of how the book came into being or came to be accepted as canonical in the Second Temple community. There are varying views on how far the material in the book comes from Ezekiel himself. The book has been seen as coming entirely from him, or as having very little to do with a real prophet in Babylon, or as containing much material from him which has been supplemented to suggest its implications for people living later. Unevennesses in the book may make the first view seem unlikely, and the second may seem a priori implausible. In the case of the third view it is difficult to know where specifically Ezekiel's work ends and the work of disciples begins, and I have not attempted to do so systematically, but I have sometimes drawn attention to examples of this approach.

The book is more clearly structured than most OT books:

Chs. 1–3	Introduction
Chs. 4–24	Warnings of Calamity to Come on Judah
Chs. 25–32	Warnings of Calamity to Come on Other Nations
Chs. 33–48	Promises of Judah's Renewal and Protection

J. B. Taylor, W. Eichrodt, W. Zimmerli, J. Blenkinsopp, L. C. Allen, and M. Greenberg have written useful commentaries on Ezekiel (see Bibliography). Taylor, Eichrodt, and Blenkinsopp are briefer; Zimmerli, Taylor, and Greenberg are on a larger scale. Taylor, Eichrodt, Zimmerli, Blenkinsopp, and Allen are overtly Christian; Greenberg is overtly Jewish. Taylor, Blenkinsopp, and Greenberg work with the text as we have it; Eichrodt, Zimmerli, and Allen are also interested in distinguishing between Ezekiel's own words and the process of subsequent expansion. Where these commentators are referred to simply by name, the allusion is to their treatment of the passage being discussed.

Ezekiel is at point after point like other prophets, only more so.

1. Other prophets had visionary experiences; Ezekiel's are technicolor, wide-screen, virtual reality as he is again and again dazzled by awesome manifestations of Yahweh's splendor. Other prophets were aware of this dazzling splendor; Ezekiel speaks of it nineteen times. It is difficult to distinguish between what Ezekiel experienced in his own mind or spirit and what he experienced outwardly. Presumably he alone saw the throne vision (though others might have seen the weather phenomena) and heard the voice; no one else would have seen the scroll he was aware of eating (and no one else in Jerusalem would have been aware of his subsequent "visits" there?), but people could have been aware of the extraordinary movements of 2:2; 3:12-15, like their equivalents in the stories of Elijah and Elisha (whom at points Ezekiel resembles more than he does the other well-known prophets). It might be that aspects of Ezekiel's behavior seemed as strange to his audience as it may to us. Yet that audience would also recall the oddness of the stories told of Elijah and Elisha. Ezekiel stands in an odd but honored tradition.

2. Other prophets felt God's presence, and some were seized, shaken, gripped, and impelled by the powerful, heavy, irresistible hand of Yahweh; this happens seven times to Ezekiel at key moments in connection with his being overwhelmed by extraordinary visions (1:3; 3:14, 22; 8:1; 33:22; 37:1; 40:1). He is again and again taken by the scruff of the neck, whisked from place to place, bowled over, and jerked to his feet. The delivery of Ezekiel's message involves a four-act drama (chs. 4–5), preaching to an absent audience (ch. 6), scattergun poetry (ch. 7), and testimony to visionary transportation (chs. 8–11).

3. Other prophets had a sense of being propelled by the dynamic, unpredictable, irresistible spirit of Yahweh, which for Ezekiel is associated with the experience just noted or is another way of describing it. The fact that *ruaḥ* refers to breath, wind, and spirit is especially important in Ezekiel (see ch. 37), and it is sometimes difficult to be sure which English word to use (see 8:3; 11:1).

4. Other prophets acted as messengers, sensing that the word of Yahweh "came" to them (more lit. "was/became/happened") for passing on to its intended recipients; Ezekiel speaks nearly fifty times of such a concrete experience of a message reaching him from the (heavenly) king which he is to pass on to his fellow subjects. Other prophets also act as heralds, commanding people to "listen to the word of Yahweh" (most frequently Jeremiah; cf., e.g., 22:2, 29) in the manner of a royal herald bringing the monarch's words to people who are subjects or who are treated as such (e.g., Isa 36:13). In adopting this form of speech, Ezekiel adapts it to his speaking in the name of *sovereign* Yahweh. He uses it even though he

is never physically facing those he overtly addresses (e.g., 6:3), so that it becomes a means of authoritative address to his actual audience in Babylon.

5. Other prophets used fables, folktales, and parables (e.g., 2 Samuel 12; Isaiah 5). Ezekiel turns a folktale motif into an allegory which occupies over four pages (ch. 16). Jeremiah includes a paragraph of critique of Israel's leaders as shepherds of Yahweh's flock (Jer 23:1-4); Ezekiel includes a sustained five-point allegorical exposition of this metaphor, turning it into a critique of shepherds and their flocks, a divine commitment to shepherding, and a promise of a faithful shepherd and of divine provision and protection for the flock (ch. 34). Something similar happens with Amos's talk of an "end" having come (Amos 8:2); see Ezekiel 7. "Amos states that in one brief, bulky menacing phrase. Our prophet shapes the same theme into a fugue" (Eichrodt). Elsewhere his words come in the form of sustained poetic expositions of an image (e.g., chs. 19, 27).

6. Other prophets communicated via mimes or acted parables (e.g., Isaiah 20). As his speaking not only conveys information but puts Yahweh's will into effect, so Ezekiel's mimes not only illustrate his message but embody that will and thus further contribute to its implementation. Ezekiel's mimes are particularly vivid, his allegories particularly complex. "As his visions outdo those of other prophets in their intricacy, so his symbolic actions are not to be tailored and trimmed along the simple lines of theirs. The possibility must be allowed that Ezekiel, the authentic Ezekiel, was baroque" (Greenberg: 219). Jeremiah senses Yahweh putting words in his mouth (1:9) and speaks in metaphor of enjoying the taste of Yahweh's words; a metaphor in Jer 15:16 becomes an allegory in Ezekiel 2–3.

7. Other prophets concerned themselves with the destiny of the whole people. Ezekiel is more systematically concerned for "the house of Israel." Earlier prophets had more often used the title "Israel" for the northern tribes. Ezekiel addresses a community comprising merely a deported remnant of the southern tribe, Judah, but he addresses it as "Israel." They are the embodiment of Israel rather than mere castoffs, though he also envisions a glorious destiny for a truly comprehensive Israel (see chs. 36–37).

8. Other prophets naturally looked for themselves to be recognized and for Yahweh to be recognized. In Ezekiel this theme of recognition becomes of central significance. The phrases "they/you shall know that I am Yahweh" and similar expressions appear over seventy times. The knowledge for which Ezekiel, like other prophets, is concerned is not mere awareness of facts but acknowledgment of Yahweh which recognizes in life that Yahweh is the sovereign whose authority must be accepted (see on ch. 6). Ezekiel's concern for Yahweh's name also parallels and exceeds that of other prophets. He wishes to see Yahweh acknowledged by Israel and by the nations for the sake of Yahweh's own name.

9. Other prophets became aware of the strange resistance of the community to Yahweh's word, and may even have been aware of it when they were commissioned. Ezekiel knows from the beginning that the community is a stubbornly resistant, impudently hostile one (not only "house of Israel" but "house of rebellion") and sees its resistance as characterizing its life from the very beginning (chs. 15; 16; 20; 23).

10. Other prophets were ignored. In part this was because the essence of their vocation was to say things that went contrary to the community's own instincts. This applied to Ezekiel during his earlier ministry when he was claiming that there was worse trouble to come than the community had yet experienced. When that calamity arrived, it also applied when he brought the community unbelievable good news. When he began his ministry the community had the excuse, or lived with the further dilemma, that it knew of many prophets and that they all contradicted each other (see Jeremiah 27–29, stories told about this period). Beyond being ignored, other prophets pay a price for the exercise of their ministry. Ezekiel becomes himself a "sign" for Israel. In his own being he is an embodiment of their threatened fate (12:6; 24:24).

11. Other prophets indict the people and declare judgment on the community; Ezekiel acts as a lookout warning of imminent danger (ch. 3) with a message of judgment that is so extensive it fills both sides of God's scroll (2:10); Ezekiel can take four chapters (chs. 8–11) where others might take four verses. Other prophets portray Israel as God's unfaithful wife (see, e.g., Hosea 1–3). Ezekiel turns this portrayal into a late-night mini-series which respectable people hesitate to admit viewing, and after doing so go to bed with a bad taste in their mouth (see chs. 16; 23). Other prophets see Yahweh as smelting Israel to burn away the dross; Ezekiel sees smelting as establishing that dross is all there is (22:17-22).

12. Other prophets spoke of a glorious future the other side of judgment. Some of Ezekiel's most elaborate visions picture the wondrous restoration of Davidic shepherding, the miraculous resuscitation of the people, and especially the laying out of a new temple at the center of a newly allocated land. This last vision is the focus of his most sustained influence on early Christian writers: see Revelation.

13. Other prophets affirm the sovereign lordship of Yahweh; Ezekiel uniquely uses the phrase "sovereign Yahweh" as his characteristic title for God. Translations such as "Lord GOD" obscure the fact that it combines the word for "sovereign" with God's actual name, combining a sense of privilege and nearness in knowledge of God's name with a sense of awesomeness because the name itself suggests something of the unpredictable enigma of the active presence of Yahweh. Ezekiel is the boldest of the prophets in attributing all that happens to Yahweh's sovereignty. This includes the apostasy of the righteous (3:20), the delusion of the prophet (14:9), and the guidance offered by Babylonian divination (21:22-23). His apparently being often addressed by a heavenly aide rather than directly by God perhaps links with his sense of Yahweh's transcendent awesomeness and his own earthly vulnerability. Yahweh's correlative characteristic title for Ezekiel is "mortal man," lit. "son of man," a less odd term in Hebrew than in English. While other prophets are directly addressed by Yahweh, no one else is directly addressed so frequently; yet whereas some other

prophets are addressed by name, Ezekiel is always addressed by this idiomatic expression meaning "human being." Set over against "Lord Yahweh," it suggests humanity in its creatureliness and frailty.

14. Other prophetic books provide us with chronological information. Ezekiel gives us a series of precise dates in terms of the deportation of 597 BC (1:2; 8:1; 20:1; 24:1; 26:1; 29:1, 17; 31:1; 32:1, 17; 33:21; 40:1). This is a new phenomenon in prophetic books, and Ezekiel is the only prophet who is said himself to give us dates (usually they come in the third person, like those in vv. 2-3, making explicit that it is editors who provide them). Chronological precision was often important to priestly ministry, though it would be important to prophets whenever they wanted their words recorded before witnesses against the moment of their fulfillment (e.g., Isaiah 8). It also conveys an impression of actuality (this is an event real enough to be dated) and a reminder that God's word tends to be specific to particular moments and needs to be understood in relation to them.

The point at which we started is the major point at which Ezekiel is unlike most of the other prophets. He is a priest. This makes a most significant contribution to the nature of his prophetic ministry.

1. He is preoccupied by Yahweh's holiness, which for him means Yahweh's otherness or extraordinariness (see on 36:22-38). "The key to Ezekiel's proclamation of God is this: *God will not be mocked.* God will not be presumed upon, trivialized, taken for granted, or drawn too close. God takes being God with utmost seriousness" (Brueggemann 1978: 53; his emphasis). That is God's holiness.

2. He is appalled at specifically religious wrongdoing, though also at the violence which characterizes the community (for the combination, see, e.g., ch. 18).

3. He sees calamity as lying in Yahweh's abandoning of the temple and in the temple's destruction. It is for this calamity, a truly community-destroying event, that he seeks to prepare his people in Babylon who do not believe it can ever happen. The other side to this coin is that he sees restoration as lying in the renewing of the temple and in a reallocation of the land which now has the temple at its center.

COMMENTARY

Introducing 1:4–3:15 (1:1-3)

The book opens by relating an experience which came to a priest "in the thirtieth year" — presumably of his life, and therefore the year in which he might have taken up his ordained ministry (cf. Numbers 4). But he is not in Jerusalem to do that; he is a member of a refugee community in Babylon, one of the priests deported there among the Judean leadership in 597 BC (2 Kgs 24:10-16; Jer 29:1). It is the fifth year since that event, and high summer (on the assumption that the year starts in the spring).

Ezekiel's community lives near the Chebar canal, part of the water system near Nippur in southern Babylonia, though he is elsewhere when he has his visionary experience (3:14-15). A community of refugees would provide a context in which a priest could exercise his ministry. The traditional sanctuary focus of a priest's ministry would make him a standing reminder of the calamity which had come upon Jerusalem. Yet the moment which would see his beginning his ministry but does not do so (a sign of God's judgment) sees his being granted a vision of God (a sign of God's mercy).

Ezekiel's experience is described in visual, aural, and physical terms. 1:1 introduces especially its visionary aspect, which is central in vv. 4-28a. Vv. 2-3 introduce its aural and physical aspects, which are interwoven in 1:28b–3:15.

Ezekiel before God as Visionary (1:4-28a)

A huge storm cloud approaches, ringed by the sun's bright light and pierced by flashing lightning. It comes from the north, a natural meteorological fact, but this is also the direction from which invaders often came. More significantly, it is the traditional location of the divine dwelling (Ps 48:2; Isa 14:13). The cloud, light, and fire, too, suggest God's presence, but the point and the centrality of 1:4 will not become explicit until vv. 26-28. The vision might have been prompted by scriptures which speak of God's presence in terms of cloud, light, and fire (Exod 13:21-22; 20:18-21; Ps 18:7-15) and/or by actual weather phenomena. The awesomeness of God's appearing is suggested by the impossibility of describing it — the vision focuses on the mere penumbra of God's active reality (Job 26:14). Thus as 1:4-28 unfold, the fuller the description, the less significant the thing described; the briefer the description, the more the thing matters. Ch. 10 will add to our understanding of this vision.

From the cloud emerge four exotic creatures, each with four wings and four faces belonging to the highest of the natural species. Four crisscross wheels stand alongside them. All these features emphasize the mobility of the entourage, which faces and moves in any direction effortlessly, along the ground or in the air. It does so as a single united entity despite the fact that creatures, wheels, and throne are not physically linked; they are held together by one "spirit" or will. The description with its repetitions conveys the awesomeness of the vision, the richness of its elements, and the thunder of the sound as the creatures' wings beat.

Standing above the creatures, wheels, and linked wings is a gleaming platform and a sapphire-blue throne seating a humanlike figure of fiery, rainbow-like splendor. 1:1 anticipatorily announced that this would be so, v. 4 hinted at it in its imagery, and vv. 5-25 built up anticipation of it, yet only now is the figure explicitly identified as a bodily representation of Yahweh's own majesty. At this moment it thus meets the appropriate response from the priest (v. 28).

Ezekiel and Genesis, Then and Later

For God to be humanlike when appearing links with the Israelite conviction that humanity itself is Godlike. That conviction is explicit in Genesis 1, a passage which may be suggestively set alongside Ezekiel 1. The two chapters come from similar priestly circles in Babylon, and both address the refugee community under pressure. Both preface old Israelite tradition with a new vision which sets the familiar in a new context. Genesis 1 provides the traditional creation story with a fresh preface that sets it in a much more all-embracing perspective in its concern with God's creative activity in the whole cosmos. Ezekiel 1 provides the traditional understanding of a prophet's call with a fresh preface, setting it, too, in a much wider metaphysical perspective in its vision and suggesting the sovereign Yahweh's capacity to appear in divine splendor anywhere, to implement heaven's purpose or to meet with heaven's agents.

The two passages' venturesome flights of revelatory imagination led to both becoming suggestive stimuli to meditation over many centuries. Their influence can be seen in Jewish apocalypses, in rabbinic writings of the talmudic period, and in medieval Jewish mystical writings. For anyone interested in what we would call theology (not least theodicy) or science, they provided an inexhaustible invitation to reflection and discovery. After the fall of the Second Temple the circle of Yohanan ben Zakkai developed the mystical study of the passages, though also placing restrictions on their study, apparently because of the fancies it could engender and the possibility of encroaching on God's own dangerous realm. In medieval times only people of Ezekiel's own age or older were allowed to study Ezekiel 1. (See *m. Ḥag.* 2:1; Gruenwald 1980.)

Ezekiel 1 provided Daniel 7 and 10 with ways of envisioning and portraying visionary manifestations. At the end of the Second Temple period it gave a Christian prophet means of envisioning and portraying the person and presence of God (Revelation 4). It is a statement both of the possibility and of the limitations of that knowledge of Yahweh to which human beings have access.

Ezekiel before God as Messenger (1:28b–3:15)

In 1:28–3:15 there is an interweaving of the mainly experiential and physical (1:28–2:2; 2:8–3:3; 3:12-15) with the verbal and aural (2:3-7; 3:4-11).

The three physical experiences involve first collapsing and being raised upright, then eating a scroll with gloomy words but sweet taste, then being lifted up and deposited back with the refugee community. We have commented in the Introduction on the characteristic form of address, "O mortal." The entering of a spirit into Ezekiel to bring him back to life suggests another link with the Genesis creation story.

Whereas the throne vision has no necessary connection with a prophetic call, each of these experiences links more obviously with such a call. Ezekiel is raised upright to be addressed, eats a scroll containing words to be uttered, and is transported back to the community with which he is to share Yahweh's words. Ezekiel is not merely a visionary or mystic who can be satisfied with keeping Yahweh's company. Yahweh appears to him in order to send him.

The picture of the written scroll would suggest that Yahweh's words came to Ezekiel directly from heaven. Yet Ezekiel's words are distinctive to him and quite distinguishable from Isaiah's or Jeremiah's. Perhaps the image of his eating and regurgitating the scroll's contents itself hints at the idea that his prophecies come via his personality. But the explicit point of the image lies elsewhere, in the contrast between Ezekiel's response to Yahweh's words (he finds them sweet despite their harshness) and the people's response to them.

The two passages which focus on the verbal and aural in turn do declare that Yahweh is sending Ezekiel, but they make this point quite briefly. Even their emphasis is not so much on the prophet's call as on the rebelliousness of the people to whom he is sent. The first (2:3-7) additionally stresses that Ezekiel is nevertheless not to fear them, and the second (3:4-11) that Yahweh will personally steel him so that he can stand firm before them.

When an account of a prophet's call appears in a prophetic book, it is not to describe an experience which the audience is also expected to have. It is one which is unique to the prophet, which thus provides the reason why the audience must take seriously the prophet's words which the book contains and why it is guilty if it fails to do so. It also commonly advertises key themes in those words. Here Ezekiel is commended to us as someone who was granted the most transcendent vision of God and was then called to speak. He was supernaturally dispatched and equipped with the words. We are indirectly pressed to take him at his word, for his words issue from his having assimilated Yahweh's word. At the same time, the audience is offered an assessment of itself as resistant to Yahweh's word. Its deportation is not the mysterious affliction of a group committed to Yahweh but the deserved chastisement of a group resistant to Yahweh.

Ezekiel among the Community as Lookout (3:16-21)

A week later Ezekiel had another kind of experience, of the word of Yahweh "coming" to him — literally "happening" to him. Whereas the earlier account implies one form of religious experience, an awareness of the personal presence of God speaking, this description implies another form, when one is simply aware of words.

The words underline the solemn significance of his call, making more explicit its implications (see further 33:1-9). As well as a visionary who sees God and is astonished, and a messenger who hears God and passes on what he hears, he is a lookout, identified with the community. A lookout's job is to keep watch in an elevated place, from where one could see anyone coming (cf. 2 Sam 13:34; 18:24; 2 Kgs 9:17-20). If the lookout fell asleep and neglected to sound the alarm to warn the city of danger (Isa 56:10; Jer 6:17), so that people failed to find refuge in it or take flight or close the city's gates to an approaching army, the people's death would be the lookout's responsibility. A prophet is the people's lookout, able to see Yahweh's judgment approaching.

Ezekiel has his attention drawn to a distinction within the community between the people who characteristically live right lives and those who do not (see also ch. 18). The distinction is then admittedly deconstructed: it becomes one between people who do wrong (but might stop) and people who do right (but might stop). It is of no use to have people reassuring themselves that they belong to the law-abiding group unless they are thoroughly consistent in their commitment.

Yet there is a difference between the approach Yahweh's word takes to habitual and to occasional wrongdoers. There is no specific reference to the possibility that the former may turn — there is something fixed about their character. There is specific reference to the possibility that the latter may turn — there is also something consistent about their character. So Ezekiel's ministry to the two groups has different functions. In relation to the former, it is to vindicate Yahweh's fairness in punishment; in relation to the latter, it is to halt them between intent and action so that they do not incur punishment. From the difference in people's response to him it has been inferred that he explicitly ministered to individuals, but more likely this is no more the case than it is with a lookout (Greenberg).

If Ezekiel fails to make his warning heard in the ears of people who have long done wrong or who now turn to doing wrong, and they as a result lose their lives (e.g., suffer untimely death), he is in effect guilty of murder and is liable to the same fate. If he does warn them, they are responsible for their own fate. A stumbling block (3:20) is something which makes someone fall; the word appears more in Ezekiel than in the whole of the rest of the OT. Here it might simply mean that Yahweh sends the calamity which brings judgment on the wrongdoer (cf. the related verb in 33:12). But it would be characteristic of Ezekiel to mean that Yahweh also sent whatever led the person into wrongdoing (like planting the tree of knowledge in Eden; and cf. 14:9). That is how seriously Ezekiel takes Yahweh's sovereignty. It is part of his explanation of the mystery of human perversity whereby we are capable of making such manifestly foolish choices. Yet he takes human responsibility seriously; we are challenged and able to resist temptation.

Ezekiel among the Community as Prisoner (3:22-27)

Ezekiel is continually harried. Yahweh had first seized him near the Chebar; then, when he had hardly recovered from this experience, he confronted him at home and commissioned him to speak like a lookout; then, when he had hardly had opportunity to fulfill this commission, he compelled him out into the open country; then he appeared to him and seized him there, only to tell him to go home, a strange location for a messenger or lookout. Except when Yahweh gives him freedom and words to speak, here he is to stay restrained and speechless. It is again a strange restriction for a lookout, more likely a sign of God's judgment on the rebellious house whom Yahweh declines to address than an indication of human opposition since the book never refers to the latter. By his silent and inactive presence Ezekiel is a sign of judgment on a rebellious house, which does not lack a prophet, yet lacks prophecy. The end of this restraint will come at 24:25-27; 33:21-22, when the judgment falls and the time of hope begins. We do not know how literal or how permanent were the means of restraint in 3:25, though in the course of his ministry as the book reports it, Ezekiel never leaves home — again, oddly for a prophet/lookout. The cords will point to the constraints of siege (cf. 4:8); perhaps the confinement itself also does so.

Yahweh's tough stance in relation to the community (see esp. 3:27b) recalls the words of Isa 6:9-10. In Matthew, Jesus identifies with both in his critique of the community of his day (see, e.g., 13:9, 15-16, 43); in Revelation 2–3, John similarly applies Ezekiel's phrase to the churches. Their assumption is like that which underlies 3:16-21: Yahweh's word will shape people, but they are responsible for their destiny, as their outward response to the prophet will reveal their inner openness or closedness.

We have noted a number of links between 3:16-27 and what follows in chs. 18, 24, 33, and 37, all key passages. Vv. 16-27 function along with 1:1–3:15 as part of the introduction to the book as a whole, offering an anticipatory summary of Ezekiel's ministry. This may be part of the explanation for the hectic sequence in ch. 3.

A Drama in Prospect (4:1–5:4)

A messenger or a lookout uses words, but Ezekiel's vision has already hinted that he may be more than a wordsmith. There follows an extended drama by means of which he will begin to fulfill his calling as a lookout. Word and action vie for prominence in this book.

Actions can reinforce words or implement words. Symbolic actions such as giving someone a candle at a baptism or putting on a ring at a wedding help people to understand what is going on and to believe in it; they also contribute to making it happen, because God chooses to work that way. Some prophets, too, undertook symbolic actions with similar significance, this being (they claimed) God's way of working through them (see, e.g., Jeremiah 13; 19; 28; Mark 3; Acts 21:10-11). In this sense symbolic actions parallel what is popularly known as magic, though the prophets would see themselves as means of Yahweh's acting in accordance with Yahweh's will rather than as able to effect what they themselves determined.

Here Ezekiel sets the scene with a dramatized version of the coming siege of Jerusalem (4:1-3). He will go on to dramatize Israel's past 390 years of guilt and punishment — and Judah's coming forty years (4:4-8). He will sustain himself on the food and drink of a man under siege or of a refugee (4:9-17). He will portray the fate of the people of Jerusalem (5:1-4). The themes and the action in these dramas overlap rather than appearing separately. The model of 4:1-3, for instance, is still present in 4:4-8, so that there Jerusalem's coming siege and the state's ongoing punishment (past and future) are all before people's eyes. In 4:9-17 Ezekiel's 390 days' guilt-bearing continues as he adds different representations of both the deprivations of Jerusalem's siege and the pollution of its people's transportation. Again the audience is forced to confront all three realities simultaneously and driven to face them and come to terms with them. In 5:1-3 once more siege, fall, and aftermath all appear. As will later happen in John's Gospel, Ezekiel then explains the significance of his "signs" (5:5-17).

A Dramatized Siege (4:1-3)

Ezekiel portrays Jerusalem on a clay brick (no doubt while it is still somewhat soft) such as was in regular use for figures and inscriptions in Mesopotamia, and makes it the focus of a representation of its siege. This brings home the threat with its implications for the refugee community and contributes to making it happen. We need not think of a huge realistic model to represent the extensive scene to which 4:1-3 refers. Like symbols, such a portrayal need not offer a realistic representation (compare the fourth sign in 5:1-4). The iron griddle which here is unexplained is Yahweh's own iron-hard hostility (see 5:5-17).

A Dramatized Punishment (4:4-8)

Ezekiel now plays the part of the people experiencing Yahweh's punishment, identifying with them in their sin, guilt, and punishment as Jesus will at his baptism. The 390 years might make the audience think first of the whole history of the temple, then when Ezekiel goes on to refer to Judah as opposed to Israel it might also make them think of the whole history of northern Israel's independent existence (periods which actually began about 970 BC and 930 BC, though such knowledge on their part could not be presumed). Both are long years of guilt and liability to punishment (*'awon* covers wrongdoing, guilt, and punishment). Northern Israel's years of actual punishment might be seen as beginning with the state's subservience and fall between 733 and 721; thus LXX reads 190 years here. The imminent forty years for Judah takes up a standard symbolic/round figure. There may also be something symbolic about the 390 years, for 390 and forty add up to the 430 years of Egyptian oppression (Exod 12:40-41). It is characteristic of biblical numbers to reflect resonances such as this at least as much as to imply precise historical calculation.

Neither figure should thus be pressed chronologically. Both will end at the same time, when both peoples are restored (cf. ch. 37), though in Ezekiel's dramatization they were acted out separately (4:6). The effectiveness of the drama does not require his literally lying on his side for the whole of 390 days. In a film or play, dramatic time and real time do not coincide, and we have ways of conveying the faster passage of the former.

The focus remains the threatened siege of Jerusalem, which will end the 390/190 years and begin the forty years; that is the central topic.

Dramatized Deprivation and Defilement (4:9-17)

While people are still reminded of the 390 years of guilt and liability to punishment, they are also confronted by the thinness of the siege diet, a two hundred–gram loaf of rather inferior ingredients, and less than a liter of water. Worse will be the way the food has to be cooked after the people's subsequent transportation. Cooking on animal dung is normal in the Middle East. Human dung would work as well, but it might be more repulsive and would be ritually polluting. God's command for its use makes the point about the inevitable defilement involved in transportation to a foreign land. Issuing the command is enough; as is often the case, God is then flexible in response to human protest. Perhaps 4:16-17 imply that in any case God's aim in giving the command was to engender the fear and dismay expressed in v. 14 — when that has been achieved, the command does not need to be implemented. On the defilement referred to in v. 14, see, e.g., Lev 17:10-16.

Dramatized Decimation (5:1-4)

Shaving and cutting hair would in themselves suggest death and humiliation (e.g., Jer 48:37-39). The sign points to the coming fate of the city's people: a third will die in the siege, a third will die in battle around the city, and a third will be scattered. From the last third a few will seem to be preserved, though even they will remain vulnerable (cf. Isa 6:13). This last is a worrisome message for Ezekiel's audience (see further 6:8-10). In the event the results of the city's fall were somewhat less fearsome. As in 4:12b, God's actions are not necessarily as fearsome as God's words.

The Drama in Retrospect (4:1–5:4)

Placing ourselves in the position of Ezekiel's audience for 4:1–5:4, we might imagine ourselves in a besieged city, with armory menacing, life endangered, movement prevented, supplies cut, surrender ultimately inevitable, suffering the greater the longer surrender is postponed, and a conviction that the city's fall is actually God's will, so that pleas for deliverance get no further than the ceiling (4:1-3). The city is destined to fall not just for a week, a month, a year, or a decade but for a whole generation, God's personal energy is bent on its destruction, and it is not merely to be trampled by foreign nations but to endure continuing subjugation and humiliation (vv. 4-8). Siege reduces people from luxuries to necessities, then these are halved, then halved again; people are foraging for food from rubbish tips and are lowered to behavior revolting to describe and disgusting to the people themselves in time of peace (vv. 9-17). A third of the people die in the city's siege, a third die in the desperate battle with its attackers, and the rest are scattered in all directions; only a proportion of the final third are kept safe for a while, then decimated once more (5:1-4). We must not imagine that this is some remote ancient event but our own city. The people who are suffering and dying are our contemporaries, our friends, our families, ourselves. We must imagine that we are not merely imagining. A prophet is portraying these events before our eyes, and not merely illustrating them but effecting them since they symbolize God's acts in the real world.

A Drama Interpreted (5:5-17)

When Ezekiel enacted the signs of 4:1–5:4, he may have first allowed them to speak for themselves. Unless he shared Yahweh's words to him (e.g., 4:1), people would be free to assume that he was picturing judgment on Babylon, until the devastating "this is Jerusalem" of 5:5. The sermon now warns of the coming calamity more prosaically (and in line with Leviticus 26) but more scarily, and claims to reveal its background. Ezekiel implies that other peoples knew something of Yahweh's expectations but that Judah knew more. It is by Yahweh's initiative that they are set in the middle of the world so that it might be drawn to recognize Yahweh's revelation through them. Given that special position, they are the more guilty for their disobedience, which cannot be ignored. Indeed, in its extremeness the punishment corresponds to the privilege.

Ezekiel's God is one who asserts absolute power in the world, is a lawgiver expecting obedience, is especially concerned about religious matters (5:11; see further chs. 8; 11), is revolted by the repulsiveness of people's actual religious behavior, and is consumed by passionate and pitiless fury when not obeyed. Different readers find his God impressive, reassuring, austere, thought-provoking, frightening, and offensive. Christian readers troubled by this God have to come to terms with similarities in the way Jesus speaks (see, e.g., Matt 8:11-13; 11:20-24). By means of shock treatment Ezekiel seeks to shake the community out of its laid-back assumption that things will soon get better and the deportees will soon be home.

Signs Which Lead to Recognition (Ch. 6)

Signs and words of judgment are not confined to Jerusalem. First, Ezekiel's hostile look (6:2) now dramatizes Yahweh's punishing the mountains which dominate Israel (and for which deportees would perhaps feel homesick, set in the flat Babylonian vale). These literal "high places" are also symbols of the "high places" located among them. These were Canaanite shrines which became Israelite ones, places where Yahweh was worshiped, but in ways that prophetic faith deplored (e.g., in the company of other gods, by means of images, and with sexual rites designed to ensure the fertility of people and land). Shrines were located in exalted positions as churches often are; they pointed to heaven as the home of the one to whom sacrifices were offered and incense ascended.

A second sign (6:11) accompanies a taunt expressing Yahweh's triumphant act of judgment; the cry *aḥ* here might suggest something like "hurrah" as much as "alas," but either way it is an exclamation by means of which Ezekiel dramatizes Yahweh's response to Israel rather than one by which Ezekiel expresses natural feelings of his own. Ezek 20:13-26, 35-36 and 2 Kgs 25:6-7, 18-21 make clear the grim connotations of "from the wilderness to Riblah" (6:14).

The events will mean "you/they will know that I am Yahweh." The phrase recurs in Ezekiel's warnings and promises; it is the aim of judgment and restoration. To appreciate its significance, first one needs to recall that in the OT "know" often covers "acknowledge" or "recognize"; it involves will as well as mind. Second, the phrase implies an ellipse. To acknowledge that "I am Yahweh" implies a recognition that Yahweh is a person of such power in heaven and on earth as to be the sole heavenly entity who seriously deserves to be called God. People in general come to this realization through judgment (6:14). So does the refugee community (vv. 7, 13). In their case the realization also comes through the mysterious interweaving of communal calamity, divine mercy, serious reflection which begins to face facts, awareness of divine hurt at people's inner and outward attitudes, and horrified, grieving remorse (vv. 8-10). The word for "reflection" is "remembering," which includes recollection of past acts but goes on to "a genuine grasping of a reality which then becomes a new living and present fact" (Zimmerli). God's hurt feelings have to be set alongside God's vindictiveness in ch. 5; both are aspects of the personal passion of Ezekiel's God. The vision of a change of heart can also be set alongside the vision of the fearsomeness of the city's fall; it, too, is an expectation not fulfilled. Thus all this is not Yahweh's last word addressing the mountains or describing the process of renewal (see ch. 36).

The Terror of Yahweh's Day and the Exposure of Human Securities (Ch. 7)

In a number of ways ch. 7 complements ch. 6.

1. Signs and straight prose are complemented by more rhythmic and vigorous language and parallelism; the NRSV prints ch. 7 as verse. The "impressionistic, episodic" chapter (Greenberg) uses metaphor (v. 10), simile (v. 16), and concrete imaginative description (e.g., vv. 12, 14, 17-19, 26-27). It utilizes similarities between very different words or meanings of words: in vv. 12-13 wrath is *ḥaron,* vision *ḥazon,* and "return" and "be revoked" are the same form of the verb *shub.* It uses some rare words otherwise known only in poetry (it has especially close links with Isaiah 13, Jeremiah 4, Amos 5 and 8 [see below], and Zephaniah 1). By "grim irony" (Taylor) the familiar form of titles for God such as "Yahweh who sees/provides" becomes "Yahweh who strikes" (v. 9). While ch. 6 was not exactly cool and collected, ch. 7 is more visionary, jerky, and urgent. Its effect is intensified by its repetitions, of individual words such as "the day," phrases such as "the end has come," and whole sentences in vv. 3-4 and 8-9. It is intensified by the piling up of synonyms

for anger and disaster. It is "a piece of music circling round in mighty sweeps, and again and again returning to the one theme" (Eichrodt).

2. The vertical perspective on the land in ch. 6 (mountains and ravines) is succeeded by a horizontal perspective (the four corners, 7:2). Both emphasize the totality of the disaster to come, a prospect underestimated both in Jerusalem and in Babylon. "Land of Israel" is "ground/soil of Israel" rather than "country of Israel" (*'adamah,* not *'ereṣ*). The expression hints at the earthiness of Israelite attachment to the land. Its frequency in Ezekiel reflects refugees' natural distinctive attachment to the land.

3. "The four corners of the *'ereṣ*" would more easily suggest the four corners of the world. 7:2 thus also points to a catastrophe which is worldwide, not merely Israel-wide. Talk of an "end" and a "day," too, suggests an event of chronologically ultimate, final significance and not merely one episode in the history of the people (cf. Gen 6:13 with its talk of the "end" of humanity). Far from being preserved when other peoples are under judgment, Israel is at the epicenter of worldwide universal judgment.

4. In addition, the geographical perspective (mountains) is succeeded by a theological one. The "country of Israel" is the entire land which Yahweh had chosen and promised (20:5-6). Most of it had been the location of those 390 years of guilt and punishment, but it is still "the country of Israel." Conversely, the people Israel remains defined by its relationship with this land. The bad news is that its theological identity may seem to have been preserved only to be now finally destroyed.

5. The country-wide or provincial perspective of ch. 6 is also succeeded by an urban, capital-centered perspective with its focus on commerce, army, wealth, leadership, and temple.

6. The religious abominations of ch. 6 are complemented by moral and social abominations, particularly the accumulation of wealth through violence (7:10-11, 23-24). Again this parallels the flood story with its stress on violence (Gen 6:11, 13). The Noah story is a frightening warning to Ezekiel's community as it will be to Jesus' (Matt 24:38-41) (Blenkinsopp). Each is to be swallowed up by flood-like judgment instead of escaping it.

7. The "future" verbs (as they are translated) are complemented by "past" and "present" verbs: the end "has come" (7:2, 6, 7, 10, 12); it "is upon you" (vv. 3, 5, 6, 15). The certainty of what the prophet describes thus comes vividly before the audience's eyes and ears. It reappears in Jesus' declaration that God's rule "has arrived" or "is here."

8. The down-to-earth, literal language of ch. 6 (battle, destruction) is complemented by more metaphorical or mythic language which first came in Amos. The "end" is coming (cf. Amos 5:18-20): Ezekiel even uses the same wordplay as Amos ("the end" is *hakkeṣ;* "has awakened" is *hekiṣ*). The "day [of Yahweh]" is coming (Amos 5:18-20); here, too, the day which people thought would be a joy will be a horror (7:7). "End" and "day" do not point to different events from those mentioned in ch. 6 (e.g., more far-off ones) but indicate the ultimate, absolute, dreadful destructiveness and terror of the historical events which are about to overwhelm the land.

The pursuit of wealth without principle (7:10-11, 23), more general involvement in business (v. 12), the security of one's patrimony (v. 13), the assumption that defense or escape is possible (vv. 14-16), people's control of their own bodily functions (v. 17), their concern for money as the means of having enough to eat (v. 19), the making of images as aids to worship (vv. 20-21), trust in God's presence (v. 22), the security of one's home (v. 24), the insight of prophet, priest, and adviser as people who might help find a way through the crisis (v. 26), and the power of leadership (v. 27) — all are replaced by paralyzing panic and its results, and by invasion and death. Even for subsequent audiences that do not see themselves threatened by equivalent disasters, the relativizing of these apparent human securities and resources is significant; it also urges us to face what disasters might be about to overwhelm us.

Paradoxically, all this issues in recognition of Yahweh (7:27); it does not seem to be a very comforting recognition.

The State of Religion and Life in Jerusalem (Ch. 8)

The new date (in our terms, 592 BC) introduces the long vision in chs. 8–11. Ezekiel is at home (cf. 3:24-27); if people wish to discover what he has to say in Yahweh's name, they must wait there until Yahweh allows/compels him to speak. Chs. 8–11 again focus on the fact and the nature of coming judgment, but initially they speak of its reasons.

From time to time Ezekiel faces Jerusalem to address it, or addresses Jerusalem as if he were there, or beholds a visionary Jerusalem, all because of Jerusalem's significance for the deportees. Here he goes on a tour of the temple area. It is unnecessary to speculate that he must have been physically in Jerusalem. Visions do sometimes involve being taken to some far-off location; nor is this a sign that the visionary is mentally disturbed. Indeed, the vision hardly portrays a scene that one could actually have witnessed in the temple area at one moment, and 8:7-13 explicitly relate to rites people practiced in private and presumably at home. We have no other indication (e.g., from Jeremiah) that such rites were practiced in the temple area in this period, and apparently the vision summarizes or epitomizes Jerusalem's wrongdoing over the centuries as well as in the present, suggesting that it was all done in the awareness of Yahweh and in despite of Yahweh.

That it is God who appears is not explicit at first to the reader or (presumably) to Ezekiel (in 8:5 the NRSV makes matters more explicit; see the margin). What he sees is a fiery figure, no doubt humanlike, as heavenly beings who appear on earth are regularly humanlike (in v. 2 this is explicit in the Greek text but not in the Hebrew: fire is *'esh,* human being is *'ish*). He is lifted by this figure and carried off — surely by the "wind" rather than by the "spirit" (v. 3; on *ruaḥ,* see the Introduction, 623).

It was a sign of mercy and hope that Yahweh would appear in divine splendor in Babylon, and it is a sign of mercy and hope that Yahweh in the same divine splendor would still appear in Jerusalem (8:4), though this sign will turn into something more equivocal as the vision progresses. "Brightness" in v. 2 is *zohar,* the word which provides the title for the most important work of medieval Jewish mysticism *(kabbalah)*; see the comments above on Ezekiel 1 and Genesis 1.

The word "temple" may suggest simply a building like a church. The OT characteristically thinks of the temple building itself in the context of the wider temple area. Its modern descendant is the huge, paved, grassy, parklike enclosure and complex of buildings surrounding the Dome of the Rock, occupying thirty-four acres. Around the side were cloisters, stores, offices, and apartments, ringing a spacious open courtyard. Walled inside is an inner courtyard with the sacrificial altar in it. Inside that is the chapel-like main temple building.

In different parts of this area Ezekiel sees four scenes whose repulsiveness (religiously, personally, or morally) increases as they take place ever closer to the main temple building.

1. In the outer courtyard he sees an "image of jealousy" (8:5-6). Comparison with 1 Kgs 15:13; 2 Kgs 21:7; 23:6; 2 Chr 33:7; Jer 44:17-30 suggests that this was a jealousy-provoking image of a goddess of love and marriage who was understood to be Yahweh's wife. While there had once been such an image literally in the temple, in this period Jeremiah 44 locates her worship elsewhere in the city and surrounding country.

2. In the inner court Ezekiel sees the people's leadership worshiping serpent and animal deities (8:7-13). The seventy elders chillingly recall and contrast with Exodus 24 and Numbers 11, as does the role of Jaazaniah with that of his father in 2 Kings 22 (see also Jer 29:3; 36:12). These cults were actually practiced in private at home (hence the digging through the wall in order to see what people did in secret). There is some contradiction between their secrecy and their claim to believe that Yahweh cannot see them, which the vision is disproving; and whereas they are wrong in saying that Yahweh has abandoned the land, they are about to become right — their words are "ironically prophetic" (Greenberg).

3. Nearer the main temple building he sees women taking part in mourning rites before a god of the underworld (8:14-15). The god's descent there symbolized the dying of the plant world during the long, withering summer (the time of Ezekiel's vision), and his return symbolized its resuscitation with the coming of rain.

4. At the very door of the main temple building he sees a group of men turning away from it to worship the sun, a chilling parody of the stance and the practice expected in Joel 2:17 (Ezek 8:16).

These religious irregularities are exceeded in loathsomeness by the violence with which people fill the land (again cf. Gen 6:11, 13) (Ezek 8:17; we do not know what v. 17b refers to).

Rites such as those in 8:5-16 had a long history in the land. They antedated the worship of Yahweh which the Torah and the prophets approve, and kept surfacing through Jerusalem's history. They appealed to people by reason of their links with everyday life, and were encouraged by political considerations (they provided common ground with the nation's political overlords in Babylon or potential allies in Egypt). Ezekiel's conviction is that they constitute the people's turning from Yahweh, which goes along with moral and social disorder (v. 17) and has the effect of driving Yahweh away (v. 6).

Divine Violence, Minority Grief, and Prophetic Plea (Ch. 9)

The scene of killing and marking forms a horrifying parody of the Passover story, another device perhaps designed to shake people out of complacency. In Exodus 12 Yahweh by means of an agent of destruction passed through Egypt, killing men, women, and children. Here Yahweh passes through Jerusalem doing the same by means of six agents of destruction, like a special army unit of trained killers; the nature of the siege and war is to make women and children pay the price as much as men. The destroyers "might be thought of as a projection of the negative energy of the deity, the anger, grief, and frustration generated by unreciprocated love" (Blenkinsopp). "Basically, the enemy was God" (Greenberg). As Deuteronomy 7 warned, if the community behaves like those who were displaced in its favor, it will be treated like them. Far from the temple being a place of safety or refuge, killing will begin there (cf. 1 Pet 4:17). It was the point of central loathing at which ch. 8 ended, but also the point which saw the city's violence as the cause of its violent end (v. 9). The movement of v. 3a is the beginning of a frightening withdrawal which takes place through chs. 8–11.

Israel's inclination to "abomination" also went back to the exodus period. There something yet further had been established. As Yahweh's role was to declare the intention to destroy, a prophet's task was to challenge Yahweh not to do so (Exodus 32–33); cf. v. 8 here. Identified with Yahweh in loathing and in commitment to judgment, Ezekiel is also identified with the people in their pathetic helplessness, and for that matter with Yahweh in working out a purpose via Israel. Even divine violence as a response to violence begets only death, not life.

In response to Moses' intercession Yahweh appeared as the God compassionate and gracious, slow to anger and forgiving — though not clearing the persistently guilty or their children (Exod 34:6-7). Here there are to be no exceptions and no pity for the guilty — though the response "too late" may be designed (like many prophecies) to jolt people into a response which makes it self-falsifying.

But in Exodus 12 Israelite dwellings were marked so that the destroyer would pass by them. Here Yahweh commissions a marking by a figure dressed like a priest but bearing the equipment of a scribe or minister who writes down and implements a king's decisions. The worship and violence of ch. 8 are not the whole story. Elsewhere in the city are people who grieve over it. In English theological usage we may speak of them as a "faithful remnant," though the Hebrew word for remnant usually does not have this connotation. In his prayer Ezekiel had used the word "remnant" in its usual Hebrew sense; it means simply "people who are left" (after disasters such those of as 721 BC and 597 BC). The "people who are left" may *then* become the faithful remnant. Here in reverse the faithful minority are to become the remnant which survives. Whether the faithful belonged to particular groups we do not know; it is as likely that this constitutes a promise that there will be such people and/or a challenge that there must be as that it is a piece of information regarding their identity.

The Temple and the Throne Vision (Ch. 10)

Chs. 8 and 9 have already presupposed that Ezekiel's temple vision included the presence of the same exalted throne of Yahweh in splendor as he had seen in ch. 1. Here the split-screen nature of his presentation becomes more overt and the balance alters, the throne element becoming more prominent than the description of events "on the ground." Admittedly "split-screen" is a misleading image insofar as the temple's inner sanctuary was the place where Yahweh deigned to dwell among Israel. It represented on earth God's heavenly dwelling. In Ezekiel's vision and/or in his subsequent reflection the two come together as one.

This fact is symbolized by the figures of the cherubs. "Cherubim" is a hebraism which has the advantage of avoiding the connotations of the English word "cherubs"; these are not rosy-cheeked baby angels (see Gen 3:24). In the temple's inner sanctuary the cherubs were winged figures sculpted of olive wood and overlaid in gold, five meters high, their wings spread and touching so that they extended wall to wall across the inner sanctuary over the covenant chest (the "ark"). They are the invisible Yahweh's attendants and bearers (Pss 18:10; 80:1; 99:1), in appearance part animal and part human; the chest was perhaps thought of as Yahweh's footstool. Cherub figures were also carved on the temple walls, doors, and furniture. They and other features of the temple furniture in 1 Kings 6–8 (see also Exod 25:10-22) overlap with the creatures, wheels, and throne of Ezekiel's vision and presumably suggested its imagery in the same way as the visions in Amos 7–8 or Jer 1:11-13 started from the prophets' knowledge and experience.

Only now is the link specifically made between the temple cherubs and the creatures Ezekiel saw by the river (10:15). The audience could perhaps guess at the identification of Yahweh's splendor as Ezekiel saw it and Yahweh's dwelling in the sanctuary, but the holding back of this explicit identification makes for dramatic impact. It is underlined by the substantial repetition from ch. 1 which features in ch. 10. The elders now know more clearly that the God who has appeared to Ezekiel and who through Ezekiel speaks to them is the very Yahweh who was enthroned in the temple, on the same throne; there is reassurance and awesomeness in that fact. To put it the other way around, the very Yahweh who was enthroned in the temple and could be approached there has moved to appear in Babylon; there is solemnity and reassurance about that. With further solemnity, the vision takes further the motif of Yahweh in splendor withdrawing from the temple (vv. 4, 18-19).

So the heavenly throne and its cherubs are one with the earthly throne and its cherubs. The man in linen is sent to collect live fire from among them, and Ezekiel can move between the two scenes in 10:1-2 without a sense of transition because they are one scene. We now realize that the fire of ch. 1 is also the fire of the incense altar in the temple. From this twofold fire, the one representing the other, the man in linen took fire and then simply "went out," as v. 7 with extreme brevity puts it (cf. John 13:30). What is the significance of this fire? Gen 19:24 points one way, to the judgment which ch. 9 spoke of, as if the coals are incendiary devices; Isa 6:6-7 points another, to the refining which Ezekiel would prefer. The fact that we do not hear of its being actually outpoured again reminds us that the future remains open. The vision need not be fulfilled.

Politicians Planning but Paying the Price (11:1-13)

The scene, including Ezekiel's prophesying and Pelatiah's death, continues to take place within Ezekiel's vision, designed to address the refugee community. It parallels rather than follows what has preceded (the killing of ch. 9 has not yet taken place). The text does not say whether these are the same twenty-five men as those in 8:16-18, but they, too, are on the east of the temple, though located further away outside the inner court. They comprise the city's political leadership discussing how to cope with the prospect of another siege. Like the earlier twenty-five, they are implicated in the violence defiling the city (religious persecution? social disorder? political strife? the result of invasion, for which they are blamed?), taken to be the world's archetypal sin (v. 12). The understanding of sin here complements the stress on sin in relation to God in chs. 8–9. Yet they believe that they are safe in the city and formulate wicked political strategy accordingly.

Both halves of it (11:3) are enigmatic (RSV mg. thus turns "the time is not near" into a question). Addressed to Jerusalemites, v. 3a presumably denotes the priority of bracing themselves for further conflict; v. 15 might imply that there is no need to build houses — they have the ones the deportees abandoned. V. 3b then warns people to face the fact that they are like meat in a cooking pot. But the vision is intended for the deportees, and the words may rather apply to them, ridiculing the idea that they need to settle down for a long stay in Babylon (cf. Jeremiah 29, set in the same context). The second clause then expresses faith in the meat's security in the pot.

That understanding of the pot is presupposed by Ezekiel's reworking of their words in 11:7-11. The death of Pelatiah in the vision is the beginning of the fulfillment of his warning (cf. 9:6-7). Like those deaths, this death functions as a stimulus to further prophetic prayer (cf. 9:8). If the prophecy was ever reported in Jerusalem, it was designed to function there as a warning which would become self-falsifying if the men in the vision heeded it. We are not told what response Ezekiel's prayer received or whether Pelatiah actually died (contrast Jer 28:17). For intercessors and for politicians, once again that suggests the openness of events and the possibility of change.

The Vision's Implications for the Refugees (11:14-25)

As happened after the four signs, after the four-scene vision Ezekiel offers some teaching. Perhaps 11:14-21 answer the question in v. 13, but more obviously they make explicit the relevance of the message about Jerusalem to the deportee community. Contrary to the view in Jerusalem, leaving temple and land does not imply leaving Yahweh's presence, and staying in the land does not imply guaranteed possession of it. Yahweh's presence is among the refugees (v. 16). The prophet and the people *knew* that Yahweh met with them there, whereas Ezekiel can *see* Yahweh's splendor withdrawing from the Jerusalem temple to hover over the Mount of Olives (vv. 22-23). Yet Yahweh stops there as if hesitating finally to leave. For all the finality of the vision, the city has opportunity to turn.

So a priest with his commitment to the Jerusalem temple makes a bold declaration which disputes any theology claiming that people are essentially closer to Yahweh in Palestine than elsewhere and reasserts the old conviction that Yahweh is as present and active in places such as Mesopotamia and Egypt (see Genesis and Exodus).

And Yahweh will give them the land. No reason for Yahweh's choice of the deportees is given except the fact that they are the apparently rejected. Ezekiel thus agrees with other strands of OT thinking (again see the ancestor stories in Genesis). The deportees are no more responsive to Yahweh than the Jerusalemites. Their chosenness is like that of Israel's ancestors and of Israel itself (Deuteronomy 7). It reflects Yahweh's instinct always to do things differently from what is expected. But their mind will be renewed, and they will purify the land of the abominations portrayed in the vision (note the recurrence of the verb "remove" in 11:18-19). Frighteningly, only then will there be a "my people — their God" relationship (v. 20); apparently there is not one now (cf. 14:11; and compare and contrast Isa 40:1).

These promises are only outlined at this point, before the final fall of the city. They will be expanded after it (e.g., ch. 36). Compare Jeremiah 24; 27–29.

Dramatized Deportation (for People Who Cannot See) (12:1-20)

Ezekiel tells the deportees all he has seen in this vision (11:25). In the light of 11:19 (their minds have the flexibility of rock; cf., e.g., 2:3-7) neither he nor we expect them to listen (see vv. 1-3a). But prophets continue to minister even while speaking of their audience's being quite set against turning (see Isa 6:9-10; 43:28; Jer 5:21; also Mark 4). It is never over until it is over (12:3b). Ezekiel is to revert to the drama of 4:1–5:4, which followed the account of his first vision of God.

As in chs. 4–5, however, drama may not speak for itself (cf. Jesus' parables); it is followed by interpretation. Preaching is both inadequate and indispensable to the opening of deaf ears. Was Ezekiel's refugee journey a warning of another deportation, or a reminder of their sad leaving of Jerusalem a while ago, or even a promise of their beginning the journey back to the promised land? Next morning reveals that it was none of those. For Jerusalem, the worst is still to come. Once again Ezekiel's ministry involves a systematic focus on present and coming events in Jerusalem, designed to shake the deportees to their senses.

The dramatization of the experience of deportation may have several backgrounds.

1. Ezekiel and his community know from personal experience and from customary practice in the Middle East about the minimal contents of a refugee's luggage, the furtive breaking through mud-brick walls (or the scrambling through fallen ones), the advisability of fleeing by night, the humiliation of leaders reduced to doing the same as ordinary mortals, and the petrified fear which affects everyone.

2. There are points at which the dramas conform specifically to what actually happened in 587 BC. Ezekiel's visionary gift enabled him to have the foresight for that, and/or his relating of the dramas was subsequently conformed to the nature of the events themselves. Instances would be the capture and blinding of the fleeing Zedekiah (2 Kgs 25:1-7), who will arrive in Babylon unable to see.

3. There are elements of symbolism in the dramas. Darkness (12:6-7) suggests disaster and gloom, and when combined with 10:7 completes the anticipation of John 13:30. Covering the face suggests grief, shame, and humiliation. Avoiding looking at the the land when leaving emphasizes finality of loss.

4. Ezekiel's characteristic theological convictions appear in abhorrence at Jerusalem's "abominations" and its violence, and the intention that people (the Jerusalemites, the deportees, and foreigners?) recognize that it is Yahweh who acts.

5. Two instances of paronomasia are striking. "Carry," "prince," and "oracle" are related words *(naśa', naśi', maśśa');* the language points to the idea that the ruler and the people are a burden that has to be carried by the prophet and will be carried from the city. And the word for "exile" *(galah/golah)* can also mean "reveal." Ezekiel dramatizes deportation "in their sight" — the phrase comes seven times. "The prophet must force himself on their attention" (Greenberg). The passage speaks much of refusal to see, covering of faces, and blindness, though also finally of recognition; *golah* in one sense does become *golah* in the other.

The Problems about Prophecy (12:21–13:23)

Among Ezekiel's problems with prophecy was people's skepticism about whether it would ever be fulfilled

(12:21-25). His God-imposed or selfimposed isolation does not make him unaware of what is going on in the community. He often refers to the way they are thinking, though of course we only have his word for this being how things were. "Proverb" (12:22) translates the wide-ranging word *mashal,* which can refer to anything that is *not* merely a straightforward factual statement, such as a poem, a prophecy, an object lesson, or an aphorism.

Prophecy involves both forthtelling (declaring God's demands of people) and foretelling (declaring God's intentions), the two being integrally interrelated. Foretelling may be a strength of prophecy, people imply, but it is also its weakness: prophecy is talking about the future, so how can you know whether to take any notice? Ezekiel's direct answer is simply the affirmation that he speaks Yahweh's word; they had better take notice or they will discover the truth the hard way. But the word "flattering" implies the link between forthtelling and foretelling which makes Yahweh's action bound to come. The other prophets decline to say tough things.

Ezekiel's second problem was people's alternative reaction that prophecy would never be fulfilled in their day (12:26-28). Indeed, it has commonly been assumed that prophecy refers to far-off events, and clearly there are many prophecies relating to the "last days" which were not implemented in the prophet's time. There are also many concrete prophecies in Ezekiel which have been taken to refer to specific datable events in recent Middle Eastern history, or to events which will soon happen in the Middle East. Ezekiel's contemporaries also believed that his prophecies would not be implemented for years. He himself assumes that they relate to the imminent future. Prophecy is not designed to convey information about the distant future, of no direct application to those to whom it is given. It is designed to move people to action on the basis of its direct concern with those to whom it is given.

Ezekiel's third problem (ch. 13) was the activity of other prophets, women and men, in Babylon and/or in Jerusalem, who saw the situation of the community much more positively than he did and would have supported the stance it took to Ezekiel's prophecy. We may think of them as false prophets, but the distinction between true and false prophets would have been more difficult to make at the time. Like Ezekiel they said, "Listen to the word of Yahweh," or, "says Yahweh," shared their visions, sought to build up the community, and looked for their prophecies to be fulfilled. It is too soon to know, for instance, whether they or Ezekiel passes the test of whether their words come true (Deut 18:22), and Ezekiel may look more vulnerable than they to that test (again, see 12:21-28). Ezekiel might see Yahweh's mercy in the delayed implementing of the prophetic word; other people could read it as the prophet's discrediting.

When Ezekiel describes the characteristics of the other prophets, some point toward criteria for making this distinction, but none is watertight. Jer 23:9-40 is the OT's other great treatment of this issue (see also Jeremiah 27–29). The passages differ except in tacitly assuming that people of true faith and commitment to Yahweh do recognize Yahweh's word, and that people can be held responsible for whether or not they do so (cf. John 7:17).

1. Consciously or subconsciously their words and visions come from their own imagination and are lying falsehoods; Yahweh has not sent them or spoken to them (13:2-3, 6-9, 17, 19). No doubt they said the same about Ezekiel.

2. They are willful fools not prophets, *nebalim* not *nebi'im* (13:3).

3. Instead of building up the community's defenses, they are making homes in their ruins (13:4-5).

4. They mislead the community by saying that things are well when they are not, colluding with its pretensions about the strength it is building up as if disguising mud-brick walls as stone ones (13:10). "Peace" *(shalom)* covers community well-being in the broadest sense.

5. They indulge in traditional means of guidance, sacramental observances, and prayers which are supposed to protect their adherents from trouble or from demonic forces but will actually imperil them (13:18-19).

6. They associate Yahweh with these practices and thereby discredit Yahweh (13:18).

7. They dishearten the righteous and encourage the wicked (13:22).

As a result Yahweh is against them (13:8-9). They will be excluded from the community and have no place in the land (v. 9). Their falsehood will be exposed and their lives lost (vv. 11-16, 23). People will be rescued from their influence (vv. 20-23; in ch. 13 Yahweh keeps expressing his concern for "my people"). And Yahweh will again be acknowledged (vv. 9, 14, 21, 23).

Prophetic Priestly Judgments (i) (14:1-11)

Ezekiel's talk about Jerusalem's judgment for idolatry might have made people such as these Babylonian elders complacent and self-congratulatory, and quite comfortable about coming to seek God's word from Ezekiel, who, after all, is clearly on the same side as they. The response they meet (14:3) overturns that assumption. He is, after all, a prophet in the mold of Elijah and Elisha, with a mysterious ability to see into people's minds and/or into their private lives. He does not treat them as a prophet from whom people have the right to seek Yahweh's word. They are no better than people in Jerusalem. Yahweh's response to them, with superficial self-contradictoriness, is that they will get no response but action (v. 8).

One of a priest's tasks was to provide the community with God's guidance *(torah)* about how to act in different life-contexts; a book such as Leviticus collects such guidance for priests, who mediate it to people. Vv. 1-11 and 12-23 are prophecies (they use phrases such as "thus says the Lord Yahweh") but are framed as if they were *torah* ("If/when such-and-such a thing happens, this is how to handle the situation"). Ezekiel perhaps had Leviticus 17 in particular in the back of his mind. His words then metamorphose into prophecy, with a call to turn (the literal meaning of the word rendered "repent") and the implicit prospect of escaping the law's judgment. Prophecy in the sense of words which avoid this confrontation (a sideswipe at Ezekiel's prophetic contemporaries among the deportees?) is impossible; if it comes, it must itself be part of God's judgment (vv. 9-11).

Prophetic Priestly Judgments (ii) (14:12-23)

In this second instance of a prophetic warning which begins in the form of a piece of priestly case law, at first it is not explicit where the argument is going. Ezekiel's technique again sets an example which is taken up in Jesus' parables. The speaker carries the audience along with an argument to which they will regret giving assent when they see its implications (see 14:21). The parable form will also take up the device of repetition-with-variation which builds suspense through vv. 12-20.

Noah and Job are distinctively upright and committed people in their times and contexts in the OT (Gen 6:9; Job 1:1). *Dani'el* is apparently a different person from the *Daniyye'l* (as the names are spelled) in the book of that name, who would still have been a teenager at this time. *Dani'el* looks like another ancient hero; a wise *Dani'el* appears in 28:3, and an upright king of this name features in an Ugaritic epic. All three righteous figures are thus non-Israelite, in keeping with the fact that 14:12-20 concern God's working with peoples in general.

Overall, biblical thinking is more realistically corporate than that of the modern West. It recognizes that, for better or worse, the destiny of individuals is bound up with that of families, communities, societies, and nations. It also recognizes that this can produce results that look "unfair" to individuals. Thus Abraham challenges God not to kill the righteous with the wicked in Sodom, and God agrees not to do so (Gen 18:22-33). There are surely some righteous in Jerusalem; perhaps the elders asked Ezekiel whether the city might be preserved because of them. Ezekiel implies that Jerusalem can no more hide behind that than Sodom did, and the Babylonian community cannot hope for the preservation of Jerusalem on this basis. The upright save only themselves. Once again the inevitability of the city's fall is pressed on the people who have already been deported (cf. the argument about prayer in Jer 15:1).

Could a few escape, as happened at Sodom? Yes, says Ezekiel, sons and not just daughters, looking as if he is offering a glimmer of hope (to the parents in Babylon?). If it is this, as usual in this book it is a sardonic and tough hope, of the survival of a few not because they are righteous but because by their lives they will show why judgment was inevitable (14:21-23). By implication, the presence of upright Israelite adults in Jerusalem who would be equivalent to the three Gentiles is actually inconceivable.

The Downside to Israel's Being a Vine (Ch. 15)

The vine, the olive, and the fig are the most important trees in the Middle East; all three thus feature as figures for Israel itself. So Israel is God's vine, a noble, royal plant (cf. ch. 17). But whereas the solid, hard wood of the olive is useful for furniture, the soft shoots of the vine, copiously pruned each year, are useless except as fuel. It is this aspect of the vine which Ezekiel takes up in his barbed extension of the analogy between the vine and Israel. Like Isaiah 5, it is again rather like a parable, whose significance (because it talks about wood rather than fruit) might not be immediately apparent but comes in the last part. As in ch. 17, it poses a question in the form of a teacher's riddle, designed to make the class think out something for themselves without knowing what its implications might be. Like some of Jesus' parables, it incorporates an element of allegory: the interpretation in vv. 6-8 affects the way the parable itself is formulated (see v. 4). Like Ezekiel's earlier words such as the messages in ch. 14, it begins from a familiar form of speech (there it was priestly guidance) but becomes once more a straight, confrontational prophetic declaration of divine intent.

Images of Ms. Jerusalem's Womanhood (Ch. 16)

Again Ezekiel seeks to convince the Babylonian community that Jerusalem *has* to fall, though also to promise that this will not be the end. This time he does so by putting an autobiographical story on Yahweh's lips. While the story opens without a hint of its destination, 16:1-2 already make explicit that straight accusation is to follow (Zimmerli). Ch. 16 thus contrasts with the more open beginning to the riddle in ch. 15, though the chapters' themes and aims are ultimately similar.

Ezekiel writes to shock and to shake, and reaches his most shocking so far here in his epic portrayal of the harrowing life story of Ms. Jerusalem. If it opens in the beguiling manner of a "rags-to-riches" fairy tale, it soon devastates the audience with the extent to which no one lives happily ever after (Taylor) as its camera moves from abandoned baby to nubile beauty to nymphomaniac whore to brazen adulteress to heartless child killer, a woman no better than her foreign parents and arguably worse than her sisters Samaria and Sodom (see further ch. 23). It is the prophetic equivalent to a four-hour movie blockbuster with repeated scenes of sexual violence and violence on children, which no one under 18 is allowed to see. It became another passage in Ezekiel which rabbinic leadership hesitated to have read in worship (Blenkinsopp).

Ezekiel and his hearers knew well Hosea's portrait of Yahweh as the loving but rejected husband and parent of Israel, his wife and child. Ezekiel puts those two images together in order to tell Jerusalem's life story on a grand scale in a nightmare parable. He sees it as a sordid story and makes the point by telling it in a sordid way. It is more parable than allegory in the sense that the stages in the girl's life do not precisely match the stages in Judah's life. Rather, Ezekiel presents five scenes from a melodrama.

Where the story is heading is revealed in where it begins (16:1-5), as is often the case with a story. Geographically Jerusalem is a Canaanite city, and ethnically or politically it was a Jebusite one. Israel's own version of its history told how originally they failed to conquer it; its inhabitants were incorporated within Israel rather than annihilated. It is the pagan ways of its own people which are thus reflected in the way it has since behaved. Jerusalem's sin goes back to its foreign parenthood. Ezekiel believes in the original sin of the people of God (cf. Exodus 32; Deut 9:7-8; Isa 43:27).

So the value of the city derives not from its inherent worth but from the fact that Yahweh gave it the gift of life (16:6-7). Words such as "grace" and "love" do not come here, but these notions underlie or emerge from Ezekiel's understanding (cf. the comments on Israel in Deut 7:7-8; 9:4-6).

To put it another way, Yahweh is prepared to enter into a lifelong commitment to Jerusalem (16:8-14). Whenever someone is committed in love to another person, that conveys the gift of beauty as well as the gifts of love and life. Perhaps without intending to do so, the gift of love changes the one to whom it is given.

The trouble is that the gift of beauty can in turn change the one to whom it is given (16:15-34; on this, see in turn Deut 8:11-17). Illogically it can make the loved one turn from the one whose love bestowed beauty, and turn brazenly toward the world confident in the beauty which actually depended on another. Here allegory again breaks into the parable. The real subject is not a woman but a religious community taking on religious practices of which the prophet disapproves; see vv. 16-22, which also show that implicitly allegory already featured in the detail of vv. 8-14. Jerusalem's "whorings" are more literally her "abominations," religious practices which Ezekiel finds objectionable. The prophet again portrays the people's general inclination to persist in observing the religious practices of their Canaanite context with all their colorful splendor. He notes their inclination to political dealings with the nations around, which would also involve joint religious ceremonies. He makes particular reference to the practice of child sacrifice, not a regular form of worship but one undertaken in time of crisis or at other moments when people wanted especially to signal their devotion.

Ezekiel prosecutes his attack on the city's life by means of a characteristically baroque elaboration of the metaphor of God as father and husband. The male-portrayed God of Jerusalem is first a compassionate foster-father who says, "Live." The baby is abandoned as newborn girls in particular have often been in a number of cultures. But her foster-father makes it possible for her to survive, and she grows up. As in ch. 15, there is a parallel with Isaiah 5. To a vulnerable teenager he is a protective guardian who commits himself to a lifelong relationship and showers her with gifts which bring out her beauty and draw the world's attention to her and to him. To an ungrateful lover he is then an offended beneficiary. Ezekiel presupposes the male assumption that prostitution characteristically emerges from and expresses promiscuous lust rather than economic pressure. To an unfaithful wife he is a hurt husband who insists on the harshest penalty of the law. To a heartless child killer he is the bereaved father who demands blood for blood.

Ezekiel's confrontation, corresponding theologically to Deuteronomy 6–8, has great power because it is combined with Hosea's images. That is now its problem. Ezekiel has shocked and offended particularly in recent decades as readers have become sensitized to the portrayal of family violence and to male-determined portrayals of women. Whereas he was once thought to be a catatonic schizophrenic because of his strange behavior, he may now seem a sexual pervert because of this offensive aspect to his speech.

For modern readers, Ezekiel's portrayal of Ms. Jerusalem thus raises the difficulty that it offers five male ways of looking at a woman, all objectionable, especially when treated as a whole. For Ezekiel the man, this woman is either a helpless child, or a young seductress, or a sex-mad whore, or a brazen adulteress, or a heartless child killer. We can hardly infer Ezekiel's own psychology from that, but it does overlap uncomfortably with characteristic male fantasies about women. It includes no positive image of womanhood such as a woman could comfortably identify with. That was, of course, not its concern; the portrayal utilized negative images of womanhood in order to make its point about a city. But the existence of these pejorative images may seem to imply something about manhood in general, whether or not it says something about Ezekiel in particular.

Their incorporation in prophecy then runs the risk of giving validity to those images, with implications for men and women in general. It risks encouraging men to affirm such approaches to women. Indeed, by building on them, Ezekiel's prophecy can encourage their becoming not merely a matter of subconscious mental attitude but of verbal and physical sexual violence. And it risks encouraging women to accept this portrayal of themselves with its associated negative self-image and the violence which follows as what they deserve. While a man reading the story sees himself in the hurt pride and rejected jealousy which lashes out in jealous fury until its passion is exhausted, a woman reading the story sees herself in the destructive portrayal of her womanhood.

Once we recognize all that, however, an opposite dynamic can begin to operate. The prophecy brings out into the open within the Scriptures an important aspect of male attitudes to women, which men and women can then begin to come to terms with, to own, and to confront. It has begun to spur women to say to men in the context of the study of the Scriptures, "We do not recognize or own these portrayals of ourselves. There is something other than these which constitutes womanhood. These are male fantasies which you as men need to come to terms with and to own as that." It is up to men who read Ezekiel to hear that and to let Ezekiel's prophecy have this effect as part of its functioning as the inspired word of God which is designed to lead men and women on toward maturity in Christ (2 Tim 3:15-16).

The story began by impugning Jerusalem's origins, and it returns to this theme in the last scenes (perhaps later elaborations). That Samaria should be called Jerusalem's sister is not surprising. That her parents should be Hittite and Amorite is more so. That her younger sister should be Sodom is a nice further insult (cf. Isa 1:10). Jerusalem does each of these sisters the favor of making them look relatively righteous. Given Ezekiel's sexual imagery, it is noteworthy that Sodom's sin lies in its combination of good living with social neglect (v. 49), in line with the implications of Genesis 18 itself, not in the sexual practices which have preoccupied the Christian postbiblical tradition.

Once again the story ends with sardonic hope. Yahweh's relationship with Jerusalem will be reestablished, Jerusalem will come to recognize Yahweh, and Yahweh will forgive her. Whereas Jerusalem does not remember Yahweh, Yahweh remembers Jerusalem (16:22, 43, 60) (Zimmerli). In one sense there is nothing surprising here. It was not Jerusalem's inherent attractiveness that led Yahweh to her in the beginning, but Yahweh's instinct to love and to give life. Yet when sin has been faced, regretted, forgiven, and turned away from, something of its shame may long remain. Jerusalem will learn to remember (vv. 61, 63), with some inevitable pain. Characteristically, Ezekiel turns this into something that Yahweh actually intends. The object of Jerusalem's finding forgiveness is that she may be ashamed. All that talk is an expression of a longing to shake the city to its senses, and of an attempt to shake the deportees to theirs.

Another Puzzle, Another Broken Covenant and Oath (Ch. 17)

This fable/warning rounds off chs. 15–17. It is another puzzle like ch. 15, another riposte for the breaking of Yahweh's covenant and oath like ch. 16. "Duality pervades the prophecy" (Greenberg); it involves riddle and allegory, puzzle and interpretation, fable and threat, body and coda, warning and promise, verse and prose, two words from Yahweh, two concerns with acknowledgments of Yahweh, two eagles, a cedar and a vine, uprooting and withering, covenant and oath, Babylon and Egypt, exile and death.

"Allegory" is again *mashal;* see on 12:22. This fable about birds and trees is indeed an allegory in the sense that each element has a coded significance. In a fable, creatures and plants behave like people, though perhaps not in selfevidently intelligible ways. As a "riddle" or puzzle, the fable is more subtle and teasing after that in ch. 15. Like a detective story, it offers many clues, but it relies on the audience misinterpreting them until its end, when retrospectively its meaning may seem inevitable.

Thus far the eagle has been a heavenly figure (1:10; 10:14); the "great eagle" might suggest Yahweh in person (cf., e.g., Exod 19:4), and the lesser eagle some alternative deity. The vine was just recently Jerusalem (see ch. 15), and the cedar is also an image for Israel (Num 24:6). In the phrase "land of trade," the word "trade" is actually identical with the word "Canaan." So the audience would have background which enabled it to seek to interpret the fable.

If it did, Ezekiel's interpretation is very different from what it might have expected. The active and more imposing golden eagle is Nebuchadrezzar; the soaring eagle is the king of birds, and the eagle is a common military emblem (cf. Jer 48:40). Lebanon is Jerusalem, perhaps on the basis of all its Lebanese cedars (see Jer 22:23). The cedar shoot is the Judean king Jehoiachin, offspring of the royal "tree" (cf. Isa 11:1). The land of trade is actually Babylon, as it was in 16:29. The somewhat lowly vine shoot is Babylon's puppet king in Jerusalem, Zedekiah, Jehoiachin's uncle. The second eagle, also less imposing and inactive, to which the vine shoot inexplicably turns, is the Egyptian pharaoh. See also 2 Kgs 24:10–25:7 and Jer 52:11 for the general history. Jeremiah 37 describes Egypt's involvement without referring to an initiative of Zedekiah, but Ezekiel may have anticipated such an initiative on the basis of past Judean practice (see Isaiah 30 and 31).

The interpretation shapes the parable so that the latter contains elements which are "unnatural," while at the same time there are elements in the interpretation which go beyond the parable, and indeed details in the parable which do not receive an interpretation and are present for vividness and/or to put the audience off the track.

Indeed, the most striking feature of the "interpretation" is a point which is not hinted at in the fable (see 17:19-21). It emerges in the use of the words "covenant" and "oath." "Oath" *('alah)* also means "curse"; an oath would involve a curse on oneself if it should be dishonest. "Covenant" *(berit)* covers secular treaties, marriage vows, and religious commitments. Here Ezekiel makes characteristically bold utilization of the potential of its range of application. Nebuchadrezzar made (perhaps "imposed" would be a better word) an agreement with Zedekiah whereby the Judean king ruled on Babylon's behalf. It was "his" (Nebuchadrezzar's) covenant and oath. By v. 19 it has become Yahweh's covenant and oath.

There might be several significances to this language. Any solemn commitment would invoke deity, and breaking it would involve breaking a commitment made before God which invited God's curse (cf. 2 Chr 36:13). Any political commitment would be something which interested God, part of the nation's life with Yahweh. Yahweh insisted on being God of the whole of life; breaking it must be an act Yahweh was interested in. Nebuchadrezzar in particular is Yahweh's agent, Yahweh's servant (Jer 25:9), so Judah's commitment to Nebuchadrezzar is a commitment to Yahweh, and its rebellion against Nebuchadrezzar is rebellion against Yahweh. But the language of "my covenant" and "my oath" takes up that of 16:59. In 17:11-18 the sacred language of covenant breaking has been applied to a specific political action, but it has not been left there. There is thus a threefold movement in vv. 1-21 (Greenberg). There is the fable in vv. 3-10, then the political interpretation in vv. 11-18, but it transpires that even this is not the final message, for the political point is itself a parable of the religious point made explicit in vv. 19-21. That is how the riddle becomes a *mashal.*

The fable returns to give a positive close to the chapter (17:22-24), more unequivocally positive than ones Ezekiel usually allows himself (contrast ch. 16). The Judean monarchy will be flourishingly reestablished (cf. 34:23-24; 37:24-25), where it belongs, on the mountain height of Jerusalem, which is still to fulfill its destiny as the focus and source of security for the whole world (cf. Psalm 48; Isa 2:2-3). There this monarchy will take over the worldwide significance which is also its destiny but has been lent temporarily to Nebuchadrezzar. This goes far beyond the freedom Zedekiah sought; it will not come about because such a man is seeking to find his own freedom (Zimmerli). Yahweh in person will bring it about. The acknowledgment formula (v. 24) is thus especially elaborate.

You Are Responsible for Your Own Destiny (Ch. 18)

According to a long-standing myth, Israelite thinking took a major step forward when Jeremiah and Ezekiel enabled Israel to move from a way of thinking which subsumed the individual under the community to a recognition that we stand as individuals before God, responsible for our own lives independently of our membership of families and communities. The power of the myth despite its lack of evidence doubtless stems from the way it undergirds a vital piece of our own self-understanding. Ezekiel 18 is one of the passages that is assumed to support the myth by its declaration that a new age is beginning in which people will no longer speak in the old terms but in the new ones (vv. 2-3; cf. Jer 31:29-30).

A moment's reflection reveals that it is a myth (see also on 14:12-23). First, our own human experience indicates that the children's teeth are indeed set on edge by the sour grapes their parents have eaten. Warnings such as Exod 20:5-6 match experience; children suffer as a result of their parents' hurts and wrongdoings, as they profit from their parents' joys and achievements. This is not fair (see 18:25-29), but it is so. In addition to that "vertical" effect of one generation on another, there is a "horizontal" effect of people on their peers (e.g., husbands and wives or sisters and brothers on each other) whereby they cause each other undeserved suffering or bring each other undeserved benefit. It is part of being human, part of humanity's being a corporate as well an individual reality.

Second, long before Ezekiel's day Israel knew that people stand before God as individuals and not just as members of groups, and are responsible for their individual lives. Israel's stories from Genesis onward make that assumption, its entire system of law presupposes the responsibility of the individual, and its prayers in the Psalms presuppose that people come before God as individuals as well as corporately. The punishment of Achan's house as well as Achan (Joshua 7) is the exception, not the rule.

Third, long after Ezekiel's day Israel knew that people stand before God as groups and not just as individuals, as did NT writers such as Paul with their stress on the church as a community, even as a body. Being human involves both the individual and the corporate, and therefore Christian faith involves both.

It is commonly the case in Christian theology and in the church's life, as in other aspects of human thinking and life, that we find it difficult to hold together things that stand in tension. The relationship of individual and corporate constitutes an example. For a variety of reasons, modernity is characterized by individualism, and we evade the significance of the corporate, using prophets such as Jeremiah and Ezekiel to justify our imbalance.

Ezekiel's problem was the opposite one. It suited his contemporaries to stress corporatism in order to evade their own responsibility. Like our opposite imbalance, theirs arose from religious, historical, and political factors. According to 2 Kings, the event which made Jerusalem's fall inevitable was the reign of King Manasseh (687-642 BC), with the religious policies and the slaughter he encouraged (see 2 Kings 21; 23:26-27; 24:3-4). If that view was current among Ezekiel's contemporaries, they could quite understandably see themselves as trapped by their past, unable to evade its influence (cf. Lam 5:7). Ezekiel's view of the people's history in its unity (see, e.g., ch. 16) would hardly make him speak as if they were unaffected by their relationship with the past, yet he denies that this is a reason or excuse for moral, social, and religious paralysis. Paradoxically, we acknowledge the influence of the past (and of family, community, and national awareness and experiences) in order to distance ourselves from it, if we wish. The very act gives us freedom. It thus denies us the right the people claim, to make bondage to the past the basis for claiming victim status in the present, for blaming other people or events in the past for where we are now. In seeing our relationship with the past, we gain a form of independence from it and the capacity to live in the present. Indeed, when we come to own our own wrongdoing and failure, we gain a form of independence from that, too. We are not even bound by our individual past. The question is whether the people desire that. Yahweh longs that they should.

A converse is that the positive features of the past give no protection. Our parents' faith or right living gives us a foundation on which to build for ourselves. It does not give us our own building. Indeed, our own past faith and life is a foundation on which we have to continue to build; it never becomes a self-existent edifice.

Three forms of everyday speech come together in this chapter. One is that of theological argument which presupposes the way one side will state a case and the other side oppose it (18:2, 19, 25, and 29). As is often the case with such speech, this may involve speaking in theoretical, artificially polarized terms; few people are as unequivocally righteous or wicked as the argument implies. Another is the priest's offering of answers to pastoral questions (vv. 5, 10, 14, 18, and 21). A third is the priest's declaration of someone's uprightness which makes it possible for that person to resume full life in the community and with Yahweh (vv. 9, 13, 17, and 18). To a community displaced from the temple, this is an especially striking promise: there can be "life" with Yahweh even in Babylon if there is commitment to Yahweh's ways.

As usual, Ezekiel's account of human wrongdoing comprises a striking mixture of acts which we would be inclined to separate into different categories. Canaanite-style worship, love affairs, intercourse during menstruation, acts of oppression and violence, and failures of charity or of legal justice all belong together as characterizing the life Yahweh abhors. The mixture corresponds to that in Leviticus and Deuteronomy.

The chapter constitutes and closes with an urgent challenge to a fundamental change of attitude (36:26 will need to be set alongside this; the two form another tension which we must not resolve in favor of one or the other) but also a compassionate invitation to repentance on the basis that it is possible and life-giving (18:31-32).

A Mother/Lioness/Vine and Her Sons/Cubs/Shoots (Ch. 19)

The allegorical poem about two kings in ch. 17 was written in standard Hebrew poetic meter, dominated by six-word lines usually divided 3-3. This allegorical poem about the same two kings and one of their predecessors is dominated by the less common five-word meter, a more lyrical form where the line (commonly divided 3-2) keeps being a word shorter than one expects. Hebrew compounds words more than English, but the reader can often guess how the poetry works by focusing on the important words. This form is not confined to heavy-hearted songs, but it does characterize them. It is thus appropriate to a self-confessed lamentation at someone's death (19:1). Such lamentations were sung at the occasion of people's actual death; 2 Sam 1:17-27 is a famous example. Prophets came to sing them over the nation before it died, speaking as if this "death" had happened, as powerful warnings of its imminent demise; Amos 5:1-2 is a famous example.

In some ways this fable is less of a riddle than ch. 17; 19:1 gives the reader the clue to understanding it, though that clue lies outside it and might not be initially given to Ezekiel's original audience. With or without it, the first "cub" (lions still lived in the forests of Israel in biblical times) is one who was exiled to Egypt (vv. 3-4), which clearly enough identifies King Jehoahaz (see 2 Kgs 23:31-34), also called Shallum (see Jer 22:10-12), who had succeeded his father Josiah as king. Josiah and Jehoahaz were long dead, but Jehoahaz's mother Hamutal was still alive to be deported to Babylon with her grandson Jehoiachin (2 Kgs 23:31; 24:15) and no doubt became a powerful figure in the Judean community there.

The identity of the second figure is less certain. Jehoahaz was deposed by the Egyptians and succeeded by his brother Jehoiakim (609-597 BC). According to 2 Chr 36:6 he was taken to Babylon at one stage, but not permanently, and he had a different mother from Jehoiakim (see 2 Kgs 23:34–24:6). He was succeeded by his son Jehoiachin, who was exiled to Babylon (see 2 Kgs 24:6-17; also Jer 22:24-30). There could be reason for jumping from Jehoahaz to Jehoiachin to focus on people who had been deposed and exiled, but the emphasis on his achievements in 19:7 does not fit Jehoiachin, who like Jehoahaz reigned only three months before also being deposed. It better fits the last king Zedekiah (597-587 BC), who was another son of Josiah and Hamutal. If so, vv. 8-9 are a frightening prophecy. Zedekiah was currently reigning in Jerusalem. The people might have hoped that he would have a long reign like Jehoiakim, die in bed, and need no lamenting. Ezekiel rather brackets him with his predecessor who reigned but three months before being deposed and exiled.

Perhaps in Ezekiel's day the identity of the second king was clear; for us its unclarity draws our attention to the fact that in any case it is the last part of the fable which contains the sharpest point, and the allegory resembles Daniel's four empires and Jesus' parables in which it is the beginning and end that matter.

There is no doubt that the third prince is Zedekiah. This does not exclude the possibility that he is also the second, for the symbolism changes (but scholars such as Zimmerli and Eichrodt think 19:10-14 are a later addition). For this portrait his mother becomes a vine of which he is a stem rather than a lioness of which he is a cub. The second image makes a more overt link with ch. 17, though both images come together in Gen 49:9 along with talk of a scepter, the symbol of royal power. This puts us on the track of another question.

We began by noting that ch. 19 is less of a riddle than ch. 17, but it turns out to have a parable's characteristic lack of straightforwardness. Its introduction talked about the kings, and the chapter has given most space to them. But the lamentation itself began with their mother (v. 2; cf. v. 5), and she reappears when the figure changes from animals to plants (v. 10); it is the vine's fate with which the chapter closes (v. 14). It is the mother who holds the passage together; its concern is her fate more than that of her sons/cubs/shoots. So is the mother really Hamutal? In Gen 49:9 Judah is like a lioness, and in passages such as Hosea 2 and Ezek 23:2 the nation is the mother. The lamentation needs rereading against the possibility that it concerns mother Judah and her royal line rather than a specific queen and her offspring.

Elsewhere the OT is capable of being highly critical of all these kings. A striking feature of Ezekiel 19 is the absence of overt criticism. Admittedly the killing and devastation of vv. 3 and 6-7 and the loftiness of v. 11 could be read that way, but being carnivorous and growing tall are the business of lions and vines. Of course the unfortunate Jehoahaz and Jehoiachin, aged 23 and 18 respectively, hardly had opportunity to act very reprehensibly before being deposed. Zedekiah had more time for that (see 2 Kgs 24:20b). Yet oddly no explanation of the vine shoot's fall is given in the terrible account of its uprooting, withering, stripping, burning, and transplanting. Indeed, it may be that this underlines the devastating significance of the wasting brought to the vine itself by this stem. Mother Judah and her royal line are finished. There is no hope at the end of this chapter. To end with such complete gloom constitutes another attempt to drive the audience to see sense.

The Past as an Anticipation of the Present (20:1-44)

The people have now been six years in exile (the date is 591 BC); nearly a year has passed since 8:1. The consultation recalls the one in ch. 14 and will have similar results. We are not told its subject, and guesswork probably misses the point. In whatever connection the elders were seeking Yahweh's guidance, they experience brisk rejection.

What Yahweh wishes to say to them explains why Yahweh is more interested in asking than in answering questions, more interested in indictment than in behaving as if the relationship was in good order, more interested in exercising authority than in engaging in a consultation (20:4). At first sight the balance of the contents in Yahweh's accusation is puzzling. The section comprises one of Ezekiel's reviews of Israelite history. Reviews such as chs. 16 and 23 focus on the people's history in the land, especially on the behavior of Jerusalem. In contrast, most of 20:1-44 relates to the people's life centuries ago in Egypt and in the wilderness before they even reached the land. This might seem an odd preoccupation for a prophet who emphasizes that the ancestors' sins are not visited on their descendants (ch. 18).

Yet consideration of the past is commonly designed to enable us to see ourselves mirrored there. History has to repeat itself because no one is listening. Wherever Ezekiel looks, the past is the sound of which the present is the echo. Ezekiel's audience are people who now live in a new Egypt, and he wants to talk about a new wilderness experience that Yahweh intends for them, and a new entering into the land. The way out of the negative side to that is a change of religious life (20:30). They are inclined to follow their ancestors, but they are free to distance themselves from them, as ch. 18 has presupposed. Thus in vv. 31, 35-36 Yahweh once more declares an interest in confrontation, not consultation.

After the introduction the sections thus concern Yahweh's relationship with

- the people in Egypt (20:5-9)
- the first wilderness generation (20:10-17)
- the second wilderness generation (20:18-26)
- the people in the land (20:27-29)
- the people now in Babylon (20:30-32)
- the people about to be in the wilderness again (20:33-38)
- the people back in the land after that (20:39-44).

In his attack on the people's life, here Ezekiel focuses entirely on religious practices, particularly worship by means of images and the use of alternative places of worship. It is this which constitutes the people's "rebellion" against Yahweh. In this respect ch. 20 again parallels ch. 14. Once more Ezekiel refuses the elders the option of combining recourse to Yahweh with these religious practices, but he adds to the basis of his confrontation by setting their religious life in the context of the community's religious life as a whole over the centuries.

It is not so much a history of salvation as a history of sin, or only a history of salvation in that it involves Yahweh's repeatedly declining to act in anger and giving despite the people's lack of response. It parodies the way Israel would have told the story of Yahweh's mighty acts of salvation on an occasion such as Passover. It corresponds by anticipation to the large-scale narrative version of that history of sin in Kings which would be completed soon after, and to overtly confessional versions such as Psalm 106, except that it takes the form of accusation rather than narrative or prayer. In this Acts 7 will follow it (Eichrodt). It begins with a reminder of Yahweh's revelation as the one who brought them out of Egypt (20:5), but it will go on to subvert any inclination on their part to make that their security.

Ezekiel has a scheme for understanding the history of Israel as a whole which recalls the scheme in Judges. In the period up to the people's entry into the land this cycle recurs:

- Yahweh makes an act of commitment (20:5-6, 10, 17)
- Yahweh reveals expectations of the people (20:7, 11-12, 18-20)
- They rebel against these (20:8a, 13a, 21a)
- Yahweh contemplates annihilating them in anger (20:8b, 13b, 21b)
- Yahweh spares them "for the sake of my name" (20:9, 14, 17, 22)
- Yahweh acts in chastisement (20:15-16, 23-26).

Judges applies its "scheme" with much flexibility; the features which the stories have in common and the ones where they differ are both interesting. The same is true with Ezekiel's scheme.

On the one hand there is a repeated emphasis on Israel's rebelliousness, Yahweh's wrathful anger, and concern for Yahweh's name as a reason for mitigation. All these go back to Egypt in a way which does not characterize the Exodus story; thus the scheme again implies Israel's "original sin," though its immediate object is to facilitate the drawing of parallels between the original Egypt and the present "Egypt" in which people live.

On the other hand, there are dynamic features in the way the scheme is worked out:

1. Yahweh's acting in self-commitment is emphasized more at the beginning of the story. This is the only point at which Ezekiel ever speaks of Yahweh's "choosing" Israel. To emphasize parallels between past and current experience, there is no reference to oppression in Egypt; the focus is on the gift of land in its splendor.

2. The extent and the nature of Yahweh's expectations develop. In Egypt these focus on the abandonment of idols. This, too, appears here as it does not in Exodus because idolatry characterizes the people's life in their present "Egypt." In the wilderness, at stage one there is the gift of all Yahweh's statutes and ordinances, and the gift of Yahweh's sabbaths (which are gifts, not impositions or burdens). On the usual historical view, the Babylonian community was responsible for collecting Israel's "statutes and ordinances," while in its context in a foreign land the sabbath became of increased significance as an expression of Yahweh's grace and of commitment to Yahweh's way. Ezekiel's account of the wilderness period is again shaped so as to make links with his community's own position. At stage two there is then the "gift" of a regulation for the offering of firstborn (cf. Exod 22:29b). While it might have seemed perverse of the people to understand such a command to require literal fulfillment, other peoples' practice of child sacrifice might make this seem quite a plausible understanding. Yahweh's command thus brought death, not life. Paul will in due

course reckon this to be true of all God's commands (Rom 5:20). He is thus following Ezekiel in being willing to see Yahweh's strange intention in such a process; this attitude to Yahweh's sovereignty also featured in ch. 14 (see v. 9). Most references to the sacrifice of children come from the years just before and during Ezekiel's day (e.g., Jer 7:31, with a different theological interpretation); again the telling of the story is shaped to show its relevance to the present.

3. The extent and the nature of Yahweh's chastisement also develop.

4. At the beginning Yahweh's oath relates to Yahweh's being personally known to Israel in a relationship which would be expressed in the gift of freedom and land (20:5-6); later it relates to the reversal of that (vv. 15, 23).

There has been continuing variety in the tone of Ezekiel's portrayal of the future, moving from lyrical promise (ch. 17) to a challenge which puts the onus on the people (ch. 18) to hopelessness (ch. 19). Ch. 20 returns to the more paradoxical stance of ch. 16 which envisages wondrous restoration on Yahweh's part, but restoration with attitude.

1. Yahweh is simply not willing to have the people go off on their own; so they might as well give up trying even if this seems a reasonable response to Yahweh's treating them as other peoples are treated (20:32). It is a "vehement assertion of the irrevocability of God's election" (Greenberg), taken up by Paul in Romans 9–11, though often subsequently denied by Christians who speak of the church as the "new Israel" which as such has replaced the old Israel.

They will be brought out of their scattering among the peoples and taken into the wilderness, but that itself will be an act of anger as well as power, designed to make a proper confrontation possible (20:33-36). Yahweh's insistence on being "king," unique in Ezekiel, links with their insistence on being like other peoples (cf. 1 Samuel 8).

3. Once more they will be brought into covenant relationship, but not on an obviously voluntary basis (20:37).

4. Once more Yahweh will annihilate rebels (20:38).

5. Once more they will enter the land and offer right worship, but not worship to bring them unalloyed pleasure (20:40-44).

The contradiction between 20:32 and 39 again brings out an important aspect of the aim of much of the prophecy. It seeks to be self-falsifying. The aim of denying people choice is to encourage them to exercise choice. The aim of threatening anger is to shake them into response. The aim of warning about future confrontation is to get the community to settle for confrontation now rather than putting it off.

There is a play on words in v. 29: *bamah* (high place) is treated as divisible into two words, *ba'* ("go") and *mah* ("what").

Swords Drawn for Slaughter (20:45–21:32)

Verses 40-45 make a somewhat enigmatic ending to ch. 20, especially in the NRSV. Why is Ezekiel promising a forest fire in the Negeb, the desert area in Israel's far south? Even if there were more trees there in biblical times, these hardly comprised a forest, and why focus on the Negeb? For us, as for his prospective hearers, Ezekiel again seems to be acting as a composer of *meshalim,* a dealer in anything but straightforward factual statements (v. 49; see on 12:22; and compare ch. 17). In printed Hebrew Bibles, however, it is 20:45 which begins a new chapter, encouraging us to read vv. 40-45 in the light of what follows. They are in fact a riddle which receives its interpretation in 21:1-7. Perhaps the English chapter division was encouraged by the new introduction in 21:1, which presumably indicates a time interval between Ezekiel's receiving of the riddle and its interpretation.

In any case, "forest" more naturally suggests the Judean hills than the southern desert, and/or suggests the city of Jerusalem with its veritable forest of cedarwood (1 Kgs 5:6; 7:2). It stands for the Jerusalem temple with its various sanctuaries. The green and dry are the righteous and wicked; fire stands for the sword. In 20:46-47 the word *negeb* does not denote *the* Negeb at all — not "the South" but simple "south," as in 21:4; it is one of three words for "south" in 20:46. From his location in the home of the northern enemy, once again Ezekiel threatens a disaster such as would overwhelm Jerusalem in 587 BC. He does so by first trading on the fearsome connotations of the image of a forest fire, perhaps a more terrifying experience than the more literal image of the sword. It has even more irresistible destructive power, all the more so when Yahweh kindles the fire (v. 47). The fearsomeness of the sword itself is then underlined by the assertion that it is Yahweh's sword, drawn from its sheath by Yahweh in person and not to return there (21:5). As we read on, we discover that the motif of the sword drawn for slaughter runs through 20:45–21:32 as a whole.

Once again Ezekiel's hostile look represents Yahweh's, as is the case with the words which the stare accompanies and strengthens (cf. 4:3, 7; 6:2). Once again Yahweh warns of a judgment which will affect the whole people, righteous and wicked alike (as in chs. 4–5). To underline the severity of the judgment there is no reference here to the possibility of some survivors (as in ch. 9), nor of righteous people escaping (as in ch. 18). Once again the aim of what happens is that people may recognize Yahweh's act (20:48; 21:5). Recognition by "all flesh" comes only here in Ezekiel, but 21:4 suggests that "all flesh" means "all Israel," not "all the world." Once again even Ezekiel's emotional reactions are what they are because Yahweh says so (21:6-7; cf. 24:16). We learn of the coming of this word from Yahweh in the order in which Ezekiel experienced it; his original audience presumably began with 21:7.

In 21:8-17 the preparing and wielding of a sword is portrayed and commissioned. It is an efficient, frightening, destructive means of expressing Yahweh's anger. Placed after 20:45–21:7, this powerful, intense poem becomes all the more awesome an account of the drawing of Yahweh's sword against Israel. The poem itself has an efficient, frightening, destructive power as it commissions this sword to do its work, and the poet's own horror (21:12) adds to this effectiveness. At the same time it is designed once again to drive Israel to its senses before it is too late (so explicitly v. 13 if the NRSV's translation is right; but the Hebrew in vv. 10 and 13, and elsewhere, is difficult and the text may be in disorder).

As the chapter goes on, the focus becomes ever clearer. In the first unit the sword is prepared for use against Israel in general. In the second it is brandished specifically against Israel's leaders (21:12). In the third (vv. 18-27) the one who wield's Yahweh's sword is specifically the king of Babylon and its victim is one specific leader, the present king (Zedekiah). Ezekiel dramatizes the Babylonians' seeking to decide whether to turn left for Amman or right for Jerusalem (cf. the drama in ch. 4). Which of the two cities is to be punished for their shared rebellion against Babylon? The Jerusalemites make fun of the variegated pagan procedures for seeking divine guidance, as in a sense is right. They think they are safe in "Jerusalem the fortified," but they are wrong. Apparently Yahweh can even use pagan divination to guide a pagan ruler in fulfilling the calling he does not realize he has, that of serving Yahweh; once again Ezekiel reveals his radical convictions regarding Yahweh's sovereignty. The event will lead to the deposing of the faithless Zedekiah (see the preceding *mashal* in ch. 17). Indeed, it will bring Zedekiah's personal day of Yahweh (21:25). As the NRSV renders v. 27 with its allusion to Gen 49:10, it will also prepare the way for the rightful king (v. 27b); the poem does not make clear whether that would be the exiled Jehoiachin or some Davidic ruler still to come. But in any case the allusion to Gen 49:10 is probably more sardonic. The agent of God referred to is again Nebuchadrezzar, and v. 27b continues to refer to judgment, not restoration.

21:28-32 round off the sword chapter in a number of ways. The description of the sword follows that in vv. 8-17; the sword is now turned on the people who escaped it in vv. 18-27. The threat that Israel will be remembered for ill (vv. 23-24) is succeeded by a threat that Ammon will not be remembered at all. The reference to divination takes up that in vv. 18-27 and again declares that Ammon's escape will not be a final one. Then the Babylonian sword is returned to its sheath, no longer a threat; it is rather to be judged itself. "God's ultimate purpose is not that the sword should be unsheathed, but that it should come to be put back in its sheath" (Zimmerli). The reference to fire takes up the image in 20:40–21:7 and turns this, too, on Israel's enemies. In this sense the note of negativity without mitigation in the earlier units is qualified in the last, in accordance with a common pattern.

The Judeans in Babylon know from what is happening around them that the Babylonian army is setting off to put in their place the empire's rebels beyond the southwestern horizon. They could speculate and hope that its sword would focus on more imposing enemies than little Judah and that Yahweh's faithfulness would protect Jerusalem. Actually, the final siege of Jerusalem is about to begin. Ezekiel concentrates all his power as prophet, preacher, and poet to disabuse his community of false hopes.

City, Land, and People Characterized by Violence, by Irreligion, and as Dross (Ch. 22)

The focus moves back from the sword which will bring judgment to the reasons for this judgment (contrast ch. 21). Here the focus is all on the present (contrast ch. 20). The chapter comprises three separate messages from Yahweh concerning the shortcomings of the city (22:1-16), the people (vv. 17-22), and the land (vv. 23-31). Together they offer a sustained indictment regarding what makes judgment inevitable.

The first and third units both list a variety of specific ills. Ezekiel again interweaves moral/social and cultic/religious sins (cf. ch. 18). Sometimes the same act might have been seen through both lenses; offering human sacrifices to other gods (16:20-21) would be an example, as would some sexual acts. In other cases, we might characterize the wrongdoings as belonging to one category or the other, though Ezekiel does not separate them in this way, any more than do God's commands to Noah (and therefore the world in general) in Genesis 9, or the Ten Commandments, or the teaching in Leviticus 17–26 with which Ezekiel shares a common perspective, or the indictment in Rom 1:18-32. "Both the contempt for the ordering of the sanctuary and the ruthless denial of the neighbour's right to live . . . break up any relationship with God" (Eichrodt).

Thus on one hand Ezekiel is indignant about violence, civil disorder, dishonesty, robbery, extortion, the taking advantage of people who are experiencing economic hardship, false accusation and bribery of witnesses which lead to people's death, abuse of power, breakdown in family relations, and neglect or oppression of immigrant, orphan, and widow. The drift of the attack is indicated by the eightfold occurrence of the word "blood." "Faithful city" or "righteous city" or "holy city" (Jerusalem's destiny in Isa 1:26; 48:2) has become "bloody city," like Nineveh (Nah 3:1), and is liable to a similar judgment.

Ezekiel is also offended by religious sins, the use of images in worship, the observance of traditional rites of folk religion which he sees as incompatible with faith in Yahweh, the abuse of holy things, the profanation of the sabbath, irregular sexual relations, and neglect of the distinction between holy and common, stained and clean.

In 22:23-31 the focus is more on the guilt of the leadership in encouraging or conniving with both sets of ills. These leaders include rulers (if we follow the Greek rather than the Hebrew text in v. 25, with the NRSV), priests, officials, prophets, and landowners ("the people of the land" in v. 29). The past tense in v. 31 may suggest that vv. 23-31 come from after the city's fall. Its wording follows the indictment of the community's leadership in Zephaniah 3 as well as echoing ch. 13; both warnings have been terribly fulfilled. Like the last unit in ch. 21, it also links with earlier aspects of its own chapter and thus seems designed to round it off: "it" (v. 24) is the bloody city, the word "within [the city]" keeps recurring, the indictment follows that in vv. 1-16, and the pouring out of the fire of Yahweh's wrath echoes vv. 21-22 as well as the repeated complaint at the pouring out of blood.

The two sets of ills result in loathsomeness, guilt, defilement, danger, disgrace, shame, infamy, and lewdness. The city has forgotten Yahweh (22:12), the land is like one polluted upon which no cleansing rain has fallen (22:24), and no one is prepared to take the lead in urging reform and thus in being able to stand before Yahweh on the land's behalf (v. 30; cf. 13:5). They will therefore find that on the day Yahweh acts, their courage and strength will fail. In theory, being separated from the nations should have made them distinctive, but the theory has not worked; perhaps being scattered among the nations will work better. This will mean their profaning (according to the Hebrew text in v. 16) or even Yahweh's profaning (according to the Greek text which the NRSV follows), but then both are profaned already by what has been going on. It will also mean their being purged and forced to face facts. The gesture of v. 13 is one of dismissal — not a mere gesture but a means of effecting that dismissal.

The middle unit offers not specific critique but a single image to pass judgment on the people. Whereas they were supposed to be precious metal, or at least useful metal, they are actually slag. By being contained in the smelting furnace which Jerusalem is about to become rather than by being scattered, they are about to be smelted down as such. Characteristically, Ezekiel picks up a common prophetic image (smelting the people so as to refine away the slag) and takes it to its radical conclusion (smelting establishes that slag is all there is). Israel had begun its life in a smelting furnace in Egypt from which Yahweh rescued it. It will end it in a smelting furnace in Judah where Yahweh will do the opposite.

A Sordid Tale of Political Miscalculation as Sexual Excess (Ch. 23)

While comparable with ch. 16, the story of Oholah and Oholibah goes well beyond it to become the most pornographic chapter in Scripture. Before considering this aspect of it, we will look behind the imagery to the realities Ezekiel is referring to.

The two cities in some sense belong to one family or one people and have a common history (23:1-4). Ezekiel again portrays that history as revealing a failure in commitment which goes back to its very beginnings and reaches into its inner depths. The story of Israel's stay in Egypt in Exodus 1–12 does not put the point in the same terms as Ezekiel does, but it, too, declines to be romantic about the people's original state. But whereas Exodus 1–12 sets the people's resistance to Yahweh in the context of their plight in Egypt, Ezekiel 23 speaks only of the people's wrongdoing there. Unlike the "love" story in ch. 16, this chapter contains no recollection of a period of divine grace and love at the story's beginning.

It is not clear what we are to read into the actual names Oholah and Oholibah. The word *'ohel* means "tent" and could refer to an ordinary bedouin dwelling tent (e.g., Genesis 18), or to Yahweh's dwelling tent (e.g., Exodus 33), or to the equivalent tent at another god's shrine, or to a marriage tent (2 Sam 16:22). Any of these connotations might come into people's minds when they heard Ezekiel use the two names, but he offers no interpretation of them, and names such as these are common without their having deep significance. They may just be names.

Two sections, then, deal with the two cities which the sisters stand for (23:5-10 and 11-35). Each section is concerned with the city's involvement with major foreign powers, which would involve both political subservience and some acceptance of their religious practices. Ezekiel's emphasis on the attractiveness of their warriors and cavalry, however, draws attention to the military benefits which the cities hope to gain through subservience to or alliance with foreign powers. Several religious, theological, or ethical issues emerge here. One is the inclination to take false responsibility for one's destiny and to trust in foreign powers rather than in Yahweh's power (cf. Isaiah 30–31). Another is the inclination to engage in warfare on the same basis as other peoples and on the basis of mere considerations of power rather than regarding war as Yahweh's business. Related is OT suspicion of sophisticated military hardware. A fourth issue is the recurrent further suspicion of culture and civilization and of human impressiveness in general.

The fate of Oholah/Samaria (23:9-10) corresponds rather literally to the actual fate of women when a city was taken. In the succeeding section Oholibah/Jerusalem is dealt with at much greater length; it is more directly relevant to the hearers. Like that on Samaria, the section begins with Jerusalem's involvement with Assyria (see, e.g., Isaiah 7) and notes its failure to learn from Samaria's fate. In vv. 14-18, again relating to its hearers' circumstances, it moves on to the city's involvement with Babylon, with its own impressiveness, youthfulness, and strength; vv. 14-15 presumably refer to carvings the exiles could see. In vv. 19-21 the section moves back to Egypt, addressing contemporary Judean policy of seeking alliance with Egypt as the city's fall to Nebuchadrezzar drew near. Again Egypt is no longer the place where Israel once met God and knew God's marvelous grace and deliverance but the place of temptation and sin.

After the paragraph concerning Jerusalem's policies (23:11-21) comes one concerning its prospective fate (vv. 22-35). Under Manasseh and his successors, Jerusalem did its best to play international politics as the political scene changed during the last years of the Assyrian Empire, the Chaldeans' coming to power in Babylon, and the Babylonians' becoming the major Middle Eastern power. Jerusalem thus turned its political allegiance this way and that as circumstances seemed to point. Technically the Babylonians are the indigenous people of Babylon and the Chaldeans are an Aramean group from further east who gained political power there at the end of the seventh century. The names of Pekah, Shoa, and Koa recall those of other Aramean peoples from the eastern part of the Babylonian Empire, but they also sinisterly recall Hebrew words for "punish," "cry," and "shriek" (Eichrodt). Through them the city will discover the well-known but generally ignored political fact that today's allies and benefactors are tomorrow's enemies and oppressors. Acceptance of responsibility for one's destiny and trust in other peoples turn out to be unwise;

the hardware and the sophistication turn against you. The trust is misdirected not merely because of the direction it took but because of the God it avoided and deliberately put out of mind, and it will be judged not merely by failure but by Yahweh's positive act (vv. 25, 35).

The final section (23:36-49) recapitulates both cities' wrongdoing and punishment. The more specific account of wrongdoing in vv. 36-39 recalls that in ch. 22 with its two aspects. Both cities are condemned for what went on in the Jerusalem temple: Ezekiel regards the nation as one and treats northern Israel as responsible for wrongs in the temple, as it will be the beneficiary of the whole people's restoration. The foreign peoples' relationship with the two cities (vv. 43-44) again suggests the cynicism of political involvements. Great powers use smaller powers in whatever way they choose, and smaller powers are extraordinarily naive in not seeing that this is what happens. Whereas the culture and civilization of the foreign powers has been emphasized earlier, now they are merely "a riff-raff of desert-dwellers or drunkards" (Taylor). For all that, they are "righteous" judges in the sense that they bring about Yahweh's just judgment on the two cities (v. 45), which pay for their miscalculation with their lives as they are assailed by missiles, sword, and fire (vv. 46-49).

To bring this message home, Ezekiel again takes up a well-known prophetic motif and develops it on a baroque scale. Folk religion sometimes thinks of a relation between heaven and earth which is like marriage and which as such enables the earth to be fruitful. This notion was applied to Yahwistic religion within popular Israelite faith, but was opposed by prophets such as Hosea. It lies more distantly in the background than was the case in ch. 16, being subordinated to a presentation in terms of "the complete humanity of the two women" (Zimmerli).

This gives the story its modern, immediate, scandalous, pornographic character. The reason, however, lies in the concentrated focus on the issues of history and politics rather than the issues of nature and fertility. As in ch. 16, the motif of sexual promiscuity provides Ezekiel with a powerful image to convey the abhorrent nature of Jerusalem's wrongdoing. Here he uses it to suggest more radically the way Jerusalem's failure reaches to the depths of its being. Whereas ch. 16 attributed promiscuity to Ms. Jerusalem only after Yahweh's marriage to her, in ch. 23 the two women are promiscuous from youth. The OT's willingness to tell this daring story about Yahweh's marriage to a pair of promiscuous women has provided African Christians with reason to question whether polygamy could have been so wrong that missionaries were right to insist on the dissolution of polygamous marriages.

The male prophet thus has resort to an image which is natural to a man, though hard for a woman, and in the end destructive for a man. It works by utilizing male distaste for female promiscuity to express and encourage distaste with contemporary political policies in Jerusalem. No doubt the formulation of such policies was largely undertaken by men; it was men Ezekiel had to get through to. The difficulty is that it risks colluding with male fascination with the idea of such promiscuity.

Male concerns become clearer as the chapter unfolds; in 23:36-49 the personifications of Samaria and Jerusalem give way to a concern with individual women and the dangerous temptation they are to men. The use of the image can imply that promiscuity is women's problem rather than men's and that women are inherently inclined to promiscuity in a way that men are not. Once again as men and women we have to note that this is not so. And the opening of the chapter has suggested that Ezekiel knew that. He began by telling us that the two sisters indulged in extramarital sex (v. 3a; "played the whore" is an overtranslation). But he explicated this in terms of what was done to them by men rather than by what they themselves did. The chapter thus makes clear that men have a problem with their inclination to sexual promiscuity.

On the Eve of the Fall of Jerusalem (Ch. 24)

A turning point is reached. The date is 15 January 588. Jerusalem's final fourteen-month siege has begun. Apparently Ezekiel discovers this by revelation or extrasensory perception, not through word coming by messenger (24:1-2). He is to write it down so that his claim to speak by Yahweh's revelation will be buttressed when news of the siege arrives by ordinary routes.

Now that the picture in 21:18-21 has come true, it is time for a new one. Characteristically, the picture Ezekiel is to offer the community in his cooking pot song with its choice meat and marrow bones (24:3b-5) is enigmatic. Did it promise a feast and thus imply the arrival of good news? Or were hearers expected to recall the previous appearance of a cooking pot symbolizing a city in 11:3?

The further words from Yahweh in 24:6-8 and 9-14 make the picture's meaning more explicit but take the interpretation in different directions from any implicit in the picture alone, again characteristically. The meat in the pot in 11:7 is the bodies of the slain. Here, too, reference to the pot's meaty contents (24:6b) leads to a further indictment of the "bloody city" of ch. 22. This indictment suggests or is suggested by another possible accompaniment to the meaty contents of a cooking pot, a rusty scum. In picture and word, the red of meat, the red of blood, and the red of rust come together. The meat is neither safe in the pot nor destined to be roasted there, but it is spoiled and indiscriminately thrown away (v. 6). What spoils it is that other redness, rust/blood. Jerusalem's life of violence has been lived openly and flagrantly and the blood shed there cries out for vengeance (cf. Gen 4:10).

The second word makes the same point by focusing more on the rusty pot itself. Its contents are cooked (24:9-10), but the pot is left on the fire to see if its rust and filth can be burned away (v. 11). Any cook knows that this does not work (vv. 12-13).

The frightening picture is accompanied by a frightening experience (24:15-17) and a frightening drama (vv. 18-19) with a frightening message (vv. 20-24). Apparently Ezekiel's wife's death came out of the blue; v. 16a does not suggest that she was already ill. Presumably her death comes about through some physically describable illness or accident, yet she dies suddenly and by Yahweh's will. There is no suggestion that Ezekiel was an unfeeling person who would have found his personal experience and that of the city easy to cope with; rather, the opposite. She *is* "the delight of his eyes" (v. 16); so is the Jerusalem sanctuary (vv. 21, 25). Yahweh knows that, knows the pain to be inflicted on Ezekiel (there is no reference to awareness of the rights of his wife). Yet the laconic report in v. 18 also suggests the steely submission to Yahweh's will which suspends personal feelings. The loss of the wife he loves is a sign of their losing the city they love and losing the families who will be killed there. These losses are guaranteed by the actuality of what was already happening in Ezekiel's life.

What is imminent for the city is terrible but deserved. To prepare his community for it, what now happens to Ezekiel and his wife is terrible but undeserved. Marriage and ministry are interwoven for them as they are in different ways for prophets such as Hosea, Isaiah, and Jeremiah. Yahweh's sovereignty does not stop short of their dearest relationships. It is precisely people's dearest relationships, with inexhaustible potential for happiness, self-giving, selfishness, and loss, that show inexhaustible potential for setting forth Yahweh's message. To be drawn into Yahweh's service involved these relationships being part of the proclamation.

In Ezekiel's community, mourning involved groaning, lamentation, weeping, the setting aside of formal dress and footwear, veiling, and abstention from one's usual food (24:15-17). The combination of such an inner emotional and outward physical response appears in many cultures, though that response is expressed in different cultural forms. Yet there are times when loss is so great that its shock inhibits mourning, or that no mourning is adequate. Jerusalem's fall will likewise be so terrible as to be paralyzing or incapable of appropriate response (vv. 19-24).

Yet it will also be freeing. It will end the constraint Yahweh imposed on Ezekiel at the beginning of his prophetic ministry (24:25-27; see on 3:22-27). For the people, too, the falling of judgment will mean that the time for a message of promise will come, not because the community have now seen sense and have changed but because the blood has been covered. The form of expression in vv. 25-27 is confusing. Ezekiel perhaps means that a messenger will leave Jerusalem on the day it falls, and that Ezekiel will be free to resume normal relationships on the day he reaches the community in Babylon with the news; there will, of course, be a significant gap between these days (cf. 33:21-22).

Judgment on Other Nations (Chs. 25–32)

Chapters 25–32 function in the manner of a chorus or interlude in a Greek or Shakespearean drama. After ch. 24 has brought the book to its turning point, chs. 25–32 play for time. With the deportee community, readers wait for the arrival of news concerning Jerusalem's capture. In this way chs. 25–32 fulfill a different function from the equivalent blocks of prophecies in Amos 1–2 (which soften up Israelite hearers before indicting them), Isaiah 13–23 (which bridge the book's concern with Judah in chs. 1–12 and with the whole world in chs. 24–27), and Jeremiah 46–51 (where they virtually close the book). Like the prophecies in Amos 1:3–2:5 they concern seven peoples, which hints at a similar worldwide concern to that in Isaiah 13–27 as a whole. They fit into a pattern which the OT recognizes begins outside Israel in the work of the prophet Balaam (Numbers 22–24); it runs through the OT prophets and continues in the NT in the prophecies on Babylon/Rome in Revelation. They thus contrast with the strand of more positive, less tough concern for other peoples which also runs through both OT and NT.

The prophecies have a broadly common subject but vary in focus and in form, combining down-to-earth prose and vivid poetry. They begin with Judah's four immediate neighbors to the east and south, treated clockwise (ch. 25), but give least space to these peoples about which Judah had strongest feelings. The prophecies then move to two powers further north (chs. 26–28), which had also been Judah's allies. They give much more space to the first of these two peoples because of its significance in terms of current international events. Finally, they come to the major international power to the far south and give the most space to it (chs. 29–32); in the light of earlier chapters, we are not surprised that Egypt is the power about which the community needs to think most. Tyre and Egypt are the two powers in Judah's region about which Nebuchadrezzar will have to think most and thus which have most prospect of providing Judah with the satisfaction of seeing Babylon defeated.

There is no prophecy against Babylon itself; contrast the lengthy treatments in Isaiah 13–14, where it comes first, and in Jeremiah 50–51, where it comes last. Babylon is here on the side of the angels, the agent of these peoples' punishment (explicitly of Tyre and Egypt; e.g., 26:7; 30:24). The parallel with Amos perhaps also suggests that the declaring of judgment on Judah's neighbors does function to soften up the community for what Yahweh has to say about Tyre, and especially about Egypt.

The prophecies form a bridge between chs. 1–24 and 33–48 by their content as well as their position. They resemble what has preceded by continuing to declare Yahweh's judgment. They differ from it by changing the object of judgment, and their promising judgment on other peoples enables them to form a bridge toward what follows in chs. 33–48 with their promise of restoration for Israel. Chronologically, they come from during the siege of Jerusalem or after, but the dates also show that they are arranged by subject rather than by date. As we have it, their editing must postdate the last of the prophecies (see 29:17), but it shows no awareness of the decline and fall of Babylon.

The prophecies against other nations presuppose that Yahweh is sovereign over the whole world. They presuppose that other nations are subject to moral and social demands, or that the moral and social demands presupposed in Israel are not merely Israel's cultural peculiarities. They also presuppose that these nations ought to have recognized the significance of Yahweh's dealings with Israel.

the nations are on equal terms with Judah, for that is Yahweh's purpose in acting in judgment on Judah, too, and in restoring Judah.

Judgment on Judah's Near Neighbors (Ch. 25)

Judah had lived in uneasy coexistence and recurrent conflict with its Ammonite, Moabite, Edomite, and Philistine neighbors over its entire lifetime, as the community's tradition ever reminded it. In this sense the prophecies of judgment start where the community is, with the peoples who were significant for it in terms of geography and tradition. No doubt these peoples' prophets uttered oracles of judgment against Judah for its hostility to them, such as Moab sought from Balaam in Numbers 22–24.

The prophecies in ch. 25 presuppose that Jerusalem's fall has actually happened. No doubt Judah's neighbors did gain some satisfaction when Judah got its comeuppance (vv. 3, 6, 8) and did take the opportunity to settle old scores (vv. 12, 15), though we have little specific information on this. They were in any case only acting in conformity with the judgment of prophets such as Ezekiel, and Judah would no doubt have done the same if the circumstances had been reversed.

All four peoples did cease to exist sooner or later. Whether one sees that as coincidence and Ezekiel's declaration of judgment as justified depends on theological convictions. Is there something special about the Jerusalem temple, the land of Israel, and the house of Judah (25:3, 6, 8, 12)? If so, God can hardly stand by in the end, when they are treated as just another sanctuary, land, and people.

We have more concrete (Israelite) evidence for hostile actions in this period on the part of Ammon and Moab (see, e.g., 2 Kgs 24:2). But it is the second pair of prophecies that focus on actions rather than words, though the offense is simply a general seeking of vengeance. This may suggest that the problem about these peoples came as much from within Judah's own spirit as from their actions themselves. They are the externalization of Judah's own guilt, fear, and shame. They would in any case also be a prominent topic of Judah's prayers; see the many pleas for the punishment of enemies in the Psalms (e.g., 74; 79), and indeed specifically Ps 137:7; also Lam 4:21-22. Prophecies such as these are the response from Yahweh which the prophet offers to such expressions of communal grief and loss. Whereas other nations will be the means of Yahweh's judgment on Ammon and Moab, Israel will itself then execute Yahweh's "punishment" of Edom (the NRSV's "vengeance" gives a misleading impression of the meaning of *neqamah*), and Yahweh will apparently punish Philistia directly.

Behind the question why Judah is special is a question about God. Is there something special about Yahweh? All these warning prophecies aim at the peoples' acknowledging Yahweh as the real God (25:5, 7, 11, 14, 17). Clearly there are limitations to the acknowledgment of God which can be forced by the executing of punishment, but at least in this drive to such acknowledgment

Judgment on Tyre and Sidon, Two More Ex-Allies (Chs. 26–28)

The city-state of Tyre sits in an imposing position on the Mediterranean coast between northern Israel and modern Beirut. The Phoenician peoples on this coast were much involved in exploring, trading, and empire building across the sea and were well known for their wealth and culture. Tyre was the greatest of these cities. Now linked to the mainland, in OT times it comprised a rocky island ("Tyre" means "Rock") and a further city on the shore, each with a harbor (see 27:3), with an area of dependent villages inland (cf. 26:6). It was a flourishing trading city (see 27:1-25) which had had a long-standing relationship with Israel (see 2 Sam 5:11; 1 Kings 5; 9:10-14, 26-28).

At first the declaration of judgment on Tyre in 26:1-6 looks like another in the sequence which occupies ch. 25, and the judgment on Sidon in 28:20-23 forms a pair with it. Tyre and Sidon (just to the south) appear in Jer 27:3 along with Edom, Ammon, and Moab, apparently as involved with Judah in rebelling against Babylon. The date in 26:1 presumably locates the judgment on Tyre after the fall of Jerusalem (587 BC), which is presupposed by 26:2, which means it must belong at the end of the "eleventh year" — perhaps "in the eleventh month" has dropped out of the text because of the similarity of the words. The Judean community imagines Tyre rejoicing in Jerusalem's fall because of the possibility of inheriting the trade or the political significance of Jerusalem as a city which had become a major crossroads. There is irony here; the Judeans are rather fanciful about their city's significance compared with Tyre's. The description of Tyre's threatened fall (26:3-6) matches the city's location, as did those in ch. 25, and the object is again the acknowledgment of Yahweh (26:6); so also with the judgment on Sidon (28:22, 23). The specificity of the Tyre prophecy matches that of the Ammon and Moab prophecies, while the generality of the Sidon prophecy matches that of the prophecies against Edom and Philistia, though it opens (28:20) more like that against Ammon.

The six judgments are then closed off by a paragraph declaring their significance for the Babylonian community (28:24-26). Scattering, insecurity, and shame will give way to restoration, at-homeness, safety, dignity, Yahweh's manifestation to other peoples, and Yahweh's acknowledgment in the community.

Set into the framework of two judgments which close off the series against Israel's neighbors and allies is a much bigger body of material concerning Tyre (26:7–28:19). The opening of this material (26:7) points to the reason for its inclusion, the particular resistance Tyre offered to Nebuchadrezzar (a form arguably closer to the Babylonian *nabu-kudurri-usur* than Nebuchadnezzar). Resistance was the stance sometimes taken in Jerusalem, and presumably also in the Babylonian community.

Tyre's setting made it possible for its people (or at least its leadership and upper class) to hole up in their island fortress when necessary, as the Jerusalem community could in their city. Able steadfastly or stubbornly to resist Babylonian siege for more than a decade, Tyre epitomizes resistance to the historical will of Yahweh whose agent Nebuchadrezzar is, resistance also urged and practiced in Jerusalem.

The material comprises units of varied form and nature, arranged into two pairs: a set of short prophecies about the fall of the city of Tyre in 26:7-21 and a lament at this event in ch. 27, then a matching prophecy about the fall of the king of Tyre in 28:1-10 and a lament at this event in 28:11-19.

We do not know what ended the Babylonian siege of Tyre in 574. In some way Tyre did submit to Babylon, but it was not forcibly conquered until Alexander the Great's campaigns in 332 BC. The development of these oracles on Tyre has sometimes been linked with Alexander's conquest. It was during Alexander's siege that the causeway was built which silted into a permanent neck of land joining Tyre to the mainland. But the oracles lack concrete evidence of connection with the Greek period to match the concrete indications of a sixth-century context. In 29:17-20 Ezekiel himself notes that the prophecy here has not come about and indicates what Yahweh intends to do instead.

A Warning of the Siege, the Fall, and the Drowning of Tyre (26:7-21)

Ezekiel begins by portraying the nature of a siege (26:7-14). For the most part the portrayal is conventional and not directly applicable to the particularities of an island-city. He then envisages the smaller cities around appalled at the city's fall (vv. 15-18). Here the picture is more oriented to the particularity of a maritime power. Finally, he imagines the island being drowned in the sea (vv. 19-21). The element which seemed to be its protection becomes its downfall. At this climax Yahweh is explicitly and emphatically the agent of what happens. As in Gen 7:11, the Deep which God restrained (Genesis 1) is once again let loose, here in a concrete political event. The further image of drowning again starts from the particularity of Tyre's position, which suggests the figure of the city going down to the mythical watery underworld. The alternative image of a Pit is suggested by the alternative literal reality of people being buried in a communal grave, cave, or pit. There when they die people join their family in a place of dissolution and nothingness from which no one returns. This is Tyre's destiny.

A Lament at the Wreck of the Mighty Merchant Ship Tyre (Ch. 27)

In ch. 27 another funeral lament over Tyre follows. As with other prophetic funeral laments (see on ch. 19), the subject's coming death is brought home with particular power by being talked about as present fact. Tyre is dead enough to be buried. Even more force is added by the lament's being not only commissioned by Yahweh (27:1) but composed by Yahweh (v. 3).

Typically, when Ezekiel sets mind and imagination to composing a serious funeral lament, it is on a gargantuan scale. He envisages Tyre's natural pride at its position and imagines it as a giant oceangoing merchant ship made of the finest imported raw materials and served by the best local and international crew and staff (27:1-11). Tyre's exquisite beauty (a reference to its majestic position) forms an *inclusio* around the whole (vv. 3, 11). While v. 3 might be read as sinful pride, it could be sober self-assessment; v. 11 affirms its truth. The cataclysm about to be reported is described more with a combination of respect, sadness, and horror than with the implication that it is just what Tyre deserved.

This cataclysm will be reported in due course. Meanwhile 27:12-25a suspend the metaphor, heighten the lament's suspense, and deepen the sense of terrible reversal involved in the cataclysm by moving to a catalogue of Tyre's trading connections and activity, which occupies the full middle third of the chapter. The catalogue shows how Tyre mediated between the lands of all the known world, peoples to the east and south and peoples across the Mediterranean: Spain (v. 12), Ionian Greece (Javan and Dedan/Rhodes) and the area of the Greek colonies in northwest Turkey (vv. 13-15), Syria and Palestine (vv. 16-18), Arabia (vv. 19-22), and Mesopotamia (vv. 23-24). Tyre's economic wealth was based on this commercial activity, which its position made possible. There passed through its harbors metals, slaves, bronze ware, horses, iron and ebony, turquoise and purple, embroidery and fine linen, precious stones, agricultural produce, wool, wrought iron, cassia and sweet cane, saddle cloths, sheep, spices, garments, clothing, carpets, and a host of other goods. The list reminds one of the successive streets in an oriental bazaar, a many-colored panoply of all that anyone could ever want to buy or sell. Human slaves are just one item of trade among others, and Judah and Israel are just two trading powers among others; economics relativizes ethics and theology. The catalogue perhaps has some earlier background than its present position and some earlier function; it has often been reckoned an insertion here.

Returning to the picture, Ezekiel portrays the ship of Tyre, loaded with all these wares, cataclysmically sunk (27:25b-36). Its rowers propel it to the high sea where it can take advantage of the east wind blowing strong off the desert, but this turns into a peril instead of a resource. The description of the shipwreck is briefer than one might have expected after the vivid specificity of vv. 1-25a. A different effect is achieved by the thrice-repeated "in the heart of the seas" (vv. 25b-27). The phrase first came in v. 4, where it suggested the impressiveness of Tyre's position. Now Ezekiel notes how the "ship" was loaded in the heart of the seas, capsized there, and sunk there. As with the wind, the element which Tyre thought was its life, protection, and livelihood turned out to be its betrayal, downfall, and death. The repetition also points to the sea as one of the embodiments of mythical powers of chaos, destruction, and death (cf. 26:19).

At noticeably greater length Ezekiel imagines the response of Tyre's former neighbors and trading partners, who also gained their livelihood from the sea (27:28-36). Having envied Tyre its position and prosperity, they are now saying, "There but for the grace of the gods. . . ." The hiss of v. 36 looks like a whistle of horror rather than a gesture of contempt. The reaction recalls the fascinated, maudlin horror of modern reaction to disasters such as air crashes — or the wreck of the *Titanic*. There is no reference to this wreck coming about by an act of God. It comes about through "natural causes," the result of a freak storm. But Yahweh had announced it in advance, and by describing it in anticipation, Ezekiel subverts any inclination on the part of the community in Jerusalem or in Babylon to envy Tyre its achievements and its capacity to resist Nebuchadrezzar in a way that Jerusalem itself finally could not.

A Warning about the Fall of the King of Tyre (28:1-10)

In 26:7–27:36 the fate of the city of Tyre is in focus rather than any critique of the city. In the matching prophecies against the king of Tyre Ezekiel does come to a critique, of which the king rather than the people is thus the object. In part this corresponds with the way prophets hold Israelite kings responsible for the wrongdoing which will issue in disaster for the people, though that critique is commonly directed against specific monarchs such as Jehoiachin and Zedekiah. Here there is no mention of a specific king of Tyre such as Ethbaal II, who reigned at the time of Tyre's siege. While he may be presupposed, the polemic also presupposes the regular responsibility of the leadership for a people's wrongdoing and failure, as leadership yields to its inherent temptations (cf. e.g., 1 Samuel 8). It parallels that against the king of Babylon in Isaiah 14 and uses some similar motifs.

The first prophecy against the king of Tyre does confront him about a sin which would particularly characterize the leadership of this particular city-state with its worldwide economic significance, his pretension to a godlike wisdom evidenced by his economic success. Wisdom is of course a necessary attribute of leadership, not least for its economic benefits. Thus once the monarchy is accepted in Israel, Solomon's story emphasizes the king's need and receiving of this gift. But it emphasizes that for all the human effort to acquire it, paradoxically it nevertheless comes as God's gift. The besetting temptation of leadership is to assume the credit for the gift and thus to see itself as godlike (28:2). Israelite tradition also emphasized that the wisdom that counted was linked with just management of the affairs of state as well with right attitudes to God; it was not merely a matter of shrewd business acumen. The king of Tyre's sin thus has nothing to do with the city's attitude to Israel (contrast ch. 25). It has to do with its attitude to God. On the wise Dani'el, see on 14:12-23. Dani'el was specifically a figure in texts which we know from the Phoenician coast on which Tyre lay. These refer to his just ruling rather than his wisdom. Perhaps wisdom was assumed to go with that, as in OT thinking; or perhaps there is irony here.

In the manner of a standard prophecy of judgment Ezekiel then proceeds with a "therefore" to declare the fall which will follow, in terms similar to those of 26:19-21 with its use of the mythic motifs of a descent into the Deep and into the Pit. Once again disaster falls "in the heart of the seas" (28:8), with new appropriateness because here that is also the place of sin (v. 2). The certainty of what will happen is emphasized by the strong reminder of whence it issues (v. 11b).

A Lament at the Fall of the King of Tyre (28:11-19)

Finally, the lament in 28:11-19 is again not only commissioned by Yahweh but composed by Yahweh (vv. 11, 12; cf. 27:3). This lament also in turn imagines that the king's fall has actually happened and goes through the motions of grieving over it. Like the previous lament it adds to its force by the vivid liveliness of its imagery. It begins from two epithets with which we have become familiar, Tyre's wisdom (cf. 28:4, 5, 7) and beauty (cf. 27:3-4; 28:7), its exquisite natural position, and the intelligent way it had exploited it (cf. v. 17). The references to wisdom complicate the poetry; they belong to lines which are longer than the characteristic 3-2 meter of a lament (see on ch. 19). The poem has perhaps been adapted to fit the context here.

The point is now put with the aid of a further set of mythical motifs, those of the Edenic paradise garden which is the very dwelling place of God. This overlaps with the Eden garden of Genesis 2 but has extra features, some of which recall later chapters in Genesis, others evidently coming from existent myths and/or from Ezekiel's imagination. The king of Tyre becomes the Adam figure in this poetic presentation, decorated with all precious stones and wholly committed to Yahweh's ways, like Noah in Gen 6:9 ("blameless," 28:15). His "fall" comes through that business activity which issued from his beauty and expressed his wisdom. The assumption that the original sin consisted in the violence of human beings to one another corresponds to a conviction underlying Genesis 4 and 6:11-13. Ezekiel 28 complements Genesis 4 by linking that violence with business and society rather than with worship and the family. It complements Genesis 6 with its portrayal of a king who went from wholeness to violence as opposed to a man who stood out in wholeness over against contemporary violence.

Whatever might or might not be possible in theory, in practice Tyre lived a successful business life only by abandoning scruple and trampling on people. If the reference to violence is another addition to the original form of the poem (Zimmerli), this again shows how it has been adapted to fit its present context and to provide a more comprehensive critique of the characteristic attitudes of a great power and its leadership. The motif fits the stress on the sin of violence earlier in Ezekiel (e.g., 7:23). Leadership's high call puts it in the way of temptations which take it through the experience of the Garden of Eden twice, once that of human beings in general, once the distinctive one which belongs to leadership. It also puts it in the way of an equivalent twofold calamity, that which belongs to all humanity and that which is the special downfall of leaders.

Judgment on Egypt, the Last Temptation (Chs. 29–32)

The date (588 BC) takes us behind that in 26:1. The previous prophecies against other nations have presupposed that Jerusalem has already fallen to Nebuchadrezzar and raised questions about their destiny in the light of that event and of their reaction to it. The prophecies against Egypt begin in the period when Jerusalem's siege is still under way, go on to a period decades later, then return to the siege and the period after the city's fall. Like the prophecies against the nations as a whole, they are thus arranged not by date but by subject, by the issues they raise for the Judean community in Babylon. Egypt, like Tyre, is the great obstacle to its facing up to judgment, turning to repentance, and finding mercy (Eichrodt).

Pharaoh, the Vulnerable Crocodile (29:1-16)

Like the last prophecies against Tyre, the first prophecies against Egypt focus on the king (for whom "pharaoh" is an Egyptian title), and the king remains prominent through the series. Two features of Ezekiel's polemic against Egypt soon surface.

One is equivalent to a motif in the Tyre prophecies, the king's pretentious self-confidence. Tyre's notable natural assets (illogically) made its king proud. Egypt's equivalent natural asset was the river Nile.

The Nile's significance for Egypt suggested its leader's characterization as the great Crocodile (*tannin;* NRSV, "dragon"; 29:3), a seriously impressive and frightening wild creature (Gen 1:21) which as such could symbolize a concentration of threatening wild power that could overwhelm the entire order of human life (Ps 74:13; Isa 27:1; 51:9) yet in its natural state, like the hippopotamus or rhinoceros, could in other contexts become a figure of fun and thus undermine the threat of disorder (Ezek 32:2; cf. Isa 30:7).

In Israel people had to rely on the vagaries of rain for water and thus for their crops. In Egypt surely nothing could stop the Nile from flowing; people simply had to channel it so that it irrigated their crops. The pharaoh is irrationally proud of this asset, as if he had created it. He assumed he could control it, in the way modern states control water supplies by means of dams and reservoirs; the modern dam at Aswan/Syene (29:10) is a spectacular example. Yet from time to time we find nature reasserting itself, and Ezekiel declares that the Crocodile will find itself captured, fish sticking to its scales (allegorically, the pharaoh takes his people with him to their death), thrown onto the unirrigated open country, and becoming carrion for animals and birds.

As a result, its actual vulnerability will be exposed (29:6-7). Here lies the second feature of Ezekiel's polemic against Egypt. The Judean community was periodically and naturally impressed by the power of this nation to the south (cf. Isaiah 30–31). In Ezekiel's day the community thought Egypt might rescue it from Nebuchadrezzar, and politically it had some grounds for thinking that. Egyptian forces have just forced the Babylonians to lift the siege of Jerusalem (see Jeremiah 37). But the community needed to see Egypt as a stick which, when you lean on it, breaks and lets you down or impales you. Politically that was just realism. For years Egypt had simply not been big enough to match the power of the great empires to the north.

The point is remade prosaically at the end of 29:8-16; see v. 16a, perhaps the main point of those verses, for we must keep recalling that these prophecies against other nations are made for Israel's benefit. Talk of Egypt's scattering is designed to drive Israel away from a stupid reliance on Egypt. In the light of 2,500 years' further history of great empires based in Asia, Europe, and America, we are now in a stronger position to recognize the advantages to keeping powers small (v. 15). A further point emerges from vv. 8-16. The description of desolation, forty-year scattering, and restoration is strangely parallel to the destiny envisaged for Judah itself (cf. ch. 4), like Ezekiel's characteristic desire for the people properly to acknowledge Yahweh (vv. 6, 9, 16). Either Judah is thereby further debased, or Egypt is implicitly exalted as in Isa 19:18-24, Jer 46:26, or both.

A Change of Plan regarding Nebuchadrezzar, Tyre, and Egypt (29:17-21)

Ezekiel returns to Tyre's destiny because of its implications for Egypt; this prophecy continues the theme of Egypt's humiliation.

This latest-dated prophecy in the book comes from 571 BC, after the raising of the siege of Tyre in 574. The very frequency of dates in the Egyptian oracles may reflect the desire to verify and authenticate predictions made during the critical period during and just after the siege of Jerusalem (Blenkinsopp). One might then have thought that the failure of Tyre's siege would have been an embarrassment to Ezekiel and to people who preserved his prophecies, but there is no overt trace of such embarrassment. There is no concern about his being implied to be a false prophet. If there is an implicit concern, it is a theological one, with questions about Yahweh's fairness and reliability.

Tyre having stood firm, Ezekiel does not merely declare that his prophecies of its fall will come about one day, though he may have assumed that. One does not get a sense that there is any kind of difficult question to be faced because Ezekiel is working with an assumption about how events work out in a world which preempts such difficulties. Alongside his emphasis on God's sovereignty, he simply assumes that human beings exercise real freedom in the world and need not cooperate with God's will. On this occasion at least, when Tyre declines to lie down and die because that is Yahweh's purpose,

Yahweh's response is not to overwhelm it but to change plans. Nebuchadrezzar is Yahweh's agent and must have his wages; if he cannot have Tyre, Yahweh will give him Egypt instead.

Ezekiel's assumption about the relationship between Yahweh's will and human resistance or initiative is similar to that presupposed by stories told of someone such as Moses, Amos, or the king of Nineveh, who prevail upon Yahweh to have a change of mind (see Exodus 32; Amos 7; Jonah 3). When Yahweh announces an intention, we might have reckoned that this was the last word. It is sometimes only the beginning of a debate in which what eventually happens is quite different from what Yahweh first "proposed." Both Yahweh's proposals and human responses contribute to what happens. Admittedly, to solve one theological problem is often to raise two more, and so it is here. Ezekiel's ploy may seem to subvert the very notion of Yahweh's sovereignty and of a prophet being in a position to declare what will happen, and to undermine the seriousness of the considerations that led to declarations of judgment on Tyre. Perhaps one has to be prepared to take the long view. Yahweh will in due course, one way or another, see that the divine purpose expressed in the divine word is implemented, and that justice is done.

For Ezekiel's Israelite audience, the focus lies elsewhere. The prophecy is another warning not to think that Egypt can be relied on as a bulwark against anyone else, and another promise that the exposure of their false hopes is not Yahweh's last word to them. As Egypt surrenders its strength, Israel will regain its, Ezekiel will indeed be vindicated, and all will again work toward the final object that Yahweh may be acknowledged (v. 21). As far as we know, this is Ezekiel's last prophecy; it is an appropriate note on which to finish.

Yahweh's Day Comes for Egypt (30:1-19)

Ezekiel has spoken of Yahweh's day about to fall on Israel, especially in ch. 7. As there, the language here is vigorous and repetitive and the portrait episodic. The meter is less regular, and sometimes we cannot tell whether to see it as free verse or as prose using parallelism.

In ch. 7 Ezekiel, like Amos before him, was turning the idea of a coming day of Yahweh from an encouragement to a terror. Here in one sense that is reversed again; Yahweh's day (30:3), the day of clouds and darkness (vv. 3, 18), is a day of international crisis (v. 3) and judgment for the nations (vv. 4-5, 9) because it is the day of Egypt's doom (v. 9), a day of wrath and judgment (vv. 14-15). For Israel the ultimate, absolute, dreadful destructiveness and terror of the historical events which are about to overwhelm Egypt as they have overwhelmed Judah ought to come as good news. Because they see Egypt as a key ally against Babylon, ironically it would feel like bad news.

Here there are familiar statements about the object of judgment on Egypt (30:8, 19) and its reasons (vv. 6, 18), and brief comments on the basis for its certainty (v. 12), but the focus is a vision of what it will actually be like, down-to-earth though still poetic and dynamic. It will mean death and decimation, anguish and bereavement, cloud and darkness, agony and loss, fire and destruction, fear and defeat, occupation and exile, shame and desolation. The concreteness of the picture is noteworthy. Egypt's key neighbors and allies are named (v. 5), as are ten of its key towns (vv. 6, 13-18), though in unordered fashion such as would be intelligible on the part of someone in Babylon.

After the introduction, 30:2b-5 warn in general of judgment on Egypt and its allies, without any specific statement of means. Instead Ezekiel simply declares, and repeats, that judgment will come by the sword (vv. 4, 5, 6; also vv. 11, 17). Ch. 30 thus takes up ch. 21 as well as ch. 7. The sword wielded against Judah will also be wielded against Egypt. Who wields the sword is not explicit, but it will become clear that, as there, its bearer is Yahweh, and on Yahweh's behalf Nebuchadrezzar. The allies include Cush/Nubia/Ethiopia, Put/Cyrenaica (part of Libya), Lud (apparently settlements of mercenaries from Lydia in Turkey), and Cub (see the NRSV margin; another term for Libya, perhaps a textual slip). The NRSV's "all Arabia" involves a slight emendation of the Hebrew text which says "all the mob," which may be correct! "The people of the allied land" may be "the people of the land of the covenant" (Blenkinsopp), Jewish mercenaries. The prose in v. 5 with its list looks like an expansion of the poetry to give more concrete detail.

The messenger formula in 30:6 may then be merely a resumptive one; the formula is not an infallible guide to the beginning of a new prophecy. Vv. 6-9 focus more directly on Egypt's allies and close off where vv. 2b-4 began, with another prose comment which may be an elaboration of the original text, portraying Ethiopian messengers taking their frightening news up the Nile in the opposite direction to the one traveled by their predecessors in Isa 18:1-2, whose wording is taken up here. Vv. 2b-9 as a whole thus work out as a chiasm, a common feature of OT poetry.

As happened in the Tyre prophecy in ch. 26, this general proclamation is followed in 30:10-12 by a more concrete statement of the way events will come about. Yahweh will act, and specifically via Nebuchadrezzar. The interrelationship of this double agency is expressed by the interwovenness of the forms of expressions: "I by the hand of him," "he," "I," and "I by the hands of them."

30:13-19 then make another aspect of judgment more concrete, listing the individual places in Egypt which will experience it. Memphis/Noph on the edge of the Nile delta was the earlier capital of Lower Egypt and center of the worship of the creator-god Ptah and the bull-god Apis. Pathros, Syene/Aswan, and Thebes/No (modern Karnak/Luxor, the capital of the whole country for many centuries and the center of the worship of Amon) are in Upper Egypt. Zoan/Tanis, Pelusium/Sin, On/Heliopolis, Pi-beseth/Bubastis, and Tahpanhes/Daphnai are in the Delta itself and nearer Palestine. The list reflects major centers of power and probably the location of Jewish exiles (cf. Jer 44:1; in addition, Syene was the location of a subsequently famous Jewish settlement at Elephantine). It suggests that for all their strategic or religious importance or their impressive antiquity and history, none of Egypt's cities will survive the sword of Yahweh and Nebuchadrezzar. It might add a worrying aspect to the prophecy of judgment for Jewish exiles in these areas, especially on the reading of v. 5 noted above.

The closing references to the day and to cloud in 30:18 form an *inclusio* with the opening references in vv. 2b-3.

A Political Comment (30:20-26)

It is relatively rare for a prophet's words to relate to a specific political event. This reads almost like an editorial comment in the Babylonian community newspaper. The date is April 587 BC, nine months into the siege of Jerusalem. Pharaoh Hophra had come to the city's aid, the Babylonian army had withdrawn, and the siege had been relieved (Jeremiah 37). The city eventually fell to the Babylonians, so this relief was but temporary, as Jeremiah and Ezekiel said it would be. News has apparently reached the community of this eventual withdrawal of the Egyptian forces.

No doubt there were Judean prophets, priests, and politicians who invited people to see the raising of the siege as Yahweh's work in fulfillment of promises of Jerusalem's preservation. Others (Jeremiah and Ezekiel at least) invited them rather to see the renewal of the siege as Yahweh's work. They have no doubt which side Yahweh is on in contemporary politics. The community sat in the middle not knowing whom to believe.

This contextual prophecy is located here because it led to another declaration of total defeat for Egypt. Pharaoh is like a man who has broken one arm in a fight. Yahweh is a ruthless boxer who will now go for the other, or a ruthless manager who will train his own protégé so that he can go for his opponent in his area of weakness. Specifically the sword motif links this prophecy to 30:1-19. Pharaoh cannot wield Yahweh's sword; Nebuchadrezzar will do so. Hophra died shortly afterward in a civil war, but we do not know of any defeat or scattering of Egypt by Babylon or of its coming to recognize Yahweh in the way Ezekiel spoke. The language of injury, defeat, and scattering is the language used of Judah adapted for Egypt; it is conventional and should not be pressed as if it reflected something like second sight.

Pharaoh and His Army: A Mighty Tree Ignominiously Felled (Ch. 31)

The date (587 BC) indicates that Jerusalem's siege has been under way for nearly a year. Jerusalem was about to surrender (see 2 Kings 25), but Ezekiel and his community did not know that, and Judeans in general looking around for something to hope in will still have had only the Egyptians to cast in the role of the Seventh Cavalry about to ride over the hill to their rescue and relief. Ezekiel thus remains in the business of disabusing them of empty hopes and making them face facts.

This time he does so by utilizing the image of the Great Tree. A tall, impressive, graceful, stately tree such as a Lebanese cedar, towering over other trees around, flourishing and always green as one nourished by plentiful water (the image suggests resourcing from the Deep below, but the emphasis on this motif also makes hearers recall the the way the Nile and its irrigation streams water Egypt), offering hospitality or protection to all that lives around, was a common image in the Middle East and elsewhere for the living, transcendent, graceful, stately, preeminent, alive, life-giving, protective, sustaining Cosmos or Reality or Godhead itself. A sacred tree at the center of the world symbolically links heaven and earth. In the OT a tree of life thus grows in God's garden; as in ch. 28 Ezekiel uses his imagination or his knowledge of Middle Eastern myths to elaborate the picture of Eden in a way parallel to that which appears in Genesis 2. A nation is like a tree or is an embodiment of it; so in particular is a king (e.g., Isa 4:2; Lam 4:20; Ezekiel 17; 19:10-11; Daniel 4). Both are treelike in relation to their peoples or the world as a whole.

Here the embodiment of the Great Tree is initially Assyria, the first great Middle Eastern empire, which had collapsed within the lifetime of Ezekiel and his contemporaries. Like the modern British, Russian, and American empires, it would once have seemed indispensable and unassailable (31:3-9). It had thought so itself, and that was why it had fallen — or rather been felled (vv. 10-14a). It had thought it could reach up into the world above, and it had therefore been cast into the world below, the world of death; it shares the destiny of all humanity, to their consternation as well as its own (vv. 14b-17). The resourcing Deep becomes a drowning Deep (cf. the threat to Tyre in 27:17-21).

Often Ezekiel would have told a fable such as this without making explicit his point until the end. Here its application is announced at the beginning (31:2), though only in part, for vv. 3-9 are all admiration, like the vast bulk of Ezekiel's portrait of the good ship *Tyre* in 27:3b-25. The way the prophecy opens gives no hint that there is bad news to come, though it would hardly be Ezekiel if there were not, and an intelligent audience would be waiting for it. The "therefore" of 31:9 is thus a surprise but not a surprise. The tree's impressiveness was bound to imply arrogance, and that in turn was bound to imply judgment.

There may be another rhetorical trick that Ezekiel is playing on his hearers. The word "Assyria" is very much like the word for "cypress." Ezekiel's hearers thus had the option of hearing the whole chapter as directly concerning Egypt and anticipating its fall instead of reflecting on Assyria's fall. Either way, if Jerusalem trusts Egypt, or the Babylonian community does so on its behalf, it is trusting a tree rotten at the roots and about to be felled. This further aspect of the fable's application is duly made explicit at the end (31:18). Egypt leaves the company of the high and mighty for the company of outcasts.

Ironically the actual feller of Assyria and the designated feller of Egypt is one who will itself soon have this image turned on it (see Daniel 4). Perhaps there is no empire or leader who will ever finally resist the temptation to think it has walked through heaven's gates. 31:14 points to the theological generalization that none will actually be allowed to do so. All fall one after another, as Daniel's visions of successive empires in Daniel 2 and 7 suggest, not by some inner inevitability but by Yahweh's will.

A Lament for a Doomed Dragon (32:1-16)

This time the date (586 BC) takes us to a period only weeks after the arrival of news that Jerusalem had indeed fallen (see 33:21). The ancient Greek, Latin, and Syriac translations have a variety of slightly earlier dates than the Hebrew represented in the NRSV. It seems that they were aware that 33:21 will go back to the time of the news arriving, and that they assumed that the prophecies must be in chronological order (Taylor). We have seen that they are sometimes arranged by timing, sometimes by subject.

Even after the Babylonian army's success and Egypt's implicit failure to enable Jerusalem to escape capture, Egypt's might is still described in larger-than-life terms. Perhaps the exiles were now entertaining the hope that Egypt would not give up the idea of exercising power in Syria-Palestine and would seek to regain control there, thus freeing Judah from Babylonian power (Allen). Or perhaps Ezekiel assumes that the community now at last has to give up the pretense that Egypt might be Judah's savior, so that talk of judgment on Egypt will now have different significance, perhaps becoming a reassurance that Yahweh's act of judgment against Judah was part of a commitment to sovereignty over the whole world (Eichrodt).

We have become familiar with the prophetic funeral lament (e.g., ch. 27), which in a distinctive 3-2 meter purports to grieve over someone's death when he or she is still very much alive. 32:1-16 describe themselves as a lament at the beginning and the end (see vv. 2a, 16). The mourning women (see Jer 9:17-20) are the Israelite equivalent to modern funeral directors, experts who look after aspects of a funeral for the bereaved. But the verses then keep us on our toes by taking a different form for much of the material in between. Traditional critical scholars suggest that an original (short?) lament has been expanded by other material (see, e.g., Zimmerli).

As they stand, however, 32:1-16 are "an ironic obituary for an arrogant world power" (Allen). As a way of "grieving" over a "dead" pharaoh, they begin by imagining the living pharaoh as someone who thinks he is unassailable as a lion but has actually become like a hunted crocodile (see ch. 29), thrashing about in the water (v. 2b). Instead of going on with a lament, the prophecy then announces that it will bring an explicit message from Yahweh (see v. 3a; also v. 11a, and the formulae at the end of vv. 8, 14, and 16). In the Hebrew the verbs are equivalent to the future tense rather than in the past tense of a lament; they utter a threat that the crocodile will be captured and, once the sport is over, left as carrion (vv. 3-4). What was announced as a lament turns out to be "virtually a reissue of 29:3-6" (Allen).

While 32:2b-4 might be simply a straightforward description of a crocodile hunt, a net is an odd means of capturing a crocodile, and Ezekiel's audience in Babylon will be in a particularly strong position to recall Marduk's use of a net to capture the sea monster in the Babylonian creation myth *Enuma elish.* The description in vv. 4-6 also fits this monster's fate in the myth. Ezekiel takes over this familiar myth and applies it to Yahweh in such a way that it becomes a means of speaking about contemporary events. Yahweh is like Marduk, while Egypt is like the slain monster. So vv. 4-6 are simultaneously lament, prophecy, myth, metaphor, literal description, and hyperbole in their threat of the fall of the pharaoh's people.

The description of cosmic and international reactions to this event in 32:7-10 follows other familiar OT descriptions of Yahweh's day and invites the audience to see Egypt's judgment (like its own) as an implementation of that day. Immediately that is juxtaposed with a warning of the nature of the grim literal political reality (vv. 11-15), with its strange aim (v. 15b). Ultimate ("eschatological") events are not separated from present, political ones, nor vice versa.

The Grim End Which Awaits Egypt as Much as Anyone Else (32:17-32)

Something more like a lament closes the prophecies against Egypt. It is a cry of woe which as God's word actually sets Egypt on its way to death (32:17-19). It also refers to a range of other nations, including Edom and Sidon, and this makes it an appropriate close for the prophecies in chs. 25–32 as a group. Chronologically the NRSV makes it earlier than 32:1-16 by following the LXX (see v. 17 and the note), but the month may as likely still be the twelfth and the date thus a fortnight later than vv. 1-16.

This prose prophecy gains power from poetic devices such as repetition with variation, which is sometimes characteristic of Hebrew poetry. Certain expressions keep recurring, but in changing combinations. Other similar but not identical phrases recur (e.g., referring to the "uncircumcised"). The "theme and variations" effect drives points home relentlessly but in a way which is never monotonous or entirely predictable. Hearers can never relax, sure what will come next, but neither are they confused by ever-new images or content.

The point that is driven home is a somber one. Everyone is going to die, even those who try to evade the fact. In the modern world, concern with evading death is mostly an individual matter, though nations and groups also assume that they will last forever and are troubled at the idea that they may not. In traditional societies the balance may be the other way. Here Ezekiel confronts Egypt's national pretension to immortality. It is going the same way as the great but finished Mesopotamian powers Assyria and Elam, more remote powers such as Meshech and Tubal (see chs. 38–39), and peoples nearer to Palestine such as Edom (in Israelite eyes, its most violent neighbor) and Phoenicia ("all the Sidonians") to the north. All have lived by violence. No matter how impressive or powerful or frightening a nation, it will end up in the same place as every other nation. Although Egypt is cast from earthly honor to one of the lower-class areas of Sheol (32:19), when the same fate comes to Egypt as to everyone else, this fact will be a strange kind of consolation for the pharaoh (v. 31).

The Israelites knew that death did not mean ceasing to exist; people went to join their ancestors in a family tomb. Here this-worldly distinctions continued. A commoner's grave, a hero's grave, and a king's grave were quite different. An uncircumcised person would not be buried with Israelites, any more than he would live a full this-worldly life with them. Someone killed in battle would be likely never to reach the family tomb; nor would someone who had died by the shame of execution. The Israelites thought of the world of the dead in general as a large-scale version of that, with its class and geographical divisions. It was not a place of punishment, but one of nothingness — like the grave itself. Here Ezekiel is interested in nations who arrive in Sheol not merely because they have died but because they have been killed; the expressions "killed/fallen by the sword" keep recurring. Those who spread terror by the sword have fallen by the sword. The prophecies against the nations thus conclude with another implicit critique of the very notion of the existence of nations which come into being and keep themselves in being by violence (see 29:8-16 and the comment).

A New Beginning for a New/Old Ministry (Ch. 33)

Ezekiel 33 marks the beginning of a new stage in Ezekiel's ministry, though its structure obscures that at first. It is arranged as another chiasm.

Ezekiel's ministry in Babylon (vv. 1-9; cf. 3:16-21)
  Ezekiel warns of judgment (vv. 10-20)
    Ezekiel receives news of the city's fall (vv. 21-22)
  Ezekiel warns of judgment (vv. 23-29)
Ezekiel's ministry in Babylon (vv. 30-33; cf. 3:22-27)

The key to the chapter is thus vv. 21-22; the material on either side has to be understood in relation to that. The outside elements restate motifs from Ezekiel's original commissioning.

Talk of the hypothetical possibility of Yahweh's bringing a sword upon a land might raise a wry smile. The word "sword" appeared seventeen times in ch. 32 alone, much more than in any other single chapter in the OT. The allegory in 33:2b-9 thus might continue to reflect on matters which affect a people such as Egypt. But vv. 1-2 have told us that we have entered another stage in Ezekiel's prophecies. He is once again to speak to his own people. It becomes clear with vv. 7-9, where the allegory is interpreted, that Ezekiel is not now speaking to them about how Yahweh deals with other peoples, but about how Yahweh deals with the Judeans in Babylon themselves. More recent talk of a sword for other nations cannot be allowed to make us forget the sword Yahweh put in the hand of the king of Babylon (30:24-25; 32:10-11), which stands poised over Judah. It has been a frequent topic of earlier prophecies (e.g., chs. 5; 6; 14; 21).

This takes us back to the image of a lookout in 3:16-21 (see the comments there). Here 33:7-9 restate 3:17-19 (scholars disagree as to which version is original), so that this image stands as a bracket round chs. 4–32. It provides a retrospective summary of Ezekiel's ministry so far which forms a bridge to what will follow after the turning point of 33:21-22. The repetition also implies a claim to have fulfilled this lookout ministry throughout chs. 4–32; Ezekiel dares anyone to disagree and blame him rather than themselves if they have failed to turn.

In the restatement, 3:20-21 does not appear. The possibility of there being righteous people who might turn away is so remote as to be not worth raising; the people are wrongdoers through and through. This leads directly into what follows in 33:10-11, which evidently presuppose the city's actual fall. At last they recognize the fact, though in a way which might suggest more remorse than repentance, a move from blind confidence to blind hopelessness. Their assessment and question recall the psalms of lament and especially Lamentations, a book which indicates how the deportees' contemporaries in Jerusalem were thinking and praying after the city's fall. Vv. 10-11 hint at the community gathering to pray and talk, and Ezekiel responding to them with his theological arguments in the context of that worship.

Ezekiel's response in 33:11 recalls 18:23. The deportees' attitude implicitly attributes a character to Yahweh which Christians often attribute to the God of the OT as compared with the God of the NT, as if Yahweh is someone who enjoys punishing people for their wrongdoing. Actually Yahweh is a God of love who enjoys having people turn from their wrongdoing and find new life. The recollection of 18:23 takes Ezekiel into another restatement in vv. 12-20, this time a less straightforward restatement of parts of ch. 18, especially 18:21-30 (see the comment); again scholars differ as to which is original. Blind hopelessness is as pointless and destructive as blind confidence. The question is, Are they going to *do* something — namely, turn? The passage again makes clear that this turning or repentance is a matter of action, not feelings of sorrow. Ezekiel's challenge provides another reminder (parallel to that in 29:17-21) that when Yahweh makes an announcement about the future, whether of trouble or of blessing, this does not mean that what Yahweh says will definitely happen. It depends on the human response to the announcement.

"The prophet is fighting on two pastoral fronts. On the one hand he has to counter despair and demoralization among the exiles; on the other, he has to do it in such a way as not to encourage moral indifference and a false sense of security. The complexity of his message is occasioned not only by his pastoral situation but also by a traditional tension in Yahweh's self-revelation, . . . that he is both gracious savior and moral judge" (Allen). Both come together here, appropriately at this turning point. A prophet, counselor, or pastor may not want to say hard things to people, and may prefer being encouraging to being negative. It is preferable to show unqualified and unjudging acceptance toward people whose sin often results from unloving, judgmental, unaccepting attitudes shown to them in the past. These instincts have to be set in the context of the warnings about a lookout's responsibility. Prophets, pastors, and counselors bring the tough good news that facing up to our failures and committing ourselves to change is the way to life.

In terms of the story itself, 33:21-22 carry straight on from ch. 24. The date (586 BC) suggests eighteen months after the city's fall (see 2 Kings 25). Six months is a more plausible period; some textual witnesses have "eleventh year," which might have been assimilated to the dates in ch. 32, or perhaps a different calendar is used here. The arrival of the shattering yet vindicating news from Jerusalem, which the previous night he knew was about to come, is a turning point in Ezekiel's ministry. He can now speak freely, abandoning the restraint reported at 3:22-27.

Yet the warning which follows (33:23-29) looks as if he carries on business much as before, despite the fact that the country is now in ruins. The point is illustrated by contrasting Ezekiel's disallowing of appeal to the example of Abraham with the encouraging of this appeal in Isaiah 51. There will come a time for claiming the promise to Abraham, but the mere fact that the city has fallen has not changed circumstances that much. It has not brought people to a changed life. The people believe that now the city has fallen, the worst is over, and perhaps their own survival proves that they are all right with Yahweh.

There may have been more material or ideological reasons for "claiming" the promise. It may have provided a basis for appropriating land, perhaps that of people who had been deported to Babylon. Perhaps it provided a basis for the claim that in general the Judean rather than the Babylonian community were the heirs to Abraham's promise, the real Israel. There are times when the people of God can "claim" some promise of God for themselves and times when they cannot. Ezekiel bids the Judeans to examine themselves to see whether they are the kind of people for whom God can fulfill promises.

The Babylonian community, too, is perhaps interested in God's word of promise in this new situation, attentive this time to the contemporary prophet's word now that Ezekiel is free to speak and looking for something to encourage them for the future (33:30-33). Or perhaps they enjoy hearing Ezekiel telling them how wicked the Judean community is. They have their own ways of mis-hearing Yahweh's word. Ezekiel "finds many to listen but few to obey" (Zimmerli). The news has not brought people to an attitude to the prophetic word which has changed in the sense which mattered, and flippancy over prophecy implies flippancy over God. The watershed (vv. 21-22) is one that has so far made little substantial difference to people or prophet.

Dealing with the Problems of Shepherds and Sheep (Ch. 34)

Ezekiel squeezes every ounce of allegory out of the notion of Israel as a flock of sheep, perhaps inspired in part by Jer 23:1-2 (and what follows there?). The chapter contains not the systematic exposition of an idea but the systematic exposition of a metaphor. 34:1-16 concentrate more on the shepherds, and vv. 17-31 more on the sheep. Vv. 1-2 form an introduction with a focus on the first, v. 31 a conclusion with a focus on the second. In both halves, declarations of judgment (vv. 3-10, 17-20) are followed by promises of restoration (vv. 11-16, 21-30). Vv. 23-31 are often reckoned later additions.

Israel's kings are its shepherds, they have failed in their leadership, and they are to be dismissed (34:1-10). In the Middle East kings were regularly pictured as shepherds of their people. In a traditional society it is not a romantic image. Shepherding is a familiar, everyday, straightforward, tough, stressful occupation like engineering, farming, or mining. Its demands and dangers are implicit in the description of what the shepherds have failed to do: for example, wandering over miles of hostile desert terrain looking for sheep, or protecting them from the attacks of wolves or lions. Its temptations are also implicit in this description: for example, sheep stealing or failing to care for ailing sheep. It was not a pastoral job in the sense in which we use the word, and if we are to understand and profit from Ezekiel's vision, it will help if we set aside for a while the NT's adaptations of the shepherd theme. In the OT it applies more directly to leadership in society.

Like any job, shepherding combined service with reward. Ezekiel's problem is that these have become out of balance. Israel's shepherds consider only what they get out of the job, not doing the job for the sake of the people.

In earlier chapters Ezekiel criticized the community in general more than its leadership, and challenged people individually to take responsibility for their destiny. In their review of the history of the community, 1 and 2 Kings are inclined to blame the kings when things go badly (and credit them when things go well); Ezekiel now does the same. Here the description of the flock's hardship might address the situation after the fall of Jerusalem when the fabric of economic and community life in Judah will have collapsed, so that contemporary leaders might be seen as the shepherds. In addition, Ezekiel's audience would be likely to recall prophetic critique of kings, not least in their lifetime (see chs. 17 and 19 and the comments there), and see them poetically addressed as if gathered before Yahweh. Jehoiachin had of course long been in Babylon, and Zedekiah joined him there after being deposed.

Now Yahweh intends to act as Israel's shepherd and fulfill the task the human leaders failed (34:11-16). Again it was as natural in the Middle East to think of the deity as shepherd as to think of the deity as king or the king as shepherd. Again the image suggested absolute authority and the power of life and death, even if you also hoped it would mean that this authority and power were your provision and protection (cf. Psalm 23). The king/shepherd was responsible for the fair organization of the community and for taking action in cases of unfairness and dishonesty. It was not a cozy metaphor.

God ought at least to be more trustworthy than a human leader. Israel had known a time without monarchs when Yahweh was its king and shepherd, and a significant strand of its thinking always saw this as the natural arrangement. The monarchy's failure would have earned an "I told you so" from the likes of Samuel. Yahweh now promises a return to the "natural" situation in which Yahweh does the shepherding, fulfilling the king's commitment to justice (34:16), which is the point at which the kings have failed. It is a shepherding that Yahweh exercises specifically in the day of clouds and thick darkness (v. 12). That is an image for the day of Yahweh, the day of judgment (see 32:8 as well as Ps 23:4; Joel 2:2; and Zeph 1:15). It promises that Yahweh will rescue the flock from the consequences of Yahweh's own judgment. In v. 16, the talk of destruction introduces the theme of vv. 17-22; the Greek, Syriac, and Latin versions imply "watch over" *('eshmir)* rather than "destroy" *('ashmid),* and some modern translations have taken this as the original text.

There are also problems within the flock itself, and Yahweh will judge between the sheep (34:17-24: not between sheep and goats, but between fat sheep and goats and lean sheep and goats). It is a common enough human experience that adversity such as is described in vv. 1-10 sets the victims against each other. In the disorder in Judah after the city's fall, it would be every man for himself and the survival of the fittest. If vv. 1-16 refer back to the years leading up to 587 BC, vv. 17-22 may also recall the way the better-off even then lived at the expense of the poor. Yahweh will now set one trustworthy shepherd over the flock (vv. 23-24). What has been described in vv. 17-22 is what happens in the absence of human leadership which exercises some responsibility for what goes on in society (see Judges). If the verses refer to the period after 587 BC, the community is only experiencing what had led to the monarchy's introduction in the first place. Yahweh's shepherding without human shepherding did not work. So Yahweh will give them a better servant-prince. Whether the text refers to a literal return of David or the gift of a new David is not explicit.

The final picture of provision and protection for the flock (34:25-30) realizes the promises of Lev 26:4-13 and recalls the idyllic vision in Psalm 72 where the flourishing of nature, the provision of justice, and the rule of a king work together to bring the fulfillment of Yahweh's purpose for the benefit of the community and the praise of Yahweh. Whether 34:25-30 come about is implicitly the test of whether any putative David has fulfilled the servant role of vv. 23-24.

Prophecies to Two Mountains (35:1–36:15)

For Ezekiel "mountains" is a natural way to speak of the land of a country itself — at least in the case of the hilly countries of Syria-Palestine. Here he addresses the mountain ranges on either side of the Jordan as a way of speaking about the destiny of countries and peoples.

Mt. Seir is the range where the Edomites lived, east of the Jordan and southeast of Judah (see 35:15). Ch. 35 is thus superficially similar to 25:12-14, though the parallel also brings out the distinctiveness of both. There Edom was but one of a number of peoples who formed Judah's political horizon, and its prophecy sat in the shadow of the more extensive treatment of the more significant Tyre and Egypt. The prophecies declared Yahweh's sovereignty over these peoples' destinies without making systematically explicit their importance to Israel. Here the horizon is narrower and Ezekiel focuses on the people identified with Israel's twin brother Esau (see particularly Gen 36:8-9), with whom Israel kept up a longstanding and sharp family quarrel. Edom was near enough to be an ongoing thorn in Israel's side and to profit from its misfortunes.

The reversal of Israel's destiny implies the reversal of Edom's (see Obadiah; Psalm 137). Restoration for Israel and trouble for Edom are two sides of a coin. In 35:1–36:15, then, the promise of judgment on Edom is set in the context of promises of Israel's restoration rather than of promises of Yahweh's worldwide assertion of sovereignty. Edom's prospective fate is parallel to Judah's. So both parts of the prophecy are also correlative to the prophecy against the mountains of Israel in ch. 6.

The taking out of this hostile neighbor apparently seemed a necessary precondition of a secure reestablishment of Israel. Alongside that, the explicitly theological motivation of the warnings to Edom is prominent and variegated (35:4b, 9b, 10b, 11b, 13, 15b; 36:5b). In addition to these concerns, which are narrowly theological (they concern Edom and God), a number of other principles underlie the prophecies, such as the hostility which issues in violence and killing, the greed which appropriates the victim's land, the special nature of Israel's land to Yahweh, and the fact that the punishment is to be inflicted by Yahweh in person rather than by Israel — which is Edom's protection.

The words to the mountains of Israel in 36:1-15 first make the same declaration of judgment from the converse perspective (vv. 1-7) and then promise the correlative reversal, Israel's restoration (vv. 8-15). What is promised is unimaginable and unrealistic from the perspective of any neutral — or hostile — observer. It involves the dispossession of a still-powerful mighty neighbor and the restoration of irreversible devastation. It also implies a transformation of the land's own nature since for all its beloved "mountains and hills, watercourses and valleys," its terrain was proverbially tough. For that point, we must compare Num 13:32 with 36:12-15, which again shows how comments here attributed to other peoples externalize attitudes that lay in Israel's own heart. But the land's traditional dangerousness was not merely "natural." Its capacity to cause people to stumble (v. 15) in part issued from the mountains being also the "high places" in the religious sense ("heights" in 36:2 is *bamot;* see further the comments on ch. 6), which tempted Israel into the Canaanite ways that caused the land to vomit out Israel as it had their predecessors (Lev 18:25-28).

The "soon" of 36:8 perhaps suggests that at least part of these prophecies come some years after the city's fall, when Ezekiel seemed no longer inclined to promise a quick restoration as he did before the fall.

We do not know how far Ezekiel's portrayal of Edom's acts and attitudes bears any relationship to the acts and attitudes of actual Edomites. It may be only the needed dark backcloth for the promises that follow. It is needed partly because it gives concrete external expression to Israel's own inner demons. It makes explicit Israel's real or felt vulnerability, and promises Yahweh's protection. If Ezekiel could know what was happening in Jerusalem, he could know what was happening in Edom, but in the exercise of his ministry what people in Babylon or Judah feared the Edomites were saying may have been more important than what they were actually saying. Ezekiel's strategy is not to tell them not to be so silly but to promise them that Yahweh will deal with such demons. The feelings attributed to Israel's enemies are thus the fears of Israel itself, shamed by its desolation and crushing, unable to imagine that there can ever be restoration or that building, agriculture, and husbandry will ever be possible again. And the repeated declaration that the people will come to recognize Yahweh perhaps corresponds to Ezekiel's own fear that this will never happen, no matter what Yahweh does.

So Edom becomes a figure for destructive powers such as were in a position to destroy the Jewish people, and specifically a figure for Rome as the Jewish people's great oppressor six hundred years later. The demonizing of enemies makes reconciliation impossible and real conflicts more likely. On the other hand, the fact that the modern age saw a concerted attempt to eliminate the Jewish people makes it impossible to dismiss the fears of Ezekiel 35–36 as inherently irrational fantasy.

Holiness and Profanity, Cleanness and Defilement (36:16-38)

The idea of the land vomiting out its inhabitants points us toward a cause-effect understanding of what happens in the world. Events come about for good or ill through "natural" processes built into the way God's world is. At another extreme in Ezekiel that model stands alongside the very personalistic one of world events being directly caused by God's own act as God pours out anger in personal response to human acts (36:18) or personally instructs the crops to grow (v. 29), or the judicial one of God's acting in judgment on wrongdoing (v. 19).

In this further promise of restoration, there also runs through the thinking of Ezekiel as a priest the antitheses of holy/profane (*qadosh/ḥalal*) and of clean/defiled (*ṭahor/ṭame'*). They are antitheses which reflect different categories of thinking from the ones people assume in the modern world. Neither pair has to do directly with the antithesis right/wrong, though they can be brought into association with these.

The holy is what is different from the everyday and ordinary. God's holiness is God's distinctiveness over against humanity, God's extraordinariness. Things that belong to God come to share God's holiness/distinctiveness/extra-ordinariness; they must therefore not be treated as if they were ordinary. That applies to Israel as a people, the sabbath as a day, and the animals sacrificed in the temple. To treat them as if they were everyday is to "profane" them, to ignore their special nature.

One way for people in the modern world to be able to sense the antithesis between the clean and the defiled is to think of the latter as what makes people shudder or say "U-u-gh." Blood often does that, and for men that is often especially true of menstrual blood. The thought of homosexual behavior does that for many people. Certain kinds of living creatures (e.g., snakes, rodents, worms, or insects) may do it. Obviously people prefer to avoid the defiled; the clean is more comfortable. There is nothing rational about all this, and nothing objective — what counts as clean or defiled differs from culture to culture.

Here Ezekiel uses the category of clean/defiled to describe what Israel did to its land. In addition to being wrongs that provoke anger and punishment, Israel's religious and social disorder make God shudder. They are things that repel God (36:17-18: "uncleanness" is the noun related to the verb "defiled," so "defilement" would have been a better translation). They are abominations that provoke loathing and generate shame (vv. 30-32). Ezekiel uses the category of clean/defiled further to describe the people's restoration. They are stained as by blood or muck and are therefore repulsive. Yahweh will wash the stain off them so as to be able to enjoy being with them and having them in the land again (vv. 24-25, 29, 33).

Ezekiel goes on to use the categories of holy/profane not for the people's acts which led to their deportation but to the consequences of Yahweh's own acts. Yahweh's involvement with them was supposed to witness among the nations to Yahweh's distinctiveness, but by forcing Yahweh to expel them from the land they have given the nations the opposite witness. They have made Yahweh seem ordinary rather than showing Yahweh to be a special God (v. 20). Yahweh's concern to be known among the nations as a special God, not an ordinary one, is thus the basis of the restoration which is coming (36:21-23; here "sanctify" is the verb related to the noun "holy"). In this sense restoration comes for Yahweh's sake, not for theirs (vv. 32, 36). Its end is that they finally resemble a holy flock (v. 38 mg.); Yahweh's original purpose can be fulfilled.

Perhaps we need this category of holiness to understand the distinctive promise in 36:26-27. The cleansing operation of v. 25 gives the people a new start but guarantees no better a performance than they offered the previous time. Something needs to be done to them from the inside. An inert, stone-dead mind will be replaced by one which is more like living flesh, vital and lively, or spirited (any antithesis between flesh and spirit is quite foreign to Ezekiel, as his going on to promise the physical renewal of the land also shows). The spirit of Yahweh the holy one will bring this about, so that Yahweh's distinctiveness is reflected in the distinctiveness of the people.

The antithesis of clean/defiled may also underlie this concern with an obedient mind and spirit. Underlying our sense of what is clean or unclean (e.g., bodily emissions such as blood or spit) may be our need of a sense of order and structure in the world and in life, a sense that things are in their place and that boundaries (such as that between inside and outside) are recognized. We also apply these categories in the moral sphere. One of the significances of sorting out the problem of idolatry and violence and replacing them with conformity to Yahweh's ordinances is that this restores order to Israel's life. That order can then be reflected in the order of nature (36:30, 33-36).

Dem Bones, Dem Bones (37:1-14)

The introduction (37:1a) indicates this prophecy's importance: compare at key points 1:3; 3:14, 22; 8:1; 33:22; 40:1. Up to 587 BC the community as reported in Ezekiel had taken a bullish attitude to its future, even if it was whistling in the wind and saying things would work out OK in order to bolster its own courage and hide from the fear that they would not. Even more surprisingly this attitude continued after the city's fall (33:24; contrast 33:10). Since then we have had allusions to the community having a hard time, being consumed by internal strife and by neighbors taking advantage of its weakness. But we have heard nothing of its own thinking.

The starting point for this prophecy's origin lies in 37:11. In Israel's lament we discover what was going on in its spirit, at least that of the community in Babylon (v. 12). It has indeed moved from one extreme of blind confidence to another extreme of abject hopelessness. It sees itself as an army slaughtered in battle, its bones plucked clean by the vultures and whitened by the scorching sun. That is how hopeless is its state. As is the case in other such laments, as far as we can tell this "prayer" is not actually addressed to God, for hopelessness makes prayer impossible; it is a groan addressed to no one in particular (cf. Isa 40:27). The prophecy which responds indicates that as prayers addressed to Yahweh sometimes do not reach their addressee (e.g., Isa 1:15), so groans with no addressee sometimes reach Yahweh (cf. Exod 2:23-25).

Ezekiel is encouraged to see this groan as a fair assessment of the situation of "the whole house of Israel" — presumably north and south, in Judah and Babylon. As metaphor becomes allegory it is a typically extravagant and bizarre picture. Ezekiel envisages the bones becoming skeletons, the skeletons corpses, and the corpses once again a living army. The interpretation does not suggest that there is great significance in the two stages of the revivification (37:4-8, 9-10).

The interpretation in 37:12-14 shows that this is not a picture of the literal resuscitation of dead people, nor of the spiritual renewal of a community, nor of future resurrection. These were familiar ideas in the Middle East, but they are not Ezekiel's concern. It is a picture of bringing back to life a community that thought it was dead, and in a sense was dead. The process is like the one which took place at the first creation whereby God's life was first breathed into it (cf. Gen 2:7). It has hope because it can go home. Throughout the picture one needs to keep in mind the fact that the Hebrew word *ruaḥ* can mean wind, breath, and spirit; the dynamic of the picture issues in part from its capacity to move between these meanings, but the English translation cannot express this.

A Conjuring Trick Whereby Two Sticks Become One (37:15-28)

If 37:1-14 manifestly requires a miracle, 37:15-28 perhaps less obviously requires a bigger one.

In Romans 9–11 Paul discusses the destiny of the Jewish people in the light of their not recognizing Jesus as their messiah and of the development of a largely Gentile church. He might well have inferred that God had ceased working with the Jewish people. To use his image, they have cut themselves out of the olive tree which represents Yahweh's people. Although Paul is a contextual theologian, for him context is not everything, and he also has to take into account the commitment God made to the Jewish people long ago. If God is to continue to be God, this requires faithfulness to that ancient commitment. Somehow the Jewish people is secure with God and will find salvation.

As a contextual theologian, Ezekiel could even more easily have decided that northern Israel had cut itself out of the olive tree. Instead he, too, affirms that Yahweh cannot have finished with it. Not only the northern Israelites who had associated themselves with Judah and thus kept in touch with the king and the temple, but northern Israel as an entity, must have a place in the future of God's people. After all, God gave that land to Jacob and through him to the descendants of his twelve sons, not just to one or two of them. It is part of God's acting for the sake of the name that God should continue to be faithful to people even when they have not been faithful. That is why it is inevitable that 37:24-28 "foresees a fourfold honoring of ancient promises — ruler, land, covenant, and temple" (Blenkinsopp).

It was not clear then and it is not clear 2,500 years later how that commitment can be worked out for the Jewish people or for the Christian church. Both are riven by divisions: orthodox, conservative, liberal; Orthodox, Catholic, Protestant, Pentecostal; liberal, fundamentalist. One group refuses to accept the validity of another's religious practices. As some divisions fade away, others develop. There are no grounds for hope of anything better except Yahweh's commitment to the nations' ultimately being able to recognize that Yahweh alone is God. D. C. Greenwood called Ezekiel's predictions regarding the restoring of the Northern Kingdom "perhaps the most conspicuous example in the [OT] of patently false prophecy" ("On the Jewish Hope for a Restored Kingdom," *ZAW* 88 [1976]: 384; as quoted by Allen). It deserves comparing with the prayer for the church's oneness in John 17, perhaps the most conspicuous example of patently unanswered prayer.

The Last Great Battle (Chs. 38–39)

The people have returned to their land, but "after many days" they will once more be invaded from the north by an alliance of shadowy, far-off powers, yet Yahweh's splendor, greatness, and holiness will be manifested in the comprehensive annihilation of these invaders, and from that day forward Israel will truly know Yahweh as their God. That summary of the "plot" of chs. 38–39 begins to open up some of the issues it raises.

First, is it eschatological? That is a confusing word with many meanings. The point is illustrated if we rephrase the question to "Is it about the end?"; to which the answer is, "It depends what you mean by the end." In one sense Ezekiel 38–39 talks about the end only in the sense Amos does. What is different about Ezekiel 38–39 is its much more detailed account of the last great battle. It is envisaging a decisive break in history; the powers of evil are finally defeated and Israel finally comes to recognize Yahweh. On the other hand, it is expecting ordinary earthly history to go on "from that day forward" (39:22). The end is not followed by nothing, or by heaven, or by something unimaginable.

Second, is it apocalyptic? That is another confusing word with many meanings. In modern parlance "apocalyptic" suggests a coming crisis characterized by all-out war, the collapse of social structures, and perhaps cosmic upheaval; one can see a parallel with part of the scenario in Ezekiel 38–39, though here the upheaval is the backcloth to a positive portrayal of a restoration of fortunes. As a literary form, an apocalypse is a revelation like those in Daniel and Revelation; Ezekiel 38–39 is no more an apocalypse than other sections of Ezekiel — indeed, less so than some of them. As theology, apocalyptic emphasizes themes such as the battle between good and evil, the importance of God's acts rather than human acts, the prospect of resurrection, and the role of angels in mediating between earth and heaven, and it often works out a timetable of events which are to pass in connection with the end; Ezekiel no more emphasizes those than many other books. As rhetoric, apocalyptic uses vivid imagery, elements of myth, neo-Babylonian astronomy, and other material, combining these into a portrait which to the modern reader may seem esoteric and bizarre; that is true of Ezekiel 38–39. As a sociological phenomenon, apocalyptic assures people who are powerless or oppressed that this is not the ultimate or final reality and that a moment will come when they are freed and find power; this fits Ezekiel 38–39, but it also fits, e.g., Second Isaiah.

The later apocalypses develop literary forms which use rhetorical devices to express theological convictions all of which utilize elements we can see in Ezekiel, but that does not make Ezekiel apocalyptic or proto-apocalyptic in the sense that these developments were the inevitable flowering of seeds which are here.

Third, do the chapters come from Ezekiel himself? In many ways the motifs and theology fit those of the rest of the book. They emphasize the initiative of God's sovereignty bringing foreign peoples to their doom (38:3-4). They also look forward to the vindication of God's holiness (38:16, 23; 39:7, 25, 27). The chapters are concerned for the cleanness of the land and thus for proper burial (39:11-16). Ezekiel's characteristic phrases appear: the title "Lord Yahweh," the address "mortal," and the aim that people may "know that I am Yahweh." Other motifs such as the hiding of Yahweh's face (39:23-24, 29) do not appear elsewhere, but this need not work against their coming from Ezekiel; we must allow him to think a new thought.

On the other hand, there are pointers to a significantly later perspective than that of the 580s. The prophecy speaks to a situation after the restoration (38:8, 14). It looks back to prophecy's heyday, in the manner of Zech 1:6 (38:17). It implies a sense that the fulfillment of prophecy has been long delayed (39:8). Further, attempts to identify a structure in these chapters as a whole have issued in less agreement than with most other sections of the book. Phrases that one might think were structural markers (such as "Thus says the Lord Yahweh") do not seem to work as markers. Scenes tumble after one another as in a kaleidoscope. The picture follows a broadly logical sequence, but the corpses of the invading army are pictured first as becoming carrion, then as being properly buried, and then as being carrion again (39:4-5, 11-16, 17-20).

All that suggests that a number of people who thought like Ezekiel have contributed to these chapters over the decades, but there is no consensus on the distinction between different contributions.

Fourth, whom is it talking about? Most of the specific places appear in Genesis 10 as founders of nations among the immediate descendants of Noah's sons Japheth and Ham (in other words, the non-Semitic peoples), and/or appear in Ezek 27:10-14 in the list of peoples with whom Tyre did business. Those two connections suggest two significances of these peoples. Some are figures from prehistoric antiquity with an almost mythical significance. Some are impressive distant contemporary peoples, a number fairly familiar: Persia; Dedan in Arabia; Cush, Put, and Sheba in North Africa; and Tarshish across the Mediterranean.

The only half-known ones (for us, and as far as we know for the prophecy's audience) are in Turkey or the area just to its east and north. Gog has been linked with a seventh-century king in Lydia in Turkey called Gugu. Magog we know only from Gen 10:2. Meshech and Tubal are tribes in Turkey whom 27:13 tells us were involved in slave trading, which might in part explain their appearance here; in 32:26-28 they lie in shame in Sheol in the company of Assyria and Elam. Gomer is the Cimmerians, north of the Black Sea, one-time foes of Gog's Lydia but now in frightening alliance with him; Beth-togarmah is Armenia. Such people are appropriate ones to be designated the contemporary embodiment of the northern enemy who had long been the symbol of threat and destruction for Judah (see Jeremiah 4–6), partly because that was the direction from which most enemies (e.g., Assyria and Babylonia) inevitably approached Israel. And if they are in part almost-mythical figures from the past, back from the dead, that adds to the frightening power of the prophecy, like that of modern horror movies.

Fifth, if the prophecy relates to what will happen "after many days," might its fulfillment lie in events in the twentieth century? In his millions-selling book *The Late Great Planet Earth,* Hal Lindsey sees the invasion of Israel from the north described here as an attack soon to be undertaken by Russia ("chief" in 38:2 is *ro'sh*) from its capital Moscow *(meshek).*

One objection to this is that it makes the prophecy quite irrelevant to OT people, whereas one gets the impression it was supposed to speak to them. Yet the expectation that Ezekiel 38–39 would be fulfilled in one's own day has repeatedly surfaced through Jewish and Christian history. In the second century BC the northern foe was Antiochus Epiphanes, for the Targum it was Rome (cf. also Revelation), for Augustine it was the Goths, and for Luther it was the Turks. This process of reidentification can hardly be faulted in principle. There is enough appeal within the OT itself to similarity of words (e.g., Abram/Abraham — ancestor of a multitude) to make it difficult to object to a linking such as *ro'sh* and Russia. And Ezekiel 38–39 is in Israel's scriptures in the conviction that it has something to say beyond its original context. As other marginalized and disappointed peoples find themselves threatened by overwhelming powers, Ezekiel 38–39 is designed to be their encouragement. God will see that evil does not have the last word, that it overreaches itself and meets its downfall.

The difficulty with an application of the chapters such as Lindsey's is that it is undertaken by the world's greatest power as a way of putting down its rival. It thus works against the spirit of Ezekiel 38–39, which was designed to encourage a small power surrounded by big powers. Citizens of big powers and big churches have to see their danger as *being* Gog, not Gog's victims. God's promises are given to people who believe that God's face is turned away and who long to see that face again (cf. 39:23-24, 29), to people who believed that God was fulfilling every promise and find out that things do not work out as they expected (38:8-9, 11-12, 14). They are promised that God is exercising initiative even when things look the opposite, and that God will fulfill promises, will protect, and will defeat.

In 39:23-29 the Gog prophecy fades into the background, indeed virtually disappears from view, and the section provides a resumptive conclusion to chs. 33–39 which enables the hearers to take stock and draw their breath before the great final vision in chs. 40–48.

A Visionary New Temple (Chs. 40–42)

The full introduction in 40:1-4 highlights another new turn in Ezekiel's prophecies and opens up the final long section of the book. It reports a visionary visit to his homeland in 573 BC, at Passover time (if he presupposes a spring new year) or on the Day of Atonement (if he presupposes an autumn new year). The passage forms a positive counterpart at the end of the book to chs. 8–11, and it has a similar beginning. "In stark contrast to the cultic aberrations and consequent judgment stands an edifice whose symmetry spells decent order and which brings only glory to the holy God, keeping at bay all that is profane" (Allen). At the same time the vision of a place of Yahweh's dwelling given as the people looks forward to returning to its land corresponds to the plan for such a dwelling given to Moses at Mt. Sinai as the people pause on the way to their land (see Exodus 25–31).

The temple complex which Ezekiel visits is also in recognizable continuity with the actual First Temple, and the picture may be illuminated by being read alongside 1 Kings 6–7. The measurements come in terms of the long cubit, just over half a meter, and the use of this "old" cubit (cf. 2 Chr 3:3) suggests the continuity of the "new" visionary temple with the old faith. But the neat symmetry of this plan distinguishes it from anything Israel has known before.

The actual scene, like that in chs. 8–11, is something other than anyone would ever physically see. That is advertised at the beginning by the description of the citylike structure as set on a very high mountain, for Zion actually stands lower than the hills around; its elevation is theological rather than geographical (cf. Ps 48:1). In Ezekiel's vision its geographical height comes to match its theological significance (cf. Isa 2:2). Taking up 37:26-28, the vision constitutes the divine architect's concrete promise concerning a transformed dwelling place to replace the one which has been devastated.

As a vision, it need portray neither what God literally intends to do nor what the recipients are literally to attempt to implement, though it does suggest something which is already existent to God and is real enough to be seen in vision. The chapters offer a concrete imaginative realization of God's purpose for the future, to function both as a promise (Yahweh is committed to dwelling among the people) and as a spur to action such as the builders of the actual Second Temple undertook — so that their work can be seen as seeking the fulfillment of the vision even though it did not (and could not) correspond architecturally to it. Chs. 40–48 as a whole thus combine promises regarding what will be done and regulations for what must be done, divine gift and human commitment (Zimmerli). Yahweh will see that the temple is renewed; the community must accept its responsibility for ensuring that it is ordered aright. More immediately, they must begin to live their lives in the present in the conviction that this is truly God's vision for the future, as really as people who could more directly feast their eyes on Zion's beauty and strength, and then talk about this to others, in Psalm 48.

Ezekiel describes the temple complex in the order in which he is conducted around it by a humanlike supernatural figure (as in earlier chapters, an original vision may have been expanded, e.g., in 42:1-14):

1. The substantial perimeter wall which establishes a firm boundary between profane/ordinary space and holy/special space (40:5), to which he returns at the end (42:15-20) and again at 43:12 in affirming the supreme special nature of the whole complex.

2. The steps and eastern gateway, like that of an actual city rather than that of a temple, with alcoves for the Levites who stood as gatekeepers (40:6-16). In the past the city, and especially the palace, had tended to subsume the temple. In this vision the temple subsumes the city as well as eliminating the palace; this temple is no royal chapel adjacent to the king's court. The significance of the gateways in general in the vision will emerge in 44:4-8: the special character of the temple area depends on watch being kept on who enters it (cf. Psalms 15 and 24). The significance of the prominent eastern gateway in particular will emerge in 43:1-9; 44:1-3 (again cf. Psalm 24).

3. The elevated courtyard through the gateway, surrounded by rooms or porticoes where people such as

priests, Levites, prophets, scribes, musicians, elders, officials, and ordinary worshipers could meet, work, sleep, talk, and eat (40:17-19); cf. accounts of the First and Second Temples in Ezra 8:29; 10:6; Nehemiah 13; Jeremiah 35–36.

4. The matching northern and southern gateways to the courtyard (40:20-27).

5. The further steps and gateways from this outer court to a more elevated inner courtyard (40:28-37) with associated room for preparing sacrifices (40:38-43) and rooms for priests on duty (40:44-47). Reference to the singers' chambers in v. 44 is odd; the LXX has the word for "two" (chambers), in Hebrew *shtym,* which could have become confused with the word for "singers," *shrym.* The LXX also assumes that the second chamber is at the south not the east gate, which makes better sense. No wall for the inner courtyard is mentioned and a ramp is thus implied, though a wall might be presupposed.

6. The yet more elevated actual temple building with its narthex, pillars, nave, and sanctuary, having progressively narrower entrances (40:48–41:4). "Nave" *(hekal)* is the word for a royal palace, reapplied to the dwelling of the divine king; it appears more often in ch. 41 than anywhere else in the OT. It underlines the fact that Israel's king is Yahweh and that the one palace in the new Jerusalem is the divine king's. Only Ezekiel's guide actually enters the "most holy place" (lit. "holy of holies"); he has confined himself to conducting and measuring through 40:5–41:3a, but here in 41:3b for the first time he speaks, highlighting the climactic significance of this moment, which comes at the center of the three chapters.

7. Its walls, storerooms, and yard, whose function is no doubt partly practical but probably partly to provide a buffer zone to safeguard the sanctity of the temple (41:5-15a).

8. Its inner decoration and furnishings (41:15b-26). The brevity of the description and the simplicity of the decoration as in the gateways offer a contrast to the abhorrent portrayal in ch. 8 and even to that of the First Temple proper.

9. The priests' vestries and refectories to its north and south (42:1-14).

For the most part what Ezekiel offers is nothing more than a floor plan, which he is apparently required to sketch out in 43:11. There is no reference to the height of the many buildings, and little explanation of their purpose, while many of the sacred objects such as the covenant chest are unmentioned. The emphasis thus lies on the systematic thoroughness of Yahweh's architectural planning. The measurements' precision and the plan's symmetry suggest careful calculation on the prophet's part as well as visionary openness. It is striking that everything works together to produce one hundred-cubit multiples; there are few fours, sevens, or twelves.

Yahweh's Splendor Returns to the Temple (43:1-12)

At great length the scene has been set and the suspense deepened for the drama which now follows, back where we began. The palace having been prepared, the king can now enter it in majesty from the direction he had left it (chs. 10–11), following the same basic path that Ezekiel's guide and Ezekiel and we as readers have already trod in chs. 40–42. So this king enters to sit in the sanctuary with his metaphorical throne and footstool (the covenant chest, more concretely Yahweh's footstool, is unmentioned, as elsewhere in the prophets; cf. Jer 3:16-17). The down-to-earth anthropomorphic expressions "exclude all doubt about the reality of his presence" (Eichrodt). To the correspondence with chs. 8–11 noted in connection with chs. 40–42, 43:3 adds a correspondence with chs. 1–3. We have accepted the guidance and words of Yahweh's assistant for much longer than in chs. 8–11; at last we hear Yahweh's own voice affirming that this is a return that will be followed by no more leaving.

The point about the divine king's palace crowding out the human king's palace becomes more explicit in 43:7-9. Yahweh's palace cannot have its special nature compromised by the too close proximity of the kings' dwelling (see 1 Kings 6–7), let alone by these kings' funeral shrines in their palaces (43:7-9). The word for "corpses" may denote "memorials"; it is usually assumed that kings were not regularly buried near the palace and thus near the temple, but the burial of the likes of Manasseh there with the kind of shrine this would involve (cf. 2 Kgs 21:18) would be enough to engender the loathing indicated here.

Yahweh unilaterally intends to dwell among them forever (43:7), but they are required to put away practices which compromise Yahweh's holiness (v. 9). This is as much a consequence of that intention as a condition of it (cf. the argument of Romans 6). Yahweh's continuing words (vv. 10-12) form a further bridge between the motifs of divine gift and human commitment, as they do between chs. 40–42 and what will follow. People are to have the temple plan explained to them so that they may implement the regulations it requires. One aspect of this process is the paradoxical expectation typical of Ezekiel that an awareness of shame is an aspect of restoration (cf., e.g., 36:32). There is further a paradoxical two-way interrelationship between knowing about the new temple and experiencing this shame. Knowing about God's gracious act of restoration enables people to own their previous failure (43:10), and owning failure opens them to God's act of restoration (v. 11a).

Regulations for the Temple's Altar and the Gate (43:13–44:3)

The altar's location was established in the outline plan at 40:47. Its stepped design might remind an audience in Babylon of a ziggurat, and thus of the true "mountain" whose ascent led the way into God's presence. Its monumental size with its hewn stone and the necessary steps for the priest to climb onto it contrast with Yahweh's earlier requirements in Exod 20:25-26: the principle of splendor and impressiveness is now allowed to override that of simplicity. The steps are to the altar's east, so that the priest climbing the altar faces the temple itself; there is to be no more of the practice described in 8:16.

The arrangements for the altar's dedication in turn recall those prescribed for the desert tabernacle, with Ezekiel playing the part of Moses. On the offerings, see Leviticus 1–7. But whereas accounts of the consecration of the tabernacle altar and the First Temple altar emphasize anointing and whole offering more than atonement (e.g., Exod 30:28; Leviticus 8; 1 Kings 8; 2 Chronicles 7), here all the emphasis lies on purification (lit. "de-sinning") and atonement (lit. "covering" or "wiping away"); indeed, the ritual compares with that for the Day of Atonement in Leviticus 16. The implication is that this time the altar needs not merely to be taken from the realm of the everyday to that of the sacred but to be taken from the realm of the sinful to that of the pure. God's commission promises that there is a way for this to happen. Once again the awareness of being polluted emphasized by earlier portrayals of the temple (see esp. chs. 8–11) influences the insight regarding what needs to be done to renew the community's worship.

Parallel considerations lie behind Ezekiel's confining of ministry at the altar henceforth to the family of Zadok, excluding the rest of the Aaronic line as well as the rest of the tribe of Levi (cf. 40:45-46; 44:10-15).

If the altar's shape may have recalled that of a ziggurat, the closing of the temple complex's main entrance to anyone but Yahweh may have recalled the closing of a great Babylonian temple gate to anyone but Marduk. But it commemorated the fact that Yahweh had entered the temple once and for all by this entrance. It had thus become as sacred as the sanctuary. Admittedly the ruler (the word is *naśi'*, NRSV "prince," implicitly a disempowered version of a king) was to be allowed to eat in its western vestibule. This strange privilege recalls the privileged status of the monarch in the First Temple period, but perhaps underlines how limited that privileged status now is.

The Ministry of the Temple (44:4-31)

The initial reprise of Ezekiel's vision (44:4-5) forms a bridge with what has preceded, introducing 44:6–46:18. The account of the prophet's visionary experience thus forms the basis for something more like regulations, beginning with ones concerning the temple's ministry. With the most pointed stipulations yet in the prescriptions for the new temple, Ezekiel issues three requirements. A number of convictions underlie them.

First, the custom of having non-Israelites working as temple servants must be abandoned (44:6-8). The foreigners are perhaps people of Canaanite origin living within Israel, but perhaps also people from the surrounding countries who found themselves in Israel for one reason or another; compare the role of the Gibeonites (see Josh 9:27) and the Carites (2 Kings 11), the story of Ruth, and the many references to non-Israelites in Ezra, Nehemiah, and Isaiah 56–66. Talk of abominations and of breaking the covenant suggests the conviction that they were a means whereby unacceptable religious practices were introduced into the temple, though talk of their being uncircumcised in mind deconstructs such a drawing of distinctions between Israelite and foreigner, for this was Israel's state too (Jer 9:25-26): Ezekiel has not used the term "uncircumcised," but it is clearly his assessment of Israel. But talk of their being physically uncircumcised points to the fact that irrespective of the question whether they were a bad influence, foreigners compromised the distinctiveness of the Israelite people. Unless they accepted circumcision and thus became Israelites, they profaned Yahweh's sanctuary, making it seem like any other place.

Second, most members of the tribe of Levi have their temple role redefined (44:9-14). They now have the privilege and responsibility of the actual killing of animals in sacrifice, which formerly could be undertaken by lay Israelites. On the other hand, their role is to be confined to such subordinate ministerial tasks. Whereas Exodus 32 praises the tribe of Levi for the rigor of its commitment to Yahweh at Mt. Sinai, and in the Second Temple period Chronicles emphasizes the significance of their role in leading worship in activities such as prophecy and music, Ezekiel sees them as especially implicated in Israel's idolatry during the First Temple period. In being henceforth confined to subordinate roles in leading worship, like deacons rather than priests, they will bear continuing punishment and shame.

Ezekiel's stance regarding the Levites and the priests needs to be set in the context of the variety of attitudes to this subject elsewhere in the OT. Unfortunately the evidence concerning this, and its implications for the history of the Levites and the priesthood, is complicated and controverted. Leviticus distinguishes between the ministerial role of Levites in general and the specific role of Aaron and his descendants in matters such as sacrifice (cf. also Numbers 18). A differentiation of role is similarly emphasized here in Ezekiel 44. The story of Josiah's reforms has been reckoned to fit with this and to provide some of its historical background in its description of Josiah's demotion of the former priests of shrines outside Jerusalem (2 Kgs 23:8-9), who might be identified with the (non-Aaronite) Levites. This would also fit with the comments in 44:10-14. The demotion of most of the Levites may explain their lack of interest in returning to Jerusalem from Babylon (Ezra 8:15-20).

Third, priestly roles in the narrow sense are to be confined to the members of the tribe of Levi who were descended from Zadok (44:15-31). In contrast to the parts of the OT just noted, Deuteronomy speaks as if all Levites are priests. While it may be concerned to minimize the difference between the two, it may be using the word "priest" in a broader sense, and may not exclude a difference of role between Levites in general and a priestly group in the narrower sense. This is supported by the fact that the narrative in Samuel-Kings (which shares many of Deuteronomy's theological emphases) moves in a different direction since it describes Yahweh as coming to reject one group within Aaron's descendants, the line of Eli and Abiathar. The more specialized priestly roles were henceforth confined to the other group, the line of Zadok (see 1 Sam 2:27-36; 2 Sam 8:17; 1 Kgs 1:7-8). It is this principle which Ezekiel advocates in 44:15-16. In his account, the Zadokite line contrasted with the whole of the rest of the tribe of Levi in remaining faithful to orthodox ways when the people as a whole did not.

Various regulations concerning the priests are outlined in 44:17-27. The section combines their tasks, their lifestyle, and their support, and especially recalls Leviticus 10 and 21. It is concerned to safeguard their sanctity and thus Yahweh's own special nature, and as part of that to avoid practices associated with other religions. At the end of this chapter vv. 28-31 in turn form a further bridge to ch. 45. The function of these bridging sections compares with that of 42:15-20 and 43:10-12.

It is natural to ask whether 44:4-31 reflects the interests of groups who urge these regulations. Their being buttressed by claims to divine revelation also buttresses the pursuing of these groups' interests. Ezekiel, after all, is an Israelite, not an alien; a member of the tribe of Levi, not a layman; a member of the family of Aaron, not of one of the other families in that tribe; and (it has been assumed) a member of the line of Zadok, not that of Abiathar. He benefits from the regulations he advocates in Yahweh's name. It is not obvious that the tribe of Levi or the family of Aaron or the line of Zadok was immune from influencing Israel into alien ways and compromises of Yahweh's holiness as effectively as foreigners. Their effectiveness in doing so was to be repeated in the history of the Christian church: after priesthood had been metaphorically transferred to Christ and to the church, the church reestablished priesthood and established episcopacy and papacy within itself for the sake of its discipline, but all these proved capable of corrupting the church as well as preserving it. These developments, too, buttressed the position of people who fulfilled the role of priests, bishops, and popes. But they perhaps safeguarded the church from worse fates than it experienced, and the Levites and Zadokites may have done the same for Israel.

The Head of State and the Temple Worship (Chs. 45–46)

Ezekiel's visions and regulations for the new temple recall the vision Moses is given for a sanctuary when Israel is first on its way to its land. The regulations in chs. 45–46 look like a miscellany rather than a coherent unity of their own, and they probably came into being by a gradual process. As a whole they offer a series of exhortations and regulations supplementing those associated with Moses. The latter made virtually no reference to national leadership, and a concern which runs through Ezekiel's visions and regulations is to make explicit the place of the ruler in relation to Israel's worship, which is not an issue in the Torah.

Ezekiel is keenly aware of the existence of the monarchy and lives among a community which apparently has two deposed kings living in its midst. Most people no doubt expect the monarchy to be reestablished as part of any reestablishment of the Israelite state. Once the monarchy had come into existence, it had developed a close involvement in Israelite worship which then focused on a temple which was a royal establishment, as well as involving itself in people's lives (e.g., in imposing taxes) in ways which as often meant oppression as freedom. Ezekiel is concerned to formalize parameters for the community's rulers and for any involvement in worship in the future. Thus this is the angle from which most of the regulations which follow approach their question. It explains why a number of matters are oddly ignored — for instance, Pentecost in 45:18-25 and the evening offering in 46:13-15. The ruler ("prince") is demoted from being king; the term applied to him was used for the Persian Empire's agent when the people were given the opportunity to return to Jerusalem (see Ezra 1:8), and it is one which could naturally be applied to subsequent figures such as Nehemiah; Blenkinsopp notes many parallels between features of chs. 45–46 and aspects of life as described in Ezra-Nehemiah.

Succeeding paragraphs presuppose a hardheaded stance regarding the ruler's likely behavior, informed by the experience of actual kings. The expectations of this ruler in the future thus emphasize realism and practicality in a way which contrasts with ch. 34 as well as with the impracticality of the plans for the temple in chs. 40–42. "Henceforth Israel is to be not a nation-state in the usual sense of that term but a temple-community" (Blenkinsopp). To some extent this is what happened.

45:1-8 concern an aspect of the (re-)allocation of the land to the people in connection with the establishment of the new temple. Again Ezekiel's prophecies recall the story of Israel's first origins as a people, which came to a climax with the land's allocation to the tribes. Ezekiel will come to the land's allocation as a whole in chs. 47–48; this anticipation focuses simply on a revision of the arrangements for the heartland. An area 25,000 cubits (nine miles) square centering on the sanctuary belongs especially to Yahweh. Two-fifths is occupied by the priests. Two-fifths is occupied by the Levites, a different arrangement from that prescribed in Numbers 35. The Levites are now exempt from the rule that they cannot own land. While this is a privilege, it is also a sign of their relative demotion from "proper" priesthood. The final fifth is occupied by the city with its needed agricultural land. Outside this square, the rest of the 25,000-cubit belt across the land is to belong to the ruler.

One can see here the same concern to safeguard the separateness of the sanctuary as appeared in chs. 40–42 (here separateness from both city and ruler), the same privileging of the priesthood to which Ezekiel belonged, the same concern to put the city in its place (it is an adjunct to the temple rather than vice versa), and the same concern to put the ruler in his place with a provision which might seem generous but was evidently designed to constrain him (45:8); cf. the complaints of Isa 5:8 and Jeremiah 22 and the stories in 1 Kings 21 and subsequently Nehemiah 5. The climactic significance of the last point is underlined by the fact that here Yahweh speaks rather than being spoken of (contrast vv. 1 and 4). The arrangement pays no more attention to the demands of physical geography, or the actual needs of the city, than does the floor plan for the temple in chs. 40–42.

The even more prophetic style ("thus says sovereign Yahweh") of 45:9-12 then compares with 44:6-8 in its context. It underlines the point made in v. 8; cf. the polemic of ch. 34. Weights and measures can easily be falsified, as is reflected in the fact that this is the subject of admonition in the prophets and the wisdom books (e.g., Prov 11:1; Amos 8:5) as well as the Torah (e.g., Deut 25:13-16). Here 45:10-12 imply that the ruler must take responsibility for the proper regulating of weights and measures. In the present context the weights and measures relate especially to the offerings, but the point is first generalized. The ephah is a dry measure for grain, the bath a liquid measure; their equivalent in our measures is uncertain. But ten ephahs or baths comprise a homer, which recalls the word for a donkey (*hamor*) and might suggest a donkey load. The gerah-shekel-mina system covers weights. There is variation between the Hebrew and Greek texts in v. 12; the Greek text presupposes a mina of fifty shekels, which corresponds to other OT evidence. This variation reflects differences in the system in different areas and over the centuries. A shekel weighed 11.4 grams; it was only during the Second Temple period that coinage was introduced and the shekel became a coin.

45:13-17 continue the talk of measurements, but in such a way as to introduce the ruler's obligations regarding the provision of the regular offerings, which are described in Leviticus without reference to the king. The only explicit reason why the people should pay taxes to the ruler is to provide for offerings to Yahweh. Once again the ruler is firmly subordinated to the temple; in any case he has his own allocation of land to supply his own needs. In the same way 45:18-25 as a whole concern the ruler's obligations for most of the major festivals outlined in, for example, Leviticus 23; the "you" of 45:18 is singular. Thus the notion of the ruler imposing taxes on the people is ratified but turned into a system whereby the people's obligations regarding offerings are fulfilled. While the passage links with Leviticus 16, as in 43:13-27 Ezekiel lays special stress on atonement in connection with the offerings, an emphasis which corresponds to the awareness of guilt which characterized the period after 587 BC and in particular to Ezekiel's own stress on the pollution of the temple (see esp. chs. 8–11). The good news is once again that this pollution is not the last word; Yahweh provides for the temple's cleansing.

46:1-15 concern the ruler's involvement in weekly, monthly, and daily worship, for which compare Numbers 28. Here he thus had further responsibilities of provision, and further privilege on the sabbath and the new moon in terms of access to the threshold of the inner court where the altar was — but no further (vv. 1-8); contrast the practice in, for example, 1 Kgs 8:22. A further feature of these regulations is an increase in the dimensions of the sabbath sacrifices, marking increased enthusiasm for the sabbath from Ezekiel's day. On other days the ruler was subject to the same requirements as other people (46:9-10). Other regulations for his offerings follow (vv. 11-15). The ruler thus fulfills none of the priestly roles undertaken by kings elsewhere, and perhaps in First Temple Jerusalem.

46:16-18 return to the ruler's property rights, mentioned in 45:8-12. Here exhortation again becomes regulation. On the one hand, the regulation in v. 17 alongside the permission in v. 16 ensures that the ruler's land allocation (45:1-8) remains in the family. The year of liberty might be the seventh year or the year of jubilee (Leviticus 25). The point of the regulation lies in 46:18; the other side of the coin is that he has no reason or right to appropriate further land, or even to acquire extra land through quite legal means such as purchase (from people who become poor?).

46:19-24 are in content an appendix to the material on the temple and its offerings, relating more directly to 42:13-14. In form they return from the issuing of priestly regulations and the declaring of prophetic words to the guiding of the man with the measuring reed. The priests have dedicated kitchens for cooking the offerings that were confined to them and must be kept separate. There are then kitchens at the four corners of the outer court for the Levites to cook the offerings which lay people shared.

The Transforming River Flowing from the Temple (47:1-12)

Anyone who stands at the eastern perimeter wall of the actual First or Second Temple stands at the great divide between the relatively well-watered western slopes of the Judean hills and the all-but-dry eastern slopes. The difference is very clear to the naked eye as one turns from west to east. On the east there are sizable canyons of the kind that elsewhere could contain flowing rivers, but they contain no water except on the odd occasions when a storm throws a flash flood down them. The descent to sea level and beyond to the river Jordan, a thousand-meter fall, sees the land becoming drier and drier. In traditional Orthodox paintings of Jesus' baptism, which took place here, fish are swimming in the river, but in reality no fish swim there. The river debouches into the Dead Sea, or Salt Sea in Hebrew; both names are accurate and telling. Nothing can live here, given the concentration of minerals in this lake from which there is no departure except by evaporation. Only alongside the one or two streams such as the Qelt and around small oases such as En Gedi do trees grow (En Eglaim is probably a similar small oasis to the east of the Dead Sea). Only around the huge oasis at Jericho do flowering and fruit trees flourish on a large scale and at all times of the year.

In the wondrous transformation within Ezekiel's vision, it is as if the course of the river Jordan is changed so that it flows not from northern Galilee but from Jerusalem, bringing with it the fertility that surrounds it in the north, or as if the fish of the Sea of Galilee or of the Mediterranean itself are transferred to the barren east, or as if the sources of water in Eden turn the land into a new paradise garden (see Gen 2:10, 9) — without totally eliminating the salts useful for preserving and seasoning food (47:11; cf. 43:24). Once again an image, suggested by the reality of the Gihon spring (see, e.g., Pss 36:8-9; 46:4; Isa 8:5), has become an allegory. The very land is transformed, and therefore the lives of the people. More obviously than anywhere else in chs. 40–48 we are here in the realm of visionary imagination, of pictorial promise. The water's source is now the temple itself, and the picture vouchsafes that the renewed holy place and its worship will become the source of a healing and renewal of the land's whole life. Rev 22:1-3 provides an influential instance of the ongoing life of vv. 1-12 (Zimmerli and Blenkinsopp give further examples).

In terms of the narrative in this vision, 47:1-12 follows on from 43:1-5. In context, the transition from the practicalities of ch. 46 is striking. For Ezekiel and his followers there is no tension between these two; Yahweh is the God of both. The detailed practical regulations are both God's way of implementing the vision and human beings' way of laying the fuel for God's lighting the fire.

The Reallocation of the Land to the Tribes (47:13–48:35)

"If chaps. 40–48 begin with theological architecture, they end with theological geography" (Allen). Once more Ezekiel envisions the people on the way to the promised land. The visionary move from the temple to the well-watered land in 47:1-12 facilitates a closing transition to a bidding in prophetic style (see the opening of 47:13) concerning the allocation of the land as a whole. The renewed land can have a new start. The theme of the land's allocation is also a prominent feature of the climax of the story of Israel's origins, dominating as it does the second half of Joshua. Here as there Yahweh's giving of the land is a fulfillment of a promise to Israel's ancestors (47:14; cf. 20:42; Josh 23:14; and, e.g., Gen 12:1-3). As in Genesis rather than in Joshua, no reflection is offered on how the people will acquire the land from its present occupants, any more than how the topography of Zion will be rearranged to make the temple plans realizable.

In modern terms, the bounds of the land include southern Lebanon and the Golan but not the part of the State of Jordan east of the Jordan once occupied by some of the tribes, and not the area down to Eilat (47:15-20); the account in Numbers 34 is similar. It broadly corresponds and works out the detail of the description of the bounds of the land in Solomon's day (1 Kgs 8:65), and thus (like other parts of chs. 40–48) makes promises that lay far beyond the bounds of human possibility for the little Babylonian community or the Second Temple Judean community which treasured and probably elaborated Ezekiel's visions in faith.

A place is to be given to people who have settled among the tribes sufficiently permanently to have had children there (47:21-23). It is perhaps implicit that they thus have a different status from the foreigners referred to in 44:6-9; cf. 14:7. The Torah's positive concern for immigrants and its openness to their full participation in the community's life of faith and worship (e.g., Deut 10:19; 26:11) is thus here taken for granted. Indeed, it is taken further, if this is the first explicit advocacy of their rights to a share in the land (cf. Isa 56:1-8).

In the allocation in which Levi will receive land near the temple, the twelveness of the tribes is to be preserved by treating Joseph as two, Ephraim and Manasseh (47:13-14). In the account of the areas given to the different tribes (48:1-35), the tribes descended from "senior" sons such as Benjamin and Judah have allocations nearer the center, while the sons of concubines appear further away. For the most part the tribes' earlier positions are thus ignored; even Benjamin and Judah are reversed. The width of the strips is not stated; that might mean that this is the kind of practical question which did not concern the visionary or might mean that the strips were all of the same size, which could have egalitarian implications, fitting other aspects of the Torah's vision.

Information on the allocation of the heartland is repeated and expanded from 45:1-8. The repetition and the prominence here in relation to the allocation to the tribes emphasizes the significance of this element in the picture. The fact that the allocation of the land is structured around the location of the temple is a wholly new feature over against the traditional accounts of Israel's origins, where the temple is a not-very-inspired afterthought (see 2 Samuel 7). The place of the ruler has a similar status (see 1 Samuel 8), though it is more equivocal even here (see chs. 45–46 and the comment). At the center of the land is Yahweh's "portion" (*terumah,* 48:8), a technical term usually applied to offerings. It suggests that the dedication of this area to Yahweh, this "choice portion of the land" (48:14), frees the people to enjoy the rest of the land themselves, as the dedication of a portion of crops, herds, and flocks to Yahweh frees them to enjoy the rest of these.

Much extra detail is given concerning the city and its twelve gates, a picture taken up (as is so much of Ezekiel) in Revelation (see 21:12-14). The focus on the city at the book's close is surprising given the focus on the city-like temple complex earlier, and 48:30-35 may thus reflect another hand and another theology, one which has more in common with the stress on city than temple in Isaiah 40–66. It leaves the book closing with a nice bringing together of city and temple, sacred and secular, in a new symbolic statement (Blenkinsopp). Commentators often observe that the closing declaration of the city's name, *Yahweh shammah* ("Yahweh is there"), is a fine actual ending to the book, "a correct definition of what was the essential content of the age of salvation in the eyes of Ezekiel and also of his disciples, and those who transmitted his writings" (Eichrodt).

Bibliography. Allen, L. C. 1994 and 1990, *Ezekiel,* 2 vols., Dallas: Word • Blenkinsopp, J. 1990, *Ezekiel,* Louisville: John Knox • Brueggemann, W. 1978/1992, *Hopeful Imagination,* Philadelphia: Fortress and London: SCM • Eichrodt, W. 1970, *Ezekiel,* Philadelphia: Westminster and London: SCM • Greenberg, M. 1983, *Ezekiel 1–20,* Garden City, N.Y.: Doubleday • Greenberg, M. 1997, *Ezekiel 21–37,* New York: Doubleday • Gruenwald, I. 1980, *Apocalyptic and Merkabah Mysticism,* Leiden: Brill • Lindsey, H. 1970/1971, *The Late Great Planet Earth,* Grand Rapids: Zondervan and London: Marshall • Taylor, J. B. 1969, *Ezekiel,* London: Inter-Varsity and Grand Rapids: Eerdmans • Zimmerli, W. 1979 and 1983, *Ezekiel,* 2 vols., Philadelphia: Fortress.

Daniel

Iain Provan

INTRODUCTION

The book of Daniel is an unusual biblical book in that it is written only partly in Hebrew (1:1–2:4; 8-12), the remainder coming down to us in Aramaic (2:4–7:28). It is a book whose final form appears to date from around the middle of the second century BC, although many would date at least the mainly Aramaic section in chs. 1–7 much earlier (around the sixth-fourth centuries BC) and some continue to argue that the whole book is an early exilic composition. It draws on the history of the struggle of the people of God under the domination of the rulers of the present world order with a view to encouraging the same people to faithfulness in their present time of "exile" (whether physical or more metaphorical, as in Heb 11:13 and 1 Pet 1:1). It also prophesies about a future time which will be different. Its message to the present is that God's people should seek to live peaceably, where they are able, with the powers of the world, but should be prepared, in holding onto the different vision represented by the kingdom of God, for confrontation and consequent suffering. Such confrontation is often required in the present, and certainly shall be so in the future, in the period when the long-running battle between the kingdoms of this world and the kingdom of God comes to resolution, and God's Messiah finally overcomes the wicked anti-Messiah. Faithfulness in the midst of trial, however, brings deliverance for God's people. Proclaiming such a message, the book of Daniel was important not only to Jewish readers living during the periods of Hellenistic and Roman domination of Palestine but to early Christian readers as well. So it is that Daniel is often referred to or alluded to where the NT writers are advocating Christian faithfulness in the present (e.g., Heb 11:33-34) or outlining their own vision of the future, with its picture of the Messiah Jesus who comes at the end of time to combat the anti-Messiah (i.e., antichrist) and finally to bring in the kingdom of God (e.g., Mark 13; 2 Thessalonians 2; Revelation). The book has remained a vibrant source of comfort and hope within the Christian tradition throughout the succeeding centuries, whether in the broad sweep of its message or in its rather more dubious employment as source material for the construction of a detailed timetable of the "events of the end times."

COMMENTARY

1:1-7 The circumstances under which the four particular Israelites chosen by the authors to represent "the people of God in exile" arrived in such exile are first explained: King Nebuchadnezzar of Babylon brought them there, probably in the aftermath of his crushing victories over the Egyptians in 605 BC, when King Jehoiakim of Judah (2 Kgs 23:31-35; 2 Chr 36:1-4) may have offered Nebuchadnezzar his allegiance and had hostages taken to ensure his future good behavior. The significance of the place of exile is brought out by the use of "Shinar" in 1:2 — the location of the tower of Babel, a symbol of opposition to God (Gen 11:1-9), and the place where wickedness is at home (Zech 5:11). This is a land in which faith and uprightness will be under threat. However, it is not a land into which the exiles have come by chance (1:2). Nebuchadnezzar may think that he has conquered the God of the Jews since he has defeated them and placed the Jerusalem temple vessels in the treasury of his god. In fact, he acts only by divine permission — something which will become even clearer as chs. 1–4 progress. The exiles need not despair. They may be compelled to live for a time in this foreign land. Their identity may come under threat, as in token of their change in status from Judean nobles to royal servants they are renamed (v. 7). God is still God, however. Nothing fundamental has changed.

1:8-16 The first event next described is closely tied to 1:1-7 by the use of the Heb. verb *yasem,* which appeared in v. 7: "the palace master gave them (*yasem lahem,* "set upon them") other names." V. 8 now tells us that "Daniel resolved (*yasem ʿal-libbo,* "set upon his heart") that he would not defile himself." Daniel's response to the Babylonian attempt to redefine their identity through setting new names upon them is to set his heart against cooperation. It is probably not simply that the Babylonian food is regarded as ritually unclean, for there are no OT purity laws which might explain Daniel's avoidance of wine. The connection between vv. 7 and 8 suggests that there is an element of political resistance as well. Daniel is determined not only not to break the law in the specific matter of religious purity but also not to compromise himself in general by accepting his redefinition as a Babylonian. It is the question of allegiance; for to eat someone's food in this context is to give allegiance to him (as it is in 11:26, where the same Persian word for food, *pat-bag,* is used). Daniel is prepared to accept his new role in Babylon to a certain extent. He is not prepared, however, to surrender his soul to the Babylonian king without a struggle.

Since God is the moving force behind the scenes in all that is happening (1:2), it is no surprise that God is now responsible for the favorable response that Daniel receives to his request for a different diet. The chief eunuch being naturally reluctant to allow Daniel to demonstrate his allegiance to Yahweh without some evidence that this will not result in the loss of his own head, a test is devised. Lying beneath the surface is the question also addressed by the other stories in Daniel: Who is really the Lord in the situation of exile — the foreign king or Yahweh? The vegetable test settles the matter, for God vindicates the four for their faithfulness.

1:17-21 The chapter comes to a conclusion with a brief summary statement which takes us through the remainder of the "three years" mentioned in v. 5 — in the light of 2:1, evidently a round figure referring (consistent with Hebrew usage) to a period of one full year and fractions of two others. This was the period of education that was to end with the four youths standing before the king. The emphasis falls characteristically, however, not on the quality of the Babylonian education system but on the work of God. It is because God has been involved in their lives that when our heroes appear for their final examinations, they excel. In particular, Daniel has a gift for understanding visions and dreams. In all this, they are vastly better qualified than any of their Babylonian counterparts. Babylonian education, like Babylonian food, has nothing to offer which Israel's God cannot match and surpass. The final verse of the chapter presents us with a puzzle, being argued by some to suggest that Daniel stopped exercising his talents in Babylon in 539 BC — the first year of Cyrus, and the date of the first return of the Jews from exile — and returned to Palestine. It would be difficult, then, to reconcile 1:21 with either 6:28 or 10:1. 1:21 could simply mean to say, however, that Daniel operated throughout the Babylonian era (the period of Israelite exile), without meaning to say that he did *not* operate during the Persian era as well.

How did the Jews of these stories come to be in Babylon? How did they come to be in the Babylonian civil service? How did they come to have Babylonian names? These are all questions that the first chapter answers, thus functioning as an introduction to the whole book. In addition, it introduces us to what will be the main themes of these stories. God is with his people in the midst of their situation under foreign domination; and God will vindicate and prosper his people in this situation if they remain faithful to him — for he, not the foreign king, is Lord. Specifically, it introduces us to Nebuchadnezzar and to Daniel. For the moment the king prospers and his god is (from his perspective) dominant. He has no reason to suspect that the God of Daniel, the God of the Jerusalem temple, is of any great consequence. He is as yet unaware of God's nature, or his claims upon all humankind. The succeeding stories will bring about a marked change to this state of affairs. Daniel appears as one skilled in visions and dreams, not (as the Babylonians might suppose) as a result of their training but as a result of God's gifting. The contrast between Daniel's wisdom and the wisdom of others is also crucial to the later stories, including that in ch. 2.

2:1-11 Chapter 2 opens a couple of years after Daniel and his friends have arrived in Babylon, when they have completed their apprenticeship. We discover that Nebuchadnezzar is a king troubled by dreams. He therefore summons his various servants, summarized as "Chaldeans" (since the end of v. 2 is better rendered, not "and the Chaldeans" [NRSV], but "that is, the Chaldeans"). This term has already appeared in 1:4 in an ethnic sense (meaning simply "Babylonians"), but here it has a narrower sense, indicating that for which the Babylonians were famous in the rest of the ancient Near East (i.e., astrology, divination, etc.). The mention of Babylonian magicians and enchanters is important since 1:20 has informed the reader that the Israelites were ten times wiser than all these. We do not expect to find them of much help to the king. There is indeed an unpleasant surprise in store for the Chaldeans. Whether because he has forgotten it, or simply because he wishes to test their mettle, Nebuchadnezzar wants from them not simply the interpretation of the dream, but an account of the dream itself! Their counteroffer in 2:4 rejected, we sense a more desperate tone in v. 7; but Nebuchadnezzar has realized that to give an interpretation is not to demonstrate knowledge of the world beyond that which most mortals possess. He is in fact convinced that his wise men will concoct stories designed to divert trouble in the short term until the crisis passes and the king is not quite so angry (v. 9). Only if they can tell him the *dream* can he trust the *interpretation*. This is, however, humanly impossible — indeed, what he asks is unprecedented, presumably because sensible people know that it is impossible (vv. 10-11). The readers of the story, on the other hand, strongly suspect that there *is* someone on earth who can meet the king's demand, precisely because they know from ch. 1 that God had given Daniel understanding in all visions and dreams (1:17). Thus the stage is set for the entrance of Daniel himself.

2:12-30 Although ch. 1 tells us that the four Israelites had finished their apprenticeship as wise men, it nowhere tells us that they were simply incorporated into the band of "magicians and enchanters" at the royal court (cf. 1:20, where we are told not that they were wiser than the *other* "magicians and enchanters," but simply that they were wiser than the "magicians and enchanters"). The text certainly implies that all magicians and enchanters were considered wise men by the Babylonians; it does not imply that all wise men were considered magicians and enchanters. It is not as surprising as it might at first appear, then, that Daniel and his friends are not consulted by the king in the first instance in ch. 2. Their success in training has not at this point put them in the inner circle of royal advisers whose job it is to interpret the king's dreams. It is nevertheless the case that the king's anger with the Chaldeans threatens to undo all the wise men in general (v. 12). It is in such circumstances that Daniel manages to buy from Nebuchadnezzar a little further time (v. 16). He uses this time to pray with his friends (v. 18); and in response to this prayer God gives him the insight that the Babylonian wise men lack (v. 19). His action in praying, the words of his thanksgiving to God (vv. 20-23) and the opening words of his speech to the king (vv. 27-30) all underline an important truth that the chapter as a whole seeks to drive home — that wisdom comes from God, and is not the possession of mortal beings. So important is this truth that Daniel actually digresses in his speech to the king to emphasize it, the words of vv. 29-30 forming a parenthesis between vv. 28 and 31 and delaying the detail of the dream until all possible misunderstanding about the source of the revelation has been removed.

This truth about the source of wisdom and understanding is, however, only an aspect of a larger truth — that in Daniel's God Nebuchadnezzar is dealing with an incomparable and all-powerful Person who controls not only revelation but also the very course of history. This, too, has already been intimated in Daniel's thanksgiving prayer (2:21). Here we receive our first hint as to what the king's dream is about — the passing of empires in succession under the sovereign hand of God. The king had required of his counselors something that they could not deliver, and they were right to object that no one could reveal it except the gods (v. 11). Daniel later underlines the point (vv. 27-28). Nebuchadnezzar will in due course be compelled, in acknowledging the truth of what Daniel says, to acknowledge not just Daniel's wisdom but also the incomparability of Daniel's God.

2:31-45 The description of both the dream and the interpretation now follow. It is to be noted that Daniel's interpretation of the dream, like that in ch. 7, adds details not at first described in recounting the dream itself — a way of maintaining the reader's interest and avoiding too much repetition (e.g., in 2:40, 41, 45). The interpretation takes as its starting point the head of gold — Nebuchadnezzar himself (v. 38). Two further kingdoms will arise after his, signified by the inferior metals of silver and bronze (v. 39), and then a fourth kingdom, made of iron, which will break and crush all the preceding kingdoms (v. 40). The iron and clay of the feet represent the division or composite nature of this fourth kingdom, its partial weakness and partial strength, and intermarriage between its two parts or the mingling of its populations (vv. 41-43). In the days of these kings, God will set up a kingdom (represented by the stone) which shall never be destroyed, and which will bring to an end the other kingdoms. Historically, there have been two main ways of understanding the succession of empires thus described.

Some interpreters argue that the empires mentioned are Babylon, Media, Persia, and Greece. In the book of Daniel as a whole, they note, Nebuchadnezzar and Belshazzar give way to Darius the Mede, who gives way to Cyrus the Persian; and the focus of the book's attention then switches to the Greeks. The contents of 2:36-45 fit well into the history of the Greek Empire. The iron and the clay represent the Seleucid and Ptolemaic (roughly northern and southern) parts of the Greek Empire ("a divided kingdom," v. 41), the Seleucid being ultimately stronger than the Ptolemaic ("partly strong and partly brittle," v. 42). From time to time these two kingdoms linked themselves through intermarriage, although such alliances never lasted (v. 43). The fifth kingdom is either the Jewish state which followed on from the Maccabean revolt against the Greeks in the middle of the second century BC, or the Christian church/ kingdom of God.

A second popular view is that the succession of empires is Babylon, Media-Persia, Greece, and Rome. "Divided" in 2:41 does not necessarily mean "divided in two"; it may mean only that the kingdom is partly weak, partly strong, as in v. 42. The emphasis is not on geography, but on the fact that this kingdom is only *apparently* strong — in reality it has feet of clay. V. 43 need not imply intermarriage, but only the doomed attempts of this empire to hold within its borders in a peaceful way the diverse peoples that it contains. There is, moreover, an inherent weakness in the "Greek hypothesis" — that the book of Daniel nowhere explicitly says that there was a Median Empire. It only says that Babylon was ruled for a while by a king of Median extraction, who is said to have applied the laws of the Medes *and* the Persians (6:8) and may well have been the same person as Cyrus the Persian (if the end of 6:28 is translated "the reign of Darius, that is, the reign of Cyrus the Persian"). Media and Persia are two parts of the same empire in Daniel — the two horns on the single ram of ch. 8. The fourth empire on this view is not named in the book, but thought of as coming after Greece (i.e., Rome). The fifth empire is the Christian church/the kingdom of God.

The view taken in this commentary is close to the second position described, namely, that Greece is understood as the third rather than the fourth empire. The fourth empire is not Rome, however, but simply an empire to come, at some point after the Greek empire has passed away, during which the events of the end times occur. The NT actually uses the name Babylon of this empire in alluding to the book of Daniel while articulating its own vision of the future, rather than any of the other names mentioned (cf., e.g., Rev. 14:8; 16:19; 17:5; 18:10). The emphasis of Daniel in fact falls upon the nature and significance of these events rather than upon any timetable for their occurrence.

2:46-49 The chapter ends by relating Nebuchadnezzar's response to Daniel's speech and what happened afterward. Nebuchadnezzar falls on his face and worships Daniel, and through Daniel his God, who is now seen to be God of gods and Lord of kings. Daniel is given the highest civil post under the king, and requests that his three companions be similarly elevated. They go out into the province of Babylon, while Daniel remains at court; and so the scene is set for ch. 3, which will concern Shadrach, Meshach, and Abednego alone.

The story in ch. 2, in emphasizing the wisdom of Yahweh and Daniel's dependence upon Yahweh in being wise, is reminiscent of the Joseph story in Genesis 40–41, and it may be that there is some intention to bring the two into association in the reader's mind — to urge comparison and contrast between Daniel and Joseph in their struggles to live faithfully in a foreign land. The major theme of the chapter is the sovereignty of Daniel's God over all things, including kings. This sovereignty will in the end bring about the destruction of all the world's kingdoms and their replacement by the kingdom of God. In the short term, God's sovereignty is already causing his people in Babylon to prosper; and even when a new threat confronts them in ch. 3, they shall discover his protection again.

3:1-12 Chapter 3 opens with King Nebuchadnezzar's

construction on the plain of Dura of a golden statue about ninety feet high by nine feet wide, and his summoning for worship of this statue all the officials of his empire, from the satraps — the top men in the provinces — down to more minor officials such as justices and magistrates. As vv. 12 and 28 make clear, not just political but also religious allegiance is involved in worshiping at the feet of this statue — and thus a challenge immediately faces the new Jewish recruits to this governmental system. The king's edict meets with the absolute obedience of all concerned — something which is emphasized by the clever structuring of the opening verses of the chapter (vv. 2-7). They seem repetitious and unnecessarily long-winded, but their purpose is to make clear the absolute power of the king to command the acquiescence of his subjects in every detail. Disobedience is unthinkable. The question facing the three Jews is whether, as a result of their promotion, to go along with the crowd, or whether to stand up (literally) and be counted. Vv. 8-12 make clear that they adopt the latter course. They are duly reported to the king, and face the penalty for non-compliance with the royal command (v. 6): death by burning.

3:13-18 The king whose wrath the three must now face is as yet unaware of the limitations of his power, as v. 15 reveals. His arrogance in face of the gods is perhaps unexpected, given his experience with Daniel in ch. 2, and his confession in 2:47. He has evidently either forgotten what happened before, or has not really understood it. Whatever is the case, he is clearly presented in ch. 3 as a king without a true understanding of God; and readers of the book to this point know that he is being set up for a fall. For they know that there is indeed a God who is able to deliver Shadrach, Meshach, and Abednego from the flames.

The response of these three to the king in 3:16-18 probably implies that they know it too, although their words in v. 17 are not without ambiguity. The Aramaic may be literally rendered as follows: "If (there is) our God whom we serve, he is able to deliver us from the burning fiery furnace; and from your hand, O king, he will deliver us." Both the NRSV translations of this line (main text and footnote) understand it as concerning the ability of God to deliver his people from the fire and the king, the difference between them lying only in the level of certainty expressed that divine ability will be followed by divine action ("let him deliver us"; "he will deliver us"). They thus interpret the Aramaic particle *'itai* ("there is") simply as emphasizing the "if," rather than as having any independent force. Both context and syntax, however, favor understanding the words in a rather more robust way. We do not expect the three men, first, to meet Nebuchadnezzar's taunt about the inability of gods to deliver anyone with an admission that their own God might not be able to deliver either. The Aramaic of Daniel in general, secondly, supports a full rendering of *'itai* and thus a reference to God's existence in v. 17 rather than simply his power (e.g., 2:28: "there is a God in heaven," *'itai 'elah bishmaya'*). A better translation, then, is: "If our God whom we serve exists, he is able to deliver us . . . and from your hand, O king, he will deliver us." If God exists at all, he is certainly able to accomplish the relatively minor task of delivering his people in this instance. The three thus meet Nebuchadnezzar's misunderstanding head-on: if gods are gods at all rather than simply figments of the human imagination, of course they can deliver people out of his hands. Whether Israel's God will choose in fact to do so in the particular instance is another matter; but his choice on that specific point makes no difference to Shadrach, Meshach, and Abednego's choice of the God they will worship. They will remain faithful to the living God, who is able to save even if he chooses not to save, rather than abandon him for the idols and images of the Babylonians, who could not save even if they were sufficiently alive to wish it (v. 18).

3:19-30 The spirited opposition of the three is not well received by a king with pretensions to sit among the gods and accustomed to implicit obedience. The furnace is made seven times hotter than usual (an idiomatic way of saying "as hot as possible"), and the three men tied up and, still fully clothed (although the precise nature of all the clothing is unclear), pushed into the furnace. It is now that Nebuchadnezzar discovers that the faith of his three Jewish officials corresponds to reality. Although the fire is apparently fierce enough to have consumed both the royal servants who push the Jews into the fire and the only thing which Nebuchadnezzar himself has sent into the fire (the ropes), it has no effect on the men themselves or their clothing. They walk around in the middle of the fire, accompanied by a fourth man whose appearance is divine — an angel sent by God (as 3:28 makes clear), to whom Shadrach, Meshach, and Abednego owe their deliverance. The king thus gains a new respect for this God. As in ch. 1, a refusal to compromise leads to vindication and success; for ch. 3 ends with the promotion of Shadrach, Meshach, and Abednego to still higher positions.

Daniel 3 is often described as a metaphor of the whole Jewish experience of exile in Babylon. Retaining Jewish identity was difficult and carried with it certain risks. The people of God characteristically suffer under regimes that require a conformity that they cannot, in all conscience, give. God would not necessarily prevent the suffering that obedience might bring, but he would be with his people in the middle of the fire and would ensure that they came out unscathed. The story is above all about the importance of guarding the purity of God's self-revelation, lest Israel (or any Gentile king) confuse its own image with that of God. This is a theme to which the OT often returns (e.g., in the Decalogue, Exod 20:1-6; in the story of the golden calf, Exodus 32; and in the stories of Jeroboam, 1 Kings 12, and of Sennacherib, 2 Kings 18–19). It is indeed the central human folly that mortals should imagine themselves to be gods rather than simply made in the image of God (Genesis 1–3). As ch. 3 closes, Nebuchadnezzar himself is still suffering to some extent from this delusion.

4:1-18 Ch. 3 leaves us with a king impressed by the God of Israel, but whose personal attitude to him is ambiguous. His last word to the peoples of his empire in 3:29 had been that they should not speak anything against this God. He neither states that his own allegiance has changed, nor does he command his subjects to worship this God. As ch. 4 opens, however, we find him writing again with quite a different tone, even alluding to Scripture (cf. v. 3 with Ps 145:13). It seems clear, taking the chapter as a whole, that what is in view here is nothing less than the conversion of Nebuchadnezzar to the Jewish faith. What has led to this amazing state of affairs? He has had another dream (v. 4). We receive a hint already in this verse of what this dream is about, and what its interpretation will be. For the king is "prospering" (Aram. *ra'anan*) — a word almost always used in the OT of plants that flourish. When we go on to read of a mighty tree cut down to size, we already guess that the tree is this king who flourishes in his palace, apparently without a care in the world.

Being a slow learner, Nebuchadnezzar once again calls in the wise men of Babylon to explain the dream. They are completely unable to interpret it. As before, Daniel arrives to rescue the situation — an enlightened person, in the king's opinion, with access to the divine realm in a way that the other wise men are not (4:9). A description of the dream follows: the great tree assaulted by the angel (a "holy watcher" — the earliest reference in Jewish literature to the idea that angels are "watchful ones," ever vigilant where the affairs of the earth are concerned), who nevertheless stops short of complete destruction, leaving the stump of the tree bound with a band of iron and bronze (possibly reflecting a custom of protecting stumps by putting a metal band around them). The "stump" is to be put outside where the animals live, his mind changed from that of a man to that of a beast (v. 17); and he is to remain in that state for seven periods of time (perhaps years). All this is to happen so that everyone may know that history is in the hand of Daniel's God, and that he may do as he wishes (v. 17).

4:19-27 Daniel seems reluctant to say what the dream means, which is not surprising to the reader who has already guessed that it concerns the downfall of Nebuchadnezzar. He cleverly prefaces his message with an affirmation of personal loyalty (v. 19). The dream does not, of course, concern Nebuchadnezzar's enemies, but the king himself. The imagery of trees cut down is often used in the OT of the dismantling of proud political power by God (e.g., Isa 10:33-34). Conversely, the flourishing of trees is often used as a picture of the rule of the Messiah (e.g., Isa 11:1-3). It is Nebuchadnezzar who will be driven out among the animals and made to eat grass until he realizes the truth of his existence as king: that heaven rules (4:26). At that time he will regain the kingdom that will have been kept for him (represented by the stump). Daniel's speech ends in v. 27, with some advice for the king that goes beyond the dream and its interpretation and the purpose of which is unclear. Is it offered in the hope that the king's punishment will be averted (cf. v. 19, and the fact that v. 29 suggests a year's respite in which Nebuchadnezzar might have reformed his ways)? Or is it intended for the period after the punishment, the object being to ensure the long reign of Nebuchadnezzar after his recovery from illness? In either case he is urged to "break off your sins by practicing righteousness" (v. 27).

4:28-37 As a matter of fact Nebuchadnezzar fails to avoid the fate described. As he surveys his empire from the roof of his palace, congratulating himself on his power, his majesty, and his self-sufficiency, he hears a voice from heaven that echoes the words of the dream and the interpretation (vv. 31-32). Immediately he is driven out into animal country, where he becomes like an animal (or, more accurately, like a combination of an ox and an eagle). He who thought himself a god has become a beast, so that he should understand absolutely that God is God, and he himself a mere mortal man. It is this understanding which finally arrives in vv. 34-37 (note again the scriptural language: Job 9:12; Pss 115:3; 145:13; Isa 14:27; 40:17), and with it the return of sanity and kingdom. In an interesting twist to the story, he tells us that "still more greatness was added to me" (4:36) — the success motif which has appeared in every story so far of our Jewish heroes is now connected with Nebuchadnezzar himself, indicating his change of sides from pagan antagonist to worshiper of the true God.

Nebuchadnezzar has for the first time experienced God's power at first hand, and has understood what the reader has understood from ch. 1 onward. Israel's God is not just a revealer of mysteries; he is not just the powerful God of the Jews. He is the Most High God who is sovereign over the kingdom of mortals and gives it to whomever he will (4:17). It is only with this final shift in perception by Nebuchadnezzar that his part of the story ends — the story of a pilgrimage from a sense of being a god to a sense of God himself. Daniel 1–4 are thus stories not merely about the faithfulness of believers in trying circumstances, and their vindication from God, but also about God's workings in the world through these believers and independently of them to bring others to faith. It is possible to hope that in the short term world empires will be converted, even if in the long term the people of God will truly know security only when world empires have passed away and the kingdom of God has truly come.

5:1-16 With the final two stories of Daniel the scene changes, and we find ourselves in the presence of two new kings — Belshazzar and Darius. Ch. 5 opens somewhat abruptly and probably with the purpose of inviting a comparison between Belshazzar and Nebuchadnezzar; ch. 3 also has an abrupt introduction (cf. 3:1, "King Nebuchadnezzar made," with 5:1, "King Belshazzar made"). Certainly the content of 5:2-4 invites such comparison. Nebuchadnezzar had taken the temple vessels from Jerusalem (1:2), but he had recognized their sacred character, placing them in his own temple in Babylon. Belshazzar, on the other hand, does the unthinkable: he brings these vessels out for use in a bout of drinking, in the course of which he and his guests praise gods other than the true God. Here is sacrilege of the highest order. In light of what has happened to Nebuchadnezzar in chs. 3–4 we expect some correspondingly worse fate to befall Belshazzar. The sign that such punishment is to fall is seen immediately in the disembodied hand writing on the wall, illuminated by the lampstand mentioned in 5:5. Among the signs of panic induced in the king, the NRSV suggests that "his limbs gave way" (v. 6). This is, however, a rather coy translation of the Aramaic meaning, "the knots of his loins were loosened." It is much more likely that the phrase refers to the loss of control of the bladder under stress.

In the midst of his perplexity the king does what Nebuchadnezzar had done before him (5:7), promising the successful interpreter on this occasion clothing in purple (the color of royalty), a gold chain, and promotion. It is not clear from the Aramaic that a numerical position in the line of command is intended (cf. NRSV's "rank third in the kingdom," after Belshazzar and one other — Nabonidus, the king in whose absence Belshazzar was exercising power, or the queen mother?), but high officialdom certainly is. It comes as no surprise, however, that the Babylonian wise men are unable to read or interpret the writing. Daniel, whose position at court has perhaps not survived the change in king or is perhaps not summoned because Belshazzar fears to summon him when he has been abusing the sacred vessels from the temple of his God, is duly introduced in vv. 10-12 by the queen (or perhaps the queen mother, since the king's wives are already present in 5:2-3; cf. v. 10). She, at least, knows of Daniel's powers, describing him cleverly as one who "loosens knots" (NRSV, "solves problems," v. 12). Part of the king's response to the writing on the wall was also to loosen knots, but of a different kind (v. 6)! Daniel's "loosening," claims the queen, will be more constructive.

5:17-28 Daniel's first move is to spurn any offer of reward — he is an independent voice and cannot be bought (cf. Amos 7). What he goes on to say to Belshazzar bears this out, for it is hardly flattering of the king. Once again Belshazzar is contrasted with his predecessor. Nebuchadnezzar, when he became proud, was disciplined by God until he understood the true nature of things (5:21). Belshazzar has failed to learn from this, honoring idols rather than the God in whose power is his breath and whose are all his ways (cf. Rom 1:23). It is for this reason that God has sent the hand to place the inscription on the wall (5:24-25), which Daniel now renders into Aramaic. The words in themselves probably refer to weights of various kinds (the mina, the shekel, and then two half-minas or two half-shekels — PERES meaning simply half of something). Daniel's interpretation, however, involves a play on words throughout rather than a literal reading. The second MENE of v. 25, which does not feature in the interpretation of vv. 26-28, is presumably to be regarded as emphatic of the fact that God has ordained the end of the kingdom ("God has numbered," Aram. *menah*). TEKEL is straightforward enough ("you have been weighed," Aram. *teqiltah*). PARSIN, on the other hand, is the plural of the singular form PERES which appears in double interpretation in v. 28 (the kingdom is to be "divided," Aram. *perisat,* and given to the Medes and the *Persian,* Aram. *paras*). Belshazzar may have imagined that he could operate independently of the Most High God — that he alone was sovereign over his empire. He no doubt had numbered his days well ahead, into his old age; he had weighed his wealth and his power, and found it to be unimaginably great and unassailable; his empire had appeared a coherent and united entity, able to withstand whatever pressure it came under. But Belshazzar's assessment counted for nothing in the end. In a moment, the Most High God had numbered the days of the kingdom and brought it to an end; Belshazzar had been weighed in the only scales which mattered, and been found wanting; his mighty empire had been divided up and given to others to rule (cf. Luke 12:13-21). The writing was truly on the wall for Babylon.

5:29-31 Chapter 5 ends with a description of the respective fates of Daniel and of Belshazzar. As usual, Daniel comes out of the whole affair well. He receives all the honors promised by Belshazzar in v. 7 (reward being acceptable after the principle upon which Daniel operates has been established). Belshazzar, on the other hand, is killed that very night, and the kingdom passes to Darius the Mede. Not for the first time, the servants of God succeed. For the first time in the book of Daniel, however, the king who opposes God meets a bitter end. And here the contrast between Nebuchadnezzar and Belshazzar, which has been drawn throughout the chapter, comes to its natural conclusion. Not all kings who oppose God are given the chance of repentance. To some the word of judgment comes, immediately to be followed by the judgment itself. The God of Daniel, like the God of the rest of the OT, is not a God who is tied to human rules, who always behaves in the same way. Nebuchadnezzar and Belshazzar stand as evidence of this. If it seems that this divine freedom operates only in respect of the wicked — that he is more consistent with his own people, always rewarding faithfulness with divine protection and earthly success — then this is only because we have not yet reached the end of the book (cf. 11:33-35).

6:1-15 The sixth chapter opens with Darius the Mede's reorganization of the kingdom. Daniel, as always, prospers in the royal service, attaining to one of the top three administrative positions, and is on the verge of still greater success until the other royal servants conspire against him (the Aram. verb *rgsh,* v. 6, means "to assemble, to conspire together, to be in a rage or uproar," and captures well the picture of an angry mob converging in commotion on the king with a view to subverting their rival). They decide that the only weak spot in Daniel's armor is his religion, and this is where they decide to attack. They display some economy with the truth in making their charge (v. 7), for it is clearly not true that *all* the presidents of the kingdom agree with what they say (Daniel knows nothing of the idea). Nor is it clear that the prefects, counselors, and governors have been consulted either. Darius accepts the claim, however, that there is unanimity among his administrators on the point, no doubt flattered by their concern for him and attracted by the prospect of being a god for a month. His naivete and vanity seal Daniel's fate, since the law of the Medes and Persians cannot be revoked. Daniel's response is to carry on as before — to pray three times a day (probably at dawn, at midday, and in the evening, cf. Ps 55:17, a practice taken over both by later Judaism and by the early church, *Didache* 8), facing Jerusalem as the location of the temple (1 Kgs 8:30). Being in violation of the new law, he is duly reported to the king (6:12).

6:16-23 The den of lions is a pit underneath the floor

with a small opening capable of being covered with a stone. The stone covering is here laid over the opening (v. 17), and the king and his nobles place their seals upon it (i.e., make a mark with their rings on some soft substance, probably clay, which has been placed around the stone, in order to prevent anyone from tampering with it — since any movement of the stone after this sealing would break this seal and be obvious to the observer). The king is evidently fully conscious of his own failure to rescue Daniel, and as conscious as the reader that only God can now do so (v. 16). That he is a troubled man is indicated by the fact that he spends a sleepless night without food; and as early in the morning as possible he returns to the lions' den to see what has happened. The question of v. 20 is not of the sort which allows for the answer, "No"; and this is certainly not the answer readers of the story expect in the light of their reading of the book thus far. Daniel's answer in fact stresses two things (v. 22). In the first place, it points up the difference between Daniel's God and Darius. Darius is by no means a wicked king as portrayed in ch. 5 — he is portrayed relatively sympathetically by the narrator. And yet he is only a mortal; he is entirely unable to rescue his servant from his fate. He is forced to participate in the sealing of the mouth of the pit when what is really required is the sealing of the mouths of the lions. Only God can do this, as Darius himself recognizes. The second thing that the language of Daniel's answer emphasizes (although obscured by the NRSV translation) is the connection between the deliverance from the lions and Daniel's innocence before the king. The lions have done Daniel no harm (NRSV, "not hurt") because Daniel has done the king no harm (NRSV, "I have done no wrong"). Daniel's claim is not just that he is blameless before God. It is also that, though he may be guilty of breaching the royal edict, he has nevertheless done the king no harm. His survival of the ordeal by lions proves that this is so. He is innocent on all fronts.

6:24-28 The royal retribution upon Daniel's enemies is swift and savage (v. 24). As if to emphasize that Daniel's escape had nothing to do with the lions' lack of appetite, we are told that the lions started on these unfortunate people before they even hit the floor of the pit. It is difficult to imagine this since they number 122 (120 satraps and two presidents), now consigned to the lions with their families. It seems more likely that the lions would be crushed to death than that they would inflict any real damage on the falling bodies. One suspects the narrator of a rather fantastic, if grim, sense of humor. It does nothing to diminish this suspicion when it turns out that the Aramaic that lies behind the word "accused" in the NRSV of 6:24 is literally "ate the pieces." The men who had "eaten the pieces" of Daniel now find themselves eaten to pieces by the lions. The narrator's sense of humor has had the better of his sense of taste.

It is no surprise that as a result of his experience with Daniel Darius should write an open letter to the empire (6:25-28; cf. Nebuchadnezzar's actions in chs. 3–4). Darius's letter, however, represents the climactic point of the Daniel stories. The Nebuchadnezzar of ch. 3 had only instructed his subjects not to speak against the Jewish God; the Nebuchadnezzar of ch. 4 had only testified to his own experience of this God. The Darius of ch. 6 makes a decree that his subjects should tremble and fear before the God of Daniel. This looks very like the conversion, not just of the king, as in Nebuchadnezzar's case, but of the empire as well. Here we have come full circle from ch. 1, which described the apparent defeat of the God of the Jews at the hands of Babylon and the exile of his people. But what has been the consequence of this exile? The faithful witness of Daniel and his companions in Babylon has gradually led non-Jews to see the truth. Daniel's God is far from defeated. He is, in fact, the sovereign Lord of the universe, and all mortal kings are under his power. Exile has thus in the end been a redemptive experience for the captors as well as the captives.

7:1-14 With the seventh chapter of Daniel we leave behind the stories about Daniel and his friends at the court of Gentile kings, and move on to a series of visions dated during the period covered by the narratives: ch. 7 to the first year of Belshazzar, ch. 8 to the third year of the same king, ch. 9 (with its long preceding prayer) to the first year of Darius, and chs. 10–12 to the third year of Cyrus. Here is the future hope to be held onto while the faithful life is lived out in exile.

Chapter 7 tells of four great beasts from the sea. The first is lionlike but with the attributes of both an eagle and a human being. The second is like a voracious bear, crouched and ready to spring ("raised up on one side"), ferocious in appearance or already feasting on a previous victim (depending on whether it has tusks or ribs in its mouth). The third is like a leopard, but winged and many-headed. And the fourth is the worst of all — unimaginably awful and destructive. Initially it has ten horns, five times as many as one would expect, illustrating its strength and power. The arrogant eleventh horn that arises in the middle of these ten and disposes of three of them also has human attributes. During the period of this "horn's" dominion the heavenly court meets in judgment, perusing the books containing the records of human deeds (vv. 9-10). It is presided over by an old man, his hair and clothing white, and his throne a throne of flames — an image of God himself (cf., e.g., 1 Kgs 22:19; Ezekiel 1).

Daniel is distracted from this heavenly vision, however, by the arrogant speech of the little horn, and notices the consequences on earth of the divine judgment in heaven: the death and destruction of the fourth beast and the loss of dominion (though not the death — their lives are prolonged for a limited duration) of the other beasts. They lose their dominion because it passes to one like a human being (lit. "one like a son of man," v. 13), who receives it from the Ancient of Days as an everlasting dominion which shall not pass away — unlike the dominion of the beasts (v. 14). This figure is thus to be contrasted with the first three beasts, who were "like a lion," "like a bear," and "like a leopard." He is also to be contrasted with the little horn, whose only similarity to a human being was in his eyes (v. 8). His precise identity is not clear, but the fact that he comes with the clouds of heaven suggests that he is in some sense divine, for clouds (like fire) are often associated with God's appearing to mortal men in the OT (e.g., Exod 16:10). It is to a supernatural being, "like a man," that everlasting dominion is therefore given — a kingdom with a human face.

7:15-28 The interpretation of the vision comes from one of the bystanders (presumably one of the angels of v. 10) who is standing before the throne. The four beasts are four kings who shall ultimately give way to the "holy ones of the Most High" (vv. 17-18). In response to Daniel's request for more information about the fourth beast, and in particular the little horn which he can now see in a flashback (vv. 21-22) battling with the holy ones of God and prevailing against them, the angel expands on this brief summary. The ten horns on the fourth beast are ten kings from the fourth kingdom, and the little horn is an eleventh who will put down three of the others. His arrogant words are directed against God (v. 25); and in his war against the holy ones, he will attempt to change both the festival calendar and the law. This struggle will last for 3.5 periods of time (the precise meaning is unclear), and then his dominion will be taken away and given to the people of the holy ones of the Most High.

It seems clear that the structures of the visions in chs. 2 and 7 are similar, and that the first beast is once again intended as Nebuchadnezzar and Babylon. It was Nebuchadnezzar who spent some time as a "beast," but later became "human" again when his reason was restored (cf. 7:4). The whole is once again constructed around a "three, then a fourth" pattern (cf. Amos 1) whose purpose is not to provide the reader with an eschatological timetable, but simply to tell us that when awful kingdom has been succeeded by awful kingdom there will come an ending which will be the beginning of the kingdom of God. The view taken here is that the second and third beasts are Media-Persia and Greece, and the fourth a future unspecified kingdom that gathers up all the wickedness of its predecessors in its unimaginable wickedness. The emphasis in the case of the little horn that arises from the fourth beast likewise falls not upon his identity but upon his nature as the incarnation of all that is wicked about kings who oppose God. He is (v. 25) an arrogant blasphemer (like, e.g., Sennacherib in 2 Kings 18–19), and he tries to change the sacred seasons and the law (like, e.g., Jeroboam in 1 Kgs 12:25-33).

The demise of the final beast and its final king results in the holy ones of the Most High possessing the kingdom forever and ever and ever (v. 18). Although in principle these could be angels (Dan 8:13), the context clearly favors understanding them as human beings (as in Ps 34:9) — the "people of the holy ones" in 7:27 in particular is most naturally taken as a synonym of "holy ones" in v. 18, and these "people" are most likely the people of God. It is they who inherit the kingdom, exercising the dominion that they had been denied while oppressed by the beasts. It has been a common view among commentators that the "son of man" imagery (v. 14) stands for the same entity as the "holy ones" imagery, but it would be difficult then to account satisfactorily for the divine aspect of a human figure (v. 13). The background to the imagery of vv. 13-14 is in fact to be found in Canaanite mythology, where the god Baal (the son of the high god El) is sometimes described as one who rides on the clouds. Although an Israelite writer would not have had polytheistic Canaanite mythology directly in mind, there was one figure in the ancient Near East who was generally regarded as divine, namely the king, and some Israelite thinking about the king shows evidence of a similar view, the king (God's anointed one, Heb. *mashiaḥ,* from which comes our English "Messiah") being described as one in the closest possible relationship with God (e.g., Pss 2:7; 110:1). The verses are therefore best taken as reflecting a royal enthronement festival, the one "like a human being" being a future messianic king who functions as the channel through which the divine rule is mediated to the people of God.

The NT has made extensive use of Daniel 7 in articulating its vision of the future, when Jesus the Messiah (one of whose titles in the Gospels is "Son of Man") returns in glory to vanquish the powers of darkness and to take possession with his church of the kingdom (cf., e.g., Matt 24:30; 26:64; Rev 1:7, 13-15; 5:11; 11:7; 12:3, 14; 13:1-8; 14:14; 17:3, 8, 12).

8:1-27 Chapter 8 describes a vision, interpreted by the angel Gabriel, in which Daniel finds himself in Susa, the capital of the Median province of Elam (one of the most important cities of the Persian Empire). It concerns the time of the end (v. 17), when the wrath that the people of God are experiencing in the world will come to an end. The ram that Daniel sees represents in its two horns the kingdoms of Media and Persia (v. 20), implying that these are thought of in the book as two aspects of one entity (and therefore that Greece is not regarded as the fourth and final beast/kingdom). Historically, Persia rose to power after Media and superseded Media in power, and it is this reality that is reflected in vv. 3-4, with their imagery of the higher horn coming up later than the lower. The goat that charges this ram and tramples it is Greece (v. 21), and we deduce that the great horn that is its first king is Alexander the Great. This "horn" was "broken" at the height of Greek power (v. 8), in that Alexander died when his empire was at its greatest extent.

Four horns (kingdoms) are then said to replace the great horn (8:8, 22), and here matters become a good deal less clear. They have often been correlated with the four kingdoms into which the Greek Empire was ultimately divided after Alexander's death. Yet it is unclear in the Hebrew that they are intended as *Greek* kingdoms at all, and unclear also whether they have dominion successively or contemporaneously. In the end they issue in the "little horn" figure (v. 9) already seen in ch. 7 — the final anti-Messiah who will arise when the sins of the "four kingdoms" have reached their full measure (v. 23), and about whom we now hear much more. He is of bold countenance (he looks hard or insolent) and devious (v. 23), destructive (v. 24) and arrogant, even to the point of rising up against the Prince of princes (v. 25) — making a blasphemous attack on God himself. Here is a god challenging the true God, as kings characteristically do in the OT, with no awareness of this God's true nature. The particular example chosen to illustrate this truth is his assault on the beautiful land (i.e., Palestine, v. 9), the Jerusalem sanctuary and its sacrificial worship (vv. 10-14). This latter passage is difficult both because of uncertainties in the Hebrew and because of the mixture of metaphor and more straightforward language that it contains. At one level it again concerns arrogant action against heaven, the "host of heaven" being a phrase often used of the heavenly army of angels (e.g., 1 Kgs 22:19-20) or simply of the sun, moon, and stars (e.g., Isa 34:4). The anti-Messiah is someone of great ambition, reaching for the stars and throwing them down (cf. Isa 14:13-14), confronting the prince of the host (God himself? one of his angels?) in doing so. At another level, however, the passage seems to concern physical warfare on earth — the battle results in real consequences for Jerusalem. The spiritual and physical realms are linked in warfare in Daniel as elsewhere in the Bible (e.g., Josh 5:14; Dan 10:20; 11:1; 12:1; Eph 6:10-20) — what happens in one realm affects the other. It is perhaps not surprising to find such a reality reflected in 8:10-14 as well — but it does make interpretation of the passage difficult.

What can certainly be said is that the anti-Messiah is accused of vanity, ambition, and sacrilege (cf. Rev 11:2; 12:4 for echoes of Dan 8:10, 13). He has some success in his assault, at least partly because of the wickedness of God's people, and is able to bring the daily morning and evening sacrifices (Exod 29:38-42) to an end. He sets up in the temple "the transgression that makes desolate" or "appalls" (8:13, with the help of 11:31; the Hebrew verb can refer both to physical and emotional desolation). The Hebrew of the whole phrase is *pesha' shomem;* and its choice may owe something to the events of 167 BC, when the Greek king Antiochus IV erected in the Jerusalem temple an image of and an altar to the Greek god Zeus, known to the Syrians as Ba'al Shamem. *Pesha' shomem* is probably a wordplay on this divine name, which means "god of heaven" (cf. the analogous change in the name of Saul's grandson, who is Meribbaal in 1 Chr 8:34 but Mephibosheth in 2 Samuel 9, the Hebrew word for "shame" replacing the name of the god Ba'al). The reign of the wicked king will not, however, last forever (8:14): the time of his oppression is restricted to a set period — either 2,300 days or the number of days which it takes to offer 2,300 morning and evening sacrifices (1,150). The latter is perhaps to be preferred as correlating more closely with the "time, times and half a time" of Dan 7:25 (perhaps 3.5 years — 1,150 days is 3.19 years if we follow chronological custom in ancient times and take a year as comprising 360 days). The days of the anti-Messiah, like the days of Belshazzar, are numbered. He will come to a sudden end, broken "not by human hands" (8:25). Here we have a reference back to 2:34, 45, where the stone cut out by no human hand (the kingdom of God) brings to an end the fourth and final world kingdom. The reign of the little horn is thus evidently seen by the author of Daniel 8 as immediately before the advent of the messianic kingdom of chs. 2 and 7. The NT authors also took this view (e.g., Mark 13:14-27).

9:1-19 The book of Jeremiah promises that the exile of the Jews in Babylon will last only seventy years, after which Babylon will be judged and the Jews return to Palestine (Jer 25:8-14; 29:10-14). It is hardly surprising that Daniel, in the first year of Darius the Mede (i.e., immediately after the last of the Babylonian kings), should be found reflecting on this prophecy, for he is evidently still in Babylon and Jerusalem is still a ruin (9:2). Reflection leads on to a prayer of confession. The fate of Jerusalem and of the exiled people of Judah is explained in terms of the people's sin against their God. Daniel now asks God to stop being angry.

9:20-27 The divine response to Daniel's prayer is a further vision in which the angel Gabriel comes to explain the true significance of the Jeremiah prophecy. Daniel has been praying for an end to the desolation (Heb. *shamam,* vv. 17-18) of Jerusalem, referring in the first instance to the ruined state of the city during the period of physical exile. The word that comes to him from God, however, concerns not only this but also the ending of all the appalling things (desolations) which have happened to this city — an allusion to the abomination of desolation already mentioned in ch. 8. After the exile, when the city has long been rebuilt (9:25), further desolations are decreed (v. 26). The "exile" that Jeremiah had in mind (seventy years) has now been extended: Jerusalem's desolations will not truly cease until the decreed end is poured out on the desolator (the anti-Messiah of chs. 7 and 8; cf. esp. 8:13 with 9:25-27) and the messianic kingdom has arrived at the end of "seventy weeks" (9:24).

As with the other numbers in Daniel, there have been many attempts to correlate these "seventy weeks" with a specific time-period and thus to arrive at a detailed timetable of events. They are most often understood in the light of Lev 25:8. If seven weeks of years comprise 49 years (as there), then seventy weeks of years should comprise 490. It is most improbable, however, that the author means us to think literally of 490 years. It is more likely that it is precisely the parallels with the sabbatical years which should guide us as to meaning, for the 49 years of Leviticus are followed by the jubilee, when there is rest from toil and social justice is enacted (Lev 25:10-55). The 490 years should likewise be taken simply as a way of speaking about the present age of toil and trouble, which is to be followed by the era of the kingdom of God. 9:24 first summarizes by means of three pairs of phrases what is to happen during the present age. "The transgression which appalls" will be removed and a period of eternal right-doing replace a period of apostasy. God will indeed put an end to *all* sin, and perhaps to visions and prophecy as well. This last point, however, is not clear since the imagery of sealing might refer either to finishing (as the sealing of a letter is the last act in writing a letter) or to giving the stamp of authenticity (visionaries and prophets will receive the seal of approval — everything will come to pass as they promised). Finally, all sin will be accounted for and pardoned, and someone or something holy will be anointed (Heb. *mashaḥ*). Since in both the occurrences of the Heb. *mashaḥ* in vv. 25-26 a *person* is involved, it is likely that this is the case also in v. 24 — that this is another reference to the Messiah figure of ch. 7 (an anointed king) who comes to set all things right. The structure of v. 24 implies, in fact, that it is this figure that will be involved in "atoning for iniquity."

In 9:25-27, the 70 weeks are further broken down, although the nature of the breakdown is a little unclear. It is possible that we are to envisage periods of 7, 62, and 1 weeks (NRSV), 7 weeks preceding the coming of an anointed one (*mashiaḥ* — this would perhaps then be a reference to the Davidic line of kings being reestablished after the exile) and a further 62 weeks preceding a time in which a second anointed one is cut off. Alternatively, we might envisage periods of 69 and 1 weeks, after which a single anointed one is cut off. The starting point is the time when the word went out to rebuild Jerusalem (v. 25) — a word of Jeremiah, perhaps (e.g., Jer 30:18-22), or the decree of Cyrus in Ezra 1:1-4, or the word of Artaxerxes in Neh 2:1-8. What is clear is that the rebuilding of Jerusalem does not lead to a time of quiet, but rather to a "troubled time" (9:25) — the city is not yet free of "desolations" in the broader sense. At the end of the 69 weeks, disaster strikes. The "anointed one" suffers a violent death, not further specified, and the city and the sanctuary are destroyed (v. 26). Here we have a new idea in relation to the picture in chs. 7–8: that before the time in which the Messiah conquers the anti-Messiah, he suffers a reverse at his hands. The rightful prince, the Messiah (Heb. *mashiaḥ*), is displaced by the prince who comes to destroy (Heb. *yashḥit*). The play on words is designed to reinforce the point. The final week of the seventy then follows, with war and desolations throughout. The wicked king wins many to his side in this period (9:27), and is able to carry on his anti-God crusade successfully for half of it (the time, times, and half a time of ch. 7 [= 3.5, or half a period of seven], or the 1,150 days of ch. 8). Then the decreed end comes, however (9:27), Heb. *kalah,* "end," being related to the "finishing" of the transgression in v. 24 — the transgression which appalls will be finished when the anti-Messiah comes to his "end" in the "flood" of v. 26.

It is not difficult to see why later Christian interpreters saw in this material a prophecy of Jesus Christos (the Greek equivalent of Heb. *mashiaḥ*) — a Messiah suffering a violent death, atoning for the sins of the world, before returning (as in chs. 7–8) in power and glory to vanquish the forces of evil.

10:1–11:20 Daniel's last vision, which occupies the final three chapters of the book, involves a human figure whose description (vv. 5-6) at the same time recalls Ezekiel's vision of God in Ezekiel 1. It is possible, then, that we are meant to think again of the humanlike yet divine figure of 7:13-14 (cf. 10:16, 18). It is this figure who comes to help the terrified Daniel understand what is to happen to the people of God "at the end of days" (10:14). The first part of his description relates to the period of Greek domination of Palestine, after the passing of the Persian Empire (11:2). The "three, then a fourth king" in v. 2 is once again not necessarily meant literally, but may reflect the literary pattern noted above (7:15-28), the advantage of which is that it enables a significant stretch of Persian history to be compressed into a small space. The wealthy king who will stir up all against Greece is most likely the famous Xerxes I, and the warrior king who comes later (11:3) is probably Alexander the Great, whose possessions in land were dispersed after this death. The focus of attention then moves to the period in which two of the kingdoms arising out of these Alexandrian possessions disputed and battled over Palestine itself — the Syrian Seleucid kingdom in the north, and the Egyptian Ptolemaic kingdom in the south. Vv. 5-20 offer us a fairly detailed account of some of the main events of this period down to the death of Seleucus IV in 175 BC: the establishment after the battle of Ipsus in 301 BC of the power of Seleucus I (who had previously fought with Ptolemy I against common foes, v. 5); the marriage in 253 BC of Berenice the daughter of Ptolemy II to Antiochus II and subsequent events (vv. 6-9); and various happenings during the reign of the Seleucid Antiochus III (vv. 10-19), who had won control of Palestine so decisively by 199 BC that it remained under Syrian domination from this point on, until the Romans took control during the middle part of the first century BC. It is Antiochus's disastrous confrontation with the Romans on his western boundary and his subsequent death that are alluded to in vv. 18-19. He was succeeded by his son Seleucus IV (v. 20), who sought to confiscate the treasure of the Jerusalem temple to pay off his debts and was in due course murdered by his prime minister Heliodorus.

11:21-35 This passage has been a focus of controversy among commentators. Many have argued that it identifies the anti-Messiah figure of chs. 7–9 with Seleucus IV's successor Antiochus IV — a notorious oppressor and persecutor of the Jews in Palestine. It is certainly the case that there are many points of connection between this passage and both the earlier Daniel texts and what is known of the reign of Antiochus. At the same time, however, there is nowhere near the same match between text and history in 11:21-45 that we find in vv. 5-20. All agree that this is the case in vv. 40-45, which bear no relation to history. Many also find vv. 36-39 problematic. Even in the case of vv. 21-35, however, it is exceedingly difficult to understand the text *in toto* in relation to Antiochus. Little of vv. 21-28, for example, fits him well. His accession to the throne was neither particularly unexpected, nor did it require intrigue and the unparalleled distribution of funds. It is entirely unclear in what sense a prince of the covenant might have been swept away and broken before him. Although he did, like many of his predecessors, wage war with Egypt, he did not provoke the conflict with Egypt in 170-169 BC (v. 25); there is no evidence that the Egyptian king was undermined by plots among the royal servants after the campaign had begun (vv. 25-26), nor that he was "broken" (v. 26 — cf. Heb. *shabar* in 8:7-8, 22, 25; 11:4, 20, 22, all of which imply that he passed away to be succeeded by another); nor any evidence of reciprocal lying (11:27). It is in fact much more likely that we are to understand vv. 21-45, not as an account of the events of Antiochus's reign, but as an account of the reign of the anti-Messiah of the end times, to which Antiochus's reign in part corresponds and for which the authors have perhaps taken the Antiochene reign as a partial model. Antiochus thus foreshadows the final anti-Messiah, as all wicked biblical kings in part do, in the same way that good biblical kings like David foreshadow the final Messiah.

The reign of the anti-Messiah is now described in much greater detail than previously, although connections everywhere appear with what has gone before. He seizes the kingdom unexpectedly and through intrigue and the unparalleled and wise distribution of money, apparently not being of the royal line (11:21, 23-24). He is a clever strategist (v. 24), victorious in battles, not least in relation to an Israelite prince ("prince of the covenant," v. 22) and at least initially in relation to the king of the south (cf. the use of Heb. *shatap,* "swept away," in both vv. 22 and 26). He is above all a king who has his heart "set against the holy covenant" (vv. 28-31) — and here we do find clear echoes of Antiochus IV, who attacked Jerusalem and plundered the temple on the way home from his first Egyptian campaign, returning after a failed second campaign (frustrated by the "Kittim" — a general designation in the OT for the lands and peoples of the Mediterranean, and primarily for Cyprus, but possibly here in part an allusion to Rome's influence on events) to wreak even more havoc. It was on this second occasion that his forces abolished the regular burnt offering and set up in the temple "the abomination that makes desolate" (v. 31; cf. chs. 8–9) — an altar to Zeus upon which pig's flesh was offered. It is this kind of assault on orthodox religion that the anti-Messiah will also initiate. The task of the people of God under such circumstances will be to behave in much the way that Daniel and his friends behaved in Babylon — to stand firm, depending on the wise among the people for understanding, and to persevere in the midst of persecution until the end (11:32-35). It is now clear, however, that the people of God, seeking to be faithful like the heroes of the Daniel stories, will not always be delivered from the fire and the lions of persecution. Faithfulness does not always result in immediate deliverance (vv. 33, 35).

11:36–12:4 In the short term, Daniel is told, things will only become worse. As Antiochus IV took his divinity very seriously — the addition of the term "Epiphanes" to his name indicated an especial identification with deity — so also the anti-Messiah will have pretensions to divinity. He will turn his back on the ancestral gods, and indeed on all gods, including the obscure god loved by women (v. 37), and he will worship an equally obscure new "god of fortresses" (vv. 38-39). He will achieve impressive domination, with a final victory over Egypt (vv. 40-43); yet he will come to a swift end while at the very height of his power and while threatening Jerusalem (vv. 44-45, echoing the events described in 2 Kgs 19:35-37). A time of unparalleled anguish will follow (12:1 — if this is not simply intended as a summary statement for the whole preceding period); but ultimate deliverance is at hand. If it is true that faithfulness does not always result in divine rescue from trouble, yet perseverance to the end does bring its own reward, as the dead are raised and brought to judgment (12:2-3). Those who have resisted the powers of darkness rise to everlasting life and light. Those who have embraced the darkness rise to shame and everlasting contempt.

12:5-12 A brief postscript brings the book to a close. It is reiterated that the awful days at the end of time are not endless, but limited by divine decree. We have already been told this in 7:25, 8:14, and 9:24-27, which together suggest that the period of immediate distress, from the assault on orthodox religion until the end of everything that needs to be accomplished, will be a period of half a week in relation to the 70 weeks of ch. 9 (3.5 periods of time in 7:25; 1,150 days = 3.19 years in 8:14; half a week in 9:27). In ch. 12 the same period is in view, but it is described in three different ways: as a time, two times, and half a time (= 3.5 "days" of the "week," v. 7); as 1,290 days (= 3.58 years, v. 11); and as 1,335 days (= 3.71 years, v. 12). The difference between the last two figures may be connected with the fact that history continues for a while after the demise of the anti-Messiah (12:1); but the point of the numbers is in any case not to allow mathematical calculations in regard to the end times. It is to bring assurance that God is in control and to urge perseverance to the very end, whenever that may be.

The NT picks up various ideas from this final vision. Rev 1:13-15 certainly does understand the figure in Dan 10:5-6 as the "son of man" figure of ch. 7, and Rev 12:7 takes up the "warfare in heaven" theme developed in Dan 10:13, 20. The anti-Messiah is described in such passages as 2 Thess 2:1-12; 1 John 2:18-25; and Rev 13:5-10. The unparalleled time of anguish described in 12:1 is correlated with the placing of the abomination of desolation in Matt 24:15-31, and both are said to precede the coming of the Son of Man in power and glory. The aftermath of the time of anguish is described in passages like Matt 13:42-43; 25:46; and Rev 7:14. Throughout we find the same conviction that underlies the book of Daniel: that the time of the forces of evil is short and in the hands of the God who has called his people to faithfulness (Rev 12:10-12).

Select Bibliography. Davies, P. R. 1985, *Daniel,* Old Testament Guides, Sheffield: JSOT • Fewell, D. N. 1988, *Circle of Sovereignty,* JSOTSup 72, Sheffield: Almond • Goldingay, J. 1989, *Daniel,* Word Biblical Themes, Waco, Tex.: Word • Goldingay, J. 1987, "The Stories in Daniel: A Narrative Politics," *JSOT* 37: 99-116 • Humphreys, W. L. 1973, "Life-style for Diaspora: A Study of the Tales of Esther and Daniel," *JBL* 92:211-23 • Longman III, T. 1999, *Daniel,* NIVAC, Grand Rapids: Zondervan • Sims, J. H. 1993, "Daniel," in L. Ryken and T. Longman III, eds., *A Complete Literary Guide to the Bible,* Grand Rapids: Zondervan, 324-36 • Talmon, S. 1987, "Daniel," in R. Alter and F. Kermode, eds., *The Literary Guide to the Bible,* Cambridge, Mass.: The Belknap Press of Harvard University, 343-56 • Towner, W. S. 1984, *Daniel,* Interpretation, Louisville: John Knox.

Hosea

Grace I. Emmerson

INTRODUCTION

Hosea's prophetic ministry took place in the Northern Kingdom broadly within the third quarter of the eighth century BC. It is significant that there is no allusion in the book to the fall of the Northern Kingdom to the Assyrians in 721. One of Hosea's main concerns was the degenerate worship of the time, marred by syncretistic tendencies which led to the confusion of Yahweh with the Canaanite god Baal. The prophet condemned the proliferation of the externals of worship, of altars and pillars, at the expense of faithful commitment to the covenant with Yahweh. He castigated the priests for their overconcentration on sacrificial rituals and their failure to instruct the people in Yahweh's law. His second main concern was the increasing social and political instability of the period. Violence and bloodshed disrupted society, and a series of palace revolutions and assassinations betrayed the tensions and corruption at court.

The book of Hosea falls into two distinct parts, chs. 1–3 and 4–14. Chs. 1–3 encapsulate in compact form the message of the whole, from judgment to salvation. They are, however, distinctive in their prominent use of feminine symbolism to represent apostate Israel, which is noticeably absent from the rest of the book.

COMMENTARY

Hosea 1:1-5

The form of the title given in 1:1 is of immediate interest. The preponderance of Judean kings in the dating of a book which relates to a northern prophet is remarkable and suggests the presence of later Judean editorial activity. The periods specified are, moreover, not coextensive; Jeroboam II (c. 786-746 BC) was contemporary only with Uzziah. It seems unlikely, to judge from the content of the book, that Hosea's ministry extended as far as Hezekiah's reign, but it certainly was not restricted to Jeroboam's time. It is reasonable, then, to suggest that the reference to Jeroboam related originally to a limited section of the book, probably to the events narrated in ch. 1.

Yahweh's first word to the prophet is clearly intended for public proclamation. It marks the beginning of Yahweh's speaking *through* the prophet (the preposition is significant). Hosea is to proclaim the message by means of a fourfold symbolic action intimately bound up with his personal domestic life, namely, his relationship with Gomer and the naming of their three children. In this respect, as also in the absence of visionary experiences, Hosea differs from his near contemporary Amos. Immediately the reader becomes aware of diversity between the prophets; each retains his individuality. There has been no attempt to systematize their message or experience.

Hosea was commanded to take "a woman of whoredom." Some have understood this to mean that Hosea was to marry a prostitute who already had children ("children of whoredom"). Others see a reference not to what Gomer is but to what she will become. A well-known theory, based on a combination of chs. 1 and 3, is that Hosea married a woman who became a prostitute, strayed into slavery, and eventually had to be bought back by Hosea (see 3:2 and the comments there).

In deciding between these possibilities the following point is relevant. Since the marriage between Hosea and Gomer was to symbolize Yahweh's relationship with Israel, a woman who was already promiscuous would not appropriately represent Israel when Yahweh found her like "grapes in the desert." It was only at a later stage that Israel proved unfaithful to Yahweh "and became detestable like the thing they loved" (9:10).

The symbolic naming of Hosea's first son, Jezreel, conveys both accusation and judgment. It alludes to the massacre at Jezreel by which Jehu came to the throne of Israel (see 2 Kings 9–10). The reference to "the house of Jehu" indicates that this oracle is to be located either in the reign of Jeroboam himself or in the short, six-month reign of his son Zechariah, with whose assassination the dynasty of Jehu came ultimately to an end. The judgment envisaged will spell the downfall of the Northern Kingdom and its military might, an event that finally occurred in 722 BC.

Hosea 1:6-9

The names given to the second and third children signify the rupture of the covenant relationship between God and Israel. They carry no implications as to the legitimacy or otherwise of the children so named, a point illustrated most clearly in the naming of Ichabod, "the glory has departed," which refers expressly not to the newborn child but to the capture of the ark by the Philistines at the time of his birth (1 Sam 4:21).

The positive attitude toward Judah (1:7), which contrasts strongly with the negative attitude towards the Northern Kingdom, is often adduced as evidence that this sentiment derives from later Judean editing of the book. There is, however, no compelling reason to deny v. 7 to Hosea. It is arguable that, although a northerner, Hosea regarded the Davidic line as the legitimate monarchy and deemed the secession of the northern tribes after

Solomon's death, with its disastrous results for the religious and political life of the Northern Kingdom, as nothing short of apostasy (8:4). The emphasis on deliverance solely through Yahweh's intervention without military assistance (1:7) reflects an ancient theme of the OT (cf. Judg 7:2, 22; Isa 31:1-3).

The third symbolic name, "Not my people," indicates a reversal of the covenant. The declaration "I am not your God" (lit. "I am not I AM for you") negates God's self-revelation to Moses, "I AM WHO I AM . . . this is my name forever" (Exod 3:14-15). Hosea's words of judgment convey not a denial of that awesome name but a poignant statement of Israel's self-exclusion from the relationship. The whole passage is a remarkable interweaving of the public and the private in its proclamation to the nation of the Lord's word by means of the prophet's personal domestic circumstances. It is reasonable to assume that this fourfold symbolic action spanned five or six years since children were customarily weaned at two or three years of age.

Hosea 1:10–2:1

At the very moment when hope seems gone there comes the promise of a future. There is no need to regard these verses as secondary, for elsewhere words of hope are integral to Hosea's message (Emmerson 1984: 11-20). The arrangement, however, is undoubtedly editorial. The ancient promise given to the patriarchs (e.g., Gen 32:12) is restated, and the symbolic names of judgment become symbols of hope. The expression "the living God" marks the contrast between Yahweh and the lifeless idols of Canaanite religion (cf. 8:5). Jezreel ("God sows") becomes a shout of triumph as Israel, to continue the agricultural metaphor, "sprouts up" from the land (cf. 2:23). The schism which divided north from south at the time of Solomon's death will be healed by the appointment of one leader. There is no compelling reason to deny to Hosea himself this far-sighted hope of reconciliation. The hostility between north and south which continually tore apart the people of God was alien to prophetic aspirations. The emphasis here on a leader appointed by popular acclamation (1:11) is explicable in view of the many violent seizures of the throne by palace revolution in Hosea's time.

The plural "brothers" and "sisters" (2:1; see the NRSV footnote) indicates a break with 1:1-8. The children are no longer in mind. The prophet's thought is focused entirely on the nation and the possibility of a future glad celebration of its restored relationship.

Hosea 2:2-13

Although 2:1 and 2 have superficial similarities which no doubt account for their juxtaposition, they are distinct in content. V. 1 affirms God's forgiveness; v. 2 returns to warning and judgment against the unfaithful wife. The whole of vv. 2-15 constitutes a thinly veiled allegory. The accusations in v. 5 relate, not to Gomer's situation, but to the nation's devotion to Baal as guarantor of its material prosperity. Since this is poetry, logical consistency is not to be expected. The "children" are in one instance ordered to call their "mother" to account (rather than "plead"; the verb has legal connotations; cf. REB), at another they are regarded as guilty by association (v. 4). Thus the prophet's thought moves between the nation as individuals responsible for recognizing the community's sin and the people as a guilty entity.

The purpose of the denunciation seems at first to be reformation rather than condemnation. There is an element of hope, even though the husband/wife relationship is ended. The practice of shaming an adulteress by stripping is known from a number of ancient Near Eastern texts. Whether it was practiced in Israel is uncertain. All the OT references occur in allegorical contexts (e.g., Jer 13:22; Ezek 16:39; 23:26). In the legal texts the death penalty is stipulated for adultery (Lev 20:10; Deut 22:22). But hope of willing repentance soon becomes enforced reformation. Cut off from her lovers and their gifts, the woman in her desperation will be driven back to her "first husband," albeit in self-interest, not repentance.

Feminist studies have emphasized that throughout this indictment the woman is voiceless. She has no opportunity to state her case. Her words are mediated by the injured husband. The symbolism which represents the unfaithful nation as an adulteress is characteristic of the patriarchal perspective of the OT.

2:6-13 is judgmental throughout. At first the allegory continues, but by the end of v. 8 it is in the main discarded, and it becomes clear that it is the nation and its devotion to Baal which are castigated. Sin brings due punishment. There is an inescapable logic in these verses. Israel is determined to pursue her lovers; *therefore,* Yahweh will frustrate her search (v. 6). Israel has failed to acknowledge the source of her blessings; *therefore,* Yahweh will withdraw them, a sign not only of the abandonment of a husband's obligations (v. 9) but of his control over the bounties of nature (v. 12). In the ensuing deprivation Israel's sacred festivals will be no more. The severity of the judgment is spelled out at length, its cause explained with solemn brevity: "me she forgot, says the LORD." "To forget," when used in theological contexts in the OT, signifies more than absent-mindedness, an excusable human weakness. It is willfully to ignore the LORD, to live as if there were no God.

Hosea 2:14-15

A third "therefore" follows, and with it an unexpected break in the logical sequence of sin and punishment. Instead of judgment God promises a new initiative of salvation. The threefold "therefore" has moved from correction (2:6), through punishment (v. 9), to renewal and restoration (v. 14). Because Israel has forgotten Yahweh, *therefore* he will cause her to remember (Clines 1979: 83-103), not by punishment, but by "speaking to her heart" (cf. Ruth 2:13). His is the initiative, Israel's the response (cf. Jer 2:2). Her story with Yahweh will have a new beginning. Israel had reached a point of no return, hence the profound insight that only by divine grace, such as Israel experienced at the time of the exodus, can the relationship be restored.

Hosea 2:16-20

The description of the promised salvation now becomes more specific; false deities abandoned, peace in society and in the world of nature, knowledge of God and fruitful harmony between heaven and earth, and finally the reaffirmation of the covenant formula, "You are my people . . . You are my God" (v. 23). The change from "you" (v. 16) to "her" (v. 17) to "them" (v. 18) and back to "you" (v. 19) suggests that we have here a loose collection of sayings rather than a literary unit. The marriage terminology continues in v. 16 with a play on the two Hebrew words for "husband," *'ish* and *ba'al*. The latter, which denotes also the name of the Caananite fertility god Baal, is unacceptable as a designation of Yahweh. Israel had been guilty, not of blatantly substituting Baal for Yahweh, but of undiscerning syncretism which failed to recognize the incomparability of Yahweh who, out of sheer grace, rescued them from Egypt and brought them into covenant relationship with himself. A cosmic covenant embracing the natural world and humanity is envisaged (v. 18). Free from danger, Israel will indeed "lie down in safety." At last they will know the LORD.

Hosea 2:21-23

This picture of restored prosperity is the antithesis of 4:3, where, the covenant broken, the land mourned in desolation. Jezreel ("God sows") becomes a shout of triumph (of 1:11). The judgment-bearing names Lo-ruhamah, "Not pitied," and Lo-ammi, "Not my people," are reversed (cf 2:1), and the relationship, broken in ch. 1, is finally restored in the reaffirmation; "'You are my people . . .'; 'You are my God.'"

Hosea 3:1-5

The relationship between chs. 1 and 3 has been the subject of much discussion. Here the woman is unnamed. Is she Gomer or not? The text is intentionally vague and provides no definitive answer. On balance, however, the former seems the more likely, hence the NIV's interpretive rendering, "Go, show your love to your wife again." The problem of identifying the woman is a salutary reminder that the book's primary concern is not the prophet's personal life but the LORD's message to his people Israel. In one respect, however, ch. 3 is less ambiguous than ch. 1. This woman is openly described as an adulteress (an entirely different expression from the circumlocution of 1:2). Whereas the first symbolic action represented Israel's unfaithfulness, this second symbolic act represents the persistence of Yahweh's love in the face of rejection. The word "love" occurs four times in 3:1, twice of faithful and twice of illicit love, Hosea's love versus a lover's, and Yahweh's love versus Israel's love of "raisin cakes." Although these were an acceptable food (2 Sam 6:19), in this context they have cultic implications, hence the explanatory description as "sacred" (NIV) and "offered to idols" (REB).

It was in response to the command to love that Hosea bought the woman from prostitution. But this love appears at first in a strange guise, manifesting itself not in an affectionate welcome but in restraint on the part of both parties for "many days," the necessary discipline of commitment. The end of Hosea's story is not told, nor is any hint given whether a loving, permanent relationship was subsequently established. The focus of the narrative is solely on Israel's future deprived of the traditional leaders of society and of familiar religious institutions. Yet, in the light of 3:1, all this is to be understood as the outworking of a love which guarantees the future. The nature of this future is then spelled out; it involves commitment to Yahweh and to the Davidic king. The inclusion of a reference to the Davidic line is often regarded as secondary. Yet arguably it is integral to Hosea's message since its combination of the political and the religious forms a parallel to the previous verse. Whereas the symbolic acts of ch. 1 signified the ultimate rupture of the covenant relationship (1:9), the present chapter offers the prospect of a return to the LORD and to his goodness.

Hosea 4–14

In contrast to the previous chapters there is nothing of the biographical in what follows, apart from the reference to "the prophet" in 9:7. Nor does the metaphor of the unfaithful wife recur to symbolize the estrangement between Yahweh and his people. Throughout these chapters all reference to Israel is in the masculine, often in the plural, although this fact is obscured in some English translations. Hosea's language, however, is rich in metaphor and irony, and the themes of adultery and promiscuity continue in both a literal and a metaphorical sense.

Structurally there is a recurrent pattern. As chs. 1–3 begin with judgment and end in promise, so do chs. 4–11 (11:12 begins ch. 12 in the Hebrew text) and 12–14.

Hosea 4:1-3

4:1-3 form an introduction to what follows, setting out in comprehensive terms both accusation and judgment, to be spelled out in greater detail in the following chapters. The summons to "hear the word of the LORD" (cf. 1:1) underlines the solemnity of what follows. This is nothing less than a breach of the covenant, hence the legal terminology. Yahweh is bringing an "indictment" *(rib)* against his people Israel. Although formal legal elements are not emphasized here as they are, for example, in Isa 1:2, Yahweh is both prosecutor and judge. The malaise in society is symptomatic of the failure to acknowledge God. Loyalty (*ḥesed*, v. 1), the basis of commitment both to God and to humankind, is lacking (cf. 6:4, 6). Particularly significant is the inclusion here of three, possibly four, of the Ten Commandments ("swearing" and "lying" taken together are the equivalent of false witness), thus reinforcing arguments for the existence of the Decalogue at an early date. Devastation is threatened, more complete than that at the Flood (Genesis 8–9), for not only land but sea and sky, too, will be denuded of life in a total reversal of creation. The contrast with the joy in God's creation of Ps 24:1 is chilling.

Hosea 4:4-6

4:4-6 move from the general to the particular. Whether the accusation is directed against an individual priest (vv. 4-6 are in the singular) or priests in general is unclear. The seriousness of the accusation and its far-reaching consequences (v. 6) suggest the latter, as do the plural verbs of vv. 7-8. There is no escape from Yahweh's judgment. An interruption from the prophet's hearers is summarily dismissed; "it is my quarrel," says Yahweh, "and it is with you, the priest" (so REB, adopting a widely accepted emendation), and the reason? Not neglected sacrificial rituals but failure to teach God's law. This is culpable "forgetting," not momentary human weakness. The isolated and somewhat intrusive reference to the prophet (v. 5) probably reflects a later period (cf. Jer 23:11, where prophets and priests are closely associated). Nevertheless, as the text now stands the inclusive expressions "day and night," "mother and children," indicate how comprehensive is the threatened judgment.

Hosea 4:7-10

The prophet addresses another group in his audience. The accusation is stark: more priests mean more sin! English versions differ as to whether 4:7c continues the accusation (so NIV, slightly amending the Hebrew and taking "Glory" as a designation of Yahweh; cf. Jer 2:11) or expresses Yahweh's judgment (so REB). The accusation here concerns not neglect of duty but abuse of privilege. The priests were entitled to a share in certain sacrifices (Lev 6:26; 7:28-36), but their greed had encouraged the proliferation of sacrifice to their own advantage. Yet the people, too, were not free of responsibility; "people and priest will fare alike" (4:9, REB), experiencing not fertility but futility. The first word of v. 11, "whoredom" (better "immorality," as in the REB) should be taken with v. 10. This unexpected turn of phrase, literally "to keep/observe immorality," is a unique and shocking variant of the familiar expression "to keep/observe the covenant."

Hosea 4:11-14

This section begins and ends with proverbial sayings on the causes and dangers respectively of lack of understanding; the latter, "a people so devoid of understanding comes to grief" (REB), is enlivened with alliteration (*'am lo' yabin yillabeṭ*). The theme of what follows is not drunkenness per se but the resultant insensitivity which delights in promiscuity. The designation of Israel as "my people" (4:12) highlights the irony of Israel's search for guidance from a wooden idol. Metaphorical and nonmetaphorical uses of "promiscuity" are interwoven. Unfaithfulness to Yahweh, their covenant God, issues in sexual impurity.

Hosea 4:15-19

The extension of Hosea's strictures to Judah (4:15b) is secondary, evidence of later reapplication of the prophet's message to the Southern Kingdom. The meaning of v. 15 as a whole, however, is problematic. Some understand it as an outright condemnation of the northern shrines at Gilgal and Beth-aven (Bethel), but the inclusion in the condemnation of the traditional sacred oath, "as the LORD lives," is problematic. More likely Hosea, like Malachi in a later century (Mal 1:10), is warning the nation against defiling their ancient shrines and sacred oath while they persist in "promiscuity." The use of the term "whore" (v. 15, NRSV) is misleading. This is not a continuation of the unfaithful wife metaphor; the Hebrew throughout is masculine, not feminine.

The picture of Yahweh as the shepherd of Israel is a traditional OT image (cf. Ps 80:1). Hosea, in response to his audience, asserts that the nation resembles a stubborn heifer. Yahweh will treat them as such. The themes of drunkenness and illicit sex link the difficult, and often emended, 4:17-18 with vv. 11-14. Behind the obscure Hebrew may lie a reference to an unnamed goddess, probably Asherah, thus accounting for the otherwise inexplicable feminine singular forms which occur in the Hebrew of vv. 18-19 (Emmerson 1974: 492-97). The general sense, however, is clear: all will end in futility.

Hosea 5:1-7

5:1-7 contains a threefold accusation (vv. 1-2, 3-4, 5-7), in which Yahweh is prosecutor, judge, and plaintiff. No witness is found for the defense; there is only Israel's arrogance which testifies for the prosecution (v. 5). Even the king, ideally the guarantor of justice (cf. Psalm 72), is guilty. It is impossible to identify the crimes associated here with Mizpah, Tabor, and Shittim (the last by emendation, reading *weshaḥat hashshiṭṭim he'emiqu*, "they dug deep a pit of (in) Shittim," for *weshaḥṭa śeṭim he'emiqu*, "revolters have gone deep in slaughter"), but clearly the hunting metaphors signify inescapable disaster (cf. Pss 7:15; 91:3).

The parallelism in 5:3-5 is characteristic of Hebrew poetry. The names Ephraim and Israel both designate the Northern Kingdom (in v. 5 Judah is secondary as in 4:15). The theme of "promiscuity" in a metaphorical sense continues. This is not a repetition of the unfaithful wife symbolism of chs. 1–3; the term "whore" (v. 3; cf. v. 4) is misleading in this respect (better "promiscuous"; cf. REB) since Israel is masculine throughout chs. 4–14. The children they have fathered are "strange sons" *(banim zarim)*, alienated and hostile rather than illegitimate (Eidevall 1996: 72-73). What should have been a joyful new moon festival (cf. Ps 81:1-3) will instead bring disaster.

Hosea 5:8-15

A new section begins with warning of danger. The context is the Syro-Ephraimite war of 734-732 BC in which Ephraim (with Syria) and Judah were protagonists (see Isa 7:1-9). Both Israel and Judah are rotten to the core, says the prophet (5:12). Hosea's bold metaphors are theologically profound. Yahweh, the savior, is also the destroyer, whether through silent decay (v. 12) or through dramatic destruction (v. 14). Lion imagery is frequently associated with kingship, for example, in Prov 19:12 and is, therefore, appropriate in this context which carries the implication that Israel ignores its true king and has sought help instead from the "great king," a standard epithet for the king of Assyria. Yet after the utter devastation of 5:14 Yahweh offers future hope (v. 15). There is still for the penitent a way of salvation.

Hosea 6:1-6

6:1-6 consists of two sharply differentiated sections, vv. 1-3 and vv. 4-6. Much discussion has centered on the connection between them, an issue which depends on the interpretation of vv. 1-3. Do these verses represent true repentance or false complacency? The answer turns on whether the theology expressed here is genuinely Yahwistic, a vehicle of repentance framed by the prophet for the people in response to 5:15, or whether it is in essence mechanistic and manipulative, reflecting Canaanite ideas and denying Yahweh's sovereign freedom. The negative evaluation of both Ephraim and Judah in vv. 4-6 suggests that the latter is the correct view. Implicit in v. 1 is the image of Yahweh as a shepherd binding up his injured sheep (cf. Ezek 34:4, 16), but here ironically Yahweh himself is the lion who has wounded the flock. Both lion and shepherd imagery in the OT are royal symbols. The language of v. 2 is often thought to reflect the mythology of a dying and rising god. It may, however, refer simply to the prospect of imminent healing as in the story of Hezekiah's healing where remarkably similar expressions occur (2 Kgs 20:5, 7).

6:4-6 are both lament and accusation. The negative response to the rhetorical questions of v. 4 forms a striking contrast to the similar questions in 11:8. At issue in v. 6 is not the abolition of sacrifice but the emptiness of ritual actions without corresponding commitment (*ḥesed*).

Hosea 6:7–7:2

There follows a "catalogue of crimes" (Ward 1966: 127). Adam, a city in the Jordan valley, was noteworthy for its association with the deliverance of Israel from Egypt (Josh 3:16). It is impossible now to determine the specific crimes referred to. The description moves from the literal, the accusation against the priests (6:9), to the metaphorical, the accusation against the nation (v. 10). All is symptomatic of their rejection of Yahweh, described as a "horrible thing" (v. 10; cf. the similar context of Jer 2:12, where "be shocked" represents the cognate verb). Judah, too, will reap what has been sown (v. 11). The words are ominous. Yet Yahweh's will is to heal. The prophet sees the irony of the situation. As soon as Yahweh's compassion breaks through it is frustrated by the determined obstinacy and complacency of his people (7:2). Once again the language is rich in implied metaphor. Yahweh is prosecutor and judge, and the witnesses called are Ephraim's evil deeds.

Hosea 7:3-7

The theme changes. Here the wickedness condemned centers on the machinations at the royal court in which kings were both instigators (7:3) and victims (vv. 5, 7) of the palace revolutions which marred Israel's history in the years following the reign of Jeroboam II. The image of the baker's oven signifies both the secret danger of smoldering conspiracy (vv. 4-6) and the sudden conflagration of open violence. The imagery is vivid, but it is extended metaphor not allegory, and questions as to the identity of the "baker" (v. 4) are inappropriate. Adultery, drunkenness, and anger are both cause and symptom of their sick society. Rulers are "eaten up" (v. 7) and kings fall, six of them between the years 746 and 724 BC, mostly by violence (see 2 Kgs 15:8-31). There is an ironical progression in these verses; the king applauds his courtiers' wickedness (v. 3), blind to their subterfuge ("mockery") (v. 5), until finally he himself falls victim to their scheming (v. 7).

Hosea 7:8-10

The metaphor of baking is sustained in 7:8 and 9, although the subject has changed to that of international relations. Ephraim "mixes" himself (*balal,* a verb usually associated with mixing ingredients; Exod 29:2; Lev 2:4-5) with the nations. In so doing the nation loses its identity and becomes no better than a half-baked cake (a sentiment matched by 7:16 and 8:8), and a moldy one at that! (a more appropriate metaphor than "grey hair," which was held in high respect in Israel; cf. Prov 16:31) (Andersen and Freedman 1980: 467). There is a downward progression in these verses. In 5:6 Israel sought Yahweh through cultic rituals but failed to find him. Here in 7:10 they do not even seek him.

Hosea 7:11-13

Despite the uncertain meaning of 7:12b, the threat of doom is clear. Yahweh the helper has become Yahweh the destroyer. This kind of terminology is not peculiar to Hosea (cf. Ezek 12:13). Against doom such as this the nation is helpless. Like a fluttering dove (here an unusually disoriented one since doves were credited with a good sense of direction; Eidevall 1996: 119), the nation "flutters" between Egypt and Assyria, the two great powers of the day. An example of such a policy, and of its consequences, is found in 2 Kgs 17:3-6. The bird metaphor continues in v. 12; the REB's "I shall take them captive when I hear them gathering" makes good sense of the difficult Hebrew.

Hosea 7:14-16

Yahweh's forgiveness is frustrated by the nation's obduracy (cf. 7:1, 13), a reminder of human freedom to rebel and of its fearsome consequences. Yet his yearning over his people breaks through (cf. 11:3). The image of "a bow gone slack" (REB) to represent Israel's ineffective efforts suggests that 7:15 is also a military metaphor of discipline and training. But, as often, the prophet's thought moves quickly from the metaphorical to the literal. Death by the sword awaits those who have failed to cry to Yahweh, preferring rituals of mourning and self-mutilation (v. 14). The passage opened with contrasting modes of speech, crying to Yahweh versus wailing on their beds; it concludes in similar vein. Those whose haughty speech expressed their rage will find themselves merely "babbling" in a foreign land (v. 16).

Hosea 8:1-6

The command given to the prophet is terse, lit. "a trumpet to your lips." The following phrase, "like a vulture [or eagle, *kannesher*] over the LORD's house," is generally understood to refer to military threat. The Hebrew is, however, grammatically difficult. A slight emendation produces a summons to the prophet "like a herald (*kennaśśar*) against the LORD's house" (cf. Isa 58:1) (Emmerson 1975: 700-704). The people claim Yahweh as their God, affirming their identity as Israel, the chosen people who acknowledge him (8:2), the very point with which Hosea has already taken issue (cf. 4:1; 6:6). The reality, however, is otherwise. Both their king making and their idol worship are symptoms of their departure from God. The prophet plays on words: Israel has spurned the good (*zanaḥ,* v. 3); their calf-god, a human artifact, is spurned (*zanaḥ,* v. 5).

Hosea 8:7-10

There is powerful imagery here: sowing futility (the wind) they will reap calamity (the whirlwind). A proverbial saying reinforces the prophet's somber warning of invasion and pillage to come. Image is piled on image. Foreigners swallow up the corn; Israel is swallowed up by the nations (the same verb is used of Sheol swallowing up its prey; Prov 1:12). The prophet is not worried about mixed metaphors. The image changes again. In a play on the Hebrew words, Ephraim (*'eprayim*) is compared to a wild ass (*pere'*), restless for want of a mate. Thus does Ephraim seek for "lovers," not this time fertility gods (contrast 2:10-13) but foreign allies, notably Assyria (8:9). The animal imagery continues. Yahweh will "round them up" (REB; cf. Mic 2:12 for a similar use of this verb). The metaphor ends. The bargaining for "lovers" becomes paying tribute to the "king of princes" (so the Hebrew), the Assyrian overlord.

Hosea 8:11-14

From international relations the prophet turns again to the emptiness of sacrificial rituals when God's law is ignored. In a striking double entendre the prophet plays on two meanings of a single verb (*ḥaṭa'*), "to sin" and "to make a sin offering." Israel's altars, destined for sin offerings, "have become altars for sinning" (NIV). The reason follows. Yahweh's laws, even though in written form, are regarded as alien, "irrelevant" (REB). The result is disaster, a reversal of the exodus story (8:13) and utter devastation (v. 14; cf. Amos 2:5). The theme of remembering and forgetting recurs from 4:6, though with a difference. Israel has forgotten its maker, but the LORD will remember its sin. Yahweh cannot be bought off, as the prophets so often reminded their hearers, by ritual acts. Sacrificial offerings cannot save (v. 11), nor can massive fortifications protect (v. 14).

Hosea 9:1-6

The reference to harvest and the threshing floor implies that the context is the great autumn festival of Tabernacles (Booths), traditionally the occasion of joyful celebration (cf. Deut 16:14). The prohibition of rejoicing is, therefore, doubly ironic. Whereas the psalms call other nations to share Israel's rejoicing (e.g., 97:1), here Israel is excluded even from their joy. Although the nation's sin is described in terms of sexual immorality, the translation "whore" and "prostitute" (9:1, NRSV) is misleading. This is not a continuation of the unfaithful wife symbolism of chs. 1–3. The passage is masculine throughout. The people have prostituted themselves to Baal and have "loved the corn you thought he paid you with" (v. 1b, GNB). Their trust is misplaced; futility, not fertility, awaits them (vv. 2-3). Egypt will become not the scene of deliverance but of burial, a sad reversal of the exodus tradition. Their tents, no longer the symbol of a journey to freedom, will stagnate with the inactivity of death (v. 6). In alien lands, cut off from the customary offering of first fruits to the LORD (Deut 26:1-11), their food will be ritually unclean. The comparison with mourners' bread underscores the element both of uncleanness and of death and bereavement (Deut 26:14).

Hosea 9:7-9

These verses contain the only autobiographical note found in chs. 4–14. The prophet tells of the scornful hostility he faced even within the temple precincts, a consequence probably of his words of judgment pronounced against the temple (8:1). The contrast between the popular perception of the prophet as a madman and the reality of his calling as God's watchman for the safeguarding of the nation is total. God through the prophet has become their enemy (REB; cf. 7:12; Ps 91:3). All that can be described as "great" in this chapter is the nation's iniquity and hostility. In a refrain which echoes the words of 8:13, Hosea emphasizes the inevitability of punishment. Different though their sin is from the sordid violence of Gibeah (Judg 19:20-30), it is no less evil in God's reckoning (v. 9).

Hosea 9:10-17

At first sight this section seems to lack a recognizable structure. It is poetry, however, neither logical argument nor a haphazard collection of sayings. Beginning with Israel's idyllic past (9:10) the section ends with the sad contrast of its hopeless future, both described in agricultural terms. This suggests that a similar figure of speech, Ephraim as a young palm tree, may lie behind the difficult Hebrew of v. 13 (so the NRSV, adopting a slight emendation). Sections 10-13 and 15-17 both begin by condemning notorious incidents in Israel's history, at Baal-peor (v. 10) and at Gilgal (v. 15). Each is followed by the threat of childlessness (vv. 11-13 and 16), an implicit affirmation that it is Yahweh's sole prerogative, not Baal's, to grant fertility and thus to safeguard the future. The whole section pivots on v. 14, a strangely "inverted blessing" (Eidevall 1996: 153; cf. Gen 49:25).

The striking expression "grapes in the desert" (9:10) gives an unexpected twist to the conventional figure of Israel as a vine (see Isa 5:4; Jer 8:13). It emphasizes how precious Israel was to Yahweh, as fruit in an oasis to a weary traveler. The contrast with v. 10b is total. The prophet's words are replete with irony; "they consecrated themselves [the verb is *nzr;* cf. "Nazirite," Num 6:2] . . . and became detestable like the thing [i.e., Baal] they loved." The word "detestable" (REB, "loathsome"; *shiqquṣ*) expresses sheer horror. It is the term used of the "*abomination* of desolation" in Dan 11:31. Their "glory," which is Yahweh's presence (cf. 1 Sam 4:21-22), will fly away.

The language of 9:15, "I will drive them out of my house. I will love them no more," suggests at first sight a return to the symbolism in chs. 1–3 of the unfaithful wife divorced from her husband. Against this, however, it should be noted that, in contrast to those earlier chapters, Israel here is referred to consistently in the plural. The occurrence of similar terminology in Judg 11:2 and 7, where Jephthah complains of having been driven from home by those who hated him, suggests that we have here a picture of God as a parent (cf. 11:1) disinheriting his rebellious son. In any case, this is but one metaphor among many varied figures of speech, in contrast to chs. 1–3 where a single metaphor is consistently maintained. "My house" (9:15) is itself metaphorical and signifies expulsion from the land, elucidated in nonmetaphorical terms in v. 17.

Hosea 10:1-8

The main theme of these verses is criticism of Israel's worship in its substitution of splendid ritual for commitment, and devotion to its calf-god in place of Yahweh. The passage ends where it began with the destruction of the external symbols of worship. The image of Israel as a vine is traditional (cf. Ps 80:7-14). Isaiah pictures Israel as a disappointing vine producing only wild grapes (5:4). Hosea sees it otherwise. Israel is a flourishing vine, but wealth was lavished on the accoutrements of worship, unacceptable to the Lord because their heart was false (lit. "slippery"). The threat of destruction (10:2) is heavy with irony; their altars will be "broken," a term more commonly applied to breaking an animal's neck (Isa 66:3).

The word "king" occurs four times in 10:3-8, and several other expressions relating to kingship indicate that this is a prominent concern of the prophet. The historical context of v. 3 is difficult to determine, but it appears to reflect the self-satisfied arrogance of those who have achieved a palace revolution, of which there were several in Hosea's time. The kingship of Yahweh, too, is rejected. This disloyalty to oaths of allegiance, whether to the earthly reigning king or to Yahweh, issues in the poisonous disorder of litigation. Their substitute "king," the calf of Beth-aven (Bethel), is powerless to help, merely a "thing" to be taken as tribute to the "great king," the king of Assyria. In v. 5 the calf image is described as a "dweller in Samaria," a deliberate reminiscence of the designation of Yahweh as "dweller in Jerusalem" (Ps 135:21), a point obscured by the translation of the phrase as plural in the NRSV and the REB. Moreover, the expression "its glory that has departed" is reminiscent of 1 Sam 4:21-22, where the captured ark, the symbol of Yahweh's presence, is described in similar terms. 10:7, too, heaps scorn on the calf image, "Samaria's king." The figure of a chip of wood swept along by the current is more immediately appropriate to the calf-god than to a human king. Rejection of Yahweh results in ultimate despair (v. 8). The mountains associated with God's presence (Ps 121:1) become in 10:8 a way of escape by death.

Hosea 10:9-15

The passage is a somber one, beginning and ending with the threat of war (10:9-10 and 14-15), and in between the poignant picture of a happier past (v. 11a). The expression "days of Gibeah" alludes to the sordid events of Judges 19. That ancient sin is compounded ("doubled") by Israel's present iniquity. The former was avenged by intertribal conflict (Judg 20:34-5); from the latter warfare yet more brutal and conquest by foreign nations will ensue (10:14-15). The incident at Beth-arbel and the identity of Shalman are unknown.

Israel, the "trained heifer" of past happier days, is contrasted with Israel, the rebellious heifer of Hosea's time (cf. 4:16). 10:11b is best taken, not as a threat but as Yahweh's original purpose for his people. But Israel has neither sown nor reaped God's intended crop, justice and loyalty (REB), but wickedness and injustice (v. 13) (the paragraph division in the NRSV between vv. 12 and 13a is misleading). The prophet emphasizes cause and effect; the consequence of dependence on brute force is brutal destruction. The last words are ironical. Yahweh promised help "when the morning dawns" (Ps 46:5). At dawn their king (whether god or human) will face utter destruction (10:15).

Hosea 11:1-10

This chapter is remarkable for its emphasis on God's initiative in salvation despite the nation's sin. It tells of past, present, and future, of deliverance from Egypt, of the reversal of the exodus tradition in self-inflicted judgment (11:5), and ultimately of the reversal of that reversal, "they will come . . . like birds out of Egypt" (v. 11, REB). Strict justice is overwhelmed by divine compassion, from One whose holiness is manifested not in judgment but in salvation. The erstwile disoriented dove (7:11) will find its way home.

Beginning with Yahweh's love as a parent/mother tending the child's bruises as it learns to walk (11:1-4), the passage ends with divine mercy which far transcends human rationality. But the divine love is obstinately rejected (v. 2). The metaphor of parent and child, with a very slight emendation of the Hebrew (reading *'ul,* "child" for *'ol,* "yoke") continues through v. 4 (so the NRSV and the REB; contrast the RSV and the NIV).

In 11:5-7 the prophet plays on the word *shub,* a rich term in Hebrew which signifies "to return" and "to repent": "they shall return *(shub)* to Egypt . . . because they have refused to return *(shub)*" to me (= repent). V. 7 is textually difficult, but the general meaning is clear; like a pendulum they swing (again from the Hebrew root *shub*) away from Yahweh, only to find that Baal is powerless to rescue them (REB).

With 11:8-9 we come to a notable paradox, one of the most anthropomorphic passages in the OT, yet at the same time emphatically a contrast between the divine and the human. Here in the tension between strict justice and divine compassion God debates with himself, changes his mind, and having changed it will not "turn back" *(shub)* to destroy Ephraim as Admah and Zeboiim, cities of the plain associated with Sodom and Gomorrah, were overthrown (*hapak;* Deut 29:23). This time it is Yahweh's heart which is overthrown *(hapak),* turned from judgment to mercy.

11:10 is generally regarded as secondary. Nevertheless, as the text stands it belongs closely with v. 11 despite the rather bizarre juxtaposition of lion and bird imagery. There are several instances in the OT where these two images appear together (see esp. Isa 31:4-5). Yahweh is no longer the destroying lion (5:14; 13:7-8), nor is Israel a disoriented dove (7:11). Yahweh roars in majesty (cf. Amos 1:2) and the appropriate response to a theophany is awe and trembling, even when Yahweh acts in salvation.

The final verse of ch. 11 belongs in the Hebrew text with ch. 12.

Hosea 11:12–12:14

11:12–12:14 (ch. 12 in the HB) signals the start of a new literary unit, such is its discontinuity with the words of hope expressed in the previous verses. It is fraught with problems and bids fair to be the chapter in Hosea which has provoked the most discussion among biblical scholars. A glance at several English translations will indicate the difficulties involved in interpreting even the opening verse. Is Ephraim's deceit contrasted with Judah's faithfulness (NRSV, JB) or are both condemned alike (REB, NIV)? One problem is the ambiguity of the word translated "Holy One" (NRSV) or "the idols he counts holy" (REB). Since the word is plural, the latter translation is possible. If it is understood, however, as a plural of majesty, the meaning "Holy One" is both possible and preferable (see Prov 9:10 for a similar usage). The decision a translator makes on this point inevitably shapes the interpretation of the verb, either "walks" (NRSV) or "is restive" (REB). There is no compelling reason why this positive attitude to Judah should be attributed, as some suggest, to a later Judean compiler with a complacent attitude toward his own country (cf. 1:7). It can reasonably be argued that in a time of great instability in the Northern Kingdom, with political factions and assassinations at court, Hosea saw in Judah, with its stable monarchy, a source of hope for the future.

There is no mistaking, however, the prophet's criticism of the Northern Kingdom. The theme of deceit and falsehood pervades the chapter. Their activity was both foolish, "herding the wind," and dangerous, "pursuing the east wind," the dry and devastating sirocco blowing from the desert (cf. 13:15). They were busy establishing trading and political treaties with the great international powers of the day, Assyria and Egypt, but all in vain. Pro-Assyrian and pro-Egyptian factions vied with each other, contributing to the country's instability.

Hosea 12:2-6

In 12:2, as the text now stands, Judah is included in the indictment. This is undoubtedly a later substitution for "Israel," for vv. 3 and 4 play, not on the name "Judah," but on Jacob and Israel, with no further mention of Judah. V. 3 refers to the Jacob stories in Gen 25:26 and 27:36, and 12:4 to the strange incident in Gen 32:28. The later substitution of the name Judah is not the work of a complacent Judean editor but the reapplication of the message to the Southern Kingdom at a time when Judah, too, faced threat of deportation.

There has been much debate whether the portrayal of Jacob (12:3-4, 12) is intended to be negative or positive. Vv. 3-4 suggest that the portrayal is deliberately ambiguous. Jacob, deceiver and supplanter from birth, is also the one who struggled with the angelic visitant by night in his determination to receive a blessing (Gen 32:22-30). It was he, too, whom God encountered and addressed at Bethel (12:4, REB; cf. Gen 28:11-22; 35:1-7). Hosea's account of these ancient traditions is essentially the same as that found in Genesis. The apparent differences arise from the conflation of the incident at Peniel with the closely related story of Jacob's subsequent meeting with Esau when Jacob wept and sought his favor (Gen 33:4-10). The conflation of the two incidents is probably due to the fact that both refer to "the face of God" (= Peniel; 32:30 and 33:10). Thus four separate incidents are alluded to briefly for an audience who knew intimately the details of these sacred traditions. The ambivalent portrayal of Jacob, their eponymous ancestor, is significant for the nation, guilty themselves of deceit, yet with hope for the future grounded in their relationship with God. The Jacob traditions to which Hosea referred encompass a considerable period in Jacob's life, hence the exhortation to Israel in v. 6 to wait patiently for God, acclaimed here by his solemn and exalted title, the LORD the God of Hosts."

Hosea 12:7-9

Hosea now turns his attention from the patriarch to the nation guilty of deceit, oppression (12:7), and complacent arrogance (v. 8). But now a lesson is drawn not from Jacob but from the exodus story. God, who brought them from slavery to the promised land, threatens to reverse his saving action. The tent dwellings of the feast of Booths will become not a ritual celebration of their ancestors' desert journey but a present reality (v. 9).

Hosea 12:10-14

At first sight there seems little connection between these verses. The opening words, however, suggest that the thought centers on the prophets, their role, and the nation's lack of response. 12:10 and 13 spell out two aspects of a prophet's task, to be the messenger of God's judgment and the protector of the nation. Beginning with the judgmental role of prophets, Hosea's thought moves to the sins of the nation (the objection to sacrifice at Gilgal may reflect a later standpoint when sacrifice was centered on the Jerusalem temple). He then takes a broad sweep of history, from Jacob to Moses and to the contemporary situation. The brief allusion of v. 12 encompasses the ambivalence of Jacob's character. Having tricked his father Isaac (Gen 27:41-45), he fled for his life to a foreign land, where he was himself tricked and served long and loyally for Rachel, his chosen wife (Gen 29:15-28). Jacob "guarded" sheep (Gen 30:31), and by Moses Israel was "guarded." The connection between 12:12 and 13 consists not only in the repetition of "guarded" but also in the story of Israel's history, stretching from Jacob's flight *to* a foreign land (Aram) to Israel's deliverance *from* a foreign land (Egypt). As in vv. 3-4, the very familiarity of the traditions is reflected in the brevity of the allusions. Yet after these centuries of history in which God has been at work, Jacob's descendants have mistreated his messengers, the prophets (cf. 9:7-8), hence the judgment threatened in v. 14. The passage ends where it began.

Hosea 13:1-16

The theme throughout this most horrific of chapters is sin and its consequences. It begins with an allusion to Ephraim's past guilt and its penalty; it ends with the contemporary sin of Samaria, Ephraim's capital city, and its dire consequences in the future.

There are textual difficulties, but the most problematic feature is its depiction of God under the figure of brutal wild beasts against which there is no defense. The only respite from the tale of death and destruction (v. 5) relates to a relationship now ended, all because the people in their arrogance have forgotten the LORD. The chapter falls into two parts, the first concerned with cultic sins, the second with political power and the rejection of Yahweh as king.

Hosea 13:1-3

The allusion behind 13:1 is unclear. It refers to the tribe of Ephraim, which eventually gained sufficient prominence to give its name to the Northern Kingdom. They gave allegiance to Baal in place of Yahweh, a false choice of which they were guilty throughout their history. The exact nature of the objectionable cult practices referred to in v. 2b is unclear. The NRSV indicates that Jeroboam I offered sacrifice to idols and kissed the calf images set up at Dan and Bethel (for a similar practice see 1 Kgs 19:18). The natural meaning of the difficult Hebrew, however, hints at an altogether more sinister practice, that of human sacrifice (see the REB and the NIV). Against this, however, is the unlikelihood that the prophet would dismiss so serious an infringement of Yahweh's will in this summary fashion. The images of v. 3, morning mist and dew, are reminiscent of 6:4. There, however, they represented Israel's wavering loyalty; now they are used as a threat of Israel's fate.

Hosea 13:4-8

The contrast is poignant between the delightful picture of Yahweh's care for his people in the desert (13:4-5) and the horrifying metaphors of vv. 7-8, images of swift, unseen, and irreversible destruction. The key to the transition lies in v. 6, in the self-satisfaction and arrogance which leave no room for the Lord. It is as if all the disappointment, rejection, and frustration of the previous chapters is concentrated here in a final portrayal of human hopelessness without God. Thankfully this is not the final chapter of the book. There is hope to follow, reminiscent of ch. 2 where Israel's forgetfulness of the Lord (v. 14) is followed by Yahweh's renewed wooing of his bride. The comparison between these two passages is a reminder that there is no cheap and easy grace. God is sovereign; his people can only wait in dependence on his mercy.

Hosea 13:9-11

The implication of 13:10 that Israel is without a king suggests the period c. 724 BC when their last king, Hoshea, was imprisoned and Samaria beseiged (2 Kgs 17:4-6). This verse reflects the antimonarchical tradition of 1 Sam 8:4-7, 19-20, where the institution of monarchy is understood to imply the rejection of Yahweh's kingship. It is arguable that Hosea here rejects the whole concept of monarchy, not simply that of the Northern Kingdom. However, the frequentative tense of the verbs in v. 11 indicates rather Hosea's attitude to the palace intrigues which marred the later years of the Northern Kingdom. The implied allusion to 1 Samuel 8 may be intended as a reminder that God still holds the initiative in the rise and fall of human monarchs (cf. 8:4, which gives the human point of view).

Hosea 13:12-14

The prophet's irony is palpable. What Ephraim treasures sufficiently to bind up for safekeeping (a practice for which there is archeological evidence) is his iniquity. Then immediately the metaphor changes; uniquely here the pangs of childbirth relate not to a woman who gives birth but to an infant who refuses to be born, symbolic of Ephraim's stubborn refusal to seize the opportunity of life. By implication Yahweh is the midwife, bringing to birth, a metaphor which occurs in more explicit form in Isa 66:9. Significantly the imagery of the wife, so prominent in chs. 1–3, is still absent even in this context where it could so easily have been appropriate.

The rhetorical questions of 13:14 are reminiscent ironically of 11:8. There Yahweh's compassion prevailed; here he puts it out of his sight (REB). The NIV translation of v. 14 as Yahweh's determination to ransom his people, although grammatically defensible, is inappropriate in the context.

Hosea 13:15-16

The precise allusion of 13:15, which appears to refer back to the situation envisaged in v. 1, can no longer be recovered. The REB's "Though he flourishes among brothers" is preferable to the NRSV's "rushes" (reading *'aḥu* for *'aḥim*), which, although appropriate to the following metaphor, contributes nothing to the meaning. In this reference to the sirocco we have a rare use of "Yahweh's *ruaḥ*" (wind/spirit) as destructive, not creative. With v. 16 the prophet moves abruptly from image to reality and the fearful brutality of war (cf. 2 Kgs 8:12). It is in this context of the actuality of war that the horrific metaphors applied to Yahweh in vv. 7-8 are to be seen. All this is the consequence of Israel's rejection of God, their sole Savior.

Hosea 14:1-3

Chapter 13 has plumbed the depths of brutality and despair. Yet there is hope, for the possibility of returning to God remains open. The prayer of penitence, suggested not actual, is reminiscent of 6:1-3 yet with a significant difference. Instead of the easy complacency of that earlier approach to God there is acknowledgment of sin, a plea for the removal of guilt, and the resolve to abandon dependence on purely human resources which leaves no room for faith. Israel, God's called and chosen "son" (11:1), has voluntarily, in rejecting the divine parent, assumed the status of "orphan." To such God's mercy is available. These words of contrition are themselves regarded as an offering (14:2), yet there is a hint in the strange Hebrew of the text that the offering of animal sacrifice is not excluded (see the NRSV footnote).

Hosea 14:4-7

Yahweh's response is not directly addressed to the suppliants but is comparable in form to the oracle of assurance in Ps 91:14-16. It promises not the ignoring of past disloyalty but its healing. Yahweh's love is not commensurate with his people's repentance but freely offered and generously given (14:4). This is the OT equivalent of God's grace in the NT. The violent theriomorphic imagery of the previous chapter has gone. In its place is the attractive symbolism of vegetation, luxuriant and fragrant, nourished by Yahweh's life-giving dew. Similarities to Cant 4:10-16 suggest that here, too, we have love poetry. Yet it is significant that still the prophet refrains from portraying Israel as a bride. The contrast with the feminine symbolism of chs. 1–3 is maintained to the end.

Hosea 14:8

The prophet's message concludes with God's final plea to his people to break with their substitute gods and recognize his uniqueness as sole protector and sustainer. In imagery drawn from Canaanite sources Yahweh is represented uniquely here as an evergreen tree. Behind the prosaic statement of v. 8b may lie a yet more daring allusion drawn from Canaanite religion. The names of Anat and Asherah, two goddesses of the Canaanite pantheon, are evoked by the resonances of Heb. *'aniti wa'ashurennu'.* Although translated blandly as "It is I who answer and look after you," they carry the bold nuance "I am your Anat and Asherah." There is no place in Israel's future for any deity other than Yahweh alone.

Hosea 14:9

The later compiler of the prophet's words gives advice to the reader after the manner of wisdom writings such as Proverbs. The Lord's message has been given through Hosea at a particular time and in specific circumstances. But his ways are relevant for all times and places, and those who read must do so with discernment and make their own response.

Select Bibliography. Andersen, F. I., and D. N. Freedman. 1980, *Hosea,* AB, New York: Doubleday • Bird, P. 1989, "'To Play the Harlot': An Inquiry into an Old Testament Metaphor," in P. L. Day, ed., *Gender and Difference in Ancient Israel,* Minneapolis: Fortress • Clines, D. J. A. 1979, "Hosea 2: Structure and Interpretation," *StudBib 1978: 1. Papers on the Old Testament and Related Themes,* Sheffield: JSOT • Davies, G. I. 1992, *Hosea,* NCBC, London: Marshall Pickering/Grand Rapids: Eerdmans • Davies, G. I. 1993, *Hosea,* Old Testament Guides, Sheffield: Sheffield Academic • DeRoche, M. 1981, "The Reversal of Creation in Hosea," *VT* 31:401-9 • Eidevall, G. 1996, *Grapes in the Desert: Metaphors, Models, and Themes in Hosea 4–14,* Stockholm: Almqvist & Wiksell • Emmerson, G. I. 1974, "A Fertility Goddess in Hosea IV 17-19?" *VT* 24:492-97 • Emmerson, G. I. 1975, "The Structure and Meaning of Hosea viii 1-3," *VT* 25:700-710 • Emmerson, G. I. 1984, *Hosea: An Israelite Prophet in Judaean Perspective,* Sheffield: JSOT • Hubbard, D. A. 1989, *Hosea,* TOTC, Leicester: Inter-Varsity • Keefe, A. A. 2001, *Woman's Body and the Social Body in Hosea,* Sheffield: Sheffield Academic • Morris, G. 1996, *Prophecy, Poetry and Hosea,* Sheffield: Sheffield Academic • Ward, J. M. 1966, *Hosea: A Theological Commentary,* New York: Harper and Row • Winn Leith, M. J. 1989, "Verse and Reverse: The Transformation of the Woman, Israel, in Hosea 1–3," in P. L. Day, ed., *Gender and Difference in Ancient Israel,* Minneapolis: Fortress • Wolff, H. W. 1974, *Hosea,* Hermeneia, London: SCM.

Joel

Anthony Gelston

INTRODUCTION

The opening verse of the prophecy, effectively its title, gives us practically no information to enable us to determine its date and historical context. His father's name enables us to distinguish the prophet from the more than a dozen other individuals in the OT named Joel. The content of the prophecy makes it virtually certain that he lived and prophesied in Jerusalem. Beyond that we are reduced to speculation based on inferences from the book's contents, and it is not surprising that this has led to a wide variety of opinions. Questions about the unity of the book only compound the difficulties in the search for its historical context. For instance, 3:4-8 appear at first sight to offer some promising clues, but if, as many suppose, they are a later addition to the main prophecy they are of no help in dating the latter. One feature suggesting the unity of the main body of the prophecy is the recurrence of the "day of the LORD" theme in all sections (1:15; 2:1, 11, 31; 3:14), although this may be the result of redaction rather than of derivation from a single prophet.

Three aspects of the contents of the book perhaps offer some useful indications, although they fall short of certainty. The fact that the king is nowhere mentioned, particularly in a passage like 2:15-17 where many categories of the community are listed, is thought by many to indicate a postexilic date (an interesting variation is Rudolph's dating in the reign of Zedekiah, not regarded as the legitimate king), which may be supported by the lack of any references to the Northern Kingdom. Most scholars think that the fact that the temple cult is evidently being practiced excludes a date within the period of the exile. Most promising of all, perhaps, is the fact that there are a number of parallels with other biblical passages in this book (cf., e.g., 1:15 with Isa 13:6 and 2:32 with Obadiah 17). Mason's argument (1994: 115) that it is far more probable that Joel has drawn on earlier material than that it became a source of citation for many different biblical writers has considerable weight, and may be supported by "as the LORD has said" in 2:32, which may point to a specific quotation from Obadiah. Nevertheless, it is rarely possible to determine with certainty the direction of dependence in parallel passages, and there is no reason to suppose that Joel is either always the source or always the borrower.

Other at first-sight-promising clues prove illusive. For instance, it is by no means clear that 2:31 presupposes a solar eclipse, while the references to hostility on the part of Egypt and Edom in 3:19 are so general as to imply nothing more specific than traditional enmity (Mason 1994: 116). No argument can be based on the position of Joel within the Twelve Prophets, since this is different in the HB and the LXX. It is best to accept the fact that we do not know the historical context of Joel and to approach the interpretation of the book in the light of its own content and the wider biblical background. The most that can be said with any probability about the date of the book is that it is most likely postexilic.

COMMENTARY

Joel 1:2–2:27

Almost two-thirds of Joel is concerned with a plague of locusts. These insects are notorious for their tendency to multiply and for their systematic feeding in large groups, leaving whole areas stripped of vegetation. To a fragile natural economy like that of ancient Israel they represented a serious threat to human subsistence, and it is only in modern times that effective countermeasures such as the aerial spraying of insecticides have emerged. One of the plagues of Egypt at the time of the Exodus consisted of locusts (Exod 10:1-20), while they figure in the list of natural disasters associated with famine in the prayer attributed to Solomon at the dedication of the temple (1 Kgs 8:37). A plague of locusts was thus seen as a natural disaster fit to occasion a religious response in the form of a communal fast, while it was always possible that it might be interpreted as a divine judgment on the people for their sins. A good example may be seen in the first of Amos's visions (7:1-3), where the threatened judgment takes the form of a plague of locusts, in response to which the prophet intercedes that the plague may be averted since it would threaten the survival of the people.

There is no means of identifying the particular plague of locusts which occasioned the material in Joel, but this does not matter greatly since both the plague and the prophet's response to it can be seen in a characteristic or representative role. In other words, what may have originated in a particular experience has led to more generalized considerations about sin, judgment, repentance, fasting, prayer, and divine deliverance that are relevant to a much wider range of situations. While it is easy and natural to allegorize the locusts (e.g., the Targum takes the imagery of an impending army as a key to its interpretation of 2:25), there seems no good reason not to take a literal plague of locusts as the original occasion and basis of this material.

One further point needs to be taken into account before we consider the detailed contents of this passage. It has often been noted that laments characteristically include a number of different kinds of adversity in the same prayer for help, possibly so that a particular lament may serve on different occasions for suppliants in need of different kinds of help. A good example may be seen in Ps 22:12-18, where it is hardly likely that any individual would suffer from all these adversities at the same time, although allowance also has to be made for metaphorical language (e.g., the hostile animals may be an alternative way of referring to human enemies). This makes it less easy to be certain that a lament is occasioned by a specific instance of adversity. On the other hand, there are certainly laments that are occasioned by a specific instance of adversity (e.g., Psalm 137 clearly reflects the exile). Joel 1–2 contains expressions that suggest other causes of the present famine than the plague of locusts: drought is mentioned in 1:10, 12, 17-18 and fire in 1:19-20; 2:3, 5. On the other hand, the references to the locusts persist as a sustained theme throughout the passage, and the expressions implying drought and fire are readily intelligible as poetic descriptions of the effect of the plague, perhaps inspired partly by the characteristic style of laments in general. The prominence and persistence of the theme of the locust plague probably indicate that this was the original occasion of the passage.

The material in this section is not presented as a single continuous sequence, as may be seen from such overlaps and parallels as 1:9 and 13, and particularly the parallel summons to observe a solemn communal fast in 1:13-14 and 2:15-17. There is, however, one major division within the section at 2:18, where the divine response to the people's fast and lament is given. This is particularly interesting in the light of the "prophetic oracle of salvation" often discerned in the Psalms (e.g., at 20:6). In this case the prophetic oracle, uttered by the prophet in God's name, may be clearly seen in 2:19-20, flanked by an introductory statement making it clear that this is God's response to his people and by the people's own ejaculation calling attention to the fact that God has done great things. Whereas in the Psalms the prophet is always anonymous and his role may well have been cultic, there is no reason to doubt in the present case that it was the prophet Joel who both summoned the people to fasting and prayer in the first place and subsequently mediated to them the divine answer in the oracle of salvation. This may be seen as a classic case where the roles of the cultic prophet and the individual prophet merge and overlap.

One of the characteristics of laments is the description of the plight of the suppliants. This section contains some vivid description of the locusts and the devastation they cause. Interpreters are divided over the question whether 1:4 describes four different species of locusts or four stages in the life cycle of each locust. What is clear beyond doubt is that, by the time the locusts move on, the entire vegetation of the area has been consumed and a whole harvest has been lost. The effect on the inhabitants is loss of the food on which they depend, and even the temple cult is affected for lack of materials for the grain offering and drink offering. The empty granaries, the domestic and wild animals dazed by the vain search for pasture, the ruined farmers, the frustrated partygoers — all contribute to the general picture of desolation. The most vivid description is that of the locusts themselves advancing like an invading army, moving forward in disciplined ranks, surmounting every obstacle, and consuming everything in their path. This imagery is sustained in 2:2-11, but recurs at other points such as 1:6 and 2:20, 25.

In fact, it is the description of the locusts as an invading army and the interpretation of the plague in terms of "the day of the LORD" that give theological and religious significance to the disaster. The origins of the concept of "the day of the LORD" are lost in obscurity and have been the subject of much speculation. There is no doubt, however, that one of the images that came to be associated with this concept was that of an invading foreign army (see esp. Zeph 1:14-16). It is equally clear that in the teaching of the classical prophets from Amos onward (see Amos 5:18-20) "the day of the LORD" was conceived in terms of a day of judgment, often of judgment of Israel or Judah themselves. Joel clearly interpreted the plague of locusts as at least a preliminary warning of the kind of judgment the people could expect (as in Amos 4:9; 7:1-3), if not as the judgment itself. See the recurrent use of the concept of "the day of the LORD" in 1:15; 2:1-2, 11.

It is equally clear, however, that Joel does not envisage this judgment as final and destructive. On the contrary, it provides an urgent impetus to the people to repent, and it issues in a divine intervention to remove the locusts and restore the prosperity of the people. In this light it is probable that the permanent relevance of the prophet's teaching about repentance and related matters is one of the main reasons for its preservation. Unlike many prophets, Joel does not draw attention to specific sins. The general sinfulness of the community is presupposed, and the plague of locusts is interpreted as an interim judgment. It affords an opportunity for repentance, and if this is taken the judgment will be removed. Otherwise it must be seen as a precursor of a final and ineluctable judgment.

The prophet's teaching on repentance is concentrated in 2:12-17. Clearly the observance of outward penitential rites is envisaged. The whole community is to be involved and to attend a public liturgy. Fasting is a prominent element, as are other mourning customs such as weeping and the rending of clothing. At the same time the sincerity of the people in observing these penitential rites is of paramount importance. As elsewhere the essential term for "repent" is "return." It is not so much the expression or even the feeling of regret for past sin that matters but rather the change of will in a deliberate return to God (2:12). This teaching is reminiscent of Jer 29:13-14 and Deut 4:29-31; 30:2-3. Above all, the communal penitence is to be expressed in prayer offered by the priests. The formula quoted in 2:17 is characteristic of laments, asking God to spare his people and using the argument that God's own reputation may be at stake if his people are allowed to perish (compare Pss 79:10 and 115:2). The most important element in the prophet's teaching on repentance is the presupposition of the nature of God as gracious and merciful (2:13). Here there seems to be a direct allusion to the revelation of the nature of God to Moses in Exod 34:6-7. It is this conviction that inspires repentance and the hope that God will indeed forgive his people and come to their rescue, but there is no presumption that human repentance will automatically result in divine forgiveness (2:14). God is sovereign in both judgment and deliverance.

God's immediate answer to his people's prayer is contained in 2:19-20. The following seven verses bring the section as a whole to a conclusion by amplifying the themes of the divine answer. The land, the animals, and people are summoned to abandon their fears and to rejoice in the turn in their fortunes which God has wrought. In place of the threatened famine there will now be an abundant harvest; in place of the threatened drought abundant rain. God will restore the prosperity lost through the devastation wrought by the plague of locusts, and Israel will no longer be embarrassed by appearing in the eyes of other peoples to be devotees of an ineffectual God (compare the prayer in v. 17). The climax of this picture of renewed security and well-being is the knowledge that God, the only God, is in the midst of his people, and this conviction is reaffirmed by God's action in responding to his people's prayer for deliverance from the plague of locusts. This passage, too, though rooted in the particular events which occasioned the section as a whole, contains teaching about the nature of life in a community under God's care, which is of far more general application.

Before leaving this section I should draw attention to two uncertainties in the meaning of the text. In 2:23 the word translated "early rain" occurs twice, but it is slightly different from the usual word and identical with a similar word which means "teacher." Some of the ancient translators understood it in this sense on its first occurrence in this verse, and some scholars have linked it with the "Teacher of Righteousness" in the Qumran writings. It is interesting that the ideas of teaching and rain also occur together in 1 Kgs 8:36. In the present context, however, "early rain" is by far the most natural and appropriate meaning. In 2:25 it is sometimes objected that a single plague of locusts is hardly likely to have devastated more than one year's harvest, and some scholars suggest revocalizing the word translated "years" to obtain the sense "double." This, however, can hardly be achieved without further modification of the text, for which there is no evidence in the manuscripts or ancient versions. It is best to regard the plural "years" as a poetic expression, possibly with an allusion to Pharaoh's dreams in Genesis 41.

Joel 2:28-32

This is the best-known and most important passage in the book. In the Hebrew Bible it is reckoned as a separate ch. 3, ch. 3 in the English Bible being ch. 4 in the Hebrew Bible. There is both continuity and discontinuity with the earlier and later parts of the book. The continuity is indicated most clearly by the continuing treatment of the "day of the LORD" theme, while the discontinuity is marked by the vague indications of time sequence in "afterward" in 2:28 and "in those days and at that time" in 3:1, both indicating events in a remoter future than the removal of the locust plague. Another marked difference from the earlier part of the book is that, whereas there the focus was on the judgment of Judah herself, in the later part it is Judah's foreign attackers who undergo judgment, while Judah herself experiences divine salvation and restoration.

This passage itself comprises three sections. In 2:28-29 the theme is the universal outpouring of the spirit of God, resulting particularly in visions and prophecy. This is one of the relatively few passages in the OT where there is a direct link between prophecy and the spirit of God. It is reminiscent particularly of Num 11:16-17, 24-30, where seventy elders of Israel receive the spirit and prophesy, including two who had been designated but had not gone out to the tent with the others. When Joshua protested, Moses expressed the wish that all the people of God might receive his spirit and prophesy. In Joel this concept is extended even further to include not simply designated leaders but all levels of membership in the community, including specifically the slaves. The use of the expression "all flesh" carries at least a further implication that the outpouring of the spirit would not be restricted to the people of God but extend to all humankind, even if this is not explicitly drawn out in the prophecy itself.

2:30-31 predict natural portents as an indication of the imminence of the "day of the LORD." This is traditional imagery, with overtones both of divine theophany and of judgment, although the sequel shows that the latter is the primary connotation here. 2:32 promises salvation to a certain group who will escape the coming judgment. They are defined as those who call on the name of the LORD, but the passage makes clear that they are also those whom God himself calls, and that the place where this community is to be found is Mt. Zion (i.e., the temple). The original intention of the prophecy is probably to indicate that a "remnant" of the chosen people will experience salvation rather than judgment at the "day of the LORD," while the expression "everyone who calls on the name of the LORD" is clearly patient of a more universal interpretation.

This brings us to the citations of the passage in the NT. Practically the entire passage is quoted in Acts 2:17-21, where it is said to be fulfilled in the events of the Pentecost immediately after the resurrection of Jesus. It is quoted in the course of Peter's address to the multilingual gathering of diaspora Jews and proselytes, to account for the phenomena attending the outpouring of the Spirit on the first Christians. The points of immediate relevance in the quotation in this context are the actual outpouring of the Spirit and the universal scope of the gift. The quotation breaks off at the beginning of Joel 2:32, with the offer of salvation to everyone who calls on the name of the Lord, for this is the point that Peter develops in his address to the crowd. Toward the end of the address (Acts 2:39) he alludes to the final words of the prophecy. The first clause of Joel 2:32 is cited in a similar context specifically justifying the Gentile mission, Rom 10:13.

Joel 3:1-21

The twin themes of this last chapter of Joel are the coming judgment of all nations and the security of the people of God. The opening verse, with its vague time reference, suggests that the passage is to be seen as a continuation of 2:28-32, where the salvation of God's people has already been announced. The traditional formula of "restoring the fortunes" of God's people has often been understood in terms of the return from exile, although this is almost certainly a secondary development of its meaning. It is apt in the present case because the judgment announced on the other nations specifically relates to their treatment of Israel, and particularly the dispersion of God's people among the nations. The restoration of their fortunes in such a context is focused particularly on their reoccupation of the promised land.

Whereas the theme of judgment in the earlier part of the book was concerned with the judgment of God's people themselves, the judgment envisaged here is clearly universal, with a summons of all nations to the valley of Jehoshaphat. This location has not been identified, nor is there any obvious reference to the king of that name. The name "Jehoshaphat" itself, however, simply means "Yahweh has judged," and it may be that the "valley of Jehoshaphat" in 3:2 and 12 and the "valley of decision" (where "decision" may denote the verdict) in v. 14 are simply poetic expressions for a place where God's judgment is to be executed. The crimes for which the Gentile nations are to be judged are, according to vv. 2b-3, those of maltreatment of God's own people.

The core of the first part of the chapter is to be seen in 3:1-3 and 11-12, and consists of the summoning of all the nations to God's judgment. Vv. 9-10 suggest that the judgment is to take the form of warfare, in which the guilty will be defeated. V. 10 forms a stark contrast with the well-known prophecy common to Isa 2:4 and Mic 4:3, but need not be a conscious reversal of that prophecy. It might easily be a standard expression in the context of a call to arms, of which the prophecy common to Isaiah and Micah is itself a deliberate reversal. Other traditional imagery of judgment is that of the harvest reaping in v. 13 and the failure of the sun, moon, and stars in v. 15 (for which cf. 2:10, 31). The theme of the "day of the LORD" is picked up again in v. 14.

3:4-8 are often thought to be a later addition to the original prophecy. While in the rest of vv. 1-15 all the nations are summoned to judgment, here the Phoenicians and Philistines are singled out. The crimes of which they are accused are looting and kidnapping. The mention of Greeks as purchasers of Israelite slaves in v. 6 is sometimes seen as evidence of a late date, but there is a similar indictment in Ezek 27:13. In reality there is nothing sufficiently specific in these verses to determine their historical context, and kidnapping and trading in Israelites is already introduced in v. 3. The theme of requital is common to the whole passage, and it is impossible to determine whether these verses are a later supplement or not. Similarly, Egypt and Edom are singled out in the second part of the chapter (in v. 19), but the maltreatment of the Judeans of which they are accused is in very general terms, and probably simply reflects traditional enmity. It is interesting that in v. 8 the Judeans themselves are to be agents of the divine judgment.

The focus changes at 3:16 to the theme of the sovereignty of Yahweh and, as its corollary, the security of God's people. The tradition of Zion or Jerusalem as God's earthly dwelling and the symbol of security for his people (for which see, e.g., Pss 46 and 48) underlies this passage, as does the conviction that there is a sharp division between the holy people of God and the guilty foreigners who will never again be allowed to invade the holy city. God's judgment is seen primarily in terms of avenging the maltreatment of his own people, while they will be compensated by security and material prosperity in the promised land. The motif of the fountain from the temple irrigating the Wadi Shittim (either a general term for wadis in the wilderness of Judea or a reference to the lower part of the Kidron valley) in v. 18 is reminiscent of Ezek 47:1-12, while the earlier part of that verse has some material in common with Amos 9:13. These parallels, however, are not verbally close and probably reflect dependence on common tradition rather than direct literary dependence. The main emphasis in the second half of the chapter is on the sovereignty of Yahweh and its consequences in salvation for his people and judgment for the other nations. Against this needs to be set the clear emphasis in the first section of the book that God's own people have to face judgment too.

Bibliography. Barton, J. 2001, *Joel and Obadiah,* OTL, Louisville: Westminster/John Knox • Coggins, R. J. 2000, *Joel and Amos,* NCB, Sheffield: Sheffield Academic • Crenshaw, J. L. 1995, *Joel,* AB 24C, New York: Doubleday • Mason, R. 1994, *Zephaniah, Habakkuk, Joel,* Old Testament Guides, Sheffield: JSOT • Rudolph, W. 1971, *Joel, Amos, Obadia, Jona,* KAT 13/2, Gütersloh: Gerd Mohn • Stuart, D. 1987, *Hosea-Jonah,* WBC 31, Waco: Word • Wolff, H. W. 1977, *Joel and Amos,* trans. W. Janzen, S. D. McBride Jr., and C. A. Muenchow, Hermeneia, Philadelphia: Fortress.

Amos

M. Daniel Carroll R.

INTRODUCTION

Amos's stature as one of the first writing prophets and the ongoing relevance of his social message continue to draw readers to this powerful prophetic text. The words "let justice roll down like waters" (5:24) have stirred those from across the theological spectrum to seek a better world for the less fortunate (Martin-Achard 1984: 161-271; Carroll R. 2002: 26-30, 53-72).

It is difficult to specify the background of the prophet (Martin-Achard 1984: 13-45; Hasel 1991: 29-55). According to the heading (1:1), the prophet was from Tekoa. Although some postulate a northern site, most commentators agree that this town was in the hill country of Judah, a few miles south of Jerusalem. Amos, then, would have been a Judahite, who spoke for God in neighboring Israel. The response of the priest Amaziah demonstrates that not all appreciated this stinging message of judgment coming from the lips of a foreigner (7:12). The heading also mentions that Amos ministered during the reign of Jeroboam II — that is, during the first half of the eighth century. One can only conjecture why Amos is not mentioned in the account of this king in the Deuteronomistic history (2 Kgs 14:23-29). The earthquake, recalled centuries later in Zech 14:5 and which apparently can be connected to the destruction level at Hazor, locates his activity c. 760 BC.

In 1:1 Amos is called a "shepherd," but this is not the usual term for this profession. It appears elsewhere only in 2 Kgs 3:4 in reference to Mesha, king of Moab ("sheep breeder"). On the basis of Mesopotamian and Ugaritic sources some have understood this word to refer to some sort of cultic functionary. Amos's focus on Israel's holy places and rituals also might imply that he was attached to a sanctuary. Neither the comparative information nor the textual data, however, requires this interpretation. 7:14 states that the prophet was a "herdsman," indicating that his "flock" would have included both cattle and sheep. In addition, he is called a "dresser of sycamore trees," a species of tree not grown in the region of Tekoa. These data suggest that Amos was no poor farmer. He could have been an owner of various properties with several sources of income. And, if the prophet were the person who actually put these words to writing, his book's literariness could point to some sort of formal education and so underscore a higher social status.

Commentators disagree, too, on the interpretation of the tense of 7:14a and its implications for Amos's prophetic ministry. Should the verse be translated with the past tense (NIV, JB, KJV), in which case the idea is that he had left his other work altogether to take on the mantle of a prophet? Or does the present tense better capture the sense (NRSV, JPSV, NEB)? Amos would therefore be saying that he is not a prophet by profession and prophesies without economic motivation; he has another livelihood and now speaks out only by the will of God. Both translations are reasonable alternatives, but perhaps the latter better expresses Amos's unique compulsion to act: he has no other reason to prophesy than the force of the divine command. Scholars also debate whether "seer" (7:12) and "prophet" (7:14) are synonymous or technical terms for divine spokespersons from Judah and Israel, respectively. Finally, some attempt to coordinate Amos's call and ministry with the visions (7:1-9; 8:1-3; 9:1-4; see further at 7:1-9). In sum, to construct a clear picture of his person is problematic. One is left with the book that bears his name.

Critical scholars have posited a number of theories concerning the composition of this prophetic text (Martin-Achard 1984: 49-74; Hasel 1991: 17-27, 91-99; Carroll R. 2002: 14-20, 31-35). Many envision a core of oracles attributable to the prophet, some early additions (such as the third person narrative of 7:10-17) by a group of disciples, other, later expansions to the message before and during the exile to include Judah in the message's purview (e.g., 1:2; 2:4-5; 6:1a), and finally a postexilic word of hope (9:11-15). Nevertheless, several recent commentators have argued for the substantial authenticity of the book on historical and linguistic grounds (note especially Paul 1991). Literary approaches have demonstrated a high degree of artistry and cohesiveness (Andersen and Freedman 1989; Carroll R. 1992; Bovati and Meynet 1994; Carroll R. 2002: 24-26, 43-47) that could weaken the force of a theory of various redactions spanning centuries. For instance, the book exhibits a number of series of five and seven items and utilizes several chiastic structures. A recent commentary tries to combine a critical stance with a sensitivity to this literary craft (Jeremias 1998). This commentary will deal with the canonical text (Carroll R. 1992: 140-75). On the one hand, it is the message of the entire book that has impacted religious communities for millennia. On the other hand, its poetics are sufficiently strong to warrant careful attention as over against hypothetical reconstructions of possible stages of production.

The sharp attack on social injustice and the criticism of religious ritual are the aspects of the message of the book of Amos that usually draw attention. Recent studies have attempted more sophisticated analyses of Israel's social ills by utilizing sociological and anthropological theories and comparative data from the ancient Near East to try to specify with more precision the object of the prophetic invective (Sicre 1984; Fleischer 1989; Carroll R. 1992: 22-47; 2002: 20-24, 41-43). Opinions differ, but these efforts do serve to give the prophet's words more concreteness (see further at 2:6-16).

In relationship to the cult, earlier scholars proposed that Amos demanded the eradication of corrupt rituals and championed an ethical monotheism (cf. 4:4-5; 5:4-6, 21-25; 7:12-17; 9:1). This perspective is inadequate for two reasons. First, in the ancient Near East religion without ritual would be inconceivable. What the prophet decries is a cult divorced from divine social imperatives and national realities. This condemnation is all-encompassing: everyone, regardless of social standing, participated in these celebrations.

Second, the religious picture is more complex than simply unacceptable Yahwistic rituals. The text also hints at the existence of syncretistic popular religion (e.g., 5:26; 8:14). Scholars often respond to this observation by taking one of two views. Some claim that allusions to syncretism are later additions that reflect the introduction of other deities after the Assyrian conquest (cf. 2 Kgs 17:30). In contrast, others propose that religious polemic was the very essence of Amos's message, which was part of a broader prophetic movement against Baalism. The archeological data evidence widespread syncretism in eighth-century Israel and thus make the first option tenuous (King 1988: 88-107, 137-61; Barstad 1984). Nevertheless, the book's message cannot be limited to an attack on Baalism.

This prophetic word, while including social concerns and attacks on unacceptable rituals and syncretism, ultimately focuses on the person of Yahweh and his name. Yahweh rejects the social construction of reality called Israel, which claims to be his, and will one day build another society on the devastation left by judgment. The book draws upon covenant, wisdom, and cultic traditions for its message (Martin-Achard 1984: 75-97; Hasel 1991: 71-81; Carroll R. 2002: 14-18).

The book can be divided into three principal parts: the Oracles against the Nations (1:2–2:16), the Announcement of Judgment (3:1–6:14), and the Visions of the End (7:1–9:15).

COMMENTARY

The Heading (1:1)

This extensive heading mentions the time frame and occupation of Amos (see the Introduction). It can also be referring to the book's content by alluding to the two main sections of the book: "the words" to the oracles of chs. 3–6 and "which he saw" to the visions of chs. 7–9. Several passages may describe destruction by earthquake (e.g., 3:13-15; 8:8; 9:1). Its mention here would serve to authenticate this prophetic word, while the two-year time frame may convey that Amos's ministry was brief.

The Oracles against the Nations (1:2–2:16)

The phrase "the words of Amos" in 1:1 are followed by the announcement of the roar of Yahweh (1:2; cf. Joel 4:16). This juxtaposition connects the prophet's words with God's. On the one hand, this verse serves as an introduction to the entire prophetic text. The catastrophic impact of Yahweh's voice announces an ominous tone that will pervade the rest of the book, while Yahweh's roar, the lack of rain, thirst, and Carmel will surface again later. The word translated "wither" can also be taken as "mourn," a threat of the death to come through judgment (5:16-17; 8:8, 10; 9:5; cf. 5:1; 8:3). At the same time, this verse leads into the oracles against the nations. The description echoes ancient Near Eastern terminology for the manifestation of a warrior god, and war will be a key theme in the oracles.

Scholars debate the historical events behind the oracles, the oracles' authenticity, provenance, structure, and theological significance (Martin-Achard 1984: 126-42; Hasel 1991: 57-69). To begin with, it is difficult to identify with certainty the events to which the oracles refer. Suggested contexts range primarily from the Syrian resurgence of the ninth century to events contemporary with the prophet. Though perhaps the referents might have been obvious to the original audience, their vagueness now pushes the modern reader to focus more on the oracles' theological importance.

Some question the authenticity of the oracles against Tyre (1:9-10), Edom (1:11-12), and Judah (2:4-5) for historical and theological reasons. Scholars also point out that these have shorter decrees of judgment and no concluding formula. Adequate explanations for each of the historical points are available, however, and an appreciation of the linking of adjacent oracles by catchwords, the alternating structural pattern of pairs of oracles with and without the longer decrees and closing formula, and the graded numerical sequence (see below) demonstrate amazing literariness (Paul 1991: 7-30; Andersen and Freedman 1989: 341-70; Carroll R. 1996).

Several sources for the literary and theological background of the oracles have been proposed, such as execration texts from Egypt, the Yahweh war traditions, clan wisdom circles, and curses from ancient Near Eastern treaties. The more important challenge is to interpret their present function within the book. Here again theories abound. One notion is that these nations were at one time members of the Davidic empire and thus had mutual commitments of peace; Tyre, though, was never formally a member of the empire, just an ally. Others contend that the nations are condemned for having mistreated the people of God; yet some of the references cannot be limited to crimes against Israel, 2:1-3 extend the ethical concerns beyond Israel's borders, and Israel itself is judged (2:6-16). What is clear is that 1:3–2:3 highlight atrocities committed in war: irrational cruelty (1:3, 11, 13), the buying and selling of the vanquished (1:6, 9), and the violation of the dead (2:1). Within this context, at one level it makes better sense to say that the oracles refer to infractions against commonly accepted codes of warfare within the ancient world. The theological undergirding will be discussed below.

The phrase "I will not revoke its punishment" is used in the opening verse of each oracle. Literally the Hebrew reads, "I will not cause it to return" (NRSV note). To what does "it" refer? To the people cited in the oracle, the word of punishment, or the divine wrath which follows? The text is ambiguous, but the menacing tone is inescapable. God sovereignly directs the nations and their chastisement.

Each oracle begins with a graded numerical sequence (x/x + 1; x = 3). Unlike the similar pattern in Proverbs 30 (vv. 15-16, 18-19, 21-23, 29-31), the text does not list all four items. Some hold that what is singled out is the worst crime or the one that oversteps the limits of Yahweh's patience; others posit that the point is to add three and four to make seven, thereby communicating the fullness of sin. In some cases, however, more than one item is mentioned (e.g., 1:11), and the common phraseology in vv. 6-10 might imply a shared heinous project. Perhaps no satisfactory explanation is possible. The x/x+1 pattern can be extended to the whole series (now 7/7 + 1). This literary device could have had the original audience expect a climax at the seventh oracle (Judah, 2:4-5) but forces it ultimately to the Israel oracle (vv. 6-16), which indicts the nation for its rebellion.

Seven transgressions against defenseless people are listed (2:6-8); the sin, in other words, is comprehensive. The poor are doomed into slavery because of debts (v. 6b; cf. 8:4-6; Exod 21:2-11; Lev 25:39-43; Deut 15:12-18) and suffer perversion of justice in the courts (2:7a; cf. 5:10,12; Exod 23:1-8). Some kind of sexual impropriety against a helpless maiden is probably meant in 2:7b (the term "girl" disallows the possibility of reference to cultic prostitution), and worship is tainted by further abuse of the poor through the utilization of distraints from defaulted loans (Exod 22:25-26) and of money from inappropriate fines (2:8). What was the socioeconomic system that allowed such oppression? Some propose "rent capitalism," an arrangement in which rural peasants are dependent on urban moneylenders and merchants and fall into debt in order to pay for seed and tools. The dynamics of the marketplaces allow for corruption across the gamut of social classes. Here some of the poor own property and can afford to pay at least some taxes. The oppressors could include merchants, as well as state officials and elders involved in judging cases at the city gates. Thus the prophet might be defending a particular group among the poorer classes (such as the peasantry). The picture is not clear, but readers should appreciate that Amos is driving at hard realities and not sharing simply a vague ethical message.

2:9-12 detail Israel's rejection of Yahweh's historical acts of favor (vv. 9-10; note the *inclusio* with "Amorite") and its refusal to heed and respect his representatives (vv. 11-12; cf. 7:10-17). The last three verses of the oracle describe the subsequent inescapable judgment. Once again a series of seven appears: seven types of soldiers, signifying total defeat.

The preeminent theological theme throughout these oracles is the absolute sovereignty of Yahweh. His word reveals the sin and decrees punishment. He is actively involved in the nation's past, present, and future history. Yahweh moves to punish all peoples for crimes against humanity, whether in war or social injustice, which are grounded in hubris and greed. The punishment will be to suffer cruelty in return. The structure of this section communicates that Yahweh's people are part of this broader human reality, but Israel stands as more guilty because of its special relationship to God.

The Announcement of Judgment (3:1–6:14)

This next major section can be subdivided into two parts: 3:1–4:13 and 5:1–6:14. Each of these larger pieces can be further broken down into three subdivisions. The segments of this first part are 3:1-8, 3:9–4:3, and 4:4-13.

The Devastation of Israel (3:1–4:13)

A new section of the book begins at 3:1-2. These lines continue the expression of comprehensiveness found in 2:14-16 but now concern guilt. This is communicated through the repetition of "all" and the use of "whole" (lit. "all"). The allusion to the saving miracle of the exodus (cf. 2:10; 4:10; 5:17; 9:7) and Yahweh's intimate knowing is ironic: the historic relationship demands chastisement.

An *inclusio* ("has spoken") joins 3:1-2 with 3:3-8. This passage is structured so that vv. 3-5 contain five questions of one pattern and v. 6 two of another (5 + 2 = 7). The lines move progressively from a meeting of vague meaning to others representing the death or setback suffered by one of the two parties: a prey by a lion, a bird by a human trap, humans by Yahweh. Some see v. 7 as an intrusion, but it is connected to the previous line by several terms and serves as a transition to v. 8. The disaster of v. 6 is revealed to Yahweh's prophets (whom Israel silences, 2:12), who transmit his announcement of judgment. The purpose of 3:3-8, however, is not to authenticate the prophetic task; the focus is on Yahweh. He is the lion who has roared (1:2; 3:8; cf. King 1988: 128-30), but now the reader realizes that the roar signifies that he has his prey (v. 4) and that what awaits Israel is loss.

3:9–4:3 open with a call to gather witnesses (v. 9a), the detailing of transgressions (vv. 9b-10), and a decree of judgment (v. 11). Surprisingly, Yahweh appeals to other nations to observe the sin. Even these oppressive peoples would be appalled at what is happening inside the capital city Samaria! As in 2:6-8, names are given neither to those committing evil nor the victims. The social setting is described only as violent. The "strongholds," which appears frequently in chs. 1–2, could refer to the fortified part of the palace (King 1988: 70). Therefore, the target is not only the more fortunate but also the monarchy — that is, not only a specific social stratum or economic structure but also the sociopolitical system. The entire social construction of reality that is Israel is rife with sin.

The hinge verse 3:12 (for interpretive options, see Andersen and Freedman 1989: 408-10) connects the demolition of the fortresses with the destruction in vv. 13-15. The earlier picture of the ferocious lion is reinforced, as only bits and pieces are left as evidence of a sheep (a people) destroyed (cf. Exod 22:10-13 [Heb. 22:9-12]). The juxtaposition of the social and religious surfaces again (cf. 2:6-8, 11-12), as the punishment will bring the tearing down of luxurious homes and Bethel's altars. 4:1-3 exposes the self-indulgence of the powerful who live off the nation's misery. These wealthy women will march out single file through the breaches in the city walls to somewhere beyond the nation's borders (for translation issues in 4:2-3, see Paul 1991: 129-36). 3:9–4:3 underscore that those in power and the society's institutions are the special objects of Yahweh's wrath. In agreement with the oracles of chs. 1–2 and 3:11, the fate that awaits Israel is invasion. Judgment is irrevocable, sealed by Yahweh's oath (4:2).

The last segment, 4:4-13, develops the religious critique hinted at earlier (2:8: 3:14). It begins in vv. 4-5 with a parody of the priestly call to worship (cf. Pss 96:8; 100:2, 4). Once more a series of seven appears: seven imperatives to worship. The irony lies in the invitation to come to Israel's historic sanctuaries of Bethel (cf. Gen 28:10-22; 35:1-15) and Gilgal (cf. Joshua 3–4; 1 Samuel 11), but to sin! A careful look at the offerings mentioned reveals that none is for transgression. For example, the "sacrifice" is probably the peace offering, which was to celebrate blessings sent by Yahweh; it provided a banquet for the worshiper and the priest (cf. Lev 3:1-17; 7:11-18, 28-36). Not only are worshipers then involved in this pious delusion; the cult personnel are as well (cf. 7:10-17). V. 5b discloses the primary motivation of this worship. The participants come to satisfy their own religious impulses, disregarding Yahweh's demands for worship inseparable from obedience and morality.

There is a stark contrast at 4:6, with Yahweh declaring what he brings them. He sent covenant curses (vv. 6-11; cf. Lev 26:18-20, 23-26; Deut 28:20-24, 29-30, 38-42; 1 Kgs 8:33-37), yet in a fivefold refrain he says that Israel refused to return to him. Each of these curses is emphatic in its own way: the twofold use of "all" in 4:6, the lengthy repetitiveness of vv. 7-8, the citing of various trees in v. 9, the vivid description of war in v. 10, and the allusion to the tradition of Sodom and Gomorrah in v. 11 (Genesis 19). All of this demonstrates that religion is far removed from national realities: even while the nation endures all manner of reversals, the sanctuaries are full of those rejoicing in God's goodness. This is not an extensive polemic against non-Yahwistic worship of fertility gods (Barstad 1984: 47-75), although some of this might lie in the background (note, too, the "heights" or high places in 4:13); nor is this a call to worship only in Jerusalem. This passage is an indictment of a religion oblivious to the actual nature of Yahweh (Carroll R. 2000). Accordingly, what follows is another invitation, an invitation to meet the true God (vv. 12-13).

4:13 is the first of three hymnic passages (cf. 5:8-9; 9:5-6). Scholars dispute their possible date of composition and whether these are fragments of one hymn or three separate hymns (Martin-Achard 1984: 59-63; Hasel 1991: 83-89). Each describes the absolute power of Yahweh, the Creator God, and highlights his "name" to forcefully distinguish his person from the Yahweh Israel worships according to its own tastes. This first doxology is a series of five participles (cf. Job 9:5-10; Isa 45:18; Mic 1:3-6). The epithet "the LORD, the God of hosts" appears nine times in several combinations (3:13; 4:13; 5:14-16, 27; 6:8, 14; 9:5). "Hosts" (Heb. *ṣᵉbā'ôt*) has military overtones (*NIDOTTE* 3:733-35): the divine judge coming across the high places of the earth to chastise his people is the warrior god who will punish through invasion.

The Death of Israel (5:1–6:14)

This section can be subdivided into three segments: 5:1-17, 5:18-27, and 6:1-14. Each is structured chiastically — that is, as a concentric ring whose climax comes at the middle of the passage and whose mirrored parts correspond to one another. In 5:1-17, vv. 1-3 go with vv. 16-17, vv. 4-6 with vv. 14-15, v. 7 with vv. 10-13, v. 8 with v. 9. The center is at "the LORD is his name" (v. 8).

5:1-3 are a lament for Israel, who has fallen in battle with horrific losses (cf. 4:10). What is worse, not only can Israel not get up, there is no one to lift it up . . . not even Yahweh. Vv. 16-17 emphatically describe the extensive mourning by concentrating on Yahweh's name and repeating "all." He will pass through by the human instrument of an invading army, and death will be everywhere (cf. Exod 11:4; 12:12, 29-30).

A smaller chiasm, whose center is at "or cross over to Beer-sheba," encompasses 5:4-6. Beer-sheba was in Judah. This indicates that the popular religion went beyond the national sanctuaries to embrace pilgrimage sites elsewhere. These verses, which exhort the nation to seek Yahweh himself (not the sanctuaries, 4:4-5) to live, raise another important issue within the book. In light of the inescapable judgment and staggering loss of life, is it possible to sustain that Amos offers a legitimate hope to Israel (Martin-Achard 1984: 143-59; Hasel 1991: 105-9, 112-16)? Is the word of devastation hyperbole, designed to spur the nation to repentance? Is the judgment to be limited to only the guilty? Were these words of hope added later to soften the original prophetic message? Or is there a hope for a remnant after the divine visitation? The corresponding vv. 14-15 provide an answer. Whatever hope might exist is for the "remnant of Joseph" — that is, those surviving the destruction (cf. 3:12; 6:9-10; 9:11). The descriptions of total devastation, then, are best not taken too literally but rather in light of ancient war annals, which commonly speak of absolute losses to signify comprehensive victory or defeat; the aim is not to communicate that no one at all survives. 5:7 suggests that the chance of a positive response by the nation as a whole to Yahweh's exhortation is slim, while vv. 10-13 narrow the accusation to elders and government officials. These leaders will suffer the forfeiture of what has been extorted.

The second doxology surrounds the center of the chiasm (5:8-9). The Creator, who controls all nature, also intervenes in history to dismantle military pride and might. This incomparable God, whose name is Yahweh, will bring the nation to wailing. All the people are in some way guilty as participants in this religious, economic, and political world called Israel, although particular groups within the nation are most responsible for sealing its fate.

The next two segments, 5:18-27 and 6:1-14, develop two fundamental themes of 5:1-17: unacceptable worship and death, respectively. The chiasm in 5:18-27 has its center at v. 24, with vv. 18-20 corresponding to vv. 26-27 and vv. 21-23 to v. 25.

The book's first woe (NRSV, "alas") begins 5:18-27 and is addressed to the nation. The wordplay with a similar term in the laments of vv. 16-17 suggests that those now spoken to are those to be mourned. They are reprimanded for a misguided conception of the day of the LORD, probably believing that the future held the certainty of victorious divine intervention (Barstad 1984: 89-108; Hasel 1991: 109-12). But that day would bring judgment and darkness (cf. 5:8) from which there would be no escape (cf. 2:14-16; 3:3-6; 9:1-4); to long for it was suicidal (5:18-20). Vv. 26-27 clarify that that day meant going into exile by Yahweh's hand. History shows that deportations began even before the fall of Samaria to the Assyrian Shalmaneser V in 722 BC (2 Kings 17); some occurred during the western campaigns of his predecessor Tiglath-pileser III in 734-732, and therefore not too long after Amos's ministry. An intriguing note concerning the march into exile appears in 5:26. This is the most difficult verse in the book to interpret, as a comparison of the English versions easily attests. Most likely the reference is to Mesopotamian astral deities. Though some commentators date such syncretism to the Assyrian conquest (2 Kgs 17:30; e.g., Wolff 1977: 265-66; Jeremias 1998: 105-6), a good case can be made for this religious mix during Amos's day (Barstad 1984: 118-26; Paul 1991: 194-98; Carroll R. 2000). These deities would helplessly accompany Israel into the exile decreed by the sovereign God.

5:21-23 and v. 25 censure Israel's worship. Whereas 4:4-5 ridiculed the celebrations at the sanctuaries and 5:4-6 urged the nation to seek Yahweh, vv. 21-23 declare his rejection of every aspect of their religious observance. This sort of empty ritual was not what the nation had offered Yahweh in the wilderness (v. 25). Instead of the self-satisfying hypocrisy that is their worship, Yahweh desires justice, a social reality perverted in Israel's day-to-day life (cf. v. 7). The twisting of their understanding of the person of Yahweh and the abandonment of morality reflected in Israel's theology and ritual would bring it to ruin.

The last segment (6:1-14), also a woe, has vv. 9-10 at the center of its chiasm. Vv. 1-3 correspond to vv. 13-14. These verses criticize a complacent leadership confident in the military prowess that had achieved victories and secured national borders (cf. 2 Kgs 14:25). Until now they had been able to postpone the "evil day" of Yahweh's judgment (cf. 3:6), but their self-delusion is obvious in the wordplays (6:13): they rejoice over Lo-debar ("no thing") and Karnaim ("horns"; cf. the fate of the horns in 3:14). Soon the "first of the nations" would be oppressed from border to border by a more powerful nation (v. 14).

Archeology has discovered that the *marzeaḥ* feast described in 6:4-7 was known for centuries across the Mediterranean basin (Barstad 1984: 127-42; King 1988: 137-61; Jeremias 1998: 110-12). This was a religious fellowship gathering renowned for its drinking and lavish consumption (cf. 4:1). This association is a testimony of another kind of syncretism at higher social levels which were callous toward the people's sufferings. The corresponding verse in the chiasm points to the nonsensical nature of this perversion (6:12; cf. 5:7).

The two verses which envelope the center of the chiasm (6:8,11) emphasize Yahweh's deep emotional reaction to this society, for which he decrees destruction by invasion. The center dramatically portrays the death toll in a scene where a kinsman burns the bodies of survivors, perhaps to avoid plague because of the impossibility of burying the quantity of corpses (vv. 9-10; cf. 5:3, 16-17). The command to be quiet in 6:10 is not out of fear of Yahweh's return, but a final act of defiance (cf. 4:6-11). In their minds they had suffered betrayal at the hands of their God of blessing and triumph. Why turn to a God who could not be trusted? Yet irony reigns: the name, the true nature of Yahweh, is what the hymnic passages celebrate (4:13; 5:8; 9:6)!

Visions of the End (7:1–9:15)

The Immediate Future as Judgment (7:1–9:10)

This section contains five visions (Martin-Achard 1984: 107-19; Auld 1986: 16-24; Andersen and Freedman 1989: 611-738). The first four can be subdivided into pairs (7:1-3, 4-6 and 7:7-9; 8:1-3). Visions three through five are each followed by explanatory expansions. Some commentators propose that the visions predate Amos's ministry; others, that the last one(s) occurred after the confrontation with Amaziah (7:10-17); still others, that each vision can be coordinated with a different stage in his work. All such reconstructions are hypothetical.

The first two visions (7:1-6) show the prophet interceding for Israel to avoid a major catastrophe; each attempt is more desperate in tone (note the change from "forgive" to "cease"). In contrast to Israel with its self-deluding confidence, Amos realizes that the nation is "so small." It is in a pitiable state, vulnerable to natural disasters and militarily helpless. The third (vv. 7-9) and fourth (8:1-3) visions add new elements: Yahweh questions Amos about what he sees and then expounds the visions' meaning. It is better to translate the term "plumb line" (7:7-8, NRSV) as "tin." The image would be that of Yahweh standing on a tin wall, tearing off a piece, and throwing it into their midst. The implication is that this metallic wall, which from a distance seems strong, is actually weak. All their pretense is vain; their defenses will come down. V. 9 declares that the religious and political institutions are finished, a reality vividly portrayed by the wordplay in 8:2 (NRSV note) and the ubiquitous mourning (v. 3; cf. 5:16-17; 6:9-10).

The primary aim of 7:10-17 is not biographical, although it does shed some light on Amos's background (cf. the Introduction). The goal is to illustrate national obstinacy and substantiate the futility of continuing to intercede. This connection with the third vision is evident in the repetition of a number of words from vv. 8-9 in vv. 10-17. Amaziah counters the indictment by defending both the monarchy and the temple (vv. 10-13). The reality that both institutions are inseparably linked is manifest in Amaziah's interpretation of Amos's activities as treasonous (prophets had participated in political changes before; cf. 1 Samuel 16; 1 Kings 14; 2 Kings 9), his desire to silence the prophet (cf. 2:11-12), and the demand that Amos leave the country. Ultimately what is at stake is the inviolability of Yahweh's word, which stands over against the priest's commitment to the status quo. The end decreed for the nation's institutions (7:9) is now individualized for Amaziah and his family (v. 17), reflecting once more the general-particular nature of guilt and punishment that runs throughout the book.

Even as 7:10-17 develop the third vision, so 8:4-14 do the fourth. It pictures the sin that brings the end as well as the awfulness of that future. Vv. 4-6 hark back to the theme of the abuse of the poor (2:6-8) but provide more details of the economic exploitation. Religion is a facade (5:21-25); greed the driving force; corrupt dealings the method (cf. Deut 25:13-15; Prov 11:1). Yahweh's response is swift and sure, as again he swears by himself to bring punishment (7:7; cf. 4:2; "pride of Jacob," unlike at 6:8, refers to Yahweh's glory; cf. Mic 5:4 [Heb. 5:3]). Formulas about that day (cf. 2:16; 4:2; 5:18-20) subdivide 7:9-14 into three shorter pericopes, each of which draws on earlier material. Vv. 9-10 are reminiscent of 5:8, 16-17, 23 and 8:3. Vv. 11-12 echo the hunger in 4:6 and are a contrast to the rejection of Yahweh's word in 2:11-12; 7:10-17. Vv. 13-14 return to the themes of thirst (4:7-8) and syncretism (see above at 5:18-27). Scholars disagree (Barstad 1984: 143-201) concerning whether these are references to other gods (NRSV, "Ashima") or different appellations for Yahweh at various sanctuaries (in this case read "the guilt of Samaria") and thus allusions to the golden calves (1 Kgs 12:26-33) and the pilgrimage to Beer-sheba (5:5). Either way, this desperate search for divine help is misdirected and too late.

The fifth and final vision (9:1-4) is followed by a hymn (vv. 5-6) and a response to those who would believe that no such disaster could befall Yahweh's chosen people (vv. 7-10). The vocabulary shared by these three passages underscores their interconnectedness. In the vision Yahweh stands on the altar and brings down the temple (probably Bethel; cf. 3:14; 5:5) in a manner similar to the third vision, where he demolishes the fortifications and institutions which provided confidence and ratified Israel's understanding of the world (7:7-9). Yahweh's instrument here could be an earthquake, but the repetition of "the sword" in these passages suggests destruction in warfare. The vision poetically reinforces the message that violent judgment is inescapable. Amos five times uses a technique called merism, in which two extremes are cited to include everything in between: there will be no place to hide (2:14-16; 5:18-20; cf. Ps 137:7-9), as the all-powerful Yahweh is sovereign over every sphere, whether the earth, the heavens, or the sea (9:5-6).

This section closes with 9:7-10. Yahweh underlines the reality of his involvement in the history of all nations, no matter how distant (Cush; cf. Isa 18:1-2) or if historic enemies, such as the Philistines (1:6-8) and the Arameans. If Yahweh can reverse the latter's exodus out of Kir (see 1:3-5), so, too, can he reverse Israel's exodus, because it is numbered among the sinful kingdoms. As in the case of those nations, some survive the destruction of sociopolitical and religious life and the death of their leaders; some go into exile; others are sold into slavery (chs. 1–2). That some would also survive Israel's punishment had already been hinted at (e.g., 3:12; 5:14-15; 6:9-10). Was this Yahweh's final word for Israel?

The Ultimate Future as Reconstruction (9:11-15)

While scholars debate the authenticity of these verses (Martin-Achard 1984: 63-70; Hasel 1991: 116-20), a careful reading demonstrates this text's conscious effort to show that beyond the judgment lies a reversal of fortunes. From the ruins of that devastation (3:14-15; 4:2; 6:8-11; 9:1) Yahweh will raise up a different kind of nation (contrast 5:2), a "booth," not one based on abusive and sinful institutions. There is no mention of fortresses, palaces, or temples, just the rebuilding of the cities and the replanting of crops. Instead of hunger and thirst (4:6-9) and the selfish indulgence of the powerful (4:1; 6:4-6), there will be plenty for all; instead of invasion and exile, there will be security in the land. The nations at war, and Edom in particular (chs. 1–2), will become members of a kingdom designed according to the Davidic ideals of the past (Acts 15:15-17 cites the LXX of 9:11-12). This very different picture is to be Israel's ultimate end, a promise from one no longer called "LORD of hosts" but "the LORD your God." The final word is that Yahweh, who demands that all recognize his sovereignty and champions social justice, is also the God of peace (Carroll R. 1998; Carroll R. 1992: 278-306)

Bibliography. Andersen, F. I., and D. N. Freedman. 1989, *Amos: A New Translation and Commentary,* AB 24A, Garden City, N.Y. : Doubleday • Auld, A. G. 1986, *Amos,* Old Testament Guides, Sheffield: JSOT • Barstad, H. M. 1984, *The Religious Polemics of Amos: Studies in the Preaching of Am. 2,7b-8; 4,1-13; 5,1-27; 6,4-7; 8,14,* VTSup 34, Leiden: E. J. Brill • Barton, J. 1980, *Amos's Oracles against the Nations,* SOTSMS 6, Cambridge: Cambridge University • Bovati, P., and R. Meynet. 1994, *Le livre du prophète Amos,* Rhetorique biblique 2, Paris: Cerf • Carroll R., M. D. 1992, *Contexts for Amos: Prophetic Poetics in Latin American Perspective,* JSOTSup 132, Sheffield: Sheffield Academic • Carroll R., M. D. 1995, "Reflecting on War and Utopia in the Book of Amos: The Relevance of a Literary Reading of the Prophetic Text for Central America," in M. D. Carroll R., D. J. A. Clines, and P. R. Davies, eds., *The Bible in Human Society: Essays in Honour of John Rogerson,* JSOTSup 200, Sheffield: Sheffield Academic • Carroll R., M. D. 1996, "God and His People in the Nations' History: A Contextualized Reading of Amos 1–2," *TynBul* 47:39-70 • Carroll R., M. D. 2000, "'For so you love to do': Probing Popular Religion in the Book of Amos," in M. D. Carroll R., ed., *Rethinking Contexts, Rereading Texts: Contributions from the Social Sciences to Biblical Interpretation,* JSOTSup 299, Sheffield: Sheffield Academic • Carroll R., M. D. 2002, *Amos — The Prophet and His Oracles: Research on the Book of Amos,* Louisville: Westminster John Knox • Fleischer, G. 1989, *Von Menschenverkäufern, Baschankühen und Rechtsverkehren: Die Sozialkritik des Amosbuches in historisch-kritischer, sozialgeschichtlicher und archäologischer Perspektive,* BBB 74, Frankfurt-am-Main: Athenäum • Hasel, G. F. 1991, *Understanding the Book of Amos: Basic Issues in Current Interpretations,* Grand Rapids: Baker • Jeremias, J. 1998, *The Book of Amos: A Commentary,* Louisville: Westminster/John Knox • King, P. J. 1988, *Amos, Hosea, Micah — An Archaeological Commentary,* Philadelphia: Westminster • Martin-Achard, R. 1984, *Amos: l'homme, le message, l'influence,* Geneva: Labor et Fides • Paul, S. M. 1991, *Amos: A Commentary on the Book of Amos,* Hermeneia, Minneapolis: Fortress • Polley, M. E. 1989, *Amos and the Davidic Empire: A Socio-Historical Approach,* New York: Oxford University • Sicre, J. L. 1984, *"Con los pobres de la tierra": La justicia social en los profetas de Israel,* Madrid: Cristiandad • Stuart, D. K. 1987, *Hosea-Jonah.* WBC 31, Waco, Tex.: Word • Wolff, H. W. 1977, *Joel and Amos,* Hermeneia, Philadelphia: Fortress.

Obadiah

Anthony Gelston

INTRODUCTION

Jerome's statement that this book is as difficult as it is short is often quoted. The first verse identifies the prophet as Obadiah and the topic as Edom. Obadiah is a common Hebrew name, meaning "Worshiper" or "Servant of Yahweh," but there are no grounds for identifying this prophet with any of the dozen or so individuals of this name in other parts of the OT. Much of the prophecy is undoubtedly concerned with Edom, but questions arise over the unity of the material and over the possibility of dating the prophecy. The most promising passage in the quest for a date and historical setting is vv. 10-14, which has often been related to the fall of Jerusalem in 586 BC, although such a setting cannot be regarded as more than a likely hypothesis. It is, however, far more likely than any of the other historical settings that have been suggested, and the chief difficulty in the way of accepting it is to determine whether any particular historical setting is reflected, and whether the relation between Israel and Edom is not rather set forth in more general terms with reference to a possible confrontation in the future. This is an example of the way in which questions of interpretation about the literary nature of the material bear on historical questions about its origin and background. It is advisable first, therefore, to take a brief look at the wider treatment of Edom in the OT.

The basic tradition underlying the OT view of Edom is that it was a people related to Israel, their respective ancestors being the patriarchal twin brothers Esau and Jacob, the sons of Isaac. The tradition of antagonism between the two peoples is traced back to the sibling rivalry of these ancestors in the patriarchal narratives of Genesis 25, 27, and 32–33. Already in Gen 25:23 their relationship is explained before their birth in terms of the political struggle between the nations to be descended from them, and it is striking in this light how positive is the portrayal of Esau's character in these narratives. Whatever the historical basis of this tradition of the ultimate relationship of Israel and Edom, during the monarchy they were often in conflict with each other.

A number of passages suggest that Edom behaved treacherously toward Judah at the time of the fall of Jerusalem. The most explicit of these, if this is the correct interpretation, is Obad 10-14. V. 10 stresses the treachery between "brother" nations that makes Edom's behavior so ignominious. V. 11 suggests that the Edomites stood aside at the time when the Babylonians conquered Jerusalem. When they might have rallied to Judah's defense, they appeared rather to side with the enemy. Even so, they are not accused of actually joining in the attack, but rather of gloating over Judah at the time of their defeat. The worst specific atrocities alleged are looting the property of Judeans and preventing fugitives from escaping. A difficulty which is not apparent in the NRSV is the translation of the series of clauses in vv. 12-14 as "you should not have. . . ." The Hebrew literally means "Do not gloat . . . ," and so on. This is crucial to the interpretation of the passage. Some commentators, envisaging a future rather than a past outrage, interpret these clauses literally as a warning to Edom not to indulge in such treacherous behavior, in view of the "brotherly" relationship between the two nations. There are, however, two strong arguments in favor of the NRSV's interpretation, assuming that the prophet is presenting his indictment in the form of an imaginary dramatic intervention at the time. One is the concrete nature of the acts of treachery envisaged, which at the same time fall a good way short of total identification with the enemy attack, despite the end of v. 11. The other is the context of the prophecy as a whole, which is certainly more in keeping with a pronouncement of judgment on sins actually committed than with a warning not to commit them in the future (see esp. v. 15b, which many commentators believe really belongs with vv. 10-14).

Although most of the prophetic references to the crimes of Edom are too general to allow specific historical inferences and seem essentially to reflect merely the general kind of attitude and behavior too be expected of enemies, there are a few further passages that are compatible with the tradition of Edomite treachery at the time of the fall of Jerusalem. Ezek 35:5 seems to relate specifically to the fall of Jerusalem considered as the "time of their final punishment," and its indictment is similar to that of Obad 14. Ezek 35:15 also reflects the same kind of *Schadenfreude* as Obad 12. Ps 137:7 ("Remember, O LORD, against the Edomites the day of Jerusalem's fall, how they said, 'Tear it down! . . .'") reflects a similar encouragement of the Babylonian attack as distinct from active participation in it, and this psalm is generally dated to the beginning of the exile, and therefore nearly contemporary with these events. These passages, together with the concrete details of the indictment in Obad 10-14, may be considered sufficient evidence for specific treacherous behavior on the part of Edom at the time of the fall of Jerusalem. The restraint in the specific allegations, in view of the evidence of Jer 40:11 that a number of Jewish fugitives successfully sought refuge in Edom, also speaks in favor of their historicity. At the end of the day individual readers must assess the balance of the evidence for themselves. The view taken here is that Obad 10-14 most probably does refer to the actual treachery of Edom against Judah at the time of the fall of Jerusalem, with the corollary that this enables us to date at least this part of the prophecy shortly after that time. For a judicious survey of the evidence, coming to a more negative conclusion, see Bartlett 1989: 151-57.

The other major problem in the interpretation of Obadiah is the question of its unity. Here it must be said at once that there is insufficient evidence to reach any certain conclusions. There does seem, however, to be a major break in v. 15. Apart from the title and introduction in the first part of v. 1 and the first part of v. 15 (which seems to be an introduction to the second part of the prophecy), there is certainly a thematic unity and continuity in vv. 1-15. There is also a degree of formal unity, in that most of the passage is represented as directly addressed by God to Edom. Yet there are signs that behind this unity in the final form of the material lie several originally disparate prophetic utterances. The clearest evidence for this is to be found in vv. 1c-5, to which close parallels are to be found in Jer 49:14-16, 9, and in which, despite the fact that Jer 49:7-22 is also a collection of prophetic material directed against Edom, Edom itself is not directly mentioned. That the parallel passages occur at different points and in reverse order in Jeremiah 49 suggests that, rather than either passage having been the direct source of the other, both are drawing on a common stock of anonymous prophetic material which had come to be regarded as directed against Edom, and therefore came to be incorporated into two collections of prophetic oracles against Edom. If this conclusion is correct, we have little indication of the date or original context of any of the contents outside vv. 10-14.

COMMENTARY

The main points in Obad 1c-5 may be briefly indicated. There is to be a multinational attack on the nation (unnamed in these verses), instigated by God and intended as a judgment against the pride of the nation, which had considered itself impregnable because of its geographical location. Theologically the thought is closely similar to the concept of Assyria as the instrument of divine judgment in Isa 10:5-15 and to the theme of divine judgment against all manifestations of pride in Isa 2:12-17. The prophet is concerned to assert the sole sovereignty of God in international relations and the divine judgment awaiting the nation that presumes on its independence. The reference to living in the clefts of the rock (Heb. *sela'*) in v. 3 has often been linked with the place of that name in 2 Kgs 14:7, which in turn has sometimes been identified with Umm el-Biyara at Petra in Edom. Bartlett 1989: 51-52 has pointed out, however, that there is no positive evidence for the identification of Sela with Umm el-Biyara, and that it is in any case not clear that "the rock" in Obadiah is a proper name, or, even if it is, that it is identical with the Sela of 2 Kgs 14:7. At most one can say that the phrase in Obad 3 *may* reflect the identity of the unnamed nation in vv. 1c-5 as Edom, but there can be no certainty in the matter. The point of the obscure v. 5 is probably the completeness of the destruction envisaged, going beyond the usual ravages of pillagers.

In v. 6 Edom is mentioned for the first time since the introduction in v. 1. As elsewhere in this prophecy the nation is named here after its ancestor Esau, no doubt to stress the traditional relationship with Israel and to underline the treachery of Edom's conduct as spelled out in v. 10. Before the indictment, however, the prophet emphasizes in vv. 6-9 the completeness and inescapability of the judgment awaiting Edom. The past tenses in vv. 6-7 are probably to be explained as examples of the Hebrew idiom called the "prophetic perfect," where the use of a tense suggesting completed action reflects the certainty of the events predicted. V. 6 gives the impression of a definite application to Edom of the less specific threat of v. 5. V. 7 indicates that at the time of its judgment Edom will itself be betrayed and let down by its supposed allies, just as Edom has betrayed Israel. The principle set forth in v. 15b is the basis of the judgment here pronounced on Edom. The additional words "those who ate" in the NRSV are an attempt to explain the obscure phrase in the light of the idiom found in Ps 41:9, reflecting the custom that the sharing of a meal established a relationship of a quasi-covenantal character (see also Gen 31:54).

Obad 8 introduces another theme, that of the "wisdom" of Edom. It is interesting that this is mentioned also in Jer 49:7, although there are no verbal parallels of the kind that are found in vv. 1c-5. It is often suggested that Edom was renowned for her wisdom practitioners, and attempts have been made to link the origins of the book of Job with Edom. Unfortunately there is virtually no actual evidence to establish the existence of a specifically Edomite wisdom tradition. Obad 8 and Jer 49:7 may simply be referring to wisdom as one of the resources with which any nation might hope to deal with political threats. At any rate, it is likely that statecraft is the particular form of wisdom that is in mind. (For the background of such wisdom see McKane 1965.) Edom's astute politicians will no more be able to rescue her from the coming judgment than her geographical situation (vv. 3-4) or her military prowess (v. 9). The whole of vv. 6-9 stresses the finality and inescapability of the judgment awaiting Edom.

The reasons for this judgment are spelled out in vv. 10-14, the indictment against Edom. It consists in their treacherous behaviour toward their traditional "brother-nation" Judah, probably, though not certainly, at the time of the fall of Jerusalem. In v. 10 Judah is named "Jacob," reflecting the view that Judah is now the sole survivor of the former Israel. The name is no doubt chosen here primarily to draw attention to the theme of conflict between the brothers Jacob and Esau, the traditional ancestors of Judah and Edom. The actual specific charges are less serious than might have been expected. In v. 11 they are accused of virtually identifying themselves with Judah's conquerors, standing passively by when they could have come to the rescue. In v. 12 they are accused of *Schadenfreude.* In vv. 13-14 they are accused of looting and of helping to prevent Judean fugitives from escaping. All of this, introduced by the general term "violence" in v. 10, is a serious breach of the obligations of "brotherhood." As such it merits divine judgment, which is applied on the *lex talionis* principle (v. 15b).

Verse 15 is the major turning point in the book. The

scope of the prophecy widens as the proximity of the day of the LORD is announced against all the nations, including Edom, but not exclusively against Edom as in the first part of the prophecy. Many scholars think that the two halves of the verse have become inverted, v. 15a introducing the new topic and v. 15b forming an effective climax to the indictment against Edom in vv. 10-14. The English translation does not indicate that the "you" in v. 15b is singular, as in vv. 10-14, suggesting that the reference is still specifically to Edom and not yet to "all the nations." There is, however, no textual evidence that such an inversion has occurred in the transmission of the prophecy, and it is perhaps more likely that we should see the mingling of themes in v. 15 as an indication of the editorial unity of the final form of the prophecy. The specific judgment against Edom, still prominent in the last section, is seen against the wider background of God's judgment on all the nations.

At all events the "you" in v. 16 is plural, and the reference now seems to be to the nations which had attacked and exploited Israel (cf. Zech 1:15). The theme of vv. 16-18 is the reversal that will result from the judgment. Those who appropriated Israel's territory will themselves be appropriated by Israel. The mention of "drinking" in v. 16 seems to allude to the tradition of the cup of divine judgment from which the nations had to drink in turn (see esp. Jer 25:15-29). V. 17 reflects the sacral traditions of the holiness and security of Mt. Zion, the site of the temple (for which compare particularly Isaiah 36–37). There is a close parallel to v. 17a in Joel 2:32, where "as the LORD has said" may indicate that Joel is citing Obadiah. There can, however, be no certainty in tracing the literary relationships between different prophecies, and in any case the dating of Joel is as uncertain as that of Obadiah. The mention of "those that escape" suggests the Isaianic concept of the "remnant" of Israel, while for Edom there will be no survivors. V. 21 seems to envisage the establishment of a theocracy in Jerusalem, incorporating in particular the former territory of Edom. The climax of the prophecy is the assertion of Yahweh's sovereignty as the final outcome of his "day" of judgment against all the nations. Vv. 15 and 21 thus constitute the theological kernel of the prophecy.

Obad 19 and 20 indicate in some detail which areas of territory will be reoccupied by which groups of Israelites, including those who will have returned from exile. This is a kind of expansion of v. 17b and may be a secondary addition to the original prophecy.

At first sight the historical obscurities of this short prophecy, together with the vengeful attitude toward Edom expressed so forcibly in it, might suggest that it has little relevance for the modern Christian reader. The prophecy does, however, affirm the basic principles of the ultimate sovereignty of God in this world and the impartiality of divine judgment, which none can evade by drawing on their own resources and supposed natural advantages. The condemnation of treachery in particular is trenchant and relevant to all human relationships.

Bibliography. Bartlett, J. R. 1989, *Edom and the Edomites,* JSOTSup 77, Sheffield: Sheffield Academic • Barton, J. 2001, *Joel and Obadiah,* OTL, Louisville: Westminster/John Knox • Coggins, R. J. 1985, *Israel among the Nations: A Commentary on the Books of Nahum and Obadiah,* ITC, Grand Rapids: Eerdmans and Edinburgh: Handsel • Mason, R. 1991, *Micah, Nahum, Obadiah,* Old Testament Guides, Sheffield: JSOT • McKane, W. 1965, *Prophets and Wise Men,* SBT 44, London: SCM • Raabe, P. R. 1996, *Obadiah,* AB 24D, New York: Doubleday • Rudolph, W. 1971, *Joel, Amos, Obadia, Jona,* KAT 13/2, Gütersloh: Gerd Mohn • Stuart, D. 1987, *Hosea-Jonah,* WBC 31, Waco: Word • Wolff, H. W. 1986, *Obadiah and Jonah: A Commentary,* trans. M. Kohl, Minneapolis: Augsburg.

Jonah

David Gunn

COMMENTARY

Flight from God (1:1-17)

While Jonah is often dated by scholars to the postexilic period, the circumstances of this book's authorship are largely unknown. The story plunges in with little explanation. God (here Yahweh in Hebrew, the LORD in English) summons Jonah to a task, reminding us of the commissioning of prophets such as Jeremiah (Jeremiah 1) or Isaiah (Isaiah 6). As it happens, a prophet called Jonah ben Amittai appears in another story, in 2 Kgs 14:25. There he announces the restoration of (northern) Israel's borders several decades before the Assyrians finally destroy the Northern Kingdom in the seventh century BC. If we assume that our Jonah is the same person, an Israelite prophet, then it is clear that he has a difficult task since Nineveh is a city of powerful Assyrians who have incorporated Jonah's own country into their empire.

Yahweh's instruction contains an echo of Abraham's encounter with Yahweh in Genesis 18–19, where God speaks of the cry of Sodom and Gomorrah that has come to him and of the gravity of their sin. Abraham pleads for the city: "Perhaps there are fifty innocent [or righteous] within the city: Will you really sweep them away and not spare the place for the sake of the fifty innocent in it?" Despite having bargained God down to ten innocent, Abraham soon witnesses the destruction of the cities. Abraham the intercessor and Yahweh the destroyer. We shall come back to this story.

What is Jonah's mission? He is to "call out against [or proclaim concerning]" Nineveh. God seems to be telling the prophet to proclaim the evil city's doom.

A complication arises. While Isaiah and Jeremiah, like Moses in Exodus 4, raise an objection to God's call, Jonah does not wait to argue the point. Whereas Abraham presses God to reconsider, Jonah simply arises and flees to the farthest corner of the Mediterranean from Yahweh's presence. Why does he flee? Why not call out against Nineveh? Perhaps he is simply too afraid to take a hostile message to a feared nation.

So Jonah arises but only to go down. He goes down to the port of Joppa, onto a ship, and, as a storm breaks, into the "innermost part" of the ship, where he falls into a "dead sleep." Thrown into the sea by the sailors, he sinks to the roots of the mountains, the belly of Sheol, the Pit of Death. Only at the door of death does he find words to pray. Some understand his flight as a metaphor of a journey of personal or spiritual decline.

What of the other seafarers? The captain's religion seems a reality; he anxiously demands that Jonah call upon his god. The fearful sailors hasten to determine (divine) the cause of their trouble, and the lot falls upon Jonah. He responds cryptically: "I am a Hebrew; and I fear Yahweh, the God of heaven, who made the sea and the dry land."

By professing his "fear" of Yahweh Jonah may mean simply that he is a Yahweh worshiper. The sailors, however, seem to take him literally: he is "afraid" of his god and that makes them "exceedingly afraid." They, too, are god-fearing men. They apparently conclude that the runaway has offended his god and the storm is the result. "What is this that you have done!" they exclaim.

Jonah's use of a familiar liturgical phrase to describe his god may strike a reader as ironic. Yahweh, affirms Jonah, is the creator of the world, heaven and earth, the sea and the land. Yet here is Jonah, attempting to flee from him! As the psalmist puts it: "Where shall I go from your spirit [wind!]? Or where from your face [your presence] shall I flee? If I ascend to heaven, there will be you! Or if I bed down in Sheol, behold — you!" (Ps 139:7-8).

The sailors ask Jonah what they should do to him to avert the danger. He apparently offers them a way out, acknowledging that he has caused their trouble. Is he genuinely sacrificing himself or hoping they will do the decent thing and refuse to drown him. When the sailors disregard his invitation and try to row back to the shore, their own motivation is also unclear. Do they act out of respect for the stranger's life? Or are they afraid that throwing him overboard may help Jonah's final escape from his god and make his god even more angry.

The storm intensifies. The sailors realize that Jonah's god is forcing immediate action ("We beg you, let us not perish for this man's life"). They must hurl Jonah overboard, *forced* to do so by the divinity ("and lay not on us innocent blood, for you, Yahweh, have done as it has seemed good to you").

So Jonah is hurled and the storm ceases, confirming to the sailors the presence of a god. Even more fearful now, they hastily make the appropriate (conventional) religious response: "and they offered a sacrifice to Yahweh and made vows." These god-fearing men have become specifically Yahweh-fearing. Inadvertently the reluctant prophet has helped "convert" these strangers to the worship of his own god. As we shall see, this turn of events foreshadows what is to come in ch. 3.

Fish and Temple (2:1-10)

Yahweh appoints a great fish to swallow up Jonah. Realizing that he cannot escape from his god, distress overtakes him, and he prays to Yahweh his god from inside the fish (2:1). He has sought the security of the innermost part of the ship, glimpsed the belly of Sheol, and found himself in the belly of the fish. He has fled the insecurities and contradictions of the outside world only to be faced with the ultimate security and certainty of death. He recoils. There is a dark side to "enclosure."

His prayer takes (largely) the conventional form and language of a psalm of thanksgiving. It is modified, however, so as to contain a story within it, a flashback. While at first sight the fish seems to be just another disaster for Jonah, the flashback tells a different story. Jonah begins his prayer in 2:2 by recalling that he had cried out to Yahweh from the belly of Sheol (in the depths of the sea), and God had answered him. Then, with v. 3, he begins to recount what happened from the point where Yahweh (actually the sailors, but at Yahweh's behest) had cast him into the deep. Sinking down to the Pit of Death, he "remembered" Yahweh and prayed — which is what he recalled in v. 2. We now see that the belly of Sheol is the cause of distress, the belly of the fish the cause of gratitude. The fish is the answer to Jonah's cry as he finds himself at death's door. Safely inside the fish he prays to Yahweh, his rescuer, this hymn of thanks (i.e., a psalm of thanksgiving). It recounts his rescue and includes a vow to make sacrifices in the temple in due course. What looked at first like oppression has turned out to be deliverance.

In the deep Jonah confronts what looks like an irrevocable consequence of his act of defiance: "I am cast out from your presence; / how shall I again look upon your holy temple?" (2:4). His flight from God had turned into his being cast out by God. For Jonah, the divine presence is bound up, above all, with the temple. (The poetry even suggests that "holy temple" may be a metaphor for Yahweh's presence.) Facing physical death ("as my life was ebbing away"; 2:7, NRSV) and the reality of being disowned by God, he yearns again for the divine presence; he "remembers" Yahweh. His prayer of distress breaks out and comes, he knows, to God, "into your holy temple." Clearly Jonah's devotion to God and temple is deep-seated.

Concluding his hymn of thanksgiving, Jonah turns to sacrifice and vow-making (2:8-9), activities associated with psalms of thanksgiving at the temple. Jonah knows intimately the regular forms of worship. Indeed, his point in v. 8 is that his own religious loyalty (*ḥesed*) to Yahweh is ingrained. He can be relied upon to maintain his religion, unlike others who are accustomed to worship "vain idols" and who will therefore readily abandon what should be true loyalty (*ḥesed*), namely, to Yahweh. (Here Jonah sounds much like the psalmists who protest their rectitude over against the failure of others.) Who are these others here? They seem to be the foreign sailors who feared Yahweh and went on to offer sacrifices and make vows (although, strictly speaking, Jonah did not witness the latter). True *ḥesed* (loyalty), Jonah seems to be saying, means the fear of God; true *ḥesed* is a product of established worship; the *ḥesed* produced by short-lived fear will not last — the sailors will never know the presence of Yahweh in the temple.

By the end of his thanksgiving Jonah's story of distress has turned into a protestation of his own religious commitment. Thus, though the psalm ends by affirming that deliverance belongs to Yahweh, ironically its focus has turned to Jonah and the quality of his religious life. From another point of view, however, the final phrase could be translated, "Victory is Yahweh's!" Jonah is acknowledging that his attempted flight has failed. Yahweh has won the first round.

Nineveh and Yahweh Repent (3:1-10)

So Jonah is vomited out onto the dry land (2:10), the world he tried to flee. When the divine word confronts Jonah a second time, he behaves as a prophet should: he arises and goes (3:1-3).

As Jonah nears the city's center he calls out, "Forty days more, and Nineveh shall be overturned" (3:4). Is this the message Yahweh intended ("proclaim to [Nineveh] the proclamation that I tell you"), or is Jonah is getting ahead of himself? (Why does he not say, "Thus says Yahweh . . ."?) Has Jonah assumed that he knows what God intends and that the message is one of judgment? Jonah uses the word "overturned," the very word used in Genesis to describe God's overturning of those other wicked cities, Sodom and Gomorrah (Gen 19:21, 25, 29). Certainly a message of judgment fits a view of God's world as one where evil is punished and good rewarded.

But the plot takes another surprising — or even absurd — turn. Without so much as a whisper of disbelief, "The people of Nineveh believed God" (3:5). All, including the king, proclaim ("called out") a fast and put on sackcloth. The king, moreover, decrees a ritual of penitence which involves even the beasts. All turn from their habitually evil ways, put aside the violence that is in their hands, and cry mightily to God (3:6-9).

God is impressed: "and God repented of the evil which he planned [lit. "said"] to do to them; and he did not do it" (3:10). So God had indeed intended judgment against the city, although it is still unclear whether Jonah was told this explicitly. The expression "said to do" here may mean "promised himself to do" ("said [to himself]"), or "planned."

The narrator is quoting from the story of the golden calf in Exodus: "And God repented of the evil which he planned to do to his people" (Exod 32:14). In that story the unrepentant Israelites are spared when Moses intercedes for them. In this story Jonah proclaims judgment upon the Ninevites, who proceed to repent extravagantly. We may remember that in the Sodom story Abraham, too, played the role of intercessor rather than of judge.

Watching What Happens in Nineveh (4:1-11)

God repents of the evil he was planning to do to Nineveh. But, the narrator continues, "That was evil to Jonah, exceedingly evil!" (4:1). And Jonah is angry! Without hesitation this time, he prays to Yahweh a complaint (vv. 2-

3). Here at last is his stated reason for fleeing in the first place. It was not that he feared the Ninevites' evil (or so he claims) but that he feared that Yahweh would not pay them the evil that was their due: "for I knew that you were a gracious God and compassionate, slow to anger, and abounding in steadfast love [*ḥesed,* loyalty], and you repent of evil." And, sure enough, here is Yahweh taking notice, not of their habitual evil but of some superficial rituals of repentance. It is the situation of the sailors writ large. To Jonah such divine behavior strikes at the basis of right religion and justice. How can God expect the faithful to persevere with religious rectitude and justice when evil escapes punishment merely because of a moment's convenient "repentance"? Given such behavior, he avows, he would rather die than live (contrast Moses in Exod 32:32).

Jonah uses words from Exodus again, words spoken by Yahweh about himself. For Jonah it is a serious problem that Yahweh is "compassionate and gracious, slow to anger, and abounding in *ḥesed,* forgiving iniquity and transgression and sin" (Exod 34:6). Moses, on the other hand, seizes on Yahweh's claim to forgive iniquity to press God to exercise mercy right there and then (34:9).

Commentators are prone to pass judgment on Jonah. For some, he is interested only in preserving his reputation as a prophet — since, if the criterion of true prophecy is fulfillment (Deut 18:21-22), then God's sparing the city marks out Jonah's prophecy of its overturn (understood as "destruction") as false. (Of course, the irony is that "overturn" is precisely what does take place, howbeit in an unexpected sense.) Others claim that Jonah represents an alleged "narrow" postexilic religion which denies that Gentiles (non-Jews) merit God's gracious mercy — he represents "nationalism" as opposed to "universalism." Yet others argue that Jonah fails to respond in love to the repenting foreigners: his passion for a just world will not allow him to see love and mercy as the hallmarks of Yahweh. The present reading suggests that not only justice is at stake for Jonah, but also order and right religion.

Yet is Jonah's frustration at God's change of mind totally unwarranted? Yahweh may be a God of *ḥesed* (steadfast love), but Jonah might well ask, How long will it be before these repenting Ninevites forsake *their* true *ḥesed* (loyalty)? Are we really to believe that the overnight conversion of the whole of evil Nineveh — including the animals — is not a farce? Perhaps Jonah sees only "skin-deep" repentance, produced, like the conversion of the sailors, by the "fear" (terror, not awe) of the moment. He believes it will prove short-lived. Why should Yahweh compromise his role as the just and orderly creator and ruler of the universe in order to offer *ḥesed* (mercy) to those who will profess *ḥesed* (loyalty, worship) today but forsake it tomorrow? Yahweh shifts the issue: "Do you do well to be angry?" (cf. Aaron in Exod 32:22).

Outside the city Jonah encloses himself in a booth, a substitute temple. From its comforting shade and security he can look out on a chaotic world of evil and shallow repentance. The booth cools him and his anger. There is strength as well as weakness in Jonah's religion. He sits in the booth in the shade, "till he should see what would happen in the city" (4:5). The translation "happen in" understands Jonah to be expecting to see a change of mind on Nineveh's part (and no doubt, then, on Yahweh's). Come the forty days and no destruction — maybe much earlier — and all will be back to normal. Nineveh will revert to being evil, and Yahweh will mete out judgment.

But Yahweh surprises him: "And God appointed a plant and made it go up over Jonah, to be a shade over his head, to save [or deliver] him from his discomfort [lit. "evil"]. And Jonah was happy about the plant, exceedingly happy" (4:6). The plant is to the booth as the fish was to the ship. The plant will save Jonah from his "evil." Jonah's conviction has been that "evil" is something he finds elsewhere; "evil" is what others do. We remember the self-righteousness in his psalm: "others will forsake you, but *I* will remain your faithful worshiper." For a brief moment the plant is the tree in the Garden, the desirable tree, the tree of the knowledge of good and evil (Genesis 3).

But this tree, like the one in the Garden, has its worm (4:7). God sends a worm to kill the plant and Jonah, faint, once more exclaims that it is better for him to die than to live (cf. 4:3 and contrast 2:7). Just as the great fish had secured him, been the occasion of thanksgiving, and then put him back on dry land, so the plant has shaded him, been the occasion of his rejoicing, and then left him "high and dry" again. The "enclosures" provided by God (God's response to Jonah's religious needs?) echo those chosen by Jonah himself in their offer of security, but their intention is not security or comfort but to be a gateway back into the world, the dry land, the world where Yahweh makes demands and subverts good order. The reality with which Jonah must live lies beyond the well-ordered, dependable garden. And Jonah is once again angry.

Once again God asks Jonah about his anger (4:9): "Is it good. . . ?" "It is good. . . ," Jonah replies. Does he resent the death of the plant simply because it results in his own personal discomfort (cf. 4:8)? Yahweh's response to him — "you pity the plant . . ." (4:10) — suggests something more. That the plant should grow, serve a high purpose (shading him, Jonah, the prophet of Yahweh) and then be so suddenly and (apparently) pointlessly destroyed is inimical to his sense of good order, elicits his pity for the vulnerable plant, and (as the sun beats down upon him!) provokes his anger.

Of course, his response to the plant's destruction is undercutting him. His newfound pity is misplaced. Yahweh presses the moral (4:10-11): if a single plant — God-given and truly ephemeral — is to be pitied in its withering, how much more a great city of 120,000 people (and their cattle) in its destruction? The addition of cattle underlines the point. If Jonah can pity one plant, can he not do the same for all those cattle, whatever his problem with the people?

The story has reached its end, yet it is a curiously unfinished end. Does Jonah understand and accept Yahweh's disturbing action and unsettling *ḥesed?* Does Yahweh forgive Jonah for his "evil"? Does the city of Nineveh retain its newfound *ḥesed* to God? Reading this story in the light of the great story from creation to the exile (Genesis–Kings) — the story that makes mention of Jonah ben Amittai — we know that within a few decades Nineveh would destroy Jonah's (northern) Israel and within a few generations be destroyed itself. So did Yahweh, the compassionate God, destroy those more than 120,000 persons who did not know their right hand from their left — and also much cattle? And was the ghost of Jonah still sitting there, outside the city, watching with some satisfaction?

Bibliography. Ackerman, J. S. 1987, "Jonah," in R. Alter and F. Kermode, eds., *The Literary Guide to the Bible,* Cambridge, Mass.: Harvard University, 234-43 • Allen, L. C. 1976, *The Books of Joel, Obadiah, Jonah and Micah,* NICOT, Grand Rapids: Eerdmans • Bickerman, E. 1967, *Four Strange Books of the Bible: Jonah, Daniel, Koheleth, Esther,* New York: Schocken • Bolin, T. M. 1997, *Freedom beyond Forgiveness: The Book of Jonah Re-Examined,* Copenhagen International Seminar, Sheffield: Sheffield Academic • Craig, K. M. Jr. 1993, *A Poetics of Jonah: Art in the Service of Ideology,* Columbia: University of South Carolina • Fretheim, T. E. 1977, *The Message of Jonah: A Theological Commentary,* Minneapolis: Augsburg • Gunn, D. M., and D. N. Fewell. 1993, *Narrative in the Hebrew Bible,* Oxford Bible Series, Oxford: Oxford University • Lacocque, A., and P.-E. Lacocque. 1990, *Jonah: A Psycho-Religious Approach to the Prophet,* Studies on Personalities of the Old Testament, Columbia: University of South Carolina • Limburg, J. 1993, *Jonah: A Commentary,* OTL, Louisville: Westminster/John Knox • Magonet, J. D. 1983, *Form and Meaning: Studies in Literary Techniques in the Book of Jonah,* Bible and Literature 8, Sheffield: Almond • Marcus, D. 1995, *From Balaam to Jonah: Anti-Prophetic Satire in the Hebrew Bible,* BJS 301, Atlanta: Scholars • Person, R. F. Jr. 1996, *In Conversation with Jonah: Conversation Analysis, Literary Criticism, and the Book of Jonah,* JSOTSup 220, Sheffield: Sheffield Academic • Sasson, J. M. 1990, *Jonah,* AB, New York: Doubleday • Trible, P. 1994, *Rhetorical Criticism: Context, Method, and the Book of Jonah,* Guides to Biblical Scholarship, Minneapolis: Fortress • Sherwood, Y. 2000, *A Biblical Text and Its Afterlives: The Survival of Jonah in Western Culture,* Cambridge: Cambridge University.

Micah

John W. Rogerson

INTRODUCTION

It is rare for a prophet to be mentioned in the OT outside the book attributed to him. There is no mention, outside of their books, of Hosea, Amos, Jeremiah, or Ezekiel, for example. Micah is an exception. In Jer 26:1-19, some unnamed "elders of the land" defend Jeremiah against those who are demanding his death because he has prophesied that God will destroy the Jerusalem temple. They cite the example of Micah. They point out (Jer 26:17-19) that Micah prophesied the destruction of the temple during the reign of Hezekiah, and that the latter, far from seeking the prophet's death, took his words seriously and turned to God in penitence. This otherwise unrecorded incident sheds a little light on Micah and his times, and shows that, over a hundred years after his death, he was remembered and appealed to, probably by elders from the provincial south of Judah, Micah's home area.

Micah's town of Moresheth (1:1) has been identified with Tell el-Judeideh, a large site a little north of Beit Jibrin, on the ancient main route from Bet Shemesh to Lachish. Although this identification is not without problems, the poem in 1:10-16 mentions Gath, Adullam, and Lachish, indicating that Micah came from this general area. His ministry is dated in 1:1 to the reigns of Jotham, Ahaz, and Hezekiah, that is, the period roughly 750 to 700 BC, although a more realistic view would place it in the period 725 to 700.

It is widely accepted by scholars that only chs. 1–3 contain material deriving from Micah, a view not followed here. Although it is obvious that the text as it has come down to us has been subjected to editorial expansion and interpolation, I will argue that genuine Micah material can also be found in chs. 5–7. One of the criteria that has been used in this debate is the view that Micah spoke only words of judgment, and that all the passages promising salvation are thus later additions. While generalizations of this kind must always be treated with caution, it is a fact that, in its final form, the book of Micah is structured in terms of alternating passages of judgment and salvation, according to the following scheme:

Judgment	*Promise of Salvation*
1:1–2:11	2:12-13
3:1-12	4:1-8
4:9–5:1 (Heb. 4:9-14)	5:2-9 (Heb. 5:1-8)
5:10–6:16 (Heb. 5:9–6:16)	7:1-20

Among what is disputed, one thing is crystal clear. Micah was an implacable opponent of what he regarded as the inhumane policies of the rulers of the Jerusalem of his day. He believed that they put the maintenance of their own interests above the needs of the people whom they governed, especially those in the provinces of Judah. He proclaimed that because of this, God would judge Jerusalem and cause its temple to be destroyed. This was a deeply unpopular message; but according to Jer 26:1-19 it produced results and was still remembered a century later.

COMMENTARY

The Introduction (1:1)

The location of Moresheth and the dates of Micah's ministry have already been discussed. Most of his words were directed against Jerusalem.

Judgment against Samaria (1:2-7)

The passage begins with God summoning the peoples and the earth as witnesses to the judgment that he is about to execute on Samaria. This disputation pattern is common in the prophets (cf. Isa 1:1; Jer 6:18-19; Joel 1:2). God will come from his true temple, the one in heaven (1:2-3), and his coming will bring turmoil to the mountains and valleys. The principal target is Samaria, the magnificent capital of the Northern Kingdom, Israel, established around 870 BC by Omri, and which finally fell to the Assyrians only after a three-year siege in 722/721. This fact provides a date for the prophecy against Samaria, probably around 725. The language of v. 6 is vivid, envisaging the total clearance of the site of its monumental buildings, so that it can be devoted wholly to viticulture. The city's crime is not only that of idolatry (v. 7a) but the misuse of power and the abuse of the poor that was bound up with fertility religion and sacred prostitution (v. 7b). In v. 5 a later editor has added a remarkable gloss, in which Jerusalem is called a high place. High places, in the official theology of Jerusalem (cf. Deut 12:2-7), were illegal sites of which God strongly disapproved. Jerusalem is called one of these!

Warnings to the Cities of Judah (1:8-16)

Samaria was not only well fortified, but it was situated in the heart of the northern hill country and served by routes that could easily be defended. This was not true of Judah. The Shephelah, or lowlands, was a transitional area between the coastal plain and the Judean hill country and a soft underbelly for any potential invader. It was here that Micah lived, and it was this area that the Assyrians overran when they attacked Judah in 701 BC. They recorded their capture of Lachish on that occasion on the memorable reliefs now in the British Museum in London. The present passage probably predates these events. We can presume that Samaria had now fallen and that Micah expected the next blow to fall on Jerusalem. He knew what this would mean for his own area of southern Judah, and he warned of the coming catastrophe in a stunning poem full of puns on place names in the region. In order to bring out the force of this a translation such as the following would be necessary:

> In Dustville, roll yourselves in the dust (1:10b).
> Do not go out, citizens of Out-town (1:11b).
> Harness the chariot to the horse, citizen of Horseville (1:13a).
> The homes of Deceitville are deceitful (1:14c).

Lachish, Judah's second city, receives special treatment (v. 13) and is accused of harboring the corrupt practices of both Jerusalem and Samaria.

Misuse of Power Denounced (2:1-5)

2:2 denounces people who appropriate the lands and houses of others. There could be two reasons why this was done. It could be simply the amassing of wealth for its own sake (cf. Isa 5:8), or it could be part of the militarization of the area in preparation for an Assyrian attack. With the word "therefore" in 2:3 the pronouncement of judgment is introduced. The precise form of the judgment is described in the song of lamentation introduced in v. 4. Unfortunately, the Hebrew of this verse, as the NRSV footnotes indicate, is very obscure. Against the NRSV, a possible rendering is "We are utterly ruined. The portion (or field) of my people is measured out (for distribution) and there is no one to restore it. Our fields are parcelled out." The sense may be that as citizens of Judah have taken land from their fellows, so an enemy will take their land in turn.

Threats against the Prophet (2:6-11)

Even if the prophet's stand was honorably remembered a century later, it did not escape hostility during his lifetime. 2:6-11 is a carefully crafted passage that begins with a threefold repetition of the Hebrew verb *nṭp,* rendered as preach by the NRSV but "rant" by the NEB. The verb normally means "to drip," and perhaps "spout" would be close in English. The same verb, rendered by the NRSV as "I will preach" and "the preacher" in v. 11, concludes the poem. While it is clear from v. 6 that Micah is being told not to prophesy, there are some obscure verses, which have been considerably emended by editors. V. 7 may be a continuation of the opponents' speech: "Is the house of Jacob cursed? Is the LORD's patience exhausted? Are these his doings? Are not his words good to those who walk uprightly?" In v. 8 this protestation of innocence is answered: "You rise up against my people as an enemy." The phrase "my people" in vv. 8 and 9 is important. The oppressive rulers are not only abusing their own people; they are harming God's people, which is why the oppressors are condemned by the prophet; they are warned to flee, but not before the prophet has bitterly accused them of wanting to hear only people who preach the virtues of wine and strong drink.

A Later Promise (2:12-13)

These verses assume that the judgment has already fallen and that Israel is now scattered abroad. It promises that God will lead the people out of captivity through the broken walls of where they were once confined (2:13). This later addition is an appropriate conclusion to the language about "my people" in vv. 8 and 9. Even if the coming judgment affects the innocent as well as the guilty, God will never give up on "his people."

Judgment upon Wicked Zion (3:1-12)

Micah 3 falls into three stanzas of roughly equal length, with the first and third being introduced by the command "Listen" (v. 1) and "Hear this" (v. 9) — in fact, the same Hebrew phrase on both occasions. In v. 1 the "heads of Jacob" and "rulers of the house of Israel" are addressed. Strictly speaking, these were the rulers of the Northern Kingdom, Israel, and it may be that the passage predates Samaria's fall in 722/721. But the language may also be ironic. If the passage is later than 722/721, Micah may be insulting Judah's rulers by calling them Israel's rulers, implying either their wickedness or the certainty that they will share the fate of Israel's rulers. The description of how the rulers treat "my people" (note this phrase again in vv. 3 and 4) employs some of the most violent imagery in the prophetic literature, as the rulers are accused, in effect, of cannibalism.

3:5-8 address the prophets whose activities are determined solely by personal financial gain (v. 5). Because theirs is an entirely human activity, they will have nothing to contribute when an answer is sought from the living God. Micah himself claims to be filled with power that comes from God in his denunciation of the sins of Jacob and Israel (v. 8). As with v. 1, this reference to the rulers of the Northern Kingdom can be taken in more than one way (see on 3:1).

3:9-12 begin by referring to the rulers of the house of Jacob and the chiefs of the house of Israel as those who build Zion with blood and Jerusalem with wrong. Here, at least, the reference to Israel's leaders must be an ironic way of describing the rulers of Judah. Their chief offense is their belief that, whatever they do, God will defend Jerusalem at all costs. The phrase "the LORD is with us" (v. 11) is probably an allusion to "Zion theology" as found, for example, in Ps 46:7. Micah turns this theology on its head. If God is with anyone, it is with those he calls "my people" — those who are mistreated by Zion's rulers.

Consequently, Jerusalem will be destroyed and will remain uninhabited for so long that a forest will establish itself where the temple ("the mountain of the house" of v. 12) once stood. A more final word of judgment could not be envisaged.

Zion's Future Hope (4:1-5)

Did Micah say nothing more? Many interpreters believe that his words end at 3:12, whereas I will argue later that they resume at 5:2 (Heb. 5:1). What intervenes is undoubtedly the work of later editors, and 4:1-3 is, in any case, almost identical with Isa 2:2-4. While it has been argued that the Isaiah passage is dependent on that in Micah, and vice versa, and Mic 4:4 certainly seems to provide a better conclusion to the whole passage, the likelihood is that editors have added the passage in both Micah and Isaiah. At first sight the passage seems to contradict what precedes it. Micah envisages a destroyed temple that is never rebuilt; 4:1 mentions the "mountain of the . . . house" (cf. 3:12) as though rebuilt. This can be explained in two ways. First, the temple *was* destroyed (in 587 BC) but later rebuilt (in 515). Perhaps the editors are saying that Micah was right about the temple being destroyed but wrong about it not being rebuilt. The second explanation takes us deeper. The temple described in 4:1-4 is not a Zion rebuilt by humans, but a Zion created by God. It is built not on violence and corruption, but on the desire of the nations to learn God's laws and to replace the weapons of war with agricultural tools symbolizing peace. There is thus a profound contrast between the human Zion of ch. 3 and the divine Zion of 4:1-4. This latter Zion is one of which it can be truly said that God is with it, and it is for this reason that nations will want to make pilgrimage there, and long for its God to arbitrate their disputes (v. 3). It is a noble passage in its own right, but one whose sublimity is enhanced when placed next to the harsh and violent language used by Micah in ch. 3. The editors have thus created a way of enabling both passages to be appreciated in a new way.

Further Promises to Zion (4:6-8)

This is another later passage, and it is similar in thought and language to 2:12-13. Pastoral imagery, that of lame and rejected sheep, abounds, but God promises to gather these outcasts together and to make of them a mighty nation. In 4:7, editors alter "the LORD will reign" to "I will reign" in accordance with the general sense of the verse. The situation in v. 8 is one of disadvantage to Zion (is the city destroyed?), but she is promised that she will enjoy her former power and independence.

Jerusalem Besieged? (4:9–5:1; Heb. 4:9-14)

This passage is divided into three stanzas of unequal length, each introduced by the word "now" (at 4:9, 11 and 5:1). Some of the language of 4:13 is very similar to that in Isa 41:15-16, and the mention of Babylon in 4:10 suggests that the material comes from the century after Micah. The precise situation cannot be determined. Does the phrase "Is there no king in you?" mean that there is still a king, or is the sense "Is it because there is no king in you?" In the first instance Jerusalem may be surrounded by the Babylonian armies (cf. v. 11); in the second case the city's capture lies in the past. If 5:1 is an integral part of the passage, then an actual siege seems to be in progress. However, 5:1 contains wordplays, for example, "with a rod (*shebeṭ*) they strike the ruler (*shopeṭ*)," that are reminiscent of 1:10-16, and there is a strong possibility that material deriving from Micah which foresaw Jerusalem's siege has been worked over and adapted to the later times of the actual siege. 4:11-12 are similar to Psalm 2, where nations gather against Zion but do so in vain because ultimately they cannot frustrate God's plans. This whole passage, then, is not easy to interpret, except to say that it continues and confirms the thought of vv. 6-8 and reassures Zion that God will ultimately not abandon "his people."

The Promised Ruler from Bethlehem (5:2-6; Heb. 5:1-5)

This passage is probably one of the two best-known parts of Micah (the other being 6:6-8) because it is quoted in Matt 2:6 and read regularly at Christmas in connection with the visit of the Magi to Bethlehem. It is usually dated to the exile or later, and it cannot be denied that 5:4 is similar to Isa 40:11 and that an exilic setting would be appropriate. It is arguable, however, that 5:2 derives from Micah and that it originally followed 3:12 (or even 5:1), for it has to be asked how the prophet conceived the existence of God's people ("my people") following his vision of Jerusalem's destruction. A plausible answer would be that he foresaw a new beginning based on Bethlehem, the true city of David. This would certainly be consistent with Micah's situation as an inhabitant of provincial southern Judah. Ephrathah in this verse refers to a "clan" that lived in Bethlehem of Judah (cf. Ruth 1:2) to distinguish the town from another Bethlehem (Josh 19:15) some seven miles northwest of Nazareth. This detail, which presumably would make sense only if the Northern Kingdom still existed or had only recently been overrun, may be a further reason for connecting the verse with Micah himself. It may also be the case that Micah expected the unnamed ruler from Bethlehem to defeat the Assyrians, if his words can be recovered from 5:5-6 as follows:

> When the Assyrian comes into our land
>   and treads upon our soil,
> he shall deliver us from the Assyrian
>   when he comes into our land
>   and treads within our border.

In its present form, the whole passage has been reworked by later editors even to the point of suggesting that Israel will produce rulers over Assyria (vv. 5-6). In what may be conjectured as Micah's original words, he foresaw a radical rejection of Jerusalem and the existing Davidic dynasty (represented by the apparently exemplary Hezekiah — see 2 Kgs 18:3!) and a completely new start beginning from Bethlehem.

Promises to the Remnant of Jacob (5:7-9; Heb. 5:6-8)

A future promise to *Jacob* has already occurred at 2:12, while the meaning of the references to the heads of Jacob in 3:1, 9 has already been discussed. Presumably, in the present passage "Jacob" is a way of referring to the whole people as descended from Jacob, that is both the Northern Kingdom, Israel, and the Southern Kingdom, Judah. Similarities between this passage and Isaac's blessing of Jacob in Gen 27:27-8 have been pointed out. Both refer to dew (Mic 5:7; Gen 27:8), and both envisage that Jacob (or his remnant/offspring) will rule over nations (Mic 5:8-9; Gen 27:29). The passage can therefore be taken as an allusion to, or a version of, the tradition about a blessing to Jacob, which functions here to reassure the people that it has a future in spite of being in exile. Whether or not it was originally connected with 5:10-15 cannot be said; but the context provided by these verses is important. Taken alone, vv. 7-9 could be read as a divine resolve to resume and ennoble Jacob come what may. Vv. 10-15 indicate that there is a moral dimension to this hopeful future.

A Purified Nation (5:10-15; Heb. 5:9-15)

As pointed out immediately above, this passage adds a moral dimension to 5:7-9. If God rescues his people from exile, it will not be so that they can resume their former ways. God will have removed everything that symbolized trust in human resources and that detracts from reliance on God alone: military hardware (horses and chariots), fortified cities, practitioners of occult arts, images that represent false gods. In vv. 14 and 15 slight emendations produce a more consistent text:

> I will uproot your sacred poles
> from among you
> and destroy your idols,
> In anger and wrath I will
> execute vengeance on the
> pride that does not obey.

God's Dispute with His People (6:1-8)

This passage falls into three sections. In the first, 6:1-2, God summons the mountains and hills as well as earth's foundations to hear the case that he wishes to bring against his people (cf. 1:2). 6:3-5 contain the accusation: that Israel's response to all God's gracious actions has been one of ingratitude and rebellion. In vv. 6-8 a first person speaker replies on behalf of the people. Without answering the charges directly, he expresses profound regret by saying, in effect, that no offering, however great, would be an appropriate way of coming before God. The prophet replies in v. 8 by specifying precisely what God requires.

The question of the passage's date turns on theories about the growth of the Pentateuch into its present form. 6:4-5 contain one of the few references to figures such as Moses and Aaron outside the Pentateuch, and v. 5 in particular assumes knowledge of the story of Balaam and Balak in Numbers 22–24, as well as of the grievous sins committed by the Israelite at Baal-peor and recorded in Numbers 22–25. If 6:4-5 were an integral part of the composition from the outset, and if the view is correct that Numbers 22–25 reached its present form in the postexilic period, then the whole passage must date from then. Such a date would suit 6:6-7. It is often said that, following the catastrophe of the destruction of Jerusalem in 587, the postexilic community had a deep sense of sin and guilt, and this certainly seems to be the case here also. The first person reply uses highly exaggerated language — "thousands of rams," "ten thousands of rivers of oil," the sacrifice of the firstborn son — although this may be a way of saying that God does not require such things (cf. Ps 50:7-15). If the passage reflects a true encounter with God and a resultant feeling of utter unworthiness on the part of the person or persons involved, the verses will be saying that no way of approaching God can ever be appropriate to the unbridgeable gulf between the compassion of God and the waywardness of humanity.

The famous reply in 6:8 states that the gulf can be bridged. Justice to others, the cultivation of loyal and unfailing live to God and to others, and a life lived in humble but informed dependence on God (walking with him) are appropriate and acceptable responses to his mercy. There is no mention of sacrifice, but the answer does not rule it out. It sets forth a particular way of life (the idea of walking with God expresses this concretely) that has to be realized in the details of daily living, and for a member of the Jerusalem community of the postexilic period, this would involve the celebration of fasts and festivals and the communal rituals associated with birth and mourning. In the world of the Bible, as opposed to today's Western world, religion was not merely a matter of intellectual opinions; it was a distinctive way of life, and that fact must be borne in mind when reading v. 8.

The Outcome of Wickedness (6:9-16)

This is a difficult passage to translate, as the NRSV footnotes indicate, yet its message is clear. Wickedness will not go unpunished. It will be counterproductive, and immoral actions devoted to the accumulation of wealth will produce exactly the opposite: poverty and hunger. As such, the passage is similar to treatments of this problem in the book of Proverbs and in psalms such as 37 and 73. In actual life, as the OT fully recognizes (cf. Ecclesiastes!), things are not so clear-cut. We can see how, in today's world, the mindless exploitation of natural resources can have catastrophic results; but it is not often that those directly responsible have to bear the resultant burdens. These fall on the poorest and weakest members of society. It was probably no different in ancient Israel. Sentiments such as those expressed here thus take on an eschatological dimension. They express a hope for a better world, one that ultimately only God can bring about.

The references to the statutes of Omri and the works of Ahab (6:16) are the only mention of these kings of Israel in the OT outside the books of Kings and Chronicles. These kings, who reigned from roughly 880 to 853 BC over the Northern Kingdom (see 1 Kgs 16:15–22:40) are regarded as two of the most evil kings in OT tradition. It is on this tradition that 6:16 draws in denouncing the people. In modern terms, it is like accusing people of the worst abuses of fascism or Stalinism. The whole passage probably dates from the postexilic period, and to a time, perhaps in the late sixth or early fifth centuries, when dishonesty was rife.

A Lament over the State of Things (7:1-7)

For the first time in Micah we have an extended passage in the first person. Whether it comes from Micah himself or a later prophet is disputed. Whatever its date, it is a dire description of a state of affairs in which all honesty and decency have vanished, no one can be trusted, and even families are an arena for strife. The poetry is powerful, from the opening description of the prophet looking in vain for justice as a hungry man might look for food after all the fruit trees had been harvested, to the likening in 7:4 of the most upright of the people (the Hebrew has the sense of being straight) to a thorn hedge (the Hebrew has the sense of being twisted and intertwined). The prophet may, of course, be exaggerating. Can *no one* be trusted? Are *all* families in a state of perpetual feud? Yet it is sometimes necessary to portray things in terms of absolute black and white. Reality is mostly grey, a color which enables evil to merge with the background.

A Song of Fallen Jerusalem (7:8-10)

The first person address is no longer that of the prophet but of a city, most likely Jerusalem. The city recognizes that its present plight, that of destruction, is deserved punishment from God. The recognition and acceptance of this is the ground of hope for restoration; for the city's plight is an indication not of the absence of God but of his presence, and of his continuing relationship with her. The opening words, 7:8, are used by Christian in Bunyan's *Pilgrim's Progress* after he has been felled by Apollyon.

A Prophecy of Restoration (7:11-13)

Fallen Jerusalem is promised that it will be rebuilt and that its power will be vastly extended. This is a far cry from the noble vision of 4:1-5, where power is seen in terms of a universal search for peace and justice!

A Prayer for Future Prosperity (7:14-17)

The mood changes from that of a request for power to one of grateful astonishment at God's limitless mercy. The beautiful images used to describe God's forgiveness are a worthy response to 6:6-8. That the gulf between God and humanity can be bridged is an occasion for awe, wonder, and gratitude.

Bibliography. Mason, R. 1991, *Micah, Nahum, Obadiah,* Old Testament Guides, Sheffield: Sheffield Academic • Smith, R. L. 1984, *Micah-Malachi,* WBC, Waco: Word • Weiser, A. 1959, *Die Propheten: Hosea, Joel, Amos, Obadja, Jona, Micha,* ATD 24, Göttingen: Vandenhoeck & Ruprecht • Wolff, H. W. 1980-82, *Dodekapropheten: Micha,* BKAT 14.12-14, Neukirchen: Neukirchener.

Nahum

John W. Rogerson

INTRODUCTION

There are at least two ways of reading Nahum. The first is to follow the lead given by the two opening Hebrew words in 1:1, "An oracle concerning Nineveh," and to see the whole book in this light. It then falls into three main parts: 1:2-15 portray God coming in awesome majesty to judge Nineveh, the capital of Assyria, the poem being interspersed with words of comfort for Judah at 1:12-13 and 1:15. Ch. 2 describes Nineveh's panic as an unnamed destroyer (NRSV, "shatterer") comes up against the city, while ch. 3 is a divine denunciation of the wickedness perpetrated in her, followed by a declaration of the futile nature of any attempt to avoid Nineveh's downfall.

The second approach takes seriously the fact that, in the Hebrew numbering of the book, ch. 2 begins at 1:15 in the English, that is, with the address to Judah. This, then, implies that the shatterer has come up against Judah, not Nineveh, although it has to be allowed that the references to "squares" and "river gates" in 2:4 and 6 make good sense when applied to Nineveh and little sense when applied to Jerusalem. However, the references to Judah at 1:12-13 and 1:15, if they are not simply later additions, suggest that complex literary processes underlie the book's production, and it has been plausibly argued that material that originally concerned Jerusalem has been reused and applied to Nineveh, especially in parts of chs. 1 and 2.

This matter affects estimates of the date of Nahum. If the entire book (apart from what must be regarded as later additions referring to Judah) originally concerned Nineveh, then there are two main possibilities. Either the composition is a prophecy of Nineveh's downfall made by an otherwise unknown prophet sometime between the destruction of Thebes (3:8) by the Assyrians in 663 and the fall of Nineveh in 612, or it is a celebration of the city's destruction after 612. The latter view could also allow that some parts were genuine prophecies before the event. If the more complicated literary approach is taken, the poem of 1:2-15 may originally have been one of encouragement to Judah to expect deliverance from its Babylonian oppressor in the century after Nineveh's destruction (cf. 1:15 with Isa 40:9 and 52:7), while chs. 2–3 either predated or postdated Nineveh's fall to the Babylonians in 612. Whatever line is followed, the book contains magnificent imagery as it contrasts the awesome majesty of God with the ultimate nothingness of some of the highest achievements of human civilization up to that point in human history. As in today's world, those achievements had their destructive side, as technology was applied to the tasks of war (2:3-5) and human life was cheaply valued, not only in wartime (3:3) but in peacetime also (3:4). In the LXX Nahum follows the book of Jonah, where a very different Nineveh is portrayed, one which repents in the face of Jonah's preaching. That Hebrew tradition could accommodate two such radically different views of the same city is a reminder both of the tradition's enormous creativity and of the need for interpretation to try to be adequate to that creativity.

COMMENTARY

The Superscription (1:1)

Depending on whether the straightforward or the complex view of the book's composition is taken, we either have one introduction (the text as we have it) or the verse originally read, "The book of the vision of Nahum . . . ." The second possibility does not rule out the likelihood that Nahum's vision was concerned with the forthcoming destruction of Nineveh. Of the prophet himself we know nothing, nor has Elkosh been identified. If Nahum indeed foresaw Nineveh's downfall between 663 and 612, there are two reigns of kings of Judah during which he could have spoken out, that of the pro-Assyrian Manasseh (699-643 BC) and that of the anti-Assyrian Josiah (640-609 BC). If the argument is cogent that the reference to the destruction of Thebes (in 663) would be meaningful only if it was of recent occurrence, this suggests Manasseh's reign as the more likely setting; in that case Nahum was a prophet who must have put himself in considerable danger by denouncing Assyria at a time when it was still very powerful, and when Judah was a vassal state pledged to allegiance to Assyria.

The Divine Coming in Judgment (1:2-15)

That this passage may fall into two parts, 1:2-9 and 1:10-15, is indicated by two considerations. Vv. 2-9 contain an incomplete acrostic in the Hebrew, with vv. 2a, 3b, 4a, 5a, 5b, 6a (second word), 6b, and 7a beginning with successive letters of the first half of the Hebrew alphabet, continuing possibly, but less obviously, into vv. 8 and 9. It is also noticeable that until at least v. 8 the sentiments are expressed in general terms. God's coming in judgment on the clouds of the storm brings terror to seas and rivers, and to forests and mountains. Because v. 3 falls outside the acrostic scheme and is either a quotation from, or a reference to, a tradition found also at Exod 34:6-7 and Ps 103:8, it is probably a later addition. 1:2-8 (9) may thus be part of a longer, complete, acrostic poem which continued the sentiments of the extant verses. In v. 9 a question is addressed to unspecified persons in the second person plural in Hebrew, followed by a statement in v. 10 in the third person plural. From here on the text becomes disjointed. In vv. 11 and 12-13 God addresses someone, most naturally a town or country (presumably a different one in v. 11 from that in vv. 12-13), in the second person feminine singular, whereas the "you" addressed in v. 14 is a masculine second person singular. When we add to these observations the addresses to Judah in vv. 12-13 and 15, vv. 10-15 constitute a heavily edited or interpolated passage. In its present, canonical, form the whole section (vv. 2-15) emphasizes the compassion of the otherwise awesome and terrifying God for his own people, Judah.

The Destruction of Nineveh (2:1-13; Heb. 2:2-14)

Although there is no allusion to Nineveh until 2:8 and, in the Hebrew, the whole passage begins with the reference to Judah at 1:15, it is best to take the whole chapter as a description, before or after the event, of Nineveh's destruction in 612. V. 3, which is placed in brackets in the NRSV, is clearly a later addition which disturbs the flow of the poem. The description of the battle is best taken as kaleidoscopic rather than as an ordered description of the actual course of events. Thus, in v. 4 the chariots of the enemy are already in the city (not the suburbs outside the walls), whereas v. 5 described preparations for the assault upon the walls. In v. 5 "stumble" is hardly appropriate for an attacking force, and editors either add a negative, "they do not stumble," or emend to a verb meaning "rushing" (so NEB). The "mantelet" is a portable wooden structure designed to protect siege engineers who are undermining the wall from missiles thrown down upon them by the defenders. It is not clear whether the opening of the river gates (Nineveh had considerable protection from canals and moats) is the result of a successful assault, an act of treachery from within the city, or a sign of the city's capitulation. However, from v. 7 the results of defeat are described. The comparison of defeated Nineveh with waters running away in v. 8 may be an allusion to her citizens fleeing. The first line of v. 10 is an excellent attempt to echo the wordplay in Hebrew: *buqah, umebuqah umebullaqah.* In vv. 11-12 the references to lions may be symbolic, with the Assyrian kings being likened to lions whose destructive days are over. But we know that lions were hunted and kept in Nineveh in the seventh century (cf. also the lions' den in Daniel 6), and there could possibly be an allusion to the fear that the Ninevites would have if the lions were let loose.

The Impossibility of Avoiding Defeat (3:1-19)

3:1-3 are especially vivid in the Hebrew, with a succession of two-word phrases conveying a breathless scene of the noise and confusion of battle. Recent excavations at the Halzi Gate in Nineveh have discovered a number of tangled skeletons on the partly cobbled roadway (Stronach and Codella 1997), although this does not necessarily mean that the prophet was an eyewitness. Wars, unfortunately, have many common features, including piles of corpses. In vv. 4-7 the mood passes to a future prediction of the city's end, on account of its wickedness, and there then follows a series of oracles that emphasizes that there can be no escape from the coming judgment. Thebes (Heb. No-Amon, from Egypt. *niw(t),* city of [the god] Amun), was a very large site some 340 miles upstream from Cairo on both sides of the Nile, including the temples on the eastern bank known today as Karnak and Luxor. Although the city itself was not protected by water (cf. v. 9, which conveys the opposite impression), the Nile was well defended against passage along it by invaders. The point is thus well made in vv. 8-10 that, in spite of her relative inaccessibility for an invader, the city was destroyed (by the Assyrians under Ashurbanipal in 663). Nineveh cannot expect to be more fortunate. The concluding verses proclaim vividly that however numerous its defenders may become (vv. 15b-16) and however thoroughly preparations may be made for a siege (v. 14), all will be in vain. Ultimately, excessive cruelty produces, at the human level, corresponding cruelty, with no room for pity or sympathy (v. 19).

Bibliography. Coggins, R. J. 1985, *Israel among the Nations: A Commentary on the Books of Nahum and Obadiah,* ITC, Grand Rapids: Eerdmans and Edinburgh: T&T Clark • Driver, S. R. 1906, *The Minor Prophets, Nahum, Habbakuk, Zephaniah, Haggai, Zechariah, Malachi,* Century Bible, Edinburgh: T. C. & E. C. Jack • Elliger, K. 1959, *Die Propheten: Nahum, Habakuk, Zephanja, Haggai, Sacharja, Maleachi,* ATD 25, Göttingen: Vandenhoeck & Ruprecht • Mason, R. 1991, *Micah, Nahum, Obadiah,* Old Testament Guides, Sheffield: Sheffield Academic • Smith, R. L. 1984, *Micah-Malachi,* WBC, Waco: Word • Stronach, D., and K. Codella. 1997, "Nineveh," in E. M. Meyers, ed., *The Oxford Encyclopedia of Archaeology in the Near East,* New York: Oxford University, 4:144-48.

Habakkuk

Anthony Gelston

INTRODUCTION

Nothing is known of the person or life of the prophet beyond his name. Many exegetes, however, have dated at least the first part of the prophecy with some confidence to the period shortly before the battle of Carchemish in 605 BC since this fits the announcement in 1:6 that God is about to raise up the Chaldeans, or neo-Babylonians, as his agent of judgment. There may also be an allusion in 2:17 to Nebuchadrezzar's exploitation of the forests of the Lebanon. This period in the reign of Jehoiakim also fits the picture of social injustice reflected in the prophet's initial complaint.

The prophecy reflects a much greater degree of coherent order and arrangement than most of the prophetic literature. This may, of course, be due to the work of a later editor, but since it permits the exegesis of the text as a logical development of themes, there is much to be said for the working hypothesis that the book does reflect the message of the individual prophet as a whole, and that it is therefore to be set against the background of the closing decades of the kingdom of Judah.

The paucity of specific allusions to datable contemporary events inevitably leaves the book open to a wide area of speculation about both its date and its unity. Mason 1994 gives a clear overview of the main positions that have been held.

One important element in the history of interpretation arises from the *Pesher on Habakkuk* discovered at Qumran (1QpHab). See Vermes 1997: 478-85. Although it covers only the first two chapters of the text, this is one of the earliest examples of a phrase-by-phrase commentary on an OT book, and it is interesting that the exegesis is in terms of the events of the Qumran sectaries' own time, which they believed to have been predicted in the biblical text, and whose fulfillment they traced in the experience of their own community. This provides an interesting background to some of the comments on OT passages found in the NT.

COMMENTARY

Habakkuk 1:2–2:5

The first main section of the book consists of a dialogue between the prophet and God. The prophet speaks to God in 1:2-4, and God replies in vv. 5-11. The prophet speaks again in vv. 12-17, while the dialogue closes with God's further reply in 2:1-5. In 1:2-4 the prophet complains to God about the rampant injustice in Judean society in his time. The form of the complaint is that of the "individual lament," familiar from the Psalms, but the prophet may well be speaking less as an individual than in an intercessory role on behalf of the society to which he belongs. There are obvious parallels to some of the "confessions" of Jeremiah (e.g., Jer 12:1-4; 18:20), but with the difference that there is no direct suggestion that Habakkuk, like Jeremiah, is himself the victim of oppressors. One may also compare the kind of prayer envisaged in 1 Kgs 8:28-32.

The prophet's protest voices the theological problem that has vexed the ages: Why does God allow evil and not intervene to rescue the victim from the oppressor? "Violence" in 1:2 seems to be a traditional cry for help (like "Thief!" or "Fire!") and is found again in Jer 20:8 and Job 19:7. The language of 1:2 and 3 suggests both actual litigation and the conflicts that lead up to it. Part of the trouble is that the judicial system is perverted by the powerful influence of wrongdoers. It is tempting to see in "the law becomes slack" (v. 4) an allusion to the ineffectiveness of the Deuteronomic law after the death of Josiah and a reflection of the disappointed hopes of the reform party during the reign of Jehoiakim, whose injustices are attested in Jer 22:13-17. The prophet's questions "How long?" (v. 2) and "Why?" (v. 3) express the anguish of those whose prayers appear to have remained long unanswered, while violence and wrong appear to go scot-free.

The passage which follows as a divine response to the prophet's plea in the present structure of the dialogue was probably originally an independent saying, since the imperatives in 1:5: "Look . . . see! Be astonished! Be astounded!" are plural in the Hebrew and were thus presumably addressed to a wider audience than the prophet himself. They introduce the announcement of a strange, almost incredible divine intervention in international affairs. In the present context this divine intervention constitutes God's response to the prophet's plea in 1:2-4. Drawing on the theme so clearly set forth in Isa 10:5-15, the prophetic message identifies the rising Chaldean or neo-Babylonian power as the divine instrument for executing judgment on the wrongdoers within Judah. The description of the advancing power in vv. 6-10 follows traditional lines, but stresses the selfish aggrandizement of the new conquerors and draws out the irony of the fact that those whom God proposes to use to judge those who practice violence within Judah are themselves bent on the pursuit of violence (v. 9).

The word translated "impetuous" in 1:6 may refer to Nebuchadrezzar's pursuit of the Egyptians to Hamath after the battle of Carchemish in 605 BC and his subsequent speedy return to Babylon to secure his own succession as king. In v. 8 "wolves at dusk" is a less likely interpretation than "wolves of the steppe" (the same applies at Zeph 3:3, where the apparent contrast with morning may have influenced the interpretation). The overriding impression of the description of the Chaldeans is that of a ruthless pursuit of their own aims without regard to the rights or authority of anyone else. They themselves epitomize the violence that they are supposed to be punishing as God's agents of judgment.

1:11 is obscure: the verbs in the Hebrew are singular, and it is possible that this verse is not part of the description of the Chaldeans. Roberts 1991: 91-100, for instance, revocalizing the consonantal text of only one word, obtains the translation: "The spirit passed on. It departed, and I was astonished: 'This one (takes) his might as his god!'" If this interpretation is correct, v. 11 reflects the prophet's own amazement at the divine message he has received and stresses particularly the fact that the Chaldeans own no god other than their own military might.

At 1:12 the prophet himself turns again to God in prayer, and his response continues until the end of the chapter. Vv. 12 and 13 are crucial, but their interpretation is by no means certain. It is clear that the first part of v. 12 and the last part of v. 13 are questions, and it is probable that the second part of v. 12 should also be interpreted as a question. The prophet is asking God if he is really intending to use as his instrument of judgment the Chaldeans, who are even worse practitioners of violence than those they are appointed to punish! Would not the cure be worse than the illness itself? V. 13 in particular affirms the moral integrity of God and asks how God can overlook the crimes of the executioners, which are even more serious than those they are appointed to punish. The persons described as "more righteous than they" (v. 13) are thus most probably the "wicked" within Judah mentioned in v. 4, who are nevertheless less guilty than the Chaldeans appointed to punish them. The "silence" of God (v. 13) in the face of such a triumph of injustice is an even graver problem now than it was in v. 2.

The statement "You shall not die" in 1:12 is one of a small number of passages where, according to Hebrew tradition, the original text had been modified out of reverence. The Hebrew text now reads "We shall not die." It was thought that the very suggestion that God might die, even though it was immediately denied, was verging on the blasphemous. Thus the text was modified to an affirmation that the people of God, the eternal one, would not die.

1:14-17 revert to further description of the aggrandizement practiced by the Chaldeans, ending in v. 17 with the question whether they are to be allowed to go on indefinitely victimizing others. Human beings are being reduced to the level of fish, caught in a net with no opportunity to escape. The Chaldeans are interested only in their own advantage and prosperity. There is an interesting variant reading in v. 17 in 1QpHab, "his sword" in place of "his net," with the difference of only one consonant in the Hebrew. The verb translated "emptying" is also regularly used of "unsheathing" a sword, and it is quite possible that this is the original reading. According to this variant, v. 17 reads: "Is he then to keep on unsheathing his sword, and destroying nations without mercy?"

The climax of the prophet's dialogue with God comes in 2:1-5, although unfortunately textual obscurities make it unclear exactly where and how it ends. In 2:1 the prophet states his determination to wait expectantly for God's answer to his complaint or "reproof" (as it might be translated). He uses the traditional image of a watchman for a prophet (see particularly clearly the "sentinel" in Ezek 3:17-21; 33:1-9, and, for the term "watchpost," the "watchtower" and "post" in Isa 21:8). For another example of a prophet having to wait some time for an answer from God, see Jer 42:7. 2:2 records God's answer quite plainly in the form of an instruction to write the message clearly on tablets (as in Isa 30:8). The last clause is often explained in terms of writing so large that a runner passing by may read it without stopping, rather like a modern road hoarding. Another possible meaning is that the writing is to be so clear that the reader may read it rapidly and without hesitation.

The reason for recording prophetic messages was sometimes so that the records would serve as evidence of the prophecies when they were later fulfilled, thus vindicating the authority of the prophet. The written records of prophecies also served as encouragement during the period before their fulfillment. In the present case part of the reason for the record seems to be to publicize the message. 2:3 makes clear both that there is an appointed time in God's purpose for the fulfillment of the prophecy and that that time has not yet come. Delay in the fulfillment of prophecies sometimes engendered doubt as to their genuineness. For a similar assurance that fulfillment will come, even if it seems unduly delayed in the present, see Ezek 12:21-28.

After this impressive introduction comes the prophetic message itself, the divine answer to the prophet's complaint about the unseemliness of the agents of judgment being even more violent than the violent ones they were sent to punish. Unfortunately, however, at this point the uncertainties of text and interpretation combine to make the answer obscure. 2:4 seems to state a contrast between two categories, those whose spirit is not upright and those who are described as "righteous." The meaning of the word translated "the proud" is quite uncertain, and the word may be intended rather to state what happens to those who are not upright. At all events, the "righteous" shall live by their faith or their "faithfulness," the marginal translation probably being the more appropriate. It refers to their own steadfastness and consistency, perhaps with overtones of their confidence in God's ultimate purpose despite his apparent nonintervention at the time.

2:5 is probably an addition to the placarded slogan made by the prophet himself. The reading "wealth" makes more sense in the context than "wine," and v. 5 is probably intended to apply the negative statement of the first half of v. 4 to the Chaldeans in particular. The second and third parts of the verse seem to reflect the aggrandizement depicted in the earlier descriptions of the

Chaldeans. If this interpretation of the passage is correct, God's answer to the prophet's complaint is that the Chaldeans will not ultimately succeed in their ambition and that in the meantime the "righteous" must patiently endure their oppression, fortified by their loyalty to, and confidence in, God. This is the secret for their "life."

The last clause of 2:4 is quoted in the NT out of its context. In Rom 1:17 and Gal 3:11 Paul quotes it in a slightly different form, where "faith" appears as an abstract principle rather than "their faith" in particular. He uses it in the different context of his message about justification by faith. Yet it may reasonably be claimed that he is penetrating to the basic principle stated in Habakkuk and drawing out its universal significance. In Heb 10:37-38 parts of Hab 2:3-4 are quoted in a version closely similar to that of the LXX but in a slightly different order (the two halves of v. 4 are reversed) and in such a way as to stress the difference between the fidelity of the "righteous" and the "shrinking back" of others, where "who shrinks back" is the LXX's rendering of the obscure word rendered "the proud" in the NRSV at 2:4. In its stress on the faithfulness of the "righteous" the quotation in Hebrews comes close to the meaning of the clause in Habakkuk. The NT citations underline the fact that the essential part of the divine answer to Habakkuk's complaint is to be found in the second part of 2:4, where the textual uncertainties are least.

Habakkuk 2:6-20

This section, consisting basically of five "Woes," is loosely attached to the preceding by references to "such people" and "them" in 2:6, suggesting that the Chaldeans are the object of the judgment sayings in this collection. It is not clear who is envisaged as pronouncing the woes, but perhaps the most natural interpretation in the context is to regard the speakers as the "nations" and "peoples" of v. 5, in other words those victimized by the Chaldeans. The victims will pronounce judgment on their oppressors in the form of taunting sayings.

Each of the five "woes" begins with the exclamation translated "Alas" in the NRSV (2:6b, 9, 12, 15, 19). In itself the exclamation is probably neutral and intended simply to excite attention. Occasionally it is used in a positive sense, as in Isa 55:1, where it is translated "Ho." More characteristically it is used in dirges, as in Jer 22:18. From this usage it seems to have been adapted in a number of prophetic sayings, where it is used to depict both the crimes and the ensuing judgment of those to whom it is addressed. The present collection of woes is a good example of this. For a similar series see Isa 5:8-23 (where the exclamation is translated "Ah" in the NRSV).

The first woe (2:6b-8) focuses on the aggrandizement of the Chaldeans. It draws attention to the way they take possession of what is not their own (as in 1:6) and to the violence and bloodshed that accompany their rapacity (cf. 1:3, 9). The woe looks forward to the time when those they have plundered will plunder them, an application of the principle of the so-called *lex talionis* (e.g., Lev 24:17-20).

The second woe (2:9-11) might seem at first sight to refer to individuals who build fine houses for themselves at the expense of those whom they exploit. The reference to "cutting off many peoples" in v. 10, however, makes clear that the reference is still to the aggrandizement of the Chaldeans, perhaps more specifically to Nebuchadrezzar's building program in Babylon, or possibly his attempt to build his own dynasty (the word "house" can often mean "dynasty"). At all events, the grandiose schemes will result not in security but in disgrace and ultimate loss, while the very buildings themselves will act as a witness against the extortions of the conqueror.

The third woe (2:12-14) also seems to refer to the Chaldeans' grandiose schemes, using language similar to that of Mic 3:10 and Jer 22:13, 17. As in these passages, the primary point of v. 12 seems to be criticism of the exploitation of the builders. Vv. 13 and 14 are difficult to interpret. They seem to consist of slightly variant quotations from Jer 51:58 (13b) and Isa 11:9 (14), while v. 13a may be intended as an introduction to the quotations. In this case the whole of vv. 13 and 14 may be a later addition to Habakkuk's original woe, suggesting that these other prophetic sayings are fulfilled in the futility of the Chaldean building schemes, whereby the labors of the subject peoples are wasted and the only ultimate result will be the universal knowledge of God's glory (with an implicit condemnation of the Chaldeans' ambitions to rule the world). See the first part of Jer 51:58, where the destruction of the city of Babylon is clearly envisaged.

The fourth woe (2:15-17) is at first sight a condemnation of alcohol abuse and reminiscent of the incident in Gen 9:20-25. The language, however, is metaphorical. The intoxicating drink is the wrath of the oppressor, and the nakedness is the stripping away of the defenses of the victims, the despoliation of their land, and the shameful treatment of the conquered population. 2:16 also contains a clear allusion to the theme of God's cup of judgment, which guilty nations must drink (the classic instance of this is in Jer 25:15-29). As earlier in the woes, the Chaldeans will receive the same treatment as they have meted out to others. There is an interesting variant in 2:16, where some witnesses read a word meaning "be uncircumcised" (here in effect "show your uncircumcised organ") in place of "stagger," where the difference in the two Hebrew words is merely that of the order of two of the consonants. Both readings make sense in this context (cf. Lam 4:21). The Chaldeans' nakedness would be an appropriate penalty for gloating on that of their victims, while staggering would indicate the effect of drinking the cup of divine judgment (see Isa 51:17). Put in more prosaic terms, in place of the magnificence of outward show the Chaldeans will experience contempt for their injustice and exploitation. In a similar way in 2:17 Nebuchadrezzar's exploitation of the forests of the Lebanon in pursuit of his grandiose building schemes may be exposed as an affront to nature, with interesting ecological implications.

The fifth woe (2:18-20) is concerned with idolatry. Very possibly in the background is the fear that the rapid growth of the Babylonian Empire reflects the superior power of their gods. To this the prophet replies by drawing attention to the fact that idol images are mere human artifacts. The references to teaching are perhaps more probably allusions to oracular direction; these nondeities can give no useful direction — at least any direction they give will be false. The sheer folly of depending, as on a superior being, on something one has made oneself is the traditional prophetic denunciation of idolatry. This woe has two unusual features. The introductory "Alas" does not come until the beginning of v. 19, raising the suspicion that vv. 18 and 19 may have been displaced, or that v. 18 is a secondary comment. Yet the continuity of thought is close, and the prophet may have felt that the abrupt question at the beginning of v. 18 was an effective variation in the proclamation of his message. The other unusual feature is the absence of a pronouncement of judgment, but the solemn statement of God's majesty in v. 20, itself pointing forward to the theophany in ch. 3, may again have been felt to be an effective variation of the normal pattern. Over against the nonentities of idolatry stands the true and living God, who rules over all creation and to whom the most fitting response is an awed and reverent silence.

Habakkuk 3:1-19

The many obscurities over details in this chapter make its interpretation difficult. The first verse is an editorial title, indicating that the rest of the chapter is a self-contained composition, similar to the Psalms and Lamentations. Shigionoth, like *Selah* in 3:3, 9, and 13, is an unknown technical term, probably of musical or liturgical meaning.

3:2 introduces the prophet's prayer with a clear reference to his knowledge of God's mighty deeds in the past, which fill him with awe. The prophet goes on to ask God to "revive" his work and "make it known," in other words to do similar mighty works again in the present situation. The repeated phrase translated in the NRSV as "in our own time" would be more literally rendered "in the midst of [the] years," or possibly (with revocalization of the Hebrew consonants) "as [the] years draw near" (for which cf. 2:3). The word translated "wrath" has a wide range of meaning and may also denote "tumult." The prophet may even intend both senses of the word, asking that, in his righteous anger and the tumult this necessarily brings about, God will also remember his purpose of mercy, as he revives his activity in the world.

3:3-7 describe the theophany, or vision of God. It is cast in essentially traditional terms of a storm, with God appearing from the general direction of Sinai. The closest parallels are in Deut 33:2, Judg 5:4-5, and Ps 68:7-8. The word translated "praise" in 3:3 might more appropriately be interpreted in this context as "splendor." The rays coming forth from God's hand in v. 4 have been explained in the light of ancient iconography: the storm deity is represented as holding forked lightning in his hand. V. 5 represents God as attended by a "military escort" of pestilence and plague, the word translated "plague" being "Resheph," which is elsewhere the name of a West Semitic god of plague. Vv. 6 and 7 describe the radical disturbance wrought by the advent of God on both the natural order and human nations. Cushan and Midian are probably singled out as among the first areas to be affected in God's progress from the Sinai region to Judah, the tents and tent curtains referring to the nomadic population of this region.

At 3:8 the prophet intervenes with a question. Is God's wrath directed aginst the natural order? The mention of rivers and sea suggests that in the background lies the concept of the rebellion of the watery chaos monster (see Pss 74:13-15; 89:9), hence the suggested capitals in the NRSV footnotes. This imagery persists intermittently until 3:15, but it becomes clear that the immediate object of God's wrathful expedition is the nations (v. 12), and in particular those who oppressed his own people (vv. 13-14). The advent of God spells judgment for the nations but salvation for his own people (v. 13). The "anointed" in v. 13 is most probably the king of Judah at the time, although it might just possibly denote the chosen people as a whole, as in Ps 105:15. The Hebrew word is actually "messiah," but it is unlikely to have any futuristic overtones in this passage. The opponents of God's people are described as the "wicked house" without being identified more specifically, but in much of the passage the dominant imagery seems to be that of a wild beast whom God will slay, perhaps again drawing on traditional imagery of the chaos monster. There may also be overtones of the Exodus tradition, particularly the destruction of the Egyptian army in the sea (Exodus 14). The uncertainties of text and interpretation in this passage are so many that it is difficult to produce a convincing translation, let alone an explanation of the development of thought. The crucial point, however, is clear beyond doubt: that God will intervene in judgment and that this will result in the salvation of his people. It is reasonable, therefore, to follow those exegetes who find here the final divine answer to Habakkuk's second complaint (1:12-17), in the form of the vision for which he was told to wait in 2:3.

3:16 records the immediate effect of the vision on the prophet in strongly physical terms (for which cf. Job 4:12-16). The last part of the verse expresses the prophet's determination to "wait quietly" for God's judgment to overcome those who attack his people. This indicates that he is now confident that God has heard and answered his complaint. The word translated "wait quietly" more commonly denotes "rest," but Roberts 1991: 146 helpfully compares the use of the same word in 1 Sam 25:9, where it refers to messengers stopping speaking while they wait for a reply (the word is actually translated "waited" in the NRSV), and in Dan 12:13, where it is used of resting while awaiting a set time in the future. 3:17-18 continue the note of the prophet's determination to rejoice in God despite adverse circumstances. The agricultural failures described are not such as to be directly attributable to devastation on the part of a hostile invader, and many suspect that v. 17 is a later supplement. The context, however, requires a concessive clause of this kind to introduce v. 18, and its content may perhaps be explained to some extent by the general characteristic of lament poetry to include allusions to kinds of adversity other than those immediately pressing. V. 19 expresses the prophet's confidence with traditional terminology (cf. Ps 18:33). The effect of the vision, with its assurance that God will intervene in judgment and salvation, is to restore the prophet's present confidence and joy in God.

Bibliography. Andersen, F. I. 2001, *Habakkuk,* AB 25, New York: Doubleday • Mason, R. 1994, *Zephaniah, Habakkuk, Joel,* Old Testament Guides, Sheffield: Sheffield Academic • Roberts, J. J. M. 1991, *Nahum, Habakkuk, and Zephaniah,* OTL, Louisville: Westminster/John Knox • Rudolph, W. 1975, *Micah, Nahum, Habakuk, Zephanja,* KAT 13/3, Gütersloh: Mohn; Smith, R. L. 1984, *Micah-Malachi,* WBC 32, Waco: Word • Vermes, G. 1997, *The Complete Dead Sea Scrolls in English,* London: Penguin (1QpHab is on pp. 478-85).

Zephaniah

Anthony Gelston

INTRODUCTION

The opening verse, effectively the title of the book, presents an unusual feature in that the prophet's ancestry is traced back for four generations. Two of the names of his forebears have occasioned comment. His father's name could also be understood as a gentilic name, a Cushite or Ethiopian. While the possibility that his father was a foreigner cannot be excluded, the fact that the three earlier ancestors listed all have Yahwist names makes it very unlikely. The last name in the list, that of the prophet's great-great-grandfather, is identical with that of the king of Judah at the end of the eighth century. If, however, the prophet was of royal descent, it is remarkable that attention is not drawn to the fact. It is interesting that a few Hebrew manuscripts and the Syriac version read "Hilkiah" rather than "Hezekiah" (the difference of a single consonant in Hebrew), although chronological factors exclude an identification with either Jeremiah's father or the high priest who discovered the "book of the law" in 2 Kings 22. Zephaniah's unusual pedigree has stimulated speculation but throws no real light on the prophet's background. It does, however, clearly distinguish him from his namesake the priest, mentioned several times in Jeremiah. Nothing further is known of the prophet beyond what may be inferred from the contents of the book.

The dating in the reign of Josiah has been widely accepted. Most commentators think that the picture of Judean society reflected in the prophecy is consonant with the earlier part of Josiah's reign, before his reforms, while the prophet's own stance is sympathetic with that of the reform movement. Such a dating is consistent with the prediction of the fall of Nineveh in 2:13, an event which occurred in 612 BC, toward the end of Josiah's reign. We are, therefore, in a better position to determine the historical context of Zephaniah than that of a number of prophets but have still to be content with general probabilities rather than with certainties.

The exegesis of Zephaniah is complicated by three further factors in the literary form of the book itself. One is the difficulty of disentangling what might be the original message of the prophet from later additions; in this case the "final form" of the book is so closely woven that there has been little agreement among modern interpreters in distinguishing earlier forms of some of its contents. This in turn leads to a further difficulty in delineating the sections into which the book is divided, beyond the obvious collection of sayings against other nations in 2:4-15. Finally, there are a number of textual and lexical obscurities which make the interpretation uncertain at some crucial points.

COMMENTARY

Zephaniah 1:2–2:3

The overall theme of this section is divine judgment, primarily against Judah but with clear universal dimensions in 1:2-3, 18. The universal scope of the judgment in vv. 2-3, embracing not only humans but also animals and even birds and fish, is reminiscent of, and indeed even more extensive than, that of Noah's flood. Nothing less than the destruction of the whole earth is envisaged (v. 18). In vv. 4-6, however, the focus is on Judah and particularly Jerusalem, and here it is the people's apostasy from Yahweh that is particularly in view. Positively the prophet denounces the syncretistic worship practiced by the people, reminiscent of the religious practices proscribed by Josiah in 2 Kings 23. The "remnant of Baal" hardly suggests a date after Josiah's reforms, but rather that Baalism will be stamped out "without remainder." The first half of 1:5 refers to astrological cults. The word translated "idolatrous priests" always has this connotation in the OT. In the Hebrew text the ordinary word for priests is added to suggest that all classes of priests are condemned. Milcom was the god of the Ammonites. The Hebrew text vocalizes the word slightly differently so as to mean "their king," but even if this is the correct reading, the context makes it probable that the reference is to the strange god worshiped alongside Yahweh. The real indictment is the negative one, that of apostasy from Yahweh, reflected in the attitude expressed in v. 12, where the people complacently disregard Yahweh as a force with whom there is no need to reckon.

The message of impending judgment is enhanced by two vivid images. The first is a parody of a cultic invitation to a sacrifice and sacrificial meal (1:7-8), in which the people themselves will be the victims. This is reminiscent of the ironical "sacrifice" to Baal organized by Jehu in 2 Kgs 10:18-28. The following verses contain further indictments. The mention of officials and sons of the king in 1:8 without mention of the king himself is often thought to reflect the period of Josiah's minority, or alternatively the prophet's recognition of Josiah's fidelity. The allusion to foreign attire suggests a desire on the part of the ruling classes to be like other nations, while leaping over the threshold is probably a pagan practice, implying a belief that demons lurked there. The people are clearly priding themselves on their commerce and wealth, accompanied in some cases by violence and fraud (1:9), but material wealth will be no protection against the threatened judgment (v. 18).

The other vivid image is the traditional concept of the

"day of the LORD," already familiar from the prophecies of Amos and Isaiah and used here in 1:7 and 14 (twice). Amos seems to be the earliest prophet in the OT to use the term, but it is clearly already familiar to his hearers, and Amos is concerned to give it an interpretation diametrically opposed to that popularly held, probably centering in the conviction that it will bring divine judgment not only on Israel's enemies but on Israel herself as well. There has been much speculation on the origins of the concept, including Mowinckel's suggestion that it derived from the putative "enthronement festival" at the new year. There is, however, no hard evidence for the meaning of the concept before its use by Amos, and we can only infer its meaning from the use he and later prophets made of it. (See Van Leeuwen's survey of theories about the background to the concept in *OTS* 19.) The two aspects of this concept emphasized in Zeph 1:14-16 are those of darkness (for which cf. esp. Amos 5:18, 20) and military defeat (consistent with von Rad's explanation of the origin of the concept of the "day of the LORD" in the sacral war traditions). This passage inspired the medieval hymn *Dies irae*.

The first three verses of ch. 2 probably belong here rather than to the collection of pronouncements against other nations in the rest of that chapter. The shameless nation addressed in v. 1 is clearly Judah. What is surprising here is the implicit summons to Judah to repent while there is still time, before the judgment is executed. The appeal is addressed more specifically in v. 3 to the "humble" of the land (an expression found often in the Psalms), with which may be compared the "remnant of my people" in 2:9 and the "remnant of Israel" in 3:13. The concept of a division within the people of God is beginning to emerge: the faithful remnant are distinguished from the apostate majority. It is probable that the concept of the "remnant" in Isaiah 1–39 is reflected in these passages. Even so, only the possibility ("perhaps" — 2:3) of exemption from the judgment is held out to them. For this cautious note compare Amos 5:15 and especially Joel 2:14.

Zephaniah 2:4-15

The three larger prophetic books (Isaiah, Jeremiah, and Ezekiel) each contain a section of several chapters comprising a collection of prophecies against several non-Israelite nations. Zephaniah is almost unique among the shorter prophetic books in containing a similar, though much shorter, collection in the middle section of the book. Other books contain prophecies against particular nations (e.g., Obadiah against Edom), but the only other example of a group of prophecies against a number of nations in the shorter prophetic books is the collection at the beginning of Amos, which is in any case distinctive in that the series leads to a climax in a prophecy of judgment against Israel herself.

The prophecies against the nations in Zephaniah 2 are in some cases abrupt to the point of obscurity, raising the suspicion that there has been a loss of material in the course of transmission. The prophecy against Ethiopia in v. 12 lacks any indictment as a basis for the sentence pronounced on it. V. 11 stands out from the rest of the passage in that it is addressed to all the nations and appears to envisage a universal recognition of Yahweh as implicitly the only real God. It is noteworthy that this acknowledgment of Yahweh is to be made by each nation in its own homeland. This verse appears to be an isolated saying, perhaps included here simply because it comes under the general heading of prophecies against other nations. It may be compared with 3:9-10.

The remainder of the section can be divided clearly into three distinct prophecies. The first, in 2:4-7, is directed against the Philistines, who are directly addressed with the characteristic "Ah" (v. 5), which more commonly opens prophetic judgment sayings. The word "For" at the beginning of v. 4 may be an editorial link with the previous section, suggesting that the universality of the coming judgment is one motive for the appeal to seek Yahweh while there is still time. V. 4 is remarkable for the mention of four of the five Philistine cities: Gath is also missing from the similar lists in Amos 1:7-8 and Jer 25:20, perhaps suggesting that it had already been conquered. There is a verbal play on the names of Gaza and Ekron in the Hebrew verbs used to describe their fate. The reference to Ashdod's people being driven out at noon may imply that the battle to capture the city would be over by midday, so weak would be the resistance offered. The Cherethites were a group within the Philistines who probably traced their origin to Crete. The prophecy ends with the occupation of the Philistine coastal plain by Judah as part of the reversal of their fortunes (cf. 3:20 and see the note on Joel 3:1 on the meaning of this phrase).

2:8-10 contain a prophecy against the Moabites and Ammonites, whose ancestry was traditionally traced to Lot, Abraham's nephew (Gen 19:30-38). They are charged with pride and scorn toward God's people. The last clause of 2:8 suggests that this took the form of encroaching on Judean territory. Their fate will be destruction like that of the legendary Sodom and Gomorrah (Gen 19:24-25), while their territory will be occupied by the remnant of Judah, implicitly in compensation for the ill-treatment they had suffered at their hands.

2:13-15 contain the final prophecy in the series, probably placed here as a climax, directed as it is against Assyria, at this time the principal enemy of Judah. Although strictly speaking Assyria was situated to the northeast rather than the north of Judah, the only practical approach to Judah was directly from the north, so that it is not surprising that Assyria came to be regarded as situated essentially to the north. It is not clear whether the reference in v. 13 is to the nation Assyria or to the city of Asshur, which would make a more exact parallel to the subsequent mention of Nineveh. Asshur was destroyed in 615 BC and Nineveh in 612 BC. Much of v. 14 is obscure, but the gist is clearly the same as in v. 15b, occupation by wild creatures underlining the extent of the desolation. V. 15a draws attention to the pride and vaunted self-sufficiency of the city, shortly to be reduced to ruins by Yahweh's judgment. Passing travelers will no longer be in awe of it, but will merely treat it as an object of scorn and derision.

This is a traditional element in the threat of destruction; compare a poignant example in Lam 2:15-16.

Zephaniah 3:1-20

Although this section probably contains several originally distinct prophetic sayings, they are combined in the present form of the text into a sequence in which there is no natural break until the end of 3:13. The beginning of the passage is clearly demarcated from the prophecies against foreign nations, since it is evident from vv. 2, 4, and 5 that the city denounced in v. 1 is Jerusalem. Read in isolation from its sequel, however, the opening verse could be taken as the denunciation of Nineveh implied in 2:15, and this is how it is in fact taken by the ancient Syrian translator, who prefaces it with "and says." This is a good illustration of the unusual difficulty encountered in disentangling the original prophetic sayings in this book. The mistaken identification of the city with Nineveh was helped by the Hebrew words translated "defiled" (which is homonymous with the commoner word meaning "redeemed") and "oppressing" (which is identical with the proper name "Jonah"). These together suggested an allusion to Nineveh's redemption from destruction as a result of its repentance in response to Jonah's preaching (see Jonah 3–4).

Such an exegesis is shown to be false by the introductory "Ah," characteristically opening a prophetic pronouncement of judgment, and by the clear indication of the rebelliousness of the city and its inhabitants in the following verses. The clear references to Yahweh as the God of the city in 3:2 and 5 indicate that only Jerusalem can be envisaged, and this is reinforced by the mention of prophets, priests, and Torah in v. 4. The indictment is fundamentally that of rebellion against Yahweh (cf. Jer 7:28), characterized more specifically by the corruption of the secular and religious authorities, who abuse their position to exploit the weaker citizens (cf. Ezek 22:23-31). Yahweh by contrast is presented as a just judge, administering justice every morning (for which see 2 Sam 15:2 and Ps 101:8), despite the shamelessness of the corrupt officials.

The exegesis of 3:6-13 is rendered difficult by textual and lexical obscurities and by the possibility that originally distinct prophetic sayings have been adapted to form the present sequence. As it stands, v. 6 seems to revert to the theme of Yahweh's judgment of foreign nations, while v. 7 expresses his hope that Judah might take warning from this, a hope that was to be disappointed. The command "wait" at the beginning of v. 8 is plural in the Hebrew, but it is not clear to whom it is addressed. Generally this word is used in contexts implying expectation of a favorable divine intervention. If this is the meaning here, it is most probable that the encouragement is addressed to the faithful remnant depicted clearly in vv. 12-13, and that the intervention for which they are encouraged to wait is a particular instance of divine judgment that will result in the removal of their unjust rulers (v. 11). The sequence of thought, however, is not straightforward. V. 8 reverts once more to the theme of universal judgment, while vv. 9 and 10 appear to introduce the concept of the conversion of Gentiles to Yahweh (cf. 2:11), although "my scattered ones" might alternatively suggest a reference to the Jewish diaspora. Some exegetes think that 3:9 and 10 in particular are a separate saying. The authenticity of vv. 12-13, on the other hand, is supported by the similar material in 2:3.

The summons to rejoice in 3:14 marks a new departure. It is clearly addressed to the Jerusalem community, and the grounds for joy are spelled out in v. 15. The divine judgment in the form of enemy attack has been taken away, and Yahweh has demonstrated his presence as king in their midst (a traditional belief — see Mic 3:11; Jer 14:9), with the corollary that their security is guaranteed. The same belief underlies 3:16 and 17. The fact that God's presence in the city now guarantees salvation, in contrast to the judgment of v. 5, indicates that these verses refer to a period beyond the judgment and are addressed presumably to the purified remnant of vv. 12 and 13, who have survived the judgment. The content of these verses is very similar in tone to the message of Second Isaiah; note particularly the repeated affirmation that the community no longer has any need to fear (Isa 41:10 and often).

Once again lexical and textual uncertainties make the interpretation of the end of 3:17 and 18 obscure (see the footnotes in the NRSV). Vv. 19 and 20 deal in general terms with the theme of the "reversal of fortune" (as in 2:7). For the "dealing with" Judah's former oppressors, compare in particular Zech 1:15. The beginning of 3:20 predicts a return from exile and dispersion, while vv. 19 and 20 both indicate a change in the status of Judah among the nations.

It is hardly surprising that many scholars have regarded the closing verses of the book as postexilic. What has emerged with greater clarity in recent years is the redactional unity of ch. 3, suggesting that the last seven verses should not be seen as a postscript but rather as an integral part of the composition of the book. This probably implies that, as in the case of most of the prophetic books, the final redaction took place in the early postexilic period. At the same time the possibility must not be ruled out that the prophet himself envisaged that a purified remnant would survive the coming judgment and experience a new era of salvation beyond it.

Bibliography. Berlin, A. 1994, *Zephaniah,* AB 25A, New York: Doubleday • Mason, R. 1994, *Zephaniah, Habakkuk, Joel,* Old Testament Guides, Sheffield: Sheffield Academic • Roberts, J. J. M. 1991, *Nahum, Habakkuk, and Zephaniah,* OTL, Louisville: Westminster/John Knox • Rudolph, W. 1975, *Micah, Nahum, Habakuk, Zephanja,* KAT 13/3, Gütersloh: Mohn • Smith, R. L. 1984, *Micah-Malachi,* WBC 32, Waco: Word • Van Leeuwen, C. 1974, "The Prophecy of the YOM YHWH in Amos v 18-20," *OTS* 19:113-34 (esp. 118-28).

Haggai

John W. Rogerson

INTRODUCTION

The book of Haggai shares with Zechariah 1–8 the unusual distinction of being provided with exact dates on which prophecies were given. The dates occur at 1:1, 15; 2:1, 10, 18, 20 and Zech 1:1, 7; 7:1. In Haggai the dates range from 29 August 520 (according to modern time-reckoning) to 18 December 520, and in Zechariah from October 520 to 7 December 518 (see the table in Meyers and Meyers 1987: xlvi). While one should be grateful for such dates which, on the face of it, make unnecessary the kinds of speculation about the dates of materials that have to be made for most of the rest of the prophetic literature, they are not without problems, as we will see. Nonetheless, it is clear from the content of Haggai that he falls within the latter part of the second half of the sixth century BC and that he played a decisive role in the rebuilding of the temple at that time.

Our information concerning events of that period comes from Ezra 1–6, although not everything is clear. Following the decree of Cyrus in 540/539 (Ezra 1:2-4), a party of exiles, headed by a certain Sheshbazzar, "the prince of Judah," sets out from Babylon to Jerusalem to rebuild the temple. By ch. 3 of Ezra Sheshbazzar has vanished from the scene and the initiative has passed to Jeshua the priest and Zerubbabel the son of Shealtiel. Haggai and Zechariah are mentioned in connection with this work at Ezra 5:1. An immediate question is raised by the fact that the book of Haggai dates the activity of Joshua *(sic)* and Zerubbabel to 520, that is, around eighteen years after Sheshbazzar's expedition to Jerusalem. There is no information about why nothing appears to have been done to restore the temple during that time. Ezra 4 suggests that there was opposition from "the adversaries of Judah and Benjamin" (4:1), but the letters cited in Ezra 4 pertaining to this opposition are dated to the reign of Artaxerxes in the following century, and, in any case, Hag 1:2 gives no hint of any such opposition.

The book of Haggai itself consists of at least two types of material: prophetic oracles (1:4-11; 2:3-9, 12-14, 15-19, 21-23) and editorial material into which the oracles have been inserted. This method of composition raises questions about the dating scheme. The date at 1:15 does not seem to refer to anything (this is more obvious in the Hebrew than in the English, where it is tacked onto 1:12-14). A very old suggestion is that 1:15 was originally followed by 2:15-19. Whether or not this is accepted, it draws attention to the fact that there is a logical progression to the oracles that is obscured in the book as we have it.

1:4-11 The prophet denies that the time is not right to rebuild the temple, and argues that the current drought is divine punishment because the people have concentrated on their own houses and neglected God's house.

2:15-19 Work has now commenced, and God promises that from now on he will bless the people's farming.

2:3-9 Progress has been made, but the results are poor in comparison with the former temple's splendor. God encourages Joshua and Zerubbabel and promises that the rebuilt temple will enjoy a greater splendor than its predecessor.

2:12-14 A consultation with the temple's priests on purity rules leads to a verdict on the offerings of the people.

2:21-23 God promises that he is about to shake the heavens and the earth and to destroy mighty kingdoms. Zerubbabel will be like a signet ring.

Because of the apparent logical progression of the prophetic oracles, the view I will take in this commentary is that there is no need to interpret Haggai in terms of the dates provided in the book. According to these dates, Haggai's words fit into a period of only four months. The possibility cannot be ruled out that his ministry lasted longer than this, even if the origin and purpose of the dates is not known to us.

COMMENTARY

Editorial Introduction (1:1-3)

Darius became king of Persia in 522 BC, and ruled until 486. A dating in terms of his reign suggests that the compiler/editor of Haggai had access to or moved in Persian administrative circles. The name Zerubbabel probably means "the offspring of Babylon," indicating his place of birth. He was the grandson of Jerusalem's last king, Jehoiachin (cf. 1 Chr 3:16-18), who was exiled to Babylon in 597, where he lived for nearly forty years. The title "governor of Judah" probably means that he was in charge of administration. Joshua was the son of the priest Jehozadak, whom Nebuchadrezzar exiled to Babylon (1 Chr 6:15). It is noteworthy that Zerubbabel and Joshua have titles which they are not accorded in Ezra 3 and 5, and that Joshua is probably the first priest to be described as "high priest" (the title is applied anachronistically to Hilkiah at 2 Kgs 22:4). The formal titles given to Zerubbabel and Joshua reinforce the suspicion that the editorial framework comes from official administrative circles. As an introduction to Haggai's words in 1:4-11, vv. 1-2 are clumsy in that it they make Zerubbabel and Joshua the recipients of the oracle ("these people say . . ."), whereas the prophet's words are clearly addressed to the people.

The First Oracle (1:4-11)

Haggai's words are in prose, whereas prophetic oracles are normally in poetry. Haggai may have spoken in prose, or we may have his words in reported speech. The purpose of the oracle is clear. Poor harvests are the result of preoccupation with the people's own houses, to the neglect of God's house. There is no hint of opposition to the rebuilding and, incidentally, no reference to Cyrus's decree eighteen years earlier ordering the rebuilding. Instead, the prophet, who passionately advocated rebuilding, used the occasion of a drought (1:11) to urge a turning of the people to God that would involve working on the temple.

The Result (1:12-15)

As a result of Haggai's words Zerubbabel and Joshua begin work on the temple. If it seems odd that Joshua was content to be high priest of a ruined temple, and needed a prophet to persuade him that rebuilding was necessary, this may be the fault of the editorial framework rather than a reflection of the reality. Perhaps Zerubbabel and Joshua were in favor of rebuilding but opposed by a hostile or indifferent populace. Perhaps Haggai's main contribution was to persuade the people, not their leaders. The phrase "remnant of the people" has been much discussed, and it has been referred to the returning exiles or to the people who remained in the land. More likely it denotes the small, post-exilic community. The dating in 1:15, unusually, concludes the section, and while this is defended by Meyers and Meyers, many commentators believe that it originally went with 2:15-19.

Introduction to the Second Oracle (2:1-2)

If the dates of the oracles can be relied upon, the second oracle was delivered about seven weeks after the first, on 17 October 520. The question of the dates affects how the oracle is read, for if work had been going on for seven weeks, or, on the assumption that 1:15 (21 September 520) marks the beginning of the work, for around four weeks, not very much would have been achieved. If the date is ignored, progress could have been greater. Again, the introduction is clumsy in that 2:3 is addressed in the first instance to the people, whereas Haggai is told to speak to Zerubbabel and Joshua and the people.

The Second Oracle (2:3-9)

On the view that these words were spoken seven or four weeks after work had begun on the temple site, 2:3 contrasts what is still presumably a ruin with what the temple must have looked like once. If the dating is not followed, the reference could even be to the completed rebuilding. Either way, the point is clear. What is seen now cannot compare with what once existed. Assuming the date of 520 for the oracle, and given that the temple was destroyed in 587, anyone present who was as old as, say, seventy-five could have remembered the former temple. It has been suggested that these included Haggai himself, but there is no evidence for or against this view. The contrast between then and now is the basis for encouragement for the people. God is with them, and is about to intervene on a cosmic scale, so that both people and temple enjoy prosperity on a scale greater than ever before. The language hovers on the borderline between events that will happen in the world as it is, and what will happen in an eschatological future.

The Third Oracle (2:10-14)

In this passage the reported nature of Haggai's words is particularly apparent, and only the bulk of 2:14 gives any access to what Haggai might have said. Until v. 14 the logic of the passage is clear. Haggai engages in what might be called a type of prophetic symbolism in that he deliberately seeks rulings from "the priests" so as to give point to the special word from God in v. 14. Again, we may be forgiven for wondering at the existence of priests who could give authoritative answers on matters of ritual cleanness or uncleanness but who had operated with a ruined temple and with no incentive to get it rebuilt until only a few months previously. The upshot of the consultation is that consecrated meat (commentators suggest that it had been offered on the temporary altar mentioned at Ezra 3:3) cannot make other food items holy, whereas what is unclean can convey defilement to anything that it touches. This leads to the divine word of 2:14; but what does it mean? Who is this nation whose work and offerings are unclean? There are two main possibilities: the postexilic community in Jerusalem, and some group of unspecified outsiders such as the "Samaritans." The latter suggestion owes something to Zech 7:1-4, which records how people came from Bethel to seek rulings from the Jerusalem priests about fasting. With the rebuilding work under way, it is suggested, news spread to the former Northern Kingdom, and people from there came to join in with the work. Haggai, however, was inspired to say that the presence of these people made the whole enterprise unclean. Unfortunately, this involves reading too much into the text, and the simpler explanation is that the holy work of rebuilding the temple being undertaken by the people can be made unclean. How that can be done is not stated, but it could be that the people were tolerating injustice while doing the rebuilding.

The Fourth Oracle (2:15-19)

In the text as we have it, this is a continuation of the third oracle, and it is possible to interpret the enigmatic

2:14 in the light of the continuation. Vv. 15-19 say, in effect, that before the rebuilding began, the community was experiencing agricultural disaster (cf. v. 17 with Amos 4:9). Since the foundation was laid, things have changed. If 2:15-19 are linked with v. 14, then the latter passage refers to the community before the rebuilding began. This might even constitute a case for dating the third oracle to the period prior to the beginning of the building work. However the saying is taken, its meaning is clear. A dividing line has been crossed, from which point onward God will bless his people.

The Fifth Oracle (2:20-23)

The date already met in 2:10 and 19, 18 December 520, is repeated, as is the promise that God is about to shake the heavens and the earth (cf. 2:6-7). Suggestions have been made about the occasion of the oracle, for example, that Zerubbabel (who alone is addressed) had received an embassy from powerful and neighboring opponents of the rebuilding. Also, it has been suggested that the uncertainties that had surrounded Darius's accession to the throne in 522 following a revolt against the previous ruler Cambyses by an impostor claiming to be Cambyses' brother were still being deeply felt, so that the idea could easily be entertained that the world order was about to topple. Suggestions such as these only indicate how little is known about Haggai and his book. The final verse, v. 23, addresses Zerubbabel as God's servant, in language that suggests his investiture to royal dignity (cf. Zech 6:9-14 and the commentary there).

The book of Haggai leaves much unanswered. We know nothing about him other than that he exercised a prophetic ministry for a mere four months (if the dates are accepted). Was his subsequent silence due to death, or to imprisonment by neighboring or imperial authorities? And what of Zerubbabel, for whom he saw such an important future? What happened to him? We do not know. All that we can say is that at a particular point in his people's history Haggai became a catalyst and played a decisive part in ridding the people of their inertia and impelling them to rebuild the house of God.

Bibliography. Coggins, R. J. 1987, *Haggai, Zechariah, Malachi,* Old Testament Guides, Sheffield: Sheffield Academic • Driver, S. R. 1906, *The Minor Prophets Nahum, Habakkuk, Zephaniah, Haggai, Zechariah, Malachi,* Century Bible, Edinburgh: T. C. & E. C. Jack • Elliger, K. 1959, *Die Propheten: Nahum, Habakuk, Zephanja, Haggai, Sacharja, Maleachi,* ATD 25, Göttingen: Vandenhoeck & Ruprecht • Grabbe, L. L. 1992, *Judaism from Cyrus to Hadrian,* vol. 1: *The Persian and Greek Periods,* Minneapolis: Fortress • Meyers, C. L., and E. M. Meyers. 1987, *Haggai, Zechariah,* AB 25B, New York: Doubleday • Smith, R. L. 1984, *Micah-Malachi,* WBC, Waco: Word • Wolff, H. W. 1986, *Dodekapropheton, Haggai,* BKAT 14, Neukirchen: Neukirchener.

Zechariah

John W. Rogerson

INTRODUCTION

Fourteen chapters long, the book of Zechariah is the largest of the twelve Minor Prophets. Critical scholarship, however, is virtually unanimous in regarding it as a compilation and in separating it into three sections: chs. 1–8, 9–11, and 12–14. While it is too simple to say that the three sections represent the work of three different prophets from three different periods, there is general agreement that chs. 1–8 are to be connected with a prophet, Zechariah, who was alive in the last quarter of the sixth century BC, from roughly 520. The main reasons for dividing the book in this way are as follows:

1. Chs. 1–8 contain chronological datings of Zechariah's oracles from the second to the fourth years of the Persian king Darius I. No such datings are present in chs. 9–14.
2. Chs. 1–8 contain eight visions initiated and interpreted to the prophet by an angel. Chs. 9–14 contain no such visions.
3. Chs. 1–8 are written in prose, 9–11 in poetry, and 12–14 mainly in prose.
4. Chs. 9 and 12 are prefaced by a heading, "An Oracle," which suggests the beginning of a new section.

It has to be admitted that none of these reasons offers conclusive proof that Zechariah should be divided into three sections; but scholars who have investigated both the thematic links between the various sections and the style and vocabulary of the book have supported the division. The most recent exhaustive study concludes, "In considering the relation between Zechariah 1–8 and 9–14, we have found almost nothing that would argue for a unified editing of the book, let alone common authorship. There *are* similarities of theme, theology and language, but these seem to be adequately explained on the basis of a continuing tradition which was well versed in the prophet's work and in the older traditions of Israel that he also knew" (Butterworth 1992: 304). In what follows, chs. 1–8 and 9–14 will be treated separately.

COMMENTARY

Introduction to Zechariah 1–8

On the basis of Neh 12:4, 16, where a Zechariah is mentioned as the head of the ancestral house of Iddo, a priest (or Levite) who returned from Babylon to Jerusalem with Zerubbabel (c. 525 BC and cf. Zech 1:1, "Zechariah son of Berechiah son of Iddo"), it is normally assumed that Zechariah was a priest who was born in Babylon. A good proportion of the material in Zechariah 1–8 is in the first person (e.g., 1:8, "In the night I saw a man riding . . ."), but it is likely that the present form of chs. 1–8 with its chronology (which is begun in Haggai) is the work of an editor whose date cannot be determined.

The fact that chs. 1–8 contain eight visions, which are interpreted by an angel, has aroused controversy about the genre of this material. Amos 7–9 contains visions but no interpreting angel. Dan 7:12 contains both visions and heavenly interpreters. Such material is often defined as "apocalyptic." Whether this is helpful or not is arguable. It is certainly not helpful where scholars believe that "apocalyptic" must emanate from particular social backgrounds and then use this belief to "locate" material that they define as apocalyptic. It is safer to note the character of the material than to speculate on its origins.

The historical situation that occasioned Zechariah 1–8 was the return of the Jews from exile following the defeat of the Babylonians by Cyrus, king of Persia, in 540 BC. In recent years, the notions of "exile" and "return" have attracted much criticism, criticism that is justified if these terms conjure up the idea of Judah as an empty land from 587 to 540, which was repopulated by the descendants of those who had been deported to Babylon in 597, 587, and 582. Judah was not an empty land during this period. However, the temple in Jerusalem remained in ruins, and those who lived in the land had little or no opportunity to organize themselves politically as a national entity. What the "return" offered was the possibility of renewed, organized national identity, albeit within limits prescribed by the Persians. The OT writers saw this possibility of national renewal as a gift of God via his servant Cyrus (2 Chr 36:22-23; Ezra 1:1-4; Isa 44:28; 45:1); and the fact that Zechariah's prophecies are dated to the reign of Darius I (521-486) can be taken as an indication of a pro-Persian attitude in the book. It does not require a great deal of imagination to picture the hopes and expectations of those who were given the opportunity to reorganize national life after 540. These hopes and expectations, as well as the practical problems they engendered, will be borne particularly in mind in the commentary.

Introduction (1:1-6)

The opening of the book, dated to 520 BC, contains an oracle in the third person. It reminds the prophet's hearers (the "them" of 1:3) that their ancestors refused to heed the former prophets (this phrase later became a technical term for the books of Joshua to 2 Kings) and that God's judgment overtook them. It is strange that the prophet's hearers should need this reminder since evidence of God's judgment, for example, in the ruined temple, was abundantly at hand. Further, Cyrus's victories indicated that God was already being gracious to his people. The call to repentance may therefore mirror an internal struggle among those who are reordering the national life, such as that recorded in Haggai, over whether or not to rebuild the temple (Hag 1:1-11).

The First Vision (1:7-17)

The first vision, and presumably also the other visions, is dated three months after the first oracle. The abrupt transition from third person to first person speech in 1:7-8 indicates the editorial nature of the dating. It could, therefore, be that the visions were all seen on one particular night; or they may have been witnessed on different occasions. Whether the prophet saw, or dreamed, the visions, whether they are literary compositions drawing upon various types of imagery, or whether they resulted from a combination of these processes, cannot be determined; in any case, this question does not affect the meaning of the visions.

There are three principal characters in the first vision: the prophet, the man with a horse standing among the myrtle trees (presumably the leader of the horsemen), and the angel. Although there may be some confusion between the leader and the angel in 1:11, and while the exact colors of the horses and the significance (if any) of these colors are matters of debate, the meaning of the vision is clear. The horsemen (perhaps modeled on Persian patrols) report that the whole earth is at peace. It is implied that this is God's doing, whereupon the angel intercedes on behalf of Jerusalem and the cities of Judah which have suffered God's anger (i.e., have remained desolate) for seventy years. The period 587-520 BC is near enough to seventy years, even though this latter figure may be symbolic. The prayer brings the divine reply that God will have mercy on Jerusalem, that the temple will be rebuilt, and that the other cities will enjoy prosperity. Aspects of the passage echo other OT texts. The patroling function of the horses (v. 10) is described with the same Hebrew verb used of Satan's roving function in Job 1:7. Whereas in Job Satan requests God to afflict Job, the angel in Zech 1:12 intercedes for God to be gracious to Jerusalem. The vision puts the priestly Zechariah firmly on the side of those who see an intimate connection between the rebuilding of the temple and the reorganization of national life.

The Second Vision (1:18-21; Heb. 2:1-4)

The prophet sees four horns, presumably made of iron. The horn as a symbol of pride and aggression is familiar in the OT, deriving from its use in fighting by bulls and other horned animals. Whether the number four is to be connected with the four winds of heaven (6:5) or whether they are to be identified with successive empires (Assyria, Babylonia, Persia) is disputed. When 1:19 is repeated in v. 21, Israel and Jerusalem are not mentioned and may well be later additions to v. 19. The blacksmiths, of which there are again four, may partly represent Persia as the nation that defeated Judah's oppressor (Babylon); but precise clarity is not to be expected in visions. The visions could both refer to the present deliverance that Judah enjoys thanks to the Persians and look to a future, more extensive deliverance.

The Third Vision (2:2-5; Heb. 2:5-9)

In the third vision the interpreting angel seems unaware of what is happening. The prophet sees a man with a measuring line who says that he is going to measure the dimensions of Jerusalem. He may well represent those who argued that it was more important to rebuild the city's walls than to rebuild the temple. While the interpreting angel stands talking with the prophet (reading, with the LXX, "was standing" for "came forward") another angel comes forward and tells the interpreting angel to run after and forestall the man with the measuring line. In the future, Jerusalem will require no walls; God's presence will ensure its safety and make possible a limitless population. The priestly language of v. 5 ("glory"; "wall of fire" — cf. the pillar of fire in the wilderness at Exod 13:21-22) suggests that once the temple is built and God's glory (presence) resides there (cf. Ezek 43:1-5) no physical protection will be needed. This is a bold conception. Even Ezekiel's visionary restored temple has walls!

Intervening Oracle (2:6-13; Heb. 2:10-17)

The general sense of this passage is clear even if some details are obscure. Because Jerusalem will be able to accommodate limitless numbers (2:1-5), the exiles still in Babylon are urged to return to Zion. A further reason for a return is that God will punish the nations that had afflicted his people. Further, the time is coming when other nations will join the people of God, and God will dwell in their midst.

The first obscurity is the phrase "spread you abroad" in 2:6, for which the Greek has "I have gathered you." A possibility is to understand the Hebrew to mean that God has (or will) spread the people around in abundance. The idea that he has scattered them is not appropriate to the context. In v. 8 the phrase "after glory he sent me" has been called the most problematic in the whole book, and the NRSV, "after his glory sent me," makes little sense. Assuming that the phrase is not a gloss, it has to be admitted that no really convincing translation or explanation has yet been proposed. The third problem is to identify the speaker in vv. 9 and 11, ending with "you shall know that the LORD has sent me." This is best taken to mean Zechariah, with two provisos: first, that the "I" of the first part of these verses refers to God and, second, that the prophet, whose vocation may be being questioned by his opponents, expects the speedy fulfillment of his expectations to vindicate his claim to speak in God's name.

The Fourth Vision (3:1-10)

The fourth vision is unlike the other seven. Instead of symbols which the interpreting angel has to explain, the prophet sees an actual person, the high priest Joshua, while the function of the angel is not to explain but to be an active protagonist in a dispute. This angelic function is even more fundamental if the ancient Syriac version of

v. 2 is correct, which makes the angel of the LORD the one who rebukes Satan. The incident is visionary, of course, in the sense that the scene is enacted in the heavenly court in a way strongly reminiscent of Job 1–2; but the manifest difference between the fourth vision and the others has led many commentators to argue that Zechariah had, or wrote, seven night visions and that the fourth vision has been added to their number. This does not, of course, diminish its importance.

A plausible context for the fourth vision is the dedication of the rebuilt temple in 515 BC (Ezra 6:15). The heavenly scene authenticates the priesthood led by Joshua, with Satan (who is not yet the leader of an angelic order opposed to God, as in later Judaism and Christianity) voicing the opposition. He is rebuked by God (or, following the Syriac, the angel), after which Joshua is clothed with new apparel. The meaning of Joshua's "filthy clothes" (Zech 3:3, 4) has been much debated. The simplest explanation is that the provision of new apparel is an act of priestly renewal and reconsecration, appropriate for the rededicated temple. The vision legitimates the new temple and its priesthood.

The resumption of temple worship is not, however, an end in itself, if 3:8-10 are taken as part of the vision (by no means all commentators agree that it should be). It is the beginning of a process that will lead to the coming of the Branch (v. 8), presumably a royal figure who will restore the kingship and inaugurate a new age (v. 10). The meaning of the stone with seven facets (lit. "eyes" — some read the word as "springs" or "fountains") has given rise to so many speculations that any interpretation can only be guesswork. The stone has been linked with the foundation stone of the temple or the stone in the high priest's diadem, to mention only two theories. Minimally, it can probably be said that the stone contains a name or phrase ("its inscription," v. 9) which promises the coming age when the whole land and its people will be cleansed of all guilt (v. 9).

The Fifth Vision (4:1-14)

As awakened from sleep, the prophet sees a lampstand with seven spouts surmounted by a golden reservoir of oil and flanked by two olive trees. The description of the vision, however, does not come until 4:10b-14, being interrupted by an oracle (vv. 6-10a) which proclaims that Zerubbabel will complete the temple and that those who doubted the possibility (those who despised the day of small things) will rejoice. Zerubbabel will achieve this by means of God's spirit (v. 6), and the bringing out of the final coping stone (some commentators link this with the mysterious stone of 3:9) will evoke shouts of admiration ("Grace, grace to it") directed to either the stone or the completed building or both.

The interpretation of the vision resumes at 4:10b by identifying the seven branches of the lampstand with the seven eyes (cf. 3:9) of God that rove the earth (cf. 1:11). While the connection between lampstand branches and the all-surveying eyes of God may not be obvious, it must be remembered that it is a vision that is being described. On the basis of 4:14, where the two olive trees that flank the lampstand are identified with "two anointed ones" who stand beside God, the lampstand is a symbol of the divine presence, in which case the seven branches can be understood as God's seven eyes.

Who are the two anointed ones (4:14)? While almost all commentators identify them with Zerubbabel and Joshua, van der Woude 1984: 95 emphasizes the fact that the word translated "anointed" (lit. "sons of the fresh juice") is not connected with the word for oil, the substance used to anoint kings and priests. He identifies the "anointed ones" with the Branch (3:8) and a future high priest, the fresh or new juice indicating a coming new age. The possibility must be reckoned with that a vision about the future was understood either by the prophet or the book's editor in terms of the contemporary figures Zerubbabel and Joshua. This would explain the presence of the material about Zerubbabel in 4:6-10a.

The Sixth Vision (5:1-4)

The prophet sees a flying scroll of enormous dimensions, twenty by ten cubits (thirty by fifteen feet). The two-to-one dimension of the scroll (a completely open scroll, such as those discovered at Qumran, would be much longer than it was wide) has raised the question whether it was only partly open; but this is a vision, and perhaps such details should not be pressed too far. The content of the scroll is limited, dealing on one side with stealing and on the other side with perjury. The intention of the passage may well be that the writing on the scroll would be so large as to be visible, and legible to any who could read.

The restriction of the content to two types of offense can be taken in many ways. Elliger 1959: 111-12 refers the offenses to those who had appropriated exiles' land during their absence in Babylon. Others see echoes of the clauses of the Decalogue concerning theft and perjury. Another possibility is to link the scroll with the discovery of the lawbook in Josiah's reign (2 Kgs 22:8) and trace the development of the written Torah in postexilic Judah. Whatever is intended, the vision looks forward to divine action in purifying the land from moral evil (cf. 3:9).

The Seventh Vision (5:5-11)

The prophet sees an ephah, a measuring basket used for such things as grain, in which a woman is sitting. Discussions concerning the capacity of the ephah and whether it would be large enough to hold a woman seems to overlook the fact that an overly large scroll in vision 6 could well be followed by an overly large ephah in vision 7. The woman represents Wickedness, and her removal from the land of Judah to Shinar (Babylon) by means of two storklike women symbolizes the cleansing of the land (cf. 5:4; 3:9). Modern readers will naturally question why Wickedness is symbolized by a woman. Possible answers draw attention to the fear of goddesses as sources of evil and corruption in the view of official Israelite religion, as well as passages in the OT that attribute disaster to women, such as Solomon's foreign wives (1 Kgs 11:1). Elliger 1959: 112 notes that individual acts of wrongdoing derive from an underlying cause which must be rooted out. In modern times it is possible to draw attention to the way injustice, oppression, and inhumanity have insinuated themselves into the very structures of society, so that merely to deal with individual wrongdoers is to treat the symptoms rather than the causes. If the seventh vision looks forward to a new order in which the structural and social causes of evil are eradicated, it will be a condition in which there will be no reason to associate women with Wickedness any more than men.

The Eighth Vision (6:1-8)

The final vision, which is reminiscent of the first, sees four chariots coming out from between two bronze mountains. These mountains are mentioned nowhere else in the Bible, but presumably denote God's dwelling place. Each chariot is accompanied by distinctly colored horses (the AV and RV translate the Hebrew literally: "in the first chariot were red horses . . .") who presumably draw either coupled or as a foursome. As an instrument of war and the carriage of kings and those in power, the chariots represent the power of God. They are also described as four winds (or spirits) controlling the whole earth. In 6:6 the reader expects to learn the direction in which each chariot goes, but only three of the four chariots are mentioned and a different direction for each one is obtained only by emending the translation of the Hebrew from "go after them" to "go toward the east . . . ." The text appears to have suffered damage in the copying process. The textual damage continues into v. 7, where the Hebrew means literally "the strong ones went out" (NRSV, "when the steeds came out") and a color is expected. The phrase in v. 8 rendered as "set my spirit at rest" can mean either "have satisfied my anger [against Babylon]" or "have made my spirit settle there," the former being the more likely. Like several of the visions, the final one affirms that God's sovereignty extends over the whole earth. Even if Judah's fortunes owe their improvement to the power and generosity of the Persian Empire, that empire is ultimately nothing compared with the power of God, the ultimate arbiter of Judah's fortunes.

Historical Appendix (6:9-15)

The prophet is told to collect silver and gold from several newly arrived exiles from Babylon, to take this to a certain Josiah (whether he is a priest or a metal worker is disputed), and to make a crown or crowns. The traditional Hebrew text has the plural, but some manuscripts and ancient versions have the singular. Scholars adopt one or the other reading depending on what is their view of what is going on in the passage. Of those who favor the plural, one view is that Zerubbabel as well as Joshua is to be crowned (cf. 6:13, where a priest is at the side of a ruler). Another view is that one crown will be used for Joshua (v. 14), while the other will be kept in the temple. Among those who favor the reading "a crown . . ." are those who hold that the words "the high priest Joshua . . ." of v. 11 have replaced an original "Zerubbabel son of Shealtiel." Two groups of commentators thus believe that the text originally referred to a crowning of Zerubbabel, and several theories are proposed to explain his absence from the text as we have it. One view is that he died before the coronation took place; another, that the Persian authorities suspected an attempt to make Zerubbabel king and removed him from the scene before this happened. Bound up with these theories is the identification of Zerubbabel as the Branch (cf. 3:8; 4:6-10; 6:12). Another question is whether Joshua the high priest is actually crowned in his own right or whether the placing of the crown on his head is a prophetic acted symbol of the crowning of the Branch in the future. With so much scholarly disagreement, it is clear that certainty is impossible. Among points made by commentators, the following are noteworthy.

Meyers and Meyers 1987: 350 point out that two crowns are supported by the two materials silver and gold. They argue that one crown would not be made of two materials. If this is correct, we may suppose that the silver crown was placed upon Joshua's head and that the gold crown was to be kept until it could be placed in the (or a future) temple. Van der Woude 1984: 116 emphasizes that the Hebrew word for temple in 6:12-14 is *hekal* and not *bayit* (house), as in 4:9. This leads him to deny any link between the building of the house (temple) at 4:9 and the building of the temple at 6:13. The reference to the Branch in v. 12 (as in 3:8) is thus to a future coming ruler who will inaugurate a new age, which will include building a new temple. In favor of this line of interpretation is the fact that the Jewish community living among the ruins of Jerusalem can hardly have thought of the restoration as already complete. They could only entertain hopes and act out prophetic signs in order to confirm and strengthen those hopes.

A Question about Fasting (7:1-7)

The incident in this passage is dated to Darius's fourth year, to 518 BC, three years before the completion of the temple. It must be remembered that the temple was an open courtyard or courtyards whose holy place, or sanctuary, was probably the only roofed building. It was possible, therefore, for worship to take place in the temple before the sanctuary had been completed. This explains the questions directed to the priests of the temple before its completion. Its services were already, at least partially, in operation. The identity of the bearers of the question about fasting is problematic. Sharezer and Regemmelech are evidently Babylonian names; the Hebrew which mentiones Bethel (7:2) is sufficiently awkward for the plausible suggestion to have been made that Bethel should be combined with Sharezer to form a personal name. This leaves uncertainty as to whether a delegation comes from the northern sanctuary of Bethel or whether the delegation is a Babylonian one.

Unless political conclusions are drawn (e.g., about rivalry between Bethel and Jerusalem), the origin of the questioners is secondary to the answer given about fasting in the fifth month(to commemorate the burning of Jerusalem, Jer 52:12-13) and the seventh month (in memory of the murder of Gedaliah, Jer 41:1-3). The answer is addressed not only to the questioners but to all the "people of the land" (either all the inhabitants of Judah, or the descendants of those not exiled to Babylon, in which case a particular group is being targeted for judgment). The reply, in the spirit of the "former prophets," is that religious observances are valuable only if undertaken with the right motives and in the right spirit. The implication is that fasts and festivals during the exile (v. 5) were not carried out in the right spirit, and that this behavior was no better than that of the generation whose indifference to God caused the destruction of Jerusalem and the exile.

Further Elaboration (7:8-14)

Some commentators take 7:8-14 with 7:4-7. Certainly the passage elaborates the "reply" of vv. 4-7 with particular stress on the need for kindness and mercy, and support for the poor and needy. The implied pessimism of the passage, that the people are still indifferent to God in spite of the improvement in their fortunes, complements the message of the visions, which sees God as the only agency that can truly purify the land (cf. 3:9; 5:11).

Jerusalem's Future (8:1-8)

In ch. 8 the phrase "Thus says the LORD" occurs ten times (vv. 2, 3, 4, 6, 7, 9, 14, 19, 20, 23), a "decalogue of promises" (Driver 1906: 220). Whether this is fortuitous or a deliberate device is unknown. In vv. 1-8 the repeated phrase highlights the promises to Jerusalem, that it will be prosperous in the sense of being populous and joyful. The picture of the city's (few) open spaces (NRSV, "streets") being full of boys and girls playing is especially evocative. The hopes expressed in these verses contrast with the implied pessimisms of 7:8-14.

Further Reassurance (8:9-17)

Whether or not this passage is a sermon, perhaps delivered in the uncompleted temple, or a set of prophetic oracles, it links the work on the temple with the hope of an imminent prosperity that will contrast signally with an immediately preceding period of economic depression. This kind of thinking is deeply rooted in the covenant ideology of the ancient Near East and finds expression in OT passages such as Deut 28:1-4. No one living in today's world can deny a link between morality and the wider environment; the destruction of the latter and the grotesque differences in wealth between the First and the Two Thirds worlds have their roots in human greed and inhumanity. However, as many psalms indicate with grave honesty, there is not always an automatic link between faithful service to God and material blessing. Was Zechariah right to attribute the recent problems of the community (8:10) to its neglect of the temple? We cannot say. We can only try honestly to look for "answers" to the specific problems that face us, in the hope that if we get things wrong God will weave our errors into a wider pattern of ultimate good.

More on Fasting (8:18-19)

It has been suggested that these verses are the actual answer to the question about fasting posed in 7:1-3 in the fifth and seventh months, although most commentators do not follow this line. The passage could well be a prophetic answer to another query about fasting. The fasts of the fourth and tenth months commemorated respectively the breaching of Jerusalem's wall (2 Kgs 25:3-5) and the beginning of the siege of Jerusalem (2 Kgs 25:1). The proclamation that these should no longer be fasts but become occasions of joy and gladness is a striking way of saying that the past is less important than the opportunities presented by the present and the future, especially a present and future placed trustingly in God's hands. It helps Zechariah's message of hope to achieve a fitting climax.

Jerusalem's Universal Appeal (8:20-23)

The closing verses move the focus from Jerusalem as the recently ruined capital of the small group within the vast Persian Empire, to a vision of the city as the center of the hopes of the nations. The justice and compassion to others that God seeks from his people (7:8-10; 8:16-17) are qualities longed for by all who desire a peaceful world. If God's people can manifest those qualities, they will become a beacon and magnet for other nations, who will want to serve Israel's God. Whatever may have been the disagreements about building or not rebuilding the temple among the postexilic community in Jerusalem, these were ultimately not simply local disagreements. We owe it to prophetic insight that they were also perceived to have universal and eschatological implications.

Introduction to Zechariah 9–14

If most commentators agree that chs. 9–14 come from a different prophet (or prophets) and period (or periods) than chs. 1–8, agreement ends when it actually comes to dating the chapters. Datings from the late sixth to the late fourth centuries are confidently maintained, with the supporting arguments depending on detailed aspects of interpretation of particular passages. The method adopted in what follows will be to indicate where appropriate the major issues of dating that arise in connection with each passage discussed.

Oracles against Israel's Neighbors (9:1-8)

In these verses mention is made of Hadrach (a place in northern Syria, sixteen miles south of Aleppo), Damascus, Hamath, Tyre, Sidon, Gaza, Ekron, Ashkelon, and Ashdod. These places, it is affirmed, will be punished by God. Their ability to harm God's people will be ended, and they will be joined to Judah and enjoy God's protection. The main issue of interpretation is whether this is a generalized vision for the future, or whether it mirrors particular historical circumstances. Those favoring the latter view suggest an event such as Alexander the Great's conquest of Syria and Palestine following his defeat of the Persians at the battle of Issus in 333 BC. Certainty is impossible. Even if it comes from a different prophet/period, the passage complements chs. 1–8 in proclaiming the universal scope of the God whose special concern is with the people of Judah.

The Coming King (9:9-10)

9:9 is probably the best-known verse in Zechariah on account of its being cited in Matt 21:5 and John 12:15 in connection with Jesus' triumphal entry into Jerusalem. Who the speaker is depends on whether the translation of the

Hebrew, "I will cut off," or the Greek, "He will cut off" (so the NRSV), is read at the beginning of v. 10. If the Hebrew is followed, the speaker is God; if the Greek, it is a prophet or (so Elliger 1959: 149) a chorus. This decision also affects the understanding of the role of the coming king. The "I" translation implies that it is God who will make wars to cease, thus establishing a peaceful world over which the king will then rule, while the "he" translation means that the king will first defeat all enemies and then preside over the peace. Which of these views is correct further depends on the translation of the words rendered "triumphant and victorious" by the NRSV in v. 9. The first word, *ṣaddiq*, means "just" or "righteous" and is rendered this way by the AV, RV, and NIV. The second word, literally "saved," is translated "having salvation" by the AV and RV.

It is difficult to decide which line to follow and best to be aware of the two possibilities. What is absolutely clear from the passage is that at a time when Jerusalem has no king, a future king is promised, the language undoubtedly drawing upon hints in the OT about coronation rituals (see 1 Kgs 1:33, where Solomon is made to ride on David's mule). However, what is envisaged is not just a king for Jerusalem, nor a renewal or enlargement of David's empire. The authority of the king will extend "to the ends of the earth," and its purpose will be to put into effect the peace and justice that only God can bestow.

Revenge for Judah (9:11-17)

This very difficult passage is joined to the two preceding verses by the second person feminine singular pronoun "you," referring to "daughter of Jerusalem" (9:9). Its subject matter, however, could hardly be different from that of vv. 9-10, with the focus not upon a universal peaceful reign of a king but upon Judah's and Ephraim's being instruments of war that God will use against their enemies. The language of victory over foes in v. 15 is problematic for many modern readers. Two phrases call for special comment. "The blood of my covenant with you" (Heb. translation, the blood of your [feminine singular] covenant) may be an allusion to the covenant ceremony recorded in Exod 24:3-8 or to Israelites who laid down their lives fighting on behalf of the covenant people. Van der Woude 1984: 179 interprets the phrase in terms of the sufferings of the covenant community in the exile. In any case, the point is that God is faithful to the people of the covenant made with him, and will set their prisoners free and deliver the people from their enemies.

The phrase "your sons, O Greece" has aroused much discussion about the date of the passage. Most probably the phrase is an addition from the time after 333 BC when Judah was under the hegemony of the successors of Alexander the Great. However, if the passage is regarded as original, two possibilities arise: first, that the whole passage is to be dated to the period after 333 BC; second, that the passage dates from the Persian period (540-333), during which time the Greeks were often at war with Persia.

Sheep without a Shepherd (10:1-2)

The point of these verses seems to be that the people, perhaps during a time of drought, have sought hope and guidance not from God but from the practitioners of the occult (10:2). This is because the people lack proper leadership, the shepherd being a well-known symbol in the ancient Near East for the king. The oracle, which is impossible to date, urges the people to turn to God and regrets the lack of a suitable leader.

The Restoration of the People (10:3-12)

The interpretation of this passage depends upon the identification of the "shepherds" and "male goats" (NRSV, "leaders") in 10:3. Are they foreign kings and rulers who have oppressed Judah or are they Judah's own leaders who have failed the people (cf. 10:1-2)? Advocates of both views can be found among the commentators. In favor of the view that Judah's leaders are meant is the fact that a prominent theme throughout Zechariah 9–11 is leadership within Judah, in 9:9-10, 10:1-2, and (see below) 11:4-17. The likely sense is therefore that God will punish the existing leaders and, because of his special concern for Judah, will produce the leadership (the cornerstone, the tent peg, and the battle bow of 10:4) from the house of Judah. The NRSV renders the Hebrew "from him," that is, the house of Judah, as "from them" in v. 4 to avoid gendered language. However, it is not simply the new leaders who will deliver Judah. A whole series of promises spoken by God in the first person ("I will strengthen" and "I will bring back" in v. 5; see also vv. 8, 10, and 12) make it clear that only God's power will suffice to gather the people from their places of exile in ways that recall the exodus (v. 11). This, again, is a passage that cannot be dated. The similarities with Isaiah 40–55 are obvious, yet there is no mention of Babylon! We have to be satisfied with ignorance.

Destruction of All That Is Proud (11:1-3)

These difficult verses center on three regions famed for their natural qualities: Lebanon with its cedars and Cilician firs (NRSV, "cypresses"; cf. Zohary 1982: 106-7), Bashan (today the Golan Heights) with its evergreen oaks, and the Jordan valley with its forested thickets, the home of lions. At its simplest, the passage is saying that these areas will be stripped of the features that make them special. What is not clear is who will be responsible. Some commentators regard the destruction as a result of war, others as a clearing of forested land to allow more returning exiles to settle. A comparison with Isa 2:13, which mentions the fate of Lebanon's cedars and Bashan's oaks on the day of the LORD, suggests that the verses are directed against natural features that arouse awe among humans. These features will not be able to withstand the might and majesty of God when he acts against all things in which humans glory apart from God.

Good and Bad Shepherds (11:4-17)

The allegory of the shepherds in Zechariah seems to have knowledge of the similar allegories in Jer 23:1-4 and Ezek 34:1-31, but whereas those passages, having condemned the bad shepherds (rulers) of Israel, promise that God will himself shepherd his people and raise up for them faithful shepherds, Zech 11:4-17 can only promise a future bad shepherd. The reason for this pessimistic view and the identification of the bad shepherd are not known.

The allegory begins with God commanding the prophet (reading "the LORD said to me" instead of "Thus said the LORD my God" in 11:4) to become a shepherd of the flock doomed to slaughter by the actions of their existing leaders, as described in v. 5. V. 6, if not a later gloss, is a parenthesis, and the action continues in v. 7 with the prophet taking the two staves carried by a shepherd, one for warding off wild animals and one for directing the sheep. The NRSV is probably wrong in translating that the prophet acted "on behalf of the sheep *merchants*" (v. 7). The admittedly awkward "oppressed of the flock" (NIV) is better. The meaning of the staff named "Favor" appears to be explained when it is broken in v. 10. It symbolizes an agreement with the surrounding nations to enable the people to live in peace. The staff named "Unity" (see v. 14) symbolizes the desirability of unity between Judah and the Northern Kingdom, Israel. These actions of the prophet are acted signs, designed to convey to the leaders of the people what God requires them to do.

The reference to "the three shepherds" in 11:8 is highly problematic. Some commentators regard the phrase as a later gloss, while others identify three Israelite or foreign rulers, from Saul, David, and Solomon at one extreme to Seleucus IV, Heliodorus, and Demetrius I (in the period 185 to 150 BC) at another extreme. While no attempt will be made here to identify the three shepherds, they do appear to be important in the allegory; otherwise there is no reason for the prophet to resign dramatically from his post. The "disposing" of the three shepherds may be a further piece of acted symbolism.

The symbolic ending of the prophet's role as shepherd is further demonstrated when the merchants (11:11 in the NRSV follows the Greek here; the Hebrew rendering is "the oppressed of the flock") give him a paltry wage (thirty shekels of silver), which he throws either into the treasury or, as some commentators suggest, into the furnace that melts down precious metals. This passage is quoted in Matt 27:9-10 (with some variations from what is found here, and ascribed to Jeremiah!) in connection with the money paid to Judas Iscariot to betray Jesus. The second staff is broken.

The final symbolic act involves the prophet taking the implements of the worthless shepherd (what they are or how they indicate worthlessness is not specified) to indicate the grim time that faces Judah under such leadership. If the whole passage is extremely pessimistic, its element of hope is that God is aware of and not indifferent to the sufferings of his people. He is afflicted in their affliction (Isa 63:9, NRSV mg.) and will not ultimately forsake them.

War, Mourning, and Hope (12:1–13:1)

There is disagreement among commentators about whether 12:1 to 13:6 is a unit or whether it should be broken into smaller units such as 12:1, 2-9, 10-14; 13:1, 2-6. Certainly 12:1 could be an originally separate (or fragmentary) piece of material including as it does a poetic hymnic clause similar to what is found in Amos 4:13. The passage then describes a divine action in which Jerusalem will be besieged and God strikes the horses and riders of Jerusalem's enemies with panic. In 12:2 it is not clear whether Judah will actually take part in the siege against Jerusalem or will also be affected by the siege. At any rate, after God's intervention Judah will join in the battle and will benefit from divine help (vv. 5-7). Commentators who see Judah as being initially against Jerusalem then seek social or historical circumstances when this might have been so; but such conclusions, drawn from a passage which has probably been expanded by numerous glosses, are precarious. The repeated formula "on that day" (vv. 3, 4, 6, 8, 9, 11, 13:1) indicates that future, eschatological, events are being referred to, and that the passage is using the themes of battle and victory to assert the ultimate triumph of God's purposes.

Following the victory (12:9) there will be a period of reflection and mourning (v. 10), centering on someone pierced. This passage is quoted in John's passion narrative as "They will look on the one whom they have pierced" (John 19:37) and may be alluded to in Rev 1:7. The Hebrew translation reads "they will look upon me, whom they pierced," the verb translated "pierced" having the sense of "thrusting through with a sword (or javelin)"; see 1 Sam 31:4, where Saul requests his armor bearer to thrust him through with a sword. It is hard to see what it could mean to have pierced through God, and if this were the correct text we would expect the continuation to say that they shall mourn "for me" and weep bitterly "over me," whereas the rendering of the Hebrew is "for him" in both cases. Modern versions mostly prefer "look on him" or "look on the one," which is apparently read by some Hebrew manuscripts. Various attempts have been made to identify the pierced one, with the lack of agreement indicating that the problem is insoluble. It is also difficult to know why the inhabitants of Jerusalem should have pierced (or killed) someone for whom they now mourn with an intensity that deeply affects families (vv. 12-14) and rivals the (pagan?) mourning for Hadad-rimmon, assuming the latter to have been a fertility god whose "death" was mourned annually. Attempts to explain the piercing range from the theory that the king in preexilic Israel was ritually "killed" and "resurrected" at a New Year festival to the view that a child had been offered in sacrifice to God as a plea for deliverance from defeat (cf. 2 Kgs 3:27). Again, no convincing solution has been proposed. It is just possible that the "they" of "they have pierced" refers not to the inhabitants of Jerusalem but to Jerusalem's enemies, in which case the pierced one would be a leader in Jerusalem or a figure representative of all those who had perished.

Looking at the passage generally, one can say that even symbolic or eschatological battles must have casualties on the "winning" side and that no contest with evil can be fought without cost. Sometimes the most bitter battles are fought *within* a community, and prophetic figures persecuted or even killed before that are later seen to have been right. Whatever it may mean, 12:10-14 are a necessary complement to all the language in Zechariah and elsewhere in the Bible about war, even when that language is figurative or indicates God's victory over evil. War involves great pain and suffering, especially for the innocent people who happen to be in the wrong place when wars are fought. Language about war must never be glib, and it is arguable that in 13:1 it is not the victory but the mourning that opens the fountain by which the house of David and Jerusalem's inhabitants cleanse themselves of sin and impurity.

No Idols or Prophets (13:2-6)

Commentators are divided over whether this passage is part of what precedes or whether it consists of two separate oracles (13:2-3 and 4-6). The continuation of the introductory formula "on that day" from the previous chapter (vv. 2, 4) can support either position. There is also disagreement about the significance of the harsh words uttered against the prophets. Are *all* prophets condemned, or only "false prophets"? If all are condemned, does the passage come from a time when predictive prophecy was under great suspicion or a period when oral prophecy was being replaced by scribal interpretation of older prophetic texts? Or is the point that "on that day," that is, in the eschatological future, there will be no need for prophecy so that anyone claiming to be or suspected of being a prophet will by definition be a deceiver? Each of these possibilities has found advocates. However, the view that connects the saying with the eschatological future is probably closest to the text.

What can be said with reasonable certainty is that the passage provides incidental information about the dress adopted by (some) prophets, and that it appears to draw upon other parts of the OT. The mantle (13:4) reminds one of the cloak (the same word in Hebrew) worn by Elijah and inherited by Elisha (2 Kgs 2:8, 13), while Elijah's garment is hairy (2 Kgs 1:8; cf. also the description of John the Baptist in Mark 1:6 as clothed with camel's hair). The chest wounds (v. 6; Hebrew meaning, "these wounds between your hands") are usually taken to be self-inflicted wounds administered during periods of ecstasy (cf. 1 Kgs 18:28).

The most obvious OT passage alluded to is Amos 7:14, where Amos's denial that he is a prophet by profession, as opposed to by divine call, becomes here an absolute denial of ever having been a prophet. Other passages which may be alluded to include Deut 18:20-21 and Jer 23:30-40. The problem of distinguishing between true and false prophecy, so evident in Deuteronomy and Jeremiah, may well be behind this vision of the dispensability of prophecy in the eschatological future.

The Smitten Shepherd (13:7-9)

At first sight, these verses (probably in poetry) do not belong with 13:2-6; and many commentators link them with 11:17. There, it will be remembered, the sword is invoked to strike (there is no actual verb in the Hebrew) the worthless shepherd, while here (13:7) the sword is called upon to awake and to strike (there is a verb in the Hebrew here!) God's shepherd and associate. The NEB actually transposes 13:7-9 to follow 11:17. While it is possible that 13:7-8 originally belonged with 11:17, it can also be argued that these verses make sense following 13:1-6. In the eschatological future when prophets will be unnecessary, human leaders (shepherds) will also be unnecessary. All human dependencies will be drastically destroyed, the people will be leaderless, and only drastic divine action will restore the people of God (v. 9d) following a painful process of destruction and purification. Allusions to passages such as Ezek 5:1-4 (v. 8) and Hos 2:23 (v. 9d) have been plausibly suggested.

As was said in connection with 12:1-14, language about war should not be read or used glibly. The images used in 13:7-9 are alarming and violent, and it can be legitimately asked whether God can root out evil only by such drastic means. Perhaps the answer is Yes; and certainly it must be a process involving some kind of suffering. In Matt 26:31 the passage about smiting the shepherd is quoted by Jesus (cf. also John 16:32) as he faces his passion, and it thereby receives a deeper meaning. The pain and suffering necessary to root out evil are not experienced by the wicked alone. The Good Shepherd himself is smitten, and the divine bearing of the pain and suffering contribute to the creation of the people of whom God says, "They are my people."

War and Peace for Jerusalem (14:1-21)

Zechariah 14 continues the theme of chs. 12–13, of war preceding peace for Jerusalem in the eschatological future. The phrase "on that day" occurs at 14:4, 6, 8, 13, and 20, and the whole chapter begins with the statement that a day is coming (v. 1).

The "you" of 14:1 is the feminine singular in Hebrew, indicating that the city of Jerusalem is addressed. There follow descriptions of the aftermath of the fall of the city (v. 2) followed by a remarkable passage in which the feet of God are depicted as physically standing on the Mount of Olives. This divine appearance will cause the Mount of Olives to split in two from east to west, with one half going northward and the other to the south. The purpose of this drastic rearrangement of the physical geography of the Jerusalem area is not apparent, unless those commentators are correct who render v. 5 in such a way that the valley of Jerusalem (the Kidron valley?) will be stopped up. This involves retaining the consonants of the Hebrew and revocalizing them. What we are then to envisage is that the topography of the area will be flattened out (cf. v. 10). As this cataclysm occurs, as frightening as an earthquake (cf. v. 5; earthquakes are common in the region), the people will flee. Then God will arrive with his "holy ones" (either angels or God's redeemed people), and the city will enjoy perpetual day (v. 7), waters will flow east and west from Jerusalem (cf. Ezek 47:1-12), and Jerusalem will dominate a landscape that has become a plain. The city will never again be destroyed (14:11).

Those nations that fought against Jerusalem will be subjected to great plagues (14:12-15), but those who survive from the nations will come annually on pilgrimage to Jerusalem at the festival of Booths (or Tabernacles). Thus the outcome of this transformation is universal in scope, and the passage can be compared with Isa 2:2-4 (Mic 4:1-4). Yet even here there is a hint of discord in the transformed world (cf. Rev 12:7). Nations that decline to make the pilgrimage will be deprived of rain (14:17) and subjected to the plagues that afflicted Jerusalem's enemies. The special mention of Egypt in vv. 18-19 may be no more than an association in the biblical tradition between Egypt and plagues.

The closing verses (14:20-1) describe a sanctified Jerusalem in a ritual sense. Anything that could be deemed to make the city unclean, such as bells on horses, cooking utensils, or traders in the temple, will either be removed or sanctified.

Bibliography. Butterworth, M. 1992, *Structure and the Book of Zechariah,* JSOTSup 130, Sheffield: Sheffield Academic • Driver, S. R. 1906, *The Minor Prophets, Nahum, Habakkuk, Zephaniah, Haggai, Zechariah, Malachi,* Century Bible, Edinburgh: T. C. & E. C. Jack • Elliger, K. 1959, *Das Buch der zwölf kleinen Propheten,* vol. 2: *Nahum, Habakuk, Zephanja, Haggai, Sacharja, Maleachi,* ATD 25, Göttingen: Vandenhoeck & Ruprecht • Hanhart, R. 1998, *Sacharja* 1.1–8.23, BKAT 7.1, Neukirchen: Neukirchener • Jones, D. R. 1962, *Haggai, Zechariah, Malachi,* Torch Bible Commentaries, London: SCM • Mason, R. 1977, *The Books of Haggai, Zechariah and Malachi,* CBC, Cambridge: Cambridge University • Meyers, C. L., and E. M. Meyers. 1987, *Haggai, Zechariah 1–8,* AB 25B, New York: Doubleday; Meyers, C. L., and E. M. Meyers. 1993, *Zechariah 9–14,* AB 25C, New York: Doubleday • Mitchell, H. G., J. M. P. Smith, and J. A. Bewer. 1912, *A Critical and Exegetical Commentary on Haggai, Zechariah, Malachi and Jonah,* ICC, Edinburgh: T. & T. Clark • Petersen, D. L. 1995, *Zechariah 9–14 and Malachi,* OTL, London: SCM • Rudolph, W. 1976, *Haggai — Sacharja 1–8 — Sacharja 9–14 — Maleachi,* KAT 13.4, Gütersloh: Gerd Mohn • Saebø, M. 1969, *Sacharja 9–14: Untersuchungen von Text und Form,* WMANT 34, Neukirchen: Neukirchener • Smith, R. L. 1984, *Micha-Malachi,* WBC, Waco: Word • Stuhlmueller, C. 1988, *Haggai and Zechariah,* ITC, Grand Rapids: Eerdmans • van der Woude, A. S. 1984, *Zacharia,* De Prediking van het Oude Testament, Nijkerk: Callenbach • Zohary, M. 1982, *Plants of the Bible,* Cambridge: Cambridge University.

Malachi

M. Daniel Carroll R.

INTRODUCTION

In both the Jewish and Christian canons the book of Malachi is placed last among the prophets. The Christian OT closes with Malachi, which in the NT is perceived as anticipating the ministries of John the Baptist and Jesus.

Some scholars question whether "Malachi" (Heb. *mal'aki*) is a proper name. The word literally means "my messenger" (or "my angel") and appears nowhere else in the OT. The term thus could be an appellative rather than the name of a historical figure. The LXX translates "by the hand of *mal'aki*" (1:1; NRSV, "by Malachi"; cf. Hag 1:1, 3) as "by the hand of his angel" (or "his messenger"). The targum does likewise and then adds, "whose name was Ezra the scribe." In addition, the opening phrase ("An oracle. The word of the LORD") is similar to the headings of Zech 9:1 and 12:1, suggesting to some that a redactor of the Book of the Twelve (i.e., the Minor Prophets) introduced three originally independent oracles with the same phrase. Those of this persuasion usually hold that the name probably was borrowed from 3:1.

In reply, it can be said that the names of other writing prophets do not appear outside the books ascribed to them (e.g., Habakkuk). It is possible that this name is a contracted form of *mal'akiyah* ("messenger of Yahweh"; cf. *'abi*, 2 Kgs 18:2; *'abiyah*, 2 Chr 29:1). Moreover, careful comparison of Mal 1:1 with Zech 9:1 and 12:1 demonstrates some differences. For instance, the phrase in Zech 9:1 does not function as a superscription to the following material as in the other two verses, and only Mal 1:1 has "by the hand of." There is then no need to discount the possibility that Malachi could be the name of an actual prophet. Interestingly, this name would connect his ministry with that of the coming messenger of 3:1, as well as contrast it with the failures of the priests in the present (2:7).

Although the book does not provide clear clues of personal background, the textual data can be related to a general historical context. The focus on the temple and worship points to the postexilic period after the construction of the Second Temple in 515 BC. The denunciation of the corruption of the priesthood (1:6–2:9), intermarriage with other peoples (2:10-11), and the negligence of the tithe (3:8-10) find an echo in Ezra 9–10 and Nehemiah 13. Interpreters differ regarding whether the prophet's ministry would have prepared the way for the Ezra-Nehemiah reforms, followed Ezra but preceded Nehemiah's arrival (assuming the canonical order reflects the historical sequence), or occurred between Nehemiah's two visits to Palestine. Perhaps the most that can be said is that Malachi's activities probably can be located sometime within the first half of the fifth century.

Recent studies have sought to ascertain the social setting of the book of Malachi with more precision. Some try to position Malachi in relationship to the attitudes toward priests expressed in the Priestly Code (Leviticus 19–26) and Deuteronomy (presupposing a late date for both) and utilize Malachi as a hypothetical reconstruction of the history of the priesthood; others identify a conflict in the text between various priestly factions. The terminology in Malachi, however, does not lend itself to this sort of exactitude (see further at 2:4-9).

The suggested time frame places Malachi within the Persian period. The term for "governor" in 1:8 (*peḥah;* cf. Hag 1:1; Neh 5:14) could refer to the imperial appointee over the province of Judah. The book's concern for intermarriage and the temple perhaps can be linked to exigencies of Persian foreign policy (Hoglund 1992), although the particulars are difficult to pinpoint. Where did the Persian authorities stand in relation to the mixing of ethnic groups through marriage? Were they encouraging this practice to improve the productivity of resettled peoples, or were they discouraging it in order to better control the distinct populations in the region? Would the Persians strategically support the Jews' passion to maintain the temple as part of a larger effort to buttress Palestine against internal unrest and foreign intervention (which at that time would have come from Egypt or Greece)? More research is needed before Malachi can be placed confidently against a clear sociohistorical background.

The book, excluding the epilogue (4:4-6 [Heb 3:22-24]), can be divided into six disputations or diatribes (1:2-5; 1:6–2:9; 2:10-16; 2:17–3:5; 3:6-12; 3:13–4:3 [Heb 3:13-21]), in which an accusation is made by God or the prophet, and then the people respond. This interaction reveals a people under foreign rule, who question the divine hand of blessing and God's justice while also defending their manner of life and worship. These disputations can be structured chiastically, with the concerns of the first mirrored by the sixth, the second by the fifth, and the third by the fourth (Hugenberger 1994: 24-25).

The prophetic word centers on the person of God. The book is full of divine first person speech. The disputations underscore the importance of the deity's name (1:6, 11, 14; 2:2, 5; 3:16) and his sovereign activity in the past, present, and future. The people are to fear Yahweh, honor him in the cult, and reflect covenant values in their daily lives. Their religious leaders are held especially accountable as those who should model the virtues God desires. This interest in the priesthood and proper ritual could suggest that the prophet came from priestly circles.

The theme of worship and its connection with the call for exemplary leadership make the book of Malachi ever relevant. Today there is much interest in liturgical renewal. Liberation theology, for example, has stressed the inseparable link between worship and praxis. What is more, in an age of so much scandal among those in positions of religious authority, many look for those who might represent integrity and sound moral values.

Critics have sometimes suggested that a number of verses in the book are secondary additions. These will be pointed out at the appropriate places, but the comments will concentrate on the canonical form of the prophetic text.

COMMENTARY

The Heading (1:1)

The Hebrew word translated "oracle" is *massa'*. Many understand this term, which is derived from the root "to lift up," to convey an idea akin to "to lift up the voice" — in this context, a prophetic utterance (cf. 2 Kgs 9:25-26). Other commentators prefer the rendering "burden" ("that which is lifted up") and suggest that this nuance expresses the weightiness, so to speak, of the message of judgment which is to follow.

This divine message comes through the prophet and is directed at Israel. "Israel" (1:1, 5; 2:11, 16; 4:4 [Heb. 3:22]) connotes the entire nation in Palestine after the exile. "Judah" (2:11; 3:4), "Jacob" (2:12), and "children of Jacob" (3:6) are also used, but apparently in these cases, too, the people of God as a whole are in view.

The First Disputation: The Meaning of Divine Love (1:2-5)

If the term "oracle" inherently has a nuance of dread, then the first verse of this section comes as a surprise. Yahweh declares his love for Israel. Indeed, it is Edom who will be judged. Why then do the people respond by questioning this divine love (1:2a)?

Historically the answer could lie in the nation's discouragement with postexilic realities. Hope in a restored nation with a glorious temple under their own king (Ezekiel 40–44; Haggai 2; Zechariah 1–8) had been met with disappointment. Had disillusionment or indifference affected even the worship of God? The reader as yet does not know but is quickly confronted by Yahweh reaffirming his love in two ways — by an appeal to tradition and then to a historical event (1:2b-4).

The patriarchal narratives said that God had preferred Jacob over his brother Esau (Gen 25:19-34; 27:1-29). The love-hate contrast spoken of here traditionally has been understood in the comparative sense of regarding one over the other (cf. Gen 29:30-33; Matt 10:37; Luke 14:26). Through their ancestor Jacob, Israel was God's elect, not because of any inherent worth but as a manifestation of his grace (Deut 7:7-8).

According to the biblical account Esau was not eliminated from divine concern (Gen 27:30-40; cf. Deut 2:4-5), but Edom, his descendants, did become enemies of Israel. Several prophets decried Edom's complicity in the Babylonian destruction of Jerusalem and spoke of a day of reckoning (Isa 34:5-17; Jer 49:7-22; Ezek 25:12-14, 35:1-15; Joel 3:19 [Heb. 4:19]; Obad 9-14). The words of 1:3-4 also reflect the language of covenant curses. Perhaps, then, the "hate" is stronger than simply a rhetorical device of comparison. Malachi proclaims that God had already judged Edom. Scholars have associated this event either with a possible Babylonian invasion of Edom sometime after 586 BC or a supposed later Nabatean destruction in the fifth century, but it is impossible to specify to what the prophet refers. This divine decree on Edom is proof of Yahweh's love, a love that Israel will eventually recognize. In the future doubts would be transformed into confession of the awesomeness of Yahweh, who is great in mercy and judgment over all nations (v. 5).

These opening verses set the tone for the rest of the book. The series of interchanges between Yahweh and the people aim to move Israel to a different perception of God and thus to another quality of life and worship. Sometimes this goal is placed against the broader canvas of universal significance, as Yahweh's majesty extends beyond the confines of Palestine (1:5, 11, 14). Divine love is not simply sentimental affection; it is the expression of a covenant relationship by Yahweh *Ṣᵉba'ot* (NRSV, "LORD of hosts") that demands commitment. To affirm love for Israel, therefore, does not mean that this people will not be judged. Israel has been and will be severely chastised, but punishment will not be unceasing as it had been for Edom (cf. 3:6). The sixth disputation (3:13–4:3 [Heb 3:21]) returns to the theme of the judgment of the wicked and the vindication of the righteous.

Is the characterization of Israel as a dissenting and disobedient people a fair description of the actual state of affairs? Or does it, literally, put words into their mouths for its own purposes? From the perspective of this book and other postexilic texts (e.g., Ezra and Nehemiah), Yahweh was pleased with neither Israel as a whole nor significant elements within that society.

The Second Disputation: Accusations of Inadequate Worship (1:6–2:9)

This section can be divided into two parts. The first details the cultic practices that Yahweh condemns (1:6-14); the second describes the punishment of the priesthood for failing to fulfill properly their traditional mandate (2:1-9). If the opening lines of the book declare Yahweh's love, this disputation will make abundantly clear that what is expected in return is proper worship. This concentration on the cult explains the narrowing down of the addressees to the priests. The first part of this section can be further broken down into two parallel segments (1:6-11; 1:12-14). Each opens with an indictment, relates Yahweh's reaction, and closes with a contrast between Israel and the nations.

The first segment continues the metaphor of the familial relationship hinted at in 1:1-5 but broadens the imagery to underscore the seriousness of the charge by juxtaposing son/father (cf. Exod 4:22; Deut 32:6; Hos 11:1) with servant/master and by the using the title Yahweh *Ṣᵉbā'ōt* to refer to Israel's God (cf. 1:4). The elevenfold appearance of this title in this section (1:6, 8, 9, 10, 11, 13, 14; 2:2, 4, 7, 8) emphasizes that it is the omnipotent God who demands respect. The term "name," which alludes to his character, occurs eight times (1:6 [twice], 11 [three times], 14; 2:2, 5). These various literary devices demonstrate that it is the person of Yahweh who is dishonored by Israel's worship.

The priests are accused of despising his name by offering inappropriate animals for sacrifice (1:6-8a), something forbidden in the law (Lev 22:13-33; Deut 15:21). Though the complaint is met with counterclaims, Yahweh expresses his frustration by declaring that no human governor would countenance such imperfect gifts. How much less Yahweh *Ṣᵉbā'ōt!* He would rather suspend all cultic activity than continue with this hypocritical charade (1:8b-10).

This initial segment concludes with the sharp contrast between Israel's rejected worship and the pure offerings of the nations (1:11). Because the universalism of this verse and v. 14 seems to contradict the book's preoccupation with Israel, some consider all or parts of vv. 11-14 a secondary addition. The parallel structures of 1:6-11 and 1:12-14, however, demonstrate that these lines are integral to the argument. In addition, this breadth of vision had already been referred to in v. 5. What is the import of turning once more to the nations?

There are two interrelated issues of interpretation in 1:11. First, to whom does this verse refer? Second, since the most disputed clause has no verb, should it be translated by a present ("my name *is* great among the nations"; NRSV, NEB, NJPS) or a future tense ("my name *will be* great among the nations"; KJV, NIV)? Those who opt for the present tense fall into two groups. Some consider this an allusion to diaspora Jews (e.g., the Elephantine colony in Egypt) or to contemporary Gentile proselytes. Others suggest that here is either a recognition of a growing monotheism among other nations (note "the God of heaven" in the Persian edicts of Ezra 5–7) or the acknowledgment that sacrifices offered in sincerity to a high god by non-Jews would be acceptable in God's sight. These possibilities, however, do not fit well into the text's message. Neither the (sometimes syncretistic) worship by Jews elsewhere nor the earnest adoration of others to a god of any another "name" can cohere with a book so stridently concerned about the proper veneration of Yahweh *Ṣᵉbā'ōt* at the temple in Jerusalem.

A better option is to translate the phrase with the future tense. The adoration of Yahweh by the nations in the latter days is a common prophetic theme (Isa 2:1-4; 19:18-23; 25:6-9; 66:18-23; Zeph 2:11; Zech 8:20-23). Whereas in 1:5 the reference to the nations serves as a motivation to respond to Yahweh, here the future worship by other peoples is a rebuke of Israel's present practices. The mention of pure worship in the future also anticipates warnings to consider the impending consequences of improper worship and its purification in that "day" (3:1-4).

In the next segment (1:12-14) some of the same vocabulary and themes are repeated, but the indictment is more explicit. The priests "sniff" at the LORD's altar and allow others to keep more fitting animals for themselves (vv. 13-14a). Likewise, the notion of worldwide acknowledgment of God is reiterated and broadened: Yahweh *Ṣᵉbā'ōt* is a great king (note the use of "great," vv. 5, 11), who will be feared among the nations. Many passages extol Yahweh as king of Israel (e.g., Isa 33:22; 43:15; 44:6) and over all the earth (e.g., Pss 47:2, 7-8 [Heb. 47:3, 8-9]; 95:3), and several non-Israelites in the biblical tradition, such as Rahab (Joshua 2), Ruth, the sailors and the Ninevites (Jonah 1, 3), and foreign rulers (Dan 2:47; 4:37; 6:26-27), had feared Yahweh. Someday the entire world would praise the sovereign king (1:14b). There could be no greater condemnation of Israel than this stark contrast with her contemptible worship.

2:1-9 continue Yahweh's indictment of the priests. The text returns to the themes of God's glory (v. 2; cf. 1:6) and his name, but turns now to specify the judgment on the religious leaders. These verses can be subdivided into two parts. 2:1-3 detail the curse that will come upon the priests, while 2:4-9 appeal to tradition to demonstrate how far they have strayed from the ideals of service to God.

The notion of curse (cf. 1:14) points to covenant language and anticipates 2:4-9. The effect of the curse will be fourfold, all of which would disqualify the priests: their pronouncements of blessing (Num 6:23-27) will be negated and the priestly lineage (NRSV, "offspring"; lit. "seed") terminated; they will be made unclean by contact with dung and removed from the holy place like the offal of sacrificial animals (Lev 4:11-12; 8:17; 16:27).

Instead of listing punishments, the next pericope mentions Levi and a covenant as the basis of divine accusation. Some understand these verses to be making a moral distinction between different groups of religious leaders — more particularly, contrasting the faithfulness of the Levites (hence the appeal to Levi) and the waywardness of the priests who traced their line back to Zadok. The reference to purifying the descendants of Levi in 3:3 makes this view problematic. Others attempt to place Malachi within a possible historical development of the priesthood by seeking certain technical distinctions in the book's vocabulary in comparison with other passages in the Pentateuch and elsewhere. Whatever the plausibility of such differentiation, the text is either unaware of them or not concerned (O'Brien 1990; Glazier-McDonald 1987: 73-78; Verhoef 1987: 258-61).

A simpler solution is that 2:4-9 are an appeal to a venerable tradition. This allusion to an ideal past (cf. 1:2-5), even as the previous reference to a different future (1:11, 14), serves to highlight the deficiencies of the present. Levi, the text asserts, had a different attitude toward God's name and righteously fulfilled his duties as the messenger of Yahweh. What is this covenant of Levi, which is mentioned three times? The making of this covenant is nowhere explicitly cited in the OT, although it is presupposed in Jer 33:20-21 and Neh 13:29 (cf. Exod 32:26-29; Deut 33:8-11). The language here is similar to that of the covenant with Phinehas the son of Aaron

(Num 25:11-13). The point is to stress the failures of the priests in comparison with the zeal of those of an earlier time. Even as they despise the things of God (1:7, 12), the priests will be despised before the nation.

The fifth disputation (3:6-12) will come back to the issue of cultic improprieties. There, too, God's dealings will impact the nations. The next two disputations turn their attention to moral failures.

The Third Disputation: Violation of the Bonds of Marriage (2:10-16)

Because of the parallelism, most commentators agree that the "father" of 2:10 is God (instead of Abraham or another patriarch). Most also understand the "covenant of our ancestors" to be a reference to the Sinaitic covenant. An important term for this disputation is "be faithless" (vv. 10, 11, 14, 15, 16), but scholars' opinions differ regarding the nature of the violation in the passage.

Some believe these verses condemn idolatry. Therefore, the "abomination" is religious, "the daughter of a foreign god" (2:11) a goddess, and the weeping a reference to non-Yahwistic ceremonies (v. 13; cf. Ezek 8:14). In this view the "wife by covenant" (2:14) would be Yahweh, who has been deserted by Israel but does not desire the relationship to be severed (v. 16).

Though the context does have cultic overtones, a better alternative is to interpret this section as speaking of human marriage. The argument falls into two parts. First, the infidelity to the relationship with Yahweh is evidenced in marriages with women of other faiths (2:11-12). Even as Yahweh is Israel's father, those women worshiping other deities would be "daughters of a foreign god." The problem fundamentally is not ethnic but religious: no sort of syncretism was to be tolerated (Exod 34:11-16; Deut 7:3-4; cf. Ezra 9:1-6; 10:18-19; Neh 10:30; 13:23-27).

The second act of unfaithfulness is divorce: their infidelity to one another corresponds to their lack of loyalty to Yahweh (2:13-16). The gravity of this charge is underscored by Yahweh's rejection of their offerings and by the reminder that marriage is a covenant relationship (Prov 2:17; Ezek 16:8; Hugenberger 1994 — not taking "wife by covenant" to mean that the women are fellow Jews). It is not necessary to hold the two transgressions in a causal sequence, that men were divorcing their Jewish wives to marry the women of 2:11-12. This could very well be a separate violation. Acceptable worship was inseparable from an ethical commitment to the marriage relationship.

Several interpretive decisions are required to make sense of 2:15-16. To begin with, who is the "one" of v. 15? Some Jewish interpreters explain this as a reference to Abraham: "Did not the one [Abraham] do this [take Hagar, a non-Jew, for a wife]? Was not his purpose to acquire a son for the line of promise?" Israel, though, would have no such excuse and stands condemned. Others identify God as the "one" who made the woman and desires a righteous offspring from marriage (NRSV, NJPS).

Our approach distinguishes the referents of the two uses of "one" and would translate the relevant clauses in 2:15: "Did he [God] not make [them/you] one? And what did the one [God] desire?" (NRSV note). If this is correct, then the text is alluding to Gen 2:23-24 and to that primeval union as the basis of the inviolability of the marriage bond. The theme of godly children was a major concern in the postexilic community (Ezra 10:3, 44; Neh 13:23-25).

Another interpretive crux in 2:15 is the word translated "flesh" (NRSV, NIV, NEB). This represents a repointing of the term "remnant" (NRSV note; NJPS). Although this emendation would fit nicely within the creation scheme, it finds no support among the ancient versions. The "remnant of spirit was his" could mean that God had enough creative power to have given the original man more than one woman for a wife. But "spirit" *(ruaḥ)* can also mean the breath of life (Ps 104:29-30; Eccl 12:7; cf. Gen 2:7). In this case, those putting away their wives adversely affect their own lives. This term reappears twice in the next few lines, where the men are warned to watch their "breath" (NRSV, "yourselves").

Many consider 2:16 to be the strongest condemnation of divorce in the OT. The opening verb is often translated in the first person ("I hate") with God understood as the subject. This rendering, however, requires a change in the Hebrew. An alternative that coheres with the Hebrew syntax would read: "If one hates and divorces . . . then he covers his garment with violence" (cf. Hugenberger 1994). The garment can symbolize the wife (Ruth 3:9; Ezek 16:8) or the man himself (Ps 109:18). Either option underscores that divorce is destructive. What is criticized here is divorce on the grounds of mere aversion. The reprehensibleness of disregarding the covenant of marriage in this fashion is emphasized by twice mentioning divine speech with two distinct titles for God and by the repetition of the warning of v. 15b. What is *not* said is that Yahweh prohibits divorce under any circumstance (note, e.g., Exod 21:10-11; Deut 21:1-14; 24:1-4).

The Fourth Disputation: The Purification of Worship (2:17–3:5)

This disputation continues the denunciation of the nation's lifestyle and worship. The new element of Israel's retort is to question Yahweh's integrity (2:17). To the challenge "Where is the God of justice?" Yahweh answers that he is sending a messenger to prepare for his coming (3:1). Unlike Isa 40:1-11 and its proclamation of comfort, here the messenger heralds the arrival of God for judgment. Opinions differ concerning whether the "Lord" and the "messenger of the covenant" are two different individuals. The parallelism ("whom you seek"/"in whom you delight"; "will come"/"is coming") suggests that the two are one and the same. This close identification between Yahweh and his messenger or angel is not uncommon (e.g., Gen 16:7-14; Exod 3:2-5; Judg 6:11-12).

The day of his coming is to be a time of purification (cf. Amos 5:18-20; Joel 1:15; 2:1-2). There is no need to see the refining of the priests as an interpolation (3:2-4). The concern for purer offerings had been a concern earlier

(1:6-14), and the reference to "former years" could be another allusion to the idealized period of Levi's service (2:4-6). The insistence that judgment begin with the priesthood is a consistent theme of the book, as is the juxtaposition of the people's lack of morality (3:5) with the cult. This rejection of worship dissociated from ethics is a major biblical emphasis (Psalms 15; 24; Isa 1:10-20; Jeremiah 7; Hos 6:6; Amos 4:4-5; 5:21-24; Mic 6:6-8).

The Fifth Disputation: Unacceptable Offerings (3:6-12)

The concentration on worship continues, but two new elements are introduced. First, Yahweh offers the possibility of staying judgment if the people repent of their consistent hypocritical worship (cf. Deut 30:1-10; Zech 1:2-6). So desirous is Yahweh of change that he invites the nation to test him (cf. Exod 4:1-9; Judg 6:36-40; Isa 7:11-12) — a surprising challenge since testing Yahweh was usually considered something negative. The second new item is the tithes. The second disputation had denounced corrupt offerings, but here the tithes for the support of temple staff are probably meant (Lev 27:30-33; Num 18:21-32; cf. Neh 10:32-39, 13:10-14).

The refusal to contribute to the temple is tantamount to robbing God (some change the term "rob" to "deceive" and thus produce a wordplay on "Jacob," 3:6; JB, NEB, NJPS). A different response would arrest covenant curses and bring blessings of agricultural bounty (Deut 28:8-14). This change in fortune would be a testimony to the nations (3:12). No longer is a reference to other peoples to spur Israel to reform (1:5, 11, 14). Transformation would make Israel a land of "delight" (contrast "no pleasure," 1:10), even as she supposedly "delights" in God.

The Sixth Disputation: Vindication of the Righteous (3:13–4:3; Heb. 3:13-21)

The beginning of this final disputation is similar to the opening of the fourth (2:17). With whom is Yahweh in dialogue? Some interpreters consider the entire passage to come from the mouth of God fearers, who voice their consternation at the apparent futility of obedience (3:14-15) but are subsequently reassured by Yahweh of divine recognition. Others who perceive the change in tone at v. 16 postulate that vv. 13-15 are an addition. The connections between these opening lines and previous disputations, however, indicate that 3:13-15 concern those who earlier questioned divine justice. Their refusal to respond properly to the challenge of 3:6-12 and this even more blatant denial of Yahweh's justice spark his final stern rebuke.

A smaller group within the nation — the God fearers, who revere his name (cf. 2:5) — now appears (3:16). They do not question Yahweh but speak only among themselves. To these God reacts favorably and promises three things (vv. 17-18) to be accomplished on that "day." First, they will be registered in a book, probably the book of life (cf. Exod 32:32-33; Ps 69:28 [Heb. 29]; Isa 4:3). Opinions differ over whether this book corresponds with the record of the deeds of all humankind (Isa 7:11-12; Isa 65:6; Dan 7:10). Second, this group will be Yahweh's special possession. This term once was applied to the entire nation (e.g., Exod 19:5; Deut 7:6), yet in the future the God fearers shall be the basis of a renewed community.

Third, in that day Yahweh will differentiate between sinners and the servants of God (contrast with 1:6; 3:14). This distinguishing between the righteous and the wicked can hark back to the first disputation (1:2-5), although here the difference is not across national boundaries but within Israel itself. 4:1-3 add that for the faithful there will be joy (not gloom, 3:14) and no participation in that judgment. (This is not the fire of purification of 3:2-4, but the common prophetic theme of judgment as a consuming fire.) They shall also experience the "sun of righteousness" (4:2). Even though this phrase has a long tradition of being interpreted as a reference to Messiah and ultimately Jesus (cf. Jer 23:5-6 with Luke 1:76-79), in context the meaning is probably that the righteousness of God will shine forth on that day of vindication (Ps 37:6; Isa 58:8). This figure could be drawn from the winged disk of the ancient Near East (however, to see here an allusion to the worship of Yahweh with solar imagery stretches the evidence).

The Epilogue (4:4-6; Heb. 3:22-24)

On the basis of vocabulary and form, some commentators see this section as a later addition designed to serve as the conclusion to the Law and Prophets in the Hebrew canon. This passage, however, is also an appropriate close to the book, reemphasizing as it does the demand for service and worship without duplicity in order to avoid judgment on the day of the LORD.

The call to observe "the teaching of Moses, the statutes and ordinances" (4:4) points back at least to what was received at Sinai/Horeb (Exod 19:1-8; 24:3-8). In the postexilic period these traditions clearly were in document form (Ezra 7:6; Neh 8:1; cf. Josh 8:30-32). To this final mandate for covenant faithfulness is added a warning connected with Elijah (4:5-6). That this prophet literally would come again is made possible by the report of his being miraculously taken away before tasting death (2 Kgs 2:1-11). Joel also declares that prophetic activity would accompany the day of the LORD (2:28-32 [Heb. 3:1-5]).

The similarities between 3:1-2 and 4:5 suggest that Elijah is that messenger of the covenant. On the one hand, his mission reinforces both the judgment of 3:1-5, 16–4:3 and the notion of "turning" (or "returning") to God in 3:7-11. On the other hand, the nature of his ministry is difficult to specify: Is Elijah to reconcile the generations within the families of Israel (cf. 2:10-16), or is he to seek continuity of covenant fidelity with earlier times (cf. 2:5-6; 3:4)? Either way, 4:6 anticipates the same powerful effect as when that prophet forced Israel to confess that Yahweh alone was God (1 Kings 18).

In the NT John the Baptist is presented as that one who heralded the ministry of Jesus (Matt 11:11-15; Mark

9:11-13 and par.; Luke 1:17), and Elijah reappears with Moses on the Mount of Transfiguration (Mark 9:2-8 and par.). An allusion to Elijah appears also in Rev 11:3-12 in the description of the two prophets testifying before the second coming of Christ.

Bibliography. Achtemeier, E. 1986, *Nahum–Malachi,* Interpretation, Atlanta: John Knox • Baldwin, J. 1972, *Haggai, Zechariah and Malachi,* TOTC, Downers Grove, Ill.: InterVarsity • Glazier-McDonald, B. 1987, *Malachi: The Divine Messenger,* SBLDS 98, Atlanta: Scholars • Hill, A. E. 1998, *Malachi,* AB 25D, Garden City, N.Y.: Doubleday • Hoglund, K. G. 1992, *Achaemenid Imperial Administration in Syria-Palestine and the Missions of Ezra and Nehemiah,* SBLDS 125, Atlanta: Scholars • Hugenberger, G. P. 1994, *Marriage as a Covenant: A Study of Biblical Law and Ethics Governing Marriage, Developed from the Perspective of Malachi,* VTSup 52, Leiden: Brill • Kaiser Jr., W. C. 1984, *Malachi: God's Unchanging Love,* Grand Rapids: Baker • O'Brien, J. M. 1990, *Priest and Levite in Malachi,* SBLDS 121, Atlanta: Scholars • O'Brien, J. M. 1995, "Malachi in Recent Research," *CR:BS* 3:81-94 • Petersen, D. L. 1995, *Zechariah 9–14 and Malachi,* OTL, Philadelphia: Westminster • Redditt, P. L. 1995, *Haggai, Zechariah, Malachi,* NCBC, Grand Rapids: Eerdmans • Smith, R. L. 1984, *Micah–Malachi,* WBC 32, Waco: Word • Verhoef, P. 1987, *Haggai and Malachi,* NICOT, Grand Rapids: Eerdmans.

Tobit

Lester L. Grabbe

INTRODUCTION

Text

The text of Tobit exists in two major forms. One has been long known in Greek in the great uncial manuscripts of Vaticanus and Alexandrinus (= shorter text), generally represented by the English translations of the AV, RV, and RSV. In the last century, however, the discovery of the Sinaiticus manuscript presented the scholarly world with a rather different Greek text (= longer text), usually followed in the more recent English translations such as the NRSV, NEB, REB, JB, and NJB. It should be remembered, however, that the English translations are not necessarily consistent in following one particular manuscript even when they do so as a general rule. See Hanhart for critical editions of both texts. The verse numberings of the various editions and translations differ slightly; I follow the verse numberings in Hanhart. It had been thought that the book was originally written in a Semitic language, and that the Greek text was only a translation. The new Sinaiticus text looked more like a translation of the Semitic original, and most scholars have tended to see it as more original (Fitzmyer 1995a). The shorter text of Vaticanus is also in more elegant Greek and seems therefore to be a revision of a longer, Semiticized text similar to Sinaiticus (Thomas 1972).

In the 1950s it was announced that fragments of several manuscripts had been found among the Dead Sea Scrolls (DSS). These have only now been officially published (Fitzmyer 1995b). There are four manuscripts in Aramaic and one in Hebrew. It is not absolutely clear whether the original language was Hebrew or Aramaic, but scholars tend to favor Aramaic since the Sinaiticus text looks more like a translation of Aramaic than Hebrew (Thomas: 471). The Semitic manuscripts also tend to be closer to the Sinaiticus manuscript (= longer text), confirming the thesis that it is generally more original than the text of Vaticanus/Alexandrinus.

The Old Latin (OL) version is usually close to Sinaiticus and is thus a valuable aid in correcting copyist errors in the latter. In his preface to the Vulgate (Vg) edition of the book, Jerome claimed to have translated his version of Tobit from an Aramaic manuscript. If so, it may well have been a late translation from Greek; in any case, it appears that he was not particularly careful and expanded or paraphased some passages to fit his own views on such matters as celibacy and sexual practices. On the whole, though, the Vg is in the tradition of the shorter text. Some extant medieval manuscripts in Aramaic seem to be retranslations from the Greek and not close to the original. (On the various versions of Tobit, see Fitzmyer 1995a.)

Time and Place of Writing

Despite firm statements in some handbooks, the time and place in which much early Jewish literature was written are unknown or can be determined only approximately. Tobit is no exception. The story is set in the diaspora, but it begins in the land of Israel. The writer seems to have knowledge of the diaspora, though his knowledge of the geography of Mesopotamia appears to be deficient (see on 5:4-6). It could have been written almost anywhere in the ancient Near East. Egypt is presented as a very distant country (8:3), which might suggest that it was less likely as the home of the writer (though Egypt was clearly a long way from Ecbatana, wherever the story was written). Although somewhere in Syria or Mesopotamia is perhaps the most likely place of origin, there is nothing so far to rule out its having been written by a Jew living in Palestine.

The time of writing is no more certain. The author knows of the rebuilding of the temple under Zerubbabel and Joshua the high priest (14:5) around 500 BC; on the other hand, he seems to have no knowledge of its desecration under Antiochus IV (168-165 BC). This puts the composition of the book in the rather broad period between 500 and 200 BC. The book makes no reference to events during or after Alexander's conquest and shows no knowledge of Greek rule. The language of the Aramaic fragments does not look particularly early, being standard Qumran Aramaic, tending to rule out the early Persian period (though we cannot be absolutely sure that Aramaic was the original language; see under "Text" above). There does not seem to be anything to rule out a composition in the late Persian period (i.e., before 330 BC) but a date in the third century is probably more likely because of the language.

Literary Structure and Elements

The literary genre of Tobit is not so easy to ascertain as might first be thought. It has many of the features of a classic folktale or even fairy tale, but it is also a literary work with elements not normally associated with a folktale (Soll 1988; Wills 1995: 68-92). This may well be explained by its origin, which is often thought to have been a folktale (see below under "Tradition History"), but the story in its present form has been developed by the incorportion of didactic, hymnic, and prophetic elements which are not usually found in a folktale. This means that the present form of the story can be called a "Jewish novel" (Wills). The Jewish novel has characteristics in common with the Greco-Roman novel or romance (e.g., *Daphnis and Cloe*) but differs in some respects (e.g., being shorter and de-emphasizing the erotic element).

The main feature of the book is the two parallel stories of misfortune, one of Tobit and the other of Sarah. Tobias, with Raphael as his helper, is the hero who resolves both. (Soll sees three elements — Tobit's poverty, Tobit's misfortune, and Sarah's misfortune — though the first two have overlapping elements.) Yet Tobit is clearly the chief character even if he is not the chief actor. It is he who is the model of piety and who gives wise advice and religious instruction to Tobias. Thus the book of Tobit differs from the folktale model and has an aim beyond the resolution of the two misfortunes into a happy ending. The entertainment value of the story needs no defense, but it goes beyond that; it is a tale with a moral, indeed a tale with a theological message.

What strikes the modern reader is the presence of a number of ironic or satirical passages in the book. Several recent studies have seen these as a device of the author/editor (Moore 1996: 24-26; Wills: 76-83). I am not persuaded that these were consciously inserted by the final author/editor, whose concern I see as being primarily that of an earnest expounder of the pious life; rather, they are the "reader-response" of a modern audience used to seeing the dour religion of our Puritan heritage made the butt of satire and comic spoofs. There is nothing so funny as the earnest but humorless preacher who caricatures himself while failing to see the joke. I do not believe that the author/editor of Tobit saw Jewish religion and piety as a laughing matter, but that does not hinder our seeing a good deal of irony and humor in the book — irony and humor which are even more entertaining because of having found their way there unconsciously. These passages will be pointed out at the appropriate place in the commentary (e.g., 8:9-10).

References to the story of Ahiqar form a significant structural element in the present story of Tobit. Although these references are brief and allude only to the Ahiqar story, they occur at crucial points in the Tobit narrative. This intertextual perspective brings in the Ahiqar story alongside that of Tobit at these points. In the Aramaic story of Ahiqar (and the many other versions which have come down to us — see Conybeare, Harris, and Lewis 1898) he was an advisor to the Assyrian king Esarhaddon. He was betrayed by his adopted nephew Nadin and supposedly executed; however, he escaped and hid until rehabilitated and called on by the king to get him out of an international crisis. Ahiqar took his revenge on his nephew by locking him up in his own former hiding place to let him starve to death, in the meantime reciting a series of admonitions and proverbs about the proper way to live.

The story is not recited in Tobit, but the story just outlined seems more or less presupposed. The main difference is that Ahiqar is Israelite (and indeed a relative of Tobit) and thus similar to Esther, Daniel, and other Jews who attained high office in one of the great Near Eastern empires. Tobit himself works for a time as a buyer for Shalmaneser the king (1:12-15). Although he clearly does not rise as high as such other Jewish diaspora heroes as Daniel, Esther, and Joseph, for a short period of time he has a position of sufficient success to accumulate a large sum of money. Bringing in the Ahiqar story may be a way of suggesting this success in the official administration via the family rather than Tobit personally.

Tradition History

It is widely agreed that Tobit contains earlier story elements (see the summary in Deselaers 1982: 280-92; Moore 1996: 11-14). The main question is whether a single author, influenced by these earlier traditions, created a new entity which we know of as the "tale of Tobit" in much its present form or whether the present work grew up through several editions from an earlier version of the story. Three of these are "The Tale of the Grateful Dead Man," "The Bride of the Monster" (or something similar such as "The Dangerous Bride"), and the Ahiqar story. The tale of Ahiqar has already been considered above ("Literary Structure"). "The Tale of the Grateful Dead Man" is known from a variety of cultures. In outline, the story tells of a man who finds a corpse and buries it; later the spirit of the dead man appears to him and rewards him for his charitable act. In "The Bride of the Monster" or "The Dangerous Bride" the hero and his helper make a journey to the afflicted princess. On the way the hero obtains a magic sword to slay the monster afflicting the princess. In some versions, the helper is slain and brought back to life by a sacrifice on the part of the hero.

While some of these stories are in some way parallel to Tobit, this does not mean that they are the origin of elements in the Tobit story; some may be, but not necessarily all. Yet the study of these antecedents and parallels may be helpful in throwing light on aspects of Tobit. For example, Tobias's enigmatic dog has often been explained as a holdover from an earlier version even though it seems to be extraneous in the present story. Nevertheless, there is a danger in assuming hypothetical developments which are by no means certain. The present version of the story has its own structure, integrity, and message, which go behind the mere sum of possible antecedents. Any analysis of the tradition history must keep that in mind.

Various attempts have been made to sort out a tradition history of the book in which a base text is edited and expanded several times to result in the present story. The most recent such study is that of Rabenu (cf. also Deselaers), but there is presently a tendency to be unimpressed with the results of traditio-historical analysis, at least in English-speaking scholarship. The reason is that they often seem highly subjective and even speculative. The general acceptance that the text has a long history behind it does not mean that that history can easily be sorted out now. Although parallels and possible origins may be noted in the commentary, the emphasis here will be on the story of Tobit in its present form as found in the longer version (represented by the Sinaiticus and Qumran texts).

Theological Themes

Perhaps the most important aim of the book is implicit rather than explicit. This is the question of theodicy or why God allows innocent suffering. This has been a major concern of theology in the past two thousand years, but it was not so often discussed in early Jewish literature. The book of Job is the most important book on the subject and probably the most sophisticated treatment of the subject in antiquity; however, Ecclesiastes (Qohelet) also relates to the subject in its own way, and several Mesopotamian works are concerned about the problem (*Ludlul bēl nēmeqi* ["I Will Praise the Lord of Wisdom"]; *The Babylonian Theodicy;* see Lambert 1960 and *ANET*). Like Job, Tobit is an innocent sufferer who is blinded in the act of doing a good deed, and Sarah is afflicted by a demon through no fault of her own. Tobit's answer is typical of literature of this time (God will eventually put it all right) and does not recognize the deep contradictions experienced by many people in life; nevertheless, despite not having the greatness of Job, it has asked and answered the question in its own way.

Most of the explicit themes within the book serve to reinforce its theological message. One of the most important of these is that of family. Most of the actors are related (or supposedly so, such as the angel Raphael, who assumes the form of a kinsman). The question of duty to the family and responsibility to help out relatives appears several times. The need to marry those related is all-important (though it is not entirely clear whether this is with fellow Israelites generally or within one's own tribe specifically). Although the family is a social matter, it cannot be separated from the practice of religion.

An emphasis which we might find a bit puzzling is that on burial. Various passages stress the importance of proper burial not only for one's parents (4:3-4; 6:15; 14:11-13) but also for the anonymous Jews whose bodies are left in the streets (1:17-19; 2:3-8). One might think this was in some way related to an expectation of a resurrection or an afterlife, but neither of these is hinted at anywhere in the book. The general view throughout much of the OT is that there was no afterlife; although some sort of shadowy existence might continue into the underworld, it was not the full person who had ceased to exist at death. Only in a very late book such as Daniel is a resurrection envisaged, though belief in the survival of the soul after death was already around in other early Jewish writings (e.g., *1 Enoch* 22). Yet alongside the view of no afterlife, there is evidence of a cult of the dead in ancient Israel, which could mean that some believed in the survival of the dead (cf. Bloch-Smith 1992; Schmidt 1994).

Various aspects or types of Jewish piety are the subject of specific admonitions or are exemplified in the text. One of the main ones is that of almsgiving (1:16-17; 2:14; 4:8-11; 12:8-9; 14:10-11), even though that is how Tobit loses his sight. Another is burial of the dead, though this is a sort of almsgiving. Other themes are observance of the festivals (2:1-5), observance of the food laws (1:11), angelology and demonology (3:8, 17), and the Golden Rule (4:15). Other points which come up are an appeal to the authority of the Scriptures (the "book of Moses" and the prophets are specifically mentioned [1:8; 2:6; 6:13; 7:11-13; 14:3]), as well as a prophecy of the destruction of Solomon's temple and the rebuilding of a new temple (14:3-7). Although many of these points are general ones relating to the practice of Judaism, they are specifically related to the situation of Jews in the diaspora. They provide examples of how Jews can survive and even succeed while surrounded by a (potentially hostile) Gentile environment. When warned about the fall of Nineveh, Tobias takes his family east into Elam rather than west back to Palestine, probably because of the prophesied fall of Jerusalem. The ultimate goal is implied to be the return to the land, but there seems to be no hurry.

COMMENTARY

Tobit in Israel and as an Exile (Tobit 1)

This is a very important chapter because it sets the scene for the entire book. It especially establishes the character of Tobit, whose exemplary life and innocent suffering are a model of piety for Jews everywhere. Tobit is of the tribe of Naphthali, not one of the better-known tribes of Israel. This might suggest that Tobit was a real person rather than a fictional character. This is possible, but Naphthali also appears in the *Testament of Naphthali,* which is one of only two books of the *Testaments of the Twelve Patriarchs* known from Qumran. In other words, there may have been reasons, currently unknown to us, why Naphthali was a significant tribe of origin for figures in Jewish tales. Naphtali had settled in the region northwest of the Sea of Galilee (Josh 19:32-39).

Tobit's character is established by the following data:

1. Although he was part of the Northern Kingdom which rejected Davidic rule and lived near the cult site of Dan, he went up yearly to worship at Jerusalem and brought the required priestly dues and tithes.
2. Nevertheless, he was taken captive because of the sins of the Northern Israelites.
3. Yet even in captivity he did not eat Gentile food.
4. He served his fellow Israelites by feeding the hungry and clothing the naked.
5. He risked his life to bury those unjustly killed by the Assyrian king, and he lost everything but his wife and son when he was found out. This righteous attribute has drastic consequences in Tobit 2.

1:1 Although the name "Tobit" is found in the Greek text, we now know from the Aramaic fragments that the original name in the story was "Tobi" and his son "Tobiah" (4Q200 fr. 4). The traditional Greek forms will be used here.

1:2 The book is dated to the time of Shalmaneser (V [726-722 BC]), Sennacherib (704-681 BC), and Esarhaddon (680-669 BC). The writer does not seem to realize that the reign of Sargon II (721-705 BC) occurred between those of

Shalmaneser and Sennacherib. This suggests that the author's knowledge of Assyrian history is derived from the biblical text and not from an independent knowledge of the subject. According to 2 Kgs 15:29, it was Tiglath-pileser III (744-727 BC) who took Naphtali captive, though the rest of the northern tribes were exiled by Shalmaneser. However, the niceties of the distinction seem to have escaped the author. In his inscriptions Sargon II claims to have conquered Samaria and deported its inhabitants in his first year of reign (*ANET*: 284-85), but this seems impossible. It is possible that he could have done so in his second year or later, but the *Babylonian Chronicle* 1.1.27-30 (Grayson 1975: 73) ascribes the taking of the city to Shalmaneser. Shalmaneser must have died just about the time of the conquest of Samaria, however, and it may be that Sargon carried out the deportation.

1:4 The time that the Northern Kingdom revolted from the Davidic dynasty was after the death of Solomon, some two centuries before Shalmaneser and the Assyrian captivity. Unless this verse is to be understood in some way at odds with its plain sense, the writer clearly has little sense of chronology.

1:6-8 This passage is an important source on the question of tithes and priestly dues. According to the Sinaiticus version, which probably follows the original, there were two tithes: the first tithe went to the priests and Levites; a second tithe was saved for the annual festivals, but in the third and sixth years of a sabbatical cycle it was distributed to the poor (NEB, REB). According to Vaticanus, however, two tithes were saved each year, for the priests and for the festivals respectively; in the third and sixth years, though, an additional (third) tithe was saved for the poor (AV, RSV, NRSV, JB). Although the Sinaiticus version is more likely to correspond to actual practice (two tithes, the second with two separate uses), some other sources do suggest three tithes in some years. For a more detailed discussion of tithes and other dues, see Grabbe 1993: 66-72.

1:8 This verse makes the statement that it was a command of his grand*mother* which led to his piety; this seems to be because he had been left an orphan, implying that normally his father would have taught him. Nevertheless, it confirms those texts which talk of heeding the instructions of one's mother as well as one's father (e.g., Prov 1:8; 6:20; 31:1). According to Sinaiticus in this verse, Tobit's father was named Hananiel (JB). This seems to contradict v. 1, which makes his father Tobiel and his grandfather Hananiel. A number of English translations emend the text from "father" to "grandfather" (NEB, REB).

1:10 Naphtali was supposedly one of the first tribes taken captive by the Assyrians (2 Kgs 15:29; Isa 9:1). They were deported to Assyria, but we are not told what specific part of the country. It would not be surprising if a writer chose the capital Nineveh as a well-known Assyrian city even without any specific information on the location, but we know from Assyrian inscriptions that some deportees were transported to Nineveh as well as other parts of the Assyrian Empire (Oded 1979: 28, 30).

1:21 2 Kgs 19:36-37 suggests that Sennacherib was slain by two of his sons shortly after his return from Jerusalem in 701 BC. In fact, it was twenty years later, in 681 BC. According to the *Babylonian Chronicle* 1.3.34-35 (Grayson: 81) and a recent republication of a text identifying the assassin (Parpola), only one son was involved in the assassination. The author of Tobit seems to be following the biblical tradition and, again, seems to have no direct knowledge of Assyrian history.

1:21-22 The theme of kinship appears again. Although Ahiqar plays only a brief role in the book as such, there are cross references to the Ahiqar story at certain crucial points in the book of Tobit (see under "Literary Structure," 736-37).

How Tobit Becomes Blind, in Spite of His Piety (Tobit 2)

This chapter continues the theme of piety begun in Tobit 1. Tobit's special trait is burying the murdered Jews who are left exposed and unburied. As a result of his unselfish actions, he lost all his possessions in Tobit 1; in this chapter he loses his eyesight. The art of the storyteller is concentrated on picturing Tobit as the innocent sufferer whose troubles come about because of his piety. Although not on the same level of sophistication, the story has much in common with the book of Job and in some ways tackles the same theme, that of theodicy (see above under "Theological Themes," 738).

2:1-5 Tobit and his family celebrate one of the main festivals, that of Pentecost, whose name derives from Greek *pentēkostē*, "fiftieth," because it was the fiftieth day after Wave Sheaf Day. The designation of Pentecost seems to occur only in Greek sources (e.g., 2 Macc 12:31-32; Acts 2:1; 20:6). In Lev 23:15-21 it has no special name; in Exod 34:22, Deut 16:10, 16, and 2 Chr 8:13 it is called *Ḥag Shabu'ot*, "Feast of Weeks," and the name *Shabu'ot* is common in later Jewish literature. *Jub.* 6:17-22 describes the festival, calling it "feast of weeks." The Aramaic text of Tob 2:1 has the name partially preserved: *ḥg shbw['y']*, "feast of wee[ks]."

2:4-9 An important part of Jewish religion, in this as well as later times, was the matter of ritual purity. Even though Tobit had no access to the temple, he is presented as carefully observing the law. However, the situation here is unclear. According to Num 19:11-22, one who buried a corpse became ritually unclean for a week. From all indications this had become a widely or universally observed rule in reference to the temple in the Second Temple period (cf. 11QTemple 49–50). But then why was Tobit able to transport the body from the street into the house without contacting impurity, and why did he become unclean and remain outside the house lest he transmit impurity to the dwelling and his family members once he did bury the body? These few verses raise a number of questions about the regulations relating to purity laws and their application at this time. First, was contacting impurity by burying a body a universal cultic rule from an early time? The chances are that it was since the separation of death and related conditions (illness, etc.) were fundamental to the Israelite cult. But this brings up a second question: Were the cultic rules applicable once one was too far from the temple for them to be of practical use? Later Jewish practice (at least from the Mishnah on) does attempt to apply them in everyday life in the absence of a temple (cf. Neusner 1973b). However, this may have been a Pharisaic innovation in which the rabbis were attempting to duplicate the temple conditions in their own home (cf. the many writings of Jacob Neusner, such as *From Politics to Piety* [1973a]). If this is true, applying many of the purity rules away from the temple may have been a late tradition that became universal only long after the time of Tobit.

The Sinaiticus text (no Semitic text is preserved) makes no connection between burying a body and spending the night out of doors (NRSV, NEB, REB, JB). Therefore, there is no suggestion that Tobit had to sleep outside. If so, there is no contradiction between his handling the body in 2:4 and returning to the festival meal, and his burying the body but not returning home. In other words, he slept outside for a reason other than ritual impurity, perhaps simply that he did not want to disturb the occupants of the house or that it was a warm night. On the other hand, the shorter Greek text (= AV, RV, RSV) makes an explicit connection between sleeping outside and his handling of the corpse in stating, "And in that night I returned from burying [the body] and, being unclean *(memiammenos)*, I slept by the wall of the courtyard" (2:8). This may represent a secondary interpretation in the light of later practice, but it is always possible that this is an early interpretation or even part of the original text. The whole question of ritual purity is a difficult one (see further Grabbe 1993: 49-62).

2:10-14 The passage contains a whole complex of literary, social, and psychological overtones. Like a good relative, Ahiqar supports Tobit and his family for two years, but then he leaves the area. Anna his wife now supports them and is accused of stealing a kid. From Tobit's point of view, for Ahiqar to support him was a loss of status but acceptable within the family. However, for him to have to be supported by his wife was humiliating, not to mention their reduction in living standards. He believed she had even stooped to stealing, which was contrary to his notions of right behavior, however great their poverty. From her point of view, she had done what she had to do when his relatives no longer gave them help and at considerable cost to herself physically and emtionally. The kid was a reward for a job well done. Tobit's lack of trust was, therefore, even more devastating.

This scenario has a very modern ring to it. A man loses his job; the woman who had previously taken care of the home goes out to work, though not at a wage equal to his. She works hard and comes home exhausted, not expecting that she should have to continue the domestic duties as well. The man's finds that his self-respect is heavily tied up with his job, which is now gone, and he finds it difficult to reverse roles and take on the domestic side of things, especially in a culture which may look on that as a further process of emasculation. And, to add to all the tension, they are having to pinch pennies and forgo many of the recreations and luxuries formerly taken for granted. The conflict of the man's pride even in adversity versus the woman's pragmatic efforts to keep things going is a commonplace in literature, perhaps best exemplified in Ibsen's *A Doll's House.*

This passage reminds one of the exchange between Job and his wife in Job 2:9-10. In the *Testament of Job* the story is developed in a way even closer to that of Tobit. Job's wife Sitis has to become a servant to support them (*T. Sol.* 21:1-2). In Tob 2:11 Anna voices what the narrative has already implied: Tobit has been scrupulously obedient and done many acts of charity and piety, yet his reward is his own blindness and the suffering of his family in poverty. This draws attention to the fact that Job and Tobit address much the same problem of theodicy: What is the good of being good since there is no guarantee of a reward or even freedom from suffering? Job's treatment of the subject is much more sophisticated, but Tobit's answer is one which has resonated more strongly with pious Jews and Christians through the ages.

The Prayers of Tobit and Sarah (Tobit 3)

In many ways, this chapter forms the climax of the book from a dramatic point of view because the happy ending is anticipated. Tobit prays a heartfelt prayer to be allowed to die. At the same time, a new actor and location are introduced — Sarah in Ecbatana — but the situation is parallel. Her plight is cast into her face by a serving girl. The force of this insult may not be immediately apparent in our egalitarian times, but it would have been an extreme of humiliation in a socially stratified society to be so treated by an inferior. This is why Sarah, like Tobit, prays for death, or at least to be freed from the insults being suffered. Her prayer takes place at the same time as Tobit's (3:11), and God hears both (v. 16). We now know that everything will be resolved, though we have yet to find out how. The writer or editor of the story is not bothered that the end is anticipated, suggesting that keeping the reader in complete suspense was not an aim of the composition. Some of the dramatic tension is lost, but the reader can relax in knowing that it will end happily and can enjoy the unfolding of God's solicitude for the two suffering individuals. The ultimate moral purpose is better served by this anticipation and is more important than the loss of dramatic tension. This is why a purely literary analysis of the story would be insufficient; the theological and moral aspects have to be given their due weight.

3:11 Sarah's contemplation of suicide is an interesting perspective on a controversial subject. Suicide has generally been looked upon with abhorrence by both Judaism and Christianity (cf. Droge 1992), but we have a number of examples in Jewish literature which make the matter more complex. Josephus and his companions consider suicide instead of surrendering to the Romans, and most of them went through with it, but Josephus himself escaped (*J.W.* 3.8.4-7 §§355-91). The suicide of the defenders of Masada has become famous in modern times (Josephus *J.W.* 7.8.6–9.1 §§320-401). In some cases, martyrdom is not far removed from suicide. We know of several examples in which individuals had the opportunity to surrender or to defend themselves but allowed themselves to be killed (1 Macc 2:31-38; Josephus *Ant.* 14.15.5 §§429-30). In this case, Sarah shows no religious antipathy to suicide but holds back because of the effect on her family; instead she asks God to take her life, which is not much different from suicide, and of course Tobit does the same.

3:17 Raphael is not mentioned in the HB nor in the NT, but this is probably accidental. He features strongly in a number of Jewish writings, at least as early as *1 Enoch* 10:4 and 22:1-6 (probably 3d cent. BC) and is regularly one of the archangels alongside Gabriel and Michael (also named in *1 Enoch* 9:1, but additionally mentioned a little later in Dan 8:16; 9:21; 10:13, 21). His presence here suggests an important mission since God did not send an ordinary angel to take care of the situation. The demon Asmodeus (3:8, 17; the precise origin of the name is uncertain) is also possibly one of the first examples of a named evil spirit, depending on whether Tobit is dated before *1 Enoch* or not. Their presence in this book is testimony to the development of angelology and demonology in the first few centuries of the Second Temple period.

Tobit's Admonitions to Tobias (Tobit 4)

The text of this chapter is somewhat problematic because vv. 7-12 are absent from Sinaiticus. The text of Vaticanus (= shorter text) is normally used to fill the gap. A few verses of a Hebrew text from Qumran (4Q200) are partially preserved for this section (4:3-9).

The first and last verses set the theme for the rest of the story (4:1-2, 20-21), for Tobias is about to be sent on a journey which will change all their lives. Tobit needs to recover a considerable sum of his money on deposit with a relative, not only for his own burial but also so that his son will not have to live in poverty. But much of this chapter is taken up with Tobit's admonitions to Tobias about life in general. Some modern readers may find this an intrusion into the story, but it was common to have pious instructions delivered to children or grandchildren, especially when the patriarch thought he might not have long to live (cf. the *Testaments of the Twelve Patriarchs*). One of the writer's aims seems to be to pass on to readers such traditional admonitions, and this time, just before Tobias is to be sent on a possibly dangerous journey, is a good point in the story to introduce these important (from the writer's point of view) considerations. From our point of view this chapter tells us a good deal about traditional piety in Judaism at this time, which includes:

- Give a decent burial to parents.
- Honor one's mother (as well as one's father).
- Do not deliberately sin but live righteously in all one's ways.
- Give alms generously but according to one's means.
- Avoid fornication and marry someone from among one's own kindred.
- Avoid idleness.
- Do not withhold the wages of a hired worker.
- Do not do to anyone what you would yourself hate.
- Do not drink to excess.
- Ask advice of the wise.
- Bless and call on God frequently.

4:12-13 The theme of taking a wife from among one's own kin is an important emphasis of the book of Tobit. Specific reference is made to the "father's tribe." Does this mean that Israelites were to marry from within their own tribe? This may be in the mind of the writer, but it is unlikely. Nowhere else is it ever suggested that Israelites had to marry only within their own tribe, suggesting that "tribe" here is being used generally to mean the broader Israelite community. As a beleaguered minority in Mesopotamia (and many other sites in the diaspora), the Jews would have been in danger of losing both their ethnic and their religious identity if they married with their Gentile neighbors.

4:15 Although easily overlooked, this verse contains the sentiment of the golden rule, though in its negative formulation (sometimes called the negative golden rule or even the silver rule). It contains the same idea as the golden rule but expressed differently. The sentiment is ascribed to Jesus in the Christian tradition (Matt 7:12; Luke 6:31) and to Hillel in the Jewish (*b. Shab.* 31a), but the idea is clearly earlier than both of them. Famous sayings are often ascribed to religious heroes even if they did not originate them. A saying not to do anything which others would find hurtful was probably much older than Tobit. Already the Akkadian *Counsels of Wisdom* (perhaps dating before 1,000 BC) states, "Do not return evil to the man who disputes with you; requite with kindness your evildoer; maintain justice to your enemy; smile on your adversary" (translation from Lambert 1960: 101). The Tobit saying is in the same category as loving one's neighbor (Lev 19:18). Interestingly, no special emphasis is placed on this rule; it takes its place alongside the admonition not to drink wine to excess or to engage in fornication.

4:17 Neither Sinaiticus nor the Aramaic is preserved for this verse. Vaticanus reads literally, "Pour your bread [OL has "wine"] upon the grave/tomb of the righteous and do not give to the sinners." Various suggestions have been made as to its meaning, and the varying translations of the different English versions are an attempt to make sense of a difficult passage. What does seem to be clear, however, is that this is borrowed from the *Proverbs of Ahiqar* (Greenfield 1981: 332). The proverbs were not originally Jewish but were apparently taken over by the Jews at some point. This is probably why what was likely to have been a reference to a pagan rite is quoted in a Jewish writing.

Raphael Is Chosen as Tobias's Traveling Companion (Tobit 5)

This chapter sets the scene for Tobias's journey and explains how it is that Raphael is able to accompany him without any suspicion of his identity as an angel. The first thing Tobit does when Tobias brings Raphael home is to ask about his family and ancestry. When Raphael tells him that he is from a related family known for its piety, Tobit feels that this is sufficient to entrust Tobias to him and does not need to inquire further. His mother still fears for his safety, as any mother would, but the reader will easily spot the unwitting irony of Tobit's assurance to his wife that "a good angel will accompany" Tobias (5:17, 22).

The major theme of looking to fellow Israelites is continued in this chapter. It is emphasized that an Israelite is one who can be trusted, this time as a traveling companion. Once Tobit knows that "Azariah" is a relative, he accepts this as already giving sufficient indication of the character and reliability of the person who will be responsible for his son's safety. It is "Azariah's" lineage (5:14: "of good and noble lineage") which tells Tobit all he needs to know. The concept that "blood will out" is still understood as a saying in the British Isles today, even if there are few who would actually subscribe to the sentiment expressed. Indeed, the extent to which personality and character traits are inherited, as opposed to being formed by environment and upbringing, is still debated today, even more so with the rise of modern genetics.

5:3 The practice of cutting a document of agreement in two, with each of the parties taking one part, so that neither could take unilateral action is well known in medieval and modern law. For example, agreements of apprenticeship and loan documents were commonly treated this way not all that long ago. Tobit shows that that concept goes back at least two and a half millennia.

5:4-6 In the days before the widespread availability of maps, one could not simply plan a journey to an unknown place and expect to arrive without incident. As it was, this was a journey of some 525 kilometers (c. 325 miles) as the crow flies — and much longer by land — just to reach Ecbatana, and it needed someone with knowledge. Thus, although the acquiring of Raphael as a companion is a literary device to advance the plot line, it also filled a practical need; it was also not just Tobias's youth which necessitated the traveling companion. Raphael claims to be a kinsman. At first he identifies himself as simply an Israelite (5:5), but then he claims a closer relationship through Gabael (v. 6). This is a sign of the ambiguity throughout the book, which, on the one hand, seems to claim kinship with all Israelites yet, on the other hand, makes all the characters apparently from the same tribe. See further at 4:12-13. The geographical accuracy of the text is rather lacking here. Ecbatana is about 325 kilometers (c. 200 miles) from Rages, which is more like a ten days' journey rather than two; cf. Plutarch *Alexander* 42). If this passage is original (though some think it is not), it shows that the author/editor was not necessarily from Mesopotamia.

The Journey to Ecbatana (Tobit 6)

Several elements within this chapter are vital for the story, primarily catching the fish which provides the solution to the problems of both Tobit and Sarah, and Raphael's telling of Sarah's existence to Tobias. This anticipation of the story's resolution does not seem to bother the narrator. Evidently, the loss of tension was compensated for by other benefits, one of these perhaps being the assurance that the story would end happily. For the eventual use of the fish parts, see 8:2-3 and 11:11-13.

6:2 One of the most puzzling features of the book is the purpose of Tobias's dog. It is a basic rule of storytelling that actors have a function somewhere in the story, yet the dog seems to have no value for the story line; at least, no one has yet come up with a convincing suggestion as to why the dog should be mentioned. In modern society, the dog is seen as a pet and companion to humans, but no such picture emerges from the OT. Dogs existed in Israelite society, but they are usually presented negatively as examples of unclean habits and a menace (1 Kgs 21:19, 23, 24; Ps 22:17, 21; Prov 26:11; Isa 56:11; Jer 15:3). Tobit is the first example in biblical literature of a dog being a companion (though Job 30:1 indicates their use to guard sheep). Most commentators have seen the dog's presence as a surviving redactional relic from an earlier version of the story in which the dog had an integral function in the story (see "Tradition History" above, 737-38).

6:4-9 As already noted, the saving of the fish heart, gall, and liver anticipates crucial junctures in the story; indeed, their use is spelled out in detail so that the reader knows specifically how the fish giblets are going to be used. This passage is an indication that there was no clear separation between magic and medicine in antiquity (Kee 1986). Although some substances were recognized as having medicinal properties, it was also widely believed that many illnesses were caused by demonic spirits of one sort or another. This is well known from such NT passages as Mark 9:17-27 par. Matt 17:14-18 par. Luke 9:38-42 and Luke 13:11-16 in which an illness was thought to be caused by demonic possession. In the same way, many medicines seemed to have symbolic and magical properties rather than being thought to work by biochemistry alone. There was also the question of illness being the consequence of sin (Luke 5:20-25; John 9:1-3; Jas 5:14-16); in the case of the 4Q*Prayer of Nabonidus,* the king's illness is healed when an *exorcist* forgives his sins. Thus sin, demonic possession, and illness are all connected in the cultural thinking of the time. Sin is not explicitly involved in either the blindness of Tobit or the deaths of Sarah's husbands, but there is a strong contextual implication that both Tobit and Sarah are absolved of their difficulties because of their righteousness.

6:11-13 These verses introduce a point of legal custom which features fairly prominently in the story: the fact that Tobias had a legal right and responsibility to marry Sarah. Deut 25:5-10 gives the pentateuchal law on levirate marriage, in which an unmarried brother was required to marry his widowed sister-in-law and raise up an heir to his deceased brother. A similar custom is presupposed by the story of Tamar, Judah's daughter-in-law, in Gen 38:6-26. Levirate marriage does not apply here, however, because (a) Tobias was not a brother of the previous husbands and (b) the nonconsummation of the marriage might have annulled the idea that the previous men married by Sarah had been husbands in a full sense. A better parallel is found in the book of Ruth, which contains the idea that the nearness of the relationship determined who had the most right to marry a widow (cf. Ruth 3:9-13). In this case, Tobias is alleged to be her nearest of kin after her parents. In Ruth the question of inheritance of property of the dead husband is also an issue, as it is here (cf. Ruth 4:3-10).

6:12 When Raphael lists Sarah's good qualities, it is interesting to notice the order: first she is wise *(phronimon),* then courageous *(andreion),* and only then very beautiful *(kalon lian).*

6:13 The statement that Raguel could not give Sarah to anyone else without incurring the death penalty "according to the decree of the book of Moses" is puzzling. What is this "book of Moses"? Is it the Pentateuch? This is a reasonable interpretation since a good deal of the book of Tobit seems to presuppose knowledge of the contents of our present Pentateuch (cf. Gamberoni 1977). But if so, no such rule as laid out here exists in the Pentateuch; however, it may represent an expansion of the law of levirate marriage. It is not uncommon for people in a society to find sanction for a societal custom from their sacred books, even if no such explicit support occurs. Creative exegesis can always be called on to find what one is looking for. Raphael's reference to a "decree of the book of Moses" may in fact be a reference to a particular exegesis or interpretation of the law on levirate marriage or some similar passage. As noted above, this was not a case of levirate marriage, anyway.

6:18 One hears of "marriages made in heaven," but it is not often that one's spouse was "set apart for you before the world was made," as here.

Tobias Meets Raguel and Arranges to Marry Sarah (Tobit 7)

This chapter concerns the negotiations for marriage and the agreement reached beween Raguel and Tobias. A significant theme, though, is that in an important way Tobias grows up in this chapter. Heretofore he has come across as a somewhat callow young man, perhaps only in his early to mid teens. In Tobit 6 his resolve to marry Sarah seems to have its stiffening from Raphael who pushes him in Sarah's direction in fairly direct language, but in this chapter Tobias moves quickly from asking Raphael to negotiate with Raguel for Sarah's hand to taking up matters for himself. At first Tobias asks Raphael to carry on the negotiations (7:9); however, when Raguel proposes to postpone discussion until after dinner, Tobias asserts himself and says that he will not eat until the matter is settled. From this point on, he carries on by himself rather than through an intermediary. Thus, by the end of the chapter he appears as a fully mature individual, confident and ready to take on the responsibilities of marriage and setting up a household. In 6:14-15 Tobias expresses concern about the danger to his life if he marries Sarah; by contrast, in this chapter Tobias is not the least bit deterred by the experiences of the previous husbands, even though warned by Sarah's father, as he becomes the eighth potential victim. Although his confidence clearly comes in part from Raphael's assurances in 6:16-18, it is also a component of the transformation of character which is evident in this chapter.

7:12-14 A written marriage contract is envisaged here. Once again the "book of Moses" is invoked, only this time the marriage will take place "according to the law and decree written in the book of Moses" (vv. 12, 13). The Pentateuch appears to be in mind here. The phrase occurs frequently in later Jewish marriage certificates. Although formal marriage contracts are known from cuneiform texts at least as far back as the early second millennium BC, most marriages in the ancient Near East were contracted through oral agreements. There is no suggestion in Tobit that a written document was required, but we also know that written agreements were not unusual by this time. A number of marriage certificates in Aramaic have been found among the Elephantine papyri of the fourth and fifth centuries BC. None of these mentions the law or book of Moses; as early as 218 BC, however, a Jewish marriage certificate in Greek from Egypt uses the phrase, "according to the decree of the Law of Moses" (cf. Moore 1996: 224), and we find a similar phrase in an Aramaic marriage certificate from the first century AD *(Murabbaʿat* 20:3), as well as in the traditional Jewish marriage certificate *(ketubah)* of rabbinic and later times (Milik in Benoit et al. 1961: 112; Dalman 1927: 4).

The Marriage and Wedding Night of Tobias and Sarah (Tobit 8)

The real test finally arrives in this chapter: Will Tobias survive his wedding night? Yet there is not a lot of tension because it has already been made rather clear earlier that the demon will not succeed this time. This probably explains why little space is devoted to the critical event itself. A fairly bald statement is made that the liver and heart of the fish are burned and the demon is driven away into Egypt. Why the smell of burning fish innards drove away only the demon and not Tobias and Sarah is not discussed — but that is probably a modern query. For the original readers, magic was serious business, and this was a magical deed, though it was followed up by Raphael's actions in pursuing the demon and binding him. Human and divine actions to achieve the same ends were not necessarily seen as mutually exclusive; see below at 11:14. What happened to the demon afterward is not stated; the binding of wicked angels is a theme in *1 Enoch* 10 and the *Testament of Solomon.*

8:4-8 The piety of Tobias and Sarah is shown by their prayer before the consummation of the marriage. Tobias says that he is taking Sarah "not because of lust, but with sincerity" (8:7). The Greek word for "lust" *(porneia)* is commonly used of illicit desire or sexual relations (hence the English word "pornography"), but the underlying Aramaic may have been more neutral (perhaps a word like *ʿdynh* or *ʿdn,* "pleasure," though the Aramaic text is not preserved here). There are several possible meanings, but one interpretation seems to be that Tobias is asserting that he is not taking Sarah out of "desire." If so, this represents the development of a certain ascetic motif with regard to sex even in marriage. Up to this point in Judaism, there is no indication that celibacy or abstinence was considered an act of piety. Asceticism is not generally a characteristic of Judaism, but there is evidence that it was practiced by some groups. Judith fasts all her days except for the sabbaths and festivals and the preparation days for them (Jdt 8:6). The Pharisees were alleged to fast two times a week (Luke 18:12). The Essenes — or at least part of them — were celibate (Philo *Hypoth.* 11.14-17; Josephus *J.W.* 2.8.2 §§120-21; *Ant.* 18.1.5 §21; Pliny the Elder *Nat. Hist.* 5.73).

8:6 The appeal to the story of Adam and Eve may seem natural to us, but it is actually unusual. The story of Adam and Eve is told in Genesis 1–5, but nowhere else in the canonical and deuterocanonical books is it referred to apart from here (Adam's name is mentioned in the genealogy of 1 Chr 1:1; Eve's not at all). Later a strong extrabiblical tradition develops, known to us from the *Apocalypse of Moses,* various *Books of Adam and Eve,* and traditions found in other early Jewish writings (e.g., *Jubilees* 3).

8:9-10 This is probably the most humorous passage in the book to anyone with a sense of irony. As already noted (see at "Literary Structure," 736-37), there are a number of passages in Tobit which lend themselves to an ironic interpretation. Some have thought that this was deliberate on the part of the author. I myself do not see evidence of conscious irony here because the context is careful to rationalize Raguel's action, but it is a prime example of unintended irony, at least to a modern reader. First, there was the smell of burning fish parts driving away the demon but not the bride and bridegroom (8:2-3). Now, having feasted his son-in-law and seen him off to the marriage bed, Raguel has a grave dug for him. To us this is hilarious, but there is no evidence that the author took it as anything but sober and logical. In fact, it is not clear that Raguel expected Tobias's death (cf. v. 10 with v. 16); the digging of the grave seems to have been only a precaution because of how another death might look to the neighbors who were Gentiles. To have lost seven previous husbands on their wedding night was unfortunate; to lose an eighth could be considered gross carelessness.

8:19-21 Once he sees that Tobias is still alive, Raguel demonstrates his generosity and good nature as well as his relief and happiness by having a fourteen-day wedding celebration, twice as long as normal (Gen 29:27; Judg 14:12). He also immediately hands over half of his possessions to Tobias, far more than would be required as a dowry. However, because Sarah is his only child, it seems that Tobias becomes his heir, since the other half of Raguel's goods will come to Tobias when Raguel and Edna are deceased (8:21; 14:13).

Raphael Is Dispatched to Fetch Tobit's Deposit of Money (Tobit 9)

This chapter demonstrates Tobias's respect and concern for his parents. By sending "Azariah" (Raphael) to collect the money deposited with Gabael, he not only sees that the mission commissioned by his father is fulfilled but he also makes sure that his return to his parents is not delayed any longer than necessary. He must take part in the two-week celebration because of Raguel's insistence, but he knows any delay will be a cause of worry to his parents (9:4). Interestingly, although Tobias's mother's anxiety is given greater textual prominence (5:18-23; 10:1-7), Tobias himself here emphasizes his father's concern. Considering the great distance from Nineveh to Ecbatana and on to Rages, it is hard to see how an exact number of days could be reckoned for the journey. Raphael is able to journey to Rages and back before the two weeks of the wedding feast are up, a rather unlikely short period of time for the distance (see on 5:6).

Tobias and Sarah Take Their Leave of Raguel and Edna (Tobit 10)

The poignant portrayal of human emotions in this chapter demonstrates the author's artistry (10:1-7). Tobit had sent Tobias off with assurances of safety (5:21-23), but his mother Anna had feared that she would see him no more. Now the time of his return has arrived, but there is no Tobias. Tobit puts on a brave face — there are many reasons why his son might have been delayed — but he is beginning to worry. His mother's fears from the beginning are only confirmed; on the one hand, she watches anxiously for him but, on the other hand, she is already mourning for him. Similarly, the interaction between Raguel, Edna, Tobias, and Sarah is touching and contradicts those who argue that women were seen only as chattels. While we may not always agree with the status or treatment given to women in that culture, the concept of a man's love and respect for his wife or daughter is not a late twenth-century invention.

10:7-13 Tobias is not even willing to trust messengers to take the good news back to his parents, but he insists on going himself, despite Raguel's entreaties to stay longer. Raguel delivers admonitions to both Tobias and Sarah, while Edna does the same to Tobias. As in Tobit 4, when Tobit was sending Tobias on his journey, so here when Tobias and Sarah are bidding farewell, the author has an occasion to give instructions on living. Once again this illustrates the author's primary aim of religious and moral teaching. He is not just out to tell a good story; on the contrary, the story itself has many moral examples, and others are added in the form of direct instructions and admonitions. In this case, they have to do with relationships between members of the extended family: daughter to parents-in-law, husband to wife, son-in-law to parents-in-law. Although the command to honor one's parents-in-law as one does one's own parents (10:12) has no exact counterpart in the HB, it would probably have been taken for granted.

Tobias Returns Home with Sarah, and Tobit Is Healed (Tobit 11)

Another dramatic resolution occurs in this chapter: the cure of Tobit's blindness. As in Tobit 8, however, the scene has been so well anticipated that it comes as no surprise. The emotions of Anna and Tobit at seeing Tobias's safe return are once again expressed in a most touching scene, with Anna's stating that she could now die happily and Tobit's stumbling out into the courtyard to meet Tobias rather than waiting for him to come in the door. In the same way, Tobit's welcome of Sarah to his household is one of love and joy (11:17), hardly the reaction of one engaging in a mere commercial transaction.

11:4 This second reference to the dog is rather startling to the alert reader. As noted at 6:2, its presence seems to be a surivor from an earlier version of the story where the dog had a more central role.

11:11-15 As noted earlier (6:4-9), it has often been discussed whether the application of the fish gall to Tobit's eyes is medicinal or magical, but that is a modern distinction. It is not always easy to define magic or to distinguish it from religion, but by any definition the burning of the fish innards to expel the demon was a magical act (8:2-3). Why should the application of the fish gall be any different? Healing in antiquity before the treatises of Hippocrates and Galen, who tried to set medicine on a scientific basis, often combined the medicinal and the magical. We have no evidence that these were considered distinct procedures. This is further evidenced in Tobit's response to his healing: he immediately proceeds to ascribe the cure to God (11:14-15), despite the obligatory mechanical application of the fish gall. See further at 6:4-9.

11:17 At the end of this verse is a very surprising statement: there was rejoicing among all the *Jews* in Nineveh. But there were probably no Jews in Nineveh at this time! Tobit had been taken captive by the Assyrians when they conquered Samaria in 722 BC; he was from the Northern Kingdom of Israel, not the Southern Kingdom of Judah (1:1-10). Assuming that Tobit was about twenty when he was taken captive, the episode in this chapter would be about 680-675 BC. The main Jewish captivity began three-quarters of a century later in 597 BC, fifteen years *after* Nineveh had been destroyed, never to be rebuilt. The matter is somewhat more complicated than this, however, in that Sennacherib claims to have taken a large number of captives in 701 BC (*ANET*: 287-88). Since Sennacherib did not actually conquer Jerusalem by his own admission (2 Kgs 19:35-36 claims divine intervention), the question of whether he took Jewish captives or how many is not easy to answer. Nevertheless, the best explanation of Tob 11:17 is that the author is really concerned about the Jewish diaspora during his own time, that is, the Persian or Greek periods, long after Assyrian rule. Except for this verse, Tobit refers to the community as "Israelites" (1:18; 5:5, 9; 13:3).

11:18 The mention of Ahiqar again is a reminder of the importance of that story for the author of Tobit. It is interesting that Ahiqar's nephew Nadab/Nadin is mentioned here in an apparently positive manner since the Ahiqar story known to us makes him go on to betray his uncle who had done nothing but good for him (cf. 14:10; see also under "Literary Structure" above, 736-37).

Raphael Reveals his True Identity (Tobit 12)

Another example of Tobit's and Tobias's piety is given in this chapter, this time their fairness and generosity. "Azariah" had agreed to accompany Tobias for a standard wage, though Tobit had promised a bonus for the successful completion of the journey (5:15-16). Now Tobias acknowledges that his companion has done much more than promised and that much of his success was due to that individual, even to the cure of his father's blindness. Therefore, it is entirely logical to him and Tobit to feel that he should divide all that he had gained with "Azariah," not excluding the half of Raguel's possessions which really came to Tobias as an inheritance.

12:6-15 We have known of Raphael's true identity all along, so this revelation does not represent much of a denouement. Interestly, it serves as another occasion for the author to deliver a set of moral precepts. The main topics are:

- Honor and praise of God
- Prayer
- Honor of the king
- The doing of good as a way of avoiding evil
- Almsgiving

The theme of almsgiving, so emphasized in the first part of the book, is brought out once again. The concept of keeping the king's secret is expressed in 12:7, 11. Exactly what is meant is not explained, though v. 11 indicates that it was some sort of known proverb whose origin one can readily understand: it was wise to be careful what you said about the king, and betraying a secret of his would be doubly dangerous (cf. Eccl 10:20). The idea that the king should be feared along with God is found in Prov 24:21.

12:13 The idea that Tobit suffered as a test is a clear parallel with Job. Their afflictions were not due to any sin on their part; rather, God chose to test them. In the case of Tobit, this test was in the very context of his most obvious pious act, that of burying the dead. Just as righteous Job had been afflicted by Satan (not a demonic leader at that time but the heavenly prosecutor), so Tobit was allowed to suffer while doing his good deed.

12:15-22 Raphael's revelation to Tobit and Tobias is also the occasion to provide further information about himself. He claims he is one of seven angels who serve in God's presence. He is not here called an archangel, but he has this title in other Jewish sources. For example, according to *1 Enoch* 20, Raphael is one of seven archangels, the other six of whom are Suruel, Raguel, Michael, Saraqael, Gabriel, and Remiel. According to Tob 12:12, one of his duties was to bring human prayers and the record of their pious deeds to God's attention. The human reaction to being in the presence of an angel is typically that of fear and prostration or even fainting (cf. Matt 28:2-4; Rev 1:17-18), to which the angels usually respond by saying, "Fear not," and by raising them from their position of obeisance (Dan 10:4-11). As themselves servants of God, angels tell humans to direct their praise and worship to God. Tob 12:19 seems to be the first passage to deny any human needs to angels. The HB has passages where heavenly messengers eat and drink (e.g., Gen 18:1-8), though in Judg 6:19-24 the food presented to the angel is consumed by fire. The story of the fallen angels was widespread among the Jews of this period (known mainly from *1 Enoch* 6–9, but also *Jub.* 4:21-23). In this case, they engage in sexual intercourse with human women, which is considered a violation of the divine command for heavenly beings. Mark 12:25 (par. Matt 22:30) denies marriage to angels. According to Tobit, the conduct of angels also excluded eating and drinking.

tion of an eschatological building still in his own future. This interpretation is given support by the content of the next chapter, especially Tob 14:5, which speaks of two rebuildings. The author was already familiar with the one rebuilding but was anticipating a glorious rebuilding still to come.

Tobit's Prayer (Tobit 13)

Tobit's prayer has essentially two themes: praise of God (13:1-8) and the restoration of Jerusalem (13:9-17), with a brief blessing on God at the very end. Vv. 7-10a are missing from the Sinaiticus manuscript, and most modern commentators resort to the OL as well as to the Greek text in Vaticanus (elsewhere in the chapter Vaticanus is usually fairly close to the text of Sinaiticus). However, we are fortunate that now a good portion of this chapter is available in the Hebrew and Aramaic fragments from Qumran. There are many small variants even from the Sinaiticus text, showing that the Greek tradition does not reflect the original in all details in this chapter; however, the sense is usually the same even if there are small differences.

13:1-8 Mixed in with praise of God are references to the scattered nature of Israel. This scattering was done as a punishment for sin (13:2, 5), and God will soon show mercy (v. 6). All that has to be done is to turn to God with a whole heart (v. 6). This theme then carries on into the next section on Jerusalem.

13:9-17 The emphasis in Tobit has been the captivity and exile of Israel which had taken place in 722 BC with the fall of Samaria, yet it is clearly the Jewish captivity which is the real concern, as already pointed out above (see at 11:17). From the perspective of the story, the fall of Jerusalem was still almost a century in the future. Tobit's prayer is in the nature of a *vaticinia ex eventu*, a prophecy after the event — a pseudo-prophecy which was actually written after the events it pretends to foretell. It is not presented as a prophecy here, but the content is of something which could not have taken place as yet, which means that this section of the prayer anticipates his more direct prophecy in the next chapter (Tobit 14). The prayer speaks both of the rebuilding of the city and its walls and of the restoration of the temple. Therefore, the author had to have been writing after the fall of Jerusalem in 587/586 BC, and also after the return of many Jews from captivity and the rebuilding of the temple (Ezra 1–6). This shows that the book of Tobit could have been written no earlier than about 500 BC.

13:16-18 The prayer ends with the building of an idealized Jerusalem made of precious stones and pure gold. Such an eschatological city is perhaps best known from Rev 21:10-21, though we have other passages of idealized Zion in the prophetic literature (Isa 2:2-4 par. Mic 4:1-5; Isa 54:11-14; Ezekiel 40–48). Does this mean that Tobit is perhaps anticipating the rebuilding of Jerusalem in a way which never took place? Is this then a genuine prophecy, with mythical elements which were never fulfilled? Although such an explanation is always possible, it seems more likely that the author knew of an actual rebuilding of the city and temple but uses it as an anticipation of an eschatological building still in his own future.

Tobit's Last Words and Death (Tobit 14)

Much of this chapter is Tobit's "testament." The final words of a patriarch, his testament, make up an important genre of Jewish literature. Some writings (e.g., *Testaments of the Twelve Patriarchs*) are devoted entirely to such testaments, but we also have testaments as a section in another genre of writing such as *1 Enoch* 91–105 and here in Tobit. A common feature of such testaments is a deathbed speech to children, grandchildren, and the like, often with admonitory material but sometimes containing special information or even prophecy. After delivering the final words, the patriarch dies in peace at a great age.

14:1-2 Tobit's ages when he became blind and when he died vary considerably in the different Greek and other versions. In this case, 62 as the age when he became blind in Sinaiticus (= NRSV, NEB, REB, JB) is not supported by the Aramaic text, which has 58 (agreeing with Vaticanus [= AV, RSV]). Both Sinaiticus and the Aramaic agree on 112 as his final age (NRSV, NEB, REB, JB). This does not conform exactly with any other patriarchal age, but it is similar to those of Joseph (110 [Gen 50:26]), Moses (120 [Deut 34:7]), and Joshua (110 [Josh 24:29]). This reversion to great ages seems to be a characteristic of some of the early Jewish literature; for example, Judith is alleged to have lived to 105 (Jdt 16:23). After the patriarchal ages, which extend as far as Moses and Joshua, the ages of figures tend to be fairly conventional. David lives only 70 years (1 Kgs 2:11), and this is taken to be the normal expectation of the length of life (Ps 90:10). Therefore, this return to patriarchal life spans for both Tobit and Tobias (117 years [Tob 14:14]) looks a bit strange, but it may have been intended to draw them into the patriarchal framework. It also reinforces the importance of piety and almsgiving.

14:3 The number of Tobias's children is not given in the Sinaiticus manuscript (= RSV, NEB, REB, JB, GNB), but the original text probably had "seven" (NRSV, NJB): although Vaticanus has "six" (AV, RV), the OL has "seven" and the fragmentary Aramaic is most easily restored with the reading "seven." If so, this indicates another example in which Sinaiticus differs from the original text. The number "seven" was a significant number in the ancient Near East, being found in many biblical and extra-biblical texts. For Tobias to have seven sons would be an ideal number with symbolic value.

14:3-4 The Sinaiticus reference to the prophecy of Nahum (NRSV, NEB, REB, JB) is undoubtedly correct (compared with the "Jonah" of Vaticanus [= AV, RV, RSV]) since it is the OT book which describes an actual fall of Nineveh. Although Jonah predicted a divine destruction of Nineveh, it did not come to pass because the people repented.

14:3-11 Tobit's entire prophecy in this section is extremely interesting. He says repeatedly in a single verse that the words of the prophets and God will not fail (14:4). He then predicts the captivity of those living in the "land of Israel," that the "land of Israel" will be desolate, and that Samaria and Jerusalem will be desolate and the temple destroyed. This is all very puzzling because Israel in the sense of the Northern Kingdom had already been taken captive and Tobit himself was part of that captivity. That captivity also included Samaria. The reference to the destruction of Jerusalem and the temple is what we would expect since it is still future with respect to the time of Tobit's death. By saying that the land and the city of Jerusalem would be desolate, the writer indicates his belief in the "myth of the empty land" (cf. Barstad 1996) such as we find in 2 Chr 35:20-21 and the books of Ezra and Nehemiah. "Israel" (in 14:5, at least) is apparently being used in a broad sense to include Judah and Jerusalem. The prediction that the temple would be rebuilt but not as at first fits the picture in Ezra 6. Thus far this is a "prophecy after the event" (see on 13:9-17), but then a genuine prediction is made: when the "time of times" is fulfilled, all the exiles will return and rebuild Jerusalem and the temple as foretold by the prophets, and all the earth will turn to God, fear him, and destroy their idols. This glorious rebuilding is not the rebuilding described in Ezra but an eschatological event such as is also spoken of in Tob 13:17-18.

14:15 If Tobias died at the age of 117 years, he would not only have lived through the destruction of Nineveh but also that of Jerusalem. That is, from the data in the book itself, he was approximately twenty when he married (about 680-675 BC; see above at 11:17). The author was probably not too precise in his own mind about how the story fitted the historical background of the time. The one who is said to have conquered Nineveh is "Achiacharos" according to the Sinaiticus text, but this seems to be a form of the name Ahiqar. We know from cuneiform and Greek sources that Nabopolassar of Babylonia and Cyaxeres (Akk. *Umakishtar*) king of the Medes conquered and destroyed Nineveh (*ANET*: 304-5). Some of the English translations emend the text to Cyaxeres here (NRSV, JB), but there is no textual justification for doing so. The preserved portions of the text from the Qumran manuscripts unfortunately do not contain this verse. The reading "Nebuchadnezzar and Ahasuerus" (RSV; or just "Ahasuerus," NEB, REB) of the Vaticanus is not of any help since these are simply familiar names, easily taken from the biblical text. Although a genuine historical name may have been in the original text, the impression one has is the same as noted several times earlier (e.g., on 1:2; 1:21): the author's knowledge of Mesopotamian history for this period is not very great.

Bibliography. Barstad, H. M. 1996, *The Myth of the Empty Land: A Study in the History and Archaeology of Judah during the "Exilic" Period,* SO 28, Oslo and Cambridge, Mass.: Scandinavian University • Benoit, P., et al., eds. 1996, *Les grottes de Murabba'at,* DJD 2, 2 vols., Oxford: Clarendon • Bloch-Smith, E. 1992, *Judahite Burial Practices and Beliefs about the Dead,* JSOTSup 123, JSOT/ASOR Monograph Series 7, Sheffield: JSOT • Bloch-Smith, E. 1992, "The Cult of the Dead in Judah: Interpreting the Material Remains," *JBL* 111:213-24 • Conybeare, F. C., J. R. Harris, and A. S. Lewis. 1898, *The Story of Ahikar: From the Syriac, Arabic, Armenian, Ethiopic, Greek and Slavonic Versions,* London: Clay • Dalman, G. 1927, *Aramäische Dialektproben,* Leipzig: Hinrichs; repr. with Dalman, G. 1960, *Grammatik des jüdisch-palästinischen Aramäisch,* Darmstadt: Wissenschaftliche Buchgesellschaft • Deselaers, P. 1982, *Das Buch Tobit: Studien zu seiner Entstehung, Komposition und Theologie,* OBO 43; Freiburg: Universitätsverlag • Droge, A. J. 1992, "Suicide," in *ABD:* 6:225-31 • Fitzmyer, J. A. 1995a, "The Aramaic and Hebrew Fragments of Tobit from Cave 4," *CBQ* 57:655-75 • Fitzmyer, J. A. 1995b, "Tobit," in J. VanderKam, ed., DJD, vol. 19: *Qumran Cave 4: XIV Parabiblical Texts, Part 2,* Oxford: Clarendon • Gamberoni, J. 1977, "Das 'Gesetz des Mose' im Buch Tobias," in G. Braulik., ed., *Studien zu Pentateuch: Walter Kornfeld zum 60 Geburtstag,* Vienna: Herder, 227-42 • Grabbe, L. L. 1993, *Leviticus,* Old Testament Guides, Sheffield: JSOT • Grayson, A. K. 1975, *Assyrian and Babylonian Chronicles,* Texts from Cuneiform Sources 5, Locust Valley, N.Y.: J. J. Augustin • Greenfield, J. C. 1981, "Aḥiqar in the Book of Tobit," in M. Carrez, J. Doré, and P. Grelot, eds., *De la Tôrah au Messie: Études d'exégése et d'herméneutique bibliques offertes à Henri Cazelles,* Paris: Desclée, 329-36 • Hanhart, R. 1983, *Tobit,* Septuaginta 8/5, Göttingen: Vandenhoeck & Ruprecht • Kee, H. C. 1986, *Medicine, Miracle and Magic in New Testament Times,* SNTSMS 55, Cambridge: Cambridge University • Lambert, W. G. 1960, *Babylonian Wisdom Literature,* Oxford: Clarendon • Lichtheim, M. 1973-76, *Ancient Egyptian Literature,* vols. 1-3, Berkeley and Los Angeles: University of California • Lindenberger, J. M. 1983, *The Aramaic Proverbs of Ahiqar,* Baltimore: Johns Hopkins • Moore, C. A. 1992, "Tobit, Book of," in *ABD:* 6:585-94 • Moore, C. A. 1996, *Tobit: A New Translation with Introduction and Commentary,* AB 40A, New York: Doubleday • Neusner, J. 1973a, *From Politics to Piety,* Englewood Cliffs, N.J.: Prentice-Hall • Neusner, J. 1973b, *The Idea of Purity in Ancient Judaism: The Haskell Lectures, 1972-1973,* with a critique and commentary by M. Douglas, SJLA 1, Leiden: Brill • Nickelsburg, G. W. E. 1988, "Tobit and Enoch: Distant Cousins with a Recognizable Resemblance," in D. J. Lull, ed., *Society of Biblical Literature 1988 Seminar Papers,* SBLSP 27, Atlanta: Scholars, 54-68 • Nowell, I. 1988, "The Narrator in the Book of Tobit," in D. J. Lull, ed., *Society of Biblical Literature 1988 Seminar Papers,* SBLSP 27, Atlanta: Scholars, 27-38 • Oded, B. 1979, *Mass Deportations and Deportees in the Neo-Assyrian Empire,* Wiesbaden: Reichert • Parpola, S. 1980, "The Murderer of Sennacherib," in B. Alster, ed., *Death in Mesopotamia: Papers Read at the XXVI[e] Rencontre assyriologique international,* MESOPOTAMIA: Copenhagen Studies in Assyriology 8, Copenhagen: Akademisk, 161-70 • Rabenau, M. 1994, *Studien zum Buch Tobit,* BZAW 220, Berlin and New York: de Gruyter • Schmidt, B. B. *Israel's Beneficent Dead: Ancestor Cult and Necromancy in Ancient Israelite Religion and Tradition,* Forschungen zum Alten Testament, Tübingen: Mohr (Siebeck) • Soll, W. 1988, "Tobit and Folklore Studies, with Emphasis on Propp's Morphology," in D. J. Lull, ed., *Society of Biblical Literature 1988 Seminar Papers,* SBLSP 27, Atlanta: Scholars, 39-53 • Thomas, J. D. 1972, "The Greek Text of Tobit," *JBL* 91:463-71 • Wills, L. M. 1995, *The Jewish Novel in the Ancient World,* Myth and Poetics, Ithaca and London: Cornell University • Zimmermann, F. 1958, *The Book of Tobit,* Dropsie College Jewish Apocryphal Literature, New York: Harper.

Judith

Gerald West

INTRODUCTION

The book which bears her name seems at first to have nothing to do with Judith, the main female character. Male characters and apparently male matters abound. Equally disconcerting is that the book begins with Nebuchadrezzar, a real ruler of the Neo-Babylonian Empire (605-562 BC), engaged in a military campaign against Arphaxad, an imaginary king of the Medes. Out of this strange setting where history and fiction merge the story of Judith and her people slowly emerges.

Like the biblical books of Ruth and Esther, the book of Judith takes its name from the main female character. However, while Judith is a central character whose actions are crucial to the plot, as are Ruth and Esther in their respective books, it could be argued that her role, and theirs, is more that of helper rather than that of heroine (Milne 1993: 54). Yet in no other book is a woman praised so explicitly and profusely (Schuller 1992: 240); from her entry into the story in 8:1 to her exit in 16:25 Judith is acclaimed. Uzziah's promise to Judith that "Your praise will never depart from the hearts of those who remember the power of God" (13:19) has been fulfilled in that the praise and remembrance of Judith have continued throughout the centuries in various forms (Schuller 1992: 240).

The story may originally have been written in Hebrew, though there is no manuscript evidence for this. The book we have has been transmitted in three slightly different Greek versions, two Latin versions, and a Syriac version. In addition, versions of the story have circulated in Aramaic and Hebrew. The book of Judith was well known in the early Christian church, where Judith was praised for her chastity and was presented as evidence that "women, empowered by God's grace, have performed deeds worthy of men" (*1 Clem.* 55:3, 4). The story was very popular in medieval art, poems, and dramas (see Stone 1992). Judith has even appeared as the queen of hearts on playing cards (Schuller 1992: 240)!

The official reception of Judith has been more cautious. The book was excluded from the Hebrew canon, is not mentioned in the Qumran literature (QL) or in the writings of Philo or Josephus, and had a mixed reception in the early church (Moore 1985: 86-90). The modern era has also been ambivalent about the story of Judith. "Painters have transformed her into a courtesan; moralists and pietists are shocked by her decision to lie and murder in order to accomplish an admittedly noble purpose; feminists criticize her blatant use of physical beauty and sexual wiles" (Schuller 1992: 240). But ordinary readers of the Bible do not, in fact, encounter Judith very frequently. As an apocryphal book, it is not part of the core of Protestant or Jewish religious instruction, and in the Catholic community the story does not appear in the lectionary cycle of scriptural readings (although a section, 8:2-8, can be selected for feasts of widowed saints) (Schuller 1992: 240).

The author, place of writing, and date of Judith are not easy to determine. The author is anonymous, and the reconstructions of scholars have few clues to follow. Because Judith is fictional, with a number of historical and geographical inaccuracies, it is difficult to date its composition, and so scholars' estimates range from the fifth century BC to the second century AD (Enslin and Zeitlin 1972: 26-31 and Moore 1985: 67-70). However, the issues implicitly and explicitly addressed by the narrative, together with linguistic and historical indicators, strongly suggest that the book should be located within the theological discussions of the latter part of the second century BC.

Whatever the uncertainties of its origins, the book of Judith in its final form is a powerful, compelling, and somewhat unsettling narrative. The sixteen chapters of Judith are structured in two parts or acts: chs. 1–7 and chs. 8–16. Strangely, Judith herself does not appear and is not mentioned until the second act. Nebuchadrezzar, king of Assyria, and other mighty men are the central characters of the first act. It would be a mistake, however, to see chs. 1–7 as simply a clumsy preface to the story proper (LaCocque 1990: 33). As a careful reading of Act 1 (chs. 1–7) will demonstrate, Act 1 is an integral part of the narrative.

COMMENTARY

Act 1 (1:1–7:32)

Scene 1 (1:1-16)

The opening words of Act 1 introduce "one of the most infamous characters of the Bible" (LaCocque 1990: 31), Nebuchadrezzar, the Babylonian king who captured and pillaged Jerusalem, burned the Temple, and took the upper echelons of the Judean population into exile in Mesopotamia. However, no sooner has his name been mentioned than the reader is told that he "ruled over the Assyrians in the great city of Nineveh" (1:1). Clearly something is amiss! This, and numerous other historical and geographical blunders, suggest that the reader should proceed carefully, for all is not as it seems. The inaccuracies are too many and are repeated too often to be accidental. Not only is Nebuchadrezzar repeatedly referred to as "king of the Assyrians," but in 1:14 he is credited with the capture of the capital of Media, Ecbatana, a city that was captured by another king (the Persian Cyrus) at another time (half a century later, in 550 BC) (LaCocque 1990: 31).

What, then, is the purpose of the first scene? The obvious historical and geographical discrepancies not only place the reader firmly in fictional rather than historical territory but they also set the ironic tone of the story. Most readers would recognize that much of what they have read so far, and much of what is still to come, does not make sense historically or geographically. Nebuchadrezzar ruled in Babylon, not Assyria, and at the time when Judea was taken into exile, not at their return! "From the very first verses one is alerted that this work is not what it appears to be, and one is thus prepared for irony and double entendre in what follows" (Schuller 1992: 241). It is as if the narrator is saying to the reader: "Imagine a situation in which the following happened. . . ."

The extensive historical and geographical details of Scene 1 also serve another purpose. Nebuchadrezzar is portrayed as the most powerful person in the entire area, whether real or imaginary. Juxtaposing two great kings, one real and one imaginary, 1:1 sets the scene for the contest that forms the framework of Scene 1. The splendid and massive fortifications of Arphaxad are described in detail in vv. 2-4, their very presence being an affront to the great Assyrian king Nebuchadrezzar (v. 5). V. 6 lists the peoples and places that align themselves with Nebuchadrezzar, while vv. 7-11 establish those people and places that refuse his summons. Nebuchadrezzar's oath of vengeance against those who were foolish enough to refuse his summons (v. 12) is given terrible force by his ruthless rout of the military might of King Arphaxad (vv. 13-15). The impregnable and splendid city of Ecbatana is despoiled and reduced to abject ruin (v. 14), and Arphaxad is captured and killed by Nebuchadrezzar (v. 15).

Does a similar fate lie in wait for those other people and places who have refused Nebuchadrezzar? This is the question that the dreadful oath of vengeance (1:12) and the final ominous picture of "a vast body of troops" relaxing and feasting portend (v. 16).

The scene is set. The stage is that of world history, of empires and great battles. Nebuchadrezzar, with his military might, reigns supreme. Those who oppose him are destroyed, and a similar fate is promised those who ignore him. In all this, the attentive reader would have noticed, Judea and Jerusalem are mentioned only in passing, as two of the nations in the list of those who refuse King Nebuchadrezzar's summons. In the grand historical and geographical scale of this opening scene Israel hardly warrants a mention. All power is Nebuchadrezzar's; Israel is of no account — this seems to be the messsage.

Scene 2 (2:1-13)

In the second scene King Nebuchadrezzar is still at center stage. He summons his officers and nobles and commissions his second in command, Holofernes, to implement his threat of vengeance. Nebuchadrezzar is in control, summoning, commanding, and sending. While the focus will shift to Holofernes in the scenes that follow, this scene makes it quite clear that he has been called, commanded, and sent by Nebuchadrezzar.

The ironic tone introduced in the first scene continues in this scene. The opening words of this scene, "In the eighteenth year," allude to the year 587 BC, when Jerusalem fell (for the first time!) to King Nebuchadrezzar of Babylon. In the postexilic narrative time of the story Jerusalem is under Israelite rule (4:8), but under threat (once again!) from Nebuchadnezzar. Furthermore, the strangeness is sustained through the names of the main characters. The commander-in-chief of the Assyrian army is Holofernes (1:4), and he is accompanied by Bagoas, a eunuch "who had charge of his personal affairs" (12:11). Both names are Persian, not Assyrian or Babylonian, and their characters are probably based on men who actually took part in the campaign of the Persian king Artaxerxes III against Egypt in about 341 BC (Diodorus Siculus *Hist.* 31.19; see also LaCocque 1990: 31). "Earth and water" (2:7) were typical signs of submission demanded by Persian, not Assyrian or Babylonian, kings (see Herodotus *Hist.* 6.48). The storyteller manipulates the time, people, and place for narrative (and theological) purposes.

Scene 3 (2:14–7:32)

A threefold chiastic pattern characterizes the structure of the third scene (Craven 1983: 47-64; Craven 1989: 572):

(a) The campaign against the disobedient nations; the people surrender (2:14–3:10)
(b) Israel hears and is "greatly terrified"; Joakim orders preparations for war (4:1-15)
(c) Achior tells Holofernes about the Israelites; Holofernes expels Achior from the Assyrian camp (5:1–6:13)
(c′) Achior is received by the Israelites into Bethulia; Achior tells the Israelites about Holofernes (6:14-21)
(b′) Holofernes orders preparations for war; Israel sees and is "greatly terrified" (7:1-15)
(a′) The campaign against Bethulia; the people want to surrender (7:6-32)

(a) 2:14–3:10

Just as Nebuchadnezzar's instructions to Holofernes are described in great detail in the previous scene (2:5-13), so, too, the preparations of Holofernes are fully recounted (vv. 14-19). These detailed descriptions serve to slow the action of the story and consequently to build tension as the reader is forced to wait for the fulfillment of Nebuchadrezzar's oath of vengeance. The tension is accentuated by the contrast between Holofernes' immediate obedience to the summons of Nebuchadrezzar and the dismissive disobedience of the western region. Although Holofernes is now the main actor, Nebuchadrezzar is always in the background — quite literally (v. 19). He is still the preeminent presence.

The slow description with which this scene opens allows the reader time to take careful note of how well prepared and vast the army of Nebuchadrezzar is. Implicitly, the question is posed: Who can stand against such a force? The sense of impending doom is made more dreadful by the almost casual comment that accompanying the disciplined and well-equipped army was "a mixed crowd like a swarm of locusts, like the dust of the earth — a multitude that could not be counted" (2:20). Ancient (and even more modern) armies were commonly accompanied by militarily untrained or semitrained accomplices who literally fed off the scraps left by the army in its wake.

The ironic tone already noted continues as the geographical particulars are indicated. The march described in 2:21-27 includes real and imaginary places, unlikely routes, and the impossible image of Holofernes' massive army (and its ragtag followers) marching from Nineveh, the capital of Assyria, through at least three hundred miles of terrain to the plain of Bectileth, an unidentified site north of Upper Cilicia in southeastern Asia Minor (Dentan 1973: 78 and LaCocque 1990: 32).

The subjugation and devastation of large parts of the western region are briefly but vividly described (2:21-27). There is no mention of any form of resistance. Whereas earlier the western region had treated the envoys of Nebuchadrezzar with contempt (1:11), his envoy Holofernes now evokes fear, dread, and terror (2:28). Having dismissed the envoys of Nebuchadrezzar, they now send their own envoys to Holofernes to sue for peace (3:1). Having sent Nebuchadrezzar's envoys away empty-handed (1:11), they now welcome his envoy "with garlands and dances and tambourines" (3:7).

Holofernes' response is, as he was instructed by Nebuchadrezzar (2:10), to occupy the territory (3:6). But he goes further (3:8): "he demolished all their shrines and cut down their sacred groves; for he had been commissioned to destroy all the gods of the land, so that all nations should worship Nebuchadrezzar alone, and that all their dialects and tribes should call upon him as a god" (3:8). The LXX has *oria,* "boundaries" or "borders," but most modern translations follow the Syriac's "shrines." While "boundaries" echoes Nebuchadrezzar's order that Holofernes capture all the *orion* of the disobedient nations (2:10), "shrines" seems to fit the sense of 3:8 as a whole. The language used here is reminiscent of texts such as Daniel 3 and 6 and, more indirectly, of 1 Macc 1:10–2:26 and 2 Maccabees 6–7.

That Nebuchadrezzar should be worshiped as a god is another historical anachronism, "for, historically, no Mesopotamian or Persian king was deified. Such a claim was first made by successors of Alexander the Great, two centuries later" (LaCocque 1990: 32). However, historical accuracy is not the primary concern of the narrator; history is reworked for theological purposes. Up to this point the ambitions of Nebuchadrezzar have been ostensibly political, but as any Palestinian reader would know, politics and religion are inseparable. What was implicit is now explicit, and the dramatic tension and sense of foreboding are heightened, particularly as the very next move Holofernes makes is toward Judea (3:9). But before the tension can be released, there is another ominous pause, reminiscent of the pause at the end of the first scene (1:16), as the pace of the narrative is slowed even further while Holofernes and his army rest and reprovision (3:10).

(b) 4:1-15

"Throughout the first three chapters the reader is overwhelmed with the seemingly invincible power of Nebuchadnezzar and his general Holofernes. One by one all the nations are destroyed or submit as vassals, leaving Judea to face the Assyrian giant alone" (Schuller 1992: 241). The focus now shifts to Judea, and remains on Judea for the remainder of the narrative. World events recede into the background.

The report that reaches the ears of the Israelites emphasizes the religious dimensions of the destruction (4:1). Like the nations around them, the Israelites are terrified, particularly as they contemplate the fate of Jerusalem and the temple of the Lord their God (v. 2).

The statement that "they had only recently returned from exile" (4:3) is another example of the deliberate distortion of time by the narrator. Historically, Nebuchadrezzar had been responsible for their captivity and exile (alluded to in 2:1), from which they had returned about fifty years later under the Persian Empire, which had succeeded the Babylonian Empire (see Ezra 1:1-3). Yet here it is plainly stated that the Israelites have recently returned from exile, reunited with those who had remained in Judea, and rededicated the temple. How can Jerusalem and the temple be under threat from Nebuchadrezzar again? The reader is once again left floundering for secure historical footing. But again the historical disorientation has a narrative and theological purpose; the reader is asked to imagine Nebuchadrezzar standing before Jerusalem and the temple once again, to imagine the destruction of their social and religious structures again, to imagine being separated from their land and faith. Such imaginings are too appalling to bear, and so present readers in their present contexts are challenged to resist Nebuchadrezzar and his like. Such an abomination cannot happen again.

Within the story, the immediate response of the Israelites is twofold: they send out a warning to every part of the territory and prepare for and plan resistance (4:4-7), and they cry out to God in prayer and fasting (vv. 9-15). Joakim and the council, who coordinate these military and religious activities (vv. 6-8), fulfill roles first encountered in Maccabean times. Not only did a senate or council *(gerousia)* not exist until Maccabean times (1 Macc 12:6 and 2 Macc 11:27), but Joakim's role is suggestive of the responsibilities held by Jonathan, brother of Judas Maccabee, in 153 BC (see 1 Macc 10:18-21) (Craven 1989: 574 and LaCocque 1990: 32). It has been argued that the use of the term *gerousia* here indicates that Judith was composed prior to the time of John Hyrcanus II (67 BC) when the term *synedrion* was used to designate the Jerusalem senate (Craven 1989: 574).

The inclusion of Samaria (4:4) in the list of places to which Israel sent words of warning is another anachronism since the people of Judea and the Samaritans were separate and increasingly anatagonistic communities in the postexilic era. However, by including Samaria in the narrative setting, the author may be adding his/her voice to Israel's ongoing debate concerning ethnicity (see the discussion of 14:10 below). The name of the high priest, "Joakim" (4:6), is probably derived from Neh 12:26. The identification of Bethulia (4:6) remains a puzzle to scholars, with some suggesting that it is a pseudonym for Shechem (see 7:18 below).

The extent and detail of the people's anguish are clearly recounted. The whole community participates in crying out to God through fasting, sackcloth, ashes, and regular and freewill burnt offerings. Everyone wears sackcloth, including resident aliens, laborers, and slaves (4:10). The crisis is felt by all, regardless of class. Even the cattle and altar are draped in sackcloth (vv. 10-12). The fear that drives their cries to God is graphically described (v. 12).

In the midst of their prayer and fasting we are told that "The Lord heard their prayers and had regard for their distress" (4:13). Yet nothing actually happens to change their predicament! "This is the only sentence in the book where God is the active subject" (Schuller 1992: 241), but while God hears, God does not act. The cries continue (vv. 14-15). The word of hope in v. 13 is surrounded by sackcloth. So this section ends somewhat ambiguously. Both the characters within the story and the reader are forced to wait in order to find what form God's response will take. Is even God unable to act against the might of Nebuchadrezzar?

(c) 5:1–6:13

Of all the people of the west it is Israel alone that resists Holofernes (5:4). The response of Holofernes is a mixture of anger, consternation, and perhaps some concern (5:2-4). Who is this people that dares to oppose him? The reader, who knows full well who Israel is, would probably be experiencing similar emotions, but for different reasons. How can Holofernes not know Israel? With supreme irony the narrative satisfies both Holofernes and the reader. Achior, an Ammonite officer in the "Assyrian" army, recounts to Holofernes Israel's history (5:5-19).

Although Achior does not mention Nebuchadrezzar by name, his account of Israel's history includes the real Nebuchadrezzar's destruction of the Jerusalem temple in 586 BC and the rebuilding of the temple in 515 BC. By imaginatively reordering the people, time, and place the narrator portrays Jerusalem and its temple as once again under threat by Nebuchadrezzar. The concerns, however, are of another, albeit related, people and place. The phrase "the God of heaven" (5:8), for example, was used by Jews during the Persian period and later (see Tob 10:11 and Ezra 1:2).

Achior does not stop, however, with an account of Israel's history; he adds a prophetic warning (5:20-21). Ironically, Achior has more faith in "their God" than the Israelites themselves. The response of first Holofernes' officers and soldiers and then Holofernes himself is one of outrage (5:22–6:9). The officers and army scoff at the military capabilities of Israel (vv. 22-24). The retort of Holofernes is more considered; he resents Achior's prophecy and rejects the implication of Achior's warning that there is any god besides Nebuchadrezzar (6:2). He accuses Achior of treason, of being a "mercenary of Ephraim" (i.e., Israel) (vv. 2, 5), and banishes him to the hill country to await the same fate as Israel (vv. 5-9).

In this section the word of Achior (5:20-21) is set against the word of Nebuchadrezzar (6:4) and the word of Holofernes (6:9). The question raised by this juxtaposition is: Who has spoken the truth? Is Achior a prophet? Is Achior a "brother of light," as his name suggests? There is also some rather macabre irony here when Holofernes says to Achior that he will not see his face again until he, Holofernes, has taken vengeance on Israel (6:5); when Achior next sees Holofernes' face it has been severed from his body (14:6).

The section ends with Achior being escorted to Bethulia and handed over to the Israelites (6:10-13). The ease with which Holofernes' slaves infiltrate Israel's territory seems to vindicate the low opinion Holofernes and his officers have of Israel's military capabilities. If Israel's defenses can be penetrated so easily, who can save Israel from the might of Nebuchadrezzar?

(c′) 6:14-21

The chiastic pattern of Scene 3 now becomes evident in the inversion of the ordering of action. Having been expelled by Holofernes (6:10-13), Achior is received by the Israelites (v. 14). Having been questioned by Holofernes (5:2-4), Achior is questioned by the Israelite leadership (6:16). Having told Holofernes about the Israelites (5:5-21), Achior tells the Israelites about Holofernes (6:17). The attentive reader is drawn into the narrative weave of the story.

The report of Achior is narrated briefly (6:17), as the pace of the narrative appears to pick up. Although brief, Achior's report contains both what he said to Holofernes, including presumably his prophetic warning, and what Holofernes said in reply. Achior's report draws two responses from the Israelites. The first response is clear; they cry out to God (v. 19) when they hear of Holofernes' boast (v. 4). Their second response is more difficult to interpret: "Then they reassured Achior, and praised him highly" (v. 20). If the first response is a response to the plans of Holofernes and his council, then the structure of these verses suggests that the second response is a response to Achior's prophetic proclamation. The Israelites are perhaps reassuring Achior that they, too, have faith in their God, and are commending him for his faith in their God.

The final verse in this section (6:21) is also puzzling, but perhaps can be interpreted as a development of the two responses. Uzziah, the chief elder of Bethulia, hosts Achior and offers a banquet in his honor. The Greek word used here for feast is *potos,* which is literally "a drinking party" (Craven 1989: 574). The literary context suggests that the "banquet" is a form of celebration, and this can be understood only as a celebration of Achior's prophetic faith in God's presence. The second sentence in v. 21 ("and all that night they called on the God of Israel for help") then signals a calling to God in hope rather than in despair. Despair, it seems, has turned to hope because of the faith of a foreigner.

Although the section ends with no overt action from

God, there is a further foreshadowing of hope; Uzziah, we are explicitly told (6:15), is of the tribe of Simeon, and so is Judith (see 9:2).

(b′) 7:1-5

Holofernes marches toward Bethulia with an army enlarged by fifty thousand soldiers (see 2:5, 15). The immensity of Holofernes' forces is emphasized in numerical and spatial terms (7:3). The preparations ordered by Joakim (4:4-7) seem paltry in comparison to these preparations. Earlier they had heard about Holofernes' advance (4:1); now they are able to see his advance with their own eyes (7:4). The sight of Holofernes' vast army recalls the image, already used (2:20), of locusts who "strip clean the whole land" (7:4). The Israelites are once again "greatly terrified" (7:4; see 4:2). All they can do is stand at their posts and wait.

The spring, which is the water supply to Bethulia, is mentioned here for the first time (7:3). In the following section the spring becomes a key element in Holofernes' strategy.

(a′) 7:6-32

Earlier in Scene 3 Holofernes launched his military campaign against the western nations, who eventually sue for peace and surrender (2:14–3:10). In this section of the scene Holofernes launches his military campaign against the Israelites. Will they, too, be forced to sue for peace and surrender?

Just when the action of the story has begun to accelerate, the pace of the narrative is slowed once again by detailed descriptions of the Assyrian tactics (7:6-18) and the deliberations of the Israelites (vv. 19-32). Tension mounts.

The plan by some of Holofernes' commanders to take control of the water supply to Bethulia (7:8-17) appears to be an unnecessary repetition, given that the water supply had already been seized by the cavalry (v. 7). It may be that there was more than one water supply to Bethulia and that those who know the locality, the Edomites, are aware of these other sources. The decision to lay siege to Bethulia rather than to attack it directly has the effect of prolonging the narrative tension. The storyteller's creative and dramatic use of time is evident once again.

"The Edomites" (7:8, 18) have not been mentioned previously, but were traditional enemies of the Jews (see Obad 18). The localities referred to in v. 18 have all been identified with sites in the vicinity of Shechem, which has led some scholars to suggest that Bethulia may be a pseudonym for Shechem (see 4:6).

Encircled by their enemies, the Israelites cry out to God again. The Assyrian plan to cut off their water supply is working (7:20-22). God, it seems, has handed them over to the Assyrians (v. 25). The people put enormous pressure on the leadership to surrender, believing that they are being punished by God and that their only hope lies in surrender and slavery (vv. 26-29). But Uzziah believes that God will show mercy and will not abandon them, and so he urges his people not to give up hope in God's deliverance. He asks them to wait for five more days (v. 31). The section, the third scene, and Act 1 ends with the Israelites waiting, but waiting in "great misery" rather than hope (v. 32). Whatever hope Achior's prophetic faith may have kindled (see above) has been extinguished by subsequent events.

Act 2 (8:1–16:25)

The ironic mood established in Act 1 is immediately evident in Act 2. Act 1 ends with each man at his military post and the women and children at home. Act 2 begins by introducing the reader for the first time to the woman warrior who will completely change the tide of events. Since ancient scrolls probably did not have titles, this is the first suggestion of a female hero (Schuller 1992: 241).

Act 2, like Act 1, Scene 3, has a chiastic structure organized around a central scene in which Judith overcomes Holofernes. The structure of Act 2 can be schematized as follows (Craven 1983: 47-64; Craven 1989: 573):

(a) Introduction to Judith (8:1-8)
(b) Judith plans to save Israel (8:9–10:10)
(c) Judith overcomes Holofernes (10:11–13:11)
(b′) Judith plans the destruction of Israel's enemy (13:12–16:20)
(a′) Conclusion about Judith (16:21-25)

(a) Scene 1 (8:1-8)

Judith (the name means "Jewess") is introduced at length; in fact, she is given the longest genealogy of any woman in the Bible. As we might expect by now, Judith's lineage is a mixture of fiction and history; other than Israel himself, Judith's ancestors cannot be identified. The narrative point, however, is clear — Judith is directly descended from the ancestor Israel. While the genealogy links Judith firmly to the male world of her husband, she is also relatively independent in that she is a widow who has property and is financially secure. The reference to her beauty (8:7) reminds us, however, that Judith can never fully escape the categories and values of the patriarchal culture of which she is both a product and a part. Above all, the text emphasizes, she is "a deeply religious woman" (vv. 6, 8).

In this introduction to Judith we have the first of numerous allusions to other women in the Bible. The opening description of Judith recalls "the good wife" of Proverbs 31, and other allusions follow. The book of Judith "is an anthology of texts about, and allusions to, other women in the Bible: Miriam, Deborah, Jael, Sarah, Rebekah, Rachel, Tamar, Naomi, Ruth, and Abigail, among others. Parallels with Esther and Susanna also are clear. In fact, the cumulative effect is striking; it amounts to a panegyric of the biblical woman" (LaCocque 1990: 35; White 1992).

(b) Scene 2 (8:9–10:10)

In this scene Judith is no longer an object being described; she is now an active subject. She sends her maid to summon the elders to her home (8:9-10); she rebukes the elders for putting God to the test and offers her own theological analysis of events (vv. 11-27); she listens to Uzziah defend his compromise and to his request that she pray for rain (vv. 28-31); she implicitly dismisses his temporary solution and proposes instead her own plan to deliver Israel (vv. 32-34); she receives the blessing of the leadership (vv. 35-36); she prays to God (9:1-14); she bathes and grooms herself (10:1-5); she goes to meet with the elders at the town gate (v. 6); she receives their blessing again (vv. 7-8); she orders the gate opened (v. 9); and with her maid she leaves Bethulia (v. 10).

As this brief summary of Scene 2 indicates, Judith is now the central character. Judith does not seem to have been present when the community and its leaders agreed to set a time limit for their deliverance (8:1, 9). This is somewhat strange given her reputation in the community (see v. 29). Her absence is probably a narrative strategy to delay her entry into the story until the last possible moment. However, having at last entered the story, Judith now takes over! The plot is propelled by her presence.

Judith is never alone, however. She has a female companion, an unnamed woman "who was in charge of all she possessed" (8:10) and who is her faithful "maid" throughout the story. The nature of their relationship is not explicitly explored in the narrative. The maid is sent on errands (v. 10), is assumed to be present (v. 33), assists in grooming (10:2), carries bags (v. 5), accompanies her mistress (v. 10), prepares food (12:19), is excluded from the action (13:3), takes what she is given (v. 9), is ignored in subsequent accounts of the action, and is set free once she is no longer of use to Judith (16:23). The maid is a prop in Judith's story; she is an object whose story remains to be told. Whatever the gender consciousness of the story (see the discussion below), there is little consciousness of class.

Judith's long theological discourse with the elders (8:11-27) on the relationship between faith and suffering is reminiscent of the book of Job (Dancy 1972: 99). However, while Judith does offer a different theological understanding of their predicament, the conclusion she comes to is not that different from that already reached — they must wait and see whether God will deliver them (v. 17), though she does argue that there are good theological grounds for hope (vv. 18-27). Ironically, having criticized the elders for usurping God's role in human affairs (v. 12) and having called them to wait and pray (v. 17), she herself follows only the last part of her advice. She prays, but she does not wait; rather, she takes action in a way that could be seen as usurping God's role in human affairs! Perhaps her theology is more radically different from that of the elders than it seems at first sight.

Judith not only rejects the theological position of the elders, but she also refuses the role they offer her (8:31). She has a reputation for wisdom and prayer (vv. 28-31), but she refuses to be limited by this reputation. Judith is about to step beyond the boundaries of her reputation, but she will not say how. Her long prayer (9:1-14) slows the action somewhat and increases suspense as the reader is offered tantalizing clues concerning her proposed plan: her plan includes deceit (vv. 10, 13), and the allusion to her ancestor Simeon (v. 2), who avenged the rape of Dinah (Gen 34:25-26), indicates that violence is a distinct possibility. The prospect of violence is confirmed by another allusion, in 9:10. The allusion here is to Judg 9:52-54, where Abimelech, mortally injured by a woman, asks his armor bearer to kill him with his sword lest it be said, "A woman killed him." Judith seems to revel in the irony of being the agent of such an ignominious act.

The reference to "the evening incense" in the preface to Judith's prayer (9:1) may indicate that there were regular prayers in the temple at this time of day. Even while remaining in her home, Judith joins with those who are praying in the temple. Her piety is emphasized. The prayer itself offers further insight into Judith's theology. If God is involved in and has knowledge of all things past and present, and if God's ways are prepared beforehand and present themselves at the appropriate time (vv. 5-6), then perhaps Judith has "read" the signs of the times and has seen God's plan, in which she plays the principal role. Ironically, however, having declared that God knows all things, she then goes on to describe the situation regarding the Assyrians to God (v. 7). While Judith is concerned about the fate of her people, particularly the most vulnerable, at the hands of the Assyrians (v. 2), her primary concern seems to be for the fate of the temple, God's sanctuary (vv. 8, 13).

Unlike later readers, Judith apparently has no scruples in praying for divine assistance in order to be deceitful (9:10, 13), and the narrator seems quite comfortable with this part of the prayer as well.

In drawing particular attention to herself as a widow (9:4, 9), Judith deliberately situates herself in the category of those whom she herself claims are close to God (v. 11). The mention of her widowhood also reminds the reader of other famous widows in the Bible, particularly Abigail (1 Sam 25:39, 42), Bathsheba (2 Sam 11:26-27), and Ruth (see LaCocque 1990: 35-38). However, although Judith calls upon God as "the God of the lowly, helper of the oppressed, upholder of the weak, protector of the forsaken, savior of those without hope" (9:11), and although here and elsewhere in the story women are remembered as protagonists of God's purposes, the prayer of Judith, and the story as a whole, remain within a nationalistic and patriarchal framework. In her prayer Judith speaks in praise of the violent revenge of her male ancestor Simeon against those who abused his sister (Gen 34:1-29), but omits any mention of Dinah by name. Furthermore, Judith actually commends God for giving the wives and daughters of Hamor and his son Shechem to others to abuse (9:2-4) (Schuller 1992: 243).

It appears from 10:2 that Judith prayed on the roof, where she apparently lived in a tent (8:5). Having prayed, she goes down to her house, puts aside her widow's garments and sackcloth, which are her usual form of dress (see also 8:5), and beautifies herself (10:3-4). "In addition to her wisdom and piety, Judith now draws upon her beauty as she adorns herself with the finest clothing and perfumes" (Schuller 1992: 242). The purpose of this process of beautification is clear: "to entice the eyes of all the men who might see her" (10:4); a further element of Judith's plan now becomes apparent. Her beauty, like her words, is to be used to deceive.

By adding that God gave her supernatural beauty because her motive in adorning herself was virtuous rather than lustful (Dentan 1973: 87), the Latin version of Judith belabors what is obvious to any attentive reader of the Greek text (Moore 1985: 201). In the midst of these preparations which are designed to entice and beguile, Judith does not neglect to prepare a bag of ritually pure food and to take vessels for cooking her food, in accordance with Jewish dietary laws (10:5). Judith's actions all take place within the framework of a rigorous piety (see also 8:6).

The altered appearance of Judith has its desired effect on the elders of the city when she meets them at the city gate (10:7), and on every man she meets subsequently! Whether they discern the details of her plan at this point is not clear, and they do not probe; they simply give her their blessing. The men of the city hand over their fate to God and Judith (v. 8a). Judith, however, deflects attention from her own role by acknowledging God (v. 8b). Prayer and acts of religious observance accompany every one of Judith's decisive acts.

The scene ends dramatically with Judith ordering the elders to open the city gates, which are closed against the Assyrian invaders, and setting off to execute her plan. In a profoundly ironic final moment "the men of the town" watch as two women, a widow and her maid, disappear in the distance to save them (10:9-10).

(c) Scene 3 (10:11–13:11)

The proximity of the Assyrians is emphasized by how quickly Judith and her maid are arrested when they leave Bethulia (10:11-12). The first words Judith utters on being questioned are deceitful words (vv. 12-13; see 9:10, 13). Judith begins to implement her plan immediately. Her beauty, another aspect of her plan, has its intended effect and is recognized and praised by the sentries who arrest her (10:14), by the Assyrian soldiers in the camp (v. 19), and by Holofernes and his servants (v. 23). The male gaze is firmly fixed on Judith.

Now that Judith stands before Holofernes the focus shifts from deceiving looks to deceiving words. Holofernes insists that his intentions are peaceful, but that it is the Israelites who have provoked him (11:1-4). Judith asks Holofernes to accept her words, promising that she will say nothing false (v. 5). In words full of irony and double meanings, she assures him that if he follows her words, "God will accomplish something through you, and my lord will not fail to achieve his purposes" (v. 6). Holofernes is deceived, believing he is her lord, but Judith and the reader know that her lord is God, not Holofernes. In the rest of her lengthy and carefully constructed speech Judith continues to flatter (vv. 7-8) and deceive (vv. 9-19).

The structure of 11:7 is unclear in the Greek, and consequently most English translations are awkward. The general thrust, however, is clear. Judith flatters both Holofernes and Nebuchadrezzar, though the focus of her flattery is Holofernes.

The deception in the remainder of her speech is delightfully ironic, and demonstrates her, and the author's, sense of humor. Judith does not simply lie to Holofernes; she plays with words and in so doing plays with him (see Craven 1983: 95). She reminds Holofernes of the words of Achior (5:5-21) and reaffirms them (11:9-10). She then offers an elaborate and, in the context of a siege, plausible account of Israel's imminent transgression of God's dietary laws (11:11-15; see Exod 23:19 and Lev 27:30). Her argument thus far is clear. Holofernes must heed the words of Achior and so must not attack Israel until they have sinned against God. But, she assures him, Israel is about to sin and so will become vulnerable.

The key question that remains concerns timing: When will Israel sin? In the final section of her speech Judith makes sure that she is in control of the timing. Having lied about the reasons for leaving her people, Judith declares with deep irony that "God has sent me to accomplish with you things that will astonish the whole world wherever people shall hear about them" (11:16). The manipulation of truth and falsehood does not stop here, for Judith goes on to assert that she is religious, which we know is true, and that she will pray to God every night, which is true, to find out when Israel has sinned, which is false (vv. 17-18). By telling him that she will pray in the valley, outside the camp, every night, Judith is already preparing a ruse for her eventual escape (v. 17). She concludes her speech by promising Holofernes that she will lead him through Judea; this she will do, but not in the way he imagines (v. 19).

There is another reference in this speech to the council in Jerusalem (11:14), the supreme religious authority of later Judaism (see 4:6-8).

Holofernes is duped; her words have deceived, and her beauty has beguiled (11:20-23). Holofernes is so taken in by her beauty and her words that he is unable to discern her duplicity. In refusing to eat the food offered by Holofernes she confirms not only her piety but also her story (12:1-2). When Holofernes worries about her supplies running out, Judith reassures him, saying "As surely as you live, my lord, your servant will not use up the supplies I have with me before the Lord carries out by my hand what he has determined" (v. 4). Her reassurance is full of irony! But the reader is reminded that time and supplies are running out for the the people of Bethulia.

Over the next three days Judith confidently uses the time to establish a pattern of piety (12:5-9). The reference to Judith bathing in the very spring that used to provide water for her people until it was captured by the Assyrians (7:7, 12, 17) is a daily reminder of their hardship (see 7:20-22; 8:30-31), and so each time she finishes her ablutions she prays for God to guide her in the deliverance of her people (12:7-8).

The narrative tension is almost unbearable by this time; only two days remain of the deadline (see 7:30). Judith has been patiently waiting her opportunity, or, more precisely, waiting for God to direct her (12:8). Both initiating and waiting have a place in her theology. On the fourth day (v. 10) an opportunity presents itself (see 9:6). Holofernes, who has been "waiting for an opportunity to seduce her" (12:16), summons Judith to a banquet. His intentions are clear: "it would be a disgrace if we let such a woman go without having intercourse with her" (v. 12). The Greek verbs used here clearly suggest seduction and forced sexual relations (Craven 1989: 575).

The plot now picks up pace. Judith pretends to be

pleased by his obvious amorous intentions (12:13-20), but even in the midst of the passion and pretense, piety is not forgotten; Judith observes the dietary laws of her people (v. 19). Holofernes' desire and Judith's deception are continually contrasted: Judith claims that her life means more to her on this day than on any other day since she was born (v. 18); and Holofernes drinks more wine in one day than on any other day since he was born (v. 20). While Judith retains her dignity and her sense of destiny throughout, Holofernes becomes more and more ridiculous in the eyes of the reader. The ironic tone of the narrative has had its effect; the collusion of Judith, the narrator, and the reader at the expense of Holofernes has shown him to be full of hubris (LaCocque 1990: 34).

While Holofernes is not able to put his plan into action, being overcome with wine (13:2), Judith, having carefully prepared for this moment (vv. 3-4a) and having prayed for God's strength, executes her plan with terrible purpose (vv. 4b-10a). There is an allusion here to 1 Sam 17:51, where David uses Goliath's own sword to decapitate him, suggesting perhaps that Judith is a female David (LaCocque 1990: 35). The book of Judith does not allude only to heroic women but also to heroic men.

With macabre irony the severed head of Holofernes is placed in the food bag, which until now has contained nothing unclean (13:10a). Even her food bag is part of a well-laid plan.

The central third scene began with Judith arriving in the Assyrian camp; the scene ends with Judith leaving the Assyrian camp. Once again, her meticulous preparation is demonstrated as she and her maid leave the Assyrian camp as was their established habit (13:10b; see 11:17; 12:7-8). Unhindered, they go all the way to the gates of Bethulia.

(b′) Scene 4 (13:12–16:20)

At the end of Scene 2 Judith commanded the elders to open the city gates so that she could fulfill God's purposes (10:9); she now stands before the same gates again, commanding that they be opened because God's purposes have been accomplished (13:11). Much has happened in this carefully constructed narrative since the city gates were closed behind her. Judith has been in control throughout Scene 3, and she remains in charge throughout this scene until victory is complete.

Judith's first response is to give praise to God; her hand has been the instrument, but it is God who has directed it (13:11, 14; see 9:5-6, 10, 12:8; 13:4). Judith is both heroine and helper of God (Milne 1993). That the people marvel at her return (13:13) is an indication of how little hope they had at her departure (see 10:10); their amazement increases as she dramatically pulls the head of Holofernes out of her food bag. Clearly the elders and the people did not expect God to work in this way, but Judith holding the head of Holofernes is convincing proof! Like Judith, the people turn to God in praise (13:17). Their words of praise emphasize the humiliation of their enemy (see 9:10).

Judith's account is brief and vivid, consisting as it does of showing and telling. She, too, emphasizes the humiliation of Israel's enemy. Her selection of detail is significant; she emphasizes the ignoble end of Holofernes (13:15). He died in his bed, while drunk, at the hand of a woman (see 9:10). Holofernes and the Assyrians have been humiliated (13:17b). She also quickly reassures her listeners that though it was her face that deceived Holofernes, she herself was not deceived or defiled (13:16).

Uzziah's blessing of Judith recalls the words spoken by Jael under similar circumstances (Judg 5:24) as well as Melchizedek's greeting to Abraham (Gen 14:19-20, LXX) (Moore 1985: 233). No other biblical woman receives such high praise.

But Judith does not allow her unfinished plan to be distracted by this praise. Using words she has used before, she instructs the people to listen to her (14:1; see 8:11, 32). She immediately begins to organize the second phase of her plan (14:1-4). She is the one who plans and directs the pursuit and final slaughter of the Assyrians. Once again her plan is based on subterfuge (v. 2).

Prior to the implementation of her plan, however, Judith calls for Achior to come and identify the head of Holofernes (14:5). This interruption is a little unusual at this point in the narrative. In the Latin version of the story, v. 5 is omitted and vv. 6-7 are placed before vv. 1-4 (Dentan 1973: 92; Moore 1985: 234). The actual identification is full of irony; Achior, a seasoned Ammonite warrior, faints at the sight of Holofernes' head, severed by the hand of a woman (v. 6) (LaCocque 1990: 33; Moore 1985: 235). Furthermore, the full irony of the situation is evident when we remember that Achior had been told by Holofernes that he would not see his face again until the day of his, Holofernes', vengeance (6:5).

Achior's amazement offers Judith the opportunity to tell him, and her people, all that has taken place until this moment (14:8). This is an important narrative moment, and is perhaps the reason for the present literary location of this episode; the reader knows what Judith has been doing outside the city walls, but the hearers within the city walls do not. So the narrator uses this strategy to update the narrative addressees, placing them on equal footing with the reader. The ironic collusion between the narrator and the reader is coming to an end just as the narrative itself is drawing to a close (see the discussion of 12:13-20 above).

But this does not mean that the ironic purposes of the narrator are finished; a final irony in this scene is the conversion of Achior, an Ammonite (14:10). Israelite law explicitly forbids the conversion of an Ammonite (or a Moabite) (Deut 23:3). This time the irony is shared by all — narrator, reader, and characters. Such blatant irony can only be deliberate, and must signal something of the purpose of the book of Judith (see Roitman 1992). Such bold irony probably cost the book of Judith its place in the Hebrew canon (Enslin and Zeitlin 1972: 235; Moore 1992). A secondary purpose of the Achior interlude at this point in the narrative is the slowing of the dramatic action. The reader is able to pause before the final frenetic moments of the rout of the Assyrian army.

All of this scene has taken place at night (see 13:1). With the arrival of dawn the second phase of Judith's plan is put into effect (14:11). As Judith had planned, the threatening military movements of the Jews lead to the discovery of the headless Holofernes (vv. 11-19). The relaying of the message of Israel's military preparations is depicted in comical detail — the message makes its way from the edge of the Assyrian lines to Holofernes' tent at the center of the Assyrian camp where the full array of Assyrian officers wait for the appearance of the (headless) head of their army! An Israelite audience would revel in this graphic, ironic, and humorous portrayal. The words of Bagoas capture the full humiliation visited on the Assyrian army (v. 18): they have been tricked by slaves (see also v. 13); worse, they have been disgraced by one, Hebrew, woman!

The leaders of the Assyrian army tear their tunics and cry out in dismay, while the rest of the army is overcome with "fear and trembling" and flees (14:19–15:3a). The phrase "fear and trembling" appears twice in Judith; here the Assyrians experience what they had induced in others (2:28). Particular mention is made of the Edomites and Ammonites, "who had camped in the hills" (15:3; see 7:18).

As with so many of the geographical details in this story, the locations of Betomasthaim, Bebai, Choba, and Kola have not been identified (15:4). The remaining details, however, accurately depict the northeastward flight of the Assyrian army as they flee between Gilead on their eastern flank and Galilee on their western flank, beyond Damascus and back toward Assyria (v. 5).

The rout of the Assyrians and the plundering of the camp are described in graphic detail (15:3b-7), as is the honoring of Judith (vv. 8-10). The juxtaposition of these episodes vividly portrays the very different fates of those who oppose God, on the one hand, and those, on the other hand, who serve God. Judith is a heroine because she is God's helper (v. 8).

Judith's religious devotion remains exemplary. Her personal plunder, the canopy from the bed of Holofernes (13:9, 15), and the plunder the people give her (15:11) are not taken for personal gain; they are later dedicated to God (16:19). Ironically, the very silver dishes Judith ate off in Holofernes' presence (12:1) are now offered to her as plunder (15:11).

For the first time in the narrative other women appear as subjects (15:12-13). Men and one extraordinary woman have dominated the narrative, but now that the crisis has passed life returns to its normal order and women resume their normal roles. The story of these women remains to be told; has Judith empowered them, or is she the exception that confirms the rule? Clearly, they revel in her prominence, and for a brief time the men are in the background (v. 13b).

The branches Judith gives to the other women (15:12b) are symbols of celebration and praise (Ps 118:27), especially in situations of God's deliverance (1 Macc 13:51; 2 Macc 10:7). The reference to the wearing of "olive wreaths" (15:13) is another indication of the late date for the book, as the custom is Greek, not Jewish (Moore 1985: 247).

As the procession that Judith and the women lead makes its way to its destination, the temple in Jerusalem (16:18), Judith sings a hymn of thanksgiving, which is taken up by the people (vv. 1-17). Just as Moses led the people of Israel in a song of triumph and praise after the deliverance from Egypt (Exod 15:1-18), so Judith leads her people in song. However, although there is a clear allusion to the song of Moses, Judith's hymn of thanksgiving and victory, which is a liturgical poem in form (see Craven 1983: 105-12), functions in the narrative to remind the reader of Judith's proper place in the narrative. Prominent though her role is, God is the real deliverer (16:1-3). It is Israel, personified as a woman, who sings the psalm; Judith herself is referred to only in the third person (v. 7).

As one might expect, the hymn of thanksgiving has many allusions to the Psalms. For example, the phrase "a new song" (16:1, 13) is found in a number of Psalms (see Pss 96:1; 98:1; 144:9). If the reference to "the sons of the Titans" (16:6) refers to the divine children of Uranus (the heavens) and Ge (earth), then it assumes that the readers would be familiar with Greek mythology; however, in the LXX, *titanes* is used in 2 Kgs 5:18, 22 to translate Heb. *rp'ym,* which evidently refers to mortals (Moore 1985: 248). The reference to "giants" (16:6) may allude to very tall mortals (see Deut 2:11, 20; 3:11; 2 Sam 21:16-22) or to semidivine creatures called "Nephilim" who are the offspring of divine beings and human women (see Gen 6:1-4) (Moore 1985: 248). The theological perspective on sacrifice (16:16), which contrasts sacrifice with moral obedience, is a trajectory of OT religion, particularly in later times (1 Sam 15:22; Pss 40:6-8; 50:8-15; 51:16-17; Hos 6:6). The phrase "fire and worms" (16:17) is also found in Isa 66:24 and Sir 7:17. As in Dan 12:2, the punishment of those who oppose God's people is eternal (16:17).

The scene ends with feasting before the sanctuary, which is now safe from Israel's enemies. Appropriately, the people spend three times as long feasting in Jerusalem as they did plundering the camp of the Assyrians (cf. 15:11 and 16:20). What Judith has started, Judith has finished (16:20b).

(a') Scene 5 (16:21-25)

A final concise scene concludes the narrative. The action of the narrative is complete. The threat to the temple in Jerusalem has been overcome, and victory has been celebrated. All that remains is a final word about the heroine. God has not been usurped by Judith, as the liturgical hymn of thanksgiving constantly reminds the worshiping community (16:1-17). But as a faithful helper of God, the narrative seems to suggest, Judith deserves the final word. The remainder of her life is briefly sketched (vv. 21-24), with every detail bringing honor to her name. Judith returns to her hometown, where she continues to live her independent but devout life (v. 21). She remains a widow, lives a full and long life, distributes her property according to the Mosaic law (Num 27:11), sets her faithful maid free, and is buried in the cave of her husband. All is tidy, all is ordered, everything seems in its place — or is it? Judith both affirms the traditions of his faith and disturbs them.

The final line of the story offers a short epitaph. Judith's memory, like her life, continues to offer protection to her people "for a long time after her death" (16:25).

Conclusion

The memory of Judith persists into the present, which is remarkable considering that the book is apocryphal and occupies the margins of the lectionary. Yet readers return to read and reread this story, using a variety of interpretative resources. Historical-critical, literary, feminist, psychoanalytical, and folklore approaches have been brought to the interpretative task (Levine 1995: 208). Judith eludes our grasp; she disturbs and unsettles received readings; she both draws and repels us; she confuses (Bal 1995: 263). Once the book is read, the memory of her lingers. Does she keep terror at bay, as she did for her people, or does her story condone untold terrors? What we make of Judith depends to a large extent on what reading resources and what life experiences we bring to the text and whom we read the text with.

Bibliography. Bal, M. 1995, "Head Hunting: 'Judith' on the Cutting Edge of Knowledge," in A. Brenner, ed., *A Feminist Companion to Esther, Judith and Susanna,* Sheffield: Sheffield Academic, 253-85 • Craven, T. 1983, *Artistry and Faith in the Book of Judith,* Chico, Calif.: Scholars • Craven, T. 1989, "Judith," in R. E. Brown, J. A. Fitzmyer, and R. E. Murphy, eds., *The New Jerome Biblical Commentary,* London: Geoffrey Chapman, 572-75 • Dancy, J. C. 1972, *The Shorter Books of the Apocrypha,* Cambridge: Cambridge University • Dentan, R. C. 1973, "Introduction and Annotations for Judith," in H. G. May and B. M. Metzger, eds., *The New Oxford Annotated Bible with the Apocrypha,* New York: Oxford University • Enslin, M. A., and S. Zeitlin. 1972, *The Book of Judith,* Leiden: E. J. Brill • LaCocque, A. 1990. *The Feminine Unconventional: Four Subversive Figures in Israel's Tradition,* Minneapolis: Fortress • Levine, A.-J. 1995, "Sacrifice and Salvation: Otherness and Domestication in the Book of Judith," in A. Brenner, ed., *A Feminist Companion to Esther, Judith and Susanna,* Sheffield: Sheffield Academic, 208-23 • Milne, P. J. 1993, "What Shall We Do with Judith? A Feminist Reassessment of a Biblical 'Heroine,'" *Semeia* 62:37-58 • Moore, C. A. 1985, *Judith,* Garden City, N.Y.: Doubleday • Moore, C. A. 1992, "Why Wasn't the Book of Judith Included in the Hebrew Bible?" in J. C. VanderKam, ed., *"No one spoke ill of her": Essays on Judith,* Atlanta: Scholars, 61-71 • Roitman, A. D. 1992, "Achior in the Book of Judith: His Role and Significance," in J. C. VanderKam, ed., *"No one spoke ill of her": Essays on Judith,* Atlanta: Scholars, 31-45 • Schuller, E. M. 1992, "The Apocrypha," in C. A. Newsom and S. H. Ringe, eds., *The Women's Bible Commentary,* London: SPCK and Louisville: Westminster/John Knox, 235-43 • Stone, N. 1992, "Judith and Holofernes: Some Observations on the Development of the Scene in Art," in J. C. VanderKam, ed., *"No one spoke ill of her": Essays on Judith,* Atlanta: Scholars, 73-93 • White, S. A. 1992, "In the Steps of Jael and Deborah: Judith as Heroine," in J. C. VanderKam, ed., *"No one spoke ill of her": Essays on Judith,* Atlanta: Scholars, 5-16.

Greek Esther

John Jarick

INTRODUCTION

In the Septuagint (LXX) the book of Esther is a longer and more explicitly religious work than the Hebrew version of this story. Most striking is the inclusion of six blocks of material which add a number of facets to the tale, including a prophetic dream and its interpretation, the texts of royal correspondence and of earnest prayers, and a central dramatic scene in which the heroine Esther courageously takes her life in her hands for the sake of her people. But also sprinkled throughout the Greek version of the story are small notices about the activities of God and the special nature of the Jewish people, aspects which are not explicitly mentioned in the Hebrew text.

The additional passages appear in the Greek manuscripts at the relevant stages of the unfolding narrative (before 1:1; and then after 2:13; 4:17; 8:12; and 10:3), but because they were all grouped together at the end of the book in the Vulgate (Vg) and subsequently given sequential chapter-and-verse numbers in that arrangement, there is now potential confusion about how to refer to them. The NRSV Apocrypha places them in their proper Greek positions, labeling them "Addition A," "Addition B," and so on, but at the same time retains the Vg chapter-and-verse numbering from 10:4 (the beginning of Addition F, which the Vg placed before Addition A) to 16:24 (the end of Addition E), while mentioning in the footnotes the alternative scheme of applying individual verse numbers to each Addition. In the following comments, all references to the Additions will give both forms of versification, with the Vg-derived system in parentheses: e.g., A:1 (11:2).

Before proceeding to concentrate on the unique material represented in the Additions, it is well to note certain variations in those sections of the Greek book that are paralleled in the Hebrew version of the story. A good number of variations are simply due to the tale now being told in Greek, such as changes in the form of names of many of the protagonists (e.g., Artaxerxes rather than Ahasuerus in 1:1), or are due to the storyteller setting forth matters more clearly, such as details about dates and customs (e.g., the extra information about the celebration of Purim in 9:19). Sometimes the Greek text includes an element of which there is no sign in the Hebrew text (e.g., Mordecai's words in 4:1), but there are also instances where the Greek completely lacks an element to be found in the Hebrew (e.g., the letter-sending activity of 9:30). There are also times when a variation between the two versions raises an interesting question about the activities of certain players in the drama, as may be seen by comparing 2:1 in the Hebrew text (the king remembers his erstwhile wife) and the Greek text (he forgets all about her), or by comparing the texts of 9:10 (do the Jews indulge in plunder or not?).

Particularly noticeable, in view of the fact that the Hebrew story of Esther never mentions God, are the occasions when the Greek version does precisely that: Esther is a God-fearing woman (2:20) who is urged to call upon her Lord (4:8), the same Lord who acts upon her husband (6:6) and protects her former guardian (6:13). Mention is also made of the Jewish laws which she and her people follow (2:20; 8:11). All of these matters receive further and fuller treatment in the Additions, but even in the portions of the book that are shared with the Hebrew version, the Greek book of Esther overcomes one of the major misgivings many readers have had about the story of Esther in a biblical context, namely, its perceived lack of overt religiosity.

COMMENTARY

Addition A (A:1-17 = 11:2–12:6)

All the action in the Greek book of Esther takes place within the framework of an initial prophetic dream (in Addition A) and the subsequent interpretation of that dream (in Addition F). The events between these opening and closing accounts are thus pictured as being part of a grand divine plan, as is explicitly stated in A:11 (11:12) and F:1 (10:4), and not some chance events with perhaps a secular moral. Certain repetitions in the opening section drive home the religious dimensions of this story: nothing less than the fate of "the righteous nation" (A:6, 8 [11:7, 9]) is at stake here, and none less than "God" himself (A:9, 11 [11:10, 12]) is the chief protagonist.

The dreamer is Mordecai, introduced to us in the very first verse. In the Hebrew book there is no mention of this man until the twenty-seventh verse (2:5), along with Esther in the twenty-ninth verse (2:7), but in the Greek book he is there right from the start (A:1 [11:2]), well before the first appearance of Esther in the forty-sixth verse (2:7). Given that already in A:15 (12:4) Mordecai is busy "writing an account" of his deeds and that later he is seen "recording these things in a book" (9:20), and indeed that the last words of definitive interpretation in Addition F will be from his mouth as well, this story might almost be called "the book of Mordecai" rather than "the book of Esther." We are told that he is "a great man" (A:2 [11:3]) and "beloved to his whole nation" (10:3), so if these descriptions purport to arise from Mordecai's own account of matters, then it seems that modesty —

along with due deference to Queen Esther as the true savior of her people — is not one of his attributes, despite his protestations to the contrary (C:5-7 [13:12-14]).

Esther herself came to be honored by the rabbis as one of the seven prophetesses of the Hebrew Bible (*b. Meg.* 14a), but in the Greek version it is Mordecai who is the prophet. Since God does not act without revealing matters to prophets (Amos 3:7), it is only right that he should show his servant Mordecai beforehand what he has determined to do (A:11 [11:12]), even though the human recipient of the message does not fully understand it until after events have unfolded. The dream itself is a gem of apocalyptic imagery, with a reiterated vision of "tumult on the earth" (A:4, 7 [11:5, 8], recalling prophetic oracles like Isa 22:5 and Ezek 7:7), "darkness and gloom" (A:7 [11:8], recalling passages of the style of Joel 2:2 and Zeph 1:15), and no fewer than "two great dragons" ready to do battle (A:5 [11:6], recalling the appearance of dragons or dragon-like creatures in such visionary utterances as Isa 27:1 and Ezek 29:3). Comparisons may also be made with certain NT apocalyptic imagery, as in Mark 13 and parallels (various tumults on the earth) and Revelation 12–13 (the vision of "a great dragon"). Most of the images will be given a specific interpretation in Addition F, but their use already in Addition A alerts the reader to interpret the forthcoming story as one which is predetermined and overseen by God. What might otherwise look like a tale of court intrigue is labeled from the beginning as a drama of cosmic significance.

But there is court intrigue as well, and a little more of it in the Greek version than the Hebrew, for mention is made twice of Mordecai uncovering a plot against the king, first here in A:12-17 (12:1-6) and then again in 2:21-23. The storytelling sequence (note "after this" in 1:1 and "after these events" in 3:1) suggests that these are two separate plots by two different pairs of court eunuchs, thus making the king doubly beholden to Mordecai, although only on the first occasion does he "reward him for these things" (A:16 [12:5]). Reward for the second piece of intelligence that again saves the king's life will wait until 6:1-11, but the two events and indeed the larger scheme of things are linked by the narrator. It will be said (in 2:21) that the later plot arises because of Mordecai's reward for uncovering the earlier plot, and the larger scene is set at the end of Addition A (in A:17 [12:6]) by the explanation that Haman's forthcoming grand plot against the Jewish people likewise stems from Mordecai's undoing of the initial plot against the king. These matters will be spelled out more fully in Addition E, but the advance notice here at the outset of the tale reveals that Haman does not have the king's interests at heart, whereas Mordecai does — even at this time when he is not related by marriage to the throne (in contrast to the occasion of the second plot to kill the king).

Addition B (B:1-7 = 13:1-7)

The Greek version provides for its readers a full account of the king's two decrees concerning the Jews (the second decree will be set forth in Addition E). The king had also issued two earlier decrees in this story, namely, in 1:22 and 2:8 (and a further decree seems to be implied in 2:18). Despite the importance of those pronouncements in demonstrating the silliness of the monarch and in bringing Esther to her crucial position, however, they are not deemed as significant as this royal incitement to genocide and the later renunciation of that program.

Haman's letter in the king's name (3:12 made it clear that Haman is the scriptwriter here) bombastically sings the praises of both the king and Haman himself, but in such a way that the reader of this book knows that the assertions made in the letter are quite false. The king is praised for his reasonableness and kindness (B:2 [13:2]), yet this is the same monarch whose autocratic excesses have been well documented in previous chapters, along with his failure to reward Mordecai for that subject's second act of loyalty to the throne. Haman is praised for his goodwill and fidelity (B:3 [13:3]), yet this is the same courtier who apparently sided in secret with the insurrectionists (A:17 [12:6]) and who now seeks the destruction of an entire race on spurious grounds.

What the letter says about the nation that Haman has determined to destroy (B:4-5 [13:4-5]) reiterates in greater detail his earlier stated opinion (3:8). This chilling concoction of half-truths has resonances with certain details in the rest of the book. The contention that the Jews follow a different manner of life is supported by the report in 2:20 (reiterated by the queen herself in C:26-28 [14:15-17]) that neither Mordecai nor Esther compromised their Jewish mode of life, and similarly the idea that this one nation stands over against all the other nations of the empire is asserted by the narrator both at the beginning (the repeated depiction of "the righteous nation" in A:6, 8 [11:7, 9]) and at the end (the setting of "the people of God" on the one hand and "all the nations" on the other hand in F:7 [10:10]). But Haman's concomitant contention that this represents a danger to the kingdom has been obviously undermined in the story by the two Jewish protagonists, for both Mordecai and Esther have demonstrated complete loyalty to the king — except in one particular, namely, that Mordecai has not done obeisance to Haman (3:2), a matter of intense irritation to the self-styled "second father" of the kingdom (B:6 [13:6]) but hardly constituting a "continual disregard" of all royal ordinances (B:4 [13:4]). In fact, Mordecai's double salvation of the king has shown the exact opposite of the "illdisposition" and "harm" Haman alleges (B:5 [13:5]).

The real danger to the kingdom is of course this very Haman himself. When his letter ends in expressing the desire that "our government" be left "completely secure and untroubled hereafter" (B:7 [13:7]), the discerning reader knows that Haman means his government rather than the king's, for the Jewish mode of life poses no threat to a just king and proper governance but only leaves Haman feeling insecure and troubled in his own self-importance. It is Haman and not the Jewish nation who plans to upset the tranquility and peacefulness of the kingdom (B:2 [13:2]), but it will be left to the next decree in Addition E to set matters right.

Addition C (C:1-30 = 13:8–14:19)

The Greek version of events had pictured Mordecai as advising Esther to "call upon the Lord" (4:8), so it is not surprising to find that both he and she do just that in Addition C. Mordecai himself is the swifter in his devotion (C:1-10 [13:8-17]), but Esther is not outdone in her piety (C:12-30 [14:1-19]), and indeed the entire Jewish nation cries out to God (C:11 [13:18]).

Both petitioners begin by acknowledging the God of the Jews as their only true King (C:2, 14 [13:9; 14:3]), a title they repeat at the midway point of their prayers (C:8, 23 [13:15; 14:12]), and they both proceed to remind this King of the special relationship that has existed between him and his people (C:8-9, 16 [13:15-16; 14:5]), taking care to make the point that if he allows his people to be destroyed there will no longer be any nation singing his praises (C:10, 20 [13:17; 14:9]). Esther's prayer makes the penitential concession that the Lord should not be accused of injustice in what he has allowed his people to suffer thus far (C:17-18 [14:6-7]), but suggests that the annihilation of the Jewish nation would cause the other nations to make certain theological deductions (C:21 [14:10]). In all of this these prayers call to mind similar petitions elsewhere in the Bible, such as those of Jehoshaphat (2 Chr 20:6-12) and Daniel (Dan 9:4-19) and various psalms (e.g., Psalms 79 and 106); accordingly, their prayers locate Mordecai and Esther solidly in the traditions of piety of their people. Particularly noticeable is the repetition of the word "Lord," eight times in Mordecai's prayer and seven times in Esther's. She will later address her husband the king as "my lord" (D:13, 14 [15:13, 14]), but her true Lord and King is the God of Israel.

The devotion of the two petitioners is underlined in each case by a vigorous defense against a charge of impiety that might be raised. In Mordecai's case we had earlier learned that he alone refused to do obeisance to Haman, but no actual reason for his refusal was given (3:2); now the refusenik reassures the readers, as he reassures his God, that he acted for reasons of piety and not pride (C:5-7 [13:12-14]). In Esther's case we had earlier learned of her marriage to Artaxerxes and her nondisclosure of her nationality (2:18, 20); now the queen reassures the readers, as she reassures her God, that this has involved no compromise of her religious principles and no embracing of a pagan lifestyle (C:26-29 [14:15-18]). Presumably God does not require such matters to be expressed for his benefit, since he already "knows all things" (C:5, 26 [13:12; 14:15]), but some readers may have had their doubts, despite the additional words of reassurance that the Greek storyteller had inserted in 2:20. Whether the queen's claim that she has "had no joy" in any aspect of her royal life (C:29 [14:18]) sits entirely comfortably with the narrator's reference to "every part that she loved to adorn" (C:13 [14:2]) is open to question, but the repeated request for courage (C:23, 30 [14:12, 19]) sets the scene well for her forthcoming entry into the den of "the lion" (C:24 [14:13]).

Addition D (D:1-16 = 15:1-16)

Addition D follows straight on from Addition C in the Greek text, and replaces 5:1-2 in the Hebrew text. The action moves more slowly than in the shorter Hebrew version of events, and therefore builds up more suspense as the queen makes her faltering way to the presence of the all-powerful king, through "all the doors" (D:6 [15:6]) that stand between her chamber and the throne room. She is absolutely terrified (D:5 [15:5]), and he is "most terrifying" (D:6 [15:6]); she is "majestically adorned" (D:2 [15:2]), but he is even more so (D:6 [15:6]); she has just "two maids" with her (D:2 [15:2]), while he has "all his servants" around him (D:16 [15:16]). The odds seem stacked against her, and therefore also against her people.

Esther indeed fears the worst (D:5 [15:5]), in view of the imperial policy she had outlined to Mordecai in 4:11 and in terms of the possible outcome she had expressed in 4:16. But now, having prayed for courage (C:23, 30 [14:12, 19]) for no less than three days (D:1 [15:1], in keeping with the plan mentioned in 4:16), she again calls upon her God to help her (D:2 [15:2]) — and when she eventually reaches the throne room, her divine King does come to her aid at the vital moment, changing the human king's response to this unsummoned appearance in his presence from one of initial anger (D:7 [15:7]) to one of subsequent gentleness (D:8 [15:8]).

The catalyst for the king's sudden change of heart is that the queen collapses in front of him (D:7 [15:7]), which leads him to speak tenderly to her. The all-powerful ruler whom she addresses as "my lord" (D:13, 14 [15:13, 14]) styles himself as "your brother" (D:9 [15:9]). The NRSV paraphrases this latter expression as "your husband," but in the context of this royal marriage — coming as it does after the perfunctory dismissal of a previous wife who had allegedly not given the proper honor and respect that a "husband" expects (1:20, 22) — the title "husband" perhaps loses something of the intimacy and solidarity that "brother" carries (comparable to the use of the expression "my sister" in the lover's talk of the Song of Songs [e.g., Cant 4:10; 5:2]).

Before she had set her face toward the king's presence, the queen had requested of God, "Give me courage" (C:23 [14:12]); now the king soothes her with the words, "Take courage" (D:9 [15:9]), and assures her that she will not be put to death for seeking an audience with him (D:10 [15:10]). He issues two invitations, "Come near" (D:10 [15:10]) and "Speak to me" (D:12 [15:12]), at which point the reader may reflect that events would not have turned out in this manner if Esther had not first drawn near and spoken to the heavenly King. Indeed, the queen's first words to the earthly king — no words between them have been reported until this moment in the story — draw an analogy between her temporal "lord" and "an angel of God" (D:13-14 [15:13-14]). Her respectful language, pandering to the royal ideology, will have the desired effect of disposing the king toward granting her request (5:3), especially when Esther's little speech is coupled with a repeat of her earlier effective action of collapsing in front of the throne (D:15 [15:15] as a reprise of D:7 [15:7]). She and her people will rise again.

Addition E (E:1-24 = 16:1-24)

As was the case with the king's first decree concerning the Jews (set out in Addition B), the Greek version provides a full text for the second decree. This one is twice the length of the first, and totally renounces the previously issued policy, but both letters follow a similar pattern, with opening formalities (B:1 and E:1 [13:1 and 16:1]), a preamble about the lamentable state of affairs (B:2-5 and E:2-16 [13:2-5 and 16:2-16]), and the decree outlining what is to be done to set things right (B:6-7 and E:17-24 [13:6-7 and 16:2-16]). Both decrees also culminate in an ominous pronouncement about what is to happen to the enemies of the kingdom (B:7 and E:24 [13:7 and 16:24]).

It seems that Esther is the scriptwriter this time (perhaps assisted by Mordecai, though 8:7-8 in the Greek version does not include his name), and she addresses the letter, as did Haman in the earlier epistle, to all the provincial governors; however, unlike his formula "and to the officials under them" (B:1 [13:1]), she uses the phrase "and to those who are loyal to our government" (E:1 [16:1]), implying that Haman's disloyalty may be shared by some others among the kingdom's officials, though it is now primarily those of Macedonian blood (E:10, 14 [16:10, 14]) rather than Jewish blood (B:4-5 [13:4-5]) who stand accused of being ill-disposed to Persian rule. Haman had himself spoken of "our government" (B:7 [13:7]), but his governance is now roundly denounced (E:2-14 [16:2-14]). He had accused others of seeking to harm the kingdom (B:5 [13:5]), while all along it was he who sought to harm the king's subjects (E:3 [16:3]) and even to kill the king himself (E:12 [16:12]) and those most loyal to him (E:13 [16:13]). The one who had styled himself as excellently wise, good, and loyal (B:3 [13:3]) is now unmasked as proud and arrogant (E:2, 12 [16:2, 12), wicked and deceitful (E:7, 13 [16:7, 13]), a "thrice-accursed man" (E:15 [16:15) in that he plotted the deaths of three preeminent figures — Artaxerxes, Mordecai, and Esther — as well as an entire innocent nation (E:12-13 [16:12-13]).

The nation in question had not actually been named in the first decree; instead it was said that they were indicated in other letters written by Haman (B:6 [13:6]), which may have been a device to excuse the king from full knowledge of matters. But the second letter names the Jews twice (E:15, 19 [16:15, 19]), and upholds their previously maligned laws (B:4-5 [13:4-5]) as righteous and permissible (E:15, 19 [16:15, 19]). It also names the Macedonians twice (E:10, 14 [16:10, 14]), a people who had not yet been mentioned in the story but whose rivalry with the Persians makes them seem a fitting foil in this imperial struggle. In his letter Haman had of course failed to reveal any non-Persian identity on his part, but the story had twice identified him as a "Bougean" (A:17 [12:6]; 3:3), an otherwise unknown group which might similarly have been a byword for opposition to Persian hegemony. The identities "Macedonian" and "Bougean" now become somewhat interchangeable in the story (9:10, 24), but the Jews are off the hook, the label of Enemies of the State having been effectively shifted onto other shoulders.

Although Haman has now been fully unmasked, the king's reputation remains mostly intact. He possesses "sincere goodwill" toward all nations (E:6, 11 [16:6, 11]) and desires that his kingdom be "quiet and peaceable for all" (E:8 [16:8]), as indeed Haman's letter had said (B:2 [13:2]). The king's only fault has been that he was too trusting of those he had entrusted with government, and he had been "beguiled" by that treacherous and evil man (E:6 [16:6]). The royal resolve to be more judicious in the future (E:9 [16:9]) is the only implication Esther's letter makes of blameworthiness on the part of the monarch for the decree of annihilation that had gone out in his name. But that decree is now effectively annulled (E:17 [16:17]), and the tables are turned (E:20 [16:20]). Indeed, not only are the Jews given the wherewithal to withstand their enemies, but it almost seems as though the entire kingdom is to commemorate the event each year — unless the "you" in E:22-23 (16:22-23) is meant as an aside to the Jewish people alone among "those who are loyal to our government" (E:1 [16:1]) and "those who plot against us" (E:23 [16:23]), both of which kinds of citizens are enjoined to take note.

Also noteworthy in this second letter are the plentiful references to God. This is none less than "the living God" who has a "chosen people" (E:16, 21 [16:16, 21]). Haman's wife and friends had warned him that such was the case (6:13), so the undoing of both him and them should have come as no surprise (E:18 [16:18]). Artaxerxes may be — and Haman may notionally have been — ruling over 127 provinces from one end of the known world to the other (E:1 [16:1], echoing 1:1; 3:12; B:1 [13:1]; and 8:9), but the one who is the true ruler over this vast kingdom (E:16 [16:16]) and who indeed "rules over all things" (E:18, 21 [16:18, 21]) is the almighty God. The godless Haman had not mentioned God once in the letter he had scripted (Addition B), but the God-fearing Esther shows appropriate piety in her own literary effort in the king's name.

Addition F (F:1-11 = 10:4–11:1)

After all the events have unfolded (and after the Hebrew book has come to an end), the Greek version rounds matters off with Mordecai's account of the fulfillment of the dream that had been related in Addition A. When he had first had the dream, Mordecai had sought "to understand it in every detail" (A:11 [11:12]), but it is only now that he is able to interpret the various images in terms of the protagonists in the drama. The emergent river of A:9 (11:10) is Queen Esther (F:3 [10:6]), the two dragons of A:5 (11:6) turn out to be Mordecai himself and his antagonist Haman (F:4 [10:7]), and the twice-mentioned "righteous nation" of A:6, 8 (11:7, 9) is the now twice-mentioned "Israel" (F:6, 10 [10:9, 13]). The first and last of these interpretations come as no surprise, but the middle revelation that Mordecai is one of the dragons whose roaring precipitated the cataclysmic events (A:5-6 [11:6-7]) is less straightforward, in view of the usual dragon imagery of a force opposed to God's rule (see the references given in the comments to Addition A), but is in keeping with the role that Mordecai's opposition to Haman and others played in the genesis of Haman's plot against the Jews (A:17 [12:6]; 3:5-6). The interpretation does not select any protagonists for the "light" and "sun" (F:3 [10:6], as in A:10 [11:11]), seeming rather to conflate those images with the riverine queen, but the general picture of an outcome of "joy and gladness" (F:10 [10:13]) is clear enough.

What the Greek version also makes abundantly clear is that the one who stands behind all of these marvelous developments is God. The word "God," which does not occur at all in the Hebrew text of Esther, but which already made an appearance in the dream of Addition A (to be followed by many occurrences throughout the Greek text), is now mentioned no less than seven times in the dream-interpretation of Addition F, as well as a twofold "Lord" in F:6 (10:9). In their prayers to this Lord (C:1, 12 [13:8; 14:1]), Mordecai and Esther had each twice reminded him about his "inheritance" (namely, the Jewish people, so styled in C:8, 10 [13:15, 17] in Mordecai's prayer and in C:16, 20 [14:5, 9] in Esther's), and now Mordecai can triumphantly announce that God has indeed remembered his "inheritance" (F:9 [10:12]). All along God held "two lots," one for the Jews and one for the Gentiles (F:7 [10:10]), so that the fate of his people was never really in doubt. This was what Mordecai's dream had ultimately meant, even though these "two lots" as such had not appeared in the dream. Because of these divine lots, the paltry lots cast by Haman (3:7; 9:24) could never have brought about the annihilation of the Jews, who in celebrating the festival of Lots, or Purim (9:26), can rejoice in their status as God's chosen people (F:10 [10:13]).

The final verse of Greek Esther is a short postscript on the transmission and translation of the book (F:11 [11:1]). Interestingly, it calls the document to which it is appended not "the Book of Esther" but "the Letter about Purim," which is what Esther and Mordecai are depicted as writing in 9:29. Several other names are mentioned in this postscript, but they do not help to pin down any firm dates for the book's composition, since several Egyptian rulers named Ptolemy and with wives named Cleopatra had reigns of at least four years apiece in the late second and early to mid first century BC. An otherwise unknown Jerusalemite named Lysimachus is credited with the translation work which brought us what we now know as the Greek Book of Esther.

Bibliography. Bechtel, C. M. 2002, *Esther,* Interpretation, Louisville: John Knox • Clines, D. J. A. 1984, *The Esther Scroll: The Story of the Story,* JSOTSup 30, Sheffield: JSOT • Day, L. 1995, *Three Faces of a Queen: Characterization in the Books of Esther,* JSOTSup 186, Sheffield: Sheffield Academic • Dorothy, C. V. 1997, *The Books of Esther: Structure, Genre and Textual Integrity,* JSOTSup 187, Sheffield: Sheffield Academic • Fox, M. V. 1991, *The Redaction of the Books of Esther,* SBLMS 40, Atlanta: Scholars • Levenson, J. D. 1997, *Esther,* OTL, London: SCM • Moore, C. A. 1977, *Daniel, Esther, and Jeremiah: The Additions,* AB 44, New York: Doubleday.

The Wisdom of Solomon

A. Peter Hayman

INTRODUCTION

Date and Place of Origin

There is a general consensus among scholars (with only a few dissentient voices) that the Wisdom of Solomon was written in Greek, in Alexandria, Egypt, around the turn of the era — late first century BC. to early first century AD. Alexandria is where the Greek Bible was translated and put together. What we know of the Jewish community there fits in well with what we can deduce from our text about the audience for which it was written. It shares an outlook similar to that of other texts such as 4 Maccabees, the *Letter of Aristeas,* and the works of Philo, which all came from this community. One specific indication of Egyptian origin is the author's use of Egyptian imagery of the goddess Isis to describe personified Wisdom as a divine female figure. Another is the very clear interest in Egypt revealed in the third section of the book (chs. 10–19). Ch. 10 begins a review of Israel's history but never gets beyond the exodus story, where the text indulges in a sharp polemic against idolatry in its particular Egyptian manifestation, that is, the animal cult (see 12:24; 15:18-19). And one cannot help seeing behind 19:13-17 a reaction to the way in which the native Egyptians received the Jewish immigrants, not only at the exodus but also when the Jewish community in Egypt was being formed in the aftermath of the Greek conquest of Egypt (331 BC) and after the crisis in Palestine caused by the Maccabean revolt in 168 BC (Barclay 1996: 19-47).

There are no clear allusions to contemporary historical events in the book, so one can suggest only an approximate date for it. Since the author quotes from most parts of the LXX version of the OT, he cannot have been writing much before the middle of the second century BC. Winston 1979: 20-25 argues that the earliest date for the book can be more precisely fixed as sometime after the Roman conquest of Egypt in 30 BC on the grounds that 14:16-20 is an allusion to the emperor cult begun under Augustus. He confirms this conclusion by an analysis of the thirty-five Greek words in the Wisdom of Solomon which are not attested in other Greek literature before the first century AD. Larcher 1983: 1:141-61 argues that the book was composed over a period of time between 31 and 10 BC. The latest possible date for the work is more difficult to fix than the earliest. Most scholars feel that Wisdom predates Philo and was also used by some NT authors, particularly Paul and the author of the Epistle to the Hebrews. This would make it no later than, say, the early first century AD. Winston dates it precisely to the reign of Caligula (AD 37-41) when the Alexandrian Jewish community underwent a particularly severe crisis which he feels is reflected in the harsh anti-Gentile tone of the book. Larcher is not convinced of this later dating. It is safest to say that the Wisdom of Solomon was probably written about thirty years either side of the turn of the era.

Genre

The Wisdom of Solomon is usually classified as part of Israelite wisdom literature. However, since it was written in Greek and is really part of Greek literature, it should, strictly speaking, be classified as belonging to the genre called the Exhortatory Discourse. There are several examples of this genre of didactic exhortation extant in Greek, one of the most famous being Aristotle's *Protrepticus,* a eulogy on the life of reason. The Wisdom of Solomon also draws heavily for its literary features on the Hellenistic diatribe, which it resembles far more than it does the philosophical treatise. Among the forms in the book which reflect this genre are:

1. personified abstractions (Wisdom throughout the book, Justice in 1:8, Death in 1:16, etc.).
2. speeches of an imaginary adversary (chs. 2 and 5).
3. rhetorical antitheses — particularly frequent in the second half of the book, e.g., 11:1-9.
4. accumulation of adjectives (7:22-24 is the most prominent example).
5. elaborate similes (e.g., 5:10-12).
6. exhortation (e.g., 6:1-11).
7. invective (chs. 13–15).

The Literary Sources of the Book

The author's primary source was the OT in its Greek, LXX version, and in particular the wisdom literature and the book of Isaiah. He was also in touch with, and influenced by, the sort of books and ideas which are found now in the Apocrypha and the Pseudepigrapha, particularly *1 Enoch.* There is a very clear allusion to *Enoch* in 4:10-15. He was conversant with, and uses, ideas from a wide range of Greek literature. Probably he received at least some of his information secondhand from compendia of Greek philosophy rather than directly from the original works. Estimates of the author's use of Greek literature and ideas vary from scholar to scholar, but none can deny a certain measure of such influence.

The Author's Audience

The Wisdom of Solomon emerged from a Jewish religious community which was facing an intense challenge to its political, social, and intellectual survival. Translated from the security of the homeland into an alien cultural environment, the Jewish community seems to have been losing members to the vibrant, new, and dominant Greek culture, alongside which Judaism seemed to be a primitive backwater. In Alexandria Jews confronted a problem which was to trouble them for the next two thousand years: how to hold themselves together as a viable socioreligious community in a virulently anti-Jewish environment, in particular, in a situation where their religious beliefs were challenged by what appeared to be a superior intellectual culture. Wisdom aims to make its readers, and perhaps particularly its young readers, proud of their cultural heritage and ready to resist the temptation to water down their ancestral beliefs.

The Literary Structure of the Text

A great deal of scholarly work has been done to uncover the literary devices, such as inclusion and chiasm, used by the author to structure the text. For an accessible summary of this work and references to the detailed studies see Grabbe 1997: ch. 1.

COMMENTARY

Wisdom 1:1-15

This section is delimited by the use of the word "righteousness" in 1:1 and 15, while the phrase "those who are fit to belong to his company" similarly marks out the next section from 1:16 to 2:24. The author makes considerable use of this device of inclusion both to mark out the sections of his argument and to bind his text into a unity. Keywords are also used as "flashbacks" to remind the reader of earlier parts of the argument. All too often English translations obscure these literary devices, which are clearly visible in the original Greek text. Ch. 1 divides into three subsections (1:1-5, 6-11, 12-15). 1:1-5 are dominated by the positive/negative contrast "righteousness" (v. 1) and "unrighteousness" (v. 5), vv. 12-15 by the negative/positive contrast "death (v. 12) and "immortality" (v. 15). The inclusive use of the word "tongue" (in vv. 6 and 11) is probably the verbal clue to the unity of the central section.

1:1-5 The opening address, which is repeated in 6:1, is probably conventional, harking back to the older setting of wisdom within the royal court (Prov 25:1). Prov 8:15-17 cannot have been far from the author's mind. The real addressees are the author's contemporaries and, in particular, those who were not thinking of the Lord "in goodness" or with "sincerity of heart." Essentially the verses are a restatement of the older motto of Israelite wisdom: "the fear of the Lord is the beginning of wisdom" (Job 28:28; Prov 1:7). Correct thinking depends on righteousness; "foolish thoughts" (better, "senseless reasoning," 1:4) are the result of moral turpitude. The first mention of wisdom in v. 4 presupposes what will be developed in detail later on: wisdom is a cosmic power which pervades the whole universe (8:1). It enters people from outside; it is not a mere human attribute developed by learning and education. But it cannot dwell with those who do not (from the author's viewpoint) think or behave correctly (v. 5). The polemic against alternative ways to truth prevalent in the author's cultural environment lies only just below the surface. This is no dispassionate philosophical treatise.

1:6-11 By the time this short section is completed the author has clearly dropped any pretense of addressing the "rulers of the earth." His words are clearly aimed at those within his own community whom he regards as "blasphemers" (1:6), whose "counsels" are "ungodly" and deeds "lawless" (v. 9). What they are actually saying which has so upset him does not become apparent until the next chapter. But how he will deal with them is already clear: they will be condemned but not logically refuted. In calling wisdom "a spirit" (v. 6) the author is continuing a process which may have begun in Sir 24:3 if, as seems likely, that is interpreting Gen 1:2. In the Wisdom of Solomon the Spirit/Holy Spirit/Spirit of the Lord/ Word of the Lord/Wisdom are largely interchangeable (see 7:22; 9:1-2, 17, and cf. *1 Enoch* 49:3). This assimilation of Wisdom and the Spirit in pre-Christian texts like the Wisdom of Solomon was an important influence on the NT writers and the early fathers (see Kelly 1960: 18, 95). In 1:7 we meet our first example of the author's attempt to restate the Jewish faith in the language of its new Greek environment. The thought of God's omnipresence (with which he is attempting to frighten his opponents) is found in the OT (Ps 139:7; Jer 23:24), but when the text goes on to describe the Spirit of the Lord as "that which holds all things together," it is using a Stoic technical expression (*to synechon* — "which holds together") for the Logos or World Soul.

1:12-15 At this point the author brings in the antithesis LIFE/DEATH, the principal theme of the following chapters. He draws on a number of biblical texts such as Prov 8:35-36 and Ezek 18:32; 33:11. Further in the background lies the ancient Israelite mythic pattern in which Yahweh defeats and controls the forces of chaos (Day 1985). These forces, symbolized by Mot/Death, the shepherd of the dead in Sheol (Hades in Greek mythology), are always seeking to rise up from the underworld to overwhelm the inhabited world. Using Isa 28:15 as a peg on which to hang his thoughts, the author accuses his opponents of being in league with Death and releasing these destructive forces into the world. He adapts this old mythological language for his own purposes and takes what is, in effect, the dualist option (see 2:23-24). God is on the side of life; he has created order out of chaos in order that life may flourish (1:14). This provides the theological basis for the belief in the immortality of the soul. But v. 13a directly negates the widespread OT belief, still pushed forcefully by Ben Sirach, that death was decreed for human beings by God (see Job 14:1-2; Ps 90:10; Sir 17:1-2; 41:1-4 and Barr 1993: 21-47). Probably to the author's chagrin, his opponents, as cited in ch. 2, are able to draw on OT language to support their views about death.

Wisdom 1:16–2:9

After his introduction the author begins his argument proper by first setting up the views of his opponents and then proceeding to denounce them. The practice of ascribing imaginary speeches to one's opponents is a constituent element of the genre of the Hellenistic diatribe upon which the author seems to be modeling his text. The opposing position, as described in these verses, seems to be the kind of practical atheism condemned in the OT, for example, Pss 10:4; 14:1; 73:11-12, and cf. *1 Enoch* 102:6-8. In 2:12 and 3:10 its proponents seem to be described as renegades from the Jewish faith. For the group criticized in texts like these, it seems as if belief in God's maintenance of justice in the world has receded, along with, in some cases, the belief that he can or will do anything at all. Like the gods of the Epicureans, he is relegated to some far-off corner of the universe, neither interfering in human affairs nor being in any way affected by them. Scholars have discussed at length the precise identity of our author's opponents but without reaching any agreed conclusion. "What the author is depicting in the wicked's negative judgment on death is not so much a particular group of apostates as the reasoning process which leads to positions that . . . threaten the community" (Kolarcik 1991: 123). Many parallels to the sentiments expressed here can be found in Greek sources, but much is also drawn from the OT, especially Ecclesiastes. With 2:1 compare Job 10:20-21 and Eccl 2:22-23; 9:5, 10; with 2:3, Eccl 12:7; with 2:4, Eccl 2:16; and with 2:6 and 9, Eccl 2:24; 3:12; 5:18; 9:7-9 and especially Isa 22:13.

Wisdom 2:10-20

Beginning at 2:10 the ungodly draw conclusions which do not seem to follow logically from the attitude to life expressed in vv. 1-9. The author seems to be succumbing to the perennial temptation to parody the opinions of one's opponents in order to make them easier targets. Seeley argues that he has been influenced by a theme from popular Greco-Roman philosophy according to which "a pious or godly figure preaches at the ungodly (who fail to see the divine behind the phenomena around them) and with surprising speed is confronted with active hostility" (Seeley 1990: 71-72). Such hostility may escalate to the point of murder. The fate of Socrates would be a case in point. Nickelsburg argues that the Wisdom of Solomon is dependent on an earlier, widespread literary genre of the Wisdom/Court Tale. Examples of this genre are the story of Joseph and his brothers (Genesis 37–45), the story of Ahikar, the book of Esther, Daniel 3 and 6, and the story of Daniel, Susanna, and the elders (Nickelsburg 1972: 48-92). Nickelsburg thinks that Isa 52:13–53:12 reflects the same pattern, and hence the use in Wis 2:13 of the word *pais* (child) just as in the LXX of Isa 52:13. The author certainly has Isaiah in mind at this point; 2:12a is taken almost word for word from the LXX of Isa 3:10. The author of the Wisdom of Solomon is implying by this use of the book of Isaiah that in this life the righteous should expect to share the lot of the Servant of the LORD, but that in the future life they will be vindicated, as is the Servant in Isa 52:13-15; 53:10-12. In *1 Enoch* 102:4–104:8 exactly the same pattern and argument are used.

Traditionally in the Christian church these verses have been interpreted as a prophecy of the death of Jesus, and Ziener 1956: 113-21 still advocates this interpretation. Larcher 1983: 262 sees here an anticipation or prefiguration of certain aspects of Christ's passion. But if it is a prophecy, it is not a very good one. 2:16 hardly squares with the picture in the Gospels of Jesus as the friend of "publicans and sinners" who associated with all classes in society. The picture given here of the fate of the just man is ideal in nature and has a remarkable parallel in Plato's *Republic* 362A.

The idea of the fatherhood of God (2:16, 18) appears in the OT and was widespread in late Second Temple Judaism (see Pss 68:5; 103:13; Prov 3:12; Isa 63:16; Tob 13:4; Sir 23:1, 4; 3 Macc 6:3). The righteous man's claim to be God's son (*huios,* 2:18) is probably a democratization of one of the titles of the Israelite king (see Pss 2:7; 89:20, 26-27). (The politically correct translation "child" for *huios* in Wis 2:18, NRSV, conceals the fact that this is a different word from *pais* in 2:13.) Jews in the tradition of the Wisdom of Solomon, the book of Daniel, and the book of *Enoch* claimed for themselves the relationship with God claimed much earlier by the Israelite king. The close parallel between vv. 16-18 and Matt 27:43, which has furthered the christological interpretation, is probably to be explained by the fact that both the Wisdom of Solomon and Matthew drew upon Ps 22:8.

Wisdom 2:21-24

Having completed his attempt to describe his opponents' point of view, the author now turns to begin his refutation of them. He argues that they have completely misunderstood the way in which God deals with human beings. Not only is there a definite recompense for being righteous, but, in saying that death is the end, the apostates are unaware of God's purpose in creating humankind. The righteous fulfill this purpose by sharing in the immortality which is part of God's own nature. Only the wicked experience death in any real sense; the righteous only "seemed to have died" (3:2). In 2:22 the text connects back to the earlier view of Israelite wisdom teaching that there is a definite reward for being righteous and wise (Prov 10:27; 22:4), albeit one in this life. But the books of Job and Ecclesiastes had denied this connection between piety and earthly blessing. However, our author can bypass this critique of Job and Qohelet by stressing that, yes, there may be no reward for righteousness in this life, but there certainly will be after death.

2:23-24 represent a milestone in the development of Jewish theology, for in conflict with the OT tendency to make God the author of both good and evil (cf. Isa 45:7), Wisdom here promotes Mot/Death into the devil and lays on him the responsibility for bringing death into existence (see on 1:12-15). The Greek word behind the translation "devil" is *diabolos,* and that translates Heb. *śatan* in the LXX. To identify the serpent of Genesis 3 as Satan/the devil or as the devil's agent (the serpent is not explicitly mentioned) and then attribute to him the origin of death is certainly a new move in Jewish theology. But already in the more mythological OT version of creation Leviathan and Yam/Sea (which, like Mot/Death, represent the powers of chaos) are depicted as serpentine (Job 26:12-13; Ps 74:13-14; cf. Isa 27:1 and Wyatt 1996: 81-101). In the OT Satan appears as a member of the heavenly court whose function reflects his name — the Accuser (see Job 1:6-12; Zech 3:1). In 1 Chr 21:1 he is depicted as a more active inciter toward evil (cf. the anonymous spirit in 1 Kgs 22:19-23). It is the combination of the mythology connected with the Canaanite gods Mot/Yam and the OT figure of Satan which gives rise to the Christian figure of the devil. By the time we reach the NT this process has transformed a morally neutral legal function in the heavenly court into a powerful, angelic adversary of God — Paul's "the god of this world" (2 Cor 4:4) and the satanic dragon of the book of Revelation (Rev 12:7-9). We meet the combination for the first time in the Wisdom of Solomon.

In 2:23 we should follow the reading in the NRSV mg. ("in the image of his own nature"), which has the support of the major Greek uncial manuscripts. The Wisdom of Solomon is not going beyond Genesis 1–3 but is offering a quite reasonable interpretation of it along the lines that humans were not created immortal but could have become so had they not sinned. They were ejected from the garden in order to *prevent them* from becoming immortal (Gen 2:22). Wis 2:23b does not specifically make the possession of eternal life the point of comparison between God and humans but merely substitutes *aïdiotētos* (own nature) for the words "image" and "likeness" used in Gen 1:26-27. See Barr 1993: 61, nn. 9 and 10, for a critique of the view taken here of 2:23.

In Wis 10:1-3 the sin of Adam is passed over, and Gregg 1909: 22-23 has argued against the view that 2:24 has Genesis 3 in mind rather than the first actual death recorded in Genesis 4 (the murder of Abel by Cain). Other commentators have found this unconvincing.

Wisdom 3:1-12

Wis 3:1–4:20 is structured by means of a series of contrasts between the relative fates of the righteous and the wicked, constituting together a direct refutation of the views placed in the mouth of the author's opponents in 2:1-20. Here 3:1-9 proclaims the blessed state of the righteous while 3:10-12 (introduced by the "but" in v. 10) contrasts this with the miserable present and future state of the wicked. In his refutation of his opponents the author makes use of the belief in the immortality of the soul. But this concept is clearly a new one for him, one which he has not fully absorbed, because two earlier OT concepts of immortality are clearly at the back of his mind. These are (1) the idea that people live on through their children, who keep their name in existence (cf. 2 Sam 18:18); and (2) the idea that immortality consists of the enduring good reputation which people leave behind them (cf. Ps 112:6; Prov 10:7; but especially Sir 44:8-15). In old Israel these two ideas were easily combined, but our author keeps them separate. He conducts a polemic against the first (3:12–4:6), while the second concept still has a very strong hold on him (4:1-2; 8:13). The seam between the new and the old can be clearly seen in the middle of 8:13. Another old Israelite belief which the author holds onto but does not integrate with his new belief in immortality is that of the day of the LORD/the Last Judgment/the Messianic Age. This appears in 3:7-9 and ch. 5, but no attempt is made to harmonize it with the new belief in the immortality of the soul.

In Palestine the belief in a worthwhile life after death took the form of the resurrection of the dead (see Dan 12:3-4) because this fits in with the OT idea that the human body and soul form a unity. The OT has no concept of a disembodied soul; any real life without a body was inconceivable for the OT writers and for many (though not all) Palestinian Jews (despite the arguments of Barr 1990). But our author lived in, and was influenced by, a Greek environment where a radical dichotomy between body and soul was an accepted cultural assumption. These Greek ideas appear in 1:4 and 9:15, and especially in the idea of the preexistence of the soul (8:19-20; 15:8). Naturally, then, the author makes use of the idea of the immortality of the soul; there is no trace of the concept of the resurrection of the body in the Wisdom of Solomon. Clarke's attempt to deny the presence of a body/soul dualism in the text is unconvincing (Clarke 29; see also di Lella 1966).

3:4-6 are a direct refutation of the Deuteronomic and earlier wisdom view that one could deduce people's "state of grace" from the suffering they were undergoing or the material blessing they were enjoying. 3:4a appears to attribute to the author's opponents the conservative dogmatic note of Job's comforters. However, by the time that the Wisdom of Solomon was written Judaism had taken the point made by the book of Job and by Qohelet and adopted on a widespread basis the explanation for suffering which we see here (cf. Sir 2:1-5; 2 Macc 6:12-16; and *1 Enoch* 108:9). This "vale of soul-making" theodicy is adumbrated in the OT (see Job 5:17-19; Prov 3:11-12; Dan 11:35). However, the same explanation for suffering can be found in Greco-Roman philosophy. In 3:7-9 we get the traditional apocalyptic imagery of the day of the Lord (cf. Sir 36:1-22). The righteous join the host of heaven and become the holy ones/sons of God/stars. Israel rules over the other nations, with God as their king (cf. Dan 7:27; 12:3; and *1 Enoch* 104:2-6; see further on 5:5). Where the righteous are before "the time of their visitation" we are not told — which precisely reveals the seam between the old and the new in the Wisdom of Solomon. It does not attempt to systematize its eschatology by, for example, introducing the notion of an intermediate state. 3:10-12 outlines the fate of the author's opponents, which will be spelled out in much more detail in ch. 5. 3:11-12 are a reversion to older OT ideas that the consequences of sin work themselves out in this life and are transmitted through the generations (cf. Exod 34:7; Sir 41:5). However, these ideas had already been refuted by Ezekiel (see Ezekiel 18 and 33), and they raise in acute fashion the problem of free will and determinism. Here, too, our author seems to be confused and muddled in his thinking; 12:10 reveals the extent of his confusion.

Wisdom 3:13–4:6

This section contains two sequences of the basic pattern: the blessings of the righteous in contrast to the afflictions of the wicked. Within the section the switch from positive to negative evaluations is clearly marked by the "but" in 3:16 and 4:3. Verbally the contrast of "fruit" (3:13) and fruitlessness (4:5) and the theme of childlessness with virtue perform the same unifying function. The author is opposing the older OT belief that having a lot of children was a great blessing and a sure sign of divine favor (cf. Pss 127:3-5; 128:3-4). At the same time he uses approvingly the older idea of immortality, that one lives on in the good reputation preserved in the memory of those left behind. So in 3:13-14 and 4:1 he rejects the shame felt by the barren woman in Israelite and Jewish society (Gen 30:23; 1 Sam 1:5-8; Luke 1:25). Sterility was seen in the OT as a punishment (see 2 Sam 6:23; Hos 9:11, and especially *1 Enoch* 98:5: "barrenness has not been given to the woman, but on account of the deeds of her own hands she dies without children"). For the social disabilities suffered by eunuchs see Deut 23:1-2. However, our author prefers the more enlightened attitude of Isa 56:3-4 to that of Deuteronomy. Nevertheless, in 3:16-19 and 4:3-6 he virulently maintains the age-old prejudice against illegitimate children. For parallel sentiments to the Wisdom of Solomon here see Sir 16:1-3. Illegimitate children were, and still are, severely disadvantaged by Jewish law. It is the inevitable consequence of a patriarchal society about which Ben Sirach is quite open (Sir 23:23-25).

The author's positive attitude toward female spirituality has led some scholars to see parallels with the Therapeutae, the contemplative community described by Philo in his *De vita contemplativa.* Within this Egyptian group male and female Jews seem to have lived and worshiped on a considerable level of equality. The *Testament of Job,* a text probably contemporary with the Wisdom of Solomon and also from Alexandria, is similarly more positive about women's religious role (see *OTP,* 1:833-34). Accordingly, the Wisdom of Solomon and the *Testament of Job* have both been related by some scholars to the Therapeutae (Schroer 1995: 26-28). Philo specifically mentions "aged virgins" as part of this group. Could our author have had such people in mind as he was writing this?

Wisdom 4:7-20

Here the delimitation of the switch from the positive evaluation of the lot of the righteous to the negative position of the wicked is less clearly marked than in 3:1–4:6. However, 4:16, with the introduction of the word "ungodly," seems to mark the fulcrum of the unit. It also marks in advance the theme of ch. 5. Like 3:12–4:6, this unit is concerned to refute a deep-rooted OT idea, namely, that to live to a ripe old age and to die "full of years" is a sure sign of God's blessing, with the corollary that to die early would be a sign of God's disapproval. To illustrate the thesis that early death need not be a disaster, or a sign of God's disfavor, the author draws on the example of Enoch (Gen 5:24). He depends on the LXX text which has "Enoch pleased God" where the Hebrew has "Enoch walked with God" (cf. Sir 44:16). The example of Enoch was an important influence on the development of belief in a worthwhile life after death in the late Second Temple period (Barr 1990: 15). The Greek of 4:10-14 refers only to a single person; the "politically correct" plurals used in the NRSV have obscured the reference to Enoch. The RSV translation is much better. Vv. 16 and 18-20 introduce a theme which will be developed at length in the next chapter. The vindication of the righteous involves a confrontation with the wicked after death in which the latter confess the error of their ways and reverse the judgment they made during their lives on the fate of the righteous.

Wisdom 5:1-23

This section is delimited as a unit by the opposition "will stand" (*stēsetai,* 5:1) and "will rise against them" (*antistēsetai,* v. 23). It is loosely structured internally by the positive/negative contrasts which marked the previous major section (3:1–4:20). The turning point is the "but" in 5:15. The point of vv. 1-14 is similar to that made in Jesus' parable of Lazarus and the rich man (Luke 16:19-31), though there the conceptual framework is a little different. Here our author had in mind the traditional idea of the Day of Judgment, not that of an immediate postmortem judgment, which seems to be envisaged by Luke. As we have seen, the Wisdom of Solomon shows little interest in systematizing its eschatological timetable, and it says nothing about the fate of the wicked from the time of their deaths up to the Last Judgment. The author is concerned only to stress their complete error with regard to the apparent fate of the righteous. For a more consistent presentation of this type of eschatology see 4 Ezra 7:36-38. 4 Ezra sharpens up the point being made here in the Wisdom of Solomon: one of the blessings of the righteous on the Last Day will be to observe the punishment of the wicked (4 Ezra 7:93)! 5:1-14 are consciously written as a reversal of the opinions quoted in 2:1-20. 5:3-5 in particular pick up and reverse 2:12-20. Yet again, as in 4:10-14, the NRSV with its pluralizing translation has completely obscured the allusion back to 2:10-20 in the original text. 5:5 refers to the apocalyptic notion that after death/the Last Judgment the righteous become angels/stars = sons of God. In the OT the sons of God and the holy ones/saints are the angels (see Gen 6:2; Deut 33:1; Job 38:7). This combination of ideas is found at Qumran (1QH 3:19-23) and feeds into the NT at Luke 20:34-36. 5:8-14 reflect the author's continued reliance on the older concept of immortality as an enduring good reputation. The wicked express dismay at this advantage which the righteous have over them (v. 13).

In 5:15-23 the author restates his belief in the reversal after death of the fates of the righteous and the wicked, but this time using traditional OT imagery of God as the divine Warrior. The whole section represents an elaboration of Isa 59:17, but compare also Isaiah 13 and 24. After having acknowledged that the righteous were right and they were wrong, the wicked are subject to a wholesale onslaught in which they seem to be utterly destroyed. 5:16 alludes to the idea mentioned above in connection with 2:16, 18, namely, the democratization of beliefs originally attached to the Israelite kings (cf. also 3:8). At God's coming the righteous will attain the kingly stature which goes with the title "son of God" (cf. Ps 89:20-27). A close parallel in *Sib. Or.* 3:702-31 (*OTP*, 1:377-78) throws light on the general scenario which the author seems to have in mind in these verses.

Wisdom 6:1-21

This section is delineated by the inclusion "kings" (*basileis*, 6:1) and "reign" (*basileusēte*, v. 21). It defines the beginning of a new set of themes by recalling the appeal to the rulers of the world with which the book begins (see 1:1). But whether it should be seen as the conclusion to the first major section of the book or as the beginning of the central section is a moot point among commentators. A consensus around the latter appears to be emerging from more recent commentators. The decision hinges on the significance we should attach to the change in 6:22 to the first person singular, which continues to the end of ch. 9.

In chs. 6–9 the author attempts to give us some idea of what he thinks wisdom is. In doing this, he is still expanding on the theme of chs. 1–5. For, according to him, immortality is obtained through possessing wisdom (6:19-20; 8:13, 17). It is, therefore, essential to know what wisdom is and how to get hold of her. These chapters contain the most extensive speculation on the figure of personified Wisdom to be found in Jewish wisdom literature. They are, however, anything but a model of clarity. To understand them it is necessary to be aware that the author is in debate with two opposing positions: (1) the view outlined in ch. 2 that traditional Judaism really has nothing much worthwhile to offer "enlightened" Jews or Gentiles living in cosmopolitan Alexandria; (2) a narrow, nationalistic definition of Judaism, expressed in the identification of Wisdom and the law of Moses. This view is adumbrated in Deut 4:6, and worked out in Sirach 24 and Bar 3:9–4:4. This narrow definition of Wisdom explicitly excluded the cosmic dimension that is emphasized in the book of *Enoch* by saying that Wisdom is in heaven, and not here on earth (*1 Enoch* 42:1-4). Our author definitely sides with those who locate Wisdom in heaven (see 9:1-4). However, the author's position on the universalism/particularism divide is not easy to specify since the second half of the work (chs. 10–19) is, at times, harshly nationalistic in tone (see Barclay 1996: 181-91).

The author bases his reply to these positions on the structure of the story in 1 Kings 3, where Solomon prayed for wisdom and was granted riches and honor beside it. He is saying to his first set of opponents that you cannot even get those worldly things which you desire unless you enter into a relationship with wisdom. This is the purpose of 6:1-21. The example of Solomon shows us that we should start with wisdom, and the rest will then follow. To the proponents of the second position he offers a broad definition of Wisdom (7:15–8:1) which he knows is necessary if Judaism is to survive in an environment dominated by Greek culture.

Like 1:1, 6:1 is more likely to be addressed to those holding power within the author's own community, who perhaps aspired to obtain political power beyond its boundaries, rather than to actual Gentile rulers. The argument of vv. 1-11 would certainly work only with Jews because it appeals to late OT notions about God's providence. But vv. 12-21 attempt a not very successful logical argument based on a Greek rhetorical device called "sorites." However, a well-educated Jewish audience living in Alexandria would need to be convinced by both types of argument. 6:3 states the basis upon which vv. 1-11 rest. This is a doctrine which appears in some late passages in the OT (1 Chr 29:12; Dan 2:21; Sir 10:4). It is specifically a Jewish rather than an Israelite belief — a belatedly recognized corollary of the changed perception of Yahweh in the Second Temple period. He is no longer seen as just the tribal God of Israel (Judg 11:24) but as the God of all the earth (cf. Rom 13:1-7).

The text is deliberately ambiguous over the meaning of "law" in 6:4 (there is no definite article in the Greek) and "her laws" (v. 18). Is it referring to the law of Moses or something like the principles of natural justice? This ambiguity fits in with the overall tendency in the Wisdom of Solomon to veil its Jewish origins in coded language as part of its attempt to present a universalistic front to the Greco-Roman world. This literary device becomes particularly clear in chs. 10–19, but see already 4:10-14. However, earlier Israelite wisdom literature (before Ben Sirach) is similarly ambiguous over what it means by "law" or "instruction." At 6:12 Wisdom, personified as a female figure, enters the scene and dominates the book until ch. 11. The description in vv. 12-16 is probably based on Prov 1:20-33 and 8–9.

As mentioned previously, 6:17-20 are based on the Greek literary device called "sorites." This is "a cumulative series of syllogisms, in which the conclusion of each becomes the premise of the next, until the main conclusion is reached" (Gregg 1909: 60; cf. Rom 5:3-5). The construction is, however, somewhat unsatisfactory, since the conclusion (6:20) hardly follows from the premises, but derives much more from the story of Solomon which controls the overall structure of these chapters. Kloppenborg (1982: 75) shows convincingly that the language of vv. 20-21 reflects the influence of the cult of Isis. This had been going through a process of democratization similar to that which our author carries through for the title "son of God." In its Hellenized form the Isis cult now offered its devotees what had earlier been on offer only to the Egyptian kings, namely, immortality. Our author wishes to assure the Jews that whatever was on offer in the Isis cult (a kingdom and immortality) can just as well be found within Judaism.

6:22-25 Having announced the importance of knowing wisdom and the benefits such knowledge confers, the author switches now into first person mode and, in the guise of Solomon, begins to provide that instruction which leads to immortality. The section is loosely attached to 6:1-21 by the keyword "wisdom" in vv. 21b and 22a. In vv. 23-24 the author may be contrasting his approach here either with that of the adherents of the Greek mystery religions or with that of secretive Jewish sects like the Essenes who claimed to possess esoteric knowledge which they would reveal only to the initiated. Goodrick 180 aptly quotes Plato's *Republic* 473c to illustrate 6:24.

Wisdom 7:1-6

This unit is defined by an inclusion which is hardly discernible in English translation: "like everyone else" (*isos hapasin,* 7:1) and "for all . . . one" (*pantōn . . . isē,* v. 6). It contains a polemic against the old oriental idea, so readily taken up by the Greek and later Roman rulers, that kings are different from ordinary human beings. Either they are gods, or they stand in a special relationship to the gods. They can then claim to be especially endowed with wisdom and knowledge (cf. 2 Sam 14:20). The "therefore" with which 7:7 commences the next section shows that vv. 1-6 are designed to show that kings by virtue of their position cannot automatically expect to be wise; they have to pray for it like everybody else. In ch. 8:17-21 this theme is developed against the background of the belief in the preexistence of the soul. Not even the superior soul which kings can expect will necessarily give them wisdom. For the details about the ancient knowledge of embryology reflected in 7:1-2 see Winston 1979: 162-65.

Wisdom 7:7-14

The boundaries of the subunits within chs. 7–8 are somewhat unclear after 7:6. 7:7-14 is closely based on Solomon's prayer for wisdom in 1 Kgs 3:3-14. It probably draws also on Prov 3:13-18, where we find the same pattern of first disparaging wealth in comparison with wisdom (Prov 3:14-15) and then stating that she brings riches and honor anyway (7:16). With wisdom you can have your cake and eat it! — which seems to be the point of the rather obscure v. 12b. The idea that wisdom secures for human beings friendship with God (v. 14) appears in 7:27 and 8:18. The terms on which it can be obtained are, however, obscured by the NRSV translation of 7:14b. V. 14 should be translated as follows: "for it is an unfailing treasure for mortals; those who make use of it obtain friendship with God, being recommended (to him) by the gifts which come from instruction."

Wisdom 7:15-22a

Here the author begins to give some content to his concept of Wisdom. It embraces, first of all, the craftsman's skill (7:16), and this reflects the root meaning of the Hebrew word for wisdom (*ḥokma);* see Exod 31:3, where "ability" in the NRSV translates *ḥokma.* Then it encompasses a knowledge of cosmology and physics (7:17), chronology and astronomy (vv. 18-19), zoology, meteorology, psychology, and botany (v. 20). This is the kind of all-embracing knowledge sought by the seer in apocalyptic texts like *1 Enoch.* Wisdom in the Wisdom of Solomon is a concept which includes under its umbrella all types of knowledge, not purely religious knowledge. In fact, our author makes no distinction between religious and other types of knowledge; they all seem to come by a process of revelation (v. 17a). 7:7, 15-16 and the prayer in ch. 9 all suggest that Collins 1977-78: 139 is wrong to deduce that in our text Solomon's "knowledge follows from the use of his natural reasoning." Rather, knowledge is a gift of God which comes only to those who possess the correct religious and ethical qualifications. In the Wisdom of Solomon we find the root idea upon which the Judeo-Christian culture of the West before the Enlightenment was based: religion, philosophy, and science are different routes to the same indivisible truth. Yet its synthesis is not entirely novel, for it is restating here in contemporary language the older Israelite view as seen, for example, in Prov 8:22-31, that Wisdom is not only a human quality but also has a very significant cosmic dimension. In fact, Wis 7:22a probably alludes to the LXX reading of Prov 8:30, which sees Wisdom as the "master workman/craftsman" by whose agency God creates the world. Wisdom knows the secrets of creation because she helped to make it (Prov 3:19). Note that, unlike Prov 8:22-23 and Sir 24:9, the Wisdom of Solomon does not say that God "created/acquired/begot" Wisdom. She seems to be primordial, as in Bar 3:32, 36.

Wisdom 7:22b–8:1

This section, the kernel of chs. 6–9 and perhaps of the book as a whole, represents the author's attempt to tell us precisely what he thinks Wisdom is. He does it first, in 7:22b-24, by giving us a list of the 21 (3 × 7) attributes of Wisdom; then in vv. 25-26 he describes her by means of five metaphors; the implications of the metaphors are then spelled out in the rest of the section. To express what he wanted to say the author draws heavily on Greek philosophy, especially on terms used by Plato and the Stoics, such as World Soul or Logos. Like all theology it represents analogical or metaphorical thinking and therefore lacks precision. We have to attempt to see the pictures in his mind if we are to follow his train of thought.

In 7:22b the first two epithets ("intelligent, holy") neatly illustrate the author's method. The first word, *noeros* (intelligent), though found in Plato, became a Stoic technical term for the possession of the ability to think and reason. The second attribute, by contrast, comes from the OT. The next two epithets ("unique, manifold") are Stoic terms used of the unchangeable World-Soul which is yet manifested in individual people (like wisdom in v. 27). Likewise the terms "pervades and penetrates" (v. 24) were used to describe the diffusion of the World-Soul. So what the Stoics claimed for their Logos our author claims for the figure of Wisdom in Jewish tradition. The apologetic appeal here is: what Greek philosophy offers is already available within our own tradition.

The five metaphors in 7:25-26 are: mist/vapor, outpouring/emanation, light, mirror, and image:

1. "mist/vapor" (*atmis);* "breath" in v. 25, NRSV. The picture here is of Wisdom as like God's breath visible on a cold day. The same image, applied to the Word which is the Wisdom of God, occurs in Sir 24:3. The Wisdom of Solomon expresses the thought less anthropomorphically than does Ben Sirach, in line with the general trend of Alexandrian Jewish theology. Hence the substitution of "the power of God" for Ben Sirach's "the mouth of the Most High." Is there more

to this than just a metaphor, that is, is the author suggesting that wisdom has some kind of material nature? Most commentators think not. But the Stoic Logos was conceived of as a kind of rarified fire which permeated the whole of the universe and held it together (Annas 1992: 43-47). This verse suggests that the author may have had something like the Stoic concept in mind.

2. "emanation/effluence" *(aporroia)* of the glory of the Almighty." This word was to have a long history in Greek philosophy, especially in Neo-platonism. Here the background is more likely to be in the OT image of the glory of God, made visible in the pillar of fire which accompanied the Israelites in the wilderness (Exod 16:10). In 10:17 Wisdom is identified with this pillar of fire. Since Ben Sirach also identifies Wisdom with this visible glory of the Lord which descended into the sanctuary as the sign of God's presence (Sir 24:10), it looks as though Sir 24:2-3 is as much behind Wis 7:25-26 as is Greek philosophy.
3. "reflection" (NRSV), "brightness" (NEB) *(apaugasma).* This word can mean either the light streaming from its source (= NEB) or the reflection of such a light (= NRSV). The commentators differ, as do the translations here, though most opt for "reflection," noting that the ideas of a mirror and its image follow in the rest of the verse. The discussion of the meaning of the text here is to some extent bedeviled by the fact that the author of the Epistle to the Hebrews, probably borrowing from Wisdom, uses this word in 1:3 to describe the relation of Jesus to the glory of God. In Heb 1:3 the NRSV and the NEB adopt the same translations as they do here in the Wisdom of Solomon. The theological point at stake is how closely Wisdom and hence the Son in the Trinity is related to God.
4. "mirror" *(esoptron).* This image is the basis for the teleological argument presented in 13:1-9. Wisdom is the visible reflection of God's presence in the universe, perceived in its order and beauty, as in God's saving work of which Wisdom is the agent (chs. 10–19).
5. "image" *(eikōn).* This is a platonic metaphor — the world as an image of the unchanging reality (the forms) underlying it. This term, too, had a long history before it in trinitarian theology (see Col 1:15).

In 7:27-28 the phrase "while remaining in herself, she renews all things" is better translated by the NEB: "herself unchanging, she makes all things new." We have an interesting combination here of Greek and Hebraic thought. "Herself unchanging" reflects Greek notions of divinity as impassible, not subject to change. But the phrase "she makes all things new" reflects the role of the Spirit in Ps 104:30. We have already encountered in 7:14 the idea that those who make use of wisdom obtain God's friendship. In the OT only Abraham bears the title "God's friend" (2 Chr 20:7; Isa 41:8). Most commentators accept Gregg's argument (1909: 77) that this theme has been derived from Greek philosophy. It was known in Alexandria, as Philo shows when he says: "all wise men are friends of God" (*Quis rerum divinarum heres sit* 21). But Ben Sirach says, "The Lord loves those who love her [Wisdom]" (Sir 4:14). Perhaps the author of the Wisdom of Solomon is extending Abraham's title to all who, like him, live with wisdom and are, therefore, beloved by God. Since in Gen 20:7 and, by inference, in Ps 105:15 Abraham is called a prophet, he may similarly be extending Abraham's title of prophet. With 8:1 compare what is said in 1:7 about the cosmic role of the Spirit of the Lord. Here Wisdom is seen not only as God's instrument in creation but also as the means by which he exercises his providence. The terminology used here — *diateinei* (reaches mightily), *dioikei* (orders) — has connections with platonic and Stoic ideas about the World Soul. Cf. Plato *Timaeus* 34B: "and in the midst (of the Cosmos) he set Soul, which he stretched *(eteinē)* throughout the whole of it." It also connects with Egyptian ideas about the cosmic role of the wisdom goddess Isis (see Kloppenborg 1982: 69).

Wisdom 8:2-16

Chapter 8 returns us to the pseudonymous framework of this central section of the book, and here Solomon describes Wisdom as a bride whom he woos, marries, and brings to his home (cf. Sir 15:2). In the original version of the poem which ends his book (51:13-20a in 11QPs[a] 21:11-17), Ben Sirach plays on the erotic analogy of the reception of Wisdom as a bride. Behind the analogy lies the experience that knowledge is its own reward and provides satisfactions comparable with or better than those of marriage — which must be the implication of 8:16 (Wisdom is no nagging wife!) Again Kloppenborg argues that "Wis 8:2-9 contains a dense configuration of attributes of Sophia which bear a significant correlation to attributes — indeed principal attributes — of Isis" (1982: 78). In 8:3 Wisdom is described as God's female consort; for this see on 9:4. In 8:4 Wisdom is a peg on which the author hangs a speculation on the role of knowledge or intellect in the mind of God, similar to that of Philo in *De ebrietate* 30. "Initiate" *(mystis)* in this verse is a term from the mystery religions and an epithet of Isis. V. 7 reflects the notion of the four cardinal virtues in the Stoic version. Philo's allegorical exegesis of the Garden of Eden with a river flowing from it which divides into four heads produces the same teaching (*Leg. all.* 1.63). In v. 8 Wisdom does all the things traditionally regarded as the role of the wise man (Sir 39:1-5). With 8:13 compare 6:19 and 8:17. What kind of immortality does the author have in mind here? The second clause and the context suggest that he has Solomon in mind and so is really thinking of the immortal reputation which the supremely wise man leaves behind him. But 6:19 and 8:17 suggest that he has the more substantial idea in mind, as in chs. 3–5. Both concepts of immortality are present simultaneously — the new and the old; see above on 3:1-12.

Wisdom 8:17-21

This section is marked out by the inclusion "heart" (8:17b and 21b). In v. 17a the author is alluding to the common Greek idea of the kinship between men and the gods, usually expressed by the philosophers in terms of the common possession of the mind/soul identified as the reasoning faculty (cf. Philo *De opificio mundi* 145–46).

There has been a great deal of disagreement among scholars over the interpretation of 8:19-20, some holding that the author clearly accepts the idea of the preexistence of the soul and others denying it (see Goodrick 377-88 and Winston 1979: 25-32). There is no trace of such an idea in the OT, but Jewish texts close in time and orientation to the Wisdom of Solomon do accept it (see 4 Macc 18:23 and *Pseudo-Phocylides* 102–8 [*OTP*, 2:577-78]). Josephus attributes to the Essenes belief in both the preexistence and immortality of the soul (*J.W.* 2 §§154-58), and there is a close parallel to this text in Philo *Leg. all.* 3.85. The main point which the author is making in these verses is quite clear and emerges in v. 21, namely, that however well endowed people may be, in body and soul, this still will not ensure for them the possession of wisdom. Wisdom is a gift from God and has to be prayed for; it is not a natural constituent of human nature.

Wisdom 9:1-18

This "prayer of Solomon" exhibits careful literary structuring with both inclusions (wisdom/humankind, 9:2 par. people/wisdom, v. 18) and chiastic patterns. In vv. 1-2 the assimilation of God's word and wisdom is very similar to that in Sir 24:3. It enables the author to identify the Word with which God creates in Genesis 1 (see also Ps 33:6) with Wisdom in its cosmic role as we see it, for example, in Ps 104:24 and Prov 3:19; 8:22-31. 9:2 seems to be based on Gen 1:26-28 and Ps 8:5-6, but again the closest parallel is with Ben Sirach (17:1-4). The epithet *paredros* (that sits by your throne), used of Wisdom in 9:4, is a striking example of personification since it is used in nonbiblical Greek for subordinate deities (Winston 1979: 202). This passage has been used by some scholars to argue that belief in a female consort of Yahweh (well attested in the preexilic period — see Olyan 1988) has influenced the development of the concept of Wisdom. For others this word reflects language used of Isis in Egyptian religion. For the events reflected in 9:7-8 see 1 Kgs 3:7; 5:4-5. It is unnecessary to argue with Gregg and others that in 9:8b the platonic theory of the forms has influenced the Wisdom of Solomon here. The idea that the Jerusalem temple is the copy of a heavenly archetype is deeply rooted in OT and Jewish tradition (see Exod 25:9, 40; 26:30; Ps 11:4). In fact, this attitude to temples can be traced far back in ancient Near Eastern thought. There seems to be a delicate balance in 9:9 between the cosmic approach to wisdom and more traditional law-oriented Judaism (see on 6:4). With 9:10 compare Sir 24:4, 8; Bar 3:37–4:1 and contrast *1 Enoch* 42:1-4.

9:13-18 reemphasize the point made in 7:1-7 and 8:19-21, that Wisdom comes only as a gift from God. The theological concepts of this paragraph are close to the outlook of both some parts of the DSS and that of the NT. All three share the idea that human nature is such that it cannot know the ways of God of itself, nor can people attain righteousness by their own efforts. To achieve both moral purity and correct spiritual knowledge human beings require the gift of the Holy Spirit sent down from on high. In the DSS and the NT this is part of the "flesh versus the spirit" complex of ideas; in Wisdom's Greek environment this common Jewish notion is heading toward the radical body/soul dualism that was to emerge later in gnosticism. 9:15 has a close parallel in Plato's *Phaedrus* 81c ("the body is burdensome, and heavy and earthy: by the possession of it such a soul is oppressed"); see also Philo *De gigantibus* 7. Our author's way of expressing himself here is the inevitable consequence of the dualistic anthropology which he adopted from his Hellenistic environment. Rabbinic Judaism did not share this loss of faith in human nature, as the OT does not share this dualistic anthropology (see Hayman 1984).

Wisdom 10:1-21

The transition to the third major part of the book is signaled by the phrase which concludes ch. 9: "and were saved by wisdom." Chs. 10–19 use the pentateuchal history of salvation to illustrate themes already presented in chs. 1–9, though two major excursuses introduce new themes. In the OT these reviews of salvation history are usually presented in the form of praise (e.g., Exodus 15; Judges 5; Nehemiah 9; Psalms 105–106, 135). Our author intends to use his for apologetic and instructional purposes, but the pull of the genre very quickly takes over; by 10:20 he is directly addressing God precisely at the point where he is thinking of Exodus 15. The contemplation of what God has done for his people impels him into the "praise mode," and thereafter he finds it difficult to extract himself from it. By 11:4 he has given up trying. So why in the first place does he attribute to Wisdom the active role in Israel's salvation? Kloppenborg's convincing answer is that the author is attempting to make a claim for Jewish tradition through the figure of Wisdom everything which Isis was believed to offer to her adherents (Kloppenborg 1982: 67-72). The author is no pioneer in attributing this role to Wisdom. Already Ben Sirach and the author of Bar 3:9–4:4 had blazed the trail by using "non-wisdom traditions of the Torah . . . to teach wisdom like that of the biblical tradition" (Sheppard 1980: 16). The direct influence of Ben Sirach can be seen in Wisdom's identification with the pillar of cloud and fire which accompanied Israel in the desert (Wis 10:17 and Sir 24:4b; cf. Philo *Quis rerum divinarum heres sit* 203–4).

Wisdom 10–19 continue the practice we observed in 4:10-14 (see on 6:1-21) of avoiding any specific mention of OT characters and events, leaving the readers to make their own identifications. This may have been intended to enhance the universalistic feel of the text — to put a universalistic gloss on what is really a very partisan Jewish work. But chs. 10–19 are also using the salvation history to illustrate and enhance the contrast established in ch. 15 between the respective natures and fates of the righteous and the wicked. The anonymity of the actors in the story has the effect of dehistoricizing them and turning them into types. This typing process leads in Wisdom 10 to a character like Lot being described as righteous (10:6); if he was saved, he must be righteous. Cain must perish because he is ungodly (10:3) despite the lack of any suitable OT reference (but see *Jub.* 4:31). For the same reasons the Wisdom of Solomon has little interest in accurately recounting OT history; such material is used solely for the author's own apologetic ends. Hence Adam's transgression in the Garden is glossed over (10:1; see also

Sir 49:16), and Cain is made the direct cause of the flood (10:4), passing over the difficult account of the fall of the angels (Gen 6:1-4). Inevitably this moralizing and chauvinistic attitude to history leads the author into logically inconsistent statements. When Israel is persecuted her oppressors become the ungodly (10:15 and 10:20), but when Israel does the same to the Canaanites the author has to wriggle and squirm with embarrassment, coming up with nonsense like 12:10-11.

For 10:1-2 see Gen 2:7–4:16, for 10:4 Genesis 6–9, for 10:5 Genesis 10–22, for 10:6-8 Genesis 19, for 10:9-12 Genesis 27–33, for 10:13-14 Genesis 37–47, and for 10:15-21 Exodus 1–15. The chapter is held together, and its units marked out, by the repeated use of the pronoun *hautē* (she — translated "wisdom" in the NRSV) in vv. 1, 5, 6, 10, 13, and 15. Each unit contains the word *dikaios* (righteous) once.

Wisdom 11:1-14

The clue to the overall structure of chs. 11–19 comes at 11:15, reprised at 18:8. They consist of a series of seven contrasts between the fate of the Egyptians at the exodus and that of the Israelites, whereby the one is punished by the same element with which the other is blessed. The primary theme of the whole book — the contrasting fates of the righteous and the wicked — is thus approached from another angle. As Reese 1970: 91-98 has demonstrated, it is incorrect to classify these chapters as "midrash" as some commentators have done; rather, they exhibit the pattern of the Greek rhetorical technique of *synkrisis* (comparison). Two large excursuses (11:15–12:27 and 13:1–15:19) interrupt this series of contrasts after the first has been completed. See Winston 1979: 224 for a detailed plan of these chapters.

The verb "prospered" *(euodōsen)* in 11:1 can be either transitive or intransitive. If it is taken as intransitive ("their works prospered"), then 10:21 would be the last mention of Wisdom as the key player in the Israelite drama of salvation, and the transition to the "prayer mode" in 11:4 would be less harsh. The commentators are divided on this, and on whether 11:1 rounds off ch. 10 or begins a new section. Whichever view is correct, it remains the case that the disappearance from 11:4 onward of personified Wisdom exposes our author's failure to produce a satisfactory synthesis of natural and revealed theology. The Stoic Logos and the OT Yahweh do not make comfortable bedfellows. Some acute and unresolved theological tensions underlie the rest of the book, as do the undoubted social and political tensions in Alexandria and elsewhere in Egypt between the Jews and the rest of the population (Barclay 1996: 181-91).

The first of these tensions appears in 11:9-10. If the author is going to explain the torments of the Egyptians as just retribution for the way in which they have treated the Israelites, how is he going to account for the sufferings which the latter undergo both in Egypt and the desert? He resorts to the tried and tested explanation (already mentioned in 3:5-6 and argued at length by Elihu in Job 32–37) that the sufferings of the righteous are God's chastisement to bring them back to the straight path. But the actual sufferings of both the righteous and the wicked look remarkably similar. How do we know which is which? Here the author makes an interesting move. He says that it is the psychological attitude of those undergoing the suffering which enables us to distinguish the good from the bad. The sufferings of the wicked are so much worse ("a twofold grief," 11:12) because they realize that their suffering is for the benefit of the righteous (v. 13). They "feel thirst in a different way from the righteous" (v. 14). For the biblical texts behind vv. 1-14 see Exod 7:14-24; 15:22–17:13. Note how our author conveniently "censors" the biblical text in order to play down the rebelliousness of the Israelites in the wilderness; compare 11:4 with Exod 17:2-7. He has to play up the wickedness of the Gentiles and gloss over that of the Israelites in order to get his required contrast. But, as the following excursus shows, overemphasizing the wickedness of the Egyptians and the Canaanites has the added advantage of ameliorating the "scandal of particularity" — explaining why they get such a raw deal according to the OT and why the Israelites are selected for blessing.

Wisdom 11:15–12:27

11:15-16 begins the second of the series of contrasts (plague of strange animals), but is interrupted by the two excursuses and is resumed only at the end of ch. 15 and the beginning of ch. 16. The argument of this first excursus is best considered as a whole, though it can be broken up into smaller sections: 11:15–12:2; 12:3-18; 12:19-22; 12:23-27. Reese 1970: 116 describes this and the following excursus as portraying "God's loving kindness toward all mankind." If this is the intention, it is not achieved; 11:24 and 12:4, 10 are in acute tension. The purpose of these digressions is revealed by the resumptive "therefore" in 16:1. They are designed to demonstrate that the Egyptians and the Canaanites received only what they deserved.

The digression which begins at 11:17 appears to have two aims. One is to develop further the disciplinary explanation for suffering adumbrated in vv. 9-10 in the context of the theological problems presented by the belief in Israel's election; the other is to explain certain features of the text of Exodus. Why were there ten plagues, gradually escalating in seriousness, and not one knockout blow of which God was certainly capable (vv. 17-20)? Why does Exod 23:28-30 say that God sent hornets/wasps in advance of the Israelite invasion of Canaan and then only gradually expelled the Canaanites (12:8)? One immediate explanation for the first nine of the ten plagues is the author's sophisticated version of the *lex talionis* (11:16; reprised in 12:23), but the real answer is that God was allowing these nations the same opportunity for repentance as was given to Israel. For, after all, these nations are also God's creatures, and mercy is an essential element of the divine nature (11:23–12:2). However, the argument does not work, and the author knows it, because, if the Egyptians and Canaanites had actually responded to the opportunity given for repentance, there would have been no exodus, no promised land, and no chosen people. The doctrine of election requires that God willed beforehand to exterminate the Canaanites to make room for his chosen people. The only way to justify this is to say that they were incorrigibly evil from their origin (12:10); in that case, however, both the statement that God loves all that he has made and the argument that he always gives an opportunity for repentance are negated. Our author is in an inextricable tangle; hence the cry of frustration in v. 12. The sentiment of this verse — who are you to criticize the actions of God? — is the last resort of most failed arguments in the Judeo-Christian (and Islamic) traditions (cf. Rom 9:14-21). We can certainly deduce from this verse that such questions were being asked either by the kind of anti-Jewish authors cited in Josephus's *Against Apion* or by apostate Jews in Alexandria. The arguments of the latter could be the "insolence among those who know" God's power mentioned in 12:17b. Other Jewish attempts to justify the extermination of the Canaanites (see Winston 1979: 238) presuppose that the Jews felt sensitive to criticism on this point.

12:19-22 now confronts the obvious problem that if the Egyptians and Canaanites could never have been allowed to take up the opportunity for repentance (and thereby frustrated all salvation history), the whole thing would have been a charade. God might as well have finished them off with one blow. The author's response to this is that God was using the experience of the Gentiles to teach the Jews how to moderate judgment with mercy (v. 22). Perhaps conscious of the weakness of this argument also, he does not pursue it but quickly moves to the much safer ground of righteous fulmination against the wickedness of the Gentiles (vv. 23-27), picking up where he left off in 11:15. Maybe the author says more than he intended when in 12:25 he says that God sent his judgment in order to "mock" the Gentiles! (He is really wrestling with the meaning of Exod 10:2.) The argument ends in as confused a fashion as it has been carried on throughout. The last part of 12:27 makes sense only if we assume that what the text really means to say is that because the Egyptians and Canaanites did not respond to the "children's games of censure/rebuke" (the literal meaning of the Greek behind "the warning of mild rebukes" in v. 26, NRSV), that is, the milder first nine plagues and the hornets, only then did the serious punishment begin: the death of the firstborn and the Israelite invasion of Canaan. The historical importance of this excursus is that it represents one of the first attempts to harmonize and reconcile the OT doctrines of creation and election, to wrestle with those intractable problems bequeathed to Judaism and Christianity by the book of Deuteronomy.

Wisdom 13:1-9

This section is marked out by the inclusion "were unable" (*ouk ischysan,* v. 1) and "had the power" (*ischysan,* v. 9). The general argument is closely paralleled in Philo in many places (see especially *De decalogo* 52–66) and summarized by Paul in Rom 1:20 (perhaps dependent on the Wisdom of Solomon, certainly on the Hellenistic-Jewish apologetic tradition of which it is a part). Estimates of the level of knowledge of Greek philosophy here displayed vary among the commentators; contrast Reese 1970: 50-62 with Goodrick's Appendix D: 404-10. It is not precisely clear who the author has in mind in these verses. Is it nature worshipers (13:2) or Greek philosophers or both? The reference in v. 9 to those who "investigate the world" suggests that it is the philosophers; for the divinity of the elements in early Greek philosophy see Guthrie 1965: 114. Gilbert 1973: 1-52 has argued at length that the author's primary target here is Stoicism.

The problem with this pericope is that the author does not grasp that natural theology on its own is not sufficient to allow people to reach the level of religious awareness he regards as adequate. He is not really conscious that he knows the "Author of beauty" (13:3) primarily through revelation. God's existence and nature are so self-evident to him that he cannot understand why others do not see things as he does. Hence he vacillates over the philosophers' level of guilt since he recognizes that their search for truth is genuine (v. 6) but feels unable entirely to excuse them (v. 8). See the close parallel in Philo *De decalogo* 66. But is he also drawing back from an outright attack on the cultural icons of his age because he might thereby alienate his potential audience? It is not difficult to deduce from his attitudes elsewhere in the book that, faced with contrary views to his own, his natural instinct is not to argue rationally but to question his opponents' morality. This is the implication of v. 1 ("foolish by nature"); see on 1:1-5. But Egyptians, Canaanites (11:15–12:27), and idolaters (13:10–15:19) are easier targets for this line of attack than philosophers are. As we read on, it becomes clear that the actual literary function of 13:1-9 is to heighten the contrast between the relative obtuseness of the philosophers and the guilt and utter worthlessness of the real idolaters discussed in the rest of chs. 13–15.

Wisdom 13:11–15:19

This section is an excursus on idolatry. Wright 1967: 180-82 has argued that it has a ring structure which emphasizes the central statement on the origin and evils of idolatry in 14:12-32. As elsewhere, the author has used the device of inclusion to mark out the literary structure of the text. Not all of Wright's analysis is convincing, especially, as he himself admits, in 14:7-31. However, the overall pattern seems fairly clear:

- a. Introduction (13:10; inclusions: "dead, hands, work").
  - b. Carpenter and wooden images (13:11–14:2; inclusions: "skill/artisan," "make/built" in 13:11 and 14:2).
    - c. Appeal to God (14:3-6; inclusion: "steers/guides" in vv. 3 and 6) plus transition (14:7-11).
      - d. The origin and evils of idolatry (14:12-31).
    - c′. Appeal to God (15:1-3) plus transition (15:4-6).
  - b′. Potter and clay images (15:7-13; inclusion: "soft earth/earthy matter," "vessel/vessels" in vv. 7 and 13).
- a′. Conclusion (15:14-19; inclusions "dead, hands, make" in v. 17).

Wisdom 13:10–14:2

The description of the carpenter constructing wooden idols is based on Isa 44:9-20 supplemented by a few other OT references such as Jer 10:1-16. As in the OT polemics against idolatry, the material is for internal consumption only, reinforcing a Jewish sense of superiority over the Gentiles. It cannot be addressed to non-Jews since it takes no account of Gentile explanations of what they thought they were doing when worshiping images (for which see Winston 1979: 262). The point of 13:13 seems to be that the idol maker is not a professional sculptor. He is doing this in his spare time, in contrast to the picture presented in Isa 44:13. Less well-attested readings for the words "leisure" and "idleness" (see NRSV, note *r*) make him seem more of a professional. 14:1 obviously draws on Jonah 1:5, though the point being made in 14:1-2 is not immediately clear. V. 2 emphasizes the professional intent and high level of skill which goes into shipbuilding, so much so that the author "apparently credits Sophia (like Isis) with the invention of the maritime trades" (Kloppenborg 1982: 81 n. 115). Yet, by contrast, sailors in distress call upon a wooden idol made from offcasts in the carpenter's spare time!

Wisdom 14:3-6 plus 7-11

Mention of boats immediately carries the author's thoughts to the biblical story of Noah and the flood (Genesis 6–8). There we have an example of wood which, in contrast to the images, was put to good use, and a trust in God which was really vindicated, over against useless appeals to idols. For the appeal to God as Father in v. 3, see on 2:10-20. The allusion in 14:6a to the Jewish form of the myth of the revolt of the Titans reflects the version known in other late Second Temple period texts (Sir 16:7; Bar 3:26-28; 3 Macc 2:4) rather than the toned-down version which appears in Gen 6:1-4 (see Sheppard 1980: 86 nn. 4-5). V. 8 brings us back from this minor digression to the topic at hand. For the potential conflict between 14:9 and 11:24, see above on 11:17–12:27 and below on 15:18-19. The term "visitation" *(episkopē)* in 14:11 recalls 3:7 (though the same Greek expression occurs in 2:20b); the language used comes from Jer 10:15. The author has in mind the kind of eschatological appearance of God at the Last Judgment which is reflected in 3:7-11 and ch. 5; cf. Sir 36:1-22.

Wisdom 14:12-31

Along with other Jewish writings (cf. *Jub.* 11:4-5), the Wisdom of Solomon assumes that idolatry was not primeval but had a beginning in time. To account for its origin the author derived one explanation from observation of some religious practices current in his Greco-Roman environment, while another he adopted indirectly from the theories of Euhemerus of Messene (c. 300 BC). Infant mortality levels were very high in his time, and various methods of assuaging the pain and grief caused had sprung up. Some amounted almost to deification of the child (see Winston 1979: 273-77). Euhemerus had accounted for the origin of the Greek gods by arguing that they were deified kings worshiped after their deaths by their grateful subjects. This euhemeristic explanation of the existence of the gods was already known in Jewish circles before the Wisdom of Solomon, as can be seen from the allusions to it in the *Epistle of Aristeas* 134–137 and *Sib. Or.* 3:110-16; see also *Pseudo-Eupolemus* in *OTP*, 2:881-82. Euhemerus's explanations would have gained added currency from the apotheosis of Alexander and his successors and, if the Wisdom of Solomon was written in the imperial age, from what was beginning to be attributed to the Roman emperors.

14:12a at first sight seems strange, but in the background lies the rich metaphorical use in the OT of the term "fornication/prostitution" for religious apostasy (see Jer 2:20; 3:2, 9; Hos 4:12; 5:4; 6:10). The parallelistic structure of the verse reinforces this less specific meaning of the term "fornication" (the idea of making idols parallels the invention of them; the beginning of fornication parallels the corruption of life). In 14:21c some commentators have seen an allusion to the practice of not pronouncing the divine name Yahweh. But idolaters were hardly likely to be calling their gods by such a name, and the more universal term *theos* is almost certainly what the author had in mind (cf. Isa 42:8). 14:22b has been taken to be an allusion to the Pax Romana. The NRSV slightly obscures the meaning of 14:29. It is because the wicked are so sure that their gods are lifeless that they swear false oaths (so v. 30) and do not, therefore, expect to suffer any untoward consequences, in contrast to Exod 20:7. 14:31a is concerned to emphasize that it is not the power of the gods represented by the idols which brings retribution on perjurers, while the Greek of v. 31b evokes the personification of Justice *(Dikē)* relentlessly pursuing wrongdoers.

Wisdom 15:1-3 plus 4-6

In 15:1 "all things" is similar to the "all things" in 11:24, that is, we have an apparently universalistic statement where the context immediately makes clear that, in reality, the reference is only to Israel. The text alludes to Exod 34:6 and its many parallels in the OT but stops short of any overt mention of Exod 34:7, though "even if we sin" in 15:2 may have been evoked by it. The contradiction between v. 2a and v. 2b is generated by the polemical context. Even though the author knows in theory that Israel has sinned, the context requires an absolute contrast between the behavior of God's people and that of idolaters. Again, as in the first excursus in 11:15–12:27, logic is displaced by the requirements of the doctrine of election; Exod 34:9 LXX is resonating in the author's mind ("we will be yours").

For the metaphorical use of the word "root" in 15:3b see 3:15. The author clearly has in mind here the substantive concept of immortality as in 3:4 and 8:17, not the immortality of an enduring reputation (4:1). "Knowing God's power" is the equivalent of "kinship with wisdom" in 8:17, but present also is the strong connection between immortality and God's power to raise the dead so insisted on in 2 Maccabees 7. V. 4a can only be a reference to the behavior of the Jews in the author's own time unless, once again, the polemical context leads him to overlook completely the many references in the OT to Israel's turning aside to idolatry.

Wisdom 15:7-13

This is a hard-hitting critique of the cynical process of exploiting people's religious gullibility by producing for them *kibdēla* (counterfeit/fraudulent goods — v. 9). Idols made of clay are dressed up to make them look like gold, silver, and bronze, but fall apart when handled (v. 13). The manufacturers know that the whole business is a profitable game (v. 12), but "one must make a living." Their cynicism reinforces the author's critique by demonstrating that those involved in the business know that idolatry is a lucrative fraud. The notion of life/the soul as a debt which has to be repaid at death (v. 8d) was widespread in the Greco-Roman world. This text reinforces the Hellenizing concept of the soul which appears in 3:1; 8:19-20, and later in this chapter at v. 16; soul and body are detachable before and after death.

Wisdom 15:14-19

This section marks the conclusion of the second excursus. The NRSV translation of v. 15a obscures the reproach which the author particularly wishes to hurl against the Egyptians: "they thought that *all* the idols of the nations were gods." He is especially accusing them of what was, in fact, a widespread phenomenon of the entire Greco-Roman world — the interchange and intermingling of gods and goddesses, cultural assimilation on a grand scale. What, however, distinguishes Egyptian idolatry above all is the worship of animal gods (vv. 18-19) — moreover, the most odious of animals (from the author's perspective): jackals, crocodiles, snakes, falcons, and the like. Compare Philo *De decalogo* 76–80 for a close parallel to this part of the Wisdom of Solomon. But yet again, the polemical intent of the author leads him into contradicting his earlier, all-embracing statement of 11:24. 15:19b alludes clearly to Gen 1:21, 25, 31 and implicitly excludes these animals from the Creator's approval. Some animals appear to have been created bad just as in 11:15–12:27 the Egyptians and Canaanites seem to have been born evil. At the intellectual level our author is a monist, but at the emotional level a dualist. The two levels are not harmonized in his mind, nor does he seem overly concerned to reconcile them. This text is more *ad hominem* polemic than philosophical treatise.

Wisdom 16:1-4

This resumes the second contrast, which was abandoned at 11:15-16. Ch. 15:18-19 has prepared the way for the transition from the two excursuses back to the comparison/contrast structure. The two verses recall 11:15-16 and 12:23-27 and then prepare us for the contrast which comes at 16:2. 16:1-4 is clearly marked out as a separate section by the inclusion "tormented" in 16:1 and 4. Unfortunately, the NRSV obscures the basic element of the contrast which is being made, namely, "strangeness." The animals that the Egyptians worship are strange and odious (15:18-19 and 16:3), whereas the Israelites' appetite is assuaged by quails whose "taste is strange" (16:2 — the phrase is omitted in the NRSV). The "therefore" of v. 1 recalls 11:15-16 and is joined to "it was necessary" of 16:4. Because the Egyptians worshiped strange and odious animals, it was necessary for them to be punished by means of such animals, "that they might learn that one is punished by the very things by which one sins" (11:16). Note how our author has censored out all mention of the people's rebelliousness, which is associated in Exod 16:1-21 and Numbers 11 with the events being referred to here.

Wisdom 16:5-14

In the third contrast the Egyptians are killed by the bites of locusts and flies, but the Israelites are saved from the serpents' bites. This is certainly a separate section, marked out by an inclusion (discernible only in the Greek text), "came upon" (v. 5) and "departed" (v. 14). However, commentators differ as to whether it should be regarded as the third contrast in the series or as an appendix to 16:1-4 dealing with the possible objection that Israel, too, was assailed in the wilderness by strange animals — the serpents of Num 21:4-9. Moreover, 16:5-14 lacks the keyword *anti* (instead of) which provides the hinge of most of this series of contrasts (11:6, 15, translated "in return for"; 16:2, 20; 18:3, translated "therefore"). But then, so does the seventh in the series (18:5–19:22). The element of contrast in 16:5-14 is certainly present in the "but" with which v. 10 begins. Nevertheless, it is certainly the case that the section is generated by the author's realization that the plague of serpents is a potential objection to the argument he presents in 16:1-4. He counteracts it with the same disciplinary explanation for Israel's suffering which he deployed in 11:9-10 and 12:19-22. The negative "not by the thing beheld" (v. 7) betrays an element of embarrassment at the apparently apotropaic function of the bronze serpent in Num 21:4-9 and, as with the incident of the quails, any reference to the complaints which triggered the plague of serpents (Num 21:5) is carefully glossed over.

Wisdom 16:15-29

We find here the fourth contrast. This is driven by the comparison between the fire which proves wholly destructive to the Egyptians (Exod 9:24) and that which is wholly beneficial to the Israelites when used to bake the manna (Exod 16:23). The contrast is then made the basis for a general principle (16:17b, 24-25) which adds some specificity to the Jewish belief in God's providence. In v. 16 the note of "strangeness/unusualness" continues from 16:1-4 and is mixed with the notion of paradox in v. 17 ("most incredible"; lit. "most paradoxical"). The author is marveling over Exod 9:24 (as does Philo in *Vit. Mos.* 1.118). 16:18 seems to presuppose that the plagues of frogs, flies, gnats, hail, and lightning were simultaneous, perhaps influenced by their contiguity in Ps 105:30-32. The statements about the manna in 16:20-21 have many parallels in later Jewish midrashim where the text of Ezek 16:19 can be seen interacting with Exod 16:4, 31 and Num 11:8. The purpose of this midrashic-type expansion on the biblical text becomes clear when we reach 16:24-25; the manna is an example of how a natural substance (albeit the food of angels! — Ps. 78:25) accommodates itself to the wishes of the elect, just as nature as a whole transforms itself to suit their needs. The use of the word *hypostasis* (sustenance) in 16:21 has occasioned some discussion among commentators. Does it mean only "sustenance," or does it refer either to the divine substance (as in later Christian theology) or to the underlying essence of the manna whose outward qualities change according to the desires of those eating it? Most recent commentators and translations take the first option. V. 23 (which is taken up again in the conclusion at 19:21) seems to refer to the fact that the fire did not destroy the manna but only exuded as much heat as was required to bake it (Exod 16:23). The miraculous nature of this phenomenon is demonstrated by the fact that at another time only "a fleeting ray of the sun," never mind direct heat, was enough to melt the manna (16:27 drawing on Exod 16:21). 16:24 develops this thought into a general principle expanding on the statement at the end of v. 17 that "the universe defends the righteous." This principle is further developed in 19:6, 18-20. For the philosophical background to the language used here see Winston 1979: 300. There are parallels in *Sib. Or.* 3:712 and Philo *Vit. Mos.* 1.201. We now have a more specific idea of what the author means when he says that Wisdom "orders all things well" (8:1). 16:28 draws a midrashic lesson from Exod 16:21, finding in a fact of nature (the melting of the manna) support for the well-known Jewish practice of early morning prayer (Sir 39:5; Josephus *J.W.* 2 §128; Philo *De vita contemplativa* 89; *m. Ber.* 1:2). Miss prayers and your manna will have gone rotten!

Wisdom 17:1–18:4

Chapter 17 begins the fifth contrast. The bulk of this section of the text is given over to a rather imaginative and somewhat overblown description of the plague of darkness (Exod 10:21-23). Naturally, the metaphorical connotations of "darkness" and "light" are fully exploited, especially in the climax reached at 18:4. After a summary statement introducing the section (17:1), v. 2 provides an exemplification of the principle stated in 11:16. "Forgetfulness" (*lēthē*) in v. 3 could be an allusion to the river Lethe in Hades, but cf. Ps 88:12. The connection between darkness, death, and Hades is explicit in 17:14 and 21. In v. 6 the word *pyr* (fire) may retain its ancient Homeric meaning "funeral pyre," thus presaging the death of the magicians (v. 10) and maybe even the eternal darkness and flames of Hades (v. 21). Since v. 5 has stated that ordinary fires gave off no light, this fire must be a supernatural phenomenon. 17:7 probably alludes to the confounding of the Egyptian magicians (Exod 9:11). 17:10a is a problem since the Exodus narrative does not record the death of these magicians or indeed of anyone during the plague of darkness. However, Josephus (*Ant.* 2 §308) has a parallel tradition. The difficulty could be obviated by taking the word "perished" idiomatically — "dying of fright." The word "powerless" in v. 14a is ironic; it is primarily the Egyptians' self-generated fears which hold them prisoner (the "prison not made of iron" in v. 16). "Powerless" in v. 14b refers back to 1:14. Darkness and the powerlessness of its inhabitants are principal characteristics of Sheol in the OT (Ps 88:12; Isa 14:9-11). "The same sleep" (17:14c) is probably the same sleep as that of the inhabitants of Hades, an implied comparison which is finally brought to the surface in v. 21. 17:20-21a is a deduction made from Exod 10:23. 17:17c seems to allude to the even more serious moral and intellectual darkness encompassing the Egyptians.

18:1-4 highlights the contrasting situation of the Israelites, first during the plague of darkness when the sun still shone on them (Exod 10:23), then in the wilderness when the "flaming pillar of fire" accompanied their journey (Exod 13:21-22). The Greek behind the word "therefore" in 18:3 is literally "instead of them." Here the keyword *anti* indicates the essential contrast in the situation of the two peoples: instead of the horrors of darkness so flamboyantly described in ch. 17, Israel travels by the supernatural light of the pillar of fire. The comparison of the law to light (18:4c) is found in the OT (Ps 119:105). In contrast to the rather ambiguous use of the word *nomos* (law) in 6:4, 18, the reference here is certainly to the law of Moses (cf. Bar 4:1). This text with its attribution of imperishability to the law points forward to the apotheosis of the law which will emerge in rabbinic Judaism, a development clearly anticipated by Philo (*Vit. Mos.* 2.14). For Israel's role as the teacher of the nations see Isa 2:2-3; 42:1-7. Nothing is said about how the law was to be communicated to the world. The statement is as theoretical as the rabbinic legend about how the law was offered to the nations prior to Israel's acceptance of it at Sinai (*Mekilta Baḥodesh* 5).

Wisdom 18:5-25

In the sixth contrast the Egyptian firstborn are destroyed but Israel is saved from the wrath of the destroyer in the desert. The section is divided into two parts marked off by the inclusions "destroyed/perished" (same word in Greek) in vv. 5 and 19, and "experience/test" (the same word in Greek) in vv. 20-25.

18:5-19 The events alluded to here are the killing of the Hebrew male children, the rescue of Moses, the slaughter of the Egyptian firstborn, and the drowning of Pharaoh's army in the sea (Exod 1:15-22; 2:1-10; 12:29; 14:21-31). The element of talion, already present in the biblical text, was widely recognized by readers of Exodus from an early time (cf. *Jub.* 48:14). "That night" (18:6) is the night of the first Passover (Exod 12:21-27). 18:8 exemplifies the principle stated in 11:16. In the first half of 18:9 the author seems to have telescoped the events of Passover night and the reception of the law at Sinai (Exod 24:7), while at the end of the verse he has the Israelites already anachronistically reciting the Hallel (Psalms 113–118). This final phrase is problematic (hence the variant reading in NRSV, note *p*) and could also refer to the Israelites recalling the stories of the patriarchs and the promises made to them. But the statement was probably evoked as much by the literary need for a contrast with the desolate cries of the Egyptians (18:10) than by reading back contemporary events into the past. V. 13 draws on Exod 4:22-23 (cf. Hos 11:1). The statement goes beyond the actual text which is presumably being referred to (Exod 12:31), but throughout chs. 10–19 the Wisdom of Solomon routinely embellishes the biblical text for rhetorical effect. Here 18:13b is created by the need to contrast the status of the Israelites with that of the Egyptian firstborn.

The personification of the Word of God in 18:15-16 is striking and unexpected, and the reasons for its appearance here have occasioned much comment. At the least we might have expected personified Wisdom to reappear, as in ch. 10. Earlier in the book she, too, is described as "all-powerful" (7:23) and comes from God's throne down to earth (9:4, 10, 17; Sir 24:3-12). The Word is undoubtedly pictured here in imagery reserved in the OT for the Angel of the LORD (1 Chr 21:16; 2 Kgs 19:35), though some see the author's language influenced by the *Iliad* 4.443. Probably the author is trying to reconcile the apparently conflicting statements of Exod 12:23, where the death of the firstborn is attributed both to God himself and to the mysterious "destroyer." Assimilating the "destroyer" to the Angel of the LORD makes it easier to harmonize the two halves of the verse. The kind of actions performed here by the Word have already been attributed to God as the "man of war" in 5:17-23 (cf. Exod 15:3; Isa 42:13). In the OT God's word has a similar irrevocable action (Ps 147:15; Isa 55:10-11, and note the reference to God's "stern word" in Wis 12:9). The semi-allegorical nature of the imagery here is suggested by the language of 18:16a where the Greek places "the sharp sword" in apposition to "your authentic [better "irrevocable"] word," thus identifying them. Two contradictory impulses seem to be at work here: a desire to reconcile apparent problems in the biblical text and partially allegorize it while at the same time using mythological language for rhetorical effect.

18:20-25 As in 16:5-14, the author moves quickly to cut off a possible objection to the scenario outlined in 18:5-19. Did not the Israelites suffer the same sort of affliction in the desert (Num 16:41-50) perpetrated by a similar demonic force (the "wrath" of Num 16:46)? Does not this undermine their status as "the righteous" (18:1)? The potential objection is turned around to become a reinforcement of the author's argument: no one came to save the Egyptians, but Aaron's censer "held back the wrath" (v. 23). In his description of this episode the author is content to leave unallegorized the impersonal "wrath" of Num 16:46; indeed, his language in 18:22 and 25 even enhances the personification. It has the effect of distancing God from the action and fits in with the text's avoidance of any mention of Israel's "murmuring" which led to the plague (Num 16:41). Israel comes out as innocent and God as not involved in punishing them. See on 16:1-4. Yet again the author presents us with a carefully censored biblical text. For the high priest's robe, breastplate, and turban (v. 24) see Exod 28:1-39. The Wisdom of Solomon alludes here to a cosmological interpretation of these vestments (and of the temple) which was widespread in contemporary Judaism (see Hayman 1986: 178-79).

Wisdom 19:1-22

The seventh contrast shows the Egyptians drowned in the sea, but the Israelites passing through on dry land. The chapter divides into four paragraphs: 19:1-5, 6-12, 13-17, and 18-21, plus a concluding summary of the central theme of chs. 10–19 (v. 22).

At first sight the logic of 19:1 seems strange. The anger (of God) is pitiless because he knew in advance how the Egyptians would behave. They are therefore punished before they commit the crime! Is this in dialogue with 12:10, or were the Egyptians given no "opportunity to repent" because God knew that this would be a waste of time? Or is 19:1b an attempt to make sense both of Exod 3:19 and the theme of the "hardening" of Pharaoh's heart in the Exodus story (Exod 4:21 through to 14:4, 8, 17)? The coy phraseology of 19:4 makes the latter seem more likely. Here the author substitutes for the philosophically difficult "hardening" theme the more rational-sounding "Fate/Necessity," though he still makes the latter the subject of active verbs. This term would resonate much better with an audience educated on Greek literature and, like the use of the terms "avenger" and "destroyer" in 18:20-25, has the useful effect of distancing God from the action. Faced with the same theological dilemma but against a Palestinian cultural background, the author of *Jubilees* makes Mastema, the chief of the evil spirits, the agent of the hardening of the Egyptian hearts (*Jub.* 48:12). Both authors are trying to absolve God from actively causing evil, but the Wisdom of Solomon is more careful here in, at least, seeming to avoid the danger of dualism. As we have seen, at 1:12-15 and 2:23 it is less cautious.

19:6-12 contrast the miraculous experiences of God's people with the "strange death" (v. 5) of its foes. The text presents the events recounted in Exodus 14 as a kind of new creation in which the current order of this world is reversed. It uses philosophically sounding language in 19:6a, as it has previously in 16:24-25, and as it does in more detail in 19:18-21. God reshapes anew the "formless matter" from which the world was created (11:17), interchanging the basic elements (three of which are mentioned in 19:7) to produce the desired result of keeping his children unharmed (v. 6b). The physical theory presupposed had been first formulated by Anaxagoras in the fifth century BC (see Guthrie 1965: 2:266-338) and had become a commonplace of Hellenistic philosophy by the author's time. Philo has a similar explanation for these miracles (*Vit. Mos.* 2.267). "Dry land emerging" in 19:7 alludes to Gen 1:9 and reinforces the theme of miracles as exhibiting the same power as God used at creation. The "grassy plain" echoes Gen 1:11-13. 19:10-12 continue the theme of this new creation which reverses the pattern of events expected under the old creation.

On the surface 19:13-17 contrast the behavior of the Sodomites and the Egyptians toward strangers to the detriment of the latter. But many scholars have seen beneath the surface an allusion to the poor relations between the Jews and their neighbors in the author's own time. The reference to the Jews having "already shared the same rights" (v. 16) is particularly evocative of the changed situation in which they found themselves after the Roman conquest of Egypt in 30 BC (see Barclay 1996: 48-51, 191). V. 13a probably draws on Ps 77:17-20, v. 14a refers to Gen 19:4-9, and v. 14b to Gen 45:16-20 and Exod 1:8-14.

19:18-22 form a fitting conclusion to the book, drawing together and summarizing elements from the later chapters and finishing with a concise statement of the theme of the major part of the book. The precise nature of the musical analogy in v. 18 is rendered uncertain by difficulties in the text (see NRSV, notes *y* and *z*). Most commentators can only make sense of the verse either by emending the text or by giving the Greek words used meanings which they do not have elsewhere. However, the general point being made is clearly the same as in vv. 6-12. At its simplest level the analogy may have been: as the same set of notes can produce different tunes depending on how they are combined, so God arranged the same elements (air, fire, earth, water) in one way at creation, but in another at the miracle of the crossing of the Red Sea. V. 19a possibly refers to the Israelites (land animals) traversing the sea like fish! V. 19a certainly refers back to v. 10 and the plague of frogs, v. 20 to 16:17, and v. 21 to 16:18, 27.

Bibliography. Annas, J. E. 1992, *Hellenistic Philosophy of Mind,* Berkeley: University of California • Barclay, J. M. G. 1996, *Jews in the Mediterranean Diaspora,* Edinburgh: T&T Clark • Barr, J. 1990, *The Garden of Eden and the Hope of Immortality,* London: SCM • Barr, J. 1993. *Biblical Faith and Natural Theology,* Oxford: Clarendon • Clarke, E. G. 1973, *The Wisdom of Solomon,* CBC on the NEB, Cambridge: Cambridge University • Collins, J. J. 1977-78, "Cosmos and Salvation: Jewish Wisdom and Apocalyptic in the Hellenistic Age," *HR* 17:121-42 • Day, J. 1985, *God's Conflict with the Dragon and the Sea,* Cambridge: Cambridge University • di Lella, A. 1966, "Conservative and Progressive Theology: Sirach and Wisdom," *CBQ* 28: 139-54 • Gilbert, M. 1973, *La critique des dieux dans le Livre de la Sagesse,* AnBib 53, Rome: Biblical Institute • Goodrick, A. T. S. 1913, *The Book of Wisdom,* London: Rivingtons • Grabbe, L. L. 1997, *The Wisdom of Solomon,* Guides to Apocrypha and Pseudepigrapha, Sheffield: Sheffield Academic • Gregg, J. A. F. 1909, *The Wisdom of Solomon,* Cambridge: Cambridge University • Guthrie, W. K. C. 1965, *A History of Greek Philosophy,* vol. 2, Cambridge: Cambridge University • Hayman, A. P. 1984, "The Fall, Freewill and Human Responsibility in Rabbinic Judaism," *SJT* 37:13-22 • Hayman, A. P. 1986, "Some Observations on Sefer Yesira: (2) The Temple at the Centre of the Universe," *JJS* 37:176-82 • Kelly, J. N. D. 1960, *Early Christian Doctrines,* London: A. & C. Black • Kloppenborg, J. S. 1982, "Isis and Sophia in the Book of Wisdom," *HTR* 75: 57-84 • Kolarcik, M. 1991, *The Ambiguity of Death in the Book of Wisdom 1–6,* AnBib 127, Rome: Pontifical Biblical Institute • Larcher, C. 1983-85, *Le livre de la Sagesse ou la Sagesse de Salomon,* 3 vols., Paris: Librairie Lecoffre • Nickelsburg, G. W. E. 1972, *Resurrection, Immortality and Eternal Life in Intertestamental Judaism,* HTS 26, Cambridge, Mass.: Harvard University • Olyan, S. M. 1988, *Asherah and the Cult of Yahweh in Israel,* SBLMS 34, Atlanta: Scholars • Reese, J. M. 1970, *Hellenistic Influence on the Book of Wisdom and Its Consequences,* AnBib 41, Rome: Biblical Institute • Schroer, S. 1995, "The Book of Sophia," in *Searching the Scriptures: A Feminist Commentary,* London: SCM, 2:17-38 • Seeley, D. 1990, "Narrative, the Righteous Man and the Philosopher: An Analysis of the Story of the *Dikaios* in Wisdom 1–5," *JSP* 7:55-78 • Sheppard, G. T. 1980, *Wisdom as a Hermeneutical Construct,* BZAW 151, Berlin: Walter de Gruyter • Winston, D. 1979, *The Wisdom of Solomon,* AB 43, New York: Doubleday • Winston, D. 1993, "Wisdom in the Wisdom of Solomon," in Leo G. Perdue et al., eds., *In Search of Wisdom: Essays in Memory of John G. Gammie,* Louisville: Westminster/John Knox, 149-64 • Wright, A. G. 1967, "The Structure of the Book of Wisdom," *Bib* 48:165-84 • Wyatt, N. 1996, *Myths of Power: A Study of Royal Myth and Ideology in Ugaritic and Bblical Tradition,* Ugaritisch-Biblische Literatur 13, Münster: Ugarit-Verlag • Ziener, G. 1956, *Die theologische Begriffsprache im Buche der Weisheit,* BBB 11, Bonn: Peter Hanstein.

Sirach

John Snaith

INTRODUCTION

The book of Sirach exists in the Apocrypha in the Greek translation of the Hebrew original made by Sirach's grandson in Egypt — the circumstances and date of the translation being adequately described in the Prologue his grandson wrote to his translation and the commentary on it below. Two matters require comment here: the circumstances of Sirach's composition of the original Hebrew and the fragments of the original Hebrew that we have.

The circumstances in which Sirach wrote are reasonably clear: his praise of Simon as high priest in 50:1-24 leads us to assume that he had personally experienced Simon's priesthood: Simon held office from 219 to 196 BC. The tone of 50:1 implies that Simon had already died when Sirach wrote. So Sirach probably wrote the Hebrew after 196, yet he shows no knowledge of the Maccabean revolt in 167, nor of the unpopular intensification of Hellenism by the decree of Antiochus IV, who reigned from 175. He does show knowledge of pressure for Greek ways, however, as he seeks to find a way for pious Jews to use Greek medical knowledge in 38:1-15. We can thus confidently say that Sirach wrote between 196 and 175 BC. Many scholars suggest a date about 185.

The original Hebrew did not survive with the Hebrew books of the OT because it was not part of the Hebrew Bible (HB): the Greek translation is part of the Roman Catholic canon, and it is often called "deuterocanonical." No complete Hebrew text is extant, but fragmentary manuscripts have been found in various places: substantial fragments from the storeroom of an ancient synagogue in Cairo (the famous Cairo Genizah) and fragments found in the fort at Masada and in the settlement at Qumran. Such widespread use of the book shows how, even if it was not regarded as part of the Hebrew canon of the Bible, it was highly appreciated and valued.

COMMENTARY

The Prologue

The Greek background of the grandson's translation is well illustrated by this preface, which resembles the historical prefaces written by classical authors like Herodotus, Thucydides, and the later Hippocrates who wrote on medical matters — and not least the preface written by St. Luke for his Gospel in the NT. It is written in good, flowing koine Greek rather than the somewhat stilted style used for his rather literal translation of his grandfather's Hebrew. The references to the "Law, the Prophets, and the others that followed them" and "the Law, the Prophets, and the other books of our ancestors" show that, by the time the grandson wrote, the number (canon) of books of the OT was fixed for the Law and the Prophets, but the contents of the Writings were still uncertain. Just as Sirach had written his exposition of Jewish faith and tradition when Jewish confidence was at a low ebb just before the Hellenistic reform (see the Introduction, this page), so his grandson, on settling in Egypt, discovered that Jews who had settled there were falling away from their ancestral traditions in their new Greek environment and failing to live "according to the law." The book thus takes its place among various "evangelistic" works in Greek like the writings of Josephus and Philo, representing Judaism to the Greeks.

In the second paragraph we should notice the grandson's impressive honesty over the difficulties of translating from one language to another. I doubt whether even today experienced translators could put it any better!

"The thirty-eighth year of the reign of Euergetes," when the grandson migrated to Egypt, was probably 132 BC. He found that the Jews who had settled there were in widespread ignorance of Jewish law and tradition, and saw the possibility of translating his grandfather's work to build up Jewish self-awareness among "those living abroad" in Egypt away from their homeland, Palestine/Israel.

Wisdom and Some of Its Human Manifestations (1:1–4:10)

Before moving into more detailed, practical topics, the opening section (1:1-20) deals with two basic themes of wisdom literature: wisdom in general as God's gift in vv. 1-10, and the fear of God in vv. 11-20; v. 20 then concludes the section neatly with echoes of the beginning — a literary device known as "inclusion" which Sirach uses quite often to conclude a section, sometimes with a specifically religious sentiment, as here in v. 20. "Wisdom" here does not mean detailed knowledge of accumulated regulations or of human experience in the world, but the intelligent purpose of God that lies behind creation: God's wisdom far exceeds such accumulated knowledge — it exceeds even "the sand of the sea" and "drops of rain," which humans cannot count. The rhetorical questions in vv. 2 and 3 emphasize God's unquestionable greatness — a style used in Job (chs. 38–41) with the same intent. God's wisdom is described as impenetrable to human beings: "There is but one who is wise — the Lord" (1:8). Although an attribute of God, wisdom is God's free gift, which he lavishes on those who love him.

By "the fear of the Lord" Sirach means reverence practiced in everyday living — what is, in fact, "the beginning of wisdom" (1:14). This term in the book of Proverbs often seems colorless and insipid. Sirach brightens it up, describing it as "glory and exultation," giving "gladness and joy and long life." The insipid term has become one of warmth, "making peace and perfect health to flourish" (v. 18).

In 1:22 Sirach turns from the general to the particular. Whereas much wisdom literature in the ancient Near East gathered proverbs in an often random way like much of the book of Proverbs, Sirach gathers them together rather more under subjects. So here vv. 22-24 deal with anger before he returns to the fear of the Lord in v. 27. One particular feature of Sirach's work that crops up again and again is his identification of true wisdom with the law: hence "if you desire wisdom, keep the commandments" (v. 26). This is even more noticeable in v. 28 where disobeying "the fear of the Lord" probably means disobeying the law.

At the beginning of ch. 2 Sirach turns to the need for "testing" people who seek "to serve the Lord." The need for such testing had already been examined at length in the book of Job. Here Sirach counsels a steady, well-balanced attitude to life that will not give way to "impetuous" behavior "in time of calamity." Following the lead of the book of Job, Sirach advises patience "in times of humiliation," accepting with calm faith "whatever befalls you." Such testing is illustrated by the mention of refining "gold" in "fire" — an image popular with ancient Jewish writers; indeed, v. 5 may well quote a traditional phrase around which Sirach has built this section on testing.

Sirach then passes on to sections on assurance of success to the faithful (2:7-11), forecasting disaster to people who are inadequate for life (vv. 12-14) and expressing approval of "those who fear the Lord" (vv. 15-17) before he rounds off the section with a spiritual appeal to his readers (v. 18). The passage is bound together by threefold patterns of repetition in "you who fear the Lord" in vv. 7-9 and 15-17, and "woe to . . ." in vv. 12-14. Such repetition is a helpful aid to memory in oral teaching and is found in the Mishnah as well as in non-Israelite proverbial literature. However, the question in v. 10 begs a very real question: historians can easily point to people who did "trust in the Lord" only to "be disappointed"! Josiah, king of Judah, for example, was faithful to the law and purified the Jerusalem temple, only to die prematurely in battle in 609 (2 Kgs 22–23). However, Sirach's answer is "not one," and he backs this up later in chs. 44–50 by surveying the past history of the Jews and finding there massive support for faith in God. We should note how he frequently concludes a section of proverbial lore with a statement of God's protective love, as in 4:10, 28; 6:17, 37, and so on.

Chapter 3 opens with a form of address typical of wisdom teachers throughout the ancient Near East. Sirach addresses his readers as "children" (v. 1), like "my child" in 2:1, and he describes himself as their "father." Such terms were used in Proverbs, as in 4:1: "Listen, children, to a father's instruction, and be attentive that you may gain insight." But family relationships meant more to Sirach than this formal mode of address. Here he devotes sixteen verses to the respect due to one's parents. He is here very much in line with Jewish tradition, as one of the Ten Commandments bids people to honor their father and mother (Exod. 20:12), and the books of Ruth and Tobit also mention respect for parents. "For the Lord honors a father above his children" means that God requires children to give their father due honor, and their mother the same. Paternal respect can even "atone for sins" (3:3). To "have long life" (v. 6) was particularly important for Sirach: as he had no belief in an afterlife, a long, happy mortal life was the greatest reward on offer. To serve "parents as their masters" (v. 7) anticipates later rabbinic statements that a man stood in the same relation to his father as a slave to his master. The style and balance of biblical Hebrew poetry means that vv. 9 and 11 refer to "blessings" and "curses" of both "father" and "mother." V. 10 shows up filial rivalry when some think they can gain credit by dishonoring their father. Sirach's injunction for special care of a father "even if his mind fails" (v. 13) shows wide knowledge of the difficulties that can arise in families. As before, care is taken to set the whole question of family relationships in a religious context at the end of the chapter (v. 16).

Such discussion leads on naturally to the problems of humility and pride in 3:17-28. Humility and the fear of the Lord are often linked in Proverbs. Readers should "reflect upon what you have been commanded" and not "meddle" in "things beyond" them (vv. 22-23) — a warning against Greek speculation in scientific matters. In v. 26 he turns from intellectual pride to "stubborn" arrogance which reflects on people with no humility.

True humility shows itself in "almsgiving" which "atones for sin" (3:30). In ch. 4 Sirach concentrates readers' attention on giving to the needy. Before the Maccabean revolt the gap between rich and poor had greatly increased because of "tax farming." Individual tax collectors gathered more than was required by their overlords, keeping the excess for themselves, cheating "the poor of their living." The OT had already stressed the importance of care for the poor and oppressed (cf. Deut 15:7-8 and Amos 2:6-7), but the current situation led Sirach to emphasize it. "Almsgiving" became an important feature of later Judaism. Rabbi Akiba of the second century AD even remarked that "God placed the poor on earth in order to save the rich from Hell!" Note that to "endear yourself to the congregation" (4:7) does not mean for Sirach ingratiating oneself with powerful people but being known for listening to the poor and rescuing "the oppressed from the oppressor." Yet Sirach is realistic enough to stress the need for being firm "in giving a verdict" (v. 9). Again the section is rounded off with a specifically religious comment in v. 10.

Wisdom and Her Warnings (4:11–6:17)

The next section is bounded here and in 6:16-17 by wisdom and the fear of the Lord — another example of inclusion. The link with the previous section is made by the catchword, "children," echoing "son" in 4:10. Wisdom is here personified and deeply concerned about the welfare of her children (us). Echoes of the earlier book of Proverbs abound here. But Sirach takes things a step further in v. 14: those who follow wisdom's lead "minister to the Holy One" in the love of "the Lord." V. 15 seems to imply that those who "judge the nations" all "obey" wisdom — no doubt wishful thinking! The theme of testing appears again in the "tortuous paths" (v. 17) she leads them in, tormenting "them by her discipline until she trusts them" — a passage which again echoes the experiences of Job. The phrase "she will test them with her ordinances" is a reminder that true wisdom for Sirach is the Jewish law.

After this general introduction Sirach moves in 4:20 to advice on particular situations in life. Jews should not be "ashamed" of themselves whatever happens in the political world. But he does not advise caution all the time: no "partiality," true, but no "deference" either (v. 22): you should not be afraid to speak "at the proper moment" (v. 23), as "wisdom" can be "known" only "through speech" (v. 24). Stopping "the current of a river" (v. 26) seems a strange thing to do! A similar phrase occurs in the Syriac proverbs of Ahikar: struggling against a forceful flow of water is applied to trying to do the impossible. Better to "fight to the death for truth" with God's help (v. 28). The chapter closes with three strong comments on everyday life: we should not talk big and do little (v. 29) nor roar around the house like "lions," making our "servants" afraid of us. Finally, we have in v. 31 a splendidly concise proverb on generosity, a theme which leads onto the perils of undue self-confidence in ch. 5.

In traditional Jewish thought of OT times wealth had been thought of as God's reward for piety (*pace* the book of Job, which challenges this). By Sirach's time Hellenization had brought riches to a part of the population of Israel: this situation is illustrated by 5:1-8. In such conditions it is all too easy to "rely on" one's newfound "wealth" — a warning equally relevant to all situations of sudden prosperity — even today. There is then a very real temptation to "gratify every impulse" and follow up all the "desires of your heart" (v. 2). Such cockiness leads to various unwise thoughts listed in vv. 3-6, where "do not say" means "not think to yourself." Lack of immediate punishment for sin can cause one to sin much more — after all, "The Lord is slow to anger" (v. 4), is he not? so why not "add sin to sin, confident of forgiveness"? The new Hellenistic aristocracy was in danger of being too confident of forgiveness. God's "mercy" goes with his "wrath" — two sides of the same coin — and his wrath "will rest on sinners": his mercy must not be presumed upon.

Hence "Do not delay to turn back to the Lord" or "postpone it" daily (5:7), for the Lord's "wrath" comes "suddenly," and "you will perish at the time of punishment" (cf. the various explanations of Job's disaster). "Wealth," whether "dishonest" or honest, will not help you: v. 8 (note the inclusion with v. 1) sums up the dangers of the get-rich-quickly mentality of pre-Maccabean Judaism. The temptation is to "winnow in every wind" and "follow every path" (v. 9), that is, to try every possible way out of the calamity that has hit you. Rather, you should be reliable, taking care to "stand firm for what you know," keeping "your speech consistent" (v. 10). V. 11 is echoed in the NT in Jas 1:19: "Let everyone be quick to listen, slow to speak," and also has a parallel in Egyptian wisdom literature.

Sirach clearly felt strongly about "double-tongued" speech (5:14), as the term occurs three times in as many verses (5:14, 15; 6:1). Speech is a responsible matter since it can bring about people's "downfall" (v. 13). The images in v. 14 are all too familiar: "double-tongued" means saying different things to different people maliciously: laying "traps with your tongue" can easily lead to your "downfall" (v. 13).

The next unit (6:2-4) on "the grip of passion" introduces a passage on true friendship in 6:5-17. By its hard grip passion tears a person apart as "a bull" rampages beyond control. The picture then changes to "a withered tree" (v. 3), hardly the result of a raging bull, but it picks up the reference to a eunuch as a "dry tree" in Isa 56:3. Just as an unwatered tree withers in a scorching summer, so "evil passion destroys those who have it" (6:4).

Friendship was a favorite topic in Hellenistic literature, where a frequent phrase occurs on "advisers" being "one in a thousand" (6:6). Seven verses are given to the need to test friends carefully (vv. 7-13) — sentiments needing little further comment as the same is true today. The Babylonian Talmud remarks that "At the door of the rich all are friends; at the door of the poor there are none." The section on unreliable "friends" ends with a splendid couplet in v. 13: Are they really "friends" if you have to "be on guard" with them? Suspicions surrounding friendship were widely discussed in the ancient world: the Egyptian *Instruction of Amenemhet* says: "Trust not a brother, know not a friend, make no intimates, it is worthless." In vv. 14-17 the worth of true friendship is emphasized by threefold repetition of "faithful friends" at the beginning of vv. 14-16 — a frequent means of emphasis in biblical poetry.

Occasionally such practical matters are interrupted by a general poem on wisdom: the book started with such a passage in 1:1-20; there is another in 4:11-19. Here a similar poem fills the rest of the chapter from v. 18.

Searching for Wisdom (6:18-37)

The frequent form of address, "my child," is natural here as the author is encouraging young people to seek wisdom, so that they have it when they become old with "grey hair" (6:18). Cultivation of wisdom is likened to "harvest" (v. 19), yet is a "heavy stone" to carry (v. 21) with "fetters" and "collar" (v. 24). But on its attainment the "collar" becomes "a glorious robe, her yoke a golden ornament, and her bonds a purple cord" (vv. 29-31), where purple is probably the color of royalty. By v. 32 the hard effort to acquire wisdom is over; the pupil enjoys listening "in the company of the elders" (v. 34) to whom he attaches himself. Again the section closes with a religious sentiment (v. 37).

Warnings about Sin in Social Life (7:1-36)

The first three verses of this section introduce a collection of proverbs on how evil and sin may befall you in public life. In 7:1 Sirach uses a play on words to make the general point at the head of the section: "evil" stands equally for bad things you may "do" and for bad things that can "overtake you." He is usually more down-to-earth than this in his advice! Would that it were always true that if you "do no evil" it "will never overtake you" (v. 1), as well as a guarantee that if you "stay away from wrong" then "it will turn away from you" (v. 2). In practice this does not always happen: Sirach seems to be expressing an unrealistically pious hope! In v. 3 he speaks of "a sevenfold crop" — using the number "seven" for success, as often in the Bible.

With 7:4 he lists a series of undesirable things to do, starting with ambition "before the Lord" and "the king" (vv. 4 and 5) and desire to be "a judge." In the pre-Maccabean period many people enjoyed political prestige and economic advantage through practicing oppression and abuse and being "partial to the powerful." Riches and a "great number of gifts" (v. 9) do not impress God. There follows another sequence of advice as relevant today as it was then. Prayer and almsgiving were both important parts of religious life for the Jew (v. 10). In v. 14 he hardly proscribes formal prayer, but probably refers to "heaping up empty phrases" as in Matt 6:7. Sirach's advice in v. 15 about "hard labor" probably reflects the urban sophistication of his day when many people gathered from rural areas to the city. Life on the land had lost its appeal since the prescription to Adam (Gen 3:17-19).

In 7:18 Sirach turns to family life. "Ophir," probably in Arabia, was well known for "gold." Wives (v. 19) are mentioned later, and similarly "slaves" (especially 33:25-33). In 7:21 he refers to the law's stipulation that after six years' service slaves should be set free. In vv. 22-28 he goes through all the members of the household, even "cattle," ending with "parents." The religious duties of vv. 29-31 reflect Sirach's love of temple ritual and are followed (vv. 32-36) by certain noteworthy social actions like caring for "the poor," generosity, mourning with mourners and visitation of "the sick." Sirach valued liturgical detail, but the need of practical living won out in the end!

Times to Avoid (8:1-19)

Sirach begins this section with warnings against quarreling with the hope of getting greater "resources," whether of influence or money: you do not stand a chance of winning! This is even more true if you "argue with" the loud-mouthed: you will only add fuel to "their fire." Insults to "your ancestors" (8:4) may result from mocking "one who is ill-bred." It is often inappropriate to criticize others for conditions we know ourselves; hence "reproach for one who is" already "turning away from sin" forgets we all are sinners (v. 5); "disdain" for the old forgets we all grow "old" (v. 6); rejoicing "over anyone's death" forgets "we all must die" (v. 7). The series of verses beginning "do not . . ." continues with disrespect for tradition handed down from "sages" and "the aged" (vv. 8 and 9): the *Sayings of the Fathers (Pirqe 'Abot)* in the Mishnah said, "He who learns from the old" is like "one who eats ripe grapes and drinks old wine." The financial advice of vv. 12-13 includes advice on giving "surety"; this means giving financial guarantees for people in debt, not unlike going bail for people today. Some advice here is self-evident; for example, going "to law against a judge" (v. 14) is obviously risky, as is picking "a fight with the quick-tempered" (v. 16). Advice for caution with "fools" and "strangers" leads on to discouragement to "reveal your thoughts to anyone" at all for the sake of your own contentment.

Relationships with Various People (9:1–10:5)

This section starts with advice on relationships with dangerous women (9:1-9) — a common topic for wisdom teachers (cf. Prov 6:24-26). Sirach returns to the topic again in 25:13–26:12, but there he ends with praise of a virtuous wife (26:13-18). Some advice here is obvious; for example, the danger of loose women or "prostitutes" (vv. 3-6), wandering in deserted "streets of a city" (v. 7), or gazing at "a shapely woman" (v. 8). More perspicacious is the warning against being "jealous of" your own "wife" (v. 1): you might encourage her in ways you could regret. Dining "with another man's wife" is seen as a possible prelude to adultery, for which a husband seeks revenge "in blood" (v. 9).

In 9:10 Sirach returns to "friends," a subject already treated in 6:5-17 and 7:18 (cf. 37:1-6). Note that "a new friend, like new wine," improves in time before he can be enjoyed fully — whence it is unwise to "abandon old friends." Pre-Maccabean court intrigues may provide the background for his remarks on the danger of "death" in v. 13: both Ptolemaic and Seleucid monarchs had the absolute right of life or death over their subjects. The book of Proverbs is full of advice against "stepping among snares" (v. 13): Sirach here follows the imagery of the wisdom tradition. He then describes the danger of keeping company with potential murderers as "walking on the city battlements," exposing oneself needlessly to attack from the enemy. V. 17, with its praise for "the skill of the artisan" and the "words" of the "people's leader" shows that Sirach approved skill with both hands and "words," but greater danger lies in "the loud of mouth" and the "reckless in speech" (v. 18).

Chapter 10 introduces public officials: poetic parallelism probably indicates that the persons mentioned in the two halves of v. 1 are the same: an intelligent magistrate. In pre-Maccabean Jerusalem his remarks on "an undisciplined king" (v. 3) would have been dangerous (he wrote only shortly before the Maccabean revolt!), as also his statement that God "will raise up the right leader for the time" (v. 4). But he covers himself by saying that "human success is in the hand of the Lord" (v. 5).

Pride and Honor (10:6–11:6)

The "arrogance," "injustice," and "insolence" of 10:6-8 start on the personal level, but by v. 8 become the reason for "sovereignty," passing "from nation to nation." This may well refer to the battles of Raphia and Panium, both fought in Sirach's lifetime: at Raphia in 217 BC the Seleucid Antiochus III tried to retrieve Palestine from Egypt but was defeated; at Panium in 198 BC Antiochus attacked the Egyptian army successfully, and Palestine became part of the Seleucid empire. The close connection between vv. 8 and 9 means that the decay of "dust and ashes" (v. 9) refers to the disasters befalling Ptolemaic and Seleucid kings, both of whom claimed divinity but were "dust and ashes" like other humans. This leads to the grimness of vv. 10-11, verses which are further explained in vv. 12-17: the worst punishment in Sirach's eyes was that God "erases" their "memory from the earth" (v. 17). This introduces in v. 19 a discussion of offspring "worthy" and "unworthy of honor," where the answer Sirach gives underlines his Jewish orthodoxy: he who "fears the Lord" (v. 24) is "greater" than princes and judges.

10:26-27 attack boasting — better to work hard for "bread" than to boast and have nothing. V. 28 makes a telling point: "honor yourself with humility" — a notable contrast to the people mentioned above. The remaining verses of the chapter draw out the contrast, but the real climax of this passage comes in 11:1, where true greatness is seen in "the wisdom of the humble." This leads Sirach to discuss true honor: it is not to be found in wealth. People should not be praised or loathed because of "their looks" (v. 2); "the bee" (v. 3) "is" certainly "small" but "produces the best of sweet things" — a far cry from those who "boast about wearing fine clothes" (v. 4). Human honors are truly topsy-turvy with "kings" dishonored "rulers disgraced," and nobodies wearing "crowns" (vv. 5-6). God's "works are concealed from humankind" in this way.

Attitudes toward Work and True Prosperity (11:7-34)

11:7-9 can be summed up in: Do not speak out of turn. You can be (wrongly!) so sure of your opinion that you put the cart before the horse: finding "fault before you investigate," criticizing before you "examine," answering "before you listen," interrupting others speaking, and arguing about matters irrelevant to you (vv. 7-9). Much of this arises through overcommitment to too many "activities" (vv. 10-11): better to concentrate on lifting people "out of their lowly condition" (v. 12) and raising "up their heads" (v. 13), as does God. Riches and success come "from the Lord" — true! — but how long can a mortal "feast on" his "goods" before he "leaves them to others" at death (v. 19)?

11:20-28 treat financial and spiritual rewards. V. 20 in particular is the boast of many elderly men who have supported their own firms all their lives: "trust in the Lord and keep at your job" (v. 21) is a good motto. Note a particularly neat comment on "prosperity" and "adversity" in v. 25. Vv. 26-28 pose a puzzle, as Sirach did not believe in life after death: the Greek version of v. 28 ("through his children a person becomes known") seems to fit Sirach's beliefs better, but, as the main NRSV text reads, it means that "a person's" character is "known by how he" dies.

To compare inviting guests "into your home" (11:29) to "a decoy partridge in a cage" (v. 30) seems hard! The decoy lures another bird into the cage through a small entrance which closes with a spring on entry, preventing escape: if you have enticed someone with hospitality, you can then "observe" their "weakness," "turning good into evil." On the other hand, it is unwise to "receive strangers into your home" (v. 34), for they could "stir up trouble," making "you a stranger to your own family." Hospitality has its dangers either way.

Choice of Friends (12:1–13:24)

12:1 implies that benevolence should be directed only to people known to you (what price Third World need?); no such benevolence is received by "one who persists in evil" or "does not give alms" (v. 3). The advice in v. 5 "not" to "give to the ungodly" but "hold back their bread" in case they "subdue you" and you "receive twice as much evil" for any "good you have done to them" seems reasonable enough but is flatly contradicted by Matt 5:43-47, where Jesus commands Christians to love their enemies. We can compare Prov 25:21-22, where readers give their hungry enemies food to eat and water to drink — not for good reasons, certainly, but to "heap coals of fire on their heads"! This is another example of Sirach being pragmatic.

The point of 12:8 is that you do not discover who your friends are when all is going well: it takes "adversity" to reveal them, and even then they sometimes disappear (v. 9). "Wickedness" grows "like corrosion in copper" (v. 10). Mirrors were then made of metal, not glass: if your reputation is not polished carefully and frequently, it loses its shine and becomes rusty; so keep your mirror well polished and maintain a good reputation. Extreme watchfulness is required: if you let your enemy "take your seat, you will realize" (too late) "the truth of" Sirach's "words and be stung by" them (v. 12). Being stung leads naturally to the "snake-charmer" being "bitten" (v. 13). Going "near wild animals" is likened to associating "with a sinner" with resultant involvement in his sins. His words do not represent the thoughts of "his heart," and he weeps only crocodile tears (v. 16), waiting to "trip you up" and then "show his true face" (v. 18). Shaking the head in the OT often means mocking, but here the enemy is pretending to be friendly; nevertheless, if you touch "pitch" it will make you "dirty," and so will association with a proud person diminish you.

13:2-23 examines friendship with various types of people. Keeping company with a man "richer than you" is like lifting "a weight too heavy for you" (v. 2), or a "clay pot" striking against an "iron kettle": it will be smashed to smithereens. On doing "wrong a rich person" can add "insults" to injury, whereas "a poor person" can only apologize (v. 3). "A rich person" can choose: he can "exploit you" or "abandon you" according to your usefulness to him. If you have possessions, "he will live with you" and "drain your resources" without conscience; but "when he needs you" (v. 6), he will deceitfully "smile" and "encourage you," pretending to be helpful — until he has no further use for you. Then he will "laugh at you" (v. 7) and "shake his head" in derision whenever he sees you. Several verses follow on the difficulties regarding invitations from "an influential person" (v. 9): neither being forward nor standing aloof will work (v. 10). You cannot "trust his lengthy conversations" or "smiles" because he is testing you (v. 11): you could be "walking about with your own downfall" (v. 13).

"Like" naturally associates with "like," and "every person" with his "neighbor" (13:15-16). In v. 17 he quotes the proverb, the wolf living with the lamb, from Isa 11:6 to show that "the sinner" has little in common with "the devout." "Rich" and "poor" are natural enemies, like the "hyena" and the "dog" (v. 18): each is an "abomination" to the other (v. 20). Contrasts between people's differing attitudes to the "rich" and "humble" continue to v. 24, which takes a step back and sums the situation up.

Happiness and Wealth (13:25–14:19)

In this section Sirach starts with true happiness in 13:25–14:2, and then turns to those who see happiness only in accumulating money (14:3-10), which leads him to consider the end of wealth in death (vv. 11-19). By "the heart" of a person (13:25) changing his "countenance for good or for evil," Sirach means his inward, moral and spiritual state rather than the amount of money he has. One wonders how far his personal experience lies behind the remark that devising proverbs requires painful thinking (v. 26)! The verse is rather a general comment on discretion since the next verse (14:1) speaks of not blundering "with" one's "lips" and thus avoiding "remorse for sin." A clear conscience is best: your heart does not "condemn" you — and "hope" remains.

In the following poem on the use of wealth, 14:3-10 concentrates on the negative side, miserly treatment of money, and vv. 11-19 concentrate briefly on the positive side of wealth before you lose it all on death. The first section is marked by inclusion, the "miser" being mentioned at the beginning and the end (vv. 3 and 10). The "miser" denies himself pleasure only to hand his riches over to others on his death. He will neither "enjoy his riches" nor "be generous" to others (v. 5) — being "grudging to himself" will constitute his "punishment" (v. 6). Any good he does is "by mistake" (v. 7). In fact, dissatisfaction "with his share withers" away his soul; even bread "is lacking at his table" (v. 10).

Turning in 14:11 to the good uses of wealth, treating oneself well goes together with presenting "worthy offerings to the Lord." Enjoyment is important because you do not know the day of your" death." "Hades," the Greek name for the afterlife, is misleading since Sirach believed in no afterlife; a better translation is the REB's "the hour of your appointment with the grave is undisclosed." Consequently his advice is to "treat yourself well" and "do good to friends before you die" (v. 11) — otherwise you leave all your goods "to another" or "to be divided by lot" (v. 15). In v. 17 "the decree from of old 'You must die!'" comes from the Garden of Eden story in Gen 2:17. The phrase "flesh and blood" in 14:18 became a technical term for "human, mortal," in rabbinic literature. Sirach here stresses that death is the end — his firm belief.

Another Poem on Wisdom (14:20–15:10)

Another general poem in praise of wisdom comes next: practical conduct must always be based on careful thought. For "reasons intelligently" in 14:20 the NEB has "uses his brains to think," which makes the point forcefully. Wisdom is here pictured as dwelling in a house, where the student "peers through windows" and "listens at doors," even "fastening his tent peg to her walls" (vv. 23-24). The chapter division may disguise the fact that "will do this" in 15:1 refers to the actions of the wise man in 14:20-27; there is in this verse another identification of "wisdom" with "the law." Wisdom is as close to the wise man as one of the family (15:2) and supplies the "bread" and "water" (v. 3) of daily life — terms used in later Jewish literature for spiritual sustenance through faith. One rabbi said that non-Jews converting to Judaism would "find in Israel the bread of the Torah (Law)." Wisdom will "make him eloquent" in the "assembly" — a better translation than "open his mouth" (v. 5). Sinners are precluded from uttering "praise," as then it does not come "from the Lord" (v. 9). The poem ends in v. 10 with yet another closing reference to the Lord's work.

Sin and Freewill (15:11–16:23)

This section, not as closely integrated as usual, starts with two popular objections to God's attitude to sin. In 15:11 the original Greek is to be preferred: "you ought not to do what he hates." In fact, God does not "lead" people "astray" because he has "no need" to bother with "the sinful" anyway (v. 12): God has no part in human sin. If man follows evil, it is his "own free choice" (v. 14). This is followed up in vv. 16-17 with examples of "fire and water" and "life and death": this doctrine of free will is found in Deut 30:19 with almost the same wording. His comments on sin close with an inclusion in v. 20 echoing v. 11.

Large families were considered a sure sign of prosperity in Jewish thought; but "a multitude of worthless children" was not desirable, particularly if they were "ungodly" (16:1). They are no joy "unless the fear of the Lord is in them" (v. 2); "one" who fears the Lord is "better than a thousand" (v. 3). There may lie behind v. 4's reference to "one intelligent person" a reference to Simon, the high priest of Sirach's own time, whom he praises in 50:1-31 and who stood firm against the wicked Tobiads. He would have "seen" his exploits "with" his "own eyes," which would give point to v. 5.

He then lists disasters to sinners. The "assembly of sinners" (v. 6) probably refers to the rebellion of the sons of Korah in Numbers 16, when God "kindled fire" against them. "Wrath" blazed up "in a disobedient nation" at Taberah in Num 11:1-3. The "ancient giants" are probably those of Gen 6:1-4. "The neighbors of Lot" (v. 8) refers to the people of Sodom in Gen 19:4-5, whose crime was sexual deviation rather than "arrogance." "The doomed nation" (16:9) is probably the Canaanites "dispossessed" by the Hebrews. "The six hundred thousand foot soldiers" (v. 10; Exod. 12:37) represent those whom Moses led in the desert after the exodus. After this short roll call of sinners, Sirach turns to more positive things in v. 14: in spite of God's antagonism to sinners, he "makes room for every act of mercy." The remaining verses of the section stress God's almightiness in a series of impressive poetic comparisons.

Divine Wisdom and Mercy (16:24–18:14)

16:24 and 25 form an introduction to the next section, written in the traditional style of wisdom writers. For precisely in v. 25 the Greek has "by weight," giving a good idea how Sirach ponders his work before putting it on paper.

He then starts a didactic poem on God's control of the universe, interrupted in 17:15-32 by answers to objections and a consequent appeal for repentance. In 16:26-28 the emphasis lies on the orderliness of creation: God has "determined" the "boundaries" of his heavenly works (v. 26) and "arranged" them "in an eternal order" (v. 27). The reliability of nature is emphasized, but living beings are not eternal: they have to "return" to the earth in the end (v. 30). As already noted, Sirach did not believe in life after death; this is underlined in 17:1 — "human beings return" to the earth "again." Although humans thus have only "a fixed number of days," they have "authority" over all "the earth" (v. 2): they are in God's "image" and are superior to all "beasts and birds" (vv. 3-4). They have God-given powers of intellect (vv. 5-6). Vv. 6-8 cover all kinds of physical and intellectual gifts, culminating in "the law of life" (v. 11), which probably means the (Jewish) law that gives life. God's gifts here close with the "eternal covenant" (v. 12), seeing God's "glorious majesty" and hearing "the glory of his voice" at Sinai (v. 13). V. 14 summarizes the Ten Commandments as love of God and love of one's neighbor. The meaning of v. 17 is unclear: probably Sirach is saying that other nations have secular rulers whereas Israel has God as sovereign; in his day Israel had had no king as head of state for several centuries.

The reference to "almsgiving" as "a signet ring" (17:22) shows Sirach's background of traditional Jewish piety and reminds the less tolerant of us of the basic "kindness" of Judaism: one's "signet ring" was very private and often hung around one's neck. Although Sirach did not believe in an afterlife, he still foresaw judgment at death, as he speaks of God rewarding people at death for their conduct (11:26); thus he speaks of "recompense" in v. 23 and repentance in v. 24. Vv. 25-28 seem to imply that repentance and "return to the Most High" are necessary before one can "sing" his "praises." "The dead" (v. 28) are truly of no use, and not everything is "within human capability" (v. 30) because of human mortality. After all, even "the sun can be eclipsed" (v. 31). Yet the difference between "the host of heaven" and the "dust and ashes" of human existence remains huge!

This last contrast leads into a hymn (18:1-14) extolling God as a righteous and merciful judge. Humans can neither "proclaim his works "nor "measure his power" (vv. 4-5). This hymn is added to emphasize God's compassion, just as the hymn in 14:28–15:10 emphasized the happiness of the wise man. But the size of God's compassion can be appreciated only when one realizes his power and majesty. Hence the opening verses concentrate on "the wonders of the Lord" (v. 6) and "his majestic power" (v. 5) before turning to the weakness of "human beings." When they "have finished, they are just beginning" (v. 7)! Even a life of "one hundred years" (v. 9) is like "a drop of water" to God (v. 10). So even the great Creator God is "patient with them" and "grants them forgiveness" (v. 12). His "compassion" is so much greater than human compassion, and he treats humans "as a shepherd his flock" (v. 13).

Warnings on Ordinary Life (18:15–19:17)

Various short sentences follow, of which the first (18:15-18) concerns generosity, leading on from God's generosity in the previous section. Mixing reproaches with "good deeds" and spoiling gifts with "harsh words" (v. 15) make for confusion: "a" personal "word" face to face "is better than a gift," just as "dew" relieves "scorching heat" (v. 16). Vv. 19-21 warn of the need for previous anticipation of various things: learning before speaking, caring for "health" before feeling "ill," self-examination before "judgment," and awareness of the need for "repentance" when you sin. The need for being circumspect continues in vv. 22-26, particularly in "paying" and "making" vows — think of God's "wrath" and "vengeance." Be prepared for "hunger" and "poverty" (v. 25) because "conditions" can "change" very "swiftly," even "from morning to evening." Vv. 27-29 sum up many of the sentiments in the preceding sections in a way very typical of wisdom writers; indeed, v. 29 could almost be a motto for the whole work:" those who are skilled in words . . . pour forth apt proverbs."

Before the next group of verses the Greek text (unusually) gives a heading: "Self-Control." First, Sirach warns against giving way to "base desires" (vv. 30-32) and "luxury" (v. 32); also, "feasting with borrowed money" can ruin you (v. 33). Such indulgence leads to poverty; the phrase "wine and women" (19:2) has become proverbial. "Decay and worms" (v. 3) means untimely death — some think this means venereal disease through sexual license, but there is no textual evidence. In 19:4 he turns to gossip, arising through trusting "others too quickly" and even rejoicing "in wickedness." V. 8 takes exception to repeated conversation: keeping silent "unless it would be a sin for you" refers to legislation in Lev. 5:1 where people are "subject to punishment" if they "have heard a public adjuration to testify, and do not speak up." Sensible people will normally remain silent; only "fools will suffer birth pangs" to repeat "gossip" (vv. 11-12). But "birth pangs" lead to the baby being born and the end of the pain, whereas "gossip inside a fool" sticks "like an arrow stuck in a person's thigh" (v. 12).

The repetitive style of 19:13-17, each verse starting with the imperative "Question," draws attention to v. 16, which starts a different way. The question in that verse thus gains emphasis: "Who has not sinned with his tongue?" Again a religious sentiment concludes the group of proverbs: "let the law of the Most High take its course" (v. 17).

The Paradox of Wisdom and Folly (19:20–20:11)

A catchword, "the law," links this section with 19:17: that all "wisdom is fear of the Lord" and "fulfillment of the law" (v. 20) further shows Sirach's Jewish orthodoxy. Even "knowledge of wickedness" is undesirable (v. 22), and "cleverness is detestable," sometimes "merely" lacking in "wisdom" (v. 23). You cannot assume "cleverness" is good (v. 23), for "the highly intelligent" is rejected for "the" simple "God-fearing" because they "transgress the law": this is highly significant in a Hellenistic context that admired intelligence. V. 25 introduces several verses on deceitful behavior when outward appearances belie inward thoughts, all results of Sirach's acute psychological observation. Though appearances can deceive, you can know much about another person by noting his clothing, his "laughter," and "the way he walks" (vv. 29-30). As Crenshaw remarks, some books "can" be judged by their covers!

With ch. 20 Sirach turns to speech and silence, another favorite topic for Egyptian wise men; indeed, in Egypt the professional sage was sometimes called "the silent one." The Greek writer Plutarch said, "A sage thing is timely silence, and better than any speech." To many thinkers silence was golden. But things are not straightforward: to fume in silence is bad (v. 2), and silence can indicate "nothing to say" as well as knowing "when to speak" (v. 6). Recognizing "the right moment" for speaking can be very important (v. 7). "Too much" talking "is detested," as is one who in his speech "pretends to authority" he does not have (v. 8).

20:9-17 interrupt the passage on speech with proverbs on jumbled subjects: an unexpected "windfall," which can lead to "good fortune" or "loss" (v. 9), gifts "to be paid back double" (v. 10), and bargains for which you later pay seven times over (v. 14) — like some secondhand cars! A fool is tight in lending and loud in complaint; therefore it is no surprise that he has "no friends" and gets "no thanks" (vv. 15-16).

20:18 returns to the subject of speech, this time regarding folly. V. 18 echoes a proverb of Zeno of Citium, a Stoic who lived from 335 to 263 BC: "Better to slip with the foot than with the tongue"; Sirach builds on it, claiming that "the downfall of the wicked" is just as speedy. Even when a fool utters a proverb, the timing is wrong. V. 21 changes the topic to poverty and shame: "poverty" can prevent one from "sinning." Losing one's "life because of human respect" (v. 22) sounds odd; perhaps Sirach meant that attempts to win "respect" in Hellenized society meant compromising one's religious faith and thus incurring "shame." In v. 23 broken "promises to a friend" cause needless enmity. Vv. 24-26 prefer "a thief" to "a habitual liar." Vv. 27-31 contain varied proverbial sayings; the "sensible" person who "pleases the great" (v. 27) probably refers to wise courtiers like Ahiqar and Daniel (cf. also v. 28). "Hidden wisdom" is no good to anyone (v. 30).

Sin, Wisdom, and Folly (21:1–22:18)

In this section on sin (21:1-10), Sirach opens with the invitation to "forgiveness for your past sins." He then moves to the vivid image of the bite of "a snake": on the analogy of the Garden of Eden story snakes were often used to symbolize the onset of sin and temptation, as in Prov 23:32, where too much wine "bites like a serpent." The image of sin as a "lion" was used in 1 Pet 5:8, where "like a roaring lion" "the devil prowls around looking for someone to devour." Also proverbial was the "two-edged sword" (21:3), which slashes in both directions; this image is used for "a loose woman" in Prov 5:4 and for the faithful executing vengeance in Ps 149:6-7. In Sirach's view "the prayer of the poor" is heard by "God," who answers "speedily" (v. 5). Sirach here rejects the traditional view that poverty is a mark of sin and God's disfavor (cf. Job again). Boasters "are widely known" for untimely speech, but "the sensible person" realizes it "when they slip" (v. 7). Building a "house," that is, becoming wealthy, at the expense of "others," often by oppressing the poor, resembles "gathering stones" for one's own "burial mound" (v. 8). The images of "tow" and "burning fire" (v. 9) suggest an unpleasant "end" for "the wicked," whose "way" may be "paved with smooth stones" but ends in "Hades" (v. 10).

21:11 moves to "wisdom," for Sirach "the" Jewish "law." His shrewd personal observation detests "a cleverness that increases bitterness." Vv. 13-14 use imagery of water: the "flood" of v. 13 is a life-giving image — not the flood of Noah's day (shown by the parallel of "life-giving spirit" and the opposite, the fool's "broken jar"). Contrasts between "the fool" and "the intelligent" continue until the end of the chapter. Of particular notice are the braying laugh of the fool and the quiet smile of the wise (v. 20), and their differing behavior at the "door" of "a house" in vv. 22-24. The fool talks without thinking; the sage thinks before talking (vv. 25-26). "An ungodly person" is his own worst enemy (v. 27), as is the gossipy "whisperer." Coarse imagery is used in 22:1 to describe "the idler": the "filthy stone" possibly refers to the ancient use of smooth stones for cleaning oneself after a bowel movement — he is therefore "like the filth of dunghills," to be gotten rid of at the earliest opprtunity.

In 22:3-6 we see Sirach's misogynist views — not uncommon for that time. What made "the birth of a daughter" a "loss" is uncertain, but Sirach may well have in mind the cost involved in obtaining a husband for her. In 42:9-14 he complains that daughters are "a secret anxiety" to their fathers, and "a headstrong daughter" may make him "a laughing stock." 22:6 perhaps reads strangely in this context, but the "thrashing and discipline" may refer to the difficulty of bringing daughters up; the verse forms a useful link to the discussion of fools which follows in v. 9.

Sirach uses strong images to describe fools: a broken pot glued together is useless because it comes apart too easily — it cannot be trusted, just like a "sleeper" suddenly roused from "deep slumber" (22:9). "A fool" listens to a "story" like "a drowsy man" (v. 10), taking nothing in. Weeping "for the dead" lasted seven days in Jewish custom, but when a fool's "intelligence" is "left behind" it does not return, is "worse than death," and lasts "all their lives" (vv. 11-12). If you do not keep clear, you will "be spattered" with his filth "when he shakes himself" (v. 13) like a dog. The fool is "heavier than lead," and "sand, salt, and iron" are more acceptable "than a stupid person" (vv. 14-15). Architectural metaphors follow (vv. 16-18): firmly fixed "wooden beams," smooth "stucco decoration" over rough bricks, and "fences" of heaped pebbles to keep wild animals out of a garden.

Friendship and Self-Control (22:19–23:27)

People upset each other in many ways: this section specifies some ways in which this can happen. 22:19-22 describe various ways of treating friends badly: pricking "the eye" and throwing stones (vv. 19-20) are good images for ways of destroying friendships. Friendships may survive physical violence (v. 21) and verbal criticism (v. 22), but in cases of "arrogance," giving away "secrets," and treacherous blows, friends will disappear. Many friendships fail through careless speech and gossip; hence the need for a "guard" and "effective seal" (v. 27) on one's "mouth." A gossip's tongue is self-destructive!

The "seal" leads to the need for self-control, expressed in general terms in 23:2-6 before Sirach turns in v. 7 to "Discipline of the Tongue." From v. 9 he enumerates ways in which people "are tripped up" in talk. Swearing by uttering "the name of" God is strongly condemned, particularly if it is habitual (vv. 9-11). Habitual "coarse, foul language" (blasphemy) is "comparable to death" (v. 12); even "if he swears in error" (v. 11), he continues in sin. No such speaking should be heard in the Jewish community ("the inheritance of Jacob"; v. 12). When people rise in social status, they sometimes forget their "father and mother" and "behave like" fools, losing all self-respect and frequently "using abusive language" (vv. 14-15).

Sirach introduces "fornication" and adultery in 23:16 with a numerical proverb. Such proverbs were frequently used by wisdom writers. The last number is emphasized most, here the "third"; Prov 6:16-19 is a good example. Sirach uses the same technique again in 25:7-11, 26:5-6, and 50:25-26. The phrase "bread is sweet" (23:17) is a deliberate reference to "bread eaten in secret is pleasant," words of the foolish woman in Prov 9:17. 23:18-21 discuss the psychology of the adulterer and the rationalization he makes to dull his conscience and to feed his insatiable appetite for sex. Sirach charges the adulteress with breaking divine law by betraying the marital relationship and bearing unwanted children — things in which his sexist view ignores the man's part! The woman's punishment is much more open to public view than the man's and will affect "her children" (v. 25). The section closes on its religious base with "the fear of the Lord" and his "commandments" in v. 27.

In Praise of Wisdom (24:1-34)

A major poem now occurs in which Sirach makes explicit his identification of wisdom with Jewish law. 24:1 and 2 seem to place wisdom in the heavenly court, but it soon becomes clear that wisdom dwells particularly in Israel. The first verse of Wisdom's speech (v. 3) tells how she "covered the earth like a mist" — a reference to the darkness before creation mentioned in Genesis. "Her throne" is described as "in a pillar of cloud" (v. 4), like the cloud that accompanied the Israelites in the Sinai desert after leaving Egypt. Wisdom traveled over "the vault of heaven" and "the depths of the abyss" in her creative act — all this in search of "a resting place" (v. 7), which she found "in Israel" (v. 8) ("Jacob" is another name for Israel.) Because of her ministry "in the holy tent" and in "Zion," Sirach links true wisdom with the cultic life of Israel, and her "resting place" with "Jerusalem." True wisdom thus "took root in an honored people" — Israel. Wisdom's presence in the land of Israel is then filled out by mention of various native trees: "a cedar in Lebanon" and "a cypress" on "Hermon" (v. 13), "a palm tree in Engedi" and roses "in Jericho" (v. 14 — both near the Dead Sea). She "gave forth perfume, myrrh," and various rich spices, ending with sacrificial "incense" (v. 15). The "terebinth" (v. 16) was probably valued for its essential oil. The final words of the speech appeal to satisfying bodily appetites.

In 24:23 Sirach makes the clearest identification of wisdom with "the covenant," the Mosaic "law," Israel's special "inheritance." This is expanded by various poetic images of refreshing water (vv. 25-27). The "Pishon" is the first river flowing from Eden (Gen 2:11); the "Tigris" in Mesopotamia was especially full in spring, "the time of the first fruits": seasonal flooding becomes an image for wisdom overflowing "with understanding." "The Jordan" and "the Nile" are also subject to flooding, like "the Gihon," the second river in Eden. "The first man" (v. 28), Adam, "did not know wisdom fully" because the law was not yet revealed. No one can contain "the sea," yet wisdom's "thoughts" are "more abundant" than it and "deeper than the great abyss" — a reference to Gen 1:2. These watery metaphors conclude with Sirach's picture of himself as "a canal" leading off from "a river" to water "a garden" (24:30). The flow of wisdom opens like the "sea," its light shines out "like the dawn" (vv. 31-32), as "teaching" pours out "like prophecy" for seekers of "wisdom" in "all future generations" (vv. 33-34).

Some Numerical Proverbs (25:1-12)

Next comes a group of numerical proverbs like those of 23:16ff.: the first two (25:1-2) lack the climactic emphasis on the last item (see below). The "harmony" of husband and wife relates to the family values discussed at length in 25:13–26:18. 25:2 criticizes "three kinds of people" whose behavior is inappropriate: "pauper who boasts" over nothing, "a rich" man "who lies" needlessly, and "an old fool" who, supposed to be a model of sobriety, "commits adultery" — a point rammed home in vv. 3-6. The next proverb (vv. 7-10) reverts to the usual pattern of heavy emphasis on the last, the tenth: the "one who find wisdom" leads on to the "one who fears the Lord," because "fear of the Lord surpasses everything" (v. 11) — again Sirach's religious faith is the culminating priority.

Family Relationships (25:13–26:27)

Sirach's misogynist attitude comes into its own in this section: bad wives and daughters occupy twenty-seven verses compared with only ten for good wives! He exaggerates a good deal to make his points. Poetic parallelism is used to make the opening statement in 25:13. The antipathy increases in v. 14, culminating in the "snake's venom" of v. 15. (Sirach definitely did not like women!). This heavy bias continues in the rest of the chapter: even lions and dragons are preferable to "an evil woman," who at times resembles a "bear," known for its ferocity as in 47:3. "Her husband" sighs bitterly "among the neighbors." Hyperbole heightens the bias in v. 19: Sirach must have known that in Israel's history men caused much more evil than women. The point of v. 20 is that climbing a mound of sand is difficult for "the aged" because the footing is insecure, so a quiet man is always slipping about with "a garrulous wife," never knowing where he is. A man should not marry "a woman" for her "beauty" or wealth (v. 21). The "disgrace" of a husband supported by his wife (v. 22) speaks of a bygone day, though the gloom and distress noted in v. 23 can be true enough! V. 24 refers to Eve as the origin of sin — contrary to most rabbinic thought, which blamed Adam (more anti-feminine prejudice!). The solution suggested in v. 26 is divorce, a right assumed in Mosaic law .

A short interval of four verses (26:1-4) then describes the "good wife" — a universal theme of proverbs — but even so she is not praised in her own right, but only in relation to her "husband." She is one of "the blessings of the man who fears the Lord" (v. 3); she makes him always "cheerful" and "content."

Sirach then returns to a numerical proverb in 26:5. The first things that frighten him all relate to shame in public life. These are bad enough, but the fourth, worst woe is a wife's jealousy of a "rival." We note that this climactic element also lies in the public view, because "tongue-lashing" makes it widely known in the community. "A chafing yoke" is a constant irritation, but "taking hold of" a "bad wife" resembles "grasping a scorpion" (v. 7), and "a drunken wife cannot hide her shame" (v. 8) in public. "Headstrong daughters" (v. 10) are also a worry: they grab all the "liberty" they can. Drinking "from any water" (v. 12) recalls the phrase "stolen water," used of adultery in Prov 9:17, and opening "her quiver to the arrow" is an obvious euphemism for vagina and penis.

For a while Sirach turns to the good "wife" in 26:13-18. Charm and good cooking work wonders, together with silence, "self-discipline," "modesty," and "chastity" (vv. 13-15). Two physical comparisons follow: a "shining lamp" expresses "a beautiful face" well, but "golden pillars on silver bases" for "legs" and "feet" sound odd! One needs to remember that vv. 17 and 18 use comparisons from the temple: "the shining lamp on the holy lampstand" may then represent the *menorah,* the seven-branched candelabrum/a(?).

There follows a passage absent from the Greek of Sirach and occurring only in the Hebrew and Syriac versions. 26:19-24 warn young men against erotic adventures with wild women; but again Sirach tends to discuss mainly the women involved.

Personal Integrity (26:28–27:15)

This section starts with another numerical proverb: three people who rouse Sirach's anger. Regarding the second and third persons mentioned, the point is clearly the antithesis between intelligence and contempt and between "righteousness" and "sin." "A warrior in want through poverty" hardly seems like a real antithesis unless Sirach thinks a soldier can always get that he wants — by force if necessary!

The next four verses (26:29–27:3) deal with moral dangers inherent in money matters and commerce, a veritable invitation to dishonesty! Gandhi once said, "It is difficult but not impossible to conduct strictly honest business. What is true is that honesty is incompatible with the amassing of a large fortune," with which most would agree. Any merchant is tempted to look the other way sometimes, and Jews were necessarily tempted to use unethical practices, as were their Gentile colleagues. Again "the fear of the Lord" concludes the topic (27:3).

In testing people (26:4-7), Sirach uses three images illustrating everyday life in ancient Palestine. The metaphor of the "sieve" seems odd; usually such metaphors are used to show how good grains are separated for use from the chaff, all "refuse" being caught in the sieve. A person's "faults" appear clearly "when he speaks": "the kiln tests the potter's" work, revealing imperfections; in the same way unguarded "conversation" tests "a person." V. 6 assumes naively that a well-tended "tree" produces its fruit reliably, thereby showing careful "cultivation." V. 7 sums up the process of testing someone by his conversation.

In 26:8-10 pursuing "justice" does not mean rushing to the law court at the least provocation: the word is used here as a quality — almost as a synonym for righteousness. Wearing justice "like a glorious robe" recalls words used in 6:31. "Birds" and "lions" are used as personifications of "honesty" and "sin" (vv. 9-10).

26:11 again takes up the theme of testing by "conversation," summing it up. But the topic changes rapidly to "the fool," whose changing moods are rather less regular than those of "the moon." The ancient Hebrews knew all about "hair" standing "on end" (cf. Job 4:15); the same happens today!

Relations with Others (27:16–28:26)

Following on abusive speech in 27:14-15, deceitful speech is treated at length around a section on God's vengeance in 28:1-7. 27:16-21 deplores betrayal of "secrets" — a good way to lose friends (vv. 16-18): they vanish as quickly as "a bird from your hand" or "a gazelle from a snare" (vv. 19-20). Betrayal of "secrets" is even worse than "wounds" and "abuses," which can be healed by bandaging and "reconciliation" (v. 21). The friendly-appearing hypocrite of vv. 22-23 is aptly described, particularly how he trips you "with your own words." In vv. 25-26 there are excellent illustrations of how evil "will roll back upon" its perpetrators: these phrases probably come from a rich stock of proverbs, but are very aptly chosen.

In 27:30 he turns to vengeance, both human and divine. 28:2-5 requires anyone desiring the Lord's forgiveness first to show that forgiveness to human enemies — a sentiment familiar to the NT but occurring generally in Jewish literature also. He concludes his remarks on this subject with a reference to the Ten Commandments (vv. 6-7). "The covenant of the Most High" leads you to "overlook faults" in other people. Sharp words must not escalate to blows: just as fires "burn" according to the amount of "fuel" they are given, so "strife increases" in proportion to "obstinacy"; similarly, "anger," "strength," and, notably, "wrath" (v. 10) increase through "wealth" — a comment rather against the traditional view of wealth as indicating God's favor!

The section on "slander" (28:13-26) has many sayings common to all wisdom writers. Warnings of the results of slander are widespread and well expressed; but most notable is v. 18, which claims that many more "have fallen because of the tongue" than "by the edge of the sword." The tongue's blow even "crushes bones" (v. 17); and the slanderous tongue is pictured as having an iron "yoke" (v. 20), "bronze fetters," and a "death" worse than "Hades" (v. 21). Among these dire results of slander is not "power over the godly"; only "those who forsake the Lord" are subject to it. Sirach here pulls out all the stops on his literary organ to describe its unpleasant results: slander will "mangle" people as a "lion" or "leopard" will; its fire cannot be quenched (v. 23). Taking care "not to err with your tongue" (v. 26) requires much preparation: "your mouth" needs "a door and a bolt"; you need "balances and scales" for what you say, just as you keep "silver and gold" under lock and key. And the whole matter is bedeviled by people "lying in wait" for you to put a word wrong.

Management of Money (29:1-28)

Here four poems on money matters are grouped together. In 29:1-7 Sirach discusses lending money. Lending money to neighbors had been strongly condemned in Prov 17:18 and sundry other places, but Sirach's view is quite the opposite: he urges giving loans responsibly — you "lend" in "time of need" and "repay when a loan falls due" (29:2). There is no mention here of the Jewish law's prohibition against charging interest (Exod 22:25; Lev 25:36-37); he ignores it completely. Delay in repayment, however, is strongly criticized (29:5-6). Kissing hands does not help — it may become a matter of "needlessly making enemies" (v. 6). This remark gains irony if one translates literally: "[you gain an enemy] at no extra charge." A change in this general principle is indicated by "nevertheless" in v. 8: the poor are in a quite different category from unreliable borrowers. You should "help" them and fulfill "the commandment" (v. 9). Sirach's concern for the poor is shown by six verses commending their support (vv. 8-13). "Treasure" is thus laid up in a spiritual repository, not left in a hidey-hole to rust away. Such treasure is more valuable "than gold"; "almsgiving" will fight for you better than military weapons (v. 13). Going "surety" for other people may be a "good" thing to do (v. 14), but shameless people break the rules. A guarantor's "kindness" should not be forgotten, nor should his property be wasted. This whole section on surety shows Sirach's considerable experience of life: more comes through than mere repetition of traditional proverbs.

It is better to be independent (29:21-28), and not "go from" rich "house to" rich "house." It is necessary to have "the necessities of life" (v. 21) in your own house rather than make a living by "being a guest" (vv. 22-24). The wise make themselves content with what they have rather than look longingly at "sumptuous food in the house of others" (v. 22). You may then be pressed into service as a wine waiter without thanks (v. 25) and be ordered about, and if someone more important arrives, then it is off with the "stranger" and in with the host's "brother," the "honored guest" (v. 27). The remarks in v. 28 about "scolding about lodging and the insults of the moneylender" bind the whole chapter together.

Children and Health (30:1-25)

This chapter covers two main topics, vv. 1-13 being concerned with rearing children. To "whip" a son "often" (v. 1) does not seem to us a good way to bring a "son" up, but we should remember that severe treatment of children was common throughout the ancient Near East, not least in Israel; see, for example, Prov 13:24 and 23:13-14. Sirach's point is that, as there was no afterlife, the only way a man's memory could survive death was in reputation and in leaving behind "one like himself" (v. 4). A good son would clear matters up on his father's death, that is, avenge his "enemies" and "repay the kindness of his friends" (v. 6). Coddling a "son" will make a parent alarmed at "every cry" in the street (v. 7). Sirach takes a strong line: a father should not "play" or "laugh with" a son or it will not be the children's teeth set on edge on account of parents but the parents' teeth because of children (vv. 9-10). Sirach here reverses the proverb cited in Ezek 18:2 and Jer 31:29. To "make" a son's "yoke heavy"

(30:13) seems hard, but the emphasis is on parents not being caught up in a son's shame.

30:14 turns to the value of physical health: Of what use is wealth if you are too "afflicted in body" to enjoy it (v. 14)? Better is "death" than "chronic illness" (v. 17). Vv. 18-20 link the section on health with vv. 21-27 on the equable spirit and food. Sirach's shrewd psychological insight is revealed in his advice in vv. 21-24, where a shortened "life" and "premature old age" are to be avoided — particularly if no afterlife follows, as Sirach believed.

Wealth and Proper Etiquette (31:1–32:13)

31:1 and 2 expand on 30:14-15; that financial "anxiety prevents" sleep is stated three times in two verses for emphasis. Does this imply that too much money necessarily means a bad conscience, or is it just too much worry, as for an unmarried daughter in 42:9? Both "rich" and "poor" toil over their possessions with opposite results: pleasure for "the rich," a "meager living" for "the poor" (31:3-4). But the balanced rhythm of these two verses is interrupted in v. 5 by concentration on the dangers and temptations of wealth which dominate until v. 12, when the subject turns naturally to greed in public. In v. 5 the word "justified" is perhaps used in a theological sense, but it is better to unpack the term and translate: "will never be free from sin." "Gold" is "a stumbling block" (v. 7); initially attractive, it trips you up if you are not careful. V. 8 turns to the proper use of wealth and the prosperity that follows from it: it is possible to be "rich" and "blameless" without going "after gold" — it is, in fact, "a ground for boasting" (v. 10). But notice that in v. 11 "the assembly" proclaims not what he has acquired but rather "his acts of charity." How a rich person behaves and uses his wealth becomes all-important, and to that Sirach turns in v. 12.

Much of his advice in this section strikes us as common courtesy. Seven verses are given to behavior "at the table of the great" and the danger of inept remarks (31:12). Yet again Sirach's remarks on greed and social behavior are as relevant today as in his time: not "crowding your neighbor at the dish" (v. 14), "judging" his "feelings by your own" (v. 15), not chewing greedily (v. 16), not "helping yourself before" others (v. 18), and so on. "Healthy sleep," "nausea," and "colic" all come into it, even avoidance of overeating by vomiting (vv. 20-21). In vv. 25-31 Sirach reveals his true temperance over "wine." Wine taken in moderation is good (v. 28), but being "drunk to excess" leads to all kinds of distress, such as those listed in vv. 29-31. It is necessary, therefore, if "master of the feast" to "take your place" only after taking "care" of the guests; then you might "receive a wreath" for your good leadership (32:1-2). Sirach's advice on behavior at banquets gains significance in the light of the Greek custom of the symposium where there was musical entertainment and clever speeches: a strong hand from the president was sometimes needed. Senior people should speak (v. 3) but only relevantly, and they should not "interrupt the music" provided. In other words, behave tactfully! He then endues the value of such entertainment with expressions like "a ruby seal in a setting of gold" and "a seal of emerald in a rich setting of gold" (vv. 5-6): such was his appreciation of Hellenistic banquets! He gives excellent advice, even to leaving "in good time," not lingering but getting "home quickly." V. 10 poses a problem: we can appreciate how "approval" by good reputation "goes before one who is modest"; but how is this like "lightning" traveling "ahead of thunder"? Di Lella thinks it describes "the modest youth who receives immediate and deserving recognition" — modest meaning creates a good impression on immediate impact! Yet again Sirach closes a section with a religious invitation to "bless your Maker, who fills you with his good gifts," including pleasurable banquets.

Living by God's Wisdom (32:14–33:19)

This section starts with a kind of primer on how to live with God. You must "accept his discipline"; then you "will find favor" with him (v. 14). Sincerity is important in fulfilling the law: "the hypocrite," who says he follows it but in fact does not, "will stumble at it." Fear of the Lord "will kindle righteous deeds" just as "a light" sets alight things near it. In v. 17 "shun" is weak for how a "sinner" treats "reproof"; the Greek implies that he deliberately and rudely pushes it out of his way. In v. 19 to think before acting is a frequent adage, but there is a fresh twist to the second half of the verse: "do not regret it" afterward, that is, allow no second thoughts to hold you back. On a hazardous "path" you learn the obstacles and do not stumble twice. V. 23 finishes this group of sayings with a reference to "keeping the commandments" — a theme repeated in v. 24 but balanced by the experience of him who "trusts the Lord": he suffers no "loss."

The thought is taken further in 33:1, where Sirach's assertion flies in the face of reality, following the somewhat simplistic theology of the wisdom writers. The Lord and the law are at least steady and reliable: they do not toss you about "like a boat in a storm" (v. 2). By the "divine oracle" (v. 3) he probably means the Urim and Thummim, when the priest throws dice to reveal the divine will (1 Sam 14:36-42). This practice had ceased by Sirach's time, but the language illustrates the traditional faith dear to Sirach. 33:5 and 6 contain several images for "fools": "a cartwheel," like a "turning axle," keeps turning incessantly, revolving in circles but getting nowhere. Similarly, "a mocking friend" shows no discrimination: "like a stallion" he "neighs" at whoever rides him, acting impulsively whatever the occasion.

In 33:7-15 Sirach tries to explain why people fall into two groups, wise and foolish. It is part of God's ordering of creation. All days seem alike, but they are "distinguished" into "different seasons and festivals" by him (v. 8). Similarly, all humans come "from the ground," created from "dust" according to Genesis. Then God handles them according to his desire, treating some well and others badly, molding them "like clay in the hands of a potter" (v. 13). God's "works come in pairs" and opposites; but this does not mean God predestines humans:

he gives them the ability to choose for themselves good or evil.

Next we meet a brief autobiographical note (33:16-19): Sirach describes himself as a watchman, keeping "vigil" against Hellenistic attacks on traditional Jewish belief and practice. He has filled his book with the riches of Jewish tradition (especially in chs. 44–50), like a vintager filling his "wine press."

Independence and God's Protection (33:20–34:20)

Sirach here discusses independence and slave ownership, followed by reliance on dreams and the hazards of foreign travel. Regarding actions before death (33:20-24), to "give your property to another" too early gives him power over you; he may "take your place" (v. 21). Keep your children dependent on you till you die (v. 24). Note Sirach's habitual prejudice against daughters; here he omits them entirely! — even slaves are given extended treatment (vv. 25-33). A single slave should be treated well: the "blood" for his purchase probably means that he has been bought with your life savings.

"Dreams" (34:1) may "be sent" from "the Most High," in which case they must be taken seriously. Most "divinations," "omens," and "dreams are fantasies" (v. 5); "the law will be fulfilled" without such things, and they affect "wisdom" not a jot (v. 6).

Moving onto the subject of God's protection, Sirach includes four verses on the value of education. Clearly he had experienced the broadening experience of foreign travel for himself, and so he knew "what he was talking about": he had seen many things in his travels, even to the extent of being "in danger of death." As often with much-traveled people, his fund of knowledge was "more than" he could express (34:12-13). Foreign travel today opens the mind: how much more in those days when people met with more unfamiliar customs and unforeseen obstacles to the private traveler! He underlines safety in the fear of the Lord in vv. 14-20; it will stop people from being "timid" or "playing the coward" (v. 16). The Lord becomes his "strong support" and "shelter" from dangers that seem like "scorching wind" and burning "noonday sun" (v. 19). On the positive side the Lord "lifts up the soul," making "eyes sparkle" and giving "health and life and blessing" (v. 20).

Sacrifices (34:21–35:26)

The discussion now moves from the dubiety of dreams to abuses in sacrificial offerings (34:21-27) and insincerity in religious rites (vv. 28-31). He starts by deploring "the offerings of the ungodly" (v. 23). "Ill-gotten goods" (v. 21) are not acceptable; nor are "a multitude of sacrifices," though people think that the quantity of offerings makes a vital difference. Sacrifices "from the property of the poor" he considers to be tantamount to murder! Depriving "the needy of bread," "taking away a neighbor's living," and "depriving an employee of wages" (vv. 25-27) amount to murder too! A rabbinic author wrote, "Everyone who withholds an employee's wages is as though he deprived him of his life." So too with insincerity before God. Vv. 28-29 use the image of builders, one building and another tearing down, to illustrate actions working at cross-purposes with inner attitudes. If "one prays and another curses," to whom does God "listen"? It is like "washing after touching" an unclean "corpse" and then "touching it again" (v. 30): What is the gain? Exactly the same happens when "someone fasts for his sins" and "does the same things" again (v. 31): Who will take notice of him and "who will listen to his prayer"? The clear implication is that God cannot be mocked! Only those who stop sinning obtain forgiveness: on its own fasting does not work!

With ch. 35 Sirach stresses at some length the ethical component of the sacrificial cult; the sacrificial cult is in no way to be understood as a substitute before God for good works. Indeed, good works may be considered of equal worth to a sacrifice: "one who returns a kindness" may be said to offer sacrificial "choice flour," and "one who gives alms" makes "a thank offering" (vv. 3-4). Even so the cult is important: readers are encouraged to "be generous" in worship and not to "stint the first fruits" — in fact, to show gladness when they dedicate their tithe (vv. 10-11). Critics could accuse Jews of offering rich sacrifices in hopes of getting a good return from God, and Sirach does say in v. 13 that God "will repay you sevenfold"; but v. 13 comes only after twelve verses emphasizing cheerful giving with no particular stress on return.

In 35:14 he turns to the negative side: people must not offer God "a bribe" or "rely on a dishonest sacrifice." When Sirach speaks of "the Lord" as "judge" showing no "partiality to the poor" (vv. 15-16), he seems inconsistent just like the OT prophets, who spoke in harsh terms of God's judgment on humans but showed marked sympathy with the poor, widows, and orphans (vv. 17-18). What matters is that a person's "service" be "pleasing to the Lord": "his prayer" will be heard. In response "the Lord will not delay" his reaction. The rest of the chapter describes vividly divine punishment against the guilty: the Lord "repays vengeance on the nations" and "destroys the insolent" (v. 23). His reference to "the scepters of the unrighteous" may be to the contemporary political chaos under the Seleucid rulers; if so, it is suitably disguised in traditional terminology. Following v. 23 with its promise of destruction for the insolent comes the neutral v. 24 where God "repays" all "according to their deeds" and "thoughts," and the more positive v. 25 where God "makes" his people "rejoice in his mercy." The chapter ends with a reference to the Lord's "mercy," "welcome in distress," which provides a suitable link to the prayer for national deliverance which follows in ch. 36.

A Prayer for National Deliverance (36:1-22)

As already suggested, this prayer for deliverance follows naturally upon the statement of God's care for his people and vengeance on his enemies in the previous chapter. To include such a prayer is strange to the wisdom tradition:

no such prayers appear in Proverbs, Ecclesiastes, or Job; but Sirach's work does not fit so neatly into any category. The prayer is written in the tradition of the psalms of lamentation, although there is here no praise of God as so often at the end of those psalms. In 36:1 "all the nations" refers to all the Gentiles and probably to the Seleucid overlords in particular, who are the "foreign nations" of v. 3. God used Israel to "show" his "holiness" to the Gentiles by punishing Israel in his hatred of evil. So Sirach hopes he will punish the Gentiles for their oppression of Israel, his holy people. In v. 6 God is implored to "give new signs" to save his people as in the deliverance from Egypt. "The appointed time" (v. 10) is probably the moment of deliverance from Syrian overlordship, his language carefully disguised for reasons of safety, and the "hostile rulers" (v. 12) are that same royal line. In v. 13 he asks God to "gather all the tribes" dispersed in exile and restore to them "their inheritance" as in former times. God is further asked to "bear witness to those created in the beginning" (v. 20), probably Abraham, Jacob, and Moses. "Those who wait for you" (v. 21) are probably the faithful Jews still living in Jerusalem under foreign rule, looking for independence.

On Making Choices (36:23–37:31)

After this rather idealistic prayer Sirach comes down to earth with advice on serious matters of everyday life. His remarks on choosing the right person to marry start with mundane thoughts on choice of food (36:23-24)! One woman is "preferable to another" (v. 26) just as "one food is better than another" (v. 23), and "an intelligent mind" sorts out different women just as "the palate" distinguishes "kinds of game" (v. 24). In the arranged marriages of Sirach's day "a woman" would "accept" any husband! But his misogynist view concentrates on advice given to choosing wives. Even so husbands are fortunate if their wives are good (vv. 27-29), and bachelors are seen as unfenced "property" (v. 30).

Choice of friends comes next (37:1-6), with emphasis on unreliable friends. Such unreliability is seen most in the difference between words and deeds. "A friend" who "says" he is "a friend" may be a friend "only in name," and when a good "friend turns into an enemy" it is almost like a bereavement (v. 2). The "inclination to evil" in v. 3 refers to the rabbinic doctrine of the two inclinations (good and evil) in human minds. Fair-weather friends also are unreliable (v. 4): they "rejoice" when things go well for you, but turn against you when "trouble" comes. A true friend may "help" you for the sake of a good meal, yet he will carry his shield in battle beside you, helping you unselfishly; you should do the same for him (v. 6) and remember him generously in victory.

Counselors also need to be chosen carefully (37:7-15): too many "give counsel in their own interest" (v. 7) and "take thought for" themselves first (v. 8). Ask advice in such a way that you "hide your intentions" from the counselor (v. 10). The long list in v. 11 of people with whom you should "not consult" covers a large number of people who could give biased judgment for various reasons, mainly self-interest or flaws in character. Interestingly, Sirach commends "the counsel of your own heart" as the most faithful to your own interests, "better informed" than even "seven sentinels on a high watchtower" (v. 14). As usual, "prayer to the Most High" concludes the section in v. 15.

"Every work" requires discussion and counsel beforehand, as "the tongue" rules "good and evil, life and death" (37:16-18). People in public life can be "useless to themselves" even though they "be clever enough to teach many" (v. 19). "A skillful speaker" without "charm may be hated" and thus destitute (vv. 20-21). V. 25 seems to strike a slightly discordant note: following on the high praise "heaped upon" the wise person in v. 24, the following verse emphasizes the mortality of even a wise individual as against the community of Israel, whose "days are without number": v. 25 thus serves to emphasize the following verse. Vv. 27-31 probably all refer to overeating, as vv. 29-31 makes plain. These last verses make an apt link to the longer section on sickness that follows.

Doctors and Mourning (38:1-23)

The verses on mourning (38:16-23) seem to be added to those on doctors (vv. 1-15) because of the dangers to health of excessive grief (v. 18). Regarding health Sirach lived between two worlds: the traditional Jewish belief that sickness was due to sin (cf. the great debate in the book of Job) and the fastspreading Greek ideas on health and medicine more akin to our practices today. In Hellenistic Palestine doctors belonged to the Greek world. Sirach tries hard to hold both attitudes together. A good example of the traditional view is 2 Chr 16:12, where King Asa of Judah has some serious ailment in his feet and is condemned for consulting doctors rather than just trusting God to heal him. Sirach favors consulting doctors; after all, God "created them," and their skill is a gift from God (38:1-2). As an example of how God "created medicines out of the earth" (vv. 4-5), he cites one incident during Israel's wandering in the desert when Moses purified bitter water by throwing a log into it (Exod 15:23-25); if plants possess healing power, the Creator must have intended it. It is through God's "marvelous works" that the doctor "heals and takes away pain" (vv. 6-7).

When death occurred, relatives had to "lay out the body" (38:16) and make due mourning: too much mourning "saps one's strength" (v. 18). "One day or two" is sufficient, says Sirach, even though the statutory period was seven days; perhaps he means intensive mourning. To be realistic, if death is the end as he believed, "you do the dead no good" and only "injure yourself." "Let his remembrance rest" after the due period, and "be comforted" (v. 23). So, as elsewhere, common sense prevails in Sirach's interpretation of religious matters.

The Scribal Profession (38:24–39:11)

Sirach introduces discussion of the professional scribe by contrasting various other professions which demand too much "business" for someone to "become wise": leisure is required (v. 24). An earlier Egyptian work, the Maxims of Duauf, had followed the same theme as Sirach, but the contemptuous satire in Duauf's work is absent here: Sirach does not despise those who work with their hands. He goes through such workers: farmers, craftsmen, blacksmiths, potters, and so on (vv. 25-30). All are useful to society — they "maintain" God's handiwork (v. 34) but do not practice more intellectual tasks (v. 33).

Very different is the scribe who devotes himself to "study of the law" of God (38:34). Rather than concentrating narrowly on a single activity like the artisan (38:26), he deals with a wide range of subjects (39:2-3). He has to appear before high dignitaries and travel in foreign parts (as an ambassador?). Such high-profile public life requires direction from and devotion to God. In his absence of belief in resurrection of the dead it becomes highly significant that the scribe's "memory will not disappear" and that his name will live through all generations (v. 9). His wisdom will be celebrated by the "nations," that is, the Gentiles, and "the" Jewish "congregation" also will praise him.

A Hymn in Praise of the Creator (39:12-35)

Before the hymn comes a personal introduction (39:12-15), and it closes with a personal epilogue (vv. 32-35); thus, like much in this work, traditional forms are given the very personal imprint of Sirach himself. His remarks in v. 12 recall his remarks in 24:30-34, where the canal of his teaching became a river and then a sea because he had so much to express! His students are invited to soak up his teaching "like" roses "growing by" streams "of water" (v. 3); he had already compared himself to a rose bush in Jericho in 24:14. He pictures himself as putting "forth blossoms like a lily" and sending "out fragrance," not like a flower but like "incense," thus revealing his love of priestly ritual so prominent in his praise of Simon, the high priest, in ch. 50. Flowers, incense, "harps," and human "lips" all combine to "give thanks" and praise to God (39:15).

The hymn starts with echoes of the creation account in Genesis: "all" God's "works are very good" (v. 16). Everything has been allotted its "appointed time" (v. 17) — a comment repeated in v. 33. The allusion to "the waters" standing "in a heap," used sometimes of God's victory over the Egyptians at the Red Sea, refers here rather to the "reservoirs" or storehouses of water at creation (Gen 1:9; cf. Ps 33:7). God's overall view is unlimited, and everything is "created" in detail "for its own purpose."

39:22 sees God's blessing likened to the Nile and Euphrates Rivers, both of which through flooding and irrigation provide fertility in arid terrain; but God can turn a watered land into salt as in Sodom near the Dead Sea (Gen 13:10; 19:24-28). The created world was readily provided with life's necessities listed in v. 26, each of which mav be used for good or evil (v. 27). In vv. 28-31 nine destructive creatures counterbalance the good things mentioned in vv. 25-27: "fire" destroyed Gomorrah (Gen 19:24); "hail" was the seventh plague in Egypt (Exod 9:13-26); "famine and pestilence" were God's punishments for infidelity in Jer 24:10; "wild animals" tell their own story, and "scorpions" are an image of chastisement in 1 Kgs 12:11, 14. All these destructive forces of nature "delight in doing [God's] bidding" (v. 11) unfailingly (different from humans!)

The epilogue expresses Sirach's own conviction of the truth of all this: "everything" being "good in its appointed time" (v. 34).

Wretchedness and Shame (40:1–42:14)

Following hard on the preceding hymn in praise of creation comes a passage expressing human reactions to such sentiments, reactions we all feel at times. Creation is not all that good: everyone has to do "hard work," and from birth to death humans live, as it were, under a "heavy yoke" (40:1). "The mother of all the living" is the opposite of the "mother's womb" and refers to the end of life in the grave; it echoes the story of the creation of Adam and Eve from the dust of the earth, and identifies Eve as the "mother" of all living persons. Death dominates the thoughts of all, from kings to paupers (vv. 3-4). V. 5 lists many of the aspects of life that worry people — in sleep or in waking hours, concentrating in vv. 6 and 7 on the horrors of bad sleep: a person's sleep may be full of imagined struggles and dreams. Notice particularly Sirach's first-class understanding of the workings of the unconscious mind in nightmares and the way one wakes up suddenly to find one's fears groundless. He piles on disasters in v. 9, with a side comment in v. 8 that such disasters happen "to sinners seven times more": they were even responsible for the flood (v. 10)!

The contrast between what "is of earth" and what is "from above" (40:11) is spelled out in the contrasts of vv. 12-17. "Bribery and injustice" do not last, but like "the wealth of the unjust will dry up" like a wadi flowing only seasonally. "Generous" people "rejoice," "law breakers fail" completely. "Roots" on "rock" without soil symbolize "children of the ungodly" — not fertile ground (vv. 14-15). Passersby may pluck "reeds" on any "river bank," but "kindness" and "almsgiving" last for a long time like a well-tended "garden" (vv. 16-17).

Ten sayings in 40:18-27 compare "the better" with "the best," culminating in "the fear of the Lord" in v. 27 — following another pattern of proverb common in Egyptian wisdom literature. "Finding a treasure" (v. 18) is balanced by finding "wisdom" in v. 19. Similarly, "a blameless life" is "better than cattle" or "orchards." Few items on this list require comment, but worth notice is the fact that the seemingly misogynist Sirach commends "a sensible wife" in v. 23. Note also the old favorites: almsgiving and fear of the Lord in vv. 24 and 26-27. Piety was all-important to Sirach, "better than any glory."

In 40:28-30 he advises against beggary, taking up the topic of 29:24-27. He particularly stresses the hypocrisy involved: self-effacement masking a "fire" of resentment.

The fear of "death," already mentioned in 40:2-5, is taken up in 41:1-13: death is "bitter" to one "at peace" and rich with "nothing to worry about," who still enjoys "food." Yet to the "needy" and weak, the old and "anxious," it is "welcome" (41:2). "The Lord's decree" of "death" is the same "for all flesh" — why then try to deny it? It is "the will of the Most High." In any case, no questions are "asked in Hades," the Greek word for Sheol, where all distinctions disappear. His thoughts on death here lead rapidly to reflection on those left behind — "children," particularly "children of sinners" (vv. 5-7). Children were to Sirach the only access to any kind of life after death. Although "children of sinners are abominable" with "perpetual disgrace," Sirach is not wholly against them. They may "suffer disgrace" through "an ungodly father" — so the fault is not theirs but inherited. "The ungodly" who forsake "the law" of God (v. 8) are probably the Hellenizing Jews of Sirach's day who adopted Greek practices and customs, thus compromising their Jewish faith. Addressing them in vv. 8-9, he prophesies "calamity" and "groaning" for their "children" and a "curse" when they die, though "lasting joy" (presumably for others) when they "stumble" seems hard; perhaps a contrast is intended to the feelings of sympathy suitable for the righteous.

41:11-13 emphasize the value of a good reputation: "a virtuous name" lasts much longer than a "human body." "Your name," that is, your fame or reputation, "will outlive you longer than" any amount "of gold": "a good name lasts forever." The introduction (vv. 14-16) to the following section on shame includes two verses from 20:30-31 with additions, notably v. 16 with its advice to pay attention, as shame "is not good in every circumstance" — inserted possibly as a caution to what follows.

Then follow eleven verses on shame. Some occasions for shame are obvious: "sexual immorality" hidden from your parents, "lies" before officials, "crimes" before judges and law-breaking before ordinary people, "unjust dealing" before people close to you, "theft where you live," and "breaking oaths." Then a real surprise: be ashamed of "leaning on your elbow at meals" (41:19)! He then mentions "surliness in receiving or giving," keeping silent when people "greet you," even "looking at a prostitute," "rejecting" an "appeal" within the family circle, "taking away" a "gift" from the recipient, "gazing" hard "at another man's wife," "meddling with a servant-girl" (even approaching "her bed"), "abusive words" to "friends," and "insulting" someone "after making a gift." Finally (42:1), do not "repeat what you hear" and "betray secrets." All this is seen as preserving "proper shame" to everyone's approval.

Then Sirach gives a list of things "not" to "be ashamed" of. In 42:2 the Jewish foundations of "law and covenant" are followed by the realism of not "rendering judgment to acquit the ungodly." One should not "be ashamed of keeping accounts" with colleagues or of "dividing an inheritance," or ensuring "accuracy" in weighing, of making justified profits "with merchants" or of frequently "disciplining children." Then comes a harsh reminder of the age Sirach lived in: do not be ashamed of drawing blood "from the back of a wicked slave" when punishing him. Seals and locks (v. 6) are commended to prevent theft (even by one's wife!), similarly "counting" and "weighing" money deposited with someone else: "put it all in writing" (v. 7). Correction of "the stupid or foolish" is not shameful, nor of aged sexual perverts. Then the whole list is summed up as showing "sound training" to the approval of "all."

42:9-14 reveal Sirach's feelings about daughters: a daughter is a "secret" worry that keeps the father awake at night, whether she is "married" or not! Before marriage she may "become pregnant" at home through seduction (v. 10); after marriage "she may go astray" or remain "barren." So "strict watch" is to be kept lest "she make you a laughingstock to your enemies" or "a byword" in public. Her room is to have "no lattice" window from which she can see "the approaches to the house" to spot likely visitors. Conversation "among married women" should be avoided, as well as any opportunity to "parade her beauty" before men. To say that "woman's wickedness comes from a woman" (v. 13) is unjust and disallows any male element in women's sin! . . . and the closing remarks of v. 14 are unspeakable!

The Wonders of Creation (42:15–43:33)

This majestic hymn on creation precedes the longer hymn on God's revelation of himself in history in chs. 44–50. Creation "by the word of the Lord" (42:15) with the light of the sun (v. 16) recalls Gen 1:1-31. Not even the angels can "recount" it fully. "The abyss" (v. 18) of primeval times and "the human heart" are both open to God's inscrutable control. Time is no barrier to him even in the minds of humans. In v. 24 he takes up the idea of pairs and opposites again, already mentioned in 33:15; here they signify variety, leaving "nothing incomplete" but supplementing "the virtues" of other things to a baffling extent.

In 43:1-26 Sirach specifies many wonders of creation, starting with "the heavens" (v. 1) and ending with "the sea" (vv. 23-26). The astronomic phenomena lead off the list with "the clear vault of the sky," the arched metal firmament believed in ancient times to hold back the (blue) upper waters in the sky. "The sun" is praised for "its burning heat" — surprisingly as it parches the land, "three times" hotter than "a furnace"; but even so it moves under orders from "the Lord who made it." "The moon" occupies several verses (vv. 6-8) and is emphasized because it determines the festal days of the religious calendar, which a pious Jew like Sirach would observe punctiliously. The moon outshines even "the hosts on high" (v. 8). "The stars" in their "glittering array" have "their appointed places" (vv. 9-10). "The rainbow" was often used to symbolize spectacular beauty (cf. Ezek 1:28; Sir 50:7). Sirach might have been expected to refer to its significance as a sign of the covenant with Noah after the flood (Gen 9:12-17), but he surprisingly omits this.

In 43:13-26 he specifies various elements in nature, each performing its due function. Thunderstorms, accompanied by lightning, were viewed as a foretaste of God's judgment of the world. These phenomena were pictured as kept in God's "storehouses" (v. 14) until they were needed — an image also mentioned in Deut 28:12

and Job 38:22. "Snow" is scattered like flying "birds," settling on the earth "like locusts" (43:17). "Frost" is "like salt," "icicles" resemble "pointed thorns," and "water" dons "ice" just "like a breastplate"; after intense heat "mist quickly heals" things and "dew" provides "refreshment" (vv. 20-22). In vv. 23-26 he describes the majesty of the sea and the emergence of "islands"; "we marvel" to hear the stories told by sailors (even now!): its "marvelous creatures" and "huge sea-monsters."

The whole catalogue is amazing and indescribable: we can never do justice to it all. In 43:27 Sirach turns quite naturally to praise and "glorify the Lord" and his power: when you have glorified him "as much as you can," you still cannot praise him enough (v. 32). Sirach has "seen" only a "few of his works" but enough to say that God "has made all things" and "given wisdom" for understanding "to the godly" (v. 33).

Hymn in Honor of Israel's Ancestors (44:1–49:16)

Following the hymn on the wonders of God's creation comes a longer hymn on the wonders of God's guidance of the Jews in history. Starting with Enoch in 44:16, Sirach surveys the Jews' heroes one by one. It is interesting to note which he praises at length and which he omits altogether. Before he starts on individuals in 44:16 there comes a famous passage praising Israel's ancestors in general. Other biblical passages, like Psalm 78, list ancient heroes similarly, but not even Wis 10:1–12:27 is as long as this passage.

General Praise of Famous Men (44:1-15)

As previously noted, for Sirach there was no personal immortality or resurrection. People lived on only in name and reputation: "famous men" were given "great glory" by the Lord (44:2), those who had "made a name for themselves" by "valor" or counsel. Although rulers and heroes have pride of place in v. 3, notably more space is given to those who gave "counsel," "spoke in prophecy," or were skilled in instruction and composed music or poetry (vv. 3-5). These, together with prominent "rich" citizens, "were honored in their generations, the pride of their times" (v. 7). These can be celebrated since they "left behind a name" (v. 8), but Sirach does not forget "others" of whom "there is no memory" (v. 9) — a notable remark from an author for whom names were so important! — yet he spends eight verses on them.

The Patriarchs (44:16-23)

First an omission: the first man, Adam, occurs only in the summing up at the end of the list in 49:16. Why Adam, there described as "above every other created being," is here omitted, we do not know. Instead we have "Enoch," hardly mentioned in the Bible but much revered in intertestamental literature for heavenly journeys and remarkable wisdom (cf. the long book of Enoch): he is here called "an example of repentance" (v. 16). Perhaps participation in heavenly journeys led to undue pride? Sirach here uses nonbiblical tradition.

"Noah" (44:17-18) was "perfect" in the wicked generation of the "flood" and "kept the race alive" in the ark. The rainbow served as a reminder of the covenant made by God with him (Gen 9:8-17).

"Abraham" (44:19), "father of a multitude of nations" (Gen 17:4), "kept the law of the Most High" (44:20) before the law was given at Sinai — a way of stressing his faithful obedience. "The covenant in his flesh" refers to circumcision.

On "Jacob" Sirach emphasizes the division into twelve tribes found in the poetic blessing in Gen 49:1-27.

Moses (44:23–45:5)

Omitting Joseph, Sirach turns to "Moses," using in 45:1 the words "whose memory is blessed" — probably intended as a variant of the traditional rabbinic benediction, "May his name be blessed." Surprisingly he devotes much less space to the lawgiver than to the priestly characters Aaron and Phinehas. This reveals Sirach's intense interest in the levitical priesthood; cf. the attention given to his contemporary high priest, Simon, in 50:1-21. The "miracles" (45:3) include the signs Moses performed to help the Hebrews trust and believe in him (Exod 4:1-9) as well as the "plagues" in Egypt before the exodus. His glorification before "kings" (v. 3) plainly refers to his confrontation before Pharaoh in Exod 7:1-7 and throughout chs. 7–10. V. 5 concerns his ascent of Mt. Sinai to receive the tables of the commandments in Exodus 19. The emphasis here is clearly on the law rather than on Israel's deliverance from Egypt, which is not mentioned — nor is there any mention of the Passover!

Aaron (45:6-22)

"Aaron" receives seventeen verses because of Sirach's strong interest in the levitical "priesthood" (v. 7). He describes in detail all the priestly garments specified in Exod 28 as "symbols of authority" (v. 8), omitting only the girdle. He emphasizes the "pomegranates" and "golden bells" ringing as the high priest walked around the sanctuary, as "a reminder to the people" of his intercession for them (v. 9); but nothing detailed is said about the sacred lot, the "Urim and Thummim." In vv. 14-17 he turns to Aaron's priestly duties (the earlier rivalry between Zadokites and Aaronites seems to be finally settled), but v. 18 mentions the conspiracy of "Dathan," "Abiram," and "the company of Korah" from Num 16:1–17:15 as a contrast to Aaron's faithfulness. He concludes by alluding to "the Lord himself" as Aaron's "portion and inheritance" (v. 22); this probably means the legitimate portions of offerings to the priests, possibly as compensation for Levi's omission during the allocation of the land to the twelve tribes.

Phinehas (45:23-26)

"Phinehas" is "third in glory" after Moses and Aaron. Sirach says this emphatically to settle contemporary disputes on the succession of the high priest between the Oniad and Tobiad families. Phinehas and his descendants are to hold "the dignity of the priesthood forever" (v. 24). The point is underlined in v. 25, where Sirach states that "the heritage of Aaron" is limited to his family just as the royal succession is limited to David's line (although there had not been leaders of David's line for many generations!) The prayer in v. 26 invokes God's blessing on the priestly line before turning to political leaders more familar to his readers.

Joshua (46:1-10)

The book of Joshua, following on the exodus from Egypt and the Sinai wanderings, attributes the conquest of Canaan largely to "Joshua" as "the successor of Moses" (46:1). Sirach makes clear the pun on his name in the Hebrew: *yehoshua'* is composed of *yeho,* short for Yahweh/Jehovah, and *(ye)shua',* from the root *yasha',* "he saved"; thus "the LORD is savior." "The enemies that rose against them" were the Canaanites, who thus threatened "Israel" and tried to keep them from occupying Canaan as their "inheritance." When Joshua "lifted up his hands" (v. 2) before the city of Ai, he was probably giving his soldiers the signal to attack (Josh 8:18-23). He was reputed through intercession with God to have made "the sun" stand "still" and caused a powerful storm of "hailstones" (46:4, 5). But his major achievement was overwhelming the Canaanites "in battle." His Amorite enemies were fleeing down "the slope" of Beth-horon when they were struck by hailstones (v. 6; cf. Josh 10:10-15).

The Judges and Samuel (46:11-20)

Several of "the judges" did fall into "idolatry," notably Gideon and Samson, and Sirach was probably right not to mention names since both Gideon and Samson, though religiously unstable, won important victories, and it was military valor that distinguished the judges. The prayer that "their bones send forth new life" (46:12) refers to the belief behind the story in 1 Kgs 17:20-21, where Elisha's bones revivified a corpse. As noted previously, it was Sirach's belief that immortality was attained only by "names" living "again" in "children."

Samuel, the main early prophet, "established the kingdom" by anointing Saul and David (46:13). He was recognized "as a trustworthy seer" (v. 15) by his accurate prophecies (cf. 1 Sam 9:6). Sirach carefully records the period when the Philistines pressed Israel in battle, Samuel "offered in sacrifice a suckling lamb," and "the Lord thundered from heaven" in reply (v. 17). In v. 19 "his anointed" signifies the Lord's choice of king, Saul, rather than the Messiah of Christian times. In v. 20 "fallen asleep" indicates Samuel's death. After his death Samuel was consulted by Saul through the witch of Endor (1 Sam 28:8-19); he told Saul that he was doomed and would be killed by the Philistines. This happened later in the battle on Mt. Gilboa (1 Samuel 31).

David (47:1-11)

Mentioning Nathan in 47:1, Sirach seems to make David fit into a prophetic succession: Nathan's exploits are decribed in 2 Sam 7:4-17 and 12:1-15. The preeminence of David is likened in v. 2 to "the fat" of the sacrifice lifted off for priestly consumption. A skillful hunter, he mastered "lions" and "bears" as confidently as domestic animals (v. 3) and even killed the "giant" Goliath when only a youth (v. 4). He was praised by local women "for the tens of thousands he conquered" (v. 6), and completely wiped out "the Philistines" (v. 7), whose defeat was permanent "to" Sirach's "own day." In vv. 8-10 Sirach concentrates on David's contribution to worship, particularly in music. Again we note omissions — of the unpleasant aspects of David's character: adultery with Bathsheba and murder of her husband Uriah. In a hymn of praise Sirach preferred to dwell on David's virtues, and his last word (v. 11) is one of praise: the hereditary "covenant of kingship."

Solomon (47:12-25)

When he turned to Solomon he did not make the same mistake! Because of David's achievements Solomon "reigned in an age of peace" with secure "borders," and thus had time to build the temple in Jerusalem. He praises Solomon's wisdom "when" he was "young" — as full of "understanding" as "the Nile." Solomon's attributes are listed one by one: "proverbs" (whence many wisdom books are attributed to him), "songs," and "parables" (47:17); his success in trade, collecting "gold" and "silver" like common metals (v. 18). V. 19 introduces the bad side: he slept with foreign women (1 Kgs 11:1-10). Thus he "stained" his "honor" and "defiled" his "family line." Solomon's rule is seen as responsible for the division of his kingdom into two: Israel (here called "Ephraim") and Judah. Since Solomon was the hero of the wisdom tradition (both Proverbs and the apocryphal Wisdom of Solomon were attributed to his patronage), it is surprising — and much to Sirach's credit — that he gives such an objective view of him.

This objective view continues with Solomon's son Rehoboam, who succeeded him, "broad in folly" (playing on Heb. *raḥab,* "was broad") and "lacking in sense" (47:23). His attitude was: "My father disciplined you with whips, but I will discipline you with scorpions" (1 Kgs 12:11); he thus split David's kingdom into Israel in the north under Jeroboam I and Judah in the south. "Leading Israel into sin" is the usual biblical phrase for deserting the Jerusalem temple: Sirach thought that this led to their exile in Assyria in 721 when "vengeance came upon them" (v. 25).

Elijah and Elisha (48:1-16)

The sins of the Northern Kingdom led to the dramatic appearance of Elijah, "a prophet like fire" whose powerful "word burned like a torch" (v. 1). He prophesied "a famine" in the reign of Ahab (1 Kgs 18:2). His "zeal" was legendary (1 Kgs 19:10, 14). "Three times" he "brought down fire" from heaven as punishment (48:3): to consume the sacrifice on Mt. Carmel in 1 Kgs 18:38 and to consume two separate groups of fifty soldiers with their captains in 2 Kgs 1:10, 12. In v. 5 he is praised for "raising from death" the son of the widow from Zarephath (1 Kgs 17:17-22). Sirach refers to the theophany of 1 Kgs 19:8-18 somewhat ambiguously, seemingly unable to distinguish between "Sinai" and "Horeb" (v. 7). "Kings" were "anointed" by Elijah (v. 8) only indirectly through Elisha, but he mentions Elijah's ascension by chariot "in a whirlwind of fire." He prefers to note Elijah's miracles rather than his opposition to Baal worship — another significant omission! In v. 10 the words "it is written" are the usual formula for citing scripture, here Mal 4:5-6; but the later popular tradition, based on those verses in Malachi, that Elijah would return before the Messiah comes, receives no mention here — another of the notable omissions by Sirach, who seems to show no knowledge of the coming Messiah.

Elisha was Elijah's successor as prophet, "filled with his spirit" (v. 12). Sirach states that Elisha "performed twice as many signs" as Elijah did. He cites the account in 2 Kgs 2:9-10 where Elisha asks "to inherit a double share" of Elijah's spirit — a misunderstanding! Elisha is claiming the double inheritance that the eldest son of a family receives; thus Elisha claims to be Elijah's successor. "His" dead "body prophesied" (v. 13) when a corpse was thrown into Elisha's grave and came to life again when he touched the bones (2 Kgs 13:21).

But Israel did not accept prophetic rebuke and were "carried off as plunder from their land" (v. 15) to Assyria in 721, the beginning of the dispersion, when they "were scattered [over] all the earth." The Southern Kingdom of Judah was left, "few in number" but still with a Davidic "ruler" (v. 15).

Another wordplay introduces Hezekiah, who "fortified" (Hebrew *ḥizzaq*) Jerusalem, digging a tunnel (usually identified as the Siloam tunnel) to conserve water in a cistern against a siege (v. 17; cf. 2 Kgs 20:20). Assyrian threats against Jerusalem are described in 48:18-20 together with the city's deliverance. The miraculous predominates in the description of Isaiah: "in" his "days the sun went backward" (v. 23). Comforting "the mourners in Zion" (v. 24) probably refers to Isaiah 40:1: Sirach, of course, had no knowledge of the later prophet of the exile in Babylon (Isaiah 40–55).

Josiah and After (49:1-16)

Sirach then skips nearly fifty years to Josiah, omitting entirely the idolatrous reigns of Manasseh and Amon — an omission apposite to his purpose. Following the idolatrous "abominations" of his predecessors, it is natural to liken Josiah's "name" to "blended incense" (49:1), "as sweet as honey" in one's memory. He acted rightly in "reforming the people" and "removing the wicked abominations." It is thought that the discovery of the lawbook in the temple in the course of Josiah's reform (2 Kgs 23:24) led to the publication of the book of Deuteronomy in his reign. The "lawless times" of Manasseh and Amon ceased with Josiah's reform.

"All" of the kings had been "great sinners" apart from "David," "Hezekiah," and "Josiah": they had tried to ingratiate themselves with Assyria and Babylonia by worshiping their gods, and after Josiah they "abandoned the law of the Most High," probably for political reasons. This did not work, and so "the kings of Judah came to an end," giving power and "glory to a foreign nation," and Babylonians "set fire to" Jerusalem and its temple, depopulating the city "as Jeremiah had foretold" (v. 6). V. 7 recalls phrases from the book of Jeremiah: in Jer 1:5, 10 the LORD said he "formed" Jeremiah "in the womb" for him "to pluck up" and to pull down, to destroy and to overthrow, "to build and to plant."

In his allusion to Ezekiel Sirach refers (49:8) to the vision of "the chariot" (Ezek 1:4-28); here again Sirach refers to apocalyptic traditions current later than the close of the OT canon. After the exile only three people are mentioned: Zerubbabel and Jeshua/Joshua, who rebuilt the temple, and Nehemiah, who rebuilt the city walls (49:11-13). Nothing on Ezra! Brief mention of the ascension of Enoch, Joseph, whose corpse was taken to Palestine, and Adam concludes the list.

Simon the High Priest (50:1-24)

Finally, there is a lengthy panegyric on Simon, son of Onias, Sirach's contemporary as high priest, who died in 196 BC, shortly before Sirach wrote his book. His death is implied by the words "who in his life repaired the house" in 50:1. Following similar building works by Hezekiah, Josiah, and Nehemiah, he "repaired" the temple structure and added fortifications, laying "foundations" for the "retaining walls of the temple enclosure." He also dug a large new "reservoir" for storing water (v. 3). Such building works are vouched for by Josephus and illustrate the great political power in the hands of the high priest at that time: his task as a leader was to defend "the city against siege" (v. 4). More important for Sirach were his duties in the religious sphere, which he describes at length in a long series of similes in vv. 6-10. These are introduced by a description of his "glorious" appearance as he "came out of the house of the curtain" (v. 5), that is, the innermost, holiest part of the temple sanctuary. The richness of this description leaves us in no doubt about Sirach's enthusiasm for the temple liturgy and ceremonial. In vv. 11-13 the circle of priestly attendants hand Simon carcasses for "the Lord's offering" like slender "palm trees" surrounding a handsome "cedar on Lebanon." The description of the ritual is easy to follow and concludes in v. 20 with the high priest blessing the congregation using the ineffable name of God. Sirach adds an ascription of praise and prayer for peace in vv. 22-24.

Two Additions (50:25-29)

The first of the additions is a numerical proverb like 23:16-18; 25:7-11; 26:5-6 and 28 enumerating "three nations" Sirach detested. "Those who live in Seir" are the Idumeans of Edom, loathed by the Jews because they devastated Judah after the Babylonian conquest; "the Philistines," subdued by David, here probably has the later meaning of Jews in Palestine who accepted Hellenism and paganism; "the foolish people that live in Shechem" are the Samaritans, condemned by Sirach as "not even a people" (v. 25). The term "Samaritans" seems to have been used for the mixed population drafted into the Northern Kingdom after its destruction by Assyria in the eighth century.

Then comes a personal postscript (50:27-29) in which the author gives his full name together with encouragement to "put" the advice in his book "into practice," and so "be equal to anything" — that is, overcome the temptations of Hellenism (on the brink of the Hellenistic reform). The chapter ends with Sirach's beloved topic of "the fear of the Lord" (cf. 1:11-30).

Sirach's Prayer (51:1-12)

There follow twelve verses entitled "Prayer of Jesus Son of Sirach" in the Greek text. This prayer of thanksgiving uses many general phrases taken from the Psalms to describe subjection to verbal abuse, feelings of despair, and remembering the Lord's mercy. How far we can rightly detect in this poem the author's own experiences is uncertain — the poem may be a literary piece using traditional phrases for similar experiences. Did Sirach, for example, really suffer from a "slanderous tongue" and "lips that fabricate lies" (51:2)? We do not know; but some phrases clearly are only literary images: "grinding teeth," "choking fire," and "the deep belly of Hades" (the underworld) (vv. 3-5) are clearly not intended literally, although it is possible that the lengthy attention given to "the slander of an unrighteous tongue" may recall some crisis over no "human assistance" (v. 7). As often in biblical psalms of lament, this psalm closes in vv. 11-12 with thanksgiving and praise.

After 51:12 comes a litany of praise without verse numbers, which occurs only in the Hebrew and not in the Greek. The psalm is completely biblical in its phraseology, using familiar titles like "the shield of Abraham" and "the mighty one of Jacob."

51:13-30 contain a seemingly autobiographical poem, originally an acrostic, each verse beginning with the next letter of the alphabet in order, as shown by the original version found at Qumran. There seems no reason to doubt the personal statements made in verses like 13-14: personal remarks occurred earlier in the book (cf. 33:16-18). Since other proverbial books of the Bible were written under the aegis of Solomon, it is refreshing to find a real author giving an account of himself in a more modern way! So ends this comprehensive account of how Sirach saw the religious life.

Bibliography. Di Lella, A. A., and P. W. Shehan. 1987, *The Wisdom of Ben Sira,* AB 39, New York: Doubleday • Coggins, R. J. 1998, *Sirach,* Sheffield: Sheffield Academic • Crenshaw, J. L. 1997, "The Book of Sirach," in *The New Interpreter's Bible,* 5:601-867, Nashville, Abingdon • Mack, B. 1985, *Wisdom and the Hebrew Epic: Ben Sira's Hymn in Praise of the Fathers,* Chicago and London: University of Chicago • Wright, B. C. 1989, *No Small Difference: Sirach's Relationship to Its Herew Parent,* Atlanta: Scholars.

Baruch

John J. Schmitt

INTRODUCTION

The book of Baruch is one of the sacred books of the Jews of Alexandria, but the Jews of Palestine did not make the same judgment. Baruch is an essential part of the OT for those Christians who hold to the Greek canon. Thus the Roman Catholic and most Orthodox churches see Baruch as canonical. The book bears the name of a figure from the seventh century, but all internal evidence suggests that the time of writing was the second century BC. The relative precision is based on Baruch's use of Ben Sirach (c. 180 BC) and the use of Bar 4:36–5:9 by the *Psalm of Solomon* 11 (mid-first century BC).

Other writings from approximately the same time were attributed to Baruch as well, but this book is not apocalyptic as most of the others are. Baruch takes up themes and phrases from the Bible and applies them in a new configuration to a new generation in a later historical setting. The book appears as a compilation of several smaller pieces: 1:1–3:8 (a prose narrative about a letter sent to Jerusalem from Babylon about sacrifices and prayers, including an inserted prayer of repentance), 3:9–4:4 (a poem on wisdom), 4:5–5:9 (poetry of lament and encouragement), and 6:1-73 (a tirade against the worship of idols — a piece that sometimes is considered a separate book, the Letter of Jeremiah). All parts of the composite book could originally have been written in Hebrew, even though the oldest surviving versions are in Greek.

The general mood of the piece emerges from this joining of parts of those earlier sacred writings that seemed applicable in the time of the authors. Each of the segments of Baruch is inspired by many different sections of the Bible. The prayer freely uses Daniel 9, Deuteronomy 28, and Jeremiah 11. The poem on wisdom incorporates ideas from Job 28 and Ecclesiasticus (Ben Sirach) 24. The poetry of 4:5–5:9 is dependent on Isaiah 40–66. And, finally, the harangue against idolatry borrows mostly from Jeremiah 10 and Isaiah 44.

When the different parts are taken together, the resultant meaning is an affirmation that God is still with the chosen people. There is no need to seek wisdom or security in the various options that present themselves to a Jew of the second century BC. The punishment for sin is past, and Israel must now continue to serve God fully and only. This service to God is accomplished by the study of Torah.

COMMENTARY

I. Narrative and Prayer of Repentance (1:1–3:8)

Activity in Babylon (1:1-9)

The opening of the book assures the reader of its credibility by its claim that this work was written by Baruch, a scribe of the seventh century. (It may be worthwhile to recall that "book" here means "scroll"; books with pages [codexes] are a creation of a later time.) Baruch appears in the book of Jeremiah as a kind of secretary for that prophet and presumably his friend as well. According to the book of Jeremiah, Baruch faithfully records in writing the words of that prophet two times (Jer 36:4, 32). Here the claim is not to write down the prophet's words but to share the writer's own ideas. The only evidence for the existence of Baruch is the book of Jeremiah, and there are strong arguments that this figure in the book of Jeremiah was created by the tradition. The name itself is a fairly common one.

The figure, however, became quite popular, and other works from this general time are attributed to this "scribe." The genealogy given in the text corresponds to that in the book of Jeremiah (32:14). The date given in 1:2, five years after the capture of Jerusalem, would perhaps seem a plausible time and situation in Jerusalem to the mind of the reader of the second century BC. But the city as it lay in ruins in Jeremiah's day would not seem to have had quite the organization depicted here, for those who had survived the destruction and not been exiled were the lowly and the untrained (2 Kgs 25:12). It is striking that the author specifically mentions that the Babylonians burned Jerusalem since the date itself would have been enough to remind the reader of the event ("five years after the capture"). 2 Kings does point out that the Babylonians burned the temple and "all the houses of Jerusalem; every great house he burned down" (2 Kgs 25:9). The reference to the offering of money and the temple equipment continues the attempt to connect this book with the events of the seventh entury. But the rest of the book fails to give true seventh-century interests. Mention of the fasting endorses this later dating, for it highlights one of the practices of ancient Israel that came into greater prominence in the time after the exile.

Preliminaries (1:10-13)

The message of the letter implies that the temple has been rebuilt and that the sacrificial system has been restored. The historical time of the exile is the context that the author is attempting to paint for the reader. But the author also wants the reader to apply these words to the reader's situation. There may indeed have been some similiarities between the two situations, since the writer has in mind either readers in the Jerusalem that had once been desecrated by Antiochus IV or readers living in the diaspora.

The writer does have some new ideas. The prayer for the king of Babylon is quite uncharacteristic for prayer in ancient Israel. Even though Cyrus is called the anointed (*christos* or "messiah") of God in Isa 45:1, the Hebrew Bible (HB) stops short of praying for an enemy general. The idea of praying for a foreign ruler is not even found in the letter of Jeremiah to the exiles (Jer 29:7) where one is encouraged to pray for the city itself.

This openness to the foreign city clearly suggests that the author is perhaps living some distance from Jerusalem and has accepted the idea of exile as a somewhat permanent concept. The writer is ill informed about the dynastic succession in Babylon. Nebuchadrezzar was not the father of Belshazzar. Nabonidus, who became king of Babylon not by inheritance but by usurpation, was the father and predecessor of Belshazzer. The writer agrees, on the other hand, with the major part of the previous biblical tradition in attributing the fall of Jerusalem and the accompanying exile to the sinfulness of the people, and not to the political weakness of the kingdom of Judah.

The Letter: Early Sins (1:14-22)

The requirement of a public reading of this writing on festal occasions suggests that the author has in mind the weekly gathering of the Jews (which was later called synagogue). Public worship and confession, which had to occur apart from the temple and its sacrificial system, may have seen their beginning stages in the author's time. This section spells out the specific ways in which the author acknowledges the sin of the people: all generations of Israelites from the time of Moses on were not faithful to the commands and invitations of the Lord. This penitential confession seems similar to other prayers from this time. 1:15-18 are related quite closely to Dan 9:7-10. Some modifications occur in the verses from Daniel. In Daniel, God is addressed directly, while here God is referred to in the third person. This change might be compared to the Jewish practice of not pronouncing the sacred name of God out of respect or out of fear.

1:15-16 are explicit in the list of people now put to shame: the men of Judah, the citizens of Jerusalem, the kings and rulers, prophets and priests, and the forefathers. The present plight of the people is clearly attributed to the wrongheadedness of the people and their refusal to heed the miraculous signs and prophetic warnings God had sent. One can only wonder what the phrases "serving other gods" and "doing what was evil in the sight of the Lord" might have meant to the author. They are stock phrases in the language of the Deuteronomistic school. But in the Hellenistic era, these phrases would now apply to the temptations of the Greek-influenced culture and the adoption of the practices of the Hellenistic world — emphasis on athletic competition, on philosophical speculation, and on a diet that did not follow the regulations of Torah.

Continued Sins and Punishments (2:1-10)

This section continues the description of the suffering that the infidelity of the people has brought upon themselves. The text is perhaps implausible to the modern reader when it claims that "under the whole heaven no such things have been done as were done in Jerusalem." But the author is insistent that the tragedy that has befallen his people should be seen as the just action of God. The worst of the dire threats of Torah has fallen upon the people. Cannibalism toward one's own children appears as an occasional element used in the description of ultimate disaster (cf. 2 Kgs 6:28; Lam 2:20). The author acknowledges his sinfulness and the justice of the punishment. He also repeats the idea that righteousness and justice belong to God but shame is due the people who had neglected, ignored, rebelled against, and abandoned the God who had been so good to them. God's punishment of the people was serious but not as severe as what they had merited.

Prayer for Deliverance (2:11-26)

The author now addresses God directly. Despite the sinfulness of the people, the author is emboldened to plead with great urgency for mercy from God. God had done wondrous things for this people in the past. Surely he will have pity on his people now. The prayer for deliverance is made for God's sake. For "Israel and his posterity are called" by the name of this God (2:15). This is a surprising idea, for the Israelite name of God (Yahweh) was no longer pronounced by the people at the time of this writing. Various substitutions were made instead; "the Lord" was the most frequent replacement. No doubt the author simply means that Israel and God are a pair, and their fates are joined together.

The author becomes impassioned in this prayer for mercy. The prayer employs traditional imagery of God living in heaven and possessing eyes and ears in order to move both the reader and God. The traditional idea that the dead can no longer praise God evokes the idea that Israel is nearly expired. The figure in 2:18 is probably Israel himself, gaunt and gasping. If mercy is granted this wretch, praise will not be able to be contained (v. 18).

There are no human grounds on which to trust. This idea contrasts with the later Jewish idea of "the merits of the fathers." Only the mercy of God is possible. The author links together various stipulations God had made in different parts of the book of Jeremiah. These commands were not observed, and the people are justly punished. In addition, refusal to obey the king of Babylon is given as the reason for the disaster. Ultimately, the temple, "the house that bears your name," has been desecrated.

God's Mercy (2:27-35)

The pleadings for mercy continue and now challenge God to be moved by his mercy. In a quotation, again drawn from various sources, the claim is made that God will use the exile as a moment of reawakening. God has predicted a change of heart from the people, and he will bring it about. They will eventually turn to God. God will respond by bringing them back to the land of promise. The promise of a new covenant (Jer 31:31) will be fulfilled, and Israel will again be God's people in the land God promised them.

Final Plea (3:1-8)

The pleading reaches a peak: the cries of those who suffer humiliation and even the cries of the men ("dead," as in the NJB, seems a misreading by the Greek translator from a Hebrew original; the NAB reads "few") of Israel rise before the merciful and all-powerful God. (3:1 and 4 contain the only occurrences of the divine title "the Almighty" [*ho pantokratōr*] in the book of Baruch; the Greek word carries with it implications beyond any Hebrew expression for God in the HB.) The just punishment has been received. This punishment includes exile and scattering to other lands. Suffering Israel suffers justly, but, in the plea of the author, must not die out.

II. Praise and Desirability of Wisdom (3:9–4:4)

With an abrupt change, the reader moves from the impassioned pleading for mercy to a serene, almost detached, reflection on the possession of wisdom with which Israel has been blessed. The poem in praise of wisdom, however, does begin with the recognition that Israel is in a foreign land, growing old, and surrounded by those who have fallen and died. It should be noted that the same personification of Israel is found here as in the first part (2:15): Israel as a male individual. This is truly a striking image — Israel growing old (better than the REB, "grown old"). Israel is in a foreign land against his will because he had not observed that wisdom which is equivalent to "God's ways." (This identification of wisdom and Torah is Ben Sirach's thought as well.) Israel has rejected the only source of wisdom. But there is hope if Israel will learn wisdom, the source of life and happiness.

There follows a poem about the dwelling place of wisdom and the human search for the way to find her. The poem is patterned on Job 28:12-28 as well as Ben Sirach 24. Wisdom is not an easy acquisition or an obvious discovery. Even those peoples famed in antiquity for having wisdom really did not have access to her. And their descendants have not attained this goal.

But Israel is special and knows the God of wisdom. God's universe is immense, and no one can know it all. It is unclear whether "the giants of old" (3:26) means the fallen angels (who appear in *1 Enoch* 7) or the physical giants who lived in Canaan before the Israelites came in (Num 13:28). Even they did not have true wisdom and hence are no more. One might search the entire earth and even the heavens and not find wisdom. God alone can bestow wisdom. And it is to Israel that he has given her.

"After that, wisdom appeared on earth and lived among men" (3:37). This passage was especially meaningful to the fathers of the early Christian church. Paul says that Christ is the wisdom of God, and the early Christian thinkers took this passage in Baruch as a prediction of the incarnation. One cannot insist that the author of this part of Baruch had any idea of incarnation. Rather, this passage agrees with many Jewish writers of that time who emphasized that the Jews were given wisdom and that their dispersion allowed for other people to access that wisdom according to their own capacities. This idea that wisdom appeared on earth is found in more than one place. One form of the idea has wisdom appear on earth but be rejected by people and return to heaven (*1 Enoch* 42:1-2).

Baruch identifies wisdom with the Torah that is contained in "the book of God's commandments." Israel is called to return to its purity of observing this Torah, this wisdom. And a beatitude is enunciated: happy is Israel for its possession of Torah (4:4). Israel is blessed in knowing exactly what is pleasing to God. The chosen people know that wisdom resides in the book of the law that God had given through Moses. The author is among those who insist on this doctrine.

III. Poetry of Consolation (4:5–5:9)

Basis for Courage (4:5-29)

The text now shifts gears and presents a passage that is intended to be a consolation for the afflicted. Israel is addressed and told to reflect on his own history. (4:5b reads better as a parallel imperative, "Remember, O Israel," as in the NAB.) Israel is told that the suffering they have endured is appropriate punishment because they had ignored the source from which they came. The Israelites forsook the eternal God who nourished them, and grieved Jerusalem who fostered them (vv. 7-8).

Two things are noteworthy. This is the first time that God is described as "the eternal God" (4:8) (and later, simply "the Eternal" — 4:10, 14, 20, 22, 24, 35; 5:2). One can note that ancient Israel probably did not have the concept of eternity current today. This author may indeed be influenced by Hellenistic thought that saw the divine in the realm of the eternal and not the temporal (as did ancient Israel). (The popularity of the term "the Eternal" for God in Jewish piety and language seems to have been influenced by Moses Mendelsohn's use of it in his translation of Torah in 1783.) A second distinctive thing in these verses is that here Jerusalem's relation to Israel is enunciated and delighted in. Jerusalem had fostered Israel, as a mother fosters a son. (There is no explicit statement of joint parentage of God and Zion for Israel, but this is the logical conclusion if Zion is their mother [4:10; 5:5-9] and God is their father [4:7-8]. The prophets give various references for the marital relationship between God and a capital city: Jerusalem [e.g., Jer 2:2], or Samaria [Hos 2:2], or both [Ezekiel 16 and 23].)

There follows a description of Zion, in her own words, a description of the widowed city who has lost her children as well as her husband (4:9b-16). Her speech to her neighbors (smaller towns, no doubt) is explanatory of her condition. But her speech to her children is moving: she cannot save them — God alone can (vv. 17-21).

She tells them that their time of suffering is ending

and that, if they return to God, God will surely restore great joy to them. The theme of joy replacing suffering is replayed in a number of ways. But she is confident that her children will turn back to God, cry for mercy, and receive it (4:21-29). This maternal image of Zion is highlighted here as strongly as it is in Isaiah 40–66.

Address to Zion (4:30–5:9)

Now Jerusalem is addressed directly. "He who gave you your name" (4:30) is a surprising designation for God in that most prophetic books (as well as earlier and later verses in Baruch) want to change Jerusalem's name, as if she had a wrong or improper name. Here the claim is that God had originally given her her current name. This name change could simply be proleptic for the renaming in 5:4. All those who wished evil on her have stopped that evil longing.

Most specifically, Babylon (although unnamed), Jerusalem's chief rival, will be pained at her own demise (4:32-35). She who in her pride had taken such joy in Jerusalem's capture now will herself become desolate and the haunt of demons. These statements recall the competition between Lady Jerusalem and Lady Babylon in Isaiah 44–47 and 51. The rivalry between women cities can also be seen in Mic 7:8-10 (between Zion and Babylon) and in Isaiah 17 (between Zion and Damascus).

Jerusalem should look eastward for salvation. This direction is taken over from Isa 41:2 and 43:5, and the direction there is a reference to Persia, the land from which Cyrus was on the move to overturn the Babylonian Empire. Now Jerusalem can put on a new garment, as a bride, to show her joy in the glory of the Lord. With various phrases and ideas from Isaiah 40–66, the author addesses Jerusalem/Zion about the restoration she will experience, a restoration to her former glory.

This section ends, however, with a return to the thought of Israel, for whose sake this exalted language is employed. God himself will come to lead Israel to safety and security. The exile is real, but God remains Israel's true guide.

IV. Letter of Jeremiah

The Letter (6:1-73)

This letter probably dates from the second century BC, as do the previous five chapters. This piece deals almost exclusively with the religious practices of the Babylonians, especially their use of statues or idols. The Bible, and in particular this distillation of biblical thought on the matter, is clear on the idea that idols cannot be divine, for they are so obviously made by human beings. Yehezkel Kaufmann proposed that ancient Israel fully misunderstood the religions of other peoples because no human thinks of a handmade statue as actually a god, but rather as a symbol for the god.

Perhaps the reality lies between the two views. The ancient Mesopotamians seemed to see the handmade idol as the place in which that deity chose to reside and by which to be symbolized. The deity is that in which one puts one's ultimate value, and the idol is the representative of that value. In this way one can view the condemnation of idols as the condemnation of a misplaced supreme value and of that which represents and symbolizes it.

The chapter is structured as ten warnings against this false worship; all but the first and the last end in a refrain. The specific arrangement is sometimes based on a word or idea that is linked to the preceding warning. The sum total of thought here naturally is that only God, the God of Israel, must be worshiped, and that God alone.

Bibliography. Burke, D. G. 1982, *The Poetry of Baruch,* Chico, Calif.: Scholars • Moore, C. A. 1977, *Daniel, Esther, and Jeremiah: The Additions,* AB 44, Garden City, N.Y.: Doubleday • Steck, O. H. 1993, *Das Apokryphe Baruchbuch,* FRLANT 160, Göttingen: Vandenhoeck & Ruprecht.

Additions to Daniel

John W. Rogerson

INTRODUCTION

In the Greek version of the book of Daniel there are three additions to Daniel as it appears in the Hebrew Bible (HB). They are The Prayer of Azariah and The Song of the Three Jews (inserted between 3:23 and 3:24), Susanna (ch. 13), and Bel and the Dragon (ch. 14). In the HB Daniel has twelve chapters.

It is more correct to speak of Greek versions in the plural, because the Septuagint (LXX) varies considerably at some points from Hebrew and Aramaic Daniel in the HB. For this reason the Bible in Greek that was adopted in the early church incorporated not the LXX of Daniel but the translation of Theodotion, a Jewish translator from Ephesus active in the mid-second century AD. This translation, which evidently expanded on an earlier translation or translations, was much closer to the Hebrew/Aramaic Daniel of the HB, and was adopted for this reason in preference to the LXX. With regard to the Additions to Daniel, English translations have rendered Theodotion. However, there are differences between the LXX and Theodotion versions of the Additions, and these will be noted where they are significant. The complicated relationship of the LXX and Theodotion versions of the Additions to each other are most comprehensively dealt with by Kottsieper 1998. A less comprehensive treatment in English will be found in Moore 1977.

COMMENTARY ON THE PRAYER OF AZARIAH

Daniel 3 of the HB is the story of the refusal of Shadrach, Meshach, and Abednego to fall down and worship the golden statue set up by King Nebuchadnezzar. They suffer the penalty prescribed for such refusal by being thrown into a furnace of blazing fire. The content of the Prayer of Azariah (vv. 26-45 [Greek], 3-22 [English]), which is offered by one (or, according to the LXX version, all three) of those cast into the fire seems to be strangely at odds with this situation. It is largely a confession of the unfaithfulness of God's people, and an acknowledgment of the justice of God in punishing his people by giving them into the hand of their enemies. The prayer describes the dire plight of the people and asks God to restore them, so that their enemies will know that the God of Israel is powerful in the world. It can, of course, be argued that the Prayer is appropriate for the situation of the Jews in exile in Babylon, which is the setting of Daniel 3; but most commentators believe that the prayer most likely comes from the period when Antiochus IV prohibited the practice of Judaism (c. 169/8–165/4). This certainly makes good sense of v. 38 (15):

> In our day we have no ruler, or prophet or leader,
> no burnt offering or sacrifice, or oblation, or incense,
> no place to make an offering before you and to find
> mercy.

In 1 Macc 2:59 Hananiah, Azariah, and Mishael are mentioned as models of faith.

It is likely, then, that this prayer, originally written in Hebrew, was composed and used during the prohibition of Judaism, although it must also be noted that, like many of the lament psalms in the HB, it contains no specific details that could tie it absolutely certainly to a particular set of events.

Detailed Comments

24-25 (1-2). The introductory verses do not introduce the addition particularly skillfully into Theodotion's Greek version of Daniel. 3:23 in the Greek uses the Babylonian names Shadrach, Meshach, and Abednego for the three heroes of faith, whereas the Addition uses Abednego's Hebrew name Azariah. The anchoring of the Addition is achieved more successfully in the LXX, which also attributes the Prayer not only to Azariah but to all three heroes. The GNB seems to combine the LXX and Theodotion versions of v. 24 (1) in order to give a more informative beginning to the Addition.

V. 40 (17). The meaning of the Greek rendered as "and may we unreservedly follow you" is uncertain, and has been explained as a misunderstanding of an original Hebrew phrase, "to satisfy your anger." If this is indeed evidence that the prayer was composed in Hebrew, it must be noted that Daniel 3 is written in Aramaic.

COMMENTARY ON THE SONG OF THE THREE JEWS

The Song (vv. 52-90 [29-68]) is introduced by a fragment of what may have existed as a different version of the story of the furnace of blazing fire. In the version in the HB the three heroes walk unharmed in the furnace accompanied by a mysterious divine fourth person (Dan 3:25). In the Greek version the heroes survive the heat because an angel makes the inside of the furnace cool (vv. 49-50 [26-27]). In the one version the men miraculously survive the heat; in the other the heat is miraculously diminished. The theology of the two versions thus differs. In the one version God enables the heroes to withstand what would normally be fatal; in the other he neutralizes the threat.

The Song is preceded by a benediction (vv. 52-56 [29-34]) which praises God who is enthroned in his temple (Jerusalem) and over all the world, and which leads into the Song with its call for all creation to praise God. The prominence of the temple has given rise to the suggestion that the benediction is the work of priestly circles in Jerusalem.

The Song is divided into nine stanzas each of three topics or areas, which are called upon to praise God: 1, the heavens and angels; 2, the heavenly powers (i.e., sun, moon, stars; v. 64 [42] does not fit into the scheme and may be a later addition); 3, winds and temperatures; 4, precipitation (i.e., dew, snow, and rain). This pattern is not clear in the English translations which follow Theodotion. The LXX has a clearer order, as do some manuscripts of Theodotion which, for example, reverse the order of vv. 67 and 68 (45, 46). The LXX order according to the English numeration is 46, 49, and 50. For 5, light and darkness, the LXX order is again to be preferred, that is, vv. 47, 48, and 51; 6, the earth, its physical features and plant life; 7, the water and its creatures; 8, the earth, its animals and birds, and humankind (vv. 80-82 [58-60]), 9, Israel and its temple officials. Vv. 86-89 [64-67] stand outside the schema and are designed to enable the narrative of Daniel 3 to be resumed, while v. 90(68) is the closing verse of the original Song.

The Song, known by the opening word of its Latin translation, *Benedicite,* became a canticle in Christian liturgical worship and is sung in the Greek monastic tradition at Lauds, the dawn office. The English Prayer Book of 1549 appointed it as an alternative to the *Te Deum* during Lent — an odd provision given the celebratory nature of the Song and the fact that Lent is a solemn ecclesiastical season. Although the restriction to Lent was removed in later Prayer Books, the tradition of singing the *Benedicite* at matins during Lent persists today in some English cathedrals and parish churches. It is also used in the Roman Catholic Divine Office for Morning Prayer for the First Sunday of the Four-week Psalter.

COMMENTARY ON SUSANNA

The story of Susanna in the Greek Bible is preserved in the version of Theodotion (see above) rather than the Septuagint (LXX). The two versions differ considerably, and where they have material in common, it is evident that Theodotion translated a Semitic original that was dependent upon a version translated by the LXX, if not precisely the LXX version that is extant. However, Theodotion's Semitic original was also a thoroughgoing revision of the LXX's Semitic original with the aim of producing a more coherent and explicit story. As opposed to the sixty-four verses of the Theodotion version, Susanna's story in the LXX amounts to around only forty-three verses. The two versions are printed in parallel columns in Kottsieper 1998. An English translation of the LXX (not in a parallel column) can be found in Moore 1977. Because a consideration of the differences yields clues about the growth of the tradition, both versions will be described in what follows.

The LXX version is framed by a piece of poetry, probably originally in Hebrew, the first part of which is also partly used by Theodotion (v. 5b). The words "Lawlessness came from Babylon by way of elders, from judges who seemed to govern the people and to whom came cases from other cities," come at the beginning, while the LXX story ends with

> Therefore young men will fear God;
> And there shall be in them a spirit of understanding
> and of insight for all eternity.

This framework establishes the purpose of the LXX version, which is not so much to focus upon Susanna as to underline the superiority of "young men" (epitomized by Daniel) over elders who hold power. This no doubt reflects a power struggle, most likely during the Hellenization crisis and the Maccabean revolt and its aftermath (c. 170-130 BC), without it being possible to be more specific. It is noteworthy, however, that the conclusion of the poem alludes to Isa 11:2 whereas its beginning is reminiscent of Isa 10:1-2. It therefore expresses messianic hopes and expectations and may derive from faithful Jews who saw in the actions of a young leader the promise of the imminent establishment of God's kingdom. It is possible that in an earlier version of the story, now preserved in the LXX, Susanna was not named (her name appears in the LXX only in vv. 7 [the Greek indicates an awkward insertion] and 29-30), but remained, like the two elders, anonymous.

The Theodotion version begins with a polished introduction which names Susanna, her husband, and her father (Theodotion names Susanna nine times), and emphasizes Susanna's upbringing (according to the law of Moses) and her husband's wealth. Because of the latter, the house of Susanna's husband becomes the place where the two elders, who are also judges, hear cases on a regular basis. In this way they see Susanna regularly, and their desire for her grows. In the LXX version the two elders see Susanna apparently by chance and, their lust being aroused, each determines to confront Susanna without telling the other. In pursuance of this aim, they meet unexpectedly, confess their purpose to each other, and decide to approach Susanna together.

The Theodotion version sets up the confrontation scene by describing how Susanna decides to bathe, and, having sent her servants away, is confronted by the elders, who tell her that if she does not have intercourse with them, they will accuse her of committing adultery with a young man. The LXX contains nothing of this. It says simply that the elders harassed her; and it is Susanna herself who says that she will fall into their power if she refuses their request (Theodotion vv. 22-23, "For if I do this . . . ," reproduces the LXX at this point).

The elders now take their revenge. In Theodotion this happens on the following day when they hold their usual legal sessions at Susanna's husband's house. In the LXX the elders go immediately to the local synagogue where they call together all the Israelites *(sic)* who live in the town. The language suggests that this is a town in which Jews live together with non-Jews. In both versions Susanna, having been summoned, appears accompanied by her parents and children (the LXX says that there were four children) but, not, apparently, her husband (the LXX adds five hundred male and female servants). The charge brought against Susanna is similar in both versions, except that in the LXX the elders claim that the imaginary young man fled before they could get to him, while in Theodotion they claim to have caught him but were not strong enough to detain him.

Susanna is condemned to death (cf. Deut 17:6-7; 22:22) but is delivered by the intervention of Daniel, who is described as a young man in the LXX but as a young boy (NRSV, "young lad") in Theodotion. In Theodotion this is in response to Susanna's prayer to God (vv. 42-43; the prayer is taken from the LXX, where it occurs *before* the elders state their charges against Susanna). In the LXX an angel intervenes and grants Daniel the spirit of insight. Daniel interrogates the elders separately, and they disagree over the type of tree under which the supposed adultery was committed, thus showing themselves to be false witnesses.

In vv. 54-55 and 58-59 the Greek words for the trees are used by Daniel to provide puns for the fate that will befall each elder. In vv. 54-45 "mastic tree" (Gk. *schinos*) is punned as "cut in two" (Gk. *schisei*); in vv. 58-59 "evergreen oak" (Gk. *prinos*) is punned as "split in two" (Gk. *katapris̨ę*). These Greek puns have given rise to much discussion about the original language of Susanna, and have been taken as evidence against its having originally been written in a Semitic language. The general opinion, however, is that the LXX translator reproduced in Greek puns that were in the original (probably) Hebrew. That puns can be reproduced in other languages (at the expense of strict accuracy) is indicated by the REB translation: "clove tree" — "cleave in two" and "yew tree" — "hew you down." The elders, having been shown to be false witnesses, suffer the fate that would have befallen Susanna had not Daniel intervened (cf. Deut 19:18-19). In Theodotion they are put to death (v. 62), while in the LXX they are thrown into a ravine where, presumably, they will have boulders pushed down onto them so that they are stoned to death. Theodotion ends with Susanna being praised by her family and with the statement that Daniel henceforth enjoyed a great reputation.

In comparing the two versions it becomes apparent that, in the LXX, Susanna's function is the secondary one of providing the context for the conflict between the corrupt and lying elders and the young, inspired Daniel. As already remarked, this no doubt mirrors a struggle between two groups in second-century-BC Palestine. In Theodotion, Susanna has moved much more onto center stage and, although necessary, Daniel has become less important. Theodotion's story centers on a pious Jewess from a wealthy family whose faithfulness to the law of Moses brings her to condemnation and the threshold of execution. She is delivered because of her piety and her prayer to God; and the message of the book is that of the importance of obedience to the law, whether on the part of individuals or in the administration of justice. Susanna, in Theodotion, could serve as a model for the whole Jewish people to be obedient to the law in the face of temptation, with the promise of God's deliverance if this faithfulness brings danger.

These contrasts enable me to suggest a broad outline of the growth of the book. The motif of the woman slandered as an adulteress by an unsuccessful suitor is common in folk literature (see Thompson 1966: K2112) and was used as the context for contrasting the young, inspired Daniel with the corrupt elders. The evidence from Ezek 14:14, Qumran, and the Additions to Daniel indicate that there were many popular stories centering on Daniel in the centuries before the coming of Christ. The Hebrew version used by the LXX reached something like its present form by the addition of a name and family details for Susanna and other additions to produce a more coherent, if not flawless, narrative. This was subjected to a thoroughgoing revision which now placed the emphasis on Susanna and her piety. Whether it is possible to draw conclusions about the Hebrew writer or writers responsible is debatable. On the basis of the references to the law of Moses and the fact that Susanna and her family are described as very wealthy, some have drawn the conclusion that the Hebrew writer belonged to aristocratic Sadducean circles (so Kottsieper). This may be correct; but the descriptions of Susanna's wealth may be literary devices — would the story be so arresting if Susanna were poor and unimportant? — and the Theodotion version could also be seen, along with stories in the book of Daniel in the HB, as encouragement to all Jews to remain faithful in the face of harassment.

COMMENTARY ON BEL AND THE DRAGON

Daniel 14 in Greek contains three stories: Daniel's demonstration of the deceit of the priests of Bel (vv. 3-22), his destruction of the dragon (vv. 23-30), and Daniel in the lions' den (vv. 31-42). The third episode was evidently the basis for the better-known version in Dan 6:1-24. Although the stories about the dragon and the lions' den may originally have been separate, they were integrated together and associated with a prophecy or scroll of Habakkuk to make up a complete story. This is evident from the beginning of Bel and the Dragon in the Septuagint (LXX), which reads "from the prophecy of Ambakoum [Habakkuk] the son of Jesus of the tribe of Levi." Habakkuk reappears in the story in vv. 34-39, as can be seen in the English translations, which are based on Theodotion. Although the Semitic original (probably Aramaic) translated into Greek by Theodotion was dependent on the Semitic version translated by the LXX, the Theodotion version omitted the opening reference to Habakkuk.

A comparison of the LXX and Theodotion combined with an examination of the internal structure of the LXX version indicates that the story of the priests of Bel (vv. 3-22) was added to the original account that combined the dragon and lions' den stories. In the latter stories, according to the LXX, Daniel is a priest whose wisdom enables him to kill the dragon by giving it food to which it is violently allergic. The theme of dragon-slaying is well known in folk literature and probably the origin of the story here. Could the Babylonians, as the story implies, have kept a dragon-like creature as a kind of domesticated divine animal? Because the likely answer is "no," it has been plausibly suggested that the figure of the dragon is deliberately used to allude to the Babylonian myth according to which the god Marduk killed the monster Tiamat. If this is correct, the implicit claim of the story could be either that it was a priest of the God of Israel who killed the monster, or, if the dragon personifies the cult of Marduk, that that cult was inferior to the religion of Israel. On the ground that the cult of Marduk was severely restricted by Xerxes I in 482 BC following a Babylonian uprising against Persian rule, the story has been dated to the late sixth century and has been seen as similar to the polemics against idols in Isaiah 40–55. The link with the prophet Habakkuk has been seen to point in the same direction. The function of Habakkuk in miraculously journeying from Judah to Babylon to provide Daniel with food while he is in the lions' den is not clear, except to emphasize that the God of Israel is faithful to his servants.

The story of the exposure of the deceit of the priests of Bel has all the marks of a good detective story. The idol (v. 3) may have been a statue in the temple of Marduk. At all events, the food placed daily before it (forty sheep, for example!) would have required enormous resources of provision, not to mention consumption, and is a literary device to emphasize the grandeur of the cult and the credulity of its adherents. The descriptions of the food may be based on Ezek 46:13-15 with appropriate multiplication. The story is less easy to date and place than the other ones, but its message is clear, that the gods of nations that are much more powerful than Israel have no real existence, and are sustained only by deceit and human gullibility.

Bibliography. Kottsieper, I. 1998, *Zusätze zu Daniel,* ATDA 5, Göttingen: Vandenhoeck & Ruprecht, 211-328 • Moore, C. A. 1977, *Daniel, Esther and Jeremiah: The Additions,* AB 44, New York: Doubleday • Plöger, O. 1973, *Zusätze zu Daniel,* Jüdischer Schriften aus hellenistisch-römischer Zeit, Gütersloh: Gerd Mohn, 63-85 • Thompson, S. 1966, *Motif-Index of Folk Literature,* 6 vols., Bloomington: Indiana University.

1 Maccabees

John R. Bartlett

INTRODUCTION

The books of 1 and 2 Maccabees were written within the Jewish community about 100 BC but became part of the Christian rather than the Jewish scriptures. 1 Maccabees, originally written in Hebrew, was preserved in a Greek translation in the fourth-century Codex Sinaiticus and the fifth-century Codex Alexandrinus, in the eighth-century Codex Venetus, and in an Old Latin (OL) translation now known from two ninth-century manuscripts. It was perhaps first translated into Greek for the benefit of the Alexandrian Jewish community (as were other Hebrew books like Ecclesiasticus [Sirach]), though it may have been translated in Jerusalem and subsequently taken to Egypt, as was the Greek version of Esther. The OL tradition stems from the second century AD and so witnesses to an early form of the Greek text. Josephus, writing in the first century AD, knew 1 Maccabees in a Greek translation, but he paraphrased rather than copied it. The Hebrew text probably lapsed from use early, for it was not accepted as scriptural by the rabbis. Jerome's reference to it leaves us uncertain whether he personally knew the Hebrew version or knew that there had been one. 1 Maccabees has been largely unknown since the Reformation, being relegated in the Reformed tradition to the Apocrypha, but it is of particular interest to scholars for its information on Hellenistic Judea and to others for its stirring theme of Jewish independence.

1 Maccabees tells the story of the Maccabean revolution from the time of the Seleucid king Antiochus IV (175-164 BC) to that of the Hasmonean John Hyrcanus I (135-104 BC). The author names no sources, except certain archival documents (cf. 14:49) and the high-priestly annals from Hyrcanus's time (16:24); he probably used similar annals from the high priesthoods of Jonathan and Simon, other Jewish archives (e.g., relating to diplomatic involvement with Rome), and some official Seleucid source or chronicle valuable for its dating of Seleucid events. Folk memory and oral tradition probably provided material for stories about Mattathias and Judas, dead for at least half a century before the author wrote of them.

The book was carefully composed. A prologue (1:1-10) gives the background to the apostasy that culminated in Antiochus IV's decree and the response of the faithful led by Mattathias (1:11–2:70). The first main part of the work (3:1–9:22) tells the story of Judas, beginning with a eulogy (3:1-9) and ending with a short lament over him (9:21). The narrative between is divided into two halves (3:10–6:63 and 7:1–9:18) (see p. 811). The story of Judas is balanced and contrasted by the story of Jonathan and Simon in the second part of the book (9:23–16:23). Possibly the author originally intended to end the work with the eulogy of Simon (14:1-15) to balance the opening eulogy of Judas (3:1-9), but felt the need to add the public record of Simon's work (14:25-49) and other material about Simon's diplomatic successes (14:16-24), his later campaigns, and his death, with a short conclusion introducing his son John Hyrcanus. In spite of this slightly jumbled ending, the author has clearly worked hard to organize the material coherently, and the attention given to chronology shows an orderly and disciplined historian's mind at work.

However, the chronological data present difficulties. The author dates events by the years "of the kingdom of the Greeks" (1:10), that is, by the Seleucid era, which was dated from Seleucus I's capture of Babylon in the sixth year of the reign of Alexander IV, son of Alexander the Great. By our calendar Seleucus I's first year began in April 312 BC. But while Babylon and the east began their year in spring, the first month being Nisan, the western part of the Seleucid Empire began the year in the autumn (the first month would be the Jewish Tishri). Official Seleucid dates given in 1 Maccabees seem to use the autumnal system, and Jewish dates employ the spring calendar (cf. 10:21, where the reference to the feast of Tabernacles in the seventh month suggests the use of a spring dating). Further, according to some scholars some dates are given according to an era beginning in spring 311 (not 312) BC. Most dates in 1 Maccabees appear to work well if we assume an era beginning in spring 312 BC for Jewish dates and in autumn 312 BC for official Seleucid dates, though this leads to the conclusion that the desecration of the temple lasted from December 168 to December 165 BC (not 167-164 BC, as is usually given). Some scholars prefer to use the era dating from spring 311 BC for Jewish dates. All systems have their problems, especially in the case of 10:1, 21 (see p. 822).

The author is a serious historian, concerned both to record and interpret events. He is aware of the outer world, and not opposed to Judah's links with it, but a staunch supporter of Judah's independence and of the Hasmonean monarchy. The Hasmonean family have defended the law and the sanctuary (13:3); salvation comes to Israel through this family alone (5:62), but through their courage and faith, not through dramatic miracles, as in 2 Maccabees. The Maccabees are not seen as messianic figures, and they are not expected to be martyrs finding their reward in resurrection (as in 2 Maccabees). The author despises renegade Jews who accept Hellenistic culture (1:11; 3:15; 6:21-27, etc.), and hates Gentile adversaries of the Jewish law (1:49; 2:48; 3:20, etc.). A threat to the temple was a threat to the nation; Judas and his followers are fighting for the people and the sanctuary, for the law, and for Jewish religious practices such as sacrifice, fasting, the sabbath, and circumcision. The author is theologically conservative, but not a theologian at heart. The end is not yet; there is more history to come under the successors of John Hyrcanus, in whom the author has obvious confidence. The author's kingdom is undoubtedly of this world.

The author is an educated Jew, writing Hebrew but able to translate and incorporate Greek documents and perhaps indebted to Hellenistic as well as to Hebrew historiography. He knows the law and the prophets, but shows more sympathy for politicians than for priests and possibly more for Sadducees than for Pharisees. His heroes are buried in a massive Hellenistic tomb. Momigliano dates the book to c. 130 BC, but a date c. 100 BC is more likely. Absence of any hostility toward Rome confirms a date of composition before 63 BC.

Select Bibliography. Abel, F.-M. 1949, *Les Livres des Maccabées,* Paris: Gabalda • Arenhoevel, D. 1967, "Die Eschatologie der Makkabäerbucher," *TTZ* 72:257-69 • Bartlett, J. R. 1998, *1 Maccabees,* Guides to Apocrypha and Pseudepigrapha, Sheffield: Sheffield Academic • Bickerman, E. J. rev. ed. 1980, *Chronology of the Ancient World,* London: Thames & Hudson • Bringmann, K. 1983, *Hellenistische Reform und Religionsverfolgung in Judäa,* Göttingen: Vandenhoeck & Ruprecht • Fischer, T. 1992, "Maccabees, Books of," in *ABD,* 439-42 • Goldstein, J. 1976, *1 Maccabees,* AB 41, Garden City, N.Y.: Doubleday • Martola, N. 1984, *Capture and Liberation: A Study in the Composition of the First Book of Maccabees,* Acta Akademiae Aboensis, Series A, vol. 63, no. 1, Abo: Abo Akademi • Momigliano, A. 1980, "The Date of the 1st Book of Maccabees," in *Sesto contributo alla storia degli studi classici e del mondo antico,* Rome: Storia & Letteratura 150, 2:561-66 • Pfeiffer, R. H. 1949, *A History of New Testament Times,* New York: Harper • Schunk, K.-D. 1954, *Die Quellen des I und II Makkabäerbuches,* Halle: Niemeyer.

COMMENTARY

The Author's Introduction (1:1–2:70)

From Alexander to Antiochus IV (1:1-10)

The author of 1 Maccabees was a serious historian who believed in being direct and precise. He introduces his history of a forty-year war for independence with a thumbnail sketch of the preceding 156 years, from Alexander the Great (d. 323 BC) to the Seleucid king Antiochus Epiphanes (ruled 175-164 BC), all in ten verses. He rightly begins with the career of Alexander the Great, whose conquest from Macedonia (the land of Kittim) eastward as far as the borders of India avenged the Persian conquest of Greece in the fifth century BC and replaced the Persian Empire with a brave new world which had immediate and lasting effects on the little province of Judah. Alexander died in Babylon in June 323 BC on his way back from India, leaving his kingdom (according to Arrian) "to the strongest." In fact his chief officer Perdiccas ruled, and under his chairmanship the empire was put into the hands of Alexander's generals. These, the "successors" (Gk. *diadochoi*), began to eliminate each other, until after the battle of Ipsus (301 BC) there remained Cassander in Macedonia, Demetrius in parts of the Aegean and southern Turkey, Lysimachus in Thrace and northern Turkey, Ptolemy in Egypt, and Seleucus in Syria and Mesopotamia. Antiochus Epiphanes was a descendant of Seleucus; he had been taken to Rome as a hostage for the good behavior of his father Antiochus III, the Great, when Rome defeated him at Apamea in 188 BC. He escaped from Rome in 175 BC on the death of his brother Seleucus IV and seized the throne, adopting the real heir, his young nephew Antiochus, as co-regent and later murdering him. The author dates this in the 137th year of the kingdom of the Greeks, probably counting from autumn 312 BC, though possibly from spring 312 BC or spring 311 BC (see the Introduction above, 807).

Our author makes clear that Alexander and his Seleucid successors were a bad thing. Alexander, like other rulers before him (cf. Isa 14:12-21), acted with what the Greeks called *hybris* (pride); his successors caused evil (1:8). It was from this "sinful root" that Antiochus IV came (v. 10) — and so the reader should not be surprised at what followed.

Select Bibliography. Green, P. 1990, *Alexander to Actium: The Hellenistic Age,* London: Thames and Hudson • Mørkholm, O. 1966, *Antiochus IV of Syria,* Copenhagen: Gyldendalske.

N.B. To save unnecessary repetition in every Select Bibliography, readers should note the following important commentaries: Abel, F.-M. 1949, *Les Livres des Maccabées,* Paris: Gabalda • Bartlett, J. R. 1973, *The First and Second Books of the Maccabees,* CBC, Cambridge: Cambridge University • Dancy, J. C. 1954, *A Commentary on 1 Maccabees,* Oxford: Blackwell • Goldstein, J. 1976, *1 Maccabees,* AB 41, Garden City, N.Y.: Doubleday.

The Beginning of the Troubles (1:11-15)

The Greek rulers were bad, but the author specifically blames Jewish "renegades" as being the immediate cause of the troubles. Exactly who these people were 1 Maccabees does not say; 2 Macc 4:7-17 identifies the usurping high priest Jason as their leader. According to 1 Maccabees, they asked the king for a gymnasium in Jerusalem. A gymnasium, along with the *ephebeum* (the military school for the young men, cf. 2 Macc 4:9) and the *palaistra* (the wrestling arena, 2 Macc 4:14), was essentially the educational and recreational training ground for the citizens of a Greek city. The proposal broke no Jewish law, and its supporters justified it by pointing to the political and economic advantages of belonging to the wider Hellenistic world. Cultural change, however, affects religious practice; 1 Maccabees paints this request in terms of apostasy, and its supporters as renegades or apostates (for an even more emotive presentation, see 2 Macc 4:11-17). Removal of the marks of circumcision (1:15) must have been limited to the few wealthy Jews engaging in games abroad and can hardly have been a widespread practice.

Select Bibliography on Hellenism and the Jews. Bickerman, E. J. 1988, *The Jews in the Greek Age,* Cambridge, Mass., and London: Harvard University • Feldman, L. H. 1986, "How Much Hellenism in Jewish Palestine?" *HUCA* 57:83-111 • Harrison, R. 1994, "Hellenization in Syria-Palestine: The Case of Judea in the Third Century BCE," *BA* 57:98-108 • Kuhrt, A., and S. Sherwin White, eds., 1987, *Hellenism and the East: The Interaction of Greek and Non-Greek Civilizations from Syria to Central Asia after Alexander,* London: Duckworth • Hengel, M. 1974, *Judaism and Hellenism,* London: SCM • Smith, R. H. 1990, "The Southern Levant in the Hellenistic Period," *Levant* 22:122-30 • Tcherikover, V. 1959, *Hellenistic Civilization and the Jews,* Philadelphia: Jewish Publication Society of America; Jerusalem: The Magnes Press, The Hebrew University.

Antiochus's First Dealings with Jerusalem (1:16-40)

According to 2 Macc 4:21-22, Antiochus had been well received in Jerusalem shortly after the coronation of Ptolemy VI Philometor in Egypt (probably 172 BC). The support of Jerusalem was important to Antiochus when in late 170 BC he invaded Egypt to counter the aggressive policy of the young Ptolemy VI's guardians. He defeated them at Mons Casius, near Pelusium, and took over the Delta region apart from Alexandria, which he besieged unsuccessfully. In autumn 169 BC he had to withdraw from Egypt, leaving Ptolemy VI as ruler in Memphis with a rival ruler in Alexandria, but covered his limited success by taking to himself the title *Nikephoros,* "Victorious." On the way home he visited Jerusalem and helped himself to the temple treasures. Since he was not at war with the Jews, his motive was almost certainly financial, not political or religious; in this he was following the precedents of Seleucus IV, who tried to rob the Jerusalem temple (2 Maccabees 3), and Antiochus III, who died robbing a temple in Susa. Antiochus probably had no idea of the outrage the entrance of a Gentile into the temple would cause in Jerusalem. 1 Maccabees colors Antiochus IV's action by accusing him of bloodshed and arrogance, and adding a poetic lament.

Things changed, however, for the worse when "two years later" Antiochus sent a tribute official (probably the Apollonius of 2 Macc 5:24) backed up by military force, which unexpectedly plundered, burned, and destroyed the city, took women and children captives, and rounded up the livestock. They built a fortress, garrisoned it (apparently with "renegades," i.e., Jews loyal to Syria), storing there arms, provisions, and loot, and it became a threat to the temple, discouraging attendance there. This fortress, the *akra* or citadel, was to remain in place for another twenty-seven years until Simon finally captured it and ejected the garrison. Its position is much disputed. Clearly it controlled access to the temple, and it has been located at almost every point around the temple. Modern scholarly consensus places it in the southern or southeastern area of the present temple platform surrounded by Herod's walls.

1 Maccabees does not explain why Antiochus ordered this attack, and there has been much speculation. In 168 BC Antiochus again invaded Egypt. He was unlucky in his timing. In June 168 BC the Romans defeated King Perseus of Macedonia at Pydna, and the Roman legate, C. Popilius Laenas, hastened from Delos to order Antiochus out of Egypt. With Roman legions free to turn to Egypt, Antiochus had no choice. He retreated north. According to 2 Macc 5:1-26 it was at this point that in Jerusalem the former high priest Jason (previously ousted by Menelaus) attempted to regain his position by force. He failed and fled; Antiochus, however, hearing that his protégé Menelaus was forced to take refuge in the citadel, assumed that Jerusalem was in revolt, took the city by storm, massacred the citizens, plundered the temple, and then sent Apollonius to kill the remaining men and enslave the women and children. This last event appears to be another version of the attack described in 1 Macc 1:29-35, and 1 Maccabees (which says remarkably little about the high priesthood, omitting all references to the high-priestly rivalries in Jerusalem between Onias, Jason, and Menelaus) may have omitted these intervening events. (Some scholars think that 1 Maccabees has also wrongly transferred Antiochus's temple plundering from 168 BC to 169 BC, but on this point 1 Maccabees' dating is probably right.) However, there is little doubt that Antiochus or his generals attacked Jerusalem viciously in autumn 168 BC, perhaps partly in reaction to the humiliation in Egypt and partly to demonstrate sharply to other subjects that this was no time to rebel against Antiochus. But while the poet in 1 Macc 1:36-40 laments the effect the citadel came to have on regular worship in the temple, there is as yet no indication that Antiochus intended anything like religious persecution.

Select Bibliography on the Chronological Problems of the Egyptian Campaigns. Bringmann, K. 1983, *Hellenistische Reform und Religionsverfolgung in Judäa,* Göttingen: Vandenhoeck & Ruprecht • Bunge, J. 1976, "Zur Geschichte und Chronologie des Untergangs der Oniaden und des Aufstiegs der Hasmonäer," *JSJ* 6:1-46 • Grabbe, L. L. 1991, "Maccabean Chronology: 167-164 or 168-165 BCE," *JBL* 110:59-74 • Hanhart, R. 1964, "Zur Zeitrechnung des I und II Makkabäerbuches," *BZAW* 88:49-96 • Mørkholm, O. 1966, *Antiochus IV of Syria,* Copenhagen: Gyldendalske • Skeat, T. C. 1961, "Notes on Ptolemaic Chronology, II: 'The Twelfth Year Which Is Also the First': The Invasion of Egypt by Antiochus Epiphanes," *JEA* 47:107-12 • Swain, J. W. 1944, "Antiochus Epiphanes in Egypt," *CP* 29:73-94.

Religious Persecution (1:41-62)

There is no doubt that Antiochus did attack the Jewish cult. The earliest, almost contemporary evidence is from Dan 11:29-35, where it is said that following Antiochus's humiliation in Egypt the king, enraged, took action against the holy covenant; his forces occupied and profaned the temple and fortress, abolished the regular burnt offering, and set up the abomination that makes desolate. 1 Macc 1:45-49, 54-61 give greater detail. All the major Jewish religious practices are forbidden (sacrifices and offerings, sabbaths and festivals, circumcision and reading and possession of the law), and non-Jewish practices are demanded. The Jews were compelled to break two fundamental requirements of the law: first, the prohibition of idolatry (Deut 5:8-10), and second, the requirement that sacrifice could be offered only in Jerusalem

(Deuteronomy 12). An inspectorate was appointed to enforce these drastic requirements. The climax came with the erection of a "desolating sacrilege" on the altar of burnt offering, which stood immediately outside the main doors of the temple, and the offering on it of a sacrifice (presumably pagan) ten days later. The "desolating sacrifice" may be a punning reference to the Syrian Baʿal Shamem, "god of heaven," but as sacrifice was offered upon it rather than to it, the artifact described was probably a pagan altar rather than a statue. 1 Maccabees records that "many" from Israel accepted this, but "many" chose rather to die. (2 Macc 6:1-11 describes Antiochus's demands differently. The Jews were to forsake their law and rededicate the Jerusalem temple to the Greek Olympian Zeus. The temple was further desecrated by debauched behavior. Jews had to offer sacrifice on the king's birthday and process in honor of the Greek god Dionysus.)

It is most unlikely that Antiochus required the many peoples of his empire to give up their particular customs (1:41-42), and there is no evidence that they did. In spite of 1 Maccabees' attempt to portray Antiochus as a universal villain, this persecution was limited to the Jews in Judea. The problem is why Antiochus adopted this policy. Though given to occasional social eccentricity, he was not a political eccentric, or religiously intolerant. There is no evidence that he tried to impose Hellenism generally throughout his empire, or that he was persuaded by a Hellenizing party in Jerusalem to persecute conservatives on religious or cultural grounds. His purpose was surely political. Possibly he wished to compensate for his Egyptian humiliation by demonstrating his complete control over his Jewish subjects (Gruen 1993: 260-64), but such bullying would hardly impress anyone. It is perhaps more likely that Antiochus saw the Jews as rebels threatening the stability of the province of Coele-Syria and Phoenicia, and simplistically tried to remove the threat by destroying the religion which sustained it (Green 1990: 516). If that was Antiochus's hope, he misjudged badly.

This chapter has been carefully constructed by its author. The historical background is explained and the faults of the Seleucids made clear (1:1-10). The policy of the Jewish renegades (vv. 11-15) and Antiochus's Egyptian campaign (vv. 16-19) led to a series of disasters: Antiochus's attack on the temple (vv. 20-23), the attack on Jerusalem (vv. 29-35), and the religious persection (vv. 41-62). Each disaster is followed by a poetic lament (vv. 27-28, 36-40, and 2:7-13), the final lament being put into the mouth of the priest Mattathias.

1 Macc 1:54, 59 date the climax of these events to December of year 145, usually given as December 167 BC, but by the Seleucid era beginning spring or autumn 312 BC, possibly Dec. 168 BC (Bringmann 1983: 28). The rededication of the temple can thus be dated to December 165 BC, which allows time for Antiochus to have news of it and of Judas's subsequent activities (6:5-7) before his own death in November/December 164 BC (6:16; Sachs and Wiseman 1954: 202-12; Grabbe 1991: 59-74).

Select Bibliography on Antiochus's Persecution of the Jews. Bickerman, E. J. 1937, *Der Gott der Makkabäer*, Berlin: Schocken and Judischer; ET H. R. Moehring. 1979, *The God of the Maccabees*, Leiden: Brill • Bringmann, K. 1983, *Hellenistische Reform und Religionsverfolgung in Judäa*, Göttingen: Vandenhoeck und Ruprecht • Bunge, J. 1979, "Die sogenannte Religionsverfolgung Antiochus IV Epiphanes und die griechischen Stätte," *JSJ* 10:155-65 • Grabbe, L. L. 1994, *Judaism from Cyrus to Hadrian*, London: SCM • Gruen, E. S. 1993, "Hellenism and Persecution: Antiochus IV and the Jews," in P. Green, ed., *Hellenistic History and Culture*, Berkeley, Calif., and London: University of California, 238-74 • Hengel, M. 1974, *Judaism and Hellenism*, London: SCM • Millar, F. 1978, "The Background of the Maccabaean Revolution: Reflections on Martin Hengel's *Judaism and Hellenism*," *JJS* 29:1-21 • Mørkholm, O. 1966, *Antiochus IV of Syria*, Copenhagen: Gyldendalske • Rowley, H. H. 1953, "Menelaus and the Abomination of Desolation," in *Studia Orientalia Ioanni Pedersen septuagenario a collegis, discipulis, amicis dicata*, Hauniae: E. Munksgaard, 303-15 • Sachs, A. J., and D. J. Wiseman. 1954, "A Babylonian King List of the Hellenistic Period," *Iraq* 16:202-12 • Tcherikover, V. 1959, *Hellenistic Civilization and the Jews*, trans. S. Applebaum, Philadelphia: The Jewish Publication Society of America; Jerusalem: The Magnes Press, The Hebrew University • Wenham, D. 1992, "Abomination of Desolation," in *ABD*, 1:28-31.

The Jewish Response: Mattathias and His Sons (2:1-70)

This chapter is also carefully constructed. Through the story of Mattathias and his sons, the author presents different Jewish responses to the persecution. This narrative is linked to ch. 1 by Mattathias's opening lament on the situation (2:7-13; see above), and the final commendation of his sons Simon and Judah (2:65-66) prepares for the two following major sections of the book (3:1–9:22; 9:23–16:24).

Mattathias comes from a priestly family of Judah listed in 1 Chr 9:10. Modein (modern Ras Medieh) is near Lod, thirty-two kilometers northwest of Jerusalem, on the hills overlooking the maritime plain toward Jaffa. The five sons reappear in 1 Maccabees, but not in the order of this list, and (Judas and Eleazar apart) without their nicknames. The meaning of these names is obscure, though Maccabeus suggests "hammer." Where the author found this list is unknown.

The heroic activities of Mattathias now recounted can hardly derive from archival material, either Jewish or Seleucid, and probably came from oral folklore about the Maccabees or from the author's own composition. There are three separate narratives. In the first (2:15-26), the author illustrates the requirement of 1:51 that the individual towns of Judah offer sacrifice and so indicate their loyalty. Mattathias, as an honored leader, is invited to be the first to obey the king and win royal recognition and other rewards, but Mattathias refuses to compromise, quoting Deut 5:32. Another Jew, less scrupulous, accepts the invitation; Mattathias's reaction is compared directly with that of Phinehas, who in Israel's early time of temptation in the wilderness had killed an apostatizing Israelite (Num 25:7-8; Ps 106:30). At this point 1 Maccabees sets the withdrawal of the Maccabees to the hills to begin their campaign; 2 Maccabees, however, puts this event before Antiochus's religious persecution (2 Macc 5:27–6:2).

In the second narrative (2:29-41), again the author distinguishes between the right and wrong response to the situation. Mattathias's group was zealous for the law and covenant (2:27); a second group of Jews, "who were seeking righteousness and justice," also withdrew to the wilderness. When they refused, on religious grounds, to fight the Seleucid forces on the sabbath, they were killed. Mattathias and his friends, hearing of this, decided that it was right to defend themselves on the sabbath. The story is essentially didactic; there is no detail here to point to a specific occasion or place. The author is producing apologetic for Maccabaean military practice.

The third narrative similarly mentions no specific occasion, but points to the correct response to the situation by the Hasideans and the friends of Mattathias. (These two narrative sections are linked by the reference in each to the friends (not sons) of Mattathias, and so perhaps distinct in origin from the surrounding sections of ch. 2, which speak of Mattathias and his sons.) The Hasideans are here portrayed as "mighty warriors" who reacted forcibly to the persecution, organizing an army and killing "sinners" and "renegades"; the Maccabean party with similar force tore down altars and circumcised the children of parents who had obeyed the king's demands. The sympathy of the author of 1 Maccabees lies clearly with these militaristic groups. The name "Hasideans" is a Greek form of Heb. *ḥasidim,* the pious Israelites of Pss 79:2; 149:1, but 1 Maccabees knows them as a distinctive group or company (Gk. *synagogē*), and connects them (7:12) with a group *(synagogē)* of scribes who go to the high priest Alcimus and the Syrian general Bacchides naively seeking just terms. 2 Macc 14:6 identifies the Hasideans as a group under the leadership of Judas Maccabeus himself, keeping up war and stirring up sedition. In 1 Macc 7:12 the author appears to be distancing them from Judas and the Hasmoneans; the author of 2 Macc 14:6 appears to be linking Judas with them, perhaps to improve Judas's image.

The final section of the chapter (2:49-70) gives Mattathias a deathbed speech. Similar speeches are credited to famous Israelites like Jacob (Genesis 49), Moses (Deuteronomy 33), and Samuel (1 Samuel 12). Mattathias's speech shows similarities with the praises of famous men in Sirach 44–50 (a book which could have been familiar to the author). The list of heroes of faith in Hebrews 11 belongs to the same genre. Mattathias holds up to his sons the examples of Israel's ancestors — Abraham for his faithfulness under test, Joseph for keeping the commandment, Phinehas for his zeal, Joshua for fulfilling the command, Caleb for testifying, David for his mercy, Elijah because of great zeal for the law, Hananiah, Azariah, and Mishael for their belief, Daniel for his innocence. (It seems likely on this evidence that the author is familiar with the five books of the Torah, the Deuteronomistic history, and the book of Daniel.) Mattathias's sons are similarly to be courageous and to grow strong in the law. Finally, Mattathias commends Simon as counselor and Judas as warrior. This is how 1 Maccabees portrays them, but in reverse order. The final admonitions perhaps summarize the author's own ideology. The date, the 146th year, with the list of Mattathias's family and the reference to the tomb at Modein (cf. 13:27-30), gives some hard information in a chapter composed mostly of *haggadah.*

Select Bibliography. Davies, P. R. 1977, "Hasidim in the Maccabaean Period," *JJS* 28:127-40 • Kampen, J., *The Hasidaeans and the Origin of Pharisaism: A Study in 1 and 2 Maccabees,* SBLSCS 24, Atlanta: Scholars • Sievers, J. 1990, *The Hasmoneans and Their Supporters from Mattathias to the Death of John Hyrcanus I,* Atlanta: Scholars.

The Acts of Judas (3:1–9:22)

On grounds of literary analysis alone, N. Martola divided 1 Maccabees into the preparation (chs. 1–2) and the story of the first generation of the Hasmoneans (chs. 3–16), the latter being divided into two halves. The first half tells the story of Judas, but it is not a simple chronicle of events. It is a carefully constructed, balanced narrative, beginning with an introductory notice and a poem in praise of Judas (3:1-9) and ending with a short poetic lament at his death and a formal conclusion (9:19-22). Between these points, the story is told in two balanced halves. In the first (3:10–6:63) we meet Judas, King Antiochus IV, and his generals Gorgias and Lysias. Judas wins a series of battles, regains and purifies the temple courts, and fortifies Mt. Zion and the town of Beth-zur; Antiochus IV dies, and the Seleucids offer peace but then regain Mt. Zion and Beth-zur. In the second we meet Judas, King Demetrius, and his generals Nicanor and Bacchides. Judas defeats Nicanor in one battle and kills him in the next, but then he is defeated and killed himself by Bacchides. In each section, Judas is at first successful and then suffers a setback (in the second half, finally). In each half, the author has incorporated an originally independent block of material for which there was no certain known date or context; in their present positions ch. 5 (campaigns against surrounding Gentiles) and ch. 8 (diplomacy with Rome) clearly interrupt the sequence of the surrounding narrative. The account of Judas, therefore, shows clear signs of the author's construction, and we should not be surprised to find that it raises some questions of sequence and dating.

Select Bibliography. Martola, N. 1984, *Capture and Liberation: A Study in Composition of the First Book of Maccabees,* Acta Academiae Aboensis, Ser. A., vol. 63, no 1, Abo: Abo Akademi • Neuhaus, G. O. 1974, *Studien zu den poetischen Stücken im 1 Makkabäerbuch,* Würzburg: Echter-Verlag • Schürer, E., rev. G. Vermes and F. Millar. 1973, *The History of the Jewish People in the Age of Jesus Christ (175 B.C.–A.D. 135),* Edinburgh: T&T Clark, 1:164-73.

In Praise of Judas (3:1-9)

The eulogist, probably the author of 1 Maccabees, draws Judas in terms of earlier Jewish heroes — possibly David in 3:3 (cf. 1 Sam 17:39), more certainly Judah in 3:4 (cf. Gen 49:9), perhaps Joshua as described in Ecclus 46:1-6, and certainly Phinehas in 3:8, which quotes Num 25:11. The poet emphasizes that Judas attacked two groups of people already identified in ch. 1 as the cause of the troubles: Israelite lawbreakers and apostates (3:5, 6, 8), and foreign kings (v. 7). C. F. Burney (1920: 319-25) argued that in the original Hebrew the opening letters of each verse formed an acrostic of the name "Jehudah the Maccabee." This eulogy of Judah at the beginning of the book is balanced by the eulogy of Simon toward the end in ch. 14:4-15. Judah and Simon are the author's two main heroes (cf. 1:65-66).

Select Bibliography. Burney, C. F. 1920, "An Acrostic Poem in Praise of Judas Maccabaeus," *JTS* 21:319-25.

The Campaigns of Judas against Apollonius and Seron (3:10-26)

In the next major section of the work (3:10–4:36) the author describes four campaigns of Judas, against increasingly important Syrian generals. The first pair of campaigns is separated from the second pair by an account of Antiochus's reaction to Judas's preliminary successes (3:27-37).

Of the first campaign (3:10-12) 1 Maccabees knows little. Apollonius was presumably governor of Samaria, as Josephus guesses (*Ant.* 12 §287). There are no details of place or time; the author notes only that Judas took Apollonius's sword and used it thereafter, a clear reference to David's use of Goliath's sword (2 Sam 17:51). The second campaign (3:13-26) is told at much greater length, though with little circumstantial detail. The campaign was initiated by Seron, an ambitious Syrian officer (v. 14). His army included Jews loyal to Syria (v. 15), perhaps replacing Syrian regulars who were on parade in 166 BC at Antiochus's army review at Daphne near Antioch. Judas routed Seron's army at the pass of Beth-horon, a favorite place of ambush (cf. Josephus *J.W.* 2 §521). The author seems more interested in pointing out the lessons for the Jewish reader: Judas's soldiers are faithful Jews, Seron's army includes godless Jews (i.e., Jewish apostates) (vv. 13, 15). Judas's troops are few and Seron's many, but victory depends not on numbers but on heavenly support (vv. 17-19; cf. 1 Sam 14:6). Seron's troops come to destroy the Jews; Judas's troops are fighting for their lives and their laws (vv. 20-21). The fear and fame of Judas spread abroad, as once David's had (1 Chr 14:17). The comparison of Judas with David in this section is obvious.

The Policy of Antiochus (3:27-37)

The author here tries to interpret for his Jewish readers the situation in which Antiochus now found himself. There are some historical facts here: Antiochus "gathered all the forces of his kingdom" for a review at Daphne in 166 BC. He was always short of money. He was well known for his lavish giving — for example, to Rhodes, to Delos, and especially to Athens (Mørkholm 1966: 51-63). Lysias was probably one of the king's Kinsmen (an honorary title; cf. 10:89) rather than a relative by birth (3:32), in charge of the western empire, and the guardian of Antiochus's son, the future Antiochus V. (Some argue that 2 Macc 9:25 and 11:16-21 require that Antiochus V was now made royal co-regent with Antiochus IV, but in 166 BC he was only a boy aged six.) Antiochus IV marched east in the year Sel. Mac. 147 (i.e., autumn 166–autumn 165 BC; probably in spring 165 BC) through the "upper" (i.e., inland) provinces. In fact he campaigned in Armenia, along the Persian gulf, and in Elymais (Mørkholm 1966: 166-80).

The rest of this passage is interpretation. 1 Maccabees implies that Antiochus gathered his whole army in response to minor setbacks in Judah, credits Antiochus with the belief that his shortage of money was due to his abolishment of Judah's laws, and states his intention of wiping out the Jews, banishing memory of them by settling aliens there and redistributing the land. All this is inaccurate and unlikely, but it represents the Jewish demonization of Antiochus that had already appeared in the book of Daniel, and would reappear in 2 Maccabees.

Select Bibliography. Altheim, F., and R. Stiehl. 1970, "Antiochus IV Epiphanes und der Osten," in F. Altheim and R. Stiehl, eds., *Geschichte Mittelasiens im Altertum,* Berlin: de Gruyter, 553-71 • Bunge, J. G. 1976, "Die Feiern Antiochus IV Epiphanes in Daphne im Herbst 166 v. Chr.," *Chiron* 6:53-71 • Gruen, E. S. 1976, "Rome and the Seleucids in the Aftermath of Pydna," *Chiron* 6:73-95 • Mørkholm, O. 1966, *Antiochus IV of Syria,* Copenhagen: Gyldendalske.

The Campaigns of Judas against Gorgias and Lysias (3:38–4:35)

1 Maccabees now describes, at greater length than the earlier campaigns, Judas's defense against two serious invasions of the Seleucid forces, led by senior generals. Again, the narrative is compounded by historical details and editorial coloring. Ptolemy son of Dorymenes, one of the king's Friends, was the governor *(stratēgos)* in charge of Coele-Syria and Phoenicia (cf. 2 Macc 8:8), and was probably responsible for the appointment of Nicanor and Gorgias. In 1 Maccabees, Nicanor plays no further part in the campaign; the active general appears to be Gorgias (4:1, 5, 18; cf. later 5:59), who is named in 2 Macc 10:14-15 and 12:32-37 as governor of Idumea. In a similar campaign in 2 Macc 8:10-29, however, Nicanor is the active general and Gorgias the silent partner. There may be some confusion here; 1 Macc 7:26-50 suggests that Nicanor's activity as the leading Seleucid general took place under Demetrius I. Both 1 Macc 3:41 and 2 Macc 8:10-11, 25, 34 note that the Seleucids expected to make money out of selling Jewish captives into slavery, a common fate of defeated armies (see Bar Kochva 1989: 246).

The Jewish army marched to Mizpah (3:46), north of Jerusalem; Gorgias camped at Emmaus (4:3). It seems that while Gorgias and a detachment of picked troops climbed some twenty-three kilometers up into the hills (probably via the Beth-horon pass) to attack the Jewish camp at dawn, Judas and his picked men marched by a slightly longer, more southerly route to a point just south of Emmaus to attack the Seleucid camp. (Bar Kochva [1989: 257-59, 262] argues that 3:57 in its present position interrupts the sequence of preparatory events at Mizpah, and properly belongs after 4:4.) Gorgias found the hills around Mizpah empty; Judas caught Gorgias's main army by surprise at Emmaus and pursued them west to Gazara and through the plains of Idumea to Azotus and Jamnia. When Gorgias's detachment reappeared from the hills to find Judas's army in full possession of the plain, it fled, and Judas's men plundered the Seleucid camp.

These factual details are few, and briefly told. 1 Maccabees colors them with biblical material and Jewish nationalism. The enemy aim is to destroy the Jews (3:42, 52); the Jews are fighting for their people and for the sanctuary (vv. 43, 51, 58-59). Judas brings the army together as a congregation at Mizpah, as in the days of the judges and Samuel (Judg 20:1; 1 Sam 7:5), to approach God with prayer, fasting and penitence, to inquire of the law, and to present offerings (3:44-53; cf. Judg 20:26-27). Assisting them were the specially consecrated Nazirites (cf. Numbers 6); the Nazirite Samson who fought against the Philistines may be in mind. Trumpets are sounded, as described in Num 10:9 and Judg 7:18, 22. Judas appointed leaders as Moses had (cf. Exod 18:21, 25; Deut 1:15), and picked his men in accordance with Deuteronomic law, sending home certain categories of men (Deut 20:5-8). Judas gives a homily (3:58-60; cf. 2 Chr 20:15-17), and another just before battle (4:8-11), reminding his men of how God had saved their ancestors from Pharaoh at the Red Sea, and after victory the army sang hymns and praises to Heaven, quoting Ps 136:23-24. The passage ends (4:25) with allusions to Judg 15:18 and 1 Sam 14:45. Judas has done everything, so to speak, in accordance with the book. The author of 1 Maccabees underlines the importance of the situation by the inclusion of a poetic lament (3:45) and a prayer (vv. 50-53).

After this lengthy account, the report of the fourth campaign, led by Lysias, the man with overall political and military responsibility for the whole of the western Seleucid empire, is surprisingly brief and lacking in detail. "The next year" is presumably year 148 of the Greek kingdom (cf. 3:37), that is, the year beginning spring or autumn 165 BC. Lysias, with sixty thousand picked infantry and five thousand cavalry, invades Idumea, camps at Beth-zur, and meets Judas with ten thousand men; the imbalance is made clear. Judas prays, recalling God's past saving acts by the hands of David and Jonathan (4:30-33). Lysias loses five thousand men, and, observing Jewish determination, retreats. The lack of detail suggests to Mørkholm (1966: 153-54) and others that this account is a doublet of Lysias's later campaign to Idumea and Beth-zur (see 6:28-63).

A careful reading of the accounts of these four campaigns thus suggests that the author is being forced to make the best of limited source material. For the first campaign, the author knows only the name of the enemy commander, and for the second, only the name of the enemy commander, the place of battle, and the number of enemy fallen. The account of the third campaign has much more circumstantial detail and in general outline seems highly credible. The fourth campaign may be a doublet, though the evidence of Lysias's letter dated year 148 (2 Macc 11:16-21) suggests that something had happened sufficient to persuade Lysias that peace talks were necessary, and a defeat of Lysias at this stage is not ruled out (cf. also 1 Macc 6:6). These four campaigns have been heavily colored by material portraying Judas in biblical terms, and none of them contains any reference to dates, whether from the Seleucid or Jewish calendar, apart from the phrase "the next year" in 4:28. The author dates these campaigns by placing the first two between the death of Mattathias in year 146 (2:70) and Antiochus's departure for the east in year 147 (3:37), and the second two between that event and the rededication of temple in the month Chislev of year 148 (4:52). These points suggest that the author has drawn on Jewish oral sources for the contents of the stories, has elaborated them from biblical material, and dated them by relating them to other known events. The details of the early career of Judas are less certain than is often assumed.

Select Bibliography. Bar-Kochva, B. 1989, *Judas Maccabaeus: The Jewish Struggle against the Seleucids,* Cambridge: Cambridge University • Mørkholm, O. 1966, *Antiochus IV of Syria,* Copenhagen: Gyldendalske • Wallach, J. L. 1979, "The Wars of the Maccabees," *Revue internationale d'histoire militaire* 42:53-81.

The Cleansing and Dedication of the Temple (4:36-61)

1 Maccabees sets the rededication of the temple after the retreat of Lysias (4:35) and before Judas's attacks on the surrounding Gentiles who were harassing the Jews (ch. 5) and the death of Antiochus (ch. 6). Between the retreat of Lysias and the temple rededication there may have been some negotiations, to judge from the correspondence preserved in 2 Macc 11:16-21, 27-33, and 34-38 (see below, p. 844). The rededication is dated to the month Chislev in year 148 (4:52), which is usually reckoned as December 164 BC but may well rather be December 165 BC (cf. Bringmann 1983: 26; Grabbe 1991: 59-74). This would give sufficient time for news of this event and of Lysias's defeat to reach Antiochus IV in the east before his death (6:5-7), as well as for the various campaigns described in 1 Maccabees 5. The date of Antiochus's death is firmly located between 19/20 November and 18/19 December 164 BC by the information given by a Babylonian cuneiform tablet preserved in the British Museum (Sachs and Wiseman 1954: 202-12). The sequence of events given by 1 Maccabees is to be preferred to that given by 2 Maccabees, in which the temple rededication follows the death of Antiochus. 2 Maccabees has much less concern for chronology than 1 Maccabees, and its material has been carefully structured so as to bring its first half to a climax with the establishment of the annual celebration of the temple cleansing (2 Macc 10:8), and the second half similarly with the establishment of the annual celebration of Nicanor's day (2 Macc 15:36).

Mt. Zion was an old name for the city of David (2 Sam 5:7), and had become a synonym for "the holy mountain," the site of the temple (Ps 2:6; Joel 2:1). The temple and sanctuary appear to have fallen into disrepair after three years' neglect, though Menelaus was still high priest (cf. 2 Macc 11:29) and priests were available (1 Macc 4:42). Bickerman (1937: 109-11) argued that the site had been changed into a Gentile temple enclosure complete with a grove of sacred trees, but 1 Maccabees does not suggest this. The burning of the gates is mentioned here and in 2 Macc 1:8, where it is credited to Jason, presumably in his attack on Jerusalem (2 Macc 5:5-6), and in the narrative of 2 Macc 8:33. The event must therefore be dated to 168 BC; it left a deep impression. For the lamentation of 4:39-40, compare 3:45-53. While Judas's soldiers prevented attack from the Seleucid citadel on the southern wall of the temple courts, priests cleansed the sanctuary. Deut 12:2-4 made clear that pagan sites of worship must be totally destroyed, but the priests hesitated to destroy the temporarily profaned Israelite altar of burnt offering. They therefore stored its stones provisionally to await some prophetic insight on the problem. The author of 1 Maccabees believed that prophecy had ceased, at least for the present (9:27), but was aware of the expectation of a prophet to come (Deut 18:15; cf. John 1:21). According to 1 Macc 14:41, the Jews appointed Simon leader and high priest "until a trustworthy prophet should arise"; similarly, in Neh 7:65 certain families were excluded from the priesthood "until a priest with Urim and Thummim [i.e., the tools of oracle giving] should come." The replacement altar is fashioned according to the law of Exod 20:25 (cf. Josh 8:31). Instructions for the table, the vessels, and the lampstand are found in Exod 25:23-40, and for the altar of incense in Exod 27:1-8. The curtains of the ancient sanctuary are described in Exod 26:1-10, 31-35. For the bread of the presence (twelve loaves offered to God every sabbath and later consumed by the priests) see Lev 24:5-9.

The dedication of the new altar took place on 25 Chislev in year 148, that is, probably December 165 BC, appropriately on the third anniversary of the first pagan sacrifice on the old altar (1:59). Similar music (4:54) was used at the dedication of the walls of Jerusalem by Nehemiah (Neh 12:27). The eight-day celebration recalls Hezekiah's purification of the temple (2 Chr 29:12-19) as well as Solomon's dedication of the temple in the seventh month (1 Kgs 8:65-66; cf. 2 Chr 7:8-9), at the time of the feast of Tabernacles (cf. Lev 23:33-43). 2 Macc 1:18 and 10:6 compare this festival of purification with Tabernacles; it seems natural that this new December festival borrowed from this autumnal feast, at which people offered sacrifices and processed with branches of palms and other trees. 2 Macc 10:7 says that the Jews carried both "ivy-wreathed wands *(thyrsoi)* and beautiful branches and also fronds of palm." Wands *(thyrsoi)* and ivy wreaths were carried in procession at festivals in honor of the Greek god Dionysus (2 Macc 6:7), which this feast of Dedication (Heb. *ḥanukkah*) was perhaps partly intended to counter.

1 Macc 4:59 provides for the continuance of this feast; 2 Macc 1:7 and 9 refer to its celebration in the years 169 and 188, and associate it with lighting the lamps (2 Macc 1:8). In the first century AD Josephus called the feast "Lights." The festal letter of 2 Macc 1:10–2:18 associates the feast of purification with the miracle of fire from heaven (2 Macc 1:18; 2:9-11; see 2 Chr 7:1). John 10:22 refers to this as the winter feast of rededication (Gk. *enkainia;* cf. *enkainismos* 1 Macc 4:56).

The author reverts to military matters: Judas fortifies the temple area to negate the strategic control of the *akra* with its Gentile (i.e., Seleucid) forces, and Beth-zur in order to control the approach to Jerusalem from the south (cf. 4:29).

Select Bibliography. Abel, F.-M. 1946, "La Fête de la Hanoucca," *RB* 53:538-46 • Bickermann, E. J. 1937, *Der Gott der Makkabäer,* Berlin: Schocken/Jüdischer • Bringmann, K. 1983, *Hellenistische Reform und Religionsverfolgung in Judäa,* Göttingen: Vandenhoeck & Ruprecht • Grabbe, L. L. 1991, "Maccabaean Chronology: 167-164 or 168-165 BCE," *JBL* 110:59-74 • del Medico, H. E. 1965, "Le cadre historique des fêtes des Hanukkah et de Purim," *VT* 15:238-70 • Schaumberger, J. 1955, "Die neue Seleukidenliste BM 35603 und die makkabäische Chronologie," *Bib* 36:423-35 • VanderKam, J. C. 1987, "Hanukkah: Its Timing and Significance according to 1 and 2 Maccabees," *JSP* 1:23-40.

Wars with Neighboring Peoples (5:1-68)

The material of ch. 5 breaks the obvious continuity of chs. 4 and 6, as is clear from 4:7, where Antiochus hears news of the events of 4:26-61 but nothing of campaigns in Transjordan. Its insertion here is probably the work of the author, who makes an obvious connection in 5:1 and a more subtle connection with the opening attack on Idumea (v. 3; cf. 4:61). Chapter 5 has obviously been carefully constructed. It has a core in vv. 9-64, which is enclosed by two balancing pericopes. In vv. 3-5, 6-7 Judas first attacks the descendants of Esau in Idumea and the sons of Baean, and then the Ammonites, taking Jazer; and in vv. 65, 66-68 Judas attacks first the sons of Esau in the south, striking Hebron, and then the Philistines, attacking Azotus. The central core is even more obviously structured:

5:9-15 Pleas for help from Jews in Gilead and Galilee
5:16-20 Plans are made:
- (1) Simon will go to Galilee (v. 17)
- (2) Judas (and Jonathan) will go to Gilead (v. 17)
- (3) Joseph and Azariah will defend Judea (v. 18-19)

5:21-62 Action is taken:
- (1) Simon in Galilee; battles; Jews brought back to Judea (vv. 21-23)
- (2) Judas in Gilead; battles; Jews brought back home (vv. 24-54)
- (3) Joseph and Azariah defeated, pursued back to Judea (vv. 55-62)

5:63-64 Judas and brothers are honored in Israel and among Gentiles

There is no reference anywhere to the date of these events. 1 Maccabees may be right in setting them between the rededication in 165 BC and the death of Antiochus in 164 BC, but this will not work if both the rededication and Antiochus IV's death were, as most scholars believe, in 164 BC. 2 Maccabees locates fragments of these campaigns elsewhere (see pp. 843, 845). Inevitably, therefore, question marks remain about the date and context of these campaigns.

As before, events in this chapter echo famous events from the Hebrew scriptures. Judas, like David (2 Sam 8:13-14; 10:1-14), attacks the Edomites (descendants of Esau) and Ammonites; like Saul (1 Sam 11:1-11), he rescues Jews from Gilead; like Gideon (Judg 7:15-23), he attacks by night, dividing his army into three companies and terrifying the enemy with trumpet blasts; like Moses (5:48; cf. Num 20:14-21), he requests safe passage through enemy territory and captures Jazer and its villages (5:8; cf. Num 21:32). Joseph and Azariah disobey Judas as the Israelites disobeyed Moses (Num 14:39-45), and suffer similarly. The Jews are threatened with annihilation by the Gentiles "in a single day" (5:27; cf. Esth 3:13) and rejoice when rescued (5:54; cf. Esth 9:17-19); but Judas annihilates his Gentile enemies completely (5:28, 35, 44, 51), as the law (Deut 7:2) had commanded and Joshua had done (Josh 11:16-20). The author again portrays Judas as a biblical hero, fulfilling the law's requirements.

In 5:3-7 Judas attacks the sons of Esau, the sons of Baean and the sons of Ammon (the same Greek word, *huioi,* "sons," is used in each case). The sons of Esau, the biblical Edomites, are not unnaturally connected with the Hellenistic region of Idumea, on Judea's south and southwestern borders. Josephus (*J.W.* 2 §235; 4 §551) located the toparchy of Akrabattene in Samaria, near Shechem, which is far from Idumea, and scholars have therefore attempted to link Akrabattene with the "ascent of Akrabbim" (Num 34:4) near the northwest end of the Dead Sea. This identification is convenient but unconvincing. The name sits uneasily in the Greek text; the Syriac and Latin versions emended to make passable sense. The Baeanites are otherwise unknown, and their location uncertain (except that they lived west of the Jordan; cf. 5:6); it is tempting to think that the place name Akrabattene might originally have belonged with them, but there is no suggestion of this in the text. The Ammonites of this period lived in Ammanitis, around modern Amman. The campaign described here against Timothy, with the capture of Jazer, may be identifiable with that given in 2 Macc 10:24-38. Timothy, leader of the Gentile troops (5:11, 37, 40), reappears in a summary of this campaign (1 Macc 5:22-44 par. 2 Macc 12:10-31) in 2 Macc 8:30-33. On the identification of Timothy and the possibility of the existence of two enemy leaders with this name, see below, pp. 843, 845.

The core narrative begins in 5:9. In vv. 9-20 the problem is stated in dramatic terms: the Jews in Gilead and Galilee are under threat of annihilation from the Gentiles. The Jews in Gilead are besieged in Dathema, the Jews in the land of Tob have been massacred, and the Jews in Galilee are under threat from the Gentiles of Galilee, Ptolemais, Tyre, and Sidon. Galilee had been known as "Galilee of the nations" for centuries (cf. Isa 9:1); its population was forcibly circumcised by Aristobulus in 104/3 BC. In the second century BC Galilee was largely controlled by the coastal cities of Ptolemais, Tyre, and Sidon, independent but friendly to the Seleucids. The hostility of Ptolemais to the Jews is indicated by 2 Macc 6:8. The land of Tob (cf. Judg 11:3), Dathema, and most of the Transjordanian places named in this chapter remain uncertainly located. The author heavily underlines the threat to the existence of the Jewish diaspora, and describes the division of the Jewish forces into three, giving Judas the largest part (5:20).

5:21-54 recount the rescue of the diaspora Jews. Simon's contribution, the rescue of Jews from Galilee and Arbatta (unknown, but possibly between Mt. Carmel and Caesarea), is described in three verses (vv. 21-23), while the victorious campaign of Judas is told at ten times the length (vv. 24-54). Judas is associated with Jonathan at vv. 24 and 55, but Jonathan's contribution is unmentioned, and Judas gets all the credit.

Judas's army crossed the Jordan eastward and marched for three days (perhaps 100 km.) "into the wilderness," where it met the Nabateans. (Aretas, "ruler of the Arabs" [2 Macc 5:8], was probably one of their early kings.) The Nabateans belonged to southern Transjordan; by the first century BC their capital was Petra. The army "turned back" — presumably northward — "by the wilderness road" to Bozrah, about 110 kilometers south of Damascus on the Damascus-Amman-Hedjaz road. Bozrah became a Nabatean city second only to Petra, and later the capital of Roman Arabia (see *ABD,* 1:775). From here a night's march brought Judas to the besieged stronghold of Dathema, and from there to Maapha (or Alema; the reading is uncertain), Chaspho, Maked and Bosor (cf. 5:26). Vv. 37-43 describe a clash at Raphon, unknown but apparently near the ancient sanctuary of Carnaim (v. 44; cf. Amos 6:13) near the modern Syrian-Jordanian border. Bozrah and Carnaim give us the only two secure points for locating Judas's activity; the other places mentioned are unknown. Judas gathers his refugees and returns to Jerusalem via Ephron (5:46), usually located east of the Jordan from Beth-shan (v. 52).

The author knows no details of the disastrous attack on Jamnia led (against orders) by Joseph and Azariah, and the story is clearly told to underline the role of the Maccabean family in the deliverance of Israel. 2 Macc 12:8-9 has an account of an attack on Jamnia by Judas.

The chapter ends with another brief account of Judas's campaigns against Idumea (5:65; possibly a doublet of the campaign of v. 3 above) and Philistia (vv. 66-68). Marisa (v. 66; cf. 2 Macc 12:35; biblical Mareshah, Josh 15:44, and modern Tell Sandahanna) was an important Hellenistic town, later captured (like Azotus, 5:68) by John Hyrcanus (Josephus *J.W.* 1 §269; *Ant.* 14 §364). 1 Maccabees has little respect for the priests "who wished to do a brave deed"; success in battle was reserved for the Maccabean family. Azotus (Ashdod) was an important city from the Middle Bronze Age to the Roman and Byzantine periods. The author of 1 Maccabees emphasizes Judas's destruction of its pagan cult; it was important to him to demonstrate Judas's religious devotion as well as his military success.

Select Bibliography. Bar-Kochva, B. 1989, *Judas Maccabaeus: The Jewish Struggle against the Seleucids,* Cambridge: Cambridge University.

The Death of Antiochus Epiphanes (6:1-17)

This section combines material based on information from some Seleucid source (6:1-4, 14-16) with the author's own editorial linkage (vv. 5-7) and romantic invention (vv. 8-13). Vv. 5-7 summarize 3:38–4:61, and vv. 8-13 give the author's picture of what, in the circumstances, Antiochus ought to have thought. At least he makes Antiochus regret some of his past acts; his view of Antiochus is less uncharitable than that of 2 Maccabees 9. For a different view of Antiochus, see Polybius *Hist.* 30.25-26.

Polybius says that Antiochus, in need of money, attacked the temple of Artemis in the region of Elymais (biblical Elam; cf. Isa 21:2; our author wrongly makes Elymais a city, not a region, 6:1). The local people repulsed him, and he retreated, fell ill, and died at Tabae on the borders of Persia and Media (cf. v. 56). 1 Maccabees appears to follow Polybius in essentials. 2 Macc 1:10-13 and 9:1-29 give more dramatic versions of the story.

Antiochus's real concern at this time was not (as 1 Maccabees suggests) the rebellion in Judea but the problem of succession (6:14-17). Antiochus apparently nominated as regent and guardian of his son and heir Antiochus V not Lysias, to whom he had previously entrusted Eupator (3:33), but Philip, a Friend (6:14) and courtier (*syntrophos,* 2 Macc 9:29; cf. Acts 13:1, of Manaen). (2 Macc 9:29, however, does not suggest that Philip was appointed, though Goldstein [1984: 372-73] suggests that the Philip of 2 Macc 9:29 is a different Philip.) Lysias, who had possession of Antiochus's son, on hearing of Antiochus's death naturally usurped Philip's place as regent and guardian, naming the boy Eupator ("of a noble father") (6:17; cf. v. 55). On the evidence of a Seleucid king list found at Babylon Antiochus's death was reported at Babylon sometime between 19/20 November and 18/19 December 164 BC (Sachs and Wiseman 1954: 202-12). "Year 149" indicates that 1 Maccabees' dating here is based on a Seleucid era beginning in spring or autumn 312 BC.

Select Bibliography. See under 4:36-61 above.

Judas's Attack on the Citadel (6:18-27)

In the year 150 (6:20), probably in spring or early summer 163 BC, Judas mounted a siege of the citadel, which from 168 to 165 BC had controlled access to the temple, and which remained capable of "hemming Israel in around the sanctuary" (v. 18). Members of the garrison, probably Seleucid troops and pro-Seleucid Jews, appealed to Antiochus V, reminding him of their earlier loyalty (cf. 1:43b) and pointing out that Judas had already fortified the sanctuary itself and the city of Beth-zur on the borders of Idumea (4:60-61).

Select Bibliography on the Akra (Citadel). Bar-Kochva, B. 1989, *Judas Maccabaeus: The Jewish Struggle against the Seleucids,* Cambridge: Cambridge University, Appendix D, pp. 445-65 • Shotwell, W. 1964, "The Problem of the Syrian Akra," *BASOR* 176:10-19 • Tsafrir, Y. 1975, "The Location of the Seleucid Akra in Jerusalem," *RB* 82:501-21 • Wightman, G. 1989-90, "Temple Fortresses in Jerusalem, Part I: The Ptolemaic and Seleucid Akras," *Bulletin of the Anglo-Israel Archaeological Society* 9:29-40.

Lysias's Second Campaign (6:28-63)

The Seleucids could not afford to relinquish their control of Jerusalem by leaving the citadel undefended, and the Seleucid reaction was inevitable, prompt, and on a massive scale, if the information of 6:29-30 is accurate. Lysias probably marched in summer 163 BC. The Jews tried to block his advance at Beth-zur, holding out against siege "for many days" (v. 31). At this point we should probably read vv. 39-40, which seem misplaced after v. 48. Hunger compelled the Jews to agree to terms and evacuate the town "because they had no provisions there to withstand a siege, since it was a sabbatical year for the land" (v. 49; see North 1953: 502-15). The sabbatical year (for the institution, see Exod 23:10-11; Lev 25:2-7) began autumn 164 BC; no crops would have been sown and reaped in spring and summer 163 BC, and the harvest of summer 164 would already have been eaten. There was therefore no food to be had either from stores or from the fields, either for besieged or besiegers. It made sense for both sides to make peace. (2 Macc 13:18-22 gives a very different picture of this event, suggesting that the Seleucid attack was a failure, at least until helped by a Jewish informer.) After the fall of Beth-zur, the Seleucid forces were free to march north toward Jerusalem; Judas blocked their way at Beth-zechariah (Khirbet Zakariya, 9 km. north of Beth-zur).

1 Maccabees gives a vivid picture of Lysias's army (6:32-41). Bar Kochva (1989: 327-28) argues that the Seleucids advanced northward up the Wadi Shukheit, claims to have shown by experiment that the early sunlight from the east could reflect off the shields to the Jews on the hills above as described by v. 39, and offers a modern parallel. The application of alcohol (presumably, v. 34) to excite the elephants for battle sounds risky and on other known occasions was disastrous to their owners' side (cf. 3 Macc 5:1-10; Josephus *Ag. Ap.* 2 §5; Maxwell-Stuart 1975: 230-33). Towers on elephants' backs (6:37) are well known from ancient illustrations; they carried four soldiers, not thirty or thirty-two as in some mss. The error arose from an early misreading of a Greek *delta* (= four) for a *lambda* (= 30). The phalanx (v. 38), introduced by Philip of Macedon and his son Alexander the Great, consisted of heavy infantry in sixteen parallel columns, sixteen ranks deep, armed with swords and long spears (*sarissai*). Their weight and close order made them invincible until challenged by the Roman legion, and for a single foot soldier to penetrate deeply into their close order (v. 45) was a real achievement. However, the light-armed Jews stood no chance against the phalanx in open battle, and the daring but mistaken bravery of Judas's brother Eleazar (cf. 2:5) could hardly save the day. The author has to admit that, though inflicting six hundred casualties, the Jews fled (v. 47).

The next stage was the Seleucid attack on the fortified sanctuary (6:51-54; cf. 4:61), using all the usual Hellenistic war machines (v. 51; see Bar Kochva 1989: 340). Shortage of food caused by the sabbatical year reduced the Jewish ranks (vv. 53-54), but the threat of a coup by Philip in his rear, together with a shortage of supplies and the strength of the Jewish position (v. 57), forced Lysias to offer terms. Lysias proposes that the Jews be allowed to return to the *status quo ante,* in which they lived by their own laws (vv. 58-59), on condition that they evacuate the fortified sanctuary (v. 61). This proposal may be reflected in the letter of Antiochus V to Lysias given in 2 Macc 11:22-27 (see below, p. 844). The author has a clear grasp of the political realities, as demonstrated by the speech he credits to the pro-Seleucid supporters in 6:22-27 and the revision of policy he ascribes to Lysias in vv. 57-59. However, in the event the Seleucids pulled down the walls of the Jewish fortifications, to leave their own citadel once again in full control of the temple area (v. 62).

Select Bibliography. Bar-Kochva, B. 1989, *Judas Maccabaeus: The Jewish Struggle against the Seleucids,* Cambridge: Cambridge University • Maxwell-Stuart, P. G. 1975, "1 Maccabees VI.34 Again," *VT* 25:230-33 • North, R. 1953, "Maccabaean Sabbath Year," *Bib* 34:502-15 • Rahlfs, A. 1934, "Die Kriegselefanten im 1sten Makkabäerbuche," *ZAW* 52:78-79 • Sekunda, N. 1994, *Seleucid and Ptolemaic Reformed Armies 168-145 BC*, vol. 1: *The Seleucid Army,* Stockport: Montvert.

Demetrius, Alcimus, Bacchides, and Nicanor (7:1–9:18)

The arrival of Demetrius, son of Seleucus, in year 151 (beginning spring or autumn 162 BC) inaugurated a new political period for the Seleucids, and marks a new section in 1 Maccabees. Antiochus V and Lysias leave the stage, replaced by Demetrius, Bacchides, and Nicanor, and for the first time 1 Maccabees mentions and names a high priest, Alcimus. In this section of 1 Maccabees, Judas makes it impossible for Alcimus to govern the country; Nicanor is sent against Judas and is defeated in one battle and killed in the next. Bacchides is sent, and now Judas is killed. Into the midst of this material is inserted an independent account of the Romans, and Judas's diplomatic dealings with them (ch. 8).

Demetrius, Alcimus, and Bacchides (7:1-25)

Demetrius (born 186 BC) was the son of Seleucus IV and had been a hostage in Rome since 175 BC. On Antiochus IV's death, the Roman Senate had refused Demetrius's request for recognition as heir. In 162 BC a Roman commissioner, investigating Seleucid rearmament, ordered the destruction of the elephants and the navy, and was assassinated. This was an embarrassment to Antiochus V and Lysias, and Demetrius, perhaps seeing his opportunity, escaped from Rome with some help from the later historian Polybius and landed, probably in autumn 162 BC, at Tripolis (2 Macc 14:1) with sixteen men (so Polybius; 2 Macc 14:1 makes them an army and a fleet). Clearly the army supported him and killed Lysias and Antiochus.

The new king was immediately petitioned by Seleucid supporters in Judea, protesting the anarchy brought about by Judas. Their leader, Alcimus, was apparently a priest of the Aaronide (though not the Zadokite) family (7:14), and acceptable to both the pro-Seleucids and the scribes and Hasideans (v. 12; for the stance of the Hasideans see above, p. 811). However, 1 Maccabees disapproves of him, presenting him as ambitious for power and treacherous; 2 Macc 14:3 strangely accuses him of some earlier act of self-defilement, which would presumably make him unfit for high-priestly office, but what this was is not clear. (Alcimus has not previously been mentioned in 1 Maccabees; Josephus puts his appointment under Antiochus V rather than Demetrius I. He could not have been appointed until after Lysias had executed Menelaus [2 Macc 13:3-8], probably in 163 BC.) 1 Maccabees in fact ignores previous high priests, condemns Alcimus, and only with the appointment of Jonathan allows any credibility to the office. For the author of 1 Maccabees, high priesthood belonged to the Maccabean family alone.

Demetrius clearly takes the situation in Judea seriously, for with Alcimus, whom he now appoints high priest, he sends Bacchides, the successor of Lysias as the governor of the whole Trans-Euphrates province, to attend to affairs personally. They were approached by some scribes (i.e, lawyers) in pursuit of justice (i.e., the regularization of the legal position?), and by Hasideans (formerly militant; cf. 2:42) in pursuit of peace. What happened to the scribes we are not told; some sixty Hasideans were executed, presumably because Alcimus did not trust them. (This execution shows that in official eyes the Hasideans were, as 2:42 and 2 Macc 14:6 suggest, linked with the Maccabees; the author of 1 Maccabees, however, sees the Hasideans as ready to compromise.) Goldstein (1976: 332-33) argues that the Greek text credits the words of the quotation in 7:17 to Alcimus himself and that therefore Psalm 79 was written by Alcimus himself with reference to the events of 169 or 168 BC. Psalms 74, 79, and 83 have often been dated to the Maccabean period. Alternatively the author may understand the unnamed subject of the verb "wrote" (Gk. *egrapsen*) to be God. Bacchides withdrew to Beth-zaith, six kilometers north of the Seleucid garrison at Beth-zur, and followed Alcimus's executions with his own execution of Jewish deserters (hardly deserters from his own troops, as some readings suggest). The new Seleucid policy is hard-line and repressive (cf. 7:26); the policy of peace has disappeared with Lysias. Not surprisingly Alcimus, though controlling the land, comes under pressure from a newly militant Judas (cf. 2 Macc 14:3-14) and is forced to apply to Demetrius for help.

Judas and Nicanor (7:26-50)

Nicanor, possibly but not certainly the Nicanor of 3:38, is not here given particularly high rank, but in 2 Macc 14:12 is commander of the elephants, and is made governor of Judea. 2 Macc 14:18-25 show Nicanor attempting a policy of friendly persuasion toward Judas; 1 Maccabees, however, sees Nicanor as treacherous from the start, as full of hatred toward Israel as the Gentiles of ch. 5. A battle is fought at Caphar-salama, possibly Khirbet Selma ten kilometers northwest of Jerusalem, or Khirbet Erha or the nearby Khirbet Deir Sellam ten kilometers north-northeast of Jerusalem (Goldstein 1976: 339, following Abel); Nicanor lost five hundred men. 2 Maccabees does not mention it, and 1 Maccabees knows nothing more of it. The author now further blackens Nicanor's character through a story describing his behavior on a visit to the temple (7:32-38; cf. 2 Macc 14:31-33 for a close parallel). The priests and elders demonstrate their loyalty by pointing to the burnt offerings made twice daily on the king's behalf (cf. Ezra 6:10; it was the cessation of such sacrifices on behalf of Rome that were taken to mark the beginning of hostilities in AD 66; Josephus *J.W.* 2 §409). Nicanor showed contempt, perhaps even spitting on the priests ("defiled them"), and threatened to burn the temple (2 Maccabees: to rededicate the temple to Dionysus) unless Judas were handed over to him. The priests stood before the altar and the temple (cf. Joel 2:17) and made lament (7:37-38), their words alluding to 1 Kgs 8:29, 33-34. The author is engaging in propaganda: the Jews are loyal to the king, but Nicanor is a blaspheming bully. However, the fact that 2 Maccabees also knows the story perhaps supports its basic historicity.

Nicanor's governorship in Judea ends in his death. After his defeat at Caphar-salama and loss of face in Jerusalem, Nicanor retreats with his army northwest to Beth-horon, and Judas gathers his army at Adasa (Khirbet 'Adaseh; Abel 1924: 377-80), about ten kilometers from Beth-horon, intending or at least expecting battle. His prayer (cf. 2 Macc 15:22) refers to the destruction of the Assyrian invaders in 701 BC (cf. 2 Kgs 19:35; Isa 37:36); the Assyrian king's blasphemy was his denial that the Lord could deliver Jerusalem (2 Kgs 18:35; 19:6). Nicanor's comparable wickedness lay in threatening the sanctuary. 1 Maccabees dates the battle on 13 Adar, the last month of the Jewish year (i.e., March). The last previous date mentioned was the year 151, when Demetrius arrived from exile (1 Macc 7:1), probably autumn 162 BC, and the next date is the first month of the year 152, when Bacchides arrives in Judea for the second time (9:3), which would be spring 161 BC if we are dating by an era running from spring 312 BC. The battle against Nicanor therefore probably took place on 8 March 161 BC. Some scholars think that this date does not allow enough time for the events of ch. 7, though not much time is needed for Bacchides' first visit (7:8-11, 19-20), which 2 Maccabees seems to ignore. Judas probably dispatched his embassy to Rome (8:17) shortly after Nicanor's death. Bacchides arrived soon afterward, and Judas died in April 161 BC before his ambassadors returned (there is no indication that Judas welcomed them back with their good news). (If Bacchides' arrival is dated by the era running from spring 311 BC, then Bacchides arrived in Judea in spring 160 BC, and Judas died thirteen months after Nicanor, which would have allowed plenty of time for the embassy to make its round trip in the summer months of 161 BC.)

Nicanor's troops fled westward some thirty kilometers to Gazara, as many armies had fled before (cf. 1 Sam 14:31). The day was made a feast day, and is mentioned in *the Megillat Ta'anit,* the "scroll of fasting," which lists days on which fasting was not allowed. In 2 Maccabees this victory, and the establishment of the feast day, appear as the climax of Judas's career and the Maccabean war, and we hear nothing of Judas's subsequent defeat and death. Historically, the importance of Judas's victory was that it gave Judas the confidence to send his embassy to Rome.

Select Bibliography. Abel, F.-M. 1924, 1925, 1926, "Topographie des campagnes machabéennes," *RB* 33:201-17, 371-87; 34:194-216; 35:206-22, 510-34 • Bar-Kochva, B. 1989, *Judas Maccabaeus: The Jewish Struggle against the Seleucids,* Cambridge: Cambridge University • Mölleken, W. 1953, "Geschichtsklitterung im 1 Makkabäerbuch (Wann wurde Alkimos Hohenpriester?)," *ZAW* 65:205-28.

On the Hasideans, see above, p. 811.

The Romans and the Jews (8:1-17)

If ch. 8 had been omitted, no modern reader would have missed it. Nevertheless, "it is an essential part of our author's narrative" (Goldstein 1976: 346). 9:1 follows on very easily from 7:50. Later references (12:1-4, 16; 15:17) to the renewal of the friendship with Rome, however, reveal the earlier presence of the story, which is neatly linked to its context by the Roman letter to Demetrius (8:31-32). The Jewish readers of 1 Maccabees, c. 100 BC or soon after, would have known the Romans as the major power in the eastern Mediterranean; after the invasion of Pompey in 63 BC, their attitude to the Romans would not have been one of friendship. In the *Psalms of Solomon* (1st cent. BC) and the Gospels (1st cent. AD), the Romans appear in less favorable light.

A Eulogy of the Romans (8:1-16)

The author clearly favors the Romans and is anxious that the Jews should be on good terms with them. Their power, along with their support for and good faith with their friends and dependents (8:1, 12-13), is underlined. This passage is a literary piece, using conventional pro-Roman arguments (Timpe 1974: 141), probably written by the author to accompany the account of the treaty making in vv. 17-30. There may also be a hint of a comparison with the Hasmonean rulers, who were themselves beginning to make conquests in surrounding lands.

The conquest of Gallia Cisalpina (i.e., Gaul south of the Alps) took place in 222 and 190 BC; the conquest of Gallia Transalpina did not begin until 125 BC and might have been known to the author. Carthage controlled Spain until the end of the Second Punic War (218-201 BC); the Roman exploitation began with Cato's campaign in 195 BC. It took another two centuries for Roman control to become complete. The kings of 8:4 are listed in the following verses. Philip V of Macedon was defeated in 197 BC and Perseus of the Macedonians (Gk. *Kittim;* cf. 1:1) in 168 BC at Pydna, thus making possible the Roman intervention in Egypt in that year (2 Macc 5:1). Antiochus III "the Great" (with 54, not 120 elephants) was defeated at Magnesia in Asia Minor by Scipio Africanus in 189 BC. He was not captured, but by the terms of the Treaty of Apamea had to cede his holdings north and west of the Taurus Mountains (but not India, Media, or Lydia); the chief beneficiaries were Pergamum (King Eumenes) and Rhodes. 8:9-10 speak of the Roman conquest of the Greek Peloponnese in 146 BC, in which Rome supported Sparta against the Achean league and mercilessly destroyed Corinth; this, however, was after Judas's time. The writer recognizes that Roman control lasted firmly until his own day (v. 10). The remaining kingdoms and islands will have included Carthage (146 BC), Pergamum (133 BC), Sicily (227 BC), and perhaps Euboea (146 BC). The Romans (doubtless in their own best interests) supported Eumenes of Pergamum (v. 8), Ptolemy VI of Egypt against Antiochus IV, and Antiochus V against Demetrius (cf. 7:1-2). According to 8:31-32, Rome intervened on behalf of the Jews at Demetrius I's court. The author underlines Rome's republican constitution (vv. 14-16), though noting 320 senators instead of three hundred, and (more surprisingly) one consul instead of two. The approval shown for the Roman avoidance of royal trappings may hint at disapproval of the adoption of them by Jonathan (10:20, 62, 64) and Simon (14:43), and similarly the final note that they all heed the one man without envy or jealousy may hint at the problems faced by Hyrcanus or Jannaeus.

An Alliance with Rome (8:17-32)

Neither Judas nor his delegates had any official standing in the government of Judea (which was still under Seleucid rule), and they apparently speak in the name of Judas and his brothers and of "the people of the Jews" (8:20). An earlier contact with the Romans may have been on the same basis, for the Roman response of 2 Macc 11:34-38 is addressed solely to "the people of the Jews." Eupolemos son of John son of Accos may have descended from the priestly family of Hakkoz (1 Chr 24:10; Ezra 2:61); 2 Macc 4:11 suggests that his father John was also a diplomat. Eupolemus is often identified (on circumstantial evidence only) as the Jewish writer who c. 158-157 BC wrote a history of the kings of Judah. Jason son of Eleazar is otherwise unknown, though his son Antipater later serves on a similar mission (12:16; 14:22). Both Eupolemus and Jason have Greek names, though their fathers' names are Hebrew. The purpose of the mission was to win Roman support for freedom from the Seleucid yoke, which included payment of tribute. Under Demetrius, Seleucid control had been firmly reasserted (cf. above, p. 817). The very long journey would have taken over a month, probably through April into May 161 BC.

The request was for a treaty of *philia kai symmachia*, "friendship and alliance" (8:20). The proposal was accepted, and the treaty inscribed on bronze plaques, a copy of which (but not the plaques) was sent to Jerusalem with the envoys. The return of the envoys via the island of Cos is witnessed by a commendatory letter preserved in Josephus (*Ant.* 14 §233) from C. Fannius (Strabo), who was consul at Rome in 161 BC (Niese 1906: 817-29).

The text of the treaty, or of the senatorial letter (8:22) conveying the decree of the Senate, is given in vv. 23-30 (or vv. 23-32). It is often compared with a treaty made between Rome and the island of Astupalea in the Sporades in 105 BC (*CIG*, no. 2485). The standard format for such treaties of friendship and alliance began by establishing peace, friendship, and alliance between the two parties. The second section prohibited the two parties from allowing enemy access through their land to the other party and from offering the obvious forms of assistance (food, arms, money, and ships) to the enemy. A third section required mutual assistance in case of foreign aggression. Lastly, provision was made for alterations (Goldstein 1976: 361-62, after Täubler 1913: 47-62). Our treaty (vv. 23-30) follows this pattern closely enough; the phrases "as Rome has decided" (vv. 26, 28) either corresponds to Lat. *censuere* signifying senatorial approval to each clause (in which case the phrase should be placed at the end of vv. 26 and 28), or indicates slight deviations from the norm required by the fact that Judea was not a free, independent state but already under heavy obligations to her Seleucid rulers (for details see Goldstein 1976: 362). V. 29 may be an intrusive gloss on the text.

8:31-32 append a report to the Jews of a letter from the Romans to Demetrius, indicating Roman support for their new friends and allies. Some suspect this to be the author's invention, such a Roman threat being unlikely. Others affirm it. If it was authentic, Demetrius does not seem to have taken it seriously.

Select Bibliography. Briscoe, J. 1969, "Eastern Policy and Senatorial Politics 168-146 B.C.," *Historia* 128:49-70 • Fischer, T. 1974, "Zu den Beziehungen zwischen Rom und den Juden im 2 Jahrhundert v. Chr.," *ZAW* 86:90-93 • Giovanni, A., and H. Muller. 1971, "Die Beziehungen zwischen Rom und den Juden im 2 Jahrhundert v. Chr.," *Museum Helveticum* 28:156-71 • Gruen, E. S. 1976, "Rome and the Seleucids in the Aftermath of Pydna," *Chiron* 6:73-95 • Liebmann-Frankfort, T. 1969, "Rome et le conflit judéo-syrien (164-161 avant notre ère)," *L'Antiquité Classique* 38:101-20 • Niese, B. 1906, "Eine Urkunde aus der Makkabäerzeit," in C. Bezold, ed., *Orientalische Studien Theodor Nöldeke zum siebigsten Geburtstag gewidmet*, Giessen: A. Töpelmann, 2:817-29 • Smith, M. 1978, "Rome and the Maccabaean Conversions: Notes on 1 Macc. 8," in E. Bammel and C. K. Barrett et al., *Donum Gentilicium: New Testament Studies in Honour of D. Daube*, Oxford: Oxford University, 1-7 • Täubler, E. 1913, *Imperium Romanum: Studien zur Entwicklungsgeschichte des Römischen Reichs*, Leipzig and Berlin: Teubner, vol. 1 • Timpe, D. 1974, "Der Römische Vertrag mit den Juden im 161 v. Chr.," *Chiron* 4:133-52.

The End of Judas (9:1-22)

It is clear from ch. 7 that Nicanor's chief concern was to lay hands on the person of Judas. If this could not be done by treachery or by threatening the priests (7:26-38), and battle on the hills had failed (7:39-50), the obvious remaining possibility was to draw Judas to formal battle against overwhelming odds (cf. 9:4-5) on the open plain. Understanding Bacchides' campaign depends upon the precise identification of the topography (Gilgal, Mesaloth in Arbela [v. 2], "against Jerusalem" [v. 3], Berea [v. 4], Elasa [v. 5], Mt. Azotus [v. 15]). Most commentaries, following Josephus *Ant.* 12.421, have assumed that Arbela referred to Arbela on the western edge of the Sea of Galilee and have therefore emended Gilgal to Galilee (following Josephus). Mesaloth has been understood as a noun meaning "heights" and thus connected with caves in the hills near Arbela. "Against Jerusalem" probably suggests that Bacchides encamped near, or within sight of, Jerusalem, thence moving to Berea, perhaps Beer (Judg 9:21), that is, al-Birah near Ramallah. The Jews encamped at Elasa, only a kilometer from al-Birah. Azotus (Ashdod) has no mountain, and in 1778 J. D. Michaelis proposed for Heb. *'ad har 'ashdod*, "to the mountain of Ashdod," an original *'ad 'asedot hahar*, "to the slopes of the mountain," which has been widely accepted (see Goldstein 1976: 373).

A campaign ranging from Galilee to Ashdod makes little sense, and the key to it has perhaps been provided by Bar Kochva (1989: 376-402, 552-59). He rejects Josephus's location of Arbela in Galilee (since Simon's campaign recorded in 5:21-23 there were presumably no Jews left to kill in Galilee), and retains the reading Gilgal.

Mesalot (Gk. *maisaloth*) is a transliteration of Heb. *mesillot*, "trails," anciently misconstrued as a place name. The Gk. *Arbelois*, usually translated "Arbela," is a transliterated version of an original Heb. *har bet 'el*, "Mount Bethel" (Bar Kochva 1989: 383). The "slopes of the mountain" suggested by Michaelis are "the eastern sharp inclines of the central mountain ridge" (Bar Kochva 1989: 396). Thus Bar Kochva reconstructs Bacchides' march as proceeding via the Gilgal road from the Jordan valley to their camp at the trails or crossroads of Mt. Bethel. From there they marched to within sight of Jerusalem, and then drew back to al-Birah near Ramallah. Judas followed them to Elasa (modern Il'asa) a kilometer away. The battle took place on "the two kilometre wide plateau where the towns of Ramallah and al-Birah are situated" (Bar Kochva 1989: 387). The final pursuit took place down the steep slopes of the hills to the east (nowhere near Ashdod, which was over a day's march to the west). This attractive solution makes good sense of the campaign. In the battle itself, Bacchides, leading the right wing of his forces, seems to have withdrawn (probably intentionally) to lure Judas forward; Bacchides' left wing then swung around behind Judas, closing the trap. Judas was among the fallen. In such a situation, his troops were no match for the professional Syrian army (as many of Judas's troops recognized, v. 6). The Seleucid military machine had won at last.

Judas was buried, with due lamentation, at the family tomb at Modin (9:19; it was later turned into a magnificent Hellenistic monument by Simon, 13:27-30). The lamentation deliberately echoes David's lament over Jonathan (2 Sam 1:19) and the language used of the ancient judges (cf. Judg 3:9), and in closing Judas's career the author imitates the formulae of the books of Kings (cf. 1 Kgs 11:41; 1 Macc 16:23).

Select Bibliography. Bar Kochva, B. 1989, *Judas Maccabaeus: The Jewish Struggle against the Seleucids*, Cambridge: Cambridge University • van den Henten, J. W. 1983, "Der Berg Asdod: Überlegungen zu 1 Makk. 9.15," *JSJ* 14:43-51.

The Acts of Jonathan, Simon, and John (9:23–16:24)

This third major section of 1 Maccabees (9:23–16:24) describes the continuing political and military resistance of the brothers Jonathan and Simon, and of Simon's son John, against the Seleucids. The two brothers are taken together and act in concert against Bacchides (9:62-69) and against Apollonius (10:74-85), as high priest and governor respectively (11:57-59), in fortifying Jerusalem and Judah (12:35-38). When Jonathan is captured, Simon tries to ransom him; when Simon retires, he invites his sons to take his place and his brother's (16:3). The section as a whole balances the major section dedicated to the acts of Judas. The opening eulogy of Judas (3:3-9) is balanced by the closing eulogy of Simon (14:4-15).

This section seems fairly simply structured. Jonathan and Simon deal in succession with Bacchides, Alexander Balas, Ptolemy, Demetrius II, and Trypho — and finally Simon's son John deals with Antiochus VII. The author's original plan may have been to end the work of Simon with the eulogy of Simon, but at some stage the author added further material, confusing the sequence and the chronology. The sections concerned with the Jews' diplomacy with Rome and Sparta (12:1-23; 14:16-24; 15:15-24) fit awkwardly into the narrative. The official decree about Simon from the Jerusalem archives seems to have been added as an afterthought; if it was part of the author's original plan, it might have been more naturally placed before the eulogy. But the final section on the contribution of Simon's son John has been previously signaled by references to John in 13:53 (cf. 16:1-10, 18-22, 23-24), and indicates the author's concern for the continuance of the Maccabean dynasty and its contribution to his own day. The author is legitimizing Hyrcanus.

These chapters differ from the earlier chapters about Judas. The focus now is on politics and diplomacy rather than on the temple and the Jewish religion. There are fewer prayers and less poetry, and more letters and archives. The Maccabees are now developing political independence and moving in an international context, and the author is proud of their presence on this wider Mediterranean stage.

Select Bibliography. Martola, N. 1984, *Capture and Liberation: A Study in the Composition of the First Book of Maccabees*, Acta Academiae Aboensis, Ser. A, vol. 63, no. 1, Abo: Abo Akademi • Sievers, J. 1990, *The Hasmoneans and Their Supporters from Mattathias to the Death of John Hyrcanus I*, Atlanta: Scholars.

Jonathan Succeeds Judas (9:23-31)

Just as trouble began with the Seleucid rulers (1:1-10) and the "renegades" (1:11), so the renegades (now the supporters of Alcimus) and the Seleucids (in the person of Bacchides) reappear here at the beginning of this major section of the history. Possibly the words of Ps 92:7 are in mind here (Goldstein 1976: 376). The fact of famine, so soon after a sabbatical year, inevitably made the people turn to the government (9:24b, 25), thus weakening support for the Maccabees and making them more vulnerable to informers. In this situation it is not surprising that the friends of Judas appointed a new ruler and leader (as the elders of Gilead appointed Jephthah in Judg 11:8), though it is surprising that Simon was passed over in favor of the younger Jonathan (cf. 2:5). For the author of 1 Maccabees, this represented the lowest ebb of the postprophetic age. Alcimus and his supporters were no friends of prophecy (cf. v. 54).

Select Bibliography. Schürer, E., rev. G. Vermes and F. Millar. 1973, *The History of the Jewish People in the Age of Jesus Christ (175 B.C.–A.D. 135)*, Edinburgh: T&T Clark, 1:174-88 • Sievers, J. 1990, *The Hasmoneans and Their Supporters from Mattathias to the Death of John Hyrcanus*, Atlanta: Scholars, vol. 1.

Jonathan and Bacchides (9:32-73)

9:32-49 become intelligible only after careful examination of the sequence of events and the topographical details. Two stories have been awkwardly combined. The first is Bacchides' pursuit of Jonathan, Simon, and their forces into the wilderness south of Jerusalem and a subsequent engagement at the Jordan; the other concerns a dispute between the Maccabees and a Nabatean tribe and a subsequent act of revenge.

The flight of Jonathan and Simon to Tekoa (cf. Amos 1:1) on the edge of the Judean wilderness makes good sense; Abel (1949: 167) identifies the pool of Asphar with cisterns at or near Khirbet Bir ez-Safaran five kilometers south of Tekoa. 9:34, which follows, makes little sense at this point and is generally agreed to be a gloss based on v. 43. In v. 35 Jonathan sends his brother, who on the evidence of v. 33 should be identified with Simon but who turns out to be John (v. 36); this suggests that v. 35 introduces a new episode not originally connected with vv. 32-33. This whole episode (vv. 35-41) took place in the region of Medeba east of the Jordan; it is the author who has linked it with Jonathan's flight to Tekoa and the Judean wilderness. The tale of revenge runs smoothly, except that "Canaan" is either a corrupt local place name (Goldstein suggests an original Maʿon, 7 km. southwest of Medeba) or an attempt to identify the nobles with Israel's ancient enemy ("the old name excuses the massacre"; Dancy 1954: 135), and Nadabath is otherwise unknown; it could be a corruption of Medeba (but why should this obvious name become corrupted here?). In v. 41 the author illustrates the story with a reference to Amos 8:10. The problems begin with 9:42, where the author returns the Jews to the marshes of the Jordan (unmentioned so far in the story).

9:43, 44, and 48 give a confusing account of a battle on the banks of the Jordan. In which direction does Jonathan cross the river in v. 48? The Gk. *eis to peran* in this context usually suggests eastward, in which case the battle was fought on the west bank; Jonathan retreated back across the Jordan, and Bacchides did not cross the Jordan (v. 48). Bacchides almost certainly arrived (v. 43) at the west bank of the Jordan. This in turn allows us to make sense of v. 44. "Battle in front of us" refers to Bacchides and his army; "battle behind us," however, seems unlikely, for if Jonathan was hemmed in by a river, a marsh, and a thicket, a flanking movement by Bacchides to attack Jonathan's rear would be impossible. The NEB repunctuates and translates, "the enemy in front, the water of Jordan behind, to right and left marsh and thicket" (also Goldstein 1976: 378). Thus in v. 44 Jonathan has already crossed the Jordan from the east and has the river behind him, faces Bacchides in front, and has the jungle of the *zor* on either side.

The author has put the whole sequence together from several constituent pieces: the flight of the Maccabees from their usual haunts northwest of Jerusalem to the wilderness of Judea; their defeat at the banks of the Jordan by Bacchides and their escape eastward across the river; the attack of the Jambrites and the subsequent act of revenge. This latter story is originally an independent and undated piece of tradition.

In 9:50-53 the author incorporates a brief list of Bacchides' military dispositions in Judea. The fortress at Jericho controlled the fords from the east; Emmaus, Beth-horon, and Bethel controlled the routes to Jerusalem from the northwest and north; Timnath, Pharathon, and Tephon secured the hills to the northwest and north toward Samaria. Gazara controlled the foothills and coastal plain to the west, and Beth-zur the southern approaches. The citadel controlled Jerusalem itself; here Bacchides imprisoned the sons of leading citizens as hostages.

In the second month of year 153 (i.e., May 160 or 159 BC), the high priest Alcimus died of a stroke. The author clearly implies that this is divine punishment for his destruction of "the wall of the inner court" of the sanctuary. This is either the wall separating the outer court of the Gentiles from the inner courts reserved for Jewish men and women and priests or perhaps the wall within the inner courts separating male Israelites from priests (Goldstein 1976: 391-93). Why this wall should be called "the work of the prophets" remains unclear unless it refers to the rebuilding of the temple under Haggai and Zechariah c. 516 BC.

With Jonathan driven across the Jordan, the land heavily garrisoned, and Alcimus dead, Bacchides may have felt that all was under control (9:57). An attempt by pro-Seleucid Jews quietly to round up known Maccabean supporters backfired (vv. 58-61), though the Greek of v. 61 does not identify the subject of the verb "seized," and "Jonathan's men" is conjecture. Jonathan, Simon, and their friends withdrew to Bethbasi, perhaps Khirbet Beit Bassa, two kilometers southeast of Bethlehem, where Bacchides besieged them. Vv. 65-68 describe how Simon and Jonathan successfully attack the besiegers from the front and rear respectively. Vv. 66-67 are hard to understand; Jonathan "struck down" the tribesmen of Odomera and the people of Phasiron (both otherwise unknown), but in v. 67 "they" (NRSV's "he" is an attempt to reconstruct the sense) began to attack. Presumably Jonathan has enlisted their help against Bacchides, which is how Josephus understands the passage (*Ant.* 13 §28), and perhaps the Greek should read *epetaxen* ("summoned") for *epataxen* ("struck") (Goldstein 1976: 395).

The exchange of prisoners after the minor engagement of 9:64-68 was hardly an event of sufficient importance to result in the total Seleucid withdrawal implied by vv. 72-73. Bacchides himself may not have reappeared, but the Seleucid garrisons remained, and the hostages in the citadel were not returned (cf. 10:9). Government remained in Seleucid hands, in spite of the author's idealized picture of Jonathan as a "judge" of the people (v. 73). There is no indication that the Seleucids appointed a successor to Alcimus until Alexander Balas appointed Jonathan in 152 BC (10:20) (though Josephus [*Ant.* 12 §414] wrongly gives Judas a stint as high priest, and H. Stegemann [1971: 213-20] and others have suggested that the gap was filled by the "Teacher of Righteousness" known from some Qumran documents). After the problems caused by the appointments of Jason, Menelaus, and Alcimus, the Seleucids may have preferred to leave the office vacant, thus keeping control firmly in their own hands (cf. Burgmann 1980: 135-76).

Select Bibliography. Bunge, J. 1975, "Zur Geschichte und Chronologie des Untergangs der Oniaden und des Aufstiegs der Hasmonäer," *JSJ* 6:27-43 • Burgmann, H. 1980, "Der umstrittene Intersacerdotium in Jerusalem 159-152 v. Chr.,"

JSJ 11:135-76 • Stegemann, H. 1971, "Die Entstehung der Qumrangemeinde," Ph.D. diss., University of Bonn.

Jonathan's Dealings with Demetrius I and Alexander Balas (10:1-89)

1 Maccabees' narrative has passed over some seven years, during which we must assume that Demetrius I continued to rule Judea through his officials and loyal Jewish subjects, and that Jonathan and his followers remained quiet since their suppression by Bacchides, his army, and his garrisons. The political situation was changed by the arrival in 152 BC of Alexander Epiphanes, also called Alexander Balas, as a pretender to the Seleucid throne. Claiming to be Antiochus IV's son, he first won the support of Attalus II, king of Pergamum (158 BC), and then of Rome (153-152 BC; Polybius *Hist.* 33.15-18). When Alexander struck, Demetrius was losing popularity both at home and abroad by political misjudgments and personal arrogance (cf. Josephus *Ant.* 13 §35). The position was further complicated by Ptolemy VI Philometor's permanent ambition of regaining Coele-Syria and Palestine from the Seleucids. Jonathan was well placed to take advantage of this situation.

Select Bibliography. Green, P. 1990, *Alexander to Actium: The Hellenistic Age,* London: Thames and Hudson, 435-52.

Alexander Challenges Demetrius (10:1-2)

The dates given in 10:1 and 21 pose a chronological problem. Most scholars believe that the date in v. 1 is based on the Seleucid Maccabean autumn 312 BC era. On this dating year 160 began in autumn 153 BC. V. 21 says that Jonathan assumed the high priesthood in the seventh month of year 160, at the feast of Booths. If this date is based on the Seleucid Babylonian spring 312 BC era, Jonathan assumed high priesthood at Tabernacles 153 BC, within a fortnight of Alexander's arrival at Ptolemais (assuming he arrived in autumn at the beginning of year 160). This is not impossible, but it seems unlikely. If then v. 21 uses the Sel. Bab. spring 311 BC era, Jonathan became high priest in autumn 152 BC, Alexander having arrived at Ptolemais in autumn 163 BC or perhaps more likely in spring or summer 152 BC (still within year 160 of the Sel. Mac. autumn 312 era). If both dates are based on a spring 312 BC era, then Alexander perhaps arrived in summer 153 BC, and Jonathan assumed high priesthood in autumn 153 BC; if both dates are based on a spring 311 era, then both events happened one year later. Most scholars accept that Jonathan's high priesthood, at least, began in autumn 152 BC.

Demetrius Enlists Jonathan's Support (10:3-14)

The authority to raise and arm troops (even to manufacture arms, according to Kasher 1990: 13) gives Jonathan a new official position. The status of ally rather than subject gives Judea a new standing within the empire, underlined by the release of the hostages (cf. 9:53) and by the departure of the garrison troops of Bacchides' strongholds (cf. 9:50-52). Judas's new authority to raise troops naturally worried those who had hitherto seen him as a rebel (10:8), and particularly the troops manning the citadel. Jonathan loses no time in rebuilding Jerusalem's walls, destroyed by Apollonius in 168 BC (1:31), and the Mt. Zion area, destroyed by Lysias in 163 BC (6:62). The squared stones (10:11), smaller than the large Herodian blocks, are probably those to be seen today on the east wall of the temple enclosure, thirty-two meters from the southeast corner. The Seleucid presence remained, however, in three key places: the citadel, Beth-zur, and Gazara, all later captured by Simon (11:66; 13:43; 13:49-53).

Alexander's Counter Offers (10:15-21)

Alexander flatters Jonathan by calling him "brother" (10:18), but Jonathan as yet has no formal title. He offers the high priesthood (following the precedent set by Antiochus IV and Demetrius I), and makes Jonathan a Friend, that is, one of his advisers (later promoting him to a chief Friend, 10:65; cf. 11:27). A purple robe was the mark of a king's Friend, and the gold crown a gift. The high priest also wore a blue or purple robe, and a linen turban with a rosette of pure gold (cf. Exod 28:36, 39) rather than a gold crown. However, it is unlikely that Alexander was sending Jonathan high-priestly robes, or that Jonathan could wear such robes from a Gentile source. Jonathan in fact put on "sacred vestments," clearly different from Alexander's gifts, at the festival of Booths (see above). Apparently going beyond Alexander's offers, he recruited and armed further troops (10:21).

Demetrius's Response (10:21-47)

Demetrius's long letter (10:25-45), addressed to the nation of the Jews, not to Jonathan, contains a remarkable list of concessions. It is important to compare these concessions with those subsequently offered by Demetrius II to Jonathan (11:30-37) and to Simon (13:36-40), and by Antiochus VII to Simon (15:2-9) (for a detailed table see Bartlett 1998: 89). Demetrius makes some concessions which reappear under Demetrius II and Antiochus. Thus he offers exemption from salt tax and crown levies (10:29), the remission of grain and fruit collections from Judah and three other districts (v. 30), tithes and revenues from Jerusalem and environs (v. 31), and the cancellation of previous debts (v. 43). He adds a number of lesser fiscal concessions which do not reappear: the cancellation of taxes on the freeing of slaves (v. 33a), on livestock (v. 33b), and on pilgrims traveling to Jerusalem immediately before and after a major feast (vv. 34-35). Incredibly, he also offers control of the citadel to the high priest (v. 32), the gift of revenues from the city of Ptolemais (no friend of the Jews) to provide for the temple (v. 39), and an annual gift of fifteen thousand silver shekels from his own purse (v. 40). But above all he appears to offer cancellation of annual tribute (v. 29) (though Goldstein [1976: 405-6] thinks that the Greek phrase indicates only salt and crown taxes). Other substantial offers are made in vv. 41-45, including the rebuilding and restoration of the sanctuary and of the walls of Jerusalem and Judah at royal expense.

Demetrius I's offers seem extravagant compared with those of Demetrius II, and are highly suspicious. J. Murphy-O'Connor (1976: 400-420) has observed that this letter combines two genres of writing. 10:29-30, 32, 33, 34(?), and 39-40 are in the first person singular, and these verses contain the most unlikely offers, including the cancellation of tribute and major tax exemptions, the handing over of the citadel, the gift of Ptolemais and its lands, and the annual grant of fifteen thousand shekels. 10:31, 34(?), 35, 36-38, and 41-45 are expressed in impersonal style and contain more plausible concessions (tax freeedom and inviolability for Jerusalem, immunities for pilgrims, permission for Jews to enlist in the army, the transfer to Judea of three Samaritan districts, government support for the temple and remission of tax on temple revenues, release for those in asylum on account of debt to the king, and the rebuilding and restoration of the sanctuary and of the walls of Jerusalem and Judea. Many of these would be appropriate to Demetrius's situation (e.g., winning Jewish favor by support for the temple, its personnel, and its worshipers), and some are substantial (e.g., rebuilding walls; but Demetrius may have had no intention of fulfilling such an offer). However, this group of concessions falls short of the cancellation of tribute and the handing over of the citadel, which would really mean the independence of Judea. Murphy-O'Connor is thus suggesting that these latter offers form the substance of the original letter; the verses cast in the first person making extravagant offers have been brought forward from a later situation and incorporated into Demetrius I's letter. Release from tribute is not granted until Simon's time (15:37), and the Seleucids never returned the citadel; Simon captured it from them (13:49-52).

It is not surprising that the Jews did not believe these offers (10:46), even if limited to those cast in impersonal rather than personal style. The rebuilding and restoration of the sanctuary and the city walls (not to mention other walls in Judea) would have seemed an extravagant price to pay in itself for Jonathan's support against Alexander, and the Jews probably rightly doubted Demetrius's good faith.

Select Bibliography. Mittwoch, A. 1955, "Tribute and Land-Tax in Seleucid Judaea," *Bib* 36:1-21 • Murphy-O'Connor, J. 1976, "Demetrius I and the Teacher of Righteousness (1 Macc x.25-45)," *RB* 83:400-420 • Sievers, J. 1990, *The Hasmoneans and Their Supporters from Mattathias to the Death of John Hyrcanus I,* Atlanta: Scholars • Wise, M. O. 1990, "A Note on the Three Days of 1 Maccabees X.34," *VT* 40:116-22.

Alexander, Ptolemy, and Jonathan (10:48-66)

10:48 clearly continues from v. 2; the author, as elsewhere, has inserted large sections of material into a narrative framework. The battle is described in Josephus (*Ant.* 13 §§58-61), possibly from Polybius, but the battleground is unknown. The NRSV footnote indicates that some ancient texts read (v. 49) that Alexander fled and Demetrius pursued; according to Josephus, on the left wing Demetrius's troops put Alexander's to flight, but on the right Demetrius was killed after fierce resistance. The present NRSV text suggests that Alexander had the upper hand from the start. Alexander sent word to Ptolemy VI Philometor announcing his possession both by inheritance and by conquest of the Seleucid throne, and proposing an alliance strengthened by diplomatic marriage. He did not want Ptolemy to align himself with Demetrius's descendants. Ptolemy responded diplomatically, proposing Ptolemais for the wedding. Ptolemais (formerly Akko) received its Greek name from Ptolemy II Philadelphus and was a symbol of Egyptian presence on the coast. Alexander and Cleopatra Thea were married in year 162, that is, autumn 151-150 BC in the Sel. Mac. era, so perhaps in summer/autumn 150 BC. When Ptolemy became disillusioned with Alexander, he promised Cleopatra to Demetrius II (11:9-10). After Alexander's death, she married Demetrius; when Demetrius was captured by the Parthians, she married Antiochus VII. She finally became regent of her son Antiochus VIII; she tried to poison him, was discovered, and was forced to take the poison herself.

Jonathan and the people made the right choice (10:46), and Jonathan now openly joins the Alexander-Ptolemy alliance in spite of the inevitable displeasure of the pro-Seleucid party (v. 61), who mistrusted both Jonathan and Egypt. Jonathan, already high priest and Friend of King Alexander, becomes one of the chief Friends (v. 65), but more importantly is made general (*stratēgos*) and governor of the province (*meridarchēs*), that is, military and civil governor of the province of Judea. Jonathan now has an official place as provincial ruler within the Seleucid Empire. In a sense, the Maccabees have arrived; but it seems that the Syrian garrison remained in the citadel and in Beth-zur, and Alexander's control of the Seleucid Empire was not secure.

Select Bibliography. Sievers, J. 1990, *The Hasmoneans and Their Supporters from Mattathias to the Death of John Hyrcanus I,* Atlanta: Scholars.

The Defeat of Apollonius (10:67-89)

Three years later, in year 165 (i.e., autumn 148–autumn 147 BC), Demetrius, son of Demetrius I, arrived from Crete with the support of Lasthenes (cf. 11:32) and mercenary troops, probably in spring or summer 147 BC. Josephus says that he landed in Cilicia, on Syria's northwest border; Alexander therefore returns from Ptolemais to Antioch to counter Demetrius's move. Demetrius appointed Apollonius (probably the Kinsman [*syntrophos*] Apollonius known to us from Polybius *Hist.* 31.11.19; 13.21) as governor of Coele-Syria (originally the deep valley between the Lebanon and the anti-Lebanon, but later linked with Palestine to refer to most of the Levant region). (The word "governor" is not in the Greek text, but it probably restores the intended meaning.) Apollonius moved south to Jamnia, presumably to threaten both Ptolemais and Jonathan (Alexander's ally).

Apollonius's message is intended to lure Jonathan and his army into the plain, where Apollonius's cavalry and the support of the coastal cities in the rear would give him the advantage. The words, however, are from the author of 1 Maccabees, who has in mind 1 Kgs 20:23-28 (cf. the reference to the plain, 10:71, 73). In 10:72 Apollonius perhaps refers to Jewish defeats at the hands of the Philistines (1 Sam 4:2, 10). 10:73: the plain is advantageous to cavalry and offers neither ammunition (stones or pebbles; cf. the story of Goliath, 1 Sam 17:40, 49) nor concealment. Jonathan (again, with Simon at his side) responds by attacking and gaining possession of Joppa, where Apollonius had a garrison, and so gaining Maccabean access to the sea (see 11:6; 13:11; 14:5, 34; and 15:28). Apollonius drew Jonathan south into ambush near Azotus, but his cavalry tired and Simon's forces came to Jonathan's rescue, defeating Apollonius's phalanx, which now lacked the customary protection of the cavalry on its flanks. The temple of Beth-dagon at Azotus and its idol appear in 1 Sam 5:2-5; in 1 Macc 5:68 Judas burns the carved images of the Philistine gods at Azotus. This episode presents Jonathan as conquering Philistine territory and purging Philistine religion as Judas and the Israelite ancestors had done before him. The important harbor of Askalon (10:86), another former Philistine city, welcomed Jonathan; Ekron (v. 89), also a former Philistine city, was given to Jonathan by Alexander, along with a decoration (cf. 11:58) indicating his promotion to "Kinsman." Alexander had every reason to be pleased with his ally, while Jonathan had every reason to be pleased with his new access to the coast.

The End of Ptolemy and Alexander (11:1-19)

Syria, with Demetrius and Alexander contending for power, was weak, and Ptolemy was ambitious. His real intent is variously calculated; 1 Maccabees' explicit statement (11:1) is softened by Josephus, who claims that Ptolemy set out as Alexander's ally but changed his mind after a plot against his life at Ptolemais (Josephus *Ant.* 13 §§106-8). If Ptolemy had really intended to help Alexander, he might have acted sooner, in year 165 (cf. 10:67); the present campaign appears to belong to year 167 (11:19). Ptolemy declined to condemn Jonathan for his work at Azotus (cf. 10:84), needing his support. Jonathan marched with him some two hundred kilometers from Joppa to the northern boundary of Coele-Syria and Phoenicia at the River Eleutherus before returning to Jerusalem in order to avoid direct conflict with Alexander. Ptolemy completed his march (now clearly a conquest) as far as Antioch's port at Seleucia, and here contacted Demetrius II, offering him marriage with Cleopatra, hitherto Alexander's wife (see above, p. 823), and accusing Alexander of trying to kill him (according to Josephus, *Ant.* 13 §§106-7, by the hand of Alexander's friend Ammonius). Inevitably this finally ruptured Ptolemy's relationship with Alexander. The climax of Ptolemy's march was his entry into Antioch, where (according to 1 Macc 11:13) Ptolemy put on the crown of Asia (in fact, a white woolen band, often visible on Seleucid coins); according to Diodorus, however, Ptolemy declined the Seleucid Empire, preferring to annex only Coele-Syria, probably for fear of inviting attack from Rome. His action forced immediate battle, which led to the death of both kings, Alexander probably at the hands of two of his generals while seeking sanctuary with Zabdiel, and Ptolemy from surgery upon his wounds. To judge from v. 18, the coastal towns had no time for Egyptian rule, and Egyptian involvement in Seleucid affairs ended here, as Demetrius took the throne in year 167 (autumn 146-145 BC; probably summer 145 BC).

Select Bibliography. Green, P. 1990, *Alexander to Actium: The Hellenistic Age,* London: Thames and Hudson, 435-52.

Jonathan and Demetrius II (11:20-37)

With Ptolemy and Alexander dead, it was time for political realignment, and Jonathan needed political assets. Jonathan therefore attacked the citadel; when he was ordered to desist (the pro-Seleucid party having complained) and report to Ptolemais, Jonathan had the siege continued, and with support from the elders and priests addressed Demetrius personally, winning his support. According to 11:27-28, Demetrius confirmed Jonathan's high priesthood and other honors, and consented to release Judea and the three added districts of Samaria (cf. 10:38) from tribute — if correct, an enormous concession, amounting to independence for Judea. But this summary is careless, as the following letter shows. The letter (quoting Demetrius's memorandum to his chief minister Lasthenes) confirms the transfer of the three districts to Judea from Samaria (11:34) (the three hundred talents of v. 28 may have been in lieu of the annual tribute from the three districts to Antioch). The punctuation and meaning of v. 34 are debated; the NEB and REB say that the three districts were transferred for the benefit of the priesthood ("those who offer sacrifice in Jerusalem"; cf. 10:38); the RSV and NRSV connect these words with the release from various taxes (11:34-35), including those on crops and fruits, and the salt and crown taxes (cf. 10:29-30). But Demetrius offers neither release from tribute nor the withdrawal of the citadel garrison, which were Jonathan's real aims.

The Appearance of Trypho (11:38-59)

Here as elsewhere the author skillfully inserts one episode (Demetrius's appeal to Jonathan for help against insurrection, 11:41-53) into another (the coup of Trypho and Antiochus VI, vv. 38-40, 54-59). Demetrius, perhaps on Lasthenes' advice (for Lasthenes was the unscrupulous general of the Cretan mercenaries in mind in v. 38; cf. on 10:67), dismissed his Syrian troops, so losing their loyalty. Seeing this, Trypho (the name means "self-indulgent"; he was born Diodotus), a former governor of Antioch, collected Antiochus, the young son of Alexander and Cleopatra Thea, from his guardian Imalcue (possibly Zabdiel's son; cf. 11:17) with the intention of making him king in place of his dead father Alexander.

Meanwhile (11:41-53) Jonathan requested removal of Seleucid troops from the citadel (clearly his attack [vv. 20-21] had failed) and from other fortresses in Judea; Demetrius agreed on condition that Jonathan would help him against his own rebellious troops. Unrest spread to the citizens of Antioch; the Jewish troops (among other mercenary troops, according to Diodorus 33.4.2-4) put down the disturbance with much bloodshed (hurling missiles on the crowds from the rooftops above, according to Josephus *Ant.* 13.135-40), won due credit from the king, and returned home with much booty. However, Demetrius failed to keep his promises and jeopardized his alliance with Jonathan (v. 53).

The final paragraph of this section begins with 11:54. Trypho appeared with Antiochus, who was proclaimed king as Antiochus VI Epiphanes Dionysus. Demetrius was ousted by his own troops, but remained in control of the eastern parts of the empire. In Syria, Trypho "captured the elephants and gained control of Antioch" (v. 56). Antiochus VI confirmed Jonathan as high priest and set him over the four districts. Three of these have been mentioned (Aphairema, Lydda, and Ramathaim; cf. 10:30, 38; 11:34); the fourth is a puzzle (possibly Akrabattene in Samaria; cf. 5:3). Jonathan is again given, with other gifts, the golden buckle, marking him out as one of Antiochus VI's "Kinsmen" as he was earlier one of Alexander's (cf. 10:89). But more importantly, Antiochus makes Simon governor of the whole coastal region, the Paralia, "from the Ladder of Tyre to the borders of Egypt" (cf. Cendebaeus, 15:38), just as his father had made Jonathan governor of the neighboring province of Judah (10:65). Presumably the Maccabees accept this new allegiance.

Select Bibliography. Fischer, T. 1972, "Zu Tryphon," *Chiron* 2:210.

Campaigns of Jonathan and Simon against Demetrius (11:60-74; 12:24-38)

These two sections clearly belong together; 11:74 is continued in 12:24, but the author has inserted between these two halves a curious account of alliances with Rome and Sparta, to which we will return. The two sections describe Jonathan's campaigns to Askalon and Gaza (11:60-62); Simon's capture of Beth-zur (vv. 63-66); Jonathan's campaign near the waters of Gennesaret (vv. 67-74); Jonathan's campaign in Syria (12:24-32); Simon's capture of Joppa (vv. 33-34); and, lastly, Jonathan's (and Simon's) construction work in Jerusalem and Judea. The editorial hand and the chiastic arrangement are obvious. Again, Jonathan and Simon work in cooperation, Simon in the south and Jonathan (apart from 11:60b-62a) in the north. In 11:67-76 Jonathan is in Galilee and in 12:24-32 in Syria, in each case apparently fighting Demetrius's troops. It seems unlikely that he would have returned to Jerusalem (11:74) only to set out immediately (12:25) for Syria within what appears to be the same season (though the author gives no dates); this must be an editorial arrangement to allow for the intervening diplomatic engagement with Rome and Sparta (also undated).

11:60 has Jonathan rather surprisingly operating within the whole province "beyond the river" (i.e., west of the Euphrates) with the help of "all the army of Syria" (presumably Trypho's troops), though there is no evidence of their presence in the following accounts. Jonathan ranges from Askalon (v. 60) to Damascus (v. 62), which he does not actually reach until 12:32. Askalon, a trading port, was always compliant; Gaza, on the borders of Egypt, was always resistant (it held out against Alexander the Great for two months). Simon captured Beth-zur (garrisoned by Seleucid troops; cf. 9:52; 11:41). Demetrius sent an army (foreigners, 11:68, 74, i.e., mercenaries) to Kedesh (cf. Judg 4:6; Tell Qades in the upper Jordan valley, north of the Sea of Galilee) against his new enemy; Jonathan marched to the plain of Gennesaret, on the northwest shore of the Sea of Galilee, and the armies met at Hazor (cf. Josh 11:10-11). Jonathan managed to turn the battle around after being ambushed, and the enemy fled. Judas's commanders Mattathias and Judas are otherwise unknown. Unless the campaign of 12:24-32 takes place in the following year (no dates are given), Jonathan probably (in spite of 11:74 and 12:25) continued directly to the region of Hamath on the River Orontes to tackle Demetrius's regrouped army ("he gave them no opportunity to invade his own country," v. 25). The Syrian army is hardly impressive (in spite of v. 24), and uses a well-known stratagem to retreat across the Eleutherus River, southwest of Hamath, to the coastal strip, which was under Demetrius's control. Abel (1949: 226) locates the Zabadeans northwest of Damascus.

Jonathan already controlled Joppa (10:75-76; cf. 11:6), but its loyalty was clearly doubtful. Simon now garrisons it, and later (13:11) expels its population to gain full control. Jonathan (now governor of Judea; cf. 10:65) has authority to convene the elders and plan military defenses. Jerusalem's walls, destroyed by Apollonius in 168 BC (1:32) and partly rebuilt in 152 BC (10:11), are now heightened and repaired (the name "Chaphenatha" remains unexplained); the blockade of the citadel marks the beginning of its end (cf. 13:49-52). Adida (12:38) lay between Modin and Lydda; control of it would help secure the route from Jerusalem to the garrison at Joppa.

Alliances with Rome and Sparta (12:1-23)

This section is clearly intruded into its present context (see above) in the author's usual way, and connects with 14:16-24 and 15:15-24. The author intertwines Maccabean dealings with Rome and Sparta, creating some confusion for the historian. Thus in 12:1-4 the author sketches Jonathan's mission to Rome to renew the friendship and alliance made in 161 BC (cf. 8:17-30), but in 12:2 adds a note mentioning sending "letters to the same effect" (renewing alliances?) to the Spartans and others; curiously, it is only in the letter to the Spartans (12:5-18) that the delegates to Rome are named (v. 16). This letter is surely a diplomatic fiction concocted by the author of 1 Maccabees; its description of constant prayer for the Spartans is insincere (vv. 11-12), and its reference to Jewish sufferings without any sign of understanding of recent Spartan difficulties in the Achean war both tactless and inappropriate (vv. 13-14). The reference to sending diplomats to Rome "and also to you" (v. 17) is equally tactless.

At the heart of this letter lies a reference to a letter sent "in time past" from the Spartan king Arius to the Jewish high priest Onias (12:7-8). The author then appends a copy of this letter (vv. 19-23); a slightly extended version of it appears in Josephus *Ant.* 12 §§225-27, which may suggest that it was known independently to Josephus and therefore perhaps derived from a source used by both 1 Maccabees and Josephus. However, this letter also has its problems. If King Arius is Arius I (309-265 BC), Onias must be Onias I, c. 300 BC, or perhaps Onias II. Arius I might possibly have been able to speculate about Jewish-Spartan kinship from Herodotus (*Hist.* 6.53; 2.91) and Hecataeus of Abdera (*History of Egypt,* c.

300 BC, preserved in Diodorus Siculus *Bib. Hist.* 40.3), but why Arius should have wanted to contact Judea, remote and subject to Ptolemy, is hard to say. Josephus identifies the addressee as Onias III (murdered 172 BC), which is more likely, except that there was no contemporary Spartan king called Arius (probably the Jewish writer used the name of the only Spartan king known to him). The references to Abraham (v. 21) and to reciprocal property rights (v. 23), apparently borrowing from 1 Kgs 22:4 or 2 Kgs 3:7, suggest a Jewish author. Such property arrangements seem most unlikely between Spartans and Jews, but they might be accepted as an understood fiction.

These letters are diplomatic inventions; knowledge of the latter prompted the author of 1 Maccabees to create the former to suit his purposes. The diplomatic contact to which they witness, however, was real. It was relatively common for Hellenistic cities to claim relationship on historical or legendary grounds (cf. examples in Dancy 1954: 166). If this letter was addressed to Onias III, his successor Jason might have found it useful when he fled to Sparta (2 Macc 5:9). In Hellenistic times, such travel and contact were regular; in Simon's time the Romans sent a letter of support for the Jews to the Spartans and other Mediterranean destinations (1 Macc 15:22-23).

Select Bibliography. Cardauns, B. 1967, "Juden und Spartaner: Zur hellenistisch-jüdischen Literatur," *Hermes* 95:317-24 • Ginsburg, M. S. 1934, "Sparta and Judaea," *CP* 29:117-22 • Katzoff, R. 1985, "Jonathan and Late Sparta," *AJP* 106:485-89 • Schüller, S. 1956, "Some Problems Connected with the Supposed Ancestry of Jews and Spartans and Their Relations during the Last Three Centuries B.C.," *JSS* 1:257-68.

On relations with Rome, see above, pp. 818-19.

Trypho Captures Jonathan (12:39-53)

Trypho's ambition to rule the empire is now clear (v. 39), and 1 Maccabees emphasizes Jonathan's potential danger to Trypho. Beth-shan (Scythopolis, 2 Macc 12:29-30) was an imposing city commanding an important route across the Jordan valley. Trypho's flattery is patent, but Jonathan was accustomed to accepting such honors from Trypho's predecessors (10:20, 62; 11:26-27) and to making political bargains at Ptolemais (10:59-65; 11:24-28), and accepted Trypho's proposals too readily (though not without some obvious precautions, v. 47). Trypho, however, had clearly prepared his ground at Ptolemais, whose people were hostile to the Jews (cf. 5:15; 2 Macc 6:8; 13:25). Trypho's attempt to destroy Jonathan's army, probably in the "great plain," that is, the valley of Jezreel from Beth-shan to Ptolemais, failed. All Israel mourns Jonathan (though he is not yet dead), as it did Judas (cf. 9:21); by contrast, all the nations around, as in 3:35 and 5:2, threaten to destroy Israel totally (cf. 13:6). "The poetic form of the sentence suggests that it is inserted more for dramatic than for historical purposes" (Dancy 1954: 170).

The Rule of Simon (13:1-53)

No date has been given since the accession of Demetrius II in year 167 (i.e., 145 BC; 11:19), probably because the author has nothing to record from the official Syrian archives for this period. The next date given is the removal of the Gentile yoke three years later in year 170 (i.e., 143 or 142 BC; 13:41). The events detailed in 1 Macc 11:20–13:40 presumably belong between these dates, but greater precision is difficult, not least because we are dependent on the author's arrangement of separate episodes. (For an attempt at dating Trypho's career, see Fischer 1972: 210.) If Jonathan's northern campaigns (11:63-74; 12:24-32) belonged to 144 BC, his capture was perhaps 143 BC, and his death in the winter (cf. 13:22) of 143-142 BC, but we cannot be sure. Simon would thus take over in summer or autumn 143 BC, which, for an era beginning autumn 312 or spring 311 BC, would be in year 169.

Simon gathers the people, and the author produces a speech underlining familiar themes such as devotion to the law and temple and the Maccabean contribution to the wars (13:4-5 assume the death of Jonathan as well as of Judas, Eleazar, and John). "I alone am left" reminds us of Elijah's words (1 Kgs 18:22). Simon's words in 13:6 and the people's response (vv. 8-9) echo Mattathias's final words in 2:67-68 and the appointment of Jonathan in 9:28-31. Jonathan was appointed by Judas's friends (9:28), but Simon by the whole people (13:8-9), an indication of the political change. Simon's first acts are to complete the fortification of Jerusalem and to make Joppa a secure military base and seaport by expelling the civilian population. This act heads the list of achievements in the eulogy of Simon (14:5).

Trypho invaded from his base at Ptolemais, probably in autumn 143 BC. Simon advanced to the recently fortified Adida (cf. 12:38). Trypho alleged that Jonathan had not paid his dues for appointments held, demanding a hundred silver talents and Jonathan's two sons as hostages. Simon had no choice but to meet the demand; he could not trust Trypho, but he dared not risk loss of public support at home (13:17-18). Trypho predictably retained Jonathan, and attempted to attack Jerusalem via Adora, a Hellenistic town southeast of Marisa in Idumea, but Simon marched to counter his attempts. (The Jews also held Beth-zur, the key to the southern approaches.) Those besieged and hungry in the citadel (v. 21; cf. 12:36) suggested that Trypho should attack through the Judean wilderness to the southeast, but he was prevented by a snowfall and marched on across the Jordan to Gilead. Jonathan (with his sons?) was finally killed in Baskama, whose location is unknown.

Jonathan (unlike Judas and Simon) receives no eulogy from 1 Maccabees, though he had ruled in various capacities for some eighteen years. By diplomatic skill he had won personal position and recognition, and with the military skills of Simon he had taken control of Beth-zur and Joppa and rebuilt the walls of Jerusalem. But his achievements were limited; he still paid tribute to Syria, and he could not oust the garrison in the citadel. He probably relied on Simon as his advisor (cf. 2:65). Simon rebuilt the family tomb in royal Hellenistic style (compare the later tombs of the kings or the Tomb of Absalom in Jerusalem, and the Nabatean monuments in Petra), with polished stone, pyramids, columns, trophies, and carved ships, the latter perhaps indicating Maccabean ambitions of emulating Solomon (cf. 1 Kgs 9:26-28; 10:11-12, 22). If the ships were to be visible at sea, some twenty kilometers away, the monument was very large; Goldstein (1976: 471) therefore translates "carved ships, intended to be seen by all who sailed the sea."

With Jonathan dead, the author at last turns his full attention to Simon. Simon's contribution has already been great, but his work now reaches its climax. While Trypho killed Antiochus VI and claimed the Seleucid crown (probably 142 BC; his first year of reign was 142/1 BC), Simon looked to Judea's defenses (13:33; these seem always to have been his special care) and approached King Demetrius II. Demetrius's reply is formally addressed both to Simon and to the elders and nation of the Jews (cf. 11:30). Simon is courteously addressed as high priest (perhaps Demetrius is thus quietly confirming the assumed appointment) and perhaps as Friend (for the Greek phrase is not the regular one, and the title does not usually appear in the address). Demetrius thanks them for gifts received, offers peace, and — the all-important clause — grants release from tribute. This declared Judea's independence from Seleucid rule. The grants (13:38) are perhaps the three districts transferred to Judea (11:34). The strongholds were probably at Joppa, Beth-zur, Adida, and elsewhere (13:33), and Demetrius was in no position to recapture them. The crown tax, with other taxes, had already been remitted (11:35), but apparently some was outstanding. The final clause apparently welcomed Jewish soldiers to the king's prestigious bodyguard.

The release from tribute — "the removal of the yoke of the Gentiles" — took place in year 170. (If crown tax and tribute are identical, the event may be referred to in *Megillat Ta'anit,* which says that the withdrawal of the crown tax from Judah and Jerusalem was celebrated on 27 Iyyar, i.e., 21 May.) Year 170 is probably to be reckoned on the basis of a Sel. Bab. era, either from spring 312 or spring 311 BC, and so year 170 here dates from either spring 143 or spring 142 BC. Simon actually took control on Jonathan's capture in the autumn of 143 BC, which would be the beginning of Sel. Mac. year 170, whose era began autumn 312 BC. How immediately the people realized that a new era of independence was dawning is hard to say because no contemporary documents or contracts (13:42) reflecting this appear to have survived. It should also be noted that Demetrius's letter said nothing about the citadel, and that Gazara remained a Syrian stronghold. Simon already held the positions of "high priest" (to which the author has added the adjective "great") and "commander"; the title "leader" *(hēgoumenos)* is perhaps to be identified with the "ethnarch" of 14:47. These titles are again Seleucid titles; Simon has not yet selected an independent styling.

The Capture of Gazara and the Capture of the Citadel (13:43-53)

Gazara is a correction for the Greek text's Gaza, which Jonathan had attacked (11:61) but not captured, and it remained independent of Judea until taken by Jannaeus in 96 BC (Josephus *Ant.* 13 §§358-64). Gazara (the ancient city of Gezer) occupied an important site between Joppa and Jerusalem. It had been garrisoned by Bacchides (9:52), and was an obvious thorn in the Judean side. The author's description of its capture emphasizes the inhabitants' wickedness and the Maccabean concern to suppress idolatry (cf. Judas's and Jonathan's treatment of Azotus, 5:68; 10:84). Simon settled loyal Jews in it, strengthened its fortifications, and built a house for himself there. Later his son John lived in Gazara (13:53; 16:1). Excavation there by Macalister (1902-9) revealed an inscription (from a prisoner?) calling for fire to descend on Simon's palace (Macalister 1912: 1:210-12).

Those besieged in the citadel also sued for peace, and Simon similarly expelled them and ritually cleansed the building. This major event is given a precise date — the twenty-third day of the second month of year 171, that is, early June 142 or 141, depending on whether one counts from spring 312 or 311 BC — and was to be celebrated annually (the date is listed in *Megillat Ta'anit*). 13:52 and 14:47 indicate that Simon and his men occupied the fortifications of the temple hill but settled a garrison in the citadel (Josephus *Ant.* 13 §217 and *J.W.* 1 §50 wrongly state that Simon demolished it). 13:53 introduces Simon's son, the later John Hyrcanus (cf. 16:1-24).

Select Bibliography. Macalister, R. A. S. 1912, *The Excavation of Gezer, 1902-1905 and 1907-1909,* London: Murray, vols. 1-3 • Schürer, E., rev. G. Vermes and F. Millar. 1973, *The History of the Jewish People in the Age of Jesus Christ (175 B.C.–A.D. 135),* Edinburgh: T&T Clark, 1:189-99 • Seger, J. D. 1976, "The Search for Maccabaean Gezer," *BA* 39:142-44 • Sievers, J. 1990, *The Hasmoneans and Their Supporters from Mattathias to the Death of John Hyrcanus I,* Atlanta: Scholars.

Capture of Demetrius (14:1-3)

The author uses his Seleucid sources to provide the date: year 172, that is, from autumn 141 BC. Demetrius was still master of most of the Seleucid Empire, Trypho's control being limited to the region of Antioch. The Parthians, however, had taken over Media and Persia in the mid-150s; in 141 BC Arsaces VI (= Mithridates I) invaded Mesopotamia and took Seleucia-on-Tigris. Demetrius, in spite of problems in the west, marched east and regained Babylonia, but after some early success further east he was captured and taken to Arsaces in Hyrcania (139 BC). Arsaces treated him well, with an eye to future political events. It was perhaps not until this point that Trypho proclaimed himself sole king (*pace* 1 Macc 11:54).

Eulogy of Simon (14:4-15)

This poetic eulogy crowns the account of Simon's career and balances that prefacing the work of Judas in 3:3-9. The author subsequently added a copy of an official decree in honor of Simon (14:25-49), further material about Jewish diplomacy with Rome and Sparta (14:16-24; 15:15-24), and an account of the threat from Antiochus VII (15:1-14; 15:25–16:10) before closing with the death of Simon (16:11-24) and a note about John Hyrcanus (16:23-24).

14:4-7 summarize Simon's political gains: he brought peace (v. 4), he captured the harbor of Joppa (13:11, but cf. 10:76 and 11:6), he "extended the borders" of Judea, presumably by settling Jews in Joppa and Gazara (but Jonathan had added three districts from Samaria by his diplomacy, cf. 11:34), and he occupied Gazara (13:48), Beth-zur (11:66), and the Jerusalem citadel (13:52). 14:8-15 present Simon's Judea in more idyllic and scriptural terms drawn from Lev 26:4; 1 Kgs 4:25; Ezek 36:33-36; Mic 4:4; Zech 8:4, and elsewhere. 1 Maccabees emphasizes Simon's care for law-abiding Jews and his destruction of renegades (cf. the work of the Hasideans and Mattathias in 2:42-48) and his benefactions to the sanctuary (14:15; cf. v. 42), but gives no details.

Select Bibliography. Neuhaus, G. O. 1974, *Studien zu den poetischen Stücken im 1 Makkabäerbuch,* Würzburg: Echter-Verlag.

Diplomacy with Rome and Sparta (14:16-24; 15:15-24)

These passages, separated by the official decree in Simon's honor (14:25-49) and the advent of Antiochus VII (15:1-14), belong together in content and continue the theme of 12:1-23. They help to disentangle the threads of Rome and Sparta. Thus in 14:16-24, the correspondence with Sparta (vv. 20-23) is clearly distinct from the surrounding verses, and the phrase "and as far away as Sparta" was inserted into v. 16 when vv. 20-23 were incorporated here. In 14:16-19, on hearing of Simon's succession, the Romans write on bronze tablets (these would normally be used for memorial plaques, not letters) renewing the established friendship and alliance (cf. 12:1, 3-4). (Such an initiative from Rome is generally regarded as highly unlikely.) Simon responds by sending his envoy Numenius (cf. 12:16) to Rome with an incredibly large offering of gold, inappropriate for such a small state, to Rome to confirm the alliance. The narrative so far is suspect on three counts. Numenius returns (15:15-24) with a letter announcing Rome's support of the Jews to various Mediterranean kings and countries. The letter, from one Lucius, a Roman consul, is clearly related to the senatorial decree proposed by the praetor Lucius Valerius and preserved by Josephus (*Ant.* 14 §§145-48), but dated by Josephus to the ninth year of Hyrcanus II (63-40 BC). If 1 Macc 15:14-24 is an original part of 1 Maccabees, written c. 100 BC, Josephus must have misdated the letter. A Lucius Valerius Flaccus was consul in 131 BC, and so praetor, probably c. 134 BC, which is too late for a decree at the beginning of Simon's reign (which seems to be confirmed by the mention of Roman approval for Simon's envoys in the decree belonging to Simon's third year, 14:40, if this passage was an original part of the decree). Josephus's attribution of the letter to L. Valerius Flaccus may thus also be suspect. Bickermann (1930: 358; cf. Timpe 1974: 133-52) suggested that the consul Lucius was Lucius Caecilius Metellus, consul in 142 BC; the date fits well enough with the death of Jonathan, probably spring 142 BC.

The sequence seems to be confused. The real sequence was probably as follows: the shield (perhaps of lesser value than that quoted, though Josephus's version of the letter gives a similar value of fifty thousand gold pieces) was sent with the original envoys, as both versions of the Roman letter (Josephus *Ant.* 14 §147; 1 Macc 15:17-18) suggest; in response the Romans renewed the alliance and advised the kings and countries of the fact. 1 Maccabees has confused matters by splitting the story into two halves, anticipating the arrival of the Roman response in Jerusalem in 14:19 (thus creating two arrivals of the renewal in Jerusalem), and misplacing the sending of the shield (v. 24). It was probably only when Numenius arrived in Rome, probably early summer 142 BC, with the shield and the request for treaty renewal that the Romans heard of the death of Jonathan (v. 16).

The Roman circular letter (15:22-24) is addressed to Ptolemy (i.e., Ptolemy VIII Euergetes II, 145-116 BC). Copies were sent to Demetrius II of Syria, Attalus II (159-138 BC) of Pergamum, Ariarathes V (162-131 BC) of Cappadocia, and Arsaces of Parthia (cf. 14:2). The remaining names are place names and well known apart from Sampsames (possibly Samsun on the Black Sea; Gk. *Amisos*). They are interesting as indicating both the extent of Roman interest and of the Jewish diaspora in the second century BC and (by their order) 1 Maccabees' limited sense of Mediterranean geography.

The letter to Sparta (14:20-23) continues into Simon's time the contacts apparently made in Jonathan's (cf. 12:2, 5-23). This letter is hardly any more authentic than that in 12:5-18, to which it is linked by the naming of the envoys in 15:22. The author is clearly much concerned to associate the Maccabean state with Spartans as well as Romans, perhaps because of their reputation for their laws and their military skills. The author's concern to treat the Romans and the Spartans together has left clear traces in the narrative both in 12:1-23 and in 14:16-24; 15:15-24 and is partly responsible for the confusions noted above.

Select Bibliography. See above, pp. 819, 826.

Official Honors for Simon (14:25-49)

These verses contain, according to the author, a copy of the record, publicly displayed on bronze tablets on Mt. Zion, of a proclamation honoring Simon. The initiative came from the people (14:25); the text appears to have been accepted by "the great assembly of the priests and the people and the rulers of the nation and the elders of the country" (v. 28). Very little is known of "the great assembly"; for another postexilic assembly see Ezra 10:9-14. The author claims to give the text of the decree (14:27b-45), which begins with a date (the eighteenth day of the month Elul, year 172, i.e., 13 September 141 or 140 BC, counting from spring 312 BC or spring 311 BC) that is the third year of Simon (cf. 13:41, where year 170 is Simon's first year). The phrase "in Asamarel" is unintelligible but is perhaps a corruption of a transliterated Hebrew title, "prince of the people of God." In 14:28 the personal reference "was proclaimed to us" reads strangely in a document otherwise cast in the third person; the original document probably began simply with the date.

Honorific decrees are well known from the Hellenistic world (and the presence of this one shows how much Jerusalem had learned from the Hellenistic world by 140 BC). They usually begin by recording the honorand's achievements, in clauses introduced by the preposition "whereas" *(epeide),* following this with the actual decree ("it seemed good to . . ."; Gk. *edoxe*). Simon's achievements are listed in 14:29-40, beginning with a clause introduced by "since" (v. 29; Gk. *epei*), but the following verses form a continuous narrative of Simon's achievements rather than a series of "whereases." They include a report that the people had already made Simon leader and high priest (v. 35), and that Demetrius had confirmed Simon in the high priesthood (v. 38), before giving the resolution of the Jews and their priests (v. 41) that Simon should be leader and high priest forever, and governor, with various powers. Presumably this is the major public and formal ratification of what has already happened. The final verses (vv. 46-49) report the direct speech of the decree as it affected the people and the priests.

1 Maccabees thus appears to be partly quoting, partly reporting the decree, and there are some indications that the author has developed the original text in the light of his own historical narrative. 14:27b-28, apart from the final phrase, are probably a direct quotation, as are vv. 29-34 (though the reference in v. 30 to Jonathan seems strange in a decree honoring Simon, and the author, who consistently shows Simon and Jonathan acting in tandem, may have imported it). V. 35 (which speaks of the action of the people rather than of Simon) interrupts the sequence of vv. 34 and 36, which clearly belong together, and vv. 38-40 record the action of Demetrius in confirming Simon's high priesthood, but the Jews would hardly wish to proclaim publicly the dependence of the office on a foreign king. V. 40 also betrays the author's interests; he wished to include reference to Simon's good standing with Rome, and achieves it by reporting it as part of Demetrius's motivation! This obvious insertion from the author has somehow affected the continuity of the text, for in the Greek v. 41 appears as a continuation of what Demetrius had heard.

The original document, therefore, contained a date (14:27-28), a general introduction (v. 29), a description of the political background (v. 31) (which refers to the earlier part of the Maccabean struggle but does not mention Judas), and an account of Simon's achievements (vv. 32-34, 36-37). (The reference to professionalizing the Jewish army in v. 32, not mentioned elsewhere, is particularly interesting; Simon, like other Hellenistic rulers, pays for this from his own funds.) There followed the actual decree that made Simon leader and high priest forever (i.e., probably for life), and governor, with power to appoint various officials and responsibility for the sanctuary (v. 41). (The repeated reference to this last role suggests some minor textual confusion.) Simon was to command general obedience, to be the authority behind all contracts, and to have the sole right to dress royally (cf. vv. 43, 44). Finally, his position is carefully safeguarded (vv. 44-45). However, Simon is not given the absolute power of a monarch, nor the promise of dynastic succession (even though copies of the decree are available to Simon and his sons, v. 49); there remains the possibility that a prophet might come and order otherwise (v. 41). The bronze tablets are displayed in the temple area, and copies are kept in the treasury.

Select Bibliography. Schürer, E., rev. G. Vermes and F. Millar. 1973, *The History of the Jewish People in the Age of Jesus Christ (175 B.C.–A.D. 135)*, Edinburgh: T&T Clark, 1:193-94.

Antiochus VII and Simon (15:1-14, 25-36)

Antiochus VI was dead, Demetrius II was captive in Parthia, and his younger brother Antiochus VII Sidetes (named after his former home Side in Pamphylia; cf. 15:3) probably claimed the Seleucid kingdom in 139 BC. His letter (vv. 2-9), probably from the Aegean, confirms privileges granted by his Seleucid predecessors to Simon (v. 5). He gives Simon the privilege of minting copper coins (within the empire only the king might mint gold or silver coins), but in fact this privilege is soon withdrawn (v. 27), and there is no certain evidence that Simon made use of it. Antiochus grants freedom to Jerusalem and the sanctuary (cf. the promise of Demetrius I in 10:35); Antiochus's original text may have meant rather that Jerusalem was to be "sacred and having the right of asylum" (Goldstein 1976: 514). Simon might retain his arms and military bases; debts would be cancelled (15:7-8). Clearly Antiochus assumes that Judea is still part of his empire (if Judea were independent, the various concessions, and especially the concession to mint coins, would be meaningless).

In year 174 (beginning autumn 139 BC), Antiochus invaded Syria, probably landing at Seleucia. According to Josephus (*Ant.* 13 §§221-22), Cleopatra Thea, currently wife of Demetrius and formerly of Alexander Balas, now invited Antiochus to marry her, which he did. Trypho fled south to Dor, on the coast south of Mt Carmel, where Antiochus besieged him by land and sea. The statement of 15:25 that Antiochus besieged Dor "for the second time" *(en tę̄ deuterą̄)* is strange, as there has been no suggestion that the first attempt had ended, and the phrase may have entered the text as a marginal note indicating resumption of the story after the author's typical intrusion of a different subject in 15:15-24.

The relationship between Simon and Antiochus is ambiguous. Antiochus assumes Simon's allegiance (15:2-9), and Simon, for all his independence, sends military aid (v. 26). Antiochus refuses it, cancels any former agreements, and sends Athenobius to bargain with Simon. Joppa, Gazara, and the citadel were indeed Seleucid possessions before Simon captured them, and Antiochus might rightly require their return, with lost tribute money, or compensation in lieu. These places did not fall, in Antiochus's view, into the category of Simon's strongholds (v. 7). The alternative of compensation suggests that Antiochus was open to negotiation. Simon entertains Antiochus's diplomat, and with deliberate provocation shows him the vessels given by Trypho's puppet Antiochus VI (cf. 11:58). Simon claims with some justification that the citadel (which must be meant in 15:33-34) was part of his people's inheritance, and that Joppa and Gazara, as Seleucid fortresses, had caused damage to the Jews and their land. Simon had a case, especially with regard to the citadel, but his offer of a hundred talents was derisory. Athenobius and Antiochus perhaps had some right to be angry.

Select Bibliography. Gera, D. 1985, "Trypho's Sling Bullet from Dor," *IEJ* 35:153-63.

The Campaign of Cendebeus (15:37–16:10)

While Trypho escapes by sea to Orthosia in Phoenicia (and ultimate death), pursued by Antiochus, his general Cendebeus is given command of the coastal region in place of Simon (cf. 11:59). Antiochus is firmly reasserting Seleucid control of the land. Cendebeus based himself at Jamnia (as Gorgias had, 5:58), and built up Kedron, perhaps the village of Qatra, seven kilometers south-southeast of Jamnia, as a forward base for attack on the high roads of Judea, in particular the main routes up into the hills.

At this point the author interrupts the story of Cendebeus to describe the transfer of power from Simon to his sons (16:1-4). His son John, strategically placed at the disputed fortress of Gazara (13:53), can inform Simon of Cendebeus's movements. Simon announces his retirement — if he was already wise in counsel at the beginning of the struggle (2:65), thirty years later he would have been well into his fifties, and his sons would be mature fighters. "My brother's" probably refers to Jonathan, with whom 1 Maccabees always links Simon. For Simon's words cf. 9:30; 13:8-9. The theme of the transfer of power within the Maccabean family runs through 1 Maccabees from beginning to end: Mattathias to his sons Simon and Judas (2:65-69), from Judas to Jonathan (9:28-31), from Jonathan to Simon (13:1-9), and from Simon to John (16:1-3, 23-24). As the author remarks, it was only through the Maccabean family that deliverance was given to Israel (5:62).

The account of the campaign raises several minor problems. In 16:4 the NRSV identifies the unnamed leader of the campaign as John, but many scholars believe Simon is still in control. Judas and John appear only in v. 9, where Judas is wounded and John then leads the pursuit. The campaign begins in Modein, where the Maccabean revolt started (2:15-28). After the descent to the plain and the crossing of a stream (1 Maccabees emphasizes the quality of leadership, 16:6), the armies meet. The Jewish tactics are original (which may support the view that Simon was in command); the cavalry are drawn up, not on either flank of the infantry but "in the center" of the infantry (v. 7), presumably to avoid their having to face the more experienced and heavier Seleucid cavalry on equal terms. (Goldstein [1976: 520] argues that the cavalry was not located in a single block in the middle of the infantry, but divided between smaller units of infantry along the line.) The surprising tactics apparently paid off, and Cendebeus's troops fled back to Kedron. V. 10 is difficult; Jonathan had already burned Azotus (cf. 10:84); perhaps this time he burned "them," that is, the towers (cf. Abel 1949: 280).

The Murder of Simon and His Sons (16:11-17)

One of Simon's daughters married a certain Ptolemy, son of Abubus. Ptolemy (Ptolemaios) is Greek in origin, and Abubus Semitic (cf. Eupolemos son of John, and Jason son of Eleazar, 8:17). Ptolemy's wealth, it is explained, came from Simon, whose wealth probably came from conquests and diplomatic gifts, as well as dues accruing to the high priest. Ptolemy had been appointed governor *(stratēgos)* over the Jericho region, presumably by Simon, but, ambitious for wider power, he had to remove Simon and his sons. It seems that, in spite of professions of retirement (16:1-3), Simon was still taking at least some major responsibility (v. 14). His son Judas has been mentioned (vv. 2, 9); Mattathias, hitherto unmentioned, was probably named after his grandfather, and might therefore have been the firstborn. The dating (the eleventh month, Shebat, year 177) is surely from a Jewish, not Seleucid, source and thus based on the spring era beginning either Nisan 312 or 311 BC; the date is thus either late January-February 135 or 134 BC. Dok is probably the fortress on the top of the "Mount of Temptation" above the spring 'Ain Duq, overlooking Jericho.

John Succeeds Simon (16:18-24)

Ptolemy sent information of these events to the king (Antiochus VII), which suggests that Judea's independence of the Seleucid Empire was still somewhat uncertain. Ptolemy at least was ready to serve under the Seleucids, perhaps recognizing that he did not have the personal authority to win over the country. He tried to assassinate his obvious rival, the remaining son of Simon, gain the support of the army by bribery, and occupy Jerusalem. Someone ran ahead to John at Gazara (some 55 kilometers as the crow flies), and, according to Josephus, John reached Jerusalem ahead of Ptolemy, who was driven away by the people when he tried to enter by another gate. The people supported John "because of his father's good deeds and the masses' hatred of Ptolemy" (Josephus *Ant.* 13 §229). Ptolemy retreated again to Dok, and after being besieged by John fled to Philadelphia (modern Amman).

The final verses of 1 Maccabees (cf. the end of Judas's career, 9:22) imitate the summaries familiar from 1 and 2 Kings. The walls completed by John may have been those rebuilt after their destruction by Antiochus VII (Josephus *Ant.* 13 §247; Diodorus Siculus *Bib. Hist.* 34.1.5). The author clearly thinks highly of John, but has no intention of writing an account of his life, which is apparently in the past, though his death is not mentioned. It has often been suggested that 1 Maccabees indirectly supports the Hasmonean rule of John Hyrcanus (who was not popular with everyone) by presenting such a glowing account of his father and uncles. Our author notes John's further achievements recorded in the annals of his high priesthood; any such annals were probably destroyed in 63 BC, or, if not then, in AD 70 when the Romans destroyed the temple.

Select Bibliography. Schürer, E. rev. G. Vermes and F. Millar. 1973, *The History of the Jewish People in the Age of Jesus Christ (175 B.C.–A.D. 135)*, Edinburgh: T&T Clark, 1:200-215 • Sievers, J. 1990, *The Hasmoneans and Their Supporters from Mattathias to the Death of John Hyrcanus I*, Atlanta: Scholars.

2 Maccabees

John R. Bartlett

INTRODUCTION

All modern texts and translations of 2 Maccabees depend basically on Codex Alexandrinus and Codex Venetus. These are Greek manuscripts from the fifth and eighth centuries respectively, descendants of the original Greek text of 2 Maccabees. The Old Latin (OL) version (second-third centuries) and the Vulgate (Vg) version (perhaps pre-Jerome) derive from the Greek, as does the Syriac translation. The Armenian translation has been influenced by the Latin tradition. For details see Abel 1949: liii-lix; Goldstein 1984: 124-28.

2 Maccabees consists of an abbreviated version (cf. 2:23) of a five-volume work by an otherwise unknown Jason of Cyrene. The original book of the abbreviator (or the "Epitomist") consists of 2 Macc 2:19–15:39, within which 3:1–15:37 is the Epitomist's reworking of Jason's five volumes. Certain passages are clearly the Epitomist's rather than Jason's work: the preface (2:19-32), the epilogue (15:38-39), and probably several reflective comments (4:17; 5:17-20; 6:12-17). Possibly 12:43-45 and 14:37-46, together with the story of the seven brothers and their mother (7:1-42), all emphasizing the resurrection belief, come from the hand of the Epitomist rather than from Jason (Habicht 1976: 173); Goldstein (1984: 49) thinks that the accounts of the deaths of Eleazar, the seven brothers, and their mother, and of Antiochus (6:18–7:42; 9:1-10) draw on a legendary source. Goldstein (1984: 35-37) also proposes a source (the *Memoirs* of Onias IV) favoring the Oniad priesthood. The four letters preserved in 11:16-37 are clearly not from the hand of Jason or the Epitomist; the letter credited to Antiochus in 9:19-27 may have been adapted or invented by the Epitomist from an archival model. The two letters of 1:1-9; 1:10–2:18 were prefixed from other sources at an early stage in the book's history.

Of Jason of Cyrene we know nothing except what can be deduced from the Epitomist's version. Cyrene in modern Libya was a cultural and intellectual center which included the poet Callimachus and the geographer Eratosthenes among its more famous citizens, but Jason, presumably a Hellenistic Jew, is more likely to have written his work in Alexandria (as the two pre-fixed letters suggest) than in Cyrene. As Jason's five volumes have not survived independently, it is impossible to know the full extent of his work (an *epitome* was customarily from a third to a fifth of the original; Doran 1981: 81), or how the Epitomist abbreviated it or selected his material, or how far the Epitomist has preserved Jason's viewpoint or overlaid it with his own. The Epitomist was happy to leave details to the original compiler and concentrate on "the outlines of the condensation" (2:28), preferring brevity to exhaustive treatment (2:31). He clearly had his own axe to grind; how far he was grinding Jason's axe is less clear. Goldstein argues, admittedly inconclusively (1976: 78-89; 1984: 82), that Jason wrote deliberately to contradict 1 Maccabees wherever possible, because it supported Hasmonean claims to royal and high-priestly legitimacy.

The Epitomist is less concerned with the factual details and sequence of events than with the preservation of Judaism and the Jewish nation. The Epitomist underlines the central importance of the temple, the law, sabbath observance, loyalty under persecution, God's mercy to his covenant people, God's miraculous power to save Israel, and a firm belief in resurrection. But "the Lord did not choose the nation for the sake of the holy place, but the place for the sake of the nation" (5:19). The nation's sufferings were punishments for apostasy (4:13-16), designed not to destroy but to discipline the people (6:12); salvation was achieved, however, by the faith and prayers of Judas and his followers (8:1-5; 15:7-11), which brought victory (15:20-27). The Epitomist, unlike the author of 1 Maccabees, is uninterested in political independence and the continuing Hasmonean dynasty, pointedly ignoring it; what matters is Judas's victory over the apostasy and blasphemy represented by Nicanor (cf. 15:20-36).

2 Maccabees has customarily been assigned to the genre of "pathetic" or "tragic" historiography, which attempted to entertain its readers by it contents and engage their emotions by its style and rhetoric. Doran has demonstrated that tragedy and history had long been interrelated, that there was no such separate thing as "tragic history" and that in fact the Epitomist (or Jason) was a typical Greek historian: "Herodotus enjoyed a good story, and even Thucydides evoked emotion in his readers" (Doran 1981: 86). 2 Maccabees' epiphanies (3:24-28; 5:2-4; 10:29-31; 11:8-11) and reflective digressions (4:16-17; 5:17-20; 6:12-17) have good precedents in Greek historiography. The author has Judaized his Greek models; Greek gods or heroes have become angels, the themes of Tyche (Fortune) or *hybris* (arrogance) have been taken over by the Jewish themes of sin followed by punishment, repentance, and salvation, the Greek deities are replaced by the covenant God of Israel, the righteous God who punishes but seeks reconciliation and turns martyrdom to resurrection. The center of 2 Maccabees' presentation is Jerusalem, its people and its temple, and their deliverance from the ungodly, whether Jewish or Gentile.

Jason was a historian, and his Epitomist, though

more concerned with religious loyalty than historical detail, has preserved much valuable information from him about the Seleucid Empire and its officers, and about the politics of Jerusalem in the reign of Antiochus IV. We might evaluate it better if we knew more of Jason. He perhaps wrote not too long after Judas's death in 161 BC. The date of the Epitomist is even harder to assess. The first pre-fixed letter is dated to 124 BC, but Momigliano's thesis (1975: 81-88) that 2 Maccabees was written to accompany this letter is not supported by any explicit reference from the author. Suggestions that Jason wrote to discredit or refute 1 Maccabees (Goldstein 1976: 72-89; 1984: 82; Toki 1977: 69-83) require a date after 1 Maccabees (whose date is itself uncertain; see p. 808). The views that the Epitomist wrote against the policies of John Hyrcanus I (Doran 1981: 112) or Jannaeus (Goldstein 1976: 85), if correct, give no basis for any precise dating. The Epitomist implies in 4:11 and 15:37 that in his time Jerusalem was not subject to any external power, which suggests a date before 63 BC when Pompey captured Jerusalem. The Epitomist wrote, probably in Jerusalem but possibly in Alexandria, between the publication of Jason's work (whether mid-second or late-second century BC) and 63 BC.

Select Bibliography. Fischer, T. 1992, "Maccabees, Books of," in *ABD,* 4.439-50 • Doran, R. 1979, "2 Maccabees and Tragic History," *HUCA* 50:107-14 • Doran, R. 1981, *Temple Propaganda: The Purpose and Character of 2 Maccabees,* Washington, D.C.: The Catholic Biblical Association of America • Momigliano, A. 1975, "The Second Book of Maccabees," *CP* 70:81-88; Toki, K. 1977, "The Dates of the First and Second Books of the Maccabees," *AJBI* 3:69-83.

COMMENTARY

Two Letters to Jews in Egypt (1:1–2:18)

The compiler's preface to 2 Maccabees appears at 2:19, and is itself prefaced by two festal letters from the people of Jerusalem and Judea encouraging fellow Jews in Egypt to keep what later became known as Hanukkah. Similar letters are found at 2 Chr 30:1-9 and Esth 9:20-22, 29-32. Jewish mercenaries had settled in Upper Egypt as early as the sixth century BC and by the fifth century had their own temple at Elephantine; Jewish captives had settled in Lower Egypt from the time of the first Ptolemies, and in the mid-second century Onias IV, son of high priest Onias III, built a Jewish temple at Leontopolis in the Delta region. The existence of this latter temple, highly irregular from the viewpoint of the Jerusalem hierarchy, may provide important background for the first letter. Most scholars, following Grimm (1857: 35), take the phrase "in the one hundred and eighty-eighth year" (1:9) as ending the first letter; some, following Torrey (1940: 119-50), take it as beginning the second and date the first letter to the year 169 (v. 7). Others have identified three letters here, the first ending with the date in 1:7a, the second with the date in 1:9, and the third beginning with 1:10.

The Letter of Year 188 (1:1-9)

This letter, from the whole Jewish community, has no one signatory. The opening verses, a lengthy prayer on behalf of the addressees (cf. Phil 1:9-11), are full of warmth but convey unmistakably that, seen from Jerusalem, the addressees are short in devotion to the law and need peace, reconciliation, and help in time of evil. The writers may be hinting that the Egyptian Jews should turn away from their allegiance to the illegal temple at Leontopolis, and so be reconciled both to God (cf. 7:33; 8:29) and to the Jerusalem community. If the date of this letter is year 188 (i.e., 125/124 or 124/123 BC), the time of evil and the prayer for peace may reflect the political difficulties between Ptolemy VIII and his sister Cleopatra II (whom the Jews supported).

1:7-8 appear to quote a letter written in the year 169, that is, probably 143 BC, when the Jews were subjects of Demetrius II and before they dated documents by Simon (cf. 1 Macc 13:42). In this letter they had referred to the first celebration of Hanukkah (cf. the lamplighting of 1:8) after the troubles brought about by Jason's revolt "from the holy land and the kingdom." This letter saw Jason primarily as a religious apostate; cf. 2 Macc 4:7-13, "ungodly, and no true high priest." Jason's burning of the gate (1:8; cf. 1 Macc 4:38) and bloodshed probably refer to the events of 2 Macc 5:5-10. After this quotation and flashback to the time of Jason, 1:9 comes to the point: "and now" (a regular formal feature of Hebrew correspondence), in the year 188, the Egyptian Jews are to keep "the festival of booths in the month Chislev" (cf. 2 Macc 10:5-8). Though held in mid-December, the celebration of the temple purification took on features of the autumn festival of Tabernacles or Booths.

The Letter to Aristobulus (1:10–2:18)

This letter, like the first one, is apparently from the Jews of Jerusalem and Judea to the Jews in Egypt, but the signatories include Judas, and the leading addressee is Aristobulus, who is said to be of the high-priestly family and a teacher of King Ptolemy. An Aristobulus was tutor to Ptolemy VI (180-145 BC); he was a philosopher who claimed that Greek philosophy derived its inspiration from Moses (the only known fragments are quoted by Clement of Alexandria *Strom.* 5.97.7).

The letter thanks God for driving out those who fought against Jerusalem and for bringing judgment upon Antiochus (1:11-17). It invites the addressees to celebrate the temple purification ("the festival of booths and the festival of the fire") (v. 18), and explains this fire's origin by reference to legends about Nehemiah and Jeremiah, to the fire consuming Solomon's sacrifice at the eight-day dedication of his temple (2 Chr 7:1, 8-9), and to the heavenly fire consuming offerings in the wilderness (Lev 9:24). These things had been recorded in the (temple) archives (2:13; cf. 2:1) and in the memoirs of Nehemiah (2:13), whose concern for books is also credited to Judas (2:13-15). The letter ends by encouraging the addressees to observe the festival, noting that God has saved his people and returned the inheritance, the kingship, the priesthood, and the consecration to all, and hoping for the return of the Jewish diaspora to God's holy place (2:16-18).

If this letter is authentic (Wacholder 1978: 89-133; Fischer 1980: 86-100), it belongs to the period between the recapture and rededication of the temple in 165 or 164 BC (see above, pp. 813-14) and the death of Judas. But it is doubtful that this letter, with its back reference to Judas's collection of books lost on account of the war (2:14) and its claim that God has returned the land, the kingship, the priesthood, and the consecration (2:17), could possibly date from those difficult days (cf. Goldstein 1984: 188), when the land was under Seleucid control, there was no Jewish monarchy, and the high priests Menelaus and Alcimus were anathema to the Hasmoneans. Time must also be allowed for the development of the biblical and legendary associations of the festival so visible in this letter. Goldstein (1984: 159-60; but see Doran 1981: 11-12) argues that the festival, mentioned directly only in 1:18 and 2:16, was not the principal focus of interest in this letter; the real concern was rather to support the holiness of the Jerusalem temple against the challenge from Onias IV's temple at Leontopolis. Thus the Jerusalem temple could claim possession of the genuine altar fire, restored by Nehemiah. Goldstein believes the letter was written at a crisis time for Egyptian Jews, in 103 BC, when their protectress Cleopatra III was under pressure from the invasion of Ptolemy IX. The letter was addressed appropriately to Aristobulus as a representative of the Oniad house (the Leontopolis temple being founded by Onias IV).

However, the festival of purification, mentioned at the beginning and end of the central portion of the letter, is clearly the focus for the letter writer, who is demonstrating for Jewish readers the festival's links with former temple rededications under Nehemiah and Solomon, and offering an important precedent in an event in the foundational wilderness period (cf. 2:10-11). The editor, who associated this letter with the first letter (1:1-9) and with the following abridgement of Jason of Cyrene's work (which begins with a reference to the purification of the temple and the dedication of the altar, cf. 2:19), clearly thought that its subject was the festival of purification. The date of the letter remains uncertain unless, as Torrey thinks, the year 188 (ch. 1:9) should be associated with it, but the reference to the restoration of land and kingship (2:17) might indicate a date in the early years of Jannaeus (103-76 BC), who put the title "king" on his coins and enlarged his kingdom to its biblical boundaries.

Some details of the letter require explanation. Antiochus IV died having fallen ill after an abortive attempt at raiding the temple of Artemis (a Greek equivalent of the Mesopotamian Nanaea, goddess of love and fertility) in Elymais (Polybius *Hist.* 31.9; cf. 1 Macc 6:1). The writer (1:13-17) has improved the story, perhaps building on Antiochus's sacred marriage to the goddess Atargatis at Bambyce (Mørkholm 1966: 132). The postexilic temple and altar were built long before Nehemiah came to Judah in 444 BC; the origin of this legend is unknown. Jonathan (v. 23) may have been taken from Neh 12:11. The prayer of 1:24-29 is a good example of Second Temple prayer; the petition for the gathering of the diaspora is reflected in the final words of the letter (2:18). The Persian king's interest in the volatile liquid is matched by a story that Alexander the Great experimented with it, nearly killing a boy (Strabo *Geog.* 16.1.15). The name "nephthar" derives from the Akkadian word *naptu;* the dubious etymology "purification" (1:36; cf. Goldstein 1984: 181; Doran 1981: 9) helps link the story with the theme of the festival. The Jewish leader Nehemiah is credited with discovering this valuable substance, as in other Jewish Hellenistic writings Abraham is the founder of arithmetic and astronomy and Moses the inventor of naval, architectural, and military devices. The legend of Jeremiah's preservation of the ark from the preexilic temple appears in Eupolemus c. 160-150 BC (Bartlett 1985: 71); other legends about Jeremiah have been preserved in the third-second-century-BC *Letter of Jeremiah* (of which 2:3 is virtually a summary) and the later *Paralipomena of Jeremiah.* The origin of the information about the libraries of Nehemiah and Judas (vv. 13-14) is not clear; essentially the writer is claiming support for his story. The reference is interesting for our knowledge of the development of the Hebrew canon in the second century BC. The memoirs of Nehemiah are presumably our book of Nehemiah in some form. The books about the kings and prophets may be 1 and 2 Kings and the writings of David the Psalms, but the "letters of kings about votive offerings" remain unidentified — possibly the Persian documents preserved in Ezra 1–7.

Bibliography. Bartlett, J. R. 1985, *Jews in the Hellenistic World,* Cambridge Commentaries on Writings of the Jewish and Christian World, 200 BC to AD 200, Cambridge: Cambridge University • Bickermann, E. J. 1933, "Ein Judischer Festbrief vom Jahre 124 v. Chr. (II Macc. 1.1-9)," *ZNW* 32:333-54 (= E. J. Bickermann, 1980, *Studies in Jewish and Christian History,* Leiden: Brill, 2:136-58 • Doran, R. 1981, *Temple Propaganda: The Purpose and Character of 2 Maccabees,* CBQMS 12, Washington, D.C.: The Catholic Biblical Association of America • Fischer, T. 1980, *Seleukiden und Makkabäer,* Bochum: Studienverlag Brockmeyer • Grimm, C. L. W. 1857, *Das zweite, dritte und vierte Buch der Makkabäer,* in O. F. Fritzsche, ed., Kurzgefasstes exegetisches Handbuch zu den Apokryphen des Alten Testaments, Leipzig: Hirzel • Torrey, C. C. 1940, "The Letters Prefixed to Second Maccabees," *JAOS* 60:119-50 • Wacholder, B. Z. 1978, "The Letter from Judah Maccabee to Aristobulus: Is 2 Maccabees 1.10–2.18 Authentic?" *HUCA* 49:89-133.

The Preface to the Abridgement of Jason's Five Volumes (2:19-32)

Not all biblical authors reveal much of themselves, but the author of 2 Maccabees, like the authors of Ecclesiasticus and of the Third Gospel, introduces the work to the reader in a preface. The author (often called the Epitomist, i.e., abbreviator) claims that for the reader's pleasure and profit he has worked hard (2:24-27). Similarly the grandson of Jesus son of Sirach (Ecclesiasticus, Prologue) speaks of his diligence and labor in translation, the evangelist Luke (Luke 1:3) of his careful investigation, and the Greek historian Thucydides of the labor involved in sifting different accounts of events (*Hist.* 1.23).

Our author begins directly by picturing for the reader the contents of the work. Five themes or *topoi* are listed: the story of Judas Maccabeus and his brothers, the purification of the temple (already underlined by the two prefixed letters, 1:1–2:18), the dedication of the altar, the wars against Antiochus IV and V, and the divine epiphanies that inspired those who fought for Judaism (e.g., 3:23-40). These, like the contrast between "those who fought for Judaism" and "the barbarian hordes," and the liberation of Jerusalem (2:21), are themes to attract the reader, not a synopsis or précis of the book. (To a Greek, *barbaroi* were those who spoke a non-Greek language; to a Greek-speaking Jew, the word clearly carried further connotations. Abel [1949: 311] notes the author's audacity in contrasting Jews, not Greeks, with barbarians.) The work is an abridgement of the "flood of statistics" and "mass of material" (though the Greek phrases carry no pejorative overtones) which made up Jason of Cyrene's five-volume history. Who Jason was and exactly what his history comprised we do not know. He probably worked in Jerusalem, where his sources would be available, and he was known in Jerusalem (where he was not the only Jason; cf. Jason the high priest) by his place of origin, the important city of Cyrene (in modern Libya), which had a large Jewish population (cf. 1 Macc 15:23; Mark 15:21) and was the home of the geographer Eratosthenes (276-194 BC) and the poet Callimachus (c. 310-240 BC). We know even less of Jason's abbreviator, except that he was Greek-speaking Jew and had a sense of Greek style and rhetoric. He compared himself to Jason of Cyrene as a decorator to a master builder (2:29), though his point here is that the latter must attend to the details of the whole structure, and the former only to highlighting the main points. For the abbreviator's final comment on his work, see his conclusion (15:38-39).

Select Bibliography. See Introductions to commentaries by Abel, Bartlett, Goldstein, Grimm, and Habicht listed in the Bibliography • Doran, R. 1981, *Temple Propaganda: The Purpose and Character of 2 Maccabees,* Washington, D.C.: The Catholic Biblical Association of America.

The Abridgement of Jason's Work (3:1–15:36)

The author arranges his abridgement clearly into two similarly structured parts, each divided into three sections, as follows:

Part I (a): Attacks on the Jewish Temple and Religion under Seleucus IV and Antiochus IV; Antiochus's threat to the Temple and Persecution of the Jews (3:1–6:17)
(b): The Martyrdoms of Eleazar and the Seven Brothers (6:18–7:42)
(c): The Defeat of Nicanor, the Death of Antiochus, and the Purification of the Temple (8:1–10:9)

Part II (a): Attacks on the Jews under Antiochus V and Demetrius I: Nicanor's Threat to the Temple (10:10–14:36)
(b): Suicide of Razis (14:37-46)
(c): The Defeat of Nicanor, the Death of Nicanor, and the Celebration of Nicanor's Day (15:1-36)

Part I (a): Attacks on the Jewish Temple and Religion under Seleucus IV and Antiochus IV; Antiochus's Threat to the Temple and Persecution of the Jews (3:1–6:17)

The Story of Heliodorus (3:1-40)

This episode illustrates well the Epitomist's artistic, religious, and historical emphases. It is similar to other accounts from the Greek or biblical world of deities appearing to defend their city (Doran 1981: 47-48). The story begins with the holy city peaceful and law-abiding under a pious high priest (Onias III; cf. 15:12), with Seleucus IV (187-75 BC) continuing Antiochus III's policy of contributing to the expense of the sacrificial system (see Josephus *Ant.* 12 §§138-44), as had Persian kings in earlier times (cf. Ezra 7:20-24). The city, high priesthood, and temple are as they should be, and the Seleucid regime is friendly. Trouble begins with a certain Simon. The Greek texts and the main Latin texts give his tribe as Benjamin (so NRSV), but some Latin texts and the Armenian tradition connect him with the priestly family of Bilgah (1 Chr 24:14; Neh 12:5, 18). A man from such a priestly family would be more likely than a non-priestly Benjaminite to become *prostatēs* (chief administrator) of the temple (a verb from the same root is used to describe the powers of the high priest Simon in 1 Macc 14:47). Simon's importance is also shown by his dispute with the high priest over the administration of the market (3:4); the high priest naturally had an interest here because large numbers of animals were required for the temple sacrifices. Given the financial implications, the scope for disagreement was inevitably wide. What really brought trouble to Jerusalem was Simon's report of the matter to the governor of the province, Apollonius of Tarsus. ("Tarsus" here is a correction of the Greek *tharsiou* or *thrasaiou,* translated "son of Tharsios/Thrasaios," made on the grounds that the governor was not Apollonius son of Tharsios but Apollonius son of Menestheus [4:4, 21], but it is possible that this was a later governor.) Simon pointed to monies in the Jerusalem temple treasury over and above the account for sacrifices. Seleucus, on hearing this, sent his chief minister (no less) to confiscate excess funds (he would not wish to alienate the Jews by clawing back money he had given for sacrifices, or taking money legitimately dedicated to temple purposes).

On Heliodorus's arrival in Jerusalem, the high priest accused Simon of misrepresentation, explaining that apart from properly accountable temple funds, the only other monies were private deposits held for widows and orphans, and the personal funds of Hyrcanus, son of Tobias, the son of Joseph of the Tobiad family. (Joseph had been a tax collector for Ptolemy III Euergetes of

Egypt, 246-221 BC [cf. Josephus *Ant.* 12 §§160-222; Tcherikover 1966: 128-29]. The ruins of a palace or temple associated with this family [cf. Josephus *Ant.* 12 §§229-35] still exist at ʾIraq el-Emir 20 km. west of modern Amman; the name Tobiah is inscribed beside two cave entrances on the cliff face nearby.) The inviolability of temples would hardly be a deterrent to a dynasty notorious for robbing temples, and Heliodorus arranged to inspect these funds.

So far 2 Maccabees tells a totally credible story, which may conceal deeper political rivalries below the surface. Onias and Hyrcanus probably had Egyptian rather than Seleucid sympathies, and Simon may have been exploiting them. However, 3:14b-21 evidently convey an overly dramatic picture of the response in Jerusalem, and vv. 22-34 resolve the crisis by divine intervention. The text appears to combine two versions of the story (though see Doran 1981: 20-21). In one version, Heliodorus and his bodyguards are confronted by a magnificent, rearing horse and a terrifying, golden-armored rider (vv. 24-25; the author of 2 Maccabees promises such appearances [2:21] and makes regular use of the apparition of horse and rider with golden weapons or accoutrements; cf. 5:2-4; 10:29-30; 11:8); in the other version (3:26) Heliodorus is beaten unconscious by two strong young men ("gloriously beautiful and splendidly dressed") who reappear (vv. 33-34) to tell Heliodorus that he has been saved by Onias's concern for him and then vanish. This latter story may be nearer the truth; the high priest (v. 32) perhaps rightly feared the king's suspicions of foul play, duly prompted by Simon (4:1). Onias plays an important role as an intercessor (the spiritual quality of an intercessor was important; cf. 15:14 and Jer 15:1), and as high priest, like any priest, he could make expiation by means of a sin offering for the unintentional sin of a ruler (Lev 4:22-26).

Heliodorus, duly chastened, returned to the king declaring the power of God, as instructed (3:34). Heliodorus is made to pass ironic judgment both on himself (for it was Heliodorus who later killed Seleucus IV) and on the power of the Jewish God (vv. 37-39; cf. Nicanor, 8:36, and Antiochus, 9:17). The Epitomist indicates the end of the episode (3:40).

Select Bibliography. Bickermann, E. J. 1939-44, "Héliodore au Temple de Jérusalem," *Annuaire de l'Institut de Philologie et d'Histoire Orientales et Slaves* 7:5-40 (= 1980, *Studies in Jewish and Christian History,* Leiden: Brill, 2:159-91) • Doran, R. 1981, *Temple Propaganda: The Purpose and Character of 2 Maccabees,* CBQMS 12, Washington, D.C.: The Catholic Biblical Association of America • Tcherikover, V. 1959, *Hellenistic Civilization and the Jews,* Philadelphia: The Jewish Publication Society of America; Jerusalem: The Magnes Press, The Hebrew University • Zayadine, F. 1997, "ʿIraq el-Amir," in E. M. Meyers, ed., *The Oxford Encyclopedia of Archaeology in the Near East,* Oxford and New York: Oxford University, 3:177-81.

Simon and Onias (4:1-6)

In spite of the closure to the Heliodorus episode, this next section picks up the theme begun in 3:4 and suggests serious political undercurrents. Ch. 4 is perhaps the section of the book most discussed by scholars because it contains much information about the political background of the Maccabean rebellion not given in 1 Maccabees. In the absence of independent sources offering a cross check, the historian's problem is how to assess its accuracy and allow for its particular bias. In v. 1 the author almost certainly means that Simon (as chief administrator of the temple) was slandering Onias (the high priest) to his fellow Jews, probably to turn the spotlight from himself. The author's attitudes toward Onias and Simon respectively are clear (vv. 2-3); what murders were committed we do not know. Onias, realizing that the governor Apollonius (the description "son of Menestheus" here is a correction of the Greek based on v. 21 below; cf. also 3:5) supported Simon, appealed to the king in person; the author defends his motives (4:5-6). Leaving Jerusalem at this stage, however, was a political error.

The High Priesthood and Reforms of Jason (4:7-17)

In 175 BC, Heliodorus killed Seleucus IV, and Seleucus's brother Antiochus intrigued his way into the kingdom (cf. Dan 11:21), bypassing the real heir, Seleucus's son Demetrius, who was a hostage in Rome, and in turn assassinating Heliodorus, his subsequent deputy Andronicus (cf. 4:31, 38), and Seleucus's other son, Antiochus's own nephew and co-regent Antiochus. He took his title "Epiphanes" in 173/172 BC (Mørkholm 1966: 48).

Onias's brother Jason (the name was adopted by Jews as a Greek version of the Hebrew for Joshua) approached the king (whether by letter or in person is uncertain; Gk. *enteuxis,* 4:8, could suggest either), offering to increase the annual tribute from three hundred talents of silver annually (for this figure see Goldstein 1984: 227) to 360, and to add a further eighty talents (presumably annually) from some other source. This would be to impose a considerable burden on a poor state like Judah, whose revenue depended on agricultural produce, possibly supplemented by earnings from pilgrims to Jerusalem. Jason, however, probably had a realistic eye for financial affairs, as his offer of 150 talents for authority (v. 9) — presumably by virtue of office — to establish a gymnasium and ephebeum shows. (2 Maccabees suggests that this proposal came from Jason alone; 1 Macc 1:11-15 attributes it to "certain renegades" and "some of the people.") A gymnasium provided a wide range of educational activities, including physical training. The ephebeum, originally a department of the gymnasium where the young men *(epheboi)* trained in military skills, was the entrée to citizenship for upper-class young males (cf. 4:12), "the noblest of the young men." Jason probably hoped that he or the city would profit from this development, as also from his proposal "to enroll the people of Jerusalem as citizens of Antioch" (v. 9). This meant either that a privileged few would be enrolled as "Antiochian citizens from Jerusalem" (cf. 4:19), forming a separate corporation *(politeuma)* within the wider population, or that the adult men of Jerusalem would be turned into citizens of a new Greek city called "Antioch at Jerusalem," with all that might imply for the city's status and privileges within the wider Greek world. Either way, Jason and his supporters wanted a new constitution, with power in the hands of the aristocracy, in which the priests would be well represented (as they were in the gymnasium, v. 14).

Such a change could be interpreted in different ways, and the author makes his views clear in 4:10-17. (For John, father of Eupolemus, and the alliance with Rome, see on 1 Macc 8:17.) The "existing royal concessions to the Jews" set aside by Jason (4:11) are probably those referred to in Antiochus III's letter to Ptolemy, governor of Coele-Syria and Phoenicia, preserved in Josephus *Ant.* 12 §§138-44, the most important concession being that "all the members of the nation shall have a form of government in accordance with the laws of their country" (*Ant.* 12 §142, Loeb trans.). There were also tax concessions for the senate, priests, scribes, and temple singers; a general three-year exemption for inhabitants and returning residents; and freedom and restoration of property for Jews recently enslaved. An additional decree supported Jewish laws protecting the holiness of the temple and the city of Jerusalem. But which of these concessions did Jason abolish? The institution of the gymnasium ("right under the citadel," i.e., south of the temple area; see above, pp. 808-9) was not in conflict with Jewish law. Did the enrollment of the population as "citizens of Antioch" imply the abolition of government in accordance with Jewish law? There is no evidence that Jewish law ceased to be constitutional until Antiochus IV's decree in 168 or 167 BC. 2 Maccabees shows little evidence of "new customs contrary to the law"; it is unlikely that Jews (especially the priests) exercised naked in Jerusalem; presumably those who tried to conceal their circumcision were preparing for participation in Hellenistic games abroad (see Goldstein 1984: 229-30). However, 2 Maccabees probably reflects the feelings of the conservative Jew confronted by the more open Hellenistic city ethos. The author uses or even invents (v. 13) a neologism, *hellenismos*, "imitation of the Greeks," to describe what he meant (cf. *Ioudaismos* in 2:21).

Select Bibliography. Bickermann, E. 1937, *Der Gott der Makkabäer,* Berlin: Schocken/Judischer; ET 1979, *The God of the the Maccabees,* by H. R. Moehring, Leiden: Brill • Bickermann, E. 1988, *The Jews in the Greek Age,* Cambridge, Mass., and London: Harvard University • Cohen, G. M. 1994, "The 'Antiochenes in Jerusalem.' Again," in J. C. Reeves and J. Kampen, eds., *Pursuing the Text: Studies in Honor of Ben Zion Wacholder on the Occasion of His Seventieth Birthday,* JSOTSup 184, Sheffield: Sheffield Academic, 243-59 • Bringmann, K. 1983, *Hellenistische Reform und Religionsverfolgung in Judäa,* Göttingen: Vandenhoeck und Ruprecht • Grabbe, L. L. 1994, *Judaism from Cyrus to Hadrian,* London: SCM • Grabbe, L. L. 2002, "The Hellenistic City of Jerusalem," in J. R. Bartlett, ed., *Jews in the Hellenistic and Roman Cities,* London and New York: Routledge, 6-21 • Hengel, M. 1974, *Judaism and Hellenism,* London: SCM • Millar, F. 1978, "The Background of the Maccabaean Revolution: Reflections on Martin Hengel's Judaism and Hellenism," *JJS* 29:1-21 • Mørkholm, O. 1966, *Antiochus IV of Syria,* Copenhagen: Gyldendalske • Tcherikover, V. 1959, *Hellenistic Civilization and the Jews,* Philadelphia: The Jewish Publication Society of America; Jerusalem: The Magnes Press, The Hebrew University.

Events of Jason's High Priesthood (4:18-21)

The new situation introduced by Jason is illustrated by the behavior of the Jewish envoys at the games held at Tyre in honor of the god Melkart (Gk. Hercules), to whom the competitors would sacrifice on the opening day. The date is unknown but is probably between 174 and 172 BC. These envoys are Antiochian citizens of Jerusalem but scruple to offer sacrifice to Melkart and offer the three hundred drachmas (a drachma was the daily wage for a workman) to the city for its shipbuilding. Jason's personal policy is unknown; there is no evidence that he quarreled with the envoys' decision.

4:21-23 touch on Antiochus's relations with Egypt. The event of v. 21 (*prōtoklisia;* the meaning of the word is debated) was probably a banquet at which the young Ptolemy VI Philometor made his first formal royal appearance rather than a coronation. The Seleucid governor of Coele-Syria and Phoenicia reported back to Antiochus his observations on Egypt's plans; Philometor's ministers, Eulaios and Lenaios, were reasserting Egypt's rights to Coele-Syria and Phoenicia lost to the Seleucids at the battle of Paneion in 200 BC. Antiochus, "for his own security" (v. 21), promptly made his presence felt in Joppa and Jerusalem, where he was loyally welcomed by a torchlight procession. The people of Jerusalem seem to have accepted Antiochus and Jason happily enough.

Menelaus and Lysimachus (4:23-50)

Simon had caused trouble for Onias (3:4; 4:1), and now Simon's priestly brothers Menelaus and Lysimachus caused trouble for Onias's brother Jason. 2 Maccabees makes clear that rivalries between priestly families played their part in the origin of the Maccabean rebellion. Menelaus and Lysimachus were well-known Greek names (Menelaus was king of Sparta and husband of Helen of Troy; Sparta was the intended final refuge of the high priest Jason, 5:9). Probably in 172 BC (after holding office for three years), Jason sent Menelaus to Antiochus to settle financial matters, but Menelaus followed Jason's example and made a larger bid for office, raising the earlier offer by three hundred silver talents. When he failed to keep up the regular payments, he and the captain of the citadel, who had the responsibility of collecting the tribute for the king, were summoned to Antioch, leaving deputies in Jerusalem. It was at this point that things began seriously to go wrong.

Tarsus (famous as Paul's home city) and Mallus were in Cilicia, across the Gulf of Iskanderun from Antioch and Seleucia. They objected to being given as a gift to a woman. Cities were often given by patrons to clients; Demetrius I offered Ptolemais to Jerusalem (1 Macc 10:39), Alexander Balas gave Ekron to Jonathan (1 Macc 10:89), and Mark Antony gave Jericho to Cleopatra. The king's deputy, Andronicus, is probably the Andronicus who murdered Seleucus IV's son and heir for Antiochus (Diodorus Siculus *Bib. Hist.* 30.7.2). Menelaus's theft of the temple vessels aroused Onias's public protest from his sanctuary at the temple of Apollo and Artemis at Daphne and led to his death; subsequent sacrilegious thefts of temple vessels led to riots in Jerusalem and the death of Lysimachus (4:32-39). Some of the vessels were given to Andronicus, perhaps by way of bribery, and others were sold in the coastal cities, presumably to provide money to pay what was owed to Antiochus. Lobbied by the Jews of Antioch (a Jewish community had existed there from early Seleucid times), the king had Andronicus humiliated (the purple robe denoted his status as King's Friend; cf. 1 Macc 10:20) and executed. The emphasis on appropriate retribution (4:38) is typical of 2 Maccabees (cf., e.g., the cases of Jason, 5:10; Nicanor, 8:35; Antiochus, 9:28; Menelaus, 13:8; and again Nicanor, 15:32-33).

It is usually assumed that the incident of 4:39-42 took place in Menelaus's absence in Syria. The text does not say this, but rather suggests that Lysimachus was his brother's agent in a continuing series of sacrilegious acts. Menelaus's complicity was known (vv. 39, 43). That the temple robber (apparently but not explicitly Lysimachus) was killed near the temple treasury in the women's court of the temple suggests that Lysimachus was attacked in an enclosed space, which may help explain why the crowd with only stones, blocks of wood, and ashes from the altar fire could put to flight armed soldiers. Even so, three thousand men seems excessive. The author never misses an opportunity to improve the story.

The case against Menelaus, the high priest, was brought by three delegates of the Senate (this council of elders is named in contemporary documents; cf. 1 Macc 14:28; 2 Macc 11:27). This fact, and the fact that Menelaus would have been lost without bribery, show that under Seleucid rule a high priest could not take immunity for granted and that Menelaus was not a popular choice. Ptolemy, son of Dorymenes, was a successor to Apollonius as governor of Coele-Syria and Phoenicia (cf. 8:8; 1 Macc 3:38); he might have put to the king that a verdict against Menelaus would weaken the king's authority in Judah, and that any replacement for Menelaus might be less loyal to Seleucid interests and financially less profitable. The author comments that Menelaus remained in office "because of the greed of those in power" (4:50). The Tyrians (known for their interest in profit) and the Scythians (known as the greatest barbarians in behavior) come out well by comparison.

Jason Attempts a Coup (5:1-10)

The struggle between the two priestly families continues, with Onias dead on the one side and Lysimachus on the other. There must have been considerable bitterness between the contestants, which may explain Jason's subsequent assault. 2 Maccabees dates this event to the period of Antiochus's second invasion of Egypt (5:1), in 168 BC (see above under 1 Macc 1:16-40). Some scholars date Jason's attack and Antiochus's response (2 Macc 5:11-14) to 169 BC, identifying it with the event of 1 Macc 1:20; this passage, however, refers to Antiochus's pillage of the temple only, not to the major sack of Jerusalem, which all sources show happened after Antiochus's humiliating eviction from Egypt by the Romans in 168 BC (Dan 11:30-31; 1 Macc 1:31; 2 Macc 5:11-14). On this point 2 Maccabees' dating is correct; but 2 Maccabees has incorrectly linked with this occasion Antiochus's pillaging of the temple, which happened in 169 BC, on his return from his first Egyptian expedition (1 Macc 1:20-23; see Bartlett 1998: 57-65).

The author, as elsewhere, marks the occasion with an apparition of heavenly cavalry (cf. 3:25; 10:29-30; 11:8). For similar visions of horsemen symbolizing divine victory, see Zech 1:8-11; Rev 6:2-8; but such visions occur also in Roman literature, as in Pliny *Nat. Hist.* 2.148 (with reference to the year 103 BC), and Tacitus *Hist.* 5.13. The period of forty days would remind the Jewish reader of divine appearances on Sinai and Horeb (Exod 24:18; 1 Kgs 19:8-18). The author is suggesting that this was a time of crisis, in which divine intervention was the only hope.

2 Maccabees describes a vicious assault on Jerusalem by Jason which apparently captured the whole city except the Seleucid citadel (cf. 4:28), presumably the predecessor of the one built later in the year as a response to this event (cf. 1 Macc 1:33). 2 Maccabees may be exaggerating Jason's impact (cf. v. 6), for Jason was soon forced to flee to Ammanitis (see above, p. 815) and then to Egypt, an obvious refuge for a member of the Oniad family. Where Jason actually died is not stated; his intention of going to Sparta may be connected with Maccabean interest in relations with Sparta (1 Macc 12:1-23; 14:16, 20-23). (Aretas was perhaps a founding member of the Nabatean dynasty well known from monuments and inscriptions at Petra; cf. Schürer, rev. Vermes and Millar, 1973: 1:574-86.) 2 Maccabees sheds no tears over Jason, Oniad though he was.

Antiochus's Treatment of Jerusalem (5:11-26)

The author's perception that Antiochus took Jason's attack on Antiochus's appointee Menelaus as a sign of revolt may be correct up to a point. Antiochus, fresh from his enforced withdrawal from Egypt, surely wished to establish promptly his total control of this important border area and to demonstrate the point to the rest of his empire. However, the author is more concerned to portray Antiochus as an arrogant oppressor (cf. 5:21) than as a pragmatic ruler of the empire, and he draws the picture of a relentless massacre (vv. 12-14), exaggerated when compared with its 1 Maccabees counterpart (1 Macc 1:20), though it must be admitted that the added comment of 1 Macc 1:24-28 also suggests bloodshed on this occasion. It is only from this point that 2 Maccabees' narrative overlaps with that of 1 Maccabees. The disagreements in sequence and chronology between the two have led to much divergence of opinion between scholars. It is clear that both authors have arranged events and episodes to suit their own schematic presentation, but the order of 1 Maccabees is controlled by a sequence of dates largely drawn from some Seleucid archival source; 2 Maccabees gives very few precise dates. The author prefers judgmental comment (cf. 5:6-10) to chronological exactitude (cf. v. 1, "about this time").

This applies also to 5:15-20, where Antiochus's raid on the temple is narrated with a minimum of historical detail (though the king's entry to the temple is confirmed by 1 Macc 1:21) and a maximum of theological coloring. The temple is the most holy temple in the world, Menelaus a traitor to laws and country, and Antiochus's hands polluted and profane. Antiochus avoided the retribution that came upon Heliodorus (3:22-28) only because the Lord was using him to punish the inhabitants of Jerusalem. (The reference to flogging in 5:18 suggests that the author knows this to be the heart of the event in 3:22-28; cf. 3:34.) The comments that the sanctuary was chosen for the sake of the nation, not vice versa, and that the misfortunes of the sanctuary itself derived from the failings of the nation (5:19-20) are the author's reflections on the meaning of events; cf. the author's comment in 6:12 that these punishments were intended to discipline, not destroy the people (cf. Doran 1981: 53-54).

Eighteen hundred talents (if an accurate record, 5:21) represents a considerable increase on the four hundred silver and two hundred gold talents allegedly available under Seleucus IV (3:11); one can only speculate on its origin. The note that Antiochus left Philip at Jerusalem and Andronicus at Gerizim (cf. 6:2; John 4:20) as governors (probably military commanders of the garrisons controlling the city and temple) rings true. Phrygia, in central Asia Minor, was ceded by Antiochus III to Pergamum under the terms of the Treaty of Apamea (188 BC). Philip may have been a mercenary under Seleucid employ. The author cannot resist caricaturing Philip and accusing Menelaus of tyranny, and Antiochus of malice, toward the Jews (5:23-24), again coloring his narrative with prejudiced comment. The story of Apollonius (vv. 24-26) is paralleled in 1 Macc 1:29-35, where "a chief collector of tribute" came to Jerusalem, deceitfully spoke peaceable words, and then suddenly fell on the city, destroying it and its walls, enslaving its women and children, and taking its livestock. The Greek phrase for "chief collector of tribute" *(archonta phorologias)* would translate into Hebrew as *sar missim,* in unvocalized Hebrew spelling *sr msym.* This phrase, however, might also mean "captain of the Mysians," that is, of mercenary soldiers from Mysia in Asia Minor. This interpretation makes better sense than "chief collector of tribute," at least to judge from the ensuing action (5:24, 26). The author increases the wickedness of the event, however, by making the Seleucid take advantage of the sabbath for the slaughter.

Select Bibliography. Doran, R. 1981, *Temple Propaganda: The Purpose and Character of 2 Maccabees,* CBQMS 12, Washington, D.C.: The Catholic Biblical Association of America.

The Appearance of Judas Maccabeus (5:27)

2 Maccabees sets this event before Antiochus's persecution, 1 Maccabees 2 after it. 2 Maccabees says nothing of Judas's father or brothers, or of the event at Modein (1 Macc 2:15-26), or of the other incidents recorded in 1 Maccabees 2. The precise nature of "the defilement" avoided by Judas is not clear; it may be a general reference to the new situation brought about by Antiochus (cf. 6:2, the pollution of the temple). It is important to the author that Judas should not be defiled by it. Judas next appears in 8:1.

The Suppression of Judaism (6:1-11)

Again, 2 Maccabees is vague about dates ("not long after this"; cf. the preceding note "about this time," 5:1). There are certain differences between the two accounts on the persecution. While both accounts agree that Jews were required to forsake their ancestral law (6:1; cf. 1 Macc 1:49), to sacrifice forbidden offerings (6:5; cf. 1 Macc 1:47, which mentions swine), to ignore or profane festivals and sabbaths (6:6; cf. 1 Macc 1:43), to leave sons uncircumcised (6:10; cf. 1 Macc 1:48, 60-61), all on penalty of death for noncompliance (6:10, 11, 18; cf. 1 Macc 1:49), 1 Maccabees adds that the regular daily offerings prescribed by the law were to be stopped, and that Jews found in possession of the law would be condemned to death. In addition, Jews were forced to sacrifice to idols (1:43), to defile the sanctuary and the priests (1:46), to build altars, precincts, and shrines for idols (1:47), and to accept the imposition of a desolating sacrilege (probably some form of pagan altar) on the altar of burnt offering. These latter requirements went beyond prohibiting Jewish practices; they introduced non-Jewish worship. 2 Maccabees lists a different set of non-Jewish practices prescribed for the Jews: the rededication of the temple to the Greek Olympian Zeus (just as the Samarians had their temple at Mt. Gerizim dedicated to Zeus Xenios, i.e., Zeus, the Friend of Strangers, 6:2), the celebration of the king's birthday and participation in the sacrifices of the day (v. 7), and finally participation in the ceremonies of festivals in honor of the Greek god of the vine, Dionysus (Roman Bacchus) (v. 7; 2 Macc 10:7 suggests that at least one of the customs associated with Dionysus remained in practice after the purification of the temple). In comparison with 1 Maccabees, 2 Maccabees emphasizes the Greek aspects of Antiochus's decree: Antiochus sent an Athenian senator or an Athenian called Geron (either translation is possible) to enforce his changes; Zeus Olympios was the major Greek deity; Dionysus was an eastern deity adopted by the Greeks; surrounding Greek cities were urged to enforce this policy on their Jewish residents and kill those who refused to change over to Greek customs. (This last item was either the proposal of the people of Ptolemais, who had no love for the Jews, cf. 1 Macc 5:15, or of Ptolemaeus, governor of Coele-Syria and Phoenicia, cf. 4:45.) 2 Maccabees earlier speaks of the policy of shifting to the Greek way of life (4:10) and of the resultant "extreme of Hellenization" (4:13). The author, writing in the time of the early Hasmonean monarchy, makes clear that he does not approve of Greek influence in Jerusalem. Finally, 2 Maccabees notes the temple's abuse by Gentiles (6:4); that is, the temple was open to non-Jews. This was a traumatic infliction on Jewish custom.

6:11 is vaguely reminiscent of 1 Macc 2:31-38, but here the point is that these Jews met to keep the sabbath, not to plan rebellion in the wilderness (cf. Heb 11:38).

The Author's Comment (6:12-17)

These verses are probably the personal work of the author, not his abbreviation of the sentiments of Jason. Compare similar comments in 4:16-17; 5:17-20. The author interprets the appalling troubles of Israel as an early discipline to forestall the final destruction which is the lot of wicked nations; cf. Ps 94:12-15; Prov 3:11-12. The author likes using a concluding marker for his paragraphs; see, for example, 2:32; 3:40; 4:17; 4:38; 7:42; 15:37.

Select Bibliography. Bunge, J. 1979, "Die sogennante Religionsverfolgung Antiochus IV Epiphanes und die griechischen Stätte," *JSJ* 10:155-65 • Gruen, E. S. 1993, "Hellenism and Persecution: Antiochus IV and the Jews," in P. Green, ed., *Hellenistic History and Culture*, Berkeley, Calif., and London: University of California, 238-74 • Vander Kam, J. C. 1987, "2 Macc 6,7a and Calendrical Change in Jerusalem," *JSJ* 12:52-74 • Wenham, D. 1992, "Abomination of Desolation," in *ABD*, 1:28-31. See also the Bibliography on p. 810.

Part I(b): The Martyrdoms of Eleazar and the Seven Brothers (6:18–7:42)

The author has signaled the end of one section in 6:12-17, and marks the end of the present section at 7:42. Between lie the accounts of two different martyrdoms, each presenting a different understanding of the meaning of the deaths.

The Martyrdom of Eleazar (6:18-31)

The author follows his account of the persecution with two exemplary stories of the martyrdom of Jews compelled to eat pork (forbidden by Jewish law; cf. Lev 11:7; Deut 14:8; cf. Isa 65:3-4). Such compulsion is not mentioned in 6:1-11, but the use of swine in sacrifices (a Greek practice) appears in 1 Macc 1:47. Eleazar is otherwise unknown; cf. Eleazar Avaran, brother of Judas, killed beneath an elephant (1 Macc 2:5; 6:43). The Greek word *splanchnismos* used here for sacrifice (6:21; cf. also v. 7) in fact suggests the eating of the more edible entrails, customarily done at the beginning of the feast. Eleazar's response to the invitation to accept the easy way out is noble (vv. 24-28); the reference to Hades (the Greek afterworld, comparable to the Hebrew Sheol, v. 23) and the view that in life or death one is equally subject to God's punishment (v. 26) convey no suggestion of the resurrection doctrine so vividly portrayed in ch. 7. Eleazar's stance has been compared to that of the Greek philosopher Socrates, who similarly preferred to die as an example to posterity rather than to betray his principles (cf. Plato *Apology*; for a detailed comparison see Goldstein 1984: 285). The author — whether Jason or his Epitomist is uncertain — finally describes Eleazar's death simply as "an example of nobility and a memorial of courage" to the nation, including its young (contrast the idea expressed in 7:38), and in ch. 7 shows how the example was followed.

The Martyrdom of Seven Brothers (7:1-42)

This episode has all the marks of the storyteller's art. It has no particular setting in time or place. Goldstein (1984: 296-98) suggests that the story has a literary rather than a historical origin, being developed from the description of a mother bereaved of her seven children (Jer 15:5-9) coupled with the story of Zedekiah's children executed in front of their parent (2 Kgs 25:6-8; Jer 52:9-11). Goldstein (1984: 299) further suggests that the seven martyred sons are to be understood as a counter to the seven sons of Mattathias (the five of 2 Macc 2:1-5, together with Joseph and Azariah of 1 Macc 5:56, seen as half-brothers). The story is more clearly related to that of Taxo and his seven sons in the *Assumption of Moses* (Charles 1913: 407-24; Nickelsburg 1972: 43-45, 97-111). In contrast to the pro-Hasmonean 1 Maccabees (cf. 1 Macc 2:39-41), 2 Maccabees shows strong support for the unresisting martyrdom of those who put their obedience to the law before their obedience to the king (7:2; cf. 6:18-31; 14:37-46).

The story in 2 Maccabees tells of seven brothers, brought before the king, gruesomely martyred one after the other (the story reappears in 4 Maccabees, which describes the tortures in even grislier detail). The accompanying speeches expound the martyrs' belief in their own resurrection and their oppressors' punishment. After six sons have died, the mother speaks; Antiochus urges her to advise the seventh, youngest son to see reason, but she encourages him to accept death. This last son's lengthy, climactic speech is quickly followed by his death and his mother's death. The theological themes are developed as the story proceeds. The first son states the basic situation: "we are ready to die rather than transgress the laws of our ancestors" (7:2). His fate is shared by the other six brothers: each loses his scalp, his tongue, his hands, and his feet before being fried. As the first is killed, his family quote from Deuteronomy 32 ("the song that bore witness against the people to their faces"; see esp. vv. 15-33). Deut 32:36 says that the LORD will have compassion on his servants "when he sees that their power is gone, neither bond nor free remaining." The second brother, presumably addressed in Greek, responds in Hebrew; with his last words he addresses King Antiochus as an accursed wretch, contrasting him with the King of the Universe who will raise to an everlasting renewal of life (the phrase in Greek appears to reflect Dan 12:2) his subjects who have died for his laws. The third brother, displaying his tongue and hands, declares that he expects to get these back again — the resurrection will be bodily. The fourth also cherishes the hope of resurrection for himself, but denies the possibility of resurrection for life to Antiochus. The fifth brother underlines the king's misuse of human authority, contrasting it with divine power, in language which may reflect Dan 8:24-25. The theme of Antiochus's arrogance is vividly illustrated in 5:21 and 9:8-12. The torture prophesied for Antiochus reaches fulfillment in 9:5-12, cf. 9:28. As for his descendants, Antiochus V was murdered by Demetrius's army (1 Macc 7:4; 2 Macc 14:2); his supposed son Alexander Balas was beheaded by Zabdiel (1 Macc 11:17); Alexander's son Antiochus VI was killed by Trypho (1 Macc 11:39-40). The sixth son picks up the point already made by the author at 5:17 and 6:12-16, that the Jews are suffering by reason of their own sin. The idea that the suffering of the Jewish people was punishment for the people's sin was already well established in Jewish literature (cf. Isa 40:1-2) and is strongly expressed in Dan 9:4-20. The sixth son adds, however, that Antiochus himself will be punished for trying to fight against God — the sin of pride and arrogance, which receives its punishment in 9:5-12, where Antiochus is forced to admit that mortals should be subject to God, not claiming equality with God (9:12).

This thematic progression is now taken up by the

mother. Her thoughts (7:22-23) are a more subtle version of the third son's hope (v. 11). They begin from her meditation on the origin of life in the womb (cf. Job 10:10-12; Ps 139:13-14; and esp. Eccl 8:17; 11:5; Wis 15:11), and proceed to the idea that God, who first fashioned life, will in his mercy give life and breath again to her son. God, who gives life at the beginning, will give life at the end. The phraseology in 7:22-23 owes as much to the Greek world of thought as to the Hebrew; instead of the biblical phrase "breath of life" (Gen 2:7) the mother says "breath and life" *(to pneuma kai tēn zōēn)* (which the NRSV text reverses into the modern expression "life and breath"). The phrase "set in order the elements within each of you" (Gk. *tēn hēkastou stoicheiōsin . . . dierrythmisa)* is drawn from Greek analysis of the makeup of the material world; the word *stoicheia,* "elements," "component parts of matter," is first used in this sense by Plato (*Theaetetus* 201E).

Antiochus offers wealth and position to the youngest son if he will turn from his ancestral loyalty, and attempts to enlist the mother's support (7:24-26). The author thus prepares for the climax in vv. 30-38. The mother's second speech (vv. 27-29), addressed to the son in response to Antiochus's plea, continues the theme begun in the first. The words of v. 28 appear to raise an issue discussed by ancient philosophers: Epicureans such as Lucretius (1st cent. BC) argued that nothing could be made from what did not exist; it was not possible to make something out of nonexistent matter, and one did not need to postulate a creator deity to explain the existence of the universe, which is everlasting. The mother, with a different purpose in mind, argues that God did not create the heavens and the earth, or the human race, out of preexistent matter. A God who can thus create the human race where nothing previously existed can *a priori* re-create the mother's son. (The mother's concern is for the possibility of resurrection, not for the doctrine of *creatio ex nihilo.*)

The son (7:30-38), however, turns back to earlier thoughts. He restates the view already expressed by the author (6:12-17) and in the speeches of the fourth and fifth brothers (7:14, 16-17) that while the brothers in particular and the Jews in general are being disciplined by reason of their past sins and for the sake of future reconciliation, the arrogant Antiochus will receive his reward (cf. 9:5-12). In 7:36 the NRSV makes sense of the phrase in the genitive, "of ever flowing life," by reading *pepōkasi* ("have drunk of") for the manuscripts' *peptōkasi* ("have fallen"); Goldstein (1984: 317) attempts to resolve the problem by arguing that *peptōkasi* can mean "have fallen heir to." The climax of the speech and chapter comes in vv. 37-38, with an important interpretation of this event. The brothers' voluntary martyrdoms for the ancestral laws are to be instrumental, as an appeal to God to show mercy, in ending the wrath of God that has justly fallen upon the Jewish nation. Their suffering was more than an example and a memorial (6:31); it was an effective appeal to God's mercy (7:37-38). (Doran [1981: 54] comments that whether or not the idea of vicarious atonement is present here, these deaths form a watershed in 2 Maccabees, after which God's mercy abounds.) This suffering will also compel Antiochus to acknowledge God (7:37), as in 9:12-13 Antiochus is made to do. The chapter ends quickly, with Antiochus's rage, the execution of the son, the death of the mother, and the author's note marking the end of the section (7:42).

Select Bibliography. Charles, R. H. 1913, "The Assumption of Moses," *APOT,* 2:407-24 • Doran, R. 1981, *Temple Propaganda: The Purpose and Character of 2 Maccabees,* CBQMS 12, Washington, D.C.: The Catholic Biblical Association of America • Nickelsburg, G. W. E., Jr. 1972, *Resurrection, Immortality and Eternal Life in Intertestamental Judaism,* HTS 26, Cambridge, Mass.: Harvard University; Oxford: Oxford University • Tabor, J. D. 1992, "Martyr, Martyrdom," in *ABD,* 4:574-79.

Part I (c): Judas's Defeat of Nicanor, the Death of Antiochus, and the Purification of the Temple (8:1–10:9)

After a long section on the decree of Antiochus and the resultant martyrdoms, the author returns to the story of Judas briefly opened at 5:27. 8:1–10:9 form the third section of Part I of 2 Maccabees, later balanced by 15:1-36 in Part II (see 2 Maccabees above, p. 834). This section follows the sequence (i) the defeat of Nicanor (8:1-36, minus vv. 30-32, 33); (ii) the death of Antiochus (9:1-29); and (iii) the celebration of the purification of the temple (10:1-9). (A similar sequence appears in Part II, section (c), with the defeat of Nicanor, the death of Nicanor, and the decree for the celebration of Nicanor's day.) While 1 Maccabees recounts four campaigns of Judas west of the Jordan, the cleansing of the temple, and a series of wars with neighboring peoples before recounting the death of Antiochus, 2 Maccabees gives an account of one campaign only before that event, preceded by a few verses on the start of Judas's rebellion.

Select Bibliography. Doran, R. 1981, *Temple Propaganda: The Purpose and Character of 2 Maccabees,* CBQMS 12, Washington, D.C.: The Catholic Biblical Association of America.

The Opening of the Revolt (8:1-7)

These verses provide an alternative to 1 Maccabees 2 as an introduction to the story of the rebellion. The account of Judas enlisting supporters through the villages and attacking towns and villages by night to frighten people already threatened by Antiochus's persecution (8:1, 6-7) is entirely credible, though it has received rhetorical enhancement in vv. 2-5. In v. 5 the author introduces the theme of 7:37-38.

The Campaign of Nicanor (8:8-36)

Where 1 Maccabees describes a sequence of four campaigns led against Judas by Apollonius (3:10-12), Seron (3:13-26), Ptolemy, Nicanor, and Gorgias (but essentially Gorgias, 3:38–4:25), and Lysias (4:26-35), 2 Maccabees presents just one campaign led by Nicanor, appointed by Ptolemy (8:8-36, apart from vv. 30-32, 33, which are intruded from elsewhere). 2 Macc 8:8-36 and 1 Macc 3:38–4:24 have some things in common (Ptolemy, Nicanor, and Gorgias; the slave traders, and the departure from the Jewish side of the fainthearted), but 2 Maccabees appears to know nothing of the topographical details of the campaign.

Philip, the governor of Jerusalem (cf. 5:22), writes to Ptolemy, the governor of Coele-Syria and Phoenicia, probably the son of Dorymenes (4:45). Ptolemy (not Lysias, as in 1 Macc 3:38) takes responsibility for the Seleucid response, and sends Nicanor son of Patroclus and Gorgias "to wipe out the whole race of Judea" (8:9 and 1 Macc 3:42) — in reality, to control Judas and his supporters. In 1 Maccabees the active general is Gorgias (1 Macc 3:38; 4:1); in 2 Maccabees the "thrice-accursed" Nicanor (cf. 8:34; 15:3) appears as Judas's opponent throughout the rebellion, Gorgias here (8:9) being merely an associate of Nicanor with no observable role (though he reappears in 10:14 and 12:35). In 1 Macc 3:41 the slave traders come spontaneously; in 2 Maccabees invited by Nicanor, in hope of profit. (If Nicanor really hoped to raise two thousand talents, at the price of ninety slaves for a talent, he had to sell 180,000 slaves, which is improbable. At the more normal price of fifteen slaves a talent, he would still have to sell thirty thousand slaves. The tribute due to the Romans by the treaty of Apamea in 188 BC, however, had long been paid.) In 1 Macc 3:56 Judas sends the fainthearted home; in 2 Macc 8:13 the cowards desert. Judas's speech in vv. 16-18 includes some obvious rhetoric (v. 17), an allusion to Ps 20:7 (v. 18), and a reference to 2 Kgs 19:35 (cf. 1 Macc 7:41, where Judas uses this reference in praying for help against Nicanor). The battle (otherwise unknown) with the Macedonians against the Galatians (Gauls who arrived and settled in what became Galatia in 278 BC) may have involved Jewish mercenaries like those settled by Antiochus III in Lydia (Josephus *Ant.* 12 §§148-53). Judas's point is that with divine help a small number may defeat a large number and take much booty.

8:22-23 raise difficulties; Joseph is not known elsewhere as a brother of Judas, and the Greek text leaves the role of Eleazar (in the Latin text, Ezra) less certain than the NRSV translation suggests. The identity of Judas's brothers may have varied in different traditions (cf. the varying lists of the disciples of Jesus). Joseph and Azarias (i.e., Ezra) appear as a pair of Maccabean commanders in 1 Macc 5:55-62; cf. Joseph in 2 Macc 10:19 and Esdris in 2 Macc 12:36). The battle is barely described (contrast 1 Macc 4:6-25); what matters to the author is the army's readiness to die for their laws and country, the reading of the holy book, the observance of the sabbath, the distribution of the spoils among those tortured and unable to fight as well as among the warriors (following a precedent set by David, 1 Sam 30:24-25), and the final prayer for reconciliation with the merciful God (8:21-29). The account continues and concludes with vv. 34-36 (for vv. 30-33, see below). Nicanor is appropriately humiliated (cf. 4:38 and the note there) by having to jettison the cloak and hat which indicated his status as King's Friend, flee back like a slave to Antioch, and there proclaim that the Jews were invulnerable, divinely protected by reason of their obedience to their laws.

8:30-32 belong to another context, perhaps summarizing 2 Macc 12:10-31 (see Bar Kochva 1989: 511-12, 514). 8:33 is another independent fragment. The burning of the gates is mentioned at 2 Macc 1:8 and 1 Macc 4:38, but it is not clear that all three passages refer to the same incident. The reference to Callisthenes in v. 33 involves some muddled syntax and may be an intrusion.

Select Bibliography. Bar Kochva, B. 1989, *Judas Maccabaeus: The Jewish Struggle against the Seleucids,* Cambridge: Cambridge University • Doran, R. 1981, *Temple Propaganda: The Purpose and Character of 2 Maccabees,* CBQMS 12, Washington, D.C.: The Catholic Biblical Association of America.

The End of Antiochus Epiphanes (9:1-29)

The death of Antiochus IV is recounted in 1 Macc 6:1-17 and in 2 Macc 1:13-16; see above, pp. 815-16, 833. In 1 Maccabees 6, Antiochus dies in Persia, seriously depressed by news from Judah. In 2 Maccabees 1, the king dies in Persia raiding a temple. In the present story, these themes are further developed. Antiochus attacks the temples of Persepolis itself and dies "among the mountains in a strange land" while hurrying from Ecbatana in Media to Jerusalem (cf. 9:4) in order to level it to the ground. In 1 Maccabees Antiochus realizes that his misfortunes are due to his maltreatment of Jerusalem and Judah (1 Macc 6:12-13). In 2 Maccabees Antiochus appears full of remorse, vowing to make recompense to the Jews (9:13-18) and writing a remarkable letter to them (vv. 19-27). In 1 Maccabees, the death of Antiochus follows the cleansing and dedication of the sanctuary and the wars against the surrounding nations (4:31-61; 5:1-68); in 2 Maccabees, the death of Antiochus immediately precedes the purification of the temple and the decree for the annual celebration of the event at the end of the first part of the book, just as at the end of the second part the death of Nicanor immediately precedes the decree for its annual celebration (see above, p. 834). There are signs that this arrangement is deliberate; 10:1-8 (which probably followed 8:36 in the author's source) has clearly been inserted between 9:29 and 10:9, thus placing the purification of the temple after Antiochus's death (though, curiously, immediately before the original conclusion to the story of Antiochus's death in 10:9).

2 Maccabees' presentation of this episode differs greatly from 1 Maccabees', particularly in the characterization of Antiochus himself and in the emphasis on his painful death as an appropriate reward for his treatment of the Jews. In 1 Maccabees, Antiochus receives news of the successes of Judas, including the refortification of the temple area (1 Macc 6:5-7); in 2 Maccabees Antiochus hears of the defeat of Nicanor (9:3; the reference to Timothy appears to be an addition, caused by the intrusion of 8:30-32 to the text; see this page). In 1 Macc 6:8 the king is astounded, shaken, and disappointed by the news; in 2 Macc 9:4 the news induces rage and desire for revenge upon the Jews. The following verses (4, 7, 8, 10, 11, and 12) portray the king's arrogance, with allusions to Isa 14:13-15 (the pride of the king of Babylon) and Isa 40:12 (the contrast of human and divine power). The same concept was expressed by the Gk. *hybris* (violence to others based on pride), which met its *nemesis* (divine vengeance). The story develops with a certain inevitability: Antiochus

tries to rob temples and is humiliated; he plans to make the Jews suffer for it (9:4) and orders his charioteer to drive faster; bowel pains follow, whereupon he urges even greater speed, which causes an accident (v. 7), which breaks his spirit (v. 11), leading him to final humility (v. 12) in words which expressed a common Greek thought (cf. Aeschylus *Persians* 820). The author enjoys describing the king's sufferings. Appropriately, he suffers the pains he has inflicted upon others (vv. 5-6). The theme of tyrants being eaten by worms (v. 9) is related by Herodotus (*Hist.* 4.205) of Pheretima, widow of Battus of Cyrene, by Pausanias (*Description of Greece* 9.7.2) of Cassander, one of the successors of Alexander the Great, and by Acts 12:23 of Herod Agrippa.

In 9:13-18 the author underlines Antiochus's penitence by crediting him with a series of unlikely vows: that he would give freedom to Jerusalem (which he had threatened to turn into a cemetery) and make the Jews equal in status to citizens of Athens (one of whose citizens Antiochus had employed to enforce the Jews to forsake the Jewish law, 6:1); that he would restore and reequip the sanctuary (which he had formerly plundered); and even that he would become a Jew and mount a worldwide mission on behalf of the Jewish God, whom by his arrogance he had challenged (compare Nebuchadrezzar's confession, Dan 4:37). Antiochus is being made to make appropriate recompense for his sins.

The following letter (9:19-27), however, raises many questions. It does not read as the apologetic supplication intended by the author (v. 18), which suggests that the author has not invented it. Its point is not to promise performance of the vows just made but to announce the appointment of a successor (Habicht [1976: 1-18] suggests that the letter was adapted from the kind of letter addressed to the king's army in such situations). The tone suggests the continuation of good relationships previously obtaining; if it was genuinely intended to gloss over the recent disastrous relationships described by 2 Maccabees, vv. 21a, 26-27 would be laughable. Doran (1981: 60) suggests that the letter is written to underline that the Jewish community as a whole is loyal and trustworthy (as distinct from individuals like Simon and Menelaus). Alternatively, this letter might fit a situation in which Antiochus is writing to his supporters in Jerusalem, Antiochene citizens (cf. v. 19), who were happy with Seleucid government and saw the Maccabeans as rebels dangerous to the community's peace and prosperity. If this is the case, however, Antiochus's announcement of his son as his successor, and the notice in 9:29 that Philip fled to Egypt for fear of Antiochus's son, must be weighed against 1 Macc 6:14-15, where Antiochus nominates his courtier Philip (if this is the same person) as regent and guardian of Antiochus. If, as Goldstein (1984: 373) thinks, the courtier Philip of 2 Macc 9:29 is not to be identified with the King's Friend of 1 Macc 6:55, 63, there remains the fact that the letter makes no mention of a guardian or regent for Antiochus V, a boy of about seven years old. In short, this letter is puzzling whether it is authentic or not.

Antiochus III named Seleucus IV his son and heir (9:23) in 189 BC, well before his departure for the east, probably 187 BC. Antiochus IV knew well that Egypt was watching for an opportunity, but he too went east in 165 BC (165 BC). Ptolemy Philometor's rule began in 180.

Select Bibliography. Dagut, M. 1953, "2 Maccabees and the Death of Antiochus IV Epiphanes," *JBL* 72:149-57 • Doran, R. 1979, "2 Maccabees and Tragic History," *HUCA* 50:107-14 • Doran, R. 1981, *Temple Propaganda: The Purpose and Character of 2 Maccabees,* CBQMS, Washington, D.C.: The Catholic Biblical Association of America • Mendels, D. 1981, "A Note on the Tradition of Antiochus IV's Death," *IEJ* 31:53-56 • Mørkholm, O. 1966, *Antiochus IV of Syria,* Copenhagen: Gyldendalske • Sachs, A. J., and D. J. Wiseman. 1954, "A Babylonian King List of the Hellenistic Period," *Iraq* 16:202-12 • Schaumberger, J. 1955, "Die neue Seleukidenliste BM 35603 und die makkabäische Chronologie," *Bib* 36:423-35.

The Purification of the Temple (10:1-9)

As is clear from 10:9, which belongs with 9:1-29, 10:1-8 have been intruded here as the climax of the first part of the work (3:1–10:9), which now ends with the decree for the annual celebration of the purification of the sanctuary, just as the second part (10:10–15:37) ends with a decree for the annual celebration of the death of Nicanor. Whereas 1 Maccabees relates the temple rededication before the death of Antiochus, 2 Maccabees reverses the sequence; but the reference to "a lapse of two years" (v. 3) between the desecration and the purification of the sanctuary may betray that in fact 1 Maccabees was right on this point. 2 Maccabees' dating is not precise but nevertheless designates the desecration "not long after" (6:1) the events "about" the time of the second invasion of Egypt (5:1). 2 Maccabees' scheme therefore probably thought of the desecration in 168 BC or perhaps 167 BC, the purification being two years later. This might agree with Bringmann's (1983: 26) and Grabbe's (1991: 59-74) dating of the purification in 165 BC; but the death of Antiochus was not until November/December 164 BC. 2 Maccabees has thus clearly inverted the order of events. The perhaps deliberate contrast between Antiochus IV's retreat and death (9:1) and Judas's entry to Jerusalem and the temple (10:1) has often been noted.

1 Maccabees details the cleansing of the sanctuary, the replacing of the defiled altar of burnt offering, the rebuilding of the sanctuary and temple, and the importing of new vessels, a lampstand, an incense altar, and a showbread table. In addition, 2 Maccabees notes the recovery of the city as well as of the temple, and the destruction of foreign-built altars in the public places and of the sacred precincts (i.e., the illicit shrines, 1 Macc 1:47). While 1 Maccabees emphasizes that the new altar was built of new stones, 2 Maccabees emphasizes that new fire was struck out of flint (though 2 Macc 1:19-35 traces the fire back to that preserved from the first temple in the form of petroleum jelly ignited by the sun). The use of incense, lamps, and the bread of the Presence implies the replacement of the appropriate furniture, as in 1 Maccabees. The purification (2 Maccabees) or dedication of the altar (1 Maccabees) took place on 25 Chislev and lasted for eight days; 1 Maccabees notes the use of songs, harps, lutes, and cymbals, and 2 Maccabees the singing of

hymns of thanksgiving with the carrying of ivy-wreathed wands (Gk. *thyrsoi*), beautiful branches, and palm fronds, "in the manner of the festival of booths" (cf. 1:9; 2:18, and see notes on 1 Macc 4:36-61). The two versions therefore have much in common (in particular, the date), and perhaps used a common source.

Select Bibliography. See under 1 Macc 4:36-61.

Part II (a): Attacks on the Jews under Antiochus IV and Demetrius I; Nicanor's Threat to the Temple (10:10–14:36)

As we have seen (p. 834), the second half of 2 Maccabees follows the same pattern as the first part. Part II (a), describing attacks on the Jews and their temple under Antiochus V and Demetrius I, parallels Part I (a), describing attacks on the Jews and their temple under Seleucus IV and Antiochus IV. In Part II (a) the author has set material which in 1 Maccabees is found in 4:28-35 (Lysias's campaign), ch. 5 (Judas's campaigns in Gilead), 6:18-63 (Eupator's campaign), and ch. 7 (Alcimus's and Nicanor's campaigns), though the sequence of events in 2 Maccabees is not entirely the same as that in 1 Maccabees, and the episodes differ in detail. The author has added material not found in 1 Maccabees, notably the correspondence of negotiations in 11:13-38, the incidents at Joppa and Jamnia (12:2-9), the story of the dead soldiers found to be wearing idolatrous tokens (12:39-45), and the story of the death of Menelaus (13:3-8).

The Accession of Antiochus V (10:10-13)

10:10 introduces the new section, but the author gives no date for the beginning of Eupator's reign. Eupator, rather than Lysias, appears to be in charge, though at Antiochus IV's death Eupator was only seven years old. In 2 Maccabees (contrast 1 Maccabees) Eupator appoints Lysias, and all Lysias's activities are set in Eupator's reign. Lysias is apparently made both chief minister (Gk. *epi tōn pragmatōn*) and "chief governor of Coele-Syria and Phoenicia," an unusual and unlikely combination. According to 1 Macc 3:32, Lysias was "over the king's affairs (Gk. *epi tōn pragmatōn tou basileōs*) from the river Euphrates to the borders of Egypt," of which Coele-Syria and Phoenicia would be a part. The title "chief governor" (*stratēgon prōtarchon*) is also unusual, and Goldstein (1984: 387) makes Protarchos the name of the governor of Coelesyria and Phoenicia. The following sentence about Ptolemy is introduced by the Greek word "for" and appears to be an explanation of the appointment of Lysias (or Protarchos). Ptolemy Macron, known from Polybius, was the Egyptian governor of Cyprus until 168 BC, when he took Seleucid allegiance. Some official relationship with the Jews is implied but not made explicit by 10:12. Ptolemy's career and pro-Jewish policy earned official mistrust which led to his suicide. Did the author see the appointment of Lysias (or Protarchos) in place of Ptolemy as indicating a new hard line toward the Jews? In that case, was Ptolemy Macron the successor to Ptolemy son of Dorymenes (cf. 4:45; 8:8, and 1 Macc 3:38) as governor of Coele-Syria and Phoenicia?

A Campaign in Idumea (10:14-23)

For Judas's campaign in Idumea see 1 Macc 5:3-5, 65; for Gorgias see 1 Macc 4:1; 5:59. The two towers or strongholds of 10:18-23 are perhaps the towers of 1 Macc 5:5; Joseph and Zacchaeus perhaps relate in some distant way to the commanders Joseph, son of Zechariah, and Azariah described in 1 Macc 5:18-20, 55-62. If Simon here is Judas's brother, 2 Maccabees discredits him utterly; but if this Simon is included among the traitors killed, the identification falls. In 1 Maccabees this material belongs before the rededication of the temple and the death of Antiochus IV. 2 Maccabees again gives no clear idea of time or place, seems to exaggerate the numbers involved, and underlines the qualities of Judas. The account is evidently further from reality than that of 1 Maccabees.

Judas Defeats Timothy (10:24-38)

This account is also related to material in 1 Maccabees 5, probably being a developed account of Judas's attack on the Ammonites under their leader Timothy described briefly in 1 Macc 5:6-8. Gazara in 10:32 is probably an error (induced by the Idumean context) for the original Jazer of 1 Macc 5:8. (Goldstein [1984: 394] suggests that the story of Timothy's advance into Judea [10:24] developed because Jason misread Jazer as Gazara.) 2 Maccabees has turned the story of a small Jewish attack east across the Jordan against a local chief into a major Seleucid invasion of Judea by mercenary troops and cavalry led by Timothy. The reference to an earlier defeat of Timothy (*ho proteron hēttētheis,* 10:24) presumably refers to 8:30-32, in which case these verses were built into their present context at an early stage of the book's composition (though clearly out of place there). Goldstein's translation (1984: 395) of the variant textual reading of this phrase (*ho proton hēttētheis*) as "the first of the two by that name to be defeated" is unconvincing, even if two Timothys may be reconstructed from the several accounts involving a Timothy. (Timothy, Chaereas, and Apollophanes are all Greek names.) The author says nothing, as usual, of the tactics of the battle, but includes an account of the Jewish prayers, the motivation of the two armies, and the demoralizing vision of horsemen (cf. 3:25-26; 5:2-3; 11:8) seen by the enemy (10:25-31), and emphasizes the enemy's blasphemies (vv. 34-36). The episode ends with appropriate thanksgivings to the Lord.

Select Bibliography. Bar Kochva, B. 1989, *Judas Maccabaeus: The Jewish Struggle against the Seleucids,* Cambridge: Cambridge University, 508-15.

Lysias Besieges Beth-zur (11:1-12)

2 Maccabees here presents Lysias in action for the first time (1 Macc 4:28-35 places this event immediately before the rededication of the temple in 4:36-59). With eighty thousand infantry, thousands of cavalry, and eighty elephants Lysias invades Judea via Beth-zur, which he apparently besieges (11:5, 6), but is defeated and put to flight, losing eleven thousand infantry and sixteen hundred cavalry. (1 Maccabees gives sixty thousand infantry and five thousand cavalry but no elephants, and records Lysias's infantry losses as five thousand; Lysias encamps

at Beth-zur but does not on this occasion besiege it.) Beth-zur is twenty-eight kilometers south of Jerusalem by road and so is about "five *schoinoi*" (so Swete 1912: 692) rather than "five stadia" (v. 5) from Jerusalem, if a *schoinos* is about thirty stadia, the stadion being about two hundred meters.

The author here notes that Lysias is the king's guardian (cf. 1 Macc 3:33; a fact ignored so far) and kinsman (a title of honor; cf. 1 Macc 10:89; 11:31). Lysias's intention of making the city a home for Greeks is a new idea in 2 Maccabees, though Greek ways, both secular and religious, have already been introduced (4:12-16; 6:1-9). His intention of levying tribute on the temple may have been realized, for later Demetrius I promises relief on this (1 Macc 10:42; 11:34). The annual sale of the high priesthood is not evidenced in Judea, though Jason and Menelaus had already in effect purchased their office. As in 10:11-13, the author suggests that Lysias at first intends to introduce a harsher regime; after his defeat (10:13) Lysias changes his mind.

The author as usual improves the narrative; Lysias advances, elated with the power of his army (11:4), and ends humilated in flight (v. 12); on the other hand, Maccabeus and his men pray for angelic help (v. 6), and a horseman appears to lead them (v. 8).

Select Bibliography. Bar Kochva, B. 1989, *Judas Maccabaeus: The Jewish Struggle against the Seleucids,* Cambridge: Cambridge University.

Negotiations and Correspondence (11:13–12:1)

Lysias initiates negotiations, and, according to 2 Maccabees, the king granted everything requested in writing by Judas. 2 Maccabees would have us believe that these negotiations took place in the reign of Antiochus V Eupator, after the death of Antiochus IV. However, if 2 Macc 11:1-12 and 1 Macc 4:28-35 recount the same campaign (Lysias's first campaign), on 1 Maccabees' dating these negotiations belong before the death of Antiochus IV. This is supported by the dates given in three of the following letters.

The first letter (11:16-21) is from Lysias to the people of the Jews and is dated "the one hundred forty-eighth year, Dioscorinthius twenty-fourth." The official Seleucid year 148 (Macedonian dating) ran from autumn 165 to autumn 164 BC. The month name is otherwise unknown. Some scholars identify it as Dios (the first month, i.e., October), others as Dioscouros (a Cretan autumnal month name), and others as Dystros (appproximately February), but it is not clear how these two last names were converted into Dioscorinthios. Lysias says that he has received a Jewish communication (carried by John and Absalom, who cannot certainly be identified) that he has informed the king (Antiochus IV) of everything necessary, and that the king has agreed to what was possible. Details are to be discussed. This letter is generally agreed to be authentic; it may be dated between October 165 BC and February 164 BC, or perhaps later in summer-autumn 164 BC (Habicht 1976: 1-18). It thus certainly belongs before the death of Antiochus IV.

The second letter (11:22-26) is from Antiochus's son Eupator (cf. v. 23) to Lysias. It is undated, but must be from after Antiochus IV's death. It offers the Jews friendship, the return of their temple (which in fact the Jews have already taken for themselves), and the freedom to live in accordance with Jewish law. The obvious date, therefore, is at the beginning of Eupator's reign, before fighting starts again. Some think it a forgery, on the grounds that it is too sympathetic to the Jews, that the young king would not be allowed to make such generous policy changes (but why not, if the policy was really Lysias's?), and that the Jewish author of 2 Maccabees could have no access to a letter from the king to his chief officer (but the policy was appropriate to the situation and might have been made public for the sake of support).

The third letter (11:27-33) is addressed formally from King Antiochus to the senate of the Jews and the other Jews. It is dated to the 148th year, Xanthicus 15, that is, 12 March 164 BC. The king therefore is Antiochus IV (though Goldstein [1984: 418-21] argues for Antiochus V as coregent in Antiochus IV's absence in Persia). Menelaus is still apparently high priest, and the king believes him acceptable to the Jews (v. 32). The letter offers an amnesty; those who go home (from involvement in Jewish resistance) by Xanthicus 30 (i.e., 27 March 164 BC) may enjoy their food (*dapanēmata;* but perhaps better *diaitēmata,* "customs") and their laws as before. The time allowed for the amnesty seems too little if the letter leaves Antioch on 15 Xanthicus; Habicht (1976: 1-18) thinks the letter originally belonged to the preceding autumn, the date in v. 33 being misapplied from the following letter (cf. 11:38), but Goldstein (1984: 418-19) does not find the dates incredible and links the letter to *Megillat Ta'anit's* statement that on 28 Adar (= Xanthicus) "the good news came to the Jews, that they did not have to depart from the Torah." This letter, then, and its amnesty might follow the negotiations mentioned in the first letter (vv. 16-21) and belong to March 164 BC. If the Jews accepted the terms of this letter, and if the date is correct, the persecution ended in spring 164 BC, several months before the death of Antiochus IV in November/December.

The fourth letter (11:34-38), from Roman envoys to the Jewish people, appears to relate to the first (cf. vv. 35-36) and to have been written shortly after it. If so, however, it can hardly have been written as late as Xanthicus 15 (i.e., early March 164 BC) because by then the matters Lysias had earlier referred to the king (vv. 18, 36) had probably been returned for discussion by the Jews — but the Romans have as yet had no word of it (v. 36). In some Latin texts the scribes seem to have noticed this and applied the month's name of the first letter (v. 21). In any case, the original letter presumably had a Latin, not a Seleucid date. Quintus Memmius is otherwise unknown; the name Titus Manius is suspect, appearing in Codex Venetus as T. Manius Ernius. Niese identified the envoy as Manius Sergius (known from Polybius as a Roman ambassador to Antiochus IV and to Eumenes II of Pergamum in the mid-160s), but the Codex Venetus reading remains unexplained, and the envoy remains unidentified. This letter is the earliest witness to any formal contact between the Jews and the Romans.

These letters are important but difficult evidence for diplomatic events in 165-163 BC. While both 1 Macc 6:55-63 and 2 Macc 11:13-15 date negotiations to Eupator's reign, after a campaign by Lysias via Beth-zur to Jerusalem, three of the letters (11:16-21, 27-33, 34-38) date at least some negotiations to the year 148 (i.e., autumn 165-64 BC), before the death of Antiochus IV, with further negotiations under Eupator in 163 BC (2 Macc 11:22-26). "This agreement" (12:1) refers back to 11:15.

Doran (1981: 67) rightly questions why the author of 2 Maccabees, not given to archival or antiquarian concerns, preserved these letters; the answer is that they demonstrated that the Jews are not haters of other nations but simply wish to follow their own way of life and laws (cf. 11:24-25, 30-31).

Select Bibliography. Bringmann, K. 1983, *Hellenistische Reform und Religionsverfolgung in Judäa,* Göttingen: Vandenhoeck & Ruprecht • Doran, R. 1981, *Temple Propaganda: The Purpose and Character of 2 Maccabees,* CBQMS 12, Washington, D.C.: The Catholic Biblical Association of America • Habicht, C. 1976, "Royal Documents in Maccabees II," *Harvard Studies in Classical Philology* 80:1-18 • Schunk, K.-D. 1954, *Die Quellen des I und II Makkabäerbucher,* Halle (Saale): Niemeyer.

Incidents at Joppa and Jamnia (12:2-9)

By Timothy (12:2) the author can hardly intend the Timothy of 11:24-37, who was killed (11:37), but the Timothy of 12:10-25. Since the author has clearly redistributed material arranged differently in 1 Maccabees, it seems likely that he has created two Timothys out of one, who operated east of the Jordan. Some, however, distinguish a local chief called Timothy (1 Macc 5:6-8; 2 Macc 10:24-37) from a Seleucid commander called Timothy (1 Macc 5:11-44; 2 Macc 8:30-32; 12:2, 10-25) (Goldstein 1976: 296-97; 1984: 339). The other names in 12:2 are unknown, and the author has no further information about them.

The population of the coastal towns and ports like Joppa (modern Tel Aviv-Jafo 50 km. from Jerusalem), Jamnia, Azotus, Ptolemais, and others was largely Gentile, with some Jewish residents. Their hostility to Jews was understandable in the light of recent Jewish attacks (cf. 1 Macc 5:58, 68). Judas does not capture the town, whose gates were closed against him, but only the harbor, as also at Jamnia. (Twenty years later Simon "to crown all his honors took Joppa for a harbor," 1 Macc 14:5; cf. 12:33.) 1 Maccabees does not mention these particular incidents, though both 1 and 2 Maccabees connect attacks on the coast with attacks on the Transjordanian region, and both emphasize the Gentile intention of destroying the Jews (cf. 1 Macc 5:14; 2 Macc 12:8).

Judas's Campaign in Gilead (12:10-31)

Clearly this narrative is closely related to that in 1 Macc 5:24-54, which 1 Maccabees sets between the rededication of the temple and the death of Antiochus IV, and 2 Maccabees in the time of Antiochus's successor. In 2 Macc 12:10 the author's grammar and geography fail badly. In v. 9, Judas is at Jamnia; in v. 10, though only a mile or more away, Judas is being attacked by Arabs, and the following verses, with reference to Caspin, Charax, and Carnaim (cf. 1 Macc. 5:24-54), suggest that northern Transjordan is in mind. In 12:10, the Greek grammar makes it clear that it is the Arabs (not Judas's forces) who are moving to attack. This section thus shows signs of being imported from elsewhere and clumsily linked with its present context. It might originally have told of a campaign against Timothy prior to that in which he was killed (10:24-38); if so, there is no need to postulate the existence of two Timothys.

12:10-12 are perhaps another version of Judas's meeting with the Nabateans (cf. 1 Macc 5:25). The fortified town of Caspin is perhaps the Chaspho of 1 Macc 5:26, 36, possibly Khisfin fifteen kilometers east of the Sea of Galilee (Abel 1949: 436). Charax is in the region of the Jews called Toubiani (cf. 1 Macc 5:13; cf. "the land of Tob," Judg 11:3), which Abel (1949: 436) locates between Bozrah and Dera'a in Syria (though this is much less than ninety-five miles from Khisfin); but the Greek word *charax* means a palisade or a stake used in making palisades and perhaps referred originally to a camp rather than a known town. Carnaim (12:21; cf. 1 Macc 5:43-44) is well known and identified with Sheikh Sa'd; the sacred precincts (1 Macc 5:43) are probably the temple of Atargatis (2 Macc 12:26). The Hellenistic name Atargatis incorporates two ancient Semitic goddesses, Ashtaroth (Astarte) and Anath; Ashtaroth was worshipped at Tell 'Astara, the biblical Ashtaroth-karnaim (= Ashtaroth near Karnaim; Gen 14:5. See *ABD,* 1:509). From Carnaim Judas marched to Ephron and Scythopolis (= Beth-shan, 1 Macc 5:52), and so to Jerusalem (see 1 Macc 5:45-54).

2 Maccabees' account is close to that of 1 Macc 5:24-54 and may derive indirectly from it or share a common source with it. 2 Maccabees exaggerates the size of the enemy army (cf. 12:20) and the numbers of enemy slain ("untold numbers," v. 16; "thirty thousand," v. 23; "twenty-five thousand," vv. 26, 28). The enemy are insolent and blasphemous (v. 14), sinners (v. 23), and possessed of great guile (v. 24). Judas's use of prayer to the Sovereign before battle is stressed (vv. 15, 28), and a divine manifestation strikes panic into the enemy troops (v. 23). However, at the beginning of the campaign Judas agrees to make peace with the Arabs, perceiving their usefulness (v. 12), and at the end he responds appropriately to the Gentiles of Scythopolis who have shown their goodwill (vv. 30-31).

Select Bibliography. Avi-Yonah, M. 1962, "Scythopolis," *IEJ* 12:123-34 • Bar Kochva, B. 1989, *Judas Maccabaeus: The Jewish Struggle against the Seleucids,* Cambridge: Cambridge University • Carroll, S. T. 1992, "Atargatis," in *ABD,* 1:509.

Judas Defeats Gorgias (12:32-45)

2 Maccabees follows the Gilead campaign with an attack on Gorgias in Idumea. How this relates to the similar sequence in 2 Macc 10:14-24 and 1 Macc 5:55-62 is not clear. The reference to Jamnia in 12:40 suggests a link with the account of 1 Macc 5:58, but the reference to Marisa (12:35) has suggested to some a link with that of 1 Macc 5:65-68. Bacenor (12:35) is otherwise unknown, and a possible correction of the Greek text suggests that Dositheus (cf. 12:19, 24) was rather "one of the Toubiacenoi" or "Tou-

bianoi" (12:17). Esdris of 12:36 is perhaps to be identified with Eleazar of 8:23 and Azariah of 1 Macc 5:55-62. There seems to be a conflation and confusion of traditions underlying the account of 2 Maccabees here. The author is concerned to emphasize Judas's custom of prayer before battle and use of the ancestral language (presumably Hebrew; cf. 2 Macc 7:8), which lead to victory (12:37), as well as the purificatory rites (cf. Num 13:13-30) and sabbath observance after the battle (12:38).

The following story (12:39-45) may have some connection with the reference to priests who went out to do battle unwisely in 1 Macc 5:67. The priests' lack of wisdom may have lain in their quest for glory; in the present story, the deaths are seen to be due to looting the "sacred tokens of the idols of Jamnia" from Gentile temples in contravention of the law of Deut 7:25-26. This is interpreted as an unintentional sin of the whole congregation (cf. Lev 4:13), the atonement of which required the sin offering of a bull (Lev 4:14-21). Judas took up a collection (a very large collection) to pay for it. However, this act needed explanation because in most minds the sin would have been expiated by death. For the author, the explanation lay in his belief in the resurrection; expiation for these sinners was required because the dead would rise again. (It would not be needed for those who had died in godliness [12:45], and in their case it was a holy and pious thought.) This passage, witnessing to the idea of prayer for the dead, has been the cause of much Protestant reluctance to accept this and other apocryphal books as Holy Scripture.

Select Bibliography. Bar Kochva, B. 1989, *Judas Maccabaeus: The Jewish Struggle against the Seleucids,* Cambridge: Cambridge University.

The Campaign of Antiochus V and Lysias, and Negotiations (13:1-26)

This chapter appears to give 2 Maccabees' version of 1 Macc 6:28-63, with the addition of the account of the death of Menelaus (13:3-8) and of a night attack at Modein. V. 1 contains one of the few dates in 2 Maccabees, dating the campaign to the 149th year, whereas 1 Macc 6:20 dates it to the 150th year. The Seleucid Macedonian year 149 ran from late September 164; the Seleucid Babylonian year 150 (if we count from spring 312 BC) ran from spring 163. This campaign, therefore, probably began in summer 163 BC. According to 1 Maccabees, it was the Seleucid reaction to Judas's siege of the citadel in Jerusalem. For the description of Lysias (v. 2) see 11:1; for the description of the army, compare 1 Macc 6:30.

The high priest Menelaus, under pressure since Judas took control of the temple, hoped for new support from Eupator. According to 11:27-33, Menelaus had been involved in negotiations between the Jews and Antiochus IV in spring 164 BC. Lysias realized Menelaus's contribution to the political problem (in ousting Jason, raising the tribute, and stealing temple vessels to pay it) and had him executed in Beroea (Aleppo). Politically, at the beginning of Eupator's reign, this was probably a shrewd move. Death was probably by asphyxiation (cf. Herodotus *Hist.* 2.100). For the author, what mattered was its appropriateness.

2 Maccabees introduces a night attack near Modein (13:9-17), omitting reference to the battle at Beth-zechariah. V. 9 resumes v. 2, but the picture of Eupator as barbarously arrogant and harsher than his father conflicts with the letter of 11:22-26; however, if this campaign is the equivalent of that of 1 Macc 6:28-63, then Eupator has the excuse that Judas has attacked the citadel. The author has no scruples in demonizing Eupator, though only a boy of eight, and making Judas a devout protagonist for the laws, temple, city, country, commonwealth, and God (13:10-14). The campaign begins with a night attack on the king's tent, the killing of two thousand men in the camp, and the stabbing of the leading elephant and its rider. In spite of this, Eupator advanced to Beth-zur (v. 19). The sequence of events at Beth-zur in vv. 19-22 is confused and confusing (cf. 1 Macc 6:31, 49-50), but the siege seems to end with negotiations as in 1 Macc 6:49. 1 Maccabees says that Eupator took the city, while 2 Maccabees states that Eupator withdrew, attacked Judas and his men (presumably the battle of Beth-zechariah is in mind), and was defeated (1 Maccabees makes clear that it was Judas who was defeated). In short, 1 Maccabees 6 and 2 Maccabees 13 give quite opposite impressions of the result of the campaign. Vv. 23-26 should be compared with 1 Macc 6:55-63; they agree in making Philip's doings (differently represented) in Antioch the reason for the Seleucid offer of peace and withdrawal from Jerusalem, but 1 Maccabees notes that the king broke his oath and tore down the walls of Mt. Zion, while 2 Maccabees emphasizes Seleucid generosity to the holy place and the king's reception of Maccabeus. 2 Maccabees further notes events at Ptolemais. A new governor, Hegemonides (possibly the soldier commemorated in a monument at Dyme in Greece), is appointed as governor "from Ptolemais to Gerar." If "Gerar" is correct, this would be the coastal strip over which Simon was later put in command (1 Macc 11:59); but Goldstein (1984: 468-70) corrects it to "the Gerrhenes" (from Gerrha, a region in Lebanon). The implications of this for Ptolemais are not clear, but they may have felt their position weakened in some way; they also objected to the Seleucid peace with the Jews, to whom they were hostile (cf. 6:8; 1 Macc 5:15), and had to be appeased by Lysias.

Select Bibliography. Bar Kochva, B. 1989, *Judas Maccabaeus: The Jewish Struggle against the Seleucids,* Cambridge: Cambridge University, 291-346 • Habicht, G. 1958, "Der Stratege Hegemonides," *Historia* 7:376-78.

Alcimus Speaks against Judas (14:1-14)

For the events described in 2 Maccabees 14 and 15, see 1 Maccabees 7 and the commentary on that chapter. 1 and 2 Maccabees have fairly similar accounts of the struggle betwen Judas and Nicanor (though 2 Maccabees omits the reference to Bacchides' cooperation with Alcimus in 1 Macc 7:8-25). In 1 Maccabees Nicanor begins by treacherously inviting Judas to a meeting; but Judas, suspecting treachery, declines a second meeting and defeats Nicanor in battle (1 Macc. 7:26-32). Nicanor visits the temple, threatening to burn it unless Judas is delivered to him. The battle of Adasa follows, Nicanor is killed, and an annual celebration decreed. In 2 Maccabees, the battle precedes the meeting, from which mutual friendship develops until Demetrius requires Judas's arrest. Nicanor visits the temple, threatening to replace it with a temple to Dionysus unless Judas is delivered to him, and there follows (after the patriotic suicide of Razis and Nicanor's failed attempt to attack the Jews on the sabbath) the final battle, the death of Nicanor, and the agreement to celebrate the day annually.

These events belong to the rule of Demetrius I, who arrived from Rome in autumn 162 BC (see on 1 Macc 7:1-25). 2 Maccabees dates the event "three years later" than Eupator's invasion in the year 149 (13:1), but Alcimus visits Demetrius in "about" the year 151 (14:4; cf. 1 Macc 7:1). 2 Maccabees' dating here as elsewhere is vague or careless. The reference to Alcimus's former high priesthood and self-defilement in the times of separation (*ameixias* [v. 3; cf. 38], perhaps "separation from the Gentiles") is strange; Alcimus could not have been appointed until after Menelaus's recent death, and it is apparently this defilement which now prevents his access to the altar. The author's meaning remains unclear. (Once in office, Alcimus had not shrunk from treachery and bloodshed [1 Macc 7:16], but 2 Maccabees equally strangely makes no mention of it.)

The author puts into Alcimus's mouth a smooth speech, linking Judas with the Hasideans (see the commentary on 1 Macc 2:1-70) and blaming them for the continuing troubles. Demetrius appoints his elephant commander Nicanor (probably the Nicanor of 8:9 is intended) to settle the problem (v. 12).

Select Bibliography. Sievers, J. 1990, *The Hasmoneans and Their Supporters from Mattathias to the Death of John Hyrcanus I,* Atlanta: Scholars.

Nicanor's Dealings with Judas (14:15-36)

The author begins the preliminaries to the final victory of Judas over Nicanor by contrasting the present ominous gathering of the Gentiles led by Nicanor with the permanently established people and the ever upheld heritage (cf. Deut 32:9) of the God who manifests himself. This antithesis between Jews and Gentiles has been a mark of the book, as has the series of divine manifestations. Dessau (14:16) is possibly a corruption of Adasa, where Nicanor fought his last battle (cf. 1 Macc 7:40), but the incident at Dessau (of which 2 Maccabees says virtually nothing) might rather be 2 Maccabees' version of the battle near Capharsalama (1 Macc 7:31-32). The place Dessau and its variant Lessau (the Greek uncial letters *delta* and *lambda* are very similar) are both unknown. Simon appears briefly as a failure beside Judas (14:17).

Nicanor avoids bloodshed and tries diplomacy. 1 Maccabees presents Nicanor as deceitful (7:29-30); 2 Maccabees presents Nicanor's friendship as genuine (cf. 14:24-25, 28). The envoy Mattathias bears a Jewish name; Theodotus was a name common with Jews. What terms were proposed 2 Maccabees does not say; if 2 Maccabees here presents fact, not fiction, then the Maccabees' acceptance of Alcimus as high priest might have been traded for acceptance of Judas as governor of Judea in succession to Nicanor (cf. v. 26). Alcimus's mistrust of this development led to representations to Demetrius, orders for Judas's capture, and Judas's retreat into hiding. Nicanor (as in 1 Maccabees) puts pressure on the priests of the temple to betray Judas; in 2 Maccabees' version (cf. 1 Macc 7:35), Nicanor now threatens to replace the Jewish temple with a temple for Dionysus, whose festival had earlier been imposed on the Jews (cf. 6:7). The priests note God's self-sufficiency (cf. 1 Kgs 8:27; Ps 50:9-15; Isa 66:1-2) and his habitation in the temple (cf. 1 Kgs 8:12-13), and they pray for the temple's preservation from defilement (not, as in 1 Macc 7:38, for vengeance upon Nicanor). Their prayer is echoed by the people after Nicanor's death in 15:34.

Select Bibliography. Bar Kochva, B. 1989, *Judas Maccabaeus: The Jewish Struggle against the Seleucids,* Cambridge: Cambridge University, 347-58 • Doran, R. 1981, *Temple Propaganda: The Purpose and Character of 2 Maccabees,* CBQMS 12, Washington, D.C.: The Catholic Biblical Association of America.

Part II (b): The Self-Martyrdom of Razis (14:37-46)

For the place of this episode in the structure of the book, see above, p. 834. Razis's self-sacrifice on behalf of Judaism is to be compared to that of Eleazar and the seven brothers in 6:18–7:42. Razis is not known as a Jewish name; Goldstein (1984: 492) suggests its origin in a Hebrew phrase in Isa 24:16. "Father of the Jews" (14:17) is a title given to Razis for his goodwill; cf. "father of orphans," Ps 68:5; "father to the needy," Job 29:16. The story is inevitably improbable in its details. Razis is a larger-than-life figure who evades arrest by five hundred men, climbs a tower, tries to commit suicide on his sword, but having merely wounded himself climbs a wall, leaps down into the courtyard, runs bleeding through the crowd to tear out his entrails before hurling them at the crowd, while calling for their restoration in resurrection (cf. 7:11)! The author offers his readers superhuman heroism, gory details, religious loyalty, and the resurrection hope, as in chs. 6–7. This brief but dramatic example of how to die for Judaism provides a pause in the action and prepares for the defeat and death of the archenemy Nicanor.

Part II (c): The Defeat of Nicanor, the Death of Nicanor, and the Celebration of Nicanor's Day (15:1-36)

In Part I Antiochus IV was the villain; in Part II that place is taken by Nicanor. As in Part I Antiochus was punished for his arrogance, so now the arrogance of Nicanor is established to precede his fall. Nicanor's demonization begins in Part I (cf. 8:34, "the thrice-accursed Nicanor") and is developed in Part II; in 14:28-33 he attacks the temple, and in 15:1-5 "the thrice-accursed wretch" shows disrespect for the sabbath and, like Antiochus (cf. 9:12), sets himself up as an earthly sovereign in opposition to the sovereign, the living Lord himself. In 1 Macc 2:32-41 (cf. 9:43) the Maccabean supporters agree to defend themselves on the sabbath if necessary; 2 Macc 15:1 suggests that the Jews had not so agreed, or that the author did not approve of that policy.

The author gives much space (15:6-19) to the Jewish preparation for the final battle. Nicanor's boastfulness and arrogance are contrasted with Judas's reliance on God. Judas reminds his followers of God's help in former times, supporting his case from the Law and the Prophets (the two main parts of the Jewish scriptures; cf. the prologue of Ecclesiasticus). Jewish courage is contrasted with Gentile perfidy (as in 14:19-22). Judas then recounts his vision of the former high priest Onias III. 2 Macc 3:1 describes Onias's Jewish virtues — his piety and hatred of wickedness — and the peaceful observance of the laws under his priestly rule; 2 Macc 15:12 appears to portray the qualities of a Greek gentleman before describing Onias's intercessory activity for the Jews (cf. his earlier intercession for Heliodorus, 3:31-33). In the vision Onias introduces another intercessor, a man of age, dignity, and authority (cf. Eleazar, 6:18), the prophet Jeremiah. Jeremiah seems to have been important to the final compiler of the book (cf. 2:1-8). Judas is thus supported by the prayers of both a high priest and a prophet (both dead), as well as by the sword of God, given him in the vision by Jeremiah. The sword, like the armor and bridles in previous visions (3:25; 5:2; 10:29; 11:8), is golden. The final point made in preparation for battle is that the Jews are fighting for the city, the sanctuary (omitted by some scholars from the text), and the temple, seen as far more important than families. These preliminaries, entirely lacking in 1 Maccabees 7, underscore the ultimate importance of this final battle.

The battle itself is reported in 15:20-27. Nothing is said of the date or place (contrast 1 Macc 7:39-50, which locates the battle between Beth-horon and Adasa; but 2 Maccabees speaks of animals (almost certainly elephants, as in the NRSV; cf. 1 Macc 1:17; 4:28; 6:30-38; 2 Macc 11:4) and cavalry on the flanks of the infantry, as usual in Hellenistic battles, and of trumpets and battle songs. (For details of the Seleucid use of elephants, see Sekunda 1994: 27-28.) 2 Maccabees omits all reference to the flight of Nicanor's army, fully described in 1 Macc 7:44-46. Both accounts, however, contain Judas's prayer referring to the angel's destruction of 185,000 Assyrians in Hezekiah's time (15:22; cf. 1 Macc. 7:41), which suggests that a common source has been used. 2 Maccabees underlines, as elsewhere, that victory is by the might of God's arm, not of human arms (15:21, 24), and speaks of God's manifestation (vv. 27, 34; cf. 10:29-30 and 11:8-10), though without describing any such intervention.

The greatest amount of space is given to Nicanor's death (15:28-36), which in 1 Maccabees occupies two verses (1 Macc 7:43, 47). 2 Maccabees' version is nothing short of theatrical (compare 1 Macc 7:47 with 2 Macc 15:30-35; for the exposing of corpses and heads, cf. 2 Sam 21:10; Ezek 39:4; Jdt 13:15; 14:1). Judas brings Nicanor's head to Jerusalem, as once David had brought Goliath's (1 Sam 17:54). Nicanor is presented as above all an enemy of the temple (15:32-34; cf. 14:31-33), which is defended by God (15:34; cf. 14:34-36). The references to the citadel (15:31, 35; see the note on 1 Macc 1:33) suggest Judas's control over the Seleucid garrison in Jerusalem, though in fact the citadel remained under Seleucid control until Simon captured it (1 Macc 13:49-51).

The date (15:36; cf. 1 Macc 7:43, 49) is 17 March 161 BC (or perhaps 160 BC), though 2 Maccabees does not state the year. Adar was the twelfth month and final month of the year, which began with Nisan in spring. 2 Maccabees associates the day with "Mordecai's Day" (otherwise the Feast of Purim, Esth 9:26-28). According to Esth 8:12; 9:1-2, on 13 Adar the Jews were allowed to gather in their cities to lay hands on their persecutors; the following 14 and 15 Adar were to be days of feasting and gladness (Esth 9:18, 21). 2 Maccabees thus makes Nicanor's Day, the climax of the book, similarly celebrate the death of a persecutor. The author, not quite accurately, states that from Nicanor's death the city was in Jewish hands; but see 1 Macc 13:41-42.

Select Bibliography. Bar Kochva, B. 1989, *Judas Maccabaeus: The Jewish Struggle against the Seleucids,* Cambridge: Cambridge University, 359-75 • Doran, R. 1981, *Temple Propaganda: The Purpose and Character of 2 Maccabees,* CBQMS 12, Washington, D.C.: The Catholic Biblical Association of America.

The Compiler's Epilogue (15:38-39)

These final verses match the preface in 2:19-32. The author makes clear that the chief aim of the book is to please the reader's ear (all reading was done aloud) rather than to instruct the reader's mind (cf. 2:25); the detailed history is the concern of the original historian (2:30). 2 Maccabees contains some valuable historical evidence, but 1 Maccabees is the more precise historical work.

Bibliography. 1 and 2 Maccabees: Editions of the Greek and Latin Texts. Gryson, R., and R. Weber, eds. 1984, *Biblia Sacra iuxta vulgatam versionem,* 4te Auflage, Stuttgart: Deutsche Bibelgesellschaft • Hanhart, R., ed. 1959, *Maccabaeorum Liber II, Septuaginta, Vetus Testamentum Graecum Auctoritate Societatis Litterarum Gottingensis,* vol. IX/2, Göttingen: Vandenhoeck & Ruprecht • Kappler, W., ed., 2d rev. ed. 1967, *Maccabaeorum Liber I, Septuaginta, Vetus Testamentum Graecum Auctoritate Societatis Litterarum Gottingensis,* vol. IX/1, 2d rev. ed., Göttingen: Vandenhoeck & Ruprecht • Swete, H. B., 4th ed. 1912, *The Old Testament in Greek according to the Septuagint,* vol. 3, Cambridge: Cambridge University.

Translations and Commentaries. Abel, F.-M. 1949, *Les Livres des Maccabées,* Paris: Gabalda • Abel, F.-M., and J. Starcky. 3d ed. 1961, *Les Livres des Maccabées,* La Sainte Bible, Paris: Les Editions du Cerf • Bartlett, J. R. 1973, *The First and Second Books of the Maccabees,* CBC, Cambridge: Cambridge University • Dancy, J. C. 1954, *A Commentary on 1 Maccabees,* Oxford: Blackwell • Goldstein, J. 1976, *1 Maccabees,* AB 41, Garden City, N.Y.: Doubleday • Goldstein, J. 1984, *2 Maccabees,* AB 41A, Garden City, N.Y.: Doubleday • Grimm, C. L. W. 1853, *Das erste Buch der Maccabäer,* in O. F. Fritzsche, ed., Kurzgefasstes exegetisches Handbuch zu den Apokryphen des Alten Testaments, Leipzig: Hirzel • Grimm, C. L. W. 1857, *Das zweite, dritte* *und vierte Buch der Maccabäer,* in O. F. Fritzsche, ed., Kurzgefasstes exegetisches Handbuch zu den Apokryphen des Alten Testaments, Leipzig: Hirzel • Habicht, C. 1976, *2 Makkabäerbuch,* in W. G. Kümmel, ed., JSHRZ, Band 1, Lief. 3, Gütersloh: Mohn • Moffatt, J. 1913, "2 Maccabees," *APOT,* Oxford: Clarendon • Oesterley, W. O. E. 1913, "1 Maccabees," *APOT,* Oxford: Clarendon • Tedesche, S., and S. Zeitlin. 1950, *The First Book of Maccabees,* New York: Harper.

Other Important Works. Abel, F.-M. 1924, 1295, 1926, "Topographie des campagnes machabéennes," *RB* 33:201-17, 371-87; 34:194-216; 35:206-22, 510-34 • Abel, F.-M. 1946, "La Fête de la Hanoucca," *RB* 53:538-46 • Abel, F.-M. 1949, *Les Livres des Maccabées,* Paris: Gabalda • Altheim, F., and R. Stiehl. 1970, "Antiochus IV Epiphanes und der Osten," in F. Altheim and R. Stiehl, eds., *Geschichte Mittelasiens im Altertum,* Berlin: de Gruyter, 553-71 • Arenhoevel, D. 1967, "Die Eschatologie der Makkabäerbucher," *TTZ* 72:257-69 • Avi-Yonah, M. 1962, "Scythopolis," *IEJ* 12:123-34 • Bar-Kochva, B. 1989, *Judas Maccabaeus: The Jewish Struggle against the Seleucids,* Cambridge: Cambridge University • Bartlett, J. R.1973, *The First and Second Books of the Maccabees,* CBC, Cambridge: Cambridge University • Bartlett, J. R. 1985, *Jews in the Hellenistic World,* Cambridge Commentaries on Writings of the Jewish and Christian World, 200 BC to AD 200, Cambridge: Cambridge University • Bickermann, E. J. 1933, "Ein jüdischer Festbrief vom Jahre 124 v. Chr. (II Macc. 1.1-9)," *ZNW* 32:333-54 (= E. J. Bickermann, 1980, *Studies in Jewish and Christian History,* Leiden: Brill, 2:136-58) • Bickermann, E. J. 1937, *Der Gott der Makkabäer,* Berlin: Schocken/Judischer; ET 1979, *The God of the Maccabees,* by H. R. Moehring, Leiden: Brill • Bickermann, E. J. 1939-44, "Heliodore au Temple de Jerusalem," *Annuaire de l'Institut de Philologie et d'Histoire Orientales et Slaves* 7:5-40 (= 1980, *Studies in Jewish and Christian History,* Leiden: Brill, 2:159-91) • Bickermann, E. J., rev. ed. 1980, *Chronology of the Ancient World,* London: Thames and Hudson • Bickermann, E. J. 1988, *The Jews in the Greek Age,* Cambridge, Mass., and London: Harvard University • Bringmann, K. 1983, *Hellenistische Reform und Religionsverfolgung in Judäa,* Abhandlungen der Akademie der wissenschaften zu Göttingen, Philologische-historische Klasse, 3te Folge, no. 132, Göttingen: Vandenhoeck & Ruprecht • Briscoe, J. 1969, "Eastern Policy and Senatorial Politics 168-146 B.C.," *Historia* 128:49-70 • Bunge, J. 1975, "Zur Geschichte und Chronologie des Untergangs der Oniaden und des Aufstiegs der Hasmonäer," *JSJ* 6:27-43 • Bunge, J. 1976a, "Zur Geschichte und Chronologie des Untergangs der Oniaden und des Aufstiegs der Hasmonaer," *JSJ* 6:1-46 • Bunge, J. 1976b, "Die Feiern Antiochus IV Epiphanes in Daphne im Herbst 166 v. Chr.," *Chiron* 6:53-71 • Bunge, J. 1979, "Die sogennante Religionsverfolgung Antiochus IV Epiphanes und die griechischen Stätte," *JSJ* 10:155-65 • Burgmann, H. 1980, "Der umstrittene Intersacerdotium in Jerusalem 159-152 v. Chr.," *JSJ* 11:135-76 • Burney, C. F. 1920, "An Acrostic Poem in Praise of Judas Maccabaeus," *JTS* 21:319-25 • Cardauns, B. 1967, "Juden und Spartaner: Zur hellenistisch-jüdischen Literatur," *Hermes* 95:317-24 • Carroll, S. T. 1992, "Atargatis," in *ABD,* 1:509 • Charles, R. H. 1913, "The Assumption of Moses," in *APOT,* 2:407-24 • Dagut, M. 1953, "2 Maccabees and the Death of Antiochus IV Epiphanes," *JBL* 72:149-57 • Davies, P. R. 1977, "Hasidim in the Maccabaean Period," *JJS* 28:127-4 • Davies, W. D., and L. Finkelstein, eds. 1989, *The Cambridge History of Judaism,* vol. 2: *The Hellenistic Age,* Cambridge: Cambridge University • del Medico, H. E. 1965, "Le cadre historique des fêtes des Hanukkah et de Purim," *VT* 15:238-70 • Doran, R. 1979, "2 Maccabees and Tragic History," *HUCA* 50:107-14 • Doran, R. 1981, *Temple Propaganda: The Purpose and Character of 2 Maccabees,* CBQMS 12, Washington, D.C.: The Catholic Biblical Association of America • Feldman, L. H. 1986, "How Much Hellenism in Jewish Palestine?" *HUCA* 57:83-111 • Fischer, T. 1972, "Zu Tryphon," *Chiron* 2:210 • Fischer, T. 1974, "Zu den Beziehungen zwischen Rom und den Juden im 2 Jahrhundert v. Chr.," *ZAW* 86:90-93 • Fischer, T. 1980, *Seleukiden und Makkabäer,* Bochum: Studien-verlag Brockmeyer • Fischer, T. 1992, "Maccabees, Books of," in *ABD,* 4:439-50 • Gera, D. 1985, "Tryphon's Sling Bullet from Dor," *IEJ* 35:153-63 • Ginsburg, M. S. 1934, "Sparta and Judaea," *CP* 29:117-22 • Giovanni, A., and H. Muller. 1971, "Die Beziehungen zwischen Rom und den Juden im 2 Jahrhundert v. Chr.," *Museum Helveticum* 28:156-71 • Goldstein, J. 1976, *1 Maccabees,* AB 41, Garden City, N.Y.: Doubleday • Grabbe, L. L. 1991, "Maccabaean Chronology: 167-164 or 168-165 BCE," *JBL* 110:59-74 • Grabbe, L. L. 1994, *Judaism from Cyrus to Hadrian,* London: SCM • Grabbe, L. L. 2002, "The Hellenistic City of Jerusalem," in J. R. Bartlett, ed., *Jews in the Hellenistic and Roman Cities,* London and New York: Routledge, 6-21 • Green, P. 1990, *Alexander to Actium: The Hellenistic Age,* London: Thames and Hudson • Gruen, E. S. 1976, "Rome and the Seleucids in the Aftermath of Pydna," *Chiron* 6:73-95 • Gruen, E. S. 1993, "Hellenism and Persecution: Antiochus IV and the Jews," in P. Green, ed., *Hellenistic History and Culture,* Berkeley, Calif., and London: University of California, 238-74 • Habicht, C. 1958, "Der Stratege Hegemonides," *Historia* 7:376-78 • Habicht, C. 1976, "Royal Documents in Maccabees II," *Harvard Studies in Classical Philology* 80:1-18 • Hanhart, R. 1964, "Zur Zeitrechnung des I und II Makkabäerbuches," *BZAW* 88:49-96 • Harrington, D. J. 1988, *The Maccabean Revolt,* Wilmington, Del.: Glazier • Harrison, R. 1994, "Hellenization in Syria-Palestine: The Case of Judea in the Third Century BCE," *BA* 57.2:98-108 • Hengel, M. 1974, *Judaism and Hellenism,* London: SCM • Kampen, J. 1988, *The Hasidaeans and the Origin of Pharisaism: A Study in 1 and 2 Maccabees,* SBLSCS 24, Atlanta: Scholars • Katzoff, R. 1985, "Jonathan and Late Sparta," *AJP* 106:485-89 • Kuhrt, A., and S. Sherwin-White, eds. 1987, *Hellenism and the East: The Interaction of Greek and Non-Greek Civilizations from Syria to Central Asia after Alexander,* London: Duckworth • Liebmann-Frankfort, T. 1969, "Rome et le conflit judéo-syrien (164-161 avant notre ère)," *L'Antiquité Classique* 38:101-20 • Macalister, R. A. S. 1912, *The Excavation of Gezer, 1902-1905 and 1907-1909,* London: Murray, vols. 1-3 • Martola, N. 1984, *Capture and Liberation: A Study in the Composition of the First Book of Maccabees,* Acta Akademiae Aboensis, Series A, vol. 63, no. 1, Abo: Abo Akademi • Maxwell-Stuart, P. G. 1975, "1 Maccabees VI.34 Again," *VT* 25:230-33 • Mendels, D. 1981, "A Note on the Tradition of Antiochus IV's Death," *IEJ* 31:52-56 • Millar, F. 1978, "The Background of the Maccabaean Revolution: Reflections on Martin Hengel's *Judaism and Hellenism,*" *JJS* 29:1-21 • Mittwoch, A. 1955, "Tribute and Land-Tax in Seleucid Judaea," *Bib* 36:1-21 • Modrzejewski, J. M. 1995, *The Jews of Egypt from Rameses II to Emperor Hadrian,* trans. R. Cornman, Edinburgh: T&T Clark • Mölleken, W. 1953, "Geschichtsklitterung im 1 Makkabäerbuch (Wann wurde Alkimos Hohenpriester?)," *ZAW* 65:205-28 •

Momigliano, A. 1975, *Alien Wisdom: The Limits of Hellenization,* Cambridge: Cambridge University • Momigliano, A. 1975, "The Second Book of Macabees," *CP* 70:81-88 • Momigliano, A. 1980, "The Date of the 1st Book of Maccabees," in *Sesto contributo alla storia degli studi classici e del mondo antico,* Rome: Storia & Letturatura 150, 2:561-66 • Mørkholm, O. 1966, *Antiochus IV of Syria,* Copenhagen: Gyldendalske • Murphy-O'Connor, J. 1976, "Demetrius I and the Teacher of Righteousness (1 Macc x.25-45)," *RB* 83:400-420 • Neuhaus, G. O. 1974, *Studien zu den poetischen Stücken im 1 Makkabäerbuch,* Würzburg: Echter-Verlag • Nickelsburg, G. W. E., Jr. 1972, *Resurrection, Immortality and Eternal Life in Intertestamental Judaism,* HTS 26, Cambridge, Mass.: Harvard University; Oxford: Oxford University • Niese, B. 1900, "Kritik der beiden Makkabäerbücher nebst Beiträgen zur Geschichte der makkabäische Erhebbung," *Hermes* 35:268-307, 453-527 • Niese, B. 1906, "Eine Urkunde aus der Makkabäerzeit," in C. Bezold, ed., *Orientalische Studien Theodor Nöldeke zum siebigsten Geburtstag gewidmet,* Giessen: A. Töpelmann, 2:817-29 • North, R. 1953, "Maccabaean Sabbath Year," *Bib* 34:502-15 • Pfeiffer, R. H. 1949, *A History of New Testament Times,* New York: Harper • Rahlfs, A. 1934, "Die Kriegselefanten im 1sten Makkabaerbuche," *ZAW* 52:78-79 • Rowley, H. H. 1953, "Menelaus and the Abomination of Desolation," in *Studia Orientalia Ioanni Pedersen septuagenario a collegis, discipulis, amicis dicata,* Hauniae: E. Munksgaard, 303-15 • Schäfer, P. 1977, "The Hellenistic and Maccabaean Periods," in J. H. Hayes and J. M. Miller, eds., *Israelite and Judaean History,* London: SCM, 539-604 • Schäfer, P. 1997, *Judeophobia: Attitudes towards the Jews in the Ancient World,* Cambridge, Mass., and London: Harvard University • Schaumberger, J. 1955, "Die neue Seleukidenliste BM 35603 und die makkabäische Chronologie," *Bib* 36:423-35 • Schüller, S. 1956, "Some Problems Connected with the Supposed Ancestry of Jews and Spartans and Their Relations during the Last Three Centuries B.C.," *JSS* 1:257-68 • Schunk, K.-D. 1954, *Die Quellen des I und II Makkabäerbuches,* Halle: Niemeyer • Schürer, E. 1885-1891, *A History of the Jewish People in the Time of Jesus Christ,* Edinburgh: T&T Clark; rev. Eng. ed., *The History of the Jewish People in the Age of Jesus Christ (175 B.C.–A.D. 135),* vol. 1 (1973) and vol. 2 (1979), ed. G. Vermes, F. Millar, and M. Black; vol. 3 (1986) and vol. III.2 (1987), ed. G. Vermes, F. Millar, and M. Goodman, Edinburgh: T&T Clark • Seger, J. D. 1976, "The Search for Maccabaean Gezer," *BA* 39:142-44 • Sekunda, N. 1994, *Seleucid and Ptolemaic Reformed Armies 168-145 BC.,* vol. 1: *The Seleucid Army,* Stockport: Montvert • Shotwell, W. 1964, "The Problem of the Syrian Akra," *BASOR* 176:10-19 • Sievers, J. 1990, *The Hasmoneans and Their Supporters from Mattathias to the Death of John Hyrcanus I,* Atlanta: Scholars • Skeat, T. C. 1961, "Notes on Ptolemaic Chronology, II: 'The Twelfth Year Which Is Also the First': The Invasion of Egypt by Antiochus Epiphanes," *JEA* 47:107-12 • Smith, M. 1978, "Rome and the Maccabaean Conversions: Notes on 1 Macc. 8," in E. Bammel and C. K. Barrett et al., *Donum Gentilicium: New Testament Studies in Honour of D. Daube,* Oxford: Oxford University, 1-17 • Smith, R. H. 1990, "The Southern Levant in the Hellenistic Period," *Levant* 22:122-30 • Stegemann, H. 1971, "Die Entstehung der Qumrangemeinde," Ph.D., Bonn • Swain, J. W. 1944, "Antiochus Epiphanes in Egypt," *CP* 29:73-94 • Tabor, J. D. 1992, "Martyr, Martyrdom," in *ABD,* 4:574-79 • Taübler, E. 1913, *Imperium Romanum: Studien zur Entwicklungsgeschichte des Römischen Reichs,* Leipzig and Berlin: Teubner, vol. 1; Tcherikover, V. 1959, *Hellenistic Civilization and the Jews,* Philadelphia: Jewish Publication Society of America; Jerusalem: The Magnes Press, The Hebrew University • Timpe, D. 1974, "Der Römische Vertrag mit den Juden im 161 v. Chr.," *Chiron* 4:133-52 • Toki, K. 1977, "The Dates of the First and Second Books of the Maccabees," *AJBI* 3:69-83 • Torrey, C. C. 1902, "Maccabees (Books)," in T. K. Cheyne and J. Sutherland Black, eds., *Encyclopaedia Biblica,* cols. 2858-79, London: Black • Torrey, C. C. "The Letters Prefixed to Second Maccabees," *JAOS* 60:119-50 • Tsafrir, Y. 1975, "The Location of the Seleucid Akra in Jerusalem," *RB* 82:501-21 • van den Henten, J. W. 1983, "Der Berg Asdod: Überlegungen zu 1 Makk. 9.15," *JSJ* 14:43-51 • VanderKam, J. C. 1987, "Hanukkah: Its Timing and Significance according to 1 and 2 Maccabees," *JSP* 1:23-40 • VanderKam, J. C. 1987, "2 Macc 6,7a and Calendrical Change in Jerusalem," *JSJ* 12:52-74 • Wacholder, B. Z. 1978, "The Letter from Judah Maccabee to Aristobulus: Is 2 Maccabees 1.10–2.18 Authentic?" *HUCA* 49:89-133 • Wallach, J. L. 1979, "The Wars of the Maccabees," *Revue internationale d'histoire militaire* 42:53-81 • Wenham, D. 1992, "Abomination of Desolation," in *ABD,* 1:28-31 • Wightman, G. 1989-90, "Temple Fortresses in Jerusalem, Part I: The Ptolemaic and Seleucid Akras," *Bulletin of the Anglo-Israel Archaeological Society* 9:29-40 • Wise, M. O. 1990, "A Note on the Three Days of 1 Maccabees X.34," *VT* 40:116-22 • Zayadine, F. 1997, "'Iraq el-Amir," in E. M. Meyers, ed., *The Oxford Encyclopedia of Archaeology in the Near East,* Oxford and New York: Oxford University.

1 Esdras

Hugh G. M. Williamson

INTRODUCTION

The first book of Esdras (the Greek form of the more familiar name Ezra) seems at first to present us with a Greek translation of several parts of the HB, namely, 2 Chronicles 35–36, Ezra, and Neh 8:1-12. Closer examination shows, however, that some other material has been added to this (principally the story of the three bodyguards in 3:1–5:6 but also some other small sections such as 1:23-24) and that there has been some rearrangement even of the biblical narrative, especially at 2:16-30 (see the commentary below). When we add to these facts the observation that both the beginning and the ending of the work are somewhat abrupt, the scene is understandably set for considerable scholarly controversy concerning the scope and purpose of this otherwise rather neglected work.

At one extreme are those who would deny that it is really a book in its own right at all. They regard it as merely a fragment of the translation of the last part of the work of the Chronicler (see esp. Pohlmann 1970). On this view, the Chronicler's work extended into Ezra and also included Nehemiah 8, which tells of Ezra's reading of the law. All the material about Nehemiah himself was added only much later. 1 Esdras is then not particularly important in its own right but gives us valuable information about the original form and later development of the Chronicler's work. Discussion of its purpose is therefore beside the point. On this view, of course, the story of the three bodyguards must have been added only secondarily and later (and have been the cause of some of the other rearrangements), and indeed its inclusion may have been part of the reason why this part of the translation of the Chronicler's work was preserved when the beginning and ending were lost.

For a number of reasons, however, this view now seems less attractive than it once did (though cf. Schenker 1991 and Böhler 1997). The view that the Chronicler's work included Ezra and Nehemiah is not as popular now as it once was. Since Chronicles and Ezra-Nehemiah have their own translations in the LXX, it seems to imply a curious duplication of effort to postulate a separate translation at roughly the same time, especially for a work which many regard as somewhat marginal within the Bible. In addition, there are some indications that 1 Esdras already knew Ezra-Nehemiah in roughly its present form and that its author has simplified the form of the Hebrew text at a number of points; it would be strange if the development of the text in the HB had complicated what was once straightforward. (Some of these points will be mentioned at appropriate points in the commentary below; for a fuller discussion see Williamson 1996). Finally, there is a strong element of special pleading in the argument that any additional material now found in 1 Esdras must have been added only later. It therefore seems preferable to hold that 1 Esdras represents a conscious selection and arrangement of source material in what was intended to be a book in its own right.

If that is so, it still leaves unresolved the question of whether it is complete or only a fragment. The latter has been the dominant opinion for many years and leaves the question of theme and purpose difficult of resolution. Recently, however, van der Kooij 1991a and b has mounted a strong challenge to this view, and his arguments are partly summarized and followed in the commentary below. Accordingly, we shall adopt the view that 1 Esdras is complete and in the form that its author intended. Why, then, did he write it?

Various attempts have been made to answer this question by fixing on a specific historical situation that he addressed, such as that he wrote to comfort people during the Maccabean crisis (Gardner 1986) or to gain favor from Antiochus III in return for Jewish support for him (Myers 1974). Such views generally build on the present Greek form of the work and its literary and linguistic affinities, but the possibility also needs to be considered that 1 Esdras is itself the translation of an earlier Semitic (Hebrew or, more probably, Aramaic) work. The most recent research on this controversial issue argues forcefully that the story of the three bodyguards and the material which connects this with the rest of the narrative is based on an Aramaic original (Z. Talshir 1999 and 2001; Z. and D. Talshir 1992). By extension, an Aramaic original for the whole work becomes most likely. If that is correct, then the approach which has usually been taken to resolve the question of setting and purpose is invalid and the date of the original work becomes even harder to determine.

Perhaps an alternative approach may be suggested, namely, that 1 Esdras is an early form of a type of literature which scholars call "rewritten Bible." These works, such as the later Genesis Apocryphon, Pseudo-Philo, and parts of the works of Josephus, follow Scripture for the most part, but sometimes with substantial supplements and interpretative developments. Because they are oriented primarily toward the biblical text rather than the specific circumstances of the author's own day, their date and purpose are more difficult to tie down. The most that we can hope to do is to observe some of the major concerns that emerge from the presentation.

Regarding 1 Esdras, the significant innovation is that it would represent for the first time a narrative continuity between the fall of Jerusalem to the Babylonians (including the destruction of the temple and the exile of the people) on the one hand and the account of the postexilic restoration on the other. And, as we shall see, this accounts well for the choice of the starting point and conclusion for the present form of the work. Following this initial clue, we shall not be surprised to find that most of the material selected for inclusion focuses on the restoration first of the temple and then of the community, both climaxing in a major celebration at a festival, paralleling the opening account of Josiah's Passover. Such a narrative would be an encouragement to Jews facing particular hardship or opposition at almost any date.

Along with this, we may note that at a number of points there is a much greater focus on the role of Zerubbabel, the Davidic descendant, in the restoration: he is the victor in the contest of the three bodyguards, a fact which leads to the promise of aid in the rebuilding of both temple and city (see 4:42–5:3), and his name is more prominent in the following narrative as well (see Japhet 1983). He also seems to have taken over some of Nehemiah's successes, as already noted. It is difficult to treat this emphasis in a "messianic" sense (after all, there are several passages where the benevolence of the Persian king is stressed even more strongly than in Ezra-Nehemiah, and Ezra the priest and scribe is clearly another of our author's heroes). Rather, as becomes clear from other sources such as Sir 49:11-13, where Zerubbabel and Nehemiah are praised but not Ezra, those involved in the restoration were variously valued by later generations. That our author should have presented his favorites in a particular light is no guarantee that he had polemical intent; it is but another example of the inevitable bias which enters any form of biblical interpretation, including that of "rewritten Bible." Other particular emphases will be noted in the commentary which follows.

COMMENTARY

Josiah (1:1-33)

1 Esdras begins with an account of the last part of Josiah's reign, based on 2 Chronicles 35. This seemingly abrupt opening has been used to argue that the work as we have it is not complete (see the Introduction, 851), but it may be noted that the narrative part of Chronicles itself begins equally abruptly at 1 Chronicles 10, while 1:23-24 and 33 suggest that the perspective of the present work is of an account which starts midway through Josiah's reign (cf. van der Kooij 1991b).

Assuming that this is correct, the opening scene presents us with a portrait of Israel in its ideal state, with all the people gathered together in worship according to the prescriptions of the law at the Jerusalem temple. This ideal already begins to be broken at the end of Josiah's reign, and events move quickly thereafter to the catastrophe of the fall of Jerusalem, the destruction of the temple, and the exile of the people. The remainder of 1 Esdras then recounts the gradual restoration of all these elements so as to conclude with a description of the renewed community which in many ways parallels the opening.

Comparison of the text here and elsewhere in 1 Esdras with that in Chronicles and Ezra reveals many differences. Some of these are the deliberate work of the author, and the more important examples will be noted. Many others, however, are either stylistic, or the result of an alternative way of reading the (unvocalized) Hebrew text, or the result of later corruption to the parent Hebrew text; for a discussion of these, the reader is referred to the notes in Myers's commentary.

1:23-24

In contrast with "these acts" (1:25), which refers to the Passover just described, these verses reflect more generally on Josiah's reign. He himself is assessed positively, unlike his subjects, whose wickedness grieved him (not "the Lord"); this parallels the description of Ezra later (8:71-72). The details in 1:24 are probably a summary of 2 Chronicles 34 (2 Kings 22), and since they are said to have been recorded in the past there is an implication that they were not, therefore, included by our author in his selection. The sharp contrast between king and people goes further than in the earlier biblical books, but it seems to reflect the same tradition of interpretation as that found in Sir 49:2-3.

1:25-32

The death of Josiah marks the start of the decline toward exile. Josiah's guilt is heightened slightly in 1:27 (contrast 2 Chr 35:21) and especially in 1:28, where Jeremiah the prophet (cf. v. 32), and not just the foreign Pharaoh Necho, is said to have warned him against fighting.

1:33

There is an interesting interpretation of "first and last" in 2 Chr 35:27, whereby a distinction is introduced between the things that are "now told" (i.e., the Passover and Josiah's death) and "the things that he had done before" (as recorded only in Kings and Chronicles) — another reflection of the fact that our author's account began only halfway through Josiah's reign.

The Last Kings of Judah (1:34-58)

The author here follows his source (2 Chr 36:1-21) closely. Even the apparently most significant difference, at 1:38, is usually explained as due to no more than misunderstanding or textual error. As with the account of Josiah's death, however, there are hints that in the process of translation the author was inclined to heighten the culpability of the people (e.g., at vv. 42, 50, and 51). With the passage of time, history becomes more rigidly "black and white," and the author wants to present in the starkest form how low the nation had sunk in order that in the remainder of his work this might more effectively point up the contrast with the steady unraveling of the work of restoration of all that is here described as lost.

The Restoration under Cyrus (2:1-15)

Basing himself closely on Ezra 1 and omitting the overlap between the end of Chronicles and the beginning of Ezra, our author here for the first time in Hebrew literature directly connects the late monarchic, exilic, and restoration periods. The theme of continuity between the first and second temples had frequently been made before in various ways, but this bold narrative presentation goes about as far as is possible in the direction of relativizing the radical disjuncture caused by the exile. Within the framework thus provided, the continuity themes of the earlier narrative, such as, in this passage, the prophetic word (2:1; cf. 1:28, 50, and 57) and the return of the temple vessels (2:10-15; cf. 1:41, 45, and 54), receive even greater emphasis.

The author could thus achieve his purpose by a new narrative setting and so had little need to change the text of his source. It is not clear, therefore, whether the variant form of the list of vessels in 2:13-14, in which the total number equals the sum of the parts (unlike the case in the obscure Ezra 1:9-11), is due to a superior text or is the result of secondary harmonization in the course of translation.

Opposition to the Rebuilding (2:16-30)

We come now to the first major deviation in 1 Esdras from the order of events in Ezra. The latter continues here with a list of those who returned from exile (Ezra 2) and an account of the start of the rebuilding program (3:1–4:5). In 1 Esdras, this material is included later. There are two reasons for this rearrangement, and they may be viewed as complementary. First, 1 Esdras includes the story of the three bodyguards (3:1–5:3), which presupposes that Zerubbabel came to Jerusalem only in the time of Darius (522-486 BC). Clearly, therefore, Zerubbabel's journey and involvement in the first stages of rebuilding in the earlier reign of Cyrus (538-530 BC), as implied by Ezra 2–3, required correction. At the same time, Ezra 4 (on which our passage in 1 Esdras is based) is itself confusing, for it places between the reigns of Cyrus and Darius correspondence from the time of the even later reign of Artaxerxes (465-423 BC). This may have been due to its author's thematic rather than chronological ordering of his material. What is more, the confusion is compounded by the fact that the correspondence in Ezra 4 relates to the rebuilding of the city and its walls and so is out of place in a context which refers only to temple building.

The author of 1 Esdras probably tried to sort out the conflicting versions of his two principal sources. First, he decided to move all the Zerubbabel material to the reign of Darius (see ch. 5). Second, the present passage came next in his Ezra source, so he included it here but modified it in various ways to make it fit its present context better. (a) He completely omitted Ezra 4:6, which refers to correspondence in the time of Xerxes (486-465 BC). He may have (mistakenly) thought that an Artaxerxes reigned between Cyrus and Darius (though contrast 5:73), but clearly he could not admit two intervening reigns. (b) He conflated what is in fact the introduction to two separate letters in Ezra 4:7-10 at 2:16, as the names clearly show (others are either misunderstood or omitted), thus making the whole passage far simpler. (There are also some simplifications of the narrative elsewhere, especially at vv. 26-29.) (c) Most importantly, he introduced into the accusation two references to the temple building (vv. 18 and 20) which help to integrate the passage into the general flow of his wider narrative. The effect of this is that v. 30, which speaks of a suspension in the work of temple building, could be retained as the next chronological event, whereas Ezra 4:23-24, on which it is based, has in its own context to be regarded as a resumption of the narrative interrupted at 4:5.

The result of this reordering of material for the overall narrative in 1 Esdras is to give the impression that no significant work was done on the temple before the reign of Darius, despite Cyrus's decree, and that, in contrast with Ezra 3, not even the regular services were resumed on the ruined site. This throws into sharper relief the difficulties which faced the first generation of returning exiles (cf. 2:15) and so sets the scene effectively for the great change in fortunes which Zerubbabel achieved. The vital importance of the new material about him included in the next two chapters is thus highlighted.

2:17

"Coelesyria and Phoenicia" is the regular equivalent in 1 Esdras for "Beyond the River" in Ezra (e.g., 2:24, 27). The latter was the official title for the province in the Persian Empire, while the former became a standard description for the same area in the Greco-Roman period. Such updating of geographical terms is a familiar feature of ancient translations.

The Story of the Three Bodyguards (3:1–5:3)

This is by far the longest passage in 1 Esdras for which there is no parallel in the HB, and consequently it has attracted most critical attention. Opinions are widely divergent both about its origins and about its role in the book. At one extreme are those who think that the whole of 1 Esdras was written with the sole purpose of recording this story, the rest of the book merely giving it a familiar context, while at the other extreme a number of scholars have maintained that it is a secondary interpolation and thus not part of the original work. The latter view is usually (though admittedly not always) held by those who regard 1 Esdras as a translation of the original ending of the work of the Chronicler, a view not shared in this commentary (see the Introduction, 851), while the former suggestion does not satisfactorily explain why so much other material is included, particularly the account of Ezra's ministry in chs. 8–9. Rather, a middle position seems preferable: we have already begun to see that the inclusion of this story, with its dating of Zerubbabel's return to Jerusalem in the reign of Darius, is a major factor in the author's reordering of the chronology of events in the opening chapters of the book of

Ezra, while at the same time we shall see that the story itself contains several features which would have made it conducive to the author's wider purposes in recounting the progress of the postexilic restoration.

The heart of the story, in which the three bodyguards each give what they consider to be the wisest answer to the question "What is strongest?" (3:5), is almost certainly a traditional tale; indeed, there are strong indications in 3:19, 21 and 4:14-16 that the present order of their answers — wine, the king, and women — was originally the king, wine, and women. There are parallels of a general sort for this type of contest in a number of ancient cultures, both Greek and "oriental," so that it is idle to speculate about ultimate origins.

To this story, the passage about truth (4:33-41), which trumps all three of the previous answers, seems to have been added subsequently (though prior to its inclusion in 1 Esdras, of course). Its earnest moral tone contrasts with the more lighthearted nature of the first three answers, it presupposes the present, secondary order of those answers (see 4:37), and it is certainly awkward to find that the third speaker has no sooner given one answer (about women, 4:13-32) than he goes on to add another, in contradiction to the rules of the contest as initially established (3:5). Nevertheless, when read in a biblical context this pattern of 3 + 1 is a not unfamiliar device for drawing particular attention to the last in the series (see Amos 1–2; Prov 30:15-33), and it is often thought to be a characteristic of the wisdom writers. This is perhaps the first clue that a "pagan" story has here been adapted for use in a Jewish context, to which others will be added below.

3:1-3 and 4:42–5:3

The introduction to the story and its conclusion serve to integrate the story into its present narrative context. It is noteworthy that both reveal contacts and parallels with other biblical passages, so that the possibility should be considered that they have been composed by the author of 1 Esdras himself. (The words "and this was Zerubbabel" in 4:13 are the only such contact within the earlier story itself, and it is likely that they, too, have been added to it by our author, if not by a later glossator.)

There are further supporting arguments for this suggestion. Assuming that the text and translation of 3:3 are sound (both have occasionally been challenged), the statement that Darius "went to sleep, but woke up again" is in clear contradiction with the implication of 3:8-9 and 13; it may have been suggested by Esth 6:1. It is probable that 3:1-3 draws on stereotypical descriptions of scenes at the Persian court (see esp. Esth 1:1-3; Dan 5:1), while the definition of the size of the empire has further parallels at Esth 8:9 and Add Esth E:1 (= 16:1). The introduction to the story, therefore, establishes a context which will have been familiar to later readers as one in which a faithful Jew triumphs against the odds in a pagan court to the benefit of his people.

Using similar devices, the conclusion builds strongly on this point. The reward promised by the king (4:42) goes further than what was originally envisaged by the three bodyguards themselves (3:5-7; cf. Esth 5:3, 6; 7:2). Zerubbabel's response (4:43-46) is somewhat reminiscent of that of Nehemiah (cf. Neh 2:5-8), and this becomes more marked as the scene develops (cf. esp. 4:47 with Neh 2:7 and 5:2 with Neh 2:9 — a point of contrast with Ezra's return journey, according to Ezra 8:22). This is part of the evidence on which some scholars build their case that there were rival appreciations of the course of the postexilic restoration, one of which, including this one, played down the role of Nehemiah by ascribing some of his successes to Zerubbabel. (It will be recalled that 1 Esdras does not include an account of Nehemiah's activities.) This is uncertain, however, for in this passage as a whole there are, in fact, equally clear allusions to several other parts of the restoration narratives, such as Ezra 3:7 (at 4:48), Ezra 6:6-12 and 7:12-26 (at 4:50-55), and Ezra 8:27-28, where Ezra responds with praise for the king's benevolence rather as Zerubbabel does here in 4:60. When these observations are coupled with the fact that Zerubbabel requests and receives permission to rebuild both the temple and the city as well as to return the temple vessels (cf. 4:43-45, 47-48, 51, 55, 63), steps which are taken more in progression through the books of Ezra and Nehemiah, it looks as though our author has drawn upon the whole of the earlier account indiscriminately. While this may be the result of a looser approach to history than we are accustomed to (there are some other minor inconsistencies even with his own account; e.g., there is no reference elsewhere to Darius's vow mentioned in 4:43, and contrast 4:45 and 50 with 1:55), it nevertheless makes the point effectively that this was the real turning point in the fortunes of the postexilic community. Unlike the account in Ezra, the return under Cyrus was referred to almost in passing (2:15) and was immediately confronted by opposition (2:16-30), so that effectively nothing of major significance happened before the reign of Darius. With this story of the three bodyguards as used by our author, however, everything begins to unfold from this point on, and everything of significance is included in embryo in the dialogue between Zerubbabel and the king in these concluding paragraphs. Viewed with theological hindsight, the restoration is a single act of God in the life of his people, not a haphazard series of chance events. In this, 1 Esdras develops to its extreme a movement of thought already attested marginally in Ezra and Nehemiah (cf. Ezra 6:14; 7:1; Neh 12:26, 47, etc., and Williamson 1987: 79-81). Small wonder that Zerubbabel responded with praise (4:58-60) and the people with extravagant rejoicing (4:62-63; 5:2-3).

3:4–4:32

The original narrative of the story (3:4-17) with its three answers to the question "What one thing is strongest?" (vv. 18-24; 4:1-12, 13-32) is relatively straightforward and requires no detailed comment. When the probability is recalled (see above) that the original order of the answers was the king, wine, and women, it can be seen that each of the second two answers builds on the previous ones: the king is first, as might be expected, but even he is reduced to the level of his subjects by wine (4:19), while women are the master of both (4:14-16). It may be the development of this theme especially in terms of the king (4:28-31) which led to the inverted order of the first two items. Whether the original tale was a satire on the pretensions of royalty cannot now be determined, though it is attractive to suppose so, and as such it could be applied to many political figures.

That the themes of the speeches are also the subject of interest to the writers of the OT wisdom literature is not surprising (for many parallels, see Crenshaw 1981) and should not be made the basis for theories about the story's origins. Such topics are of universal concern, and parallels may be drawn from widely different sources. Nevertheless, these similarities will have helped make the story acceptable to a Jewish writer.

3:33-41

The additional speech in praise of truth has been analyzed in detail by Hilhorst 1992, developing the earlier work of Pohlmann 1970: 35-52. He explores the apparent ambiguity of the passage regarding the question whether it is a hymn to truth or to the God of truth (as 4:40 seems to suggest at the end). He agrees with others that the last clause of 4:40 must be a later interpolation, but then goes on to show that the presentation of truth in this passage (including its personification and close relationship with justice) has points of contact with ideas widely current at the time — in Greece, Persia, and Egypt as well as in Israel — though the notion of personified truth ruling supreme is unique. Naturally, this would suggest God to a Jewish reader, but the expression is sufficiently subtle to satisfy audiences with different religious ideas. The narrative continuation of the contest shows clearly which way the author of 1 Esdras understood the presentation, and it may be that he was himself responsible for adding 4:40b. But even without that, the passage gives us another good example of a sensitive adaptation of an originally pagan story to a new Jewish context.

A List of the Returning Exiles (5:4-46)

Following Zerubbabel's success in the contest of the three bodyguards, the account of the restoration now picks up momentum. Although the text generally follows that in Ezra quite closely from this point on, the chronological presentation is quite different for the first part (1 Esdras 5). Unlike the account of the ups and downs in Ezra 1–4, that in 1 Esdras has already moved the "negative" part of the narrative up to the days of the first return (2:16-30). Concomitantly, all the "positive" material is moved down to this present setting in the later reign of Darius, with the result that the restoration can move forward from this point on without serious interruption.

The chronology of the actual course of events remains a matter of dispute among scholars, and the author of 1 Esdras was right to perceive that the nub of the issue concerns the date of Zerubbabel's return to Jerusalem. Despite the clear implication of Ezra 1–6 that he returned and began work in the reign of Cyrus only to resume it after a lengthy interruption, many believe that the order of 1 Esdras, in which he enters the scene only with Darius, is more probably correct. Whether or not this is the case, it is clear that 1 Esdras should not be cited as independent evidence of this. There can be no suggestion that he had any sources other than those of the HB at his disposal, together with the originally unattached story of the three bodyguards. Out of this material alone and his identification of one of the bodyguards with Zerubbabel, he has worked with his own form of logic and with broader theological intent to recast his sources into the present narrative.

The list of the exiles who returned, which introduces the restoration account, is based on Ezra 2 (with its parallel in Nehemiah 7). There are many small textual differences between the two, as indeed there are between the two Hebrew forms of the list themselves and their later Greek renderings (for detailed comparisons, see Myers 1974). In the course of translation and copying of such material this is not at all surprising. The deviations can nearly all be ascribed to such technical reasons, together with some attempts at harmonization. There is certainly no need to suggest that tendentious factors were at work, nor to propose that the list is different because it is now dated to Darius's, rather than Cyrus's, reign.

5:4-6

This is the author's own introduction, joining the list to the previous narrative, as 5:6 makes clear. In view of the prominence which he has given everywhere else to Zerubbabel, it is striking that the priestly leaders are mentioned first (v. 5), before Zerubbabel himself. This may unconsciously reflect the dominance which the priesthood had attained by the writer's own day (so Coggins 1979). The text of v. 5 seems to be confused. The name Joakim is always associated elsewhere with the priesthood, and nobody of that name features among the known sons of Zerubbabel (cf. 1 Chr 3:19-20). Moreover, we certainly expect to find Zerubbabel himself as a leader of the return, not one of his sons. While proposals to deal with this difficulty vary, it is clear that Joakim should be included with the priestly names in the first part of the verse, leaving Zerubbabel himself as the primary lay leader; see, for instance, the NEB.

On the date at the end of the paragraph, Clines 1993: 1734 notes, "The author knows that the building of the temple was halted until *the second year of the reign of King Darius* (2.30), so that the contest is dated to *the month of Nisan, the first month* of that year to explain how Zerubbabel came to be appointed as director of the temple works." This is the only indication that our author considered the story of the three bodyguards to be chronologically prior to the end of ch. 2.

5:40

"Attharias" is not a personal name, but a Greek rendition of the *tirshatha* (probably "governor"; see the NRSV footnote), who is mentioned unnamed at the parallel Ezra 2:63. This title is referred elsewhere to Nehemiah (cf. Neh 8:9; 10:1), and this probably caused our author to add his name here as well. A Nehemiah is mentioned among the leaders of the return in 5:7 above, so that it is not absolutely certain that his more famous namesake is intended here. However, it is most probable that he is, and that this is another example of the chronological telescoping for theological reasons noted at 4:42–5:3 above.

The Restoration of Worship (5:47-55)

Those returning from exile move quickly to restore worship at the hastily prepared altar even before the temple itself is built. While the account follows Ezra 3:1-7 quite closely, the setting is, of course, in the time of Darius, not the earlier Cyrus as implied in Ezra. This may account for the addition of the words "in writing" in v. 55: whereas in Ezra the returnees were the direct recipients of Cyrus's decree, here they are considered to be at one remove from the time at which it was issued.

5:50

Contrary to Ezra 3:3, 1 Esdras here seems to indicate a measure of support from "the other peoples of the land," though the translation of the verse is not certain. This could be a reference to those who, in this writer's view, had returned previously with Sheshbazzar (2:15), or it may be another attempt to cast these events in an even more positive light.

The Rebuilding of the Temple (5:56-73)

In Ezra 3:8–4:5 and 24, on which this passage is closely based, there is an account of the laying of the foundations of the temple in the days of Cyrus and of the opposition which prevented this continuing with the building of the temple itself until the reign of Darius. Here in 1 Esdras, as seen above, much of the account of the opposition (Ezra 4:6-23) has been moved up to the time between the reigns of Cyrus and Darius (2:16-30). Consequently, there is no need for the distinction maintained in Ezra between foundation laying and actual building, and by some very small changes this account therefore becomes one of the building of the temple itself, all in the reign of Darius. As in Ezra, it starts with the foundations, naturally enough (5:56-57), but thereafter references to "the foundation" are omitted, and the temple itself is the object of building (contrast vv. 58b, 62, and 63 with Ezra 3:10, 11, and 12). Once again, this is an example of how our author views the restoration as moving forward unstoppably after Zerubbabel's triumph at the Persian court.

Viewed from this perspective, the events in 5:66-72 as well as in ch. 6 become "flashback" incidents in the course of the basically uninterrupted process of rebuilding the temple. This is a familiar narrative technique in the Bible, whereby the main conclusion is stated first and thus given greatest prominence, before simultaneous or anterior details of no lasting significance are "mopped up" in the sequel. In contrast with the situation in Ezra, therefore, the opposition in vv. 66-72, though formidable, is only a temporary setback. It was "the completion" (v. 73) of the work which was held up for a while ("two years"), not the fundamental undertaking.

5:73

Even allowing for the points just made, this verse still presents us with insoluble problems. It implies that the work of building as led by Zerubbabel began in Cyrus's reign, which is contrary to the main presentation of events in 1 Esdras in which Zerubbabel does not return to Jerusalem until the reign of Darius, and it also suggests that only two years separated Cyrus and Darius, which is completely wrong: Cyrus's son Cambyses (530-522 BC) reigned for some seven years before Darius, and in any case according to Ezra the work on the temple began many years before Cyrus's death. The situation is made worse when it is recalled that according to 2:16-30 the author of 1 Esdras envisaged the reign of Artaxerxes (did he identify him with Cambyses?) coming after that of Cyrus, and that it was during *his* reign that the first abortive attempt to build the temple was made and stopped. While it is difficult to be sure how to account for such confusion unless it be complete incompetence, it seems most probable that our author has here tried to work in and harmonize a reference to Ezra 4:5, and especially 4:24, by turning its "second year" into "for two years." It does not work, of course, as we have seen, but even through the confusion the point emerges that he is trying to cover over a lengthy interruption in the work as portrayed in Ezra and to reduce it to only a short delay in a single operation (Klein 1988: 773-74 even thinks that the text may originally have read "two months," limited to Darius's reign, and that the present text is a later partial assimilation to that in Ezra). By the same token, the earlier attempt at building (2:30) is dismissed as of no significance by being more or less completely forgotten.

The Completion and Dedication of the Temple (6:1–7:15)

From this point on (until 9:36) 1 Esdras follows Ezra 5–10 quite closely and without any further major chronological alterations. The steady progress of restoration, which it was his purpose to present by his earlier rearrangements, is well served by the Hebrew (and Aramaic) version of the narrative which he is following. The following comments can therefore be relatively brief, since most matters are dealt with in the commentaries on Ezra itself.

6:1-22

Whereas in Ezra the work in the second year of Darius represents virtually a fresh start on the temple building, here it is but a resumption of what has already been started only shortly before (5:56-73). The inquiry by Sisinnes (Tattenai, Ezra 5:3) does not cause any further delay (6:6). In line with earlier tendencies in 1 Esdras, where less distinction is made between the building of the temple and of the city (e.g., 4:43-45), Jerusalem itself is given slightly greater prominence in 6:8-9 than in Ezra 5:8. More significantly, Zerubbabel's name is added to that of Sheshbazzar in v. 18 (contrast Ezra 5:14), underlining his greater importance in 1 Esdras's account of the restoration.

6:23-34

On the basis of the find of a memorandum by Cyrus, Darius authorizes the work to continue with full financial support. Once again the general substance of this follows Ezra (6:1-12) closely. Whereas Ezra 6:2b-3 seems to give a verbatim transcript of the introduction to an official memorandum, with title, heading, and so on, a fact which has caused the commentators some difficulty (and consequently unnecessary emendation; cf. Williamson 1985: 68, 71, 74-75), here the author has rewritten the text in a more freely flowing style. As at 2:16-17, it looks very much as though he was no longer aware of the tight conventions which governed Aramaic epistolography in the Persian period. It is once again revealing that he twice adds the name of Zerubbabel to the text (6:27, 29), on the first occasion with the further honorable title "the servant of the Lord" (contrast Ezra 6:7, 8, but cf. Hag 2:23).

7:1-9

For the completion and dedication of the temple, 1 Esdr 7:1-9 follows the account in Ezra 6:13-18 closely, though it stresses the involvement of the provincial officials more strongly (see v. 2). The apparently anachronistic reference to Artaxerxes (v. 4) is retained. In Ezra 6:14 it may summarily refer to his patronage of Ezra himself in the chapters following; if our author even thought about it, he may have had in mind his apparent (and mistaken) insertion of a reign of Artaxerxes between that of Cyrus and Darius (2:16-30), though his decisions as recorded there were scarcely beneficial to the Jews. The completion of the temple on the "twenty-third" of Adar (v. 5) was probably also the original reading at Ezra 6:15, which has been corrupted to the "third." Since Adar was the last month of the year, a week's dedication celebration would then lead neatly to the new year festivities as the start of the resumed temple services.

7:10-15

The celebration of Passover soon afterward (cf. Ezra 6:19-22) will have been of particular significance to our author, for it recalls the Passover celebration under Josiah with which his account began (1:1-22). Although there is more of the restoration account still to follow, it is clear that for him the completion of the temple and the resumption of its services and festivals will have marked a truly major step in the process. There is a sense in which at this point, due to Zerubbabel's leadership under God, much that had been lost in the decades following Josiah has now been restored.

The Ministry of Ezra (8:1–9:55)

Although a considerable amount of time separated the completion of the temple from the work of Ezra, 1 Esdras follows Ezra 7:1 in bridging this gap with a casual "After these things" (8:1). History is again viewed from a theological rather than a political perspective, so that even events far distant in time can be closely related when seen as the next stage in God's plan for the restoration of his people.

More clearly even than in Ezra-Nehemiah, the crowning purpose of Ezra's ministry is here portrayed as the presentation of the law to the community which has previously been purified by the dissolving of all mixed marriages. This is achieved by the complete omission of the Nehemiah narrative, with the result that the reading of the law in Nehemiah 8 follows in close sequence upon the rest of the Ezra material (9:37-55; see further below). This gives strong narrative expression to the point that the law does not come first in the life of the community of God's people, with membership then dependent on obedience to it, but rather the law is given as a crowning gift to the people whom God has already so signally acted to restore and purify. The law does not create the community, but it is received with joy as God's final benevolent act toward them. This is a far cry from the legalism with which postexilic Judaism has often been charged.

The bulk of the story of Ezra follows Ezra 7–10 closely. Numerically, the largest number of differences again comes in the various lists of names and numbers which pepper the account. Other noteworthy points include the greater emphasis on Ezra as a scholar of the law of God (8:3, 8-9), on the fact that he is to act even more on his own authority to teach it (v. 23), and on the graciousness of the Persian kings toward the Jews (vv. 80-81). As we have already seen, this latter point is emphasized in 1 Esdras even more than in Ezra-Nehemiah, where it is already prominent.

9:37-55

The situation with regard to this final section of the Ezra narrative raises, perhaps, the most interesting questions as far as 1 Esdras itself is concerned. First, those who think that the book represents merely a Greek translation of the original ending of the Chronicler's work (see the Introduction, 851) use 1 Esdras as part of their argument that in that work Nehemiah 8 originally followed Ezra 10 directly, before the later addition of the Nehemiah material. For a number of reasons, however (see, e.g., Torrey 1910: 252-84), it seems more likely that in the original Ezra memoir the material now included in Nehemiah 8 stood between Ezra 8 and 9 and that it was rewritten for its present setting as part of the process of combining the stories of Ezra and Nehemiah. The purpose of this rearrangement will have been primarily theological, to make the same point as that emphasized just above about the present narrative shape of 1 Esdras. In that case, 1 Esdras was not making a wholly novel point here, but by his selection of material (principally the omission of the Nehemiah account) he drew it into even greater prominence. Concomitantly, as we have seen (see on 4:42-53 above and elsewhere), he anticipated some of the major achievements of Nehemiah, such as the rebuilding of the city, elsewhere in his narrative. This fits with our conclusion that he consciously selected from and arranged the material at his disposal for didactic reasons of his own.

Secondly, what are we to make of what looks like a

very curious ending to the work as a whole, "And they came together" (9:55)? Since these words are a translation of the opening of Neh 8:13, it seems at first sight as though the text has been broken off at this point. Many scholars have therefore concluded that 1 Esdras was originally longer than it now is and that its ending (as well as its beginning) has been lost in the course of transmission. If that is true, it would, of course, make very difficult any discussion of its original theme or purpose. Recently, however, van der Kooij 1991a has reexamined the Greek syntax of this verse and shown that the translator has introduced some slight changes vis-à-vis the underlying Hebrew so that the words under consideration become an integral part of the preceding sentence, no longer a detatched fragment as in the NRSV. We might better translate "both because they were inspired by the words which they had been taught and because they had been gathered together." Coupled with our comments on the opening of the work, this means that it is no longer necessary to regard 1 Esdras as a fragment.

Finally, we should not fail to note the consequence of this appreciation for interpretation. The work ends on a note of rejoicing in the gathering together of the community at a festival — just as it had begun (see Gardner 1986: 19)! The restoration of the community is therefore completed (for the hope of the gathering of the people as an element in restoration, see 2 Macc 2:18). Far from being a mere torso, 1 Esdras traces the history of loss and recovery in a manner that requires no further continuation. It is a retelling of a key period in the history of the people of God, told at a later time for their encouragement and strengthening in faith.

Bibliography. Böhler, D. 1997, *Die heilige Stadt in Esdras α und Esra–Nehemia,* Freiburg: Universitätsverlag and Göttingen: Vandenhoeck & Ruprecht • Clines, D. J. A. 1993, "1 Esdras," in W. A. Meeks, ed., *The HarperCollins Study Bible,* New York: HarperCollins, 1723-45 • Coggins, R. J., and M. A. Knibb. 1979, *The First and Second Books of Esdras,* Cambridge: Cambridge University • Crenshaw, J. L. 1981, "The Contest of Darius' Guards," in B. O. Long, ed., *Images of Man and God: Old Testament Short Stories in Literary Focus,* Sheffield: Almond, 74-88 • Eskenazi, T. C. 1986, "The Chronicler and the Composition of 1 Esdras," *CBQ* 48:171-85 • Gardner, A. E. 1986, "The Purpose and Date of 1 Esdras," *JJS* 37:18-27 • Hanhart, R. 1977, "Zu Text und Textgeschichte des ersten Esrabuches," in I. A. Shinan, ed., *Proceedings of the Sixth World Congress of Jewish Studies (Jerusalem 1973),* Jerusalem: World Union of Jewish Studies, 201-12 • Hilhorst, A. 1992, "The Speech on Truth in 1 Esdras 4,34-41," in F. García Martínez, A. Hilhorst, and C. J. Labuschagne, eds., *The Scriptures and the Scrolls: Studies in Honour of A. S. van der Woude on the Occasion of His 65th Birthday,* Leiden: Brill, 135-51 • Japhet, S. 1983, "Sheshbazzar and Zerubbabel, II," *ZAW* 95:218-29 • Klein, R. W. 1988, "1 Esdras," in J. L. Mays, ed., *Harper's Bible Commentary,* San Francisco: Harper & Row, 769-75 • Myers, J. M. 1974, *I and II Esdras,* Garden City, N.Y.: Doubleday • Pohlmann, K.-F. 1970, *Studien zum dritten Esra: Ein Beitrag zur Frage nach dem ursprünglichen Schluß des chronistischen Geschichtswerkes,* Göttingen: Vandenhoeck & Ruprecht • Rudolph, W. 1949, *Esra und Nehemia samt 3. Esra,* Tübingen: Mohr • Schenker, A. 1991, "La Relation d'Esdras À au texte massorétique d'Esdras-Néhémie," in G. J. Norton and S. Pisano, eds., *Tradition of the Text: Studies Offered to Dominique Barthélemy in Celebration of His 70th Birthday,* Freiburg: Universitätsverlag and Göttingen: Vandenhoeck & Ruprecht, 218-48 • Talshir, Z. 1999, *1 Esdras: From Origin to Translation,* Atlanta: Scholars • Talshir, Z. 2001, *1 Esdras: A Text Critical Commentary,* Atlanta: Society of Biblical Literature • Talshir, Z. and D. 1992, "The Original Language of the Story of the Three Youths (1 Esdras 3–4)," in M. Fishbane and E. Tov, eds., *"Sha'arei Talmon": Studies in the Bible, Qumran, and the Ancient Near East Presented to Shemaryahu Talmon,* Winona Lake: Eisenbrauns, 63*-75* (Hebrew) • Torrey, C. C. 1910, *Ezra Studies,* Chicago: University of Chicago • van der Kooij, A. 1991a, "On the Ending of the Book of 1 Esdras," in C. E. Cox, ed., *VII Congress of the International Organization for Septuagint and Cognate Studies,* Atlanta: Scholars, 37-49 • van der Kooij, A. 1991b, "Zur Frage des Anfangs des 1. Esrabuches," *ZAW* 103: 239-52 • Williamson, H. G. M. 1985, *Ezra, Nehemiah,* Waco: Word • Williamson, H. G. M. 1987, *Ezra and Nehemiah,* Sheffield: Sheffield Academic • Williamson, H. G. M. 1996, "The Problem with First Esdras," in J. Barton and D. J. Reimer, eds., *After the Exile: Essays in Honour of Rex Mason,* Macon: Mercer, 201-16.

The Prayer of Manasseh

Philip R. Davies

INTRODUCTION

History of the Prayer

According to 2 Kings 21, Manasseh was a wicked king, of whom no repentance is recorded. However, 2 Chronicles 33 adds that during his reign he was taken to Babylon and "While he was in distress he entreated the favor of the LORD his God and humbled himself greatly before the God of his ancestors. He prayed to him, and God received his entreaty, heard his plea, and restored him again to Jerusalem and to his kingdom. Then Manasseh knew that the LORD indeed was God" (vv. 12-13). Whether the Chronicler already knew of the text of a prayer, or merely provided a pretext for later writers to create one we cannot know, though the majority of scholars favor the latter. A prayer of Manasseh is also mentioned in the first-century-AD *2 Baruch* (64–65), which nevertheless emphasized his evil, suggesting that he prayed but did not truly repent. The *Ascension of Isaiah* (2:1-6; probably from around the same time) also has a negative evaluation of this king.

Most scholars date this Prayer to the second or first century BC, basing their conclusions on the reference in *2 Baruch*. But this Prayer is not the only one bearing the name. In 1986, Eileen Schuller published two manuscripts of noncanonical Psalms (in Hebrew) from Qumran (4Q380 and 4Q381), one of which bears the heading "Prayer of Manasseh, king of Judah, when the king of Assyria imprisoned him" (4Q381, frag. 33, ll. 8ff.). The text of this hymn is quite different, though the genre, from what has been preserved, seems to be the same; Schuller rightly concludes that "there does not seem to be any concrete relationship which can be established between this Hebrew psalm and the Greek prayer" (Schuller 1986: 160). The existence of this different Hebrew "Prayer of Manasseh" makes it hard to date the apocryphal Prayer of Manasseh except on the basis of its earliest manuscript attestations.

In fact, the Prayer was not included in two of the three great early Christian Bible codices, Vaticanus or Sinaiticus, and was included in Alexandrinus only among a collection of Odes appended to the Psalter (most, but not all, of which consist of biblical passages). Its first appearance is in the *Didascalia*, a second- or third-century Christian writing that later formed part of the *Apostolic Constitutions*. Here it actually forms part of a narrative about Manasseh. Thus, the Prayer of Manasseh was never truly regarded as part of the Christian Bible (and thus should strictly not be considered part of the LXX). The Council of Trent did not include this book in its OT, but regarded it (like 1 and 2 Esdras) only as apocryphal. Luther included it in his Weimar Bible edition as the last book of the Apocrypha. The Tyndale and Coverdale Bibles did not include it; the first English Bible to include it was Matthew's Bible of 1537. But while the Prayer has been preserved in Christian tradition, it is unmentioned in any rabbinic or postrabbinic Jewish writings.

Structure, Genre, and Text

This prayer falls into parts — praise (vv. 1-4), acknowledgment of the mercy of God (vv. 5-7), confession (vv. 8-10), supplication (vv. 11-13) — and ends with a statement of trust and praise (vv. 14-15). Like many of the biblical psalms, it thus exhibits the typical features of the genre of "individual lament." The lament genre has been studied by Werline, who unfortunately omits all discussion of the Prayer on the grounds that it is directed at the restoration of the individual rather than the community (Werline 1998: 2).

The individual lament, however, can fall into two kinds. In one of these the suppliant asks for relief from affliction. Here it is not always forgiveness that is asked for, but rather the help that God's commitment to Israel demands (e.g., Psalms 12, 22, 40). Only where the suppliant's sin is seen as the cause of the affliction (e.g., Psalms 32, 38, 51) is forgiveness asked for. It is precisely because the Prayer of Manasseh is that of an individual penitent that it was preserved among Christians, for whom all humans are guilty of sin and do not deserve divine grace merely as children of Israel.

Whether or not it was composed originally in Greek (as many scholars believe) or in Hebrew or Aramaic, the Prayer of Manasseh has been preserved in Greek and Syriac, as well as in a Latin translation (possibly medieval: it was not in the Vg but was added in the sicteenth century), Armenian, and Ethiopic. Equally uncertain is whether it was composed in Palestine or elsewhere; but it is now generally agreed that the work is a Jewish composition, without any recognizable trace of Christian authorship. Possible Christian additions to some manuscripts may be detectable in vv. 1 and 7, but these do not affect its thoroughly Jewish theology.

Rhetoric and Theology

It is important to remember that the biblical prayer of individual lament, to which this Prayer conforms, is a negotiation. The argument and the rhetoric are carefully calculated to induce the desired result. Thus the point of magnifying God at the outset is to offer him due respect. The difficult part of the negotiation that follows admits that God has every right to be angry (as he is assumed to be), yet no sooner is this justified anger mentioned than God's mercy has also to be introduced and then dwelt upon. This part of the negotiation should be undertaken in such a way that the power, anger, and mercy all seem to belong together within God's nature. Because he is so powerful, he can also be merciful.

The next stage is to direct attention toward the speaker. Just as God's might has been glorified, so the speaker's sin must now also be acknowledged as a dramatic contrast. But this acknowledgment is already a sign of contrition, and so the prayer flows smoothly into a plea for forgiveness. Finally, in a kind of recapitulation, the prayer now moves back through the topics of divine anger, then mercy, and finally divine glory, to end with the promise of proper gratitude through praise. The right relationship will be restored: that of true patronage, where the client (Manasseh) confesses fault and pledges all loyalty and gratitude for the future, while the patron (God) puts aside anger and agrees to be magnanimous. The Prayer, then, is rhetorically elegant and effective, combining flattery, obsequiousness, an appeal to magnanimity, and finally a promise of gratitude, in conformity with the requirements of the genre and of the relationship between a patron deity and a client worshiper. That the speaker of the prayer is also an Israelite king, a descendant of God's most illustrious client David, underlines the character of the relationship to which this kind of prayer appeals.

The main idea of the prayer, and presumably the reasons for its inclusion first in Christian liturgy and then among the Apocrypha, is that of God's infinite mercy toward even the most wicked sinner who shows true repentance — an obviously fitting subject for Christian prayer. However, it is worth noting that in this late Second Temple prayer there is no clear suggestion of *eschatological* judgment, unless we give weight to the phrase "that they may be saved" (Gk. *eis sōtērian*), which is a very Christian-sounding phrase. Possibly the absence of any explicit mention of final judgment is explained by the historical fiction of Manasseh's authorship. But if the prayer was intended to have a contemporary resonance, such a warning might have been expected, if the author believed in such a final judgment.

COMMENTARY

Praise (vv. 1-4)

In Codex Alexandrinus, the word "heavenly" is added after "Lord Almighty," which, if original, provides an interesting resemblance to the beginning of the Lord's Prayer: "O Lord Almighty, in heaven" (see Matt 6:9). Similarly, "Yours is the glory for ever. Amen" recalls Matt 6:13, "the kingdom and the power and the glory are yours for ever. Amen" (but this phrase is also absent from some ancient NT manuscripts!). It seems unlikely that there is any deliberate Christian addition here in 1:1. But the resemblances in wording at the beginning and end of the Lord's Prayer offer another reason for this prayer to have been embraced by Christians. The two themes of creation and the patriarchs which follow would also perhaps remind Christian readers of Paul's words on these matters in Galatians 3 and Romans 4. But both, of course, are standard attributes of God in the OT: the creator of the world and the one who chose the people of Israel through their ancestor. The reference to "righteous offspring" is nevertheless of some significance, going as it does explicitly beyond the OT assertions of Israel's election by eliminating the wicked — a qualification generally implicit but mostly unstated in the Scriptures. Manasseh is made to represent himself, then, as outside the promises of God until his repentance is accepted and he is forgiven. Yet again we have a statement, then, that is compatible with a Pauline interpretation of the covenant with Abraham (through faith), though it is not expressed in Pauline terms and probably should not be taken as a piece of Christian theology inserted into this Prayer.

The "deep" (or "abyss") refers to the subterranean waters on which the earth rests and from which the dry land was separated at creation. The "sealing" of the deep by means of the "name" may build on the biblical notion of God setting a bound to the limits of the ocean (e.g., Job 38:8-11), but also suggests the magical power of the divine name, alluded to in Tob 8:5 and in the numerous incantation bowls that Jews owned in antiquity, inscribed with names of God. The idea here is surely that God sealed up the sea by some kind of spell, using his own name.

Acknowledgment of God's Mercy (vv. 5-7)

The linking of God's creative power and his mercy, the rhetorical aim of this section, is also an important theme in the book of Jonah, where the prophet first boasts of his God's power over nature (ch. 1) and then upbraids his God for being merciful and compassionate to repentant sinners who are not Jews (and whom, God replies, he also created; ch. 4). Here, of course, the repentance and forgiveness of non-Jews is not the issue, as the association of creation with election in the previous section makes clear. The theme moves gradually from God's power to the fear that this power invokes, and then focuses on the fear that a sinner must have in the face of righteous divine anger. But at v. 6 occurs a quite abrupt change: using adjectives that express the infinity of divine attributes ("unbearable" [NRSV, "cannot be borne"], "unendurable"), the author moves to God's "immeasurable" and "unsearchable" promised mercy. Here the language echoes Jonah 4:2 but also Joel 2:12-13 (using the words of the LXX). However, there is a careful amendment. Where both OT texts speak simply of "repenting of evil," meaning a divine intention to exact something evil, here the "evil" is that of wicked humans. The writer, perhaps, does not bring himself to say that God does something bad (let alone repent of it!).

Another interesting idea is "appointing" repentance." The verb may, once more, echo the language of Jonah, where God "appoints" (Heb. *manah*) a great deal. Many texts of the late Second Temple period (especially the DSS) express the view that all sinners and righteous are predetermined (see 1QS 3 and CD 2), so that repentance itself must also be allowed only to those chosen. But the sense here may rather be that repentance is a procedure that has been *sanctioned* by God for the benefit of any who wish to avail themselves of it (see below on v. 8). However, the second half of v. 7, from "O Lord" to "be saved," is absent from Codex Alexandrinus and could be suspected as an addition, though the motivation for this would be unclear, as it adds no specific doctrinal amplification or correction and leads well into the content of the next verse.

Confession (vv. 8-10)

What is the point of the statement that repentance is not appropriate for the righteous? It was held by some writers at this time (e.g., in the book of *Jubilees*) that the patriarchs were perfect keepers of the law. Perhaps the writer wishes to explain why no cases of patriarchal repentance are described in the Bible, or indeed why the Mosaic law does not prescribe any ritual of penitential prayer. Is this possibly a hint that temple sacrifice was already at an end, and that forgiveness was now accorded in response to noncultic acts?

Just as Manasseh's words magnify the divine forgiveness, so they magnify (or at least underline) the magnitude of his own sin. The reference to his own captivity, though rooted in his own story in Chronicles, could well be intended to allude to the "captivity" of Israel, something which, according to many writers of the period (*1 Enoch*, Daniel, and several DSS such as 11QMelchizedek, the *Damascus Document*), had not really ended with the so-called "return": God was still angry with Israel, and this anger would be terminated only at the end of history when sinners would be destroyed and the land restored fully. A reference to such an "exile" is certainly a common feature of Second Temple *communal* penitential prayer (see Nehemiah 9; Daniel 9; 4QDibHam).

Supplication (vv. 11-13)

The shift from acknowledgment to supplication is accompanied by a change of posture: at this point kneeling is appropriate, and the Greek reads literally "bend the knee of the heart" at v. 11, a clumsy phrase but one perhaps emphasizing that what counts is not outward behavior but inward attitude. Just as he twice says "I have sinned," so he twice asks for forgiveness.

The translation "do not condemn me to the depths of the earth" follows the Latin version. But the Greek suggests rather "do not condemn me *in* the depths of the earth." In either case, what is denoted is the Underworld (Heb. *Sheol*), where all the dead were supposed to go after death. Depending on the translation preferred, several interpretations are possible here: (1) That the wicked who do not repent and are forgiven are condemned to this place. But what, then, is the different lot of the righteous? (2) That the wicked go to the *remotest area* of this Underworld. But there is no hint elsewhere in biblical or early postbiblical literature of degrees of remoteness in Sheol as a kind of reward or punishment; the phrase "lowest parts of the earth" in the OT means simply "the Underworld" (see Ps 139:15; Isa 44:23). (3) That there is some possibility that access to God is not denied the righteous even in Sheol. This might be hinted at in Ps 139:8. (4) That Manasseh is referring to an immediate or premature death. In Hebrew "death" is sometimes used to denote a life of misery or a life threatened by extinction, and thus God can be asked to save the psalmist from death or praised for saving him from Sheol (Ps 16:10; Jonah 2:6). This may be the sense here: the wicked come to a miserable and premature death, while the righteous live a long and honorable life, dying with honor, wealth, and posterity, a belief that the book of Proverbs declares and the book of Job grapples with.

Statement of Trust and Praise (vv. 14-15)

This section really begins with the last line of v. 13: "For you, O Lord, are the God of those who repent." A final statement of confidence in the outcome of the petition is a common feature of the lament genre in the Bible. In return for the expectation of the plea being heard, the psalmist may offer to praise God for the rest of his life (e.g., Ps 52:9; 61:8). Again, no question of an afterlife is raised; but Manasseh expects to live a long life as a reward for his penitence. And this is precisely what the Bible records of him, giving rise to this penitential psalm.

Bibliography. Editions, translations. Baars, W., and H. Schneider, eds. 1972, "Prayer of Manasseh," in *Vetus Testamentum Syriace,* 4, Leiden: Brill (Syriac text) • Charlesworth, J. H. 1985, "Prayer of Manasseh," in J. H. Charlesworth, ed., *The Old Testament Pseudepigrapha,* New York: Doubleday, 2:623-25 • Dancy, J. C. 1972, *The Shorter Books of the Apocrypha,* CBC, Cambridge: Cambridge University, 242-48 • Rahlfs, A. 1935, "Prayer of Manasses," in *Septuaginta* 2, Stuttgart: Privilegierte Württembergische Bibelanstalt (Greek text) • Ryle, H. E. 1913, "Prayer of Manasses," in R. H. Charles, ed., *Apocrypha and Pseudepigrapha of the Old Testament in English,* Oxford: Clarendon, 2:612-24 • Schuller, E. 1986, *Non-Canonical Psalms from Qumran: A Pseudepigraphic Collection,* HSS, Atlanta: Scholars, 146-62 (Qumran "Prayer of Manasseh").

Studies. Bogaert, P. "La Legende de Manasse," in *Apocalypse de Baruch,* SC 144-45, Paris: Cerf, 296-319 • Charlesworth, J. H. 1981, *The Pseudepigrapha and Modern Research: With a Supplement,* SBLSCS 7S, Chico, Calif.: Scholars, 156-58 (with bibliography) • Werline, R. A. 1998, *Penitential Prayer in Second Temple Judaism: The Development of a Religious Institution,* SBLEJL 13, Atlanta: Scholars.

Psalm 151

Alison Salvesen

INTRODUCTION

The canonical collection of psalms known to Judaism and Western Christianity numbers only 150. But the Septuagint Psalter includes Psalm 151, and the same work is found among the Syriac apocryphal psalms. Latin, Armenian, Arabic, Ethiopic, and Georgian versions also exist, and like the Syriac these were all translated from the Greek (Wigtil 1983: 407). However, two closely related compositions in Hebrew have been discovered among the Dead Sea Scrolls (DSS), in col. 28 of the Psalm Scroll 11Q5 (= 11QPs[a]). These are two consecutive psalms, each with its own superscription, and together covering more or less the same material as LXX Psalm 151. They are therefore termed Psalms 151A and 151B. However, only the opening lines of 151B have survived.

Psalm 151A

Hallelujah. Of David, son of Jesse.

1. I was smaller than my brothers, and younger than the sons of my father.
He made me shepherd of his flock, and a ruler over his kids.
2. My hands have made a pipe and my fingers a lyre.
I have rendered glory to the Lord; I have said so in my soul.
3. The mountains do not testify to him, and the hills do not tell (of him).
The trees praise my words and the flocks my deeds.
4. For who can tell and speak of, and recount the works of the Lord?
God has seen all, he has heard all, and he listens to all.
5. He sent his prophet to anoint me, Samuel to magnify me.
My brothers went out to meet him, beautiful of figure, beautiful of appearance.
6. They were tall of stature with beautiful hair, yet the Lord did not choose them.
7. He sent and took me from behind the flock, and anointed me with holy oil as a prince of his people, and a ruler among the sons of his Covenant.

Psalm 151B

The first display of David's power after God's prophet had anointed him.

1. Then I saw the Philistine taunting [from the enemy lines] . . .

(translation by G. Vermes, *The Dead Sea Scrolls in English*, Allen Lane: Penguin, 1997, 302)

The date of the original composition behind Psalm 151 is very uncertain. The handwriting of the Psalm Scroll 11Q5 is dated to the first half of the first century AD, and so is of little help. Although the language of Qumran Psalm 151A and B is based on biblical models, it also has late features and probably belongs to the Second Temple period (Hurvitz 1967: 82-87). As for the Greek version, though the LXX Psalter is generally dated to approximately the third century BC, we cannot be certain that Psalm 151 was included so early since we have no early citations of it. Furthermore, the superscription suggests that it was added after the main collection of 150 psalms was complete.

It is clear that Greek Psalm 151 must have been based on a Hebrew text resembling that of 11Q5. However, opinion differs as to whether the Greek or the Qumran Hebrew is closer to the lost original. Haran (1988: 171-82) and Smith (1997: 186) argue that the Qumran Psalm compositions represent the development and embellishment of a single shorter Hebrew text. In contrast, Sanders (1965: 59) and Strugnell (1966: 257-72, 278-81) believe that the Greek cannot be understood except by reference to Qumran Psalms 151A and B, which must therefore be very close to the original form.

Many of the ideas and much of the language of the psalm are drawn from 1 Samuel 15–18, and especially from chs. 16–17 (Smith 1997: 195-97). Similar emphases are found in the versions of David's story found in Sir. 47:2-11 and Ps.-Philo, *Bib. Ant.*, chs. 59–62 (Strugnell 1965: 207-16).

COMMENTARY

Superscription

The Greek acknowledges that the psalm is "outside the number," but defends its inclusion on the ground that it is *idiographos,* an authentic composition of David. Qumran Psalm 151A is entitled simply, "A Hallelujah of David, the son of Jesse." For the reference to David's fight with Goliath (described in v. 7 [Eng.] of the psalm), compare the Hebrew superscriptions of canonical Psalms 3, 18, 34, 51, 52, 54, 56, 59, 60, 63, 67, and 142, all referring to events in the life of David.

Verse 1

Lit. "small I was . . . and young"; cf. 1 Sam 16:11; 17:14, though the NRSV renders the Hebrew word "small" as "youngest." By placing the words "small" and "young" first in each phrase, the writer emphasizes David's insignificance in worldly terms (Rabinowitz 1964: 199), in preparation for the climactic conclusion of the psalm, which in the Greek version is David's killing of Goliath and his vindication of the entire people. (In the Hebrew version of 151A, the conclusion of the psalm is different, so the contrast there is with David's later status as ruler of the nation.)

In the Greek, David tends his father's sheep, but the Hebrew has David's father as subject: "he made me shepherd. . . ." The Hebrew syntax rather implies that David was given this menial task because of his lowly status within the family.

Verse 2

The context suggests that David began his musical activity while out pasturing the flocks. The Hebrew has more material at this point (151A:2-3), but scholars are still far from agreement as to its precise meaning. This is in part because the script of the scroll does not distinguish clearly between the letters *waw* and *yodh,* with the result that the forms for "my" and "his" are largely undifferentiated. See Sanders (1967: 100-103; 1984: 169, 176) for various attempts at rendering the text.

Taking one line of interpretation of the Hebrew, then, David complains that "the mountains do not bear witness for me, nor the hills, the trees will not report my words on my behalf, nor the flock my deeds" (Rabinowitz 1964: 193-200), the suggestion being that God alone hears David's praise of him. Another view is that David contrasts his praise of God with the muteness of nature: see, for example, Skehan (1963: 407-9): "I had said to myself, the mountains cannot witness to Him, nor the hills relate: neither the boughs of trees, my words, nor the flock, my compositions." But the first part of the stanza would then seem to contradict the common biblical notion that the natural world does praise God (e.g., Pss 96:11-12; 97:1; 145:10; 148:3-10; Isa 44:23; 55:12). Cross's translation (1978: 69) ("O that the mountains would bear Him witness, O that the hills would tell of Him, the trees [recount] His deeds, and the flock His works!") is in closer accord with biblical norms, but dependent on what is probably an anachronistic occurrence of a particular word (*lw'* understood as precative, "I wish!" "O that . . . !" rather than as the negative particle "not"). Dupont Sommer (1964: 37) preferred "Do the mountains not witness to Him . . . ? The trees esteemed my words, and the flock, my poems." He argued that the entire reference to nature was omitted in the Greek text because of the perceived Orphism of the psalm: the idea of nature responding to David's music was too close to the Greek myth in which Orpheus's playing entranced the animals (Dupont-Sommer 1964: 37-39; cf. Sanders 1965: 61-63). However, given the textual difficulties of the Hebrew text, it would be unwise to conclude that it was heterodox ideas that led to the omission of the section in the Greek translation. The many gaps and omissions in Greek may be mechanical, or a deliberate attempt to shorten the text, or simply due to misunderstanding of the Hebrew original.

Verse 3

The meaning of the English translation, based on the Greek, is unclear. Some Greek manuscripts have "(who hears) everything," which makes more sense. The corresponding Hebrew (151A:4) is much longer. Rabinowitz (1964: 194) and others have pointed out that the Hebrew could also be read as ". . . O that someone would report my deeds! The Lord of All saw. . . ." It is very likely that the shorter Greek text is due to haplography: the eye of an early scribe skipped a line.

Verse 4

The "messenger" presumably refers not to an angel (the Greek word *angelos* can refer to either) but to the prophet Samuel, who comes to David's town of Bethlehem in 1 Sam 16:4. (151A:5 is much more explicit: "He sent his prophet . . . Samuel. . . .") The subject of the rest of verse 4, "he took me . . . he anointed me," could be either Samuel or the Lord. In 1 Sam 16:13 it is Samuel who performs the anointing, though the Lord could be said to be the originator of the action. The first phrase could also refer to Samuel's request that David be fetched from his duties as shepherd, but it corresponds very closely to 2 Sam 7:8, where the Lord is the subject: "I took you from the pasture, from following the sheep."

In the Hebrew, the narrative order differs, with the brothers being introduced before the anointing. The subject of 151A:4 is clearly the Lord, and there are two more lines to round off Psalm 151A describing the Lord's removal of David from following the flock shepherding and his anointing as "prince," *nagid,* a word used of the leader of the nation. The passage bears a strong resemblance to Ps 78:70-71. Such sentiments form a triumphant parallel to David's appointment as a lowly shepherd in the Hebrew of v. 2.

Verse 5

Saul is also described as tall and handsome (1 Sam 9:2), and David's brother Eliab evidently impresses Samuel with his height and looks (1 Sam 16:6-7). The Hebrew (Ps 151A:5b-6) is fuller, and uses expressions found of Rachel in Gen 29:17 and Joseph in Gen 39:6. Implicit in both versions is the belief that the Lord looks on the heart and does not take into account the outward appearance (1 Sam 16:7).

Verses 6-7

The Greek alludes to the events of 1 Sam 17:40-51. As in 1 Sam 17:43, Goliath curses David by his gods, and as in 1 Sam 17:51 David beheads the fallen champion, but there is no reference in Psalm 151 to David using a sling against him. The idea of removing the disgrace of Israel occurs in 1 Sam 17:26, and here marks the climax and end of the psalm in Greek.

The corresponding Hebrew is found in Psalm 151B of the Qumran Psalm Scroll. However, the text is damaged, and the only words that can be deciphered refer to David's first sight of Goliath: we do not know how the Hebrew treated David's victory.

Psalm 151 as a Whole

The Qumran psalm has been described as a "poetic midrash" on 1 Sam 16:1-13 (Sanders 1965: 56), and the same is true of the Greek version. Both are examples of inner-biblical interpretation, where a later biblical writer reworks an earlier passage from the angle of the theology and literature of his time; the treatment of material in Kings as reworked by the Chronicler and the view of Israel's history in Psalm 78 are more familiar examples.

Both versions of Psalm 151 are interested only in the boyhood of David and his anointing as leader of the nation, followed by his triumph over Goliath, but they ignore his later and better-known role as mighty king. The Qumran psalm has one theme from outside 1 Samuel 16–17, David's psalmody to the Lord (only his skill in playing the lyre being mentioned in ch. 16). The author or editor no doubt understood 1 Sam 16:7 ("the LORD looks on the heart") in terms of David's personal piety and linked it to the tradition of his composition of Psalms. His praise of God in humble circumstances is rewarded by divine election to the leadership of the nation. The Greek psalm, in contrast, presents God's elevation of David as his sovereign choice for the deliverance of Israel. Whatever the origin of the differences between the two versions, their effect on the religious message of each is considerable.

Bibliography. Cross, F. M. 1978, "David, Orpheus, and Psalm 151:3-4," *BASOR* 231:69-71 • Dupont-Sommer, A. 1964, "Le Psaume CLI dans 11QPs[a] et le probléme de son origine essénnienne," *Sem* 14:25-62 • Haran, M. 1988, "The Two Text Forms of Ps 151," *JJS* 39:171-82 • Hurvitz, A. 1967, "The Language and Date of Psalm 151 from Qumran" (Hebrew), *ErIsr* 8:82-87 (Eng. summary *70-*71) • Rabinowitz, I. 1964, "The Alleged Orphism of 11QPss 28.3-12," *ZAW* n.s. 35:193-200 • Sanders, J. A. 1965, *The Psalm Scroll of Qumran Cave 11 (11QPs[a])*, Oxford: Clarendon, 54-64 • Sanders, J. A. 1967, *The Dead Sea Psalms Scroll*, Ithaca: Cornell University, 100-103 • Sanders, J. A. 1984, "A Multivalent Text: Psalm 151:3-4 Revisited," *HAR* 8:167-84 • Sanders, J. A, with J. H. Charlesworth and H. W. L. Rietz. 1997, "Non-Masoretic Psalms," in J. H. Charlesworth, ed., *The Dead Sea Scrolls: Hebrew, Aramaic, and Greek Texts with English Translations*, 4A: *Pseudepigraphic and Non-Masoretic Psalms and Prayers*, Tübingen: Mohr and Louisville: Westminster John Knox, 163-69 • Skehan, P. W. 1963, "The Apocryphal Psalm 151," *CBQ* 25:407-9 • Smith, M. S. 1997, "How To Write a Poem: The Case of Psalm 151A (11QPs[a] 28.3-12)," in T. Muraoka and J. F. Elwolde, eds., *The Hebrew of the Dead Sea Scrolls and Ben Sira: Proceedings of a Symposium Held at Leiden University, 11-14 December 1995*, Leiden: Brill, 182-208 • Strugnell, J. 1965, "More Psalms of David," *CBQ* 27:207-16 • Strugnell, J. 1966, "Notes on the Text and Transmission of the Apocryphal Psalms 151, 154 (= Syr. II) and 155 (= Syr. III)," *HTR* 59:257-72, 278-81 • Wigtil, D. N. 1983, "The Sequence of the Translations of the Apocryphal Psalm 151," *RQ* 11:401-7.

3 Maccabees

Philip S. Alexander

INTRODUCTION

Preserved only by the Greek, Syriac, and Armenian Churches, 3 Maccabees seems to have been unknown in the West before the time of the Reformation. The work is oddly named, given that it does not once mention the Maccabees and, in fact, purports to record events in the time of Ptolemy Philopator (Ptolemy IV, 221-203 BC), over forty years before the Maccabean revolt. It may have acquired its title simply because it was placed in a stichometry or in one of the great Greek Bible codices immediately after the first two books of Maccabees. The name, however, is not entirely inappropriate since there are numerous similarities between the story of the book and the history of the Maccabean rebellion.

3 Maccabees purports to be history, but it is history heavily worked in a rhetorical and novelistic style, rich in pathos, melodrama, and miracle, and topped off with a liberal garnish of apologetic. The author has drawn on a variety of sources, which he has not always adapted fully to his own account (see, e.g., 1:2 and 2:25), nor always interpreted correctly (see, e.g., 2:27-30 and the curious double celebration of the festival at 6:30-40 and at 7:17-20). As a result, his narrative occasionally lacks clarity, and the links between events are unconvincing. For his account of the battle of Raphia and Philopator's visit to Jerusalem (1:1-28), and possibly for other information about the Ptolemaic court and the king's Friends (a class of court official), he may have drawn on Ptolemy of Megalopolis's lost history of the reign of Ptolemy Philopator, a source which Polybius also employed in Book 5 of his *Histories*. His account of the measures against the Jews in 2:25-30 is probably derived, as the text hints, from an actual decree of Ptolemy Philopator, recorded in the form of a public inscription, which, however, he appears to have misunderstood (see below). Some of the phrasing used there may record the precise wording of the decree. Philopator's plan to kill the Jews by having them crushed by drunken elephants (5:1–6:21) is almost certainly based on an incident recorded also by Josephus in *Against Apion* 2.53-55. If Josephus is to be believed (and in this case he probably is), the incident occurred in the reign not of Philopator but of Ptolemy Physcon (Ptolemy IX, 146-117 BC). Physcon, angry at the Alexandrian Jews because they had backed Cleopatra rather than him after the death of Philometor, arrested them and threatened to have them trampled by elephants. However, the combination of an apparition and the entreaties of his favorite concubine dissuaded him from carrying out his threat, and "that" concludes Josephus, "is the origin of the well-known festival which the Jews of Alexandria keep, with good reason, on this day, because of the deliverance so manifestly vouchsafed to them by God." The author of 3 Maccabees probably conflated an Alexandrian festival of deliverance dating from the reign of Physcon with an earlier festival of deliverance dating from the reign of Philopator, which may have originated in Ptolemais (see on 7:17). The dating of the Alexandrian festival to Physcon's reign may have been less clear in his than in Josephus's source. He may have assumed that the two festivals celebrated the same events. (This conflation possibly survives in the curious double celebration of the festival in 3 Maccabees, once in Alexandria and once in Ptolemais.) Finally, the author of 3 Maccabees doubtless used folk traditions circulating within the Jewish community, and consulted the inscription at Ptolemais mentioned at 7:20, which may have contained a brief history of the festival it commemorated. He took all these sources, pondered them, made inferences, and wove them together with embellishments supplied by his own fertile imagination to create the present tale.

Despite much muddle, implausibility and outright fiction, 3 Maccabees, like the book of Esther, almost certainly contains a historical core, though isolating that core is far from easy. It seems to have been written to explain a festival which Jews in Egypt had been celebrating for some time. The center of this festival, which ran from 7-13 Epiphi (= 1-7 July), appears historically to have been the town of Ptolemais in the Fayum. The events which the festival originally celebrated were probably linked in some way to the decree mentioned in 3:27-30. That decree, which is almost certainly genuine (though misinterpreted), would have affected all Egyptian Jews, but for some reason the flash point of Jewish opposition to it must have been the Fayum. The Jews of this region, or their representatives, were hauled off to Alexandria for punishment, but in the end they were released unharmed and allowed to return home. Their deliverance was recorded in their hometown in an inscription, in the dedication of a new synagogue and in an annual festival (7:17-20). 3 Maccabees, which must have been written long after these events, recounts the origins of the festival and draws out its religious lessons. Like the book of Esther on Purim and (much later) the Scroll of Antiochus on Hanukkah, 3 Maccabees may have been intended as a kind of *megillah* for public reading on this festival. However, it does more than simply record the origins of the festival: it attempts actively to promote it and to urge its observance upon all Egyptian Jews. It even links it with events in faraway Jerusalem. At first reading the Jews in the country *(chōra)* seem peripheral to the story: the action begins in Jerusalem, spreads to Alexandria, and eventually implicates the country Jews. But a closer reading shows that, in fact, it is the Jews of Alexandria who from 4:12 onward are marginal and the country Jews who hold center stage. The author of 3 Maccabees' confusion of a local Ptolemais festival dating from the time of Philopator with a similar local Alexandrian festival from the time of Physcon may have encouraged him to involve the Jews of Alexandria more fully in the story. 3 Maccabees tries to suggest that the persecution had, in fact, embraced all Egyptian Jews and that, therefore, the deliverance should be commemorated by all.

Why should 3 Maccabees have promoted a local festival in this way? It is possible that when it was written the Jews of Egypt were once again under threat, and the festival's message was deemed to be relevant, to encourage them to stand firm and to hope for divine deliverance. Some have argued that its composition should be linked with the reorganization of Egypt as a Roman province in 24 BC. This might have threatened the civic status of the Jews by making them subject to poll tax, which was paid only by those who did not have full civic rights. This suggestion focuses attention on 2:28, where the Jews are threatened with registration for poll tax *(laographia)* and with reduction to servile status. However, it is religious rather than civic issues that dominate the book — loyalty to the ancestral traditions and resistance to idolatry. Others link the composition of the book with the dispute over the status of the Jews in Alexandria in AD 38 during the reign of Caligula, when the local Greeks rioted against the Jews and tried to force them to set up statues of the emperor in their synagogues. The Roman governor Flaccus sided with the Greeks and declared the Jews to be aliens (the story is told in Philo's *In Flaccum* 41–46 and *Legatio ad Gaium* 132–35). But 3 Maccabees does not create the impression of having emerged from so specific a crisis. "No specific persecution is needed to explain the composition of an aetiological romance of this sort in the constantly tense Jewish community of Alexandria at any time after the mid-second century BC" (Schürer 1986: 540). The book's general moral of loyalty to the community would always be seen as relevant by the leadership of an ethnic minority struggling to maintain its identity. What may have provoked the reinterpretation of the festival was not a political but a literary event, the arrival in Egypt of two Jewish works promoting "foreign" festivals of a rather similar nature — the book of Esther (Purim) and the Second Book of Maccabees (Hanukkah). Local pride, not to say rivalry, may have led the author of 3 Maccabees to remind Egyptian Jews that their ancestors were no less zealous than their co-religionists in Jerusalem or Persia in resisting tyranny and in defending their ancestral laws; they had their own local heroes to celebrate. Whether or not he intended to promote the Egyptian festival *instead of* either Purim or Hanukkah is less clear. However, the absence of any reference to the story of Esther, which the author of 3 Maccabees must surely have known, is eloquent and suggests that he disapproved of Egyptian Jews adopting this festival. (Mordecai's letter in Esth 9:20 enjoining the observance of Purim was sent to "all the Jews who were in all the provinces of King Ahasuerus"; as Esth 1:1 makes clear, this would have included Egypt.)

The affinities between 3 Maccabees on the one hand, and 2 Maccabees, the *Letter of Aristeas,* and Greek Esther on the other, suggest that it belongs to the same period and emanates from broadly the same circles. A date of between 100 and 75 BC is very probable. The author was clearly an Egyptian Jew, and, given his knowledge of the topography of Alexandria, probably a native of that city, though the possibility that he hailed from Ptolemais, where the festival originated, should not be totally discounted. If he was a "country cousin," this might explain his general religious conservatism, his unpolished Greek style, and his apparent indifference to any of the distinctive developments of Alexandrian Jewish thought. Lexically his Greek is rich and shows a considerable level of Greek education, and his narrative powers are by no means negligible (the narrative perspective of 5:48ff. is masterly), but his general style is poor and bombastic and his book contains numerous minor textual and linguistic problems which have never been satisfactorily solved and which probably go back to his inadequate command of language.

3 Maccabees deals with issues of assimilation that, as contemporary documents such as the *Letter of Aristeas* show, were exercising the minds of Egyptian Jews. It advocates a dual loyalty — to God and to the king — but if these loyalties came into conflict, then loyalty to God takes precedence: martyrdom should be contemplated, though in this case it was avoided by divine intervention in response to prayer. The book envisages three distinct audiences. First, the Jews of Egypt, whom it exhorts to hold fast to their ancestral way of life and to avoid the pressures, political or cultural, to assimilate. For the author assimilation is idolatry. A focus of this rededication to Judaism was to be the universal observance of the Ptolemais festival. Second, it addresses the non-Jews of Egypt, and particularly the ruling class, asserting robustly that the Jews are loyal, law-abiding citizens who contribute in all sorts of ways to civic life. They are not a threat to the state and should not be discriminated against or persecuted. Third, it obliquely addresses the Jews of Jerusalem, showing them that although the Jews of Egypt live in exile and may go to Greek schools, they are no less zealous than the Jerusalemites for the law of God.

Like the book of Esther, 3 Maccabees reads chillingly in the perspective of Jewish history. Though in an exaggerated and, to some extent, fictional way, it addresses the problem of genocide. It explores the mentality of tyranny and of racial hatred. The charges leveled here against the Jews were to become the stock-in-trade of anti-Semitism. Its nuanced descriptions of the reactions of non-Jews to the anti-Jewish measures (see especially 3:1-10), of the state's exploitation of popular anti-Jewish resentment in order to further its policies (2:26; 3:2; 4:1), and of the bureaucratization of mass murder (4:14-15) show uncanny prescience. And if its claim that God would directly intervene to protect his people is too pat and would be falsified time and again in the subsequent sorry history of Jewish persecution, it was doubtless sincerely meant and based, as the author would have argued, on good historical precedent.

COMMENTARY

A Tale of Two Cities: Events in Jerusalem (1:1–2:24)

Though 3 Maccabees is concerned with the Jewish community in Egypt and Alexandria, its action begins in another country and another city — Jerusalem. Events in Jerusalem trigger events in Alexandria. The reason is simple: both cities have Jewish populations. Philopator, having been frustrated by the Jews of Jerusalem, decides to take his revenge on the Jews of Alexandria (2:27). He acknowledges a link: the fundamental identity of the two communities is affirmed and their destinies inextricably intertwined. The parallelism between Jerusalem and Alexandria, expressed in the parallelism between the two halves of the book, is one of the themes of 3 Maccabees: the Jews of Egypt are shown as no less zealous for the traditions of their ancestors than their coreligionists in Palestine, and are no less saved by divine intervention. The author of 3 Maccabees is, perhaps, making here a subtle intracommunal point: he and other Egyptian Jews like him may have acquired a Greek education and have studied Greek wisdom, but that does not mean that they have sold out to Hellenism — they remain loyal Jews.

The parallelism between Jerusalem and Alexandria also resonates, somewhat awkwardly, in another context. 3 Maccabees is, in part, about the civil rights of the Egyptian Jews. However, the reference to Jerusalem reminds the reader that the Jewish homeland is elsewhere. Jews in the diaspora often displayed great pride in Jerusalem and its temple (see, e.g., the *Letter of Aristeas*) and clearly believed that it bestowed prestige on them in the eyes of their non-Jewish neighbors: Philo calls Jerusalem the "mother city" *(mētropolis)* of the Jews and the far-flung diaspora communities her colonies (*In Flaccum* 46). But a possible effect of this is to reinforce the metic status of the Jews, to remind the reader that they are foreigners. 3 Maccabees to a degree counters this by stressing the unswerving loyalty of the Alexandrian community to the local administration. They are as loyal politically to Ptolemy, and as solicitous for his welfare, as they are loyal religiously to their ancestral way of life.

The Battle of Raphia (1:1-7)

The battle of Raphia explains how Philopator came to visit Jerusalem. The battle was a real battle, known from the Greek historian Polybius (5.79-86), which took place in spring 217 BC. It was part of the constant skirmishing between the Seleucids of Syria and the Ptolemies of Egypt to decide who would control Palestine. The Antiochus mentioned at 1:1 is Antiochus III (224-187 BC). Raphia is the biblical Raphiah, modern Tel Rafah, twenty miles southwest of Gaza, a town seen in ancient Jewish texts as marking the southern border of the land of Israel and the site of several battles throughout history.

The author of 3 Maccabees treats the battle more fully than is necessary in order to get Philopator to Jerusalem. However, his expansions of the story allow him to make some points which are useful within his overall argument and which add pathos and human interest to the narrative. The first expansion deals with the attempt by Theodotus to assassinate Philopator. The details of this in 3 Maccabees are obscure, and it is uncertain what prior knowledge the author is presupposing on the part of the reader. Polybius deals with this episode at length (5.81) and makes it clear that Theodotus was a deserter from Ptolemy who had gone over to Antiochus's side some time before and served him well. 3 Maccabees only hints at this by referring to Theodotus "crossing the lines" (*diekomisthē,* 1:2). 1:2 should probably be translated, "he took with him the best of the Ptolemaic armor which had previously been assigned to him"; that is to say, he dressed up in his old Ptolemaic regimentals, in order to insinuate himself into the Ptolemaic camp as a high-ranking Ptolemaic officer and thus get close to the king. Polybius says that Theodotus took two companions with him, but 3 Maccabees implies that he acted alone: he alone conceived the plan, and he alone was to kill the king. The element of personal treachery is thus highlighted: the issue would not be decided in manly fashion on the field of battle, but by a renegade's dagger in the darkness of the night. Polybius also confirms that the plot failed, but he says nothing about the role of Dositheus in frustrating it. It is unlikely that 3 Maccabees totally invented Dositheus: if it had, it would surely not have made him an apostate Jew (for its attitude toward apostates, see 7:10-15). Dositheus is a plausible Jewish name (very common in the Jewish papyri from Egypt; cf. also Greek Esther 11:1 and Josephus *Ag. Ap.* 2.49, who mentions two Jewish generals of Ptolemy Philometor, Onias and Dositheus). In fact, a Dositheus, son of Drimylus, is mentioned in *P. Hibeh* 90 (dated 222 BC) (*CPJ* 127e). He appears to have been a Jew influential at court in the reign of Ptolemy III Euergetes (246-221 BC) (*CPJ* 127a-e). That he would have continued to advise Philopator, Euergetes' successor, is entirely believable. 3 Maccabees seems to have adapted its source, which was also used by Polybius. According to Polybius, it was Andreas, the king's physician, who was killed; the implication is that the assassination was botched in the darkness of the night, and the wrong man murdered. 3 Maccabees, however, has it fail because of a clever stratagem devised by Dositheus. But if this was the case, Dositheus could hardly have proposed that the king's physician should sleep in the king's bed, so the substitute had to become "a mere commoner," "an insignificant person." Dositheus is a foil to Theodotus. Like Theodotus, he is a renegade, in his case from his ancestral religion (in *P. Hibeh* 90 he holds the exalted position of priest of Alexander and the deified Ptolemies, which would not have won the approval of a traditionalist like the author of 3 Maccabees); but, unlike Theodotus, he is totally loyal to his political master. Like Joseph, he was a court Jew, an adviser to the king. Like Mordecai in Esther, he protects the king against a treacherous courtier. He is indicative of the real political loyalties of the Jews.

3 Maccabees' second expansion of the battle story recounts Arsinoë's exhortation to the Ptolemaic troops. That Philopator took Arsinoë (here correctly designated his sister, but later, in pharaonic fashion, to become his wife) with him on the campaign is confirmed by Polybius, but whereas Polybius has her and her brother address the troops and promise rewards before the battle, 3 Maccabees heightens the drama by stating that she alone intervened, while the battle was raging and when the issue was in doubt. And her entreaties and promises of money (two gold minae, or two hundred drachmae, is a very substantial sum per person) proved effective. The princess's exotic behavior and disregard for social norms ("with braided hair hanging loose") points up the extreme peril of the situation. 3 Maccabees again uses unconventional behavior by women at 1:18-20 and at 4:6 (in the latter case forced upon them) to bring home the gravity of the events, to heighten the drama, and to generate pathos. And if, as seems likely, there is a strong intertextuality between 3 Maccabees and the book of Esther, then Arsinoë provides the sort of female interest in the former that Queen Esther does in the latter, just as Dositheus son of Drimylus in 3 Maccabees plays the role of Mordecai in Esther.

That Philopator should have toured Palestine after his victory to secure its loyalty is likely, but when we again compare 3 Maccabees with its source, which we can access through Polybius, we detect a subtle "spin" being given to the story. Polybius, faithfully reflecting the source, stresses the gifts which the subjects gave to the king, but in 3 Maccabees it is the king's gifts to his subjects that are to the fore: he is shown as a pious ruler who honors the gods of his people and respects their cults.

Philopator Tries to Enter the Sanctuary (1:8-15)

The Jews take the initiative in approaching Philopator and offering their congratulations. The delegation comes with the highest authority — from the Jerusalem *gerousia* (just which body is indicated here is far from clear). It is reminiscent of the delegation that, according to Jewish tradition, went out from Jerusalem to meet Alexander the Great (Josephus *Ant.* 11.329-39; cf. *b. Yoma* 69a; *Lev. Rab.* 13.5; the *Scroll of Fasting* 9). When Philopator first arrives in Jerusalem he behaves impeccably, offering sacrifices and thank offerings to the "greatest God" (*theos megistos,* a divine title used also in 1:9, 16; 3:11; 4:16; 5:25; 7:22 and in 2 Macc 3:36), and attributing his recent victory to the God of the Jews. 1:9 does not mean that Philopator personally offered the sacrifices; that would have been sacrilege. Rather, he ordered the sacrifices to be offered on his behalf and, presumably, at his expense. This would have been an effective means of gaining the favor of the local population, and certainly the Jerusalem priesthood would have had no qualms about making sacrifices on the king's behalf. It is only after the sacrifices have been offered that he actually enters the temple. The word "place" *(topos)* in 1:9, commonly used in Alexandrian Jewish Greek to denote the Jerusalem temple (2 and 3 Maccabees, the *Letter of Aristeas,* and elsewhere), refers to the temple as a whole, and not the sanctuary. Philopator is impressed by the temple's architecture and organization. The compliment to the temple is obvious: Philopator had a reputation as a connoisseur of the arts and had, of course, seen the mighty temples of Egypt. But then things started to go wrong: he wanted to explore and to enter the sanctuary (the holy of holies). The allusion to the Day of Atonement, the sole occasion on which the high priest alone could enter the sanctuary, shows that it is the innermost sanctum that is in view (Exod 30:10; Lev 16:34; cf. Heb 9:7). That Philopator tried to violate the sanctuary, plausible though it is in itself, is not corroborated by other texts, and it is suspicious that, apart from 3 Maccabees, this dramatic episode has left no mark on Jewish sources (such as the book of Daniel; see Dan 11:11-12). A similar incident is recorded by Josephus as having occurred in 63 BC, when the Roman general Pompey entered the sanctuary (*J.W.* 1.152). Some have suggested that the Pompey incident was the model for 3 Maccabees here (which, if it were true, would have implications for the date of the work), but this is far from certain. It is just as easy to suppose that Pompey shows how any conqueror of Jerusalem would have been tempted to behave, if backed by his legions. The Jews cite their custom and quote to the king their law (cf. Exod 30:10; Lev 16:34) to dissuade him from violating their sanctuary, but to no avail: he has entered every other sanctuary, why should he not enter this one as well? 1:14 is puzzling. The Greek is obscure, but it seems to imply that the king was provoked by an undiplomatic remark of one of the bystanders (it should probably be translated, "someone thoughtlessly said that he [the king] did wrong to take this [his safe entry into other sanctuaries] as a portent"). It lifts a little of the blame from the king's shoulders, but still leaves him behaving like a spoiled child. The background to the comment may lie in the wisdom tradition, with its exhortations, especially relevant to royal counselors, to guard the tongue (Prov 13:3; 21:23).

The Jerusalem Jews Oppose Philopator (1:16-29)

Jewish opposition to Philopator's intention to violate the sanctuary ripples out from the priests to embrace the whole people. No longer certain that they can sway the king, the priests turn to God to avert the wicked deed. The fact that they are in full ceremonial dress adds solemnity to their supplications. The behavior of the women is used to show how Jewish zeal for the law transcends both nature and social norms. Brides forsake the bridal canopy (Gk. *pastos* = Heb. *huppah,* as also in 4:6) in order to join in the protest. Mothers and nurses forsake their newborn charges. Young women who would normally not be seen out of doors, at least unveiled, rush into the street bareheaded. The king's own counsellors (= "the elders around the king," 1:23) make one last attempt to change his mind, but when they fail, they too join with the Jews in supplicating the Jewish God. The king is left isolated in his arrogant defiance of the universal will and of the law of God. 1:29 provides a vividly imagined climax: the hubbub of supplication reverberates so loudly around the temple courts that it seems as if the building itself is crying out in protest. The temple as a locus of public protest is well attested in Second Temple Jewish history. The episode here closely resembles the description of Jewish opposition to Heliodorus's attempt to remove the gold from the temple treasury in 2 Macc 3:14-35, and it is very likely that the author of 3 Maccabees knew this passage.

1:22 makes a telling point: Jewish zeal for the law may result in armed rebellion. The hotheads call for their compatriots "to take up arms and die courageously for the ancestral law." They are restrained by the "old men and the elders" (variant reading: "old men and the priests") and are in the end content to join in nonviolent protest. There is a definite, if veiled, warning to the authorities here: push the Jews too far and they may revolt — no idle threat given that 3 Maccabees was almost certainly written after the Hasmonean rebellion. But there is also a warning to the Jews not to resort to arms; rather, they should pray to God, who is well able to defend his own cause. 3 Maccabees is infused by zeal for the law, but as a political tract it is pacifist: it advocates a kind of Gandhian principle of passive resistance to tyranny, involving, if need be, martyrdom (this is the probable meaning of 1:29, "all at that time preferred death to the profanation of the place"). It thus stands at the opposite end of the political spectrum to the *War Scroll* at Qumran, which envisages and plans for a real war against the enemies of Israel.

The Prayer of Simon the High Priest (2:1-20)

The focus of the action shifts dramatically. Ch. 1 leaves us with a crowd scene and general uproar. Ch. 2 focuses on a single individual and a single, dignified voice. The high priest Simon (i.e., Simon II, "the Just," 219-199 BC; cf. Sir 50:1-24), on his knees, with hands outstretched in supplication, becomes the embodiment of Jewish opposition to the king.

The text of Simon's prayer has been specifically composed for the occasion (note especially 2:2 and 2:14), but it closely reflects Jewish liturgical style both inside and outside the Bible (see Gaster 1978 and Hadas 1953 for a partial list of examples) and is simpler and less bombastic than the narrative framework; interestingly, the author's grasp of liturgical style is much more assured than his grasp of historical style. As the Dead Sea Scrolls show, the late Second Temple period was one of the most creative in the history of Jewish liturgy. The author of 3 Maccabees skillfully constructs a moving and effective prayer which stresses a number of themes appropriate to the situation: (1) God is ruler, creator, and judge. The majesty of God, "the king of the heavens, and sovereign of all creation," puts the posturing of the earthly king in perspective and rebukes his arrogance. The king is reminded that God is not indifferent to what goes on in his world but judges wrongdoers.

(2) Examples from history of arrogance that was punished by God. The first example is the giants. There is an allusion here is to an interpretation of Gen 6:1-4 which identified the Nephilim as the monstrous and gigantic offspring of the fallen angels (the sons of God) and mortal women (the daughters of men). This tradition was widespread in Second Temple literature (LXX Gen 6:4; *1 Enoch* 7:1-6; 10:9; *Jub.* 5:1-10). All the sources agree that the giants oppressed humankind and that they contributed mightily to the evil conditions that finally necessitated the flood, but the view, apparently taken here, that God brought the flood specifically to destroy the giants was not universal. It is implied in some rabbinic texts (though the giant Og, who became king of Bashan, was said to have survived by riding on top of the ark!). According to *1 Enoch* and *Jubilees,* however, the giants were killed by divine intervention in response to the entreaties of oppressed humanity before the advent of the flood, a scenario which would have equally fitted the context here, but which is not as dramatic as invoking the flood. Greek mythology also had a tradition about giants, which probably influenced the Jewish development of the theme, and, significantly, in the Greek tradition the arrogance of the giants, and their rebellion against the gods, is emphasized. The second example is the people of Sodom (Gen 18:16–19:29). The Sodomites were certainly a byword for vice, but hardly for arrogance. However, they may have been chosen here because they were sinners who suffered a dramatic, catastrophic punishment, like the generation of the flood, or possibly because they provided an oblique allusion to the sexual mores of the Ptolemaic court (cf. 2:26). The statement that they "were made an example to those who should come after them" might allude to the salt formations at the southern end of the Dead Sea (like "Lot's Wife"), which were seen by later travelers as a permanent memorial to the destruction of Sodom. The final, climactic example is especially apt: it is the Pharaoh of the Exodus — in a sense a predecessor of Philopator. The clause "and when they had seen works of your hands, they praised you" alludes to the Song at the Sea in Exodus 15.

(3) The third theme of the prayer is God's choice of Jerusalem and of the temple as his earthly dwelling where he manifests his presence, and where he meets with his people and listens to their prayers. This highlights the enormity of the sacrilege which Philopator is about to commit. 3 Maccabees seems to suggest that God's choice of Jerusalem and of the temple goes back to the creation of the world (see 2:9). There may be a distant echo here of the idea that Jerusalem, and specifically the rock within the present-day Dome of the Rock (on which, according to tradition, the high altar once stood), is the navel of the earth — the first-created point, from which the rest of the world grew like a fetus from the umbilicus (*Jub.* 8:19; Tanḥuma, *Qedoshim* 10, ed. Buber, 4:78).

(4) The final theme of the prayer is confession of sin. At first sight this is surprising since the sin at issue would appear to be the terrible sacrilege that Philopator is about to commit, and not the sins of Israel. But the prayer finds a subtle connection between the two. Philopator is able to act as he does because Israel is at present subjected to her enemies, and that subjugation is a direct result of her sin. Because through her sins she has opened the door to the present wicked deed, Israel is indirectly responsible for it. Hence the plea to God not to lay the deed to her account, but to forgive her sins and to deliver her from her oppressors.

God Punishes Philopator (2:21-24)

In 2 Macc 3:25-26 Heliodorus is attacked by supernatural agents (a horse and his rider, and two young men), and in

2 Macc 9:7 Antiochus has a stroke and falls from his chariot. The affliction that befalls Philopator here reads like a rather precise description of an epileptic seizure. The author would, of course, like most of his contemporaries, have regarded such attacks as evidence of divine displeasure. Both Heliodorus and Antiochus are carried off in litters, in a comparatively dignified fashion. Philopator is "dragged" away. The scene is grimly comic: the king who at 1:26 was advancing so confidently to enter the sanctuary is now pulled unceremoniously away by his panic-stricken courtiers. 3 Maccabees is careful to note that Philopator did not repent. Like Pharaoh at the time of the Exodus, he hardened his heart, despite the evident sign of divine displeasure.

Events in Alexandria (2:25–7:23)

Events now move to the main theater of action, Egypt, and especially to Alexandria. They oscillate between the city and the country, and build to a dramatic climax, which is twice delayed. The Jewish community, threatened with annihilation, is finally saved and restored to its former position. As in the first part of the book, though details are obscure, the general narrative is clear and vigorously told, with clever use of documents and direct speech to vary the texture, and with dramatic changes of perspective.

Hostile Measures against the Jews of Alexandria (2:25–3:1)

The blackening of the king's general character is in accord with the ancient sources, but is somewhat unexpected in context. Certainly in the earlier narrative he is portrayed as acting arrogantly, but he is not without redeeming features (see 1:7). Here he is depicted as totally debauched and immoral. And the "previously mentioned drinking companions and comrades" of 2:25 are not, in fact, previously mentioned in the extant form of the book. The most probable explanation of these inconsistencies is that 3 Maccabees is here slavishly following a source and failing to adapt it to its own narrative. The alternative explanation, that the "drinking companions" were originally mentioned in the lost beginning of the book, is less convincing.

The king's attack on the Jews begins with anti-Jewish propaganda (the probable meaning of 2:26): the content of the "evil reports" that were circulated can doubtless be filled out from 3:2, 7 and 22-24. But he then moves to judicial measures. 2:27-30 probably have a historical core. They show considerable knowledge of Ptolemaic administrative practice and language. The posting of decrees in the form of inscriptions or of *stelai* is well documented. And some of the phrasing of the decree sounds authentic. The "tower" mentioned is probably the citadel on the peninsula of Lochias in Alexandria, which served as the Ptolemaic palace. However, there is undoubtedly considerable incoherence in the narrative, perhaps caused by the author of 3 Maccabees' not fully understanding his source. It does not make sense to say that it was the Jews who *refused* to participate in the state cult who were to be branded with the ivy leaf of Dionysus when that brand was surely meant as a sign of acceptance of the cult. Being branded was a sign of apostasy from Judaism, not of loyalty to it. Perhaps the author of 3 Maccabees viewed the branding with such abhorrence as a physical mutilation that he assumed it was intended as a punishment, or he linked it with the practice of branding runaway slaves. 3:20 offers a reprise of the events recorded here and points to a rather more plausible scenario, which our author has garbled. After his return from the victory of Raphia, Philopator probably decided to extend certain civic rights to non-Greeks, including the Jews. This is believable: he had used Egyptians to good effect in his phalanx, and as 3:21 hints, Jews were playing a significant part in the army and the administration (see also 1:3). Civic rights and religion were, however, closely linked: full citizenship was open only to those who took part in the state cult, which functioned, like swearing allegiance today to the monarch or the state, or saluting the flag, as a basic test of loyalty. Philopator probably felt there was a need for such a cult to create a sense of cohesion and national identity among the diverse ethnic groups which made up his kingdom. The state cult was centered on the worship of Dionysus (the "mysteries" mentioned at 2:30). The interest of the Ptolemies in general, and of Philopator in particular, in the cult of Dionysus is well documented: Philopator issued coins (drachmas and didrachmas) which display an ivy-crowned head of Dionysus. Those who were "initiated into the mysteries" and participated in the state cult were branded with the ivy leaf of Dionysus — a crude but highly effective way to keep track of those who did or did not conform.

Those who did not conform suffered a threefold penalty. (1) First, they lost whatever rights and privileges they may have had as citizens. Citizenship in Egypt was complex, but it is probable that numbers of non-Greeks, including Jews, in virtue of their wealth, education, and social position, enjoyed *de facto* if not *de jure* citizenship. (It is unlikely, despite the claims of Josephus, that the Jews as a group had full citizenship.) The new measures would have had the effect of clarifying a rather murky situation and of determining who was and who was not a full citizen. In the case of the Jews, it would have meant a return to "their former limited status," that is, to the status they occupied before they were emancipated by Ptolemy II Philadelphus, 283-244 BC (*Letter of Aristeas* 12–27). With the loss of privilege went loss of social standing, something hard for the politically marginalized to bear. (2) Second, dissenters suffered a financial penalty: they became subject to the poll tax, which was paid only by non-citizens (this is the probable implication of *laographia* in 2:28). (3) Third, they were forbidden to practice their own cults (2:28). The state cult was not exclusive: it allowed the worship of other gods, provided their devotees also participated, in typical polytheistic fashion, in the state religion. This would have hit the monotheistic Jews particularly hard. Many of them probably did not exercise even *de facto* the privileges of citizenship and were already paying poll tax, so they would have had nothing to lose on these two counts, but forbidding them their own form of worship would have touched them all to the quick.

The measures were probably not historically aimed at the Jews specifically, but Jews would undoubtedly have formed the main group that would have refused to participate in the state cult; 2:28, "that all Jews shall be subjected to a registration involving the poll tax and to the status of slaves," is probably not a direct quotation from the decree but an interpretation of its inevitable results. Jewish reaction to the decree, as described in 2:31-33, rings true and has been repeated a thousand times throughout the long history of Jewish oppression. Some Jews compromised for the sake of social advancement. The majority, however, held firm and attempted to bribe the corrupt officials (tyrannies [cf. 3:8] are usually corrupt) to ignore the fact that they were continuing to observe their own religion, though they did not support the state cult — an act of defiance punishable by death. This is probably the meaning of 2:32: "But the majority acted firmly with a courageous spirit and did not abandon their religion; and by paying money in exchange for life they confidently attempted to save themselves from the registration." The decree did not actually compel everyone to join in the state cult; one could opt out and take the (admittedly severe) consequences. The one point where Jews were certain to fall foul of the regulations was in continuing their ancestral worship without supporting the state cult. "The registration" here and in 2:29 was registration as devotees of Dionysus. From the perspective of history the words "they remained resolutely hopeful of obtaining help" are poignant. They played for time and hoped the trouble would pass. They put the compromisers under the ban *(ḥerem)*, withdrawing from all religious, social, and commercial intercourse with them, thus denying them the possibility of having the best of both worlds, namely, participating in the state cult and at the same time retaining their links with their own ethnic and religious community.

The king, learning of the Jews' attempts to subvert his decree, decides on a policy of genocide: all Jews are untrustworthy, and all must be put to death. Just as his anger against the Jews in Jerusalem spilled over into anger against the Jews of Alexandria, now his anger against the Jews of Alexandria spills over into anger against the Jews in the country (the *chōra*, the area outside Alexandria). Though the motivation is hardly plausible, the determination of the status of the Jews of Alexandria was bound to affect the status of the Jews throughout Egypt. By far the largest Jewish population was in Alexandria, but significant numbers of Jews also lived in the Fayum.

The Attitude of the Jews' Neighbors (3:2-10)

In an important aside the author of 3 Maccabees explores the attitude of the non-Jews toward the anti-Jewish measures. He acknowledges that many hated the Jews, and implies that this hatred made them complicit in the attempted genocide. Judeophobia was common in the ancient Mediterranean world. It centered, as here, on two charges: first, Jews were atheists; that is to say, they disregarded the gods of the state — indeed, they denied their very existence and worshiped only their own God. The charge of atheism naturally evolved into a charge of disloyalty toward the state. Second, they were misanthropes; that is to say, they kept themselves to themselves and did not integrate socially with the Gentile population. The basis of this social separation was the Jewish dietary laws. Both of these charges had a clear basis in fact which 3 Maccabees does not attempt to deny. However, in defense it urges that the Jews should be judged by their deeds. In actual fact they maintained goodwill and unswerving loyalty toward the state (2:2), and they behaved honestly and uprightly toward their non-Jewish neighbors (2:5). There is a real and deeply felt issue here. 3 Maccabees' apology for the Jews is comparable to similar apologies in the *Letter of Aristeas* and elsewhere, which reply to pagan attacks on the Jews, one of the earliest of which was in the *History of Egypt* by the Egyptian priest Manetho (fl. 280 BC).

3:2, which should be translated "an occasion being afforded for the charge that they [the Jews] were preventing them from observing the laws," contains an accusation specific to this case: the Jews, by suborning the officials, were frustrating the implementation of the king's decree (= the laws). Bribery of officialdom always carries this risk.

3 Maccabees, however, significantly, acknowledges that not all Gentiles were anti-Jewish. Alexandria was a cosmopolitan city which contained many "races" *(phyloi,* 3:6). Of these the Greeks are singled out as more kindly disposed toward the Jews. The reference must be to ordinary Greeks who were "neighbors, friends, and business partners" (3:10) of the Jews, rather than to the Greek ruling class, who were the source of the Jews' woes. 3 Maccabees goes out of its way to exonerate these Greeks. 3:8 implies that popular anti-Jewish riots had broken out (a common enough event in Alexandria; cf. the disturbances under Caligula), and in the face of overwhelming numbers decent citizens could do little to help. Besides, these Greeks lived under a tyranny which was fanning the anti-Jewish flames: their options were limited to private expressions of sympathy and support. Again the reaction of these decent Greeks resonates strongly within the history of Jewish persecution. Whether or not the precise events recorded here actually happened, the behavior of the Greeks is well observed and probably based on experience.

Philopator's Decree to Arrest the Country Jews (3:11-30)

Philopator now issues a decree, in the form of a letter, to arrest all the "country" Jews and send them in chains to Alexandria. It is somewhat puzzling why the decree should single out the country Jews, but this is the implication of 4:12-13. It is only at this latter point that the city Jews get included in the action. The letter has certainly been composed by the author of 3 Maccabees. Ptolemy III would not have used his epithet Philopator in a document such as this; this practice only came in later, as did the salutation "greetings and good health" *(chairein kai errōsthai)*. But it is a convincing piece of work, which shows a nice sense of appropriate chancellery style. 3 Maccabees has sufficient artistic integrity to allow Philopator to express a persuasive case in justifying his action. His case is simple: the Jews are the enemy within;

the state cannot trust them and must take preemptive measures to protect itself (3:24). As proof of the Jews' innate ill will toward him Philopator cites first the incident in the Jerusalem temple. The irony should not be missed. Philopator claims that it was benevolence which motivated him to enter the sanctuary in Jerusalem; it was benevolence that stopped him from punishing the Jews when they thwarted him. The reader, of course, knows from chs. 1–2 what "really" happened, and that Philopator is being somewhat economical with the truth. The second instance of the Jews' ill will toward him is their rejection of the offer of full citizenship and of participation in the royal cult. And they compounded their fault by ostracizing those who were willing to accept the king's gracious offer. The Jews of Alexandria behaved like the Jews of Jerusalem: in classic anti-Semitic fashion the king blackens the nation as a whole. They are incorrigible: they are a "wicked people, who never cease from their folly" (3:16); "they are unwilling to regard any action as sincere" (v. 19); their malice is innate and "they incline constantly to evil" (v. 22); their way of life is "infamous" (v. 23).

The letter depicts Philopator as cunningly doing everything he can to make his subjects complicit in his genocide. Anyone aiding the Jews would suffer the same fate, together with their families, and their houses would be laid waste for all time (a stern deterrent to the "decent" Greeks who had privately offered help [3:8-10]). Informers, however, were to be rewarded by being granted the property of their hapless victims, a substantial payment from the royal treasury, and "their freedom." The final element of the offer may indicate that the informers were expected to come from the Egyptian serf class, perhaps slaves of the Jews who were betrayed. However, the reference is rather abrupt and a simple emendation yields the sense, "and will be honored at the Eleutheria" (i.e., the festival of Dionysus). Philopator's letter, as we noted, is concocted, and 3 Maccabees, if not totally fictional, is, at best, a highly embellished account of historical events. However, the encouraging of informers by offering them a share in their victims' property is well attested in the annals of oppression. It is hardly surprising that the Jewish community down through the ages has shown a particular loathing of informers.

The Country Jews Are Deported to Alexandria (4:1-10)

The king's decree allows the Gentiles to express openly the hatred for the Jews that they have long cherished in private. They celebrate, at public expense, the Jews' downfall. Feasting plays a major part in 3 Maccabees, as it does in the book of Esther: the feast here is "reversed" by the feast of 6:30-34. The suffering of the Jews is described with full pathos. Again the fate of the young brides is used to elicit sympathy (cf. 1:19). The language is exaggerated and, as Hadas notes (1953: 55), the high-flown, melodramatic tone from here on in 3 Maccabees is closer to romance than to history. In fact, as emerges incidentally from 4:12 and 18, not only were the Jews of Alexandria not involved in this roundup, but not even all the Jews in the country. The Jews are taken to Alexandria by boat, presumably down the Nile or along the canal, which were the country's main arteries of transport. This would make particular sense if the author of 3 Maccabees is thinking particularly of the deportation of the large Jewish community in the Fayum.

The Action Extends to Include the Jews of Alexandria (4:11-21)

The text reveals a detailed knowledge of the topography of Alexandria. Schedia was the dock area of Alexandria, about three miles from the city, an obvious terminus if the prisoners are being brought into the city by boat. The hippodrome was beside the eastern or Canopic city gate, which was linked to Schedia by a canal (Strabo *Geog.* 17.1.10, 16). Incarceration within the hippodrome allows Philopator to make an example of the Jews to those streaming in and out of the adjacent gate (important for propaganda purposes), and sets the scene for the grim events of ch. 5. At the same time it isolates the Jews. Jews are dangerous and must be kept from contact with the king's troops (lest, presumably, they suborn them; cf. 2:32 along with 4:19, which tellingly reveals the king's paranoia on this point). Their pariah status is symbolized by the fact that they are not to be allowed to enter the city, even as prisoners; the probable translation of the end of 4:11 should be, "to prevent them from communicating with his forces and to deny them the protection of the city walls."

4:12ff. reveals, almost casually, that the action so far had affected only the Jews in the country. The solidarity of the city Jews with their suffering country compatriots enrages the king and leads him to extend the action to include them as well. The motivation is hardly convincing, but once again the point is made that all Jews, whether in Jerusalem or Alexandria or the "country," stand or fall together.

According to 4:14, the registration was initially intended to be "for the hard labour that has been briefly mentioned before." It makes sense if the Jews, as threatened in 2:28, were to be reduced to the status of slaves. But even when the plan is changed, the registration goes incongruously ahead. This obsession with administrative efficiency, so typical of the Ptolemaic state, underscores the planning and premeditation. It bureaucratizes the genocide and echoes chillingly in the perspective of history. At the same time the registration allows the author to remind the reader (in what may, like 1:22-23, be a veiled threat) that the Jewish community in Egypt is very large. Jewish writers, for political reasons, were inclined to exaggerate the Jewish population of Egypt. The *Letter of Aristeas* 27 claims that in the mid-third century BC they numbered 120,000. Philo *In Flaccum* 6 maintains that in the first century AD there were one million Jews in Alexandria alone. The registration also allows the author to record a minor miracle (the pens and paper running out), which he sees as a sign of God's providence and a portent of the dramatic divine intervention that was to come.

4:16's depiction of the king carousing with his companions, praising his idols and blaspheming the true God, is a standard Jewish picture of a dissolute oriental monarch, a veritable Sardanapulus. It should be compared with the picture of Ahasuerus in Esther (Esth 1:5-9) and of Belshazzar in Daniel (Dan 5:1-4).

Two Attempts to Kill the Jews Are Thwarted (5:1-47)

The reference to "the great colonnade" at 5:23, obviously a well-known feature of the city, continues to give topographical verisimilitude to the story. And the Ptolemies' and Seleucids' use of war elephants, as a kind of animate battle tank, was famous, though the round figure of five hundred animals mentioned in 5:2 is surely exaggerated: Philadelphus had three hundred, and Philopator himself deployed only 73 at Raphia. (The "beasts" of *Pesher on Habakkuk* from Qumran [1QpHab 3:10] may be war elephants, though this is disputed. War elephants "clad in coats of mail," however, are clearly mentioned in the *Scroll of Antiochus* 46–47.) The arming of the elephants' legs with blades (5:45; cf. 5:23, 38), analogous to the arming of chariot wheels, is probably correct, as may be the use of drugs to induce frenzy in them. There are reports of elephants being drugged prior to tiger hunts in India. But the historicity of the whole episode is highly suspect. It is remarkably similar to a story told by Josephus (*Ag. Ap.* 53–55) in which Ptolemy Physcon exposes the Jews of Alexandria, with their wives and children, "naked and in chains," to be trampled by drunken elephants (see above).

The tale is vigorously told in 3 Maccabees (the naming of the keeper of the elephants, Hermon, adds a human touch), but it teeters on the edge of farce. The first attempt to execute the Jews is thwarted by the fact that the king oversleeps — a sleep, to be sure, providentially induced by God (5:11). He is still asleep at the middle of the tenth hour (3:30 p.m. by Egyptian usage; 4:30 p.m. by Roman) and has to be "nudged awake" (5:14) and reminded that the banquet is prepared and his guests are waiting. There may be an "in" joke here since Philopator seems to have had a reputation as a lie-abed. He then proceeds to act in a confused fashion and has to be put right by his Friends. The second attempt is thwarted by the fact that when the king wakes up on the second morning he has forgotten (again due to divine intervention, 5:30) his anger against the Jews and instead threatens to throw the hapless Hermon and his family to the elephants. He has to be reminded, rather tetchily, by the Friends, who are not to be denied their sport, of his original plans. Their trump card, significantly, is to threaten him with civil disorder if he denies the mob's lust for Jewish blood. The reader is offered a lively but "off-the-shelf" picture of a deranged oriental tyrant who, for the benefit of Greek readers, is twice compared (5:20 and 42) to Phalaris, the notorious sixth-century tyrant of Agrigentum who slowly roasted to death his enemies inside a brazen bull, so that he could hear them bellowing in anguish (Polybius *Hist.* 12.25). Equally stock-in-trade is the picture of the king's dissolute Friends (the word is used throughout 3 Maccabees in its technical sense of a courtier of a certain rank; the Kinsmen of 5:39 are, technically, courtiers of a higher rank). The image of the courtiers trying to keep the king on the straight-and-narrow of villainy, and of their staying awake all night to devise insults to hurl at the Jews as they are trampled to death, is more likely to provoke ridicule than horror. And the narrator's grasp of the narrative detail is not entirely assured. At 5:5 the Jews are bound. This highlights their plight and makes the point that only a miracle can save them now. But according to 3:25 and 4:9 they were already bound, and in the subsequent story they behave in a decidedly unbound way (5:25 and 49-50).

5:43 offers a significant flashback, which reminds the reader of how the tale began, and, incidentally, of the solidarity of the Jews. When Philopator has dealt with the Jews of Egypt he will go and settle the score with the Jews of Jerusalem, devastating Judea, destroying the temple that had been "inaccessible to him," and terminating its cult.

The Prayer of Eleazar (5:48–6:15)

The third attempt to massacre the Jews is vividly imagined from the standpoint of the Jews themselves, incarcerated and helpless in the hippodrome. A cloud of dust coming from the direction of the city gate gives them early warning of the approach of the elephants, soldiers, and spectators. Pandemonium breaks out among the prisoners. The parallelism with chs. 1 and 2 is unmistakable. Here as there the general cries of supplication are silenced, and the single voice of the priest Eleazar (an appropriate name meaning "God has helped"; cf. 2 Macc 6:18; 4 Macc 6:5; 7:1; Letter of Aristeas 41) leads the intercessions. He is described as "famous among the priests of the country" (cf. 7:13). This may be intended to link him with the Jewish temple at Leontopolis in Egypt — anachronistically since the Leontopolis temple was founded by former high priest Onias IV only in the 160s BC. If this is the meaning, then it helps to date 3 Maccabees, and the lack of any perceived rivalry between the Jerusalem and Leontopolis temples would be striking.

Eleazar's prayer is simple, affecting, and in good liturgical style. Like Simon's in 2:1-20, its language contrasts with the bombast of the surrounding narrative. Eleazar, like Simon, quotes biblical examples, in this case to illustrate how God has delivered his people in dire circumstances in the past. The first, appropriately, is the deliverance of Israel from Pharaoh, "the former ruler of this Egypt" (6:4). The second is the deliverance of Jerusalem from the Assyrian Sennacherib (cf. 2 Kgs 19:35). The third is the deliverance of the three Hebrews from the fiery furnace; the verbal echoes here of the story as told in the book of Daniel are particularly strong (cf. 6:6 with Dan 3:27, and for "turning the flame against all their enemies" see The Prayer of Azariah 24-25 [an LXX addition to Dan 3:23], itself probably suggested by Dan 3:22). The fourth example is Daniel's deliverance from the lions' den (Dan 6:24). 3 Maccabees' retelling of examples two to four curiously makes no mention of the angelic agents who, according the biblical story, were involved in each of these acts of deliverance. In 2 Kgs 19:35 it is the "angel of the LORD" who destroys the Assyrians. In Dan 3:25 Nebuchadnezzar sees a fourth figure in the fiery furnace whose appearance is "like a son of the gods." And in Dan 6:22 Daniel tells King Darius, "My God sent his angel and shut the lions' mouths." The author of 3 Maccabees has nothing against the idea of angelic intervention: he himself is just about to introduce angels to deliver the Jews of Alexandria. He may have avoided bringing them in here so as not to blunt the dramatic impact of the climax. Eleazar's final example from Jonah (cf. Jonah 1:17–2:9) is at first sight surprising. However, it is possible that he takes Jonah as a symbol of Israel. Jonah tried to flee from the presence of the LORD, but found that wherever he went, even to the depths of sea, God was still there to hear his prayer and to save him. This would chime well with the ending of Eleazar's prayer with its quotation of Lev 26:44, "When they are in the land of their enemies, I will not spurn them, neither will I abhor them so as to destroy them utterly and break my covenant." The one example conspicuous by its absence is the story of Esther. This might be because 3 Maccabees predates Esther. However, more probably the omission is deliberate: although the author of 3 Maccabees knew the story of Esther and freely adapted some of its motifs, he deplored its lack of conventional piety and of an overt religious message.

Like an OT prophet Eleazar disputes with God. Like Simon in 2:1-20, he acknowledges the sin of the people ("the impieties of our exile," 6:10), but obliquely pleads the merits of the patriarchs (v. 3) and argues that the defeat of the Jews, God's "people" and "consecrated portion" (v. 3), will be a victory for idolatry and call into question God's universal power. He concludes by reminding God of his own promise not to neglect his people even when they are in the land of their enemies (cf. Lev 26:44).

Two Angels Deliver the Jews (6:16-21)

God, who has hitherto worked invisibly to help the Jews (2:22; 5:11, 28), now intervenes in a terrifying epiphany which is all the more effective because it is unique within the book. God "reveals his face." There is probably an allusion here to Exod 33:20, "You cannot see my face; for man shall not see me and live." The title "the most glorious . . . God" (6:18) is carefully chosen: God's "glory" and his "face" are linked (cf. Exod 33:18 with 33:20): they are the effulgence of his power and majesty and are destructive of sinners. (God is called "the Great Glory" in *1 Enoch* 14:20 and *T. Levi* 3:4.) The manifestation of God's glory is embodied in two divine agents, possibly Angels of the Face. It is because the epiphany is destructive and judgmental that the Jews are spared it (6:18), not because the author of 3 Maccabees has any reservations about the doctrine of angels. (The Jews must, therefore, within the logic of the narrative, have learned of the apparition from the Egyptians.) Angelic manifestations in such situations are common in the cognate literature; see 2 Macc 3:24ff.; 10:29; Wisdom 17:3, 15; 18:17; Josephus *Ag. Ap.* 2.53-55. Emmet 1913 notes parallels from Greek sources, such as the apparitions at Marathon and Salamis. The Angel of Mons is the classic modern example. Normally, however, the situation is reversed: it is the heroes who see the vision and are encouraged by it, but not their foes. The terrifying vision causes the king to shake uncontrollably (cf. 2:22) and transfixes his soldiers to the spot in fear, where they are trampled by the stampeding elephants. There is an element of measure for measure in this: the soldiers shackled the Jews to make them easy prey (5:5-6); now God shackles the soldiers for the same purpose (5:19).

The King Reverses His Decision and the Jews Are Delivered (6:22-41)

The king's accusation that his courtiers are guilty of treason and responsible for the debacle rings hollow in the light of his earlier actions (1:26-28; 2:24-25; 3:1, 11-30; 4:12, 16; 5:1, 18, 20, 37-38, 42-43, 47), but 3 Maccabees has stressed enough the role of the Friends in the anti-Jewish plot (2:25-26; 5:21-22, 34, 39-41, 44; 7:3) to lend some credibility to the diplomatic ploy of blaming not the king but his advisers for the wrongs that had been done. And history records that Philopator was, in fact, very much in thrall to his Friends, who were infamous for their immorality. He acknowledges the loyalty of the Jews and their role in the defense of the country (cf. 1:3; 3:6, 21; 7:7; further *Letter of Aristeas* 13, 36; Josephus *Ant.* 12.8: Jews had been used for garrison duty in Egypt ever since the Persian period, when they manned the border post at Elephantine). Once again he recognizes the role of the God of the Jews in his affairs and attributes the stability of the Ptolemaic state to his providence (cf. 1:9). He orders the Friends personally to untie the Jews and to beg their forgiveness.

At the king's suggestion and at royal expense the Jews hold a feast to celebrate their deliverance in the very hippodrome where they were supposed to die. The precise dating of the events in 6:38-40 recalls the similar precision of Esth 9:22. Pachon (= 26 April-25 May) and Epiphi (in the papyri Epeiph = 25 June-24 July) are Egyptian months. The feasting runs for seven days (cf. the eight-day festival of Hanukkah) from 7 to 13 Epiphi (= 1-7 July). This period is ordained as an annual festival for the Egyptian Jews. No name is given for the festival, and it is not otherwise mentioned unless it is the same festival which Josephus refers to as commemorating similar events in the reign of Ptolemy Physcon (*Ag. Ap.* 2.53-55; see above). However, there is no good reason to doubt that there was some such Egyptian Jewish festival of deliverance, and that 3 Maccabees was an attempt to explain its meaning. Such festivals were common at the period not only among Jews (cf. 1 Macc 4:56; 6:59; 13:50; 2 Macc 10:6; 15:36; Jdt 16:25 [Vg]; Esth 9:22) but among non-Jews as well (see Emmet 1913). They were an obvious way for ethnic groups in a cosmopolitan society to reinforce their identity and to boost communal morale. 6:32 and 35 seem to suggest that singing and dancing marked this particular festival in some special way. 6:32, "they raised their ancestral chant, praising God, the deliverer and worker of wonders," suggests that the author has some particular text in mind, perhaps Exodus 15 or Psalm 106.

Philopator's Letter of Behalf of the Jews (7:1-9)

Philopator's second letter, offering protection to the Jews, totally reverses his first, which decreed destruction (3:12-29). However, the general tone of the second letter is less convincing than that of the first: its overly hearty endorsement of Judaism is implausible, and the reference to "children" in the salutation is probably a historical slip since Philopator did not have a son and heir till 208 (the implied date of the letter is 217 BC). Ptolemy blames his

Friends for the attack on the Jews, accusing them of "Scythian" cruelty (cf. 2 Macc 4:47; 4 Macc 10:7). The charge against the Friends is clarified: it is not so much that the Jews were treated cruelly, but rather that the due process of the law was ignored: "they tried without examination or inquiry to put them to death" (7:5). The king reaffirms his belief in the Jews' loyalty, acknowledges that they are under the particular protection of the God of heaven (so anyone thinking of attacking them should beware), and forbids his subjects to do them any harm.

The Community Is Restored (7:10-23)

The final section of 3 Maccabees records the triumphant restoration of the *status quo ante.* But before this can be done a serious matter of communal business needs to be attended to: the Jewish renegades, who have breached the community's code and destroyed its solidarity, have to be dealt with. The Jews obtain from the king permission to put the renegades to death. The Jews in Egypt, like Jews elsewhere in the diaspora, had their own courts, which tried communal cases according to Jewish law. This was doubtless allowed by the Ptolemies. What the state, however, would not normally have permitted was that these communal courts should exercise capital jurisdiction. Hence the need for a special faculty in this case. The argument used by the Jews to gain permission to exercise capital jurisdiction, namely, that the loyalty to the state of those who transgress the laws of God must be deeply suspect, would, as Hadas notes, have played well to a Roman audience (see Polybius *Hist.* 6.56.6-15), but was more unusual in Greek political thought. There is no implication here that the renegades were treated to summary justice, or that lynch law applied (this would have been highly ironic in the light of 7:5). Due process of law by the Jewish courts is probably envisaged. The precise violation of God's law alluded to in 7:10 could be Deut 13:6-11 or even 13:12-18, which clearly involve capital crimes. Unlike the Esther story (9:1-17), 3 Maccabees has no general settling of scores. The Gentile enemies of the Jews are not punished, only the Jewish renegades, and they number only three hundred. A strong intracommunal point is being made here, a warning to traitors and informers that they will be dealt with severely. 7:15 seems to imply that the seventh day of the unnamed festival specially commemorated the destruction of "the profaners."

The alternative ending to the story in 7:17-20 suggests that 3 Maccabees is combining different sources. According to 6:30, the Jews celebrated their deliverance for seven days in the hippodrome at Alexandria. Here, however, they celebrate it for seven days at Ptolemais, probably not the city of that name in the Thebaid in Upper Egypt, but Ptolemais Hormos (Ptolemais Harbor) in the Fayum (in the Arsinoite Nome). This Ptolemais, which stood on the canal some eleven miles southeast of Arsinoë, the principal city of the region, was a major entrepôt through which goods passed into and out of the Fayum. Its epithet, "rose-bearing," is not otherwise attested but was probably added to distinguish it from other cities of the same name. It shows, once again, the author of 3 Maccabees' topographical knowledge of Egypt. The Jews dedicate an inscription and a synagogue *(proseuchē)* to commemorate the events. Significantly we know of three synagogues in nearby Arsinoe, one of them dating to the late third century BC (Horbury and Noy 1992: 117). We touch here probably the historical core of 3 Maccabees: it writes up a festival annually celebrated by the Jews of Ptolemais to commemorate their deliverance from some official persecution, which may have been a rather limited and local affair, and attempts to turn it into a national festival for all the Jews of Egypt, a festival with echoes of Purim and Hanukkah, both of which were being strongly promoted from Palestine.

7:21-22 implies that the transfer of Jewish property alluded to in 3:28 had actually taken place. It is now returned, and the Gentiles treat the Jews with respect and fear.

The concluding benediction, "Blessed be the Deliverer of Israel through all times! Amen," might indicate that 3 Maccabees was intended to be read publicly at the festival, like Esther on Purim and (much later) the *Scroll of Antiochus* on Hanukkah. For somewhat similar concluding formulae see Tob 14:15 and 4 Macc 18:24.

Bibliography. Alexander, P. S. 2001, "3 Maccabees, Hanukkah and Purim," in A. Rapoport-Albert and G. Greenberg, eds., *Biblical Hebrew, Biblical Texts: Essays in Memory of Michael P. Weitzman,* Sheffield: Sheffield Academic, 321-39 • Anderson, H. 1985, "3 Maccabees," in J. H. Charlesworth, ed., *The Old Testament Pseudepigrapha,* Garden City, N.Y.: Doubleday, 2:509-29 • Cousland, J. R. C. 2001, "Dionysus *theomachus?* Echoes of the Bacchae in 3 Maccabees," *Bib* 83, no. 4, 539-48 • Emmet, C. W. 1913, "The Third Book of Maccabees," in R. H. Charles, ed., *Apocrypha and Pseudepigrapha of the Old Testament,* Oxford: Clarendon, 1:155-73 • Gaster, T. H. 1978, "3 Maccabees," in A. Kahana, ed., *Ha-Sefarim ha-Hitzonim,* 2d ed. 1956, repr. Jerusalem: Makor, 2:231-57 (Hebrew) • Hadas, M. 1953, *The Third and Fourth Book of Maccabees,* Jewish Apocryphal Literature, New York: Harper, 1-85 • Horbury, W., and D. Noy. 1992, *JIGRE = Jewish Inscriptions of Graeco-Roman Egypt,* Cambridge: Cambridge University • Kasher, A. 1985, *The Jews of Hellenistic and Roman Egypt,* Tübingen: Mohr-Siebeck • Schürer, E. 1986, "The Third Book of Maccabees," in E. Schürer, *The History of the Jewish People in the Age of Jesus Christ,* vol. 3.1, rev. and ed. G. Vermes, F. Millar, and M. Goodman, Edinburgh: T&T Clark, 537-42 • Tcherikover, V. A., A. Fuks, and M. Stern, eds. 1957-64, *Corpus Papyrorum Judaicarum (CPJ),* Cambridge, Mass.: Harvard University, vols. 1-3.

2 Esdras

John J. Schmitt

INTRODUCTION

2 Esdras is part of Holy Scripture in the strict sense of the term for only a certain percentage of the world's Christians. (The Greek Orthodox Church considers it fully part of the Bible, while the Russian Orthodox Church holds it to be biblical but of less authority than the major part of the Bible. The Vulgate included it as apocryphal, calling the whole work 4 Esdras.) The book has, nevertheless, fostered the devotion and faith of Christians in many times and places.

It was quoted by various church fathers of the early centuries AD (Clement of Alexandria and Ambrose of Milan). Christopher Columbus used it in his appeal to the Spanish crown for funds to discover other lands. (His claim was that the world is only one-seventh water and sixth-sevenths dry land, as 2 Esdr 6:42 states. He knew there was more land than had yet been accounted for.) The book also furnished the basis for the words "Requiem aeternam dona eis, Domine" ("Grant them eternal rest, O Lord," a rephrasing of 2 Esdr 2:34), which are the opening words of the traditional "Requiem Mass" offered for the deceased in the older Roman Catholic liturgy.

Actually, close examination shows that 2 Esdras is a composite work, resulting from a juxtaposition of three different writings that come from different times. 2 Esdras 3–14 (sometimes referred to as 4 Ezra) is a Jewish work that stems from the end of the first century AD. Chs. 1–2 of 2 Esdras (sometimes called 5 Ezra) in their current form are of Christian origin and come from perhaps the mid-second century AD. And 2 Esdras 15–16 (or 6 Ezra) are Christian, originating in the third century AD. This more specific terminology of 4 Ezra, 5 Ezra, and 6 Ezra will be used below.

The book as a whole survived in the West in Latin and in the East in various languages: Syriac, Coptic, Georgian, and Ethiopic. All translations seem to be dependent on a Greek version that is no longer extant. 4 Ezra was most probably written in Hebrew and later translated into Greek, but neither the Hebrew nor the Greek versions have survived. 5 Ezra was probably composed in Latin (surviving in two rather different manuscript groups), while 6 Ezra was likely written either in Greek or in Latin.

The purpose of the book, accordingly, is multiple. 4 Ezra was written in response to the catastrophe of AD 70 when the city of God, Jerusalem, and the temple of God were destroyed by the Roman Empire. The Jews had risen up and revolted against the Roman Empire because of the treatment they were receiving from it, but they suffered a humiliating and faith-challenging defeat. What would existence mean for the Jewish community after this disaster? Was there any hope? Surely Rome would eventually fall and its oppression cease. In the meantime the Jews had been given Torah to live by, and the author emphasizes that Torah came through dictation to Ezra. Torah should still be relied on as the way God was leading the chosen people.

The Christian author of the second century prefaces (with what is called chs. 1 and 2) this earlier work, thereby asserting that the Christian community is the real successor to ancient Israel, and not the Jewish community. The Christian Messiah was predicted, the author feels, in this very work of Ezra, just as clearly as in the other books of ancient Israel that later Christians called the OT. The judgment that 4 Ezra assigned against the wicked in general is now turned against those who had not accepted the promised Messiah. The earlier work found its fulfillment, then, in the mind of this second writer, in the Christian faith and among its community. The author wrote in order to explain and argue that idea in the two introductory chapters.

Another Christian writer, this one of the third century, saw the need to update the work with an appendix in order to show that God was still acting in history, even the history that had not been spelled out in the original work. This writer added specific details (chs. 15 and 16) with warnings against the persecutors of the new people of God and promises for those who remain true to the way of life that God had revealed.

In terms of literary genre, the original Jewish work was clearly written in the style and structure of many other apocalyptic works of the first century. This form of writing and thinking, which in modern times people have called apocalypticism, arose in a time of perceived oppression. The apocalyptic author promises that fidelity to the revealed way of life will bring with it an eternal reward even if present circumstances do not of themselves suggest this. Apocalyptic writings use various devices, such as visions and symbolism, to convey this conviction that the powers of evil will be defeated and God will bring the faithful to fulfillment. The apocalyptic writer of 4 Ezra does exactly that.

The two Christian writers respected these apocalyptic ways of thinking and writing and passed them on with their own interpretations and applications. Since the faith expressions of first-century Judaism and first-century Christianity were generally close enough to each other (since both were interpreting the traditions and writings of ancient Israel), the Christian writers felt no real contradiction in the work they accomplished.

The theology of all the parts have the basic conviction that God continues to act in history, as was believers' experience in the past. All three writers were convinced that the recent past indicated that the powers of darkness would not win out, but would be roundly and permanently defeated by God. The reward of the faithful was spelled out by each of the writers in ways appealing to their own readers. All three writers encouraged their readers to full fidelity and submission to God. Their conviction of the victory of God over the forces of evil should speak even to the modern reader.

COMMENTARY

5 Ezra = 2 Esdras 1–2

Introduction and Call to Prophesy (1:1-11)

The author creates a genealogy using both the biblical book of Ezra (Ezra 7:1-5) and the apocryphal 1 Esdras (1 Esdr 8:1-2). Ezra is identified as a prophet, indicating that he is, for the writer and the readers, no longer only "a scribe learned in the law of Moses" (Ezra 7:6) but now a spokesperson for God. The author knows well his Bible, both Hebrew Scripture and the Christian writings, and freely uses words and ideas of the prophetic and Deuteronomistic books (Deuteronomy, Joshua through Kings, and parts of Jeremiah), as well as the Gospels. The theme is that Israel has turned away from God despite all that God had done for the chosen people. (A curious misconception of the author [1:11] is the location of and time of destruction of Tyre and Sidon, cities on the Mediterranean, not provinces in the East.)

The Guilt of Israel's Nonresponse (1:12-34)

Now Ezra receives words from God, here called "the Lord Almighty," a term used only in 5 Ezra 1:14, 21, 27, 32; 2:9, 31 and 6 Ezra 16:63. These words address the Israelites directly: you have not lived up to the promises, benefits, protection, and special care I have given you, even showered on you. Your lack of positive response means that your special status of being the chosen people of God will be given to others (1:24). The author connects the Israelites and the Christians by means of the idea of replacement. This kind of thinking seems to place the author in the mid-second century. Later on, some Christian writers (such as Marcion) proposed no connection between ancient Israel and the church. Some scholars have seen in 1:26 a charge against the Jews as being responsible for the death of Jesus (see Matt 27:25).

The author uses many varied comparisons to depict God as disappointed. Some of those comparisons are taken from the NT (especially Matt 23:30-38). The likening of God to a mother and the Israelites to daughters is quite striking and perhaps found nowhere else. The charges and accusations against the Jews abound. For the murder of the prophets (a tradition prominent at the time [Matt 23:30, 34], although the Bible does not describe any murder of a canonical prophet) and the neglect of the commandments, Israel will be forsaken.

A New Nation to Replace the Old (1:35–2:14)

The nation "coming from the east" will represent the fulfillment of what the sinful nation was not. This surprising idea of the Christian people as "easterners" shows that the author is using images of redemption and liberation in the HB, Isa 41:2; 43:5; and 46:11 (where God calls a liberator from "the East"), and especially Bar 4:36-37 and 5:5 (where Zion's children return from that quarter). The Christian people or peoples (the plural in 1:24 occurs in one group of Latin manuscripts, the singular in the other) will now be what God calls "my people."

The author makes personified Zion (Jerusalem) speak as the mother of the Israelites. Her words of sorrow at the plight of her children hold no word of hope for them, but she does encourage them to seek the mercy of God (2:2-4).

Again the author argues for a judgment on Israel and claims that the punishment will be that they will be replaced by the Christians. The author freely uses passages from the OT and NT showing that this new people of God will replace the old one. Among the judgments is a woe against Assyria. This name is probably a cipher for Rome, the major political power at the time. Alternatively, the intent of the text might be to refer to the ancient, cruel military regime of Mesopotamia that eventually was conquered by the Babylonians. Sodom and Gomorrah (or often just Sodom alone) are symbols of destruction due to many different kinds of sins in the HB (e.g., arrogance, Isa 3:9; general wickedness, Jer 23:14; pride, gluttony, and neglect of the poor and needy, Ezek 16:49).

The New People as a Woman (2:15-32)

In this section the focus is on the new people personified as a woman — the church or the fulfilled Zion. Curiously, the first word to her is that her deceased children will be raised. Perhaps this reference is to the martyred Christians or at least those who died a natural death before the parousia (cf. 1 Thess 4:15-17). She is promised that the prophets Isaiah and Jeremiah will come to her. These two prophets were selected perhaps as the prophets who were regarded as those who spoke more fully of the coming of Jesus. The REB inserts the phrase "to be my people" in 2:18. This insertion seems to disturb the consistent imagery in 2:15-32, for all these words are addressed to Mother Zion, completely in the singular "you" in Latin. Normally "my people" would be a reference to Israel, who is consistently personified as male in the Bible. Israel is the son of Zion (see the commentary on 2 Esdras 10), and so the "twelve trees" and the "twelve fountains" are indeed the replacements for the twelve tribes of Israel. City imagery and imagery for Israel are related but not interchangeable.

Mother Zion is encouraged to care for all peoples, not only her own children. She will be the new caretaker of humanity, and God will protect her. God will ultimately raise her dead children to new life. And God promises to come and bring mercy and grace (2:32)

The New People Will Be Composed of Gentiles (2:33-48)

Now the Gentiles are addressed as the potential new people. If they are ready, they can received the rewards of being this new people. The test will be the sending of a Savior. What is required is to receive this Sent One with joy and thanksgiving. The author foresees many who have made that acceptance. Enthusiastically, the author addresses Mother Zion again and bids her to count the multitude who will be saved.

Then Ezra reports his vision of a multitude. In the midst of this multitude of those who have taken on immortality stands one who towers above them all. Ezra, in good apocalyptic style, asks an angel the identity of this tall young man awarding palms to the crowds. The response is, "He is the Son of God." This title for Jesus is found already in Paul and the Gospels (Matt 14:33; Rom 1:3). The expression had multiple meanings in ancient Israel, and if this passage was written in the early second century, the title probably would not have carried the full weight of unqualified divinity as it did in later centuries.

Thus end these two introductory chapters, clearly of Christian origin in their present form. They were probably written as a preface to 4 Ezra to show that the Christian church is the true fulfillment of ancient Israel. For this author, there is no debate about the identity of the people who were called from the beginning of creation (2:41). For this writer, Christians form that people. This claim seems to relate to the idea expressed at 6:55, namely, that the world was created for the sake of Israel. Christians of the second century thought they had full and exclusive claim to and true understanding of the truth of the biblical tradition.

4 Ezra = 2 Esdras 3–14

The First Episode (3:1–5:19)

The author (re-)identifies himself as Ezra (3:1), whom the writer takes to be the same person as Salathiel, the Greek form of Shealtiel. Shealtiel (1 Chr 3:17; Ezra 3:2; Hag 1:1) was the son of Jehoiakin (the king of Judah who died in 597, three months before the city surrendered to the Babylonians). Shealtiel, however, lived at least a century before Ezra. Since the author is appropriating the figure of Ezra, the additional assumption of Shealtiel adds royal authority to the scribal authority of Ezra. The REB inserts the word "Jerusalem" in place of the simple "the city." The author assumes that the reader will immediately know "the city" as Jerusalem (3:1). The words "on my bed I was troubled" and "filled with perplexity" depict the initial stage of inspiration as presented by this writer. "The Most High" (v. 3) as a designation for God is the divine epithet found in various parts of the HB that are usually connected with Jerusalem (e.g., Gen 14:18-20; Ps 46:5). The name occurs 68 times within chapters 3–14, the original work, but not in the added initial and closing chapters.

The first content of the revelation given Ezra is the desolation of the holy city and the plight of the exiles. The seer addresses God directly in response to his own grief. The author makes Ezra, not an activist, but rather a thinker who contemplates the whole of history as he knows it. Ezra ponders the whole history of God's dealings with Israel from the beginning of creation. He starts where the Bible begins — with God speaking (3:4). From the creation of the world by the divine word and the creation of Adam by a command to the earth, through the sin of this first human and the sins of all humans, until the flood and beyond, Ezra paints an unattractive picture of humanity's sin-filled story (v. 8). One note of hope is the sparing of Noah (v. 11) and his descendants.

Even the arrival of Abraham in this recital (3:13) and the beginning of God's special people do not improve the situation, for this people, too, sinned, just as the others had sinned. It is remarkable that this author emphasizes that both sin and death came to humanity through the sin of Adam. (Striking, also, is the omission of Eve from this summary of human history.) But there is a hopeful item with Abraham, for with him God made an "everlasting covenant" (v. 15) and God promised never to abandon the descendants of Abraham. (A curious, apocalyptic feature is that God is said to have revealed to Abraham "how the world would end" [v. 14]; the idea of this kind of revelation to Abraham also appears in some rabbinic literature.)

The story of the deliverance from bondage in Egypt is told rather quickly — and this without mention of Moses. Although Moses is not mentioned here as the receiver of the revelation and of the theophany, he is the figure to whom Ezra is often implicitly compared. God's passage through the four gates (3:19) adds further mystery to the story, borrowing the phenomena from 1 Kgs 19:11-12. Then the author focuses on the wickedness in the human heart (3:21). The author states ideas that parallel those later taken up both in the Christian dogma of original sin, that is, the proclivity to sin that comes with the very creaturehood of humanity, and in Judaism with the idea of "the evil impulse," found in rabbinical literature. Along with the innate tendency to sin, God's law existed within the hearts of humans. Sin, nevertheless, won out. The absences both of Eve and of the serpent remain striking.

David is mentioned by name as the one who builds "the city that bears your name" (3:24). Jerusalem does not literally carry the name of the God of Israel, but rather "houses" the name or glory of God — the city where God chose to place the divine name (Deut 12:5). (The city's name actually contains the name of the Shalem, a different deity, and this embarrassing name is perhaps the reason why several prophetic books insist that God will change the name of Jerusalem to something else; see, e.g., Isa 62:2, 4; Jer 3:17; 33:17). The inhabitants of the city also fall into sin, and the city is handed over to the power of the enemy.

Ezra asks the rhetorical question whether Jerusalem fell to Babylon because Babylon was the better city with truly devout residents. But he argues the complete opposite: evil doings abound there too. Babylon, the wicked, thrives, while Jerusalem, the city of God, is punished because of its lesser evil. (This contrast between the two cities recalls the competition that is depicted between Jerusalem and Babylon in Isaiah 40–55.)

The question, "Has any nation except Israel ever known you?" (3:32), is a challenge for the modern reader.

Writings from around the time of this one had already suggested that there is only one God and that that God is worshiped under many names. This author may be attempting to use the mentality of the time of Ezra as the writer imaged it. There is poignancy in the claim that Ezra has traveled far and compared different peoples to see if any of those peoples observed the laws of the Lord better than Israel did. He is sure that there is none as faithful as his own people. Here and there perhaps a truly wicked person exists within that people, but such a person would be the exception. Israel has been faithful and does not deserve this punishment.

Rather than coming to respond to Ezra, God sends an angel (4:1). This angel even has a name. Uriel means "God is my light." Then begin the continuing conversations that make up most of the book of 4 Ezra. Oddly enough, Uriel is sent initially to propound riddles to Ezra, not simply to give answers. He starts with three from "the ways of the world" but quickly overwhelms Ezra with the knowledge of his own ignorance. If Ezra cannot know the world which he sees, how could he expect to understand God and the ways of God toward the world?

Uriel tells Ezra a parable to drive home to him the futility of attempting something in which one is unable to win (4:12-21). The trees and the sea compete in a quaint little story to show that Ezra's own understanding will get him nowhere. Revelation of secret knowledge is needed, a good apocalyptic thought.

Ezra persists in his puzzlement. How can he understand Israel's suffering? All the favor Israel had received is now lost sight of because of the ridicule and oppression they experience from other peoples. Even "the written covenants are made a dead letter" (4:23). It is so bad that "we pass from this world like a flight of locusts; our life is but a vapor" (v. 24). Uriel's words in response only confuse more: "The present age is passing away" (v. 26). This is a most gripping thought in apocalyptic literature. The writer and the reader are captivated by the concept of the end time. Not only is time marching on; its march here seems to suggest an imminent halt. Evil will only increase before the end (vv. 28-30). The evil that Adam brought on will rise to an unbearably horrible moment.

Not surprisingly, Ezra asks, "How?" and "When?" (4:33). Uriel replies that God, too, waits and is anxious for the end to come. Everything is on time, for all things have been decided and determined from of old (cf. Dan 11:36). This apocalyptic conviction about fixed times dominates the speech. God has measured out all things; nothing will deviate from that measurement (4:36-37). How humans are to relate to this idea, how they are to act in relation to it — this is the task of the author to explain.

Ezra says that perhaps the end time could be delayed somewhat. But Uriel says that delay is just as impossible as is delay when a woman is in labor pains. There is nothing that can hold back the birth. All the souls are in storage, as it were, ready for their rebirth in the end time (4:41-42). (It is interesting to note that this metaphor of the inevitability of the birth moment is also found in ancient Hittite literature from the twentieth century BC.)

Ezra is a bit insistent in his wanting to know both the time of his life's end and that of the world's end. Will the end take as long to come as the present moment took to come (4:45)? Uriel's response is that, indeed, there was a lot more time past than what will be. But as to his own time, he is not given authority to tell him.

Then Uriel begins to list some of the signs of the end (5:1). His catalogue contains many of the signs that apocalyptic literature of the first centuries AD assumed would precede the end. As regards human beings, two thoughts are primary: few will believe, and evil will increase. One can recall the NT conviction that faith will be slight in the end time (Luke 18:9).

The idea of the increase of evil appears already in Dan 12:4. (This reading in Daniel depends on a correction of the traditional Hebrew text [from the Middle Ages] which reads, "knowledge will increase." The difference between the words "knowledge" and "evil" in Hebrew is only one letter. The letters ר and ד are quite close, and a copyist could easily misread and miscopy the letter. This correction, which is supported by the Greek, is adopted in the NRSV but not in the REB.) In 5:3, Uriel announces the fall of "the country you observe ruling over the world" — a designation, of course, for Rome. This prediction was surely a word of comfort for Jews living in the conditions that led to the Jewish revolt against the Roman Empire and the devastating defeat of the Jews and the destruction of Jerusalem. (It was probably that defeat and especially the defeat in the Second Jewish Revolt against Rome in 133-35 that led the Jews to lose interest in apocalyptic literature, including this work. It was Christians who continued to read and expand the apocalypses.)

Some of the other signs are truly frightening. Many involve reversals of natural phenomena, such as the sun shining at night and the moon in daylight. The Dead Sea will produce living fish (5:7). Friends will be enemies (v. 9). All that is governed by natural laws will fall into disorder. The critical time of pregnancy will become fearsome because monsters could be born (v. 8). (This idea is parallel to, and explains, the NT's "Woe to those who are pregnant" [Matt 24:19; Mark 13:17; Luke 21:23].) The author makes sure that he describes a tumultuous and terrifying time.

Even those things that make human beings human will have fled away: reason, justice, and hope. These things that human beings had actually pursued are now gone. Of the horrible things that will happen only this much "I am allowed to tell you" (5:13). More than this, who could bear? The final command, besides to pray, is to weep and to fast (v. 13).

Ezra awakens and is terrified (5:14). Uriel's physical and moral assistance enable Ezra to face the next experience, brief though it is. Phaltiel is introduced as a "leader of the people" (v. 16). He wants Ezra to do his job as the guide to whom Israel has been entrusted, for now they are as sheep threatened by wolves. Ezra, the shepherd, asks Phaltiel to return in seven days (5:19).

The Second Episode (5:20–6:34)

After seven days of fasting, Ezra is ready for more revelation. He directly asks the Most High the future fate of Israel. The past had shown God's decision to choose and

God's actual choice of the one vine, the one plot, the one lily that is watered by the river which gladdens the one chosen city of Zion, the one dove (5:26). Chosen are only one sheep, and only one people to whom God gave a special way of life, one root, and one "unique one." The sequence of the nouns seems to be six references to the chosen city: the vine, the plot, the lily, the river, Zion herself, and the dove (in 2:15 also the word "dove" refers to Zion). Then there are four references to Israel: the sheep, the people (who is named Israel), the root, and "the only one," a term for one's only offspring, as in Gen 22:2.

With this emphasis on God's act of choosing Zion and Israel, this narrowing down to the chosen, the writer thinks it odd that now the relationship is reversed: the one is given over to the many — the one root is trampled on by others. Israel is undergoing severe trials as "your only one" (who is later explicitly identified as "your firstborn," 6:58). Israel first appears in the Bible as the son of God in Exod 4:22. The author proposes that God owes his people direct dealings rather than treatment at the hands of other nations. If Israel is to be punished, it should not be the other peoples who execute that sentence; rather, the God of Israel and his own punishing hand (5:30) should act.

Uriel returns and challenges Ezra, saying that he really does not love Israel as much as God does (5:33). But Ezra's love does not help him understand why God allows the prolonging of Israel's humiliating experience. Ezra in abject puzzlement wonders with Job (Job 3:3) and Jeremiah (Jer 20:14) whether his birth was a mistake (5:35), at least in respect to seeing Israel's current condition. Uriel tries a different approach; he quizzes Ezra about those things in the realm of nature that Ezra is ignorant of. Again the figure of Uriel fades into that of God, and Ezra wonders whether it would not have been better if all people of all ages were not living on earth at the same time (v. 43). In that way there could be a much quicker judgment than this long-drawn-out ordeal that Ezra and Israel are experiencing.

Uriel uses the metaphor of the earth as mother (as earlier at 4:41) who bears many children sequentially (5:46-49). It takes time for the conception, gestation, and birth of each child individually. Moreover, the world is growing old now (v. 55). Little time remains. Ezra asks how God will actually judge creation. God explains that just as the world started, developed, and was brought to its current fullness through him, so the world will end only through him. He is totally in charge and in control (6:1-6). Moreover, the change from one age to the next is without break, just as one generation passes to the next. Ezra asks for knowledge of the final sign before the end. In a solemn address, for which Ezra must stand, God says that the world will be transformed. And the voice that will sound will be like "the sound of a mighty torrent" (v. 17). When "Zion's humiliation" (v. 19) is over, then the things of the end will occur. (Here the reader might think the author thought of a truly imminent end; ch. 14 of the book, however, suggests a significant time before the end.)

Then the books will be opened (6:20). Children will be born with a precocious ability to speak. Certain pregnant women will give birth prematurely to children who can already dance (v. 21). The trumpet blast is also standard imagery for the end (v. 23). Streams will stop their flow. All things will be turned around in this end time. "Whoever is left after all I have foretold will be saved" (v. 25), and those who left the earth without dying will appear. Earth's people will repent. Moreover, the faithful will be rewarded, and truth revealed.

After this speech of God, the earth itself where Ezra stood began to reel as a sign of the end of that vision (6:29). Ezra is told to resume fasting. Perhaps more revelations will be given. Ezra is commended for his chaste life (v. 32). He is not to belittle the past so that he will not be mistaken about the future.

The Third Episode (6:35–9:25)

After the usual week of fasting, Ezra is ready to pour out his soul to the Most High. Ezra recalls the full six days of creation with thoughtful reflections on each of them as they appear in Genesis 1 as well as in popular Jewish thought of that day. This narration stresses that God created by word only, and the narrator dwells on Behemoth and Leviathan, creatures that do not appear in Genesis 1 but in Job 40–41. The author proposes that God assigned each of these creatures to a different part of the world: Behemoth to part of the land (six sevenths of the world) and Leviathan to the water (one seventh of the world) (6:42, 47, 52). This creation account curiously omits God's rest on the seventh day, perhaps because Ezra wants God to act now.

A major thrust or goal of the passage is to show that the world was created for the sake of Israel (6:55; see 7:11). All of creation is simply the backdrop for the life of Israel, and now, Ezra says, this life is more difficult for Israel than would seem necessary. The questioning is impassioned: the Gentiles are now ruling over Israel; the one for whom the world was created is suffering unbearably. The author uses a series of titles for Israel (6:58), much like those for Isaac in Gen 22:2 and for Israel in Exod 4:22.

Ezra had made his speech and posed his questions to God, but the response comes from the angel Uriel. Israel is straitened now because suffering and difficulty are part of the scenario for the end time. Two parables describe this condition: a narrow approach to a wide sea (7:3-5) and a treacherous approach to a city (vv. 6-9). Both show that what is difficult now for Israel will eventually give way to a far more enjoyable fulfillment. The angel repeats the idea that the world was created for the sake of Israel. But creation was tarnished by the sin of Adam, and because of that, life is indeed very difficult. The angel advises, however, to look not at the present but at the future and the reward to come.

Ezra insists, addressing the angel again with the words he uses toward God, that Torah assures the faithful that their good deeds will bring a happy life (7:17-18). But the respondent seems to charge Ezra with really questioning and accusing God of inconsistency in those promises. Torah was given, and the world should perish before one would dishonor Torah (v. 20). The angel asserts that there is a time for true rewards for the faithful, and that such a time has been set up for the next world. Sinners will indeed receive their just deserts, and the just, who follow the law (presumably both that given to all humans and that given to Israel), will be rewarded. All will receive what is due them: "Emptiness for the empty, and fullness for the full!" (v. 25).

Then the angel or God confides that after the signs there will be the revelation of the city and of the Messiah (7:26-28). "The invisible city" and "the hidden country" are mysterious terms (as mysterious as is the whole of the writing), and they in some sense refer to Jerusalem, the heavenly Jerusalem, the land of Israel, and messianic times. The mention of the redeemer figure here is the first of several occurrences (also 11:37–12:1; 12:31-34; 13:3-13; 13:25-52; and 14:9). This particular appearance of the Messiah is striking in that he does only one thing here, namely, he rejoices with those who have been delivered, and then he dies (7:28-29).

The title "my son the Messiah" (7:28) in Latin is surprising for the time of writing. There are strong reasons to think that the Latin reading here, "son," is the result of Christian translators' rendering of the Greek word, which regularly means "servant" or "child." If the original Hebrew term were "son," the occurrence would surely make 4 Ezra an exceptional document. "Son of God" is not a regular title for the messianic figure in the HB. The activity of the Messiah here is quite limited: he rejoices with those who have survived for four hundred years (v. 28), and then he dies (v. 29). The idea of the death of the Messiah is quite a surprise (cf. John 12:34). Only one Jewish writing of this time can be interpreted as expecting the Messiah's death (*2 Apoc. Bar.* 30:1; Stone 1990). The length of the reign of the messianic figure is specified here as four hundred years (7:28). This number of years of rejoicing, perhaps, is meant to counterbalance the four hundred years of oppression that Israel experienced in bondage in Egypt (Gen 15:13; Exod 12:40).

The cosmic upheaval or silence referred to here is seven days, paralleling the seven days of creation (7:30). After those days, the new era of creation will commence. The first thing to happen in the new age will be judgment. All will arise for judgment, either for reward in the place of rest and joy or in "the place of torment" (v. 36). The belief in resurrection was widespread in the Judaism of that time. Dan 12:2 has a similar sequence of resurrection, judgment, and reward.

The depiction of the judgment day has all who have lived come before a throne from which mercy has departed (7:33). All persons will have their deeds reviewed, to see whether they were good or wicked (v. 35). The places reserved for the faithful and for the wicked will be revealed (v. 36). The divine judgment will address all nations and bid them see the place of joy and rest over against the place of fire and torment (vv. 37-38).

The reader may notice that at this verse a double verse-numbering in the REB begins to appear. This numbering difference results from the fact that in most of the Latin manuscripts of 2 Esdras 7, vv. 36-105 do not appear. These verses seem to have been excised in an early Latin manuscript from which most copies were made, but they survive in two Latin manuscripts and in the copies in the eastern languages. The reason for omitting these verses was probably that they appear to be too pessimistic about the number of those to be saved and about the fate of the wicked, specifically, whether they can be helped by another's prayer for them after death.

Time and all things connected with time cease their progression (7:39-42). Only the glory of the Most High is seen, and all things are seen in it (v. 42). Ezra, in conversation with the angel, learns that there are very few who will be saved (v. 51). This idea is a common thought in apocalyptic mentality. One finds it in various places in the NT, for example, Matt 7:14 and 22:14. Moreover, the wicked, who are wicked because of the evil inclination in human beings, will be separated from the just in the world to come. This differentiation is currently hidden in humanity. But God made two worlds, and in the next world the just will be segregated from the wicked (7:50). To emphasize the value of the few who are to be saved, the author creates a parable about the metals of the earth (vv. 54-58). The rarer metal is more valuable than other metals. A similar phenomenon occurs among humans: the saved are few and precious (vv. 59-60). The comparison of the wicked with transitory things such as vapor, flame, or smoke (7:61) should not give the impression that they will escape the torments. Such comparisons are meant simply to show the wicked to be of little value, and one can find such images elsewhere in Scripture (Job 7:7; Ps 144:4; Hos 13:3).

Ezra addresses the earth who brought forth human beings into this place of trial in which few can be victorious (7:62-69). To the moving question, Why did God allow only so few to be saved? the angel replies that the joy over those who are saved is all the greater. But the future of those who have chosen not to obey God will depend on their own past choices. They had been free to accept God's conditions or to reject them. God was more than patient with them (v. 74).

The dominant thought in the next section is the contrast between the faithful and the wicked during the interim period of existence before judgment (7:74-99). The author spells out the seven ways of existence or reasons for the misery of those who are destined for punishment because of their sinfulness (vv. 81-87). The sinful will suffer in seeing the joy of the blessed (v. 83) and in the knowledge that their own fate cannot change (v. 82). Seeing God, the faithless cringe (v. 87). Equally, seven states of joy for the righteous are enumerated. The faithful, on the other hand, who have served God the Most High in all the difficulties that life presents, will go from one degree of blessedness to another. The list begins with the joy that results from resisting the "evil impulse" (v. 92; cf. 3:21) to the very beatifying and eternal vision of God (7:98). This is the first time an author in the biblical tradition has attempted a nuanced description of the afterlife, and, in this sequence, existence after death and before the resurrection and final judgment.

Ezra finally asks a question that has bothered him deeply: Can those who have died receive any aid from those who have not yet died? The angel is perfectly clear that the answer is "No" (7:104-5). One's fate is sealed at death; nothing after that matters regardless of what one might do for the soul that had died. This seemingly harsh position is in contradiction to 2 Macc 12:44-46, where prayer for the dead is invoked as efficacious in freeing the dead from their sins (a text that is an important source for later Christian practices).

Ezra proffers the examples of intercessory prayer to the angel. Many passages in the Bible contain examples of individuals who prayed for others: Abraham for Sodom, Moses and Joshua for Israel, even Elijah for rain for the people (7:106-11). The reply is equally simple: the irreversibility begins with the day of judgment. There are two worlds that differ in nature: the present world is subject to change and corruption; the world to come is eternal and will not change. Then "unbelief will be eliminated, justice full-grown, and truth will have risen like the sun" (7:112-15).

Is there then no reason to be born? Ezra asks. Adam sinned, and we all have become sinners because of him. Is there any hope of salvation for people mired in sin? Revelation itself is for naught for those in this plight (7:116-26). The picture of Ezra pleading in this way perhaps appeals to the modern person, especially one influenced by existential thought. Have we been condemned by birth?

But the answer of the angel is not especially sympathetic. Yes, the test is severe, but the battle can be won. The angel invokes the book of Deuteronomy and its divine injunction to "Choose life!" (Deut 30:20) and the means to it. The Israelites may have ignored this command, but right now fidelity is possible (7:127-31).

Ezra reflects on the goodness and mercy of God, without which humanity would indeed have no chance of being spared. The list of titles for God is taken from Exod 34:6-7 with little variation. This list of divine attributes appears in various places in the Bible, for example, Joel 2:13 and Jonah 4:2. The exegesis of these verses from Exodus here is the only clear example in 4 Ezra of an attempt to exegete or explain in some detail a biblical passage (7:132-40).

The angel repeats one of his favorite thoughts, that there are two worlds. There are many souls alive in this world, but only a few will be saved in the next. The author has interesting direct addresses to the earth in different parts of the work. Here the angel encourages Ezra to "inquire of the earth" (8:1-3). The thought is persistent and irradicable: justified souls are as rare as gold.

Ezra prays fervently to God. He invokes the frailty of humanity and elaborates on the time and care that it takes for a human being to evolve from conception to full growth and maturity (8:4-14). With these thoughts he hopes to move God. And he applies such thoughts directly to Israel (vv. 15-19).

Ezra commences a magnificent prayer, beginning with the majesty of God and sweeping down to the lowliness and sinfulness of humanity. (This prayer has a title, which shows that it sometimes functioned independently. Its power and beauty led to its being used in public worship. It was copied and arranged with other solemn hymns from the Bible in Latin in the Middle Ages.) With liturgical cadence, Ezra praises the greatness of God and indicates that the divine majesty should be careful in expecting too much from humanity. Humankind is weak, and not one person has avoided sin. Some persons were just and observant, and God is asked to look on these. Mercy should be called forth by the knowledge of human weakness. In this prayer, even though the word "covenant" appears, the thought and expressions are applicable to all of humanity (8:20-36).

The angel or God replies that he, too, has to focus, when viewing humanity, on those who are just. God sows the seed, but he knows that not all seed sprouts, takes root, and grows to maturity (8:37-41). But Ezra becomes even more bold and, using the imagery of the farmer and the sown seed, seems to reproach God for being totally responsible for the actions of humans. He even invokes Genesis 1 in its claim that humanity was created in the image of God. God is responsible for all that humans do; how then can any person be punished by God when some evil is committed? It behooves God to spare his own creation (vv. 42-45).

In response he tells Ezra not to confuse the issue. Just as this world is different from the next, so, too, is God's love for creation much greater than Ezra's. But now Ezra is chided for counting himself among the unrighteous. He is indeed among the godly (8:46-51). For such righteous ones, heaven and the new age lie open, and the speaker lists the various images for the end-time fulfillment (vv. 52-54). He should not worry about the others who are not faithful. God certainly does not want any to be lost. But if some refuse to follow God, lost they will be, even if they are many. The cause for their loss is not God but their own misuse of free will (vv. 55-62).

Ezra then asks the question that many ask in this regard: When will it be? (8:63). The response is that the end and judgment will be preceded by signs, some of which have already occurred (9:2). The list of problems and disasters he gives as "signs" are such as occur in much apocalyptic literature and the kinds of things that are applicable to almost any era. But the author asserts that the time is close. The time has indeed been determined, and what has been planned by God is on its way irretrievably. The trials that will arise as the end approaches occur frequently in apocalyptic texts. These are the "messianic woes" that precede the time of fulfillment. These tribulations serve to separate the faithful from the faithless, the sinner from the saved.

The point of life is to remain true to God and to the divine commands, for the divine plan is to save those who are to be saved. "All who come safely through" (9:7) refers to those few who choose to hold fast the faith, accepting God as their leader. The author uses terms like "good deeds" and "faith" (v. 7) but does not make any kind of contrast between the two; rather, he sees them as a unity. A person who trusts and reveres God simply does the divine commands. Where an individual will be in the next world — this work continually emphasizes — is entirely up to the individual and the individual's response to God's claim.

The rewards for being a "survivor" will be given in the Lord's land (9:8). The land of Israel is quite important for the author, and he seems to think that "seeing the salvation of the LORD" (cf. Exod 14:13) will be possible only there. To "show my salvation" is a phrase from Ps 91:16. This expression was given an eschatological interpretation in other writings from around the time of this author. Those who fail to recognize and follow the way of the Lord will be consigned to torments, but the faithful will be saved in the world that was created for them. Ezra is warned again not to worry about the lost, but to focus on the reward for the righteous (9:13).

Ezra repeats his concern with the ratio between the lost and the saved (9:15). The angel tries again to explain to Ezra that God's plan is to plant a wondrous garden of different flowers. But when the creative work was progressing, human choice began to corrupt the project. The image of what could be saved, "one grape out of a cluster" or "one tree out of a large forest," is striking for the small percentage involved (v. 21). These are painful metaphors for the fewness of those to be saved. But Ezra is told to ready himself for another vision. He gets a seven-day wait, this time without fasting. Once in the flowery field, however, he should abstain from meat and wine but eat all the flowers he cares to (vv. 23-24).

The Fourth Episode (9:26–10:59)

The week-long vegetarian diet of Ezra parallels the eating habits of Adam and Eve and their descendants before the flood. It is also reminiscent of Moses' forty-day fast during the revelation on Sinai. But Ezra's regime here seems halfway between the total fast before his previous visions and his lack of a fast in his later ones. The moment is a turning point in the book and in the development of the figure of Ezra, especially now that Ezra seems fully consoled about the destruction and punishment that are due and inevitable.

Ezra addresses the Almighty again with words about Israel and its lack of obedience to the law that God had given (9:29-32). The seed imagery returns with God planting the seed of the law with Israel and it not bearing the desired fruit because they had not protected and fostered it (vv. 33-36). The author catches himself to point out that the failure is Israel's fault and not due to any deficiency in the seed itself. The law in itself is indestructible and glorious (v. 37). This affirmation is a strong witness to the Torah piety of that time and the centuries to follow, the piety that will be encouraged and underscored in ch. 14.

Ezra sees a woman in tatters (9:38-40). The woman is described as dressed in the traditional mourning attire. Ezra begins to inquire of her the reason for her mourning. His reaction to her continues the transformation of Ezra, the change that marks a turning point in the book. Ezra begins to act differently from the manner in which he had behaved thus far, taking on the role of the instructor after he had been the instructed one for all the preceding chapters. In response to Ezra's request (v. 42), the woman tells her story.

The woman's story of her marriage and her son (9:43–10:4) has some similarities to Ezra's own story in this book. She was barren thirty years; he was three years in exile before this revelation. She is overwhelmed with grief in a loss, as was he. The story also has elements that are not developed later on: the husband, the neighbors, even the upbringing of the child. Yet other features clearly parallel biblical stories: the barren woman who finally conceived (Sarah, Hannah), and the young husband who dies on his wedding night (Tobit).

Later in the chapter, the reader learns that the woman who tells about her son is Zion. Her son seems to be the personification of all her children. Zion's children appear with some regularity in Isaiah 40–66, but also elsewhere in the HB and in the deuterocanonical books, such as Bar 4:10-12, 21, 25, 27-29, 37; 5:5. In Lamentations (especially Lam 1:11-22) Zion/Jerusalem laments the loss of her children with the destruction of the first temple and the devastation of the city by the Babylonians. The destruction of Jerusalem by the Romans five centuries later was just as much a shock to devout believers. The woman's son is Israel, who has suffered defeat and near extinction in the Jewish revolt against Rome (AD 66-72).

The personification of Zion as a mother is an image that recurs with some regularity in the HB. The image, of course, is part of the standard personification of cities as women. Probably one of the most memorable passages with such a personification is Ezekiel 16, where Jerusalem is raised and married by her divine finder. The personification of two cities simultaneously occurs in Ezekiel 23 and a passage in Jeremiah that seems dependent on Ezekiel 23, namely, Jer 3:6-18.

The details of the story of the woman and her son are not as important as the general thought of the woman's speech. The woman is beside herself and determines never to reenter the city, but rather to stay in the field mourning and fasting (10:4).

Ezra, giving up his previous questioning and complaining, verbally attacks the weeping woman. He rails at her for weeping for the loss of one son while Zion, "the mother of us all," is lost (10:7). Ezra includes all of humanity. His previous concerns return when he tells the woman of all those who will be lost, all those that the earth has given birth to but who are destined for destruction. He even anticipates the possible claim of the mother that it is her own flesh and blood that she has lost. He says that mother earth, too, is losing what she had painfully brought forth (vv. 9-14).

He tells her that she should accept her own loss and stop mourning publicly. If she can do this, she will receive her son back and be restored to a place of honor among women. But she insists that her sorrow is great and that she will remain there till death (10:15-18).

Ezra cannot believe that the woman is not moved by the tremendous loss of Zion. There is an intentional irony here. Ezra had only recently become a believer in God's justice determining the course of events in this world and preparing rewards in the next world for the faithful. He feels he has to convince this woman of the catastrophe that has happened to Zion. In reality, the woman is (or is the personification of) Zion. Ezra becomes eloquent in describing this loss. The poetic structure of his description in 10:21-23 is carefully wrought. The center of 10:22 contains the main concern: "the name which God has conferred on us is disgraced." The words of 10:23 are the crushing climax. This description of Zion's defeat parallels those in Lam 1:4-5 and 1 Macc 2:7-9

(Stone 1990). Ezra prays to God that the woman might have a change of heart and that she might find favor now and later (10:24).

Then a marvelous thing happens, an extraordinary, perhaps surrealistic scene, unique in this book. The woman becomes radiant, cries out in a fearsome voice, and is transformed before Ezra's eyes into a city that is spacious and well founded. Ezra is so astounded at the sight and power of the experience that, confused and shaken and fearing his demise, he calls out for the angel who had taken him this far (10:25-28).

Uriel comes to strengthen and raise up the collapsed Ezra. Uriel resumes his teaching and interpreting role. Ezra is so confused that he wonders whether this could all be an ephemeral dream. Uriel says that Ezra has served the Most High well in his life and by mourning the loss of Zion. The angel assures Ezra that God is willing to reveal secrets to him (10:38).

Uriel explains the whole vision to Ezra. First there is a touching exchange between Ezra and Uriel over Ezra's feeling of abandonment in this extraordinary experience (10:29-39). It may be noted that the angel, in addressing Ezra in 10:39, maintains the distinction between "your people," namely, Israel, and the city, Zion. In the explanation, the loss of the son is the virtual demise of Israel. The mother, Zion/Jerusalem, laments that destruction by the Romans (10:40-54).

Uriel continues to explain the speech of the woman: the story she tells of herself and of her son is the story of Zion. Her barrenness of thirty years represents the three thousand years during which there were no sacrifices in Zion. This length of years is in striking agreement with the general biblical understanding of the age of the world. The author is thinking that Zion began with creation and became inhabited only at the time of Solomon. The author mentions Solomon rather than David (although neither of them founded the city, but rather expanded its size). He is focusing on the sacrificial system of Israel that became effective only in the temple that Solomon built (1 Kgs 8:62-64).

The further imagery of the allegory is not clear. Occasionally the Bible uses marital imagery for the relation between God and the personified city. Here the imagery is not limited to that image. The city has a son who marries. Interpreters differ on the identity of the son. Perhaps since the text mentions only Solomon, he may be meant as a symbol of Zion's son, personified Israel. The death of the son would symbolize the cessation of the sacrificial system in Jerusalem when it was conquered, first by the Babylonians in the sixth century BC, and then by the Romans in the first century AD. More important is the glory of the heavenly Jerusalem which is now revealed to Ezra in the wonderful city, as explained by Uriel.

Ezra is told to experience and savor this glorious city (10:55). This enjoyment of transformation is symbolized by Ezra's walking into the city. This is the future that awaits Israel if all Israel will follow Torah (that revelation of God's will which was lost in the confusion of Zion's defeat but will be revealed a second time in ch. 14). Ezra is given this wondrous revelation so that the reader of this book can understand that the election of Israel is still in effect and that a reward awaits those who follow the way of the Lord.

Ezra prepares for the next episode by taking two nights of sleep.

The Fifth Episode (11:1–12:39)

While still asleep, Ezra has a vision with dramatic symbolism. The eagle rising out of the sea is a fairly transparent symbol. The sea is often a biblical symbol of chaos (Job 26:12; Ps 89:10), and the eagle was emblematic of the Roman Empire (in Roman literature and archeology). The author was most conscious of the Roman armies' destruction of Jerusalem. Even if there had been many mercenaries who served in Rome's troops, the destruction happened under Rome's aegis.

The details of the bird with its various wings (twelve before others start to grow) and heads (three at first) are not easily identifiable (11:1). Surely the reader of the book in the first century understood the references to specific emperors or regional rulers. Apocalyptic authors were writing for their contemporaries and had no idea that later generations would need more clues than the people of their own time to penetrate the specifics of the symbolism.

Some of the symbolism (clouds, wings, heads, voices) comes from the book of Daniel, especially ch. 7. Some scholars have proposed that part of the enigma in this scene is due to various levels of editing and revising. This reasoning might be correct. It is curious that the eagle addresses part of its own body (11:8-9). The voice from another source is heard in vv. 16-17 announcing the inevitable end of the empire.

The severity of Roman rule is expressed in well-chosen words. "This head got the whole earth into its grasp, establishing an oppressive regime over all its inhabitants and a worldwide kingdom mightier than any of the wings had governed" (11:32). The yoke of Rome lay heavy on the Jews of the first century AD.

The scene builds up to the appearance of another symbol from the animal kingdom, a lion who is given a human voice (11:37). The lion was a traditional symbol for kingship in the kingdom of Judah. Here the symbol is employed for the great kingly figure to come, the Messiah.

There were already various understandings among Jews of the manner in which the time of fulfillment would come. The *Testament of Moses* (about contemporary with 4 Ezra) 10:1 reads, "Thus his kingdom will appear throughout his whole creation," and this without any intermediary. Another expectation was that God would use a figure, like the kings of old, to usher in the kingdom. Such an intermediary was sometimes a priestly figure. And sometimes both the kingly and the priestly figures appear together (as at Qumran). Here in 4 Ezra the messianic figure directly addresses the eagle. The scene is the future final assessment of the Roman Empire in the mind of this author.

The speech of the lion refers the reader to the book of Daniel, the second half of which is the only fully apocalyptic work in the canon of the HB. It was a standard practice of writers of apocalyptic literature to make direct and indirect references to previous writings. These writers knew their Scriptures well, and they expected their readers also to be familiar with the images and standard vocabulary of such writing. The lion asserts to the eagle itself that the eagle is the last of the four beasts (of Daniel 7) (11:39-41). He accuses the eagle of oppression and deceit. Because of virtually all kinds of evil, the lion inveighs against the eagle. Most dramatically he announces that the end of the ages of anticipation has come. The eagle, too, must now come to an end. Then at last the earth will relax and rejoice (11:46). The end, when it comes, will be definitive.

In his dream vision Ezra sees the eagle go up in flames (12:1-3). This vision is so frightening that he prays to God to help him understand this terrifying vision. The angel responds — again in the continuing interchangeability between God and the angelic figure. The angel also refers to the book of Daniel, this time by name, calling that seer a "brother" to Ezra (v. 11). His interpretation of the dream is no surprise. In the list of rulers, Caesar Augustus (27 BC–AD 14) is clearly recognizable as the second in the list after Julius Caesar (vv. 14-15). He has things to say about some of the twelve wings or emperors. This number, of course, does not identify individuals. There are not exactly twelve Roman emperors from Julius Caesar to the time of the writer. But the writer does use convincing imaginative detail to depict that final end of this monstrous affront to humankind. There have been proposals that the author uses "the three sleeping heads" (12:22) to refer to the Flavian emperors (Vespasian [69-79], Titus [79-81] and Domitian [81-96]) who ruled in the years leading up to the writing of this book.

The angel explains that the lion is the Messiah. God had kept him in reserve for the end time. He is descended from David (a curious concept if he has preexistence) (12:32), but his role in this writing is not to rule but rather simply to accuse the guilty and then to destroy those sinners (v. 33). The faithful he will reward at the end, giving them freedom and joy. This role of the Messiah does indeed differ from some of the other depictions of the Messiah. The emphasis in this presentation of the end time, one might say, falls on God and not on the instrument God uses.

Ezra receives instructions to write down the revelation that he has received and to keep it in a safe hiding place (12:37). Only to the wise can these revelations be disclosed. The wise will be able to keep them for the right time. This device of calling the writing "hidden" is widespread in these apocalyptic writings. This hiddenness enhances the dignity of the book, but it also serves to explain why this writing had not been widely known before. The reason why it had not circulated before is that, although the book was revealed back in the time of Ezra, some five centuries before the time of the writer of 4 Ezra, only now is it taken from hiding and shared with the faithful. With these instructions given, the angel leaves Ezra (v. 39).

This episode ends with reaction to the crowd of people around Ezra. They are distressed that Ezra has or will abandon them, for they see him as their last prophet, a last hope they have for survival in this storm-tossed world (again like the crowd worrying about Moses when he is gone) (12:41-45). This reaction of the people inspires Ezra to address the people and, through them, personified Israel. He tells Israel to take heart and not think that God has abandoned them (vv. 46-47). They should go home, and they will all meet again. After the people have gone, Ezra prepares for the next vision through the same vegetarian fast as before (vv. 50-51).

The Sixth Episode (13:1-58)

In another dream vision, Ezra sees a human figure (13:3). The words which introduce this figure in our translations are dependent on the Syriac and other early versions. The Latin has about twelve words missing, and those other versions show that the author was using ideas and phrases from Daniel 7. There "one like a son of humanity" (that is the meaning of "son of man") comes with the clouds of heaven. The figure in 4 Ezra is clearly messianic, while the figure in Daniel 7, according to most contemporary commentators, did not represent the Messiah at that time.

This awe-inspiring figure arouses hostility in a large horde of people gathered from throughout the world (13:8). The crowd who was intent on attacking the figure is not met with sword or force but simply with "a stream of fire, a breath of flame, and a great storm" (v. 11) from the mouth of the man. And the entire throng is consumed.

Then Ezra sees the man call to himself a different crowd of people, people who had been captives and are now free (13:12-13). Their joy and rejoicing seem to awaken Ezra, but he is terrified. He prays for an explanation of this dream vision (vv. 14-15). He is still puzzled and worried by the fact that some will be saved and others will be lost (vv. 16-19). Should one hope to survive and witness the end (v. 20)?

Yes, is the reply. The one who has faith and good works will receive the reward that all hope for. Indeed, those who survive will be more blessed than those who have died (13:24). But the vision showed that the Messiah, whom God calls his son, will be revealed after having been held all this time in hiding. The Messiah will bring about the undoing of all those who have plotted against God and his Anointed (v. 28). The role, then, of the Messiah here, as in other places in this book, is rather simply to bring about the judgment of all peoples and to reward those he finds faithful (vv. 33-34). The judgment will occur at Mt. Zion, the holy city already revealed. Part of that judgment by fire is the law that was earlier mentioned (13:38).

The explanation continues with an identification of the crowd of people that the man had assembled, and the explanation is quite surprising. They are the ten tribes that had been exiled with the fall of the Northern Kingdom in the eighth century BC (13:40). The Bible generally has little to say about those Israelites who had been deported to northern Mesopotamia. The author must have been troubled by this unresolved tension in the HB. The time of fulfillment must include the return of these people as well as some reflection on their absence from the biblical text. The author has the interesting view that those tribes after their deportation realized that it had occurred because they had not followed the laws God had given. They resolved to go farther still into a distant realm to there live fully those laws to which they had earlier been unfaithful (v. 42). To enhance their journey, the author even has the mighty Euphrates become stopped up while they pass (vv. 43-44). This miracle as they return imitates the miracle at the Jordan as Israel first entered the land of promise (Josh 3:1-17).

With this peaceful group from beyond the Euphrates are those other faithful who are now in the land, "inside my sacred borders" (13:48). There is a promise that at the end of time there will be "countless portents" (13:50).

Ezra asks an explanation of the man (the Messiah) coming from the sea. The answer is that, just as the sea is mysterious, so is God's decision regarding the time and manner of the appointed event. Indeed, no one is able to see the Messiah until that time of revelation (13:52-54). Only Ezra has been given this preliminary revelation because of his devotion to the law and to wisdom (perhaps equating the two, as some other writings of this time do). One of his images has a different twist from the way it appears in the Bible. In Proverbs the young man is to seek wisdom as if it were a beautiful, attractive woman; here Ezra has taken wisdom as his mother (v. 55). Ezra prepares three days for the final episode of 4 Ezra (v. 58).

The Seventh Episode (14:1-47)

The divine voice that Ezra hears from a bush is another subtle likening of Ezra to Moses (14:1). Then the comparison is again made explicit. Just as Moses had secrets revealed to him of things that would occur in the future and at the end of time, so it is with Ezra (vv. 5-8). The world is getting old (v. 10), and the time of the end hastens. It has been pointed out that the author does not really seem to anticipate an immediate end of the world (Esler 1994). At the time of Ezra, according to the book, about 80 percent of earth's allotted time has past (nine and a half twelfths, v. 11). If the writer thinks the world was about six thousand years old at the time of Ezra, then he would have thought that about fifteen hundred years remained.

God tells Ezra to prepare to die, for Ezra will go to live with God and his son (14:9) until the end time. There are signs of that time: evil will increase, truth will be remote, and falsehood will be near at hand (vv. 16-18). Ezra asks if he can leave behind him some written document that would furnish for the remaining generations some guide for their path in the encroaching darkness. The law, he says, had been consumed in the flames (without saying which ones, but no doubt it is the conflagration of Jerusalem in AD 70) (vv. 21-22).

The divine response is a command to Ezra to absent himself from the people for forty days (as did Moses) (14:23). He must make ready a full complement of writers, that is, he should make a selection of five scribes, a number parallel to the five books of Moses, Torah (v. 24). Some writings will be made public, others will be hidden away (v. 26). Ezra addresses the people as "Israel" and recites some of their history from Egypt to the land of promise and gift (vv. 28-29). The people sinned and were punished by the loss of the land (vv. 30-33). He encourages the people to redirect their minds to help them do the right things, so that they will escape a negative judgment after death (vv. 34-35). Then he excuses himself for his dictation session (v. 36).

Ezra and his five scribes retire to the field to await instructions. The next day Ezra has knowledge and memory poured into his mind from a cup that is given to him. The liquid looks like water but has the color of fire (14:39). Under this inspiration and with direct access to the divine words, Ezra dictates the ninety-four books of revelation (v. 44). Twenty-four are to be made available to the public, for these are the books of the Hebrew canon, to be read by all (v. 45). The remaining seventy books are to be hidden ("Apocrypha" means "hidden"), and these latter are only for those who will be able to understand them at the right time. The author has high respect for these "extra" books, for he calls them "a stream of understanding, a foundation of wisdom, a flood of knowledge" (v. 47). This is truly a fine encomium for this book itself, for the present book was, as it were, one of the "hidden books." Torah has been given again through this new Moses.

One should remember that here is where the first-century Jewish document ends. It is a work written to encourage people to remain true to their calling and to the demands of Torah, so that they can enjoy the age to come.

5 Ezra = 2 Esdras 15–16

2 Esdras 15 and 16 are, as noted earlier, probably a Christian composition that was presumably added to supplement the ideas in 4 Ezra. The author tries to warn the reader of the trials to come but also assures the reader that faith, fidelity to good behavior, and confession of sins will bring to God's elect the rewards that come from God alone.

The Punishment That Is Due (15:1-27)

The author begins by having God address him, the author — in the context of the whole book, Ezra — and bid him write down these words of prophecy. These are significant words, "for everyone who does not believe will die because of his unbelief" (15:4). The divine speech warns of the coming terror for the world. Human violence and evil have multiplied on the earth, and God can no longer be a simple observer (vv. 5-9). God is concerned for the people of God.

The author depicts them as living in Egypt (15:10). It is unclear whether this refers to people physically living in Egypt. Or, perhaps more likely, Egypt is a symbol for all that oppresses the people of God. God will repeat the wonders he did against the Egyptians of Moses' time by sending blight, hail, and storm against them (v. 13). The massive disturbance of the end time is described in imagery and words that resemble the NT (Mark 13) and other literature of the time (15:14-19).

The image of God bringing the armies of destruction

is, of course, biblical (Isaiah 13). God brings them to do against the enemy of God's chosen what that enemy had itself done against the elect (15:21). God is presented as unmerciful to sinners and frighteningly vengeful, the divine anger "consuming sinners like burning straw" (v. 23). It is curious that the author has God say that the sinners "pollute my sanctuary" with their presence (v. 25). It is unclear if this expression is purely rhetorical or meant to refer to some physical reality or simply the people of God.

Specific Threats (15:28-63)

The vision becomes specific: two enemy groups come from the East under the imagery of dragons and boars (15:29-33). Storm clouds, too, enter the imagery, and the destruction adds up to a disaster beyond imagination (vv. 34-35). Virtually all interpreters read this section (vv. 28-44) as referring to the invasions of Odenathus of Palmyra and Shapur I of Persia into Syria, a province of the Roman Empire, in the mid-third century AD. This interpretation shows that the author was imitating the apocalyptic writers' technique of referring to past events in an attempt to determine what has already happened. The forces work their way to Babylon (Rome) and bring about her demise. Even survivors will be taken captive (v. 45).

Asia, too, the Roman province of that name in what today is western Turkey, has everything to fear in that day (15:46). The author presents Asia as a woman, a whore who has taught her daughters to be whores (v. 47). Woeful disaster will come upon them. God says that mercy might have been available, but the woman "always killed my chosen ones" (v. 53). This seems to refer to persecution, but the details are insufficient to be specific about the reference.

The taunt against Asia continues in feminine imagery. Her punishment will be severe because of her cruelty against God's chosen. Again the author mixes many different biblical images (Rev 17:3-5; 18:3) with various other examples of destruction and humiliation (15:54-63).

Individual Warnings (16:1-34)

In 16:1, some different and some already mentioned parts of the Roman Empire are singled out. Babylon, again, is a cipher for Rome itself. Asia is again addressed. Egypt and Syria are roughly the lands by those names today, without emphasis on specific boarders. The author emphasizes the inevitability of the day with vivid metaphors (16:6-11), somewhat similar to those in Amos 3:3-8. The author depicts the coming disasters and calamities in the image of a sword already in motion. The hard times and destruction ahead are as inevitable as an arrow leaving its pulled string. The whole earth trembles (16:12) at what seems to be the final catastrophe. Fire consumes the earth's foundations (v. 15).

The author cries out, "Alas for me!" (16:17). The reader wishes the author would have given away more of his identity than this unique self-reference. The disaster mounts. "Famine, plague, suffering, and hardship" (v. 19) — who could conceive of worse times? But people will not give up their evil ways. All sinners will die, with no one to mourn for them. (This is the meaning of the curious phrase in the REB, "no one will give them the last rites," v. 23.) Vast desolation is in store for the earth. The author again picks phrases from the Bible to convey the horror (Isa 17:6; Amos 5:3; Matt 24:40-41) (16:24-32). Some of the most touching of human experiences will be brought to nothing (vv. 33-34).

The faithful are told that they should not fear (16:35-36). The end is near, with the inevitability of a woman giving birth (v. 38). When disaster comes, one must be ready for it. One must leave the occupation that engages that person when the time comes (vv. 41-47). Only the virtuous will escape the disaster.

The author uses an interesting and prolonged personification of justice and wickedness (16:49-51). The rivalry between these two women personifications recalls the rivalry between city women elsewhere in the Bible. Ultimately justice will reign, as ultimately Zion will reign instead of Babylon (Isaiah 47 and 49).

Warnings to God's People (16:35-67)

Next the author implores the sinner to confess his sins, for God knows all that happens (16:53). The author recalls that God is the one who created all things, and gives a review of creation, somewhat in the words of Genesis 1 and of other parts of the Bible. Sinners who try to hide their sins fool themselves (16:66). God will judge. If one confesses his sins and throws himself on the divine mercy, God will set him free (v. 67).

Reward for the Faithful (16:68-78)

Sinners will be utterly destroyed, but the faithful will be tested as gold is (16:73). God has chosen some, and these he will rescue. The faithful should have no fear. If one is a follower of God and the commandments, one has victory awaiting. But unrepentant sinners await destruction by fire (v. 78).

This apocalyptic writer, just as the author of 4 Ezra, wants the reader to be true to the faith, for the faithful will have an eternal reward. Thus ends a book which, though perhaps not fully biblical, did influence some significant figures in Western civilization.

Bibliography. Esler, P. E. 1994, "The Social Function of 4 Ezra," *JSNT* 53:99-123 • Humphrey, E. M. 1995, *The Ladies and the Cities: Transformation and Apocalyptic Identity in Joseph and Aseneth, 4 Ezra, the Apocalypse and the Shepherd of Hermas,* JSPSS 17, Sheffield: Sheffield Academic • Knibb, M. A. 1978, in *The First and Second Books of Esdras,* CBC, Cambridge and New York: Cambridge University • Longenecker, B. W. 1995, *2 Esdras,* Guides to Apocrypha and Pseudepigrapha, Sheffield: Sheffield Academic • Myers, J. M. 1974, *I and II Esdras,* AB 42, Garden City, N.Y.: Doubleday • Stone, M. E. 1990, *Fourth Ezra: A Commentary on the Book of Fourth Ezra,* Hermeneia, Minneapolis: Fortress.

4 Maccabees

David A. deSilva

INTRODUCTION

4 Maccabees drinks deeply of Hellenistic philosophical ethics and artistic rhetorical form in order to promote strict observance of Torah among Hellenistic Jews. It designates itself as a philosophical demonstration of the thesis that "devout reason is sovereign over the emotions" that hinder virtue (1:1), using specific regulations from Torah, examples from Scripture, and, most prominently, the praiseworthy examples of the martyrs of the Hellenization crisis of 167-166 BC to prove that it is in fact the devout, Torah-observant Jew who achieves the Greek ideal of virtue and the philosophical ideal of the wise person or sage. The title, which is surely not authentic, reflects its association with 1 and 2 Maccabees, particularly on account of the similarity of setting and the interest in the martyrs. This well-crafted oration encourages Jews living in the midst of the often critical, sometimes scornful, Greco-Roman culture to renew their commitment to their ancestral heritage as the noblest way of life and surest path to honor and self-respect.

Author, Date, and Provenance

The identity of the author is lost to posterity. Beginning with Eusebius (*Hist. Eccl.* 3.10.6), the work was attributed to Josephus and was passed down in collections of his writings. Differences in style, inconsistencies in the narration of the same events, and the highly contrastive stances taken with regard to accommodation to Gentile culture, however, make this identification highly unlikely (Williams 1987; Townshend 1913). The anonymous author possessed a high level of linguistic sophistication (reflected in his invention of compound words, his use of the rather rare optative mood, and his ornate syntactical style), was adept at rhetorical ornamentation and techniques (such as *prosopopoeia*), paid more than passing attention to popular philosophical ethics, and displayed a passionate commitment to the law of the God of Israel.

The date of the book has been much debated, and the ingeniousness of the cases advanced testifies to the lack of clear and direct evidence. The probability that the author has used 2 Maccabees (his free handling of that source is not surprising given the liberty he takes when retelling the biblical story of David's thirst; cf. 4 Macc 3:6-16 with 2 Sam 23:13-17; 1 Chr 11:15-19) and the author's explanation that the high priesthood used to have lifetime tenure (4 Macc 4:1) indicate that the work was written after 63 BC, after which the high priesthood was no longer held for life. Dupont-Sommer 1939, Breitenstein 1978, and van Henten 1986, arguing from stylistic considerations and from the growth of eclecticism late in the first century AD, have favored a date as late as the reign of Hadrian (AD 117-38). The strongest case so far has been made by Elias Bickerman. Pointing to the tendency to read one's contemporary political arrangements back into the history one writes, he finds the author's linking of Syria, Cilicia, and Phoenicia under a single governor (4 Macc 4:2 vs. 2 Macc 3:5) to reflect the linking of those regions under one governor from AD 19 to 54. Allowing for van Henten's correction that this arrangement persisted to AD 72, I conclude that 4 Maccabees was composed sometime in the middle half of the first century AD.

Provenance is similarly difficult to determine. Earlier generations of scholars gravitated toward Alexandria (Townshend 1913), due more to their familiarity with Alexandria as a prominent Jewish center than to any data internal to the text. Indeed, everything points rather to Asia Minor as the place of composition. First, 4 Maccabees displays the ornate style that came to be associated with this region (Norden 1923). Second, interest in (and even veneration of) the martyr-heroes of the book was most intense in Syria and Asia, especially Antioch, which came to be associated with their burial place (Dupont-Sommer 1939). Finally, and most convincingly, the literary epitaph for the martyrs provided by the author in 17:9-10 resembles most closely the funerary inscriptions found almost exclusively in the southern parts of Asia Minor (van Henten 1994). A provenance in an urban center with a significant Jewish population somewhere within Syria or Cilicia is therefore to be preferred.

Setting, Purpose, and Occasion

The author addresses fellow Jews (18:1) living in the midst of the dominant Greco-Roman culture. It is highly unlikely that the text responds to an outbreak of anti-Jewish persecution (known or unknown), addressing rather the everyday tensions experienced by Jews who, on the one hand, seek to preserve their particular ancestral culture and, on the other hand, are surrounded by and imbued with Greco-Roman values and thought. This tension was exacerbated by strains of anti-Judaism within Greco-Roman culture: the Jews' exclusive devotion to one God and denial even of the reality of others struck at the heart of Greco-Roman piety and looked like atheism; the peculiar customs of the Jews (e.g., sabbath observance, avoidance of certain foods, and circumcision) and their tendency to form communities in the midst of the larger city were interpreted by many Gentile authors as barbarism and "hatred of outsiders" (see 3 Macc 3:3-7; Josephus *Ag. Ap.* 2.121, 258; Diodorus Siculus *Hist.* 34.1-4; Tacitus *Hist.* 5.1-5; Juvenal *Sat.* 14.100-104). Strict adherence to the Jewish Torah would frequently bring one into disfavor and dishonor in the eyes of one's Gentile neighbors — two things greatly to be avoided in a world where one's honor and access to patronage were primary priorities. Some Jews resolved the tension by apostatizing and assimilating fully into Greco-Roman culture. Such Jews could themselves become critics of Torah as a flawed, human, ethnic body of laws with no ultimate value (see Philo *Vit. Mos.* 1.31; *Conf. ling.* 2).

4 Maccabees speaks to Jews living in the midst of such tensions, offering a strong voice in support of Torah observance as the God-given path to live nobly, fulfilling the highest virtues prized by Greco-Roman ethicists (prudence, courage, justice, and temperance). The author does not reject Hellenism, to be sure. His fluency in Greek, use of rhetoric, and interpretation of Torah observance in terms of Greek virtues and ethical philosophical topics show a high degree of penetration by Hellenization, but the author uses these resources to promote strict adherence to the particularistic laws and practices of Judaism. His purpose is not merely to gain assent to the philosophical thesis that begins the speech, but rather to reinforce commitment to the Jewish way of life, the way of life defended courageously by the martyrs with their lives, the way of life that best fulfills the Greek ethical ideal of reason's mastery of the passions, enabling the life of virtue. The author chooses the martyrs as his exemplars because their extreme contest will facilitate the more moderate contest faced by his own audience in their everyday lives (although, should hostility escalate, they will be ready to give the last measure of devotion).

While we know of purely "literary speeches," and while 4 Maccabees came to be disseminated as a written text for a broad audience beyond its oral delivery, this oration gives several hints that it was composed for a specific occasion, speaking of being delivered "on this anniversary" (1:10) and called for by "the present occasion" (3:19). Hadas 1953 and Dupont-Sommer 1939 suggest that it was delivered on the anniversary of the martyrs' deaths, but, although Christians would commemorate these martyrs with a feast day, there is a striking lack of evidence that Jews did the same (especially as early as the first century). The feast of Dedication (Hanukkah) would have provided an appropriate occasion for celebrating those loyal Jews whose commitment to Torah caused God's anger to turn from Israel (see 2 Macc 7:33, 37-38; 8:5; 4 Macc 6:27-29; 17:21-22). Lack of attention to the Hasmonean military heroes would not be surprising given, first, the widespread disillusionment with that dynasty and, second, the greater appropriateness of commending as examples those who showed resolute steadfastness toward Torah rather than those who took up arms against the Gentile authorities. Certainty about the occasion cannot be ascertained, however, since the festivals celebrating the giving of the law (e.g., Pentecost or *Simḥat hattorah*) would be equally appropriate settings for promoting the virtues of Torah observance and for praising those who died rather than abandon that way of life.

Form, Structure, and Strategy

4 Maccabees combines elements of the philosophical demonstration and the eulogy, or commemorative address. In both aspects, the oration belongs to the genre of epideictic rhetoric, which is largely concerned with the maintenance of the audience's commitment to values central to the survival of the culture. He sets forward an ethical thesis in the first verse, namely, that "devout reason is sovereign over the emotions," proceeds to define his terms (1:13-30), and sets about proving his thesis first by showing how specific regulations in Torah temper the passions and providing brief examples from the Jewish Scriptures of those who held fast to virtue rather than yield to the passions (1:30–3:18). The remainder of the work is dedicated, however, to what the author calls a "narrative demonstration" of his thesis (3:19), seen in the firmness and courage of the nine martyrs. After each episode of martyrdom, the author will return to confirm his thesis (7:16-23; 13:1-5; 16:1-4), but it is clear that the martyrs provide more than mere proofs of a thesis. The praise of the martyrs' virtuous choices and character will rouse emulation in the hearers, who will be moved both by argumentation and praise to persevere in their commitment to Torah as the way of life that leads to virtue and a lasting, praiseworthy remembrance. In this regard, 4 Maccabees is strikingly similar to Seneca's *De constantia sapientis.* Both are discourses aimed at promoting a certain "philosophy" (a "way of life") by demonstrating a thesis that captures some ethical advantage promised by the philosophy and by including extended consideration and praise of those who have embodied that way of life.

A way of life that embodies the cardinal virtues is considered an honorable one, and if a course can be shown to be honorable and praiseworthy, it will be considered advantageous and desirable (see *Rhet. Her.* 3.3.4-7; Aristotle *Rhet.* 1.9.35-36). The author therefore proceeds to show how keeping Torah, rather than lead away from virtue, trains and perfects one in every virtue. He even shows quite specifically how particular regulations, like the dietary laws of Torah that are frequently the object of Gentile scorn, train the devout Jew in virtues such as temperance. If their neighbors mock them, therefore, it is due to Gentile ignorance. The author's narration of the history of the Hellenization crisis in 3:19–4:26 also advances his protreptic goals: the example from history demonstrates that assimilation to Gentile culture and abandonment of Torah lead not to advancement but to the destruction of the peace and divine protection enjoyed by the Jewish nation when its members adhere closely to God's law. Finally, in his presentation of the martyrs, the author creates a deliberative environment in which the audience hears the advice given by Antiochus, representing the unsupportive Gentile culture, and the rebuttals given by the martyrs. Because Antiochus's point of view can be characterized as error stemming from lack of knowledge of God, and the martyrs' decisions and deliberations praised as leading to their eternal honor in God's court, the audience will be moved in their own setting to reject the arguments and enticements to assimilation and pursue lasting honor and God's continued favor through devotion to their ancestral law. They are enabled to maintain their self-respect as Torah-observant Jews in the midst of a Gentile world that finds their ways dishonorable and incomprehensible.

Influence

While exhibiting little influence on other Jewish writings, 4 Maccabees exercised a significant influence on the early church. The author's interpretation of the martyrs' deaths as acts of obedience that reconcile God and the people, serving as an atoning sacrifice for the people's sins and a "life in exchange for others" (6:27-30; 17:21-22), resonates deeply with the early church's interpretation of the obedient death of Jesus (cf. the language used in Rom 3:24-25; 1 Cor 15:3; 1 Tim 2:6; 1 Pet 1:19; 1 John 1:7). This oration may also provide a window into a neglected aspect of the Judaizers' appeal to the Galatians, namely, the promise that submission to Torah will provide the needed guidance to rule the "passions of the flesh" and live a virtuous life. While the Judaizers need not have relied on 4 Maccabees directly, to be sure, our text displays the kinds of arguments for Torah observance that the Gentile might well have found persuasive. This would also explain Paul's need to show how "his gospel" already provides a better way to counter the "passions of the flesh" (Gal 5:16-24; see Barclay 1991).

There are a number of points of contact between 4 Maccabees and the Pastoral Epistles as well. The elevation in the Pastorals of "self-control" and "piety," the recognition that the passions are the chief impediment to virtue (2 Tim 2:22; 3:6; Tit 2:12; 3:3), and the focus on fidelity to God and God's standards as a "noble contest" (1 Tim 6:12; 2 Tim 4:7) raise the possibility that the Pastor has learned from our author. The Epistle to the Hebrews also recalls 4 Maccabees both at the level of language and syntax (compare Heb 12:2 with 4 Macc 6:9; Heb 3:6, 14 with 4 Macc 17:3-4), as well as in the promotion of loyalty toward God and God's promises ("faith" in both texts) as ultimately more advantageous than seeking temporary release from tension with the host society (Heb 10:32-39). Revelation shares with 4 Maccabees an emphasis on "endurance" and faithful testimony, as well as the presentation of martyrdom as the path to an honorable victory over a human tyrant (Rev 15:2) rather than a degrading defeat.

With regard to the NT, 4 Maccabees at least provides a host of comparative material displaying the topics and strategies employed by both Jewish and Christian minority cultures to promote perseverance to their way of life, as well as attesting to traditions that played an important part in the first decades of the early church. As one moves into the second century, the direct influence of 4 Maccabees, particularly with regard to the development of an ideology of martyrdom and to the continued promotion of faithfulness in the face of death, is unmistakable. The letters of Ignatius, the *Martyrdom of Polycarp,* and Origen's *Exhortation to Martyrdom* bear indications of direct dependence on this oration (and not merely on 2 Maccabees, as has frequently been suggested; see deSilva 1998). Origen's use of athletic metaphors as well as his interpretation of martyrdom as the fitting act of reciprocity for God's many benefits bears the clear stamp of 4 Maccabees (see 6:10; 12:11; 13:13; 16:16-23; 17:11-16). Interest in this oration and in its martyr heroes outlasted the period of the church's persecution, and both John Chrysostom and Gregory of Nazianzus devote sermons to their witness (the latter referring to "the book that philosophizes concerning Reason being supreme over the passions"). It remains a testament to the unassailable dignity of the human person, who need never compromise his or her self-respect or values for any external compulsion.

COMMENTARY

The Principal Thesis and Proofs from Scripture (1:1–3:18)

The Philosophical Thesis (1:1-6)

The author opens his speech with a promise to demonstrate a "most philosophical" proposition, and his audience would probably recognize the "mastery of reason over the passions" as, in fact, a common theme for philosophical discourse (see Plutarch *Mor.* 440D; *Letter of Aristeas* 221–22, 256; Plato *Phaedo* 93–94; Seneca *Ep. Mor.* 116.1). The "passions" cover a broad range of human experience, including the emotions, desires, and physical sensations. These were viewed by ethicists as the foremost threat to virtuous behavior: the emotion of fear or the physical experience of pain could subvert a courageous action; the fires of lust could undermine a temperate respect for the bonds of matrimony. The heart of ethical philosophy lay, therefore, in setting forth arguments which would arm the rational faculty to choose the path of virtue and not yield to the pull or pressures of the passions (see Cicero *Tusculan Disputations* 4:83-84).

Opening with the promise to aid the hearers in their quest for such knowledge as will enable a life of virtue makes a strong claim on the attentiveness of the hearers (the principal aim of the introduction of a speech); the unusual venue by which the author approaches the topic of Torah observance additionally assures the hearers that they will hear more than worn platitudes calling them to remain steadfast. The author distinguishes his discourse by adding the adjective "devout" to "reason." As the oration progresses, it will become clear that this signifies "reason" wholly committed to following Torah, trained by constancy in obedience to God's law (see 2:21-23; 5:19-26; 18:1-2). It is this rational faculty — that of the pious Jew — that possesses the necessary knowledge to live virtuously and honorably.

The topics announced in 1:3-4 will be developed in 1:30–2:6a, where the author shows how Torah controls the self with regard to desires for food and sex; 2:6b–3:18, where the author develops how Torah observance teaches moderation of greed, anger, and desire in favor of acting justly; and 5:1–17:6, where the examples of the martyrs themselves will show how dedication to the God of Israel enables courage and overcomes fear and pain.

1:5-6 is occasionally regarded as an interpolation (see Dupont-Sommer 1939), but these verses are integral to the exordium. At the outset, the author prevents misunderstandings of his point and distances himself from objectionable views (Klauck 1989). A number of prominent Stoics argued that the goal of the sage was the excision of the passions (so Cicero *Tusc. disp.* 3.22; 4.38, 57), while Plato, Peripatetics, and more moderate Stoics argued that moderation or control of the passions, rather than extirpation, was the goal (see Renehan 1972; Plutarch *Mor.* 442D, 443D). The author of 4 Maccabees, like the author of *The Letter of Aristeas* (221–22), aligns with the latter school of thought, probably on account of his conviction that the passions were part of God's design of the human and that the harmonious relationship between the parts of the human being fulfilled God's design (see 2:21-23; 3:2-18).

The Martyrs as Praiseworthy Exemplars of Jewish Philosophy (1:7-12)

Examples function as inductive proofs in classical rhetoric. The martyrs will provide the best "proof" of the thesis in that the passions they faced and overcome were certainly the most intense that could be endured by any human. Their physical torments, gruesomely depicted by our author, signify the extremes of fear and pain, while the inner emotions of seeing one's family thus mistreated and killed are also the most intense (affection for offspring and love of siblings being the strongest emotional attachments in classical ethics). The martyrs' ability to overcome both internal and external compulsions does indeed, therefore, demonstrate that "devout reason" can "master the passions."

Equally significant about the author's choice of example is the fact that these figures preferred death to assimilation at the cost of transgressing points of Torah observance. The martyrs also demonstrate also that attaining the highest degree of virtue as the Greek would define it is not incompatible with fidelity to Torah. Indeed, the more committed one is to Torah, the more equipped one is for virtue. The author in fact applies the highest terms of praise within the dominant culture ("excellence," *aretē,* 1:8; "nobility and goodness," *kalokagathia,* 1:10) to those who resist assimilation to that culture where Torah is concerned.

The author presents the martyrs' deaths not as the Gentile king intended them to be, namely, a shameful example of what befalls the one who refuses assimilation, but rather a noble death. They embody courage (1:8), the endurance of "fearful things," even "disgrace or pain," "for the sake of what is noble" (Aristotle *Nic. Eth.* 3.1.7; 3.7.2). Their deaths bring benefit to the nation, defeating the tyrant Antiochus (1.11). This notion of defeating an assailant by being able to endure more blows than the opponent can give recalls a common philosophical discussion of the sage's victory over external compulsions (see Seneca *De constantia* 9.4; Philo *Prob.* 26–27). The honor that accrued to the martyrs (within the Jewish community, but also enjoyed by them in God's realm; 13:17; 17:5) makes their way of life a model for emulation by those who seek to maintain and increase their own honor. These martyrs are therefore "blessed" in the same way that the fallen soldiers' deaths were considered "fortunate," for "having received mortal bodies, [they] left behind an immortal memory arising from their valor" (Lysias *Orat.* 2.81).

The exordium of the oration (1:1-12), then, establishes the two ways by which the author will accomplish his protreptic purpose: through the demonstration that it is *devout* reason that regulates the passions and enables one to choose virtue, and through the celebration of martyrs who perfected virtue and attained everlasting honor, he will confirm the audience's commitment to Torah observance as indeed the most noble and advantageous way of life.

Definition of Terms (1:13-30a)

The author proceeds to define "reason" and provide a sort of taxonomy of the passions. This section is artfully bracketed by two statements of the thesis which act as an *inclusio* (1:13, 30a). 1:15-17 develops a chain of definitions. Reason is defined not ontologically but functionally. "Reason" is evidenced by its effects, namely, when the mind acts in accordance with "sound logic" to choose a "life of wisdom." The term "sound logic" frequently appears in philosophical texts as that which leads the soul to choose virtue over vice (Plato *Phaedo* 93E). Epictetus regards the possession of "sound logic" as the whole goal of philosophy itself (*Diss.* 4.8.12). The definition of "wisdom" is, word for word, what one finds in Greco-Roman philosophers (see Cicero *Tusc. disp.* 4.26.57; Philo *Congr.* 79; Seneca *Ep. Mor.* 89.5; Renehan 1972), but the author shows his particular allegiance to Jewish "philosophy" in his identification of the source of this "knowledge." True to the Jewish wisdom tradition, it is the "fear of the LORD" and, specifically, observance of the Torah that provides this knowledge of how to relate to God and human beings prudently (see esp. Sir 1:26: "if you desire wisdom, keep the commandments"; also 15:1; 19:20; Wis 6:17-20). The author thus continues to promote fidelity to the Jewish way of life as the way to attain the respected goals common to ethical philosophers. The remainder of the oration will demonstrate how commitment to this way of life perfects "wisdom" in terms of its four species, namely, the cardinal virtues of Greco-Roman ethicists enumerated in 1:18. The author's claim that "prudence," or "rational judgment," holds first place among the four virtues (see 1:2), which reflects the view of Zeno of Citium (see Plutarch *Mor.* 441A), arises from the focus on the contest between the mind and the passions. The virtue of prudence enables one to choose the virtuous path even against the demands of the passions.

Contrary to his preview in 1:14, the author does not provide an actual definition of "emotions" or "passions." Instead, he proceeds directly to present rather elegantly the "types" of passions, following Aristotle's twofold classification of the emotions based on "pleasure" and "pain" (see *Rhet.* 2.1–2.1.1) rather than the Stoic fourfold taxonomy of desire, pain, pleasure, and fear (Diogenes Laertius *Lives* 7.110; Cicero *Tusc. disp.* 4.9-22). The definition of anger as a mixture of pleasure and pain is particularly Aristotelian (see *Rhet.* 2.2.1-2). Pleasure is not, however, evil in and of itself. Only when pleasure is sought in excess, or in ways that are not licit or just (i.e., in ways that reach beyond the boundaries inscribed in God's law), does it become a danger. Thus the role of reason is not to uproot pleasure (or the other passions; see Cicero *Tusc. disp.* 4.57), but to prune away or weed out what is excessive and to cultivate and moderate what remains (see Philo *Det. pot. ins.* 105; *Leg. all.* 1.47). The discussion that follows (1:30b-2:20) demonstrates how, in specific ways, Torah leads and enables reason to accomplish its task.

Self-Control (1:30b–2:6a)

The author regards self-control as a principal resource in the mastery of the passions, reflecting here the cumulative judgment of centuries of Greek and Roman philosophy (see Plato *Gorg.* 507C; Aristotle *Virt.* 5.1; Cicero *Tusc. disp.* 4.22). The first proof he brings forward for his thesis is the ability of Jews to keep observing the dietary restrictions of Torah when their passions lead them to desire any of the forbidden foods (the author recalls specifically Lev 11:4-23, 41-42; Deut 14:4-21). His use of the first person plural ("we") strategically involves the audience: as they keep these regulations they bear witness to reason's rule over their passions, giving them a ground for self-respect. This would be all the more significant in light of the dominant cultural evaluation of Torah's food laws, which is overwhelmingly negative (see Josephus *Ag. Ap.* 2.137; Tacitus *Hist.* 5.4.3; Juvenal *Sat.* 14.98-99). Like other Hellenistic Jews, the author defends the dietary laws of Torah on the basis of their benefits, specifically the cultivation of self-control (see Philo *Spec. leg.* 4.100; cf. *The Letter of Aristeas* 128–29, 144–69). It will become especially clear from 2.6b-9 and 5:22-26 that the author regards Torah as God's means of training the rational faculty and taming the passions: Torah provides specific exercises to master specific passions and vices.

Next he produces the example of Joseph (see Gen 39:7-12), who on the basis of his refusal of Potiphar's wife becomes the model of temperance in intertestamental Jewish literature (see especially *T. Jos.* 2.7–10.4). The author had mentioned in 1:29 that "habits" (*ēthē*) were to be tamed along with the "passions" (*pathē*), and here he touches briefly on how the two work together. Aristotle discussed the predispositions that are peculiar to the various stages of life as "habits" (*ēthē*; see *Rhet.* 2.13), and here our author notes how the young are particularly susceptible to the passions of sexual desire. The Torah provides proof from example and from command that mastery of the passions is possible. In a manner strikingly contrary to Paul's use of the tenth commandment (see Rom 7:7-24), the author affirms that the prohibition of coveting is itself proof that the passions can be mastered. He assumes that the Torah commands not what is impossible but only what is possible (see Deut 30:11). Philo also elevates the tenth commandment as a safeguard against desire, the only passion that attacks reason from within (*Decal.* 142–43; *Spec. leg.* 4.84).

Justice (2:6b-14)

The author moves on to consider how Torah trains the devout Jew in the virtue of justice, now treating the various injunctions contained therein as specific remedies and exercises to curtail injustice and breed justice in human relationships. The law-observant Jew acts as the sage who, according to Epictetus (*Diss.* 3.12.7-11), engages those activities and creates those exercises that will most address the virtues lacking in his or her soul and help the sage overcome his or her intemperate desires or inclinations. The author finds in the commands to lend without interest (Exod 22:25; Deut 23:19-20), to cancel debts in the sabbatical year (Deut 15:1-2, 9), and to provide welfare for the poor by not gleaning one's own fields (Exod 23:10-11; Lev 19:9-10) Torah's means of curbing love of money and greed. Following Torah, one gives to each his or her due (the essence of justice), as God has defined that due; one also gives God God's due by honoring God's right to regulate relationships among God's creatures.

Closely related to the laws that govern the Jewish community are the laws that curb the emotion of enmity (2:14; the author alludes specifically to Exod 23:4-5; Deut 20:19-20, 24). The affirmation that Torah teaches kindness and humaneness toward one's enemies is an important answer (addressed also in the *Letter of Aristeas* 169; Philo *Virt.* 116–19; Josephus *Ag. Ap.* 2.221–22) to the dominant cultural critique of Torah as a body of xenophobic laws (see Diodorus Siculus *Hist.* 34/35.1.1-4; Tacitus *Hist.* 5.5; Josephus *Ag. Ap.* 2.121). The author reminds his hearers to do good to outsiders, thereby perhaps to undermine anti-Jewish prejudice through beneficence (cf. Paul's advice in 1 Thess 3:13; 5:15).

Torah also allows reason to prevail over what would generally be considered to be positive emotions, namely, love for one's family and friends (2:10-13). The Jewish sage will never fail to do what is just because he or she is swayed by even one of these positive emotions. 2:12 in particular reflects the author's knowledge of the injunctions to chastise the disobedient child (Prov 13:23; 19:18; 23:13-14; 29:15, 17). The author goes on to give dramatic proofs of reason's mastery of filial and fraternal affection in 8:1–17:1.

Anger (2:15-20)

As an example of reason's ability to master the more violent passions of the soul, the author cites Moses' refusal to act out of anger when his authority was challenged by the power-seeking Dathan and Abiram (see Numbers 16). Rather than take vengeance upon them himself (the goal of anger according to Aristotle *Rhet.* 2.2.1), he asked God, to whom vengeance properly belongs, to adjudicate the matter. Anger did not move Moses, therefore, to act contrary to justice (arrogating to himself God's privileges).

The second "proof" comes from Jacob's deathbed censure of Simeon and Levi (quoting Gen 49:7 in 2:19) for their refusal to accept any means of reconciliation from the Shechemites for the seduction of their sister Dinah (see Gen 34:1-31). Anger led them to act contrary to justice in light of the peace that was made by Jacob and the terms offered by Shechem. The fact that Jacob uttered this curse is taken as proof that human beings are capable of, and responsible for, mastering anger.

Living in Accordance with Nature (2:21-23)

In these three brief verses the author presents his anthropology as well as his view of "living according to nature" in the sense of the divine order and purpose for the human being. Reason, the passions *(pathē)*, and habits (or character traits — again the author includes the *ēthē* in his discussion) are all part of God's planting in the human soul. God has, however, given a clear hierarchy to these aspects of human being: the passions and inclinations are to be subject to the mind, or reason, and the mind is to be subject to God's Torah. Because they are given by God, the passions are not to be uprooted, but rather moderated and used only to fulfill their God-given purposes. Thus the "solitary gormandizer" and "glutton" are censured (2:7), but the one who shares a meal with others for the preservation of health and the nurturing of community moderates the desire for food and channels it toward God's purposes.

The author continues to promote diligent observance of Torah in philosophical terms. Following Torah is the means by which one lives in accordance with one's divinely implanted nature; it is the means to the cultivation of a life of virtue; finally, it promises to the devotee the "kingship" that is familiar from Stoic discourse, namely, the exercise of perfect rule over the passions and enjoyment of the fruits of virtuous governance of one's life (see Diogenes Laertius *Lives* 7.122; *Stoicorum veterum fragmenta* 3.617-19; Philo *Migr. Abr.* 152).

Clarification of Thesis (2:24–3:18)

The author returns to the possible objection to his thesis that he had already raised in 1:5-6a, namely, reason's inability to master the passions of forgetfulness and ignorance that assail the mind, but he shares with Philo (see *Migr. Abr.* 206) the view that such things, being beyond human control, are also beyond human responsibility. He leaves this undeveloped, however, in order to return to his main point of clarification, namely, that the goal of reason is the control rather than the extirpation of the passions (similar positions are expressed in Seneca *Ep. Mor.* 11.1; 116.1; Plutarch *Mor.* 442D, 443D; in contrast to Cicero *Tusc. disp.* 3.22; 4.38). Philo would also disagree that it is "impossible" to uproot the passions, for he credits Moses, the "perfect human being," with this achievement (*Leg. all.* 3.129-32), but he would concur that the rest of humanity would achieve enough simply to attain Aaron's mark of mastery of the passions.

The story of David's thirst (see 2 Sam 23:13-17; 1 Chr 11:15-19, although with significant differences) provides the proof of this clarification. Thirst after a day of battle is not a blameworthy passion, but it becomes "irrational desire" when David refuses the water that God has provided close at hand and longs only for the water guarded in the enemy camp, attainable only at great danger to life and limb. When David refuses the drink his courageous soldiers bring to him, he acts justly, not allowing his desire to lead him into an act of *hybris* (pride) that would affront God. The water that cost the potential loss of life was too valuable to be used for a human being, and could be used rightly now only to honor God in a libation. He thus avoids the danger that Agamemnon steps into (see Aeschylus *Agam.* 920–47). Although David still experiences thirst (hence cannot extirpate the passion), he does not allow it to lead him into injustice (hence he masters it).

A Lesson from History (3:19–4:26)

The author provides a highly condensed version of the story found in 2 Macc 3:1–6:11. Several episodes and characters are conflated; many others are ignored. The author's goal, however, is not to provide another history of that period but rather to set the stage for the martyrs' contests as well as to provide a relevant lesson from history. The juxtaposition of a story about God's protection of the temple (3:20–4:14) and a story about God's lack of intervention when Antiochus attacks the city (4:15-26) provides a historical example in support of the continuing validity of the blessings and curses of Deuteronomy 28–31. Torah observance on the part of the Jewish people makes for the peace of their community, prosperity, and even the respect of outsiders (3:20). As the hearers keep Torah, they act honorably in accordance with the harmony and peace of their civic group, which is held in very high regard in the ancient world (see Dio *Orat.* 48.15-16). While the people adhere to the Deuteronomistic covenant, they enjoy God's patronage and protection, such that God readily vindicates them (here, their holy place) from antagonists (compare the very similar story in 3 Macc 1:8–2:24).

Jason, however, regards assimilation to Gentile culture and polity as the path to advantage and prosperity for the Jewish people. His annulment of Torah as the constitution of the land in favor of a Greek constitution, far from bringing the hoped-for advancements, instead brought about God's wrath. He has acted, in cooperation with the Jerusalem elites, disloyally against Israel's divine Patron, who uses the Gentile king Antiochus IV to chasten the people that turned from the covenant (see Deut 28:49-50) just as he had used Nebuchadrezzar in 587 BC. This sets the stage for the last item in the disobedience-punishment-return pattern articulated in Deuteronomy. God will regard the steadfastness of the martyrs' loyalty to Torah (see Deut 30:2-3) as repentance on behalf of the people, such that, after their deaths, God's favor is restored, the tyrant punished, and Torah observance is revived in the land, and, with it, peace (17:20-22; 18:4).

This reaffirmation of Deuteronomy's ongoing effectiveness supports the author's main goal by orienting the hearers toward performance of Torah's requirements as the way to contribute to the peace and advance the prosperity of the Jewish community, and toward weakening or abandonment of Torah observance in the hope of preferment in the dominant culture as an ignoble act of sedition against the common good.

The Martyrdom of Eleazar (5:1–7:23)

Antiochus's Challenge to Eleazar (5:1-13)

Antiochus is portrayed throughout the oration as a stereotypical tyrant, a most negative figure in the Greek environment that prized freedom, democracy, and frank speech. His use of extreme and inventive tortures (see Thucydides *Hist.* 6.57.4; Diogenes Laertius *Lives* 9.26, 58-60; Seneca *De ira* 2.23.1), his arrogance (see Lucian *Tyran-*

nicide 26), and his destruction of time-honored laws (Lucian *Tyrannicide* 10; Dionysius of Halicarnassus *Rom. Ant.* 4.41.2) are all part of this stereotype. This characterization allows the author to present the martyrs in the also familiar role of the philosopher who rises above the tyrant's threats and attempts at compulsion.

Antiochus utters a deliberative speech in support of assimilation, relying on the topics of the pleasant, the beneficial, and the necessary (see Anaximenes *Rhetorica ad Alexandrum* 1421b21-1422b12). He criticizes the Torah for running contrary to the law of nature (see Dio *Orat.* 80.5-7 and Epictetus *Diss.* 1.13.5 on the relativizing or rejection of ethnic laws in favor of the universal law of nature), particularly in the matter of eating pork (see the widespread ridicule of this restriction: *Letter of Aristeas* 128–130; Josephus *Ag. Ap.* 2.137; Plutarch *Mor.* 669E-F; Juvenal *Sat.* 14.98-99). Rejecting nature's gift is unjust, since it shows ingratitude toward her provision, and imprudent since it shows ignorance concerning what is truly allowable and what is shameful. Antiochus challenges the very virtue of Judaism as a way of life. His final case involves the blamelessness of yielding to him in the face of the compulsions he is about to apply (see Aristotle *Nic. Eth.* 3.1.7; 3.5.7). Eleazar will demonstrate, however, that disloyalty to Torah and God belongs to that class of crime which must be resisted even in the face of torture unto death (see Aristotle *Nic. Eth.* 3.1.8).

Eleazar's Defense of Torah Observance (5:14-38)

Eleazar's speech not only addresses the tyrant's critique but also speaks directly to the audience with regard to the reasons for remaining loyal to their ancestral customs and laws. He retorts that virtue is the most compelling force for the devout Jew. In particular, justice requires that Torah be strictly observed and not transgressed for any temporal advantage or relief. Eleazar speaks specifically of the obligations to uphold the vows made by his ancestors (5:29; cf. Exod 24:3, 7), to preserve the honor of his nation (5:18), to uphold existing laws (5:16, 34), and to repay the Divine Patron with honor and obedience rather than insult (5:20-21), all of which would be familiar topics of justice (*Rhet. Her.* 3.3.4; Aristotle *Virt.* 5.2). It is a common error to suppose that Eleazar supports a distinction between serious and light sins in 5:20-21 in contrast to the Stoic doctrine that all sins are equal, for Eleazar's point is explicitly the equal gravity of all transgressions of Torah as affronts to God equally to be avoided, whether or not the matter be considered an unimportant one (like the eating of pork; cf. *'Abot* 2.1).

He counters Antiochus's challenge to Judaism's status as a noble philosophy with the functional proof that obedience to Torah trains the Jew in the universally honored virtues of self-control, courage, justice, and its corollary, piety (5:22-24). Since Torah observance provides what ethical philosophy seeks to attain, it is simply wrong for Gentile critics to dismiss it as senseless. The author includes here an implicit criticism of Gentiles who do not "worship the only living God," for their idolatry and polytheism shows that they, and not the Jews, have a "vain opinion concerning the truth" (v. 10; see 3 Macc 4:16; *Letter of Aristeas* 139, 142).

Stoics sought to live "according to nature," meaning, to live in accordance with the divine ordering of creation such that one attains one's proper end or goal. Because the human being contained a spark of the divine mind, living according to nature meant following reason and not the baser instincts and passions. Eleazar counters Antiochus's criticism of Torah's variance with nature by affirming Torah's origin in the mind of the Creator of nature itself. The giving of the law was an expression of divine kindness and sympathy, containing the repository of knowledge concerning what indeed is allowable and what unsuitable (5:25-26). As the oration will demonstrate later, nature is in itself a fallible guide to virtue (see 13:27; 15:25); because the devout Jew has a more reliable guide in the Torah, he or she can perfect virtue where the Gentile would fail (7:18-19; 9:18).

Eleazar's determination both to speak his mind freely and to act in accordance with his own moral principle rather than succumb to any compulsion exhibits the freedom of the sage that was the ideal of Stoic philosophy (see Epictetus *Diss.* 1.25.21; 3.24.71; 4.1.1, 60-87; Philo *Prob.* 25, 30; Seneca *De constantia* 5.6–6.8). Indeed, those who have not been trained by Torah remain vulnerable to the subversion of their virtue by external compulsions (5:38; see Philo *Prob.* 60, 97; Epictetus *Diss.* 1.12.9), but the devotee of Torah attains the full mark of the Stoic sages, who will "do nothing of which they can repent, nothing against their will, to do all things nobly, consistently, prudently, rightly" (Cicero *Tusc. disp.* 5.80-81).

Eleazar's Contest (6:1-30)

Eleazar must immediately prove his resolve and the viability of his philosophy. The author is concerned to emphasize that, while the treatment of his body reflects the dishonor that the dominant culture's representatives ascribe to him and his way of life, Eleazar's true honor remains intact. His virtue gives him dignity, even as his clothes are stripped away (6:2). He keeps his "reason upright" even though his body falls beneath the beating (v. 7; see Epictetus *Diss.* 4.8.12). This recalls the platonic concept that one's real honor is reflected only in the state of the soul, and not by the trappings that cover the body (*Gorg.* 523D-525A). Despite brutal sufferings, the author claims the victory for Eleazar, the "noble athlete" (6:10), since he was able to hold onto his moral purpose in the face of whatever injuries his assailants could inflict, "despising the compulsions" insofar as he resisted their force to overcome his will (see Philo *Prob.* 26–27; Seneca *De constantia* 9.4). Because he remains true to his commitment to Torah even to death, he has won (see Seneca *Ep. Mor.* 67.16).

During a brief respite from torture, Eleazar is enticed to save his life by a ruse. In terms strongly reminiscent of ethical discussions concerning the importance of preserving honor rather than saving life by means of a cowardly or dishonorable course of action (see Thucydides *Hist.* 2.42.4; Aristotle *Nic. Eth.* 3.8.3; *Virt.* 4.4; Isocrates *Ad Demonican* 43), Eleazar rejects this plan. He knows that by dying well he will do more good than by saving his life; he will preserve his own honor rather than lose everything he had lived for (see Epictetus *Diss.* 3.20.4-6), and leave a powerful model of commitment to virtue for those who come after him (see Epictetus *Diss.* 4.1.168-69). His answer reminds the hearers that the devout Jew is called to bear witness to fellow Jews and to Gentiles concerning the value of Torah observance. Eleazar's spirited rejection of an ignoble course especially resembles Socrates' rejection of the escape his friends had planned for him (Plato *Crito*). Neither character would consent to add a few years to his life at the cost of preserving the virtue of that life unblemished (5:36; 6:18-21; see Epictetus *Diss.* 4.1.163-65; Plato *Crito* 52A-54C). Eleazar's life must remain a testimony to the value of keeping Torah, and his brave example invites the audience to join in his resolve.

Eleazar's last words ask God to accept his voluntary death suffered out of obedience to Torah as a ransom for the nation, a concept the author will develop at 17:21-22. Clearly it is not the blood of the martyrs that itself atones for the sins of the nation, but rather their obedience to God even to the point of death. The author combines Deuteronomy's prescription for reversing the experience of God's wrath (namely, a response of obedience to the covenant; see Deut 30:1-5) with the sacrificial language of Leviticus (e.g., 17:11) as a means of interpreting the significance of these martyrdoms. Isa 52:13–53:12 may have particularly informed this author's interpretation of the significance of the suffering righteous ones (deSilva 1998). Greek drama, frequently featuring voluntary deaths as "sacrifices" that allow others to live or a nation to survive (see Euripides *Iphigenia at Aulis* 1553-56; *Heraclidae* 529-34; *Phoenician Women* 997-98, 1013-14), also offers an instructive background.

Resumption of Thesis and Encomium for Eleazar (6:31–7:23)

The fearsome detail with which the author describes Eleazar's torments makes the martyr's steadfastness in the face of such torment all the more impressive and lends force to the author's claim now to have shown that "devout reason" can master even the fiercest "external agonies" (the sensate experience of pain, a passion of the body as opposed to the soul; see Cicero *Tusc. disp.* 5.76). We return here to the function of chs. 5 and 6 as a "narrative demonstration" (3:19) of the thesis (1:1). Very quickly, however, the author moves into the language of encomium and returns to his protreptic (rather than merely demonstrative) purpose.

The author uses a series of images familiar from popular ethical philosophy to praise Eleazar's achievement. Reason is often likened to the pilot of a ship (Euripides *Trojan Women* 686-96; Philo *Leg. all.* 223–24; *Migr. Abr.* 6), and Seneca uses both the images of the cliff withstanding the surf and the city withstanding siege warfare to illustrate the contest between reason and the passions (*De constantia* 3:5; 6:4-8). The author artfully employs the device of apostrophe, or direct address, in 7:6-10, 15 to heighten the emotional effect on the audience of Eleazar's struggle and achievement. Death "perfects" and places a "faithful seal" on Eleazar's life (7:15) because he preserved his honor and virtue intact to the end, and now these are unassailable forever.

The comparison between Eleazar's martyrdom and Aaron's act of atonement (Num 16:41-50; Wis 18:20-25) underscores both the former's courage and the expiatory significance of his death. Both priests courageously took a stand in a place of great danger for the sake of the nation (for Eleazar, the arena of tortures, for Aaron, the advance of the plague and the "destroyer"), and both sought to bring an end to God's just wrath against the disobedient.

The effect the author desires the Eleazar episode to have on the audience can be discerned from 7:9, 17-21. His willingness to die for his way of life makes Eleazar a proof that Jewish philosophy delivers all that the author promises. The author hopes that it will indeed confirm the hearers' loyalty to that way of life, especially as Torah provides the devotee with all he or she needs for the reason to fulfill its divinely appointed function. Indeed, while mastery of the passions is possible for all, only the devout Jew achieves this ideal (7:18; 9:18), in part because the hope of eternal reward in the presence of God greatly outweighs any temporal enticements to sacrifice virtue for safety or temporary gains (7:19; see 16:25; Josephus *Ag. Ap.* 2.217-18). Undermining the sting of death by some means is an essential aspect of achieving the philosophical ideal (Seneca *De constantia* 8.3).

The Martyrdoms of the Seven Brothers (8:1–14:10)

Antiochus's Invitation to the Seven Brothers (8:1-26)

Just as the aged were able, through adherence to Jewish "philosophy," to overcome the impediments of their time of life (7:13-14; this again introduces the *ēthē* into the discussion alongside the emotions), so now the author will demonstrate how the young were able to do the same (cf. 2:3-4). The seven brothers are described as possessing the Greek ideal of male beauty and skill; it is not for lack of potential that they will not take part in Greek culture. Antiochus offers the brothers his personal patronage if they will accede to his demands. If they assimilate, their future honor and careers in the dominant culture would be assured as "friends" of the king. Such an offer would be seen as immensely generous and valuable within the dominant culture, and most would give the king the obedience, honor, and allegiance that patrons expected from their clients; to refuse such an offer and persist in disobedience would be seen as stark ingratitude and result in anger (8:9; cf. Aristotle *Rhet.* 2.2.8) and vengeance (9:10). The king also returns to the topic of necessity and the assurance that such compulsions as he will exercise upon them would remove them from blame (see 5:6-13), as well as the topic of the pleasant (5:8) in opposition to the unpleasant (5:9, 11).

Jews were enticed toward assimilation by both the promise of broader networks of patronage (and, with this, access to wealth, power, and protection) and by the negative pressure of anti-Jewish slander and sporadic abuse. The response that the brothers might have made (8:16-26), but did not, no doubt resembles the potential response of many Jews to their Greco-Roman environment. The author seeks strongly to discredit this way of thinking as cowardly, and his whole discourse aims at affirming to the hearers that their way of life is not "vain opinion" and that loyalty to God is not a "vain resolve" bringing "hollow pride" but rather the only honorable course, the only source of true self-respect, and ultimately the profoundly more advantageous course (see 13:13-17).

The Brothers' Noble Response (8:27–9:9)

The brothers' courageous response in the face of extreme hardship, together with their mutual encouragements throughout the remainder of the oration, should shame those Jews wavering in the face of their lesser contest and embolden the audience as a whole to persist in preserving God's laws as their own path to virtue. Just as the brothers exhibit the praiseworthy quality of unity and harmony (8:29; see Dio *Orat.* 48; Aristotle *Nic. Eth.* 9.6.3), so the author hopes his hearers will be of one mind concerning their commitment to Torah. The brothers show an awareness that the contest is much larger than the one facing the present generation: many scores of generations have nobly fought before, and their honor is at stake with each new generation. This, again, will weigh on the audience's own assessment of their options. Like Eleazar, the brothers regard safety without honor as worse than death with honor, thus exhibiting the Greco-Roman ideal of courage (Aristotle *Virt.* 4.4; *Nic. Eth.* 3.8.3; Tacitus *Agricola* 34). Similarly, they claim that the tyrant is powerless to injure them, the audience being expected to supply here the context of the sage's freedom from injury (see Seneca *De constantia;* Plato *Apol.* 30C) in the sense that his or her virtue and moral faculty remain unassailable by external assaults. The author introduces the expectation of postmortem, eternal reward and punishment as the rationale for their position. In light of God's justice and its eternal consequences, enduring torment now for the sake of eternal honor and peace is far preferable to living unjustly now and encountering eternal punishment. The postmortem punishment of tyrants, a common theme in antiquity (see Seneca *Hercules Furens* 731-46; Lucian *Tyrant* 25-28), runs throughout this oration (see 9:24, 32; 10:11, 15, 21; 11:3; 12:11-14).

The First Brother's Contest (9:10-25)

The author continues to use the technique of vivid description *(ekphrasis)* to heighten the hearers' admiration for the endurance of the martyrs enabled by their commitment to God. Like Eleazar, the young man is able to endure more than the torturers can inflict (9:12; see the note on 6:10). His denunciation of Antiochus (9:15) recalls the central argument of Plato's *Gorgias* that inflicting unjust injury is worse than suffering unjustly since the former leaves the soul in jeopardy of eternal loss. The physical affronts ascribe no dishonor to the young Jew, but only to Antiochus who is acting contrary to justice (see Seneca *De constantia* 16.4). Despite the power the tyrant displays over the young man's body, he remains free with regard to his "reason" (9:17), recalling a well-known philosophical topic that physical instruments of coercion cannot shackle the mind or moral faculty (see Epictetus *Diss.* 1.18.17; 1.29.5-8; the same thought is expressed at 4 Macc 10:4, which may, however, be a later addition). He dies encouraging his brothers, but also the hearers, to continue the battle for which he gave his life; the hope that the innocent suffering of God's righteous ones would provoke God to intervene on behalf of God's people is grounded in the familiar hymn of Moses (Deut 32:36-43).

The Second Brother's Contest (9:26-32)

Subjected to new torments, the second brother also displays the virtue of endurance (an aspect of courage). Ethical discussions of courage encouraged endurance of fearsome or painful things if this was necessary to fulfill one's duty toward one's country or family or "whatever justice commands us to respect" (see *Rhet. Her.* 3.3.5), and the brother's maxim reflects this quite closely (9:29; cf. Horace's maxim, "How sweet and fitting it is to die for one's country"). The notion that virtue brings joy to lighten pain but that vice makes one perpetually miserable again recalls Plato's *Gorgias* (470E-471A, 507B; see also Plutarch *Mor.* 498C-E; Cicero *Tusc. disp.* 2.31; 5.51-67, 73-72), where Socrates pronounces the virtuous person suffering undeserved torture happier than the vice-ridden tyrant inflicting the agonies. Once again it is God's judgment that will reveal who was truly acting to his or her own benefit; it is the devout and obedient Jew, and not the prosperous but erring Gentile, who will know the greater joy in this life and the next.

The Martyrdoms of the Third and Fourth Brothers (10:1-21)

Both brothers enter the arena armed with the resolve to preserve their noble family ties by showing the same courage and steadfastness as their older brothers (10:2-3, 15-16). They regard it a source of honor to be part of such noble and virtuous stock. Moreover, the honor achieved by the virtuous martyrs is enjoyed also by those who continue to live out their kinship with them through devotion to Torah and loyalty in all things to the one God. Such words will challenge the audience to consider that their honor comes from living up to the examples of virtue found in their own tradition rather than advancing in Gentile power structures. The fourth brother also rejects the evaluation of his brothers' deaths made by the representatives of the dominant culture. These were not "insane" deaths but "blessed" deaths, for in God's sight the martyred brothers will have eternal honor and joy. These considerations will continue positively to insulate the audience from the opinion of the dominant culture, pointing them away from Gentile evaluations of their honor and toward God's estimation of them. Finally, the fourth brother draws attention to the fact that Antiochus assaults not a disobedient subject, but God's faithful client — one who properly honored his divine Patron with worship. God will surely act to avenge this assault on God's own household.

The Fifth Brother's Contest (11:1-12)

In the fifth brother's challenge to Antiochus can be heard the retort spoken to any Gentile who has slandered or physically assaulted a Jew on account of the Jew's commitment to his or her ancestral law and religion. The charge of "hatred of the human race" frequently leveled at the Jew is here turned back against those who persecute the Jew (11:4) merely because of his or her different religion. Antiochus applies the grossest physical punishments to people who have not committed any real crime, showing his own ignorance concerning what deeds are just and what unjust. He is in the basest state of slavery and wretchedness, according to Plato (see *Gorg.* 472C), and is unable to form a true evaluation of the honorable and shameful. The Jew places a higher value on piety (revering the one God) and virtue (living obediently to God's law) than on life itself. Assaulting or slandering such a person only shows the darkness clouding the judgment of the slanderer. The hearers may thus be assured that, as long as they remain committed to Torah, they are acting honorably; if their neighbors fail to recognize that, it should not injure their own self-respect or erode their commitment (see Epictetus *Diss.* 1.29.50-54).

This brother, who had earlier refused Antiochus's patronage along with his family, now points ironically to his torments as the only "favors" the pious Jew can accept from the tyrant. They are, from a philosophical point of view, truly "favors" insofar as they provide the Jew the opportunity to demonstrate the steadfastness of his or her commitment to Torah and virtue, the opportunity to be "proven" virtuous (see Seneca *De constantia* 3.4; 9.3; Epictetus *Diss.* 1.6.37). Those among the audience are encouraged to view any pressures and hardships that the dominant culture might impose upon them not as an impetus to assimilate but as an opportunity similarly to prove the genuineness of their piety and their loyalty to God, thus transforming the debilitating experiences that might undermine their piety into a source of self-respect.

The Sixth Brother's Contest (11:13-27)

A new motivation for perseverance in the Jewish way of life is brought forward: the Jew thus fulfills the purpose (the end) inherent in his or her birth and education. Even martyrdom, and so certainly the lesser contests that the audience might face, can be viewed as the meaningful goal toward which one's life had been shaped, whereas apostasy would mean an unnatural disruption in the course of one's life, a breach of the integrity or wholeness of life from birth to death. This brother also introduces a fair amount of athletic imagery into the interpretation of the experience of the martyrs ("contest," "arena [lit. gymnasium] of sufferings"). This kind of image runs throughout the oration (see 9:8, 23; 12:11, 14; 16:16; 17:11-16), and appears very frequently in the literature of philosophers and the writings of other subcultures or countercultures as a means of interpreting the experience of hardship at the hands of the dominant culture (see Pfitzner 1967; Dio *Orat.* 8.11-18). Just as athletes, for the sake of a praiseworthy victory, submitted to physical assaults, endured insults and jeers from the crowd, and disregarded the opinion of the many in favor of the opinion of their trainer, so the pious Jew or devotee of philosophy could ennoble the hostility he or she experienced as the necessary hurdles to a crown of victory (see Dio *Orat.* 18; Epictetus *Diss.* 1.18.21; 1.24.1-2; 3.15.1-5; 3.22.52-56).

By turning victims into competitors, athletic imagery facilitates the presentation of resistance unto death as victory over the tyrant. Because the brothers have not yielded to a course of action contrary to virtue and their own consciences, they remain undefeated (11:20). Their ability to hold fast to the course dictated by reason, as opposed to the course of capitulation to which the passions (i.e., the experience of fear and extreme pain) would drive them, enacts the achievement prized by Stoic and Platonic ethical philosophy (see Seneca *Ep. Mor.* 67.16; *De constantia* 5.6-7).

The Last Brother's Contest (12:1-19)

The pathos of the scene is heightened by the author's claim that even the tyrant felt for this last and youngest of the brothers. The king repeats his offers of personal patronage to the youngest brother, and enlists the mother's aid in persuading her last son to accept his offer. The author's source, 2 Maccabees, does in fact provide a speech for the mother at this point in the story (also emphasizing the use of the Hebrew language, no doubt to prevent the tyrant's understanding her words but also perhaps as a linguistic token of resistance to the radical Hellenization being enforced). When this author provides the mother's speech "a little later" (16:16-23), however, she is no longer addressing merely this one son but all her children together.

The youngest brother denounces the king on two cogent grounds. First, he expresses the conviction that all human beings, whether Jew or Gentile, as recipients of God's gifts (see Seneca *Benef.* 7.31.2-4; Matt 5:45; *Letter of Aristeas* 181, 190, 210, 281) owe God loyalty, reverence, and obedience. Kings in particular were held to have received their power and authority from God (see Dan 4:25; *Letter of Aristeas* 15–16, 19, 37, 224; John 19:11) and ought therefore to honor God and serve God through their office (Rom 13:1-7). Antiochus, however, has acted shamefully by assaulting God's loyal clients, the very people that he, as God's client himself, ought to have assisted and protected. Second, Antiochus has shamelessly violated the universal bond of humanity joining all people together (see Epictetus *Diss.* 1.13.3-5; Wis 7:1-3; Acts 14:15; Ign. *Trall.* 10) by his brutal torture of those who share his own human nature. In this passage the two charges frequently leveled against Jews, namely, not giving the gods their due (atheism) and hatred of foreigners *(misoxenia)*, are turned back upon Antiochus and, with him, all Gentiles who act unjustly toward Jews and fail to honor the one God who benefits all.

Resumption of Thesis and Encomium for the Brothers (13:1-18; 14:2-10)

The story of the seven brothers serves as further proof for the author's thesis (13:1-5). After returning to the image of the fortified wall withstanding the surf as an apt analogy for reason withstanding the onslaught of passions and allowing the soul to arrive at the perfected port of virtue (vv. 6-7; see comment on 7:5), the author upholds for special praise the concord of the brothers (v. 8; 14:3, 6-8). Unanimity is respected in the classical world: it is the mark of the honorable city or community (see Dio *Orat.*

48) as well as the essence of the friendship of noble and virtuous people (Aristotle *Nic. Eth.* 1556b6-7, 1559b1-7). The solidarity of the seven is given special notice here as the source of the victory of each individual martyr (14:7-8), and the author desires that the audience, moved by the praise of the unity of the brothers where fidelity to Torah is concerned, should themselves exhibit the same praiseworthy harmony on this point, reinforcing one another's individual determination to remain committed to the Jewish way of life. The honor of the Jewish community is itself enhanced by their common commitment to Torah, just as it is eroded by division on this point.

This solidarity is manifested in the brothers' mutual encouragements (13:9-18). The courage of the three young men who, in Daniel 3, preferred death in a fiery furnace to idol worship, as well as of Isaac, who would have submitted to death for the sake of God's command, is lifted up for imitation (see also 16:20-21; 18:11-12). Most effectively, the brothers remind one another of the debt they owe God for the gift of life itself (see 16:18-19). Such an immense benefit merits the fullest measure of gratitude (see Seneca *Ep. Mor.* 81.27 for a powerful discussion of true gratitude). Even though loyalty to the divine Patron will have fearsome consequences in this life, it will receive eternal reward and honor from those whose opinion matters most and lasts forever (i.e., the ancestors who have already crossed over). The brothers' weighing of the dangers attending fidelity to God and apostasy from God (13:14-15) bears a striking resemblance to Matt 10:28 (see also Sophocles *Antigone* 72–77, 459–60). These exhortations will also impact the audience, calling them so to live in their circumstances as to preserve the honor of their faithful ancestors, give to God a fitting return for God's gift of life itself, and secure their own safety in light not of temporary difficulties but eternal judgment. The hearers are explicitly drawn into the discourse as spectators (14:9), and their natural response will be to examine themselves concerning their ability to defeat the pressures calling them to assimilate, but they will also be inclined to rise to the mark set by the brothers as they hear these martyrs lauded (see Thucydides *Hist.* 2.35; Aristotle *Rhet.* 2.11.1; deSilva 1998).

Reason Masters Fraternal Affection (13:19–14:1)

The emphasis in 14:3-8 on concord or harmony reflects part of a larger discussion concerning the nature of "fraternal affection" *(philadelphia)* and the bond between siblings, with which the author appears to have been quite conversant. Almost every detail in this passage has a counterpart in Plutarch, "On Fraternal Affection" (*Mor.* 478–90) or Aristotle (*Nic. Eth.* 8.12), who considered fraternal love a subset of friendship (see Klauck 1990). The distinctive element here is the brothers' "discipline in the law of God" (13:22, 24). Although a positive emotion, such affection could have become an obstacle to these brothers in their commitment to Torah since, for the sake of one another, they might rather have chosen safety than endure the loss of one another (see Plutarch *Mor.* 253D-E). Because of their superior education (Torah), however, they rise above even this passion and even fulfill the ideal of friendship by spurring one another on in the virtuous path (14:1; 13:9-18) rather than allowing each other to succumb to enticements or pressures (Aristotle *Nic. Eth.* 8.8.5), even though it means such grievous loss.

Their agreement and mutual support is set forth as a model to the Jewish audience, which is also called to replicate such "concord" and noble friendship in their community by means of diligent attention to, and mutual support in, fulfilling, Torah (see 3:21).

The Mother's Contest (14:11–17:6)

Reason Masters Even Parental Affection (14:11–15:28)

The climactic passion or emotion conquered by pious reason is "affection for offspring" *(philostorgia)*. The author includes lengthy reflections on the power of this feeling (14:11-19; 15:4-10), which again show points of contact with Greco-Roman texts on parental love in every detail (see especially Plutarch *Mor.* 493B-496A; Aristotle *Nic. Eth.* 8.12.2-3), including the comparison with birds to highlight the natural instinct to protect one's young and the emphasis on the mother's greater cause for sympathy with children on account of her greater role in giving birth and providing nurture to the young. The author's amplification of the potency of this emotion makes the mother's resistance to the pull of this passion all the more astounding (15:11, 23, 32; 16:4), and thus the equipping power that Torah gives the rational faculty all the more impressive. Extended periods of "vivid description" *(ekphrasis)* mark this passage (see 15:14-22), heightening the audience's experience of the same sense impressions that assaulted the mother and roused her maternal feelings to a feverish pitch so that their appreciation of her achievement (and Torah's ability to perfect mastery of the passions) will be greater.

The author provides a window into the internal deliberations of the mother as she considered the "two courses" (15:2) open to her and which of "two ballots" to cast (v. 26). The dominant topic in her reasoning is the weighing of advantages (see *Rhet. Her.* 3.3.4; Quintilian *Inst.* 3.8.33) according to the categories of "temporary" (15:2, 8, 27) and "eternal" (15:3; cf. 16:13). Capitulation now would bring temporary safety but engender eternal loss since it would provoke God; by honoring God now with their lives, they will endure temporary hardship but gain eternal honor and life. This rhetorical strategy, by which commitment to the minority culture is secured despite temporal hardship, is prominent in Jewish and Christian discourse (see Susanna 22–23; 2 Cor 4:16-18; Heb 11:24-26). Once again "Nature" appears as an unhelpful counselor, since nature calls for the preservation of one's children (15:25). It is only her education in Torah that allows the mother to decide for virtue (piety, courage) rather than release from pain.

Praise of the Mother and Resumption of Thesis (15:29–16:13)

The author returns to the device of apostrophe (directly addressing the mother) to heighten the pathos, or emotional effect, of the speech. This time the author uses an image from the Jewish Scriptures, namely Noah's ark, to illustrate the contest of reason (the ship) and the passions (the floodwaters; see Philo *Quaest. Gen.* 2.18 for a very similar interpretation). As he had after narrating Eleazar's struggle and the martyrdoms of the seven brothers, so here the author returns to declare that he has proven his thesis (16:1-4). Torah observance does, he reaffirms, provide the mastery over the passions that he asserted at the outset, and the mother's victory should silence all doubt that Jewish philosophy achieves the highest marks in this regard.

Mirroring his treatment of the seven brothers (see 8:16–9:9), the author tells the audience how the mother did not react or speak (16:5-11) before giving her actual, virtuous response (vv. 12-25). The lament in vv. 6-11 suggests yet again how deeply immersed in classical culture this author was, for almost every phrase of the lament (every cause for grief) has a parallel in the speeches of mothers in Euripidean tragedies (see *Trojan Women* 380-82, 504-5, 758-60). The author stresses that the mother did not grieve in this manner (compare 1 Thess 4:13) because such grief would be inconsistent with her own evaluation of advantage in her situation. She knows, unlike Andromache, that her pregnancies are not without profit, for in fact she is now "giving rebirth for immortality" to all her children. Though she feels the pains intensely (14:20; 15:6-7, 11, 16, 22), she does not betray her conviction that death with loyalty to God was indeed the beneficial course of action. If, then, the mother could hold firm her hope (17:4) and accept such monumental hardship as benefit, the audience should be emboldened to accept lesser hardships for their uncompromising loyalty to God and Torah in the same spirit.

The Mother's Noble Counsel and Death (16:14–17:1)

The praise of the mother's courage recalls the encomiastic stories told by Plutarch concerning "The Bravery of Women" (*Mor.* 242E-263C), in which again women bested men in terms of embodying courage. The mother urges her sons on to fight the enemy rather than surrender dishonorably (16:15-16), just as the women of Chios urge their husbands (*Mor.* 245A); she becomes a "soldier of religion" credited with driving out the tyrant (v. 14), recalling the women of Argos who themselves took up arms against the enemy (*Mor.* 245D-E); like the brave Megisto, she prefers to witness the death of a child than give up her country's freedom (*Mor.* 252A-C). While Thucydides thought that woman to be most honored of whom there was least talk among men (*Hist.* 2.45.2), Plutarch believed that great benefit was derived from elevating the virtues of women as of men, so that the nature of virtue itself would become clearer. The author of 4 Maccabees concurs with Plutarch, as he finds "courage" (*andreia,* from Gk. *anēr, andros,* "man"; see thus the striking pun in 15:30) given its fullest expression in the mother's example.

The audience has already been led to identify this mother as, in some sense, "the mother of the nation" (15:29) and benefactor of the people through her courage and sacrifice. Her words to her natural children cannot fail to have an impact on her extended family as well. She interprets Eleazar's encounter with the tyrant as a "noble contest" (see Plato *Rep.* 608B; *Gorg.* 526D-E) in which all her children are called to compete. Remaining faithful to God and God's law in the face of strong opposition constitutes a noble victory and bears a fine testimony to the honor of the Jewish people as a whole. The hearers are called thus to see their lives as an opportunity to bring distinction to themselves and their people through their loyalty to the Jewish way of life. The chief motivation is, again (see 13:13; 2 Macc 7:11, 23), maintaining the gratitude and loyalty owed to God for God's benefits (Aristotle *Nic. Eth.* 8.14.1; *Rhet. Her.* 3.3.4). The mother introduces a number of examples of devout Jews who, rather than avoid danger or death, preferred to show loyalty ("have the same faith" [16:22] may be rendered "show the same loyalty") and obedience to God's command. Daniel and the three young men are especially apt examples since they chose the prospect of brutal execution rather than violation of piety (see Dan 3:17-18; 6:7-16). Belief that loyalty to God now leads to life with God for eternity (16:25; see 7:18-19; Josephus *Ag. Ap.* 2.217-18) undergirds the martyrs' assessment of advantage and emboldens them to face temporal hardship. The audience is called to chart its course by the same compass points.

The mother takes her own life to avoid being sullied by alien hands. Her suicide would have been regarded as a noble death, motivated by an intense concern for chastity (see 18:7-9a) and desire to avoid disgrace (see 1 Sam 31:1-6; Josephus *J.W.* 7.324-34, 377; 2 Macc 14:41-46).

An Apostrophe to the Mother (17:2-6)

The author seeks to vindicate the mother's evaluation of advantage and her hope, portraying her reunited with her sons in heaven, fixed there unmovable and unassailable (like the stars which were, according to ancient cosmology, immobile), and enjoying the honor that befits their commitment to virtue. The praise of her family as "true descendants of our father Abraham" contains an implicit challenge to the hearers: Will they prove equally true to their heritage and show themselves worthy of being included in the noble family of Abraham? The hearers' ambition will be redirected toward this goal.

Epilogue (17:7–18:24)

Commemorative Tableau and Epitaph (17:7-10)

Quintilian (*Inst.* 6.1.32; see also Lucian *Peregr.* 37) knows of the practice of bringing a depiction of a crime into the courtroom to sway an audience's emotions, and this author uses an imaginary painting to do the same. He then proposes a literary epitaph for the martyrs (see Euripides *Trojan Women* 1188-91; Lysias *Orat.* 2.1; Demosthenes *Orat.* 60.1). The emphasis on the sacrifice made by the martyrs to preserve "the Jewish way of life" should encourage the hearers not to relinquish that way of life now in the face of lesser hardships and enticements. Rather, they are called to carry on the battle left to them by the fallen martyrs, vindicating their nation against Gentile critics and Jewish apostates, both of which seek to undermine the credibility of the Jewish philosophy.

The Achievement of the Martyrs (17:11–18:5)

Returning to athletic images (see comment on 11:13-27), the author celebrates the way in which the martyrs proved the worth of the Jewish way of life before the whole world. The remainder of the section praises the martyrs as benefactors and saviors of their nation. Their deaths are ennobled by the benefit they brought to others (see *Rhet. Her.* 3.7.14; Quintilian *Inst.* 3.7.10-18), liberation from tyranny being an especially valuable benefit (see Lucian *Tyrannicide* 4, 7). The Hasmonean family is not given a place in this victory (vs. Townshend 1913 on 18:4-5), which is achieved rather by the martyrs who, by their noble resolve, awaken zeal for Torah throughout the land and thus restore peace (v. 4; 3:21). Their deaths are interpreted in terms of an atoning sacrifice (17:21-22; see comment on 6:27-29) since their obedience unto death turned aside God's wrath (17:22) that had been provoked by the apostasy of Jason (4:19-21). The exhortation of 18:1 makes explicit the protreptic purpose of the whole oration.

A Final Instruction from the Mother and Her Husband (18:6-19)

Although some scholars (Freudenthal; Deissmann) would excise this speech as an interpolation, it provides a fitting and integral conclusion to the oration. The mother first articulates principles upholding the female virtue of chastity (cf. Thucydides *Hist.* 2.45.2; Philo *Spec. leg.* 3.169; Euripides *Trojan Women* 645-53), a virtue rooted in the author's reading of the creation story. The woman's body (the "rib") was entrusted to her to be protected by a single husband; unchastity repeats the primal sin of Eve's seduction by the serpent (see Sir 18:8 for a similar reading of Gen 3:13). She then recounts the basic curriculum taught by the father of the martyrs which prepared them for their contest. To the familiar examples of Isaac, Daniel, and the three young men (see notes on 13:9-18; 16:16-23), the father adds the example of Abel and Cain, in which the one who did not please God assaults the one who does please God. This example sustains the pious Jew who encounters opposition, assuring him or her that the one who inflicts hardship actually stands under God's disfavor. Joseph endured imprisonment rather than transgress God's law, and Phinehas exemplifies the religious zeal that purges the community from apostasy within (Num 25:1-9), encouraging vigilance against assimilation.

The string of quotations from Scripture encourages perseverance in hardship for the sake of God. Isa 42:3 promises protection for those called to undergo hardship; though the martyrs are indeed burned with fire, such a path leads to their immortality and ultimate safety (9:22). David's Psalms (Ps 34:19 is cited) prepare the righteous to expect hardship but also to trust in God's deliverance, while Prov 3:18 announces the prize of immortality for the obedient (see Gen 3:22; Rev 2:7; 22:1-2). Ezekiel's vision teaches that God will give new life even to the dead; even those who are "burned to the very bones" (6:26) will not fail to enjoy God's reward. The last quotation is a combination of Deut 32:39 and 30:20. The Song of Moses (Deuteronomy 32; see Rev 15:1-8) celebrates God's vindication of God's people after periods of punishment. The word order in the quotation is significant in light of the juxtaposition with Ezekiel's vision: after bringing about death, God then gives life again. The hymn thus gives further support for belief in life after death. In its original context (Deut 30:20), the second half of the verse appropriately promotes obedience to God's commandments and remaining loyal to God as the cause of "length of days," which are now extended to eternity. The hearers are dismissed soon after this final reminder of that ultimate ground for remaining true to God and Torah in their own settings, whatever difficulties those may bring upon them.

Peroration (18:20-24)

As is typical for perorations to speeches, the author seeks to leave an impression on the emotions of the audience (here, through the recapitulation of the brutal tortures, 18:20-21). The final verses remind the hearers of the ultimate considerations that should guide their own deliberations and cement their own commitment to Torah, namely, the reward of honor and immortality to be enjoyed in the presence of God and the faithful who have gone before, assuring them that, as they remain true to the just course of action, God will also vindicate them for any dishonor or abuse they suffer now.

Bibliography. Anderson, H. 1985, "4 Maccabees (First Century A.D.): A New Translation and Introduction," in J. H. Charlesworth, ed., *The Old Testament Pseudepigrapha,* Garden City, N.Y.: Doubleday, 2:531-64 • Aune, D. C. 1994, "Mastery of the Passions: Philo, 4 Maccabees and Earliest Christianity," pp. 125-58 in Wendy Helleman, ed., *Hellenization Revisited: Shaping a Christian Response within the Greco-Roman World,* Lanham, Md.: University Press of America • Barclay, J. M. G. 1991, *Obeying the Truth,* Minneapolis: Fortress • Bickerman, E. J. 1976, "The Date of Fourth Maccabees," in E. J. Bickerman, *Studies in Jewish and Christian History,* Leiden: E. J. Brill, 1:275-81 • Breitenstein, U. 1978, *Beobachtungen zu Sprache, Stil und Gedankengut des Vierten Makkabäerbuchs,* Basel/Stuttgart: Schwabe • Deissmann, A. 1900, "Das vierte Makkabäerbuch," pp. 149-76 in E. Kautzsch, ed., *Die Apokryphon und Pseudepigraphen des Alten Testaments, Teil II,* Hildesheim: Georg Olms • deSilva, D. A. 1998, *4 Maccabees,* Guides to the Apocrypha and Pseudepigrapha, Sheffield: Sheffield Academic • deSilva, D. A. 2002, *Introducing the Apocrypha: Message Context, and Significance,* Grand Rapids: Baker Academic • deSilva, D. A. 1995, "The Noble Contest: Honor, Shame, and the Rhetorical Strategy of 4 Maccabees," *JSP* 13:31-57 • Dupont-Sommer, A. 1939, *Le Quatrième Livre des Machabées,* Paris: Librairie Ancienne Honoré Champion • Freudenthal, J. 1869, *Die Flavius Josephus beigelegte Schrift über die Herrschaft der Vernunft (IV Makkabäerbuch), eine Predigt aus dem ersten nachchristlichen Jahrhundert,* Breslau: Grass, Barth, & Company • Hadas, M. 1953, *The Third and Fourth Books of Maccabees,* New York: Harper • Klauck, H.-J. 1989, *4 Makkabäerbuch,* Jüdische Schriften aus hellenistisch-römischer Zeit 3.6, Gütersloh: Gerd Mohn • Klauck, H.-J. 1990, "Brotherly Love in Plutarch and in 4 Maccabees," in D. L. Balch, E. Ferguson, and W. A. Meeks, eds., *Greeks, Romans, Christians,* Minneapolis: Fortress • Lebram, J. C. 1974, "Die literarische

Form des vierten Makkabäerbuches," *VC* 28:81-96 • Moore, S., and L. Alexander. 1998, "Taking It Like a Man: Masculinity in 4 Maccabees," *JBL* 117:249-73 • Norden, E. 1923, *Die antike Kunstprosa vom VI. Jahrhundert v. Chr. bis in die Zeit der Renaissance,* Leipzig: B. G. Teubner • O'Hagan, A. 1974, "The Martyr in the Fourth Book of Maccabees," *SBFLA* 24:94-120 • Pfitzner, V. C. 1967, *Paul and the Agon Motif: Traditional Athletic Imagery in the Pauline Literature,* Leiden: Brill • Redditt, P. D. 1983, "The Concept of *Nomos* in Fourth Maccabees," *CBQ* 45:249-70 • Renehan, R. 1972, "The Greek Philosophic Background of Fourth Maccabees," *Rheinisches Museum für Philologie* 115:223-38 • Townshend, R. B. 1913, "The Fourth Book of Maccabees," in R. H. Charles, ed., *The Apocrypha and Pseudepigrapha of the Old Testament,* Oxford: Clarendon, 2:653-85 • van Henten, J. W. 1986, "Datierung und Herkunft des Vierten Makkabäerbuches," in J. W. van Henten, H. J. de Jonge, et al., eds., *Tradition and Re-interpretation in Jewish and Early Christian Literature,* Leiden: Brill, 136-49 • van Henten, J. W. 1994, "A Jewish Epitaph in a Literary Text: 4 Macc 17:8-10," in J. W. van Henten and P. W. van der Horst, eds., *Studies in Early Jewish Epigraphy,* Leiden: Brill, 44-69 • van Henten, J. W. 1997, *The Maccabean Martyrs as Saviors of the Jewish People: A Study of 2 and 4 Maccabees,* Leiden: Brill • van Henten, J. W. 1993, "The Tradition-Historical Background of Romans 3.25: A Search for Pagan and Jewish Parallels," in M. C. De Boer, ed., *From Jesus to John: Essays on Jesus and New Testament Christology in Honor of Marinus de Jonge,* JSNTSup 84, Sheffield: Sheffield Academic, 101-28 • van Henten, J. W. 1995, "The Martyrs as Heroes of the Christian People," in M. Lamberigts and P. van Deun, eds., *Martyrium in Multidisciplinary Perspective,* Leuven: Leuven University, 303-22 • Williams, D. S. 1987, "Josephus and the Authorship of IV Maccabees: A Critical Investigation," Unpubl. Ph.D. diss., Hebrew Union College • Winslow, D. F. 1974, "The Maccabean Martyrs: Early Christian Attitudes," *Judaism* 23:78-86.

Introduction to the Pseudepigrapha

James R. Mueller

The word "Pseudepigrapha" means literally "falsely ascribed writings." This anachronistic term describes a variety of ancient noncanonical Jewish documents from the Hellenistic and Roman periods (c. 250 BC–AD 200). The texts are not a part of the Hebrew Bible (Protestant OT) or the OT Apocrypha (roughly equivalent to the Roman Catholic Deuterocanonicals), but such a delineation does not do justice to the fluidity of this "modern" category. There is no widespread agreement as to what texts should be included in this corpus, for there is no consensus on the criteria for inclusion. A maximalist view includes nearly any text associated with a character, or passage, from the OT, whether the text is considered Jewish or not, and whether the text derives from the Hellenistic and Roman periods or not (e.g., *Vision of Ezra*). Minimalists would tend to restrict the category to those works that are clearly Jewish, and almost certainly date from c. 250 BC to AD 200. Confusion arises in that a sizable majority of the texts often included in the Pseudepigrapha were clearly transmitted and altered by Christians, thus making strict categorization impossible.

Though not included in any of the major Western canons of Scripture, these texts, along with the Dead Sea Scrolls, are important for any attempt to understand the religious, political, and social world at the turn of the eras. They represent the multifaceted Jewish responses to the encroachment of Hellenism, the establishment of Maccabean power, Roman conquest and hegemony, the destruction of the Jerusalem temple, and the rise of Christianity. Christian preservation and adaptation of nearly all of these texts also enhance our knowledge of Jewish-Christian relations in the first several centuries AD. In addition, many theological notions present in embryonic form in the OT are explored and expressed with increased sophistication within the Pseudepigrapha, making this literature an invaluable resource for the study of both early rabbinic Judaism and Christianity. For example, the NT book of Jude includes an extracanonical prophecy attributed to the antediluvian figure Enoch found only in the noncanonical *1 (Ethiopic Apocalypse of) Enoch.* Judging from the context, the author of Jude clearly approved of this writing. He may even have considered this pseudepigraph "canonical." Jude's use of *1 Enoch* helps us to understand the processes of canonization of both the OT and the NT.

Many, but not all, of these texts are associated with a figure or character from the Hebrew Scriptures such as Enoch. He was a prime candidate for "authorship" because of the OT's description of his fate (Gen 5:24). The ancient authors expanded on this passage and built a significant interpretative framework in which Enoch becomes a scribe in heaven, recording both the secrets of creation and of the eschaton, and then revealing these secrets to a select group. The characters Ezra and Baruch are also employed because of their historical connection with the destruction of the first Jewish temple by the Babylonians. Later authors, attempting to come to grips with the destruction of the Jerusalem temple by the Romans in AD 70, used Ezra and Baruch to draw parallels between the two disastrous events. However, instead of envisioning a historical restoration as in the Persian period when the Jews were allowed to return from exile and rebuild the temple, the authors of the later pseudepigrapha look forward to a final, eschatological restoration. (For a more complete treatment of *1 Enoch* see the contribution by Daniel C. Olson below.)

As one might surmise, many other documents are associated with great heroes of Israel, including Adam, Abraham, Isaac, Jacob, Joseph, Moses, Elijah, and Jeremiah.

Other texts attempt to fill in gaps in specific OT stories, or to smooth over theological problems perceived to be present in such stories. One of the best examples of this type of pseudepigrapha involves the marriage of Joseph and Asenath. In the OT, Asenath is described as the daughter of an Egyptian priest (Gen 41:45). The text does not address the theologically thorny issue of a marriage between a foreign woman and a Jewish man, a union heavily discouraged in other parts of the OT (cf. 1 Kgs 11:1-4; Neh 13:26-27), but a later author composed a full narrative that details Asenath's conversion to Judaism, followed by her marriage to Joseph. The expansion of the biblical story eliminates the problem of Joseph having entered into a potentially corrupting marriage to a foreigner. Other such narrative expansions, or rewritings, include the story of Adam's ritual atonement for eating the forbidden fruit in the Garden of Eden (he stands up to his neck in the Jordan River for forty days; *Life of Adam and Eve*), a narrative that relates Abraham's discovery of the worthlessness of his father's idols *(Apocalypse of Abraham),* deathbed testamentary speeches by Jacob/Israel to each of his twelve sons *(Testaments of the Twelve Patriarchs),* tales about the Egyptian magicians who opposed Moses (Jannes and Jambres; cf. 2 Tim 3:8-9), and a full and graphic description of the martyrdom of seven sons and their mother that is presented in abbreviated form in

This essay is reprinted by permission from the *Eerdmans Dictionary of the Bible,* ed. David N. Freedman, Allen C. Myers, and Astrid B. Beck, © 2000 Wm. B. Eerdmans Publishing Company.

2 Maccabees 6–7 (4 Maccabees). Each "new" story tends to address issues of concern for the actual author's contemporaries, concerns directly related to the text being expounded and/or to the unstable religious and social situation of the period.

In addition to expansions or retellings of limited portions of the OT, some texts offer nearly complete reworkings of whole sections of the biblical text. *Jubilees* recounts the history of Israel from creation to the giving of the law to Moses on Mt. Sinai. This pseudepigraphical text recasts, supplements, and sometimes eliminates the familiar stories of the OT so that its narrative supports the reckoning of dates according to the solar calendar (as opposed to the lunar/solar calendar which predominated within Judaism). Pseudo-Philo's *Liber Antiquitatum Biblicarum (Biblical Antiquities)* describes the period from Adam to David, interweaving adaptations of the biblical text with legendary elements in order to emphasize the law and its eternal validity. It is by the law that God will judge the whole world at the eschaton. The righteous will be granted peace and happiness in the age to come, while the wicked will be destroyed. Beyond any attempt to understand the particular theological and religious emphases of the individual pseudepigraphical works described here, it is also important to note the freedom with which the Hellenistic and Roman period authors treated the texts of the OT. The biblical texts were not considered untouchable or final, but instead served as starting points for these new narratives.

Still other biblical texts served as models or templates for several of the Pseudepigrapha. This is most evident in the hymns, prayers, and wisdom texts generally included in the corpus. The eighteen *Psalms of Solomon,* which clearly imitate the biblical psalms, describe the lawlessness of those who have established a non-Davidic monarchy and who have profaned the temple, but also relate the anticipation of the righteous as they await the appearance of the Messiah. *The Prayer of Manasseh* (sometimes classified among the OT Apocrypha), based on 2 Chronicles 33, provides the content of the wicked king's penitential prayer in which he details his own abominable actions and prays for divine forgiveness. Several apocryphal psalms, some of which are found in a Qumran scroll interspersed with biblical psalms (11QPs), highlight the fluidity and malleability of the biblical canon in this period. Several wisdom texts included among the Pseudepigrapha (e.g., *Pseudo-Phocylides, Syriac Menander, Aristobulus*) clearly incorporate Hellenistic traditions, often concealing by means of style and substance any distinctive Jewish elements. In such cases the authors may very well have been trying to demonstrate the compatibility of Jewish and Greco-Roman wisdom traditions.

At least a few other pseudepigrapha consciously imitate Greek epic poetry. The *Sibylline Oracles,* for example, are claimed to be the ecstatic prophecies of a legendary character from the distant past. The Jewish and Christian oracles focus on both ritual and ethical violations that have led, or will lead, to punishment by God, although they also contain some hope for future restoration. Several other fragmentary poetic texts, preserved only in later Christian works, include a history of Jerusalem *(Philo the Epic Poet),* an extended reworking of the story of the rape of Dinah in Genesis 34 *(Theodotus),* a dramatic rendering of the Exodus story *(Ezekiel the Tragedian),* a reconstruction of the life of Job based on the Greek version of the canonical story *(Aristeas the Exegete),* to name just a few.

As is evident from this survey, the Pseudepigrapha covers a wide range of theologies within Hellenistic and Roman period Judaism. This diversity incorporates attempts to contemporize traditional biblical stories as well as efforts to reconcile Hellenistic and Jewish philosophical notions. However, the most persistent theme within the corpus is the eschatological hope centering on the renewal of all creation by God or God's Messiah. In nearly every genre represented in the Pseudepigrapha, the hopelessness of the present is balanced by the expectation that God will judge the world, punishing the wicked and those who oppress Israel, and will reward the righteous for their steadfast faithfulness to the commandments.

Bibliography. Charlesworth, J. H., ed. 1983, 1985, *The Old Testament Pseudepigrapha,* 2 vols., Garden City, N.Y.: Doubleday • de Jonge, M. 1995, *Outside the Old Testament,* Cambridge: Cambridge University • Nickelsburg, G. W. E. 1981, *Jewish Literature between the Bible and the Mishnah,* Philadelphia, Fortress • Sparks, H. F. D., ed. 1984, *The Apocryphal Old Testament,* Oxford: Oxford University • Stone, M. E., ed. 1987, *Jewish Writings of the Second Temple Period,* CRINT 2/2, Philadelphia: Fortress.

1 Enoch

Daniel C. Olson

Never before has *1 Enoch* appeared in a Bible commentary. This is not surprising since the book is not found in any English Bibles and is missing from even the most generous editions of the Apocrypha (such as the one included in the NRSV). *Enoch* is therefore a unique member of the present volume and requires special treatment. Not only does its unfamiliarity demand a fuller introduction than is needed for the proto- and deuterocanonical writings, but even the bare fact of its inclusion at all in this commentary calls for an explanation.

The *Book of Enoch* is part of the canon of Scripture in the Ethiopian Orthodox Church; in fact, the book is often called "Ethiopic Enoch" since the complete work survives only in that language. (Another common title, "1 Enoch," is intended to distinguish it from two later Enoch books.) *Enoch* is also reckoned canonical among Ethiopian Jews. As such, a biblical commentary seeking truly ecumenical and international scope might justify its inclusion on these grounds alone. However, other books unique to the Ethiopian canon are not treated in the present volume, so there are obviously other considerations at work. A historical survey may be the simplest way to explain *Enoch's* long journey from the netherworld of exotic Judaica to general Bible commentary.

It has always been known that the *Book of Enoch* enjoyed a high reputation among the early Christians. The NT epistle of Jude even provides a citation of *Enoch* 1:9, respectfully prefaced: "Enoch, in the seventh generation from Adam, prophesied, saying" (Jude 14-15). If we scan the Christian literature of the second and third centuries we find no lack of *Enoch* quotations and allusions, and these are uniformly favorable, occasionally indicating that the author accepted *Enoch* as authoritative Scripture. However, by the fourth century the book began falling out of favor in the church, mainly due to: (1) awareness of the exclusion of *Enoch* from the Jewish canon; (2) consternation over *Enoch's* understanding of the "sons of God" in Gen 6:1-4 as angels; and (3) the usefulness of the book to heretics. Although *Enoch* was known and still read for several centuries more, eventually it ceased to be copied and was lost to most of the world, surviving only in a few scattered quotations.

The book fared worse in the synagogue. A high regard for *Enoch* is evident in late Second Temple writings such as *Jubilees*, the *Testaments of the Twelve Patriarchs*, and documents known only from the Dead Sea Scrolls (DSS), but the rabbinic Judaism which came to dominate public religious life among Jews after the disastrous first and second revolts (AD 66-70 and 132-135) took a dim view of apocalyptic literature such as *Enoch*. Although there is plenty of evidence that the angel legends found in *Enoch* were remembered as a kind of folklore, the book itself ceased to have any influence as a serious religious text except among some of the more esoteric schools of Jewish mysticism. *Enoch* was never a candidate for scriptural canonicity among the rabbis, and it appears that Jews lost track of the book long before Christians.

Reports began circulating in Europe as early as the beginning of the seventeenth century that the lost *Book of Enoch* had survived in the Ethiopian church, but it was not until 1773 that copies were obtained, and then another half-century elapsed before an English translation appeared in 1821. After this slow start, however, scholarship proceeded rapidly. No fewer than five German editions were published between 1833 and 1901. Newly discovered Greek manuscripts of portions of the book were published in 1844 (*Enoch* 89:42-49) and 1892 (*Enoch* 1–32), and a Latin version of *Enoch* 106:1-18 appeared the following year. A second English *Enoch* came out in 1882. Many more Ethiopic manuscripts began to surface; a 1906 critical edition collated almost two dozen, and that same year saw the publication of an important French *Enoch*. But it was chiefly the translation and commentary of R. H. Charles (Oxford: Clarendon, 1893; 2d ed. 1912) which ensured the book a permanent place in the scholarly spotlight. The inclusion of this landmark work in the highly successful *Apocrypha and Pseudepigrapha of the Old Testament* (ed. R. H. Charles et al.; 2 vols.; Oxford: Clarendon, 1913) made Charles's *Enoch* available to a wide readership.

From the 1920s until the early 1970s scholarly treatments of *Enoch* focussed primarily on the book's messianology, or more particularly on the mysterious "Son of Man" figure described in one of its sections. Owing to its obvious potential for illuminating the "Son of Man" title in the Gospels, this feature of *Enoch* tended to crowd out interest in other parts of the book.

Meanwhile, more raw data continued to come to light. In 1930 a fourth-century-AD Greek manuscript covering most of the final booklet of *Enoch* was found (*Enoch* 97:6–107:2, minus ch. 105). Total Greek fragments now covered a third of the book. Small Coptic and Syriac fragments were published in 1960 and 1968. Fresh Ethiopic manuscripts of *Enoch* were discovered and became available on microfilm in the 1970s, some of which rank among our oldest known copies. The most sensational development, however, came in the 1950s when J. T. Milik announced that he had identified Aramaic portions of the *Book of Enoch* among the recently discovered DSS. After a tantalizing delay, the fragments were finally published in 1976. Tattered remains of eleven different copies had been recovered, representing four of the five constituent booklets that make up *Enoch*.

Although scanty, covering less than 5 percent of the book by one estimate, these Qumran finds have nevertheless revolutionized *Enoch* scholarship. Certain copies of the first and third booklets (the Book of the Watchers and the Astronomy Book) are datable to roughly 200 BC, indicating a third-century-BC date of composition for these booklets *at the very latest*. They are thus the oldest extracanonical Jewish religious writings known (Stone 1978), forcing us to rewrite the history of Jewish apocalypticism, and this at the same time that the importance of precisely this thought stream of Judaism for the understanding of Christian origins has received fresh emphasis in NT scholarship, as summed up by Ernst Käsemann's widely quoted dictum: "Apocalyptic . . . was the mother of all Christian theology."

More generally, the DSS have challenged old stereotypes and fostered a new appreciation for the vitality and diversity of Judaism in the late Second Temple period. The Qumran literature reveals a thoroughgoing apocalyptic mentality happily coexistent with fervent Torah loyalty, all within a dissident Jewish sect that nevertheless evidences surprising connections of thought with both early Christianity and nascent rabbinic Judaism. Since Qumran, old tags like "Pharisaic legalism" and "early Christian charisma" no longer distinguish anything very well. The Scrolls also raise questions about the extent of the Jewish canon during the first century AD, since not only the familiar Hebrew scriptures but also books like *Enoch* and *Jubilees* appear to have enjoyed authoritative status at Qumran. These factors, along with the actual *Enoch* fragments themselves, have stimulated unprecedented interest in the book.

All of this has led to an avalanche of scholarly literature devoted to *Enoch* since the mid-1970s (García Martínez-Tigchelaar 1989), and the editors' decision to include this work in the *Eerdmans Commentary on the Bible* may simply reflect the fact that a critical mass has been reached: familiarity with *Enoch* is no longer optional for serious Bible study. We might even say that Charles's bold assessment nearly a century ago has been vindicated: "To the biblical scholar and to the student of Jewish and Christian theology 1 Enoch is the most important Jewish work written between 200 B.C. and 100 A.D." (Charles 1912: vi).

INTRODUCTION

The Enochic Tradition

The *Book of Enoch* is a collection of five booklets and two appendices written within a distinct tradition of Jewish apocalyptic thought over a period of at least three hundred years — probably longer. Although there is room for debate on some points, the majority of scholars today believe the corpus was originally written in Aramaic, the Aramaic translated into Greek, and the Greek into Ethiopic.

Most of the *Enoch* booklets are composite, and as many as a dozen authors might be represented altogether. The book is therefore best thought of as an anthology, the chief literary depository of the "Enochic tradition." Like other apocalyptically minded Jews, the Enochians believed that God would openly break into history in the near future and usher in a new age after a day of wrath and reward, but more specifically they saw this Last Judgment as profoundly connected with the first (and heretofore only) universal judgment — the Genesis flood. Thus the days of Noah were expected to yield clues for understanding the current scene.

With this in mind, we go to Gen 5:24 and read that Enoch, in the seventh generation from Adam, "walked with God; then he was no more, because God took him." A few verses later we come across an equally cryptic passage relating how the "sons of God" took wives from among the "daughters of humans" and begot children, "the heroes that were of old, warriors of renown" (6:1-4). Immediately following, Noah is introduced and the flood narrative begins.

These seemingly unconnected texts are fleshed out in the first section of *Enoch*, the Book of the Watchers, where we learn that Enoch learned both the secrets of the cosmos and the future fates of humankind in his various "walks with God." He is allowed to return in order to give instruction to the "chosen and righteous," preparing them in this way to face the coming judgment. Alongside the story of Enoch is an elaboration of the Gen 6:1-4 pericope. We learn of a rebellion led by a group of angels known as "Watchers" (cf. Dan 4:13, 17, 23), who sire with human women a race of violent giants and who compound this crime by spreading knowledge of the occult arts and forbidden technology. Only Enoch's great-grandson Noah will escape with his family when the corrupted world is drowned.

The theological ramifications of these strange tales occupied Jewish minds for centuries and found expression in a stream of writings, mostly apocalypses, and mostly attributed pseudonymously to Enoch himself. To the seminal first booklet were added these later works which expand on its themes in a wide variety of ways, so that the finished *Enoch* represents a full-scale attempt to account for the growth of evil in the world, how it manifests itself, and how God intends to deal with it in the future.

Though *Enoch* arrived at its present form in piecemeal fashion, the corpus exhibits a real unity in that virtually everything in it relates to one or the other of two interwoven and contrasting myths which are already well developed in the first book:

1. the righteous man who ascended to heaven, became like one of the angels, received true wisdom, and passed on his revelations to his godly offspring for their salvation;
2. the wicked angels who fell from heaven, became like mortals, produced demonic offspring, propagated worthless mysteries, and now stand condemned to perish.

These neatly complementary myths find their resolution in the Last Judgment — a ubiquitous presence in *Enoch* — when God will consign to all players their final reward or punishment. The Enochic authors also exploit to great effect the typology of Genesis flood/Last Judgment (and Noah/latter-day righteous), allowing the readers to see themselves and their world within the antediluvian scene and therefore to use the twin myths as a lens for interpreting reality in their own time.

Because it is possible to read everything in *Enoch* as in some way elucidating either the Enoch myth or the Watcher myth (or both), it is profitable in an *Enoch* commentary to make frequent recourse to these paradigms, allowing us to see "Enochic theology" at work.

Dates and Provenance

R. H. Charles's division of *Enoch* into five major sections has stood the test of time, and the DSS have furnished some solid paleographical data for dating the individual booklets. The components of *Enoch* are now conventionally organized as follows:

1. The Book of the Watchers
   (**BW**) chs. 1–36 3d cent. BC or earlier
2. The Parables (or "Similitudes") of Enoch
   (**PE**) chs. 37–71 1st cent. BC to late 1st cent. AD
3. The Astronomy Book
   (**AB**) chs. 72–82 3d cent. BC or earlier
4. The Dream Visions
   (**DV**) chs. 83–90 165-160 BC
5. The Admonitions (or "Epistle") of Enoch
   (**AE**) chs. 91–105 2d cent. BC

The two appendices (chs. 106–7 and ch. 108) are usually lumped in with the AE, although their secondary status is universally recognized and their dates of composition are unknown (cf. The Appendices below).

New controversy flared up regarding the dating of the PE once it became known that this section alone was not represented among the DSS fragments (Suter 1981). By the early eighties this debate had spent itself, however, and all *Enoch* specialists have rejected Milik's arguments for a late, Christian origin for the book, while a consensus has emerged which sees the PE as wholly Jewish and probably written between the late first century BC and the destruction of the temple in AD 70 (Black 1992: 161-62). Some scholars hold out for a late-first-century-AD date, largely because the booklet is missing from the Scrolls, but most critics rightly reject that argument, finding a number of different reasons for this non-appearance. In particular, the clear evidence that the Qumran community had begun to lose interest in the *Enoch* literature in its latter days (Milik 1976: 7, 139) adequately explains the absence there of a relatively late Enochic writing like the PE.

The question of provenance is more difficult, since the Enochic tradition originally sprang from unknown quarters. The Essenes (or "pre-Essenes"), a disgruntled band of levitical priests, the elusive "Hasidim" mentioned in the books of Maccabees, and even the Samaritans have all been assigned paternity for this apocalyptic child by various modern scholars, but solid evidence is lacking. The dates of the booklets allow us at least to organize the growth of the tradition into three phases: (1) the BW and the AB are certainly pre-Maccabean, with many scholars looking for their genesis early in the postexilic period; (2) the DV and the AE belong to the second century BC and reflect the first years of the Maccabean crisis and events just prior to it; and (3) the PE gives us a glimpse of the Enochic tradition a century or two later, but probably still pre-70 AD.

The two oldest booklets suggest a priestly and scribal origin, and nothing in either work indicates sectarianism, as is sometimes claimed. The priestly element is most obvious in the extensive attention given to the calendar in the AB. It is true that this distinctive, 364-day solar calendar has sometimes been called sectarian since it was used by the Qumran community and contrasts with the luni-solar calendar employed by the temple establishment in the Hellenistic period, but in fact no one knows when this latter system first came into official use. Some scholars have argued that the solar calendar is actually the older one, used in Jerusalem before the exile and possibly for some time afterward, because it seems likely that the same 364-day calendar was used by the priestly editors of the OT (cf. AB Introduction below, 926-28). If so, the Enochic system can hardly be labeled sectarian.

The scribal element, on the other hand, is more obvious in the BW. Clearly the authors of this book were educated and well versed in the Scriptures, and their hero is described as "Enoch, scribe of righteousness" (12:4; 15:1). As with the AB, nothing here suggests sectarian origins. Parts of the BW read like a veiled criticism of the Jerusalem priesthood, but this hardly proves that the Enochic authors categorically rejected the national cult: OT prophets, early and late, castigate unfit priests at least as harshly. There is a stratum of the BW which still respects the old northern shrine of Dan as sacred territory (13:7-9), but the finished booklet makes Jerusalem the center of the world (26:1). In both the AB and the BW the transgressions of the "wicked" may all be understood as those of the Gentiles or of real apostates from Torah Judaism, and the "righteous and chosen" (1:1) and the "plant of righteousness" (10:16) do not appear to be anything less than the whole nation of Israel (Collins 1984: 56-63).

The second-century booklets (the DV and the AE) evidence a shift in perspective from the older writings. Each of these features a historical survey faulting Israel's religious observance since before the exile (89:73-74; 93:8-9), and each speaks of a smaller group within Israel exemplifying the purer faith (90:6-7; 93:10). We now have an alienated and self-conscious group, disputing with some other Jewish groups on the one hand (the AE) and throwing in its lot with those who supported the Maccabean uprising on the other (the DV).

The latest *Enoch* booklet, the PE, speaks of a "congregation" described variously as "chosen," "righteous," and "holy" (38:1; 41:2; 45:1; 46:8; 53:6; 62:8), suggesting continued self-consciousness among the Enochians as a group distinct from the larger nation long after the Maccabean crisis. This congregation is either being persecuted or anticipates imminent persecution (ch. 47), a feature also found in the AE. There are interesting new theological developments in the PE, particularly in its messianology, but as in the earlier booklets, we are not given sufficient clues to identify the Enochians with any known sect.

A crucial consideration in any attempt to place this tradition within the matrix of early Judaism is the fact that, as a religious book, *Enoch* is not enough to live on by itself. Every section exhorts its readers to righteousness, but very little detail is provided as to what this entails, and when we add to this *Enoch's* intimate knowledge of the canonical Hebrew Scriptures, a knowledge the authors presume their readers share since they rely wholly on allusions rather than quotations, it is clear that they never divorced themselves radically from the Jewish nation or its framework of religious law. Even when they had come to disregard the Second Temple sacrifices as impure, as in the DV, the Enochians put forward no new Torah. They supplement but do not supplant.

Putting the facts together, we have a Jewish tradition of unknown antiquity with its roots in a scribal/priestly milieu. Its adherents unwaveringly considered themselves a loyal part of Israel, but by at least the second century BC this group had become a sometimes persecuted reforming movement outside the main temple establishment and continued thus until their demise, perhaps at the time of the first Jewish revolt. In NT times their writings were widely respected and found a cordial reception in the church which lasted for centuries.

All translations of *Enoch* in the following commentary are by Daniel C. Olson and Archbishop Melkesedek Workeneth.

COMMENTARY

The Book of the Watchers (Enoch 1–36)

Introduction

The first Enochic booklet is itself clearly composite and divides into the following sections:

Introductory Oracles	chs. 1–5
The Fall of the Watchers	chs. 6–11
The Call of Enoch	chs. 12–16
Enoch's First Journey	chs. 17–19
Enoch's Second Journey	chs. 20–36

The BW is especially important since it is probably the oldest Enochic composition, not the AB as we are now routinely told. This prevailing view is based primarily on the relative ages of the oldest DSS scraps of each work, a difference of perhaps fifty years. However, there is no reason to believe these are fragments of the autographs rather than copies, so the Scrolls actually tell us nothing about which book was composed first. It is also suggested that the end of the BW (chs. 33–36) contains summarizing allusions to the AB, but it is just as easy to understand the latter as a subsequent expansion of the former, incorporating for this purpose actual pseudoscientific documents known to the authors of both booklets but only alluded to in the BW.

In favor of its priority is the obvious fact that the BW is foundational. It narrates the two legends which inspired the entire tradition, and it provides background information presupposed in all the other sections of *Enoch*. This includes the AB, which opens with an unnamed narrator explaining that the astronomical data to follow were shown him by Uriel, "the holy angel who accompanied me" (72:1). The author *assumes* that the reader already knows it is Enoch who is speaking and that he is a veteran of some kind of cosmic tour requiring angelic escort. This information comes from the last section of the BW. The AB reads most naturally, then, as a self-conscious sequel to the BW (cf. AB Introduction below, 928).

The Introductory Oracles (chs. 1–5)

In their present position these chapters serve as a preamble to the entire *Book of Enoch*, but the Qumran fragments suggest that they originally belonged to the BW as an independently circulated work. They consist of three items: (1) an introductory superscript (1:1-3a); (2) a theophany (vv. 3b-9); and (3) a discourse contrasting nature's obedience with human perversity, coupled with a prophecy of doom for sinners and salvation for the righteous (chs. 2–5).

(1) *The Introductory Superscript:*

> 1:1. The Blessing of Enoch: The words with which he blessed the chosen and the righteous, who will be present on the Day of Tribulation when all the godless are removed and the righteous are delivered. 2. He took up his parable and spoke, "[Oracle of] Enoch, a righteous man, whose eyes were opened by God himself, and who saw a vision of the Holy One and of heaven, which he revealed to me, and I heard everything from the words of the Watchers and the holy ones, and so I fully understood what I saw. I do not speak to the present generation but to a remote one still to come."

(Restore "Oracle of" in v. 2 with Matthew Black [Black 1985: 103-4].) These verses are closely modeled on both the blessing of Moses (Deut 33:1) and the Balaam oracles (Num 24:3-4, 15-17), creating a curious hybrid, a figure combining prophetic authority both from Judaism's most revered leader and from a shady pagan seer. The choice of the latter is prophetic in itself: just as the portrait of Balaam in Numbers is deeply ambivalent, so later Judaism will not know what to do with the exalted figure of Enoch, or with the whole phenomenon of apocalypticism so closely associated with him. Rabbinic Judaism will dismiss both, but the Qumran finds have raised up inconvenient old ghosts, demonstrating how very Jewish the apocalyptic mind was. The Balaam ambivalence afflicts modern Christian writers too, with some finding in *Enoch* a happy means to recovering a lost spirituality (Barker 1988) and others openly regretting the attention now lavished on such puerile relics (Malan 1983).

The concept of election appears in the very first verse, and Enoch will address the "chosen" often thereafter, but it is a mistake to speak of "rigid apocalyptic determinism" here or anywhere else in *Enoch* (see the comments on 98:4 below). For example, even though in the BW "the righteous" and "the chosen" apparently mean Israel, this book also looks hopefully for the conversion of the Gentiles — as do four of the five *Enoch* booklets (10:21; 50:2; 90:30, 33; 91:14), and we will see that the BW presumes human moral choice (cf. 8:4 below).

Similarities to that other fountainhead of Jewish apocalypticism, Daniel, appear also here at the beginning of the BW. The "watchers and the holy ones" are an obvious link, and this species of angel enjoys an unusually high degree of independent authority in both books (cf. Dan 4:17). Despite the tendency to merely equate the word with the wicked angels, "Watchers" is a neutral term — there are good and bad Watchers in *Enoch* (cf. 6:2; 12:3). Also like Daniel is Enoch's remark that his oracles are intended for a far-off generation (cf. Dan 8:26; 12:4).

(2) *The Theophany* (1:3b-9) draws on a variety of OT models, especially Deut 33:2, Mic 1:3-4, and Zech 14:5. Enoch predicts here not the flood, as one would expect, but the Last Judgment, thrusting this theme dramatically before the reader already in the book's opening paragraphs. Notably, the fallen Watchers, whose story we will shortly read, are expected to be active again before the end (1:5), our first clue that the antediluvian scene will replay itself in the last days. The theophany ends with the famous verse quoted in Jude 14-15, taken as a prophecy of the Second Coming of Christ.

(3) *The Prophetic Discourse* (chs. 2–5) is ingeniously constructed in three parts: first is a homily glorifying the regularity and harmony of the natural world (2:1–5:3); next comes a blunt denunciation of the stubborn, hardhearted sinners who defy this pattern (5:4a); then comes a prophecy of the doom of these sinners and the salvation awaiting the chosen (vv. 4b-9). We have *A* contrasted with *B* (as they now are), and this *B* is then contrasted with *C* (as they will be). Thus, the righteous in the future (*C*) are put in parallel with the obedient creation observable now (*A*) by contrasting each of these with the wicked (*B*). The subtle, underlying idea is that the future can be read in the existing cosmos — a concept unprecedented in Jewish thought but common in *Enoch* (chs. 17–32; 43–44; 80–81; 101:1–102:3) and therefore an example here of the wisdom uniquely bestowed upon the man who walked with God. The narrative immediately following (chs. 6–8) will speak of a more sinister approach to divining the future from the created world.

The Fall of the Watchers (chs. 6–11)

This section demands detailed attention as it is among the oldest and most fundamental passages in *Enoch*. Curiously, there is no mention of the patriarch in these chapters, and most scholars believe they are excerpted from an even older "Book of Noah," known from allusions found in other writings (cf. *Jub.* 10:13; 21:10). Whether or not this is so, these chapters provide the essential legend of the fallen angels. The narrative falls into two distinct parts: (1) the double crime and its results, and (2) heaven's reaction and response. Chapters 6–8 cover the first part and have an earthly setting; chapters 9–11 cover the second and have a heavenly setting.

(1) *The Double Crime and Its Results* (chs. 6–8):

> 6:1. And it came to pass in those days, when the children of men had multiplied, that there were born to them daughters fair and beautiful. 2. And the Watchers, the children of heaven, looked at them and desired them; and they said to each other, "Come, let us choose for ourselves wives from the daughters of men, and let us beget children for ourselves." 3. But Shemihazah, who was their leader, said, "I worry that you may not be willing to go through with this deed, and I alone may end up paying the penalty for committing a great sin." 4. They all answered him, "Let us all swear an oath, binding one another with solemn imprecations, that we will not deviate from this plan until we commit this deed." 5. So they all swore together, binding each other by solemn imprecations. 6. There were two hundred of them who descended in the days of Jared on the summit of Mount Hermon. They called it "Mount Hermon" (*ḥermon*) because it was there that they "swore" (*ḥerem*) and bound one another with imprecations. [The names of the twenty leaders of the two hundred angels follow here, including Shemihazah in the first place and Asael in the tenth.]
>
> 7:1. These then, and the others, all took wives for themselves from whomever they chose; and they began to go in to them, and they defiled themselves with them. They began teaching them sorcery and spell-casting, and they showed them the cutting of roots and herbs. 2. The women became pregnant by them and bore to them gigantic offspring (of three kinds): Giants were born to them, and the Nephilim were born to them on the earth, and the Elioud were their offspring. 3. These devoured the entire produce of the toil of humanity, but people were still unable to sustain them. 4. The Giants then turned against them and began killing humans. 5. They also began to sin against the birds and beasts of the earth, the reptiles that creep along the ground, and the fish of the sea. They began to devour their flesh and drink their blood. 6. Finally the earth laid accusation against these lawless ones concerning all that was being done upon it.
>
> 8:1. Asael taught men to make swords of iron and breastplates of bronze. He revealed to them the metals of the earth, and how to fashion gold into jewelry and silver into bracelets for women. He taught them about antimony and about making eyeshadow, and about all kinds of precious stones, and about colored dyes. And the world was changed. 2. The result was great wickedness on the earth. Men committed fornication and went astray, becoming corrupt in all their ways.
>
> 3. Shemihazah taught spell-casting and the cutting of roots. Hermoni taught the release from spells, magic, sorcery, and successful techniques. Baraqel taught how to read the signs of the lightning. Kokabel taught how to read the signs of the stars. Ziqiel taught how to read the signs of the comets. Arataqoph taught how to read the signs of the earth. Shamshiel taught how to read the signs of the sun. Sahriel taught how to read the signs of the moon. And they all began revealing secrets to their wives. 4. There came death upon the earth for part of

humankind, and because of this their cry went up to heaven.

Scholars agree that there are two different stories interwoven in these and the following chapters. In one, Shemihazah and his gang of two hundred angels take human brides, teach occult arts, and father giants. In the other, Asael teaches humanity forbidden technology and thus corrupts the world. Many have argued that the Shemihazah myth originally lacked the teaching element and received it here by "contamination" from the Asael material, but the teachings are not all alike: arts of civilization are consistently associated with Asael, and sorcery and divination with Shemihazah and company (Newsome 1980: 314). Perhaps both myths always included a distinctive forbidden teaching motif.

There is also disagreement about the obvious literary relationship between *Enoch* 6 and Gen 6:1-4. A few scholars hold that the *Enoch* passage is older than the final redaction of Genesis and that the biblical text is directly dependent on *Enoch* here, but most think it is *Enoch* which expands Genesis. The question is whether the elaboration is faithful to the original myth truncated in the Genesis account, or it is a late concoction of "foreign" elements and pure imagination. There are reasons to favor the first option. First, there is strong evidence that both the BW and Genesis draw independently on some of the same ancient Mesopotamian material in their portraits of the patriarch Enoch himself (Kvanvig 1984), demonstrating that at least in some cases the Enochians knew what Genesis knows and did not simply fill biblical gaps with novel inventions. Secondly, the Genesis account is clipped to the point of near incoherence and seems therefore to presume that its readers know the story well enough to be satisfied with a mere allusion, while the Enochic elaboration is by far the oldest "full" version we have and apparently enjoyed unqualified acceptance for at least three centuries before a rival interpretation of the Genesis passage is even known to have come into existence.

These legends have been traced variously to Persian, Mesopotamian, Canaanite, and Greek sources, with the Greek parallels unquestionably the closest in form, but the basic motifs — gods mating with women and producing half-breeds; superior beings teaching humanity the arts of civilization in primeval times — are found in mythologies around the world. We have in Gen 6:1-4, and elaborated fully in *Enoch,* the Jewish form of an international myth, perhaps influenced by Greek models at the time of written composition, but not a new creation of the Hellenistic age.

Turning to the narrative itself, we find the two crimes of the Watchers well articulated: illegal marriages and illegal teaching. In regard to the marriages, we learn that angelic wedlock is itself the cause of two evils. First, the unions constitute "defilement" in themselves (7:1). Second, they produce vicious monsters who lay waste to the earth (vv. 2-6). The defilement is mentioned four more times in the chapters to follow (9:8; 10:11; 12:4; 15:3-4) and will explain why the angels cannot be readmitted to heaven: their action is simply irreversible, and they cannot be forgiven (12:6; 13:1-2; 14:5; 16:4). The second evil, the rapacity of the giants, is more than humanity is able to sustain (7:3), and threatens the existence of the earth itself (vv. 5-6). When the breach of purity and the violent results are taken together, it becomes clear that the sin of the angel marriages is grave indeed: like an incurable cancer, the evil cannot be undone which seeks to undo creation. There is therefore no hope of working evil out of the world by human effort through normal historical developments, nor can something so deadly be accepted as merely an unpleasant given within a larger worldview. It cannot be withdrawn, and it cannot be endured. As we discover in chs. 9–11, the only remedy is a dramatic intervention by God in history, ending the old world and creating a new. The Genesis flood is the archetype of apocalyptic eschatology.

The other great crime of the Watchers involves illicit teachings, and again the crime is the cause of two evils: occult practices and dangerous technology (7:1b; 8:1-3). Few readers in the Judeo-Christian tradition will be surprised to find the black arts condemned, and the same may be true regarding such pandering luxuries as colored dyes, jewelry, and cosmetics. But it is jolting to find metallurgy per se damned as the revelation of a fallen angel (8:1), even though the idea is already shadowed forth in Gen 4:22 (metalworking discovered by the cursed line of Cain). Enochic theology consistently takes a negative view of this craft for four reasons: metals are used (1) for accumulating wealth and power, leading to injustice (52:7; 97:8-9; 98:2 [Gk.]); (2) for waging war (8:1-2; 52:8); (3) for fashioning idols (65:6-7; 99:6); and (4) for seduction and ostentation (8:1-2; 98:2). (Note that antimony, from which eyeshadow was manufactured in ancient times, is also a metal.)

In the BW, dismissal of certain arts of civilization (metallurgy, cosmetics, jewelry, dyes) is part of a general contrast between the opposing kinds of wisdom found in the two paradigmatic myths: the wisdom of Enoch includes an appreciation of nature just as it exists (e.g., chs. 2–5); the wisdom of the Watchers involves exploitation and perversion of created things for unworthy purposes (e.g., 7:1a; 8:1). In view of the human tendency to turn every technological discovery to wicked ends, our BW author seems to suggest that we would have been better off without some of this knowledge.

The other aspect of the illicit teaching — the occult — also provides a contrast between the two types of wisdom, but in a less obvious way. Many of the skills taught by the Watchers involve divination by reading the "signs" of various natural phenomena (8:3), yet by the time we finish the BW it becomes clear that Enochic wisdom also reads the future in the existing structure of the created world (cf. notes on chs. 2–5 above). The difference is that the Watchers teach *techniques,* putting the adept in the role of initiator, whereas Enoch's wisdom, including his knowledge of the future, comes by *revelation,* with God as the initiator (cf. 1:2). Nowhere in the Enochic corpus does Enoch practice any kind of theurgy in order to coax the mysteries of heaven out of the extant cosmos; rather, he is taken, he is shown, and holy angels interpret for him.

The roles of ordinary humans in all of this can be gleaned from the wording of 8:4, which hints in context that there are two types of people during this era, those who accept the illicit arts of the Watchers (vv. 1-2) and those who are victimized and killed by the same, perhaps after refusing the forbidden knowledge (vv. 3-4). With this, the author solves the moral problem of the total extermination of humanity in the flood. It turns out that only the wicked drown; all the righteous (except Noah) have been martyred!

We are also told that these unjustly slain humans cry for vengeance, a point made frequently in the BW (8:4; 9:10; 22:5-7, 12; cf. also 27:1-4). This theme is taken up again in the PE and the AE (47:1-2; 97:3, 5; 99:3, 16; 104:3; cf. also 90:7-11 in the DV). In contrast to classic Deuteronomic theology, the Enochians consistently see persecution and martyrdom as the expected lot of the righteous in this world, and consequently the vindication of these souls becomes an important part of God's agenda at the Last Judgment.

(2) *Heaven's Reaction and Response* (chs. 9–10): The scene changes to heaven, and we learn that the four archangels, Michael, Sariel, Raphael, and Gabriel, are distressed by events taking place on earth. Impatient, they rehearse the situation before God (9:1-10), concluding: "But you know all things before they happen. You see all of this, and yet you leave them alone! You say nothing to us about what we ought to do with them concerning these things" (v. 11). God responds by assigning a mission to each of the four. Sariel is to warn Noah about the impending flood: "Instruct the righteous one, the son of Lamech, what he should do in order to escape and keep himself alive. Planted from him will be a plant established throughout the generations of the world" (10:3). Note that already the reader is receiving an implicit offer of identity: be one of that established plant, show yourself to be of the righteous seed.

God next addresses Raphael:

> 10:4. . . . Go, Raphael, and bind Asael hand and foot, and cast him into the darkness. Make an opening in the desert which is in Dudael, and throw him into it. 5. Place rough, jagged rocks over him, cover him with darkness, and let him stay there for all time. Cover his face so that he may not see the light. 6. On the Day of the Great Judgment he will be led away into the fire. 7. Heal the earth, which the Watchers have corrupted. Announce the healing of the earth, that the wound may be healed. The children of men will not utterly perish by the secrets which the Watchers have disclosed and taught to their children, 8. but the whole earth has been devastated by the practice of the teachings of Asael. To him ascribe all sin.

Though some scholars deny it because of the dissimilarity in the names, this passage identifies Asael with *Azazel,* a mysterious denizen of the desert to whom a goat is dispatched bearing the sins of the people on the Day of Atonement (Lev 16:8-26; cf. especially v. 22 with *Enoch* 10:8b). Later Jewish sources allow us to identify the "rough, jagged" place and probably also the name "Dudael" as the destination of the goat sent off to Azazel (*m. Yoma* 6:8; *b. Yoma* 67ab; *Tg. Ps.-Jon.* Lev 16:10). Two Qumran texts, including a passage from a lost Enochic writing known as the "Book of Giants," also explicitly link Azazel to the fallen angel myth found in *Enoch* (*4Q203* 7 i 5-6; *4Q180* 1 7-8). Even the multiple references to "covering" in *Enoch* 10:5 may be allusions to the "Day of Atonement" (lit. "day of coverings"; *yom hakkippurim*). The BW author is here identifying the infernal source to whom the people of Israel, on Yom Kippur, symbolically give back their rejected evil.

Gabriel is sent to destroy the giants, the "bastard offspring, the children of fornication" (10:9). He is also told that the Watchers will present requests for clemency and immortality for their children, but in vain (v. 10). Interestingly, Gabriel has only to send out these giants to battle among themselves, and the results are apparently assured. The author suggests that evil, because of its violent nature, has an inherent ability to destroy even itself. This is the one glimmer of hope that the incurable cancer can, in fact, be cured, but only if directed by heaven's intervention: Gabriel must muster the giants. This principle is seen on a larger scale in the coming flood, which, though orchestrated by God, is similarly an example of evil overwhelming itself. The primeval waters, often a symbol of godless chaos in the OT, were divided and assigned their place at creation (Gen 1:6-9), but later released to drown the world in Noah's day (Gen 7:11; cf. also Ps 104:5-9).

Michael's assignment is similar to Raphael's. He is first to announce to Shemihazah and his companions that their children are doomed and that they will witness their destruction, and then he must "bind them for seventy generations in valleys of the earth until the Great Day of their condemnation" (10:12). At that time both they and wicked humanity will be cast into an eternal abyss of fire (vv. 13-14). Later passages in the BW supply more details about this terrible place (21:7-10; 27:2). We encounter here for the first time in literature the notion of hell as a bottomless pit of fire originally intended for the fallen angels (cf. Matt 25:41).

Having dealt with the various rebels, God now promises that a "plant of righteousness" (10:16) will appear and a paradisical world will emerge after the flood. Humanity will enjoy plenty of food and "beget thousands of children" (v. 17). It is predicted that all of humankind will worship God (v. 21), and the section concludes with the promise that "Peace and Truth will be united through all the days and all the generations of eternity" (11:2).

Puzzlingly, this is *not* a picture of eschatological bliss but a description of the postdiluvian world, the one in which *Enoch's* readers now live. Obviously something has gone wrong and spoiled — or, rather, delayed — the fulfillment of God's promises! Basic Enochic typology is at work, since conflating the realized kingdom of God with the era following the flood also forces the mind to conflate the events which mark the beginning of those two eras: the deluge and the Final Judgment. We readers are left to suppose that the postponement of the kingdom must be due to a fresh incursion of evil, since we now live under the shadow of a badly needed second Judgment, after which the promises of chs. 10–11 may presumably be fulfilled. In some sense, then, the Watchers must be among us again (cf. 1:5), and in some sense the wisdom of Enoch is yet available as a guide (cf. 1:2). Later Enochic authors (the PE, the AE) will so conclude, but the concepts are already implicit in this oldest stratum of the tradition.

The Call of Enoch (chs. 12–16)

"Now before these things, Enoch was taken" (12:1a). The second myth is introduced, a foil to the fall of the Watchers as well as a commentary on it. *Enoch* 6–11 elaborated Gen 6:1-4; these chapters perform like service for Gen 5:22-24:

> Enoch walked with God after the birth of Methuselah three hundred years, and had other sons and daughters. Thus all the days of Enoch were three hundred sixty-five years. Enoch walked with God; then he was no more, because God took him.

The double reference to walking "with God" (or "with the angels"; *'et ha'elohim*) was taken to mean that before his final translation Enoch enjoyed many such walks. The episode of *Enoch* 12–16 begins during one of these earlier voyages and consists of three movements: (1) Enoch condemns the Watchers (12:1–13:2); (2) Enoch intercedes for the Watchers (13:3-7); and (3) Enoch again condemns the Watchers (13:8–16:4).

(1) *Enoch Condemns the Watchers* (12:1–13:2): These chapters assume from the beginning a remarkably exalted, even angelic status for Enoch, who is after all a mere human. Beginning with 12:3, Enoch speaks in the first person and relates how he was once abruptly interrupted in his worship of God ("Enoch! Scribe of righteousness!") and told by certain angels to go down and address the Watchers who had mingled with women: "You have wreaked terrible destruction upon the earth; you will have neither peace nor forgiveness." Enoch is also informed that the Watchers' children will die before their eyes, no matter how much they might protest. This makes Enoch a herald of Michael's actions in the previous section (10:11-13). Enoch goes and first tells Asael that he is to be bound forever, without hope of clemency, because of his forbidden revelations to humanity (again a herald, this time to Raphael's mission in 10:4-8).

(2) *Enoch Intercedes for the Watchers* (13:3-7): The righteous Scribe finds the main group of Watchers huddled in terror and ashamed even to lift their eyes toward heaven. They beg Enoch to take back a petition asking for forgiveness for themselves and their children (yet again Enoch works in conjunction with the archangels: Gabriel expects a similar petition [10:10]). Enoch agrees to the Watchers' request, and goes off to "the waters of Dan (in the land of Dan, which is southwest of Hermon)" and falls into a trance while reading their petition (13:3-7).

(3) *Enoch Again Condemns the Watchers* (13:8–16:4): Dreams and visions come over him as he lifts up his eyes "to the gates of heaven" (13:8), and he is told a second time to reprimand the Watchers. When he awakes, Enoch finds them gathered and mourning in either Abel-maim or Abilene (the text is corrupt), located "between Lebanon and Senir," another name for Mt. Hermon (cf. Deut 3:9; for Abel-maim, cf. 2 Chr 16:4). The precise and accurate geographical terms in these verses indicate that at least this section of the BW was composed in the upper Galilee region by someone who still recognized the sanctity of the holy place at Dan (Nickelsburg 1981b: 582-86).

The long section following consists of a "Book of the Words of Truth: The Reprimand of the Eternal Watchers, in Accordance with the Command of the Great Holy One in the Dream Which I Saw" (14:1), in other words, our Scribe's authentic transcript of his heavenly visions, subsequently read out before the rebel angels. After repeating again their sentence and reporting the utter failure of their embassy (14:4-7), Enoch explains:

> 14:8. This was all shown to me in a vision as follows: "Behold, clouds were calling to me in my vision, and thick clouds were crying out to me; shooting stars and flashes of lightning hastened me onward and drove me. Winds, in my vision, lifted me aloft, raising me upwards, carrying me, and they brought me into heaven. 9. I continued to go in until I drew near to the wall of a building made of hailstones, with tongues of flame surrounding it on all sides, which began to scare me. 10. And I went into those tongues of fire and drew near to a great house built of hailstones. The walls of this house looked like flagstones, but all were made of snow; also the groundwork was of snow. 11. The ceiling was like shooting stars and lightning flashes, with fiery cherubim among these, and their heaven was water. 12. Burning flame surrounded all its walls; even its doors were ablaze with fire. 13. I entered into that house. It was hot as fire and cold as snow. There were no delights of life in it. Terror overwhelmed me, and trembling seized hold of me. 14. I was shaking and trembling, and I fell on my face. And I saw a vision: 15. And behold, a door was open before me — another house! Greater than the first one, it was entirely built of tongues of flame. 16. So glorious, so splendid, so magnificent was its excellence in every way that I am utterly unable to describe to you its glory or its grandeur. 17. Its floor was of fire. Above, there were lightning flashes and shooting stars. Its ceiling also was flaming fire. 18. I looked and I saw, inside, a lofty throne, its appearance like ice crystals, and its wheels were like the shining sun! And the sound of cherubim! 19. And from underneath that throne came rivers of blazing fire — I was unable to look upon it further. 20. And the Great Glory sat thereon, his robes brighter than the sun, whiter than any snow. 21. No angel was able to enter this house or look upon his face so magnificent and glorious, and no flesh could behold him. 22. Blazing flames surrounded him, and a great fire rose before him; none of those around could approach him. Ten thousand times ten thousand they stood before him, but he had no need of counsel: in his every word was a deed. 23. The most holy of the holy ones who draw near to him do not turn away by night or by day, never departing from him."

Whatever this remarkable passage owes to Ezekiel 1 and 10, its account of an actual ascension and its detailed description of heaven are unprecedented in Judaism and became models for later "Merkavah" mysticism. Striking similarities between the latter part of this vision (vv. 18-23) and Dan 7:9-10 have also long been noted, but the direction of likely literary dependence has reversed since the DSS indicate a pre-Maccabean date for this first *Enoch* booklet. Within the BW itself, however, the narrative function of this throne-vision is chiefly to authenticate Enoch's message in the eyes of the Watchers, since they would surely detect the fake if his heavenly descriptions were not accurate (Nickelsburg 1981c: 52-53).

The passage continues:

> 14:24. ". . . Then the Lord called me with his own mouth, saying, 'Come near to me, Enoch, and hear my word.' 25. And there came to me one of the holy ones, who raised me to my feet and brought me to the doorway, but I bowed my face low. 15:1. He spoke to me; I heard his voice, 'Do not fear, Enoch, righteous man, scribe of righteousness! Come near to me and hear my voice.'"

The superiority of Enoch's wisdom over that of the Watchers is again an unspoken theme: the righteous Scribe is granted full access where "no angel" and "no flesh" dares to go (v. 21), but only the holiest of the holy ones (v. 23). The revelations granted Enoch there must surely be superior to whatever knowledge the Watchers might boast.

God then characterizes the fallen Watchers as deficient priests by remarking that they should be interceding for humanity — not vice versa (15:2), a reference to Enoch's labors on their behalf and still another way he serves as a foil to them. Priestly identity also explains the continual characterization of the Watchers' sin as "defilement" (cf. the comments on chs. 6–8 above). God goes on to explain that the angels have violated their created nature by taking wives "as the children of earth do" (15:3). Only mortals need to procreate, while spiritual beings, being immortal, have no such need (15:3-7). (Exactly the same logic is implicit in Jesus' teaching about marriage in the resurrection age; cf. especially Luke 20:34-36.)

The BW author next accounts for the mysterious persistence of evil after the flood, after all guilty parties involved in the fall of the Watchers would appear to have been neutralized by the four archangels in chs. 9–10. It is revealed to Enoch that the souls emerging from the slain giants will remain upon the earth as "evil spirits" (15:8-12), and that these demons will torment humanity "without incurring judgment" until the "Day of the End," when the Watchers and the wicked will be condemned (16:1), a date already set as seventy generations hence (10:12).

Knowing that Enochic Jews well before NT times expected the destruction of demons as an eschatological event throws welcome light on earliest Christian demonology. The genealogy of Luke 3:23-37 places Jesus exactly seventy generations after Enoch, and Matt 8:29 presupposes a set time limit to the demons' depredations. Jesus' exorcisms are taken in both these Gospels as a sure sign of the inbreaking of God's kingdom (Matt 12:28; Luke 11:20). Beyond the NT, the demonology found in *Enoch* 15:8–16:1 became standard among Christian writers of the second and third centuries, and could still be appealed to by Eusebius in the fourth (*Commentary on Isaiah* 13).

God entrusts Enoch with one more, final, message to the Watchers:

> 16:3. "'Though once you were in heaven, every secret had not yet been opened to you, and those which you did know were the rejected ones. These you have made known to women through the hardness of your hearts, and by these secrets the women and men multiply evils upon the earth.' 4. Tell them therefore, 'You will have no peace.'"

What began as a proud rebellion (6:2-6) ends in utter humiliation. Only now do the Watchers learn that their wisdom encompassed far less than they thought, and that what little they did know was essentially worthless. Even the exasperated archangels of ch. 9 did not know this secret, believing that Asael had "revealed the eternal mysteries created in heaven" (9:6). God was a step ahead all the time.

Enoch's First Journey (chs. 17–19)

In this section Enoch claims to have seen by divine revelation things normally inaccessible to any human. They reveal a less well-known side of pre-Christian Judaism, returning a positive answer to scriptures which question whether any human can plumb the secrets of nature (e.g., Job 36–38; Prov 30:4; Jer 31:37). The Enochians believed that such knowledge is available if God so chooses to bestow it.

(1) *Chapters 17:1–18:5:* The first journey moves rapidly. In thirteen verses Enoch is taken on a comprehensive cosmic tour, including such things as the chambers of the stars, thunder and lightning, various mythical and semi-mythical rivers, the fountains of the Deep, the winds, the foundations and cornerstone of the earth, and the "paths of the angels." Greek and Mesopotamian parallels for many of these items have been adduced, but the author is also heavily dependent on Job and the Psalms, creating a surrealistic panorama by taking biblical cosmological imagery with eerie literalness.

(2) *Chapters 18:6–19:3:* Going south (18:6 Ethiopic), Enoch encounters seven mountains made of precious stones, laid out as two ranges of three mountains each and with the larger seventh in between, looking "like the throne of God" (18:6-8). This throne will be described in more detail in the second journey (see below). Beyond these Enoch sees a great abyss full of fiery columns (vv. 9-12a), and beyond that he sees an even more dreadful sight:

> 18:12. I saw a place: no vault of heaven was above it, no foundation of earth was beneath it, there was no water upon it, and there were no birds; but a desolate place it was, and terrible. 13. And there I saw seven stars, like great mountains of fire, and concerning these, when I

> made inquiry, 14. the angel said to me, "This is the place where the heavens and earth end; this has become the prison of the stars and of the hosts of heaven. 15. The stars which turn in these flames — these are they which transgressed the commandment of the Lord from the beginning of their rising, so that there is an empty place outside of heaven; for they did not come out at their appointed times. 16. He was furious with them, and he bound them until the time of their punishment comes to an end: ten thousand years."

The angel Uriel concludes the tour by explaining that this astral prison also serves for the fallen Watchers:

> 19:1. Here those angels who mingled with women will remain, but their spirits, taking on various forms, defile humankind and lead them astray into sacrificing to demons — as if to gods — until the Great Judgment arrives in which they will be condemned — until they are finished.

Enoch also learns that when these angels are no more their human wives will finally "have peace" (i.e., be released from their husbands' authority, following the Ethiopic of 19:2; the Greek says they will become sirens).

Enoch finishes boldly with what may be the conclusion of an early version of the BW: "And I, Enoch, alone saw the vision: the ends of all things. Not one other man has seen as I have seen" (19:3). The righteous Scribe has seen the unseen world at its extremities, all undiscovered by others because it is either too remote or in another dimension. This privilege Enoch enjoys uniquely: the BW writer wants it clearly understood that the supplemental wisdom found in the Enochic tradition is not available elsewhere.

The visit to the prison of the angels and "seven stars" underscores the certainty of future judgment by letting Enoch see the places of punishment prepared in advance and already existing in this world, even if they are located where "the heavens and the earth end" (18:14). The future can be read in the created universe, provided one is privy to God-given revelation. This contrasts with the unauthorized methods of augury introduced by the Watchers in ch. 8. The worthlessness of these prognostic arts is nowhere more obvious than in the Watchers' ignorance of their own future. Enoch must spell out the doom of the Watchers to them again and again, both in plain statements (e.g., 13:1-2; 14:3-7; 16:4) and in a vision report like this in ch. 18, which is formally still part of the reprimand against them begun back in 14:4.

In condemning the "seven stars" the author is probably condemning the widespread ancient worship of the seven planets (Sun, Moon, Mercury, Venus, Mars, Jupiter, Saturn). Their transgression, enigmatically dated to "the moment of their first rising," leaves "an empty place outside of heaven" (18:15). This explains why the visible luminaries are still there and functioning properly: they are innocent and obedient (cf. 2:1), but in a parallel realm "outside of heaven" the skies are blackened since the seven planetary angels, who have perhaps been accepting worship as gods (cf. 80:7 in the AB), are cast down and bound, awaiting final punishment. Notice that Enoch is not only transported great distances during his journeys, but sometimes into another dimension. It is not always easy to distinguish the two in *Enoch.*

We learn in 19:1 that the spirits of the Watchers still roam about, even though they themselves are bound. Such bifurcation is apparently possible since they assumed a flesh-and-blood existence unnaturally. These spirits lead humanity into worshiping demons as gods. Demons are the Watchers' own beloved offspring, and by passing them off as gods the Watchers attempt to achieve for their children the immortality requested in their petitions (10:10) but denied (14:6-7). Enochic demons now come in two varieties: the spirits of the original two hundred Watchers and their demonic seed. Before the Enochic tradition expires, a third kind will be added (cf. 40:7 below).

Enoch's Second Journey (chs. 20–36)

The second journey duplicates much of the first, but mostly in reverse order (21:1-6 = 18:12-14; 21:7 = 18:11; 21:8-10 = 19:1; 23:2-4 = 17:4-5; 24:1-3 = 18:6-7). It also expands the elements it duplicates and includes a good deal of original material as well, such as the sections on Sheol, Zion, and the Trees of Life and of Knowledge. An important thematic difference is that this tour gives us information about the fates of righteous and wicked humanity as well as the angels.

(1) *Chapter 20* lists the holy archangels and their respective duties. To the angels already introduced in chs. 9–10 (Michael, Sariel, Raphael, Gabriel) and ch. 19 (Uriel) are added Raguel and Remiel, for a total of seven. These will act as Enoch's tour guides during the second trip, although the original text seems to have been altered so that three of these angels are not used (Sariel, Gabriel, and Remiel), while Raphael and Uriel take their places by appearing twice and three times respectively. This alteration may have been the work of a general editor to the entire corpus who wished to reserve three guides in order to supply the identities of the three angels of 86:3 in the DV and the three angels of 81:5 in the AB (later Ethiopic texts only; earlier texts of 81:5 read "seven").

(2) *Chapters 21–22:* Chapter 21 duplicates the account of the prison in 18:12-14, adding little, but ch. 22 supplies a description of Sheol which has no counterpart in the first journey. In the extreme west, Enoch is shown a mountain with four caverns, the abodes of the souls of all human dead. First of all, however, he notices the spirit of a man making complaint and learns from Raphael that this is Abel, crying for vengeance against the seed of Cain (22:5-7). Enochic authors were fully aware of the presence of evil in the world before the fall of the Watchers. Abel's murder is mentioned here, there is a reference to Adam and Eve's sin later (32:6), and we have also learned of an astral rebellion taking place in primeval times (18:15). The Watchers' sin is therefore not offered in the BW as an explanation of the *origin* of evil, as has sometimes been claimed, but simply as the most devastating irruption.

Enoch, meanwhile, has asked about the four caverns, and Raphael explains each, giving us the first instance in

Jewish literature of clear moral distinctions among the dead in Sheol. The first cave contains a bright fountain of waters and is reserved for the righteous (22:8-9; cf. Luke 16:24). The second is for those sinners who escape all retribution in their earthly life, who "die and are buried" (cf. Luke 16:22), and who now suffer here in anticipation of the everlasting torments they will receive at the Last Judgment (22:10-11). The third cavern holds those spirits who have never had their case heard and await judgment concerning wrongful death (v. 12). The purpose of the fourth cavern (v. 13) is difficult to decipher because of the obscure text:

> 22:13. That one there has been created for the spirits of humans who are not righteous, but rather sinners — wholly impious. And they will become closely allied with the lawless ones. But these spirits — since those who are afflicted here are punished less than they are [i.e., the lawless ones] — will not incur further damages elsewhere on the Day of Judgment. Neither, however, will they be raised from there.

Apparently the fourth cavern holds utterly depraved individuals who are like the giants themselves ("the lawless ones"; cf. 7:6). But we know that the demonic spirits of the giants run free until the close of the age (16:1), while these equally wicked humans are punished even now. Lest this seem unfair, we are told that these human spirits actually suffer less in the long run: come the Day of Judgment they will not receive any further punishment but will remain in Sheol. In this case, denial of resurrection is a blessing, since they would surely be raised only to be thrown into flaming pits with the demons (10:12-15; 16:1).

(3) *Chapters 23–25:* In chs. 23 and 24:1-2 we meet again the fiery river of 17:4-5 and the seven mountains of 18:6-7, but beginning with 24:3 new details emerge, many of them taken from Ezek 28:13-14. We discover that the central mountain throne of God is also verdant with fragrant trees (24:3), among which one in particular stands out for beauty and pleasant smell (v. 4). When Enoch remarks on these things, the angel Michael interprets the entire tableau for him: the mountain is indeed God's throne, where he will sit "when he descends to visit the earth with goodness" (25:1-3). The tree is apparently the Tree of Life. It is presently off-limits, but in the future it will be transplanted to the house of the Lord, and the chosen will be permitted to eat from it and even to enter the holy place, and they will live long and happy lives, "such as your ancestors also lived in their days" (vv. 4-6). This passage recalls the blessed postdiluvian existence promised in 10:17–11:2, but here that worldwide scene is concentrated and located in a new garden of Eden, which is also God's mountain throne and his holy house.

(4) *Chapters 26–28:* Enoch's next stop is Zion, the "center of the earth" (26:1), although the pseudonymous author is careful not to anachronistically imply the existence of a city there in Enoch's day. Chs. 26 and 27 give a brief but accurate description of the mountains of Zion and the valley of Hinnom ("a ravine deep and dry" [26:4]). As Enoch marvels at these things, the angel Uriel explains that this will be the site of the Great Judgment and that the "accursed valley" (27:2) in the south is destined for the "eternally accursed." Although there is a vague hint in Isa 66:24, this is the first clear identification in Jewish literature of the Valley of Hinnom, or "Gehenna" in Greek, as the eternal destination of the wicked.

Again Enoch is taken away, this time southeast. He sees a rushing watercourse, apparently connecting Zion with a lush oasis in the Judean desert (28:1-3). These details remove any doubt that the whole scene of chs. 25–28 is inspired by Ezekiel 47, with its eschatological vision of a new Jerusalem and a river flowing out of it to the southeast, flanked by vivifying trees and transforming the Dead Sea area. *Enoch* has modified its source in several ways: (1) the many trees of Ezek 47:12 are reduced to a single tree; (2) this tree is clearly the Tree of Life; (3) it is located now at the holy place instead of outside the city as in Ezekiel; (4) its fruit is promised for the elect alone; and (5) their entrance into that holy place is explicitly mentioned. The author of the book of Revelation also draws heavily on Ezek 47:12, but significantly he adopts all of these Enochic modifications as well (cf. Rev 22:1-2, 14).

(5) *Chapters 29:1–33:1:* Enoch is off once more, this time along the spice routes to the east. The very brief chs. 29–31 are dotted with curious details about various aromatics and where they grow, although none of these locales can be positively identified. Many of these aromatics are necessary ingredients in sacred incense (cf. Exod 30:34-38), raising the possibility that the intense interest in Jerusalem in the preceding chapters continues here in the form of priestly concern about temple supplies.

Finally, Enoch crosses the Erythraean Sea (Persian Gulf) and arrives at the Paradise of Righteousness (32:3), where again he sees a magnificent tree, beautiful, fruitful, and fragrant (vv. 4-5). This time he is able to identify it: the Tree of Knowledge, "the fruit of which they eat and know great wisdom" (v. 3). Naively echoing Eve's temptation in Gen 3:6, Enoch exclaims, "How beautiful this tree is! What a delight to the eye!" (v. 5). Raphael, Enoch's guide at this point, affirms Enoch's identification, but has nothing positive to say about the tree: "This is the Tree of Knowledge, from which your father of old and your mother of old did eat; and they learned knowledge, and their eyes were opened, and they understood that they were naked, and they were driven out of the garden" (32:6). This is the closest *Enoch* ever comes to a bald biblical citation, and the closest the wise Scribe ever comes to foolishness: Enoch forgets that he is already possessed of "great wisdom" without recourse to forbidden fruit.

The description ends with a look beyond the garden, even further east, to the ends of the earth, where curious birds and animals are seen (33:1); but Enoch does not linger over them and persists eastward to the very "ends of the earth, on which the heavens rest" (33:2).

(6) *Chapters 33:2–36:4:* These short final chapters of the BW present in summary form material more fully supplied

in the AB. Uriel shows Enoch the gates of the stars and of the winds at the four points of the compass, and the BW then ends with a fitting doxology:

> 36:4. And with every observation I offered continuous praise. And praise I will the Lord of Glory, who has created great and glorious wonders, that he might show forth the greatness of his work — to his angels, to spirits, and to humanity, that they might praise his deeds, all of his creation, that they may see the working of his might, praise the great work of his hands, and bless him forever!

Enoch has broken out into doxologies like this after every major scene throughout the second journey (22:14; 25:7; 27:5), providing a more liturgical atmosphere than we find in the earlier sections. Again the contrast: while Enoch's revelations inevitably lead to the praise of God, we recall that the revelations of the Watchers pander to selfish pursuits. No wonder he is deemed a better priest than they (cf. 15:2). By ending on this doxological note, the BW author also brings us full circle, returning Enoch to precisely the activity he was engaged in before his call to confront the Watchers back in ch. 12.

The chapters describing Enoch's second cosmic journey have spread unseen mysteries and eschatological apparatus all over the cosmos: the place of the dead is in the extreme west; the mountain throne of God and the Tree of Life are in the deep south, and even further south are the fiery pits and astral/angelic prisons (not north; cf. Beckwith 1981: 395-96); the future sites of the Tree of Life and of the Last Judgment are at Zion in the "center of the earth"; and the old Paradise of Adam and Eve, with its Tree of Knowledge, is in the extreme east. The certainty of future reward and punishment are built into the architecture of the universe, but no ordinary human being can ever hope to match an expansive itinerary like this one; wisdom generally thought denied to humans has been bestowed on this one exceptional individual, and the esoteric wisdom of the Watchers, with its auguries, root chopping, and eyeshadow recipes, is made to seem puny and foolish by comparison.

The Parables of Enoch (Enoch 37–71)

Introduction

The booklet known as the Parables of Enoch follows second in the *Enoch* corpus as it now stands, although it was probably the last one written. It falls neatly into five sections:

Prologue	ch. 37
The First Parable	chs. 38–44
The Second Parable	chs. 45–57
The Third Parable	chs. 58–69
Epilogue	chs. 70–71

Also called the "Similitudes of Enoch," the PE actually supplies its own name: it is Enoch's "second vision" and styles itself a "vision of wisdom" (37:1); that is, the PE is a sequel to the BW and consists of further heavenly revelations. These are in the form of three "parables" given to Enoch during one of his raptures (37:5), and they are explicitly marked off in the text (38:1; 45:1; 57:3; 58:1; 69:29). The three parables have in turn been bequeathed to Noah, who adds a few revelations of his own near the book's end (65:1–68:1). This much is simple enough, but the PE is difficult to outline in further detail, being a rather loose collection of three kinds of material which alternate with each other to create a patchwork effect: (1) *Enoch's eschatological visions:* As in chs. 17–32, Enoch visits the future destinations of both the wicked and the righteous and hears what the Last Judgment will be like, but unlike his experience in the BW, he also sees actual visions of this event; (2) *cosmological secrets:* these portions resemble the AB and chs. 33–36 in the BW, but although they are still part of Enoch's travel itinerary in the PE, they differ from the other visions in that they depict the current order, not scenes of the future; (3) *Noah materials:* the various descriptions of the Final Judgment are interspersed with passages related directly to the Genesis flood, reinforcing the now-familiar Enochic typology.

Scholars like George Nickelsburg and David Suter have been able to discern some linear organization in the PE; for example, the first parable is roughly patterned on the BW, information about the Messiah figure leads gradually up to a climax, and various sections of the PE mirror and anticipate each other. Despite such efforts, however, a convincing organizational key to the book as a whole remains elusive. Perhaps we should not look for one: the kaleidoscope of rotating motifs produces a hallucinatory atmosphere well suited to the apocalyptic genre, and only a skimpy narrative framework is needed.

The most original feature of the PE is its expansion of the cast of characters found in the older BW, introducing logical counterparts to the main players in the two Enochic legends and thereby giving a sociopolitical application to the Watcher myth on the one hand and a deeper mysticism to the Enoch myth on the other. Concerning the angel myth, it is true that scholars have argued that even in the BW the author has particular religious and political targets in mind (Nickelsburg 1981c: 52, 54), but at best we are given only hints; the BW is more concerned to narrate the myth merely, inviting future readers to apply it to new historical situations as they arise (Collins 1984: 39). As for the second myth, the BW casts Enoch in an astonishingly exalted role without explaining how this came to be, leaving an open door to speculation on this side as well. The PE author exploits both of these opportunities. Noticing that the one story features angels as its main characters (the Watchers) and that the other features a human being (Enoch), the PE author furnishes *earthly* counterparts to the spiritual beings of the first myth and a *heavenly* counterpart to the flesh-and-blood man of the second. Thus the notorious sinners of the PE, known most often as the "kings and mighty," are counterparts of the fallen Watchers and their offspring, while the mysterious and powerful Messiah in the PE, most often called the "Chosen One" and the "Son of Man," turns out in the end to be the heavenly double of Enoch himself. And the author sees to it that these counterparts behave in exact parallel: in the BW a man is the agent of God's condemnation against sinning angels at the time of the first world judgment; in the PE a heavenly figure is the agent of God's condemnation against sinning humans at the time of the second world judgment.

Nevertheless, the PE should not be reduced to a one-to-one system of rigid parallelisms. For example, the holy ones in heaven, the angels, have their counterpart in the holy ones on earth, the righteous (cf. 38:4; 39:5; ch. 61); but the luminaries of heaven are also counterparts to the righteous (ch. 43), and the Messiah — the Righteous One, the Chosen One — is obviously linked intimately with his namesake "righteous ones" and "chosen ones" on earth (cf. especially ch. 47). Such fluidity is typical of the PE; hence in any place where we find a parallel between a particular earthly and a particular heavenly reality, it is important to allow for other correspondences as well.

Prologue (ch. 37)

This brief chapter echoes both the beginning and the ending of the first half of the BW. Vv. 2-3 are clearly modeled on *Enoch* 1:2-3, but the claims to exclusive wisdom in v. 4 remind us of *Enoch* 19:3, a passage which reads like a conclusion to the whole BW up to that point. Thus the author of this sequel cleverly evokes the full oracular context of chs. 1–19 in the older work:

> 37:2. Here is the beginning of the words of wisdom which I lifted my voice to speak, declaring to those who dwell upon the earth, "Hear, you who are of old, and see, you who are of later times, the words of the Holy One which I will speak in the presence of the Lord of Spirits! 3. It is proper to declare such things to those of former times, but even those of later times will not be denied the beginning of wisdom. 4. Until the present day the Lord of Spirits has never given me such wisdom as I have now received, as my insight allows and in accordance with the will of the Lord of Spirits, from whom the inheritance of eternal life has been given to me." 5. Three parables were entrusted to me, and I lifted my voice and told them to those who dwell upon the earth.

"Lord of Spirits" is the usual title for God in the PE, occurring more than a hundred times. It is a paraphrase of "Lord of Hosts," as the reworked trisagion of *Enoch* 39:12 makes clear: "Holy, holy, holy, is the Lord of Spirits; filled with spirits is the earth." The author's interest in both the secrets of heaven and of the people "who dwell upon the earth" (37:2, 5; the phrase occurs 19 times in the PE) is consistent with this book's portrayal of the universe: every mundane reality has a spiritual counterpart, and vice versa, and neither is more "real" than the other.

The First Parable (chs. 38–44)

(1) *Chapter 38:* Enoch starts off with a question:

> 38:1. The First Parable: When the congregation of the righteous appears, and sinners are judged for their sins, and driven from the face of the earth, 2. and when the Righteous One appears before the faces of the righteous and chosen, whose works depend upon the Lord of Spirits, and light appears for those righteous and chosen who dwell upon the earth; where then will be the dwelling place for the sinners? Where will they eventually come to rest, those who have denied the name of the Lord of Spirits? It would have been better for them not to have been born.

Enoch goes on to promise future judgment without mercy on the wicked (vv. 4-6), but the question raised here — *where* will they end up? — is not answered in this first parable, which is actually dominated by a concern with the dwelling place of the *righteous* (38:4; 39:4-8; 41:2; 43:4). Regarding the destination of evildoers, it is enough for the present to know that "when the secrets of the Righteous One are disclosed, sinners will be judged, and the wicked will be driven from the presence of the righteous and the chosen" (38:3).

Much of the PE author's distinctive vocabulary and many of his key players and favorite themes are on display at the beginning of this first parable. In fourteen places the wicked will be called, as they are here, "mighty kings" (38:5), or words to that effect. V. 2 tells us that these sinners deny the name of the Lord of Spirits, a frequent accusation in the PE (41:2; 45:2; 46:7; cf. 48:10; 60:6; 63:7; 67:10). Holy people are called here "the righteous" and "the chosen," and collectively "the congregation of righteousness" — all standard monikers in the PE. They are also known as "the holy ones" (vv. 4-5), a common term in the PE for both humans and angels, whereas elsewhere in *Enoch* "the holy ones" refers almost exclusively to angels. (Note that even in a detail like this we see a dominating concern to parallel things heavenly and earthly.) Perhaps most interesting of all, we are already introduced here to "the Righteous One" (v. 2).

"Righteous One" is the rarest of the three names given to the Messiah in the PE; indeed, owing to textual variants in the Ethiopic manuscripts ("Righteous One"/"righteous ones"/"righteousness") and to suspected use of the term as a collective singular (i.e., "the righteous one" = "any righteous person"), the only certain occurrence of this name in the PE is in 53:6, where it forms part of a compound title: "the Righteous and Chosen One" (VanderKam 1992: 170-71). "Righteous One" derives from Isa 53:11 (cf. also Isa 24:16; Wis 2:12, 18), near the end of the famous series of "Servant of the Lord" songs embedded in Isaiah 41–53. That the Isaianic servant is also (and more commonly) known as "the Chosen One" clinches the identification (Isa 41:8, 9; 42:1; 43:10, 20; 44:1, 2; 45:4; 49:7).

(2) *Chapter 39* begins with a striking narrative fragment: "And it will come to pass in those days that the chosen and holy children from the high heavens will descend, and their seed will become one with the sons of men" (v. 1). Nothing more is said on the subject. Since the original fall of the Watchers took place in the days of Enoch's father, this passage would appear to predict an entirely new angelic transgression in the future. The author is elaborating *Enoch* 1:5, part of the theophany at the beginning of the BW, which implies that the Watchers will be

active again in the last days. For the author of the PE, the "kings and mighty" who are troubling the "congregation of righteousness" are these latter-day incarnations of the fallen Watchers, or perhaps their offspring (cf. 56:1-4 below). The PE author is not the only one mulling over this prophecy; Jude, in the NT, likewise identifies his contemporary opponents (in his case, false teachers) with the latter-day wicked described in the same BW theophany (Jude 14-15, quoting *Enoch* 1:9).

Enoch next describes his ascension to the "end of the heavens" (39:3) for another of his famous walks. He sees a vision of "the dwellings of the holy and the places of rest for the righteous" (v. 4). He witnesses the angels and the righteous praying together on behalf of humanity on earth, and he sees there also "the Chosen One of righteousness and of faith," learning that "in his day, righteousness will prevail, and the righteous and the chosen will be innumerable in his presence for ever and ever" (vv. 5-6). This second messianic title — the "Chosen One" — occurs in all three parables (about 16 times total). As already noted, it is drawn from the Servant Songs of Isaiah. The names themselves make it clear that there is a close bond between the "chosen" community on earth and this heavenly figure. Enoch learns that this blessed place will eventually be his home as well, and he readily joins his doxology to the perpetual songs of praise offered to the Lord of Spirits (vv. 9-14).

(3) *Chapter 40:* We are now given a description of the angelic hosts surrounding the Lord of Spirits, and four angels in particular with specific assignments. The first three spend their time blessing God and interceding for humanity (40:1-6), but the fourth is occupied with "fending off the satans, forbidding them to come before the Lord of Spirits with their accusations against those who dwell upon the earth" (40:7). Obviously based on Job 1–2, this passage pluralizes the solitary Satan of Job into a distinct class of evil spirits, to be added to the spirits of the Watchers and the demons described in the BW. As an individual, however, Satan himself will also be briefly mentioned later on (see 54:6 below).

The four angels are identified by Enoch's guide, a certain "Angel of Peace" (from Isa 33:7), as Michael, Raphael, Gabriel, and Phanuel (40:9). These are the same as the four in chs. 9–10 of the BW, except that "Sariel" has become here "Phanuel," a name probably derived from Gen 32:30-31 and understood as the name of Jacob's wrestling partner (as in certain Samaritan traditions). This substitution is not haphazard: "Sariel," too, is identified in early Jewish literature as the angel who renames Jacob (*Tg. Neof.* Gen 32:25; *The Ladder of Jacob* 3–4 [*OTP*, 2:408-9]). Connecting "Phanuel" with the angel at the Jabbok will be helpful in interpreting ch. 71 at the end of the PE (see below).

(4) *Chapter 41* provides a list of the "secrets of the heavens," beginning with a presentation of material elaborated more fully later on in chs. 60–63 (Suter 1979: 140-41). It is simply a capsule summary of the judgment which will separate finally the sinners from the holy (41:1-2, 9), and it is oddly interrupted by a disquisition on the orderly conduct of heavenly phenomena like wind and weather, sun and moon (vv. 3-8), a passage reminiscent of chs. 2–5 in the BW. This insertion of a second body of material into another, always near (but not at) the end of the first, is an editorial oddity found all through the PE:

38:1-6 *(39:1-2a)* 2b;
41:1-2 *(3-8)* 9;
52:1-9 *(53:1-6)* 7;
54:1-6 *(7–55:2a)* 2b–56:4;
60:1-6 *(7-24)* 25;
chs. 62–64 *(65:1–69:25)* 69:26-29;
65:1-6 *(7-8)* 9-12.

Though confusing, this quirk is probably intended to remind the reader that the author is never talking about just one thing in the PE: everything is an analogy — a *parable* — of something else.

(5) *Chapter 42:* At this point the author inserts a short poem on Wisdom:

42:1. Wisdom found no place where she might dwell;
A dwelling for her came to be in heaven.
2. Wisdom set out to make her dwelling among the sons of men,
And found no dwelling place.
Wisdom returned to her place,
And found refuge among the angels.
3. Iniquity went forth from her chambers;
Whom she did not seek, she found;
And she has dwelt among them
Like rain in a desert,
Or dew upon a thirsty land.

As has often been noted, this tart lyric succinctly captures the apocalyptic attitude toward true Wisdom: it is not to be found on earth and is therefore inaccessible without divine disclosure. The Enochians stand here in sharp contrast with those Jews who believed Wisdom had taken up permanent abode among the people of Israel in the law and temple (Sir 24:1-12; Baruch 3–4).

(6) *Chapters 43–44:* The first parable ends with a description of the lightning flashes and the stars of heaven, which are each called by name, pay heed to God, perform their functions obediently, and "keep faith with each other" (43:1-2). When Enoch asks his angelic escort what he is seeing, the reply is revealing: "The Lord of Spirits has shown you an image — one which is theirs: these are the names of the holy who dwell on the earth and believe in the name of the Lord of Spirits forever and ever" (v. 4). As this is the only place in the PE (indeed, in all of *Enoch*) where one of its images is explicitly interpreted, we may conclude that in the Enochic typology of this author the preeminent counterpart to the righteous on earth is the starry host (cf. Dan 12:3). A similar concept is already implicit in chs. 2–5 of the BW (see above).

The Second Parable (chs. 45–57)

(1) *Chapter 45:* According to its opening statement, the second parable concerns those who deny the names of both

the Lord of Spirits and the congregation (or dwelling) of the holy ones (45:1). Like the first parable, however, this one wanders into other subjects as well. The manuscripts are confused in the passage which follows, but we seem to start off with a description of how the Chosen One will sit enthroned, encouraging the righteous and eventually dwelling among them "on that day" when sinners are judged and creation is renewed. Concerning these sinners:

> 45:2. Into heaven they will not ascend, nor to the earth will they come; such will be the inheritance of those sinners who have denied the name of the Lord of Spirits, who are thus kept for the day of suffering and distress.

We finally get an answer to the question leading off the first parable: the dwelling place of the sinners is neither heaven nor earth but apparently a kind of non-place. Probably the author is thinking of the dread netherworld described in 18:12-16 of the BW. The reason sinners have not so much as a corner of the cosmos to themselves becomes clear presently: "On that day . . . I will transform heaven and make it forever a blessing and light; I will transform the earth and make it a blessing, and I will settle my chosen ones there; but those who commit sin and wickedness will not set foot upon it" (45:4b-5). The author of the PE expects a renewed heaven and earth both, not merely one or the other, and evil must therefore be expelled into an outer limbo. Small wonder that "it would have been better for them not to have been born" (38:2).

(2) *Chapter 46:* The author rests the title "Chosen One" and takes up a new designation for the Messiah in one of Enoch's most remarkable visions:

> 46:1. And in that place I saw one who had a "head of days": his head was white, like wool, and with him was another whose face had the appearance of a man; it was a face full of graciousness, a face like one of the angels. 2. So I asked the particular angel who went with me, who revealed to me all hidden things, concerning the one who was born of men: Who was he? Where did he come from? Why did he accompany the Antecedent of Days? 3. And he replied to me:
>
> "This is the Son of Man, to whom belongs righteousness, and with whom righteousness abides; he will reveal all the treasures of that which is hidden. For the Lord of Spirits has chosen him; his destiny is to triumph before the Lord of Spirits in eternal justice. 4. And this Son of Man whom you have seen will rouse the kings and mighty up from their soft beds, and the powerful from their thrones! He will loosen the reins of the powerful and break the teeth of sinners. 5. He will hurl down the kings from their thrones and kingdoms, because they neither exalt nor praise him, nor humbly acknowledge where the gift of their kingdoms came from. 6. He will cast down the faces of the powerful and fill them with shame. Darkness will be their dwelling, and worms will be their bed; and from these beds they will have no hope of rising, because they do not exalt the name of the Lord of Spirits.
>
> 7. "There they are: magistrates of the stars of heaven! Raising their fists against the Most High! But they tread upon the earth, and that is where they dwell. All their deeds exhibit iniquity (indeed, are iniquity itself), and their power rests upon their wealth. Their faith is in the gods which they have fashioned with their own hands, and they deny the name of the Lord of Spirits. 8. They persecute the houses of his congregation and the faithful who depend upon the name of the Lord of Spirits."

This passage is clearly inspired by the night vision of Daniel 7, as can be seen by use of the terms "Son of Man" and "Antecedent of Days" (lit. "head of days," harking back to the Danielic "Ancient of Days"). 46:3 leaves no doubt that this "Son of Man" is identical with the "Righteous One" and the "Chosen One," and there are also more echoes from the Isaianic Servant Songs here (vv. 3-5; cf. Isa 43:10; 45:1, 3; 49:7). Ch. 46 tells us, then, that the Messiah is not only the Isaianic Servant but the Danielic "son of man." We also pick up some valuable clues about the villainous "kings and mighty" in vv. 7-8: (1) they are arrogant to the point of blasphemy; (2) with their many gods they must be pagan rather than Jewish; and (3) they persecute the household of faith (some manuscripts say they "will be driven out" of these houses, a less convincing reading). The author also draws on Isa 14:9-14 in his prediction of these arrogant rulers' downfall (46:5-7), a natural scriptural allusion in such a context.

(3) *Chapter 47:*

> 47:1. In those days, the prayer of the righteous, and the blood of the Righteous One, will have ascended from the earth into the presence of the Lord of Spirits. 2. In those days, all the holy ones who dwell above in the heavens will supplicate and pray with one voice — glorifying, giving thanks, and praising the name of the Lord of Spirits — on behalf of the blood of the righteous which has been shed, and that the prayer of the righteous may not come to nothing before the Lord of Spirits, and that there might be judgment on their behalf, and that their long-suffering may not be endless.
>
> 3. In those days I saw the Antecedent of Days as he sat down on the throne of his glory, and the Books of the Living were opened before him. All of his powers, which are in heaven above, and his council stood before him. 4. Then were the hearts of the holy ones filled with joy; for the sum total of righteousness had approached completion, the prayer of the righteous had been heard, and the blood of the Righteous One had been found fully acceptable before the Lord of Spirits.

This short chapter is a midrash on Deut 32:43, a verse which in turn can be interpreted as referring to an ultimate Yom Kippur ritual performed by the Lord himself:

> Praise, O heavens, his people;
> worship him, all you gods!
> For he will avenge the blood of his children,
> and take vengeance on his adversaries;
> he will repay those who hate him,
> and cleanse the land for his people.

(So the NRSV; but the first line can as easily be rendered, "Rejoice, O heavens, with him," while the last line is more literally, "and he will make atonement [*wekipper*] for the land of his people"). The PE author's motivation in providing a midrash on Deut 32:43 becomes clear only a few chapters later when we are told that the Chosen One will sit in judgment on Azazel (55:4; cf. comments on "Asael" in 10:4-8 above). Since the climax of the Day of Atonement is precisely the Azazel goat ritual (Lev 16:8-26), it would be natural for an Enochic author to see the final judgment of Azazel/Asael in the eschatological Yom Kippur of Deut 32:43.

Enoch 47 seems to envision the "the blood of the Righteous One" as the instrument of this ultimate atonement. Such an interpretation, if acceptable, would have obvious relevance for NT studies, although the imprecise dating of the PE casts its usual shadow here. Most *Enoch* scholars insist, however, that although the PE draws heavily on Isaiah's Servant Songs, it does not portray a suffering Messiah. The phrase "the blood of the righteous one," appearing twice in this passage (47:1 and 4), is taken as a collective singular (i.e., "every righteous one") in view of the explicit plurals in v. 2 (and, we may add, in Deut 32:43). But this does not explain why an author would oscillate confusingly between explicit plurals and collective singulars, nor does it do justice to the fact that "the Righteous One" is originally taken from the Isaianic Servant's grimmest song (Isa 53:11). Besides, if it is a question of possible influence on NT messianology, it is irrelevant whether the author of the PE intended an individual or a group in "the blood of the Righteous One"; early Christian authors interpreted Scripture with no more concern for authorial intent — in the modern sense — than the Qumran commentators or the later rabbis.

As Matthew Black notes, it seems most natural to read in ch. 47 a deliberate inclusion of *the* Righteous One in the sufferings of *every* righteous one (Black 1985: 209). "The blood of the Righteous One" would then refer only to a vicarious suffering with the righteous martyrs, just as the stricken Righteous One of Isaiah 52–53 can be interpreted as a cipher for the suffering Remnant of Israel. In that case, *Enoch* 47 is like *Enoch* 62 in the third parable (see below), and both passages anticipate the point made by the parable of the sheep and goats in Matt 25:31-46. It happens that this is the one Gospel passage widely conceded by even the more cautious *Enoch* scholars to be dependent on the PE. Furthermore, if we allow that the first Evangelist knew the PE, it may be relevant to our discussion of ch. 47 that some good NT manuscripts have Pilate washing his hands of "the blood of this righteous one" at Jesus' crucifixion (Matt 27:24).

(4) *Chapters 48–49:*

48:1. In that place I saw a fountain of righteousness which was inexhaustible, and around it were numerous fountains of wisdom. From these all the thirsty drank and were filled with wisdom, and their dwellings were with the righteous, the holy, and the chosen. 2. At that hour, that Son of Man was named in the presence of the Lord of Spirits, and his name before the Antecedent of Days. 3. Before ever the sun or the heavenly signs were created, before the stars of heaven were made, his name was named before the Lord of Spirits. 4. He will be a staff to the righteous, that they may lean on him and not fall, and he will be the light of the Gentiles and the hope of those who are troubled in heart. 5. All who dwell on the earth will fall down and worship before him and will praise and bless and celebrate with song the name of the Lord of Spirits. 6. Because of all this, he has been chosen and hidden in his presence before the creation of the world and forever. 7. But the wisdom of the Lord of Spirits has revealed him to the holy and the righteous, for he has preserved the inheritance of the righteous because they have hated and despised this world of iniquity, and hated all of its works and ways in the name of the Lord of Spirits. For in his name they will be saved, and he will be the avenger of their lives.

8. "In those days, the kings of the earth, and the powerful who possess the land through the deeds of their hands, will be shamefaced; for in the day of their anguish and affliction they will not be able to save themselves. 9. I will give them over into the hands of my chosen ones: as straw in the fire, so will they burn before the face of the holy; as lead in the water, so will they sink before the face of the righteous. Not a trace of them will be found."

10. On the day of their affliction there will be rest on the earth, and they will fall down before him and not rise up again. There will be no one to grasp them in his hands and raise them up, for they have denied the Lord of Spirits and his Messiah. Blessed be the name of the Lord of Spirits!

In 48:1 we discover that wisdom, which could find no place on earth in chapter 42, is found in abundant fountains for the righteous here in the heavenlies (cf. Isa 55:1). The author then continues to mine Isaiah's Servant Songs for more information about the Son of Man. 48:2-8 plainly parallel Isa 49:1-7, which tells how the Servant is called, named, hidden in the shadow of God's hand, made a light to the Gentiles, and destined to have kings and princes bow down before him. Notably, the PE takes the Servant's call from birth (Isa 49:1) as virtually a case for his preexistence (48:3). Also new is the idea that his hidden identity, known by God from the beginning, has now been revealed to the "holy and righteous" (v. 7). The same concept is found in 1 Pet 1:20.

The word "Messiah" (i.e., anointed one) appears explicitly for the first time in the PE in 48:10; it will appear only once more (52:4). The context is significant, for the reference to the kings and the powerful denying "the Lord of Spirits and his Messiah" probably alludes to Ps 2:2, an enthronement psalm. A third important facet is therefore added to the messianic portrait: he is the Davidic king as well as the Danielic son of man and the Isaianic servant. This is confirmed beyond doubt in the next chapter, which repeats that wisdom flows like water in the presence of the Lord of Spirits and the "Chosen One" (49:1-2; the alternate title is again taken up), and that within him "dwells the spirit of wisdom, the spirit which gives understanding, the spirit of knowledge, and of power, and the spirit of those who have fallen asleep in righteousness" (49:3). This is a clear allusion to Isa 11:2, a passage not from the Servant Songs but from a prediction about the "shoot" out of "the stump of Jesse" — the idealized Davidic king. Some scholars find yet further evidence of royal messianism in the PE at 61:8 (see below).

(5) *Chapters 50–51* return us to the lot of the righteous, with new information about the future. Chapter 50 presupposes a time of relief and prosperity during which "the others" (i.e., the Gentiles) may repent and "abandon the works of their hands" after seeing the glory and honor bestowed on the righteous on Judgment Day (50:1-2). This fits awkwardly with ch. 63 in the third parable, which implies that it is too late for repentance when that great day arrives. The two can be reconciled if one distinguishes between a preliminary "day of the sword" (cf. 48:8-10 above), in which overt sinners like the kings and mighty are punished, and a later inauguration of a new heaven and earth (cf. 45:4-6), allowing for an interval during which ordinary Gentiles may repent and join the righteous. This eschatological scheme also fits the picture found in weeks 8–10 of the "Apocalypse of Weeks" (part of the AE; cf. 91:12-17 below). The invitation to conversion is remarkable: "Although they will have no honorable standing through the name of the Lord of Spirits, yet through his name they will be saved" (v. 3). Passages like this make it clear that "chosen ones" does not imply any kind of fixed predestination in the PE (cf. notes on 1:1-2 above).

Chapter 51 explicitly teaches that bodily resurrection of the dead is part of the plan: "In those days, the earth will give up that which has been entrusted to it, Sheol will give up that which has been deposited there, and Perdition will return that which it owes" (v. 1). The author may have surmised this doctrine from the BW by combining the physicality of the restored world in chs. 10–11 with the immortality of the soul and implied future resurrection in ch. 22 (cf. also 20:8). Enoch tells us that "in those days" the Chosen One will sit upon the throne of the Lord of Spirits and preside over the judgment of the resurrected dead (vv. 2-3). The notion that a single throne can belong to both God and his vicegerent is found in both the OT and the NT (1 Chr 29:20, 23; 2 Chr 9:8; Rev 22:2).

(6) *Chapter 52:* Enoch is now whisked off in a "chariot of wind" (52:1) for a series of new visions, much less poetic in style, but full of striking, concrete details. In ch. 52 he is shown in the west a series of six mountains of various metals, reminiscent of the six which surround the mountain throne of God in the BW (18:6; 23:1–24:1). Thanks to a helpful interpreting angel, Enoch learns that the Lord of Spirits has destined these mountains to melt away "like wax" before the Chosen One (52:6). The PE author is linking the six lesser peaks from Enoch's journeys in the BW with the melting mountains mentioned in the theophany at the beginning of that same book (1:6). Significantly, in the BW they melt away utterly in the presence of *God* when he appears; here they do so at the appearance of *the Chosen One.* They will be utterly "under the dominion of his [God's] Messiah, that he may be in command and hold power on the earth" (52:4). The six metal mountains represent the kingdoms of the world, possibly inspired by the vision of the metallic statue in Dan 2:31-45. If so, the author may be hinting that the missing seventh peak — the mountain throne of God — is the one found in Dan 2:35. The PE author also takes this opportunity to reaffirm the curious disdain for metallurgy found in the BW (cf. comments on 8:1 above), citing the fate of these mountains as proof of the worthlessness of metals (52:8-9).

(7) *Chapters 53:1–56:4:* Next Enoch sees three similar visions of punishing angels bringing forth shackles for the wicked and of the deep abysses into which these sinners are to be hurled at the time of their judgment. The first (ch. 53) is for the kings and mighty, the second (54:1-6; 55:3-4) is for the hosts of Azazel along with the kings and mighty, and the third (ch. 56) is for the "chosen and beloved ones" of Azazel and company. Many commentators believe these "chosen and beloved ones" (56:3) are again the kings and mighty, but more likely these are the demonic offspring of the Watchers, which are described in the BW as their "beloved ones" (10:12; 14:6). It is objected that this would then be the only mention of the demons in the PE, but that is not sufficient to deny the identification. The dispute may not matter: given the PE author's passion for parallels between earthly and heavenly reality, the ambiguity could be intentional. Judgment of demons and of kings is the same judgment.

Two statements particularly arrest our attention in these brief scenes. First, Azazel and his associates are being judged "for their iniquity in becoming servants of Satan and leading astray the inhabitants of the earth" (54:6). We learn here for the first time that the Watchers were not acting solely on their own initiative but as agents of a sinister anterior power, projecting the source of evil back another step in the cosmic scheme of things (and, not unimportantly, facilitating the easy incorporation of *Enoch* into Christian theology). Satan is not again mentioned in *Enoch,* and this tantalizing new dimension goes unexplored. Second, we also hear God declare that the kings and mighty "must look upon my Chosen One as he sits on the throne of glory and judges Azazel, all of his associates, and all of his hosts" (55:4). This is the first clear incorporation of the Watcher myth into the PE's messianic dioramas. Also, as noted earlier, this decisive judgment on Azazel confirms the suspected allusion to Yom Kippur in ch. 47.

These three tableaux are interrupted by a so-called "Noah fragment" (54:7–55:2) describing the preparations for the flood beforehand and quoting the Antecedent of Days' pessimistic assessment afterward — the destruction was "in vain" (55:1). By now, juxtaposing the first and last judgments is a familiar Enochic motif, and here we are reminded that the need for a second judgment, such as these chapters describe, is already apparent at the conclusion of the first (as even Gen 8:21 hints). These "Noah fragments" are therefore not so intrusive as critics sometimes claim, and in two PE passages (54:1–

56:4 and 64:1–69:12) they help create a tri-part pattern similar to Isa 24:17-23: (1) judgment on the earth; (2) flood imagery; and (3) punishment of both heavenly hosts and earthly kings (Suter 1979).

(8) *Chapters 56:5–57:3:* The second parable concludes with a prediction of an invasion of "the land of my chosen ones" by the Parthians and the Medes, foiled because "the city of my righteous ones" proves to be "an impediment to their horses." The invaders then destroy one another and are swallowed up in Sheol (56:5-8). After this, in a passage based on Deut 30:4, the dispersed population is miraculously gathered together "in a single day" (ch. 57).

This is one of the only places in the PE where we find historical clues for dating the book. Scholars often see in ch. 56 an allusion to the brief Parthian (Persian) occupation of Jerusalem in 40 BC, yet the author implies that they will *not* occupy the city, and the internecine conflicts and eschatological events which the author goes on to describe hardly fit the period following 40 BC either. But ten years earlier (51-50 BC), the Persians invaded Syria as a preemptive strike against Roman military ambitions, and an invasion of Israel seemed imminent at that time. It was also known that the Persian cavalry had done poorly in seiges against walled cities up to that point. This seems a more likely setting for *Enoch* 56 (Bampfylde 1984). Some scholars think this kind of analysis asks for more historical detail than apocalyptic imagery is meant to give, but at bare minimum the author believes that Jerusalem can successfully turn away cavalry, and this presupposes a walled, defensible city. That is enough to convince most scholars that the PE must have been written before AD 70.

The Third Parable (chs. 58–69)

The third parable announces itself as "concerning the righteous and the chosen" (58:1), but like the others it actually deals with all the PE themes, moving from one to the other in the author's usual desultory manner.

(1) *Chapter 58* is a sunny blessing upon the righteous, a promise of future glory which includes an invitation to "explore the mysteries of righteousness, the inheritance of faith; for it has become bright as the sun upon the earth, and darkness has passed" (v. 5). We are reminded of the wicked and worthless mysteries revealed by the Watchers (ch. 16 above). These were shunned by the righteous, and their reward will be the privilege of learning true wisdom without restriction, as already implied in 48:1 above. They all become little Enochs, so to speak.

(2) *Chapter 59:* Enoch learns more about the secrets of thunder and lightning, adding to his already considerable store of cosmological knowledge. This little chapter provides an excellent example of how an Enochic writer distills practical wisdom about nature from biblical data. The PE author makes three observations, stressing first the ambivalent role of lightning (v. 1: "for blessing or curse"); second, the penetrating sound of thunder and its function as the voice of God (v. 2: "When it peals in the heavens above, the sound is heard even in the shelters of the earth . . . the voice of the thunder bodes for peace and blessing, but if it involves a curse, it is by means of the voice of the Lord of Spirits"); and third, the essentially benign character of lightning when one comes to understand the whole (v. 3: "All of the secrets . . . were afterward shown to me: It is for blessing and satisfaction that they light up"). The author has surmised these three statements from a close reading of the three references to thunder and lightning in Job 36–38, which carry similar thematic undertones (Job 36:30-33; 37:5, 13; 38:25-27).

(3) *Chapter 60* is a Noah apocalypse, clumsily altered to read "Enoch" rather than "Noah" in its opening statement. The references in v. 1 to the five hundredth year in the life of Enoch (who had only 365) and in v. 8 to "my great-grandfather . . . the seventh from Adam" give the game away. The chapter is structured as an odd kind of chiasmus in which the second part of each pair does not mirror the first but simply continues an interrupted narrative:

A1 60:1-6
  B1 60:7-10
    C 60:11-22
  B2 60:23-24
A2 60:25

Enoch (= Noah) collapses in terror as he sees the heavens shaking in agitation and has a vision of the Antecedent of Days upon his throne surrounded by angels and the righteous (vv. 1-3). Michael sends an angel to help him up and then asks him why he is so shaken; after all, a day of reckoning for sinners and reward for the righteous has long been planned, and that day has finally come (vv. 4-6). The narrative breaks off here and concludes at v. 25, where it is explained that although God's punishment is severe, it is followed up by mercy. The verse plays on a double meaning of "rest" (i.e., lie and desist), which happens to work in English as well:

> ". . . in order that the punishment of the Lord of Spirits may 'rest' upon them, and that this punishment may not be issued in vain, children will be slain with their mothers, sons with their fathers. But when the punishment of the Lord of Spirits upon them all 'rests,' judgment in accordance with his mercy and his forbearance will follow."

Such a pun comes naturally in a Noah apocalypse, since "Noah" means "rest, respite" (cf. Gen 5:29).

60:7-10, 23-24 narrate a strange myth about Leviathan and Behemoth, the legendary beasts best known from the latter chapters of Job. The two were separated from each other in primeval times and assigned different homes — the female Leviathan to the sea and the male Behemoth to a wilderness called "Dundayin" (= the "Dudael" of 10:4?), located east of the Garden "where the chosen and righteous are and where my great-grandfather was taken" (60:7-8). We are reminded of the strange menagerie east of Paradise which Enoch mentions in passing in the BW (33:1). The speaker wonders about the power of these creatures, but the angel tells him only that they are "prepared for the Great Day of the Lord, to become food" (vv. 9-10, 23-24), alluding to a widespread Jewish legend that these beasts will provide the main entree at the great eschatological feast (2 Esdr 6:49-52; *2 Apoc. Bar.* 29:3-4; *b. B. Bat.* 75a; Theodotion's version of Ps 74:14). The reason for including this myth in the PE is not clear, but it does echo the general apocalyptic theme of resolving unsettled primeval affairs in the last days, and perhaps the images of sea and dry land in connection with themes of separation, judgment, and the day of the Lord resonated well in a Noah apocalypse.

The lengthy midsection of this chapter consists of another catalogue of cosmological information, mostly involving wind and weather (60:11-22). The overall message is that every aspect of nature is governed by its own particular spirit (or "wind" — the word is the same), and that strict supervision by these spirits is essential to maintaining proper balance in nature. Along with *Enoch* 69:13-24, this is one of two passages in the PE reflecting what today might be called ecological consciousness. Particular attention is given here to precipitation in all its forms (rain, dew, hail, and snow), perhaps a reminder that Noah's flood involved an *unleashing* of forces, a simple withdrawal of God's carefully imposed order (cf. ch. 66 below).

(4) *Chapter 61:1-5.* With this chapter we return to Enoch's visions:

> 61:1. I saw in those days long cords given to two angels, and they each took their sections and flew off in the direction of the north. 2. I inquired of an angel, "Why have they taken these cords and left?" He replied to me, "They have gone to take measurements."

These verses are most closely modeled on Zech 2:1-2, but the idea of taking measurements under angelic supervision is a common convention in visionary literature (Ezek 40:2-3; 5Q15 [the New Jerusalem]; Rev 11:1; 21:15). All of these texts involve finding the dimensions of Jerusalem, but in *Enoch* 61 the cords are to be given to the righteous "that they may lean upon the name of the Lord of Spirits forever and ever. The chosen will begin to dwell with the chosen, and these are the measurements which will be given — for faith, and for the strengthening of righteousness" (61:3-4). The ropes serve another function as well:

> 61:5. These measuring cords will also reveal all that is hidden in the depths of the earth: those who have been destroyed by the desert, those who have been devoured by the wild beasts, and those who have been devoured by the fish of the sea; that they may return, relying on the Day of the Chosen One; for no one will turn out to be destroyed before the Lord of Spirits, and no one, in fact, can be destroyed.

As in ch. 51, expectation of a physical resurrection is unmistakable. Thus, in an apocalyptic vignette where the presence of a stock motif leads us to expect a vision of the New Jerusalem, we are given instead glimpses of mystic unity between the righteous dead and the righteous living and assurance of their reunion through resurrection on the "Day of the Chosen One." By this bait-and-switch is the author lecturing us on the true significance of the City of God?

(5) *Chapters 61:5–64:2:* Now that the dead are raised we can commence the final Judgment. The enthronement of the Chosen One on his glorious throne, prophesied three times already (45:3; 51:3; 55:4), is here depicted as a witnessed event. The explicit statement that "the Lord of Spirits placed the Chosen One upon the throne of glory" (61:8) has reminded many critics of Ps 110:1, believed to be a royal enthronement psalm; if so, we have another example of Davidic messianism in the PE.

First to be judged are the holy angels in heaven (61:8-9). Not surprisingly, they fare rather well, so that vv. 6-13 are largely devoted to an ecstatic outpouring of praise before the Lord of Spirits by what seems to be every variety of angel known to the author (v. 10). Included in this choir are "the chosen ones who dwell in the Garden of Life" and "all flesh" (v. 12). Based on what can be gathered from 60:8 and 70:4, the former are probably to be understood as the righteous antediluvian ancestors (cf. also 37:3), while the latter are the dead raised at the beginning of the chapter.

The judgment of the mighty by the Son of Man, another event promised earlier (ch. 46), follows immediately. It is the dramatic highpoint of the PE:

> 62:1. And after this, the Lord commanded the kings, the mighty, the exalted, and those who occupy the earth, saying, "Open your eyes, lift your eyebrows — see if you can recognize the Chosen One!"
>
> 2. The Lord of Spirits seated him [emended; all mss.: "sat himself"] on the throne of his glory, and the spirit of righteousness was poured out upon him. The word of his mouth slays all the sinners, and all the lawless are destroyed before his face.
>
> 3. On that day, all the kings, the mighty, the exalted, and those who occupy the earth — all these will stand up and look, and they will recognize him and that he is sitting on the throne of his glory. Righteousness is judged before him, and in his presence there is no empty talk. 4. Then agony will overtake them as it does a childbearing woman in hard labor, at the moment that her child enters the mouth of the womb, and delivery is painful. 5. Half of them will look at the other half, and they will be terror-stricken, and their faces downcast, and they will be gripped with pain when they see that Son of Man seated on the throne of his glory. 6. Then the kings, the mighty, and all who possess the earth will praise, glorify, and exalt him who rules over all — the One who was hidden. 7. For from the beginning, the Son of Man was hidden, and the Most High preserved him in the presence of his power, but he has revealed him to the chosen. 8. The congregation of the chosen and the holy will be sown, and all the chosen will stand before him on that day.
>
> 9. And all the kings, the mighty, the exalted, and those who rule the earth will fall down before him on their faces and worship, placing their hopes in that Son of Man, petitioning him and pleading for mercy from

him. 10. But the Lord of Spirits will inspire such panic in them that they will rush to escape from his presence. Their faces will be filled with shame; the darkness in their faces will grow deeper. 11. And he will turn them over to the angels for punishment, to execute vengeance upon these who have oppressed his children and his chosen ones.

12. It will provide a spectacle for the righteous and for his chosen. They will rejoice over them, for the wrath of the Lord of Spirits rests upon them, and his sword is drunk with them. 13. The righteous and the chosen will be saved on that day, and never again will they see the faces of the sinners and the lawless. 14. The Lord of Spirits will remain over them, and with that Son of Man they will eat, and lie down, and rise up, forever and ever. 15. The righteous and the chosen will have risen from the earth, their faces no more downcast. They will be clothed with garments of glory. 16. (And this will be *your* garment: a garment of life from the Lord of Spirits. Your garments will not wear out, nor will your glory fade away before the Lord of Spirits.)

63:1. At that time the kings and the mighty who possess the earth will plead with the Angels of Punishment, to whom they are delivered up, to grant them a brief respite, so that they may yet fall down and worship in the presence of the Lord of Spirits, confessing their sins before him. 2. And they will praise and glorify the Lord of Spirits, saying, "Blessed is the Lord of Spirits and the Lord of Kings, and the Lord of the Mighty and the Lord of the Rich, and the Lord of Glory, and the Lord of Wisdom. 3. And in every hidden thing your power shines, from generation to generation, and your glory is forever and ever. Deep are all your secrets, and numberless, and your righteousness beyond all calculation. 4. We have learned our lesson now: We should glorify and praise the Lord of Kings and him who rules over all rulers."

5. They will also say this: "O that we might be granted some respite, that we might glorify, praise, and profess our belief before his glory! 6. And now we long for a little rest, but do not find it. We pursue but cannot get hold of it. The light before us has disappeared, and darkness will be our dwelling place forever and ever. 7. Because until now we have not professed belief, nor glorified the name of the Lord of Spirits — and of kings! Nor glorified *our* Lord, but our trust has been in the scepters of our kingdoms and in our glory. 8. So now in the day of our suffering and distress he does not save us, and we find no respite in which to profess our belief that our Lord is true in all his works, his judgments, and his justice. And his judgments show no respect of persons. 9. And so we pass away from his presence, thanks to our works. All of our sins have been scrupulously totaled."

10. Then they will say to themselves, "Our souls are glutted with ill-gotten gains, but they will not prevent our descent into the pit of Sheol." 11. After this, their faces will be filled with darkness and shame before that Son of Man; and they will be banished from his presence, and in their midst and before his face the sword will abide.

12. Thus says the Lord of Spirits, "This is the decree and the judgment with respect to the mighty, and the kings, and the exalted, and those who possess the earth, before the Lord of Spirits."

64:1. Then I saw other Presences hidden in that place. 2. I heard the voice of an angel saying, "These are the angels who descended to the earth and revealed what was hidden to the children of men, and led astray the children of men into committing sin."

Although this passage fairly swims with biblical allusions, George Nickelsburg has identified the basic judgment scene as a traditional reworking of Isaiah 52–53; traditional since a similar handling of the same text is found in Wisdom 4–5: both expand the last Isaianic Servant Song with material from Isaiah 13–14, and both feature the exaltation of a formerly persecuted righteous man (Wisdom 4–5) or patron of the persecuted righteous (*Enoch* 62) in the presence of the persecutors, who react in each case with terror and despair as they recognize him, learning too late that their wealth can do them no good and confessing their guilt, even though they realize that they have no hope of escaping punishment (Nickelsburg 1972: 70-74).

The challenge to the kings and mighty to recognize — "if you can" — the Chosen One (62:1) implies that he is someone they formerly knew but did not then recognize. The most likely interpretation is that it is the *Chosen One* they were oppressing whenever they persecuted any of the *chosen ones* (which they did, according to 62:11). A similar identification of a heavenly figure with an earthly community is found in Daniel's night vision (cf. Dan 7:14 and 27), so the switch in terminology from Chosen One to Son of Man in 62:5 is not inappropriate. As noted in the discussion of ch. 47 above, Matt 25:31-46 makes the same point. In addition to the thematic similarity, the Matthean parable begins with the Son of Man coming in glory and sitting upon "the throne of his glory" (25:31), using the same phrase found here (62:3). This phrase also occurs in Matt 19:28, where it is virtually identical with the wording of *Enoch* 62:5 ("when the Son of Man is seated on the throne of his glory"). As these are the only texts of their time which speak of a messianic figure sitting on a glorious throne, direct literary influence is not unlikely.

The unavailing repentance of the kings and mighty reminds us of the situation of the fallen Watchers in the BW, whose petition for mercy is likewise rebuffed (chs. 13–15). Lest we miss the point, the author draws attention to the parallel rather explicitly with a ghostly little vision following the judgment scene (ch. 64).

The short passage on the salvation of the righteous in 62:13-16 forms an interlude in a scene otherwise wholly devoted to the fate of the wicked. Vv. 14-16 present the two themes of the messianic banquet and garments fit for God's presence, drawing language and imagery from Deut 8:4; 29:5; Isa 52:1-2; and Zeph 3:13. Exactly the same two themes are combined back-to-back in yet another Matthean parable (22:8-13).

(6) *Chapters 65–68:* Chapter 65 begins a second Noah apocalypse, undisguised this time, although where it ends is not clear: either 68:1 or 69:25.

> 65:1. In those days, I, Noah, noticed that the earth had warped downward, and that its destruction was near! 2. I picked up my feet and dashed to the ends of the earth, and I shouted to my great-grandfather Enoch. Three times I cried bitterly, "Hear me! Hear me! Hear me!"

The idea that Enoch is still available for consultation in emergencies is found also in the first appendix of *Enoch* (chs. 106–7), the lost "Book of Giants," and the *Genesis Apocryphon* (1QapGen). Possibly this motif provides a clue to the phenomenon of pseudepigraphy: Did these authors believe they were in actual contact with Enoch? If so, it may have been convenient that Enoch never died since writers could freely claim that the righteous scribe himself had inspired them without incurring charges of necromancy, forbidden under Mosaic law (Deut 18:11)!

Like the interpreting angel of ch. 60, Enoch appears to Noah and asks him why he is so shaken (65:5), explaining that God is preparing to bring judgment on those "who dwell on the earth":

> 65:6. For they have acquired knowledge of all the secrets of the angels and of all the wrongdoing of the satans, with all their powers — the most arcane secrets — and all the powers of those who practice sorcery, the power of spells, and the powers of those who fashion molten idols for the entire world.

Typically, the PE is far more interested in the "forbidden teaching" motif of the Watcher myth than the "forbidden marriage" one. This is not surprising since the earthly enemies in the author's view are Gentile rulers rather than fellow Jews. Sexual defilement would be the more potent metaphor in a dispute with the latter, while the theme of false wisdom lends itself nicely to condemnation of gentilic sorcery and idolatry, as here.

After firing yet another shot at metallurgy (65:7-8), Enoch comforts Noah with assurances of his preservation through the coming judgment:

> 65:11. . . . But as for you, my son, the Lord of Spirits knows that you are pure and blameless concerning these secrets. 12. He has established your name among the holy ones, he will save you from among those who dwell upon the earth, he has established your righteous seed both for kingship and great glory, and from your seed will come forth a fountain of the righteous and holy; they will be numberless for eternity.

This Noah apocalypse serves to bring back to the fore the basic Enochic tales, contrasting here the wicked teachings of the fallen angels with the true wisdom of the Enochic tradition. For much of the PE the fundamental myths have been present only subliminally.

The vision ends after Noah is given a glimpse of the Angels of Punishment holding back the waters of the flood and awaiting God's signal (ch. 66). Then, in a fresh vision, Noah is told that there are angels "working with wood," which God will use to preserve the "seed of life." This seed will "not prove unfruitful on the face of the earth; rather, they will be blessed, and they will multiply on the earth in the name of the Lord" (67:1-3). It is remarkable that in these passages the author of the PE recasts the Noachic covenant of Genesis 9 so as to resemble the more well-known Abrahamic covenant (cf. Gen 13:15; 15:5).

There follows a unique vision which draws an ironic parallel between the hot springs used for medicinal purposes by the kings and mighty and the subterranean rivers of molten fire tormenting the imprisoned angels (67:4-13). Palestine is the site of many such thermal springs, and Roman officials were indeed fond of them. Josephus gives a detailed account of Herod the Great's attempts to relieve his gruesome ailments in the waters of Callirhoe, east of the Dead Sea (*Ant.* 17 §§171-72 and *J.W.* 1 §§656-58). Many think that these verses in the PE may be an allusion to Herod's unsuccessful medical treatments; if so, *Enoch* 67:4-13 was probably written about the time of the birth of Christ. As for its function within the context of the PE, this episode again removes any possible doubt about who the Watchers' counterparts are, and it also blends ingeniously imagery from the first and the last universal judgments, the one by water and the other by fire.

Chapter 68 begins with a verse explaining how Enoch's Parables were bequeathed to Noah, evidence that these latter Noah chapters were added to an already extant work. We then eavesdrop on a conversation between Michael and Raphael. Appalled at the severity of the judgment God has decreed, Michael lets it be known that he has no intention of interceding before such an angry Deity on behalf of idolatrous humanity (vv. 2-5). We may note from this incidental conversation that Enoch the scribe is more compassionate than the archangels, for in the BW he was willing to act as mediator before God even for the fallen Watchers (chs. 13–15)!

(7) *Chapter 69* begins with two lists of fallen angels. The first is simply copied from 6:2 in the BW, but the second gives cryptic information about five angels who are often identified by critics as the elusive "satans" of 40:7 and 65:6, since the first of these (Yeqon) is said to have "led astray the angelic sons, bringing them down to the earth and leading them astray through the daughters of men" (69:4), while the second (Asbeel) "recommended to the angelic sons an evil plot, leading them astray so that they might defile their bodies with the daughters of men" (v. 5). The "angelic sons" (lit. "sons of angels" — likely the *bene ha-'elohim* of Genesis 6) are clearly the Watchers, and we have to do here with an evil presence who led them astray. From 54:6 we learned that in fact the Watchers became servants of Satan, so it is indeed plausible that in context these five are represented as satans. However, it may be that this list was originally an alternative Watcher list assimilated into this late *Enoch* booklet, since some of these satans' functions look suspiciously like ones attributed to the Watchers in chs. 6–8. For example, we are told that the third angel Gadriel, who "led Eve astray" (v. 6), also introduced all the weapons of war, as does Asael in *Enoch* 8:1.

The fourth satan is Penemue, who introduced among other things the art of writing. This may seem a strange thing for our righteous scribe to attribute to an evil angel, but he elaborates: "For humans were not born for such a practice as confirming their faith with pen and ink" (69:10). It seems that writing is evidence of humanity's degeneracy; between honest parties the spoken word should be sufficient (cf. Matt 5:37). The author builds on this point with a ringing affirmation of human free will:

> 69:11. Humans were not, in fact, created any differently than the angels in that they ought to live continually pure and righteous lives. Death, that destroyer of all things, would never have touched them, but thanks to this knowledge of theirs they are perishing.

When we compare a passage like this with the stark double predestination found in the famous "Instruction on the Two Spirits" in the Qumran *Manual of Discipline* (1QS 3–4), we can appreciate another reason why the Dead Sea sect may have deliberately ignored the PE.

The fifth satan (Kasdeya) is in charge of abortions and miscarriages (69:12), one of the most durable types in world demonology. Here he seems to be identified with the dread midday demon of Ps 91:6 (LXX).

69:13-15 are very obscure, but they seem to tell of a misguided plot by a former high-ranking angel named Kasbeel to cajole out of Michael the secret name of God in his possession, in order that he might then combine it with the secret name — or "oath" — in his own keeping and by doing so terrify the Watchers into submission. Whether or not this is the correct interpretation, we are next treated to a splendid song describing this cosmic oath. It holds the universe together, preserving and ordering all things, "from the creation of the world, and for eternity" (vv. 16-25; cf. Pr Man 2-3). The hymn climaxes with a burst of joyful praise to the Lord of Spirits (v. 24), but then concludes on a quieter note: "This oath holds dominion over them, and through it they are kept; their paths are kept also, and their ways do not come to ruin" (v. 25). This serves as a transitional statement to the endpiece of the third parable:

> 69:26. Great joy was theirs! They blessed and glorified and exalted; for the name of that Son of Man had been revealed to them, 27. and he sat upon the throne of his glory, and the sum total of the judgment was given to that Son of Man, and he will eliminate and destroy from the face of the earth those who have led the world astray. 28. They will be bound in chains, and their congregation of corruption will be imprisoned, and all of their works will disappear from the face of the earth. 29. From then on there will not be found anything corruptible. For that Son of Man has appeared and has seated himself on the throne of his glory, and before his face all evil will pass away and be gone; for the word of that Son of Man will be powerful in the presence of the Lord of Spirits. This is the Third Parable of Enoch.

Several parallels with the Gospel of John suggest themselves immediately (John 5:22, 27; 12:48), and the Son of Man on his glorious throne reminds us again of Matt 19:28. It has frequently been suggested that this passage is out of place and may originally have followed 62:16 or 63:12, but in ch. 41 a cosmic oath passage (41:1-8a) passes directly into a description of the Final Judgment (vv. 8b-9), exactly as here.

These verses may imply in context that the "name of that Son of Man" is parallel to (identified with?) the Cosmic Oath — or Name — which sustains all creation. In any event, it is clear that knowledge about the Messiah, divinely bestowed upon the righteous and chosen, includes especially his identity (48:2, 7; 62:7; 69:26), and this wisdom assures them a place in the renewed world of eternal light and joy about to dawn upon them (48:7; ch. 58).

Epilogue (chs. 70–71)

Many scholars believe that these chapters are a later addition by a different hand, mostly because Enoch appears to be identified with the Son of Man in 71:14. This is thought to contradict the rest of the PE, where Enoch has been viewing this messianic figure with no hint that he is seeing himself; furthermore, the Son of Man appears to be preexistent, whereas Enoch was born seventh from Adam. These and other objections do not hold up well under scrutiny, however, and there is no convincing reason to regard chs. 70–71 as secondary (VanderKam 1992: 177-85). In particular, the *Prayer of Joseph,* a first-second-century-AD mystical account of Jacob's encounter with the angel in Genesis 32 (*OTP,* 2:699-714), provides an excellent parallel to the PE. The author of the *Prayer* did not think it impossible for earthborn mortals to be simultaneously "created before any work," or that a human could have an angelic heavenly double and yet be unaware of this — or at least forget it until being reminded.

Any discussion of the identification of Enoch and the Son of Man in 71:14 must also take into account the pervasive influence of both *Enoch* 14 and Daniel 7 throughout this whole epilogue. The PE author has not chosen at random two unrelated texts: the throne visions in *Enoch* 14 and Daniel 7 bear a close relationship to each other (cf. ch. 14 above), and it cannot be denied that Enoch the scribe, summoned by storm clouds and carried on the winds into heaven (14:8), and standing before God on his dazzling throne (14:18-23), bears a strong resemblance to Daniel's "son of man," "coming with the clouds of heaven" and standing before a divine throne described in almost the same language as in *Enoch* (Dan 7:9-10, 13). Already in the BW, then, it may be hinted that Enoch and the Danielic "son of man" are the same person.

> 70:1. Afterward it came to pass that the immortal name of that Son of Man was exalted in the presence of the Lord of Spirits above all those who live on the earth. 2. He was raised aloft on a chariot of wind, and his name became a household word.
>
> 3. "From that day, I was no longer numbered among them, but he placed me between two winds — between the north and the west — located where the angels had taken cords to measure for me the place of the chosen and the righteous ones. 4. And there I saw the first forebears and the righteous ones of old, dwelling in that place."

(The translation of *Enoch* 70:1 follows a minority reading now found in four of our oldest *Enoch* mss., three unpublished [Olson 1998].) Enoch's ascent follows a three-stage process as he is lifted first to the Paradise of his forebears (70:1-2), described with language which recalls ch. 61, then secondly to the lower heavens (71:1-4a), where he sees the angels and the secrets of the cosmos under the guidance of Michael, and then finally to the "heaven of heavens," where the seer describes God's fiery, crystalline house in language much like that of *Enoch* 14:18-22 (71:4b-7). The vision then reaches its climax:

> 71:8. "And I saw countless angels encircling that house — thousands upon thousands and ten thousand times ten thousand — and Michael, Raphael, Gabriel, and Phanuel, and the holy angels who are above the heavens, all going in and out of that house.
>
> 9. "Then Michael, Gabriel, and Raphael, and many holy angels without number emerged from that house. 10. With them was the Antecedent of Days. His head was pure and white as wool, and his garments indescribable. 11. I fell on my face; my whole body melted, and my spirit was transformed. Then I cried out with a loud voice, in a spirit of power, blessing, glorifying, and exalting. 12. These blessings which came forth from my mouth were well pleasing before the Antecedent of Days. 13. And then the Antecedent of Days approached, with Michael, Gabriel, Raphael, Phanuel, and thousands and ten thousands of angels without number.
>
> 14. "Then that one approached me and spoke a greeting, and he said, 'You are the Son of Man who is born to righteousness, and righteousness has remained with you. The righteousness of the Antecedent of Days will not forsake you.' 15. He also said to me, 'He summons forth peace for you in the name of the world to come; for since the creation of the world, peace has come from there, and therefore it will be yours forever, and forever and ever. 16. And everyone will walk in your ways, since righteousness never forsakes you. Their dwelling places will be with you, and with you their inheritance; and they will never part from you, forever and ever.'"

The angels here enjoy free access in and out of the heavenly palace (71:8), but in the otherwise similar scene of *Enoch* 14 no angel could enter there (14:21). The author may be deliberately drawing our attention to this anomaly so that we might notice another: Michael, Gabriel, Raphael, and Phanuel enter the house in 71:8, but when they emerge, along with a host of other angels and the Antecedent of Days (v. 9), Phanuel is missing (at least in most of the best mss.). A scribal error? Or is Phanuel staying behind for some unknown purpose? At any rate, by v. 13 he has rejoined the group. A figure designated only as "that one" (many mss. have "that angel") then steps forward in the next verse to tell Enoch, "You are the Son of Man." Thus Enoch receives a new name from a conspicuously unnamed angel. Most likely "that one" is Phanuel, the angel whose name derives from Gen 32:30-31, the wrestler with Jacob who bestowed upon him his new name while refusing to disclose his own. We recall that the closest literary parallel to Enoch in the PE is Jacob in the *Prayer of Joseph*.

The faint echo of Genesis 32 is no fluke. It has been noted that all the messianic titles in the PE (Son of Man, Chosen One, Righteous One) designate in their original biblical contexts heavenly representatives of the community of saints on earth; they are "ciphers" for the redeemed (Black 1992: 150). Unlike Daniel's "son of man," however, the mystical heaven-to-earth dynamic of the Chosen/Righteous One in the Isaianic Servant Songs is closely bound up in those passages with the Servant's name: he is repeatedly called "Jacob" and "Israel" (e.g., Isa 41:8; 44:1-2, 21; 45:4; 49:3), even though he is also *distinguished* from Jacob and Israel (49:5-6). Daniel has no concern for the name of his "son of man" figure, but the PE equates him with the Isaianic Servant and so naturally shows great interest in his name (48:2-3; 69:26). Through a subtle allusion to Genesis 32, the author attaches to the Danielic "son of man" the same Jacob-Israel mysticism already associated with the Isaianic Chosen/Righteous One. Such a move may have been partially inspired by an earlier *Enoch* booklet; the DV also represents its Messiah figure as the true Jacob, although he is not there identified with Enoch (see the notes on 89:11-12; 90:37-38 below).

Enoch's glorification in the PE is intended to encourage the faithful within the Enochic tradition. The PE author believes that the Watchers have begun the fresh assault vaguely prophesied in the BW (1:5; cf. 39:1). Some of the righteous are already facing martyrdom (ch. 47). It is naturally expected that Enoch will again play a crucial role in the coming events, just as he did before the flood, but is he up to the present crisis? An avid student of Scripture, the PE author has strengthened Enoch's credentials as God's chosen agent by collecting Danielic, Isaianic, and royal Davidic traits into one heavenly figure and by identifying this Messiah as Enoch's mystic double, just as the earthly patriarch Jacob discovers a numinous identity which betokens his role in history and sets him far above his peers.

The PE closes on this confident note: "And so there will be length of days with that Son of Man. The righteous will have peace, and the righteous will have a path of justice, in the name of the Lord of Spirits, forever and ever" (71:17).

The Astronomy Book (Enoch 72–82)

Introduction

A relic of ancient pseudo-scientific literature, the AB provides sketchy descriptions of the movements of the sun and moon, a simple solar calendar, plus information about the winds, geography, and the angels who govern the stars and seasons. Having acquired this material from the angel Uriel, Enoch bequeaths it to his son Methuselah and offers predictions about the future based on his perusal of "the tablets of heaven."

This the shortest of the five *Enoch* booklets has clearly suffered in transmission, especially the latter half (chs. 78–82), where the material is disordered and incomplete in the Ethiopic version — the only form in which the book has survived. The damage can be undone to some degree: a scanty DSS fragment allows us to put chs. 78–79 in order, and it has always been widely agreed on literary grounds that the last chapter is backward (82:7-20 should precede 82:1-6). Unfortunately, if we stop here, we are still left with an intolerable mess, and going further requires a certain amount of conjecture in order to recover an acceptable form for the book. Recognizing the provisional nature of any reconstruction, the following outline may be suggested as at least closer to the original AB than the order as it now stands in the *Book of Enoch:*

Superscription	72:1
Sun and Moon	72:2–74:9
The Calendar	74:10–75:3
The Portals of the Heavens	75:4–76:14
Geography	77
More Solar and Lunar Data; the Lunar Year	78:1-16 (79:3-5); 78:17
The Seasons and the Stars	79:1-2 (82:7-20); 79:6–80:1
The Tablets of Heaven	81:1-4
Enoch's Instructions and Prophecies	81:5–82:6; 80:2-8

The Qumran fragments of the AB correspond to the Ethiopic text less exactly than the fragments of other parts of *Enoch.* Most probably, the version that has come down to us is only an abridged summary of a longer work. Evidence suggests that the Aramaic AB was a hefty scroll containing a day-by-day account of the movements of the sun and moon, fully synchronized with each other. The solar and lunar information in the Ethiopic AB, on the other hand, is far briefer, and the two cycles are treated separately. In addition, original information about the movements of the stars has been totally lost in the Ethiopic version, along with descriptions of two of the four seasons. Nevertheless, while the Ethiopic booklet must be treated with caution, it does fit reasonably well the apparent allusions to the AB found in two second-century-BC sources, *Jub.* 4:17 and Pseudo-Eupolemus (*OTP,* 2:881).

With its plodding descriptions of uranological phenomena, much of the AB makes dull reading. The book is far more interesting for what it represents. Because of its distinctive calendar and proven antiquity, many scholars use the AB in their attempts to piece together the history of Jewish sects and priestly rivalries during the third through fifth centuries BC, the most obscure phase of Israel's history. The Enochic solar calendar consists of twelve thirty-day months, with an extra day added at the end of each third month, making an annual total of 364 days. Being exactly divisible by seven, a 364-day cycle allows sabbaths and other feasts to fall on the same dates every year — an attractive feature. The more familiar calendar in use among Jews during the later Second Temple period (and the one still in use) was basically a lunar calendar of 354 days, with an extra month added about every three years in order to recalibrate it against the solar year. It could not be a matter of religious indifference which calendar was used: feasts and sabbaths were fixed by God's revealed word just as surely as the world he had created, and employing a wrong calendar for cultic purposes would invalidate all observances and lead to gross sabbath violations. At least by the second century BC, there were sharp solar-lunar disputes among Jews (*Jub.* 6:23-38; cf. CD 3:14-15), with *Jubilees* and the ultra-conservative Qumran sect both opting for the Enochic solar calendar. However, the AB itself pre-dates these solar-lunar debates since it describes the lunar year and the movements of the moon with no polemic against lunarists. Instead, the AB repeatedly criticizes those who fail to correctly add the four quarterly days to the solar 360-day calendar (74:10-11; 75:1-2; 82:4-6). These people must have started with a 360-day calendar and either added no extra days at all or did so by some other pattern. Such schemas are unattested in Judaism but *are* found elsewhere: the Egyptians and Persians used a 360-day calendar (twelve thirty-day months) and added a string of five days at year's end, while the Babylonians had among their ancient calendars a 360-day year which may not have been intercalated at all. The AB can plausibly be read as a defense of Israel's distinctive solar calendar against Gentile solar calendars at a time when no one in Israel had yet suggested use of the lunar system for cultic purposes.

That these AB Enochians were not sectarians is further indicated by an extraordinary fact: no solitary, precisely dated activity in the OT falls on a sabbath if we use the AB system, with the exception of the Purim festival in Esth 9:13-22. (Interestingly, Esther had difficulty getting into the canon and is the only OT book not found at Qumran, where Purim was ignored.) There are nearly one hundred such dated events in the OT altogether, so the statistic is significant. Anywhere exact date formulae occur in the OT, they are routinely attributed to priestly editorial work, beginning in the Pentateuch with the so-called "Priestly Source" (P). At the same time, a link between Enoch and the solar calendar is already hinted in Gen 5:23-24, where the patriarch ascends at the unusually young age — for antediluvians! — of 365. This passage is also assigned to P. It seems, then, that P not only used the 364-day calendar but is our first witness to the Enochic astronomical tradition in at least a rudimentary form (VanderKam 1979). That being so, the trend toward a preexilic date for P in the wake of groundbreaking studies by A. Hurvitz and J. Milgrom carries weighty implications for the antiquity of the Enochic AB material. It also tends to undercut the theory that the AB originated among diaspora Jews exposed to Babylonian astronomy, and more especially so since the centerpiece of the AB, the 364-day calendar, has no true Babylonian parallel. All things considered, it is entirely possible that the AB represents the official calendar of preexilic Israel.

Evaluated as an *Enoch* booklet, we find the AB all but ignoring the Watchers and expanding instead the Enoch myth. Here the fabled wisdom of the righteous scribe consists primarily of insight into natural phenomena, especially astronomy. Similar material, in smaller doses, is found in some of the other booklets as well (chs. 34–36; 41:3-8; chs. 59–60; 83:11), but in the AB it dominates until the final chapters. Instructed by the angel Uriel, our visionary becomes an authority on such topics as the regularity of nature and the details of the proper calendar, knowledge of which enables readers to live their lives in harmony with God's creation and the liturgy of the heavens. Enoch's spiritual heirs, living according to this true calendar, can be confident that they reflect the divine order even now during their earthly sojourns. They are lockstep with the holy angels.

The absence of the fallen angel theme is less surprising when we remember that the AB was probably written as a sequel to the BW (cf. 72:1 below): the author expected both works to be read together and may have believed that the BW had adequately covered the subject. A few items in the AB, however, do reflect this strand of the tradition. The BW lists astrology among the worthless arts taught by the Watchers (8:3). Its foolishness is amply demonstrated in the AB, since there the heavenly bodies follow a rigid and unvarying scheme from year to year; obviously, nothing about the future can be learned from observing them, and the planets and the zodiac are not even mentioned. The BW also tells of a primeval rebellion by seven stars, parallel with the fallen angels, who "transgressed the commandment of the Lord from the beginning of their rising" (cf. 18:12-16 above). Ch. 80 of the AB possibly alludes to this (vv. 6-7); but if it does, it is a satirical reinterpretation: the luminaries are innocent and on schedule; it is sinners deluded by faulty calendars who mistake ordinary astronomical movements for evidence of autonomous activity and worship stars as gods. For this author, human weakness and folly are the immediate sources of sin in the world (cf. 81:5).

Superscription (72:1)

> 72:1. The Book of the Courses of the Luminaries of Heaven: the positions of each one in respect to their classes, their dominions, their seasons; and in accordance with their names, their starting points, and their months; as revealed to me by their leader Uriel, the holy angel who accompanied me. He revealed to me all of their regulations, exactly as they are for all of the world's years until eternity; that is, until the new creation is established which will endure forever.

As noted, the AB reads like a continuation of the first book (cf. also the Introduction to the BW, 907). Readers are expected to know already who the speaker is. In fact, Enoch's name will not appear in the AB until 80:1.

The current order of nature is described as only temporary pending a new creation, a theme picked up in later *Enoch* booklets (45:4; 91:16). Although often cited as a quintessentially apocalyptic idea, the concept is halfway there already in Ps 102:25-27 and fully present in Isa 65:17; 66:22.

Enoch learns about the cosmos through the angel Uriel. About 180 BC, Ben Sirach will explicitly deny that angels are given such roles (Sir 42:17). If this is an attack on the AB, perhaps Sirach is motivated by his enthusiasm for the lunar calendar (Sir 43:6-7).

Sun and Moon (chs. 72:2–74:9)

The author divides the horizon into twelve portals, six on the east and six on the west, through which the sun enters and exits each day as it makes its way across the dome of the sky (72:2-7). New Year begins immediately after the vernal equinox, when the sun shifts to gate four, and it keeps to the track between the fourth eastern and western gates for thirty days, during which time the day length increases daily and the night length decreases nightly, until by the end of the first solar month the day is ten units long to the night's eight (vv. 8-11). This curious division of each full day into eighteen parts is probably borrowed from Babylonian astronomy (VanderKam 1984b: 93-94). The remainder of the chapter methodically plots the sun's shift each month from one pair of matching gates to the next and the simultaneous augmenting and diminishing of day and night lengths during the course of the year. Every third month has thirty-one days, for a total of 364 at year's end (v. 32).

There is little correspondence between this artificial system and observable astronomical fact. *Enoch* 72 is a purely schematic presentation of the solar calendar and a stylized illustration of the orderliness of the heavens.

The treatment of the waxing and waning of the moon (73:1–74:4) is a bit closer to observational reality, but it still remains more mechanical than natural. The lunar surface is divided into fourteen sections, and each of these fills with light, one per day, until full moon on day 14 (in twenty-nine-day lunar months) or day 15 (in thirty-day lunar months). The surface then goes dark section by section over the next fifteen days, completing the month. All of this is presented in tortured and obscure syntax, and what begins as a detailed description of the process cuts off abruptly after describing only the first day (73:4-8). What then follows is a mutilated account of lunar positions on the horizon at the times of moonrising and setting (74:1-9).

The Calendar (74:10–75:3)

The author compares calendars, demonstrating the trouble lunarists can get into if they try to synchronize their calendar to a wrong solar version. Unadjusted, the lunar system will be thirty days behind a naked 360-day calendar in five years (74:10-11), but thirty days behind the 364-day calendar after only three years (and fifty days after five years; eighty days after eight years) (vv. 13-16). The point of these seemingly trivial calculations becomes clearer after the next paragraph, which informs us about certain angelic leaders with a special task:

> 75:1. And the leaders of the chiefs over thousands — which leaders are put in charge of the entire creation and of all the stars — have also to do with the four additional days. They are inseparable from their stations, corresponding to the computation of the year: they themselves render service on the four days which are not counted in the computation of the year. 2. Because of this people fall into error, for in truth those luminaries render service in these cosmic stations: one in the first gate of heaven, one in the third gate of heaven, one in the fourth gate, and one in the sixth gate, and so the year is completed precisely in 364 individual cosmic stations.

The first, third, fourth, and sixth gates (75:2) are those used by the sun in the third, sixth, ninth, and twelfth months (72:13-32), that is, the months when an extra day is added. Here we are told that these four days are "not counted in the computation of the year," and apparently the angels who "render service" on those special days are not common knowledge; hence someone using a lunar calendar might naively think the solar calendar has only 360 days and add an extra thirty-day month every five years instead of every three, and thus "fall into error." Neither will recourse to some kind of three-, five-, and eight-year cycle of intercalation save the lunarist from error when working with the Enochic calendar. The Greeks were using such a system (called an *octaeteris*) by at least the sixth century BC, but it works only when synchronizing the lunar year with a solar 365¼-day year.

This intriguing passage implies that true astronomical knowledge depends not only on empirical observation but on divine revelation. The cultic calendar was the province of those who knew about the "leaders of the chiefs over thousands" and the exact handling of the four extra days. The author may be worried here about foreign solar calendars (Egyptian, Persian, and Babylonian) and foreign methods of intercalation (the Greek *octaeteris*), which could foul up attempts to synchronize the lunar and solar cycles. Because certain details of the Enochic year were secrets, amateurs might easily become confused.

Another piece of carefully guarded esoteria must have been the method of adjusting the 364-day system to fit the true solar year of 365¼ days. The Qumran sect used the 364-day calendar for two centuries, so some system of intercalation surely existed, but either this information is among the sections of the AB lost to us or the priests were reluctant to commit this secret to writing.

The Portals of the Heavens (75:4–76:14)

Uriel briefly describes the numerous sets of gates and portals in the dome of heaven. Some are used by the various luminaries, some are heat ducts, and some are weather ports (75:4-7).

Chapter 76 details the twelve gates encircling the horizon through which the winds blow. Winds coming from the cardinal points of the compass are beneficial, but those coming through the remaining eight — toward the corners — bring devastation, locusts, and foul weather. Again, the picture is so artificial and schematic that the author of the AB cannot possibly be representing this as accurate meteorology. Readers may be intended to search for eschatological or allegorical significance, as perhaps did the author of Revelation, who speaks of "angels at the four corners of the earth, holding back the four winds of the earth so that no wind could blow on earth or sea. . . . angels who had been given power to damage earth and sea" (Rev 7:1-2).

Geography (ch. 77)

We learn about the four quarters of the earth through Hebrew/Aramaic puns on the names of the four directions. The earth is also divided into three sections, with only one assigned to humanity (v. 3), and Enoch also sees seven mountains, seven rivers, and seven islands (vv. 4-8). Again we have a mixture of the real and the schematic, reminding us of the mystical geography in Enoch's BW travels.

More Solar and Lunar Data; The Lunar Year (chs. 78:1-16 [79:3-5]; 78:17)

The DSS indicate that *Enoch* 79:3-5 originally preceded 78:17 (Milik 1976: 294), but it is also obvious that 79:3-5 is the second half of a description of the lunar year, while 78:15-16 is the first half. Thus, the text must originally have been arranged as suggested here.

Enoch 78:1-2 lists the various names of the sun and moon, rather corrupt in the Ethiopic but mostly recognizable as transliterations of Hebrew words for these luminaries in the OT. Vv. 3-9 essentially repeat material already found in chs. 72–74, an indication that the AB may have been conflated from two earlier astronomy texts containing some overlapping data. An account of the filling and emptying of the lunar disc with light and the peculiar appearance of the moon in the daytime sky (78:10-14, 17) is interrupted by a sketch of the full lunar year (78:15-16; 79:3-5), important evidence that the author of the AB had no quarrel with the lunar system per se.

The Seasons and the Stars (79:1-2 [82:7-20]; 79:6–80:1)

Enoch pauses and tells his son Methuselah, the recipient of all this heady material, more about his impressive source of information:

> 79:1. Now, my son, I am showing you everything, and the calculation of all the stars in the heavens will be completed. 2. He showed me all of their calculations for each day, each period of exercising dominion, each year, and the procession of every one according to its regulations, for each month and each week. (82): 7. And their account is accurate and their recorded computations precise, for Uriel (whom the Lord of the whole created world gave instructions on my behalf concerning the hosts of heaven) has breathed on me and revealed to me the luminaries, the new moons, the feasts, the years, and the days. 8. He has authority in heaven over night and day, in order to make the light shine on humankind — the sun, moon, stars, and all the powers of heaven which go around in their circuits.

Enoch's angelic guide is not a detached observer but actually is entrusted with power to maintain the systems he is describing. This adds weight to Uriel's claims about the stability of the cosmos in the AB's superscription (72:1).

The data on the stars and feasts promised here are not delivered in the Ethiopic AB, but a DSS fragment preserves part of the lost description of the stars (Milik 1976: 296-97). It is likely that in the missing section the movements of the stars were synchronized with the sun.

Enoch goes on to detail the angels who govern the days, months, and seasons of the year, with the agricultural characteristics of each season, although after spring and summer the text quits (82:9-20). The same Qumran fragment just mentioned also appears to contain some of the lost account of winter.

> 79:6. Such is the appearance and diagram of all the luminaries, shown to me by the great angel Uriel, who is their leader. 80:1. So in those days, the angel Uriel addressed me and said, "You see, I have shown you every-

thing, Enoch. I have revealed to you everything so that you might see the sun and the moon, and the leaders of the stars of heaven, as well as all those who turn them, their tasks, their seasons, and their processions."

The portrait of creation draws to a close. The cosmos has been presented as obedient and harmonious, but Uriel is not finished, and he now turns Enoch's attention to another sphere.

The Tablets of Heaven (81:1-4)

81:1. Then he said to me, "Enoch, look at the tablets of heaven; read what is written upon them, and note every individual item." 2. So I looked at the tablets of heaven, reading everything written there. And I understood everything. I read the book of all the deeds of humanity, all the children of flesh upon the earth throughout the generations of the world. 3. Immediately I blessed the Great Lord, the King of Glory forever; for he has fashioned all the works of the world. I exalted the Lord because of his forbearance, and wept on the earth because of the children of Adam. 4. Afterward I spoke: "Blessed is everyone who dies righteous and good, against whom a record book of iniquity will neither be written nor be found on the Day of Judgment."

Scholars commonly dismiss chs. 81 and 80:2-8 as later additions to the original AB, primarily because these passages carry an ethical emphasis foreign to the "scientific" atmosphere of the rest of the AB. But humans, too, are part of the created world and therefore a logical inclusion in Uriel's survey, while the contrast between orderly nature (i.e., the AB so far) and disobedient humanity is a fundamental and indispensable Enochic theme, featured in every one of the other booklets (chs. 2–5; 41; 60; 83:10–84:6; 100:10–101:9); it should hardly be surprising, then, to find morality brought up when people enter the picture. Without these chapters it is doubtful whether there would have been an Enochic Astronomy *Book* as opposed to a loose collection of pseudo-scientific documents in Enoch's name.

Enoch's Instructions and Prophecies (chs. 81:5–82:6; 80:2-8)

81:5. Then the seven holy ones brought me and placed me upon the earth before the door of my own house. And they said to me, "Tell your son Methuselah everything, and make all your children see that no flesh is righteous in the sight of the Lord, for he is their Creator. 6. We will leave you with your son for one year, until once again you have given them your last instructions, so that you may teach your children, write it down for them, and bear witness to all of them. In the second year, you will be taken from all of them.

7. "Be strong of heart! For the good will proclaim righteousness to the good, the righteous will rejoice with the righteous, and they will exchange salutations among themselves. 8. But the sinner will die with the sinner, and the apostate will drown with the apostate. 9. Those who do what is right will also die, thanks to the actions of humanity, and be gathered in, because of the deeds of the wicked."

10. And so in those days they finished their conversation with me; and I came then to my people, blessing the Lord of the world.

The author is writing up this scene as the real conclusion to the tour which began in the latter part of the BW (chs. 20–36). The "seven holy ones" are the angelic guides of ch. 20. The "one year" Enoch will be left to instruct his family must be his 365th (Gen 5:23), and this means Enoch is currently 364. Perhaps this is an attempt to provide some kind of harmony between the two solar numbers associated with Enoch (VanderKam 1995: 19).

The grim remark that "no flesh is righteous in the sight of the Lord, for he is their Creator" (81:5) seems to clash with the free will and moral choice presupposed elsewhere in *Enoch,* but it makes sense in the context of the AB, which argues that there are limits to unaided human inquiry into the cosmos, the parade example being the correct intercalation of the solar calendar (cf. 74:10–75:3). People fall into error because they ignore their creaturely limitations, their dependence on divine wisdom (cf. 80:7 below). In fact, the key phrase here could even be translated, "nothing fleshly is reliable."

82:1. "And now, my son Methuselah, I am recounting to you and writing down for you all of these things. I have shown you and given you written accounts of all these things. My son, preserve the writings from the hand of your father, so that you may pass them on to the generations of the world. 2. I have given wisdom to you and to your children, and to your children yet to be, that they may in turn pass this wisdom on to their children for generations — and to all those who have wisdom. All who are wise will sing praises, and wisdom will rest with their thoughts. 3. They will not sleep but understand, and they will listen with their ears that they may master this wisdom; those who feed on it will find it more satisfying than rich food.

4. "Blessed are all of the righteous! Blessed are all who walk in the path of righteousness and commit no fault, as do the sinners, in their tabulation of their days as the sun traverses the sky. It comes in and goes out through the portals for thirty days, along with the chiefs of thousands (of the orders of the stars), together with the four additional ones which separate the four seasons of the year — who lead them and come in with them for the four days. 5. In respect to these there are some who go wrong by not counting them in the complete reckoning of the year. Such people are mistaken, not reckoning them correctly, 6. for they belong in the calculation of the year, and they are truly recorded forever: one in the first gate, one in the third, one in the fourth, and one in the sixth. So the year is completed in 364 days.

(80):2. "In the days of the sinners the years will be cut short, their seed will go late to their lands and fields, and everything on the earth will be turned back and not appear in its times; the rain will be held back, and the heavens will stand still, (5b.) and famine will reach the extremities of the Great Chariot in the West. 3. In those times the fruits of the earth will be late, and will not grow in their season. Indeed, the fruits of the trees will be withheld in their season.

4. "The moon will alter its order and not be seen at its proper times, 5a. and in those days it will be seen in the sky 5c. shining too brightly for the proper order of light.

6. "Many of the chiefs of the stars will stray from what is prescribed, and these will alter their courses and functions, not appearing at the seasons prescribed for them. 7. The whole order of the stars will be closed off to sinners, and the thoughts of those on earth will fall into error concerning them; they will turn from their ways, fall into error, and take them to be gods.

8. "Evil will be multiplied upon them, and punishment will come upon them so to destroy them all."

Readers of the AB are implicitly offered in 82:1-3 a stream of tradition in which to find themselves. The Enochic tradition boasts a wisdom which embraces true righteousness and a reliable calendar. The author feels no instinct to differentiate between the two; indeed, calendrical error is tied to sin here in 82:4-6 (especially v. 4), forging a crucial link between the science of the main body of the AB and the moral urgency of chs. 80–81.

The passage 80:2-8 immediately precedes ch. 81 in the Ethiopic AB, but it is clearly out of place there. It probably belongs *after* the whole section 81:1–82:6 since Enoch would not know that people in the future would mistake stars for gods (80:7) if he had not first read the tablets of human destiny (81:1-2), and the remarks of 80:2 follow naturally on those in 82:5-6.

The agricultural and uranological chaos described in 80:2-5 indicates not a breakdown of the natural order but the illusion thereof, the disastrous results of blindly following the wrong calendar! Enoch has already assured us that the cosmos is in good hands (82:7-8) and will endure until the new creation dawns (72:1). The ironic intent of this passage is apparent when we note that all its examples of cosmic catastrophe involve *timing* ; there is no real blood and thunder in this "apocalyptic" meltdown. It is precisely because the true order of the stars is "closed off to the sinners" (v. 7) that they fall prey to bad calendars and misjudge the planting seasons, resulting in the panicky misperceptions satirized here.

The final verse of the passage (80:8) ties us firmly back into a classic Enochic context, whether or not this constitutes the actual close of the AB. The language of universal judgment is reminiscent of the flood, a motif otherwise missing from the book.

The Dream Visions (Enoch 83–90)

Introduction

The fourth *Enoch* booklet consists of two visions Enoch received early in life, before his marriage (age 65, according to Gen 5:21) and before his career as heavenly scribe (he is still learning letters; 83:2). The first vision is a brief glimpse of the violent collapse of the world. The second, which accounts for 88 percent of the DV, is a lengthy allegory, often called the "Animal Apocalypse" (*An. Apoc.*), in which historical events from the creation of Adam to the advent of the kingdom of God are acted out by animals. The *An. Apoc.* can be outlined in various ways, but the simplest organization is temporal: a three-part division of history into past, present, and future ages (Tiller 1993: 15-18).

First Dream Vision: Universal Cataclysm	83:1–85:1
Second Dream Vision: The Animal Apocalypse	85:2–90:42
The Past Age: Adam to the Flood	85:2–89:8
The Present Age: Noah to the Final Judgment	89:9–90:27
The Future Age: The Messianic Kingdom	90:28-42

The *An. Apoc.* can be precisely dated to the opening years of the Maccabean revolt (165-160 BC; see the notes on 90:9-12 below). It has much in common with the "Apocalypse of Weeks" in the fifth Enochic booklet (see 93:1-10; 91:11-17 below), which predates the *An. Apoc.* by less than a decade. These secondcentury writings evidence a group self-consciousness for the first time in *Enoch:* the Enochians are now alienated from the official Jerusalem cult and are distinct from other Jewish groups (cf. above, Introduction: Dates and Provenance, 906). Naturally enough, some Enochic authors were moved to reflect on how this fragmented state of affairs came to be. On this subject the *An. Apoc.* and the Apocalypse of Weeks are remarkable for their substantial agreement with each other, and they allow us to see an Enochic philosophy of history for the first time.

In true Enochic fashion, the *An. Apoc.* makes creative use of the traditional twin motifs of Enoch's wisdom and the fallen angels. Regarding the former, we already knew from the older booklets that Enoch had been given knowledge of human destinies (chs. 22, 27, 81), but there were few details beyond descriptions of the Last Judgment, and no account was given of the phenomenon of Israel. The *An. Apoc.* fills this gap as Enoch becomes a privileged witness to the full tapestry of human history, using as main sources the historical material in the OT and the BW. As for the fallen angel theme, the DV (like the later PE) adds a political dimension to Enochic angelology in order to explain what is going on behind the screen of earthly events. The *An. Apoc.* introduces a group of seventy wicked shepherd-angels who are assigned governance of Israel as punishment for her sins from the time of the Babylonian conquest until God's intervention, a period neatly divided into seventy "hours" (89:59–90:19). Whether these seventy are parolees from the original two hundred Watchers or a different angelic caste is not clear, but they enable the author to offer a new interpretation of Israel's sad postexilic experience: disastrous international military and political events are really steered by human surrogates for these seventy shepherds (89:59–90:19) rather than by God directly, thus accounting for excessive Jewish suffering during these centuries. These angels also serve as a warning to the author's contemporaries: apostate Jews ("blinded sheep") will share the same fate as the Watchers and these wicked shepherds (90:24-27), a clear tie-in with the eschatology of the BW (10:6, 13).

The *An. Apoc.* gives us valuable insights into Enochic theology as articulated by a representative of that tradition during the turbulent Maccabean period. The author rejects the sacrifices at the rebuilt temple after the exile as "polluted and impure" (89:73), and Ezra's reforms are entirely ignored. There is hardly any interest in the Mosaic law received at Sinai, although the figure of Moses himself is clearly revered as leader of the exodus (89:15-38). Such views represent very different emphases from those to which we are accustomed in conventional reconstructions of early Judaism. The *An. Apoc.* reveals a dissident tradition claiming that mainstream Israelite religion has not been properly on track since before the exile. The author has often been connected with the Hasidim ("pious ones"), a reform-minded group which already existed at the outbreak of the revolt and which lent support to the Maccabees. It is possible that the author of the *An. Apoc.* was one of the Hasidim, but we know too little about this group to be sure.

Notwithstanding serious criticisms of official Judaism, this Enochic writer was a patriot who supported the Maccabees during the war of independence against Greek tyranny, and it is here that the single most remarkable feature of the *An. Apoc.* emerges: writing in the first years of the uprising, the author yet believed that the separation of the human race into Jew and Gentile was a *negative* thing which the Messiah would eventually abolish (see notes on 90:37-39 below). The Jewish author of the *An. Apoc.* envisioned a messianic kingdom where there would be only one human family, and he committed this lofty hope to writing at a time when hatred for Gentiles surely could not have been easier.

First Dream Vision: Universal Cataclysm (83:1–85:1)

> 83:1. My son Methuselah, I will now show you all of the visions which I have seen by narrating them in your presence. 2. I saw two visions before I took a wife, and the one bore no resemblance to the other. The first was while I was still learning how to write, and the second also was before I took your mother as wife.
>
> First, I saw a terrible vision, and I made supplication to the Lord concerning it. 3. I was lying down in the house of my grandfather Mahalalel, and in a vision I saw the heavens flung down, wrested loose and collapsing onto the earth! 4. And when they fell to the earth, I saw the earth swallowed up in a deep abyss, with mountains suspended over mountains, and hills sinking down upon hills. Lofty trees were ripped up by their roots and cast down, sinking also into the abyss! 5. At this, a word fell into my mouth, and I took it up, crying, "The earth is destroyed!"

Enoch tells his grandfather what he has seen (83:6-7a), and Mahalalel interprets the nightmare as a prophecy: "You have dreamed a powerful vision: the sins of the whole world. It is about to collapse into the abyss in utter destruction" (v. 7b). He suggests that Enoch, since he is "a faithful man," implore God for the survival of a remnant of humanity through the coming catastrophe (83:8-10).

In context, this vision must be describing the Genesis flood, but, curiously enough, it does not mention a drop of water! Once again an Enochic author is using literary tricks to conflate the first and last universal judgments in the readers' minds (cf. chs. 10–11 in the BW; chs. 53:1–56:4 in the PE).

After this unnerving revelation, Enoch goes out under the aerodome of the pre-dawn sky and is relieved to see the luminaries yet moving in orderly fashion along their set courses (83:11). The description is reminiscent of the AB. He then offers up blessings and intercessions (ch. 84) modeled on the prayer of the four archangels in chs. 9–10 of the BW. God's sovereignty is acknowledged (84:2-3), and Enoch then admits that "the angels of your heavens are doing wrong, and your wrath is directed against human flesh until the Great Day of Judgment" (v. 4), a succinct summary of the first half of the BW. Enoch begs God to spare a righteous remnant as a "plant of the eternal seed" (vv. 5-6; cf. 10:16).

Brief as it is, the author of this first dream vision provides the DV with unmistakable echoes of major themes from the older *Enoch* booklets, including the contrast between orderly nature and rebellious angels and humans. The punishment Enoch foresees fits the crime: perverse, disordered souls inherit a creation allowed to return to its original chaos.

Second Dream Vision: The Animal Apocalypse (85:2–90:42)

(1) *The Past Age: Adam to the Flood (85:2–89:8)*

Enoch announces a second dream vision to Methuselah, which he likewise saw in his youth (85:2-3):

> 85:3. Before I married Edna your mother, I saw a vision while lying on my bed. And behold a bull emerged out of the earth, and that bull was white. Next there emerged a heifer, and along with her came two bull-calves, one of which was black and the other red. 4. The black bull-calf struck down the red one: it pursued it across the land. From then on I could not see the red calf. 5. But the black calf grew up, and a heifer accompanied it. I saw that many cattle issued from it which all resembled and followed after it. 6. Then that female cow — the first one — left that first bull and began searching for that red calf, but she could not find it. She lamented greatly over it and continued her search. 7. I watched until that first bull came to her and calmed her, and from then on she stopped crying. 8. Later she bore another white bull, and after him many black bulls and cows. 9. I watched that white bull in my sleep, and it likewise grew up and became a great white bull, and from it issued many white bulls which resembled it. 10. These also began to sire numerous white bulls which in turn resembled them, one after the other.
>
> 86:1. Again, while looking upward in my sleep with my eyes, I saw heaven above me, and behold a particular star fell from heaven down into the midst of those large cattle, where it began eating and grazing among them. 2. After that I noticed that the large and the black cattle began to make changes in their pastures, their stables, and their calves; and they began to attack one another. 3. Once again looking up to heaven in my vision, behold I saw many stars descending, casting themselves down from the heavens to that first star. They turned into bulls among those calves, and they were grazing with them in their midst. 4. As I watched,

> behold they all let out their private parts like horses and began to mount the heifers of the bulls. All the heifers then became pregnant and bore elephants, camels, and donkeys. 5. All of the cattle were afraid and terrified of them; they began to bite with their teeth and to devour and to gore with their horns. 6. Furthermore, they started to eat the cattle! And behold all of the children of the earth began trembling and shaking in their presence, and they were fleeing. 87:1. Again, I saw how they began to gore and devour each other until the entire earth began to cry aloud.
>
> 2. Then I turned my gaze once again to heaven, and in my vision behold I saw descending from heaven beings who were like white men: a group of four came out and three others with them. 3. Those three who had emerged last seized me by the hand and took me up away from the children of the earth, and they lifted me up to a lofty place. They showed me a tower high above the earth: all the hills were lower. 4. Then they told me, "Remain here until you witness everything that is to happen to those elephants, camels, and donkeys, and to those stars, and to the cattle — all of them."
>
> 88:1. Then I looked at one of those four who had emerged first, and he seized that first star that had fallen from heaven. He bound him hand and foot and hurled him into an abyss — an abyss narrow and deep, desolate and dark.
>
> 2. Another one drew a sword and gave it to the elephants, camels, and donkeys. These proceeded to attack each other, and because of them the whole earth trembled.
>
> 3. I looked as my vision continued, and behold one of those four who had emerged came down from the sky and gathered up and took away the many stars whose private parts were like those of horses, and he bound them all hand and foot, and he hurled them into a chasm of the earth.
>
> 89:1. Then one of those four went to one of the white bulls and taught it a mystery without him trembling. Though born a bull, he became a man. And he built for himself a ship, and he stayed on board along with three other bulls who also entered the ship. And the ship was closed up and provided them cover.

We recognize without difficulty the Genesis account from Adam to Noah, with the BW tale of the fallen Watchers reproduced in its correct chronological setting. There are notable differences here between the *An. Apoc.* and Genesis. Most glaringly, the sin of Adam and Eve is ignored. The Enochians were certainly aware of Genesis 3 (cf. *Enoch* 32:5-6), but in their view the fall of the angels in Gen 6:1-4 had far greater universal impact. There are also extrabiblical traditions included, such as Eve's mourning for Abel (85:6) and the glorification of Seth (85:9), which can be paralleled in folklore preserved elsewhere in noncanonical Jewish and gnostic literature (Klijn 1978: 147-59).

Certain liberties have also been taken with the BW materials. Asael's descent and corruption of humanity is narrated separately and placed prior to the descent of the other Watchers, and Shemihazah's leadership has been ignored entirely (ch. 86). Thus the tendency to focus on Asael/Azazel's central role in corrupting the earth, a trend already visible in the BW itself (e.g., 8:1-2; 10:8), continues to gain momentum in this later booklet. The order of the four archangels' missions as found in *Enoch* 10 has also been rearranged so as to put Sariel's contact with Noah into a more logical position just before the flood narrative begins (89:1). Noah is transformed into angelic status (i.e., becomes a man, in the allegory's code). Noah's supernatural qualities will figure also in the first Appendix to the *Enoch* corpus (chs. 106–7), although there he is *born* as an angelic figure. The author of the *An. Apoc.* feels free to reinterpret as well as pass on his inherited traditions.

The symbolism of the dramatis personae of the *An. Apoc.* which we find here will remain consistent throughout the allegory: people are always animals, the Watchers are stars (cf. *Enoch* 21), and angels are men. The offspring of the Watchers are "elephants, camels, and donkeys" (86:4). Not only is this clever use of allegory since these animals would indeed be monsters if born from cattle, but the words themselves in Aramaic are puns and anagrams for the "Nephilim," "Giants," and "Elioud" of *Enoch* 7:2 (Milik 1976: 240). The author also makes some use of color symbolism, but this is minimal and of an obvious sort: the line of promise is that of white bulls (Adam to Seth to Noah), while wicked Cain is a black bull and the martyred Abel is red.

The flood narrative immediately follows (89:2-8), and from this point on the *An. Apoc.* sticks much closer to its biblical sources. Noah, like Adam, has three sons, one of which (Shem) is white like himself (v. 9), so it appears that Enoch's prayer after his first dream vision for the survival of a righteous remnant has been answered, and we move into the postdiluvian era, what the author would consider the present age.

(2) *The Present Age: Noah to the Final Judgment (89:9–90:27)*

Except for the freak offspring of the Watchers (stars) and their wives (heifers), humanity has been represented up to this point by cattle, with the line of promise indicated by color. Now, after the flood, a variety of animal species are born to Noah's sons:

> 89:10. They began to engender all the the beasts of the fields, and birds, and from them arose every kind of species: lions, tigers, wolves, dogs, hyenas, wild boars, foxes, rock badgers, swine, falcons, vultures, kites, eagles, and ravens. And among these there was born a white bull.

Most of these animals will reappear in the course of the narrative as symbols of various enemies of Israel (e.g., the wolves are the Egyptians, the dogs are the Philistines, etc.). The white bull who is born among them is Abraham, now not only the representative of God's chosen line but an entirely separate species from his neighbors.

As the allegory continues, Abraham sires both a white bull-calf (Isaac) and a wild donkey (Ishmael; cf. Gen 16:11-12), but Isaac turns out to be the last bull. He sires a black boar (Esau) and a white *sheep* (Jacob), who in turn engenders twelve white sheep, and so a new set of symbols is introduced (89:11-12). Throughout the remainder of the narrative, until the future age predicted by the author, Israel is symbolized as a flock of sheep harassed by wild animals.

The shift from bulls to sheep cannot be explained as the author's way of distinguishing Jews from Gentiles, because Abraham and Isaac have already been pictured as white bulls among the wild beasts. Moreover, the fact that a messianic white bull appears again near the end of the allegory (90:37) proves that the bovine species has not been dropped but rather suspended. Most likely the allegorist is thinking of the mysterious change in identity from Jacob to Israel (Gen 32:26-28; 35:10). Perhaps the author is suggesting that the Messiah to be born in the future, and not (or not merely?) the earthly son of Isaac, is in fact the "true" Jacob, the next white bull (see comments on ch. 71 above).

A long passage follows which summarizes the biblical narrative from Joseph's Egyptian sojourn to the Babylonian conquest (89:13-59), using transparent animal symbolism throughout. There are several points of interest. The giving of the law at Sinai scarcely appears (89:29), suggesting that the Mosaic Torah was not a central concern for the author of the *An. Apoc.* The entire period of the Judges is covered in a single verse (89:41). The attitude of the author toward Solomon's Temple is positive:

> 89:50. Then that house [Jerusalem] grew large and spacious — built for those sheep. A great and lofty tower [the temple] was erected upon that house for the Lord of the sheep. The house was not high, but the tower was elevated and lofty. The Lord of the sheep stood upon that tower, and they spread before him a full table.

The sheep immediately begin to go astray, killing the prophets sent to them by God (v. 51). The translation of Elijah is mentioned, and he is brought up to stay with Enoch (v. 52). The author moves from this to the Assyrian and Babylonian conquests (which are not here distinguished) in just two verses, ignoring Josiah's and Hezekiah's reforms. The passage ends with the Lord of the sheep handing over the flock and their house and tower to the lions and other wild beasts (89:54-58).

At this point the author sets forth a bold new interpretation of exilic and postexilic history: the Lord of the sheep summons "seventy shepherds" and turns the care of the sheep over to them. They are to shepherd the flock, one at a time, for a single "hour" each. Besides tending the sheep, they are to kill a specific number of them as punishment, but God knows in advance that these shepherds will destroy far in excess of their commission, and he appoints an unnamed angelic auditor to keep track of the shepherds' depredations, without their knowledge, instructing him to record everything carefully but without interference (89:59-64).

These shepherds may be an adaptation of the traditional seventy guardian angels of each of the seventy Gentile nations (cf. the "table of nations" in Genesis 10, which totals seventy, and Dan 10:13, 21-22, which implies that each nation has its angel); but if so, this spatial image has been freely turned into a temporal one, probably inspired by Jeremiah's division of the exile into seventy periods (Jer 25:11). Periodization of history based on jubilees (forty-nine years), or sevens and seventies is a common feature in intertestamental literature (Tiller 1993: 56-57).

The author of the *An. Apoc.* thinks in terms of four empires ruling Palestine from the time of the exile: Babylonian, Persian, Greek Ptolemaic, and Greek Seleucid. The periods of the seventy shepherd-angels are likewise divided into four segments of twelve, twenty-three, twenty-three, and twelve "hours" (89:65–90:12). If one "hour" equals seven years, the numbers actually do come out about right for these four empires in real history, but only if one assumes "hours" of three-and-a-half years for the last period, a temporal device used by the DV author's apocalyptic contemporary, the final redactor of Daniel (Dan 12:7).

An important event occurring during the second (Persian) period is the rebuilding of the house and tower (89:72-73), but in the author's view, all of the bread laid upon the altar of this tower (= temple) is "polluted and impure" (v. 73), a critical indicator that the second-century Enochians found the Second Temple deficient even from its beginnings, although the reasons why are not stated.

The beginning of the fourth period brings us to the real author's own day and the early stages of the Maccabean revolt:

> 90:6. But behold the white sheep gave birth to lambs! And these began to open their eyes, and to see, and to cry out to the sheep. 7. But even though they cried out to them, the sheep did not listen to their words. No, they were deaf in the extreme, and their eyes were extraordinarily and severely blind. 8. Then in my vision I saw how the ravens [Seleucid Greeks] swooped down on those lambs, and they seized one of them [Onias III?; cf. 2 Macc 4:33-36]. They dashed the sheep to pieces and devoured them. 9. And as I continued to look on, horns grew upon those lambs; but the ravens crushed their horns. I watched until a large horn sprouted on one of the sheep [Judas Maccabee], and this opened their eyes. 10. They had vision — their sight had returned. That sheep cried out to the flock, and the rams saw it and all rallied to it. 11. In spite of all this, those eagles, vultures, ravens, and kites continued to tear at the sheep, swooping upon them and devouring them. The sheep kept silent, but the rams protested and cried aloud. 12. Then the ravens battled and contended with that sheep. They wanted to eliminate its horn, but they did not prevail against it.

This passage dates the allegory: Judas's ascendancy to leadership of the revolt is described (165 BC), but not his death (160 BC; note that the ravens "did not prevail" against him). The younger generation of reformers mentioned here (the lambs who try to rouse the blinded sheep [v. 6]) is probably the group with which the author most identified, and they may be the Hasidim mentioned in 1 and 2 Maccabees (Tiller 1993: 109-15). If the seventy weeks-of-years scheme conforms to real history, as suggested above, with foreshortened weeks in the last period, and if the date of the *An. Apoc.* is 160, then the author sees himself as writing at the onset of the seventieth week, and we pass after these verses from *vaticinia ex eventu* into genuine prophecy.

The next verses describe in two parallel passages the final assault on the sheep by the predatory birds. Comparing the "doublets," it seems likely that the original allegory (90:16-18) was updated shortly after its composition (vv. 13-15) to include late-breaking developments in the Maccabean conflict: the unexpected victories at Beth-zur (early 164) and at Carnaim (mid-163), during which battles visions of an angel and of God himself were reported (2 Macc 11:6-12; 12:20-23) (Tiller 1993: 63-79). Like the author of the Qumran *War Scroll,* this author expected God and his angels to personally join the fray at the last battle and finally turn the tide against the Gentile aggressors. Here God indeed appears and routs the enemies (90:15, 18), and he gives a special sword to the sheep so that they may assist in the defeat (90:19). The way is now prepared for the Last Judgment:

> 90:20. Then, as I watched, a throne was erected in the pleasant land, and the Lord of the sheep seated himself upon it, and he received all of the sealed books. And they were opened in the presence of the Lord of the sheep. 21. Then the Lord summoned those men — the first seven white ones — and commanded them to bring those stars before him, beginning with the first one who had preceded the stars whose private parts were like those of horses. And they brought them all before him. 22. Then, speaking to that man who had been writing in his presence (who was himself one of those seven white ones), he said, "Seize those seventy shepherds, to whom I delivered the sheep, and who, having received custody of them, killed far more than they were commanded." 23. And behold I saw all of them bound, and they all stood before him.
>
> 24. Judgment was first held over the stars, and they were judged and found guilty. Off they went to the place of damnation, and they were cast into an abyss full of blazing flames and fiery pillars. 25. Then those seventy shepherds were judged and found guilty, and they too were cast into that abyss of fire. 26. And I saw at that time that a similar abyss, full of fire, was opened up in the middle of the land. Then were brought those blinded sheep, and they were all judged and found guilty, and they were cast into this fiery abyss and were burned up. (This abyss was located south of that house.) 27. I saw those sheep burning; even their bones were burning.

Many scholars have suspected influence from this scene on the parable of the sheep and goats in Matthew 25. Enoch here actually sees in a vision the judgment described to him as a future event in the BW (*Enoch* 27). The *An. Apoc.* now passes to the age to come.

(3) *The Future Age: The Messianic Kingdom* (90:28-42)

> 90:28. Then I stood up to watch as he folded up that old house! All the columns were removed, and all the beams and ornaments of that house were folded up along with it. It was taken out and deposited in a certain place in the southern part of the land. 29. I watched until the Lord of the sheep brought out a new house, greater and loftier than that first one, and he set it up on the site of the former one which had been folded up. All its columns were new, its beams new, and its ornaments new and larger than those of the first, the old one which had been removed. And all of the sheep were within it! 30. I saw all the sheep which were left, and all the beasts of the earth and all the birds of heaven were prostrating and bowing down before those sheep, making petition to them, and obedient to them in everything.
>
> 31. After this, those three who were clothed in white (the ones who had brought me up earlier) seized me by the hand — and also the hand of that ram, who was holding on to me — and they lifted me up and set me down in the midst of those sheep who were free of condemnation. 32. All of those sheep were white, with their wool thick and pure. 33. And all who had been destroyed and dispersed, along with all the beasts of the field and all the birds of heaven, gathered together in that house, and the Lord of the sheep rejoiced with great joy because they had all become good, and they had returned to his house. 34. As I continued watching, they laid down the sword which had been given to the sheep. They returned it to his house and sealed it up in the presence of the Lord. All of the sheep enclosed themselves within that house, but it was not able to contain them all. 35. And the eyes of all of them were open, and they saw clearly; there was not one among them that did not see. 36. I observed that the house had become large and spacious, and it was very much full.
>
> 37. Then I saw that a certain white bull was born, and it had large horns. All the beasts of the field and all the birds of heaven feared it and made continual petition before it. 38. As I watched, all of their species were transformed: they all became white bulls! The first one became a *nagar* among them, and that *nagar* in turn became a great beast with large black horns upon its head! The Lord of the sheep rejoiced over these and over all of the cattle. 39. And as for me, I fell asleep among them, and I awoke. And I witnessed everything.

A great many of the details found here will eventually make their way into Christian eschatology. God himself builds the new Jerusalem (house) to replace the old (cf. Heb 11:10), and there is no temple (tower) in the new city (cf. Rev 21:22). We learn that Enoch and Elijah return to the city during these end times (v. 31), a tradition that will live on in Christian expectation beginning already with the "two witnesses" of Rev 11:3-12, which have been consistently interpreted by Christian writers as Elijah and *Enoch* (not Moses) since earliest times (Black 1978: 227-37). Other notable features of the scene include the resurrection of the dead and the conversion of the Gentiles (v. 33).

Remarkably, *after* these events a white bull is born, often interpreted as a Messiah figure. He is perhaps to be seen in continuity with the unbroken string of white bulls from Adam to Isaac, the real heir to this original line (cf. comments on 89:10-12 above). His only task is somehow to act as a catalyst whereby all animals become white bulls, thus eliminating not only sinful or secondary status among Jews (no black or red bulls in sight), but even the distinction between Jew and Gentile (the sheep/wild animal phase of the allegory is finished). With the elimination both of national distinctions and of evil in general, humanity returns to Eden.

At this point the text is corrupt. "The first one" (apparently the white bull) becomes a *nagar* ("word," "thing") and then a great beast of some kind. Many solutions to this textual absurdity have been proposed, most of them suggesting an animal of which *nagar* is a mistranslation, going back through the Greek to the Aramaic. "Wild ox" and "lamb" are among the more plausible suggestions. If "lamb" is right, the Messiah may be understood as an idealized human figure who nevertheless sprang from Jewish stock before his exaltation as a beast above all other animals (Lindars 1976), but the interpretation must be tentative.

The DV concludes with Enoch waking from sleep and blessing the Lord of righteousness, but later he weeps for all the sorrows of history which — from his antediluvian viewpoint — are still to come (90:40-42).

The Admonitions of Enoch (Enoch 91–105)

Introduction

The last section of *Enoch* has gone by a variety of names. Currently the "Epistle of Enoch" is the most common, but it now seems unlikely that the whole book constitutes Enoch's "epistle," and one of the older titles, "Admonitions," more adequately suits the contents.

The AE suffers from severe textual confusion in its initial chapters, the result of two separate problems. First, the opening oracle, known as the "Methuselah Apocalypse," was probably intended to serve originally as a conclusion either to the DV or to the AB. If the latter, it was artificially separated from the AB when the later DV was inserted between the third and fifth booklets. Second, sometime during the long transmissional history of the text it seems likely that a page with *Enoch* 92:3–93:10 on the front and 91:11–92:2 on the back was flipped over, radically disordering this section. (The chapter and verse numerations of *Enoch* are modern.) With the help of DSS fragments, the original sequence can be recovered with a fair degree of confidence (Olson 1993).

The Methuselah Apocalypse	91:1-10; 92:3-5
The Apocalypse of Weeks	93:1-10; 91:11-19
Enoch's Letter	92:1-2; 93:11–105:2

Each of the three pieces is presented as a farewell address by Enoch to his sons before his final ascent (cf. ch. 81 in the AB). The AE would certainly qualify as a *testament* — a popular literary genre during the intertestamental period — except that in a testament the patriarchal main character delivers his speeches from his deathbed, and Enoch never died!

The exact date of composition is unknown. The "Apocalypse of Weeks" (*Apoc. Wks.*) was probably written no later than about AD 170, but many scholars think that the rest of the AE is a later work which incorporated this apocalypse, although the arguments in favor of this view are not compelling (García Martínez 1992: 79-84). But even if we accept multiple authorship, the difference in years is not great since the Qumran fragments indicate a latest possible date for the AE not much past 100 BC.

The AE is in many ways a surprising inclusion in the *Book of Enoch.* The author of the main body of the AE ("Enoch's Letter") has nothing more to say about the fallen angels; in fact, this half of the tradition appears to be *discounted* to the extent that it distracts from human responsibility for evil (98:4). We also find here a different view of the afterlife. Despite a great emphasis on postmortem judgment, there are no references in the "Letter" either to a future earthly kingdom or to a bodily resurrection, and the future fates of human souls are spoken of in entirely spiritual terms (e.g., 103:4; 104:2). Finally, the author demonstrates an interest in socioeconomic issues far beyond anything found in the other booklets. The Enoch of the AE is an angry prophet in the style of an Amos or a Jeremiah.

Nevertheless, we should not exaggerate the idiosyncrasies. The *Apoc. Wks.* includes a (temporary) earthly reign for the elect (91:12-15), it mentions the condemnation of the Watchers (91:15), and in the original Aramaic version the phrases "earth will have rest" followed by "all generations forever" are found at the end of the description of the eternal kingdom of God (91:17), indicating some sort of physical aspect to the world to come — which may in turn imply a bodily resurrection. Even if it be allowed that the *Apoc. Wks.* comes from a different hand than the rest of the AE, the author/editor of the main booklet apparently saw no reason to edit this material out before incorporating the *Apoc. Wks.* into the finished work. Then, too, the "Letter" may be alluding to the Watchers when it condemns not only sinners but *those who associate* with sinners (97:4), echoing the Enochic teaching — found in all four of the other booklets — that human associates of the fallen angels share in their judgment (10:14; 67:4-13; 80:6-8; 90:24-26). Again, a verse like *Enoch* 96:8 is virtually a synopsis of chs. 7, 10–11 in the BW and would be suitable in that first booklet as a direct address to the giant offspring of the angels: "Woe to you, the powerful, who forcibly oppress the righteous; for the day of your destruction is coming, and the day of your destruction will be the beginning of many and good days for the righteous!" Like the giants of old, the wicked in the AE are guilty of eating blood (98:11; cf. 7:5), perhaps to be understood not merely as a purity violation but also as emblematic of economic exploitation. It may be argued that by the very act of writing a booklet in the name of Enoch the author has given a supernatural, angelic dimension to the social evils denounced in it. The AE author drops no heavy-handed hints linking the wicked with the rebel hosts (as in books 2 and 4) because such a connection can be taken for granted if the speaker is Enoch.

Other aspects of the AE make it clear that we are firmly within the Enochic tradition. Charles produces an impressive list of unique similarities between the AE and the BW, including phrases like "you will have no peace," "plant of righteousness," and railings against blasphemy and eating blood (Charles 1912: 219). In the AE, Enoch's prophetic knowledge and authority are still derived from his heavenly sojourns (93:2; cf. 1:2-3), he is supremely wise (92:1; 93:11-14), and possession and acceptance of the Enochic writings are seen as a hallmark of the righteous (104:1-6, 10-13). The AE is certainly more interested in the theme of Enoch's wisdom than in the fallen angel myth, but the same can be said of the AB.

The Methuselah Apocalypse (91:1-10; 92:3-5)

> 91:1. Now, my son Methuselah: call to me all of your brothers. Gather here before me all the children of your mother, for the word calls me, and the spirit has been poured out upon me, that I might reveal to you all that is to happen to you until eternity.

Methuselah obeys, and Enoch urges his children to stick to the path of truth and virtue despite the fact that iniquity is bound to increase, culminating in first one, and later another, universal judgment (91:3-7). Enochic typology again links the two. The flood allusion provides no details ("a great punishment will be executed upon the earth"), but the second judgment is described as a fiery destruction of every vestige of paganism, cutting off iniquity and deceit from their very roots (vv. 8-9). Beyond this lies the resurrection of the righteous and a life of sinlessness, grace, and goodness (91:10; 92:3-5). The original reading of these concluding verses is not clearly distinguishable among the textual variants of the Ethiopic manuscripts, and it is just possible that the passage also alludes to a resurrection of the "Righteous One," who in turn gives gifts of grace, power, and truth to each "righteous one."

The Apocalypse of Weeks (93:1-10; 91:11-19)

This much-discussed piece, like the *An. Apoc.* in the DV, consists of a panorama of world history, in this case divided into ten "weeks" and ending with the establishment of a "new heaven" in place of the "first heaven" which "will pass away" (cf. Rev 21:1). Significantly, the *Apoc. Wks.* shares the same dim view of postexilic Israelite religion as the *An. Apoc.*, evidence for common historical perspectives among Enochic authors.

The *Apoc. Wks.* is important as the first of many Jewish apocalypses to use the pseudonym of an ancient worthy in order to "prophesy" the future. It is also the first "historical review" type of apocalypse, presenting a schematized pattern of time periods all the way up to the consummation of God's kingdom. These devices effectively serve to encourage the faithful by demonstrating God's control of history and the assured outworking of his will in the end.

Enoch intends this revelation for all his children, not simply his biological descendants but "the chosen ones of the world," "those who have sprung up from the plant of truth and righteousness." His cites for his prophecy a threefold authority, having seen everything in a vision, having heard it from the holy angels, and having read it on the tablets of heaven (93:2). The *Apoc. Wks.* then begins:

> 93:3. And so, again, Enoch took up his parable and spoke: I, Enoch, was born the seventh in the FIRST WEEK, and until my time judgment was held back [i.e., upon the Watchers].
>
> 4. After me the SECOND WEEK will come, in which falsehood and violence will spring up. In it will be the First End, but in it a man will be saved [Noah]. After that has ended, iniquity will increase, but an orderly arrangement will be made for sinners [tower of Babel and division of nations].
>
> 5. After that, in the THIRD WEEK, and as it reaches its close, a man will be chosen as a plant of righteous judgment [Abraham]; and after him will come forth a plant of eternal righteousness [Israel].
>
> 6. After that, in the FOURTH WEEK, and as it reaches its close, visions of the holy ones and of the righteous ones will be seen, and a rule for all generations, and an enclosure, will be made for them [Sinai, the law, and the land of Israel].
>
> 7. After that, in the FIFTH WEEK, and as it reaches its close, the House of Glory and Dominion will be built forever [Solomon's temple].
>
> 8. After that, in the SIXTH WEEK, all who are living then will go blind; and the hearts of all of them will godlessly forget wisdom. In that week a man will ascend [Elijah]; and as it reaches its close, the House of Dominion will be burned with fire, and the entire race of the chosen root will be scattered [exile].
>
> 9. After that, in the SEVENTH WEEK, an apostate generation will arise. They will do a great many things — all of them apostate! 10. And as that week reaches its close, the chosen from the eternal plant of righteousness will be elected to serve as witnesses to righteousness, and sevenfold wisdom and knowledge will be given to them [probably the *Book of Enoch*]. (91):11. They will uproot the foundations of violence and the structure of deceit which is on it, and so execute judgment [the author's own time].
>
> 12. After that the EIGHTH WEEK will come: the week of righteousness in which all the righteous will be given a sword, so that they may execute a righteous judgment on all the wicked, who will be delivered into their hands. 13. And as that week reaches its close, they will gain riches righteously. And the royal temple of the Great One will be built in splendor, for all generations forever.
>
> 14. After that the NINTH WEEK will come, in which justice and true judgment will be revealed to all the children of the entire earth. All the workers of iniquity will wholly vanish from the entire earth; they will be cast into the Eternal Pit, and all men will look to the path of everlasting righteousness.
>
> 15. After that the TENTH WEEK will come, and in the seventh part of it the eternal judgment — indeed, the time of the Great Judgment — in which vengeance will be executed among the angels. 16. At that time the first heaven will pass away, and a new heaven will appear, and all of the powers of heaven will rise, shining for all eternity with sevenfold brightness. 17. After this there will be many weeks — endless and without number — forever. They will practice goodness and righ-

teousness in these, and sin will never again be mentioned.

The *Apoc. Wks.* boasts a well-crafted chiastic structure (VanderKam 1984a: 518-23): weeks one and ten refer respectively to the first and last judgments on the Watchers; weeks two and nine respectively to the first and last judgments on humanity as well as to the scattering and the unification of humanity; weeks three and eight to the eternal establishment of the righteous and their roles as instruments of judgment; weeks four and seven respectively to dual divine revelations — Mosaic and Enochic; and weeks five and six to the first temple, built and then destroyed (Barker 1987: 59).

This section concludes with Enoch urging his children again to walk in the paths of righteousness and shun the ways of iniquity (91:18-19), perhaps an editorial addition uniting this piece with the Methuselah Apocalypse, which also features this "two-ways" theme.

Enoch's Letter (92:1-2; 93:11–105:2)

(1) *Introduction* (92:1-2; 93:11-14): This long "Letter" begins with a superscription assuring us that this is Enoch's own writing, entrusted to Methuselah and through him "to all future generations: to everyone who dwells upon the earth and practices goodness and peace" (92:1). The tacit invitation to identify with the Enochic tradition is plain. Following on this is a short poem (92:2; 93:11-14) implying the same grand claims for Enoch's wisdom that we find in other booklets (e.g., 19:3; 37:1-4). The queries found in OT passages such as Job 38, Prov 30:3-4, and Jer 31:37 — all of which essentially ask, "Who can know the hidden things of the cosmos?" — are taken not as a rhetorical questions expecting the response, "No one," but as *riddles* to which the AE author knows the answer. Indeed, any reader of the *Book of Enoch* knows who this is.

(2) *Woes and Exhortations* (94:1–101:3): After yet another "two-ways" admonition for his children (94:1-5, 11), Enoch launches into a lengthy series of alternating "woes" for the wicked and exhortations for the righteous, much of it written in classic OT prophetic style (94:6-10; chs. 95–100). Sprinkled among these warnings and encouragements are descriptions of the future day of reckoning with its judgments and rewards, the basis for Enoch's certainty (97:5-6; 98:6-8; 99:3; 100:4-6). The "apocalyptic message" of the AE is that even though the existing world is admittedly unjust, with the wicked prospering and the righteous suffering, a day of judgment is coming which will correct this situation, bringing certain punishment for evildoers and vindication for the faithful (Nickelsburg 1977b).

There are also signs by which the wise will understand that the last days are fast approaching. Enoch warns that "at that time, the nations will be thrown into confusion" (99:4), and he adds:

> 100:1. At that time, and in the same place, fathers and sons will strike one another down, and brothers with one another will fall in death, until their blood flows like a stream. 2. For a man will not withhold his hand from killing his sons, nor his son's sons. The sinner will not withhold his hand from the worthy, nor from his brother, but from dawn until dusk they will kill each other. 3. The horse will wade up to its breast in the blood of sinners, and the chariot will sink to its axles.

Lines like these have a familiar ring to Bible readers. *Enoch* makes use of a common stock of doomsday imagery encountered frequently in the apocalyptic rhetoric of the centuries surrounding the turn of the era.

The author is zealous to accentuate human responsibility for evil, and to this end the fallen angel myth is almost brushed aside at one point:

> 98:4. I swear to you sinners: just as a mountain has never, and will never, become a slave, nor a hill the handmaid of a woman, so also sin has not been sent onto the earth; rather, people have created it themselves, and those who commit it will be subject to a great curse.

This passage does not really contradict the rest of the Enochic corpus, however, since nowhere in *Enoch* is human moral responsibility denied just because the Watchers have introduced a raft of wicked options into the world. In the BW there is a distinction between the righteous who resist the Giants (and are martyred) and the wicked who embrace the forbidden arts of the fallen angels (8:4). The supposedly fatalistic "tablets of heaven" mentioned in the AB (81:1-4) are invoked without embarrassment in the AE (93:2; 103:2), which encourages its readers to "choose for yourselves righteousness and an elect life" (94:4). Even in the middle of a description of the corruptions brought about by the fallen angels, one of the authors of the PE tells us that human beings "were not, in fact, created any differently than the angels in that they ought to live continually pure and righteous lives" (69:11).

"Enoch's Letter" describes the wicked in more detail than in the other books. Most of their crimes are social justice issues, abuses of wealth and power (94:6-7; 96:4-8; 97:8-10; 98:1-3). Some of these "woes" aimed at the rich resemble the words of Jesus as recorded in the Gospel of Luke:

> 94:8. Woe to you, O rich, for you have trusted your riches, but from your riches you will be separated, because you have not remembered the Most High in your days of affluence.

> 97:8. Woe to you who gain gold and silver unjustly, and say, "We have grown very wealthy and have amassed possessions, and we have acquired everything that we desire. 9. Now let us do whatever we wish, for we have hoarded silver in our treasure storerooms, and lots of good things in our houses." 10. But they will be poured out of there like water! You are deceived, for your riches will not last. Rather, they will quickly take flight from you; for you have amassed all of it unjustly, and you will be given over to a great curse.

Compare Luke 6:24; 12:16-21. It is quite possible that a real connection exists between the AE and the third Evangelist (Nickelsburg 1979).

Other infractions of the wicked in the AE are more

strictly religious, such as committing blasphemy and eating blood (94:9; 96:7; 98:11). It is difficult to identify these "sinners" since some passages imply that they are pagans, while others accuse them of perverting the Jewish scriptures: they are idolaters (99:7; 104:9), but they "tamper with the words of truth and distort the eternal covenant" (99:2) and lead others into error (98:15). In all probability the "sinners" of this booklet include both powerful Gentile rulers and worldly-wise Jewish collaborators willing to compromise their religion for pragmatic gain.

(3) *Parable of the Sea Captains* (101:4–102:3): One of the literary gems of the *Book of Enoch,* this short parable manages to evoke a wide array of Enochic themes, including the flood, the contrast between the obedience of nature and the defiance of sinners, God's power to bind and control chaos, the ties between knowledge of the natural and of the spiritual realms, and the familiar first/last Judgment typology:

> 101:4. Observe the sea captains who sail upon the sea. Their ships are tossed by the waves and shaken by tempests. Distressed 5. and battered by the storm, they are afraid and jettison all their goods and possessions into the sea, for they have forebodings in their hearts: the sea will swallow them up, and they will perish in it! 6. But is not the entire sea, with all of its waters, and all of its turbulence, the work of the Most High? Has he not determined its limits, bound it, and fenced it in with sand? 7. At his rebuke, *it* is afraid! It dries up, and the fish and everything in it die. But you sinners on the land, *you* are unafraid of him! 8. Did he not create heaven and earth, and everything in them? And who gave understanding and wisdom to all those who traverse the seas? 9. Do not the sea captains fear the sea? Yet sinners do not fear the Most High!
>
> 102:1. In those days, when he throws at you a wave of blazing fire, where will you flee to escape? When he launches his voice against you, will you not be shaken and terrified at the mighty sound? 2. Heaven and all the luminaries will tremble with terror! All the earth will be shaken and trembling and alarmed! 3. The angels will carry out their commands, and the children of the earth will tremble and shake, seeking to hide themselves before the presence of the Great Glory! And you — sinners eternally accursed — you will have no peace.

(4) *Debate concerning Ultimate Destinies* (102:4–104:9): The wicked in the AE seem to deny any afterlife. Here, toward the end of the book, the author engages in a mock debate with self-satisfied and comfortable sinners who feel that the misery of the so-called righteous vindicates their own philosophy of life, while these righteous for their part are so discouraged that they are ready to quit, having concluded that the curses of the Mosaic covenant (Deuteronomy 28) have perversely fallen upon themselves. Against all this the author argues with enormous vigor that justice is manifested only in the afterlife, that sinners will there inherit blazing torments (103:7-8; cf. 100:9), and that the righteous must keep their hopes of immortality alive:

> 104:1. I swear to you that in heaven the angels memorialize you — for good — in the presence of the glory of the Great One. 2. Take courage! In the past you have been worn out with evils and afflictions, but now you will shine like the luminaries of heaven! — shine and be gazed upon! And the portals of heaven will be opened to you. 3. Your cry *will* be heard, and the judgment for which you cry will also appear. Insofar as it will be helpful to you, there will be an investigation by the angels concerning your afflictions, even concerning all those who joined with those who oppressed and devoured you. 4. Be hopeful! — do not cast your hope away; for great joy will be yours, like the angels of heaven. 5. What obligation will you have? *You* will not need to hide. Calamities on the day of the Great Judgment, indeed, you will absolutely not encounter. (You — the sinners — *will* be troubled, and there will be an eternal judgment executed on you for all the generations of eternity!) 6. Fear not, you righteous! And when you see the sinners growing strong and prospering, do not be their companions; but distance yourselves from all of their wickedness, and you will become the companions of the hosts of heaven!

(5) *A Prophecy and a Commission* (104:10–105:2): Pseudo-Enoch finishes with a remarkable (because correct!) prophecy that his writings will be preserved and translated, although he worries that this process of transmission may introduce inaccuracies:

> 104:11. If only they would write down all my words — accurately, and in their languages — without omitting or altering any of them, but writing down accurately everything which I testify to them! 12. But now, another mystery I know! My books will be given to the righteous, the holy, and the wise, for joy in the truth, and for abundant wisdom.

A brief chapter, difficult to interpret, closes the book.

> 105:1. "And in those days," says the Lord, "they will summon the children of earth and testify to them. And reveal your wisdom to them, for you are their guides, and rewards upon all the earth. 2. For I and my son will forever be united with them in the paths of righteousness, during their lives, and you will have peace. Rejoice, you children of truth!" Amen.

This appears to be an exhortation from God himself to the Enochians to spread abroad their wisdom. Possibly the quotation ends with v. 1, and Enoch is the speaker in v. 2, referring to Methuselah ("my son"), a plausible view since the "Letter" makes no other reference to a Messiah figure (but cf. 91:10; 92:3-5 in the Methuselah Apocalypse). If, however, God is the speaker in both verses, a messianic interpretation cannot be ruled out, since the idea of the Messiah as God's son appears elsewhere in Jewish apocalyptic (2 Esdr 7:18-29; 14:9). Either way, the missionary emphasis of the AE's conclusion demonstrates a desire by the author to win over the "children of earth" to the Enochic tradition.

The Appendices (Enoch 106–8)

The First Appendix: The Birth of Noah (chs. 106–7)

The DSS prove that by the end of the first century BC the first appendix (chs. 106–7) was already attached to the AE, although in the Aramaic fragments they are separated by a noticeable gap. In these chapters Enoch tells the story of the supernatural birth of his great-grandson Noah, who emerges from the womb with a radiance that fills the room, praising God already in the hands of the midwife (106:2-3)! Understandably frightened, Noah's father Lamech asks his own father Methuselah to seek out Enoch at the "ends of the earth" (106:8; cf. 65:2) and find out what this omen means. Enoch responds to Methuselah with a brief rehearsal of the Watcher tale and a warning about the imminent flood, plus reassurances about the newborn. He is to be named "Noah," and he will assure the survival of a remnant of humanity. Included in this is a prediction of a later growth of wickedness and another judgment someday (106:13–107:1), all familiar Enochiana by now.

There are striking similarities between this narrative and part of the *Genesis Apocryphon* (1QapGen 2–5), a lost work partially preserved among the DSS, as well as certain resemblances to the birth of Melchizedek in *2 Enoch* 71, a later Enochic writing. Clearly a common "wonder birth" tradition was adaptable to more than one narrative situation. The purpose of this story here at the end of *Enoch* is to amplify the biblical narrative and to emphasize the continuity of the Enochic traditions. Latter-day recipients of these traditions may be confident that they, like Noah, will survive the coming wrath.

The Second Appendix (ch. 108)

Missing from both the Aramaic fragments and the sole Greek copy of the AE, this chapter is an independent Enochic apocalypse of unknown date. In a vision inspired by *Enoch* 18:13 and 21:1-6 in the BW, Enoch is shown the fate awaiting sinners in an awful netherworld while an interpreting angel tells him what he is seeing (108:3-7). The righteous, however, have a bright future:

> 108:8. Those who love God have loved neither gold nor silver nor any of the good things which are in the world; rather, they have given over their bodies to torture. 9. From the time they came into being, these have not craved earthly food but have instead counted themselves as a breath that passes away, and this they have preserved. And the Lord tested them much, but their spirits have been found pure so that they might praise his name. 10. I have recounted all their blessings in the books. He has assigned them their reward, for they proved to be those who loved heaven more than their life in the world.

To each of these is promised a "throne of honor" (v. 12), while sinners are destined for a dark place "where days and seasons are prescribed for them" (v. 15). Charles rightly comments: "The object of this chapter is to encourage the righteous still to hope on despite the long delay of the advent of the kingdom" (Charles 1912: 269). As such, it makes a fitting end for a book which waited a long time for its own rebirth.

Bibliography. Bampfylde, G. 1984, "The Similitudes of Enoch: Historical Allusions," *JSJ* 15:9-31 • Barker, M. 1987, *The Older Testament,* London: SPCK • Barker, M. 1988, *The Lost Prophet: The Book of Enoch and Its Influence on Christianity,* Nashville: Abingdon • Beckwith, R. T. 1981, "The Earliest Enoch Literature and Its Calendar: Marks of Their Origin, Date, and Motivation," *RevQ* 39:365-403 • Black, M. 1978, "The 'Two Witnesses' of Rev. 11:3f. in Jewish and Christian Apocalyptic Tradition," in *Donum Gentilicium,* Oxford: Clarendon • Black, M. 1985, *The Book of Enoch or 1 Enoch: A New English Edition,* Leiden: Bril • Black, M. 1992, "The Messianism of the Parables of Enoch: Their Date and Contribution to Christological Origins," in *The Messiah,* Minneapolis: Fortress • Charles, R. H. 1912, *The Book of Enoch or 1 Enoch,* Oxford: Clarendon • Collins, J. J. 1984, *The Apocalyptic Imagination,* New York: Crossroad • Collins, J. J. 1982, "The Apocalyptic Technique: Setting and Function in the Book of Watchers," *CBQ* 44:91-111 • Davies, P. R. 1983, "Calendrical Change and Qumran Origins: An Assessment of VanderKam's Theory," *CBQ* 45:80-89 • García Martínez, F. 1992, *Qumran and Apocalyptic,* Leiden: Brill • García Martínez, F., and E. J. C. Tigchelaar. 1989, "*1 Enoch* and the Figure of Enoch: A Bibliography of Studies 1970-1988," *RevQ* 14:149-74 • Glessmer, U. 1996, "Horizontal Measuring in the Babylonian Astronomical Compendium MUL.APIN and in the Astronomical Book of 1En," *Henoch* 18:259-82 • Hanson, P. D. 1977, "Rebellion in Heaven, Azazel, and Euhemeristic Heroes in 1 Enoch 6–11," *JBL* 96:195-233 • Hartman, L. 1979, *Asking for a Meaning: A Study of 1 Enoch 1–5,* Lund: Gleerup • Horowitz, W. 1996, "The 360 and 364 Day Year in Ancient Mesopotamia," *JANES* 24:35-44 • Klijn, A. F. J. 1978, "From Creation to Noah in the Second Dream-Vision of the Ethiopic Henoch," in *Miscellanea Neotestamentica,* Leiden: Brill • Kvanvig, H. 1988, *The Roots of Apocalyptic,* Neukirchen-Vluyn: Neukirchener • Lindars, B. 1976, "A Bull, a Lamb and a Word: 1 Enoch XC.38," *NTS* 22:483-86 • Malan, J. C. 1983, "Enochic (Apocalyptic) and Christian Perspectives on Relationships: A Tentative Comparison of Striking Aspects and Underlying Lines of Thinking Revealed in 1 Enoch and the New Testament," *Neot* 17:84-96 • Milik, J. T. 1976, *The Books of Enoch,* Oxford: Clarendon • Neugebauer, O. 1985, "The 'Astronomical' Chapters of the Ethiopic Book of Enoch (72 to 82)," in *The Book of Enoch or 1 Enoch: A New English Edition* (Appendix A, 386-419), Leiden: Brill • Newsom, C. 1980, "The Development of 1 Enoch 6–19: Cosmology and Judgment," *CBQ* 42:310-29 • Nickelsburg, G. W. E. 1972, *Resurrection, Immortality, and Eternal Life in Intertestamental Judaism,* Cambridge, Mass.: Harvard University • Nickelsburg, G. W. E. 1977a, "Apocalyptic and Myth in 1 Enoch 6–11," *JBL* 96:383-405 • Nickelsburg, G. W. E. 1977b, "The Apocalyptic Message of *1 Enoch* 92–105," *CBQ* 39:309-28 • Nickelsburg, G. W. E. 1979, "Riches, the Rich, and God's Judgment in 1 Enoch 92–105 and the Gospel According to Luke," *NTS* 25:324-44 • Nickelsburg, G. W. E. 1981a, "The Books of Enoch in Recent Research," *RelSRev* 7:210-17 • Nickelsburg, G. W. E. 1981b, "Enoch, Levi, and Peter: Recipients of Revelation in Upper Galilee," *JBL* 100:575-600 • Nickelsburg, G. W. E. 1981c, *Jewish Literature between the Bible* *and the Mishnah,* Philadelphia: Fortress • Nickelsburg, G. W. E. 2001, *1 Enoch 1,* Minneapolis: Fortress • Olson, D. C. 1993, "Recovering the Original Sequence of *1 Enoch* 91–93," *JSP* 11:69-94 • Olson, D. C. 1998, "Enoch and the Son of Man in the Epilogue of the Parables," *JSP* 18:27-38 • Stone, M. 1978, "The Book of Enoch and Judaism in the Third Century B.C.E.," *CBQ* 40:479-92 • Suter, D. W. 1979, *Tradition and Composition in the Parables of Enoch,* Missoula, Mont.: Scholars • Suter, D. W. 1981, "Weighed in the Balance: The Similitudes of Enoch in Recent Discussion," *RelSRev* 7:217-21 • Tiller, P. 1993, *A Commentary on the Animal Apocalypse of I Enoch,* Atlanta: Scholars • VanderKam, J. C. 1979, "The Origin, Character, and Early History of the 364-Day Calendar: A Reassessment of Jaubert's Hypotheses," *CBQ* 41:390-411 • VanderKam, J. C. 1984a, "Studies in the Apocalypse of Weeks (*1 Enoch* 93:1-10; 91:11-17)," *CBQ* 46:512-23 • VanderKam, J. C. 1984b, *Enoch and the Growth of an Apocalyptic Tradition,* Washington D.C.: The Catholic Biblical Association of America • VanderKam, J. C. 1992, "Righteous One, Messiah, Chosen One, and Son of Man in 1 Enoch 37–71," in *The Messiah,* Minneapolis: Fortress • VanderKam, J. C. 1995, *Enoch: A Man for All Generations,* Columbia, S.C.: University of South Carolina.

The Hebrew Bible in the Dead Sea Scrolls

Daniel C. Harlow

When the Dead Sea Scrolls (DSS) came to light in 1947 through 1956, a whole new window was opened onto the study of the Bible, early Judaism, and Christian origins. The vast majority of scholars recognize the Scrolls as the library holdings of a group of Essenes who established themselves at Qumran, off the northwest shore of the Dead Sea, around 100 BC. This consensus has survived several competing explanations posed over the last decade or so, such as those that identify the Qumran sectarians as Sadducees; those that interpret the site at Qumran as not a religious community center but a military fortress, a country villa, a commercial entrepôt, a fortified farm, or a center for ritual purification used by various Jewish groups; and those that think the Scrolls represent not the library of a particular group, but a cross-section of early Jewish literature from the temple archives in Jerusalem. Despite these alternate theories, the Essene hypothesis remains intact as the most persuasive explanation of the available data. Various methods of determining the date of the Scrolls, including paleography, carbon-14, and accelerator mass spectrometry, have established their antiquity, and archeology has confirmed that the site and the eleven nearby caves that yielded scrolls are indeed related to one another.

The Essenes were a Jewish movement that emerged alongside others such as the Pharisees and Sadducees in the latter half of the second century BC. In 152 BC, the Hasmoneans, the heroes of the Maccabean revolt, ushered in a period of native Jewish rule whose combination of royal and priestly authority splintered Judaism into sects, that is, rival political-social-religious interest groups, at a time when there was no official, normative Judaism. The Essenes at Qumran may have been a breakaway group or else a subset of the wider Essene movement. A celibate group with priestly origins and leadership, they pulled out of Jerusalem in protest over how the temple was being run. The Scrolls indicate that they objected to the temple's worldliness, the calendar in use there, the stance on ritual purity taken by its leadership, and the illegitimacy and impiety of its current high priesthood (e.g., CD 3:12-17; 4:13-19; 20:22-23; 4QMMT). They eventually withdrew to the desert to practice an ascetic lifestyle in preparation for the end of the age and devoted themselves to communal prayer, study, worship, meals, and ritual purity, as a surrogate temple (e.g., 1QS 5:4-7; 8:4-10; 9:3-6). An apocalyptic sect with a strongly dualistic and deterministic worldview, they considered themselves the only true Israelites, whom God would vindicate and exalt when he visited the earth in judgment.

There are around 100,000 DSS. This is a staggering number, but the vast majority of the Scrolls are fragments. Together they represent the remains of some 930 manuscript copies of approximately 350 different literary compositions. The vast size of the library likely owes to the intense interest of the group in studying sacred literature over the course of more than a century and a half. Some have suggested that the collection's magnitude may also indicate that the group met the literary needs of the wider Essene movement as a kind of publishing house.

The Hebrew Scriptures at Qumran

The contents of the library of Qumran may be divided into three general categories: (1) biblical texts (Hebrew Bible/Old Testament); (2) nonbiblical (from our modern point of view) but nonsectarian texts valued by many different Jewish groups ("apocrypha" and "pseudepigrapha"); (3) sectarian texts, the in-house literature not just copied but also composed by and for members of the Qumran community. A recent count has set the number of biblical manuscripts at 222 (205 from Qumran, seventeen from other sites in the Judean Desert), or a little over a fourth of the library. The current estimate is not final, since ongoing assessments have to face the difficulty of distinguishing a biblical fragment from one preserving a biblical paraphrase. The majority of the biblical manuscripts (140) come from Cave 4. As with the library in general, the state of their preservation varies widely. At one end of the spectrum, only one scroll preserves the complete contents of a biblical book — the first Isaiah scroll from Qumran Cave 1 (1QIsa[a]), and only one other preserves most of its contents (11QPs[a]). At the other end, all that survives of the books of Chronicles is one small fragment. Between these extremes lie scroll fragments in varying states of preservation, those representing a fraction of a book, a few chapters, a few paragraphs, or a few lines.

The Essene library at Qumran contained copies of virtually every book of the Hebrew Bible, with the sole exception of Esther and possibly Nehemiah, although the latter may be represented *in absentia* if the books of Ezra and Nehemiah were originally one book. The oldest biblical manuscripts (4QSam[b], 4QJer[a], 4QExod[b]) date to the end of the third century BC and are therefore more than a thousand years older than the oldest previously known manuscripts. Among their library holdings, the Qumran Essenes had multiple copies of most scriptural books. The most popular books were the Psalms (36 copies), Deuteronomy (30), and Isaiah (21). (These happen to be the very ones most often quoted in the NT.) Other popular books at Qumran were Genesis (20), Exodus (17), Leviticus (15), Daniel (8), and the Minor Prophets (8). Some biblical books are represented by only one (Ezra, Chronicles) or two (Joshua, Proverbs, Ecclesiastes) fragmentary copies. Also in the collection are witnesses to the text of Leviticus and Job in the form of targums, which are Aramaic translations and paraphrases of the Hebrew text. The text of passages in Exodus and Deuteronomy has also been preserved in tefillin (phylacteries) and mezuzot, which are small capsules or compartments containing tiny slips of parchment inscribed with passages from the Torah. Tefillin were strapped to the forehead and/or left arm during the morning weekday prayers; mezuzot were attached to the doorposts of houses.

Textual Development

The first thing that the biblical scrolls from Qumran have helped clarify is that there was no "Bible" before the end of the first century AD. There were of course collections of sacred writings ("scriptures") but no official *canon,* that is, no closed list of books accepted as authoritative and normative for all Jews, and no fixed textual form for each book. This fact is not so odd, considering that today there are different Bibles or biblical canons — with different textual forms of different books in different orders — in use among different religious groups (Jews, Catholics, Protestants, Greek Orthodox, Russian Orthodox, etc.). At the turn of the eras, there was even greater variety; the textual form of each book as well as the identity, number, and order of books considered sacred varied from Jewish group to Jewish group.

Thus both the interior, textual forms and external, canonical shapes of the collections of Scriptures were pluriform at the turn of the eras, up until about AD 100 or even as late as the end of the second Jewish revolt against Rome (AD 132-135). Not until that time can we speak of textual and canonical uniformity, since only by then did the three major surviving religious groups that laid claim to the literary heritage of ancient Israel — Rabbinic Judaism, Christianity, and Samaritanism — end up with a particular text for each book and decide which books were to be included in which order for their respective canons of Scripture. The Samaritans, Jews, and Christians chose their books according to their religious beliefs and practices, but they seem to have adopted whatever textual form they happened to have for each book, or, if they had more than one form at their disposal, they evidently chose the one that enjoyed the greatest established usage in their respective communities of faith. The result was the compilation of what would become the MT by rabbinic Jews, the SP by Samaritan Jews, and the LXX by Christians. However, neither the MT, the LXX, nor the SP is a unified text type but a disparate collection of varied textual forms of the various books, each of which has different features and is of varying textual value.

When manuscripts share several distinct wordings, phrasings, spellings, scribal errors, and other features, text critics recognize a textual group or family. The Scrolls have revealed that during the late Second Temple period, several different text types were in circulation among various Jewish groups, including the one at Qumran. To explain this variety, scholars have proposed different theories of how the biblical text developed. A theory of "local texts" was initially proposed by W. F. Albright and further refined by Frank M. Cross. According to this schema, different textual traditions for the books of the Pentateuch arose and developed in different geographic regions — the (proto) SP (minus its sectarian features) in Palestine, the (proto) MT in Babylon, and the LXX in Egypt. All three text types eventually found a place in Palestine and made their way into the Qumran library.

Emanuel Tov, following the lead of Shemaryahu Talmon, has dispensed with the notion of only three basic text types taking shape in three distinct regions and has recognized a much greater degree of variety among the biblical scrolls. On this reckoning, the biblical scrolls from Qumran can be grouped into at least five broad textual categories. (1) *Proto-Masoretic* texts are those that resemble the text of a particular book in the developing MT tradition. By Tov's calculation, some fifty-seven, or 47 percent, of the Qumran biblical scrolls fall in this category, among them 1QIsa^{b}, 4QJer$^{a, c}$, and 4QEzra. The actual figure, however, may be much lower, since twenty of the twenty-four Pentateuchal texts placed by Tov in this category are equally close to the SP. (2) *Proto-Samaritan* texts are those bearing affinities with the text of the SP. Qumran Scrolls in this category comprise around 6.5 percent of the Qumran Pentateuchal manuscripts or 2.5 percent of all the biblical scrolls and include such manuscripts as 4QpaleoExod^{m}, 4QExod-Lev^{f}, and 4QNum^{b}. (3) *Septuagintal* texts look like the putative Hebrew text behind the Greek translation of a particular book in the Septuagint. Texts in this group represent only some 3 to 4 percent of the Qumran biblical scrolls and include 4QDeut^{q}, 4QSam^{q}, and 4QJer^{b}. (4) *Non-aligned* texts have no strong affinity with any of the above text types. This group is, in fact, a broad rubric for numerous forms of the biblical text. Qumran scrolls that fall into this category number approximately fifty-seven or 47 percent, including 4QDeut$^{b, c, h}$, 4QIsa^{c}, and 4QDan^{a}. (5) Tov has also proposed a fifth group, comprised of texts written in a distinctive *Qumran practice,* as evidenced by such features as long orthography (*plene* or "full" spelling), distinctive morphology, frequent errors and corrections, and a free approach to the text. In this group he would place some twenty-seven manuscripts, including 4QExod^{b}, 4QDeut^{j}, 1QIsa^{a}, 4QIsa^{c}, and 11QPs^{a}. The isolation of this category has not met with as wide an acceptance among scholars as have the previous ones, and Tov himself has recently refrained from treating it for statistical purposes as representative of a separate textual affiliation.

Eugene Ulrich has proposed a theory of multiple literary editions. The identification of a distinct literary edition of a book centers on recognizing large-scale patterns in the variants in a manuscript or manuscripts. Many biblical books evidently were the product of a long, complex literary process involving numerous authors, editors, and copyists through several generations and even centuries. In other words, these books "grew" over time in organic, developmental fashion. Some books seem to have reached a final compositional form fairly early on and been copied rather faithfully; others, though, were expanded, contracted, and altered in various ways while they were being copied to suit the interests of different scribes and their communities. In several cases, then, the stages of composition and transmission (copying) of a book overlapped. This process resulted not only in numerous variations in wording among manuscripts and in different textual families but also in different literary editions of some biblical books. Sometimes, though not always, a new edition of a book replaced an older one.

Among the biblical scrolls from the Judean desert, variant literary editions are most evident for Exodus, Numbers, Joshua, Jeremiah, and Psalms. Most of the seventeen Exodus scrolls from Qumran have a text that is very close to the MT, but 4QpaleoExod[m] shares many features with the text of Exodus in the SP. Among the eleven fragmentary copies of Numbers is one manuscript (4QNum[b]) that shares several longer readings with the SP and that therefore attests the existence of different editions of the book. Before the discovery of the Scrolls, the book of Joshua was extant in two editions, one preserved in the MT, the other in the LXX, with the LXX preserving the shorter, earlier version of the book. A still shorter, earlier text is now manifest in 4QNum[b]. Similarly, two editions of the book of Jeremiah were known before the Scrolls came to light — a longer, later edition preserved in the MT and a shorter, earlier version preserved in the LXX. The earlier version, which is about 13 percent shorter than the other version, is now attested in two Jeremiah manuscripts from Qumran, 4QJer[b] and 4QJer[d].

The book of Psalms is the most amply attested work among the DSS. The Masoretic Psalter, with 150 Psalms, is attested in the MT, the LXX, and the second Psalms scroll from Masada (MasPs[b]), though the LXX includes Psalm 151. Three psalms scrolls from Qumran, 11QPs[a], 11QPs[b], and 4QPs[e], seem to reflect an alternate version of the Psalter. The great Psalms scroll from Cave 11 (11QPs[a]) contains portions of forty-one psalms known from books four and five of the Masoretic Psalter, from Psalm 101 to the end, but in a different order. It also contains Psalm 151 (at the very end) plus two other Psalms previously extant only in Syriac (Psalms 154, 155) and a poem related to Sir 51:13-20b, 30. Further, 11QPs[a] contains a poem identical to 2 Sam 23:1-7 (the last words of David), three previously unknown psalms — a "Plea for Deliverance," an "Apostrophe to Zion," and a "Hymn to the Creator" — and a prose list of David's compositions. In all, then, 11QPs[a] has a peculiar arrangement and a total of nine texts not present in the Masoretic Psalter. Although some scholars continue to regard 11QPs[a] as only a liturgical collection intended for study or worship, the witness to this same psalter in 11QPs[b] and 4QPs[e] suggests that it is a bona fide variant edition of the Psalter and the main one in use at Qumran.

If Ulrich is right in his assessment of the Qumran biblical scrolls along with that of the other available textual evidence, then half or more of the books of the Hebrew Bible — at least twelve, perhaps as many as sixteen — may have circulated in different literary editions. All in all, the variety of textual forms exhibited among the DSS suggests that the Essenes at Qumran, and very likely other Jewish groups in the Second Temple period, did not assign sacred status or authority to only one textual form of certain scriptural books but to the book or tradition as such.

Canonical Formation

The official rabbinic canon eventually had three divisions: the Law (*Torah*), the Prophets (*Nebi'im*), and the Writings (*Kethubim*). Such a threefold division, or perhaps even a fourfold one, may be attested, albeit not very clearly, in the halakic document 4QMMT (*Miqṣat Ma'aśe hattorah*), a pre-Qumran work from the second century BC that speaks of "the books of Moses" and "the books of the Prophets" and that mentions "Davi[d]" (a reference to the Psalter?) and "[the events] of ages past" (a reference to the historical books Joshua–2 Kings and/or Chronicles, Ezra, and Nehemiah?).

By the latter part of the Second Temple period, most Jews recognized the five books of Moses (the Torah or Pentateuch) as authoritative, and this was certainly the case at Qumran. But not all Jewish groups necessarily limited the Mosaic Torah to only five books (Genesis to Deuteronomy). The Qumran Essenes evidently regarded *Jubilees*, the *Temple Scroll*, and the so-called *Reworked Pentateuch* as sacred books of Moses. This seems to be the case in light of their contents (they purport to be divine revelation), the number of copies of them in the Qumran library, and the quotation formulae used to refer to them in the sectarian Scrolls (e.g., "it is written"; "as God said"). In the case of *Jubilees*, for example, we have a document extant in fifteen manuscripts that purports to be teaching revealed to Moses either directly by God (ch. 1) or through an angel of the presence, and that is cited as authoritative in CD 16:2-3 and perhaps in 4Q228.

Most Jewish communities also recognized the books of the Prophets as sacred scripture. Here again, the Essene group at Qumran was no exception, as both the number of copies of prophetic books and the existence of commentaries on them attest. However, it is not clear which books and how many books each group put in this category, or in what order they put them. For example, some Jews evidently regarded the book of Daniel and the Psalms as prophetic books, while others classified them among "the other books" or "the rest of the books" (what would later be "the Writings" in the rabbinic canon). The Qumran Essenes evidently joined other, "Enochic" Jews in regarding *1 Enoch* as a scriptural book of the Prophets. All parts of *1 Enoch* except for the *Similitudes* (chs. 37–71) have turned up in the Qumran library in Aramaic, in some twelve scroll fragments. The scriptural status of *1 Enoch* at Qumran seems assured given its large number of copies, its presentation as divine revelation, its advocacy of the calendar that came to be preferred at Qumran, and its possible quotation in a pesher on the *Apocalypse of Weeks* (4Q247).

It is unclear whether a third distinct category of books (such as the Writings in the rabbinic canon) existed before about AD 100. If it did, it did not necessarily contain only or all of the books included in the rabbinic canon (Psalms to Chronicles). This caveat seems appropriate, at least for the Qumran covenanters, given that not all the books later included among the Writings are formally cited in the sectarian scrolls. Among the books whose scriptural status was disputed by Jews were Esther, the Song of Songs, and Ben Sira.

The Enhanced Value of the Septuagint

The LXX is a collection of ancient Greek translations of the Hebrew Scriptures undertaken in Egypt by different translators between the third century and first century BC. The LXX version of a book is not the only nor always the most reliable witness to the Old Greek (OG) text of a biblical book. Yet the Scrolls have enhanced the value of the Septuagint for certain books, as indeed they have of the proto-Samaritan tradition. Some Hebrew biblical manuscripts among the Scrolls resemble what the parent Hebrew text behind the Septuagint must have looked like. Evidently, the Greek translators did not always freely alter the text while translating from the Hebrew but faithfully rendered the Hebrew text that was in front of them, which happened to differ from the emerging Masoretic textual tradition. As noted above, the LXX version of the book of Jeremiah is about one-eighth shorter than the MT's. Four of the six Hebrew manuscripts of Jeremiah from Qumran reflect the longer text, but 4QJer^{b} and 4QJer^{d} have the shorter text represented in the Greek version. Another example is provided by 4QSam^{a}, which contains many agreements in wording with the LXX of 1 Samuel in ch. 1 (the story of Samuel's birth) and chs. 17–18 (the story of David and Goliath). Although it is not clear that the book of Samuel as a whole existed in different literary editions, the Qumran manuscripts seem to indicate that there were variant editions of particular passages in existence for this book and others as well (e.g., Daniel).

Superior Readings in the Scrolls

The Scrolls have provided dozens of superior readings (words, phrases, sentences, verses) for passages in the OT. Some modern English translations indicate in footnotes those instances where the wording of a Qumran biblical manuscript has been preferred over against the wording of the MT. For example, the NRSV translation committee has adopted some twenty readings from the Qumran scrolls for the book of Isaiah and around forty for the books of Samuel. A few examples culled from various books of the Hebrew Bible may illustrate the contributions made by the Scrolls:

Exod 1:5 on the number of Jacob's descendants who came with him to Egypt

MT: seventy descendants
LXX: seventy-five descendants (cf. Acts 7:14)
4QExod^{a}: seventy-five descendants

Deut 32:8 on the number of ? according to which God divided the nations/peoples

MT: sons of Israel
LXX: angels of God (some manuscripts)
LXX: sons of God (other manuscripts)
4QDeut^{j}: sons of God

1 Sam 17:4 on the height of Goliath

MT: six cubits
LXX: four cubits
4QSam^{a}: four cubits

Isa 21:8 on who cries out from the watchtower

MT: Then a lion (אריה) called out, "Upon a watchtower I stand, O Lord. . . ."
1QIsa^{a}: Then the watchman (ראה) called out: "Upon a watchtower I stand, O Lord. . . ."

Ps 22:16 on the psalmist's hands and feet

MT: like a lion (כארי) are my hands and feet
LXX: they have pierced my hands and feet
5/6HevPs: they have pierced (כארו) my hands and feet

A missing verse from Psalm 145

Psalm 145 is an acrostic psalm in which each line begins with a different letter of the Hebrew alphabet. In the MT there is no line for the Hebrew letter *nun* (נ = n). This line has been known from the LXX and the Syriac version, and it has now turned up in Hebrew between vv. 13 and 14 of the psalm in 11QPs^{a}. The line reads "God is faithful in his words and gracious in all his works."

A missing paragraph in 1 Samuel

The Scrolls have made possible the restoration of an entire paragraph in the book of Samuel that evidently dropped out of the developing MT tradition. Between 1 Sam 10:27 and 11:1, the NRSV restores a small paragraph not found in the traditional Masoretic Hebrew text of 1 Samuel (see, e.g., the NIV). The restored text is supplied by 4QSam^{a}, a fragmentary copy of the book of Samuel from Qumran Cave 4. The first-century Jewish historian Josephus Flavius knew the material in this paragraph; he paraphrases it in his retelling of Israelite history (*Ant.* 6.5.1), so his Greek text of Samuel must have had it, and so therefore must the Hebrew parent text of his Greek text. The restored material explains that the Ammonite king Nahash attacked the Israelite city of Jabesh-Gilead because the city had harbored fugitives from the conquered tribal lands of Reuben and Gad. Why did the paragraph drop out of the proto-Masoretic textual tradition? Probably because of scribal error: a copyist's eye skipped from the phrase "and he held his peace" (ויהי כמחריש) to the phrase "about a month later" (ויהי כמו חדש) — phrases that look almost identical in Hebrew. When the scribe continued copying he proceeded to write down the material after the second phrase, with the result that he accidentally omitted all the intervening material.

Scriptural Interpretation in the Scrolls

Greek and Aramaic Translations

Fragments of Greek renderings and of Aramaic paraphrases in targums among the DSS provide examples not only of translation of the Hebrew Scriptures but also interpretation of them. As noted above, the Septuagint is not a single, unified translation of the Hebrew Scriptures but a collection of translations of very uneven quality. Some books in the LXX look like very literal renderings of their Hebrew parent text. Others subtly change the meaning of Hebrew words and phrases by choosing Greek terms that introduce Hellenistic concepts into the text. For example, the LXX often translates the proper divine name YHWH and the divine title *Elohim* with the generic nouns *kyrios* ("lord") and *theos* ("deity"), respectively. "I am who I am" becomes in Greek "I am the Being"; "sons of God" becomes "angels"; "You shall not revile *Elohim*" is transformed into "You shall not revile the gods"; "Who has known the Spirit of the Lord?" is translated "Who has known the mind of the Lord?"; "Moses went up to God" becomes "Moses ascended the mount of God"; "Behold, the young woman is with child" changes to "Behold, a virgin shall conceive"; "I shall not see Yahweh in the land of the living" yields to "I shall never again see the salvation of God in the land of the living." In many of these cases, the LXX translators reworded anthropomorphic depictions of God in accord with Greek philosophical conceptions of Deity. Other Greek translators incorporated traditions of interpretation into their renderings or else sought to clarify ambiguities through various translation techniques. Still others produced more a paraphrase than a translation. There are even cases in the LXX where the Greek translator obviously had no idea what the Hebrew word or phrase in front of him meant.

Qumran Cave 7 yielded only Greek papyrus fragments, including two Septuagint fragments, one of Exodus and one of Leviticus, and one fragment of the Letter of Jeremiah (7Q2), a letter purporting to be from Jeremiah to the exiles in Babylon that is not contained in the Hebrew version of the book. Cave 4 provided two fragmentary LXX manuscripts of Leviticus (4Q119, 120) and one each of Numbers (4Q121) and Deuteronomy (4Q122). The text of the Leviticus and Deuteronomy manuscripts is generally close to that of the LXX textual tradition, but they do contain variant wordings. The LXX Numbers manuscript appears to reflect the revision of an earlier Greek version to make it conform to the proto-Masoretic textual tradition.

A few Aramaic paraphrases of the books of Leviticus and Job have also become available. All that survives of the Leviticus Targum (4Q156 or 4QtgLev) is the text of Lev 16:12-15, 18-21, a passage dealing with the Day of Atonement ceremony. The Aramaic follows the Hebrew closely, but at times its renderings attempt to clarify the meaning of the Hebrew, as in the case of the translation "cover" instead of "mercy seat" for the Hebrew word *kaporet,* and in its addition of "house of" to the word "holiness" to make clear that the temple is in view. Two fragments from a targum of Job from Cave 4 preserve the text of Job 3:5-9 and 4:16–5:4. The Cave 11 Job Targum (11Q10 or 11QtgJob) is one of the longest and most complete of the Dead Sea Scrolls, preserving portions of Job 17:14–42:11. It gives a rather literal rendering of its parent Hebrew text, which appears to have been close to the later MT of Job. The targum does have interpretive renderings, though. For instance, it sometimes adds pronominal suffixes for clarity, it has "angels of God" instead of "sons of God" at Job 38:7, it finds ways to avoid the suggestion of disrespect toward God and to enhance the image of Job, and it interprets the Hebrew word *ḥyl* to mean "wealth" rather than "strength" at Job 21:7.

Plain-Sense Commentary

A few Qumran scrolls engage in a type of interpretation that the rabbis would later call *peshat* exegesis — a straightforward interpretation that tries to clarify or explain details of the text that are either unclear or puzzling. A good example is provided by 4Q252 (or 4QpGen[a]), the *Commentary on Genesis,* a work that comments only on selected passages in the book. The approach of the biblical text in this work ranges from simple explanation to the more expansive genre typical of "rewritten Bible." One passage in 4Q252 retells the biblical story of the flood and attempts to square its chronological notices with the solar calendar used by the Qumran community. In its commentary, it often supplies straightforward explanations of puzzling features in the text. A ready example comes in its explanation of why Noah cursed his grandson Canaan instead of his son Ham, when Ham and not Canaan was the one who uncovered his father's nakedness (Gen 9:21-24). The commentator explains that Noah did so because God had already blessed Noah's sons, including Ham, a divine act that prevented the patriarch from cursing him.

Paraphrases and Reworkings

Some Qumran manuscripts present the text of a biblical passage but make additions, omissions, rearrangements, and other changes. Some texts paraphrase the biblical text (e.g., 4Q422 paraphrases passages in Genesis 1–4, 6–9). One of the best examples of a thoroughgoing revision is 4Q364-367, the so-called *Reworked Pentateuch* (4QRP). This document covers the complete Pentateuch but periodically changes the sequence of material, at times adding interpretive elements that range from a word or two through several lines. For example, before Gen 28:6, 4QRP adds six lines of material for dramatic emphasis. The added material relates Rebecca's parting words to her son Jacob before he flees for his life from his brother Esau, and Isaac's words of consolation to Rebecca; in the latter instance, it draws upon material in Gen 27:45 and the book of *Jubilees.* At Exod 15:20-21, 4QRP inserts seven lines of text to produce a Song of Miriam to match the Song of Moses in the biblical text. At Lev 23:2–24:2, it introduces additional laws concerning an offering and a festival not commanded in the Pentateuch — a wood offering and a festival of new oil. 4QRP's new material here is based in part on other biblical passages (e.g., Nehemiah 10) and other works deemed authoritative by the Qumran sectarians (e.g., 11QTemple; 4Q calendar texts).

Harmonizations of Legal Passages (Halakhic Midrash)

Yet another type of biblical interpretation found in the Scrolls comes in the form of harmonizing exegesis, when one text is brought into relation with another text. This type of midrashic interpretation (from the Hebrew word מדרש/*midrash,* meaning "exposition, explanation") was especially popular in the treatment of legal (= "halakhic," from הלכה/*halakhah,* meaning "law, legal ruling") material in the Hebrew Scriptures. In some cases, the intent was to harmonize apparently contradictory legal passages. In others, it was to combine legal passages from the Scriptures to formulate a new sectarian legal principle. This sort of exegetical activity occurs frequently in the three main legal texts among the Scrolls — the *Damascus Document* (CD), the *Rule of the Community* (1QS), and the *Temple Scroll* (11QTemple). A good example of a new sectarian legal principle being derived via halakhic midrash comes in CD 9:2-8. In this passage, three scriptural verses, two from Leviticus and one from Nahum, are brought into relation to produce a new law pertaining to how the Qumran covenanters should deal with disputes among themselves. The gist of the new law is that, if a Qumran sectarian accuses his fellow sectarian of a crime without first going through the community's "due process" of issuing a complaint in front of witnesses, then he is liable to the same penalty that would have fallen on the accused. Interestingly, an actual case in which this law may have come into play at Qumran is found in a fragmentary text from Cave 4 (4Q477).

Rewriting and Expansion of Narratives

Another genre of biblical interpretation in the DSS has come to be known as "rewritten Bible." It involves the wholesale expansion and recasting of scriptural narratives based on a perceived need to explain puzzling or disturbing features of the narrative, to fill in its gaps and silences, or to embellish it with expansive details so as to make it more entertaining.

Without a doubt, the best preserved example of this type of biblical exegesis among the Scrolls is the *Genesis Apocryphon* (1Q20 or 1QapGen). This Aramaic document, probably of pre-Qumran origin, retells select stories in Genesis. The most legible portions of the scroll concern the birth of Noah (col. 2) and the exploits of Abram (cols. 19-22). The material relating to Noah describes the alarm of his father Lamech on seeing such a marvelous infant. Lamech suspects and then accuses his wife Bathenosh of having committed adultery with one of the Watchers or fallen angels (the "sons of God" mentioned in Gen 6:1-4). Bathenosh protests her innocence, assuring Lamech that he is indeed the father of Noah, and reminding him of the pleasure she enjoyed in bed with him. Lamech, still flummoxed, implores his father Methuselah to consult with his father, Enoch. Unfortunately, the column breaks off at this point, so readers never receive Enoch's revelations (but cf. *1 Enoch* 106-7). The extensive Abraham material elaborates on the text of Genesis 12–15. The columns focusing on this patriarch seem to have been composed on the basis of different sources, as is evidenced by the switch from first-person narration ("I [Abram] . . .") to the third person ("Abram wept . . . camped . . . said . . ."). One of the most interesting passages in this section seeks to justify Abram's decision to pass Sarai off as his sister. In Genesis Abram's deed looks like a cowardly lie to save his own skin — and at great risk to the purity and safety of his wife, who ends up in Pharaoh's harem! 1QapGen improves the portrait of Abraham by having him divulge to Sarai a dream vision he has had about a cedar tree (representing himself) and a palm tree (representing her). Abram also prays for Sarai's safety during the two years she is in Pharaoh's harem. Eventually, Abram performs an exorcism on Pharaoh, whom God has afflicted with an evil spirit to keep him from having sexual relations with Sarai.

Pesher Exegesis

A final type of biblical interpretation practiced at Qumran is pesher exegesis (the word פשר/*pesher* means "interpretation"). In this method, the commentator cites a scriptural verse, follows it with the phrase פשרו/*pishro* ("its interpretation is") or פשר הדבר/*pesher ha-dabar* ("the interpretation of the passage is"), and then presents an explanation that relates the ancient prophetic text to events in the life of the Qumran community. Some seventeen pesharim that together comment on a total of seven scriptural books appear among the Scrolls. The underlying assumption in this type of exegesis is that the ancient Hebrew prophets did not really understand their own statements, since their oracles were actually predictions of experiences of the Qumran sect living at the end of days. The Qumran Essenes believed that God had revealed the true meaning of the sacred books to their community's founder, the Teacher of Righteousness. This conviction, and the assumptions informing it, is stated explicitly in one of the pesharim — 1QpHab 6:12–7:6.

> *I will take my stand to watch and will station myself upon my fortress. I will watch to see what He will say to me and how [He will answer] my complaint. And the Lord answered [and said to me, "Write down the vision and make it plain] upon the tablets, that [he who reads] may read it speedily"* (Hab 2:1-2). . . . and God told Habakkuk to write down that which would happen to the final generations, but He did not make known to him when time would come to an end. And as for that which He said, *That he who reads it may read it speedily:* interpreted this concerns the Teacher of Righteousness, to whom God made known all the mysteries of the words of his servants the Prophets. (trans. Vermes)

One type of pesher interpretation, often called "continuous pesher," is represented in works that provide a running, verse-by-verse commentary on a scriptural book or part thereof. Three examples may illustrate the genre. The *Nahum Commentary* (1Q169 or 1QpNah) is distinctive for actually mentioning historical figures by their real names: Demetrius (probably the Seleucid king Demetrius III Eukerus, who ruled Palestine 95-88 BC) and Antiochus (either Antiochus III or IV). It also uses cryptograms to refer to various groups and figures — "Seekers after Smooth Things" (the Pharisees), "Kittim" (the Romans), and "the Young Lion" (probably the Hasmonean ruler Alexander Jannaeus, 103-76 BC). The *Habakkuk Commentary* (1Q33 or 1QpHab) is remarkable for focusing on key moments in the history of the community and for mentioning some important figures in Qumran history under symbolic names: the sect's leader ("the Teacher of Righteousness"), its principal opponent ("the Wicked Priest"), and a personage (the "Liar") who may have led a rival faction of the sect ("the House of Absalom"). The *Psalms Commentary* (4Q171, 173 or 4QpPs) interprets Ps 37:32-33 as a prophecy of the struggles between the Wicked Priest and the Teacher of Righteousness. It mentions a "law" that the latter "sent" to the former, a document that has been identified with either 11QTemple or 4QMMT. And most intriguing of all, it speaks of the Wicked Priest's attempted assassination of the Teacher of Righteousness.

Another type of pesher, the so-called thematic pesher, is found in works that cluster different biblical texts around a common theme, usually eschatological, and then expound upon them. Three main examples may be cited. The *Florilegium* or *Midrash on the Last Days* (4Q174 or 4QFlor; cf. the related text 4Q177 or 4QCatena A) engages in messianic exegesis of 2 Samuel 7, Psalm 2, and other scriptural passages. Among its hallmark features is its description of three temples — the current temple in Jerusalem; the Qumran community as a substitute, spiritual temple; and the eschatological temple to be built by God in the new age. It is also important because it is one of the Qumran texts that mentions two messiahs, a royal one ("the Branch of David") and a priestly or prophetic one ("the Interpreter of the Law"). The *Testimonia* or *Messianic Anthology* (4Q175) offers a collection of proof-texts that culls various scriptural passages, most without commentary, for use in teaching about the messiah(s). In a passage it shares with an *Apocryphon of Joshua* (4Q379), it refers obliquely to an incident in the Hasmonean era, a father's loss of two sons. The figures in question have been identified with Simon and his two sons, who were murdered at a banquet in Jericho in 134 BC; and, alternately, with John Hyrcanus, whose son Antigonus murdered his brother Aristobulus I and then died shortly thereafter in 103 BC. 11QMelchizedek (11Q13 or 11QMelch) presents an eschatological midrash on Lev 25:13, Deut 15:2, Isa. 60:1, and other scriptural passages. The three main biblical passages speak, in turn, about the year of Jubilee, when properties revert to their original owners; the remission of debts every seventh (sabbatical) year; and the eschatological liberation of captives. 11QMelchizedek brings these texts into association to formulate a teaching about the release of captives from Belial, when God will grant victory to the heavenly forces of good over the cosmic forces of evil, through the leadership of a heavenly savior or messiah figure called "Melchizedek." This heavenly figure is probably the archangel Michael (see 4QAmram; cf. 1QS 3; 1QM 17). Among his tasks are to atone for and forgive the sins of the Sons of Light. In the midrash, Melchizedek is associated with Ps 82:1 and is in fact identified with the *Elohim* (divine being) mentioned in that passage: "*Elohim* [NRSV: "God"] has taken his place in the divine council; in the midst of the gods he holds judgment." Beyond these two types of pesharim, the continuous and the thematic, isolated pesher interpretations appear in other genres of sectarian literature. They are especially prominent in the *Damascus Document* (e.g., CD 4:14-19 on Isa 24:17).

* * *

To many a modern reader, the status and treatment of "the Bible" at Qumran pose a paradox. How is it that a group who so highly valued the inspiration and authority of the Scriptures could allow itself to treat the biblical text in such a seemingly arbitrary manner? Specifically, how is it that a group who so manifestly revered the Scriptures was nevertheless glad to have them in different textual forms and different literary editions? And how is it that a community so concerned with exact observance of the Torah could feel free to engage in conscious revisions of it and to indulge in interpretations that more often than not ignored the historical, contextual meaning of the text? Only partial and tentative answers to these questions are possible, and even then only by drawing inferences from the texts themselves. The Qumran group's penchant for a variety of textual forms and literary editions may simply have risen from their conscious awareness of living in an age when the biblical text was in fact still fluid. On the principle "the more the merrier" they may have understood their production and study of these pluriform texts as a contribution to a creative literary enterprise. When it comes to their contemporizing, actualizing modes of interpretation, the Qumran covenanters evidently approached their task in the conviction that the Scriptures were a *living* tradition whose proper appropriation had recently been revealed to them through the inspiration of their founder, the *moreh ha-ṣedeq*, the Right — the Sole, Legitimate — Teacher. They apparently considered themselves to be standing within an ongoing, Spirit-inspired tradition. The age of revelation was not over. This realization, combined with their intense awareness of living at the end of days, evidently predisposed them to see themselves within the pages of Scripture. In this respect, the Jews of Qumran were no different from the early Christians who produced the New Testament. Finally, it is important to recognize that in the history of both Judaism and Christianity, concern with Scripture's historical, contextual sense is a relatively modern preoccupation.

Bibliography. Abegg, M. G., P. W. Flint, and E. Ulrich. 1999, *The Dead Sea Scrolls Bible*, San Francisco: HarperSanFrancisco • Flint, P. W., and J. C. VanderKam, eds. 1999, *The Dead Sea Scrolls after Fifty Years: A Comprehensive Assessment*, 2 vols., Leiden: Brill • Magness, J. 2002, *The Archaeology of Qumran and the Dead Sea Scrolls*, Grand Rapids: Eerdmans, • Schiffman, L. H., and J. C. VanderKam, eds. 2000, *The Encyclopedia of the Dead Sea Scrolls*. 2 vols., Oxford: Oxford University • Tov, E.

2d ed., 2001, *Textual Criticism of the Hebrew Bible,* Assen/Maastricht: Van Gorcum; Minneapolis: Fortress • Trebolle Barrera, J. 1998, *The Jewish Bible and the Christian Bible: An Introduction to the History of the Bible,* Leiden: Brill; Grand Rapids: Eerdmans • Ulrich, E. 1999, *The Dead Sea Scrolls and the Origins of the Bible,* Grand Rapids: Eerdmans; Leiden: Brill • VanderKam, J., and P. Flint. 2002, *The Meaning of the Dead Sea Scrolls,* San Francisco: HarperSanFrancisco • Vermes, G. 1997, *The Complete Dead Sea Scrolls in English,* London/New York: Penguin.

The History of the Tradition: New Testament

James D. G. Dunn

1. Introduction

The New Testament (NT) is made up of twenty-seven documents of varying lengths and types. Their range is somewhat similar to that of the Old Testament (OT):

- four Gospels, as primary in character for the NT as the five books of Moses for the OT;
- a book of history (but only one in the NT);
- a sequence of letters interpreting the primary traditions (the gospel) somewhat as the prophets interpreted the Torah;
- and an apocalypse (the Apocalypse of John = Revelation) equivalent to the OT's Daniel.

The most glaring lack of parallel is the absence of psalms in the NT (but psalms and hymns do appear in various other NT books) and the absence of wisdom writings (though James could qualify as such).

On this point the NT is more closely parallel to the OT than it is to the Apocrypha, or to the Dead Sea Scrolls (DSS), or to the Pseudepigrapha. The point highlights an important feature of the NT — what might be called the tension between continuity and discontinuity in the NT's relation to earlier Jewish writings, including the writings which were already regarded as "scripture." On the one hand, the NT can properly be classified as the literary product of what at least began as a Jewish sect (the Nazarenes). The indebtedness of its writings to the OT in particular can be documented on page after page. C. H. Dodd subtitled his study of the use of the OT in the NT, "The Substructure of New Testament Theology." At the same time, however, the NT writings do not appear simply as a supplement to the OT (like much of the Apocrypha) or simply as an interpretation of the OT (like many of the DSS), or simply as a rewriting of the OT (like several pseudepigrapha). In its present "shape" the NT is more like the OT itself, more a complement than a supplement, as we might say, more, indeed, like an alternative collection gathered around its own primary traditions.

For the task of clarifying how these documents and the NT took their historic and present shape, the more important difference between OT and NT is the time span covered by the process. In the case of the OT, the time span from the earliest traditions to the last of the OT writings (Daniel), and to a widely recognized Hebrew Bible (OT canon; cf. Sirach prologue), covered a millennium or more. In contrast, in the case of the NT the time span from Jesus' first utterance to the latest of the NT writings (2 Peter?) was probably less than a century, and the NT canon was more or less finalized within a further three hundred years (see, e.g., Kümmel 1975: pt. 2). Consequently it is relatively easier in the case of the NT to trace the history of the tradition which now constitutes the NT documents and the NT itself.

Given the importance of Jesus himself for the NT and of the Gospels within the NT, it will be necessary to spend the most time on what is usually described as the history of the Jesus tradition — that is, the traditions of teaching from Jesus and stories about Jesus which now make up the Gospels. But the rest of the NT is also tradition, and it will be important to trace out its history too.

2. The Gospels

2.1. From Jesus to Tradition

The NT begins with Jesus. It was the impact of his ministry or mission, of his teaching and life, which forms the beginning of the history of the tradition which now makes up the Gospels. We can readily imagine these earliest traditions. They would be quite diverse. At one end they would consist of the reports and rumors regarding things Jesus said and did which circulated around Galilee and Judea and perhaps more widely. Typically they would consist of versions of stories he told (parables), of memorable sayings and teachings (e.g., proverbs), of striking acts of healing (particularly exorcisms). From the present character of the tradition (particularly the Synoptic Gospels) we can be sure that the main emphasis of his preaching (on the kingdom of God) would have been known, as well as the controversial nature of his dealings with those popularly regarded as "sinners." Reports and tales, we may speculate confidently, would be told and retold in the marketplace, around campfires, in homes and places of assembly. The seminovelistic presentation by Gerd Theissen of *The Shadow of the Galilean* gives as good a "feel" for this process as we are likely to be able to reconstruct now.

It is important to recognize at once that the traditions which come down to us attest and reflect the impact made by Jesus from the first. We do not have traditions which have come down through Herod or Pilate, through Pharisees or Sadducees (with possible but uncertain and minimal exceptions in Josephus *Ant.* 18.63 and *b. Sanh.* 43a). We do not have traditions preserved by dispassionate or uninvolved spectators who happened to hear or see something which accidentally lodged in their memory. We have only those traditions which made sufficient impact on audiences for them to be remembered and passed on. That is to say, their effect is already indicated in the very fact of their preservation and retelling, and is already embodied to some extent at least in the form in which they were retold and passed on. Alternatively expressed, we today have access to these sayings and events only because they became "tradition."

The corollaries to this insight are important. For it means, first, that the ideal sometimes maintained by scholars, that it should be possible to hear and encounter the historical Jesus as a disinterested spectator might have done in the year 30 or so, is wholly unrealistic. The preaching of Jesus does not come to us because he wrote it down or as a tape recorder or video recorder might have preserved it. It comes to us only because it made the impact it did on the witnesses and only as it was experienced and remembered by them. In other words, the hearing (and witnessing) was what Paul calls faith-creating hearing (Rom. 10:14, 17), hearing with faith (Gal 3:2, 5). Those who did not have "ears to hear" (Matt 11:15; 13:9, 43) heard and saw nothing of major or lasting significance. So they remembered nothing of importance (for them), they formulated no continuing tradition, and so we have no access to "the historical Jesus" through them. The tradition we have is faith tradition, or disciple tradition, and we have it because what was seen and heard created that faith and made disciples of those who thus heard, disciples through whom the tradition was remembered and passed on. This is not to say, of course, that what Jesus did and said had a uniform impact on his first disciples or that there was a uniform attempt to recall and pass on these remembrances of Jesus; the diversity of tradition in the Gospels no doubt reflects in some measure at least the diversity of impact which Jesus had on those who can be called "disciples." Nonetheless, the basic point remains: the Gospels are disciple tradition.

The other corollary worth noting at this point is that Jesus must have said and done far more than has been recorded in the Gospels. Even for a three-year ministry, on the usual reckoning, it could hardly be otherwise (Mark's Gospel can easily be read in a single evening). This also means that not everything Jesus said and did was memorable, which is also to say that not everything Jesus said and did was remembered. The thought may be surprising or even offensive to some — that anything Jesus said or did might be considered not worth remembering. But the thought quickly degenerates into a false piety. It was the things Jesus did and said and which created faith which were remembered, and they were remembered precisely because of their faith-creating power. To look outside that circle of witness on the assumption that there must be other faith-creating nuggets to be discovered is simply to fail to realize that the Gospel tradition is locked into and dependent on the circle of faith from the first. The point has been given weight at the end of the nineteenth century by Martin Kähler, and now again, a century later, by Luke Johnson.

That is not to say that the Gospels themselves exhausted the complete stock of remembered tradition of what Jesus did and said. There are several sayings of Jesus preserved outside the Gospels which seem to belong to that same first circle (see, e.g., Hofius 1991). We may assume that the evangelists were selective even among the traditions available to them. But the number of these individual sayings are few and, if anything, strengthen the view that the Synoptic writers in particular provide a full and thorough representation of the traditions as remembered from the first.

2.2. Remembering Communities

The forming and passing on of the Jesus tradition was not the work of individuals as such. The impact made by Jesus was lasting because it was disciple making, which is also to say that it was community forming. The individuals influenced by Jesus were drawn together by their shared experience and by their shared discipleship. And that which bonded them together included, not least, the impressions and remembrances which they shared and which continued to motivate them as disciples. We can deduce this from a number of factors.

For one thing, sociology has made us aware that in group formation, foundation tradition plays a critical role in determining the identity and boundaries of the group. The members of the group have to be able to explain, to themselves as well as to others, what it is that constitutes them a distinctive group. In this case the foundation tradition would certainly include the shared remembrances of what Jesus did and said.

This is confirmed by the evidence we have of the first names given to the groups of Jesus' disciples. Early on they evidently thought of themselves simply as "the disciples" (Acts 6:1, 2, 7; etc.) or as followers of "the Way" (Acts 9:2; etc.) — that is, disciples of *Jesus,* followers of the way *indicated by him* (cf. 4:13; 18:25-26). By others they were known as "the sect of the Nazarenes" (Acts 24:5, 14; 28:22), that is, they were identified by their association with Jesus of Nazareth, the prophet/teacher/messiah from Nazareth (cf. 4:10). Subsequently the name "Christians" emerged in Greek at Antioch — a group designated by their belief in Jesus as Messiah/Christ. In each case that which marked the first believers out was their relation to and belief in Jesus. Such a group would be bound to explain and define themselves by reference to Jesus — that is, by using the traditions regarding Jesus.

For another, group dynamic would insure that some within the group assumed or were charged with the responsibility to remember and rehearse these traditions for strangers, for newcomers, and for celebrations of the group. In villages it would be typically the older members, the elders. In the assemblies of disciples of Jesus we soon hear of just such "teaching" (Acts 2:42) and of "teachers" (Acts 13:1; Gal 6:6; Jas 3:1) whose responsibility it must have been to tend to the teaching.

Of course, the process of group formation really got under way only after Jesus' death and resurrection. This climax of Jesus' ministry seems to have made more impact than his earlier ministry, at least on the central core of disciples. And very soon the conversion-effecting impact was that of the message *about* Jesus rather than that *of* Jesus himself; the tradition became the point of impact rather than its effect, or, alternatively expressed, the tradition of Jesus' teaching and life, death and resurrection, mediated the impact which Jesus himself had formerly made directly.

At the same time the process presumably already got under way at least to some extent during Jesus' ministry. Jesus early on is remembered as having taught his disciples a prayer (the Lord's Prayer) to function as the badge of their discipleship, that is, no doubt, to be said by them together (Luke 11:1-4). Prominent in the impact of Jesus was his own attitude to the teachings and traditions of the past — particularly his ability to cut through secondary issues to the heart of the matter (e.g., Matt 5:21-30; Mark 2:23–3:5; 7:5-13) — an attitude to revered text and tradition and prioritizing in teaching and action which his disciples presumably sought to follow in their discipleship more or less from the first. And Matthew can even include a code of church discipline already within the Jesus tradition (Matthew 18). Most of the sayings tradition preserved in Q (a source which most agree was used by Matthew and Luke) could have been taught and passed on without reference to Jesus' death and resurrection, and so may already have been gathered before these final events. And at one or two points we catch tantalizing glimpses of active groups who were not part of the main stream of discipleship (Mark 9:38-41; Acts 19:1-7) and who had a patchy or fragmentary knowledge of the much larger shared deposit of foundation tradition.

This raises a further intriguing question: whether the impact made by Jesus was much more diverse than is reflected in our Gospels; whether, that is, there were, more or less from the beginning, other groups/churches which remembered different aspects of Jesus' ministry, or remembered solely Jesus the teacher (and not Jesus the crucified and risen). The issue has been raised in recent years by the discovery and subsequent reflection on the significance of the *Gospel of Thomas.* We will return to the issue below; suffice it to say here that the amount of reliable or authentic Jesus tradition outside the canonical Gospels (i.e., tradition which begins from the hearing and witnessing of what Jesus said and did) seems to be very limited (see again Hofius 1991 and further Tuckett's "Introduction to the Gospels," 990 below). Anyway, our primary task is to trace the history of the tradition which came to form the NT.

2.3. Oral Tradition – The How

One of the important insights about the early tradition is that it was not conceived as something fixed — a memory of something Jesus said which had to be preserved and paraded in a precious casket, as it were, reverenced as said by Jesus at such and such a time and place, a memory of something he did which had to be retold in just this and not that way. All the evidence we have indicates otherwise. The most immediate evidence is that of the Gospels themselves, particularly the three Gospels which share so much of the same material (the Synoptics). Of course, they preserve the tradition in a later, written form. But the forms of the tradition reflect earlier usage, and the way in which the tradition was handled at the written stage may not have been so different from the oral use.

This oral usage can be illustrated in a number of points. First, most of the traditions of Jesus' sayings and actions do not display any concern to remember time and place of saying or doing — one of the preliminary insights behind the development of "form criticism" (see below 2.4; 5.4). And if they now give the impression of chronological and geographical sequence, that is usually because of the editorial work of the evangelists in so sequencing them. In other words, the stories were retold because their point and continuing value was independent of original time or place (e.g., Mark 2:18, 23; 3:31; 4:21; etc.). We should add that such a conclusion says nothing for or against the historical value of these traditions; it simply observes how the traditions were remembered.

Second, similar traditions were put together, presumably for ease of remembering and retelling. For example, Matthew 13 and Mark 4 look as though they are the end products of quite a process of gathering together parables of Jesus, including some reflection on their significance. A sequence of Jesus' sayings about his exorcisms has been brought together, it would appear in overlapping collections (Mark 3:22-30; Luke 11:14-26). The same is true of a number of sayings about discipleship (Matt 8:19-22 par. Luke 9:57-62). And a group of miracle stories around the lake of Galilee seems to lie behind Mark's sequence in Mark 4:35–5:43 and 6:30-56. Again, this is not to imply any casualness in the remembering process, but the manner and priorities in the process — the continuing benefit of these remembered words and deeds for the communities of faith.

Third, we can see how readily stories about Jesus could be told in different versions. We may compare, for example, Mark 2:23-28 with Matt 12:1-8 and Luke 6:1-5, and Mark 5:21-43 with Matt 9:18-26 and Luke 8:40-56. Material could be and was added or subtracted, expanded or curtailed. There was evidently a sense that the substance and value of the story did not depend on its being told and retold with slavish or pedantic accuracy. More generally, E. P. Sanders has shown that the detail of tradition evidently "developed" both by elaboration and by abbreviation.

Fourth, not surprisingly, stories about Jesus could be told from different angles to bring out different points for the attentive assemblies. The best example is the story of Jesus' encounter with the centurion and healing of his slave (Matt 8:5-13; Luke 7:1-10). Behind the two versions is evidently a shared memory of a single event. The heart of the shared memory is the actual encounter between Jesus and the centurion, the dialogue between them, where, noticeably, the words are in close agreement (Matt 8:8-10 par. Luke 7:6b-9). But both evangelists seem to have taken a theme from the common core and elaborated it to bring out their respective points: Luke emphasizes the centurion's humility (so in his account the centurion does not come personally — Luke 7:2-6a); and Matthew focuses on the centurion's faith (so he climaxes his account by attaching a saying of Jesus from elsewhere — Matt 8:11-12 par. Luke 13:28-30). Here again we observe the same combination of respect for the tradition's substance and core and a certain freedom in reusing the tradition.

All this tells us something about the tradition and about the remembering. The tradition was a living tradition, of contemporary value, not an attempt simply to recall a heroic figure now dead and gone. Likewise the remembering was a means not so much of recalling the past as of bringing the tradition into the present. If we are to appreciate the history of the Jesus tradition, it is vital that this character of it as living tradition be properly grasped. Too much ink has been wasted in debate about the Jesus tradition in posing as sharp opposites either a scrupulous fidelity to historical facts and details or a complete freedom to create and elaborate. The evidence of the Synoptic Gospels, illustrated above, is that the transmission of early Christian tradition was neither, but was rather a combination of respect and adaptation, a genuine concern to recall the teaching and example of Jesus blended with a concern that the tradition should continue to speak to the developing churches and changing situations of the time.

Much of this is borne out by the researches of Kenneth Bailey into oral tradition processes in Middle Eastern village communities in the middle of the twentieth century — as close as we are likely to get to the tradition culture in the villages of upper Galilee, closer, at any rate, than the oral epics of Yugoslavia and Greece, on which Albert Lord built his not dissimilar conclusions regarding oral tradition. Bailey observed the same phenomena as described above — stories of memorable visitors or incidents, told often in different versions, but characteristically with the core of the story fixed, the substance and point of the story constant, while the supportive details could be elaborated or abbreviated as circumstances allowed or necessitated. It is the same kind of popular/formal or semipopular/semiformal transmission of tradition which seems to be reflected in the tradition which makes up the Synoptic Gospels.

2.4. *Oral Tradition – The Why*

The other side of the same process is the purpose to which these traditions were put. Here, too, we can gain a fairly clear idea of why the traditions were retained and retold.

In terms of the history of Gospels research we have now reached the phase at which the Synoptic tradition was analyzed into different "forms" (hence "form criticism") (esp. Bultmann 1963). This research recognized the living character of the tradition by envisaging tradition molded to the situations for which it was being reused (*Sitz im Leben* = "life setting") and by observing and arguing that much of the tradition took what might be called "standard forms." The working assumption was that in order for the tradition to be used in the churches it would naturally fall into the forms characteristic for different kinds of material. The clearest examples are miracle stories (trouble signaled, decisive word or act indicated, result described), pronouncement stories (climaxing in a memorable saying of Jesus), and the epigrammatic character of wisdom sayings. Unfortunately, however, the concept of the "form" itself became too much the focus of debate, the conception of tradition formation and tradition transmission became too stereotyped and formalized (the "laws" of transmission), and the appreciation of the living character of the process, of the malleability of the forms from the first, was largely lost to sight.

More valuable was the attempt of C. F. D. Moule to turn the question around and to focus on the different contexts in which and purposes for which the tradition was maintained and used. For example, we need not doubt that worship was at the heart of the early Christian assemblies. Nor can we doubt that tradition deriving directly from the remembered Jesus was very much at the heart of that worship. We need only think of the Lord's Prayer, whose slightly differing versions (Matt 6:9-13; Luke 11:2-4) tell the same story of tradition cherished, but cherished by the using, and adapted in the using to be the more useful. Jesus' own example of praying to God as "Abba, Father" was evidently also cherished, as the preservation of the Aramaic term into Greek-speaking worship, as a prayer betokening sonship shared with Jesus, surely indicates (Rom 8:15-17; Gal 4:6-7). The same is true of the words of institution of the Last/Lord's Supper (cf. Mark 14:22-25 with Luke 22:17-20), whose regular usage in the earliest churches is confirmed by Paul in 1 Cor 11:23-26. Many scholars have deduced from the fact that the passion narrative is a continuous block of material that it was put together for liturgical purposes, presumably to be recited afresh at each anniversary of Jesus' passion.

A second obvious case would be material for teaching within the assemblies of believers and for catechizing inquirers or new converts. The clearest example here is probably the Sermon on the Mount (Matthew 5–7). The fact that most of the parallel material in Luke is scattered throughout Luke strongly suggests that the Sermon has been put together as a teaching device, to gather appropriate teaching material from the remembered words of Jesus, and to frame it in a way that made it the more easily remembered by those taught in turn. Once again this is not to say that the account of Jesus sitting down on the mountain and teaching (Matt 5:1-2) is a later creation. No doubt Jesus quite often sat on a Galilean hillside to teach. It is simply to recognize that the early Christian teachers grouped and edited the Jesus tradition not so much in accord with any particular remembered where and when of Jesus speaking (as though that was the primary consideration) but in accord with the most effective remembrance and usage of the tradition.

The "little apocalypse" of Mark 13 probably came to Mark as the end product of a text of Jesus tradition much used by assemblies when they came to reflect soberly on the end to come. And we can easily envisage many a story about Jesus or sequence of Jesus' teaching providing means of edification and cause for pause at the breakings of bread alluded to in Acts (2:42, 46) and the Lord's Suppers and other gatherings for worship indicated in 1 Corinthians 11–14.

If evangelistic preaching usually focused on the death and resurrection of Jesus (as both Acts and the Pauline letters imply — e.g., Acts 2:23-36; 4:2; 17:18; 1 Cor 15:1-11; 2 Cor 5:18-21; Gal 3:1), apologetic in a Jewish context probably drew more immediately on the tradition of Jesus' words and actions itself. This is clearly suggested by the block of tradition used by Mark in 2:1–3:6, a collection of some five controversy stories in which Jesus' authority to act in ways judged by many to be controversial is asserted. Since they touch on such matters as healing, eating with sinners, fasting, and how to conduct oneself on the sabbath, we can easily see that they would have provided important precedents for the earliest Jewish believers. In other words, Mark 2:1–3:6 looks as though it was put together to provide early Jewish believers with arguments to counter the criticisms they may have received for following the teaching and lifestyle of Jesus as remembered in the tradition.

2.5. *New Tradition?*

Thus far we have spoken only of tradition as the remembrances of Jesus' first disciples. But many interpreters assume that much if not most of the tradition in the Synoptics is the work of the post-Easter churches. Rudolf Bultmann 1963 and Ernst Käsemann 1964: 60, for example, argued that traditions quite different from the original remembrances poured into the Jesus tradition from the wider Hellenistic world and from Christian prophets active in the early Christian assemblies. The counter-attempt, by Birger Gerhardsson in particular, to argue for a greater fixity in the tradition from (later) rabbinic methods of rote learning and memorizing has not proved an adequate response. For one thing, the evidence illustrated above on how the Synoptic Gospels handle the tradition, and the relative freedom with which they have done so, hardly bears witness to fixed tradition passed on by memorizing. Bailey's "middle way" of "informal controlled oral tradition" makes better sense of all the evidence. And for another, the basic scenario of prophets functioning in assemblies (as well as teachers) and speaking in the name of Jesus, possibly even in an "I" form (speaking in Jesus' words), cannot be dismissed out of hand. Prophets and prophesying are certainly attested in Acts (11:27; 13:1; 15:32; 21:9-10) and Paul (Rom 12:6; 1 Cor 11:4-5; 12:28-29; 14:29-32; 1 Thess 5:20), and a text like Matt 18:20, which seems to presuppose a later setting of established "churches," has all the appearance of a prophetic saying received as a saying of Jesus himself.

What has been forgotten, however, as Dunn 1977-78 has pointed out, is that the heritage of prophecy made both Jews and Christians highly sensitive to the danger of false prophecy. In the OT we need think simply of the classic cases of Micaiah ben Imlah in 1 Kgs 22:1-40 and of Jeremiah in Jeremiah 28. And Paul was alert to the danger from the first, as his repeated reminder that prophecies must be tested and evaluated indicates (1 Cor 12:10), whether by the recognized prophets in particular (1 Cor 14:29) or by the congregation as a whole (1 Thess 5:19-22). There had also been much reflection on effective tests for false prophecy. One of the most effective within the assembly of Israel presumably was the appeal to what we might call the foundation tradition:

> If prophets . . . appear among you and promise you omens or portents . . . and they say, "Let us follow other gods" (whom you have not known) "and let us serve them," you must not heed the words of these prophets . . . ; for the LORD your God is testing you, to know whether you indeed love the LORD your God with all your heart and soul. (Deut 13:1-3)

In other words, a prophet might make an accurate prediction, but if that prophet counseled departure from Israel's foundation confession, in Deuteronomy classically summed up in the Shema (Deut 6:4), he was to be judged a false prophet.

Paul follows the same pattern: the prophet who fails to acknowledge the primary confession, "Jesus is Lord," is a false prophet (1 Cor 12:3). And 1 John subsequently indicates the same sure test: the prophet who denies that Jesus Christ has come in the flesh is false (1 John 4:1-3). Given the depth of this experience of false prophecy in Jewish scripture, confirmed early on in the Pauline assemblies, it is unlikely that the reappearance of prophecy as a living experience of the earliest assemblies would have caught these assemblies unprepared for the problem of false prophecy. As soon as prophets began to speak in "I" terms in the assemblies there would almost certainly have been those who asked whether the prophecy was indeed from God. In those circumstances what test would they use to decide on the authenticity of the inspired words?

One of the most obvious answers is, the foundation tradition on which their assembly was built (Gerhardsson 1986 speaks of "inner tradition"). In other words, these assemblies almost certainly did not gather tradition indiscrminately from all quarters. They had their core material, the remembered words and actions of Jesus which had first drawn them together, or, in the case of later assemblies, the tradition which had first converted them and brought them together as "church." This would be their foundation tradition, the yardstick remembrances which they would particularly cherish and which they would almost certainly use when the issue of true or false prophecy came up. The measure would be clear: if the teaching accorded with the primary tradition, it would be acceptable; but if not, the teaching or prophecy would probably have been rejected.

This proves a useful rule of thumb for those today concerned as to whether and how much new (post-Easter) tradition has crept (or flooded) into the Jesus tradition. Where there is teaching which clarifies or explains previous tradition, that is the sort of supplementation or elaboration of the earlier tradition which would prove acceptable. One of the best/most plausible examples is Mark 13:10. But where there is material in the Synoptic tradition which is distinctively different from other early tradition, it must be judged unlikely that that material was added later; for it is just such material, even if produced by a prophet or a teacher, which would most likely have been deemed to be at odds with the already accepted and revered tradition. For example, a distinctive self-reference like "the son of man," or distinctive emphasis in regard to the kingdom of God (either its presence or its imminent approach), is almost certainly part of the original Jesus tradition; for it would be just such a new tradition which would have been judged to fail the test of foundation tradition.

A nice in-between example is the birth narratives of Matthew and Luke (Matthew 1–2; Luke 1–2). Interestingly enough, we observe the same storytelling features in these chapters. For both accounts focus on a central core: Jesus' birth was such that, from the beginning, he was both Son of David and Son of God (Matt 1:20, 23; Luke 1:32, 35). But beyond that they are completely diverse, with hardly any other common features. These stories cannot be strictly described as foundation tradition. But they attest an interest in the life as well as the teaching of Jesus which could evidently not be resolved without some account of his birth; this is frequently the case with figures early on recognized to have historic or epochal significance, such as Alexander the Great. In this case the accounts as they emerged, whether in much briefer or in their present form, were deemed to be consistent with and an acceptable elaboration of the primary tradition of Jesus' ministry, death, and resurrection.

2.6. From Aramaic to Greek

In any attempt to trace the history of the Gospels tradition the next phase has to be the transition from Aramaic to Greek, when tradition which initially circulated in Aramaic (the language which all assume was the principal language of Jesus) was put into Greek (the principal *lingua franca* of the Eastern Mediterranean world). We do not know when this happened, but we can assume that it must have begun to take place quite quickly. For the traditions about Jesus would undoubtedly have aroused interest in the Greek-speaking/Hellenistic cities of the region. And we soon hear of a body of disciples in Jersalem itself, within months rather than years of Jesus' death and resurrection, who were known as "Greek-speakers" (Acts 6:1). Since their very designation must indicate that they could function effectively only in Greek (as opposed to the Hebrew/Aramaic speakers – Acts 6:1), they must have heard and used the Jesus tradition in Greek more or less from the first.

The transition would be bound to have an effect on the Jesus tradition. Modern translators know that there is no translation from one language to another which does not involve at least some interpretation. Since the nearest equivalent words in different languages rarely have identical semantic ranges, and since idioms are usually distinctively different among languages, good translations of the Aramaic tradition into Greek would inevitably involve some shift of emphasis and tone.

The point, however, should not be exaggerated. For, as we have already seen, the Aramaic tradition was not fixed; vocabulary and idiom would vary between regions; and the teachers and retellers of the Jesus tradition insured its continuing flexibility (living tradition). Nor should we assume that the transition was immediate, widespread, or final. For many years, even decades, no doubt, the tradition continued to be used in Aramaic in Aramaic-speaking churches. Indeed, one can fairly say that the still continuing Syrian churches are the direct heirs of the early Aramaic-speaking churches. In other words, the transition would be long-drawn-out and always partial, the first expansion of the Jesus tradition into other languages rather than a transfer of it *en bloc* from one language to another.

Nevertheless, those who are interested in the history of the tradition need to remind themselves that it is only as a result of this transition that we today have immediate access to the tradition. We today have no NT text in Aramaic, and reconstruction of Aramaic forms is always a hazardous business. Given that we have to be content with the Greek translations, it is only a few scattered words (like "Abba") which put us in touch with the words whose syllables Jesus actually pronounced.

2.7. From Oral to Written Tradition

Even more important than the transition from Aramaic to Greek was the transition from oral to written tradition. We are even more in the dark as to when this transition began to take place. It is by no means impossible that there were written versions of sayings and stories of Jesus circulating during his life (as suggested by Ellis). Who can say what scribal activity literary disciples, or government spies(!), engaged in to help circulate news about the Nazareth prophet or potential troublemaker? Possibly the first literary collections or epitomes were attempts to put the tradition into Greek for those who could not understand the Aramaic teachers and storytellers.

Whenever the transition began to take place, and in whatever forms, it is sometimes assumed that the transition was something epochal, from highly flexible oral tradition to a script fixed in writing (Bultmann 1963: 3), "frozen into a static condition" (Kelber 1983: 94). Such a view exaggerates both the flexibility of oral tradition and the degree of fixity of written tradition. The former, as we have seen, retains core, substance, and shape, even while the secondary, complementary, or interpretative details are varied. The latter, as the literary relations between the Gospels themselves confirm, allow quite as much flexibility in transmission. And as we shall see, even when the written text is beginning to be regarded as sacred, the processes of scribal transmission allow for variation, elaboration, and correction. Those who have studied the processes of oral tradition most closely point out the difficulty of making clear and consistent distinctions between oral and written tradition in terms of fixity and flexibility (Ø. Anderson 1991).

And as with the transition from Aramaic to Greek, so the transition from oral to written did not take place overnight, or all in one place. It was neither once and all, nor, once it had happened in any place, did it mean that the new literary community somehow ceased to be an oral community. The oral community assuredly did not jettison its oral tradition when and because it had received a proto-Gospel or complete Gospel. Rather, we have to assume a quite lengthy process of tradition being increasingly put into writing, probably in Aramaic but certainly in Greek, while at the same time the same and other material continued to circulate orally and to be used in both Aramaic and Greek in oral forms. Well into the second century, when presumably the transition was well advanced, there were still those inquiring about oral traditions which must still have been circulating and not all "reduced" to writing. We need recall only the words of Papias (c. 130) cited by Eusebius:

> If anyone chanced to come who had actually been a follower of the elders, I would inquire as to the discourses of the elders, what Andrew or what Peter said, or what Philip, or what Thomas or James, or what John or Matthew or any other of the Lord's disciples; and the things which Aristion and John the elder, disciples of the Lord, say. For I supposed that things out of books did not profit me so much as the utterance of a voice which liveth and abideth. (*Hist. Eccl.* 3.39.4)

All this needs to be remembered when we consider the more familiar next phases.

2.8. From Forms to Written Sources

The process by which written sources emerged is still fairly speculative for the twentieth-century inquirer. Presumably the passion narrative was early on put into writing, in one or more versions, for different churches' use. Certainly the relatively sustained character of the narrative and the stability of the sequence of events in the two main Synoptic versions (Matthew par. Mark and Luke) suggest a narrative well established by repeated use, where the distinction between oral and written becomes immaterial. Similarly, it is quite possible that the collections of Jesus' teaching, such as the Sermon on the Plain in Luke 6:17-49 and the collections on parables mentioned earlier (Mark 4; Matthew 13), were put into writing at some early stage.

Gospels research of the last 150 years has concluded that our present Gospels drew on two main sources — Mark as the earliest of the written Gospels, and Q as a collection of sayings of Jesus which Matthew and Luke drew heavily upon (see again Tuckett, "Introduction to the Gospels," 993-96 below). But Mark may well have had earlier blocks of written material to use (the group of controversy stories in 2:1–3:6, the collection of parables in ch. 4, the collection of miracle stories in chs. 4–6, the material behind "the little apocalypse" in ch. 13, and the passion narrative running from chs. 14 to 16). And Luke in the preface to his Gospel speaks of many orderly accounts of Jesus' ministry attempted before he himself took the task in hand (Luke 1:1). Alternatively, the putting into writing of the tradition in Mark's Gospel, with the ordering, shaping, and editing involved, may have been mostly his own work.

In terms of the process of tradition transmission it need not have made very much difference how many layers or phases there were in the process before the tradition reached its present shape in the Synoptic Gospels. Earlier research tended to assume that there must have been innumerable layers between the present Gospels and any original words of Jesus or witnesses to Jesus. On this view, every telling of the tradition, every transcription of the tradition was another layer, each with its own emphases, elaborations, or abbreviations, each with its own peculiar characteristics, which in principle at least might be stripped away, like layers of old paint or wallpaper, or layers of varnish, dirt, and alterations obscuring the work of some old master, to reveal the original, authentic masterpiece, pristine fresh once again. Not unnaturally, no one thought the in-principle possibility was very realistic. As one attempted to penetrate through each successive layer, more and more would become less and less certain, and in the end, at best, there would be a few sayings or actions which one could confidently trace back to Jesus himself (Bultmann traced only about forty sayings to the earliest layer of tradition).

But the imagery itself is wrong. Above all, it depends too much on an outmoded model of literary tradition — as though it was all a process of cutting and pasting, in which one by extreme diligence might actually be able to peel away and identify the authorship of each phrase or sentence. Or, indeed, as though analysis of Gospel tradition was something like tracing a tradition through a nineteenth-century writer's dependence on Shakespeare, through a medieval chronicler available now only in fragmentary condition, and back to some long-lost classical text. But we have already noted how much of the process we have been tracing was a process of *oral* tradition rather than of literary dependence. We have also noted that the character of oral tradition likely to have been followed was not a matter of one teacher building a fresh layer on another but rather of a teacher retelling the settled core and substance of a respected tradition. The variation and elaboration of any such retelling did not constitute a fresh layer to be carried forward to the next retelling; any particular retelling may have been quite ephemeral. It was the stable core and substance and overall shape of the tradition which was passed on, to be freshly elaborated in the next telling.

In other words, in the the process of tradition transmission, the original emphases and features of the sayings and doings of Jesus are unlikely to have become obscured and lost to view by layers of overtelling. On the contrary, it was precisely the original emphases and features which were fixed by the process of retelling because it was these emphases and features which encapsulated the original impact and which the process was designed to preserve and maintain. Furthermore, that character of oral transmission has been carried over into the written tradition, as the relationship of tradition between the Synoptic Gospels confirms. For, as we have seen, it is precisely that same respect for tradition, its core and point, together with variation in the use to which that tradition is put, which is such a manifest feature of the Synoptic tradition.

2.9. The Gospels

We need not pursue the transmission process further in any detail. For the next phase is the written Gospels themselves, and enough detail is given concerning them and their use of the tradition in the pages which follow. It is important to observe, however, that the evangelists forwarded the traditioning process by the way they themselves shaped the tradition which came to them in ways indicated above. In the history of Gospel research we have now reached the phase of "redaction criticism," where attention began to turn from the evangelists as collectors of earlier forms to their own role as editors (below 5.5). Some obvious examples are Mark's use of the Caesarea Philippi confession and transfiguration narrative as center and turning point of his Gospel (Mark 8:27–9:13), Matthew's ordering the traditions of Jesus' teaching into five large blocks (chs. 5–7, 10, 13, 18, 24–25), quite possibly in deliberate echo of the five books of Moses, and the way Luke has inserted a perhaps surprising amount of traditional material within the framework of the journey to Jerusalem (Luke 9:51–19:27).

In addition, there are a number of more general points of relevance worthy of note. One is the way in which the Gospels seem to have fixed the nature of a "Gospel" — that is, as an account of Jesus' ministry which climaxes in his death and resurrection. This seems to have been an early extension of a use of the term "gospel" already established in Paul's writings (e.g., Rom 1:1, 9, 16; Gal 1:6-7, 11; 2:2, 5, 7). We see the transition from "gospel" = good news of Jesus' life, death, and resurrection to "Gospel" = written account of Jesus' life, death, and resurrection already in the opening of the earliest written Gospel (Mark 1:1). And since it was Mark's outline ("a passion narrative with extended introduction") which provided the framework for the other three Gospels, we can probably credit Mark with establishing the definitive Gospel shape. In the same connection it is notable that the Q material (a collection only of Jesus' teaching) was not preserved as such, but within the Gospels only as incorporated into the Markan outline. Q as such was evidently not judged to be a "Gospel." This Markan outline evidently became the "canonical shape" of the Gospel and was no doubt a factor in the subsequent decisions of the emerging catholic church to reject other would-be Gospels which lacked that shape (see again Tuckett, "Introduction to the Gospels," 995-96 below).

Another point deserving of note is what the evangelists' use of traditions tells us about the character of the Gospels themselves, and whether the achievement of written Gospels marked a significant change in the character and function of the tradition. The point here can be summarized in terms of the debate on whether the Gospels may properly be described as biographies. In the heyday of form criticism (see again below, 5.4) it was strongly asserted that the Gospels were *not* biographies (typical was the reaction of Bultmann 1934). This was in reaction to the late nineteenth-century abuse of the Gospels by those anxious to write Lives of Jesus which explored his spiritual development and self-consciousness. And the criticism made at that time remains valid: that such a Life of Jesus can only be written by filling in the gaps by imaginative reconstruction (Kähler 1964). For the Gospels were not written to provide such information, and they themselves did not express such interest. But to acknowledge this is simply to recognize that the Gospels do not share the interests of the modern biographer. Bultmann and others of his generation would have been more accurate if they had asserted the Gospels were not *modern* biographies. In contrast, however, they can be adequately classified as *ancient* biographies. For they share the ancient biographical interest in depicting the hero's character by telling stories about him and reporting the sort of things he said. To be precise, the Gospels are *sui generis*. But it nevertheless remains true that they are closer in genre to ancient biographies than to anything else (Burridge 1992).

The point is that as a type of ancient biography the Gospels do confirm a continuing interest in the life of Jesus, that is, in what he said and did, and that one of the primary reasons for writing the Gospels was indubitably to preserve and spread that tradition.

Add to this the strong evidence of consistency between the traditions as recorded in the three Synoptic Gospels — all the more noteworthy in view of the renewed appreciation of the evangelists as editors and theologians in their own right (see again below, 5.5). For all their variation in structure and individual emphasis, the amount of substantially shared tradition (in character and emphasis as well as detail) far outweighs the amount of variation. To repeat: the respect shown by oral tradition to retain core and substance and shape within the variation of each retelling remains a feature of the tradition as "fixed" by the Synoptic Gospels.

To be noted here, too, is the evidence provided by the Gospels as to how widely the tradition had spread around the Eastern Mediterranean. Matthew is usually linked with Syria; Mark has traditional links to Rome; the Q material has links with Egypt; and we might also mention John, which is traditionally linked with Ephesus. Even if these geographical associations are speculative and far from securely grounded, they are a reminder of what must have been the case — that is, that the tradition which they embodied was widely dispersed and in its coherence and consistency provided a solid base of foundation tradition for the many churches throughout the region which treasured and made use of that tradition.

All this highlights one other point worthy of some emphasis. Many explorations of the Gospels tradition seem to work on a series of questionable assumptions: (1) that the traditions of each church or group of churches were distinct and discrete from the traditions of other churches; (2) that the Gospels were written exclusively for their own group of churches and reflect these churches' distinctive interests (the Matthean churches, the Q community); (3) that when a Gospel like Mark or Matthew reached a more distant church, that was the first time the church would have heard most if not all of these traditions; and (4) that the relations between the different versions or collections can be understood only on the model of literary interdependence.

But everything we have considered so far speaks against these assumptions. The reality is much more likely to have been the reverse: (1) that churches possessed a considerable amount of shared foundation tradition — the tradition which the church founders (apostles) would regard as essential for the church to know and be able to use in its own evangelism and apologetic, nurture and worship (see below, 3.4); (2) that the Gospels were able to draw on tradition which was not exclusive to one or other group of churches and were written as an evangelistic, apologetic, catechetical, and/or liturgical aid for a wide range of churches (Bauckham 1998); (3) that when any Gospel first reached such churches, they were able to compare their own versions of much if not most of the traditions which that Gospel contained; and (4) that many if not most of the variations within the Synoptic tradition are to be explained precisely because of these variations between written Gospel and still oral tradition being incorporated into further copies of these Gospels.

2.10. *John's Gospel*

Finally, we should consider the Fourth Gospel, John's Gospel. For it may seem to call in question several of the features and conclusions drawn above. The reason is that John's Gospel does not seem to be simply an extension of the traditioning process evident in the Synoptics. The Synoptic traditions, consisting of linked short sayings characteristic of wisdom teaching and independent of particular miracles, seem to have been wholly replaced by the long Johannine discourses characteristically linked to some typical miracle presented as a "sign." The characteristic emphases of the Synoptic Jesus' teaching on the kingdom of God, with little self-reference, seem to have been wholly replaced by the complete Johannine contrast of characteristic self-proclamation with little reference to the kingdom.

At the same time, however, John's Gospel retains the characteristic ("canonical") Gospel shape noted above. Like the other Gospels, but unlike subsequent claimants to the title, John's Gospel drives single-mindedly toward the climax of Jesus' death and resurrection, and the whole Gospel is to be read in that light. Moreover, closer examination of John's material reveals a consistent pattern, where the distinctively Johannine discourse begins from a typically Synoptic-type incident or saying and proceeds to draw out its significance in characteristic Johannine style (cf., e.g., John 3:3, 5 with Matt 18:3; see Dunn 1991). The point remains valid even if John's Gospel was able to draw directly on one or more of the Synoptic Gospels as such (rather than on similar versions of the Synoptic traditions), as many believe. In other words, even John's Gospel retains the earlier features of the original oral tradition — a core saying of Jesus at the heart, with the overall Gospel shape of the tradition.

The distinctive Johannine elaboration of the tradition seems to draw particularly on the earlier Jewish wisdom tradition (see Scott below, 1161). This way of conceptualizing and presenting Christ and his significance was already well developed in first- and second-generation Christianity, as passages like 1 Cor 8:6, Col 1:15-20, and Heb 1:2-3 indicate. In John's case the wisdom Christology has been meshed both with the more Hellenistic concept of the creative Logos (rational power) of God (John 1:1-18) and with the more characteristic Jewish concept of the divine agent sent by God, as typified by the prophet in particular. That the endeavor thus to fill out the significance of Jesus as expressed in the Jesus tradition seemed to some to take on docetic-like features (Jesus only seeming to be human) was more a hazard of the type of elaboration on which John embarked than any part of John's obvious intention (Dunn 1991/1998).

Particularly noteworthy is the addition of John 21, generally reckoned as a (slightly) later appendix. Notable is the way it seems to commend the holding together of potentially diverging patterns of tradition, the one looking to Simon Peter for authentication (Mark, Matthew), the other to the beloved disciple (John). This appendix is a further indication of how earlier tradition could be elaborated, but it also possibly indicates an emerging self-consciousness of the need to assert (and maintain) the coherence and consistency of a developing pattern of tradition. Other indications of a similar consciousness may be the commendation of Luke and Mark in the same breath in 2 Tim 4:11 and the commendation of Paul's letters in 2 Pet 3:15-16.

John's Gospel should probably be seen, therefore, as a bold retelling of the tradition which in the event was judged to be acceptable as part of the fourfold Gospel (see, e.g., Dunn 1990: 296-97). Somewhat like the birth narratives, its detail is not to be recognized as part of the foundation tradition as such. Rather, it was an elaboration of the tradition which was seen to be consistent with the foundation traditions, to supplement them, and to draw out their fuller significance. As midrash on these traditions, as reflections and meditations on things that Jesus said and did, as still manifestly "Gospel," they have provided invaluable insights into the meaning of Jesus for further generations. Not least, John's Gospel reminds us of the character of the tradition as living tradition, of the charge laid upon the ministers of the tradition not simply to reverence and repeat rigid and unchanging forms but to retell it in ways which enable its power to be experienced afresh.

We break off the history of Gospel tradition at this point, not at all because that history "ceased" with the writing of the Gospels. Quite the contrary, as we shall see (4 below). But having reached this stage in tracing the tradition process in the case of Jesus tradition, we pause to let the rest of the NT tradition "catch up."

3. The Rest of the New Testament

The history of tradition in the rest of the NT is both easier to trace and more difficult to trace. It is easier because, as Christian tradition, it is post-Easter; if the Gospels tradition begins with Jesus, other NT tradition begins with the first Christian Easter. So the other NT documents are nearer to the beginnings of their tradition, and the modern inquirer into the history of that tradition does not have to embark on the difficult task of tracing tradition to the far side of Easter, to the period before the Gospel shape and context had even been provided. At the same time, however, the tracing of the post-Easter tradition is more difficult. For, as we have seen, one of the strengths of the Gospels tradition is the coherence and consistency among the Synoptic Gospels. The post-Easter tradition, however, comes to us in a wide variety of documents, none of which were designed as tradition carriers as the Gospels were, and from which it is often difficult to disentangle the earlier tradition as such.

Nevertheless, a considerable amount of study has been devoted to these traditions, most of which is still of value, and we can draw on that work a good deal more confidently than with much of the equivalent work carried out on the Gospels tradition. The fact is that the NT writings bear testimony in many ways to earlier tradition and how it was used, both by themselves and by the churches to which these writers belonged. Nor should we fall into the trap of thinking that tradition is to be defined solely as that which lies behind these writings. For as the Gospels are themselves forms which the Jesus tradition took/was given at the time of writing, so the other NT writings are themselves the different forms which the tradition took/was given in a variety of instances. The fact that all these writings were retained for posterity attests to the acceptability of these forms to the churches and church leaders who preserved and cherished them.

3.1. Early Kerygmatic Tradition

To avoid the confusion caused by overuse of the term "gospel" it is convenient to use the alternative "kerygma" to denote the proclamation of the good news or the good news itself. The best-known investigation at this point was that of C. H. Dodd, who correlated the accounts of sermons in Acts with references by Paul to his earlier preaching which had given rise to the churches to which he now wrote. Even from Paul alone a common outline could be discerned — the apostolic kerygma. Dodd summarized it as the assertion of fulfilled prophecy and the new age inaugurated by the coming of Christ, an outline of Jesus' birth, death, resurrection, and exaltation, and the affirmation of his coming again in judgment (Dodd 1936: 17). Key texts behind this excerpted summary were Rom 1:3-4, 1 Cor 15:3-5, and 1 Thess 1:9-10 — 1 Thess 1:9-10 because it comes from what most interpreters regard as the earliest NT writing and actually describes the preached gospel which proved successful in Thessalonica; Rom 1:3-4 because it is Paul's description of "the gospel of God" which confirmed his *bona fides* to the Roman believers; and 1 Cor 15:3-5 because it is Paul's fullest explicit statement of the gospel which he preached and on which his churches were founded —

- Rom 1:3-4 — ". . . descended from the seed of David in terms of the flesh, and appointed Son of God in power in terms of the Spirit of holiness as from the resurrection of the dead";
- 1 Cor 15:3-8 — ". . . that Christ died for our sins in accordance with the scriptures, and that he was buried, and that he was raised on the third day in accordance with the scriptures, and that he appeared to Cephas, then to the twelve. . . ."
- 1 Thess 1:9-10 — "You turned to God from idols, to serve a living and true God, and to wait for his Son from heaven, whom he raised from the dead — Jesus, who rescues us from the wrath that is coming."

Dodd's work has been qualified and improved in various ways (cf., e.g., Evans 1956 and Dunn 1990: ch. 2). For example, there has been much debate about the sermons in Acts and whether they contain earlier tradition or simply indicate what Luke thought should or might have been said on the occasion narrated. In the event, careful analysis of sermons like those in Acts 2, 3, and 10 does seem to demonstrate the use of earlier tradition. This is indicated, for example, by the liveliness of the eschatology in 2:16-17 and 3:19-21 (less typical of Luke elsewhere) and by the use of primitive-sounding Christology in 2:22, 36; 3:13-15; and 10:38, 42. Other features are more appropriately dealt with in the next section.

Two points worthy of particular note emerge from this. One is the watershed formed by the resurrection of Jesus or, as some prefer to say, by the earliest conviction that God had raised the crucified Jesus from the dead. Whatever preparation or lack of preparation there had been among Jesus' disciples for this epochal (eschatological) event, it was this event which made the decisive difference — the decisive difference between a tradition which was essentially the remembrance of a dead teacher and a tradition which itself continued to speak of a living Master — the decisive difference of perspective which transformed the tradition from a recycling of Jesus' proclamation to a proclamation of Jesus himself, from good news preached by Jesus to the gospel about Jesus, and subsequently to the Gospel according to Mark, to Luke, to Matthew, to John. The very fact that the Acts sermons and the echoes of Paul's evangel in his letters are *not* simply restatements of Jesus' teaching (as though it was the impressiveness and impact of that teaching which were the real source of the resurrection faith) but focus on the significance of Jesus himself (his death and resurrection in particular) should be enough proof that the kerygma of Jesus' death and resurrection marked a decisive new phase in the history of tradition behind the NT (see also Pokorný 1987).

The other point worthy of note is how central was the interplay with (OT) scripture in the first formulations of this new faith. "According to the scriptures" (1 Cor 15:3-4) should be taken with full import. Psalms like 16, 22, 89, and 110 and prophecies like Isaiah 53 and Dan 7:9-14 very quickly (in at least some cases immediately) became luminous for the first believers (Lindars 1961; Juel 1988). It was not so much that the first disciples came to a belief and then sought out and discovered confirmation in scripture (though there was no doubt some of that). Nor indeed the direct converse, that certain scripture gave rise to a kind of wish fulfillment (otherwise resurrection appearances would probably have taken the form of Jesus "coming on clouds," as Dan 7:13 would have suggested). It was rather that such scriptures provided the metaphor and analogy in which the conviction could be expressed, provided the imagery and conceptuality which clothed the experience of Christ as risen in communicable language. However the point is put, it is unlikely that this first and most essential element in distinctively Christian faith (the resurrection of Jesus) would have become established among devout Jews had it not been for the confirmation and language which the scriptures provided. The tradition was taking a tremendous step forward, but unless its roots in and continuity with the already sacred tradition of the OT could be affirmed and were secure it must remain doubtful whether the new development would have taken and become established so quickly.

It perhaps also needs to be reemphasized that, though the resurrection of Jesus marked a decisive new stage in the traditioning process which gave rise to the

NT, the gulf(?) between pre-Easter tradition and post-Easter kerygma should not be exaggerated. For as the mid-century debate in the Bultmann school on the relation of the historical Jesus to the kerygmatic Christ brought out, the Gospels are not other than kerygma, are not simply pre-kerygma, but are themselves kerygma. It would be odd, then, to affirm the continuity of NT with OT (as above) and not also to affirm the continuity between kerygma/gospel and Gospel, when, after all, the gospel shape (both gospel and Gospel) focuses and climaxes precisely in the death and resurrection of Jesus.

3.2. Liturgical Tradition

Closely related to kerygmatic tradition is the tradition evidently used in earliest Christian worship and teaching. Throughout the twentieth century the task of uncovering and identifying this tradition was a continued topic of interest in NT scholarship (e.g., Hunter 1961, Kramer 1966). The Pauline letters proved especially valuable since they are themselves evidence of the lively character of mid-first-century church life and of the interchange between churches.

In particular, a series of confessional formulae can be readily identified — identified because they are so frequently echoed or alluded to within the Pauline letters and elsewhere in recognizable forms. The most obvious/used are: "God raised him from the dead" (e.g., Acts 3:15; Rom 4:24-25; 10:9; 1 Cor 6:14; 1 Pet 1:21); "Christ died for us" (e.g., Rom 5:6, 8; 2 Cor 5:14-15; 1 Thess 5:10); "He was handed (or handed himself) over (for our sins)" (e.g., Rom 8:32; 1 Cor 11:23; Gal 1:4); "Christ died and was raised" (Rom 8:34; 2 Cor 13:4; 1 Thess 4:14); and confessional formulae like "Jesus is Lord" in Rom 10:9. Here again we see the tradition process in full flow: new beliefs coming to formulation, formulations becoming formulaic by regular use and repetition, formulae becoming so established that they can simply be alluded to or "quoted" to summarize beliefs which have thus become central to and part of the foundation tradition.

"The church at worship" (Moule 1981) was another obvious focus of interest. Here hymnic tradition has attracted considerable scholarly attention. How soon was it that the canticles preserved by Luke in his birth narrative — the *Magnificat* (Luke 1:46-55), the *Benedictus* (1:68-79), the *Gloria* (2:14), and the *Nunc dimittis* (2:29-32) — began to be used regularly in Christian worship? The thought that these songs may have been regular features of Christian liturgy for almost as long as Christianity has existed must surely give food for reflection on the character of NT tradition and the mode of its preservation. Certainly they as much as any other tradition within the NT evidence the character of a living tradition, of a tradition which lives through worship and is not simply maintained by worship.

More fragmentary in their influence have been the doxologies, or rather shouts of praise, which have been preserved in Revelation: acclamations of God (4:8, 11; 7:12; 11:17-18; etc.); acclamations of the Lamb (5:9-10, 12); acclamations of God and of the Lamb/Christ (5:13; 7:10; 11:15; 19:6-8). What fervor did they originally express? What fervor have they provided expression forever since!

Less durable as hymns, if they ever were hymns, have been the much discussed passages Phil 2:6-11 and Col 1:15-20, possibly even John 1:1-18. Certainly if they were hymns, they have not had the sustained liturgical influence of the Lukan canticles. Other passages like 1 Tim 3:16 and Heb 1:3 are frequently classified as early Christian hymns, as also the fragmentary exhortation, Eph 5:14. In truth it matters not whether they were hymns as such or not. Their value is in showing that tradition took many forms, that some took poetic or hymnic form, and that as such they lent themselves to being quoted in communication between churches. More to the point, several of these hymnic passages were on the cutting edge of reflection on the significance of Christ. In other words, it may have been the poetic or liturgical expression of tradition (and the relative freedom which such a format facilitates) which made it possible for the tradition to develop as it did.

There is evidence also of what in later terms can be called sacramental tradition. It is clear that the use of a regular baptismal formula quickly became established — "in the name of" (Acts 8:16; 10:48; 19:5; 1 Cor 1:13). It is also clear from Matt 28:19 that this early formula was soon elaborated into a three-fold name formula — "in the name of the Father and of the Son and of the Holy Spirit" — to become the regular formula of catholic Christianity more or less from then on (already *Did.* 7:1). Rom 10:9 is widely regarded as (one of) the earliest baptismal confessions, quoted with that in mind by Paul. Many other passages (e.g., Col 1:12-20; 1 Thess 1:9-10) and even whole letters (Ephesians; 1 Peter) have been linked to baptism, on the assumption that baptism was one of the primary loci around which tradition would have gathered. But since it is unclear how quickly baptismal liturgies developed, such speculation needs to be restrained (Dunn 1990: 142-43). Nevertheless, the assumption is probably more sound than our evidence actually demonstrates.

Eucharistic tradition is attested as remarkably fixed already in 1 Cor 11:24-25 (cf. Luke 22:19-20 and the only slight variation from Matt 26:26-28 par. Mark 14:22-24). At the same time elaborations are evident in comparing the three Gospel texts and 1 Corinthians 11: the switch in emphasis from the significance of the cup (new covenant) to the content of the cup (blood); the emphasis on repeating the act ("Do this in remembrance of me"); and the Pauline interpretation ("As often as you [do this], you proclaim the Lord's death until he comes" — 11:26) (Dunn 1990: §40). Here again we see the characteristic of fixed core and elaborated (and varied) significance, as also the indications of developing appreciation of the significance of the original words and acts. It is little wonder that the Eucharist and the eucharistic formulations have provided the living heart of the living tradition for so many Christians and for so many centuries.

3.3. Ethical Tradition

Perhaps the widest and most diverse range of earliest Christian tradition in terms of source and influence is to be found in the ethical teaching preserved in the NT letters.

In the first place, there was evidently a widespread

appreciation of some of the moral forms and even of the ethical standards upheld in some of the philosophies and by some of the Greco-Roman moralists of the day. The use of vice lists in condemnation of unacceptable social behavior was comon to all religious and ethical systems (in the NT, e.g., Mark 7:21-22; Rom 1:29-31; 1 Cor 6:9-10; Gal 5:19-21; 2 Tim 3:2-5; 1 Pet 4:3). In the second generation of Christianity use of *Haustafeln* (household codes/rules) became common, in direct reflection of the widespread belief that the household was the core unit of society, on whose stability the common good and flourishing of society depended (see esp. Eph 5:22–6:9; Col 3:28–4:1; 1 Pet 2:18–3:7). But already in the first generation Paul showed appreciation of Stoic values ("what is contrary to nature," "what is fitting" — Rom 1:26, 28) and was quite ready to appeal to the broadest categories of "good and evil" and conscience (Rom 2:7-10, 14-15) and to what would generally be regarded as "virtue" and "praiseworthy" (Phil 4:8-9). Here, in other words, were little communities (a new sect) not setting themselves apart, as though to be fully themselves as Christians they had to be wholly different, but fully prepared to draw on the common wells of human experience and wisdom. To be good ethical tradition it did not need to be distinctively Christian.

Within that broader range of ethical tradition, however, the first believers were able to draw more fully and most consistently on the wells of Jewish wisdom. The Letter of James, as a handbook of good, practical advice, is thoroughly Jewish in content and character (e.g., Bauckham 1999). Paul's advice in passages like Rom 12:14-21 and 1 Corinthians 5–7 (Rosner 1994) is heavily dependent on the OT and Jewish wisdom. Perhaps most striking is the fact that although Paul regarded himself as free from the Torah (law) in one sense, his regular commendation of the law (Rom 3:31; 7:12; 8:4; 13:8-10) can only be explained by the degree to which he found Judaism's traditional ethical wisdom still basic and sound in directing the lives and lifestyles of his churches. The most notable examples of this are his sustained hostility to sexual license and to idolatry (e.g., 1 Cor 6:18; 10:14), which did indeed set Christian morality in direct contrast to Hellenistic morality. Paul sat loose to such Jewish traditions as food laws and the sabbath, but not because he was opposed to Jewish tradition as such; on matters ethical the continuity and contribution of Jewish tradition to Christian tradition was too important to be sidelined (Dunn 1998: §§23-24).

In some ways most significant for the present inquiry is the evidence of the importance of and use made of Jesus tradition in Christian parenesis (exhortation). There are clear signs of this, for example, in James (1:5, 17, 22-23; 4:12; 5:12), in *Didache* 1, and at several points in Paul (e.g., Rom 12:14; 14:14; 1 Thess 5:2, 4, 13). In the last case Paul's failure explicitly to cite Jesus as the authority for the teaching (apart from 1 Cor 7:10-11 and 9:14) has caused much bewilderment. But such bewilderment reflects a failure to appreciate the character of the traditioning process. The probability, as we have already mentioned and will document below, is that each new church was established on a foundation of Jesus tradition (also kerygmatic and confessional tradition). This tradition would inevitably have formed part of the regular diet of teaching and reflection in the gatherings of these churches — the process, indeed, which we have outlined in the first section above.

This also means that much of this tradition would have become part and parcel of their communal discourse; as living tradition it would be a present factor in their communal meditations and so also in shaping and determining the character and detail of their own daily living. Paul could thus simply allude to various elements in that tradition with every confidence that the audience gathered for the Lord's Supper or worship would recognize the allusion — much as generations of preachers (or schoolteachers) have been able simply to refer to "the Good Samaritan" or "the Prodigal Son" without further detail and could be confident that their point was sufficiently made by the bare allusion. In such discourse, the possibility of communication by abbreviated reference and allusion is one of the things which gives the discourse its bonding force and which confirms the sense of belonging for those engaged in the discourse. This last is one of the most important roles of tradition in any ongoing community.

3.4. The Pauline Letters

As the history of tradition behind the Gospels came to fruition in the Gospels themselves, so the history of tradition behind the other NT documents came to fruition in the NT letters, the Acts of the Apostles, and Revelation. And once again not as tradition becoming something other than tradition, but tradition becoming crystallized in particular documents and formulated for particular occasions. The most interesting for our purposes are the Pauline letters, because of their number and range of situations addressed and because the Pauline corpus (by widespread consensus) extends beyond the first generation.

Of immediate interest for us are, first of all, the confirmation which Paul explicitly provides that the passing on of foundation tradition was regarded as an essential part of the establishment of a new church (1 Cor 11:2; 15:3; Col 2:6; 1 Thess 4:1; 2 Thess 3:6); and, second, the indications of how Paul himself contributed to the development of the tradition which he inherited and passed on. For the latter, it will suffice if we take examples from each of the three categories already discussed.

So far as kerygmatic tradition is concerned, the point is highlighted by the tension between the assertions of 1 Cor 15:1-3 and Gal 1:12. In the one case Paul insists that his gospel was given him directly by God; in the other he is equally clear that his gospel came to him as already established Christian tradition. This tension can be resolved only if we recognize that Paul's gospel was indeed the gospel shared by all the churches but also recognize Paul's conviction that he had been specially commissioned to take this gospel to the Gentiles (Rom 11:13; Gal 1:15-16; 2:7-9). It was evidently the slant which this conviction gave to the shared gospel (not requiring circumcision of Gentile believers) which made Paul's gospel so controversial for many of his fellow Jewish believers

(Galatians 2). Here again we see the character of living tradition — the same core formulations shared by the range of apostles/missionaries (1 Cor 15:1-11), but adapted to the new circumstances and challenges of a gospel for Gentiles as well as Jews.

In the case of liturgical tradition we might mention the way Paul seems to have taken up the tradition of an expected baptism in Spirit, stemming originally from John the Baptist (Mark 1:8 and pars.), already adapted by the Jesus tradition to depict Jesus' own death as a baptism (Mark 10:38-39; Luke 12:49-50), and now further extended to speak of believers as being baptized into Christ's death and body (Rom 6:4-5; 1 Cor 12:13). With regard to the tradition of the Lord's Supper, we have already observed how Paul elaborates the institution tradition in 1 Cor 11:26, both strengthening its reference to Jesus' death and injecting a fresh eschatological note. We might also note the debate on what seems to be a traditional formula on Jesus' death in Rom 3:24-26, as to whether and to what degree Paul may have elaborated and modified it (Dunn 1998: 174). In any case, the character of tradition for Paul as living tradition is further illustrated.

As far as ethical tradition is concerned, the most interesting examples are provided by the two cases where Paul actually does attribute teaching explicitly to Jesus (1 Cor 7:10-11 and 9:14). For what emerges from a closer examination of both cases is, once again, Paul's readiness to affirm the tradition but also to adapt it as circumstances required. In the former case, the instruction of the Lord seems clear: as a rule, no divorce or separation of husband and wife should be allowed. But the situation of a believer married to an unbelieving partner was new; and in these circumstances Paul ruled that if the unbelieving partner chose to separate, the believer should accept it (7:15). Similarly, the Lord's command was clear in the case of missionaries being supported by those to whom they ministered (9:14). But, once again, in the circumstances of his own mission Paul chose to disregard the tradition and to maintain himself by the work of his own hands, despite the authoritative tradition (9:15-18). Here again, then, we see clear statements of principle derived from the tradition, principles whose authority Paul deliberately restates; evidently he had no quarrel with the tradition itself; he reaffirms the point and authority of the tradition. At the same time, however, he adapts its reference and application to the changing circumstances of his own missionary work and churches. Once again, then, we see the character of living tradition, core and substance sustained but adapted, stability with flexibility.

We could say more on Paul's use of scriptural tradition, but we have probably said enough. Particular reference should be made, however, to the work of Richard Hays, who through careful investigation of the resonances of intertextuality in the Pauline letters has given further demonstration of the pervasiveness of the influence of tradition and of the subtle ways in which traditional narratives and texts shape new discourse and are themselves given fresh life by and through the new formulations which they have in part inspired and informed.

On a different front of contemporary interest in Pauline scholarship is the similar evidence of the way Paul has taken over contemporary epistolary and rhetorical traditions and adapted them. Exploration on this front would take us too far from our immediate concern. But it is worth noting how, for example, Paul adapted the traditional pattern of the letter opening — the traditional Greek "greeting" *(chairein)* changed to the distinctive Christian "grace" *(charis)* and combined with the traditional Jewish greeting "Shalom" (peace). Also how he made effective use of the Greek philosophical school format of the diatribe — conversation with an imaginary opponent or interlocutor — in Romans (2:1-5, 17-24; 3:1-8; etc.). Paul had no hesitation in drawing on and adapting traditional forms and content where they proved effective vehicles for his message.

Finally, we need to note how at the far end of the Pauline corpus (the Pastoral Epistles) the traditioning process has become more structured and deliberate. There is a clearer sense of the need for carefully formulated teaching to be affirmed and adhered to — for example, "the faith" (11 times), the "sound teaching" (1 Tim 1:10; 2 Tim 4:3; Tit 1:9; 2:1), and the "faithful sayings" — the last, interestingly, falling into the same three categories: kerygmatic (1 Tim 1:15; 2 Tim 2:11; Tit 3:5-8), ecclesiastical (1 Tim 3:1; or is the reference to 1 Tim 2:15?), and ethical (1 Tim 4:8-9; 2 Tim 2:11-13). Very striking is the image of the tradition as *parathēkē,* "deposit, goods left in trust with someone" (1 Tim 6:20; 2 Tim 1:12, 14). The image is rather static, and the complementary idea of "protecting" it (the same verb is used each time) encourages the picture of something retained and returned in the form in which it was first received. It is this image which probably above all gives the impression that the Pastorals mark a new phase in the traditioning process, the impression of a theology concerned more to preserve than to develop, of a faith tied to earlier formulations and discouraged from seeking fresh expression. The living tradition is beginning to lose some of its vitality. Also notable is the window suddenly opened to us in 2 Tim 2:1-2 to the traditioning process toward the end of the first century — in this case from Paul to Timothy, through many witnesses, from Timothy to faithful people, "faithful people who will be able to teach others also" — perhaps three or even four generations in all. The traditioning process is stretching out, but still an extension of the same process we have been examining from the first.

3.5. *The Rest of the New Testament*

The main outlines of the tradition process which resulted in the NT have now been illustrated with sufficient detail. The scope of the tradition is further indicated by the other NT documents, the other letters, the Acts of the Apostles, and the Apocalypse (Revelation) of John. But to gain a "feel" for the history of the NT tradition and its character it is unnecessary to review them in any detail.

The other letters display an interesting variety of tradition: James, with its strongly Jewish character and Jesus tradition enmeshed in it, in effect an extension of the older Jewish wisdom tradition; 1 Peter with the fascination of its Pauline character under the name of Peter; Jude and 2 Peter with their unique mutual relationship, use of Jewish pseudepigrapha (Jude 14-15 referring to *1 Enoch* 1:9), and unique echo of the Gospels transfiguration narrative (2 Pet 1:16-18); 1-3 John, both extending the character of the Johannine elaboration of the Jesus tradition and bearing witness to the way the kerygmatic tradition was also being elaborated in the face of new challenges (1 John 2:22-23; 4:1-3; 2 John 7); and the extraordinary letter to the Hebrews, with its extended elaboration of the otherwise slim tradition of Jesus as heavenly intercessor (Rom 8:34), its confirmation of a widespread interest in the figure of Melchizedek at the turn of the millennia, and its ability to express a Jewish apocalyptic perspective in language meaningful to a Hellenistic audience.

In the case of the Acts, the debate on the sources of Luke's tradition has never been satisfactorily resolved (Dupont 1964). Was there, for example, a "Hellenist" source behind Acts 6–8 and 11:19-30, possibly even a Hellenist tract used for Stephen's speech in ch. 7? Does the "we" form of much of the later narrative indicate Luke's personal eyewitness involvement in what he records or dependence on some travel journal available to him? Whatever the precise facts, we need doubt neither that Luke had sources of information to draw upon nor that he shaped them to his own ends. Both points need to be given due weight. In the case of the much discussed speeches in Acts, for example, we have already noted, on the one hand, the evidence of primitive features (above, 3.1); at the same time, however, no one disputes that the speeches are in Luke's style, complete little cameos (three or four minutes in length) of what Luke no doubt judged to be the substance of the gospel for the occasion. Again, Luke had good information about various significant phases of Paul's work; but he deliberately (we may assume) chose both to pull a veil over more controversial aspects of it (no hint of a crisis at Antioch or with the Galatian churches, for example) and to stress Paul's positive attitude to his ancestral faith (e.g., Acts 18:18; 21:26) in a way that leaves readers of Paul's letters somewhat bemused. Here once again we see that respect for tradition does not mean a slavish reproduction of it, but creative use of it to bring out the point of the past for the benefit of the present.

Finally, with regard to the Apocalypse of John (Revelation), we need simply note its presence in the NT. Here was a means of inscribing and expressing the experience of revelation, of eyes opened to the mysteries of God's purpose, expressed in terms of visions of strange and weird beings, which had gained currency in late Second Temple Judaism (Charlesworth 1983, 1985). It was not regarded as rendered unnecessary or unacceptable in the light of the primary revelation of Christ. On the contrary, it gained fresh inspiration from the mode (apocalypse) and from the stock of apocalyptic images available in Daniel and other Jewish apocalypses, and it adapted them to a fresh vision of heaven in which Christ had the central place (with God). The genre and outcome are not the same, but in its use and reuse of tradition Revelation also bears witness to an essentially similar traditioning process.

4. The Ongoing Tradition Process

It is important to recognize that the tradition process did not cease when the writings of the NT were completed. As the formulation of the Gospels themselves did not mark the end of the oral tradition, so the writing of the other NT books did not mark a closure of the tradition process which lies behind them. On the contrary, in every case the documents are to be regarded as a stage in the process, a crystallization of the process at various points in the course of the first and second generations of Christianity. We begin to move beyond our brief at this point, but its importance for our understanding of the history of NT tradition and of the place of the NT as such within it warrants at least a few more words. The key point can be put thus: when NT scripture is set over against tradition, the impression is often given that the NT is fixed whereas tradition is ever fluid and developing; that is misleading. The NT shares at least something of the flexibility (the not-easy-finally-to-tie-down-ness) of tradition. The point can be documented briefly.

4.1. In Search of the Text

In every case of a NT document, we can obviously affirm that the document was written down at some point in time. Do we have that document? Strictly speaking, No! Was there an "original"? Not necessarily, since multiple copies may have been made from the first dictation. The intended recipients no doubt preserved the copy they received, and probably further copies were made for further distribution. We have no idea whatsoever what happened to the originals. As the document became better known and more widely used, more and more copies were made and circulated. The earliest copies available to us are products of that process, several generations removed from the originals, various fragmentary scrolls from the second and third centuries and more extensive manuscripts from the fourth century onward.

All this brings us into the realm of text criticism, the science of reconstruction of the "original" text; at least that is how the science was at first conceived. The point, of course, is that these multiple copies contain very many variations, and the textual critic has to decide which is the "best" reading. Most of the variations are relatively minor and can be attributed to scribal errors in copying. But in a good number of other cases what we encounter in these variations is the evidence that the tradition process was ongoing; the text was subject to modification, elaboration, and correction as part of a deliberate scribal enterprise. In other words, the scribes were not merely copying a fixed tradition, but were doing (in a more modest way) what the storytellers of oral tradition were doing before them — retelling the story in the text, with the sort of modifications, elaborations, and improvements which the oral performance had much more readily facilitated. It would be accurate, indeed, to speak of the scribal task as not simply issuing copies of the text, but as providing something more like versions and editions of the text. The traditioning process at this point is in essence not very different from the process which gave rise to what we might call the sequence of editions of Moses' or Isaiah's or David's or Paul's works (Meade 1986), or indeed from the fresh editions of Esther, Daniel, and Ezra in the LXX. In the case of the NT tradition it would be all the more marked when translation of the Greek "originals" into different languages (Latin, Coptic, Georgian, etc.) was involved.

A few examples will suffice to illustrate the ongoing character of the tradition process. The Lord's Prayer, in its slightly different versions, was already a good example of a living tradition — a prayer not simply remembered as part of Jesus' instruction but used, and in the using shaped by the liturgical usage. But the process did not stop with the forms fixed by Matthew and Luke (Matt 6:9-13; Luke 11:2-4). For the textual apparatus at the foot of the Matthean text (or margin of the English translation) indicates that the familiar conclusion ("for yours is the kingdom, the power and the glory, forever") was soon added (already in a transitional form in *Did.* 8:2). In other words, the traditioning process of liturgical usage provided a more and more suitable liturgical form — a fluidity of tradition which continues to the present day in the use of various/variant forms of the Lord's Prayer in different churches. Here is a preeminent case of the character of the tradition process: few doubt that the prayer in its basic form and substance goes back to Jesus; but the use and reuse of the tradition have allowed for a variation of forms whose extent is amazing for such a few lines in such regular use.

Other familiar examples of the problems turned up by textual criticism are the ending of Mark's Gospel, the poor attestation of Luke 22:43-44, the location of the famous pericope about the woman taken in adultery usually to be found as John 7:53–8:11, the much elaborated version of Acts to be found in Western texts, the multiple positioning of the doxology in Rom 16:25-27 (also after 14:23 and 15:33), and so on. If Mark chose to end his Gospel abruptly at 16:8, the scribes and teachers who used it evidently soon became dissatisfied and attempted to improve it by adding different extended endings. Luke 22:43-44 looks like the sort of pious elaboration which later generations delighted in. Presumably the account of the woman taken in adultery was a "loose" tradition, a kind of rogue oral element which for a time had no settled place within the written tradition. The scribes behind the Western texts of Acts seem to show the same old storytelling impulse to try to tell the same story better (e.g., Acts 8:37). And the various positions of the doxology in Rom 16:25-27 attest the circulation of abbreviated versions of the letter. But these should not be thought of simply as text-critical "problems." They are more positively to be reckoned as evidence of how the tradition process continued, evidence that the NT itself was part of that process. In his study *The Orthodox Corruption of Scripture,* Bart Ehrman demonstrates how much the textual tradition was affected by the struggles between "orthodoxy" and "heresy" in support of christological doctrine (see also Parker 1997).

As has become clearer in more recent decades, the outcome of textual critical reconstruction is not the "original" text of the NT. At best the text used by NT scholars is eclectic, made up of innumerable decisions (by majority vote) on innumerable details, with its form changing little by little from one edition to another. Of course we can be confident that it is more or less what Matthew, Paul, and the like wrote, in, say, 95 percent of significant cases. The eclectic text is substantially what the NT writers dictated. But the text is not as "hard," not as "fixed," as some would like to think when they appeal to the NT over against later tradition. For it shares in something at least of the flexibility of the traditioning process.

4.2. The Emergence of the Canon

Another important part of the ongoing tradition is the emergence of the canon (details again in Kümmel 1975: pt. 2). The canonization process should not be oversimplified — as though some third- or fourth-century church council overnight declared some documents canonical and from that moment gave them an authority they had not previously possessed. The process was a good deal more drawn out and consists rather of the NT documents themselves becoming widely known, used, and respected in the churches of the Mediterranean region. They were seen to be authoritative witnesses to Christ and expressions of the common faith. In other words, canonization was a recognition of intrinsic authority, or of the continuing impact of these documents on congregations, rather than the bestowal of an ecclesiastical authority not previously possessed.

Several aspects of the process are relevant for a better understanding of the history of NT tradition. One is the point just made, which relates back to what was said at the beginning. For the word had not merely to be spoken and the document dictated. It also had to be received. As the Jesus tradition began not so much with what Jesus said and did but with how he was heard and seen (the impact he made), so the canonization process began with the NT writing being heard and responded to, circulated more widely, read frequently, and treasured more deeply. This again attests the living character of tradition and the tradition process — the tradition (Gospel, letter, etc.) not simply prized and displayed in a locked cabinet, as it were, but influencing conduct and shaping faith, and being itself shaped in the process. The tradition process takes the form of an ongoing interactive dialogue between Scripture and the *sensus fidelium,* summed up early on in "the rule of faith" and then in the creeds.

Here we should also simply note the fact that as the text of Scripture is not as fixed as many assume, so the canonization process is not quite as closed as many assume. The facts that Luther regarded certain NT documents as of secondary value, and that most denominations have to reckon seriously with the reality that they operate effectively with a canon within the canon, have to be set alongside the continuing confusion regarding the status of the OT canon (with or without the Apocrypha?) and the fact that one Christian church (Ethiopic) regards the OT pseudepigraphon, *1 Enoch,* as part of the canon. In other words, once again we see repeated that typically traditional feature of an agreed and firm core and substance together with a flexible form, and variation in subsidiary detail and scope.

Of course, a primary function of the NT canon was to

provide a norm and yardstick by which to judge which forms and variations of the tradition were acceptable within the churches. For all the flexibility we have seen, there emerged a clear consensus *(sensus fidelium)* that there were elaborations of Gospel and other teaching which modified the core and transformed the character of the tradition too much. For example, the birth narratives of Matthew and Luke were evidently regarded as a primary elaboration of the earliest gospel tradition, properly expressive of faith, whereas the subsequent elaborations (e.g., the *Protevangelium of James;* see Elliott 1993) were judged to be too far beyond the foundation tradition to be counted as foundation tradition; they were not recognized as part of the NT canon. This canonical (normative) function remains a primary function of the NT as such within the traditioning process.

For that reason also, most people will want to resist attempts to reinsert a reconstructed Q into the current stock of Christian tradition, or to give the *Gospel of Thomas* a place alongside the canonical Gospels. For insofar as Q and *Thomas* ever had a place within the process, they were judged unfit to retain that place; they failed the test of the process itself, being neglected and then lost as far as the great body of churches were concerned. They simply ceased to be effective parts of that tradition which informed faith, stimulated worship, and instructed conduct. In the "natural selection" of the evolution of tradition, they simply did not survive — primarily, we may guess, because they did not assume the normative "Gospel" shape (climaxing in Jesus' death and resurrection) established by Mark and his three most immediate successors. Historical reconstruction (hypothetical Q) or chance discovery in a desert cache (*Thomas*) does not change the verdict of that history.

At the same time it should be noted that the NT did not canonize simply the unity of the tradition; it also canonized the diversity of the tradition (Dunn 1990: ch. 15). To overemphasize the former is to overemphasize once again the ideal of a fixed and uniform tradition rather than a common core and substance with varied and variable detail and elaboration. To overemphasize the latter is to lose both the unity and the continuity of tradition, and consequently to lose also its power to hold together the diversity and to maintain the full richness of the tradition as a resource rather than as a threat.

4.3. Hearing the Tradition

Finally, a word to connect this outline of the history of the NT tradition to the next essay ("Hermeneutical Approaches to the New Testament Tradition," 972ff.). For as Joel Green will indicate, attention has recently switched from the attempt to understand the history of the tradition to the attempt to appreciate how the tradition was/is received. This is important for an understanding of the history of the tradition since it is the second side of what, as I have tried to indicate, has always been a two-sided process — hearing and responding to the tradition is as fundamental to the process as telling and enacting the tradition.

This ongoing process of the living tradition has always been well appreciated in the Orthodox churches of the East — that the NT is not something separate from the church or its liturgy, cannot be read and understood apart from the church and its worship, and can be appropriated only through and with the church (cf. Meyendorff 1978). In the Catholic West the process has become too formalized and, from a Protestant perspective, too restricted to and by the magisterium. The resulting dispute about the respective roles of Scripture and tradition, which the Reformation occasioned, has resulted in an unfortunate polarization which for many generations lost sight of the history of tradition and the tradition process described above. But perhaps we are now in a better position to appreciate what both sides of that dispute counted as important.

On the one hand, the fluid and flexible character of the process, of the retelling and reusing of the NT tradition, of the hearing and responding to the tradition, needs to be underlined. No one within a Western cultural tradition truly hears the NT as an entirely new experience. The culture has been so shaped by the NT and its resultant tradition that those who are influenced by that culture in any degree (through education, literature, moral values, etc.) have already encountered much that has been derived directly from or through the NT and the ongoing tradition, their preunderstanding shaped by it. Even more so, the responsive hearer cannot stand above the tradition as though divorced from it, but stands already in the stream of tradition, part of the continuum formed by the living, ongoing tradition, and informed by it (Gadamer 1990). Here the distance between the retelling of the earliest oral tradition within the setting of some first-century house group/church and the reading of Scripture in some twenty-first-century congregation is not as great as we might at first assume. For it is the same core tradition, the same foundation tradition which was/is being retold each time; and it is in principle the same kind of expositions and elaborations of the tradition which were/are being heard, each reflecting in various degrees the ongoing tradition of the retelling and the changing circumstances in which the retelling is taking place. In the recognition of the NT as part of a living process of tradition, and of the church as the context within which the NT is heard and understood, the millennial gap between East and West is further narrowed.

On the other hand, an appreciation of the traditioning process allows the Protestant concern for the canonical authority of the NT to be given proper weight within that process. The reason why Protestantism emphasized the importance of Scripture over against tradition was the realization that the tradition, the church, can become corrupt. NT scripture provided a norm against which the larger tradition could be checked and any abuses identified. One thinks only of St. Francis's hearing again the call to gospel poverty, or the Reformation's rediscovery of justification by faith, or the West's denunciation of its own horrific history of Christian anti-Semitism. In effect, this function of the NT as the determinative core which provides a check and control on the flexibility and elaboration of subsequent retellings, as *norma normans* within the overarching tradition, is simply a continuation of the process of tradition from the first. Of course, hearing the NT both within the tradition of the church and in its critical role within the tradition involves a subtle dialectic, in which NT scholarship has an important part (though only a part) in setting the text into its original context of vocabulary, syntax, and idiom — but no more subtle than the hearing which recognized the authority of these writings from the first and the hearing which resulted in their being accorded canonical authority. The tradition still lives (see also Dunn 1982).

5. Investigating the Tradition

It was originally the intention of the Editors to have a separate article on "Methods for Studying the Tradition." But it soon became apparent that a description of the history of NT tradition was bound to cover most of the same ground. And so it has proved. Methods for studying the tradition have been developed steadily in the West since the Renaissance. They have provided a steadily clearer view of the history of the NT tradition as the investigations plumbed deeper into that history. What we have done above is in effect to reverse the process: drawing on the insights and findings of generations of investigative scholarship, we have been able to trace the history of the NT tradition using both well-informed historical imagination and consensus critical conclusions. It is appropriate, then, to round off this account of the history of the NT tradition by outlining briefly the steps by which the stages of that history became clearer to NT scholarship.

5.1. *Textual Criticism*

The publication of Erasmus's *Greek New Testament* in 1516 marks the beginning of the modern period of NT scholarship. For it signaled the beginning of the now centuries-long quest for the original text of the NT, or, as it would now be expressed, the search for the text which will be closest to the sort of NT text being read and heard in the first few generations of Christianity. The recovery of that text, and its translation into the lingua franca of different countries, in Europe and then more widely, became the first priority and primary task of all NT scholarship, basic to all that might properly be said thereafter in explanation or exposition of the text.

Over the intervening centuries the number of manuscripts of the Greek NT catalogued, in part or whole, amounts to several thousand. Add to that the manuscripts in other languages (translations from the Greek) and quotations in early Christian writers, with all the thousands of variations attested, and the task of reconstructing an "original" might seem impossible. The early text critics quickly deduced basic rules whose logic still holds good.

Clearly it was not enough simply to count manuscripts in favor of any particular reading. For later manuscripts were all dependent on earlier manuscripts, and some well-supported reading in later manuscripts could easily have been derived from some much earlier scribal mistake or improvement. A classic case is the longer ending of Mark: what seems to have been a second-century improvement to Mark's more abrupt end at 16:8 quickly established itself in the scribal transmission of Mark.

Two other rules quickly developed: *lectio brevior* (shorter reading) and *lectio difficilior* (more difficult reading). The logic is again clear and convincing: it is more likely that scribes added to the text (by way of elaboration or clarification) than that they omitted part of the sacred text; and it is more likely that a scribe will have improved a more difficult reading than that he will have made more difficult a reading which was straightforward. More details can be found in any textbook on textual criticism (e.g., Aland and Aland 1989).

The consequence is that all commentators on NT texts really do need to check what text they are commenting on. If it is unsatisfactory for a would-be scholar to work solely from one or more translations, it is also inadequate simply to assume that the Greek text consulted records the text as it was first dictated by Paul, Mark, or the other NT authors. In the same way it is inadequate to assume that the text, whatever it was precisely, was either intended by the writer in a wholly unambiguous way or heard by the first circle(s) of recipients in just one way. As noted above, however fixed the text might have been from the first, the way it was heard was not fixed. The uncertainty with regard to the text, which the task of textual criticism highlights, should serve as a constant reminder of this fundamental degree of flexibility in the tradition from the beginning. A word which finally escapes our attempts to tie it down (and thereby control) is a word which can address us with fresh and unexpected authority.

5.2. *Historical Criticism*

A second important concern and principle also derives from the Renaissance, that is, from the emerging sense of the pastness of the past: that the past was not only *distant* from the present, but was also *different* from the present. The rediscovery of the Greek and Latin classics brought home to Renaissance men and women that the world revealed in these texts was very different from the late medieval Western world. The manners and customs, the mode of government and law, the way of conceptualizing the cosmos and thinking about society were not as they are now. Significant change had occurred, and if these texts were properly to be understood the differences and changes had to be recognized and taken into account.

The appropriate method as it first emerged was that of historical philology: such texts had to be set in their correct historical context and their language read in accord with the grammatical and syntactical rules of the time. By the careful analysis of meanings of words and sentences and by reference to the way these words and such sentences were used at the time of writing, these texts could be understood as what they were — historical texts, written in what was an ancient and foreign language. It was this principle and method which enabled humanist scholars to expose medieval documents masquerading as classical authorities for the forgeries they were (notably the "Donation of Constantine"). The result was the great lexicographical studies on which modern NT scholarship still builds.

For the Reformers this awareness of historical distance and method of documenting historical difference became the means by which the corruptions of medieval Catholicism could be identified and shown up for what they were. On the question of Scripture and tradition, and who determines the meaning of the text, they replied by maintaining that the text should be expounded in terms of its *plain meaning* as seen in its historical context. Of course they recognized that the "plain meaning" may include allegory or symbolism when the particular text in question is "plainly" allegorical or symbolical. But they were sufficiently confident of the perspicacity of Scripture, that is, of its sufficiency to indicate its own interpretation when read in accord with its plain meaning.

This historical awareness of the character of the NT text is the heart of historical criticism. With the Enlightenment it was developed in accord with the paradigm of the emerging scientific method to appear as the historical-critical method. That is to say, it assumed an objectivity to the past, as though facts were like archeological artifacts to be dug out from under layers of history. It assumed that human reason was a sufficient measure of true and false facts. And it assumed that the cosmos was an intricate machine following immutable laws, a closed system of cause and effect whose explanation required no God hypothesis or divine intervention.

If the above analysis of the history of NT tradition has been followed, however, it will hardly need saying that the historical-critical method thus defined has come under severe questioning in recent decades. Each assumption has been tested and found wanting. The ideas of a cosmic system whose future events are all inherently predictable, that reason alone is a sufficient arbiter of values and complex relationships, and that the observing subject can be wholly divorced from the observed object, no longer have much currency or leverage. So in literature, the rediscovery of the reader and of the act of reading in the communication and formation of meaning have become integral to the hermeneutical enterprise. At the same time, the earlier principles of historical criticism remain valid, and the role of the NT read as historical text in historical context to provoke fresh hearings and to criticize received readings can still be asserted. In fact, the balance made possible by a recognition of the NT as tradition, and of what the tradition process has involved and still involves, would have prevented such excesses; that balance needs to be more fully recovered in the present.

5.3. *Source Criticism*

With the next phase of European cultural history came a romantic interest in origins, appreciation of the inspiration of the creative moment of authorship being seen as the key to understanding and appropriating what emerged from that moment. In terms of NT scholarship this interest translated into a desire to appreciate the religious experience and consciousness of Jesus as the *fons et origo* of Christianity and (if anything, more important) of the Christian values and insights which still endured. And since Jesus himself left no written record, that meant getting back as close as possible to the historical Jesus in terms of the records in which he featured.

Out of this concern emerged the century-long inquiry into the sources of the Gospels. This has been alluded to above (2.8) and is treated in more detail by Christopher Tuckett ("Introduction to the Gospels," 993-96 below). He will also indicate the somewhat similar debate regarding sources for the Fourth Gospel. We should simply note here, however, one of the benefits of having three of the NT Gospels so obviously in a literary relationship, with one (Mark) as the source for the other two (Matthew and Luke) and with the possibility of reconstructing in some degree a second source for Matthew and Luke (Q). I refer to the benefit that analysis of these relationships yields us clear insights into the tradition process both prior to the writing of these Gospels and indeed subsequent to their being "reduced to writing." Likewise, the benefit of the Fourth Gospel and the very difficulty of tracing sources behind it is a salutary reminder that the retelling of the Gospel story can absorb (in the retelling) the very sources on which it drew so completely that they can no longer be disentangled with confidence.

On sources for Acts we have already said enough above. As might be expected, the Gospels and Acts are the only NT writings which have raised in a substantial way the question of traceable sources. For the rest the immediacy of the letter format and of the Apocalypse (Revelation) hardly invites much if any source criticism.

5.4. *Form Criticism*

Form criticism emerged in the early decades of the twentieth century as a way of getting behind the earliest *written* sources to the earlier *oral* traditions on which the sources drew. As with source criticism, the chief focus of interest was the Jesus tradition. Here, too, enough has probably been said by way of description above (2.4). Unfortunately the potential benefits of the new tool were clouded by two factors. One was the translation of the Germ. *Formgeschichte* (history of the form) into the Eng. "form criticism." The former emphasized the process nature of the oral tradition prior to its writing down; the latter invited the reduction of the task to the rather sterile labeling of forms uncovered by (quasi-archeological) form-critical analysis. The other was that the literary model of analysis of the tradition process encouraged the image of layer upon layer of tradition being built on top of each other. Consequently, the early model of form-critical analysis was largely negative in its results — the impression usually being given that form criticism enabled penetration through only a few layers and left the researcher in inescapable confusion regarding how much of the tradition could be traced right back to Jesus (see again above, 2.8). The earlier analysis of the history of tradition (above) has been an attempt to counter that impression by undermining its assumptions and by demonstrating that a "retelling of tradition" model allows more positive conclusions regarding the retentiveness and stability as well as the flexibility and adaptability of the Jesus tradition.

We have also noted that form criticism had a much wider role to play than source criticism in regard to the

NT epistles (above, 3). If Bultmann is the name to conjure with in regard to form-critical analysis of the Synoptic tradition, Dibelius is the one who most effectively pointed out its wider value beyond the Gospels. In particular, it was Dibelius who more clearly emphasized the purposes to which the various forms were put. Dibelius's insight at this point is neatly summed up in the aphorism: "In the beginning was the sermon" (1934: chs. 2 and 9). The insight was elaborated by Marxsen in his description of the NT itself as "the oldest extant volume of the preaching of the church" (Marxsen 1972: 46). By means of such insights the living character of the tradition process from its individual form to the NT as a whole is retained, and form criticism prevented from lapsing into the "archeological dig" model, to inform our appreciation of the history of the NT as tradition.

5.5. Redaction Criticism

For the sake of completeness I should mention briefly four further stages in the history of critical analysis of the NT tradition before passing the reader on to Green's contribution.

The first is the reaction which followed the emphases of the early form critics. In focusing attention on the form and its identifiability, some of the early form critics overemphasized the evangelists' role as (simply) collectors of the forms (e.g., Dibelius 1934: 3). The lapse was natural, but it indicated clearly enough that they had not fully grasped the character of the tradition process which they were trying to uncover. For the flexibility of the oral tradition, as indeed revealed by the variations in the forms uncovered, should have alerted them to the likelihood that the evangelists would probably have been equally as flexible in their use of the earlier oral forms. As noted above (2.8), the assumption that the transition from oral tradition to written tradition meant a fundamental alteration in the traditioning process (oral = flexible, written = fixed) has been at best misleading and has severely inhibited the recognition of the character of the NT as living tradition (or as sermons, if you like).

Whatever the rights and wrongs of the case, the reaction was almost inevitable. For the evangelists clearly could not be credited simply as collectors of tradition. They had to be recognized as editors and authors in their own right. It does not take much comparison among the Synoptic Gospels to recognize both how stable the basic tradition was and how adaptable it was to each evangelist's different emphases and concerns. In the sequence of "criticisms" it was natural to designate this last addition to the pile of critical tools as "redaction criticism," that is, the study of the way in which the evangelists redacted the tradition which came to them. The litany of names recited at this point always includes Bornkamm (Matthew), Marxsen (Mark), and Conzelmann (Luke).

The value of redaction criticism for an understanding of the history of tradition is precisely its confirmation that the process of passing on the tradition involved creative ordering, adaptation, and elaboration of the tradition. The tradition at the stage of literary dependence was still not fixed but adaptable to the needs of the churches as perceived by the evangelists. At the same time we need to note again the weakness of the assumption which came in with redaction criticism — namely, that the evangelist in his redaction had in view only or primarily the needs of a particular community. Such an assumption runs counter to the indications of a commonality or even large-scale consensus of Jesus tradition across many/(most/all) churches in the Mediterranean region (2.9). The more appropriate image is not of different composers of different works, but of different variations on the common themes, outlines, and emphases of the shared foundation tradition.

5.6. Narrative Criticism

Another weakness of redaction criticism has been its tendency to focus attention on the points of redaction as the surest and clearest indications of the evangelists' theological and ecclesiastical concerns. The result here, too, was inevitable and predictable: the Gospels should rather be treated as a whole, the emphases of particular passages determined more by the function of these passages within the whole (within the individual Gospel's "plot") than by comparison of these passages with the parallel passages in other Gospels. The point has been well made, and "narrative criticism" has produced its own textbooks in turn (e.g., Powell 1990). Indeed, the end of the twentieth century sees a whole scholarly and publishing industry in the business of producing "readings" of the various books of the NT.

The danger in this case is that the heavy focus on the particular document in itself will abstract it too much from the process of tradition. It is all very well to emphasize "the world of the text" as the primary context for exegesis of individual passages, as long as the world of the text is itself not abstracted from the historical context within which the text emerged. Nor can (or should) readings of the text divorce themselves from the history of tradition and from the history of the text's influence (*Wirkungsgeschichte*), since it is often this awareness of the history of the tradition which gives the text its resonance for the informed reader/hearer.

A form of narrative criticism can also be applied to the rest of the NT writings — Acts obviously (Tannehill 1986, 1990), but also the epistles. In the latter case, the narrative in view is the story of God's dealings with humankind, Israel in particular, climaxing in Jesus and the inauguration of the new epoch of salvation (e.g., Hays 1983 and Witherington 1994). Here the resonances of tradition are deep indeed, often beyond normal hearing. In this case the danger is that the narrative can become a composite construction or abstraction compiled from other texts which then provide a kind of control over how the NT text should be heard.

5.7. Rhetorical Criticism

Equally active in the last two decades of the twentieth century, and particularly in reference to the NT epistles, has been rhetorical criticism (e.g., Betz 1979, Kennedy 1984). The primary concern in this case has been to bring to bear on the letters the light which ancient rhetorical practice provides. In what ways, with what tricks and techniques did, for example, Paul endeavor to persuade his audiences in churches around the Aegean and further afield? Here the value for us is a further means of clarifying and coming to a better understanding of how and why Paul adapted his traditions, including his own formulations in earlier letters. The tradition was "hellenized" not simply in conceptual terms (as increasingly became the case during the patristic period), but also and already in the communicative idiom in which it was expressed by Paul and the other writers of the NT letters.

The dangers here have been similar to those in form criticism, particularly in regard to the various forms of persuasive speech — judicial (to persuade in relation to the past), deliberative (to persuade in relation to the future), or epideictic (usually in praise or blame of someone). For there has been a tendency to assume that these were fixed forms, with Paul's intention in disputed passages too much determined by that assumption. A clearer appreciation of the living character of Paul's gospel and tradition, however, would have facilitated a sounder recognition of Paul's readiness to adapt form as well as content to the situation addressed. Equally misleading has been the assumption that there was a uniform rhetorical system in antiquity; for example, Betz himself did not know what to make of the parenetical section in Galatians, since there was no place for exhortation in what he took to be an example of judicial rhetoric. In actual practice, however, as R. D. Anderson has pointed out, ancient rhetoric was much more supple. In rhetorical analysis the interplay of topoi or motifs is much more significant for understanding the dynamic of Paul's theological handling of earlier tradition than the possibility of giving the letter a particular rhetorical label.

5.8. Canonical Criticism

Finally, we should mention "canonical criticism." In one sense it actually spans the history of the modern investigation of NT tradition. For since so much of the early modern history of NT scholarship is Protestant in character, it is not surprising that an important early concern was to demonstrate the authority of the NT writings. It was, after all, the authority of the NT which provided the counter to the authority of Catholic tradition. So the early great commentaries on the NT documents saw it as important to be able to establish that the writings had been deservedly recognized as canonical. And if the traditional criteria of apostolic authorship proved questionable (Who wrote Hebrews? was an unresolvable question), that simply encouraged the scrutiny of external attestation as well as internal characteristics. In this, of course, it was being assumed that church tradition, the tradition of the document's reception within the churches of the patristic period, could help establish the authority of the document within the churches and their tradition. Modern commentators rarely feel the need to redo all this work since it was done so well by their predecessors; that is one of the reasons why the older classic commentaries still hold an honorable place within the libraries of theological institutions.

In its more recent usage, however, "canonical criticism" is usually understood as referring to an interpretation of the individual NT document which reads it within the NT as a whole (particularly Childs 1985, and differently J. A. Sanders 1984). In it the definitive moment within the NT tradition is consciously shifted from the moment of composition (the intention of the author) and the moment of reception (how it was received by the original recipients) to the "moment" of canonization, or, better, to the context provided by canonization. In so doing it is assumed that the canon provides the determinative interpretative context: that, for example, readings of 1 Corinthians which do not take account of the Pastoral Epistles, or readings of the Synoptic Gospels which do not take account of John's Gospel, should by that token command less authority; or indeed that OT monotheism has to be understood as the starting point and context for NT Christology; or that the OT prophetic concern for the poor remains a constant for NT ethics.

Such canonical criticism may in effect be assuming a roundedness of the NT (the Holy Spirit building in checks and balances in the composition of the NT, as it were) which is less than clear. And it may invite the mistake in turn of abstracting the NT from the flow of the history of the tradition. We have already noted the ongoing debate about the limits of the NT; if the text of the NT is not as fixed as some would like to be able to assume, neither are the boundaries of the canon (4.2); Childs himself speaks of "the church's ongoing *search* for the Christian Bible" (1992: 67). At the same time, the wisdom which recognized the importance of canonizing the diversity of the NT witness, including four versions of the Gospel (Dunn 1996) and the Apocalypse of John within the one canon, has to be commended. Both the process of canonizing the NT and the canon itself, properly appreciated, are valuable witnesses to the character of Christian tradition, both in the tentativeness of some of the judgments made (regarding canonical status of particular documents) and in the firmness with which the *sensus fidelium* has affirmed the others. Ambiguity and fuzziness around the edges are an integral and essential part of Christianity's canonical tradition and heritage.

6. Conclusion

One of the most striking features to emerge from this study is the amazing consistency of the history of the NT tradition, the tradition which gave birth to the NT, the tradition which is the NT, and the tradition *(Wirkungsgeschichte)* as which, within which, and through which the NT continues to be heard meaningfully.

(1) We began with a tradition which was the verbalized impact both of the ministry of Jesus and of a consequently fresh encounter with the OT tradition. From the first, in other words, the tradition was a matter of hearing and retelling. It encapsulated the impact made by Jesus, first by his life and teaching and then by his death and resurrection, and effected to convey that impact to others.

(2) If the process described above has any closeness to reality, the mode of retelling, of transmission, combined a stable core and substance with variation and variety for

the particular occasion. Typically, the particularities did not become part of the tradition (fresh layers of tradition) but examples of how the tradition might be retold; typically the retellings would be fresh remintings of the core and substance. In consequence the heart and fundamental thrust of the tradition and its various expressions were maintained through the process of transmission.

(3) The same features (stable core with occasional variations) can be seen in the post-Easter tradition (kerygmatic, liturgical, and ethical). They appear in the Gospels themselves — presented to us precisely not as four Gospels but as the one gospel according to four fundamentally coherent and complementary versions, united by common tradition and common Gospel shape. They appear also in the rest of the NT writings, exemplified by Paul in his several expressions of a gospel which is both coherent and contingent (Beker 1980). And they appear, not least, in the continuing history of the NT tradition, where it is precisely the NT which encapsulates the stable, coherent, and normative core within the ongoing tradition.

In other words, (4) the traditioning process did not alter in essential character throughout the history of the NT tradition. The various transitions — from one language to another, from oral to written text, from source to document, from individual writings to canon — affected the tradition in various ways and over all mark an increasing stability in the tradition. But the flexibility of the retelling (in preaching, teaching, and practice), which was there from the first, and the possibility of a revelatory moment which was always there from the first in the hearing even of older forms of the tradition, has remained a consistent feature of the history throughout.

These observations have important theological implications. For they remind us that the revelatory word of God is not something fixed and final, is not to be simply identified with particular words or with a particular form of the tradition frozen in time (even the NT as such). Were it so, then the tradition would have been something fixed and final, beyond modification and improvement, simply to be transmitted lock, stock, and barrel from one generation to the next. Were it so, then hearing would be simply reception of words with univocal meaning, there would be no room for diverse interpretations, and the different hearings of the different denominations and different ages would be heresy and blasphemy.

In contrast, the history of the NT tradition reminds us that while the core and substance of the tradition remains stable through time and multiple retellings, the forms it takes are diverse and variable. And precisely because there must be hearing as well as retelling if the tradition is to be received, there is inevitably a degree of intangibility in the word of God, a coming to be as authoritative word in each effective hearing. It is just this appreciation of the history of tradition as a dynamic process which helps prevent the written or spoken word from becoming an idol which is overvalued and frees the hearing to be open to the word within the words, the good news which still comes through the tradition in all its various forms.

Bibliography. Aland, K. and B. 2d ed. 1989, *The Text of the New Testament,* Grand Rapids: Eerdmans • Anderson, Ø. 1991, "Oral Tradition," in H. Wansbrough, ed., *Jesus and the Oral Gospel Tradition,* JSNTSup 64, Sheffield: Sheffield Academic, 17-58 • Anderson, R. D. 1996, *Ancient Rhetorical Theory and Paul,* Kampen: Kok Pharos • Bailey, K. 1991, "Informal Controlled Oral Tradition and the Synoptic Gospels," *Asia Journal of Theology* 5:34-54 • Bailey, K. 1995, "Middle Eastern Oral Tradition and the Synoptic Gospels," *ExpT* 106:363-67 • Bauckham, R. 1998, "For Whom Were Gospels Written?" in R. Bauckham, ed., *The Gospels for All Christians: Rethinking the Gospel Audiences,* Grand Rapids: Eerdmans, 9-48 • Bauckham, R. 1999, *James,* London: Routledge • Beker, J. C. 1980, *Paul the Apostle: The Triumph of God in Life and Thought,* Philadelphia: Fortress • Betz, H. D. 1999, *Galatians,* Hermeneia; Philadelphia: Fortress • Bornkamm, H. G., G. Barth, and H. J. Held. 1963, *Tradition and Interpretation in Matthew,* London: SCM • Bruce, F. F. 1997, *Tradition Old and New,* Exeter: Paternoster • Bultmann, R. 1934, *Jesus and the Word,* New York: Scribner's • Bultmann, R. 1963, *The History of the Synoptic Tradition,* Oxford: Blackwell • Burridge, R. A. 1992, *What Are the Gospels? A Comparison with Graeco-Roman Biography,* SNTSMS 70, Cambridge: Cambridge University • Charlesworth, J. H. 1983, 1985, *Old Testament Pseudepigrapha,* London: Darton, Longman & Todd • Childs, B. S. 1985, *The New Testament as Canon: An Introduction,* Philadelphia: Fortress • Childs, B. S. 1992, *Biblical Theology of the Old and New Testaments,* London: SCM • Conzelmann, H. 1960, *The Theology of Saint Luke,* London: Faber and Faber • Dibelius, M. 1934, *From Tradition to Gospel,* London: Nicholson and Watson • Dibelius, M. 1937, *A Fresh Approach to the New Testament and Early Christian Literature,* London: Nicholson & Watson • Dodd, C. H. 1936, *The Apostolic Preaching and Its Developments,* London: Hodder & Stoughton • Dodd, C. H. 1952, *According to the Scriptures: The Substructure of New Testament Theology,* London: Nisbet • Dunn, J. D. G. 1977-78/1998, "Prophetic 'I'-Sayings and the Jesus Tradition: The Importance of Testing Prophetic Utterances within Early Christianity," *NTS* 24: 175-98, repr. in *The Christ and the Spirit,* vol. 2: *Pneumatology,* Grand Rapids: Eerdmans/Edinburgh: T. & T. Clark, 142-69 • Dunn, J. D. G. 1982, "Levels of Canonical Authority," *HBT* 4:13-60, repr. in *The Living Word,* London: SPCK; Philadelphia: Fortress, 141-74, 186-92 • Dunn, J. D. G. 2d ed. 1990, *Unity and Diversity in the New Testament,* London: SCM • Dunn, J. D. G. 1991/1998, "Let John Be John: A Gospel for Its Time," in P. Stuhlmacher, ed., *The Gospel and the Gospels,* Grand Rapids: Eerdmans, 293-322, repr. in *The Christ and the Spirit,* vol. 1: *Christology.* Grand Rapids: Eerdmans/Edinburgh: T. & T. Clark, 345-75 • Dunn, J. D. G. 1991, "John and the Oral Gospel Tradition," in H. Wansbrough, ed., *Jesus and the Oral Gospel Tradition,* JSNTSup 64, Sheffield: Sheffield Academic, 351-79 • Dunn, J. D. G. 1996, "John and the Synoptics as a Theological Question," in R. A. Culpepper and C. C. Black, eds., *Exploring the Gospel of John,* D. M. Smith Festschrift, Louisville: Westminster John Knox, 301-13 • Dunn, J. D. G. 1998, *The Theology of Paul the Apostle,* Grand Rapids: Eerdmans/Edinburgh: T. & T. Clark • Dunn, J. D. G. 2003, *Christianity in the Making,* vol. 1: *Jesus Remembered,* Grand Rapids: Eerdmans • Dunn, J. D. G. 2003, "Altering the Default Setting: Re-envisaging the Early Transmission of the Jesus Tradition," *NTS* 49:139-75 • Dupont, J. 1964, *The Sources of the Acts,* New York: Herder/London:

Darton, Longman & Todd • Ehrman, B. D. 1993, *The Orthodox Corruption of Scripture: The Effect of Early Christological Controversies on the Text of the New Testament* (New York/Oxford: Oxford University • Elliott, J. K. 1993, *The Apocryphal New Testament,* Oxford: Clarendon • Ellis, E. E. 1978, "New Directions in Form Criticism," in *Prophecy and Hermeneutic in Early Christianity: New Testament Essays,* Tübingen: Mohr/Grand Rapids: Eerdmans, 237-53 • Evans, C. F. 1956, "The Kerygma," *JTS* 7:25-41 • Gadamer, H. G. 2d ed. 1990, *Truth and Method,* New York: Crossroad • Gerhardsson, B. 1961, *Memory and Manuscript: Oral Tradition and Written Transmission in Rabbinic Judaism and Early Christianity,* Lund: Gleerup • Gerhardsson, B. 1964, *Tradition and Transmission in Early Christianity,* Lund: Gleerup • Gerhardsson, B. 1979, *The Origins of the Gospel Traditions,* Philadelphia: Fortress/London: SCM • Gerhardsson, B. 1986, *The Gospel Tradition,* Lund: Gleerup • Hays, R. B. 1983, *The Faith of Jesus Christ: An Investigation of the Narrative Substructure of Galatians 3.1–4.11,* Chico: Scholars • Hays, R. B. 1989, *Echoes of Scripture in the Letters of Paul,* New Haven: Yale University • Hofius, O. 1991, "Unknown Sayings of Jesus," in P. Stuhlmacher, ed., *The Gospel and the Gospels,* Grand Rapids: Eerdmans, 336-60 • Hunter, A. M. 2d ed. 1961, *Paul and His Predecessors,* London: SCM • Johnson, L. T. 1996, *The Real Jesus: The Misguided Quest for the Historical Jesus and the Truth of the Traditional Gospels,* San Francisco: Harper • Juel, D. 1998, *Messianic Exegesis: Christological Interpretation of the Old Testament in Early Christianity,* Philadelphia: Fortress • Kähler, M. 1892, 1964, *The So-called Historical Jesus and the Historic Biblical Christ,* Philadelphia: Fortress; Käsemann, E. 1964, "Is the Gospel Objective?" in *Essays on New Testament Themes,* London: SCM • Kelber, W. H. 1983, *The Oral Tradition and the Written Gospel,* Philadelphia: Fortress • Kennedy, G. A. 1984, *New Testament Interpretation through Rhetorical Criticism,* Chapel Hill, N.C.: University of North Carolina • Kramer, W. 1966, *Christ, Lord, Son of God,* London: SCM • Kümmel, W. G. 1975, *Introduction to the New Testament,* Nashville: Abingdon/London: SCM • Lindars, B. 1961, *New Testament Apologetic,* London: SCM • Lord, A. B. 1978, "The Gospels as Oral Traditional Literature," in W. O. Walker, ed., *The Relationships among the Gospels,* San Antonio, Tex.: Trinity University, 33-91 • Marxsen, W. 1969, *Mark the Evangelist,* Nashville: Abingdon • Marxsen, W. 1972, *The New Testament as the Church's Book,* Philadelphia: Fortress • Meade, D. 1986, *Pseudonymity and Canon: An Investigation into the Relationship of Authorship and Authority in Jewish and Earliest Christian Tradition,* WUNT 39, Tübingen: Mohr-Siebeck • Meyendorff, J. 1978, *Living Tradition: Orthodox Witness in the Contemporary World* (Crestwood, N.Y.: St. Vladimir's Seminary • Moule, C. F. D. 3d ed. 1981, *The Birth of the New Testament,* London: A. & C. Black • Parker, D. C. 1997, *The Living Text of the Gospels,* Cambridge: Cambridge University • Pokorný, P. 1987, *The Genesis of Christology: Foundations for a Theology of the New Testament,* Edinburgh: T. & T. Clark • Powell, M. A. 1990, *What Is Narrative Criticism?* Minneapolis: Fortress • Rosner, B. S. 1994, *Paul, Scripture and Ethics: A Study of 1 Corinthians 5–7,* Leiden: Brill • Sanders, E. P. 1969, *The Tendencies of the Synoptic Tradition,* SNTSMS 9, Cambridge: Cambridge University • Sanders, J. A. 1984, *Canon and Community: A Guide to Canonical Criticism,* Philadelphia: Fortress • Tannehill, R. C. 1986, 1990, *The Narrative Unity of Luke-Acts: A Literary Interpretation,* Philadelphia: Fortress • Theissen, G. 1987, *The Shadow of the Galilean: The Quest of the Historical Jesus in Narrative Form,* London: SCM • Trocmé, E. 1973, *Jesus and His Contemporaries,* London: SCM • Wansbrough, H., ed. 1991, *Jesus and the Oral Gospel Tradition,* JSNTSup 64, Sheffield: Sheffield Academic • Witherington, B. 1994, *Paul's Narrative Thought World,* Louisville: Westminster/John Knox.

Hermeneutical Approaches to the New Testament Tradition

Joel B. Green

1. Introduction

"Texts" — whether in the form of newspapers or road signs or e-mail — permeate our lives, so that we are continually, though typically unknowingly, in an interpretive mode. Those squiggly lines on a page or computer screen demand decoding, understanding. Most of the time, this process of interpretation seems natural enough, with few obstacles. At other times, though, we encounter a news story about a developing situation unknown to us that leaves us puzzled, or we find references to people or habits or events of which we have scant knowledge. At these and comparable points, texts come to us in all of their ambiguity, demanding a different, more exacting level of interaction and engagement if perception is to be achieved.

For at least two reasons, the attribution of the heading "Scripture" to these particular texts, OT and NT texts, raises the stakes on how we hear them. This is because, first, they have a peculiar, formative role to play in the life of those communities that regard them as Scripture. How can these texts be heard as Scripture? How might they be appropriated in our many and diverse settings? Thus, we can never be content with accruing "information" as the goal of reading these texts as Scripture, since the role of Scripture is a formative and transformative one. As David Kelsey has noted, the authority of Scripture relates fundamentally to what the Scriptures *do* as Scripture. He insists that "part of what it means to call a text 'Christian scripture' is that *it functions to shape persons' identities so decisively as to transform them*" (Kelsey 1975: 90-92). These issues are exacerbated by a second observation — namely, these texts derive from a different time and place than our own. They speak of people and places that are foreign to us and incorporate assumptions that sometimes escape us. The NT, after all, was written in Greek. And the ease with which we recall and accept this truism masks the reality that with such an array of modern translations, the NT is so readily accessible to us that we perhaps too easily assume that its words, familiar to us in translation, also carry commonplace meaning from our world. We too easily merge the horizons of our world with those of the NT world, presupposing that all people in all times and places experience life as we do. If, as the church believes, these texts mediated the divine voice in *those* times and places, the question remains, How might they function thus in our own? Such considerations bring to the surface concerns not only of *method* but also, and even more fundamentally, of *hermeneutical approach.*

"Method" has to do with any of a range of interpretive strategies with which one might engage a text. These might focus on the exploration of possible meaning or meanings:

- *behind the text* — in the history assumed by the text, the history that gave rise to the text, and/or the history to which a text speaks;
- *in the text* — the text in this case understood as a self-contained attempt at interpretation;
- *in front of the text* — with particular attention paid to the perspectives of its readers and/or reading communities, together with the effects texts have on their readers; and/or
- *at the interface of two or more of these levels.*

Underlying reading strategies of this nature are commitments of a hermeneutical sort, commitments that help to determine what method or methods might best be employed. Different hermeneutical aims call for different interpretive strategies.

While "method" refers to the practice of reading texts, then, "hermeneutics" is the theory of interpretation. In biblical studies, hermeneutics is concerned with the appropriation of texts in ever new contexts, a concern that necessarily includes issues of how to read texts.

2. Hermeneutical Approaches

The distinction just made, between "hermeneutics" and "method," is a relatively recent one. In the period leading up to the nineteenth century, the process of reading texts had as its sole aim the recognition of a single valid meaning. In reaction against biblical interpretation in the medieval period, the Protestant reformers emphasized the one meaning of Scripture; from this emerged the quest for the original meaning of NT texts. Handbooks for hermeneutics focused on criteria for achieving legitimate readings, including philology, study of the historical circumstances governing the meaning of words, and reference to the intent of the author. At the turn of the nineteenth century, however, the twin concepts of cultural context and cultural relativism were introduced into hermeneutical thought. As a result, biblical (and other, especially classical) texts came to be understood with reference to the distance between text and reader, with this distance construed along historical and cultural (and not only theological) lines. To a significant degree, hermeneutics came to focus its energies on the exploration and/or mediation of this distance. Interests of this nature understandably gave rise to the forms of historical inquiry that have largely characterized biblical studies since.

Beginning early in the twentieth century, innovations in hermeneutical theory began to shift the weight of emphasis from interpretation as the achievement of understanding toward interpretation as the production of meaning. In this evolving hermeneutic, emphasis is placed on the process whereby "the right of the reader and the right of the text converge in an important struggle that generates the whole dynamic of interpretation" (Ricoeur 1976: 32). Hans-Georg Gadamer (1990) moved hermeneutics in this direction by viewing the radical separation of subject and object as a kind of "fall from grace." In his formulation, the scientific quest for truth, based on the experimental method, is not the only path to truth; art, for example, is "known" through a hermeneutical "game" in which we are transformed in relation to it. With regard to texts, Gadamer analogously calls for a type of hermeneutical consciousness whereby the act of understanding is imagined as a fusion of one's own horizon (i.e., confronting one's own historicality) with the historical horizon embodied in these texts from the past.

Accordingly, one's historical and cultural distance from the text is not to be seen as a barrier to but as a necessary factor in the process of interpretation. "Meaning," according to this way of thinking, is not so much something to be stalked and captured as to be made manifest, embodied, and proclaimed. A further innovation in hermeneutics in the latter half of the twentieth century has developed in conjunction with this theory of interpretation, however. Some have argued that texts, including biblical texts, are not simply to be embraced and appropriated but must be exposed for their latent ideological commitments. This "hermeneutics of suspicion" distrusts the underlying presumptions of both texts and the history of their interpretation. Today, numerous hermeneutical approaches are championed, including refashioned versions of previous theories, newer theories that locate meaning solely or almost solely in the experience of the audience, and theories that question the capacity of any particular text to divulge a single, congruous understanding of itself.

Of course, such modifications and transformations in hermeneutical theory as we have sketched do not sweep the interpretive table clean. To at least some degree, each builds on the previous one, typically with an approach developed to address the perceived excesses or lacunae of a prior one. Moreover, at least within contemporary circles of biblical interpretation, the introduction of fresh interpretive approaches does not always signal the rejection of earlier versions. In fact, at the turn of the twenty-first century the hermeneutical landscape is characterized by an unruly heterogeneity. It may be helpful to characterize the lay of the land with reference to the contemporary embodiment of four "modes of reading": precritical, scientific, contextual, and reactive (cf. Padilla 1981).

2.1. *Reading in a Precritical Mode*

The Bible reading conducted by many people today can be characterized as "precritical" insofar as it advances on the basis of the unexamined presumption that a NT text written, say, in the late-first-century AD continues to possess an immediate and straightforward relevance in new times and situations. The text, it is assumed, is transhistorical and transcultural. For persons operating in a precritical mode, the idea of "interpretation" is itself problematic since, as it is often repeated, one needs only to read the NT in order to apprehend its message. "The Bible says it. I believe it. That settles it."

On the positive side of the ledger, this mode of reading helpfully underscores the importance of the faithful appropriation of Scripture. It also suggests the accessibility of Scripture to all persons rather than to those who possess accredited skills only. Moreover, at certain levels of relative abstraction, such a reading has pragmatic value. It remains true, for example, that the people of God are to practice love for one another, even if one might go on to insist that the precise content and shape of practices that communicate and exhibit neighborly love might shift from one context to the next.

On the negative side, precritical readings of Scripture overlook the sociolinguistic reality that all language is embedded in culture, together with its direct corollary that a message oriented toward one context may have a quite different meaning in a new one. At the specific linguistic level of the usage of words, for example, such terms as "gay" or "bum" do not carry over well from one contemporary English-speaking people to another. Problems of translation multiply exponentially when the twenty-first-century person from Los Angeles or Edinburgh is to grapple with NT texts written in Koine Greek in the Roman Mediterranean of two thousand years ago. Sometimes the only way to say the same thing is to use different words, a process that dictates interpretation and translation. Furthermore, some NT texts seem so culturally embedded in their first-century contexts as to be of little or no immediate relevance. Not many of us regularly practice the holy kiss, for example, in spite of clear scriptural admonition (Rom 16:16), nor do we often engage in footwashing, the clarity with which Jesus instructs his followers to do so notwithstanding (John 13:14).

We all choose to embrace some NT texts as possessing particular relevance while not sanctioning others, at least in the direct way demanded by a traditional or precritical mode of reading. From the perspective of hermeneutics, this is problematic since it leaves open the question, How is it decided when a text is to be read as directly relevant for us? As will become clear below, perhaps even more pressing is the question, Who decides when a text is to be taken in such a straightforwardly relevant way?

2.2. *Reading in a Scientific Mode*

In some ways, "scientific" modes of reading developed as a reaction to traditional readings of biblical texts, not least in response to certain interpretations of Scripture that were perceived to accord privilege to the institutional church or church hierarchy as interpretive authority. As a control on the construal of the meaning of Scripture, the scientific method turns away from traditional creeds or ecclesiastical offices. Instead it places a premium on the study of historical context. According to the promise of scientific hermeneutics, if we were able to understand enough about the historical situations in which NT texts were penned, then we could achieve the singular meaning of each of those texts. "Meaning," then, is an attribute that coheres not so much to the texts of the NT as to the histories that gave rise to those texts.

Unlike precritical hermeneutics, scientific readings take seriously the historical rootedness of biblical texts. Moreover, they do so in ways that are open to verification by other "scientists" — that is, by other academically endorsed interpreters. Although this is helpful with respect to the objective of hearing NT texts better on their own terms, it is also true that scientific hermeneutics has tended to define "meaning" in historical terms that preclude or at least diminish concern with the appropriation of those texts for new audiences. Moreover, as with the scientific method more generally, so also its utilization in biblical studies has generally proceeded on the basis of an alleged objectivity on the part of the reader. Biblical scholars as "scientists" imagined themselves as persons concerned with the data as it exists in and of itself, failing to realize that interpreters always construe data in relation to themselves, according to their own categories of thought and analysis. Persons reading in a scientific mode have thus failed to account for the fact that their own historical concerns are themselves manifestations of a particular historical moment. Finally, by seeking to maintain scientific distance from the text, such interpreters often valued readings of Scripture that were not oriented toward or useful for those persons and communities who looked to the NT as Scripture. Not surprisingly, the rise of the scientific method in the study of Scripture is easily correlated with the development of study of the Bible in university departments unrelated to religious instruction or ministerial education. Sundered from issues of faith and faithful existence, biblical texts could more easily be molded into objects to be examined and studied but without a voice of their own with which to call into question or to shape their interpreters.

2.3. *Reading in a Contextual Mode*

A way beyond the impasse propagated by scientific hermeneutics was signaled already by the image made famous by Karl Barth of the preacher with one hand clutching the Bible and the other the newspaper. According to this reading scenario, both the context of the reader and that of the ancient text are to be given due consideration. For contextual modes of reading, cultural setting is important at both ends of the hermeneutical enterprise since the message of Scripture is always and necessarily embedded in particular situations. In order to communicate a particular message of Scripture, then, one must inquire into the meaning of a given text in its historical context, then turn to the question of how that same message might best be communicated in different cultural settings.

Contextual hermeneutics may at first appear to be a throwback to a form of scientific reading, with the exception that the importance of the appropriation of biblical texts today is again highlighted. Such an approach to biblical interpretation might have three steps (observation, interpretation, and application) or two (determine what it meant, then determine what it means), and would employ strategies that promise uses of Scripture that provide us with an objective base from which to launch discussion of contemporary significance. Accordingly, as it is often asserted, a text cannot mean what it did not at first mean, for meaning (then) determines significance (now). Clearly, however, this is not the direction a fully context-sensitive hermeneutic can go, for such an approach assumes the impossible: it asks interpreters to shed their modern clothing in order to stand nakedly on a nonexistent ledge of neutrality and objectivity where they might delineate the "original meaning" of a biblical text.

Indeed, one of the pivotal contributions of feminist hermeneutics in the late-twentieth century was its fundamental challenge to professed "objectivity" in interpretation. Feminist hermeneutics, like other liberation hermeneutics (see below), raises sensitivities about the pervasiveness of oppression in society and especially about how the Bible has been and continues to be used to reinforce unjust relationships and social systems. The first principle of such a hermeneutic, then, is suspicion, and the second is the rejection of the notion of objectivity. Different social contexts lead to different sets of questions and different vantage points from which to ask them, and thus to different understandings of biblical texts. *Who* is doing the reading? This becomes a pivotal question since all interpretation is influenced and conditioned by the interests and social location of the interpreter.

Of course, liberationist hermeneutics is not the only source for this dis-ease with the scientific paradigm. Philosophical hermeneutics in the twentieth century has likewise given birth, as it were, to the significance of the reader. According to earlier perspectives, readers "received" meaning from texts; now the role of the reader in the production and actualization of meaning is increasingly recognized. This means, minimally, that "interpretation" and "application" cannot be simply classified as discrete steps in the hermeneutical enterprise. Texts are effecting cognitive and affective responses in their readers already in the midst of the reading, just as readers are either deliberately or unselfconsciously shaping how they hear a text by bringing with them to it their own interests, needs, and assumptions about God and the cosmos.

Even though this concern with original context can be overstated, however, the value of the impulses behind this paradigm should not escape us. They helpfully point to the importance of our taking seriously the contextual framework in which the biblical texts were generated and first read. Nevertheless, to take seriously the role of context in hermeneutics is also to bring into the foreground the inescapable truth that all reading is done from the perspective of the reader's historical situation and lifeworld.

2.4. *Reading in a Reactive Mode: Hermeneutics at an Impasse*

Biblical interpretation at the beginning of the new millennium is faced with a critical challenge. A Chinese feminist theologian such as Kwok Pui-lan (1995) can invite forms of hermeneutical inquiry indigenous to Asia and Asian women while at the same time rejecting modes of reading common in the West on account of their roots in the matrix of the (alien) Western intellectual tradition. Gerald West (1995), on the other hand, can inquire into what hermeneutical approach might be followed so that Scripture becomes a truly liberating force in South Africa's black community. And these are only two examples of what has become more and more commonplace — namely, the admission that NT interpretation is influenced keenly by the contextual locations and presuppositions of readers. For some, it is only one small step from one's awareness of such conflicted, even competing interests to a hermeneutic that might best be described as "reactive." "Reactive readers," recognizing that no reading is innocent or devoid of ideology, formulate the reading experience as a battleground whereby readers seek to overturn the perspectives of both the text and the history of its reading in order to replace them with one's own.

Clearly, admissions of this nature may make room in biblical studies for anthropological reality, but they also raise important questions of their own. The most pressing is, If our own lifeworlds are of necessity the starting point for reading these texts, will we not find in them only that for which we were already looking? If NT reading is so influenced by one's cultural presuppositions, can the biblical text have any function other than that of a mirror? Is "meaning" something to be discovered or generated, or can it only be imposed? By refusing to aim for an impartial reading of a NT text, and indeed by denying even the potential of neutrality, have we not already compromised the primary aim of biblical hermeneutics? To put it differently, Can we as readers have interests and remain open to challenge?

These are portentous questions, especially given the ease with which religious communities historically have found in their readings of the Scriptures divine legitimation for their sometimes heinous practices. One has only to reflect on the forms of biblical interpretation undergirding apartheid in South Africa, classism in Britain, the treatment of Native Americans in the United States, or the almost global disparaging of women, to name only four cases, in order to discern the import of facing squarely and honestly the hermeneutical challenge of these considerations.

3. The Hermeneutical Challenge

Not least given the magnitude and multiplicity of related issues, summarizing a way forward in NT hermeneutics is not easy, so many are the questions and so few are the assured results. How does one navigate through shifting sands? The opening of the new millennium is nonetheless a creative moment, one well suited to the exploration of fresh prospects for grappling with the task of biblical hermeneutics. Before sketching a mode of hermeneutical inquiry appropriate to the challenges we have outlined, it is necessary to introduce other contenders.

3.1. *Possible Resolutions*

Some scholars today propose a mode of reading that bears remarkable kinship to the "dogmatic hermeneutics" whose heyday persisted into the Middle Ages. Characteristic of dogmatic hermeneutics is the presence of systems (theological, philosophical, or sociological) or precepts beyond the biblical text that are not only involved in the interpretive enterprise but are actually determinative for establishing the authentic meaning of the text. A hermeneutics of this sort is very much in evidence today when a predetermined position (or, alternatively, an unexamined assumption) is allowed to constrain the possible meaning or range of meanings available to readers of biblical texts. Within Protestantism, the "rule of faith" has generally centered on the doctrine of "justification by faith" — so much so that recent attempts to rethink the meaning of those biblical texts on which this doctrine has been based have been met in some quarters with stiff resistance. Similarly, for many charismatics in the twentieth century, a prior commitment to the experience of a second blessing or second outpouring of the Holy Spirit as the normal Christian autobiography has been determinative for the interpretation of certain NT texts. In some feminist circles today, interpretation of particular biblical texts is circumscribed by a prior commitment to a reconstructed "community of equals."

Such an approach is ultimately unsatisfying since to read the NT as Scripture is to leave open at every turn the possibility that our interpretive traditions are erroneous and in need of reformation. As Gadamer argues,

> A person trying to understand something will not resign himself [*sic*] from the start to relying on his own accidental fore-meanings, ignoring as consistently and stubbornly as possible the actual meaning of the text until the latter becomes so persistently audible that it breaks through what the interpreter imagines it to be. Rather a person trying to understand a text is prepared for it to tell him something. That is why a hermeneutically trained consciousness must be, from the start, sensitive to the text's alterity. (Gadamer 1990: 269)

We come to Scripture again and again, in humility, not only with our questions but with an openness to its questions — open to the possibility that this text will speak a word over against our interpretive communities, resisting the nagging temptation to which we so easily succumb of substituting our word for God's Word.

One may counter that all reading is shaped by such external commitments and, indeed, that explicit recognition of the commitments of one's reading community is a positive response to the reality that the Word of God is always scandalous in its specificity. The word of God came to John in the wilderness at a certain time, in the context of a particular politico-religious framework (Luke 3:1-2). Paul wrote to the Philippians, a particular people in a particular place, at a particular time for particular reasons. Even if the gospel embraces the whole cosmos and is universal in its claims, life in light of the gospel is lived by persons living in economically deprived southeast Dallas, on wheat farms in Kansas, and in the suburbs of Manchester — so the specific demands of faithful living cannot be predetermined or engineered for distribution to the masses. The relevance of Scripture for Christians seeking to live out their vocations in diverse settings must be worked out by Christians interpreting Scripture in those diverse settings.

This is not to allow, however, that each local congregation or interpretive tradition is self-legitimating when it comes to biblical interpretation. Nor is it to deny the wisdom of a teaching office at supralocal levels of church life. The particularity of revelation requires engagement with Scripture at the local level and within communities of interpretation but also threatens the development of myopic vision, ingrown and un-self-critical faith. Local congregations and other communities of readers must be in conversation with biblical interpretation among others seeking to be faithful disciples — across time and across lines of all kinds, be they generational, urban or suburban or rural, gender related, racial, national, political, and so on. Local congregations need the whole body of Christ, global and historical, in order to remain open to the authority of Scripture to speak in voices not usually heard in their own contexts.

As a prophylactic against drafting the NT to one's own ends or to the agenda of a particular interpretive community, many today continue to insist on the ongoing necessity of a scientific hermeneutics. That is, they continue to insist on the basic division between "what it meant" and "what it means" with respect to the biblical message. Although we have already visited some of the reasons for caution with regard to this proposal, this is not to discount the presence and appropriateness of some restraints on the significance of a biblical text. Attending to the co-textual location of a given text is itself an exercise in the control of meaning, since the co-text (i.e., the location of a text in a narrative or epistolary argument) exerts considerable pressure on meaning. Moreover, since all language is embedded in culture and since biblical texts will have been generated within particular discourse situations, it behooves modern interpreters to engage as fully as possible in an exploration of the cultural presuppositions biblical writers shared with their contemporaries. What is more, the location of NT writings in their function as "canon" also reminds us that the canon itself serves as a context within which the church construes the meaning of particular biblical texts.

3.2. *Reading in a Discursive Mode: A Proposal*

With these considerations in place, we are now in a better position to outline an interpretive process that takes seriously the hermeneutical questions and gains of the past century. Given that no interpreter comes "clean" to Scripture, that all of us bring with us to the NT our own commitments and interests, what is to keep the interpretive enterprise from degenerating into self-legitimating pragmatism? How can we affirm not only the anthropological fact but also the interpretive significance of readerly interests *and* continue to speak of the formative role of Scripture? It has become increasingly evident that the practice of biblical hermeneutics must locate itself within communities of biblical interpretation that take seriously a range of conversation partners.

Ultimately, then, a hermeneutical model capable of addressing contemporary concerns must be "discursive" in its fundamental profile. That is, it must attend to a range of overlapping and interlocking levels of discourse — some represented by and in NT texts themselves, some derived from the history and contemporary practice of interpretation of the NT, and some that take seriously the location of the church within the world created and redeemed by God (Green 1997). Conversation with and about Scripture, then, must be:

- *cross-cultural* — taking seriously the historical, cultural contexts both within which NT texts were produced and within which contemporary interpretation takes place, in order to inhibit the wholesale cultural imperialism that surfaces when we assume all people everywhere and in all times believe and act as we do;
- *canonical* — taking seriously that, within the canon, one finds a diversity of voices that sometimes balance and counterbalance one another, all of which are canonical, and so which legitimate a certain range of diversity within and among the people of God;
- *historical* — taking seriously that we are not the first persons to read Scripture, that our own readings of Scripture are, for good or bad, at least partially formed by previous interpreters, and that our mothers and fathers in the faith may contribute positively to our attempt to articulate the significance of the gospel in our worlds;
- *communal* — taking seriously that the biblical witness is itself concerned with the formation of faithful communities of God's people, and that biblical interpretation, in order to be authentically *biblical,* must take place in the context of faith(ful) communities;
- *global* — taking seriously that our faith communities, which keep us from developing private and idiosyncratic interpretations, are themselves subject to tunnel vision and self-legitimation, and thus need the witness of believers who are "not like us" as conversation partners; and
- *hospitable* — taking seriously that, even as God's grace extends to all people, so we may learn from those whose lives seem not at all to be oriented around God — persons, then, who may be able to remedy our tendencies toward interpretive arrogance.

If the hermeneutical agenda thus outlined seems daunting, this is understandable. This is not cause for despair, however, but should rather provide the necessary impetus for such dispositions as openness and humility. If in the early days of the Enlightenment people may have seemed intoxicated with the promise of secure knowledge, global understanding, and assured results, the twilight years of modernity are marked instead by a chastised human awareness of ambiguity, anomaly, and complexity. The degree to which we need each other — people in southern and northern hemispheres, churches in the East and West, communities past and present, and so on — has never been more apparent if we are to engage in a biblical hermeneutics the object of which is the formation of faithful communities.

4. Interpretive Strategies

The hermeneutics outlined above does not function as a telescopic lens, focusing the interpretive enterprise narrowly on one or two interpretive strategies. It has the opposite affect, performing rather as a prism that opens our sensitivities to a multiplicity of methods.

4.1. Setting the Stage

Contemporary concern with method in NT interpretation cannot be painted without reference to the enormous upheavals that shook the foundations of biblical study in the last third of the twentieth century. Among these the most noticeable is the fallen hegemony of the historical-critical paradigm and concomitant disillusionment among students of Scripture concerning the promise of isolating the single, "intended," correct meaning of a biblical text.

The historical-critical paradigm shares with earlier modes of reading a fundamental emphasis on the history to which a text gives witness. Earlier modes of reading, however, focused primarily on the biblical "text," but took "text" and "event" as co-terminus. Thus, whatever the Gospel of Matthew reports of Jesus was thought actually to have happened in precisely that way. Historical-critical readings made no such assumptions about the historical veracity of the text but rather assumed the necessity of isolating history from text. Three principles have served as guidelines in the process: (1) every historical statement is open to doubt; (2) the possibility of accepting historical statements as true must be worked out in analogy to our own experience of what is historically possible; and (3) historical events are governed by the laws of natural cause and effect.

If many events in the Gospels and Acts were consequently dismissed from consideration as having actually happened, however, this did not rule out their being studied by historians. Historical-critical scholarship has been interested in events but also in the traditions by which events are interpreted and/or by which particular interpretations have accrued to persons like Jesus in the Gospels or Peter in Acts. With reference to the study of the historical Jesus, these interests gave rise to a series of criteria for determining the relative authenticity of sayings and practices attributed to Jesus. More broadly, historical criticism has been concerned with the historical realities assumed by NT texts and to which those texts address themselves.

In the waning years of the twentieth century, the foundations of this form of historicism have been shaken rigorously. There is now a growing recognition that the textualizing of historical events is itself always historically inspired. History recounts what has been determined to be significant by a community or society and, then, by a historian, with the incontrovertible corollary that historical events are remembered and reported always not with reference to "the truth, the whole truth, and nothing but the truth," but in relation to those doing the remembering and recording. Historical investigation, then, can never escape the element of the subjective, and all historical narrative is inherently partial, both in the sense of being incomplete and in the sense of bringing to expression certain commitments on the part of the historian.

Again, these considerations do not have as their inevitable sequelae the suspension or rejection of historical inquiry. They do intimate strongly the need for more nuanced ways of construing notions of "history" and "historical," however, and they invite forms of interpretation that highlight aspects of the text in addition to those events and traditions to which texts give testimony.

For a brief period and in selected quarters, it appeared that the hyperconcern with historical meaning characteristic of the last two centuries of NT study might be replaced with a narrow focus on the text itself. If, according to the historical-critical paradigm, the meaning of a text cannot be equated with how it affects the reader ("The Affective Fallacy"), according to the literary turn in interpretation, neither can reports of an author's original intention be regarded as germane to criticism ("The Intentional Fallacy"). After all, in the case of the NT writings, we are physically incapable of checking our interpretations against the intentions of their writers. Even if we could interview these authors, though, such discussion could never guarantee that the texts they produced represent nothing more or less than what they had originally intended to say. In the end, readers have before them to consult only the literary text itself, and, in "new criticism" and its incarnations in various "formalisms," the text itself is regarded as a self-sufficient verbal artifact. Accordingly, the text is presumed to be the unique and privileged source of meaning and interpretive value, available to the interpreter via careful attention to its language.

New criticism has attracted only guarded support in NT studies for at least three reasons. First, it was unable to contend with the powerful inertia built up by two centuries of historical inquiry; the academy had little room for self-styled "ahistorical" readings. Second, fast on the heels of new criticism in literary studies came the rediscovery of the reader. Claude Lévi-Strauss, supporting a formalist approach to interpretation, had spoken of a work of art as "an object endowed with precise properties, that must be analytically isolated, and this work can be entirely defined on the grounds of such properties." For him, one should approach a work of art, like a literary text, "as an object which, once created, had the stiffness — so to speak — of a crystal; we [confine] ourselves to bringing into evidence these properties." In reply,

Umberto Eco observed, "A text is not a 'crystal.' If it were a crystal, the cooperation of the reader would be part of its molecular structure" (Eco 1979: 3-4, 37). For Eco, a text not only calls for the cooperation of its reader in the construction of meaning but also summons the reader to make a series of interpretive choices. One could never surmise, then, that a text existed as a self-sufficient verbal artifact. Third, as has been increasingly appreciated, literary texts participate in, legitimate, perpetuate, and criticize, the lifeworlds within which they were generated. Texts are therefore "cultural products" which can be understood only in part when read without reference to the cultural settings in which they took shape.

As with historical criticism, the now widely acknowledged limitations of new criticism have not led to the complete debunking of the close readings of texts characteristic of literary approaches. Rather, literary readings are increasingly viewed as important points of departure in need of the supplementation of other interpretive approaches.

Evidence abounds everywhere in biblical studies of a search for aims and approaches that are not tethered to the historical mode of critical inquiry that has characterized biblical scholarship in the nineteenth and twentieth centuries. As we have suggested, the meaning of biblical texts is itself more and more regarded as polyvalent, with different methods oriented toward locating textual significance behind the text, treating the text as a window into the historical events and processes informing the text; in the text, according privilege to the text itself as literature; and in front of the text, accounting for the reality that different readers and reading communities often hear a text and construe its significance differently. Variation at this junction has yielded a dazzling array of strategies for engaging biblical texts (see Green 1995). To representatives of this variety we may now turn.

4.2. Social-Scientific Readings of the New Testament

Given contemporary hermeneutical sensibilities, one of the chief considerations that must inform any responsible reading of the NT is this: these documents originate from a time and place distinctive from our own, and they take for granted social values and contexts not all of which are natural to us. Social-scientific readings of NT texts orient themselves toward situating those texts within the social conditions and real lives of persons in first-century Palestine and the larger Roman world. They remind us that the letters of Paul, for example, were not delivered as advanced theological seminars but were meant to address the particular lives of people and communities struggling with such issues as community definition, the nature of authority, the ramifications of the good news for relationships of all kinds, and the like.

Early in the twentieth century, concerns with history and the historical began to move onto center stage the question, What was the occasion of the NT documents? This query opened up concerns with life in the Mediterranean world, including questions of population, economics, political structures, and the like. Such interests could have led into social-scientific investigation. Instead, with few exceptions, attention was redirected to the world of ideas and the internal life of the communities of faith to which those NT documents were first addressed. Similarly, a particular species of historical criticism concerned with the "forms" by which materials were shaped and handed down in the tradition, "form criticism," took an interest in how various patterns of literature were bound to and shaped by specific "settings in life." Such concerns were particularly popular through the middle of the twentieth century and might have brought to the surface a genuine social-scientific interest. Under the influence of an existentialist hermeneutic, however, form criticism turned away from what might have become social-scientific investigation in order to locate the traditio-historical basis of the Gospel traditions in the life of the early church. That is, the impulses of form criticism were not toward a community's social setting or cultural horizons per se, but rather toward particular community practices such as worship, catechesis, and missionary apologetic. Consequently, the rise of social-scientific criticism in NT interpretation can be traced most easily to the later third of the twentieth century, a time when a more general commitment to understanding the social embeddedness of values and experiences of all kinds achieved prominence in many arenas.

Social-scientific readings have usually been divided into two broad categories. The first is "social description." Here the aim is to understand and report as fully as possible the conditions of life in a given locale, or even throughout the Roman Empire. What was the population? What ethnic mix characterized this city? What were the means of income? Demography, economics, social class, and the like — these are the stuff of attempts to describe the visible features of a target society. According to this typology, the second major sociological approach to NT interpretation takes its departure from social and cultural anthropological theory. In this case, models are constructed, often from other cultures, then employed by way of filling in the gaps of what is taken for granted within a NT text. In this way, evidence is gathered and analyzed within a theoretical framework. Utilization of theoretical models, for example, has resulted in major questions being raised against the modern, Western tendency to read into the NT a concern with an individual-oriented, subjective experience with God. This is because the Roman world is now understood more as a "dyadic culture," where personal identity is constructed always in relationship to one's group of reference, one's larger kinship group. Attempts are now being made to understand better the communal and social nature of Christian life in the NT era (and since).

Once our sensitivities have been sharpened by them, social-science or cultural questions that might be directed toward texts multiply easily: How are group boundaries drawn? Who are the insiders? Who are the outsiders? What threatens these definitions? How are boundaries maintained? How are certain people addressed? With kinship terms — such as "loved ones" or "sisters" or "children"? Or with terms of authority — such as "slave" or "sir"? Who is in charge? On what basis? Who wears what kind of clothes? What do they signify? What kinds of behavior does this text seem to reinforce?

To what sources of authority does the text or a character within the text appeal? And so on. (See Kee 1989: 65-67.)

Why does our interpretation need to be informed by social-scientific sensibilities? Primarily, this is because people from a particular social group employ the forms of communication indigenous to that culture without thought — spontaneously, un-self-consciously, colloquially. Typically, they do not, except fleetingly, recognize that there are any "concepts" involved at all since, in their communities, ideas and the realities they inform are naturally and indissolubly bound up together. Social-scientific questions such as those just enumerated help to identify and make plain the taken-for-granted meanings in communication that might otherwise pass our notice. They also help to remind us that we have our own taken-for-granted values and meanings that, unless recognized, are simply downloaded into texts to which they might be quite foreign. As cultural anthropologists have observed, "The juxtaposition of alien customs to familiar ones, or the relativizing of taken-for-granted concepts such as the family, power, and the beliefs that lend certainty to our everyday life, has the effect of disorienting the reader and altering perception" (Marcus and Fischer 1986: 111). The effect is that we are able to see the text, and ourselves, through new, more candid eyes.

This does not mean, however, that the work of social-science readings of NT texts is complete when one has filled in the terrain of the NT world. If it is true that NT texts "absorb" the values of the cultures within which they were generated, it is also true that those same texts are capable of overturning even major aspects of their social world. Hence, by "world of the NT" we have reference to at least three phenomena. There is, first, the "world" assumed by a given NT text — in the case of the Gospels, Galilee, Jerusalem, and the larger world of Palestine; in the case of the Pauline letters, the world of Rome, Corinth, Philippi, and so on. It must be admitted, though, that individual NT accounts cannot capture the many and diverse ingredients of the real world of first-century Palestine or even first-century Corinth. Hence we have recourse, second, to the world actualized by a given NT text — that is, the world as it is portrayed by a particular NT book. Given limited space, with what ingredients of the real world did each writer choose to interact? The world as represented by a NT writer will overlap with but will not be identical to the real world since the author shapes his message by emphasizing what he regards as of particular importance. Luke and John emphasize the presence and significance of Samaria and Samaritans, but Matthew and Mark are silent on these. In literary terms, this second sense of world is sometimes referred to as the "narrative world" of the author; it is the world at the level of the discourse as this is represented by the author.

Third, "the world of the NT" signifies the world of hope. This is the world to which a NT writer points, the vision of a new era, the new world that is breaking into the old. That is, an evangelist like Mark is not content to present the world "as it really is," but purposefully shapes his writing in such a way that some of its facets are undermined, others legitimated. So, although it is helpful to know as much as we can about the world of Mark (in the first sense), it is just as critical if not even more so to see how that world fares in his hands. If we are concerned with the world of Mark, then, we must attend to how his narrative represents and challenges the world of the first-century Mediterranean. Consequently, we will be interested above all in reading the Second Gospel on its own terms, albeit against the backdrop of what we otherwise know about the first-century world it purports to portray. The text is thus given a chance, as it were, to speak back to, as well as within, its own world. At the same time, in grappling with how Mark embraces and critiques the commonly held views and respected cultural institutions of his day, we may well find our own conventional wisdom brought under suspicion, our own prior understandings and pet convictions assailed.

4.3. *Narrative Readings of the New Testament*

Beginning with a subtle distinction between "story" and "narrative," narrative readings concentrate on the total shape of those writings presented in narrative form in the NT. Obviously, this includes the four Gospels and the Acts of the Apostles; to a lesser degree, narrative criticism can be applied with profit to the book of Revelation, and some insights from narratology have also proven relevant to study of NT epistolary literature. Elements of the narrative study of NT texts include plot, point of view, the development of characters, settings, conflict, time, perceived gaps in the narrative, the use of irony, and so on. Though often branded as a "formalist" approach and thus dismissed by some as ahistorical, narratology is actually quite flexible in its cultural sensibilities. Clearly, it is open to the effects a narrative might have on readers; in addition, narratology can be exercised in ways that attend fully to the potential of narrative both to represent and to challenge the culture within which it is written.

It is nevertheless true that narratology assumes that the focus of study is the biblical narrative in its final form. Unlike historical-critical research, then, it is not at all concerned with sources and the development of the tradition. Instead, NT narratives are to be appreciated as complete wholes, as internally coherent and interactive. Hence, although narratology is capable of establishing links between the narrative text and the values, institutions, and practices of which the wider culture consists (see Greenblatt 1990: 226-27), narrative readings do not depend on historical reconstruction. Instead, priority goes to the analysis of the literary artistry of a narrative text, to its capacity to define an internally coherent world, and to its power to persuade readers to embrace its understanding of reality.

Narrative analysis features two interrelated assumptions about the way narratives work. The first has to do with the aforementioned distinction drawn between "story" and "narrative." We may tend to use these terms interchangeably in ordinary discourse, but in narratology they are quite distinct. "Story" refers to the *content* of narration, while "narrative" refers to its particular *expression;* story refers to the "what," narrative to the "how." This distinction assumes that the elements of a story, a set of events, might be told in any number of ways but that each of these ways would differ in meaning from the others. Narratology thus emphasizes how those events are arranged and expressed in a given narrative, with reference to the order of events, and causal relationships between events. As Aristotle observed, "narratives" are characterized by temporal sequence and an orientation toward the realization of an objective or the resolution of a dilemma — that is, they possess a beginning, a middle, and an end. The NT Gospels might be regarded as case studies for representing the difference between story and narrative since, in two, three, and sometimes in all four of these books, the same events appear, but they are recounted within narrative sequences that provide these same events with new significance.

The second assumption in narratology is the model of the communicative process. This process can be represented as follows:

real author → text → real reader

↑

implied author → narrator → narrative → narratee → implied reader

According to this configuration, actual, flesh-and-blood readers have direct access only to the text, but this text embodies an important series of connections. Thus the real author speaks through the voice of the implied author, who advances the narrative through the mouth of a narrator created for this task. These divisions are easier to imagine in recent novels than in NT narratives since, for the most part, with reference to NT narrative literature we cannot distinguish between the real author, the implied author, and the narrator; they all speak with the one voice. Of course, in the case of Luke-Acts the narrator can speak of himself in the first person, as in the prologue (Luke 1:1-4) and "we"-sections in Acts (Acts 16:10-17; 20:5-15; 21:1-18; 27:1–28:16). Similarly, Mark's readers can be addressed directly: "Let the reader understand" (Mark 13:14). Even where this distinction seems unnecessary, however, it is an important reminder that NT narratives are in fact anonymous and that almost everything we know about their authors (e.g., their skill in Greek, their predilection for urban life, or whatever) comes to us via a close reading of these narratives themselves; but this, of course, gives us not so much access to the "real authors" as to the authors as they are known to us from the texts — that is, the "implied authors."

Similarly, we have no direct access to the actual, real readers of the Gospels and Acts. We know nothing in particular of their needs or concerns, nor anything about how they might have heard these narrative texts. What we do have access to is the sort of reader that the text seems to presume — that is, the implied reader. From the information provided by the text itself, we can extrapolate the sort of reader imagined by the narrative, and even follow the narrative in order to see how it seems to be calling forth responses on the part of its implied reader. From the standpoint of narratology, the goal of reading is for the real reader, as it were, to become the implied (or model) reader — that is, to enter into a kind of interpretive dance whereby one is able to deal interpretively with the text in a way that corresponds to how the author has dealt with it generatively. This, in fact, becomes a test for validity in narrative interpretation: Does the text itself provide the basis for anticipating that the reader should respond in this way?

The practice of narrative reading calls for attention to a number of elements within the narrative that contribute to its overall dynamic — six of which we can mention and briefly develop here. (1) Chief among these is the establishment early on in the narrative of a fundamental *aim,* the potential achievement and/or frustration of which creates tension within the narrative and drives the narrative forward. Concentration on the identification and attainment of this aim on the part of the reader draws attention to two aspects of the Gospels and Acts that are often lost in other forms of reading — namely, the degree to which NT narratives are about God and the achievement of God's aim, and the urgency with which the reader is confronted to align him- or herself for (or against) this aim. In this reckoning, for example, the Gospel of Luke and the book of Acts are not so much about Jesus and his witnesses as they are about the ancient purpose of God now coming to fruition. According privilege to the issue of narrative aim also brings into the foreground the motif of conflict as characters and institutions within the narrative arrange themselves over against the aim of God and against those who serve him.

(2) Additionally, narrative analysis concentrates on the *sequence of events* as they are arranged within the text. The import of order is highlighted by the fact that, when reading narrative texts, readers encounter and judge the significance of each event in the light of those events that have preceded it. Narratives typically work not only with a pronounced sense of teleology, with events rushing toward an aim, but also with attention to causal relations; prior events are understood in some sense to set the stage and provide the basis for later ones.

(3) The progression of events is also related to issues of *timing.* Sometimes the evangelist will pass over scenes quickly, providing summaries that indicate what is typical and expected. At other points, the crucifixion scene for example, the writer will retard the narrative pace, providing time indicators and a wealth of detail in order to prompt the reader to linger over an event. At still others, the evangelist will recount a series of similar events or sayings, or even call attention to an event repeatedly, either in prospect or retrospect; in these and other ways, significance is allocated through the use of the narrative devices of frequency and duration.

(4) The identification and formation of *characters* within the narrative are also crucial to narratology, and the evangelists draw on a substantial repertoire for indicating the nature of the persons they introduce: brief character references, access to inner thoughts, reports of characteristic activity, and the like.

(5) Also of consequence is the *point of view* from which statements are made. Because of the esteem with which God is held in the Gospels and Acts, messages that represent the divine point of view — whether they be from angels or the Scriptures or God's own voice — become the benchmarks of valid interpretation within the narrative.

Moreover, because the narrators of the Gospels and Acts so fully align themselves with God's point of view, their assessments are to be taken at face value. This is not true of everyone within the narrative, however, since Jesus' opponents, the wicked within parables, and sometimes even Jesus' disciples themselves are depicted as unreliable.

(6) Narratology is also characterized by a concern for *presuppositions* — including, first, the initial assumptions a narrative makes about its audience and, following this, the building of presuppositions within the narrative itself. From this vantage point, it is noteworthy that the Gospel of Mark opens with the assertion, which it never attempts to prove, that Jesus is the Messiah and Son of God. Apparently, the Second Evangelist can assume that his audience will embrace this characterization of Jesus, even if the narrative he then relates is decidedly oriented toward shaping in what sense his audience might understand the nature of Jesus' messiahship and divine sonship. This illustration also draws attention to how a narrative is able to provide new definitions for old concepts, and thus to build for its audience a new lexicon of meaning as fresh information is provided about taken-for-granted values and conventions. Thus, the Second Evangelist may not devote his narrative to proving that Jesus is the Messiah, the Son of God, but he does go to great lengths to shape how his audience might come to understand the content of this inaugural affirmation.

Within the Gospels and Acts, one of the expectations that comes most to the fore is that audiences will already have become intimate with the Scriptures of Israel. Through direct citation of OT texts, or allusions, or even sometimes faint echoes, Israel's Scriptures provide added texture to the significance of these narrative texts.

In the last decades of the twentieth century, some scholars have begun to bring the insights of narrative analysis to the Pauline epistles. This is not because they confuse, say, the Letter to the Romans with the Gospel of Matthew with respect to the identification of genre. Literary theorists, we may recall, make a basic distinction between *story* and *narrative,* with "story" referring to the content, the "what" of narrative. "Story" has to do with a series of events and characters without reference to causality or plot. "Narrative," or what we may now refer to as "discourse," on the other hand, refers to the communication of that content, now construed so as to reveal purpose and plot. If story refers to the *what,* discourse refers to the *way* a medium is used to present that *what.* At the level of discourse (or "performance"), the elements of story are construed in relation to each other, with a variety of literary devices (such as the ordering or even repetition of events) employed to mark the relative emphasis of the parts and the overall significance of the whole.

Taking these methodological distinctions to an exploration of the Pauline correspondence, we can discern underlying the letters of Paul the one story of redemption. This story has a number of key components — including, but not limited to:

- the creation of the world and of humanity;
- the transgression of Adam which marks the invasion of sin and death;
- the communication of God's purpose in covenant with Abraham;
- the election of Israel and the revelation of the law;
- God's sending his Son, Jesus Christ, to redeem humanity and usher in the new epoch;
- the achievement of God's purpose in the death and resurrection of Jesus;
- the life of the church in the temporally anomalous present — cruciform, hopeful, Spirit-empowered, mission-oriented; and
- the final transformation, the new creation, marked by Jesus' return.

In his correspondence with various churches, Paul arranges elements of the story, relating some in temporal and causal ways while omitting others altogether. The Thessalonians, for example, have upset the temporal logic of the story as Paul understands it and so misconstrue their present vocation. Concern about those who have "died in Christ" is addressed by a reminder that Jesus' return remains a future event. Today ought therefore to be characterized by sobriety and faithfulness (1 Thess 4:13–5:11). Similarly, in his dealings with the Corinthians, Paul repeatedly attempts to situate the Corinthians temporally back at the proper place in the ongoing story of redemption. Apparently, he must remind the Corinthians that the Lord has *not* yet returned, and that the present is reserved for proclaiming the Lord's death "until he comes" (1 Cor 11:26). In his correspondence to the Galatians, on the other hand, Paul seems vitally concerned that these followers of Jesus have regressed to a former moment in the continuing story. Having begun to be persuaded regarding the importance of circumcision, they have effectively located themselves in an earlier period of redemptive history when circumcision was seen as the hallmark of the identity of God's people.

In such cases, clearly Paul's missives are not made the raw materials for the narratologist. Instead, insights borrowed from narrative readings of narrative texts have been brought to bear on nonnarrative literature.

4.4. *Rhetorical Readings of the New Testament*

Inasmuch as contemporary hermeneutics is oriented toward the effects of the interpretive process, renewed interest in rhetoric is well justified. Notwithstanding its popular association with pompous, pretentious verbosity and exaggerated reasoning, rhetoric, understood as the study and practice of persuasion, has a long and distinguished history. In rhetorical criticism we are interested above all in how texts function or might have functioned to convince others of their truth and to move them to embrace it.

Of the plethora of methods by which readers of the NT work with these texts, attention to artistry and argument is perhaps the most indigenous to the NT world. The practice of oratory predates Homer in the eighth or ninth century BC, and by the fifth century BC manuals on rhetoric circulated among those charged with making their cases in the public forums of law and politics. In the fourth century BC Aristotle wrote his treatise *The Art of Rhetoric,* and this was followed by handbooks on rhetoric that date from the NT era. Indeed, during the Greek and Roman periods secondary education had as its "core curriculum" the theory and practice of rhetoric — proficiency in which was a baseline requirement for public life. Whether Jesus, his first followers, or such writers of NT books as Paul and the author of Hebrews had actually been schooled in rhetoric is less important than the certainty that they were reared in a culture already permeated by the rhetorical tradition.

The revival of rhetoric in NT interpretation has taken several forms, one of which is the recovery of the canons of rhetoric from the Greek and Roman periods. Credit for contemporary interest among students of the NT in classical rhetoric belongs largely to the work and influence of G. A. Kennedy (1984). Drawing on classical texts by Aristotle, Cicero, and Quintilian, Kennedy thinks of rhetorical criticism as a step-by-step process. First, one must determine the rhetorical unit to be explored. Rhetorical units might be as small as five or six verses or in some cases encompass an entire letter; each must have a beginning, a middle, and an end, and thus be capable of analysis on its own terms. Following this, one defines the rhetorical situation. What is the rhetorical problem facing the writer? What events, persons, and setting are necessary for understanding the context of that problem? Definition of the rhetorical situation is intimately related to the determination of the species of rhetoric employed in a given situation. Classical rhetoric works with three species of argumentation: Forensic speech accuses or defends someone regarding past actions, addressing the question, Are the charges brought against this person just? Deliberative discourse attempts to exhort or dissuade an audience regarding future behavior, asking, Is it appropriate and beneficial? Epideictic rhetoric celebrates or condemns someone or a course of action in an attempt to affirm or undermine a commonly held value, asking, Is it laudable?

Having identified the nature of the rhetoric of a text, one should consider the arrangement of the material within the rhetorical unit and investigate what devices of style are utilized, how the parts are structured within the whole, and their overall persuasive effect. Finally, one is in a position to evaluate the overall effect of the rhetorical unit on the rhetorical situation.

A return to the classical rhetoricians is only one of three primary manifestations of the contemporary renaissance in the study of the rhetoric of NT texts. Practitioners of the "New Rhetoric" (see Perelman and Olbrechts-Tyteca 1969) concentrate less on a text's logic and more on the capacity of the text and the values it embodies to seize its readers in order to secure from them commitment and action appropriate to its message. Rhetorical criticism in this key is still concerned with arguments, but syllogistic reasoning is not as clearly in focus as are appeals to conventional wisdom and attempts to reenvision the nature of things. By means of what rhetorical strategies does the text undermine the reader's prior commitments and provide the impetus for new behaviors structured around a transformed image of reality? These are among the practical foci of New Rhetoric.

Finally, rhetorical criticism in biblical study is sometimes defined and practiced as a means for revealing and valuing a text's literary artistry. As in narratology and other forms of literary approach, the reader attends to the properties of a text — style, structure, use of metaphor, and so on — by which its author generates meaning and (the author may hope) recruits a following.

Rhetorical criticism may therefore seem baffling in the diversity of its contemporary expressions or, in the case of the reformulation of classical rhetoric under the tutelage of Kennedy and others, highly technical. From the vantage point provided by the state of hermeneutics at the onset of the new millennium, this would be unfortunate. At its best, Christian proclamation has always been concerned with something more than understanding, this "something more" being amplified with reference to persuasion and motivation to greater faithfulness before God. The turn from meaning-based hermeneutics to a hermeneutics of formation and transformation brings into serendipitous alignment the aims of the Christian message and the objectives of contemporary hermeneutical theory. Rhetorical criticism, with its fundamental interest in patterns of persuasion, seems particularly well suited to reading the NT in these conditions.

4.5. *The Reader and the New Testament*

As we will rehearse momentarily, philosophical considerations contribute to the prominence of the reader, but so also do the challenges provided by texts themselves. Four of these merit immediate mention (Green 1995: 4-6). First, language is linear. Texts present information in a specific sequence, left to right in English (and Greek). In reading texts or hearing texts read, we are unable to get the whole picture at once but must rely on progressive disclosure of information as one paragraph gives way to another and on fading memories of information increasingly distant from what we are currently reading. Perhaps it is in this way, partly, that "a picture is worth a thousand words" since in a landscape portrait we are able to see the whole at once; describing that landscape to someone else via words, however, introduces an inescapable linearity.

Of course, with respect to NT texts, the problem of linearity can actually benefit interpretation since it raises the question of the arrangement of material. What comes first? Last? Linearity leads to sequence, and sequence draws attention to particular connections that open interpretive possibilities.

Second, language is selective. Not every detail can be presented, with the result that readers are left with work to do. In fact, one can trace an inverse relationship between the amount of detail and cohesiveness provided by the writer and the degree of interpretive work required of the reader. Some gaps in literary detail occur because of the assumptions of the writer. Others function as invitations for readers to participate imaginatively in the production of meaning.

Third, language is ambiguous. Words often carry multiple meanings, giving rise to potential ambiguities whether one is reading or hearing read. Umberto Eco illustrates the ambiguity of symbols with reference to a picture of a ranch-style house with an old wagon wheel leaning against the front exterior wall. Is this a picture of a movie set for a western film? A snapshot from a ghost town? A restaurant serving country-style food? An antique shop? The workshop of a blacksmith? An actual ranch house? Like this picture, language is capable of many and diverse readings, and a way must be found for sorting through the possibilities. Finally, language is culturally embedded, and, as we have already noted, words spoken in the first-century Mediterranean world often carry meanings that are not readily apparent to us and our contemporaries.

With regard to philosophical considerations, the influence of René Descartes (1596-1650) on modern study of the NT is difficult to exaggerate. His perception of knowledge in terms of a mind grasping a subject has led to the representation of traditional interpretation along the lines of the objective reader who finds the meaning already inherent in the text. Traditional methods of interpretation, then, were engineered to manipulate the text in order to extract from it the intention of its author. The seeds for a surprisingly radical reformation of this portrait of the reading process were introduced in the philosophy of Immanuel Kant (1724-1804), who contended that the knower contributes something to the object of knowing. Until the final decades of the twentieth century, Cartesian approaches to interpretation have generally carried the day in biblical study. The application of additional insights has led to the broadening realization that we are simply incapable of grasping the text as it is in and of itself, that texts are construed always in relationship to the human mind engaged in the process of reading. Recognition of the importance of the reader in NT studies, then, grows from the acknowledgment that meaning is not so much repeated or reproduced in the experience of reading; rather, reading constitutes, at least in some sense, the production of meaning.

The phrase "at least in some sense" at the end of the last paragraph is meant to draw attention to the reality that there is today no one way of thinking about the role of the reader in NT study. "Reader-Response criticism" is not so much a method as a conglomerate of approaches that share a common, basic rejection of any portrait of the reader as nothing more than the potential receptacle for meaning. This heterogeneity is marked by the diversity of ways in which "readers" are represented (Rabinowitz 1994). There is, for example, the "implied reader" — that is, readers whose moves are charted out by a given text and are largely controlled by the author; the "model reader" — that is, readers who are able to deal interpretively with the text in a way that follows how the author has dealt generatively with that text; the "competent reader" — that is, a reader whose moves are plotted by her general culture, whose knowledge of readerly and cultural conventions allows her to make sense of literary texts; the "authorial audience" — that is, readers presumed by the author when the text was being written; the "informed reader" — that is, readers for whom the text's meaning emerges from perceiving it through the eyes of a reader whose characteristics are assumed by the author; and, of course, "real readers," whose inferences from the text are more or less unpredictable and uncontrollable.

Ambivalence regarding the "identity" of readers is related to how one construes the interpretive process generally, and specifically to the role one gives the text in the production of meaning. Many portray readers and texts as involved in a kind of performance, with the text manifesting gaps and ambiguities that invite the participation of the reader in the production of meaning. According to this expression of reader-response criticism, the reader has an active role to play, but it is a role circumscribed by the responsibility of the reader who is to receive the text. Readers may actualize the text, but it is *this* text that they are actualizing.

Others take a more radical view of the reader's role. They resist any and all restrictions on the making of meaning, from both texts and traditions of interpretation. The reading experience has no frontiers. As no boundaries are placed on the reader, so can no reading be judged as more or less valid than the next. Some who take such a view do so on pragmatic grounds. Forsaking any pledge to neutrality, they maintain that texts have no aims but only uses. Achievement of the goal of reading is measured, therefore, with reference to the production of interesting or serviceable readings. Others who follow this more radical construal of the role of the reader do so on the grounds of the indeterminacy of hermeneutical inquiry. Texts are complex systems of codes capable of yielding an infinite multiplicity of meanings. According to this form of reader-response theory readers have replaced authors in the historical-critical paradigm as those solely responsible for the generation of meaning.

The presence of plurality in readerly approaches to the NT is thus marked by concerns with the definition of the reader and with the aim of reading. Judging that texts include signals and invitations for the reader, some readers read in order to be led, persuaded, and/or enlarged in their interaction with the text. Others, less sympathetic to the promptings of the text, experience reading as a process of interrogating the text, overrunning its claims with the interests they bring to the text. Additionally, persons concerned with the role of the reader struggle to account for the perspective from which reading occurs. That is, the question is not only what one means by "reader" but also the perspective from which the reader does the reading. It is to this issue of "perspective" in NT study that we may now turn.

4.6. Liberationist Readings of the New Testament

A plurality of liberationist hermeneutics has arisen in many global contexts in response to the use of Scripture as a tool of oppression. For those who have participated in the history of biblical interpretation, this may come as a surprise, especially for those who have operated with hermeneutical commitments derived from Cartesian categories. Since, in this formulation, interpretation is nothing more than the process of discerning a meaning already resident in the text, the possibility of "the use of Scripture" as an instrument of anything, positive or negative, will seem remote. This, however, is precisely the starting point of liberationist hermeneutics — namely, the recognition that all textual inquiry is shaped by the contextual presumptions of the reader. Taking this recognition seriously leads liberationists to read Scripture in fresh ways at the same time that it raises for them a fundamental critique of the practice of biblical interpretation in the modern period.

The heading "liberationist readings" encompasses a great variety of approaches to the NT, but all of them share some basic premises. First, no interpretation is objective since the presuppositions, biases, and needs of readers and reading communities help to determine how a text will be read. Indeed, even the (failed) attempt to read biblical texts from the perspective of "objectivity" reflects the prominence of cultural forces that can be traced back to Descartes (see above). Second, liberationist readers take as their starting point a hermeneutics of suspicion. For some, this means operating with a presumption of distrust vis-à-vis interpretive traditions since, for example, in many Third World contexts the Bible was introduced as a means of justifying colonialism and the systems of oppression that accompany it. Thus, images of the "suffering Christ" were introduced in Latin America as a model worthy of emulation for indigenous peoples, while Spanish conquistadors adopted for themselves the portrait of the "royal, theocratic Christ." For others, distrust reaches behind the history of interpretation and is directed toward the biblical texts themselves. For this latter group, even the biblical texts are the fruit of oppressive societies, and the culture of oppression has placed its stamp on the pages of these texts themselves.

A third assumption of liberation hermeneutics is that interpretation of Scripture does not belong primarily in the hands of academically well-trained and accredited scholars. Rather, the text belongs especially to communities of the oppressed, so that the only way to hear fully the message of these texts is to hear them as they are comprehended by those who live on the underside of history. Fourth, the goal of interpretation is never the construction of abstract theories about God and the world. Instead, the aim of interpretation must be the generation of dispositions and behaviors oriented toward liberation. Those who read the Bible faithfully, according to a liberationist hermeneutics, will be challenged to join in the struggle for the liberation of the oppressed.

Apart from these basic principles, liberationist readings of the NT take many forms. This is only to be expected, given the potent relevance of context to the interpretive process. African-American biblical interpretation, for example, takes its starting point from the reality that, within the context of an oppressive society, the Bible has played a formative role in assisting the survival of African-American communities. Scripture has been a source of identity and hope. The Scriptures have functioned in this way in spite of the widespread presence of predominantly Eurocentric interpretive practices — practices which, from this hermeneutical vantage point, have not accounted for minority cultures within the predominant culture; which have been erroneously possessed by the ideal of achieving the one, critical meaning of the text by means of historical analysis; which have failed to articulate the importance of proactive responses to the liberating word of God; and which have not exhibited an understanding of the importance of narrative, either in Scripture or in the believing community. Attempts to formulate a distinctive African-American biblical interpretation have taken at least four avenues: (1) allowing African-American experience the role of seminal influence on how communities of interpretation understand notions of authority and truth; (2) recovering indigenous resources for engaging Scripture from within the historic practices of the African-American church (e.g., worship and preaching); (3) recovering the place of Black Africans within the Bible itself; and (4) reading and rereading biblical texts from African-American perspectives (Felder 1991).

Although feminist approaches to Scripture are generally catalogued along with liberationist hermeneutics, for many feminists a crucial distinction must be advanced. For many communities involved in liberative readings of Scripture, the source and promise of emancipation are found in the pages of the Bible; this is not always true for women since Scripture contains texts that allege a qualitative contrast between men and women, at times allowing women a lesser role in the community of God's people. The multiplicity characteristic of feminist readings of the NT reflects this disparity, and attempts at feminist interpretation have included at least five strategies. (1) Feminist interpretation challenges biblical translations that accord privilege to the male and masculine while moving the female and feminine further into the shadows. (2) Feminist interpreters work to document the case for liberation for women within Scripture as well as draw attention to those texts that embody and perpetuate patriarchal patterns and commitments. (3) Feminist interpreters seek to raise the visibility of women who are sometimes invisible in Scripture as the beneficiaries of divine deliverance. (4) Feminist interpretation attempts to reconstruct the history of the early Christian movement in order to bring to the surface the important roles shared by women — roles that have often become obfuscated in the textual tradition. (5) Feminist interpreters work to undermine and overturn the history of biblical interpretation when it champions (mis)interpretations that are themselves androcentric, patriarchal, and sexist (cf. Schneiders 1991: 183-86).

Liberation hermeneutics from Latin America works with the presumptions shared by other forms of liberation hermeneutics sketched above, but articulates these in a context marked by economic injustice. In order to be faithful to the Bible and to the Latin-American situation, then, biblical interpreters must embrace as a precommitment a belief in God's preferential option for the poor. This leads, first, to a socioeconomic analysis of the Latin-American context. Because this inquiry typically advances through the employment of the categories and tools of Marxism, this social situation is expounded principally in terms of class struggle, pitting the wealthy (who possess the means of production) against peasants (who do not). Second, Latin-American hermeneutics invites biblical and theological reflection on Latin-American reality. Because of its precommitment to solidarity with the poor and because of its thoroughgoing commitment to Marxist categories, Latin-American exegesis is unusually resistant to spiritual readings of NT texts. Religion is not and cannot be relegated to matters of the heart, for the Word of God as this is construed via Latin-American hermeneutics can speak most clearly only in political terms.

As a final example of liberation hermeneutics, we may refer to South African readings of Scripture. Again, one finds a diversity of approaches — a phenomenon that is hardly surprising given both the role of the church (and thus, readings of Scripture) in perpetuating apartheid and the capacity of Black South Africans to find in the pages of Scripture itself the resources for hope and social reformation (see West 1995). One of South Africa's most articulate prophetic voices, A. A. Boesak, affirms the authority and relevance of the biblical tradition for the South African situation. This mode of liberative interpretation takes as its starting point a mode of reading from within a particular community of struggle, the oppressed community of Black South Africans. It then explicitly refuses to divorce the ancient story of the people of God expressed in Scripture from contemporary existence: *that* story is *our* story, so the struggle for liberation in the biblical text is linked across time and space to the struggle for liberation in South Africa. Finally, Boesak self-evidently accords privilege to the text of Scripture itself — not to its prehistory or the traditions to which it might give access but to its literary and thematic coherence and to its location within the canon as a whole.

A quite different mode of reading is proffered by I. J. Mosala, a South African whose point of departure is the prehistory of the biblical story, and who finds in that prehistory a power struggle that has given rise to the text in its final form. It is here, in this prehistory of struggle, that Mosala finds correspondence with the struggle for liberation in South Africa. For Mosala, then, the text is problematic because it masks the struggle for liberation; it covers over the class conflicts that lie behind the production of scriptural materials.

Where Boesak and Mosala agree marks one of the key elements of all liberation hermeneutics — namely, their common commitment to reading Scripture *from* within communities of struggle and oppression *for* the purpose of participating faithfully in the struggle for freedom.

4.7. Validity in Interpretation

At the turn of the twenty-first century, NT study may seem to be in a state of disarray, given the diversity of approaches now practiced and championed. Though unruly in appearance, this is actually a creative moment for reading the NT. Older methods and assured results are experiencing the twilight years of their hegemony, and the onslaught of new approaches and findings is signaling a corrective to forms of study that too easily allowed particular communities of interpretation to coopt the meaning of Scripture for their own ends.

What has become increasingly clear is that we need more voices, not fewer, to be involved in the interpretive enterprise. What has also become clear, though, is that this new pluralism of methods and approaches renders increasingly problematic the question of validity in interpretation. Apart from openness to the readings of others, on what basis can we believe that a particular reading is appropriate or legitimate? On this point the struggle continues — first, among those looking to the texts themselves, or to their sociohistorical contexts, or to their underlying traditions, or to some combination of these, for canons of sound interpretation; and second, with those who reject even the concept of validity in interpretation, who maintain that all readings, however disparate and contradictory, are equal.

We do not need to consult a prophet to know that the question of validity will continue to be the center of heated discussion. In the interim, we are able to suggest considerations and criteria for validity (see Schneiders 1991: 165-67). At the outset it is important to underscore, however, that "valid" must not in this case be confused with "right." "Cogent" and "convincing" are more accurate descriptions of an interpretive process whose goal belongs more to the realm of the "plausible" than to that of "proof." This means that it will often be easier to determine those interpretations that are unsupportable or erroneous than to certify that some other is legitimate. It also means that one must always leave room for multiple, though not infinite, possible meanings. An interpretation can be said to be valid when it: (1) accounts for the text in its final form, without depending on a cut-and-paste job that refabricates the text in order that it might fit a prior theory; (2) accounts for the text as a whole and is consistent with the whole of the text without masking unfortunate aspects of the text that continue to haunt the interpreter; (3) accounts for the cultural embeddedness of language, allowing the text to have its meaning fashioned in light of the sociohistorical assumptions of its own day; and (4) is consistent with itself and with the methodological approach chosen by the interpreter — though in this instance we should also recognize that the notion of "valid" interpretation must not be mistaken for any idea of a "complete" interpretation since different methodological frameworks will continue to turn the spotlight on different aspects of the text.

5. Reading the New Testament: Text, Church, and World

Persons and communities concerned with the contemporary significance of the NT face an abundance of obstacles, perhaps the most important of which are not related directly to the methodological glossolalia to which we have drawn attention. We have already mentioned the cultural and chronological distance separating us from the worlds of the NT. To push further at this point, we may go on to recognize both that the NT texts contain material seemingly far removed from our lives and that we face issues about which the NT has nothing immediate to say. The ramifications of the cloning of sheep, the question of the ordination of homosexuals — these exemplify issues about which the NT has nothing directly to say. Similarly, few of us struggle today with hairstyles in worship or the moral implications of meat sacrificed to idols, though these were important enough to attract the reasoned attention of the writers of some NT books.

The phenomenon of distance is an interpretive obstacle especially for those who are only or primarily interested in the *content* of the NT ("what the text says about *x*"). For others, the significance of the NT as Scripture extends further than *what* it teaches to include *how it engages in cultural and moral discourse*.

To take seriously the role of culture in the generation and interpretation of NT texts is to be open to the possibility that we are to engage in appropriation of the biblical message not simply (and sometimes not at all) by reading the content of its message into our world but also (and sometimes only) by inquiring into how the biblical writers have themselves engaged in the task of theology and ethics. This is true above all because the biblical writers were universally concerned to fashion a community that discerns, embraces, and serves the divine purpose more than they were to outline in precise detail the beliefs and habits of that community. In writing the Third Gospel, for example, Luke bears witness to the divine visitation that makes redemption and redemptive community possible and invites persons to participate as co-workers in this redemptive aim — not to render his audience dependent on him as a kind of "teacher of righteousness."

To pursue the example of the Gospel of Luke further, we might ask, How can the Third Gospel be situated in and reflect its own, particular sociohistorical environment while at the same time working to undermine that environment? How can Luke gain for his narrative a hearing among a people whose understanding of "the way the world works" is itself being subverted by that narrative? What strategies does he adopt? How has he engaged in theological and ethical reflection? How has he invited his audience into the reflective and constructive task of discourse on discipleship? To what authorities does he appeal? What vision of "the new world" does he present; and how does he solicit contemplation on and service in that world? In other words, to learn "Lukan theology" is to grapple with more than the content of the Lukan message; it is also to explore how Luke engages in the theological task and the strategies by which he engages his audience in transformative discourse.

Through attending to the ways the biblical materials themselves engage in the theological task of shaping authentic witness in particular cultural settings, we gain access into how Scripture provides a methodological framework for our struggle to work out the implications of the good news in our own cultural settings. In reflecting critically on Christian witness, we attend to Scripture again in order to evaluate the authenticity of our witness — to determine, so to speak, whether we have got our theologizing "right."

To give Scripture this role in the life of the community is to beg the question how these texts might best speak. Alternatively, we might inquire into our greatest need from Scripture. Historically, Christians have appealed to Scripture in an assortment of ways; various modes of discourse can be found within NT texts, and these are represented in attempts to appeal to Scripture for guidance. (1) Scripture provides "commands of God" — direct rules, both negative and positive, that speak to particular behaviors. (2) Scripture provides "principles" or "values" requiring implementation in ever new contexts. (3) Scripture provides exemplars of persons and courses of action worthy of emulation, or to be avoided. And (4) Scripture provides a vision of the world that shapes the categories through which we interpret reality and formulate faithful discipleship. Since each of these modes of discourse is well represented in the NT, there is neither need nor basis for dismissing any of them. Nonetheless, it remains true today that humanity's greatest need is not for catalogs of regulations and indices of behavior, but for a transformed imagination.

How might this happen? One of the most prominent practitioners of reflexive sociology, Pierre Bourdieu (1991), has employed the term *habitus* in his effort to present a theory of the practical character of social interaction. This allows him to highlight sets of dispositions that incline agents to perform in certain ways. Dispositions engender practices, perceptions, and attitudes which are typical, neither consciously coordinated nor subject to any preplanned blueprint. Dispositions are acquired through a gradual process by which they assume the status of second nature, reflect the social conditions within which they are acquired, are ingrained so that they operate at a preconscious level, and can be transposed to new settings where they might produce alternative practices. Accordingly, practices, or behaviors, grow out of the interplay of *habitus* and the specific social contexts in which we find ourselves. What makes this model immediately relevant to the hermeneutical task is that human dispositions are shaped in relation to a particular understanding of the world. And this gives rise to the question, How might our readings of the NT reform our "dispositions" and so influence our practices in the world?

In fact, one of the major efforts of NT documents is directed here, toward the reformation of the imagination, the reconstruction of persons' visions of God and the nature of the redeemed cosmos. One might expect this of such "visionary literature" as the book of Revelation, a primary purpose of which is the recovery of a notion of God that will engender hope and active faithfulness in the midst of the Roman Empire. But the same can be said of Paul, who hopes to reconstruct life around the cross of Christ — life, then, that is constrained by the love of God and that replicates in new contexts the selflessness of the death of Jesus. The Gospel of Luke, too, especially in its central section, the long journey from Galilee to Jerusalem, is oriented toward the exposition of God, portrayed as the gracious benefactor, the Father whose care for his children opens the way for them to leave the way of Mammon, to embrace the poor as though they were family, and to engage in lives of service. And so on. Seen in this way, NT hermeneutics is grounded in the transformative power of Scripture to evoke new ways of listening and seeing, a new vision of reality.

At the same time, it is doubtful that any "procedure" can guarantee the faithful appropriation and reappropriation of the NT. Certain tasks seem inescapable, however: engaging the text closely on its own terms and in relationship to its sociocultural mores; locating the text in conversation with other canonical voices; correlating the ancient community of God's people with our own community so as to hear that ancient word in fresh and relevant ways; and embodying that message in our lives personally and communally (see Hays 1996). The apparent linearity of this presentation of tasks is deceptive since they must never be conceived nor can ever be practiced as discrete steps, one leading to the next. Rather, the one feeds back on and informs the other with the consequence that, in an important sense, the community of interpretation that is working with NT texts is itself the community that has been formed and continues to be formed through interaction with those texts.

Nevertheless, sketching the hermeneutical tasks in this way allows important issues to surface for further reflection. Of these, one of the pressing complications facing persons and communities concerned with the contemporary appropriation of Scripture is the diversity represented within the twenty-seven books of the NT. On any number of issues, we can find multiple voices within the NT itself. Sometimes this diversity occurs between different authors — as is the case with the question of eating meat sacrificed to idols, on which Paul's counsel stands in tension with the witness of Acts and the book of Revelation (see Acts 15, Romans 14, 1 Corinthians 6 and 8, and Revelation 2–3). Sometimes this diversity appears in one author — as is the case with the implications of the gospel with respect to possessions in Luke-Acts (compare Luke 18:18-30 [total renunciation]; 19:1-10 [almsgiving and restitution]; and Acts 4:32–5:10 [economic community]).

If the NT fails to speak with a consistent voice on such issues, how can we hope to appropriate its message faithfully? Several interrelated considerations emerge. It is crucial, first, simply to allow those tensions within the canon to stand. To do otherwise is to select one voice to serve in a canonical way and the other to be muzzled artificially. Moreover, it is often true that we choose to bring into the light those parts of Scripture most congenial to our commitments and practices, while relegating to outer darkness those parts of Scripture that question or challenge us the most. In many instances, these different voices reflect attempts already within the NT era to draw out the meaning of the good news for persons and communities facing different challenges in different sociohistorical contexts. Sensitivity to issues of context demands that we allow the message to take different shapes in different circumstances. Second, different voices within the NT may profitably be brought into conversation. Sometimes, after all, one voice is raised so as to keep the other from becoming unbalanced, and in different times and places the people of God continues to need to hear each of them. Third, the diversity of voices within the NT attests to the reality that such consistent values as "love for one another" and "oneness" cannot be equated with any consistent experience of "agreement" within the community of God's people. At times we can fall victim to a kind of primitivism that upholds the church in the NT era as an entity in pervasive agreement on theological issues and moral concerns of all kinds, but this portrait is not well represented within the pages of the NT. Indeed, we may find in this collection of books, the NT, much-needed resources for learning to live more faithfully in the midst of diversity today.

In the end, appropriation of the text is part art and part science, part imaginative participation in the text and part critical discourse with the text. Disciplined method in biblical study aids this process, in an important sense, by constructing a wall between the text and the reader which must ultimately either be scaled or razed. However temporary, this wall has an important function, for it guards the text from the reader and the reader from the text. Protection for the text is necessary because of our tendency to find in Scripture what we want to find and to draft the NT into a role supportive of our own presumptions. We need protection from the text as well. Inasmuch as the message of NT texts derives from contexts that are not our own, our allowing that message an immediate voice into our present circumstances would sometimes result in nonsense and other times havoc. As Jesus discovered in the wilderness, in diabolic hands even the Scriptures can be cited out of turn, inappropriately read into new contexts (Luke 4:1-13). Apart from faithful attention to the world of the NT, together with faithful consideration of the location of phrases and sentences within their larger literary framework, NT texts are too easily spurned as irrelevant or come to serve too easily as bully bats.

From the standpoint of turn-of-the-century hermeneutics, this need for a wall of protection can never be the last word spoken. There is a further, crucial sense in which what is needed is not critical aloofness but an encounter with this text on contemporary grounds, with all of its implications for our lives together, where we are able to address our questions to the text as well as to hear its questions of us. Also involved are openness and surrender. This is the willingness to enter imaginatively into the world of these texts, to experience them as works of art and as utterances of the God who is in love with his people. This form of appropriation defies critical exposition but is related to the communal and personal encounter with Scripture in worship, in meditation, and in prayer. "Meaning," we may recall, is more than the end result of the quest for "what a text says"; it also has to do with the formation and transformation of persons and communities, and this is a process that is cognitive, to be sure, but also affective and social.

Bibliography. Baird, W. 1992, *History of New Testament Research,* vol. 1: *From Deism to Tübingen,* Minneapolis: Fortress • Baird, W. 2003, *History of New Testament Research,* vol. 2: *From Jonathan Edwards to Rudolf Bultmann,* Minneapolis: Fortress • Bourdieu, P. 1991, *Language and Symbolic Power,* Cambridge, Mass.: Harvard University • Eco, U. 1979, *The Role of the Reader: Explorations in the Semiotics of Texts,* Advances in Semiotics, Bloomington: Indiana University • Eco, U. 1990, *The Limits of Interpretation,* Advances in Semiotics, Bloomington:

Indiana University • Felder, C. H., ed. 1991, *Stony the Road We Trod: African American Biblical Interpretation,* Minneapolis: Fortress • Gadamer, H.-G. 2d ed. 1990, *Truth and Method,* New York: Crossroad • Goldingay, J. 1995, *Models for Interpretation of Scripture,* Grand Rapids: Eerdmans • González, J. L. 1996, *Santa Biblia: The Bible through Hispanic Eyes,* Nashville: Abingdon • Green, J. B. 1997, "Biblical Authority and Communities of Discourse," in E. C. Goodwin, ed., *Baptists in the Balance: The Tension between Freedom and Responsibility,* Valley Forge: Judson, 151-73 • Green, J. B., ed. 1995, *Hearing the New Testament: Strategies for Interpretation,* Grand Rapids: Eerdmans • Green, J. B., and M. Turner, eds. 2000, *Between Two Horizons: Spanning New Testament Studies and Systematic Theology,* Grand Rapids: Eerdmans • Greenblatt, S. 1990, "Culture," in F. Lentricchia and T. McLaughlin, eds., *Critical Terms for Literary Study,* Chicago: University of Chicago, 225-32 • Hays, R. B. 1996, *The Moral Vision of the New Testament: A Contemporary Introduction to New Testament Ethics,* San Francisco: HarperCollins • Kee, H. C. 1989, *Knowing the Truth: A Sociological Approach to New Testament Interpretation,* Minneapolis: Fortress • Kelsey, D. H. 1975, *The Uses of Scripture in Recent Theology,* Philadelphia: Fortress • Kennedy, G. A. 1984, *New Testament Interpretation through Rhetorical Criticism,* Chapel Hill: University of North Carolina • Kwok, P. 1995, *Discovering the Bible in the Non-Biblical World,* The Bible and Liberation Series, Maryknoll, N.Y.: Orbis • Marcus, G. E., and M. M. J. Fischer. 1986, *Anthropology as Cultural Critique: An Experimental Moment in the Human Sciences,* Chicago: University of Chicago • Morgan, R., with J. Barton. 1988, *Biblical Interpretation,* Oxford: Oxford University • Padilla, C. R. 1981, "The Interpreted Word: Reflections on Contextual Hermeneutics," *Themelios* 7:18-23 • Perelman, C., and L. Olbrechts-Tyteca. 1969, *The New Rhetoric: A Treatise on Argumentation,* Notre Dame: University of Notre Dame • Rabinowitz, P. J. 1994, "Reader-response Theory and Criticism," in M. Groden and M. Kreiswirth, eds., *The Johns Hopkins Guide to Literary Theory and Criticism,* Baltimore: Johns Hopkins University, 606-9 • Ricoeur, P. 1976, *Interpretation Theory: Discourse and the Surplus of Meaning,* Fort Worth: Texas Christian University • Schneiders, S. M. 1991, *The Revelatory Text: Interpreting the New Testament as Sacred Scripture,* San Francisco: HarperCollins • Thiselton, A. C. 1992, *New Horizons in Hermeneutics: The Theory and Practice of Transforming Biblical Reading,* London: Collins; Grand Rapids: Zondervan • Toolan, M. J. 1988, *Narrative: A Critical Linguistic Introduction,* London: Routledge • Watson, F. 1994, *Text, Church and World: Biblical Interpretation in Theological Perspective,* Grand Rapids: Eerdmans • West, G. 2d ed. 1995, *Biblical Hermeneutics of Liberation: Modes of Reading the Bible in the South African Context,* Maryknoll, N.Y.: Orbis • Yeo, K. K. 1998, *What Has Jerusalem to Do with Beijing? Biblical Interpretation from a Chinese Perspective,* Harrisburg, Pa.: Trinity Press International.

Introduction to the Gospels

Christopher M. Tuckett

1. "Gospel"

The word "gospel" is often used today to refer to the four books of the NT bearing that title and associated with the names Matthew, Mark, Luke, and John. "The Gospels" are often thought to refer to these four, and just these four, literary documents. Moreover, these texts are in many respects very similar to each other. All four purport to give relatively extended reports of the life and ministry of Jesus; they all conclude with a relatively lengthy account of his trial and crucifixion, and they all follow this with some narrative (though with varying length) relating, or implying, his appearance alive to others after his death. As such, then, the four NT Gospels are clearly different from other NT texts: they are neither accounts of the life of the early church (as is Acts), nor letters from one individual to a community (as are the Pauline epistles), nor do they purport to be visions of the heavenly realm (cf. Revelation).

The focus of attention of this article will be primarily on these four literary texts. However, we should make a number of preliminary observations. First, the term "gospel" (Gk. *euangelion*) as a description of these documents can probably be traced back relatively early to some time in the second century AD. (The more precise date is disputed. Hengel [1985: 64-84] argues for a time around the first quarter of the second century, on the basis of the titles of the Gospels; Koester [1980: 35-36] argues that Marcion in the middle of the century was the first person to refer to these texts as "Gospels.") However, such terminology cannot clearly be traced back much earlier than the second century. It is *possible* that one or more of the Gospel writers themselves referred to his work as a "Gospel," but this is by no means certain. (The theory is perhaps strongest in the case of Matthew; cf. Matt 26:13, which may be a reference to Matthew's own literary text [see Stanton 1992: 16-18]. It is not clear if Mark's use of the word *euangelion* in his title verse Mark 1:1 refers to his literary text or not. Neither Luke nor John uses the word explicitly in his own Gospel, though Luke does use the cognate verb "to evangelize"; see also below on Acts 10:36.)

Second, we may note that the word "gospel" seems to have been used rather differently in the first century by early Christians, notably by Paul. Within first-century Christianity, the term "gospel" was used to refer to the Christian kerygma centering in the death and resurrection of Jesus. The word *euangelion,* or "good news," is unusual and rare in Greek. Its somewhat specialized use by Christians may owe a lot to the use of the cognate verb "evangelize" (Gk. *euangelizomai,* meaning to "bring good news") in passages in Deutero-Isaiah, notably texts such as Isa 52:7; 61:1. Thus the "good news" preached by Christians is implicitly being claimed as the fulfillment of the hopes of the good news proclaimed by Deutero-Isaiah in the past. The noun and the verb are often used by Paul but apparently have little to do explicitly with giving information about Jesus' pre-Easter life and ministry. (Cf. 1 Cor 15:3: the "gospel" of which Paul reminds his Corinthian readers has to do with the basic Christian claim that "Christ died for our sins according to the scriptures," that he was raised, and that he was then "seen" by a whole series of other people.) Moreover, the "gospel" is something that is preached and proclaimed, and it is received by being heard and believed; it is not apparently something which is written or read. Above all, the "gospel," for Paul at least, is unique; there is, and can be, only one gospel, and any other alleged "gospel" cannot be the true gospel but must be counterfeit (cf. Gal 1:6). Thus, in moving from the first to the second century, the word "gospel" undergoes a significant semantic shift in meaning.

Thirdly, we should note that once this semantic shift had taken place, the word "gospel" was not attached to only these four documents which finally made their way into our NT. We now know of a considerable number of other documents which evidently styled themselves, or were called by others, "Gospels." Some of these we now have available through the discovery of the codices from Nag Hammadi. These include the *Gospel of Thomas,* the *Gospel of Philip,* the *Gospel of the Egyptians,* and the *Gospel of Truth.* We also have a *Gospel of Mary,* as well as excerpts from a *Gospel of Peter.* Further, there is evidence in some church fathers (in the form of quotations) of other Gospels whose text is not extant in any manuscript; thus, for example, Jerome quotes from a text which he calls *"The Gospel of the Hebrews"*; clearly such a text existed although no manuscript of it has survived.

These other Gospels are generally very different in form, or genre, from the four Gospels which were later to become canonical. The *Gospel of Thomas* comprises a string of sayings of Jesus, prefaced at most only by a simple "Jesus said" (or perhaps "Jesus says"); there is no narrative at all, hence no account of Jesus' miracles, and nothing about Jesus' passion, his death, or explicitly his resurrection appearances (at least in narrative form; it is possible that the sayings of Jesus recorded are intended as a series of sayings of the resurrected Jesus, so that the Gospel has the form of an extended resurrection appearance). The *Gospel of Mary* has the form of a so-called "resurrection dialogue," being an extended conversation between Jesus and his disciples after his resurrection. The *Gospel of Truth* has the form of an extended meditation on the nature of the divine and of salvation, and has no explicit reference to Jesus at all. Thus the Gospels which were finally placed in the NT canon are rather different in kind from the ones that were not. It is therefore in one way sensible and appropriate to distinguish the four Gospels of Matthew, Mark, Luke, and John from the other Gospels we know about, and to consider them as a separate group, not only on the basis of their being later canonized and the other Gospels being excluded from the canon but also by virtue of their nature and contents.

The dating of these other Gospels is disputed. However, most are almost certainly younger than the canonical Gospels, dating from the second century or later. As such, they have probably styled themselves Gospels by dependence on the canonical texts, perhaps at a time when a fourfold Gospel canon had already been established. They probably therefore have prime value in witnessing to the beliefs of certain groups of Christian believers at a later period in Christian history.

The chief possible exception to this is the *Gospel of Thomas,* about which there has been fierce debate ever since the discovery of the full text of the Gospel among the Nag Hammadi texts in 1945. Many have argued that the *Gospel of Thomas* may be (or may preserve) a very early form of the tradition of Jesus' sayings, independent of the canonical Gospels, and hence may provide potentially reliable information about Jesus. Others, however, have argued that the *Gospel of Thomas* represents a secondary form of the tradition, dependent (at perhaps more than one stage removed) on the canonical Gospels, and thus a witness primarily to the form of the tradition after the NT documents were written. There is not space to debate the issue here in detail. (See the full discussion in Fallon and Cameron 1988.) It is, however, not certain whether the text was originally termed a "Gospel." (The title *"Gospel of Thomas"* now appears as the colophon, that is, the final phrase, in the one manuscript of the text which we now possess. This manuscript is a fourth-century production and written in Coptic. We cannot therefore be certain that the colophon has not been added at some stage in the textual history of the document.) What is clear is that the *Gospel of Thomas* in its present form is quite *un*like the form of the present canonical Gospels: with no narrative at all and its exclusive focus on Jesus' sayings, given for the most part without any historical context, it is clearly different in literary terms from the canonical (and many other) "Gospels."

For the most part, attention will be focused here on the canonical Gospels. This is in no sense because of any value judgment in relation to the worth or otherwise of noncanonical texts (cf. Koester 1980). Nevertheless, the canonical status which the four Gospels subsequently achieved means that, historically, these four Gospels have been the focus of more attention and exerted more influence than other Gospels. Further, on literary grounds, these four documents are clearly different from other documents claiming the same title.

Given that the four canonical Gospels are similar to each other and radically different from other so-called "Gospels," can we say anything more about what kind of documents the four canonical Gospels are? We face then the complex problem of the genre of the canonical Gospels.

2. Gospel Genre

The importance of genre in literary-critical studies is universally recognized. We cannot really understand a literary text properly unless we have some idea of what kind of text it is. We need to know if a text, or part of a text, is intended to be fiction or nonfiction, prose or poetry, a serious novel or a lighthearted detective story, if we are to interpret it appropriately. If we make a mistake at this level, we are liable to misunderstand what is said. Thus "all understanding of verbal meaning is necessarily genre bound" (Hirsch 1967: 76).

That said, however, it is sometimes very hard to define the genre of a work, at least with any precision, though the issue can be discussed at many different levels. We can work at a very broad, general level; for example, we can say that a text we are reading is a "story." Alternatively, we could seek to be very much more specific: we could claim that our text is "seeking to tell the true story of the whole life of an individual in such a way as to commend all the values which the individual stood for and represented" (perhaps to be classified by some such term as "laudatory biography"). We can then distinguish a very broad genre from a much more specific genre.

A realization of the importance of genre has been recognized ever since the time of Aristotle. At the risk of making too sweeping a generalization, one can perhaps say that ancient theorists regarded genre in very prescriptive terms. A genre represented a set of constraints within which one *must* work in producing a literary text. Later studies recognized that life is not always so simple and suggested that genre is a matter of description rather than prescription: genre simply represents the abstraction of common features from a number of texts which we choose to classify together and regard as generically similar. Today most scholars would argue that these two different approaches — genre as prescriptive and genre as descriptive — are probably both too one-sided. Writers can and do deliberately modify an existing genre, at times precisely in order to make a point. In such cases, however, the fact that a writer is deviating from a prior pattern has to be recognized if the point is to be seen. Thus one recent writer has suggested that genre is a "set of expectations" (Kermode 1979: 162) which writers and readers may share, but which does not constitute a set of immutable rules. Rather, the shared expectations provide the common framework within which creative adaptation can, and frequently does, take place and which provides the backdrop to enable such creativity to be recognized and appreciated for what it is.

How does all this relate to the canonical Gospels? What kind of documents are they? To what genre should we assign them? As we have already noted in passing, it is in one sense easier to say what the Gospels are not: they are clearly not "letters," they are not sonnets, they are not epic histories of world history, they are (probably) not apocalypses, they are not autobiographies of their authors, and so on. But specifying more precisely what they actually are has proved more difficult and more controversial within biblical scholarship.

In the nineteenth century, it was very popular to defend the view that the Gospels were biographies. Many writers used the details from all the Gospels to concoct a modern biography of Jesus, supplying where necessary psychological explanations of Jesus' motives and filling in the gaps which the present accounts left out. Thus, for example, Peter's confession at Caesarea Philippi was seen as a great watershed in Jesus' life, Jesus turning away from the crowds to give more detailed instruction to his disciples about his impending suffering and death. Many such "lives of Jesus" were constructed in the nineteenth century on the basis of such assumptions about the nature of the Gospels. This "old quest for the historical Jesus" effectively came to an end at the beginning of the twentieth century with the work of W. Wrede on the messianic secret (ET 1971), who showed that several of the secrecy elements in Mark (on which so many of the older lives of Jesus had been based) were not historical at all. The work of A. Schweitzer (ET 1954) was also very important: Schweitzer showed unmercifully how fanciful, and unjustified by the evidence, many of these reconstructed "lives" were. Nevertheless, the view that the Gospels were biographies continued to be held: in 1915 an influential article by C. Votaw strongly defended the view that the Gospels were biographies, comparing the Gospels with ancient biographies such as Philostratus's *Life of Apollonius of Tyana* and Xenophon's *Memorabilia*. Certainly, too, in one of the early references to the Gospels in the Christian church, Justin Martyr (c. AD 155) refers to the Gospels as the "memoirs [Gk. *apomnēmoneumata*] of the apostles" (*1 Apol.* 66:3; 67:3, and many references in his *Dialogue with Trypho*), almost certainly intending to draw a positive correlation with Xenophon's *Memorabilia* (Gk. *apomnēmoneumata*), a "biography" of Socrates.

Such a view of the biographical nature of the Gospels was severely attacked by the form critics in the early part of the twentieth century. (See, e.g., the influential discussion of R. Bultmann ET 1963: 368-74.) According to these form critics, the Gospels are not to be compared with the "highbrow" literary products of the ancient world: they are not *Hochliteratur,* but *Kleinliteratur,* popular writings of a low-grade literary quality, the product of Christian communities rather than of highly literate authors. Further, the Gospels show no interest in historical or biographical details such as Jesus' personality, his origins, his education or development, or his appearance. Moreover, the Gospels are mythical, determined above all by the Christian "myth" of Jesus as Son of God and Lord, and they grow out of the Christian cult as cult legends of Christian worship. Thus the Gospels are not to be seen as biographical but as developments of the Christian kerygma. As such, they have no real analogies in the ancient world. They thus represent a totally new literary genre; in relation to other literature of the time they are *sui generis.* Such a claim dominated Gospel studies in the first half of the twentieth century, and it is still influential today.

Some have sought to go further by arguing that the roots of the Gospel narratives may still be visible in the kerygmatic preaching of the early church as witnessed in Peter's speech recorded in Acts 10. There, Peter's preaching incorporates as part of the "Gospel" message (cf. v. 36, where the word "evangelize" is used) a brief summary account of Jesus' life and ministry (vv. 37-38). The "Gospel" texts thus represent a filling out of the primitive gospel preaching — hence their distinctive character and their (appropriate) description as "Gospel." (Cf. Guelich 1991.)

This last theory must remain a little uncertain. It is, for example, not clear how far the speeches in Acts represent reliable historical accounts of the preaching of early Christians or how far they are due to Luke's own composition. For many today, Luke's own contribution may have been far more influential in the composition of these speeches in Acts than others have allowed in the past. The summary of Jesus' ministry in Acts 10:37-38 may then be as much a summary of Luke's own Gospel narrative given in his first volume, which in turn is probably dependent on the account in Mark (cf. below). Thus it is by no means certain that the summary in Acts 10:37-38 allows us a glimpse of the earliest roots of Gospel literature; rather, this may simply reflect rather more Luke's own perspective at a later date, *after* the time that such literature had been established.

More generally, the assertion about the generic uniqueness of the Gospels is not easy to accept in literary terms. At one level it is of course true but virtually trite: each individual literary text is unique in the sense of being not identical with other texts. Moreover, one can also justifiably say that the Gospels are unlike other biographies of the ancient world in that Jesus is not regarded in the same way as other subjects of ancient biographies. Any account of Jesus' life is thus not going to be the same as an account of the life of Socrates or Moses, for example. Further, the Christian claims about Jesus are radically different from others' claims about the importance and significance of figures like Socrates, Julius Caesar, or Apollonius of Tyana. There is, for example, nothing in the ancient world that is quite the same as Christians' claims about Jesus' "resurrection." So, too, no other figure becomes the center and focus of religious faith and commitment in the way that Jesus does for Christians; nor is the significance which comes to be attached to Jesus' death really comparable to the significance seen in the deaths of other figures of antiquity. In this sense, therefore, the Gospels can rightly be said to be unique.

However, at a slightly higher level of abstraction, or in terms of a more "broad" genre, the claim that the Gospels are *sui generis* becomes rather harder to sustain, as recent studies have made clear (cf. esp. Aune 1987; Burridge 1992). First, one must distinguish between ancient and modern biography. Thus, in seeking to determine whether a text from antiquity can fit the category of "biography," one should not use modern ideas associated with the term. For example, the Gospels contain no details of Jesus' origins, education, development, or whatever, but the same is also true of much ancient "biography." So while the Gospels might not fit a modern idea of a contemporary biography, that is not to say that they may not fit the category of ancient biography. (On the differences between modern and ancient biography, see Stanton 1974: 117-36.)

Second, the form critics' general view of the Gospels as *Kleinliteratur,* and as reflecting primarily the situations and beliefs of early Christian communities rather than individual authors, has been implicitly questioned in recent years by the rise of so-called "redaction" criticism. Redaction-critical studies of the Gospels have put the spotlight much more on the individual authors of the Gospels, and many today would argue that the evangelists are to be seen much more as self-conscious authors, perhaps even "theologians" in their own right, with their own distinctive characteristics and perhaps theological agendas. The Gospels are now seen as much more than just the (almost mindless) conglomeration of smaller units which simply reflect the beliefs and activities of early Christian communities. The rehabilitation of the evangelists as authors has had its effect on the study of the genre of the Gospels. This is not to say that the evangelists are necessarily high-powered literary geniuses in the ancient world. Their literary standing would probably have been judged to be a little second rate by the more literate people of the time. Nevertheless, the old distinction between *Hochliteratur* and *Kleinliteratur,* or between literate individual authors and amorphous Christian communities as "authors," is probably not easily sustainable any more in relation to the Gospels.

Third, the theory that the Gospels are *sui generis* has been increasingly regarded as one which is rather uncomfortable to sustain in literary terms. Given the nature of genre as a "set of expectations" shared by writer and reader alike to enable communication to take place, any claim that a text has no generic analogy at all looks increasingly odd: if a text were really *sui generis,* there would be no common set of expectations and the text would effectively be almost totally incomprehensible. Without some kind of generic framework, a text is virtually unintelligible. And nothing really indicates that the evangelists thought that their books were totally unintelligible enigmas!

In recent years, therefore, there has been something of a revival of the theory that the Gospels can appropriately be seen as fitting within the broad parameters of ancient biography. It is now recognized that ancient biography was quite broad in scope, encompassing a wide range of different writings (cf. Aune 1987; Burridge 1992). Further, one should take note of the way in which authors *did* write "lives" of other people rather than simply look at what ancient theorists said was the way in which authors *should* write such "lives." One can take as a rough working definition of biography that of David Aune: "Biography may be defined as a discrete prose narrative devoted exclusively to the portrayal of the whole life of a particular individual perceived as historical" (Aune 1987: 29). Despite one or two caveats (chiefly focused on the word "whole" here: not all Greco-Roman biography dealt with the *whole* life of its subject, nor do all the Christian Gospels), if such a definition may be accepted, then the Christian Gospels can be seen as falling within such parameters. Above all, Richard Burridge has shown that, on the basis of a wide range of different considerations and possible comparators, the Gospels are quite at home within such a broad category of biography and can be seen to be similar in kind to other examples of ancient "biographical" writings (Burridge 1992). In terms of length, subject matter, and a range of external and internal features, the Gospels can be seen to be similar to biographies of the ancient world to such an extent that the identification of the Gospels as biographies is, at a relatively broad level, both meaningful and defensible. As such, then, the claim that the Gospels are *sui generis* should probably be discounted as an oddity in literary-critical terms and not sustainable.

However, we should not lose sight of the fact that the Gospels remain highly unusual documents, even within the broad category of ancient biography. For example, unlike other biographies, the Christian Gospels are all anonymous: however much we may now wish to stress the individuality of the evangelists, none of them identifies himself explicitly. (The only exception might be John 21:24, though there the identification of the author of the *rest* of the Gospel as the beloved disciple is apparently made by a third party testifying to him.) As such, this feature sharply distinguishes the Gospels from other Greco-Roman biographies. Further, as already said, the claims made by Jesus' followers about Jesus, particularly in relation to the significance of his death, are quite different from the claims made of other figures whose biographies were written by their followers and/or admirers (or detractors!). The very form of the narrative in the Gospels is thus unusual, with an excessive concentration on the account of Jesus' suffering and death. Hence the well-known categorization of the Gospels as "passion narratives with extended introductions" (Kähler ET 1964: 80, originally intended to *distinguish* the Gospels from other biographical writings of the ancient world).

Nor should we assume that the possible identification of the Gospels as biographies has the same kind of hermeneutical significance as others have perhaps assumed in the past. In the nineteenth century, the claim that the Gospels were biographical was implicitly used to justify the claim that they could be used as accurate sources for a chronologically arranged life of Jesus. Such, however, was not necessarily the case for all Greco-Roman biography, and hence, ipso facto, it is not necessarily the case with the Gospels. A number of other biographies reflect as much the situation and the outlook of their authors as of the person about whom they are ostensibly written. So, too, we must remember the differences between ancient and modern ideas about the nature of biography. Thus any recognition of the Gospels as biographical cannot be used immediately to establish anything about the historical reliability of the Gospels. The work of form criticism and redaction criticism, which has enabled us to recognize the ideas of the early Christians quite as much as the historical Jesus in the Gospels, cannot be bypassed by some sleight of hand of genre criticism.

The identification of the genre of a text is an important aid to its interpretation. We can interpret a text properly only if we have some idea of what kind of text it is. However, the hermeneutical value deriving from the identification of a genre is effectively proportional to the degree of specificity of the genre: the more broad, or general, the level of the generic identification, the less help it may be in enabling us to interpret the text appropriately. And one has to say that, if one does accept the notion that the Gospels may be seen as "biographies," this can only be at a relatively high level of abstraction and generality, with a correspondingly low yield in terms of hermeneutical gain. Thus although one may avoid what is probably something of a nonsense in literary-critical terms in talking of a text as *sui generis,* the gain may not ultimately be very great in terms of aiding our understanding of the Gospels themselves by regarding them as biographies. The fact remains that the use to which the general "biographical" form is put by the evangelists in writing their Gospels as (presumably) part of the Christian kerygma about Jesus is radically different from the uses made of other ancient biographies by their writers. But this simply reflects the special nature of Jesus for Christians vis-à-vis claims made about others in the ancient world. In this sense the Gospels are unique, though the uniqueness arises more out of the claims made regarding Jesus by his followers, rather than the formal nature of the documents themselves (cf. Guelich 1991).

3. The Relationships between the Gospels

We have noted on a number of occasions already that the four Gospels in the NT are in some ways very similar to each other and, in turn, distinct from other "Gospels." The level of similarity in fact varies within the fourfold Gospel canon. The Fourth Gospel, while sharing some notable characteristics with the other three, also differs in other ways from them, at times significantly, as we shall see. The other three Gospels are extremely close to each other, so close indeed that one can usefully put them side by side and look at them together: hence their description as the "Synoptic" Gospels (from Gk. *syn,* meaning "with," and "optic" relating to looking). How then are we to explain the similarities between the Gospels?

The question is best approached in two separate stages: (a) how to explain the similarities between the Synoptic Gospels themselves, and (b) how to explain the relationship between John and the other three. I consider first the question of the relationship of the Synoptic Gospels to each other, the so-called "Synoptic Problem."

3.1. The Synoptic Problem

The close similarity between the Synoptic Gospels applies at all levels: the order of events in the three Gospels is often the same; and at the points where the Gospels are evidently parallel, that is, recording what is ultimately the same original tradition, they do so in very similar if not identical wording. Indeed, the relationship is so close at times as to demand a *literary* relationship between the three Gospels: one evangelist has used one or more of the others as a written source, or the evangelists have used common source material which they share.

Occasionally attempts have been made to explain the relationships between the Synoptic Gospels on the basis of common oral tradition, but these seem unconvincing. The agreements between the Gospels is at times far closer than one would normally expect if simply a common oral tradition underlies the three accounts. For example, in Mark 2:10 there is a small grammatical "hiccup" in the narrative: a speech by Jesus is slightly interrupted as the addressees change from the scribes who have questioned Jesus' authority to the paralyzed man who is about to be healed. This change is marked by a parenthetical remark by the narrator, "he said to the paralyzed man." The Greek is slightly awkward, reflected, too, in many English translations by parentheses, or dashes, placed around the extra phrase. Now in fact exactly the same unevenness in the narrative occurs in all three Synoptic Gospels at exactly the same point in the story. Such a detail is not what one would expect to be preserved in oral tradition. Oral tradition might well preserve accurately a memorable saying such as the claim that Jesus as the Son of Man has the authority on earth to forgive sins; but the break in the narrative at precisely the same point in all three Gospels seems to demand a literary relationship to explain it.

The most widely held theory today is that, of the three Gospels, Mark's is the earliest and was used as a source by Matthew and Luke, the theory of "Markan priority."

3.1.1. Markan Priority

Mark's Gospel is certainly much shorter than the other two, and virtually all of the material in Mark appears in either Matthew or Luke, much of it in both. The theory of Markan priority is widely held, but not universally so. (The classic defense of the theory is Streeter 1924; for a more recent discussion, see Fitzmyer 1970; see also the essays in Bellinzoni 1985.) In recent years there has been a strong upsurge of support for the "Griesbach hypothesis," arguing that Matthew's Gospel was written first, Luke came second, and Mark was written last of the three, using the other two as sources. (See Farmer 1964, Dungan 1970, and the essays in Dungan 1990; for a discussion, see Tuckett 1983.) Nevertheless, not many have been convinced, although the renewal of the debate has focused attention on the nature and the value of the arguments used to defend one or other of the possible hypotheses. If nothing else, the modern debate has highlighted the inconclusive nature of many of the traditional arguments. In the past it was thought that some arguments could logically prove the theory of Markan priority beyond reasonable doubt. It is now seen that this is too optimistic. Most arguments are reversible and depend ultimately on weighing up probabilities and judging possible likelihoods rather than dealing with cast-iron certainties.

One argument thought to work in favor of the Markan priority is the appeal to the fact that practically all of Mark's content appears in either Matthew or Luke, or often in both. The evidence is certainly consistent with the theory of Markan priority, and it makes good sense on such a scenario. It is, however, theoretically equally possible that Mark came last and deliberately chose material that was in one of the other two Gospels, mostly choosing material in both. But one must then raise the question of how likely this is. Why would Mark have omitted so much material from his sources even if he were restricting himself mainly to material in both his alleged sources? Why omit the ethical teaching in the Sermon on the Mount/Plain? Why omit the Lord's Prayer? Further, Mark often takes many more words to tell the same story (cf. the relative lengths of the story of the Gerasene demoniac in Matt 8:29-34 par. Mark 5:1-20 par. Luke 8:26-39). Why then omit so much from the sources but expand the material that is retained, at times quite significantly in terms of length but with little real extra substance? No obvious reason seems forthcoming. On the other hand, if Mark came first, a more plausible scenario emerges. Matthew and Luke take over most of Mark; at times they abbreviate Mark's rather wordy account, partly perhaps in order to make space for other material they have from other sources.

In purely formal terms, either theory is possible; neither is totally impossible. For many the theory of Markan priority seems more plausible — but that is all that we can say. It may be, for example, that Mark did come last and had a clear set of reasons for choosing the material he did, but those reasons have not yet been correctly identified by the modern scholar. Nevertheless, until such reasons are identified, the theory of Markan priority will remain more favored by many.

A second argument concerns the order of events in the Gospels. Frequently the order of events is the same in all three Gospels in the material they share in common. And if either Matthew or Luke fails to agree with Mark, the other supports the Markan order. Many have claimed in the past that this shows that Mark's order must be foundational, Matthew and Luke alternately (and occasionally) departing from it.

Others have pointed out an important logical fallacy in this argument if it is claimed that the evidence can be explained only by the theory of Markan priority. For example, the Griesbach hypothesis can explain the facts just as well: Mark may follow the order of both Matthew and Luke when they agree, but choose to follow one or the other when they disagree.

Nevertheless, a more concrete approach, looking at the actual differences in order among the Gospels, may again be more fruitful (cf. Tuckett 1984; for the whole question of arguments from order, see Neville 1993). For advocates of the Griesbach hypothesis, it becomes quite difficult to explain precisely why Mark switches back and forth between his two main sources in the way the hypothesis presupposes he must have done. Conversely, defenders of the theory of Markan priority have generally found it quite easy to explain the differences in order as due to Matthew's or Luke's changes of the Markan order. The majority of Matthew's differences from Mark serve to enable Matthew to collect a block of miracle stories in chs. 8–9, a section that Matthew seems to create deliberately to place alongside the Sermon on the Mount in chs. 5–7, thereby showing Jesus as the Messiah of both word and deed. Luke's main difference from the Markan order concerns the placing of the story of the rejection of Jesus in Nazareth (Luke 4:16-30; cf. Mark 6:1-6). Luke places this story right at the start of Jesus' ministry, where it functions in Luke's Gospel as a programmatic summary of the whole story that is to come. Again there is little difficulty in explaining the difference in order as due to Luke's redaction of Mark.

Much the same phenomenon occurs at the level of the detailed wording within each pericope: Matthew and Luke frequently agree with Mark's wording, but rarely agree with each other against Mark. Nevertheless, there are a number of exceptions to this general rule, the so-called "minor agreements" which have always been felt to constitute a difficulty for the theory of Markan priority. For example, in their parallels to Mark 14:65 in the story of the mockery of Jesus by the soldiers, both Matthew and Luke have the soldiers put to Jesus an extra question: "Who is it who hit you?" (Matt 26:68 par. Luke 22:64). The agreement between Matthew and Luke extends to five words which are identical in Greek, a fact which is very surprising if Matthew and Luke are independently using Mark as a source.

These minor agreements have been much debated. There are potentially a rather high number of such texts, suggesting to some that Luke may have known Matthew as well as Mark (cf. Goulder 1978, 1989); for others, they call into question the whole theory of Markan priority (cf. Farmer 1964). They do, however, vary considerably in importance. A number are relatively insignificant and not at all unexpected. For example, Matthew and Luke often link clauses with the normal Greek particle *de,* where Mark has a rather clumsy *kai* (cf., e.g., Matt 12:2 par. Mark 2:24 par. Luke 6:2); Matthew and Luke often use a normal aorist tense in narrative where Mark has a historical present tense (e.g., Matt 9:12 par. Mark 2:17 par. Luke 5:31). In cases such as this, independent but identical changes of Mark by Matthew and Luke are perfectly plausible. Thus the genuinely significant minor agreements may be relatively few in number; in any case, most can be explained quite easily as due to Matthew's and Luke's changes of Mark (cf. Neirynck 1974). One should also note that these texts are by no means easy to explain on other hypotheses. If they are due to Luke's knowledge of Matthew as well as Mark, one has to explain why the agreements between Matthew and Luke are often so minor in nature. Alternatively, the Griesbach hypothesis would have to explain why Mark, contrary to his usual procedure elsewhere, suddenly decided in these texts to avoid the common witness of both his sources. The "minor agreement" texts clearly constitute a bit of a problem for the theory of Markan priority; but probably they are equally problematic for many other alternative source hypotheses.

The most convincing argument for the priority of Mark is probably that which is based on an examination of many actual parallels among the Gospels, looking often as much at the differences as at the similarities and asking the question in which direction the tradition is most likely to have changed. There is no time to discuss many examples here, and so I focus on two of the most famous instances in this context.

In Mark 6:5-6, Mark says that Jesus was unable to do any miracles in Nazareth and marveled at the unbelief of the people there. Matthew's parallel (Matt 13:58) simply says that Jesus did not do many miracles because of the unbelief of the people there. It looks very much as if Matthew has had difficulty with Mark's suggestion that Jesus was unable to perform miracles; hence he has changed the tradition by deleting any idea of impotence on Jesus' part and attributing the failure of Jesus to perform miracles to the people's unbelief rather than to any deficiency by Jesus. The opposite change is very difficult to envisage: Why would Mark change Matthew's simple note to one which appears to attribute a lack of power to Jesus?

The second example concerns the wording of Peter's confession at Caesarea Philippi. In Mark, Peter says simply, "You are the Christ" (Mark 8:29). In Matthew, Peter says, "You are the Christ, the Son of the living God" (Matt 16:16). On the theory of Markan priority, there is a plausible scenario: Matthew has expanded Mark's shorter version by adding a reference to Jesus as the Son of God, a term which is clearly significant for Matthew's Christology. But the term "Son of God" is just as significant for Mark's Christology (cf. Mark 1:1, 10; 9:7; 15:39). If Matthew came first, and Mark knew Matthew, a rather implausible line of the development results: Why should Mark delete the reference to Jesus as the Son of God in this story which, on any showing, is a key one in his narrative? There seems to be no reasonable explanation.

However, one should note that, in cases such as this, we cannot *prove* anything with mathematical finality. It might be that Mark did change Matthew in the texts above, for reasons which are not at present apparent to us. All we can say is that it seems highly unlikely to many. But we cannot exclude the alternative possibility completely. Nevertheless, it is for reasons such as this that many today regard the theory of Markan priority as reasonably well founded and a viable basis for further study, for example, redaction-critical analysis of the Gospels.

3.1.2. The Theory of Q

The theory of Markan priority explains only some of the agreements among the Synoptic Gospels. There is, for example, a further substantial body of non-Markan material in which Matthew and Luke agree with each other. Often this is explained by Matthew's and Luke's use of common source material, usually known as "Q." The main sources behind the Synoptic tradition are thus Mark and Q, giving rise to the name of the overall hypothesis as the "Two Source Theory."

The existence of Q is debated, some denying its existence completely and explaining the Matthew-Luke agreements by Luke's knowledge and use of Matthew. (Cf., in addition to defenders of the Griesbach hypothesis who would seek to explain Luke as dependent on Matthew alone, the views of Goulder 1978, 1989, who would maintain Markan priority but seek to explain the remaining Matthew-Luke agreements by Luke's dependence on Matthew. For arguments defending the existence of Q, see Catchpole 1993: 1-59, Tuckett 1996: 1-39, as well as Bellinzoni 1985.) The main arguments for the existence of some kind of Q source are largely negative, denying the theory that Luke could have known Matthew. (A theory that Matthew was dependent on Luke is scarcely ever advocated today.) Given then the at times verbatim agreement between Matthew and Luke (cf. the preaching of John the Baptist in Matt 3:7-10 par. Luke 3:7-9, or the teaching about prayer in Matt 7:7-8 par. Luke 11:9-10), some theory of dependence on a common source seems necessary to explain the texts.

Among the negative arguments against Luke's use of Matthew, one may refer to the fact that Luke never seems to know any of Matthew's substantive additions to Mark in Markan passages (cf. Matt 12:5-7; 16:17-19; 17:19, 24-25). Further, Luke never has the non-Markan material he shares with Matthew in the same order relative to Mark (at least after the opening section). Yet Luke rarely changes Mark's order. If he knew Matthew as well, he must have radically changed Matthew's order at almost every point but been extremely conservative in relation to the Markan order. Such a procedure seems inconsistent, and it is easier to suppose that Luke did not know Matthew, the different orders of the material being due to *Matthew* changing things to collect his account of Jesus' teaching into the five large "blocks" he creates from thematically similar material. Finally, it seems that neither Matthew nor Luke consistently offers the most original form of the individual sayings they do share in common: sometimes Matthew is more original, sometimes Luke. For examples of Luke's greater originality, one can compare parts of the versions of the beatitudes in Luke 6:20-23 (cf. Matt 5:1-11), the Lord's Prayer in Luke 11:2-4 (cf. Matt 6:9-13), or the doom oracle in Luke 11:49-51 (cf. Matt 23:34-36). (There is no space to discuss the details here; more detailed discussion can be found in the works cited above.) For reasons such as these it has therefore seemed implausible to many that Luke knew Matthew. Hence both depend on common source material, usually known as "Q."

The nature of Q is debated, even by those who would espouse some sort of Q theory. Was the Q material unified in a single source prior to being used by Matthew and Luke? Or should we be thinking of a rather more disparate body of material, perhaps from a variety of different sources? In fact considerations of the order of this material may suggest that Q did exist in a more unified form. When allowance is made for Matthew's policy of collecting similar material into his five discourses, the order of Q material in Matthew and Luke is strikingly similar. Hence it may be sensible to think of Q as a single source (now lost) lying behind Matthew and Luke. Further, the fact that the Matthew-Luke agreement is at times so close in Greek suggests that Q may have been a written Greek source. Further discussion of Q would take us too far afield here. Many scholars today would want to argue that Q displays a form of the Jesus tradition that has many distinctive and characteristic features, perhaps reflecting the beliefs of a specific "group" of Christians within early Christianity (cf. Kloppenborg 1987, Jacobson 1992, and Tuckett 1996). Some would even go further and claim to be able to trace developments in the history of Q and to isolate two or three strata within Q (cf. especially Kloppenborg 1987, whose arguments have been very influential). So, too, the nature of Q is debated: Is it some kind of "sayings collection"? Or should one refer to it as a "Gospel" (cf. Jacobson 1992 and others)? The latter possibility seems a little optimistic in view of the earlier discussion here: if Q is a "Gospel," it is certainly *un*like the present New Testament Gospels since it (apparently) had no passion narrative and relatively little narrative element elsewhere. Perhaps it would be least confusing to call Q a "sayings collection," though recognizing that Q contains a few narrative elements as well (cf. the temptation narrative or the account of the healing of the centurion's servant).

3.1.3. Other Sources?

The remainder of the material in the Synoptic Gospels is virtually all found in Matthew alone or Luke alone. (There is very little in Mark alone.) This is often referred to as "M" and "L" material respectively. Whether M and/or L constituted separate sources is very difficult to say. Undoubtedly some of this material came to the evangelists from sources; other parts may be due to their own redaction, for example, the so-called "formula quotations" in Matthew, where the narrator says that specific events fulfill specific OT texts: these may well be due to the evangelist himself (cf. Stanton 1992: 348-63). Certainly the "M" material seems to be quite disparate, some of it reflecting a very "conservative" Jewish-Christian point of view (cf. Matt 23:2, advocating obedience to *all* the scribal tradition) which is at times hard to square with Matthew's own viewpoint (cf. Matt 15:6). It is probably best, therefore, to assume that this M and L material represents a collection of possibly disparate material available to each evangelist separately.

The main theory explaining the agreements among the Synoptic Gospels is thus the Two Source Theory, although, as already noted, some scholars would in various ways question each plank of the overall theory.

3.2. John and the Synoptics

We noted at the start of this section that the three Synoptic Gospels are much closer to each other than they are to the Fourth Gospel. All four Gospels have a number of similarities. But there are also wide differences at many levels. For similarities, one can refer to the fact that all four Gospels start with the figure of John the Baptist; all four finish with a lengthy account of Jesus' death; in between are a number of stories common to John and the Synoptics (e.g., the feeding of the five thousand and the story of Jesus' anointing).

Yet there are many differences at many levels. In terms of chronology, Jesus spends far more time in Jerusalem in John than the final hectic week implied in the Synoptics. Jesus' ministry seems to last for three years rather than the one year implied by the Synoptics. In terms of details, Jesus' death takes place on the eve of Passover rather than on the feast day itself (as the Synoptics imply). So, too, John's account of the last supper does not record any institution by Jesus of the Eucharist. More generally, the whole tone of Jesus' ministry is quite different in John. There are no exorcisms in John; the miracles generally tend to be more "stupendous" (cf. the raising of Lazarus, or the changing of water into wine at Cana). Further, the teaching of Jesus in John is quite different in both style and content from that in the Synoptic accounts: the Johannine Jesus no longer teaches in short sections, often with parables, but delivers long discourses, at times almost rambling in their structure. And Synoptic themes such as the "kingdom of God" tend to be replaced with new categories such as "eternal life" and "light and darkness." Above all, the Johannine Jesus seems to point to himself as the focus of commitment in a far more explicit and exalted way than is the case in the Synoptics where, for the most part, Jesus points away from himself to God as the focus of attention.

Most interpreters would say that, in general terms, the Synoptic Gospels give us better access to the historical Jesus: the teaching of Jesus recorded in the Synoptics is probably closer to that of Jesus himself. This is not to deny that some details of John may be historically valuable; for example, the references to a longer time spent by Jesus in Jerusalem, the note that Jesus may have undertaken a baptizing ministry alongside John the Baptist (John 4:1), and *perhaps* the dating of the crucifixion in relation to the feast of Passover. But for the most part, the presentation of Jesus in John is thought to reflect more the views of John than of the historical Jesus.

What, then, is the relationship between John and the Synoptics? (For a survey of the debate, see Smith 1992.) The dominant theory today is probably that John and the Synoptics are independent of each other. There are a number of small details in which John agrees with one or other of the Synoptics, for example, in the reference to two hundred denarii in the story of the feeding of the five thousand (John 6:7; Mark 6:37 and pars.), or the use of the very rare Greek adjective *pistikos* to refer to the ointment used at Jesus' anointing (John 12:3; Mark 14:3). But it is hard to see these small details as outweighing the enormous differences which exist between John and the Synoptics. Most scholars have therefore been content to explain the small common features as reflecting links in the earlier history of the traditions used by the evangelists rather than as indicating direct knowledge of the Synoptics by John. (Dependence the other way around has hardly ever been advocated.)

There has, however, been something of a revival in recent years of the view that John may have known one or more of the Synoptics (cf. Neirynck 1992 and other essays in Denaux 1992). One can, for example, point to features in the Synoptics which may be redactional and which reappear in John. For example, the way in which the story of Peter's threefold denial of Jesus is split up and placed around the account of Jesus' trial before the Jewish authorities in Mark may be due to a typically Markan "sandwiching" technique (Mark 14:53-72), and a very similar arrangement appears in John as well (John 18:15-27).

Nevertheless, one must still say that any such details are very small. Such a theory of dependence of John on the Synoptics also has to presuppose great freedom on John's part in using his alleged sources as well as in using relatively insignificant, odd phrases and words in at times quite different ways and contexts. On any showing John's presentation shows considerable creativity since it is very hard to trace the distinctive features of John's account of Jesus' teaching back to the historical Jesus himself. But given this, there is probably not a lot to be gained by postulating John's dependence on the Synoptics.

Clearly, too, there are other traditions which John has used and which cannot have been derived from the Synoptics (cf. the stories peculiar to John: many of the miracles as well as distinctive features of Jesus' teaching). John must then have had access to independent traditions besides the Synoptics. Some have sought to be more precise about the nature of the sources or traditions used by John. For example, it has long been argued that John used a separate source for his miracle stories (the so-called "signs source" [cf. Bultmann 1971; Fortna 1970, 1988; on this see Lindars 1972]). Reference is also often made to some of the place names in John as being predominantly from southern Palestine; John may therefore have had access to traditions associated with the south, in contrast to the predominantly Galilean traditions reflected in the Synoptics. Whether John knew the Synoptics must therefore remain uncertain. The dominant view remains that John is independent of the Synoptics; but even if dependence is asserted, this will probably not help a great deal in interpreting the Fourth Gospel. John remains a striking testimony to his own peculiar understanding of the significance of Jesus for Christian belief and practice.

It is also worth noting that although John gives a highly distinctive presentation of Jesus, it is no less the case that each of the three Synoptic evangelists gives us an equally distinctive presentation. Modern redaction criticism has highlighted the ways in which all four evangelists have shaped the material available to them to present their own peculiar version of their "Gospel." All, then, present some of the richness of the tradition in a way that they thought was both relevant and meaningful for their own contemporary situations. The challenge they present to us as readers is perhaps to make that tradition equally relevant in our own situations.

4. The Fourfold Gospel Canon

Why, then, were these four Gospels privileged and placed in a canon of Scripture? Why were other Gospels excluded? Why four Gospels? Why these four?

Such questions are ultimately intractable and unanswerable. The process whereby eventually twenty-seven documents were isolated from others and included in a "canon" of "Scripture" was very long and complex (Kümmel 1975: 475-510). Indeed, the debates about some documents continued for a very long time. Doubts about the canonicity of the book of Revelation were being expressed as late as the ninth century (cf. the so-called Stichometry of Nicephorus); equally, other texts not now regarded as canonical were included in lists of scriptural books, or were copied in Bibles, for a long time too. For example, Codex Sinaiticus (4th cent.) contains the texts of the *Epistle of Barnabas* and the *Shepherd of Hermas;* Codex Alexandrinus (5th cent.) contains the texts of *1 Clement* and *2 Clement.* Certainly no single public decision was made at a specific point of time determining the limits of the canon. Athanasius's Festal Letter of 367 is often referred to in this context, for Athanasius lists the twenty-seven books now in our NT as canonical; but he is in part simply reflecting standard practice of his day, and in any case debates about texts on the fringes of the canon continued well after 367, as already noted.

Yet despite debates about the fringes of the canon, one can also say that the fourfold Gospel canon consisting of Matthew, Mark, Luke, and John was established relatively early and never seriously questioned in later debates. By the end of the second century the fourfold Gospel canon seems well established, and no one questions it explicitly.

One must, however, be wary of the dangers of anachronism. In the earliest Christian communities, "scripture" was a term which referred above all to Jewish scripture, the body of literature which later Christians termed the "Old Testament." Over a long period of time, a collection of Christian writings were gradually accorded the same status as the Jewish scriptures, so that a "New Testament" was placed alongside the "Old Testament." However, that process was a very long one. Moreover, a decision about whether a book was canonical was not necessarily the same as whether it contained valuable material and was worth reading. Some books were ultimately not regarded as scriptural but nevertheless were thought to be worth reading and consulting. The time around the end of the second century and the beginning of the third century represents a time of considerable flux in this process. Thus, for example, writers such as Clement of Alexandria and Origen in the early third century can still happily refer to traditions of Jesus' sayings found in books outside the four canonical Gospels without any apparent embarrassment and without ever questioning the fourfold Gospel canon, which was probably firmly established by then (cf. below).

In relation to the Gospels, it is clear that significant developments occurred in the second century. Certainly by the end of the century, Irenaeus (c. 180) can defend the existence of a fourfold Gospel canon as almost self-evident. In his famous argument in his *Adv. Haer.* 3.11.8 he appeals to a variety of phenomena to justify the existence of a fourfold Gospel canon: there are four corners of the earth and four winds, the cherubim are four-faced, reflected in the four living creatures around the divine throne in Rev 4:7, and so it is right and fitting that there should be four and only four Gospels.

It seems highly likely that Irenaeus is writing in part polemically and seeking to set limits around the Gospel canon in the light of two tendencies. We know of the existence of Gnostics in the second century who expanded the "Gospel" literature with several more of their own texts claiming the title "Gospels" (cf. above). Some of these were no doubt intended to provide the content of esoteric teaching of Jesus, now available for the chosen few (perhaps given during the period — extended by the Gnostics — when the risen Jesus met with his disciples before his final departure from earth). Irenaeus's restriction of the canon to just four Gospels thus serves to exclude other so-called "Gospels."

Such concerns might have led more naturally to a restriction to a single authoritative Gospel account. There is evidence of worries by Christians at times about the differences among the Gospels, so that the plurality of the Gospels was evidently regarded as in some sense problematic. We know, too, of one famous attempt to reconcile the Gospel narratives into a single story: Tatian (c. AD 170) sought to write a single narrative of the Gospel events, the so-called *Diatessaron,* working together the accounts in all four canonical Gospels (and possibly using another source as well). Only parts of Tatian's work have survived, mostly in translated form in other languages or available to us only indirectly. But his *Diatessaron* was clearly very influential over a wide area.

There was, however, another prominent figure in the mid-second century who may have influenced matters considerably. This was Marcion, who was influential in Rome c. AD 150. Marcion took some of Paul's statements about the contrast between law and grace to an ultimate extreme, denying any positive value to Judaism and the "old" dispensation. In line with this he had to cut out large parts of Paul's letters which showed a more positive attitude to the Jewish tradition, claiming that such parts had been added by later Judaizers. So, too, Marcion believed that Paul's reference to the one true gospel referred to a single *book.* (Marcion may have been the first to use the word "gospel" to refer to a book in this way. So Koester 1990: 35-36, though see above.) This he believed was the Gospel of Luke. But as with Paul's letters, Marcion believed that Luke's Gospel had been added to by later Judaizers; the true Gospel thus had to be recovered by excising some sections from the present text of Luke (e.g., the birth narratives with their very positive presentation of Jewish piety). For Marcion there was therefore one and only one true Gospel, that of Luke (suitably edited!). Irenaeus's insistence on a *four*fold Gospel canon thus serves to include (rather than exclude) other Gospels in the face of Marcionite tendencies.

Irenaeus's argument may therefore have both an exclusive and an inclusive function. It seeks to allow plurality but to exclude total, unfettered license.

What sorts of criteria were applied in deciding to fix on just four Gospels, and these four? The fact of the matter is that we simply do not know. The rather artificial nature of Irenaeus's appeal to "fourness" in creation (four is not the most obvious sacred number to choose; three or seven might be more natural candidates) suggests that he is in part reflecting a situation that has already been established rather than arguing for a totally new position. (See also Stanton 1997.) At best we can make educated guesses, partly bearing in mind some of the arguments used by later writers about other books whose place in the developing canon was disputed, but remembering, too, that attitudes may well have varied over both space and time (cf. Meade 1986: 203-7).

One test was some kind of doctrinal "orthodoxy" or propriety (though how that might be assessed is not always clear!). Thus Eusebius tells a story about a bishop Serapion in the second century who heard of one of his congregations using a *Gospel of Peter:* Serapion is in principle quite happy with this; but, on learning of some of its contents, he banned its use because of its *doctrinal* deficiencies (Eusebius *Hist. Eccl.* 6.12). (It seems to advocate a docetic Christ, who did not really suffer on the cross.) It is above all this that is evidently regarded as the crucial factor.

Many have argued that authorship — specifically apostolic authorship — was a critical factor in deciding on canonicity. It is, however, doubtful whether this was always the case. Serapion's rejection of the *Gospel of Peter* was made independently of any consideration, positive or negative, concerning the accuracy of the ascription of the Gospel to Peter. In any case, in relation to the four canonical Gospels, two of them — Mark and Luke — are traditionally not written by apostles, even if the tradition links them closely with the apostles Peter and Paul respectively. These Gospels are thus at best "apostolic" only at one stage removed. But there is little evidence that this factor was thought in itself to be directly relevant.

For Irenaeus it was probably more relevant that the Gospels were historically reliable and trustworthy as historical records. Von Campenhausen has shown that this was the most important aspect for Irenaeus in his discussion with the heretics of his day, rather than any status held or claimed by their authors (Von Campenhausen 1973: 204-6). And the link with the apostles by, say, Mark and Luke was important not necessarily because this gave added status to the authors themselves but because this insured their historical accuracy as accounts of the life of Jesus. (The irony today is of course that, by such a criterion, none of the four Gospels might have passed such a test!)

It is possible, too, that the age of a document was important. For example, the Muratorian Canon (probably dating from around the end of the second century) rejects some books such as the *Shepherd of Hermas* on the grounds that they were written only "recently." So, too, it was important that documents be related to the *whole* church. (Hence the Muratorian Canon has to work a little harder to justify including Paul's letters, which are addressed to individual people or communities; and in the end Paul is accepted by comparison with the letters of Revelation, taken as written to the whole church!) Yet whether this affected the situation regarding the Gospels we do not know. It *may* have been that some of the other Gnostic Gospels were rejected because they gave only secret teaching of Jesus directed to a select few, though the same could be said of a text like the Gospel of Mark (cf. Mark 4:10-12)! The fact remains that from the time at which any such discussions in relation to the Gospels must have been taking place (if indeed they occurred at all), the evidence of any such discussions simply has not survived. All we can say with any confidence is that by the end of the second century a fourfold Gospel canon seems firmly established and is virtually never explicitly questioned subsequently. Other traditions about Jesus are cited at times, evidently taken from other Gospels. For example, Origen cites with approval the saying, "He who is near me is near the fire; he who is far from me is far from the kingdom" (*In Jerem. hom. Lat.* 20.3) as a saying of Jesus he has from some (unspecified) source. The saying now appears in the text of the *Gospel of Thomas* 82 (though it is not clear whether the *Gospel of Thomas* itself is Origen's source of information). But such instances never seem to threaten the position of the fourfold Gospel canon. Certainly by the end of the second century one begins to get codices probably containing all four Gospels together in a single volume. Moreover, we have no codices containing a noncanonical Gospel alongside one of the canonical ones. It is clear that, from a very early time, Christians regarded these four texts as both valuable and separable from other literature — hence on the way to becoming part of "canonical" "scripture" (cf. Stanton 1997, who also suggests very plausibly that the use of the codex form itself — as opposed to a scroll — for carrying around the texts of the Gospels may have been a very influential factor in this whole process).

Many of the criteria and arguments used in the past seem strange to us today. Or at least if we applied the same criteria, we might end up with a different canon! It is probably true to say that, in terms of historical accuracy, the NT Gospels provide us with our best sources of evidence for recovering information about Jesus. (The one exception may be the *Gospel of Thomas,* though even that Gospel has almost certainly been overlaid in its present form by an influx of Gnostic-type sayings; at best, only *parts* of the *Gospel of Thomas* may give us access to primitive Jesus traditions.)

Nevertheless, all Gospels scholars today recognize that none of the Gospels gives us immediate and direct access to Jesus. Each of the evangelists has imposed his own ideas on the tradition. In the case of John, this has been accepted for a long time; but it is now increasingly recognized that what applies to John applies equally to the Synoptic evangelists. They, too, have their axes to grind and their own agendas to pursue in telling the Jesus story in the way they have.

The four Gospels in the NT almost certainly give us the *earliest* Gospels we possess. (There may have been others which were earlier still, but, if so, none has survived.) They also provide us with the best sources of information about Jesus which we have. But they also provide us with glimpses of the ways in which Christians struggled to make the traditions about Jesus relevant to their own day and their changed situations. For those who struggle to do the same in the present, the ways in which the Gospels show us earlier Christians grappling with this hermeneutical problem may be in the end just as, if not more, theologically rewarding than simply providing us with sourcebooks for recovering Jesus.

Bibliography. Works Cited in §1. Fallon, F. T., and R. Cameron. 1988, "The Gospel of Thomas," *ANRW* 2.25.6:4196-4251 • Hengel, M. 1985, "The Titles of the Gospels and the Gospel of Mark," in *Studies in the Gospel of Mark,* London: SCM, 64-84 • Koester, H. 1980, "Apocryphal and Canonical Gospels," *HTR* 73:105-30 • Koester, H. 1990, *Ancient Christian Gospels: Their History and Development,* London and Philadelphia: SCM and Trinity Press International • Stanton, G. N. 1992, *A Gospel for a New People: Studies in Matthew,* Edinburgh: T. & T. Clark.

Works Cited in §2. Aune, D. E. 1987, *The New Testament in Its Literary Environment,* London: James Clarke • Bultmann, R. 1963, *The History of the Synoptic Tradition,* ET Oxford: Blackwell • Burridge, R. A. 1992, *What Are the Gospels? A Comparison with Graeco-Roman Biography,* Cambridge: Cambridge University • Guelich, R. A. 1991, "The Gospel Genre," in P. Stuhlmacher, ed., *The Gospel and the Gospels,* Grand Rapids: Eerdmans, 1991, 173-208 (original 1983) • Hirsch, E. 1967, *Validity in Interpretation,* New Haven, Conn.: Yale University • Kähler, M. 1964, *The So-called Historical Jesus and the Historic Biblical Christ,* ET Philadelphia: Fortress (original 1896) • Kermode, F. 1979, *The Genesis of Secrecy: On the Interpretation of Narrative,* Cambridge, Mass., and London: Harvard University • Schweitzer, A. 3d ed. 1954, *The Quest of the Historical Jesus,* ET London: A. & C. Black • Stanton, G. N. 1974, *Jesus of Nazareth in New Testament Preaching,* Cambridge: Cambridge University • Votaw, C. W. 1915, "The Gospel and Contemporary Biographies," *AJT* 19:45-73, 217-49; repr. as *The Gospels and Contemporary Biographies in the Graeco-Roman World,* Philadelphia: Fortress, 1970 • Wrede, W. 1971, *The Messianic Secret,* ET Cambridge and London: James Clarke (German original 1901).

Works Cited in §3. Bellinzoni A. J., ed. 1985, *The Two-Source Hypothesis: A Critical Appraisal,* Macon, Ga.: Mercer University • Bultmann, R. 1971, *The Gospel of John,* ET Philadelphia: Westminster • Catchpole, D. R. 1993, *The Quest for Q,* Edinburgh: T. & T. Clark • Denaux, A., ed. 1992, *John and the Synoptics,* BETL 101, Leuven: Leuven University & Peeters • Dungan, D. L. 1970, "Mark — The Abridgement of Matthew and Luke," in *Jesus and Man's Hope,* Pittsburgh: Pittsburgh Theological Seminary, 1:169-81 • Dungan, D. L., ed. 1990, *The Interrelations of the Gospels,* BETL 95, Leuven: Leuven University & Peeters • Farmer, W. R. 1964, *The Synoptic Problem: A Critical Appraisal,* New York: Macmillan • Fitzmyer, J. A. 1970, "The Priority of Mark and the 'Q' Source in Luke," in *Jesus and Man's Hope,* Pittsburgh: Pittsburgh Theological Seminary, 1:131-70; repr. in Fitzmyer, 1981, *To Advance the Gospel: New Testament Studies,* New York: Crossroad, 3-40 • Fortna, R. 1970, *The Gospel of Signs: A Reconstruction of the Narrative Source Underlying the Fourth Gospel,* Cambridge: Cambridge University • Fortna, R. 1988, *The Fourth Gospel and Its Predecessor,* Edinburgh: T. & T. Clark • Goulder, M. D. 1978, "On Putting Q to the Test," *NTS* 24:218-34 • Goulder, M. D. 1989, *Luke — A New Paradigm,* Sheffield: JSOT • Jacobson, A. D. 1992, *The First Gospel: An Introduction to Q,* Sonoma, Calif.: Polebridge • Kloppenborg, J. S. 1987, *The Formation of Q,* Philadelphia: Fortress • Lindars, B. 1972, *Behind the Fourth Gospel,* London: SPCK • Neirynck, F. 1974, *The Minor Agreements of Matthew and Luke against Mark,* BETL 37, Leuven: Leuven University • Lindars, B. 1992, "John and the Synoptics: 1975-1990," in Denaux 1992: 3-62 • Neville, D. J. 1993, *Arguments from Order in Synoptic Source Criticism: A History and Critique,* Macon, Ga.: Mercer University • Smith, D. M. 1992, *John among the Gospels,* Minneapolis: Fortress • Stanton, G. N. 1992, see Works cited in 1 above • Streeter, B. H. 1924, *The Four Gospels,* London: Macmillan • Tuckett, C. M. 1983, *The Revival of the Griesbach Hypothesis,* Cambridge: Cambridge University • Tuckett, C. M. 1984, "Arguments from Order: Definition and Evaluation," in C. M. Tuckett, ed., *Synoptic Studies,* Sheffield: JSOT, 197-219 • Tuckett, C. M. 1996, *Q and the History of Early Christianity,* Edinburgh: T. & T. Clark.

Works Cited in §4. Koester, H. 1990, see Works cited in §1 above • Kümmel, W. G. 1975, *Introduction to the New Testament,* ET London: SCM • Meade, D. G. 1986, *Pseudonymity and Canon,* Tübingen and Grand Rapids: J. C. B. Mohr and Eerdmans • Stanton, G. N. 1997, "The Fourfold Gospel," *NTS* 43:317-46 • Von Campenhausen, H. 1973, *The Formation of the Christian Bible,* ET London: A. & C. Black.

Matthew

Anthony J. Saldarini

INTRODUCTION

Name, Authorship, Composition, and Date

The modern English name "The Gospel According to Matthew" arose from a variety of titles, called superscriptions, placed above the beginning of the Gospel text in ancient manuscripts. Two of the most reliable manuscripts, Sinaiticus and Vaticanus, have the simple superscription "According to Matthew." The early Christian author Papias (c. AD 125, quoted by the fourth-century historian Eusebius) refers to Matthew as the author of a collection of Jesus' Hebrew/Aramaic sayings or oracles (*logia*). Irenaeus of Lyons (c. 180) speaks of Matthew as the author of a Hebrew Gospel which Irenaeus views as a source of the Greek Gospel According to Matthew, which he possessed. No Hebrew or Aramaic collection of Jesus' sayings has survived, so its existence must remain hypothetical. However, Irenaeus testifies that by the late second century the Greek Gospel of Matthew was available and accepted as authoritative.

The author of the Gospel does not identify himself within the narrative. Tantalizingly, the tax collector who followed Jesus is named "Levi, son of Alphaeus" in Mark 2:14 (cf. Luke 5:27), but is named "Matthew" in this Gospel (9:9). Levi the tax collector does not appear in the lists of the twelve apostles, but the name "Matthew" does; in the Gospel of Matthew the list of the twelve identifies "Matthew" as a tax collector (10:3), while the other lists simply give the name (Mark 3:18; Luke 6:16; Acts 1:13). Some commentators hold that the author of this Gospel subtly substituted his own name, "Matthew," for the otherwise unknown Levi. Others suggest that Levi the tax collector changed his name to Matthew after he began following Jesus (cf. Simon's new name "Peter" in 16:18). Still others propose that the author of this Gospel replaced the otherwise unknown Levi with a symbolic Greek name *Maththaios* ("Matthew") which sounds somewhat like the Greek word for disciple, *mathētēs*. In the end neither the external nor the internal evidence explains satisfactorily the origin of the title "Gospel According to Matthew" or identifies the author of the Gospel. This, however, is not unusual. First-century society valued ancient and traditional writings much more than contemporary Western culture does and cared less about the personal identity and accomplishments of authors. Thus the author of the Gospel remains anonymous without affecting the credibility or authenticity of his work. In this commentary the anonymous author of the Gospel will be referred to interchangeably as "the author of Matthew," "the author of the Gospel," or "Matthew." No claim is made that the apostle Matthew was the author. One other piece of evidence may clarify the author's social setting. He may hint that he is a learned scribe when he compares the scribe of the kingdom to a householder who brings old and new things out of his storeroom (13:52) and when he praises the prophets, wise men, and scribes whom God has sent (23:34).

The Gospel's literary characteristics and its relationships with the other two Synoptic Gospels (Mark and Luke) provide probable evidence dating the Gospel and for the process by which it was composed. The Synoptic Gospels share many sayings and stories, which are often found in the same order. The most convincing hypothesis for their literary relationships concludes that the Gospel According to Mark was composed first and then was used independently by the authors of the Gospels of Matthew and Luke. Since Mark probably was written around the time of the destruction of Jerusalem (AD 70), the Gospel of Matthew must be dated after that. And since Ignatius of Antioch (died c. 107) seems to have cited the Gospel of Matthew, it was probably written in the last two decades of the first century. The Gospel of Matthew drew on a number of oral and written sources besides Mark. Since the Gospels of Matthew and Luke share a number of teachings of Jesus and a couple of stories which are not derived from Mark, both authors probably had available a collection of sayings of Jesus, conventionally designated "Q" (from the German word for "source," *Quelle*). Many scholars have reconstructed and commented on Q, but this commentary will attend only to Matthew.

Social and Historical Setting, Audience, and Community

The Gospel of Matthew has often been placed in the city of Antioch in Syria, the third largest city in the Roman Empire, because it had large Jewish and Christian communities, provided a literate Greek-speaking milieu for the composition of the Gospel, and was the home of Ignatius, the bishop of Antioch, who probably quoted the Gospel in the early second century. However, any city of several thousand people in the eastern Mediterranean would provide the cultural context for the composition of the Gospel, and many of those cities contained a significant Jewish population. Thus scholars have suggested a number of other cities for the origin of the Gospel, including Caesarea, Tyre, and Sidon on the Mediterranean coast, the cities of the Decapolis in Transjordan, and the Galilean cities Tiberias and Sepphoris. No city has gained widespread support. Recent research into the development of Second Temple and early rabbinic Judaism suggests a city near Galilee or Judea. The legal discussions and arguments developed in Matthew's narrative correspond to the legal agenda found in Second Temple Jewish writings such as the Dead Sea Scrolls and *Jubilees* and in the early layers of the Mishnah isolated by Jacob Neusner. The author of Matthew knows and participates in late-first-century Jewish discussions of law, so he probably had contact with the early rabbis who a century later (c. 200) produced the Mishnah, a detailed exposition of Jewish law. Since the rabbis were only a small, local Judean and Galilean group in the late first century and had not become widely influential yet, Galilee or an area contiguous with Galilee or Judea becomes a more probable home for the Gospel of Matthew than Antioch.

The Gospel's author, like the authors of the other NT books, addressed a concrete first-century community or communities of followers of Jesus. No NT writings are missionary documents addressed to nonbelievers. Scholars have argued over the composition of Matthew's community. The majority have held that author was a Jew and his audience/community contained many Jews who had become followers of Jesus (so-called "Jewish Christians"). Since the author shows a special concern for Gentiles (lit. "the nations," used to refer to non-Jews), many have held that the community had a large Gentile membership as well. A minority have argued that the author and audience were virtually all Gentiles. More recently some scholars have argued that the Matthean community was virtually all Jewish and that one purpose of the Gospel was to urge the Jewish followers of Jesus to reach out to Gentiles with the good news about Jesus. This understanding of the author and audience as Jews who followed Jesus depends on a new appreciation of the variety of Jewish communities and movements in the first century. Neither the first-century Jews nor the early followers of Jesus can be defined as unified "orthodox" communities. Rather, Jewish communities included a number of reform movements, messianic and apocalyptic worldviews, political stances toward the imperial authorities, supportive and critical attitudes toward the temple, and interpretations of biblical traditions and laws which competed for followings in Judea and Galilee as well as in diaspora cities. In this context the author of the Gospel of Matthew seems to be a Jewish teacher who believes in and follows Jesus, who teaches and guides his own community of Jewish followers of Jesus, and who tries to refute other Jewish leaders with different views and practices. Thus the Matthean group in the late first century did not differentiate itself as "Christians" in opposition to "Jews." (In other places at the same time communities of Gentile followers of Jesus probably did make such a distinction.) This scenario explains the sharp and often intemperate polemics against the Jewish leaders for which Matthew's Gospel is notorious. The attacks make most sense not as a rejection of "Judaism" by a "Christian" but as an attempt of one teacher and leader to blunt the influence of other leaders and their teachings. These polemics, however, which call the Pharisees hypocrites (23:13-36) and blame the people in Jerusalem for Jesus' death (27:25), have subsequently been used in anti-Semitic attacks which have resulted in discrimination, injury, and death for Jews.

Approach and Limitations of the Commentary

This commentary will stress the Gospel as a literary unity. It will link the stories and teachings to one another in order to explain the purpose of each element in the Gospel as a coherent whole. The commentary presupposes that the late first-century author of the Gospel made use of a variety of early traditions, including the Gospel of Mark, the sayings source Q mentioned above, as well as a number of teachings, stories, and sayings passed on orally or in writing. In composing this Gospel the author rewrote Markan stories and teachings to improve the Greek, make them more concise, and emphasize aspects of Jesus' character, work, and thought which were important to him and his audience. The author of Matthew, like the other three evangelists, interprets and adapts the Jesus tradition to the needs of his audience. He is a relatively conservative and reliable tradent but not a modern historian or archivist recording traditions from the mouth of Jesus.

This commentary will omit some valuable approaches common in larger commentaries, mostly due to limitations of space. It does not proceed verse by verse, explaining words, odd expressions, ancient customs, physical realities, historical events, and unfamiliar outlooks as they occur. Rather, it concentrates on larger units of expression and the most important aspects of the narrative and neglects some of the minutiae of the text. More significantly, the commentary does not consistently compare Matthew's narrative with the parallel and often differing presentations in the other two Synoptic Gospels, Mark and Luke. Though much can be learned from this essential task, describing and explaining each of the differences takes an inordinate amount of space incompatible with a brief commentary. Surprisingly to some, the commentary will not try to determine which teachings may go back to the historical Jesus. For some readers and scholars the identification of such sayings and of the "historical Jesus" constitutes the apex of Gospel study. However, the Jesus tradition has given the church four very different Gospels, all of which were written by second-generation followers of Jesus. Attempts to reconstruct the teachings "behind" the four Gospels are necessarily hypothetical and in fact have not resulted in a broadly acceptable consensus. In addition, the status of each saying and each story must be argued at length. Similarly, no attempt is made to construct the original form of the sayings source (Q) because this task, too, is a very hypothetical and fragile enterprise. At the level of philosophical and theological principle, to locate some kind of privileged truth about Jesus in the pre-Gospel tradition is to narrow the scope of truth excessively and to concede too much to modern skepticism about the kind of literary and theological interpretation found in the Gospels. This commentary concentrates on one authoritative first-century author's interpretation and presentation of Jesus, to understand it in its context and to make it available to Christians and other interested readers today.

Structure and Genre

Outlines of Matthew's Gospel come in several types. Some summarize the content in greater or less detail; others mark off the larger literary units and sub-structures which give the narrative its shape. Still others focus on the narrative action surrounding Jesus, the central character of the Gospel. A few literary observations will provide a general orientation to the movement of the narrative and its contents. The first four chapters introduce Jesus as the Messiah and the Son of God in telling the story of his birth and infancy (chs. 1–2) and the beginning of his public activity (chs. 3–4). The last three chapters recount the climax of Jesus' life, his arrest, condemnation, suffering, and death (chs. 26–27), and his resurrection and final instruction to his disciples to "make disciples of all nations" (ch. 28). The most striking feature of the twenty-one chapters between are Jesus' five "sermons," which are thematic collections of his teachings. The most famous, the Sermon on the Mount (chs. 5–7), summarizes Jesus' teachings. The others instruct disciples how to spread Jesus' message (ch. 10), explain the kingdom of God in parables (ch. 13), teach communal love and forgiveness (ch. 18), and encourage vigilance and hope in the second coming of Jesus and the final judgment (chs. 24–25). The intervening chapters recount Jesus' healings (chs. 8–9), describe the opposition he faced (chs. 11–12; 21–23), and trace the ongoing instruction of his disciples (chs. 14–17; 19–20).

These actions, teachings, and evaluations of Jesus are contained in a narrative which resembles to a limited extent an ancient Greco-Roman "life" (Gk. *bios*) of a famous person. Such a "life" emphasized the virtues and accomplishments of the subject and his moral meaning for the reader. The goal of an ancient "life" was not to attain detailed historical accuracy and completeness as in a modern biography, but to encourage the reader to a life of virtue. In some ways, Jesus' "life" in the Gospel of Matthew resembles ancient "lives of the prophets" which stress their call by God, the role or task to which the prophets are dedicated, and often the sufferings which they must undergo. Some scholars have fruitfully compared the Gospels to aspects of the so-called Greco-Roman "romances" or "novels" which stress the interaction of the hero or heroine with the gods and their escapes from danger. On the other hand, the Gospels lack the highly emotional and erotic motifs common to this literature. Granted these literary similarities, the four canonical Gospels have more in common with one another than with Hebrew or Greco-Roman literary types and constitute an identifiable genre of their own.

Symbols, Themes, Thought, and Theology

The Gospel of Matthew does not discuss or allude to the kind of systematic theology which modern Christians are used to, with its clearly defined, abstract categories such as Christology, justification, salvation, eschatology, and ecclesiology. Commentators have sometimes imposed these categories on the Gospel narrative to the detriment of its vital message and communicative immediacy. On the other hand, the narrative's major symbols, themes, characters, and actions require some kind of organized exposition and interpretation.

Though Jesus is the main character in the Gospel, God is the primary force behind the narrative and in the world as the author of Matthew understands it. As a background character, God is always present and active. Most of the actions and goals of the characters relate positively or negatively to God's purposes and activity. Jesus' birth, mission to Israel, death, and resurrection take place according to God's will. God controls history from creation to the final judgment when the Son of Man will appear. Through it all God is faithful to his people and merciful to them when they sin and fail. God appears most clearly as the Father of Jesus, who is himself the Son of God; and Jesus is reciprocally a cipher for God, God's agent on earth and the mediator between humans and God. Jesus' birth, powers, and wisdom make him more than a prophet or simple representative of God. As Son of the Father, apocalyptic Son of Man, and Messiah, Jesus functions as a heavenly being (cf. the last scene — 28:16-20) who is plenipotentiary for God, that is, "Emmanuel," meaning "God with us" (1:23).

God the Father and Jesus his Son form the center of the web of kinship relations which hold the author's narrative and community together. God as Father to Jesus the Son supports the relationships of love and mercy which hold together the brothers and sisters of Matthew's community. The story of Jesus' birth implies that he is not Joseph's son but God's, and at crucial moments God reveals that Jesus is his Son, especially at the baptism and transfiguration (3:17; 17:5). In turn Jesus acknowledges the importance of knowing and recognizing the Father (11:25-27), especially when Peter, who speaks for the disciples, calls Jesus the Messiah and Son of God (16:16-17; cf. also 14:33). The apocalyptic phenomena at the death of Jesus make clear even to the Roman centurion and his soldiers, who are "neutral" observers, that Jesus is the Son of God (27:54). Satan (3:17) and the demons (8:28-29) know that Jesus is the Son of God through their otherworldly knowledge.

Because the title "Son of God" carries with it connotations of trinitarian theology for modern Christians, it is important to review the first-century Jewish understanding of this term which Matthew actualized in his narrative. The Judean kings, preeminently David, were the sons of God in a special way. God promised to treat David's son as his own son and not reject him (2 Sam 7:14). This stress on royal kinship merges divine with human rule in Israel. Ps 2:7 extends the hope of divine and Israelite rule over all the earth: "The LORD said to me, 'You are my son.' . . . I will give you the nations for an inheritance." That the hopes found in these two passages were alive among Jewish groups in the first century can be seen in the Qumran midrash on the last days (4Q174, also called *Florilegium* or *Eschatological Midrashim*), which quotes 2 Samuel 7 and Psalm 2 together. The themes of divine election, sonship, and eschatological royal power are also found in the so-called "Son of God text" found at Qumran (4Q246 or 4QpsDan ar[a]) in which a king is being addressed and promised that his son "shall be hailed (as) the son of God, and they shall call him son of the Most High." Second Temple literature recognizes a wider sense of the Son of God as a righteous person. The righteous one helps his fellow humans, endures suffering from the unjust, and in the right circumstances rules wisely as God wills (Sir 4:10 [Heb.]). Such righteousness in responding to God fits Matthew's stress on obedience to the law and God's will. God's care for the just, like his care for the king, is expressed in kinship terms which transcend the present. The book of *Jubilees* has God predict to Moses that Israel will return to God and keep the commandments. Then "I shall be a Father to them, and they will be sons to me. And they will all be called 'sons of the living God.' And every angel and spirit will know and acknowledge that they are my sons . . . and I shall love them" (*Jub.* 1:24-25; cf. also *Pss. Sol.* 17:26-27). The just sons of God are frequently persecuted by the wicked, but vindicated by God (Wis 2:16-18; 5:5), as is Jesus when threatened by Herod (Matthew 2). In Second Temple Judaism the son obeys God faithfully and can depend on God for favor, protection, or, in the case of persecution, vindication.

Jesus is also the Christ, a Greek word which translates the Hebrew *Mashiaḥ* (Messiah), meaning "anointed one." The title "Messiah/Christ" was the earliest and preeminent title used for Jesus by his followers. As early as Paul's letters (the fifties of the first century) Christ is treated as part of Jesus' name as well as a title; similarly in Matthew it is both a name (1:1) and a separate title (1:17). In the HB kings and high priests were anointed when appointed to office. In Second Temple Jewish apocalypses a Messiah is a powerful figure sent by God to intervene in an evil world on behalf of those faithful to God. This intermediary may be designated as an anointed king like David who will war against evil and rule once it is destroyed or an anointed priest or may be a similar kind of figure such as a prophet like Moses (Deut 18:18) or an angelic warrior. Contrary to many Christian understandings of the Messiah, not all Jews were expecting a Messiah. Some first-century Jews did not accept the relatively recent teachings about the end of the world; others expected God to intervene directly without the use of an intermediary. Those who hoped for a messianic figure had a variety of expectations. The early followers of Jesus had to integrate into this web of apocalyptic hopes something new, a Messiah who had suffered, been executed, and risen from the dead.

In the Gospels Jesus frequently refers to a figure called the "Son of Man"; the literary context makes it very clear that Jesus is referring to himself. However, this figure and the term or title "Son of Man" are so ambiguous that their meanings and connotations have been greatly disputed. Jesus uses the expression "Son of Man" of himself when speaking, but the author of Matthew never uses it when he describes Jesus. Outside the Gospels "Son of Man" appears only three times in the NT (Acts 7:5; Rev 1:13; 14:14). Later Christian writers dropped the expression when referring to Jesus, probably because it had so little specific content that it could not stand on its own and because the Greek expression, literally "the son of the man," is unidiomatic and awkward. Thus the dynamics of the narrative and associated titles, allusions, and metaphors are needed to give shape to the meaning of "Son of Man."

In later Aramaic dialects, *bar '[e]nash[a']* ("son of man") is an idiomatic way of saying "human being." Some scholars claim that this is the primary meaning of the expression in the first century, but direct evidence is lacking. In many cases Matthew uses the title "Son of Man" in an apocalyptic context (13:41; 16:28; 19:28; 24:30; 25:31 are proper to him and not derived from Mark). This usage depends on the heavenly, royal figure in Daniel who is described as "one like a son of man" (Dan 7:13; cf. Mark 14:62; Matt 26:64) who comes to rule God's kingdom after evil is destroyed. In Daniel this figure is either an angel or a symbolic representation of the people of Israel. A Son of Man appears in 4 Ezra 13, the *Similitudes of Enoch* (*1 Enoch* 37–71), and the *Apocalypse of Abraham* (A 12-13, B 8), where he fulfills eschatological roles as a redeemer, ruler, or judge. He fulfills similar functions in some places in Matthew (10:23; 24:3, 27; 26:64) and is treated as authoritative in others (9:6; 12:8). However, the Son of Man also suffers (17:9, 22; 20:18) and is rejected (8:20; 11:19; 12:32). Consequently, some commentators understand the expression "Son of Man" to connote Jesus' humanity more than his apocalyptic and authoritative roles.

The kingdom of God is the central symbol in the teachings of Jesus. The author of Matthew most often speaks of "the kingdom of heaven"; in this expression "heaven" is used as a euphemism for God. This use of metonymy (substituting a related item for the one being spoken of; e.g., calling a king "the crown") was common in early Judaism. Similarly, the metaphor "kingdom" refers to God's rule over humans and the created world, not to a limited territory or to a circumscribed period such as the end of the world. The Gospel of Matthew conceives of God's kingdom as both present and future. God rules actively in and through Jesus and his followers, who are faithful to God (cf. 3:2; 4:17; 10:7; 11:12; 12:28, 41-42; 13:16-17). God's kingdom or rule will be fully revealed and realized when God intervenes at the end of the world, judges and destroys evil, and transforms the world (6:10; 8:11; 16:28; 25:1, 34). Many other passages about the kingdom treat it as both present and future. The author of Matthew, along with the HB and the other Gospels, understands God's rule (kingdom) as an ongoing relationship with the created world and humanity. He concentrates on clarifying Jesus' authoritative role as God's representative and on the disciples' and crowds' reception of and adherence to the kingdom through obedience to God's will.

Scholars have long disputed over whether the late-first-century author of the Gospel expects an imminent end of the world or sees the end as delayed. Warnings concerning the coming judgment, threats of punishment against those who do evil, and apocalyptic imagery suffuse the Gospel. Thus the author of Matthew orients his readers toward the coming of the Son of Man and the judicial evaluation of human activity. On the other hand, the Gospel of Matthew attends to the ongoing life of the church community in a way which suggests that the end may not be near. This double thrust in the narrative indicates that the modern question concerning the imminence of the end may be foreign to the Gospel. The author encourages a fervent dedication to Jesus and to his new, politically powerless and vulnerable movement. Such dedication requires both an enthusiastic engagement with a community which follows Jesus and a wider vision which offers hope that God will prevail over the hostile powers of the Roman Empire and the local opponents of the community. Thus the seemingly contrary emphases on establishing a community and waiting eagerly for the end work together to stabilize and encourage Matthew's group of followers of Jesus.

Jesus' disciples constitute a corporate character which symbolizes the faithful followers of Jesus after Jesus' death, including the Matthean community. They are the most important characters in the Gospel narrative after Jesus. In the Gospel of Mark the disciples frequently misunderstand Jesus completely and are harshly criticized. The Gospel of Matthew portrays them more positively. When they misunderstand, they seek instruction from Jesus and learn (13:10-11, 36, 52; 15:15-16; 16:12). When they lack faith (6:30; 8:26; 14:31; etc.), Jesus instructs and encourages them. Their very designation as disciples indicates that they are learners attached to their teacher and master Jesus. The status of disciple is so permanent that even after Jesus has died, they do not use the usual titles of rabbi, father, and master because Jesus and God retain these roles (23:8-12); they remain disciples. At the end of the Gospel Jesus commands them to do for all nations what he did for them, that is, to make them disciples (28:19). The disciples replicate Jesus' work in their lives: they heal (10:1, 8; unsuccessfully in 17:14-20), teach (10:7; 28:20), and exercise authority (16:17-19; 18:15-20). Jesus requires these faithful followers to be just or righteous (*dikaios*), that is, to obey God's will as revealed in the Bible and in Jesus' teaching (1:19; 3:15; 5:6, 10; 6:33; 12:18, 20; 21:32; etc.). As a result of their responsiveness to God they are the righteous or just who will be vindicated at the judgment (12:37; 13:43, 49; 25:37, 46). Matthew does not use the term "righteousness" in the same way as Paul, nor does he see any tension between righteousness and biblical law. Rather, in Matthew Jesus obeys the law and teaches his followers to do the same. Jesus in the narrative and the author of the Gospel in his own time dispute with other Jewish leaders over the proper interpretation of biblical law. Thus the Gospel of Matthew contains a number of extended arguments defending Jesus' interpretation of the law as Matthew understands it (5:20-48; 12:1-14; 15:1-20; 23:16-26).

Two other salient characteristics of the Gospel require comment: its frequent use of Scripture and its polemical attacks on the Jewish authorities. Though all four Gospels quote and allude to the Hebrew and Greek Scriptures frequently, the Gospel of Matthew does so more formally and self-consciously. He introduces approximately a dozen quotations with a formula which explicitly claims that Jesus has fulfilled a prophecy or Scripture in general. These fulfillment prophecies are not empirical proofs, but they do link Jesus to the ultimate source of authority in the Jewish tradition, Scripture. Because of variations in the formulae used, scholars differ in the number of passages they call fulfillment quotations. Granted variations in formula, the following are frequently cited: 1:22-23; 2:5-6, 15; 2:17-18; 2:23; 3:3; 4:14-16; 8:17; 11:10; 12:17-21; 13:35; 21:4-5; 26:31; 27:9-10. The fulfillment of Scripture without a specific quotation is mentioned twice (26:54, 56). In addition to the formal quotations, the Gospel contains numerous other quotations from Scripture and allusions to passages and biblical figures such as Moses, Elijah, and David. This rich biblical texture links the Gospel narrative to the biblical tradition and to Israel, and most especially to God who reveals himself through them.

Finally, the Gospel of Matthew includes a series of notoriously harsh attacks on the Jewish leaders in the narrative who opposed Jesus. The author refers symbolically to the community leaders opposing him in the late first century, but Christians have applied these attacks to all Jews for centuries. The Jerusalem crowd's acceptance of responsibility for the execution of Jesus, whom they understood to be a threat to their community ("His blood be upon us and our children"), turned into a monstrous charge of blood libel against all Jews which in turn led to the death of many Jews in the Middle Ages and the modern period. Matthew's polemical condemnation of the scribes and Pharisees as "hypocrites" has so formed the consciousness of Western Christians that "Pharisaic" and "hypocritical" are synonyms in English dictionaries. Generations of Christians have confidently, but mistakenly, asserted that the Pharisees were legalistic and insincere, despite historical evidence to the contrary. The first-century Jewish author of the Gospel of Matthew did not reject or condemn all Jews. He sought to blunt the influence of the leaders who opposed his own community and, in his view, Jesus before him. The author of Matthew was not an outsider condemning Judaism, but a Jew arguing with his fellow Jews. Polemics like these abound in the Dead Sea Scrolls, especially in the scriptural interpretations ("Pesharim") and the *Damascus Covenant*. For example, in the Qumran interpretation of Hab 2:8 (1QpHab) the verse "concerns the last priests of Jerusalem, who amass wealth and profit from the plunder of the peoples; but at the end of days their wealth together with their booty will be given into the hand of the army of the Kittim [Romans]," and it also concerns the "Wicked Priest [an unidentified Jerusalem high priest], whom — because of wrong done to the Teacher of Righteousness [a leader of the Qumran community] and his partisans — God gave into the hand of his enemies to humble him with disease for annihilation in despair, because he had acted wickedly against his chosen ones [the Qumran community]." These attacks among Jewish leaders are no less harsh than those in the Gospel. However, even though the author of the Gospel of Matthew was not an anti-Semitic Gentile, the harm done by his words is not lessened. Polemics among Jews caused deaths in the first century, and those words, transposed to a new setting, have done even greater harm. Gentile Christians of later centuries used the words of brothers fighting with one another to denigrate and nihilate the whole Jewish people and Judaism itself. The communal reading of the attacks against Jewish leaders in the Gospel remains a permanent peril to Jewish lives and Christian souls.

The presence of Jewish thought and culture in the Gospel of Matthew invites comparisons of Jews and Christians. Many interpreters have read the narrative as a progressive rejection of Jesus by Jews and of Jews by the author of the Gospel. According to this view, God's purpose in history, to save all humans, began with Israel, but in Jesus "salvation history" left Israel behind and continued to develop in the Christian community. Regrettably this theological scheme has often silenced and denigrated Jews. For many Christians "the Jews" are God's people in the OT, that is, the HB, up to the time of Jesus. From Jesus on God turns his eyes on Christians and gives them his love, care, and guidance. Israel is no longer the people of God. Jews, Judaism, and Israel all cease to be relevant. This dangerous supersessionism still lives at the heart of many Christian theologies. In this scheme Christianity is the completion, fulfillment, development, improvement, or broadening of Judaism. However, such an inaccurate portrayal of Jews and Judaism only establishes an inauthentic Christian identity at a terrible price, namely, portraying Judaism as an abstract caricature and as the inadequate religion Christians left behind. The reality is quite other. God remains faithful to Israel in Matthew. Jesus works within Israel, seeking to instruct and reform its people according to a new revelation from God. The author of Matthew does the same in his generation. Suggestions that the Gospel or Jesus rejects "Judaism" can be sustained only by the imposition of artificial dispensations of salvation. The author of Matthew lives in a more messy and unfinished world where God still works vitally with both the people of Israel and Gentiles.

Bibliography for Introduction and Commentary in General. Aune, D. E., ed. 2001, *The Gospel of Matthew in Current Study,* Grand Rapids: Eerdmans • Carter, W. 1996, *Matthew: Storyteller, Interpreter, Evangelist,* Peabody, Mass.: Hendrickson • Davies W. D., and D. C. Allison. 1988, 1991, 1997, *The Gospel According to St. Matthew,* 3 vols., ICC, Edinburgh: Clark • Hagner, D. A. 1993, 1995, *Matthew,* 2 vols., WBC, Dallas: Word • Harrington, D. J. 1991, *The Gospel of Matthew,* Collegeville, Minn.: Liturgical Press, Glazier • Keener, C. S. 1999, *A Commentary on the Gospel of Matthew,* Grand Rapids: Eerdmans • Kingsbury, J. D. 2d ed., 1988, *Matthew as Story,* Philadelphia: Fortress • Koester, H. 1990, *Ancient Christian Gospels: Their History and Development,* Philadelphia: Trinity Press International; London: SCM • Levine, A.-J. 1988, *The Social and Ethnic Dimensions of Matthean Salvation History,* Lewiston: Edwin Mellen • Overman, J. A. 1990, *Matthew's Gospel and Formative Judaism: The Social World of the Matthean Community,* Minneapolis: Fortress • Saldarini, A. J. 1994, *Matthew's Christian-Jewish Community,* Chicago: University of Chicago • Saldarini, A. J. 1997, "How Do We Understand Early Jews and Christians? A New Paradigm," in *Removing the Weeds of Hatred from Jesus' Garden of Love,* Philadelphia: American Interfaith Institute, 25-37 • Saldarini, A. J. 1997, "Understanding Matthew's Vitriol," *BibRev* 13:32-39, 44-45 • Sim, D. C. 1996, *Apocalyptic Eschatology in the Gospel of Matthew,* SNTSMS 88, Cambridge: Cambridge University; Sim, D. C. 1998, *The Gospel of Matthew and Christian Judaism: The History and Social Setting of the Matthean Community,* Edinburgh: T&T Clark • Stanton, G. N. 1992, *A Gospel for a New People: Studies in Matthew,* Edinburgh: T & T. Clark.

COMMENTARY

Introduction to the Infancy Narrative (Matthew 1–2)

The genealogy and dramatic birth stories introduce Jesus, the main character of the Gospel, by connecting him with the biblical narratives and their main characters. They authenticate him as God's representative promised by the Bible. Jesus relives the stories of Jacob/Israel going down into Egypt, Moses leading the people of Israel out of Egypt, and David ruling over the people as God's anointed king. The biblical language, stories, and allusions introduce many motifs, symbols, and narrative patterns found throughout the Gospel. Scholars dispute whether the author of Matthew created these introductory stories through meditation on Scripture or gathered a series of traditional stories or revised a preexistent narrative, but all agree that Matthew has shaped the stories to serve his overall narrative purposes.

Jesus Christ's Genealogy (1:1-17)

The first four Greek words of the Gospel are literally, "The book of the genesis of Jesus Christ." The genesis of Jesus may refer to his genealogy (1:1-17; cf. Gen 5:1) or to his story (Gen 2:4), either the story of his birth (chs. 1–2) or his life (the whole Gospel). A book (Gk. *biblos,* closely related to *biblion*) may refer to a document (Jer 32:10-16), a letter (Jer 29:1), a record, or an account as well as what we call a book or scroll (Jeremiah 36; Acts 7:42). Thus this type of heading, common in ancient books, introduces the genealogy (the meaning supported in the NRSV and NIV) as well as the birth narrative (chs. 1–2) and the whole story of Jesus. The phrase "the book of the genesis" is used in Gen 2:4 and recalls the Greek title of the biblical book of Genesis. The Gospel of Mark may have a similar resonance with Genesis when it speaks of "The beginning of the gospel" (Mark 1:1).

The name Jesus will be treated under 1:21. Christ is the Greek translation of Heb. *mashiaḥ* (Messiah), meaning "anointed one." In Jewish apocalyptic literature of the Second Temple period people expected divine intervention either by God directly or through an intermediary identified as an anointed one, an angelic warrior, a son of man, a descendant of David, a specially anointed priest, or a prophet like Moses (Deut 18:18). The dramatic final events and roles of these intermediaries varied considerably. The title "Messiah/Christ" was the earliest and preeminent title used for Jesus by his followers. Here the title seems to be treated as part of Jesus' name, though elsewhere it is clearly a separate title (1:17).

From all the names in the genealogy two are chosen to be placed in the heading, David and Abraham. During the Second Temple period the designation "son of David" and similar expressions like the "shoot or root of Jesse" (Isa 11:1, 10) were associated with expectations of a new, anointed Davidic king (a Messiah) to relieve Israel's suffering. Matthew uses "son of David" nine times (1:1, 20; 9:27; 12:23; 15:22; 20:30, 31; 21:9, 15), much more than any other NT book. The infancy narrative identifies Jesus as a messianic king through the genealogical relationship with David and his birth in Bethlehem. "Son of Abraham" affirms Jesus' place as a Jew within the biblical narrative about God's people Israel and implicitly refers to the promises made to Israel through Abraham. Just as David brought the promises of land, people, and blessing to their high point by establishing an independent kingdom, Jesus will restore Israel in a new way. The genealogy elaborates Jesus' initial identification as Christ, son of David, and son of Abraham and repeats the identification in the final verse (1:17), where the three are named in chronological order to form an inclusion which concludes the genealogy.

The author of Matthew has constructed a genealogy explicitly said to contain three groups of fourteen ancestors extending from Abraham to Jesus (1:17). In fact, the last group has only thirteen members, like many traditional numbered lists which often have less or more members than they claim. The reason for groups of fourteen is not clear. The Hebrew letters of the name "David" *(dwd)* have the numerical value fourteen, which fits Matthew's emphasis on David but would not be an obvious message to a Greek-speaking audience. Fourteen is double seven, which is a favorite biblical number, but the text contains groups of fourteen, not seven. A later rabbinic chain of tradition in *m. 'Abot* 1 has fourteen members in some versions. Perhaps the author began with the fourteen members of the first group, who are all well attested in the Bible, and then organized his remaining materials into two more groups of fourteen.

The genealogy begins with the common ancestor of Israel, Abraham, and is divided into three groups ending with the reign of David, the founder of the first dynasty, with the destruction of the Jerusalem and its temple, which marks the end of the Davidic dynasty, and with Jesus. The promises of land, people, and blessings to Abraham reach their high point in the kingdom established by David and their low point in the loss of sovereignty and exile of many of the people by the Babylonians. Implicitly, the genealogy points to the reestablishment of God's rule (the kingdom of heaven) through an anointed king, Jesus.

The names in the first group of fourteen ancestors come from 1 Chronicles 1–2 and are well known. Those in the second group come from 1 Chr 3:10-15 with the omission of three unworthy kings (Joash, Amaziah, and Azariah). The sequence of names in the third group is not found in any biblical genealogy, though they are common Jewish names. The final group may depend on an unknown genealogical source or may have been constructed by Matthew to link the biblical genealogies with Jesus as the Messiah and successor to David. In general, people map out genealogies to accomplish political, social, or religious purposes such as to explain how peoples are related to one another or to legitimate a political union of groups and peoples or to authenticate leadership status for certain families. They often begin with a common ancestor, finish with the immediate ancestors of the person making the genealogy, and are abbreviated or have variations in the middle.

The names of four women are included in the list: Tamar (Genesis 38), Rahab (Joshua 2), Ruth of the book of Ruth, and Bathsheba (2 Samuel 11–12). Each of them may be, or have been thought of as, a Gentile who joined Israel, and each of them marks a disruption in the ideal genealogy one would want for an ideal Davidic king. But each was committed to Israel. Tamar saw to the carrying on of the name of Er, according to Jewish law, by tricking Judah his father into marrying her. Rahab saved Joshua's spies and aided in the conquest of the land of Israel. Ruth bound herself willingly to Israel as Boaz's wife, and Bathsheba, who was seduced by David, bore his successor Solomon and intervened to assure Solomon's succession to the throne (1 Kings 1). Since first-century interpreters probably considered these women to be proselytes, they may have symbolized Gentile proselytes joining Matthew's group of Christian-Jewish followers of Jesus. They also prepare for the end of the genealogy where the succession suddenly shifts from Joseph to Mary and then Jesus.

At the end of the genealogy (1:16) the author prepares for the story of Jesus' conception by the Holy Spirit in identifying Joseph, not as "the father of Jesus" (the pattern of the genealogy), but as the husband of Mary, the fifth woman named in the genealogy, "of whom [Mary] Jesus was born, who was called Christ." Joseph's non-fathership of Jesus is made explicit in the following story and in his dreams when the angel twice tells him to "take the child and his mother" to Egypt and back to Israel (2:13-14, 20-21). The genealogy is Joseph's because he is the legal parent of Jesus and descent is traced through the male side. The theory that an original genealogy has Jesus as the son of Joseph and was later changed has no foundation in the text.

Jesus' Origin (1:18–2:23)

The story of Jesus' conception and birth (1:18-25) begins and ends with Jesus Christ's name (in the Greek), as does each of the first two chapters. Together these chapters explain who Jesus is, where he comes from, and his relationship with God. Jesus' conception without a human father implies that Jesus is God's Son and the Davidic king of the Jews. The early tradition about Jesus' virginal conception (which appears in a different form in Luke 1:31-35) may have provoked accusations that Jesus was an illegitimate child as it certainly did in later polemics. If so, the stories of Jesus' origin defend against this charge.

The story of Jesus' marvelous conception and birth as

a divinely chosen leader brings religious figures from the East ready to recognize Jesus' kingship (2:1-12) and provokes violent opposition from the notorious king who held power in the first century BC, Herod the Great (2:1-23). These stories are bound together not only by narrative sequence but also by characters, literary patterns, and biblical typology. All the action takes place around the infant Jesus and his mother, but they are passive characters all the way through, in contrast to Luke 1–2 where Mary is a major actor in a series of scenes. Joseph initiates the action as an ideal Matthean character, a just man (1:19) who follows the law and other expressions of God's will. He is the recipient of three dream revelations from a divine messenger, and his obedient response to instructions leads to his marriage to Mary, their escape from danger into Egypt with their child, and their return to Israel and Nazareth. The three dreams which give divine guidance (1:20-23; 2:13-14, 19-21) have a common structure: an introduction, the appearance of an angel, and a message including a command and a supporting reason.

Biblical, Near Eastern, and Greco-Roman typology have all influenced the stories of Jesus' origins. Stories of marvelous births of future leaders were common in the ancient Near East and Greco-Roman world. For example, the story of Moses' birth and escape from danger is similar to an older story of Sargon of Akkad, the (legendary) originator of the Akkadian dynasty. The story of Mary's virginal conception through God's power recalls God's intervention in the births of Isaac (Gen 18:9-15), Jacob (Gen 25:19-26), and Samuel (1 Samuel 1) to overcome their mothers' barrenness. These kinds of stories emphasize divine legitimation for the leader's life, decisions, and actions.

The author of Matthew draws upon biblical and postbiblical traditions about Moses to clarify and establish Jesus' teaching and authority through his close relationship with God. The threat to Moses from Pharaoh, the evil Egyptian king, matches the threat to Jesus from Herod. Dream visions guide Moses' and Jesus' parents. Both Moses and Jesus escaped danger and were later ordered to return respectively to Egypt and Israel. The author of Matthew has provided five explicit citations from Scripture (1:23; 2:6, 15, 18, 23) introduced by a special formula in order to make the typological dimension clear.

The story begins with a pregnant Mary engaged to Joseph. According to Jewish custom, when Joseph and Mary were engaged, their families signed a marriage contract which regulated the transfer of property and set out the rights and duties of each party, including food, clothing, ransom from captivity, and provision for the wife and child if the husband died. Babatha's Aramaic marriage contract (early 2d cent. AD) and other Aramaic and Greek contracts found in the wilderness of Judea contain such stipulations. Unlike engagement in contemporary Western culture, engagement in the Near East was a serious and final commitment; voiding the contract required a divorce document which freed the woman to marry another. Mary's pregnancy required Joseph to separate himself from a woman supposedly carrying another man's baby. The audience knows that the child has been conceived by God's power through the agency of the Spirit rather than by sexual intercourse, but Joseph does not until informed by a dream vision. The author declares Joseph "just," that is, one who follows God's law (see 5:20). First he chooses private divorce rather than public denunciation (Num 5:11-31) as the preferred legal solution, and then he obeys the dream vision: "He took his wife" (literal translation), which probably means that he took Mary, who was already his wife through the marriage contract, home to his house.

The author explicates these extraordinary events through an interpretation of the name Jesus and the citation of a passage from Scripture. The angel commands Joseph to name the child "Jesus" because he will save his people from their sins (v. 21). A change of name often accompanies a call by God (Abram to Abraham in Genesis and Saul to Paul in Acts). Here the name Jesus *(Iēsous)* is a Greek rendition of the Hebrew name *Yehoshuaʿ*, which is shortened to *Yoshuaʿ* (Joshua) and later to *Yeshuaʿ*, Jesus, which was a common Jewish name during the Second Temple period. The first part of the name *(yeho, yo, ye)* is an abbreviated form of God's proper name, *YHWH*, usually vocalized Yahweh. The second part of the name, transliterated as Heb. *shuaʿ* or Gk. *sous*, is probably from a group of similar words (*shuaʿ* etc.) which mean a cry for help. By the first century AD the names Joshua and Jesus were popularly associated with a similar-sounding Hebrew verb *yashaʿ*, "to save" (e.g., Sir 46:1 and Philo *Mut. nom.* 121), and that understanding of the name appears here. Matthew specifies salvation *from sins* (cf. 9:2, 10-13; 20:28), a task which Jesus will accomplish by his death at the end of the Gospel.

A quotation from the Bible introduced by a fulfillment formula (v. 22) provides the second explanation for Jesus and the events surrounding his birth. Matthew's unique formal introductions stress prophecies which Jesus fulfills and lend the authority of Scripture to Jesus' words and deeds. The quotation from Isa 7:14 gives Jesus a second, symbolic Hebrew name, "Emmanuel," which means "God with us." This name establishes Jesus' status as a divine representative on earth, a role which reaches its climax at the end of the Gospel when Jesus tells his disciples that he will be with them until the end of the age (28:20). The quotation, with its mention of a virgin conceiving, also corroborates Mary's virginal conception of Jesus. The Hebrew original speaks of an *ʿalmah,* which is a young woman of childbearing age who has not yet had a child and who may be an unmarried virgin or a married young woman. The Greek translation of the Bible, the LXX, chose the Greek word for virgin *(parthenos)* to translate the Hebrew and so provided an opportunity for Matthew's interpretation. The final verse of the chapter further verifies Jesus' virginal conception by noting that Joseph did not have sexual intercourse with Mary until she gave birth. The Greek expression for "until" neither affirms nor denies that she remained a virgin for life, as patristic and medieval interpretations affirmed.

The first chapter put Jesus into the context of Israel's history; ch. 2 locates him in the political, social, and geographic world of the first century. Herod the Great was appointed king of Israel by the Roman senate in 40 BC and ruled until his death in 4 BC. He was brave in battle, politically astute, loyal to his Roman masters, and energetic in his building projects and benefactions in Israel and elsewhere in the Roman Empire. He was also an autocrat with effective secret police who ruthlessly killed or suppressed anyone who might threaten his power, including his favorite wife, some of his sons, other members of his family, and the Judean governing class. Matthew sharply contrasts Herod, the Roman client king who ruled the Jews in Jerusalem, Judea, and the surrounding areas, with Jesus, the true "king of the Jews" (2:2), just as he contrasts the Roman authorities with Jesus the "King of the Jews" at the end of the Gospel (27:11, 29, 37). Only at the beginning and end of his life does Jesus go to the Jerusalem area in this Gospel, and both times his life is endangered by the political authorities. In both cases the social, political "facts" have a major impact on Jesus but do not control the movement of history as a whole nor blunt God's goals, which are fulfilled through Jesus even as he is executed.

The stories in ch. 2 locate Jesus within the geography of the Near East, especially as it is reflected in the Bible. The first verse informs us that Jesus was born in Bethlehem. In contrast to Luke, Matthew does not have Joseph and Mary travel to Bethlehem but assumes that they live there in a house (2:11), as descendants of David. Jesus and his family escape danger from Herod by fleeing to Egypt, just as Jacob/Israel and his family escaped famine by migrating to Egypt (Genesis 46). After Herod dies and the danger to Jesus ceases, Jesus is called out of Egypt, as were Moses and Israel after Pharaoh died (2:23; cf. also 4:19; Exodus 3–15), and returns to the land of Israel, but this time to Nazareth in Galilee, which was well ruled by Antipas, one of Herod's sons (2:22-23). In Galilee Jesus lives his whole life, according to Matthew, except for the trip to Jerusalem which leads to his execution. Matthew leads his readers to Galilee, where they will see and hear Jesus heal and teach near the shores of the Sea of Galilee (chs. 3–20).

The Magi from the East precipitate the conflict between Herod and Jesus. *Magus* is from a Persian word for the learned religious leaders of Zoroastrianism, the traditional Persian religion until the Islamic conquest in the seventh century. In Greek and Latin this word was used for any religious wise man who represented a non-Greco-Roman religion and in a pejorative sense for a magician or charlatan. Magi were widely associated with astrology and knowledge of the stars as they are here. All stories about where they came from and what they were like are later Christian legends. In the text the "east" may refer to the Arabian desert, or Mesopotamia, or Persia. In Matthew the Magi are foreigners who recognize Jesus as a king through their interpretation of the stars. They enter Herod's court in Jerusalem like ambassadors seeking to make contact with a foreign king, but ironically not with Herod. Thus they threatened Herod and "all Jerusalem" (meaning the governing classes allied with Herod). The Jerusalem authorities thus meet to confront the potential danger to Herod's rule because in the Bible what we call religion and politics were one integrated whole which defined the nation and people of Israel. When Jesus taught a different interpretation of Israel's beliefs and way of life, he became a political threat and evoked a violent response. As a foreshadowing of that, his presence here provokes a violent response from Herod, who was noted for his vigorous and even paranoid attacks on any hint of opposition.

The learned priests and scribes do what Matthew does to find "the anointed one" (the Christ): they interpret Scripture. In this case Mic 5:1, 3 says that a ruler who will shepherd (meaning "rule," 2 Sam 5:2) Israel will come from Bethlehem and that the authorities will unwittingly confirm Jesus' royal status, since he has already been born in Bethlehem (2:1). With their help and the star the Magi find Jesus, and they complete their "embassy" by paying due homage to him and presenting their gifts. Though some translations say that they worshiped him, the Greek word means to show due honor to a king, as well as to God. Thus homage probably fits the narrative better here, though Matthew plays on the double meaning. Their embassy done, the Magi blunt Herod's strategy for finding and killing Jesus through a divinely given dream (like Joseph) and return home.

The Magi symbolize the subtle but powerful forces arrayed against Herod and his fellow leaders as they try to exclude Jesus, and they foreshadow Jesus' unusual victory over his opponents at the end of the Gospel. They are extraordinary Gentiles who join with Jesus' parents in recognizing his God-given status and role as Messiah. Similarly, Matthew's community is composed of Jews and some Gentiles who accept Jesus as Messiah. The Magi are not active political, military leaders who can bring force to bear to save Jesus against Herod, but they can, with divine guidance and help, contribute to his life and work. Similarly, Matthew's community is a minority within a larger Jewish and Greco-Roman world which finds divine guidance and help through the teachings, life, and death of Jesus.

After the Magi leave, Herod continues his attack against Jesus in a way similar to Pharaoh's attack against Israel and Moses in Egypt. The result is inevitable: Jesus escapes and lives to lead his people. The three quotations introduced by Matthew's fulfillment formula give the final stages of this story a unique biblical depth. Jesus' flight into Egypt resembles that of Jacob and his family faced with famine as well as Jeroboam escaping Solomon (1 Kgs 11:40) and the prophet Uriah escaping Jehoiakim (Jer 26:21). However, Matthew understands Egypt not as a refuge but as a place Israel and Jesus must leave, with God's help, in order to return to the land of Israel. Thus he anticipates the return of Jesus at the end of the story. The source of the quotation, Hos 11:1-4, speaks of God's maternal love for Israel, and the first verse applies perfectly to God's care for the child Jesus: "When Israel was a child, I loved him, and out of Egypt I called my son." The second quotation (Jer 31:15 in Matt 2:18) addresses the horrible deaths of the children of Bethlehem at Herod's hand in an elliptical and suggestive fashion. Matthew follows a later biblical tradition that the tomb of Rachel, the mother of Benjamin and Joseph (from whom come the northern tribes Ephraim and Manasseh) is at Ephratha near Bethlehem (Gen 35:16-20; 48:7). He has Rachel mourning the deaths of the children killed in Bethlehem, who are actually descendants of Judah, her sister Leah's son.

Disputes over the location of Rachel's tomb and the identity of the people being mourned blur the scene of Rachel mourning. According to an early biblical tradition, Rachel's tomb was in the tribe of Benjamin (one of her children) at an (unknown) place called Zelzah (1 Sam 10:2). It was probably later identified with an Ephratha located north of Jerusalem near Kiriath-jearim; later it was confused with the Ephratha, located near Bethlehem. This confusion of places serves Matthew well because Rachel can mourn the children of Bethlehem. In using Jer 31:15 in this way Matthew has changed the object of Jeremiah's oracle. In Jeremiah, when the inhabitants of Jerusalem and Judea are taken into exile to Babylon (586 BC), they are gathered for transport at Rama, five miles north of Jerusalem (Jer 40:1). Thus the mention of Rama suggests sorrow for the Judean exiles. However, in ch. 31 Jeremiah, anticipating the return of all Israel in a new exodus, refers explicitly to Ephraim, Rachel's grandchild (Jer 31:18-20). As a result of these ambiguities and transformations Matthew identifies the children of Bethlehem with all Israel in its suffering and exile and implies Israel's need for a savior, who is God in Jeremiah and Jesus sent by God in the Gospel.

The final fulfillment quotation is vaguely attributed to "the prophets" and authenticates Jesus as a resident of Nazareth: "He shall be called a Nazarene *(Nazōraios)*" (2:23). However, neither the prophetic books of the Bible nor nonbiblical Jewish literature contains this statement. Significantly, the place name "Nazareth" does not appear in the HB. Archeological exploration suggests that it was a very small settlement of a few hundred people located on a ridge in lower Galilee above the Jezreel valley. The meaning of the name of the village is unknown. Scholars have looked to biblical themes and wordplays on biblical words as the source for Matthew's "quotation." The most popular is to understand the first three consonants in Nazareth as Heb. *nṣr,* which in Isa 11:1 is a branch or shoot *(neṣer)* from the roots of Jesse, David's father, who will be an ideal leader of Israel. Thus Matthew understood the name of Jesus' village in relationship to his being an anointed successor to David. The Messiah is often symbolized as a branch or new growth (Zech 3:8; 6:12). A less successful explanation connects Nazarene with the biblical nazirite (Num 6:1-21). Nazirites took a temporary vow to abstain from alcoholic drinks and from having their hair cut and offered sacrifices at the temple when their vow was completed. However, this pattern of behavior has no relation to Jesus except at an abstract level of holiness or dedication. In the end this saying remains obscure. However, Nazareth in Galilee provides a foundation for the activities of Jesus the Nazarene, who teaches and cures people in Galilee throughout the rest of the Gospel.

Bibliography. Brown, R. 1977, 2d ed. 1993, *The Birth of the Messiah,* New York: Doubleday • Davis, C. T. 1971, "Tradition and Redaction in Matthew 1:18–2:23," *JBL* 90:404-21 • France, R. T., 1981, "The Formula-Quotations of Matthew 2 and the Problem of Communication," *NTS* 27:233-51 • Nolan, B. M. 1979, *The Royal Son of God: The Christology of Matthew 1–2 in the Setting of the Gospel,* OBO 23, Göttingen: Vandenhoeck • Powell, M. A. 2001, *Chasing the Eastern Star: Adventures in Biblical Reader-Response Criticism,* Louisville: Westminster John Knox • Soares-Prabhu, G. M. 1976, *The Formula Quotations in the Infancy Narrative of Matthew,* Rome: Biblical Institute • Stendahl, K. 1960, "*Quis et Unde?* An Analysis of Mt 1–2," in W. Eltester, ed., *Judentum, Urchristentum, Kirche,* Festschrift J. Jeremias, BZNW 26, Berlin: Töpelmann, 94-105; repr. 1995 in G. N. Stanton, ed., *The Interpretation of Matthew,* Philadelphia: Fortress.

Introduction to Jesus, the Teacher and Healer (Matthew 3–4)

Matthew 3 and 4 introduce Jesus the adult by narrating his preparation and inauguration as a teacher and healer. First, John the Baptizer, who prepares the way for Jesus through his own teaching and call to repentance, baptizes Jesus. Then Jesus is tested by the devil and by the arrest of John in Judea before he returns to Galilee, where the people recognize him as a powerful healer and authoritative teacher. Jesus' independent work in Galilee is marked off literarily by the phrase "From that time . . ." (4:17). The same phrase appears again in 16:21, another transition where Jesus turns his attention to his death in Jerusalem. The first stage of Jesus' work, his teaching in the Sermon on the Mount and his healing in a series of miracles (chs. 5–9), is summarized in almost identical fashion at the end of this introduction (4:23-25) and after the recital of Jesus' words and deeds (9:35).

John the Baptizer and Jesus (3:1-17)

All four Gospels associate John the Baptizer with the beginning of Jesus' public life. Historically, John was probably a Judean teacher of repentance and reform, popularly recognized like Bannus later in the first century (Josephus *Life* 11–12). Matthew associates John strongly with the prophetic tradition since his clothing is like Elijah's (v. 4; 2 Kgs 1:8), as is his presence in the desert (3:1; 1 Kgs 19:4). Like Elijah the prophet he attacks Israel's leaders (3:7-10), and he fulfills the prophecy in Isa 40:3 which is cited in 3:3. John's food, locusts and wild honey (v. 4; cf. 11:18), is traditionally eaten by bedouin in the wilderness. His rough clothing and life in the wilderness (an area lacking water and agricultural cultivation) mark him out as an ascetic protesting the social and political status quo. John is also an apocalyptic teacher through his identification with Elijah, who was popularly expected to return at the end of the world (3:11; Mal 4:5; Sir 48:10; Matt 11:14; 17:10-13), and through his teaching of an imminent judgment (vv. 7, 10-12). Finally, the wilderness imagery and the quotation from Isa 40:3 (in v. 3) echo the exodus from Egypt and the new exodus of Isaiah 40–55.

The story of John and Jesus answers the same questions concerning Jesus' work which the first two chapters answered about his origin. Both Jesus and John proclaim the same message of the kingdom and repentance (3:2; 4:17), but in different places and times: John in the wilderness of Judea, and Jesus after him in the towns of Galilee. John baptizes and lives as an ascetic, but Jesus does not (11:7-19). Interestingly, Matthew drops Mark's description of John's message as "for forgiveness of sins" (Mark 1:4), reserving that phrase for Jesus (Matt 26:28).

Contrary to many anti-Jewish theological schemes which attribute corporate depravity to the Jews of Jesus' day, the author of Matthew gives no special reason for the people's need to repent from sin. He turns John's harsh attack away from the people and toward their leaders (3:7-10), in contrast to Luke and Q, where John aims his vitriolic rhetoric ("brood of vipers") at the crowds. The author presumes the hostility of the Pharisees and Sadducees (v. 7), as he does throughout the Gospel, even though they have done nothing up to this point. John threatens them with God's "wrath" *(orgē)* against evil, which destroys sinners on the prophetic "day of the Lord" (Isa 13:9; Jer 46:10; Ezek 30:3; Joel 2:1; 1 Cor 5:5; 1 Thess 5:2) and the apocalyptic day of judgment (Daniel 7; 10–11; Matthew 24). Fear of judgment gives rise to the idea of flight at the coming of the Lord (Zech 14:5; *Pss. Sol.* 17:25; Matt 24:20; Rev 6:15-16; 12:6), which appears here also (3:7). The other imagery used against the Judean leaders derives from sectarian polemics in which the faithful community is compared to a fruitful plant, vine, or tree and their unfaithful, unfruitful opponents to flora which are uprooted and burned (cf. Matt 7:16-20; 12:33; 13:8, 26; 21:18-19, 33-45). 3:9, which interrupts the development of the imagery in vv. 8 and 10, differentiates faithful from unfaithful Israelites, as do the Dead Sea Scrolls (1QS 1–4; CD 1–8; 1QpHab) and many other Second Temple documents such as *1 Enoch.* The children of Abraham made from stones (3:9) do not symbolize a rejection of all Jews and their replacement with Gentiles, as many commentators hold. Rather, the author of Matthew attacks the leaders' reliance on descent to the detriment of observance of the commandments.

In the rest of the chapter (3:11-17) John's teaching, with its apocalyptic and sectarian imagery, explains the emergence of Jesus as a powerful, authoritative, divinely appointed leader. Historically, Jesus probably began his public activities as a disciple of John in Judea (3:13; 4:12), though this relationship has been obscured by the author's concern to show that Jesus is superior to John (3:11-12, 14-15; 11:2-6). John's water baptism for repentance (3:3) cannot compare to Jesus' apocalyptic baptism with the Spirit and fire (vv. 11-12, 16). Water baptism in the Spirit, which is constitutive of the Matthean community (28:19), looks forward to the end of the world when it will receive its fulfillment through Jesus' "baptism" of fire at the judgment. Perhaps the leading image of an apocalyptic baptism of the Spirit and fire explains why Jesus is not shown baptizing with water in Matthew, in contrast to John, where Jesus does baptize (3:22, 26; 4:1-2).

John recognizes Jesus' superiority to himself and his baptism of repentance (3:14-15), but since John is God's spokesperson at this point in the Gospel, Jesus submits himself to John and his baptism as being in accordance with "righteousness" (v. 15). Righteousness in Matthew refers to doing God's will by obeying the commandments and other manifestations of divine governance (cf. 5:20 below). John's baptism of Jesus accords with God's will and prompts approval by God's voice and by God's Spirit manifested as a dove (3:16-17). (The origin and meaning of the dove symbol is unclear. One recent commentator lists sixteen theories, none particularly convincing.) Like the kings and prophets of the Bible, Jesus receives God's Spirit and is called God's Son (2 Sam 7:14; Pss 2:7; 110:3 [LXX 109:3]). Two texts from Qumran connect the title "son of God" with the apocalyptic leader (messiah) to be sent by God (4Q246 [= 4QpsDan ar[a]]; 4Q174 [= 4QFlor]). The characterization of Jesus as "the Beloved *(agapētos)* in whom I am well pleased" comes from the variant Greek text of Isa 42:1, which is quoted in full by Matthew later (12:18). The beloved figure is the servant of God in the Greek text of the first of Isaiah's four Servant Songs (Isa 42:1-4; 49:1-6; 50:4-11; 52:13–53:12). (In Hebrew the servant is designated as "chosen" *[baḥir]* rather than "beloved.") Thus Matthew's choice of text identifies Jesus as both the Son and servant of God. Another possible allusion may be found in the Greek version of Abraham's binding of Isaac for sacrifice, which refers to Isaac as Abraham's "beloved" son (Gen 22:2; the Hebrew has "only" *[yaḥid]* son). These statements and allusions progressively raise the status of Jesus in the reader's eyes. At the beginning of the baptism story John had described Jesus as stronger than he (3:11; cf. Isa 11:1-2 on the "might" of the "shoot from the stump of Jesse"), but by the climax a heavenly voice and dove and scriptural allusions make very clear Jesus' close relationship to God and possession of Godlike attributes.

Bibliography. Gibbs, J. A. 2002, "Israel Standing with Israel: The Baptism of Jesus in Matthew's Gospel (Matt. 3:13-17)," *CBQ* 64:511-26 • Kazmierski, C. R. 1996, *John the Baptist: Prophet and Evangelist,* Collegeville, Minn.: Liturgical • Meier, J. P. 1980, "John the Baptist in Matthew's Gospel," *JBL* 99:383-405 • Meijer, J. P. 1994, *A Marginal Jew,* New York: Doubleday, 2:19-233 • Murphy-O'Connor, J. 1990, "John the Baptist and Jesus: History and Hypothesis," *NTS* 36:359-74 • Webb, R. L. 1991, *John the Baptizer and Prophet: A Socio-Historical Study,* Sheffield: JSOT • Wink, W. 1968, *John the Baptist in the Gospel Tradition,* SNTSMS 7, Cambridge, U.K.: Cambridge University.

The Temptation of Jesus (4:1-11)

The exodus story has strongly influenced the accounts of Jesus' baptism, forty-day fast, and temptations. Just as Israel passed through the Reed Sea into the desert or wilderness (*midbar* in Hebrew), where they were tested for forty years by hunger, physical dangers, and idolatry, so Jesus passes through the water in baptism, goes into the wilderness, fasts for forty days, and faces the same temptations as Israel. Jesus' forty-day fast corresponds symbolically not only to Israel's forty years in the wilderness but also to Moses' forty-day fast on Mt. Sinai (Exod 34:28; Deut 9:9) and to Elijah's forty-day fast on his trip to Mt. Horeb (1 Kgs 19:8). Unlike John the Baptizer, who proclaims the kingdom, baptizes in the wilderness, and lives as an ascetic (3:1-6), Jesus is not generally known as one who leaves inhabited areas and demands fasting (Matt 11:19). Rather, during a limited period in the wilderness (4:1-2) he prepares himself for his work in the villages of Galilee, just as Israel, after their sins in the wilderness (Exodus 32; Num 20:7-13), prepared themselves through hardship to enter the promised land. In Exodus the wilderness is a place of testing and preparation, and in later tradition it is also the place where evil spirits live.

In Matthew the devil tempts Jesus *after* his forty-day fast, when he is physically weakest but spiritually most prepared. (Contrast Mark 1:13 and Luke 4:2, where Jesus is tempted *during* the forty days.) Appropriately the devil begins with Jesus' hunger and then moves to the insecurity of life and finally to the attractions of idolatry as a solution (4:3-10). Unlike Israel in the wilderness Jesus overcomes his temptations. When the Israelites feared starvation in the desert, they complained to God until fed with manna and quails (Exodus 16), but Jesus refused to turn stones into bread. When they faced hostile peoples, they lost confidence in God (Numbers 13–14), but Jesus refused to test God's care by jumping from the temple pinnacle. When Israel lost confidence in God at Sinai, they worshiped a golden calf (Exodus 32), but Jesus refused to worship Satan. The three temptations also correspond to the later rabbinic interpretation of Deut 6:5 according to which the command to love God with all one's heart refers to the good and evil inclinations, corresponding to the temptation to make bread from stones. "Soul" refers to life itself and corresponds to the temptation to jump from the temple pinnacle. "Might" refers to possessions and corresponds to the temptation to rule the whole world by worshiping Satan (*m. Ber.* 9:5; Sipre Deuteronomy #32). Deut 6:5 is part of the Shema, the central Jewish prayer composed of three biblical passages (Deut 6:4-9; 11:13-21; Num 15:37-41), and it is likely that this liturgical tradition influenced telling of the temptation story as well as later rabbinic exegesis.

In responding to the devil's temptations Jesus quotes Scripture three times from Deuteronomy 6–8, three chapters which review Israel's experience in the wilderness. Deut 8:1-5 give an interpretation of Israel's wilderness experience as a time of testing. The stories of the baptism and temptations recapitulate and reinterpret Israel's experience in reference to Jesus so that Jesus' rejection of the temptations affirms the Deuteronomic covenant and commandments. The devil uses Jesus' identity as the Son of God (cf. 3:17) in the first two temptations (vv. 3, 6) to prompt Jesus to demand food and protection from God. But Deut 8:3 values the word of God, meaning God's commandments (cf. Deut 8:2; Matt 5:17-48), above manna and bread, and Deut 6:16 reaffirms God's role in testing Israel and Jesus and God's rule over them. Jesus' acceptance of hardship foreshadows his acquiescence to his own death in the garden (26:36-46). The repartee between Jesus and the devil, including the use of Scripture three times by Jesus and once by the devil (Ps 91:11-12 in Matt 4:6), is typical of debates in Second Temple Jewish and later rabbinic literature.

In the final temptation the devil substitutes himself for God as the ruler of the world and offers Jesus the whole world in exchange for recognizing and submitting to him. This offer attacks the fundamental covenant relationship which binds God to Israel, so Jesus counters it with the central monotheistic theme of Deuteronomy, "Worship the Lord your God, and serve only him" (Deut 6:13, LXX; Matt 4:10). Ironically, because of his fidelity to God here, Jesus will become ruler of the world after his death and resurrection in the final scene of the Gospel: "All authority in heaven and on earth has been given to me" (Matt 28:18). In both scenes Jesus is on a mountain with power, authority, and teaching at stake. Similarly, the Sermon on the Mount (5:1-2) and Mt. Sinai (Exodus 19–24) involve the same conjunction of mountain, God, and authority.

Bibliography. Fitzgerald, J. T. 1972, "The Temptation of Jesus: The Testing of the Messiah in Matthew," *ResQ* 15:152-60 • Gerhardsson, B. 1966, *The Testing of God's Son* (Matt 4:1-11 and pars.), ConBNT 2/1, Lund: Gleerup • Porkorný, P. 1973-94, "The Temptation Stories and Their Intention," *NTS* 20:115-27 • Przybylski, B. 1974, "The Role of Matthew 3:13–4:11 in the Structure and Theology of the Gospel of Matthew," *BTB* 4:222-35 • Stegner, W. R. 1967, "Wilderness and Testing in the Scrolls and in Mt 4:1-11," *BR* 12:18-27.

The Beginning of Jesus' Work (4:12-25)

The notice of Jesus' move to Galilee (v. 12) continues a series of place names supported by scriptural texts: Bethlehem (2:1-6), Egypt (2:14-15), Nazareth (2:22-23), and here Capernaum by the Sea of Galilee (4:13-16). The author assumes that Jesus remained in Judea for an indefinite period until John the Baptizer was arrested, but he does not say what he did. Perhaps Jesus worked with John or on his own (cf. John 1:28-43). In this Gospel Jesus' real work of announcing the kingdom begins in 4:17 after he "withdrew into Galilee" (v. 12). "Withdraw" *(anachōreō)* has the connotation of escaping danger (2:22; 12:15; 14:13).

The places named in the quotation from Isa 9:1-2 are the territory of the tribe of Naphtali next to the western shore of the Sea of Galilee; Zebulun, whose territory was west of them in the middle of the valley of lower Galilee; the "way of the sea" on the shore of the Mediterranean; and Gilead across the Jordan, south of the Sea of Galilee. This territory, along with the whole Northern Kingdom of Israel, was conquered and annexed by the Assyrians in the late eighth century (BC). Isaiah promised Israel relief ("light") from oppression, a promise which Matthew sees fulfilled in Jesus. Matthew is especially interested in the final geographical expression, "Galilee of the nations" (Matt 4:15 from Isa 9:1, *galil ha-goyim*) since Jesus comes from and works in Galilee. The meaning of "Galilee of the nations" is much disputed. *Galil* derives from a Hebrew root for circular *(gll)* and refers to a circumscribed area or district. The expression "Galilee of the nations" in Isaiah may refer to the district conquered and settled by the nations (the Assyrians and their armies). For the author of Matthew it hints at the conclusion of his Gospel when Jesus sends his disciples to teach and baptize all the nations (28:19). Historical and archeological evidence suggests that in the first century Galilee was heavily Jewish, not Gentile. Certainly for Matthew Galilee was heavily Jewish because Jesus directs his teaching to Jewish crowds in Galilee (10:5-6).

The editorial transition, "From that time Jesus began to proclaim," signals the beginning of Jesus' work as a teacher and healer in Galilee. A similar transition signals the movement toward his suffering and death in Matt 16:21. Jesus' message here repeats John the Baptizer's "Repent, for the kingdom of heaven is at hand" (3:2). Jesus' disciples later announce the same message (10:7, without the imperative "repent"). For the author of Matthew the kingdom (designated as the kingdom of heaven most often but also as the kingdom of God, kingdom of the Father, and simply kingdom) is the root metaphor and central symbol of Jesus' teaching and work. The Gospel refers to the kingdom throughout, especially in the sermons (chs. 5, 7, 13, and 18). Kingdom refers not to a place, such as heaven, but to God's eternal rule over all creation including the human world. The kingdom's characteristics emerge from the narrative and teaching of Jesus gradually throughout the Gospel. God's rule over the world (the kingdom) is present now, even though imperfectly known and accepted, but it will be fully revealed and actualized at the end of the world when evil is destroyed and good vindicated at the divine judgment. The verb "come near" (*ēngiken*) implies either that the kingdom is imminent but not yet present, or that it is emerging in the present but the process is not complete. In one place Jesus says that the kingdom of God has come (12:28, using *ephthasen*). The modifier "heaven" is a pious circumlocution for the more holy name "God." Thus "heaven" is not a reference to the place above the world which appears in apocalyptic literature but a synonym for "God."

Jesus first recruits four followers to help him as messenger and proclaimer of the kingdom of God (4:18-22). The story, taken from Mark, is stripped to the essentials and lacks all psychological detail. Jesus commands Peter and Andrew, James and John, to follow him, and they do so immediately, leaving behind their work and families no matter what the disruption of the social order (cf. also 8:21-22; 10:21). Though in reality Jesus may have known his first followers for some time before they left home (cf. John 1) and they may have had a variety of motives for following Jesus, in the end call and response define the transaction between Jesus and his followers. Similarly, the story assumes rather than discusses the discipline and renunciation required for James and John to leave their father (v. 22) and Peter his wife and family (8:14-15), especially in a traditional society with strong social and economic kinship relations. Later instructions concerning leaving home, family, work, and wealth make clear the renunciation required of disciples (8:19-22; 10:38; 16:24; 19:21, 27-28; 27:55).

Jesus' calling of these followers incorporates and symbolically transforms both the sea where they work (4:12, 15, 18) and their skill at fishing, so they become "fishers of humans" in the world rather than of fish in the sea (v. 19). The metaphoric meaning of fishing relies on major features of Galilean society and geography. The Sea of Galilee is really a freshwater lake (Gk. *thalassa* means both "sea" and "lake"), about thirteen miles long, which was known by a number of names (Gennesaret in Luke 5:1 and in 1 Macc 11:67; Tiberias in John 6:1 and in Josephus *J.W.* 4, §456; and Taricheae in Pliny *Nat. Hist.* 5.15.71). Fish in the Sea of Galilee probably included talapia (called St. Peter's Fish), carp, and catfish. As fishermen, the four followers were neither indigent, as patristic writers later imagined, nor "middle class," as some modern commentators claim. They with their families owned equipment (nets and boats), just as farmers owned land, and they probably earned a subsistence living from their craft.

A compact summary of Jesus' activities and effect on people (4:23-25) introduces the subsequent detailed accounts of his teaching (chs. 5–7) and miracles (chs. 8–9). The first sentence of the summary, that Jesus taught in synagogues, proclaimed the good news of the kingdom, and cured illness (4:23), is repeated almost verbatim in 9:35 to close this long section of the Gospel and is abbreviated in 11:1 to describe Jesus' continuing activities. Here the teaching about the kingdom is for the first time referred to as "good news" or "gospel" (v. 23; also 9:35), which will be proclaimed to the whole world (24:14; 26:13). Jesus teaches about the kingdom in "their" synagogues (v. 23 and 9:35), a phrase that is usually understood as symbolizing the author's estrangement from the Judaism of his own day. However, in these summaries "their synagogues" does not connote hostility but simply the local assemblies of village Jews in which they learned Torah. In other cases Jesus meets hostility from various opponents in "their synagogues" (10:17; 12:9; 13:54; 23:34). Archeological evidence for dedicated synagogue buildings comes mostly from the third century AD on, so probably village assemblies met in a large house, a public assembly hall, or outside and were presided over by the village elders. (Rabbis begin to emerge as teachers and community leaders only after the destruction of the temple in AD 70, when they controlled the schools but not the synagogues.)

The final two verses (4:24-25) locate the geographical origins of the crowds which follow Jesus and testify to his growing reputation as a Near Eastern popular holy man who heals and teaches. Syria probably does not refer to the Roman province of Syria, which included modern Syria, Lebanon, Jordan, and Israel. It connotes either the broad geographical area in which Galilee and the places mentioned in v. 25 are found or the area north and east of Galilee, centered in Damascus. The regions mentioned (Judea, Galilee, and Transjordan) all had large Jewish populations, in keeping with Matthew's Jesus, who announces the kingdom to his fellow Jews. The Gospel omits places with a non-Jewish population such as Samaria, the seacoast, and northern Syria. The impressive list of maladies healed by Jesus (v. 24) emphasizes the necessity and centrality of healing to the work of ancient popular teachers and holy men in the Near East. The crowds who followed Jesus are a permanent feature of the Gospel (8:1; 12:15; 14:13; 19:2; 20:29; 21:9).

Bibliography. Abogunrin, S. O. 1985, "The Three Variant Accounts of Peter's Call: A Critical and Theological Examination of Texts," *NTS* 31:587-602 • Gerhardsson, B. 1979, *The Mighty Acts of Jesus According to Matthew* (Lund: Gleerup • Kingsbury, J. D. 1978, "The Verb *Akolouthein* ('To Follow') as an Index of Matthew's View of His Community," *JBL* 97:56-73.

Introduction to the Sermon on the Mount (Matthew 5–7)

Matthew's initial summary of Jesus' teachings and works at the end of ch. 4 is illustrated by an extended section of Jesus' teachings (chs. 5–7, called the "Sermon on the Mount" in the modern period) and a collection of Jesus' miracles (chs. 8–9). The Sermon on the Mount is the first of the five collections of Jesus' teachings (chs. 10, 13, 18, 24–25) created by the author of Matthew using teachings from Q, the sayings source he has in common with the Gospel of Luke, and from other unknown sources in order to describe the fundamental attitudes and behaviors which should characterize and unite his community of followers of Jesus. The instructions and exhortations of the Sermon on the Mount reflect the Jewish cultural context of Matthew's late-first-century community and of the early followers of Jesus. The author articulates his interpretation of the teachings of Jesus in order to give guidance to his community.

The teachings in chs. 5–7 have been grouped by theme and literary form. The eight beatitudes (5:3-12) and the sayings following them (vv. 13-16) introduce the main teaching section (5:17–7:12), which itself is followed by a series of warning and exhortations (7:13-27). The instruction on keeping the law (5:17-20) and the summarizing golden rule (7:12) bracket the main section, whose teachings may be divided into three sections: a series of six interpretations of biblical law (5:21-48); instruction on three pious practices (6:1-18); and a less cohesive series of sayings centered on trust in God and social relations. Scholars have proposed other principles of organization none of which has achieved a broad consensus. For example, the three sections of teachings have been associated with the scribes, Pharisees, and disciples or with the three pillars on which the world stands: Torah, worship, and deeds of lovingkindness (*m. 'Abot* 1:2). Others have linked the parts of the sermon with the petitions of the Lord's Prayer, for example, "Thy will be done" with the six interpretations of biblical law (5:21-48) or "Give us this day our daily bread" with the instruction to trust God, not mammon (6:19-34). Others have linked only the second half of the sermon (6:19–7:27) with the Lord's Prayer. These comparisons illuminate the thematically rich, self-referential texture of the sermon but do not explain its order and contents.

The attitudes and behaviors promoted by the sermon have seemed very idealistic or otherworldly to some commentators. The blessing of the poor (5:3) and the promise that the meek will inherit the earth (v. 5) clash with the competitive quest for wealth in modern capitalist society. The blessing of peacemakers (v. 9) and the command to love one's enemies (v. 44) pale before violent quests for power by nation-states and ethnic groups. Some commentators have restricted the ethics of the sermon to the Christian community rather than society at large, or to the first century when Christians expected the imminent end of the world and thus could briefly embrace the stringent requirements of the sermon. Others see in it a personal call to ascetic and spiritual perfection for all Christians or special groups within the Christian community. Theologians have stressed the sermon as a call to God's grace in the face of evil and human weakness, and social reformers have understood it as a validation of the poor, powerless, and marginalized in the eyes of God.

The author of the Gospel addresses a small community (or communities) and teaches that God's rule (kingdom) is making its presence felt in the present, preparatory to its final and full expression at the end of the world. Thus the small community of followers of Jesus ought, in his eyes, to be bound to one another and God by the ideals, attitudes, norms, and behaviors taught in the sermon. The application of these teachings to Christian communities within a global society composed of large, anonymous, and diverse nations requires a complex process of interpretation which begins with the Bible and utilizes the riches of Christian tradition and human understanding.

Beatitudes and Introductory Teachings (5:1-16)

Jesus ascends the mountain in 5:1 and descends in 8:1, both times accompanied by crowds. In between he teaches without interruption in such a way as to astound the crowd with his authoritative teaching. The setting on the mountain alludes to Moses on Mt. Sinai and to the authoritative teaching he received there and passed on to Israel. The narrator identifies the sermon's audience somewhat unclearly as the crowds and then the disciples. The crowds are around Jesus and presumably prompt him to teach (5:1). They react positively to his teaching at the end (7:28-29) and follow Jesus as he leaves the mountain (8:1). But the author gives Jesus' disciples special place in the narrative, sitting near Jesus as he teaches (5:1). Some claim that this sermon, like the other four (chs. 10; 13 from v. 36 on; 18; 24–25), is addressed to the disciples primarily.

The sermon begins with eight or nine blessings ("blessed" or "happy" are . . .), traditionally called "beatitudes" (5:3-12). Blessings in Jewish prayers usually begin with the Hebrew participle *baruk,* addressed to God as well as to humans. However, the kind of beatitudes here, which are introduced by *'ashre* in Hebrew and *makarios* in Greek in the Bible and Second Temple Jewish literature, are never addressed to God, but refer to human beings, either in the second or third person. In wisdom literature they exhort people to wise, good behavior or to the avoidance of foolish, evil behavior. In narratives they express joy over good fortune or hope for consolation in times of suffering, and in apocalyptic literature they express hope in a time of oppression. The Matthean beatitudes conform to this type. They refer to humans, the first eight in the third person and the final one in the second person. They console, exhort, and promise eschatological vindication.

The eight beatitudes are actually nine in number, but since the last two concern enduring persecution (in the third and second person respectively), they are usually treated as one. The first and the eighth (5:3, 10) have the same reward ("for theirs is the kingdom of heaven"), so that they form an inclusion bracketing the list. Some commentators divided the list in half, with the first half concerned with the needy (the poor, mourners, the powerless, and the unjustly treated) and the second with wise and good activity (mercy, peacemaking, purity of heart, and fortitude in unjust persecution). The beatitudes structurally contrast the seven curses or woes in ch. 23. (Luke 6:20-26 has parallel lists of four beatitudes and woes together.) The content of the beatitudes has been influenced by Isaiah 61, which mentions the poor in 61:1, comfort for mourners in 61:2, righteousness in 61:3, 8, and 11, and healing of the brokenhearted (similar to the pure of heart) in 61:1. Inheriting the land is found in Isa 61:7 as well as in Ps 37:11, and the kingdom of heaven is functionally equivalent to the preaching of the good news in Isa 61:1. A list of beatitudes found at Qumran (4Q525) shares the form and content of Matthew's beatitudes, as do the Hebrew version of Sir 14:20-27 and 15:1-2 and some parts of the *Hymn Scroll* (1QH 13–14[Puech 5–6]).

The beatitudes set the tone and agenda for the Sermon on the Mount. Much effort has been expended in arguing whether they are ideals, ethical demands, eschatological promises, gifts of God's grace, or entrance requirements for the kingdom. Many of these discussions derive more from later theological disputes than from Matthew's message. For the Matthean community the beatitudes simultaneously refer concretely to the difficulties faced by the author's community, suggest attitudes and goals to guide the community, and contain promises of eschatological reward. They also serve to articulate the dimension of the rule (kingdom) of God in the world at large, especially vis-à-vis the needy and the just.

The first and third beatitudes, concerning the poor and meek, are probably variants of one another since both Greek words translate the Hebrew for "poor" (*'anawim*). Poor in the Bible and Second Temple literature refers not only to those lacking wealth but also to the powerless, oppressed, and needy members of society. These "poor," "meek," and powerless people are under the special care of God, like the poor, widows, and orphans (Isa 10:2) to whom God gives victory over the powerful (Isa 16:6). The poor may be Israel oppressed by a foreign empire (*Pss. Sol.* 5:2; 10:6) or a community within Israel oppressed by the authorities (1QpHab12:3; 4Q171 [Ps[a]] 2:9-11, "the congregation of the poor"). This outlook opposes the standard wisdom position that the rich are blessed and the poor wretched, as found in Prov 10:15, "The wealth of the rich is their fortress; the poverty of the poor is their ruin," and in a Qumran wisdom text, "What is more insignificant than a poor man?" (4Q417 2.1.10). Matthew's phrase, "poor *in spirit,*" does not weaken the blessing of the poor found in Luke 6:20, but enlarges the category to include all those faithful to God, as in the Qumran *War Scroll*, where the poor in spirit are contrasted with the hard of heart (1QM 14:7). The third beatitude comes from Ps 37:11, "the meek shall inherit the land," which is interpreted in the Dead Sea Scrolls as referring to the congregation of the poor which will inherit the land (4Q171 [Ps[a]] 2:9-12). The expression "inheriting the land" recalls Israel's inheriting the land of Israel in the Bible, but in the beatitudes as in apocalyptic literature the just or the chosen inherit the whole world at the end when God judges good and evil (*1 Enoch* 5:7). Matthew uses the word *"earth" (gē)* to refer to the whole world, not just the land of Israel. Thus God's rule (kingdom) in the first beatitude and inheriting the earth in the third are complementary.

The second beatitude concerns the just who mourn over their oppression and suffering at the hands of the wicked (Isa 61:2; 4Q525, the Qumran Beatitudes; and 4Q417 2.1.10-12, a wisdom text). In response God turns the sorrow of the just into joy at the end (Isa 60:20; Bar 4:23). The fourth beatitude praises those who seek righteousness (justice — *dikaiosynē*), that is, what is just according to God's will and law (3:15; 5:20; 6:33). The metaphor "hunger and thirst" may denote physical privation, but it is vague enough to include those suffering other kinds of ill treatment too. Those seeking justice in any sense are satisfied by the kingdom of God (5:3; 6:33), so that these two symbols aptly summarize Matthew's understanding of Jesus' teaching.

The fifth through seventh beatitudes (5:7-9), found only in Matthew, promote dispositions and behavior proper to the kingdom of God. Mercy, which includes loyalty to God (Matt 18:33; 9:13 = Hos 6:6), inner purity (Ps 24:3-4; Matt 15:10-11, 17-20), and peace (10:13), characterizes God and God's rule in the Bible. These characteristics bring the person successively closer to God through reception of God's mercy, seeing God, and becoming a son of God. This intimacy with God takes place in the present and more fully in the apocalyptic future. The themes of mercy, purity, and harmony appear frequently in the Gospel when it stresses God's and Jesus' mercy for humans and humans for each other (9:27-31; 17:14-18 and miracles generally; 9:13; 23:23), integrity of the inner person in contrast to hypocrisy (6:1-18; 23:23-36), and communal harmony (5:21-26, 38-47; 18:21-22). Mercy, purity, and especially peacemaking contrast starkly with the persecutors in the final beatitude. These practices apply to social relationships both within the community and with the world at large.

The last beatitude, first in the third person (v. 10) like the previous beatitudes and then in the second person (vv. 11-12) as in Luke (and Q), encourages the followers of Jesus in the face of social rejection and aggression. As threatened or oppressed minorities, the early followers of Jesus and the late-first-century Matthean community struggled to remain faithful in adversity. The change from third person to direct, second person address (v. 11) underlines the communal and personal exigency of persecution and martyrdom. This grammatical change also makes a transition to the subsequent sayings in direct address (vv. 13-16). In addition, the eighth beatitude repeats the themes of the first and fourth beatitudes, the kingdom of God and justice or righteousness, thus providing a coherent ending. The repetition in direct address specifies the persecution as both verbal (being reviled or dishonored and being slandered) and physical. The persecutors are not "people" as in the NRSV, but simply "they," that is, unnamed enemies or perhaps implicitly the opponents of Jesus and the Matthean community throughout the Gospel. The polemical charge that "they" killed the prophets is a favorite in Matthew, the NT, and early Christian literature (Matt 13:57; 21:35-36; 22:6, 29-37; Mark 6:4; 12:2-5; Acts 7:51-52; Rom 11:3 = 1 Kgs 19:10; Heb 11:32-38), though historical records do not support allegations of this pattern of behavior.

The introduction to the Sermon on the Mount ends with metaphors about salt and light to characterize the work of Jesus' followers (5:13-16). Salt was valued in antiquity because it had many uses in seasoning and preserving food, and light symbolizes the impact of Jesus' followers and teachings in the Sermon on the Mount on the world. Those teachings like salt must be kept pure to have their desired effect, and they must be exposed to the world like light. Consonant with Matthew's emphasis on righteousness as doing God's will, the disciples will spread Jesus' teachings through their good deeds so that "the world" and "others" may give glory to God (v. 16). This concise summary agrees with the final instructions that Jesus gives his disciples in the last scene of the Gospel (28:16-20), to teach all nations "to obey everything I have commanded you."

Jesus' Interpretation of the Law (5:17-48)

Many interpreters contrast the "new" teachings of Jesus with the "old" teachings of Judaism which they abrogate or supersede. Others claim that Jesus' teachings have a radical and unique character which distinguishes them from commonly accepted understandings of Jewish law. Contrasts of the spirit of the law to the letter, purity of motive to outward observance, or God's true will to legalistic conformity import later anti-Jewish theology into Matthew and homogenize diverse first-century Jewish communities into a caricatured opponent to Christianity. In reality, the author of Matthew eagerly combats the view that Jesus abolishes or changes the law. Using a general statement (5:17-20) and six cases (vv. 21-48), he argues that Jesus changes nothing in the law itself (the Bible, especially the Pentateuch or Torah), not even an "iota" or "horn, hook," that is, neither the smallest letter of the alphabet (*iota* in Greek and *yod* in Hebrew) nor any of the strokes used in forming the letters in Hebrew. The law remains in force until the end of the world when all things have been accomplished (v. 18). (It is contrary to the context for the phrase "until all things have been accomplished" to refer to the death and resurrection of Jesus, as some have argued.)

In Matthew's view Jesus has come to "fulfill" the law and the prophets (5:17) by his actions and teachings. He constantly argues that Jesus fulfills the words of the prophets (1:22; 2:15, 17; 26:54, 56; and frequently). Both here and at the end of the teaching section of the Sermon on the Mount (7:12), as well as in the commandments to love God and neighbor (22:40), Matthew treats Jesus' teaching as coextensive with the law and the prophets (the HB). The metaphor "fulfill" is open and ambiguous, but it means that Jesus not only upholds and establishes the law but also interprets it correctly so as to bring out its intended meaning. This polemical claim combats the interpretation of the law by other Jewish groups (symbolized by the scribes and Pharisees in 5:20) who disagree with Jesus and the author of Matthew. Strikingly, the sanction for departing from Jesus' interpretation of the law, becoming least in the kingdom of heaven (v. 19), contrasts sharply with hell, fire, darkness, weeping, and gnashing of teeth (5:22, 29, 30; 8:12; 10:28; etc.), the usual punishment for rejecting or disobeying the substance of God's law. Consequently, the author here opposes those in his community who disagree with his understanding of Jesus' teaching about biblical law, not hardened sinners who reject God's law.

Matthew introduces six interpretations of law (5:21-48) with references to righteousness (v. 20) and ends them with exhortations to perfection (v. 48). Righteousness in Matthew refers to doing God's will, that is, to keeping God's law (3:15) and interpreting it correctly (v. 20). "Righteousness" is both the core characteristic of God's rule (kingdom) (5:6; 6:33) and a polemical term which differentiates Matthew's group, with its own distinctive teaching and practice, from other groups of Jews and followers of Jesus. The Qumran community similarly claims that it is righteous and its Jewish opponents are not (e.g., 1QS 1–4). The exhortation to be perfect (*teleios*) as God is perfect (v. 48) continues the polemic. At Qumran the community aspires to be perfect (*tam*) in numerous poetic and legal texts. Perfection refers to integrity (Job 1:1, where Job is *tam* — "perfect" — in Hebrew, or *alēthinos* — "genuine" — in Greek) and authenticity or faithfulness (Deut 18:13, where Israel is called to be *tam/teleios* in relation to God).

The six cases interpreted by Matthew (5:21-48) all come from the legal agenda which was being debated in first-century-BC through second-century-AD Judaism. The six topics (murder-anger; adultery–sexual desire; divorce; oaths; retaliation; and love-hate) appear in the Dead Sea Scrolls, Pseudepigrapha, and Mishnah in one form or another. Though Jesus speaks authoritatively ("but I say to you"), he is not replacing the old law with a new law but interpreting biblical law in debate and dialogue with other Jewish teachers. Most commentators agree that the teachings on murder and adultery intensify or expand the scope of the law. Some have claimed that Jesus changes or contradicts biblical law in one or another of the other four cases on divorce, oaths, retaliation, and loving enemies. However, the Gospel's staunch affirmation of the law in vv. 17-19 suggests that it is interpreting the law with its own nuance according to the teachings of Jesus. The formula "You have heard that it was said" introduces biblical commands from God ("It was said" is an indirect way of invoking God as author). The continuation, "but I say to you," is not a negation or contradiction of the laws since the Greek word translated "but" is a connective that can also mean "and yet" or "in addition." Thus Jesus speaks as an authoritative divine spokesperson whose interpretations of God's law extend beyond details to clarifications of the overall intention of the Bible and God's will. His teaching actualizes the potential meaning of the law by intensifying in some cases, stressing inner attitudes in others, and adapting the laws to the needs of his new community of followers of Jesus.

The six cases address threats to the harmony and survival of a new, small community. Since the author of Matthew shares this agenda with other Second Temple and early rabbinic groups, he is probably attacking his adversaries' competing interpretations of biblical law. The full introductory formula, "You have heard that it was said to those of ancient times," occurs before the first and fourth cases (5:21 and with the conjunction "again" in v. 33), dividing them into two groups of three. The first two cases (vv. 21-30) address the commandments against murder and adultery (Exodus 20; Deuteronomy 5). Matthew moves from the observance of these commandments, which was not in dispute, to the attitudes and behaviors which might promote or impede infractions. Anger and insults easily lead to violence, especially in a culture which highly valued public honor and demanded a response to its infringement. Thus the commandment against murder entails avoiding conflicts and resolving disputes expeditiously (a view widely held in wisdom literature and the Dead Sea Scrolls, e.g., 1QS 6:25–7:5) and exceeds in importance even offering sacrifices (cf. Sir 34:21-27 on proper dispositions for sacrifice). Note that Matthew does not distinguish just from unjust anger, as many later Christian teachers have done, but forbids anger entirely (5:22), presumably because of its danger to the community. Similarly, because uncontrolled desires easily lead to sexual relations outside of marriage, the author recommends mastery of desire (v. 28), a virtue greatly valued by Greeks, Jews, and Christians. The hyperbole of excising one's eye or hand if it leads to sin is a metaphoric application of the principle of measure for measure (Lev 24:19-20). These teachings about anger and self-control were common in the first century, but Matthew establishes their authenticity through the Ten Commandments as interpreted by Jesus because disregard for them would threaten the peace and integrity of his community of followers of Jesus.

Many take the prohibitions against divorce and oaths (5:31-37; also treated in 19:3-12; 23:16-22) as changes in biblical law. However, the Bible does not positively command the practice of divorce (Deut 24:1-4), oaths, and vows (Lev 19:12; Deut 10:20; 23:21-23). It assumes that they exist and pragmatically regulates them. The NT disapproves of these practices and so regulates them differently. In Jewish law a woman had to be provided for by a man (a father first, then one's husband, and if he died, a son, brother, etc., or a new husband). Thus families arranged marriages for the economic welfare of their daughters, and the husband married and divorced his wife (but not vice versa). In order to provide legally and economically for a divorced woman, biblical law requires that a man divorcing his wife give her a divorce document which frees her to marry another man. In the NT the Synoptic Gospels and Paul forbid remarriage after a divorce (here and 19:3-9 in Matthew; Mark 10:2-12; Luke 16:18; 1 Cor 7:10-11). This early, widely accepted teaching, which probably came from Jesus, safeguards the integrity of the community, which could easily be fractured by divorces among its members. (The arguments for the prohibition of divorce and the exception in Matthew — "except on the ground of unchastity" — will be discussed in ch. 19.)

Oaths and vows were common in legal, religious, and personal relationships, and their abuse was often condemned in ancient literature. An oath bound the person to tell the truth or perform some action; a vow bound a person's property to God or some sacred purpose. In Leviticus swearing falsely (19:12) is associated with profaning God's name, stealing, lying, defrauding, robbing, and withholding wages. The *Damascus Covenant* (15:1) forbids the use of certain forms of God's name, as do Matthew (5:34-35; 23:16-22) and the Letter of James (5:12). The discussions of vows and oaths in Second Temple and rabbinic literature testify to the danger of deception in social relationships. Against this the early Jesus tradition advises direct honesty and commitment in all social interchanges as a way of preventing strife in the community.

The last two cases grapple with the conflicts, wrongs, and injuries which divide community members from one another and provoke retaliation or hostility (5:43-48). Conventionally, people defended their public honor by verbally, socially, or physically injuring those who injured them and by rejecting those who were their social enemies or inferiors. But insulting behavior (v. 39) and legal proceedings (v. 40) divide communities. Thus NT traditions (Luke 6:27-36; Rom 12:19-20; 1 Cor 6:7; 1 Thess 5:15; 1 Pet 2:23), along with Greco-Roman and later rabbinic literature, sought to promote social harmony by humility instead of pride, along with deference to one another rather than getting even. Accommodation even extends to the Roman government, which could demand labor from colonial subjects (v. 41 — "if anyone forces you to go one mile, go also the second mile").

Christians interpreters have often mistaken the rule of measure for measure ("an eye for an eye") as an example of justice without mercy or love (5:38; Exod 21:24-25; Lev 24:20; Deut 19:21). However, this ancient rule, found in Mesopotamian law, limited the response to injury and insult to a proportionate punishment and brought an orderly end to blood feuds. As interpreted in the Second Temple period, satisfaction was customarily sought through monetary compensation rather than mutilation. Here the followers of Jesus are to promote positive social relations and reconciliation by giving way to others, even when not required, and by lending and giving alms generously (5:42). These instructions presume a personal social context (e.g., a village) in which offering the other cheek or offering one's cloak (thus leaving the person virtually naked) would shame the litigant in front of his neighbors and encourage more generous behavior through social pressure. Though theologians have used the metaphor of turning the "other cheek" (v. 39) and the command to love enemies (v. 44) to argue for personal and institutional pacifism, this was not its original meaning.

The commandment to love one's enemies (5:43-48) concludes the six cases with the thematic Matthean emphasis on love, mercy, and faithfulness. The Bible does not contain the command cited by Matthew, to "hate your enemy" (v. 43); God's command that Israel destroy its enemies (Deut 7:2) and the sentiment that Israel should hate those who hate God (Ps 139:21-22) make the lines between neighbor and enemy clear. The sectarian *Rule of the Community* of the Dead Sea Scrolls expects community members to love and accept those whom God approves and hate and reject those who oppose God (1QS 1:4, 10; 9:21-22). In contrast, Matthew encompasses enemies in the love command, including persecutors of Jesus' followers. Disciples who pray for their enemies and persecutors act like sons of the Father who cares for all (v. 45; analogously 6:26-30) and become perfect like him (v. 48). This openness to hostile outsiders supports the turn to the Gentiles at the end of the Gospel.

Cultic Instruction (6:1-18)

The next section in the Sermon on the Mount contains a triad of concise teachings on authentic almsgiving, prayer, and fasting (6:2-4, 5-6, and 16-18) and a version of the Lord's Prayer (vv. 7-15) different from that in Luke 11:2-4. The instructions on giving to the poor, prayer, and fasting are probably a pre-Matthean instruction reinterpreting traditional Jewish practices according to the teachings of Jesus. The same group of three practices is found in Tob 12:8, and they are found individually in many Jewish writings. Here they are literarily parallel, each introduced by the formula "Whenever you . . ." give alms, and the like, and divided into two halves. The first half describes how not to act, and the second commands proper behavior. The negative examples are "hypocrites" (6:2, 5, and 16) who draw attention to their good deeds so they will be praised by people in contrast to community members who hide their deeds so that only God knows of them. Hypocrisy here pertains to a public pretense of virtue or piety in order to win honor and recognition, not to inner self-deception. The author does not identify the hypocrites as a particular group, in contrast to ch. 23, where he attacks the scribes and Pharisees as hypocrites.

The crisp style of these instructions communicates a sincere, no-nonsense approach to the essential self-control required by biblical morality. The first verse announces Matthew's theme, that good deeds which receive a human reward do not merit a divine reward in the future. Thus those who hide their actions receive honor and reward from God in the kingdom (cf. numerous rabbinic discussions of reward and punishment in this life and the world to come). The instructions themselves teach conventional concern for fellow humans through almsgiving, for God through prayer, and for one's own human desires and weakness through fasting. The biblical tradition testifies amply to each of these practices. The lengthened instruction on prayer, which includes the Lord's Prayer, was probably inserted by the author of Matthew so that the Lord's Prayer would stand at the midpoint of the Sermon on the Mount.

Biblical injunctions to leave the corners of the fields unreaped, fallen sheaves on the ground, and stray olives and grapes on the branches for the widow, orphan, and stranger and to collect a tithe to feed the poor (Deut 14:28-29; 24:19-22) support the practice of giving to the poor. The book of Proverbs blesses those who are kind to the poor (14:21, 31), and Tobit highly values helping the poor (Tob 1:8, 17; 2:2-3; 4:7-8, 16; 12:8-9). This special status of the poor before God underlies Matthew's first beatitude on the poor in spirit (5:3) as well as this passage (6:2-4).

Prayer (6:5-15) pervades the HB and Second Temple Jewish literature. The narratives, prophets, and psalms are filled with expressions of praise, thanksgiving, lament, and petition. In the Second Temple period hours for prayer began to emerge (Dan 6:10), though the form of the prayers has not survived. The Dead Sea Scrolls testify to a wide variety of psalms of praise and requests for divine help. Ezra-Nehemiah, Daniel 9, and Baruch 1–3 contain striking communal expressions of repentance. Other religions in the Roman Empire similarly employed prayer in a variety of circumstances and forms.

The author of Matthew warns against two types of inauthentic prayers: ostentatious prayers which seek public approval and the wordy, repetitious, incantational prayers common in the Greco-Roman world (6:5-8). He recommends a brief prayer, the Lord's Prayer, which is oriented toward the central elements of God's kingdom and human life. The Lord's Prayer probably was recited in the author's community. Since the forms of oral prayers were not fixed in this period, another version has survived (Luke 11:2-4). The Lord's Prayer shares themes and terminology with the ancient and central Jewish prayers, the Eighteen Benedictions (the Amidah) and the Qaddish, which may have been recited by Jews in some form during the first century.

The prayer addresses God as "Our Father," a metaphor which appears in Third Isaiah (63:16; 64:8) and in the Eighteen Benedictions. In addition, many biblical and extrabiblical texts understand Israel as God's child and thus God implicitly as Father. Because Christians have consistently confessed Jesus as the Son of God, the father-son relationship has been central to Christian theology and prayer. J. Jeremias claimed that the Aramaic for father, *'abba'*, which Jesus would have used, was an intimate address like the English "Daddy" and thus a qualitative theological advance. However, the word *abba* is the normal word for father and is used as a nominal title for adults who have fathered sons. Christianity's theology of God's fatherhood does not derive from this one word.

The present and future actualization of God's kingdom on earth and in heaven governs the content of the Lord's Prayer. The holiness of God, God's rule (kingdom), and the implementation of God's will in the first three petitions all point to the kingdom, which is the central theme of the Gospel's understanding of God. The mention of heaven at the beginning and end of the first half

(6:9-10) marks it off from the second half of the prayer (vv. 11-13), where the focus is on the petitioners ("we," "our") who need "daily" bread, forgiveness, and protection from evil forces. "Daily" *(epiousios)* bread probably refers to bread for the next day, though it has been understood as bread for the present day, the bread needed to sustain life, or the bread of the heavenly banquet at the end of the world. If *epiousios* refers to the next day's ration, the prayer is in slight tension with the admonition not to be anxious about tomorrow (6:34). In both cases, however, the speaker presumes trust in God's care.

The final two petitions (6:12-13) continue the eschatological orientation of the prayer, though less obviously than the first half. The "debts" *(opheilēmata)* are most probably sins (hence the traditional translation "trespasses") to be forgiven by God, especially at the judgment at the end of the world. However, the metaphor of debt may also encompass real debts and other obligations between humans in the present since human society demands reciprocal reconciliation on many levels. The author of Matthew picks up this theme in his comment at the end of the Lord's Prayer (vv. 14-15; cf. Mark 11:25), where he explicitly reaffirms the criterion of measure for measure and demands that humans forgive sins *(paraptōmata)* against one another so that God may forgive them their sins. Matthew stresses forgiveness and reconciliation in his instruction against anger (5:23-26) and in his sermon on community order (18:10-35). The Lord's Prayer ends with a double request to be protected at the end of the world from "[the time of] testing" (not "temptation" in general, found in the traditional translation of the Lord's Prayer) and from the "evil one" (i.e., the devil, a more probable translation than "evil" in general). All through the Gospel, Matthew stresses, in conjunction with God's rule over humans, his judgment of them at the end of the world. The temptations, conflicts, and evils faced by humans derive ultimately from evil forces beyond the visible human world. As the beginning of the prayer invoked God as Father, the end rejects the "evil one," the devil, as a fatal threat.

Many motives and goals for fasting may be found in Jewish literature, for example, repentance for sins, preparation for prayer or for a visionary experience, petition for help in need, or intercession with God in a time of crisis. Matthew does not mobilize that rich tradition to support a regular practice of fasting, nor does he give fasting a prominent role in his community's life. Jesus fasted when tested in the wilderness (4:2), but he does not demand that his disciples fast during his lifetime (9:14-15), though they will fast after he dies. Matthew assumes fasting as a practice (6:16-18), but he does not specify times or reasons for it. His main goal is to combat ostentation and pretense by his opponents and to promote modest, sincere behavior among his group of followers of Jesus.

Economic and Social Relationships (6:19–7:12)

The final section of teachings contains wisdom instructions and exhortations which are not tightly unified, though some have related them to the contents of the Lord's Prayer. The two instructions concerning wealth (6:19-21) and judging others (7:1-2) are each followed by a teaching about the eyes (6:22-23; 7:3-5), a second teaching (6:24; 7:6), and an exhortation to trust in God (6:25-34; 7:7-11). The golden rule (7:12) summarizes and concludes the teachings. Many of the sayings are poetically balanced and based on contrasting metaphors such as heaven and earth, light and dark, health and sickness, and God and mammon (wealth).

Matthew counters the natural desire for security through wealth with the reliability of God's care for the world and humans in the present (6:25-34) and the promise of permanent treasure in heaven (6:19-21). Trust in God requires clear, healthy vision (6:22-23) and an inner commitment to God's kingdom and righteousness (6:21, 24-25, 33) rather than a false confidence in impermanent wealth. In antiquity people assumed that sight arose from an inner light within the eye, in contrast to the modern understanding of the eye as a receiver of light waves. Thus a good or healthy eye would send out light, and an evil, diseased eye would be dark (vv. 22-23). The warning against trying to serve two masters (v. 24), God and mammon ("wealth" in the NRSV), personifies wealth as a power opposed to God. Mammon, the Aramaic word for wealth, appears in the Hebrew Dead Sea Scrolls — 1QS 6:2; CD 14:20 — as well as in Greek here and in Luke 16:9, 11, and 13.

The same awareness of human limitations above mediates personal relationships with others in the next section (7:1-12). In the face of human imperfections and the natural tendency to judge one another, Matthew reminds his community that all will be judged measure for measure (vv. 1-2) and compares obstructions to ocular vision to the inevitable faults in all human beings, both the judge and the judged (vv. 3-5). Yet, while insisting on self-awareness, Matthew accepts the necessity that his community judge whether a person has the proper attitude to be instructed in its teachings (v. 6; cf. 18:15-17). Since people often get into conflict over things they need or desire, Matthew finishes this section of the Sermon with an exhortation to ask God for any necessities (7:7-11). Unified by the assumption that God responds to requests for help with good things (vv. 7, 11), this threefold instruction to ask, search, and knock parallels humans' care for their children with God's care for humans. Implicitly in this comparison and explicitly in the golden rule which follows, the author emphasizes human care and love as the keys to the just relationships which he seeks in society at large and in his community. The golden rule as a criterion of measure for measure is formulated in various ways in many cultures. It is found frequently in Jewish literature (Tob 4:15; Sir 31:15; *Epistle of Aristeas* 207; *T. Naph.* 1:6), most often in a negative version. (Claims that Jesus' positive version is a new, higher ethic are overblown.) The golden rule and the Sermon on the Mount presume that society binds people together, even when they are in conflict. The only path to harmony and justice runs through a forgiving, deferential attitude which accepts human faults and seeks reconciliation at the deepest level, that of love of one's neighbor and enemy based on the love of God, who cares for all creatures. The claim that the golden rule summarizes the law and the prophets (7:12; see also *b. Shab.* 31a) which Jesus came to fulfill (5:17) is one of a number of way of summarizing the Torah in one principle. Interestingly, the Talmud suggests "the righteous one will live by faith" (Hab 2:4), a verse made famous by Paul and his interpreters as a summary of the Torah. Here the golden rule, to treat others as you would be treated yourself, complements the other summary of the law at the end of Jesus' teaching, the double commandment to love God and one's neighbor (22:34-40).

Final Warnings and Conclusion (7:13-29; 8:1)

A series of four concluding instructions warns the audience to take the Sermon on the Mount seriously. The metaphor of the "two ways" (7:13-14) is the common ethical heritage of the eastern Mediterranean found in Hesiod's *Works and Days* 286-92 and in Deuteronomy's command to walk in God's way and not go astray (Deut 11:26-28; 30:15-18). Among Second Temple writings the *Rule of the Community* from the Dead Sea Scrolls has an extended instruction on the conflict between the spirits of good and evil, the ways of dark and light, truth and falsehood, and so on (1QS 3:13–4:26). The Qumran Beatitude text (4Q525) begins with the metaphor of the two ways, blessing those who adhere to God's laws and avoid "perverted" and "insane paths." Many other hymns and wisdom texts allude to this tradition. The Wisdom of Solomon (1st cent. BC or AD) contains a confession of the wicked admitting that they strayed from the way of truth to paths of lawlessness and destruction (Wis 5:6-7). In the *Testament of Asher* (found in the *Testaments of the Twelve Patriarchs*) the first five chapters expound a version of the two-ways doctrine, beginning with "God has granted two ways to the sons of men, two mind-sets, two lines of action, two models, and two goals. Accordingly, everything is in pairs, the one over against the other. The two ways are good and evil; concerning them are two dispositions within our breasts that choose between them" (*T. Ash.* 1:3-5). Extended accounts of the two ways are also found in the early Christian writings, the *Didache* (*Teaching of the Twelve Apostles*) 1–3, and the *Epistle of Barnabas* 18–20.

Here the two ways are combined with the two gates. The two metaphors communicate the same message and can be seen as complementary. In another reading the two ways may lead to the two gates, which are the entrances to cities. Given Matthew's emphasis on the end of the world, judgment, reward and punishment, the heavenly city, and hell probably lie in the background. However, in the Sermon on the Mount the two ways encourage observance of the commandments and teachings which have been expounded in chs. 5–7. Matthew warns that the just way of life he proposes is difficult to live in contrast to the broad and easy road to destruction. He proposes that disciples do whatever it takes, whatever Jesus teaches, and whatever God wants.

The attack on false prophets (7:15-23) uses the traditional polemical language of good and bad fruit found elsewhere in Matthew (3:8-10; 12:33-36; 21:19, 43) and in the HB as well (Jer 8:8-13; Ezek 17:8-9, 22). However, the identity of the false prophets remains obscure, as does the phenomenon of early Christian prophecy as a whole. Matthew counted prophets among the leaders of his community (10:41; 23:34) but expected false prophets at the end (24:11, 24). Paul opposed traveling teachers who disagreed with him (Galatians; 2 Corinthians), and the *Didache* regulates charismatic, itinerant prophets. Probably Matthew here rejects prophetic teachers who oppose his interpretation of the teachings of Jesus and the Bible. Some identify the false prophets with Pauline Christians who reject the law which Matthew defends, but this hypothesis lacks clear evidence. Others with equal lack of evidence point to Jewish Christians opposed to bringing Gentiles into the Matthean church. Neither of these proposals nor other less popular ones are certain because the polemical language is so stereotyped and general that it fits a number of possible situations. The view that 7:15-20 refer to one group and vv. 21-23 to another is improbable because of the thematic and linguistic ties between the two paragraphs. In both the author of Matthew seeks to discern true from false leaders in his community using traditional sayings of Jesus.

The final parable of the Sermon on the Mount praises those wise people who will respond to Jesus' teaching and predicts disaster for those who reject it. The storm and flood which destroy the fool's house have apocalyptic overtones, and the stable rock of the responsive person's house looks forward to the rock on which the church is built (16:18). The narrator concludes with the people's affirmation of Jesus' teaching authority and an attack on rival teachers symbolized by the scribes. The end parallels the beginning with its allusion to Moses on Mt. Sinai (5:1) and its claim for a righteousness greater than that of the scribes and Pharisees (5:20). Jesus then comes down from the mountain followed by crowds (8:1), just as he had ascended earlier (5:1).

Bibliography. Commentaries. Allison, D. C. 1999, *The Sermon on the Mount: Inspiring the Moral Imagination,* New York: Crossroad • Betz, H. D. 1995, *The Sermon on the Mount,* Hermeneia, Minneapolis: Fortress • Guelich R. 1982, *The Sermon on the Mount: A Foundation for Understanding,* Dallas: Word • Lambrecht, J. 1985, *The Sermon on the Mount,* Wilmington: Glazier • Strecker, G. 1988, *The Sermon on the Mount,* Nashville: Abingdon.

Articles. Allison, D. C. 1987, "The Structure of the Sermon on the Mount," *JBL* 106:423-45 • Davies, W. D., and D. C. Allison. 1991, "Reflections on the Sermon on the Mount," *SJT* 44:283-309 • Kingsbury, J. D. 1987, "The Place, Structure and Meaning of the Sermon on the the Mount within Matthew," *Int* 41:131-43 • Stanton, G. 1993, *A Gospel for a New People,* Louisville: Westminster/John Knox; Edinburgh: T. & T. Clark, ch. 12, "Interpreting the Sermon on the Mount," 285-306; and ch. 13, "The Origin and Purpose of the Sermon on the Mount," 307-25.

Introduction to Jesus' Miracles (8:2–9:38)

The bulk of chs. 8 and 9 consists of nine miracle stories, grouped into three triads (8:2-22; 8:23–9:17; 9:18-38), with teachings and events interspersed. Some commentators enumerate ten miracle stories by counting the summary statement in 8:16 as a story; others list ten miracles by treating the double cure of the ruler's daughter and the woman with a hemorrhage in 9:18-26 as two miracles. This cluster of miracles responds to the author's summary of Jesus' activity as teaching, announcing the kingdom, and healing (4:13). The Sermon on the Mount elucidated Jesus' teachings; chs. 8 and 9 recount his healings. Together they disclose the full range of Jesus' activities as a popular holy man in Galilee and provide a basis for subsequent recognition of Jesus as the Messiah and Son of God by his followers and for opposition to him by the authorities. Jesus and his activities, in turn, reveal the nature and requirements of the kingdom of God. Some interpreters have attributed theological themes to each of the three cycles: Christology in 8:2-17; discipleship (and separation from Israel) in 8:18–9:17; and faith in 9:18-38. However, so many themes are intertwined with the miracle stories that divisions on the basis of the thought or emphasis are very subjective and questionable. For example, teaching about discipleship follows each of the three cycles.

Under the influence of rationalism and a mechanistic view of the physical universe, miracles have been defined as events that are exceptions to the laws of nature. Science treats physical exceptions to the laws of nature as impossible. If they occur, the "laws of nature" must be reformulated to account for the newly observed phenomena. This view of natural law is not present in the Bible. "Deeds of power" (*dynameis,* the Greek word used for Jesus' "miracles" in the Synoptic Gospels) encompass a wide range of actions which are out of the ordinary and so are attributed to the effects of God's power. The Gospels' stories about these deeds of power have a stereotyped form which differs from many Greco-Roman accounts of miracles. They stress the petitioners' faith in Jesus, Jesus' desire to help humans in a multitude of ways, especially by curing and exorcising them, and the recognition of Jesus' God-given power by the crowds and those cured. Biblical miracles take place only in a context where they are sought and recognized by people who trust in God and, in the Gospels, Jesus. Jesus cures by a simple command and/or touch, without the elaborate rituals and incantations common in Greco-Roman texts. Jesus thus fits the general profile of Near Eastern holy men who were expected to teach wisely and perform miracles. Note that, contrary to many modern treatments of miracles, the Gospel writings do not try to prove Jesus' divinity by way of miracles, but rather to show his God-given authority and power.

Bibliography. Brown, C. 1984, *Miracles and the Critical Mind,* Grand Rapids: Eerdmans • Hull, J. M. 1974, *Hellenistic Magic and the Synoptic Tradition,* SBT 2.28, London: SCM • Kahl, W. 1994, *New Testament Miracle Stories in Their Religious-Historical Setting,* FRLANT 163, Göttingen: Vandenhoeck & Ruprecht • Kee, H. C. 1983, *Miracles in the Early Christian World: A Study in Sociohistorical Method,* New Haven: Yale University • Kee, H. C. 1986, *Medicine, Miracle and Magic in New Testament Times,* SNTSMS 55, Cambridge, U.K.: Cambridge University • Meier, J. P. 1994, *A Marginal Jew: Volume Two: Mentor, Message, and Miracles,* New York: Doubleday, 507-1038 • Theissen, G. 1983, *The Miracle Stories of the Early Christian Tradition,* Philadelphia: Fortress • Twelftree, G. H. 1999, *Jesus the Miracle Worker,* Downers Grove: InterVarsity.

The First Cycle (Three Healings) (8:2-22)

The first cycle of cures covers the full range of social relationships, including the healing of a Jew, a non-Jew, and a family member. The cure of a leper (8:2-4) continues the theme of the Sermon on the Mount, obedience to God's law. Leprosy (Gk. *lepra*) is not Hansen's disease but a general word for a number of scaly skin ailments (Heb. *ṣaraʿat*) treated in Leviticus 13–14. Biblical law required lepers to separate from the community because they were "unclean" (Lev 13:45-46). Since most scaly skin conditions are not medically contagious, the uncleanness concerns ritual fitness of the individual and community to worship God, who is holy; it has no connection with medical contagion or moral status. Besides leprosy, a number of "abnormal" conditions, such as bodily discharges, could render a person unfit for worship and transmit impurity to other people and things, rendering them unfit as well. According to biblical law, a priest decides when a person is sufficiently recovered to be "clean" once again (Lev 14:2-32). Since Matthew portrays Jesus as obedient to God's law, Jesus does not declare clean the man whom he has healed nor allow him to speak to people. Jesus sends him to a priest to be certified "clean" and to offer the appropriate sacrifice before rejoining society.

The relationship between Jesus and the leper concisely summarizes the essential action of all healings, a person's need and Jesus' response (10:8; 11:5). The leper initiates the encounter by expressing faith and confidence in Jesus' power and goodwill (8:2). Jesus in turn speaks, in this case touches him, and effects the cure (v. 3). Touching a leper is not sinful in biblical law, but it would lead to uncleanness. However, Matthew pictures power going forth from Jesus to affect the unclean disease rather than the uncleanness affecting Jesus.

The relationship between Jesus and those in need continues in the story concerning a non-Jew, a centurion in the Roman army (8:5-13) stationed at Capernaum, a city which was Jesus' home (4:13) and a customs post on the route to Damascus (9:9). The centurion intervenes on behalf of his *pais,* which in Greek means "young boy" in the sense of either a son or a slave who is a house servant. (Luke 7:2 refers to this character as a servant/slave — *doulos;* John 4:46-54 call him a son — *huios.*) In this case the faith and confidence of the master mediate for the young boy. The dialogue between Jesus and the centurion concerning healing at a distance and power over subordinates emphasizes that this representative of imperial power acknowledges Jesus' God-given power to cure. The terms "faith" and "believe" in connection with healings refer to confidence that Jesus has the power and benevolent will to help; it does not signify full acceptance of Jesus by a dedicated follower. (See the healing of the Canaanite woman's daughter in 15:21-28 for the same meaning.) Jesus heals only when the petitioners have confident faith in him. In the case of these Gentiles, faith overcomes Jesus' restriction of his efforts to Israel (10:5-6; 15:24). If Jesus' reply that he will go and cure the boy is read as a question (possible in the Greek of 8:7), then Jesus here also initially challenges the appropriateness of the centurion's request.

The author of Matthew puts this story to work to explain for his late first-century community why some Jews have not accepted Jesus and some Gentiles have (8:11-12). The scene is the apocalyptic heavenly banquet, with God attended by the patriarchs and implicitly all of faithful Israel. A number of biblical passages suggest that the nations will join Israel in recognizing God at the end of the world, so they are probably the "many . . . from east and west" who will attend the banquet. The "many" may also refer to diaspora Jews returning to the land at the end. The author of Matthew uses the story as a polemic against Jews ("sons of the kingdom") who reject Jesus, but he does not imply that Israel as a whole has been rejected by God, contrary to many commentators. Rather, he adds to the story, compared to the version in Luke 7:1-10 (from Q), the names of Abraham, Isaac, and Jacob, making clear that the banquet has Israel at its center, even if some of Israel are unfaithful. In contrast to those who enjoy the pleasure and security of God's banquet (which is characterized by light), those who reject Jesus will be put out of the house into the dark (cf. 22:13; 25:30), where they will weep and gnash their teeth in frustration at their loss. Matthew uses this weeping-and-gnashing formula to signify apocalyptic judgment at the ends of five parables (13:42, 50; 22:13; 24:51; 25:30).

In the final miracle of the cycle Jesus simply and swiftly cures a member of his inner circle, Peter's mother-in-law, with a touch and without even being asked (the only case in the Gospel — 8:14-15). A summary report of numerous exorcisms and healings ends the first cycle of miracles, along with a passage from Isaiah's fourth Servant Song which explains that God's servant will bear Israel's sickness (vv. 16-17; Isa 53:4). A pair of encounters (8:18-22) teach that following Jesus requires extraordinary dedication. Jesus confronts a scribe who addresses him as "teacher" with the homelessness required of a disciple. In Matthew only outsiders, that is, nondisciples, address Jesus as teacher; thus the scribe is not a true follower. Though Jesus teaches, his teaching and goals require recognition that he is more than a teacher and demand the total commitment of a disciple. In the second encounter Jesus urges a disciple to put him and his fellow disciples before his family (cf. Matt 12:46-50). By contrast, when Elijah called Elisha, he allowed him to go home to kiss his parents good-bye and to offer a sacrifice (1 Kgs 19:19-21). Respect for the priority of family obligations is more in keeping with Near Eastern sensibilities, but the radical demand for commitment characterizes new, small groups like Jesus and his disciples which operate as fictive kinship groups. Jesus and the Gospel do not reject families totally, but they do insist that the group devoted to the kingdom (rule) of God receive priority over kinship.

Bibliography. Bockmuehl, M. 1998, "'Let the Dead Bury Their Dead' (Matt. 8:22/Luke 9:60: Jesus and the Halakhah," *JTS* 49:553-81 • Held, H. J. 1963, "Matthew as Interpreter of the Miracle Stories," in G. Bornkamm et al., eds., *Tradition and Interpretation in Matthew,* Philadelphia: Westminster, 165-299.

The Second Cycle (Three Sea Miracles) (8:23–9:17)

The second cycle of miracles clusters around the Sea of Galilee (8:18, 23, 28; 9:1). As in the first cycle, Jesus helps members of his inner group, Gentiles, and a Jew by demonstrating his control over natural forces, evil spirits, and bodily impairments. This cycle emphasizes the responses of Jesus' audiences: his disciples are amazed at his calming of a storm at sea (8:27); the Gentiles across the sea ask Jesus to leave after he exorcises two possessed men (8:34); the Jewish crowd in Capernaum expresses awe and glorifies God after the healing of a paralytic (9:8); but the scribes and Pharisees criticize Jesus for his teaching (9:3) and behavior (9:11).

The story of Jesus and his disciples on the lake in a storm (8:23-27) has long been read by the Christian church as a symbol of itself in a hostile world. However, the hostile sea threatening to swamp the disciples' boat because of an earthquake (v. 24; not a "windstorm" as in the NRSV; contrast Mark 4:37, which does refer to a windstorm) recalls the Near Eastern myths of a battle between the sky god (order) and the sea goddess (chaos). Earthquakes also connote the apocalyptic end of the world and resurrection (Matt 24:7; 27:51; 28:2; and Rev 6:12). The boat in a storm recalls Israel crossing the sea (Exodus 15), the terrors of evil (1QH 3[Puech 11]:6, 13-18; 6[Puech 14]:22-25; 7[Puech 15]:4-5), and the story of Jonah on a ship sinking in a storm. Jesus' control over the waves thus implies control over cosmic evil as well, and marks him out as greater than Jonah (12:41). Thus Jesus is an object of amazement to "the men" (8:27 — not "they," as in the NRSV, or "the disciples," as we would expect) in the boat. Jesus, the "Lord" who saved them (v. 25), is depicted as greater than a mere human and is contrasted with the disciples, who have "little faith," that is, who lack full confidence in Jesus' power to rule the universe and who thus have not yet accepted him as the Son of God (cf. 14:33 at the end of the other storm miracle).

The second miracle of the second cycle is the first exorcism story in the Gospel (8:28-34), though the fact that Jesus exorcised has been mentioned previously. Ancient society took demons and demon possession for granted and attributed to them a wide variety of ills, including some sicknesses. Jesus as a powerful holy man would be expected to control both natural forces and evil spirits which afflict humans. The author of Matthew has abbreviated Mark's vivid, complex version of this story (Mark 5:1-20) to put attention squarely on Jesus, not on the spectacular character of the exorcism of the possessed. The demons recognize Jesus as the "Son of God" at a stage in the Gospel when the disciples still do not (8:27) and fear an early judgment, which is why they ask for reprieve in a herd of pigs. Jesus grants their request, but ironically he torments them when the pigs stampede into the water.

The presence of a herd of pigs indicates that Jesus is interacting with Gentiles, even though Jews lived across the sea where Jesus traveled. The name of the city has been garbled in the manuscripts. The best reading in the Gospel of Matthew is Gadara, a city six miles southeast of the Sea of Galilee. Since the story must take place near the water, the author probably understands the territory of the city to reach the shore of the Sea. (Mark 5:1 and Luke 8:26 in the best manuscripts refer to Gerasa, a major city of the Decapolis which is over thirty miles inland.) Typically of Matthew, Jesus exorcises two possessed men instead of one (8:28 in contrast to Mark 5:2; cf. Matt 9:27; 20:30 for similar doublings of Markan cures). Jesus' trip across the lake comes to nothing because the people of the area inhospitably ask him to leave. This outcome coheres with Matthew's plot, which restricts Jesus' work to Israel and has no real place for Jesus' trip to Gentile territory. In contrast, Mark and Luke give an excuse for the Gentiles' inhospitality, that they feared Jesus, and they have Jesus leave the exorcised man there to testify to what Jesus has done. In Matthew Jesus merely recrosses the lake to his own town, Capernaum (9:1).

As Jesus arrives at Capernaum, some people carry to him a man who is unable to walk, presumably near the shore, in the hope that Jesus will heal him (9:2-8). In Mark 2:1-12 and Luke 5:17-26 the man is lowered to Jesus through the roof of a house, but Matthew has simplified and relocated the scene. Before Jesus heals the man he encourages him and forgives his sins. The belief that sickness could be a punishment for sin was widespread in antiquity (Lev 26:14-33; Deuteronomy 28; Isa 1:5-6; John 9:34), but it does not seem to be operative here. Rather, the story extends Jesus' powers and efforts from the physical to the inner world, so that the healing of a physical disability symbolizes the healing of a person's relationship before God. Interestingly, Jesus directly forgives the sins of humans in only one other story in the Gospels, that of the sinful woman (Luke 7:48), but the underlying theme of forgiveness of sins spans the Gospel of Matthew from Jesus' birth (1:21) to his final meal with his disciples (26:28). Jesus' reference to the "Son of Man" (v. 6) implies divine power communicated by God to God's emissary, Jesus. The more general expression of this power at the end of the story, when the crowds marvel that God had given such power to "men" (plural — v. 8), supports Matthew's view that the church community can forgive sins (16:13-19; 18:15-20).

The smooth flow of the healing narrative from request to fulfillment is interrupted by a conflict between Jesus and some scribes, who are probably community officials or teachers who object to Jesus' claim to forgive sins. (Note that the scribes, the Pharisees, and John the Baptist's disciples challenge Jesus one after another here and in the following two stories.) The scribes do not challenge Jesus publicly but complain privately that he has blasphemed (9:3), that is, injured God's reputation (Lev 24:16), by claiming God's prerogative to forgive sins. But Jesus knows what they are saying and challenges them publicly to a debate, which he wins. The author enhances Jesus' power and dominance of the institutional scribes through Jesus' extraordinary knowledge of their thoughts and manifest power to heal the lame man's body.

Teachings about Jesus' activities and discipleship (9:9-17) follow the second miracle cycle, as they did the first, but here with an emphasis on forgiveness. Jesus calls as a disciple Matthew, a collector of customs in Capernaum. Since tax collectors worked ultimately for a foreign government, the Roman Empire, and since they often aggrandized themselves by collecting excessive taxes, they were socially despised in Israel. Thus in calling Matthew (v. 9) and eating with tax collectors and sinners (v. 10), Jesus transgressed social propriety in favor of the ostracized. Though eating with Jewish sinners and tax collectors is not against the law, it transgresses the normal boundaries maintained by social pressure. However, associating with socially marginal people is typical of a new group which seeks to recruit those rejected by society at large. The Pharisees, who appear here for the first time, challenge Jesus because they were a group who highly valued holiness and the biblical purity laws. Against their interpretation of the biblical law (righteousness), Jesus affirms his calling to aid sinners by citing a proverb about a physician tending to the sick and by quoting Hos 6:6 (also cited in 12:7), which teaches that God values mercy above all (9:11-13).

The name of the toll collector varies in Matthew and Mark. In the Markan version of this story Jesus calls a toll collector named Levi, son of Alphaeus (Mark 2:14). Some commentators speculate that this person had two names; others think that the author of the Gospel of Matthew changed the name Levi to Matthew because Levi appeared in none of the lists of the twelve apostles or because the name Matthew sounds similar to the Greek word for disciple, *mathētēs.* Still others identify the toll collector Matthew as the author of the Gospel of Matthew. In the end the reason for the variation in names remains uncertain.

After the conflict over a meal, John the Baptist's disciples, who live an ascetic life of repentance, challenge Jesus' "different" behavior in not fasting regularly (9:14-17). Jesus does not reject regular fasting (6:6-8), which was probably practiced on Mondays and Thursdays by the early Christians, but further qualifies its appropriateness here (cf. 11:19 also). Jesus defends his practice with the metaphor of a wedding feast, an allusion to his coming death, and two comparisons between old and new. The comparisons (9:16-17) defend new behaviors for new situations, though the author at the very end promotes saving both old and new teachings and customs (cf. 13:52). This compact discussion probably reflects early church disputes over fasting practices.

The Third Cycle (Three Miracle Stories) (9:18-38)

The third and final miracle cycle contains three progressively shorter stories involving four miracles affecting five people. The raising of the ruler's dead daughter encloses the healing of a hemorrhaging woman, a double story from Mark 5:21-43. In Matthew's abbreviated version of the story, the ruler is not identified as Jew or Gentile, nor is his name given, in contrast to Mark's version where he is Jewish and named Jairus. Both the ruler and the woman express unusual faith in Jesus. The ruler trusts that Jesus can bring life back to his daughter who has just died, and the woman who just touches the "fringe" ("hem," "tassel") of his cloak trusts that he will "save" her. ("Fringes" were required on garments by Num 15:38-41 and Deut 22:12.) Jesus makes the woman's unspoken attitude explicit when he tells her that her faith has saved her. The Greek verb "save" (9:21, 22 [twice]) means "cure" here and is so translated in the NRSV, but has wider connotations in Matthew. The faith of the woman and of the leader who came to Jesus contrasts sharply with the attitude of the mourners, who laugh at Jesus' confidence that the girl will awaken. The author plays on the word "sleep," which is a euphemism for death, so that it suggests that in this case death is not final. Despite rationalist hypotheses that the girl was not really dead, in Matthew's narrative she has died (v. 18, in contrast to Mark 5:23 where she is on the point of death), people mourn her, and Jesus raises her from death, a messianic activity listed later in 11:5. The disciples who accompany him (9:19) witness his accomplishment, and the whole land (area, district) hears of it.

The author of Matthew retells the last two healing stories (9:27-34) in different versions later on (20:29-34; 12:22-24). The story of the two blind men emphasizes confidence (faith) in Jesus' power to heal (9:27-31), and the story of the possessed man who is mute contrasts appreciation and opposition to Jesus' healing activity (vv. 32-34). Though the very request to be cured of blindness implies confidence in Jesus' power to heal, as it does in other healing stories, here Jesus explicitly asks the two blind men if they believe he can cure them. Their positive response and addressing Jesus as "Lord" (v. 28) make exquisitely clear the underlying transaction between Jesus and those in need of his extraordinary power. Here, as elsewhere, two people are cured (8:34; 20:30). They address Jesus as "Son of David," a title which identifies Jesus not only with David as an anointed leader (i.e., Messiah) but also with David's son and successor Solomon, who was known in the Jewish tradition for his wisdom and healing powers (cf. also 12:23, 15:23; 20:30-31; 21:15). Jesus' command that the men not speak about their cure fits Matthew's view of Jesus as a modest, low-key helper (12:15-21).

The final miracle story (9:32-34) merely reports that the possessed man was exorcised and could speak. Because he is possessed, the man is *kophos,* a Greek term which can mean deaf and/or mute. In Matt 11:5 it is used for the deaf, but here it refers to inability to speak. The contrasting reactions of the crowds and Pharisees conclude the miracle cycles and foreshadow opposition to Jesus and his disciples. The amazement of the crowds (see 8:27; 15:31) and their judgment that "never has anything like this been seen in Israel" (v. 33) serve as a climactic summary to Jesus' healing all through chs. 8–9. The mention of Israel prepares the readers for the disciples' ministry to Israel in ch. 10. The Pharisees acknowledge Jesus' power but undercut it with an accusation that Jesus' power over demons is itself demonic (9:34; cf. 10:25; 12:24). Their negative appraisal prepares for the opposition to the disciples described in ch. 10 and the growing hostility to Jesus in chs. 11–12.

The final verses of ch. 9 (vv. 35-38) bring chs. 5–9 to a close and begin the transition to the missionary instruction in ch. 10. Strikingly, 9:35 repeats the opening summary in 4:23 almost exactly and ties together Jesus' teachings in the Sermon on the Mount and his powerful deeds in chs. 8–9. Matthew's introduction of Jesus the teacher and miracle worker is complete. Now the author turns his attention to the disciples' responsibility to teach and heal as Jesus did (ch. 10) and to Jesus' further efforts to teach the kingdom of God to Israel (chs. 11–13). According to the author, the situation is critical. The crowds (Israel) are "harassed and helpless" because they are badly led (9:36) and in danger of being lost like an ungathered harvest. Only Jesus' compassion for them and the advent of new workers sent by God will result in their being gathered and preserved (vv. 37-38).

Bibliography. Bornkamm, G. 1964, "The Stilling of the Storm in Matthew," in G. Bornkamm, G. Barth, and H. J. Held, *Tradition and Interpretation,* Philadelphia: Westminster, 52-57 • Chilton, B. D. 1982, "Jesus *ben David:* Reflections on the *Davidssohnfrage,*" *JSNT* 14:88-112 • Craghan, J. 1968, "The Gerasene Demoniac," *CBQ* 30:522-36 • Duling, D. C. 1977-78, "The Therapeutic Son of David: An Element in Matthew's Christological Apologetic," *NTS* 24:392-410 • Feiler, P. F. 1983, "The Stilling of the Storm in Matthew: A Response to Günther Bornkamm," *JETS* 26:399-406 • Gerhardsson, B. 1979, *The Mighty Acts of Jesus According to Matthew,* Lund: Gleerup • Heil, J. P. 1979, "Significant Aspects of the Healing Miracles in Matthew," *CBQ* 41:274-87 • Hill, D. 1977, "On the Use and Meaning of Hosea vi.6 in Matthew's Gospel," *NTS* 24:107-19 • Kiley, M. 1984, "Why 'Matthew' in Matt 9,9-13?" *Bib* 65:347-51 • Kingsbury, J. D. 1978, "Observations on the 'Miracle Chapters' of Matthew 8–9," *CBQ* 40:559-73 • Kingsbury, J. D. 1988, "On Following Jesus: The 'Eager' Scribe and 'Reluctant' Disciple (Matthew 8:18-22)," *NTS* 34:45-59 • Robbins, V. K. 1987, "The Woman Who Touched Jesus' Garment: Socio-Rhetorical Analysis of the Synoptic Accounts," *NTS* 33:502-15 • Thompson, W. G. 1971, "Reflections on the Composition of Mt 8:1–9:34," *CBQ* 33:365-88.

Introduction to the Missionary Sermon (Matthew 10)

When Jesus sends his disciples to teach and heal as he did (10:1; cf. 4:23–9:35), he formally acquires a stable group of followers which foreshadows the Matthean community to whom this Gospel is addressed. The instructions to the disciples, especially from 10:16 on, anticipate the persecution and opposition experienced by the early Jesus movement and by Matthew's community. Following Jesus and recruiting other followers entail necessary and inevitable rejection, oppression, persecution, and suffering. The theme of persecution has been anticipated in the eighth beatitude (5:10-12) and will be actualized in the disputes and hostility in chs. 11–12. The theme reaches its fulfillment in the passion predictions and instruction beginning in 16:21, the conflicts with the Jerusalem authorities in chs. 21–23, and Jesus' passion and death. The end of the missionary sermon may be divided into three parts, each concluding with a saying initiated by the formula "Truly I say to you" (10:15, 23, 42).

Sending Out the Twelve (10:1-15)

Jesus answers his own prayer for harvest workers at the end of ch. 9 by sending his twelve disciples/apostles (10:1, 2) to exorcise and heal (vv. 1, 8; cf. 4:23; 9:35) and to announce the kingdom (v. 7; cf. 4:17), just as he has done in chs. 4–9. The group of disciples whose names are listed here is most often referred to as "the twelve"; only at the beginning of this sermon are they called the twelve apostles (10:2) and at the end the twelve disciples (10:1; 11:1). ("Twelve disciples" in 20:17 is an uncertain reading in the Greek mss.). The common Christian use of the term "apostles" for the twelve derives from Luke-Acts. Here they are designated "apostles" because they are "sent out" (the literal meaning of apostle) by Jesus. Matt 10:2-4 and Mark 3:16-19 list the same twelve names; Luke 6:14-16 and Acts 1:13 replace Thaddeus with Judas (Jude), son of James. The twelve as a designated group appear in Matthew here (10:1; 11:1), and as judges over the twelve tribes of Israel at the end (19:28), while traveling to Jerusalem (20:17), and at Jesus' final meal and arrest (26:14, 20, 47). In each case they have a formal task (mission, judgment, and witness). Otherwise, in dozens of passages, the Gospel refers to Jesus' followers, both the twelve and others, as disciples, that is, as students of Jesus the teacher. Throughout the Gospel the author of Matthew emphasizes Jesus' instruction of his disciples.

The sermon begins with concrete directions about where to go (10:5-6), what to do (vv. 7-10), and how to respond to the people they meet in Jewish villages in Israel (vv. 11-15). Like Jesus, the disciples confine their efforts to "the lost sheep of the house of Israel" (v. 6; cf. 9:36); efforts to teach non-Jews will begin after Jesus' resurrection (28:16-20). The disciples do as Jesus did; they proclaim the kingdom, heal, exorcise, and even raise the dead (10:7-8). They are not to profit from their work, but to accept food and lodging from those they instruct and help (vv. 8-10). In some villages they will be put up in someone's house, but in others they will be rejected (vv. 11-14). These instructions fit the lower Galilean countryside in the Esdraelon valley where agricultural towns, villages, and hamlets were numerous and close to one another. A traveling teacher might be well received by one rural community and avoided as suspicious or troublesome by others. If rejected in one town, he could walk to another in an hour or less. He would always be close to his home or a friendly dwelling, and so he would not need money, extra clothing, or even a staff. The judgment against villages which reject Jesus' disciples (v. 15) begins with the solemn formula, "Truly [Amen] I tell you." Here and elsewhere (cf. 5:18, 26; 6:2, 5, 26; 8:10, and frequently) it marks a teaching or warning as important and fraught with serious consequences.

Persecution (10:16-23)

The judicial proceedings and punishments and the communal and family hostility against the followers of Jesus described in this section of the sermon pertain historically to the early followers of Jesus after his death rather than to the disciples' experience during his lifetime. The author of Matthew conceives of opposition, rejection, and persecution as a permanent dimension of following Jesus, and tries to strengthen his community to accept it. Disciples of Jesus will flee and endure danger, but they will never totally escape it. They must be sheep among wolves who are wise as serpents and innocent as doves (10:16). Conflict over following Jesus will incite family members to betray one another to the courts and execution. In Gentile courts the disciples will give testimony with the help of the Spirit (vv. 18-20). Matthew's assembly *(ekklēsia)* of followers of Jesus will be hated by all to such an extent that only endurance and flight will bring salvation (v. 22; cf. Matt 24:13, 20). The themes of flight, social conflict, family discord, and endurance come from Mark's description of events near the end of the world (Mark 13:9-13), but Matthew has integrated them into the ongoing life of the community, perhaps because of the intracommunal conflict in Israel before, during, and after the war with Rome (AD 66-70). The climactic and concluding saying of this section of the sermon, that the Son of Man will come before the disciples finish visiting all the towns of Israel (v. 23), probably refers to Matthew's attempt to recruit his fellow Jews in Galilee and contiguous territories where Jewish communities were numerous. Though some commentators have tried to associate the coming of the Son of Man with the resurrection or the destruction of Jerusalem in AD 70, the expression refers here as elsewhere (e.g., Daniel 7) to the full coming of God's kingdom.

Advice for Facing Persecution (10:24-42)

The last section of the sermon on discipleship is less tightly organized than the previous two. It consists of proverbial advice, thematically connected but not tightly wound like modern discursive prose. The author of Matthew drew materials from the Jesus traditions with which he was familiar and arranged the sayings for his own purposes. All proverbial material requires a reflective, imaginative reading which associates revealed or traditional wisdom with contemporary experience so that they mutually illuminate one another. The juxtaposition of proverbs, instructions, and exhortations in ch. 10 further enriches the context for their interpretation.

Previously, Jesus has instructed the disciples to teach and heal as he has done and to expect rejection and persecution likewise. Now he gives them a reason for the persecution: a disciple or servant can expect the same treatment as his or her master (10:24-25). The metaphor of a household underlies Jesus' relationship to his disciples as well as the author's to his late-first-century community. Jesus' opponents reject not just Jesus but his whole household by demonizing master and servants. In calling Jesus "Beelzebul" they attribute his power and his disciples' as well to the devil (v. 25; cf. 9:34; 12:24). Beelzebul is a mocking, derisive name meaning "Lord of dung"; Beelzebub, a less-well-attested manuscript variant, means "Lord of flies" (cf. Baal-zebul in 2 Kgs 1:2). These names are a wordplay on an old epithet for the Canaanite sky-god, "Prince" or "Exalted One" (*zebul* or *zabul*). In the Gospels Beelzebul is synonymous with Satan (12:34, 36).

In response to pejorative labeling and active opposition the disciples are told, "Do not fear" (10:26, 28, 31). Their fear, which might impede them from disclosing Jesus' teaching (vv. 26-27), is groundless because human opponents can kill only the body, not the soul, and because God, who cares for sparrows and knows the number of hairs on people's heads, will care for them (vv. 28-31). Matthew's instruction to trust in God repeats some of the themes of the Sermon on the Mount (6:25-33) and draws sayings from Q (Luke 12:2-9). His advice to be courageous goes far beyond emotional well-being in that it entails public acknowledgment of Jesus in the face of resistance. For this reason, one's acknowledgment or rejection of Jesus entitles the disciple to similar treatment by Jesus at the judgment (10:32-33).

The comforting reminder of God's care for birds and humans does not change the harsh realities of following Jesus, nor does it bring about social peace. Joining Jesus and his "household" causes disruption and conflict within one's family (10:34-36; cf. Luke 12:51-53 and Q, which depend on Mic 7:6), as already predicted in this chapter (10:21-22). Contrary to the most fundamental social values of the Near East, those who follow Jesus must love him more than their parents or children and take up his cross, that is, be willing to suffer violent and dishonorable death and all that goes with it (vv. 37-38). Though the imagery is familiar through frequent repetition, the author of Matthew envisions a catastrophic loss of everything which is humanly valuable and necessary for social and individual survival. He rebukes those who would preserve ("find") their lives and promises that those who lose their life will find it in return (at the end). This rigorous instruction pertains most properly to violent persecution and to the end of the world (Mark 8:34–9:1; 13:12; *1 Enoch* 56:7; 100:1-2; 4 Ezra 6:24), but it implies a demanding way of life in preparation for such sufferings.

This last, long section of the missionary sermon ends as it began, with attention to the treatment of Jesus and his followers (10:40-42; cf. vv. 24-25). The success of the disciples' mission in the narrative and of the Matthean community in the late first century depends on the reception they receive from the people whom they approach. Thus the fundamental principle of the whole chapter is concisely and clearly articulated, that receiving a follower of Jesus means receiving both Jesus who sent the disciples and God who sent Jesus (v. 40). This crucially important first step, accepting Jesus and his disciples, will result in a commensurate reward (vv. 41-42). The distinctive roles of Jesus' followers invoked here, prophets, righteous persons, and little ones, are somewhat obscure. Some commentators refer the three terms to all members of the Matthean community, while others reserve them for specially dedicated members who spread the good news about Jesus. Still others suggest that the community recognized the specialized roles of prophets, teachers, and missionaries (see "prophets, sages, and scribes" as members of Matthew's community in 23:34 and the implied role of prophets in 7:15). If so, their functions and the structure of the Matthean community still remain obscure. "Little ones" is a symbolic name here associated with disciples (10:42) and used as a name for the members of Matthew's community in the sermon on communal order (18:6, 10, 14).

The sermon ends in 11:1 with the formula "when Jesus had finished instructing his twelve disciples." Jesus, like his disciples, goes on to teach and proclaim his message. Interestingly, the Gospel contains no account of the disciples' return because in the author's view the task to which Jesus sent his disciples has not yet been completed and continues on in his own day. The disciples have not yet gone to all the towns of Israel (10:23), nor has "this good news of the kingdom" been "proclaimed throughout the world, as a testimony to all the nations" (24:14). These tasks must be accomplished before the end will come, according to Matthew. In the meantime, in the narrative the disciples are with Jesus in his teaching and healing (11:2–16:20) and in his death and resurrection (16:21–28:20).

Bibliography. Beare, F. W. 1970, "The Mission of the Disciples and the Mission Charge: Matthew 10 and Parallels," *JBL* 89:1-13 • Brown, S. 1978, "The Mission to Israel in Matthew's Central Section (Mt 9:35–11:1)," *ZNW* 69:73-90 • Combrink, H. J. B. 1977, "Structural Analysis of Mt 9,35–11,1," *Neot* 11:98-114 • Luz, U. 2d ed. 1995, "The Disciples in the Gospel According to Matthew," in Stanton, G. N., ed., *The Interpretation of Matthew,* Philadelphia: Fortress • McDermott, J. M. 1984, "Mt. 10:23 in Context," *BZ* 28:230-40 • Weaver, D. J. *Matthew's Missionary Discourse: A Literary Critical Analysis,* JSNTSup 38, Sheffield: JSOT • Wilkins, M. 1988, *The Concept of Disciple in Matthew's Gospel,* NovTSup 59, Leiden: Brill, repr. 1995 as *Discipleship in the Ancient World and Matthew's Gospel,* Grand Rapids: Baker.

The Deeds of Jesus and John the Baptizer in Israel (11:2-19)

John the Baptizer's inquiry concerning Jesus' identity (11:2-3) raises the question of the Messiah and uses the word "Messiah/Christ" as an explicit title for the first time since the story of the Magi (2:4). (It will next be used when Peter and the disciples identify Jesus as Messiah in 16:16.) Jesus' reply sums up his activity since it began in 4:23. John's question comes from the fortress at Machaerus, east of the Dead Sea, where John had been imprisoned by Herod Antipas the ruler of Galilee, whom John had rebuked for an illicit marriage (cf. 4:12; 14:1-12).

John heard of "the deeds *(erga)* of *the* Christ [Messiah]" (11:2, literally translated) and sent his disciples to inquire about Jesus. The term "deeds" refers to Jesus' teachings and miracles just narrated in chs. 5–10, that is, to what people "hear and see" (v. 4). Jesus refers later in this chapter to wisdom (identified with Jesus) being known by her deeds (v. 19), to his powerful deeds *(dynameis),* that is, healings (vv. 20-21), and to the revelation and light yoke offered to his followers (vv. 25-30). Thus Jesus' activities identify him, if correctly interpreted. The list of six types of deeds done by Jesus (v. 5) has been drawn from several passages in Isaiah (26:19; 35:5-6; 61:1; also 29:18; 42:7, 18) and together the types fairly characterize Jesus' work in the previous few chapters of the Gospel. The citation of Isaiah turns the audience's attention again to the fulfillment of Scripture (5:17); in the next chapter Matthew will once again use Isaiah to identify Jesus and his works (12:17-21, using Isa 42:1-4).

The interaction of Jesus and John in ch. 3 began Jesus' public role; here it begins a new stage of the Gospel. In Matthew's narrative John's inquiry about the Messiah stems from sincere doubt since John expected the Messiah to inaugurate imminent, direct intervention in the world and divine judgment (3:10-12). In addition, Jesus' approach to the reformation of Israel differs from John's, as he points out later in this chapter. John fasts and Jesus does not; Jesus heals and John does not (vv. 18-20). Thus John, in common with many first-century Jews, did not expect a Messiah like Jesus. Some Jews did not expect an anointed leader at all. Among those who did, some pictured him as a priest, and others as a prophet, an angelic figure sent from heaven by God, or a military leader who would defeat the Romans. Jesus recognizes John's confusion and warns against rejecting him (being scandalized – v. 6) because he does not meet some of the current expectations. Jesus' blessing of those who accept him (v. 6) as he is described in Isa 61:1 recalls the initial list of blessings (beatitudes), several of which are also linked to Isa 61:1 (cf. 5:3-10). For Matthew, Scripture correctly interpreted describes the behavior of the Messiah and of those who enter the kingdom.

The blessing (11:6) is also a polemical challenge to Jesus' opponents who play major roles in chs. 11–12. If even John the Baptizer questions Jesus, certainly the leaders such as the Pharisees and scribes as well as some of the people in the villages will be "tripped up" by Jesus' teachings and deeds and reject him. Jesus interprets John as a challenge to the crowds and as a precursor of the Messiah (vv. 7-15). John lives in the wilderness, away from normal Jewish life. He does not bend like a reed on the shore of the Jordan River nor wear luxurious clothing (cf. 3:4), but, like a prophet (11:7-9), he criticizes Jewish society. Because he and Jesus are both reformers, the Gospel connects John to Jesus and enlarges his role. John is greater than a prophet (v. 9) or any figure in Israel (v. 11). He is a messenger sent to prepare the way for Jesus (v. 10; Exod 23:20; Mal 3:1; Mark 1:2), the legitimate inheritor of the law and prophets (v. 13). In early Christian interpretation John is also the prophet Elijah returning before the coming of the Messiah (v. 14). Since Elijah was taken up to heaven in a fiery chariot (2 Kgs 2:11), he was thought of as still alive and available to return to earth just before the day when God would intervene to bring justice to the world (Mal 4:5-6). The linking of Elijah with the Messiah appears for the first time in the Gospels (Mark 9:12-13; Luke 1:17; John 1:25; etc., but contrast John 1:21) as part of the early church's reflection on Jesus as the Messiah. Here the author of Matthew makes the identification of John the Baptizer with Elijah explicit as a summary of John's role (11:14). To the early followers of Jesus John was a figure linking Jesus with the biblical tradition. Historical schemes which argue about placing John outside the time of Jesus (v. 11) or within it (vv. 9, 12-13) miss the point that in Matthew John stands with one foot in traditional Judaism and the other in the type of renewal of Judaism taught by him and Jesus. According to an enigmatic saying (v. 12), the kingdom announced by John and Jesus provoked a violent reaction among their opponents. The Greek verb for "suffering violence" and the noun for "violent ones" (v. 12) have pejorative connotations, so the observation about the violent taking the kingdom by force is not praising people who forcefully seek the kingdom. Rather, those who reject God's rule violently attack those who accept it. In this context the saying alludes to the opposition which Jesus is about to face and to the deaths of John and Jesus.

The proverbial story of children taunting one another while playing a funeral game and a wedding game (11:16-17) trivializes the opposition to Jesus and John as arbitrary and inconsistent. To "this generation," that is, the hypercritical leaders and their followers who oppose Jesus and John, Jesus' normality appears as license (v. 19) and John's asceticism seems demonic (v. 18), a charge which is made against Jesus' powerful deeds (10:25; 12:22-32). Jesus' opponents accept nothing and reject all the deeds of the Messiah (v. 2) and of wisdom (v. 19). (The phrase "this generation" recalls "this evil generation" in Deut 1:35, i.e., the generation which distrusted God in the wilderness.) In response to these critics, the author of Matthew identifies Jesus with wisdom at the end of this unit, just as he identified him as the Messiah at the beginning, in order to authenticate his teachings and deeds. As personified wisdom appealed to young men to accept her, but some refused (Proverbs 1–9), Jesus and John have appealed to this generation with mixed results. The pattern has continued for the author and his community at the end of the first century, and the narrative will illustrate this opposition in subsequent encounters.

Jesus' Appeal to Galilee (11:20-30)

The cities in which Jesus did most of his deeds of power (*dynameis,* a Greek term used for miracles), Chorazin, Bethsaida, and Capernaum, are near each other in northeast lower Galilee, near the shore of the Sea (11:20). The narrative connects these deeds of power with wisdom's deeds in the previous verse and the deeds of the Messiah at the beginning of the chapter (v. 2). The rejection of Jesus' miracles by those living in his region matches the rejection of Jesus' "wisdom and deeds of power" by his neighbors in his hometown, Nazareth (13:54). Though Jesus spent most of his time in this small area of Galilee near Capernaum, the majority of the people had not repented (11:20) and reformed their lives under the rule of God. This admission probably reflects Jesus' failure to reform Galilean society in his lifetime as well as the failures of his early followers and of the late-first-century Matthean community to win over a majority of their fellow Jews.

Jesus prophetically condemns Chorazin, Bethsaida, and Capernaum with two parallel judgment oracles (11:21-24) consisting of direct address, an indictment, and a verdict (see parallels in Isa 5:11-17; Mic 2:1-5). Chorazin and Bethsaida compare unfavorably with Tyre and Sidon, two Gentile port cities on the Mediterranean coast. The Bible usually condemns Tyre, which culturally influenced the mountainous regions of upper Galilee (Isaiah 23; Ezekiel 28). This judgment oracle, however, imagines Tyre and Sidon as repentant, like Nineveh in the book of Jonah, in contrast to Israel, which has not responded to God's prophets. People customarily mourned or did penance in "sackcloth [rough animal skins usually used to make sacks] and ashes" (11:21). The second oracle similarly compares Capernaum, Jesus' "own city" (9:1), to Sodom, the notoriously evil city destroyed by fire and brimstone (Genesis 19), which was frequently used as an example of corruption and total destruction (Deut 32:32; Isa 1:10; 13:19; Zech 2:9, etc.; Matt 10:15; Rom 9:29; Rev 11:8). The oracle also draws upon language in Isaiah's oracle against Babylon, the destroyer of the temple (Isa 14:11, 13, 15). These oracles more directly attack Jesus' opponents than the wisdom sayings about the children which precede.

Jesus completes his appeal to Galilee by thanking God for revealing "these things" to him and by inviting those in need to follow him (11:25-30). He speaks like Wisdom in Proverbs, inviting the foolish and uneducated to gain wisdom and virtue. He also subtly continues his polemic against his opponents by claiming that God has hidden these things from the "wise and intelligent," that is, the educated leaders of the Jewish community, and revealed them through Jesus to "infants" (v. 25). Jesus' wisdom, identified only as "these things" *(tauta)*, presumably concerns the kingdom of God as clarified by Jesus' actions and teachings. The infants, who are uncharacteristically wise and favored, are the followers of Jesus and the members of Matthew's community who elsewhere are called "little ones" and the "least" (18:3-4, 6, 10; 25:39, 45). They, like Jesus here, are meek and humble (11:29; 5:5; 18:4), weary and burdened (11:28), and need rest (vv. 29-30). For them Jesus has "all things . . . handed over" to him by his Father (v. 27); the term "handed over" suggests tradition — in this case, as revelation and its interpretation. Jesus immediately offers all the things he has received to the needy by inviting them to take up his easy yoke and light burden (vv. 29-30). The yoke metaphor refers to observance of the commandments. The author of Matthew contrasts Jesus and implicitly himself with rival Jewish teachers who have not really recognized (NRSV, "know") and accepted Jesus' interpretation of the commandments (v. 27; cf. Exod 33:12-23, esp. 12-13). The identification of Jesus as wisdom and as the teacher of the law who knows God, like Moses in Exodus 33, solidifies his position as God's unique representative. For Matthew's community Jesus' promise of rest (11:28-29; cf. Exod 33:14) addresses their suffering and oppression. Within the narrative the lightening of burdens, easy yoke, and rest point concretely to Jesus' interpretations of sabbath law which follow immediately (12:1-14) and anticipate the author's interpretation of Jesus as the gentle servant of God (12:17-21).

Bibliography. Cameron, P. S. 1984, *Violence and the Kingdom: The Interpretation of Matthew 11.12,* Frankfurt: P. Lang • Deutsch, C. 1987, *Hidden Wisdom and the Easy Yoke: Wisdom, Torah and Discipleship in Matthew 11,25-30,* Sheffield: JSOT • Deutsch, C. 1996, *Lady Wisdom, Jesus and the Sages: Metaphor and Social Context in Matthew's Gospel,* Valley Forge, Pa.: Trinity Press International • Lambrecht, J. 1980, "Are You the One Who Is to Come, or Shall We Look for Another?" *Louvain Studies* 8:115-28 • Moore, W. E. 1975, "BIAZO, ARPAZO and Cognates in Josephus," *NTS* 21:519-43 • Moore, W. E. 1989, "Violence and the Kingdom," *ExpTim* 100:174-77 • Suggs, J. 1970, *Wisdom, Christology and Law in Matthew's Gospel,* Cambridge: Cambridge University • Verseput, D. 1986, *The Rejection of the Humble Messianic King,* Frankfurt: P. Lang.

Jesus' Interpretation of the Law (12:1-21)

Jesus disputes twice with the Pharisees over sabbath observance (12:1-14). The precise arguments and conclusions reflect the author's interpretation of Jesus' teachings about sabbath law. Some commentators on Matthew 12 have argued that Matthew, like Jesus before him, rejects a "legalistic" or "ritualistic" observance of the sabbath. However, neither addresses such polemical abstractions. Matthew focuses the discussion on two precise points: what kinds of activity could override the sabbath rest and what principle was more important, keeping the sabbath or caring for human needs. The topics of debate and the types of argument proposed were common in Jewish legal discussions in the first century. The author of Matthew was familiar with Jewish discourse on law and took part in it by defending Jesus' positions as he interpreted them.

In the first case the disciples have picked heads of grain to assuage their hunger as they walked through the fields on the sabbath (cf. Deut 23:25), and the Pharisees have accused them of harvesting, a forbidden type of work on the sabbath. In recounting the story, the author of Matthew begins with an explicit disclaimer that Jesus' disciples were hungry (12:1). This foreshadows the argument based on David and his men's hunger (vv. 3-4) and the principle of mercy (v. 7; Hos 6:6) adduced later on and defuses the charge of wanton disregard of the sabbath. The Pharisees' position, that casual picking of grain as a snack was forbidden, was probably based on the principle that food for the sabbath should be prepared the day previous (Exod 16:22-30; *Jub.* 50:9). Matthew defends his more permissive interpretation of sabbath law by citing an inexact biblical parallel, David feeding himself and his men with the Loaves of the Presence from the sanctuary at Nob as they fled Saul (1 Samuel 21). Since David's case does not concern sabbath observance but eating consecrated loaves, Matthew adds another argument which he did not find in Mark 2:23-28. In the temple priests engage in activities forbidden on the sabbath in order to carry out sabbath sacrifices required by the law (Matt 12:5-6; cf. Num 28:9). Matthew applies the temple service precedent to the case of the disciples by comparing Jesus to the temple and finding him greater than the temple. Therefore, the disciples' actions, like those of the priests, are allowed according to the well-known principle of arguing from the lesser to the greater *(qal waḥomer)*. But this claim is not patently cogent. If Jesus is greater than the temple, then the disciples might be justified in serving *him* the way priests serve the temple; but the disciples serve themselves in their hunger and do not feed Jesus.

Matthew invokes two other principles to support Jesus' teaching, mercy and Jesus' divinely given authority. The foundation of Matthew's case rests on the principle of mercy found in Hos 6:6 (12:7), a verse which is quoted elsewhere in Jewish literature to support atonement through prayer (1QS 9:3-5) and the value of acts of lovingkindness in place of the lost temple sacrifices (*Fathers According to Rabbi Nathan*, A, ch. 4). Here the author of Matthew uses this "weightier" commandment of mercy (cf. 23:23) to define what is allowed and forbidden on the sabbath. He meets a real but not life-threatening (for the principle of "saving a life," see *m. Yoma* 8:6) need by ruling, contrary to the Pharisees, that the casual picking of another's crops on the sabbath to assuage immediate hunger was allowed. Perhaps the distinction between a casual snack and reaping in Deut 23:25 prompted Matthew's distinction, but he does not make this clear. He gives the principle of mercy in response to human need a higher priority than his opponents do and thus authorizes assuaging hunger on the sabbath even if the food has not been previously prepared. The second principle, "the Son of Man is Lord of the sabbath" (v. 8), reflects Matthew's recognition of the authority of the risen Jesus to interpret Scripture and teach in God's name (28:18).

The second sabbath controversy over whether Jesus should cure a man with a withered hand on the sabbath (12:9-14) continues the theme of mercy for humans in need, but this conflict is sharper because the Pharisees confront Jesus in "their synagogue" (v. 9) in order to entrap Jesus (v. 10). The battle over interpretation of the law begins in scholastic fashion when the Pharisees ask Jesus whether it is permitted (*exestin* in Greek; *mutar* in Hebrew) to heal on the sabbath. (Mark's question, "Is it permitted on the sabbath to do good or to do harm, to save life or to kill?" [3:4], is much too broad and imprecise for Matthew.) In response Jesus argues for healing on the sabbath by comparing the case of lifting a sheep out of a pit on the sabbath to the case of curing the man with a withered hand. Though some did not allow lifting an animal from a pit (CD 11:13-14), Jesus and the Pharisees both accepted it, and so Jesus argues from the lesser to the greater (v. 12) as he did above (v. 6). He then appeals to the general principle of doing good on the sabbath, but without reference to the custom of doing things before or after the sabbath whenever possible (cf. Luke 13:14). Rather, Jesus here implicitly appeals to the principle of mercy (12:7; Hos 6:6) and applies it to the suffering of animals and then humans. Matthew thus interprets doing good as giving priority to human needs in the application of biblical law. The Pharisees and Jesus do not resolve their differences, but both take action according to their convictions. Jesus heals the withered hand and leaves to continue healing the crowds which follow him (12:13, 15). The Pharisees plot to destroy Jesus (v. 14), a reaction which foreshadows Jesus' arrest and conviction at the end of the narrative. Jesus responds by leaving the area to avoid conflict and by urging the crowds not to publicize him (vv. 15-16).

The author of Matthew reinforces his main argument in the sabbath controversies, the principle of mercy, by reflecting on Jesus' person and work using the longest biblical quotation in the Gospel, the first Servant Song from Isaiah (12:18-21 from Isa 42:1-4). He adapts the Hebrew and Greek texts to mirror more exactly Jesus' attitudes and activities as he understands them. The servant of God in this quotation does not wrangle or cry in the street (12:19), just as Jesus did not engage in a prolonged public squabble with the Pharisees (vv. 15-16). The servant does not break a bruised reed or quench a smoldering wick (v. 20), just as Jesus had an easy yoke and light burden for his followers (11:28-30). The term for servant, *pais*, may mean child, servant, or son. Here it alludes to Jesus as the Son of God as well as the suffering servant of God in his crucifixion (cf. Isaiah 53). The servant is chosen and beloved, as is Jesus at his baptism and transfiguration (3:17; 17:5), and he has God's Spirit, contrary to the charges of demon possession which Jesus' opponents will raise against him in the next encounter (12:22-37). The servant both proclaims and effects justice (vv. 18, 20), especially for the Gentiles (vv. 18, 21), as does Jesus in this Gospel. This richly significant biblical passage summarizes and solidifies the figure of Jesus in the narrative against the increasingly frequent attacks of his opponents.

Bibliography. Beaton, R. 2002, *Isaiah's Christ in Matthew's Gospel*, SNTSMS 123, Cambridge: Cambridge University • Cohn-Sherbok, D. M. 1979, "An Analysis of Jesus' Arguments concerning the Plucking of Grain on the Sabbath," *JSNT* 2:31-41 • Hicks, J. M. 1984, "The Sabbath Controversy in Matthew: An Exegesis of Matthew 12:1-14," *ResQ* 27:79-91 • Neyrey, J. H. 1982, "The Thematic Use of Isaiah 42:1-4 in Matthew 12," *Bib* 63:457-73 • Robbins, V. 1989, "Plucking Grains on the Sabbath," in B. Mack and V. Robbins, eds., *Patterns of Persuasion*, Sonoma, Calif.: Polebridge, 107-41.

Discerning Jesus from Satan (12:22-50)

The healing of a possessed man (12:22) initiates a dispute over whether the origin of Jesus' power to exorcise and heal is divine or demonic. The narrative assumes that evil spirits are real and powerful and can cause illness such as the man's blindness and deafness and that only superhuman power can overcome them. When the crowds wonder if Jesus is the "son of David," they may refer to Jesus as both a Messiah like David and as a successor to Solomon, the son of David, who possessed the power to heal and exorcise according to extrabiblical traditions. In contrast, Jesus' opponents attribute his power over demons to the most powerful of demons, Beelzebul (v. 24; cf. 10:25 for this title) or Satan (v. 26). Jesus refutes the charge that he is allied with evil spirits using three arguments, that Beelzebul would divide his kingdom if he gave Jesus power to expel other demons (vv. 25-26), that other Jewish exorcists accepted by the Pharisees cast out demons (v. 27; cf. Tob 8:1-5; Acts 19:13-16), and that Satan's (the strong man's) house can be plundered through exorcism only after he is neutralized (12:29). These arguments lead to three conclusions, that Jesus exorcises through God's Spirit, that the kingdom has arrived (v. 28), and that they must choose Jesus or Satan (v. 30).

The sharp conflict between good and evil implicit in the exorcism leads to a series of warnings and observations concerning evil and the judgment at the end of the world (12:31-37). Many are drawn from the common wisdom tradition of Judaism and the Near East. Blasphemy (injuring God's reputation; cf. 9:3) against the Spirit of God cannot logically receive forgiveness because God communicates through his Spirit, whom the sinner has already rejected (vv. 31-32). The polemical metaphor of good and bad fruit (v. 33) has already been used to distinguish Jesus' followers from his opponents (7:15-23); John the Baptizer called his opponents a brood of vipers as does Jesus here (12:34; 3:7); the correlation of inner integrity with good speech (12:34) will appear later (15:17-19), as will the metaphor of bringing good things out of one's treasury (12:35; 13:52). The warning against sins of speech (vv. 36-37) recurs often in the Bible and other eastern Mediterranean wisdom literature (Prov 15:1; 16:26-27; 25:23; 29:11; Sir 5:13-14; 28:11-22; Jas 1:19-20; 3:1-12). Matthew links speech with justification and condemnation at the judgment (v. 37), where one must give an account for careless words (v. 36). *Argon,* translated as "careless," also means idle and useless; it is the opposite of *ergon,* the word for an (effective) deed (Jas 2:20), and may be an implicit play on words.

The teachings on evil and judgment (12:27, 32, 36) connect loosely with the judgment oracles against this evil generation and further teachings about exorcism (vv. 38-45). Jesus' opponents again make a controversial comment (v. 38; previously in v. 24) which initiates several teachings bound together by a reference to "this evil generation" (vv. 39, 45; cf. 11:16), a phrase which refers here to the leaders opposing Jesus and to those rejecting him in general. The addition of the epithet "adulterous," a metaphor for idolatry in the HB, makes explicit their unfaithfulness. The sign *(sēmeion)* which the scribes and Pharisees seek from Jesus (v. 38) is not a reflectively apprehended miracle, as in the Gospel of John (e.g., 2:11), but a spectacular act, like Aaron's signs before the Hebrews (Exod 4:30-31), which will provide patent and irrefutable proof of Jesus' divine authority. However, in demanding a sign from the "teacher," a form of address used only by outsiders who do not follow Jesus, his opponents implicitly reject the authenticity of all his deeds recounted in chs. 8 and 9. Jesus instead offers them a paradoxical sign from the prophets, Jonah's journey in the belly of a fish for three days and nights (Jonah 2:1; Heb 1:17), as a symbol of his burial for three days and nights (v. 40). This sign, like the signs in John, demands faith in Jesus for a correct interpretation of the allusion to Jesus' resurrection. Since the questioners do not accept the sign, they are condemned by two judgment oracles based on Jonah and the queen of the South (Sheba) which contrast them negatively with the Ninevites who repented when confronted by Jonah, and the queen who came to Solomon to learn wisdom (vv. 41-42). Ironically the scribes and Pharisees, who have rejected Jesus, a greater prophet than Jonah and wisdom personified (cf. 11:19, 25-30), will be condemned by the Ninevites and the queen at the judgment.

The final two narratives of the chapter stress the necessity of choice and commitment to Jesus (12:43-50). Commentators have debated the meaning of the strange story of the unclean spirit which is exorcised but then returns with other spirits to repossess its empty "house," that is, the person who was exorcised (vv. 43-45). The possibilities for this narrative are endless, but in this Matthean context it refers back to the exorcised person with whom this discussion began (v. 22). If the healed or exorcised remain "empty" instead of filled with the good spirit through adherence to Jesus' teachings, the evil which had been expelled may repossess them as it has possessed Jesus' opponents of "this generation" (v. 45). Jesus' concluding comments on his family define those who accept Jesus (vv. 46-50). The author of Matthew drops Mark's claim that Jesus' family thought he was out of his mind (Mark 3:21) but uses their arrival as a moment for teaching that his "real" mother and brothers, his fictive family, are those who follow him in doing the will of his Father (12:49-50). Righteousness, that is, doing God's will, which Matthew so strongly emphasizes, makes a person a son of God like Jesus. The author does not reject family entirely, but relativizes its claim on a disciple in favor of following Jesus. Thus disciples must be ready to leave their families (4:21-22; 8:22; 10:34-37) and become eunuchs for the kingdom (19:12). The instruction to do God's will and belong to Jesus' family leads appropriately to an extended sermon on the parables on the kingdom of God (13:1-52), which is followed by another story about Jesus' family and hometown (13:53-58).

Bibliography. Boring, M. E. 1976, "The Unforgivable Sin Logion Mark III 28-29/Matt XII 31-32/Luke XII 10: Formal Analysis and History of the Tradition," *NovT* 18:258-79 • Duling, D. C. 1978, "The Therapeutic Son of David," *NTS* 24:392-409 • Edwards, R. A. 1971, *The Sign of Jonah in the Theology of the Evangelists and Q,* London: SCM • Robbins, V. 1989, "Rhetorical Composition and the Beelzebul Controversy," in B. Mack and V. Robbins, eds., *Patterns of Persuasion,* Sonoma, Calif.: Polebridge, 161-93.

The Parables of the Kingdom (13:1-52)

The third of five sermons contains seven parables (beginning in 13:3, 24, 31, 33, 44, 45, and 47) plus another parable used in the final instruction (v. 52). Three interpretations (vv. 18-23, 36-43, and 49-50) and three comments (vv. 10-17, 34-35, and 51-52) explicate the parables. Scholars have proposed a number of structural outlines for the chapter without forming a consensus. At a minimum the parable of the sower with its discussion and interpretation (vv. 3-23) constitutes one unit, and the withdrawal of Jesus and his disciples into a house away from the crowds (v. 36) marks the transition to another unit in the narrative. The parables all point to the kingdom, that is, God's rule in Israel and the world, a symbol which appears thirteen times in the chapter (vv. 11, 19, 24, 31, 33, 38, 39, 41, 43, 44, 45, 47, 52). The first, second, and seventh parables (sower, weeds-wheat, and dragnet) describe good and bad responses to God's rule (the kingdom of God); the other four parables illustrate salient characteristics of God's rule. The first three parables use the metaphors of sowing and seed. The second and seventh parables (weeds-wheat and dragnet) characterize the judgment of good and evil as a sorting. The third and fourth (mustard seed and leaven) stress large effects from a small beginning, and the fifth and sixth (treasure and pearl) emphasize the value of the kingdom.

The English term "parable" comes from the Greek word *parabolē,* which in the Bible often translates the Hebrew word *mashal.* Both terms point to some sort of comparison and are used for a variety of literary forms. The most commonly recognized parables in the NT are narratives which challenge listeners by their paradoxes and ambiguity, suggest new apprehensions of life, and demand reflection and decision. However, the terms for "parable," *parabolē* and *mashal,* stand against a complex literary background. In the NT a *parabolē,* besides being a narrative parable, may be a comparison (Luke 5:36), a proverb (Luke 4:23), a riddle or question (Mark 3:23; 7:17; Luke 6:39), a symbol (Heb 9:9; 11:19), or a rule (Luke 14:7). Similarly, in the HB a *mashal* is primarily a proverb, that is, a compact and easily remembered observation or judgment which is widely held to be true. It may also be a long didactic poem (Ps 49:4 [Heb 5]), an account of Israel's history (Ps. 78:2 [*mashal,* translated "parable" in the NRSV]), a long discourse (Job 27:1), a taunting song (Isa 14:4), an example of misfortune (byword) (Ezek 14:8), a riddle (Judg 14:10-18), an allegory (Ezek 20:49 [Heb. 21:5]) or a prophetic saying (Num 23:7). In summary, a *mashal* is a popular, oral form of wisdom teaching which is multivalent. Simple on the surface, these extended metaphors and similes, which contain vivid imagery and unusual narrative characteristics, demand subtle interpretation because they are suggestive and undetermined. They often speak of daily life and appeal directly to listeners, but they equally often include observations, characters, or plots which shock the audience out of their comfortable assumptions about society, God, and life. They invite new applications to different contexts. Thus, though the parables may have been taught by Jesus, they have been contextualized in the Gospel narrative and subsequent interpretation in unique and creative ways.

At the beginning of the parables chapter Jesus leaves the house where he was teaching "on the same day" in order to address the crowds (13:1; cf. 12:46). The chronological marker is vague, referring back at least to the instruction concerning family at the end of ch. 12 and perhaps to the cure of the blind mute man (12:22). In any case, the parable sermon about the growth of the kingdom refutes the charge that Jesus works for Satan's kingdom and roots him securely in God's kingdom (12:24-28).

The parable of the sower (13:3-9; the name appears in v. 18) really concerns the four types of soil in which the seed is sown and their different yields, not the sower, who appears only in v. 3, nor the seed, which is presumed to be vital in all cases. The narrative reflects practical agricultural problems in the rocky soil of Galilee and Judea. Paths were tramped down through fields, only a thin layer of soil covered limestone in places, and thornbushes clung to the hillsides. The results of sowing such land are predictable: seed is lost on the ground of the paths, and plants wither in thin soil and are choked by bushes; but the seed flourishes in good soil (vv. 4-7). The sower's largesse in scattering the seed probably reflects the agricultural practice of sowing seed everywhere and then plowing it under. The parable itself has a polemical edge since discussions of unfruitfulness in Jewish religious literature imply criticism of those adhering to conflicting views and practices (3:7; 7:15-23; 12:33; cf. 4 Ezra 8:41; 9:31-37).

Despite Jesus' exhortation to listen (13:9), the parable does not have an obvious determinate meaning. Consequently, it stimulates a discussion concerning teaching in parables (vv. 10-17) which itself implicitly interprets the parable of the sower and prompts Jesus to explain the parable explicitly for his disciples (vv. 18-23). The disciples' question about Jesus' strategy of teaching the crowds "many things in parables" (vv. 10 and 3) presumes that people find the parables challenging and hard to understand. Jesus answers the disciples' initial question directly: he teaches through parables because the people do not really perceive, listen, or understand what he says (v. 13). The parables stymie those who refuse to listen and stimulate those who seek to understand. Thus, knowing the "mysteries (Gk. *mystēria;* NRSV, "secrets of the kingdom") which the parables teach divides the disciples from outsiders ("them" in v. 11). The term "mystery" in Second Temple Jewish literature refers to God's plan for humanity and the world, especially in regard to their ultimate destiny at the end. The urgent need to decide for or against Jesus and the kingdom in the previous chapter (12:30-50) carries over into the warning that those who lack understanding will end up with nothing (13:12; cf. Matt 25:29; Mark 4:25; Luke 8:18; 19:26).

Isaiah 6:9-10 explains the resistance to Jesus' teachings in the narrative, and implicitly to the author's teachings in the late first century (vv. 14-15), as a lack of perception and understanding usually referred to as a "hardening." The NT uses this image drawn from Isaiah in several places (John 12:40; Acts 28;26-27; Rom 11:8) to explain (away) the majority of Judeans and Galileans who did not commit themselves to Jesus and his teachings. The Gospel uses the passage as a warrant for the necessity of rejection and misunderstanding, no matter how disheartening to Jesus' followers. In contrast to the majority of the people, the disciples will, in this chapter, understand Jesus (13:51) through the special instruction (here and vv. 36-50). The disciples are even more blessed than the prophets and righteous of the Bible (v. 17; cf. 11:11-13) because through Jesus' teaching they attain a greater righteousness (5:20) than their predecessors.

Jesus begins explaining the parable of the sower to his disciples with an admonition: "You therefore hear the parable of the sower" (v. 18, literal translation). The command to hear (with understanding) fulfills the exhortatory command in v. 9 and contrasts sharply with those who "hearing do not hear" (v. 13, literal translation). Though the parable itself addresses the four types of soil and their yields (vv. 3-9), the partly allegorical explanation of the parable assumes that the seed is Jesus' teaching of the "word of the kingdom" and that Jesus is the sower. It also somewhat confusingly identifies the seed with the individuals who hear the word with varying results. In the interpretation of the parable the soil and other agents play a larger role in the fate of the seeds which die. An outside force, birds, interpreted as the evil one (Satan — 6:13), interrupts any chance for the growth of the seeds on the inhospitable path (13:19). The rocks under shallow soil limit the response by seeds which cannot endure adversity (vv. 20-21); thorns overwhelm growing seeds the way work and wealth overpower other interests in life (v. 22). In contrast the seeds in good soil (and listeners who understand) produce satisfactory results (v. 23). This interpretation applies the parable of the sower to the mixed response experienced by Jesus in the narrative as well as by the early followers of Jesus in Israel and the Matthean community in the late first century.

The next three parables (13:24-33) presumably address the crowds which stand before Jesus on the shore (vv. 2, 34). Like the parable of the sower, the parable of the weeds and wheat has an interpretation taught privately to the disciples later in the chapter (vv. 36-43). In the parable itself a weed (*zizanion* in Greek, *zun* in Hebrew; perhaps darnel, which resembles wheat) has flourished with the crop and presented the farmer with a dilemma (vv. 24-26). Pulling the weeds may damage the wheat (v. 29), but leaving them to grow will presumably lessen crop yield. The farmer opts for a patient strategy of sorting the weeds and wheat at the harvest (v. 30). Though the spontaneous growth of weeds is a common problem, the parable unexpectedly introduces an "enemy" as the sower of the weeds (vv. 25, 28). The conflict of the farmer and his enemy suggests an allegorical interpretation (vv. 37-43; the parables in vv. 31-36 will be treated below) which briskly links the parable with the cosmic battle between the Son of Man (v. 38, identified with the householder) and the devil (v. 39, identified as the "enemy"; cf. the "evil one" in v. 19) which will end with a judgment and the subsequent punishment and reward of evil and good (symbolized here and often by a harvest). Since in this reading the field is the world (v. 38; Gk. *kosmos*), the parable points to the judgment of all people, a favorite theme of Matthew which is at the center of the final parable of the dragnet as well. Some commentators think that the parable may also refer to good and evil people within the author's community. However, the Gospel contains procedures for expelling members who fail in their responsibilities (18:15-17) and so does not counsel waiting for the end in such cases.

The third seed parable, the mustard seed (13:31-32), is paired with another parable of extraordinary growth, the leaven (v. 33; NRSV, "yeast"). Both contrast a small beginning (a seed; a small amount of leaven) with eventual great size (a mustard bush; a raised batch of dough). Mustard seeds, though not literally the smallest seeds, are often used to illustrate smallness (Matt 17:20; Diodorus Siculus 1.35.2). Leaven, probably old fermented dough, was used like yeast to raise bread dough. Since leaven causes fermentation, that is, the breakdown of organic compounds, it could be a symbol of corruption (Matt 16:6; 1 Cor 5:6-8), but here it is a life-giving force which provides enough bread to feed a hundred or more. The product of the mustard seed is also unusually large since mustard bushes can grow six to ten feet high. The clause concerning birds nesting in the mustard bush's branches like those of a tree (13:32) is drawn from Dan 4:10-12, 20-22 (LXX 4:7-9, 17-19) in which the tree which Nebuchadnezzar of Babylon sees in a dream symbolizes his rule over the earth. Thus the mustard bush understood as a tree is an apt symbol for God's kingdom. Finally, both parables may also allude to the hiddenness and surprise of the kingdom since both the seed and leaven work out of sight to produce great effects (the verb used for mixing the leaven in with the flour can also mean "hidden" — v. 33).

The narrator authenticates and summarizes Jesus' teaching in parables (13:34; cf. vv. 3, 10) by citing Ps 78:2. The verse has been slightly modified by Matthew to refer to things "hidden" from the foundation of the world which are revealed in parables (13:35). Though the "hidden things" allude to the hidden meaning of the parables which the crowds do not understand (vv. 10-17), the psalm verse declares that the parables reveal God's kingdom. In order that the revelation may continue, Jesus leaves the crowds, enters the house (v. 36; cf. 12:46 and Peter's house in 8:14), and answers his disciples' question (cf. also v. 10) about the meaning of the parable of the weeds and wheat. (This interpretation of the weeds and wheat has been analyzed above.) The final three parables are taught to the disciples only. The twin parables of the treasure in the field and the extremely valuable pearl (vv. 44-46) testify to the importance of the kingdom of God and to the total commitment necessary to gain it. Both the farmer who unexpectedly found the treasure in a field and the merchant who was searching for fine pearls used all their resources to acquire the single most valuable and important object of their desire. Though commentators have discussed the morality of hiding the discovered treasure, buying the field, and then taking possession of it, the parable itself assumes that the finder has a right to it and praises his single-minded and effective action.

The final parable of the dragnet which catches all kinds of fish to be sorted into edible foodstuff and inedible waste on the shore (13:47-50) recalls the parable of the inedible weeds and edible wheat growing together to be separated at the harvest (vv. 24-30). The sea is the world containing good and bad who are separated only after being gathered, just as the harvest was gathered earlier. A brief interpretation of the parable (vv. 49-50) compares the sorting of the fish to the separation of the evil and good at the end of the age (the judgment). Both the dragnet and wheat-weeds parables emphasize the punishment of evil with fire (cf. the burning of the weeds in v. 30 and the interpretation of it as punishment with fire in v. 42). The sermon concludes with an inquiry whether the disciples have understood (v. 51; in contrast to the people in vv. 10-17). When the disciples affirm that they have understood, Jesus implicitly compares them to scribes (educated persons) who are trained to teach about the kingdom. A brief comparison (a parable of another kind) likens these teachers to a householder who brings both new and old things out of his storeroom. The author of Matthew may be referring both to Jesus and to himself as teaching the news about the kingdom along with the laws and prophecies of the HB.

Bibliography. Carter, W., and J. P. Heil. 1998, *Matthew's Parables: Audience-Oriented Perspectives,* CBQMS 30, Washington: Catholic Biblical Association • Crossan, J. D. 1973, *In Parables: The Challenge of the Historical Jesus,* New York: Harper • Gerhardsson, B. 1972, "The Seven Parables in Matthew xiii," *NTS* 19:16-37 • Kingsbury, J. D. 1969, *The Parables of Jesus in Matthew 13,* London: SPCK and Richmond: Knox • Lambrecht, J. 1991, *Out of the Treasure: The Parables in the Gospel of Matthew,* Louvain: Peeters; Grand Rapids: Eerdmans.

Facing Adversity (13:53–14:36)

The narrative continues with the concluding formula of the sermons, "When Jesus had finished these parables" (13:53) and with Jesus leaving for a visit to his "hometown" (Gk. *patris,* meaning native country, region, or town — vv. 54, 57), elsewhere identified as Nazareth (2:23; 4:13). Jesus' encounters with his family before the parable sermon (12:46-50) and with his neighbors immediately after enclose the sermon and contrast the links that bind family and town with dynamically developing relationships within the kingdom of God. The townsfolk react at first like the crowds, with amazement at Jesus' wise teaching and powerful deeds (miracles). However, when they assess Jesus as a member of a local family, they are offended (lit. "scandalized" — v. 57) and skeptical that he could be that different from them (vv. 54-57). They ask, literally, "How all these to him?" a question which reflects the envy of villagers toward one another when one person has gained an advantage in a society of limited resources. Jesus responds to this folk attitude with a proverb about Israel's rejection of the prophets with whom he has already been identified. The author ends with the explanation which implies that the unbelief (*apistia,* used only here in Matthew) of Jesus' townsfolk prevented him from performing miracles because they depend on faith (v. 58).

The little we know of Jesus' family comes from this passage. His father (Joseph in 1:16, 19) is a carpenter (*tekton,* meaning also "builder," "mason," "woodworker," or "artisan"), his sisters live in the town, his brothers are James, Joseph (Hellenized as Joses in Mark 6:3), Simon, and Judas, and his mother is Mary (or "Miriam" — 1:16, 18). The very natural listing of Jesus' brothers and sisters conflicts prima facie with the later Christian belief that Mary remained a virgin. Some ancient and modern commentators have held that "brother" often denotes a cousin. This is true in Hebrew, but not in Greek. Others have identified the brothers as children of Joseph from an earlier marriage. The mention of a Mary the mother of James and Joseph/Joses looking on at the crucifixion (Matt 27:56; Mark 15:40) could be a reference to Jesus' mother Mary, but it is more likely that Matthew would have identified Jesus' mother directly. Whatever the historical facts and doctrinal developments, the author of Matthew seems to have assumed that Mary had children with Joseph after Jesus' birth (see the ambiguous expression "until" in 1:25).

Along with the residents of Nazareth, Herod Antipas, the ruler of Galilee (technically, *tetrarch,* a term often used of a dependent ruler in the Roman Empire), wonders about Jesus' powers (14:1-2). He resolves his anxiety by identifying Jesus as John the Baptizer, whom he had executed and who now had returned to life. Antipas's views serve to bring John back into the narrative and introduce a flashback to John's arrest and execution (vv. 3-12). Perhaps Antipas's interest in Jesus is also meant to motivate Jesus' later withdrawal to the wilderness (v. 13) and to patch over a notorious chronological lapse by the author. After John's death his disciples are said to have informed Jesus of Antipas's action so that Jesus took cover against the threat of Herod (vv. 12-14; cf. 11:2-6 for earlier contact). But the execution and burial of John (14:10-12) are a flashback to an earlier event, so that Jesus could not have just been informed of it in the narrative present (vv. 12-13) and taken action. But thematically the narrative as written transfers the danger and rejection from John to Jesus. Similarly, John's execution prepares for Jesus' similar death, and Herod's view that Jesus is John risen from the dead foreshadows the resurrection.

In telling the story of John's arrest (14:3-5), the author of Matthew merely alludes to a well-known dispute over Herod Antipas's marriage to a woman who was both his brother's ex-wife and his niece. Sexual relations with a living brother's wife were explicitly forbidden in Lev 18:16; 20:21. Marrying a niece was not explicitly forbidden, but was frowned upon (CD 5:6-11; 11QTemple Scroll 66:16). The identification of Herodias's first husband as Philip (v. 3), the tetrarch of Trachonitis and son of Herod the Great and Cleopatra of Jerusalem, is erroneous. In fact Philip married Herodias's daughter, Salome. Herodias had first married Herod, son of Herod the Great and Miriamne the daughter of Simon the high priest, and then divorced him to marry his half-brother, Antipas, son of Herod the Great and Matthace a Samaritan. Herodias was thus both the wife and niece of both her husbands since she herself was the daughter of Aristobolus, a son of Herod the Great and Miriamne, daughter of Hyrcanus the Hasmonean. (The Byzantine Herodian family relationships, with frequent repetition of names, may be found in Josephus *Ant.* 17.1.3 §§19-22; 18.5.4 §§130-42; *J.W.* 1.28.4 §§562-63; 2.11.6 §§220-22. The mixup in the story used by Mark and Matthew is easily understandable.) John's challenge to the legitimacy of Herod Antipas's marriage undercut Antipas's authority as a Jewish ruler and provoked a violent response. Josephus says that Antipas also feared John's great popularity as a threat to his rule and so imprisoned him in the palatial fortress Machaerus, east of the Dead Sea. The lurid story of John's execution and the presentation of his head on a platter to Herodias's daughter (unnamed in the Gospel accounts) highlights the hostility and corruption of the political leadership (vv. 6-11), which will eventually kill Jesus. The version of the story in Mark 6:17-29 presents Antipas as a reluctant executioner manipulated by Herodias, but Matthew pictures Antipas himself as hostile to John and in fear of the crowd (v. 5), perhaps in order to increase the parallelism between the stories of John and Jesus.

After the story of John's death, both before and after Jesus' feeding of the crowds and calming of the storm (14:15-33), the author of Matthew confirms the pattern of Jesus' work: Galilean crowds follow him, and he heals them (vv. 13-14, 34-36; cf. 4:23-25; 9:35; 12:15; 15:30). Jesus cares for the crowds by healing, in contrast to the parallel in Mark 6:34 where Jesus only teaches the crowd. In this part of his Galilean ministry in Matthew Jesus teaches his disciples, continues to dispute with his opponents, who resist his views, and heals the crowds. The crowds follow Jesus as usual, even as he withdraws from the familiar villages of Galilee to an uninhabited spot (vv. 13, 15). Since food was not readily available there, the disciples raise the necessity of seeking food in surrounding villages (v. 15). Strangely, Jesus asserts that the crowds need not leave if the disciples will feed them (v. 16). This unrealistic solution to the problem prompts the disciples to raise the scarcity of provisions consisting of five loaves and two fish. More importantly, this interchange alerts readers that the story has implications beyond mere words and actions and that something unusual will happen. Jesus resolves the problem by providing food for a crowd of five thousand men, plus women and children who may have outnumbered them, by multiplying the five loaves and two fish. This story is one of the few to appear in all four Gospels, probably because of its rich, multivalent symbolism and association with the early Christian celebration of the Lord's Supper. The wilderness setting and the miraculous availability of food associate Jesus with Moses, who fed Israel in the desert with manna provided by God (Exod 16:13-35). Multiplying a small amount of food to feed a crowd also recalls Elisha's feeding of a hundred men with twenty loaves and fresh ears of grain (2 Kgs 4:42-44) and Elijah's feeding of himself, his widowed host, and her son with a handful of meal and a little oil until a famine ended (1 Kgs 17:12-16). Within the Gospel narrative the simple meal of bread and fish for hungry crowds, eaten while reclining on the grass (14:19), contrasts starkly with Herod's elaborate banquet during which John the Baptizer was executed (vv. 6-11). The meal, associated in the narrative with healing and following Jesus, foreshadows the banquet of the just in God's kingdom, which symbolizes eternal life with God (Isa 25:6; 1QSa 2:17-22; Matt 8:11-12; 22:1-10). Most importantly, the feeding of the crowds foreshadows Jesus' final meal with his disciples, which was celebrated as the Lord's Supper (Eucharist) in the earliest communities of Jesus' followers (Matt 26:26-29; 1 Cor 11:23-26). The blessing over the bread, the breaking of the loaves, and giving it to the disciples who distribute it to the crowds anticipate the account of the last supper and ritual practices in the later Christian meal. Significantly, the distribution of the fish is omitted from the account. The twelve baskets of leftovers symbolize the ample produce promised to the twelve tribes of Israel (Deut 8:10) to whom Jesus has been sent (10:5-6). The feeding story, like the parables in the previous chapter, points to the future development of God's kingdom even as it actualizes it in the narrative.

The story of Jesus walking on the water at night to rescue his disciples in a storm follows the feeding of the five thousand in all four Gospels; so the two miracles must have been paired in pre-Gospel traditions. Like the feeding of the five thousand, the walking on the water was highly symbolic for the early followers of Jesus. It reveals Jesus more clearly as a divinely sent and empowered emissary who is intimate with God in prayer, can rule the sea and winds, and evokes recognition as the Son of God from his disciples (v. 33). In the prelude to the storm, Jesus sends both the crowds and his disciples away so he can pray alone (vv. 22-23). The disciples' destination, "the other side," seems to be somewhere south of Capernaum on the coast of the Sea of Galilee, since they eventually land at Gennesaret (v. 34). (Mark 6:53 says they traveled toward Bethsaida, northeast of Capernaum, first, but Matthew drops this destination because the direction of travel is inconsistent.) Jesus prays alone in this story only in Matthew, though he prays publicly once (11:25-27), seeks to pray with three disciples in the garden of Gethsemane (26:36-46), and gives instruction on prayer in the Sermon on the Mount (6:5-15). The author of Matthew gives no hint of Jesus' motive or the content of the prayer, but the act of praying stresses Jesus' intimacy with God preceding his exercise of divine attributes on the sea. The place of prayer, a mountain, furthers the sense of closeness to God, who appeared at Sinai (cf. also the Sermon on the Mount, the transfiguration, etc.).

The disciples reenter the story "early in the morning" (v. 25), literally, "the fourth watch" (3:00–6:00 a.m.), about twelve hours after they set sail. Their battle in the dark against the wind and the waves provokes Jesus to approach them walking on the sea. In the Near East people attributed power over the sea to the sea gods or to the sky god who had conquered the sea god (e.g., Marduk's victory over Tiamat in the Babylonian epics). Influenced by this worldview, the disciples interpret Jesus as a superhuman power or apparition, a "ghost" *(phantasma)* which they fear. Their reaction matches that of those who receive apocalyptic visions in dreams or from a divine messenger (Dan 7:1, 15; 10:7-12, 18-19), and Jesus responds exactly like such a visionary messenger by telling them not to fear and identifying himself (14:26-27). His self-identification, "it is I" in the NRSV, reads literally "I am" in the Greek. This expression characterizes God at the burning bush (Exod 3:14; Deut 32:39) and is invoked as a sign of divine help and reassurance against fear (Isa 4:4; 43:5, 10-11). Peter as representative of the disciples tests the two hypotheses, that the apparition is a ghost or really Jesus, by asking Jesus to call him (14:28-30). Jesus the human shares his divine domination of the sea by enabling Peter to join him in walking on the water. This striking theophany bridges the divine-human divide. Of course, when Peter becomes humanly fearful again, he loses contact with the divine power and sinks until Jesus saves him by grabbing him and taking him into the boat (vv. 31-32). Peter's cry to be saved is the same as the disciples' cry in the similar storm scene earlier in the Gospel (8:25). The verb "to save" means to heal as well (v. 36) and has a strong symbolic resonance of asking God for help (cf. Ps 69:1-3 for sea imagery and a request for salvation). In this scene Peter plays the role of protagonist and representative of the disciples, as he does frequently in Matthew (15:15; 16:16-19; 17:24-27; 18:21-22). His role in the Gospel attests to his symbolic importance to the late-first-century Matthean community.

The denouement of the story reinforces both Jesus' special status and the need for human acknowledgment of it. Jesus accuses Peter of "little faith" (v. 31), a frequent failing of the disciples in Matthew (6:30; 8:26; 16:8; 17:20), which persists even to the end of the Gospel (28:17). Only faith, that is, adherence to, confidence in, and thorough commitment to Jesus, differentiates the disciples from the crowds. The struggle for faithfulness and for confidence in Jesus and God goes on throughout the Gospel. (The later, widely held understanding of the church as a ship in a storm saved by Jesus responds to this major theme.) In the narrative the disciples respond appropriately by prostrating themselves before Jesus, that is, reverencing or worshiping him, and by acknowledging him as the Son of God (v. 33; contrast their misunderstanding in Mark 6:51-52). Jesus had been revealed as the Son of God earlier (1:18-25; 2:15; 3:17; 4:3, 6; 8:29), but for the first time his disciples recognize him as such because he has exercised powers reserved for God alone.

The author of Matthew continues Jesus' work in Galilee through another summary of his healing of the crowds (14:34-36; cf. vv. 13-14). In contrast to the faith of the disciples and the hostile question of the Pharisees and scribes which follows is the welcome Jesus receives from the crowds, who accept his healing (salvation). The fringe of Jesus' garment which people touch to be cured (cf. 9:20) suggests that Jesus observes the law (cf. the requirement of "fringes" in Num 15:38-41; Deut 22:12), in contrast to his opponents, whose charges follow immediately.

Bibliography. Fowler, R. M. 1981, *Loaves and Fishes: The Function of the Feeding Stories in the Gospel of Mark,* SBLDS 54, Chico, Calif.: Scholars • Furfey, P. H. 1955, "Christ as *Tekton,*" *CBQ* 17:324-35 • Heil, J. P. 1981, *Jesus Walking on the Sea,* Rome: Biblical Institute Press • Temple, P. J. 1955, "The Rejection at Nazareth," *CBQ* 17:229-42.

Dispute over Interpretation of the Law (15:1-20)

The Pharisees and scribes who come from Jerusalem to rebuke Jesus (15:1; similarly the Pharisees and Sadducees in 16:1) punctuate Jesus' work with the Galilean crowds who have come to Jesus for healing (14:13-14, 35-36). In their interpretation of the biblical commandments they were stressing observance of dietary and purity laws in order to make Israel holy for God and as a way to maintain communal boundaries. The author of Matthew acknowledges the purity and dietary laws as part of biblical law (see also 23:27-28) but stresses the centrality of the Ten Commandments, the commandments to love God and neighbor (Deut 6:5; Lev 19:18), and his own interpretation of "justice, mercy, and faithfulness" (23:23). Matthew argues that the Pharisees' "tradition of the elders" (v. 2), that is, their interpretations of biblical law and their practical program for observance of law, has not been commanded by the Bible. Matthew, of course, develops his own tradition for interpreting the Bible in his Gospel. The author of Matthew also accuses the scribes and Pharisees of subverting biblical commandments with their practices. All these polemical charges are typical in sectarian disputes over law and practice in first-century Judaism.

The laws governing purifying one's body for ritual actions or for eating food dedicated to God and the temple are extremely complex and especially pertain to priests and their families (e.g., Leviticus 11–15; 19). However, the Pharisees had interpreted these laws so that they might be observed by non-priestly Israelites. Their motive was to encourage Second Temple Jews in the land of Israel to live a holy life closely linked to God and God's law. In this case the first point at issue is washing (i.e., ritually purifying) one's hands before meals so that the food eaten will not be rendered impure (unfit to eat). The Bible mentions hand washing (Exod 30:19-21; Lev 15:11; Deut 21:6), but not as a general obligation to be undertaken before meals. Customs and interpretations varied; for example, the Essenes immersed themselves before eating (Josephus *J.W.* 2.8.5 §129). The extension of hand washing to other contexts can be found later in the Mishnah and Talmud, but even there it is disputed because it is only loosely founded on biblical law (*m. 'Ed.* 5:6; cf. also *b. Soṭa* 4b; *m. Ber.* 8:2-4; *t. Ber.* 5[6]:25-30). The dispute found here in Matthew and in Mark 7:1-23 probably reflects conflicts over the observance of purity and dietary laws among the early Jewish followers of Jesus and between them and the larger Jewish community.

Jesus' response to the rebuke of his disciples for not ritually purifying their hands before eating shifts the argument, for the time being, from hand washing to vows (15:3-6) in order to raise a more fundamental issue, the distinction between biblical law as a whole and particular human interpretations and customs. Since vows are allowed by the Bible but not mandated, the author of Matthew argues that commitments made by a vow to God should be subordinated to the explicit commandments of Scripture, in this case the command to honor one's parents (v. 4; Exod 20:12). "Honoring" a parent in antiquity entailed supporting them and caring for them in their old age. Matthew charges that the Pharisees teach that a son might dedicate his property to God and thus escape the obligation to use it to support his parents (for similar polemical charges of subverting divine law with human law in Jewish literature, see *T. Levi* 14:4; *T. Ash.* 7:5). The accuracy of this charge and the rules for revoking imprudent or illicit vows in the first century remain largely unknown. The author of Matthew expounds the problem as a conflict of two obligations, that vows should be kept and that parents in need should be supported; the question is how the two are to be reconciled. The author of Matthew argues polemically that the Pharisees misinterpret the law through lack of inner integrity by stressing vows, purity, and hand washing over the Ten Commandments. Given the Pharisaic devotion to law, this global charge is unlikely. Rather, for the Pharisees, for Matthew, and for the tradition, imprudent or excessive vows were a constant problem (cf. Judg 11:29-40; Numbers 30). A century after Matthew the Mishnah still argued whether a person could be released from a vow for the honor of his parents (*m. Ned.* 9:1; cf. also *m. Ned.* 2:1-2; 3:1-4). The rabbis recognized a serious weakness in their code: "[Rules for] release from vows hover in the air and do not have anywhere upon which to land" (*m. Ḥag.* 1:8). It is likely that later in the first century, before the Mishnaic laws were developed, the problem of release from vows was acute. The author of Matthew attacks the whole system by subordinating it strongly to the Ten Commandments, in this case, honoring one's parents (15:6), and by attacking his opponents as "hypocrites" (v. 7) condemned by Isa 29:13. He also changes the Greek version of Isa 29:13 so that it more explicitly rejects the Pharisaic "tradition of the fathers" (15:2) and condemns them for "teaching [as] teachings the precepts of men" (vv. 8-9, literal translation).

After his confrontation with the Pharisees and scribes Jesus addresses the people with his own teaching about purity in general (not about hand washing in particular, which is resolved in 15:20): "Listen and understand: not what goes into the mouth defiles a person, but what comes out of the mouth, this defiles a person" (vv. 10-11). Matthew writes more precisely than Mark 7:15 concerning what enters and leaves the *mouth,* not what goes into and comes out of a person. The mouth is associated with both speech and food, to which hand washing before meals is related. Jesus provides no explanation of his teaching, nor are the implications of this proverbial saying unpacked, so the disciples need further instruction after another polemical exchange. The Pharisees immediately see the implications of Jesus' teaching and are offended ("scandalized" — v. 12). The author of Matthew attacks them with his favorite polemical imagery, which appears often in Jewish literature, good and bad plants: "Every plant which my heavenly Father has not planted will be rooted up" (v. 13; cf. 3:10; 7:16-20; ch. 13). The polemical epithets "blind guides" (15:14) and "hypocrites" (v. 7) foreshadow the climactic polemic against the scribes and Pharisees in ch. 23 and are part of the author's programmatic attack on opposing interpretations of biblical law.

When Peter asks Jesus to explain his teaching to the disciples, he appropriately refers to it as a "parable" (v. 15, Gk. *parabolē*), that is, an aphoristic saying, like Heb. *mashal,* whose meaning requires thought and interpretation. Appropriately the disciples, who do not understand the parable, respond by seeking further instruction. Jesus' explanation, based on Mark 7:15-19, has been carefully crafted by the author of Matthew to avoid Mark's conclusion that Jesus invalidated all the biblical laws about purity and diet (Mark 7:19) and to support the validity of biblical commandments. Matthew defuses the dangerous edge to Jesus' teaching (15:11, 17-18) by shifting its focus to moral attitudes and behaviors and leaving the purity and dietary restrictions in a lesser, but still secure, position. He contrasts the permanent nature of moral evil with the passing effect of food. Food passes into the stomach and is "passed on into the outhouse" (v. 17, lit.). Matthew does *not* say here, in contrast to Mark 7:18-19, that whatever goes into a person cannot render him unclean. He says only that it passes through and is gone, leaving the meaning of the saying gnomic and vague. Since the whole dispute concerns hand washing before eating, Matthew concentrates on the mouth: what comes out of the mouth shows what is in a person's heart, and what is in the heart renders a person impure. The products of one's mouth are enlarged to include several kinds of disobedience to the commandments: "evil thoughts, murder, adultery, fornication, theft, false witness, slander" (15:19-20). Matthew tones down the clash between purity and ethical commandments so that he can stress the ethical without rejecting purity. In addition, he emphasizes inner dispositions, as he did in the Sermon on the Mount and in a previous saying, "You brood of vipers! How can you speak good things, when you are evil? For out of the abundance of the heart the mouth speaks" (12:34). In conclusion, Jesus finally answers the Pharisees' challenge (15:2) by teaching that eating with unwashed hands does not defile a person (v. 20)

Bibliography. Booth, R. P. 1986, *Jesus and the Laws of Purity,* Sheffield: JSOT.

Caring for the Needy (15:21-39)

As he does frequently in the narrative, Jesus returns to healing and caring for the crowds after his conflict with the Pharisees. Here he exorcises the daughter of a woman from Tyre and heals and feeds crowds near the Sea of Galilee before moving on (v. 39) and confronting the Pharisees and Sadducees (16:1). The themes of the stories continue and subtly comment on the dispute over food and purity. Jesus responds (reluctantly) to a Gentile woman who is outside the sphere of Israel's purity and holiness (vv. 21-28), cares for the crowds in their need (vv. 29-31) in contrast to the vows which impeded care for elderly parents (vv. 3-6), and feeds a crowd of over four thousand (15:32-38; cf. 14:13-21 earlier). The dispute with the Pharisees and scribes over purity (vv. 1-20) and the story of the Canaanite woman's faith parallel the cure and purification of the leper and the story of the centurion's faith at the beginning of the miracle cycle (8:2-13).

In one of Jesus' few journeys away from the Galilean shore he travels "into," or perhaps "toward" *(eis)*, the territories of Tyre and Sidon near the Mediterranean shore (15:21), and a Canaanite woman comes out from that region to seek help for her possessed daughter (v. 22). Though the text is ambiguous, Jesus probably does not enter Gentile territory in Matthew, in contrast to Mark 7:24, where he enters a house in Tyrian territory. Staying at a home might imply eating unkosher food with Gentiles and possibly contracting some kind of ritual impurity. The woman is identified by the first-century ethnic designation "Syrophoenician" in Mark 7:26, but the author of Matthew calls her a "Canaanite," the ancient biblical name for the non-Jewish residents of the area and a group from whom Israel was supposed to remain separate. Matthew thus shows Jesus helping the needy woman without breaking the purity and dietary rules and explains his reluctance as obedience to the biblical commandment to stay apart from the Canaanites. The Canaanite woman approaches Jesus with the ideal dispositions for a person seeking aid: she requests help (15:22, 25), prostrates herself before (worships) Jesus (v. 25), and humbles herself before Jesus' objections (v. 27; cf. 5:3, 5). She has so robust a faith that she is praised by Jesus (15:28), as was the Gentile centurion (8:10). She approaches Jesus as the Son of David, which here probably refers to Solomon, who was known in folk wisdom as a healer and exorcist (9:27; 12:23; 20:30). Jesus, who has healed the Galilean crowds, refuses to help her and puts her off until she overcomes his objections in debate (vv. 23-27). Though Jesus' reluctant response contradicts the usual picture of a universally merciful Jesus, in this Gospel Jesus has been explicitly sent to "the lost sheep of the house of Israel" (v. 24; 10:6) and remains obedient to that mission. Directly confronted by the woman, Jesus explains his position with a blunt parable which compares the Gentiles to dogs in contrast to Israel as God's children (vv. 25-26). The woman's riposte, that dogs eat crumbs at their masters' table, defeats Jesus in debate (v. 27), the only time this happens in the Gospel. Her confidence in Jesus and her ability to make a case for Gentiles prepare for the final command for the disciples to teach and baptize the nations (28:16-20).

When Jesus returns to Galilee he continues healing the Jewish crowds, who respond with amazement and praise for God (15:29-31). Jesus' location, on a mountain, recalls Moses on Sinai, the Sermon on the Mount (5:1), Jesus' transfiguration on a mountain (17:1), and people gathering on Mt. Zion on the day of the Lord (Isa 35:5-6; Jer 31:7-14; Ezek 34:25-31). Jesus' care for the crowds climaxes with the feeding of four thousand men plus women and children (vv. 32-38) who have been with Jesus for three days. This story is a variant of the feeding of the five thousand in 14:15-21. Because it seems to occur in Gentile territory in Mark 8:1-10, some commentators have identified the four thousand as Gentiles. However, in Matthew the place and people are Galilean. The same symbolism underlies both feedings: manna in the desert, miraculous feedings by Elisha and Elijah, the heavenly banquet, the last supper, and the eucharistic meal. (See the commentary on 14:15-21.) Details differ, of course. Here Jesus, not his disciples, raises the problem of feeding the crowds, whose need is very acute since they have been with Jesus for three days. Jesus and his disciples do not raise the option of sending people to neighboring villages because they might faint on the way. Seven loaves and a few fish satisfy the crowds and produce seven baskets of leftovers. (The numbers do not seem to be symbolic.) The feeding story is probably repeated because it recalls the most important cultic practice of the early followers of Jesus, the communal meal of thanksgiving.

After the feeding Jesus and his disciples move on by boat, as they did after the previous feeding story, but without the storm and appearance by Jesus (15:39; cf. 14:22-25, 34). Their destination, Magadan, is unknown (15:39); Mark 8:10 has them travel to Dalmanutha, also unknown. Among the manuscript variants for the name of the destination, Magdala, modern Taricheae, on the coast of the Sea of Galilee between Capernaum and Tiberias, is the most likely.

Bibliography. Levine, A. J., ed. 2001, *A Feminist Companion to Matthew*, Sheffield: Sheffield Academic • Neyrey, J. H. 1981, "Decision Making in the Early Church: The Case of the Canaanite Woman (Mt 15:21-28)," *ScEs* 33:373-78.

Warning against the Teachings of Jesus' Opponents (16:1-12)

A dispute with Jesus' opponents and more instruction of his disciples follow the feeding of the four thousand, as they did the feeding of the five thousand (16:1-12; cf. 14:15–15:20). Jesus' opponents, here the Pharisees and Sadducees, test Jesus (16:1) as Satan tested him earlier (4:1), and they ask for a sign as the scribes and Pharisees did earlier (12:38). The request for a sign implies distrust or misunderstanding of Jesus' teachings and miracles, which the author of Matthew has used to manifest his identity (cf. 16:13-20 below). The nature of the sign sought is vague, but it might include a heavenly voice, a divine appearance, or a prophetic act designed to mark Israel's spiritual or political deliverance. Matthew speaks of supernatural signs in connection with the end of the world (24:3, 30), but some of these are false (24:24). Perhaps Jesus' opponents wanted an irresistible, eschatological sign from God. Jesus implies in his response that the clues to his work are as obvious as the signs of good and bad weather in the sky (16:2-3; these verses are missing in a number of good manuscripts and may have been added). The only sign left is the greatest and final one which he has already promised, the sign of Jonah which symbolizes his resurrection (v. 4; 12:39-40). Implicitly, signs will not help Jesus' opponents because they have refused to recognize Jesus; they are a culpable, evil, unfaithful generation (16:4; 12:39, 45) who ironically have not seen because they have not believed.

The symbolism of the feeding miracles continues in Jesus' instruction of his disciples (16:5-12) after yet another boat trip to an unidentified location (v. 5 — "the other side"). The disciples lack provisions, as did the crowds in the two feeding miracles, but here Jesus responds with a symbolic evaluation of the Pharisees' and Sadducees' teaching (vv. 11-12). The disciples, who are worried about a lack of bread, have little faith (v. 8; cf. 6:30; 8:26; 14:31; 17:20) because they have not penetrated the physical bread to its symbolic meaning (v. 11). Jesus prompts them to reflect and learn with a warning against the yeast (lit. "leaven") of the Pharisees and Sadducees (v. 2), and they finally understand that yeast refers to teaching since both are permeating forces which cause considerable change. Yeast or leaven is often seen as corrupting agent (1 Cor 5:6-8; Gal 5:9), especially since it must be removed from the house at Passover; thus it is applied to the teaching of the Pharisees and Sadducees. In addition, the author of the Gospel probably refers covertly to those teachers with whom he disagrees in the later first century.

Jesus' True Identity (16:13–17:13)

All Jesus' previous activities in Galilee and the Gospel writer's interpretations of him as teacher, healer, Messiah, and Son of God come to a climax in Jesus' dialogue with his disciples about his identity (16:13-20). Immediately after the disciples' first explicit recognition of him as Messiah (v. 17), Jesus initiates a major shift in his instruction by speaking about his arrest and death (v. 21). Jesus' interrogation of his disciples begins with popular views of Jesus as a prophet like John the Baptist (brought back to life — cf. 14:2), or Elijah who was carried off to heaven in a fiery chariot and expected to return (2 Kgs 2:11; Mal 3:1-23), or Jeremiah, a favorite of Matthew (2:17; 27:9; cf. also allusions in 7:15-23; 11:28-30; 23:37-39). While the author of Matthew links Jesus with the prophets constantly, readers already know that Jesus is the Son of God and the Messiah, and Peter in the name of the disciples already has acknowledged Jesus as the Son of God (14:33). Here for the first time Peter, acting for the disciples, affirms that Jesus is "the Christ" ("anointed one"; in Hebrew "messiah"). Since first-century Jews understood the "anointed one" in a variety of ways, the additional title "Son of God" (16:16) specifies further Jesus' high status before God. When Jesus blesses Peter for the revelation he has received from God (v. 17; cf. 11:25-27), he also approves of the identification of himself as Messiah and Son of God as accurate and adequate.

The place where Peter receives his revelation, Caesarea Philippi (v. 13) at the northern border of Israel near Mt. Hermon in the tribe of Dan, is the place where Enoch receives revelation as well (*1 Enoch* 12–16). Caesarea Philippi had a shrine dedicated to the Greek god Pan and had been rebuilt by Herod the Great's son Philip as a Hellenistic city dedicated to Caesar Augustus. Ironically, despite its Greco-Roman culture and its location at the extreme edge of Israelite territory, it is here that the disciples finally and definitively recognize Jesus. In honor of this revelation Jesus' disciple, Simon son of Jonah (identified as "son of John" in John 1:42; 21:15-17), receives a new symbolic name, Peter (16:18). Though the author has used the name Peter previously, only here does a character in the narrative call him by that name. In Greek the name *Petros* comes from *petra,* the word for "stone" or "rock." The Aramaic version of this wordplay is also pertinent: *kepa'* means "rock" or "stone" and is used as a name or nickname. Simon's renaming signifies an important turning point in the narrative (cf. the renaming of Abraham in Gen 17:1-8). Rock as a metaphor for divine or communal stability appears often (Ps 118:22, used in Matt 21:42, Acts 4:11, and 1 Pet 2:4-8; Matt 7:24-27; 1QH 6[Puech 14]:24-28). Jesus identifies Simon as a rock in response to Simon's identification of Jesus as Messiah and Son of God in order to establish a community (v. 18) which will endure after Jesus' death. (Jesus' death becomes the main theme of the Gospel with the first passion prediction in 16:21.) This blessing and promise to Peter appears only in Matthew (vv. 17-18), but the Aramaic influences on the language of the passage make it probable that it derives from an early tradition of the Jesus community. The Greek contains a transliteration of Simon's Aramaic name, "Simon bar Jonah," and uses the Semitic idiom "flesh and blood" for "human." The focus on Peter as spokesperson and leader of the disciples in the Gospel of Matthew testifies to the late-first-century importance of Peter as an authority and foundational figure in the worldview of the Matthean community.

In the Greek Bible *ekklēsia* (church — 16:18) usually translates Heb. *qahal,* a term used for the community of Israel. The Qumran community in Second Temple times also used *qahal* to describe itself (1QM 4:10; 1QSa 2:4; CD 7:17, etc.). These terms are closely related to the congregation (*'edah*) of Israel, usually translated into Greek as "synagogue" (*synagogē*). Both *ekklēsia* and *synagogē* refer to various kinds of assemblies of people, without denoting the highly articulated institutions referred to today as churches and synagogues. Possibly the author of Matthew, who alone among the Gospel writers uses the word *ekklēsia,* sought to differentiate himself from his opponents in the Jewish community who had named their assemblies "synagogues." In any case, just as Jesus' identity and status are rooted in the divine world, so the Matthean assembly partakes of a power and authority which transcend this world. The "gates of Hades," from which the community is protected, refer literally to the gates which open into the realm of the dead in the underworld (*Sheol* in the HB; Hades in Greek literature). Symbolically they connote the forces of evil which will oppose Jesus' assembly and followers (cf. 1QH 5[Puech 13]:20-39; 6[Puech 14]:22-29; Rev 9:1-11) until defeated by God. Since heaven was similarly conceived of as having gates or doors (*1 Enoch* 9:2; *T. Levi* 18:10; for keys to the temple, see *2 Bar.* 10:18; *Para. Jer.* 4:4; for heaven as a place, see Matt 7:21; 23:13), Peter receives the keys to the kingdom of heaven (v. 19), along with protection from the gates of Hades. The image of keys connotes ruling authority (cf. Isa 22:22 on keys as the powers of the king's prime minister; Rev 1:18), as does the metaphor of binding and loosing (16:19). Binding and loosing may refer to decision making, adjudicating what is permitted and forbidden by law, judicial power, exorcism, and so on (cf. the comments below at 18:18). Here it probably supports the teaching and governing authority of the Matthean community broadly understood. For the author's late-first-century readers, the promise of divine protection and guidance through divinely appointed leaders addressed the threats they felt from their minority status in the Jewish community and the Roman Empire.

Since God and Jesus have revealed Jesus' identity and the community's divinely sanctioned origins to the committed disciples, the disciples are to keep the teaching private from the crowds and Jesus' opponents (16:20). Since Jesus' messianic role requires extensive explication, it begins immediately with the transition phrase, "From that time on" (v. 21; cf. 4:17), followed by a thematic statement of the content of the rest of the Gospel: Jesus teaches his disciples that God has willed that Jesus suffer, die, and be raised from the dead in Jerusalem. Jesus teaches the disciples how to reconcile his suffering and execution with his traditional roles as Messiah and Son of God.

As usual in the Gospel, Jesus' difficult and unusual teaching produces confusion among his disciples. Peter immediately rebukes Jesus for his prediction of "disaster," that is, his death, and expresses an elliptical hope that it will not happen: "(May God be) merciful to you, Lord!" (16:22, lit.). Peter's very human reaction to the thought of Jesus' death conflicts sharply with God's will ("He must go . . ." — v. 21), so that he is a stumbling block (lit. "scandal") and a tempter ("satan") for Jesus because Peter does not understand divine wisdom and purposes (v. 23). This very human resistance and confusion concerning the meaning of Jesus' death motivates and guides the rest of the teaching and narration in the Gospel. Jesus begins instructing his disciples with a group of paradoxical sayings about self-denial, suffering, death, and life after death (vv. 24-28; cf. 10:38-39). Jesus' prediction of his death has provoked consternation in his disciples, but as always Jesus' teachings and deeds demand obedience and following from his disciples. The cross, first explicitly mentioned as the instrument of Jesus' death in 20:19, serves here as a metaphor for self-denial (16:24). Similarly, losing one's life serves as a paradoxical metaphor for saving and finding life (v. 25), which is the fundamental and greatest value (v. 26). This improbable and countercultural view of life finds its fulfillment and vindication in the final judgment and rule of the Son of Man (vv. 27-28; cf. 13:41; 20:21). Matthew's reference to "on the third day" as the time of the resurrection alludes to "the third day" in biblical passages as the time when God resolved crises (see Hos 6:2 and Jonah 1:17). Thus the death and resurrection of Jesus and his disciples' acceptance of death and resurrection in their own lives find their context in the major theme of the Gospel, the coming of God's kingdom.

The story of Jesus' transfiguration into a divine-like being (17:1-8 — lit. *metamorphoō* in Greek, i.e., "changed in outward form") verifies what the Gospel has taught about Jesus' high status as Messiah and Son of God in the preceding stories and sayings. The story resembles divine visions and epiphanies which were common in Second Temple Judaism and in the Greco-Roman world, but the author of Matthew has used significant motifs from the ascent of Moses to Mt. Sinai (Exodus 19–24; 32–34) and visions common in Second Temple apocalypses. The chronological note "after six days" (17:1 from Mark 9:2), one of the few in the Synoptic Gospels, does not clearly refer back to a specific incident. Rather, it alludes to Moses' six days on Mt. Sinai, after which he saw the glory of God on the seventh (Exod 24:15-16). Like Moses, Jesus ascends a high mountain, traditionally identified with Mt. Tabor in Galilee. (This site is improbable because it was occupied as a Roman outpost in the early first century.) Peter, James, and John, who accompany Jesus (17:1), match Moses' three companions, Aaron, Nadab, and Abihu (Exod 24:1, 9). Jesus' face shines as did Moses' after being in the presence of God (17:2; Exod 34:29-35), a bright cloud overshadows the mountain, and a heavenly voice speaks (17:5), just as a cloud covers Moses on Sinai and God's voice is heard in thunder (Exod 19:16, 19; 24:15, 18). Jesus' clothes become white as light (17:2, lit.); analogously, Moses' face shone after he was with God on the mountain (Exod 34:29-35). Though the stories of Moses on Sinai and Jesus on a high mountain are very different, motifs from the Sinai account lend authority to Jesus' teaching, as do the appearances of Moses and Elijah symbolizing the Law and the Prophets so often referred to in the Gospel. Jesus gains stature by comparison with Moses, the most authoritative teacher in the HB and the one who had the closest contact with God. The divine command to "hear him [Jesus]" (17:5) may identify Jesus with the prophet like Moses promised in the Torah (Deut 18:15-18). Finally, Peter's odd suggestion that he set up three tents for Jesus, Moses, and Elijah (17:4) may allude to the tent of meeting where God's presence dwelt and to the Second Temple conception of God's presence ("Shekinah," from the word for "dwell" and "tent"). There, too, a cloud covers the tent of meeting when Moses speaks with God (Exod 33:9-11).

The divine voice which proclaims Jesus as the Son of God (17:5) reaffirms the identification made in the narrative of ch. 1, the baptism (3:17), the calming of the storm (14:33), and Peter's revelation (16:16). The judgment that God is well pleased with Jesus alludes to the first of the suffering servant songs in Isaiah (42:1-4) and to Jesus' impending death. Jesus' radiant face and garments, along with the divine phenomena, portray him as one of the heavenly intermediaries (angels, ancient figures like Enoch, etc.) so common in Second Temple apocalyptic literature and narratives (cf. also Matt 1:20; 28:3; etc.). The disciples' paralyzing fear and need for reassurance from Jesus (17:6-7) correspond to the reactions of apocalyptic visionaries (e.g., Dan 8:15-19; 10:5-11). The author of Matthew interprets the transfiguration as a vision (17:9 — *horama*) and has interpreted Jesus in an apocalyptic context which points ahead to the second coming of Jesus.

The transfiguration was preceded by sayings concerning the judgment and the coming of the kingdom (16:27-28), and here it is followed by a discussion of the role of Elijah as a forerunner of the Messiah or Son of Man (17:9-13). As was noted in the commentary on Matt 11:14, the linking of Elijah with the coming of the Messiah appears first in the Gospels and is not a widespread Jewish expectation. Similarly, the identification here of John the Baptizer with Elijah and Jesus with the Messiah obviously derives from the early Jesus movement. Elijah, John the Baptizer, and Jesus all suffer persecution due to their fidelity to God and promote God's rule (kingdom). The mention of the resurrection (17:9) after the vision of Jesus as a heavenly being prepares the disciples to accept Jesus' death.

Bibliography. Brown, R. E. et al., 1973, *Peter in the New Testament,* New York: Paulist; Minneapolis: Augsburg • Chilton, B. D. 1980, "The Transfiguration: Dominical Assurance and Apostolic Vision," *NTS* 27:115-24 • Kingsbury, J. D. 1979, "The Figure of Peter in Matthew's Gospel as a Theological Problem," *JBL* 98:67-83 • Marcus, J. 1988, "The Gates of Hades and the Keys of the Kingdom," *CBQ* 50:443-55 • Nickelsburg, G. W. E. 1981, "Enoch, Levi and Peter: Recipients of Revelation in Upper Galilee," *JBL* 100:575-600 • Taylor, J. 1991, "The Coming of Elijah, Mt 17,10-13 and Mk 9,11-13: The Development of the Texts," *RB* 98:107-19.

Strengthening the Disciples (17:14-27)

The story of the healing of the epileptic boy (17:14-20) presumes and further demonstrates Jesus' divinely given power and authority so recently manifested in the transfiguration. However, like most of the stories and instruction in chs. 16–18 which concern the proper way of understanding and following Jesus, the healing story addresses the disciples' faith. While Jesus and three disciples were on the mountain, the rest of the disciples failed in their attempts to exorcise a boy who was "moonstruck" (v. 15), even though they had already been given authority over unclean spirits and sickness (10:1). Similarly, Gehazi fails to raise a child from the dead in the absence of his master Elisha (2 Kgs 4:31). The boy's symptoms, being moonstruck, suffering terribly, and falling to the fire and water (vv. 15, 18; see the more elaborate description in Mark 9:17-22), have led commentators to interpret the disease of being "moonstruck" as epilepsy. The disciples' failure to cure the boy is just one more obstacle to understanding Jesus and acting as his true followers. The disciples have struggled to understand the feeding of the five thousand (14:15-17), Jesus' power over the sea (14:26-32), the teaching on purity (15:15-16), the leaven of the Pharisees and Sadducees (16:5-12), the prediction of Jesus' death (16:22), the vision on the mountain (17:4), and the role of John the Baptizer (vv. 10-13). Their problem is "little faith" (v. 20; previously in 6:20; 8:26; 14:31; 16:8), that is, a lack of confidence in Jesus and God's power and an inadequate understanding of Jesus' role as God's emissary as the Messiah and the Son of God. The disciples' difficulties parallel the more acute failure of a "faithless and perverse generation" (17:17; see Matt 11:16; 12:39, 45; 16:4 and Deut 1:35; 32:5, 20 for similar language) to understand and accept Jesus. In contrast to them the father approaches Jesus with words and gestures proper to prayer when he genuflects and requests: "Lord, have mercy on my son" (17:15). His behavior affirms Jesus' close relationship to God just revealed to his three disciples on the mountain. In response Jesus immediately exorcises and cures the boy. The disciples subsequently find out that inadequate faith explains their failure (vv. 18-20), for even the smallest amount of real confidence in God, as small as a mustard seed (cf. 13:31-32), will move mountains (a divine prerogative). This proverbial teaching on faith recurs in the story of the withered fig tree (21:20-22). Matt 17:21, which attributes successful exorcism to prayer and fasting, does not appear in the best manuscripts and was probably added under the influence of Mark 9:29 and Matt 21:22, which refer to the necessity of prayer.

A second prediction of Jesus' death and resurrection (17:22-23) follows the disciples' instruction in faith and tests it further. The place and time, "as they were gathering in Galilee" (v. 22), are vague; the last place name was Caesarea Philippi (16:13). Perhaps the author implies that the transfiguration and exorcism of the epileptic boy took place in the far north of Israel, around Caesarea Philippi. Or the verb, which also means to gather around, may refer to the disciples gathering around Jesus in Galilee for private instruction. Previously the disciples protested Jesus' prediction of his death (16:22), but here they are distressed (v. 23), indicating that they have understood and to some extent accepted what Jesus has said.

The final story before Jesus' fourth sermon on community relations in ch. 18 takes place at Jesus' base of operations, Capernaum. The collectors of the didrachma, the double drachma or half-shekel yearly tax to support the temple, question whether Jesus fulfills his duty as a faithful Jew by paying the tax (17:24-27). This temple tax was not clearly mandated by the Bible, but was indirectly derived from a voluntary one-third shekel tax collected yearly by Nehemiah (Neh 10:32) and a half-shekel "ransom for their lives" given to the sanctuary by the Israelites during a census in the wilderness (Exod 30:13). The members of the Qumran community disputed the legitimacy of this tax because they interpreted the half-shekel tax as a once-in-a-lifetime obligation (4Q*Ordinances*), and some rabbinic opinions questioned it as well (*m. Sheqal.* 1:4). After the Romans destroyed the temple in AD 70 they collected the tax to support the temple of Jupiter Capitolinus.

Peter immediately defends Jesus verbally, even though the narrative assumes that Jesus has not paid the tax (17:25). Jesus argues that he need not pay the tax but does so in order to not give offense (scandal). Since the author of Matthew always portrays Jesus as faithfully obeying Jewish law, Jesus' decision to pay the tax is not surprising. Jesus' argument that he is exempt from the temple tax presumes and supports the Matthean teaching that he is the Son of God. Since the temple is God's house and God's subjects pay for its upkeep through taxes, Jesus, who is God's Son and a family member, is not a member of the populace liable for taxes (vv. 25-26), but a recipient of the taxes. The attitude toward taxes here, that they should be paid for the sake of social order but that they are not pertinent to God's kingdom, fits the common NT attitude toward civil authorities (cf. Matt 22:15-22; Rom 13:1-7; 1 Pet 2:13-17; Titus 3:1). The story probably provided a rationale for some of the early followers of Jesus to remain connected to the temple and in good standing with Jewish communal authorities by paying the tax and may have provided others with a reason (Jesus' special status before God) to stop paying it.

Introduction to the Sermon on Community Relations (18)

The center of the Sermon on Community Relations contains procedures for reconciling or expelling a sinful community member (18:15-17). They are similar to those known from the Dead Sea Scrolls. The presence of these rules suggests that the late-first-century Matthean community was struggling with divisions and conflicts which threatened its integrity. The rest of the sermon teaches concern for one another and merciful forgiveness, both of which support reconciliation and communal unity.

Care for Community Members (18:1-14)

The Sermon on Community Relations begins with the disciples' question about the greatest in the kingdom of heaven, a question found frequently in Matthew (and in a different context in Mark 9:33-34). In the author's view the one who keeps the least commandments and teaches others to do so will be great in the kingdom (5:19). The least member of the kingdom is greater than John the Baptizer (11:11). The one who wishes to be great must serve others (20:26; 22:39), but the greatest commandment is to love God (22:36-38). Consonant with these comparisons, the greatest in the kingdom is a person who "humbles himself" like the child Jesus has placed before them (18:4). The connotations of the child metaphor have been unduly developed by commentators, especially under the influence of Romanticism. The text itself does not support the usual appeals to the innocence, sinlessness, simplicity, trust, dependence, or openness of children, though these characteristics may be drawn from the parable interpreted out of context. The humility which Jesus recommends refers most properly to the social station of a person in a hierarchical society; thus it is not native to nor appreciated as a virtue in modern societies which stress equality. Children, especially in ancient society, were without power and status; Jesus teaches that those who live under God's rule (in the kingdom) must all give up their claims to status and position in deference to God and treat each other as equals. Thus Jesus advises welcoming children (v. 5), something he himself does in the next chapter (19:13-15). These instructions about children and the subsequent teaching about "little ones" (18:6-14; cf. 10:40-42) implicitly identify the disciples with these "children," as do later references to the disciples as "least" (25:40, 45). The warning against doing harm to "these little ones who believe in me," symbolized as scandalizing, that is, placing "stumbling blocks" in someone's way (18:6-7), refers to people who were discouraging, misleading, or impeding members of the author's group. The problem might have been community strife over teaching, or observance, or authority, or persecution (13:21; 26:31), or causing others to lose their faith (18:6), or despising members in trouble or of lower social station (v. 10), or doing wrong to another (v. 15). Threats to faithful following of Jesus can come from people themselves as well as others (vv. 8-9; cf. 7:3-5). The hyperbolic images of drowning with a millstone and excising a hand, foot, or eye (cf. 5:29-30) testify to the author's fear of some serious threat to the community and its members.

These warnings against scandal and sin end with a consoling expression of confidence in divine protection (18:10, 14) and the parable of the lost sheep. The man searching for his lost sheep recalls Jesus' description of his task, to go to the lost sheep of the house of Israel (10:6). Since the shepherd and his flock is a common biblical image for God, Israel, and its leaders, the parable of the lost sheep mandates that community members make every effort to bring back those who are losing heart and leaving the community because of scandal or the "stumbling blocks" just mentioned. This concern for one another's welfare and for the integrity of the whole community leads to an instruction on reconciling community members who are in conflict.

Bibliography. Addley, W. P. 1976, "Matthew 18 and the Church as the Body of Christ," *Biblical Theology* 26:12-18 • Crossan, J. D. 1983, "Kingdom and Children: A Study in the Aphoristic Tradition," *Semeia* 29:75-95 • Duling, D. C. 1999, "Matthew 18:15-17: Conflict, Confrontation, and Conflict Resolution in a 'Fictive Kin' Association," *BTB* 29:422 • Robbins, V. K. 1983, "Pronouncement Stories and Jesus' Blessing of the Children: A Rhetorical Approach," *Semeia* 29:43-74 • Schweizer, E. 1973, "Matthew's View of the Church in His 18th Chapter," *AusBR* 21:7-14.

Reconciliation of Community Members (18:15-35)

The firm procedures for correcting sinful behavior in the community (18:15-17) resemble those used by the Qumran community (1QS 5:24–6:1; CD 9:2-8, 16-22). A biblical law against nursing resentment and anger which might divide a family or town has guided the formation of the rules in the Dead Sea Scrolls and the Gospel: "You shall not hate in your heart anyone of your kin; you shall reprove your neighbor, or you will incur guilt yourself" (Lev 19:17). In accordance with this general rule the Gospel requires a community member to make every effort to correct, reconcile, and forgive the offending party while protecting the integrity and authority of the community as a whole. If a community member knows that another has sinned, he must first confront him privately to win him back (v. 15). (The NRSV translates "sins against you" in v. 15, but "against you" is missing from the best manuscripts. The offense may be any behavior objectionable to community norms and goals.) If the offending member will not reform, the next step in the process, also guided by biblical law (Deut 19:15), requires that the complaint be witnessed by two or more members. If this produces an unsatisfactory response from the offender, the whole church (*ekklēsia* — "assembly") adjudicates the matter and as a body refuses to have any more relationship with the sinner. Expulsion from the community or shunning (later called "excommunication" by Christians) was practiced at Qumran and in Pauline communities (cf. 1 Cor 5:1-5; 2 Thess 3:6-15). Minority groups within a culture depend for their existence on the active involvement and cohesiveness of their members, so they especially need to maintain standards and boundaries.

Matthew follows the disciplinary process with a defense of the community's underlying authority to judge and to expel or forgive its members. The traditional Jewish metaphor for authoritative legal decision is binding and loosing (cf. the discussion concerning Peter in 16:19), a power which the community exercises with divine endorsement (18:18). The power of decision may be exercised even by two disciples who agree in deciding a case (v. 19). The Greek verse says literally "agree on earth about any matter [or perhaps "case" — *pragmatos*] concerning which they might ask." The NRSV seems to understand the clause as a reference to prayer ("if two of you agree on earth about anything you ask"; cf. 7:7), but in this context the power to decide refers to judges deciding cases or interpreting law. The following verse (18:20) is the most general of all, promising that Jesus will be present with a gathering of two or three of his followers. This understanding of Jesus' presence was implied at the beginning of the Gospel (2:23) and is reaffirmed and broadened at the end (28:20). Rabbinic literature finds God similarly present when people study Torah together (*m. 'Abot* 3:2, 3, 6). The three related sayings in Matthew (18:18-20) establish the divine authorization of Matthew's small group of Jewish followers of Jesus and articulate the consequences of the risen Christ's presence in the community.

Peter responds to Jesus' teaching with a question concerning the limits of forgiveness (18:21; cf. v. 15). Should people forgive others seven times? (Seven is a common round number in the Bible.) Jesus' hyperbolic reply, seventy-seven times (or seventy times seven — the Greek is ambiguous), connotes an unlimited number (v. 22). His answer is drawn from Gen 4:24, where it connotes unlimited blood feuds among Lamech and the descendants of Cain and it opposes the usual attitude that at some point justice limits mercy.

The concluding parable of the sermon (18:23-35) starkly contrasts the mercy and forgiveness proper to God's rule with unjust and irresponsible lack of care for others. References to the kingdom at the beginning of the sermon (18:1-4) and here at the end (v. 23) form a thematic inclusion which holds it together. The hyperbole of the narrative emphasizes God's mercy and forgiveness. The slave (or, perhaps better, a high official) owes his king ten thousand talents, an impossibly large sum communicated by the largest Greek numerical unit available, ten thousand, and the largest unit of value for money, a talent (originally a measure of weight for precious metals). The king proposes the usual punishment for indebtedness, the sale of the slave and his family to pay the debt. Of course, measured against the enormous debt the value of the slave's family would be minimal. (Some commentators have suggested that the debt was originally ten thousand denarii.) Nevertheless selling a debtor to recoup a loss was common in the ancient world (cf. the allusion to it in 5:25-26). In the Bible a thief may be sold to make restitution for his theft (Exod 22:3) and children are sold into slavery if the family cannot repay its debt (2 Kgs 4:1; Neh 5:1-13). Later Jewish law allows a man to be sold for debt but does not allow a man's wife to be sold (*m. Soṭa* 3:8), presumably because she would be violated sexually.

When the slave pleads for time to pay (18:26), an unrealistic aspiration given the size of the debt, which was equivalent to billions of dollars, the king takes pity on him and frees him from what he suddenly and tactfully calls a "loan" (*daneion* rather that *opheilē*, "debt"). At this point in the Gospel the king's generosity and the slave's need inevitably recall God's merciful forgiveness of human sinners, which has been a theme since the infancy narrative (1:21).

The slave's subsequent unmerciful behavior toward a fellow slave (18:28-30) contradicts the treatment he received. He unrealistically demands immediate payment of a debt of hundred days' wages (a denarius was about a day's wage), which could only be paid over time, and jails his debtor who could not comply. His upset colleagues report to the king, who judges the forgiven slave wicked for having ignored the norms of measure for measure (6:14-17; 7:2) and of mercy (18:33; cf. 5:7; 23:23; Hos 6:6 in Matt 9:13 and 12:7). The king's next action, torture until the payment of the impossibly large debt (18:34), is yet again unrealistic but leads smoothly to the application of the parable to Matthew's community. God punishes unforgiving community members at the final judgment if they do not forgive one another.

Bibliography. Carmody, T. R. 1989, "Matt 18:15-17 in Relation to Three Texts from Qumran Literature (CD 9:2-8; CD 9:16-22; 1QS 5:24–6:1)," in M. P. Horgan et al., eds., *To Touch the Text: Biblical and Related Studies in Honor of Joseph A. Fitzmyer, S.J.*, New York: Crossroad, 141-58 • Duling, D. 1987, "Binding and Loosing: Matthew 16:19; Matthew 18:18; John 20:23," *Forum* 3:3-31 • Thompson, W. G. 1970, *Matthew's Advice to a Divided Community: Mt. 17,22–18,35*, AB 44, Rome: Biblical Institute.

Introduction to Households of Disciples (Chs. 19–20)

Matthew's group of Jewish followers of Jesus probably met in small assemblies (*ekklēsiai* — churches) composed of a few families which gathered in a house for prayer and instruction. Large public buildings dedicated to worship became common only in the third and fourth centuries in the eastern Roman Empire. Thus, after working out the attitudes and formal procedures which should govern his assemblies in ch. 18, the author of Matthew explores the relationships which affect the unity and fidelity of the families of disciples, including the marriage bond, children, wealth, suffering, competition, and understanding of Jesus' teachings. Since the teaching on marriage and divorce ends with the option of remaining unmarried and the story of the rich young man with a defense of poverty, all in obedience to the demands of the kingdom and perfection, ch. 19 became the biblical source for development of monastic life with its vows of poverty, chastity, and obedience.

Family and Wealth (19:1–20:16)

After his instruction concerning community relationships (ch. 18), Jesus returns to Judea from Galilee for the first time since the beginning of his Galilean ministry (4:12). Jesus heals the crowds, but he does not teach them (in contrast to Mark 10:1) until he is in the temple (21:23; 23:1). Rather, the Pharisees immediately test him on the laws for divorce, which were debated in first-century Judaism (cf. Satan in 4:1 and the Pharisees in 16:1; see also 22:18, 35). The double discussion of this problem (5:31-32 and here) testifies to Matthew's interest in it. He alters the question in Mark 10:2 about whether divorce is permitted to a more precise Second Temple Jewish question concerning the grounds for divorce: "Is it permitted for a man to divorce his wife *for any reason?*" (19:3). In traditional Near Eastern law men take women in marriage and release them from marriage by divorce. The woman does not take the man. When Mark 10:12 mentions women divorcing their husbands, he addresses a possibility deriving from Roman law. Concerning the grounds for divorce, Deut 24:1 says only that a man may divorce his wife for "indecency of a matter" (*'erwat dabar*), a vague phrase concerned with sexual impropriety. *'erwat* refers to "nakedness," "the sexual organs," and then "sexual matters" and "sexual shame" in general. According to rabbinic literature, the school of Shammai (1st cent. AD) took the phrase narrowly to refer to a case of sexual impropriety, most probably adultery. The school of Hillel focused on the word *dabar,* which means "thing," "matter," or "word," and so taught that a man could divorce his wife for any reason, "even if she spoiled his dish of food" (*m. Giṭ.* 9:10). Probably the Hillelite position stressed marriage as a voluntary and loving relationship; if anger over a burnt dinner produced a desire to divorce, then the relationship had effectively ended anyway. Matthew enters this argument by taking a position similar to that of the Shammaites, that a man may divorce his wife only for *porneia* (19:9), a very general Greek term referring to sexual impropriety or irregularity, roughly equivalent to the Hebrew expression *'erwat dabar.*

Commentators continue to disagree over the sexual irregularity to which Matthew refers, with most opting for adultery, even though the technical Greek term for adultery is not used. According to the Mishnah, an adulteress is forbidden to her husband and lover (*m. Soṭa* 5:1; cf. *m. Ned.* 11:12 for a priest's wife who has been raped). The woman's irregular sexual relations force her husband to divorce her. This view underlies Joseph's initial decision to divorce Mary (1:19), and Abraham's fear, in the *Genesis Apocryphon,* that Pharaoh will have intercourse with Sarah (1QapGen 20:15). Sexual irregularity which would render a woman impure and unfit to continue in a marriage may extend to involuntary intercourse due to rape, captivity and the like. Others suggest that the irregularity which would void a marriage is a blood relationship between the spouses forbidden by Scripture (see the dispute in CD 5:7-10). The underlying cultural assumption is that a woman must be sexually pure to continue in a marriage. Even when divorce is permitted because of sexual irregularity (*porneia*), it is unclear whether Matthew allows remarriage while the spouse is alive. Certainly the woman affected by sexual irregularity, if forbidden to her husband by law and custom, would be forbidden to another man also. Thus she could not remarry, but the status of the husband is unclear. The *Temple Scroll* may address a similar issue, but like Matthew it is unclear. "[The king] shall not take another wife in addition to [his wife], for she alone shall be with him all the time of her life. If she dies, he may marry another" (11QTemple 57:17-19). This passage may forbid royal polygamy (see also 11QTemple 56:18-19) or it may forbid him (and implicitly all Israelites?) to remarry while his divorced wife lives. In the early Christian tradition, the patristic writers taught that remarriage after divorce was forbidden, but many Reformation and modern authors have allowed it, albeit with hesitation.

As usual, the author of Matthew has reorganized and nuanced the arguments for the prohibition of divorce which he found in Mark 10. Though the HB takes divorce for granted in Deut 24:1-4, Jesus turns back to the creation story to argue that God made male and female "one flesh" (Gen 2:24) from the very beginning as a norm for marriage (19:5). The Pharisees counter with the obvious objection, that the biblical procedures for divorce assume its legitimacy (v. 6), but Jesus argues that divorce is a later concession contrary to the original normative arrangement in Genesis, not a law positively taught by the Bible (v. 8). In returning to the original divine law expressed in Genesis, Jesus overturns two biblical practices, divorce and polygamy, though the latter was not widely practiced in the Second Temple period. In response Jesus' disciples protest the rigorous prohibition of divorce and remarriage with the objection that it might be better not to marry at all (v. 10). (The disciples and others object, ask questions, etc., in 19:13, 25, 27; 20:20, 24, 31.) Jesus retorts that not everyone can "accept this teaching" (*logos* — 19:11), but that everyone who can "accept" it should "accept" (v. 12). "This teaching" probably refers to the prohibition of divorce and remarriage, though it also hints at the disciples' suggestion that celibacy may be better than marriage (v. 10; cf. 1 Corinthians 7 for Paul's views). The metaphor of a eunuch (19:12) links the discussion of divorce and remarriage to the requirements of God's kingdom, but the meaning of the saying has been as much debated as the prohibition of divorce. Within the inclusion based on the verb "accept" (vv. 11-12) Jesus admits that only some can accept his teaching and explains this by a threefold distinction of eunuchs: those born physically defective; those (slaves) castrated, usually to work in their owners' harems; and those who are voluntary eunuchs "for the sake of the kingdom of heaven." Since Scripture forbids voluntary castration, Matthew refers metaphorically to those who remain unmarried, either totally (v. 10) or after a divorce (v. 9), in accordance with Jesus' teaching. The teaching on divorce, which almost certainly goes back to Jesus, stresses fidelity, unity, and permanence in marital relations as a reflection of God's relationship with humans in his kingdom. In the late first century the health and stability of Matthew's small, threatened community depends on stable, enduring family relationships.

The defense of marriage leads naturally to concern for children who are brought to Jesus so that he can lay his hands on them and pray over them (19:13-15). Jesus does not take them in his arms, as in Mark 10:16, and the disciples seem to rebuke the children (lit. "them" in Greek, not the "people" as in the NRSV). Thus Matthew probably understands the children to be older than in Mark, perhaps young members of the crowd gathering around Jesus. The author does not say here why theirs is the kingdom of heaven (but cf. 18:2-5), but in this context the children have a place as part of the family structure which the author defends.

The young man (19:16-22; *neaniskos* in vv. 20 and 22) who refuses to follow Jesus contrasts with the children *(ta paidia)* who sought Jesus' blessing (v. 13). The young man is not evil since he keeps the commandments (v. 20). Rather, he seeks instruction on what good deed will lead to eternal life (v. 16) beyond the commandments (v. 20). Jesus offers him perfection (v. 21; cf. 5:48), which requires relinquishing his wealth (19:21) in favor of wholehearted trust in God (cf. 6:19-34), from whom real wealth and treasure comes. Like God and Jesus, the young man must also care for the poor (19:21). The invitation to follow Jesus without possessions (cf. 8:20) demands the dedication of a disciple (cf. the four disciples in 4:18-22; Levi in 9:9). The young man could exchange wealth for heavenly treasure, but he refuses this teaching (*logos,* as in 19:11) in order to hold onto his wealth (vv. 21-22). The narrative appreciates the young man as obedient to God's commandments and worthy of eternal life and does not condemn him as evil. However, the dialogue between Jesus and his disciples which follows treats him and all rich people more harshly. The rich can enter the kingdom of God, that is, live under God's rule now and in the next world, only with great difficulty (v. 23) to the point of impossibility (v. 24 with the hyperbole of a camel going through the eye of a needle). Matthew probably fears that the comfort and security of wealth detract from trust in God (6:31-33) and commitment to God's rule (6:21, 24; 13:22). This radical demand implies that few will be saved, though an addendum offers the vague comfort that God will work it out (19:25-26). A question by Peter on behalf of the disciples elicits an explicit promise of reward for those who endure poverty for Jesus (v. 27; cf. 5:3): the twelve will join the Son of Man in judging Israel at the end of the world (19:28). The Son of Man as judge and the twelve tribes of Israel appear in various scenarios of the end. "The renewal" (v. 28; *palingenesia*) is a term used in Greek Stoic philosophy for the cyclical destruction and then rebirth of the universe. Some hold that Matthew envisions a judgment for Israel separate from the judgment of the Gentiles in the parable of the sheep and goats (25:31-46), but it is doubtful that Matthew means to separate the judgment of Jews and Gentiles chronologically. Some NT texts distinguish Jews and Gentiles (Rom 2:9-10) or believers in Jesus from nonbelievers (1 Cor 6:2-3; 1 Pet 4:17) without clearly separate judgments. Second Temple Jewish literature envisions the destruction of oppressors and the vindication of the just who were faithful to God at the end of the world, but the process seems to be one continuous action of doing away with evil and then establishing God's rule (*1 Enoch* 91:12-14; *Pss. Sol.* 17:26-32; 4 Ezra 13:29-50; 2 *Bar.* 72–74).

In addition to the special role given to the twelve, all disciples who have followed Jesus by leaving their houses, families, and fields (described in a symbolic list of seven items) will ultimately not lose anything but receive them back a hundredfold and inherit eternal life (19:29). Intriguingly, Jesus, who had already told the young man to keep the commandments in order to inherit eternal life (v. 17), here promises a similar reward to those who leave their possessions (v. 29). The prior warning that the rich will find it hard to gain eternal life and this response to the disciples weights Jesus' teaching heavily in favor of detachment from family and land in order to follow him. The young man who rejected Jesus because he was unwilling to give up his wealth contradicts the teaching of Jesus from the Sermon on the Mount on and cannot stand for a type of follower of Jesus (or Christian). To observe the commandments does not suffice; Matthew demands that his entire audience follow Jesus. On the other hand, Jesus does not attack or condemn the young man the way he does the Jewish leaders; thus the young man does not symbolize the rejection of Israel, as some commentators have claimed. The young man is an observant Jew doing God's will according to the biblical commandments and thus worthy of eternal life. The author of Matthew has no clean solution to this dilemma. He acknowledges the admirable obedience of many of his fellow Jews, but he argues that their response to God is incomplete without obedience to God's Son and his teaching. He does not reject the crowds or the young man totally because he still hopes to attract them to Jesus and because they remain faithful to God in the traditional way. The final saying of this group of teachings, that the first and last will reverse positions (v. 30, repeated in 20:16; cf. Luke 13:30), expresses well the paradoxical situation in which the author finds himself as well as the dramatic reversal which is expected at the end for the powerless and oppressed.

The parable about the compensation of the vineyard workers (20:1-16) continues the discussion of wealth and success in relationship to the kingdom. The landowner, unlike the rich young man, makes good use of his wealth. The question of who or what is good appears in both stories (19:16-17; 20:15), and both end with the paradoxical saying about the first being last which supports the priority of the needy over those who have accumulated wealth (19:30; 20:16). The unusual decisions of the landowner drive the plot, but the reactions of the laborers make its point. The landowner hires repeatedly during the day, even employing laborers for the last hour of work (vv. 6-7) and promising to pay all "whatever is right" (v. 4; *dikaios,* meaning "just"). He pays the most recently hired first ("the last shall be first") with great dramatic effect because he gives them a full day's wage (a denarius). Those who have worked the longest expect to get paid more than the contractual amount which has been paid to those with shorter hours (v. 10). They are guided by the pragmatic, rational expectation of equal pay for equal work, a variant of "measure for measure" in Jer 10:24; 13:25; 30:11; Lam 5:22; Matt 7:2; and 1 Thess 2:16 applied to judgment and punishment; and in 2 Cor 4:17; Eph 4:7 contrasted with God's immeasurable gifts. When they complain to the owner that they received only their contractual amount (20:11-12), they implicitly charge that he has not done "what is right" in "making them equal to us" who have worked all day. Two ancient assumptions about socioeconomic relations hide beneath their complaint. First, those who achieve more ought to receive more honor, status, and recognition than those who have not. Thus the owner has dishonored them and denigrated their efforts by treating everyone equally. Secondly, ancient society conceived of the world as having limited goods. Thus if one person gets more pay, produce, or honor, then the other person inevitably gets less. Those who worked all day fear that they have lost what belongs to them because the owner gave it to the group hired later.

The owner's reply attacks the laborers' charges and presuppositions. He has kept his contract with them, paid them a living wage, and thus has not "done them wrong" (20:13 — *adikō*). In addition, he has legitimately dispersed his abundant resources as he chose by giving a full day's wage, sufficient to feed a family, to all the workers (vv. 14-15). Common practice does not constrain his generosity. Finally, he attacks the workers' outlook with an evil eye accusation which reads literally, "Or is your eye evil because I am good?" (v. 15). The NRSV correctly associates the "evil eye" with envy, resentment at the success of another tinged with an aggressive desire to see loss or harm come to the envied one. In contrast to these "evil" attitudes (cf. 6:23, where the NRSV's "unhealthy eye" is literally the "evil eye") the owner is "good," that is, generous and not coerced by the narrowness of others.

This challenging parable has stimulated many responses from commentators. Within the Gospel the owner's generosity supports love of neighbor expressed through generosity and the type of nonhierarchical, mutually supportive social relations envisioned in ch. 18 and 23:1-12. Since it is applied to the kingdom of God (20:1), it affirms God's abundant resources available to all, the need for trust in God's generosity (6:19-34), the requirement that all people be cared for, and the teaching that wealth be used well. The owner's anxiety that the grapes be harvested and the story's setting in the vineyard (often used to symbolize Israel) recall Jesus' metaphoric plea for more workers in the harvest, that is, more disciples to teach Israel (9:37-38). The workers whom no one else had hired near the end of the day may allude to the tax collectors and sinners whom Jesus seeks out in his work (9:11; 11:19; 21:31-32). The single wage for all the workers parallels the single goal and single reward of those who follow Jesus, no matter what their status: entry into the kingdom of God and eternal life. The owner's fidelity to his contractual obligations and his generosity mirror the justice and mercy of both God and Jesus. This parable ends the discussion of family and wealth and material loss and gain, but leads to a more demanding lesson on the greater loss of life itself.

Understanding Jesus' Death (20:17-34)

The third passion prediction (20:17-19; cf. 16:21; 17:22-23 for the first two) is the most detailed and emotionally charged because Jesus and his disciples are on their way to Jerusalem. The author stresses that Jesus is fully conscious of what will happen to him and goes forward voluntarily. Jesus goes to Jerusalem with his disciples ("we are going"), and the disciples do not respond negatively to his prediction as they did previously and do in Mark's version (Mark 10:32). Similarly, Matthew attributes the misunderstanding about the qualifications for ruling the kingdom not to James and John (Mark 10:35), but to their mother (20:20-23). The request for places of honor and power next to Jesus when he rules (v. 21) fits the apocalyptic scenarios of the Son of Man ruling the universe (Daniel 7) but ignores God's ultimate authority over the kingdom and Jesus' teaching about serving one another and suffering. The metaphoric cup which Jesus offers them (20:22) symbolizes the destiny of a person, especially if it involves suffering (Pss 11:6; 75:8). Though James and John accept the cup, they do not understand, nor do the rest of the twelve, who become jealous and angry at the brothers' attempt to gain special power and honor. (Note the thematic parallel to the parable of the vineyard workers above.) Their misunderstanding prompts a brief instruction (20:25-28) on ruling through service to one another, an approach exemplified by Jesus all through the Gospel, a further interpretation of the reversal of the first (cf. first and last in 19:30; 20:16) as a slave (v. 27) and a rejection of hierarchical rule (v. 25; cf. 23:1-12). Here as elsewhere the author contrasts the behavior of the followers of Jesus with life in the Roman Empire. The teaching on suffering and service ends, as it does in Mark, with the pithy and undeveloped interpretation of Jesus' death as a ransom for "many," a Semitism for "all" (20:28; Mark 10:45; Isa 53:11). "Ransom" refers to freeing a slave or prisoner of war by payment of money and issuance of a legal document. Its precise meaning here is not worked out, though most interpreters associate ransoming or redemption with freeing of humans from the power of sin on the basis of Matthew's interpretation of Jesus' death (26:28, "for the forgiveness of sins"). The giving of one's life also recalls the heroes and martyrs of Jewish history, especially the Maccabean period, who gave their lives for others (1 Macc 2:50; 6:44; 2 Maccabees 6–7) and the Greco-Roman stories of the noble deaths of virtuous leaders.

The healing of two blind men (20:29-34) repeats more fully the healing of the two blind men recounted earlier (9:27-31; consult the commentary there for the basic story). Here the healing of blind men provides an ironic commentary on the blindness of the disciples, who do not fully understand and accept Jesus' present goal, to go to Jerusalem and die according to God's will. Despite opposition from the crowd, the two blind men insist on getting a hearing from Jesus (20:30-31) because they understand clearly that he provides them a unique opportunity to be healed. They have confidence in Jesus, Jesus responds with compassion (v. 34 as in 9:36; see also 14:14; 15:32), and the cure is done. More strikingly, they alone among those healed in the Gospel follow Jesus (20:34). They symbolize the faith and sight/understanding appropriate to followers of Jesus. Their response encapsulates the proper attitude and behavior of a disciple of Jesus, and their following propels the narrative toward the completion of the journey to Jerusalem in the next chapter.

Bibliography. Bockmuehl, M. 1989, "Matthew 5.32; 19.9 in the Light of Pre-Rabbinic Halakhah," *NTS* 35:291-95 • Carter, W. 1994, *Households and Discipleship: A Study of Matthew 19–20*, JSNTSup 103, Sheffield: Sheffield Academic • Elliott, J. H. 1992, "Matthew 20:1-15: A Parable of Invidious Comparison and Evil Eye Accusation," *BTB* 22:52-65.

Introduction to Conflicts with the Jerusalem Leaders (21–23)

The action in the last eight chapters of Matthew takes place in Jerusalem, except for the final scene, Jesus' appearance in Galilee (28:16-20). The author recounts Jesus' conflicts, teachings, and activities within a richly symbolic matrix reaching back into the HB and forward to the end of the world. In chs. 21–23 Jesus enters Jerusalem with popular acclaim, criticizes the Jewish leadership in a series of confrontations (21:12–22:46) and parables (21:28–22:14), and attacks them at length in a long discourse to the crowds and disciples (ch. 23). Jerusalem as God's chosen city and the seat of government lends greater meaning to all these materials and to the Eschatological Sermon which follows (chs. 24–25).

Jesus Enters Jerusalem as a Humble King (21:1-27)

Jesus formally enters Jerusalem for the first and only time against a background of ironic contrasts. He is treated symbolically as king, but destined to die. Jesus, the son of David (21:9, 15), appears as a humble, not a powerful king (v. 5). The crowds which acclaimed him as king (vv. 8-9) will eventually denounce him for execution (27:20-25). Jesus approaches Jerusalem from the Mount of Olives, a ridge overlooking Jerusalem to the east where God will stand when he appears as king of the earth (Zech 14:4, 9). He rides on a donkey the way Israel's king will upon entering Jerusalem (21:5-7, from Zech 9:9 combined with Isa 62:11). Though riding on a donkey may seem strange to people in Western cultures, biblical leaders rode on donkeys (Judg 5:10; 10:4; 12:14; 2 Sam 17:23) and mules (2 Sam 13:29; 18:9; 1 Kgs 1:33). The people spread garments before Jesus as for a king (21:8; 2 Kgs 9:13), and branches as in the festivals of Tabernacles (Lev 23:39-43) and Hanukkah (1 Macc 13:51; 2 Macc 10:7). They greet him with the acclamation used for God, "Hosanna" (lit. "save us"), and bless him as the one coming in the name of the Lord (21:9; from Ps 118:25-26), an allusion to his coming both here and at the end of the world (cf. 23:39). Matthew is so anxious to link Jesus with these biblical prophecies that he understands the "colt, offspring of a donkey" (21:5) as two animals (v. 7) and seems to say that Jesus rode both beasts, which is hard to envision. Jesus as the "humble" (*praüs*) king has been foreshadowed by his self-designation as humble (11:29) and his praise for humility in the beatitudes (5:5).

The author of the Gospel stresses the effect of Jesus' arrival on the Passover crowds and the national leaders in Jerusalem. A large crowd on the road and the children in the temple recognize Jesus as a popular leader associated with the Davidic traditions of anointed kingship (21:9, 15); the people in general see him as a prophet (vv. 11, 26, 46). With Jesus' coming the whole city, meaning the people, was "shaken" (v. 10), just as at Jesus' birth Herod and "all Jerusalem with him" were frightened" (2:3). These Davidic and prophetic traditions were alive and influential in first-century Jewish society, as the messianic claims of revolutionaries show. Athronges, a shepherd (Josephus *J.W.* 2 §§60-65), and Simon, Herod's slave (Josephus *J.W.* 2 §§57-59), proclaimed themselves kings; Judas and Zadok, the founders of the revolutionary philosophy, proclaimed God alone as leader and master (Josephus *Ant.* 18 §§4-10, 23-25); others proclaimed themselves prophets.

Jesus' first act in Jerusalem, expelling those engaged in commercial enterprises from the temple compound (21:12-13), was a symbolic prophetic action (v. 11). Though commentators often impute unjust prices or greedy motives to the money changers and merchants, Matthew only vaguely suggests the problems in the temple by quoting Isa 56:7. This verse suggests that Jesus' program for renewal requires God's house to "be called a house of prayer," but the temple priests and officials have countenanced injustice and social disorder in making it "a den of robbers." In themselves the sale of sacrificial animals and the exchange of secular coins for aniconic Jewish coins were essential for conducting the temple cult. But Jesus uses these transactions as symbols of venality. He promotes order and social health by healing in the temple and by calling for a renewed, perfected worship according to the will of God. Similarly, the Qumran community protested irregularities in priestly marriage, the calendar used for festivals, and sacrificial procedures (cf. *Pesher on Habakkuk*, Isaiah, Psalms, Nahum, etc.). The author of the first-century-BC *Psalms of Solomon* called for reform (17:30), as did some prophetic texts (Zech 14:21; Mal 3:1-5). Matthew may associate Jesus' action with that of the eschatological prophet expected to guide Israel at the end (Deut 18:15, 18). Some commentators have interpreted Jesus' confrontation with the businessmen in the temple as a curse and a sign of the temple's approaching destruction, but the equally ancient tradition of purifying the temple is better attested. The conflict caused by

Jesus' action may have contributed to his eventual arrest, but the story is so brief and heavily symbolic that the political and social causes and consequences may only be imagined.

Jesus, as the son of David, has also been identified with Solomon, who was the builder of the temple and according to later tradition a healer (cf. the comment on 9:27). Jesus' healing in the temple (21:14) continues his work begun in 4:23, but here it also restores the wholeness and health of Israel in God's house. Biblical laws restricted the participation of priests with sicknesses and disabilities in the temple worship (Lev 21:18-20), and the communities of the Qumran *Community Rule* (2:5-22) and the *Damascus Covenant* (15:15-17) similarly restricted membership in their assemblies in order to preserve an integral, pure and holy people for God. Jesus addresses this problem so that children in the temple acclaim him as the adults did earlier (21:15).

These activities lead to the first of several hostile encounters between Jesus and the national authorities, culminating in his trial and death. The temple authorities (chief priests and scribes) protest the popular interest in Jesus as inappropriate (21:15-16), but Jesus defends the children with the Bible using Ps 8:3, which refers to "infants" (21:16; cf. 11:25 for the disciples as "infants"; Luke 19:39-40). In a second encounter the next day (21:23-27), the authorities (chief priests and elders of the people) challenge his authority and the power by which he does "these things" (v. 23) because he is a popular, unauthorized holy man. Jesus is presumably teaching, announcing the kingdom of God, an activity in which he has been engaged since the beginning, as well as healing (4:17, 23). Jesus counterquestions the authorities with the case of a better-known Judean holy man, John the Baptizer, causing the officials to back off since the people accepted John as a prophet and would not let his God-given authority be impugned. Between these two stories Jesus engages in another prophetic symbolic action which implicitly attacks the temple authorities. On his way back to Jerusalem from Bethany (two miles east of Jerusalem) Jesus curses a fig tree that had no fruit, causing it to wither immediately (21:18-22). In Mark 11:12-14, 20-26 the two-part story which brackets the purification of the temple criticizes the running of the temple more clearly than in Matthew (cf. Jer 8:8-13). Matthew retains but softens that critique by turning it into an awkward didactic narrative concerning faith, prayer, and the power to work miracles (21:20-22), thus rejecting the potential interpretation of the fig tree as symbolic of Israel's cursing and rejection. Rather, the position of the story between visits to the temple, the polemical image of fruitlessness (to appear later in the parable of the tenants), and perhaps the topic of prayer suggest but do not specify the failings of Jesus' authoritative opponents who mislead Israel. The following three parables, told to the authorities in the temple, will suggest other failings among them as well.

Bibliography. Evans, C. A. 1989, "Jesus' Action in the Temple: Cleansing or Portent of Destruction?" *CBQ* 51:237-70 • Telford,W. R. 1980, *The Barren Temple and the Withered Fig Tree,* Sheffield: JSOT.

Three Parables against the Leaders (21:28–22:14)

Three parables of the kingdom all refer to sons. The first two involve vineyards and their owners; the last a king and his subjects. The parable of the two sons (21:28-32) seems to imply that the Jerusalem leaders have pledged obedience to God's laws but not actually observed them. By contrast the sinful tax collectors and prostitutes who originally rejected God's laws have in the end observed them. However, the situation is more complex. In ancient society the second son, who refuses to obey his father but then relents, has offended the honor code which requires respect for the head of the family. Thus some Greek manuscripts choose the son who respectfully agrees to obey his father but does not go to the vineyard as the one who did the will of the father by not shaming him to his face. In the end, though, Matthew sides with the son who obeys, that is, does the law ("the way of righteousness"). Matthew also invokes John the Baptizer to justify repentant sinners like the tax collectors, in contrast to the leaders who saw but did not change and believe in John.

A second vineyard parable drives home the leaders' nonobservance of God's will, bad leadership, and hostility to Jesus with the metaphor of refusing to pay rent (21:33-46). According to the standard interpretation the tenants represent Israel rejecting and killing Jesus, with the result that the kingdom (the vineyard) is taken from Israel and given to a "nation" *(ethnos)* producing fruit (v. 43), that is, to the Christian community composed of Gentiles (or sometimes Jews and Gentiles) who believe in Jesus. This interpretation fits the later Christian supersessionist rejection of Judaism, but contradicts both this Gospel's concern for Israel and the parable itself.

Matthew, like Isaiah before him, is concerned about Israel's response to God. In Isa 5:1-7, as here, Israel is a vineyard planted by God. Strikingly, in Isaiah Israel as a whole sins against God by producing foul grapes, identified as bloodshed and a cry (by the oppressed), rather than good fruit, judgment, and justice. Isaiah predicts that God will knock down the hedge and wall and let natural forces destroy the vineyard. But even then, Israel is only being punished, not permanently destroyed or rejected. Note the contrast between the narratives in Isaiah and Matthew: in Isaiah the vines, the people of Judah, are unfruitful; in Matthew the vineyard itself and the vines are fruitful. The tenants, who symbolize the Jewish authorities, not the people, are at fault for not paying their dues to the owner, God. At the end of the parable the chief priests and Pharisees recognize that the parable is directed against them (21:45). Thus the thesis that a new nation (Christianity) replaces an old nation (Israel) arose from later Christian theology and has no foundation in the Gospel.

What of the *ethnos* (usually translated as "nation") which will receive the kingdom and produce fruit (21:43)? Since this *ethnos* replaces the chief priests, elders, and Pharisees, it must be a new leadership group for Israel. Significantly, the Greek word *ethnos,* besides its most common meaning "nation," can also refer to guilds and trade associations in the Petrie papyri of the third century BC. *Ethnos* can refer to a social class of people or to a caste or other political subdivision. Plato used *ethnē* for the various groups who have different functions and stations in his ideal city (*Republic* 421c). An order of priests is referred to as a holy *ethnē*. Finally, in idiomatic Hellenistic Greek *ethnē* can mean the rural folk in contrast to the urban population.

The vineyard parable clearly refers to Jesus' eventual death at the hands of the Jerusalem leadership and thus prepares the way for the climactic charge of murder against the scribes and Pharisees in 23:29-33 and the story of Jesus' arrest and condemnation to death in chs. 26–27. The tenants first beat and kill two groups of the owner's slaves who come to collect the rent (21:34-36) and then kill the owner's son so that they can inherit the vineyard in his stead (vv. 37-39). Their punishment in the parable, to be killed and replaced by new tenants, alludes to the destruction of Jerusalem and its leaders in AD 70. It also reflects the author's hope in the late first century that his community will become the leaders of a Jewish community which acknowledges that God sent Jesus, his Son, to rule over them. The charge that the leaders do not pay rent to God, that is, do not observe the law and follow God's will, strikes at the heart of the Pharisees' and priests' programmatic concentration on observance of the law. Thus, when they realize that the parable speaks of them, they want to arrest him but cannot because of his popular support (vv. 45-46).

The third parable, concerning a king inviting guests to his son's wedding banquet (22:1-14), continues the themes of the previous parables: son, kingdom, leader/subject relations, and violence. The banquet is a standard metaphor for life in God's kingdom (v. 2; cf. 8:11; Isa 25:6; Rev 19:7, 9). Commentators have often understood the rejection of the invitation by the guests and the subsequent gathering of people in the "main streets" or, better, on the roads leading into the countryside (*diexodoi*) as a rejection of Israel in favor of the Gentiles (outsiders). However, the ungrateful guests correspond to the Jerusalem leaders, who are still being addressed in this parable. In fact, Matthew has molded this story as a parallel to the preceding parable of the wicked tenants. The owner and the king each send two groups of slaves (22:3-4; 21:34, 36), who are treated violently (22:6; 21:35-39). The owner and king respond violently to the provocation (22:7; 21:41; cf. 8:12). The attack on the king's servants (22:6) and his response ("the king was angry, and he sent his troops and destroyed those murderers and burned their city" — 22:7) clearly does not fit comfortably into the story of a king inviting people from his own city to his son's wedding, but it does match nicely Matthew's view that Jerusalem and its leaders died at the hands of the Roman emperor because they rejected Jesus (cf. 27:25). Matthew has modified the parable to turn it against the leaders. In Luke (14:15-24) and the *Gospel of Thomas* (#64) a rich man who is not a king gives a banquet. The context in the *Gospel of Thomas* addresses the dangers of wealth (cf. #63), as does Luke, who includes among the second group of invitees the poor, maimed, blind, and lame (Luke 14:21).

In contrast Matthew focuses on governing power and authority. In the parabolic narrative the guests invited to the royal wedding feast would be wealthy, powerful, high-ranking leaders of the kingdom. Thus the original invitees who reject the king represent not all Israel, but the leaders of Israel. Since their rejection of the king's invitation shamed him and challenged his rule, the king took violent action against them and in their place invited other subjects, the farmers in the rural villages subject to the city and people on the roads. These secondary invitees do not symbolize Gentiles but the "lost sheep of the house of Israel" (10:6), that is, the villagers to whom Jesus sent his disciples. Though the parable contrasts the proper invitees with undistinguished people in the street, all are subjects of the one king. If the king represents God, then the invitees are Israelites, consistent with Matthew's narrative up to this point. As in 23:13, 15, Matthew wishes to attract Israel to the banquet (i.e., the kingdom which is both present and future) and to free Israel from its resistant leaders who do not accept Jesus.

The end of the parable and the appended narrative (22:10-14) address the presence of good and bad people among those accepting the invitation to the banquet/kingdom. This new topic does not fit smoothly with the parable thus far and originally may have been independent. The author of Matthew emphasizes that invitation into the kingdom demands conformity to the requirements of the kingdom, symbolized by a proper wedding garment (vv. 11-12). This concern with righteousness as obedience to God's will which is necessary for the kingdom began in the Sermon on the Mount (5:6, 20) and is sanctioned by the ever present theme of judgment (22:13-14).

Bibliography. Brachter, R. G. 1989, "Righteousness in Matthew," *Bible Translator* 40:228-35 • Kingsbury, J. D. 1986, "The Parable of the Wicked Husbandmen and the Secret of Jesus' Divine Sonship in Matthew: Some Literary-Critical Observations," *JBL* 105:643-55 • Lemcio, E. E. 1986, "The Parables of the Great Supper and the Wedding Feast: History, Redaction and Canon," *HBT* 8:1-26 • Meyer, B. F. 1990, "Many (= All) Are Called, But Few (= Not All) Are Chosen," *NTS* 36:89-97 • Richards, W. L. 1978, "Another Look at the Parable of the Two Sons," *BR* 23:5-14 • Snodgrass, K. 1983, *The Parable of the Wicked Tenants,* Tübingen: Mohr.

Disputes with the Jerusalem Leadership (22:15-46)

While he is in the temple, Jesus engages in four final debates with the Jewish leaders. The Pharisees try to "entrap him in speech" (22:15), followed by the Sadducees and a Pharisaic lawyer. In the final confrontation Jesus interrogates the Pharisees until at last "no one was able to give him an answer, nor from that day did anyone dare to ask him any more questions" (v. 46) and the plot moves on to Jesus' arrest and execution. These disputes continue the hostile relations between Jesus and the temple authorities initiated in ch. 21. The topics of the four disputes move from governmental authority in this world to life in the next and from Torah to the identity of the Messiah. At a more general level, these exchanges address the important themes of the Gospel — Jesus' teaching, authority, and messiahship — using the kinds of riddling (v. 17), mocking (vv. 24-28), ethical (v. 36), and exegetical (v. 42) questions which are common in biblical, rabbinic, and Greco-Roman wisdom literature.

The first exchange (22:16-22) attempts to confound Jesus on the horns of a dilemma. The Roman Empire collected a head tax on each citizen. Though people resented the tax, almost all complied, however unwillingly, since opposing it was a form of revolt. The question put to Jesus, "*Is it permitted* to pay the head tax to Caesar or not?" (literal translation), asks for a technical interpretation of what is permitted and what forbidden according to Jewish law (v. 17). If Jesus answers yes, the disciples of the Pharisees (v. 16) and the crowds who perceive Jesus as a prophet, especially the more revolutionary-minded, will reject him as an inauthentic popular teacher who is not "true" and does not teach "the way of God in truth" (v. 16). If he is bold and frank in his speech, according to the Greco-Roman rhetorical ideal (v. 16), and says outright that Jews have no obligation under Jewish law to pay taxes to Caesar, then the political supporters of Herod Antipas (v. 16), his ruler in Galilee, will denounce him to the governmental authorities. Jesus sidesteps the question by reducing the emotionally loaded question of the foreign head tax to an interpretation of the imperial coin with which the tax was paid. The image of the emperor on the coin distinguishes it sharply from "God's things." Jesus implicitly supports the conventional solution of limited cooperation with the empire (cf. Rom 13:1-7; 1 Pet 2:17) but avoids giving a controversial answer. This exchange does not support a sharp division between church and state, though Christian theology later based its teaching on this verse. In fact, the vague reference to "God's things" potentially includes all of life since God created everything and everything belongs to God. A revolutionary interpretation of Jesus' answer might hold that nothing really belongs to Caesar. Even in the most restricted reading of Jesus answer, humans must dedicate ("give") their whole selves to God (Matt 22:37 quoting Deut 6:5), in contrast to returning a Roman coin to Caesar. This kind of challenge and response is typical of controversial literature and stories of wise men. The disciples of the Pharisees and the Herodians test Jesus (22:18; cf. 16:1; 19:3), and he responds with a concise, clever answer which avoids the unacceptable alternatives and justifies the practical, mediating position taken by most: to pay the imperial tax but remain faithful to God. The disciples of the Pharisees and the Herodians have insincerely called Jesus "sincere" (lit. "true" in v. 16); in response Jesus accurately calls them hypocrites for their deceitful pretense (v. 18). Jesus wins the contest because his opponents have no retort but leave in shock.

The next three confrontations depend on interpretations of Scripture. In the first century many Jews, including the Sadducees who asked the question, had not embraced belief in the resurrection of the dead. Except for Daniel 12:1 the HB has no explicit statement supporting life after death; thus resurrection was a new belief among Jews. In the narrative the Sadducees try to ridicule resurrection with an extreme case of Levirite marriage (22:23-33). According to Deut 25:5-6, if a man died childless, his brother residing in the same place was required to marry his deceased brother's wife so she could bear a son who would carry on the dead man's name. The Sadducees postulate a woman who was married to seven brothers successively, each dying in turn. Logically, in the next world she will have seven husbands. Though polygamy was allowed in the Bible, polyandry was not; thus her marital relationships with seven men after they rose from the dead would be unlawful. Jesus solves the problem by excluding sexual relationships after the resurrection, in accordance with various apocalyptic traditions according to which humans become divine-like beings (stars, angels) in heaven with God (Dan. 12:2; *1 Enoch* 62:13-16; 104:4; *2 Bar.* 51:10). He then argues for resurrection by quoting Exod 3:6, which, if analyzed extremely literally, can be made to speak of the dead patriarchs as living. (Compare this interpretation with the clever answers based on Scripture which Jesus gives the devil in the temptations [4:4, 7, 10].)

In the third controversy the Pharisees return to the attack a final time by asking a question about law (the Torah); Jesus responds by challenging them to a fourth controversy with a question about the Messiah. The Pharisee's question about the greatest commandment in the law (22:36) forces the respondents to reveal their interpretation of Jewish life and its symbolic center (cf. *b. Mak.* 24a and *b. Shab.* 31a for Talmudic examples). Jesus answers with the double love commandment (22:37-39) derived from Deut 6:5 and Lev 19:18. In this Gospel love provides a coherent perspective for understanding, interpreting, and observing biblical law. Since the author of Matthew contrasts his view with that of the scribes and Pharisees, he replaces Mark's friendly scribe who is praised by Jesus (Mark 12:28-34) with a Pharisee who tests him (22:35). (The word "lawyer" used to describe the questioning Pharisee is missing in some ancient versions and manuscripts and may have been an early addition reflecting Luke's references to lawyers.)

The double love commandment, coming near the end of Jesus' life, recalls his teaching on love for enemies in the Sermon on the Mount at the beginning of his public work (5:43-48). The love commandments give further definition to the notion of just social relations and attitudes promoted by the Gospel. The demands of the law and the prophets can be summarized by the golden rule (7:12; cf. Hillel in *b. Shab.* 31a) or by the love commandments (22:40; cf. also 19:19; 24:12). Though many Christian interpreters have understood love as a rejection of Jewish law (understood as legalistic and meaningless), Matthew is more concrete and demanding. Though love, especially faithful love (Heb. *ḥesed*), cannot be directly legislated, its framework may be outlined with laws. The love commandments serve as the center of the law, giving to the Bible and Jesus' teachings an order and thrust which characterize Matthew's community and distinguish it from other Jewish communities and movements.

Jesus initiates the final controversy (22:41-46) with

the Pharisees in this Gospel and decisively settles the question of his authority by posing a question which refers back to his entry into Jerusalem when he was acclaimed son of David. He asks whose son the Messiah is and receives the conventional response, David's son. He then brings up a scriptural "contradiction" by quoting Ps 110:1 in which (according to an early interpretation of Jesus' followers) David, the inspired author of the Psalms, refers to the Lord (i.e., God) enthroning David's Lord at his right hand. Clearly David's Lord, enthroned at God's right hand, is not David and cannot be David's son (i.e., subordinate). If David is not the Messiah's father, then God must be. Thus the Messiah, traditionally called David's son, is really of higher status than David and receives his ruling authority from God. Since the crowds have proclaimed Jesus as the Son of David and since the reader already knows that Jesus is the Messiah and the Son of God (16:16), Jesus' status is clear. The unclear affirmations of the crowds when Jesus entered Jerusalem have been clarified, the objections of the rulers in Jerusalem have been answered, and the ruling authority of Jesus has been established. This conclusion lays the foundation for Jesus' final attack on the authority of the Jewish community leadership in ch. 23 and for the rejection of all titles for Matthean leaders (23:8-12).

Bibliography. Hay, D. M. 1973, *Glory at the Right Hand: Psalm 110 in Early Christianity,* Nashville: Abingdon • Hultgren, A. J. 1974, "The Double Commandment of Love in Mt 22:34-40: Its Sources and Composition," *CBQ* 36:373-78 • Perkins, P. 1982, *Love Commands in the New Testament,* New York: Paulist.

Jesus' Final Attack on His Opponents (23:1-39)

This uninterrupted attack on the Jewish leaders in the presence of the crowds and his disciples is not counted as one of the Gospel's five sermons because it does not conclude with the usual formula (7:28; 11:1; 13:53; 19:1; 26:1). The vitriolic tone and detailed charges in this climactic polemic suggest that the author of Matthew is addressing the conflicts he and his community faced within the Jewish community near the end of the first century.

The chapter begins by acknowledging the de facto authority and influence of the scribes and Pharisees but immediately undercuts it by rejecting their titles, laws, and intentions. Though the instruction to do what the scribes and Pharisees do and teach (23:3) has troubled many commentators, the author is merely advising prudent acceptance of their power and social station. The metaphor of sitting on "Moses' seat" (v. 2) alludes to Moses' status as teacher of the Sinai revelation (Exodus 19–24, etc.) as a basis for communal authority. Archeological evidence does not support the common view that "Moses' seat" was the name of an item of synagogue architecture in the first century. The scribes and Pharisees symbolize for Matthew the emerging coalitions of teachers and leaders seeking control over Jewish communities after the destruction of the Jerusalem leadership by the Romans in AD 70. Second Temple Pharisaic and scribal groups joined with priests and landowners to form the early rabbinic movement; other groups gradually coalesced as well. Even while acknowledging their influence, the author of Matthew levels against them his favorite charge of pretense and deception for failing to practice what they demand of others (23:3b) and for doing "all their deeds to be seen by others" (v. 5; cf. 6:1-18). In a general sense he uses them as negative examples for how community leaders should act. Their interpretations of the law impose burdens on people (v. 4) in contrast to Jesus' light burden and yoke (11:28-30). They wear phylacteries at prayer and fringes on their garments pretentiously to gain notice (23:5). Phylacteries were leather-covered boxes with Scripture passages inside which were strapped to the forehead and arm during prayer. Phylacteries have been found at Qumran. This custom was based on a literal reading of Exod 13:9 and Deut 6:8 and 11:18. In Greco-Roman terms they were a kind of amulet (the meaning of Gk. *phylaktērion*). The command to wear fringes on garments also comes from the Torah (Num 15:37-39; Deut 22:12) and was widely practiced (cf. Jesus in 9:20; 14:36). Consistent with his emphasis on hypocrisy, the author of Matthew charges his opponents with putting them to deceptive, selfish uses to achieve their own goals of public honor and respect (23:6-7).

The last honor sought by the social leaders, to be called "Rabbi," symbolizes the outlook Matthew opposes and leads to his instructions for a new type of leader in his own community. The Hebrew "rabbi," which means literally "My Great One," was originally a general term of respect equivalent to "Sir" or "Mr." After the destruction of the temple it was used of teachers (23:8; John 1:38; 3:2), especially the teacher in an emerging reform group which eventually produced the Mishnah. Other titles such as "Father" and "Instructor" were common in the Near Eastern social hierarchy. "Father" was used for elders in a community and for the founders of a people or movement. "Instructor" *(kathēgētēs)* may mean "Teacher" or "Master" but here perhaps has the connotation of "tutor." Matthew forbids the use of such honorific titles because Jesus is the one teacher, God is the one Father, and all his followers are brethren (23:8-12). The members of the group are to be "servants" to one another (v. 11; 20:26; Mark 9:35; 10:43). This resistance to hierarchically structured roles plus the emphasis on equality is typical of new groups and reform movements. All the members have begun a new life together and are to participate fully and equally in the emerging community outside the traditional framework controlled by the elders of established communities. Humility, not human recognition and power, leads to God-given honor and respect (23:12; Luke 14:11; 18:14).

The seven woe oracles (23:13-36), which curse the scribes and Pharisees seven times (23:13, 15, 16, 23, 25, 27, 29), are the centerpiece of Matthew's attack on the Jewish community leadership. (Matt 23:14 is rejected by most textual critics. It is missing from many manuscripts, interrupts the topical arrangement of the woes, and increases the number of woes, from seven to eight, perhaps to match the eight beatitudes in ch. 5.) A woe oracle is a mild form of curse which functions as a public denunciation. They appear frequently in prophetic literature, either individually (Amos 5:8; 6:1; Isa 1:4; 3:11; 10:5) or in series (Isa 5:8-24). The exclamation "woe" (Heb. *'oy*) is usually followed by a participle describing the criticized action or by a noun giving a negative characterization of a person. Here the formula, "Woe to you, scribes and Pharisees, hypocrites," used six times (23:16 has "Woe to you"), drives home the contrast between inner attitudes and outward behavior, a contrast also found in the Sermon on the Mount. The metaphor of blindness, repeated five times (vv. 16, 17, 19, 24, 26; cf. 15:14), undercuts the scribes' and Pharisees' teaching authority. Matthew does not attack Judaism or all Jews. He is a Jew who attacks certain local leaders of his ethnic group. This kind of conflict occurs many places in Second Temple literature (*Psalms of Solomon* 4; 1QpHab, etc.). In addition, Greek rhetorical disputes, which frequently appealed to a contrast between appearances and reality, have influenced Matthew's thematic charge of hypocrisy. This vitriolic polemic has led some Christians to embrace anti-Semitism and persecute Jews. However, the author of Matthew does not deny the fundamental legitimacy of Israel, its law, and its community structures, as many commentators have claimed. Rather, he attacks the personal integrity and legitimacy of Israel's leaders as well as their interpretations of Jewish law and the divine will.

These seven woe oracles are not a random selection of complaints but a structured series of charges aimed at the thought and practices of Matthew's opponents. The first two woes (23:13, 15) concern the competition between rival ways of living as Jews. In Matthew's view when his rivals prevent fellow Jews from entering Matthew's community, they exclude them from the kingdom (v. 13). The locked door to the kingdom stands in diametrical opposition to the keys of the kingdom possessed by Matthew's assembly (*ekklēsia* in 16:19). Matthew also charges that when his rivals attract Gentiles to their Jewish way of life, they remove Gentiles even farther from Matthew's community and the kingdom of God (note the metaphor of "twice as much a child of Gehenna" — 23:15), in contrast to God's will that Jesus' disciples should teach all nations to observe God's commands (28:16-20). In fact, active Jewish proselytizing was probably infrequent during the first century. However, many Gentiles were interested in the Bible, attended synagogues, and observed some Jewish practices without becoming Jews. Thus Matthew may refer to this group of Gentiles, often referred to as "God-fearers."

The next three woes promote alternative legal (oaths), economic (tithes), and cultic (purity) practices and understandings (23:16-26) which give the community its identity and help maintain its boundaries. The Sermon on the Mount already rejected the popular ancient custom of taking oaths (5:33-37). However, once a person takes an oath, Matthew, like his contemporaries, treats it as binding (cf. 15:3-6). Here in the third woe oracle he mocks a series of rules for deciding which oaths are valid as illogical and devious (23:16-22). Similar criticisms and examples of oath language appear in Jewish and Greco-Roman literature (*m. Ned.* 1–9; Sir 23:9-11; Epictetus *Enchiridion* 33.5). The fourth woe oracle (vv. 23-24) relativizes, but it does not repeal Jewish laws concerning tithing herbs. The author of Matthew turns the argument against the integrity of his opponents, a theme which will continue in the last three woe oracles. A tithe is a tax of one tenth (or some other determinate portion) of produce, animals, money, and the like, which is to be given to God through the temple or other institution. The Bible mandated tithes on grain, wine, oil, fruit, and animals (Lev 27:30; Num 18:12; Deut 14:22-23). The Mishnah (AD 200) reflects the expansion of tithing to include all growing things, including vegetables and herbs (*m. Ma'as.* 1:1), a development to which the Gospel of Matthew testifies in the late first century. Matthew affirms that "mint, dill and cummin," which were used as spices and medicine, should be tithed because his community observes the law as interpreted by Jesus. However, he stresses "the weightier matters of the law, justice and mercy and faith," consistent with Jesus' interpretation of the law elsewhere in the Gospel. The charge that his opponents ignore the heart of the law, justice and faithfulness to God, hardly fits the Pharisees, Essenes, or any other historical group we know of, but in the narrative it initiates the type of *ad hominem* attack common in controversial literature.

The fifth woe oracle (23:25-26) subordinates purity in eating food, a defining characteristic of the Jewish community, to moral purity. The distinction of "pure/impure" or "clean/unclean" in the HB does not refer to physical cleanliness or to the moral status of something. To be impure is not to be sinful, but rather to be unprepared to enter or function in a holy place or to eat food which has been rendered holy by being offered to God. To be pure or clean is to be in the proper state for doing activities specified by the Bible. If a person is impure or unclean, he or she must go through a prescribed ritual to remove the effects of the impurity. Impurity could also affect food and the containers and implements used for food. In raising the problem of impurity of the outsides and insides of cups and plates, Matthew accurately alludes to a dispute between the schools of Hillel and Shammai in *m. Kelim* 25:1, 7-8 over the interpretation of biblical injunctions (Lev 11:29-35; 15:1-12; Num 31:19-24). This sophisticated argument concerns whether impure drops of water on the outside of a cup will render the contents of the cup impure also. The Hillelites held that the outside is always unclean and does not affect the inside. The Shammaites, whose position is reflected in Matthew (23:25), sought to keep the outside as well as the inside ritually clean because for them the one affected the other. The author of Matthew uses this dispute about inside and outside as an occasion to contrast outward behaviors with inner dispositions and to accuse his opponents of bad faith and lack of integrity ("greed and self-indulgence" in v. 25).

The sixth woe oracle continues the contrast between the inside and outside, this time in reference to tombs (23:27-28). In the Near East tombs were whitewashed outside, in accordance with Jewish custom. Matthew contrasts the nice-looking exterior with the inner contents of the tomb, bones and the like, which are impure. The charge of hypocrisy and *lawlessness* (v. 28) against the scribes and Pharisees, who interpret, create, and promote a distinctive set of Jewish laws, is noteworthy. The author accuses them of lawlessness because they do not discern and do the will of God as the Matthean community understands it.

The theme of tombs continues into the final woe oracle (23:29-36), where it leads to a charge of murder, the sin par excellence (cf. Gen 4:3-10). Matthew refers to the tombs of prophets and righteous which had been constructed along with the tombs of kings near Jerusalem. The prophets and righteous symbolize those who are faithful to God (cf. 10:41; 13:17) and truly observe the law, in contrast to the opponents who, the author claims, lack righteousness (23:28, 30-31). The Gospel alludes to nonbiblical traditions that prophets had been martyred in Jerusalem, traditions loosely based on biblical assassinations of prophets (Uriah in Jer 26:20-23; Zechariah in 2 Chr 24:20-22) and elaborated in Josephus (*Ant.* 10.3.1 §38), the *Martyrdom of Isaiah* 5, and the NT (cf. 5:12; 23:37; Luke 13:33-34; Acts 7:52). The murder charge leads to a prophetic and apocalyptic judgment oracle (23:32-36) which foreshadows Jesus' death and predicts the persecution of his followers. The references to the murders of Abel and Zechariah encompass all the unjust killings in the whole of biblical history and compare the deaths and persecution of these just and faithful prophets, priests, and leaders to the fate of Jesus and the Matthean community (v. 34, "prophets, sages, and scribes"). The disciplinary measures taken against Matthew's community, scourging and expulsion (v. 34), fit synagogue practice (cf. 10:17). The charges of "killing" and "crucifying" are appropriate to the Roman authorities and recall Jesus' death but were not part of Jewish communal discipline. The ironic curse "Fill up the measure of your fathers" (v. 32) and the final verse (v. 36) warn of imminent judgment. The verb "fill up" is elsewhere translated as "fulfill" *(pleroō)* when it is used to describe Jesus' relation to the Bible and Jewish history and to legitimate his views and standing on the basis of the Bible. Here ironically the same word undercuts the legitimacy of the Jewish leaders.

Lament over Jerusalem (23:37-39)

Jesus' lament over Jerusalem connects the attack on the leaders with the instruction on divine judgment (chs. 24–25). Jerusalem, the symbolic center and seat of government for Israel, will be destroyed along with its government. Here and in ch. 24 Jesus' life and death (c. AD 30), the destruction of Jerusalem by the Romans (AD 70), and the expected end of the world are inextricably linked. The intensity of the author's feeling is transmitted by his transliteration of the Hebrew form of Jerusalem's name, *Ierousalēm,* rather than the usual Hellenized form, *Hierosolyma.* The image of gathering under God's wings appears frequently in the HB (Pss 17:8; 36:7; 57:1; 63:7; Isa 31:5). Despite Jerusalem's tragedy, Matthew raises the hope that at the end the crowds will again bless Jesus (23:39; Ps 118:26), as they did when he entered Jerusalem (Matt 21:9). The tragedy of Jerusalem will be made explicit in the first three verses of the next chapter (24:1-3) and the coming of the Son of Man soon after (21:29-31).

Bibliography. Garland, D. E. 1979, *The Intention of Matthew 23,* Leiden: Brill • McKnight, S. 1991, *A Light among the Gentiles: Jewish Missionary Activity in the Second Temple Period,* Minneapolis: Fortress • Neusner, J. 1976, "'First Cleanse the Inside': Halakhic Background of a Controversial Saying," *NTS* 22:486-95 • Saldarini, A. J. 1992, "Delegitimation of Leaders in Matthew 23," *CBQ* 54:659-80 • Viviano, B. T. 1990, "Social World and Community Leadership: The Case of Matthew 23:1-12, 34," *JSNT* 39:3-21.

Introduction to the Eschatological Sermon (24–25)

The Gospel narrative fittingly ends with Jesus' death and resurrection. However, the author and his audience know Jesus as their risen Lord and look forward to the end of the world when Jesus will return as judge. Consequently, Jesus' last sermon addresses these expectations by instructing the disciples concerning these future events. Within the flow of the narrative, the discussion of Jesus' second coming gives his death a cosmic significance. Immediately "after Jesus had finished saying all these things [chs. 24–25]" (26:1), he tells his disciples again that he will be handed over to be executed at Passover, and the plot against him begins (26:2-3).

The first part of ch. 24 (vv. 4-31) alludes symbolically and metaphorically, but somewhat indistinctly, to the events which will precede the end, to the destruction of Jerusalem and to the coming of the Son of Man. Commentators disagree about which predictions and warnings refer to what. Frequently vv. 4-14 are related to the present, vv. 15-28 to the fall of Jerusalem (especially if the commentator holds that Matthew or his source was written before AD 70 when Jerusalem was destroyed), and vv. 29-31 to the coming of the Son of Man. But such a precise chronology is doubtful. The end of ch. 23 and beginning of ch. 24 already merge the destruction of Jerusalem and the end of the world into a single, complex topic (23:37-39; 24:1-3). For the late-first-century author of Matthew the destruction of the temple had already occurred. In response to this and to Jesus' death and resurrection he weaves together these events and the end into one rich, symbolic matrix in which God's kingdom triumphs. The author makes extensive use of scenes and metaphors from apocalyptic literature, especially those describing holy war and apocalyptic crises (see *1 Enoch* 99:4-7; 4 Ezra 4:51–5:13; 8:63–9:6; *2 Baruch* 25–27; 1QM [the *War Scroll*]). The sermon may be divided into two large sections, the instructions about events leading to the end (24:4-31) and nine parables concerning watchfulness for the end and preparation for judgment, which are supplemented by warnings (24:32–25:46).

Bibliography. Burkitt, F. W. 1981, *The Testimony of Jesus-Sophia: A Redaction-Critical Study of the Eschatological Discourse in Matthew,* Washington, D.C.: University of America Press • Gaston, L. 1970, *No Stone on Another: Studies in the Significance of the Fall of Jerusalem in the Synoptic Gospels,* NovTSup 23, Leiden: Brill • Lambrecht, J. "The Parousia Discourse: Composition and Content in Mt. XXIV–XXV," in M. Didier, ed.,

L'Évangile selon Matthieu: Redaction et théologie, BETL 29, Paris: Gembloux, 309-42 • Hartman, L. 1966, *Prophecy Interpreted: The Formation of Some Jewish Apocalyptic Texts and of the Eschatological Discourse Mark 13 Par.,* Lund: Gleerup • Sibinga, J. S. 1975, "The Structure of Apocalyptic Discourse: Matthew 24 and 25," *ST* 29:71-79 • Thompson, W. 1974, "An Historical Perspective in the Gospel of Matthew," *JBL* 93:243-64.

Signs of the End and the Coming of the Son of Man (24:1-31)

Jesus, who had entered the temple area in 21:23, leaves it in the first verse. When his disciples advert to the beauty of the temple compound, just as tourists marvel at the Dome of the Rock and El Aqsa Mosque on the Temple Mount today, Jesus predicts the temple's destruction. This shocking prediction prompts his disciples to inquire further about the temple, the sign of Jesus' coming (*parousia,* used only in Matt 24:3, 24, 37, 39) and the end of the age. Jesus responds to his disciples privately while sitting on the Mount of Olives (v. 3), which is where the Messiah is to appear at the end of the world (Zech 14:4).

Warnings against deception ("Beware that no one leads you astray") begin and end the review of the events which precede the coming of the Son of Man (24:4-5, 23-28). False messiahs (vv. 5, 23-24) and false prophets (vv. 11, 24) will lead many astray, including the elect, that is, the members of Matthew's community (vv. 4-5, 11, 24). The Matthean community acknowledged legitimate prophets (10:41; 23:34) and had had trouble with false prophets (7:15-23). Attempts to identify the false prophets exactly or to distinguish those in 24:11 from 24:23-26 are dubious, just as it is difficult to identify separately those referred to in 7:15-20 and 7:21-23. The author's labeling of some as false prophets and messiahs testifies to serious disagreements over teaching and interpretation of Scripture and tradition within both the Matthean community and the Jewish community at large.

Disagreements over teaching, claims to messiahship, and the natural, social, and political disorder of the end times lead to conflict and violence. Matthew anticipates both external and internal threats to his community of the just. The external threats are common in apocalyptic literature: international warfare and hostility, famines, earthquakes, persecutions, and executions (24:6-9). The hardships and distress from this extreme adversity and persecution (*thlipsis* in vv. 9, 21) will cause apostasy, betrayal of one another, and corresponding hostility or hatred (vv. 9-10; cf. 10:22) within the Matthean community which will lead to lawlessness and a lack of love (v. 11). Since observance of the law (righteousness) and love are the keys to Matthew's teaching, these critical trials threaten the very constitution of the group (cf. the similar family strife in 10:21, 35-36). The author of Matthew encourages his audience by noting that these hardships must take place for the end to come (hence the image of labor pains in 24:8). Because the end has not yet come (vv. 6, 8), salvation depends on endurance (v. 13; cf. 10:22; 13:21). Finally and strikingly, Matthew teaches that the end will come when the good news about God's rule has been announced to all the nations throughout the world (24:14). Matthew was probably thinking in terms of years or decades, though Christian history has been more extended.

The next section of this instruction (24:15-28) concerns the more intense crises which will immediately precede the return of Jesus as Son of Man to judge humanity. Here again the author uses traditional imagery from apocalyptic literature, beginning with the desolating sacrilege (or abomination of desolation) which first appears in second-century-BC Jewish literature (Dan 9:27; 11:31; 12:11; 1 Macc 1:54). The Syrian Greek king Antiochus IV Epiphanes and the Jewish priests who supported his policies, introduced the worship of Syrian deities into the temple in 167 BC. Faithful Jews referred to this worship of *ba'al shamayim* (Hebrew for "Lord of the Heavens") using a Hebrew parody of the name *(shiqquṣ meshomem)* translated as "abomination which makes desolate." Luke 21:20 explicitly associates the abomination of desolation with the siege of Jerusalem, but Matthew does not. For him the abomination of desolation suggests the final war between good and evil, when all that is holy will be desecrated and destroyed. Even though the temple had already been destroyed by the time the author of Matthew wrote, its memory was fresh and the symbolic meaning of the abomination of desolation retained its power. It signals a time of "great suffering *(thlipsis),* such as has not been from the beginning of the world until now, no, and never will be" (24:21; cf. Dan 12:1; Rev 7:14), a time in which Judeans must flee the final battle so quickly that they will not pick up their cloaks in the fields nor pack up anything as they run from their houses (24:16-18). The Gospel of Matthew, depending on Mark and perhaps an earlier source, envisions an all-out battle near Jerusalem, as did the Qumran *War Scroll* before him. The special difficulties for women with infants and the rigors of flight in winter symbolize the acute danger and stark physical reality of these sufferings (vv. 19-20). Matthew refers to flight on the sabbath because his law-observant community of Jewish followers of Jesus would be reluctant to flee on the sabbath when travel was forbidden (v. 20). The author emphasizes the destructive nature of the final conflict by a prediction that no one would survive if God did not shorten the conflict for the sake of the faithful. (For more specific timetables of the end, see Dan 7:25; 8:13; 9:27; 12:11-12.)

The author of Matthew returns to his primary fear for his community, deception by false leaders such as messiahs and prophets (24:23-24). To counteract them he affirms the public and manifest coming of the Messiah using metaphors of lightning and vultures in the sky, as opposed to the esoteric revelations often associated with apocalyptic literature (vv. 26-28). When the Son of Man comes, he will appear in the sky after the heavenly bodies have been destroyed (cf. Dan 7:13-14, 26-27) and after his "sign" appears in heaven (vv. 29-31). "Sign" *(sēmeion)* probably refers to a military banner or standard ("signal" in Isa 11:12; 18:3). The *War Scroll* from Qumran (1QM 3:13–4:17) has an elaborate description of the banners or military standards of the angelic army of God at the end. The signs of the Son of Man will affect all people on earth, meaning those not faithful to God and Jesus. By contrast, the coming Son of Man will gather his elect wherever they are (cf. 24:22, 24, 31). Note that this account, like Dan 12:1-3, emphasizes the gathering of the just and implies but does not elaborate on the particulars of judgment.

Bibliography. Ford, D. 1979, *The Abomination of Desolation in Biblical Eschatology,* Washington, D.C.: University Press of America • Stanton, G. N. 1989, "'Pray That Your Flight May Not Be in Winter or on a Sabbath' (Matthew 24:20)," *JSNT* 37:17-30, repr. 1992 in *A Gospel for a New People,* Edinburgh: Clark, 192-206 • Taylor, J. 1989, "The Love of Many Will Grow Cold," *RB* 96:352-57.

Nine Parables about Watchfulness and Judgment (24:32–25:46)

A series of nine parables specify the requirements and consequences of judgment by the Son of Man (24:30-31) by teaching about the time of the end, vigilance, responsible behavior while waiting, and the criteria used in judgment. Five short parables or comparisons (the root meaning of *mashal,* the Hebrew word for proverb and parable) begin this section: the fig tree (24:32-33, from which we learn a *parabolē,* i.e., a "parable," translated in the NRSV as "lesson"); the days of Noah (vv. 37-39); the two men in the field (v. 40); the two women grinding (v. 41); and the owner and the thief (vv. 43-44). Four longer narrative parables follow: the faithful slave, the ten bridesmaids, the talents, and the sheep and goats (24:45–25:46). The author of Matthew derived the first parable about the fig tree from the Gospel of Mark (13:28-32) but then went his own way with the remaining eight, most of which are taken from the sayings source (Q) and found also in the Gospel of Luke (chs. 12, 17, 19).

The first parable, about a fig tree, and the three sayings which follow it (24:32-36) answer the disciples' initial question about the time and signs of the end (v. 3). The fig tree's stage of growth marks the coming of summer, just as the signs in 24:4-31 mark the coming of the Son of Man. (Earlier in 21:19 a fig tree which failed to produce fruit in a timely fashion symbolized the failures of the temple leadership.) Matthew balances this lively expectation of an imminent coming (the Son of Man is at the gates in 24:33-34) with a warning that no one knows the exact time of the end (v. 36), and supports this speculation about the time of the end with a parenthetical assertion that Jesus' words will not pass away (v. 35; cf. 5:18, where not one letter or stroke of a letter of the law will pass from the law until heaven and earth pass away).

The next three brief parables counsel vigilance and diligence while waiting for the end (24:42). Most people are inattentive (and implicitly at fault?), like the generation totally unprepared for the primeval flood which only Noah and his family survived (vv. 37-39; cf. Genesis 6–9). Many men work the fields and women prepare food, but only some will be "taken," that is, gathered as the elect by Jesus' angels (24:40-41; cf. v. 31). A fifth, longer parable illustrates the need for vigilance by a shocking comparison of the Son of Man with a thief (vv. 43-44).

The final four narrative parables (24:45–25:46) stress responsible behavior in the present while the master is away and alert expectation of his sudden return to evaluate his subordinates. The first parable (24:45-51) contrasts a faithful and wise slave (cf. the wise virgins in 25:2) with a wicked one in their administration of the master's household while he is away. The faithful slave fulfills his responsibilities and so is blessed (24:46; cf. 5:3-12) and given further responsibility (v. 47; cf. also the slaves in 25:21, 23). He serves as an ideal type for the responsible leader in Matthew's group and the Jewish community at large. The wicked slave, by contrast, loses sight of his responsibilities (24:48-50; cf. v. 36), a failure the author of Matthew perceives in the "mis-leaders" whom Matthew excoriates all through the Gospel. The penalty for such failure is shockingly severe, to be cut in pieces (v. 51, also in Luke 12:46 from Q); this metaphor suggests the slaughter expected in the final battle between good and evil. Less probably the image of cutting may suggest excommunication, a penalty which is found in the Qumran *Community Rule* (1QS 1:10-11; 2:16-17; and several times in the laws in cols. 6-8). For Matthew such a wicked leader is a "hypocrite" (cf. 6:1-18; 22:18; ch. 23).

The next two parables (25:1-30) stress even more the need for wise and provident behavior and accountability and the need for vigilance while waiting for the return of the householder or master. The parable of the ten virgins (Gk. *parthenoi,* paraphrased loosely as "bridesmaids" in the NRSV) is explicitly linked with the kingdom of God/heaven (25:1; see ch. 13; 18:23; 20:1; 22:2). The place where the virgins wait for the wedding procession of the bride from her home to the groom's after the wedding is unclear; they seem to have gone out from the groom's house to meet the procession. In contrast to the wicked slave in the previous parable, none of the virgins engages in sinful activities forbidden by the commandments (25:1-13). The five foolish virgins simply did not anticipate and prepare for a delay in the wedding procession, in contrast to the wise virgins ("wise" is Gk. *phronimos,* meaning "prudent"). However, foolishness and wickedness are interchangeable in the book of Proverbs and in the parable of the two houses (Matt 7:24-27). Foolishness can cause irreparable harm, just as carelessness can cause a devastating injury. In this narrative the foolish virgins who failed to prepare properly for their duties in the procession had to separate themselves from the group to secure more oil. (Presumably the whole village was awake for the wedding procession, so someone was able to provide oil for their needs.) When they are finally ready, the opportunity to join in the celebration has been lost, and the householder hosting the banquet, which symbolizes the kingdom of God (cf. 8:11; 22:1-14), rejects their request to be let in (25:11-12). Their address to him, "Lord, Lord," is the equivalent of "Mister" or "Sir," but here it has a further connotation: Jesus is Lord of the kingdom of God, but those who call "Lord, Lord" without doing the will of God will not enter the kingdom of heaven (7:21-23). The problem faced by the virgins was not falling asleep because all ten fell asleep, but not anticipating and providing for the delay. Thus the warning to stay awake which follows the parable (25:13) does not fit the context literally, but does metaphorically encourage alertness while waiting for the coming of the Son of Man (see other versions of these themes and materials in Mark 13:33-37; Luke 12:35-38; *Did.* 16:1). The author of the Gospel of Matthew seems to address a decline in commitment within his community already alluded to as "love grown cold" and a disinclination to "endure to the end" (24:12-13). The parable may also be an attack on the early rabbis, who were nonapocalyptic in their orientation and so did not stress waiting for the Messiah.

The parable of the talents (25:14-30) begins with a cryptic formula ("Just as a man . . .") which does not tell us what is being compared to the story. The themes of the story are the master's extended absence, proper behavior while waiting for his return, and the master's criteria for judging the work of his slaves. In the context of chs. 24–25 the master is the Son of Man or Jesus, his return is the end of the world, and the accounting of the slaves is the final judgment. Matthew has set this story within the context of a household, which symbolizes his community and the Jewish community at large, in contrast to Luke, who speaks of a ruler who strives to manage his kingdoms (Luke 19:11-27). The slaves are relatively independent managers of substantial properties (a talent was probably 50 to 75 pounds of silver), and the master's harsh insistence that the slaves not just preserve but increase his wealth accords with modern economic attitudes. The metaphors of reaping and gathering in fields not sown or cultivated (25:26; cf. 9:36-38) and the emphasis on growth and gain recall the parables of the mustard seed, treasure, net, and fields (ch. 13).

The third slave, who simply preserves his talent by burying it, like the foolish virgins in the previous parable does not violate the commandments, but is nevertheless rejected by the master and judged to be "wicked and lazy" (25:26), "unworthy (or useless)," and liable to expulsion into the "outer darkness" (v. 30) for his failure to make good use of the time and goods given to him. Interestingly, the parable does not promote love, sharing, justice, or mercy, but unsentimental, proactive preparation for the end. The master is a hard man (v. 24), gathering wealth for which he has not worked and recommending investment with "moneylenders" (v. 27; "bankers" in the NRSV). The parable points solely to the aggressive commitment needed to serve Jesus adequately. But commitment to what? Frequent sermons notwithstanding, a general exhortation to make use of one's natural talents (a peculiarly English play on the double meaning of "talents") fails the parable entirely. Since the Son of Man will come only after "this good news of the kingdom will be proclaimed throughout the world, as a testimony to all the nations" (24:14) and since Jesus will instruct his disciples to "make disciples of all nations, baptizing them in the name of the Father and of the Son and of the Holy Spirit, and teaching them to obey everything that I have commanded you" (28:19-20), the fruitful investing of the talents most probably symbolizes the obligation to convince people to follow Jesus. The unproductive slave may symbolize followers of Jesus who do not fulfill their obligations and perhaps the Jewish leaders, so often attacked by the author of Matthew because they have not enriched their form of Judaism with the teachings of Jesus.

The parable of the sheep and goats (25:31-46) really concerns judgment by the Son of Man as king (vv. 31, 34, 40). It fittingly completes the Eschatological Sermon by making explicit the criteria for innocence or condemnation at the end, and it prepares, by ironic contrast, for the unjust judgment of Jesus in the next two chapters. The narrative is as much a symbolic apocalyptic revelation about the end as it is a parable. The "Similitudes" or "Parables of Enoch" (*1 Enoch* 37–71, probably from the first century AD) contain three apocalyptic visions identified as parables (*1 Enoch* 38, 45, 58). In the third "parable" the Son of Man sits in judgment with God over the kings and the mighty and the exalted ones and those who rule (*1 Enoch* 62–63). The sinners and unjust ones beg vainly for another chance, but only the "congregation of the holy ones," "the chosen ones," are vindicated and rewarded. In Matthew's parable the separation of the good from the evil is compared to the separation of sheep from goats after they have grazed together. The use of animals to symbolize humans is common in apocalyptic literature (cf. *1 Enoch* 83–90) and the metaphor of God and the king as shepherds runs through the HB (cf. Pss 23:1; 28:9; 80:1; 2 Sam 5:2; 7:7; 2 Kgs 22:17; Ezek 34:23; 37:24). The sheep symbolize the good because they provide wool as well as meat.

The metaphor of sheep and goats is quickly dropped as the king addresses those on his right and left as responsible human beings (25:34). The criterion by which the king judges his subjects is repeated with variations four times in the dialogue (vv. 35-36, 37-39, 42-43, 44). The king rewards the righteous (vv. 34, 46) — those who have helped the needy, that is, the hungry, thirsty, stranger, naked, sick, and imprisoned — with "the kingdom" and eternal life," and condemns those who did not to "eternal fire . . . eternal punishment" (vv. 41, 46). The stress on care for one another continues and completes the Matthean emphasis on love and mercy toward others found in the Sermon on the Mount (5:38-48; 7:12); in the double quotation of Hos 6:6 ("I desire mercy, not sacrifice") in Matt 9:13; 12:7 to explain Jesus' treatment of tax collectors, sinners, and his disciples; in the allusion to Isa 35:5-6 in Matt 11:5 to describe Jesus' messianic activity; in the quotation of Isa 42:1-4 in Matt 12:18-21 to further describe his activities; and in the command to love God and neighbor (22:37-40).

Commentators have disagreed strongly for centuries concerning the scope of those being judged and the precise identity of the needy. The most common modern position is that all humans are judged according to how they have loved and cared for those most in need. This is certainly a potential meaning of the parable, especially when the parable is read without reference to its context in the narrative. However, Jesus said earlier in the Gospel that the twelve would judge the twelve tribes of Israel (19:28), and some early writings envision a separate judgment for Israel (Ezek 39:21; *1 Enoch* 91:14; *Pss. Sol.* 17:29; Rom 2:9-10; 1 Cor 6:2-3). Thus this judgment in ch. 25 may be for the non-Jewish nations only. On the other hand, the author of Matthew refers to many topics more than once so that two descriptions of the judgment probably do not imply two, separate judgments for Israel and the Gentiles.

Commentators have most frequently identified the needy as any human beings who require aid from fellow humans. However, the judge identifies himself with those needy and refers to them as "these least *(elachistoni)* brothers of mine" (25:40) and "these least" (v. 45; cf. 10:40-42). The expression "least" recalls the expression "little ones" which was used for the members of Matthew's community (10:42; 18:6, 10, 14). This suggests that if the parable is read and interpreted within the Gospel, those needing food, water, and clothes and suffering sickness and imprisonment as strangers are the members of Matthew's community suffering oppression, especially when they seek new followers of Jesus (cf. 28:19-20) in hostile environments. If this is the case, the nations are judged according to how they have received the followers of Jesus (cf. 10:11-15). A similar norm for the judgment of the nations appears in the *Apocalypse of Baruch* (*2 Baruch* 7). It is also possible that the requirement to help the needy is addressed to the members of Matthew's community, urging those with means to help those without. All of these interpretations encourage the strengthening of the social relations which keep communities together and reflect the concern for the weak and poor (the widow, orphan, and stranger) in the HB, where God cares for them.

Bibliography. Bauckham, R. 1977, "Synoptic Parousia Parables and the Apocalypse," *NTS* 23:165-69 • Catchpole, D. R. 1979, "The Poor on Earth and the Son of Man in Heaven: A Reappraisal of Matthew XXV.31-46," *BJRL* 61:355-97 • Cope, L. "Matthew XXV 31-46: 'The Sheep and the Goats' Reinterpreted," *NovT* 11:32-44 • Donfried, K. P. 1974, "The Allegory of the Ten Virgins (Matt. 25:1-13) as a Summary of Matthean Theology," *JBL* 93:415-28 • Donohue, J. R. 1986, "The 'Parable' of the Sheep and the Goats: A Challenge to Christian Ethics," *TS* 47:3-31 • Gray, S. W. 1989, *The Least of My Brothers: Matthew 25:31-46,* SBLDS 114, Atlanta: Scholars • Harrington, D. J. 1991, "Polemical Parables in Matthew 24–25," *USQR* 44:287-98.

Introduction to the Passion Narrative (26–27)

Jesus' arrest and execution at a Passover festival in Jerusalem during the governorship of Pontius Pilate (AD 26-36) was potentially disastrous for the early followers of Jesus. The shame of a public execution prejudiced the majority of society against them. Since they were a new group without widespread social standing and approval and since they were threatened with public sanction and persecution as Jesus had been, they needed to understand Jesus' death as a positive event in God's work in the world both to stabilize their own commitments to God and Jesus and to present a plausible case for Jesus to potential converts. Consequently, the author of the Gospel of Matthew closely relates the events surrounding Jesus' death with Scripture so that Jesus' betrayal, arrest, suffering, and death contribute to God's activity in Israel and the world. Because Jesus' death was foreseen and required by Scripture, it was not just another Roman execution of an obscure, potential troublemaker. Rather, Jesus died as part of a scripturally foreseen series of events through which God was saving Israel and the nations from their sins. The authoritative interpreter of Jesus' death is not the civil authorities, who judged Jesus an expendable outcast, but God, who accepts and values his death.

On the human level, Jesus voluntarily accepts his impending death as God's will and as necessary to accomplish his goal of bringing the kingdom of God to Israel. The narrative only hints at the theological interpretations of Jesus' death as sacrifice, atonement, redemption, and so on which were developed so extensively in later Christian literature. It emphasizes the sinful human injustice and hostility which led to his execution by censuring the Jerusalem leaders and more indirectly the Roman government for their malice and blindness to God's will and purposes. The violent assault on Jesus parallels King Herod's attempt to kill Jesus as a child in ch. 2.

Bibliography. Brown, R. E. 1994, *The Death of the Messiah: A Commentary on the Passion Narratives,* 2 vols., New York: Doubleday • Crossan, J. D. 1995, *Who Killed Jesus: Exposing the Roots of Anti-Semitism in the Gospel Story of the Death of Jesus,* San Francisco: HarperCollins • Heil, J. P. 1991, *The Death and Resurrection of Jesus: A Narrative-Critical Reading of Matthew 26–28,* Minneapolis: Fortress • Senior, D. 1985, *The Passion of Jesus in the Gospel of Matthew,* Wilmington, Del.: Glazier.

Passover and the Plot to Kill Jesus (26:1-46)

After the cosmic, eschatological overview of human destiny in the fifth and final sermon (chs. 24–25), Jesus summarizes his own fate by recalling the three previous predictions of his death (26:2; cf. 16:21; 17:22-23; 20:18-19). Even though Jesus is about to lose his physical freedom, he remains in control of his life by freely adhering to God's will for him. When the authorities gather to plan his covert arrest and execution, they fulfill Jesus' predictions of his own death. The time of this crisis, the Passover festival, links his death symbolically with the sacrificial system (26:2; cf. vv. 26-28), thus making it more than a simple execution of a potential troublemaker. The high priest who coordinates the plot is "Joseph who is also called Caiaphas" (Josephus *Ant.* 18 §35); he was a member of a prominent priestly family and served as high priest from AD 18 to 36. Two ossuaries recently discovered in a burial cave near Jerusalem are inscribed respectively with the names Caiaphas (Heb./Aram. *Qapa'*) and Joseph bar (son of) *Qapa'*. It is possible but not certain that this burial cave belonged to this prominent family. Caiaphas the high priest, the leaders of the priestly houses (chief priests) and of prominent Judean families (elders), and high officials (scribes) ruled Jerusalem and Judea under the Roman prefect Pontius Pilate. Generally speaking, the imperial government co-opted local leaders and gave them control over local affairs as long as they remained subordinate to the empire, kept order, and collected taxes. The Jerusalem leaders appear to have considered Jesus as a potential threat to public order and thus as someone to be taken out of circulation.

The Pharisees, who were the opponents of Jesus in Galilee, suddenly drop out of the narrative. They were a group of retainers dependent on these wealthy, hereditary leaders. Though the Pharisees had plotted against Jesus previously (12:14; 22:15), once the leaders take charge themselves, the Pharisees stand aside. The authorities seek to arrest Jesus "covertly," that is, "by deceit" or "stealthily" to avoid civil unrest because they worry that the crowds of pilgrims in Jerusalem for the festival will get out of hand and riot, as had happened before (cf. Josephus *Ant.* 17 §254). Their concern to control the crowds and avoid violence is reasonable since about thirty years later, in AD 66, when they lost control of the crowds, a war with Rome ensued which resulted in the destruction of the temple and Jerusalem. Ironically, although they wish to avoid trouble during the Passover, they finally arrest Jesus during the festival because Judas Iscariot provides them with a good opportunity (26:14-16 and 47-50) and almost cause a riot in their efforts to convince Pilate to find Jesus guilty (27:24). Contrary to this analysis of the probable political perceptions and motives of the Jerusalem leaders, the author of Matthew presents their actions as unjust and Jesus as the innocent victim of their immoral hostility.

While the chief priests plot against Jesus in Jerusalem and offer Judas thirty silver shekels (coins) for giving them access to Jesus (26:3-5, 15), in Bethany two miles east of Jerusalem Jesus is enjoying the company of his disciples in Simon the Leper's house (v. 6). But his death overshadows even that peaceful scene when an unidentified woman foreshadows Jesus' burial by pouring expensive oil or perfume ("myrrh" in its generic meaning) on his head. The oil has several symbolic meanings. Guests were often given sweet-smelling oil or perfume at formal banquets. The pouring of oil on the head of Jesus the Messiah in this narrative context (cf. 21:1-17) may also allude to the anointing of Israel's kings (1 Samuel 10 for Saul and 1 Samuel 16 for David). The anointing also foreshadows the pathos of Jesus' death, for he will be buried hurriedly without proper preparation which included spices and anointing (27:59-60; cf. Mark 16:1). Though the woman has no name in the narrative, like many women in the NT, her symbolically significant act in Matthew's narrative keeps her memory alive "wherever the gospel is preached in the whole world" (26:13; see 24:14; 28:19-20). In contrast to Jesus' awareness of his impending death, the disciples partially misunderstand the meaning of these anticipatory events. In agreement with the first beatitude (5:3) they show proper solicitude for the poor and suspicion of luxurious waste (26:8-9), but they miss the symbolic meaning of the woman's anointing of Jesus until instructed by Jesus concerning his impending death (vv. 10-12). The bittersweet atmosphere of the supper, bracketed by the plot to kill Jesus, prepares the audience to understand Jesus' memorial supper with his disciples and to endure his arrest.

Matthew and Mark refer to the day of preparation, 14 Nisan, as "the first day of Unleavened Bread" (26:17), even though the feast began only after sundown, which is the beginning of 15 Nisan. The pedestrian arrangements for eating the Passover meal manifest once again Jesus' awareness of his future, for he has the disciples tell a householder that "his time *(kairos)* is near" (v. 18). (Presumably Jesus had made arrangements to celebrate the Passover with the householder earlier.) The Synoptic Gospels disagree with the Gospel of John on the date of Jesus' meal with his disciples. In John the meal is not a Passover meal on 15 Nisan, but the evening previous to the Passover meal. These conflicting dates both have symbolic significance. In John Jesus dies on the cross during the afternoon of the preparation day (the day before Passover), at the time the Passover lambs are being sacrificed at the temple (John 19:31). In Matthew, Mark, and Luke Jesus' final meal with his disciples is on Passover evening and his death is during the daytime of Passover itself. Both accounts link Jesus' death symbolically with the Passover sacrifice. Historically, John's chronology is more probable since the arrest, hearings, and trial before Pilate and the crucifixion would be over before the beginning of the solemn observance of the Passover meal in the evening and temple observances on Passover morning. The Synoptic chronology demands, improbably, that the chief priests and the council interrupt their celebration of Passover in the evening and in the morning in order to prosecute Jesus.

The account of the meal focuses on Jesus' death and the disciples' failures (26:20-35), the same themes which ran through the account of the meal in Bethany (vv. 8-12). As they are eating, Jesus initiates a dialogue with the twelve about betrayal and then creates a ritual enactment of his death. The dialogue about betrayal (vv. 21-25) distorts the expected intimacy of the festival meal but echoes faithfully the danger of death which threatens Jesus and threatened Israel in the Passover story (Exodus 12–13); it also prepares the disciples for Jesus' death. The author subtly differentiates the disciples, who address Jesus as "Lord," from Judas, who alone addresses Jesus as "Rabbi" (26:25; cf. 23:8). Jesus' prediction of his betrayal and betrayer (vv. 21, 25) accords with Scripture (vv. 24, 31) and is fulfilled in his arrest and death. The threat of punishment against the betrayer ("Woe to that one by whom the Son of Man is betrayed" — v. 24) is fulfilled in Judas's suicide (27:5). Thus, Jesus' death is once again interpreted as a significant event foreseen and accepted by Jesus.

Jesus concludes his final meal with his disciples by turning it into a ritual enactment of his death in which the disciples are told to eat bread and drink wine, which are his body and blood. The ritual prepares the disciples for Jesus' death and demonstrates once again Jesus' voluntary acceptance of his end. The author of Matthew gives no extended explanation of the bread and wine, probably because the meal was celebrated in his community and was already understood by his audience. In the context of the Passover festival, the symbols "body and blood" refer to the Passover lamb or goat which was sacrificed to God and then eaten in each household (Exod 12:1-13; cf. Lev 11:18 for the consumption of sacrifices). In the Gospel narrative the meal transforms Jesus' tragic execution by the imperial government into a religious sacrifice and links Jesus' self-sacrifice with the sacrifices and sprinkling of blood at the ceremony validating the Sinai covenant (Exod 24:3-8) and with biblical sacrifices which forgive sins (26:28; Leviticus 4–5). The concise narrative of the meal contains instructions ("take," "bless," "break," "give" — 26:26; "take," "thank," "give" — v. 27) using formulae derived from the celebration of the Lord's Supper in Matthew's community. With slight variations, these formulae were also used in the Pauline (1 Cor 11:23-26), Markan (14:22-25), and Lukan communities (22:19-20). Matthew draws the interpretation of Jesus' death as a sacrifice for sin (26:28) from the Bible (Isa 53:12) and from his own thematic stress on forgiveness of sins (1:21; 5:23-24; 6:12, 14-15; 9:6; 18:21-35). Jesus' final statement, that he will drink wine next in his Father's kingdom (26:29), puts his death and the ritual meal in an apocalyptic context. Jesus' death will lead to God's intervention in the world, that is, the coming of God's kingdom (see ch. 24), to the end of evil, and to a final heavenly or messianic banquet with God (see Exod 24:9-11; Isa 25:6-10; *1 Enoch* 62:14; 1QSa; Matt 8:11; etc. for the metaphor of a meal with God). The hymn which ends the meal may be the psalms of praise referred to as the Hallel (Psalms 113–18).

After the meal, Jesus and his disciples walk to the Mount of Olives (26:30), a mountain ridge east of the Temple Mount. As at the supper, so on the Mount of Olives (vv. 31-46) Jesus first deals with his disciples' failure and then with the substance of his death. Jesus prophesies his disciples' abandonment of him and Peter's threefold denial (vv. 31-35; see 10:33), which will soon be fulfilled (26:56, 69-75). Yet, the author also foreshadows the disciples' eventual fidelity to Jesus and Jesus' overcoming of death by the promise that Jesus will be raised and precede them in returning home to Galilee (v. 32). The verse from Zechariah (13:7 in Matt 26:31) alludes both to the disciples' failures and to Jesus' leadership. The metaphor of "shepherd" for a king and "flock" for his subjects is common in the Near East. According to Matthew's interpretation Jesus' scattered followers will be definitively gathered and reformed in Galilee by the risen Jesus.

Jesus' acceptance of his death reaches its climax in his prayer at Gethsemane (26:36-46). "Gethsemane," which means "oil press," was probably located among the olive tree orchards on the Mount of Olives. (John 18:1 refers to a nameless garden; tradition combined them into the "Garden of Gethsemane," a name that does not appear in the NT.) Jesus' three sessions of prayer in which he accepts his Father's will that he die (26:36-45) contrast sharply with Peter's subsequent threefold denial of Jesus (vv. 69-75). The three disciples, Peter, James and John, who saw Jesus transfigured into a heavenly being on the mountain (17:1-8), now accompany Jesus when he is most human and weak. However, their threefold inability to stay awake with Jesus (26:40, 43, 45) foreshadows their abandonment of them (v. 56). Jesus' special relationship with God as Father provides the background for his sorrowful feelings (see Pss 42:6; 43:5) and request to be relieved of his duty to die (26:38-42). These very human fears foreshadow his sense of abandonment on the cross (27:46). The "cup" which he wishes to avoid (26:39, 42) is a metaphor for suffering and death (20:22-23; 26:27-28) and in other contexts for God's anger at sin by Israel (Isa 51:17, 22) or the world (Rev 14:10; 16:19). Paradoxically, in the course of revealing his fears to God Jesus accepts God's will that he die and then voluntarily rise to face his captors (26:45-46). The Gospel has stressed obedience to God's will as the substance of righteousness (6:10; 7:21; 13:50), and Jesus lives by his teaching one last time.

In contrast to Jesus the disciples do not stay watchful and pray, but sleep, thus opening themselves to temptation (26:40-41; cf. 6:13) and to failure through flight from Jesus (v. 56). The Greek word for staying awake appears also in the warnings to be vigilant for the return of Jesus at the end (24:42-43; 25:13). The disciples' failure stems from their "little faith" and their doubts, which persist until the very end of the Gospel (28:17). A proverbial expression about weakness of the flesh (26:41; see 1 Cor 7:34 and the DSS *Community Rule* [1QS], cols. 3-4) fittingly describes their attempt to follow Jesus. As Jesus is about to be arrested, the author reminds us again that the death of Jesus is foreseen and significant (26:45; see 26:18) and that sin is the cause of Jesus' death.

Bibliography. Beck, B. E. 1988, "Gethsemane in the Four Gospels," *Epworth Review* 15:57-65 • Delorme, J., ed. 1964, *The Eucharist in the New Testament,* Baltimore: Helicon • Greenhut, Z. 1992, "Burial Cave of the Caiaphas Family," *BAR* 18/5:28-36, 76 • Jeremias, J. 1977, *The Eucharistic Words of Jesus,* Philadelphia: Fortress • Maccoby, H. 1992, *Judas Iscariot and the Myth of Jewish Evil,* New York: Maxwell Macmillan International • Marshall, I. H. 1981, *Last Supper and Lord's Supper,* Grand Rapids: Eerdmans • Reich, R. 1992, "Caiaphas' Name Inscribed on Bone Boxes," *BAR* 18/5:38-44, 76.

Jesus' Arrest and Condemnation (26:47–27:26)

Recognizing an opportunity for a safe arrest at night outside the city, Judas presumably left Jesus and the disciples when they started for the Mount of Olives and called out a group from the high priest's entourage to arrest Jesus. Since numerous pilgrims were circulating around the city during the festival, the authorities needed Judas to identify Jesus (26:48). The large armed crowd sent to apprehend Jesus (v. 47) conforms to the authorities' fear that Jesus' followers might violently resist an arrest and start a disturbance. They treat Jesus as a bandit or brigand (v. 55 — *lēstēs*), that is, as a politically and economically marginalized member of the lower classes who resists (oppressive) laws, takes wealth from the government and the rich, and disrupts the social order. Usually social bandits have support from economically stressed farmers in rural villages who resent the governing classes in large cities. The Jerusalem authorities feared that Jesus the popular Galilean teacher might turn his criticism of them into political and social revolution. In fact, one of Jesus' disciples did attack and wound one of the crowd before Jesus stopped further resistance (vv. 51-53). It is likely that Jesus' followers had a variety of interpretations of how society should be changed, and were seen as a threat both during and after Jesus' lifetime. Matthew's narrative dissociates Jesus from such political machinations and puts the blame for his arrest and execution on hostile authorities.

Jesus' enigmatic reply to Judas, literally "for what you are here" (26:50), can be understood as a rhetorical or ironic question ("Why have you come?" or "For this you have come?") or as an elliptical command to "do what you are here to do" (NRSV). In either case Jesus resigns himself to his immediate apprehension and avoids a fight between his followers and the crowd. The author gives three reasons for Jesus' avoidance of violence: a proverbial truth that human violent resistance provokes violence (v. 52); an apocalyptic observation that armies of angels are available to bring about God's justice (v. 53; see 24:31 and the *War Scroll* [1QM]); and a pair of references to the necessity of fulfilling the Scriptures according to God's will (vv. 54, 56; cf. 26:24, 31). When Jesus is arrested, his disciples run away, fulfilling the prophecy from Zech 13:7 quoted in v. 31.

The crowd brings Jesus to a ruling council of scribes and elders in Caiaphas's house (26:57, 59). The council's activities begin at night with an interrogation of Jesus (vv. 57-66) and continue with the transfer of Jesus to Pilate's court in the morning (27:1-2) where the members of the council accuse Jesus (v. 12) and seek the death penalty (vv. 20-23). The opportunity to arrest Jesus provided by Judas led to a late night interrogation, not a formal trial. In the morning Pilate quickly disposed of Jesus' case in order to remove a potential threat to public order during Passover. Though Roman citizens and prominent leaders enjoyed well-articulated judicial protection, obscure colonials in the eastern empire were often treated to summary judgment just as Jesus was.

Anti-Semitic charges throughout Christian history that "the Jews killed Jesus" have led to incessant debates over Roman versus Jewish culpability for Jesus' execution. The legal status of Jesus' so-called "trial" before the Jerusalem council (26:57–27:10) has been frequently debated. Much of the discussion has been based on erroneous understandings of Roman and Jewish governance and on later theological judgments retrojected into the first century. First, Jesus was not taken before "the Sanhedrin," a word which does not appear in the NT and is correctly avoided by the NRSV. "Sanhedrin" is a second-third-century-AD Hebrew word based on the Greek word *synedrion,* meaning "council." The Mishnah tractate *Sanhedrin* (c. AD 200) envisions a number of sanhedrins of different sizes governing Israel. It also lays down rigorous procedures to be used in capital cases by the supreme Jerusalem Sanhedrin of seventy-one members. However, the Jerusalem council in the first century was not the idealized Sanhedrin of the Mishnah, but a typical Near Eastern city council in the Roman Empire. The council in Jerusalem was neither a religious body nor a sovereign Jewish political institution. It served at the convenience of the governor and emperor with broad, flexible legislative, executive, and judicial powers and a mandate to keep order and collect taxes. It did not operate under elaborate legal procedures nor according to a constitution. Practically speaking, the national council could not be clearly separated from the Roman provincial administration and governors. Contrary to the theories of some scholars who try to reconcile later rabbinic texts with the first-century evidence, there were not two Sanhedrins, one religious and one political. In antiquity religion and politics were tightly bound together so that the Jerusalem council had authority over the temple, interpreted biblical law in the religious, civil, criminal, and political spheres, and supervised routine administration.

The night meeting of the council at Caiaphas's house as described by Matthew was not a formal court in which a verdict was rendered, but an ad hoc hearing to deal with a crisis. Thus analyses of this hearing as a "trial" and comparisons with the judicial procedures here with the rules in Mishnah *Sanhedrin* a century later miss the point. When Caiaphas accuses Jesus of blasphemy (26:65-66), he does not ask the council, "What is your verdict?" (v. 66 as translated by the NRSV; "decision" in the RSV). Rather, *ti hymin dokei* is more informal and means literally, "What does it seem to you?" or "What do you think?" (NIV). The assembled elders implicitly agree with Caiaphas that Jesus' claim is blasphemous and, since they already had plotted to kill Jesus (vv. 3-5), they answer that Jesus is deserving of death. Consistent with that informal evaluation of Jesus' case, in the morning they "took counsel" in order to execute him (27:1; cf. 26:4) in a strategy session, rather than a formal court proceeding, which leads them to bring Jesus to Pilate for formal judicial proceedings, sentencing, and execution. In contrast to Matthew, Mark 14:64 says explicitly that the members of the council "condemned him as deserving death." The places where Jesus was interrogated and judged support the distinction of informal and formal proceedings. Caiaphas and the elders speak with Jesus in Caiaphas's house (26:57), which had a gateway (v. 71 — *pylōn,* often translated "porch") and a courtyard (vv. 58, 69 — *aulē*). Pilate the governor (vv. 2, 11 — *hēgemōn*) sat on a *bēma* (27:19), a raised platform, outside the governor's residence (27:27 — *praetorium*). The praetorium probably refers to the palace built by Herod the Great on the western hill of Jerusalem, near the present Jaffa gate. Thus Pilate judged Jesus in a public building following formal procedures, in contrast to the informal interrogation at Caiaphas's house. Thus, those who analyze the "legality" of the Jewish "trial" of Jesus in the Gospel of Matthew misunderstand the author's nuanced appreciation for Jewish judicial procedures. However, the author of Matthew has not suddenly exonerated the Jewish authorities of complicity in the death of Jesus. His unrelenting attack on their integrity continues unabated since he portrays them as seeking Jesus' death from the Roman court. Thus Judas's imprecise perception "that Jesus was condemned" (27:3) anticipates Pilate's verdict but is true to the unfolding of events.

The charges brought against Jesus in the hearing before the chief priests and elders are notoriously unclear. The leaders had already decided to arrest Jesus and have him executed. During the hearing they suborn perjury against Jesus (26:59-60) until finally two witnesses, the legal minimum (Deut 19:15), agree that Jesus claimed he "could" (v. 61, not that he "would," as in Mark 14:58) destroy the temple and rebuild it in three days. Since Jesus does not say this in any of the Synoptic Gospels, its meaning remains obscure. The Gospel of John 2:19-22 refers to this general tradition when he has Jesus challenge his opponents to destroy "this temple" and watch Jesus "raise it up" in three days. But Jesus' opponents in John do not treat this claim as a crime, but as ridiculous. In addition, the Johannine tradition envisions Jesus' opponents, not Jesus himself, destroying the temple. The interpretation of the saying in John 2:22 makes clear that "temple" is a metaphor for Jesus' body and "raise up" alludes to the resurrection. Matthew contains no similar interpretation of Jesus' alleged teaching. Perhaps in Matthew the charge is a political interpretation of Jesus' attack on merchants and money changers in the temple (21:12-13), or a garbled version of his teaching that the temple would be destroyed (24:2; but he taught this to his disciples privately), or an inference drawn from Jesus' hostility toward the Jewish leaders. In any case, because a threat against the temple showed disrespect for the sanctity of God and God's house, it could be designated as blasphemy (26:65; see Lev. 24:10-23); and because such talk weakened the stability of the state, the charge had social, political, and religious ramifications.

Jesus' silence in the face of the charges might be taken as acquiescence (see also 27:14 and Isa 53:7), but Caiaphas, dissatisfied with Jesus' lack of response (26:62), links the charge of threatening the temple with Jesus' messianic "pretensions." Caiaphas asks Jesus to identify himself using the terminology most central to this gospel: "Messiah/Christ" and "Son of God" (v. 63; cf. Jesus' question to his disciples in 16:15-16). Jesus responds to the high priest's question affirmatively (26:64) and clarifies his stand with a quotation from Dan 7:13 and Ps 110:1 concerning the Son of Man's reign with God at the end of the world. Just as Matthew's audience knows that Jesus is the Son of Man, Son of God, and Messiah, Caiaphas in the narrative understands the high status implied by these verses and accuses Jesus of blasphemy, that is, claiming privileges which belong to God alone (26:65-66). The other council members agree and, as they had before they arrested Jesus, decide to seek his execution. At the end of the hearing they act like a mob out of control, taunting and abusing Jesus (vv. 67-68). As the author of Matthew recounts Jesus' dealings with the authorities, he stresses Jesus' innocence and the injustice of the proceedings. He attacks the Jewish leaders in Jerusalem, as he has all through the Gospel, especially for using legal proceedings, witnesses, and oaths inauthentically. (Note Matthew's opposition to oaths in 5:33-37 and 23:16-22.) Matthew's shrill attack against Jesus' opponents probably arises from the persecution experienced by his group of disciples, who are a minority in the large Jewish community. As such, they lacked social acceptance and carried the stigma attached to Jesus' public execution. In the light of later Christian anti-Semitism, we must emphasize that the Jewish author of the Gospel does not condemn all Jews nor Jews for all time as responsible for Jesus' execution, but only the Jerusalem leaders who cooperated with the Roman governor in executing Jesus.

Peter's threefold denial of Jesus (26:69-75) and Judas's suicide (27:3-10) parallel one another and highlight the isolation of Jesus from his disciples as well as from society at large. Jesus' arrest separated him from his disciples (26:56) for the first time since ch. 4. Peter faithfully follows Jesus to Caiaphas's house to see the end (26:58 — *telos*), but fails to support Jesus.

Peter gives himself away by his Galilean accent (26:73) and, confronted by the household staff, dissociates himself from a politically dangerous situation by denying three times that he is a follower of Jesus. His denials eerily mimic the rejection of Jesus in the hearing going on inside, and he, like the false witnesses within, lies under oath (26:72). Given the Gospel's stress on persecution (ch. 10), Peter's story probably reflects the Matthean community's experience of social and political oppression. The narrative last mentions Peter as a distinct character when he recognizes what he has done and mourns it at sunrise. Similarly, Judas repents his betrayal of Jesus (27:3-10) and then testifies to Jesus' innocence before the chief priests and elders. However, while Peter's "end" is kept open and he presumably joins the rest of the disciples and Jesus in Galilee, Judas commits suicide. His payment, thirty silver coins (26:15), acquires a symbolic meaning which furthers Matthew's attack on the Jerusalem authorities. First, the chief priests acknowledge that the silver coins are blood money (27:6). Second, the author weaves his story out of Zech 11:13, an attack on the sixth-century-BC Jerusalem leaders who caused the destruction of the temple. He also alludes to images of pottery and buying fields found in Jeremiah (Jer 18:2-3; 19:1-15; 32:6-9). Matthew attributes the whole scriptural passage to the more well-known prophet Jeremiah rather than to Zechariah (27:9-10). In Zechariah the prophet plays the part of the shepherd (leader) of a flock which is to be destroyed, an allegorical reference to Judah, which is badly led by the "sheep merchants" (the Jerusalem leadership — Zech 11:7, 11) during the fifth century. The sheep merchants pay the prophet-shepherd thirty shekels of silver, which is the price for a slave gored by an ox (Exod 21:32), but he throws it into the temple as a condemnation of them (Zech 11:12-13). Thus the author of Matthew continues his attack on the leaders of the Jewish community in Jerusalem by having Judas the traitor and conspirator against Jesus condemn them with a prophetic action.

Matthew's account of Jesus' second interrogation and condemnation by Pilate (27:11-26) repeats the themes of the first, especially that Jesus is innocent and voluntarily dies according to God's will expressed in Scripture. The claim that Jesus is the Christ/Messiah (vv. 17, 22) occasions a political charge of sedition for claiming royal authority contrary to Caesar (vv. 29, 37, 42). Jesus responds to Pilate as he did to the council, with a silence (26:63; 27:12, 14) that prompts further questioning. Pilate asks three times what he should do with Jesus (27:17, 21, 22), and three times the chief priests and elders persuade (mislead) the crowds to ask for Jesus' condemnation to death (vv. 20, 21, 22). In Matthew's account Pilate knows that the Jewish leaders are framing Jesus out of envy (v. 18, from Mark), is warned by his wife's dream that Jesus is innocent (v. 19), and declares his innocence of Jesus' death by "washing his hands of the matter" (v. 24). In response all the people take responsibility for Jesus' condemnation. However, even though Matthew shifts blame for Jesus' death onto the Jewish leadership, he does not exculpate the Roman governor Pilate, contrary to some commentators. Pilate condemns Jesus to death and turns him over to be tortured by his troops even though he knows that Jesus is innocent. The author's account of Pilate's interrogation and judgment only partially masks the Roman government's involvement in Jesus' execution. Though Pilate says "see to it yourselves" (v. 24), in fact Pilate hands Jesus over to his own soldiers (vv. 26-27). The verdict corresponds to imperial policy and Pilate's own history. Pilate crucified Jesus for the best of reasons, from a Roman point of view, to keep public order, which in this case meant quieting an unruly crowd during a Jerusalem festival. Pilate was a cruel and insensitive governor who provoked resistance from Judeans a number of times during his ten-year governorship (AD 26-36) and was finally removed from office by the new emperor, Claudius, for malfeasance in office. Condemning a potential troublemaker like Jesus to death would have been business as usual for Pilate and not an occasion for hesitation or doubt.

As noted above, the author's comments on the Jewish leaders in Jerusalem probably stem from his own conflicts with the leaders of the Jewish community in the late first century. He also links the death of Jesus with the destruction of Jerusalem and the temple during the war with Rome in AD 70. In a highly stylized scene, the author of Matthew has "all the people," under the influence of the chief priests and elders, take responsibility for the verdict against Jesus (27:25). Their response to Pilate, "His blood be on us and our children," has been *the* key prooftext for later anti-Semitic charges that the Jews killed Jesus. Many interpreters have seen the shift from "the crowds" in vv. 20-24 to "all the people" in v. 25 as a theological statement by Matthew that the Jewish people as a whole rejected Jesus for all time. However, Matthew speaks concretely rather than universally here as in the rest of the Gospel. "All the people" are those Jerusalem Jews gathered before Pilate under the influence of the Jerusalem leaders. The "blood" which came upon them for their rejection of Jesus is, in the author of Matthew's view, the destruction of Jerusalem and much of its population by the Romans in AD 70. "Us and our children" refers to two generations of Jerusalemites, those active in AD 30 and their children who experienced the destruction with them forty years later. The author does not condemn all Jews in the first century for rejecting Jesus, much less Jews in later generations or alive today, but only those of his fellow Jews who opposed Jesus and his teaching.

Bibliography. Bammel, E., ed., 2d ed. 1970, *The Trial of Jesus,* London: SCM • Catchpole, D. R. 1972, *The Trial of Jesus: A Study in the Gospels and Jewish Historiography from 1770 to the Present Day,* Leiden: Brill • Brandon, S. G. F. 1968, *The Trial of Jesus of Nazareth,* New York: Stein and Day • Cargill, T. B. 1991, "'His Blood Be upon Us and upon Our Children': A Matthean Double Entendre?" *NTS* 37:101-12 • Gerhardsson, B. 1981, "Confession and Denial before Men: Observations on Matt. 26:57–27:2," *JSNT* 13:46-66 • Heil, J. P. 1991, "The Blood of Jesus in Matthew: A Narrative-Critical Perspective," *Perspectives in Religious Studies* 18:117-24 • Senior, D. 1974, "A Case Study in Matthean Creativity: Matthew 27:3-10," *BR* 19:23-36 • Winter, P. 1961, *On the Trial of Jesus,* Berlin: de Gruyter.

Jesus' Death (27:27-56)

The mockery of Jesus by the Roman soldiers (27:27-31) echoes the mockery of the members of the council (26:67-68) and of the bystanders at the crucifixion (27:39-44). Their parody of the charge that Jesus is "King of the Jews" ironically affirms that claim for Matthew's readers. The red robe thrown around Jesus was a Roman soldier's cape; the crown of thorns and reed scepter were used to mock Jesus and to cause him physical pain. The scourging administered to Jesus was a common practice to make the crucified person die sooner. Mockery degraded, dishonored, and dehumanized the condemned person in preparation for his final separation from society by execution.

The author of Matthew tells the story of Jesus' execution by crucifixion with a minimum of emotion or explanation. Romans crucified criminals and rebels outside cities. As Jesus carried the crossbeam outside the city walls, he required help, presumably because he was weak from the scourging; so the Roman soldiers impressed into service Simon of Cyrene (modern Libya), a diaspora Jew in Jerusalem for Passover (27:32). The place of crucifixion was Golgotha (v. 33), a name derived from the Aramaic word for skull *(gulgaltha).* (In Latin the world for skull is *calvaria,* hence Eng. "Calvary.") The two "robbers" crucified with Jesus are really "brigands" or "bandits" *(lęstai),* that is, political opponents of Roman rule (see 26:55). The author skips the details of crucifixion in which the executioners tied or nailed the body of the condemned to crossed pieces of wood. Usually the victim died of asphyxiation, loss of blood, exposure, or shock. Crucifixion was used on colonials and slaves; it was forbidden for Roman citizens.

The author of Matthew tells the story of Jesus' death with symbolic allusions which bring out the true significance of the event. He counters the social stigma associated with public execution by linking Jesus' death to Scripture and God's will. Jesus is offered wine twice while on the cross in accordance with Ps 69:21, "They gave me poison for food, and for my thirst they gave me vinegar to drink." "Poison," traditionally translated "gall," is a bitter-tasting substance that may be medicinal or poisonous. "Vinegar" is an inexpensive, sour wine with a taste like vinegar. Thus at the beginning of the crucifixion Jesus is offered "wine mixed with gall" to ease his suffering or hasten his death, but he rejects it (27:34), and just before he dies, one of the bystanders offers him "sour wine" (v. 48). Another series of actions is linked to Psalm 22, a prayer for deliverance from enemies. Like the psalmist (identified as David in the title), Jesus is surrounded by enemies (Ps 22:12-13, 16; verse numbers follow the English translation), pierced through his hands and feet (Ps 22:16 in the Greek), mocked (Ps 22:6-8), has his clothing divided by lot (Ps 22:18), and is finally worshiped by Gentiles (the centurion and soldiers in 27:54; Ps 22:27). Jesus also recites Ps

22:1, "My God, my God, why have you forsaken me?" (27:46). Since the citation of a first verse often implies the recitation of the whole passage in ancient literature, the author probably alludes to the whole psalm. Jesus' cry for help, then, should not be interpreted as a sign of despair, but, like the psalm itself, as an expression of his deep suffering and human fear before death and of his continuing reliance on God to save him.

The reactions of the bystanders (27:39-44) also give meaning to Jesus' death, for, as they mock him for his helplessness, abandonment by God, ineffective claims to destroy the temple, and claims to be the king of Israel and Son of God, the author and readers understand that Jesus is God's Son, will be saved, will rise from the dead, and will rule Israel. Ironically, only the Roman guards understand in some sense that Jesus is God's Son and not a common criminal (v. 54). Jesus' salvation by God and overcoming of death are foreshadowed by a series of apocalyptic allusions which surround his death. When Jesus recites Ps 22:1 in Aramaic, "Eli, Eli, lema sabachthani," the bystanders misunderstand "Eli," which means "my God," as the name of the prophet Elijah, who, in this narrative, is expected to return at the end of the world (27:46; cf. 11:14; 17:11-12). The call for God to intervene and save Jesus alludes to apocalyptic hopes for divine intervention to destroy the evil and establish justice in the world. The author of Matthew associates a number of apocalyptic events with Jesus' death, including the tearing of the curtain in front of the temple, earthquakes, the splitting of rocks, and (after Jesus' resurrection) the resurrection of holy people who appeared to many (27:51-53; cf. Ezek 37:1-14). These events foreshadow Jesus' resurrection, itself an apocalyptic event, as well as the end of the world and resurrection for judgment described in chs. 24–25.

After Jesus' death the focus turns to those who watched Jesus die. The Roman guards on watch affirm his close relationship with God ("Son of God") on the basis of the apocalyptic events which surround his death (27:54). The women from Galilee who had taken care of Jesus faithfully look on from afar (vv. 55-56); they symbolize that Jesus, though dead, has not been abandoned by God. The women also provide a positive witness to his death and later to his resurrection (28:1), in contrast to the guards at the tomb who will be bribed to lie (28:11-15) and the male disciples who have run away (26:56). The identities of the women vary in the Gospel stories of the crucifixion and empty tomb. Mary Magdalene is prominent in all accounts. The author of Matthew may have understood Mary the mother of James and Joseph to be Jesus' mother since Jesus' brothers who accompany Jesus' mother earlier are James and Joseph (13:55). In contrast, Mark identifies this Mary as the mother of James the younger, Joses (a variant of Joseph), and Salome.

Bibliography. Fitzmyer, J. A. 1978, "Crucifixion in Ancient Palestine, Qumran Literature and the New Testament," *CBQ* 40:493-513 • Hill, D. 1985, "Matthew 27:51-53 in the Theology of the Evangelist," *IBS* 7:76-87.

Jesus' Burial and Resurrection (27:57–28:20)

Jesus continues as the central focus of the narrative even after he has died. The stories of his burial, the guard at his tomb, the empty tomb, and his appearances all testify that "he has been raised as he said" (28:6) and rebut charges that Jesus' disciples stole his body. Joseph of Arimathea, a wealthy and therefore influential and well-known member of the governing class, securely buries Jesus' corpse in a new cave tomb which was hollowed out of the Jerusalem limestone. And since the tomb was new, the absence of Jesus' body on Sunday was obvious and could not be mistaken. Since the tomb was closed by a large rock, the body could not have been easily stolen (27:57-61). Joseph and the two Marys (cf. 27:55-56 and 28:1) witness the burial, know the location of the tomb, and thus can testify to the other disciples that Jesus had been buried in that particular new tomb. Joseph from Arimathea (a Judean town of uncertain location) is described as a disciple of Jesus (v. 57) in Matthew rather than as "a respected member of the council" (Mark 15:43) because Matthew has unceasingly attacked the council members.

The account of the posting of a guard at the tomb and of bribing them after the resurrection (27:62-66; 28:11-15) may originally have been an independent apologetic story meant to counter rumors that Jesus' disciples stole his body. Within the narrative the bribing of the guards testifies in a backhand way to the reality of the empty tomb. The Pharisees, who have not been mentioned since ch. 23, suddenly reappear in the narrative with the chief priests (27:62; previously in 21:45), perhaps because they believe in the resurrection of the dead (12:40) but do not accept Jesus' resurrection. They argue before Pilate that Jesus was a "deceiver" who predicted that he would rise from the dead in three days. They fear that his disciples might continue the deception by stealing his body, and intimate that Jesus is a deceptive prophet like those described in Deut 13:1-5. Pilate's authorization of a guard at the tomb does not make clear whether he gave them a detachment of Roman soldiers or told them to use their own guards. In either case the guards and a seal on the tomb secure the body and make the later charge of theft against the disciples less credible. Hence the attraction of this story for the author of the Gospel.

Many apocalypses describe resurrection from the dead as part of divine intervention at the end of the world; similarly, later works of art and Christian literature depict Jesus' resurrection in graphic detail. Strikingly, the four canonical Gospels do not describe the actual resurrection but its aftermath. Instead an angel interprets the meaning of the empty tomb to the two Marys, who had faithfully followed Jesus and come to see his grave the morning after the festival. The characters and events at the tomb resemble those found in apocalypses: a divine messenger with white garments and a fiery appearance ("like lightning" — v. 3), an earthquake, the rolling aside of the rock sealing the tomb, the frightened fainting of the guards, the fear of the women, the instruction not to be afraid, and the revelatory message that Jesus has risen from the dead (28:2-6). Jesus has not been revivified, like Lazarus in the Gospel of John (ch. 11), but has transcended earthly life. The narrative concentrates on the central point, that Jesus has risen, not on details of how it happened. The angel announces the resurrection to the two women (v. 6), tells the women to announce it to the disciples (v. 7), and anticipates the disciples' commission to teach about Jesus to the nations in the final scene (vv. 16-20).

The ending of the Gospel of Matthew grew out of the ending to the Gospel of Mark. In Mark the women found the tomb already open and were instructed by a young man in a white robe to tell the disciples that Jesus would meet them in Galilee. But strangely they went away afraid and said nothing to anyone (Mark 16:1-8). The Markan (lack of an?) ending has troubled commentators since antiquity. As usual, the author of Matthew smooths out Mark's narrative. The women are fearful, as is normal after a heavenly appearance, and joyful at the news of Jesus' resurrection. As they leave the tomb to bring the "brothers" the message to go to Galilee, Jesus appears to them (28:8-10) in order to reinforce their resolve and repeat the instruction to go to Galilee. Matthew ends his Gospel, logically enough, with Jesus' promised Galilean appearance to his disciples. The appearances of the angel and Jesus verify and authenticate the narrative's claim that Jesus has risen from the dead. Even the ending of the story of the tomb guards supports Matthew's case, for they testify to the chief priests about their experience of the angel, earthquake, fear, unconsciousness, and the empty tomb (vv. 11-15; cf. v. 4).

The chief priests and elders take counsel, bribe the guards as they did Judas, suborn perjury, and plan to mislead Pilate, just as they did earlier in the plot against Jesus (26:1-5, 14-15, 57-68; 27:1-2). This apologetic story refutes charges that Jesus' disciples falsified the resurrection by stealing the body and blames the leaders of Judea for misleading the people away one last time. The author of Matthew laments his opponents' success with a rare editorial comment that "this story [*logos* — that Jesus' body was stolen by his disciples] has been spread among the Jews to this day" (28:15). "Jews" here refers to those Jews who, unlike Matthew and his followers, have not accepted Jesus as Messiah and Son of God.

The final scene of the Gospel brings Jesus' life to a climax and initiates a new way of life for his disciples (28:16-20). Jesus meets the eleven for the first time since they abandoned him at Gethsemane and instructs them on a mountain, as he did in the Sermon on the Mount (5:1-2), in order to rally them after their defection. They prostrate themselves (v. 17), as did the women earlier (v. 9), but, true to their proclivity toward "little faith," some of them still doubt (v. 17; Gk. *hoi de* refers to part of the group). It is likely that the author of Matthew sees the same ambivalence in his own community whom he addresses in this gospel. Jesus' response to them resembles both an enthronement hymn, which celebrates the power and honor of a new king, and a commissioning narrative, which empowers the followers of a king to accomplish a task. The extent of Jesus' power is conveyed not only by his assertion that "all authority in heaven and on earth has been given to me" (by God) but also by his command to his disciples to "make disciples of all nations" and to teach them to observe "all that I have commanded" with the assurance that he will be with them "all days" (28:18-20). Though the common Gospel titles "Lord," "Christ," "Son of God," and "Son of Man" are not used, Jesus appears as God's representative and viceroy par excellence. The turn to "all nations" is not, as some have said, a rejection of the Jews as a people, but an inclusion of non-Jews with Jews as part of God's people, Israel. The phrase "all nations" has been understood by scholars as referring to Gentiles only rather than including the Jewish nation along with all other nations. In either case the Gospel affirms the place of both Israel and the nations in God's plan for the world. It is likely that the Matthean community was predominantly Jewish (10:5-6) and only beginning to enlarge their vision to include Gentiles. Thus the author of Matthew ends the Gospel by exhorting his community to recruit non-Jews aggressively as followers of Jesus.

Baptism makes a sudden appearance at the end of the Gospel as the initiation rite for the followers of Jesus. From Paul's letters, Acts, and many other early sources such as *Did.* 7:1-3 we know that baptism was an early Christian practice. The author of Matthew testifies to this practice and authenticates it in the final scene of the Gospel. The origin of this practice of baptism is unknown. John's baptism of repentance and Jesus' participation in it (ch. 3) were not an initiation rite. However, the account of John's baptism in Matthew's narrative prepares for baptism at the end of the Gospel. In a general way those being baptized imitate Jesus, who was baptized by John. When John acknowledged that Jesus did not need baptism, Jesus insisted that he be baptized "to fulfill all righteousness" (3:15), that is, to do God's will. God's will that Jesus be baptized at the beginning of the Gospel matches God's will that the nations be baptized at the end. The invocation of Father, Son, and Holy Spirit in the liturgical formula used in baptism also has roots in the story of Jesus' baptism in which the Son of God is baptized, the Father's voice acknowledges the Son, and the Spirit of God descends on Jesus. This formula does not imply the fully developed trinitarian theology of the fourth century, even though later reflection on it fostered that theology. The teaching and observance that accompany baptism (28:20) are probably the contents of the Gospel in their entirety. Jesus' final promise to be with his disciples "all the days until the end of the age" reaches back to his birth and forward to the end of the world. In the infancy narrative Jesus received the symbolic name Emmanuel, meaning "God with us" (1:23), and here he actualizes it by being authoritatively present to his followers even after he has died. The "end of the age" which is the goal of Jesus' promise has been explained in the parables (13:39-40, 49) and the eschatological sermon (24:3). This final instruction strengthens and guides Jesus' disciples and the author's community and leaves their work and life open to the future coming of Jesus at the end.

Bibliography. Bahat, D. 1986, "Does the Holy Sepulchre Church Mark the Burial of Jesus?" *BAR* 12/2:26-45 • Craig,

W. L. 1984, "The Guard at the Tomb," *NTS* 30:273-81 • Hubbard, B. J. 1974, *The Matthean Redaction of a Primitive Apostolic Commissioning: An Exegesis of Matthew 28:16-20,* Missoula: Scholars • Reeves, K. H. 1993, *The Resurrection Narrative in Matthew: A Literary-Critical Examination,* Lewiston, N.Y.: Mellen • Schaberg, J. 1982, *The Father, the Son and the Holy Spirit: The Triadic Phrase in Matthew 28:19b,* Chico: Scholars • Smyth, K. 1975, "Matthew 28: Resurrection as Theophany," *ITQ* 42:259-71 • van der Horst, P. 1986, "Once More: The Translation of *hoi de* in Matthew 28:17," *JSNT* 27:27-30 • Wright, N. T. 2003, *The Resurrection of the Son of God,* Minneapolis: Fortress.

Mark

Craig A. Evans

INTRODUCTION

The Gospel of Mark, the shortest of the four NT Gospels, tells the story of Jesus, from baptism to empty tomb, in an impressive and compelling manner. Although neglected in the early centuries of the church, this Gospel has enjoyed a great deal of scholarly attention throughout the twentieth century. This will likely continue on in the twenty-first century.

Mark and the Other Gospels

Recently certain scholars have argued that several of the noncanonical Gospels (such as *Papyrus Egerton* 2, the *Gospel of Peter,* the *Gospel of the Hebrews,* and the *Gospel of Thomas*) are independent of or older than the NT Gospels. But the evidence that has been adduced for these claims is not persuasive. Most of these writings exhibit the traits found in second- and third-century writings that are characterized by embellishment and pious imagination. *Papyrus Egerton* 2 exhibits conflation of Synoptic and Johannine elements. The *Gospel of Peter* tells a fanciful tale of the resurrection of Jesus, complete with a talking cross. Even the *Gospel of Thomas,* which enjoys the lion's share of scholarly attention, exhibits many traces of the later editing and secondary tendencies that reflect second- century, not first-century practices.

Most scholars today are rightly convinced that the Synoptic Gospels are the oldest Gospels. But which one of these three is the oldest? Augustine (d. c. AD 430) believed that Matthew was written first and that Mark is in essence an abridgment of it. Johann Jacob Griesbach in 1776 proposed that Matthew was composed first, that Luke was composed next, making use of Matthew, and that Mark was composed last, conflating and abridging both Matthew and Luke. The Griesbach hypothesis was influential for about a century, but it began losing ground to Markan priority in the years following the publication of a work by Heinrich Julius Holtzmann in 1863. Holtzmann argued that an early version of Mark ("source A") was written first and that Matthew and Luke independently of one another made use of it and another source of sayings ("source B"). The latter source eventually came to be called "Q," which is an abbreviation for the German word *Quelle,* meaning "source."

Following the influential study of B. H. Streeter in 1924, the basic principles of Holtzmann's explanation of the relationships among the Synoptic Gospels became the dominant view. Although in the last thirty-five years or so William Farmer and a small number of like-minded colleagues have vigorously argued for a return to the Griesbach hypothesis, the majority of Gospel scholars still hold to Markan priority.

Markan priority appears to be the most prudent position for several reasons: (1) Mark's literary style lacks the sophistication and polish often seen in Matthew and Luke. This phenomenon is more easily explained in terms of Matthean and Lukan improvement upon Mark rather than Markan degradation of Matthean and Lukan style. (2) In the Markan Gospel Jesus and the disciples are sometimes portrayed in a manner that appears either undignified or possibly at variance with Christian beliefs. More often than not these potentially embarrassing passages are touched up or omitted altogether by Matthew and Luke. Again, it is easier to explain the phenomena in terms of Matthean and Lukan improvements upon Mark rather than the reverse. (3) The phenomena of agreements and disagreements among the Synoptic Gospels are more easily explained in reference to Markan priority. Among other things, we observe that where there is no Mark to follow (e.g., no infancy or resurrection narratives, no "Q" material) there Matthew and Luke diverge from one another. This observation is more easily explained in terms of Markan priority and Matthew's and Luke's independence from one another than in terms of Mark writing last and making use of Matthew and Luke. Markan priority also avoids the problem of trying to explain Luke's inconsistent use of Matthew. (4) Another indication of Markan priority is in the observation that in some instances, due to omission of Markan details, Matthew and Luke have created difficulties. In some of these instances only by looking at Mark can the reader fill in the gaps created by Matthew and Luke, whose tendency is to abbreviate and streamline Mark's wordier versions of most episodes. (5) The small amount of material that is unique to the Gospel of Mark also supports Markan priority. This material consists of 1:1; 2:27; 3:20-21; 4:26-29; 7:2-4, 32-37; 8:22-26; 9:29, 48-49; 13:33-37; 14:51-52. In reviewing this material one should ask which explanation seems most probable, that Mark added it or that Matthew and Luke found it in Mark and chose to omit it. The nature of the material supports the latter alternative, for it seems more likely that Matthew and Luke chose to omit the flight of the naked youth (14:51-52), the odd saying about being "salted with fire" (9:48-49), the strange miracle where Jesus effects healing in two stages (8:22-26), the even stranger miracle where Jesus puts his fingers in a man's ears, spits, and touches his tongue (7:32-37), and the episode where Jesus is regarded as mad and his family attempts to restrain him (3:20-22). If we accept the Griesbach-Farmer hypothesis, we would then have to explain why Mark would choose to add these odd, potentially embarrassing materials, only to omit the Sermon on the Mount/Plain, the Lord's Prayer, and numerous other teachings and parables found in the larger Gospels. (6) The final consideration that adds weight to the probability of Markan priority has to do with the results of the respective hypotheses. The true test of any hypothesis is its effectiveness. In biblical studies a theory should aid the exegetical task. The theory of Markan priority has provided just this kind of aid. Not only has Synoptic interpretation been materially advanced because of the conclusion, and now widespread assumption, of Markan priority, but the development of critical methods oriented to Gospel research, such as form and redaction criticism, which have enjoyed success, has also presupposed Markan priority. In countless studies, whether dealing with this pericope or that, or treating one of the Synoptic Gospels in its entirety, it has been recognized over and over again that Matthew and Luke make the greatest sense as interpretations of Mark; but Mark makes no sense as a conflation and interpretation of Matthew and Luke.

The evidence is compelling that Mark represents the oldest surviving account of Jesus' life, ministry, death, and resurrection. What sources the evangelist Mark made use of, if any, will in all probability remain a mystery. That he made use of some written material seems likely. That he made use of some eyewitness testimony is also probable; it cannot be ruled out. How early this Gospel was written will be considered shortly. But now we must ask what Mark is literarily.

What Is Mark?

Mark is the only Gospel to call itself a "gospel" (see 1:1, "The beginning of the gospel," or "good news"). This word has its origins in Isaiah (see 40:9; 41:27; 52:7; 61:1), but also carried with it important connotations in the Greco-Roman world (see commentary on 1:1-8 below). The genre of Mark is for the most part biography, similar to the biography of Elijah and Elisha in the OT (1 Kings 17–2 Kings 9) or the popular biography found in the Pseudepigrapha (such as *Lives of the Prophets* or *Joseph and Aseneth*). The distinctive features of Mark's biography are the exclusive focus on Jesus and the emphasis on the proclamation of his message. The "good news" has been realized with the appearance of Jesus. Now the story must be told and the message must be proclaimed (see Guelich 1989: xix-xxii).

Mark may be a somewhat novel form of biography (and its novelty has sometimes been exaggerated by scholars), but one must not expect of it what we moderns usually expect of biography. Mark tells us nothing about Jesus' birth and upbringing (details which are partially supplied by Matthew and Luke). The evangelist says absolutely nothing about Jesus himself; not one word describes Jesus' appearance or personality. Apart from his teaching and one or two details, Mark tells nothing of Jesus' habits, likes, dislikes, or interests. The evangelist is principally concerned with Jesus' public ministry, the impact he had on others, and his fate in Jerusalem. But this account is not in a strictly chronological, developmental order. The order is thematic. The stories and teachings are sometimes clustered around common themes. When and where these things happened or were spoken often cannot be determined. The Markan presentation is largely guided by literary and theological interests. Jesus is presented as a remarkable, even stunning figure.

When Mark Wrote and Why

Careful study of Mark 13 (see Hengel 1985: 14-28) and a few related passages suggests that the Gospel of Mark was published in the early stages of the Jewish war with Rome (AD 66-70). Mark 13 begins with Jesus' prediction of the complete and total destruction of the Herodian temple (v. 2). The disciples ask when this will happen (v. 4), and the long discourse that follows describes various signs that will precede the coming of the "Son of Man" (v. 26). Among these signs will be the appearance of various false messiahs and false prophets (vv. 5-6, 21-22) and wars and rumors of war (vv. 7-8). But the major sign that will warn Jesus' followers that the end is near will be the setting up of the "abomination that desolates" the temple (v. 14).

The events of the 40s to 60s correspond in many ways to these signs. But if Mark wrote after 70, as many scholars maintain, then the prediction of the abomination would be unfulfillable. Sensing this problem, some interpreters argue that the abomination was the occupation of the temple precincts by the rebels, or Titus's entry into the sanctuary as it burned. But these proposals do not work. Jesus tells his disciples to flee from Jerusalem when they see the abomination set up. But as it happened, it was too late to flee the city when the rebels occupied the temple precincts, and certainly too late to flee when the Roman army stormed the Temple Mount and General Titus himself entered the sanctuary. Moreover, v. 18 urges believers to pray that this may not happen in winter. But the taking of Jerusalem and the horrors that resulted in fact occurred in the summer. On any fair reading of Mark 13, the actual events of AD 70 do not seem to lie behind these warnings.

It is more probable that Mark 13 reflects the very beginning of the war, possibly even a time shortly before the war began. It is a time of rumors of war, perhaps the early stages of the revolt itself. It reflects a time when various would-be prophets and deliverers proffered signs of salvation. It was a time when Christians believed that the abomination of which Jesus spoke would be set up in the temple, thus making worship there impossible. It would be a time to flee the city, for judgment and the appearance of the Son of Man would be quite near (vv. 14-27).

If the Gospel of Mark was indeed written in the middle 60s, then it was written at a time of severe Christian persecution at the hands of the megalomaniac Nero (ruled AD 54-68). This emperor, increasingly hated and despised by his own people, promoted his deification (which in death was denied by the Senate). More than any emperor before him, he encouraged the use of the honorific titles "god," "son of god," "lord," "savior," and "benefactor." Written in the last two or three years of Nero's life, when the Jewish rebellion was in its early stages, when persecution of Christians was severe, and when many prophets and deliverers were making themselves known, the Markan evangelist puts forward Jesus as the true Son of God, in whom the good news for the world truly has its beginning.

Mark's opening verse makes the Gospel's purpose clear: "The beginning of the good news of Jesus Christ, the Son of God" (1:1). The evangelist has very carefully chosen his language, for it deliberately echoes the language of the imperial ruler cult, as seen in an inscription in honor of Caesar Augustus: "the birthday of the god Augustus was the beginning for the world of the good news" (see commentary below). The evangelist Mark has challenged the imperial myth, claiming that the good news for the world began with Jesus Christ, the true Son of God (see Mark 15:39, where the Roman centurion admits upon seeing the impressive death of Jesus: "Truly this man was the Son of God").

From this extraordinary claim at the beginning of his narrative, to the sudden and dramatic conclusion of the discovery of the empty tomb, the Markan evangelist takes pains to show that Jesus is truly God's Son, despite rejection by the religious authorities of his time and his execution at the hands of the Roman governor. The Julian emperors, whose latest and most unfortunate manifestation at the time of the publication of Mark is the demented Nero, can provide no compelling candidates for recognition as the son of God, whose life and death are truly of benefit to humankind. To the Roman world Mark proffers Jesus and his message of the kingdom of God. By doing so he encourages the faithful to remain steadfast and enjoins the critics and opponents of the Christian faith to reconsider.

COMMENTARY

The Beginning of the "Good News" (1:1-15)

The introduction of Mark's Gospel consists of an incipit, or title (1:1), the citation of OT Scripture (vv. 2-3), a description of the person, preaching, and ministry of John the Baptizer (vv. 4-8), an account of Jesus' baptism, and the declaration of the heavenly voice (vv. 9-11), followed by the time of testing in the wilderness (vv. 12-13), and finally a summary of the substance of Jesus' kingdom proclamation (vv. 14-15). As such this introduction anchors the ministry, death, and resurrection of Jesus to the OT and to the ministry of the popular John the Baptizer, widely regarded as a prophet and martyr. John promises the coming of a "stronger one"; the sudden appearance of Jesus fulfills this promise.

Prologue (1:1-8)

Mark's opening words, "the beginning *(archē)* of the good news *(euangelion)* of Jesus Christ, the Son of God *(huios theou)*," serve more or less as the title of the work as a whole. The entire story of Jesus' ministry, including his death by crucifixion, is "good news" for the world. As the quotation of Isaiah 40 in v. 3 shows, the good news of Jesus is clarified by the Jewish scriptures. But the language of these opening words also recalls the language of the Roman imperial cult, rooted especially in the much revered Caesar Augustus (30 BC–AD 14). The oft-cited Priene inscription (9 BC) is in this instance very significant: "Providence . . . has given us Augustus, whom she filled with virtue that he might benefit humanity, sending him as a savior *(sōtēr)*, both for us and for our descendants, that he might end war and put all things in order. . . . Caesar, by his appearance *(epiphanein)*, excelled our expectations and surpassed all previous benefactors, and not even leaving to posterity any hope of surpassing what he has done . . . the birthday of the god *(theos)* Augustus was the beginning *(archesthai)* for the world of the good news *(euangelia)* that came by reason of him." Anyone acquainted with NT Christology will immediately recognize several important parallels, for the NT writers speak of the *epiphany* of Jesus (2 Thess 2:8; 1 Tim 6:14; 2 Tim 1:10; 4:1, 8; Titus 2:13), the *Savior* of the world (Luke 2:11; John 4:42; Acts 5:31; 13:23; Eph 5:23; Phil 3:20; 2 Tim 1:10; Titus 1:4; 2:13; 3:6; 2 Pet 1:1, 11; 2:20; 3:2, 18; 1 John 4:14).

Mark's language (esp. the words "beginning," "good news," and "Son of God") deliberately echoes the Roman doctrine of the divine emperor. (On its OT antecedents, see the commentary on 1:14-15 below.) In effect, the evangelist is saying to the Roman world: Caesar is neither the beginning of the good news for the world, nor is God's Son; Messiah Jesus is. As such, Mark's opening words directly challenge the Roman emperor cult (see the comments on Mark 15:39 below).

"Just as it is written in Isaiah the prophet" introduces Isa 40:3, but prefaced with Mal 3:1 (and/or Exod 23:20). Isaiah's reference to the "voice of one crying in the wilderness" provides the rationale for John's presence and preaching in the wilderness. The Baptizer's association with the Jordan River, his call for repentance, his promise of the coming of a mightier one, and the appeal to Isa 40:3 place John in the context of the various renewal movements active in the first century. The verse plays an important part in Qumran's *Community Rule* (1QS 8:12-14; 9:19-20), a work which anticipates Israel's renewal and restoration (see Marcus 1992: 12-47). One is also reminded of Theudas who during the administration of Fadus (AD 44-46) persuaded many to take up their possessions and follow him to the Jordan River. He claimed to be a prophet and that at his command the river would be parted, providing easy passage (Josephus *Ant.* 20.5.1 §§97-98). Evidently Theudas saw himself as a Joshua figure, probably as the promised prophet like Moses (Deut 18:15-19). Crossing the Jordan River was but a prelude to a new conquest of the promised land and a restoration of a theocracy based on the laws of Moses. John's presence at this river appeals to Isa 40:3 (linked to Mal 3:1), and the promise of the coming of a mighty one seems related to the hopes expressed by Qumran, Theudas, and others. The mighty one of John's expectations will baptize people "with the Holy Spirit."

Baptism of Jesus (1:9-11)

It is against the backdrop of John's wilderness preaching and baptizing that Jesus makes his appearance. He is part of the crowds that have gone to the Jordan to be baptized by John. But when Jesus comes up from the water, "he sees heaven torn apart and the Spirit as a dove descending upon him." Then a voice from heaven is heard, "You are my beloved Son; in you I am well pleased." This event sets Jesus apart from all others. It is also makes it clear that he should be identified as John's expected "mighty one" who will baptize "with the Holy Spirit."

The tearing apart of heaven and the descent of the Spirit may have been understood as a fulfillment of the prophet's prayer that God "tear apart the heavens and come down" (Isa 63:19 [Eng. 64:1]; cf. 1 Cor 2:9, where Paul applies Isa 64:4 to the revelatory work of the Holy Spirit). There is also an important parallel in the *Testaments of the Twelve Patriarchs:* "The heavens will be opened . . . and the spirit of understanding and sanctification shall rest upon him" (*T. Levi* 18:6-7). The significance of this parallel is seen in its eschatological perspective.

The descent of the Spirit "as a dove" implies that the Spirit was visible to Jesus. But it is not clear why the Spirit is said to have appeared as a dove. The suggestion that it is meant to recall the dove sent out by Noah, after the flood waters had begun to abate (Gen 8:8-12), is not persuasive.

The reference to Jesus as the "beloved Son" probably echoes Ps 2:7 ("You are my son"). The adjective "beloved" may reflect the Aramaic tradition, as preserved the *Tg.* Ps 2:7 ("You are as beloved to me as a son is to a father"), but this targum is quite late. Perhaps God's address to Jesus is meant to recall God's command to Abraham, to sacrifice his "beloved son" Isaac (LXX Gen 22:2).

The heavenly voice confirms Jesus as the "mighty one" of whom John the Baptist had preached. No greater attestation could be expected. God himself had spoken. The mighty one, upon whom the Spirit of God had descended, was now ready to be tested by God's adversary.

Temptation of Jesus (1:12-13)

Quite abruptly Mark tells us that "the Spirit drove [Jesus] out into the wilderness," where he was for forty days "being tested *(peirazein)* by Satan." The evangelist's choice of words is curious, for "drive out" *(ekballein)* is frequently used to describe the casting out of demons (cf. Mark 1:34, 39; 3:15, 22, 23; 6:13; 7:26; 9:18, 28, 38). It is not surprising, therefore, that both Matthew (4:1) and Luke (4:1) replace "drive out" with "lead." The Markan evangelist may have wished to emphasize the power of the Spirit. That is, when the Spirit moves, dramatic things happen. Just as the Spirit drives Jesus out into the wilderness, so during the ministry of Jesus the Spirit drives demons out of people.

Satan's temptation of Jesus may recall the temptation Abraham faced, when God commanded him to sacrifice his son Isaac (LXX Gen 22:1: "God tested *(peirazein)* Abraham and said to him . . ."). But the Genesis story, at least as it is preserved in the Hebrew and in the Greek (i.e., the LXX), says nothing about Satan. However, in later Jewish interpretation, Satan is understood as the motivating force behind the temptation. According to *Jubilees* (2d cent. BC), "Prince Mastema" (i.e., Satan) urges God to put Abraham to the test, to see if he is truly faithful (17:16; 18:12; the same interpretive tradition reappears in the late rabbinical writing *Pirqe de Rabbi Eliezer*). This interpretive tradition was probably inspired by the story of Satan's testing of Job.

Thus the heavenly voice, "You are my beloved Son" (1:11), probably represents a deliberate allusion to Ps 2:7 and Gen 22:1. The first OT passage links Jesus to the anointed figure of Psalm 2 who is said to be God's son, while the second passage prepares for the testing of the beloved son at the instigation of Satan, much as a similar test had been thrust upon Abraham with regard to his beloved son Isaac. The descent of the Spirit and the utterance of the divine voice which has alluded to Ps 2:7 imply Jesus' messianic identification (in that he has been anointed), which the evangelist asserted in the opening verse ("Jesus Christ").

Satan (from Hebrew, meaning "adversary" or "opponent") elsewhere in Mark is called "Beelzebul" (cf. 3:22). The "wild animals" may be part of an Adam-paradise typology, as some commentators have suggested. But they may also be part of the wilderness backdrop, perhaps even as Satan's allies (Ezek 34:5, 8, 25; *T. Naph.* 8:4 ["the devil will flee from you; wild animals will be afraid of you"]; *T. Benj.* 5:2; see the comment on 1:21-28 below). Mark's point may have been to underscore the dangers Jesus faced during his stay in the wilderness. Jesus encountered dangers from the spiritual world and from the natural world (cf. Daniel in the lion's den; Dan 6:1-28). The reference, "forty days," recalls a favorite temporal designation in biblical literature. Especially relevant is Elijah's forty-day fast (1 Kgs 19:4-8). The food that enabled the famous prophet to be sustained for so long was provided by an angel. This is probably the background against which we should understand Mark's statement that "angels were ministering to him." Thus, with angelic assistance — whose presence adds further corroboration of his divine approval — Jesus survives his natural and supernatural testings.

The Proclamation of the Kingdom (1:14-15)

With his arrest John's public ministry has come to an end. With his (implied) successful completion of the period of testing Jesus' public ministry may commence. We were told in 1:7 that John was preaching in the wilderness near the Jordan; now we are told in v. 14 that Jesus was preaching "God's good news" in Galilee. Whereas John had offered a "baptism of repentance for the forgiveness of sins" (v. 4) and had proclaimed the coming of a mightier one who would baptize with fire (vv. 7-8), Jesus now proclaims that "the time is fulfilled and the kingdom of God has come near. Repent, and trust the good news" (v. 15). The call for repentance continues an important aspect of John's message and mission. But the proclamation of the "kingdom of God" is new. How did Jesus understand the kingdom?

The Greek word "gospel" *(euangelion)* in earliest Christianity in all probability derives from Isaiah (Heb. *basar*) and not from Greco-Roman usage (though later the parallel would be exploited; cf. comments on Mark 1:1 above). Isaiah 40, 52, and 61 contributed to the substance and manner of Jesus' preaching and teaching (Matt 11:2-6 = Luke 4:16-30; 7:18-23). Isaiah had promised the good news of God's reign (52:7: "Your God reigns!"; *Tg. Isa* 52:7: "the kingdom of your God is revealed"; cf. *Tg. Isa* 40:9), which Jesus now proclaims (Mark 1:15: "the kingdom of God has come near"). The "gospel," or good news, is that the promised and awaited kingdom of God is now at hand.

Mark's use of the word *euangelion* is somewhat curious. It occurs only seven times; three times in ch. 1 (vv. 1, 14, 15), then four times in the second half of the Gospel (8:35; 10:29; 13:10; 14:9). An eighth occurrence is found at 16:15, in what is a later, secondary ending (see commentary on 16:9-20 below). All of these occurrences appear to reflect early Christianity's description of the essence of Jesus' message and later the essence of its preaching about Jesus himself. But it would be unwarranted to infer from this that Jesus did not think of his proclamation as constituting the good news of God's reign, as promised in Isaiah. Jesus' use of the Isaianic tradition, especially 52:7 and 61:1-2, and the coherence with the Aramaic diction, as seen in the Isaiah targum, are strong indications that from earliest times the proclamation of the kingdom (or reign) of God as "good news" originated with Jesus and became standard and ubiquitous in the Christian community.

If we follow the lead of the targum, then we should understand the kingdom of God as a way of speaking of the presence and reign of God. The clearest indication of this is seen in Synoptic traditions outside of Mark, where Jesus says, "If by the finger of God I cast out demons, the kingdom of God has come upon you" (Luke 11:20). Mark, however, displays only modest interest in the kingdom. More often than not, references to the kingdom have more to do with membership and who may enter the kingdom and who may not and why. For Mark, Christology is paramount. Recognizing Jesus' messianic identity and divine sonship is more important than emphasizing the kingdom.

A New Message (1:16–3:12)

This is the first major section in Mark's Gospel. It consists of Jesus' first call of disciples (1:16-20), the casting out of a demon and the onlookers' amazement at this "new teaching" (1:21-28), the healing of Simon's mother-in-law (1:29-31), the gathering of the first crowd hoping for healing (1:32-34), the departure to minister elsewhere in Galilee (1:35-39), the cleansing of a leper (1:40-45), the healing of the paralyzed man (2:1-12), the call of Levi and eating with sinners (2:13-17), the question about fasting (2:18-22), controversy over picking grain on the sabbath (2:23-28), controversy over healing on the sabbath (3:1-6), and a summary report of more healing and exorcising (3:7-12). The section acquaints the reader with Jesus' power and his magnetism. Wherever he goes, he attracts ever larger crowds. Although not identified or acknowledged by the crowds, the evil spirits know who Jesus is and they fear him.

Call of the Disciples (1:16-20)

Jesus calls his first disciples, though they will not be referred to as disciples until 2:15. There are several features about this story that are odd: (1) The call is abrupt. Why does Jesus call Simon and his brother Andrew, then later James and John? (2) What does the odd saying mean, "I will make you fishers of people"? (3) Why do these fishermen drop every thing and follow Jesus? These features evidently troubled the Lukan evangelist, who prepares for the call by telling of Jesus' teaching and the miraculous catch of fish (Luke 5:1-11). The odd saying about fishing for people is omitted.

Mark may have wished to impress upon his readers the authority of Jesus. When he extends a summons, people jump. Little or no ceremony is required. Most impressive is the comment that James and John "left their father Zebedee in the boat with the hired servants, and followed him" (1:20). The mention of the hired servants may have been meant to imply that Zebedee had no more sons; only paid workers remained. Given the values of Jewish culture, where sons were expected to assist and even support their parents, the departure of James and John to follow Jesus would strike most as bordering on irresponsibility, even disrespect. (Such criticism may be hinted at in the saying in 10:29-30.) But for Mark it once again shows the authority of Jesus.

The epithet "fishers of people" is a clever turn-of-phrase that unquestionably originated with Jesus but was not picked up and put to use by Christians in the early church. Prior to meeting Jesus, the principal occupation of these men had been the catching of fish. They have now been called to catch people, by which is probably meant bringing people into the kingdom of God, whose time has come. A parallel from *Joseph and Aseneth* is apropos: "By his [Joseph's] beauty he caught me, and by his wisdom he grasped me like a fish on a hook, and by his spirit, as by bait of life, he ensnared me" (21:21).

We should not assume that these fishermen were simple, ignorant folk. The fishing industry in Galilee was prosperous. Zebedee evidently was doing well enough that he could afford to hire workers. The Hellenistic names of Simon (later called Peter) and Andrew, moreover, points to the Hellenizing of Galilee. Far from a backwater, Galilee was a cosmopolitan center of trade and commerce. Disparaging remarks about Jesus' Galilean disciples (Mark 14:70; John 7:52; Acts 4:13) had more to do with their lack of formal religious training and to misgivings about the "orthodoxy" of the more worldly setting of Galilee.

Mark's "Sea of Galilee" is a colloquialism. This body of water is a lake, not a sea. Luke provides the correct name when he calls it Lake Gennesaret (Luke 5:1). The lake lies between Galilee to the west and Gaulanitis to the east. The Jordan empties into the lake at its north end and issues forth at its south end. The lake was ringed by several small towns and cities, many of which (such as Capernaum) were visited or occupied by Jesus and his disciples.

Exorcism of an Unclean Spirit (1:21-28)

Having withstood Satan's testings in the wilderness (1:12-13), Jesus is now in a position to launch his offensive against Satan's kingdom. By casting out unclean spirits Jesus begins to do serious damage to Satan's domain and to clear the way for the kingdom of God. The linkage between the appearance of God's kingdom and the destruction of Satan is seen in a pseudepigraphon probably penned in the early part of the first century AD: "Then [God's] kingdom will appear throughout his whole creation. Then the devil will have an end. . . . For the heavenly One will arise from his kingly throne" (*T. Moses* 10:1, 3).

The statement that Jesus "went into Capernaum" and "on the sabbath entered the synagogue and taught" (1:21) leaves one with the impression that this was Jesus' custom (cf. Luke 4:15-16). The reference to the spread of his fame "everywhere throughout all the surrounding region of Galilee" (v. 28) and the absence of even a hint of opposition, at least at this point in Mark's narrative, suggest that Jesus freely taught in the synagogue of Capernaum (whose ruins are probably those now exposed beneath the grander ruins of the third-century synagogue which stands above) and perhaps in other synagogues of Galilee.

Mark likes to portray Jesus as a teacher. Twelve times Jesus is called "teacher" *(didaskalos),* five times his "teaching" *(didachē)* is referred to, and fifteen times, in reference to Jesus, Mark uses the verb "to teach" *(didaskein).* What is of interest here is the crowd's description of Jesus' power to exorcise as a "new teaching" (1:27). This teaching is so powerful that Jesus is able to command the unclean spirits, and they, although unwilling, obey him.

Jesus is confronted by a "man with an unclean spirit *(pneuma akatharton)*" (1:23, 26). In the NT world unclean spirits were understood as demons (Mark 1:34 passim), who were numbered among the evil forces of Satan, who himself was called Belial or Beliar (1QH 2:16; 1QM 1:1; 2 Cor 6:15) or Beelzebul (Mark 3:22). In the literature of this period we find mention of "spirits of Belial" (CD 12:2), "spirits of wickedness" (1QM 15:14; 1QH frag. 5, line 4), and "spirits of error" (1QH frag. 5, line 6; 1QS 4:20). In the *Psalms Scroll* from Qumran someone prays: "Let not Satan rule over me, nor an unclean spirit" (11QPs[a] 19:15). A close Greek parallel to the wording in our passage in Mark is found in the *Testaments of the Twelve Patriarchs:* "If you continue to do good, even the unclean spirits *(ta akatharta pneumata)* will flee from you, and wild animals *(thēria)* will fear you" (*T. Benj.* 5:2); "the devil *(ho diabolos)* will flee from you; wild animals *(thēria)* will be afraid of you" (*T. Naph.* 8:4). We should recall that when Satan tested him in the wilderness, Jesus was with *thēria* (indeed, according to *T. Naph.* 8:6, over the evildoer "every wild animal *[thērion]* will dominate").

The unclean spirit's address to Jesus is a challenge. The spirit suspects that Jesus has come to destroy *them* (note the plural "us" in 1:24). "I know who you are" probably should be understood as the spirit's attempt to gain control over, or at least fend off Jesus. The spirit knows that he is Jesus of Nazareth and knows that he is the "holy one of God." In antiquity it was believed that to possess someone's name was an advantage. In supernatural dealings, to know the name was necessary if one was to manipulate a spirit or god. Jesus, however, rebukes the spirit, commands it to be silent, and orders it to depart. (It is also possible that the evil spirit's words do not constitute a challenge, but acknowledgment and surrender.) An inscription in Egypt, dating as early as the sixth century BC, has a demon through his host speak to the exorcist: "You come in peace, great God, destroyer of the evil ones. . . . I am your servant; I will depart to the land from which I came . . ." (Bentresch Stele).

Jesus' command, "Come out of him" (1:25), finds an exact parallel in the papyri concerned with exorcisms (e.g., Paris Magical Papyrus 3013; cf. Deissmann, *Light,* 256). Josephus (*Ant.* 8.2.5 §§46-49) and other authors of antiquity describe the activities of various exorcists (e.g., Philostratus *Vita Ap.* 4.20). The *Genesis Apocryphon* of Qumran describes Abram laying hands on Pharaoh's head with the result that an evil spirit is removed (1QapGen 20:28-29). Lucian of Samosata (second century AD) relates what he was told when the exorcist interrogates the possessed person: "The patient himself is silent, but the spirit answers in Greek or in the language of whatever foreign country he comes from, telling how and whence he entered into the man; whereupon, by adjuring the spirit and if he does not obey, threatening him, he drives him out. Indeed, I actually saw one coming out, black and smoky in color" (*The Lover of Lies* 16).

This is the only place in Mark where Jesus is called the "holy one" *(hagios).* The soon-to-be-conceived Jesus is called "holy, Son of God" in Luke's infancy story (Luke 1:35). Luke repeats the epithet in his parallel to Mark's account (Luke 4:34). In the Fourth Gospel the disciples confess that Jesus is the "holy one of God" (John 6:69). Before the religious rulers Peter calls Jesus the "holy and righteous one" (Acts 3:14). Later, the first Christians speak of the "holy child Jesus," whom God "anointed" (Acts 4:27). But it is not clear that "holy one" is a messianic designation (as some have argued). In the OT Aaron (LXX Ps 105:16), Elisha (LXX 2 Kgs 4:9), and Samson (LXX B Judg 16:17) are called *hagios.* In LXX A Judg 13:5, 7 and 16:17, however, the word for holy is *naziraios,* which transliterates the underlying Heb. *nazir.* The epithet may originally have been a play on words in Hebrew: "You are Jesus the Nazarene *(naṣri)* . . . the holy one *(nazir).*"

The crowd is astounded by Jesus' authority *(exousia),* or "new teaching" (1:27). Unlike other exorcists who cast out demons through incantations and rigmarole (e.g., Josephus *Ant.* 8.2.5 §§46-49), Jesus speaks and the evil spirit obeys. For Mark this is the main point of the story. Recognized by God and empowered by the Spirit, Jesus possesses authority on an order not before witnessed. He is authorized to proclaim the good news of the kingdom (vv. 14-15), to call followers (vv. 16-20), and to make war on Satan (vv. 21-28).

Healing of Simon's Mother-in-Law (1:29-31)

Jesus' effective ministry continues, even after retiring from public view. In the home of Simon and Andrew, Jesus is told that Simon's mother-in-law suffers from fever.

He takes her by the hand, lifts her up, and the fever departs. So effective is the cure that the woman is able to serve Jesus and his disciples dinner. In one rabbinic tradition healing someone with a fever was considered a greater miracle (because it is heaven sent) than the miracle of the three men who survived the ordeal of the furnace (because the fire was man-made): "who can extinguish" a fever? (*b. Ned.* 41a).

Luke's version, "he rebuked the fever" (Luke 4:39), could imply that the fever was thought to have been of demonic origin. The healing of Simon's mother-in-law, then, may have been viewed as an exorcism as much as a healing.

Healing Summary (1:32-34)

So impressive was Jesus' ministry of healing that even at sundown people brought the sick and demonized to Jesus. Indeed, Mark tells us that the "whole city was gathered together about the door." And, as in his encounter with the unclean spirit in 1:21-28, Jesus was able to cast out the demons and would not permit them to speak, because they recognized him. We are not to suppose that Jesus is trying to keep his identity a secret; rather, we should understand that Jesus shows the evil spirits no quarter. He does not wrangle or bargain with them. In effect Jesus is commanding them: "Shut up and get out!" This is the first mention of "demon" *(daimonion)* in Mark. These evil beings will be mentioned several more times (3:15, 22; 6:13; 7:26, 29, 30; 9:38; and 16:9, 17 in the secondary, long ending of Mark). On the association of exorcism, healing, and forgiveness of sins, see 4QPrNab *(Prayer of Nabonidus)*: "I was afflicted with an evil ulcer for seven years . . . and an exorcist pardoned my sins" (4Q242 2-4).

An Itinerant Ministry (1:35-39)

A busy and demanding day and evening notwithstanding, Jesus arises early in the morning and seeks a private place where he might pray. No specific purpose is given for Jesus' prayer that morning in Capernaum. We may assume that early morning prayers were his custom. This is the first reference in Mark to Jesus praying. A few other times of prayer are mentioned. After feeding the five thousand he prays on the mountain (6:46). Later he tells his disciples that certain evil spirits cannot be cast out except through prayer and fasting (9:49). When in Jerusalem Jesus will instruct his disciples on faith and prayer (11:22-25). In the eschatological discourse he enjoins the disciples to pray that the period of tribulation may not overtake them in winter (13:18). And, of course, Jesus prays in the Garden of Gethsemane only a short time before his arrest (14:32-39).

Simon and others "pursue" *(diōkein)* Jesus because "every one" is searching for him. Jesus, however, wants to go to other towns where he might preach. He explains to his disciples, "that is the reason why I came out" (1:38). He does not mean that that is the reason why he came out of the house, but rather that that is the reason why he "came out" from God and began his public ministry. Jesus' desire to preach throughout Israel (Mark 6:7-13) is why he chooses to move on. He does not want to be detained indefinitely in Capernaum. A second reason may have been a desire to remove himself from a growing crowd of enthusiasts.

Cleansing of a Leper (1:40-45)

The next person to request healing from Jesus is a man afflicted with leprosy. The stigma attached to the disease is well known, often being viewed as a judgment from God (e.g., Num 12:10; 2 Kgs 5:27; 15:5; 2 Chr 26:19; but in nonbiblical sources as well, e.g., Herodotus *Hist.* 1.138: "The citizen who has leprosy or the white sickness may not come into a town or consort with other Persians. They say that he is so afflicted because he has sinned in some wise against the sun"). Many skin ailments were called "leprosy" in late antiquity; not all were actual cases of the dreaded disease. Most manuscripts read "moved to pity" *(splanchnistheis)*, but a few read "being angry" *(orgistheis)*. If the first reading is accepted, then no explanation is required. But if the second reading is accepted (and Guelich 1989: 71-72, among others, thinks it is the original reading), then we must ask what the anger means. Is Jesus angry because of the impertinence of the leper, a man who should keep his distance? Probably not, for this stands in tension to Jesus' willingness to touch the leper and heal him. A better explanation is that Jesus was moved to anger by yet one more instance of human suffering, possibly thought to have been brought on by Satan. Angered by the man's pitiful condition and the estrangement from Israel's worship that it entailed, Jesus touches the man and heals him.

Quite apart from the question of whether Jesus was moved to pity or moved to anger, his willingness to touch the leper is remarkable. It reflects Jesus' awareness of his power to heal and that this power derives from the Holy Spirit. If the *Holy* Spirit effects healing, then cleansing indeed has occurred and no defilement can possibly have been transferred to the healer.

Two papyrus fragments preserve an interesting version of the healing of the leper: "[32]And [be]hold a leper draw[ing near to him] [33]says: 'Teacher Jesus, wandering with lep[ers] [34]and eatin[g with them] [35]in the inn, I also con[tracted leprosy]. [36]If then [you will it], [37]I shall be cleansed.' Immediately the Lord [said to him]: [38]'[I] will it; be cleansed.' [And immediately] [39]the lep[rosy de]parted from him. [40]But [said] Jesus to him, 'Go, show [41]yourself to th[e priests.] [42a]and offer for [43a][pur]ification, as Moses com[manded, and] [44a]sin no longer'" (*P. Egerton* 2 [frag. 1 recto, lines 32-41] + *P. Köln* 22 [for lines 42a-44a]).

Jesus' command that the healed man "show" himself "to the priest" complies with the requirements of Leviticus 13–14, where a person whose leprous condition has cleared up must be examined by a priest before he can reenter Jewish life without restrictions. Jesus' final words, "for a proof to the people" (v. 44), are suggestive. Proof of what? Proof that Jesus really healed the leper? Perhaps. But given the association that leprosy has with messianic healing activity (as seen in Matt 11:5 = Luke 7:22), it may be that the healed leper is proof that the Messiah, the one anointed to proclaim the kingdom, the era of God's favor (see Luke 4:16-30, where Jesus cites Isa 61:1-2 and appeals to the example of Elisha, who healed the leper), has indeed appeared on the scene and that God's kingdom power is now at work.

The command to "say nothing to anyone" in context may mean that the healed man is not to claim that he has been cleansed until he has been officially declared clean by a priest. It may also be another attempt by Jesus to quell counterproductive publicity. His avoidance of such publicity is seen in his later refusal to perform a sign in response to the demands of some Pharisees (see commentary on 8:11-12). Such injunctions to silence notwithstanding, Jesus' fame spreads everywhere.

Healing of the Paralytic (2:1-12)

When Jesus returns to Capernaum the crowds once again gather. We are told that he was "at home" (2:1). Whose home was it? Jesus grew up in Nazareth, several miles to the southwest. But Nazareth seems not to have been his base of operations (see commentary on 6:1-6a below). Jesus' home (or headquarters) evidently was in Capernaum, but whether it was his home or the home of one of his followers cannot be determined. (Given Jesus' itinerant ministry and the probability that he had no wife or children, the house was probably not his.)

As in his earlier experience in Capernaum (1:32-33, 37), Jesus once again draws large numbers of people with the result that the house in which he was staying no longer had "room for them, not even about the door" (2:2). This detail makes it clear why it was necessary for the four men to lower their paralyzed companion down through the roof of the house. On this occasion, we are not told that Jesus was casting out demons or healing anyone. We are told that "he was preaching the word to them" (v. 2). Jesus' message is called "the word" *(ho logos)* in the explanation of the parable of the sower (4:14-20), and in later Christian preaching comes to be equated with the message of the gospel (Acts 6:4; Gal 6:6; Col 4:3). Here in Mark 2:2 the word refers to Jesus' proclamation of the kingdom of God (1:14-15).

Because of the crowd the paralyzed man, lying on his pallet, is lowered through the roof (v. 4). In what sense does Jesus "see their faith" (v. 5)? In the other healing stories in Mark where faith is mentioned (5:25-34; 5:21-24, 35-43; 10:46-52) we read of people who overcome obstacles or in some sense take pains to approach Jesus. The episode of the paralyzed man fits this pattern and in fact is the first example of it. What is the object of their faith? Given the context, where the preaching of the word is mentioned, we should probably assume that their faith consists of belief in the message that Jesus proclaims. Of course, belief in the message entails belief in the messenger. But we should not read into their faith an element of Christology (i.e., that Jesus is God's Son, Israel's Messiah, or the Savior of the world). Rather, they believe that the kingdom of God approaches and that the proclaimer of the kingdom is able to make the presence of the awaited kingdom felt in tangible ways. Jesus had blessed others with healing; surely, they reason, he can heal their paralyzed friend.

The surprise in the story comes when Jesus does not simply heal the man, but pronounces his sins forgiven (v. 5: "Your sins are forgiven"). Some scribes (Luke 5:21 adds "and Pharisees") witness the event and, hearing Jesus' words, regard it as "blasphemy." They reason, "Who can forgive sins but God alone?" (v. 7). Why do the scribes think this? To answer this question, we must ask in what sense Jesus has forgiven this man's sins. Is his pronouncement an instance of the divine passive? If so, Jesus is saying, "Your sins are forgiven [by God]." But in this case, the scribes should be accusing Jesus of presumption, for assuming priestly prerogatives (e.g., "Who does this man think he is? A priest?"). Or is his pronouncement based on his own authority, in which case the scribes' thoughts of blasphemy are better founded. The answer is suggested by v. 10, where Jesus says that "the Son of Man has authority on earth to forgive sins." The self-designation "Son of Man" and the qualifier "on earth" point to Daniel 7, where a human ("one like a son of man"), coming with the clouds of heaven, approaches God (the "Ancient of Days") and receives authority (Dan 7:9-14). The "clouds of heaven" are antithetical to "on earth," with the latter presupposing the former. That is to say, because the "Son of Man" receives authority from heaven, he possesses authority on earth, among other things, to forgive sins. Only twice in Mark is Jesus accused of blasphemy, and both times Jesus identifies himself as the "Son of Man." The other passage is found in the hearing before Caiaphas the high priest. Jesus declares that he is the "Son of Man" who will be "seated at the right hand of Power, and coming with the clouds of heaven" (14:62). Caiaphas reacts in horror and calls the statement blasphemy (14:64; see the commentary on 14:53-65 below). As the human being described in Daniel 7, the human being to whom divine authority is granted, Jesus has authority to forgive sins, or, in the case of someone like Caiaphas, he has the authority to sit in judgment. Jesus has not claimed to be God (if he had, the scribes would have reacted much more violently); he has claimed to be God's vice-regent on earth, proclaiming God's rule and offering forgiveness to those who respond in faith to the proclamation.

The link between sin and sickness, forgiveness and restoration of health, is well illustrated in a later rabbinic saying: "A sick man does not recover from his sickness until all his sins are forgiven him, as it is written, 'Who forgives all your iniquities; who heals all your diseases' [Ps 103:3]" (*b. Ned.* 41a).

It is also worth noting that in the Aramaic paraphrase of Isaiah (i.e., the Targum) the suffering servant of Isa 52:13–53:12 is understood in messianic terms as one through whom Israel's sins can be forgiven. A few phrases are instructive: ". . . in that we attach ourselves to his words our sins will be forgiven us . . . before the Lord it was a pleasure to forgive the sins of us all for his sake . . . he shall beseech concerning their sins . . . yet he will beseech concerning the sins of many, and to the rebels it shall be forgiven for him" (*Tg. Isa* 53:5, 6, 11, 12).

To defend his claim that he truly does possess divine authority to forgive sins, Jesus asks his critics: "Which is easier, to say to the paralyzed man, 'Your sins are forgiven,' or to say, 'Rise, take up your pallet, and walk?'" (2:9). The word of healing is harder because it can be verified; the word of forgiveness is easier because it cannot be verified. Therefore, to prove that he really can do the easier (i.e., forgive the man's sins) he does the harder (i.e., heal the man's paralysis). Jesus commands the paralyzed man to rise, take up his pallet, and go home (v. 11). He does so, and everyone is astounded and glorifies God (v. 12). This response stands in stark contrast to the grousing of the scribes only moments earlier. "We never saw anything like this!" No, they had not, because the authorized Son of Man had never before been among them.

Call of Levi (2:13-17)

The attraction of Jesus and his teaching continue in evidence, as once again Mark tells us that "all the crowd gathered about him" (2:13). Whether in someone's house or, as in this instance, outdoors beside the Sea of Galilee, crowds follow Jesus and he teaches them.

The call of Levi (= Matthew in Matt 9:9) the son of Alphaeus, evidently a tax (or toll) collector (2:14), sets the stage for the important scene that follows. Jesus and his disciples join Levi for supper ("Levi made him a great feast" in Luke 5:29), along with "many tax collectors and sinners" (v. 15). Tax collectors (who collect tolls, not just taxes on goods and revenues) and "sinners" were regarded as non-Torah-observant persons. Many of them probably were non-observant. Not only did they fail to live up to the written commands of Moses but they failed to observe many of the oral traditions, which to Pharisaic scribes were so important.

Some "scribes of the Pharisees" observe Jesus and his disciples eating with these people and object, "Why does he eat with tax collectors and sinners?" (2:16). Whether or not we are to understand these scribes as the same ones who objected to Jesus' pronouncement of forgiveness in 2:1-12, we cannot be sure. Many of Mark's first readers would probably have assumed so. Here they object to Jesus' eating with non-Torah-observant Jews, because as a religious teacher Jesus would have been expected to avoid ritual impurity. By eating with non-observant people Jesus ran the risk of eating food that failed to meet the requirements of the food laws (especially as understood by Pharisees) and of coming into contact with impure persons (e.g., improperly washed hands and other aspects of uncleanness). The scribes may also have registered their objections out of consideration for Jesus' message and ministry (to which they probably attached some importance, at least initially). If Jesus really were the herald of the approaching kingdom of God, to which some or all of these scribes would have been sympathetic, then one should expect his standards of purity to be exemplary. Why then does he eat with such people?

In response to these criticisms Jesus compares himself to a physician: doctors are sent to the sick, not to the healthy. Jesus' comparison has its counterparts in the Greco-Roman world. One is reminded of the story about the philosopher Antisthenes: "One day when he was censured for keeping company with evil men, the reply was made, 'Well, physicians are in attendance on their patients without getting the fever themselves'" (Diogenes Laertius *Lives of the Philosophers,* "Antisthenes," 6.6). Accordingly, Jesus "came not to call the righteous but sinners" (2:17). It is important to note that Jesus does indeed regard these people as sinners. He does not take their sin lightly. He summons sinners to repentance and admonishes Torah-observant Jews to appreciate his mission.

Question of Fasting (2:18-22)

It was not unusual for religious teachers and their disciples to fast (Matt 6:16-18; Luke 18:12). According to Matthew, Jesus fasted during his forty days in the wilderness (Matt 4:2). Fasting is usually observed at times of repentance (Judg 20:26; 1 Sam 7:6; 1 Kgs 21:27; Ezra 8:21, 23; Neh 9:1; Jonah 3:5) or in times of mourning (1 Sam 31:13; 2 Sam 1:12; Neh 1:4), in times of great distress (2 Sam 12:16, 21, 22, 23; Esth 4:3), or in preparation for a time of trial or special mission (Esth 4:16; Dan 9:3; Matt 17:21; Acts 13:2, 3; 14:23; 27:33). It was self-effacing and self-humiliating, the antithesis to pride and presumption (or at least it was supposed to be).

People wonder why it is that Jesus' disciples do not fast (a sign of religious fervor, spiritual humility, and preparation for religious work) when the disciples of John and the disciples of the Pharisees fast. The question is not necessarily critical. But the lack of fasting on the part of Jesus' disciples is viewed as exceptional and in need of explanation.

Jesus' figurative reply, "Can the wedding guests fast while the bridegroom is with them?" (2:19), implies that his presence is a cause for celebration. The same idea is present in the comparison Jesus makes between John's earlier ministry and his own: "John came neither eating nor drinking, and they say, 'He has a demon'; the Son of Man came eating and drinking, and they say, 'Behold, a glutton and a drunkard, a friend of tax collectors and sinners!'" (Matt 11:18-19 = Luke 7:33-34). The wedding celebration is consistent with some of the imagery of Jewish eschatological hopes. Jesus' implied self-identification as the "bridegroom" coheres with his earlier and later self-identification as the "son of man" of Daniel 7. While he is present, announcing the good news of the kingdom of God and extending forgiveness and salvation to Israel, there can be no mourning. When he suffers and is taken from his disciples, then there will be mourning and fasting. (On Jesus as the suffering Son of Man, see comments on 10:45 below.)

Jesus illustrates his point with two more figures of speech. Both figures (old and new cloth; old and new wineskins) underscore the incompatibility of the (old) age of John and the (new) age of Jesus. Up to the close of John's preaching, it was an era of mourning, fasting, and preparation. With the presence of Jesus, it is now an era of celebration. Jesus' conduct (no fasting; rather, eating and drinking with sinners) cannot be made to fit within the context of the Baptist's earlier ministry of austerity, any more than a new piece of cloth can repair an old garment, or new wine can be placed in old wineskins.

In 2:1-12 Jesus is questioned for assuming the authority to forgive sins. In vv. 15-17 he is questioned for assuming the liberty to eat with non-Torah-observant people. Now in vv. 18-22 Jesus is questioned for not requiring his disciples to fast. Common to all three of these challenges and the replies given them is the unique authority of Jesus. He is that man (i.e., the "son of man" of Daniel 7) to whom heavenly authority has been given. He may pronounce the forgiveness of sins. He may seek out sinners and eat with them without himself becoming impure. And now his presence is so special that fasting would be inappropriate; fasting should take place only in his absence.

Picking Grain on the Sabbath (2:23-28)

This passage and the one that immediately follows it (3:1-6) involve controversy over what is permitted on the sabbath. The other references to the sabbath in Mark are innocuous (1:21; 6:2; 15:42; 16:1). Luke alone relates the healing of an infirm woman on the sabbath, which also provokes controversy (Luke 13:10-17); likewise the healing of the man with dropsy (Luke 14:1-6). The Fourth Gospel relates two other sabbath healings (John 5, 9), both of which aroused sharp criticism of Jesus. Mark 2:23-28 is also the third consecutive passage to touch on various aspects of eating. In vv. 15-17 controversy erupts over Jesus' eating with sinners, while in vv. 18-22 people wonder why the disciples of Jesus do not fast.

Of all these sabbath controversy stories Mark 2:23-28 is unique in that it does not involve a healing. The disciples of Jesus pluck heads of grain and eat them. The charge that they are doing something not permitted on the sabbath has nothing to do with theft (and we assume that the fields through which they passed were not their own), for this sort of gleaning was permitted in the law (Deut 23:25). The charge has to do with "reaping," that is, working on the sabbath (Exod 20:10; 34:21; Deut 5:14), at least according to oral tradition (e.g., *m. Shab.* 7:2; CD 10:14–11:18).

Jesus counters the criticism with an example from the life of David, at a time of disenfranchisement and hardship. David and his men entered the house of God and ate the bread of the Presence (1 Sam 21:1-6), which was supposed to be eaten by the priests only (Lev 24:5-9). The comparison is an important one, and it may provide evidence that Jesus did indeed see himself in Davidic terms. The logic of Jesus' reply suggests that the Pharisees can no more criticize his disciples who gleaned and ate on the sabbath than they can criticize David and his men who ate the consecrated bread of the Presence.

Jesus counters his critics with a second argument: "The sabbath was made for humankind, not humankind for the sabbath" (2:27). Jesus' appeal is to creation (Gen 2:1-3; Exod 31:12-17). The sabbath was recognized as a day of rest and refreshment, not as a burden and time of denial. A remarkable parallel appears in an early rabbinic midrash: "The sabbath is given over to you, not you to the sabbath" (*Mek.* on Exod 31:13). Jesus may have been alluding to a similar interpretation, or, as one Jewish interpreter has thought, the midrash in this instance echoes Jesus' words, though anonymously. (For other Jewish parallels, see 2 Macc 5:19: "The Lord did not choose the nation for the sake of the holy place, but the place for the sake of the nation"; *2 Bar.* 14:17: "Man . . . was not created for the world, but the world for him").

From the principle that the sabbath was made for people, Jesus draws a provocative inference: the "Son of Man is lord even of the sabbath" (2:28). The statement is ambiguous. It could mean "people are lord over the sabbath" (because, after all, the sabbath was made for people), or it could mean "the son of man [of Daniel 7] is lord over the sabbath" (because God gave the Son of Man authority). Given the earlier appeal to the authority of the "Son of Man" to forgive sins (see the commentary on 2:10 above), we should probably prefer the latter interpretation. As God's vice-regent, Jesus possesses the authority to pronounce judgment in many matters, including forgiveness of sins and rulings pertaining to the Mosaic code.

Healing of the Man with a Withered Hand (3:1-6)

Jesus' legal authority is witnessed yet again, this time in the healing of the man with the paralyzed and atrophied hand. Eating with sinners (2:15-17), failure to promote fasting among his disciples (2:18-22), and gathering food (i.e., "working") on the sabbath (2:23-28) had aroused the suspicions of certain religious persons, including Pharisees. It is for this reason that when Jesus enters the synagogue on a sabbath, they watch him closely. If Jesus heals someone (like the man with the withered hand), they can accuse him.

Aware of his opponents' sentiments, Jesus summons the man with the withered hand and asks, "Is it lawful on the sabbath to do good or to do harm, to save life or to kill?" The question as posed would have to be answered, "to do good and to save life." But the objection would be that no one's life was in danger; only if a life was in danger would sabbath law be overridden (*m. Yoma* 8:6). The man with the withered hand could be healed on any other day of the week; healing did not have to take place on the sabbath. Perhaps to add to the urgency and desperation of the suffering man, one second-century revision of Matthew has the man say to Jesus: "I was a mason and earned my livelihood with my hands; I beseech you, Jesus, to restore to me my health that I may not with disgrace have to beg for my bread" (*Gos. Naz.* §10, according to Jerome, *Commentary on Matthew* 2 [on Matt 12:13]). But even here, one could still argue that the man could wait one more day.

Jesus' argument has validity only in light of who he is and the message he proclaims. The kingdom of God is present; the redemptive and restorative power of God has been released. Jesus' exorcisms and healings provide evidence of this divine activity. The man with the withered hand is not merely healed, so that now he can use his hand; he is reclaimed and restored fully. In this sense his life is indeed "saved." That Jesus' argument is valid is seen in the fact that the man's hand is restored (3:5). The implicit claim that divine power is at work in Jesus has been confirmed by the immediate and effective healing. Healing on the sabbath is one more illustration of Jesus' earlier claim to be "lord of the sabbath" (2:28).

The episode ends on an ominous and ironic note. At the beginning of the scene "they watched him . . . so that they might accuse him" (3:2). Now we are told that the Pharisees and Herodians counsel together "how to destroy him" (v. 6). This plotting anticipates 15:3-4, where the ruling priests seek to "lay charges against [Jesus]."

The irony is seen when we remember Jesus' earlier question about what is lawful to do on the sabbath, "to do good or to do evil, to save life or to kill?" Jesus does good and saves life; his opponents plot his destruction.

Healing of Many (3:7-12)

This passage effectively sums up Jesus' ministry and prepares the reader to move into a new stage in the story (3:13–6:6), in which the mystery of the kingdom of God is the principal concern. Jesus' ministry has been so stunningly successful that a "great multitude" from all parts of Israel (Galilee, Judea, Jerusalem) and beyond (Idumea, beyond the Jordan, about Tyre and Sidon) follows him (vv. 7-8). The crowd is so great that it becomes necessary for Jesus to teach from a boat moored by the shore. The evangelist explains that this is necessary, "lest they should crush him" (v. 9). The reason that the crowd presses Jesus so is because of his great success in healing and the desire of many to touch him (v. 10). Indeed, many even of the crowd would be in danger of injury. The awesomeness of the scene is enhanced further by noting that "whenever the unclean spirits beheld him, they fell down before him and cried out, 'You are the Son of God!'" (v. 11). (On unclean spirits, see the commentary on 1:23 above.) Falling down before Jesus indicates their submission (as humans also do in 5:33 and 7:25). As before, Jesus orders the evil spirits "not to make him known" (1:25, 34). Given the context, where Jesus must make great effort to control the crowd and keep himself from being crushed, his silencing of the evil spirits should be understood as a further attempt to muzzle unwanted publicity (and not so much to keep his messiahship a secret until Easter).

The Mystery of the Kingdom of God (3:13–6:6)

The first major section of the Gospel of Mark had introduced to the reader Jesus the proclaimer of the kingdom of God. In this section the reader will be confronted with aspects of the kingdom, some unusual and unexpected. The section consists of the appointment of the twelve apostles (3:13-19), controversies with family and critics (3:20-35), the parable of the sower (4:1-9), the question about parables (4:10-12), the explanation of the parable of the sower (4:13-20), additional parables of the kingdom (4:21-34), the stilling of the storm (4:35-41), the encounter with the Gerasene demoniac (5:1-20), the healing of the woman with the hemorrhage and the daughter of Jairus (5:21-43), and the rejection at Nazareth (6:1-6a). Thematic to this section is the difficulty people have in understanding and receiving the kingdom. Although people eagerly seek out the blessings of the kingdom (such as healings and exorcisms), they are not always ready and willing to accept the demands of the kingdom.

Appointment of the Twelve (3:13-19)

On three previous occasions in Mark Jesus called disciples (1:16-18, 19-20; 2:14). Now he appoints twelve of his disciples as "apostles" (though they are not formally called such until Mark 6:30; cf. Matt 10:2). In Greek *(apostolos)* and in Hebrew *(shaliaḥ)* "apostle" means one who is sent, usually as a messenger, agent, deputy, or ambassador. It was understood that an apostle was commissioned by a higher authority and acted in behalf of this authority. This is the meaning here. Jesus appoints twelve apostles, sends them out to preach his message, and grants them authority. Paul's dramatic call and subsequent itinerant missionary activity well illustrate the office of apostle.

The appointment of "twelve" apostles surely symbolizes the regathering and reconstitution of the twelve tribes of Israel. The twelve apostles do not, of course, come from all twelve tribes (because some of them are brothers, this would not be possible). The association is made clearer in a passage Matthew and Luke derived from their common sayings source (or "Q"): "You who have followed me will also sit on twelve thrones, judging the twelve tribes of Israel" (Matt 19:28 = Luke 22:30; cf. Matt 10:6: "Go nowhere among the Gentiles . . . but go rather to the lost sheep of the house of Israel"). The symbolism of the twelve is so powerful that it is necessary to replace the deceased Judas (Acts 1:15-26).

The regathering of the twelve tribes coheres with other visions of redemption championed by various would-be prophets and redeemers of Israel. One immediately thinks of Theudas, who in about AD 45 summoned people to take up their possessions and join him at the Jordan River. He promised that at his command the water would part, providing easy passage (Josephus *Ant.* 20.5.1 §§97-98; Acts 5:36). Similarly, an unnamed Egyptian Jew in about AD 56 summoned a crowd to the Mount of Olives. He claimed that at his command the walls of Jerusalem would fall down, allowing his following to enter the city (Josephus *Ant.* 20.8.6 §§169-70; Acts 21:38). Common to the promises and hopes of these men is the idea of renewal, perhaps through a new conquest of the promised land, following the model of Moses in the wilderness and Joshua crossing the Jordan River and conquering the inhabitants of Canaan. The hope of a new conquest of the promised land is consistent with the messianic expectation of a work like the *Psalms of Solomon,* whose author expects great things of the Davidic Messiah: "He will gather a holy people . . . he will judge the tribes of the people . . . he will distribute them upon the land according to their tribes" (*Pss. Sol.* 17:26-28).

Jesus has commissioned the twelve to preach his kingdom message, and he has given them the authority (or power) to cast out demons. In effect, Jesus has delegated his own special power and authority to these chosen disciples. Through them his mission to Israel has been significantly expanded.

About most of the twelve we know very little: "Simon," whom Jesus named Peter (Greek) or Cephas (Aramaic), both of which mean "rock" (3:16), figures prominently in the first half of the book of Acts, is mentioned a few times in Paul's letters (e.g., 1 Cor 1:12; Gal 2:9), and is given credit for two letters in the NT (i.e., 1 and 2 Peter). "James the son of Zebedee and John the brother of James, whom he named Boanerges, that is, sons of thunder" (3:17), along with Peter, are among Jesus' closest associates. Four times in Mark these three are with Jesus (5:37; 9:2; 13:3; 14:33). The etymology of the epithet "Boanerges" is uncertain. The story of the martyrdom of James is narrated in Acts 12:1-2. The early church speculated that John may have been the "disciple whom Jesus loved" (John 13:23; 19:26; 20:2) and possibly the author of the Fourth Gospel. Little is known about "Andrew" (v. 18), Peter's brother. On one occasion he is with Jesus and the inner circle of James, John, and Peter (Mark 13:3). Apart from the appearance of his name in the apostolic lists nothing is known of "Philip" in the Synoptic Gospels, but in the Fourth Gospel he plays a prominent role (John 1:43-48; 6:5-7; 12:21-22; 14:8-9). Nothing is known of "Bartholomew" (from Aramaic, meaning "son of Tolmai"); his name appears only in the apostolic lists (Matt 10:3; Mark 3:18; Luke 14; Acts 1:13). There is no evidence that he is the Nathanael of John 1:45-46, though some have made this suggestion. "Matthew" is probably to be identified with Levi, whose call was recounted in Mark 2:14 (Matt 9:9). Apart from the call itself nothing is known of this person. The early church thought that he might have authored the Gospel of Matthew. "Thomas" is perhaps the most interesting figure among the twelve. He plays a prominent if at times dubious role in the Fourth Gospel (John 11:16; 20:24; 21:2). He is the twin brother of Jesus in gnostic circles, and the author of the *Gospel of Thomas.* Other writings are attributed to him, including the fanciful *Infancy Gospel of Thomas.* Nothing is known of "James the son of Alphaeus." He is not to be confused with "James the Lord's brother" (Mark 6:3; 1 Cor 15:7; Gal 1:19) or with "James the Smaller" (Mark 15:40). Because Levi (Matthew) in Mark 2:14 is called the "son of Alphaeus," it is possible that James and Levi were brothers. "Thaddeus" appears only in the apostolic lists of Mark 3:18 and Matt 10:3. Nothing is known of him. "Simon the Cananaean" appears as "Simon who was called the Zealot" in Luke's parallel passage (Luke 6:15) and in the list that appears in Acts 1:12-14. "Zealot" is probably meant as the Greek equivalent of the Aramaic "Cananaean" (which means "zealous"). Last on Mark's list is "Judas Iscariot, who handed him over" (v. 19). Judas is infamous as the betrayer of Jesus. Two evangelists believed that Satan influenced Judas (Luke 22:3; John 13:26-27), but little is known of the man's actual motives (see the commentary on 14:10, 43 below).

Accusations and Family Tension (3:20-35)

The success and notoriety of Jesus' exorcisms provoke diverse reactions among family and observers. This diverse but closely linked material consists of four pericopes: the accusation that Jesus is possessed by Beelzebul (3:20-22), Jesus' reply to the charge (vv. 23-27), a warning against blasphemy of the Holy Spirit (vv. 28-30), and a pronouncement on who Jesus' true family is (vv. 31-35).

The comment that the crowd was such that "they could not even eat" (3:20) suggests a very crowded house. Because there was standing room only, it would have been impossible to recline (as was Mediterranean custom) to eat (and not that Jesus and the disciples were simply too busy to stop and eat). The evangelist is once again making the point that wherever Jesus goes he draws large crowds. The truly odd feature is the notation that his family, who have come from Nazareth, respond by trying to "seize him" (v. 21). The evangelist explains that Jesus' family were saying that he was mad (lit. "outside of himself") — and it is his family who say this, not the excited crowd whom Jesus will later identify as his true family, nor the scribes who hold to a much more sinister opinion. Accusations of madness were sometimes made against prophets, exorcists, and healers. One of the Sibyls complains of being called a "crazy liar," yet she knows that she will be vindicated when her words come to pass (*Sib. Or.* 3:811-18). Too much learning, it was thought, could lead to madness (Acts 26:24: "Your great learning has driven you mad"; Alciphron *Letters of Courtesans,* "Thais to Euthydemus," 1.34.1-2: ". . . ever since you took it into your head to study philosophy you have put on airs. . . . You have gone mad . . .").

Scribes from Jerusalem accuse Jesus of being possessed by Beelzebul (from the Canaanite deity, whom Israelites derisively called "Lord of the Flies"), and suggest that "by the prince of demons he casts out the demons" (3:22; for a colorful contemporary description of Beelzebul the Prince of Demons, see *T. Sol.* 6:1-11). Jesus responds first to the charge of the scribes; later he will respond to his family. The idea that Satan would cast out "Satan" (i.e., his demonic allies) is illogical. If Jesus were truly in league with Satan, he would advance his dominion, not undermine it. "If a kingdom is divided against itself, that kingdom cannot stand" (v. 24; cf. Dan 5:28). Far from being Satan's ally, Jesus is the Evil One's fiercest enemy, as is made clear in the saying in v. 27: "But no one can enter a strong man's house and plunder his goods, unless he first binds the strong man; then indeed he may plunder his house." Satan is the "strong man," but Jesus is the stronger one, who is able to bind Satan. (Recall that the Baptist in Mark 1:7 had promised the coming of a "stronger" one.) Jesus' statement is remarkable. In essence he has claimed that he has defeated Satan, and having bound him is now able to ransack his domain (i.e., liberate the possessed and oppressed; cf. Luke 13:16, where Jesus "looses" the woman whom Satan had "bound" for eighteen years).

Jesus now adds a warning to his reply to the scribes. Their malicious misidentification of the work of the Holy Spirit as the work of Satan constitutes a serious form of blasphemy for which there can be no forgiveness (3:28-29). Instead of saying, "He has the Holy Spirit," as they should have, they made the absurd and potentially misleading statement that "he has an unclean spirit" (v. 30). If they persist in this assertion they are in danger of committing an "eternal sin" (v. 29).

Finally, Jesus has a word to say about his family. Earlier his family had tried to seize him, saying, "He is mad" (3:21). Unable to get to Jesus on account of the tightly packed crowd surrounding him, they send word. Jesus is told: "Your mother and your brothers are outside, asking for you" (v. 32). Jesus asks rhetorically: "Who are my mother and my brothers?" (v. 33). The question is indicative of the estrangement that has developed between Jesus and his family. (Luke finds it embarrassing and omits it.) Answering his own question, Jesus looks upon those sitting about him and says: "Here are my mother and my brothers!" (v. 34). The reply approaches disownment of his own family (cf. Mark 10:29-30, where Jesus consoles his disciples who have lost family and possessions as a result of following Jesus). Jesus defines his true family: "Whoever does the will of God is my brother and sister and mother" (v. 35). Jesus' use of hyperbole must be taken into account here. Has he literally rejected his family? Probably not, for his family will come to believe in him, and his brother James becomes an apostle and one of the "pillars" in the church (Gal 1:19; 2:9). But his language indicates the seriousness of his message and the need to commit to it.

Parable of the Sower (4:1-20)

Once again because of the large crowd Jesus finds it necessary to teach from a boat (3:9). The evangelist presents a cluster of Jesus' parables that relate in one way or another to the kingdom of God. The first is the well-known parable of the sower (4:3-9). The parable describes four types of soil which respond differently to the sown seed. In the explanation of the parable (4:13-20) we learn that the seed is the "word" and that each type of soil represents a person's response to the word. The first is like the hardened soil along a path. The seed lies exposed and is easily taken by birds. This person hears the word, but before it has any chance to sink in Satan snatches it away. The second is like the rocky ground, where the soil lacks depth. The seed sprouts but lacks root, and so withers in the heat of the sun. This person hears the word and receives it joyfully, at least initially. But when persecution comes, he falls away. The third is like the soil that is infested with thorns. The seed sprouts, but the thorns choke it. This person hears the word, but the cares of the world, his delight in wealth, and his materialism choke the word. The fourth is like good soil in which the seed takes root and becomes very fruitful. This person hears the word, accepts it, and bears fruit. The abundance of fruit varies from person to person.

The parable recalls words and imagery from the OT. God's word is likened to rain and snow that give seed to the sower and does not fail to accomplish the divine purpose (Isa 55:10-11). Through the prophet Jeremiah the LORD enjoins the men of Judah and the inhabitants of Jerusalem, "Break up your fallow ground, and sow not among thorns" (Jer 4:3). The closest parallel is found in 4 Ezra: "For just as the farmer sows many seeds in the ground and plants a multitude of seedlings, and yet not all that have been sown will come up in due season, and not all that were planted will take root; so also those who have been sown in the world will not all be saved" (8:41; cf. 3:20; 9:17, 31-37).

Mark's version of the parable, as well as its explanation, does not make it clear that the parable directly concerns the kingdom of God. It is for this reason that Mark's "word" (3:14) becomes in Matthew the "word of the kingdom" (Matt 13:19). But the evangelist Mark does understand the parable as teaching us something about the kingdom of God. This is seen in the fact that two of the parables he adds to the parable cluster of ch. 4 specifically mention the kingdom (4:26-29, 30-32). It is also seen in the dialogue about parables situated between the parable of the sower and its subsequent interpretation (i.e., 4:10-12). When the disciples ask Jesus "concerning the parables" (3:10), he tells them that they have been given the "secret of the kingdom of God, but for those outside everything is in parables" (v. 11). Here "parables" probably carries with it the Semitic word meaning riddle or conundrum, not the common idea of parable as clarifying illustration. The implication is that Jesus' teaching is in some way veiled from from those who are not part of his following (which in context explains why many do not respond positively to his preaching). The paraphrase of Isa 6:9-10 in v. 12 provides scriptural warrant as well as explanation for this spiritual obduracy. Refusal to heed Jesus' preaching brings on spiritual blindness. In contrast, those who follow Jesus are more able to understand the parables; and, even if they do not understand them, they receive private explanation (4:34; 7:17-23).

Parables of the Kingdom (4:21-34)

To the parable of the sower Mark appends three parables and two sayings (4:21-23, 24-25) that qualify — indeed, almost contradict — the strange saying in vv. 11-12. Lest one imagine that the purpose of Jesus' parables is to veil the truth (and the language of vv. 11-12 could suggest this), the saying in vv. 21-23 makes it clear that light is not to be hidden. The implication is that Jesus' teaching is like a lamp, and like a lamp it should be "put on a stand," not "put under a bushel or under a bed" (v. 21). The next verse (v. 22) explains that everything will be revealed. The point of this seems to be that whatever may at first seem obscure (to outsiders and even to the disciples) will become clear through spiritual insight and, as necessary, through private explanation (to the disciples). Jesus urges everyone who "has ears to hear, let him hear" (v. 23). Anyone who is willing to hear Jesus' word, to let it soak in, as it were, will gain understanding. Such a person is like the fourth type of soil in the parable of the sower. If he accepts Jesus' word, meditates on it, and does not permit it to be choked out because of the cares of the world, his understanding of it will grow.

The second saying reflects a common Jewish wisdom saying: "The measure you give will be the measure you receive" (4:24; cf. *m. Soṭa* 1:7: "With the measure one measures, it will be measured to him"). In the present context the maxim means that one's receptivity and commitment to Jesus' preaching will be rewarded with insight accordingly. The same point is made in the saying in v. 25, which could be paraphrased as follows: "To him who has [commitment to Jesus' teaching] will more [insight into Jesus' teaching] be given; and from him who has not [commitment to Jesus' teaching], even what [little knowledge] he has will be taken away." Insight into Jesus' teaching will result in an understanding of the kingdom.

The two kingdom parables make simple points. The parable of the seed and harvest (vv. 26-29) suggests that the kingdom will grow and establish itself, quite apart from human comprehension and contrivance (it grows "of itself"; lit. "automatically"). Like a crop that matures for the inevitable harvest, so the kingdom will mature until its eventual and inevitable consummation. The reference to the ripe harvest and putting in the sickle may allude to the words of Joel 3:13 ("Put in the sickle, for the harvest is ripe"). If so, the parable may be hinting at judgment that arrives with the kingdom.

The parable of the mustard seed (4:30-32) teaches that the kingdom of God begins in a small, seemingly insignificant way, yet grows to great proportions. By saying that the tiny mustard seed has been "sown upon the ground," we parallel the earlier parable of the sower and perhaps should think that the sown mustard seed refers once again to Jesus' preaching of the word. If this is so, then the parable teaches that Jesus' word, though seemingly insignificant in comparison to the world politics of his day, will someday dominate the world scene. The possible allusion to Ezek 17:23 ("it shall put out branches . . . every bird shall dwell in the shade of its branches") may have been intended to underscore this point. According to Ezekiel the day will come when God will plant a small sprig on top of a mountain (i.e., Jerusalem), which will grow into a noble cedar whose branches will shelter "birds of every kind" (i.e., the nations). Ezekiel's allegory of the cedar (17:22-24) is messianic and, if it is alluded to, adds a significant touch to Jesus' parable. (In the Aramaic paraphrase of Ezekiel, the sprig is identified as a "child from the dynasty of the house of David" through whom the "kingdoms of the nations" will be "humbled.")

Stilling the Storm (4:35-41)

The stilling of the storm gives Jesus another opportunity to display his authority. The seriousness of the situation is seen in the panicked, disrespectful shouts of the disciples: "Teacher, do you not care if we perish?" (4:38). Both Matthew and Luke are embarrassed by the disciples' tone and lack of faith, and edit accordingly (Matt 8:23-27; Luke 8:22-25). But Mark appreciates the dramatic effect and the contrast between the terrified disciples and the masterful Jesus. With two words (in Aramaic, that is) Jesus quiets the storm: "Peace, be still!" (v. 39). The wind stops and the sea becomes calm. Astounded, the disciples say among themselves: "Who then is this, that even wind and sea obey him?" (v. 41).

The disciples' question is reminiscent of the scornful remark made in reference to the stricken Antiochus IV Epiphanes, the Syrian Greek ruler who had severely persecuted the Jews in the second century BC: "Thus he who had just been thinking that he could command the waves of the sea, in his superhuman arrogance, and imagining that he could weigh the high mountains in a balance, was brought down to earth and carried in a litter, making the power of God manifest to all" (2 Macc 9:8).

In contrast to the Greco-Roman despots about whom all sorts of hyperbole were inscribed in public notices and official documents, Jesus is the genuine article. He speaks the word, and it happens. It is further evidence of the divine authority entrusted to this human, this "Son of Man."

The Gerasene Demoniac (5:1-20)

The encounter with the Gerasene (or Gergasene) demoniac surely ranks as the eeriest episode in the life of Jesus. The description of this possessed and tormented man is shocking and disgusting. He lives in a cemetery. He possesses superhuman strength, as seen in the fact that no one can bind him and, when fettered, he breaks the chains. He howls in the night and bruises himself with stones. The man is insane; he is possessed. But when he sees Jesus "from afar," he runs up to him, bows before him, and says: "What have you to do with me, Jesus, Son of the Most High God? I adjure you by God, do not torment me" (5:6-7).

Jesus' authority over unclean spirits is unequaled. Even at a distance his presence terrorizes and subdues evil. Jesus demands to know the possessed man's name. "My name is Legion; for we are many" (5:9). The alternation between the singular and the plural is interesting (cf. vv. 10-13). At one moment it is the possessed man who speaks; at another moment it is the demonic legion who speak. The name "Legion" is in itself of interest, for it would make first-century readers think of the Roman legions who enforce the will of the emperor. It also puts their number at as many as six thousand. That Jesus could take on and defeat an entire legion of demons, who tremble before him, would be very impressive to his contemporaries. Jesus knows their name; the demons, though many, cannot escape exorcism. Casting the demons into the swine, which then plunge into the sea and perish (and the demons perish with the pigs; cf. *T. Sol.* 5:11, where a demon pleads: "Do not condemn me to water"), foreshadows the grim fate that awaits Satan and his evil allies. Satan's rout at the hands of Jesus continues.

The herdsmen flee into the city and report the whole incident. Once again the deeds of Jesus attract attention. People from the city and surrounding countryside come to see for themselves. They find Jesus and the man who had been possessed now clothed and in his right man. In the presence of one so powerful as Jesus they are fearful and beg him to depart from their country. The delivered man wants to be with Jesus, so complete is his cure. But Jesus wants him to stay behind as his witness. This he does, for he begins to "proclaim in the Decapolis" (lit. "ten cities"; Greek cities founded mostly in the land east of the Sea of Galilee and the Jordan River) "how much Jesus had done for him; and all the people marveled" (5:20).

Two Healings (5:21-43)

The next story is unusual in that it intertwines two miracles (one healing and one resuscitation). Jesus has left the region of Gerasa (or Gergesa) and returned to the western shore of the Sea of Galilee (on teaching by the sea, see 2:13; 3:7; 4:1). As the reader comes to expect, a crowd gathers (5:21). But this time we are introduced to a named individual who beseeches Jesus on behalf of his fatally ill daughter. Jairus (whose name in Hebrew means "he will awaken" [cf. 1 Chr 20:5], and so may have been understood as a portent of things to come), one of the rulers of a local synagogue, asks Jesus to come and lay his "hands on her, so that she may be made well, and live" (5:23). This is the first time in Mark when there is mention of laying hands on someone who is ill (in 1:41 Jesus reaches out his hand and touches the leper, but he does not "lay hands" on him). In 6:5 he will lay hands on the sick. In 7:32 he will lay hands on the deaf mute, and in 8:23-25 he will lay hands on the blind man. In 10:16 Jesus lays hands on the children, but for blessing, not healing. The laying on of hands for healing and/or exorcism is attested in the *Genesis Apocryphon,* an Aramaic document from Qumran probably dating to the first century BC. In this scroll Abram lays hands on Pharaoh to rid him of a demon which had plagued him and his household (1QapGen 20:29). This is the earliest attestation of the ritual in Jewish sources.

On the way to the house of Jairus a woman suffering from a hemorrhage touches Jesus' clothing hoping to be healed. Elsewhere in the Gospels people touch Jesus' clothing hoping for healing (Matt 14:36; Mark 6:56; Luke 6:19). In Acts we are told that people laid the sick in the street hoping that the shadow of Peter might fall on them and restore them (Acts 5:15). Mark notes that the woman, whose condition had lasted for twelve years, had spent all that she had on physicians and had only become worse (the negative reference to physicians drops out in Luke 8:43). Quite apart from the physical difficulties, the woman's condition would have kept her in a perpetual state of impurity (Lev 15:25-28). She has heard of Jesus and believes that if she just touches his clothing as he passes by she can be healed. Her assumption is well founded. "Immediately the hemorrhage ceased; and she felt in her body that she was healed of her disease" (5:29).

Jesus perceives that healing power had gone forth, so he turns in the crowd and asks, "Who touched me?" (5:30). The woman does not immediately step forward. Her action in touching Jesus while in a state of ritual impurity would have been viewed as offensive ("How dare she presume . . ."). Her touch would render Jesus ritually impure (Lev 15:26-27; cf. *m. Ṭohar.* 5:8). Jesus looks around, not put off by his disciples' oafishness (5:31: "You see the crowd pressing you, and yet you say, 'Who touched me?'"). Finally, the woman comes forward, kneels before him, and tells the truth. Her fear is due to the divine power she has just experienced, as well as to the fact that she had presumed to touch Jesus. She receives no rebuke; rather, she is assured: "Daughter, your faith has made you well; go in peace, and be healed of your disease" (v. 34). Jesus' words imply that the disease will no longer trouble her.

The reader is abruptly brought back to the emergency of the dying daughter of Jairus. While Jesus was still speaking to the healed woman, people come from the synagogue official's home to report that the girl has died (5:35). Jesus is too late, or so they assumed. Before the father is overcome with grief Jesus assures him, "Do not fear, only believe" (v. 36). Jesus' injunction to have faith is especially appropriate here, given the healing that the woman had just experienced because of her faith. If Jairus has the faith of this woman, his daughter will live.

Jesus permits only Peter, James, and John to follow Jairus to his home. There they find mourners already gathered, weeping and wailing. Although some professional mourners may be present (as seen by the presence of flutists in Matt 9:23), most of these people were probably relatives who had been present during the girl's illness. Now that she has finally succumbed, they join the family in its hour of grief. Jesus' comment that the girl is not dead but is sleeping (perhaps hinting that for God raising the dead is no more difficult than awaking a sleeper) strikes the grieving family as silly (5:39-40). Their response makes it clear that there is no doubt that the girl has really died. As far as they are concerned, the girl is dead and nothing now can be done. Jesus puts the scornful outside, perhaps because they have no faith in Jesus. Without any rigmarole or magical ritual, he simply speaks in Aramaic, "Little girl, arise" (v. 41; Mark's "I say to you" is not in Aram. *talita qumi*). "At once" the girl arises and is able to walk (v. 42), thus signifying the completeness of the resuscitation. She not only is restored to life, but is restored to full health as well (recall the healed paralyzed man, 2:9). Jesus commands the parents to feed the girl before those outside learn of her resuscitation (v. 43). Delay in reporting her recovery would also make it easier for Jesus to slip out and continue on his way.

Rejection at Nazareth (6:1-6a)

Jesus' experience in his hometown of Nazareth stands in sharp contrast to his experience elsewhere in Galilee. In the previous stories of Jairus and the woman with the hemorrhage we witness astounding miracles facilitated by faith. In Nazareth (which is not mentioned by name) there is little faith and therefore little working of miracles.

On the sabbath Jesus began to teach, and the people were "astonished" (6:2). But their amazement is not positive. They ask a series of questions, all of which imply that they question Jesus' mission. "Where did this man get all this?" That is, where did Jesus get these notions (probably of the kingdom of God and his right to proclaim it) as well as his ability to perform miracles? This question anticipates the next two: "What is the wisdom given to him?" That is, what kind of education has Jesus acquired? Does it have any validity? What about "these mighty deeds brought about by his hands?" That is, where has Jesus acquired the ability to heal and exorcise? The residents of Nazareth ask these questions because in their view Jesus is nobody special. He is "the woodworker" (which is probably a better rendering of *tektōn,* traditionally translated "carpenter"), the "son of Mary, brother of James, Joses, Judas, and Simon" (v. 3). His sisters still live in town. Jesus comes from an ordinary family. He is from Nazareth; how can he be special? Recall the earlier tension between Jesus and his family in 3:21, 31-35. If Jesus' own family thought him mad, why would others in Nazareth think him special?

The implication is that Jesus' ministry came as a surprise to those who knew him. But it is no surprise to the reader of Mark's Gospel. Jesus went to John to be baptized, and the Spirit of God came upon him in a powerful way. He began to preach the kingdom, and his miracles demonstrated that God's kingly power was indeed present. Demons were terrified at his presence. But despite his success abroad, when Jesus returns home he is met with disrespect and unbelief. His former neighbors are offended (v. 3). To this Jesus replies with the axiom: "A prophet is not without honor except in his home country and among his relatives and in his own house" (v. 4). The parallel found in the *Gospel of Thomas* (§31: "No prophet is accepted in his own village; no physician heals those who know him") does not derive from independent tradition, but is better explained as a conflation of sayings taken from Luke's version of Jesus' experience in Nazareth (Luke 4:23: "Physician, heal yourself"; Luke 4:24: "No prophet is acceptable in his own country"). In the late first century Apollonius of Tyana complains to his brother: "Other men regard me as the equal of the gods, and some of them even as a god, but until now my own country alone ignores me, my country for which in particular I have striven to be distinguished" (*Letters to Hestiaeus* 44).

It may be true that familiarity breeds contempt, but because he performs miracles in their very presence (6:5) the unbelief of the people of Nazareth amazes Jesus (v. 6). Of course, because of their unbelief he does not perform as many or as mighty miracles as he has in other towns.

Failure to Understand the Kingdom (6:6b–8:26)

Running throughout this diverse section of the Gospel of Mark is human difficulty in understanding the presence and nature of the kingdom of God. The section begins on a promising note, with the empowerment and commission of the twelve. But the next passage describes the execution of John the Baptizer. Twice Jesus feeds large multitudes, but the disciples are unable to grasp the true significance of what Jesus has done. The Pharisees quarrel with Jesus over questions of purity and demand a sign. Even a Gentile woman debates with Jesus. The section is made up of the following several passages: sending out the twelve to preach and heal (6:6b-13), the death of John the Baptizer (6:14-29), the return of the twelve and the feeding of the five thousand (6:30-44), Jesus' walking on the sea (6:45-52), healings by the sea (6:53-56), controversy over oral tradition (7:1-23), the encounter with the Syrophoenician woman (7:24-30), the healing of the deaf-mute (7:31-37), the feeding of the four thousand (8:1-10), the demand for a sign (8:11-13), the meaning of the loaves (8:14-21), and the healing of the blind man (8:22-26).

Mission of the Twelve (6:6b-13)

Jesus leaves Nazareth and continues to teach in other towns. The twelve whom he had earlier appointed to be with him (3:14) are now commissioned to preach repentance, to cast out demons, and to heal (in 3:15 they had been given authority to cast out demons). Jesus "begins to send (*apostellein*) them out two by two" (6:7). It is from the verb "to send" that the noun "apostle" (*apostolos*) is derived. The apostles (as they will be called below in v. 30) are sent in pairs in conformity with the law's requirement that testimony be confirmed by two or three witnesses (Deut 19:15).

Jesus instructs the apostles "to take nothing for their journey except a staff" (6:8). The staff serves as a walking stick, but it may also serve as an emblem of authority. (Evidently the sons of Jacob possessed staffs, perhaps as symbols of the headship of their respective families or tribes; cf. Gen 38:18, 25.) They are to take no food or money; they are to be sustained by hospitality, but they are to be careful not to appear as freeloaders (6:10-11). To "shake off the dust" that is on their feet is to offer a very serious warning to the village or town that despises ambassadors of the proclaimer of the kingdom (cf. Luke 10:13-16).

The apostles do Jesus' bidding. They preach repentance, cast out demons, and anoint many with oil and heal them (6:12-13). They do as their master has been doing since the beginning of his ministry (though nowhere does Jesus anoint anyone with oil; cf. Luke 10:34; Jas 5:14).

Is Jesus John Raised from the Dead? (6:14-29)

Because of his own ministry and now because of its amplification through his apostles, Jesus' fame has spread throughout Galilee. Even Herod Antipas, tetrarch of Galilee (though sometimes called "king" unofficially), has heard of Jesus. Herod wonders who this person is. His advisors pass on all sorts of proposals that people are making. Some say, "John the Baptizer has been raised from the dead"; others, "It is Elijah"; still others, "It is a prophet, like one of the prophets of old" (6:14-15). Herod, however, is of the opinion that he must be John, whom he had beheaded (v. 16). Herod's opinion, evidently shared by many, is evidence that Jesus' ministry was indeed similar to John's. Since John was not known as a healer or exorcist, the similarity must lie in the content of their preaching. Both proclaimed repentance.

The reference to John's beheading occasions a digression in which the imprisonment and execution of the Baptizer may be narrated. The story is macabre, echoes OT traditions (e.g., the putting away of Vashti in Esth 1:19; the pompous offer of one half of the kingdom in Esth 5:3; 7:2), and is at points either unattested or somewhat at variance with the account in Josephus (*Ant.* 18.5.2 §§116-19). But at most points the accounts can be reconciled, and there is no good reason to give Josephus priority. Although Josephus chooses to emphasize the political dangers that John posed to Herod, and Mark chooses to emphasize the moral dimension, the two accounts are in essential agreement. Herod's disgraceful dismissal of his wife, the daughter of the king of the Nabateans, and his unlawful marriage to Herodias his sister-in-law prompted John's condemnation. John's condemnation focused on the immoral and unlawful aspects (which Mark mentions), while Herod's fears focused on the political dangers (which Josephus narrates). Later Josephus himself mentions the inappropriateness of Herod's divorce and remarriage (*Ant.* 18.5.4 §136).

Herod's thinking that Jesus is a resurrected John attests to the power of Jesus' ministry. Who could do such amazing things? Surely it must be someone like John back from the dead (cf. 2 Kgs 13:21, where the bones of Elisha are the cause of a man's resuscitation). To imagine that John himself is actually raised up is extraordinary when it is remembered that his head had been delivered to the king and had been given to the daughter of Herodias to pass on to her vindictive mother. There was no doubt that John had died; his head had been displayed on a serving platter! Herod's belief that Jesus was John raised up attests to the magnitude of Jesus' powers.

John's death surely had an impact on Jesus' thinking. From this point on he must have reckoned with the possibility that he could suffer martyrdom (for more on when Jesus begins to talk of his own death, see the commentary on 8:31-33).

Return of the Twelve and Feeding the Five Thousand (6:30-44)

When the preaching and healing mission of the twelve comes to a conclusion, Jesus and his apostles retire to a secluded place (6:30-32). The mention that they had been so busy that they had not the leisure even to eat (v. 31) prepares for the eventual need to feed the multitude. When they return by boat they see throngs of people, and Jesus feels compassion for them, for "they were like sheep without a shepherd," and he begins to teach them many things (v. 34). Mark's language recalls Num 27:15-17, where Moses petitions God that a man be appointed to shepherd God's people, lest they be "as sheep which have no shepherd" (see also 1 Kgs 22:17).

One of the important tasks of the shepherd is to find food for his flock (cf. Num 27:17, where the shepherd leads the flock out to pasture). Moses did this in the wilderness through the provision of manna (Exodus 16). Elisha did it when he multiplied the loaves for one hundred men (2 Kgs 4:42-44). Now Jesus has the opportunity to provide food for his flock.

The disciples want Jesus to dismiss the crowd (6:35-36). The day is spent, everyone is tired and hungry, and it is best that they go to nearby villages to find food. But Jesus says, "You give them something to eat" (v. 37). The disciples wonder if Jesus means for them to purchase two hundred denarii worth of food. Given that a denarius equaled a day's wage for a laborer, the amount they estimated to be necessary to provide a modest meal for everyone in the crowd was a large one. Matthew (14:16-17) and Luke (9:13) omit this reply, perhaps to spare the disciples.

The disciples are at a loss to know what to do, so Jesus asks, "How many loaves do you have?" (6:38). They have five loaves and two fish (in John 6:9 the disciples obtain this food from a boy). Elisha had been able to multiply twenty loaves for one hundred men; now Jesus will multiply a mere five loaves for five thousand! He commands the multitude to recline on the green grass, which is suitable for this purpose, in groups of fifties and hundreds, perhaps echoing biblical clusters seen in Scripture (e.g., Exod 18:21, 25; Num 31:14).

Jesus takes the loaves and fish, looks up to heaven, blesses and breaks them, and then gives them to the disciples to set before the people (6:41). The language contributes to, or perhaps reflects, the words of institution: "He took bread, and blessed it, and broke it, and gave it to them" (Mark 14:22). The miracle is astounding: "And they all ate and were satisfied" (6:42); not "most ate and some were satisfied." That these five loaves and two fish could feed five thousand is stunning enough, but when Mark notes that those who ate were five thousand "men" *(andres)* and that there were twelve full baskets of leftovers (vv. 43-44), the reader is left awestruck. The abundance of bread may have called to mind traditions about the giving of manna in the eschatological age (cf. *2 Bar.* 29:1-8).

Jesus Walks on Water (6:45-52)

Jesus sends his disciples on ahead, probably to reconnoiter and to prepare for the next stage of his itinerary. He himself dismisses the crowd and retires to a hilltop for a time of prayer (6:45-46). The separation of Jesus from his disciples sets the stage for the strange event that follows.

When evening comes, Jesus is on land and his disciples are in their boat upon the lake. Jesus observes that the disciples were straining against the oars in the face of a contrary wind. What is extraordinary is that Jesus goes to them, "walking on the sea" (6:48). The disciples are terrified and imagine that they have seen a "ghost" (v. 49). It was believed that only a divine being could walk on water. We find this in biblical literature (cf. Job 9:8 [esp. in the LXX]; 38:16; Ps 77:19; 2 Macc 5:21) and in extrabiblical literature: "Hesiod says that [Orion] was the son of Euryale, the daughter of Minos, and of Poseidon, and that there was given him as a gift the power of walking upon the waves as though upon the land" (Eratosthenes, frag. 182). To their astonishment, the disciples discover it is Jesus.

Mark says that Jesus meant "to pass by them" (6:48). The expression may imply divine power and status (cf. Exod 33:19, 22; 34:6; in these passages God "passes" before Moses; Job 9:11). Even Jesus' assurance, "Fear not" (v. 50), is reminiscent of God himself giving assurance to those to whom he appears (to Abraham in Gen 26:24; to Israel in Deut 1:21; to Joshua in Josh 8:1; to Gideon in Judg 6:23; to Judah in 2 Chr 20:15; to postexilic Israel in Isa 41:13-14). When Jesus enters the boat, the wind ceases.

The disciples are "utterly astounded" by the experience (6:51). This episode on the lake reminds the reader of the stilling of the storm (4:35-41), where the disciples ask themselves, "Who is this?" (6:41). The walk on the water suggests that Jesus is divine; he not only commands the wind and the waves but he also walks upon the water itself.

Mark brings the passage to a conclusion with a strange comment, intended to explain why the disciples were astounded: "for they did not understand about the loaves, but their hearts were hardened" (6:52). Because the disciples lack spiritual sensitivity (or, in biblical parlance, "have hardened hearts"), they fail to understand the significance of the miracle of the multiplication of the loaves (6:35-44). Bereft of understanding, they are astonished when Jesus comes to them. When Jesus later feeds the four thousand (8:1-10), the disciples will again show lack of understanding (see the commentary on 8:14-21).

Healings at Gennesaret (6:53-56)

Jesus' fame has by now become so great and widespread that people come from miles around. Any place Jesus goes people bring the sick. Indeed, they even lay the sick in the marketplaces, hoping to touch the fringe of his coat, with the result that those who touch are healed (recall 5:24-34). Jesus' healing power is so great that he is able to heal those so ill that they have to be carried on stretchers. According to Mark, there was no limit to the numbers that Jesus could heal.

On What Defiles (7:1-23)

The excitement and large crowds attract the Pharisees and scribes from Jerusalem (7:1). Jesus' activities on previous occasions had attracted the attention of these men (2:6, 16, 24; 3:6, 22), and they will again (8:11; 10:2; 12:13). Mark states that they had observed that Jesus' disciples ate with "unwashed hands" (7:2) and then explains to his readers who are unfamiliar with this Jewish sect its great concern in matters of purity (vv. 3-5). It is possible that the food that the disciples ate was the food left over from the feeding of the five thousand (6:43). According to Josephus, "The Pharisees have imposed on the people many laws from the tradition of the fathers not written in the law of Moses" (*Ant.* 13.10.6 §297). Such a distinction is made by Jesus himself at the end of his heated reply (7:9-13).

Earlier some Pharisees had objected to Jesus' free association with "sinners and tax collectors" (2:16). This time they ask Jesus why his disciples do not eat with washed hands (7:5). Both of these concerns have to do with the Pharisees' understanding of purity. Jesus does not answer the question directly; he does not say that eating with unwashed hands is permissible or that concerns with purity are unnecessary. Rather, Jesus cuts to the heart of the matter: Pharisaic teachings often go beyond the requirements of Scripture; indeed, these teachings sometimes nullify Scripture itself. Jesus appeals to Isa 29:13, where the prophet of old leveled a similar complaint against the religious authorities of his day. With biting irony Jesus chides his critics: "You reject the commandment of God beautifully, in order to keep your tradition" (7:9). By way of illustration, Jesus alludes to Exod 20:12 (= Deut 5:16) and Lev 20:9 (cf. Exod 21:17), scriptures which enjoin grown children to care for their parents. But the tradition of "corban," whereby something is dedicated to God and so is no longer available for secular use, was sometimes invoked, with the result that substance needed by elderly parents was denied them (7:12).

For readers unfamiliar with Jewish religious customs the evangelist Mark explains that corban means "given to God" (7:11). Josephus understands it similarly: "'Corban' to God — meaning what Greeks would call a 'gift'" (*Ant.* 4.4.4 §73); "Now this oath [i.e., Corban] will be found in no other nation except the Jews, and, translated from the Hebrew, one may interpret it as meaning "God's gift" (*Ag. Ap.* 1.22 §167). A first-century ossuary inscription reads: "All that a man may find to his profit in this ossuary is an offering [corban] to God from him who is within it" (see Fitzmyer 1959: 60-65).

Having silenced his critics, Jesus turns to the people and announces his understanding of purity: "There is nothing outside a person which by going into him can defile him; but the things which come out of a person are what defile him" (7:15). Jesus goes on to explain in private (v. 17) that what defiles is the evil that springs from within a person, not food that is eaten, digested, and eliminated. The implication of this, the evangelist adds parenthetically, is that "all foods are clean" (v. 19), a position taken up by Paul (Rom 14:14; 1 Cor 8:8) — himself coincidentally a former Pharisee and as such one who would have been extremely concerned about purity and food laws.

Far from impugning Jesus' teaching, the religious authorities have themselves been exposed as lawbreakers. We have witnessed yet another encounter with his critics in which Jesus has demonstrated his mastery of logic and Scripture.

The Syrophoenician Woman (7:24-30)

The story of the Syrophoenician woman is one of the most poignant in the Gospels. Although Jesus attempts to retire from public, he cannot be hid. A Greek-speaking woman, whose young daughter was possessed by an "unclean spirit" (see the comment on 1:21-28 above), fell at Jesus' feet and begged him to exorcise the demon (7:25-26). The story takes a surprising turn when Jesus rebuffs the woman, "Let the children first be fed, for it is not right to take the children's bread and throw it to the dogs" (v. 27). The apparent harshness and insensitivity argue strongly against the invention of this story in an increasingly Gentile church. On the contrary, Jesus' disposition reflects genuine tradition in which Israel enjoyed priority (cf. Matt 10:5-6; 15:24). It may strike us as rude, but Jesus' intent was not to insult the woman. Rather, he uses the analogy familiar in his culture in which children of the household are fed first, then the leftovers are thrown to the dogs in the street (cf. Luke 16:20). Jesus is still feeding the people of Israel; Gentiles will have their turn.

But the woman cannot wait; her need is urgent. Building on Jesus' analogy, she points out that the dogs under the table often eat the children's crumbs while the children are still eating. These dogs do not have to wait, as do those outside the house. Impressed with her wisdom and tenacity, Jesus grants her wish: "For this saying you may go your way; the demon has left your daughter" (7:29). Upon arriving home the much relieved mother finds her child well, the demon having departed (v. 30).

Healing of the Deaf Man (7:31-37)

The miracle of the healing of the deaf man is in some ways strange and probably for this reason is omitted by Matthew and Luke (the former vaguely alludes to it in 15:29-31). The evangelist's description of the route Jesus takes (7:31) has occasioned a great deal of debate (see Guelich 1989: 391-93). Mark's point may have been to show that following the encounter with the Syrophoenician woman Jesus was open to ministry to Gentiles, and thus travels in a northward direction (to Sidon), then eastward and southward until he is once again in the region of Decapolis near the Sea of Galilee (see 5:1-20).

A deaf man who could hardly speak is brought to Jesus. Those who brought him assume that if Jesus lays his hands upon him he will be healed (7:32). Earlier Jesus had laid his hands on the sick in 6:5, and he will do so again in 8:23-25. As he will do in 8:22-26, Jesus takes the impaired man aside (7:33). He does this probably because of the difficulty of the man's condition and the need for privacy. The odd things that Jesus does (probing with fingers, spitting, and touching his tongue) should probably also be understood in this sense. In late antiquity spitting was associated with healing (Suetonius *Vespasian* 7; Tacitus *Hist.* 4.81, where the Roman emperor restores the sight of a blind man by spitting into his eyes; cf. John 9:1-7). Jesus looks heavenward and says to the man, "Ephphatha," an Aramaic word that means "be opened" (7:34). With that the man is able to hear and speak plainly (v. 35). Those standing by were so astounded that no matter how sternly Jesus charged them to tell no one they proclaimed it all the more (vv. 36-37). Mark's point in this is that although Jesus sought no publicity or sensationalism, his ministry was so powerful, so stunning in its results that people everywhere proclaimed it.

Feeding of the Four Thousand (8:1-10)

The feeding of the four thousand is the second major feeding miracle (compare 6:35-44). Many commentators suspect that the two feeding stories are in fact versions of one original episode in the life of Jesus. Three factors support this position: (1) several common details in setting and activities suggest a common origin; (2) close parallels between Mark 8:1-10 and John 6:1-15 suggest that the feeding of the four thousand was not the creation of the Markan evangelist; and (3) it is improbable that the disciples would for a second time wonder how a large crowd was to be fed (6:37; 8:4). The Markan evangelist probably drew upon two versions of the feeding story. If the semi-Gentile setting of 7:24-37 is still in view, the feeding of the four thousand may have been intended as a Gentile counterpart to the earlier, larger Jewish feeding. The children have indeed been fed first; now the "dogs under the table" may enjoy the crumbs that fall from the children's table (see 7:27-28).

The need for food on this occasion was greater than it had been when Jesus earlier fed the five thousand. The four thousand had been without food for three days (8:2). This time the disciples have seven loaves of bread and a few small fish (vv. 5, 7); and, as before (6:43), there are several baskets of scraps left over (v. 9).

No Sign for This Generation (8:11-13)

We do not know about what Jesus and the Pharisees argued. Their request for a sign implies that they disputed Jesus' call and authority. If the demand for a sign parallels Jesus' approximate contemporaries who proffered signs of national deliverance (such as Theudas; see the comment on 1:1-8 above), then the Pharisees may have been demanding proof of Jesus' proclamation that the kingdom of God had come. The sign that they demand cannot have been simply another miracle; surely they knew of Jesus' ministry of miracles. Indeed, some miracles took place in the presence of religious teachers (as in 2:1-12; 3:1-6, 22). The sign which they seek must have been of a greater magnitude. Again, if we accept them as appropriate parallels, then we may think of Theudas, who said that the Jordan River would divide and permit dry passage, or the Egyptian Jew who said that at his command the walls of Jerusalem would fall down. These were no mere miracles of exorcism or healing, which various holy men in Israel were able to do (which is acknowledged by Jesus; see 9:38-41). These were signs, modeled after the miracles of the exodus, that would confirm the prophet's proclamation. For the sign to be "from heaven" means it was to be from God. Seeking divine proof of Jesus' credentials may have reflected the directives found in Deut 13:2-6; 18:18-22.

Jesus wonders aloud why his generation seeks a sign (which, according to Paul in 1 Cor 1:22, Jews insist upon), especially given the fact that his critics have already chosen to ignore the evidence thus far provided. Remember that when Jesus cast out demons, the religious authorities accused him of being in league with Satan (Mark 3:22, 30). We should probably assume that the intention of the Pharisees was to embarrass Jesus, either because God would not perform the requested sign, or because the sign itself would fail to impress and persuade. Jesus, however, will not play their game: "No sign shall be given to this generation" (8:12; compare Matt 12:39 = Luke 11:29, where the qualifying phrase "except the sign of Jonah" appears). Jesus' refusal to petition God for a sign is remarkable and suggests a deliberate distancing from the various would-be deliverers who from time to time appeared on the scene.

Discussion of Bread (8:14-21)

The feeding of the four thousand (8:1-10) and the dispute with the Pharisees (vv. 11-13) set the stage for the discussion about "bread." Jesus cautions his disciples to "beware of the leaven of the Pharisees and the leaven of Herod" (v. 15). Because the disciples forgot to take an adequate supply of bread with them (they had but one loaf among them), they assume that Jesus was making reference to literal bread. Hearing them discuss the point, Jesus scolds them, "Do you not yet perceive or understand? Are your hearts hardened?" (v. 17). The rebukes go on to echo the language of prophetic criticism ("Having eyes, do you not see?"; see Jer 5:21; Ezek 12:2), language that had earlier been directed against "outsiders" (see Mark 4:11-12 and Isa 6:9-10). The severity of the rebuke embarrasses Matthew (who softens the story) and Luke (who omits it).

The entire exchange is awkward and confusing. The "leaven" of the Pharisees and Herod occasions the misunderstanding on the part of the disciples, but it does not play any role in the ensuing discussion. What Jesus meant by it is never explained, and what association Herod has with the Pharisees only makes the statement more puzzling. (Matthew, in 16:6, 12, attempts to deal with the problems by substituting the Sadducees for Herod and by explaining that the leaven is the "teaching" of the Pharisees and the Sadducees. Several early Christian scribes, as seen in manuscripts $\mathfrak{p}^{45}$ W Θ 28, substitute the "Herodians" for Herod. In a different context, Luke 12:1 explains that the "leaven of the Pharisees" is hypocrisy.) Leaven (or yeast) could be use figuratively for evil (probably because of the negative role it plays in the observance of Passover; cf. 1 Cor 5:6-7; Gal 5:9). The original context of Jesus' warning about the leaven of his religious critics the Pharisees and his political enemy Herod

Antipas is probably lost (as the awkwardness of the Markan context and the different location of the Lukan context suggest). In the Markan context the leaven is probably unbelief (as seen in Herod's rejection of John's preaching and in the Pharisees' lack of faith in Jesus). The warning occasions the disciples' second failure in the aftermath of a feeding miracle.

Jesus criticizes his disciples for failing to have faith. Despite witnessing two astounding miracles, which resulted in substantial surpluses of food, the disciples are confounded by the discovery that they have only one loaf of bread with them. This lack of faith puts the disciples potentially in the company of those who reject and oppose Jesus.

Healing of the Blind Man (8:22-26)

The healing of the blind man of Bethsaida represents another odd miracle in the Gospel of Mark, one that is omitted by both Matthew and Luke. The setting reminds us of the deaf man who is brought to Jesus in 7:31-37. In the earlier episode Jesus is begged to lay his hand upon the impaired man. In the present episode Jesus is begged to touch the blind man. Like the first episode, the second episode says that Jesus made use of spittle. In fact, it says that he spat on the man's eyes and laid hands on him (8:23). Again we are reminded of Emperor Vespasian, who spat on the eyes of the blind man and healed him (Suetonius *Vespasian* 7; Tacitus *Hist.* 4.81).

What makes this healing miracle so unusual is that it is effected in two stages. Jesus asks the man if he can see anything (8:23), which according to the miracle tradition is highly unusual. The man says that he can "see people, but they look like trees walking about" (v. 24; cf. the inscription from Epidaurus, in which we find that the first things one healed blind man sees are "the trees in the holy place" [*SIG* 1168/69]). Then Jesus again lays his hands upon the man's eyes. With this the cure is complete; the man can now see everything clearly (v. 25).

Since it follows the episode in which Jesus criticized his disciples for having eyes that did not see (8:18), one wonders if the placement of the healing of the blind man, which was difficult and had to be effected in two stages, was deliberate on the part of the Markan evangelist. Was he trying to show that no matter how complete the blindness, Jesus was able to give (in)sight?

Jesus' Instruction of the Disciples (8:27–10:52)

Mark 8:27–10:52 constitutes a major section that introduces the passion narrative. In this section we find Jesus confessed as Messiah (8:27-30) but predicting his suffering and death (8:31-33) and teaching that his followers must be prepared to face the same fate (8:34–9:1). Jesus' solemn and disturbing asseveration receives divine confirmation in the appearance of Elijah and Moses and in the utterance of the heavenly voice (9:2-8). Following the transfiguration Jesus predicts his passion a second time and identifies the martyred Baptist as the awaited Elijah (9:9-13). The raising of the demon-possessed boy (9:14-29), who people supposed was dead, foreshadows Jesus' own death and resurrection. This is followed by yet another prediction of the passion (9:30-32). Questions of greatness (9:33-37) and what it really means to follow Jesus characterize the balance of this section.

Peter's Confession (8:27-33)

At Caesarea Philippi Jesus asks his disciples who people say he is (v. 27). The disciples' report, "John the Baptist; others say, Elijah; and others one of the prophets" (v. 28), recalls the evangelist's earlier summary of opinion regarding the identity of Jesus. According to Mark 6:14 people were saying of Jesus, "John the baptizer has been raised from the dead." But others were saying, "It is Elijah"; and still others said, "It is a prophet, like one of the prophets of old" (6:15). Even Herod Antipas speculates that "John, whom I beheaded, has been raised" (6:16). Public speculation that Jesus might in some sense be "John the Baptist," whether in spirit or in some sense *redivivus* (as in Mark 6:16), pays a significant compliment to Jesus. The popular wilderness prophet had been put to death by Herod Antipas, as much for political reasons as for personal reasons (see the commentary on Mark 6:17-29 above). Jesus' ministry draws so much attention and is accompanied by such astonishing deeds of power that people wonder if God has raised up John to continue the work of preparation for the kingdom. It is not surprising in light of Mal 4:5-6 ("Behold, I will send you Elijah . . .") that some thought Jesus to be Elijah. The promise that someday God would raise up a "prophet like Moses" (Deut 18:15-18) would feed speculation that Jesus could be such.

Jesus then asks his disciples for their opinion, and Peter answers, "You are the Messiah" (8:29). The Greek is "Christ" *(christos),* but this is a translation of Heb. *mashiaḥ,* from which the word "Messiah" is derived. The word means "anointed." But because the word is used in reference to anointed kings (1 Sam 15:1; 16:13; Ps 2:2), anointed prophets (1 Kgs 19:15-16; 1 Chr 16:22 = Ps 105:15; Isa 61:1), and anointed priests (Exod 29:6-7; Lev 16:32; 1 Chr 29:22), it is not certain what Peter means by it. Jesus' crucifixion as "King of the Jews" (Mark 15:26, 32) provides strong support for the traditional view that Peter confessed Jesus to be Israel's messianic King.

In 8:27-30 the evangelist takes up the most important emphasis of his narrative: the messiahship of Jesus. After some eight chapters of public ministry, highlighted by a series of astounding miracles, Jesus is now recognized by the spokesman of his followers as Israel's Messiah. With this recognition Jesus begins to speak of his suffering and death. Mark 8:27-30 in a certain sense is both the conclusion of the first half of the Gospel and the introduction to the second. Jesus' authoritative teaching and person have led to a confession of his messiahship. Now he may begin to explain what that messiahship entails.

In what must have been viewed as completely out of step with Peter's solemn confession, Jesus declares that the "Son of Man must suffer many things . . . and be killed" (8:31; on "Son of Man," see the comment on 2:10 above). Rejecting this thinking, Peter rebukes Jesus, but is rebuked in turn. His opposition to Jesus' anticipation of and willingness to suffer earns him the designation

"Satan" (i.e., adversary or opponent). Jesus does not mean that Peter is Satan, or that he has become possessed by Satan, but that he unwittingly stands opposed to God's will and so is on the side of men who typically fail to understand and obey God (v. 33).

This is the first of Jesus' predictions of suffering and death. He will predict these things again in 9:31 and 10:33-34. Did Jesus really predict his death, or did the evangelist or tradents before him create the tradition? The probability that Jesus did in fact anticipate his death is seen in his prayer in the Garden of Gethsemane: "Abba, Father, all things are possible for you. Take this cup from me! But not what I want, but what you want!" (Mark 14:36). This scene, in which Jesus expresses his dread (cf. Mark 14:34) and in which his disciples fail to keep watch and pray with him, is so potentially embarrassing for the early church that its authenticity is virtually guaranteed (see the commentary on Mark 14:32-42 below). Jesus' prayer implies that he anticipates his death and would like somehow to avoid it. The violent fate of John the Baptizer probably influenced Jesus' thinking as well. But did Jesus anticipate his resurrection also? Very probably. Not to have anticipated it would have been strange, for pious Jews very much believed in the resurrection (Dan 12:1-3; *1 Enoch* 22–27; 92–105; *Jub.* 23:11-31; 4 Macc 7:3; Josephus *Ant.* 18.1.3-5 §§14, 16, 18). Would Jesus have faced death and then, having on another occasion affirmed his belief in the resurrection (Mark 12:18-27), have expressed no faith in his own vindication? The qualifying phrase "after three days" (8:31) probably owes its inspiration to Hos 6:2, "on the third day he will raise us up." The allusion to this passage in all probability derives from Jesus himself. But his allusion may have meant no more than his expectation that his resurrection would be soon, perhaps as part of the general resurrection (see *Tg. Hos* 6:2, which reads "on the day of the resurrection of the dead he will raise us up"), because the kingdom itself was soon to appear in its fullness, and with it judgment. Perhaps we should think that when the tomb was found empty the morning of the first day of the week, his followers interpreted the phrase in a literalistic fashion.

The Way of the Cross (8:34–9:1)

Peter's opposition to Jesus' predicted fate leads to teaching on suffering. The disciples of Jesus must be prepared to face martyrdom. But the loss of everything, even one's life, is to gain eternal reward if it is in the service of the Son of Man. Jesus' saying about taking up one's cross finds an interesting parallel in Epictetus, who warns the nonconformist: "If you want to be crucified, just wait. The cross will come" (*Disc.* 2.2.20). Jesus' saying about saving and losing one's life also finds a parallel in a late-first-century source: "Because of what have men lost their life and for what have those who were on the earth exchanged their soul?" (*2 Bar.* 51:15).

Mention of the Son of Man and of his coming "in the glory of his Father with the holy angels" (8:38) leads to one of the most debated verses in Mark: "Truly, I say to you, there are some standing here who will not taste death before they see the kingdom of God come with power" (9:1). The general impression one receives from the Gospels is that Jesus assumed that the kingdom of God would come in its fullness within one generation or so (see esp. Mark 13:30). This expectation, reinforced by the resurrection, is evident throughout early Christian literature (especially in Paul). But Jesus also admits that he does not know the precise time (13:32). Do these sayings about the time of the kingdom's appearance derive from Jesus, or are these later Christian sayings that try to explain the kingdom's delay? (See the commentary on 13:28-32.)

The prediction in 9:1 coheres with the summary of his proclamation in 1:15: "The kingdom of God has arrived." It also coheres with another saying: "If it is by the finger of God that I cast out demons, then the kingdom of God has come upon you" (Luke 11:20). So, in a certain sense, Jesus understands the kingdom of God as having arrived and the exorcisms as evidence of its arrival. But why say that some of the disciples would still be alive if, having witnessed several exorcisms, they had already experienced the presence of the kingdom? The point of the saying in 9:1, that they will "see the kingdom of God come in power," seems to go beyond the saying in Luke 11:20. Given the close association of the saying in 8:28, it seems that the saying in 9:1 has to do with the *final consummation* of the kingdom. At the time of the writing of Mark this consummation had not yet taken place, and some of Jesus' followers were still living. Therefore the evangelist had no reason to think that this saying could not yet be fulfilled literally. However, the evangelist's placement of the saying in 9:1 immediately preceding the transfiguration narrative (9:2-8) suggests that he understood this unusual event as a foreshadowing of the full power of the kingdom (so Gundry 1993: 469). The partial fulfillment of Jesus' prediction in just one week of being uttered and the dramatic quality of this partial fulfillment guarantee the eventual comprehensive fulfillment.

The Transfiguration (9:2-8)

Several scholars have argued that Mark's account of the transfiguration was originally a resurrection appearance story. However, this theory has been challenged by many. Among other things, it has been observed that at many points the transfiguration account differs from the resurrection accounts found in the NT Gospels. It is not at all clear that the earliest accounts of Jesus' resurrection involved the kind of luminosity depicted in the transfiguration (see Gundry 1993: 471-73).

Many features about the transfiguration have led commentators to conclude that this episode is intended to have some sort of typological connection to Exodus 24 and 33–34, passages which describe Moses' ascent up Mt. Sinai, where he meets God and then descends with a shining face. The following specific parallels between Mark's account (9:2-8) and Exodus are evident: (1) the reference to "six days" (Mark 9:2; Exod 24:16), (2) the cloud that covers the mountain (Mark 9:7; Exod 24:16), (3) God's voice from the cloud (Mark 9:7; Exod 24:16), (4) three companions (Mark 9:2; Exod 24:1, 9), (5) a transformed appearance (Mark 9:3; Exod 34:30), and (6) the reaction of fear (Mark 9:6; Exod 34:30). Another suggestive item that should be mentioned is that in Exod 24:13 Joshua is singled out and taken up the mountain with Moses. Since "Joshua" in the Greek OT is frequently rendered "Jesus," the early church may have seen in Exod 24:13 a veiled prophecy, or typology, that came to fulfillment in the transfiguration where once again Moses and Jesus are together.

According to Mark, Jesus "was transfigured" (*metemorphōthē*) and his "clothing glistened and became exceedingly white" (9:2-3). The closest parallel is probably to the shining face of Moses (Exod 34:30), but the faces of other saints are described as shining (see 2 Esdr 7:97, 125; *1 Enoch* 37:7; 51:5; compare Luke 9:29, which specifically mentions Jesus' face). The clothing of the saints also will shine (see Dan 12:3; Rev 4:4; 7:9; *1 Enoch* 62:15; *Eccl. Rab.* 1:7 §9: "he will renew their faces and will renew their garments"). In one tradition it is said that when Elijah was born "men of shining white appearance greeted him and wrapped him in fire" (*Lives of the Prophets* 21:2). There are stories of transfigurations of the Greco-Roman gods. One thinks of Demeter, whose transfigured person filled a house with light (*Homeric Hymns* 2.275-80).

Mark's depiction of Jesus is also reminiscent of Daniel's vision of the "Ancient of Days," whose "clothing was white as snow, and the hair of his head like pure wool" (Dan 7:9). The "one like a son of man" approaches the Ancient of Days (i.e., God) and receives authority and kingdom (Dan 7:13-14). Perhaps in his transformation we should understand that Jesus, as the Son of Man, has taken on some of the characteristics of the Ancient of Days when in his presence (much as Moses' face begins to shine with God's glory). If this is correct, then the transfiguration should be understood as a visual verification of Jesus' claim to be the Son of Man who will come in the glory of his Father with the holy angels (see Mark 8:38; Dan 7:10).

Moses and Elijah are said to have appeared and to have spoken to Jesus (9:4). These two are often paired up. The two witnesses of Rev 11:3-12 could very well be Moses and Elijah (on Moses compare 9:6 with Exod 7:17, 19; on Elijah compare 9:5-6 with 2 Kgs 1:10). (However, Elijah is sometimes paired up with Enoch; see 2 Esdr 6:26; *Apoc. of Elijah* 4:7-19, which appears to be dependent on Revelation 11.) According to one rabbinic midrash, God promises in the future to bring Moses with Elijah (*Deut. Rab.* 3.17 [on Deut 10:1]). The rabbis compared Moses and Elijah at many points: "You find that two prophets rose up for Israel out of the tribe of Levi; one the first of all the prophets, and the other the last of all the prophets: Moses first and Elijah last, and both with a commission to redeem Israel. . . . You find that Moses and Elijah were alike in every respect. . . . Moses went up to heaven [cf. Exod 19:3]; and Elijah went up to heaven [cf. 2 Kgs 2:1]. . . . Moses: 'And the cloud covered him six days' [Exod 24:16]; and Elijah went up in a whirlwind [cf. 2 Kgs 2:1]" (*Pesiq. R.* 4.2). This rabbinic comparison is probably an elaboration of older traditions in which Moses and Elijah were believed to be involved in some way with the last days.

It is likely that Peter had concluded that the Last Day had arrived when some of the great events of the first exodus would be repeated (such as manna in the wilderness and God's presence among the people). To commemorate the exodus Jews celebrated the feast of Booths by living in small booths or huts for seven days (Lev 23:42-44; Neh 8:14-17). But the feast was also understood by many as looking ahead to the glorious day of Israel's deliverance.

The heavenly voice interrupts Peter (9:7) and may be partially intended as a rebuke (i.e., "listen to Jesus, not to Moses or Elijah"). The time of Moses and Elijah is over. It is time to heed the words of Jesus. The heavenly voice recalls the words uttered at the time of Jesus' baptism (1:10-11) and serves as a second divine endorsement: Jesus' talk of rejection and death has not disqualified him from his messianic task. He is still God's Son, and his message, now placed in a new light, must still be heeded.

Elijah and John (9:9-13)

The transfiguration, a foreshadowing of Jesus' resurrection and of the kingdom's power, is to be proclaimed when Jesus is resurrected. It is at this time that the disciples will proclaim Jesus' messiahship (as commanded by Jesus in 8:30). Mention of the resurrection of the "Son of Man" (9:9) prompts the disciples to ponder what this means (v. 10). From what follows we may infer that the disciples' question is as much chronological as it is logical. With regard to the latter, they wonder why Jesus must suffer and die at all. With regard to the former, they wonder when this resurrection will take place — before the appearance of Elijah, or after? Their uncertainty leads to the question about Elijah in v. 11: "Why do the scribes say that first Elijah must come?" This interpretive opinion is probably based on Mal 4:5-6, which in part reads: "Behold, I will send you Elijah the prophet *before* the great and terrible day of the LORD comes, who will restore the heart of parents to their children" (emphasis added). Jesus agrees: "Elijah does come first to restore all things" (v. 12a). Here Jesus not only alludes to Malachi, but his language is reminiscent of Sirach's praise of Elijah, who says that the great prophet is "ready at the appointed time . . . to restore the tribes of Jacob" (Sir 48:10). Sirach's hope of the restoration of the tribes finds expression in Jesus' appointment of the twelve (see the comment on 3:13-19 above). However, Elijah's ministry of restoration cannot be effected until the Son of Man suffers. "How is it written of the Son of Man? That he should suffer many things and be treated with contempt" (9:12b). But the Son of Man is not the only one who must suffer; Elijah, who has already come (here Jesus evidently identifies John as Elijah, which the Matthean evangelist explicitly and rightly states; cf. Matt 17:13), has been martyred.

The fate of John the Baptist leads Jesus to modify scribal interpretation. John, as Elijah *redivivus,* came to restore all things; Jesus, as the Son of Man, came to inaugurate God's kingdom, to wage war on Satan's kingdom. But both John and Jesus have faced or will face martyrdom. This martyrdom and the resurrection that will follow it will complete Jesus' mission.

Exorcism of the Demonized Boy (9:14-29)

The exorcism of the demonized boy provides Jesus the opportunity to demonstrate a power far beyond that of his disciples, who had earlier received authority over demons (Mark 6:7). The demon that successfully resists the disciples proves to be no match for Jesus. The exorcism also occasions Jesus' complaint about the lack of faith on the part of his contemporaries. Because no rebuke of the disciples is offered later in private (see 9:28-29), we should not assume that Jesus numbered them among the faithless.

Why was the crowd "greatly amazed" when they saw Jesus (v. 15)? Gundry (1993: 487) suggests that the afterglow of the transfiguration was still in evidence in Jesus' person. He may be correct, for "amaze" *(ekthambein)* is used in Mark 16:5-6, where the women see the young man (probably an angel) at the empty tomb, and in Mark 14:33-34, where Jesus is awestruck and troubled at the prospects of death. The exorcism of the boy takes place right after the transfiguration of Jesus, which in turn had been followed by a prediction of death. Thus all three passages are linked by aspects of Jesus' death, which in various ways and for various reasons amazes people.

Jesus' complaint, "You faithless generation, how long am I to be with you?" (9:19), underscores the importance of faith (see esp. v. 23) and hints at Jesus' impending fate. On the association of faith and deliverance (whether exorcism or physical healing), see Mark 2:5; 5:34, 36; 10:52. For teaching on faith, see 4:40; 11:22-24. The father's anguished cry, "I believe; help my unbelief!" (9:24), serves as a model for Mark's readers.

The violence of the exorcism attests to the power of the demon and the even greater power of Jesus. The convulsions (9:20) demonstrate the demon's defiance in the presence of Jesus. The disciples could not evict it; neither can Jesus, or so the evil spirit assumes. But the demon is quite wrong. Jesus commands it to leave; it does, but not without one final convulsion (v. 26a). The deathlike appearance of the boy brings the violent scene to a climax. People in the crowd comment: "He is dead" (v. 26b). Did the demon win after all? Its intention all along had been to destroy the boy (by throwing him into water and fire; see v. 22). But no; Jesus takes him by the hand and lifts him up. The boy lives; the demon has been vanquished. The episode ends with Jesus explaining to his disciples that this kind of virulent spirit can be cast out only by prayer (some mss add: "and fasting"); that is, the *disciples* must pray. *Jesus* merely commands the evil spirit and it obeys.

Second Passion Prediction (9:30-32)

For the second time Jesus formally predicts his passion (on the first prediction, see 8:31 above). The concluding part affirms that after three days "he will rise" (9:31). The word used here is the same used in describing the rising of the boy who had appeared dead (v. 27). The context suggests that the boy's rising foreshadows Jesus' resurrection. The disciples are afraid to ask Jesus to elaborate on his prediction, perhaps because they feared that further questioning and explanation would only confirm the grim pronouncement. The disciples' fear and ignorance (v. 32) stand in sharp contrast to Jesus' foreknowledge and self-assurance.

Dispute about Greatness (9:33-37)

This is the first passage in which Jesus teaches on humility. He will again in the next chapter (see 10:13-16, 41-45). Jesus overhears his men discussing something. He asks about it, but the sheepish disciples remain silent (9:33-34). His comments show that he had overheard enough to know that they had been talking about who was the greatest. (In 10:35-37 James and John will ask Jesus to grant them positions on his left and right.) Jesus pronounces, "If any one would be first, he must be last of all and servant of all" (9:35). To be "first" or "last" refers to social and political position (as opposed to merely being first or last in a line). This is seen in Josephus, who describes the leading men and ruling priests of his day as the "first men" (*Ant.* 11.5.3 §§140-41; 18.3.3 §64; 18.5.3 §121), as well as in Mark (see 6:21). The point is confirmed by the parallel between "servant" and "last." Plutarch (late 1st cent. AD) warns his contemporaries to flee the vice of the love of fame and the "desire to be first and greatest" (*Moralia,* "Public Affairs," 8).

The action of taking a child (9:36) and the saying about receiving a child in Jesus' name (v. 37) may not originally have been linked to the saying about being first and last. But the evangelist places the material here because it illustrates the kind of humility Jesus values. Powerful people often ignore the powerless, and children in any society are the least powerful. By taking the child into his arms, Jesus, who is by far the most powerful figure in Mark's narrative, demonstrates the idea of the powerful receiving the weak and marginalized. He adds that to receive such persons is in fact to receive him, and to receive him is to receive the one who sent him, namely, God himself (compare the saying in *Te'ezaza Sanbat,* where God says to personified Sabbath: "Those who honor you honor me, and those who reject you reject me"). Those who think of themselves as servants are not as likely to despise the lowly and weak in society or in the church.

Another Exorcist (9:38-41)

Jesus was not the only exorcist in first-century Palestine. According to Josephus (*Ant.* 8.2.5 §§45-49), a certain Eleazar, who followed the incantations of Solomon, could draw out demons through a person's nostrils, through use of the Baaras root (for description of the plant, see Josephus *J.W.* 7.6.3 §§180-85). The church father Origen knew of exorcists who made use of these incantations (*Commentary on Matthew* 33 [on Matt 26:63]). In material common to Matthew and Luke, Jesus responds to those who accuse him of casting out demons with the aid of Beelzebul (see commentary on Mark 3:20-22) by asking his critics: "By whom do your sons cast them out?" (Matt 12:27 = Luke 11:19). Later rabbinic legends tell us that the holy man Hanina ben Dosa banned the "queen of the demons" from inhabited places (*b. Pesaḥ.* 112b). In view of this material it comes as no surprise that there were other men casting out demons. But the disciples report that one man was exorcising in Jesus' name (9:38). This shows that Jesus' power had become so well known that exorcists were making use of his name, even as many made use of Solomon's name. (On the danger of using Jesus' name illicitly, see Acts 19:13-15, where the demon knows and respects the names of Jesus and Paul, but neither knows nor respects the opportunistic exorcists who invoke them.)

Jesus, however, commands his disciples not to forbid this man, for no one who does a mighty work in his name will soon after speak evil of him (9:39). Jesus reasons that when a person discovers the power of Jesus, she or he will join him, not oppose him. In his war against Satan, Jesus welcomes allies. The saying in v. 40 might originally have been part of this exchange, or it might have been added by the evangelist (or the tradition before him) as further clarification of the point (compare the similar saying that appears in different contexts in Matt 12:30 = Luke 11:23). The saying in v. 41 has probably been added by the Markan evangelist (compare its different location in Matt 10:42). What draws the saying to the present context is the reference to the "name of Christ." If a person shows someone kindness because he is a follower of Jesus, he will be rewarded. This is similar to the saying in 9:37 in which one is assured that receiving a child in Jesus' name is to receive Jesus himself, indeed even God. Both sayings may very well reflect the experience of the church during times of persecution (especially in the 60s AD).

Discourse on Temptations (9:42-50)

Mark rounds out Jesus' teaching on discipleship with a collection of sayings that look back to 9:36-37 and 41 and the general theme of humility. The material has probably been edited in the light of the church's experience (as seen especially in v. 42). Vv. 42-48 may originally have formed a unity, but the sayings that make up vv. 49 and 50 probably have been drawn from other contexts (compare the different contexts in Matt 5:13 = Luke 14:34).

The gruesome figurative speech that Jesus employs underscores the importance of what is at stake. To trip up anyone, including the small and marginalized, and so to cause them to sin (which could mean to fall away) will result in judgment. Better to commit suicide or to maim oneself than to be guilty of such an offense. (Again, the warning here is probably best understood in the life of the church during a time of persecution.) This sort of figurative language is also found outside of Jewish and Christian circles. According to Plato (5th-6th cents. BC), "men are prepared to have their own feet and hands cut off if they feel these possessions to be harmful" (*Symp.* 204e). Similarly, Porphyry (late 3d cent. AD) says: "Often people amputate some limb to save their lives; you should be prepared to amputate the whole body to save your soul" (*Letter to Marcella* 34).

Jesus' description of Gehenna as the place "where their worm does not die, and the fire is not quenched" (9:48; in later mss. this saying appears in vv. 44 and 46) is taken from Isa 66:24. The association of this Isaianic verse with Gehenna reflects the Aramaic tradition as seen in the Isaiah Targum, which adds: "the wicked shall be judged in Gehenna." Jesus evidently understood Isa 66:24 in a similar way and so appealed to this verse in describing the dangers of judgment.

Two "salt" sayings conclude the passage. Jesus warns that "every one will be salted with fire" (9:49), by which he means everyone will be judged (see Luke 12:49). The second saying scores a different point: "Salt is good; but if the salt has lost its saltiness, how will you season it?" (v. 50a). Here salt should be understood in reference to friendship, as we see in several sayings in late antiquity: "Homer calls salt 'divine' . . . the most truly godlike seasoning at the dining table is the presence of a friend" (Plutarch "Table Talk" 7; see also Plutarch "On Having Many Friends" 3). Philo speaks of the "salt of hospitality" (*Somn.* 2.210). The "covenant of salt" in the OT connotes the friendship between God and his people Israel (see Lev 2:13; Num 18:19; 2 Chr 13:5). Therefore, says Jesus to his disciples, you are to "have salt in yourselves, and be at peace with one another" (9:50b; see Ezek 43:24-27, where the Israelites are commanded to put salt on their "peace" offerings).

Question of Divorce (10:1-12)

To test Jesus, some Pharisees ask if it is lawful for a man to divorce his wife (10:2). The issue was as controversial in the first century as it is today (though not as common). Jesus counters with a question of his own: "What has Moses commanded you?" (v. 3). The Pharisees reply with a summary of Deut 24:1-4: "Moses permitted a man to write a certificate of divorce, and to put her away" (v. 4). The Pharisees' question does not reflect a concern for the correct answer but is a test to see how Jesus can reconcile potentially contradictory passages: Whereas Moses permits divorce, according to the prophet Malachi, God "hate[s] divorce" (Mal 2:16). The Pharisees' question, therefore, is not easily answered. But Jesus does so. He begins by qualifying Moses: laws governing divorce had to be provided on account of human sinfulness (which is what is meant by "hardness of heart"). The law was not meant to encourage divorce, but was designed to protect women, who often were victimized by it. God's true attitude toward divorce is seen in the creation account of Genesis: "God made them male and female. For this reason a man shall leave his father and mother and be joined to his wife; and the two shall become one flesh" (10:6-8; Gen 1:27 plus 2:24). (Genesis, as one of the books of Moses, would also be viewed as part of the law. Note that Gen 1:27 is cited in CD 4:19-21 to indict Jerusalem's ruling priests for divorce and remarriage.) Jesus' concluding statement, "What therefore God has joined together, let not man put asunder" (10:9), reflects his interpretation of the two passages. The Mosaic legislation in Deuteronomy 24 has to do with sinful actions of humans (not God's will), while the creation account in Genesis has to do with God's purposes. God puts a man and a woman together; sinful humans wrongly pull them apart. This idea was also expressed in part in the Gentile world, as seen when the goddess Isis says: "I have brought woman and man together" (*SIG* 3.1267).

How to Receive the Kingdom (10:13-31)

The saying about receiving the kingdom of God like a child (10:15) should be interpreted in the light of the saying in 9:37. The point does not center on how a child behaves (which is often selfish and seldom exemplary), but on the lowly position a child occupies in society. A person receives the kingdom without any presumption of worthiness.

Jesus' conversation with the rich young man (10:17-22) is a classic in the Gospel tradition. The young man runs up to Jesus, which points to the urgency of his concern, then kneels, showing profound respect. He addresses Jesus as "good teacher," and then asks what he must do "to inherit eternal life" (v. 17). Jesus' counterquestion, "Why do you call me good? No one is good but God alone" (v. 18), has nonplussed interpreters from the first century to the present. Matthew revises the question: "Why do you ask me about what is good?" (19:17). But the point made in Mark's form of the question should not be missed. In saying that only God is good, Jesus in effect makes it impossible for the young man, or anyone else for that matter, to be good. Not even by keeping the commandments written in the law can a human being attain to God's goodness. This truth is quickly illustrated when the young man is unwilling to comply with Jesus' recommendation that he sell his possessions and give to the poor. Although he has obeyed the major laws of the Ten Commandments (10:19-20; see Exod 20:12-16; Deut 5:16-20), he cannot bring himself to part with his wealth. We should recall what Jesus regards as the Great Commandment: to love God with one's whole being (which includes one's wealth) and to love one's neighbor as oneself (Mark 12:28-34). The rich man fails to love his neighbor as himself, and by implication he has probably failed to love God with his whole being. The man wants to be assured of eternal life but not if he is inconvenienced by it.

In response to Jesus' pronouncement, "How hard it will be for the wealthy to enter the kingdom of God!" (v. 23), and remarkable analogy, "It is easier for the camel to go through the eye of a needle than for a rich man to enter the kingdom of God" (v. 25), the stunned disciples ask, "Then who can be saved?" (v. 26). The question is prompted by the widespread assumption that health and wealth were signs of divine blessing, while disease and poverty were signs of judgment. It was further assumed that because God is fair the blessed surely are righteous, while the judged surely are sinners. These generalizing assumptions (and exceptions, of course, would be allowed) are rooted in Deuteronomy, which promises blessings for obedient Israel but judgment for disobedient Israel (see the summary in Deuteronomy 30).

According to Jesus, people cannot save themselves; only God can (10:27; see Philo *Vit. Mos.* 1.31 §174: "What is impossible to all created beings is possible to [God] only"). Harking back to the rich young man who was unwilling to give up his wealth, Peter cites himself and the other disciples as examples of those who have given up everything to follow Jesus (v. 28). Jesus assures his disciples that whatever they have given up for his sake and for the sake of the gospel will be paid back one hundredfold in this life (vv. 29-30; see *T. Job* 4:6-9). But his followers must also understand that persecutions will accompany these earthly rewards. But in the age to come they will receive eternal life (v. 31). In what way will Jesus' followers receive in this life houses, brothers, sisters, and land? All of these things will be gained through the new community that Jesus has begun to establish. Whatever is left behind due to the demands of the ministry or due to flight from persecution, Jesus' follower may look forward to receiving through Christian hospitality.

Third Passion Prediction (10:32-34)

Jesus now predicts his passion for the third time. This prediction is much more detailed than the previous two (see 8:31; 9:31). Jesus says: "Behold, we are going up to Jerusalem; and the Son of Man will be delivered to the ruling priests and the scribes, and they will condemn him to death, and deliver him to the Gentiles; and they will mock him, and spit upon him, and scourge him, and kill him; and after three days he will rise" (10:33-34). The fear and amazement of those accompanying Jesus heighten the sense of drama. Everything about Jesus has astounded his contemporaries, from his miracles and exorcisms to his solemn pronouncements and predictions of passion.

This third and climactic prediction summarizes the principal features of the passion of Jesus. His condemnation to death as the "Son of Man" at the hands of the high priest and ruling priests occurs in Mark 14:55-65. Jesus will be handed over to the Gentiles in 15:1. The Gentiles will mock Jesus in 15:20. They will spit upon him in 15:19 (the ruling priests also will spit on him in 14:65), and they will flog him in 15:15. As on the earlier occasions Jesus predicts that "after three days he will rise."

A Request to Sit at Jesus' Right and Left (10:35-45)

The request of James and John, the sons of Zebedee, to sit at Jesus' right and left in his glory (10:35-37) is in effect a request to occupy the preeminent positions of authority in the new government that they anticipate will be established not long after Jesus enters Jerusalem. Their request recalls the earlier dispute among the disciples as to who was the most important (see 9:33-37).

Jesus asks them if they are prepared to "drink the cup" that he will drink and to "be baptized with the baptism" that he will undergo (10:38). By this Jesus means suffering and death. ("Cup" used figuratively means fate, with or without judgment in view; see Pss 11:6; 16:5; sometimes it refers to suffering and judgment; see Isa 51:22; Jer 25:15; but the actual idiom "cup of death" is targumic and is the closest parallel to the words of Jesus; see *Tg. Neof.* Gen 40:23; *Tg. Neof.* Deut 32:1). James and John say they are able to drink this cup and to undergo the baptism that awaits Jesus (though they might not yet have been convinced that Jesus' violent fate was inevitable). Jesus assures (warns?) them that they will indeed share his fate. But the assignment of seats at his right and left is not his prerogative; it is God's.

The disciples' expectations of sitting on thrones derives from a statement that Jesus makes but is not recorded in Mark: "In the new world, when the Son of Man shall sit on his glorious throne, you who have followed me will also sit on twelve thrones, judging the twelve tribes of Israel" (Matt 19:28; see also Luke 22:28-30). The idea that the "Son of Man" will sit on a throne and that the saints will sit on thrones is derived from Dan 7:9-14, a vision in which "thrones" are set up and the kingdom is given to the human who comes with the clouds of heaven. Jesus understands himself in these terms (see the commentary on 2:1-12 above and on 14:53-65 below).

When the rest of the disciples hear of this conversation they become indignant at James and John. Jesus responds by elaborating on his earlier teaching in 9:33-37. The style and philosophy of leadership of his disciples are to be substantially different from those of rulers in the secular world. They seek power and aspire to lord it over others. But it is not to be this way with his disciples. The great among Jesus' followers are to be servants. Even the Son of Man himself, contrary to what might be inferred from Dan 7:14 ("And to him was given dominion . . . that all peoples . . . should serve him"), "did not come to be served but to serve, and to give his life a ransom for many" (10:45).

Giving "his life as a ransom for many" probably alludes to Isaiah 53 (esp. vv. 11-12; for the possible influence of the Aramaic version, see the commentary on Mark 2:1-12 above). The concept of giving one's life for Israel is attested in Jewish literature of late antiquity. One immediately thinks of the courageous sons who refused to abandon their faith, one of whom says to Antiochus Epiphanes: "I, like my brothers, give up body and life for the laws of our fathers, appealing to God to show mercy soon to our nation and by afflictions and plagues to make you confess that he alone is God, and through me to bring to an end the wrath of the Almighty which has justly fallen on our whole nation" (2 Macc 7:37-38).

Blind Bartimaeus (10:46-52)

The southward journey at last takes Jesus and his following to Jericho, some fifteen miles northeast of Jerusalem. The next major leg of the journey will take them to Jerusalem itself, a wearisome uphill trek. When he leaves Jericho he is, as almost always, accompanied by crowds of people. Among these is Bartimaeus, a blind beggar. His cry, "Son of David, Jesus, have mercy on me!" (10:47), carries with it an unmistakable messianic ring (note the forward placement of the title of honor; see also *T. Sol.* 20:1-2, where a distraught father addresses Solomon: "King Solomon, son of David, have mercy on me!"). The crowd attempts to hush the man (possibly because of the political dangers of such an epithet but more probably because he is viewed as a nuisance), but he is as determined as ever and continues to cry out, "Son of David, have mercy on me!" (10:48). Reflecting the teaching of the immediately preceding passage (vv. 40-45), Jesus demonstrates a willingness to render service to one in need. The contrast is marked: Jesus, the son of David (and, as such, Israel's first citizen), stopping to help a beggar of no account named son of Timaeus. The idea of service is made plain by Jesus' inquiry: "What do you want me to do for you?" That is, does the man want alms or something else? The blind man requests his sight, and Jesus grants it: "Go, your faith has saved you" (v. 52). With the command "go" Jesus has dismissed others whom he has healed (see 1:44; 2:11; 5:19, 34; 7:29; on being healed through faith, see 5:34). One is again reminded of the scene in which the blind man approaches Emperor Vespasian for healing (Suetonius *Vespasian* 7; Tacitus *Hist.* 4.81; see the commentary on Mark 8:22-26 above). Now able to see, Bartimaeus falls in with the procession trailing Jesus. Hailing Jesus as "Son of David" prepares for the triumphal entry into Jerusalem.

Jesus Confronts Jerusalem (11:1–13:37)

In Mark 11–13 the reader is treated to a series of scenes in which Jesus confronts Jerusalem and its temple establishment. From hopeful entry to final pronouncement of judgment and destruction, this part of the Markan Gospel traces the escalation of animosity toward Jesus and the escalation of Jesus' criticisms. Virtually every passage contributes in some way to this theme.

Entrance into Jerusalem (11:1-11)

In preparation for his entry into Jerusalem Jesus sends ahead two disciples. The instructions that he gives them and events that follow show that arrangements had been made. The Markan evangelist is not privy to these arrangements (nor is he privy to the arrangements that were made to secure the upper room; see the comments on 14:12-16). We should not assume that Jesus has demonstrated supernatural knowledge (i.e., he knew that a colt would be tethered in the street and that onlookers would surrender it if the right words were spoken). What is demonstrated is Jesus' mastery of the situation. It may also hint at his assumption of political authority, at least on a par with Roman authority.

Mark calls the animal a "colt" *(pōlos),* which may mean a young horse, not necessarily a young donkey. Mark's Roman readers would have had no reason to imagine anything other than a horse. (It is Matthew who cites Zech 9:9 and speaks of a donkey; see Matt 21:1-7.) The actions of Jesus' followers (11:8) are reminiscent of honors accorded Israel's past rulers. Throwing garments on the colt and on the road before reminds us of the royal anointing of Jehu and how the Israelites placed their garments on the steps before him (2 Kgs 9:12-13). The branches placed before Jesus recall the reception that Judas Maccabeus, Israel's great intertestamental leader, received after purifying the temple (2 Macc 10:7). Riding the colt, which may or may not have called to mind Zech 9:9, would also have been reminiscent of Solomon, David's son, who rode his father's mule and was proclaimed king (1 Kgs 1:32-48).

The shouts that meet Jesus, "Hosanna! Blessed is he who comes in the name of the Lord! Blessed is the kingdom of our father David that is coming!" (11:9-10), allude to Ps 118:26. The coherence with the interpretive tendencies preserved in the Psalms targum is especially suggestive. In v. 22 it speaks of the rejected boy (instead of stone, as it is in the Hebrew) who was a son of Jesse and is worthy to be appointed king and ruler. Although David was initially rejected by the builders (i.e., the religious authorities; see CD 4:19; 8:12; Acts 4:11), the builders will later bless him from the temple precincts: "Blessed is the one who comes in the name of the word of the LORD"

(v. 26). The ruling priests then celebrate David's kingship by sacrificing a lamb (v. 27). How ancient this Aramaic tradition is cannot be determined with certainty, but the association of Ps 118:26 with the kingdom of David suggests that elements of this interpretive tradition lie behind the words of the enthusiastic crowd. (For more on Psalm 118 in Jesus' thinking, see the commentary on Mark 12:1-12 below.) There can be no doubt that the people that make up Jesus' following anticipate the imminent appearance of a Davidic kingdom. That Jesus would only one week later be crucified as "King of the Jews" (15:2, 26) is compelling evidence that this was indeed what the crowd hoped would come about under Jesus' leadership.

The triumphal entry comes to a halting, uncertain conclusion. Jesus enters the temple, looks around, then retires. Mark notes, almost lamely, that "it was already late" (11:11). The procession ends the way it does because none of the priests greets Jesus. There are no calls of Hosanna from the temple steps. Jesus is ignored. He will not be ignored when he enters the temple the next day.

The Fig Tree (11:12-14)

Hungry, Jesus espies a fig tree in full leaf. He approaches it hoping to find edible buds (which can appear in the spring). But he is disappointed; there is nothing but leaves (11:13). (For those unfamiliar with the habits of the fig tree, the evangelist explains that it was not the season for full-grown figs. They appear later in the summer.) This prompts Jesus to utter a curse, which was overheard by his disciples: "May no one ever eat fruit from you again" (v. 14). The barren fig tree and Jesus' reaction to it foreshadow the demonstration in the temple that will take place later in the day. The barren fig tree does not, however, symbolize *Israel.* As the context makes clear, it is the *temple establishment* that is criticized and threatened.

Action in the Temple (11:15-19)

Abruptly and without ceremony Jesus enters the temple precincts and "began to drive out those who sold and those who bought . . . and he overturned the tables of the money changers and the seats of those who sold pigeons" (11:15). Not only that, he "would not allow anyone to carry anything through the temple" precincts (v. 16; see Josephus *Ag. Ap.* 2.8 §106, who says that "no vessel whatever might be carried into the temple"). On a historical level it is possible that Jesus was pursuing a line of action that arose out of his understanding of Zechariah (as seen in mounting the colt and entering the city, and now in the action he has taken in the temple). The temple action, traditionally known as a "cleansing" (though cleansing language occurs nowhere in the passage), may have been prompted by Zech 14:20-21, a passage that anticipates the day when every vessel in the temple will be pure and there shall no longer be any trader in the precincts. Shortly before his arrest, Jesus is remembered to have alluded to Zech 13:7 when he says, "I will strike the shepherd" (see the commentary on Mark 14:26-31 below). But the Markan evangelist himself shows little interest in Zechariah, having made no reference to the appropriate passages in the triumphal entry or in the action in the temple.

Mark's critical stance toward the temple establishment is reflected in Jesus' utterance in 11:17: "Is it not written, 'My house shall be called a house of prayer for all the Gentiles'? But you have made it a 'cave of robbers.'" The first part of the statement alludes to Isa 56:7, part of a larger oracle (Isa 56:1-8) that looks forward to the day when people from all over the world, including Gentiles, come to the temple to worship God. It will be a time when their sacrifices will be acceptable. But in Jesus' view the temple establishment has failed to live up to this standard; it is not prepared for the new order that will come with the kingdom of God. Instead of a house of prayer the temple has become a "cave of robbers." Here Jesus has alluded to Jer 7:11, part of a passage in which the prophet Jeremiah indicted the temple establishment of his day, warning that it would be destroyed.

Did Jesus encounter policies or activities that he regarded as corrupt, and, if so, what were they? From rabbinic tradition we hear of a first-century protest against a policy of overcharging for doves, the poor person's sacrifice (*m. Ker.* 1:7). Josephus tells us of shameful, strong-armed actions of the ruling priests against the lower-ranking priests in the years before the great revolt of AD 66-70, in an effort to steal the tithes (*Ant.* 20.8.8 §181; 20.9.2 §§206-7). Josephus relates stories of religious teachers inciting crowds to take action in the temple precincts over questions of purity (*Ant.* 13.13.5 §§372-73; *J.W.* 1.33.2-4 §§648-55; *Ant.* 17.6.2-4 §§149-67). These incidents suggest a range of disputes and practices, any one or more of which may have been at issue the year that Jesus visited Jerusalem at Passover time (on the importance of purity, see Chilton 1992, 1996).

In light of the threatening comments that Jesus will make as passion week continues to unfold (see the parable in 12:1-12, the prophecy of destruction in 13:1-2, and the accusation in 14:58) there can be little doubt that the allusion to Jer 7:11 implied that the temple of Jesus' day also stood in danger of destruction. As indicated by its linkage with the cursed fig tree, it is highly probable that the evangelist Mark understood Jesus' utterance this way.

Lesson of the Fig Tree (11:20-26)

In the morning Jesus and his disciples pass by the fig tree which Jesus the day before had cursed. They observe that it had withered to its very roots, and Peter exclaims as much (11:21). For Jesus it is an example of faith. When he spoke to the tree, he meant it, and he had faith that God heard and would act. Jesus had destroyed a tree; his disciples can move mountains. They must pray with faith, and they must forgive others while they pray. If they do, God will forgive them and, by implication, answer their prayers. Given the context, the reference to casting "this mountain" into the sea could be to the Temple Mount itself.

The cursing of the fig tree in 11:12-14 and the discovery of its withered condition here in vv. 20-21, surrounding the temple action described in vv. 15-19, foreshadow the temple's judgment and doom. If the temple establishment has no fruit to offer God, that is, no more than the fig tree had to offer Jesus, then it, too, is in danger of destruction.

Question of Authority (11:27-33)

When Jesus returns to the temple precincts he is met by a delegation of ruling priests, scribes, and elders. They demand that Jesus tell them "by what authority" he has done what he has done (11:28). They are referring, of course, to the actions and words of Jesus in the temple precincts the previous day (vv. 15-19). These representatives of Jerusalem's elite are attempting to take stock of Jesus. Whose backing does he enjoy? Whom does he represent? Does he think he is a prophet and as such speaks and acts in God's name?

Jesus counters with a question of his own: "I will ask you a question; answer me, and I will tell you by what authority I do these things" (11:29). Jesus has thrown the burden back to the priestly delegation. He asks them, "Was the baptism of John from heaven or from men?" (v. 31). They are caught in a dilemma. If they answered according to what they really believe (i.e., "from men"), the people would be outraged, for they regarded John as a true prophet and martyr (v. 32). To belittle John would reveal to the people that many of the Jewish elite are little more than collaborators with Rome and with Rome's client kings, the Herodians. However, if they adopt the political expedient and say that John derived his authority "from heaven" (i.e., from God), which would win support from the people, it would then be hard to criticize Jesus, a former associate of John, for claiming the same authority. If Jerusalem's ruling elites truly believed that John's ministry was of God, they would have to respect it. The same would apply to Jesus. But this they cannot admit.

Checkmated, the delegation responds that they do not know the answer to Jesus' question (v. 33). Recognizing the dodge for what it is, Jesus replies: "Neither will I tell you by what authority I do these things." The reader of Mark knows, of course, that Jesus' authority is from God. As the human being (i.e., "son of man") of Daniel 7, Jesus has received royal authority from God (see the commentary on 2:10, 28). Possessed of this royal authority, he may rightly be hailed "son of David" (10:47, 48), he may enter Jerusalem as a royal figure amid shouts for deliverance and the coming kingdom of David (11:9-10), and he may review the activities of the temple precincts (11:11, 15-19; see 2 Kgs 12:1-16, where temple reforms are initiated by King Josiah).

Parable of the Vineyard Tenants (12:1-12)

Immediately after telling the priestly delegation that he will not divulge to them by what authority he acts (11:33), Jesus begins his parable of the wicked tenants. Mark's chapter division is unfortunate, for it interrupts the continuation of the discussion in the temple precincts and obscures for readers the wider context. Jesus had refused to disclose the source of his authority explicitly, but implicitly he will now disclose it in the parable (i.e., he is the son of the man who owns the vineyard, which in turn implies that Jesus views himself as God's Son). The ruling priests, scribes, and elders remain to hear the parable, which they rightly perceive is told against them (12:12). The parable only escalates the growing hostilities between Jesus and the temple establishment.

The parable begins with the development of a vineyard and its leasing to tenant farmers. The details, such as the tower and the wine vat, are drawn from Isaiah's Song of the Vineyard (Isa 5:1-7), which proves to be important for our interpretation. The owner of the vineyard (which in light of Isaiah 5 must be understood as God, while the vineyard represents Israel) sends one servant after another (by which is probably meant the prophets), but the tenant farmers treat them roughly, refusing to render payment. Finally, the owner sends his own son, but he is murdered and cast out of the vineyard. "What will the owner of the vineyard do?" Jesus asks, and then provides the expected answer: "He will come and destroy the tenants, and give the vineyard to others" (12:9; see Matt 21:41, where the crowd supplies the answer: "He will put those wretches to a miserable death"). Jesus concludes the parable with a quotation of Ps 118:22-23 ("The stone which the builders rejected . . .").

The evangelist comments that the ruling priests "perceived that the parable had been told against them" (12:12). They would have liked to have arrested Jesus, but do not for fear of the crowd. How did Jesus' enemies know that the parable had been directed against them? Would they have identified themselves, the affluent and powerful, as the tenant farmers? Was not Isaiah's Song of the Vineyard directed against the "men of Judah" and the "inhabitants of Jerusalem"? The Isaiah targum interprets the tower as the sanctuary and the wine vat as the altar. When God judges his vineyard, he will destroy these items (see *Tg. Isa* 5:1-7). This narrowing of the focus of judgment from the people in general to the temple establishment coheres with Jesus' parable and its understanding of Isaiah 5. The Isaiah targum in this instance probably retains ancient interpretive tradition which developed in the synagogue, with which Jesus evidently was acquainted (see Chilton 1984: 111-14). This helps us understand why the priestly delegation sensed that the parable was directed against them. Greek papyri and other sources from late antiquity have also made it clear that the wealthy were often involved in the leasing of farms for commercial purposes (see Evans 1995: 381-406). Indeed, the only instances we know of where high-handed action was taken against powerful creditors were committed by prominent and wealthy men (e.g., see *P. Cairo Zenon* no. 59.018, which describes the physical abuse and ejection from town of servants of a powerful man who had attempted to collect overdue payments).

The appearance of Ps 118:22-23 at the conclusion of a parable that tells of the rejection and murder of a "beloved son" (12:6) is particularly interesting. The Psalms targum paraphrases Ps 118:22 thus: "The boy which the builders abandoned was among the sons of Jesse, and he is worthy to be appointed king and ruler." Although the Markan evangelist supplies us with a verbatim quotation of the Greek version of Ps 118:22-23, which speaks of the "stone" which the builders rejected, one suspects again that the interpretive tradition underlying the Aramaic paraphrase was known to Jesus and was the reason why he appealed to this passage. The Aramaic's substitution of "boy" for "stone" probably comes from the similar-sounding Hebrew words *ha-'eben* ("the stone") and *habben* ("the son"). This very wordplay seems to lie behind a detail related by Josephus, who says that when a Roman siege stone was seen hurtling toward the city, the lookouts would yell, "The son comes!" (*J.W.* 5.6.3 §272). Although the Greek words *lithos* ("stone") and *huios* ("son") bear no resemblance, the underlying Hebrew words do. The same wordplay is probably reflected in the Baptist's assertion that "God is able from these stones to raise up children to Abraham" (Matt 3:9 = Luke 3:8). There was probably wordplay originally, but in the Hebrew or Aramaic, not between the Greek words *lithoi* ("stones") and *tekna* ("children").

The linkage of Ps 118:22-23 to the rejected son of the parable, through Hebrew and Aramaic, argues against the view that the appearance of the passage is due to the Greek-speaking church (as some commentators argue). The Greek-speaking church may have been responsible for the assimilation of a non-Greek allusion to Psalm 118 to a formal quotation of the Greek OT. Moreover, the allusive presence of Ps 118:26 in the entrance narrative (11:9-10) coheres with its use here at the conclusion of the parable, lending additional support to the antiquity and authenticity of the tradition (see the commentary on 11:1-10 above). Jesus entered Jerusalem as the Davidic king, recognized as such by his enthusiastic followers, but rejected by the "builders" (on builders as religious authorities, see CD 4:19; 8:12, 18; Acts 4:11; 1 Cor 3:10; *Song Rab.* 1:5 §3; *Exod Rab.* 23:10 (on 15:11); *b. Ber.* 64a; *b. Shab.* 114a). He hints that the wicked tenants have rejected no one less than God's Son and will, as a consequence, suffer the loss of their privileged position. God will take away their stewardship and give it to others.

Question about Taxes (12:13-17)

In an effort to lure Jesus into making a dangerous statement, the Pharisees and Herodians ask whether or not it is lawful to pay taxes to Caesar. The question is a good one; many Jews in first-century Palestine pondered it. For Jesus to say "yes" would diminish his popularity (and make it easiser for the ruling priests to arrest him); to say "no" would easily lead to a charge of sedition, making Roman arrest all but inevitable (see Josephus *J.W.* 2.8.1 §117, who tells of Judas the Galilean [C. AD 6-9], who upbraided fellow Jews as cowards for paying tribute to the Romans).

Since arriving in Jerusalem, Jesus has been rumored to be a messianic descendant of David and proclaimer of the kingdom of God. As Israel's sovereign, surely he would not authorize payment of taxes to a foreign king, would he? But Jesus does not take the bait. He asks his questioners to produce a coin. They do, and by possessing it show that they have submitted to Caesar's authority. Again, Jesus responds to his critics' question with a question of his own: "Whose are this image and inscription?" "Caesar's," comes the reply. Then "give to Caesar what is Caesar's, and give to God what is God's" (12:17). Jesus' answer is clever, to be sure, but it is more than that. Lying behind it is probably the principle of conscience, a principle that will surface elsewhere in early Christian literature (e.g., in Paul's letters to Corinth and Rome). As long as one gives God what is due, it matters little what is given to Caesar.

Debate about Resurrection (12:18-27)

Having dodged a potentially dangerous political question, Jesus is now tested with a tricky theological question. The Sadducees know that Jesus, along with the Pharisees, believes in the resurrection. They themselves believe in no such thing (see Acts 23:8; Josephus *J.W.* 2.8.11-14 §§154-66), which for Mark's readers means that they would roundly reject Jesus' previous predictions of his own resurrection. They attempt to show that belief in the resurrection leads to violation of the commandments of Moses. They reason: if a woman is married successively to seven brothers (in keeping with the law of levirate marriage; see Deut 25:5-6), then in the resurrection she will have seven husbands, which of course is adulterous and unlawful.

Jesus responds by showing that the Sadducees do not know the Scriptures, nor the power of God (12:24; note the biting irony of the rhetorical question, which could be paraphrased: "Does not your confusion arise from ignorance . . . ?"; see also 12:10, "Do you not know this scripture?"). In the resurrection, human beings are angel-like; they no longer marry (see *2 Bar.* 51:10, where the righteous "will be like the angels"; and *2 Enoch* 22:10). Therefore, the levirate laws that bind men and women on earth no longer apply. As to scriptural warrant for the doctrine of the resurrection, which is the real point of contention, one may infer from Exod 3:6, where God says that he is the "God of Abraham," that the patriarchs still live; for God is not the God of the dead but of the living. Jesus' appeal to a passage taken from one of the books of the law is strategic, for only these books were recognized by the Sadducees as fully inspired and authoritative. (To have appealed to Dan 12:1-2, a passage from a book probably not recognized by Sadducees, would have been pointless.) That God is the "God of the living" is implied throughout Scripture. Many times in the creation account God creates and "living" things appear (see Gen 1:20, 21, 24, 28). God breathes into Adam and he becomes a "living" being (Gen 2:7). God is himself frequently referred to as the "living God" (Deut 5:26; Josh 3:10; 1 Sam 17:26, 36; Ps 42:2; Jer 10:10; 23:36; Dan 6:20, 26; Hos 1:10). From this close association of God and life one may infer that a similar association exists between God and the patriarchs, whose names so frequently serve to identify God (for "God of Abraham, Isaac, and Jacob/Israel," see Exod 3:15, 16; 4:5; 1 Kgs 18:36; 1 Chr 29:18; 30:6; for "God of Abraham" and "Isaac," see Gen 28:13; 31:42, 53; for "God of Abraham," see Gen 26:24; Ps 47:9).

Jesus' reply to the Sadducees, therefore, is not simply clever, based on the present tense of Exod 3:6 (i.e., "I *am* the God of . . ."), which could imply that the patriarchs are still alive (which is probably the idea underlying 4 Macc 7:19; see Luke 20:38, which alludes to this passage). Jesus has appealed to the life-giving and life-sustaining character of God. As the "living God" he would not identify himself as a God of the dead. For examples of exegetical ingenuity, in which many Scriptures are said to confirm the hope of resurrection, see *Sipre Deut.* §306 (on Deut 32:1-3), where Rabbi Simai says: "There is no scriptural lesson lacking a reference to the resurrection."

The Great Commandment (12:28-34)

Interrogation now comes from a scribe who has seen how well Jesus has answered the questions put to him. The question offered in this instance is not a trick question, nor is it designed to entrap Jesus. Unlike his response to the previous questions (12:14-15, 19-23), which Jesus countered with questions of his own, this time Jesus answers in a straightforward manner. The scribe asks which commandment is first (or most important) of all (v. 28). Jesus replies by quoting Deut 6:4-5 as the "first" (12:29-30). He then quotes part of Lev 19:18 as the "second" (12:31). Jesus' double commandment has some parallels in the Jewish literature of late antiquity and so may not be innovative (e.g., *T. Iss.* 5:2: "love the LORD and the neighbor"; 7:6: "I loved the LORD and man with the whole heart"; *T. Dan* 5:3: "Love the LORD with all your life and one another with a true heart"; Philo *Spec. Leg.* 2.63: "But among the vast number of particular truths and principles [are] two main heads: one of duty to God . . . one of duty to humans").

The scribe finds Jesus' reply succinct and compelling, commenting that to love God with all that one is and has and to love one's neighbor as oneself "is much more than all whole burnt offerings and sacrifices" (12:32-33). His comment is a remarkable admission, suggesting that Jesus' teaching potentially renders the temple activities of the priests redundant. As such, in the Markan context it represents one more criticism of the temple establishment. Jesus commends the scribe for his answer, "You are not far from the kingdom of God" (v. 34a). Having come to the point of agreeing with Jesus' answer, the scribe is now drawing closer to the kingdom.

Jesus' critics are beaten; they have been bested in argument at every point. Indeed, even one of his antagonists has been nearly converted, so powerful is Jesus' teaching and debating skills. Not until he is later arrested and brought before the high priest "did anyone dare to ask him a question" (12:34b).

How Is the Messiah David's Son? (12:35-37)

Because now no one will ask him a question, Jesus must go on the offensive. Still teaching in the temple precincts, Jesus asks, "How can the scribes say that the Messiah is the son of David?" (12:35). In rabbinic literature the messianic epithet "son of David" is commonplace, and its antiquity is attested in *Pss. Sol.* 17:21 (1st cent. BC). As is clear from v. 37, the point of the question rests in the assumption that to be the "son" of someone is to be in some sense subordinate or even inferior. Is the Messiah inferior to David? In other words, is it true that the Messiah will only be a junior David? Jesus disputes this assumption, citing Ps 110:1: "The LORD said to my lord, 'Sit at my right hand . . .'" (12:36). Jesus understands this to mean "The LORD [God] said to my lord [the Messiah]." Thus David the famous king calls the Messiah "lord"; so in what sense is the Messiah nothing more than David's son (v. 37)?

Two questions arise from Jesus' interpretation of Psalm 110: (1) If the Messiah is to be more than David's son, what then does Jesus expect him to be? (2) Was Jesus distancing himself from Davidic messiahship? Both questions are answered by recognizing that Jesus evidently defined his messiahship in terms of the vision of Daniel 7. Jesus saw himself as that human being (or "son of man" in Aramaic idiom) who received from God authority and kingdom (Dan 7:13-14) and who would sit on one of the thrones set up in heaven (note the plural "thrones" in Dan 7:9), at God's "right hand" (Ps 110:1). His authority has eclipsed that conferred upon David his ancestor, so that while it may be genetically true that Jesus is the "son of David" (as hailed by blind Bartimaeus in Mark 10:47 and 48 and assumed by Paul in Rom 1:3), it is not true that the epithet "son of David" implies subordination or inferiority in any sense. The crowd is impressed with Jesus' teaching and "hear him gladly" (12:37; compare with Josephus *Ant.* 18.3.3 §63, who says that Jesus the teacher was followed by those who "receive truth gladly").

The authenticity of the saying is supported by the improbability of the early church to make up something which could undermine the claim that Jesus was a descendant of David and had a legitimate claim to the messianic line.

Beware the Scribes (12:38-40)

Jesus continues his offensive against the temple establishment by warning of the avaricious and hypocritical conduct of the scribes. They display the trappings of piety in their clothing and relish the marks of respect in public, but "they devour the estates of widows and pray long, phony prayers" (12:40; lit. "they devour the houses of widows and with pretext pray long prayers"; see Hos 10:4). The Gentile world offers parallels to Jesus' invective: there are those who "preach for the sake of gain and glory and only for their own benefit" (Dio Cocceianus *Orations* 13.32.30) and "make a great show of virtue and never practice it" (Aelius Aristides *Platonic Discourses* 307.6).

The religious establishment was supposed to aid the widow and the orphan, not exploit them (see Exod 22:22; Deut 10:18; 14:29; 24:17, 19-21; 26:12-13; 27:19). The reference to the widow might have reminded Mark's astute reader of Jeremiah's complaints against the temple establishment of his day, in which, among other things, widows and orphans were neglected and denied justice (see Jer 7:6; recall that Jesus alluded to Jer 7:11 in Mark 11:17).

The Widow's Offering (12:41-44)

The story of the widow's offering follows right on the heels of the denunciation of the scribes, who "devour the estates of widows" (12:38-40). The context of the widow's offering suggests, therefore, that it is an example of the very thing that Jesus warned about: the "house," or estate, of the poor widow has finally been consumed.

The traditional, popular interpretation that views the widow as a model of sacrificial giving probably has missed the point. Nor is the point that the smallness of her gift is in God's sight equal to the much larger gifts of the wealthy. The point lies in the fact that the poor widow cannot afford her tiny gift, which amounts to "her whole life" (for parallels to this idea, see Julianus of Egypt *Anthologia Graeca* 6.25; *Lev Rab.* 3.5 [on Lev 1:17]), while the wealthy person who gives a large gift does not even miss it. The example of the widow's mite is a tragic example of the exploitation of a temple establishment that has become oppressive, not generous and protective.

Prediction of the Temple's Destruction (13:1-2)

Again the chapter division of Mark obscures the unfolding of the evangelist's story. Since he has just complained of the oppressive nature of the temple establishment in 12:38-40 and 12:41-44, Jesus' prediction of the fate of the temple buildings, which have been decorated from the profits of its very lucrative trade, completes the logical sequence of criticism and judgment in ch. 12. The threat of destruction, only hinted at in the parable of the wicked tenants (12:1-12), has now been made explicit; and it is regarded as unavoidable.

Impressed with the grandeur of the temple precincts, the disciples point out to Jesus the "wonderful stones and wonderful buildings" (13:1). Construction on the Temple Mount had been underway for half a century ("forty-six years," according to John 2:20) and would continue until AD 64. Many of these magnificent stones are still visible today along the Western Wall, especially at the southern corner and in the tunnel, both of which have been recently excavated. The disciples may have assumed that they would someday rule over Israel from some of these very buildings (as the promise in Matt 19:28 = Luke 22:28-30 could have led them to believe). But Jesus dashes such hopes when he says: "Not one stone will be left upon another, that will not be thrown down."

When Will These Things Be? (13:3-13)

Jesus' prediction of the destruction of the temple buildings leads the disciples to inquire, "When these things will take place and what will be the sign?" (v. 4). What follows is the second and only other lengthy discourse in Mark (the first having been 4:1-34). This discourse attempts to trace the progression of events and portents that will lead up to the coming of the "Son of Man" (13:24-27). The discourse ends with Jesus' warning that his disciples be alert (vv. 33-37), for they do not know when this time will come (v. 32).

Three major difficulties complicate attempts to interpret Mark 13. The first is that the disciples' question about when the temple will be destroyed does not appear to be answered, at least not directly. Nowhere in vv. 5-37 is anything said about the temple surrounded, besieged, taken, or destroyed (as we have in Luke 19:41-44; 21:20-24; 23:28-31). It is interesting to observe that both Matthew and Luke sense this difficulty. The former seeks to mitigate the problem by having the disciples ask Jesus about his "coming and the end of the age" (Matt 24:3), since that is what Mark 13:5-37 actually addresses. Luke deals with the problem by attempting to segregate some of the material treating Jesus' return as the "Son of Man" (see Luke 17:22-37; 21:25-33) from material that speaks of Jerusalem's destruction (as seen in the already mentioned Luke 19:41-44; 21:20-24; 23:28-31).

The second problem involves the difficulty of identifying the "abomination of desolation" in v. 14 and of determining in what way, if at all, it relates to the destruction of the temple in AD 70. The third problem derives from the observation that the signs portending the coming of the Son of Man appear to be associated with the events and upheavals that led to the Jewish revolt in AD 66-70. Do the signs that portend the coming of the Son of Man have anything to do with the destruction of the temple, and, if they do, in what way?

The position taken here is that the prediction of the temple's destruction, the disciples' question, and the ensuing discourse do in fact form a consistent and coherent unity, when the rest of Jesus' teaching regarding the coming of the Son of Man and the appearance of the kingdom of God is taken into consideration. Apart from the full context of Jesus' teaching in Mark, the problems that ch. 13 presents to interpreters cannot be solved.

In Mark 8:38–9:1 Jesus predicts that the Son of Man, when he comes in the glory of his Father, will be ashamed of any person "in this adulterous and sinful generation" who is ashamed of him and of his words. After entering the city and being challenged by ruling priests (ch. 11), Jesus threatens his enemies with the loss of their position and authority (12:1-12). The antagonism intensifies (12:13-44). Departing from the temple precincts, Jesus predicts the total destruction of the temple complex (13:1-2). Later, at his hearing before the high priest, Jesus is accused of threatening to destroy the temple (14:58). When asked if he is the Messiah, the Son of God (14:61), Jesus affirms that he is and that the high priest "will see the Son of Man seated at the right hand of Power, coming with the clouds of heaven" (14:62).

These elements help clarify the train of thought in 13:5-37. The disciples ask Jesus when his prediction of the temple's destruction will be fulfilled and what signs will precede this fulfillment. Jesus then describes various signs that will precede the coming of the Son of Man, a coming that has already been predicted in 8:38 and will be repeated in 13:26. One of the signs that will portend the nearness of the coming of the Son of Man will be the "abomination of desolation" (v. 14). This will be the time to flee, for a severe, unprecedented persecution is about to fall upon Israel (vv. 19-20). More false messiahs and false prophets will arise (vv. 21-22; others were mentioned earlier in vv. 5-6). Even the heavens will be shaken (vv. 24-25). Then "they will see the Son of Man coming in the clouds with great power and glory" (v. 26). After this the restoration of Israel will be brought to completion, as the elect are gathered from the four winds (v. 27).

When will the temple be destroyed, as predicted in 13:2 and accusingly charged in 14:58? The temple will be destroyed when the Son of Man comes in power. At this time the ruling priests "will see" him (as Jesus promised them in 14:62). And at this time the temple "made with human hands" will be destroyed and replaced with a temple "not made with human hands" (14:58, echoing the messianic vision of Dan 2:44-45). "Not one stone will be left upon another, that will not be thrown down" (13:2), so complete will be the destruction of the Herodian temple. At this time Jesus will make good on his implied threat in the parable of the wicked tenants (12:1-12). The ruling priests will lose their stewardship; it will be handed over to those who have not been ashamed of the Son of Man or of his words. The old regime will be swept aside; Israel will be regathered and restored; and a new temple will be erected. Israel's destiny will be realized; the temple will at last become a "house of prayer for all the nations," as prophesied by Isaiah (Isa 56:7, cited in Mark 11:17).

During the 50s and 60s and leading up to the outbreak of the war, the eschatological discourse probably underwent a certain amount of editing, to reflect the somewhat parallel events of this period (many points of contact will be suggested in the commentary below) and probably to reflect a growing belief among Christians that the impending war with Rome signaled the unfolding of the signs and events that Jesus had foretold. The possibility that the temple could be destroyed and Jerusalem taken probably led many to conclude that the abomination of desolation and the coming of the Son of Man were drawing near.

The discourse begins with a warning, "Watch out!" (13:5). Warnings will punctuate the discourse (vv. 9, 23, 33, 34, 35, and 37). Jesus warns his followers not to be led astray by those who come in his name, saying "I am he" (v. 6). "Name" here means "title," so coming in Jesus' name means claiming to be the Messiah (see the parallel Matt 24:5, which actually reads "I am Christ," correctly capturing the idea; see also Mark 13:21-22). Many will come making these false claims, and they will deceive many. Josephus tells of several would-be deliverers of Israel, some of whom should probably be understood as messianic pretenders. Some first-century material preserved in the *Sibylline Oracles* predicts that Beliar (normally meaning Satan, but here probably referring to Nero) will arise from the line of Caesar Augustus and will perform signs that lead people astray, including the faithful (3:63-74; see also 2 Thess 2:1-12).

The disciples will also "hear of wars and rumors of wars," but they are not to be alarmed. Jesus' language here may echo that of the prophets, who spoke of the sounds of war (see Jer 51:46; *2 Bar.* 48:34-37). It seems to be formulaic, for later — but independent — rabbinic tradition speaks of the "sounds and rumors of war" that precede the coming of the Messiah (see *Pesiq. Rab Kah.* 5:9; *b. Sanh.* 97a). Rabbinic tradition also relates stories of various signs and prodigies thought to portend the temple's destruction (*b. Yoma* 39b). Writing not long after Mark, Josephus also relates portents of doom (*J.W.* 3.8.3 §§351-52). Outside of Mark's Gospel Jesus employs the language of the prophets who described the siege and destruction of Jerusalem at the hands of the Babylonians (compare Luke 19:41-44 with Jer 6:6-21; Ezek 4:1-3; Luke 21:20-24 with Jer 20:4-6; Zech 12:3). The disturbances and disasters that attended the first destruction of Jerusalem and the temple will, perhaps as a sort of typology, portend the second destruction (for interpretations of the second destruction against the fictive backdrop of the first destruction, see 4 Ezra 3:1-2; 10:21-24; *2 Bar.* 7:1–8:5).

The disciples are warned of persecutions (13:9-13). They will be delivered up to councils (*synedria*), and they will be beaten in synagogues. We immediately think of the tribulations of the apostles as described in Acts, who on occasion were delivered up to the Jewish Council (or *synedrion*) for intimidation (Acts 4:1-21; 5:17-2) and on other occasions were beaten in synagogues and elsewhere (Acts 5:40; 16:22, 37; 21:32; 22:19). The apostles also stand before governors (Acts 23:24, 33; 25:6-12) and kings (Acts 25:23–26:32) and are even sent to Caesar (Acts 25:12, 21; 26:32).

Alluding to Mic 7:6, Jesus foretells family strife and division, some of it on account of the gospel. Indeed, his followers "will be hated by all" for his "name's sake" (13:12-13). All of these things — the rumors of war, the earthquakes, the famines, the spread of the gospel, and persecution — constitute the "beginning of birthpangs" (v. 8). Worse will follow.

Signs of the End (13:14-23)

When the "abomination of desolation" is observed, then it is time to flee; disaster is near. But what is the "abomination of desolation"? The phrase itself is taken from Dan 12:11 (with another close parallel in Dan 11:31). Dan 9:26-27 foretells the murder of Jerusalem's anointed high priest (probably Onias III; see 2 Macc 4:23-28) and the coming of a prince (almost certainly Antiochus IV Epiphanes, who dies in 164 BC), whose followers suppress proper sacrifice and set up an "abomination" that "desolates" the temple and altar (see 1 Macc 1:54, which refers to Antiochus's "abomination of desolation"; and 2 Macc 6:2, which says that Antiochus renamed Jerusalem's temple in honor of Zeus). According to Josephus (*Ant.* 12.5.4 §253), the abomination of Antiochus was a pagan altar on which swine were sacrificed (for partial corroboration, see 1 Macc 4:43; 2 Macc 6:5). The phrase occurs again in Dan 11:29-32, which tells of Antiochus's withdrawal from Egypt in 168 BC and his plundering of the temple in Jerusalem and the setting up of the abomination of desolation. This is a retelling of the event earlier described in Daniel 9. The phrase occurs again in Dan 12:11 as one of the temporal markers in the author's calculations of when the end of Antiochus will come and the restoration of the temple will take place.

Daniel is clearly oriented to the great crisis brought on by Antiochus IV. Jesus' appeal to Daniel's "abomination of desolation" should be understood in a typological sense. That is, the crisis of long ago, which threatened to bring Judaism and Israel's national life to an end, will once again threaten Israel and Jesus' followers. Jesus says that this abomination will "stand where he ought not." The masculine gender of the participle "stand" (in contrast to the neuter "abomination") suggests that the abomination is a statue or image of a pagan deity or deified man. When Jesus' followers see this desecrating thing set up, which makes it impossible for the faithful to worship in the temple precincts and continue with proper sacrifice (hence the idea of "desolation," i.e., deserted), they will know that it is time to flee to the mountains. Probably related to this tradition is the Pauline prediction in 2 Thess 2:3-4: "for that day will not come, unless . . . the man of lawlessness is revealed . . . and takes his seat in the temple of God, proclaiming himself to be

God." Mark's parenthetical comment, "let the reader understand," may be intended to alert readers to Dan 12:5-13, a passage where Daniel asks an angel, "How will it be until the end?" just as the disciples had earlier asked Jesus, "When will these things be?" (Mark 13:4). To understand what is happening, the evangelist advises his readers, one must read Daniel. The answer provided in Daniel entails, among other things, the appearance of the abomination that will leave the temple desolate (Dan 12:11). Thus the parallel with Mark 13:4-14 is structurally and thematically quite close.

The danger will be so great that people should flee without stopping to gather up possessions (13:15-16). It will be the worst possible time for pregnant and nursing women (v. 17). Jesus' followers should pray that it not happen in the winter (v. 18) when travel is more difficult and keeping warm in the countryside is a problem. The tribulation will be so great that it will eclipse all crises of biblical history (v. 19), which is quite a claim when we remember the flood, the Babylonian captivity, and the war with Antiochus. Indeed, it will be so bad that no one could survive had not God shortened the period; and this he does only for the sake of his elect (v. 20; see *1 Enoch* 80:2 for ideas about the shortening of seasons). The warnings about false messiahs and false prophets is repeated (vv. 21-22; see v. 6 above). Jesus' followers have been warned; they have been told all in advance (v. 23). Elsewhere in Jewish tradition (e.g., *m. Soṭa* 9:15) great tribulation was expected to precede the coming of the Messiah.

The Coming of the Son of Man (13:24-27)

Various cosmic signs are said to portend the coming of the Son of Man: the "sun will be darkened, and the moon will not give its light, and the stars will fall from heaven, and the powers in the heavens will be shaken" (13:24-25). We have here a paraphrase of part of Isa 13:10: "For the stars of the heavens and their constellations will not give their light; the sun will be dark at its rising, and the moon will not shed its light" (see also Isa 34:4, where we read of the fall of the host of heaven). Isaiah's oracle concerns the destruction of Babylon. This is appropriate language, given what is in store for the temple (see Hatina 1996: 43-66) when the Son of Man finally comes.

The powerful "Son of Man" will send forth his "angels" (or messengers) to gather the elect who have been scattered to the four winds (v. 27; on the salvation of the elect and the appearance of the Son of Man, see *1 Enoch* 62:13-14). The allusion is to Zech 2:6 (Heb. v. 10), which is part of an oracle that foretells the gathering of Israel's exiles. The gathering of the exiles is a messianic task (see *Pss. Sol.* 8:28; 11:1-4; 17:21-28; *Tg. Isa* 53:8; *Tg. Hos* 14:8; *Tg. Mic* 5:1-3), an idea which coheres with both the literary context in Mark and the ministry of Jesus, as seen in his appointment of the twelve (see the commentary on Mark 3:13-19 above), in the expectation of the gathering of the scattered people of Israel (Matt 8:11 = Luke 13:28-29), and in his promise that the twelve would sit on twelve thrones judging the twelve tribes of Israel (Matt 19:28 = Luke 22:30).

There may be an important parallel here with the *Testament of Moses,* composed in the early part of the first century AD. We read that a second punishment will befall God's people, so severe that it will "exceed the former one" (9:2, in reference to the Babylonian destruction and exile). "Then his [God's] kingdom will appear throughout his whole creation" (10:1). The sequence here is the same as in Mark 13: terrible tribulation followed by the appearance of God's kingdom. The only difference is that in Mark the kingdom is consummated through the coming of the "Son of Man," the person to whom God entrusted the kingdom.

The idea of someone dying and then returning in kingly power is not without parallel in late antiquity. Some believed that Nero, who died in AD 68, would or even had returned. For fear of him, and in some cases out of love for him, some people prepared for his return (see Suetonius *Lives of the Caesars,* "Nero" 6.57).

Knowing When He is Near (13:28-32)

Jesus urges his disciples to be perceptive of the signs portending the time when the Son of Man will return (which is what is implied by "he is near, at the very gates"). The saying, "this generation will not pass away before all these things take place" (13:30), is consistent with the similar prediction in 9:1 ("there are some standing here who will not taste death before they see the kingdom of God having come with power"). The generation of Jesus expected to see the things prophesied in the discourse. These predictions were partially fulfilled in the events of the first century. That generation saw the destruction of the temple and some of the signs, or at least events that paralleled the signs that will portend the coming of the Son of Man. But Jesus' generation did not see the coming of the Son of Man, nor did it see the consummation of the kingdom of God. When will these things take place? The qualification in v. 32, where even Jesus is excluded, answers our question in part: "of that day or that hour no one knows" (see 4 Ezra 4:44-52, where Ezra asks if he will be alive in the last days and the angel tells him, "I do not know"; see also *2 Bar.* 21:8, which in a prayer to God says: "You alone know the end of times before it has arrived"). As in the case of many of the prophecies of the OT prophets, some things have come to pass and some things yet remain.

It is probable that the sayings relating to when the kingdom of God or Son of Man would appear derive not from Jesus but from the early community trying to explain the delay of the parousia. Mark 13:28-32 assures Christians that the eschatological events of which Jesus spoke will take place before Jesus' generation passes away. The saying in 9:1 promises that at least some "will not taste death before they see the kingdom come in power," while the Johannine Gospel wrestles with a tradition that had predicted that the Beloved Disciple would remain until Jesus returned (John 21:22-23; cf. 2 Pet 3:4).

Watch (13:33-37)

Jesus' warning to take heed is illustrated by a parable of watchfulness and lessons that can be drawn from it (13:33-37). Taken with v. 32, where Jesus asserts that no one knows the day or the hour of the coming of the Son of Man, the principal lesson here is that Christians are to be watchful and prepared, not caught up in attempts to calculate the coming.

Jesus' Trial, Execution, and Resurrection (14:1–16:8)

The passion of Jesus comes to a speedy climax. He is anointed by a woman (14:3-9), Judas decides to betray him (14:10-11), Jesus and the disciples observe the Passover (14:12-26), Jesus prays (14:27-42), and Jesus is arrested (14:43-52). The passion comes to an end with Jesus before the high priest and members of the Jewish council (14:53-65), with Peter's denials (14:66-72), with Jesus before Pilate (15:1-15), and with the crucifixion (15:16-41) and burial (15:42-47). Mark's narrative then concludes with the drama of the discovery of the empty tomb and the message that Jesus "has risen" (16:1-8).

Mark's passion narrative portrays Jesus as in control of his destiny. His actions are deliberate and compelling. He knows that he will be put to death and that his death is "for many" (14:24). Although he has no desire to die, he is willing to accept his fate (vv. 34-36). Rome must acknowledge that Jesus, even in death, "was truly the Son of God" (15:39). Jesus cuts an impressive figure, one that should elicit respect and admiration from the Roman world (for a major study of the passion narratives of the Gospels, see Brown 1994).

Plot against Jesus (14:1-2)

The evangelist observes that it was just two days before the Passover and the feast of Unleavened Bread. The ruling priests wish to arrest Jesus, but not during the feast itself, lest it spark a riot. It would be bad enough for any Jew to be seized and handed over to the Romans, but for a popular prophet and preacher like Jesus, whom some among his following believed to be the awaited Messiah, an arrest would be especially risky.

The Passover was the great holiday in which Jews remembered and celebrated their rescue from slavery in Egypt (see Exodus 12). It was celebrated on the fourteenth of Nisan (April/May) and was followed by the feast of Unleavened Bread, which was celebrated from the fifteenth to the twenty-first of Nisan. These holidays were usually thought of as the "week of Passover." Passover week was especially worrisome for the Romans and their aristocratic Jewish collaborators. Recalling God's great act of salvation in history could inspire thoughts of revolt from Rome.

The Anointing (14:3-9)

Although anointing was a custom during feasts (see Pss 23:5; 141:5), the woman's anointing of Jesus was in this instance probably messianic (but note that the word "anoint" is not used). In John 12:3 this woman is identified as Mary, the sister of Martha. Olive oil is sufficient for such an anointing; pure nard — a very costly perfume (see Pliny *Nat. Hist.* 12.25.42) — is not required. If a new government is to be set up, as the disciples still hope, money will be needed. Moreover, giving of alms was a custom during the Passover (see John 13:29; *m. Pesaḥ.* 9:11; 10:1), and Jesus' movement should not be an exception. So why this waste of precious resources? But Jesus commends the woman. She has done a beautiful thing to him. The disciples will always have opportunities to assist the poor (and not only at Passover time). But there is little time left to show love and devotion to Jesus.

Jesus interprets the woman's action as an anointing for burial (14:8). It is hard to imagine that the woman viewed her actions in this light. If it was intended to be more than a festive anointing, in honor of Jesus, it was probably a messianic anointing. This perspective coheres with the context of Mark's narrative. Only days before, Jesus entered the city mounted on a colt, to shouts of "Blessed is the kingdom of our father David that is coming" (11:10). But Jesus has already foretold his death (8:31; 9:31; 10:33-34) and later in the evening will pray about it (14:36). In this light the people of the Roman world would have seen the anointing as an omen. Jesus tells his disciples (the "to you" in v. 9 is plural) that wherever the gospel is proclaimed, what the woman did will be told in memory of her.

Judas Makes a Deal (14:10-11)

Judas Iscariot has had enough. Jesus' insistence on dying has demoralized him. We may speculate that he had joined Jesus in the first place because he, too, longed for the appearance of the kingdom of God. But things had not gone well in Jerusalem. The ruling priests did not welcome Jesus; on the contrary, they are actively opposing him. Jesus himself now speaks of martyrdom. This was not what Judas had anticipated. It is time to cut his losses and get out. He decides to surrender Jesus to the ruling priests. They promise Judas money in exchange for arranging a quiet and effective arrest. Though they want him out of the way, they do not want to incite violence.

Celebrating the Passover (14:12-21)

The reference to the "first day of Unleavened Bread" (14:12) is to the Passover day itself (see the comments on vv. 1-2 above). Reminiscent of the arrangements for securing a colt for his entry (see 11:1-6), Jesus again has made arrangements — evidently unknown to the disciples — for observing the Passover in a private room. The clandestine rendezvous with the man carrying a jar of water (14:13) had to do with precautions that Jesus felt were necessary. He knew that he was a wanted man. But he was also determined to eat the Passover meal, and to do that he had to find a room in Jerusalem.

While reclining at table and eating, Jesus predicts that one of his disciples will betray him (14:18-19). Mark again emphasizes Jesus' predictive power. He has predicted his death on several occasions and has only recently foretold that the woman's pouring of perfume on his head was in fact preparation for his burial, and now he startles his disciples by predicting the betrayal. Predicting the betrayal softens the embarrassment and disgrace for Jesus, namely, that one of his own disciples would give him up. Far from being a discreditable reflection on Jesus, it becomes a credit to him, because he foresaw it (unlike Julius Caesar, e.g., who entered the Senate chambers and much to his surprise was attacked by his colleagues).

Shocked, the disciples each in turn ask, "Is it I?" Indeed, it is one of the twelve (as opposed to one of those of the larger following), a friend who shares food with Jesus (14:19-20; see the addition in Matt 26:25). The Son of Man will suffer the fate that awaits him, a fate foretold in Scripture, but his betrayer faces a fate far worse. In his case it would have been better never to have been born (v. 21).

Jesus' vague reference to what is written in Scripture of the Son of Man supports the authenticity of the utterance (see also 14:49). Early Christian scriptural apologetic supplied proof texts; none is provided here. Jesus may have had in mind Ps 41:9, which is probably alluded to earlier in 14:18; and Isaiah 53, which is echoed here and there in the Gospels (see the commentary on Mark 10:45 above). It is also possible, given Jesus' interest in Daniel, that Dan 9:26 ("the anointed one will be cut off") was in mind.

The Last Supper (14:22-25)

During the meal Jesus takes bread (*artos;* but we should assume that this bread is *azymos,* i.e., unleavened bread) and says, "Take; this is my body" (14:22). Given the context, in which Jesus has predicted his death and interpreted the woman's kindness as preparation for burial (vv. 3-9), one should agree with Gundry (1993: 831) that *sōma* (body) here is better translated corpse, that is, "This is my corpse." This metaphor coheres with Passover diction, as seen in *m. Pesaḥ.* 10:3: "And in the holy city they used to bring before him the body [*gup*] of the Passover offering" (see LXX 1 Chr 10:12, where *sōma* translates *gup*). Jesus offers his own body, or corpse, as the Passover offering. This tradition is witnessed in 1 Cor 5:7 and intensified in John 19:32-36, where even in the manner of his death (e.g., bloody death on Passover, legs not broken; see Exod 12:46) Jesus is the Passover lamb (see also John 1:29, 36: "the Lamb of God").

Extending the melancholy metaphor, Jesus then takes the wine and says, "This is my blood of the covenant, which is poured out for many" (14:24). The phrase "blood of the covenant" may echo Exod 24:8 and/or Zech 9:11. (Some mss. read "new covenant," which probably reflects 1 Cor 11:25 and Luke 22:21; see Jer 31:31 for God's promise that he "will make a new covenant with the house of Israel.") The words "for many" remind us of Mark 10:45 ("to give his life as payment for many"). The difference here, however, is that whereas Jesus' blood is "for" or "in behalf of" *(hyper)* many, the giving of his life is "for" or "in the place of" *(anti)* many. We have here a blending of ideas of atonement, whereby through the shedding of blood sins are forgiven, and of remembrance of the exodus, when the lamb's blood protected the Israelites from death and paved the way for their escape from Egypt. To object, as some do, that Passover was not about atonement is to overlook Paul's comment that "Christ, our Passover lamb, has been sacrificed" (1 Cor 5:7; see Rom 5:6-11, where Paul speaks of Christ's atoning death).

Traditions of commemorative meals were known in the Greco-Roman world (see Diodorus Siculus *Library of History* 4.3.4; Lucius Apuleius *The Golden Ass* §11; *P. Oxy.* 110; *P. Köln* 57).

Jesus vows that he will not drink the fruit of the vine until the day that he can drink it again "in the kingdom of God" (14:25). This saying is quite interesting in light of Jesus' prediction of death. It corroborates the authenticity of his anticipations of vindication. Jesus believes that the kingdom of God will appear soon; he also knows that he will suffer martyrdom. His death, however, will actually facilitate the coming of the kingdom and the redemption of Israel. It is probably in this sense that we should understand Jesus' statement that his death is "on behalf of many" (v. 24). By taking the blow that should fall heavily on Israel, Jesus will mitigate the severity of divine judgment and hasten the consummation of the kingdom (see the commentary on 14:7).

Prediction of Peter's Denials (14:26-31)

Singing a hymn at the conclusion of the Passover meal may have been part of the tradition in the days of Jesus (see *m. Pesaḥ.* 10:5-7); the hymn was probably drawn from one of the Hallel Psalms (i.e., Psalms 113–18) or perhaps the Hallel Hagadol (the "Great Hallel," i.e., Psalm 136), in which God is praised. With the Passover observance concluded, Jesus and his disciples leave the city and go up to the Mount of Olives.

Jesus stuns his disciples with the prediction, "You will all fall away" (14:27). "I will strike the shepherd, and the sheep will be scattered" (see Zech 13:7) refers to God's judgment on Israel. By citing it, Jesus implies that divine judgment has fallen on him, which is consistent with the words of Institution (i.e., "This is my blood of the covenant, which is poured out for many," 14:24). In being struck down, Jesus will no longer be able to protect his flock; the sheep will be scattered.

The citation of part of the oracle from Zechariah is important, for as a whole (see Zech 13:7-9) the oracle coheres with the context in which Jesus now finds himself. Jerusalem's rejection of Jesus has aroused God's wrath. The shepherd will be struck down, the sheep will be scattered, and the entire land will be judged. Only a remnant will be spared. When they call on the name of the Lord, they will be answered. The oracle summarizes the principal points of the eschatological discourse in Mark 13.

Jesus assures his disciples that after he is raised up, he will go before them to Galilee. With the Passover and weeklong feast of Unleavened Bread over, the disciples could be expected to return home. But before they do, Jesus will already be there waiting for them. As Gundry remarks, "the disciples will not leave him in a grave when they go back to Galilee" (1993: 845).

Peter makes a different prediction: others may fall away, but he will not (14:29). Jesus counters with an even more specific prediction: before the rooster crows twice, Peter will have denied Jesus three times (v. 30). Peter protests further; even if he must die with Jesus, he will not deny him. All of the disciples join in saying the same thing. As it turns out, however, it is the predictions of Jesus that come true. Mark's reader will discover that at every point Jesus had it right. The predicted betrayal (v. 20) will be fulfilled (vv. 42-46); indeed, already it has been fulfilled to a degree in vv. 10-11. When arrested, "all forsook him and fled" (v. 50). When questioned by the maidservant, Peter denied Jesus (vv. 66-72). The accuracy of Jesus' predictions only lends further credibility to his predictions of resurrection and of coming with the clouds as the Son of Man.

Praying at Gethsemane (14:32-42)

Still on the Mount of Olives, Jesus and his disciples retire to a place called Gethsemane (from *gat shemaney,* which literally means "press of oils"). Taking Peter, James, and John, he posts his other disciples as a watch while he prays. He tells the three that his "soul is very sorrowful, even to death" (14:34a). The passion, or suffering, of Jesus has now begun. But his sorrow again testifies to Jesus' predictive power. He knows that his disciples' betrayal and apostasy will soon take place.

Jesus then commands Peter, James, and John to remain nearby and watch, while he himself goes further and falls on the ground and prays that, if possible, the hour of trial might pass (14:34b-35). The prayer itself, "Abba, Father . . . remove this cup from me" (v. 35), reveals the human Jesus who recoils from the coming suffering. But it also paints an impressive picture. Jesus is fully aware of the severity of the trial that lies ahead. No aspect of it — the arrest, the abuse, the interrogations, the beatings, or the crucifixion itself — will take him by surprise. Mark's portrait is of one who is the master of the situation, not that of a fanatic who in bewilderment sees his plans go awry.

The expression "cup" reminds us of the question that earlier Jesus had put to James and John: "Are you able to drink the cup that I drink? . . . The cup that I drink you shall drink" (10:38-39). Before entering Jerusalem, Jesus had anticipated that he would have to drink the cup of suffering and death (on the OT background of "cup," see the commentary on 10:35-40 above). The implication is that his disciples (indeed, all Christians) will face the same trials. Jesus' repeated prayers and the disciples' repeated failure to keep awake put Jesus in a contrasting, complimentary light. Indeed, Peter's falling asleep three times (14:37, 40, 41) may be intended by the evangelist to parallel his later three denials. While Jesus gains strength through prayer, his disciples lose spiritual fortitude, thus becoming vulnerable to fear and faithlessness.

Jesus' prayer that God can do all things, even taking away the cup of suffering, underscores the idea that Jesus' suffering is God's will. It is not Jesus' wish but God's; and Jesus accepts it (14:36). His abrupt announcement that "The hour has come; the Son of Man is betrayed into the hands of sinners" (v. 41) again shows Jesus to be very much in control of the situation. Nothing has taken him by surprise. Ironically, it is Jesus who announces the arrival of the betrayer (v. 42), not his feckless disciples who were supposed to be keeping watch.

Betrayal and Arrest (14:43-52)

As Jesus finished speaking, a crowd came up, armed "with swords and clubs, from the ruling priests and the scribes and the elders" (14:43). Thugs similarly armed worked for the ruling priests, according to Josephus (*Ant.* 20.8.8 §181; 20.9.2 §§206-7). In the darkness it was necessary for Jesus to be identified quite specifically, lest he bolt and elude capture. This is why Judas approaches Jesus, calls him "rabbi" (master or teacher), and as a rabbi's *ḥaber* (associate or disciple) kisses him (v. 45). Thus identified, the priests' deputies seize Jesus. Seizure at night was intended to render Jesus' following leaderless and so discourage a coordinated attack (as those doing the priests' bidding may have feared). Reacting to this seizure, someone draws his sword and strikes the servant of the high priest, cutting off his ear (v. 47). (The other Gospels tell us that it was Peter who struck a servant named Malchus and cut off his right ear, which Jesus then healed.)

Preachers have often poked fun at Peter (for it is assumed that Peter was indeed the disciple who lashed out with his sword), speculating that in his rashness he did not take careful aim but only slightly wounded the man. Quite apart from whether or not the high priest's servant thought his wound was slight, such a line of interpretation is probably off target. Because the deputies were facing Jesus as they attempted to subdue him, the wound in the side of the head suggests that the aggressive disciple had attempted to intercept him. Far from missing, the disciple hit his man. But before the altercation can get out of control, Jesus rebukes those who have come out against him: "Have you come out as against a rebel, with swords and clubs to capture me?" (14:48). Jesus mocks the cowardice and villainy of his captors. He reminds them that daily he had taught in the temple precincts, in the very backyard of the ruling priests. If they had wanted to take him, why not on those occasions? No, they could not seize him in public, out in the open, lest an angry public rise up against them. They had to use stealth, bribery, and treachery to take him, thus revealing the sort of men they were.

But Jesus is unabashed; "let the scriptures be fulfilled" (14:49). Mark's reader immediately thinks of 9:12: "How is it written of the Son of Man, that he should suffer many things?"; or the more recent prediction of betrayal in 14:21: "For the Son of Man goes, even as it is written of him" (for OT passages that may have been in mind, see the commentary on v. 21 above).

Not only is Scripture fulfilled; Jesus' own predictions begin to be fulfilled. He has been betrayed by one of his, as he had said. Now all of his disciples take flight (14:50), as predicted earlier that night (v. 27: "You will all fall away"). Shortly Mark's readers will learn of Peter's denials. The complete collapse of Jesus' following is seen in the flight of the naked young man. Lane (1974: 527) suggests that what we may have here is an allusion to the picture portrayed in Amos 2:16, where in an oracle against Israel the prophet foresees that even the "stout of heart among the mighty will flee away naked" in the day of judgment. Lane is probably correct, for this idea coheres with the earlier appeal to Zech 13:7, where the shepherd is struck down and the sheep are scattered (see the commentary on 14:27 above). In rejecting its Messiah, Israel has brought upon itself the judgments described in the prophets; the Scriptures are being "fulfilled."

Hearing before the Sanhedrin (14:53-65)

In being brought before the high priest, all the ruling priests, the elders, and the scribes (14:53), Jesus now faces the most powerful men among the Jewish people. Peter, following at a safe, inconspicuous distance, enters the courtyard of the high priest, where he joins the attendants who are warming themselves by the fire. What happens to Peter will be narrated later.

Indoors Jesus is being accused by the ruling priests and by all who make up the Council (or Sanhedrin). The evangelist says that they were seeking testimony that would bring with it the death sentence but could not find any (14:55). There were many who offered false testimony, but it failed to agree (v. 56). The law of Moses requires that the testimony of witnesses be in agreement (see Deut 17:6; 19:15). Some other men stood up and accused Jesus of saying, "I will destroy this temple that is made with hands, and in three days I will build another, not made with hands" (14:57-58). The evangelist describes their testimony as "false" in v. 57, and in v. 59 he says that it did not agree. What did not agree? Their words, or something else? The disagreement does not seem to lie with the words themselves ("we heard him say"). It probably lies with the circumstances in which they were spoken and their intent. This is only a guess, but it follows the lead of the apocryphal book Susanna, a later addition to Daniel. When the two elders falsely accuse Susanna of adultery (1:36-40), their words are in agreement. But when they are questioned separately, their testimony as to the circumstances of Susanna's alleged sin does not agree (1:52-59). We may suppose that the testimony against Jesus broke down in a similar fashion.

The words themselves of the accusation very possibly approximated something Jesus had said. The clearest support for this comes from the parallel in the Fourth Gospel: "Destroy this temple, and in three days I will raise it up" (John 2:19). The probability of the authenticity of the saying, even in its Markan form, receives additional support from the likelihood that the saying reflects Dan 2:44-45: "And in the days of those kings the God of heaven will set up a kingdom which shall never be destroyed . . . just as you saw that a stone was cut from the mountain by no human hand" and broke in pieces the kingdoms of the world. We have already seen that at various points Jesus is informed by the visions and prophecies of Daniel. He is the "son of man" of Daniel 7, who receives authority and a kingdom. He may also have seen himself as the anointed one who will be cut off (Dan 9:26), and he foretells the coming "abomination of desolation" that will signal the nearness of the appearance of the Son of Man (Dan 11:31; 12:5-13). It could very well be that after his rejection in Jerusalem, Jesus began to speak of his death and of the temple's destruction (as in Mark 13:2), possibly even threatening to replace the temple built by Herod with one of heavenly origin (see the commentary on 13:3-27).

But the accusations of these witnesses do not hold up. The high priest asks Jesus to respond to their testimony; but he remains silent (14:60-61a). Then the high priest directly asks for confirmation of Jesus' identity: "Are you the Christ, the Son of the Blessed One?" (v. 61b). This time Jesus replies. His first words, "I am," have nothing to do with the divine name (i.e., Yahweh = "I AM"), but simply mean "yes." The rest of his answer qualifies in what sense Jesus is the Christ (i.e., Messiah), the Son of the Blessed (i.e., God): "You will see the Son of Man seated at the right hand of Power, and coming with the clouds of heaven" (v. 62; "Power" is another circumlocution for God). Here Jesus again alludes to the figure of Dan 7:13-14, as well as to the words of Ps 110:1, which earlier in Mark 12:35-37 he discussed in the temple precincts. On that occasion Jesus questioned the scribes' habit of referring to the Christ as the "Son of David." Jesus queried this habit in light of David's calling him "Lord." The implication is that the Messiah is more than a mere "son of David" (see the commentary on 12:35-37 above). In his reply to Caiaphas the high priest, Jesus has identified himself as the Davidic Messiah who in fulfillment of Psalm 110 will sit at God's right hand and as the figure of Daniel 7 who received from God authority and kingdom. As such, he is greater than David and greater than the high priest before whom he now stands. In light of his earlier teaching in the temple precincts, especially as seen in the parable of the vineyard tenants (see the commentary on 12:1-12 above) and prediction of the temple's destruction (see the commentary on 13:1-2 above), we should probably assume that Jesus' reply carries with it an element of threat. When next Caiaphas and his colleagues see Jesus, he will be installed at God's right hand and will be coming with the clouds of heaven, in judgment upon the temple establishment. The temple "made with hands" will be destroyed (and this probably means more than simply the physical buildings themselves, but refers to the entire establishment) and will be replaced with one of heavenly construction (compare Rev 11:19, which speaks of a "temple of God that is in heaven"; and Rev 21:22, where God and the Lamb are themselves the temple).

How can the Son of Man *sit,* which implies being stationary, and still *come with the clouds,* which entails movement? Do we have here two originally distinct traditions which have been clumsily juxtaposed? Not at all. According to Dan 7:9, God's throne has burning wheels. The throne described there, on which the Son of Man will take his seat (according to Jesus' exegesis, which draws upon Psalm 110), is none other than God's chariot throne (see Ezekiel 1, 10). Seated on this throne, at God's right hand, will be Jesus the Son of Man, coming with the clouds.

Caiaphas is outraged at this affirmation. Not only has Jesus affirmed his messianic identity, which now makes it possible to charge him with treason (for to be Messiah is to be king of Israel), but he has committed blasphemy by daring to claim that he will sit on the divine throne. No further witnesses are needed; all agree that Jesus is worthy of death (14:63-64). The ruling priests then fall upon him violently. They cover Jesus' head, strike him, and then with mockery call on him to prophesy (which means that Jesus is to identify which person has struck him; it is spelled out in Matt 26:68). The guards also begin to beat Jesus (14:65).

Peter's Denials (14:66-72)

In stark contrast to Jesus inside before the high priest, the most powerful Jew in Israel, stands Peter outside quailing before a female servant, a person of no power. Peter is recognized as having been with the Nazarene, Jesus (14:67). But he denies it without qualification. He neither knows nor understands what she is talking about. The maid again sees Peter (and the Greek suggests that it was the same maid, though see Matt 26:71, which says "another maid") and says to the bystanders: "This man is one of them" (14:69). But Peter again denies it (v. 70a). A little while later, the bystanders say to Peter that he surely must be one of the followers of Jesus, for he is a Galilean (v. 70b; in 26:73 Matthew explains that it was Peter's accent that gave him away). The maidservant's persistence has now led to several suspecting that Peter was a disciple. Perceiving the growing danger, the panicked disciple invokes a curse on himself (i.e.,"damn me if I am not telling the truth") and says that he does not know the man they are talking about (14:71). The words are hardly out of his mouth when the rooster begins to crow. Jesus' prediction is fulfilled instantly and impressively. Remembering the prediction and recognizing what he has done, Peter breaks down and weeps (v. 72).

Mark's portrait contrasting Jesus and Peter is masterful and has often been the subject of Christian preaching. Even while Jesus is inside before the ruling priests who mock him and ask him to prophesy (14:65), Peter is outside fulfilling the very prophecy of Jesus which foretold Peter's threefold denial. Peter's failing only makes Jesus look more impressive.

Jesus before Pilate (15:1-15)

At first light the ruling priests, elders, and scribes hold a council and decide to bind Jesus and send him to Pilate, the Roman governor. Pilate's question, "Are you the King of the Jews?" (15:2a), makes clear what charge the ruling priests have brought against Jesus. Jesus' affirmation of messiahship and divine sonship, understood in the Jewish context, amounts to an unambiguous claim to kingship. The Roman Senate made kings (such as Herod the Great). Self-proclaimed kings were viewed as treasonous rebels (and in recent years Israel had been plagued with several would-be kings).

In replying, "You are saying it" (15:2b), Jesus does not refuse the title "King of the Jews," but neither does he say "I am," as he had when Caiaphas asked him if he was the Messiah, the Son of God (see 14:61). That Jesus' answer was not seen as a rejection of the title is seen in his subsequent crucifixion and mockery as "King of the Jews" (15:18, 26). Jesus is indeed the King of the Jews, but not in the sense understood by Rome, her Jewish collaborators, or various Jewish would-be kings. Jesus' kingship derives entirely from God, from whom he as the "son of man" of Daniel 7 received kingdom and authority.

Jesus refuses to discuss the matter with Pilate, and he refuses to reply to the various charges laid against him (15:3-5). Pilate is amazed (v. 5a), which casts Jesus once again in a favorable light. With calm and dignity Jesus stands before his accusers.

Pilate's offer to release Jesus as a gesture of goodwill at the Passover season only heightens the hypocrisy and villainy of those who wish to destroy Jesus. Are they really concerned about law and order? Do they really have Rome's interests in mind? Evidently not, for they call for the release of one Barabbas, a rebel and murderer, a man truly deserving of the death sentence (15:6-11).

Because there is no corroboration of Pilate's Passover pardon outside the NT Gospels, some critics think that it is nothing more than a literary and theological invention. But this is very doubtful. The invention of such a story would be risky, for there would be many who would know it to be baseless. Moreover, the tradition is attested in at least two independent streams, Mark (followed by Matthew and Luke) and John (which is independent of the Synoptics).

The Gospels' portraits of Pilate as wavering, wishing to release Jesus but finally acquiescing to the demands of Jerusalem's influential elite, have often been questioned. Many assume that this portrait grew out of apologetic interests, hoping to put Jesus and early Christianity on the side of Rome. It was the Jewish leaders, after all, not the Roman governor, who desired Jesus' death — so goes the argument. That the evangelists exploited the story of the wavering, uncertain Pilate is quite probable, but its wholesale invention is doubtful. When we remember the political and social setting of Jewish Palestine in the time of Pilate, we should not be surprised that Pilate was reluctant to execute in such a public and provocative manner a popular prophet from Galilee, whose many followers were present in Jerusalem. Stringing up Jesus could very well instigate a riot, the very thing Pilate hoped to avoid. If Jesus had no military intentions, then he was little more than a pest. A beating and some jail time would suffice. But no, the ruling priests wanted him dead. So Pilate released Barabbas (whose name ironically means "son of the father") and had Jesus flogged in preparation for crucifixion. (Flogging was apparently standard precrucifixion procedure; see *Digesta* 48.19.8.3; Josephus *J.W.* 2.14.9 §306.)

The Mocking (15:16-20a)

The soldiers mock Jesus by placing on him a purple robe and a woven crown of thorns (15:16-17). They then salute him, "Hail, King of the Jews!" strike him on the head with a reed, and bow before him (vv. 17-19). What the Roman soldiers are acting out (and they are Roman, as indicated by their leading Jesus into the praetorium) is a mock salute of the Roman emperor, as is done during the celebration of a triumph. It is at such a time that the emperor would wear an ivy crown and a robe with a purple mantle. His soldiers would shout, "Hail, Caesar!" This entire scene will later be turned on its head by the Roman centurion, who will supervise the crucifixion.

The Crucifixion (15:20b-41)

With the conclusion of the mockery, the soldiers lead Jesus out to be crucified. One Simon of Cyrene is compelled to carry Jesus' cross. Having been severely beaten (15:15), Jesus is too weak to carry it. (Those condemned to the cross were normally required to carry it; see Plutarch

Mor. 554a-b.) For Mark we may have here an acting out of Jesus' warning that his followers will have to take up the cross (see 8:34).

Jesus is brought to Golgotha, the place of the skull. They offer him a numbing drink, but it is refused. Jesus is then crucified. It was the most gruesome form of execution practiced in the Roman Empire. It was designed to kill the condemned slowly and painfully (on this subject, see Hengel 1977). The soldiers gamble for what was left of Jesus' property — his clothing. Nearby, or attached to the cross itself, is the charge for which Jesus was crucified: "The King of the Jews" (15:26). Passersby (identified as ruling priests in v. 31) mock Jesus for having talked of destroying the temple and then rebuilding it in three days (v. 29; see 14:58). Why not save himself and come down from the cross? Evidently he cannot; though he saved others, he cannot save himself (15:30-31)! Let the Messiah, the King of Israel, come down from the cross, that the ruling priests may see and believe! And so goes the mockery (v. 32), which serves as a foil for the resurrection. Jesus in fact will be taken down from the cross and in his resurrection will be saved, while the prediction of the temple's destruction is foreshadowed.

At the sixth hour (i.e., noon) darkness fell over the land. At the ninth hour (i.e., 3 p.m.) Jesus cries out in a loud voice, quoting the words of Ps 22:1: "My God, my God, why have you abandoned me?" (15:34). The darkness of the land signifies judgment; that Jesus cries out the way he does suggests that divine judgment has in part fallen on him. This is consistent with his earlier allusion to Zech 13:7 in Mark 14:27. In rejecting God's Son (see the parable of the vineyard tenants in 12:1-12) God strikes his own people, beginning with Israel's shepherd.

Bystanders think that Jesus has called for Elijah (*eloi* ["my God"] approximating the sound of *'eliya* ["Elijah"]), an eschatological figure who will come and rescue the righteous. Jesus again cries out and dies. The loud shout, instead of a dying moan, tells of Jesus' power even in death. The temple curtain then tears, a second supernatural sign that probably foreshadows the doom of the temple. Impressed by the manner of Jesus' death and the signs that attend it, the Roman centurion confesses: "Truly this man was the Son of God!" (15:39). The mockery is now over. In calling Jesus the Son of God, the centurion has switched his allegiance from Caesar, the official "son of God," to Jesus, the real Son of God (on the range of meanings of this epithet, see Hengel 1976). The scene concludes with the notation of the women who witness the crucifixion. They stand in stark contrast to the disciples who had fled. They will also be the first to discover the empty tomb and to learn of the resurrection of Jesus.

The Burial (15:42-47)

When evening of the day of Preparation came (i.e., day before the sabbath), Joseph of Arimathea requested the body of Jesus for burial. Given the charges brought against Jesus, the Roman governor might very well have refused permission (see *Digesta* 48.24.1-2; 48.16.15, 3). But Jewish custom was opposed to leaving bodies hanging on gibbets or crosses overnight (see Deut 21:23; *m. Sanh.* 6:6; *b. Sanh.* 46b), but regarded burial of the dead as an act of piety (see 2 Sam 21:12-14; Tob 1:17-19; 2:3-7). Pilate, moreover, was probably only too happy to have the corpse of Jesus removed from public view. When he had ascertained from the centurion that Jesus was indeed dead, he released the body to Joseph. (Pilate's surprise that Jesus had died so quickly was due to the fact that most crucifixion victims suffered for two or three days, sometimes even longer, before succumbing; see Seneca *Dialogue* 3; Hengel 1977: 29-31.)

Jesus' body is wrapped in a linen shroud and placed in rock-cut tomb. A stone is then rolled against the opening, thus sealing the tomb. (Examples of this type of tomb can be seen in the vicinity of Jerusalem today.) The evangelist again notes that women from among Jesus' following observed where he had been buried. Earlier we were told that these women had looked on during the crucifixion (15:40-41). Women will also be the first to discover the empty tomb (16:1).

The Empty Tomb (16:1-8)

Because Jesus had been buried in haste and probably because his criminal status had placed restrictions on the burial rites, three brave women risk going to the tomb early Sunday morning to complete the burial process and to weep quietly at the tomb. They wonder who will roll back the heavy stone. It is ironic that not one of Jesus' male disciples was available to offer this assistance. (The story of the empty tomb should be viewed as historical, for a fictional account in late antiquity would scarcely have chosen women as witnesses.) But the question becomes moot; the stone has already been rolled back. Entering the tomb, they see a young man. Mark does not call him an angel, but his description probably would have made most of Mark's readers think that he was an angel (see Matt 28:2, 5, where he is explicitly identified as an angel).

The young man tells the astounded women (16:5) that Jesus of Nazareth is risen and is not to be found in the tomb. He bids them to look upon the very place where his body had lain. Jesus is indeed gone. They are to go and tell the disciples, especially Peter, that he will go before them to Galilee. There they will see him (vv. 6-7). There is an element of irony here. The disciples fled and have presumably begun their journey for home, leaving behind their dead master. But not so; Jesus will arrive in Galilee before they do.

Mark's Gospel ends abruptly with the notation that the women were so astonished that they were left frightened and speechless. It also ends with a dramatic finish emphasizing once again the awesome power of Jesus, who not only astounded people during his ministry but also astounded people in his death and in his resurrection. Did Mark's Gospel end with 16:8? The earliest manuscripts end here. But later manuscripts of Mark and the later Gospels of Matthew, Luke, and John go on to narrate resurrection appearances. The later manuscripts of Mark provide two endings, which may be briefly considered.

Appendix: Two Endings

In the ancient manuscripts that contain the whole of Mark we find four endings: (1) at 16:8, "for they were afraid"; (2) at 16:20, the so-called Long Ending; (3) at 16:8, plus the so-called Short Ending; and (4) at 16:20, plus the Short Ending. Many of the older manuscripts have asterisks and obeli marking off the Long or Short Endings as spurious or at least doubtful.

The Long Ending (16:9-20)

The traditional ending of Mark, the so-called "Long Ending," tells of Jesus' appearance to Mary Magdalene, of her report to the unbelieving disciples, of a later appearance to the eleven, and of the commission to evangelize. This commission contains some bizarre elements: picking up snakes and drinking poison and not being injured by either (16:18). The entire passage appears to have been composed from the resurrection accounts of Matthew, Luke, and John, and has even alluded to events described in the book of Acts. The most obvious parallels are as follows: v. 11: lack of belief (Matt 28:17); v. 12: the two on the road (Luke 24:13-35); v. 14: reproach for unbelief (John 20:19, 26); v. 15: the Great Commission (Matt 28:19); v. 16: salvation and judgment (John 3:18, 36); v. 17: speaking in tongues (Acts 2:4; 10:46); v. 18: serpents and poison (Acts 28:3-5); v. 18: laying hands on the sick (Acts 9:17; 28:8); v. 19: ascension (Acts 1:2, 9); v. 20: general summary of Acts.

16:14 appears in a somewhat expanded and different form in the fifth- century codex W. In this version the disciples excuse their lack of faith as due to the influence of Satan and his unclean allies. Jesus assures his disciples that Satan's time is almost over and that a fearful judgment is near.

The parallels with Acts and the other Gospels, the high concentration of vocabulary found nowhere else in Mark, the absence of these verses in our oldest copies of Mark (e.g., א B) and in the earliest fathers (e.g., Clement of Alexandria and Origen), and the awkward connection between 16:8 and 9 have led most scholars to conclude that the Long Ending of Mark was not part of the original Gospel.

The Short Ending

Some manuscripts preserve the so-called Short Ending to Mark (L Ψ 099 0112). Almost all of those that do also contain the Long Ending. The Short Ending reads: "But they reported briefly to Peter and those with him all that they had been told. And after this Jesus himself sent out by means of them, from east to west, the sacred and imperishable proclamation of eternal salvation." This ending, too, has no compelling claim to authenticity, for it contains a high precentage of non-Markan vocabulary and exhibits a rhetorical tone found nowhere else in Mark.

Bibliography. Boring, M. E., K. Berger, and C. Colpe, 1995, *Hellenistic Commentary to the New Testament,* Nashville: Abingdon • Brooks, J. A. 1991, *Mark,* NAC 23, Nashville: Broadman • Brown, R. E. 1994, *The Death of the Messiah: From Gethsemane to the Grave. A Commentary on the Passion Narratives in the Four Gospels,* ABRL, 2 vols., New York: Doubleday • Chilton, B. D. 1984, *A Galilean Rabbi and His Bible: Jesus' Use of the Interpreted Scripture of His Time,* GNS 8, Wilmington: Glazier • Chilton, B. D. 1992, *The Temple of Jesus: His Sacrificial Program within a Cultural History of Sacrifice,* University Park: Penn State • Chilton, B. D. 1996, *Pure Kingdom: Jesus' Vision of God,* Studying the Historical Jesus, Grand Rapids: Eerdmans • Deissmann, G. A. 4th ed. 1978, *Light from the Ancient East,* Grand Rapids: Baker • Donahue, J. R., and D. J. Harrington. 2002, *The Gospel of Mark,* SacPag 2, Collegeville: Liturgical Press • Dunn, J. D. G. 1990, *Jesus, Paul and the Law: Studies in Mark and Galatians,* London: SPCK; Louisville: Westminster • Edwards, J. R. 2002, *The Gospel according to Mark,* PNTC, Grand Rapids: Eerdmans • Evans, C. A. 1992, *Noncanonical Writings and New Testament Interpretation,* Peabody: Hendrickson • Evans, C. A. 1995, *Jesus and His Contemporaries: Comparative Studies,* AGJU 25, Leiden: Brill • Evans, C. A. 2001, *Mark 8:27–16:20,* WBC 34B, Nashville: Thomas Nelson • Fitzmyer, J. A. 1959, "The Aramaic Qorban Inscription from Jebel Hallet Et-turi and Mk 7:11/Mt 15:5," *JBL* 78:60-65 • France, R. T. 2002, *The Gospel of Mark,* NIGTC, Grand Rapids: Eerdmans • Garland, D. E. 1996, *Mark,* NIVAC, Grand Rapids: Zondervan • Geyer, D. W. 2002, *Fear, Anomaly, and Uncertainty in the Gospel of Mark,* ATLAMS 47, Lanham, Md.: Scarecrow Press • Guelich, R. A. 1989, *Mark 1–8:26,* WBC 34A, Dallas: Word • Gundry, R. H. 1993, *Mark: A Commentary on His Apology for the Cross,* Grand Rapids: Eerdmans • Hatina, T. R. 1996, "The Focus of Mark 13:24-27 — The Parousia, or the Destruction of the Temple?" *BBR* 6:43-66 • Hengel, M. 1976, *The Son of God,* London: SCM; Philadelphia: Fortress • Hengel, M. 1977, *Crucifixion,* London: SCM; Philadelphia: Fortress • Hengel, M. 1985, *Studies in the Gospel of Mark,* Philadelphia: Fortress • Hooker, M. D. 1991, *The Gospel according to Saint Mark,* BNTC, London: A. & C. Black; Peabody, Mass.: Hendrickson • Keener, C. S. 1993, *The IVP Bible Background Commentary: New Testament,* Downers Grove: InterVarsity • Lachs, S. T. 1987, *A Rabbinic Commentary on the New Testament: The Gospels of Matthew, Mark, and Luke,* Hoboken: Ktav • Lane, W. L. 1974, *The Gospel of Mark,* NICNT, Grand Rapids: Eerdmans • Malina, B. J., and R. L. Rohrbaugh. 1992, *Social-Science Commentary on the Synoptic Gospels,* Minneapolis: Fortress • Marcus, J. 1992, *The Way of the Lord: Christological Exegesis of the Old Testament in the Gospel of Mark,* Louisville: Westminster/John Knox • Marcus, J. 2000, *Mark 1–8,* AB 27, New York: Doubleday • Rousseau, J. J., and R. Arav, 1994, *Jesus and His World: An Archaeological and Cultural Dictionary,* Minneapolis: Fortress • Sanders, E. P. 1985, *Jesus and Judaism,* Philadelphia: Fortress • Taylor, V. 1952, *The Gospel according to St. Mark,* London: Macmillan • Witherington, B. 2001, *The Gospel of Mark: A Socio-Rhetorical Commentary,* Grand Rapids: Eerdmans.

Luke

David L. Balch

INTRODUCTION

The prologue does not name the author, although Luke 1:1, 2, and 3 use the first person pronoun. Luke 1:2 distinguishes the author from "eyewitnesses," but tradition identified the writer as Luke, Paul's companion (Phlm 24). Mark is probably one Lukan source, so that the date is post-70, indicated also by 19:43 and 21:20. Other sources include sayings common with Matthew (Q) and sayings found only in this Gospel (L). The irenic view of the Roman government and the author's failure to cite Paul's epistles, which had been collected by the early second century, indicate a first-century date, probably in the 80s. Most students consider the Alexandrian text ($\mathfrak{p}^{75}$ B) closer to the original than the "Western" text (D). Our author imitated the LXX in chs. 1–2, as contemporaries (Arrian, Lucian) imitated Attic.

Luke-Acts have been understood as biography, novel, or ancient history, literary genres that overlap. As a genre "history" narrates corporate religious and political events, whereas biographies and novels concern individuals. This commentary assumes that the two volumes are both biography and ancient history (Balch 2003b). Roman cultural ideology outlined by the historian Dionysius of Halicarnassus (see Gabba) influenced both Josephus and Luke. Dionysius arrived in Rome in 30 BC and was writing his history in 7 BC, one literary model a century later for Josephus *Antiquities of the Jews,* both written in twenty books. Both multivolume histories tell of the ancestors of Romans and/or Jews, the founder of the people ("biographies" of either Romulus or Moses), and the founder's successors (consuls and/or kings). Luke in a multivolume history also narrates three epochs, the ancestors (Acts 7 and 13), Jesus, the central epoch of history (the Gospel), and successors (Acts). In contrast to Mark's focus on Christology, Luke also emphasized ecclesiology, the epoch of the church.

These ancient historians carefully date the three Founders and narrate stories of their birth from God, so that they are the sons of God. Each taught authoritatively, appeared to witness(es) after their death, and ascended to heaven. Crucial aspects of their religious and political teaching concern the relationship between rich and poor persons and whether to "receive" "foreigners" into the people, both ecclesiological concerns in Luke.

The Gospel is structured as follows: prologue (1:1-4), infancy narrative (1:5–2:52), John the Baptist's ministry and Jesus' preparation (3:1–4:13), Jesus' Galilean ministry (4:14–9:50), the journey to Jerusalem (9:51–19:27), Jesus' teaching in the Jerusalem temple (19:28–21:38), the passion (22:1–23:56), and the resurrection (24:1-53). For outlining the structure and plot development in the following commentary, I owe much to Alan Culpepper; for critique I am indebted to Andy Mangum.

The Gospel was first read in a Mediterranean city to followers of Jesus gathered in a house church to share the Lord's Supper. This commentary makes a special effort to understand how the Lukan Christian communities gathered for worship in Greco-Roman houses would hear the Gospel as they reclined in the dining room *(triclinium)* and sat together in the courtyard (*peristylos;* see Osiek and Balch: chs. 1 and 8).

COMMENTARY

Prologue (1:1-4)

The author does not categorize this book as a "Gospel" but as a "narrative" *(diēgēsis),* which others have already attempted. Other ancient historians also used the term "narrative" of their works (Cancik: 682 n. 5). It concerns deeds that God has fulfilled "among us" — therefore, not only salvation history that happened centuries or decades earlier in the time of Moses or Jesus but also now in the time of the author and other believers.

Luke claims to write more "fully" *(akribōs)* than his predecessors (Balch: "The *Full* History"). 2 Maccabees uses similar language: the summary shortens the story told earlier by the historian Jason, who had gone through each matter "fully" (*di-akriboun;* 2 Macc 2:28). The historian Dionysius criticizes Thucydides for being "lazy" in his history and not "fully" reporting major characters' *speeches* (Dionysius *Thucydides* 14.3; 15.1). He objects that historians narrate military actions "fully"; but they do not do the same for civic seditions (Dionysius *Rom. Ant.* 7.66.3-5). Luke is observing that the predecessors (including Mark) have not given their readers Jesus' or the apostles' speeches. Since ancient historians conveyed the meaning of their narratives by inserting speeches, we must pay particular attention to them in this Gospel. Luke-Acts is a religio-political history of the Founder, that is, of the predecessors, Founder, and successors, including both their deeds and words (Acts 1:1).

Infancy Narrative (1:5–2:52)

Mark begins his "Gospel" with John the Baptist's proclamation and Jesus' baptism by him, and Luke, too, may originally have begun with John. Luke summarizes the Gospel in Acts 10:34-43 (Wilckens), a summary that also begins with John's preaching (Acts 10:37b; cf. 1:22). As ancient historians commonly did, the author may have finished writing the rest of the Gospel before adding the introduction, the infancy narratives (chs. 1–2) (Gabba: 85). This would explain similarities between the canticles of the infancy narratives and the speeches that Luke composed later for the book of Acts (Brown: 243).

The contrast in style between the elegant, balanced, periodic sentence in 1:1-4 and the following narrative is intentional: the Greek reader is immediately submerged into Semitic religious culture. Students in Greco-Roman *gymnasia* learned to imitate the styles of diverse writers. Arrian, best known for editing Epictetus's *Discourses* in the Koine Greek dialect, also wrote the story of Alexander the Great in Attic and told of India in a third dialect, Ionic. Lucian typically wrote Attic Greek, but imitated Herodotus's Ionic dialect so successfully in his work "The Syrian Goddess" that some scholars refuse to recognize him as the author! Modern authors speculate about Luke's sources for the Semiticized Greek of Luke 1–2, but Luke imitates the Greek translation of the OT. Our author wants the reader to hear Jesus' authentic Jewish origins in continuity with Scripture.

The infancy narrative serves as a transition from later priestly elements of the Hebrew Bible to the contemporary story of God's people refounded by Jesus. Quoting from the Mosaic Torah, Psalms, wisdom literature, and prophets, the author presents Jesus in continuity with the earlier (now pre-) history of God's contemporary people. Luke is abbreviating a pattern employed by Josephus, who also told the prehistory of Israel before narrating Moses' founding words and deeds, followed by the subsequent history of Israel. Josephus took the pattern from Dionysius of Halicarnassus, who a century earlier had written the prehistory of peoples emigrating to Rome, then narrated the founder Romulus's words and deeds, followed by the subsequent history of the Roman Empire.

This pattern dramatically affects the Christology. Unlike Mark and Paul, who focus exclusively on the Jesus event, Luke is narrating salvation history through the ages. Mark names Jesus Christ in 1:1. Luke first writes a preface not mentioning Jesus, tells of Zechariah's priestly service in the temple, the angel Gabriel's annunciation of John's birth, Elizabeth's conception, Gabriel's annunciation to Mary, then finally names Jesus (v. 31). Luke-Acts does not focus exclusively on Jesus the way Mark does, but is more theocentric and ecclesiastical. History does have a center in the founding words and deeds of Moses, or Romulus, or Jesus, but crucial events also occur before and after the central figure's life.

The infancy narrative has seven episodes: the two annunciations of John's and Jesus' births, Mary's visit to Elizabeth, the two stories of John's and Jesus' birth/circumcision/naming, Jesus' presentation in the temple, and his boyhood teaching in the temple. The two annunciation stories are closely parallel, and the two birth/circumcision/naming stories are also parallel, although less closely. However, the well-known canticles fit only awkwardly into various outlines, probably because they were added after the more balanced narrative text was written, a typical technique in ancient historiography of adding speeches to a narrative outline written earlier.

Speeches, here canticles, were a means used by ancient historians to clarify the meaning of the narrative for their readers. Orators' speeches were thought of as *causing* events. This overlaps with the Jewish expectation that prophecies would be fulfilled: *God's* revelatory speech to prophets causes events (Isa 55:10-11). When the Spirit moves Simeon to come to the temple, he takes the baby Jesus in his arms, quoting Isaiah (42:6; 49:6, 9) concerning this [baby] being a "light for the Gentiles," a prophecy that is fulfilled, that is causal, both in relation to the Gentile Cornelius hearing the gospel proclaimed by Peter (Acts 10) and the pagans of Antioch accepting Paul's proclamation (Acts 13).

Annunciation of the Birth of John the Baptist (1:5-25)

Luke composes freely. As a Gentile convert, the author avidly read the ancient scriptures, including the annunciation stories of Ishmael (Gen 16:7-12), Isaac (Gen 17:1-21), and Samson (Judg 13:3-22; compare the story of Samuel in 1 Samuel 1–2), all of which exhibit a similar pattern: an angel appears, the visionary responds with fear or prostration, and the message notes that the woman is or is about to become pregnant and should give the child a certain name. In response, the visionary objects or requests a sign, which is given (Brown: 156). Luke employs the biblical pattern in both annunciation stories; the material that does not belong to the pattern needs explaining (Brown: 296).

A key theme in the Lukan infancy narratives concerns whether characters "believe" the proclaimed "good news" or not. In the first annunciation, Gabriel observes that "I have been sent to speak to you and to bring you [Zechariah] this good news *(euangelisasthai),* but now because you did not believe *(ouk episteusas)* my words, which will be fulfilled *(plerōthēsontai)* in their time, you will become mute . . ." (1:19-20). But after the annunciation to Mary, Elizabeth proclaims: "blessed is she who believed *(pisteusasa)* that there would be a fulfillment of what was spoken to her by the Lord" (v. 45). Mary is a paradigmatic disciple. This pattern of males disbelieving and females believing is also central to the resurrection narratives. The women "remembered his words, and returning from the tomb they told all this to the eleven and to all the rest" (24:9). "But these words seemed to them [the male apostles] an idle tale, and they did not believe them" (24:11). In Luke, whether individuals or groups *hear* and believe the promises declared by God's messengers is finally even more pivotal than *seeing* the resurrected Christ! Seim writes in this sense of Luke's *Double Message:* the author does not portray women seeing the resurrected Christ, preaching, or holding office in the church, but they are often the ones who hear, remember, and believe, a theme that Luke employs to form an inclusion between the infancy and resurrection narratives. Luke develops the theme throughout the Gospel narrative (e.g., 8:12; 22:67; 24:25, all unique to Luke) and Acts (38 references — e.g., 4:4; 8:12 [Samaritans]; 10:43; 13:41 quoting Habakkuk, 48; 15:7; 17:11-12; 18:27-28; 24:14; 26:27). Luke has employed the old annunciation pattern with a twist:

whether one believes God's oral or written word is decisive, not religious status, gender, race, or economic/political class.

Both Matthew (2:1-12) and Luke narrate Jesus' birth in the time of Herod the Great, probably a historical fact. Whether the same is true of John's parents' priestly descent has been debated (Brown: 265-68) because it corresponds so closely to Luke's attempt to establish continuity between Jesus and Judaism in Jerusalem. Elizabeth's barrenness also corresponds to the stories of Hannah, Samuel's mother (1 Sam 1:2), and Sarah, Isaac's mother (Gen 18:11), and thus probably belongs to Luke's ability to tell a good scriptural tale.

The inaugural vision of the book occurs in the Jerusalem temple *(naos),* the central holy place for Luke. At Jesus' death, however, there is an eclipse of the sun, "and the curtain of the temple was torn in two" (23:45); later, to Stoic philosophers, Paul declares that the Creator, "the Lord of heaven and earth, does not live in shrines made by human hands" (Acts 17:24-25). This plot develops in relation to the temple!

Both kinship and gender were defined by sacrifice in the temple (see Stowers: 293-333). Who was and who was not allowed to sacrifice in the temple or how closely they might approach the holy place generated and maintained cultural/social relationships between ethnic groups and between the sexes. Antiochus III decreed: "it is unlawful for any foreigner *(allophylos)* to enter the enclosure of the temple which is forbidden to the Jews, except to those of them who are accustomed to enter after purifying themselves in accordance with the law of the country" (Josephus *Ant.* 12.145, trans. Marcus in LCL). The women's court was more distant from the sanctuary than the men's. The temple was an identity symbol for the ethnic group and for gender differentiation, but our author is writing a story the plot of which progresses toward the fulfillment of Joel 2: "In the last days it will be, God declares, that I will pour out my Spirit upon all flesh, and your sons and your daughters shall prophesy.... Then everyone who calls on the name of the Lord shall be saved" (Acts 2:17, 21). A high point of the second volume is reached when Cornelius, a foreigner (*allophylos;* Acts 10:28), is received into the people of God. This subversion of the temple's functions, this change in the identity of God's people, must be legitimated within the temple itself, which is where Luke begins and ends the Gospel (1:8; 24:53). Conflicts about ethnicity and gender are not conflicts between Judaism and Christianity, but within Judaism and within Christianity (Balch 1998).

Luke sets the story within Zechariah's service at the temple, with the multitude praying outside (1:8-10). The scene itself has all the elements of annunciations to Sarah (Genesis 16), Abraham (Genesis 17), and Manoah's wife (Judges 13). Gabriel addresses Zechariah by name, telling him that he is not to be afraid and that his prayer has been heard. Elizabeth will have a son, whose name is to be John. He will be filled with holy spirit even before birth, and his task in the spirit of Elijah will be to turn Israel to God, which the angel calls "good news." Our author often prefers "holy spirit" without the definite article. Christian readers accustomed to confessing "the Holy Spirit" as one of the Trinity should be careful not to read later theology into the early Gospels. Luke writes of the spirit that enabled Elijah to speak "the word of the LORD" (1 Kgs 17:8; 18:1; 21:17), just as "the word of the Lord came to John" (3:2). The Spirit's role is prophetic, to turn Israel to God. Zechariah goes home (1:23). Six of the seven scenes in the Lucan infancy narrative conclude, as does this first one, with a departure (Brown: 263).

Annunciation of the Birth of Jesus (1:26-38)

Luke again follows the biblical annunciation pattern, receiving a message about bearing a son to be called Jesus. These verses claim that Mary conceived as a virgin, a common means in the Hellenistic world of claiming divine origins for the founder of a philosophical school or a state. Some deny this contemporary origin for the idea because it appears to be immoral sexual activity on the part of the male deity (Brown: 523). But when one social or religious group takes over ideas or practices from another, the ideas/practices are always changed. When Christians borrowed *logos* theology from the Stoics or more probably from Hellenistic Jews, they changed it: the logos took on *flesh* (John 1:14), an absurd idea for the Stoics or the Hellenistic Jew Philo. Greeks and Romans told stories of divine fathers for Plato (Diogenes Laertius 3.1-2, 45), Alexander the Great (Plutarch *Alexander* 2.1–3.2), Romulus the founder of Rome (Dionysius *Rom. Ant.* 1.77.2-3; 2.56.6; cf. 4.2; Plutarch *Romulus* 2–4), and Augustus who (re)founded the empire (Suetonius *Lives of the Caesars* 2.94.1-7). Luke wanted to claim that Jesus, founder of the network of house churches that was growing throughout the world, was more than Plato, Alexander, Romulus, or Augustus, as well as more than John the Baptist. Were his teachings only those of a wise human being? No, for Luke Jesus and his teachings were of divine origin, so he must have had a divine conception/birth. When Luke completed the two-volume history by prefacing the infancy narrative, Luke adds Mary's virginal conception of this Son of God, just as a century earlier in his history Dionysius had narrated the divine origins of Romulus (and of Rome's fifth king, Tarquinius). "On the mother's side they [Romulus and his twin Remus] were descended from Aeneas . . . ; it is hard to say with certainty who their father was, but the Romans *believe* them to have been the *sons of Mars*" (*pepisteuntai . . . Areos huioi;* Dionysius *Rom. Ant.* 2.2.3). Luke disputes this theology: Jesus is the "Son of God," not Romulus, the founder of the state persecuting Christians, and Jesus' teachings are of divine origin, not Romulus's military policies. When Romulus appeared after his death and before his ascension to heaven, Livy (1.16.7) summarizes his key policy statement: "Declare to the Romans the will of Heaven that my Rome shall be the capital of the world; so let them cherish the art of war. . . ." But the teaching that has legitimate divine origin and authority is "love your enemies, do good to those who hate you . . ." (Luke 6:27). The ancient debate was not about whether miracles happen but about who is Lord of the world and whose religious and political policies are legitimate.

When Mary heard the angel's news, she was betrothed; the marriage was sealed. But as a virgin, she would bear the Son of the Most High, to whom God would give the throne of David. Through the prophet Nathan, God had promised David successors: "I will be a father to him, and he shall be a son to me" (2 Sam 7:14). Mary responds to the angel's announcement with a question (Luke 1:34), not very different from Zechariah's question (v. 18), but for Luke the male priest is an example of unbelief (v. 20) while Mary is a female example of a believing disciple (vv. 38, 45).

Informing Mary that her barren relative Elizabeth had conceived a son in her old age, Gabriel departs, saying, "For nothing will be impossible *(adynatēsei)* with God" (1:37). These words reflect the Lord's annunciation to Sarah that she would have a son, Isaac. Sarah hears God's promise after her menopause, "so Sarah laughed to herself, saying, 'After I have grown old, and my husband is old, shall I have pleasure?'" The LORD is offended at Sarah's laughter and asks Abraham, "Is anything too wonderful *(adynatei* [impossible]) for the LORD?" (Gen 18:13-14).

Mary Visits Elizabeth and Magnifies God (1:39-56)

The two stories of John and Jesus merge; the narrative is short, the speeches longer. Mary visits Zechariah and Elizabeth and greets the latter, at which the child leaps in Elizabeth's womb (1:41); she adds that John leaped "for [eschatological] joy" (v. 44). Elizabeth herself is filled with the Holy Spirit and speaks several oracles, three times pronouncing Mary blessed *(makaria);* the adjective "blessed" recognizes an existing state. The final beatitude is Lukan, pronouncing her blessed "who believed that there would be a fulfillment of what was spoken to her by the Lord."

Mary responds with a canticle, the *Magnificat.* Few scholars think that this and the canticles which follow were composed by the characters in the narrative, nor were they simply composed by Luke. Since speeches were often added to a narrative written earlier in order to interpret it, Luke has probably followed that practice. Since they resemble later speeches in Acts, Luke certainly chose and rewrote them, but their core seems to be pre-Lukan. Brown: 273 argues that this is not a Baptist source: nothing in them goes beyond knowledge of John elsewhere in Christian sources. The salvation announced has already been accomplished (1:69, 71), more characteristic of Jewish Christians than of other contemporary sects of Judaism (Brown: 350).

The *Magnificat* has parallels to Peter's inaugural sermon on Pentecost (Acts 2). Mary is one who "believed" that there would be a fulfillment of what was spoken to her by the Lord" (1:45), a contrast with Zechariah who did "not believe" (v. 20), a choice that is basic to Luke's two-volume work. In the hymn, Mary refers to the Lord's help to Israel "as he spoke to our fathers" (1:55). Correspondingly, Peter proclaims "what was spoken by the prophet Joel" (Acts 2:16) and what "David says" who "foresaw" events (2:25, 31); the result is that three thousand "believed" (2:41, 44).

The content of this common prophetic word is a reversal: Mary is the "slave of the Lord" (1:37), a Lord who "looks upon the humility *(tapeinōsin)* of his slave" (v. 48), but who by the strength of his arm "has scattered the proud" (*hyperēphanous;* v. 51), "put down the mighty from their thrones and exalted the humble" *(hypsōsen tapeinous;* v. 52). In the Pentecost sermon, Peter quotes David prophesying that the Lord "will not abandon my soul to Hades" (Acts 2:27 quoting Ps 15:10 LXX). Peter interprets this to mean that David "foresaw and spoke of the resurrection of the Christ," that he was not abandoned to Hades (v. 31) but was "exalted *(hypsōtheis)* at the right hand of God" (v. 33, citing Ps 109:1 LXX). Peter's keyword "exalted" is the same verbal root as in the *Magnificat* (1:52). This prophesied reversal for Mary and Jesus — from slavery or humility to exaltation, from Hades to God's right hand in heaven, and for the "proud" the opposite reversal — is the content of what Israel is to know "assuredly" (*asphalōs* [Acts 2:36], the same root as for the emphatic final word of the prologue, Luke 1:4). Thus the *Magnificat* and the Pentecost speech are closely connected by themes of faith/unbelief and prophecy/fulfillment, and by God's reversal of slavery, humiliation, and death through raising Jesus from the dead and exalting Mary.

Both the *Magnificat* and Peter's Pentecost sermon are related to the christological hymn in Phil 2:6-11, in which Christ Jesus took the form of a "slave" and "humbled" himself; therefore, God "highly exalted" him (2:7-9). Jesus' parable of the rich man and Lazarus also images God's reversals: the rich man is contrasted with a poor man, Lazarus. The latter dies and goes to Abraham's bosom, but surprisingly the rich man finds himself in "Hades" (a key term also in Acts 2:27, 31), a disaster related to not listening to Moses and the prophets (Luke 16:19-23, 31). Mary's praise of God in the *Magnificat* for favoring her, the Christology of Acts 2 and Philippians 2, and the threat to the imperceptive rich in Jesus' parable all express praise and trust in a God of reversal. The basic pattern is christological, involving Jesus' humiliation and exaltation, with parallel praise for Mary and a challenge to wealthy Christians.

Greco-Roman Christian readers would also recognize the theme of reversal in history. A dramatic example is the story of Brutus and Coriolanus from Rome's legendary beginnings (Balch 1995a: 1997). Brutus is one of the poor who revolts against wealth, the humble against the eminent (Dionysius *Rom. Ant.* 6.54.1), and the humble poor attain the new office of tribune to protect them! The poor man Brutus is elevated to one of the most powerful offices in the state. Coriolanus, the most successful Roman general of his age, opposes the humble Brutus and is banished, reduced to "nothing" because he hated the poor.

Birth of John the Baptist (1:57-80)

The first part of this unit briefly narrates John's birth, circumcision, and naming (1:57-59); the second exhibits Zechariah blessing the child, the *Benedictus* (vv. 67-79). The birth is theologically interpreted as the Lord's showing great mercy to Elizabeth. Another emphasis is on fulfillment: Zechariah was struck mute because of his unbelief "until the day these things occur" (1:20), and so now "immediately his mouth was opened and his tongue freed . . ." (v. 64). Another emphasis typical of ancient historiography is that an ethnic group maintains its own customs and laws: as Romans and Greeks kept their own customs, so John's circumcision on the eighth day was according to the law of Moses (Gen 17:12; Lev 12:3). Then the child does not receive his father's name, but is named "John": "God has been gracious." All these emphases typify the whole two-volume work.

The *Benedictus* (1:67-79) follows the pattern of Jewish blessings: initial praise of God is followed by reasons for the praise. God "visits" the people Israel to intervene (see Gen 21:1; Exod 4:31), a word that Luke uses often (7:16; Acts 7:23; 15:14). These divine visitations are political, although in Luke-Acts no longer military. For prayer against military enemies (1:71, 73) compare 2 Macc 10:26, "falling upon the steps before the altar, they [Judas Maccabeus and his men] implored him to be an enemy to their enemies and an adversary to their adversaries, as the law declares" (citing Exod 23:22). The phrase "to give light to those who sit in darkness" (1:79; cf. Isa 42:7, cited also in Acts 26:18) already hints at the controversial religious and political invitation to invite foreigners into the people of God, which climaxes in Acts 10–11, 15.

The covenant with Abraham (1:73; see Gen 12:1-3; 17; 22:17-18; Acts 3:25) and David (2 Sam 7:8-16) was an unconditional promise, fulfilled, Luke argues, in the births of John and Jesus. An emphasis on John occurs in Luke's outline of the Gospel as presented in Peter's sermon to Cornelius's household: ". . . the word . . . beginning from Galilee after the baptism which John preached . . ." (Acts 10:37-38). The *Benedictus* also has ties with Paul's sermon that focuses on the Abrahamic/Davidic covenant. God "raised up David to be king" of Israel, and "Of this man's posterity God has brought to Israel a Savior, Jesus, as he promised. . . . And as John was finishing his work, he said, 'What do you suppose that I am? I am not he. No, but one is coming after me; I am not worthy to untie the thong of the sandals on his feet.' My brothers, you descendants of Abraham's family . . ." (Acts 13:23-26). Paul's sermon continues arguing from Scripture that Jesus is the enthroned Son of David. One function of both the Benedictus and Paul's sermon in Acts is to argue that "I [John] am not he," not the Messiah, king, son of David. Luke, the ancient historian, added both these speeches, persuasive arguments, to Mark's story of the Gospel.

The hymn concludes by describing John's place in salvation history, although 1:78-79 are more characteristic of Jesus' ministry. John the prophet will prepare the way and give knowledge of salvation through the forgiveness of sins, both Lukan themes (vv. 76-77). Finally (vv. 78-79), God will give light to those who sit in darkness as well as guide us into peace — through John's call for justice (3:7-14) and Jesus' ministry (e.g., 7:50; 8:48; 10:5-6; 19:38, esp. 42-44; 24:36). Luke 19:38 interprets the *Benedictus:* at Jesus' triumphal entry into Jerusalem the people shout "Blessed is the king" who brings "peace" (quoting Ps 118:26), but Luke has Jesus refer to (Roman) "enemies" setting up ramparts around Jerusalem. The city did not recognize the *kairos* of its "visitation" (1:44). Lukan eschatology thus radically qualifies the unconditional Abrahamic/Davidic covenant.

The Birth of Jesus (2:1-20)

After a chapter preparing for it, the account of Jesus' birth takes few verses (2:6-7). Vv. 8-20 then tell of the angelic annunciation to the shepherds and their visit to the Davidic Savior. The author relates the birth of the "Lord" (v. 11; on the title see Tuckett: 76-78) chronologically to the reign of the current emperor, Augustus (v. 1), whose birth legends also claim a divine father (see the commentary on 1:26-38). The stories involve competitive claims of divine lordship and contrasting economic and social status, although historically Octavian/Augustus lived his entire reign in a comparatively simple house on the Palatine hill in Rome. Luke's attempt to give the historical date involved him in mistakes: Gabriel announced the births "in the days of King Herod of Judea" (1:5), who died in AD 4. Jesus' birth, Luke narrates, occurred when the governor Quirinius made a census of Judea, although Quirinius became legate of Syria only in AD 6. Nor is there any other record of a census of "all the world" (2:1; see Brown: appendix 7); such universalizing is a Lukan tendency. Nor in a Roman census would persons return to their birthplace, but it serves the purpose of placing Joseph and Mary in Bethlehem. Luke is an ancient, not a modern historian; as modern readers, we may see the author's interest in datable, political events and contrasts.

We learn that Jesus was Mary's "firstborn" (2:7). In Acts the author refers to Jesus' brothers (1:13) and to James (12:17; 15:13; 21:18). Luke never calls James Jesus' "brother" as Mark does (6:3, omitted by Luke), possibly to avoid giving the impression of nepotism in the church. Jesus was swaddled, as was common (see Soranus *Gynecology* 2.15.42), and placed in a "manger," probably a feeding trough.

The story that follows is of humble shepherds, a despised occupation, typical of Luke, a contrast to Matthew's intellectual magi. At Augustus's birth Publius Nigidius announced to the patrician Roman senate: "the ruler of the world has been born" (Suetonius *Lives of the Caesars* 2.94.3, 5). In the twenty-first century one may still visit the imposing senate house in the Roman forum. In contrast, an angel of the Lord announces the Messiah's birth, "good news *(euangelizomai)* of great joy for all the people *(panti tǭ laǭ)*" (v. 10), to shepherds in the field. Luke's story is so powerful that contemporary tourists may still visit this field (?), though there is no imposing building. Already in the infancy narrative, we hear what Jesus announces later in his inaugural sermon: the good news is for the poor.

The angel's song ascribes glory to God in the highest as well as peace on earth among people of [God's] goodwill, contrasting God with humans and the highest with earth. The shepherds engage in conversation with each other, then find Mary, Joseph, and the child in the manger. Luke again emphasizes the fulfillment of God's word. They find the child just as he was described, so perhaps the rest of the announcement — peace — will also come true? (Compare the *Benedictus,* 2:29, and 7:50; 8:48; 10:5; 19:3; Acts 9:31; 10:36; contrast Luke 12:51; 24:36-37; and Acts 24:2, 5!)

Presentation of Jesus in the Temple (2:21-40)

A major motif in historical works concerns the customs and laws of the people whose story is being told. In the prologue of his *Roman Antiquities* Dionysius observes that he will "describe the best customs and the most remarkable laws; and in short I show the whole life of the ancient Romans" (1.8.2; Balch 1995b). Similarly in this final section of the infancy narrative, Luke ties the paragraphs together by repeated references to Torah, five of the nine references to the law in the whole Gospel (2:22, 23, 24, 27, 39; 10:26; 16:16, 17; 24:24). Ancient historians insisted that they were not changing traditional laws precisely when from a modern perspective they were indeed changing them. Institutions change over time, but in Greco-Roman (Platonic) culture what was best (e.g., the founder's laws, whether Romulus's or Moses') could only change for the worse. Change had to be denied. Just after narrating a sedition which provided the occasion for the plebeians demanding and obtaining the *new* office of tribune to protect them against the patricians, Dionysius inserts an excursus denying that the Romans have ever changed their laws (*Rom. Ant.* 7.70-73)! Luke multiplies quotations of Torah precisely when the priest prophesies something new, a "revelation to the Gentiles" (2:32).

The *Nunc Dimittis* (2:29-35) concludes and climaxes the birth narrative. It is related to the pivotal conclusion of Paul's speech in Antioch (Acts 13:47) and with the conclusion of the two-volume work as a whole (Acts 28:28). Like Mary, Simeon calls himself a slave (2:29) and announces that his eyes have already seen God's salvation "which you have prepared in the presence of all peoples, a light for revelation to the Gentiles and for glory to thy people Israel" (vv. 31-32). The phrase "light for revelation to the Gentiles" alludes to Isa 42:6 and 49:6. This inclusive way of reading Torah, as opposed to the exclusive Priestly strand of the Pentateuch, to Ezra (9:10-15) and Nehemiah (10:28-31), and to the Maccabean books, is Luke's key to the Abrahamic/Davidic covenant. After Paul's speech arguing that Jesus is the enthroned Son of David, Luke pictures the synagogue audience as divided, and Paul responds with another speech: "Behold, we turn to the Gentiles. For so the Lord has commanded us, saying, 'I have set you to be a light for the Gentiles, so that you may bring salvation to the uttermost parts of the earth'" (Acts 13:46-47, quoting Isaiah again). Luke's scriptural citation argues an ethnically inclusive interpretation of the Torah against a Priestly/Maccabean understanding. Luke closes the two-volume work similarly: Paul "welcomed *all* [Jews and Gentiles] who came to him" (Acts 28:30).

As stipulated in the law, Jesus is circumcised on the eighth day (Gen 17:9-14; Lev 17:12) and given the name announced by the angel (2:21; 1:32). The law also requires the purification of the mother (Lev 12:1-5). After this time she was to offer a lamb, although the poor could offer instead two pigeons (Luke 2:24; Lev 12:6-8). Luke seems to assume that the whole family needed purification ("their" in 2:22), although Leviticus legislates this only for the mother.

Luke is reflecting a concern of Pharisaic Judaism: Neusner: 85-86 surveys all the literary material from Pharisees dating before AD 70 and observes that two-thirds of it concerns ritual purity of food, people, and dishes. Luke's thesis is that Jesus' parents belong to traditional Judaism, a thesis of the narrative that prepares for refutation of the charges against Stephen (Acts 6:11, 13-14) and Paul (Acts 21:21) that "Jesus of Nazareth will destroy this place and will change the customs that Moses handed on to us." From prologue to conclusion Luke's volumes are apologetic (Balch 1995b).

Simeon's blessing focuses not only on light for the Gentiles but also on the "consolation of Israel" (Luke 2:25), a prominent theme in deutero-Isaiah (40:1-2; 51:3; 52:9), consolation originally promised to Jewish exiles in Babylon but certainly meaningful for Jews living under Roman rule.

Simeon's second blessing (2:34-35) is addressed to Mary and foreshadows both the rejection and acceptance of Jesus and of the Gospel messengers. Jesus will be rejected, which occurs already as a response to his inaugural sermon (4:29), and he will also be accepted, symbolized by Simon Peter's amazing catch of fish (5:7, 9-10). The child will also "be a sign that will be opposed," literally, "spoken against," which happens as a response to Paul's preaching (Acts 13:45; 28:19, 22), so this prophecy and Acts 28 (where Paul accepts *all* who come) form an inclusion. Those interpreters are mistaken who understand Luke-Acts as finally rejecting all Jews.

Luke's narrative often includes stories of both male and female characters: Zechariah's disbelief is contrasted with Mary's belief, a contrast that will recur in the final chapter of the Gospel. The aged prophet Anna comes into the temple and, uniquely for a woman in Luke, "speaks about the child to all who were looking for the redemption of Jerusalem" (2:38). She preached, but Luke does not give us her words. We also hear of Philip's virgin daughters who prophesy (Acts 21:9), but we do not read their words. Plutarch tells of the wise and famous Eumetus, whose riddles are known as far away as Egypt, but he does not record a single word she says (*Dinner of the Seven Sages* 148B-E)! However frustrating to modern readers, this was typical of Greco-Roman values, but a contrast to early Pauline churches where women preached (e.g., Rom 16:3; 1 Cor 11:5, 13; Phil 4:3).

Anna is a model for groups of widows later in the work (Acts 9:39, 41, where they may have lived as a group in Dorcas's house). 1 Tim 5:3-16 attempts to regulate these widows. But in contrast to the deutero-Pauline author, Luke pictures Anna and the widows in Dorcas's house as ascetics without any reference to children or to remarriage (contrast 1 Tim 5:4, 10, 14; compare Pol. *Phil.* 4.3, a bishop's attempt to control wealthy widows). Luke is not afraid of wealthy, influential widows, as are the later bishops.

The infancy narrative concludes by emphasizing the accomplishment of "everything required by the law of the Lord" (2:39) and their returning to Nazareth from which they had come (1:26, 39 and 2:4, not in Matthew). 2:40, stressing Jesus' wisdom and God's grace, forms a transition to Jesus as a boy already teaching in the temple (anticipating chs. 20–21). The similarities in both content and language ("wisdom" and "grace") between 2:40 and 52 bracket the intervening narrative.

The Boy Jesus Teaching in the Temple (2:41-52)

Biographies often narrate not only the subject's birth but also the youth and education of the main character (Burridge: 146, 178-79). Childhood play and activity portend the adult. Plutarch's biography of Cato (2.5-6) shows his concern for his unjustly imprisoned playmate. When the future Roman king Tullius was "scarcely more than a boy . . . he was thought to have fought so splendidly that he straightway became famous . . ." (Dionysius *Rom. Ant.* 4.3.1). Moses, too, outstripped his teachers (Philo *Vit. Mos.* 1.21), and the young philosopher Apollonius soared above his teachers like a young eagle (Philostratus *Vita Ap.* 1.7; Burridge: 207-8). Likewise, Jesus' activity as a boy foreshadows his later teaching and activity in the temple, exhibiting "wisdom" (2:40).

The family continue to obey Torah, making pilgrimage to the Passover (see Exod 34:23). The plot of this small vignette is driven by Jesus' seeming disobedience, sharply questioned by Mary (2:48). The child Jesus responds, asserting what he "must" be doing. Luke tags a traditional conclusion onto this story of an independent child: "he came to Nazareth and was obedient *(hypotassomenos)* to them" (v. 51), similar to the "obedience" of children demanded in later household codes (Eph 6:1; Col 3:20; 1 Tim 3:4). Luke denies that youthful rebelliousness portended the adult prophet.

The story concludes with a saying, the main christological point. The first words of Jesus in the Gospel assert that "I must be in my father's" (house; or about my father's things) (2:49). Following his virginal conception, this is another claim to the status of "Son of God."

John the Baptist's Ministry and Jesus' Preparation (3:1–4:13)

John the Baptist's Preaching and Imprisonment (3:1-6)

Luke is concerned to date the events. Puzzlingly, he dates John's call to prophesy (3:1-2; also 1:5) more closely than Jesus' appearance (2:1), another indication that this Gospel is not a biography of the individual Jesus but rather a work of salvation history. Luke understands Jesus in the context of "the message he [God] sent to the people of Israel, preaching peace by Jesus Christ. . . . That message spread throughout Judea, *beginning* in Galilee after the baptism that John announced . . ." (Acts 10:36-37). Dating John's prophecy also dates the beginning of Jesus' ministry of peace to Israel.

The six references in 3:1-2 do not enable us to fix the year exactly. Luke names the fifteenth year of Tiberius, but we do not know whether this includes his becoming co-emperor with Augustus in AD 11 or 12, which would add up to AD 26 or 27, or whether this refers to his sole rule after Augustus's death in AD 14, which would yield the date AD 29. The other governors, kings, and high priests mentioned fall within this same time period.

John is called as a prophet: "in the fifteenth year of the reign of Emperor Tiberius . . . the word of God came to John son of Zechariah in the wilderness. He went into all the region around the Jordan, proclaiming . . ." (3:1-2). Compare: "the words of Jeremiah son of Hilkiah . . . to whom the word of the LORD came in the days of King Josiah . . . in the thirteenth year of his reign. It also came in the days of King Jehoiakim. . . . Now the word of the LORD came to me saying . . ." (Jer 1:1-2, 4; see Ezek 1:2-3).

Mark has no infancy narrative, so Luke begins utilizing Mark as a source for the first time in this chapter. After the first verse announcing "the gospel of Jesus Christ, the Son of God," Mark quotes Mal 3:1 combined with Isa 40:3. Luke introduces John as a prophet, drops the words from Malachi, and extends the quotation from Isaiah (40:3-5) to assert that "every mountain and hill shall be *humbled,*" a theme announced in the *Magnificat* (1:48), and adding the universalizing verse, "all flesh shall see the salvation of God" (cf. Acts 10:34-36, 38, 43; 28:28). If the infancy narrative was Luke's final addition to the two-volume work, then the original draft began with John quoting Isaiah 40 anticipating Pentecost and the conversion of the foreigner Cornelius.

The content of John's proclamation is "a baptism of repentance for the forgiveness of sins." Within a decade of Luke's writing, Josephus also refers to John "surnamed the Baptist" (*Ant.* 18.116, trans. Feldman in LCC), whom Herod had put to death. Herod's army was destroyed by Aretas, his former father-in-law, an event that many took to be God's vengeance for his killing John. Sixty years later Josephus still recalled John's popularity. He "had exhorted the Jews to lead righteous lives, to practice justice towards their fellows and piety towards God, and so doing to join in baptism. . . . When others too joined the crowds about him, because they were aroused to the highest degree by his sermons, Herod became alarmed" (*Ant.* 18.117-18). Josephus, like Luke, informs us of John's preaching of social ethics and baptism, but says nothing of John's eschatology or of any relation to Jesus. Writing in the same decade, Luke wants to subordinate John's importance to that of Jesus.

Epictetus (c. AD 50-120), a later Stoic contemporary of Luke, may refer to the conversion of a Greek to Judaism marked by the well-known ritual of proselyte baptism: "whenever we see a man halting between two faiths, we are in the habit of saying, 'He is not a Jew, he is only acting the part.' But when he adopts the attitude of mind of the man who has been baptized and has made his choice, then he both is a Jew in fact and is also called one" (*Disc.* 2.9.20, trans. Oldfather in LCC), Epictetus was speaking forty to ninety years after John preached; we cannot prove that proselyte baptism was practiced as early as John. But T. W. Manson: 44 assumes that the practice was early and concludes that John "deliberately invites the children of Abraham to submit to a rite which had been devised for the benefit of pagans." John was a prophetic critic whose mission was to prepare sinful Israel to meet God.

John's Preaching (3:7-18)

Luke reports John's eschatological preaching, which does not include a Messiah. Matthew reports the same sermon with virtually identical words, although the audiences differ. The similarity is often taken to mean that Matthew and Luke use the same source, usually called Q and dated either at AD 50 or in the late 60s during the Jewish war with Rome, a collection of Jesus' sayings by the earliest Jewish Christian community. These Jewish Christians were in high tension with other Jewish sectarian groups, reflected in their redaction and additions to Jesus' beatitudes (Matt 5:10-12 par. Luke 6:22-23). They have either repeated or ascribed to John their own critique of aspects of the Abrahamic/Davidic covenant of unconditional promise: "Do not begin to say to yourselves, 'We have Abraham as our father'; for I tell you, God is able from these stones to raise up children to Abraham" (3:8)! Ezekiel had uttered an even sharper prophetic critique (33:24-29; also 16:3, 45-46, 59-63). A similar critique occurs elsewhere in Q (Luke 13:28-29 par. Matt 8:11-12), which Luke develops in the story of the Ethiopian eunuch (Acts 8:26-40) from the "south" (Acts 8:26 = Luke 13:29; see Felder: 13).

John challenges his audience to repent, to act differently. The following ethical teaching is also characteristic of Luke, who is concerned with those who do "not have" and those who "have" possessions (3:11; cf. 7:42; 14:14; 18:22, 24; Acts 2:44; 4:35; but see Luke 19:26). Luke is also concerned with those who collect toll for the Romans (3:12; see 5:27-30; 7:29, 34; 15:1), the sort of person Jesus contrasts with a righteous Pharisee (18:10-13). But "soldiers" (3:13) are even more central to the plot as centurions, including both a story from Q that is more open to the Romans than were many in Judea in the 50s and 60s (7:2, 6) and the conversion of the centurion Cornelius (Acts 10:1, 22; also 27:1).

There Is One Mightier Than John (3:15-18)

Luke's introduction (3:15-16) to this scene has a parallel not in the Synoptics but in John (1:24-25). Luke has John himself repeat the comparison and contrast between himself and the Messiah that the reader has already heard in the infancy narrative, but John's verbal assertion goes further: he is not worthy to be a slave who unties the thong of the Messiah's sandals. This is not utterly dismissive: Jesus' parables teach that his disciples are somehow to be like slaves and to serve others (12:36-38, 42-48), so for Luke the meaning may be close to that of 7:28. The baptism of the Holy Spirit and fire (3:16) refers to John's eschatological expectation of salvation ("holy spirit," 1:15 and seven times in the infancy narrative, usually without the article; see Acts 1:5; 11:16) and judgment ("fire"; see 3:9, 17; 9:54; 12:49). Luke summarizes John's message in 3:18 as one of "exhortations" and "proclaiming the gospel" to the people, and, indeed, in Luke's story he has just announced Christ.

John's Imprisonment (3:19-20)

Luke is distinctive among the Synoptic Gospels in narrating John's imprisonment before the beginning of Jesus' ministry, even before John baptizes Jesus. This storyteller's choice separates the two ministries and moves John off stage so that readers can concentrate on Jesus, although the author will present one more Q section comparing the two (Matt 11:2-19 par. Luke 7:18-35).

Luke's story is similar to Mark's (6:17-18), with the dialogue omitted. Strikingly, Josephus tells the story of Herod's divorce from the daughter of Aretas, king of Petra, and his marriage to Herodias, the wife of his (half-) brother. Then he tells the story of Herod's murder of John, connecting the two only by explaining that the people blamed Herod for murdering John, thinking that his defeat by Aretas was divine vengeance (*Ant.* 18.109-15, 116-19). Luke does not tell two juxtaposed stories but one; Herod did not execute John for political reasons because of his rhetorical power over the people (Josephus) but because of his condemnation of Herod for marrying his brother's wife as "not lawful" (3:18, referring to Lev 20:21). For Luke both John and Jesus teach Torah.

Jesus' Baptism (3:21-22)

". . . when Jesus had been baptized and was praying . . ." (3:21). One feature of Jesus' baptism may be a model for Christians: Jesus' ministry begins and ends (22:46) with prayer (Karris: 675-721). Jesus prays when healing (5:16), before calling the apostles (6:12), before prophesying his passion (9:18), before being transfigured (9:28-29), before teaching (11:1), for Peter (22:32), when tempted (22:39-46), and on the cross (23:34, 46). The church follows this model (Acts 1:14) and also receives the Spirit (Acts 2:1-4), which Luke interprets as an event of the last days (Acts 2:17).

Luke gives another interpretation of the event in Acts 10:36, 38, "You know . . . the message . . . how God *anointed* Jesus of Nazareth with the Holy Spirit and with power; how he went about doing good and healing all who were oppressed by the devil, for God was with him." "Full of the Holy Spirit" (4:1), Jesus withstood the devil's temptation, and "filled with the power of the Spirit, returned to Galilee" and "began to teach in their synagogues" (4:14-15). Then in Nazareth he reads Isaiah (61:1-2) in the synagogue, "The Spirit of the Lord is upon me, because he has *anointed* me to bring good news to the poor . . ." (4:18).

After the baptism, from which Luke omits John's name, a voice from heaven pronounces, "You are my Son [Ps 2:7; Isa 42:1], the Beloved [Gen 22:2, 12, 16]; with you I am well pleased." Later the Western manuscript D added, "today I have begotten you," from Ps 2:7. The heaven opening is an eschatological symbol of revelation. At the transfiguration the heavenly voice again calls Jesus "beloved" (9:35). God is "well pleased" with Jesus at the Jordan, just as when the angels announced the birth of a Savior, the Messiah, the Lord, to the shepherds, they praised God and announced peace among those with whom God is well pleased (2:11, 14). And the voice from heaven affirms that Jesus is God's beloved, as Isaac was Abraham's "beloved" son (Gen. 22:2) whom he was nevertheless willing to give up. This baptismal story, then, concerns God, who recognizes a son, a beloved, with whom the heavenly voice affirms God is pleased.

Jesus' Genealogy (3:23-38)

Jesus was about thirty years old. Genealogies are a puzzle to modern persons unless the person is a member of the Kennedy clan or in the Bush or the English imperial family and thus from a political family, the same families that published genealogies in the Hellenistic world. Priests also kept genealogies, which made social/political sense in Judea, a temple state. Luke plays down hereditary status within the church by never naming James, a leader in the Jerusalem church (Acts 15:13), a "brother" of Jesus. His mother Mary is primarily a disciple who "believes" (1:45), although she, too, is influential in the later church (Acts 1:13-24, a list of church leaders). The author still wants to reaffirm the christological point that Jesus is the Son of God, the chief point of the baptismal story and the climax of this genealogy (3:22, 38).

Both Matthew and Luke trace Jesus' descent through Joseph: "He was the son (as was thought) of Joseph . . ." (Luke 3:23). The "as was thought" is common among historians when distancing themselves from their own narrative of myth. For example, Dionysius narrates the birth of the future Roman king Tullius with phrases like: "concerning his family, then, the account with which I can best agree is . . ." (*Rom. Ant.* 4.1.2). Also: "This fabulous [mythological] account, although it seems not altogether credible, is rendered less incredible by reason of another manifestation of the gods . . ." (*Rom. Ant.* 4.2.3). Luke's genealogy of the male line behind Joseph, who is not Jesus' father, flashes a warning light against relying on genealogies, and concludes not with the claim of a famous human father but the same way the baptism concludes, with a claim that Jesus is the Son of God (see Acts 17:28-29). Romans also claimed divine parentage for their ancestors (Dionysius *Rom. Ant.* 1.31.1: Evander, son of Hermes; 1.31.2: Faunus, a descendant of Mars; 1.62.2: Aeneas, of Anchises and Aphrodite; see esp. 1.76-77 and 2.56 on the birth [and death] of Romulus [and Remas] from Mars and Ilia). Therefore, Luke is contesting the authority of divine Rome and its values by claiming an alternative divine founder who has a different, authentic message. This claim follows soon after John's assertion that "God is able from these stones to raise up children to Abraham" (3:8). This reserve against hereditary status corresponds to Luke's parallel critique of the patron-client relationship in the culture (22:24-27). Still, as in the Lukan work as a whole, the salvific history of Israel remains important: Jesus is (as was thought) the son of Joseph, the son of David, the son of Abraham, the son of Adam, the son of God.

Jesus' Temptation (4:1-13)

That Jesus was "tempted" by Satan forty days in the wilderness is Markan. The rest of the story — primarily sayings — has its source in Q, a document that represents countercultural Jewish Christian preachers in Israel between AD 50 and 65, just before the Jewish war against Rome. Many in the ethnic group were preparing for war and expected that the Messiah would lead them. Luke has just established who Jesus is and now tells a story that narrates Jesus' choice about how the Messiah will and will not lead. Some expected a military leader: "See, Lord, and raise up for them their king, the son of David, to rule over your servant Israel. . . . He will gather a holy people . . . ; the alien and the foreigner will no longer live near them. . . . And he will purge Jerusalem" (*Pss. Sol.* 17:21, 26, 28, 30, trans. Wright in Charlesworth: 2:639-70). Some at Qumran anticipated a Priestly Messiah (1QS 9:11; 1QSa 2:19). Both of these are "temptations" for Jesus, as we can see not only in the *Psalms of Solomon,* but also in the *Magnificat* and the *Benedictus.*

Matthew's three dialogues climax with a temptation on a high mountain in Galilee, the place where the whole Gospel concludes. Luke's dialogue climaxes rather in the temple, where this Gospel concludes, beginning and ending with a challenge to Jesus' sonship, the theme from the baptism and genealogy. In these dialogues Jesus rejects three methods of inaugurating the kingdom of God: (1) use of extraordinary power to provide bread, (2) military dreams of world empire, and (3) a sudden appearance in the temple. Elsewhere, too, some want a sign from heaven to "tempt/test" him (Mark 8:11 par. Luke 11:16), which Jesus rejects — in high tension with the story of Jesus multiplying bread to feed five thousand (Mark 6:32-44 par. Luke 9:10-17, which echoes Exodus 16 and Num 11:31-35). In his rejection, Jesus repeatedly cites Deuteronomy (6:13, 16; 8:3), the last time after hearing the devil quote Ps 91:11-12.

The Messiah is God's servant, and the Sermon on the Plain (6:20-49) is Jesus' alternative Messianism, the demand for active merciful love toward the poor and hungry. This story is another contrast between John and Jesus, who had accepted John's baptism; the former proclaims God's judgment by fire, while the latter announces the gospel to poor, blind captives.

Jesus' Ministry in Galilee (4:14–9:50)

As in Mark but not as in the Gospel of John, Jesus' ministry occurs in Galilee prior to the journey to his passion in Jerusalem. Luke introduced John's ministry quoting deutero-Isaiah (ch. 40); now the author introduces Jesus' ministry quoting the same prophet (ch. 61). Luke follows Mark, omitting a longer section (Mark 6:45–8:26, including Jesus' feeding of the four thousand) but adding sayings from Q (e.g., Luke 6:20–8:3, including the Sermon on the Plain).

Jesus' Preaching at Nazareth (4:14-30)

Jesus' temptations had concluded in the Jerusalem temple; Luke's transition notes that he returned "in the power of the Spirit" to Galilee (4:14a). In Mark the return could be understood to have been motivated by John's imprisonment, but Luke has placed that imprisonment earlier in the narrative (3:19-20). Luke notes for the first time that the news spread through "all" (an adjective Luke employs often) the countryside (see 4:37; 7:17).

Luke does not use traditional sayings for Jesus' inaugural sermon, but delays the Q Sermon on the Mount/Plain for two chapters (until ch. 6) and constructs a sermon appropriate for the Founder of this growing body of house churches that supplies basic themes for the whole two-volume history. Luke pictures Jesus attending ("as was his custom") the synagogue (4:16) and reading scripture: "The Spirit . . . has anointed me to bring good news to the poor" (*ptōchoi;* 4:18 quoting Isa 61:1-2). The

Sermon on the Plain begins: "Blessed are you who are poor *(ptōchoi),* for yours is the kingdom of God" (6:20, echoing the same Isaiah text). The word "poor" (see 7:22; 14:13, 21; 16:20, 22; 18:22; 19:8; 21:3) refers to those who have absolutely nothing, no house in which to live. Wealthy Epicureans had debated Cynics (ancient begging preachers in some ways like medieval Franciscans) for three centuries concerning whether it was better to live in wealthy villas or to beg daily for one's food (Balch 2003a). Whether he knew of the philosophical debate or not, Jesus agrees with the Cynics. The Spirit anointed him (see Acts 10:38) for the purpose of proclaiming the gospel to the homeless, and he pronounces "blessed" those who have nothing economically. Luke adds a "parable" and two illustrations of prophetic miracles from 1 Kings 17 (Elijah) and 2 Kings 5 (Elisha). Judging by our lifestyle, virtually all modern First-World Christians agree with the Epicureans against Jesus and the Cynics: it is better to live in a (wealthy) house!

Jesus' pronouncement is a fulfillment of prophecy. The eschaton is now: "Today this scripture [Isa 61:1-2] has been fulfilled in your hearing" (4:21). "Everything written about the Son of Man by the prophets will be accomplished" (18:31, rewriting Mark 10:33). Luke also adds "in the last days" to the quotation of Joel 2 in Acts 2:17. An emphasis on fulfillment occurs in this inaugural, causative sermon, and it also concludes the Gospel: the resurrected Jesus repeatedly emphasizes this to the disciples (24:26-27, 44-46; see Acts 3:18; 17:3; 26:22-23).

The last phrase that Luke quotes from Isaiah is, "to proclaim the year of the Lord's favor *(dektos),*" or of the Lord's "acceptance" (4:19; also *Barn.* 14:9). Jesus uses the same verbal adjective later in the sermon: "Truly I tell you, no prophet is accepted *(dektos)* in the prophet's hometown" (4:24). This verbal adjective also occurs in the one sermon in Acts that summarizes the Gospel: Peter begins his sermon to Cornelius's household (and to the Jewish Christians whom he has brought with him): "I truly understand that God shows no partiality, but in every nation anyone who fears him and does what is right is acceptable *(dektos)* to him" (Acts 10:35). This adjective is related to the verb that Luke employs to observe that members are "received/accepted" into the church *(dechomai,* Acts 2:41; see Luke 9:5, 48, 53; 10:8, 10; 16:4), the verb that Dionysius employs to say that Rome "received" many nations into citizenship (*Rom. Ant.* 1.89.2-3; 3.10.4-5; see 3.11.3-4). Members are also "added" to the church (Acts 2:47; 5:14; 11:24) as foreign nations are "added" to Rome (Dionysius *Rom. Ant.* 2.16.3). Reading Luke 4 and Acts 10 together, Isaiah prophesies what Jesus announces, God's acceptance of or favor to all, and by Acts 10 readers understand that this means that God accepts or receives "all nations." For Luke Isaiah's prophecy concerns God's providential will revealed both through the Messiah's death, resurrection, and ascension and by the reception of all nations into God's people. (This has consequences for a "clean" temple that excludes foreigners.)

Another key to Luke's interpretation of Isa 61:1 and 58:6 lies in the Elisha story summarized later in the sermon: "There were also many lepers in Israel in the time of the prophet Elisha, and none of them was cleansed *(ekatharisthē)* except Naaman the Syrian" (4:27; see 5:12-13; 7:22; 10:8; 11:39, 41; 17:14, 17; Matt 5:8; 10:8; 11:5; 23:25-26; Mark 1:40-42; 7:19; Acts 10:15; 11:9; 15:9; also Num 12:10, 13; Isa 35:8). Neusner observes that fully two-thirds of contemporary material from the Pharisees is concerned with food, dishes, and people that are "clean" (see the commentary on 2:29-35). But there were different views and practices among Jews about how to relate to "unclean" outsiders. The *Epistle of Aristeas* (128–72, 173–86) tells the story of Jerusalem "elders" sent by the high priest to Egypt, who ate with the foreign king at a symposium (Tcherikover).

An analogous debate occurs within early Christianity; in other words, this is not a debate between Judaism and Christianity, but in both cases an internal debate. Acts 10:28, Peter's comment to Cornelius's household, should be read as follows: "you yourselves know that it is unlawful for a Jew[ish disciple of Jesus] to associate with or to visit a foreigner." This objection is ascribed to Peter as an orthodox Jewish Christian, not to him simply as a Jew. There was an orthodox party in the Jerusalem church who "were teaching the brothers that "unless you are circumcised according to the custom of Moses, you cannot be saved. And . . . Paul and Barnabas had no small dissension and debate with them . . ." (Acts 15:1-2). After he baptized Cornelius, the Jerusalem brothers ask Peter, "Why did you go to uncircumcised men and eat with them?" Peter then recounts hearing a revelatory voice from heaven: "What God has *cleansed,* you must not call profane" (Acts 11:9). Luke 4 is directed to *Christian* readers, to those who, like Theophilus, "have [already] been instructed" (1:4), to "believers" like those who heard Peter's sermon in Caesarea (Acts 10:23). Some Christians reading this Gospel were apparently resisting inviting just anybody to worship in the dining rooms *(triclinia)* of their house churches (see the commentary on 22:24-30). Jesus reminds Christians of Elisha's "cleansing" a Syrian leper. Nor were Syrians warmly welcome in other parts of the Roman Empire (see Juvenal *Sat.* 3.62).

The scene ends with all in the synagogue being filled with rage and wanting to kill Jesus (4:28-29), which is socially realistic. Conflict over greater inclusivity, whether it involves economic class, race, gender, religion, or sexual orientation, typically turns ugly quickly. The story concerns inter-Jewish conflict, but Luke-Acts is addressed to inter-Christian conflict over ethnic inclusivity in the church. The Nazareth story prefigures the passion stories of Jesus and Stephen and the riots resulting from Paul's sermons in Acts. It also prefigures the resurrection: "he passed through the midst of them and went on his way" (4:30). This inaugural scene presents the content of Jesus' preaching, its rejection by his hometown, and God's overcoming that rejection.

Teaching and Healing in Capernaum (4:31-44)

Jesus travels to another town, Capernaum on the Sea of Galilee, and again becomes involved in conflict. The narrator informs us that Jesus was teaching on the sabbath. With the other Synoptic Gospels, Luke mentions Jesus' authority, but our author twice emphasizes that his *word* was with power (4:32, 36), another theme of both volumes (e.g., 1:2, 4, 20; 4:22; 5:1; 6:47; 7:7, 17; 8:11-13, 15, 21; 9:26; 11:28; 24:44; Acts 2:22, 40; 4:4, 29, 31; 6:2, 4, 7; 7:22; 8:4, 14, 25; 10:44; 11:1, 19; 12:24; 13:5, 7, 26, 44, 46, 48-49; etc.).

Jesus' first miracle is an exorcism, one of four in the Gospel (see Penny and Wise: 627-50). The exorcism may be related to Jesus' mission defined by Isaiah 61 and 58, to proclaim release to the captives, to let the oppressed go free (4:18; see 7:21-22; 8:26-39; 9:1; 10:17-20). Exorcism in Jesus' ministry assumes a struggle between God and evil that has an apocalyptic or an eschatological context (Matt 12:22-30 par. Luke 11:14-23). For Luke exorcism is one of Jesus' deeds that refer back to Isaiah's prophecy (Luke 7:22, alluding to Isa 29:18-19; 35:5-6; 61:1, although exorcism is not in Isaiah's lists). High tension between good and evil is realistic, in both the first and the twenty-first centuries.

Calling and Training Disciples (5:1–6:16)

These stories concern discipleship, healing, and controversy. Some accept the call; others, often named scribes and Pharisees, refuse. Later Luke identifies the Pharisees with the rich (16:14), so that wealthy Christians reclining in the dining room of their house churches as the Gospel was read might hear themselves addressed. Luke again emphasizes that the crowd wants "to hear the word of God" (5:1). Jesus responds by teaching them from a boat in the lake of Gennesaret, followed by a command to Peter to fish.

Calling Simon, James, and John, Fisher Folk (5:1-11)

Only after his inaugural sermon does Luke present Jesus as calling and teaching disciples. Jesus does not call soldiers for the messianic army, nor the promising sons of leading citizens in nearby cities, but simple (see Acts 4:13 and Eusebius *Hist. Eccl.* 3.20.1-6) fisher folk. This unit is a pronouncement story: the final saying of Jesus (5:10b), preceded by Simon's confession (v. 8b), contains the point: "Go away from me, Lord, for I am a sinful man!" "Do not be afraid; from now on you will be catching people." In origin this may be a postresurrection appearance story, since it has many similarities with John 21:1-11 (Culpepper: 117). Luke does not want to tell such a story after Jesus' death, which involves Galilee (see Luke 24:6, 47; Acts 1:8); therefore, he moves it earlier in the narrative. There are few parallels with Mark 4:1-2, 16-20; more with Christ's call of Paul (see Acts 9:15, 17-18; 22:3, 8, 15-16; 26:15-16, 20). Both Peter and Paul are sinful, confess Jesus as "Lord," leave former lifestyles, and are sent out on mission. This explains Peter's address to Jesus as "Lord" (5:8), an address rarely used by human characters in the Gospel (Tuckett: 76-78) but common in Acts.

Cleansing a Leper (5:12-16; see 17:11-19)

As in the inaugural sermon (4:27; see Acts 10:9-43), which this healing illustrates, "cleansing" is key. Luke refers to it three times in this short story, all three taken from Mark (1:40-45). Again, Jesus is careful about Torah prescriptions (5:14). The "word about him" spread (v. 15), but Jesus withdraws to pray (v. 16).

Healing the Paralyzed (5:17-26)

Four controversy stories follow. Since the word had spread, Luke adds an introduction to the Markan (2:1-12) story: a crowd of Pharisees and teachers of the law gather "from every village of Galilee and Judea and from Jerusalem" (v. 17)! But as in Mark, "when he saw their faith [of those carrying the paralyzed man], he said, 'Friend, your sins are forgiven you'" (v. 20). Both faith (already in 1:20, 45) and especially forgiveness of sins (see 1:77; 24:47; Acts 2:38; 10:43) are central in Luke. Who can forgive sins as well as to whom God's forgiveness may be given are still controversial in the twenty-first century, for example, should it be given to gay and lesbian persons? Jesus' word of forgiveness generates the charge of "blasphemy" (v. 21; see the apologetic situation in Acts 13:45; 18:6; also 21:20-21 without the term "blasphemy"). The second volume, Acts, focuses on this same issue and climaxes in chs. 10–11, 15 with disputes around the answer.

In response to the scribes' and Pharisees' questioning, Jesus claims that "the Son of Man has authority on earth to forgive sins" (5:24). For Luke, "Son of Man" refers to Jesus and is a title used only on his own lips (except in Acts 7:56; see Rev 1:13 and Eusebius *Hist. Eccl.* 2.23.13). The source of this phrase, its use by Jesus, and its interpretation in the Gospels are disputed. It occurs in Dan 7:13 and Ezek 2:1, 3, as well as in the "Similitudes" of *1 Enoch* 37–71, for example, 46:4; 48:2; 71:17, although the date of these sections of *1 Enoch* is debated. Luke may have added it to the source in 6:22. For our author "Son of Man" refers to Jesus' salvific acts, sometimes specifically to his death and resurrection (5:24; 9:22; 19:10) and to his future role as the resurrected Lord (12:8, 40).

Luke concludes by naming these events *paradoxa* (5:26; see Philo *Vit. Mos.* 1.212 and Diodorus Siculus 1.69.2, who tells the "wonderful" customs of Egypt, which made many Greeks such as Orpheus, Homer, Pythagoras, and Solon the lawgiver eager to visit).

Calling Levi, Eating with Outcasts, and a Debate about Fasting (5:27-39)

This scene had transparent meaning for disciples in a Greco-Roman house church assembled in a dining room (*triclinium*) and spilling out into the peristyle garden listening to the Gospel read aloud. Banquets were perhaps the most important symbol of meaning and status in Judean and in Greco-Roman society; they mirrored and reinforced or they challenged everyday social structures. Jesus' parable in Luke 14 argues for status transformation, reflected in rich Lukan Christians inviting their poor brothers and sisters to dinner, which generated ostracism from wealthy peers (Braun; see the commentary below). Whether the story of Levi's banquet was heard in Judean society concerned with purity or in Roman society concerned with social status, Jesus models dining that reverses societal practice in the kingdom of God. Jesus' eating is an acted parable.

Jesus calls a "toll collector" saying, "Follow me" (5:27), and the toll collector then gives a great banquet (v. 28). Toll collectors were often corrupt and abused the system; their cooperation with the Romans made them despised in an occupied country, whether Judea, Asia, Greece, or Macedonia. Pharisees, on the other hand, were religious experts, identified by Luke with the rich (16:14); in Luke's non-Judean/Galilean setting, this makes Pharisees symbolic characters in the narrative, not a historical Judean group whose actions or piety is being described.

Levi accepted the call and "left everything" (5:28; see 10:40; 18:22-23). Lucian (*The Scythian* or the *Consul* 4–5) describes Toxaris, a Scythian who had "left" wife and children in Scythia; his countryman, Anacharsis, also will not remember his wife or children and has been willing to "leave all." Crates was persuaded by Diogenes the Cynic to turn his property into money and distribute it to other citizens (Diogenes Laertius 6.87). Being a disciple of Jesus is the ultimate commitment; family and money fall into second and third places.

The final two sayings climax the story. "I have come to call not the righteous but sinners to repentance" (5:32), a saying close to Paul's theology of a God "who justifies the *ungodly*" (Rom 4:5) and a Christ who "died for the *ungodly*" (Rom 5:6). Following Jesus does not involve alienation, even to maintain group identity, but rather association with those who differ. We good and pious Christians have difficulty hearing the negative.

Fasting was a common religious practice among both Jews and pagans (Porphyry *On Abstinence*). No other NT passage questions the value of fasting; early Christians did fast — sometimes on days other than did Jews (*Did.* 8:1), hardly the point of Jesus' aphorisms.

The metaphor of a wedding is followed by three other sayings opposing the old to the new, sayings of Jesus that were difficult for Luke who, with other historians, valued the old. The second saying images Jesus and his teachings as a new garment that cannot patch the old, but Luke wants to claim precisely that Jesus "fulfills" (old) prophecies and keeps ancient customs (see 1:1; 24:44; Acts 6:14; 21:21, 24; 26:22). The third saying, "No one after drinking old wine desires new wine, but says, 'the old is good,'" characterizes Greco-Roman values in general, that is, the values of Luke's readers. Despite Luke's preference for the ancient, the author handed on these Jesus sayings. Jesus' proclamation to the poor, toll collectors, the sick, and sinners generated celebration.

Debates about the Sabbath (6:1-11)

Controversies continue, two of them concerning the sabbath. Christian readers often focus on the legalistic demands of sabbath observance, forgetting its attractions. It is a family day of rest and celebration, not of fasting, insisting that families take time to worship God together despite other cultural and business demands. Pagans criticized the Jews' holy day (Juvenal *Sat.* 14.96-106), and some diaspora Jews also played down distinctive aspects of Judaism (Collins 1983: 11, 142-43, 162 and Heschel).

The first controversy story (6:1-5) climaxes in the pronouncement that Jesus, the Son of Man, is "lord of the sabbath" (v. 5). The reference to eating and to the Pharisees connects this story with the previous one. Jesus here argues from Scripture: King David could break the levitical laws even in the temple (1 Sam 21:1-6), and in Luke Jesus is the Son of David (3:32; Acts 2:30-36; 13:34-39).

This is often interpreted by commenting that ethics is more important than ritual, but these are modern categories. Ritual enacts the central values of the community, and in this sense Jesus, too, practiced ritual: he regularly ate and drank with sinners (5:30), an anticipatory messianic banquet which celebrated the presence of God's rule and became the central ritual of Jesus' followers, the Eucharist. Contrasting various sorts of rituals is more appropriate. Luke narrates Jesus modifying a ritual that designates one ethnic group as acceptable to God and substituting a ritual that (by the second volume, Acts) celebrates the acceptance of all sinners before God, whatever their ethnic origin.

The second sabbath controversy (6:6-11) pictures Jesus going to the synagogue to teach (v. 6) and meeting a man with a withered right hand. While the scribes and Pharisees watched, wanting to find an accusation against him, Jesus asks a question (of the reader): "is it lawful to do good or to do harm on the sabbath, to save life or to destroy it?" (v. 9) For Greek readers, "doing good" is unquestionably laudable (see 1 Pet 2:15, 20; 3:6, 17), which makes the response of the religious leaders (6:11) blameworthy. At another level, by wanting to destroy him, are not the leaders themselves doing evil on the holy day (Culpepper: 135)?

Jesus Calls the Twelve (6:12-16)

Luke places the calling of the twelve after Jesus' inaugural sermon and after several controversies in which other leaders have rejected Jesus. Jesus is forming an alternative leadership for the people of God, the (traditional) twelve tribes of Israel. Jesus now not only teaches by symbolic healings with pronouncements but prepares with prayer to name leaders. They are the "men who have accompanied us during all the time that the Lord Jesus went in and out among us, beginning from the baptism of John until the day when he was taken up from us" (Acts 1:21b-22a). They will become witnesses to "all that Jesus did and taught from the beginning until the day when he was taken up to heaven, after giving instructions through the Holy Spirit to the apostles whom he had chosen" (Acts 1:1b-2). These twelve, with some variation in the lists of names (Matt 10:2-4; Mark 3:16-19; Luke 6:14-16; Acts 1:13), were called by the historical Jesus and were symbolic figures. Some of them became leaders in the earliest Jerusalem church (Gal 2:9; Meier 1997: 635-72).

Jesus Teaching Disciples by the Sermon on the Plain (6:17-49)

Jesus had prayed on a mountain, and "came down" to teach (6:17; see Phil 2:6-8 and Luke 1:48?), a contrast to Matthew's going "up the mountain" (5:1). This information constitutes a summary (6:17-19) that includes Jesus addressing a "great crowd of his disciples and a great multitude" from a startlingly wide geographical area, "from all Judea, Jerusalem, and the coast of Tyre and Sidon" in Lebanon, where later there were assemblies of disciples (see 10:13-14; Acts 21:3-4, 7-8). Luke continues the emphasis on Jesus "healing all of them" (6:19).

The sermon is loosely structured, but it seems to have three parts divided by the address in v. 27 and the aside in v. 39, so that it is constituted by blessings and woes (vv. 20-26), exhortations (vv. 27-38), and "parables" (vv. 39-49).

Blessings on Mendicants and Woes to Rich Householders (6:20-26)

Luke's churches listened to this sermon read aloud as the wealthy believers reclined in the dining room *(triclinium)* of a Roman house and the poor sat out in the peristyle garden (Osiek and Balch: chs. 1 and 8), the setting in which Luke places Jesus' last supper (22:14, 24-30). The sermon is specifically addressed to "disciples" (6:20) divided by economic class. Luke and Matthew have taken blessings from Q; Luke's beatitudes are the first, fourth, and ninth of Matthew's, the second one having no Matthean parallel. The four woes, either from Q or formulated by Luke, are addressed to the polar opposite groups and conditions addressed by the beatitudes. Luke's blessings occur in the second person ("you") and Matthew's in the third ("they"), except for the final blessing, which is also in the second person.

"Blessed are you who are poor" (6:20) echoes the same prophetic text with which Jesus had begun the inaugural sermon (4:18; Isa 61:1), the gospel in one sentence. The kingdom of God belongs to mendicants, to those with nothing. Jesus pronounces the fulfillment of Isaiah 61. Matthew softened it to "poor in spirit" (Matt 5:3). Some modern interpreters incorrectly take "poverty" to refer not primarily to economic status but merely to "the general human condition," to an "intellectual insight" (Betz: 114-16).

In the first three centuries BC, two Greek philosophical schools — Epicureans (Metrodorus, Philodemus) and Cynics (Diogenes of Sinope, Crates) — debated whether it was better to be wealthy or poor, to have nothing at all, which included whether to live in a "house" or to be a beggar/mendicant without anything (Balch 2003a). Jesus' word for "poor" meant "the deprivation, not of many, but of all things" (Philodemus *On Wealth* 45.15). Epicurus said that his followers were not to Cynicize, not to be poor beggars (*ptōcheusein;* Diogenes Laertius 10.119). A precursor of the Cynics, Antisthenes, said to Socrates, "people's wealth and poverty are to be found not in their *house,* but in their souls" (Xenophon *Symp.* 4.34). Diogenes' follower Crates sold his lands, gave away the proceeds to his fellow citizens (Diogenes Laertius 6.87-88), and then he and his wife Hipparchia lived and slept together in public places (Musonius *Orat.* 14).

Some of Jesus' sayings are equally shocking. To the wealthy ruler, Jesus said, "Sell all that you own and distribute the money to the poor, and you will have treasure in heaven; then come follow me" (18:22; also 16:19-31). Jesus sees that some are astounded and responds, "What is impossible for mortals is possible for God" (18:26). Peter replies, "we have left our households and followed you," and Jesus "said to them, 'Truly I tell you, there is no one who has left house or wife or brothers or parents or children, for the sake of the kingdom of God, who will not get back very much more in this age and in the age to come eternal life'" (vv. 29-30). But Jesus' sayings in Luke are inconsistent: despite his demand, some followers retain their houses and property (4:38; 5:29; 9:4; 10:5, 38; see Acts 4:34; 12:12). Jesus' disciples, reclining in their dining rooms for the Lord's Supper and listening to the gospel read, knew that the Lord claimed both their souls and their property for the poor.

Hunger and weeping are related. The hungry will be fed, and, if not, the rich hear Jesus' parable of consequences (16:23). Those weeping will laugh with joy (7:13, 32, 38; 8:52; Acts 9:39).

Like the other beatitudes, the fourth is addressed to disciples, who may experience social ostracism from their neighbors; they may be hated, excluded, reviled, or defamed on account of the Son of Humanity (6:22). Braun: 113 persuasively suggests that patrons in the Lukan house churches are inviting their poor brothers and sisters to dinner (14:12-14), which generated ostracism from their wealthy, disapproving peers. This relates the fourth beatitude directly to the first, since the disciples were acting and eating according to Jesus' teaching.

Love Your Enemies (6:27-36)

The Greek ethic of Luke's readers considered it "equally shameful to be surpassed by your enemies in doing harm and your friends in doing good" (Isocrates 1.26). In Socrates' *Electra,* Orestes announces his intention "to shine out like a star against my enemies" (66); correspondingly Electra is loyal to her friends (345-46). Jesus, however, opposed vengeance and retaliation. His command to love enemies is repeated in three variations (6:27b-28); then four illustrations follow. The attitude and action are not passive; Luke uses the verb (see also 7:42, 47; 10:27; 16:13), rarely the noun (only 11:42). Disciples are to "pray for those who abuse you" (6:28). Jesus' command rejects the Greco-Roman ethic of reciprocity and benefaction, so that relationships become more than a response to an other, more than a political and economic bargain for a return, but rather a proactive doing good to others in the way that Martin Luther King Jr. and Mahatma Gandhi practiced it. But as Jesus', King's, and Gandhi's religious and political lives illustrate, this is not a passive receiving of abuse but rather a verbal and active, although not violent, reversal of evil and alienation, at least in the household worship assembly. This was symbolized in the Lukan churches by the transformed ways masters and slaves ate together (see 12:37; 14:12-14; 22:24-30), a response to Jesus' having given his body and blood "for you" (22:19-20; see Acts 21:13). But this "doing to others as you would have them do to you" in household relationships was provocative, for ancient politics suggested that the house was a microcosm of the city. Such attitudes and actions mean that the disciples in their communities will be children of God (6:35), merciful as the Father is merciful (v. 36).

Prophetic Wisdom (6:37-49)

Some of the exhortations that follow are related to wisdom literature, as much as to the prophets (Johnson: 115). The first advice, though, has apocalyptic sources: disciples are not to judge or condemn but to forgive, and they will not be judged or condemned, but forgiven — by God. Paul says something similar: "But with me it is a very small thing that I should be judged by you. . . . I do not even judge myself. I am not aware of anything against myself, but I am not thereby acquitted. It is the Lord who judges me. Therefore do not pronounce judgment before the time . . ." (1 Cor 4:3-5a). Similarly, "give and it will be given to you" — by God (6:38a).

Four "parables," virtually proverbs or riddles, follow (6:39-40, 41-42, 43-45, and 46-49). The first one ("Can a blind person guide a blind person?") hints at teachers in the Lukan house churches (see Osiek and Balch: chs. 3 and 6). "A disciple is not above the teacher, but everyone who is fully qualified will be like the teacher" (v. 40). Teachers were often employed by the head of a household; Plutarch discusses their instruction in *How to Study Poetry.* He includes ethical material much like that at the end of Jesus' sermon: "to beg *(ptōchos)* does not degrade a noble mind" (21D); "to do wrong is worse than to be wronged" and "to do evil is more injurious than to suffer evil" (36E). Luke's Greek readers would have heard such ethical maxims in their home schooling. That Jesus' sermon ends with parenesis has a parallel in similar conclusions to Paul's letters (Romans 12–13, also wisdom mixed with apocalyptic urgency).

The second "parable" is grotesque and memorable, referring to seeing a speck in a neighbor's eye, but not a log in one's own. In context, the proverb probably illustrates the previous caution about judging others. Third, the good person produces good out of the good treasure of the heart (6:45). Luke is repeatedly concerned with the human heart (1:17, 51; 2:35; 5:22; 8:12, 15; 10:27; 12:34, 45; 16:15; 21:34; 24:25, 32, 38; Acts 2:37), of which the prophet Jesus is aware (9:47). Simeon prophesies that in response to Jesus, the thoughts of many persons' hearts will be revealed (2:35).

Fourth, as Jesus' own words and deeds harmonize, Jesus asks the same of disciples who confess him to be "Lord" (6:46, a title rare in this Gospel; see Acts 2:25, 34, 36; 10:36; Rom 10:9; 1 Cor 12:3; Phil 2:11). "Hearing" is a crucial theme in this Gospel, and sometimes women hear Jesus or the word of God (8:21) when men do not, especially in the infancy and passion narratives (24:9, 11, 16, 25, 38, 41; Seim: 147-63). Jesus' emphasis on hearing and also acting on his teaching reinforces the observation that this ethic is not passive; one must do it. This leads to the comparison with a person building a house, digging deeply and laying a foundation on rock; otherwise a flooding river would wash it away. In this context, the flood may come from those hating, cursing, and abusing (6:28) the disciples, or perhaps merely from the "cares and riches and pleasures of life" (8:14-15, 18; see Johnson; Seim).

Healing the Centurion's Slave (7:1-10)

Luke takes this story from the sayings source Q, dated AD 50-65 (also Matt 8:5-13), one of only three narratives in that collection. We may imagine three audiences: Jesus' rural Galilean audience about 30, a Judean audience that included nationalists preparing for war with Rome about 50-65, and a Lukan audience in their dining room listening to the Gospel read aloud about 80. Those brave early messianic preachers in Judea who collected Jesus' sayings and this deed about AD 50 were retelling them in the context of urban terrorists *(sicarii)* murdering those not opposed to Rome (Josephus *J.W.* 2.254-57). The positive portrayal of a Gentile centurion juxtaposed to a criticism of those in Israel (7:2, 9) would have endangered the storyteller! But Luke retells the same story for a quieter domestic setting in a Greco-Roman city.

In Luke there is a tension between the Jewish elders' testimony to the centurion and his own humility; and the centurion cares for his slave. Both humility (14:11; 18:14; cf. 1:48) and care for those who cannot return love (7:2; 6:32-36) are Lukan values. The centurion is a model for householders in the Lukan community as well as a predecessor of the Gentile centurion Cornelius in Acts, who is also saved by faith (7:9; Acts 10:43; 11:17; 15:7, 9). Given that many Jews did not believe in Jesus, his statement had one meaning in AD 30, another about 80: "not even in Israel have I found such faith" (7:9).

Raising the Widow of Nain's Son (7:11-17)

Now Jesus raises the dead, an anticipation of the series of claims he makes in 7:22, this time echoing not Isaiah but 1 Kgs 17:17-24, Elijah raising the son of a Sidonian widow. In his inaugural sermon Jesus had already appealed to Elijah raising this widow's son (4:25-26), there making the point that "there were many widows in Israel in the time of Elijah, . . . yet Elijah was sent to none of them." Luke is echoing both 1 Kings 17 and Jesus' sermon in ch. 4. The raising of the widow of Nain's son resonates with Jesus' apophthegm after healing the centurion's son: God also sends prophets to foreigners who have faith (7:9), now also to a foreign woman! The disciples and the large crowd are afraid and glorify God, proclaiming Jesus "a great prophet" and saying that God has looked favorably on the people (7:16, as prophesied by Zechariah in 1:68, 78).

These two stories concern both genders, the male centurion whose slave is healed and the female widow whose son is raised, a conscious pairing that Luke does repeatedly. Zechariah and Mary both receive visitations from angels (1:11, 26-27). The male shepherd searches for his lost sheep, and a woman searches for her lost coin (15:4, 8). The Spirit comes to all at Pentecost, men and women, both of whom prophesy (Joel 3:1-5, quoted in Acts 2:17-21). In Luke this gender pairing has limits, for males preach and are leaders but women (except Anna) may do neither, a retreat from women preaching and prophesying in early Pauline churches (Rom 16:3, 6-7, 12; 1 Cor 11:5; Phil 4:3). Seim: 150, 154 observes, however, that women "see," "remember," and "believe," especially in the infancy and passion narratives (23:49, 55; 24:4, 6-7, 9), when males do none of these (24:11, 16, 25, 38, 41), although they are the preachers and leaders, a "double message," she remarks, which "nurtures a dangerous memory."

John's Question to Jesus and Jesus' Speech on John (7:18-35)

Luke has commented extensively on the relationship between John and Jesus, but in this scene they both have "disciples," as years later, after his death, John still has in

Ephesus (Acts 19:1). John refers to Jesus both as "the coming one" (7:19; see 3:16; 4:34) and "the stronger one" (3:16 again). Jesus' list of his deeds with respect to the blind, lame, lepers, deaf, the dead, and the poor summarizes the preceding narrative of his deeds and words, especially 4:18-19 (Isa 61:1-2; 58:6) and 6:20. Given much of contemporary Judaism's focus on ritual purity, that is, on separation from outsiders, Jesus' reference to "lepers cleansed" is the most surprising (despite 5:12-16). Isa 35:8 foresees no "unclean" person on the "holy way," since it is for God's people. The story of Moses praying that God cleanse Miriam of her leprosy is one of only a few such stories in the Bible (Num 12:10-15). Another concerns Elisha cleansing Naaman the Syrian, the story Jesus summarized in the inaugural sermon (4:27; 2 Kings 5). This and the previous paragraph (7:11-17) concern precisely the two scriptural stories in Jesus' inaugural, which exhibit God's power with respect to raising the dead and leprosy. In the plot of Luke-Acts, these stories even more centrally concern God's prophets raising and cleansing foreigners, a foreign destitute woman and a foreign powerful man, so that questions of race, gender, and class are all involved.

For the author of Luke-Acts and the readers, reflecting on John's question about AD 80, John distinguishes diverse hopes for "the coming one." Jesus has not proved to be "the powerful one" who baptizes with fire, the mighty savior who would save Israel from its enemies anticipated by John and by his father Zechariah (1:69, 71; 3:16), but rather one who ministered to outcasts in Israel (7:22) and who hints about God's acceptance of foreigners (4:25-27). No wonder Jesus blesses "anyone who takes no offense at me" (7:23). Nevertheless, Jesus praises John as "more than a prophet" (7:26) because he fulfills prophecies (Mal 3:1 and Isa 40:3), that is, because he is the forerunner of the Messiah, Savior of the outcasts. (Elijah as "forerunner" of the Messiah is a Christian interpretation, not an earlier Jewish idea.) Jesus' greatness also exalts John.

Although they were different, that generation accepted neither John nor Jesus. Luke has editorially inserted 7:29-30: the leaders have "rejected God's will *(boulē tou theou)* for them by not being baptized by" John; Luke is focused on discerning the will of God with respect to the history of salvation, God's will for King David, John, Jesus, Paul, and the church (see Acts 2:23; 4:28; 5:38; 13:36; 20:27). In this context Jesus was accused of being "a glutton and a drunkard" (7:34), a charge that echoes Deut 21:20, so he addresses a riddle about himself and John to the Pharisees and lawyers (7:30), who reject both: "we played the flute for you, and you did not dance; we wailed, and you did not weep" (v. 34), which could also have meaning for Luke's readers looking back at the Jewish rejection of both. But "wisdom is vindicated by all her children" (7:35; Matt 11:19), by those who hear the tune, dance, and/or weep.

Responses of a Pharisee and a Sinful Woman (7:36-50)

Many interpreters understand this as a different story from those in Mark 14:3-9 and John 12:1-8, despite striking similarities. At this point in Luke's narrative we know how a Pharisee will react to Jesus, but surprisingly he invites Jesus to share a meal. Jesus does what he had been accused of doing, for the second character in the story means that Jesus is indeed "a friend of toll collectors and sinners" (7:34). Ancient houses were more public than modern ones, so the woman may simply have walked into the house through an open front door and into the dining room *(triclinium).* At ancient *symposia* guests reclined; it was dishonorable to sit, so the woman would have had easy access to Jesus' feet, on which she poured myrrh, a scented oil. The Pharisee doubts that Jesus is a prophet, the same issue we have seen throughout this chapter (vv. 16 and 26, and now v. 39). But Jesus knows both who the woman is and the internal judgment of his host (cf. 5:21-22; 6:7-8), which again shows a division in Israel (2:35). Jesus responds to the Pharisee's thoughts with a parable of two debtors (7:41; the same word as in the parable of 16:5 and the cognate verb in the Lord's Prayer, 11:4; also 16:7; 17:10); again, such puzzles were typically debated at *symposia.* Debts and the possible forgiveness of burdensome debts were debated (Balch 1997: 129-30, citing Dionysius *Rom. Ant.* 6.63.3; 83.4). Dionysius narrates rich Roman patrons sometimes forgiving the debts of their clients as a favor, even promising it in response to a demand by the poor. Simon is familiar with the attitude and knows that forgiven clients would typically be grateful (7:43). Jesus then confronts the rich man with his lack of hospitality, in contrast with the sinful woman and her care (vv. 44-46), perhaps another of Luke's intentional gender contrasts. The climax comes in the saying of vv. 47-48: "Therefore, I tell you, her sins, which were many, have been forgiven; hence she has shown great love. But the one to whom little is forgiven, loves little. Then he said to her, 'Your sins are forgiven.'" The Pharisee has not been forgiven and has not loved. If Jesus' parable and this setting go together, which might not originally have been the case, the woman's actions demonstrate that she must already have been forgiven (the verb is perfect passive), although Jesus actually pronounces it only in v. 48. Then the guests raise the question, "Who is this who even forgives sins?" (v. 49), the theme of the following narrative. The last line emphasizes her "faith" (v. 50), the same trust at which Jesus had marveled when expressed by the centurion (v. 9), perhaps yet another of Luke's male/female pairings (Balch 1997: 123-44).

The Word of God Proclaimed, Heard, and Done (8:1-21)

The following four units concern the proclamation of God's word; some hear and act, but some reject. This is Jesus' third major speech in Luke. In Hellenistic histories, speeches clarify the meaning of the narrative (Johnson: 134); here the people are divided by Jesus' proclamation of the word of God.

Mary Magdalene and Other Women Provide for the Disciples (8:1-3; see 24:10)

Jesus, accompanied by the twelve and some women, continues proclaiming the good news of the kingdom of God, a combination listed again in Acts 1:13-14. This second list includes the eleven, certain women, Jesus' mother Mary, and his brothers, a list of church leaders. By Luke's time much of the church had become an institution led by males (Acts 1:21). In Luke 8:1-3, however, we see some of the women who were prominent in the Jesus movement, wealthy women who supported the wandering band of preachers by their means. These wealthy prominent women were a paradigm for later wealthy male householders in the Lukan communities (Seim: 79, 81, 88), but Luke reduces their stature. They are, with many others in chs. 5–8, healed or exorcised, but in this narrative the leaders and preachers are not. In Greco-Roman culture Luke did risk scandal by including them in the narrative: wandering Cynic preachers were notorious for converting and sexually abusing women (Lucian *Runaways* 18–19).

The Parable of the Word of God Growing (8:4-15)

Luke takes the parable from Mark. In Luke, the parable should also be interpreted in light of the whole two-volume history that primarily concerns the "growth" of the Word of God throughout the world (see 13:19; Acts 6:7; 7:17; 12:24; 19:20). The "word" is the primary means by which God addresses the world (1:2, 4, 20, 29; 3:4; 4:22, 32, 36; 5:1, 15; 6:47; 7:7, 17; 8:11-13, 15, 21; 9:26, 28, 44; 10:39; 11:28; 12:10; 16:2; 20:3, 20; 21:33; 22:61; and 65 references in Acts including 1:1; 2:22, 40-41; 4:4, 29, 31; 6:2, 4-5, 7; 10:36, 44; 11:1, 19, 22; 15:7, 15; 16:6, 32, 36; 17:11; 19:10; 20:2, 32, 35; 22:22). The prefaces to both the Gospel and Acts emphasize God's word. Jesus concludes the Sermon on the Plain with a parable illustrating a person who hears and does his words (6:47 = 8:15). When a person in the crowd blesses Jesus' mother, Jesus responds, "Blessed rather are those who hear the word of God and obey it!" (11:28). God sent the word of peace to Israel (Acts 10:36) that Peter also announces to the Gentile household of Cornelius; and the Holy Spirit falls on all hearing the word (10:44). The Spirit forbids Paul to speak the word in Asia (16:6), but he proclaims it in Europe and in Berea, where "these Jews were more receptive than those in Thessalonica, for they welcomed *(edexanto)* the word very eagerly and examined the scriptures every day to see whether these things were so" (17:11), a commentary on Jesus' parable in Luke 8. But when Paul returned to Jerusalem, Jews from Asia stirred up a crowd in the temple, who listen to Paul until he narrates a trance he had in the holy temple itself in which God sent him away to the Gentiles; at this "word" they shouted that Paul should die (22:22; contrast 11:1)! Luke moves Mark's citation (4:12) of Isa 6:9-10 to the end of the second volume, in Luke-Acts a comment on many (not all) Jews rejecting the word (Acts 28:26-27; cf. 13:46, 49). Luke's final note (8:15) concerns holding fast to the word despite persecutions (see 21:12-19).

This "growth" is unlike that stressed by the Priestly writer in the Hebrew Bible, where the phrase "grow and multiply" occurs a dozen times (see Gen 1:22, 28). There the Hebrew family grows without intermarriage among Canaanites (Gen 28:3; Jer 23:3). In contrast to Israelite Priestly ideology, the Roman historian Dionysius narrates Rome's "growth" through the mixing of nations, customs, and languages (Balch 2003b), and in Acts this "growth" also occurs in a context of Hebrew and Hellenist unity (Acts 6:7; 11:19-20; 19:8-10, 20). When the historian Polybius (6.43.2) compares the greatness of Athens and Rome, he dismisses Athens simply because the city did not continue to "grow"! For both ancient Romans and modern Americans and Europeans, growth is better, and Luke's readers would be assured (Luke 1:4, *asphaleia*) of God's providence in history because the church was growing. Luke has abandoned the ethnocentricity of Hebrew Priestly writers for the ethnic multiplicity of Rome. Luke's urban readers would have found this just as difficult as do modern, ethnocentric, Christian urbanites, whether in Bosnia, Europe, or America (Balch 2003b).

The Hidden and Revealed (8:16-18)

The second parable interprets the first one: no one puts a lamp under a jar or a bed but on a lampstand, so that people may "see" the light. For Luke "seeing" is as crucial as "hearing" (8:16, picking up Isa 6:9 quoted in 8:10; see 10:23-24; 11:33-36; 21:8, 30; Acts 1:9, 11; 2:33). Luke stresses the importance of "seeing" again just before denouncing the Pharisees (11:33-36, 37-54). Disciples are to "watch" so that they are not led astray by a false Messiah (21:8).

What is secret shall be "made known," just as the angels had made known Jesus' birth to the shepherds, and as God made known to David the ways of life, that is, the resurrection of the Messiah (Acts 2:28, quoting Ps 16[15]:11, interpreted by Acts 2:31). Jesus' audience is to be careful how they hear (8:18) revelation, the word of God; to take the interpretation from the previous parable, they are to watch that the devil not snatch away the word from their hearts (v. 12).

Jesus' Mother and Brothers (8:19-21)

Jesus redefines the family: his mother and brothers are those who hear the word of God and do it. In the Jesus movement, family serves the purpose of supporting discipleship, not the other way around (see 14:26-27; 18:28-30), however offensive that is to modern readers. Already in the infancy narrative, Mary is an example of discipleship (1:38, 45). Luke never names James Jesus' "brother," probably to avoid the appearance of hereditary leadership (contrast Gal 1:19).

Jesus' Powerful Deeds Evoke Faith and Prepare for Succession (8:22-56)

This section has three stories that demonstrate Jesus' power over the sea, demons, the human body, and death, another series of powerful deeds that prepare for Jesus' giving this power to exorcise and to proclaim the word to the twelve (9:1-17).

The Master Commands Wind and Water to Obey (8:22-25)

Luke continues to follow Mark's (4:35-41) order in narrating the stilling of the storm, but Luke also writes Acts 27:1–28:16, which narrates a climactic, concluding storm whose outcome is due to the divine will (Talbert and Hayes). God rules the power of the sea and calms its waves (Ps 88[89]:9). God commands the storm and calms it to a gentle breeze (Ps 106[107]:29-30). The story in Luke 8 means that Jesus exercises God's power, that he prepares to invest in the twelve (9:1). Talbert and Hayes refer to a story in Plutarch (*Life of Caesar* 38.2-4), who commanded sailors to sail through a storm, which was impossible, showing that Caesar was only a human being pretending to be a god. In contrast, Jesus rebuked the wind and raging waves, and there was a calm (v. 24), followed by a call for faith in Jesus exercising God's power. The question follows: "Who then is this . . . ?" (v. 25). Jesus is establishing supreme power before appointing leaders of the community and teaching them a way of life (Talbert and Hayes).

Son of God with Power over the Foreign Demonic "Legion" (8:26-39)

Mark has placed this story in the country of the Gerasenes (Mark 5:1; Luke 8:26), difficult since that is thirty miles south of the Sea of Galilee. Scribes substituted either Gadara, six miles away, or Gergasa, on the shore near Tiberias. Luke adds the explanation that the country of the Gerasenes "is opposite Galilee." Fortunately, the story retains its point, whatever the geography. Luke also adds that the man was from the city, for a long time had worn no clothes, had not lived in a house but among tombs (v. 27), and that he was bound with chains, which he broke, then being driven into the desert by the demon (v. 29).

In Mark and Luke, not Matthew, when Jesus asks his name, he replies "Legion," a Latin loanword in Greek referring to a military unit, the *Legio* of four to six thousand soldiers. In Luke (alone) they want Jesus not to command them to go to the "abyss," in Revelation (11:7; 17:8; 20:3) the place of the beast and later of Satan. Instead Jesus sends them into swine, who run (thirty miles!) to the lake and drown. The herdsmen proclaim (*apangellō;* see Luke 8:47; 1 Cor 14:25; and if an allegory, Luke 6:22) it in the city. The city folks come out and find the man "sitting at the feet of Jesus, clothed and in his right mind" (*sōphronounta,* 8:35; see Acts 26:25), that is, a disciple of Jesus. They are afraid (8:35, 37) and ask Jesus to leave (again, if an allegory, see Acts 16:39). Jesus tells the healed demoniac, "'Return to your home and declare *(diēgou)* how much God has done for you.' And he went away proclaiming *(kēryssōn)* throughout the whole city . . ." (v. 39). Luke describes this whole gospel as a "narrative" (*diēgēsis;* 1:1), the noun cognate with the verb "declare" used by Luke to describe the healed person's speech.

This is another hint of the coming mission to Gentiles in Acts. Mark (5:20) concludes that he "began to proclaim in the Decapolis," a phrase Luke omits. Luke must get the "order" (1:3) of salvation history correct, and the Gentile mission does not happen until Acts 10, not already in Luke 8. Nevertheless, Luke adds the hint that this proclamation and confession of the Son of God's great deeds (vv. 28, 39) occurred "opposite Galilee" (v. 26), an observation made just after the parable concerning the growth of the word of God. Both anticipate the missionary proclamation in Acts.

Theissen: 100-102 makes an astute *modern* observation about this story. Psychologically, he connects foreign rule and the rule of demons. Jews who suffered many injuries from the Romans reacted by transferring their aggressive reactions to another object, from the Romans to demons. Foreign Syrian rulers were "shepherds," demons, subjects of Satan (*1 Enoch* 85–90). Among the Essenes, too, the final war was against Belial and his hosts (1QM 1:9ff.). Mark and Luke's demons speak Latin, present themselves as "legion," a Roman unit of soldiers, and wish to stay in the country. Jesus' power is greater. Christians took comfort in "seeing" the Son of Man presently seated (or standing) at the right hand of the power of God (Luke 22:69; Acts 7:55-56). For Lukan disciples, Christ's present power was as important as his future powerful coming as the Son of Humanity.

Jesus, More Powerful Than Human Death or Sickness (8:40-56)

Mark (3:21-35) employs a "sandwich" pattern: Jesus' family charges that he is beside himself; second, the scribes say that he is possessed by Beelzeboul; and third, Jesus' family asks for him, stimulating Jesus to characterize his true family, a literary pattern that brings Jesus' family into dangerous proximity to the blaspheming scribes. Luke breaks up the "sandwich" in Mark 3, improving the image of Jesus' family, but retains the pattern here. Both stories involve "daughters" (8:42, 48) who are "saved." Jairus's "only daughter" recalls the "only son" of the widow (4:25-26; 7:11-17).

Luke omits the hemorrhaging woman's interior dialogue ("If I touch even his garments . . .") in Mark and adds Jesus "perceiving in himself that power had gone out of him," heightening the narrative emphasis on Jesus' prophetic knowledge. In Luke both Jesus' demand personally to see the healed hemorrhaging woman, and, in the second story, the omission of Jesus' Aramaic (foreign) command, *talitha koum* (Mark 5:41), distance both stories from magic, focusing the power in Jesus. Later the church is still concerned with magic (Acts 5:15; 19:11-12, 18-19, a contrast to the "word of the Lord" in 20).

Jesus tells the woman to "go in peace" (8:48; see 2:14; 7:50; 10:5; Acts 10:36), another fulfillment of Zechariah's *Benedictus* (1:79).

The Messiah's Successors, the Messianic Banquet, and the Cross (9:1-50)

In chs. 4–5 and 7–8 Luke has emphasized Jesus' spectacular power, which he transmits to the twelve (9:1), his successors as leaders of the institutional church. In Luke's work of ancient history, Jesus' power is a contrast to and competes with the form of power usually portrayed in history, that is, with Roman military victories and official administrative power throughout the empire, power that the Lukan Christians experienced. Following the investment of the twelve with "power and authority," Jesus tells them to give the crowd something to eat (v. 13) and himself feeds five thousand, the messianic banquet (vv. 1-17). Peter confesses who Jesus is, the Messiah, and hears Jesus' prophecy of suffering (vv. 18-27). Then in an epiphany God affirms who Jesus is, "God's Son, the Chosen" (vv. 28-36). Jesus rebukes another evil spirit in an epileptic boy (vv. 37-43a), another aspect of the conflict in this gospel. He again announces his death (vv. 43b-45), speaks of "receiving children" in his name (vv. 46-48), allows diverse persons to exercise power in his name (vv. 49-50), and then travels to Jerusalem, teaching the successors a way of life (9:51–19:27).

Jesus Gives the Twelve Power and Tells Them to Feed the Crowd (9:1-17)

The Christ who has demonstrated his power and proclaimed the nature of the kingdom now gives his successors "power and authority over all demons and to cure diseases, [as he sends] them out to proclaim the kingdom of God and to heal" (9:1-2). The instructions for dress and provisions given to them for their journeys would both make them appear like Cynic preachers and differentiate them from those Hellenistic moralists. Epictetus (3.22.50, 54, "On the Calling of a Cynic," trans. Oldfather in LCC) tells students that what makes a Cynic is not "a contemptible wallet, a staff, and big jaws . . . to revile tactlessly the people he meets," but rather, "he must needs be flogged like an ass, and while he is being flogged, he must love *(philein)* the men who flog him, as though he were the father or brother of them all." Jesus had also told his disciples that they are "blessed when people hate you" (6:22) and to love *(agapate)* their enemies (6:27). However, they learn here that they are not to carry a Cynic's identifying staff or bag (9:3). They are not to beg, but rather to depend on other disciples' household hospitality (v. 4).

Early Christian communities sometimes met in Greco-Roman houses, so that the owner was host both to the worship assembly and to traveling preachers. Unlike modern homes, the more crowded Roman homes were, the more powerful the household patron was perceived to be. Acts, the Pauline letters, and the *Didache* (11–13) allude to the importance of such hospitality. Some houses were wealthier, but Christ's emissaries are not to move from a poorer to a richer house (Luke 9:4). Some cities would not receive them, and Jesus gives the twelve a symbolic gesture against such urban areas, shaking off the dust of their feet against them (v. 5; see 10:11-12; Acts 13:51), an act close to Jesus' earlier "woes" (6:24-26), for the cities had rejected the kingdom of God.

Mediterranean people often assumed that they were subject to "fate," to the stars, and salvation is sometimes understood as the defeat of these heavenly powers (Eph 1:20-22; 2:2; 3:10; 6:12-13; Col 2:15, 20), also crucial for Luke (4:1-13; 6:18; 8:2, 26-39; 9:37-43). Luke repeats important scenes: there are four commissionings of the disciples in the Gospel (also 10:1-11; 22:35-38; 24:48-49; see Acts 1:6-8; 13:2-4; 14:26-27). After the seventy are commissioned and return, they celebrate that "even the demons are subject to us!" (10:17-20). And at the end of the Gospel, the eleven remain in Jerusalem until they are "clothed with power from on high" (24:49; see Acts 2:1-4; 10:44; 13:4-12).

Zeus "sends out" the Cynic preacher (Epictetus 3.22.2, 23), but on the other hand, neither philosophers nor philosophical schools were institutions that organized and sent out missionizing proclaimers. This is rather the political language of "philanthropic" states that both "receive" *(dechesthai)* immigrants and "send out" *(apostellein)* colonies to spread one's way of life (Dionysius *Rom. Ant.* 2.15.3–16.3; Josephus *Ag. Ap.* 2.255-86; see Balch 1982: 111, 118). Jesus has anticipated this missionizing effort in the parable of the Word of God planted (ch. 8) and also had already begun to describe the disciples' way of life in the Sermon on the Plain (ch. 6), a characterization that he will continue on the journey to Jerusalem going to his death (9:51–19:27).

Since "sending out" colonists was a political gesture, not surprisingly Herod the tetrarch raises a question and asks whether Elijah or one of the ancient prophets had arisen (9:8). He had beheaded John, but asks, "Who is this about whom I hear such things?" (v. 9; see the same question in 5:21; 7:19, 49; 8:25; also 9:20, 22, 35). Elijah was expected to return (Mal 4:5), but John the Baptist had fulfilled that role (Luke 1:17). Readers learn of John's fate from the first half of Herod's compound sentence (9:9a), the second half asking about Jesus. The gospel involves the cross and resurrection, thus making the highly paradoxical narrative assumption that God's great power is not defeated by the killing of God's prophets (Culpepper: 195).

The twelve return from their mission (9:10), Jesus preaches and heals the crowds (v. 11), then he feeds five thousand (vv. 12-17), events followed by Peter's confession (vv. 18-27). Assuming that Mark was one of Luke's sources, at 9:17 Luke omits Mark 6:45–8:26! The second feeding story disappears (Mark 8:1-10), as does Jesus' declaration that "all foods are clean" (7:19b), which Luke reserves for its appropriate "order" (1:1) in salvation history (Acts 10–11), not during Jesus' lifetime.

Jesus' feeding of the five thousand reflects several stories from the Bible. The most well-known story concerns God feeding Israel in the wilderness (Exodus 16–17, esp. 16:10; Numbers 11). Second is one of the series of miracles reported of Elisha (2 Kgs 4:1–6:7), the feeding of a hundred men who "have some left" in 4:42-44, the only series of prophetic miracle stories in the Bible comparable to wonders at the exodus from Egypt. Third, the language reflects words spoken at the Eucharist. After telling the twelve, "you give them something to eat" (9:13a), Jesus, "taking the five loaves . . . looked up to heaven, and blessed and broke them, and gave them to the disciples to set before the crowd. And all ate . . ." (vv. 16-17a). These verbs, except "looked up," are repeated in the ritual of 22:19 (earlier 5:30; also Matt 26:26-27; 24:30; Mark 14:22-23; 1 Cor 11:23b-24; see *Didache* 9–10; Justin *1 Apol.* 62). There may be an implied connection between this central ritual act and social ethical deeds; the later church both breaks bread together and shares possessions (Acts 2:46; 4:32-37; see Rom 15:26-27; 2 Cor 8:13-15).

Peter's Confession, Discipleship, and the Daily Cross (9:18-27)

Peter confesses Jesus as "the Messiah of God" (9:20), a title that has military implications. Peter receives the response not to tell anyone from Jesus, who prophesies instead the suffering of the Son of Humanity (v. 22) and a daily cross for followers (v. 23). Jesus' first prophecy of his suffering in Mark (8:31-33) is a total shock since it follows chapters (4–8) that contain spectacular miracles, but as a historian Luke had added speeches to the chapters of Markan miracle stories that prepare the reader for suffering discipleship (see 2:35; 6:22, 26, 29, 32; 7:42-48; 8:13-14, none of which is in Mark).

The disciples know that people are calling Jesus either John the Baptist, Elijah, or "one of the ancient prophets" (9:19). Peter, however, moves beyond prophetic categories by confessing that Jesus is "the Messiah of God" (v. 20). For Luke's Gentile audience a decade after the Jewish war against Rome, this unqualified response would need clarification, but readers know from the Sermon on the Plain that messianic discipleship involves being reviled and defamed because of the Son of Humanity (6:22). This Davidic Messiah is not a military conqueror (despite phrases like 1:52, 69, 71, and 73; and 2:26 is nuanced by 2:32). This does not mean that this Messiah will not say or do anything "political," since he speaks concerning foreigners and the poor.

Jesus responds that "the Son of Humanity must *(dei)* undergo great suffering, and be rejected by the elders, chief priests, and scribes, and be killed, and on the third day be raised" (9:22). Luke writes "must" eighteen times in the Gospel, most of them following 9:22, and again twenty-four times in Acts, a focus on the compelling will of God (2:49; 4:43; 13:16, 33; 17:25; 21:9; 22:37; 24:7, 26, 44; Acts 1:16; 9:16; 14:22; 17:3; 23:11). Scripture prophesies two events, both the Messiah's suffering, death, and resurrection and that witnesses will proclaim repentance and forgiveness in his name to all nations beginning at Jerusalem (24:44b, 46b-48) and — we learn in Acts — "to the ends of the earth" (Acts 1:8; 13:47). Scripture prophesies not only the crucified Messiah (see already Luke 4:28-30), but suffering witnesses who sow the Word of God (see already 8:4-15).

The following five sayings on discipleship follow the Markan order and are addressed to "all" (9:23), to both disciples and the crowd. Luke contemporizes the meaning of Jesus' cross for followers, who must "deny themselves and take up their cross daily . . ." (v. 24). "Daily" is not in Mark or Matthew, and is given content by the Lukan beatitudes (6:20-23), by the expectation that some cities will reject their witness (9:5; 10:10-12), divided households (12:52-53; 14:26), persecution in synagogues and prisons (21:12-19), as well as controversies over church leadership (22:24-27). For Jesus the way to life is by losing it, by experiencing the cross (9:24). The following saying denies any profit in gaining the whole world if one loses oneself (v. 25). The fourth discipleship saying links a disciple's being ashamed of Jesus and his words in the present to the eschatological coming of the Son of Humanity, who will be ashamed of that disciple (v. 26). Disciples will publicly affirm Jesus' beatitude for the poor, publicly love enemies, and publicly "sow" the Word of God, publicly confess Jesus as the suffering Messiah. In this saying Jesus seems to separate himself from the coming Son of Humanity, which the church would not have done, so many understand the saying to have originated with the historical Jesus.

A fifth saying, also eschatological, is linked to the fourth; in Luke, some will not taste death until they see the kingdom of God (9:27). The devil claims all the kingdoms of the world (4:5), but the poor have God's kingdom (6:20). The kingdom comes to the sick who are healed (10:9); indeed, it has come to those who have been exorcised (11:20). Jesus' great banquet parable exhibits the poor, crippled, blind, and lame eating bread in the kingdom (14:15, 21). After John, the kingdom is proclaimed (16:16). Responding to the Pharisees, Jesus affirms that the "kingdom of God is among you" (17:20-21). The kingdom belongs to little children (18:16) and, shockingly, to those who leave their household (house, wife, brothers, parents, and children) for the sake of the kingdom of God (18:29). The kingdom is not to appear immediately (19:11). On the apostles, Jesus confers a kingdom in order that they may eat and drink at his table in his kingdom judging the twelve tribes of Israel (22:29-30). Jesus speaks of the kingdom after being crucified and raised (Acts 1:3), and Philip proclaims the gospel of the kingdom, with the result that the city of Samaria is baptized (Acts 8:12). Paul and Barnabas tell the Christians of Asia Minor that "through many persecutions we must enter the kingdom of God" (14:22; see the Lukan beatitudes). At the end of Acts, to Jewish leaders in Rome, Paul is "testifying to the kingdom of God and trying to convince them about Jesus both from the law of Moses and from the prophets" (28:23, 31).

These verses link the kingdom of God closely to Jesus, to his words and deeds, and the latter involve Jesus' healings and exorcisms. Jesus invites the poor, blind, children, and the apostles to eat bread in the kingdom. On the other hand, the redactor of the gospel cautions that the kingdom is not to appear immediately (19:11). The kingdom is proclaimed both to nonbelievers, who are (invited to be) baptized (Acts 8:12; 28:23), and to Christians, emphasizing persecutions (14:22). Luke 9:27 is affirmed: especially the poor, blind, healed, and exorcised believers, those who have learned about Jesus from Moses and the prophets, and those who endure persecutions, do "see the kingdom of God" already in the present.

Discipleship for Those Who Misunderstand (9:28-50)

The disciples do not understand this kingdom of the poor, of children, of persecution, of a king who dies. So there is, first, confirmation of Jesus' heavenly origin and nature in the transfiguration, another conflict with the demonic world that shows what is at stake, then a second prophecy by Jesus of his forthcoming betrayal. Another key statement about discipleship follows: "Whoever welcomes *(dexētai)* this child in my name welcomes *(dechetai)* me" (9:48). The same verb is employed twice, the verb that Jesus had used in the third sermon (8:13) and that will be used again in the first story narrating the journey to Jerusalem (9:53). Just before and after this major juncture in the Gospel of Luke (the transition from the Galilean ministry to the journey to Jerusalem, 9:51), Jesus is focused on whether the messengers who proclaim the Word of God will be "welcomed" and whether the disciples will "welcome" others.

The Transfiguration (9:28-36)

Historians of Rome told stories of divine kings whose divinity was confirmed by a transfiguration story. Not only

Romulus, the founder, but also Tullius Servius, the sixth king of Rome, was born of a slave woman and a divine phantom, so that he, too, was "superior to the race of mortals" (Dionysius *Rom. Ant.* 4.2.2), and his divinity was confirmed by a transfiguration story (4.2.3-4, trans. Cary in LCC):

> This fabulous account [Tullius's birth from a human mother and a god], although it seems not altogether credible *(ou piston),* is rendered less incredible *(apisteisthai)* by reason of another manifestation *(epiphaneia)* of the gods relating to Tullius which was wonderful and extraordinary *(thaumastē kai paradoxos).* For when he had fallen asleep one day while sitting in the portico of the palace about noon, a fire shone forth from his head. This was seen by his mother and by the king's wife, as they were walking through the portico, as well as by all who happened to be present with them at the time. The flame continued to illumine his whole head till his mother ran to him and wakened him; and with the ending of his sleep the flame was dispersed and vanished.

Just as some doubted Jesus' divine sonship (Luke 4:22, 24, 29), so despite stories of his birth generated by a god, many called Tullius merely the son of a slave woman (4.1.2–2.3; 4.6.6). The transfiguration story made the birth story more believable.

These Greco-Roman assumptions are combined with the story of Moses' transfiguration (Exod 34:29-35), a story also important to Stephen (Acts 7:30-34, 37-38), to Paul and the Corinthian Christians (2 Cor 3:7-11), as well as to the Hellenistic Jew Philo (*Vit. Mos.* 1.158; 2.69-70; Ps.-Philo *Bib. Ant.* 12.1). Philo says that Moses "entered into the darkness where God was, . . . and beheld what is hidden from the sight of mortal nature," . . . that he is "a model *(paradeigma)* for those willing to copy him," adding that he was named "god and king" of the nation (*Vit. Mos.* 1.158)! For Luke, too, Moses is a type of Jesus (Acts 7:17-44). Paul is harshly critical of such stories (2 Cor 3:7, "a ministry of death"; v. 8, "a ministry now set aside"; v. 9, "a ministry of condemnation"), perhaps because he opposed a telling of the Moses story that encouraged the Corinthian Christians to think that they could follow Moses into divinization (2 Cor 12:1-10). Instead Paul stressed suffering and the cross (2 Cor 4:7-11), which Jesus also does immediately in Luke (9:44). But the transfiguration itself made it difficult for the disciples to understand (v. 45) that they would not be deified and therefore be beyond suffering, because their "model" had already been glorified before their eyes.

Peter is presented as willing to equate Moses, Elijah, and Jesus (9:33), but a voice from a cloud forbids it. "This is my Son, my Chosen; listen to him!" (v. 35), a rare contrast in Luke-Acts to the command to listen to Moses (Deut 13:3, 8; 18:15).

An Epileptic Boy (9:37-43a)

God's Son comes "down from the mountain" (9:37; see 6:17 and Phil 2:7-8?) and exorcises the son, the "only child" of a man in the crowd (9:38), because the disciples could not do it (v. 40). For some unclarified reason, Jesus is angry (v. 41), rare in Luke. Jesus rebukes the unclean spirit, heals the boy, and gives him back to the father, so that "all were astounded at the greatness of God" (v. 43). According to later texts (10:9 and 11:20), the kingdom of God has come — to one who was formerly in convulsions (9:39, 42).

Jesus' Second Prophecy of His Death (9:43b-45)

After Moses' transfiguration, God named him a "god" and gave him the two tablets of the law, but after a similar transfiguration Jesus prophesies his "betrayal into human hands" (9:44). The disciples, familiar with the story of Moses, did not understand (v. 45). They were hearing the contemporary, mystical Moses story, not the gospel of the cross.

Who Is the Greatest and Who May Be a Leader in the Church? (9:46-48, 49-50)

This final unit in the Galilean ministry concerns a value that also figures in another key speech, Jesus' farewell address (22:24-27). Here it is an "argument" among the disciples; there a "dispute" that addresses later problems of church leadership and membership. The problem of whom to "welcome" into one's city, people, or institution was extensively discussed in ancient history. Whether to "accept" "foreigners," those who speak a different language and have different cultural values, was a major "dispute," for these foreign ways would lead, it was thought, to "corruption" of the ancient, legitimate (Greek, Roman, or Jewish) way of life, or, on the other side of the argument, to renewed energy in the city/people/institution (Dionysius *Rom. Ant.* 1.89.2-3; 2.25-27; 3.10-11; contrast Josephus *Ant.* 4.126-55, 159, 183, 228, 294). Jesus takes one side in this dispute, "welcoming" children, outcasts, and the foreigner.

9:49-50 concern who may lead in the church. John, one of the twelve (probably the "John" of Gal 2:9), explains that they have seen other disciples doing what Jesus had modeled, casting out demons in Jesus' name, "and we tried to forbid *(ekōlyomen)* him because he does not follow *(akolouthei)* with us" (v. 9b). To "forbid" is formal language prohibiting institutional practices (see Mark 10:14; Acts 8:36; 28:31; 1 Cor 14:39; Josephus *Ant.* 16.41-45, 174); therefore, these two verses formally allow diversity among the leadership of early Christianity, which the apostolic council later ratifies (Acts 15:1, 7-10, 14, 19; see Gal 2:9-10; Balch 1995b, 2002b).

Jesus' Journey to Jerusalem (9:51–19:27)

After the Galilean ministry, Jesus "set his face to go to Jerusalem" (9:51), a major turning point in the Gospel. Jesus has twice prophesied his death in Jerusalem (9:22, 43b-45), and on the way, then, teaches future leaders of the community a way of life. The historical Jesus' life may well have been more complicated than residence in Galilee followed by one journey to Jerusalem, where he died, the Markan pattern; the Gospel of John has several such journeys to Jerusalem. Luke follows Mark's literary outline, but he gives very few references to any journey as such; after eight chapters, Jesus is still "going through the region between Samaria and Galilee" (17:11). A chapter later he arrives in Jericho (18:35), then in Bethpage and Bethany on the Mount of Olives (19:28-29), and finally in Jerusalem (19:41, 45).

The sayings, parables, and other material in the journey narrative are drawn largely from Q and from "L," Luke's own source(s); Luke stops following Mark (at Mark 9:40) until near the end of the "journey" (at Luke 18:15). Luke then omits Mark 9:41–10:12, but then again begins to utilize the First Gospel. The material omitted in Mark includes the paragraph on divorce (Mark 10:2-12) that is in tension with Luke's other sources (14:26; 20:34). No outline of this section has won acceptance, despite numerous scholarly proposals; Luke seems to be combining Q and L, both of them primarily Jesus' sayings mixed with some narrative, according to the pre-existing literary order of those documents (see Paffenroth).

Samaritans Refuse to "Welcome" Jesus, Whose Face Is Set toward Jerusalem (9:51-56)

"When the days were 'fulfilled' *(symplērousthai)* for him 'to be taken up' *(analēmpseōs),* he set his face to go to Jerusalem." The verb "fulfilled" is a variant of the verb in Luke's preface (1:1): "many have put their hand to organizing a narrative of the events fulfilled among us." In this instance, not only Jesus' death and resurrection have been prophesied, but also his ascension to lordship (20:41-44 [Ps 110:1]; 22:69; 24:25-27; Acts 1:11, 22; 2:33-36 [again Ps 110:1]; Rom 8:34; 1 Cor 15:25; Phil 2:9-11) and his defeat of the people's enemies (see 1:51-52, 71, 73).

The terminology alludes to Elijah's being taken up to heaven (2 Kgs 2:1). The disciples' call for fire from heaven to consume the Samaritan villagers echoes both Elijah's similar call (2 Kgs 1:10, 12) and Phineas killing those who disobey Moses' laws (see Josephus *Ant.* 4.126-55, esp. 153-55), but Jesus rebukes them for the suggestion (contrast Acts 5:1-11). Even though the Samaritans did not "welcome" him (see the commentary on 9:48), Jesus refuses to call for immediate eschatological judgment, but as the apostles are to do, he proceeds to another village (see Acts 1:8). In conclusion, Jesus ended the Galilean ministry emphasizing the "welcoming" of children (9:48), the marginal, into the community, and Luke begins Jesus' journey narrating the Samaritans' refusal to "welcome" Jesus and the apostles (9:53). The literary transition focuses on questions of the community's inclusiveness (see Acts 10–11, 15) and on the rejection or acceptance of the community's messengers who proclaim the Word, to which God will not respond by immediate eschatological judgment (see Acts 1:6-7).

Ultimate Commitment by Those Proclaiming the Kingdom (9:57-62)

Some early preachers were itinerants, as Jesus had been, and the saying in 9:58 challenges those volunteering to be messengers with the model of the itinerant Jesus, the Son of Humanity. Jesus calls a second follower, and radically characterizes the commitment to Jesus that is involved as beyond commitment to family. The saying is phrased in a way that would offend virtually all ancient value systems, which demanded burial of relatives. Precisely since family values were central in the ancient world as they are in the modern one, ultimate values were often placed in tension with valuing family (e.g., Dionysius *Rom. Ant.* 3.16-21). Jesus states that "proclaiming the kingdom of God" is more important than family relationships and responsibilities (v. 60). The third saying is similarly offensive, indeed, nearly incomprehensible: one must not only leave family, but not even say good-bye (v. 61; see 14:26). The three sayings are so radical that some place them in the category of hyperbole, dramatic sayings not meant to be taken literally; but for Christians this cannot mean that they are not to be taken with ultimate seriousness.

Jesus Sends Out Seventy Workers (10:1-16)

Jesus for a second time has prophesied his death (9:43b-46), but not understanding who he is, a Messiah who will be crucified, the disciples have quarreled over who will be the greatest, that is, the leaders (9:46-48). They tried to "forbid" others to exercise ministry (9:49-50) and prematurely called for God's eschatological judgment on hearers who reject the message (9:52-56). Despite these ecclesiastical misunderstandings and quarrels, Jesus chooses and appoints seventy others and sends them out to "cure the sick . . . and say, 'The kingdom of God has come near to you'" (v. 9; see v. 11). This is a church order instructing the messengers about how to carry out their mission and how to respond when they are accepted or rejected.

The Lord appoints seventy or seventy-two to send out (10:1, 17). The manuscript evidence for either reading is strong, although manuscript support for seventy-two is slightly stronger ($\mathfrak{p}^{75}$ B D have seventy-two in v. 1, but $\mathfrak{p}^{45}$ has seventy in v. 17). The harder choice concerns the numbers' meaning. It refers either to the list of nations in Genesis 10 or to the seventy elders Moses appointed to assist him (Exod 24:1; Num 11:16, 24); that is, it either foreshadows the mission of the church to all the nations or it concerns church leadership in analogy to Israel. To complicate the matter, the Hebrew text of Genesis 10 lists seventy nations and the Greek text seventy-two, although neither text names the number itself. The preceding Lukan context has discussed leaders, as does the text itself (10:2-5, 7, 9-12), those who want to be "greatest," but the passage itself also concerns those who welcome or reject them (vv. 6, 8), as does the following context (vv. 13-16). A chapter earlier Jesus calls the twelve together and gives them similar powers and a similar message (9:1-6); that is, it focuses on leaders. The weight of external and internal/contextual evidence favors seventy, with the analogy being to the seventy elders Moses appointed (Num 11:16).

Jesus' sending them out by pairs is reflected in Acts, for example, Paul and Barnabas (11:30; 13:1) and Paul and Silas (15:40). Some pairs probably consisted of male and female workers (e.g., Andronicus and Junia in Rom 16:7). Jesus' own itinerant entourage in Galilee and on the journey to Jerusalem included both (8:1-3; 23:49). Luke balances both individuals and groups of males and females (e.g., 2:25-35, 36-38; Acts 1:13-14; 9:36, 39, 41), and Paul asks, "Do we not have the right to be accompanied by a sister, a woman *(adelphē gynaika)*, as do the other apostles and the brothers of the Lord and Cephas" (1 Cor 9:5)? Women's relation to teaching is traditional in Titus 2:3-5, but not in the *Acts of Paul and Thecla* 3:26, "And Thecla said to Paul: 'I will cut my hair short and follow you wherever you go'"). This could explain why some of Jesus' followers were (accused of being) prostitutes (Matt 21:31). Lucian (*The Runaways* 18) satirizes some contemporary Cynic preachers who "carry off the wives of their hosts to seduce them . . . pretending that the women are going to become philosophers; then they tender them, as common property, to all their associates. . . ." On the other hand, the early Jesus movement and the earliest Pauline churches were gender-fair in ways that Luke no longer approves: there is no Thecla preaching in Luke's Acts, although, uniquely, the widow Anna does "praise God" and "speak about the child" in public (2:38). Acts (21:9) later refers to Philip's virgin daughters "who had the gifts of prophecy," but Luke does not record any words they speak in public (compare the wise but silent Eumetis in Plutarch 148 B-E, cited in Osiek and Balch: 129).

Jesus' call includes two proverbs (10:2-3), followed by instructions about positive responses (vv. 5-9) and negative ones (vv. 10-11); positive responses describe entering households (vv. 5-7) and towns (vv. 8-9). The first proverb concerns the crisis of getting in the harvest. Weather during harvesttime is potentially destructive, so more laborers are imperative (v. 2). The second proverb is a warning that the messengers, sheep, will be attacked by "wolves" (v. 3; see 6:22; 21:16-17), which include "wolves" in the church who, Paul says later, will entice disciples to follow them (Acts 20:29-30), another address to church leaders (10:17). People in that agrarian culture were typically closer to nature than are modern First-World people, closer to carnivores whose diet included other animals or humans.

On 10:4 (no purse, bag, sandals, or greetings), see the comments on 9:1-17 above, although the prohibitions — except the bag — given the twelve do not match those given to the seventy. The prohibition of sandals would make these messengers look more like Cynic preachers. Musonius (*Orat.* 19.120.32–122.11, trans. Lutz) insists that appropriate clothing strengthens and invigorates the body but is not to make it soft or approve its appearance. Musonius gives wise advice to Cynics, that they are better off not being "bound" by sandals; this takes on eschatological urgency in Luke for those who are reaping the harvest, who have no time for greetings on the road.

The first proverb envisions a positive response to the proclamation described in 10:5-9. These itinerants accepted hospitality in Greco-Roman households, in shops, atrium houses, or apartment buildings *(insulae)*. Both in Musonius and in the early Jesus movement, there is tension between being a barefoot preacher and owning a house (see Luke 18:28; 5:11). Musonius's oration continues,

> whatever a natural cave would offer, furnishing a moderate shelter for man, this our houses ought to furnish for us. . . . What good are courtyards surrounded by colonnades. . . . How much nobler than spending money for sticks and stones to spend it on men? (Musonius *Orat.* 19.122, 15-17, 18-19, 27-28, trans. Lutz)

But Jesus was ambivalent: householders could indeed offer hospitality to the messengers (10:5-7; see Acts 5:42; 11:12-14; 16:15, 31; 18:8; 20:20; 21:8; Rom 16:3-5a; 1 Cor 16:15, 19; Phlm 2). But they are to "remain in the same house," presumably not moving to a finer house that would include the pitfalls satirized by Lucian in *On Salaried Posts in Great Houses!* Such visitors may "have the noblest Romans for their friends," and are "eating expensive dinners without paying" (*Salaried Posts* 3).

Their message includes, "Peace to this household!" (10:5), a message prophesied by Zechariah (1:79), celebrated by angels (2:14), and delivered by the resurrected Christ to the eleven (24:36). Peter delivered this message of peace to Cornelius (Acts 10:36; see Eph 2:14, 17); therefore, in this context, God's "peace" announced to a Gentile is the equivalent of the final word of Jesus' inaugural, who has come "to proclaim the year of the Lord's acceptance" (*dekton;* 4:19 quoting Isa 61:2).

Not coincidentally, then, the messengers are told to "eat what is set before you" (Luke 10:8), which both Peter (Acts 10:13-14, 48; 11:7) and Paul do (Acts 16:15, 34). This Greek phrase (*esthiete ta paratithemena hymin;* v. 8) is virtually identical to Paul's instruction to the Corinthians, "If an unbeliever invites you to a meal and you are disposed to go, eat whatever is set before you" (*pan to paratithemenon hymin esthiete;* 1 Cor 10:27). With various nuances, the message is what the angel told Peter in a vision (Acts 10:13-15).

Luke repeatedly omits an idea from Mark, but narrates its equivalent in Acts (e.g., Mark 10:45 reformulated in Acts 20:28), correcting Mark's view of the history of salvation by writing a narrative that is more "orderly" (*kathexēs;* Luke 1:3). Luke omits Mark 7:1-23, especially v. 19, narrating its substance not in Jesus' lifetime, the second period of salvation history, but in the period of the church (Acts 10), making ecclesiology virtually the equivalent of Christology. Nevertheless, Luke 10:8 is a clear anticipation of Peter's vision in Acts and is verbally identical to Paul's advice in 1 Corinthians, although, inconsistently, Luke subsequently argues that Paul is orthopraxic (Acts 21:21-24).

When the messengers are not "welcomed" (10:10-12), they are to shake the dust off their feet (see the comments on 9:1-17, esp. v. 5). Here the symbolic action is followed by curses (10:12-15; see 1:20 and 2 Cor 2:15-16). Whether one receives God's "peace" or God's "woe" is related to whether the house or city "welcomes" the apostles and later the seventy who proclaim the kingdom and heal (Luke 9:5, 53; 10:8, 10) and related to "welcoming" children (Luke 9:48-49). This is the key question before and after the narrative transition into Jesus' long journey to Jerusalem (at 9:51; see 9:48-49 and 53 followed by 10:8, 10), and in volume two becomes a debate over welcoming a "foreigner" like Cornelius (Acts 10:28, 35, 36, 43). The "historians" Dionysius *(Roman Antiquities)* and Luke (Luke-Acts) both emphasize the contemporary question whether the people "welcome" foreigners into their group. Josephus emphasizes the same debate from the opposite point of view: there should be no "mixing" of Israelites with Madianites/Midianites (*Ant.* 4.126-55, 159, 183, 228, 294 retelling Numbers 25; see the comments above on 9:1-17 and 9:46-48, 49-50).

Chorazin and Bethsaida did not repent in response to "deeds of power," but Tyre and Sidon would have (10:14). Luke knows that these cities later did respond to the messengers (Acts 21:3, 7); 10:14 is virtually a "prophecy."

The final saying asserts that "whoever rejects *(a-thetōn)* you rejects *(athetei)* me" (v. 16); this verb begins with an alpha privative, an alpha that negates the verb *(a-tithēmi)*. Without the negative, the verb occurs repeatedly in Acts; instead of "rejecting" the message, persons are "added" to the church: "so those who welcomed *(apodexamenoi)* his message were baptized, and that day about three thousand persons were added *(prosetethēsan)*" (Acts 2:41; see Acts 2:47; 5:14; 11:24). Dionysius similarly remarks that Romulus "welcomed" *(hypodechesthai)* fugitives, and these "additions *(prostithēntes)* were so successful that the Roman people became inferior in numbers to none of the nations that were most populous" (*Rom. Ant.* 2.15.3 and 16.3). "Welcoming" "foreigners" brings "additions" that cause "growth," both in Rome and in Jerusalem. On the other hand, "whoever rejects me rejects the one who sent me" (Luke 10:16c).

Return of the Seventy (10:17-24)

The seventy return with joy (10:17, an eschatological joy announced already by angels and canticles in the infancy narrative in 1:14; 2:10), a joy associated with reception of Christ or the Word (8:13; 15:7, 10; Acts 8:8; 13:52; 15:3).

The demons were subject to them, they report, "in your name" (10:17), as the demons had been subject to Jesus (4:35, 41; 8:2, 29, 33; 9:1, 42, 49; 11:14-23; 13:32, the last mention of demons in the Gospel, with only one reference in Acts [17:18]). Jesus responds that he "saw" Satan fall from heaven, saw eschatological victory. Jesus must later deny that he operates by Satan's power (11:18-20). Satan has power to bind people, it is assumed, but Jesus gives freedom from bondage precisely on God's day, the sabbath (13:16). Satan influences Judas to cooperate with those who oppose Jesus, the chief priests (22:3), and demons have power to sift Peter (22:31). Satan can deceive Christians, for example, stimulating Ananias to lie to the church and to God (Acts 5:3). Most important, in Acts Luke presents Paul narrating his commission to Agrippa: Jesus sent Paul to the Gentiles to open their eyes so that they might turn from darkness to light (Isa 42:7 and 49:6, also echoed in Luke 2:30, 32; Acts 1:8; 13:47) and "from the power of Satan to God, so that they may receive forgiveness of sins . . ." (26:18; see Isa 14:12; Rev 12:7-10). 10:19 continues this apocalyptic imagery: the seventy had authority to walk on serpents and scorpions (see Luke 11:11-12; Rev 9:3). And in v. 20, this cluster of sayings concludes as it began, with rejoicing, now that their names are written in the book of life (see Rev 3:5; 13:8). For Jesus' disciples, conflict with evil means victory — with many persecutions (Acts 14:22).

10:21 and 22 are sayings Luke has in common with Matthew (Q), but it is distinctly Lukan that Jesus "rejoices in the Holy Spirit," the kind of "rejoicing" celebrated in the infancy hymns (1:14, 44) and at Pentecost (Acts 2:26, 46). Mary's "spirit rejoiced in God my Savior . . ." (1:47). At Pentecost Peter quotes King David, whose tongue "rejoiced" that God would not abandon his soul in Hades (Acts 2:26-27 quoting Ps 16[15]:9). Jesus rejoices in the Holy Spirit (10:21) in wisdom language: God's revelation comes to the simple, not to the wise (see 1 Cor 1:18-25; 3:1).

10:22, however, has been called the "Johannine thunderbolt" among Q sayings (see John 3:35; 10:14-15; 13:3). "Righteous Father, the world does not know you, but I have known you, and these know that you have sent me" (John 17:25). The exclusive claim to salvation in this Q saying is made over against those whose Messiah seeks (military) authority over the cosmos (against Rome; see 4:6), against those offended by the gospel for the poor (7:22), who say Jesus has a demon, that he has come eating bread and drinking wine (7:33-34; 11:19-20; 12:10), who reject the reign of God (10:9-10), and primarily against those who do not "rejoice" at the eschatological message of Jesus' humiliation and exaltation and at Mary's and Peter's responses at the beginning of Luke and Acts. Finally, Jesus blesses those who see and hear what prophets and kings did not (vv. 23-24).

The Son of God's Way to Inherit Eternal Life: Love of God and Neighbor (10:25-42)

Jesus, the Son who has claimed to know the Father, is now asked by a lawyer about what to do to inherit eternal life (10:25). One who knows the Mosaic law tests Jesus, not as in Matthew about individual laws but about what he must do to inherit "(eternal) life," the goal of the law (Lev 18:5). Jesus returns the question by asking him, "What is written in the law?" (v. 26). He answers by quoting Deut 6:4 and Lev 19:18, the commands to love God and neighbor. This is strikingly different from the stories in Mark and Matthew, in which Gospels a lawyer asks Jesus about the first or great commandment (Mark 12:28 par. Matt 22:36) and *Jesus* answers. In Luke, Jesus affirms that the lawyer has "given the right answer" (10:28).

The Samaritan Does What Is Written in the Law, Loving the Neighbor (10:29-37)

By means of the lawyer's third response to Jesus, "And who is my neighbor?" Luke joins the parable of the good Samaritan to this context. Jesus has determined to go to Jerusalem, but on the way he has been rejected by a village of Samaritans. He has sent out seventy healers and proclaimers, presumably in Samaria (which Matt 10:5-6 forbids), who have returned with joy.

Luke the historian narrates two stories about how life — as revealed by the Son of the Father (10:22) — is to be lived. One of the two central characters, a Samaritan, has an ancestry from mixed nations, mixed marriages, and mixed customs (2 Kgs 17:24-41; Josephus *Ant.* 9.288-91; 11.306-12, 340-47). Josephus relates the origin of the Samaritans during a time when the high priest, many priests, and other Israelites had married foreign women (*Ant.* 11.306-8, 312; see Ezra 9:12; 10:2-3, 10-44; Neh 10:30; 13:1-3, 23-31). The elders of Jerusalem, however, believed that those who wanted to transgress the laws took foreign wives and that this was the beginning of community with foreigners (*allophylous . . . koinōnias archēn; Ant.* 11.307). Samaritans are "apostates" who often deny they are Jews, confessing the truth, but when Jews experience good fortune, they grasp at community (*koinōnia*) with them and trace their genealogy back to Ephraim and Manasseh (*Ant.* 11.340-41). Josephus observes that when any Jew is accused of eating unclean food or violating the sabbath, they flee to the Samaritans (*Ant.* 11.346-47).

The Roman view of their own origins and subsequent Roman political policy was just the opposite: they mixed races, the native and the foreign, by marriages, which resulted in the mingling of customs, laws, and religious ceremonies (Dionysius *Rom. Ant.* 1.60.2-3; Philo *Legat.* 147; see Balch 1998: 31-32). Rome "welcomes" other races into citizenship, "mixing" many nations (Dionysius *Rom. Ant.* 1.90.2; 3.10.4; 3.11.5), exactly what the Jewish martyrs Eleazar and the mother with her seven sons died to oppose (2 Maccabees 6–7). This contrast between political policies in Rome and in Jerusalem led to the Jews being accused of being unfriendly (*amiktōn*) and unsocial, the enemy of all humankind (*Ant.* 11.212).

For Luke's Greek audience, Scythians would be "outsiders" equivalent to Samaritans: Aristophanes, *Thesmophoriazousai* 1082-35, satirizes Scythian archers' broken Greek and their ludicrous relation to women. But five centuries later, in Luke's time, Lucian (*The Scythian* or *Consul*) praises the Scythians' ability to become Greek, no longer satirizing them.

At the beginning of his journey to Jerusalem the Jew Jesus is teaching the disciples, including the seventy he has sent out in Samaria, that a half-breed, irreligious Samaritan has done what the Father wills in Torah, loving his neighbor (Lev 19:18), and the Samaritan will inherit eternal life, the reward promised to the covenant people (Lev 18:5). But the Jerusalem priest and Levite have not done "what is written in the law" (Luke 10:26). Jesus is indeed on the way to the cross (9:22, 43-45).

Mary, Not Martha, Does What Is Written in the Law, Loving God (10:38-42)

The argument is offensive in modern egalitarian culture, but in Greco-Roman culture as well as in ancient Judaism women were perceived as "weak" both physically and mentally (see 1 Pet 3:7). Historians sometimes used them as examples, implying that if a woman could exemplify this value, certainly men could and should. The mother whose seven sons died rather than eat the unclean pork offered by Antiochus Epiphanes is such a paradigm: "even a woman's mind despised many pains" (4 Macc 14:11; see 4:25; 16:1, 5, 12-13; 17:1-6; 18:20, 22). Lucretia, too, was such a paradigm: she was raped by Sextus, son of the Roman king Tarquinius, a crime that caused Brutus to expel the corrupt kings and institute Roman consuls to govern the city (Dionysius *Rom. Ant.* 4.63-85). Lucretia was overwhelmed with shame (4.66.1), tells of terrible wrongs, then kills herself, which struck the Romans with horror and compassion (4.67); they retell her story to generate the will to throw out the tyrants. "O admirable woman and worthy of great praise for your noble resolution! . . . After this example, Lucretia, when you, who were given a woman's nature, have shown the resolution of a brave man, shall we, who were born men, show ourselves inferior to women in courage? . . . Nay, but we must all choose one of two things — life with liberty or death with glory" (4.82).

Jesus had sent out the seventy with instructions about accepting hospitality in houses: when people "welcome" them, they are to eat what is set before them, cure the sick, and proclaim, "the kingdom of God has come near to you" (Luke 10:8-9). Martha "welcomed" Jesus into her house (v. 38) and "served" (*diakonein*) him (v. 40), which Jesus, however, saw as her being "worried (*merimnąs*) and distracted" (v. 41). Paul, too, wants the Corinthians not to be "distracted" (*amerimnous;* 1 Cor 7:32), and invites them to make the major decision concerning whether to remain single or to be married on the basis of which state is "distracting."

Mary, on the contrary, was "listening to his word" (Luke 10:39; see 5:1, 15; 6:27, 47, 49; 7:22; 8:8, 15, 18; 9:35; 10:24, 39; 11:28, 31; 16:29, 31; Acts 2:6, 33, 37). As Jesus observes later, "The queen of the South . . . came from the ends of the earth to listen to the wisdom of Solomon, and see, something greater than Solomon is here!" (11:31). Moses commanded that the people "must listen" to whatever the coming prophet tells them (Acts 3:22 [Deut 18:15-16]), and Isaiah has harsh words of judgment for those who listen but do not understand, whose ears are hard of hearing (Acts 28:27 [Isa 6:10]). Neither Moses nor Isaiah specified gender, nor does Jesus, despite the fact that a woman's role as a learning disciple was often found to be offensive in that culture. There were exceptions: Axiothea attended Plato's academy, and she even wore the philosopher's cloak "without offense as did the men" (Cancik: 689-90). Hipparchia, the companion of the Cynic Crates, is also famous, not only for listening but also for an argument putting down Theodorus the atheist (Diogenes Laertius 6.97). The "countless tales" told of her are striking partially because she has few peers. Diogenes gives us Hipparchia's argument, but Luke nowhere presents a woman's sermon. Luke does present women who are models for both men and women, especially Mary for "listening to the word" and for loving and responding to it despite social, cultural customs that would have prohibited her from listening and learning.

Jesus' Model Prayer (11:1-13)

Jesus prays at major events in his ministry (3:21; 5:16; 6:12; 22:44), as does the church at crucial points in salvation history (Acts 1:24; 6:6; 9:11; 11:5; 13:3; 14:23; 16:25; 20:36; 21:5; 22:17; 28:8). The Jewish Eighteen Benedictions were also formulated in the first century of our era, and apparently John's disciples had a structured form of prayer (11:1). It fits that Jesus, too, taught the disciples set phrases for prayer. Some of the Matthean wording may be more original, for example, "forgive us our debts" (6:12a), whereas Luke substitutes "forgive us our sins" (11:4a). But the Lukan structure is more original, without "in heaven" (Matt 6:9b), "your will be done" (v. 10b), or "on earth as it is in heaven" (v. 10c). Nor did Jesus' original prayer have the final benediction, "for the kingdom, the power, and the glory are yours forever, amen" (v. 13c).

Jesus addresses God by "Father," a Greek noun in the Lord's Prayer, which many have argued was derived from Jesus' use of the Aramaic *Abba,* an address transliterated into Greek in Mark 14:36, Rom 8:15, and Gal 4:6. Recent discussions of this address have shown that Jews at Qumran prayed to God as "Father" (4Q372 1 and 4Q460; D'Angelo: 618-19), so that Jesus was using a designation also used by other Jews in at least three ways: to address God as the refuge of the persecuted, for an assurance of forgiveness, or as the "Father" whose providence governs the world (D'Angelo: 621). D'Angelo argues that by using this address, Jesus also challenged the Roman imperial patriarchy and the patriarchal family. Readers of the Gospel of Luke must agree that Jesus did at a minimum subordinate family to the kingdom of God (18:28-29; 20:34-35).

The first petition, "Hallowed be your name," recognizes God's otherness from humanity, God's sovereignty. Isaiah hears the LORD demand: "do not fear what it [the people in Judea] fear [the kings of Damascus and northern Israel] or be in dread. But the LORD of hosts, him shall you shall regard as holy; let him be your fear, and sanctuary . . ." (8:13-14; see Ezek 20:9; 36:23-24). God is awesome and holy, and the nations who have political power over Israel are not.

The second petition, "Your kingdom come," is then similar to the first. "All the kingdoms of the world" are a temptation Jesus rejects (4:5). Rather, the poor, the utterly destitute, are promised the kingdom of God (6:20). Jesus comforts the "little flock" because "it is your Father's good pleasure to give you the kingdom. Sell your possessions . . ." (12:32-33a). There will still be a messianic banquet — for the crippled, blind, lame (14:15, 21), and children (18:16; see 22:16, 29). When Jesus sent out the seventy, they were to cure the sick and say, "The kingdom of God has come near to you" (10:9); the demonic forces of evil have and are being defeated (10:17-18). Jesus says that some who are present will not die before they see the kingdom of God (9:27); on the other hand, the author of this Gospel cautions, "The kingdom of God is not coming with things that can be observed; nor will they say, 'Look, here it is!' or 'There it is!' For in fact, the kingdom of God is among you" (17:20-21; see 19:11). In its first verses the second volume raises the question of the kingdom and interprets it in light of "the promise of the Father," the baptism "with the Holy Spirit not many days from now" (Acts 1:3-5). Similarly, Marcion's substitute for the second petition (at 11:2) was, "Let your holy spirit come upon us and sanctify us."

The three following petitions make requests for "us," for "our" bread, forgiveness, and deliverance. In both Matthew (6:11) and Luke (11:3) the petition for bread contains a Greek word *(epiousion)* of unknown meaning. Luke's verb is present tense (expressing continuous action in Greek) imperative: "(you please) be giving" us, and Luke adds "daily" to the petition. Interpreters typically ask whether this is ordinary bread or the eschatological bread of the messianic banquet (Isa 25:6-8; see Exod 16:8), but this is probably a false alternative. The first beatitude (6:20) has an irreducible economic component that some interpreters try to eliminate, and so does the petition for bread: it refers to ordinary bread for the hungry. If we interpret the Lord's Prayer in light of Jesus' first beatitude, "Blessed are you beggars, for yours is the kingdom of God," the petition for bread is also eschatological. In history written in Jesus' time, the "poor," that is, laborers and artisans, lacked "the necessities of daily life" (*ton kath' hēmeran;* Isocrates *Panegyricus* 34, 168; *On the Peace* 46; *To Philip* 120; Dionysius *Rom. Ant.* 6.23.3; 56.3), and they demanded "forgiveness of all their debts" (*pantas opheisthai tōn ophlematōn;* Dionysius *Rom. Ant.* 6.83.4). Jesus' model petition uses the same verb and participle: "Forgive us our sins, for we ourselves *forgive* every one who is *indebted* to us" (Luke 11:4a). The Lukan petition emphasizes "sins," different from Matthew's "forgive us our debts" (6:12), but Luke does retain an emphasis on "debts" (besides 11:4a see also 7:41; 13:4; 16:5, 7; 17:10). Patrons would graciously "forgive the debts" of clients, who in turn would recognize that they were receiving favors (Dionysius 6.63.3; see 7.8.1). Both the petition to God for bread and the one for forgiveness of debts have irreducible material aspects and include a reference to ordinary bread and financial debts. For First-World Christians it is shocking to hear that Jesus has a claim on money that we loan. God is to forgive our sins, we persuade God, "for we ourselves forgive every one who is financially indebted to us" (11:4b).

The final petition is for God not to "bring us to the time of trial" (11:4c). Jesus was "tempted/tried" by the devil (4:2, 13), and later he tells the disciples "to pray that you may not come into the time of trial" (22:40; see v. 46). Jesus addresses the apostles at the last supper as those "who have stood by me in my trials" (22:28). Some hear the Word and "receive" it with joy but fall away in a time of "testing" (8:13). Paul, however, through the plots of the Jews, did experience "trials" in Asia (Acts 20:19), which must refer to his difficulties in Iconium (Acts 14:5), Lystra (14:19), and Ephesus (19:9, 23-41). Thus his preaching of the Word generated urban tensions, his being stoned, public debates, and a riot. In the narrative of Luke-Acts, this petition assumes that itinerant preaching of the gospel by Jesus and Paul generates opposition, urban conflict, and "testing" for preachers and for believers associated with them (Luke 8:13; 22:28, 40; Acts 19:29). The inclusive gospel preached by Jesus (e.g., Luke 10:33, 42), Peter (Acts 11:2-3), Stephen (Acts 7:52-54), and Paul (Acts 21:21-22; 22:21-22) generates offense. During his own journey to Jerusalem, which began with rejection by Samaritans (9:53), Jesus encourages his disciples to pray that they might not have to experience such "tests" that would cause some to lose their faith (see Josephus *Ant.* 14.245-46; 16.41-45). Jesus, the apostles, and Paul and their companions are examples of those who withstood such tests.

Parable of a Shameless Neighbor (11:5-8)

"Suppose one of you has a friend," this paragraph begins, making the ancient assumption that friends have responsibilities in relation to each other, one of which is to share possessions in common. But in the parable, either the friend needing bread for a guest or the friend who is already in bed and is being asked to get up and give bread is called "shameless" (*anaideia;* 11:8), acting in a way the culture perceives to be irresponsible or immoral in the relationship (Sir 25:22; Josephus *J.W.* 1.224; *Ant.* 17.119). It is difficult to imagine that the friend asking for help is acting irresponsibly, so the friend who refuses to get out of bed must be the one accused by the powerful adjective "shameless." The parable presents a human situation and argues to the certainty that God, unlike the sleepy householder, will not be shameless, refusing to respond to prayer. Such a strong parable risks promoting magic, encouraging humans to believe that we can manipulate God by our prayers, a possibility Luke addresses in the following paragraph.

Everyone Who Asks in Prayer Receives (11:9-13)

As human beings we ask, search, and knock, three metaphors with which Jesus assures the disciples that God responds to prayer, that God gives, enables finding, and opens doors. 11:11-12 use different images than in Jesus' previous parable (vv. 5-8), but the effect is similar: as a parent will give a child what is good for that child, not what is harmful, so God will give to one praying. However, unlike Matthew (7:11), who simply says that God will give "good things" to one asking, Luke specifies "holy spirit" as the gift (11:13), both anticipating Pentecost (Acts 2) and avoiding magic, not promising whatever we desire or that prayer will extract disciples from suffering and persecution (see 22:39-46 and Acts). We pray that we not be "tested"; Acts shows that Paul was. God remains the acting subject, giving what God says we need, not whatever we feel we may need.

Either Demonic Rule or God's Rule (11:14-36)

In the narrative, suddenly Jesus is interacting with a "crowd," not with the disciples. Some in the crowd "test" Jesus, as the devil had done earlier (4:2), seeing that he was exorcising demons, but attributing the power to Beelzeboul, ruler of the demons. This section makes assumptions similar to Paul's in Rom 6:14-23: human beings are not self-sufficient but are "slaves" to one of two powers, to good or evil, God or Beelzeboul.

The crowd not only wants exorcisms but demands "a sign (*sēmeion*) from heaven" (11:16). "Signs" are common in John and in Acts (2:22, 43; 4:16, 22, 30; 5:12; 6:8; 7:36; 8:6, 13; 14:3; 15:12; see 2 Cor 12:12), but occur in the Gospel of Luke only at 11:16 and 29. Knowing their thoughts (11:17; see 2:34-35; 5:22; 7:39 [prophets know inner thoughts]; 9:47; 24:38), Jesus distrusts their demand for a sign (compare John 2:23-25). Jesus responds that a kingdom or a house divided becomes a desert. Then he asks by whom their exorcists drive out demons.

Josephus, an aristocratic, educated Jew, who like Luke writes a "history" of Judaism, makes similar assumptions. Josephus says that King Solomon excelled in prudence and wisdom and composed incantations for exorcisms (*Ant.* 8.41-45), which a certain Eleazar recited before Vespasian. He put certain roots under the nose of an affected man, and as the man smelled them, drew the demon out through his nostrils and then commanded the demon to overturn a basin of water as it left (*Ant.* 8.47-48). This proved that God favored Solomon and that he possessed great virtue. Pagans made similar assumptions. To explain Beelzeboul, Eusebius quotes Porphyry (who wrote AD 260-305), *Of the Philosophy to Be Derived from Oracles,* as follows:

> Every house is also full of them [evil daemons], and on this account, when they [pagans] are going to call down the gods, they purify the house first, and cast these daemons out. Our bodies are also full of them, for they especially delight in certain kinds of food; and this is the reason of the purification, not chiefly on account of the gods, but in order that these evil daemons may depart. But most of all they delight in blood and in impure meats, and enjoy these by entering into those who use them. (Eusebius *Preparation for the Gospel* 174d, trans. Edwin Gifford)

The objection to Jesus' exorcism is not the modern one whether demons exist, but a question about whether Jesus' power originated from evil or good power, a question that Jesus returns to them about their own exorcists.

Jesus' power is not from Beelzeboul, but "by the power of God I cast out demons." Therefore, "the kingdom of God has come to you" (11:20). The verb "has come" is past tense: this has already happened! Roman historians announce the victory of their armies; as a "historian" Luke proclaims Jesus' initial defeat of demonic evil "by the finger of God" (v. 20; see Exod 8:19 of Moses, the only other text that uses this phrase), even though society has not become a messianic utopia. Jesus is the stronger one, who has attacked and overpowered Beelzeboul's "house" or "castle" and is dividing the goods (11:21-22). One must choose sides (v. 23, a variant of 9:50). The war is not over, as Paul also agrees in Romans 6: a person who is victorious and free may still submit to demonic power. The evil demon may bring other evil spirits and repossess the person, Jesus warns (vv. 24-26).

A woman has a different response than the accusation in 11:15: Jesus' mother is "blessed" (v. 27), a blessing that Jesus corrects. "Blessed rather are those who hear the word of God and obey it!" (v. 28, a saying unique to Luke; see the commentary at Luke 8:4-15). Mary is a disciple because she "believed" the Lord (1:45), not because she bore Jesus. Similarly, Luke-Acts nowhere names James Jesus' "brother"; rather, he leads the Jerusalem church by prayer (Acts 1:14), by knowledge of the prophets (Acts 15:13-17), and by being zealous for the law (Acts 21:17-26). The word translated "obey" in 11:28 means "guard." Stephen later accuses his audience of not "guarding" the law (Acts 7:53), and James suggests a way to Paul to prove that he does "guard" the law (21:24), the Mosaic law that Jesus interprets in Luke 24:44-47.

Others wanted not an exorcism but a "sign" (11:16). All three Synoptic Gospels note that some were seeking a sign, and that Jesus responded by calling them an "evil generation" (v. 29). Only Matthew and Luke (Q) add the saying about Jonah and the queen of the South. As Jonah was a sign to the people of Nineveh, so will the Son of Humanity be to this generation (v. 30), which Matthew (12:40) clarifies by adding a reference to the Son of Humanity being "three days and three nights in the heart of the earth." Luke's vague reference may refer rather to Jonah's (and Jesus') preaching (see Luke 11:32 and Jonah 1:2; 3:2, 4), Jonah to the Gentiles of Nineveh, Jesus to the Samaritans, also not accepted as Jews (see the commentary on 10:29-37). Not only the "men" of Nineveh, however, but a woman, the queen of the South (11:31; see 1 Kings 10), "heard the word of God" (v. 28) from Solomon. As noted above, Solomon was known for his "prudence and wisdom" as well as for his "knowledge of the art used against demons . . . for healing" (Josephus *Ant.* 8.41, 45), so it is probably not accidental that Jesus the exorcist is here called greater even than Solomon (11:31), although he is misunderstood.

Sayings with the catchwords "lamp" and "light" follow, suggesting perhaps that Jesus' preaching generates this light (11:33), which is rejected because the hearers are full of darkness (vv. 34-35).

Jesus Denounces Pharisees and Lawyers (11:37-54)

In the Gospel, Pharisees do come to hear Jesus (5:17), but question and criticize when Jesus heals on the sabbath or eats with sinners (5:21, 30, 33; 6:2, 7; 7:36, 39; 14:1, 3; 15:2). They are observantly pious, not sinners (18:10-11). Some of these orthodox Jews are believers (Acts 15:5; see Acts 23:6-9), including the orthopraxic Pharisee Paul (Acts 26:5). Rejecting John, the Pharisees reject God's purpose (Luke 7:30), but, on the other hand, they assist Jesus against Herod (13:31; see Acts 5:34). A key to their identity occurs when the narrator refers to them as "lovers of money" (16:14). Luke would sometimes be read in the dining room *(triclinium)* of wealthy Greco-Roman houses, heard by Christians reclining as they ate the Lord's Supper (see 22:11-12, 24-27). Such houses were built to display and reinforce the social and economic status of their wealthy owners (Osiek and Balch: 29, 183). The Pharisees' controversies with Jesus about eating customs become transparent symbols for wealthy Christian leaders of house churches who offered space for the Lord's Supper (see Acts 5:42; 16:15, 31, 34; 18:8; 21:8). Those who heard the Gospel read would know little about the historical Jewish sect of Pharisees in early first-century Jerusalem, but they would be well aware of the "lovers of money" in their own society and house churches, who objected to riffraff eating in their beautiful, elite dining rooms! Tragically, Christians have usually read these "woes" as if Luke addressed them to outsiders, not to Christians hearing the Gospel read, an interpretation which has generated anti-Semitism. It is beyond tragic, even sinful that a Gospel written to argue for the inclusion of all has been read to exclude and vilify our Jewish forefathers and mothers through whom we Christians came to know God.

The Pharisees would ritually wash with water before meals so that they would be clean (see Leviticus 14; Numbers 19). Wealthy owners of Greek or Roman houses would go to the baths and wash, Romans around 3 p.m. and Greeks a little later, before they came home for a meal or a symposium. Paul objects that the rich would begin eating while others, perhaps the poor slaves who had fewer resources and less leisure, went hungry (1 Cor 11:20-22). The owner's slaves cooked and served the food from the kitchen, whose smells and noises were placed architecturally as far from the dining room as a large house would allow. Kitchens were "nowhere" where "dirty" "nobodies" worked (Osiek and Balch: 29-30, 199); owners, the nobly born and "clean" *(katharotaton),* would not invite the "indigent, filthy and such" to eat with them (Osiek and Balch: 204, citing Dionysius *Rom. Ant.* 8.71.3). Luke's story of Jesus eating with a Pharisee who is concerned about being "clean" (Luke 11:39-40) would be heard in Lukan house churches as a concern of the socially elite that Jesus opposes with a theological affirmation: "Did not the one who made the outside make the inside also?" (v. 40). Verse 41a has several possible meanings, literally "the inside things give for alms." This may refer to things inside the cup, or inside the person, or perhaps "because of inside things, give alms." But v. 41b concludes, "and see, everything will be clean *(kathara)* for you" (see 4:27; 10:8; Acts 10:14, 34; 11:8).

Luke then presents three woes that Jesus spoke to the Pharisees and three to the lawyers, woes like those in 6:24-26. The first woe curses the Pharisees because they tithe kitchen spices, obeying scriptural imperatives in minute matters (Deut 14:22-29; 26:12-15) but neglecting justice *(krisis)* and the love of God (11:42). Later Philip, interpreting Scripture for the Ethiopian eunuch, will present Jesus as the servant of Isaiah to whom "in his humiliation justice was denied" (Acts 8:33, quoting Isa 53:8). Similarly, Rome is typical of cities split in two, one part ruled by poverty, the other by satiety and insolence, but with modesty, order, and justice *(dikē)* in neither. Justice *(to dikaion)* in Roman society is exacted by force, like wild beasts trying to destroy the enemy (Dionysius *Rom. Ant.* 6.36.1). In opposing the poor in everything, however, a Roman aristocrat is not just (Dionysius *Rom. Ant.* 8.61.3). Again, Jesus' charges against the Pharisaic "lovers of money" would be heard in Mediterranean society as charges that ring true in an urban context. But "the love of God" had just been illustrated by a female disciple, despite opposition, listening to the Lord's word (10:27, 39).

The second woe fits this same context: patrons were given the best seats in synagogues — those hearing the Gospel read would easily hear "theaters" instead of "synagogues." The socially well-placed left their houses early in the morning in such cities exactly in order to be greeted — influential — in the marketplaces (11:43). This second woe virtually repeats 6:24, "Woe to you who are rich!"

The third woe assumes that "unmarked graves" make those walking over them unclean; in cities like Ostia and Pompeii, visitors today may still see that graves were erected outside the city. The third woe is strident: mere contact with these "lovers of money" makes one unclean, a reaction that comes dangerously close to reversing the typical clean/unclean taboos. Clearly, some in the Lukan house churches felt oppressed by rich, unjust patrons who did not love God.

The lawyers (see 7:30) feel attacked by Jesus' woes to the Pharisees and complain (11:45), and Jesus confirms their feelings: they are being criticized. Precisely a lawyer "tempts" Jesus in 10:25 with a legal question, illustrated also by 14:3 with the question whether it is lawful to cure people on the sabbath or not, disputes called "lawyers' quarrels" in Tit 3:9 (but see v. 13). Lawyers can make the law a "burden" (11:46), which others deny that it should be (Deut 30:11-14). The second woe (11:46-51) assumes that the descendants are like the progenitors: when descendants build tombs for the prophets, they must be like those who killed the prophets (see the *Lives of the Prophets,* trans. in Charlesworth: 2:379-99). 11:49 may quote the "Wisdom of God" as revealed to Jesus, may be Jesus' way of referring to himself, or may be a title for Jesus (see 1 Cor 1:24). The queen of Sheba came to hear Solomon's wisdom, and something greater than Solomon is here (11:31). Speaking in the first person, Wisdom says, "I will send them prophets and apostles, some of whom they will kill and persecute . . ." (v. 49; see Acts 7:52). These could be the "prophets of old" (1:70) or prophets in the present, either John, Jesus, or those whom Jesus sends out (1:76; 3:4; 4:24; 7:16, 26, 39; 9:19; 13:33-34; 20:6; 24:19-20). Two crucial texts connect Jesus as a prophet with death (13:33-34; 24:19-20). This, combined with the pairing "prophets and apostles," means that 11:49 probably refers to prophets in the present time (see Acts 11:27; 13:1; 15:32; 21:10-11; 1 Cor 12:28; Eph 2:20; 4:11) whom Wisdom is sending as martyrs. Jesus cites two such prototypical martyrs, Abel (Gen 4:8-10) and Zechariah (1 Chr 24:20-22). The third woe (11:52) curses those who know the law, who possess the key (10:27-28), but who will not enter (the kingdom; see Acts 14:22) and "hinder" others from entering. "Hinder" as used here is a legal term prohibiting certain practices (see, e.g., Acts 28:31; Josephus *Ant.* 16.41-45); for example, they try to hinder Jesus from healing people on the sabbath (14:3).

The end of this symposium is hostile, which was not uncommon. Lucian *The Carousal, or the Lapiths,* satirizes philosophers at a symposium that ends as a brawl! 11:53 contains a word *(apostomatizō)* that means "teach by dictation," which does not fit the present context; ancient commentators interpreted it to mean that they began to "watch Jesus' utterances closely" (BAGD) in order to trap him.

Jesus' Judgments concerning Civic Authority, Possessions, Slaves, and Family Relationships (12:1–13:9)

The Son of Humanity (12:8) will acknowledge those who do not fear civic authority, but who say rather what the Holy Spirit teaches them (v. 12), who do not value possessions (v. 15) but rather God (v. 21). They are not anxious about their life (v. 22) but are concerned rather for the kingdom (v. 32). They therefore sell their possessions (v. 33), are slaves who astoundingly will be served by their master (v. 37), managerial slaves to whom much is entrusted and from whom much will be demanded (v. 48). They will experience divided household relationships (v. 53). And they know how to interpret the present time (v. 56) and have repented in the time allotted (13:3, 5).

Do Not Fear Domestic or Civic Authority, but Rather God (12:1-12)

The warning against the Pharisees' hypocrisy (12:1) connects this section with what has gone before; the theme still concerns powerful, wealthy patrons who have the power of life and death over clients, wives, children, and slaves in their households (see, e.g., Dionysius *Rom. Ant.* 2.9; 2.25-27; 5.6-8). Theaters and theatrical masks were very popular in Greco-Roman cities, and were often used to decorate houses. Jesus accuses some of being "hypocrites," of playing the actor and wearing a mask, perhaps of acting differently "behind the doors closed" (at night? v. 3) than they did in the daytime in the marketplaces. But nothing these powerful patrons do will remain uncovered, but rather will become known (vv. 2-3). The terminology suggests revelation at the coming judgment by the Son of Humanity (v. 8). Rather, the hearers of this gospel are to fear the One who has power beyond death (v. 5), whose providential care includes even the sparrows (v. 6) and the hairs on a person's head (v. 7). Jesus assures his "friends" (v. 4), his powerless clients, that what their rich, powerful, human owners do to them "behind closed doors" (v. 3), even if this includes murder (v. 4), is seen by a providential God who cares and will judge the deeds of all humans, saving those who "confess" their "friend" Jesus publicly (vv. 8-9), who accept the proclamation of Jesus' and believers' resurrection from the dead (Acts 23:6-8). The powerless have a patron, a "friend," more powerful than their murderous human owners, whom therefore they should not "fear" (five times in 12:4-5 and 7).

12:8 has been debated extensively; most interpreters have argued that it stems from the historical Jesus and that no later disciple would have implied a distinction between Jesus and the Son of Humanity, so that this saying reflects Jesus' use of apocalyptic images from Dan 7:13-14. This assertion is disputed by Schürmann, who argues that the title "Son of Man" is redactional, not original. But in its Lukan context, if one confesses Jesus before other human beings, the Son of Humanity will confess this person before God's angels, which assumes (a) a hostile attitude toward confessing Jesus, (b) so hostile an attitude that disciples would deny him, and (c) two court scenes, first a human court, then an eschatological one before God (see 17:20-37, esp. 26-30; 21:5-36, esp. 27). This Son of Humanity saying (12:8) has been reformulated in light of persecution of the Lukan church, the kind of reformulation seen in 6:22-23, 26. In its present position, it concludes in 12:4-5, 6-7, giving motivation not to "fear" these human courts. Verse 9 is a variant without the Son of Humanity title: whoever denies me before humans shall be denied before the angels of God.

12:10 takes up the same title, making a distinction between "speaking against" the Son of Humanity and "blaspheming" against the Holy Spirit. Persecutors "hate" disciples "on account of the Son of Humanity" (6:22), call him "a glutton, a drunkard, a friend of tax collectors and sinners" (7:34), and some disciples deny him before others (12:8-9). Later in the narrative, Israelites reject the Holy and Righteous One (Acts 3:14), and the Jerusalem high priest and council want to kill the apostles who witness by the Holy Spirit (Acts 5:32-33). Stephen accuses the high priest and the council, who "always oppose the Holy Spirit, just as your ancestors used to do" (Acts 7:51). Johnson: 19-20 suggests the key to the distinction in 12:10 in Luke (although not in Matthew): the story of Moses in Acts 7 has two main stages with an interlude.

Moses is sent by God to visit the people and save them, but they are ignorant of his identity and reject him the first time. Moses is forced to go away (Acts 7:23-29), but God empowers him to return to the people a second time (7:30-34), and he leads them out of Egypt with signs and wonders. But the people reject him a second time, preferring an idol, and God rejects them (7:39-43). Moses is therefore sent twice, a striking parallel to Luke's account of Jesus, which Johnson suggests is the essential clue to Luke's overall story. This insight explains much of Luke's narrative, including the distinction made in 12:10; those who reject the gospel the second time will be rejected by God (see esp. Acts 28:25-28). Johnson's theory fails, however, to explain the acceptance of Gentiles in the narrative (the second half of Acts).

12:11-12 encourage trust of the Holy Spirit's instruction in what one says before synagogues, rulers, and authorities (v. 11; see 21:14-15 and Acts 4:8, 25, 31; 5:32; 6:5; 7:51, 55-56). Both Peter and Stephen speak in the Spirit before the authorities. The Holy Spirit encourages the mission to Gentiles, so Luke may consider resisting this extension of the mission to be blasphemy against the Spirit (see 10:45; 11:15-16; 13:2, 4, 9, 52; 15).

To Have Many Possessions with Anxiety or to Be Rich toward God? (12:13-34)

"Greed" *(pleonexia)* was a vice for Jews and Greeks, but there were very different opinions about what constitutes greed. Antisthenes, predecessor of the Cynics, said: "people's wealth and poverty are not to be found in their house but in their souls" (Xenophon *Symp.* 4.34). Diogenes of Sinope, founder of the Cynics, called himself a "homeless *(aoikos)* exile, . . . a wanderer who begs *(ptōchos)* his daily bread" (Diogenes Laertius 6.38), the same vocabulary later used by Jesus (e.g., Luke 6:20; see 9:58 [Q]). Diogenes' wealthy follower Crates sold his lands and gave the proceeds to his fellow citizens (Diogenes Laertius 6.87-88), just as Peter tells Jesus that he and the disciples have done (18:28-30). The Cynics' opponents, the Epicureans, debated whether poverty is an evil (Philodemus *On Wealth* 45.15-40), but in great contrast to our modern capitalist assumptions, even among Epicureans "no one dares to say that the possession of [only] a few things is evil" (ibid. 46.26-34; see Balch 2003a). Whether he knew the philosophical arguments or not, Jesus' evaluation of wealth in Luke agrees with that of the Cynics. Even the Epicureans admit that wealth is "easily destroyed and subject to being taken away" (ibid. 54.4-10), and thus would not "betray our souls by desire *(epithymia)* for wealth" (ibid. 58.3-9). Rather than be greedy, Epicureans wanted "quiet, peace, and the least care" (Philodemus *Concerning Household Management* 12.44–13.2; see Balch 2003a), but this meant moderate wealth, not the utter poverty pronounced blessed by Cynics and Jesus. Jesus, like the Epicureans, counseled against business troubles, struggles, being disturbed, and the labor of acquisition (ibid. 12.25-38; 13.3-8, 26-35; 14.30-37), except that the Epicureans then argued for moderate, "natural" wealth (ibid. 14.17-23) while Jesus spoke about giving it *all* away (12:35; 18:22) — a hard saying for First-World Christians.

Jesus' rejection of the role of economic arbitrator is the occasion for introducing the parable of the rich fool, one of the fourteen special Lukan parables, all of which contain dialogue and/or monologue between characters within the parable (e.g., 12:17-20; Paffenroth: 97-98). This one is not really a "parable," but an "example story." Parables refer by analogy to another reality, but example stories offer a pattern of correct or incorrect behavior. All four example stories in our Gospels occur in Luke (10:29-37; 12:16-21; 16:19-31; 18:9-14), and may originally have been parables of Jesus that Luke reformulated. In this story there is only one character conversing with himself, a monologue in the presence of God. The sole character never considers sharing his wealth, but wants only to store it for his own future: "relax, eat, drink, be merry!" (12:19). Jesus himself had a reputation for being a "glutton and drunkard" (7:34; see Mark 2:15-17), and joyful meals continued in the early church (Acts 2:46). The problem does not seem to be that the farmer wanted to enjoy himself. But in Acts these meals are eaten "with glad and *generous* hearts" in the context of having "all things in common" (2:44), a matter never considered by the character in the example story. Rather, he is among those who "store up treasures for themselves," not by being generous to others and so becoming "rich toward God" (12:21).

Cynics, Epicureans, and Jesus all associated "anxiety" with many possessions (12:15, 21-22), but many modern Christians would replace the word "anxiety" with "security." We act on our values by investing in a mutual fund. Commentators often criticize the Epicureans when interpreting this text, but their economic values were closer to Jesus' than are the values of Jesus' modern followers. Who in our modern churches would seriously debate whether it is good to have nothing at all, to be homeless, as Epicureans debated mendicant Cynics?

"Do not worry *(merimnate)* about your life. . . ." More literally translated: "Do not be anxious about your soul" *(psychē,* 12:22, the catchword used in v. 19). Already in the parable of the sower, Jesus has mentioned the seed "choked by the cares *(merimnon)* and riches and pleasures of life" (8:14). And he will warn, "Be on guard so that your hearts are not weighed down with dissipation and drunkenness and the worries *(merimnais)* of this life . . ." (21:34-35a), the kind of "worry" for which Jesus reproves Martha (10:41). In 12:22 the worry focuses on food (also vv. 24-26) and clothing (vv. 27-28). The Epicureans, too, named anxiety as a disadvantage of wealth, but argued that it would be present whether one were poor or rich. Paul likewise wants the Corinthians to be "free from anxieties" (whether married or unmarried; 1 Cor 7:32-34). Jesus uses three or four arguments to persuade: "life is more than food" (12:23), "can any of you by worrying . . ." (v. 25), again, "if God so clothes the grass of the field . . ." (v. 28), and finally a variant of the last argument, "your Father knows that you need them" (v. 30), a call for trust in God's providence. In the flow of Luke's narrative, this is not a naive trust but one that holds onto God through crises and even death (6:22; 12:5).

12:30 speaks of the concerns of "the nations of the world," a group often evaluated positively in Luke (e.g.,

24:47), so these must be wisdom sayings earlier than Luke. But instead of striving for food and clothing as do the nations, Jesus demands striving for the kingdom and promises that these things will be given as well (12:31), perhaps an allusion to Christian hospitality and almsgiving (see 9:3-4; 10:4-8). Jesus encourages the opposite of fear, assuring the disciples that it is God's good pleasure to give them the kingdom (see the comments on 9:18-27).

12:33-34 again express the alternative to v. 21: treasures for oneself or being rich toward God; sell your possessions and give alms (see 18:22; Acts 2:44-45; 4:32–5:11 and the parallels quoted above from Antisthenes and the Cynics Diogenes and Crates; Paffenroth; Balch 1998c; Malherbe: 123-35).

The Master Will Serve the Slave! (12:35-48)

The parable of the slaves watching or of the doorkeeper (see Mark 13:34-35) may originally have symbolized anticipating the kingdom of God. In Mark and Luke it becomes waiting for Jesus' coming, although Luke removes it from Mark's eschatological discourse, placing it in a different setting, warning those who are church leaders (12:1, 4, 22, 32). Later Peter asks whether the two earlier parables are for all (v. 41), and Jesus tells the story of a slave "manager" (*oikonomos,* v. 42) who beats other slaves and gets drunk. For such vicious leadership, the master will punish the slave. Originally, Jesus' parable focused exclusively on promise, not warning (Crossan: 99). When the master returns from the marriage feast to find slaves awake, "He will gird himself and have them sit ["recline"] at the table, and he will come and serve them" (v. 37)! In Greco-Roman society this is an astounding reversal, characteristic of Jesus' parables, elsewhere seen once a year at the festival of the Saturnalia (Osiek and Balch: 195-96). Jesus' slave parable is one source for Christian leaders serving as slaves at the Lord's Supper. Characteristically Luke (22:24-26; contrast the context of Mark 10:41-45) moves precisely this question of a reversal of roles into the last supper setting, and John (13:1-20) has Jesus act out such slave service, which in Greco-Roman society was not an honor!

12:35-38 narrate slaves guarding the door of the house while waiting the master's return from a wedding (see Mark 13:33-37). Jesus pronounces those who remain "awake" "blessed," just what Jesus asks on the Mount of Olives, although the disciples "sleep" (22:45-46; see 9:32). The second parable (12:39-40) changes images to a thief coming in the night (see 1 Thess 5:2), and is followed by a similar blessing for those ready for the "Son of Humanity."

Peter asks whether this parable is for all (12:41), a question Jesus leaves unanswered, except that he then either tells another parable or offers an explanation of the previous parables that concerns a "slave manager" (*oikonomos),* an important social group in the early church that gave images for church leadership. Particularly interesting are clay tablets found in the house of a banker, Jucundus, tablets preserved for us by the volcanic eruption of Vesuvius (Osiek and Balch: 77, 175). These tablets record the loan of substantial sums by one slave manager to another managerial slave; the financial transactions were handled by the slaves, not by the owners. Sometimes the sums loaned belonged to the owner, sometimes to the slave. Sometimes the slave banker would even make a loan to a free person, so that the slave was the patron and the free person the client. The slave manager's profession and social position were more important than and inconsistent with his legal status. In Jesus' parable, the slave manager "knows the will of the lord" (v. 47) and represents the owner, and thus has status and power over other slaves. The slave manager is blessed when using the position well (vv. 43-44), but judged and punished when not (vv. 45-46; Crossan).

Jesus and Divided Homes (12:49-53)

Shockingly to First-World Christians, Jesus says that he came to bring division in homes. Our value systems claim to put our families first, but consistently in the Synoptic Gospels Jesus puts families second so forcefully that interpreters debate whether sayings such as these are anti-family. Jesus speaks of his purpose, saying, "I came" (12:49), "I have come" (v. 51), and "I have a baptism with which to be baptized" (v. 50). This purpose is not peace, but conflict and division. When the Son of God from Nazareth announces the gospel for all ethnic groups to one with privilege, or when the rich hear that God blesses the poor, or when Jesus enters Mary and Martha's home, some "welcome" the message and some reject it, sometimes creating divisions in the same family (v. 53; see 2:34-35). Jesus exclaims that he is under stress until he is "baptized," which may refer to his death (Mark 10:38), acted out later in the baptism of disciples (Rom 6:4; Col 2:12). John had prophesied that one more powerful than he would "baptize you with the Holy Spirit and fire" (3:16; see 12:49-50 and Acts 1:5). This saying does not mention division between husbands and wives, although other words do (14:26; 20:34-35). Matthew (10:36; see 1 Pet 3:6 and 1 John 2:19) has an additional frightening phrase, "and one's enemies will be members of one's own household."

Recognizing the Crisis Precipitated by Jesus' Presence and Proclamation (12:54–13:9)

Jesus addresses two groups of sayings to the crowds (12:54-59), then asks two questions, giving his own answer (13:1-9). The first group of sayings concern the weather. Six months a year in Israel (winter) rains borne by clouds come from the sea to the west; rain is common and expected. The other six months (summer) are dry, and a hot wind blows from the south. People know the difference between the rainy and the dry season, "But why do you not know how to interpret the present time?" (12:56), the present eschatological crisis when "the kingdom of God has come upon you" (11:20). When hauled into court, a person understands that there is a crisis, that debtor's prison or slavery with abuse is probable (see Dionysius *Rom. Ant.* 6.26). Jesus proclaims a crisis with God that some particular audience, "hypocrites" (12:56), refuses to perceive.

Then Jesus twice asks two questions, giving answers that emphasize repentance. The first question asks whether the Galileans "are worse sinners" (*hamartōloi*) than others (13:2), the second question whether a group were worse "offenders" (*opheiletai*, v. 4), two terms used as synonyms, as they are in a petition of the Lord's Prayer, "forgive us our sins (*hamartias*), for we ourselves forgive everyone indebted (*opheilonti*) to us" (11:4; compare Dionysius *Rom. Ant.* 3.9.2; 6.83.4; 7.45.4; 8.50.3-4). Pilate's Roman soldiers have killed some Galileans, which could raise questions about revolution, about God being the sole ruler of Israel. In Luke Jesus does indeed address political questions concerning foreigners and the poor, but here he does not evaluate Pilate's Roman rule. Instead, he proclaims the need for repentance, a central Lukan redactional theme (interestingly not in 9:1-6 or 10:1-12, but see 10:13; 11:32; 15:7, 10; 16:30; 17:3-4; Acts 2:38; 3:19; 8:22; 17:30; 26:20). Similarly, there had been a tragedy at the pool of Siloam in southern Jerusalem, but Jesus does not explain theodicy; again he rather calls for repentance, as do the Lukan conclusions of three parables (15:7, 10; 16:30) and of many sermons in Acts. The following parables of the vineyard and the fig tree do not, however, continue the emphasis on repentance, but rather emphasize God's judgment, as had the sayings in 12:54-49. In the Hebrew prophets both the fig tree (Isa 36:16; Jer 8:13; Hos 2:12; 9:10) and the vineyard (Isa 5:1-7), often as a pair, represent Israel or the nations being judged. Jesus' parable represents the owner giving the fig tree a year of grace (13:8-9), which corresponds to Luke's emphasis on the delay of the parousia (e.g., 17:23, 25; 21:7-8, 12; Acts 1:6-7).

The Kingdom of God, the Purpose of Traditional Institutions (Sabbath, Jerusalem), and Newcomers from East, West, North, and South (13:10-35)

Culpepper: 272-73 observes that 13:10-17 and 14:1-35 are parallel. Luke presents a scene about the healing of a stooped woman (13:10-17) and the healing of a male with dropsy (14:1-6), typical of Luke's female/male stories. Both healings occur on a sabbath, involve controversy with a leader, conclude with a pronouncement, and invite the opponents to compare what they would do for an ox and a human being. Three parables of the kingdom follow (13:18-29, 20-21, and 22-30), and as in ch. 14 the healing is followed by teaching on humility (14:7-14) and a banquet of the kingdom (14:15-24). Both chapters end with warnings either for Jerusalem (13:31-35) or on the cost of discipleship (14:25-35).

Healing a Woman on the Sabbath (13:10-17)

Greco-Roman historians must claim to be faithful to traditional laws and institutions or explain their apparent abrogation as a return to the original meaning of the institution (Acts 6:11, 13-14; 21:21, 24; Dionysius *Rom. Ant.* 1.89-90; 3.10-11; 7.70-73; Josephus *Ant.* 6.35-39, 83-93). In this controversy, Jesus is not criticizing or annulling the traditional sabbath but rather (re)interpreting the function of that holy day (contrast Mark 2:27, omitted by Luke, and compare Mark 3:4 par. Luke 6:9).

At the midpoint of Luke, Jesus enters a synagogue for the last time (see 4:31-37; 6:6-11). Mark wrote that "the sabbath was made for humankind, and not humankind for the sabbath," a saying that Luke omitted, perhaps as too critical of a traditional, well-known holy day. When Jesus healed in the synagogue on another sabbath, he argumentatively asked, "'Is it lawful to do good or to do harm on the sabbath, to save life or to kill?' But they [the Pharisees] were silent" (Mark 3:4). Luke 6:9 repeats these words, and the thought is close to the later argument in 13:15-17: those in the synagogue would untie an ox to give it drink on the sabbath; ought not a daughter of Abraham be freed from bondage on that holy day? (The Jewish mother of the seven martyrs is also a "daughter of God-fearing Abraham"; see 4 Macc 15:28.) Jesus argues not about whether one should observe the sabbath, but about the meaning of the day. Jesus "does good" to the crippled woman on the sabbath, a woman who had a "spirit of weakness" (13:11), which may refer to an evil spirit.

Philo similarly argues that the purpose of the sabbath is "humanity and justice" (*Spec. Leg.* 2.63), that slaves should relax and look forward to liberation on this day (ibid. 67, 83-84), that land, too, should be allowed to lie fallow every seven years, every sabbatical year (ibid. 97-104), and that widows and orphans should be allowed to gather in fields and orchards during this seventh year (ibid. 108-9; see 56-139). According to Philo, these allegorical meanings should not mean the abrogation of literally resting on the sabbath (see *Migr. Abr.* 89–91)! But in Luke-Acts the spiritual/moral meaning of the sabbath is enough for Gentile converts; literally resting on the sabbath is not included in the Jerusalem church's prescriptions for a Gentile Christian lifestyle (Acts 15:19-21, 29; see Culpepper).

The Kingdom of God Is Like Mustard Seed, Yeast, and a Narrow Door (13:18-30)

The first two parables concern, again, a male/female pair, a man planting a mustard seed (13:18-19) and a woman hiding yeast (vv. 20-21; see vv. 10-17 and 14:1-6). The mustard seed, one of the smallest, "grows" into a tree two or three feet taller than a human. The verb "grow" is from Q (see Matt 13:32), not Mark. It is used in an only partially similar way earlier in Q: exhorting the disciples not to worry, Jesus says, "Consider the lilies, how they grow; they neither toil nor spin . . ." (Luke 12:27 par. Matt 6:28). In both 12:27 and 13:19, God gives the growth, but the earlier point concerns disciples not worrying, the latter the contrast between small beginnings and a tree large enough to support birds' nests. There are parallels (Ezek 17:22-23; Dan 4:10-12), however, to large trees. Equally important sources stem from Luke's current culture. Romulus wanted Rome to "grow" (Polybius 6.43.2; Dionysius *Rom. Ant.* 2.15.4), and the means was the "mixture" of races, "welcoming" foreign nations that Rome conquered as citizens. Many nations — those coming "from east and west, from north and south" — are also affirmed at the close of the final parable in the Lukan series (13:29; cf. Acts 6:7; 12:24; 19:20). But this kind of "growth" is opposed by the Priestly document in the Hebrew Bible, which prefers families within the same ethnic group having many children (Gen 1:22, 28; 28:1-3). Following Q, Luke has placed Jesus' parable in a literary context that promotes the kind of multiethnic "growth" narrated in the third parable in this series and in Acts, a value in Luke's Roman culture so basic that the readers of Acts would gain "certainty" (Luke 1:4; Acts 2:36), security, and reassurance from a narrative recording such spectacular growth.

The parable of a woman hiding yeast in a huge batch of dough (13:20-21) is ironic at several levels. Yeast was excluded at Passover (Exod 12:19), and a holy assembly eats unleavened bread (Exod 12:15-16; cf. 1 Cor 5:7). But it is precisely this unholy, unclean yeast that leavens the whole, huge lump of dough. Similarly, by "welcoming" foreign fugitives, Romulus made Rome "grow," "great from small beginnings," beginning with not more than three thousand soldiers (Dionysius *Rom. Ant.* 2.16.2; cf. Acts 2:41). Exactly "unclean" persons such as Cornelius (Acts 10:14-15, 28; 11:3, 8; 15:9) make the church grow.

A woman's work becomes transparent for God's reign. Her hands, kneading bread dough, become transparent for God's actions, for God's life-giving power (see 11:3), as transparent to God as the man's hands who sowed a mustard seed (see Schottroff: 79-90).

Luke may have constructed the third parable of the narrow door/eschatological banquet (13:22-30) from elements scattered through Matthew, that is, from Q, although the Lukan story shares only scattered words with Matthew, for example, "enter through a/the narrow door" (Luke 13:24 par. Matt 7:13). The introductory verse refers artificially to the motif of the journey to Jerusalem (see 9:51). Prior to the parable someone asks, "Lord, will only a few be saved?" (13:23). The narrative has placed Jesus in Samaria (9:51-52), not Galilee or Jerusalem, but he has been healing in synagogues (13:10), so that the reader does not know whether the question refers to a few Samaritans or to a few Jews or to both. Who are the "you yourselves" who will be "thrown out" of the kingdom (v. 28)?

Jesus begins exhorting the undefined audience to "struggle to enter through the narrow door" (13:24), which will be shut (v. 25). Those shut out remind Jesus that they ate and drank with him and that he taught them (v. 26). But Jesus calls them "workers of evil" (v. 27; for evangelistic "workers" see 10:2, 7; 2 Cor 11:13; Phil 3:2; 2 Tim 2:15). Thus the parable suddenly seems addressed to Jesus' disciples, to Christian evangelists, which suggests an audience for the whole section (see the commentary on 10:1-2). Those addressed have celebrated the eschatological banquet with Jesus (Isa 25:6-7; Luke 5:30-32; Acts 2:46; Rev 12:9). Then follows Luke's conclusion: "people will come from east and west, from north and south, and will eat in the kingdom of God" (13:29). Luke has modified Matt 8:11-12, adding "from north and south," referring to the Ethiopian south (see Acts 8:27; Felder: 13). Twenty-first-century tensions within the church between whites and blacks are not so far from first-century tensions within the church between Jews and Gentiles, Greeks and barbarians, racial tensions addressed by this Lukan parable, by other speeches in Luke (2:29-32; 4:16-20; 10:1-12; 24:44-49), and by the book of Acts (chs. 10–15; see Eph 2:11-22; 3:5-6; Col 3:11). Luke concludes with the theme of reversal (13:30).

Jerusalem in Relation to the Fox and the Mother Hen (13:31-35)

The intent of this short section is puzzling: the Pharisees, who have consistently been portrayed as hostile to Jesus (5:17, 21, 30), seem to offer him protection (13:31). Given the narrator's consistent portrayal, Johnson: 221, 223, 225-26, 239 interprets this as a temptation to Jesus to save himself from his prophesied death in Jerusalem. On the other hand, there are positive references to Pharisees in Acts: the Pharisee Gamaliel I protected Peter (5:33-39); some Pharisees have become Christians who demand that believing Gentiles be circumcised (15:5); and later in the book Paul represents himself as a Pharisee who believes in the resurrection from the dead (23:6-10).

However Pharisees are portrayed in 13:31, Jesus then makes two pronouncements, the first referring to his exorcisms and healing, "and on the third day I finish [my work]" (v. 32). For anyone who makes the Christian confession, "the third day" in this context has one clear meaning (see 9:22; 18:33; 24:7, 21, 46; Acts 10:40), referring to Christ being raised on the third day. The verb "finish" also refers exclusively in Luke to "completing" prophesied acts (see 2:39; 12:50; 18:31; 22:37). 13:32 is a summary of the gospel. Prophets are killed in Jerusalem (v. 33), a death Jesus prophesied for himself (9:22; 17:25; 24:7, 26; see Acts 7:52 and for prophets' deaths, *The Lives of the Prophets,* in Charlesworth: 2:379-99).

13:34-35 have a parallel in Matt 23:38-39. Many have argued that v. 34 was spoken by Jesus because of the reference to Jerusalem "stoning" the prophets, not the kind of death Jesus died, thus a saying not created by the later church, one of the few indications that the historical Jesus foresaw his coming death. This is followed by the image of a mother hen, probably of the divine, feminine figure of Wisdom speaking to Jerusalem (see Proverbs 8; Sir 15:1-10; 24:23, wisdom identified with the Mosaic law; Wis 6:12-25; Luke 11:49-51; 1 Cor 1:24). In this passage (13:34), Wisdom is rejected by Jerusalem (see Sir 24:28; John 1:11-12).

Therefore, Jerusalem's house is forsaken (13:35), and they will not see Jesus until they say, "Blessed is the one who comes in the name of the Lord," a chant that "the whole multitude of disciples" sing at the triumphal entry into the city (19:38 from Ps 118:26), to which the Pharisees object (19:39). Jesus weeps again over Jerusalem (19:41-44).

Whether to Invite the Indigent to Dinner (14:1-24)

As Culpepper observes, 13:10-17 and 14:1-35 are parallel. The earlier section began with the healing of a crippled woman, this one with the healing of a man with dropsy, with the Pharisees objecting to both because the events occur on the sabbath. Recently Braun: 28 has observed that Luke is not interested in the historical sect of Jewish Pharisees in Israel, except that they serve as literary figures. Dropsy, an unquenchable craving for drink even though the body is inflated with fluid, was a Cynic metaphor for consuming passion (Braun: 33). The healing is a *chreia* (a "concise reminiscence, useful for living, aptly attributed to some character"; Hock and O'Neil: 23-26) in the form of an act (14:1-6), followed by several gnomic sentences (vv. 7-14), then by a story of the great banquet (vv. 15-24), all of which is an inductive argument, a persuasive composition. Luke argues in a conventional rhetorical manner for unconventional behavior! Meals like the "great supper" typically have a conservative function, but Jesus' story argues for status transformation, crossing social boundaries (Braun: 121). The story of a banquet is not a symposium, but part of the argumentation (Braun: 136-44; Osiek and Balch: ch. 8).

Jesus' question is simple, "Is it lawful to cure people on the sabbath, or not?" (14:3), again a question concerning the meaning of the day, and, given Braun's interpretation, whether one could be cured of consuming passion on the sabbath (see the commentary on 13:10-17).

Jesus' second question, "If one of you has a child or an ox that has fallen into a well, will you not immediately pull it out on a sabbath day?" (14:5) repeats the question Jesus asked about the crippled woman (13:15), both of which go unanswered. The result is that those who follow Jesus do not also become proselytes, converts to Judaism (Acts 15:1, 20, 29; contrast Josephus *Ant.* 20.34-48). The sabbath is a holy day, not abrogated, but a day on which one is "set free from bondage" (Luke 13:16), and on which one may cure those consumed by passion or save a child or an animal that has fallen into a hole (14:5; cf. 1 Macc 2:32-41).

The following could be understood as wise advice, especially 14:8-11 addressed to the guests, although vv. 12-14 to the host would be harder to misunderstand. Verses 8-11 assume that guests chose their own place in the dining room, which would be "democratic" on the part of the host; alternatively, the host often assigned aristocrats the best places (Plutarch *Table-Talk* 615D-619A). This host mixes the two practices, only later assigning someone the best couch. Jesus gives wise advice: recline on the couch distant from the host, who may then say, "Friend, move up higher" (v. 10). Jesus concludes with the eschatological formula of bipolar reversal, "all who exalt themselves will be humbled, and the one who humbles himself will be exalted [by God]" (v. 11, a formula already in Q: Matt 23:12 par. Luke 18:14).

The second group of gnomic sayings (14:12-14), this time directed to the host, cannot be mistaken for wise advice. The patronage system was built on reciprocity, on doing favors that one expected would be returned, "repaid" (v. 12), which Jesus opposes. The host is not to invite those who could repay him, "friends, brothers, relatives, or rich neighbors," but on the contrary, the "poor *(ptōchous)*, crippled, lame, and blind" (v. 13). The word for "poor" is the one Jesus quoted from Isa 61:1 in his inaugural sermon (4:18), the same one designating those who have nothing whom Jesus pronounced "blessed" (6:20), the word describing Lazarus, whom the rich man will ignore (16:20), not those who could "repay" anything. "Poor" means that they do not have houses. Jesus is not giving wise advice but referring to bipolar reversal seen already in the *Magnificat* (1:47-48, 51-54; cf. Phil 2:6-11). Repayment will be made by God at the "resurrection of the righteous" (14:14).

Someone, "hearing this," perhaps the invitation to the "poor" (14:13), exclaims, "Blessed is anyone who will eat bread in the kingdom of God" (v. 15). Jesus responds with the parable of the great banquet (vv. 15-24), which concerns the conversion of a rich, dishonored householder who first invited his upper-class peers, then invited a new social grouping, the "indigent, filthy, and such" (Dionysius *Rom. Ant.* 8.71.3). The peers give excuses that involve concern for land and farm animals and a new marriage (see v. 26 below); they are perhaps those who have heard the "word of God" but "are choked by the cares and riches and pleasures of life" (8:14; see 6:24; 12:22-31). As an alternative to those who are anxious about their riches, the householder tells the slave, "Go out [see 9:6] . . . and bring in the poor *(ptōchous)*, the crippled, the blind, and the lame" (14:21, repeating v. 13). This patron typically wants the "house" full; many clients showed influence in that world. And the parable concludes with a threat, "none of those who were invited will taste my dinner" (v. 24), which in this context refers not to Israel but to the rich, repeating the contrasts between 6:20-21 and 24-25; 8:14 and 15; 12:22 and 23, 30 and 31.

The poor are reluctant and have to be encouraged, typical of those not accustomed to eating in great houses (14:23; see Osiek and Balch: 166-67, 211-14). The story may reflect rich Lukan Christians inviting their poor brothers and sisters to dinner, which generated ostracism from wealthy peers (Braun: 113). These upside-down Christian eating customs are reflected elsewhere in Luke (see 12:37; 22:24-27; see Braun; Hock and O'Neil; Osiek and Balch).

Conditions for Discipleship (14:25-35)

The narrator again notes that Jesus is journeying. He turns to the crowds and speaks of conditions of discipleship, that unless one hates *(misei)* father, mother, wife, children, brothers, sisters, even life itself, one cannot be Jesus' disciple (14:27). To generalize, in contemporary First-World Christianity money is first, family second, and Jesus third, so that this saying is hard to understand. In the Roman world, the state was one's primary commitment (see Dionysius *Rom. Ant.* 5.6-8). Jesus differs from both the Roman and the modern capitalist worlds by demanding primary allegiance, commitment beyond money, family, or state. Jesus includes hatred of a "wife" (v. 26), just as someone has excused himself from the eschatological banquet because of a new marriage (v. 20; see 20:34-35). Our culture so idealizes romantic love that we find this impossible to comprehend. We do not adequately interpret it by asserting that commitment to God/Jesus has "priority" over family; disciples *left* "house, wife, brothers, parents, and children" for the sake of the kingdom of God (18:29). Such radical demands must simply be left to challenge disciples, not explained away.

Further, disciples must carry the cross (14:27) and be ready to suffer the death Jesus did for proclaiming the kingdom. Two parables, imaging one person building (vv. 28-30) and one planning a war (vv. 31-33), encourage estimating the cost. Finally, Jesus demands giving up "all your possessions" (v. 34), a challenge to ancient and modern values (see the commentary on 5:27-39).

Parables of Joy at Finding What Was Lost, or Restoring a Sinner Who Was Alienated (15:1-32)

Luke edits three parables, uniting them by a common theme. The Lukan introduction has "Pharisees" complaining about Jesus "welcoming sinners" *(hamartōlous prosdechetai)* and eating with them (15:2). The common Lukan conclusion to the first pair of parables is that there is "joy in heaven over one sinner *(heni hamartōlǭ)* who repents" (vv. 7, 10). The confession of the prodigal is also, "I have sinned" (*hēmarton;* vv. 18, 21). The centrality of Luke's concern for the forgiveness of sins is clear (1:77; 11:4; 24:27; Acts 2:38; 10:43; 13:38; 22:16; 26:18, all in Lukan speeches). A sheep, a coin, and a son were all "lost" (*apollymi;* 15:4, 8, 24, 32; see 4:34; 17:27, 29; 19:10; Rom 2:12; 14:15), but the lost are "found" (15:4-6, 8-9, 24, 32; see 12:43; 13:6-7; 18:8). This "being found" would be heard by Lukan Christians — reclining in the dining rooms of their house churches and listening to the Gospel read — either as a call to "welcome" others or as the experience of having been "welcomed" (see the commentary on 4:19 and 9:1-17) into a church that is inclusive with respect to race and class (and gender?).

God "welcomes" all who fear God, Jew or Gentile (4:19; Acts 10:35), the church is to "welcome" children (9:48), and, finally, Paul "welcomes all" (Acts 28:30). Further, Luke's introduction specifies the problem: Jesus "eats" with these sinners (15:2). Elite householders in the Greco-Roman world were reluctant to "welcome" the "poor" to dinner (see the commentary on 11:37-54 and 14:1-24). One message to Luke's readers, who experienced social divisions within the household worship assembly, is to encourage reluctant Christian patrons to hear these parables of Jesus and to "welcome" the "indigent, filthy, and such" (Dionysius *Rom. Ant.* 8.71.3) into their dining rooms. This would challenge either the orthopraxic historical Pharisees with whom Jesus debated about the unclean or Luke's literary Pharisees, who are "lovers of money" (16:14), that is, who enjoyed high social status in the house churches they hosted.

Second, the challenge is not only to welcome the poor, but also to welcome foreigners. Peter observes, "you [the non-Jewish household of Cornelius] yourselves know that it is unlawful for a Jew[ish disciple of Jesus] to associate with or to visit a foreigner" (*allophylǭ;* Acts 10:28a; see 15:1-2). Peter, however, then realizes that "in every nation anyone who fears him and does what is right is acceptable (*dektos;* see the commentary on 4:19) to him" (10:35) with the consequence that Peter and the Jewish believers with him (10:23) accept the hospitality of the foreigner Cornelius for several days (10:48). Jesus' parables would be heard in Lukan worship assemblies divided by economic status and by race, and in light of Luke 10:38-42 we can add, divided by reflection on women's functions in worship.

In this setting, the poor would have to be encouraged to enter the house, and the wealthy patron would be tempted to feel social superiority and disdain. Hippolytus, for example, describes Christian patrons making significant efforts to encourage the poor to participate in Christian communal meals (Bobertz: 164-70).

The opening question asks the listener, "Which one of you . . . ?" (15:3). The house owner, who in that agrarian society would also be a farmer and owner of animals, is asked to compare himself or herself to a shepherd who has lost an animal and would be happy to have found it. The *Gospel of Thomas* 107 utterly reverses the point: "One of them [the sheep] went astray. . . . He said to the sheep, I love you more than the ninety-nine"! Thomas reinforces the Greco-Roman hierarchical value system; Jesus' parable in Q (Luke 15:1-7 par. Matt 18:12-14) challenges those values for those whom Jesus has "welcomed" to "eat."

A woman has lost a coin (15:8-10), so by editorial placement Luke has again generated a male/female pair of stories. The amount of money she has is small, and she sweeps the house herself, that is, does not tell a slave to search for her, so she is poor. After finding the coin, she calls her "[female] friends" (v. 9) to celebrate with her. Among those Christians hearing Luke's Gospel read, this parable encourages wealthy household patrons to celebrate that God has found the sinners who are eating in the patron's beautiful dining rooms.

The double parable of the dissolute, sinful son and the angry, obedient son (15:11-32) is also introduced by v. 2 ("[Jesus] welcomes sinners and eats with them") and concluded by a refrain from the first two parables ("this son of mine/this brother of yours was dead and is alive, was lost and is found"; vv. 24 and 32). The first half, the parable of the dissolute, sinful son, is related both to other Bible stories, for example, that of Jacob and Esau (Genesis 25–36) and of Joseph and his older brothers (Genesis 37–50), and to stories in the Greco-Roman tradition, for example, to the one told by Terence, *The Brothers.* One brother, Demea, belongs to the older generation, is thrifty to a fault, and works his own farm, but his expansive brother Micio lives as a citizen in Athens. Demea has two sons, Aeschinus and Ctesipho. The rich Micio is a bachelor without an heir, so he invites Aeschinus, his brother Demea's son, to Athens. Ctesipho remains with his father on the farm, is raised strictly, and becomes accustomed to hard work. On the contrary, Micio allows his young nephew Aeschinus complete freedom, and he soon develops into a fun-loving young Athenian. He seduces an honorable young Athenian woman, but Micio assists him, and they turn the scandal into a happy marriage: the lax upbringing has a good end. On the other hand, Demea's strict discipline on the farm fails: despite his father's opposition, Ctesipho carries on with a prostitute (Osiek and Balch: 68, 139).

All of Luke's special parables contain dialogue or monologue between characters, some have contrasting characters, and some reach a narrative crisis in the middle (Paffenroth: 98, 104), all true of this double parable. Luke's (ancient) history emphasizes direct speech throughout, beginning with canticles in the infancy narrative and concluding with Paul's apologetic speeches in Acts. In this parable we hear the younger son's request of the father (15:12b), the interior monologue of the dissolute son (vv. 17b-19), his conversation with the father (v. 21b), the father's order to slaves (vv. 22b-24), a slave informing the older, obedient brother (v. 27), the obedient son's angry words to his father (vv. 29b-30), and the father's challenge to his angry son (vv. 30-31).

Jesus' parable concerns, first, a "prodigal" father who has compassion on the son who has wasted household goods and, second, the father's challenge to the older son to celebrate the return of his dissolute brother. In ancient agrarian society this would have been an offensive, potentially transforming metaphor of the kingdom of God, clashing with centuries of domestic wisdom. The dissolute son has sinned against the household by wasting property. By its extravagant ending, Jesus' parable collides with this ordered agrarian world and evokes the just protest of the elder brother. As Jesus told it, the story was a parabolic metaphor that breaks through and contradicts domestic order.

As Luke tells it in the context of all of Luke and Acts, the story is a parenetic example story encouraging "welcoming sinners and eating with them," celebrating the finding of the lost, now confessing sinners in Christian households. Following Peter's Pentecost sermon, sinners are baptized and forgiven (Acts 2:38). The verb Luke uses to describe the communal "eating bread with glad hearts" (*euphrainō;* Acts 2:46) is the same verb Luke had used in this parable of the father "celebrating" the dissolute, sinful son's return and encouraging the angry, obedient son to celebrate (Luke 15:23-24, 29, 32).

There was a related dispute between the haughty and the humble, the rich and the poor in the Roman Empire, a dispute about who had offended or "sinned" against whom, whether the rich should forgive the sins of the poor as a favor, or the opposite, whether the typical acts of the rich needed rather to be pardoned by the poor (Dionysius *Rom. Ant.* 6.73.1-2; also 7.45.4; 63.1). In this dispute, many of the rich Roman patricians refuse to "celebrate" the poor sinners participating in the state, but, on the contrary, want to drive them out of Rome. The rich patricians' role is analogous to that of the angry, obedient son in Jesus' parable and would have been heard as such in Greco-Roman cities. Some readers of the Gospel could have identified the angry, obedient son with the wealthy patron of the house church, some of whom only reluctantly admitted the poor or foreigners into their houses (see Balch 1995a: 214-33; Bobertz: 170-84; Osiek and Balch; Paffenroth).

Rich People Who Love Money (16:1-31)

We have difficulty interpreting the parable of the dishonest steward for two reasons: stewards were often slaves, but the modern experience of slavery is quite unlike the ancient one; and, second, Jesus is presenting a dishonest person as one to emulate. Anyone could fall into slavery either because they could not pay debts or because of war, which means that a former neighbor or a whole nation, such as the Jews following the Jewish-Roman war of AD 66-70, could fall into slavery. Ancient slavery was not limited to one social class or to one race. The records of a banker in Pompeii, Julius Caeculius Jucundus, are fascinating in this respect: slave managers controlled large sums of money (see the commentary on 12:35-48). Similarly, the (dishonest) slave in Jesus' parable manipulated large loans to his own advantage.

Addressing the second difficulty, Beavis interprets in light of Aesop's fables, in which the slave outwits the master or mistress, doing exactly what the slave is accused of in Jesus' parable, being dishonest! Plautus, the most popular playwright of the age, amused Romans by reversing their everyday value system, also praising slaves for their roguery (Beavis: 47-48, 51).

Jesus' parable seems to end at 16:8a; that is, v. 8a is not a reference to Jesus as "Lord" *(kyrios)* but rather to the "master" of the dishonest manager. Outside the infancy narrative (see 1:43; 2:11), Luke usually distinguishes between the meaning of *kyrios* in the Gospel and in Acts. In Acts the author uses *kyrios* to refer to the resurrected Jesus, Lord at the right hand of God. But in the Gospel human characters rarely use *kyrios* in a christologically significant way (only in 12:41-42 and 19:8), but rather use the vocative, "O master" (see Tuckett: 76-78). 16:8a exhibits this nonchristological use. V. 8b is then an early Semitic, apocalyptic comment on the parable using the phrases "sons/children of this age" and "sons/children of light," a contrasted pair found in the Dead Sea Scrolls and in Paul (see 1QM; Eph 5:8; 1 Thess 5:5). The parable's conclusion praised the "dishonest manager" for acting "shrewdly," and this comment picks up this term, applying it to the "shrewd" children of this age, recommending that trait to the children of light. By the use of "dishonest wealth" (for Luke all wealth is dishonest), that is, by giving all (14:33) or some of it (8:3) away, or by the wealthy forgiving the debts of the poor (compare 16:5 and 11:4-5), one may prepare to be "welcomed" into an eternal home (16:9; see Balch 1997: 127-35).

16:10-13 collects diverse sayings about dishonesty, faithfulness, wealth, and slavery; v. 13 is the conclusion to the whole. V. 13a is similar to Paul in Romans (6:16, "if you present yourselves to anyone as obedient slaves, you are slaves of the one whom you obey, either of sin . . . or of obedience . . ."). V. 13c is Lukan interpretation ("You cannot serve God and wealth").

The Law and the Prophets on Money and Marriage (16:14-18)

Interpreters have puzzled about how the units of ch. 16 are connected. When Romulus and Moses gave their "constitutions" to Rome and Israel respectively, they outlined financial and marital laws (see Dionysius *Rom. Ant.* 2.8-10, 24-27; Josephus *Ant.* 3.269-79, 282; 4.129-64, 231-43, 244-65, 266-75, 285-89, 301), which Jesus does in this unit. Luke's collection of texts has at least two sources: Luke is redacting Mark, who presents a block of material on household-related topics: marriage and divorce (Mark 10:2-12), children (10:13-16), and possessions (10:17-31; see Osiek and Balch: 127, 137-38). From this block, Luke retains only Luke 16:18, separating this one verse from the Markan unit on the household, delaying retelling the units about children and the rich man (until 18:15-17, 18-30). Luke is less interested than Mark in the relationships within birth families, but more interested in ethical behavior in the new fictive, church families. Some discussions contemporary with Luke insisted that household management should primarily concern possessions, not household relationships (e.g., Epicurus and his later follower Philodemus: Diogenes Laertius 10.119-20; see Balch 2003a). Luke comes close to this, breaking up the Markan unit on the household.

Luke characterizes the "Pharisees" in this narrative as "lovers of money" (16:14), effectively making them symbols of such characters in Luke's contemporary society and church (see Dionysius *Rom. Ant.* 7.65.5; 8.35.4; 47.3). And these patrons ridicule Jesus' parable, suggesting that they give away their money and/or forgive debts of the poor (compare Dionysius *Rom. Ant.* 6.59.3 and 63.3; Balch 1997: 129). Such wealthy patrons characteristically thought much of themselves (16:15; compare Dionysius *Rom. Ant.* 6.59.1; 7.34.2-5; 45.4; 54.5; 63.1). But God knows human hearts (Acts 1:24). That which is "exalted" by humans is an "abomination" to God (15:15; compare v. 13), an apocalyptic contrast (see Mark 13:14; Rev 17:4-5; 21:27) that points to the kind of bipolar reversal announced in the *Magnificat* (1:47, 51-53).

Luke moves from a spatial contrast (exaltation/humiliation; Abraham's bosom/Hades) to a chronological differentiation of the times of salvation history. "The law and the prophets were in effect until John came; since then the good news of the kingdom of God is proclaimed . . ." (16:16). A great deal of ink has been spilled over whether John belongs on one side or the other of this division. Acts 10:37 says that "the message spread throughout Judea, *beginning* in Galilee *after* the baptism that John announced"; in Luke's Gospel that would be after 3:3-22, after John had been imprisoned (3:20). John proclaims the "good news," but not actually the "kingdom" (see 1:69, 77; 3:18). More crucial, God's acts that had been the center of salvation history are reduced to prehistory, to the age which anticipates the new center of salvation history. This prehistory is recounted by Stephen and Paul in Acts 7 and 13. The new center is Jesus' proclamation of the kingdom of God (16:16b; see 4:18, 43). "And everyone tries to enter it by force" (16:16c). The NRSV translation just given uses a middle voice of the verb, but it might be passive: "and everyone is compelled to enter it," which encourages a positive response to Jesus' urgent message.

Luke, like other ancient historians, insists that the ancient laws must be kept, not abolished (16:17; compare Dionysius *Rom. Ant.* 7.70-73). Even when, from a modern point of view, change happened, for example, uncircumcised, unclean Gentiles entered the people of God, Luke must insist that this was the original intention of the ancient laws, and therefore constitutes no change (see the accusations in Acts 6:13-14; 21:21, 24); on the contrary, it was prophesied in the law itself. In the Gospel this yields the story of Jesus' circumcision (2:21); in Acts it produces the unhistorical story of an orthopraxic Paul.

Finally, this unit on wealth, justice, and the law includes a law on marriage and adultery (16:18), only one verse from Mark's section (10:2-31) on the household. Seim argues that this verse not only addresses those who want to remarry after divorce but also excludes primarily the possibility of remarriage by male disciples who have left their wives behind, without necessarily divorcing them (see 18:29). This Lukan prescription, then, is quite different from Paul's, who forbids separation (1 Cor 7:10-11), assumed by Luke. Among the Gospels, Luke has the most radical critique of marriage and promotes ascetic values (see Osiek and Balch: 136-40; Carter; and Seim).

The Rich Man and the Beggar Lazarus (16:19-31)

In the parable the earthly contrast rich/beggar (*plousios/ ptōchos;* 16:19 and 22; see 6:20, 24; 10:15) is reversed after the two characters' deaths when the unnamed beggar is carried away by angels to "Abraham's bosom" (16:22), but the rich man is buried and finds himself in "Hades" (v. 23). This parable features bipolar reversal, the reversal of the roles of both rich and poor, proud and humble.

Similarly, Peter quotes Ps 16:10 (15:10 LXX), interpreting it to mean that God did not abandon Christ in *Hades* (Acts 2:27 and 31), but raised him up, where he was "exalted *(hypsōtheis)* at the right hand of God" (vv. 32-33). Peter quotes the prophets (Joel) and the Psalms to prove this resurrection from the dead (compare Acts 2:31, 32, 34 with Luke 16:30-31), followed by a demand for repentance (Acts 2:38), precisely the goal of Jesus' parable (Luke 16:30; see 15:7, 10; 17:3-4). The language in the Philippians' hymn (2:6-11) is quite similar, but the distance between the poles being reversed is the greatest possible contrast: form of God/form of a slave (*morphē theou/ morphēn doulou;* vv. 6-7)! Christ "humbled *(etapeinōsen)* himself . . . to the point of death . . . on a cross; therefore God also highly exalted *(hyperhypsōsen)* him . . . and every tongue should confess that Jesus Christ is Lord . . ." (*kyrios;* vv. 8-11). The primary contrast in these texts is not a chronological, eschatological one (although see 16:14-15), but is spatial and social: high/low, exalted/humiliated, bosom of Abraham/Hades, rich/poor, form of God/ form of a slave, and Lord/slave. The basic polarity is christological (Philippians 2; Acts 2), a contrast extended to Mary (Luke 1) that also has consequences for social ethics (Luke 16).

Culpepper: 316 describes this parable as a drama in three acts. The first act (16:19-21) introduces the characters but has no action. Bodmer Papyrus 75, dated about 200, supplies the rich man with a name: Neues. The rich man "rejoiced daily" (v. 19), where "daily" is an implicit reminder of the Lord's Prayer, which assumes that people must pray, "give us our daily bread" (11:3; see Dionysius *Rom. Ant.* 6.79.2). The rich man does not do anything overtly evil to the beggar; he simply does not open his eyes to see the poor. This scene is easily imaginable on Roman streets, where luxurious houses had commercial shops in the front if, as was often the case, they were situated on a busy street. Ancient cities were not zoned as are modern ones, on which it is even easier not to see foreigners or the poor.

The short second act (16:22) is the reversal: the poor man died and was carried by the angels to Abraham's bosom; the rich man also died and was buried, finding himself in Hades. According to Acts 2:27, 31, Hades is separated from the right hand of God, but to focus on determining the geography of the world beyond death would be to miss the point of this story.

The third act (16:23-31) questions directly addressed to the readers of the Gospel, is the longest. As is uniquely typical of Luke's special parables, dialogue occurs between the characters, in this case three exchanges between the rich man and Abraham. In the first exchange (vv. 24, 25-26), the rich man addresses Abraham as "Father," which recalls John the Baptist's insistence that "God is able from these stones to raise up children to Abraham" (3:8). Since most of the readers of the Gospel are Gentiles, at one level this may reassure them that they belong to God's people. Second, the rich man asks for mercy, which he had never shown to Lazarus, quite typical of elite attitudes toward the poor in Greco-Roman cities, as is lamented by Isocrates (*Panegyricus* 167–68; cited by Balch 1995a: 219). Third, he still assumes the arrogant attitude of a master, demanding that Abraham send Lazarus to serve him. Abraham simply replies that this typical social assumption is no longer functional, a response equivalent to the Pauline baptismal confession, "there is no longer slave or free" (Gal 3:28; see Luke 12:37). Questions of economic status are involved in this first exchange.

The second (16:27-28, 29) and third (vv. 30, 31) exchanges assume early Christian missionary activity and sermons like Peter's Pentecost address. The rich man asks Abraham to "send" Lazarus (*pempō;* v. 27; see 4:26; 20:11-13; Acts 10:22; 11:29; 15:22, 25; also *apostellō*: Luke 4:18, 43; 9:2; 10:1, 3; Acts 28:28) to his father's "house," which assumes that the Christian mission converted households (see 10:5, 38; Acts 11:14; 16:15, 31; 18:8). Abraham's final two responses (16:29, 31) assume the Christian conviction that Torah and the prophets say that "the Messiah is to suffer and to rise from the dead on the third day" (24:46; Acts 2:32). The rich man's reversal, his finding himself in Hades, means that he failed to recognize the sovereign God of reversals who cares for the poor in any century, the first or twenty-first. In the final verse, the readers of the Gospel are offered identification with the rich man's brothers: Will we listen to Moses and the prophets or to the one who has been raised from the dead?

Disciples' Forgiveness and Faith (17:1-10)

Still addressing the disciples, Jesus voices a "woe" to those who are the occasion for "little ones" to be" scandalized" (17:1). The latter term is found in Luke otherwise only in 7:23, where some might be scandalized by the kind of Messiah Jesus is, one who cleanses lepers and preaches to the poor. It occurs more often in Mark, where believers may be scandalized by eschatological crisis or persecution (4:17; see 6:3; 14:27, 29).

The "least" in the kingdom are greater than John (Luke 7:28), and the "least," the child, is "welcome" among Jesus' followers (9:48). Jesus refers to the disciples as the "little" flock, to whom God gives the kingdom (12:32). All those in Samaria, "from the least to the greatest," listened to Simon Magus (Acts 8:10), and Paul, addressing King Agrippa, says he testifies "to both small and great" (26:22). The term "little ones," then, has social connotations, referring perhaps to the urban poor and slaves, those who are not kings, which connects the term with the previous parable contrasting the rich man and the beggar Lazarus. Jesus' saying in 17:2 is then a warning to those with social status, to Christian patrons, not to be scandalized by his preaching to the poor, nor themselves to scandalize these "little ones," the children, poor, and slaves.

The second saying (17:3-4) demands that the disciples rebuke sinners, but if they repent, to forgive "seven times a day!" Matthew (18:22) colorfully says, "seventy times seven." After the holocaust, contemporary Jews have rightfully raised the question whether forgiveness means helping the sinner avoid the consequences of sins, which would often encourage repetition of the wrongs, which is not what Jesus is saying. (See Wiesenthal, *The Sunflower: On the Possibilities and Limits of Forgiveness.*)

The disciples respond by asking, "Increase our faith!" (17:5). But Jesus' response is mixed or grammatically corrupt. The saying begins with the assumption that the condition is real ("If you had faith the size of a mustard seed"), but concludes with a Greek construction indicating that the condition is contrary to fact ("you could say to this tree . . . , be planted in the sea. . . .") Although the disciples request more faith, Jesus challenges them by observing that if they had any, they could. . . .

The following parable (17:7-10) is also confrontational, hard for modern Christians to hear, since we are taught to meet our own needs. We are shocked by Jesus' parable of a slave who has duties but no rights, the legal situation of Greco-Roman slaves. Perhaps in interpretation we should pair this slave parable with the one in 12:35-38 (see the commentary above) that states the opposite of the present parable: "[he or she, the master] will have them [the slaves] sit down to eat, and he will come and serve *(diakonēsei)* them [dinner]" (12:37). As First-World Christians, typically devoted to our own pleasure and living in rich countries, we can hear the earlier parable easily because we identify with others serving us, but is not the parable of 17:7-10 an appropriate challenge for those of us who are not usually focused on seeing or meeting the needs of others in God's world? Luke's Gospel as a whole challenges readers to "welcome" and share our food with foreigners and the poor, with God's children whose needs are rarely met. This parable begins by inviting the hearer to identify with the master (17:7, "Who among you would say to your slave . . . ?"), but shifts at the end by suggesting identification with the slave (v. 10, "So you also, when you have done all that you were ordered to do, say, 'we are worthless slaves . . .'"). This shift is precisely what the author of this Gospel is suggesting for wealthy masters and leaders in the churches, that they learn to "serve" (*diakonei,* v. 8) "little ones" (v. 2) in the worship assembly (see 22:24-27; Osiek and Balch: 187-88, 204-6; Culpepper: 323).

The Samaritan Foreigner's Exceptional Praise to God for Being Cleansed (17:11-19)

The author picks up the motif (from 9:51) of Jesus' journey to Jerusalem. Seven chapters after the journey began, Jesus is still "going through the region between Samaria and Galilee," a famous phrase probably showing that the storyteller had an inexact idea of geography in Israel.

The healing story becomes a pronouncement story, so that the point is in the final saying(s), "Was none of them found to return and give praise to God except this foreigner?" (*allogenēs;* 17:18). Naaman the Syrian had also returned to Samaria to offer a present to Elisha the prophet, who had cleansed him of leprosy (2 Kgs 5:15). In Luke's Gospel the story of this foreign leper being "cleansed" prepares for the key story in Luke's second volume, the conversion of Cornelius, also a "foreigner" (*allophylos;* Acts 10:28) who was "cleansed" (Acts 10:14-15; 11:8-9; 15:9).

Not surprisingly, the pronouncement story in the Gospel concludes, "your faith has made you well" (Luke 17:19), or, more literally, "your faith has saved you." This parable of the one leper among ten who returned to praise God thus continues the emphasis on the "little ones" (v. 2) for whom Jesus and God care. Further, Luke's readers would hear the story not primarily as a critique of ethnocentrism in Israel, but as addressed at another level to their own Greek or Roman ethnocentrism (see Balch 1998a; 2003b). The "integration" of foreign ethnic groups (in the language of Acts, "welcoming" them) and disdain for racist "segregation" (for those who refuse *koinōnia*) were primary values in the Roman world, values honored even though they often were not actually practiced.

The Presence of the Kingdom of God and the Sudden Future Coming of the Son of Humanity (17:20-37)

Following the provocative either/ors of the travel narrative, it is not surprising that Jesus warns of future judgment, a warning he has repeatedly stated (see 9:62; 10:12, 15, 18; 12:2, 5, 8, 40, 49; 13:9, 25, 34-35; 14:14, 24; 16:9, 15, 23, 28). Jesus will again make a speech on eschatological concerns in 21:5-36, a text that is clearer in some ways than is 17:20-37. Most of this section is Q material. Following those sayings in the travel narrative, Jesus says that the kingdom is not something external that simply "can be observed" (17:20), and "the kingdom of God is among you" (v. 21). The Son of Humanity on his "day" will be like a lightning flash across the sky (v. 24), like an apocalypse when fire and brimstone rained to destroy Sodom (v. 30). People sharing the same daily life will be separated by swift judgment in the night (vv. 34-35). In Jesus' setting, this was an urgent appeal not to let good meals, marriages, and commerce lull them into ignoring God's demand for radical righteousness, not to be like the complacent contemporaries of Noah and Lot.

Luke's revising of the materials presents problems: What are the "days [plural] of the Son of Humanity" in 17:26? Similarly, "*one* of the days of the Son of Humanity" (v. 22) has no parallel but is probably related somehow to "the Son of Humanity . . . in his day" (v. 24). Enigmatic, too, is the concluding saying, "Where the corpse is, there the vultures will gather" (v. 37), although the question, "Where?" connects its meaning with the opening negation (v. 21). Luke took over this material from Q and anticipates an eschatological crisis, with some hints of delay (vv. 22, 25). The content of this section is primarily warning of coming judgment, not promise to the faithful, although Luke adds consolation in the following parable (18:1-8).

The "Pharisees," who consistently represent the disciples' misunderstanding, ask Jesus about the kingdom (17:20) and hear that it is not open to simple observation as if a neutral observer could point and say "here!" or "there!" (v. 21), a warning given also to the disciples (v. 23). Rather, it is presently "among you" and can be perceived in the manner that Jesus has been teaching on this journey (since 9:51). But "the [future] days are coming" when the disciples will be offered apocalyptic signs, and Jesus warns, "do not set off in pursuit" (v. 23). The future apocalypse will be sudden (v. 24), but first the "Son of Humanity must endure much suffering and be rejected by this generation" (v. 25; cf. 9:21-22). "This generation" (17:25) is wicked in Luke's Gospel (see 16:8), so the paragraph is an eschatological warning. In Noah's day, too, people were "eating and drinking, marrying and being given in marriage," and the flood destroyed all of them (17:27). The ordinary activities of living are somehow judged negatively, as in 20:34-35 and as Paul does in 1 Cor 7:29-31, "the appointed time has grown very short; from now on, let even those who have wives be as though they had none, . . . and those who buy *(agorazō)* as though they had no possessions, and those who deal with the world as though they had no dealings with it. For the present form of this world is passing away." The verb "be married" (*gamizō;* Luke 17:27 par. Matt 24:38; Luke 20:35; and 1 Cor 7:38) is quite rare, and may connect this Q saying to Corinth, indicating that Paul is teaching them these same eschatological values. The next saying concerning Lot has a similarly negative view of "buying" *(agorazō)* and "selling," as does 1 Cor 7:30.

Luke advises any disciple on the roof not to come down, a disciple working in the field not to turn back (17:31-32). The initial picture of the coming of the Son of Humanity is one of suddenness (v. 24), but inconsistently the sayings in vv. 31-32 assume that a disciple will have time to make decisions, so the Gospel writer exhorts the reader (v. 32, "Remember Lot's wife!").

Then Luke summarizes: "Those who try to make their life secure will lose it" (17:33a), as Jesus has taught repeatedly (see 12:13-21 on the rich fool; 14:25-35; 16:1-9). "But those who lose their life will keep it" (17:33b), those, for example, who "hate father and mother, wife and children . . . ," who carry the cross, and "give up all possessions" (14:26, 27, 33), challenges difficult to comprehend both for ancient and for modern followers of Jesus.

17:34-35 illustrate with two scenes drawn from daily life, two on a bed and two women grinding meal: "one will be taken, and the other left." We do not know what Luke means by "taken" unless we may fill in with a Pauline statement like 1 Thess 4:16-17, "For the Lord himself . . . will descend from heaven. . . . Then we who are alive, who are left, will be caught up in the clouds together with them to meet the Lord in the air; and so we will be with the Lord forever." But Luke never has anything this graphic (see 21:27), so we are left uncertain, except that judgment and salvation are involved.

The unit concludes with the enigmatic 17:37. "Where" recalls v. 21, thus including the whole eschatological discourse. The image may be drawn from wisdom literature: the Lord confronts Job, "Is it at your command that the eagle mounts up? . . . and where the slain are, there it is" (Job 39:26-30; Culpepper: 333). This would illustrate the combination of apocalyptic images and wisdom found in the book of Daniel. In this context, the image must refer to judgment, to those "securing their life" (17:33), doing the ordinary activities of eating, marrying

(v. 27), and engaging in business (v. 28) as if these were ordinary times, not times of decision in which one must act decisively.

The Parable of the Widow and the Unjust Judge (18:1-8)

Luke connects this parable with what precedes and what follows. In Luke's interpretation, Jesus' parable has multiple meanings: the surprising final question, suddenly reflecting on "when the Son of Humanity comes" (18:8), connects the parable with the preceding eschatological section that had repeatedly raised the same concern (17:22, 24, 30). But the introduction (18:1) focuses the meaning of the parable on prayer, the topic of the following parable (18:9-14). And although the context is further removed, this parable of an "unjust judge" (18:6) recalls another main character, the "unjust slave manager" (16:8). Jesus challenges the disciples to learn even from the actions of the unjust.

Groups of women, especially widows, are prominent in Luke-Acts, which reflects their presence in the Lukan churches (see Seim). The auditors of Luke's Gospel included groups of "widows" modeled on Anna (2:37; see Acts 6:1-6; 9:39, 41); this parable is virtually parenesis directed especially to these widows, who "worshiped there [in house churches with patrons like Dorcas?] with fasting and prayer night and day" (2:37). Differently from Luke, the author of the deutero-Pauline Pastoral Epistles wants some of these women to remarry (1 Tim 5:14).

18:1 is a redactional introduction to the parable, which is narrated in vv. 2-5. By asking two questions v. 7 gives interpretations different from the one suggested in the introduction, and v. 8b suggests yet another reading, showing a discussion of Jesus' parables in the early church comparable to rabbinic midrash that multiplied legitimate interpretations of biblical texts.

18:1 directs the parable to widows whose vocation is prayer as well as to all Lukan Christians, who are to pray "always." They are "not to lose heart," an expression that could also be translated "not to despair" in the eschatological crisis (Gal 6:9; 2 Cor 4:1, 16; Eph 3:13). This reflects Jesus' own prayer in times of eschatological "temptation" or at significant moments in the history of salvation (6:12; 9:18; 22:39-46).

Jesus' parable introduces a judge who "neither feared God nor had respect for people" (18:2). He is neither pious nor just (see v. 6); the readers learn that he is unfit to be a judge. The second character is a widow, and the verbs used of her (v. 3) indicate that she continuously was saying (see "always" in v. 1) to the judge, "Grant me justice against my opponent." We are not informed about her grievance, nor about why the judge was delaying, neither of which then can be the key to understanding the story. As is typical of almost all the parables found only in Luke, we hear the judge's interior monologue (Paffenroth: 98-99, 104), which repeats and thus reinforces the storyteller's characterization of him from v. 2. He does not fear God or respect anyone, that is, he is without piety or honor. Despite this, he decides to grant the widow justice for two reasons: she bothers him, and he does not want to be worn out, for Luke surely an allegorical reference to Christian widows' persistence in prayer (cf. 18:1 and 2:26, 30, 37, which records God's response to the persistent prayers of Simeon and Anna). 18:7 supplements v. 1: first, the persistent prayers of God's chosen will elicit "justice," and, second, God will not delay long in helping them.

Luke does not promise magic, that humans can manipulate God in order to receive exactly what we want. Luke 11:8-9 and 13 similarly encourage persistence in prayer and promise that those who ask will receive . . . "the good gift of the Holy Spirit." In the First World we often pray for our financial security, but it would be grossly inappropriate to interpret Luke this way, the Gospel that repeatedly asks us to give up our possessions. Second, God will not long delay in helping, but will quickly grant justice (18:7b-8a; see 1:17; 14:14; Acts 22:14; 24:15; contrast Luke 15:7). However, Luke's basic category in the Gospel is not "justice" but whether humans who are indeed unjust have been "forgiven" (see 18:11; 24:47). Finally, in 18:8 the author refers the meaning of the parable back to the previous eschatological section of the Gospel. The focus is no longer on persistence in prayer or on God's responding, but now on whether humans respond to God with faith, decisive when the Son of Humanity comes (see already 1:20, 45; also 24:25; Acts 2:44).

The Pharisee and the Tax Collector (18:9-14)

The author again connects this uniquely Lukan parable to what precedes and to what follows. The parable continues the theme of prayer, but it introduces the contrast (which becomes a reversal of roles) between the proud and the humble (see 18:15-25), a contrast between persons that is both religious and social. Luke introduces this parable by aiming its critique at "some who trusted in themselves that they were righteous and regarded others with contempt" (v. 9). Luke encourages the reader to think that this characterizes the "Pharisee" of the parable, but a believer hearing the Gospel read while reclining in a Roman dining room *(triclinium)* for the Lord's Supper would recognize that these words describe a whole social class of persons in Greco-Roman society.

Dionysius (*Rom. Ant.* 6.72-80) describes the conflict between patricians and plebeians in Roman society (see Balch 1995a: 221-30, esp. 223-25), a conflict between "the arrogant" *(hoi hyperēphanoi)* and "the humble" *(hoi tapeinoi;* Dionysius 6.72.3 and 76.2), exactly the two groups referred to in the parable's conclusion (18:14). In the history of the relationship between those who are proud and those who are humble, or those who are rich and those who are poor, there is a debate about which group has "offended/sinned," which group is "just" *(dikaios),* and, therefore, which group needs "pardon/forgiveness" (*amnestia* and *aphesis;* Dionysius 6.73.1-3). The proud class claim to be "virtuous" and vilify rural farmers and the poor (8.6.2-3). Characteristically, the proud/rich refuse to share their blessings, to have *koinōnia,* with the humble poor (6.80.4). These contrasts are also individualized: one of the patricians, Appius Claudius, "sets great value upon himself" (6.59.1) and characterizes the poor as "vile and humble wretches who have committed sins/offenses" (6.60.3). Another, Coriolanus, is advised to descend from his haughtiness *(hyperēphanon)* to assume the humble demeanor *(schēma tapeinon)* of one who has erred/sinned *(hēmartēkotos;* 7.45.4 and 63.1), which he refuses to do (7.67.3). When Christians reclining in the dining room of a well-to-do Roman house heard Luke's retelling of Jesus' parable, they would recognize character types in their own culture. In the introduction (18:9) and conclusion (v. 14), Luke addresses this parable to the proud wealthy patron(s) and host(s) of the Christian worship assembly. Greco-Roman culture taught them to despise the poor, who are now guests in their house church, but the Greek story cited above also calls those elitist values into question, as does Jesus' parable. The same message will be heard later in Jesus last testament at the Lord's Supper (22:24-27; see 14:7-11, which also concludes, "For all who exalt themselves . . .").

18:11 places this typical class distinction in the mouth of the "Pharisee" and has him thank God for the difference. V. 12 has him list his pieties in Jewish terms: fasting twice a week and tithing all his income. The *Didache* (8:1) also has Jews fasting twice a week; and tithing has its origin in Scripture (Num 18:21-24; Deut 14:22-26). We do not have to think of the class values as *either* Greco-Roman or Jewish. A friend, Stanley Stowers, suggests an analogy: millions today are Freudians, whether they have read Freud or not. Similarly, the economic class values narrated by Dionysius were held in Rome but also in Corinth, Philippi, and Antioch by Greeks and "barbarians," Jews and Gentiles. Luke's introduction and conclusion picture a God who will reverse the position of the arrogant elite and the humble poor (see also Mary's *Magnificat,* Jesus' parable of the rich man and Lazarus, and Peter's Pentecost sermon).

The tax collector's prayer, "God be merciful to me, a sinner" (18:13), echoes Ps 51[LXX 50]:3, 17, and in the Apocrypha, the Prayer of Manasseh 7 and 11–15.

The Little Children and the Rich Ruler (18:15-30)

The former parable was Lukan, but with this story Luke nears the end of the narrative journey to Jerusalem and returns to following the Markan sequence. The two preceding sections contrast a persistent widow and an unjust judge, a Pharisee and a tax collector. Culpepper: 344 observes that the two short stories of Jesus receiving children and of Jesus' interaction with a (rich) ruler are juxtaposed, not directly contrasted; but read together they illustrate the kingdom.

People bring infants to Jesus that he might "touch" them. This may refer to Jesus' healing touch (see 5:13; 6:19; 7:14; 8:44-47; 22:51), although the text is not explicit (he also touches an unclean sinner, 7:39). Sickness and death among infants and children were much higher in earlier societies. Half the number of babies born did not live until their fifth birthday, and only 40 percent reached age twenty; a couple needed to have five children if they wanted two of them to reach child-bearing age (Osiek and Balch: 67). Nor does the text explain why the disciples "sternly ordered them not to do it" (18:15). We may overhear some clues about why in Jesus' following two pronouncements: "let the children come *(erchesthai)* to me, and do not stop (or forbid, *kōlyō*) them; for it is to such as these that the kingdom of God belongs" (v. 16). "Truly, I tell you, whoever does not receive *(dexetai)* the kingdom of God as a little child will never enter *(eiselthȩ̄,* past tense of *erchesthai)* it (v. 17). These two sayings in Luke (and already in Mark) parallel children "coming" to Jesus and others "coming" into the kingdom. Luke has shown us shepherds coming with haste to Jesus (2:16); those who come, hear, and act on Jesus' words (6:47); others who come and are afraid (8:35); Jairus, who comes and begs for healing (8:41); a hemorrhaging woman who comes, touches Jesus in faith, and trembles as he pronounces her well (8:47); the queen of the South coming from the ends of the earth to hear Solomon, who is not as great as the Son of Humanity (11:31); the rejection of those who come to Jesus but do not hate their father and mother . . . (14:26-27); believers who come and confess their magic practices (Acts 19:18); and Roman Jews who come to Paul to hear him testify (Acts 28:23). Presumably the shepherds, Jairus, the hemorrhaging woman, the queen of the South, and those who reject their natural family have come as "babies," and Jesus insists that the disciples not forbid them, as they had attempted to forbid another exorcist (9:49-50), and as scribes by interpreting Scripture (!) had hindered others from entering (11:52). In Acts a eunuch asks if anything prohibits him from baptism (8:36), and Peter asks whether anyone can forbid water for baptizing Gentiles (10:17; see 11:17).

Some disciples of the first century attempted to forbid some sorts of people from "entering." Lev 15:19-31 legislates that a hemorrhaging woman not defile the LORD's tabernacle, and Deut 23:1 forbids any eunuch from "being admitted to the assembly of the LORD," legislation that Luke-Acts (without explicitly citing Leviticus or Deuteronomy) reverses. Any today who would forbid the wrong sorts of persons, for example, those of differing sexual orientations, from entering our assemblies would run a high risk of disobeying our Lord, who pictures all sorts of persons entering the kingdom.

The following story (18:18-23) forms a contrast with the previous one. Both ancient and modern religious communities would typically be shocked that Jesus would invite infants to come/enter the kingdom (18:10) but say that the rich cannot enter (18:25). This story about "receiving" infants, placed at the conclusion of the travel narrative, reflects another at the beginning of the journey to Jerusalem (see the comments on 9:25-50, esp. 46-50).

In Mark, a "man," whom Luke makes a "ruler" to sharpen the contrast, asks Jesus what he must do to inherit eternal life. Only late in the HB is there hope for "eternal life" (Dan 12:2). Earlier Israel hoped to inherit the land, when living according to the statutes of the covenant (Deut 4:1; 29:8-9). In Luke's day, some hoped for the resurrection of the body (2 Macc 7:9, 14, 29, 36; 4 Macc 7:19; 16:25, alluding to Exod 3:6; Luke 20:35-38, another allusion to Exod 3:6; Luke 24:41-43; Acts 23:6-9). The ruler's question assumes both that he must "do" something and that eternal life is God's gift (that one may "inherit" the blessings of the covenant). As a "teacher," John had been asked a similar question (3:12; see the poignant question in Ezek 33:10). The Pharisee Simon listened to Jesus as "teacher" (7:40; see 19:39). A lawyer had asked Jesus exactly the same question about eternal life (10:25), and Jesus had answered quoting the Torah commandments (10:26-27), which means that this question with various scriptural answers was taught in the Lukan churches. As a "teacher," Jesus may also be asked hostile questions (20:21-23, 27-28), which is perhaps what the ruler is doing in 18:18.

Jesus responds further to the ruler, quoting from the second half of the Ten Commandments and listing them in the same order Philo does (*Decal.* 12.51), *concluding* with the command to honor father and mother (Fitzmyer 1981: 1199). Surprisingly for some modern readers, the ruler responds that he has observed (*phylassō,* guarded) all these from his youth (18:21; already in Mark 10:20; compare 1 Cor 4:4; Phil 3:6). This view may not really differ from those of Luther and Melanchthon, who stressed the impossibility of obeying the *first* table of the Ten Commandments without God's grace (111-12, 125).

Only Matthew adds, "love your neighbor as yourself" (Lev 19:18; see Luke 10:27), perhaps as an explanation of Jesus' further demand to give one's possessions to the poor (one's neighbor). Jesus responds that the ruler still lacks one thing, which he indicates with four imperative verbs: sell all you have, give to the poor *(ptōchois),* come, and follow me (18:22). Jesus attaches a promise to the first two verbs ("you will have treasure in heaven"), rather than the final two verbs. These demands, which either interpret or go beyond Torah, result in the ruler's becoming sad, for he was "exceedingly rich" (v. 23). Reflecting on v. 27, interpreters often call Jesus' demands "impossible." In Greco-Roman society, however, Crates was one of the Cynic philosophers who did give away their wealth and become "poor" (Diogenes Laertius 6.87; see the commentary on 5:27-39). Despite our modern values, some ancients did what Jesus demands.

Theissen (38) observes that Jesus was "inconsistent" in his demands, telling this ruler to "sell all" but accepting financial support from other wealthy patrons (8:3; cf. Acts 4:32; 16:15, 40). His radical demand to "sell all" sometimes functioned to encourage Christians to share wealth (19:8-9), but other times, it must be admitted, it has either been ignored, especially in modern capitalist societies, or it has served as an ideology that made no practical difference. In contrast to our values, Jesus teaches that God's blessings, the kingdom of God, belong not to the rich but to the poor (6:20, 24) and to infants.

Luke has Jesus continue the theme of "entering" the kingdom of God, which for those having possessions is virtually impossible (18:24; see vv. 16, 17, 25). Wealthy householders in Lukan house churches (see Acts) would thus also feel addressed by Jesus.

Commentators have generally abandoned metaphorical interpretations of Jesus' aphorism in 18:25: Jesus refers to a (large) camel and to the (tiny) eye of a real needle. For the former to "enter" the latter is ludicrous, impossible, which the hearers understand (v. 26; see the imagery in Matt 23:24). 18:27 is then an early commentary on Jesus' images; wealthy Christian householders are reassured that what Jesus pictured as impossible is possible for God (see Gen 18:14).

Peter responds (18:28) to the commands Jesus had given in vain to the ruler (v. 22): "we" have left our personal affairs (*ta idia,* not Mark's "all things"), thus left not only whatever wealth they had but also "father, mother, wife, children, brothers, and sisters" (14:26; contrast Matt 8:14; 1 Cor 9:5; see the commentary on 5:27-39 above) and "followed" you. Jesus affirms (18:29) that whoever has left personal affairs for the sake of the kingdom of God will get back "much more" (*not* as Mark promises [10:30], "houses, brothers, sisters, mothers, children, fields, with persecutions") in this age and in the age to come eternal life (18:29-30, see v. 18). For Luke neither in this age nor in the coming one does a disciple get back a wife (20:34-36), a reflection of early ascetic tendencies in Lukan churches.

The Third Prophecy of the Passion (18:31-34)

Luke had placed Mark's first two prophecies of Jesus' passion in 9:22, 44-45, then inserted the long travel narrative, and now nine chapters later, records the third prophecy (see Mark 10:32-34). Characteristically, Luke adds an emphasis on "fulfilling all the things written through the prophets" (18:31). In Mark the disciples never understand that Jesus and they will suffer, but Luke ends his Gospel narrative with the resurrected Jesus giving them Bible lessons so that they do finally understand (24:25-27, 44-48), which legitimates them for church leadership (Acts). But in this passage the disciples accept suffering no more than the rich ruler had accepted giving up his wealth. Luke omits Mark's (10:33) reference to Jewish leaders' role in condemning Jesus to death, focusing instead on the Gentiles mocking and killing him (reflecting language from Isa 50:6), and on God's raising him on the third day (18:32-35). Both Mark and Luke place phrases from early Christian confessions (1 Cor 15:3b-5) on Jesus' lips. Jesus' own words anticipating his death may be reflected in Luke 13:34 par. Matt 23:37, which anticipates his being "stoned" as a prophet.

The Blind Beggar (18:35-43)

Luke omits the crucial section on greatness and service (Mark 10:35-45) in order to place it later in the context of Jesus' final testament at the Lord's Supper (22:24-27). The story of the blind beggar may follow as a hopeful comment on the disciples' "blindness" to suffering (see 6:39; 24:31; also 4:18; 7:21-22; 14:13, 21). Ominously, some leaders in Jesus' crowd order the blind man to be silent (18:39), as some disciples had forbidden infants to come to Jesus (v. 16). Luke places the narrative as Jesus enters Jericho (contrast Mark 10:46), in order to tell the next story of Zacchaeus in Jericho. Luke also omits his name, Bartimaeus. The blind man hears that "Jesus of Nazareth" is passing by (18:37), a name that is often associated with Jesus as a healer (4:34; 24:19; Acts 2:22; 3:5; 4:10). He then repeatedly shouts, "Jesus, Son of David, have mercy on me!" (18:37, 39). The infancy narratives already make this claim (1:27, 32, 69; 2:4, 11; 3:31; 20:41-42, 44; Acts 2:25, 29, 34; 15:16), and God's sending this Son of David is precisely an act of mercy (1:72, 78-79 ["to give light to those who sit in darkness," an allusion to Isa 42:7 and 60:1-3]). Jesus commands that the blind man be led to him and asks what he wishes. He asks to see again, which Jesus commands (18:41-42), explaining that his faith has saved him. The story exhibits a pattern: Jesus' *disciples* resisted (a) religiously marginal person(s) coming to him, (b) the person(s) have faith, and (c) they are accepted (cf. Acts 10:28-29; 11:1-3, 18; 15:1-3, 5, 19; 21:20-21, 27-29).

Jesus and Zacchaeus, a Wealthy Convert (19:1-10)

As Jesus passes through Jericho, we learn of a man named Zacchaeus, a chief tax (or toll) collector, who was rich, information the author gave us only at the end of the story of the (rich) ruler (18:18-23). Since the reader has just heard Jesus say that it is virtually impossible for a rich person to enter the kingdom of God (18:25), this information sets up clear expectations, which the story itself reverses, legitimating wealthy householders who host churches. Despite the Lukan critique of wealth, rich persons who are willing to enact the reversals of the kingdom (see 12:35-38; 22:24-27) are among the outcasts whom Jesus came to save (19:9-10). Thus, this special Lukan story at the conclusion of the travel narrative is close to the interests of Acts.

Zacchaeus, a short, rich man, ran to climb a sycamore [fig] tree, neglecting his own honor and dignity. Jesus invites him down from the tree, "for I must stay at your house today" (19:5). Zacchaeus obeys eagerly and "welcomes" him (v. 6). This cluster of terms "house," "stay," and "welcome" occur in stories referring to the missionary conversion of households (9:4-5; 10:5-8; Acts 16:15, 40; 18:3; see 21:7-8), of which this story is a prototype. But there were objections to Jesus' ascetic missionary followers being hosted by wealthy patrons, so some (Christians) grumble (19:7). This function of the story may explain commentators' debates over interpreting v. 8. Luke has transformed a story of the conversion of a rich man's household into an apology legitimating wealthy Christian patrons. V. 8 had concerned the genuineness of Zacchaeus's repentance. The present tense verb may be read as futuristic or ingressive: "Look, half of my possessions, Lord, I am intending to give to the poor (*ptōchoi*). . . ." But Luke is defending Christian householders like Lydia, Aquila, and Priscilla; if they give half their wealth to the poor, salvation has come to their house (v. 9; despite Jesus' saying in 18:25). Verse 8 becomes a protest against some Christians' exclusive emphasis on Jesus' sayings (6:24) against the rich.

Jesus' Charge to Christian Leaders: The Kingship Parable (19:11-27)

This parable challenged the ancient reader; its final vengeance offends the modern one. We in the First World like to live our prosperous lifestyles, ignoring the lethal cost to people in the Two-Thirds World and to the earth's environment, but we are squeamish about the direct "slaughter" (19:27) of anyone. Luke's eschatology, however, does include a final judgment (21:36; Acts 17:31; cf. Acts 5:5, 10).

The traditional interpretation of the parable assumes that it corrects a false opinion in 19:11, that Luke is opposing some Christians' expectation of Jesus' imminent return (see Acts 1:6-7). Johnson: 293 points out, however, that Luke's readers did not expect the narrative to include Jesus establishing the kingdom when he rode into Jerusalem, and further, that if Luke was downplaying the importance of Jesus' entry into Jerusalem as king (19:28-40), he made a mess of it. Further, the nobleman in Luke's parable does not delay a long time before returning as king.

Instead, Johnson interprets the parable allegorically in the context of Luke's narrative. The nobleman is Jesus, who indeed will immediately be acclaimed king (19:38) and who will grant authority to his servant followers (24:49; Acts 1:8, 21-26). The fellow citizens who do not wish to have Jesus as king are the leaders of the people (19:47-48; 20:1, 19; 21:37-38; 22:2, 52-53, 66; 23:10, 13, 27, 35). The parable confirms the correct expectation in its introduction (19:11).

The parable is then primarily an exhortation to church leaders. The emphasis falls on the third "slave," who is afraid and inactive (19:20-26). The twelve (18:31) and the crowd (18:36; 19:3) had been "listening to this" (19:1), which must refer at least to the story of Zacchaeus (19:1-10), but in the context of Luke's narrative it more probably refers to all Jesus' many sayings (Q and L) on the journey (beginning in 9:51), one primary audience for which has been precisely church leaders (see the commentary on 10:1-16). These church leaders have Jesus' teachings as a bank "deposit" (19:21-23; see 1 Tim 6:20 and 2 Tim 1:14, all using the root of *tithēmi,* "entrust," "deposit"). Luke's exhortation is then similar to 2 Tim 1:7-8, "for God did not give us a spirit of cowardice. . . . Do not be ashamed, then, of the testimony of our Lord. . . ." Also 2 Tim 2:24, "the Lord's slave must be an apt teacher. . . ."

Jesus Teaching in the Temple (19:28–21:38)

The Triumphal Entry (19:28-40)

Jesus arrives at Jerusalem, the goal of the long travel narrative (9:51–19:27). The journey has concluded with a third prophecy of Jesus' passion (18:31-34), Jesus' healing a blind man who calls on him as the Son of David to have mercy (18:35-43), a story legitimating wealthy (Lukan) household patrons who give their possessions to the poor (19:1-10), and with Jesus' charge to these rich household leaders to be courageous and to invest their bank "deposit" of Jesus' teaching (19:11-27). After instructing successors, Jesus enters Jerusalem and his passion.

Jesus' triumphal entry reflects a kind of event that many in that century had experienced. It includes (1) the ruler being escorted into the city, (2) accompanying hymns, (3) symbolic depiction of the ruler's authority, and (4) the ruler symbolically taking charge of the city and its temple(s) (see Culpepper 1995: 366, citing Duff in *JBL* 111 [1992]: 66). Jesus the king (1) is escorted into the city by a multitude who spread their tattered clothes on the road (19:36-37), (2) they chant a Hallel psalm (v. 38, quoting Ps 118:26), (3) Jesus demonstrates his prophetic foreknowledge by his instructions to bring the colt (vv. 29-34), and (4) he assumes authority over the city by decrying its failure to recognize its visitation by God (vv. 41-44) and by cleansing the temple (vv. 45-46). Luke omits waving palm branches (see Mark 11:8), possibly because of their association with nationalistic hopes. Referring to the "multitude" of those accompanying Jesus, Luke gives the impression of "growth" from the small group of 8:1-3 (Johnson 1991: 297; see Acts 6:7, 9:31; 12:24; 19:20). And they "praise God" (19:37), a major motif in Luke-Acts, for all the "deeds of power" they had seen (see 4:14, 36; 6:19; 8:46; 9:1; 19:13, 19; Acts 2:22; 10:38).

The Mount of Olives (19:29, 37) may refer to the expectation that the eschatological appearance of the Lord would be on that mountain east of Jerusalem (Zech 14:4-5). Matt 21:5 quotes Zech 9:9 with its reference to "your king" coming to you, "humble and riding on a donkey." Luke does not quote the text, but the same expectations are in the background. Jesus rides into Jerusalem on a donkey, not a warhorse (see Gen 49:11; 1 Kgs 1:33, Solomon rides on David's mule/donkey; 2 Kgs 9:13).

Luke mentions the Pharisees for the last time in the Gospel in 19:39 (but see further Acts 15:5; 23:6-9). They object to the multitude proclaiming Jesus as King, as Jesus' kingship parable prophesied they would (19:14).

Jesus Crying over Jerusalem and Occupying the Temple to Teach (19:41-46)

The narrative of Jesus' crying over Jerusalem has been influenced both by Hebrew prophetic laments and perhaps by Josephus's or others' stories of the city's actual burning. Jesus accuses Jerusalem of not knowing "the things that make for peace" (19:42), referring to (Roman) ramparts encircling the city (v. 43) and the horrible deaths involved (v. 44). Josephus sees Jewish revolutionaries against Rome as the cause (see Josephus *J.W.* 2.409-10); Jesus rather sees their "not recognizing the time *(kairos)* of your visitation from God" (19:44). The *kairos* would be either a time of God's salvation or of judgment. Jesus had voiced a similar lament earlier (13:34-35), as had Jeremiah (chs. 11–20). We, too, may cry bitter tears that for the next two millennia the Jews had no political home, so that their "peace" depended on the whims of Roman, Christian, or Muslim rulers.

Luke drastically simplified Mark's account of Jesus occupying the temple. Jesus simply enters the temple and drives out the ones selling things (19:45), then loosely quotes Isa 56:7. For Luke the temple will have no future significance for Gentiles, so our author drops the last phrase: "my house shall be a house of prayer" (for all peoples). The temple has been central, however, so that the salvation of Gentiles must be announced from inside the temple (see Acts 22:17, 21).

These verses are often called the "cleansing" of the temple, but the Synoptic Gospels do not actually use that verb. On the contrary, Jesus' entry is a contrast to the "cleansing" of the temple portrayed in 2 Macc 10:7, where it means that "foreigners" are excluded. Jesus' inaugural sermon (4:18-19, 27) had quoted both Isaiah 61, proclaiming the year of God's "acceptance," and 1 Kings 17, narrating the "cleansing" of a foreign leper, Naaman the Syrian. Jesus occupies the temple in a narrative moving toward the acceptance and "cleansing" of the foreigner, Cornelius (Acts 10:28), not toward the cleansing of the temple.

Jesus Teaching in the Temple (19:47–21:38)

Following Jesus' entry into the temple, the next two verses (19:47-48) both introduce him "teaching" there "daily" and tell of the division in his audience, the leaders who want to kill him, and the "people" *(laos)* who "hear" him. The first six scenes present Jesus in conflict over authority with these leaders (ch. 20), followed by Jesus praising the widow for her offering (21:1-14). The final three sections in the temple warn the disciples (21:5-36) and are followed by the conclusion, observing again that the people were listening to him (21:37-38).

On one of the days when he was "teaching the people in the temple and evangelizing," the leaders ask him the key question that the readers of the Gospel of Luke also have in mind: "Who has given you this authority?" (20:1-2). By this point in the story both the leaders in Jerusalem and the readers of the Gospel have seen and heard much of the evidence, the history of this divine king: we know his ancestors (3:23-38, concluding ". . . son of Adam, son of God"), his divine conception (1:27, 33-35), and oracles proclaiming his divine origin (3:22; 9:35). We have seen him transfigured in heavenly glory (9:29), heard stories of his miraculous heavenly power (beginning in 4:14, 38-41), seen him defeat demonic enemies (4:1-13, 33-37, etc.), and heard prophetically inspired teaching to his successors and against his opponents (e.g., 4:16-30; 9:51–19:27). All that remains is to learn of his opposition to rulers, his exemplary death, and his ascension back to heaven. Given what the "people" and the readers already know, why are the leaders still asking, "Who gave you this authority"?

Jesus responds by asking them a similar question about John, whether his baptism was "from heaven or from human beings" (20:4; see Gal 1:1). They "reason" *(syllogizomai)* among themselves and give a calculated answer (20:5-7; see 18:2). This conflict again places Jesus and the "people" on one side, and the leaders, afraid of the people, on the other. Jesus will not verbally respond to the authorities' question (v. 8). There are consequences for those who refuse to "believe" (v. 5; see 1:20, 45; 8:12; 16:10-13; esp. 22:67 and 24:25), since the answer to the leaders' question is clear to those with eyes to "see" (cf. 6:41; 7:20-23; 8:9-10, 18; 10:22-24; 11:33-36; 21:8, 29-31).

The Parable of the Wicked Tenants (20:9-19)

The disciples know the secrets of the kingdom, "but to others I speak in parables, so that 'looking they may not perceive, and listening they may not understand'" (8:9-10, partially quoting Isa 6:9-10, quoted again to the "leaders" in Rome, Acts 28:17, 26-27). Jesus tells this parable "to the people" (20:9) "against" the scribes and chief priests (v. 19). Earlier Jesus had given instruction to the future leaders of the people (see the commentary on 10:1-16; also Acts 15:14); now as a prophet speaking in the temple he condemns the present leaders of the people (see Jeremiah 7 and 26, where the prophet is condemned to die, esp. 26:8, 11, 21, as in Luke 20:14).

The image of a vineyard symbolizes Israel in all the Gospels (see Isa 5:1-7). In Luke this parable of wicked tenants caring for vines also recalls the kingship parable

(19:11-27), good or evil slaves managing cities. The earlier parable was directed to Jesus' *disciples* who are leaders. Unlike the slave master in ch. 19, the owner of the vineyard in ch. 20 went away "for a long time" (20:9), but in salvation history, this refers allegorically to the time before the sending of the beloved son (vv. 10-15). The owner's return (v. 16) refers to the time of the destruction of the vineyard, Jerusalem, an event in the past for the readers of the Gospel (21:20), not to Jesus' return *(parousia).* In Luke the owner sends three slaves (20:10-12), the first two of whom are "beaten," a verb that later describes the abuse of Jesus (22:63); then he sends "my beloved son" (20:13, recalling 3:22, which alludes to Ps 2:7; see Isa 42:1; and perhaps Gen 22:2).

Seeing the son, the tenants discuss it and decide to kill him "so that the inheritance may be ours" (20:14). The "inheritance" language does not fit the logic of the parable, but comes rather from the implicit allegory to the history of salvation, according to which Israel was to "inherit" the land (Gen 28:4; Deut 4:1; 29:8-9). Powerful, abusive, blind tenants do not inherit God's vineyard (Isa 5:5-6). Typically, Luke turns Mark's (12:6) third person report into a first person soliloquy, "What shall I do? I will send . . ." (20:13). The owner decides to give other tenants the vineyard and to remove the scribes and chief priests against whom the parable is told, a possibility that evokes the (people's) response, "Heaven forbid!" (v. 16). Jesus then quotes Ps 118:22, a crucial proof-text for early Christians that God can and will reverse elements of salvation history (cf. Acts 4:11; 1 Pet 2:7). The leaders realize that Jesus has told the parable against them and want to arrest him immediately, but they fear the people (20:19). As Christians we must remember that the subject is the rejection of abusive, blind leaders, not the church succeeding Israel. Further, Jesus had already warned leaders among Jesus' disciples (19:11-27), and Paul will do so again (Acts 20:17-35, both texts close to 2 Timothy; see the commentary on 19:11-27).

The Question about Paying Taxes (20:20-26)

Jesus had entered the temple [state], calling it a den of robbers (19:45-46), has had his "authority" challenged by the chief priests, scribes, and elders (20:1-2), and has prophesied that God will remove those priests from their rule, giving their authority to others (20:16, 19). Now Jesus' opponents raise the remaining obvious question in that society about the "authority of the [Roman] governor" (20:20).

Because of stories like this one, Luke has been characterized as pro-Roman, a basic mistake if that expression means accepting all Roman values. The Roman value system demanded allegiance to the state above all else, for example, above family. Romans told a paradigmatic story of their revolting from the mother city, Alba. The battle was fought by three Roman sons of Horatius with their three cousins, sons of the Alban Curiatius. All six cousins "esteem kinship less than honor" (Dionysius *Rom. Ant.* 3.17.5; see Livy 1.22-26). The Romans win the battle by killing their three Alban cousins. Then because he "loves his country" and punishes those who wish her ill (3.21.6), the single remaining Roman murders his sister, who mourned for one of the Alban cousins to whom she had been engaged to be married! That night the Roman father gave a banquet to celebrate Rome's victory, despite his two dead sons and three dead nephews, refusing to allow his daughter to be buried! Luke tells a story in which Jesus urges his disciples to pay taxes demanded by Rome, but our author has not taken over the Roman value of country above all else! On the contrary, the disciples owe allegiance to Jesus above any other human relationship, including the state. The disciples of Jesus can come into conflict with Rome (14:26; 18:28-30; Acts 5:29) or any other country that demands patriotism above faith.

In Luke's story, the chief priests' spies ask, "Is it lawful for us to pay taxes to the emperor, or not?" (20:22). Since God had promised King David a son on the throne forever (2 Sam 7:8-17; see Luke 1:32-33, 69; 2:11; 20:41-44; Acts 2:34; 13:33-35; 15:16), paying taxes to a foreign (Roman) ruler was religiously and politically problematic. (Compare the arguments by Jewish revolutionaries against Rome in Josephus *Ant.* 18:1-10, 23-25.)

Jesus asks for a denarius, a working person's average daily pay, a coin on which was stamped the image of the emperor and an inscription: "Tiberius Caesar, son of the divine Augustus." Jesus has been craftier than the spies, for he has brought them dangerously close to admitting idolatry, worshiping a foreign god, graver in Jews' eyes than submitting to a foreign ruler's taxes. When Stephen later recounts salvation history, including Israel's worshiping the golden calf (Acts 7:39-43), he is *accusing* Israel of the most heinous (pagan) sin possible (see Rom 1:18-23). Despite claiming to recount the entire history of Israel, Josephus *never* mentions the idolatrous golden calf! Jesus' aphorism is rather that "the things of Caesar [with his image inscribed] should be returned to Caesar, and the things of God [with God's image implanted?] to God" (20:24-25; Gen 1:26-27?). If it is implied, this would be the only reference to God's "image" in the Gospels, a term more common in Paul. In Luke this aphorism functions as an apology, arguing that one of the charges against Jesus in 23:2 is false (see Acts 16:20-22, 38-39; 18:12-16; 25:8).

The Sadducees' Question about the Resurrection (20:27-40)

This series of controversies in the temple with Jesus' opponents seems to turn on questions of religious and political authority, so the present debate would not be exclusively about ideas, but concerns who authoritatively interprets the ancient Scriptures (cf. Acts 23:6-10; also Luke 18:31; 24:25-27, 44-49; Acts 17:10-12). Historically, belief in the resurrection is a late idea, but some influential contemporary Jews read it in(to) the earlier and authoritative Torah. The Sadducees, whom Josephus associates with skeptical Epicureans (*Ant.* 18.16-17), are not legitimate interpreters; rather, the Pharisees and Jesus' disciples agree on this crucial reading of Moses. Since Rome saw the later rabbis as legitimate authorities among the Jews, this is also an argument for the legitimacy of Jesus' followers.

The Sadducees refer to Torah legislation concerning levirate marriage (Deut 25:5-10). Rather than belief in the immortality of the soul or the resurrection of the body, this practice assumes that people live on in their descendants. When a man died, his brother was obligated to have a child with his widow, and the child would take the deceased brother's name. The Sadducees construct a scenario in which seven brothers have sex with the same woman, who remains childless. Against the doctrine of the resurrection, they ask whose wife she would then be after all of them had been raised.

Along with many others in ancient Greco-Roman society, Christians had internal disputes about the value of marriage and of having children (contrast 1 Cor 7:1, 7 with 1 Tim 2:15; 5:14). The Lukan verses in which Jesus responds to the Sadducees emphasize sexual asceticism even more strongly than had Paul ("I wish that all were as I myself am" [without a marriage partner]; 1 Cor 7:7). The verbs are in the present tense, denoting continuous action: "Those who belong to this age are marrying and are being given in marriage, but those who are considered worthy of a place in that age and in the resurrection from the dead neither are marrying nor are they being given in marriage . . ." (20:34-35; cf. the *Acts of Paul and Thecla* 3:11-12, "[Paul teaches] that they should not marry. . . . Otherwise there is no resurrection for you, unless you remain chaste and do not defile the flesh, but keep it pure"). The pair of verbs in Luke ("marrying," "being given in marriage," and the second one, *gamizō*, which is quite rare) also occurs in 1 Cor 7:38, where Paul insists that marriage is not a "sin" (7:36). Paul's insistence that marriage is not a sin may be set over against the way some Corinthians were applying this very Jesus saying. The Lukan saying and the one from the *Acts of Paul and Thecla* demand a sexually ascetic lifestyle, whereas Paul, despite his ascetic preference, affirmed that "each" has a particular gift from God (1 Cor 7:7; see 17, 20, 24).

Angels were assumed not to die, and this saying of Jesus affirms that those worthy of resurrection from the dead are like angels also in this respect, that they do not die (20:36), a theological assertion that is radically different from that of Paul (see Rom 6:3-11; 1 Cor 4:8-9; 2 Cor 4:7-12), but like some deutero-Pauline baptismal texts (Eph 2:4-6; Col 2:11-13; also 1 Cor 13:1?).

Jesus argues that the resurrection is assumed in the ancient, authoritative Torah, as is shown by Moses' words in Exod 3:6 (alluded to in 20:37). When Moses was before the burning bush, God said, "I am the God of your father, the God of Abraham . . . ," assuming that the patriarchs were alive. This same Torah text is appealed to in 4 Macc 7:19 and 16:25 (see the commentary on 18:18-23), showing its importance in current debates. Some scribes affirm Jesus' argument (20:39; also Acts 23:9).

The Question about David's Son (20:41-44)

The following controversial question has neither a context nor a notice of those with whom Jesus disputed. The only context we can supply comes from similar debates in Luke-Acts. The infancy narratives compare the conceptions and births of John and Jesus; for example, John was conceived by an aging couple but Jesus by a virgin (1:18, 34). In the transfiguration narrative Peter proposes honoring Moses, Elijah, and Jesus, but a voice from heaven insists that "This is my Son, my Chosen; listen to him!" (9:33-36). When our author narrates salvation history in Acts, the story basically concerns Moses (Stephen's speech in ch. 7) and David (Paul's speech in ch. 13), so it is not surprising that a question about how to interpret Moses (Luke 20:27-40) is followed in our verses (20:41-44) by a question about David, which also extends Jesus' controversies in the temple about religious and political authority in light of Scripture. Later Peter, too, voices arguments comparing David and Jesus (Acts 2:25-36, including the same scriptural text, Ps 110:1 in 2:34-35, "David did *not* ascend into the heavens, but he himself says, 'The Lord said to my Lord . . .'"). Jesus is more than John, Moses, Elijah, and David — more than a baptizer for forgiveness of sins, a lawgiver, a prophet, and a Messiah who defeats enemies. These verses inform the church about Jesus' relation to scriptural heroes.

The Lukan churches' image of the "Lord" may best be seen in 22:69, which shows the Son of Humanity reigning in the *present,* "seated at the right hand of the power of God," or in Acts 7:55, where Stephen as he is *martyred* sees the "heavens opened and the Son of Humanity standing at the right hand of God." Stephen's Lord is hardly a Davidic Messiah who will drive the Romans out of the land of Israel.

Denunciation of the Scribes (20:45-47)

While all the people listen, Jesus speaks to the disciples (20:45). Wealthy householders, including leaders of Christian worship assemblies, could hear this as addressed to themselves, although the stated addressees are the "scribes" (v. 46). Clients came to the houses of wealthy patrons at daybreak and left with the men (probably not the women, since they went to the city square) for the day's socializing, business, and politics in the marketplace. In mid-afternoon or evening they hosted formal dinners *(symposia),* and there were often debates about where prominent guests were to be seated (Osiek and Balch: ch. 8). Luke is describing and condemning assumptions about honor in Mediterranean culture in general, which Christian householders are to reverse at community celebrations of the Lord's Supper (see 12:37; 22:24-27; and the commentary on 14:1-24).

The Widow's Offering (21:1-4)

20:47 condemns those "eating up" widows' houses and offering long prayers for appearance's sake. It may be that that Jesus' denunciation of the scribes is connected to the story of the widow's offering merely by the keyword "widow" (20:47; 21:2), but it is also possible that this next story fits the theme of the section, religious and political authority (see all of chs. 19–20). There were groups of ascetic widows in Lukan house churches (1:36-38; Acts 6:1-6; 9:36, 39, 41; see Seim: 95, 229-47, 258), and the issues of how they were treated (Acts 6:1) and their influence in the church were controversial (see 1 Tim 5:2-16; Ign. *Pol.* 4; *Phld.* 4; *Acts of Paul and Thecla* 30). Widows were often addressed as poor, but some were wealthy and had more influence than (male) leaders wanted. The final verse of ch. 20 may reflect this gendered struggle for religious and political influence.

Lukan readers could read this story of the rich and poor giving gifts in the Jerusalem temple in terms of economic divisions within their own house churches. The architecture and art of the Greco-Roman houses in which they met for worship had beautifully frescoed rooms for owners, but unpainted rooms for slaves (Osiek and Balch: 29-30, 199, 215). The story contains a characteristic Lukan contrast between rich (*plousioi,* 21:1) and poor (*penichra,* v. 2; *ptōchoi,* v. 3). The "poor" person or "beggar" is a woman, a widow, who throws in "more than all of them" (v. 3; cf. 18:22 and Philo *Therapeutae* 13, 18). Seim: 116-18 points out that women are models for males in Luke, for example, models of faith (1:45), of remembering Jesus' words (24:6, 8), and of giving financial support (8:3), even though they are excluded from official public roles such as preaching or serving as apostles or elders. The widow in our text is such a model of giving, possibly also for the rich Christians who supply domestic space in which the church can worship. The rich "contributed out of their abundance, but she out of her want" (v. 4). They contribute "gifts"; she "all she had to live on" (see 18:28-30). Against Greco-Roman cultural values, leaders are not to despise poor members of the worship assembly (see Jas 2:1-7), especially not widows.

Coming Frightful Events: Wars and Being Persecuted for the Name of Jesus (21:5-19)

For both Hebrew prophets and Greek historians, wicked leaders guide a nation to destruction. After weeping over Jerusalem (19:41-44) and after having prophesied in the parable of the wicked tenants that the scribes and chief priests would kill him (20:14-18), Jesus denounces the scribes (20:45-47). He then prophesies the future consequences for the temple (21:5-9), the disciples (vv. 12-19), and the city of Jerusalem (vv. 20-24); he also pictures the coming of redemption, the Son of Humanity (vv. 25-36).

Ancient culture was right-brained, oriented toward beauty, form, and color; people were discussing the temple and its adornment with beautiful stones and offerings (21:5). Differently from Mark (13:1), Luke has Jesus stay in the temple for these prophecies about the temple. Jesus prophesies that none of these (beautiful) stones will be left one upon the other (21:6), a prophecy that prepares for Paul's vision in the temple in Acts, which sends him away from the temple to the Gentiles (22:17-21).

Some unspecified persons ask him, "Teacher, when . . . and what is the sign . . . ?" (21:7). Since Jesus' disciples never call him "teacher," the question may come from the scribes or the people, who do later make accusations about Jesus' teaching on this subject (Acts 6:14). Both Acts (5:36-37) and Josephus (*J.W.* 6.289-309) enumerate eschatological prophets and signs, including a different Jesus, son of Ananias, who pronounced fearful woes on Jerusalem just before its destruction. The Lukan Jesus opposes false prophets and messiahs who will come and say, "I am," and "The time is near!" (21:8) The first saying is one made by the Johannine Jesus (e.g,. 8:24), the second by the historical Jesus (see Mark 1:15)! Luke is changing the teaching of Jesus himself in order to allow time for the world mission (see Acts 1:6-8), a change that includes our author not only writing about Christology (Luke) but also stressing ecclesiology (Acts).

Jesus insists that the audience not be terrified by military events, "for . . . the end will not follow immediately" (21:9-10). Further, there will be dreadful events on earth, earthquakes *(seismoi),* famines, plagues, as well as "dreadful portents and great signs from heaven" (v. 11), events meaningful to either Hebrew or Greek audiences. Jesus had been quite negative about miraculous deeds as "signs" (11:29), but the apostles' sermons mention them more positively (Acts 2:22, 43). Luke later continues with the subject (21:20), but first our author inserts an excursus to the disciples anticipating their persecutions and imprisonments narrated in Acts (vv. 12–19).

"Before all these things happen," Luke begins (21:12). This editorial addition places the disciples' persecution before the fall of Jerusalem, from which it is sometimes concluded that Luke viewed persecutions of the church as past events, not a problem at the time of writing. This is surely incorrect and overemphasizes this one adverbial phrase, neglecting the second half of Acts, the whole of which is an apology, an epideictic appeal arguing that society's negative view of Paul (and the church) is mistaken (see Balch 1995b). When the text foresees that the disciples will be brought before kings and governors, this refers not only to Jesus (23:1, 7) but also to Paul (24:1; 25:13-14), whose apologetic speeches (chs. 22, 24, 26) offer Christians a "defense" *(apologēthēnai)* in advance (21:14), arguments they might make to local officials who were harassing them. And in the Gospel of Luke itself, during the whole of the journey to Jerusalem (9:51–19:27) Jesus alternately addresses the crowds, opponents, and disciples (Johnson: 232, 254), a literary pattern that also informs us about the social situation of the readers: "rejection" by opponents was still a significant experience.

They will be arrested (see Acts 4:3; 5:18; 12:1; 21:27), handed over to synagogues (Acts 9:2 and 26:11 of the preconversion Paul only), and imprisoned (Acts 5:19; 8:3; 12:4; 16:23; an aspect of the pre-conversion Paul's activity, 22:4 and 26:10). This will give an opportunity to "witness" "for the name" (21:12-13; see Acts 4:33 and 26:27-29). They will be betrayed by parents, brothers, relatives, and, Luke adds, friends (21:16; see the commentary on 14:7-14). Some will be martyrs (Acts 7:60; 12:2; 14:19), and they will be "hated by all for my name," expectations taken over from Mark (13:12-13). In Luke lethal conflict with society could indeed be generated by aspects of the Gospel, especially receiving "foreigners" (see 4:25-27; Acts 10:28) into one's community and having masters serve slaves the Lord's Supper (22:24-27), conflicts as intense as those generated in the modern world by immigration from the Two-Thirds World into northern Europe and America.

"But not a hair of your head will perish" (21:18; see 12:7; Acts 27:34) is strange after v. 16, nor does it correspond with martyrdoms in Acts. Perhaps we should interpret its meaning by 21:19: "By your endurance you will gain your souls."

The Destruction of Jerusalem Prophesied (21:20-24)

Following Luke's excursus on the disciples' being persecuted (21:10-19), v. 20, foreseeing Jerusalem being surrounded by armies (or army camps), picks up the reference to "wars and insurrections" in v. 9. Luke changes Mark's (13:14) apocalyptic "abomination of desolation" (originally from Dan 9:27) into a reference to its historical "desolation."

Luke repeats Mark's imperative (13:14) that those in Judea are to flee to the mountains (21:21), adding that those in the city are to go out and those in the country are not to enter it. Johanan ben Zakkai did the former, leaving the city under siege in order to found a school on the coast that generated early rabbinic Judaism. A later story has Christians leaving for Pella, east of the Jordan (Eusebius *Hist. Eccl.* 3.5.3).

Those will be the "days of vengeance" (21:22) a term used by Jeremiah (51:6; see 2 Thess 1:8). Characteristically, Luke names this a "fulfillment of all that is written." Mark uses this phrase of diverse prophecies (1:2 of John; 7:6 of the Pharisees; 9:12-13 of Elijah coming again; 11:17 of the temple's perversion; 12:19 of the Son of Humanity; and 12:27 of the disciples' desertion). Luke's reading of prophecy in addition emphasizes the church's mission (3:4 of John; 4:17 of God anointing Jesus to preach; 7:27 of John; 18:31, everything about the Son of Humanity; 19:46 of the temple; 20:17 of Jesus' rejection by the leaders; 22:37 of Jesus being counted among the lawless; 24:44, everything about Jesus; 24:46, both of Jesus' suffering and resurrection *and* of the proclamation to all nations beginning from Jerusalem; Acts 1:20 of Judas's replacement; 13:29 of Jesus' death; 13:33 of Jesus' resurrection; cf. 13:47 and 15:15 of the proclamation of the gospel to Gentiles, prophecies made by the "God of our ancestors" [24:14]).

Luke, depending on Mark, notes the horrors of Jerusalem's siege for pregnant women (21:23; see Josephus *J.W.* 4.326-33). There will be great distress (*anankē;* see 1 Thess 3:7; 1 Cor 7:26) and wrath *(orgē)* against this people *(laos),* who from Luke's point of view have evil leaders.

They will fall by the sword and be taken away as "captives" among all nations (21:24), a prophecy that reverses both Jesus' (4:18) and key prophetic (Isa 11:11-12; 43:4-7; 49:18, 22-26) hopes. Jerusalem will be trampled by the nations "until the times of the Gentiles are fulfilled." This last phrase refers to the pagan occupation of Jerusalem, not to the period of Christian mission to Gentiles. The short- and long-term consequences of the fall of the temple state in Jerusalem were incalculable: after AD 70 the Jews had no political home for two millennia but became completely dependent on Roman and later on Christian and Muslim rulers, and Judaism was transformed by the rabbis into an apolitical religion.

The Coming of the Son of Humanity (21:25-36)

Earlier Jesus had refused to give a "sign from heaven" (11:16), except exorcisms (11:20); but now he speaks of cosmic "signs in the sun, the moon, and the stars" (21:25). The first such sign is narrated at the crucifixion: an eclipse of the sun (23:44-45; see the commentary). He also points to "distress among nations confused by the roaring of the sea and the waves" (21:25), an end-time reversal of creation, in which God set boundaries for the watery chaos (Job 38:8-11; Ps 73:13 LXX; 103:9; mentioned by Paul on the Areopagus, Acts 17:26; see Balch 1990: 55). People faint from fear of this undoing of creation, the shaking of the "powers of heaven" (21:26; for the Creator's power in the heavens see 4:25; Acts 2:19; 4:24; 14:15, 17).

Their seeing "the Son of Humanity coming in a cloud" (21:27) is a direct allusion to Dan 7:13, a figure Luke has referred to repeatedly (9:26; 12:8-9, 40; 17:24; 18:31). Jesus' disciples do not anticipate this with fear, but rather are to "raise your heads, because your redemption *(apolytrōsis)* is drawing near" (21:28). "Redemption" (see 1:68; 2:38; Rom 3:24; 8:23) is a metaphor referring to freedom from slavery, the deepest wish of many in Roman society.

Jesus tells a final parable: when you yourselves "see" the fig tree sprout, "know" that summer is near; so also when you "see these things" (the dissolution of creation and the coming of the Son of Humanity), "know" that the kingdom of God is near (21:29-31). Strikingly in Luke, one can "see" or refuse to "see" the kingdom of God in the present (for *blepō,* one Greek verb for "see," cf. 7:20-23; 8:9-10, 18; 10:22-24; 11:33-36; 21:8; Acts 1:9, 11; 2:33; 4:14; 8:6; 13:40-41; 28:26; for *horaō* 3:6; 9:31, 36; 13:28; 16:23; 17:23; 23:49; 24:23; Acts 2:3, 17).

Jesus says that "this generation will not pass away until all things have taken place" (21:32), which did not happen (cf. Paul's expectation in 1 Thess 4:15-17, which he modified in 2 Cor 5:9-10). Our faith does not depend on whether these time schedules are correct but on whether Jesus truly reveals the character and will of God (see the commentary on 1:26-38). Of this we have assurance, that "my words will not pass away" (21:33 from Mark 13:31). Mark (13:32) — correctly — adds that "about that day or hour no one knows, neither the angels in heaven nor the Son, but only the Father," a qualification that Luke omitted.

Luke's final exhortation warns against being "weighed down with dissipation and drunkenness and the worries of this life" (21:34). Peter, James, and John had been "weighed down" with sleep, a popular metaphor in such exhortations, during the transfiguration (9:32). Drunkenness, too, is a metaphor for those not preparing for the coming of the Son of Humanity. Luke has cautioned before about the "worries" of this life (10:41; 12:11, 22, 25-26; see 1 Cor 7:32-34), including the worry about how to defend themselves in synagogues and before civil authorities (the concern of the second half of Acts). Our author wants them instead to pray that they may escape the eschatological dissolution and stand before the Son of Humanity (see the paradigm on the Mount of Olives, 22:40, 44-46; Acts 17:30-31).

Conclusion to the Disputes about Religious and Political Authority and to Jesus' Warnings in the Temple (21:37-38)

Luke observes again (see the introduction to this section, 19:47-48) that Jesus was teaching in the temple and that the "people" were eagerly listening to him (contrast Acts 22:21-22; 26:17).

Jesus' Passion (22:1–23:56)

Luke concludes with stories of Jesus' passion, some of which are in Mark but none in Q, the source from which our author drew many of Jesus' sayings during the journey to Jerusalem. Jesus' revelation of God includes more than wise sayings: Jesus' and the disciples' sufferings and deaths are meaningful revelations of God. One Lukan emphasis concerns the devil, who had "departed" from Jesus after the temptations failed (4:13); but in the passion narrative Satan intensifies his assault on Jesus and the disciples (22:3, 31). Luke's account is different enough from that of Mark that many assume another source and/or Luke's significant editorial shaping of the stories.

The Priests' and Jesus' Preparations for Passover (22:1-13)

The Synoptic Gospels make Jesus' last supper a Passover meal, although John (13:1; 18:28; see 1:29), Paul (1 Cor 11:23-26; see 5:7), and the *Didache* (9–10) do not. Jesus was crucified during this festival, but the theologies of our NT sources interpreting his death differ among themselves. John and Paul understand Jesus as the Passover lamb crucified, killed therefore before the meal was eaten. The other Gospels rather interpret Jesus' last meal in light of this ancient holy feast that celebrated God's freeing Israel from slavery (Exodus 12–13).

The chief priests and scribes, our author says, continued to look for a way to put Jesus to death, although they were still afraid of the people (22:2; see 19:47-48 and Jesus' prophecies in 9:22; 20:14, 19). Josephus (*J.W.* 2.8-13, 223-27) does tell stories of riots at this festival.

Luke conceives of Satan as entering Judas, explicitly naming him one of the "twelve," and says that he was "called Iscariot," perhaps a "man of Kerioth," a town in Judah south of Jerusalem. The "twelve" were to be the new rulers of Israel (22:30; see 6:13; 8:1; 9:1; 18:31; Acts 6:2; 7:8). Judas's betrayal is threatening: Luke has just written two chapters (20 and 21) criticizing the present leaders of the people. Now Judas, one of the twelve, confers with these chief priests about betraying Jesus (22:4)! Not surprisingly, they are "greatly pleased" and agree to give him money (v. 5). People in power struggles need a mole on the other side, and the priests have found one. Judas then agrees (*exhōmologeō,* the usual verb for "confess"; see 12:8; Rom 14:11) and looks for an opportunity to "betray" Jesus, when the "people," favorable to him, are not present (22:6; see 19:48; 20:6, 19, 26, 45; 21:23, 38).

Jesus sent two disciples (see 10:1; 19:29-35; 24:13; Acts 13:2; 15:39-40), whom our author identifies as Peter and John (5:10; 6:14; 8:51; 9:28, 49, 54; Acts 1:13; Gal 2:9), to prepare the Passover lamb (22:7-8). Culpepper: 416 observes that the significance of their task, "waiting tables," models the servant/slave role of leaders among Jesus' disciples (see 12:35-38, 41-48; 22:24-27; Acts 6:2; Rom 1:1; Phil 1:1). They ask where to prepare (22:9), and Jesus gives detailed instructions based on prophetic foreknowledge (vv. 10-12). Luke mentions Passover six times in thirteen verses, emphasizing its importance (Johnson: 333). Jesus prepares for it despite the leaders' plans.

Jesus' Last Supper (22:14-20)

When the hour came, sundown on the fourteenth of Nisan, Jesus and the "apostles" "reclined" (22:14) as one would for a symposium. The readers of the Gospel might, however, have *sat* to celebrate the Lord's Supper (as in 1 Cor 14:30), perhaps in an open courtyard or garden, not all in the dining room *(triclinium)* of a house.

Jesus has eagerly looked forward to eating this Passover with them "before I suffer" (22:15), an allusion to his death. The verb for "suffer" *(paschō)* sounds like the noun "Passover" *(pascha),* and some early Christian authors (Melito) played on the similarity. Vv. 16 and 18 are similar; do the present tense subjunctive verbs mean that Jesus is not himself eating, or do they have a future reference, implying that he will not eat it ("again," the reading of a Western manuscript, D) until . . . ? (The subjunctive mood does not involve time, so there is no future tense in the subjunctive mood.) V. 18 has "from now on," and this seems to give the sense Luke intended, although the phrase is omitted by a few witnesses.

Jesus will not eat the Passover "until it is fulfilled in the kingdom of God" (22:16), which may refer to the coming eschatological banquet (see 13:28-29; 14:13, 15-24) and/or to meals celebrated by the disciples after Jesus' resurrection (24:30-32, 35, 42-43; Acts 2:42, 46; 10:9-16, 28, 41, 48; 11:3-10; 12:3; 14:17; 16:15, 34; 20:6-7; 21:16; 27:33-38; also 15:20, 28; 21:25; 23:14, 21). These two possibilities are not alternatives. The coming eschatological banquet will include all nations (13:29, the fulfillment of which includes the conversion of the presumably black Ethiopian eunuch from the "south," Acts 8:26-40) as well as the "poor, crippled, lame, and blind" (14:13, 21). Peter and the disciples later claim to have "left our homes" (18:28), which means that they have joined the "poor" who will be invited to the eschatological banquet. Luke also narrates the occurrence of the second option: Jesus appears to and eats with two disciples in Emmaus as well as with the eleven and their companions after his resurrection (24:30-32, 35, 42-43). Acts narrates multiple instances of "all" sharing this feast at the invitation of the risen Lord (see especially the debates around the conversion of the "foreigner" Cornelius, 10:9-16, 28, 41, 48; 11:3-10). It fits, then, that Luke concludes the second volume with Paul "welcoming *all* who came to him, proclaiming the *kingdom of God* and teaching about the Lord Jesus Christ . . ." (Acts 28:30-31). Jesus had said he "eagerly desired to eat," but not "until it is fulfilled in the kingdom of God" (22:16). Believers "see" Jesus present celebrating the kingdom banquet in Luke 14 and 24, repeatedly in Acts, and wherever the church welcomes people of all nations, genders, classes, and orientations.

According to the oldest discussion of the Passover meal (*m. Pesaḥ.* 10.1-7), there were four cups of wine. Luke mentions two cups (22:17, 20), although some "Western" manuscripts (D it) dropped out the second cup, which Jesus interprets. Jesus "takes" a cup, "gives thanks," and says, "Take this and divide it among yourselves . . ." (v. 17;

see 9:16). He also "took" a loaf of bread, "gave thanks," "broke" it, and "gave" it to them, "saying . . ." (22:19). These two verses describe ritual actions that the later church amplified in its liturgy. In several ways Luke's ritual is closer to Paul's (1 Cor 11:23-26) than to Mark's (14:22-25); for example, the cup word mentions "the *new* covenant," echoing Jer 31:31-34 instead of Exod 24:8, reflected in Mark. Only in Luke and 1 Cor 11:24 does Jesus command them to do this "in remembrance of me" (22:19; see Exod 2:24 and 6:5 of God remembering the covenant), that is, of Jesus giving his life "for you."

". . . the cup, the new covenant in my blood, is the one having been poured out for you *(hyper hymōn)* for the forgiveness of sins" (22:20). The reference to "pouring out" may echo Isa 53:12, but Luke's readers also knew other traditions of heroes "giving their life" or their "blood" "for" others (Dionysius *Rom. Ant.* 3.16.2; 6.9.2; see Rom 8:32; 1 Cor 15:3; 2 Cor 5:14-15, 21). Luke sometimes shifts key theological sentences from the Gospel to Acts, in this case from Jesus' farewell address to Paul's. Our author has moved the equivalent of Mark 10:45 to Acts 20:28, referring to "the church of God that he obtained with the blood of his own Son."

The Lukan Farewell Discourse (22:21-38)

The Gospel of John (chs. 14–17) records Jesus giving a farewell discourse, but among the Synoptics only Luke has such a speech. Jesus points to his betrayer, speaks about slave leadership, predicts Peter's denial, and revises mission instructions for his followers. As Jesus approached and taught in the temple, he engaged in controversy about religious and political authority (chs. 19–20), then gave warnings about the eschatological future (ch. 21). In the farewell discourse he continues the same theme, now discussing the character and actions of leaders among his own disciples.

Jesus Points to His Betrayer (22:21-23)

Luke has narrated controversies between Jesus and the people's leaders, who want to kill him. Following such a notice (22:2), the narrator ominously informs the reader that Satan entered into Judas, "one of the twelve" (v. 3). But whereas Mark (14:18-21) has Jesus prophesying Judas's betrayal before the last supper, Luke delays the story until afterward, reducing the readers' awareness of Judas's presence at the supper itself.

Jesus has prophesied that he would be betrayed (9:44; 18:32; 20:20), and he now refers to "the one who betrays me," saying, "his hand is on the table" (22:21). Christians reading this story celebrating the supper at their own table (see Acts 16:34) might wonder whether one among them would betray them to the society or the governor (see 21:16-17). My teacher, Ernst Käsemann, lived and preached through Hitler's rise to power in Germany, and saw many Christian theologians and pastors become Nazis. The Judas story teaches us not to be naive either about ourselves or about others who call ourselves Christians.

Jesus insists that this has been ordained (cf. Acts 2:23; 10:42; 17:26, 31) by God, but he still pronounces a "woe" on the person through whom he is betrayed (22:22). Here, unresolved, is the paradox of divine sovereignty and human freedom. As humans we are surprised and usually offended when God is present in the messy stuff of history, particularly in suffering and death, but as Christians we continue to believe our Jewish teachers: God was actively present with the Jews during their exiles in Egypt and Babylon and also in the events leading up to and climaxing in God's revelation through Jesus' death on a cross. Jesus' prophecy stimulates the first of two disputes *(syzētein)*: Who among them was about to do this (v. 23)?

The Disciples Dispute about Greatness, but Jesus Insists on Slave Leadership (22:24-30)

For the first readers, this was one of the most provocative paragraphs in the Gospel. Mark (10:41-45) placed it four chapters earlier, but our editor has delayed recounting it until Jesus' last supper. The disciples' second dispute (*philoneikia,* 22:24) concerns greatness, typical during a Greco-Roman symposium (Osiek and Balch: 194-96, 199, 205, referring to Plutarch *Table Talk* 615D-619A). The verses contain several contrasts: kings of the Gentiles, greatest, leader, the reclining diner on the one side, Gentile subjects, youngest, servant, table servant *(diakonōn),* and Jesus the table servant on the other (22:25-26). V. 26b is imperative: "let the greatest among you become like the youngest, and the leader like a table slave." For readers hearing the Gospel in a Roman dining room, this is an offensive social reversal. The houses in which Christians met for worship were designed architecturally to reinforce the social status of the owner, who "reclined" at dinner to be served by slaves. Jesus concludes by asking, "Who is greater, the [master] reclining or the table slave? The one reclining? [assuming an offensive, negative answer] But I am among you as a table slave" (v. 27). By placing Jesus' provocative questions in the context of the Lord's Supper, Luke was asking the readers to make their eucharists *frequent* Saturnalia, a Roman feast that reversed the roles of master and slaves *once a year* (see the commentary on 12:37 and 14:15-24; Lucian *Saturnalia*; Osiek and Balch: 195-96). The Lukan churches were then in high social tension with the values of their society. It was shameful to be a slave, to serve food in a Roman *triclinium;* but following Jesus' example, the early Lukan Christians learned to "serve," to be slaves to others during their eucharistic feasts, a reversal that continues into the twenty-first century! Legitimate leaders among us do not wait to be served but serve others, an anti-Roman value symbolically acted out in our worship services until the present day.

The apostles are those who have "remained" with Jesus in his "trials" (22:28; see vv. 40, 46; 4:13; 11:4; Acts 20:19), unlike the seed of Jesus' parable, who received the word with joy but in a time of "trial" fell away (8:13). As the Father conferred a kingdom on Jesus, so Jesus confers one on the apostles. Jesus, like Moses and Romulus, is a king more than a prophet. Sitting on twelve thrones, the apostles will celebrate the kingdom banquet (see the commentary on 22:16). The apostles become Jesus' successors in Acts 1–2 (see 1:3, 15-26; 2:34-36).

Jesus Prophesies the Testing of the Apostles and Peter's Denial (22:31-34)

During the journey to Jerusalem (9:51–19:27), Jesus instructed his successors, future leaders; and in Jerusalem and the temple (19:28–20:47) Jesus engages in controversy with the chief priests and scribes, the present leaders of the "people," about religious authority. He gives eschatological warnings (21:1-38); then, as king, he institutes his own eschatological banquet (22:1-20), warning that one of the twelve whom he has chosen to lead Israel and the nations will betray him (22:21-23). The other apostles dispute about which one of them was the greatest (22:24-26), showing that they understand Jesus' style of leadership no more than the chief priests and scribes; and now Jesus prophesies that Simon Peter, their "first among equals," will deny that he knows Jesus! Is this story a tragedy?

Jesus addresses "Simon" (22:31), a name Luke had used of Peter before Jesus called him and gave him the Greek name Peter (5:8; see 4:38). Jesus tells "Simon" that "Satan demanded to sift you [plural], but I have prayed for you [singular] that your [singular] own faith may not fail" (22:32). The sentence emphasizes both Jesus' prayer and Peter's faith (for positive and negative examples see 1:20, 45; 8:12-13, 50; 16:11; 20:5; 24:25; Acts 10:43). Peter protests his faithfulness, but Jesus foresees and assumes Peter's denial: "when you have turned back, strengthen your brothers." The contrast between Matthew's and Luke's narratives of this event is fascinating: after Peter denied Jesus (Matt 26:69-75; see 10:33; 23:8-12), Matthew never again mentions his name, removing it from the resurrection stories, but Luke narrates his Pentecost speech founding the church!

Peter changes between the Gospel and Acts, quite unusual in ancient literature: ancient biographies and histories assume that a person possessed a stable character that unfolded during one's lifetime, that did not change. But the Peter who denies Christ in the Gospel (22:54-62) repeatedly goes to prison for him in Acts (4:1-31; 5:17-42; 12:1-17). Ancient readers would have been surprised and asked about the sources of his transformation.

Jesus Revises Mission Instructions for His Successors (22:35-38)

In the fourth and final unit of the farewell discourse, Jesus recalls his earlier instructions (9:1-6; 10:1-12) and modifies them, an early revision of church order manuals (compare the *Didache*). In 10:4 he had instructed them "to carry no purse, no bag, no sandals. . . ." Like wandering Cynic, mendicant preachers, they lacked nothing (22:35); apparently resident householders had given them shelter, food, and drink, and washed their feet (9:4; 10:5-8). "Then, . . . but now . . . ," Jesus says (22:35-36), thus signaling that the situation had changed and that such instructions are open to revision, a real problem in the ancient world. Now they are to take a purse and a bag, and, Jesus adds, a sword, probably to take with them as they traveled, although the narrative in Acts never actually mentions one.

The textual explanation is a quotation of Isa 53:12 from one of the "suffering servant" hymns: those who preach this gospel "will be counted among the lawless." Our author constructed the apologetic in Luke-Acts to oppose such accusations against Jesus and his followers, that either according to Jewish or Roman customs they were lawless (see 23:2; Acts 6:10-11, 13-14; 16:20-21; 21:20-21; see also Balch 1995b). Luke sees Isaiah's prophecy fulfilled in both Jesus and the apostles (22:37). Thus Jesus' farewell discourse concludes with a warning of future tension between Jesus' successors and society.

Praying on the Mount of Olives Not to Come into Trial (22:39-42, 45-46)

(22:43-44 seem to be a later textual interpolation, supported by manuscripts Aleph and D, Justin and Irenaeus, but omitted by $\mathfrak{p}^{75}$, the first corrector of Aleph, A B, Clement and Origen). Readers are accustomed to the story of Jesus in "Gethsemane" and easily overlook the fact that Luke omitted this place name. Luke writes only that he "went, as was his custom [see 2:42], to the Mount of Olives; and the disciples followed him." There he urges them to "pray that you may not come into the time of trial" (22:40; see the commentary on v. 28 above). Jesus withstands his "trial" (4:13), as will Paul (Acts 20:19), but Peter will not (22:57-60). In this story, Peter's failure is related to his "sleeping" and failing to pray (v. 46). "Sleeping" is metaphorical, eschatological language; Jesus' disciples are not to be children of the "night" (see v. 53 and 1 Thess 5:6-7). Jesus withdraws, kneels, and prays a line Luke takes from Mark (14:36), a line that Matthew (6:10; contrast Luke 11:2) added to the Lord's Prayer, "not my will but yours be done" (22:42).

The Arrest of Jesus (22:47-53)

Luke reemphasizes that Judas was one of the twelve (22:47; see v. 3). Jesus rebukes him for betrayal with a kiss (contrast 7:45). But one of the primary emphases of this scene is to correct a possible misunderstanding of 22:36. When a disciple cuts off the right ear of the high priest's slave, Jesus says, "No more of this!" (22:49-50). Jesus also challenges the chief priests, officers of the temple police, and elders: they had had the opportunity to arrest him when he was teaching daily in the temple (chs. 20–21), but they were afraid of the "people" (22:52-53; see 19:48; 20:6, 19, 45; 21:38; 22:2, each reference employing the Gk. *laos* for "people"). In the present scene, the priests have brought merely a "crowd" (*ochlos*, v. 47), not the "people," whom they presumably still fear.

Peter Three Times Denies Knowing Jesus (22:54-62)

The chief priests led Jesus into the high priest's "house," where all "sit" (22:54-55). Incidentally, we see that many wealthy houses were not private, unlike modern homes. Peter, a stranger to the priests, walks into the courtyard unchallenged. Christian worship in houses also admitted "outsiders" (1 Cor 14:16, 22, 24-25), and people also "sat" (1 Cor 14:30), probably also in the courtyard, not only in the dining room, where one "reclined."

Peter is accused by a young slave girl and by two men; addressing each of them directly ("woman," "man"), three times he denies knowing Jesus (22:57-60). When the cock crows, Peter "remembers the word of the Lord" (v. 61). By remembering Jesus' word, later disciples know the truth in crises (see 24:6, 8; esp. Acts 11:16-18). On this occasion, both Jesus' presence in his glance (see 24:32; Acts 4:31; 7:55; 16:7-10) and Peter's remembering stimulate him to bitter tears (22:62, verbally similar to Matt 26:75). In contrast to Matthew's Gospel, where Peter's name disappears after his denial, in Luke-Acts Peter "turns" (22:32) and preaches the sermon that founds the church (Acts 2; see Luke 5:8-10).

Jesus Mocked and Tried before the Chief Priests, Elders, and Scribes (22:63-71)

After Peter fulfills Jesus' prophecy of betrayal, those guarding Jesus blindfold and ironically challenge him to "Prophesy! Who hit you?" (22:64). The reader remembers that Jesus has prophesied this, too (18:32; see 20:11, 14). Mocking will occur repeatedly in the passion narrative (see 23:11; 23:36). The soldiers and priests ironically set out to fulfill Jesus' prophecies. "They kept on heaping many other blasphemies against him" (22:65; see 5:21; 23:39), which the later church also experienced (Acts 13:45; 18:6; 26:11).

Jesus' death was such a shock to the disciples that, as the church reflected on the events, preachers and writers made connections both to scriptural prophecies and to Jesus' own foreknowledge, telling themselves in effect that had they read the Scriptures and "remembered the words of the Lord," they would not have been so shocked (Luke 24:25, 44-49; John 7:40-42; Acts 17:11; 1 Cor 15:3). We, too, are shocked and offended by suffering and death; these texts remind us that it is possible to begin to see meaning in our pain, that the God of Moses and Miriam, Jeremiah and Jesus is still present with us.

In the trial before the Sanhedrin, three titles are involved: Christ, Son of Humanity, and Son of God. "They" (perhaps the chief priests, officers of the temple, and elders of 22:52) ask him to say whether he is the Christ, or, in Hebrew, the Messiah (v. 67; see 2:11; 4:41; 9:20; 20:41; compare this title in the Sanhedrin's accusation to Pilate, 23:2). Jesus replies that even if they hear, they will not believe. In earlier debates about John (see the commentary on 20:8), Jesus had questioned them about their faith, and they refused to answer, of which Jesus reminds them here (22:68).

Jesus then asserts that "from now on the Son of Humanity will be seated at the right hand of the power of God" (22:69, a reference to Dan 7:13), omitting Mark's (14:62) "and coming with the clouds of heaven." Luke's omission means that the sentence focuses on the present reign of the Son of Humanity (see the commentary on 20:41-44; also 5:24; 6:5, 22; 7:34; 11:30; 12:8, 40; 17:22; 18:8; 22:22; 24:7; and 21:27 with "coming in a cloud"). But characteristic of the Gospel, this reigning Son of Humanity will die (see Jesus' prophecies in 9:22, 44; 18:31-33).

Jesus' reply stimulates their question whether he is the Son of God (22:70), as God has declared him to be (see 1:32, 35; 3:22; 10:22) and the devil has challenged (4:3, 9, 22, 41; 9:35). Jesus attributes this confession to them, "You say that I am" (22:70), and they declare that they need no further witness, for "we have heard from his own lips" (v. 71). The irony is that they have not "heard" (see only 2:18; 4:28; 6:47; 7:29; 8:8, 18; 10:24; 11:28; 15:1; 16:29, 31; 19:48; Acts 28:27-28).

Jesus' Trial before Pilate (23:1-25)

The narrator indicates a fundamental shift in the plot by noting that "all the multitude," presumably for the first time including the "people," led Jesus to Pilate (23:1; for this expression see 1:10; 5:6; 6:17). Until this point the priests have been afraid of the people, who enthusiastically followed Jesus. And "they" began to "accuse" him. The plot does not supply an adequate reason for this shift, but Luke writes for an audience who know that many (not all) of the "people" had eventually rejected a crucified Messiah. That rejection motivates our author to place the change during Jesus' trial and crucifixion.

All of Luke-Acts is epideictic apologetic, a "history" addressed to a larger public, attempting to persuade readers toward a favorable opinion of the church and its Founder, instead of the present negative one. Countering such "accusations" is then a core purpose of both volumes (see 6:7; 11:54; 23:2, 10, 14; as well as the climactic second half of Acts: 22:30; 24:2, 8, 13, 19; 25:5, 11, 16; 28:19). The fundamental charge is "perverting (misleading) our nation" by (1) forbidding *(koly-)* us to pay taxes to the emperor and (2) saying that he himself is the Messiah (23:2; cf. Acts 16:20-22). This is exactly what the Jewish revolutionaries against Rome did in AD 66, the fundamental charge Josephus (*J.W.* 2.409-10; see Balch 1995b: 13) makes against them. The charge is military sedition. Some commentators distinguish between religious and political charges, as if Jesus were not "political," but this is a modern notion. Jesus was not being tried by the Roman governor for completely nonpolitical reasons. Luke-Acts advocates certain religio-political policies related to the "poor" and to "receiving foreigners," as do other apologetic histories (see Balch 1982), but Luke-Acts denies that Jesus advocated military subversion in Judea or that the church causes violent riots in Greco-Roman cities, either of which would be a cause for Romans to suppress this Jewish "sect." The two volumes conclude on a victorious note: Paul was proclaiming the kingdom of God and teaching things about the Lord Jesus Christ, which was not forbidden (*a-koly* [the "a" at the beginning negates the verb in Greek]) even in Rome (Acts 28:31)!

Christian readers believe in Christ and are called to confess this before authorities (12:8-9), but for Jesus to claim to be a "king" before Pilate inside the plot would be awkward, since king suggests military subversion. Therefore, when Pilate asks, Jesus answers ambiguously: "You say so" (23:3). Pilate must take this either as a question or as a denial, for he tells the chief priests and the crowds that he finds no accusation ("cause") against this man (v. 4). In turn they insist that he "stirs up [*anaseiō*, "incite"; Dionysius *Rom. Ant.* 8.81; Josephus *J.W.* 5.120] the people by teaching throughout all Judea, from Galilee where he began even to this place" (v. 5). The geography outlined in the accusation is Lukan, a sketch of our author's Gospel (see Acts 10:37), but Luke's summary, on the contrary, is that God was "preaching peace by Jesus Christ . . . , doing good and healing all who were oppressed by the devil" (Acts 10:36, 38), not preaching revolution against Rome.

Only Luke reports Jesus being questioned by Herod (23:6-12). Acts 4:25-26 quote a psalm (2:1-2) that mentions the opposition of both kings and rulers, then interprets this as a prophecy of King Herod's (Antipas) and Pilate's opposition to Jesus. Later Paul is tried by both the Roman governor Felix and by King Herod (Agrippa II; Acts 24-25), possibly a reflection of the same prophetic pattern. In this case we may be seeing prophecy generate history. Pilate assumes Jesus is Galilean (23:6, ignoring ch. 2, probably added later). Herod wants to see some "sign" (v. 8; see 11:29-30) and questions Jesus, who "answered nothing," an allusion to another prophecy (Isa 53:7). The chief priests and scribes are still accusing Jesus, fulfilling Jesus' own prophecies (9:22, 32; 20:14, 19), as does Herod's mocking (18:32). Pilate and Herod become friends, possibly developed from Ps 2:1-2.

Reflecting 23:1 listing the original group that accused Jesus, our narrator notes that Pilate called the chief priests, leaders, and "people" (*laos;* v. 13), adding them explicitly to Jesus' accusers. Pilate names the charge (v. 14; see v. 2), and for the second time declares Jesus not guilty, adding that Herod had agreed. Pilate asserts that he will flog and release Jesus (v. 16). From other sources, we know that Pilate lost several battles of the will against the people of Jerusalem (Josephus *J.W.* 2.169-76); if the first readers knew Pilate's reputation for weakness, development of the plot would look ever more lethal for Jesus.

23:17 is probably a later explanatory interpolation. It is present in Aleph and Eusebius, but absent in $\mathfrak{p}^{75}$ A and B. Manuscript D includes it after v. 19.

The "whole multitude" (*pamplēthei;* see *plēthos,* 23:1) shout, "Away with this fellow! Release Barabbas for us!" (v. 18). V. 19 notes that he was in prison because he had been involved in murder during an insurrection (*stasis;* see also v. 25; Acts 19:40; 24:5). The irony is heavy, both because they have accused Jesus of precisely this crime and because of the meaning of Bar-abbas's name, "son of the father." Following Mark (15:6-14), Luke involves the accusers in utter contradictions.

For the first time they begin shouting, "Crucify him!" (23:21). Pilate a third time vainly declares him innocent (v. 22), asking helplessly, "What evil has he done?" (v. 23; see 1 Pet 2:12; 3:17) But he capitulates and grants their demand, for their voices were "stronger" (23:23). The story concludes with the absurdity of a Roman governor releasing a prisoner for insurrection and murder, but handing over Jesus, whom he had repeatedly declared to be innocent, "to their will" (vv. 24-25). The reader could hardly miss the point: the governor had reached the first conclusion, but he was criminally weak.

The Crucifixion, Mocking, Death, and Burial of Jesus (23:26-56)

Simon of Cyrene in Africa carries the cross while Jesus mourns with the daughters of Jerusalem (23:26-32); he is crucified and mocked (vv. 33-38), converses with two criminals (vv. 39-43), dies during an eclipse of the sun with crowds and women mourning (vv. 44-49), and is buried by Joseph of Arimathea before the sabbath with women witnesses (vv. 50-56).

Simon Carries the Cross, and Jesus Laments, Warning the Daughters of Jerusalem of the Fall of the City (23:26-32)

As "they" led Jesus away, seizing Simon of Cyrene who was coming in from the field, they had him carry the cross behind Jesus (23:26; on disciples carrying their cross, see 9:23-26; 14:27-33; Col 1:24?). Luke omits Mark's note (15:21) that Simon was "the father of Alexander and Rufus," presumably known to Mark's readers but not to Luke's. A "great multitude of the people" (*plēthos tou laou,* combining the terms from 23:1 and 13, but not "all" the people) and of women followed, beating their breasts and wailing for him (v. 27). The narrator does not tell us why the people changed from calling for Jesus' crucifixion (vv. 1, 13, 18 ["all the multitude"], 21) to lamenting it. If Luke means that "some" of the people wailed for Jesus, we may see them again in Acts (2:6; 5:14, 16; but see 21:36; 25:24); the people are divided.

On the way to the place called "The Skull," Jesus turns to the multitude, including the women, and utters four sayings (23:28-31). Addressing the "daughters of Jerusalem" directly, he tells them not to weep for him but for themselves and their children (v. 28), a theme from earlier sayings (19:44; 21:23; see Deut 28:32, 41, 53-57, 62). "The days are coming" when they will bless barren women (23:29), usually thought to be cursed (Gen 16:1-2; 1 Sam 1:6, 11, 19-20). Those in Jerusalem will pray that the mountains may fall on them (23:30; an apocalyptic image in Rev 6:16); Vesuvius had erupted not long before Luke wrote, and the stories of the mountain falling on Pompeii were terrifying (Pliny the Younger *Letter* 6.16). Finally, "For if they do this [crucify Jesus] when the wood is green (or moist), what will happen when it is dry?" (23:31). Jesus' final question foresees the horrors committed by some leaders during the fall of Jerusalem to the Romans.

The Crucifixion and Mocking of Jesus (23:32-43)

The word order of 23:32 is awkward: "They led away also others, evildoers, two, to be put to death with him." Ancient manuscripts did not have commas, as in the translation above, so that it would be possible to read, "two other evildoers"; therefore, some manuscripts changed the word order. Characteristically, Luke later develops a conversation between Jesus and these revolutionaries (vv. 39-43).

Luke omits the Hebrew place name "Golgotha," referring only to "the place that is called The Skull" (23:33). Then follows the simple sentence at the heart of Christian faith, "there they crucified him — and the criminals [evildoers; see v. 23], one on his right and one on his left" (v. 33; see 1 Cor 1:13, 22-25, although Paul and Mark focus more exclusively on the cross than does Luke).

"Father, forgive them; for they do not know what they are doing" (23:34a). Important manuscripts omit these words ($\mathfrak{p}^{75}$, the first corrector of Aleph, B, and D); but some good manuscripts include them (Aleph, C, a corrector of D, and many second-century church writers, e.g., Hegesippus, Marcion, Justin, Irenaeus, Clement, and Origen). The manuscript evidence alone would indicate that v. 34a is not original.

But rivalry between Christians and Jews may have led scribes to omit Jesus' prayer for the forgiveness of Jewish leaders (see Epp: ch. 2), and internally the prayer corresponds with Lukan themes, the petition for forgiveness in the Lord's Prayer (11:4). In Acts (7:60) Stephen utters a similar prayer as he is stoned. Sometimes Luke narrates similar events both in the Gospel and Acts (e.g., both Jesus and Paul are tried by "kings and governors"), but sometimes Luke moves key theological affirmations from the Gospel to Acts (e.g., the equivalent of Mark 10:45 to Acts 20:28). If Jesus does not voice this prayer, but only Stephen, our author has a very high ecclesiology.

The soldiers fulfill Scripture (Ps 22:18) by dividing Jesus' clothing (23:34b). The narrator once again distinguishes between the "people," who watch, and the "leaders," who scoff and mock, saying he cannot "save himself," even though he is "the Messiah of God, the chosen one!" (v. 35; for "chosen one" see 9:35 and Isa 42:1). All three mockings concern Jesus as Savior (also vv. 37, 39, by the soldiers and one of the "evildoers," not by the "people"). The mockers assume that a Savior on a cross is ridiculous, but Luke and the readers believe that God "saves" by a cross.

There are both Jewish and Hellenistic contexts for this faith. Despite the fact that an earlier version of the Hebrew story of salvation included conquering the land (see Deut 6:20-23; 26:1-11), the final Priestly redactors excluded stories of the taking of the land from "Torah," which includes five books of Moses, not six, not Joshua. Moses died in Moab (Deut 34:4-6), in exile, not in the promised land, just as the redactors of Torah died in Babylon (see Sanders). God saves through and in exile and suffering, not only in prosperity and blessing (see also Jeremiah and the other prophets). The God who was with Israel in the hovels of Egypt was also willing to hang on the cross. The many citations of Scripture in the passion narrative argue this point text by text: we worship the God of Moses who was with Israel through the tragedies, the low points, as well as the high points of history.

Second, the most popular goddess in the Roman world was Isis, a worship reflected in Apuleius's tale *The Golden Ass*. The first nine books are so full of (sometimes hilarious) pain and suffering that they are difficult to read, but in the final book Lucius is transformed by Isis from an ass into a human being (11.13). Plutarch remarks that Isis "was not indifferent to the contexts and struggles which she had endured . . . , but she intermingled in the most holy rites . . . representations of her experiences at that time, and sanctified them, both as a lesson in godliness and as encouragement for men and women who find themselves in the clutch of like calamities" (*Isis and Osiris* 361DEK). Do we Christians in the twenty-first century believe that God is with us as we experience suffering in our bodies and as we act out the will of God in conflict with others in our society, or do we primarily want to save our individual souls from this evil chaos, as did Lucius in Apuleius's tale? The literary question is whether Luke-Acts is religious and political history or individualistic biography or novel?

The soldiers also offer him sour wine (23:36) and call him "the King of the Jews," written as an inscription on the cross (vv. 37-38). The inscription is probably historical. "King" and "cross" may have been combined for the first time by pagans who mocked, but they were soon repeated in the earliest Christian confessions (1 Cor 15:3, "Christ died. . ."; see also Luke 9:22; Acts 2:14-36).

One of the criminals crucified with Jesus "kept blaspheming" him, for the third time mocking his ability to save himself or them (23:39). Mark (15:32) notes only that "those [plural] who were crucified with him also taunted him," a notice that Luke develops into a dialogue (23:39-43). The one who mocked was rebuked by the other, "Do you not fear God . . . ?" (v. 40; see 1:50; 12:4-5; 18:2, which shows this to be a typical contrast for Luke: some fear God, others do not; Acts 10:2). The "wrongdoer" who fears God considers himself justly *(dikaios)* condemned, but Jesus as having done nothing wrong (nothing "out of place"; 23:41).

Addressing Jesus directly, he asks, "Remember me when you come into your kingdom" (23:42). God remembers Israel in this gospel (1:54, 72), but here the Jewish revolutionary asks Jesus to remember him, as later God "remembers" the prayers and alms of the Gentile Cornelius (Acts 10:31). The criminal accepts Jesus' message, that as king (as also the inscription on Jesus' cross says) he has a kingdom (1:33; 4:43; 6:20; 7:28; 12:32; 17:20; 22:29, claimed by Jesus himself; also Acts 14:22; 28:23, 31).

Jesus responds, "Amen, I tell you, today you will be with me in Paradise" (23:43; see 2 Cor 12:2, 4). Luke has fewer (6) of these "Amen, I tell you" sayings than do Mark (13) or Matthew (31). In Luke the expression precedes assertions that many in the culture would not accept, for example, 12:37 concerning the master serving the slave dinner, 18:17 concerning only children entering the kingdom, and 18:29 concerning disciples who leave house or wife or brothers . . . getting much back. Here the "wrongdoer" is to enter paradise — today.

Jesus is a savior today (2:11), fulfills Scripture today (4:21), forgives sins today (5:26), performs cures today (13:32-33), stays in a toll collector's house today, bringing salvation to his house (19:5, 9). Among sinners, the Savior acts today, on the cross. The mockers cannot see that Jesus' cross and a "wrongdoer" and salvation "today" are compatible, the gospel of a crucified Savior forgiving in the tragic present.

Jesus' Death, the Sun, the Centurion, the Crowds, and the Women (23:44-49)

Beginning at noon for three hours, there was an eclipse of the sun (23:44-45a). In some apocalyptic texts, this is a sign of the Lord coming on the day of judgment (Amos 8:3, 9). But the day of Jesus' crucifixion is not the day on which God judged Israel or the nations, so Amos is not a relevant parallel. V. 45a, like 45b, is a comment on the meaning of Jesus' crucifixion and death. Jesus, not Romulus, is the center of history; even Moses becomes a predecessor. Like Romulus/Augustus, the alternate claimant to kingship over the world, Jesus was born miraculously of a woman without a human father (see the commentary on 1:26-38), and now at Jesus' death there is an eclipse of the sun (compare Dionysius *Rom. Ant.* 2.56.6). Then also like Romulus, he ascends to heaven, after having taught his successors how to live.

"The curtain of the sanctuary *(naos)* was split down the middle" (23:45b). The passive voice of the verb means that God is the actor. The term *naos* signifies the inner sanctuary, not the temple in general, but we do not know which curtain was intended. Several meanings of the event have been suggested. It may indicate a judgment on the temple, and/or perhaps God leaving the temple and becoming the sanctuary for all peoples (see Ezek 10:3-5, 15-19; 11:16-17, 22-24; Luke 21:5-6; Acts 7:45-51; 17:24-25, 29; Eph 2:11-22, esp. v. 14).

With a loud voice, Jesus cried, "Father, into your hands I commend my spirit," and he "breathed his last" (23:46). The difference from Mark's scene is dramatic. Mark (15:34-37) narrates a very human Jesus dying in agony, abandoned by God. Mark's Jesus also "cried out with a loud voice," but the content is: "My God, why have you forsaken me?" (quoting Ps 22:1). Luke narrates a philosopher calmly commending his spirit to God (see Johnson: 334-35, 354-55, 379). Jesus is the model for Stephen the martyr, who dies praying, "Lord Jesus, receive my spirit" (Acts 7:59).

When the centurion saw this, he both praised (gave glory to) God and declared Jesus innocent (*dikaios;* 23:47). For Luke one of the choices of those who hear the word is whether to praise God or not (compare Rom 1:18-23, esp. vv. 21, 23). The crippled woman who was healed glorified God, but Jesus' opponents did not (13:13); the Samaritan leper did, but the other nine did not (17:15); the tax collector did, but the Pharisee did not (18:43; also Acts 4:21; 13:48-52; 21:20, 27-36, including orthodox *Christians* who did not glorify God).

Luke has a clear apologetic interest in the series of declarations that Jesus is innocent in relation to Roman law (23:4, 14, 15, 22; 23:41 and now v. 47, six times in the passion narrative). In Acts (3:14; 7:52; 22:14) "Righteous One" becomes one of Jesus' titles.

The crowds who gathered for the spectacle returned home, beating their breasts (cf. 18:13). Luke has repeatedly distinguished the crowds from the leaders, except in this chapter (23:1, 13, 18, 23), where they change and shout for Pilate to crucify Jesus. But by v. 27 they are beating their breasts and wailing for him, noted again in v. 48. This is the last time the "people" appear in Luke, but a repentant people appear again in Acts (see the commentary on 23:26-32). Luke presents a division among them.

All Jesus' acquaintances stand at a distance (23:49), as had Peter when Jesus was taken to the high priest's house (22:54). The acquaintances include the women who followed him from Galilee, women named as financial supporters in 8:3 and included among the leaders of the Jerusalem church in Acts 1:13-14. They are "watching" these events (see 3:6, quoting Isaiah; 24:34; Acts 2:27, quoting Joel; 22:15).

Jesus' Burial (23:50-56)

Luke introduces Joseph of Arimathea as a "good and righteous" man, a member of the Sanhedrin but one who had not agreed with their plan to put Jesus to death (see 22:1-2, 66-71), who was rather waiting for the kingdom of God (23:50-51; for others "waiting" see 2:25, 38; 12:36; Acts 24:15). Romans did not typically release the bodies of those whom they crucified for insurrection, but Pilate did for this official. Joseph wrapped Jesus' body in linen and laid it in a rock-hewn tomb where no one had ever been laid (compare 19:30). Joseph was a pious Jew, whether a disciple or not we do not learn, for he buried Jesus on the day of preparation as the sabbath was beginning, perhaps obeying Deut 21:22-23.

The women who had watched the crucifixion (23:49) also watch Joseph bury Jesus (v. 55); when they return to anoint Jesus' body with spices and ointments (v. 56; 24:1), they will find the tomb in which Jesus was buried. Like Joseph, the women rest on the sabbath according to Moses' commandment (23:56, an emphasis on orthodox piety found also in the birth narrative).

The Resurrection Narratives (24:1-53)

This section includes stories of Jesus' empty tomb (24:1-12), his eating with two disciples in Emmaus (vv. 13-35), the appearance to the eleven in Jerusalem (vv. 36-53), and Jesus' ascension (vv. 50-53). Earlier proclamations (not narratives) of Jesus' resurrection and/or ascension occur in confessional passages in Paul's letters (Rom 1:3-4; 1 Cor 15:3-7; Phil 2:6-11). They function both to vindicate Jesus' acts and teaching and to legitimate leaders in the church. Those who have seen the resurrected Christ are the ones who teach the church (contrast Gal 1:1, 11-12). Since the leadership of the Lukan churches is male, there is no resurrection appearance to women (contrast Matt 28:9-10; John 20:11-18). The resurrection appearances and stories of ascension to heaven have contemporary analogies, especially to Romulus, the other contemporary claimant to ruler of the world (see Dionysius *Rom. Ant.* 2.56.2-3).

The Women Discover the Empty Tomb, and the Apostles Disbelieve (24:1-12)

After the sabbath is over, the women come to the tomb in which they have seen Joseph bury Jesus, bringing spices (*arōmata*) to anoint his body (24:1). The stone had been rolled away from the opening, but they did not find his body (v. 2). Two men in dazzling ("astral, flashing like lightning") clothes stood by them, at which they were terrified and bowed to the ground (vv. 4-5a). These two other-than-human persons announce the gospel to them: Jesus is not dead but living; he has been raised (v. 5b).

These two astral visitors say, "Remember how he told you, while he was still in Galilee [see 9:22, 44-45, but not 18:31-33, no longer in Galilee], that the Son of Humanity must be handed over to sinners, and be crucified, and on the third day rise again" (24:6-7). First, Luke has strongly modified Mark (16:7), where the women are told that Jesus "is going before you to Galilee," that is, Jesus will appear in the future in Galilee. This does not fit Luke's eschatology, that the preaching is to go out from Jerusalem (24:47, 49), not Galilee. Luke, therefore, changed Mark; instead of referring to the future, the announcement concerns the past. The women are to remember what Jesus said, indeed when he was in Galilee.

Second, the women "remembered his words" and told the eleven and the rest (24:6-9). Despite women not functioning as preachers in Luke-Acts, nor as apostles or elders, these verses present women as the first post-resurrection persons who heard the gospel, which they believed and announced to the apostles. This includes "remembering" Jesus' words, one of the functions of the Gospel of Luke itself. The empty-tomb narrative contains a contrast found also in the infancy narrative: women (Jesus' mother Mary and Mary Magdalene) believe (1:45; 24:8-9) but men (the priest Zechariah and the apostles, including Peter) do not (1:20; 24:11). Seim calls this Luke's subversive "double message": women believe and remember Jesus' words, but they may not be official church leaders (Acts 1:21) or preach. This is close to Jesus' message to Mary (10:42): listening to Jesus' words will not be taken away from her. All the sermons in Acts are delivered by males. "Believing" and "remembering Jesus' words" and Scripture then seem to be more important than "seeing" the resurrected Christ and becoming an official (Seim)! This qualifies the emphasis in Luke on Jesus teaching his successors, the leaders of the church.

Earlier scholars of the manuscript tradition judged that 24:12 was a later addition. More recently $\mathfrak{p}^{75}$, dating from around AD 200, was discovered, and since it contains this verse, most text critics now judge the verse authentic. Its account of Peter running to the tomb, looking in, seeing Jesus' clothes, and going home is similar to John 20:3-10, a more expanded account.

Two Share a Meal with a Stranger at Emmaus (24:13-35)

For centuries readers have found Luke's storytelling most gripping in this and in the Cornelius story (Acts 10–11); both the style and content are extraordinary. For an insightful literary commentary, I refer the reader to Culpepper's (474-83) exposition. The only similar story is the later addition to Mark (16:12-13), concerning Jesus' appearance to two as they walked into the country, who returned and told the rest, who did not believe them. The addition to Mark may well be dependent on Luke.

The two walk toward Emmaus, a village near but outside Jerusalem (24:13). Luke narrates only appearance stories in and near Jerusalem, but this one may already hint that the gospel is to go out from that city (v. 47; Acts 1:8). The resurrected Jesus himself started walking with them, while they discussed and "disputed" (*syzētein;* 24:15; also 22:23). Here "dispute" seems positive, an effort to interpret Jesus' words and deeds. Stephen and Paul engage in similar "disputes" (Acts 6:9-10; 9:29; on education in the early church see Osiek and Balch: 71-73, 158). The disputes concern "all that had happened," the subject of the whole Gospel (see 24:19; 1:3; Acts 1:1; 10:38), but particularly the events of the passion (24:20, 26). These disputes were continuing in the Lukan churches, and the Gospel addresses them.

Jesus asks what they had been debating (*antiballō;* 24:17). Cleopas asks him whether he is the only stranger who does not know what has happened in Jerusalem in these days (v. 18). The irony is that the questioner is ignorant, while the one questioned knows. Culpepper: 477 points out that in classical irony, the ignorance of the know-it-all character is exposed by the character feigning ignorance (Aristotle *Nic. Eth.* 4.7), a character played by Jesus: "What things?" (v. 19). The reply of the two runs six verses (19-24), mentioning Jesus' deed and word in one verse, the passion in five. They emphasize again the division between the "people" and the "leaders" (vv. 19-20), the women's report of "angels" who said that "he was alive" (vv. 22-23), and the others' failure to "see" him (v. 24; compare Luke's summary in Acts 10:36-43). Culpepper: 478 sees further ironies: they hoped that Jesus would fulfill Scripture, but understand his death only as a frustration of their hope (24:21). Second, Peter had not seen Jesus; now they have but still they do not understand.

Jesus shows the way to knowledge: believing all that the prophets have declared, that the Messiah "must" suffer and enter into his glory (24:26). The final phrase may refer to Jesus' resurrection or to his ascension (9:31, 51; Acts 2:34-35; 13:33-37; 24:14-15, 21; 26:6, 23). Luke summarizes Jesus' christological exegesis of Moses and all the prophets (24:27).

Culpepper: 479 observes that the meal (24:28-32) is a classical recognition scene, the *anagnōrisis,* a change from ignorance to knowledge, best arising from the actions alone (Aristotle *Poetics* 1452a, 1454b-55a). Jesus walks ahead as if he is going on (v. 28), but they urge him to "remain" "with us," and he does (v. 29). This scene, then, is of a missionary being given hospitality in a disciple's house (1:56; 9:4; 10:7; 19:5; Acts 16:15). Jesus "takes, breaks, blesses, and gives" (24:30), the verbs spoken at the Lord's Supper (9:16; 22:19). Now their "eyes were opened, and they recognized him" (24:31).

This story continues a theme from the previous one: in Luke the women did *not see* Jesus, either his dead or his resurrected body, but they "remembered his words" and told the apostles, while the males who were officially leaders considered the women's words an idle tale (24:3, 6-8, 11-12). Here the two actually *do see* Jesus without recognizing him, until they hear Jesus' christological interpretation of Scripture and eat with this stranger/sojourner (vv. 15-16, 18, 25-27, 29-32, 35). Luke plays down the centrality of *seeing* the *resurrected Lord!* That event lay in the past for the Lukan churches; how could they experience the presence of the resurrected Lord? Culpepper: 480 compares the clear hermeneutic of John (2:22; see 12:16; 20:9). Luke's hermeneutic in addition focuses on a meal with a stranger (24:18), a meal where masters serve slaves (12:37; 22:27), in which a woman, too, listens to Jesus (10:39, 42), in which all nations participate (13:29; Acts 2:42; 10:9-16, 35, 43, 48; 11:6-9; see 15:20), and where the poor are invited (14:12-14, 21), as are the religiously disqualified (15:1-2; Acts 15). In the Greco-Roman, status-conscious society and church, the Lukan narrative reveals that distinctions of citizenship, gender, race, legal, economic, and religious status are insignificant compared to the willingness of "all" to eat together worshiping the present Lord of the world, who is not Romulus or Caesar.

The Lord "disappears" (24:31). They recognize that

their hearts "burned" as they heard Scripture (v. 32). "That same hour," so on the first day of the week (vv. 1, 13), they return to Jerusalem. First, they hear a report of Jesus' appearance to Simon (v. 34), in traditional circles the first to whom Jesus appeared (1 Cor 15:5). Finally, they tell how he had been made known to them in the "breaking of the bread" (see Acts 2:42).

Jesus Eats with the Eleven, Leads a Postresurrection Bible Study, and Commissions Them to Preach to All Nations (24:36-49)

Paul records a very early tradition in which Jesus appears to "Cephas [Simon Peter] and the twelve" (1 Cor 15:5). Luke also records an appearance to Simon or Peter and to vague group, "they" (24:36). The antecedent of the pronoun is vague, but the most specific possibility is given in vv. 9-10, "the eleven and all the rest," including Mary Magdalene (see vv. 12, 22, 24, 34, 36). Acts (1:2, 4) narrows this to the (male) "apostles," but there, too, the leadership group includes the eleven "with certain women, including Mary the mother of Jesus, as well as his brothers" (1:11-14). The Gospel of Luke never narrows the group to whom Jesus appears in this passage to only the eleven (males).

Culpepper: 484 observes close connections between this Lukan story and John 20:19-29 and 21:1-14 as follows: (1) Jesus stands among them and pronounces "peace be with you," (2) he shows them his hands and invites someone to touch him, (3) one or several doubt, (4) Jesus asks for and then eats fish, (5) he commissions them, and (6) he breathes the Holy Spirit on them or promises power from on high. However, each evangelist employs the themes in diverse ways suitable to the particular Gospel.

At the end of a (long!) Sunday, Jesus stands among them and pronounces, "Peace be with you" (24:36), as he commanded in his own mission instructions (10:5-6; see 2:14; 7:50; Acts 10:36). Not astoundingly, the group is terrified (24:37), typical of angelophanies (1:11; Acts 10:30). They thought they were seeing a "spirit." Jesus chides them about their fright and doubts, offering his hands and feet to touch *(psēlaphēs-),* his flesh and bones (24:38-39), a different understanding of the resurrection body than Paul has (1 Cor 15:35-50, esp. 50: "flesh and blood cannot inherit the kingdom of God"). When Paul preaches to Stoics on the Areopagus, he proclaims the Creator, "so that they would search for God and perhaps grope for *(psēlaphēs-)* him and find him — though indeed he is not far from each one of us" (17:27). Most commentators rightly compare the Stoic Dio Chrysostom (*Or.* 12.60-61), but the author of Acts also refers back to Jesus' use of the same verb: one may grope for (touch) God in the resurrected Jesus. In the group's joy, they were disbelieving (24:41; see v. 11 and the apology in 22:45). Jesus asks for something to eat, they give him broiled fish, and he eats it in their presence (24:41-42). Similarly, when Romulus appeared after his death to Julius Ascanius, who had never told an untruth, he saw Romulus departing from Rome fully armed, hardly a "spiritual" appearance story (*Rom. Ant.* 2.63-64; see Livy 1.16 and Balch 2003b)!

Jesus' last words refer to "my words that I spoke to you while I was still with you," the ones remembered by the women (24:6), specifically his christological and ecclesiological interpretation of "the law of Moses, the prophets, and the psalms" (v. 44). Jesus taught this hermeneutic of the Bible in the passion prophecies (9:22, 44; 18:32-33), in a reading of Jonah (11:29-32), by parable (20:9-19), and in a dispute about King David (20:41-44), a reading of the Bible expanded in the speeches in Acts, especially by Peter (ch. 2), Stephen (ch. 7), and Paul (ch. 13). Whereas Mark's (8:31; 9:31; 10:33-34) hermeneutic is primarily christological, Luke's is also ecclesiological, emphasizing that "repentance and forgiveness of sins is to be proclaimed in his name to all nations, beginning from Jerusalem. You are witnesses of these things" (24:47-48; see Acts 10–11; 13:47, quoting Isa 49:6; 28:25-28, quoting Isa 6:9-10). Mark is one book, but Luke writes a second one, Acts, about the origin and growth of the church, the proclamation of forgiveness to all nations. The group has been "witnesses" of these things, a primary emphasis of the Gospel (1:2). Acts (1:15-26, esp. 21-22; see 10:39, 41) limits the official apostolic witnesses to males, but Luke 24 does not. These witnesses are to receive the Father's promise, to be clothed with power from on high (v. 49; see the commentary on 9:1-17), phrases that the readers of Acts (1:5) learn refer to the Holy Spirit. The image of being "clothed" occurs in baptismal contexts (Gal 3:27; Eph 4:24; 6:11, 14), a ritual associated with God's giving the Spirit (Acts 2:38, but not in 8:14-17 or 10:44, 47).

Jesus' Ascension (24:50-53; see the Commentary on 1:26-38)

Leading them out to Bethany, he lifted his hands and blessed them (24:50), as Moses had blessed the twelve tribes of Israel (Genesis 49; Deuteronomy 33) and as the high priest Simon blessed Israel (Sir 50:20-24). Withdrawing from them, he is carried up to heaven (24:51), again as Romulus had been. Dionysius refers to Romulus's sudden death, noting that while he was giving a speech to his soldiers a sudden darkness rushed down from a clear sky, he disappeared *(aphanē)* and was nowhere to be seen, so that some believe he was caught up into the sky by his father Mars (*Rom. Ant.* 2.56.1-3).

> The incidents that occurred by the direction of Heaven in connexion with this man's conception and death would seem to give no small authority to the view of those who make gods of mortal men and place the souls of illustrious persons in heaven. For they say that at the time when his mother was violated, whether by some man or by a god, there was a total eclipse of the sun and a general darkness as in the night covered the earth, and that at his death the same thing happened. (*Rom. Ant.* 2.56.6)

By narrating Jesus' birth as the Son of God and the eclipse of the sun at Jesus' death followed by his ascension to heaven, Luke is claiming that Jesus, not Romulus or any Roman Caesar, is the ruler of the world, that Jesus is "my Son, my Chosen; listen to him!" (9:35), not to any other claimant to divine status. The disciples do indeed worship him (24:52) and return to Jerusalem with joy, as

Jesus had instructed them (v. 49). They were continually in the temple blessing God (v. 53), as had been the characters at the beginning of the Gospel (2:25-38), Simeon and Anna.

Bibliography. Balch, D. 1982, "Two Apologetic Encomia: Dionysius on Rome and Josephus on the Jews," *JSJ* 13/1-2:102-21 • Balch, D. 1990, "The Areopagus Speech: An Appeal to the Stoic Historian Posidonius against Later Stoics and the Epicureans," in D. L. Balch, E. Ferguson, and W. A. Meeks, eds., *Greeks, Romans, and Christians: Essays in Honor of J. Malherbe*, Minneapolis: Fortress, 52-79 • Balch, D. 1995a, "Rich and Poor, Proud and Humble in Luke-Acts," in L. M. White and O. L. Yarbrough, eds., *The Social World of the First Christians: Essays in Honor of Wayne A. Meeks*, Minneapolis: Fortress, 214-33 • Balch, D. 1995b, "Paul in Acts: '. . . You teach all the Jews . . . to forsake Moses, telling them not to . . . observe the customs' (Act. 21,21)," in *Panchaia: Festschrift für Klaus Thraede*, JAC Ergänzungsband 22, Münster: Aschendorff, 11-23 • Balch, D. 1997, "Political Friendship in the Historian Dionysius of Halicarnassus, *Roman Antiquities*," in John T. Fitzgerald, ed., *Greco-Roman Perspectives on Friendship*, SBLRBS 34, Atlanta: Scholars, 123-44 • Balch, D. 1998, "Attitudes toward Foreigners in 2 Maccabees, Eupolemus, Esther, Aristeas, and Luke-Acts," in Abraham J. Malherbe, Frederick W. Norris, and James W. Thompson, eds., *The Early Church in Its Context: Essays in Honor of Everett Ferguson*, NovTSup 90, Leiden: Brill, 22-47 • Balch, D. 1999, "*akribōs . . . grapsai*" (Luke 1:3): To Write the *Full* History of God's Receiving All Nations," in David P. Moessner, ed., *Jesus and the Heritage of Israel: Luke's Narrative Claim upon Israel's Legacy*, Harrisburg: Trinity Press International, 229-50 = "The *Full* History" • Balch, D. 2003a, "Philodemus, 'On Wealth' and 'On Household Management': Naturally Wealthy Epicureans against Poor Cynics," in John T. Fitzgerald, ed., *Philodemus and the New Testament World*, NovTSup, Leiden: Brill • Balch, D. 2003b, "*Metabole Politeion*: Jesus as Founder of the Church in Luke-Acts: Form and Function," in T. Penner and C. Vander Stichele, eds., *Contextualizing Acts: Lukan Narrative and Greco-Roman Discourse*, Symposium Series, Atlanta: Scholars Press and Leiden: E. J. Brill • Beavis, M. A. 1992, "Ancient Slavery as an Interpretive Context for the New Testament Servant Parables with Special Reference to the Unjust Steward (Luke 16:1-8)," *JBL* 111:37-54 • Betz, H. D. 1995, *The Sermon on the Mount*, Hermeneia, Minneapolis: Fortress • Bobertz, C. A. 1993, "The Role of Patron in the *Cena Domenica* of Hippolytus' Apostolic Tradition," *JTS* 44:170-84 • Braun, W. 1995, *Feasting and Social Rhetoric in Luke 14*, SNTSMS 85, Cambridge: Cambridge University • Brown, R. E. rev. ed. 1993, *The Birth of the Messiah: A Commentary on the Infancy Narratives in the Gospels of Matthew and Luke*, AB, New York: Doubleday • Burridge, R. A. 1992, *What Are the Gospels? A Comparison with Graeco-Roman Biography*, SNTSMS 70, Cambridge: Cambridge University • Cancik, H. 1997, "The History of Culture, Religion, and Institutions in Ancient Historiography: Philological Observations concerning Luke's History," *JBL* 116:681-703 • Carter, W. 1999, *Households and Discipleship: A Study of Matthew 19–20*, JSNTSup 103, Sheffield: JSOT • Charlesworth, J. H. 1995, *The Old Testament Pseudepigrapha*, 2 vols., Garden City, N.Y.: Doubleday • Collins, J. J. 1983, *Between Athens and Jerusalem: Jewish Identity in the Hellenistic Diaspora*, New York: Crossroad • Crossan, J. D. 1973, *In Parables*, New York: Harper and Row • Culpepper, R. A. 1995, "The Gospel of Luke," in *The New Interpreter's Bible*, vol. 9, Nashville: Abingdon • D'Angelo, M. R. 1992, "*Abba* and 'Father': Imperial Theology and the Jesus Traditions," *JBL* 111/4:611-30 • Epp, E. J. 1966, *The Theological Tendency of Codex Bezae Catabrigiensis in Acts*, Cambridge: Cambridge University • Felder, C. H. 1989, *Troubling Biblical Waters: Race, Class, and Family*, Maryknoll, N.Y.: Orbis • Fitzmyer, J. A. 1981 and 1985, *The Gospel according to Luke*, AB 28 and 28A, New York: Doubleday • Gabba, E. 1991, *Dionysius and the History of Archaic Rome*, Berkeley: University of California • Heschel, A. J. 1951, 1975, *The Sabbath: Its Meaning for Modern Man*, New York: Noonday • Hock, R. F., and E. N. O'Neil. 1986, *The Chreia in Ancient Rhetoric*, vol. 1: *The Progymnasmata*, Atlanta: Scholars • Johnson, L. T. 1991, *The Gospel of Luke*, SacPag 3, Collegeville, Minn.: Liturgical • Karris, R. J. 1990, "The Gospel according to Luke," in R. E. Brown, J. A. Fitzmyer, and R. E. Murphy, eds., *The New Jerome Biblical Commentary*, Englewood Cliffs: Prentice Hall, 675-721 • Luther, M. 1959, "The Apology of the Augsburg Confession," art. 4 in *The Book of Concord*, trans. T. G. Tappert, Philadelphia: Fortress • Malherbe, A. J. 1996, "The Christianization of a Topos [Luke 12:13-34]," *NovT* 38/2:123-35 • Manson, T. W. 1961, *The Servant Messiah*, Cambridge: Cambridge University • Meier, J. P. 1997, "The Circle of the Twelve: Did It Exist during Jesus' Public Ministry?" *JBL* 116/4:635-72 • Neusner, J. 1973, *From Politics to Piety: The Emergence of Pharisaic Judaism*, Englewood Cliffs: Prentice-Hall • Osiek, C., and D. L. Balch. 1997, *Families in the New Testament World: Households and House Churches*, Louisville: Westminster/John Knox • Paffenroth, K. 1997, *The Story of Jesus according to L*, JSNTSup 147, Sheffield: Sheffield Academic • Penny, D. L., and M. O. Wise. 1994, "By the Power of Beelzeboul: An Aramaic Incantation Formula from Qumran (4Q560)," *JBL* 113:627-50 • Sanders, J. A. 1987, "Adaptable for Life: The Nature and Function of Canon," in *From Sacred Story to Sacred Text*, Philadelphia: Fortress, 9-39 • Schottroff, L. 1995, *Lydia's Impatient Sisters: A Feminist Social History of Early Christianity*, Louisville: Westminster/John Knox • Schürmann, H. 1994, "Observations on the Son of Man Title in the Speech Source: Its Occurrence in Closing and Introductory Expressions," in John S. Kloppenborg, ed., *The Shape of Q: Signal Essays on the Sayings Source*, Minneapolis: Fortress, 74-97 • Seim, T. K. 1994, *The Double Message: Patterns of Gender in Luke-Acts*, Nashville: Abingdon • Stowers, S. 1995, "Greeks Who Sacrifice and Those Who Do Not: Toward an Anthropology of Greek Religion," in L. M. White and O. L. Yarbrough, eds., *The Social World of the First Christians: Essays in Honor of Wayne A. Meeks*, Minneapolis: Fortress, 293-333 • Talbert, C. H., and J. H. Hayes. 1995, "A Theology of Sea Storms in Luke-Acts," *SBL 1995 Seminar Papers*, Atlanta: Scholars, 321-36 • Tcherikover, V. 1958, "The Ideology of the Letter of Aristeas," *HTR* 51:59-85 • Theissen, G. 1978, *Sociology of Early Palestinian Christianity*, Philadelphia: Fortress • Tuckett, C. M. 1996, *Luke*, New Testament Guides, Sheffield: Sheffield Academic • Wiesenthal, S. 2d ed. 1997, *The Sunflower: On the Possibilities and Limits of Forgiveness*, New York: Schocken • Wilckens, U. 1958, "Kerygma und Evangelium bei Lukas (Beobachtungen zu Acta 10 34-43)," *ZNW* 49:223-37.

John

J. Martin C. Scott

INTRODUCTION

The Fourth Gospel (= FG) is a work of great literary artistry, full of dramatic irony and poetic beauty. The medium of poetry, with which the Gospel opens (1:1-18), is appropriate to the literary-theological style employed throughout and reflects the principal background on which the Fourth Evangelist (= FE) draws, namely, the writings of the Jewish wisdom tradition.

While the FG undoubtedly alludes to a wide number of works from the Hebrew scriptures (both the prophets and often polemically the Torah), it is the wisdom writings which provide the most important materials for understanding the FE's use of the term "Logos" and the whole christological reflection which emerges from it in the body of the FG. Knowledge of the picture of Sophia (her Greek name is used to highlight the gender of Wisdom in this commentary) found in the great poetic chapters of Proverbs 1–9, Sirach 24 (also chs. 1, 4, 6, 14, and 15) and throughout Wisdom of Solomon, is fundamental for reading John's Gospel. Pictured in wisdom literature as the agent of God's communication of salvation, hope, judgment, and reproach to humanity, she provides a model for understanding the Johannine Jesus' mission in the world (Scott 1992: 83-173).

The portrayal of God's wisdom as a woman comes about at its most basic level because of the feminine gender of the Hebrew and Greek words. Yet it is not simply a linguistic accident that the portrayal develops in the way that it does in Israel's wisdom literature (Scott 1992: 36-82). The whole contrast between Sophia's call and that of the prostitute who sits at her door to entice *men* into her parlor (Prov 7:5-27; 9:13-18) depends on powerful sexual imagery. To make a direct equivalence in *incarnational* terms between the male Jesus and what is decisively a female image of God's presence in the world is not possible. In choosing Logos, a well-established but masculine-gendered synonym for Sophia, the FE is making firm the connection with the tradition while taking seriously the limitations of incarnation.

The importance of this female image of God's presence in creation, redemption, and judgment as a background for reading the story of Jesus at the start of the third millennium is highlighted by the history of interpretation of the FG. Far from letting "John Be John" (Dunn 1983), the Logos of John's Prologue was used as a significant building block for patriarchal Christology by many early church writers. The interpretation of the Logos in terms of Greek philosophical speculation, largely ignoring its primary roots in Sophia tradition, fast became the norm. It is clear, not least from the writings of Philo, the Alexandrian Jewish philosopher, that the words "Logos" and "Sophia" were quite interchangeable by the time of writing of the FG. In using the term "Logos," which acknowledges the maleness of the human Jesus, the FG still leaves open the full range of meaning of the word "Sophia."

In the Johannine Jesus we may see the fullness of God revealed, in both masculine and feminine dimensions, albeit within the limitations of incarnation in terms of human sexuality. As Elizabeth Johnson puts it: "The gender particularity of Jesus does not reveal that God must be imaged exclusively as male. In Jesus Christ we encounter the mystery of God who is neither male nor female, but who as source of both and Creator in the divine image can in turn be imaged as either" (Johnson 1985: 280).

Whether the FE intended to convey all the gender subtleties of the Sophia background (it is at least possible that it is intentional), this commentary adopts a *narrative* approach to reading the text as it stands. Little time is spent on weighing up historical matters which can be followed up in other literature on the FG (cf. Brown 1997: 362-82). We have no certain access to either the historical author or her/his audience, even if there are strong pointers to a community in crisis being addressed throughout. What may be attempted, however, is a reading of the Gospel from the viewpoint of an "ideal [or "implied"] reader," whom the text itself constructs. This hypothetical "reader" is required for the narrative to make sense, or be heard coherently (cf. Powell 1993). In endeavoring to enable the modern reader to hear the FG from such an ideal reader's perspective this commentary places emphasis on the pointers to the emergent theological meaning which the developing narrative contains.

John often uses "intertextual echo" as a means of alerting the "implied reader" to a variety of subtle connections. This takes the form of a word, a phrase, or an idea which evokes particular counterparts either internal to the Gospel (e.g., the use of "feet" in 12:1-8 evoking the later "footwashing" account), or externally in the literature of wider Jewish tradition (e.g., the opening words of the Gospel evoking Gen 1:1). Many of these echoes are crucial for understanding the christological picture which the FE paints, particularly in terms of the relationship to Sophia. Since she represented the immanence of God's wise presence in its fullest appeal to Israel, Jesus, Sophia incarnate, comes in similar manner to the whole of humanity.

Another important literary-theological technique which the FG employs is *irony.* This takes a variety of forms throughout the Gospel, sometimes overt, sometimes covert (cf. Duke 1985: 7-27), but always pressing and inviting the reader to see beyond the surface responses of Johannine characters to the twists of meaning which often turn interpretation on its head. One such twist which this commentary attempts to read in a novel way is the use of the term "Jews." Jesus, who is clearly a Jew, often speaks of "Jews" as though he were not one. For the most part this has been interpreted as part of the struggle of the Johannine community with its separation from its roots in Judaism (cf. Stibbe 1994: 107-31). Such a reading has never, however, done justice to the full spectrum of use of the term in the FG, so we will instead attempt to read it as an ironic reference to the struggle of the Johannine community with other Christian groups evidenced in the polemic of the later Johannine epistles (see the comment on 1:19).

Another ironic element of the FG's presentation is the way in which discipleship is portrayed. Far from the Synoptic picture of a central band of men who demonstrate in positive and negative manner the traits of true discipleship, it is the women of the FG who serve in a paradigmatic role (cf. Scott 1994). Given the overwhelmingly overt male language of the FG (Father-Son) and indeed the maleness of Jesus, the subtlety of Sophia's influence may perhaps be glanced in this role reversal. Certainly it provides an important alternative perspective to other NT and later ecclesiological viewpoints in this third millennium.

COMMENTARY

John 1:1-18

In the beginning the FE employed poetry to draw together the disparate themes which now find their theological focus in the Gospel's portrayal of Jesus as the Christ, the Son of God. The primary themes of the FG are laid before the reader in these verses. The genius of the FE lies in the ability to make these opening words not only point *forward* to the content of the Gospel but also hark *back* to so much that has gone before.

Many attempts have been made to reconstruct an "original" hymn lying behind this introduction to the FG. Most commentators define four stanzas, which are interrupted by the comments on John the Baptist (= JBap), though the content of the stanzas differs in the various analyses (Dunn 1989: 240). There is general agreement on the scope of the first two stanzas (1:1-2, 3-5). Brown gives good grammatical and literary reasons for seeing the next stanza as comprising vv. 10-12b, with a fourth made up from vv. 14 and 16 (Brown 1966: 1-18, 21-23). While we shall not attempt any detailed analysis of the prehistory of the hymn, we shall point to important literary blocks which may help move our theological understanding forward and inform our comment on the text as the narrative unfolds.

"In the beginning" (1:1) obviously takes the reader back to the opening of the Torah (Gen 1:1) and so to the theme of creation. It is a theme which will dominate the opening verses both in terms of the creation of the world (1:1-5, 10) and in relation to the new beginnings which become possible from the presence of the Word in the world (1:12-13, 16-17). The concern here is not with *origins,* either of the man Jesus or of the believing child, but with *connections.* The Gospel will unfold in detail the connection between the introductory Word and Jesus, the beginning of whose story this poem is. In addition to that, however, the Prologue also plays a vital role in connecting that Word back into various strands of Israel's salvation history.

Primary among the connections for the FE is that between Word (Logos) and the Wisdom of God, Sophia, whose own intimate link with both creation and salvation belongs to the most ancient literary traditions of Israel (Prov 8:22-33 — creation; Prov 1:20-33 — salvation). She was in the beginning with God (Prov 8:22; Sir 1:1, 4) and participated with God in the creation of the world (Prov 8:30; Sir 24:3-6; Wis 9:1-2). The wider scope of wisdom literature reveals Sophia's participation in the making of the world as all-inclusive: the separation of waters and dry land, the establishment of the mountains and fields, the laying out of the heavens, and finally even the creation of the human race. Like the Word, Sophia may be hailed as the one through whom "all things came into being" (1:3).

It was not the FE who first made this connection between Logos and Sophia. The process is well attested in wisdom literature (Scott 1992: 88-94). In Sir 24:3, Sophia announces that she emerges from the "mouth of the most high," at least hinting at a connection with "word." The link is made explicit in Wis 9:1-2, where the parallel between Logos and Sophia is unmistakable. Other passages in the book of Wisdom hint at the same conclusion (both proceed from the royal throne in heaven: 9:10 — Sophia; 18:15 — Logos), but the most frequent parallels are found in the many writings of the Jewish philosopher, Philo of Alexandria. Philo uses the terms interchangeably, for the most part substituting the Logos for Sophia in her traditional function as God's agent in the world (Scott 1992: 58-61, 91-94).

The literary function here (and probably also the intention of the FE) in using the epithet Logos/Sophia is surely to make connections. All that has been known in the tradition concerning Sophia (and more!) is now embodied in Jesus Christ. At the same time, the mystery of Jesus Christ can best be illuminated with reference to the known categories of Sophia. The use of "Logos" to describe the one whose prehistory comes to fruition in Christ owes its origins to Jesus' gender (see the Introduction, 1161), but constant intertextual echoes bind Jesus and Sophia ever closer as the story unfolds.

"In him was life" (1:4) seems to continue the creation theme, but the text is difficult. Brown lists five separate problems in translation (Brown 1966: 6-7), and finally opts for a direct connection to 1:3, a view which has found favor with others (Witherington 1995: 47 — "what has come into being in him was life"). The theme has strong links with Sophia, not only in terms of creation but significantly in relation to salvation. "The one who finds me finds life," she declares (Prov 8:35). Just as important is the implicit dualism of Prov 1:22-33, where the consequence of ignoring the claims of Sophia is calamity and death, in contrast to receiving her, finding security, and "living at ease" (Prov 1:33). Sirach echoes these sentiments (Sir 4:12), while in Wis 8:13, "Solomon" even goes so far as to suggest that she grants immortality! The FE elsewhere uses "life" only in the sense of "eternal life" (Brown 1966: 505-8), so it is hard to think that it means anything other here. While the whole Gospel may pick up the theme of "eternal life" in an idiosyncratic way, its seeds are sown in the wisdom tradition. The Johannine Jesus, like Sophia, brings about a crisis point in human experience, on the basis of which decisions between life and death will be made.

"The life was the light of all people" (1:4) again echoes the ancient tradition. Light is brought into being by the word of God as the first act in the creation story (Gen 1:3). The emphasis in John 1:4, however, seems closer to that in Ps 119:105, where God's word is said to illuminate the psalmist's pathway. There is a double connection here to the wisdom tradition, where Sophia is not only known as the first of God's acts of creation, but is also revered for her illuminative presence. "Solomon" chooses her before light because her radiance is greater (Wis 7:10). She is a reflection of the ever present light of God (Wis 7:26), unquenched by the night or by evil (Wis 7:29-30). The gift of light, sought as a symbol of salvation, is being opened up to all people in the person of Jesus Christ, the very embodiment of Sophia.

Light is identifiable only in contrast to darkness, as the poem goes on to state (1:5). Primeval darkness is overcome by the creation of light (Gen 1:2-3), a motif which surely informs this text. John's prior association of light with the salvation of humanity, however, leads the reader to hear the theme of conflict between good and evil behind this contrast. The word "overcome" *(katelaben)* is used again in 12:35, where such conflict is undoubtedly in mind, centered around the person of Jesus, the Light. The thought is not of an irreconcilable dualism, but rather in line with what we have noted in Wis 7:29-30, namely, that darkness/evil cannot put out the light of God's all-pervading wisdom. The brief clarification of the role of JBap which follows (1:6-8) confirms this, since he is to be seen neither as "darkness" nor as a "false" light in contrast to the true light of 1:9. We might say that JBap sheds light on the Light through his witness. In parallel with Wis 7:10, 29-30, therefore, he is eclipsed by the superior radiance.

A new block begins with 1:10, recalling the previous emphasis on the involvement of the Word in creation, but moving on to explore his ongoing relationship with the world. Given the poetic skill which lies behind this opening to the FG, it seems surprising that the high point of v. 14 — "the Word became flesh" — should be preempted by the statement "he was in the world" (1:10). Once again the echoes of Sophia tradition help with clarification, the emphasis of vv. 10-12 lying on the *reaction* of the world to the Word rather than on the *form* of his presence, which first becomes an issue in 1:14. Like Sophia, the Word comes to those most likely to recognize him, but they fail to recognize or accept him in their ignorance. Only those wise enough to believe find themselves in a familial relationship with God.

This is exactly the story of Sophia's experience with Israel. She is found proclaiming her message in the most public places: at the city gate; in the market square; in the streets (Prov 1:20-21; 8:1-3). She spans the whole earth (Wis 8:1) and sets up camp in Jerusalem (Sir 24:8-12) in order to offer her good gifts to humanity. Yet she finds little response among her own people, who ignore, despise, or scoff at her wisdom (Prov 1:22-33). Later Jewish texts speak of her withdrawal from the world because of rejection (*1 Enoch* 42:1-2). Sophia's rejection brings judgment, but to accept her is to gain life (Prov 8:35; Sir 4:12) and to enter a new relationship with God, as friends (Wis 7:27).

For the informed Christian reader, of course, these verses already foreshadow the mission of Jesus in the world. The poetic introduction to the FG wants to set this against the background of God's saving intention throughout history, to echo the continuity of God's relationship with the world since its very inception. Just as God, in conjunction with Logos/Sophia, created the world, so that same God is bringing into being a new creation through Jesus/Sophia (1:13). This is a birth brought about by no ordinary human desire but by the will of God.

The most striking claim of this opening poem now follows (1:14). Unique though the specific idea of incarnation of the Word may be, it can be seen as being in continuity with the wisdom tradition. Even the language of the FG owes something to the description of Sir 24:8, where Sophia is described as "pitching her tent" *(kataskēnōson)* in Israel — precisely the expression John 1:14 uses of the Word's descent into the world. Whereas some wisdom writers (Sirach; Baruch) talk of Sophia's confinement in the Torah, the FE instead declares that she has really taken on flesh, become flesh, in the person of Jesus, the Christ.

Incarnation requires self-limitation: the Word who was at the beginning of all things and in all things is now identified with a specific human being, limited by time, space, and gender. But incarnation is not only about self-limitation: it is also about disclosure, or revelation. The glory of God is made plain in the incarnation, a glory which Sophia was also known to reveal to those who loved her (Wis 7:25; 9:11). In the Exodus tradition, the glory of God was made visible through miraculous provision: manna; the guiding presence (cloud; fire). This lies behind John's understanding of "glory," but again it is worth remembering that the whole Exodus story is retold as the glorious, saving work of Sophia in Wisdom 10–11. The Gospel will gradually reveal the glory of God present in Jesus, initially through signs (2:11; 11:40), then the whole ministry (17:4), finally and completely through the "hour" of passion, death, and resurrection (12:23; 13:31-32; 17:1).

Despite the continued attempts of commentators to interpret the word *monogenēs* as "only begotten" (recently, Witherington 1995: 54), the word is better translated "uniquely precious," denoting the quality of Jesus' relationship with God as Father (Brown 1966: 13-14). Sophia is described in exactly this way in Wis 7:22, her epithet now transferred to the Logos as son.

The phrase "full of grace and truth" (1:14) seems to reflect the Hebrew coupling of *ḥesed* and *'emet.* These terms declare the covenant faithfulness of God, which is surely coming to new expression in the life, death, and resurrection of Jesus Christ. Since the word "grace" never appears in the body of the Gospel, it would seem that the emphasis lies more on the Word as the embodiment of "truth," a major theme of the Gospel. Truth, for John, can mean *both* the one who is ultimately real (a usage common in Greek literature), Jesus Christ (14:6), *and* the one who is completely faithful (more typical of Hebrew usage; cf. 10:11). In this usage we find another parallel to Sophia, who not only utters truth (Prov 8:6-7) but also remains utterly faithful to those who follow in her paths (Prov 8:32-36) and can be seen as synonymous with truth (Prov 23:23).

The covenant love of God, expressed anew in the Logos, encompasses human experience completely (1:16). The Psalms speak frequently of the "fullness" of God's creation (Pss 24:1; 50:12; 89:11), and rejoice in the way that God's glory "fills" all the earth (Ps 72:19). The fullness here is described in terms of "grace upon grace." Like the branches of a vine, Sophia spreads out her glory and grace (Sir 24:16). Those who lack wisdom lack God's grace (Sir 37:21). Although the language may appear strange, the text is simply picking up on the description of covenant love already begun in 1:14 and preparing the reader for the declaration of its fulfillment in the person of Jesus Christ.

The text now makes the connection complete by naming the one in whom grace comes to fruition (1:17). It is difficult not to see a deliberate contrast being made between old and new at this point: the law through Moses (old); grace and truth through Jesus Christ (new). Unlike Moses the lawgiver, the incarnate Logos/Sophia has been with God from the beginning; has assisted in creation; and by implication was there at the giving of the Torah. The one who was before Moses (and JBap, 1:15) now appears as the very embodiment of creative wisdom. Far from Sirach's assertion that Sophia is shut up in the Torah (Sir 24:23, 25), the FE declares her to be present in Jesus Christ, who supersedes the Torah because he was before it. The rest of the Gospel will set about revealing the Creator's desire for the world, direct from the heart of God (1:18), and culminating in the call to continue in life through belief in Jesus as the Christ, the Son of God (20:31).

So what of JBap, sporadic mention of whom seems to interrupt the opening poetry (1:6-8, 15)? Is his presence simply due to bad editing by the FE? Or is it because of a special polemic against a sect of disciples of JBap? Neither of these options seems likely since the material included in the poem has as its central theme *witness,* which word receives a crucial emphasis throughout the Gospel. As we noted already, he is not a "false" light, but rather is eclipsed by the true light, to whom he bears witness. His testimony is given in a nutshell in 1:15, but will be spelled out more fully in the next section of the narrative. John's purpose and his message are consistent with that of the Prologue as a whole, namely, to point to Jesus Christ as the Son of God. This is the end to which the whole story strains, from its opening words to its original close (20:31).

John 1:19-34

Having introduced JBap as the first witness to Jesus through the Prologue, the FE now turns to the content of his testimony. While it is true that the presence of JBap is a common feature with the Synoptics, there is little overlap with the presentation here. The FG makes no reference to JBap's clothing, eating habits, lifestyle, or, more significantly, his call to repentance. We do hear that he practiced baptism, but the purpose of that baptism is not discussed. Over the course of these verses the content of his "testimony" may be summarized as follows:

> There is one who is coming after me who is greater than me, because he existed before me. He is Jesus, the Lamb of God, who is taking away the sin of the world, upon whom I saw the Spirit rest and remain. He is the Son of God and will baptize with the Spirit.

For the rest, JBap spends most of his time defining himself negatively. From the narrative point of view, his denials ("I am not" — 1:20, 21) are important because they function as a foil for Jesus' frequent later declaration, "I am." The narrative assumes that some people thought of JBap as the Messiah (hence the denial in v. 20). Whether we have any historical evidence of this is irrelevant to the narrator, who is concerned primarily with the establishment of an authoritative witness to Jesus as such.

In 1:19 we first hear of "the Jews" as a group. This is a peculiar, but frequently employed, epithet applied by the FE. There is much discussion of the identity of this group, but most often it seems to denote the combination of the chief priests and Pharisees based in Jerusalem (Ashton 1993: 158). The ironic question of Pilate in 18:35 — "Am I a Jew?" — does indicate, however, that the term is more generally applied to those who obstinately refuse Jesus as the Christ. It is highly likely that the term "Jews" also relates to the time of writing of the Gospel. The common viewpoint is that it alludes to those responsible for the expulsion of Christians from the synagogue (9:22; 12:42; 16:2). I think that it may have another function toward the end of the first century, by which time the expulsion from the synagogue is some years distant. It is clear from the Johannine epistles that the community faced a crisis which caused a rift, with some leaving (1 John 2:19). It is possible that the expression "the Jews" relates more to this event. The parallel is then: those with whom we should naturally belong are no longer part of us and need to be seen as separate from us. We shall explore this crucial theme as it develops throughout the Gospel. The opponents would thus be other *Christians,* for whom "Jews" is but a cipher.

The language of 1:20 sounds like that of the courtroom. JBap is called as a witness and makes formal confession, initially concerning his own identity. He is not the Messiah: Jesus has already been announced to the reader as such in 1:17. Nor is he Elijah — sometimes thought of as the forerunner of the Messiah (Mal 4:5) and a popular figure in Jewish apocalyptic. Nor is he "the prophet" after the fashion of Deut 18:15-18, which figure was also the subject of expectation in the time of Jesus (compare 1QS 9:11). Instead JBap declares himself to be an agent after the prophecy of Isa 40:3 (here in agreement with the Synoptics). From the angle of legal testimony, Barrett is right to suggest that the quotation of "scripture" here lends authoritative status to the confession within the Jewish setting (Barrett 1978: 174).

The reference to "Pharisees" (1:24) links back to 1:19 — the "Jews" are here given an identity. Since the Pharisaic party came to real prominence only after AD 70, it is likely that this reflects such later interest, while the reference to "priests and Levites" (1:19) reflects the time of Jesus. They raise the question of baptism (1:25), a question which JBap hardly answers. The comment is only on the form of his baptism (in water), which prepares for the later statement of Jesus' baptism (in Spirit). Instead of discussing the reason for baptizing, JBap points once again to his role, now established firmly in the reader's mind, as the one who comes as a witness to his greater successor (1:26-27).

The geographical reference (1:28) to JBap's work taking place at Bethany, beyond the Jordan, has narrative significance for its subsequent appearance in 11:1 (cf. 10:40) and is dealt with there.

The scene shifts to the next day (1:29), but the texts are intimately connected by the common themes of baptism and JBap as witness. There is no description of the baptism of Jesus in the FG, but 1:32-33 may well be meant to evoke traditions concerning it. Suddenly JBap introduces a completely new description of Jesus as "Lamb of God who takes away the sin of the world!" Commentators are divided on the background against which this picture of the Lamb should be viewed. In terms of the narrative development of the Gospel, it is highly significant that the hour of Jesus' condemnation before Pilate (19:14) is precisely the hour of the slaughter of the Passover lambs in the temple. Although the Passover tradition neither views the killing of the lamb as *sacrificial* nor connects it with the wiping out of sin, these elements were connected in other parts of early Christian tradition. It is likely, then, that the primary reference in this description of Jesus is to his role as paschal Lamb, though it may also have overtones of the suffering servant motif in Isaiah (see Brown 1966: 58-63).

1:30 echoes JBap's confession during the Prologue (1:15). The theme is the preexistence of Jesus as a basis for the *authority* of his ministry. This use is echoed at a number of points throughout the Gospel, progressively pushing the time boundaries back (1:30 — before JBap; 8:58 — before Abraham) until we reach the point at which the opening poem had begun — before the foundation of the world (17:5). The point is not that the human being, Jesus, existed beforehand in heaven, but that "Christ fully embodies the creative and saving activity of God" (Dunn 1989: 212). Here we find another echo of Sophia, whose preexistence also functions as the basis of her authority and power to save. The call to listen to her (Prov 8:32-36; Sir 24:3-7) comes directly upon the recall of her part in the creative process (Prov 8:22-31; Sir 24:8-22). The recital of her salvific deeds (Wisdom 10–11) comes hard on her celebration as the maker of all things (Wis 9:1-2). It is because of this origin with God that Jesus Sophia can speak with greater authority than JBap, or anyone else (Scott 1992: 131-34).

In contrast to Jesus, JBap does not know everything (1:31, 33), and sees his water baptism as a preparation only for the full revelation of God to Israel (used in a positive light, unlike most references to "Jews"). Jesus is identified as the one upon whom the Spirit rests *permanently* (v. 32). This is qualitatively different from the intermittent prophetic insight of JBap and introduces us to another key Johannine verb: "to abide," or "remain" *(menein)*. The term is used to express the mutual indwelling of God as Father and Jesus as Son (14:10), of Jesus and the disciples (14:23; 15:4), or of the Spirit in the believer (14:17). The discussion of the development of this theme will be found at its focal point, 15:1-11. For the moment, we note that Jesus is once again seen as greater than JBap on account of the permanence of his union with God in the Spirit and his ability to pass on ("baptize in" — 1:33) that gift.

JBap finishes by reiterating his role in line with the Prologue as witness, here confessing Jesus as Son of God.

John 1:35-51

The beginnings of a disciple band in the FG come about less through a "call," the main Synoptic motif, than by the pattern of witness and "quest" (Painter 1991: 129-54). Not surprisingly, the first witness to Jesus is JBap (1:35), whose testimony to two of his own followers (v. 36) is a repetition of his previous words (v. 29). Whatever the background of this terminology, the ongoing narrative reveals that it is understood by the hearers as a *messianic* claim (v. 41).

The word of witness is sufficient to cause the two to follow (1:37), literally and metaphorically (Lindars 1972: 113). Jesus turns to challenge them (1:38), his question introducing another significant Johannine theme: seeking. As the FG drama unfolds, this motif appears at crucial points (cf. 4:27; 7:34; 8:21; 13:33; 18:4; 20:15). It is another point of contact with wisdom tradition, in which seeking Sophia is the true goal of the wise (Prov 8:17), while those who reject her cannot find her when seeking her in times of trouble (Prov 1:28).

The embryonic disciples, on the journey toward faith, can address Jesus only as Teacher (Rabbi) at this point. That the FE must translate for the ideal reader is a sign that the audience is not assumed to be Jewish. The disciples ask where Jesus is "staying" *(menein)*, and this word appears twice more in the following verse (1:39). We have already noted (cf. v. 32) the significance of this word for the FE. While on the surface it is merely a descriptive part of the story, the context also allows for an understanding of the permanence of the relationship which is part of the disciples' quest.

Jesus invites the disciples to "Come and see," a phrase which is characteristic of the discipleship picture in the FG. The whole portrayal stands again under the influence of Sophia tradition (cf. Brown 1966: 79), in particular the image of her making her daily round to gather in those who seek her (Wis 6:12-16).

We now discover the identity of one of the disciples, Andrew (1:40), the other remaining unnamed. Though some have speculated that the "other" is John, after whom the Gospel is named, there is no evidence whatsoever in the text to support this claim. Andrew and Peter were the first to be called in the Synoptics, and the narrator seems to presuppose knowledge of this by identifying *Andrew* in relation to Peter, who is only later called as a result of Andrew's witness (1:41).

After he has "'seen" Jesus, Andrew's faith is moved on to a new stage and he can now hail Jesus as Messiah. He establishes a pattern for Johannine discipleship by bringing Peter (1:42) to an encounter with Jesus through his witness. The change of name from Simon to Peter (Cephas) is known also from the Synoptics, though the circumstances surrounding it are different in each Gospel. Given the following story of Nathanael's encounter with Jesus and the fact that Simon's naming follows Jesus' "looking intently" *(emblepsas)* at him, the name would appear to be a reflection of his perceived character. Once again the reader needs a translation from Aramaic into Greek.

The Greek text opening the next quest narrative (1:43) is smoothed out by the NRSV. It is not at all clear who the subject is, the more likely solution being Peter, the immediately named antecedent. This would make some sense since Peter would then be continuing the sequence of going and seeking out another to bring to Jesus. In any case, Philip, clearly an acquaintance of the brothers (v. 44), receives Jesus' call to follow. Mark indicates Peter and Andrew's hometown as Capernaum (Mark 1:29), but the FG narrative is more concerned with the sequence of seeking and finding here.

Philip continues the succession of discipleship illustrations (1:45) by seeking out his friend Nathanael (the name means "God has given"). Philip's witness is based on an understanding of the Torah and prophets as containing messianic pointers and is more subtle than Andrew's direct confession. His identification of Jesus as the son of "Joseph" indicates that his "faith" is not yet complete, since he does not see the irony of declaring Jesus' origins.

Nathanael's response (1:46) continues the irony as he concentrates on Jesus' supposed place of origin. His reply, as a "true Israelite," may reflect an attitude of aloofness toward a perceived inferiority in a Galilean background. Philip repeats the call to discipleship, "Come and see." This leads properly to an encounter between Nathanael and Jesus (1:47) in which Jesus' supernatural insight, hinted at in the naming of Peter, becomes explicit. Although he has expressed only skepticism to this point, Nathanael is hailed as an exemplary representative of Israel. To be without "deceit" implies that his attitude, though questioning, is open to hear and to see. This is an important example for the reader, who will encounter others who apparently "believe" but whose witness is deceitful. Given the connection with Jacob in 1:51, there may also be an echo of a play on the parallel Israel = Jacob = "deceiver," Nathanael being identified as one without such deceit.

Nathanael is astonished at Jesus' remarkable insight (1:48), seeking its origin. Jesus responds with a precise picture of Nathanael's previous location. The "fig tree" may represent the place where the teacher of the Torah would sit with pupils, and would fit the picture of Nathanael as the devout Jew (cf. Brown 1966: 86-88). If so, then he recognizes the true Teacher (Rabbi — 1:49) in his confession. His response is the proper culmination of the discipleship sequence which the FE wants to illustrate. A disciple seeks and brings another potential one to an encounter with Jesus: this "seeing" leads to deepening faith in his presence, exemplified by an appropriate confession.

Nathanael's confession reveals that he, like Andrew (1:41), already sees in Jesus the presence of the Messiah. "Son of God" is the confession toward which the FG is driving (20:31), but "King of Israel" is at best ironic and a title which elsewhere Jesus avoids (6:15). His almost mocking response (1:50) indicates surprise that such a small thing should have evoked this confession, and it prepares the reader for both the immediate Son of Man saying and, more generally, for the signs which follow.

The section closes with a remarkable saying (1:51) which is a narrative echo of the vision of Jacob's ladder (Gen 28:12). Brown lists several rabbinic interpretations of the Jacob story (Brown 1966: 88-91), but the theological implication is straightforward. Just as Jacob encountered God in the place where the ladder reached the ground, so the one who is greater than Jacob (John 4:12) *is* the very place/person in whom the one with eyes to see encounters both God's revelation and presence.

John 2:1-11

The public history of Jesus begins and ends (cf. 19:25-27) with a story involving his mother (Scott 1992: 175-84). In narrative terms, her appearances form an *inclusio* in which the ministry of Jesus occurs. On either side of this *inclusio* we have introductory material (the poetic prologue; the gathering of disciples) and concluding material (burial; postresurrection appearances). This positioning makes the wine miracle at Cana a crucial story for understanding the rest of the ministry which follows.

Two further factors heighten the significance of the story. First, it is reported by the FE that this event is the first "sign" which Jesus performs. Such signs play an important role in the public ministry of Jesus, not least as a pointer to who he is. For John the signs appear somewhat ambiguous in themselves. Belief on the basis of such events may be accepted on some occasions (2:11; 4:53), while on others it is not to be trusted (2:23-25). The validity of belief based on signs is left open almost to the end of the Gospel, when Jesus declares to Thomas, "Blessed are those who have not seen and yet have come to believe" (20:29). The greater faith is that which does not *depend* on signs — an important point for the reader who can no longer physically see Jesus.

Second, the opening words point to a special status: "on the third day." Given that this was an established code for "the day of resurrection" among Christians in the late first century (1 Cor 15:3-4 has it already in a *pre-*

Pauline tradition), its intertextual echoes alert the reader to such a connection. The precise symbolism of this link is difficult to determine. Perhaps it indicates that, from the beginning, the Risen One is present in transforming power, even though his "hour" has not yet come. What follows would thus be a foretaste of what is still to come, a possibility increased by the mention of three days in the following incident as something upon which theological reflection took place only *after* the resurrection itself (2:19-22).

The opening verse seems to make Jesus' mother the principal character (2:1), since we hear only second that Jesus and the disciples were *also* there (v. 2). The identity of these disciples is not clear, but the proximity to the call stories allows the reader to assume that it is the group mentioned there. The text also offers us no indication as to the identity of the bride and groom and, although Jesus' mother later takes authority over the servants, there is no hint that it takes place in her home. Such wedding celebrations often lasted several days, so the embarrassing possibility of running out of wine was always there.

The reaction of Jesus' mother to this hiatus is interesting: she comes not with a request but a statement — "They have no wine" (2:3). The third person here indicates to the reader that it is not her responsibility to supply more. It appears, rather, that she is the one who knows where to go when the wine runs out. This echoes the disciple of Sophia, who knows her as the giver of bread and wine (Prov 9:5; Sir 24:19, 21). It would appear that Jesus' mother recognizes what the Prologue has revealed, that in her son all the fullness of Sophia is present.

Jesus' initial response may not be rude — "woman" is his most common address even to intimate female friends in the Gospel (4:21; 8:10; 19:26; 20:13) — but it is not what one expects from a son to his mother (2:4). The reply creates a distance between them, which is consistent with the Synoptic portrayals of Jesus' relations with his family (Mark 3:33-35 and pars.). Notoriously hard to put into English, it should probably read: "What concern is that to you and to me?" (Witherington 1995: 76). In what follows, Jesus' mother acts not out of family devotion, but rather as a disciple in her own right.

2:4 is the first mention of Jesus' "hour." As the narrative unfolds, the reader becomes aware that this "hour" will come to fulfillment only in the events of the cross and resurrection, which pave the way for the coming of the Spirit. As a reply to the statement about wine it seems a little enigmatic, but it is an important pointer to the interpretation of the coming "sign." The one who can supply wine will do so in a new and abundant way when the "hour" finally does arrive. For the moment, the "sign" will give a foretaste.

Despite the formality of Jesus' reply, his mother is not put off. Far from shrinking into the background, she takes control and demonstrates her belief that Jesus can supply the need by ordering the servants to "Do whatever he tells you" (2:5). In terms of Johannine discipleship, this looks like an instance of faith *before* the sign and thus marks Jesus' mother's move from familial to disciple relationship. This theme will be picked up again in her reappearance at the foot of the cross.

The dialogue is interrupted by some information from the narrator: six, apparently empty, stone water jars, used for purification rites, are in the house (2:6). In the context of a concise narrative like the FG, such details catch the reader's attention. These are no ordinary jars, but ones set aside for a specific task. It is their contents which will be transformed from the ordinary to the extraordinary, but this in turn raises a question about their symbolism for the reader. The Prologue sets up the contrast between Jesus and Torah (1:17), and this seems to be the focus of the transformation here. The old empty symbols of ritual are changed into abundant (120 gallons!) sources of celebration. Such generous provision is typical of Sophia (Sir 1:16; 24:19-21; Wis 7:8-14), as it is of the one who embodies her. It is also a prophetic symbol for the eschatological hope of salvation (Jer 31:5; Amos 9:13-14; Joel 3:18), which is becoming a reality in Jesus Christ.

The miracle is not described, but merely alluded to in 2:7-8. The servants, having been prepared for the task by Jesus' mother, obey the commands set before them. The chief steward, in typically ironic Johannine style, does not realize the full significance of his discovery of highest quality wine, even though the servants do (2:9). In the reporting of this incident we see a dramatic technique of the FE, which will surface at many crucial moments in the Gospel — a character declares the truth, though without any apparent understanding of its significance (e.g., 4:12; 9:40; 11:50; 19:19).

Like all good proverbial sayings, the remark of 2:10 functions on more than one level. It may be a good description of human nature — don't waste good things on those who are not in a condition to appreciate them. It may also, however, reflect the theme begun through the specific mention of purification jars — that the eschatological gift of God, realized in the coming of Jesus Sophia into the world, is far better than anything that has gone before, even if people are not all capable of recognizing it.

As we noted above, food and drink are known as gifts of Sophia. As such they are symbolic of the message which Sophia wants her followers to consume. The food, as the message, is better than anything else on offer. So, too, with the provision which Jesus makes and the message it conveys, which the FE reports as evoking faith from his disciples (2:11). It also reveals the "glory," announced in 1:14, even though the "hour of glorification" has not yet arrived. This adds to the feeling of this whole account as anticipatory, a foreshadowing of the situation to come after the "third day," in the new abundant age of the Spirit-filled community of disciples.

John 2:12-25

The setting now moves from Cana to Jerusalem via Capernaum, an unlikely route geographically (2:12). This is a pointer to the theological narrative which drives the FE throughout. The combination of the deliberate detour with the brevity of the stop serves to underline the fact that transitory familial ties must be left behind as Jesus moves toward the primary sphere of action, Jerusalem, and in particular the temple. For the informed reader this is borne out by the later reference to Ps 69:9, which follows reference to separation from "brothers" (Ps 69:8). As we shall see in this context, it probably also informs the emergent breach between the Johannine Jesus and "the Jews."

Jesus' attack on the temple is recorded in all four Gospels, but only in John at the beginning of his ministry. The discussion of the historical primacy of John or the Synoptics is inconclusive, both having their own dramatic reasons for giving the story its relative position (Schnackenburg 1968: 353-57). The importance for the FE as always is the christological symbolism of the event. This story connects with the previous Cana account through the common theme of the inadequacy of institutional religion (purification jars, 2:6) and its replacement in the person of Jesus.

The prominence given to this scene by placing it at this point in Jesus' ministry is consistent with the persistent picture of the Johannine Jesus appearing in the temple involved in a kind of running battle with "the Jews" over a variety of theological issues (5:14-47; 7:14–8:59; 10:22-39). The "temple" theme is already at this point a continuation from the announcement of the "tabernacling of the Logos/Sophia" (1:14).

This section is informative in terms of the implied reader of the Gospel. First, the reference to the "Passover of the Jews" (2:13; cf. 6:4; 11:55) marks the reader out as a "non-Jew" who needs such explanation. Second, the unqualified allusion to Jesus' resurrection (2:22) by way of contrast indicates a reader who is already familiar with the Gospel story, though perhaps not in its Johannine version (Moloney 1992: 20-21). However little we may know of the historical setting of the FG, it assumes a reader with insight, needing encouragement to continue in faith (see the comment on 20:30-31).

Given this factor, the purpose of placing the attack on the temple at the start of Jesus' ministry is more easily understood. From the outset the reader must recognize that Jesus' mission will bring him into conflict with "his own" and issue in his death. Although making the presentation in a much more subtle fashion, the FG is one with the Synoptics at this point in seeing the death of Jesus as consequent upon his action in the temple precincts.

John's account introduces large animals (oxen and sheep, 2:14) to the scene in addition to the pigeons of the Synoptic versions, thus heightening the drama of expulsion. The deliberate nature of the attack is also underlined through the detail of Jesus *making* the whip with which to carry it out. His motivation is alluded to as having roots in the prophetic tradition (Zech 14:21), but the FE sees no need to justify Jesus' action further.

The interpretation of the account hinges on reading "will consume" (*kataphagetai* — 2:17) as an intentional change to the future tense (Ps 68:9 [LXX] — *katephagen,* "has consumed"). Far from implying that it is *Jesus'* zeal for his Father's house which is all-consuming, it is instead the zeal of his *opponents* which will lead to the "consumption" of his body and so to the necessity of its "reconstitution/resurrection." This is confirmed by the provocative challenge to "destroy" the temple (2:19), a typical piece of Johannine irony, which is misunderstood by his opponents as a reference to the buildings. The reader avoids such confusion through the reminder of the second level meaning: the temple is in fact Jesus' body (v. 21), which will be destroyed and restored.

The use of the word "sign" is significant in this passage. Initially the shocked "Jews" demand one from Jesus as proof of the basis of his authority (2:18). Jesus responds by offering a hint of the greatest of the Gospel "signs" — his death and resurrection (v. 19). In the end, however, their marked lack of understanding and inability to discern the proper place of the "signs" lead to Jesus' refusal to entrust himself to them (vv. 23-24). The reference to the ambivalent attitude of the "Jews" functions as a link between the attack on the temple and the following series of dialogues (Nicodemus, 3:1-21; disciples of JBap, 3:22-30), which treat the theme of faith/understanding within Israel.

The role of the "Jews" in the FG is complex. Jesus himself is a Jew and positively accepts this definition (4:9, 20, 22), but for the most part he speaks as though he were not one. The shameful anti-Semitic history of interpretation should not cloud our understanding of a crucial motif in the narrative development of the Gospel. For the ideal reader the language delineates group boundaries in the context of an ever intensifying crisis. Within the larger group of "Jews" stands a group, represented by Jesus and some ideal friends, who are increasingly marginalized by the majority power-group. There is nothing wrong in being a "Jew"; simply, the reader must be aware that not all those who share that identity are to be trusted. Setting this at the end of the first century AD, we hear the echoes of an inter-*Christian* struggle, whose traces are more clearly evidenced in the epistles of the same community. In the impending fate of Jesus the seriousness of the internal conflict already presses itself upon the reader.

The division caused by the teaching of Jesus mirrors the response to Sophia in the wisdom tradition. Like her (Prov 1:20-33), Jesus knows the human condition (2:24-25) because of his origins, a central theme of the dialogue which follows.

John 3:1-21

Having heard that Jesus knows the motives of the kind of person (*anthrōpos* — 2:25) who has placed faith in him on the basis of "signs," the reader is immediately introduced to such a person (*anthrōpos* — 3:1), Nicodemus. The dialogue becomes an illustration of the discussion between those who apparently share the same identity (both are Jewish teachers/leaders) but do not read the "signs" in the same way.

The discussion of historicity in this passage is somewhat pointless given the clearly representative nature of the narrative. Both Nicodemus and Jesus address each other, as Queen Victoria once said of Gladstone, "like a public meeting"! Although the plural is by no means consistently used throughout, the dialogue is peppered with such references (Nicodemus: 3:2 — "*We* know you are a teacher"; Jesus: 3:7 — "*You* [plural] must be born from above"), as though two parties are discussing rather than two individuals. The reader is drawn into the dialogue to hear the witness of Jesus, in contrast to the supposed "witness" of Nicodemus, which type has just been disclaimed (2:25 — "he needed no one to bear witness").

The dialogue contains a number of ironies and wordplays. The first of these is the designation of Nicodemus as "ruler" (3:1). Significantly the FG uses the common Synoptic phrase "kingdom of God" only twice — both times in this story (vv. 3, 5). The so-called "ruler" does not understand the essence of the "rule" of God and has to have it explained to him. The FG avoids the language of the kingdom, replacing it with a concept of community based on the model of "friends who abide to the end" and exemplified primarily through the paradigmatic discipleship of women and the unnamed beloved disciple (Scott 1994: 180-88). This theme will be woven through the Gospel, coming to a head in the ironic crowning of Jesus as "King of the Jews" (19:19-22).

Nicodemus announces that his "party" see Jesus as a Rabbi/Teacher (3:2). The irony of this also becomes apparent later when Jesus expresses astonishment at the ignorance of this "teacher" (v. 10). The knowledgeable witness of this pillar of the establishment is seen to be utterly lacking in understanding. He also belongs in the darkness rather than the light since he comes to Jesus "by night," a motif sufficiently important to be mentioned again in 19:39. Night and day, a theme first played in the Prologue (1:5), is a common symbolic element in the unfolding drama of the FG (9:4; 11:10), reaching a crisis point in Judas's act of betrayal (13:30). The discourse returns to the contrast at the end (3:19-21), where the encounter with the light exposes people who prefer darkness. The implicit critique of the Nicodemus "party" is scarcely veiled.

The dialogue continues with a wordplay, difficult to see without the Greek text. *Anōthen* (3:3) can mean either "from above" or "again" and functions as a pivot of misunderstanding between the teachers. Jesus' second answer ("water and Spirit" — 3:5) indicates that in his first answer *anōthen* meant "from above." That Nicodemus fails to perceive this is the first indictment of his qualifications as a teacher. In taking Jesus' statement on a literal level (3:4 — *anōthen* means "again") he stands alongside a number of Jesus' interlocutors in the FG (4:8-15, 31-34; 11:11-14). While others, notably the Samaritan woman (4:11, 15, 19, 25, 29), seem to recover from a bad start, for Nicodemus matters get worse.

To be born "from above," or "of the Spirit," in this context means to enter a full and public discipleship of Jesus, to become a "child of God," as the Prologue puts it (1:12). To enter this, Nicodemus must step out of the night and into the light. Rensberger (1988: 52-63) sees the unity of ch. 3 as formed around the theme of baptism/rebirth in water/Spirit and its implications for active engagement and proper christological confession.

That rebirth is not merely an individual but a community need is shown by the use of the plural in the second occurrence (3:7). The community born of the Spirit ("*we* speak of what *we* know," 3:11) calls upon the Nicodemus "party" to join publicly with the Johannine understanding of the Christ. This again reflects the struggle of the Johannine group with others who do not share their view of Jesus as the one who incarnates the wisdom of God, Sophia — the one who has "come down from above."

There follows another wordplay, this time between "wind" and "Spirit" (3:8 — both *pneuma* in Greek). Picking up on the creation imagery of the Prologue and its insistence that God is the author of new birth (1:13), Jesus declares that, like the "wind" which is unseen and beyond human control, the Spirit brings new life beyond rational explanation. The metaphor seems to have its focus in the notion that the effects of the wind/Spirit are clear in those touched by it, most notably in their ability to "understand/believe" (another Johannine double entendre).

It is precisely here that the failure of the Nicodemus "party" becomes sharpest and is treated with irony by the Johannine Jesus (3:10). For all their claim to believe because of the "signs," there is no sign of understanding (v. 11) what has been heard (the words) or seen (the Word made flesh).

Up to 3:10 the narrative structure follows a fairly clear question and answer format. At v. 11 Nicodemus seems to melt into the shadowy background narrative world from which he emerged! The rest of the section is entirely devoted to a monologue which the Johannine Jesus addresses in the plural. A similar structure shapes the second half of the chapter (3:22-30, 31-36), where JBap (or Jesus?) addresses a christological statement to a general audience. Both of these soliloquies offer further clarification of the origin and purpose of the mission of the Son of God. In addition to the baptism/Spirit links, the narrative unity of the chapter depends on this common christological theme.

The Nicodemus "party," who believe (*pisteuō* — 2:23) on the basis of signs, do not understand (*pisteuō* — 3:12) "earthly" illustrations (birth; water; wind), and thus will be unable to grasp the "heavenly" things which follow (vv. 13-21). The reader is now included in the audience as one with potential for such understanding. The key lies in knowledge of the origins of Jesus, already outlined in the Prologue, with the introduction of Jesus as Sophia incarnate. The "earthly"–"heavenly" combination is found notably in Wis 9:16-18, where the Greek for "what is on earth" (*ta epi gēs* — Wis 9:16) almost certainly underlies the peculiar Johannine expression "earthly things" (*ta epigeia* — John 3:12). This passage introduces the picture of Sophia as the Savior of Israel in Wisdom 10–11 by indicating that knowledge of the heavens, and thus of salvation, is given only through the descent of Sophia/Holy Spirit (in parallel — Wis 9:17). It is against this background that the ideal reader of the FG recognizes again that this Jesus who speaks is none other than her full incarnation.

The Son of Man saying (3:13) continues this theme by

picking up a contrast begun with Moses in 1:17. The lawgiver (cf. 1:45) may have ascended the mountain and returned with the law, but he did not ascend into heaven. The one who descends, Jesus Sophia, speaks of what he has seen and heard already in heaven. His superiority to Moses the lawgiver is apparent, and contrasts with the view of Sirach and *Baruch* that Sophia is confined in the Torah (Scott 1992: 53-55). While the specific example of Moses is probably in view here, the polemic against "ascent" also functions as a more general guard against such ideas prevalent at the time (cf. Dunn 1983: 326-30).

The comparison with Moses continues with reference to the story of the serpent in the wilderness (3:14; cf. Num 21:8-9). Again the theme is the temporary, passing nature of Moses' action compared with the "eternal" gift of Jesus (cf. Sophia, Wis 8:13). While the serpent granted temporary extension of life when placed in a position to be seen by those bitten by the desert snakes, the "lifting up" (i.e., the crucifixion; 3:14-15; cf. 8:28; 12:32-34) of the Son of Man offers an unending source of life to all who look upon him.

The speech continues with clarification of the origin and nature of the Son's mission (3:16-17). Beloved of evangelical preachers, these verses contain much that goes to the heart of Johannine theology. It is the *agapē* of God which leads to the appearance of the Son "from above." He comes as the *gift* of God, leading to eternal life. He is *sent* by God into the world to bring life and salvation. Despite the angry exchanges and harsh language which characterize so much of Jesus' ministry in the FG, the reader is left in no doubt about the primary intention of God's goodness in approaching humanity.

Although the Son's purpose is not to judge, nevertheless judgment does take place according to the attitudes of those who encounter him (3:18). This whole sequence is illuminated by the Sophia tradition, where she is seen as the *gift* of God (Wis 8:21; 9:17), *sent* into the world from the heavens (Wis 9:10) to bring eternal life (Wis 8:13) and salvation (Wis 9:18). In her presence judgment takes its own course (Prov 1:20-33) (Scott 1992: 134-40). The one who purports to be the "teacher of Israel" clearly does not know the traditions of Israel regarding "heavenly things" well enough to recognize their presence!

The concluding verses develop the theme of light, hinted at by Nicodemus's "night" appearance. The scathing judgment of evil intent (3:19) points ironically back to him and confirms that he is anything but a "positive" character in the drama. The appearance of the light causes a crisis (Gk. *krisis* = judgment), whereby what is hidden (a nighttime visit!) will be uncovered for what it is (3:20). This is typical of the way in which *krisis* will unfold as a (realized) eschatological theme in John. Although there are hints of a future, Son of Man, judgment in the FG (5:27-30), they are but a complement to the picture of judgment already taking critical shape in the *presence* of Jesus. The reader learns that, for the one who comes genuinely seeking the truth (3:21), there is no fear in approaching the light of the world. There is no such thing as secret discipleship of Jesus, but bold confession of his true nature as Sophia incarnate leads to life.

John 3:22-36

Like the preceding part of the chapter, the material concerning JBap begins with a statement and answer and leads into a christological soliloquy. As in 3:13-21, the speaker in 3:31-36 is not clearly identified in the text: is it JBap, Jesus, or simply the Narrator? In terms of the narrative development, it would seem sensible to see the speakers respectively as Jesus (3:13-21) and JBap (3:31-36). Since JBap's primary role in the text to this point has been as a witness, he is seen here to bring his witness to a conclusion and then "decrease" (i.e., disappear!). In parallel, the Johannine Jesus, who needs no other witness (2:25), bears witness to himself before the Baptist once again clarifies his own relationship to the one "from above."

The episode opens with some introductory, scene-setting remarks by the Narrator. Jesus and his disciples enter the "land of the Jews" (Judea, 3:22), even though Jerusalem, the scene of the action to this point, is also in Judea. This emphasizes for the reader the continuing theme of inner group delineation (reliable "Jews," Jesus and JBap, over against "unreliable" ones, Nicodemus). The idea that Jesus himself baptized is later clarified as being the work of his disciples (4:2).

The theme of John as the baptizer (1:24-28) is renewed (3:23), though this time he is said to be at Aenon, near Salim. The precise location is unsure, the essential point for the reader being that JBap's and Jesus' disciples were engaged in separate baptismal missions. As with the earlier indication that the reader has prior knowledge of the story of Jesus (2:22), the FE here assumes knowledge of the story of JBap (3:24) by indicating that he was "not yet" in prison.

The scene proper begins, in parallel to 1:19, with a reminder that the true witness/disciple faces the same kind of questioning from the "Jews" (3:25 — this time in the singular, though the textual evidence is not conclusive). The question of this "Jew" concerns purification. This has only a tenuous link to the theme of John's baptism, which is nowhere in the FG referred to as a purificatory rite. There is an echo of the Cana incident, where the water in purification jars is replaced by new wine, in an illustration of the new age emerging in Jesus. It is that theme which comes up once again here in the question of the relationship between Jesus and JBap (v. 26). The reader is probably meant to hear "they came" (v. 26) as inclusive of the "Jew," with whom the initial discussion takes place.

They address JBap as "teacher" (Rabbi), echoing the earlier ironic dialogue with Nicodemus. Here, by way of contrast to the preceding story, is a teacher of Israel who understands Jesus' origins and purpose in coming "from above" (3:27), bears witness to him, and gives way to his mission. The proper response for disciples who come questioning is to do likewise. JBap emphasizes this (v. 28) by a reiteration of his original denial of messianic status (1:20) and confirmation of his temporary role ("sent before him" — cf. 1:15).

It is important not to push JBap's parabolic saying (3:29) beyond its credible limits. Some have speculated that the "bride" referred to is the Johannine community (e.g., Howard-Brook 1994: 97-98), but the point of the parable is the comparison between JBap and Jesus as "best man" and "bridegroom." It evokes the tradition (from a thoroughly male perspective!) of the friend of the bridegroom who stands guard outside the nuptial bedroom, awaiting the cry of the bridegroom successful in intercourse with his new bride (Schnackenburg 1968: 416-17). The image is thus one of complete joy, appropriate to the role and status of JBap as witness.

This is confirmed by the stepping back of JBap from his role (3:30). The swan song speech which follows in vv. 31-36 is the ultimate indicator to those who might have mistaken his role that even the primary witness must step out of the limelight to let Jesus take the center stage as his own best witness.

The teacher/witness now illustrates the role of exemplary believer/understander by recalling the main themes of Jesus' own speech (3:13-21). JBap knows Jesus' origin is "from above" (v. 31), unlike his own origins and words, which are from below ("the earth"). The statement that "no one" accepts Jesus' testimony (v. 32) is surely dramatic hyperbole, since JBap himself clearly does! It parallels Jesus' address to the Nicodemus "party" (v. 11 — plural) that none of them believes. What is at stake, however, is not merely believing what Jesus says, but the very truth of God (v. 33), whose words he speaks. The relationship between God and the Son, outlined in terms of Sophia tradition in vv. 16-18, is recalled by the primary witness here in a quasi-judicial statement (v. 34). To reject the Son is to reject God, in the same way that rejection of Sophia indicates rejection of God. It is unclear whether it is God or "the one sent" (Jesus) who gives the Spirit; both ideas are present in the FG. The statement here emphasizes the unity of God and Jesus and the abundance of their provision.

As further "proof" JBap brings forward his earlier witness (1:32-34) concerning the Spirit's relationship with Jesus. God has fully empowered the Son to act, a recurring theme of the FG (3:35 — cf. 5:22, 26; 6:37; 12:49; 17:6-19). The one who has been sent comes with authority to do God's mission.

In the same way that Jesus' earlier soliloquy ended by announcing the radical judgment which comes in his presence (3:20-21), so too JBap's final words stress the decisive nature of belief (v. 36). The present participles in Greek (lit. "the one believing"; "the one disobeying") indicate that what is in mind is a continuing way of living. This Gospel is concerned with patterns of discipleship, as the succeeding story will indicate. As the first witness falls silent (although mentioned in 5:33-36, JBap does not speak for himself again), others begin to come forward.

John 4:1-42

Since the JE has dealt with the question of faith among the people of Judea (the "Jews") and with their contrasting responses of nonunderstanding (Nicodemus) and exemplary understanding (JBap), the scene now shifts to a similar pattern outside the immediate confines of Judaism (Moloney 1980: 185-213; Scott 1992: 184-98). The story of the encounter between the Samaritan woman and Jesus is one of three great stylized dramatic interludes in the FG (cf. 9:1-41; 11:1-44), each revealing a high degree of literary skill in storytelling. The structure consists of three scenes: (i) Jesus dialogues with the woman, leading to a revelation of his identity (4:7-26); (ii) Jesus dialogues with the disciples (vv. 31-38), while the woman is off stage acting as a witness (vv. 27-30); (iii) the Samaritans encounter Jesus and confess him as Savior of the World (vv. 39-42).

The opening verses (4:1-3) make the move from Judea to Samaria consequent upon the issue raised in 3:26 — the numbers coming to Jesus. To that number will now be added outsiders, Samaritans. The scene is set around a well traditionally associated with Jacob (4:5-6), a significant figure in Samaritan theology. The well is evocative of stories of Jewish patriarchs in which potential matrimonial encounters took place (Isaac, Genesis 24; Jacob, Genesis 29; Moses, Exodus 2). There is an intertextual echo of Gen 29:7 in the occurrence of the meeting around noon (4:6 — "the sixth hour"). The reader is prepared now for the direction of this story. "Just as the Patriarch Jacob met and found a relationship with a woman at a well, so too Jesus meets with a woman at a well (Jacob's) and forms what will eventually be a 'fruitful' (4:39-42) relationship with her" (Scott 1992: 185).

The woman comes to draw water (4:7) at a strange time, the height of the day's sun when no one else is around. Since water drawing was often a communal rather than an individual activity, the reader may later understand her action in the light of her reputation (vv. 17-18), a matter which she uses as an indicator to the rest of the city dwellers in due course (v. 29). The disciples are gone, so the stage is clear for a dialogue between Jesus and the woman.

The history of bad blood between Jews and Samaritans is raised by the woman (4:9). For a Jew to share a Samaritan's drinking vessel would be bad enough in terms of cleanliness regulations, but to do so with a woman was outrageous. Later tradition shows that Jews considered Samaritan women permanently unclean ("menstruants from the cradle"; *m. Nid.* 4.1). She recognizes the irregular nature of Jesus' approach to her.

To a Jew, the "gift of God" (4:10) was supremely the Torah, alongside which Jesus places himself in offering "living water." The narrative depends for its development on the assumption that the woman might have guessed already who Jesus is. She reveals her lack of perception/faith in what follows (4:11), by echoing Nicodemus's literal interpretation of Jesus' words. The woman is not, however, without any understanding and sees the implication of Jesus' statement at least as a claim to greater authority than the cherished patriarch Jacob (v. 12). This is another case of Johannine irony, as she declares the truth about Jesus without realizing what she has done.

Jesus now reveals the nature of the gift he offers (4:13-14). The "living water" he promises is a "spring" (*pēgē*, v. 14), which replaces the need for the "well" (*pēgē*, v. 6).

The image of "living water" is thoroughly rooted in the Jewish scriptures (Jer 2:13; 17:13) and is most especially a gift of Sophia (Sir 15:3; 24:21, 30-31; Bar 3:12). The narrator later informs the reader that it symbolizes the gift of the Spirit (7:38-39). As with Nicodemus, the dialogue holds the potential for the concomitant gift of "eternal life." The woman, however, still only manages to comprehend on the material rather than the spiritual level (4:15).

The dialogue now takes a completely new turn, offering the woman a further opportunity to see who Jesus is (4:16-18). The subject of her marital history might appear a strange digression at this point were it not for the expectation already raised in the mind of the reader by the situation of a man and a woman at a well. Jesus is not going to make her an offer of marriage, but he will use her experience to push her toward understanding. The potential symbolism of the "five husbands" has been the subject of much speculation. It could relate to the gods of the Samaritans (2 Kgs 17:29-31) since the Hebrew word for husband (*ba'al*) is also a name for a god, but if this is the wordplay it is as lost in Greek as in English.

The recognition of Jesus as "a prophet" (4:19) is the beginning of a movement toward true understanding. The woman is theologically informed about the traditions of her people and engages Jesus, as a prophet, in discussion of "true worship" (v. 20). The Samaritan shrine on Mt. Gerizim was destroyed by Judea in 128 BC, a primary cause of the antagonism between Samaritans and Jews. It was the equivalent of the Jerusalem temple to the Jews, already "attacked" by Jesus (2:13-21).

Her statement (not a question!) is answered by a short discourse from Jesus (4:21-24). The focus on *place* of worship denies the real question, which is about the *relationship* which comes out of encounter with God, whether for Jew or non-Jew. The ideal reader is drawn into the discussion in a manner already seen previously in the FG. The encounter with God takes place in the present meeting with Jesus, who incarnates "truth" (1:17). This is the focus of the salvation which comes "from the Jews" but which includes "the world" (3:16; 4:42). Jesus is thoroughly and positively a Jew, not least as the living presence of Sophia, however negative the reaction of others in the FG.

The idea of God as "spirit," with its counterpart of worship in "spirit and truth," should not be read individualistically. It has radical social and political dimensions, seen in Jesus' mission here outside of Israel and in relationship to a woman. The new encounter with God, made possible in the presence of Jesus Sophia, leads to the breaking down of traditional stereotypes and boundaries. This is true salvation.

The woman shows further theological insight with her belief in the coming Messiah (4:25) as teacher (in the Samaritan outlook, the *Taḥeb;* cf. McDonald 1964: 362-71). This brings the dramatic revelation from Jesus: "I Am" (v. 26). This is a clear use of the divine name (the Greek is literally: "I am is speaking to you"). It is a frequent form of revelatory address in the mouth of the Johannine Jesus, most commonly attached to a predicate ("bread"; "light"; etc.).

At this point the woman completes her movement from lack of faith toward true understanding by abandoning the mundane task (4:28 — "left her water jar"; cf. Matt 4:20; Mark 1:18; Luke 5:11) and going about the task of calling others to an encounter with Jesus (4:29). The results of her witness are hinted at in v. 30, but become clearer in the final act of the drama (vv. 39-42). "Coming" toward Jesus is the first step to faith in the FG (6:35).

That this is a groundbreaking story is confirmed by the reaction of the disciples on their return (4:27). They are shocked to find him in conversation with a woman, revealing to the reader that issues of gender are very much on the agenda. The sidelining of any questioning of this issue is an indication to the reader that Jesus' acceptance of a woman as an equal dialogue partner is not a matter for question or dispute. The theme of women as true disciples of Jesus, often in a much better light than the traditional male ones, continues to emerge throughout the FG.

The return of the disciples marks the beginning of a new act in the drama (4:31). Johannine irony is seen at work again here. While the Samaritan woman is off doing the work of a disciple, the so-called "disciples" are receiving a discourse on the subject of mission. This is couched initially in terms of "food" supplied by Jesus (v. 32), setting up a play on the task the disciples have recently undertaken. Their misunderstanding parallels that of both Nicodemus and the woman in her first response, as their literal interpretation of Jesus' words demonstrates (v. 33). This lack of perception is characteristic of the disciple group's response to Jesus (11:11-14; 12:4-6; 13:6-11; 14:5-7; 18:10-11; 20:24-29), often in contrast to the action of women in the text.

The mission of Jesus harks back to the Prologue (1:13) through the catchword "will" (*thelēma* — 4:34). The "will of God" (cf. 5:30; 6:38-40; 7:17; 9:31) is that people should become part of the family of belief, and this task Jesus seeks to bring to completion in the company of those who understand his identity and origin ("sent" — cf. 3:16). The theme of "fulfillment" continues throughout the Johannine Jesus' mission, culminating in the climactic final word from the cross (19:30).

The interpretation of the parable in 4:35 depends on the dramatic staging of this scene for its sense. The Samaritans (offstage) are already "coming to him" (v. 30) and can be seen ("lift up your eyes") as the first fruits of the harvest by those "onstage." Instead of the normal period of waiting between planting and reaping, the disciples see the immediate effect of the Samaritan woman's missionary efforts.

The interdependence of sower and reaper is stressed in mutual celebration (4:36). Jesus has sown the seeds of eternal life in the life of the Samaritan woman, who has clearly understood him sufficiently to continue the task in others. Although her role later diminishes (v. 42), the joy is shared and her contribution is not denigrated. This has to be spelled out to the obtuse disciples (vv. 37-38), who as yet have failed to undertake the task. The "labor" in which she engages is phrased in the language of early Christian missionary endeavor (Fiorenza 1983: 327), marking the Samaritan out as a faithful disciple in the line of early witnesses.

The final scene finds the Samaritan "harvest" coming

from the city to see Jesus (4:39). We learn that they already believe because of her testimony (lit. "on account of the word") of the woman. Her witness concerns Jesus' insight into her life and is thus parallel to that of Nathanael (1:48-49). It is, however, not to be seen as inferior as an act of witness since it follows precisely the pattern outlined by JBap (3:30), as the basis of Samaritan belief shifts from the word of the woman to that of Jesus (4:42 — exactly the same phrase, "on account of the word"; cf. 17:20).

The confession of the Samaritans moves the developing understanding of Jesus on for the reader. The title "Savior of the World" is suggested neither by the self-revelation of Jesus (4:26) nor by the Samaritan woman's witness (vv. 29, 39). It relates back to 3:16-17, which we saw to be heavily influenced by Sophia tradition. This title is another pointer to Jesus' identity as the incarnation of all her qualities. "Just as the saving role of Sophia and God runs into one in the book of Wisdom, so too does that of Jesus Sophia and God in the Gospel of John" (Scott 1992: 197).

John 4:43-54

The linking verses (4:43-45) have caused much consternation to commentators. On the one hand, v. 43 links back logically to v. 3, seeing Jesus' movement here as a continuation of the journey begun there, with v. 45 pointing forward to the hopes raised of miraculous intervention. On the other hand, v. 44 seems to be in complete contradiction to v. 45, since the overwhelming witness of the FG is that Jesus' "own country" is Galilee (Jesus — 1:46; 7:42-52; 19:19; his family — 2:1; 7:3). This problem is usually resolved by seeing 4:44 as a redactional insertion tying the shallowness of the Galilean reaction (v. 48) to that of the "Jews" in 2:23. The welcome of the Galileans is thus superficial because it is based on a desire for the miraculous and not on true faith in Jesus. This may be the case, but since these verses function as a narrative link, their main effect is to emphasize the contrast between the response of the Samaritans and that previously evidenced among Jesus' own people (1:11).

The return to the wine-miracle site of Cana (4:46) brings out a literary tie with the opening of this section of the Gospel (2:1) and is designed to bring it to a close. The two framing "signs" point to the reality of Jesus as the giver of new life, the subject of much of the intervening dialogue, though the theme of "true faith" also pervades the entire narrative section.

The identity of the man as a "royal official" (from the court of Herod Antipas?) has led to comparison of the story with the Synoptic healings of a centurion's son (Matt 8:5-13; Luke 7:1-10). This in turn has often led to the assumption that the man is a Gentile (there are also many parallels with the Syrophoenician/Canaanite woman, Matt 15:21-28; Mark 7:24-30), but nothing in the text suggests this. The echo of 2:23 in 4:48 suggests rather a connection with the substandard belief of the "Jews."

The narrator presupposes that the official knows of Jesus' reputation as a healer from his work in Jerusalem (4:47). The seriousness of the child's condition is stressed, making the story literally one of life and death. The intensity of the man's desire for help is seen in his coming to Jesus rather than attempting to send for him. All of this makes the tone of Jesus' reply (v. 48) and his method of action throughout this short episode the more remarkable. Jesus exhibits frustration bordering on rudeness, with little hint of care. That is how the official, at least, interprets it, since he repeats the seriousness of the situation, emphasizing the imminence of death (v. 49). Despite the coolness of Jesus' response, the official shows his continuing respect for him by addressing him as "sir" (*kyrios* — not "Lord" here). The picture is of a man used to obedience to authority respectfully pressing for the command he desires.

When it arrives, the command is abrupt and quite dismissive (4:50). In line with his characterization to this point, the official accepts the direction and is said to "believe in the word" spoken to him. This significant phrase, used only recently with regard to the Samaritan woman's missionary efforts, indicates that the journey toward faith is very much in focus throughout the course of the story. He continues on the road home and is met by his own servants (v. 51) bringing news of the child's improvement in health.

The official asks when the child's recovery began (4:52). "The seventh hour" (one o'clock) need not be treated as symbolic. It is a narrative device to enable the verification of the miracle by the main characters. It thus becomes the basis for confirmation of the man's faith (v. 53). Echoing the earlier response of the Samaritans, not only the man himself but his whole household believe. The repetition of the phrase "your son shall *live*" serves only to underline the central Johannine theme of Jesus Sophia as the giver of life. It will be recalled more dramatically in the climactic story of the raising of Lazarus.

The story indicates the problems of the relationship between "signs" and faith. The official moves from "sign"-seeking (4:48) to belief in the "word" (v. 50). His final position of faith seems to come about when he puts the two things together (v. 53) and realizes their conjunction. However much priority is given to faith which has "not seen," the "sign" and the "word" of Jesus are closely interrelated in the FG.

The final verse stresses the sequence of "signs" and the relationship to the previous events at Cana. As has often been pointed out, the deliberate numbering frames this section of the FG as a journey from Cana to Cana (2:1–4:54). It is a journey on which the vagaries and ambiguities of faith are encountered, and the character of Jesus as the giver of life is revealed both within and outside the immediate confines of "his own people."

John 5:1-18

The scene shifts back again to Jerusalem (5:1), and we enter a new period of Jesus' ministry. Although a Jewish festival is mentioned, it is not specified which is in mind, nor that its attendance was the primary purpose of Jesus' return to the city. Instead the reader later discovers that the focus of the whole passage lies on the *sabbath* rather than on any particular feast.

The detailed description of the setting of the forthcoming miracle (5:2-3) is unusual for the FE, leading to the suggestion that the "five porticoes" are symbolic. Barrett (1978: 253) rejects symbolism on the basis of good archeological evidence for the existence of a pool exactly as described. Howard-Brook (1994: 121-22) has recently raised the possibility again, seeing a contrast between the porticoes as representative of the five books of the Torah and the utter failure to deal with the problems lying around. Given the propensity for polemic against the Torah in the FG, the suggestion is not without merit.

The story continues (5:4 is clearly a later gloss, missing from all the best manuscripts) with another odd detail, the paralyzed man's age (v. 5). This may simply be a detail of "authenticity," but given the symbolic nature of so much of the FE's writing, a connection with Deut 2:14, which measures a generation as thirty-eight years, seems plausible. The irony of the narrative is that one who has suffered a lifetime (5:6) of illness now finds wholeness in an instant — on a sabbath — when he could have waited just a little longer.

The ensuing conversation between Jesus and the unnamed man (5:6-8) shows affinity to Synoptic miracles, in particular Mark 2:1-12. Jesus' question ("Do you want to be healed?") sounds somewhat naive to a man who has suffered so long. It serves an important narrative function in allowing the man to demonstrate his complete lack of understanding/faith. Confronted with the possibility of healing in the presence of Jesus Sophia, he can only complain about the inadequacy of provision for his need at the poolside. As in previous cases of inadequate reaction, Jesus is unperturbed and commands a response.

As in the instance of the royal official's child, the word of Jesus is sufficient to effect the required cure (5:9). It becomes immediately clear, however, that the command has a double edge in provoking a confrontation with the authorities over "work" on the sabbath (v. 10). Since both Jesus and the man are evidently Jews, the reference to "the Jews" here must delineate an opponent group. The internecine conflict which will issue in the death of Jesus steps up a gear at this point of the FG, though this is made explicit only as the text unfolds (v. 16).

The dialogue between the "Jews" and the man (5:10-12) shows no interest in the preceding miracle, centering instead on sabbath observance. Unlike the Samaritan woman before him, the man has failed to recognize who Jesus is, even if he does recognize the authority with which Jesus speaks as sufficient to take the risk of "working" on the sabbath.

Strangely, the "Jews" tacitly accept the man's insistence that his decision to break the sabbath law is based on the authority of another. This leaves the narrator to explain the circumstances to the reader (5:13), if not to the "Jews"! The aside is a little confusing: Does Jesus intend to leave the man alone to face the hostility of the authorities? Jesus has himself felt the need to make a getaway (*exeneusen* — v. 13) following the healing. This is a technique adopted later when inappropriate responses by others seem imminent (6:15), but it is not the case here. The aside rather allows the FE to change the scene to the temple and heighten the sense of Jesus deliberately provoking the authorities.

Unlike previous encounters in the FG, this one has Jesus going and seeking out the man (5:14). The warning to the man concerning sin is doubly surprising here. First, there has been no connection of the sort made to this point in the story. Second, such a link is specifically ruled out in another somewhat similar context (9:3). It needs to be clear that no *necessary* connection is made between sin and illness in the FG, even though it might be read here. The "sin" is not specified, though Grayston's suggestion that it relates back to the view of God as only intermittently active as a healer (5:8) is an interesting one (Grayston 1990: 48).

The man's naiveté in returning to the authorities (5:15) leaves the reader to fill a gap in the narrator's earlier statement. Has a demand been made that the man report on the identity of his healer? Another possibility which takes seriously the narrative development of the FG to this point would be that, following on his new encounter with Jesus, the man is now in a position to return and bear witness to Jesus' true identity with clearer understanding.

Certainly the outcome of the man's "witness" to the "Jews" is an intensifying of the opposition to Jesus (5:16). Initially this is based on sabbath observance, but the real expansion of this motive in v. 18 indicates that the issues run deeper in the realm of Christology. Jesus responds to the renewed antagonism with an enigmatic statement (v. 17). If we accept Grayston's proposal regarding v. 14, this reply makes perfect sense as a rejection of the view of God as only occasionally in tune with the needs of humanity. At the same time it builds on the theme of sabbath observance. God may have "rested" on the seventh day, but God does not cease from engagement with the world and judgment of it.

The "Jews" understand (correctly!) the reference to the "Father" as a reference to God and a claim to equality with God (5:18). They are now *more* determined to kill him, though this is the first we hear of it. The two causes mentioned are inextricably linked. By "destroying" (*lyō* — same word as at 2:19!), not merely breaking the sabbath, Jesus sets himself above the law and equal to God.

To the non-Jewish implied reader this is a highly significant verse. The "Jews," the representative opposition party within the larger group, are in dispute with the Jesus party primarily over *christological* issues rather than mere questions of Jewish cultic observance. This leaves the door open to interpret their primary symbolism as part of a late-first-century inter-*Christian* dispute over the claims of Jesus, *Sophia* incarnate, the one who is equal to God.

John 5:19-30

This section is really a continuation of the preceding miracle story and is typical of a pattern in the FG which links important christological monologues with "signs." The issue of the authority by which Jesus acts has been raised by his "destruction" (5:18) of the sabbath and before it the temple. This is now clarified with reference to the relationship between Jesus and God (vv. 19-20), which in turn echoes material previously covered in the FG (1:1-18; 3:16, 35).

The mutual love of Jesus as Son and God as Father is modeled on the ancient traditions concerning Sophia (Scott 1992: 140-43). She loves God and is loved by God, and all who love her are loved by God and find life (Sir 4:11-15; Wis 8:3-4). Their mutual love comes to expression in their unity of knowledge and will, issuing in the ability to exercise judgment (Sir 4:15). The works which she performs are God's work, done in obedience to God's desire. This is precisely the relationship between Jesus and God envisaged by the FE in 5:19-30, and it also forms the basis of the authentic witness in the courtroom scene of the following section (vv. 31-47).

The allusion to "greater works" (5:20) echoes the statement to Nathanael (1:50). This is an example of a frequently employed narrative element in the FG, whereby layers of interpretation are built up incrementally. The first impression following 1:50 is that the "greater things" are represented by the wine miracle at Cana. Now we see that something yet more spectacular is being alluded to, namely, the raising of the dead (5:21). The relationship between God and Jesus points forward to the double claim that God raised Jesus and that, in Jesus himself, resurrection and life are to be found (11:25). This theme is picked up again shortly (5:25-29).

The theme of judgment is now introduced (5:22) as emerging from the intimate relationship between God and Jesus. Given the wisdom background to this text, it is a logical partner of the primary theme of life in this passage. The acceptance or rejection of Sophia brings with it a self-judgment for life or death (Prov 1:20-31). Similarly with Jesus as God's agent in the world. Witherington is correct in stressing the theme of "agency" as an important background to this section (and others) (Witherington 1995: 140-41). Like Sophia, Jesus is sent into the world (5:23) as the one who acts to bring life and deserves the honor due to God. Refusal to accord such honor has its inevitable outcome in death rather than life.

While this section is represented as an address to the "Jews," it bears the hallmarks of a christological dispute over "honoring" the true nature of the Christ which has its echoes in the Johannine epistles. As such it fits well with my contention that the primary focus of the "Jews" language is an inter-Christian dispute. At least here Brown supports this by seeing 5:23 as "part of an apologetic against some Christians of the evangelist's time who refuse to give proper honor to the Son" (Brown 1966: 214).

That life rather than judgment is the main thrust of the passage is emphasized by the eschatological outlook of what follows (5:24). The tension between the "now" and the "not yet" is not always clear in the FG, which seems more often to favor the "realized" view of v. 24. The latter view, though dominant, was clearly open to misunderstanding (21:21-23) and is balanced here by the "not yet" (5:25). The theme of "hearing" and "having life" is dramatically acted out at the climactic moment of the raising of Lazarus (11:43). As always, however, that sign is but a pointer to a greater reality in *eternal* life. Jesus Sophia, God's life-bringing agent, now actualizes that possibility (5:26).

Given that this discourse is related to the preceding miracle and the theme of sabbath "destruction," the death/life contrast offers a perspective similar to that of the transformation of water to wine at Cana. The presence of Jesus as life-bringer opens the possibility of leaving behind the enslavement to a system which denies life and freedom (cf. 8:31-32). The healing of the man trapped by illness and by the system illustrates the point now made in the "word" of Jesus.

The final verses of this section (5:27-30) add little more than emphasis to what has gone before. The Son of Man (v. 27) is also seen as an agent of God's judgment in the Synoptic tradition (Matt 13:41; Mark 13:26-27 pars.; Luke 21:36) and derives from the figure of Dan 7:13, as does the bipolar (5:29, good/evil) outcome (Dan 12:2). In reiterating the theme of common will, however, the final verse (5:30) recalls the foundational influence of Sophia speculation. Just as her purpose in entering the realm of humanity was to fulfill the will of God, so, too, Jesus seeks only to remain in tune with that same will.

John 5:31-47

Having stated the basis of his authority for action (unity of purpose with God who sent him — 5:19-30), the Johannine Jesus now moves on to a quasi-judicial defense of his actions and claims. Even if Jesus' own testimony was not acceptable to his opponents, there are others who may be relied upon (5:31-32). An impressive list of witnesses is drawn up: JBap; Jesus' works; God; the Scriptures, especially the Mosaic tradition.

The first witness has already been heard, JBap (5:33-35). Jesus' opponents sent interrogators (1:19-28) who, at least briefly, received his testimony (5:34). The dramatic narrative holds out the (vain) hope that the shared humanity of JBap and Jesus' opponents may help them to find a common mind. In denying the ultimate status of JBap's witness, Jesus is not denigrating either him or his message. Rather, he is reiterating the constant theme of the FG, that JBap is but an important witness (5:35 — *lychnos,* "lamp," an echo of Ps 132:17) and not the "real thing" (John 1:9 — *phōs,* "light"). Jesus' primary testimony is from "above" (God) and not from "below" (human beings).

The second witness is the work which Jesus does (5:36). He has declared before that this is not his own, but God's work. The source of that work should be self-evident in the healing of the man at the pool, but all his opponents have seen is a breach of a redundant legal code. Had they entered into a proper relationship with God's existing testimony (5:37) they could have understood. Mere reliance on the tradition of ancestors will not suffice in place of renewed encounter with God in their own generation (Howard-Brook 1994: 137).

Presumably the reference to the witness of God is already an allusion to Scripture. Now with classic Johannine irony, Jesus declares (5:38) that his opponents are not in harmony with the "word." Although on one level this could mean the "words" of Jesus, the reader knows that the opponents have failed to recognize the "Word," Jesus Sophia incarnate. Just as their ancestors refused her witness and fell into judgment, so, too, the present generation.

Now the Scriptures are formally called to witness (5:39). No particular text is in focus here, but the later reference to Moses suggests the Torah. That the opponents ("Jews") cannot read Jesus properly in the Scriptures fits with a group holding a different christological outlook from the FG's Sophia Christology. The failure to see is by choice (5:40 — *ou thelete*) and thus parallel to the refusal to receive Sophia, with the same result.

The contrast between Jesus and his opponents is brought out in the following verses (5:41-44). While Jesus does not accept human glorification (v. 41), his opponents crave it (v. 44); they do not know the love of God (v. 42), while Jesus is thoroughly in union with God's purpose (v. 43); they reject Jesus (v. 43; cf. 1:11) but will accept another who is engaged in his own business, not God's business (5:43). Who is meant by this is not clear, though the later choice of Barabbas (18:40) by the "Jews" echoes this.

The focus of the speech now changes dramatically, with the opponents put on trial in place of Jesus (5:45-47). It is not even Jesus who accuses them, but the one they purport to represent, Moses. Their refusal to understand/believe means that their champion becomes their judge. The scene is set for further conflict, and the reader will not be disappointed!

John 6:1-21

The whole of 6:1-71 is dominated by the theme of food, or more particularly Jesus as the Bread of Life. Following ch. 5, it is a clear example of the linking of "sign" and "word" in the FE's presentation of Jesus. The chapter's themes are thoroughly rooted in OT ideas, both the Exodus tradition and especially materials concerning Sophia.

The change of scene back to Galilee (6:1) has led some commentators to suggest that the chapter order has been confused (e.g., Bultmann; Schnackenburg). This suggestion misses the point of the ongoing narrative since the following "sign" and especially the discourse are intended as illustrations of Jesus' claim (5:46) that Moses wrote about him (Lindars 1972: 50, 249-70). The "sign" has notable parallels in the Synoptic tradition, including the connection in two other Gospels with the water-walking story (Mark 6:32-52 pars.). The use of the Roman name for the sea (Tiberias) is another possible pointer to a non-Jewish implied reader.

The crowd are still attracted by "signs" (6:2), despite Jesus' earlier scorn of such action (4:48). The ascent of the mountain (6:3) is connected with the sea-walking account in Matthew and Mark and surely evokes the Mosaic ascent of Sinai. For the FG the whole scene is to be viewed in this light, as the later speech will make clear in its explicit comparison of Jesus with Moses. The disciples rejoin the narrative at this point.

The mention of the approaching Passover (6:4) is important as a setting for both the miracle and the subsequent discourse on bread. It is also an indicator of the broad timescale of the FG account of Jesus' ministry, since this is already the second such Passover (2:23).

While the narrative demands the appearance of a crowd (6:5), the motif of "coming toward" Jesus commonly indicates the search for faith in the FG (4:35), even if its basis is still questionable. The crowd are not alone in their lack of perception, as the disciples will shortly make clear. In the Synoptic tradition it is they who ask the question which is found in Jesus' mouth in the FG. The FE explains that this is a test (6:6) for the disciple, since Jesus has already shown his foreknowledge of people and events (1:48; 2:25; 4:17-18).

Philip's reply to Jesus' question (6:7) reveals his continuing lack of understanding. It should be contrasted with the later replies of Martha (11:22, 27), where faith in the face of insuperable odds is the exemplary response of a disciple. Philip is still thinking in terms of the prohibitive cost (two hundred days' wages — a detail shared with Mark 6:37), failing to see Jesus as the potential source of food and life. Philip's fellow disciple Andrew fares little better in terms of understanding (v. 8), though he does continue his discipleship role as a bringer of others to Jesus (1:41-42). As in the Synoptic accounts, the boy has five loaves and two fish (6:9), but the FG adds that they were "barley" loaves. This echoes the story of Elisha's miraculous provision for the people (2 Kgs 4:42-44), where barley loaves provided enough and to spare for a crowd.

Jesus plays a more active role in the FG account than in the Synoptics, himself delivering the bread and fish to the crowd (6:11). This is surely hyperbole, but it points to the narrative intention of the FE, to show Jesus as the source of the food and, subsequently, as the *real* food: bread. The crowd are more than satisfied with his provision (v. 12). As in Mark's account, scraps are gathered up, but the FE reports that this is to avoid waste. Some have seen this, combined with the use of "give thanks" (*eucharisteō* — v. 11), as indicative of a eucharistic symbolism. There is no doubt that the text can be read in this way, but it need not have been the primary intention of the author that it should be.

The idea of symbolism attached to the "twelve" baskets (6:13) is commonly dismissed by commentators, but it is striking to note that the introduction of the disciple group as the "twelve" actually takes place later in this chapter (v. 67). There they appear to be those left over when others have gone, so the idea of a "remnant" twelve is not so absurd, even if the leftovers do not yet grasp what is going on around them!

The outcome of the miracle is a partial recognition of who Jesus is, albeit an inadequate one (6:14). In seeing Jesus as "the prophet who is to come," the crowd begin to open up a comparison with Moses, in whose image such a prophet was expected (Deut 18:15-19). It is immediately clear that the crowd's comprehension of the prophet, as a potential political leader (6:15), is not in line with Jesus' own thinking. His withdrawal in solitude seems to indicate that the disciples were among those who so crassly misunderstood the sign. The Johannine Jesus rejects both the language and notion of kingship throughout the unfolding drama of the FG (cf. the comment on 18:36).

The sea-walking story is often seen by commentators as unusual in comparison with other Synoptic parallels in the FG, since it might be construed as more "primitive" (e.g., Bultmann; Brown). By this is usually meant that it shows less sign of theological development. This assumption is based on the lack of some of the more obvious theological detail of Matthew or Mark. Closer inspection shows, however, that the theological sophistication of the FE's account is characteristically strong.

The disciples embark without Jesus (6:16), who has distanced himself from both the crowd and his closest followers. Although it is "toward evening," darkness falls only after some time (v. 17). Strangely we hear that Jesus had "still not" *(oupō)* joined them, despite their stated distance from the land. There appears to be an expectation that he might still arrive, which hardly ties up with their later surprise.

The mention of the rough sea conditions (6:18) hints at a potential sea rescue (as in Matt 14:22-33), but this does not feature directly in the FG account. The distance from the lakeside (c. 3-4 miles; 6:19) would place the boat about halfway across the broadest part of the lake, putting the story in line with Mark 6:47.

The appearance of Jesus has all the marks of a theophany, including the proper response of fear. Mark makes this more explicit with the allusion to "passing by." The climax of the FG account is the use of the divine name (6:20), here to be understood as in 4:26, both as an identification and a theological statement. This clarifies the relationship of the sea walking to the rest of the chapter: Jesus is no mere prophet (6:14), and certainly not a political Messiah-King (v. 15), but rather the very presence of the divine.

The remarkable nature of the sea walker is confirmed by the Johannine ending, whereby the boat is suddenly found to have reached its destination (6:21). This bypasses both the need for Jesus to enter the boat ("they wanted" [*ēthelon*] seems here to be unfulfilled) and the stilling of the storm (as in Matthew and Mark). In advance of the bread discourse the reader is reminded of the identity and authority of the speaker.

John 6:22-40

Although the theme of this section is clear — Jesus has been sent into the world as God's true life-giving Bread — the opening verses (6:22-24) are far from clear! It is only possible to speculate on the sense, as follows. The crowd become aware in the light of day that Jesus is no longer on their side of the lake; and since no boat was available after the departure of the disciples, they assume that Jesus has miraculously (?) joined his followers on the other side. They set off to find him using other boats which have arrived from Tiberias. The textual evidence suggests that the repetitive (cf. 6:11) reference "the Lord gave thanks," using the technical term *eucharisteō*, is probably a later addition to imply a eucharistic symbolism in the bread discourse.

The immediate interchange between the crowd and Jesus reveals the now familiar Johannine technique of two-level irony (6:25-27). The title "rabbi" is one of respect, but shows continuing failure to grasp who Jesus really is, as does the question "when" Jesus came, rather than "how," which seems to be the concern of the preceding verses. Jesus indicates that the crowd's interest is in their stomach rather than truth and life. His descent to earth is focused on more than physical provision, important though that may at times be.

This is immediately confirmed by another Son of Man saying (6:27), which builds on previous references to his origins and authority (1:51; 3:13). The Son of Man has come down from heaven as the agent of God's life-giving, life-sustaining power to provide a food, of which the miraculous bread was only a parabolic sign. The crowd's next question (6:28) serves only to emphasize their continuing misconception that they may possess ("work for") something temporally satisfying. Ironically there is no "work" which human beings can do other than to have faith (v. 29) — frequently the very antithesis of "works" in Pauline thought!

The response of the crowd to Jesus' call to believe (6:30) seems almost oblivious to the foregoing narration of the double sign. It again reveals the ambivalence of the Johannine "signs" and the insecurity of faith built upon them. It also takes us to the heart of Johannine political theology. The forthcoming stress on Jesus *as* Bread (not *like* bread) is not merely a "spiritual truth," but a fundamental question of life orientation. Jesus has provided bread: such provision is part of the Gospel, but it is not an easy way out of the daily struggle of life. Jesus provides the food for a life informed by and imbued with God's own wisdom, as we shall shortly hear.

The quotation of Scripture (6:31) by the crowd makes the transition to the next part of Jesus' discourse and serves as the material for exposition. There is no single OT text to which it corresponds, though Exod 16:4 and Ps 78:24 have clear claims as background. A further interesting parallel is Wis 16:20, which not only talks of bread from heaven but specifies that the people did not work for it, a prominent theme of the Johannine narrative.

The crowd's response offers the Johannine Jesus the opportunity to correct their exegesis of the tradition on three counts (6:32). The "he" in the text refers to God as the giver and not Moses; it does not refer to the wilderness manna but to the true/real bread; they should not think that it *was given* (past tense), since God *is giving* (present tense) it in the one who comes down as bread from heaven. The polemic begun in 1:17 is sharpened in this pointer to Jesus Sophia as the true embodiment of God's life-giving power.

Another example of Johannine irony (6:33) carries the question and answer session further through the ambiguity of the Greek participle *ho katabainōn*. It could mean either "*that which* comes down" or "*the one who* comes down." The crowd stumble in understanding again by choosing the former (v. 34), opening the way for Jesus' great declaration of the latter in the subsequent "I am" saying.

The "I am" sayings are one of the uniquely typical christological features of the FG. The background to this absolute use of "I Am" is complex, since it evokes several usages in Jewish literature: the name of God (Exod 3:14); the self-declaration of God in the prophetic tradition (e.g., Isa 43:3, 10-12); the first person direct speech of Sophia (Proverbs 8–9; Sirach 24). As elsewhere, however, it is the wisdom background which comes most often to the fore, not least in the *content* of the "I Am" formulae (bread; light; door; shepherd; resurrection/life; way; truth; vine), all of which reflect significant wisdom influence in their particular Johannine portrayal.

This is nowhere clearer than in the self-identification of Jesus as bread (6:35). The wisdom tradition points to Sophia as the provider of both bread and drink (Prov 9:5; Sir 15:3). The idea that the one who drinks from her wants more (Sir 24:21) is not the opposite of the Johannine saying, but points to the same truth that the FE puts forward — the bread and water which Jesus Sophia provides are indispensable for life (Scott 1992: 116-19). Taking the close connection of bread, water, and wine in the Sophia tradition with the proximity of the elements here in the FG, it is difficult to think that a eucharistic allusion is not intended (Lindars 1972: 259-60).

Neither signs nor the very presence of the life-giving Bread seems sufficient to bring Jesus' audience to faith (6:36). This is an echo of a later statement to the reader distant from the events of Jesus' ministry (20:29) and a further indication of the two-level discourse in which the FE often engages (seeing as "sight" and "faith").

It is vital to hear the continuing wisdom influence in the statements which follow (6:37-40). The FE is interested neither in the beginnings of a doctrine of predestination nor in the ideal of "once saved — always saved"! The emphasis here lies on the choice for humanity which is initiated by the presence of Jesus Sophia. Just as the descent of Sophia brings a moment of judgment and decision (Prov 1:20-33) leading to a potential for life (Prov 8:35; Sir 4:12), even eternal life (Wis 8:13), so, too, the presence of the Johannine Jesus brings a similar opportunity to all who will respond (cf. 3:15-17). While the grace of God is undoubtedly present in the movement of humanity toward God, human decision in the face of the offer of Jesus Sophia is the determining factor. The notion of resurrection may be a step beyond the wisdom tradition, but that tradition is the fundamental source of inspiration for Jesus' speech here.

John 6:41-59

Having established the life-giving significance of Jesus as Bread, the FE now turns to a discussion of how this image functions in relation to the believer. The "Jews" (6:41), here apparently part of the Galilean audience, echo their ancestors in the wilderness (Exod 16:1-8), whose "murmuring" against Moses was deemed a complaint against God. The words attributed to Jesus are a conflation of his earlier statements, indicating that the main purpose of their reiteration is to open up the exegesis of the theme.

The question of Jesus' origins (6:42) is discussed in all four Gospels (Matt 13:55; Mark 6:3; Luke 4:22), but it has a different slant in the FG because of its connection to the theme of descent from heaven. The FE betrays no interest in the idea of "virgin birth." The notion is redundant in any case, given the pushing back of christological speculation to the foundation of the world through the use of wisdom categories in the Prologue.

Like Moses before him, Jesus points to his opponents' murmuring as an issue with God (6:43-44). Unlike Moses, whom Jesus supersedes (vv. 32-35), the provision which Jesus makes is not merely temporary and physical but eternal and spiritual. The theme of being "drawn" is found in the prophetic tradition (Jer 31:3; Hos 11:4), but the Johannine imagery is much influenced by the picture of Sophia, as a woman, offering her own attractions in contrast to those of the prostitute (Proverbs 1–9). As in the preceding verses (6:37-40), the offer is open to *all* who will respond (v. 45) and not a predetermined few, a sentiment reflected in the substitution of "they" for the expression "your sons" in the quotation from Isa 54:13.

In 3:12-13 the FE has already pointed to Jesus Sophia as the one who has "come down" to reveal God and so bring life. This theme is reiterated (6:46-47) as a reminder that Jesus is superior to Moses as the provider of *true* bread. The predicate of v. 35 is restated (v. 48) to introduce a discussion of the relative merits of the old and new breads. The old bread may have sustained life for a time during the desert wanderings, but it met only a temporal need (v. 49). By contrast, the living Bread meets humanity's ultimate need, eternal life (v. 50).

If there is a hint of the eucharistic words in the phrase "This is the bread" (6:50), then it becomes clearer in the new theme of "eating" the bread/flesh (v. 51) (Lindars 1972: 265-67). This will be the subject of exegesis in the following verses. The reader is reminded again of the origin and identity of the life-giving bread (cf. 4:14), Jesus Sophia, before being pointed forward (*future* tense) to the self-giving Passion which inaugurates a life which transcends death.

There might appear to be a change in the direction of the dialogue at this point, with the emphasis on *feeding* rather than *believing* as the way to life through the Bread. Essentially the meaning is the same: it is only by complete identification with Jesus as the living Bread that sharing in the true life becomes possible. Despite the clear eucharistic allusions, there is no suggestion that participation in it is the vehicle to death-transcending life.

The "Jews" are now moved to "battle" with one another, rather than simply to murmur (6:52). As in v. 31, they misunderstand in a literalistic way, thinking that Jesus means to provide food. The word "his" is probably best left out here, making their comment an echo of Exod 16:8, where "flesh" is to be provided by God.

As on the previous occasion, so here their misunderstanding opens up the way for Jesus to clarify his meaning (6:53-55). Just as Sophia opened up the way to life through the provision of bread and wine (Prov 9:5), so, too, the one who wholly feasts on the revelatory Bread and imbibes the true Wine becomes one with God. There is a boldness of language ("munch" — *trōgein*) which aims at emphasizing the realistic nature of the commitment involved in sharing the life given by the Bread/Wine. It is not, however, intended to be taken literally!

The dialogue reaches its goal in the crucial reference to "abiding" (6:56). This anticipates the Vine imagery of 15:1-11 and is a vital building block in the FE's understanding of discipleship. The mutual indwelling of God and Jesus parallels that of Jesus and the disciple, issuing in life (6:57). In much the same way Sophia is life to those who find her (Prov 8:35; Sir 4:12), and indwells those who respond to her (Wis 7:27). Thus also Jesus Sophia gives life to those who fully feast on him. Once again a crucial Johannine theme is illuminated by its origins in the wisdom tradition.

The concluding verse of the speech (6:58) is a clever summary of the main themes: the bread which comes down from heaven eclipses the temporal provision of the past and gives the hope of transcendent life to the world. The final comment on the setting in the synagogue (v. 59) serves merely to link the passage to the controversy which follows.

John 6:60-71

The Bread of Life discourse evokes a strong response from the audience, but not this time from the "Jews." Rather, it is from among the "disciples" that opposition comes. Jesus' words are "offensive" (6:60 — *sklēros*), not merely "hard to grasp," and division is the result. He is hard to listen to and, by implication, to obey (Barrett 1978: 302-3). Once again, the Johannine Jesus displays a supernatural knowledge of the situation of his audience (6:61; cf. 1:47; 2:24-25; 4:16-18; etc.) and challenges their standpoint.

The stumbling block now emerges as the descent of Jesus Sophia from heaven (6:62). Rather than being a division over the meaning of eating the flesh, it is more fundamentally a division about the christological outlook of the disciples — the very nature of the incarnation. Just as Sophia's descent into the world brought division among her disciples and her withdrawal judgment (Prov 1:28-32; *1 Enoch* 42), so this will be the effect of the return of Jesus Sophia to his/(her) place of origin. While the language of withdrawal is the more common Johannine expression of the mode of Jesus' departure (John 7:33 — as also with Sophia), his glorification will be completed only by the full cycle of "lifting up" (crucifixion), death, resurrection, and ascension (20:17).

We are dealing here with a text which addresses the divisions of the same late-first-century audience as in the Johannine epistles (cf. 1 John 2:19), where christological matters are the root of the problems. The opposition of "disciples" parallels the FG's more common use of "Jews," indicating clearly that that term is not used in an anti-Semitic way but as an internal group boundary marker. Not all "Jews," not all "disciples" are true followers: many see the claim that Jesus is Sophia incarnate as an insurmountable offense and a focus for virulent opposition.

The comparison between flesh and spirit (6:63) has often been seen as a contradiction of the stress placed on eating the flesh of Jesus (vv. 51-58), but this is not the case. Overliteral reading of Johannine irony places the reader in the same danger as the opponents which the FG caricatures! Here such irony is used to play with the reader's understanding of the word "flesh." The same misunderstanding noted at vv. 52-54 is tackled again from a different angle here. The physical presence of Jesus must make way for his withdrawal to the place of origin, thus opening up the way to the coming of the ubiquitous, life-giving Spirit (cf. 14:25-28).

The christological divisions noted earlier now take on a highly charged association with the deadly dealings of Judas (6:64). As in the earlier material (vv. 37-40, 44), the grace of God is active in all human response to Jesus' life-giving words (v. 65), but it is the understanding/faith of the disciples, demonstrated by abiding to the end, which realizes that calling.

Such faithfulness of discipleship now becomes the focus of the final portion of this momentous chapter (6:66-71). The split is final for some (v. 66), but even the core group must face the hard question of durability (v. 67). This passage is frequently seen as the FG's version of the Synoptic account cited at Caesarea Philippi (Mark 8:27-33 pars.). That the FE intends it as such is probably most apparent in the sudden introduction of "the twelve" as a designation for the core group, whose "calling" has nowhere been hinted at in the FG. The implied reader again emerges as someone already familiar with the story of Jesus, though not yet in its *Johannine* form (cf. 2:22).

What is most striking about this reinterpretation of the Caesarea Philippi incident is the alteration to Peter's confession. The words of 20:31 indicate that "You are the Christ, the Son of God" is the ultimate confession for the Johannine believer, yet Peter quite pointedly does *not* say this. Instead that great confession, found in his mouth in the Synoptics, is reserved for a later climax, appearing there in the mouth of a female disciple, Martha of Bethany (11:27). While Peter does recognize the ultimate significance of Jesus' words (6:68), his confession indicates that his understanding is not yet complete.

The expression "Holy One of God" (6:69) appears in the mouths of the demons in the Synoptic tradition (Mark 1:24; Luke 4:34), but is nevertheless a recognition by them of Jesus' God-given power. The Johannine Jesus speaks of himself as "made holy" by God in 10:36, thus reinforcing Peter's words here. They do not, however, express fully the faith in which the FG urges the reader to continue and must therefore be seen at best as a step on the road toward full understanding.

In common with the Synoptic scene, the confession is followed by reference to the presence of the "devil" (6:70). For the FE, however, this is not Peter but Judas (v. 71), about whose duplicity the ideal reader already knows. The character assassination of Judas will intensify as the drama unfolds.

John 7:1-13

Jesus' reason for time spent in the wilderness and in Galilee generally is revealed as a desire to avoid the murderous intent of his opponents (7:1). This recalls the threats of 5:18 and is all the more poignant for its proximity to the remarks on Judas's forthcoming betrayal (6:71).

Passover, the setting of the previous chapter, and Tabernacles (7:2) are some six months apart in the Jewish calendar, leaving a large narrative "gap" at this point. The symbolism of the Tabernacles setting is probably more important than any attempt to establish a chronology of Jesus' ministry (Yee 1989: 70-82). Since this harvest festival was associated with the period of tent dwelling in the wilderness, and in particular with the themes of water and light, it makes good sense as a sequel to the period of miraculous provision in the wilderness of Galilee.

Jesus' brothers reappear for the first time since the Cana wine miracle. Their role is clearly as skeptical unbelievers here (7:3-5). It is correct that Jesus' major signs to this point have been in Galilee rather than in Judea, but he has provoked opposition by performing a significant sign at the heart of Israel's cultic homeland (5:1-18). The reader knows that the claim that he has worked only "in secret" is untrue. It serves only as evidence of the ignorance of the brothers, whose lack of insight/faith is confirmed by the evangelist.

Jesus indicates that his attitude to familial pressures remains the same as in a previous incident with his mother (2:4). His "time," here equivalent to the "hour," will be decided by his relationship with God rather than by human compulsion (7:6). The use of the word *kairos* here indicates a decisive moment. While this will come for Jesus only in his glorification through death and resurrection, the moment of decision for the unbelieving brothers is held continually open.

The hatred of the world (7:7) is a wider statement of the intense opposition already noted in the inner group of "Jews" (5:18; 7:1). It takes a turn for the worse in the events around Tabernacles, with an attempt by the "Jews" to stone Jesus (8:59). Once again the influence of Wisdom upon the Johannine portrayal of Jesus is evident in the attitude of those who oppose him. Just as Sophia's child is hated by those whose ways are wicked (Wis 2:10-20), so, too, the wickedness exposed by Jesus Sophia leads to hatred from its exponents.

The restatement of Jesus' plan concerning attendance at the festival (7:8-10), with its explanation for the reader, is notable for its play on the verb "go up" (*anabainō*). The "hour" toward which the Johannine Jesus moves inexorably forward will include his "going up" to the Father (20:17). It is striking that exactly there, the "brothers" are informed that Jesus is now ready to "go up." The narrator surely intends irony in the use of the verb toward the brothers at this point, when the plot to do away with Jesus is gathering pace.

The FE suggests that Jesus' absence from the festival was sufficiently notable to raise questions among the crowd (7:11-12). This conflicts with the earlier challenge to make himself known through signs to those in Judea (v. 3). The "murmurers" parallel the Israelites in their wilderness experience under Moses (Exod 16:2; John 6:41). The divided response is typical of that experienced also by Sophia in her call to people to follow her. Ironically, in place of the fear of God, the beginning of wisdom (Prov 9:10), the crowd shows its folly by fearing the "Jews" (7:13). Since the crowd are also Jews participating in the festival, we see clearly that the term here refers to a group, probably the authorities, within a more neutral wider group.

John 7:14-36

The appearance of Jesus in the temple halfway through the feast of Tabernacles (7:14) allows the drama of hide-and-seek between him and his opponents to be worked out. The much feared "Jews," who at this point must represent the authorities in Jerusalem (v. 15), raise the question of Jesus' fitness to teach, given his uneducated background. Jesus merely reasserts his role as the agent of God (7:16), whose teaching he delivers (cf. 3:34; 5:19). It is the testing of Jesus' teaching which provides the narrative unity to the section.

This dialogue and its subsequent partner (7:37-52) have been the subject of many redaction-critical reconstructions, with links being made back to the material of ch. 5 (cf. Bultmann [1972], who deals with 7:15-24 between 5:1-47 and 8:13-20!). It is our intention to read the text as it stands and, with Lindars (1972: 286-87), to see a clever narrative structure binding together what may previously have been diverse bits of material.

The content of Jesus' teaching is neither described nor discussed (7:17), but its character is evident as obedience to God rather than self-promotion. This becomes the test of both the freewill response of the listener, who seeks nothing other than to do God's will, and of the true (= sincere) teacher, who aims not at self-glorification (7:18) but at honoring God.

Brown (1966: 312) suggests that the word "dishonesty" (*adikia* — 7:18) provides a link to the supposed murderous intent of Jesus' listeners (v. 19) by evoking 2 Sam 14:32, which prescribes stoning for such behavior. The failure of the audience to grasp the true source of Jesus' teaching leads them to the point of breaking the very law which they claim to keep by killing him without due cause. They deny that this is their aim (7:20), accusing him of madness (cf. Mark 3:21-26). It is notable that the *crowd* and not the *Jews* protest innocence at this point. In dramatic terms this allows the FE to keep the smaller subgroup of arch-villains plotting. They will repeat a similar charge against Jesus in 8:48.

The reference to a single good deed (7:21) in this Judean context must be an allusion to the poolside miracle of 5:1-15, even though no astonishment was recorded then. That this is the case becomes immediately clear in the further discussion of the sabbath question (7:22-23). The Torah legislates for male circumcision on the eighth day after birth (Lev 12:3), and this was carried out even if the day in question happened to be a sabbath. The Johannine Jesus argues that the life-giving intention of this act is far outweighed by his life-restoring action of complete bodily healing. The reader, if not also the crowd, is parenthetically reminded, in Pauline fashion (cf. Romans 4), that the law was not exclusively the prerogative of Moses.

The dialogue comes to an initial climax (7:24) with an allusion to Isa 11:3, part of a text given messianic significance by early Christian writers (Rom 15:12). If the crowd are to judge Jesus' teaching and action, it must at least be fairly on the basis of the law to which they profess to adhere.

The second part of this dialogue is laden with irony throughout. Apparently some at least know of the threat to Jesus' life (7:25), so easily dismissed as madness earlier. His high-profile public appearance in the temple, however, raises a question as to the attitude of the rulers (v. 26), namely, whether they *know* that Jesus is the Messiah. This is ironic, the reader sensing the discomfort of these leaders who know the truth but refuse it.

The irony continues in the confidence of the Jerusalem crowd concerning Jesus' origins (7:27). They *do* know where he comes from in a literal sense (his place of birth), which would rule out any messianic claim by their preconceived notions. Yet they actually do *not* know his real origin ("from above"), which, by the crowd's own standards, precisely supports Jesus' true messianic claim. The whole question of origins is another pointer to the Johannine picture of Jesus as Sophia incarnate. Like Jesus here, Sophia's origins are a matter of speculation in the wisdom literature (Job 28:12-28; Bar 3:14-15), with God the only one who truly knows. The Sophia influence becomes clearer as the dialogue progresses.

Once again showing dramatic insight, Jesus responds publicly to the "off-stage" disputation (7:28-29). His answer is merely to point to the irony noted above, reiterate his divine origins (*alēthinos* — which here stands for "God"), and emphasize the apostolic nature of his mission as God's work. An attempt is made to arrest him (7:30), presumably for blasphemy, but in line with the determinism of the FE's understanding of God's plan, they are unable to do so. The tension, however, is markedly rising.

Once again some appear to come to belief at this point (7:31), echoing the divided reaction to earlier events (2:23-25; 6:14-15, 41-42, 59, 66). The reader is suspicious since the crowd's faith is based entirely on "signs," and they apparently know of no more than the one to which Jesus has previously alluded.

The plot thickens with an "official" attempt by the authorities, worried by the crowd's more positive response, to arrest Jesus (7:32). In quiet defiance, Jesus emphasizes his control over events by asserting that he is not going yet (v. 33)! Then using a classic Sophia (cf. 6:62) image, he indicates that his ultimate choice will be to withdraw above to God. The effect of his departure will parallel that of Sophia's exit from the world (Prov 1:28-29): he will be inaccessible (7:34) and his withdrawal will bring judgment (John 8:21).

The section ends with a further ironic question in the mouths of Jesus' opponents (7:35-36). Failing to grasp that Jesus Sophia speaks of a return to God, they suggest that he will try to escape them among the Gentiles. The reader knows that this is precisely where the primary mission of Jesus' followers has been focused, given the refusal of "his own" to accept and believe.

John 7:37-52

The second half of the dialogue at Tabernacles begins a few days later (7:37) as Jesus issues an invitation based on claims previously made by Sophia (cf. 4:13-14). The sentiment of Sir 24:21, already seen as a link to the parallel discourse on bread (6:35), surely lies behind Jesus' offer here. Just as the Passover setting was appropriate to bread, so the Tabernacles setting, with its celebration of the provision of water in the desert, is appropriate to this part of the discourse. When this is placed alongside Wis 11:4, where Sophia is hailed as the provider of water for thirst in that desert context, the circle back to the Johannine statement is complete.

The origin of the specific "scripture" is difficult (7:38). Most likely the background is again the great hymn to Sophia in Sirach (Sir 24:30-32). If this is the case, then the problem of the subject of 7:38 is alleviated. The Greek is quite unclear as to whether the water will flow from the believer or from Jesus as the speaker. Both are possible, but a connection with Sirach would make the former more likely, as does its consistency with the previous statement about never-ending supply in 4:13-14. The NRSV translation reflects such a reading.

The narrator now clarifies for the implied reader that the references to living water are symbolic of the Spirit (7:39). Since the farewell speeches will later indicate the necessity of Jesus' withdrawal/departure before the Spirit could be given, the narrator again makes the link here between the coming glorification of Jesus and the gift of the Spirit.

As in the first part of the Tabernacles speech, it is the crowd who respond to Jesus' words (7:40-44). In parallel with the wisdom tradition, they are again divided in their reaction to Jesus Sophia, some thinking him to be the Prophet like Moses (Deut 18:15-18), others directly claiming messianic status, but yet others mocking his humble origins in Galilee. If the implied reader knows the Gospel of Luke, as I think quite probable, the reference to Bethlehem, evoking Mic 5:2, is another example of Johannine irony: the crowd state the "truth" unwittingly. Again the attempt to arrest Jesus is unsuccessful, the reader already being aware that this is because the "hour" is not yet fulfilled.

The temple police (cf. 7:32) reappear on the scene at this point (v. 45). Given that the scene has shifted a few days (v. 37), we can see how the FE has gathered various elements in the construction of this speech, this verse logically following v. 36. Lindars (1972: 303) sensibly suggests that it was necessary to insert the material here in order to move more smoothly from the reaction of the crowd to that of the authorities. Unlike their bosses, the police seem impressed with Jesus' teaching (v. 46), causing the Pharisees further frustration and evoking their scorn (vv. 47-49). The question of Jesus' humble Galilean origins becomes something of a "class" divide between the crowd (perhaps better translated "mob" or "rabble"), the police, and Jesus on one hand, and the ruling authorities on the other. The Pharisees consider these others beneath them and consequently accursed (cf. Deut 27:26; 28:15-68) due to their ignorance of the Torah.

The hesitant Nicodemus makes another cameo appearance, offering a brief defense of Jesus' right at least to a fair hearing (7:50-51). The narrator reminds the reader of Nicodemus's previous role, perhaps as a pointer to a positive outcome to his unresolved faith question at that time. His eminently fair question to his colleagues serves the dramatic plot by disclosing the vindictive drive which motivates the opponents of Jesus. That they will heap scorn on one of their own number, Nicodemus (7:52), augurs badly for the one whose words and very presence rebuke them.

John 7:53–8:11

The story of a woman accused of adultery and dragged before Jesus as a test case offers a fascinating insight into the development of Gospel traditions. The text certainly did not belong to the oldest manuscripts of the FG, and it appears in various places in the later manuscripts, including notably also after Luke 21:38! The reasons for its initial exclusion and ultimate inclusion are beyond thorough discussion here, but among them would be its affinity to other Johannine stories in which Jesus and women engage sympathetically with one another; its conclusion (8:11), which shows that it illustrates the declaration of Jesus in v. 15 — "I judge no one"; and its continuation of the theme of dispute with the Pharisees over the law.

The story is intriguing as much for what it does not tell us as for what it does. The opening (7:53–8:1) is clearly the ending of another story since it bears no relation to v. 52. This probably indicates that it originally belonged to a lost collection of some kind, probably another Gospel. The setting is once again the temple (8:2), and it pictures Jesus as a rabbi seated and teaching, as though it was a normal pattern for him to hold court in this way. The scribes, never mentioned elsewhere in the FG but frequent partners of the Pharisees in the Synoptics (8:3), come together in order to test Jesus.

Several things point to a "setup." First, there was no reason to try such a case in public and certainly no need to consult Jesus — the Torah makes the verdict clear, however violent it may appear from our perspective (Lev 20:10; Deut 22:21). Second, only one partner in the crime, the woman, is brought, despite the insistence that she was caught in the very act (8:4). Third, in Johannine terms the demand for a judgment puts Jesus in an impossible position (v. 5). Either he must appear to go against the Torah or against Roman law (18:31). Fourth, the narrator removes any doubt by indicating in an aside (8:6) that the whole purpose of the incident was to entrap Jesus.

Much ink has been spilled in speculation on what Jesus may or may not have written in the sand. It seems to be more part of the drama of the story, building tension and causing the opponents (8:7) to become more insistent in their demand for an answer. Jesus' response now is to quote back an intensified version of the law which they seek to enact. It was the duty of the witnesses to a capital crime to initiate the death penalty (Deut 13:9; 17:7), but Jesus challenges their intention in executing judgment by demanding that those of pure motive begin. Witherington is right in suggesting that "without sin" means here without "moral responsibility" rather than sinless (Witherington 1995: 364). Jesus then returns to his mysterious doodling in the dust (8:8), while his chastened opponents drift away (v. 9), leaving him alone with the woman for the final scene.

For the first time in the story Jesus and the woman now address one another (8:10-11). The patent injustice of bringing only the woman is relieved by the absence of any witness against her and the refusal of Jesus, by implication the only pure-hearted witness, to judge her (cf. v. 15). Placed here in the FG, his final words are a narrative echo of 5:14 and show that the end result is not one merely of being "let off," but of healing.

John 8:12-30

The material in ch. 8 consists of a number of dialogues which continue themes already discussed in chs. 5 and 7. It also paves the way for the dramatic story of healing which follows in ch. 9. This is clear from the opening words (8:12), the second of the "I Am" sayings. The theme of Jesus as "light" was begun in the opening verses of the Prologue (1:4-5, 9) and is closely attached to the picture of Jesus as Sophia incarnate (cf. 3:19-21). There is probably also here an allusion to Isa 9:1-2, not least given the mention of Galilee in the preceding verse (7:52) and the motif of walking in darkness.

The dialogue partners turn out to be the Pharisees (8:13) rather than the "Jews," but the subject of the dispute is a continuation of the earlier question about testimony. The Pharisees throw back as a question Jesus' own words in 5:31. This initiates a quasi-judicial discussion echoing 5:31-38, with the emphasis again falling on the unity of will and purpose between Father and Son.

The claim that Jesus' witness is invalid is countered initially by oblique reference to his origins (8:14). The significance of this will be spelled out clearly in the subsequent dialogue (vv. 21-24), but for the moment Jesus' response calls into question the confidence some have expressed previously (7:40-42). Despite appearances to the contrary, as with Sophia before him (Job 28:20-21), no one knows his true origins.

Jesus goes on to challenge the basis of the judgment which his opponents make against him (8:15-16). The assertion that he "judges no one" (though consistent with 3:17 and the late insertion of 7:53–8:11) seems in direct contradiction of 5:22, 30. It is, however, immediately qualified. Jesus does indeed bring judgment in his person, but it is not his own judgment. Rather, in common with the picture of Sophia as the bringer of God's judgment (Prov 8:8; Wis 8:11; 9:3; Sir 4:15), Jesus comes as the agent of God's judgment in the world.

The validity of Jesus' testimony is now addressed more directly (8:17). In line with other polemic against the Torah, the Johannine Jesus here distances himself from the provisions of Deut 19:15, alluded to here, by calling it "your" law. He makes explicit (8:18) what has until now only been hinted at, that it is God who stands alongside him as witness. Even Jesus' own testimony is made as "I Am" *(egō eimi),* another hint of his origins and status in relation to God (cf. the comment on 6:35). The dialogue in 8:21-26 shows that the predominant influence on this use of "I Am" is once again Sophia.

There is a fascinating parallel here to Wis 2:12-24 as Jesus Sophia stands trial before his accusers as the righteous one who can call God "Father." His accusers immediately inquire about his "Father" (8:19), again echoing the discussion of 7:40-42. Jesus' response once more evokes the model of the relationship between God and Sophia (Wis 9:13-18), indicating that to know Jesus is already to know God (with its negative corollary!). The narrator ends this section of dialogue with a brief hint of the developing plot against Jesus (8:20). These disturbing claims of Jesus are made at the heart of the religious establishment, the temple (on the precise position "near the treasury," see Brown 1966: 342), and symbolically continue to strike at its users' attitude to him.

The second part of the dialogue begins with an allusion to Jesus' departure (8:21) and its consequences. This is an exact parallel to 7:34, with its echoes of the judgment which follows Sophia's withdrawal from the world (Prov 1:28-29). It results in a typical misunderstanding on the part of the listeners (8:22), who think that Jesus is talking about committing suicide. Ironically, of course, the reader recognizes that Jesus *is* talking about his coming death, but not by suicide. His response to their confusion is to stress his origin with God (v. 23), using the same contrast of "from above–from below" which informed the earlier dialogues with Nicodemus and the disciples (see the comments on 3:12; 6:62).

Jesus now goes on to explain his earlier statement concerning the consequences of his departure (8:24). What must be grasped is the nature of Jesus as "I Am." The one who has spoken in this way in the past has brought news of salvation, whether it be God's deliverance in the exodus (Exod 3:14), or the words of hope from God to the people in exile (Isaiah 43), or the reinterpretation of Israel's salvation history as guided by Sophia (Wisdom 10–11). Bultmann is correct in saying that, by his use of "I Am" here, the Johannine Jesus asserts that "he is everything which he has claimed to be" (Bultmann 1971: 349).

The result of Jesus' further self-revelation is continued misunderstanding (8:25). His interlocutors ironically assume that "I Am" still needs a predicate, even though one has only recently been supplied (8:12). Jesus' answer to their question, "Who are you?" is notoriously difficult to translate without supplying a subject. It is best read as a statement: "From the beginning (I am) what I tell you" (cf. Barrett 1978: 343). As so often in the FG, Jesus reveals only that he is what the Prologue has claimed him to be, the very presence of Sophia incarnate, whose claim to unity of will and purpose "from the beginning with God" (Prov 8:22; Sir 24:9) should be clear. This is confirmed by the restatement of some common wisdom themes (8:26): being sent by God; delivering God's judgment; speaking the truth; communicating only what God wills. The result of this restatement (v. 27) is, as usual, continued misunderstanding.

At this point in the dialogue (8:28) it becomes evident that there is another witness, which will underline the validity of Jesus' words, namely, his forthcoming "lifting up" in glorification. This will confirm him as "I Am." As with Sophia before him, Jesus' authority for teaching is not self-derived but comes from God, with whom he was in the beginning (Scott 1992: 131-34). The unity which binds Jesus to God (8:29) means that even in the moments when he appears most alone, God is both present and pleased (cf. Prov 8:30-31).

The reader is surprised by the apparent outcome of this self-revelatory statement, that "many" believe in Jesus (8:30). Given the level of misunderstanding to this point in the dialogue and the reluctance of Jesus to accept such belief on earlier occasions (2:23-25), the reader awaits the next section with interest.

John 8:31-59

Although ostensibly addressed to those who believed in Jesus (8:31), the words which follow in 8:31-59 are among the most difficult in the NT, not least because of their misappropriation as an apology for "anti-Semitism" by some Christians. We have already noted that the term "Jews" is used in different ways in the course of the FG, most commonly to denote an opponent group within a larger group to which Jesus himself belongs. We have also suggested that this mirrors the internal struggles of the *Christian* community toward the end of the first century rather than a dispute between Christians and Jews. It is in this light that the whole of 8:31-59 needs to be read.

The dialogue begins with some words about discipleship, which will later be echoed in the direct address to the disciples in 15:1-17. "Abiding" is an essential quality of discipleship in the FG. Here it is associated with knowledge of the truth (8:32), and thus with freedom. In common with the Johannine Jesus, truth is precisely what Sophia comes to reveal during her sojourn on earth (Witherington 1995: 176-77). The freedom in Jesus may also be intended to contrast here with the thought of obedience to the Torah (Psalm 119) as a path to truth and freedom.

Jesus' opponents seize on the implication that they are not yet free (8:33), taking it in a literal sense. As descendants of Abraham they understand themselves to be free to practice their faith in an unbroken line of tradition. It is patently false to imply that the Jews had never been enslaved, as the exodus story indicates, but it is all the more ironic here in a situation in which they are seen to be under slavery to Rome (cf. 19:15).

Using a short parable, Jesus now illustrates what he means by slavery (8:34-35). There are numerous textual difficulties in these verses (cf. Brown 1966: 355-56), but the general thrust of the parable seems clear. Disobedience to the Torah (sin) leads to disinheritance (slavery); so those who might have seen themselves as having a guaranteed place in the household of God now find this not to be the case. By contrast, the "son" (8:36 — probably here intended as "Son") has a permanent place and is able to grant freedom to those who are slaves. Only in this way can true freedom be achieved.

The whole argument now centers around true descent. Jesus acknowledges that his opponents are physically descended from Abraham (8:37), but their attempts to kill him indicate that they are not the patriarch's true heirs. They do not recognize Jesus Sophia as the one who has come down to reveal the truth from God (8:38). By their actions (seeking to kill Jesus) they deny their true parenthood. This is stated over again (8:39-40), with a probable allusion to Abraham's proper reception of the messengers of God (Gen 18:1-15) as a contrast to their rejection of Jesus' teaching. In this restatement, however, the Johannine Jesus makes clear what was only hinted at in 8:38, that his Father = God.

This promptly raises the question: Whose work are the "Jews" doing (8:41)? They see themselves as the true children of God and not as bastards. There is probably another (cf. 6:42) oblique reference here to the suspect nature of Jesus' origins, even if the main emphasis lies on the current dispute. The question of legitimacy launches Jesus into an extended argument against his opponents (8:42-47). They are the true children neither of Abraham nor of God (v. 42). In contrast to the child of God who loves Sophia and thus enjoys God's love (Prov 8:17; Wis 7:28; Sir 4:14), the opponents of Jesus Sophia cannot be God's children because they seek to kill Jesus rather than loving *(agapaō)* him.

The idea that Jesus "came forth" from God echoes 7:28, is equivalent to the notion of being "sent," and echoes the emergence of Sophia from the heavenly places to communicate God's wisdom on earth (Sir 24:3-12). Even if the later Nicene theologians understood this as a trinitarian indicator, it does not yet have such overtones for Johannine Christology but belongs to the sphere of wisdom influence.

Jesus' opponents appear not only lacking in understanding but completely deaf to his words (8:43). This may reflect Isa 6:9-10, which is also known in the Synoptic tradition (Mark 4:12; cf. John 12:40), but the Johannine Jesus attributes it to the parentage of his adversaries — namely, the devil (8:44)! Although the grammar is awkward (Lindars 1972: 329), the inference is clear enough: those who sin (= seek Jesus' death) are children of the devil. There is a close correspondence here to 1 John 3:7-17, which berates "children of the devil" and is the only other place in the NT where the rare word for murderer (1 John 3:15 — *anthrōpoktonos*) is used. There the opponents are clearly other "deviant" Christians, the background against which, I have suggested, the whole Johannine language of "Jews" is heard by the ideal reader.

The picture of the devil as a liar and murderer is most probably influenced by the Genesis accounts of the "tempter" (serpent) and of Cain. *Diabolos* literally means "slanderer" and fits the juridical nature of the scene. The devil is a false advocate who slanders the "true Light." As God is the "father" of the truth (= Jesus), so the devil is the "father" of falsehood (= Jesus' opponents). Jesus repeats his claim to truth (8:45), underlining it with a rhetorical challenge to refute it or come to faith (v. 46). This challenge offers another point of connection for the late insertion of 7:53–8:11.

The section of dialogue ends (8:47) with an echo of v. 43, emphasizing that the deafness of the opposition is thoroughly connected to their alienation from God. It bears a striking resemblance both to 1 John 4:6, reflecting inter-Christian strife, and to the description of deafness attributed to those who refuse to hear Sophia's voice (Prov 1:20-33).

Instead of coming to belief, Jesus' opponents now accuse him of madness (8:48), or, strictly speaking, demonic possession (cf. Mark 3:21-26). There is no easy explanation of the use of "Samaritan" as a parallel here (cf. Lindars 1972: 331-32), but the report of bad blood between Jews and Samaritans (John 4:9) confirms its use here as a term of abuse.

Far from being mad, Jesus underlines his mission as honoring to God (8:49), a repetition of a theme heard already in 5:23-24, where the question of giving honor to Jesus as God's agent was also stressed. Jesus' mission is not self-seeking, but directs glory toward God (8:50), a sign of the authenticity of his work (7:28). The reader recalls, however, that from the beginning of the FG it has been claimed that, in Jesus, God's glory is actually seen (1:14).

The benefits (and dangers) of keeping Jesus' word (8:51) are outlined in the farewell speeches (14:21, 23-24; 15:20), but ultimately "eternal life" is the goal. This saying has close parallels in the Synoptic tradition (Matt 16:28; Mark 9:1). Integrity of "hearing" and "doing" was also the sign of mutual honor between God, Jesus, and the believer in the earlier rehearsal of this theme (John 5:22-24).

The opposition begins to mount with a further accusation of madness thrown at Jesus (8:52). There is typical ironic misunderstanding, as the "Jews" take Jesus to mean physical life and death. Like the Samaritan woman earlier (4:12), they cannot see past the literal, and question (8:53) Jesus' status in relation to the great patriarch, whose lineage is already in dispute here, and the prophets.

Since the opponents echo their own question (8:25) concerning Jesus' identity, it opens the way for a further summary (vv. 54-55) of four previous points: (1) Jesus gives glory to and receives glory from God; (2) Jesus knows and is one with God; (3) his opponents do not know God and are liars if they say they do; and (4) Jesus keeps God's word. To this summary is added the staggering conclusion (v. 56) that Abraham already anticipated and rejoiced in the ministry which Jesus now exercises! This parallels Jesus' claim in a similar "trial" context (5:46) that Moses wrote about him. It is a pointer to Jesus as the goal of Israel's salvation history.

Again the opponents' narrow literalism (8:57) brings incredulity and opens the way for the climax toward which the entire set of speeches has been leading. Using the now familiar divine title "I Am" (v. 58), Jesus proclaims both his temporal and spiritual superiority even to the most revered of Israel's founders. As with Sophia, his preexistent presence with God is the ground for his authoritative speech and claims (cf. Scott 1992: 148-49).

Recognizing the full implications of Jesus' statement (8:59), and in line with the prescriptions of the Torah (Lev 24:16), Jesus' opponents immediately seek to stone him. Since his "hour" has not yet come, he vanishes unharmed from their sight.

John 9:1-41

Like the previous story of the Samaritan woman's encounter with Jesus, the story of the blind man is a carefully constructed drama with several scenes building to a decisive climax. It continues the themes of light, sight, and blindness begun in ch. 8 and functions both as a positive illustration of Jesus' role as "light" and as a negative depiction of his opponents' blindness.

The drama opens with a discussion of the reason for the man's blindness (9:2-3). In connecting suffering with sin the disciples seem to represent a view still held by many in Jesus' day, probably on the basis of OT texts like Exod 20:5, though it is clear from Ezek 18:20 that this was not the only possible view. Jesus infers that the man's blindness provides an opportunity for God's glory to be revealed, not that God caused the man to be born blind to illustrate a point! A similar idea is expressed later in John 11:4.

Using a further "light" metaphor, "night and day" (9:4), Jesus stresses his urgent need (with the disciples — "we") to engage in God's mission before "darkness" falls. Although this is an ominous warning, the reader recalls the opening affirmation that the light cannot be extinguished (1:5), a fact which is reinforced (9:5) by the recollection of the earlier "I Am" saying (8:12).

Jesus' character as "light" is immediately demonstrated in the healing miracle. As at the healing at the poolside (John 5:6), Jesus approaches the man rather than being asked for help. The technique is described in brief detail (9:6-7). It evokes the creation story in its combination of dust and water (Gen 2:6-8), and in the command to bathe it also echoes the story of Naaman's healing by Elisha (2 Kgs 5:10-14). The connection between the removal of blindness and bathing in water was interpreted from earliest times as an allusion to Christian baptism (Brown 1966: 380-82).

The main substance of the chapter is the reaction of various parties to the healing. The first of these groups is the man's neighbors (9:8). There was no indication at the outset that the man was a beggar, but this is a standard feature of such stories in the Synoptic tradition (cf. Mark 10:46) and was the only realistic option for such an invalid in Jesus' day. Confusion as to the man's identity (9:9) echoes previous uncertainties about Jesus and leads to a clear statement from the man himself. He uses the familiar "I Am" (*egō eimi*), but here it has none of the overtones of Jesus' usage.

In response to the neighbors' questioning (9:10-11) the man recalls the process of the miracle. His bland depiction of the healer ("a man called Jesus") is part of the progressive revelatory technique used in the story, whereby the man moves from a position of complete lack of understanding (blindness) toward faith (sight). This is confirmed (v. 12) by his lack of knowledge of Jesus' whereabouts.

The scene changes as the man is brought (by the neighbors?) to the Pharisees (9:13). Pharisees and "Jews" are used interchangeably to describe Jesus' opponents in this story. As in 5:9, we discover only after the miracle that it has taken place on the sabbath (9:14). Although this is significant as an "authority" question, the focus of this dispute is clearly christological. The Pharisees ask the man how he was healed (v. 15) and receive an abbreviated description. Although Jesus is not named in this, it provokes the by now customary division between opponents (v. 16). Some see the alleged breach of sabbath regulations as an indication that he cannot be God's agent, while others recognize the character of the miracle as a "sign" and hint at its godly origin. The division leads them back to the healed man for his opinion on Jesus' status (v. 17). In a close parallel to the developing faith of the Samaritan woman (4:19), he now declares that Jesus is a prophet, perhaps again evoking the work of Elisha.

Jesus' opponents introduce a new dimension with the assertion that the claimed miracle is a fraud (9:18), calling the man's parents to give evidence. The required evidence (v. 19) is given in two parts: (1) they identify their son and confirm that he has been blind since birth (v. 20); (2) they deny knowledge both of the manner of his healing and of the identity of the healer, indicating that their son is of age and can answer for himself (vv. 21, 23). They were not initially asked to name the healer, but their reason for doing so becomes clear from the narrator's aside (v. 22) — they fear expulsion from the synagogue.

Underlying this verse are issues which are crucial for understanding both this story and the portrayal of the "Jews" in the FG as a whole. First, although the parents' reply gives no hint of it, 9:22 presupposes that they both knew the identity of Jesus *and* were ready to confess him as the Christ. This is surprising, given that the man himself still does not recognize Jesus in v. 36. Second, it assumes within Jesus' lifetime a formal decision by his opponents on how to deal with his followers, a situation which seems highly unlikely from a historical perspective. This places the interpretative framework for the story in the realm of the community to which the FG is addressed. The central issues are a *christological* dispute and its real *consequences* for the marginalized group. This verse (along with 12:42; 16:2) is frequently used to contend that the Johannine community is reflecting its recent history in being expelled from the synagogue. Taken, however, with the evidence of inter-*Christian* dispute in the Johannine epistles, the overall use of "Jews" as a group-within-a-group symbol in the FG, the lack of evidence of the *community* being expelled from the synagogue, and the overall purpose of the FG as a document to encourage existing Christians to hold fast to their understanding of Jesus as the Christ (see the comment on

20:31), it is best to read this reference and all other references to "Jews" against the background of a later inter-*Christian* dispute. If that scenario is correct, the threat of expulsion for the Johannine community is really one of isolation from the emergent "mainstream" of the early Christian church.

The scene shifts again to a second "trial" of the healed man (9:24). The opponents use an exclamation echoing the oath of Josh 7:19 (cf. 1 Esdr 9:8), which was used in relation to a confession of guilt (Brown 1966: 374). They make explicit the earlier inference (9:16) that Jesus is a "sinner." The man's reply is noncommittal (v. 25), simply reasserting the fact of his healing. As before, an explanation is demanded for the healing (v. 26). Instead of repeating his earlier description, however, the healed man begins to show his own sense of humor (v. 27), sarcastically asking his inquisitors if they want to become Jesus' disciples! His answer is heavy with irony, functioning as a concise summary of Jesus' whole argument with the same opponents in ch. 8.

The man's sarcasm sparks off a hostile reaction in the opponents (9:28). They accuse him of being a disciple of Jesus and contrast this with their own allegiance to Moses. This is an unusual way of describing the Pharisees, but it evokes the comparison made in the Prologue between Jesus and the Torah (1:17), as becomes clear in the reference to God "speaking" through Moses (9:29). Ironically they confess their own ignorance of Jesus' origins — a point which has already been conceded as indicative of messiahship (7:27)!

The healed man now becomes the spokesperson for Jesus' case (9:30). His tone appears scathing as he upbraids these religious leaders for their failure to discern in such a miracle the hand of God. There is unanimity in the assertion (v. 31) that the prayers of those who willfully sin without repentance go unheard (Pss 66:18-19; 109:1-7). The opposite is surely also true, that those who are obedient to and honor God are heard. The man calls his interrogators to view the evidence (9:32): no record exists in the Jewish scriptures of any such healing of a man *born* blind, even if the prophets see it as a sign of God's coming deliverance. The phrase "since the world began" (NRSV — *ek tou aiōnos*) takes the reader back to the opening of the Prologue, linking the giving of "light" to the man with the very act of creation itself. He rests his case, that Jesus must be from God (v. 33), on the very fact that Jesus was *able* to perform such a creative act.

At this point the opponents have heard enough. They hurl abuse at the man (9:34) by implying that being *born* blind is sufficient sign of his total depravity to render his witness void. In doing so, they reveal their total lack of understanding of the point made by Jesus to the disciples at the outset (v. 3) and fail to discern God's glory. The man's subsequent expulsion is evidence that they understand his words to constitute a recognition of Jesus as the Messiah (cf. v. 22).

After a long absence, Jesus now returns to bring the final scene to a head (9:35). Once again he takes the initiative to find the man, and a cameo of the call to discipleship takes place. In framing the question about himself, the Johannine Jesus uses the title "Son of Man" (some manuscripts have "Son of God"). Lindars lists a number of reasons why this is appropriate (Lindars 1972: 350), but in terms of the developing narrative it allows for a later full confession of Jesus as the Son of God (11:27).

Whatever the Pharisees may have thought of the man's understanding of Jesus' status, his reply (9:36) reveals that he has not yet come to full faith. As a good disciple he wants to increase his knowledge and his faith. As in the case of the Samaritan woman, his role in the drama is a foil for Jesus progressively to reveal more of his identity. It is no surprise, then, that Jesus immediately does so (v. 37), this time using a variation on the "I am" theme appropriate to the circumstances: he declares that the man has now *seen* the "Son of Man." The self-identification formula follows in third person speech.

As might be anticipated, the man finally comes to full confession (9:38) and further falls down in worship before Jesus. This verse is missing from some significant manuscripts, leading to speculation that it is a later liturgical insertion (cf. Brown 1966: 375, 380-81). As it stands in our translations the verse confirms the proper conclusion of the blind man's healing in body and spirit as he comes to full faith.

The final verses reveal that, all along, the Pharisees have been listening in to Jesus' conversation with the man. This makes Jesus' statement (9:39) all the more telling. It is a paraphrase of the sentiment expressed classically in Isa 6:9-10 (cf. John 12:40), but is also much influenced by the story of Sophia's descent into the world with the resulting judgment (Prov 1:20-33). The two parties to the declaration represent two sides of the equation: the blind man, now healed and come to faith, represents those who truly see. The Pharisees, never physically impaired but increasingly obdurate, represent those who are truly blind.

With thorough Johannine irony the Pharisees, unable to see, finally protest their lack of blindness (9:40)! Jesus' reply is damning, for once taking them literally (v. 41). Their lack of physical impairment is matched by an ability also to see the truth of Jesus as the "Light," but their scurrilous refusal to accept it brings its own judgment. With these words this magnificent Johannine literary drama comes to its full conclusion.

John 10:1-21

The opening of ch. 10 brings a change in theme, but no apparent change in audience (10:1) (cf. Brown 1966: 388-90 for discussion). The setting given in 10:22 is the festival of Dedication, which recalled the Maccabean revolt against the "false shepherds" of Israel in the form of the quisling high priests, Menelaus and Jason. The reference to "thieves and bandits" may evoke such memories in an informed reader, but the clearest background is Ezekiel 34.

Two images of Jesus are presented in this passage: (1) as the shepherd who leads sheep through the door to the safety of the fold; (2) as the door by which the sheep enter. They are complementary images rather than contradictory, and may be read in the light of Bishop's remarks concerning the shepherd who lies down at night across the opening of the fold, thus becoming the "door" for the sheep (Bishop 1960: 307-9). The whole section concerns the relationship between God and Jesus and its consequences for both his followers and detractors.

The opening parable contrasts the thief with the shepherd (10:2) by comparing their means of entry into the fold. The picture of the doorkeeper (v. 3) who limits access only to the rightful entrant functions as a further guarantee of the legitimacy of Jesus' words and witness, which have been under scrutiny in the preceding chapters. As the shepherd he is, here by implication, admitted by the doorkeeper of the fold. The intimacy of relationship between leader and disciple is stressed in the notion of recognition through naming. This is beautifully illustrated later in the immediate aftermath of the resurrection (20:16).

Continuing the theme of voice recognition, the parable evokes (10:4) the classic image of the shepherd who walks ahead of the sheep, calling as they follow (Num 27:17; Psalm 23; Ezek 34:11-16). The opposite reaction is to be expected from the sheep when confronted with a strange voice (10:5). This is a jibe at Jesus' opponents, as becomes clear from the later exposition of these verses (vv. 11-13).

The narrator again draws attention to the obtuse hearers (10:6), opening the way for an expansion on both parts of the parable in the form of two "I Am" sayings (Scott 1992: 121-23). First we hear of Jesus as the "Door" (10:7 — or "Gate"). The previous "I Am" sayings have been connected with "signs" of Jesus, but here they function as explanations of the "word," the parable. The idea of Jesus as the "Door" traces several roots, including Jewish apocalyptic notions of the "gate of heaven" and the wisdom theme of Sophia as the means of access to knowledge, life, and salvation. The picture of the "Door" as the point of entry (or not!) fits well with the motif of entering the "kingdom" in the Synoptics.

As the "Door," the Johannine Jesus differs from any previous means of access, or those who have seemed to offer it (10:8). Bultmann is correct in seeing this statement not so much as directed against the Pharisees, but as an affirmation of Jesus' status as the only true, saving revealer (Bultmann 1971: 376-77). This fits well with the overall aim of the FE to present Jesus as the incarnation of Sophia, who has been seen as the "Savior" of Israel (Wisdom 10–11). It is precisely this emphasis on salvation which characterizes the repetition (10:9) of the "Door" theme. Again the life-giver stands in contrast to the thief (v. 10), who is intent only on robbery and murder. The persistent Johannine theme of Jesus Sophia as "life" is thus reiterated as a counter to all pretenders.

The focus now switches to the second image, Jesus as "Shepherd" (10:11). The word "good" *(kalos)* is here synonymous with "true" in other "I Am" sayings. The picture is firmly rooted in the image of God as the true shepherd of Israel in contrast to the false leaders who have failed the people (Ezekiel 34). "Shepherd" is used as a positive royal metaphor in relation to David (Ezek 34:23), or negatively of others in Jewish writings (1 Kgs 22:17; Jer 23:1-6). Significantly it is also used by Philo as a description of both God (*Agr.* 51) and the Logos (*Mut. nom.* 116), who replaces the function of Sophia in descending with God's revelation into the world.

Whichever background the reader finds most compelling for understanding the FG picture, what is completely new here is the slant on the shepherd as self-sacrificial. Lindars rightly sees this as a reference to the passion, as 10:17-18 also make clear (Lindars 1972: 361), and it is likely that the Johannine development owes much to the common early Christian reflection on "suffering servant" imagery from Isaiah.

Like the "Door," the true shepherd stands in contrast to that which is false (10:12). The image is a perfectly natural one drawn from "pastoral" experience, so the "wolf" is best not allegorized. The thrust is made clear by the next verse (v. 13), which stresses the "detached" nature of the hired hand over against the one who owns the sheep.

The repetition of the shepherd imagery (10:14) introduces a new theme and clarifies that "ownership" of the sheep actually implies intimacy of relationship. This familiarity is modeled on Jesus' own relationship with God (v. 15), which we have in turn seen to be parallel to that of Sophia and God. The "sheep" are shown to be those for whom Jesus lays down his life, both now (in story time) and later (in discourse time — v. 16). It is likely that the ideal reader hears "fold" here as a reference to the Jewish followers of Jesus, with "others not of this fold" signifying the Gentiles, who probably make up the majority of the community addressed by the Gospel at the end of the first century AD. The desire for unity among these different groups of disciples is indicated in the oneness of the shepherd and will later emerge as an important Johannine theme (17:20-23).

The monologue returns to the theme of Jesus laying down his life (10:17). We now hear that the intimacy between the shepherd and the sheep is based not merely on Jesus' knowledge of God, but on the *love* which God has for him. Jesus' willing obedience to the mission of God leads to his passion, but that is not the end. In Johannine thought, as Brown puts it, "resurrection is truly the purpose of his death" (Brown 1966: 399). Later we will hear that it is only in this way that the promised Paraclete can come and the believer be empowered to live the continuing life of Jesus in the world (14:15-21, 25-29). For the moment, the emphasis lies on the power which Jesus has over his own destiny (10:18). Far from the picture of Jesus as "victim," which Mark's Gospel presents, or the "good martyr" of Luke's account, the Johannine presentation is, from start to finish, one of Jesus as "victor." As Jesus fulfills God's declared mission, his fate lies in his own and God's trustworthy hands.

The customary reaction of division follows (10:19-21), with some reiterating the claim of madness (8:48, 52) and others referring back to the healing of the blind as a sign that Jesus' words cannot issue from madness. Although it is not easy to see in translation, the word for "blind" here is plural *(typhlōn)*, a reminder that the issue of blindness is wider than the man who was healed. This will become more evident as the next part of the text unfolds.

John 10:22-42

The context of the whole of ch. 10 appears to be that given here (10:22), the festival of Dedication, Hanukkah. The reference to "winter" is correct in terms of the timing of the festival, but it also has "chilling" literary overtones, as the opposition to Jesus mounts further. Jesus appears in the outer part of the temple (v. 23) and is surrounded by the "Jews" (v. 24), now evidently a unified hostile crowd rather than the divided groups from earlier. The scene has strong overtones of the trial before the high priest in Mark's passion account (Mark 14:61-62), with the united group here raising the crucial question of Johannine Christology — Is Jesus truly the Messiah? Since this question is omitted from John's trial account (18:19-23), the section takes on the character of such an event.

Jesus begins his defense with a double reference to his previous words and works (10:25). Since these have been done in God's name, his opponents' refusal to believe is a further indication that they do not belong to the "flock" (v. 26) of which he has just spoken. The recapitulation of the "sheep" theme continues (v. 27) with a reminder of the open ears (they hear) and eyes (they follow) of those who do not share the obstinacy of Jesus' opponents. Their reward for such discipleship is, as before, life, now explicitly called *eternal* life (v. 28).

The issue of eternal life is a frequent theme in the FG (cf. the comments on 3:16-20), but here it is expanded by means of an allusion to the motif of "snatching" in the previous speech (10:12). Entry by the Door, following the true Shepherd, brings a security which is unshakable. The reader knows that this will be mightily reinforced by Jesus' own passion and resurrection, but its guarantee lies also in the promise that *God* (10:29) will ensure such safety for the believer.

The grammar of 10:29 is extremely difficult (see the discussion in Lindars 1972: 369-70), but the sense appears to be that God's pledge to the believer (cf. Ezek 34:28-31) holds good because God is above all, the very origin of life. This fits well with the final declaration of Jesus (10:30), which is actually the answer to the question asked by the "Jews" in v. 24. Although God is acknowledged as greater than Jesus, their unity of will, purpose, knowledge, and mission is the basis of the security of both Jesus' own future and that of the believer. This is a fundamental theme of Johannine Christology and ecclesiology.

Jesus' claim provokes another attempt (cf. 8:59) by the "Jews" to stone him (10:31). This time Jesus does not disappear but faces his attackers with the question as to why they should want to do so (v. 32), reiterating his claim that his work is the work of God. His opponents indicate that they have understood the inference of his claim to oneness with God (v. 33) as an attempt to supplant God's sovereign position, and thus as blasphemous. As always, their reply is heavy with irony since they see Jesus as merely human and as making *himself* God. Jesus, Sophia incarnate, rather claims a unity with God which grows out of engagement in *God's* mission; thus the status accorded to Jesus is God-given, not self-proclaimed (cf. the comments on 5:18).

Jesus now defends himself against the charge of blasphemy (10:34), initially through a quotation of Scripture (Ps 82:6). Clearly this text does not come from the "law" (Torah), the term more generally used here to represent the Scriptures or indeed the opponents' general viewpoint. Jesus' argument (10:35-36) is that if the Scriptures allow that human beings may to some degree at least be thought of as gods, then how much more may he, as the one fulfilling God's mission in the world, be legitimately regarded as the Son of God. Jesus also notes the formality of his mission as "sanctified" (*hēgiasen*) or "dedicated" by God, which is probably an allusion to the setting of the scene in the festival of Dedication (Hanukkah).

The final part of Jesus' defense (10:37-38) returns to the theme of v. 25, namely, Jesus' works. The words have all the pathos of the final appeal of a defendant on trial for his life — precisely what is happening here. The "signs" which Jesus has performed to this point are sufficient evidence of Jesus' true relationship with God, for those who have eyes to see. His opponents remain in the same position as at the end of ch. 9, seeing yet utterly blind. This is evident in their attempt once more to arrest Jesus (10:39). His escape prepares the way for the last, greatest, and most decisive of the "signs."

The final verses (10:40-42) form a bridge to the stories at Bethany, recalling through mention of JBap's work and witness the earliest chapter of the Gospel. The implication is that JBap has now gone, but that his witness concerning Jesus has been shown to be true through all that has happened in between his first appearance and this point of the FG. No indication is given as to the identity of the "many" who come to belief here, but the durability of their faith will be put to the test in what follows.

Witherington is correct in noting the strong connections between this trial scene and the story of Sophia (Witherington 1995: 191). Its significance goes further than he would suggest, in that it is the *Sophia* Christology espoused by the FE which affects the situation of the community to which the FG is addressed. I have maintained throughout that the "Jews" should be seen as symbolic of other Christian groups with which the Johannine community is in conflict rather than as Jewish Christians who have "defected" back to the synagogue. The distancing of the Johannine Jesus here from his opponents ("your law" = "your viewpoint" — 10:34) is another pointer to the situation of dispute, wherein Johannine Christians are defending their christological outlook (Jesus Christ = Jesus, Sophia incarnate) over against that of others who do not share this outlook.

John 11:1-44

The drama enacted between Jesus, Martha, Mary, and Lazarus is the final great word/sign event of the "Book of Signs." It shares many of the narrative patterns set elsewhere in the FG: the conjunction of christological claim with enacted sign; the contrast between obtuse male disciples and paradigmatic women disciples; the growing anger of hostile opponents who refuse to see, reaching its climax in their deadly response (11:45-57).

The setting is Bethany (11:1), not this time "beyond the Jordan" (cf. 1:28 recalled in 10:40), but the place associated with Jesus' stopovers near Jerusalem in the Synoptics (Mark 11:1, 12). Since the place mentioned in John 1:28 is impossible to identify, it seems better to view the name there as a catchword forming a narrative *inclusio*. The place of initial public witness to Jesus is also the place where the final great sign of witness will be accomplished.

The implied reader seems to be "in" on the character setting beforehand, given the proleptic comment concerning Mary's fame (11:2). The mention of Jesus' love for Lazarus (v. 3) has provoked some to argue that he may be seen as the Beloved Disciple (Stibbe 1994: 102-3), but this is unnecessary when viewing the text from the angle of the reciprocal love shown by Sophia and her disciples (Sir 4:12-14). This view is reinforced by the emphasis on Jesus' love for all three siblings (11:5).

Jesus' initial response to the request to come and meet his friend's need might appear callous (11:4), but it shares the same sentiment as his initial reply to his mother's approach at Cana (2:4). He has come to do God's will, not to answer the call of family or friends. The verse is full of irony: Lazarus will die, but the story will not end in his death, but rather in the death of Jesus, which all along is seen as the sign of his glorification. The reader discovers this only as the drama unfolds, so Jesus remains where he is to let things develop (11:6)

Following his short sojourn beyond the Jordan, Jesus proposes a return to the scene of his earlier conflicts (11:7-8). There is no hint yet that this suggestion has anything to do with Lazarus, so the disciples recall the threat posed to his life by the "Jews" (8:59; 10:39). Unlike the rest of the two Bethany scenes, this one shows the "Jews" as the opposition group.

The theme of "light," so much a feature of the previous dialogue and healing story, now returns (11:9-10), making a narrative link between the last two great word/sign pairs of the public ministry. The parable relates closely to the one in 9:4-5 and similarly operates on two levels. Jesus is the Light (8:12; 9:5), so the disciples are safe in his presence despite their fear. Yet there is urgency because his "hour" will soon mark the end of the daylight, ushering a dangerous period of night. This sets an interpretative framework for the ironic twists of life and death which follow in the "sign" and in the passion narrative.

The attention now focuses on the real reason for the return to Judea — the death of Lazarus and his subsequent reawakening (11:11). This little cameo shows the male disciples at their most obtuse, unable to grasp that Lazarus is dead (v. 12), never mind what Jesus is about to do! The narrator deliberately draws attention to their reaction (vv. 13-14) to enable the reader to see the curious contrast between the disciples' lack of perception and the insight of Martha later in the story.

The seeming indifference of Jesus to the death of his friend (11:15) parallels his reaction in v. 4 and for the same reason. The tragedy is being played out to the full for a higher purpose, that Jesus may be fully revealed and elicit faith from his followers in the short time now remaining. Those disciples, represented by the skeptical Thomas, still do not understand what is to come (11:16). As so often in the FG, he declares the truth without realizing it as he announces the forthcoming death of Jesus.

We approach the heart of the story with Jesus' arrival at Bethany (11:17-18). The finality of Lazarus's end is underlined by the indication of the period of time since his death — decay has set in (cf. v. 39). The proximity to Jerusalem allows many "Jews" to attend, though their presence does not apparently indicate a threat (v. 19). Certainly, no attempt is made to arrest him in line with the previous decree of the rulers. The number of mourners, along with other incidental details of the two Bethany stories, probably indicates that the family group is fairly wealthy and of high social status (cf. Witherington 1995: 200).

At this point (11:20) Martha enters the drama, anxious to remonstrate with Jesus over the delay. It has often been observed that the characterization of Martha as active and Mary as the more passive sister, attentive to Jesus' feet (!), resembles the mention of these women in Luke 10:38-42. This is only partially true since the FE gives no indication that Mary's role is prized over her sister's part. Indeed, it is Martha who engages in theological discussion with Jesus, while Luke portrays Mary as the one who soaks in the proffered wisdom.

As in the previous story of the Samaritan woman's encounter with Jesus, we see in Martha's dialogue with Jesus a blossoming of faith/understanding (cf. Scott 1992: 198-207). Her initial words do seem to chide Jesus (11:21-22), but even so she indicates that in the person of Jesus she discerns the presence of God. This evokes a bold assertion from Jesus (v. 23) that the outcome for Lazarus will be life in place of death. Martha does not yet grasp the *present* reality of this claim, but shows her theological insight by representing a form of contemporary Jewish eschatological outlook (v. 24). Barrett may be correct in suggesting that her position here also corresponds to that of the Johannine community whom the FE wants to address again with the full christological claim (Barrett 1978: 395).

Jesus replies with another of the "I Am" sayings (11:25), which again demonstrates how, as Sophia incarnate, he supersedes all previous expectations. The latter part of the verse indicates that the emphasis in this phrase lies on Jesus Sophia's life-giving power and brings into dramatic focus all the previous statements, begun already in the opening verses of the Prologue, concerning life. We have noted how these correspond directly to the claims of Sophia in the wisdom tradition. Strictly speaking, the notion of resurrection goes beyond anything said before and points forward to Jesus' own experience rather than to the resuscitation of Lazarus. Since the very word "resurrection" already implies that death must have taken place, the reference to "never dying" (11:26) must be to the spiritual relationship established between Jesus and the believer.

Jesus asks Martha if she really believes what he has said. Her response (11:27) is the most astonishing piece of reinterpretation of Christian tradition found anywhere in this remarkable Gospel. Martha's confession both replaces the classic Petrine confession at Caesarea Philippi (cf. Mark 8:29) and expresses fully the faith toward which the FG directs itself (cf. 20:31). Consistent with the role of women disciples elsewhere in the FG, Martha demonstrates how a true disciple confesses faith in Jesus.

Martha now sets out to bring her sister to the encounter with Jesus (11:28). There is no hint of Jesus' having asked for Mary, so either we must assume it as an unreported part of the preceding dialogue, or it represents a "calling" to Mary. This latter suggestion is not outlandish given the setting of exemplary discipleship. If we understand it in this way, Mary's response (v. 29) is both immediate and appropriate.

What has transpired in private (*lathra* — 11:28) now becomes public (vv. 30-31) as the crowd of mourners follows Mary to meet with Jesus. She expresses exactly the same frustration as her sister concerning Jesus' tardiness (v. 32), though without Martha's additional expression of hope. This does not mean she lacks faith, as the speed of her coming to Jesus and her prostration indicate. She openly expresses her emotion (11:33), evoking a similar response in Jesus. The text literally implies that Jesus was angry *(enebrimēsato),* a strange choice of word. It is qualified by the following verb "deeply shaken" *(etaraxen)* and so is best read as an expression of the depth of Jesus' feelings in the face of the grief surrounding him. It does not represent indignation at a lack of faith, which might be construed as present in Mary.

Jesus asks to see the burial place (11:34). Lindars notes the connection between Jesus' question and the angel's words in the traditional resurrection account in Mark 16:6, allowing the reader an echo of what is to come in Jesus' own experience (Lindars 1972: 399). The reply of the mourners is ironic since it echoes the call to encounter life as disciples (1:39, 46; 4:29), but it is here used of an invitation to view death.

Jesus' emotion is again emphasized (11:35), allowing for the FE to express the by now common divided reaction of onlookers to Jesus (vv. 36-37). For some it is an expression of the depth of his *agapē* for Lazarus, still with no hint of what is to come. For others it indicates his impotence in the face of death, despite his previous power in healing the blind man. Again the FG stresses that faith built only on "signs" cannot perceive the truth about Jesus.

Jesus now proceeds to the tomb (11:38). Many of the details of this story parallel those of Jesus' own death, burial, and resurrection, the mention of the stone over the entrance being but one. Martha's shock at Jesus' command to remove the stone (v. 39) is frequently taken as proof that her earlier expression of faith was only temporary and incomplete. This view does not take the narrative seriously since to this point Jesus has given no indication to the sisters or the mourners that he intends to raise Lazarus. In his grief he is assumed to wish to view the body of his dead friend, and Martha's protest is quite natural. Only following her objection does Jesus introduce the question of faith (v. 40). It is noticeable that the precise question is one which only the disciples would recognize, since it was to them at the beginning of the story that Jesus spoke of seeing God's glory and coming to faith (vv. 4, 15). Finally, they (the disciples?) obey the command (v. 41).

The story reaches its climax as Jesus first prays then commands Lazarus to come out of the tomb. The prayer is not for power to do the miracle since it takes the form of a thanksgiving. Instead it is intended for the benefit of the as yet unpersuaded bystanders (11:42). It is both a public illustration of Jesus' oneness with God and a reminder of the purpose of his mission — sent by God into the world to evoke belief.

The miracle does not require touch but is a perfect example of the power of the Word in action. The FE describes Jesus' action as shouting out (*ekraugasen* — 11:43), a rare NT expression. It is striking that this is the verb used both of the fickle crowd in praise of Jesus (12:13) and of the crowd who demand Jesus' death in the trial scene (18:40; 19:6, 15). With a typical sense of irony the FE makes what is a word of death in the mouth of others a word of life in the mouth of Jesus. It is a precise illustration of Jesus' promise in 5:25, 28-29.

Lazarus finally emerges from the tomb (11:44). Though there are many points of similarity, unlike the risen Jesus, Lazarus is still bound in the burial clothes and has to be released. The raising of the dead man is, after all, but a sign of the truth of the christological claim (v. 25) which Jesus Sophia has already made — "the one who finds me finds life" (Prov 8:35).

John 11:45-54

The raising of Lazarus provokes the now familiar divided response among the audience (11:45-46). The portrayal of the "Jews" is still by no means uniform even at this late stage in the plot, with some believing and others acting as spies for the Jerusalem rulers. The reports of the latter group lead to the summoning of a meeting of the Sanhedrin (v. 47). Here the decisive conspiracy leading to Jesus' death is hatched and outlined.

It is not the Lazarus miracle alone which leads to the scheming, but the sum of the "signs" which calls for action. The danger is framed in political terms (v. 48), the inference being that belief in Jesus as Messiah would mean a definitive rejection of the authority of Rome. "Messiah" is thus defined as a religio-political title. Part of the irony of this account, written well after the siege and destruction of Jerusalem by Rome in AD 68-70, is that the reader knows the futility of this statement! The word "place" *(topos)* is not qualified in Greek by the word "holy," and in line with the irony outlined may well be a more general reference to the whole city of Jerusalem rather than just the temple.

The high priest, Caiaphas, now enters the scene (11:49). His contribution is the greatest irony yet in a Gospel full of it. Proclaiming the ignorance of others, he goes on to display his own, supposing his declaration of Jesus' impending death a shrewd political move (v. 50). The knowledgeable reader is already aware, however, not only of the ultimate vanity of Caiaphas's attempts to placate Rome but also that the high priest's declaration has the greatest *theological* and *soteriological* significance rather than merely displaying political adroitness. The FE makes this explicit (vv. 51-52) with a veiled reference to the "shepherding" role revealed by Jesus earlier. While this may, on the level of the unfolding Gospel narrative, refer to the scattering of the disciples, it surely also prefigures the role of Jesus in pushing the notion of the chosen "children of God" beyond the boundaries of Israel in the Gentile mission.

The finality of the plot is outlined (11:53), but Jesus retires to the boundaries of the desert, avoiding the immediate wrath of the "Jews" (v. 54). The town of Ephraim is difficult to locate with certainty, but it is probably the same as that mentioned in 2 Sam 13:23 (cf. Lindars 1972: 409-10). The scene is set for the final stages of Jesus' public ministry.

John 11:55–12:11

The story of the anointing by Mary has often been considered a hopeless mixture of sources, given its apparent combination of Mark's anointing with oil and Luke's bathing of feet. However, far from being a confused story, this is one of the most skillful of Johannine dramatic presentations, consistent with the picture of women as paradigmatic disciples found elsewhere in the FG.

The story has literal parallels with Mark 14:3 (the oil of nard; fragrance filling the house), the rare wording being cited as a compelling argument for the FE's knowledge of either Mark's Gospel itself or traditions used by Mark. The imagery, however, shows more affinity with Luke 7:38 in its description of anointing feet. Although the reader will become fully aware of the implications of Mary's action only at a later stage, she is seen here to fulfill the desire of Jesus for disciples to serve one another, expressed precisely through the washing of *feet* (John 13:12-17). The anointing becomes both a literary and a theological precursor of footwashing and needs to be read in that light (Scott 1992: 207-16).

The modern chapter division may conceal the setting of the anointing (11:55-57) from the reader. The plot to arrest Jesus reaches its head in a general "order" from the opposing authorities to betray his whereabouts. The third Passover in the FG account (cf. 2:13; 6:4) will be the time when the "hour" will be fulfilled for Jesus, so despite the massive number of pilgrims who would have come to Jerusalem for the feast, the FE wants to give the impression that Jesus is the center of attention.

Jesus returns to Bethany, where a meal is given in his honor with all the siblings present (12:1-2). The presence of Lazarus is a reminder of the preceding events and their affirmation of Jesus as the one in whom life is truly found. It might seem appropriate for Lazarus to be the one serving Jesus at this point, but it is Martha who takes the role. The verb "to serve" *(diakoneō)* is rare in the FG (cf. 12:26). By the time of writing of the FG it was an established term describing an office of ministry in some parts of the church. If taken with the precise dating on a Sunday, a eucharistic overtone may be intended for the whole event (Schneiders 1982: 42). Martha's credentials as an exemplary disciple are underlined in this brief aside.

Mary anoints Jesus' feet (12:3) in a scene described in some detail. Her action is certainly meant to appear extravagant, involving an excessive amount (a pound) of expensive perfume (*myron* is not simply "oil"). The effect is dramatic, filling the entire house with the smell. Loosing her hair to wipe the ointment implies not only a somewhat messy picture but also one with a quasi-erotic tone. It is a measure of the devotion and love of the disciple for Jesus.

The contrast between Mary's exemplary, anticipatory action as a disciple and that of the traditional male disciple Judas could hardly be more stark (12:4). Once again he is introduced as the one who betrayed Jesus, emphasizing the prior knowledge of the implied reader. His feigned (allegedly!) concern for the poor (v. 5) merely serves the narrative by pointing to the costly sacrifice which Mary has made. It also allows the narrator the opportunity for an astonishing sideswipe at Judas (v. 6). The FE never reports the Synoptic tradition concerning payment for Judas's act of betrayal, primarily because it is seen as a result of two things: first, it is a response to the "order" of the religious authorities (11:57); second, it is because of Judas's possession by Satan (13:27). The idea that he stole from the common purse may reflect a tradition that he was motivated by greed, but in narrative terms it functions as an ironic reinforcement of the contrast between true and false disciples (cf. 10:7-13)

Jesus takes up the defense of the true disciple (12:7), interpreting her action as a preparation for his death. This would be less strange if the anointing at burial was missing in the FG, but it is not (19:39-40). Lindars is thus correct in stating that Mary "has performed a prophetic act" (Lindars 1972: 419). With true Johannine irony, the one who has been given new life (Lazarus) witnesses the seal of death being set on his life-giver by his own sister. Equally so, in her self-giving, potentially humiliating action she is pointing forward to the marker of discipleship which Jesus himself will indicate around the table with his followers (13:1-20).

The final part of Jesus' response (12:8 — missing in some important manuscripts) needs to be read in the light of the whole Gospel story and not as an excuse for personal extravagance at the expense of the poor. It reflects the immediate fate of Jesus and the proper celebration of his presence. It also stands as a rebuke of the false attitude of Judas, seen as the real defrauder of the poor in the story.

The appearance of the "Jews" as seekers after Jesus (12:9-11) undermines any easy picture of the term as representing an escalating opposition group. There is a hint that their "faith" here is still inadequately based on "signs" since they also want to see the man at the center of the miracle, Lazarus. There is a double irony in their ignorance, as they now place the lives of both the miracle worker and the recipient of the miracle in peril.

John 12:12-19

The entry of Jesus into Jerusalem is one of a small number of texts which have direct parallels in the Synoptic tradition. As always the Johannine version, though sharing common features, is quite independent in its presentation, not least in its conclusion. Although this story has often been interpreted as a sign of Jesus' kingship, the purpose of the Johannine narrative is precisely to subvert, or at least reinterpret this view (cf. Scott 1994: 184-88).

Unlike the Synoptic picture, the initial focus of the story is on the crowd (12:12), who have assembled for the Passover and anticipate Jesus' arrival. It is they who "go out" (*exēlthon,* v. 13) to meet Jesus, ready to hail him as the messianic King. They carry palm branches, a detail supplied only by the FE and probably meant to alert the reader to potential political implications (cf. Witherington 1995: 220-21). Their cry is a quotation of Ps 118:26, appropriately a song of pilgrimage associated with the festival, though it may also have had some messianic overtones (*m. Tehillim* 224a).

Only after the crowd have hailed him does Jesus find a young donkey (12:14) on which to sit. This is immediately followed (12:15) by an explanatory quotation, apparently from Zech 9:9 but certainly influenced by Zeph 3:14-20, being both shortened and edited. Gone is all the warlike paraphernalia associated with a triumphant King; instead we find only reference to the young donkey. This is a symbol to the reader that Jesus enters the city in peace and without any hint of a political coup.

The narrator now interrupts the flow to offer an aside (12:16), indicating that even Jesus' closest followers misinterpreted the event as it happened. It also reveals that the application of Scripture to Jesus' ministry was very much part of the *post*resurrection community's response to the events of his life.

We now learn (12:17-18) that the crowd which has gone out to hail Jesus as king consists largely of those who had seen his "sign" at Bethany. The scene bears all the same hallmarks as the earlier attempt to make Jesus king following a "sign" (6:15), an overture rejected at that juncture. The placing of the scene immediately following the anointing story, in which *feet* rather than *head* have been the focus, is a clever editorial move by the FE, since the two stories function as a narrative comment on each other. Jesus is not anointed as king (head) any more than he claims kingship (the *crowd* do so). In a Gospel which avoids the language of "kingdom," Jesus is only ironically portrayed as King, a fact which will emerge strongly in the trial before Pilate.

The story ends (12:19) with the Pharisees once more expressing exasperation. As ever, there is irony even in this, since they declare the truth of the universal character of Jesus' mission.

John 12:20-36a

The last two sections of ch. 12 form the conclusion to Jesus' public ministry, a farewell to the world, to be followed by an extended farewell to his closest followers (John 13–17). The appearance of "Greeks" (= Gentiles) here (12:20) points to the nature of Jesus' whole mission as universal. The practice of large numbers of Gentiles attending the Passover is attested by Josephus (*J.W.* 6.427).

It is perhaps because of his Greek name that they seek out Philip (12:21), but it also functions as a narrative echo of Philip's earlier missionary role (1:45). The Greeks request to "see" Jesus, and though it might be inferred from 12:29 that they do, the text does not make it clear. Philip's reaction (v. 22) is to go with Andrew to Jesus and report the interest of the Gentiles.

The coming of the Greeks symbolizes the whole world seeking after Jesus and thus brings the decisive moment toward which the Gospel has been moving — the "hour" announced at the beginning (2:4) now arrives (12:23). What follows in the passion and resurrection will be Jesus' "glorification." This is described through a parabolic saying (12:24) about grain, applied initially to Jesus' own life and subsequently to the disciples. Given that the FE tends to introduce traditional material through the use of the "double amen" (NRSV — "very truly"), the grain saying may relate to similar (though not identical) material in the Synoptics (e.g., Mark 4:3-8). That Jesus' death will yield "much fruit" is already indicated in the symbolism of the coming Gentiles, foreshadowing the Gentile mission of the early church.

Readiness to give up all is also a feature of the true follower (12:25-26), whose model *and* goal is Jesus (Lindars 1972: 430). This theme will be much expanded in the more intimate farewell speeches, but for the moment the indication is that the disciples' task will be to continue the mission of Jesus, with all its potential pitfalls, in the world. The saying of v. 25 has numerous Synoptic parallels (Dodd 1963: 338-43), notably Mark 8:35, but the intensity of choice confronting the disciple is marked by the Johannine "love–hate" contrast. Though "service" is the image used here, the FE will later clarify that "friendship" is the model for interpreting the role of "servant" (15:15).

Much of this passage reflects the Synoptic accounts of the agony in Gethsemane (cf. Matt 26:37-38), nowhere more so than in 12:27. It opens with a quotation from the Psalms, most probably Ps 6:3 (cf. Ps 42:6). The word "troubled" ("violently disturbed" — *tetaraktai*) reflects the severity of the struggle. The Johannine Jesus, however, remains typically in control, with an almost detached semipublic pondering of his options. He seems to accept the coming passion as the goal of God's mission.

The coming glorification of Jesus will serve its true end — giving glory to God (12:28). This is a process already begun in Jesus' words and signs ("have glorified"), now being brought to fulfillment in his death ("will glorify"). The voice from heaven echoes the Synoptic baptism stories (Mark 1:11), though the purpose is different. Since the Greek word "voice" (*phōnē*) can simply mean "sound," the confusion of the crowd (12:29) is not altogether surprising. God's voice can be described as "thunder" (cf. 1 Sam 7:9-10), but this irony seems lost on the crowd. Others understand in part that it is a heavenly message of support, but fail to see that it is for *their* benefit (12:30) rather than for Jesus' edification. The FE has Jesus clarify this in much the same way as at Lazarus's tomb (11:42).

The crisis (*krisis* = judgment) point has now come (12:31), and it is the beginning of the end for the "ruler of this world." This phrase surely refers to Satan (cf. 1 John 5:19), but there may also be an ironic hint at the powerlessness of the Roman state, despite all indications to the contrary, to overcome the effect of Jesus' ministry in word and sign. It is from the world rather than from heaven that expulsion happens. The counterpart to this casting out is the "lifting up" of Jesus (12:32), making explicit the identification of Jesus with the Son of Man. Jesus replaces the present ruler, not by force but by an attractive appeal ("draw"), which will be all-encompassing ("all people"). For any readers still wavering in their faith, the narrator (12:33) makes the connection of "lifting up" with crucifixion explicit.

The misunderstanding of the crowd continues to the end (12:34), even though they seem to be aware of Jesus' impending death! The belief in a Messiah who remains forever is indicated in the intertestamental writings (e.g., *1 Enoch* 49:1), but it is already implicit in texts which the early church took to be messianic (e.g., Isa 9:6-7). The basis of the crowd's question thus seems to be: "How can someone about to be crucified be the Messiah?" He does not fit any known expectations, allowing the blind man's question to arise again (cf. 9:36).

In the final words of Jesus to the world (12:35-36a), it is the theme from the blind man's story, and indeed the Prologue, which returns — light and darkness. Jesus the Light is entering the time of darkness (passion), when even his followers will stumble. The reader, as a child of the light, knows, however, that "the darkness cannot overcome it" (1:5). Jesus Sophia, who has brought the light of God's revelation into the world, now withdraws, leaving in darkness those who will not believe.

John 12:36b-50

In line with his own previous predictions and with the pilgrimage of Sophia, Jesus withdraws from the world (12:36b). The reason for this is made immediately clear by the narrator (12:37) — the lack of proper response to Jesus' work in the world, again a direct parallel to the experience of Sophia (Prov 1:29-30; *1 Enoch* 42:1-2) (Scott 1992: 159). It is seen as a fulfillment of Scripture by the FE, who sums up Jesus' reception in two quotations from Isaiah, the first (12:38) from Isa 53:1. Part of a "suffering servant" passage, the FG understands it as an indication of the actuality of the lack of belief (Lindars 1972: 437-38).

The narrator then goes on (12:39) to supply a Scripture outlining the reason for this unbelief (the comment refers *forward* to the second quotation, while the NRSV mistakenly refers it back!). This time (v. 40) the text is from Isa 6:10, as we have already noted, a quotation fundamental to the FE's understanding of the theme of blindness (cf. 9:39). Isa 6:9-10 was widely used in early Christian literature to explain the reason for Israel's refusal to accept Jesus (cf. Mark 4:12; Acts 28:26-27). Here the FE is trying to indicate that the whole sequence of events leading to Jesus' death was far from random. Rather, it was part of the scheme by which God, in Jesus, would bring salvation to all, something seen already (12:41) by the prophet.

At this point it might appear as though no one from among Jesus' contemporaries was capable, by some divine determination, of belief in him. The FE is quick to indicate the contrary (12:42) but sees fear as the compelling motif which prevented any from intervening, despite their influential positions. This offers an explanation in advance for the lack of support for Jesus in his trial and sentencing. The repeated suggestion (cf. the comments on 9:22) that belief in Jesus would lead to expulsion from the synagogue highlights the *christological* nature of the dispute in which the Johannine community finds itself. The understanding of Jesus the Christ as the incarnation of Sophia is at stake for the reader of the FG. It is the glory *(doxa)* which she revealed from God (Wis 7:26; 9:11) which is revealed now in the Johannine Jesus (12:43). This glory far outshines the "praise" *(doxa)* which human beings offer, even if they do in some sense share a common heritage (Jew or Christian).

The final verses of the chapter offer a brief summary of Jesus' teaching, apparently addressed exclusively to the reader, Jesus having already retired from the world (12:36b). The scene is highly reminiscent of the wisdom tradition, where Sophia cries aloud (v. 44) to an unspecified audience (Prov 1:20-21; 8:1-3), offering her wisdom and the way to salvation. The content also reflects the strong parallels between the two figures.

Jesus Sophia points not to himself but to God, in whom belief is urged. He has been sent into the world (12:45) to reveal God to those with eyes to see (cf. Wis 9:10). That revelation is possible because of his character as light (12:46 — Wis 7:26), which is able to penetrate the obscurity of human failing. His purpose in entering the world is to offer salvation (12:47 — Wisdom 10–11), rather than to judge, but that judgment will ultimately take its inevitable course for those who reject the words he has spoken (12:48 — Prov 1:29-31). This is because the words which he speaks are not his own but those of God, upon whose mission he has come (12:49 — Prov 8:35-36; Sir 4:11-19; Wis 9:9-18). That mission issues in life, indeed, *eternal* life for those who believe (12:50 — Wis 8:13).

This summary, which ties Jesus so closely to traditions concerning Sophia, rounds off the first section of the Gospel. It is rightly set in a kind of "limbo" as far as the audience is concerned, since it both looks back as a précis and also prepares the way forward to the intimacy of the farewell discourses.

John 13:1-20

Having turned from public ministry in the world, the Johannine Jesus now begins the long farewell from his intimate circle of friends (John 13–17). It is important to see this series of speeches in their proper context in order to make sense of the whole. This has been well set out recently by Witherington, who rightly identifies the setting and style as that of a Greco-Roman banquet at which a Sage offers parting wisdom to his guests (Witherington 1995: 231-34). This picture fits well with our overall reading of the FE's portrait of Jesus as Sophia incarnate (cf. Prov 9:5-6, where Sophia hosts a meal for her disciples). In line with Paul's teaching in 1 Corinthians 11–14, the Johannine interpretation of the meal also subverts the rigid social stratification which characterized such events in Roman society, here through the footwashing incident.

While I value Witherington's analysis, he is wrong in his notion that the passage serves the "missionary" purpose of the FG. Since it is my contention that the FG is primarily aimed at encouraging the existing Johannine Christian to *continue* in faith (cf. comments on 20:30-31), the primary aim of the meal and discourses would be to exhort the disciple to remain true even in the face of betrayal from within, a prominent feature of the Johannine reports. There is also a call to continue in the task of witness, but this will be issued in the consciousness of potential persecution from one's own kind, of whom Judas is representative (thus "synagogue" in story time = "other Christians" in discourse time). For the Johannine community, the persecution arises out of a christological dispute, especially over the Johannine view of Jesus as Sophia incarnate.

Unlike the Synoptic meal stories, the Johannine account takes place before the Passover celebrations (13:1). This is an indeterminate designation, probably implying that its setting is the week leading up to the Passover itself, but not the Passover eve. The reason for this becomes clear in the later condemnation of Jesus (19:14-16). The reader is reminded of Jesus' love for his disciples, which goes "to the end." There is a double emphasis in this, it being true both temporally and in its extent ("to the utmost degree"). This is again reminiscent of Sophia's relationship with God (Wis 7:28) and her disciples (Prov 8:17; Sir 4:14) (cf. Scott 1992: 140-43, 199-200).

The counterpart to Jesus' love is Judas's evil intent (13:2), which runs as an undercurrent throughout the scene. It is the clearest sign yet of the *internal* nature of the Johannine community's struggle with high-profile betrayal. It is at the most intimate of occasions ("during supper") that treachery strikes. For the FE this can only be the work of the devil. Despite the presence of this evil, the whole of the Johannine passion is characterized by the image of Jesus as in control of his destiny. The narrator (v. 3) now announces that Jesus' fate is in his own hands. It is placed in the context of the overall Johannine wisdom schema of descent into and withdrawal from the world.

The footwashing itself begins with Jesus assuming the role of a servant (13:4), disrobing and donning a towel. The description of both the preparation and the execution of the act (13:5) bears close comparison with 12:3, of which it is both a narrative and a theological echo. Footwashing was a common practice in Jewish households (e.g., Luke 7:44), and it could be refused as a task by Jewish servants as too menial (*Midr. Mekilta,* Exod 21:2). It was, however, sometimes performed by the guests themselves, or on occasions by disciples in honor of their master (cf. Brown 1966: 564-65).

Peter interrupts the sequence of footwashing (13:6), incredulous at the anachronistic role reversal. Jesus' comment in reply (v. 7) both underlines the motif of disciple misunderstanding which Peter typifies in the FG, and serves to point forward to the event's significance as an act of cleansing for Peter's later denial of Jesus. To some degree this latter role is undermined by the addition of 21:15-19.

Peter now openly refuses the washing (13:8) because he cannot accept the image Jesus presents of the servant Messiah. Jesus' reply picks up the emphatic nature of Peter's rebuff by underlining that Peter can have *no* part in the legacy to come without receiving this action. The language here reflects the notion of a shared inheritance, which also emerges at other points in the following discourses (14:2-3).

The irony of Peter's response (13:9) indicates his continuing misunderstanding. He thinks that more washing will guarantee his place in Jesus' heritage, not seeing that it is symbolic of another deeper reality. This emerges in Jesus' comment (v. 10), which takes the form of a short wisdom/proverbial saying. The text is rather difficult due to manuscript variations, but its meaning turns on the illustration of the saying — "a person who has had a ritual bath at home before coming to the dinner only needs to have his feet washed on arrival" (Lindars 1972: 451).

Given the refusal of Jesus to bathe the whole body, the focus cannot be on baptism. Instead, the saying illustrates how Jesus' coming, once-for-all action in his death and resurrection obviates the need for further major cleansing! The washing of feet, a necessary daily ritual, may then be read as the need for ongoing forgiveness of sin (cf. 20:23). To underline the irony of Peter's lack of understanding, the narrator once again reminds the reader (13:11) of Judas's coming act of betrayal, which continues to mark him out as unclean, despite his washing.

Having finished washing all their feet (13:12), Jesus dresses and returns to the meal to address the group. What appears as a question in the NRSV — "Do you understand?" — is probably better read as an imperative: "Understand what I have done," since the following monologue is an explanation of his action. The disciples are right to recognize his role as teacher and leader (v. 13), another overlap of function with Sophia (cf. Scott 1992: 152-57), but this will have consequences given the nature of the action (vv. 14-15). It is not that Jesus is instituting a "rite" of some kind which the disciples must slavishly reproduce. This reading would be quite out of character with a Gospel which shows no explicit interest in ritual, sacramental acts. Rather, it is the same exemplary self-giving and humility which are called out from those who follow Jesus.

The monologue moves to underline this ethical lesson (13:16) with a traditional saying, highlighted by the "double amen." In Matt 10:24, this appears in a context dealing with the coming persecution of Jesus' followers, and these overtones may still be heard in the Johannine setting. The humility of Jesus is, after all, revealed finally in his death. To understand this and carry it through (13:17) is to receive God's benediction ("blessing").

Again attention turns to the betrayer (13:18-19), known already to the reader if not to the participants in the meal. Jesus has already shown supernatural insight concerning his followers (1:47-48; 4:17-18), so no hint can be given that he was taken unawares by Judas's subsequent action. It is the fulfillment of a scripture which speaks of the ultimate betrayal of a "bosom friend" (Ps 41:9, NRSV). The fact that Jesus can reveal this in advance is another indication of his divine claim ("I Am" — *egō eimi*).

The final verse (13:20) uses traditional material (cf. Mark 9:37; Luke 10:16) as a reminder of the God-given nature of both Jesus' and the disciples' mission. It is a further echo of the relationship between Sophia and her emissaries (Prov 9:1-6; Wis 7:26–8:18), whereby their reception mirrors her acceptance by God.

John 13:21-30

Following the footwashing, the FE recounts the horror of the intimate scene in which the betrayer finally makes his move. This has often been viewed as the Johannine version of the last supper, but this is certainly not the way that the FE presents it. Undoubtedly there is material which is directly parallel to (and probably dependent on) Mark 14:17-20, and there are many similarities of setting, but in the FG Jesus himself is broken as the Passover offering, so a symbolic representation of this would be preemptory here.

Once again Jesus is "deeply troubled" (13:21; cf. 11:33; 12:27), here over the tragedy of intimate betrayal. As usual the double amen introduces traditional material, this time a direct quotation of Mark 14:18. Jesus witnesses the announcement of the forthcoming treachery (NRSV's "declared" misses this point) in a formal, quasi-judicial manner. Still the disciples show no understanding of the situation (13:22), even if the reader understands.

At this point the "Beloved Disciple" (= BD) makes his first appearance (13:23). He is said to be "reclining" at table, a motif indicative of the Greco-Roman style of meal, albeit within a Jewish setting. No figure in the FG has been the subject of more speculation than he, various attempts having been made to identify him with John the apostle, Lazarus (most recently Stibbe 1994: 97ff.), Mark, and even the apostle Paul (for details see Lindars 1972: 31-34)!! Such efforts miss the point that the disciple is deliberately unnamed because of his literary-theological function as an ideal representative. He *may* have been a historical figure, but this is irrelevant to the narrative consideration of the FE.

Critical here is the use of Gk. *kolpos,* "bosom," a fact completely obscured by the NRSV. It is a direct narrative echo of the same word (similarly obscured!) in 1:18. Just as Jesus rested in the "bosom" of God in the beginning, so, too, the ideal disciple rests in Jesus' "bosom." It is part of the whole Johannine schema, based on Sophia tradition, of the parallel relationship between God, Jesus, and the disciple.

Peter has to inquire as to the identity of the betrayer through the aegis of the BD (13:24). The ideal disciple is consistently portrayed as in a more intimate relationship with Jesus than is Peter. No particular preference is given to Peter in the FG, his role, as we have seen, being at points considerably played down (11:27). The BD inquires of Jesus (13:25) in words reminiscent of the disciple group in Mark 14:19.

Jesus obliquely announces the identity of the betrayer (13:26), though to whom is not initially clear. The later confusion over Judas's departure suggests that it could only be, at best, the BD and Peter to whom this revelation was made. The report of dipping the bread shows a close affinity with Mark 14:20, but for the FE it is made the more poignant in that Jesus himself dips the bread rather than Judas. Lindars notes that this is a "mark of special favour" (Lindars 1972: 458), heightening the horrific intimacy of the treachery.

This is the decisive point for Judas, who is possessed by Satan (cf. Luke 22:3), and is sent out at Jesus' command to fulfill his critical "mission" (13:27). Again the FE portrays Jesus as fully in control of the situation. Astonishingly, the disciples, including Peter and the BD, still do not grasp what is happening (v. 28), though the reader is quite clear by now. Some refer back to Judas's role in 12:5-6 as the keeper of the community money box (13:29), thinking he may be making a customary Passover gift to the poor (Jeremias 1966: 54). The opinion of others, that Judas may be buying provisions for Passover, indicates that the FE sees the scene as quite clearly predating that event.

Judas goes out at Jesus' command (13:30), and, with characteristic Johannine dramatic style, the narrator informs the reader that it is "night." Darkness has finally arrived in its attempt to extinguish the light, both in the literal terms of story time and in theological terms.

John 13:31-38

The departure of Judas signals the beginning of Jesus' glorification (13:31). There is a sense of "light" in the theme of glory, which contrasts immediately with the "night" of the previous verse. God's glory has been revealed in Jesus' ministry, and Jesus now looks forward, on the basis of their mutuality of knowledge, purpose, and will, to receiving glory from God (13:32). Although it is not yet complete, it can be thought of as happening swiftly enough to be described as "at once."

The disciples are addressed intimately as "little children" (13:33), a phrase commonly used in 1 John to identify the beleaguered community of disciples. The FE deliberately takes the reader back to 8:21, but with a significant omission. The departure of Jesus does not spell disaster for the believers, as the following discourse will indicate (14:1-27). The announcement is very much in line with the picture of Jesus as Sophia, who withdraws from the world, bringing judgment on those who have not received her (Prov 1:29-31; *1 Enoch* 42:1-2). Jesus again stresses the brevity of time left before his departure, a theme which evokes the prophetic hope of God's swift salvation (Isa 10:25; Jer 51:33).

Jesus leaves a legacy with the disciples — a "new" commandment (13:34). It is not entirely "new," the substance already being firmly present in Lev 19:18! It is, however, framed very much in Johannine language, where, above all, such "love" (*agapē*) is demonstrated by Jesus (11:3, 5, 36). The prior footwashing also points to the interpretation of "love" as an *active* engagement rather than a mere emotional response.

Although the FG is addressed primarily to encourage continuing belief in the disciples, they are reminded that their mutual love will also function as an important witness (13:35) to the world around. The disciples are the continuing presence of Jesus in the world (20:22), and as such they must fully reflect his way of being.

Peter now picks up the question of Jesus' destination (13:36), using the important word *hypagein* ("go away"). Jesus' departure mirrors that of Sophia, who has been sent by God, descended to the world, and then withdraws ("goes away") from it (cf. Scott 1992: 134-40). Peter does not understand this, but the reader hears an ironic double meaning in Jesus' permission for Peter to "follow afterward." Despite his denial (soon to be announced), Peter will be both a disciple (follow) and will die the same kind of death (cf. 21:18-19).

Peter still does not understand, and the irony deepens as he firmly declares his intention to die for Jesus (13:37). Although this tradition is similar to that of Luke 22:33, it is recorded in Johannine style. It is followed by a more direct quotation (13:38), using the now common double amen introduction, echoing Mark 14:30 (= Lk 22:34). Peter's misunderstanding is complete.

John 14:1-31

The discourse of ch. 14 primarily deals with the question: "Where is Jesus going, and what consequences does this have for the disciples?" The opening is rather abrupt (14:1), the reader being left to assume that the words of comfort relate back to Jesus' announcement of departure (13:36). Jesus' basic response is, "trust me" (NRSV, "believe also in me"), and this is reinforced throughout the speech. The basis for trusting Jesus is his intimate relationship with God ("Father") and consequent knowledge of heavenly things (14:2). The image of many rooms seeks to convey the fact that God's provision is more than sufficient for all who will follow Jesus.

Jesus' departure will be for the benefit of the disciples (14:3), in contrast to those who have rejected him (8:21). The background to this scene is again the wisdom tradition, where Sophia's withdrawal from the world brings judgment on those who abandon her (Prov 1:20-33), but the FG gives it a new slant with Jesus Sophia's departure opening up the future for those who are faithful. The talk of Jesus' return is vague, specifying neither the parousia nor the resurrection as the means by which it will occur, but the latter is certainly more in focus elsewhere in the FG.

The enlightened disciple should know the "way" of Jesus (14:4). The path which Jesus takes and *is* leads to life. This idea connects again to Sophia tradition, where her path leads to life/salvation (Prov 3:17; 4:11; 8:32-36), not least in the exodus story (Wis 10:17-18). Once again, however, a male disciple, Thomas, is found wanting here (14:5). He seems to understand neither the cryptic reference to death and return, nor the path which this will open up. This confirms the earlier irony of his apparent "understanding" of the consequences of Jesus' mission (11:16).

The narrative function of Thomas's question is to prepare for another "I Am" saying (14:6). Given the subject of the question, it is clear that of the three elements in this saying, "way" is the focus: "because Jesus is the life and the truth, he is the Way to the Father" (Scott 1992: 126). As with all the other "I Am" sayings, there are clear precedents in Sophia tradition for all three elements ("way" — above; "life" and "truth," see comments on 1:4, 14 (Scott 1992: 125-28). Through his coming departure, Jesus, like Sophia, will be omnipresent as the Way, Truth, and Life (Witherington 1995: 249), opening up access to God's salvation.

The exclusivity of Jesus' role here should not be overplayed: the emphasis lies on the intimacy of Jesus' relationship with God (14:7), which we have seen to be modeled on Sophia as an intermediary figure. This corresponds to the rapport developed between Jesus and the disciples, which will be enhanced rather than diminished by his return "home."

Philip's subsequent comment (14:8) picks up on the idea that in Jesus, God can be *seen*. Jesus is still only partially understood by the disciples, whose spokesperson here offers a narrative echo of Exod 33:18, where Moses requests to see God's glory. Jesus rebukes this lack of comprehension (14:9). The reader recognizes, even if the disciples do not, that at this point the wisdom Christology of the Prologue (1:1-18) comes to fruition. There is nothing especially new in the assertion that Jesus makes God visible, given that the language of Jesus as the divine agent of God so closely parallels Sophia's story. Just as Wisdom 10–11 can retell the salvation history of Israel with Sophia in the role of divine savior and guide (an apologetic against the notion that Isis is savior and guide), so the FE can talk of Jesus as the revealer of God's saving presence.

The evidence of Jesus' relationship with God has been there for the disciples to see throughout his public ministry (14:10-11), hence Jesus' frustration with his followers at this point. Both "words" and "works" have previously been declared as nothing other than *God* at work in Jesus (8:28), the misunderstanding of Jesus' opponents being echoed here in the disciples' response. That such an echo is intended is seen in the reemphasis of 14:11, which strongly recalls 10:38, where an appeal to the witness of the "signs" falls on the deaf ears of Jesus' accusers.

The relationship depicted here should not be read against the background of later trinitarian theology, which is not the interest of the FE. Rather, it is perfectly understandable when placed alongside the picture of Sophia, whose relationship to God (cf. the comments on 3:16-18) is the basis of her authority to speak (Scott 1992: 131-34).

A word from tradition (14:12, double "Amen") begins the movement from the call to understand/believe to the promise of assistance in doing so. The departure of Jesus means that God's work will be continued by the disciples. Lindars is correct in seeing the word "greater" *(meizona)* as a reference to quantity rather than quality (Lindars 1972: 475) since the whole point of Jesus' withdrawal is that God's saving work may be expanded and completed. Jesus' commitment and continuing involvement are not in doubt since he will continue to grant the requests of disciples and make their task possible (14:13-14). So, like Sophia, on returning to the heavenly places Jesus will still bring glory to God by the empowerment of God's continuing work.

As the ongoing representatives of Jesus' work in the world, his followers must reveal the same relationship with each other ("new commandment," 13:34-35) as Jesus has with God (14:15) (Burge 1987: 137-49). For those who do, provision is made in terms of permanent support for their fulfillment of God's work through the presence of "another" Advocate (*paraklētos,* 14:16). The language here indicates that Jesus' current relationship with the disciples will find its counterpart in the Paraclete's later work. Despite the range of meanings which the word *paraklētos* can have ("comforter"; "advocate"; "helper"; "counsellor"), its *primary* meaning in the FG is probably "Advocate" (Witherington 1995: 250-52).

The Paraclete is none other than the Spirit (14:17), promised subsequent to Jesus' coming glorification (7:39). Just as Jesus is the "Truth" (14:6), so the Spirit will display this primary quality which divides the "world" from the disciples. Jesus' withdrawal from the world (13:1) indicates that it is the place of unbelief, whose occupants do not fulfill the condition of mutual love. They cannot see (believe), in contrast to the disciples in whom the Spirit permanently remains *(menein),* as God lives in Jesus (14:20, 23).

The intimate familial language continues with the insistence that the "little children" (13:33) will not be made "orphans" (14:18). That Jesus will return is initially a reference to the resurrection but ultimately to the coming of the Spirit (Burge 1987: 138), to whose care and guidance the disciples will be committed. Through this coming (both forms) the disciples will continue to see Jesus (v. 19), in contrast to the "world," whose sight of Jesus ends with his death (cf. v. 17). Jesus' departure and return is to the life-giving benefit of the disciples, his resurrection and the gift of the Spirit carrying the same possibility for the believer.

The FE uses common eschatological language ("on that day") to speak of Jesus' resurrection (14:20). His return will cement a new, three-way mutual relationship between God, Jesus, and the believer, the means of maintenance of this having already been indicated ("the Spirit/Paraclete," 14:17). By repeating the sentiment of v. 15, emphasis is given to the primacy of love *(agapē)* in the life of the believer (v. 21). The model for this love relationship is once again Sophia, whose devotees are also loved by God (Sir 4:14). Indeed, the whole relationship between Jesus and the Spirit mirrors that of Sophia and the Spirit in the wisdom tradition (Wis 1:4-6; 9:1-2, 17-18) (cf. Scott 1992: 162-65).

The appearance of "another" Judas (14:22) offers another connection between the FG and traditions found in Luke's accounts (cf. Luke 6:16; Acts 1:13). His question confirms that Jesus cannot be talking about the parousia since the "world" will not see it — so to what is Jesus referring? This allows Jesus (14:23) both to reiterate the conditions (cf. vv. 15, 21) and outline the mutuality of the relationship of indwelling which will emerge in the postresurrection period. The role of the Spirit in this will be further explicated in the verses which follow. For the moment, this section is rounded off by a return to the theme of "homes" (cf. v. 2): just as the believer finds a home with God, so God finds a home in the believer. This is true only for those who are obedient to Jesus' love commandment (v. 24), which is given not on Jesus' authority alone but is God's commission (cf. v. 10).

The last section of this speech deals with the benefits of Jesus' departure and the consequent arrival of the Spirit. There is a reminder of the short space of time which is left (14:25), but reassurance that the coming Paraclete will take on the role of "teacher" and "prompter" (v. 26). It is in Jesus' name (cf. v. 13) that the Spirit comes, being "sent" as his representative, very much after the model of Sophia's entry into the world to unfold the truth of God. It is not clear whether the Spirit is expected to reveal "new" things, the primary function being to "remind," but this is not ruled out. The speech implies that Jesus' teaching is already clear, a point much disputed, not least in Bultmann's famous dictum: "Jesus as the Revealer of God reveals nothing but that he is the Revealer" (Bultmann 1955: 2:66). Yet the reader is aware that the Johannine Jesus' whole mission has focused precisely on revealing *God,* as light, life, truth, and salvation for the world!

Part of the continuing gift of Jesus is *shalom* — the Hebrew lies behind the Greek word *eirēnē* (14:27). This holistic concept is far more than the mere removal of conflict or anxiety. Fundamentally, it is the state which results from being in a continuing relationship with God, the very thing of which Jesus has been speaking. It does not release the believer from trouble, but its presence ensures that trouble cannot overwhelm — thus the allusion back to 14:1. Since the "world" does not believe, it cannot either receive or give such "peace."

The speech now directly recalls the words of 14:3. Jesus indicates here (v. 28) that his withdrawal is for the benefit of the disciples since it completes his work and opens up the possibility of a permanent supportive presence in the shape of the Spirit. It is thus an occasion for celebration rather than sadness, the limitations of incarnation finally being overcome. Once again the emphasis is on God's preeminence in the whole sequence of events. Later trinitarian controversy categories of "subordination" are not appropriate here. The whole FG presents the incarnation on the prior model of the relationship between Sophia and God. Both she and Jesus act out of free, loving obedience to the mission of God, to reveal God's intention in the world. The Johannine Jesus is not swept along to death against his will, but acts in union with God's desire for the salvation of humanity (3:16).

Jesus reveals the good that lies ahead in anticipation of the intervening passion (14:29). His foreknowledge has been seen at numerous points throughout the FE's presentation, but now it is directed toward the confirmation of the disciples' faith in the face of the forthcoming "disaster" of crucifixion. It is important, then, for Jesus to stress again that he retains control of his destiny (v. 30) and is now ready to face it. The "ruler" has the common Johannine feature of double meaning, alluding to both the devil and the state authority (Pilate), to whom similar words will later be addressed (19:11). In the end, Jesus' purpose is clear: to reveal his love for God, and thus the veracity of his entire ministry, to the world (14:31), in fulfillment of God's goal.

The final words of the chapter reveal something of the editorial work that the FG underwent in its early formation. It is evident that at some point this chapter moved directly to the passion (18:1) and that chs. 15–17 have been inserted. In light of this it is no surprise to find that many of the themes of these subsequent chapters strongly echo the material of 14:1-31 and should be read in its light.

John 15:1-17

The second part of the farewell banquet speech begins with another "I Am" saying (15:1). The image of the vine is common in Jewish literature, but it is usually connected with the theme of judgment (e.g., Isa 5:1-7; Ezek 15:1-8), certainly not the dominant motif here. Once again the FE is drawing on wisdom tradition, where Sophia is pictured as a vine (Sir 1:20; 24:17, 19) providing "sustenance and abundance of life through the fruit of her branches" and seeking faithful disciples who will bear such fruit in contrast to the faithless (Sir 23:25) (Scott 1992: 129-31). Likewise Jesus is encouraging such productiveness in his disciples. Jesus is the "real" (NRSV, "true") vine, perhaps in contrast to the idea of Sophia as identified with the Torah (Sir 24:23).

As always Jesus undertakes the work of God, who is the gardener. Indeed, God is pictured as actively doing "pruning" work on the vine (15:2). Although it is only later in the speech that the disciples are identified as the "branches," already at the outset it is clear that Jesus is addressing the words to that group. This implies that there are those in the community of the FG who are not faithful (= bear fruit), and that even those who remain faithful need further "refining" — a fact evident to the reader who has seen the male disciples all along fail to grasp fully what is happening in Jesus.

Even if they do not yet understand, the disciples have been washed (15:3), both literally (13:10) and through their response to Jesus' word. The concern is that they will show their true allegiance to Jesus by "abiding" (15:4 — *menein*), a variation on the theme of mutual indwelling already rehearsed in the first part of the speech (14:11, 20, 23). The reason for such constancy on the disciples' part is elucidated: without it there can be no fruitfulness. Although the "fruit" is not specified, there are echoes of Jesus' earlier teaching, where the task of witness and bringing others to encounter Jesus is emphasized (4:36). While this may be in the background, it will emerge in the course of the speech that "fruit" here is in fact faithful fulfillment of the love command (15:9-12).

The repetition of "I Am" (15:5) launches discussion of the nature of the "fruit" and its producers. Yet again the fundamental need for "attachment" to Jesus is stressed. Without it a detached branch is useless (v. 6) since it cannot receive the life-giving sap necessary for fruitfulness. Fire is sometimes taken as a symbol of judgment, but this is alien to Johannine thought. It is simply a natural part of the image of vinedressing, where the discarded material is fit only for burning, being too brittle for use, for example, in woodworking.

It is important to remember that this speech is addressed to *insiders,* not to the "world." It is a further indication of the situation of the Johannine community, where some have detached themselves (we have noted this in relation to the "Jews" language elsewhere). Whatever they may claim, they cannot bear fruit of the type required. In contrast, however, the abiding disciple will be able to continue the work of Jesus (15:7), receiving from God the necessary support (cf. 14:13-14).

Since Jesus' whole mission is directed toward the glorification of God, the disciple will continue this work (15:8) by faithful commitment to the task. Only now does the nature of the "fruit" begin to emerge, with the theme of the mutual *agapē* of God, Jesus, and the disciple (vv. 9-10). This is an echo of the love command (13:34-35) which very much reflects the influence of the Sophia tradition, where love for Sophia is seen as love for God, who reciprocates (Prov 8:17; Wis 8:3-4; Sir 4:14). Jesus' love for God is shown in his obedience to God's mission and faithfulness even to this climactic "hour." The disciple's complementary compliance is the sign of love, identified now as bearing fruit. Much will happen (the "hour" of death, resurrection, the coming of the Spirit) before the disciples are in a position to fulfill their task, but speaking in advance (15:11), Jesus repeats the theme of rejoicing in the midst of the coming trouble for the hope which will emerge from it (cf. 14:28).

If there was any doubt about the connection between "fruit" and the love command, it is dispelled by its repetition (15:12), now as an introduction to an outline of its consequences for discipleship. Peter has already, somewhat impetuously and without understanding, volunteered his life for Jesus (13:37), but Jesus' words (15:13) take the reader back to the parable of the Good Shepherd, whose action on behalf of the sheep is described precisely in these words (10:12-18). Such willingness to die for others is the ultimate sign of committed love, and it is that for which, by implication, the disciple must prepare (15:14). Here, as in v. 12, the demand of Jesus is singular as against the plural of 14:15. There is but a single focus to friendship (= obedient discipleship), and that is mutual love based on the pattern of God's mutual love for Jesus.

It might appear that there is some inconsistency in the talk of "friends" (15:15) over against a "master-servant" relationship, not least since Jesus has alluded to himself as master in the footwashing scene (13:16). The setting of that episode, with its picture of humility, reveals that anything but a traditional master-servant relationship is envisaged. Here this is made explicit. Just as Jesus expects to fulfill the mission of God, so the disciple as friend will, out of loving friendship, be obedient to Jesus' demand. Jesus indicates that this friendship relationship is confirmed by his openness in sharing the things of God with them. Such intimacy is not part of a slave's expectation.

The parallel between Jesus' mission and that of the disciples is carried through in the language of commissioning (15:16). Again using the tried and tested model of Sophia's embassy in the world, Jesus likens his own experience of being chosen by God and sent out with a mission to that of the commissioning of believers. It is not their own work which they will do, but they are, as it were, under the authority of the same God who commissioned Jesus Sophia to act in the world. It is from God that strength for the task will be derived, when obedience to the love command (15:17) is maintained.

John 15:18–16:15

So much for the internal relations of the community of believers, even with its defective and defecting "branches." John now turns his attention to the response of those outside — the "world" (15:18). Presented with typical Johannine starkness, the dualistic opposite of the community love ideal is hate. It is this emotion, characteristic of opposition to Jesus' works (7:7), which now faces the continuing doers of God's work, the disciples. It is precisely because of the unity of Jesus and his disciples that they will experience hatred (15:19) since believers do not share the value system of the world at large (i.e., they *love* one another). Being chosen does not *remove* the disciple from the world, but it gives a totally different orientation which is despised by those who do not share it.

Jesus returns to the "servant-master" language (15:20), recalling his previous usage (13:16). Lindars correctly points out that this quotation above all shows that the second part of the discourse is intended as a commentary on chs. 13–14 (Lindars 1972: 493). Now the hierarchical tone can be read in the light of Jesus' designation of the disciples as "friends." If the disciples share Jesus' love and joy, as his friends they will also share his hatred and suffering.

The unity of purpose between Jesus and his followers is expressed fully in the fact that hatred toward them will not be based on a dislike of the disciples themselves, but rather on antipathy toward the mission of God (15:21), manifested in Jesus' work. More than that, as Brown points out, it is because Jesus "bears the divine name" that his disciples who use it are persecuted (Brown 1966: 697).

The culpability of Jesus' opponents, which we have already seen to parallel closely that of those who reject Sophia (cf. the comments on 1:10; 8:21), is brought to mind (15:22-24). It is not ignorance which leads to opposition to Jesus and his followers but a deliberate choice to reject the words of wisdom and works of life. Note the stress on the uniqueness of Jesus' signs and the ironic reference to "seeing." The very thing which those who hate Jesus have not done is to "see" (i.e., "believe"), yet among the signs performed was one of giving sight to a blind man. Jesus rounds off this condemnation of his opponents with a quotation from scripture (v. 25), probably from Ps 69:4 (or Ps 35:19), which shows that nothing in what will unfold is outside the control of God's plan. That Jesus should talk of "their law" is consistent with the use of such phraseology in the disputes with opponents in earlier chapters.

The speech returns now to the theme of help in the face of opposition (15:26), again using the title Paraclete ("Advocate") for the Spirit. Commentators have noted the strong parallel to Matt 10:19-20, where the scene is one of disciples on trial needing a spokesperson, or advocate. Brown may well be correct that this kind of tradition is being reinterpreted by the FE in the figure of the Paraclete (Brown 1966: 699-701). It is certainly a further comment on 14:26, where the Spirit is given by God. The later conciliar controversies over the *filioque* (Latin — "and the Son") clause, which stem from the absence of this phrase here, are not at all in view for the FE.

The purpose of the Spirit's coming is not merely to remind the disciples (14:26), but to give evidence concerning Jesus. The language is juridical, and this becomes clearer with the call for the disciples, too, to stand as witnesses (15:27). They will be able to do so through the presence of the Spirit but also because they have accompanied Jesus throughout his ministry. At this point it is especially important to remember that the whole purpose of witness is to bring others to an encounter with Jesus and so to faith. When this takes place, the reader as believer is drawn into the circle of those who have "been with Jesus from the beginning."

It will be in the confrontation with those who should be closest allies that the disciples will experience persecution, so the danger of giving up under pressure is all the greater (16:1). For the third time the FE mentions being excommunicated from the synagogue as a primary outcome of witness (16:2), but this time it is heightened by the possibility of death. The "hour" for the disciples will be similar to Jesus' own "hour," a time to share in Jesus' glory through death and, in the light of what is to come, to hope also for resurrection.

Witherington recalls that Paul saw persecution of Christians as a form of religious zeal, so the idea of "offering worship" through killing members of the Johannine community is not farfetched (Witherington 1995: 262). Here, though, we are probably dealing with other Christian groups, some of whom have left the Johannine circle, betraying that circle by suppressing them on account of their christological and ecclesiological outlook. If the FG does date from the time of Domitian (cf. 20:28), it may be that they were even betrayed to the authorities and faced death. The Johannine Jesus thus continues to maintain that they have failed to discern his true nature (16:3), and so, in classic Sophia terms, failed to see God.

Like the Spirit to come, Jesus acts here as one who reminds (16:4) in advance of the horrific circumstances of his own departure. It has not been necessary for him to speak in this way because of his physical presence, but these words open the way for him to talk further about the work of the Spirit, his continuing nonbodily presence. This raises again the question of Jesus' leaving, and strangely, in the light of 14:5, he now declares it odd that no one asks where he is going (16:5)! There is no satisfactory historical solution to this obvious contradiction (Barrett 1978: 485 stresses the *present* tense as indicating that the disciples do not ask at *this* point!), but from a narrative viewpoint the question paves the way for further reflection on Jesus' departure.

The disciples' sorrow (16:6) is an indication of their continuing failure to grasp what Jesus is saying. This leads to a further exposition of 14:28, this time making explicit (16:7) the nature of the benefit accruing to the disciples through Jesus' departure — the gift of the Spirit. Although a literal reading of the text may suggest that the Spirit and Jesus cannot be in the world at the same time, this is not the narrative intention. What is in view is reassurance for the disciples that the coming death of Jesus is not the end of everything but conversely the beginning of something greater. Jesus talks again of himself as the sender, but this is not in conflict with 15:26. The Paraclete emerges as the joint legacy of Jesus and God.

The juridical function of the Advocate is further illuminated (16:8), this time not as the defender and representative of the disciple, but as the accuser *(elenxei)* of the disciple's opponent, "the world." Three elements of this accusation are outlined in the following verses. The combination of sin, righteousness, and judgment here has greatly exercised scholars (cf. Segovia 1991: 228-35), but it need not be so difficult. Witherington's comments (Witherington 1995: 264-65) make perfect sense, and I follow them here.

The "world" is convicted of *sin* on account of its lack of belief (16:9), which has clearly been demonstrated throughout as a willful choice rather than ignorance. It is condemned in relation to *righteousness* (v. 10) because its failure to accept the ministry of Jesus as from God is shown to be negated by God's acceptance of Jesus through the glorifying events of death and resurrection. The signs and words as evidence of Jesus' righteousness are validated by God's coming action on Jesus' behalf. Lastly, the world is guilty with regard to *judgment* (v. 11) because its own judgment of Jesus (execution) is overturned by God through Jesus' resurrection. Its judgment is thus turned on its head, and it is numbered with Satan (ironically the great "Accuser"!). Whatever other subtle overtones the word "Paraclete" may have, there can be no doubt that here the function is as a legal Advocate, summing up the case for the prosecution!

The function of the Spirit as the continuing revealer of the things of God now comes under scrutiny (16:12-13). Jesus cannot reveal all now because the ensuing struggle to the death will in itself be overwhelming for the disciples, whose comprehension level is already low (vv. 17-18)! It is probably fair to the FG's whole picture to allow that the Spirit *will* continue to interpret the revelation of God anew beyond written words (whether of Torah or Christian scripture!) in continuity with the Word. This is certainly how some later groups such as the Montanists (cf. Trevett 1995) understood Johannine teaching.

The unity of Jesus and the Spirit is seen in the area of speaking the truth. Just as Jesus speaks and acts only on God's authority (8:28, 38-42; 14:10), so the Spirit will continue to act and speak in this way. As we have already noted (see the comments on 1:14), this is a further development of the tradition concerning Sophia as the bringer of truth, who not only speaks the truth (Prov 8:6-7) but leads her disciples into wise ways (Wis 9:11; 10:10).

Just as Jesus' mission has been to glorify God, so the Spirit will glorify Jesus (16:14) by continuing the mission of Jesus through empowerment of the disciples. The complete unity of God, Jesus, and the Spirit comes to expression in their one mission, continued in the world through the disciples (16:15). It is toward the recognition of this shared goal that the entire discourse has been leading. The next question is, Have the disciples really understood?

John 16:16-33

Although Jesus has spoken consistently of his departure, the reader is still unsure whether the disciples have grasped its significance. In 14:19 Jesus mentioned the "little while," but the phrasing could have implied that he was intending only to hide himself from the world, with the disciples remaining in physical contact. Now this issue is taken up directly (16:16) and the disciples' understanding tested. While the final departure and replacement with the Paraclete have been addressed, now John speaks of the immediate circumstances of the Passion and resurrection in veiled, "now-you-see-me, now-you-don't" language.

The disciples' misunderstanding is wholesale! Already Jesus has announced that they will see him no longer (16:10) and frequently spoken of his relationship to God using "Father" language. Yet they understand neither the timing nor the goal of his departure (vv. 17-18) and, almost pathetically, puzzle over Jesus' words. Their questions reflect "a comprehensive failure to understand the fundamental nature of these farewell disclosures as a whole" (Segovia 1991: 249). From the narrative point of view, however, their misunderstanding opens the way for a final summary statement of the implications of both the coming passion and the time beyond when the disciples continue Jesus' mission in the world. The FE employs the common motif of Jesus' supernatural insight (v. 19) to engage with the questions.

For the informed reader, who already knows the story if not the Johannine version, the talk of mourning turned to joy (16:20) self-evidently refers to Jesus' death at the hands of his opponents (who rejoice), followed by his resurrection. In fairness to the seemingly obtuse disciples, this is easier to understand with reader's hindsight! A traditional saying is introduced (double "amen") to illustrate the process through which the disciples will pass (16:21), though its origin is not entirely clear (Isa 26:17?). Its imagery is nevertheless appropriate, using the picture of a woman giving birth, in which the pain and struggle of labor are replaced by joy at what has come into being — life. Jesus promises that his return will bring a similar joy (16:22), precisely because it brings a similar result — life. This will take the form of a new permanent relationship with God through the Spirit, the joy of which the world cannot supplant.

Once again Jesus refers to the day of resurrection using classic eschatological language (16:23, "in that day"; cf. 14:20), indicating already that Jesus' return and the gift of the Spirit are the FG's primary understanding of the parousia. The disciples will then not need to ask any more questions (NRSV's alternative reading makes better sense here [cf. Barrett 1978: 494]), as they will then fully understand. As promised before (14:12-14), however, God will continue to provide on the basis of the relationship established through Jesus. It will be in *Jesus'* name that future requests are made (16:24). Quoting what appears to be a tradition similar to that in Matt 7:7-8, the Johannine Jesus confirms the earlier assurance (15:11) that his return and its consequences will bring a fulfilling joy to outweigh the current sorrow.

The final section of the banquet speeches (16:25-33), to be followed by a stylized prayer (17:1-26), is crucial for understanding the role of Jesus as Sophia incarnate. Witherington sums up well when he states that the Johannine Jesus is "seen as both sage and Wisdom at once, as both revealer and the content of revelation, as both means and ends of salvation" (Witherington 1995: 265). As a good sage, Jesus has spoken in proverbial language (16:25), but as Sophia incarnate he has also revealed the things of God through this, and will continue to do so openly. His revelatory work has opened up a direct line of communication with God (v. 26), to continue through Jesus' name. The content of the revelation is summed up through the theme of mutual love (16:27) which has dominated the banquet speeches. It is Jesus' work which has established this new relationship of love between God and his disciples, which Jesus' departure now cements.

Central to the continuity of the new relationship with God is understanding Jesus' origins. Here the reader, with the disciples, must recognize the thoroughgoing nature of the Sophia Christology around which the whole Gospel picture is built. Like Sophia before him, Jesus has come into the world from God (16:28) and is withdrawing again to be with God (cf. Scott 1992: 134-40). It is this modeling of Christology around the figure of Sophia which has provided the richness of Johannine imagery — and also become the focus of so much of the struggle of the Johannine community with its *Christian* peers (see my discussion of "Jews" language throughout).

Johannine irony returns as the disciples declare their understanding of Jesus' words (16:29-30). It is not that Jesus has said anything particularly new, but it is crucial for the ideal reader to hear the specific model of Sophia Christology confirmed as central from the mouth of the Johannine Jesus and confessed by the disciples. This affirms its contemporary validity and serves the overall purpose of the FG in encouraging the believer to *continue* in this faith (20:31).

In terms of the unfolding narrative it will become clear that the disciples do *not* yet understand, so Jesus questions their comprehension (16:31). Just as Peter's bold declaration of solidarity was met with realism by Jesus' response (13:38), so, too, the confidence of the group receives a practical assessment (16:32). Their corporate story has largely been one of failure in terms of both action and understanding, and the climax of the "hour" will be no different. The Johannine Jesus' words here seem to echo the Synoptic predictions of desertion (cf. Mark 14:27 pars.), which in turn echo Zech 13:7. The ideal reader at least knows that Jesus was left alone, though there will still be a surprise in store with the presence of ideal disciples at the foot of the cross (19:25-27). In any case, the group should be aware that Jesus' unity with God guarantees that he will never be abandoned — a symbolically important message to the community.

Finally, Jesus returns to the opening theme of peace in the midst of troubled times (16:33). This is a message to the disciples in the narrative, but to the current reader as well. Although the world will temporarily appear to take power over Jesus, his return and continuing presence in the Spirit guarantee that, in the midst of persecution, the gift of God's peace will sustain and bring life. As Jesus' resurrection will show, this means life out of death, even though bearing its marks (20:20).

John 17:1-26

The prayer of Jesus brings to a close the long section of farewell speeches. Its basic division is quite straightforward: he prays first for his own situation (17:1-5); then for the disciples as his continuing presence in the world (vv. 6-19); thereafter for those who respond to their witness, that is, the church (vv. 20-23), and finally for harmony and assurance of glory for all future followers. Although this prayer has often been seen as the FG's version of Jesus' Gethsemane prayer, Witherington is correct to observe its greater similarity in style and characteristics to closure passages in the wisdom writings (e.g., Prov 9:1-18; Eccl 12:9-14; Sir 51:1-30) on which so much of Johannine thought is based (Witherington 1995: 268). If there is a parallel to the Synoptic Gethsemane prayer in the FG it is in 12:27-28 (see the comment there).

The prayer begins (17:1) in a similar vein to a previous prayer at Lazarus's tomb (11:41), where Jesus' action is announced as for the benefit of those listening. This echo suggests that the same purpose is being fulfilled here: that the prayer is meant for those around, including the Johannine community and the current reader. Jesus declares that his "hour" has finally arrived and calls upon God to make it the point of their mutual glorification. This is the end toward which the whole mission of Jesus has proceeded, its outcome being, as earlier promised, eternal life (17:2) for those who believe. That goal is achieved through Jesus' God-given authority as judge (cf. 5:27) of humanity ("all flesh").

Jesus goes on to define eternal life (17:3) as knowledge of God and, astonishingly enough, Jesus Christ. It is as though he steps outside of himself to speak in the third person, a factor which leads most commentators to see this verse as an editorial aside. The epithet "one true God" certainly "splendidly voices Jewish monotheism" (Lindars 1972: 519), but more significantly for the FE, this

God is related directly to the revelation in Jesus Christ, Sophia incarnate, declared throughout the FG to be the "Truth." The Johannine community's confession is that only in this one is the true God to be known (cf. Brown 1966: 752).

Jesus is in a position to call upon God to be faithful to the promise of glory because he has been faithful in completing God's mission in the world (17:4). That work, however, will not be seen for what it truly is without the next step — the imminent passion ("now," 17:5). Jesus has another reason to call upon God to glorify him, and this relates back to the opening words of the FG (1:1-3). As Sophia incarnate, Jesus has shared God's glory from before creation (Prov 8:22-31) and will return to a full share in it. It is this which has given the Johannine Jesus both superiority and authority throughout the FG; now it "functions as a validation of his coming suffering and death as an hour of glorification" (Scott 1992: 132).

Jesus' attention now turns to the primary purpose of the prayer, concern for the disciples and those who will follow in their footsteps. Jesus declares that he has made God's "name" known (17:6), which Brown suggests may mean the use of "I Am" throughout as a translation of YHWH (Brown 1966: 754-56). This is an attractive suggestion, but it may simply be a way of summing up the (somewhat nonspecific!) revelation which Jesus has brought through his words and works. It is the disciples, albeit still in much confusion and misunderstanding, who have been faithful to God's/Jesus' commandment ("kept your word"). This is important for later readers in their imperfection to hear. The disciples' lack of comprehension and coming desertion of Jesus are nevertheless outweighed by faithfulness to the core demand (13:34-35).

The whole prayer, though placed here before the "glorification," can make sense only from a postresurrection viewpoint. Within story time, the disciples' claims to understanding have already been put in perspective by Jesus (16:31-32), but in discourse time, with the experience of resurrection, they do recognize (17:7) all Jesus' work as from God. Not just Jesus' work, but especially his words (17:8) are acknowledged to come from God, whose gift to them Jesus is. The question of Jesus' origins in God and the recognition of his divine mission are again shown to be fundamental to the Johannine understanding of belief.

The prayer now makes explicit its primary concentration on the disciples (17:9-10), though later it will include a much wider circle. The unity of God and Jesus is stressed through the recognition of the disciples as belonging to God. This should not be interpreted as a narrow sectarianism, whereby Jesus/God is concerned only with the small band. The whole point of praying for the disciples is that they will be enabled to continue Jesus' work of calling the "world" to God. The prayer in fact presupposes that many believe because of their witness in the world (17:20).

Since Jesus' work has aimed at the glorification of God, mutual indwelling will mean that the disciples will continue that work, glorifying Jesus and so God. The perfect tense ("have glorified" — *dedoxasmai*) makes sense only from a postresurrection perspective, since nothing in the disciples' behavior to this point could be said to fulfill this role. When they do glorify Jesus, however, they will surely entertain the same risk of persecution and death as Jesus' own glorifying work does, so he prays for their protection (17:11) following his departure from the world. That protection should be on the basis of Jesus' revelation of God (cf. 17:6) and involves maintaining their unity as a group. There is considerable textual difficulty with the last phrase ("they may be one as we are one"), which is missing in some crucial manuscripts. It is just possible, however, that from the perspective of the later divisions of Christian communities, already reflected in the Johannine literature, such division goes back to apostolic rivalries, though this is by no means clear.

Jesus now speaks clearly from a postresurrection viewpoint concerning the fate of the disciples (17:12). The previous predictions of falling away (Peter — 13:38; the group of disciples — 16:32) are assumed to be resolved, though the case of Judas needs special explanation. It is not that Jesus, the Good Shepherd who "guards" the sheep, has somehow failed in his responsibility. Rather, Judas fulfills the destiny outlined by Scripture, presumably Ps 41:9 (cf. John 13:18), and his fate, though never discussed by the FE, is known by the ideal reader.

If it were not already evident that the prayer is offered for the benefit of the listener, Jesus' next statement (17:13) demonstrates this. The speaker's perspective seems to fluctuate constantly between the "now" and the "not yet," so here again the joy of the disciples is still to be perfected after the passion and resurrection. Jesus talks as though he has to *pronounce* these things in order to make them come to pass. The connection with God's "word" (17:14) makes it possible that there is an allusion here to the prophetic tradition where the power of God's word going out already insures that it achieves its purpose (e.g., Isa 45:22-23). Above all, Jesus wants to stress the continuity between himself and the disciples both in terms of the message declared and the outcome to be expected — the hatred of the world ("has hated" again makes sense only in the post-Easter setting).

Jesus' concern is still with their safety in the postresurrection situation (17:15), but he knows the answer is not to remove the disciples from the reality of persecution. This is no Gnostic, world-hating, withdrawn group, but one which is engaged in active witness and challenge to the world. The disciples may share Jesus' own perspective as "not belonging to the world" (17:16), but they will face the kind of deadly evil intention which is about to take Jesus to the cross.

It is for this reason that Jesus asks God to "set apart," or "consecrate," the disciples (17:17-19) for the task. The translation of *hagiason* here requires this sense, rather than the potentially misleading "sanctify" of the NRSV. Witherington is correct in noting that the question is not one of "cleansing" but of consecration for the mission ahead, but his subsequent connection of this theme with ideas of ritual sacrifice is unnecessary (Witherington 1995: 270). This might fit with some ideas of atonement in later christological speculation, especially when applied to Jesus, but this is not the focus of the FG's understanding at this point. A more likely point of contact is with wisdom tradition, where Sophia is regarded as "set apart" ("holy"), bringing glory to those who, in serving her, serve God (Sir 4:13-14). It is precisely this type of shared mission, with its focus of glorification, toward which both Jesus and the disciples are now being set apart.

Attention turns to the next generation of believers (17:20-21), among whom are numbered the Johannine community. It is a prayer centered on the theme of unity: a unity between disciples, and generations of disciples, which reflects and is rooted in the relationship between Jesus and God. The aim of this unity is to enable others to believe. This belief comes about through the "word" of the disciples, as in the case of the witness of the Samaritan woman, whose role is thereby confirmed as one of exemplary discipleship (4:39-42).

A major facet of Jesus' relationship with God is the "glory" which emanates from it (1:14). In common with the disciples of Sophia (cf. John 17:19), it is Jesus' intention that his followers will share in this glory (v. 22), so that God may continue to be discerned in the world in accord with the whole mission of Jesus from the beginning. What the world will be able to know is summed up in two things (17:23): first, that the unity of the disciples has come about because Jesus was sent by God, thereby confirming the divine origin and authority of all of Jesus' words and work. Second, they will know that the disciples enjoy the same measure of God's love which Jesus also enjoys, thus confirming the truth of the earlier claim (3:16-17) that God's open possibility and desire is that the *whole* world may share in this relationship of love.

The concern with unity surely reflects an important theme which has run through the FG — that of the division between the Johannine community and others brought about by christological and ecclesiological difference. That this existed toward the end of the first century AD is confirmed by the Johannine epistles. The prayer reminds the community that if they are truly to reflect the mutual indwelling which has been such an important subject in the farewell speeches, there must be a unity among the disciples which mirrors that of Jesus and God.

The final verses sum up Jesus' appeal on behalf of the future mission. Ultimately the goal for disciples is unity with God and Jesus in heaven (17:24), where the glory already seen in Jesus will be fully known and shared. The unity of Jesus with Sophia is once again recalled through the reference to God's love for him/her in the beginning (see the comments on 1:1-3). Despite this display, the world still fails to acknowledge Jesus, as it also did Sophia (17:25). Yet God, who is just (NRSV, "righteous"), knows the faithful work of Jesus and that his followers recognize his origins (and with it the Sophia Christology of the FG!).

So the final words the earthly Jesus speaks to his disciples state again his role as revealer of God (17:26) and confirm the role of the disciples as the ones who will continue this purpose. The key to the success of this mission, as also its goal, is that highest of desires in the Johannine Jesus' revelation: love.

John 18:1-11

The speeches ended, the Johannine passion narrative continues by picking up the more familiar sequence of the Synoptics: arrest — trial — sentencing — crucifixion — burial. Although the sequence is similar in all four Gospel accounts, the FG is quite different in detail and in theological interpretation of the events. Throughout Jesus is pictured as the Victor, whose control over events is never in doubt.

Jesus is accompanied by the disciples through the Kidron *wadi* (18:1), which the text literally implies is in its water-filled winter state. There may well be an allusion here to 1 Kgs 2:37 (Guilding 1960: 165), which predicts the death of the king on crossing this brook. Only the FG mentions a "garden" as the place of arrest, but the FE makes clear that this was a place familiar to the disciples (18:2), and therefore to Judas.

It is Judas who leads the authorities to Jesus in order to arrest him (18:3). Both the secular and religious forces are represented here, though the suggestion that a "cohort" (Gk. *speiran*), normally 600 soldiers (!), accompanied the religious police is a piece of Johannine dramatic license. Witherington is probably right in saying that it indicates "the magnitude of the forces of darkness" (Witherington 1995: 286), who need torches to find the Light.

At the beginning of the Johannine passion (13:1), the narrator has already declared that Jesus has foreknowledge of his fate. This is underlined again (18:4) as the drama moves toward its climactic point. Throughout the Gospel the theme of "seeking" Jesus Sophia has been prominent, so there is much irony in Jesus' question to his opponents here. This is no true "seeker" group (cf. 20:15), but deadly enemies seeking his life.

The "seekers" identify their prey as "Jesus of Nazareth" (18:5), a common means of denoting Jesus. His response is to use again the divine revelatory formula, "I Am." Its use in this way, juxtaposed to Judas the betrayer, formerly one of Jesus' closest colleagues, provides the starkest of contrasts, since Judas now stands "with *them*," the powers of darkness. That it is correct to view Jesus' words here as the divine formula is confirmed by the narrator (18:6), who reports the reaction of the human authorities. Falling down in this way before a theophany is elsewhere regarded as an appropriate response (Dan 10:9; Acts 9:4; Rev 1:17). This is less a historical report than a theological comment by the FE on Jesus' authority over the "powers."

The repetition (18:7) of the previous question and answer prepares the way for a second "I Am," ironically used this time as a simple identification (18:8). Since it is Jesus alone whom they "seek," he can instruct his opponents to let the disciples go. This also implies that even the desertion of these followers stands within the control of the Johannine Jesus (cf. Lindars 1972: 542). It is striking that this "protection" of the disciples is treated by the FE as a fulfillment of a "word" of Jesus (cf. 17:12) in precisely the same way that elsewhere scriptural quotations are introduced (18:9). This is an indication of the status achieved by the words of Jesus by the end of the first century AD.

In the Synoptic tradition, the identity of the attacker of the high priest's servant is not revealed, but in the FG it is another opportunity to portray the misunderstanding of Peter (18:10). In doing so, the FE is also able to link this event with the denial (18:26), making the act a clear proof of presence. The identification of "Malchus" is also unique to the FG. Although some have tried to see this as symbolic, the lack of a translation (the name means "king") renders this unlikely.

Jesus rejects violence as an appropriate means of defense for his followers (18:11), indicating instead the necessity of fulfilling his God-given mission. The notion of the "cup" has not been brought forward by the FE before, but it is surely an allusion to Mark 14:36, part of the Gethsemane narrative. It is another pointer to the fact that the implied reader of the FG already knows the story, even if not in its Johannine version.

John 18:12-27

The arrest of Jesus by the combined forces of state and religious authority (18:12) is followed by what appears to be a "pre-trial" hearing. There are numerous historical and compositional problems in the FG account (cf. Lindars 1972: 544-47), not least the question as to why Annas (18:13), the deposed high priest, should be conducting the hearing rather than Caiaphas. There being no obvious theological interest in reporting the story in this way, it may well be that the FG retains a historical reminiscence independent of the Synoptic tradition.

Since Caiaphas was high priest for more than one year, the reference to "that year" is somewhat ironic. Witherington suggests that it reflects the temporary nature of office under Roman rule (Witherington 1995: 287). The reference to Caiaphas's part in the original plot (11:50-51) comes here (18:14) as a reminder to the reader of the salvific nature of Jesus' forthcoming trial and death.

Jesus is followed to the hearing by Peter and "another" disciple (18:15), identified as an associate of the high priest. It is unlikely that this figure should be seen as identical to the "beloved disciple," despite a similar reference in 20:2. The tag, "who was known to the high priest," is a marker similar to "whom Jesus loved." It is used here to introduce a character who in turn can explain Peter's presence in the courtyard, where public access would not normally have been allowed. It is only on this "other" disciple's cognizance (18:16) that Peter gains entry.

The gatekeeper's question to Peter (18:17 — "also") implies that the "other" disciple is known to the high priest's household as a disciple of Jesus. It is increasingly obvious that Peter *must* be a disciple, as 18:26 will reveal, but he is at pains to deny it. His words, "I am not" *(ouk eimi),* are less a contrast to Jesus' earlier "I Am" than a narrative echo of the opening words of JBap (1:20-21). The FE's skill in bringing these words at both points in the narrative allows a contrast between the faithful disciple who rightly denies an unwarranted claim (JBap) and the one who wrongly denies a truthful claim to protect his own skin (Peter). The shadowy, cold setting of this drama (18:18) offers perfect Johannine symbolism for Peter's stance with the worldly authorities ("the police") rather than with Jesus.

While Peter is denying outside, inside Jesus is facing Annas (18:19), here named as the high priest, although the FE clearly knows he is not. His questions concern Jesus' disciples and teaching, but Jesus answers only with reference to the latter. His response (18:20) evokes the whole Sophia tradition of public disclosure (Prov 1:20-21; 8:1-3; Wis 6:12-16) which dominated the public teaching of the Johannine Jesus (John 7–10). In particular it recalls the "trial and defense" which has already taken place (cf. the comment on 10:22-42). In line with proper Jewish procedure (cf. 8:17), Jesus calls (18:21) for witnesses to be brought forward.

Jesus' answer is taken by the attendant police officer as a mark of disrespect (18:22). The Synoptics report the abuse of Jesus by the authorities (Mark 14:65; Luke 22:63), with Mark using the same word (*rhapisma* — Mark 14:65), so this may be the FE's attempt to evoke this tradition. Jesus' response is again juridical in nature (18:23), calling for proper testimony to be brought forward to support, or deny, his opponents' claims. The irony here is that the reader is aware that an acquaintance of the high priest, a known disciple, is waiting outside along with another potential witness (Peter), the two witnesses required! Instead of calling these, Annas sends Jesus for a formal hearing with Caiaphas (18:24), a process of which the FE tells us nothing. The main event will be played out before Pilate, who will use it entirely to his own political advantage over the Jewish leaders, whose arraignment procedure is rendered meaningless and unnecessary to report.

The narrative now comes back to Peter's denials, sandwiching in Markan style the pre-trial hearing. The question and answer (18:25) are exactly those of v. 17, so a new witness is brought forward to test Peter — a relative of Malchus (v. 26), whose ear Peter has only recently lopped off! The audience here knows that Peter has been clearly identified, not only by his association with the "other" disciple but by his own impulsive, criminal action. It remains only for his duplicity to be confirmed, ironically with a denial (v. 27), for his complicity in the condemnation of Jesus to be complete. By a clever narrative device, the framing of Jesus' hearing before Annas with the denial of Peter, the FE allows the reader to contrast Jesus' complete openness with the disciple's secrecy and lies.

John 18:28–19:16

The trial before Pilate is the major focus of the discussion of the condemnation of Jesus in the FG. It is a highly dramatized account, moving from outdoors to indoors in a sequence of staged scenes (Brown 1966: 857-59). Pilate is a strong figure in comparison with his presentation in the Synoptic accounts, appearing to take the case of Jesus with the utmost seriousness. Although he does apparently try to have Jesus released, seeking to place the blame for Jesus' death on the "Jews" (18:35), Pilate is portrayed as a clever political schemer. The dialogue reveals that he finds the claims of Jesus absurd (19:10), but he plays along in order to "demand a high toll from the Jews" (Bond 1998: 197). By staging the condemnation at the hour of preparation (v. 14), he manipulates the Jewish leaders into rejecting not only the messianic status of Jesus but also the sovereignty of God.

In terms of its narrative function, this technique allows the FE to challenge the reader to decide between the earthly power of Caesar and the "not-of-this-world" power of Jesus, the sacrificial lamb who takes away the sin of the world. This is a notable theological reinterpretation. The result of the dramatic sequence is to place the demands of the "Jews" at center stage, and to put *them* on trial throughout. With full Johannine irony, it is those who seek to judge who are themselves judged, Pilate included.

The scene moves from the high priest's domain to the Roman praetorium (18:28) early in the morning. It is quite probable that the Prefect would have conducted judicial affairs early, but the timing makes the likelihood of defilement (presumably by entering a Gentile space) *less* rather than greater, given that there would then be opportunity for cleansing rituals to be enacted before Passover. This motif is part of the FE's preparation for the "inside–outside" drama which follows.

It is assumed that the reader knows who Pilate is (18:29), since no introduction is made. The first part of a Roman trial is establishing the charge, but Pilate's question is met with a rather haughty reply (v. 30) which gives no hint of the substance of the matter. It may be meant to infer that a judgment against Jesus had already been taken in the unrecorded Jewish arraignment. This initially leads to a dismissal from the Prefect (v. 31), until it transpires that a potential capital case is at stake. Although the evidence is not absolutely clear, the FE's assertion that the Jews had no power of capital sentence fits well with the general pattern of Roman law (for a brief summary of the arguments see Lindars 1972: 556-57). The narrator, however, makes clear (v. 32) that the *theological* significance of the decision to commit Jesus for Roman trial lay in its leading to crucifixion (= "lifting up") rather than stoning.

The scene moves indoors to a private interview between Pilate and Jesus (18:33). At once the charge becomes evident. It is the same as in the Synoptic Gospels: Is Jesus King of the Jews? The political implications of Jesus' claims were already pointed to by the Jewish authorities in 11:48, and now he must answer the state representative directly. Yet it is Jesus who takes the accuser's role here (18:34), pushing Pilate onto the defensive with his question. Pilate's response (v. 35), as will be the case throughout, is full of irony. Clearly he is not a Jew, but in terms of the negative side of the FG's picture of the "Jews," he is precisely that: one who refuses to believe and colludes in Jesus' death. Pilate tries to shift the blame onto the Jews, extending complicity to the whole nation on the basis of its leaders' accusation. He also wants to regain the initiative in the trial by asking about Jesus' actions. It is not merely the title but what Jesus has done that matters.

Jesus' reply initially seems to allow that he has a "kingdom" (18:36), but if so, it needs radical redefinition. The starting point is its *origin,* which is from above rather than taking on traditional political significance. It is not defined by violence or by human endeavor. It is important to note that whatever the Johannine Jesus may say about "kingdom" arises primarily out of Pilate's use of the word and not Jesus' own teaching in the FG.

Pilate now shows classic Johannine literalistic misunderstanding (18:37), thinking Jesus is admitting to being a king. Jesus' reply now indicates that he is not really interested in being hailed king at all, but in his origins and mission. These reflect the fundamental Johannine theme of Jesus as Sophia incarnate: sent by God into the world with the message of life and truth. With the greatest of irony, Pilate fails to see that he is in the presence of the Truth, as his question ("what" rather than "who") indicates (v. 38a). His blindness to the truth already points to the outcome of the trial.

The scene moves outside again (18:38b) in what amounts to a switch of defendant: the "Jews" are now on trial since Pilate declares Jesus innocent as charged. In common with the Synoptics, however, the FE reports the "custom" of releasing a prisoner (18:39). There is no real evidence external to the Gospels of such a tradition, but it may have been an attempt by the Prefect to appease the people at a time of high tension in the annual calendar. What is even more striking is Pilate's description of Jesus as "King of the Jews," despite his immediately preceding declaration of Jesus' innocence. It does make sense if we see this scene as part of a trial of the *Jews,* with Pilate pushing them inexorably toward their "confession" in 19:15.

A provisional judgment of the Jews takes place in their choice of Barabbas over Jesus (18:40). This accords with the Synoptic reports (cf. Brown 1966: 870-72), but it crucially evokes the Johannine description of Jesus as the Good Shepherd (see 10:1, 8 above). That image spoke of the "bandit" (Gk. *lēstēs*) who seeks to supplant the true shepherd — precisely what happens here. Since the implied reader knows the story, there is no further need to elaborate on Barabbas's release, and we hear no more of him.

Again, though not explicitly, the scene moves indoors (19:1) as Pilate delivers Jesus for flogging. Given the chiastic structure which Brown has identified in this drama (Brown 1966: 857-59), this brief scene takes on crucial symbolism as a mock "crowning" of Jesus. The royal insignia are present (v. 2) in the soldiers' action: crown (thorns) and robe in imperial colors, and their mocking acclamation (v. 3) contains all the Johannine irony of unconscious prophecy. In place of the hand of devotion, they offer the smack of ignominy.

The indoor mockery over, Pilate emerges again dramatically to present Jesus (19:4) to his accusers. Pilate's declaration of Jesus' innocence is surely mere pretense, given the method of introducing him. The mockery has simply moved outdoors as Jesus emerges in full "regalia" (v. 5) and is formally presented by Pilate. Slowly but surely, the Prefect is luring the authorities toward their own judgment, since he knows they cannot possibly accept this tragi-comic figure as an object of veneration.

Their response is predictable as they clamor for Jesus' death (19:6), but by the Roman means of crucifixion. Cleverly, Pilate mocks them by demanding that *they* crucify him, a power completely outside the scope of the Jewish authorities. Pilate has yet more to extract from these leaders before the day is done.

Only at this point does the difference between the Jews' understanding of "kingship" and Pilate's come into view. Even if Jesus is innocent of a political charge, they demand the right to have him executed on religious grounds (19:7). Their claim picks up on the earlier condemnation in 10:31-39, where an attempt was made to stone Jesus on the charge of blasphemy.

Pilate is a complex figure in these scenes: driving the Jews toward their own judgment, but driven, too, by Jesus. Nowhere is this clearer than in the fear (19:8) which possesses him, despite his protestations of power. He has been confronted by the "truth" and chosen the way of rejection. He now asks the right question — regarding Jesus' origins (v. 9), but it is too late for an answer, and Jesus remains silent. In a moment of intense irony, Pilate then claims for himself (19:10) the authority which the reader already knows (cf. 5:25-30) belongs to Jesus. In reply (19:11), "Jesus pricks the bubble of Pilate's conceit" (Lindars 1972: 568), and confirms his own prior knowledge and control (cf. 13:1-3). Whatever worldly power Pilate may have is nothing compared to the authority Jesus exercises "from above" (an implicit answer to Pilate's question of origins).

The reference to "the one who handed me over" seems to allude to Judas, though its vagueness may also include Caiaphas. It is another reminder that the whole scene is part of the plan for Jesus' glorification. Pilate is thus reduced to a mere functionary in the process, despite his lofty claims.

The tables are briefly turned on Pilate as he seeks, now apparently genuinely ("from then on"), to release Jesus (19:12). For a moment the Jews have the upper hand as they taunt Pilate about his loyalty to Caesar. Precisely in that taunt, however, they place the initiative back with Pilate, who now has the Jews starting to acclaim Roman rule. So the final act of the drama emerges in the open as Jesus is brought out for judgment (v. 13), as the Jews themselves are judged.

There is a notorious problem here as to who sits on the judgment seat. The verb *(kathizein)* can be used both transitively and intransitively, the meaning being determined by context. In this position, either reading is possible (NRSV, "Pilate . . . sat" [intransitive], with footnote, "Pilate . . . seated him" [transitive]). In line with my comments to this point, the transitive reading makes good sense, as Jesus is once more ironically placed in his rightful position, though as a further piece of mockery.

As the drama reaches its climax we are given a specific time reference — noon on the day of Preparation (19:14). This is highly significant since it was the time when the priests began the slaughter of the lambs for Passover. The informed reader now recognizes that JBap's words at the opening of the Gospel are being fulfilled (1:29). With unconscious precision, Pilate mockingly declares the Lamb on the judgment seat as King!

The Jews once again cry out for Jesus' death (19:15), and Pilate seizes the chance for which he has waited. His mock presentation of Jesus allows him to extract from the priests, who should at this very point be in the temple proclaiming the kingship of Yahweh, the ultimate blasphemy as they declare: "We have no king but Caesar." The Johannine irony is complete: the drama of the trial is over (v. 16). The Jews, who have come to judge, are judged out of their own mouths, manipulated by Pilate. The Prefect, who has sought to exercise judgment, is judged by his failure to see the truth, even when seated before him — and Jesus, the judge, is delivered to the hour of glory toward which the whole Gospel has striven.

John 19:17-30

The FG's crucifixion scene lacks many details of the Synoptic tradition, but it adds significant ones of its own. Jesus goes to his execution still in dignified control, carrying his own cross (19:17), with no hint of the tradition regarding Simon of Cyrene. The ideal reader again needs a translation of the Hebrew (actually Aramaic!), "Golgotha." Passing mention of two other victims is made (v. 18), but no elaboration of traditions of death-throes conversation with Jesus.

Much more than the Synoptics, the FE emphasizes the significance of the *titulus*. It is made and placed on the cross at Pilate's command (19:19), a sure sign of its purpose as a further mockery of *both* Jesus and the Jews. As a narrative connection, the reference to Nazareth may recall for the reader the skepticism of Nathanael (1:46), but it is highly doubtful from a historical perspective that Pilate would have been sufficiently conversant with Jewish theology to see this in itself as a mockery of messianic claims. The title as a whole, however, has its desired effect of offense (19:20). Although outside the city, it was close enough to be viewed by the large crowds approaching for Passover. Written in three main languages, its offense was as public as possible.

The offense is great enough to require a further audience with Pilate (19:21). Once again Johannine irony comes to the fore as the representative of earthly kingship refuses to tone down the accusation, preferring unconsciously to declare the very truth which Jesus' opponents wish to conceal. Pilate's insistence (v. 22) allows the *titulus* a double function, as Lindars sums up: "the title is retained, not only as the grounds for crucifixion, but also as a proclamation of the Gospel" (Lindars 1972: 576).

It was usual for crucifixion victims to be led out naked, but Jesus' case appears an exception here. This may also be the case with the division of belongings among the execution party (here four soldiers), but the evidence is scanty (Brown 1994: 952-58). The FE (19:23-24) uses the double emphasis of the Hebrew parallelism in Ps 22:18 to expand the description. The seamless robe may be the simple garment worn by most Jewish men as a kind of underclothing, or perhaps the FE intends a reference back to the "imperial robe" (19:2), of whose removal there is no indication to this point. What the quotation from Psalm 22 indirectly indicates is the deliberate nature of the Johannine reinterpretation of the passion, given the omission of Ps 22:1 from Jesus' words on the cross.

The presence of disciples at the foot of the cross (19:25) is in direct contradiction to Synoptic reports, but it provides a perfect setting for Jesus' last will. This scene is crucial for understanding discipleship in the FG (Scott 1992: 216-22), as male and female representative (unnamed!) disciples (19:26) remain faithful to the end and come together to receive Jesus' testament. His dying words to his mother and to the BD (19:27) represent "a call to mutual relationship . . . a new and interdependent relationship" (Scott 1992: 219). It evokes the relationship which is pictured between Sophia and those disciples who do not forsake her (Prov 4:6) and is a reminder of the high status given to women as equals in the task of discipleship in the FG. The image of Jesus in control at this point of excruciating agony and suffocation in crucifixion adds to the stress on the *symbolic* importance of the report.

His will delivered, the Johannine Jesus now knows his work to be complete (19:28). It may seem out of place to the reader that Jesus Sophia, the giver of an unquenchable supply of refreshment (4:14), should be thirsty, so this is clearly explained as a fulfillment of Scripture (Ps 69:21). There is further irony as the giver of fine wine becomes the recipient of poor wine (19:29), strangely delivered on a "branch of hyssop." Given the impossibility of managing this (hyssop stalks could scarcely hold the weight of a wet sponge), many have searched for symbolism here. The suggestion most consistent with Johannine Christology connects it with the reference in Exod 12:22 to the dipping of hyssop stalks in the blood of the Passover lamb. While the connection is only vague, it at least fits with the theme of Jesus as the Paschal Lamb (Brown 1994: 1074-77).

Jesus finally dies as the Victor, without a cry of dereliction (19:30). Instead he announces the completion of his ministry and, in a controlled manner, bows his head and hands over his *spirit* (to God). Although it is not spelled out, the reader may sense a hint here of Jesus' earlier promise of the coming Spirit following his death.

John 19:31-42

In the Synoptic Gospels, the death of Jesus is followed by an act of confession on the part of an onlooker. While the FG clearly is not the same, the effect of what follows is similar. Given the setting on the day of Preparation, the Jews (here, presumably, the authorities) wish to remove the bodies to avoid the risk of defilement (19:31). The Roman practice was frequently to leave bodies for days as an example to others. The conjunction, in the FE's timing, of the fifteenth of Nisan (Passover) with a sabbath made this especially inappropriate (Deut 21:22-23); thus the request to hasten death by the breaking of the victims' legs.

With true Johannine drama, the legs of the two others are broken first (19:32), leaving Jesus as the focus, but the soldiers find he is already dead (v. 33). The reason why Jesus should have expired so quickly is not addressed, though the "giving up" of his life/spirit (to God) earlier suggests to the reader an element of control even here. The subsequent scriptural allusions make this even more likely.

The spear thrust is clearly a means of certifying Jesus' death (19:34), rather than a deathblow. As further evidence, the FE mentions "blood and water," the primary purpose of which is to point to the reality of Jesus' death. Some secondary symbolism may be implied (Brown 1994: 1178-82), Barrett's explanation being the most convincing — blood signifies the *death* of Jesus, while water, a life-giving symbol throughout the Gospel (4:10-14; 7:38), signifies the *life* which issues for humanity from his death (Barrett 1978: 556-57).

The narrator's comment on the "witness" to this event (19:35) is usually taken to indicate the BD's role. It may, however, be the Johannine version of the soldier's confession (Mark 15:39 par.), since John 19:27 seems to imply that the BD has already left the stage. The use of the present subjunctive (*pisteuēte,* "you may believe") should be read in the light of the comments on 20:31, as an encouragement to *continue* in belief.

Two scriptural allusions seek to explain the details of Jesus' death (19:36-37). The first seems to allude to Exod 12:46 (cf. Num 9:12), and continues the FE's theme of Jesus as the Paschal Lamb. The second, probably to Zech 12:10, shows a typical Johannine development of tradition, whereby the "piercing" probably referred in the first instance to the nailing of Jesus to the cross. The FE now takes this to point to the spear thrust instead.

The burial of Jesus introduces Joseph of Arimathea (19:38), also known in the Synoptic accounts. The FG talks of him as a "secret" disciple, of the type earlier condemned (12:42). His clandestine discipleship may have served the dramatic purpose here of allowing him to take the body since Pilate was hardly likely to release the body to a known sympathizer. With Joseph comes Nicodemus (19:39), of whose earlier night visit the reader is reminded. The inference may be that the secret disciple is emerging from the "night," but this is far from conclusive.

A huge quantity of embalming material is provided, reminiscent of Mary's earlier effusive anointing. The body is prepared *before* the burial (19:40), thus rendering a morning visit of the women, as found in the Synoptics, unnecessary. The newness of the tomb is emphasized (v. 41), presumably because it would have been thought unsuitable to place Jesus' body in a used one. The tomb is said to be in a garden, thus preparing the way for the following drama of mistaken identity (20:15). The scene is now set for the final dramatic act to unfold.

John 20:1-18

The story of the encounter between Mary Magdalene and the risen Jesus at the tomb is a typical Johannine reshaping of Synoptic tradition. It brings together two separate stories in a fairly clumsy manner, but emerges as a superb piece of theological reflection on a number of FG themes. Especially important is the issue of discipleship, which receives a double exposition initially through the BD and then in the exemplary role of Mary (cf. Scott 1992: 222-34).

The account opens with Mary coming alone to the tomb before dawn (20:1). There is no indication of why she has come, but it is surely not to anoint Jesus as in Mark and Luke, since this has already been done (John 19:39-40). On discovering that the stone has been removed from the tomb entrance she runs to find Peter and the BD to report what has happened (20:2). Her report is simply that an unspecified "they" have taken Jesus' body to an unknown destination. This suggests that she has looked into the tomb, although this was not stated in 20:1. In terms of redaction criticism, it is interesting to note that her words are still in the plural ("*we* do not know"), indicating that the FE has narrowed the Synoptic *group* of women (cf. Mark 16:1 par.) down to an individual witness.

Mary is left behind for the moment as the two men run to the tomb (20:3-4), the BD arriving first. This detail has been taken as symbolic of the superior desire of Gentile Christianity over Jewish Christianity (cf. Bultmann 1971: 685), but this is highly unlikely, not least given that the BD is also a Jew! It is better viewed as part of the whole Johannine picture, whereby the roles of the prominent male disciples of the Synoptic tradition are played down in favor of a different kind of presentation, often involving women as examples. We are dealing with material from a group which highly regards its independent thinking in this area, as in other areas such as Christology and ecclesiology.

The BD looks into the tomb (20:5), sees the grave clothes, but will not venture in. By way of contrast, Peter goes straight into the tomb (v. 6) and notes the detail of the clothes (v. 7). The manner in which the headcovering and other bindings have been neatly separated from each other and rolled up may suggest an apologetic against the idea that Jesus' body had simply been snatched by grave robbers (cf. Lindars 1972: 601).

Despite having reached the tomb first, the BD only then joins Peter within (20:8). We are told that he "believed" — but the question is, What? If he believed that Jesus was risen, there is certainly no evidence of his having been able to convince the others of this (cf. 20:19). Much more likely is that the two men are placed here as corroborating evidence of *Mary's* report that the tomb was empty (Minear 1976: 127-28; Scott 1992: 227). In other words, they believe her. The narrator makes this clearer by saying precisely that they did *not* know the scripture (v. 9) concerning resurrection. No such text is quoted, but it has often been assumed to be Ps 16:10. In Johannine terms, the BD cannot thus have believed in Jesus' rising at this point. Further confirmation of the disciples' lack of understanding comes in the rather banal description of their return home (20:10), with no apparent haste or excitement.

With the men out of the way, the central narrative involving Mary is ready to unfold. The camera turns to find her weeping outside the tomb (20:11), though how she got back there is unstated (this is probably due to the conflation of the two stories). The four evangelists are agreed that Mary Magdalene was present at the tomb, but the FE ignores other women to focus on the role of a single disciple in Mary. Like Peter and the BD, she, too, stoops to look into the tomb, but her eyes see more than theirs. Two angelic messengers (v. 12) occupy the place where Jesus' body had earlier been placed. Their precise positioning (at head and foot) may be symbolic, though the symbolism is far from clear (cf. Brown 1966: 989 for suggestions).

The angels ask why Mary is weeping (20:13), though without the further question posed by Jesus on his later appearance. This is important because it focuses the attention on that second question (v. 15). Like the male disciples, Mary has no real understanding yet about what has happened, so she replies (this time *singular*) by repeating her earlier report to Peter and the BD. The angels disappear from the scene at this point and are replaced by Jesus, whom Mary turns to see standing there (v. 14), though as yet she does not recognize him. Failure to recognize is a common feature in such epiphany stories (Mark 6:49; Luke 24:16; John 21:4). Even when Jesus addresses her directly, she still assumes him to be the gardener (20:15). He asks her whom she seeks, a crucial concept in Johannine thinking about discipleship. Jesus has already indicated, like Sophia before him, that many will seek and not find him because of his withdrawal (8:21). Now Mary, like a true disciple, without yet having full understanding, comes seeking and will find "much more than she could ever have expected" (Scott 1992: 232). For the moment she asks the obvious question of this man, whether he has taken and hidden the body.

Jesus' reply consists of only one word — her name, "Mary!"(20:16). This is a beautiful illustration of the Good Shepherd parable, where the sheep know the Shepherd because he calls them by name (see above, 10:3). Immediately her eyes are opened, and she responds to Jesus. Her response, however, reflects the fact that her understanding is not yet complete. In her reply, "Teacher," she does not realize that "he must now be seen as more than just another conveyor of Wisdom" (Witherington 1995: 331). Full recognition of Jesus Sophia is still to come.

Mary's action in attempting to cling to Jesus (20:17 — implied by his words to her) also betrays her incomplete understanding. She thinks that she can still "recapture the conditions of incarnate life in place of the universal and abiding relationship" the risen Jesus now establishes (Lindars 1972: 607). This new state is one of familial relationships, so she must go to the "brothers" and tell of Jesus' ascension to be with their mutual parent-God. The motif of ascension is not the real focus here, or anywhere in the FG for that matter, it being a vehicle for expressing the departure of Jesus and the establishment of a new relationship which is dependent on neither sight nor touch, but on the Spirit — soon to be given.

Mary's response indicates that the eyes of faith are finally fully open, as she goes with the apostolic (cf. 1 Cor 9:1) confession, "I have seen the Lord" (20:18). Through her participation in the story, Mary thus illustrates for the reader the complete pattern of coming to faith and exercising discipleship. She is faithful to the end in coming to the tomb; she moves from little to complete understanding/faith; she responds to the intimate voice of the Shepherd; she goes out to confess Jesus to others. She well deserves the title "Apostle to the Apostles," the first witness to Christ and the symbol of true discipleship to the community which must believe without seeing.

John 20:19-31

The postresurrection appearances continue beyond Mary Magdalene's encounter with Jesus. However well she may have told her story, it would seem that the "brothers" did not fully understand since they are still fearfully behind closed doors (20:19) after her report. Jesus comes to them with the greeting he promised before the passion, "Shalom" (14:27). Although Jesus seems to enter the room miraculously without opening the door, it is clear from what follows that the reader is expected to understand his body as quite normal. Like Matthew's account of Jesus walking on the sea (Matt 14:22-33), the coming of Jesus is meant to illustrate his continuous presence, even when this appears least likely.

The disciples are said to be in fear of the "Jews" — here obviously the authorities who connived in the death of Jesus. The undertones we have noted in the previous appearances of this language continue here because it is precisely in the postresurrection situation that the community faces opposition and has fear. Jesus' greeting is to help dispel such anxiety and recall earlier teaching.

It would appear that the disciples recognize Jesus fully only when he displays his wounds for them (20:20); at least it is only then that they rejoice. The evidence of the wounds is theologically important since it dispels any notion that Jesus did not really suffer, points to the physical nature of his presence, and underlines the oneness of the crucified and risen Jesus.

The peace greeting is repeated (20:21) before Jesus launches into words of commission. All along Jesus has spoken of himself in terms of Sophia tradition as the one sent by God: it is precisely this language with which he now initiates the disciples in their new role. In order to do this, however, they need to be transformed from their current state of fear and dependence on visual contact with Jesus. So the earlier promise of help in the form of the Spirit is kept (20:22), but what is pictured is much more than just additional help. It is nothing less than a new act of creation, or a rebirth. As God breathed life into humanity (Gen 2:7 uses exactly the same form *enephysēsen;* cf. significant uses of the verb in Ezek 37:9 and Wis 15:11), so Jesus breathes his continuing life into the disciples. The imagery has strong links with the pictures of Sophia, whom we have already seen "passes into holy souls" as the very breath of God (Wis 7:25-27). As in the opening verses of the FG, with its stress on presence at creation, so, too, in the closing verses the identification of Jesus as Sophia incarnate, passing on the mission of God to the disciples, is clearly made (cf. Scott 1992: 162-65).

Despite all the tortuous efforts of scholars to harmonize Acts 2 and John 20:22 (cf. Witherington 1995: 340-41), this is the FE's representation of what Luke describes in terms equally dependent on the imagery of the Jewish scriptures. Even a scholar as conservative as Carson thinks that John's description is "best understood as a kind of acted parable" (Carson 1991: 655).

The thorny issue of the forgiveness of sins (or not!) is linked to the gift of the Spirit here (20:23). This has been interpreted in different ways by Roman Catholic and Protestant scholars, both with interests defined by an era later than the Johannine community (cf. Brown 1966: 1039-45). The verse needs to be read carefully in the light of Sophia Christology, in particular 8:21, which talks of "dying in your sin." Jesus Sophia's withdrawal leaves those who will not respond to his words without forgiveness. It is the same work to which the disciples are now commissioned, so the response of people to their promulgation of the word will be decisive. Either they will believe, and so benefit from Jesus' withdrawal, or like those who rejected Sophia's wisdom before, fail to find (eternal) life. Even if the text does address the question of internal relationships of the community, this is only a secondary consideration.

Attention now turns to Thomas (20:24), apparently absent during the initial giving of the Spirit. His characterization is consistent (cf. 11:16; 14:5) as one who is skeptical and lacking in understanding. Here again he is not prepared to accept the witness of the group (20:25), demanding to "see" and touch as a precondition to belief. He is surely an example for the community of the way in which even one so incredulous "could become not only a nominal Christian but even one who makes a full and robust confession about Jesus" (Witherington 1995: 339).

Thomas also serves an important *narrative* function in the FG, opening the way for crucial statements from Jesus. A third appearance of Jesus, exactly parallel to 20:19 in its setting and greeting (20:26), leads on to a demonstration of an essential characteristic of faith for the reader. Thomas is confronted with the reality of Jesus' presence (v. 27), and in it he can see clearly the continuity between the Jesus who died and the Jesus who now lives. This sight leads Thomas to make the climactic confession of the FG (20:28), which takes the reader, by a superbly planned narrative *inclusio,* full circle back to the beginning of the Prologue. This is the sum of the Johannine development of Sophia Christology: in Jesus, Sophia incarnate, all of God's creative and saving power is present.

It has long been recognized that Thomas's confession also hints ironically at the overcoming of the power of the world, in that the Roman emperor Domitian demanded this very title as an address (cf. Cassidy 1992: 13-16). We cannot be certain that this reference was *historically* intended, but it is certainly a fine literary-theological irony if it was not!

Jesus' final words (20:29) are directed to the future. Generations to come cannot see Jesus in the flesh, but they, the reader included, will demonstrate a greater quality of faith by their belief without "signs."

The original ending of the FG (20:30-31) attempts to sum up what has gone before. Clearly not everything that Jesus ever did has been included, but these things are written with a purpose. Much of the interpretation of the whole purpose of the FG hangs on a single Greek letter here! The textual tradition is equally divided between a present subjunctive (*pisteuēte* — "you may continue to believe") and an aorist subjunctive (*pisteusēte* — "you may come to faith"). My own conclusion throughout has been that the former is more likely. The FG is not *primarily* a missionary document, but demands a reader already well informed of the story, even if not in its Johannine version. It is, of course, part of the continuing task of the believer, in Johannine terms, to engage in mission, so there is a strong urge to be involved.

What the disciple is called upon to continue believing is the confession already expressed so clearly by Martha (11:27). This is that Jesus is the Christ, and for the FE the meaning of this is best expressed through the vehicle of Sophia language and tradition. Whatever other Christian groups may think of this, the reader is encouraged to stick with this Christology. Given its richness for inclusive imagery today, we may be thankful that some did.

John 21:1-14

The addition of this final chapter of the FG took place sometime early in its transmission. There is no textual evidence to show that the FG ever circulated without the addition, but the finality of 20:30-31 is sufficient indication of an original ending. John 21 is both tantalizing and frustrating: tantalizing because it takes us close to being able to uncover some of the later tensions of the community, reflected in its subject matter; frustrating because it seems at points almost to undermine what has gone before (cf. Scott 1992: 248-50).

An appearance in Galilee (21:1) is a new departure for the FG since the other appearances appear to take place in the environs of Jerusalem. Some seven of the male disciples, led by Peter (21:2-3), set out once again to their old trade — fishing. The list is a strange combination of Johannine (Nathanael — now we are told he is from Cana) and Synoptic figures (sons of Zebedee — nowhere else spoken of in the FG). The whole story bears comparison with Luke 5:1-11, where a similar miraculous catch of fish takes place in a preresurrection context. Despite a whole night of fishing they catch nothing at all.

Around dawn (21:4), a popular christophany time (cf. Matt 14:25), Jesus appears on the beach. As in the dawn appearance to Mary in the garden, he is unrecognized, even when he addresses them in familiar fashion (v. 5 — probably best translated "lads"). His question in Greek assumes the answer "no," perhaps hinting at Jesus' intimate knowledge of their situation. Even though they still do not realize who he is, the disciples obey his instructions (21:6) to cast the net again on the right of the boat. The result is a miraculous, overflowing catch.

Given the initial list of players, it is a little surprising to find the BD in the boat (21:7), but typically he is the one to recognize Jesus. He tells Peter, who immediately responds by covering his nakedness. This is surely an allusion to the creation story, where the man becomes aware of his nakedness in the presence of the divine. Peter wades in front through the sea, while the rest of the disciples follow in the boat (21:8) dragging the catch behind them.

On arriving at the shore they find that Jesus has already prepared a fire (21:9), has fish (!) cooking and bread supplied. There are some interesting linguistic parallels here, showing again the mixture of materials used in the construction of the story. The word used for "disembarking" is found only here and at Luke 5:2 in the NT, suggesting strongly a link with that tradition. By contrast, however, the word for fish *(opsarion)* seems to come from John 6:9, 11 — the only other place it is used in the NT. This is probably intended as an echo to take the reader back to a previous feeding miracle with its theme of Jesus as Bread.

Jesus asks them for (more?) fish to cook (21:10), so Peter again takes the initiative in hauling the large catch to shore (21:11). We are told specifically that there were 153 fish, a number surely so precise as to be symbolic. Brown lists many of the suggestions made to explain this symbolism through the centuries (Brown 1966: 1074-76), the most likely being that it bears some relationship to the number of known species of fish at that time. Even if this is not the case, the effect is to point to the abundance and probably the all-inclusive nature of the catch — presumably a symbol of casting the net of the Christian mission throughout the known world.

Jesus invites the group to breakfast (21:12-13), with himself as host. The similarity to the Emmaus Road sharing of bread is strong, and there may here be allusions to a eucharistic meal, especially when Jesus takes the bread and gives it to the disciples. There is still a hint of uncertainty, but a general acceptance of Jesus' identity with no one willing to raise a question which elsewhere came in the mouth of Jesus' opponents (8:25).

The verse concluding this part of the story (21:14) points to the problem of the way in which this appendix chapter relates to the rest of the FG. If this is Jesus' *third* appearance to the disciples (plural), then the others referred to are those in the second half of John 20. This would mean that the *primary* appearance to Mary Magdalene is ignored. The person responsible for this chapter would seem not to have understood (or accepted? or been aware of?) the overall Johannine picture of women as paradigms of discipleship (cf. Scott 1994: 169-89). The prominence given to Peter in this account, and even more so in the subsequent one, also fits badly with his portrayal elsewhere in the Johannine tradition and helps to subvert Mary's role. It may well be that this chapter represents "the first step on the ladder of misunderstanding of the Johannine traditions concerning women which prevails to the present day" (Scott 1992: 250).

John 21:15-25

The completion of breakfast leads into a conversation between Jesus and Peter (21:15-17), constructed around a repetitious question-and-answer session. The threefold question looks identical in English, but the Greek varies between *agapan* (vv. 15 and 16) and *philein* (v. 17). The word for sheep/lambs also varies between the verses, with the textual tradition far from clear which word should be adopted in each verse. There has been much argument among scholars and ingenious interpretation put forward in relation to these variations (cf. Brown 1966: 1102-6), but they are probably stylistic rather than theological variations. The two words for love are used interchangeably elsewhere in the FG, including in the name of the BD, for whom the FE normally uses *agapan,* but in 20:2 uses *philein.*

The overall purpose of the conversation between Jesus and Peter is generally accepted to be a threefold reinstatement of Peter following his threefold denial (18:17, 25-27). In the first question (21:15) Jesus asks if Peter loves him "more than these." This could be a comparative question ("more than the other disciples love me"), but this seems unlikely. What Peter is being asked is the basic question on which he failed earlier — Does his love for Jesus outstrip his desire for anything else (people or things)? Only when this is clearly seen to be the case will Peter be in a position to take on a shepherding role parallel to that of the Good Shepherd, who puts the life of the sheep before all other concerns. Peter's earlier claim to be willing to "lay down my life" (13:37) will be put to the test again, and having failed once cannot be left to chance.

The persistence of Jesus' questioning alongside Peter's positive affirmation of his love for Jesus leads to Peter feeling "hurt," but it is important for him to be tested to the limit. Jesus reveals why in a proverbial statement (21:18). A young person is free to choose much that lies ahead in life, having the energy and possibility to make and follow through such choices. An old person is often dependent on others for getting around, and choice is reduced. This is turned into a statement about Peter's future martyrdom, whereby he is "bound" and "fastened" in crucifixion, like Jesus. The narrator makes this explicit (21:19) lest the reader should not have understood. Significantly, Jesus then calls Peter to make a choice in the classic Synoptic words of discipleship — "Follow me."

Peter's testing is not yet over. The BD is also following Jesus (21:20), and this raises a question for Peter. The writer gives a lengthy explanation of the identity of the BD, almost as though the reader might not know, suggesting again the separate nature of the material in ch. 21. The effect, however, is to emphasize the intimate relationship between the BD and Jesus. Peter's question is very open-ended (21:21), but Jesus' reply indicates that it concerns what will happen to the BD. Will the BD's fate be the same as Peter's? Jesus basically indicates that the BD's fate is not Peter's concern (21:22), and that Peter must concentrate on the task of following Jesus himself. The dialogue certainly seems to reflect some of the tension between different factions related to these two apostolic figures. Indeed, this whole additional chapter is concerned primarily with a kind of rehabilitation of Peter which suggests an underlying conflict with communities in which his authority held a central role.

The narrator's comment on Jesus' reply (21:23) indicates an eschatological viewpoint (the "second coming" of Jesus) not expressed clearly anywhere else in the FG. The community would surely have been aware of such early Christian speculation, but it is not generally their understanding. The idea that Jesus' life continues through the presence of the Spirit in the life of believers is not utterly incompatible with a future eschatology, but the former is certainly the "normal" view.

The final verses of the chapter (21:24-25) claim that the whole FG stems from the testimony of the BD, but reminds the reader of the same conclusion as found in the original ending (20:30) — this is only a small fraction of the whole story of Jesus. The purpose of this statement is to try to persuade the reader finally of the validity of the witness therein contained. Given the radical nature of the Christology, the prominence of women as disciples, the lack of many traditional "sacramental" features, and the absence of traditional "kingdom" language, this was probably a claim which the writer needed to make with some urgency!

Bibliography. Ashton, J. 1993, *Understanding the Fourth Gospel,* Oxford: Clarendon • Ashton, J, ed. 1986, *The Interpretation of John,* Philadelphia: Fortress • Barrett, C. K. 2d ed. 1978, *The Gospel According to John: An Introduction and Commentary with Notes on the Greek Text,* London: SPCK • Beasley-Murray, G. 1987, *John,* Waco: Word • Bishop, E. F. 1959-60, "The Door of the Sheep — John x.7-9," *ExpTim* 71:307-9 • Bond, H. K. 1998, *Pontius Pilate in History and Interpretation,* Cambridge: Cambridge University • Brown, R. E. 1966, *The Gospel According to John,* 2 vols., AB 29a and b, New York: Doubleday • Brown, R. E. 1979, *The Community of the Beloved Disciple: The Life, Loves and Hates of an Individual Church in New Testament Times,* London: Geoffrey Chapman • Brown, R. E. 1994, *The Death of the Messiah: A Commentary on the Passion Narrative in the Four Gospels,* 2 vols., London: Geoffrey Chapman • Brown, R. E. 1997, *An Introduction to the New Testament,* New York: Doubleday • Bultmann, R. 1955, *Theology of the New Testament,* 2 vols., trans. K. Grobel, London: SCM • Bultmann, R. 1971, *The Gospel of John: A Commentary,* Oxford: Basil Blackwell • Burge, G. M. 1987, *The Anointed Community: The Holy Spirit in the Johannine Tradition,* Grand Rapids: Eerdmans • Carson, D. A. 1991, *The Gospel According to John,* Grand Rapids: Eerdmans • Cassidy, R. J. 1992, *John's Gospel in New Perspective,* Maryknoll, N.Y.: Orbis • Culpepper, R. A. 1983, *Anatomy of the Fourth Gospel: A Study in Literary Design,* Philadelphia: Fortress • Davies, M. 1992, *Rhetoric and Reference in the Fourth Gospel,* Sheffield: JSOT • Dodd, C. H. 1953, *The Interpretation of the Fourth Gospel,* Cambridge: Cambridge University • Dodd, C. H. 1963, *Historical Tradition in the Fourth Gospel,* Cambridge: Cambridge University • Duke, P. D. 1985, *Irony in the Fourth Gospel,* Atlanta: John Knox • Dunn, J. D. G. 1983, "Let John Be John: A Gospel for Its Time," in P. Stuhlmacher, ed., *Das Evangelium und die Evangelien,* Tübingen: J. C. B. Mohr, 309-39 • Dunn, J. D. G. 2d ed. 1989, *Christology in the Making: An Inquiry into the Origins of the Doctrine of the Incarnation,* London: SCM • Fiorenza, E. S. 1983, *In Memory of Her: A Feminist Theological Reconstruction of Early Christian Origins,* London: SCM • Fiorenza, E. S. 1994, *Jesus: Miriam's Child, Sophia's Prophet: Critical Issues in Feminist Christology,* London: SCM • Fortna, R. A. 1988, *The Fourth Gospel and Its Predecessors: From Narrative Source to Present Gospel,* Philadelphia: Fortress • Gese, H. 1981, "The Prologue to John's Gospel," in *Essays on Biblical Theology,* Minneapolis: Augsburg, 12-21 • Grayston, K. 1990, *The Gospel of John,* London: Epworth • Guilding, A. 1960, *The Fourth Gospel and Jewish Worship,* Oxford: Clarendon • Howard-Brook, W. 1994, *Becoming Children of God: John's Gospel and Radical Discipleship,* Maryknoll, N.Y.: Orbis • Jeremias, J. 1966, *The Eucharistic Words of Jesus,* London: SCM • Johnson, E. A. 1985, "Jesus, the Wisdom of God: A Biblical Basis for Non-Androcentric Christology," *ETL* 61:261-94 • Käsemann, E. 1968, *The Testament of Jesus: A Study of the Gospel of John in the Light of Chapter 17,* London: SCM • Lindars, B. 1972, *The Gospel of John,* London: Marshall, Morgan & Scott • McDonald, J. 1964, *The Theology of the Samaritans,* London: SCM • Martyn, J. L. 2d ed., 1979, *History and Theology in the Fourth Gospel,* Nashville: Abingdon • Minear, P. 1976, "'We Don't Know Where . . .': John 20.2," *Int* 30: 125-39 • Moloney, F. J. 1980, "From Cana to Cana (John 2.1–4.54) and the Fourth Evangelist's Concept of Correct (and Incorrect) Faith," in F. A. Livingston, ed., *Studia Biblica II: Papers on the Gospels,* JSNTSup 2, Sheffield: JSOT, 185-213 • Moloney, F. J. 1992, "Who Is 'the Reader' in/of the Fourth Gospel?" *AusBR* 40:20-33 • Painter, J. 1991, *The Quest for the Messiah,* Edinburgh: T. & T. Clark • Powell, M. A. 1993, *What Is Narrative Criticism?,* London: SPCK • Pryor, J. 1992, *John: Evangelist of the Covenant People: The Narrative and Themes of the Fourth Gospel,* London: Darton, Longman & Todd • Rensberger, D. 1988, *Overcoming the World: Politics and Community in the Gospel of John,* London: SPCK • Schnackenburg, R. 1968-82, *The Gospel According to St John,* 3 vols., London: Burns & Oates • Schneiders, S. M. 1982, "Women in the Fourth Gospel and the Role of Women in the Contemporary Church," *BTB* 12:35-45 • Scott, M. 1992, *Sophia and the Johannine Jesus,* Sheffield: JSOT • Scott, M. 1994, "The Women of the Fourth Gospel: Paradigms of Discipleship or Paragons of Virtue?" in *Festschrift für Günter Wagner,* Bern: Peter Lang, 169-89 • Segovia, F. F. 1991, *The Farewell of the Word: The Johannine Call to Abide,* Minneapolis: Fortress • Smith, D. M. 1992, *John among the Gospels: The Relationship in Twentieth-Century Research,* Minneapolis: Fortress • Smith, D. M. 1996, *The Theology of the Gospel of John,* Cambridge: Cambridge University • Stibbe, M. G. 1994, *John's Gospel,* London: Routledge • Trevett, C. 1995, *Montanism: Gender, Authority and the New Prophecy,* Cambridge: Cambridge University • Witherington, B. 1995, *John's Wisdom: A Commentary on the Fourth Gospel,* Cambridge: Lutterworth • Yee, G. A. 1989, *Jewish Feasts and the Gospel of John,* Wilmington: Michael Glazier.

Acts

John T. Squires

INTRODUCTION

Acts is half of what was originally a two-volume work of literary and theological unity (given the name "Luke-Acts" in modern scholarship), written by an unknown author (given the name "Luke" in early ecclesiastical tradition) sometime in the latter decades of the first century. The first volume (Luke's Gospel) tells the story of Jesus from his conception to his ascension into heaven about three decades later. The second volume (Acts) traces the development of the messianic Jewish movement which was begun by Jesus from his ascension to Paul's arrival in Rome about three decades later. Both volumes are written in the style of history of that time (see the Introduction to the Gospel of Luke above, 1104; Sterling 1992: 311-21, 331-39).

No clear evidence exists regarding the sources available to the author in writing this second volume of his work. It is possible that Luke knew and used sources which told of the beginnings of the movement in Jerusalem (Acts 1–7), the spread of this movement into Samaria (Acts 8), and the missionary activity of Paul (Acts 9, 13–20). Some sections of Acts include the author as one traveling in Paul's group (Acts 16:10-17; 20:5-15; 21:1-18; 27:1–28:16) and may reflect a basic record of the group's itinerary. A significant proportion of Acts is devoted to speeches made by leading characters (e.g., Peter, Stephen, and Paul). As was the custom in the history writing of the time, such speeches were not necessarily verbatim reports but creations of the author, reflecting what was appropriate to the occasion (Sterling 1992: 372-74).

Acts is known in two main textual versions; the Western text (Codex D) is 10 percent longer than the Alexandrian text ($\mathfrak{p}^{45}$, Codex B) since it has numerous stylistic and theological additions. Most scholars favor the Alexandrian text as more likely to be the original text.

Geography is important in Acts. The opening scene is in Jerusalem, the focal point of the Jewish faith. The final scene is in Rome, the center of the Roman Empire. The story which unfolds between these two scenes reveals the gradual expansion of this messianic movement as it progresses from Jerusalem to Rome. The first section (1:1–8:3) deals with the earliest community of believers; it is set wholly within Jerusalem. The second section (8:4–12:25) prepares for the "turn to the Gentiles" through a sequence of steps which initially proceed away from Jerusalem — although the final scenes in this section return to Jerusalem. The third major section (13:1–21:16) recounts the activity of Paul and some of his co-workers in establishing new communities of faith in the northeast part of the Mediterranean basin. This section begins in Antioch and moves through a series of episodes to Caesarea before ending in Jerusalem once more. The arrest of Paul precipitates the fourth major section of Acts (21:17–28:15), focusing on the trials of Paul. The geographic focus is again first on Jerusalem, but this section of the story moves relentlessly toward Rome, where it ends.

The book is traditionally known as The Acts of the Apostles. It tells of the deeds of the apostles. Luke appears to have a concern to demonstrate that the apostles represent the unbroken continuation of the ministry of Jesus in decades immediately after his public preaching and healing. There are numerous resonances between what takes place in Acts and what has already been narrated in Luke's Gospel. The appointment of a twelfth apostle, Matthias, to replace Judas Iscariot is narrated early in the book (1:15-26). This seems to signal that the group of twelve, now reconstituted, retains its leadership in the movement begun by Jesus. This is but the first of many indications that Acts may be read as a "confirmation of the Gospel" (Maddox 1982: 22-23, 180-87).

However, the work as a whole does not continue this focus on the apostles as a unified group. Most of them do not figure at all in the rest of the story, for it immediately narrows to a focus on Peter (accompanied silently by John). Neither those individuals who have some prominence in the ensuing narrative (Stephen, Philip, Barnabas, Silas, Timothy, etc.) nor the figure who comes to dominate the account (Paul) are to be numbered among the twelve apostles at all.

A conclusion which some interpreters have drawn from the prominence of Paul is that Acts ought really to be called The Acts of Paul — since his "conversion" (or, better, his commissioning) is reported no fewer than three times during the work (9:1-18; 22:1-21; 26:1-32) and since more than half of the work is devoted to the activity of Paul (9:19-31; 13:1–28:31). This claim has some merit, but it still fails to explain both how the first half of the book relates to this concern and why the book ends without reporting the ultimate fate of Paul, the alleged main character.

Others have suggested that Acts has as its focus the Spirit rather than the apostles or Paul; they believe that the work should be regarded as The Acts of the Holy Spirit. While the first major incident reported at length — the day of Pentecost (2:1-41) — does focus on the Spirit, and while the Spirit plays a significant role in parts of Acts, this suggestion still has a sense of incompleteness about it. There are long sections of the work from which the Spirit is absent; indeed, there is neither explicit mention of, nor indirect allusion to, the Spirit from the moment that Paul has determined that he will go to Jerusalem (21:11-14) until the glancing reference to the Spirit in the final scene (28:25).

Another option is to regard the book as The Acts of Jesus Christ, explaining how Jesus has been at work in the deeds of Paul, the apostles, and others throughout the book. The singular claim advanced by Peter, that "there is salvation by no one else, for there is no other name . . . by which you must be saved" (4:12), focuses attention on "coming to faith in Christ" as the key to the work. That Acts is an explicitly missionary work, recounting the early Christian mission and advocating missionary activity, is undoubted. However, the long account of Paul's arrest and trials (Acts 21–28) seems to be a peculiarly disappointing anticlimax if the missionary orientation is indeed the central focus.

The present approach to Acts will be to focus on the role which God plays in the narrative. As we note the scope of "language about God" throughout the book, we will explore the contribution that this makes to Luke's purposes. Seen in this way, the book may well be understood as The Acts of God. In Acts, Luke reveals how he understands the purposes of God are being worked out through the various people who make up the messianic Jewish movement which was begun by Jesus of Nazareth. He shapes his narrative so that it constantly unveils the workings of the divine in ordinary human events.

Such an interest in how God is at work in the events of human history is not unique to Luke. Both the historical narratives of the Hebrew Bible and the historical works of various Gentile authors provide interpretations of events in this vein. The appearances of divine beings and the occurrence of miraculous incidents through divine intervention are found often in the Pentateuch and ensuing historical writings. The Deuteronomist regularly notes how events fulfill words spoken by God (1 Kgs 2:27; 8:15-16; 8:23-24; 8:56; 12:24; 14:18; 15:29; 16:12; 16:34; 17:5; 17:16; 22:38; 2 Kgs 1:17; 4:44; 5:14; 7:16; 9:36; 10:17; 14:25; 15:12; 17:22-23; 23:16; 24:2; 24:13). The character of Yahweh dominates the scriptural narratives — and history is implicitly understood in the way articulated by Yahweh through Isaiah: "As I have designed, so shall it be; and as I have planned, so shall it come to pass" (Isa 14:24; a refrain repeated at 46:11b; see also 37:26; 55:11; Sterling 1992: 352-63; Rosner in Winter and Clarke 1993: 78-80).

Such an understanding of history is also to be found in the Greek tradition. In the works of Hellenistic historians, particular deities are understood to be the forces which guide and shape history: Pronoia in Herodotus, Fortuna in Polybius, Fate in Posidonius, Pronoia in Diodorus Siculus, and Tyche in Dionysius of Halicarnassus. Indeed, the first-century-BC Sicilian historian Diodorus describes historians as being "ministers of divine providence" (Pronoia) whose task is to demonstrate how the unifying effect of providence is made manifest in the histories which are narrated (*Hist.* 1.1.3). Similarly, in his twenty-volume history of Rome, Dionysius of Halicarnassus demonstrates that the goddess Fortune (Tyche) had bestowed upon Rome "a supremacy so great and already of so long continuance" (*Rom. Ant.* 1.5.2). Luke's contemporary, Flavius Josephus, writes his twenty-volume history of the Jews with similar intent, demonstrating that "men who conform to the will of God . . . prosper in all things beyond belief, and for their reward are offered by God felicity" (*Ant.* 1 §46). His history is permeated with references to divine providence at work among the Jews. Luke writes within the same conventions of history writing, showing that the events recounted take place within God's providential plan. He shapes his narrative so that his readers/listeners are constantly reminded of this theme (Squires 1993: 15-36; Sterling 1992: 363-69).

The story of Jesus, as retold in the speeches of Acts, is understood within the parameters of the things that "God did through him" (2:22); the most succinct summation of his life is that "God was with him" (10:38). Likewise, as the history of Israel is retold in speeches, it is always presented in the light of the claim that God shaped its history: "the God of glory appeared to our ancestor Abraham" (7:2), "the God of this people Israel chose our ancestors and made the people" great (13:17). It is God who is at the center of Luke's theological understanding (Jervell 1996: 18-25). The narrative concerning the growth and development of the messianic movement makes similar reference to God's role. To the community in Jerusalem, "the Lord added those being saved daily" (2:47). When Peter encounters Gentiles in Caesarea, he asserts, "God gave the same gift to them [Gentiles] as also to us [Jewish] believers" (11:17). The missionary endeavors of Paul and others are summarized thus: "they announced what God did with them, and how he opened a door of faith to the Gentiles" (14:27), and "God has called us to preach the good news to them [in Macedonia]" (16:10). God guides all that takes place; Paul sums up this perspective when he comments, "may the Lord's will be done" (21:14), "to this day I have had the help which is from God" (26:22), and finally, "this salvation of God has been sent to the Gentiles" (28:28). As Luke presents his story, it is clear that everything takes place under the guidance of God (Squires in Marshall and Peterson 1998: 19-39).

Luke-Acts is written to Theophilus (Luke 1:3; Acts 1:1), who represents people who know full well the customs and practices of Hellenistic society and yet have been introduced to the distinctive beliefs and practices of the messianic movement begun by Jesus, as it was found in the various communities in the eastern Mediterranean. Such people were caught in a set of tensions between established societal expectations, on the one hand, and the developing customs of the messianic movement, on the other. By addressing his work to this audience, Luke is writing in a manner best described as "apologetic."

The function of apologetic literature was to reinterpret these distinctive community customs and beliefs in such a way that they would "make sense" in the context of the wider Hellenized society. Sterling calls the result of this process an apologetic history, that is, "an extended prose narrative written by a member of the group who follows the group's own traditions but Hellenizes them in an effort to establish the identity of the group within the setting of the larger world" (Sterling 1992: 17,

378-89; see also Squires 1993: 52-55). This is an apt description of Luke's labors; he writes so that Theophilus, and others who are part of his faith community, may be strengthened in their self-understanding within the wider society.

Luke writes apologetically in order to provide certainty or reassurance *(asphaleian)* about the faith already known to his readers/listeners (Luke 1:1-4). Even as he recounts events from the past, Luke's writing is constantly oriented toward his contemporary audience. The continual references to God within the story have particular relevance to this apologetic process; they provide an important means of legitimating (or validating) the distinctive self-identity of this community within the wider context of Hellenized society. For Luke, since God has made the messianic communities to be just as he depicts them in his narrative, the story of Acts provides his readers/listeners with models of being a faith community and of exercising leadership within such a community, and it encourages such readers/listeners to follow these models (Maddox 1982: 180-87; Peterson in Marshall and Peterson 1998: 532-44). Such a purpose remains entirely relevant in the twenty-first century.

COMMENTARY

Section One: The Community in Jerusalem (1:1–8:3)

The first major section of Acts recounts the life of the community in Jerusalem, where the earliest followers of Jesus establish a pattern of faithful living through their common life, their public witness, and their persistent adherence to their Jewish traditions. The whole section is located entirely within Jerusalem (1:4, 8, 12; 2:5; 4:5; 5:16; 6:7; 8:1). The scene on the day of Pentecost begins as pilgrims gather for the festival (2:1, 5) and concludes with the daily gathering of believers in the temple (2:46). The trials of Peter and John are located on the temple grounds (3:1, 11; 4:1; 5:12, 20, 21, 42), while the trial of Stephen takes place before the temple priests (7:1) and moves to a climactic focus on the (in)validity of the temple (7:47-50).

A major theme running through this section is the relationship of the community of Jesus' followers to the Jerusalem temple. The temple is the place where God has long been understood to live (Exod 25:17-22; 29:42-46; Deut 12:5-7, 10-12, 17-18; Ps 80:1-2; Isa 6:1-3; Ezek 44:4). The priests, as functionaries of the temple, represent an established understanding of how God wishes Israel to live, through the sacrificial rituals (Ezek 44:15-16, 23-24). The community is persistent in its involvement in this set of rituals; none of its members voluntarily take themselves away from the temple or fail to perform its rituals. Nevertheless, a tension is set up between the temple and the community of Jesus' followers. Despite their regular involvement in the temple rituals, community members see their leaders being placed under intense scrutiny by the temple leadership. The section ends with a criticism of the temple, articulated by Stephen (7:44-50). However, this is not a rejection of the temple and all that it stands for, as much as a strenuous critique of the ways that the current temple leadership have misunderstood the intentions of the temple and have misinterpreted its role in Israelite life.

Throughout this tense narrative (culminating in a direct conflict), references to God, both explicit and implicit, play a key role in helping the reader to interpret the events reported. Such language about God validates the nature of the common life established in the community, indicates the sovereignty of God in the events that are told, and demonstrates the way to give faithful witness to God's sovereignty. A key theme in this section is "the sovereignty of God" (1:3). The involvement of God in the events narrated is expressed by means of explicit narrative comments (2:47; 6:7) and through epiphanies which occur in the story (1:3, 10; 2:4; 5:19; 7:55). In the eight speeches reported in this section, Luke has his characters provide an overarching framework for understanding God's providential activity. The speeches contain affirmations that God has been at work in the life of Jesus (2:22-32, 36; 3:13-15, 17-18; 4:27-28; 5:30-32) and earlier in the history of Israel (7:2-53), as well as in the events reported in the narrative itself (1:16-22; 2:16-21, 33; 3:12, 16; 4:8-12, 29-30; 5:29, 38-39).

Restoring the Community Leadership (1:1-26)

The narrative of Acts begins with a **recapitulatory preface (1:1-5)** which summarizes the Gospel of Luke and begins to prepare for the ensuing narrative about the community in Jerusalem. First, Luke explicitly acknowledges that what follows is a sequel to an earlier volume, addressed to the same recipient, Theophilus (1:1). We know this as the Gospel of Luke; here, however, the content of this Gospel is epitomized as simply "the things which Jesus began to do and to teach" until his ascension (1:1-2). This recapitulation makes valid the claim that the preface to Luke's Gospel also applies to his second volume, Acts (Marshall in Winter and Clarke 1993: 163-82; on the preface to Acts as a preface to a history, see Alexander in Witherington 1996: 73-103). An early hint at the element of divine guidance in the story is found when the Holy Spirit is identified as the means by which Jesus chose the apostles (v. 2). Then follows a summation of the various manifestations of Jesus throughout the ensuing forty days (v. 3). These appearances are akin to the string of epiphanies whose divine origin has been clearly established in the Gospel (see Luke 1:26; 2:11).

During these appearances of Jesus, he speaks of "things concerning the sovereignty of God" (*basileia tou theou,* 1:3). The theme of divine sovereignty had been the focus of Jesus' message in Luke's Gospel. It characterized his initial public proclamation (Luke 4:43), marked his teachings in Galilee (Luke 6:20; 7:20; 8:1, 10), and recurred throughout his journey to Jerusalem (Luke 11:2, 20; 13:18, 20, 28, 29; 14:15; 16:16; 17:20, 21; 18:16; 19:12). Once in Jerusalem, Jesus continued to speak of "the sovereignty of God," both in the eschatological discourse he gave in the temple area (Luke 21:31) and at his final meal with his disciples (Luke 22:16, 18).

This theme will retain its prominence throughout

Acts; it provides the content of the preaching of Philip (8:12) and Paul (19:8; 20:25 with reference to the whole of Paul's preaching activity), and is reiterated in the final scene in Rome (28:23, 31). This "sovereignty of God" is the overarching theological theme of the whole story of Acts, from its beginnings in Jerusalem to its ending in Rome.

This preface continues with a bridging section which foreshadows the events of the next chapter of the narrative. Jesus instructs the apostles not to depart from Jerusalem (1:4). This instruction keeps Luke's geographic focus on Jerusalem, in contrast to other traditions concerning the postresurrection departure of the apostles to Galilee which are inferred (Matt 26:32; Mark 14:28; 16:7) or explicitly told (Matt 28:7, 10; John 21). Remaining in Jerusalem is required so that the apostles might receive the promise (1:4), which is immediately explained as being the Holy Spirit spoken of by John (1:5; evoking Luke 3:16). The fulfillment of this promise is narrated in detail in Acts 2.

Then follows an expanded **recapitulation of the ascension (1:6-11),** an event already reported in brief at Luke 24:50-53. The ascension forms the pivotal moment in Luke's narrative; it is the hinge between volume 1 (Luke) and volume 2 (Acts), and attention is drawn to the ascension and exaltation of Jesus at a number of points elsewhere (Luke 9:51; 22:69; Acts 2:33; 3:21; 5:31; 7:56). Luke expands this second narrative account of the ascension through the explicit recording of words spoken on that occasion: the last words of Jesus to his followers and the words of the two angel-like men to the followers of Jesus after his ascension.

The dialogue between Jesus and his disciples raises the central issue of sovereignty. The disciples ask, "Lord, (may we ask) if you will at this time restore sovereignty to Israel?" (1:6) — quite rightly, for the issue of sovereignty was central to Jesus' preaching (v. 3). Here, however, the orientation of the question is concerned with the sovereignty of Israel. Jesus replies with a sequence of three clauses which stand as his last words before he ascends into heaven.

The first clause of 1:8 turns the question away from Israel, back to the primary theme of God's sovereignty, with the clear declaration that the times and seasons are under the sovereignty of God, who has "set them by his own authority" (1:7). Rather than the political independence of Israel, it is God's unfettered freedom to act in history which is crucial to his enterprise. The next clause, "you will receive power when the Holy Spirit has come upon you" (v. 8), is a promise which reinforces the key role of the Spirit, as divine agent, throughout this volume (beginning with the events of 2:1-4). The third clause introduces the important motif of witness (1:22; 2:32; 3:15; 4:33; 5:32; 10:39, 41, 43; 13:31; 22:15, 18, 20; 23:11; 26:11, 22) and provides a condensed geographical summation of the course of the ensuing events: "in Jerusalem [1:12–8:3] and in all Judea and Samaria [8:4–12:25] and to the end of the earth [13:1 onward]." The precise referent of "the end of the earth" is debated. Although *Pss. Sol.* 8:15 may suggest that it refers to Rome, it is preferable to see the reference as drawn from Isa 49:6, a verse cited at Luke 2:32 and Acts 13:47. It is thus a poetic statement about the extensive scope of the ensuing events (Brawley 1987: 28-50). These departing words of the Lukan Jesus neatly conjoin the geographical pattern and theological foundation of Acts: from Jerusalem outward, the divine Spirit will enable followers of Jesus to bear witness to the sovereignty of God.

The description of two men in white robes (1:10) evokes the epiphanic occurrences of earlier chapters: the two men in the tomb (Luke 24:4) and the transfigured Jesus in the company of two scriptural figures (Luke 9:29-31). The prominence they have at this point establishes the important role of such epiphanies throughout Acts (Squires 1993: 103-20). The words spoken to the followers of Jesus who witness his ascension stress that his return will be in the same portentous manner as his departure (1:11), although no detailed description is provided (cf. Matt 24:31; Mark 13:27; 1 Thess 4:16).

Ten days separate the ascension (forty days after Passover, 1:3) from the day of Pentecost (2:1, fifty days after Passover). Only two things are told of these ten days; already the process of selectivity which shaped Luke's Gospel can be seen in his second volume. Thus we learn only that the community had gathered on the day of ascension (1:12-14) and that at some stage in these days a replacement was found for Judas Iscariot (1:15-26).

Luke's report of the **(re)gathering of the community (1:12-14)** establishes key features of this community. First, since they returned to Jerusalem immediately after the ascension (1:12), the focus remains on Jerusalem, which retains its preeminent position as the birthplace of the movement (Bauckham in Bauckham 1995: 450ff.). Any gathering of believers elsewhere is incidental to the single-minded picture painted by Luke of the Jerusalem community as the movement's place of origin. This is the only community which matters for Luke at this moment.

Second, the description reveals that this was a community that met continuously during these ten days ("these [the eleven] all were unanimously attending constantly to prayer with the women and Mary the mother of Jesus and his siblings," 1:14). The constant and communal nature of their meetings will later become important; for the moment the emphasis rests on the line of continuity between Jesus and this group. This is secured by the reference to those present both here in Jerusalem and earlier, with Jesus, in Galilee: the women (Luke 8:2-3), the family of Jesus (Luke 8:19), and the inner group of named male followers who are identified as apostles (Luke 6:14-16; "the twelve" of Luke 8:1). Such continuity is an implicit element in God's ongoing sovereignty. The specific reference to the inclusion of women within the community continues a particular interest already unveiled in Luke's Gospel (Luke 8:1-3; 10:38-42; 23:49, 55-56; it is subsequently noted explicitly at Acts 5:14; 8:3, 12; 9:2; 17:4, 12; see Seim 1994: 18-24).

However, the recapitulation of the familiar names of "the twelve" ends abruptly with the penultimate apostle, Judas son of James (replacing Thaddeus, as found in Matt 10:3; Mark 3:18). The expected last name, that of Judas Iscariot (cf. Luke 6:16), is missing; Judas has been deleted from the company of "the twelve." This situation of incompleteness opens the way for **the reestablishment of full apostolic leadership (1:15-26).** Luke's Jesus has already signalled the significance of having precisely twelve apostles (Luke 22:30). The twelve provide continuity with the symbolic role of the twelve patriarchs of Israel, whose memory functioned to validate leadership within Israel (Genesis 49; Exod 24:4; 28:21; 39:14; Num 1:44; 17:2; Deuteronomy 33; Josh 4:1-9; 1 Kgs 18:31; Ezek 47:13). Luke's narration of this scene shows a strong concern to continue this line of continuity on from Jesus to his twelve apostles from the earliest days of the movement's life (Wilson 1973: 107-20; Jervell 1996: 75-83; Clark in Marshall and Peterson 1998: 169-81).

The episode begins with **the first speech of Peter (1:16-22)**, in which he proposes a remedy for the situation of incompleteness and provides an interpretive strategy for understanding the events which thus ensue. The remedy is the process of drawing lots to select one of the two possible candidates who "accompanied us for the whole time that the Lord Jesus went in and out among us" (v. 21). This insures that the apostolic leadership provides full and complete continuity with the activity of Jesus in Galilee and Jerusalem.

The strategy for interpreting this process is thoroughly Lukan — namely, to place it within the arena of God's sovereign activity. Thus Peter begins his speech with a triply significant note (1:16): what ensues will be a fulfillment of Scripture; it is driven by a sense of necessity (it "had to be fulfilled"); and it has been foreshadowed by the Holy Spirit through David. The drawing of lots (1:26) echoes Peter's words that an apostle is one who is "allocated a portion of this service" (v. 17) and may be an allusion to Prov 16:33, which affirms that when a lot is thrown, "the decision is the LORD's alone." The reference to scriptural fulfillment is given specificity at 1:20 in the quotations of Ps 69:25 (the desolation of Judas) and Ps 109:8 (the replacement of Judas). The statement about necessity is expanded in the detailed description of action to be taken (1:21, "therefore it is necessary . . ."). The function of the Spirit as divine inspirer of scriptural words recurs subsequently (4:25; 28:25).

The cumulative effect of Peter's first speech is thus to articulate what we recognize as the typical Lukan understanding of events taking place under divine sanction. The function of this interpretive claim is to validate the apostolic leadership — for the replacement apostle was chosen in accordance with God's ways — and to present a model of faithful leadership — since Peter shapes human community under what is understood as the divine will. Indeed, the prayer of the believers expresses their belief in divine superintendence: "You, Lord, know the hearts of everyone" (1:24).

By reestablishing the full apostolic leadership of the followers of Jesus, Luke has confirmed the continuity between Israel and the followers of Jesus, who at this stage of the story appear not to envisage any break with their Jewish heritage. A key question here is, How will these followers of Jesus live out their beliefs in the context of Second Temple Judaism? Clear signs are given that God intends these followers to live out their faith within Judaism; yet signs of tension will not take long to emerge. By the time we arrive at the closing scene, Paul is presenting the "sect" of "Christianity" to the Jewish leadership in Rome. Even at this point, there is an insistence that the movement belongs within Judaism, despite all that has gone before; yet it also indicates the relevance of the movement for life in the Roman Empire. Questions such as these will percolate throughout the whole narrative: What is the relationship between the Christian movement, which Paul represents, and the Jewish faith from which it emerged? How might this movement be placed within the Roman Empire as a whole? What might God's intentions be for this movement? In the course of the intervening chapters, these issues are constantly canvassed and explored through the narrative which Luke writes.

As a whole, the opening chapter has indicated that the Spirit is guiding, angelic figures are leading, a certain necessity is driving events as they occur, and these events can be understood as fulfilling scriptural prophecy. (The same cluster of themes can be found in the extended prologue of Luke 1–2; see Squires 1993: 27-32.) This concentration of language about God means that the narrative moment is ripe to turn immediately to the substantive events of the narrative, beginning with the day of Pentecost, when the apparently supernatural phenomena which occur (2:1-4) are immediately interpreted as being an irruption of God into human history (vv. 14-21). In the ensuing speech (vv. 22-36), the second which Peter gives, he continues what he began in his first speech and interprets events with reference to divine guidance. And so the pattern is set for the whole work.

The Day of Pentecost (2:1-47)

In the second part of the Jerusalem section, a detailed description is given of events on **the day of Pentecost (2:1-13)**. Pentecost was one of the annual festivals of the Jewish people; it was known as the festival of Harvest (Exod 23:16) or festival of Weeks (Exod 34:22; Num 28:26-31; Deut 16:9-12). The particular significance for Luke of what happened on this festival day is evident initially from its placement in the narrative as the first major event reported at length, as well as from the portentous introduction it receives, literally, "in the complete filling up of the day of Pentecost" (2:1). The phrase recalls Luke 9:51, a similarly momentous phrase in the Gospel. Many of the elements of this story will recur in later sections of the narrative, confirming the programmatic significance of the Pentecost account for the whole of Acts. This scene thus performs a function for Acts similar to that of Luke 4:16-31, which establishes the pattern for Jesus' ministry in Galilee (Luke 4–9) and Jerusalem (Luke 19–21).

The initial action, as narrated, is a portent, comprising miraculous phenomena both auditory ("a sound like the rush of wind," 2:2) and visual ("there appeared to them tongues as of fire," 2:3). Such portents would be understood by any reader in the Hellenistic context as being divine in origin (Squires 1993: 78-102). For Jews, these phenomena might evoke scriptural resonances from the story of Moses on Mt. Sinai, when God gave the Ten Commandments, accompanied by thunder, lightning, thick cloud, smoke, and violent shaking of the mountain (Exod 19:16-19).

Initially, those gathered are said to be "filled with the Spirit" (2:4). In Hebrew Scripture, the Spirit is known as a manifestation of God's actions in relation to Israel, guiding selected leaders (Moses, Num 11:16-17; Joshua, Deut 34:9; Othniel, Judg 3:10; Gideon, Judg 6:34; David, 1 Sam 16:17) and inspiring various prophets (Saul, 1 Sam 10:6; 19:23-24; Isa 42:1; 61:1; Ezek 37:1; Mic 3:8). The Spirit granted specific gifts (Num 11:25; Deut 34:9; Prov 1:23; Dan 4:8-18; Joel 2:28-29) and will rest upon the future Davidic leader (Isa 11:2-5). The Priestly writer attributed to the Spirit a role in creation (Gen 1:1-2; see also Job 33:4), and the psalmist envisioned the Spirit as playing an eschatological role (Ps 104:30). Luke has noted the strategic role of the Spirit in the lives of Jesus (Luke 4:1) and John the baptizer (Luke 1:15), as well as of John's parents (Elizabeth, Luke 1:41; Zacharias, Luke 1:67). The giving of the Spirit at Pentecost thus stands in continuity with God's actions in Israel; it also prefigures the state of many individuals later in the narrative of Acts (4:8; 6:3, 5; 7:55; 9:17; 11:24; 13:9; and cf. 18:25). The Pentecost narrative signals that the Spirit is to be an integral factor in the leadership of the messianic movement.

The action of the Spirit immediately results in ecstatic phenomena, as "they began to speak in different tongues" (2:4). This phenomenon recurs at Caesarea (10:46) and at Ephesus (19:6). Often the gift of tongues has been taken as being the key element in this narrative. In the light of the comment of the bystanders (2:7-8), it cannot be doubted that Luke understands the phenomenon to be "xenoglossy," that is, the way individuals miraculously spoke publicly in identifiable foreign languages. This is different from "glossolalia," or speaking in unknown languages in private, prayerlike communication with God, which Paul reports in 1 Corinthians 12–14; it is entirely plausible, however, that Luke has reinterpreted such a phenomenon as "xenoglossy" for his own purposes (Wilson 1973: 121-22). For Luke, the foreign languages which were spoken begin to fulfill Jesus' prediction that the message was to be preached in every nation (Luke 24:47-48; Acts 1:8). This is the program which now begins to be implemented in Acts; the spirit of prophecy gives an empowering for witness (Turner in Marshall and Peterson 1998: 327-48).

Luke 24:53 leads us to expect the location of the Pentecost story to be in the temple; certainly it soon becomes explicit that events occur in Jerusalem (2:5). The "Jews, devout men [*sic*] from all the nations under heaven," who are present are identified as having come to live in Jerusalem from the nations at the eastern end of the Mediterranean basin (vv. 9-11), in four quadrants with Jerusalem at the center (Bauckham in Bauckham 1995: 417-27). The scene already points to events later in Acts; although the particular setting is the Jewish context of festive Jerusalem, this gathering from the nations surrounding Jerusalem foreshadows the wider awareness of the Gospel which is to come. However, for the moment the focus remains strictly Jewish, both in terms of the individuals who are present ("Jews," 2:5) and in terms of how the story echoes the prophetic vision of the eschatological gathering of the nations (see Isa 2:2-4; 34:1-4; 42:1-6; 43:8-9; 45:20-23; 49:22-23; 52:7-10; 55:1-5; 60:1-7, 11, 14; 62:1-2; 66:18-24; at Isa 11:12 it is "the outcasts of Israel and the dispersed of Judah" who are gathered).

It is a deliberate narrative decision to portray God acting amid this gathering of diaspora Jews. For the crowd of pilgrims the precise action narrated is unexpected and is capable of diverse interpretations ("all were amazed," 2:12; "others sneered," v. 13). Peter offers what, for Luke, is the definitive interpretation: "this is what was spoken by the prophet" (v. 16). In speaking in this way, Peter not only refers to the prophetic words of Joel but also functions himself as a prophet, in that he sets forth the divine perspective on the events that are taking place. What has taken place is what God said he would do "in the last days" (vv. 16-17).

Peter's speech (2:14-41) locates him in the public arena, for the first (but not the last) time in Acts. His speech sets a pattern for the ensuing speeches in Acts; its contents establish many of the motifs for subsequent speeches in Acts (Squires in Marshall and Peterson 1998: 24-27). In form, it follows Hellenistic rhetorical conventions (Soards 1994: 31-32, 157-61); the note that Peter stands (2:14) is typical of public oratory (see 5:20; 11:13; 17:22; 25:18; 27:21). This speech, like all the others in Acts, is undoubtedly a Lukan creation, in the style of Hellenistic historians who crafted words appropriate for the speaker and the occasion (Thucydides *Hist.* 1.22.1; see McCoy in Witherington 1996: 3-32; Gempf in Winter and Clarke 1993: 259-303). Luke thus has Peter initiate a long sequence of speeches in which, as a whole, the larger story of Jesus and Israel is linked with the events that are taking place (Squires 1993: 63-76).

Luke has Peter speak as one who has the authority of a prophet; the unusual term *apophthengesthai* (NRSV, "addressed"; 2:4) is best translated as "declaimed," to convey the seriousness of the occasion (see also 26:25). Peter thus speaks an inspired, intelligent utterance, as the prophets did. Subsequent events confirm this view of Peter as one of the prophets. In addition to his subsequent prophet-like speeches, Peter's association with suffering (4:1-21; 5:17-41; 8:1b; 12:1-5) and with miraculous signs (2:43; 3:1-10; 4:22; 5:12; 9:32-43) are both in the manner of a prophet.

At the conclusion of the Pentecost speech, Luke describes Peter as "bearing witness and exhorting them" (2:40). Both of these terms recur in Acts to describe the public speaking of various leaders. Peter and John bear witness as they return from Samaria (8:25); the twelve apostles bear witness by the command of God (10:42). Paul likewise bears witness throughout his public activities (20:21, 24); specific instances are noted in Corinth (18:5) and in Rome (28:23). Associated Greek terms refer to the witness of others throughout Acts: the apostles (4:33; and see below on 2:32), Stephen (22:20), Paul (23:11), and Paul with Barnabas (14:3). Witness is also borne by the ancestors (7:44), the prophets (10:43), David (13:22), the Holy Spirit (20:23), and God (15:8; 23:11). Significantly, the specific term for "bearing witness" which Luke uses here *(diamartyresthai)* appears almost exclusively in the LXX as a description of the prophetic task (Exod 18:20; 19:16, 21; Deut 31:26; 32:46; 1 Sam 8:9; 2 Kgs 17:15; Neh 9:34; 13:21; Pss 49:7; 80:8; Jer 6:10; 44:23; Ezek 16:2; 20:4;

Mal 2:14). This strengthens the impression that Luke understands Peter's speech as a prophetic utterance.

In the same clause Luke describes Peter as "exhorting" his audience (2:40). Exhortation is another characteristic of leadership which is subsequently evidenced by Philip (8:31), Barnabas, the "son of exhortation" (4:36; 11:23), Barnabas and Paul (13:42; 14:22), the letter from the council in Jerusalem (15:31), Judas and Silas (15:32), and Paul (13:15; 20:1-2; 20:12; 27:33-34). Thus, the exhortation first evidenced by Peter at Pentecost also characterizes the community leaders. The term *parakaleō,* which is found often in the LXX, does occasionally describe the prophetic task (Deut 3:28; Isa 66:2; Sir 49:10); more frequently the prophets declare that it is God who carries out this task (Isa 51:12; also Deut 32:36; Judg 2:18; Pss 23:4; 71:21; 86:17; 90:13; 94:19; 119:50, 76, 82; 126:1; 135:14; Isa 40:1, 11; 41:27; 49:10, 13; 51:3, 18; 52:9; 54:11; 57:18; 66:11-13; Sir 17:24). Peter's exhortation thus continues in this prophetic stream.

Within the speech itself, Peter has referred to the fact that he speaks "with frankness" (2:29), a quality reminiscent of the prophets but also used to describe a valued way of speaking among philosophers (see 4:13). Such frank speech is to be understood as divinely instigated. It recurs after Pentecost, when in response to the community's prayer to God, the ground shakes and community members are "filled with the Spirit" and speak with "frankness" (4:31). It is also noted in the preaching of Peter and John (4:13), the teaching of Apollos (18:26), and the proclamation of Paul (9:27-28; 19:8; 28:31; with Barnabas, 13:46 and 14:3). Divinely bestowed frankness of speech thus typifies the leaders of the messianic communities.

Peter's prophetic role places him in a position of leadership within the community, and thus his speech provides a foundational model for this kind of leadership. The substance of the speech provides a template for using language about God to interpret particular phenomena. Peter is the mouthpiece for the Lukan template, which here performs three functions: to interpret the phenomena of the day, to articulate the significance of Jesus, and to introduce a definitive aspect of the nature of the community. The interpretation of each of these matters stands here in the narrative as a reference point for understanding subsequent chapters.

First of all, the speech offers an interpretation of **the phenomena (2:14-21)** which have just been experienced, through recourse to Scripture. This is Peter's second speech, and, like his first, it is grounded in Scripture. The fulfillment of prophecy which is reported here is a strong thematic strand which runs throughout Acts (Squires 1993: 121-54; Peterson in Winter and Clarke 1993: 83-104). It is the most explicit of a range of ways in which Scripture figures in his narrative; for Luke, Scripture is the matrix which will provide full understanding of the events he narrates (Jervell 1996: 61-75). The citation of "what was spoken through the prophet Joel" in vv. 17-21 already contains more than adequate points of connection with the immediate context: reference to the Spirit (vv. 17, 18; see v. 4), prophecy (v. 17; this appears to be the force of vv. 7-11), and wonders (v. 19; again, this describes vv. 2-4). It will also provide points of connection with subsequent events in other places: male prophets (11:28; 21:10-11), female prophets (21:9), the seeing of dreams and visions (9:10; 10:3, 10-12; 12:9; 16:9; 18:9; 22:17-18; 23:11; 27:23), and the granting of salvation to those who "call on the name of the Lord" (4:12; 16:31). This Scripture citation thus has a strategic significance in terms of the ensuing narrative (Wall in Marshall and Peterson 1998: 443-49).

The particular version of the scriptural text that Luke cites intensifies these connections with the immediate events, thereby highlighting the way he wishes them to be interpreted. The emphatic "God says" (2:17) makes explicit the intention of the prophetic oracle, that these phenomena are divinely given ("I will pour out my Spirit," v. 17; "I will give wonders," v. 19). In Luke's version of the text, the divine gift of prophecy (v. 17) is repeated in the phrase "and they will prophesy" after the reiteration of "I will pour out my Spirit" (v. 18), and the divine portents are emphasized through the inclusion of signs after the reference to wonders in v. 19. Each of these gifts recurs throughout the narrative of Acts: prophecy at 11:28; 19:6; 21:9-11, and signs and wonders at 4:30; 5:12; 6:8; 14:3; 15:12. Finally, the inclusion of a reference to "in the last days" (2:17) heightens the significance of the event as the beginning of eschatological fulfillment (Carroll 1988: 132-37). The interpretation which Luke has Peter provide thus uses language about God to elucidate the inner significance of the Pentecost phenomena. Interpreting the tongues and wonders as divine gifts provides a paradigm for understanding subsequent occurrences of such features in the later narrative.

Toward the end of his speech, Peter uses a number of terms to interpret the manifestation of the Spirit. It is said to be "poured out" at Pentecost (2:33). The same term recurs in the description of events in Caesarea (10:45). The parallelism between events in Jerusalem and Caesarea is reinforced when Peter declares that "they received the Holy Spirit as we also did" (10:47; see also 11:15, 17). However, it is not just this one subsequent event which is patterned on the Pentecost Day experience. The terminology of "receiving the Spirit" (2:38) occurs not only in Caesarea (10:47) but also in Samaria (8:15, 17, 19) and Ephesus (19:2), as well as in Jesus' own case (2:33).

Peter describes the Spirit as a gift (2:38); he continues to interpret the Spirit in this way in later speeches (5:32; 10:45; 11:17; 15:8). Peter also notes that such a gift is the fulfillment of the promise (2:33, 39) which was spoken of by Jesus (Luke 24:49; Acts 1:4). He associates it with the forgiveness of sins, not only in his Pentecost speech (2:38) but also in subsequent speeches (5:31; 10:43); the same link is made by Paul in Pisidian Antioch (13:38). Thus the Pentecost narrative introduces the central elements of the role accorded to the Spirit in the ensuing narrative.

The body of Peter's speech moves from the events of the day to **the life of Jesus (2:22-36).** The connection is not immediately apparent; what remains consistent across these two parts of the speech is the use of language about God. Peter thus provides a second application of the Lukan template, as he presents the message about Jesus in terms of what God did in him (vv. 22, 36). A better understanding of how God is at work in the events at Pentecost can be gained through understanding the divine will which was evident in the life of Jesus.

The Lukan template is given in three ways. First, Jesus is consistently presented in terms of God's acting in and through him. This is directly specified both at the beginning of the body of the speech ("mighty works and wonders and signs which God did through him," 2:22) and at the conclusion of the speech ("both Lord and Messiah, God has made him, this Jesus . . . ," 2:36). (The Greek text is precisely parallel in these verses; Squires 1993: 64-65.) This element is developed first of all in the statement that Jesus is "attested to you by God" (2:38); the claim is later echoed in words of Gamaliel (5:38-39) and Peter in Caesarea (10:38). Second, Peter refers to the delivering up of Jesus ("by the predetermined plan and foreknowledge of God," 2:23); this important Lukan motif is repeated by the Jerusalem community (4:28), Gamaliel (5:39), and Paul (13:36; 20:27). Third, the precise means of this delivering up is stated starkly by Peter: "you crucified him" (2:23); this is repeated in a gradually refined form over subsequent speeches ("you killed," 3:15; 5:30; "they put him to death," 10:39; "they asked Pilate to have him killed," 13:27-28). This does not, however, invalidate the divine plan; for God acts further in the raising of Jesus from the dead ("whom God raised," 2:24; cf. 3:15; 5:30; 10:40; 13:30; 17:31). The death and resurrection of Jesus thus stand at the very center of "the plan of God" (Tiede 1980: 97-125; Squires 1993; Moessner in Witherington 1996: 218-50).

A second element of the template is that Jesus is described in terms of how he fulfilled prophecy (2:25-31, 33-35). For Luke, as Peter demonstrates, the life of Jesus can readily be understood in terms of the ancient "God-talk" of scriptural prophecy. Peter first quotes Ps 16:8-11 (Acts 2:25-28) to interpret the risen Jesus as incorruptible; v. 10 is repeated in a modified form by Peter at Acts 2:31 and by Paul at Acts 13:35. Peter also quotes Ps 110:1 (Acts 2:34-35) to substantiate the claim that Jesus can be acclaimed as Messiah. This application of Scripture to Jesus is a persistent element in subsequent speeches, not only those given by Peter (3:18, 21-26; 10:43) but also by Stephen (7:2-50 *passim*), Philip (8:32-35), James (15:16-18), and Paul (13:27, 29, 33-37; 14:15; 17:11; 23:5; 24:14; 26:22-23; 28:23, 25-27). It is also a notable feature of the Lukan account of Jesus' "inaugural sermon" in Capernaum (Luke 4:18-21), in which the blended citation of Isa 58:6; 61:1-2 is said to be fulfilled by Jesus' presence in the synagogue. It is thus a consistent Lukan motif that God's plan can be known by means of Scripture (God speaking through the prophets), which is coming to fruition in the events being narrated (Squires 1993: 121-54).

The third element is that the claims made concerning Jesus are buttressed with the apostolic witness ("This Jesus God raised; of him we all are witnesses," 2:32). This witness provides a present validation which complements and continues the ancient prophetic witness. The elements in this speech are typical of the pattern which is followed in subsequent speeches. Peter often refers to the witness of the apostles (3:15; 5:32; 10:39, 41). Paul also refers to this in his speech in Pisidian Antioch (13:31), and he is subsequently identified as a specially chosen witness (22:15; 26:16).

The climactic sentence in Peter's description of Jesus (2:36) lays the groundwork for understanding the nature of **the community** which has gathered in Jerusalem (1:12-14; 2:1). Luke has Peter prepare the way for a definition of this community as a messianic Jewish community, with the declaration that "both Lord and Messiah, God has made him, this Jesus" (2:36). The claim that Jesus is Messiah will play a central role in the ensuing narrative, as this is argued — often strenuously — by Peter in Jerusalem (3:20; 5:42); by Paul in Damascus (9:22), Thessalonica (17:3), and Corinth (18:5); by Apollos in Ephesus (18:28) and — it is inferred — by Philip in Samaria (8:5). (I have translated *Christos* as "Messiah" to emphasize how it would have been understood in a first-century Jewish context; likewise *Christianoi* is translated as "Messianists.") Throughout Acts, Jesus is typically known by the title "Jesus, Messiah" (2:38; 3:6; 4:10; 8:12; 9:34; 10:36; 48; 16:18; 28:31; "Messiah Jesus" at 24:24; "Lord Jesus, Messiah" at 11:17; 15:26). Those who believe this about Jesus form communities that are messianic; eventually, they come to be known as "messianists," usually translated as "Christians" (11:26; 26:28). It is noteworthy that the first time this fundamental description of Jesus as Messiah is made, it is defined as an initiative of God ("God made him . . ."). Because of this (indirectly, at least), it is God who defines the nature of the community as messianic.

From this climactic description, Peter is prompted to prescribe the desired response from his listeners in Jerusalem (2:37-41). First, Peter instructs his listeners to repent (2:38). Such a call to repentance is a standard element in prophetic discourse; see Deut 30:1-3; 1 Kgs 8:46-53; Isa 1:16-20, 27-29; 9:13; 10:20-23; 31:6; 44:21-22; 45:22-23; 55:6-7; Jer 3:11-14; 4:1-2; 18:11; 22:1-7; 50:4-5; Dan 9:3-19; Hos 5:14-15; 6:1-3; 12:6; 14:1-3; Joel 1:13-14; 2:12-13; Amos 4:6-11; 5:4; 6; Jonah 1:1-2; 3:1-5; Mic 6:6-8; Zech 1:1-6; Mal 3:6-7. Peter's use of this typical prophetic style establishes a pattern which will recur often at the end of his speeches (3:19; 5:31-32; 8:22; 10:43; cf. 11:18), as well as in some by Paul (17:30; 20:21; 26:20). Peter also calls for his listeners to "be baptized" (2:38), signaling an action which occurs immediately (2:41) as well as at key moments later in the narrative — notably during the "turn to the Gentiles" (8:12, 16, 37-38; 9:18; 10:48) and the journeys of Paul (16:15, 33; 18:8; 19:5). Again, language about God is employed to define the process: the promise of the gift of the Holy Spirit (2:38) is offered to those whom the Lord God has called (2:39). The people's response, as described in 2:41, is both favorable ("they received his word") and abundant ("about three thousand souls"). This, too, is a pattern which will be repeated — but also significantly modified — in later incidents in Acts, when many will accept the apostolic message but others will reject it (see 13:4-12).

Peter's speech, the events leading up to it, and the response which follows from it together lead to the expansion of the community within Jerusalem. The community of messianic Jews has various characteristics, which are set forth in the first **summary description of the**

community (2:42-47). Many of these characteristics recur in the six subsequent descriptions of the community in this first section (4:4; 4:32-35; 5:12-16; 5:41-42; 6:7; 8:1b-3). The concluding verses of ch. 2 thus continue the programmatic role which we have seen in the Pentecost event and in Peter's speech. The community gathers for four inter-related aspects of their common life, which are introduced in the first verse (2:42): the teaching of the apostles, fellowship, the breaking of bread, and prayers. These four aspects, and associated ideas, provide a programmatic description of the messianic Jewish communities in Jerusalem and beyond.

The first aspect, the *teaching* of the apostles (2:42), is not only a private matter but also a public phenomenon (4:2; 5:25, 42), which will soon make the community notorious. This is made clear when the chief priest notes that "your teaching has filled Jerusalem" (5:28), despite the priests' commands to stop. Later in Acts, the focus for this typical apostolic activity shifts to Paul (15:35; 17:19; 18:11; 21:11); in his farewell speech, Paul summarizes his work as "proclaiming . . . and teaching" (20:20), while in his closing scene Luke notes that Paul's time under arrest in Rome was characterized by "preaching . . . and teaching" (28:31). The content of this teaching in the early stages concerns the resurrection of the dead (4:2) and the claim that Jesus is Messiah (5:42). From the pattern of the speeches in this section we may also reasonably conclude that Luke intends us to understand the explication of Scripture as part of the apostles' teaching (see 2:16-21, 25-28, 34-35; 3:22-25; cf. 4:25-26). Each of these elements continues in the teaching of Paul, who affirms the resurrection (17:18, 32; 23:6; 24:15, 21), confesses Jesus as Messiah (9:22; 17:3; 18:5; 28:31), and uses Scripture to explain the significance of Jesus (13:33-36; 17:2-3; 26:22-23).

Fellowship is identified as the second aspect of the community (2:42). The precise term *koinōnia* occurs only here in Acts; however, the notion of sharing or togetherness which is inherent in it is evident in other ways. Members of the community gather with one mind (2:46) in a way that will consistently characterize the community (4:24; 5:12; 15:25). They meet day by day (2:46), as is evident from the immediately ensuing events. Paul subsequently emulates this pattern of daily meetings in Berea (17:11), Athens (17:17), and Ephesus (19:9). The Jerusalem community is described by means of a philosophical ideal, as "having all things in common" (2:44; see on 4:32). The ideal is reinforced by the role models that Luke provides — the positive role model, Joseph Barnabas (4:36-37), and the negative role models, Ananias and Sapphira (5:1-11). That it remains an ideal, however, is evident from the larger movement of early Christian history.

Members of the community are to be found both in the temple and in their homes (2:46). Even though Luke writes after the destruction of the temple (Luke 19:41-44; 21:20-24), he knows well the prominent role of the temple in Jerusalem (Esler 1987: 148-54) and accurately locates the messianic community as continuing faithful to the temple cult. Thus their *public* presence in the temple (2:46) continues unabated throughout the first section (3:1, 11; 5:12, 20, 21, 42). Such a practice is continued by Paul, both in the Jerusalem temple (21:26-30, a single event which is recounted at 22:17; 24:6, 18; and 26:21) and in other public places (e.g., in Philippi, 16:13; the Athenian agora, 17:17; and the Areopagus, 17:19; see 20:20). Roman historians who wrote in the decades after Luke's writing described members of the community as "a class of men given to a new and mischievous superstition" (Suetonius *Life of Nero* 16) and as adherents of a "detestable superstition" who were "hated for their shameful deeds" (Tacitus *Ann.* 15.44). Still later, Christian apologists defended Christians against criticisms that they were secretive and therefore not to be trusted (Minucius Felix *Octavius* 8.1-4; Origen *Against Celsus* 1.1, 23; 3.50, 55; 4.23; 8.2, 17, 49). It may be that Luke's insistence on the public witness of the community meets this type of objection if it was already being raised late in the first century AD. The practice of *private* meetings in their homes is likewise continued throughout Judea and Samaria (8:3) and, as would be expected of a religious association, in dispersion communities in Caesarea (10:30; 11:12-14; 21:8) and Philippi (16:34). (On the archeological remains of houses, and the implications for the "house churches," see Blue in Gill and Gempf 1994: 119-222.) Paul continues this twofold pattern, for his activities typically take place "in public and from house to house" (20:20).

The third aspect, the *breaking of bread* (2:42, 46), was a custom of Jesus (Luke 9:16; 22:19; 24:35). While 2:46 makes it clear that this was a daily practice of the Jerusalem community, there is no further reference to the breaking of bread in this section. However, the sharing of meals is inferred at various points in the ensuing narrative (10:23; 11:12; 16:14-15, 34; 18:7). Later references demonstrate that "the breaking of bread" remained a practice of Paul, at least in Troas (20:7) and on board ship (27:35). By contrast, the fourth aspect of *prayers* (2:42) remains thoroughly characteristic of the community in Jerusalem (1:14; 4:31; 6:4, 6; 12:5, 12) as well as the community established in Antioch (13:3; 14:23). Prayer is practiced by Stephen (7:59), Peter (3:1; 8:15 with John; 9:40; 10:9; 11:5), Cornelius (10:4, 30-31), and Paul (9:11; 16:25; 20:36; 21:5; 22:17; 28:8). These prayers indicate that God is engaged within the narrative of the story, as the recipient of petitions and thanksgivings. They signal the firm link between the various messianic communities and the divine realm. The prayers of the community also indicate the continuity that runs from the life of Jesus, for he was frequently to be found at prayer (Luke 3:21; 5:16; 6:12; 9:18, 28-29; 10:21-22; 11:1; 22:31-32, 41-42, 44; 23:34, 46) (Plymale 1991).

The community in Jerusalem is further characterized by the performance of *wonders and signs* (2:43). This links back to two significant statements by Peter earlier in the chapter: his proclamation that Jesus "was attested to us by God through mighty works and wonders and signs" (v. 22) and his application to the Pentecost phenomena of the Joel prophecy concerning "wonders in the heaven above and signs on the earth below" (v. 19). In each case, language about God is used to interpret the source of the phenomena: Jesus was attested by miracles "which God did through him" (v. 22), while the wind and tongues on Pentecost were God-given portents ("I will give wonders . . . and signs," v. 19). In noting that the apostles performed miraculous deeds under the guidance of God, this summary description establishes the way that subsequent reports of miraculous happenings are to be understood: they occur as deliberate actions within the sovereignty of God. A select number of such happenings are described in detail, when performed by Peter in Jerusalem (3:1-10; 5:15-16) and Judea (9:33-35, 36-52), and by Paul in Asia Minor (14:8-10; 19:11; 20:7-12) and en route to Rome (28:8-9). Elsewhere, they are referred to by the concise phrase "wonders and signs": in Jerusalem (4:30; 5:12; 6:8), Samaria (8:6), and Asia Minor (14:3; 15:12). These ongoing instances of miracles strengthen the understanding that the messianic community lives under the overarching sovereignty of God.

A key characteristic within the community is the way members respond to the wonders and signs performed by the apostles with *fear* (2:43). The same response of fear is elicited by some rather ominous events in subsequent chapters: the retributive deaths of Ananias (5:5) and Sapphira (5:11) and the demonic overpowering of the seven sons of Sceva (19:17). The term may have a negative connotation in these latter instances; however, 19:17 is immediately glossed by the author with the note that "the name of the Lord Jesus was magnified," many converts were made, and some magicians burned their books. This infers a positive dimension to the fear thus evoked; it is in accord with the sense that "the word of the Lord grew in power and strengthened" (19:20). Such a sense of fear has already been evident in the Gospel (Luke 1:65; 5:26; 7:16; 8:37); in each case it is a response to the working of God. This is clearly the sense that is intended at 2:43, and it is akin to the response to further signs and wonders performed by the apostles at 5:12, namely: "the people held them in high esteem" (5:13). The fear that is introduced at 2:43 is thus a positive attitude toward those who are enabled by God to perform miraculous deeds. This has the same positive quality as the scriptural idea that fear of God is the attitude toward Yahweh which is inculcated by keeping the Torah (Deut 6:1-9, esp. v. 2; for the fear of God in the Scriptures, see Exod 1:17, 21; 18:21; Lev 19:14, 32; 25:17, 36, 43; Deut 6:1-2, 13, 24; 10:12, 20; 14:23; 17:19; 31:12-13; Josh 4:23-24; 2 Kgs 17:35-41; Neh 5:9, 15; Job 1:1, 8-9; 2:3, 4:6; Pss 36:1; 66:16; 96:4; Eccl 7:15-18; 8:12-13; 12:13; Jer 5:23-24; Jonah 1:9; Tob 4:21; 14:2, 6-7; Jdt 8:8). The use of the term at 2:43 prefigures the positive attitude toward God which is exhibited by "those who fear God," such as Cornelius ("a devout man who feared God with all his household," 10:2; "a centurion, an upright and God-fearing man," 10:22) and those who are addressed by Peter in Caesarea (10:35) and Paul in Antioch (13:16, 26).

The community is further described as "having grace toward the whole of the people" (NRSV, "having the goodwill of all the people"; 2:47). This introduces another term which will have significance in the narrative of Acts: *charis.* It recurs in the third summary description of the community (4:33), where it is related to the testimony of the apostles. In 2:47 it is linked with the inner life of the community as they "ate their food with glad and generous hearts, praising God and having grace toward the whole of the people." *Grace* is a characteristic which also marks Stephen, enabling him to perform "great wonders and signs" (6:8); in his speech he notes that God ascribed grace to Moses (7:10) and to David (7:46). It is this grace of God which is evident in the growing community in Antioch (11:23) and continues to be a characteristic of the community in Iconium, where once again it is evident through the signs and wonders granted by God (14:3). Such grace is regarded as the means of salvation (15:11), which enables people to believe that Jesus is the Messiah (18:27-28). This same grace of God is attested by Paul throughout his ministry (20:24, 32). It thus forms another of the characteristics of messianic communities in Jerusalem and beyond.

In this summary, for the first time Luke describes community members by using a term which will become most common for them throughout the narrative, namely, *the believers* (2:44). This term (or one of its cognates) is applied to members of the messianic communities in Jerusalem (3:16; 4:4, 32; 5:14; 6:7; 11:17; 15:5), Samaria (8:12, 13), Joppa (9:42), Syrian Antioch (11:21), Salamis (13:8, 12), often throughout Asia Minor (13:48; 14:1, 9, 22, 23, 27), around the Aegean Sea (16:5, 31, 34; 17:12, 31, 34; 18:8, 27), in Ephesus (19:2, 4, 18), as well as more generally (10:43; 13:39; 15:7, 9; 21:25; 22:19; 26:18). It is also applied to individual leaders within the communities, such as Stephen (6:5), Barnabas (11:24), and Paul (24:14, 24; 27:25). The divine origin of such faith, inferred at 4:4, is made explicit by later comments that the large number of "those who believe" were being added to the community "by the Lord" (5:14), and that "as many as believed had been appointed to eternal life" (13:48)

Salvation is a central theme in Luke-Acts from early in the Gospel (Luke 1:47, 69, 71, 77; 2:11, 30, 36). Salvation so characterizes the ministry of Jesus (Luke 7:50; 8:36, 48, 50; 13:23; 17:19; 18:26, 42; 19:9-10) that he is identified as the Savior (Luke 2:11; Acts 13:23), assuming the role once exercised by Moses (7:25) and always attributable to God (Luke 1:47). In Acts, this salvation is highlighted in the Joel citation ("those who call . . . shall be saved," 2:21); it returns at the end of Peter's speech ("save yourself," 2:40) and then is applied to community members at the end of the first summary ("those being saved," 2:47). The theme continues on throughout Acts, from Peter's programmatic declaration concerning "the name" as the means by which "we must be saved" (4:12) to Paul's final declaration that "this salvation shall be sent to the Gentiles" (28:28; see also 4:9; 11:14; 13:26, 47; 14:9; 15:1, 11; 16:17, 30, 31; 27:20, 31, 34). "Those being saved" is thus a fitting description of "the believers" throughout Acts (Jervell 1996: 84-100).

Thus we see that in providing this careful description of the community of messianic Jews in Jerusalem from the day of Pentecost onward, Luke has shaped it to introduce a number of key characteristics of the messianic communities that he will describe in later chapters. Along with the miraculous events of Pentecost and the speech of Peter, this summary description performs a programmatic role in the narrative. The most significant way in which this chapter sets the scene is reiterated in the concluding sentence, which draws this first summary description of the messianic community to a close. Once more, the emphasis is on the role of God in the community's life: "The Lord added those being saved daily to the same [group]" (2:47). The explicit use of language about God here sets the pattern for understanding later, less explicit, comments about the increasing size of the Jerusalem community (5:14; 6:7) and of messianic communities further afield (9:31; 12:24; 19:20). The communities that are established or visited in later chapters exist within this pattern, under the sovereignty of God. They continue to exemplify the best characteristics of faithful communities. Taken together, all of the communities in Acts present a coherent and persuasive picture of what it means to live with others who follow the way of Jesus. The narrative thus provides a model of community.

The Trials of Peter and John (3:1–5:42)

What follows in the next three chapters arises out of a specific incident — the healing of a lame man in the temple grounds — and largely concerns the consequences of that incident — the twofold arrest and double trial of Peter and John. These chapters contain three speeches by Peter as well as a speech by the Pharisee Gamaliel and a prayer by the Jerusalem community, each of which expresses the Lukan understanding that events take place within the sovereignty of God. The chapters also contain four summary descriptions of the community which develop the picture of community life established in 2:42-47. These descriptions punctuate the narrative at breaks in the action.

The account of how **Peter heals a lame man (3:1-11)** provides a specific instance of the "many wonders and signs" which the apostles performed (2:43). As this particular healing takes place in the grounds of the temple (3:2), the focus remains on the heart of the Jewish capital. Peter and John come to the temple to pray (3:1), in keeping with both the community practice of prayer (2:42) and of regularly attending the temple (2:46). The temple remained a focal point for prayer until its destruction in AD 70 (Falk in Bauckham 1995: 285-93). The juxtaposition of the lame man and the temple setting is striking. Lame animals were decreed to be unsuitable as offerings to God (Deut 15:21; Mal 1:8, 13), and lame people were among those forbidden from drawing near to offer sacrifice in the temple (Lev 21:18; 2 Sam 5:8). Yet in the prophets, the lame are included among the outcasts gathered by God as the faithful remnant (Jer 31:8; Mic 4:6-7; Zeph 3:19), and the vision of the return of the redeemed to Zion (Isa 35:1-10) includes the assertion that "the lame shall leap like a deer" (Isa 35:6). Jesus has followed in this prophetic tradition by healing the various categories of outcasts; by his activity, "the blind receive their sight, the lame walk, the lepers are cleansed, the deaf hear, the dead are raised, the poor have good news preached to them" (Luke 7:22 par. Matt 11:5; see also Luke 4:18; Matt 15:30-31; 21:14). In parables told only by the Lukan Jesus, the lame are included in the outcasts invited to the banquets (Luke 14:13, 21; cf. the account of how Mephibosheth, the lame grandson of Saul, son of Jonathan, ate regularly at the table of King David — 2 Sam 4:4; 9:1-13). Although no account of a specific healing of a lame person is found in Luke's Gospel (cf. John 5:1-9), the healing of this lame man (the first specific healing incident in Acts) places the apostles in continuity with Jesus, who heals the lame (Luke 7:22). A similar healing is later performed by Paul (14:8-10), while Philip is described as healing "many others who were paralyzed or lame" (8:7).

The lame man's expectation that he would receive alms (3:2-3) is reasonable; caring for the needy was integral to Jewish piety (Deut 15:7-11; and see Kim 1998: 277-81). By the Hellenistic period almsgiving had become highly valued as a religious duty (Sir 3:30; 7:10; 29:9-12; 40:24; Tob 4:7-11, 16; 12:8-10; 14:8-11; cf. Matt 6:2-4). The Lukan Jesus commended almsgiving (Luke 11:41; 12:33), and subsequent characters in Acts practice almsgiving (Cornelius, 10:2, 4, 31; Paul, 24:17; see Kim 1998: 218-33). However, as Peter and John "look intensely" at the man (3:4; on such intense scrutiny, see 14:9), they sidestep this responsibility, for the focus in this account is to be on their exercise of divine power. Peter commands the man to stand, revealing that his power comes from "the name of the Messiah, Jesus of Nazareth" (3:6). This name has already been declared as the source of salvation (2:21) and forgiveness (2:38); "the name" remains a constant emphasis in the ensuing scenes (3:16; 4:7, 10, 12, 17-18, 30; 5:40-41) and appears subsequently in connection with proclamation (8:12; 9:15-16, 27-28; 10:43; 15:14, 17; 21:13), baptism (8:16; 10:48; 19:5; 22:16), and exorcism (16:18; 19:13, 17).

As Peter raises up the lame man (3:7), he is healed and strengthened, and enters the temple (v. 8). The healed man immediately recognizes the source of this miracle, for he is portrayed as "praising God" (vv. 8, 9). The man thus joins himself with the community members, whose regular life is typified by an attitude of praise toward God (2:47). Later in the account, even the people will praise God, recognizing that God has been at work in this incident (4:21). At this point their response is one of "wonder" (3:10), a questioning attitude also displayed toward Jesus (Luke 4:36; 5:9), and "amazement" (3:10), a more insightful appreciation of the incident, as also displayed toward Jesus (Luke 5:26).

Having reported the healing, Luke shifts his focus to Peter, who provides an interpretation of what has taken place, just as he did on the day of Pentecost. **Peter's third speech (3:12-26)** begins by accusing the people of thinking "as if by our own power or piety we have made him walk" (v. 12). Peter asserts that it is God — "the God of Abraham and Isaac and Jacob, the God of our ancestors" (v. 13) — who has enabled the miracle. The speech contains key elements of the template established in Peter's Pentecost speech. The healing took place in the name of "the Messiah, Jesus of Nazareth" (3:6; see 2:36), who is here represented to the people in ways largely familiar from this earlier speech. Jesus is the one whom God glorified (3:13) and God raised (v. 15; see 2:24); he is the one of whom the apostles are witnesses (3:15; see 2:32), for of him they "see and know" (3:16). Jesus is the suffering Messiah, in fulfillment of "what God announced beforehand through the mouth of all the prophets" (v. 18). This extends the fulfillment of prophecy from Jesus' resurrection (2:25-31) and exaltation (vv. 34-35) to his crucifixion. Such a claim is important for

Luke; he has Paul make the same affirmation, that the suffering of the Messiah fulfills Scripture, at 26:23; indeed, he places its initial appearance on the lips of Jesus at Luke 24:26. (However, Peter's claim that "all the prophets" predicted this is surely Lukan exaggeration.) The speech both reprises and develops the explicit language about God of 2:22-36, as well as the prophetic and apostolic witness which characterizes the apostolic proclamation.

Luke has Peter once more evoke the response of repentance (3:19) by reference to God, as he did at 2:37-39. Repentance is portrayed as an integral element in the eschatological scenario. The eschatological hope which was often proclaimed by Jesus (Luke 4:43; 9:26-27; 10:1-16; 12:49-56; 13:22-30; 17:20-37; 19:11-27; 21:5-36) continues as an essential element in the apostolic proclamation (Wilson 1973: 59-87; Maddox 1982: 100-157; Carroll 1988; Nolland in Marshall and Peterson 1998: 63-81).

Luke reports Peter as describing the eschatological sequence in some detail (3:19-21; see Carroll: 137-54). The sovereignty of God is clearly in focus in this eschatological process: God will wipe out sins (3:19b) because people will have already repented and turned to God (3:19a); "times of refreshing" will come "from the presence of the Lord" (3:20a); and God will then send the appointed Messiah (3:20b). After this, there is an interim period, as the ascended Jesus remains in heaven (cf. 1:11; 2:33), awaiting "the time of universal restoration" which will implement what God has long ago promised (3:21). The delay occasioned by this waiting does not signal a breakdown in God's providential control of events, for Jesus remains in heaven by divine decree (he "must," 3:21; on necessity, see 1:16, 21; Squires 1993: 155-85). This concentrated eschatological proclamation thus underlines the continuing sovereignty of God, which is especially manifested at the end times.

The "times of refreshing" may refer to Jesus' teaching that "the Lord will cut short the end" (Mark 13:20, but omitted in Luke 21); the sense of "refreshing" is of a breathing space before the next event in sequence takes place (see Exod 8:15). The "time of universal restoration" transcends the earlier question of the disciples concerning the restoration of the kingdom to Israel (1:6); here resotration has a universal scope. It may thus correlate with the eschatological events which Peter has already reported at 2:17-21 (citing Joel 2:28-32; see also Mal 4:5-6). References to the eschaton also appear in Peter's Caesarea speech (10:42) and in Paul's Areopagus speech (17:31). On these occasions, however, the description of the eschaton is limited to noting the role that Jesus will perform, as the one "ordained" (10:42) or "appointed" (17:31; cf. 3:20) to execute God's judgment. Nowhere else in Acts do we find the fulsome eschatological description offered in this speech by Peter at Solomon's Portico.

The time of universal restoration which Peter declares is that which "God spoke through the mouth of his holy prophets" (3:21; cf. Luke 1:70). In addition to the exaggerated claim that "all the prophets . . . predicted these days" (3:24), Luke has Peter cite specific scriptural passages in support of his statement about the eschatological role of Jesus. Peter identifies Jesus in two eschatological roles: as the prophet promised by Moses (3:22-23, quoting Deut 18:15-16, 19) and as the one who implements the blessing in the covenantal promise to Abraham (3:25, alluding to Gen 12:3; 18:18; 22:18; 26:4). The way that Peter here expresses the eschatological role of Jesus is evocative of the prophetic words of Mary (Luke 1:54-55) and Zechariah (Luke 1:68-75). It is this still-awaited eschatological act of God which provides the springboard for Peter's demand for repentance (3:19). Peter concludes his speech by urging the people to "turn, each one, from your sins because God raised up his son and sent him as a blessing to you" (3:26, as a fulfillment of the promise to Abraham cited in 3:25). In addressing the issue posed in 3:12, Peter thus uses the affirmation that God has been at work in the healing as the basis for expounding God's eschatological actions, which will bring blessing to the people.

Conflict erupts, however, when the authorities object that Peter is teaching the people (4:2; see 2:42), primarily (in their eyes) about the resurrection of the dead (4:2). Luke has already documented the opposition of the Sadducees to this idea (Luke 20:27-40). Here they join with the priests and the temple police, the same group which Luke noted as having plotted against Jesus (Luke 22:4) and arrested him (Luke 22:52). Together they initiate **the arrest of Peter and John (4:1-3).** This is the first of many scenes of judicial conflict in Acts; the pattern has already been established in the story of Jesus (Luke 22:47–23:25). (On conflict in Luke-Acts, see Malina and Neyrey in Neyrey 1991: 97-122.) A very brief **second summary description of the community** (4:4) follows, picking up from 2:41 the motif of increasing numbers within the messianic community.

In recounting **the first trial of Peter and John (4:5-22),** Luke has the authorities return to the issue posed by Peter at 3:12. The move from "by power or piety" (3:12) to "by what power or by what name" (4:7) depicts the authorities as oblivious of Peter's explicit claims regarding the name of Jesus at 3:6, 16. Their question continues the focus on the source of the healing, provoking yet another speech in reply.

Peter's fourth speech (4:8-12) is delivered once he is "filled with the Holy Spirit" (4:8), a state which reproduces that of the messianic community at Pentecost (2:4). Peter is the first individual who is so filled; after him will come Stephen (6:3, 5; 7:55), Saul (9:17; 13:9), and Barnabas (11:24). Peter stands in continuity with individuals in the Gospel who are Spirit-filled: John the baptizer (1:15), Zechariah (1:67), Simeon (2:25-26), and Jesus himself (4:1, 14). This Spirit-filled state has the effect of reinforcing the validity of the interpretation which Peter here provides as a Spirit-filled prophet. It also reinforces his membership in the messianic Jewish community, since members of this community are typically "filled with the Spirit."

Peter answers the question posed at 4:7 by repeating his assertion of 3:6, that the name by which the healing took place was that of "the Messiah, Jesus the Nazarene" (4:10). Immediately he presents Jesus in the now familiar way, as the one whom "God raised from the dead" (v. 10; see 3:15; 2:24) and as the one who (implicitly) fulfills the scriptural description of "the stone" (4:11, alluding to Ps 118:22). This brief speech ends with an assertion of the necessity of this name for salvation (4:12). Only if it is taken out of context can this verse be seen to prescribe that a relationship with Jesus is the single necessary element of salvation. The speech as a whole has made it clear that, while the name of Jesus is the necessary means by which salvation comes, God is the source of that salvation. Indeed, such salvation has been offered prior to Jesus, as other speeches indicate (2:21; 7:25, 35-36; 13:17-19).

Luke's narrative commentary on the speech notes the "frankness" (NRSV, "boldness") with which Peter has spoken (4:13). This characteristic, already evident at Pentecost (2:29), will become a recurrent quality, evident in the prayer of the Jerusalem community (4:29, 31), the teaching of Apollos (18:26), and the proclamation of Paul (9:27-28; 19:8; 28:31; with Barnabas, 13:46 and 14:3). Frankness of speech was a quality which philosophers held to be most desirable in the wise man (see, e.g., Dio Chrysostom *Orat.* 32.11 and 77/78.37; Diogenes Laertius *Lives* 2.122-23 [on Simon the cobbler] and 6.69 [on Diogenes the Cynic]; Julian *Oration* 6), so the juxtaposition with the assertion that Peter and John were "unlettered and uneducated" (4:13) is striking.

The authorities ponder what action to take; Luke depicts them as being cowed by the power demonstrated by Peter and John, both in their speech (4:13) and in their deed of healing (4:14, 16). Peter has clearly identified this power as divine in origin (3:12-16), and the authorities even describe what has taken place as "a notable sign" (4:16), ironically using the term which has already been identified as describing divine activity (2:19). Yet they remain oblivious of the divine dimension of the event; they can see only the consequences among the general populace should they take no action. Thus they make a pronouncement banning Peter and John from speaking in the name of Jesus (4:18). Clearly, it is unlikely that they will comply with this demand, given that Peter has already indicated that the name of Jesus is the centerpoint of their claims (2:38) and was instrumental in their healing of the lame man (3:6, 16; 4:10, 12).

Accordingly, Peter and John reply (4:19-20) in a way which underlines the futility of this command in the face of God's sovereignty. To refrain from speaking out would mean that they ceased being "right before God," that they preferred "to listen to you [the authorities] rather than to God" (v. 19). The climax to the apostolic speeches in this section is articulated when Peter and John assert the necessity of bearing witness to "what we have seen and heard" (v. 20, prefiguring the way that Paul describes his commissioning at 22:15). The narrative conclusion, in noting that the apostles were released (4:21), appears to align the people with the messianic community, for as they glorify God they adopt the interpretive stance of those who praise God for events they experience: the healed man (3:8, 9) and the whole community (2:47). The influence of the community thus appears to be spreading among the people but not among the authorities. It cannot be regarded as having broken from Jewish faith; yet it is set on a collision course with the Jewish authorities. Luke's final comment repeats the description of the healing as a sign (4:22), thereby reinforcing his view that it was God who enabled this healing, as with the other signs (2:19).

This will not be the end of the matter with regard to the threat raised against the apostles. However, for the moment Luke juxtaposes an extended interlude (4:23–5:16) which gives further insight into the life of the Jerusalem community, showing them at prayer and in action. In each case, the community's dependence on the sovereignty of God underlies the text.

The prayer of the community (4:23-31) is offered in thanksgiving for the release of Peter and John. The community gathers "with one mind" (v. 24; see 1:14; 2:46) for their customary practice of prayer (1:14; 2:42). While couched as a prayer to God, the substance of the prayer indicates that its function is the same as that of the speeches delivered thus far; it expounds the sovereignty of God in events reported through explicit and implicit language about God. Thus, the prayer begins with a direct address to God as "Sovereign One" and acknowledges the sovereignty present in the creative power of "you who made heaven and earth and sea and everything in them" (4:24; similar descriptions of God are found at 14:15; 17:24).

The community continues its prayer by drawing on Spirit-given prophecy to illuminate the death of Jesus (4:25-26; for Spirit, see 1:16; for fulfillment of prophecy in Jesus' death, see 3:18). Jesus is described as the one anointed by God (4:27; see 10:38; Luke 4:18) who is dealt with under "the hand and plan" of God (4:28). Peter has already employed the characteristic Lukan reference to God's plan (see 2:23). Luke has introduced the phrase in his Gospel (Luke 7:30) and will place it, unsurprisingly, on the lips of Paul (13:36; 20:27), but also, quite astonishingly, on the lips of Gamaliel (5:38-39). The notion of God's plan is already available to Luke in the Scriptures (Isa 5:19; 14:24-27; 19:17; 25:1; and implicitly throughout Isaiah 40–55; Jer 18:11; 49:20-22; 50:45-46; Mic 4:12). The added reference to God's hand is similarly attractive to Luke. God's hand grants signs and wonders (4:30), brings salvation to Israel (7:25), has made all things (7:50, citing Isa 66:2), guides the community (11:21), and inflicts punishment on Elymas (13:11). In Scripture, God's hand was understood as being both gracious (Exod 6:1; 15:6; Deut 4:34; 2 Chr 6:15; 30:12; Ezra 7:9; 8:18, 22, 31; Pss 63:8; 145:16) and destructive (Judg 2:15; 1 Sam 5:11; 1 Chr 21:17; Isa 1:25; 5:25; Hab 2:16). This twofold nature is clear at Deut 32:39 and Job 2:10. God's hand was a symbol of God's providence (Isa 48:13; 64:8). (See Squires 1993.)

In stark contrast to the way that Jesus implements the divine plan, "the kings of the earth and the rulers stand resolutely opposed to the Lord and his anointed one" (4:26); this resonates with the recent actions of the Jerusalem temple authorities (vv. 1-22). Ironically, the community is citing scriptural words (Ps 2:1-2) whose initial reference was to Gentile rulers; now, however, such opposition emerges from within the Jewish leadership itself (Mason in Bauckham 1995: 147-58). That the Jewish residents of Jerusalem viewed the movement more favorably, however, is evident throughout this first section of Acts (2:47; 3:9-11; 4:4, 16-17, 21; 5:13; 6:7).

The community prays that they may be marked both by the frankness (4:29) which has characterized Peter and John (4:13; 2:29) and by the signs and wonders (4:30) which the apostles have performed (2:43; 4:22) under divine initiative (2:19). The content of the prayer is thus akin to that of the speeches which Peter has so far delivered, interpreting events by means of language about God.

After this prayer, Luke narrates the fulfillment of the last two requests of the prayer. First, a sign is given when "the place was shaken" (4:31a). Second, members of the messianic community speak with frankness because they have been "filled with the Holy Spirit" (v. 31b). This fulfillment is evocative of the initial sign on the day of Pentecost (2:1-4); it may even be that the comment that "they were speaking the word of God with frankness" serves to interpret the "speaking in different tongues" of 2:4. In reporting that the signs that have characterized the messianic community from Pentecost continue to be manifest, Luke continues to model the way to live in community.

A **third summary description of the community (4:32-35)** serves to introduce the next episode in the life of the community. Once more, typical features of this messianic Jewish community are evident: unity of purpose (4:32; see 2:42, 46), powerful testimony to the resurrection (4:33; see 2:24, 32; 3:15; 4:2), and the manifestation of grace (4:33b; see 2:47). The major focus in this summary description is on the first feature, which is introduced with a striking phrase: the believers were "one in heart and soul," to which is added a repetition of the earlier comment that "for them all things were common" (4:32; see 2:44). These phrases evoke the traditional Greek proverbs, "friends have one soul" and "the goods of friends are common property," which were known since the time of Aristotle (Aristotle *Nic. Eth.* 9.8.2; Cicero *De officiis* 1.16.51; Plutarch *On Brotherly Love* 490E, *How to Tell a Flatterer* 65A, and *On Having Many Friends* 96E; Iamblichus *Life of Pythagoras* 65A; Dio Chrysostom *Orat.* 34.20; Diogenes Laertius 5.20, 8.10). The Essenes were described in a similar way by Philo *Quod omnis probus liber sit* 85, and Josephus *J.W.* 2 §122 (see Capper in Bauckham 1995: 324-37; Kim 1998: 223-52). The first phrase is also reminiscent of the common Deuteronomic reference to "heart and soul" (Deut 6:5; 10:12; 11:13; 13:4; 26:16; 30:2, 6, 10).

Luke's interest in the relations between rich and poor is a central concern throughout his two volumes (Esler 1987: 164-200); the theme is particularly focused in the ensuing episode which shows **the community in action (4:36–5:11)**. The tangible manifestation of being "one in heart and soul" is that community members sell their possessions and have "all things in common" (4:32). This is evidenced in the ensuing incidents positively by Joseph Barnabas (4:36-37) and negatively by Ananias and Sapphira. Barnabas sells some of his property and lays the full proceeds from the sale of his property at the feet of the apostles (4:36-37). Ananias and Sapphira also own property (on the property rights of married women, see Seim 1994: 62-66; Reimer 1995: 2-6). With the full knowledge of Sapphira, Ananias sells some of their property but fails to lay the full amount of the sale at the feet of the apostles (5:1-11). The practice of Ananias is in accord with the normal expectations of a patron-client society; the community, however, has begun to live in such a way as to overturn these norms (Moxnes in Neyrey 1991: 241-68). This "community of possessions" implements the commands of Jesus to "sell your possessions and give alms" (Luke 12:33) and to "sell all that you have and give [them] over to the poor" (Luke 18:22). Such commands are intensified by Luke's reporting of additional sayings of Jesus on this subject (see Luke 12:13-21; 14:13, 21; 16:9, 19-31; 19:1-10).

To live in this way is thus commanded by Jesus; but the reason given for the deaths of Ananias and Sapphira indicates that their deaths have been directly authorized by God, at work through the Spirit. When Ananias refuses to obey the command to surrender his possessions, Peter declares that "Satan has filled your heart to lie to the Holy Spirit" (5:3) and interprets this as "lying toward God" (v. 4). When Sapphira is confronted with evidence of her conspiracy with Ananias, Peter likewise accuses them both of "putting the Spirit of the Lord to the test" (v. 9). This account establishes divine approval for the "community of possessions"; divine retribution awaits those who are disobedient to the vision. Such retribution is evident elsewhere in Luke's story (1:18; 12:20-23; 13:8-11; 23:2-3; see Trompf in Talbert 1984: 225-39).

This is confirmed, in each case, by the response of those who learn of the deaths of Ananias and Sapphira: they exhibit great fear (5:5b, 11) — a response which signifies that God has been at work (see 2:43). Included for the first time at this point in the narrative is the description of the community as the *ekklēsia,* or "assembly" (5:11); this term is used a further eighteen times in chs. 8–20. (Not included in this count are the occurrences which do not relate to the messianic Jewish communities: 7:38 refers to Israel, while 19:32, 39, 40 refer to the Ephesian city assembly.) *Ekklēsia* was a common Greek term for the gathering of a city's citizens; it was used extensively in the Greek translation of Hebrew Scriptures to describe the congregation of Israel (Deut 4:10; 9:10; 18:16; 23:1-3, 8; 31:30; Josh 8:35; Judg 21:5, 8; 1 Sam 17:47; 1 Kgs 8:14, 22, 55, 65, etc.). Subsequently, however, it has become firmly established with a distinctive meaning in the Christian lexicon: "church."

A fourth **summary description of the community (5:12-16)** frames the account of Ananias and Sapphira; once again the community meets "with one mind" (1:14; 2:46; 4:24). Any potential discord is banished by the ominous fate of these two dissenters. The summary picks up on the miraculous dimension of the preceding episode through the emphasis on signs and wonders (5:12; see 2:43, 4:30); specific examples of these miracles are given in 5:15-16. These healings are performed "through the hands of the apostles" (v. 12), a description which evokes the prior request to God to "stretch out your hands to heal and perform signs and wonders" (4:30). The hands of the apostles subsequently perform further signs and wonders at 14:3 and 19:11; they work for good at 8:17; 9:41; 11:30. The people exult the community (5:13), adopting an attitude which recognizes the divine at work (10:46; 19:17; Luke 1:46, 58; cf. Pss 34:3; 35:27; 40:16; 70:4; etc.).

Members of the messianic community are again identified as "those who believe" (5:14; see 2:44; 4:32), and for the third time Luke notes the growing numbers of those associated with the believers (5:14; see 2:41; 4:4). That they were added (5:14) has already been established as the work of the Lord (2:47); in contrast to the NRSV ("added to the Lord"), the better translation would thus be "added by the Lord," taking the dative case as an expression of agency.

The **second trial of Peter and John (5:17-40)** begins with their re-arrest and detention (vv. 17-18). The authorities are "filled with jealousy" (v. 17), an attitude often at odds with the divine will (13:45; 17:5; 22:3-4) and in contrast to being filled with the Spirit (see 4:8). They lay their hands on the apostles (5:18), aligning themselves with the "hands of those outside the law" who crucified Jesus (2:23). Their action contrasts with the way that miracles are performed through the hands of the apostles (5:12) and of God (4:30). This antagonism is dramatically enacted by God's immediate intervention through the epiphany of an angel of the Lord (5:19). The angel's command to the apostles, "Go and stand up and speak in the temple" (v. 20), validates their escape as an act sanctioned by divine sovereignty. Such direct command from a figure seen in an epiphany introduces yet another way in which God's sovereignty will be evident throughout the story; commands are issued in subsequent epiphanies which take place in Joppa (10:3-6), Caesarea (10:10-16), Jerusalem (12:7-11, 23), Troas (16:9), Corinth (18:5-6), Jerusalem once more (23:11), and en route to Rome (27:23-24).

The apostles resume their location in the temple and their task of teaching (5:21a), but the authorities order their re-arrest and return to the court (vv. 21b-26) on the charge of "standing in the temple and teaching the people" (vv. 25, 28), in defiance of their earlier command (4:18). A response to the charge is given in **Peter's fifth speech (5:29-32).** Although brief, this speech nevertheless reflects the elements already established in Peter's speeches, through the use once more of explicit talk about "the God of our ancestors" (5:30; see 3:13) who "raised Jesus" (5:30; see 2:24, 32; 3:15) and "exalted him" (5:31; see 2:33). There follow the standard references to repentance and forgiveness of sins (5:31; see 2:38), the apostolic witness (5:32; see 2:32; 3:15), and the gift of the Holy Spirit (5:32; see 2:33). Most striking, however, is the introductory statement, "We must obey God" (5:29). Luke justifies the apostles' action by having Peter employ this widely known Greek proverb (Plato *Apology* 29D: "I must obey God rather than you"; see also Sophocles *Antigones* 453-55; Herodotus 5.63; Epictetus *Diss.* 1.30.1; Athenaeus *Deipnosophistae* 12.502A; Livy 39.37.17; Plutarch *Conviv.* 125C). The proverb also has strong resonances with the persistent scriptural language of obedience to Yahweh. (The language is particularly Deuteronomistic and prophetic; see Gen 22:18; 26:5; Exod 19:3-6; Deut 4:30; 8:20; 9:23; 11:13, 27-28; 13:4, 18; 15:5; 26:14, 17; 28:1-2, 13, 15, 45, 62; 30:2, 8, 10, 16, 20; 1 Sam 15:17-25; 28:18; 1 Kgs 6:12; 13:21, 26; 2 Kgs 18:11-12; Ezra 7:26; Neh 9:16-17; Jer 3:13, 25; 7:23-24, 28; 9:13; 11:7-8; 22:21; 25:8; 26:13; 32:23; 34:17; 38:20; 40:3; 42:6; 43:4, 7, 23; Dan 9:9-14; Hag 1:11; Zech 6:14.) The proverb sounds forth the note of divine necessity which resonates throughout the book of Acts, providing another dimension to the language about God by which Luke validates his models (Squires 1993: 155-85). The speech is framed with references to God's effort to persuade human beings (5:29, 32) (on persuasion, see 28:24).

The authorities, however, are not yet persuaded — they seek to kill the apostles (5:33). **Gamaliel's speech (5:34-39),** which follows, refers to the Jewish uprisings under Judas and Theudas, which serve as warnings to the council (5:36-37). Josephus calls Judas the Galilean the leader of "the fourth of the philosophies" (*Ant.* 18 §23; *J.W.* 2 §433). Luke dates the activity of Judas to "the time of the census," already referred to in Luke 2:1-3. This was probably around AD 6. Josephus also refers to the uprising under Theudas (*Ant.* 20 §§97-98), but places him at the time when Cuspius Fadus was governor (c. AD 44-46). This is more than a decade after the putative date of the trial scene reported in Acts 5. Although the historical references are somewhat inexact, the apologetic purpose of this speech is clear. Gamaliel ends with a forthright exposition of the Lukan perspective: "if this is of God, we will not be able to resist them, and we may be found fighting against God" (5:39; cf. Luke 7:30; Squires 1993: 180-82). This sentence climaxes this subsection and holds the whole sequence of events in the temple (3:1–5:42) within the framework of God's overarching sovereignty. Gamaliel's success is noted succinctly: "they were persuaded by him" (5:39; see 28:24).

The **fifth summary description of the community (5:40-42)** draws this subsection to a close with yet another typical description of the community. The apostles are released after a flogging and return to the community rejoicing (5:41), a response which Luke notes as typical of a number of messianic communities (8:8; 11:23; 13:48, 52; 15:3, 31; 16:34). The community meets every day (see 2:46) in the temple (see 2:46) and in homes (see 2:46), teaching (see 2:42; 4:2; 5:21, 25, 28) and preaching that Jesus is the Messiah (see 2:36).

The Seven and Stephen (6:1–8:3)

Although sometimes regarded as the start of a new section in Acts, the story of the seven and Stephen (6:1–8:3) is better viewed as the final subsection of the Jerusalem section (Squires 1998: 608-9). The story continues to be related to the Jerusalem temple. As on previous occasions, a single incident initiates the main action of the subsection (1:6-10; 2:1-4; 3:1-10; 6:1-6). Similarly, the prominence of speeches continues; in this case, hower, it is one speech, the longest of the book (and the only one spoken by Stephen), which serves to set the events narrated within the broader framework of divine sovereignty. The subsection contains two summary descriptions which tell of significant modifications in the nature of the community (6:7; 8:1b-3).

The initial incident is the **division between Hellenists and Hebraists (6:1-6).** This takes place in the days when the messianic community is "increasing in numbers" (v. 1). A new description for community members, that of "disciple," is introduced here (vv. 1, 2); it emphasizes continuity with events of Jesus' lifetime since the term has already described all those who followed Jesus in Galilee (Luke 5:30-33; 6:1, 13, 17, 20; 14:26-27; etc.). The two groups mentioned, Hellenists and Hebrews, reflect the cultural diversity within the Jerusalem community; such diversity arises from the simple fact that different members of the community had different languages (Greek and Aramaic) as their first language (Esler 1987: 136-39; Hill 1992: 5-24). The presence of Greek-speaking Jews in Jerusalem is no surprise; the city had been exposed to Greek influence for some centuries (1 Macc 1:11-15, 41-50; see Fiensy in Bauckham 1995: 213-36). The incident reported concerns the demands made by "the daily serving of the widows" (6:1; at table, 6:2), which detracts the community leadership from their tasks of "serving the word of God" (6:2, 4 — either their ongoing preaching activity, 2:42; or their teaching, 4:2; 5:42) and of prayer (6:4; see 2:42). Luke has a special concern for widows (Luke 2:36-38; 4:25-26; 7:11-17; 18:1-8; 20:47; 21:1-4; Acts 6:1; 9:39, 41); this incident reflects the social vulnerability of those women such as widows who lack the male "protection" expected in Hellenistic society (Seim 1994: 229-48). The Greek term *diakonia* (6:1, 4) and its cognate verb (v. 2) have a general reference to waiting at table in ordinary Hellenistic Greek usage (Luke 4:39; 10:40; 12:37; 17:8), but here take on the distinctive sense which they collect in Luke-Acts, by referring to a leadership role in the community (Luke 8:3; 22:26-27; Acts 1:17, 25; 12:25; 19:22; 20:24; 21:19; see Seim 1994: 57-64, 72-77). The twelve determine to appoint as table servers (and community leaders) seven individuals who bear the desired characteristics of being "filled with the Spirit" (6:3; see the list of individuals who are Spirit-filled in the comments on 4:8) and wisdom (6:3). The first of the seven appointed, Stephen, meets these criteria and is, in addition, "full of faith" (v. 5). Each of these criteria is linked with divine sovereignty at different points in the narrative of Acts: the Spirit is a direct gift of God (2:17), as is faith, or believing (5:14); wisdom is given by God (7:10) and is linked with the Spirit (6:3, 10) and other divine gifts (grace, 7:10; power, 7:22).

The appointment of these seven is the first appointment since that of Matthias; like that appointment, this one takes place after prayer (6:6; see 1:24). The new element added here is the laying on of hands (6:6), a practice found also when some Samaritans are baptized (8:15-19), when Saul's sight is restored by Ananias (9:12, 17), and when Barnabas and Saul are commissioned by the church in Antioch (13:2-3). Such laying on of hands is a scriptural practice; when used as here, to set apart a group for a designated task, it evokes the account of the consecration of the Levites (Num 8:5-22) when they are cleansed (Num 10:5-8), the Israelites lay hands on them (10:9-10), and Aaron presents them to Yahweh as an elevation offering (8:11); cf. the commissioning of Joshua (Num 27:18-23). At Ps 139:5, the laying on of God's hand signals the divine presence with the psalmist. Most often the laying on of hands refers to a ritual action (Exod 29:10, 15, 19; Lev 1:4; 3:2, 8, 13; 4:4, 15, 24, 29, 33; 16:21; 24:14; Num 8:10, 12). In Luke's Gospel, however, the laying on of hands has a consistently negative connotation since it refers to the arresting of Jesus (Luke 20:19; 21:12; 22:53). In Acts this negative connotation is common (2:23; 4:3; 5:18; 12:1; 21:11, 27; 28:17). This echoes the scriptural use of the phrase to refer to divine judgment (Exod 7:4-5; 24:11; 1 Kgs 13:3-5; Ezek 25:12-14), political opposition (1 Kgs 20:6; Neh 13:21; Zech 14:13), and murder (Num 35:22-25; Josh 20:2-6; Job 41:8; Esth 2:21; 3:5-6; 6:2; 8:7-8; 9:1-2; Add Esth 12:1-3; 1 Macc 14:30-34). Here, however, the connotations are all positive; the appointment of the seven allows the twelve to "devote themselves" to their apostolic task of "serving the word of God" (6:4; for serving as the task of an apostle, see 1:17, 25; for devoting themselves, see 2:42).

The ensuing **sixth summary description of the community (6:7)** replicates phrases from the narrative of the scene which has just concluded. "The word of God" (v. 2) is now used to describe the community itself rather than an activity of its leadership; "disciple" (vv. 1, 2) now becomes the standard term for members of the messianic community (v. 7; and a further 25 times in chs. 9–21). The increasing numbers in the community (6:1) form the basis for the comment that "the number of disciples increased and multiplied greatly" (v. 7); the two verbs that are used here recur with the word of God in subsequent summary descriptions (12:24; 19:20; similar ideas are expressed at 9:31 and 16:5). The membership of the community now comprises "a great many of the priests" — a surprising comment in light both of the constant opposition shown by the priests to this point (4:1, 6; 5:17, 21, 24, 27) and of the role that the priests will soon play in Stephen's death (7:1; as members of the council, 6:12).

The fate of Stephen (6:8–8:1a) is now told. Out of the seven just appointed, Luke focuses first on Stephen, who is described in familiar terms as a person empowered by God. Stephen is full of grace (6:8), a mark of the community at 2:47; 4:33, and of power, a divine gift (2:22) exhibited by the apostles (4:33); he is able to perform wonders and signs (6:8), a divinely inspired capacity (2:19) exhibited by Jesus (2:22) and the apostles (2:43; 5:12). Luke notes again that he speaks with wisdom and spirit (6:10), attributes already noted as divine in origin (see v. 3); here they are qualified as being unable to be withstood by humans. This description introduces the account of **the arrest of Stephen (vv. 8-15)**. Those in conflict with Stephen are diaspora Jews who have returned to Jerusalem, where they worship in a synagogue (v. 9; Riesner in Bauckham 1995: 179-211). However, they do not make the front running against Stephen, but they conscript agitators to stir up the crowd (vv. 11-12). This is reminiscent of a detail in the trial of Jesus (Matt 27:20; Mark 15:11) which Luke omits, transferring it to Stephen's trial. Similar agitation of the crowd will later be encountered by Paul (13:50; 14:19; 17:5, 13). Likewise, the "false witnesses" who accuse Stephen of speaking against the temple (6:13) recall the false witnesses who charge Jesus with the claim that he would destroy the temple (Matt 26:59-61; Mark 14:55-58), another detail which Luke transfers to Stephen's trial. Later Luke will consciously model Stephen's death on the death scene of Jesus (7:54-60; cf. Luke 23:34, 44-46). Stephen is charged with uttering "blasphemous words against Moses and God" (6:11) which are manifest in his allegedly speaking against "this holy place and the law" (6:13). Similar charges are later brought against Paul (21:28). The charges against Stephen turn out to be ironic since in the speech which follows he will speak at length and with deep conviction about the people of Israel, to whom the law was given, and with penetrating insight about the role of the holy place of Israel.

Stephen's speech (7:1-53), the eighth speech of this section, is by far the longest of the whole book. By means of this speech, Luke matches the divinely given qualities of Stephen (6:3, 5, 8, 10) with his testimony to the acts of God in the history of Israel. The speech begins in typical Lukan fashion by defining the subject as God (7:2; cf. 2:17; 3:13; 5:30); the phrase used here, "the God of glory," is drawn from Scripture (Ps 29:3). The speech which follows rebuts the charges laid against Stephen; it demonstrates that, far from speaking "blasphemous words against God" (6:11), Stephen has a fulsome understanding of God's place in Israel's history. At the end of his speech, Stephen takes up the charge that he spoke "against the holy place" (v. 13). Luke has Stephen quote Scripture (7:49-50, citing Isa 66:1-2) in order to show that his criticism of the temple (God's "place of rest," 7:49) arises from within Jewish tradition itself. (On the relation of the charges to the speech, see Wilson 1973: 129-38.)

Stephen makes numerous scriptural allusions and quotations in this speech. In general, this seems similar to the earlier speeches by Peter, although the precise function of these scriptural elements is somewhat distinctive in this speech. Here, Scripture functions as historical narrative, whereas elsewhere in Acts it provides prophecies to be fulfilled. (The exceptions within the speech are the prophecies of 7:6, 7, which are fulfilled at 7:9-16, 36 respectively.)

Luke has Stephen provide a detailed rehearsal of significant parts of Israel's history by focusing in turn on Abraham (7:2-8), Joseph (vv. 9-16), and Moses (vv. 17-44). Then, after briefly mentioning Joshua (v. 45a), David (vv. 45b-46), and Solomon (v. 47), Stephen moves to the climactic claim of the speech (vv. 48-53). Lengthy recitals of key features of Israel's history are already found in Hebrew Scripture (Deuteronomy 26; Joshua 24; Nehemiah 9; Psalms 78; 105; 106; 135; 136; Ezekiel 20). In the present instance, the effect of the long recital of the earlier part of Israel's history is twofold. First, the historical recital reinforces Stephen's Jewish credentials. When he begins to speak critically of the temple and of the Jerusalem authorities, it is clear that he does so from within the Jewish tradition. Stephen is not an outsider but an insider, offering a prophetic critique. Second, the historical recital provides insight into a further layer of God's providential activity. Earlier speeches by Peter have interpreted the events of the life, death, resurrection, and ascension of Jesus as being within divine providence (see 2:14-41). Various features of the narrative have revealed the active involvement of God in the events that take place in the Jerusalem community. Now the undergirding plan of God is revealed within the long history of Israel. The line of continuity is strengthened between each layer; God is at work in the Jerusalem community as in the life of Jesus and as in the history of Israel (Squires in Marshall and Peterson 1998: 21-23).

Each of the leaders of Israel is interpreted in typically Lukan style to present them as the vehicles through whom God was working in history (Squires 1993: 66-67). It was to Abraham (7:2-8) that God appeared, promising him a land ("God . . . said to him," 7:2-3; cf. Gen 12:1). His move from Haran to Canaan was at the initiative of God (7:4; cf. Gen 11:35–12:5), but the fact that his descendants did not inherit this land was also God's intention (7:5; cf. Gen 17:8). Subsequently God spoke to Abraham of the promise of the covenant of circumcision ("God spoke thus . . . and God said," 7:6-8; cf. Gen 17:9-14).

Of Joseph (7:9-16), Luke has Stephen say that "God was with him" (7:9; cf. Gen 39:1-3, 21), the same phrase as is later used of Jesus (10:38). God's presence enables Joseph to exhibit grace and wisdom (7:10), characteristics with which God had also endowed Stephen (6:3, 8, 10) and Jesus (Luke 1:40, 52). As a result of his wisdom, Joseph is given authority by Pharaoh (7:10; cf. Gen 41:37-45). Joseph is brought through afflictions and is rescued by God (7:10); the same term describes God's rescue of Israel under Moses (7:34, quoting Exod 3:7-8) and of Paul (26:17). The events which follow are reported without explicit reference to God, but demonstrate the outworking of Joseph's wisdom. The ensuing famine (7:11; cf. Gen 41:53-54) leads to the two visits of Joseph's brothers (7:12-13; cf. Gen 42:1-28; 43:1–44:34). The family settle in Egypt (7:14-15; cf. Gen 45:1–47:12); subsequently Jacob and others are returned to the family grave at Shechem in Canaan (7:16; cf. Gen 49:29-32; 50:13, where the grave is located in Hebron).

The "time of the promise which God confessed to Abraham" comes to fruition under Moses (7:17-43). During the time between Joseph and Moses, the people "increased and multiplied" (7:17), the same phrase used to describe the expanding community in Jerusalem ("the number of disciples increased and multiplied greatly," 6:7) and elsewhere (12:24; 19:20). At his birth, Moses is "beautiful before God" (7:20; cf. Exod 2:2). As he grows, he is trained in wisdom in Egypt and becomes "powerful in his words and deeds" (7:22). These qualities evoke the divine enabling seen in Luke's accounts of Stephen, the apostles, and Jesus, and are in direct contrast with the scriptural description of Moses as "slow of speech and slow of tongue" (Exod 4:10). Luke has Stephen demonstrate that Moses shares other similarities with those chosen by God in later ages, especially Jesus. Despite the rejection he experiences from his kinsfolk (7:23-29; cf. Exod 2:11-22), "God through his hand gave salvation" to Israel (7:25), just as God later gives salvation through Jesus (Luke 1:69; 2:11, 30; 3:6; Acts 5:31; 13:23, 26). When this salvation takes place under Moses it is accompanied by divinely enabled wonders and signs (7:36; cf. Exod 7:3), as it does through Jesus (2:22). This fulfills the command given to Moses (7:34) when an angel appeared to him in the burning bush (v. 30) and God spoke to him (vv. 32, 33-34; cf. Exod 3:1-10). Stephen omits entirely the series of objections raised by Moses when he is called (Exod 3:11–4:17); his portrayal of Moses is that of a person who is immediately obedient to the divine call. This sequence of call (7:30-34) and obedient response (7:36) repeats the pattern seen with Abraham (call, 7:2-3; obedient response, 7:4). It is replicated in the narrative of Acts, especially with regard to Saul (call, 9:15; obedient response, 9:19b-20).

Stephen tells of Moses being mocked by his kinsfolk, who could not conceive of him as ruler and judge (7:27, 35; cf. Exod 2:14). Stephen affirms that he is rightly called ruler, infers that he is correctly regarded as judge, and adds the further title of liberator (7:35). The functions of two of these titles are attributed to Jesus (judgment at 10:42; 17:31; liberation at Luke 1:68; 2:38; 21:28; 24:21). The third function, of leader, is not directly attributed to Jesus by Luke; however, he does use the related term *archēgos* at 3:15; 5:31. A further title applied to Moses is the scriptural one of prophet (7:37; cf. Deut 18:15), which has also been applied to Jesus (Luke 7:16; 9:8, 19; 24:19) as well as to numerous individuals in the narrative of the Gospel (Luke 1:67, 76; 2:36; 7:26) and Acts (11:27; 15:32; 21:9). That it is a divinely bestowed function is evident from 2:17-18. Stephen's depiction of Moses thus resonates strongly with the Lukan understanding of Jesus, the prophet, ruler, and judge through whom God was at work enabling signs and wonders and bringing liberation and salvation for the people of Israel.

As prophet, Moses is given living oracles by yet another angel (7:38; see 7:53; cf. Exod 19:1–20:21; Deut 5:1-33). The idea that the law was mediated by angels is not found in Hebrew Scripture; it is mentioned at Gal 3:17; Heb 2:2. (On the description of Israel as an *ekklēsia*, see 5:11.) Moses in turn passes on these oracles to Israel, but they refuse to accept them and commit idolatry by making a golden calf (7:39-43; cf. Exod 32:1-35). The description of the golden calf introduces the theme of idolatry which will undergird Stephen's critique of the temple in 7:48-51. A prophetic citation (Amos 5:25-27) provides justification for God's abandonment of Israel (7:42); they had been idolaters in the wilderness (7:42-43).

Stephen then summarizes how God was at work in the conquest of Israel and the early monarchy. The presence of the tent of testimony fulfills what God commanded to Moses (7:44; cf. Exod 25:40); Joshua leads the conquest of the nations "whom God drove out" (7:45; cf. Josh 21:43-45; 23:9; 24:18); the tent remains in the land until the time of David, who "had grace before God" (7:46; on grace, see 2:47). The speech ends with Solomon's action of building a house for God (7:47). According to Stephen, this inverts the typical relationship seen in Israel's history. The Deuteronomic explanation for the building of the temple was that it was done in fulfillment of God's promise to David (1 Kgs 8:14-21). By contrast, Stephen announces that, by building the temple, Solomon acted in a way that God had not sanctioned. Solomon thus repeats the error made under Moses, when the Israelites made an idol and "revelled in the works of their hands" (7:39-41). The argument leads us to expect that Solomon would incur the same wrath as exhibited to the people under Moses (vv. 42-43). Indeed, God's opposition to Solomon's building is evident in that it is not in the temple built by human hands (v. 48) but in the world which "my [God's] hand made" (v. 50) that God is to be found. Stephen here quotes a prophetic text (Isa 66:1-2), but the message resonates with the way that Cynic philosophers mounted their critiques of idols (see Squires 1993: 67-68). The climactic moment of this speech provides a foundation for understanding the subsequent shift of focus away from the temple and toward the house-based communities that will be established during the "turn to the Gentiles." (For Lukan antagonism toward the temple authorities, see Brawley 1987: 107-32; for the temple/household contrast, see Elliott in Neyrey 1991: 211-40; Seim 1994: 118-47.)

The language about God in the latter part of this speech thus establishes a parallel set of antagonisms: between God and Israel under Moses, and between God and Israel under Solomon. A further parallel can be drawn from the surrounding narrative: there is antagonism between God and the Jewish authorities who have brought Stephen (God's agent) to trial. This antagonism mirrors both the antagonism which the apostles (God's agents) have experienced from the same Jewish authorities (chs. 3–5) and the antagonism mounted against Jesus (another of God's agents) by those authorities (Luke 19:47 onward; Acts 4:27). Paul (yet another of God's agents) will subsequently experience similar antagonism in his encounters with Jewish groups in the diaspora (9:23; chs. 13–18) and in Jerusalem (9:29, 21:27-28).

In concluding the speech, Luke has Stephen attack his accusers; he levels his own charges against them, depicting them as "resisting the Holy Spirit" (7:51). At this point Ananias and Sapphira come to mind; for a similar antagonism toward the Spirit, they were killed (5:1-11). However, the tables are turned on Stephen, for those listening to his speech interrupt him at this point. **Stephen's martyrdom (7:54–8:1a)** ensues, with narrative reinforcement of the validity of his point of view by means of language about the divine. Stephen is once again described as "filled with the Spirit" (7:55, evoking 6:3, 5). He experiences an epiphany in which he sees "the glory of God" (7:55), which aligns him with Abraham (7:2), as well as "Jesus standing at the right hand of God" (7:55-56). Stephen is also aligned with Jesus; in 7:56 his description of the heavens opening evokes the Lukan account of Jesus' baptism (Luke 3:21), and his vision of the Son of Man is similar to the apocalyptic vision which Jesus paints at his trial (Luke 22:69). Stephen's two cries "in a great voice" (7:57, 60) are reminiscent of the death of Jesus (Luke 23:46), and his dying words, "receive my spirit" (7:59), are patterned on the final words of the Lukan Jesus (Luke 23:46, citing Ps 31:6). Stephen's last cry, a petition that the Lord overlook this sin (7:60), is similarly evocative of the Lukan Jesus' forgiveness of those who crucified him (Luke 23:34). As Luke clearly interprets the death of Jesus as God's predetermined action (2:23, 4:28), this similar description of Stephen's death has at least overtones of divine authorization, even if they are not explicit.

Later in his narrative, Luke has Paul describe Stephen as God's "witness" (22:20). As already noted, the task of bearing witness is enabled by the gift of the Spirit (1:8).

There follows **the seventh summary description of the community (8:1b-3)**, the final one of this first section, in which the opposition experienced by Peter and John, and more dramatically by Stephen, is broadened to include the persecution of everyone in the Jerusalem assembly except the apostles (v. 1). This leads to the scattering of the community (v. 1b), an adversity which will come to be the primary means by which the promise of 1:8 is fulfilled — beginning here with Judea and Samaria. The summary description also notes the role played by Saul in this persecution of the assembly (8:3).

Section Two: Preparing for the "Turn to the Gentiles" (8:4–12:25)

The second main section of the narrative outlines the steps taken by members of the Jerusalem community as they continue to fulfill the prophecy of Jesus (1:8), moving out from Jerusalem and Judea to Samaria and beyond. (On the reasons for taking 8:4–12:25 as a unified section, see Squires 1998: 608-11.) Four main steps are taken in this section, recounting how selected community members begin to "turn to the Gentiles," as Paul later describes it (13:46). These steps together form a pivotal moment in the narrative; they provide initial validation for the establishment of communities which are inclusive of both Jewish and Gentile members.

The geography of this section is structured in a spiral-like fashion, moving away from Jerusalem only to return to it before the next outward movement occurs (Squires 1998: 611-14).

- In the first step (8:4-40), Philip enters the city of Samaria (v. 5) but ends by returning to Caesarea (v. 40). His actions in Samaria receive validation through a visit from the apostles in Jerusalem (v. 14).
- The second step, concerning Saul (9:1-31), begins in Damascus (v. 2) but returns to Jerusalem (v. 26) before Saul leaves for Tarsus (v. 30).
- The third step, focused on Peter (9:32–11:18), begins in Judea at Lydda (9:32) before moving through Joppa (v. 36) to Caesarea (10:1). The action moves between Joppa and Caesarea before Peter returns to Jerusalem (11:2) and recounts what has taken place in Joppa and Caesarea to the Jerusalem community.
- The final step (11:19–12:25) begins in Antioch (v. 20), where the community receives envoys: Barnabas from Jerusalem (v. 22) and Saul from Tarsus (v. 25), followed by prophets from Jerusalem (v. 27). The narrative then returns to Judea (vv. 29-30) for the delivery of the "collection" and for an account of further events in Jerusalem. A brief visit to Tyre and Sidon (12:20) precedes the return of Barnabas and Saul to Jerusalem (v. 25).

Each step includes events which demonstrate that this movement away from Jerusalem is within the divine plan while firmly retaining the link with Jerusalem. Gentiles are to be incorporated into communities which still retain their fundamentally Jewish character. The section as a whole is marked by a prominence of miraculous events, interventions by divine agents, and the working of the Spirit. The combination of these themes, along with explicit statements of God's plan, reinforces at each step the validity of the turn to the Gentiles and the establishment of inclusive communities. This section makes it clear that Luke sees God's hand resting on all that takes place as the story line turns toward the Gentiles (Squires in Marshall and Peterson 1998: 19-39).

Philip in Samaria (8:5-40)

After the **summary description (8:4)**, which recapitulates the scattering motif from v. 1, the "turn to the Gentiles" begins with an account of the activity of **Philip in Samaria (vv. 5-24)**. The movement into Samaria begins the fulfillment of the second stage of Jesus' programmatic statement (1:8; Hengel in Bauckham 1995: 67-78). The spread of communities in "all Judea" is not narrated directly, although it is assumed later in this section of the narrative when believers are introduced in Lydda (9:32) and Joppa (v. 36). The note that Philip enters a city of Samaria (8:5) signals that the spread of this movement is to be urban-based; such is the pattern followed by all subsequent leaders in Acts. Luke writes for a settled urban community; his account of the spread of faith communities is completely urban-based. This focus contrasts with the rural-based movement initiated by Jesus (Mark 6:6; 8:27), although Luke has already located Jesus in cities (Luke 4:43; 5:12; 8:1; 9:10; 13:22) as well as villages (Luke 8:1; 9:6, 12, 52, 56; 10:38; 13:22; 17:12). For the distinction between the unwalled "village" and the walled "city," see Lev 25:29-31; for a description of the preindustrial city of Luke's time, see Rohrbaugh in Neyrey 1991: 125-49.

In this Samaritan section, the lines of continuity with what has gone before are strong. The initial, concise summary notes that Philip preaches "the Messiah" (8:5), a message already announced in Jerusalem (2:36; 3:20; 5:42). His activity is characterized by signs (v. 6) — an activity consistent with that of the apostles (2:43; 4:30; 5:12) and Stephen (6:8). He casts out unclean spirits (8:7), as did Peter (5:16), and heals the paralyzed and lame (8:7), as did Peter (3:1-10, a lame man; 9:32-35, a paralyzed man) and Jesus (Luke 5:18, a paralyzed man; 7:22, the lame). As a result, Philip brings "much joy" to the city's inhabitants (8:8), akin to the emotions experienced by the Jerusalemites (3:11; 4:21). Implicit in this account is the sense that, as God guided the apostles in Jerusalem, so God guides Philip in Samaria.

This sense of God's oversight is strengthened in the ensuing conversion of Simon (8:9-13). The people of the city are amazed at the magical powers of Simon (8:9, 11); magic was considered to be a viable religious option in the first century, although (like all religious expressions) it was capable of being degraded in practice (see Philo *Spec. leg.* 3.100-101; Lucian *Lover of Lies* 15-16). Luke's view of magicians is made clearest in his portrayal of the Cyprian magician Elymas (13:6-10), where he notes that magicians are in thrall to the one whose power has, in fact, been defeated (Luke 10:18; see Garrett 1989: 37-60). In later centuries, Simon became identified as the founder of a significant branch of gnostic Christianity (Justin *1 Apol.* 1.26.1-3; Iren. *Adv. Haer.* 1.23; Origen *Contra Celsum* 6.11; Eusebius *Hist. Eccl.* 2.13-15). In Luke's account, however, Simon is acclaimed as "the power of God that is called Great" (8:10). Could this be the same power which energized the apostles (3:12-13; 4:7-10), just as it had energized Jesus (2:22; Luke 5:17)? The answer (no) is implicit in the account of Philip's conversion of Simon; the one who was acting as if he did possess such power is actually made to be subservient to the true power of God (Garrett 1989: 61-78). In bringing Simon to the point of baptism, Philip acts in the same manner as Jesus; he preaches "the sovereignty of God" (8:12), the central message of Jesus (1:3; Luke 4:43; 6:20; etc.), and performs "signs and great miracles" (8:13), as did Jesus (2:22). The specific miracles performed by Philip in 8:7 are akin to miracles of Jesus, who casts out unclean spirits (Luke 4:33-37; 7:21; 9:37-43) and heals the paralyzed and lame (Luke 5:17-26; 7:22). The people respond by undergoing baptism (8:12), paralleling what had taken place earlier in Jerusalem (2:41). Now a community of Samaritans exists in continuity with the Jewish community in Jerusalem. Even Simon becomes a member of the community through baptism (8:13).

Confirmation of God's guidance comes through both positive and negative means in the subsequent visit of Peter and John (8:14-24). Positively, the Samaritans who have already "received the word of God" (v. 14) now "receive the Holy Spirit" through the laying on of hands by the apostles (vv. 15-18), prefiguring the subsequent laying on of hands on Saul (9:12, 17; 13:3, with Barnabas). Just as the Spirit has guided the community in Jerusalem (2:4; 4:31; 6:3, 5, 10; 7:55), so guidance by the Spirit is integral to each step taken toward the Gentiles (8:17, 29, 39; 9:17; 10:19-20, 44, 46; 11:12, 15; 11:24, 28). Although the gift of the Spirit (8:17) is here separate from baptism (8:12), as also in Ephesus (19:1-7), Luke does not intend this pattern to be read as prescriptive for all situations, as other accounts of baptisms indicate (2:38-41; 10:44-48; and cf. the discussion at 19:1-7). Rather, the emphasis is on continuity with the Jerusalem experience: the apostles validate the Samaritans' experience by means of the Holy Spirit.

Negatively, this gift of the Spirit provokes the envy of Simon, who requests authority to perform the same act (8:19). Peter's rebuke accuses Simon of seeking to purchase the gift of God (v. 20) and places him in the same category as Ananias and Sapphira, since his heart is "not straight before God" (v. 21). The same type of conflict that has been evidenced in Jerusalem is now found in Samaria; once more language about God is used to define the preferred option and to validate the actions of the community leaders. This conflict is resolved, neither by imprisonment nor by martyrdom, but through means already evidenced in Jerusalem: Peter asks Simon to repent and offers a petitionary prayer to the Lord for his forgiveness (v. 22; cf. 2:39; 3:19; 5:31). This initial Samaritan passage concludes with a **summary description (8:25)** of the testimony to "the word of the Lord" undertaken by the apostles as they preach throughout Samaria.

The following incident, a conversation between **Philip and the Ethiopian (8:26-40),** moves the narrative back into Judea but involves contact with an Ethiopian. The Israelites regarded Ethiopia as the furthest extent of the earth in a southwesterly direction (Isa 11:11-12). Although the man was a Gentile, he was returning from worship in Jerusalem (8:27); he is probably thus the first of a number of proselytes who appear in the narrative of Acts (10:2; at 13:50; 16:14; 17:4, 17; 18:7). However, he would have been barred from entering the temple precincts because he was a eunuch (Deut 23:1). Philip travels south-west toward the coast, on the wilderness road to Gaza, at the urging of "an angel of the Lord" (8:26), a phenomenon already seen in Jerusalem (5:19). His encounter with the Ethiopian is both initiated by the Spirit (8:29) and ended by the Spirit, when Philip was snatched away immediately after baptizing the Ethiopian (v. 39). The content of the conversation is given in some detail; of particular interest is the fact that one of the scriptural prophecies which is fulfilled by Jesus is here identified. As the Ethiopian reads of the "lamb led to the slaughter" (Isa 53:7-8), Philip explains that this relates to Jesus, whom Philip then preaches to him (8:32-35). Such fulfillment of prophecy has already been introduced in speeches in Jerusalem (2:16-21, 25-31, 34-35, 3:18, 4:25-26) as another indicator of God's sovereignty in the events of history. The particular scriptural passage quoted is part of the fourth "servant song" (Isa 52:13–53:12); various excerpts from this song are interpreted as applying to Jesus by a range of NT writers (Matt 8:17; Luke 22:37; John 12:38; Rom 4:25; 5:18-19; 10:16; 15:21; Heb 9:28; 1 Pet 2:21-25). The scene ends with the baptism of the Ethiopian (8:38; see 2:38), thereby incorporating a person of another nationality into the extending community of messianic believers. Philip is then removed by the Spirit of the Lord (8:39); as he returns to Caesarea, he continues to preach "good news" (v. 40), a message already defined as concerning "the sovereignty of God" (v. 12).

Saul in Damascus and Jerusalem (9:1-31)

The second step in this section (9:1-31) recounts a key miracle: the complete turnaround of a persecutor, including his blinding and then restoration to sight, prior to his engagement in preaching activity among the messianic believers. The individual who experienced this miracle has been introduced in passing at the point of Stephen's death (7:58; 8:1a); the inference of this brevity may be that he was a character already well known to Luke's audience. At 9:1 the narrative returns to this individual, Saul. He will become the preeminent human character in the later narrative of Acts; for Luke he will become the model par excellence of faithfulness in the face of opposition and persecution (Maddox 1982: 66-90).

But at this moment in the narrative, Saul is simply a vigorous persecutor of "the disciples of the Lord" (9:1). The account of the **conversion of Saul (vv. 1-19a)** begins on the road to Damascus, a predominantly Jewish town in the Roman province of Syria. This location, along with the charge which is given to Saul in Damascus (v. 15), foreshadows the ultimate move into the Gentile world. In all the letters of Paul which we now have, the single reference which might locate his conversion at Damascus is Gal 1:5-17.

Luke appears to assume knowledge that Damascus contains "disciples of the Lord" (9:1). How they got there is not narrated, nor whether they were Jewish or Gentile disciples. They are described, for the first time, as being of "the Way" (v. 2), a term which recurs in later chapters of Luke's narrative (18:25; 19:9, 23; 22:4; 24:14, 22). It may owe its origins to scriptural usage in association with God's activity (Pss 5:8; 18:30; 25:9; 27:11; 37:34; 50:23; 67:2, etc.; and note the use of Isa 40:3-5 at Luke 3:4-6). The term is also appropriated in the Dead Sea Scrolls as a means of defining the Qumran community (1QS 9:17-18, 21; 10:21; CD 1:13; 2:6); this may reflect competing claims for being the authentic keepers of Torah among Jewish sects. In subsequent usage (beyond the first century) it has come to be completely overshadowed by a term used less often by Luke, that of "Christian" or "messianist" (11:26; 26:28). By using the term "the Way" for the first time here, Luke emphasizes the Jewish characterization of those communities which declare Jesus to be Messiah, even if they are in Gentile areas. It is significant that this comes at the point in the narrative when Luke introduces Saul, the person who (in his eyes) is the greatest proponent of the "turn to the Gentiles."

Saul is introduced as an opponent of "the Way." The Greek reads literally, "he breathes a murderous threat" (9:1; NRSV, "breathing threats and murder"), precisely the antagonistic threatening attitude about which the Jerusalem community has already prayed (4:29). He gains his authority from the high priest (9:1), already identified as standing in opposition to God's agents, Peter and John (4:6; 5:21, 24) and Stephen (7:1). Saul has already been described as being "in agreement with their plan" (8:1a). The scene is thus set for a continuation of the conflict narrated in Jerusalem; Luke's description of Saul's activities (9:2) imports this conflict to Damascus in tangible ways. In letters written later by Saul (under the name of Paul), he refers to this period of his life as "violently persecuting" the believers (Gal 1:13; Phil 3:6). His own references to his change of heart, to become a member of the messianic assemblies, are brief and lack any of the narrative color and detail that Luke's accounts provide (Gal 1:15-16; Phil 3:7-11; 2 Cor 4:4-6; and possibly 1 Cor 9:1).

The crucial event which takes place as he draws near to Damascus is initiated by an epiphany: an overpowering light shines and a voice speaks to Saul (9:3-6). The epiphanies which have already taken place in Acts (1:10-11; 5:19; 8:26) are described in a rather bare fashion. By contrast, this particular epiphany is recounted in detail (as is the later epiphany to Peter, 10:10-16). The divine origin of the epiphany is promptly identified: the light was from heaven (9:3). The voice which addresses Saul is that of Jesus, whom Saul (as did Stephen before him, 7:59-60) addresses as "Lord" (9:4-5).

At this point in the narrative, the ambiguity of the term "Lord" is heightened. Until now the vast majority of occurrences of "Lord" have referred to God. From this point on, the term can be used to refer to Jesus (20 times, of which 4 repeat the incident from ch. 9), although more often it still refers to God (36 times). When Luke reports that people "turned to the Lord" (9:35; 11:21) or "believed in the Lord" (9:42; 11:17; 14:23; 16:15, 31; 18:8; 20:21), the phrase appears somewhat ambiguous as to its precise referent. However, in each case the context indicates that "the Lord" is now referring to Jesus.

The later categories of christological thought (after Nicea) introduce categories not relevant for the time when Luke's text was being written. The most that can be said is that Luke never envisages any ontological unity of Jesus and God, but on some occasions (and certainly not always) there is an overlap of function — Jesus now functions as God has functioned in the past. For the most part, Luke presents Jesus as an agent of God's sovereignty, as one member among many (Peter, Philip, Stephen, Saul, Barnabas, and so on) who have functioned as agents of God's sovereignty. Occasionally Jesus is distinguished from these figures, such as when he appears as a divine messenger to Saul (9:5, paralleled at 26:15 and expanded at 22:8-10; also 9:10-17, 27).

The vision and command to Saul (9:3-6) find a parallel in the subsequent vision and command of the Lord to Ananias, instructing him to meet with Saul (vv. 10-16). That God is at work in these events is clear from Luke's narrative account; it is the divine voice (speaking through Jesus) which addresses both Saul (vv. 4-6) and Ananias when he speaks of Saul (vv. 15-16). The theme of divine necessity has already been present in the Jerusalem narrative, both with reference to events narrated (1:22; 3:21; 4:12, 19-20; 5:29) and with reference to the death of Jesus (2:23; 4:28). This theme is now articulated in both divine speeches: to Saul, who is given a general charge: "it will be told to you what you must do" (9:6); and to Ananias, who is instructed to tell Saul, "I will show him what he must suffer" (v. 16) because "he is a chosen vessel for me" (v. 15).

The key role which Saul plays in later sections of the narrative is thus signaled at this point; he is a critical agent in the execution of the necessary plan which God has for the believing communities in Jerusalem, Damascus, and beyond. Acts 13–28 is not solely about what was done by Paul (as he is then known); it is unambiguously about "what the Lord did through the activity of Paul" (14:27; 15:4, 12; 21:19). The other dimension to Saul's role will become evident by implication throughout the latter half of Acts; that is, he stands as a model for what faithful proclamation and faithful discipleship entail. All that Paul does and says, and how he deals with what he encounters, functions as a role model for the readers of Luke's narrative. This is underscored by Paul's two repetitions of this story, with alterations and elaborations, in the final section of Acts.

After being blinded, Saul is brought back to wholeness by Ananias, who acts in ways consistent with membership in "the Way." Ananias lays his hands on Saul to heal him (9:17), a divinely endowed ability (4:28) exercised by the apostles in Jerusalem (5:12) and Samaria (8:17). He tells him that "the Lord sent me" (9:17), a phrase which evokes the divine commissioning of Moses (7:34; cf. Exod 3:9-15; 4:13; 5:22-23), the sending of the angel Gabriel (Luke 1:19, 26), and the task of Jesus (Luke 4:43; cf. 4:18). Ananias then commands Saul to be "filled with the Holy Spirit" (9:17), repeating the divine action already evident in Jerusalem (2:4, 38; 4:31) and Samaria (8:15-17). Like Peter (4:8) and Stephen (7:55), Saul is now filled with the Spirit. (Philip, too, is guided by the Spirit [8:29, 39], although the precise terminology of "being filled" is not applied to him.) The association of laying on of hands with this Spirit filling is reminiscent of the account of how Joshua, "a man in whom is the Spirit," was commissioned as Yahweh directed through Moses by the laying on of hands (Num 27:18-23, esp. v. 23). Like Joshua, Saul has been given authority over God's people (Num 27:20) as "a chosen vessel" who will bear God's name (9:15). Paul is then baptized (9:18), following the pattern set for new believers by Peter (2:38) and Philip (8:16).

This action of the Spirit enables Saul not only to be able to see (9:18) but also to begin his **subsequent activity in Damascus and Jerusalem (vv. 19b-30).** He preaches to Jewish listeners in the synagogue of Damascus (vv. 20-22) and to the disciples in the Jewish city of Jerusalem (vv. 27-29). In each place, Luke demonstrates that Saul's preaching follows in the pattern already established by Peter and John in Jerusalem and by Philip in Samaria. In Damascus, Saul preaches Jesus (v. 20), identifying him as "Messiah" (v. 22), as did Peter (2:36; 3:20; 5:42) and Philip (8:5), but also as "Son of God" (9:20), a new identification which only later does he explain as having divine warrant (13:33, citing Ps 2:7). This latter title has already been applied to Jesus in the Gospel (Luke 3:22; 4:3, 9, 41; 22:70). In Jerusalem, Saul's credentials as a disciple naturally come under suspicion (9:26). However, Barnabas presents Saul's divine authorization; he explains that Saul has had an epiphany which has converted him, and that he subsequently spoke "with frankness" (NRSV, "boldly") in Damascus (v. 27), just as Peter and John had done before him (4:13). That this frankness was a divinely bestowed gift has already been made evident at 4:29, 31 (relating to the whole Jerusalem community). Saul continues to speak "with frankness in the name of the Lord" while in Jerusalem (9:28).

In his account of Saul's proclamation in both Damascus and Jerusalem, Luke establishes an important pattern that will be evident wherever Paul later preaches: a pattern of divided response to the message proclaimed. In Damascus, "all who heard him were amazed" (9:21), although Jewish opposition soon emerges (v. 23), leading to Saul's escape at night in a basket lowered over the walls (vv. 24-25). (A variant account of this incident is found in 2 Cor 11:32-33, where Paul attributes the opposition to the city ethnarch.) In Jerusalem, Paul's frankness of speech enables him to move freely among the community (9:28), although once again opposition arises, this time from the Hellenists (9:29). (Paul's reference to this visit in his own letters is strikingly different; in Gal 1:18-20 he claims to have made only a private visit to Peter and James.) In each case, Saul's opponents seek to kill him (9:24, 29), threatening him with the same fate faced by the apostles (5:33) and encountered by Stephen (7:60). Jesus, of course, had also met death at the hands of his enemies (2:23). Paul escapes to Caesarea and then returns home to Tarsus (9:30; Gal 1:21 confirms this in general terms).

In these two vignettes in Damascus and Jerusalem, therefore, Saul is aligned not only with the apostles and other witnesses but also with Jesus — each of whom faithfully carried out God's ways. The same manner of language about God which validated the activities of Jesus, the apostles, Stephen, and Philip now validates the role which Saul will play. In being elected as God's agent to go "before Gentiles and kings and sons of Israel" (9:15), Saul will play a key role in generating inclusiveness within the communities of "the Way" that are established around the northeast part of the Mediterranean basin.

Luke concludes this seminal account of the conversion of Saul, and his commissioning, with a **summary description of the community (9:31).** This summary encompasses a wider sweep of geography than in the Jerusalem section; communities are mentioned in the whole of "Judea and Galilee and Samaria." This indicates that the prediction of 1:8 is beginning to come to fruition — although no details of the Galilean communities are reported, nor was Galilee included in Jesus' prediction. The communities in Judea, Galilee, and Samaria are described in familiar terms, for they exhibit some features already seen in the Jerusalem community. They "increase in numbers" (see 2:47) and "walk in the fear of the Lord" (see 2:43). They are guided by the Holy Spirit (see 2:1-4), although the role of the Spirit is described as providing "exhortation," a role already exhibited by Peter (2:40) and later exhibited by various individuals (Barnabas, 11:23; 14:22; Paul, 13:15; 14:22; 16:40; 20:1; Silas, with Judas, 15:32, and with Paul, 16:40) as well as by the Jerusalem council (15:31).

Luke describes these communities with the term "assembly," used already for the Jerusalem community (5:11, 8:1). Here he uses the singular of the term with a collective sense to refer to a number of established communities throughout the region — a new dimension to the term which emphasizes the relatedness of individual assemblies. These communities enjoy peace, a state later explained as being the substance of Jesus' message (10:36) and evident in the Antioch community (15:33). The conversion of the persecutor (9:1-19) apparently heralds a widespread relaxation of the persecution (8:1-3).

Peter and Cornelius in Joppa and Caesarea (9:32–11:18)

The third step toward the Gentiles, focused on Peter (9:32–11:18), brings the Gentiles firmly into view (10:28, 45; 11:1, 18). While narrating this step, Luke reports two speeches by Peter — one in Caesarea, to a Gentile audience (10:34-43), and another in Jerusalem, to the gathered (Jewish) community (11:4-18). The previous step has prepared for the activity of Saul as preacher to the Gentiles, an activity which receives explicit divine authorization. In this step further divine authorization is given to this movement, in a narrative which is replete with the activity of divine messengers (angels, visions, and the Spirit). By the end of this step, Peter will be prepared to support and validate the activity which Saul (as Paul) will undertake among the Gentiles.

Before narrating these details, Luke recounts **two miracles of Peter (9:32-43)** which reestablish Peter in his role as a faithful leader. The miracles are performed on Aeneas, a male, and Tabitha, a female, reflecting Luke's penchant for paired stories featuring a male and a female (Luke 2:25-38; 4:25-27; 7:1-17; 15:3-10; 17:34-35; Seim 1994: 11-24). He comes to Lydda, where "saints are living" (v. 32), and then to the coastal city of Joppa, where disciples can be found (v. 38). The existence of these communities indicates that the second stage of the prophecy made at 1:8 has begun to be fulfilled, although its fulfillment is not narrated directly. In these Judean towns, Peter performs two miracles: he heals a paralyzed man (9:33-34) and resuscitates a dead woman (vv. 39-41). The first miracle is perhaps a reminder of the healing of the lame man (3:1-11) but more directly aligns Peter with Jesus, who also healed a paralyzed man (Luke 5:19-26) — an action explicitly regarded as an act of God (Luke 5:25-26). Peter's action awakens a response among the residents which confirms this interpretation, for when they recognized who it was that enabled the healing, they "turned to the Lord" (9:35; cf. 3:19). The second miracle likewise results in acknowledgment that God is at work, for "many believed in the Lord" (9:42); however, the claim that "all" those living in Lydda and Sharon "turned to the Lord" is surely another Lukan exaggeration (cf. 3:18). These two accounts provide reassurance that, although God has worked through Philip in Samaria and has prepared Saul for preaching among the Gentiles, nevertheless God continues to work in Judea among Jewish believers. This is reinforced by the description of Peter in Joppa, exhibiting the characteristics of community members; he prays (9:40; see 2:42) and he uses his hand (9:41), as he also did when healing the lame man (3:7; for "hand" as an agent of healing, see 5:12).

The disciple who is resuscitated in the second miracle is introduced in a significant manner. She is given two names (Aram. "Tabitha" and Gk. "Dorcas"), perhaps representing the two arenas of Jewish and Gentile believers. As a Jewish believer, Tabitha is "full of good works" (9:36), a quality she shares with Barnabas (11:24). Yet Tabitha, like Dorcas, also prefigures the kind of Gentile believer who will become important in the narrative, for she performs charitable acts as Cornelius does (10:2). Her resuscitation comes to be "known through the whole of Joppa" (9:42), just as the healing of the lame man "became known by all who live in Jerusalem" (4:16) and the defeat of the Jewish exorcists became "known to all residents in Ephesus" (19:17). Each of these events has significance beyond the immediate act performed. Indeed, the desire to "know" what God is doing frames the whole of Acts, from Peter's Pentecost speech in Jerusalem (2:14) to Paul's final speech in Rome (28:28).

The narrative then moves abruptly to Caesarea, an old city which had been rebuilt by Herod the Great to serve as the principal port for Judea; from the year AD 6 it also served as the administrative capital for the province. Luke provides a detailed account of events concerning **Peter and Cornelius (10:1-48)**, which will provide another validation of the "turn to the Gentiles." In this narrative, events are guided by a combination of divine agents: an angel, the Spirit, and a heavenly voice.

The initial part of this account concerns **Cornelius in Caesarea (10:1-8)**. He is introduced by language which presents him as already exhibiting similarities with members of the messianic assemblies. Initially (v. 2) he is described as "a devout man" (see 2:5) who "feared God" (see 2:43); Luke has already highlighted the piety of Gentiles who are attracted to Jewish religious customs and beliefs (Luke 7:5; Acts 8:27) and who are then included within the company of Jesus' followers (Luke 7:9; Acts 8:38). The historical existence of God fearers is verifiable through clear references in inscriptions and Josephus (*J.W.* 2 §§461-63; *Ant.* 14 §110; *Ag. Ap.* 2 §282; see Hemer 1989: 444-47; Levinskaya 1996: 51-126). For Luke, their narrative importance is undeniably strategic (Esler 1987: 36-45). Cornelius does "many charitable acts," as did the disciple Tabitha (9:36; on almsgiving see 3:2-3), and "prays to God constantly," an activity typical of the messianic community (1:14; 2:42; 6:6; 7:59; 9:11, 40; 10:9; 12:5; 13:3; 14:23; 20:26; 21:5). Cornelius sees a vision of an angel of God, another phenomenon experienced by community members (see 5:19). The angel gives Cornelius a command to send to Joppa for Peter (10:3-6), in the same way that the angel commanded the apostles to go to the temple (5:20) and the Lord in a vision commanded Ananias to go to "Straight Street" to find Saul (9:11). The validity of Cornelius's piety is strengthened both by the angel's confirmation of the effectiveness of his prayers and charity (10:4) and the fact that his commands are carried out by a devout soldier (v. 7). This devotion insures that what Cornelius orders to be done is consistent with the divine will.

The vision and command to Cornelius are swiftly complemented by a report of what occurs for **Peter in Joppa (10:9-16)**. While he prepares to pray (v. 9), Peter sees a heavenly vision (vv. 10-12) and hears a voice (v. 13). The divine origin of these phenomena is obvious. Peter's vision comes as the heaven opens (v. 11), a sign that revelation is about to take place (see 7:56). The sheet descends from heaven at the start of the vision (10:11) and is taken back into heaven at its conclusion (v. 16) — the same place into which Jesus was taken up (1:11; 7:55). The voice is thus identified with the divine voice which has addressed Saul (through Jesus, 9:4-6). Peter hears it while in a trance (10:10), a state of receptivity to revelation which is later to be found in Paul (22:17).

While the content of the vision and the ensuing conversation are reported in some detail (10:11b-14), the central meaning of the phenomenon is given in the terse logion, "What God has cleansed, you must not consider common" (v. 15). This moment is a crucial point in the narrative; what appears at first to be a vision with multivalent symbolism is given a specific interpretation as showing the direct leading of God. The importance of this command is indicated by its verbatim repetition at 11:9, as well as its summary, in a varied form, at 10:28.

The language of this command is purity language, and the ideas inherent in it are drawn directly from the Holiness Code in Leviticus 17–26. The importance of being "holy" in this code is affirmed at Lev 19:1-2; 20:26. Those foods considered "unclean" have already been defined in Leviticus 11, and are identified as a sign of holiness at Lev 20:25. Adherence to the rules of holiness brings assurance of God's presence (Lev 26:11-12); disobedience means that God abhors and scatters Israel (Lev 26:30-33). Jewish antipathy toward dining with Gentiles appears to have been widespread, although not universal (Esler 1987: 73-86). The saying of 10:15 thus validates a change in practice by attributing to God the role of altering these divinely given rules. The story signals that a new understanding of holiness has come into play (Neyrey in Neyrey 1991: 271-304, 361-87).

The special strength of the sequence of events in 10:1-16 lies in the report that a Gentile and a Jew each receive direct divine guidance in what will turn out to be crucial matters. This strength is reinforced by the repeated accounts of the complementary visions and commands given to each character. The characteristics of Cornelius (vv. 2-3) are summarized by his messengers: he is righteous, he fears God, and the course of action he took was revealed by "a holy angel" (v. 22). By repeating what was said in the narrative introduction of Cornelius at vv. 2-3, these words strengthen his significance, as does the added supporting claim that these characteristics were testified by "the whole Jewish nation" (yet another Lukan exaggeration). Cornelius's vision (vv. 3-6) is repeated at vv. 30-33; once more his character is emphasized through reference to his prayers (vv. 30, 31) and charitable works (v. 31). Still later this vision will be recounted again (11:13-14). The vision seen by Peter is likewise repeated (11:5-10) with a similar emphasis on the divine authorization of the breaking of the food laws (Squires 1993: 116-20). Elsewhere in Acts, epiphanies serve as the means by which a character is divinely commissioned to a specific task (1:6-10; 5:19-21; 9:1-19; 16:6-10; 23:11; 27:21-26; see Hubbard in Talbert 1978: 187-98).

Peter receives the messengers from Cornelius (10:17-23a), who appear suddenly in the manner of a portent. The words of the Spirit which follow (vv. 19-20) specifically interpret their appearance as divinely authorized: "I have sent them" (v. 20; see 9:17). It is the dramatic divine intervention of the vision (10:11-15) which now leads Peter to open his house to Gentiles (v. 23a) and thence to initiate mission among the Gentiles (vv. 34-48). The breakdown of the distinction between clean and unclean — and thus between Jew and Gentile — has been given full divine warrant. It is now expressed in a most tangible manner, in the table fellowship shared by Jews and Gentile, which is implicit in the brief comment that "Peter invited them in and gave them lodging" (v. 23a). Such table fellowship is the critical factor in the sequence of events reported in Joppa and Caesarea (see 11:3); this theme is significant enough for Luke to include numerous scenes of sharing meals throughout his narrative (Luke 5:29-32; 7:33-34, 36-50; 10:7-8; 11:37-54; 14:1-24; 15:1-2; 19:5-10; 22:14-38; 24:30, 35, 42-43; in Acts, see 2:42). The table fellowship of Peter and Cornelius's messengers serves to legitimate table fellowship in messianic communities such as Luke's own (on table fellowship, see Esler 1987: 93-109).

Peter travels to Cornelius (10:23b-33) and meets Cornelius and "his relatives and close friends" (v. 24). The conversion of this household group, which is narrated in the ensuing narrative (vv. 25-48), continues the pattern of the Lukan Jesus' household mission and establishes a pattern for subsequent household conversions in Philippi (16:11-5, 25-34) and in Corinth (18:1-11) (Matson 1996: 86-134). The moment of encounter between Cornelius and Peter establishes for Cornelius what has always been evident to Luke's readers; Peter is not a figure to be worshiped (10:25) but simply a man (v. 26) who is carrying out his divinely appointed task. For Cornelius, Peter interprets his vision succinctly and directly: "God showed me" (v. 28). Less directly and more expansively, Cornelius interprets his vision for Peter: a man stood before me with "shining clothing" (v. 30, perhaps evoking the angelic messengers at 1:10?). That God has guided both characters is evident, nevertheless, from the closing words of Cornelius: "now, therefore, we are all present before God" (10:33a). That God will continue to be at work in what is narrated is equally clear from the words given to Cornelius when he tells Peter, "we are present . . . to hear all the things commanded to you by the Lord" (10:33b). Subsequently, this speech is described as "the word of God" (11:1) and instruction given by the Spirit (11:12).

Peter's speech in Caesarea (10:34-43) begins, in the characteristic style of previous speeches, by announcing God as its subject (see 2:22; 3:13; 4:24; 5:30; 7:2). As its particular theme, it employs "the impartiality of God" (10:34), a scriptural theme (Deut 10:17; Job 34:19; Wis 6:7; Sir 35:13-15; it can also be found in *Jub.* 5:15-16; *2 Bar.* 13:8-10; *1 Enoch* 63:8, as well as in a number of Pauline letters: Rom 2:11; Gal 2:6; cf. Eph 6:9; Col 3:25). This theme reinforces the message of the vision (10:11-16), which rebutted the levitical holiness motif and validated table fellowship as being consistent with the divine will. Such divine impartiality is evident in that those who fear God and do righteous deeds can be found in every nation (v. 35). Peter's speech is thus targeted precisely to Cornelius and those like him who fear God (vv. 1, 22).

This divine impartiality is especially evident in Jesus, who can be affirmed as Lord of all (10:36). Peter interprets the life of Jesus in a consistently Lukan manner, in terms of the activity of God (vv. 37-43). "God anointed him" (see 4:27) "by the Holy Spirit" (see 4:8) and "by a mighty deed" (see 2:22). "God was with him" is also a phrase used to describe Stephen (7:9), as he "went about doing good and healing." "God raised him" (a phrase found in the earlier speeches at 2:24, 32; 3:15; 4:33; 5:30) and "gave him to be manifest" (NRSV, "allowed him to appear") as a witness to those whom the hand of God had chosen (for God's hand see 2:23; 4:28, 30; 7:25). As before, Peter affirms the apostolic witness (10:39, 41; see 2:32; 3:15; 5:32) and the prophetic witness (10:43; see 2:25-31, 33-35; 3:18, 21-25; 4:25-26); once again Luke has him make the exaggerated claim that "all the prophets testify about him" (10:43; see 3:24). The prophets testify to "the forgiveness of sins," which is essential to the proclamation (2:38; 5:31) and which will carry over into Paul's speeches (13:38). To these elements, familiar from preceding speeches, Luke has Peter add the description of Jesus as "ordained by God" to be the eschatological "judge of the living and the dead" (10:42), a concept which Paul will later express (17:31; cf. 24:15). The speech thus comprises a consistent exposition of God's activities in Jesus, extensively in the past as well as (briefly) in the future.

The response to this speech is both unequivocal and

not unfamiliar when **the Spirit falls on the Gentiles (10:44-48).** At the beginning the Spirit had instructed Peter to accompany the messengers from Cornelius (vv. 19-20) and initiate contact with this household of Gentiles in Caesarea; at the conclusion of the speech to this group "the Holy Spirit fell upon all who heard the word" (v. 44). The Spirit has twice filled the messianic community gathered in the Jewish capital, Jerusalem (at Pentecost, 2:1-4, and subsequently, 4:31). When the Spirit is poured out on the Gentiles (10:45) in this Gentile capital, it is already known that this is an act of God (2:17).

In both previous cases, God had acted through the Spirit in relation to Jews. That this current outpouring of the Spirit, outside of Judea, among Gentiles, is still an act of God is emphasized by a series of narrative comments. The Jewish believers present express surprise at "the gift of the Holy Spirit" (10:45), but the reader already knows that such a gift is from God (2:38; 8:18). They hear the Gentiles "speaking in tongues" (10:46), a phenomenon already experienced as a divine event in Jerusalem (2:11). Peter draws this connection when he interprets the event: they "received the Spirit as we also [did]" (10:47; see 2:38). Peter and his fellow Jews thus "exulted God" (10:47; see 5:13). Baptism ensues (10:48; see 2:38). The deepest significance of this moment for Luke is identified as being that "the gift of the Holy Spirit had been poured out even on the Gentiles" (10:45). That God has acted even on the Gentiles signals that the "turn" which has been anticipated since 8:4 has come about in a fulsome way. This interpretive perspective on the events in Caesarea draws them into close relationship with the interpretation of Jesus which Peter has given (here and before). The impartial God who has acted through Jesus (10:34-43) is the God who declares all things clean (v. 15), who shows this to Peter (v. 28), who gifts Gentiles by pouring out the Spirit (v. 45), and who is exulted by the people (v. 46). It is language about God which interprets the significance of the narrative at each key moment.

The consequence of this dramatic event is noted briefly: "they invited him to remain for some days" (10:48b). Table fellowship with Gentiles and the breach of the food rules were considered to be the inevitable results of God's actions (Matson 1996: 110-17).

The narrative returns once more to Jerusalem for what can rightly be called **the first Jerusalem council (11:1-18).** The council is necessary because of doubts raised in Jerusalem about Peter's activities in Caesarea — specifically, that "the Gentiles received the word of God" (v. 1). During this council, an accusation against Peter is raised from within the assembly for the first time. In reply, **Peter's speech in Jerusalem (vv. 4-17)** has the nature of an apology, although Luke refrains from employing the technical term until the Hellenistic settings in which Paul makes his defense speeches. Peter speaks in response to criticism concerning his breach of the food rules (v. 2). The criticism comes from those of the circumcision (v. 2); the use of the same phrase by Paul at Gal 2:9 suggests that James is behind the criticism. Such criticism requires an explanation "in order" (11:4; NRSV, "step by step"), in line with the overall Lukan program (Luke 1:3).

Accordingly, Luke has Peter explain events in order by turning first of all to the vision he saw in Joppa and recounting it almost verbatim (11:5-10; cf. 10:9-16). This repeated account retains the essential elements. The detailed description of the vision of the animals, reptiles, and birds is repeated (11:5-6 par. 10:11-12); a reference to "beasts of prey" is added at 11:6. The command to "kill and eat" (v. 7) parallels 10:13. Peter's objection on the basis of the food laws (11:8 par. 10:14) is modified so as to emphasize the food law requirements, placing them first in his response. The insistence that he must accept "what God has cleansed" (11:9 par. 10:15) and the note that this happened three times before being "drawn up again into heaven" (11:10 par. 10:16) are then repeated exactly. This full repetition but slightly changed order highlights Peter's vision as the primary one; by contrast, he truncates his reports of the visit of Cornelius's messengers (11:11-12; cf. 10:17-29) and the vision to Cornelius (11:13; cf. 10:1-8), as well as his own speech in Caesarea (11:14; cf. 10:34-43) and the subsequent giving of the Holy Spirit (11:15; cf. 10:44-48).

Yet Peter's speech is not simply an epitomized summary, for it offers an interpretation of these events which stresses that they took place under divine initiative. In reporting the arrival of messengers from Cornelius (11:11-12), Peter notes simply that "the Spirit said to me to go with them without criticism" (v. 12; cf. 10:19-20). His omission of many details (character traits, travel details, conversation, and personnel; even, surprisingly, the name of Cornelius) places the focus on the role of the Spirit. Cornelius remains anonymous when Peter reports the vision he saw in similar fashion, with a stark summary of what the angel had told him (11:13). The substance of Peter's speech in Caesarea is summarized as "words by which you and your household will be saved" (v. 14); the emphasis here is not on the content of the speech but on the fact that Peter was given these words to speak by the angel.

Peter's version of the outpouring of the Holy Spirit is short on factual reporting, as it were; he simply states that the Spirit fell on them (11:15). His report abounds in interpretation of the significance of the event, however. The earlier narrative of this event has already noted that the Spirit was given as a gift (10:45); Peter now reinforces the divine source of this gift as that which God gave them (11:17; see 10:45). This gift fulfills the prophetic word of Jesus, that "John baptized with water, but you will be baptized with the Holy Spirit" (11:16, quoting 1:5; cf. the similar, but longer, saying of John at Luke 3:16). Twice Peter parallels this act of the Spirit on "them" (Gentiles) with the events that happened to "us" (Jews) at Pentecost, when he notes that the Spirit "fell on them just as on us at the beginning" (11:15) and when he states that "God gave them the same gift that he gave us who believe" (v. 17). The motif of necessity concludes Peter's speech, with the rhetorical question, "Who was I that I could hinder God?" (v. 17). Such a question is a reminder of Peter's unquestioning and faithful attitude expressed at 4:19-20 and 5:29.

Peter thus validates the events in Caesarea through use of language about God. The "turn to the Gentiles" is authorized by God working through an angel and the Holy Spirit, as well as by the inexorability of Peter's response to God. This understanding (which is entirely Lukan) is further reinforced by the **concluding summary (11:18)** which follows, in which language about God defines the significance of what has taken place. Peter's audience have moved from criticism (v. 2) to silence before they now "glorify God" (v. 18), a believing response seen already in Jerusalem (4:21). Glorifying God will recur later in Antioch (13:48) and Jerusalem (21:20); it has appeared often in Luke's Gospel, as a response to Jesus (Luke 2:20; 4:15; 5:25-26; 7:16; 13:13; 17:15; 18:43; 23:47). The words of the audience concisely express Luke's understanding of the occasion: "Surely God gave repentance to life even to the Gentiles" (11:18). God's prominent role, as the one who sent the angel, gave the gift of the Spirit, and enabled the Gentiles to repent, validates what has taken place. An inclusive community has been established; this will provide a key model for preaching in the Dispersion.

"Christians" in Antioch and the Community in Jerusalem (11:19–12:25)

The fourth step toward the Gentiles (11:19–12:25) is set in Antioch and Jerusalem, thereby straddling both Gentile and Jewish arenas. It functions as a conclusion to this section of the narrative. Luke begins with yet another **summary description (11:19-21)** in which he refers back to "those who were scattered by the troubles which took place with Stephen" (v. 19; cf. 8:1). These scattered ones provide the basis for beginning the "turn to the Gentiles" from 8:4 onward. Some of these now come to Antioch in Syria, "speaking the word" (11:19; see 2:41; 6:2, 4; for "the word of God," see 4:31; 6:7). Although the message is being taken into Gentile territory, and although both Saul and Peter have been prepared to engage in preaching to Gentiles, these preachers continue the established pattern of "speaking to nobody except to Jews" (11:19). However, "some men from among them" begin "preaching to the Hellenists" (v. 20), insuring that the community in Antioch is inclusive from the very start. This community continues to be marked by characteristics of the Jerusalem community: "the hand of the Lord was with them" (v. 21; see 4:28, 30), people "turned to the Lord" (11:21; see 3:19, 26), and those who believed were "a great number" (11:21; see 6:7). What emerges in Antioch is thus presented by Luke as patterned on the Jerusalem model.

This link between **the community in Antioch (11:22-30)** and the Jerusalem community is consolidated through the sending of an emissary from "the assembly which is in Jerusalem" (v. 22) — a procedure which has already taken place in Samaria (8:14-17). The emissary, Barnabas, is "a good man"; the same word has described Joseph of Arimathea at Luke 23:50. Barnabas exhibits characteristic traits of leadership: he is "full of the Holy Spirit" (11:24; see 4:8 on Peter) and "of faith" (11:24; see 6:5 on Stephen). That Barnabas is "filled with the Spirit" has already been inferred in his juxtaposition with Ananias and Sapphira, who each oppose the Spirit (5:3, 9). He sees that "the grace of God" is evident in Antioch (11:23), as it was in Jerusalem (2:47; 4:33; 6:8), so he responds with joy, as seen in Samaria (8:8; cf. 2:46 in Jerusalem), and exhorts them all, as did Peter in Jerusalem (2:40; see also 9:31).

Barnabas has missionary success in Antioch, a city which is to become crucial in sponsoring the Gentile mission (13:1-3). This success is authorized by explicit language about God, in the narrative comment that "a large crowd was added by the Lord" (11:24, rendering the dative case as an expression of agency, as also in 5:14). Barnabas seeks out Saul from Tarsus to help with teaching the large crowd for a whole year (11:25-26). This community of disciples in Antioch is then described as an "assembly," indicating the established nature of the community (v. 26; see 9:31), and its members are described by the significant new term "Christians," or "messianists" (11:26), a term indicating a particularly Roman perception of this originally Jewish community. ("Christ" is the Greek equivalent to the Hebrew term for Messiah. The ending *-ianos* is found appended to a number of Latin names, indicating "the followers of" the person named; see "the Herodians" at Mark 3:6; 12:13.)

A further emissary now arrives from Jerusalem, a prophet named Agabus (11:27-28). Just as the Holy Spirit has already guided Barnabas and Saul as they teach in Antioch, now Agabus "predicted by the Spirit" that there would be a worldwide famine (v. 28). The comment about its fulfillment under Claudius validates Agabus as a true prophet; Josephus describes a famine in Judea in AD 46-47 (*Ant.* 20 §§51-53). The universal scope of this famine may be prophetic hyperbole (Winter in Gill and Gempf 1994: 59-69), or yet another Lukan exaggeration (cf. 3:18; 9:42). More importantly for Luke, he links this prediction with the instigation of the collection by Barnabas and Saul (11:29-30) — an enterprise which attempted to unite Jewish and Gentile churches in a common bond. Luke points to the divine initiative for this aspect of the work of Barnabas and Saul since it arises out of the Spirit-inspired prophecy of Agabus. Paul dwells on the collection in a number of his letters (Rom 15:25-29, 31; 1 Cor 16:1-4; 2 Cor 8:1-7; 9:1-5; Gal 2:10), although these refer to a visit to Jerusalem some years later than the present visit (see 20:2-3).

By following Barnabas and Saul to Judea, Luke returns to **the community in Jerusalem (12:1-19)**. The persecution of 8:1 (which appeared to be in a lull at 9:31) returns with the actions of the king. Herod Agrippa was the brother of Herodias (see Mark 6:17) and the grandson of Herod the Great (see Matt 2:1-12). When King Herod lays hands on "some who were from the assembly" (12:1), he repeats the actions of the Jewish authorities (4:3; 5:18). Yet they are intensified because he intends to cause evil (12:1), replicating the Egyptian oppression of the Israelites (7:6, 19). A second martyr, James, is noted without any elaboration (12:2); this is the only reference to this member of "the twelve" since 1:13. Once more Peter finds himself under threat from the authorities (12:3). He is arrested and placed in prison during the Passover (v. 4), evoking the paschal trials and death of Jesus (Luke 22:1, 7, 13, 15). During this intensification of the conflict, however, the assembly engages in its typical activity of prayer to God (12:5, 12; see 2:42).

At this point, during the night an angel appears to Peter, accompanied by a light (12:6-7a). A detailed (and at times comical) narrative recounts how the angel carefully guides Peter in escaping from prison (vv. 7b-11) and returning to the assembly (vv. 12-17). Although Peter initially believes that he is simply seeing a vision (v. 9), with the help of a clear portent — the city gate opens of its own accord! (v. 10) — he comes to believe that "the Lord sent his angel" (v. 11). Peter is thus rescued from the hands of Herod (v. 11; cf. v. 1). Once more, language about God interprets the narrative. Peter's departure is deliberately vague ("to another place," v. 7); Luke is preparing the way for the emergence of James as the leader of the Jerusalem community (Bauckham in Bauckham 1995: 431-41).

Subsequently, Herod is revealed as an enemy of God when an angel of the Lord strikes him down because of his antagonism toward God. When Herod "did not give the glory to God" (12:23), he failed to recognize the true nature of God (7:2, 55) and acted directly opposite to those who knew how God worked (see 11:18). This death is a reminder of the way in which God's sovereignty can be at work in punishment — as seen in the earlier fate of Ananias and Sapphira — as well as through guidance and empowering. Such angelic intervention has already been significant in the narrative (see 5:19). At three of the four steps in this section, God's guidance is evident through the intervention of angelic figures: to Philip (8:26); to Cornelius (10:3, 22, 30; 11:13); and to Peter (12:7) and Herod (12:23).

The death of Herod takes place after an audience with people from the the Phoenician towns Tyre and Sidon (12:20-23). Being eaten by worms (12:23) is a typical element in the death accounts of evil leaders in Hellenistic literature (see 2 Macc 9:9), although many more such gruesome elements are usually narrated. A much more elaborate account of his death is given by Josephus (*Ant.* 19 §§343-46). The crowd's acclamation of Herod as "a god, and not a mortal" (12:22) is immediately undercut by his death by means of an "angel of the Lord" (v. 23). For Luke, the death of Herod serves as another act of God in Gentile territory, asserting the sovereignty of God over both Jews and Gentiles.

A **concluding summary description (12:24-25)** follows in which Luke notes that "the word of God increased and multiplied" (v. 24), a generalized statement evoking the formula applied to the Jerusalem community at 6:7. Barnabas and Saul then return to Jerusalem (12:25), having "completed the service" allocated to them at 11:29. After establishing the validity of the "turn to the Gentiles" and reporting on the establishment of inclusive communities of Jews and Gentiles, Luke brings the narrative back to its central point, Jerusalem.

Section Three: Inclusive Messianic Communities (13:1–21:16)

In the third section of Acts, the narrative tells of how Paul and various co-workers established messianic communities in towns throughout Asia Minor and around the Aegean Sea. These communities contain many elements of the pattern of community life which has become evident in the first two sections of Acts. In particular, this section consolidates the inclusive character of the community, for each newly established assembly comprises Gentiles as well as Jews. In this way the section particularly builds on what has been established in the previous section.

The previous sections have reported the activity of a number of leaders: Peter, John, and Stephen in Jerusalem and Philip, Saul, Peter, Cornelius, and Barnabas in the preparation for the "turn to the Gentiles." In this section, however, the focus remains persistently on the activity of Saul. In the first missionary incident in this section, Saul is renamed Paul, the name which he keeps from this point onward. He figures in every pericope in this section, and indeed until the end of Acts. Nevertheless, Paul carries out his activities in association with a number of co-workers, most notably Barnabas (13:1–15:40), and Silas and Timothy (15:40–17:15), with additional references to Apollos (18:24–19:1), Agabus (21:10-14), and others.

The geographical arrangement of this section continues the spiral structuring of Section Two. The overall movement is based around Syrian Antioch, which has become the base for Barnabas and Paul.

- Barnabas and Paul are sent from Antioch to travel through Asia Minor (13:1–14:28). There are four "scenes" on this journey, with most attention being given to their time in Pisidian Antioch (13:14-52). In each place their message is given to Jews and Gentiles, thus insuring that the communities which are established are truly inclusive, before they return to Syrian Antioch (14:26-28).
- Paul and Barnabas then attend the second Jerusalem council (15:1-35). The decision of this council reasserts the validity of such inclusive communities and promulgates this decision more widely. Once again they return to Antioch (v. 30).
- Paul and his co-workers then visit believers in a number of locations while en route to Miletus (20:1-16), where Paul bids farewell to the Ephesian elders (vv. 16-38), and then proceeds to Caesarea (21:1-14), before returning to Jerusalem (vv. 15-16).

Although the section begins with Antioch at the center, the focus shifts back to Jerusalem for the council in ch. 15, and toward the end of the section, where the need to return to Jerusalem is extensively debated (21:1-14). However, in the middle of the extended scene in Ephesus there is already an indication that Paul must eventually travel on to Rome (19:21). This section as a whole, then, provides a bridge between Jerusalem, which has been the location for Section One (1:1–8:3) and the grounding for Section Two (8:4–12:25), and Rome, which is the inexorable destination in view throughout Section Four (21:17–28:31).

As in the previous two sections, the events narrated are interpreted by means of language about God. The activities of Paul and his co-workers are described as "what God did" (14:27; 15:4; cf. 21:19). The section as a whole is framed by the work of the Holy Spirit (13:1-3; 21:10-12). A crucial alteration of direction takes place under divine guidance (16:6-10), and the miracles which occur in this section are understood to be performed by divine action (15:12). The section ends with a direct affirmation that the divine will is at work in events still to come (21:14). These clear statements interpret the establishment of inclusive communities as being the outworking of the divine plan and provide a model for the faith communities of Luke's time.

Antioch and Asia Minor (13:1–14:28)

Barnabas and Saul begin their activities in **Antioch (13:1-3)**, after their visit to Jerusalem (11:29-30). They are described, with others, in terms typical of community leaders, as "prophets and teachers" (13:2). Their prophetic status has already been established through earlier descriptions of each as "filled with the Spirit" (Saul, 9:17; Barnabas, 11:24), while their roles as teachers has already been demonstrated in Antioch (11:26). In this context the Holy Spirit instructs the assembly to set them apart (13:2), an instruction which evokes the commissioning of Jesus, for Jesus also begins his activities under a charge from the Spirit (Luke 4:18). What follows is thus a report of activities which Barnabas and Saul undertook under explicit divine guidance.

The actions of the Antioch assembly provide a clear signal that a new phase is underway (Squires 1998: 609-11). The assembly commissions Barnabas and Saul through actions already identified with the setting apart of individuals for a specific task (13:3). In a context of fasting, they pray, as did the Jerusalem community (see 2:42); and they lay hands on them, as was done to the seven (6:6). The latter action is associated with the Holy Spirit, not only here but in Samaria (8:17), Damascus (9:17), and Ephesus (19:6). The same collection of three actions is noted toward the end of their journey, when Luke notes that Barnabas and Paul appoint elders in each assembly by "laying on hands . . . and praying, with fasting" (14:23). The reversed order creates a chiasm which functions as an *inclusio* for this journey, indicating that the means by which Barnabas and Paul were appointed were used by them and repeated in each place. Those whom they appoint as elders are appointed in accord with the divine will, as they themselves had been divinely appointed.

That Barnabas and Saul begin their journey with a clear divine sanction is reinforced by the note that they were "sent out by the Holy Spirit" (13:4). Throughout this section, they continue the stereotypical pattern already seen in Damascus (9:20), when they preach "the word of God" in the synagogues of the Jews in Salamis (13:5). This pattern can be seen subsequently in Paul's activities in Antioch (13:14), Iconium (14:1), Thessalonica (17:1), Berea (17:10), Athens (17:17), Corinth (18:4), and Ephesus (18:19, 19:8), and in Apollos's activities in Ephesus (18:26).

This **journey (13:4–14:26)** takes them to numerous towns, but Luke singles out just four "scenes" for detailed reporting. The first main scene of their journey is in **Salamis (13:4-12)**, a port town on the east of the island of Cyprus. What takes place here will strongly confirm that Barnabas and Saul enjoy God's sanction. The two visitors are thrust into a polemical situation similar to those experienced in Jerusalem (4:1-3; 5:17-18; 6:9-15; 8:1b-3; 9:1-2, 29; 12:1-5) and Damascus (9:23-24). In this scene, they encounter two very different individuals. One, the proconsul Sergius Paulus, wishes to "hear the word of God" (13:7); the other, the magician Elymas, is a false prophet (13:6) who opposes them, attempts to turn Sergius Paulus away from faith (13:8), and persists in "making crooked the straight paths of the Lord" (13:10; cf. Isa 59:8). The incident presents most sharply "a pattern of conflict betweeen good and evil, between the purposes of God and the purposes of Satan" (Garrett 1989: 79-87). From this point in the narrative, Saul is identified by his Roman name of Paul. Luke reiterates that he is "filled with the Holy Spirit" (13:9; cf. 9:17), in contrast to Elymas, who is "filled with all deceit and all wickedness" as the "enemy of all righteousness" (13:10). Paul becomes an agent of divine retribution; his words to Elymas evoke the strident judgment of Peter over Ananias and Sapphira (13:10; cf. 5:4, 9). The punishment which falls on Elymas is not, however, as drastic as in their case. Instead, it reverses the Damascus experience of Paul himself, when he regained his sight after Ananias laid hands on him (9:17-18). Similar interpretations of this portent are provided both by Paul and by Sergius Paulus. Paul declares that Elymas is made blind through the direct intervention of "the hand of God" (13:11; see also 6:6). Sergius Paulus then acknowledges that the deity is at work, for he believed (13:12; cf. 4:4; 8:12, 13; 9:42; 11:17, 21) and "was astonished at the teaching of the Lord" (13:12).

This first scene thus patterns the divided response which Paul and his co-workers often encounter (Jervell 1972: 44-49). This pattern, already seen in Damascus (9:21), will recur in Antioch (13:43-50), Iconium (14:1-4), Lystra (14:19), Thessalonica (17:4-5), Berea (17:11-14), Athens (17:32-34), Corinth (18:5-8), Ephesus (18:19-21, 19:23-40), and finally Rome (28:23-24). Such a divided response provides strong validation for the experience of the members of messianist assemblies throughout the first century (including Luke's own community). The narrative models the understanding that, although God is at work in the deeds and words of Paul and his co-workers, not all human beings respond with faith. The mixed responses, often from Jews but also occasionally from Gentiles, indicate that the plan of God is not an irresistible force which compels belief. On the contrary, God's work invites (and perhaps urges) a response of faith (Squires 1993: 177-85). It is from those who respond positively (both Jews and Gentiles) that the new communities are formed (Jervell 1996: 34-43).

After the first scene in Salamis, we learn that Barnabas and Paul were traveling in a larger group ("those around Paul," 13:13). That Paul was usually accompanied in his activities by a number of people is evident from the later reference to "many others" (15:35), the naming of specific companions (18:5; 19:22, 29; 20:4), and the use of the first person plural (16:10-17; 20:5-15; 21:7-18; 27:1–28:16). A reminder of the continuing link with Jerusalem is given with the aside that "John returned to Jerusalem" (13:13). The group move inland through Pamphilia to Pisidian Antioch, where they enter the synagogue (v. 14) and listen to the scripture readings (v. 15).

This second scene, in **Pisidian Antioch (13:14-52)**, is dominated by the report of **Paul's first speech (vv. 16-41)**, which has programmatic significance akin to Peter's Pentecost speech (2:14-41) and Jesus' own synagogue speech (Luke 4:16-30). This speech is given in answer to a request for "a word of exhortation" (13:15); indeed, Peter's final words in his Pentecost speech have already been identified as exhorting his listeners (2:40). Although exhortation was a quality for which Barnabas was known (5:36; 11:23), here it is Paul who speaks in this manner. The speech thus models the substance of such exhortation as it is subsequently given (without any details being reported) in Syrian Antioch (14:22), Philippi (16:40), Ephesus (20:1), and Macedonia (20:2). It also equates the speech with the delivery of the apostolic decree in Antioch (15:32). In the body of the speech, Paul describes what he is doing as "proclaiming the good news" (13:32), a description which will subsequently apply to his speaking in various places on this journey (14:7, 15, 21) as well as later (17:18).

The style of the speech is familiar in that language about God shapes the whole of the speech. Paul addresses "Israelites and those who fear God" (13:16), the kind of audience which Peter addressed in Caesarea (10:35; see 2:43) and in Jerusalem (2:5, taking "devout" as equivalent to "fearing God"). The subject of the speech, typically, is God, and the description of God as "the God of this people Israel" (13:17) is shaped with the immediate content in mind, as is usual. Similarly contextualized introductions have been found in earlier speeches: "God says" (2:17, when Peter quotes from Scripture) and "God made him" (2:22, when introducing Jesus); "the God of Abraham and the God of Isaac and the God of Jacob, the God of our ancestors" (3:13, Peter to the people in Jerusalem); "Sovereign, you who made the heaven and the earth and the sea and all things which are in them" (4:24, when God's mighty acts will become tangible amid the community); "the God of our fathers" (5:29, Peter to the Sanhedrin); "the God of glory" (7:2, Stephen, in a speech recounting epiphanies at 7:2, 26, 30 — but not in relation to the temple, 7:47-53; and note that this speech leads to another epiphany at 7:55); and "God is without partiality" (10:34, Peter, when this impartiality becomes manifest among the Gentiles).

The first part of the speech (13:17-22) recounts the history of Israel from the exodus to David. Paul's review of Israel's history drastically condenses that already given by Stephen (7:1-46). The story of Abraham (7:2-8) is summarized in one concise phrase (13:17a), and the story of Joseph (7:9-16) in the following clause (13:17b). Similar abbreviated references are made to the exodus (13:17; cf. 7:17-36), the wilderness years (13:18; cf. 7:36-44), and the conquest of the land (13:19; cf. 7:45). Paul adds references to the judges, Samuel, and Saul (13:20-21) before moving to the time of David (13:22; cf. 7:46).

The positive evaluation of Israel's history, evident in most of Stephen's speech (7:1-38), is also found in this speech. Paul describes Israel's history in characteristically Lukan fashion, as the outworking of divine activity: God "chose our ancestors" (13:17), "exalted the people" (v. 17), "led them out" from Egypt (v. 17), "fed them" in the wilderness (v. 18), "gave them an inheritance" in Canaan (v. 19), "gave judges" (v. 20) and then "a king, Saul" (v. 21), and finally "raised up David as king for them" (v. 22). This string of divine actions culminates in David, of whom God testifies, "he will do everything of my will" (v. 22); this statement is similar to that of Stephen, "he found favor with God" (7:46).

Rather than continuing on to the building of the temple, as Stephen had done (7:47), Paul jumps from David to one "of this man's posterity" (13:23), namely, Jesus, introduced as the Savior given to Israel by God (on Savior, see 7:25). For the first time, Luke reports Paul's understanding of Jesus in detail. Not surprisingly, it is consistent with the understanding already set forth in Peter's speeches. Paul readdresses his audience as "sons of the race of Abraham and those among you who fear God" (13:26; cf. v. 16), preparing for the immediate claim that Jesus is the fulfillment of Scripture (vv. 27-29; see 8:32). Such fulfillment is "the word of this salvation" which was "sent to you" (13:26), that is, sent by God (10:34-36). Language about God thus shapes the presentation of Jesus in this speech.

Accordingly, Jesus is described as the one whom God raised (13:30; see 2:24, 32; 3:15; 5:30; 10:40), who appeared to those with him (13:31). This can be validated by apostolic testimony (13:32; see 2:32; 3:15; 5:32; 10:39, 41) as well as prophetic witness (13:33-37). This prophetic testimony is expounded by Paul in detail, just as Peter did on the day of Pentecost (2:25-31, 33-35) and subsequently (3:18, 24; see also 10:43). Fulfillment of Scripture will continue to be a central feature of Paul's preaching in this section (13:40-41; 17:2, 11) and when he is a prisoner (24:14; 26:22-23; 28:23, 25-27). It serves to demonstrate the antiquity of the claims which Paul makes in a cultural context where antiquity is highly regarded (Plato *Timaeus* 21E-23C; Josephus *Ag. Ap.* 2 §§151-54). Here in Antioch, Paul states that Jesus is the one through whom God fulfilled "the promise to the ancestors" (13:32) when he "raised him from the dead" (13:33) in fulfillment of Ps 2:7, Isa 55:3, and Ps 16:10 (already cited by Peter at 2:27, 31). That this testimony can be trusted is assured by the reference to David as "serving the plan of God" (13:36). Paul's description of Jesus is thus consistent with that given by Peter; it is the thoroughly Lukan claim that God was at work through Jesus. The particular contribution of this speech is to demonstrate that the resurrection of Jesus culminates God's saving acts (vv. 32-33), fulfills God's promise (vv. 23, 32-33), and provides the basis for forgiveness of sins (vv. 38-39) (Hansen in Marshall and Peterson 1998: 300-307).

The climactic declaration of the speech, that "forgiveness of sins has been proclaimed" (13:38), is Lukan language, for the offer of forgiveness characterizes the Lukan Jesus (Luke 1:77; 4:18; 5:20-24; 7:47-50; 11:4; 17:3-4; 23:34) and is integral to the preaching task given to the followers of Jesus (Luke 24:47; and see Peter's speeches at 2:38; 3:19; 5:31; 10:43). The only occurrence of "forgiveness" in Pauline letters is in the deutero-Paulines (Eph 1:7; Col 1:14). Luke has Paul claim that everything which the prophetic word could not justify has now been justified (13:38-39); the NRSV avoids the language of justification *(dikaioō, dikaiosynē)* by using the translation "frees from." This is one of just four occasions in Acts when Paul uses the language of justification (see 13:10; 17:31; 24:25) — a striking difference from Paul's own writings, given the significance of this idea in two of his letters (Rom 1:17; 3:21-31; 4:2-6, 9, 11, 13, 22, 25; 5:1, 9, 15-21; 6:7, 16-20; 8:10, 30, 33; 9:30–10:10; 14:17; Gal 2:15-21; 3:6-14, 23-26; 5:2-6) and its occurrence in others (1 Cor 1:30; 4:4; 6:11; 2 Cor 3:9; 5:21; 11:15; Phil 1:11; 3:6, 9). To conclude this speech, Paul utters a warning lest the prophetic word concerning unbelief (Hab 1:5) might come to fruition (13:40-41). This is one prophecy which Luke does not wish to see fulfilled!

The **response to Paul's speech (13:42-52),** like the speech itself, is programmatic in that it depicts the typical way in which people responded to Paul's speeches. Initially this response is positive (vv. 42-43), for many of the Jews and devout proselytes are attracted by the message, as occurs subsequently in many towns (God-fearers respond positively at 13:50; 16:14; 17:4, 17; 18:7; other positive responses take place at 14:1; 17:11-12; 17:32b-34; 18:19-21; 28:23-24a). Luke comments on this positive response with typical language about God, when he notes that Paul and Barnabas "persuaded them to continue in the grace of God" (13:43; see 2:47).

However, the response of some in Antioch soon fulfills the prophetic warning (13:40-41) when it turns negative on the following sabbath (vv. 44-52), even though the expectation of some is that Paul and Barnabas will speak "the word of God" (v. 44). The crowd which gathers is large — "almost the whole city" (v. 44) — but Luke does tend to exaggerate (see 3:24; 9:35). The situation which emerges is rendered as a typical scene, representative of the encounters which Paul experiences throughout this section, as well as in Rome. A familiar antagonistic situation is created by Jews who were "filled with jealousy" (13:45), just as the priestly group in Jerusalem had been (see 5:17) and the Jews in Thessalonica would later be (17:5). The Antiochene Jews contradict Paul and Barnabas (13:45), as the Jews in Rome would later do to Paul (28:19, 22), exhibiting an attitude which fulfills the earlier prophecy of Simeon that Jesus would become "as a sign to be contradicted" (Luke 2:34).

Paul and Barnabas respond by "speaking frankly" (13:46), a mode of speech both familiar from the Jerusalem section (2:29; 4:13, 29, 31) and characteristic of Paul's subsequent speeches (14:3; 19:8; 28:31). Such frankness of speech justifies their description of what they speak as "the word of God" (13:46; see 4:31), which has already been identified as the apostolic task (6:2, 4). Their claim that it was necessary to speak first to Jews interprets the typical pattern of going first to the synagogue (see 13:5) as not simply a pragmatic decision, nor as an accident of chance, but as an integral part of the divine necessity which drives their activities. The fact that their Jewish audiences reject their message then instigates their decision to turn to the Gentiles (v. 46), a turn which will itself mark subsequent episodes in Corinth (18:6), Ephesus (19:9), and Rome (28:28).

This "turn to the Gentiles" is not to be understood as a falling away from the divine plan, however, for it is immediately justified as obedience to "what the Lord commanded" (13:47) through the quotation of Isa 49:6. This quotation contains two familiar affirmations. The first affirmation, that those whom God commanded are "set to be a light to the Gentiles," has already been articulated by Simeon at Luke 2:32. The second affirmation, that those commanded by God will be "a means of salvation unto the end of the earth," has been incorporated into Jesus' parting commission to be "witnesses . . . unto the end of the earth" (1:8). In neither case is it envisaged that activity among Gentiles would takes the place of activity among Jews. In Simeon's oracle, the "light to the Gentiles" coexists (in Hebraic parallelism) with "glory to my people Israel" (Luke 2:32); in Jesus' commission, being "witnesses until the end of the earth" takes place as an extension of (and not as a replacement of) being "witnesses in Jerusalem and all Judea and Samaria" (1:8). The turn to the Gentiles does not therefore supplant the witness to Jews, but supplements and broadens it (Green in Marshall and Peterson 1998: 83-106).

In addition to this, the notion of "turning to the Gentiles" has been extensively and thoroughly prepared for in Section Two (8:4–12:25). In no instance in this section does the "turn to the Gentiles" mean a letting go of the work among the Jews. In fact, as he prepares for the "turn to the Gentiles" in Section Two of his narrative, Luke is concerned to insure that the links with Jerusalem are maintained and strengthened (8:14, 25; 9:26; 11:2-18, 22, 27, 29-30; 12:1-19, 25). Turning to the Gentiles does not mean creating communities of Gentiles which replace the Jewish messianic communities; rather, it means including Gentiles within such Jewish communities, which thus become broader, inclusive kinds of communities.

So it is that the quoting of Scripture in order to justify an action (13:46-47) — itself a familiar element in Luke's narrative — functions both to validate the immediate action and to model the pattern for subsequent events. From this highly stylized account of the response in Pisidian Antioch, we can reasonably expect the same pattern to be replicated in subsequent chapters. This indeed takes place, as Paul and his companions go to the synagogue, proclaim the message, evoke a believing response, encounter opposition, and so declare that turning to the Gentiles is necessary and in accord with the divine will, without ever articulating any sense of universal abandonment of the Jews.

The immediate response of the Gentiles is, quite naturally, to adopt the typical stance of believers: they "rejoice" (13:48; see 13:52; 15:3; and 5:41) and they "glorified the word of the Lord" (13:48; see 11:18). That "they believe" is part of the predetermined plan of God, for those who believe have been "appointed to eternal life" (13:48; see 2:44). Thus "the word of the Lord" which spreads in the surrounding areas (13:49) is the message of the incorporation of Gentiles into the assemblies, as has already been celebrated by Jewish members of the assemblies in Caesarea (10:45) and Jerusalem (11:18).

The response of certain Jewish people in Antioch, however, is dramatically different (13:50). They institute a "persecution," a phenomenon already familiar to assembly members in Jerusalem (8:1), and "drive out" Barnabas and Paul, an action which will recur in Iconium (14:2). The pair "shake the dust from their feet" (13:51), an action similar to that which Paul performs in Corinth (18:6). This action replicates that commanded of the twelve by Jesus, where shaking dust from their feet functions as a testimony against those houses which do not receive them (Luke 9:5). Dust is used in curses signaling divine punishment in a number of scriptural incidents (Gen 3:14; Exod 9:8-10; Num 5:11-31; Deut 9:21; 28:24; 2 Sam 22:43; 2 Kgs 53:7; 2 Chr 34:4; Ps 78:27; Isa 25:12; 26:5). Shimei casts dust into the air to curse David (2 Sam 16:13). However, other actions related to dust can symbolize repentance. Joshua repents of the sin of Achan by tearing his clothes and placing dust on his head (Josh 7:6); other scriptural characters do likewise (Job 2:12; Lam 2:10; Ezek 27:29-31; 1 Macc 11:71; 2 Macc 10:25; 14:15; 3 Macc 1:18). Here in Antioch, the action of shaking off the dust may well have the function of warning recalcitrants. It does not indicate a full-scale repudiation of all Jews, but a moving on to the next town, as is evident in the fact that Paul and Barnabas leave Antioch, travel to Iconium, and immediately enter its synagogue (14:1).

The scene in Antioch ends with a note (13:52) that the disciples there enjoy the characteristic qualities of being filled with joy (5:41; 8:8; 11:23) and the Holy Spirit (see 4:8), even in the midst of such opposition.

The third scene is set in the town of **Iconium (14:1-7)**, where once again Barnabas and Paul enter the synagogue of the Jews (v. 1) and speak to an inclusive audience of Jews and Greeks (presumably God-fearers?). Opposition continues unabated, however, as unpersuaded Jews seek to remove them (v. 2). Paul and Barnabas respond in an expected manner (v. 3) by "speaking frankly" (see 13:46), "testifying to the word of his [God's] grace" (see 2:47), and "giving signs and wonders through their hands" (see 5:12). Each of these terms indicates that God is at work in very familiar ways. The ability to perform miracles is attributed to Paul on a number of occasions in Acts (14:3, 8-10; 15:12; 19:8-12; 20:7-12; 28:6-10). Although Paul himself refers to such abilities (Rom 15:19; 2 Cor 12:12), they are far more important for Luke to emphasize, in order to align Paul with the abilities demonstrated by Jesus and the apostles (Jervell 1984: 77-95). Although it is only in this scene and the next that Luke describes Paul and Barnabas as apostles (14:4, 14), the picture he paints of them is always consistent with the one he has given of the apostles in Jerusalem (Clark in Marshall and Peterson 1998: 181-90).

The workings of God in Iconium produce a typically divided response among the people (14:4; see 13:4-12), resulting in another enforced departure for Paul and Barnabas (14:5-6). However, moving on enables them to travel through a wider region, "proclaiming the good news" (v. 7), an activity which typifies the whole of their journey (see 13:32).

In the fourth scene, in the Roman colony of **Lystra (14:8-20a)**, Barnabas and Paul encounter a lame man (v. 8). The language used in this brief report provides many additional allusions that the divine power is here at work. This healing (vv. 8-10) is reminiscent of the earlier healing of a lame man in Jerusalem (3:1-11), for in both healings the man has been lame from his mother's womb (3:2; 14:8). Paul "looks intensely" at the man (14:9), as Peter did at the lame man in Jerusalem (3:4); however, this kind of intense scrutiny is more often found in people who see visions (1:10; 6:15; 7:55; 10:4; 11:6). Such intense looking is also the way in which God addresses individuals, through angels (8:26, to Philip; 12:7, to Peter) and visions (9:6, to Saul, repeated at 26:16). Paul is thus able to perceive that the lame man "had faith to be saved" (14:9).

Paul's command to the man to "stand up" (14:10) evokes Peter's commands to Aeneas (9:34) and Tabitha (9:40). The way the crowds responded to each of these healings indicated that the divine power had been tangibly manifested (9:35, 42). The response is different in Lystra, for the inhabitants exalt Barnabas and Paul as "the gods in human likeness" (14:11). This response recalls Peter's encounter with Cornelius, when he commanded him to "stand up" (10:26) because of his mistaken view that Peter was more than human. In Lystra, the misconception of the crowd is not readily corrected, for the priest of Zeus prepares to offer sacrifice to Zeus and Hermes (14:12-13). This leads to a **brief speech by Barnabas and Paul (vv. 15-17)** which sounds once more the theme of God's providential care. After explaining that "We are human beings just like you are" (v. 15; cf. 10:26) and that they are "proclaiming the good news" (14:15; see 13:32), Barnabas and Paul identify "the living God, who made the heaven and the earth and the sea and all things which are in them" (14:15; cf. 4:24). Their speech is a briefer version of the message which Paul will proclaim on the Areopagus (17:24-27), in which God's providential care for humanity is more fully asserted. Here the speech serves to mollify the priest of Zeus and distract him from his intended sacrifice (14:18).

This scene ends, not in triumph, but with renewed opposition to Barnabas and Paul (14:19), who are forced to continue their journey. As he recounts their **return to Antioch (vv. 20b-26)**, Luke notes many of the characteristics which have marked their activity on this journey. The report of these characteristics places Barnabas and Paul in continuity with leaders earlier in the story, as well as identifying the ways in which Paul will operate in subsequent scenes in this section.

The first characteristic of Barnabas and Paul, noted while they were in Derbe, is that of "proclaiming the good news" (14:21), as they have done earlier on this journey (13:32; 14:7, 15). This places them in continuity with other figures who have proclaimed good news: Philip (8:12, 25, 35, 40) and Peter (15:7) as well as Jesus (Luke 4:18, 43; 7:22; 8:1; 20:1; and probably 16:16) and the twelve (Luke 9:6). Subsequently, Paul summarizes all his activities under the phrase "testifying to the good news" (20:24); specific instances of this are later noted in Macedonia (16:10) and Athens (17:18). Secondly, Luke describes Barnabas and Paul as "making disciples" (14:21). The term "disciple" describes members of the assemblies in Jerusalem (6:1, 2, 7; 9:26), Damascus (9:1, 10, 19, 25), Joppa (9:38), Syrian Antioch (11:26, 29; 14:28), Pisidian Antioch (13:52; 14:22), Lystra (14:20; 16:1), Galatia and Phrygia

(18:23), Corinth (18:27), Ephesus (19:1, 9, 30; 20:1), Tyre (21:4), Caesarea (21:16), and generally at 15:10; 20:30.

As they travel toward Antioch, Barnabas and Paul are described as "strengthening" these disciples (14:22). This term describes another of their typical activities which becomes characteristic of Paul's speaking in other places (throughout Syria and Cilicia, 15:41; through the region of Galatia and Phrygia, 18:23; and in the general summary of 16:5). The companion term to strengthening is "exhorting" (14:22), an activity which has already characterized Barnabas (4:36; 11:23) and has already been defined at Pisidian Antioch (13:15, describing Paul's ensuing speech). This places Barnabas and Paul in continuity with Peter (2:40) and indicates another common feature of their activity. The content of their exhortation is given succinctly (14:22). The theme is "the sovereignty of God" (see 1:3), although the turn of phrase used here gives it a strong sense of a location to which entry is sought ("the kingdom of God"). That "we must enter through many trials" highlights a theme which was central to the commissioning of Saul ("he must suffer," 9:16) as well as evoking the refrain of necessity which runs throughout Luke's narrative (see 1:15, 21; Squires 1993: 155-85).

That all of these elements — proclaiming good news, making disciples, strengthening, exhorting, and preparing for suffering — are part of the divine plan is evident in the concluding comment that Barnabas and Paul have "completed the work" to which they had been "handed over to the grace of God" in Antioch (14:26), a reference to their commissioning by the Spirit (13:1-3). It is "the grace of God" (see 2:47) which has enabled them to bring their work to a satisfactory conclusion. The summary of **the journey (14:27-28)** which follows reinforces this understanding through Luke's characteristic use of explicit language about God. Their activities are best understood as "what God did with them" (v. 27); the same phrase is used to interpret their activities to the council in Jerusalem at 15:4, 12. The additional phrase, "how he [God] opened a door of faith to the Gentiles" (14:27), interprets the journey in language uncharacteristic of Luke (Paul uses it at 1 Cor 16:9; 2 Cor 2:12; see also Col 4:3). The understanding that God directed the journey is nevertheless retained in this phrase.

The Jerusalem Council (15:1-35)

After a rest in Antioch (14:28), Paul and Barnabas are summoned to Jerusalem (15:1-2) for **the second Jerusalem council (vv. 1-35)**. Paul's letter to the Galatians includes a report of this meeting (Gal 2:1-10) which differs significantly from Luke's account in overall tenor and in specific details (Hill 1992: 107-17, 126-47). While Paul presents himself as exhibiting great persuasive power in what he portrays as a strongly polemical debate, Luke emphasizes the irenic nature of the meeting and focuses more on the contributions made by the Jerusalem leaders, Peter and James. Paul omits mention of the letter which, according to Luke, the meeting produced (Acts 15:23-29), whereas Luke says nothing of the division of labor which Paul notes was agreed upon during the council (Gal 2:7-9).

In Luke's account of the council, the presenting issue is the failure of Paul and Barnabas to require circumcision in what they preached (15:1, 5). This leads to "not a little dispute and discussion" between Barnabas and Paul, in company with others of their group, and some Judean believers (15:2). As they travel to Jerusalem, they inform assemblies in Phoenicia and Samaria of their success in "the conversion of the Gentiles" (15:3), resulting in great joy in those places (v. 3; see 13:52). On their arrival in Jerusalem, a familiar refrain summarizes their activities as being "what God did with them" (15:4; cf. 14:27). As Paul and Barnabas come to the council, they embody the Lukan understanding of how the divine will has been guiding them.

Some Pharisaic believers present at the council provide a different perspective on the divine will. The sympathetic attitude of Pharisees toward the messianists is critical on two occasions in forensic settings (5:34-39; 23:9; see Brawley 1987: 84-106), so Luke sees no conflict in the idea that some Pharisees had joined the messianic community in Jerusalem. Since the assertion of the Pharisaic believers, that "it is necessary to circumcise them" (15:5), is grounded in Scripture (Gen 17:1-14, 21-27), it appears plausible that this necessity is the divine will. However, Luke's report of the debate in this council shows that this is not the case. Three speeches are reported, each of which draws on earlier events to rebut the claim advanced by these Pharisaic members.

Peter's speech (15:7-11) interprets what Paul and Barnabas have done in the light of Peter's experience in Caesarea. He uses the established Lukan pattern of interpreting what has occurred by reference to God's actions, when he explains that "God chose through my mouth for the Gentiles to hear the word of the good news and to believe" (v. 7) — a summary of the events already reported in detail at 10:1-48. In this context, such language about God serves to reinforce the validity of the activities of Paul and Barnabas and to rebut the claims advanced by the Pharisaic members. This sense is strengthened by the repetition of familiar language about God in the remainder of the speech: "God who knows all hearts" (15:8; cf. 1:24) "gave the Holy Spirit" (15:8; cf. 10:44-46; 11:17) in a way which exactly parallels "them" with "us" (15:8; cf. 10:47; 11:15, 17) and thus "did not distinguish between us and them" (15:9; cf. 11:12). To question this understanding of events would be to tempt God (15:10) and thus to encounter the fate imposed on Ananias and Sapphira (5:9). Peter concludes by urging acceptance of what Paul and Barnabas have done since those Jews who believe have received salvation "in the same way as they" (Gentile believers) — that is, "through the grace of the Lord Jesus" (15:11). In this way, he argues that the "God who is not partial" (10:34-35) has clearly been at work both in events in Caesarea, which Peter experienced, and in the activity of Paul and Barnabas throughout Asia Minor. The assemblies they established are inclusive — Gentiles belong just as much as Jews.

The second speech is reported only as a condensed summary of what Barnabas and Paul reply (15:12). This restates their earlier report of "what God did with them" (v. 4) and applies that understanding to the signs and wonders which were performed through them among the Gentiles throughout Asia Minor (v. 12). This strengthens the argument for inclusive assemblies, for just as God enabled signs among Jews (5:12), so, too, are signs given among Gentiles (15:12).

James's speech (15:13-21) demonstrates his prominence in the community at Jerusalem. He begins by supporting Peter's explanation through the use, yet again, of language about God. The claim that "God visited" (15:14; NRSV, "God looked favorably") evokes the blessing of Zechariah (Luke 1:68) and suggests, to careful readers of Luke's work, that by incorporating "a people *(laos)* from the Gentiles" (15:14) God has brought about "redemption for his people" (Luke 1:68). In Scripture, the term *laos* often refers to Israel (Exod 6:7; Deut 4:20, 34; 14:2; 26:18-19; 32:9), but the incorporation of the Gentiles into this people now reflects the promise of Zech 2:14-15: "Many nations shall join themselves to the Lord on that day, and shall be my people."

James then provides further scriptural validation of the inclusion of Gentiles within the messianist assemblies (15:15-18). He cites the agreement of a compilation of scriptural texts (Jer 12:15; Amos 9:11-12; Isa 45:21) which depicts the way that "all the nations . . . will seek out the Lord," and affirms that this process is one which "the Lord . . . has been making known from long ago" (15:18; cf. 15:8). Like the prophetic quotation by Peter at 2:16-21, this prophetic citation is strategically placed to interpret the ensuing narrative (Wall in Marshall and Peterson 1998: 449-52).

James then indicates, "I have reached the decision" that will be crucial in bringing the council to agreement (15:19). He argues that "those among the Gentiles who turn to God" (v. 19; cf. 14:15) should not be troubled, and he proposes a compromise position (15:20) which nevertheless retains a clear scriptural basis. (No idol food: Exod 34:11-17; Lev 17:8-9. No sexual immorality: Lev 18:6-29. No strangled animals: Exod 22:31; Lev 17:10-16, equating "what is torn," 17:15, with "something strangled." No blood: Gen 9:4; Deut 12:15-16, 23-25; cf. Lev 17:11, 15.) Luke's portrayal of James indicates his prominent role among the leaders of the assembly since what James decides (15:19-20) is adopted unchanged by the council (vv. 28-29). This Lukan view of the authority of James is reinforced later in his account; when Paul returns to Jerusalem, he will report directly to James (21:17-19). Indeed, the Jerusalem community accepts the four requirements without dissent (21:25).

Thus Luke's report of these council debates reaffirms the understanding already developed in the narrative of 13:4–14:27, namely, that Paul and Barnabas engage in activities among the Gentiles in accord with the divine will. The logical consequence of this perspective is thus worked out in the council's **letter to the assemblies (15:22-29)**, which is to be taken to Antioch for distribution among the "believers who are from the Gentiles" in assemblies in Antioch and Syria and Cilicia by four chosen delegates: Judas, Silas, Paul, and Barnabas (vv. 22-23). This action signals a desire by the Jerusalem community to maintain fellowship with the newly formed Gentile communities (Hill 1992: 143-46). The text of the letter asserts that it has been worked out by the council and the Holy Spirit (15:28), thus placing this decision within the stream of events which have been guided and shaped by God. The inclusion of Gentiles within the Jewish messianic assemblies is validated directly by God.

This letter is then sent to **Antioch (15:30-35)**, where the assembly rejoices (v. 31; see 13:48) and receives it as an exhortation (15:31; see 13:15). Judas and Silas, identified as prophets, then continue the work of Barnabas and Paul as they exhort and strengthen the assembly (15:32); for exhort, see 13:15; 14:22; for strengthen, see 14:22. After they leave, Paul and Barnabas continue their customary activities of "teaching and proclaiming the good news" (15:35), just as the apostles had done in Jerusalem (5:42). The end of this portion of the narrative thus presents the continuation of these characteristic activities.

Macedonia and Achaia (15:36–18:23)

Luke then provides a most significant **transition (15:36–16:10)** which reports an important regrouping of leaders, entailing the separation of Paul from one of his co-workers and the establishment of a new group associated with Paul. The first part of this transition is set in Antioch, where Paul and Barnabas separate (15:36-41) over the issue of whether John Mark will accompany them or not (v. 37). The word *paroxysmos,* used to describe their separation (v. 39), depicts the violent severing of the relationship, but no further details are provided. Paul writes of a severe conflict he experienced in Antioch, involving Barnabas (Gal 2:11-14). However, since this conflict was primarily with Peter, over the issue of his withdrawal from table fellowship with Gentiles, it is unlikely to have been the same incident as reported here by Luke.

That Paul and Silas continue to enact the divine will is conveyed by the apologetic comment that they continued their journey "after they had been handed over to the grace of the Lord" (15:40). This evokes the interpretation of their earlier activities as being within "the grace of God" (13:43; 14:3, 26; cf. 15:11; and see 2:47) and thereby as continuing to enact the divine purpose. The summary of their continued journey indicates this through the description of their activities as "strengthening the assemblies" (15:41; see 14:22).

The next part of the transition establishes a new grouping, as Paul and Silas are joined by Timothy to travel **through Asia Minor (16:1-5)**. Timothy, who is already a disciple in Lystra (v. 1), represents in himself the inclusive quality of the assemblies which have been, and will continue to be, established by Paul and his co-workers. Timothy's parentage is both Jewish ("son of a Jewish woman, a believer") and Gentile ("a Greek father"). The grouping of Paul, Silas, and Timothy brings to the assemblies they visit both the decree of the Jerusalem council (v. 4) and the experience (by now quite typical) of "being strengthened in faith" (v. 5; see 14:22) and of "increasing in numbers daily" (16:5; see 4:4; 5:14; 9:31; 12:25).

At this point the highly significant geographical shift that takes place is reported in **the move into Macedonia (16:6-10)**. This move across the northern Aegean Sea is validated by a concentration of references to God which demonstrates that Paul's separation from Barnabas and co-option of Timothy will continue his earlier work and will open up new avenues for fruitful work. Three injunctions are given; each one is from a divine source. The first of these, an instruction not to speak in the southern region of Asia, comes from the Holy Spirit (v. 6). The second direction, a prohibition against any attempt to head north and enter Bithynia, comes from the same Spirit, here described as "the Spirit of Jesus" (v. 7). The third divine interjection takes place at Troas, where a vision is seen in the night with a petition to "come across into Macedonia" (v. 9). Being guided by the Spirit and seeing visions are common occurrences in Acts. The nature of such phenomena has already been established as divine in origin (2:14-21); the move into Macedonia is thus in accord with the divine will.

This understanding is explicitly underscored as the transition ends with the succinct statement that "God has called us to preach the good news to them" (16:10). Events still to follow are thus introduced in as strong a manner as possible through the use of explicit language about God. This statement (v. 10) begins the first of the so-called "we sections" of Acts, which are narrated in the first person plural. Three of these are but brief notes concerning journeys (from Troas to Philippi, 16:10-17; from Troas to Miletus, 20:5-15; from Miletus to Jerusalem, 21:1-18). Each of these passages contains lists of the places visited and the means of travel (16:11-12; 20:5-6, 13-15; 21:1-3, 7-8, 15) and small vignettes concerning one incident that took place on the journey (16:13-15; 20:7-12; 21:4-6, 10-14). The fourth "we section"' encompasses the extensive series of journeys by which Paul travels from Caesarea to Rome (27:1–28:16). It includes mention of places and means of travel, as well as a number of particular incidents.

Scholarly opinion over the historical value of the "we sections" is divided. Some have argued that there is evidence for an ancient literary convention by which an author can alternate third person ("he," "they") and first person ("I," "we") narratives. In this view, Luke makes use of the first person narrative to strengthen the sense of unity felt between author and audience, and the characters in the events narrated (Robbins in Talbert 1978: 215-42; also Pervo 1987: 57). However, others have criticized this claim and argued that the use of "we" indicates that these passages, at least, must go back to an eyewitness (Hemer 1989: 312-34; Porter in Gill and Gempf 1994: 545-74). The likelihood of ever being able to prove that the author of Acts was himself present with Paul in these journeys is low; at best we might conclude that Luke had available to him a very brief source which may possibly have had its origins among Paul's fellow travelers (see also 20:5).

The group crosses over into Macedonia, an ancient province of Greece which had been the dominant political power four centuries earlier. They arrive in **Philippi (16:11-40)**, a city founded by Philip of Macedonia in 356 BC, taken under Roman rule in 167 BC, and declared a Roman colony (as Luke accurately notes, v. 12) in 31 BC. The group proceeds, in typical fashion, to find a place of worship on the sabbath (v. 13) — not, as expected, a synagogue (see 13:5), but "a place of prayer" (16:13) for some women. (That the place of prayer was, in fact, a synagogue is argued by Reimer 1995: 72-92.)

One of this number, **Lydia,** is singled out for attention. Lydia is a God-fearer (16:14; on female God-fearers, see Reimer 1995: 93-98), as was Cornelius (10:2) and probably the Ethiopian (8:27); what will occur here will place Lydia in a paradigmatic position akin to that occupied by Cornelius. Lydia is the first individual convert identified once Paul, Silas, and Timothy, under divine guidance, have crossed over into Macedonia (16:6-10). She thus presents a paradigm for the process of conversion and leadership; as the first convert in Europe, she models a faithful response to the message of Paul. Indeed, what takes place in this scene is directly interpreted as an act of God, for "the Lord opened her heart" (v. 14) to listen eagerly to Paul's words. The "opening of her heart" (v. 14) echoes the discoveries made by the archetypal disciples on the walk to Emmaus (Luke 24:31, 32) and by the larger group of followers gathered in Jerusalem later that day (24:45). Her "eager listening" (16:14) repeats the response evoked by Philip in Samaria (8:6).

Lydia is judged as being "faithful to the Lord" and, with her household, is baptized (16:15), in accord with the programmatic declaration of Peter's Pentecost exhortation (2:38-39). The baptism of her household follows the pattern already seen in Caesarea (10:24-48; 11:13-16) and foreshadows a pattern which will be repeated soon in Philippi (16:31-33), and subsequently in Corinth (18:8) (Matson 1996: 135-83; on the house church in Philippi as "a subversive contrast society," see Reimer 1995: 113-27).

Her belief leads to the offer of hospitality (16:15), as was also the case with the Gentiles in Caesarea (10:48); this same pattern follows in the story of the conversion of the Philippian jailer and his household (16:34). Belief, baptism, and table fellowship have also been linked in the accounts of the conversion of Saul (9:18-19) and of Cornelius and his household (10:24-48) and the events on Pentecost in Jerusalem (2:41-47). Lydia's role as a patroness echoes that of Mary, the mother of John Mark, in Jerusalem (12:12) and prefigures that of Priscilla (with Aquila, 18:13). Paul will encounter, and convince, other women of relatively high social status later in Thessalonica (17:4) and Berea (17:12).

The status of Paul as one who carries out the purpose of God is further consolidated in the following events in Philippi. A **demon-possessed slave woman (16:16-18)** recognizes Paul and his companions as "slaves of the most high God" (v. 17), just as Jesus had been identified by demon-possessed characters as "the Son of the most high God" (Luke 8:28; cf. 4:41). Their message is identified as the "way of salvation" (16:17), a phrase consistent with the terms already used to describe the movement and its message. (On "the Way," see 9:2; on salvation, see 2:21; 5:31.) The subsequent casting out of this spirit (16:18) reinforces the perception that Paul exercises the divine power, in the manner already shown by Jesus (Luke 4:41; 8:26-33), Peter (5:16), and Philip (8:7).

However, it also precipitates **the arrest, trial, and imprisonment of Paul and Silas (16:19-24).** The scene builds feverishly to the dramatic climax of their imprisonment by the local authorities, here identified as *stratēgoi* (v. 20), the same term that is used on inscriptions from Philippi. Paul and Silas are placed in stocks "in the innermost cell" (v. 24; on the poor conditions in Roman prisons, see Rapske 1994: 195-225). This is the first imprisonment for Paul in Acts; others await him (20:23; 21:27-28). Such imprisonments are also referred to in Paul's own letters (Phil 1:7, 13-14; 2 Cor 11:23; Phlm 1, 9-10, 23; and see Col 4:3, 10, 18; 2 Tim 3:11).

In the course of this scene, a fleeting reference to Roman customs is made (16:21). The crowd believes that the Jewishness of Paul and Silas places them outside of Roman customs; that they are misguided will become evident when Paul and Silas are released (vv. 37-38). Until this point in the narrative, the only explicit reference to Rome has been at Pentecost (2:11). After this point, there will be no further such reference until the very end of this section (21:16), at the moment when Paul's long journey to Rome comes into view. In this Philippi scene, then, the Roman citizenship of Paul will be established (16:37; see further on 22:25-29). The opposition he encounters from this point onward is thus to be seen in light of his Roman right of appeal to the emperor. What is established as obvious for Luke and his readers will only become gradually apparent to Paul's opponents in the narrative — in much the same way as the inexorable plan of God is worked out, scene by scene, in apparently disjointed ways which can eventually be seen within the overall plan of God.

Paul and Silas in prison (16:25-34) exhibit the typical attitude of praying (v. 25; see 2:42). Suddenly "a great earthquake" shakes open the prison doors (16:26). The universal scope of the earthquake's impact ("*all* the doors opened . . . *everyone's* chains unfastened") is striking, but perhaps it is a Lukan exaggeration (see 26:4). Although there is no explicit indication of divine guidance at this point, an earthquake was widely considered to be a portent of the divine will. The psalmist expresses the common scriptural view that God was the initiator of earthquakes: "O God, you have rejected us . . . you have caused the land to quake, you have torn it open" (Ps 60:1-2; see also Judg 5:4-5; 2 Sam 22:8-16; Pss 18:7-9; 29:3-9; 68:7-8; 97:4-5; 104:32; 144:5-6; Isa 13:13; 29:4-6; 64:1-3; Jer 4:24; 10:10; Ezek 32:7; Joel 2:10-11; Nah 1:5-6; Zeph 1:14-15; Hag 2:6-7, 20-23; Zech 14:5). The historian Dionysius of Halicarnassus articulates a view found often in Hellenistic literature when he lists among "the terrible portents sent from the gods" such phenomena as "flashes shooting out of the sky and outbursts of fire . . . the rumblings of the earth and its continual tremblings" (*Rom. Ant.* 10.2.3; for descriptions of such portents, see Cicero *De divinatione* 1.33.72–49.109; *De natura deorum* 2.5.13-14; Minucius Felix *Octavius* 7.1-6; for the theme in Hellenistic histories, see Squires 1993: 78-84). Indeed, the narrative of Acts has already reported how God can sovereignly release a person from prison (as with Peter in Jerusalem, 12:6-11). Although it is not described with explicit reference to God, the earthquake in Philippi is nevertheless a clear portent of divine providence.

The melodramatic response of the jailer (16:27) enables Paul and Silas to speak the word of the Lord (v. 32), explaining that what must be done to be saved is to "believe on the Lord Jesus" (v. 31). The ensuing scene replicates familiar elements: the jailer and his household were baptized (v. 33; see 2:38), he set a table (16:34; see 2:42, 46; also 10:23, 48), and they rejoiced (16:34; see 5:41). His conversion now makes him "one who has come to belief in God" (16:34).

The release of Paul and Silas (16:35-40) takes place, not by divine intervention, but through the invocation of Paul's Roman citizenship (vv. 37-38). Roman writers documented the prohibition against flogging a Roman citizen (Livy *Hist.* 10.9.4; Cicero *Pro Rabiro* 4.12-13). Paul makes no reference to his Roman citizenship in his letters, although there is no need for him to have done so. The name "Paul" may well have been his Roman name. Yet his claim clearly plays a strategic role in Luke's narrative at two points (here and in Jerusalem, 22:25-29), as it plants the seeds for Paul's eventual journey to Rome. This scene (as also the scene in Jerusalem) is shaped by Luke's rhetorical purposes, to put the spotlight on Paul as a positive role model (Lentz 1993: 105-38).

After an official apology (16:39), Paul and Silas leave the prison, paying a parting visit to Lydia's home where, in typical fashion, they exhorted the community members (v. 40; see 13:15). Paul's own description of his time in Philippi notes that he "had suffered and been shamefully mistreated" (1 Thess 2:2), but his letter to the Philippian believers rejoices in the fellowship that they shared with him (Phil 1:5, 7; 4:14-16).

Two "typical" scenes then ensue in **Thessalonica and Berea (17:1-15)**. Each city was of importance; the Roman governor of the region resided in the former, while the latter was the local seat of the imperial cult. Entering the synagogue in Thessalonica on the sabbath is described as being "according to the custom" which Paul practiced in each town (17:1-2; see 13:5). Here Paul argued with the synagogue attenders (17:2), a practice in evidence in his subsequent synagogue visits (17:17; 18:4, 19; 19:8) as well as in the assembly in Troas (20:7, 9) and when he is before Felix (24:25). His argument is made from the Scriptures (17:2), as was done by Philip (8:35), Peter (see 2:25-31), and Paul himself (see 13:33-37). Paul's message contains elements which are familiar not only from his own speeches but also from those of Peter and Jesus. First of all, he states that "the Messiah must suffer" (17:3; see 3:18) "and be raised from the dead" (17:3; see 5:30; 10:40). Then Paul defines the Messiah as "Jesus whom I proclaim to you" (17:3; see 2:36). Paul's message stands in clear continuity with the message that has been proclaimed from Pentecost onward.

This message brings success among the devout Greeks and leading women (17:4). Such success among God-fearers has occurred in Antioch (13:43, 50) and Philippi (16:14), and will occur in Athens (17:17) and Corinth (18:7). Women of high social status become believers in Antioch (13:50), Philippi (the description of Lydia's trade in 16:14 infers such high status), and Berea (17:12) (see Gill in Gill and Gempf 1994: 105-18). However, the pattern of divided response (see 13:4-12) continues, for opposition is stirred up by Jews who exhibit jealousy (17:5), like those who were similarly antagonistic in Jerusalem (5:17) and Antioch (13:45), and like Paul himself when he was a persecutor (22:3-4). Paul and Silas are brought before the politarchs (17:6); Luke accurately employs an uncommon term which inscriptional evidence suggests was reserved for city authorities in Macedonia only (Horsley in Gill and Gempf 1994: 419-31). A long list of such historical accuracies in Acts 13–28 can be cited (Hemer 1989: 107-58); this does not, however, remove concerns about Luke's inaccuracies at times (see 5:36-37), nor does it negate the claim that Luke's own interests shape the way that he presents and interprets events in his narrative. Thus, the accusations leveled against Paul and Silas reflect Lukan motifs. "Turning the world upside down" (17:6) has been a common theme in Luke's story of Jesus (Luke 1:46-55; 6:20-26; 9:23-24; 13:30; 14:7-11; 16:19-31; 18:9-14; 22:25-26). Acting contrary to Roman practice (17:7) was a charge leveled against Paul and Silas in Philippi (16:20-21); Paul later defends himself against this charge in Caesarea (25:8).

Paul's own description of his time in Thessalonica refers to the "distress and persecution" which he experienced (1 Thess 3:7); this appears to concur with Luke's account of opposition there. By contrast, Paul comments that the Thessalonian converts "turned to God from idols" (1 Thess 1:9) and uncharacteristically fails to quote from Hebrew Scripture in his letter to them, suggesting that they were a wholly Gentile community of believers. This differs from Luke's account of the community's origins from the synagogue.

In Berea the typical Lukan pattern is replicated: Paul and Silas enter the synagogue (17:10), speak from the Scriptures (v. 11), have success among Jews (v. 11) and Greek women (v. 12), but then encounter opposition from Jews sent up from Thessalonica (v. 13), leading to yet another forced exit — this time, of Paul only (v. 14). Paul makes no reference to this visit in his extant letters. These two scenes end with a brief geographical note about Paul's arrival in Athens (v. 15).

The same pattern will recur yet again in **Athens (17:16-34),** although much more detail is given of this encounter and a significant variation in the pattern is identified. Athens had been the capital of ancient Attica; it was renowned for its rigor of learning and range of religiosity (Sophocles *Oedipus at Colonus* 260-64; Pausanias *Attica* 1.17.1; Livy *Hist.* 45.17.11) and honored for its contributions to the legal system (Gill in Gill and Gempf 1994: 441-48). In his letter to the Thessalonians, Paul refers to being alone in Athens (1 Thess 3:1; cf. Acts 17:15-16). When Paul enters the city, the sight of all the idols on display makes "his spirit . . . provoked" (17:16; the word is related to that which describes the contention between Paul and Barnabas at 15:39). Nevertheless, he proceeds in the expected way when he enters the synagogue and argues with "the Jews and the devout persons" (17:17; see v. 2). However, Luke moves him rapidly from the Jewish synagogue to the city marketplace (v. 17), thereby placing Paul in the very middle of the city's commercial and religious life. This variation to the customary pattern enables Luke to present Paul's message as not only applicable to the Jewish context but also able to stand in its own right in the Hellenized context of the Mediterranean world. The substance of Paul's speech will confirm this aim in no uncertain terms.

In the marketplace, Paul encounters some of the philosophers for whom Athens was renowned: Stoics, named after the public colonnade *(stoa)* where Zeno had taught his pupils in the fourth-third centuries BC, and Epicureans, who studied the teaching of Epicurus in the garden where he had established his school in 306 BC. These two schools of philosophy held strongly opposing views on the question of divine providence: the Stoics exalted fate as preeminent, while the Epicureans dismissed it as an illusion (Diogenes Laertius *Lives* 7.138-39; 10.133-34). Some of these philosophers dismiss Paul as a "babbler" (17:18); the Greek term *spermologos* is a derogatory description of a person who collects snippets of ideas and strings them together willy-nilly (Philostratus *Vita Ap.* 5:20). Others raise allegations against him, that he speaks of "strange demons" (17:18; NRSV, "foreign divinities") and that he presents a "new teaching" (v. 19). Such charges were laid against Socrates at his trial (Plato *Apol.* 24B-C; Xenophon *Mem.* 1.1; cf. Josephus *Ag. Ap.* 2 §§262-68; Dio Cassius *Roman History* 52.36.1-2), and so it is entirely fitting that the philosophers take hold of him and lead him to the Areopagus (v. 19), the location for the trial of Socrates. Nevertheless, the pedigree of Paul's message is quite apparent to Luke's readers, for in the familiar way he has "proclaimed the good news" (v. 18; see 13:32), the content of which is "Jesus and the resurrection" (17:18; see 5:30; 10:40; 17:3). Paul is thus brought to trial prepared to speak in defense of his beliefs. Luke sets the scene so that Paul can assert the antiquity of his beliefs in a context where "something new" is more commonly sought (17:21). In the speech he will go on to demonstrate that the substance of his beliefs ought to be familiar to the Athenians (see 17:28).

Paul's Areopagus speech (17:22-31) is a thoroughly Lukan creation, which probably owes its shape to the development of preaching in Hellenistic Judaism (Wilson 1973: 196-215). The speech begins in apologetic style with a traditional *captatio benevolentiae* ("expression of goodwill"; 17:22); on the apologetic dimension of this speech, see Squires 1993: 71, 74-75. The theme of the speech, once again, is God. In standard fashion, Luke has Paul contextualize the theme by referring to "the unknown God" (v. 23) before identifying this god as "the God who made the earth and all things in it" (v. 24; cf. 4:24; 14:15). God then functions as the subject of the speech; God's actions encompass everything from the creation (17:24) to repentance (v. 30; see 2:38). Paul's polemic against idols (17:24, 29) repeats a motif already sounded in Stephen's speech (7:48); the theme would have been familiar to the philosophers (Heraclitus *Epistle* 4; Seneca *Ep. Mor.* 95.48). The final reported sentence in the speech adds to this God's eschatological judgment when he will establish a day for judgment (17:31), a transformation of Peter's assertion concerning the final days (3:19-21, 26). Such judgment will be on the basis of righteousness, a term used infrequently by the Lukan Paul (13:10, 38-39; 24:25), although it is so important in some of Paul's letters.

Reference to Jesus in this speech is truncated to the abrupt "man whom he chose" who will execute judgment on that day (17:31). In previous speeches God has related to humanity in the history of Israel (Paul, 13:17-22;

see also Stephen's speech, 7:1-53) but preeminently through Jesus (see 2:22-36 and 13:23-39). In Paul's Areopagus speech, God's relationship to humanity is described, without reference to Jesus, in terms of God's creative and systematizing activity (17:24-26), humanity's quest for God (v. 27), and the consequent indwelling of human beings in the divine being (v. 28). The speech is radically different from the earlier speeches in two ways: God's presence is described in philosophical rather than historical terms, and the texts cited to support the argument are drawn from Greek writers rather than the Jewish Scriptures. "Your own poets" (17:28) introduces a quotation from Aratus (*Phaenomena* 5, cited by Eusebius *Prep. Evang.* 666b), while there are affinities with Stoic writers in the clause "in him we live and move and have our being" (Dio Chrysostom *Orat.* 12.27-28). Such a claim to the antiquity of the beliefs which Paul articulates has been a consistent element in his previous speeches, although it is usually couched in terms of the fulfillment of prophecy because of his Jewish audiences (see 13:33-37). However, there is a general commonality with the earlier speeches of Acts — for each speech interprets human existence in terms of being in relation to God, whether that be expressed in Jewish terms or Hellenistic terms. Paul's Areopagus speech is thus a notable variant of the established pattern — yet it must be regarded as nothing more than a variant since it still uses language about God to shape the message (Squires 1993: 71-75).

The response to Paul's speech in Athens follows the pattern seen throughout Paul's journeys to this point, namely, a divided response of acceptance and rejection (see 13:4-12). A subtle difference here is the reversal of order; rather than first noting those who show interest in Paul's message, Luke draws attention to those who mocked (17:32a) before providing more details concerning those who sought to know more (v. 32b) and those named and unnamed individuals who believed (v. 34). Thus, rather than indicating Paul's failure in Athens (and leading to a new missionary strategy which is articulated in 1 Corinthians), as many scholars have asserted, this account emphasizes Paul's success in the cultural capital of Greece.

Just sixty kilometers from Athens was the city of **Corinth (18:1-22)**, a strategic trading city because of its two ports, one on each side of the isthmus. The old city had been sacked by the Romans in 146 BC; they rebuilt it and declared it a colony in 44 BC (Gill in Gill and Gempf 1994: 448-53). While in Corinth, Paul meets with a new set of co-workers, Aquila and Priscilla (18:2). This married couple is well known from Paul's letters, where the mention of the female, in the shortened form, Prisca, ahead of Aquila, is noteworthy (Rom 16:3; 2 Tim 4:19; see also 1 Cor 16:19). Luke notes that they are Jews who had recently moved from Italy to Corinth as a result of the expulsion of Jews from Rome under Claudius (18:2); this probably took place in AD 49 (Suetonius *Claudius* 25.4; Clarke in Gill and Gempf 1994: 466-71). They work as tentmakers (v. 3), an occupation often considered to indicate significant means (however, an alternative reading, that tentmakers were craftspeople of lower social status, is offered by Reimer 1995: 1999-208). This shared trade means that they can provide both hospitality and a place for Paul to carry out his trade while he is in Corinth. When Paul travels on, they accompany him to Syria (v. 18) and Ephesus (v. 19), where they remain while Paul continues on further; in Ephesus they instruct Apollos (v. 26).

Paul's familiar pattern (18:1-6) is evident as he argues in the synagogue on the sabbath, in an attempt to persuade his audience (v. 4). Paul here bears witness (v. 5), a typical activity of his (20:21), and he fulfills the promise made by Jesus (1:8), as also did Peter (2:32; 5:32). Paul's message is the familiar refrain: "the Messiah, he is Jesus" (18:5; see 9:22; 17:3). Just as this claim provided the foundations for the community in Jerusalem (2:36), so in Corinth the declaration that Jesus is the Messiah will form the basis for the Corinthian assembly.

Once more, in such a context of bearing witness, opposition erupts (18:6). The Corinthian Jews are described as opposing and blaspheming, evoking memories of the scene in Pisidian Antioch (13:45). Paul's response (18:6) contains three elements, none of which indicates a full-scale repudiation of the Jews. His actions and words are intended to convey the same message he has already given in Antioch (see 13:51).

The first part of Paul's response is the prophetic action of "shaking out his clothes" (18:6), a reminder of when he and Barnabas shook the dust from their feet in Antioch (13:51). Such shaking of clothes probably alludes to the actions of Nehemiah when he dealt with the unjust actions of some Israelites during a time of financial difficulty (Neh 5:1-13). Nehemiah reported how he warned the people to make restoration for all their unjust actions, and then he noted: "I shook out the fold of my garment," a symbolic action which stood as a metaphor for the impending divine judgment (Neh 5:13). This action immediately evoked a positive response: the people did as he had instructed them. Thus the action of shaking his clothes brings about repentance. For Paul, as for Nehemiah, it does not signify definitive, irreversible divine retribution.

Second, Paul makes a prophetic declaration: "Your blood be upon your heads" (18:6). This refrain is found in scriptural stories, where it usually functions as a threat of divine retribution which elicits repentance. In the earliest instance, when David hears of the deaths of Saul and Jonathan, he tears his clothes and sentences the Amalekite messenger to death, pronouncing a curse over him as he dies: "Your blood be upon your head" (2 Sam 1:16). In subsequent instances, however, the threat of divine justice evokes repentance. Solomon warns the rebellious Shimei that, as soon as he departs from Jerusalem, "your blood shall be upon your own head" (1 Kgs 2:37); Shimei thus refrains from so departing (1 Kgs 2:38b). Three times in the book of Ezekiel, this warning is uttered in order to evoke repentance. Soon after being called to be a prophet, Ezekiel is told that if he fails to warn the people of Israel of the need for repentance, he is to be held responsible: "their blood I will require at your hand" (Ezek 3:18, 20). In a later oracle, the prophet announces that the man who is a shedder of blood shall die for his sins; "his blood shall be upon himself" (Ezek 18:13). This threat is not absolute, however; it is intended to provoke repentance (Ezek 18:30-32). Ezekiel subsequently declares that for those who ignore the warning of the sentinel, "their blood shall be upon themselves" (Ezek 33:4). This also leads to an invitation to repentance (Ezek 33:11, 14). In the light of these passages, when Luke has Paul utter the phrase "Your blood be upon your heads," he has him sound a warning of divine retribution with the intention of provoking repentance.

Third, Paul repeats his assertion from Pisidian Antioch (13:46) when he declares, "From now on I will go to the Gentiles" (18:6). This also evokes his words in Antioch, "behold, we turn to the Gentiles" (13:46). As we have seen, this was not a universal declaration since Paul soon returned to the synagogues. Likewise, after leaving Corinth Paul will still return to the synagogue in Ephesus (18:19; 19:8). Turning to the Gentiles does not entail abandonment of the Jews. Luke understands that Paul's statement applies only to his time in Corinth, where he leaves the synagogue and establishes the kind of inclusive assembly which is now imperative.

The familiar pattern of a divided response to Paul's message then becomes evident in Corinth. Whereas in Antioch, after declaring that he was turning to the Gentiles, Paul was driven out of the city (13:46-51), in Corinth Paul employs a different strategy by establishing **a Corinthian assembly (18:7-11)**. This assembly draws upon those who fear God (18:7; see 2:43; 17:4) and the household of the synagogue leader, Crispus (18:8). Once more those who believed in the Lord are baptized (v. 8; see 2:38). Although established independently of the synagogue, the assembly in Corinth nevertheless shares characteristics with messianic assemblies in many other places. What begins here is not a new movement, apart from Judaism; it is rather the manifestation of the kind of inclusive community which is now to characterize messianic believers (Towner in Marshall and Peterson 1998: 417-36). Paul's own correspondence to the Corinthians indicates the difficulties that were inherent in maintaining a balance amid diverse expressions of faith in such an inclusive community; over time the Corinthian assembly was racked by internal squabbles (1 Cor 1:10-17; 11:17-34; 12:1–14:40) and pressured from outside by those with different teachings (2 Corinthians 10–13).

For Luke, however, the focus remains squarely on Paul's role as leader of the community. Once the assembly has been established, Paul is given divine reassurance concerning the validity of his witness when "the Lord" (i.e., Jesus; see 9:5) appears to him in a vision (18:9a). Visions are integral to the narrative of Acts (see 2:14-21); to this point Paul has seen two visions, each of which has commissioned him to a new task: the vision of Jesus, on the road to Damascus (9:3-7), who commissioned him to "bear my name before Gentiles and kings and the people of Israel" (9:15); and the vision of the Macedonian man who appeared to Paul in Troas, beckoning him to "Come over into Macedonia and help us" (16:9). The visions to Cornelius (10:3-7) and Peter (10:10-16) have a similar commissioning function.

The function of this vision, however, is to encourage Paul in his difficulties. The Lord Jesus exhorts him to continue speaking (18:9b) and affirms, "I am with you" (v. 10). He also asserts that none will be able to do evil to Paul (v. 10); Paul is thus to be rescued from the fate endured by the Israelites (7:6, 19), the Jerusalem assembly (12:1), and the Gentile believers in Iconium (14:2). Paul will receive two subsequent visions which will repeat this consolatory function (23:11, in Jerusalem; 27:23-24, on board ship).

In this vision the Lord refers to the nature of this new community in a distinctive manner by stating, "I have many people *(laos)* in this city" (18:10). Luke uses *laos* in its scriptural sense, to refer almost exclusively to Israel (e.g., 4:10; 7:17, 34; 13:17; 21:28; 26:17; 28:26); in this case, however, it appears to refer to Gentiles as well as Jews who have come to believe that the Messiah is Jesus (18:4-5). This distinctive usage of *laos* looks back to the key comment by James at the second council of Jerusalem, "God first chose to take a people out of the Gentiles for his name" (15:14). The composition of God's people has been notably modified to include Gentiles, but not explicitly to exclude Jews.

Having been reassured by the vision, Paul stays in Corinth for eighteen months, pursuing his traditional activity of teaching (18:11; see 11:26; 13:2, 12; 15:35; 17:19; 20:20). The content of this teaching is once again described as "the word of God" (18:11; see 13:5, 7, 44, 46). It is likely that during this period in Corinth Paul wrote what is now regarded as his earliest surviving letter (1 Thessalonians). However, Luke is consistently silent about Paul's letter-writing activities; more important for him is the preaching and teaching activity of Paul in each place he visits.

Eventually, some Jews bring Paul to **trial before Gallio (18:12-17)**, repeating the pattern of opposition seen in most places Paul visits (see 13:4-12). Lucius Junius Gallio was proconsul of Achaia in AD 52; a fragmentary inscription found early last century at Delphi records part of a letter from the emperor Claudius to Gallio at this time (Gill in Gill and Gempf 1994: 436-37). This firm date provides the starting point for reconstructing the chronology of Paul's life from the hints and implications elsewhere in Acts and throughout Paul's letters. (Many such correlations are attempted in Hemer 1989: 159-93.) The Corinthian Jews charge Paul with persuading people to worship God in a manner contrary to Torah (18:13); the reader of Acts is quite clear, however, about the fidelity of Paul's piety. The nature of the charge as stated leads Gallio to dismiss it as an internal Jewish matter (vv. 15-16); his words cannot be regarded as a verbatim report, but the speech which Luke attributes to him follows the expected judicial conventions. As Paul goes free, Sosthenes is punished in his place (v. 17).

The scene in Corinth ends with a summary of **the preaching tour (18:18-22)** which eventually brings Paul back to Antioch (v. 22) before he sets off through Galatia and Phrygia (v. 23). While in Ephesus he visits the synagogue (v. 19; see 13:5) and argues with the Jews there (18:19; see 17:2) — yet another typical scenario. On his departure from Ephesus, Paul promises that he will return "if God is willing" (18:21), an expression which indicates that Paul's travels and activities are still divinely guided.

The Greek text of v. 22 states that Paul "went up and greeted the assembly"; the NRSV (with other translations and commentators) interprets this as a visit to Jerusalem. In his summary of Paul's travels through Galatia and Phrygia, Luke notes that Paul continues the divinely given task of "strengthening all the disciples" (v. 23; see 14:22).

Ephesus (18:24–20:1)

Luke devotes much space to Paul's stay in **Ephesus (18:24–19:22)**, the city where the Roman governor of Asia was based. The wealth of the city (perhaps reflected in the thriving silversmith business, 19:24) arose from the strategic position of the port of Ephesus and the convergence of land trade routes in Ephesus from all directions. Ephesus had become the chief marketplace for the whole of Asia Minor; among the numerous Ephesian inscriptions in existence today, some include the city's self-description as "the first and greatest metropolis of Asia" (Trebilco in Gill and Gempf 1994: 302-11). Of his stay in Ephesus, Paul himself mentions only that he "fought with wild beasts" (1 Cor 15:32) and that he encountered "many adversaries" there (1 Cor 16:9).

The first figure encountered in Luke's report of events in Ephesus is **Apollos (18:24-28)**, who is introduced before Paul arrives in Ephesus. Apollos is described in such a way as to leave no doubt that he is to be seen in continuity with previous figures. Apollos is a teacher (v. 25), like the apostles (4:2, 18; 5:21, 25, 28, 42) and Barnabas and Paul (11:26; 13:1; 20:20). He knows of the movement by the title of "the Way" (see 9:2), here specified as "the Way of the Lord" (18:25). He teaches "the things concerning Jesus" (18:25), as did Paul (28:23, 31). Apollos is to be found in the synagogue (18:26), as was Paul's custom (13:5); he "began to speak frankly" (18:26), adopting the same approach as Peter (4:13) and Paul (13:46).

Luke describes Apollos as being "fervent in spirit" (18:25). The term "fervent" is rare (cf. only Rom 12:11), but conveys a sense of complete commitment to the task. The most common understanding of the phrase is to link it with being "filled with the Spirit" (see 4:8). In Ephesus, Apollos is taught further by Priscilla and Aquila (18:26); they appear to function as "sponsors" of Apollos. This is often interpreted as a corrective to, or expansion of, the inadequate understanding of the gospel which Apollos exhibits, on the basis that "he knew only the baptism of John" (v. 25). However, the baptism of John is the foundational element of apostleship (1:22; 10:37), so this still places Apollos within the movement rather than outside. Furthermore, the distinctive verb used to describe their instructional activity is striking (*exethento,* 18:26). This is the same word used of Peter's apologetic speech to the community leaders in Jerusalem (11:4) and of Paul's climactic apologetic effort among the Jewish leaders in Rome (28:23). It connotes a development, rather than a correction, of ideas.

Such "sponsorship" by a leader within the movement is not understood in such a pejorative way in other cases. Others assume a leadership role after being "sponsored" in like fashion. Matthias is chosen by lot by the eleven, with prayer (1:23-26); the seven are chosen by the multitude and the apostles, with the laying on of hands and prayer (6:1-6); after Saul's Damscus road epiphany, Ananias lays hands on him and baptizes him (9:10-19a); subsequently, Barnabas introduces Saul to the apostles in Jerusalem (9:27) and to the assembly in Antioch (11:25-26); both Barnabas and Saul are commissioned by the assembly in Antioch after being so instructed by the Holy Spirit, with fasting, prayer, and laying on of hands (13:1-3). Furthermore, Luke's portrayal of James indicates something of a "hierarchy" among the leaders since what he proposes (15:19-20) in the second Jerusalem council is adopted unchanged by the council (15:28-29), and when Paul returns to Jerusalem he reports directly to James (21:17-19). Neither of these incidents diminishes the authority of Paul in any way. (Cf. Gal 2:11-14, where Paul criticizes Peter, but not James, when Peter withdraws from eating with Gentiles under instructions from James.)

In addition, the description of Apollos evokes terms from Luke's preface (Luke 1:1-4). Apollos is "instructed" (18:25) in the same way that Theophilus is instructed (Luke 1:4); he provides "accurate teaching" (18:25) in the same way that Luke provides Theophilus with an account which is the fruit of accurate investigation (Luke 1:3). Apollos thus takes his place among the leaders whom Luke describes, those who carry out the divinely given task of teaching and proclaiming the good news. Indeed, as one who instructs with accuracy, even before he is further instructed by Priscilla and Aquila, Apollos stands in continuity with the task undertaken by Luke himself.

Apollos moves across to Achaia, with the support of members of the Ephesian assembly (18:27). The letter of recommendation he takes with him probably reflects a common Jewish practice (9:2; see also Rom 16:1-2; 2 Cor 3:1; Col 4:10; cf. 2 Cor 10:12, 18). In Achaia (i.e., Corinth — see 19:1), Apollos continues to speak in public (18:28), as was Paul's custom (20:20). His message, which "confounded the Jews" (18:28) as Paul's had earlier done (9:22), is the familiar assertion that "the Messiah, he is Jesus" (18:28; see 17:3). Apollos is thus placed firmly within the line of continuity stretching from the apostles, through Stephen, Philip, Paul, and his co-workers, each of whom exhibits similar characteristics and proclaims the same message.

After Apollos has been active in Corinth, Paul writes to the believers there and refers approvingly to Apollos as his fellow worker (1 Cor 3:5-9); together with Peter, they are "servants of Christ and stewards of the mysteries of God" (1 Cor 4:1). Paul is in no doubt about the important contribution that Apollos makes to the Corinthian community, although he is somewhat hesitant concerning the possibilities of a return visit by Apollos to Corinth (1 Cor 16:12).

The next episode reported in Ephesus takes place when Paul arrives there. The incident concerns **Paul and the twelve men (19:1-7)**, described as "disciples" (v. 1). They are thus to be regarded as already part of the messianic movement, "the Way." This brief account places "the baptism of John" and "receiving the Holy Spirit" in tension. The tension is resolved through the baptism of the men "in the name of the Lord Jesus" (v. 5). Throughout Acts, baptism is consistently "in the name of Jesus" (2:38; 8:16; 10:48). Apart from the references to "the baptism of John" (1:5, 22; 10:37; 11:16; 13:24; 18:25; 19:3-4), almost all the other occurrences of baptism in Acts which omit specific reference to the name of Jesus can legitimately be understood as being "in the name of Jesus." The Ethiopian (8:36) is baptized after learning that Jesus was the subject of the scripture citation (8:32-33). Saul is baptized after Jesus has been the agent active in the epiphanies to Saul (9:3-9) and to Ananias (9:10-16). The words of Ananias (22:16) refer to the baptism of Paul after his encounter with Jesus on the road to Damascus (9:18). The baptism of the Philippian jailer and his household (16:33) takes place in response to the exhortation to "Believe on the Lord Jesus" (16:31). The baptism of Crispus and his household (18:8) takes place after Paul preaches that "the Messiah, he is Jesus" (18:5). Only the baptism of Lydia and her household (16:15) has no explicit reference to Jesus in the immediate context.

Baptism is here accompanied by the laying on of hands (19:6), as in Samaria (8:15-16) but not elsewhere. The laying on of hands results in the Holy Spirit coming upon them (19:6), a link similar to that made in Samaria (8:15-17, 19) and Antioch (13:3-4). The gift of the Spirit leads both to speaking in tongues (19:7), as in Jerusalem (2:4) and Caesarea (10:45-46), and to prophecy (19:7), as predicted in Scripture (2:17-18; cf. 28:25). In Acts, baptism may come both prior to (2:38-42; 8:14-17) and after (10:44-48; 11:15-17) the gift of the Spirit; further, the gift of the Spirit is not necessarily linked with baptism (e.g., at 2:1-4 and 4:31). Yet, while the time sequence differs here from other patterns, the collation of similar elements implies strong continuity with events in Jerusalem, Samaria, and Caesarea.

After this singular event, Luke reports in general terms of **Paul's activities in Ephesus (19:8-12)**. The scenario is the familiar one of engagement in the synagogue (v. 8; see 13:5), where Paul "speaks frankly" (19:8; see 13:46). As is to be expected, Paul is both "disputing" (19:8; see 17:2, 17; 18:4, 19; also 20:7, 9; 24:12, where it is Paul's usual custom) and "persuading" (19:8; see 17:4; 18:4, 13; 19:26). His message is "the sovereignty of God" (19:8), the same as that spoken by Jesus (see 1:3). A division takes place (19:9; see 13:4-12), leading to the relocation of Paul's preaching in the hall of Tyrannus (19:9); the pattern replicates that which took place in Corinth (18:5-8). For two further years in Ephesus, Paul continues to make known "the word of the Lord" (19:10; see 13:47; 16:32; cf. "word of God," 18:11). That this became known by "*all* the residents of Asia" is surely a Lukan overstatement (see 9:35). Alongside this verbal activity, Luke notes that "God did miracles through the hands of Paul" (19:11), continuing to exercise the miraculous powers which God had given him (14:3; 15:12). Here he both heals diseases and casts out unclean spirits (19:12), as did the apostles (5:15-16; 9:33-34, 39-41) and Philip (8:7). Luke thus insures that his picture of Paul continues to be consistent with the apostolic picture both in word and in deed (see 2:43).

Paul's encounter with **the sons of Sceva (19:13-19)** follows hard on the heels of this general scene. These Jewish exorcists attempt to use "the name of the Lord Jesus" for their own purposes (vv. 13-14). The terminology used to describe their words and actions ("using the name," "I adjure you," "casting out," "overpowering") is that commonly associated with the practice of magic. The scene reflects the ongoing cosmic conflict between God, represented by Paul, and Satan, represented by the evil spirit (cf. Luke 4:1-13; 10:17-20; 11:14-26; 22:3-6, 31-32; Acts 8:9-25; 13:4-12; see Garrett 1989: 89-99). The exorcists fail in spectacular fashion when the evil spirit turns on them and chases them out of the house "naked and wounded" (19:15-16; cf. Luke 11:21-22). News of this becomes "known to all the residents of Ephesus, both Jews and Greeks" (v. 17), a likely exaggeration of the actual impact of their actions (cf. 9:35; 26:4). Their response of fear (19:17) is one of belief (see 2:43), as is confirmed by the additional comment that "the name of the Lord Jesus was exulted" (19:17; see 5:13). This process of having come into belief then leads to tangible expressions of repentance through public confession (19:18) and the burning of magical books (v. 19). The workings of the divine continue to be manifest while Paul is in Ephesus.

The first half of Luke's description of Paul's Ephesian sojourn ends with a brief summary (19:20) concerning the word of the Lord (see 19:10). The summary is strengthened by the insertion of the emphatic phrase, "according to might" (NRSV, "mightily"), which qualifies the formulaic comment that this word "increased and multiplied." This formula closed Section Two (12:24), and we might therefore also expect it to close Section Three. However, a new sequence of events will unfold before this section comes to an end, for immediately **Paul decides to visit Jerusalem and Rome (19:21-22)**. This decision has important geographical considerations. First of all, it will bring Paul back to Jerusalem, a move which is a consistent requirement in Luke's schema. (Paul himself describes his desire to return to Jerusalem at Rom 15:25-26, 31; 1 Cor 16:3; 2 Cor 1:16.) Second, it will open up opportunity for Paul to journey to Rome, which becomes the desired end point for Luke's narrative. (Paul indicates his intention to visit Rome in Rom 15:23-24, 28-29, 32.) This move is validated by two Lukan motifs. First, the spirit is involved in Paul's decision to return to Jerusalem (see also 20:22-23; 21:4, 10-11). Second, the journey to Rome will take place under divine impulse: "it is necessary for me to see Rome also" (see also 23:11; 26:32; 27:24; 28:19; Squires 1993: 174-77, 182-85). The dramatic tension which this decision introduces into the narrative is intensified by the long scene which follows (19:23–20:1). The underlying anticipation about Paul's ultimate fate, in obedience to the divine will, is exacerbated by the tensions in the incident which then ensues.

As Paul prepares for his return to Jerusalem, he sends on to Macedonia Timothy and Erastus, "servants" (19:22); the NRSV translation "helpers" downplays the significance of Gk. *diakonountōn,* the importance of which has already been indicated at 6:1-6. During his stay in Asia (i.e., Ephesus), Paul probably wrote the letter to Corinth which we know as 1 Corinthians (1 Cor 16:8). He twice refers in this letter to Timothy's visit to Corinth (1 Cor 4:17; 16:10).

The incident concerning Demetrius (19:23–20:1) is introduced as being "no little disturbance concerning the Way" (19:23) and concludes with reference to the potential that such a commotion had for becoming a riot (v. 40). If the climax of Paul's public speaking has been his earlier speech on the Areopagus (17:22-31), then this incident represents the culmination of his public activity of making converts. Curiously, although the narrative contains a dramatic portrayal of the events, Paul himself is absolutely silent throughout Luke's account; his one attempt to speak is blocked both by the disciples (19:30) and by some local authorities who were sympathetic (v. 31). Paul's public speaking appears to have come to an end; his point of view can be put forward only by others. The authorities who are "friendly with him" are described by Luke as Asiarchs; the term is also found in nonbiblical literature relating to Ephesus (Kearsley in Gill and Gempf 1994: 363-76). The favorable attitude of Roman officials toward Paul is a striking element throughout the latter section of Acts (21:31-35; 22:23-29; 23:17-35; 24:23; 27:1-3, 41-44; 28:16; see Esler 1987: 201-5).

The cult of Artemis thrived in Ephesus and exerted a major influence on the civic, economic, and cultural life of the city. The temple of Artemis was renowned for its splendor and size, being described on one inscription as "the ornament of the whole province" (Trebilco in Gill and Gempf 1994: 316-57). The manufacture of silver shrines of Artemis (19:24) sparks the central issue of Luke's report of this incident: whether "things made by hands" are indeed divine (19:26). It is the same issue which Paul raised in Athens (17:24, 29) and which caused Stephen to be martyred (7:48). What occurs in Ephesus thus crystallizes a current which has run underneath the public activities of Paul, his co-workers, and those of his predecessors who were active among the Gentiles. By having the silversmith Demetrius declare his concern at Paul's activities "not only in Ephesus but in almost all of Asia" (19:26), Luke presents this incident as programmatic for the whole of Paul's career. By linking the threat against Paul with the martyrdom of Stephen, Luke draws a common thread throughout the whole of his narrative. Proclaiming "the sovereignty of God" inevitably conflicts with established belief systems, be they Gentile or Jewish — as well as, of course, with the economic and social systems which are structured around the public expressions of those belief systems (see vv. 24-27).

Alexander initially tries, unsuccessfully, to defend Paul (19:33-34). A defense is then attempted by the town clerk (vv. 35-40), although he offers no theological rationale as Paul has done previously (see 14:15-17) and as he would subsequently provide before various officials (22:17-21; 24:14-18; 26:16-18). The town clerk defends those of "the Way" as being "neither temple robbers nor blasphemers of our goddess" (19:37), but naturally provides no further apologetic assertion about the beliefs which have generated such anxiety among the populace. However, the basis for Paul's defense would be evident to the reader of Acts, both from Paul's previous speeches (chs. 13–17) and his subsequent apologies (chs. 22–26). The parting comment, that the charges against Paul properly belong in the courts (19:38), provides a glimpse of impending events (21:27 onward). This insures a clear understanding that the threat inherent in Paul's activities relates not to the state as such, but to a particular religious perspective — a point which will subsequently be repeated by Roman officials.

Paul thus leaves Ephesus in safety, engaging in his familiar activity of "exhorting" (NRSV, "encouraging") the disciples (20:1; see 13:15) before he bid farewell to them.

Troas, Miletus, and Caesarea (20:2–21:16)

In the final part of this section, Paul's public activity is barely in view; Luke gives mere glimpses of Paul's participation in selected messianic assemblies during his **further travels (20:1-6)**. After leaving Ephesus, Paul first travels through Macedonia (vv. 1-2a); while here he may have written another letter to the Corinthian assembly (2 Cor 2:12-13; 7:5). Once more Luke is silent about Paul's letter writing, preferring to focus on Paul's immediate activity as he "exhorted" the Macedonian believers (20:2; see 13:15). Paul then moves to Greece, where he stays for three months (20:2-3); he may have visited the Corinthians for the third time at this stage (2 Cor 13:1). During this period, many commentators believe, Paul wrote his famous letter to the Romans; once more Luke is silent about such matters. Similarly, Luke omits any reference to the collection which, in his own letters, Paul notes that he has marshaled for his return to Jerusalem at this time (Rom 15:25-26, 31; 1 Cor 16:3). Luke has dealt with this matter much earlier in his narrative and with much less fanfare than Paul does (see 11:29-30), although a brief reference later (24:17) appears to corroborate the statements in Paul's own letters.

More significant for Luke is the fact that in Greece Paul encounters a plot by some Jews. This is not a new experience for Paul; he had once faced such a plot in Jerusalem (9:24) and would soon face it again on his return there (23:30, referring to 23:12-14). This plot means that he must travel a different way to Troas (20:4-6). The return to Troas at this point sees the narrative resume the first person plural of the so-called "we sections" of Acts (20:5-15; 21:1-18; 27:1–28:16). Tannehill remarks that the use of the "we" narrator from 20:5 to 21:18 provides "a special opportunity for us and others to enter the narrative as participants and to see ourselves as companions of Paul as he prepares the churches for his absence and resolutely approaches the danger in Jerusalem" (Tannehill 1990: 247).

In Troas (20:7-12), Paul participates in typical fashion in an assembly meeting, for he was "arguing" (NRSV, "holding a discussion") with them (20:7; see 17:2). "Those who had gathered on the first of the sabbaths" refers, in this instance, not to a synagogue meeting (as would be expected), but to the believers, since they meet to "break bread," the first reference to such a practice since Jerusalem (2:42, 46). The subsequent comment that Paul broke the bread (20:11) infers that it was a common practice for Paul (see also 27:35). This scene in Troas provides opportunity for Luke to recount Paul's ability to bring a person back from the dead (20:8-12), thus placing him in continuity with others who had performed a similar miracle: Peter (9:36-42) and Jesus (Luke 7:11-17). That it is God who enables such miraculous power is explicit in the account of Jesus' miracle (Luke 7:16); this understanding is thus implicit in the Troas narrative. Furthermore, 20:9-12 is to be interpreted by the comments on Paul's miracles at 14:3, 15:12, and 19:11, in which the divine empowering of such miracles is made explicit.

Whereas those two earlier resuscitations had brought forth a response of belief and then widespread knowledge (Luke 7:16-17; 9:42), this resuscitation takes place among believers, drawing forth the rather understated Lukan comment, "they were not a little comforted" (20:12). Rather than telling how the news spread throughout Troas, Luke has another point in mind. Swiftly he recounts how Paul journeys eventually to Miletus (vv. 13-15), skirting around Ephesus so as to leave good time to reach the goal which has now come back into focus: that of Jerusalem (v. 16).

What takes place in **Miletus (20:15-35)** is, in effect, a surrogate leave-taking by Paul of the assembly in Ephesus, which was about fifty kilometers from Miletus. Once he has summoned the elders of the assembly from Ephesus (v. 17), the scene is set for **Paul's farewell speech (vv. 18-35)**. This speech is of a different character from the predominantly "missionary" speeches which have been recounted from Jerusalem (2:14-41) to Athens (17:22-31). Luke has reported these speeches so as to provide models for those who would become witnesses of Jesus (1:8). In Paul's farewell speech, Luke has Paul present a full picture of the lifestyle required of such witnesses. The speech recapitulates Paul's activities in a thematic manner, ending with the explicit statement of its exemplary function: "I have shown everything to you" (20:35). Structurally, the speech contains an introduction (vv. 18b-21), followed by three sections each introduced by the phrase "and now": Paul's journey to Jerusalem (vv. 22-24), his commissioning of the elders (vv. 25-31), and his personal example to the elders (vv. 32-35).

While Paul's speech on the Areopagus stands as the climax of his public message concerning divine providence (indeed, it brings to a climax all the public speeches from Pentecost onward), this speech to the Ephesian elders encapsulates a broad overview of Paul's work in public as a free person. Many elements in the speech reflect the Hellenistic picture of the ideal philosopher, who holds his own life to be of little value (20:24; Xenophon *Apol.* 5; Plato *Apol.* 28E-30B; Epictetus *Diss.* 3.22.21-26), lists the hardships he has experienced (20:19; Plato *Apol.* 21E, 23A, 28A; Epictetus *Diss.* 3.22.45-51, 100-104), is concerned to benefit his listeners (20:20, 27; Dio Chrysostom *Or.* 32.5, 10), teaches in public and in private (20:20, 31; Epictetus *Diss.* 3.23.33-34; Dio Chrysostom *Or.* 77/78.38, 42), completes the task which he has received from God (20:24; Epictetus *Diss.* 3.22.23), is explicit about not desiring money (20:33; Plato *Apol.* 19E; 31B; Xenophon *Apol.* 16; Lucian *Nigrinus* 25-26; Dio Chrysostom *Or.* 32.10; 77/78.37), and exhorts his students to help the needy (20:35; Lucian *Nigrinus* 26; *Demonax* 8, 63). This list suggests that Luke is consciously modeling Paul, at the end of his public activity, in the pattern of highly regarded philosophical teachers.

Furthermore, as the speech summarizes Paul's public activity, it also looks to the end of his life. The genre of the speech is firmly in the style of farewell speeches which are found in Jewish literature: Genesis 49 (Jacob), Deuteronomy as a whole, but esp. chs. 30–33 (Moses), Joshua 23–24 (Joshua), 1 Samuel 12 (Samuel), 1 Kings 2 (David), 1 Chronicles 28–29 (Solomon); see also Tobit 14 (Tobit), *Jubilees* 21–22 (Abraham), and *Assumption of Moses* (Moses). In the NT, see also John 14–16(17) and Luke 22 for two different "farewell speeches" by Jesus; 2 Timothy and 2 Peter may be regarded as "last testaments" in epistolary form. In such a speech, the person who is facing imminent death surveys his life and teachings and provides a "last testament" for his followers. Paul's speech is certainly located in such a setting, and it contains an overall summary of the activities that he has been engaged in throughout Acts 9 and 13–20.

Paul uses a number of familiar Lukan terms to describe his activities, beginning with "service" (20:24; NRSV, "ministry"), a term which has already been applied to the apostles (1:17, 25, 6:4) and the seven (6:1-4). It is clearly broader in scope than when used to refer to the collection which Paul and Barnabas brought to Jerusalem (11:29; 12:25); here, as at 21:19, it describes the whole of Paul's activities and so links him with Jesus and his vision of service (Luke 22:26-27). This "service" has led Paul to engage in his public speaking, which he describes by various terms. He has taught (20:20; see 18:11), as did the apostles (see 2:42), and preached (20:25; see 9:22; 19:13; 28:31), as did Philip (8:5) and Peter (10:42). He has testified (20:21, 24, 26; see 18:5; 23:11; 28:31), as did Peter (2:40; 10:42; and see 4:33) and Philip (8:25), in fulfillment of the words of Jesus (1:8); and he has announced (20:20, 27; see also 14:27; 15:4; 19:18). Paul's message has comprised "repentance" (20:21), as the apostles taught (see 2:38), "faith" (20:21), as taught by Peter (3:16) and evoked by Philip (8:12, 13), Peter (9:42), and the unnamed preachers in Antioch (11:21); and "sovereignty" (20:25), a familiar Lukan description of the message, not only of Paul (14:22; 19:8; 28:23, 31) but also of Jesus (see 1:3) and Philip (8:12).

The speech also contains the verb "admonish" as a description of Paul's activity (20:31). The term was often used in pagan literature to describe the activity of the philosophers. This is the only time it appears in Acts; however, Paul uses the term in his own letters (Rom 15:14; 1 Cor 4:14; 1 Thess 5:12, 14; see also Col 1:28, 3:16; 2 Thess 3:15). There are many other points at which the speech touches the language and ideas which are found in the authentic Pauline letters, such as reference to "repentance" (Rom 2:4; 2 Cor 7:9-10), "turning to God" (1 Thess 1:9), "the good news of God's grace" (Rom 1:1, 9; 1 Thess 1:5), "the kingdom" (1 Cor 4:20; 6:9-10; Gal 5:21; 1 Thess 2:12), "building up" (1 Cor 14:3-5, 26; 2 Cor 12:19; 13:10; 1 Thess 5:11), and "the inheritance" (Rom 8:17; Gal 3:29; 5:21) of "those who are sanctified" (Rom 15:16; 1 Cor 1:2; 6:11).

Paul states that he performed these tasks in public (20:20) and from house to house (v. 20); both aspects were part of the pattern of the apostles (see 2:46). The inclusive nature of his activities is emphasized in his comment that he testified "both to Jews and to Greeks" (20:21); this has been borne out in the reports of Acts 13–20 (see esp. 14:1; 17:4, 12; 19:17).

In addition to such speaking, Paul refers to his "work" (20:35) and notes that "these hands served my needs and [the needs of] those who were with me" (v. 34). This recalls mention of Paul's trade as a tentmaker (18:3); it is a theme which Paul notes in his own letters (1 Cor 4:12; 1 Thess 2:9; 4:11; and see 1 Cor 9:3-7, 15-18). The context for Paul's activity has often been stressful in those scenes narrated by Luke, in fulfillment of the commission Paul received to "suffer many things" (9:16). The Lukan Paul alludes to this with his reference to tears (20:19, 31), trials (20:19), and the plots of the Jews (20:19; see 20:3). Paul also refers to such trials in his own letters (1 Cor 4:9-13; 2 Cor 4:8-12; 6:4-10; 11:23-29). Thus the manner of Paul's activity as well as the context in which he carried it out is depicted in this speech in such a way as to summarize the incidents which Luke has already reported. In bidding the Ephesian elders farewell, Paul distills the essence of his service throughout Asia Minor and around the Aegean Sea.

As is to be expected, the speech contains a significant amount of language about God. Paul is now able to declare that he has "announced the whole plan of God" (20:27); the comprehensive claim inherent in the adjective "whole" is made only here. The phrase "the plan of God" has not previously been used in reference to the content of Paul's speeches, but it is a most suitable Lukan way to summarize Paul's message and to place him in continuity with the earlier messages of Peter (2:23; 13:36), the sympathetic Pharisee, Gamaliel (5:38), and the Jerusalem assembly (4:28) (Squires 1993: 75-76). The plan of God appears to be equivalent to the message of sovereignty (20:25) which Paul has been preaching. His message also entails the familiar Lukan concepts of "repentance toward God" (20:21; see 2:38), "faith in our Lord Jesus" (20:21; on faith, see 2:44; 5:14), and "the good news of the grace of God" (20:24; on grace, see 2:47). Paul's message has been consistent with the Lukan program throughout Acts.

A further element of language about God which is found in the speech is the reference to the Spirit. That Paul's activities have taken place under the guidance of the Spirit has been clear from Luke's narrative, especially from 13:2, 4 onward. In this speech, Luke has Paul affirm that in what yet lies ahead of him, he will be guided by the Spirit. Thus, he states that as he goes to Jerusalem (20:22; see 19:21) he is "bound in the Spirit" (20:22; cf. 21:11-14); his natural anxiety about what might take place there is echoed at Rom 15:31. Paul affirms that "the Holy Spirit testifies to me" what is awaiting, not only in Jerusalem but in every city (20:23); his prophetic qualities are in evidence at this point in the speech (Squires 1993: 151-53). That "imprisonments and persecutions" await him in each city can only intensify his reliance on divine help.

That the Spirit will continue to be active among the Ephesians beyond Paul's departure is then noted in the reference to the "overseers . . . whom the Holy Spirit placed to shepherd the assembly of God" (20:28). Some of the language in this verse is notably rare in Lukan usage. Apart from its use in the story of the shepherds in Luke 2, the word "flock" occurs only in the parable at Luke 17:7; in Paul, only at 1 Cor 9:7; cf. Eph 4:11. "Overseers" is used only here by Luke and only once by Paul (Phil 1:1; cf. 1 Tim 3:2; Tit 1:7). The assembly is never called "the assembly *of God*" by Luke; in Paul, see 1 Cor 1:2; 10:32; 11:16, 22; 15:9; 2 Cor 1:1; Gal 1:13; 1 Thess 2:14; 2 Thess 1:4. The verb "place" is Lukan (Luke 17 times, Acts 23 times) and Pauline (13 times; and 3 times in the Pastorals). The reference to "the blood of his own Son" is traditional material known to Paul (Rom 3:25; 5:9; 1 Cor 10:16; 11:25) as well as Luke (Luke 22:20). The clause "which he obtained" is non-Lukan (only 20:28 in Acts) and reflects a post-Pauline situation (Eph 1:14; 1 Tim 3:13). Although the points of contact with the letters of Paul are strong in this speech, it is most likely that Luke's composition of the speech has been influenced by factors subsequent to the historical ministry of Paul.

The fourth section of the speech (20:32-35) includes the benedictory words, "I commend you to God and to the word of his grace" (v. 32). As the speech draws to a close, it thus shows full awareness of the broad scope of divine providence which is the ultimate context within which Paul (like all the leaders in Acts) has operated.

The **closing scene in Miletus (20:36-38)** provides an explicit interpretive comment from outside the narrative, with the note that emotions ran high because "they were about to see his face no longer" (v. 38). The "farewell" nature of the speech is thus made perfectly clear and explicit. It is fitting for Luke that Paul's public ministry closes, as it had begun, with prayer as well as physical touch (vv. 36-37; 13:3). That Paul would continue to be guided by the Spirit who commissioned him (13:2-3) has been apparent beforehand (16:6-7, and most recently at 19:21) and is affirmed, in general terms, by Paul himself (20:22-23). Yet detailed knowledge of this guidance by the Spirit still needs to be worked out in the next scene, before Paul returns to Jerusalem.

The long and detailed description of the activities of Paul and his co-workers in Asia Minor (13:1–14:28) and around the Aegean Sea (15:36–19:41) comes to a close with another travel narrative which takes Paul **back to Caesarea (21:1-14)** in two short trips. The "we narrative" resumes for these trips. Interwoven amid the straightforward notes of the itinerary are two significant incidents which concern the leading of the Spirit, an issue raised by Paul in his farewell speech (20:22-23). The function of the account of these two trips is thus to focus on whether Paul ought, in fact, to journey back to Jerusalem.

The first trip calls at, or passes by, various ports (21:1-4) before arrival in Tyre (vv. 4-7), an important port town in Phoenicia, the coastal region of Syria. The travelers meet disciples there and receive, not confirmation of their destination, but a warning "not to go up into Jerusalem" (v. 4). Were it not for the affirmation that these words came "through the Spirit" (v. 4), it would be easy to dismiss this warning. Nevertheless, Paul has already signaled that he undertakes this journey under the impulse of the Spirit (19:21; 20:22). The resolution of this tension is delayed until Caesarea (21:8-14). Though brief, this visit ends in a scene reminiscent of the highly charged emotions in Miletus (20:36-38), with prayer (21:5; 20:36), a common occurrence in the messianic assemblies (see 2:42), and farewells (20:38; 21:6). Paul's imminent fate strongly colors the account.

In the second short trip (21:7-18), departure from Tyre takes the travelers on land to the assembly at Ptolemais (v. 7) and then to **Caesarea (vv. 8-14).** The matter of divine guidance through inspired prophecy remains uppermost in Luke's mind as he reports Paul's stay in Caesarea with Philip, described here as "the evangelist" (cf. the use of the cognate verb at 8:4, 12, 25, 35, 40), "one of the seven," along with his "four virgin daughters who prophesy" (21:9; on women prophets in Luke-Acts, see Seim 1994: 164-84). However, they provide no clues as to his fate; rather, it is the visiting prophet Agabus from Judea (last encountered in 11:28) who activates his prophetic capacities to predict what lies in store for Paul. Agabus uses a prophetic gesture with Paul's belt to undergird his prediction of Paul's fate: "In Jerusalem, the Jews will bind you like this and hand you over to the Gentiles" (21:11).

The Holy Spirit has already inspired a message to Paul "not to go up to Jerusalem" (21:4). That the prediction by Agabus is genuine (despite its apparent difference from the warning at v. 4) is assured in three ways. First of all, Agabus, who speaks it, is known as a prophet (v. 10); his earlier prophecy concerning the famine has been proven true (11:28). Second, Paul accepts the prediction as being in accord with "the will of the Lord" (21:14). The fate which Agabus describes for Paul resonates strongly with the commission Paul was given in Damascus, that "he must suffer for the sake of my name" (9:16) — indeed, Paul is prepared to go beyond this "even to die in Jerusalem for the sake of the name of the Lord Jesus" (21:13). Third, therefore, the claim that the prophecy is given by the Holy Spirit (v. 11) is trustworthy. The message spoken by Agabus actually refrains from insisting that Paul go to Jerusalem; it simply identifies what will happen when he next is there. The prophetic status of Agabus is not in doubt; his prophecy is complementary with the warning Paul received in Tyre (v. 4). Paul determines his course of action in the light of these Spirit-led prophecies. The narrative refutes the notion that divine necessity leaves absolutely no room for human decision-making (Squires 1993: 177-85) and provides a Lukan caution against accepting every word of the Spirit as "genuine."

This scene in Caesarea — and this whole section of Acts — ends with a concise statement on the lips of Paul: "Let the will of the Lord be done" (21:14). Such a prayer is consistent with Paul's earlier acceptance of the divine will in Ephesus (18:21). The same idea is found in a range of literature, both Hellenistic (Epictetus *Diss.* 1.1.17; 3.21.22) and Jewish (1QS 11:10-11) and in Paul's letters (Rom 1:10; 1 Cor 4:19; 16:7). However, as Paul's own arrest is imminent (21:33), Luke probably intends Paul's prayer to be reminiscent of Jesus' prayer of obedience immediately prior to his arrest (Luke 22:42). This statement both summarizes the way that God has guided events that have taken place since Barnabas and Paul left Antioch (13:1-3) and foreshadows the continuation of divine guidance of events which will lead Paul to Rome (28:14b-16). Paul then returns to Jerusalem in the company of a number of disciples (21:15-16). Thus, his last journey as a free person brings Paul back to the center of the expanding network of messianic assemblies in Jerusalem and situates him in the right place for traveling, albeit as a prisoner, to the very center of the Roman Empire.

Section Four: Faithfulness amid Trials (21:17–28:31)

The final section of Acts (21:17–28:31) narrates the arrest and trials of Paul. The geographical arrangement of this section takes in Paul's movements from Jerusalem (21:17–23:22), through Caesarea (23:23–26:32), and on a sea journey (27:1–28:15) which leads ultimately to Rome (28:16-31).

In two ways the focus of the final section of Acts is different from what has preceded. Previous sections have been oriented toward Jerusalem. Now, however, attention shifts to Rome. Within a short time of his arrest, it becomes clear that Paul is a Roman citizen, who therefore has the right to be brought before Caesar (22:25-29). The journey which Paul undertakes to Rome is thus both understandable in political terms (25:9-12; 26:30-32) and interpreted theologically as being firmly set within the overall purpose of God (19:21; 21:14; 23:11; 27:24).

The focus in this section also moves away from that of the earlier narratives, which have reported both the establishment of numerous messianic communities and the leadership which they received from various individuals. Now attention rests solely on the fate of one individual; only Paul is in view throughout the section. In his deeds and words as a prisoner, Paul models what it means to be faithful to the charge which God gave him in Damascus, when he became a leader among the messianic communities. True leadership means not only to be "a chosen instrument to bear my name" (9:15) but also "to suffer on account of my name" (9:16). This final section of Acts narrates the outworking of this model of faithful leadership, as Paul bears faithful testimony amid his trials.

However, neither of these elements is new to the narrative; earlier chapters have told of the vigorous public witness of a number of individuals, as well as the opposition and persecution encountered by members of a number of messianic communities. The picture of Paul which is given in the final section is consistent with the portrayal of these earlier figures, who bear witness to God and endure suffering on account of their testimony.

The section begins and ends with references to God. The previous section has concluded with a direct affirmation that the divine will is at work in events still to come, as Paul leaves for Jerusalem, declaring, "Let the will of the Lord be done" (21:14). This final section begins with a retrospective summation of preceding events as "what God did among the Gentiles through his ministry" (v. 19). After his arrest, Paul's slow but inevitable progress to Rome takes place under divine guidance (23:11; 27:23-24). Upon arrival in Rome, even though he is still a prisoner and his fate is not certain, Paul "gives thanks to God" (28:15). The final scene of Acts ends with further acknowledgments of God's role, as Paul refers to "the salvation of God" (28:28) and "the sovereignty of God" (28:31). The sequence of events in this section is thus framed by indications that what takes place is in accord with the divine plan.

The narrative recounts Paul's arrest (21:27-39) and details his subsequent appearances before various audiences: the Jerusalem crowd (21:40–22:29), the Sanhedrin (22:30–23:11), the chief priest Ananias (24:1-23), governors Felix (24:24-26) and Festus (25:6-12), and Governor Festus with King Agrippa (25:13–26:32). The hearings before the Jerusalem authorities and before Festus and Agrippa are reported at greater length. Each time Luke takes the opportunity to have Paul recount his divine commission and validate his subsequent missionary activities. In the speeches he makes in these two places, as well as in other scenes, the Lukan Paul often has recourse to language about God. Paul emphasizes that he serves God (24:14) and hopes in God (24:15; 26:6). His commission was instigated by God (22:14; 26:16), and his activity among the Gentiles has been in accord with God's will (22:21; 26:17-18). In all of this, Paul affirms, he has had "the help which comes from God" (26:22).

Previous speeches by Paul have been predominantly missionary proclamation (13:16-41; 14:14-17; 17:22-31; more briefly, 9:20, 22; 17:3; 18:4). This final cycle of Paul's speeches is set within a very different context; Paul defends himself against charges in a judicial setting. Despite this different context, these speeches continue the function of interpreting events with reference to the divine will. In this section of Acts, language about God specifically undergirds the apologetic function of Paul's speeches. Language about God thus continues to play an important role in this final section of Acts.

Jerusalem (21:17–23:22)

In the scenes set in Jerusalem, Paul meets with leaders of the Jerusalem assembly before being arrested and taken before the Jewish people and the Jewish leaders.

Paul meets with James and the elders (21:17-26) on his arrival in Jerusalem. James is clearly the leader of the community (v. 18), as the earlier reference to "James and the believers" (12:17) had hinted and James's leading role at the council in Jerusalem (15:13-21) had clearly demonstrated (Jervell 1972: 185-207). This scene both reviews Paul's activities up to this point and prepares for events which will soon take place. Paul's activities in Asia Minor, around the Aegean Sea, and in Ephesus are summarized as being "what God did among the Gentiles through his ministry" (21:19, recalling 14:27; 15:4, 12). That God was guiding Paul is confirmed by the response of those who listen to Paul: "they glorified God" (21:20). The same response indicated that God was at work in events in Caesarea (11:18) and Pisidian Antioch (13:48), as it had in the Gospel (Luke 2:20; 4:15; 5:25-26; 7:16; 13:17; 18:43; 19:38). However, events will soon overtake Paul, as a charge has been leveled against him by Jewish believers (21:21). James proposes a means for defending Paul against this charge (21:22-24) which will supplement the already circulated letter to Gentile believers (v. 25). The ritual for which Paul prepares himself (v. 24) is based on the Nazirite vow of Num 6:1-21. Accordingly, Paul enters the temple to carry out a week-long purification ritual (21:26).

Toward the end of this week, Paul encounters renewed Jewish opposition. The scene reporting **the arrest of Paul (21:27-39)** looks both backward, to Paul's earlier experiences, and forward, to what lies in store for Paul. First, this scene aligns Paul's experience with earlier instances of opposition. Jews from Asia had previously opposed Stephen (6:9); Paul had experienced opposition from Jews throughout Asia (20:18-19). Once more they act against Paul (21:27), "laying hands on him" (21:27); the same phrase describes the experience of Jesus (2:23), Peter and John (4:3; 5:18), and James (12:1). The accusations they bring against Paul ("teaching against the people and the law and this place," 21:28) recall the charges laid against him in Corinth ("persuading people to worship God against the law," 18:13) and against Stephen in Jerusalem ("speaking words against this holy place and the law," 6:13). The alleged presence of Greeks in the temple heightens the charge (21:28-29). These charges will run throughout the ensuing narrative and cause Paul to develop an intricate set of defense speeches to rebut them. God will play a prominent role in these speeches.

Most immediately, however, Paul is seized and dragged by the crowd (21:30), evoking earlier scenes where he was seized and dragged before local authorities (Philippi, 16:19; Athens, 17:19; cf. the use of *epilambanō* at 8:3; 14:19; 17:6). The crowd intends to kill him (21:31), just as Jesus (3:15) and the prophets (7:52) were killed. However, the tribune intervenes and has Paul arrested and chained (21:33). Although being bound in chains and imprisoned was publicly dishonoring (Rapske 1994: 283-98), in Luke's account this arrest begins a remarkable sequence of Roman protection for Paul (see also 22:23-29; 23:17-35; 24:23; 27:1-3, 41-44; 28:16). In contrast to Jesus, who was crucified under Roman rule (Luke 23:1-25, 36-38, 47), Paul represents a new phase in relations with the authorities. Luke's depiction of Paul's positive relations with Rome encourages his readers to model themselves on Paul rather than to adopt the political model seen in the crucifixion story. Their faith is not antagonistic to good citizenship in the Roman Empire (Esler 1987: 205-11).

The second function of this scene is to point forward to what is in store for Paul. The tribune wishes to "know something certain" about Paul (21:34). This concern is repeated by the tribune in his actions after Paul's speech (22:24, 30; 23:28), and subsequently by Governor Festus when he has Paul brought before King Agrippa (25:26). These inquiries echo the fundamental purpose of the author of Luke-Acts, who undertakes his work so that Theophilus might "know the certainty" of what he writes (Luke 1:4). The speeches which Paul is able to deliver on these occasions (21:40–22:29; 24:10-21; 26:1-29) thus provide a sure basis for understanding his activities, in accord with Luke's overall apologetic purpose.

The tribune prepares to move the hearing inside (21:34) because of the threatening scene that is developing (vv. 34-36). His intention appears to be to enable a formal hearing to take place under Roman jurisdiction; Paul, however, subverts this aim. Later in the narrative, the proper execution of Roman justice will play a central role. For the moment, Paul simply asserts his Jewish credentials: "I am a Jewish man" (v. 39), thereby setting the main theme for his defense strategy (Jervell 1972: 153-83). He makes a petition that he might speak to the people (v. 39), as a result of which he is granted a public forum (22:1-2). By contrast, Paul's subsequent speeches will take place in private before Felix (24:10), Festus (25:8), and Agrippa, Berenice, and Festus (26:1-2, 24).

Paul addresses the crowd (21:40–22:29) in a speech which contains the characteristic features of a forensic speech (on this aspect of Paul's speeches in Acts 22–26, see Veltman in Talbert 1978: 243-56; Neyrey in Talbert 1984: 210-24). The introduction specifies the nature of the speech as an "apology" (22:1). The body of the speech identifies the defendant in such a way that he defends himself against the charges identified in 21:28. Far from "teaching against the people," he is one of them (22:3-5); far from "teaching against the law," he has been commissioned by the one who first gave the law (vv. 6-16); and far from "teaching against this place," he was in fact praying in the temple itself when he was seized (vv. 17-21). The speech ends with the delivery of a verdict. It is not the favorable verdict expected from the tribune, but a verdict of condemnation, announced in dramatic style (vv. 22-23) by the very people to whom Paul had requested that he might speak. However, when he is then brought inside for further examination (v. 24), Paul invokes his Roman citizenship (vv. 25-28) and thus insures that proper justice will be accorded him (v. 29). The scene closes indicating that further investigations will be required and further speeches must be made.

Language about God is an important aspect of the apologetic dimension of this speech, as also of Paul's subsequent apologies. In the first section of the speech, when he sets forth his Jewish credentials, Paul defines himself as "zealous for God" (22:3). Here he seeks to identify himself with his audience, emphasizing their common bond: "brought up *in this city* . . . educated according to the strict manner of the law of *our ancestors* . . . zealous for God *as you all are*" (v. 3). This identification is repeated in the subsequent reference to "the God of our ancestors" (v. 14); it is an ascription used earlier by Peter (3:13; 5:30) and Stephen (7:32). Such language about God is central to Paul's defense against the first charge, that he was "teaching against the people" (21:28). It continues to be central to Paul's self-identification in subsequent apologies, as one who "lives before God in all good conscience" (23:1; 24:16), "worships the God of our ancestors" (24:14), "has a hope in God" (24:15; 26:6), and "has had the help that comes from God" (26:22). Luke is consistent in having Paul define himself with reference to God, whether speaking to Jews or to Gentiles.

In the second section of the speech, Paul defends himself against the charge that he was "teaching against the law" (21:28) by recounting his encounter with the divine author of that law. The details of this encounter have already been recorded in the third person narrative (9:3-18). It is to carry out his apologetic purposes, not in order to provide autobiographical information, that Luke now has Paul speak directly of this experience for the first time (22:6-16). This section culminates with the commission of Paul which Ananias conveyed to him (vv. 14-16). In detailing this commission, Paul begins now to define himself in distinction from his audience. Here again language about God functions to define and validate Paul's role. He declares that God "appointed" him (v. 14), using language which previously in Acts has been reserved for Jesus (3:20; note similar terms at 10:42; 17:31). Paul is to "know God's will" (22:14), as did David (13:22). He is to see "the righteous one" (22:14), that is, Jesus (3:14; 7:52), as did Stephen (7:55), and to "hear a voice from [God's] mouth" (22:14), as did Peter (10:13-15). Indeed, this seeing and hearing has taken place on the road to Damascus, when Paul both sees a heavenly light (9:3; 22:6; 26:13) and hears God's voice (9:4-6; 22:7-8; 26:14-15). Through this epiphany Paul is now to undertake the task of being a witness (22:15; 23:11; 26:16), a task already given to the prophets (10:43), the apostles (1:22; 2:32; 3:15; 5:32; 10:39, 41; 13:31), Peter (15:7), and Stephen (22:20). These terms align Paul with key leaders — Peter, John, Stephen — as well as with Jesus, David, and the prophets, each of whom had an especially intensified relationship with God (Bolt in Marshall and Peterson 1998: 191-210). Paul is representative of the kind of person who obeys the divine calling to bear witness to God's actions.

Paul is to bear witness to "what you have seen and heard" (22:15), pointing to his encounter with the divine on the road to Damascus. The content of this witness is precisely the same as that given by Peter and John in Jerusalem: "we cannot keep from speaking of what we saw and heard" (4:20). Their witness reaches back to the earlier manifestation of God at Pentecost: "this which you both see and hear" (2:33). Epiphanies thus validate Paul's witness, as they validated the witness of Peter and John. The audience of Paul's witness is expressed as "all people" (22:15), a generalizing summation of his audience which avoids pressing home the offense of proclamation to the Gentiles as well as to "the sons of Israel" (9:15; 26:17, 20).

However, rather than recounting his immediate obedience to this charge, as he will do in Caesarea (26:19-20), Paul now turns to the third charge against him: that he was "teaching against this place" (21:28). He recounts how he was "praying in the temple" (22:17) when he received direct guidance from God (v. 18). Paul cannot therefore be accused of speaking against the temple when he was at prayer within it — and when he encountered God in its very midst. The effect of this further encounter with the divine is to strengthen the legitimation of Paul's commission to go to the Gentiles, for it is now given directly from God in the temple: "I will send you far away to the Gentiles" (22:21). The activities he has undertaken have been in obedience to this divine charge.

At this point uproar breaks out among the Jewish crowd, and they render their verdict (22:22-23). Despite the divine validation of Paul which he has presented, they are unanimous: death is necessary. This is underlined in three ways. The crowd shouts against Paul, as crowds had shouted against Stephen (7:57). They tear their garments, turning back onto Paul an action he had carried out in Lystra (14:14) and Corinth (18:6). They throw dust, akin to the actions of Paul and Barnabas in

Pisidian Antioch (13:51). Cumulatively, these actions reveal their antagonism to Paul. Because of this threat, the tribune reclaims Paul into the direct control of the Roman state (22:24). The actions of the respective Jews and Gentiles thus strengthen the validity of the divine call which Paul has received: he is to bear witness to "all people" (v. 15), but Jews in Jerusalem will oppose him (v. 18) while Gentiles far away will be a sympathetic audience (v. 21).

In contrast to the Jewish crowd with their unreasonable reaction, the Gentile centurion accords Paul the full rights due to him when it is revealed that he is a Roman citizen (22:25-29; cf. 16:37-38). Paul's claim that "I was born a citizen" (22:28) is historically possible; Josephus cites a decree which refers to "Jews who are Roman citizens" in Ephesus (*Ant.* 14 §228). Paul may have had a forebear who was manumitted from slavery. However, the Lukan Paul overstretches himself by making three claims about himself (that he was a citizen of Tarsus, 21:39; a Roman citizen, 22:28; and a Pharisee, 23:6) which together are rather improbable. It is likely that Luke's intention was not to make historically verifiable claims but to have Paul present himself as a person of high social status (Lentz 1993: 23-61) and thus of impeccable moral virtue (Lentz 1993: 62-104). (A contrary view is argued in Rapske 1994: 71-112.)

The centurion seeks further understanding of the situation by placing **Paul before the Jewish council (22:30–23:11)**. Paul thus follows in the footsteps of those who have been arraigned before the council in Jerusalem: Stephen (6:12–7:57), Peter and John (4:5-23; 5:21, 27-41), and Jesus before them (Luke 22:66-71). Language about God continues to play an important role in Paul's encounter with the council. Paul reiterates his good standing before God (23:1). Acting in a prophetic mode, he invokes God's judgment on the high priest (v. 3) before judiciously backing down, citing Scripture (vv. 4-5). Then Paul craftily divides the council by invoking his traditional Pharisaic belief in the resurrection (vv. 6-7); the same division on this issue had marked Jesus' final visit to the temple (Luke 20:27-38).

The scene before the Sanhedrin ends in chaos and further Roman intervention (23:10). However, the narrative climax comes in the ensuing epiphany to Paul in which the Lord exhorts Paul to "take courage" (v. 11). The epiphany reveals that the events which have taken place in Jerusalem come under the umbrella of divine providence, just as what will ensue in Caesarea and Rome will be guided by God (Rapske 1994: 393-422). Paul functions as a divinely commissioned witness in both Jerusalem and Rome. Such epiphanies have appeared at many points earlier in the narrative (see 5:20); they have performed the specific function of consoling Peter in Jerusalem (5:19-20, with John; 12:7-17) and Paul in Corinth (18:9-10) (Squires 1993: 116-20).

The tribune's withdrawal of Paul from the council leads to a resurgence of **the threat against Paul (23:12-22)**. The Jews opposed to Paul strengthen their resolve by making a plot (v. 12). Paul has already experienced Jewish opposition acting in concert against him in Damascus (9:23-24), Greece (20:3), and throughout Asia (20:19). This time, however, they conscript the Jerusalem council to act for them against the Roman tribune (23:14-15). The plot is foiled through the knowledge of Paul's nephew (v. 16) and the cooperation of the Roman centurion (v. 17) and tribune (vv. 18-22).

Caesarea (23:23–26:32)

Paul is moved to Caesarea (23:23-35) under the direction of the tribune. Caesarea was the administrative capital of the province. The tribune provides an armed guard and a horse for Paul (vv. 23-24), as well as rehearsing immediate events in a letter to Governor Felix (vv. 25-30). Antonius Felix was governor from AD 52 to 60; the reference to two years at 24:27 suggests that Paul was arrested in AD 58. Felix is addressed as "most excellent," the same form of address directed to Theophilus (Luke 1:3). This was a common way to address one's social superiors; it suggests that Theophilus enjoyed a high status, but it does not mean that he was of equestrian rank. (On social status in Acts, see Lentz 1993: 6-22.) The significance of Paul's Roman citizenship is underscored in the tribune's letter (23:27); it will play a key role in subsequent events (25:10-11, 21). Once Paul arrives safely in Caesarea (23:31-33) he is placed under guard, awaiting the arrival of his accusers (vv. 34-35). A number of scenes in Caesarea follow in which Paul speaks before Roman officials.

Paul appears before Governor Felix (24:1-23) after the arrival of the Jerusalem leaders five days later (v. 1). The charge is placed by Tertullus, on behalf of the Jewish leaders (vv. 2-8), in a speech which adheres to the standard form of a forensic speech (Veltman in Talbert 1978: 243-56; Neyrey in Talbert 1984: 210-24; Winter in Winter and Clarke 1993: 315-22). He begins with an extended *captatio benevolentiae* (vv. 2-4) begging the favor of the governor in the customary fashion, by flattering him for his good deeds. Then Tertullus repeats the earlier charges with some emotive variants (vv. 5-6). The charge that Paul was "teaching against the people" (21:28) has become "we have found this man a pestilent fellow, making an uprising among all the Jews throughout the world" (24:5); this evokes the charge against Jesus, "we found this man perverting our nation" (Luke 23:2). The second charge, that he was "teaching against the law" (21:28), is transmuted into the description of Paul as "a ringleader of the sect of the Nazarenes" (24:5). The accusation that Paul was "teaching against this place" (21:28) is reflected in Tertullus's final statement that "he even tried to profane the temple" (24:6, reflecting 21:26-27). The confirmation of the Jerusalem authorities who are present (24:9) is not unexpected.

Paul's reply (24:10-21) is the second of his speeches explicitly designated as an "apology" (v. 10); it follows the expected pattern of a forensic speech (Winter in Winter and Clarke 1993: 322-27). His defense is mounted in three ways. First, Paul directly denies Tertullus's charges that he was making any uprising (v. 12; cf. v. 5) and profaning the temple (vv. 17-18; cf. v. 6). Second, he buttresses these denials with a reiteration of his character (vv. 14-18). Once again language about God is a crucial element in this aspect of his defense; here it particularly functions to locate Paul squarely within Judaism. Paul asserts that he "worships the God of *our* ancestors" (v. 14). The description of God as "the God of our ancestors" places Paul within Judaism (see 22:14). Adherence to ancestral customs was highly valued by the Romans; Paul here expresses an element of Luke's overall apologetic purpose (Esler 1987: 214-19). Reference to the worship of God (22:14) strengthens this ancestral adherence. Luke has previously referred to such worship (see Luke 1:74; 2:37; 4:8, citing Deut 6:13; 10:20; Acts 7:7, 42; 26:7; 27:23). Paul affirms his "hope in God" (24:15); this hope he presents as standard Jewish belief accepted even by his accusers (see also 26:6-7; 28:20). Both his worship of God and his hope in God are expressions of the "sect" to which he belongs; the term "sect" *(hairesis)* is applied not only to "the Way" (24:5, 14; 26:5; 28:22) but also to other parties in the Judaism of the time (Sadducees, 5:17; Pharisees, 15:5; 26:5). Then Paul repeats his earlier claim that he has "a clear conscience toward God" (24:16; see 23:1). He cites for support the alms which he brought to Jerusalem (24:17), a passing reference to the activity mentioned in four of Paul's own letters (Rom 15:25-29, 31; 1 Cor 16:1-4; 2 Cor 8:1-7; 9:1-5; Gal 2:10). The timing of this action ("after some years") agrees with the dating which can be deduced from Paul's letters (in the late 50s AD) and is at odds with Luke's dating of the collection to an earlier time in Paul's activities, in the mid 40s AD (11:29; 12:25). As the third element in his defense, Paul makes a direct attack on the Jews who brought the charges (24:19-21a).

To conclude this brief speech, Paul reshapes the charge (24:21b) in the light of what happened at his appearance before the Jerusalem council (23:6-9). By narrowing the accusations to just the one matter — "the resurrection of the dead" (24:21b) — he makes a play to have the case dismissed as an internal Jewish squabble, as took place in Corinth (18:12-16). The governor stalls for time (24:22) but continues to provide generous arrangements for Paul's imprisonment (v. 23; see Rapske 1994: 164-72).

There follows a series of short scenes. **Paul appears again before Felix (24:24-26).** The explanation for the "more accurate knowledge" of Felix (v. 22) appears to be his marriage to Drusilla, a Jew (v. 24) who was a daughter of Herod Agrippa (12:1). The discussion ranges over pagan philosophical and Jewish topics, but ends inconclusively (24:25). Righteousness was a central issue in Jewish Scripture (e.g., Gen 15:6; 18:11-33; 1 Sam 26:23; 2 Sam 22:21-25; 1 Kgs 8:32; 2 Chr 9:8; 113 times in the Psalms; 87 times in Proverbs; 111 times in the major prophets; 15 times in the minor prophets) but was also related to the Greek concern for justice (as the NRSV here translates *dikaiosynē*). It has earlier been mentioned by the Lukan Paul just three times (13:10, 38-39; 17:31), but is central to Paul's letters to the Romans and Galatians and appears in others of his letters (see 13:38-39). Self-control *(enkrateia)* was a key philosophical ideal; Paul mentions it in stereotyped ways at 1 Cor 9:25; Gal 5:23. The coming judgment *(krima),* a topic of debate in Jewish circles, picks up on the eschatological issues of 23:6-9; 24:21. While noted in Paul's speech in Athens (17:31), this topic receives more attention in Paul's letters (Rom 2:5-10; 3:5-8; 4:10-12; 15:9; 1 Cor 3:12-15; 4:5; 1 Thess 1:10).

Felix is succeeded by Festus (24:27) in AD 60. **Jewish influence on Festus (24:27–25:5)** is initially strong in the administrative capital, Caesarea (v. 27). When in Jerusalem, however, Festus does not succumb to the renewed plotting of the local leadership (25:2-3) and determines to learn more of Paul's case (vv. 4-5). Back in Caesarea, **Paul appears before Festus (vv. 6-12)** in a scene which once more evokes the trial of Jesus. Paul is beset by false charges (v. 7); to the narrator his innocence is manifestly clear (25:8; cf. Luke 23:4, 14, 22). Paul's reply is an extremely succinct apology (25:8) which indicates that three charges were made, echoing the earlier charges of the Asian Jews in Jerusalem (21:28). That he has "offended against the law of the Jews" repeats the second charge of 21:28. That he has "offended against the temple" repeats the third charge of 21:28. That he has "offended against Caesar" is a new charge, apparently replacing the initial accusation of 21:28 that he taught "against the people." This charge is reminiscent of those raised against Jesus at Luke 23:2 and against Paul at Acts 17:7.

Festus, continuing his favor of the Jews, offers Paul a trial in Jerusalem (25:9). Paul, however, stands on his rights as a Roman citizen and insists on a trial before Caesar (vv. 10-11). The legal basis for this in Roman law appears somewhat shaky, given the evidence known today (Lentz 1993: 139-70). For Luke, however, the assertion that "it is necessary for me to be tried" before the emperor's tribunal (v. 10) emphasizes the sense of divine necessity at work in these events. Felix thus has no choice but to determine that Paul must be sent on to Caesar (v. 12).

Consequently, **Festus informs Agrippa about Paul (25:13-22).** Marcus Julius Agrippa, son of Herod Agrippa (see 12:1-4, 19-23) and brother of Drusilla (see 24:24), had become King of Judea in AD 52. Bernice, his widowed sister, accompanies him. In his speech before Agrippa (25:14-21), Festus reviews the situation that has unfolded. He reasserts the necessary procedure under Roman law: once clear charges have been made (see 22:30; 23:28-30; 24:8), an adequate opportunity must be given for the accused to make an apology (25:16; see 22:1; 24:10; 25:8). He also advises Agrippa that, in his opinion, the charges did not fall under Roman jurisdiction (25:18-19; see 23:29). Nevertheless, the invocation of Paul's Roman citizenship (25:21; see 22:25-28; 23:27; 25:10-11) has meant that he had been kept in custody since then. Agrippa responds by confirming his interest in taking up the invitation of Festus (25:22).

Paul appears before Festus, Agrippa, and Bernice (25:23–26:23) on the very next day. The scene which is set is one of great pomp (25:23). Once more Festus reviews events: some Jews made charges (v. 24), the accused appears innocent (v. 25a), but an appeal has been made to Caesar (v. 25b). What is thus sought from Agrippa is a clarification of the charges to be forwarded to Rome (vv. 26-27). Agrippa immediately grants Paul permission to speak (26:1a); what follows is yet another apology (vv. 1b, 24).

The body of the speech follows the same pattern as the apology before the crowd in Jerusalem (22:2-21). Once again the major components of a forensic speech are evident (Veltman in Talbert 1978: 243-56; Neyrey in Talbert 1984: 210-24; Winter in Winter and Clarke 1993: 327-31). Like that earlier address, this speech enables Paul to address the charges first raised against him by the crowd in Jerusalem (21:27-28) and subsequently passed on to the Roman authorities in Caesarea (24:5-6). The speech begins with an introductory *captatio benevolentiae* (26:2-3; cf. 24:2-4) in which Paul explicitly relates his case to "the customs and the controversies of the Jews" (26:3). Then, in the speech's **first major section (vv. 4-11),** Paul provides an expanded self-identification which locates him firmly within that context. His description of his preconversion antagonism to "the Way" is extensively elaborated from his earlier apologetic speech (26:9-11; cf. 22:5). The vehement and thorough opposition which Paul exhibited (26:11) was undertaken under authority from the chief priests (v. 10a; see also v. 12). Paul even infers that he was a member of the Jerusalem council (v. 10b). His Jewish credentials cannot be doubted.

In support of these claims, Luke has Paul apologetically strengthen his Jewish credentials (26:4-8; cf. 22:3-4). This is especially evident in three ways. First, reference to Paul's upbringing in Jerusalem, noted in passing when he spoke in that city (22:3), is explicitly highlighted in his speech in Caesarea (26:4). In his defense, Paul utters a typical Lukan exaggeration in his claim that "all the Jews" are witnesses to this upbringing (26:4; see 3:24; 9:35; 10:22, 34; 11:28; 13:44; 16:26; 19:10, 17). Second, Paul's earlier comment that he was "strictly educated" (22:3) is here intensified by the claim that he belonged to "the strictest sect" (26:5). This sect is then identified by name as that of the Pharisees (v. 5). Paul's adherence to this sect was a claim he first made in self-defense as he stood before the council in Jerusalem (23:6). The apologetic function of the claim continues at this point in Caesarea. (The description of Paul's zeal as a Pharisee is echoed in his own letters; see 2 Cor 11:22; Gal 1:14; Phil 3:6). Third, Paul explains his adherence to Pharisaic beliefs by referring to his "hope in the promise made by God" (26:6), which is explained as being a belief that "God raises the dead" (v. 8). This promise is at the heart of Jewish faith, for Paul maintains that "our twelve tribes hope to attain" to this promise (v. 7). The cumulative effect of these details is to identify Paul with his people and confirm that, far from "teaching against the people" (cf. 21:28), he is to be located among the Jews. For the Lukan Paul, the Jews are "my people" (26:4); he lives "as a Pharisee" (v. 5) and he hopes for what they also hope (v. 6).

At this point explicit reference to God intensifies this Jewish apologetic. Paul's Jewish self-identity can be verified by no less an authority than God. What Paul hopes for is a promise that has been made by God (26:6). The substance of the promise is that God will raise the dead (v. 8). Paul's hope in this promise has already been identified as being grounded, in general terms, in God (24:15). The context of Acts as a whole strengthens this apologetic claim, for it is clear that God has indeed guaranteed this promise by the specific act of raising Jesus from the dead. Furthermore, it is implied that the twelve tribes themselves are very close to the realization of this promise because "they earnestly worship night and day" (26:7). Such worship puts them into close contact with this very God, just as Paul has already indicated in his apologetic claim that "I worship the God of our ancestors" (24:14). This emphatic use of language about God, when added to Paul's intensified Jewish identity, strengthens the apologetic thrust of this part of the speech. Paul presents himself as a faithful Jew, sharing in Jewish beliefs and participating in Jewish actions.

In the speech's **second major section (26:12-18),** Paul recalls what happened to him on the road to Damascus. The reader of Acts is quite familiar with this sequence of events, having encountered the initial third person narration (9:3-19a) and Paul's earlier explanation, in Jerusalem, of what had taken place (22:6-16). Initially, the accounts follow approximately the same course, from Paul's initial encounter with the bright light (9:3; 22:6; 26:12-13) through the question posed by the heavenly voice (9:4; 22:7; 26:14) to the identification of the speaker as Jesus (9:5; 22:8; 26:15). At this point, however, with his own apologetic purposes firmly in mind, Luke carefully reshapes Paul's description of the charge which he is given. (Each version of this story is shaped for the context immediately at hand; Witherington 1996: 335-44.)

First, the command to "go into the city" (9:6; 22:10) is absent. Allied with this, Ananias disappears from the account (cf. 9:10-19a; 22:12-16). There is no need for Paul to be taken into the presence of a disciple (9:10) whose function was to mediate between Paul and God, for Luke is now to have Paul highlight that he received his commission directly from God (Wilson 1973: 162-67).

Second, the actual charge Paul is given is extensively elaborated. The initial narrative reported that the Lord appeared in a dream to Ananias, charging him to go to Paul (9:15) with the comments that Paul would "bear my name" (9:15) and "suffer many things" (9:16). The tasks given to Paul have a divine origin, although they are communicated to Paul quite indirectly. In his Jerusalem apology Paul had presented a more developed version, which Ananias did in fact convey to him: first, a declaration that "the God of our ancestors has chosen you" to do three things: "know his will, see the righteous one, and hear a voice from his mouth" (22:14); and then the designation of Paul as "witness" (22:15). The apologetic use of language about God at this point has already been noted. In the account of his commissioning given in Caesarea, Luke has Paul depict his charge as an immediate continuation of the initial conversation, begun on the Damascus Road (26:14-15). What follows (26:16-18) is thus conveyed to Paul immediately and directly from the Lord. Each elaboration in this version of the charge serves to strengthen the Lukan portrayal of Paul as divinely commissioned in the manner of a prophet.

(i) The command to "rise" (9:6; 22:10) is extended by the order to "stand on your feet" (26:16). In Acts, these terms indicate the stance adopted by those who publicly proclaim God's message; for "rise," see Peter (15:7) and Paul (13:16); cf. Gamaliel (5:34); for "stand," see Peter (2:14; 5:20) and Paul (17:22; 27:21). They resonate with a typical element in the scriptural narratives of the call of a prophet (Jer 1:17; Ezek 2:1-2; Dan 10:11; Hab 2:1).

(ii) The reference to a vision (alluded to in 9:16; explicit in 22:14) here functions as the primary legitimating experience: "I have appeared to you for this purpose, to appoint you as servant and witness" (26:16). Throughout Acts, it is God who appoints (see 22:14) and God's Spirit who empowers one as a witness (see 1:8; 2:4). Also throughout Acts, visions sent from God have played key roles (e.g., 10:9-16; 18:9-10). Typically a prophet sees a vision at his call (Isa 6:1-7; Jer 1:11-13; Ezek 1:4-28; Dan 10:5-8; Hab 2:2-3).

(iii) The task that is given to Paul (as an "instrument" chosen by God, 9:15; to be God's "witness," 22:15) is expanded to the declaration that he is divinely appointed as "servant and witness" (26:16; NRSV, "to serve and testify"). Each term is significant for Luke; "servant" *(hypēretēn)* aligns Paul with those identified by Luke as among his sources (Luke 1:2), while "witness" links Paul with the apostolic role (1:22; 2:32; 3:15; 5:32; 10:39, 41; 13:31) in obedience to the commission given by Jesus (1:8). The terms "servant" and "witness" are also used by Epictetus to describe the ideal Stoic (*Diss.* 3.24) and the ideal Cynic (*Diss.* 3.22). Paul's commission is one of a number of divine epiphanies that have occurred throughout Paul's public activities. This final version of his charge refers both to a vision in the past ("the things in which you have seen me") and to visions still to come in the future ("the things in which I will appear to you"). This enables the divine validation of Paul's work to be verified in a tangible way, for the narrative has already recounted the past epiphany on the road to Damascus (9:3-7) and most of the epiphanies which are future to this moment (16:9; 18:5-6; 23:11; only 27:23-24 is yet to be told).

(iv) Finally, the precise content of this charge is extensively expanded in 26:17-18 so as to emphasize that Paul, like many prophets, is to be "delivered" by God (26:17; cf. Jer 1:8, 19; Dan 3:15, 17, 28-29; 6:16, 20, 26-27) and "sent" by a divine decree (26:17; see Isa 6:8; 42:19; Jer 1:7; 26:5; Ezek 2:3-4). Furthermore, his task is typically prophetic: faced with a people in darkness, his task is "to open their eyes, to turn them from darkness to light" (26:18; for "darkness," see Isa 6:10; 42:6-7, 16; 44:18; 59:10; Jer 4:23; 5:21; 13:16; Ezek 12:2; directed to the prophet himself, Isa 29:10; Ezek 40:4; 44:5; for "light," see Isa 29:18; 32:3; 35:5; 42:6-7, 16; 43:8). This is the language of salvation, which is the crux of the prophetic message (see Luke 1:70-71; Acts 13:47) and central to the mission of the Lukan Jesus (Luke 4:18; 7:21-22).

The other terms in this expanded charge reflect Luke's hand; the language is either Lukan ("receive forgiveness of sins," Luke 24:47; Acts 2:38; 10:43; 13:38; cf. Eph 1:7; Col 1:14; "faith in God," Acts 11:23; 15:15; 27:25) or used by both Luke and Paul ("an inheritance," Acts 20:32; Gal 3:29; cf. Eph 1:14, 18; 5:5; Col 1:12; 3:24; "the saints," Acts 9:13, 32, 41; 20:32; 26:10; 26 times in Paul, 14 times in Ephesians, Colossians, and the Pastorals).

It is the explicit and implicit references to God at this point which enable Luke to have Paul rebut the earlier charge that he was "teaching against the law" (cf. 21:28). As he has been commissioned by the one who has given this law, such a charge is not possible. Indeed, an additional divine comment added to this account ("it hurts you to kick against the goads," 26:14) strengthens the divine impulse with overtones of a well-known Greek proverb (Euripides *Bacchae* 794-95; Aeschylus *Prometheus* 324-26; *Agamemnon* 1624-25; Pindar *Pythian Odes* 2.93-96; Philo *Det. pot. ins.* 46; Julian *Orations* 8.246B; see Lentz 1993: 84-87). This saying evokes the theme of divine necessity which has run consistently throughout Luke's account of Paul's activities (Squires 1993: 173-77).

The sending of Paul to the Gentiles (26:17-18) is not offensive to Agrippa, as it was to Paul's audience in Jerusalem (22:17). This then allows the speech's **third major section (26:19-23)** to follow. In Jerusalem, it was important to have Paul assert that, far from "teaching against this place" (cf. 21:28), he was in fact praying in the temple itself when he was seized (22:17-21). In speaking to Agrippa and Festus, the issue is different; the focus is on the immediate divine origin of the charge which Paul received while he was on the road to Damascus. The temple, which was the place of divine commissioning according to 22:17-21, now becomes simply the location for seizing Paul (26:21). In this version of the speech, Luke has Paul emphasize his obedience to the commission he received (vv. 19-20). Once again language about God functions apologetically, to legitimate Paul's proclamation; it has taken place in obedience to the heavenly vision (v. 19).

At this point in the parallel speech in Jerusalem, Paul had offended his audience such that they vigorously interrupted him (22:22). No offense has yet been given here, however, allowing Paul to complete his speech with emphatic reference to the role played by God in his activities. First, he makes a claim which is programmatic for the whole of his public activity throughout Luke's narrative: "To this day I have had the help which is from God" (26:22a). Once again language about God serves to validate Paul's activities as a witness. Then, Paul summarizes the content of this witness with a typical Lukan reference to the way that the words of the prophets have been fulfilled (26:22b-23). Luke has often had Paul buttress his argument with reference to the antiquity of his beliefs (see 13:33-37; 17:28). This use of language about God is similarly programmatic. The prophets, God's spokespersons, have pointed to the suffering of the Messiah as well as to the proclamation of light to the people and the Gentiles (26:23). Such fulfilled prophecy also serves to authorize Paul's witness; the truth of the prophetic words has been manifested in Paul's own proclamation "in Damascus and in Jerusalem and all the countryside of Judea and to the Gentiles" (26:20). The speech thus concludes with strong divine validation of Paul. (On this theme in the speech as a whole, see Squires 1993: 32-35.)

In recounting the **response to the speech (26:24-32),** Luke reiterates its apologetic nature (v. 24) and has Paul describe it by an unusual term which emphasizes its significance (*apophthengomai,* 26:25; see 2:14). This term is best translated "I am declaiming" or "I am solemnly declaring"; the NRSV translation, "I am speaking," is quite inadequate. He then notes the varied responses of the chief characters in the audience: Festus declares Paul "mad" (26:24), whereas Agrippa admits that he is "almost persuaded" (v. 28). Paul's reply to Festus continues the apologetic direction of the scene by claiming that he exhibits the highly prized virtue of self-control (v. 25;

NRSV, "the sober truth"; see Lentz 1993: 68-91) and by citing the well-known Greek proverb "these things were not done in a corner" (26:26; Plato *Gorg.* 485CE; Aulius Gellius *Attic Nights* 10.16-18; Epictetus *Diss.* 1.29.54-57; see Malherbe 1985-86: 193-210). As he turns his attention to Agrippa, he invokes Agrippa's support through his belief in the prophets (26:27) and states his apologetic aim most explicitly: "would that not only you, but all who hear me today, might become like me" (v. 29). This aim is buttressed by one last reference to the divine ("I pray to God," v. 29). The speech achieves as much as it can; Agrippa sends Paul on to Rome, convinced of his innocence (v. 31) but constrained by his earlier appeal to Caesar (v. 32). Thus the summoning of the divine has once more proved an effective apologetic strategy.

The Journey toward Rome (27:1–28:15)

Like the passion narrative which comes near the conclusion of Luke's Gospel (Luke 22:1–23:56), the account of Paul's sea journeys (Acts 27:1–28:15) is a cohesive literary unit, which presses on relentlessly from one incident to the next. The account must be treated as a whole, and its various thematic elements dealt with each in turn. The mass of details appears to provide historical credibility, but the use of themes common in the popular literature of the time warns against a ready acceptance of historicity. The careful literary shaping of the account raises the tension: Will Paul survive or not? Will he be "saved" or will he perish?

Paul's journey to Rome looms as the final threat to the satisfactory implementation of the divine plan. As he journeys on a number of ships, he is constantly under the shadow of death, culminating in the moment when one of these ships is run aground by the elements. Eventually, however, he is brought safely — and triumphantly — through Malta, to Rome. The last section of the narrative concludes with clear signals that the divine plan remains on track.

Details of the journeys flow thick and fast at the beginning of this section of the narrative. The centurion who guards Paul is identified as Julius (27:1), and another passenger is named as Aristarchus (27:2; perhaps the same as Paul's companion at 19:29; 20:4?). The nautical details of the first two legs of the trip include mention of the difficulties in sailing past the islands of Cyprus (27:4) and Crete (v. 7) as well as the visits to the ports of Myra (v. 5) and Fair Havens (v. 8). Reports of subsequent sections of this sea journey provide similarly detailed accounts. In noting the ship's progress off Crete (vv. 13-16), Luke includes careful reference to wind changes; when it drifts in the Sea of Adria (vv. 27-29), he reports the depth soundings taken. When the ship is forced to land on Malta (vv. 39-41), Luke provides a step-by-step account of the crew's actions; on the final stage from Malta to Puteoli (28:11-13), the details include the ship's nationality and distinctive features, the length of stay in Syracuse and Rhegium, and the wind directions encountered off Rhegium.

Such details are in contrast to the studied vagueness of many of the earlier sections of Acts. Much longer journeys have been described far more briefly, such as those from Pisidian Antioch to Syrian Antioch (14:24-25); through Phrygia and Galatia (16:6); from Caesarea, via Jerusalem, to Antioch (18:22); and through Galatia and Phrygia (18:23). Large spans of time have been dismissed in a few words, notably "for a considerable period of time" in Corinth (18:18); "for three months" in Ephesus (19:8); "for two years" in Ephesus (19:10); and "after two years" in Caesarea (24:27). Numerous time references have been very vague ("one day," 3:1; "during those days," 6:1; "that day," 8:1; "after some time," 9:23; "about that time," 12:1; "one day," 16:16; "about that time," 19:23; and "after these days," 21:15). The numerous details reported in this sea journey from Caesarea to Puteoli are reminiscent of similar details given in earlier "we" passages (16:11-12; 20:3-6, 13-15; 21:1-4, 7-8). These sections are notable for the impression of verisimilitude which they convey.

Literary Characteristics. However, the difficulties encountered in the sea journeys include many of the standard elements found in stories of sea journeys in the literature of the period. The first such commonplaces occur when the risky decision is taken to set sail even though the winter season, when sailing was not possible, is imminent (27:9-13), and when it is clear that one of the passengers knows better than the crew (Paul, at v. 10). Then follow accounts of being abandoned to a fierce wind (vv. 14-19); a threatened shipwreck (v. 29); an aborted mutiny (vv. 29-32); and ultimately an actual shipwreck (vv. 39-41), leading to the potential death of the hero (Paul) (v. 42). After the miraculous saving of the ship's company (v. 44, as predicted at v. 24) there follow encounters with strange local peoples and the performance of further miracles (28:3-6, 8-9). Such elements are common in Hellenistic travel literature (Pervo 1987: 50-57).

As the sea journey is recounted, the accumulation of such threatening details slows the pace of the narrative and focuses attention firmly on the possibility that Paul will fail to arrive in Rome, as promised. Sailing into the winds off Cyprus (27:4) and Crete (v. 7) means that progress is slow and the boat is caught at sea just as the nonsailing season of winter is beginning (vv. 9, 12). A violent wind off Crete (vv. 15-16) and a pounding storm (v. 18) mean that the ship's tackle must be thrown overboard (v. 19). The darkness of the storm (v. 20) and the diminishing food supplies (v. 21) lead to a sense of hopelessness. The threat of being washed onto the rocks sees even the pagans praying (v. 29), before their fear gets the better of them (v. 30) and the ship's small boat is lost (v. 32). Off Malta, shipwreck looms and the threat of death is acute (vv. 41-42). Once the ship is run aground, a dangerous swim to shore must follow (vv. 43-44). At any point Paul's life may be ended and the prophecy that he will see Rome (23:11) will be proven false. The integrity of divine providence is at risk at each of these points in the sea journey.

Paul's Speeches on Board Ship. Yet as these barriers to safe arrival in Rome rise up, one after another, Paul remains resolute in his confidence in God's providential care. He is the only character whose speeches are reported throughout the sea journey. His words are uniformly confident and encouraging. In his **speech at Fair Havens (27:9-10)**, he utters a prediction which ultimately turns out to be true in almost all respects; only the loss of human life fails to come about. With hindsight Paul is again validated as a prophet. Ironically, however, his words are swiftly dismissed by the centurion, who places his trust (not surprisingly!) in the experienced seafarer rather than the doom-saying prisoner (v. 11).

As the ship drifts aimlessly on the Sea of Adria, Paul makes three speeches. His **first speech,** when the food supplies are low (27:21-26), emphasizes God's faithfulness in the midst of danger. In this speech he reports the last in a long series of divine epiphanies which have taken place in Acts. While Paul is on board ship, an angel has given him a comforting message: "Do not fear . . . God has looked favorably upon you and all who are with you" (vv. 23-24). Earlier epiphanies had given Paul similar assurances that he would receive divine assistance in the face of persecution in Corinth (18:9-10) and as he stood before the Jerusalem council (23:11) (Rapske 1996: 419-22). Many other epiphanies throughout Acts and the Gospel of Luke have already imbued the story with a strong sense of divine guidance (Squires 1993: 112-20). The sense of divine necessity which drives this journey is also expressed in the words of the angel, "you must stand before Caesar" (27:24), as is the sense of divine providence in the assurance that "God has given to you all those who are sailing with you" (v. 24).

Paul's **second speech** on the Sea of Adria takes place when the soldiers threaten to mutiny. His brief statement (27:31) refers to "being saved" — a term which appears frequently in this section of the narrative (Acts 27:20, 31, 34, 43, 44; 28:1, 4). The term describes being rescued from the imminent dangers posed by the elements, but it has resonances with the overall program of "salvation" which runs throughout both of Luke's volumes (see Acts 28:28; Tannehill 1990: 330-43).

Paul's **third speech** comes toward the end of the same night. He urges all to have a last meal before the remaining wheat is thrown overboard to lighten the ship (27:33-34). Paul, the prisoner, continues his encouragement of the crew and the Roman guard by citing a saying about God's providential care during distress, which was spoken also by Jesus (v. 34; Luke 21:18). The meal with these Gentiles contains a further resonance with the story of Jesus, at his last meal before his death (Luke 22:14-20). As Jesus "took a loaf of bread, and when he had given thanks, he broke it and gave it to his disciples" (Luke 22:19), so Paul "took bread, and giving thanks to God in the presence of all, he broke it," and the whole company of 276 people shared in this meal (27:35-37). The pattern that is repeated here is the normal pattern for beginning a Jewish meal and need not be regarded as specifically eucharistic (see Luke 9:16; 24:30; Dunn 1997: 341). The ensuing events (27:39-44) climax with the statement that "all were brought safely to land" (27:44), demonstrating that God is faithful to the word of promise; as predicted, not one has lost even a hair from their heads (27:34). God's providential care remains effective.

Paul's Miracles on Malta (28:1-10). The narrative of Acts (and the Gospel) has included numerous portents through which God's ongoing involvement in the story has been clear. The last portents in this series take place on Malta, where Paul survives a snakebite (28:3-6). The mistaken perception of the inhabitants of Malta is that Paul is a god (v. 6). The same mistake had been made by the residents of Lystra (14:11-13); in that instance Paul and Barnabas immediately correct the crowd (14:14-18). On Malta, however, Paul is in a different situation; as a shipwrecked prisoner, still in Roman custody, he is constrained to maintain polite relations with the locals. His acceptance of hospitality (28:7) and his healing of the local official's sick son (v. 8) open up the possibility for him then to heal "the rest of the people on the island who had diseases" (v. 9). These healings cement Paul's status as a benefactor who is accorded many honors (v. 10). The effect of these portents is to reinforce Luke's view that, even though he is a prisoner, Paul continues to be validated by manifestations of divine power.

Arrival in Italy (28:11-15). The final stage in the sea journey, from Malta to Puteoli (vv. 11-13), takes place without a problem; indeed, the sense of divine guidance is heightened by the note that the necessary south wind sprang up after only one day (v. 13). After landing at Puteoli, the travelers meet with a company of believers there (v. 14). When Paul finally enters the city of Rome (v. 14), his arrival is marked with a prayer to God expressing gratitude for his safe arrival (v. 15). This draws the journey to a close with a suitably prominent action. The prayer is a final reminder of Luke's view that the whole journey has taken place under the providence of God.

Rome (28:16-31)

The final scene is introduced with the brief geographical comment, "When we came into Rome" (28:16). This reprises the comment of v. 14, at the end of the previous subsection, emphasizing that the geographic goal of Acts (stated in 19:21; 23:11; 26:32) has been achieved. Paul is held under house arrest (28:16) in an accommodation which rents privately (vv. 23, 30); he is guarded by a solitary soldier (not a centurion, v. 16) and is chained (v. 20). Throughout the two years he spends in custody in Rome, he is permitted visitors (vv. 17, 23, 30; on the arrangements for Paul's Roman custody, see Rapske 1994: 173-82, 227-42). Although Luke provides no report of his legal encounter with the emperor, he concludes his second volume by detailing two meetings between Paul and the local Jewish leadership (vv. 16-28). In these two meetings Paul summarizes events from previous chapters in the familiar Lukan manner, using language about God as the chief interpretive lens.

In Paul's **first meeting** with Roman Jews (28:17-22), as he reports his arrest in Jerusalem and his delivery to the Romans, he apologetically emphasizes his Jewishness one more time (vv. 17, 20; see 22:3, 14; 24:14; 26:4-8). Continued Jewish opposition has meant that he was "compelled to appeal to Caesar" (28:19). This bare report thus continues the interpretation of events with reference to God, in that Paul experiences the divine necessity to act as he does.

Even though it is the last scene of the book, Luke has still placed Paul within a Jewish context; he continues to testify to "the hope of Israel" despite being bound in chains at the instigation of his fellow Jews (28:20). Paul has already defined this hope as being a belief in the resurrection, as he declared in Jerusalem (23:6) and in Caesarea (24:15; 26:6-8). Yet the scene ends with Paul's statement that salvation is now sent, not to the Jews, but to the Gentiles (28:28).

The three occasions in Acts when Paul states that he goes to the Gentiles are often seen as forming a connected series which culminate in a final rejection of the Jews because of their failure to accept the Gospel. (Sympathetic readings in this vein are found in Brawley 1989: 68-78 and Tyson 1992: 174-89.) However, the progression of audiences in these scenes is noteworthy: "almost all the city" in the synagogue in Pisidian Antioch (13:44), including numerous Gentiles (13:48); a crowd in the Corinthian synagogue which includes "both Jews and Greeks" (18:5); and finally, in Rome, a group of "many" (28:23) drawn exclusively from "the local leaders of the Jews" (v. 17). The movement from a predominantly Gentile audience in the first scene to an exclusively Jewish audience in the third scene gives the lie to the interpretation that by the end of Acts Paul has turned finally and definitively away from the Jews, and fully and irrevocably toward the Gentiles alone. Whenever the break between Judaism and Christianity comes, it still has not occurred at the end of Luke's writings (Squires 1998: 614-16).

In his **second meeting** with Roman Jews (28:23-28), Paul bears testimony to God's actions, as the one who is both sovereign (v. 23) and Savior (v. 28). Paul has typically proclaimed "the sovereignty of God" in his public proclamation (19:8; 20:25); here he further develops this central theme by propounding the fulfillment of scriptural prophecy in the life of Jesus (28:23) and in the failure of many of the Jews to accept the gospel (vv. 25-27, quoting Isa 6:9-10). This latter prophecy is further described as a statement made "by the Holy Spirit through the prophet Isaiah" (28:25, quoting Isa 6:9-10), thus picking up the role of the Spirit described in the opening scene of Acts (1:16).

Also typical is the divided response among his listeners: "Some were persuaded by what he was saying, but others did not believe" (28:24; see 13:5-12). The persuasion which occurs here is more than the offering of a sympathetic ear by the Jewish listeners; it indicates persuasion such as leads to full faith in Jesus as Messiah (17:3; 18:5). This is how the word is used earlier in scenes in Pisidian Antioch (13:43) and in Corinth (18:4), as well as in Thessalonica (17:4) and in the programmatic description of Paul's activities, given in Ephesus ("this Paul has persuaded and drawn away a considerable number of people," 19:26).

As the divided audience breaks up, Paul cites at length a prophecy from Isaiah. The first clause of the quotation underlines the prophetic charge given to Isaiah when it begins, "Go to this people *(laos)* and say" (28:26a). By beginning his quotation in this way, Luke explicitly aligns Paul with the task which was being carried out by Isaiah; the prophet speaking to Israel is now Paul. His task is to confront the people with the evidence of their sin: "You hear and hear but do not understand; you look and look but do not perceive" (v. 26).

This part of the scripture citation is familiar to the readers of Luke's two-volume work, for Jesus has already quoted a much-truncated, variant version of it immediately after he has told the parable of the sower (Luke 8:10). There, as in the Synoptic parallels (Mark 4:12; and in the full version at Matt 13:14-15), it indicates the incapacity of the crowds to penetrate the parables of Jesus; they have not been given "the mystery of the sovereignty of God" (Mark 4:11; Luke 8:10 par. Matt 13:11). The full citation, however, is reserved by Luke for this final scene. Here Luke extends the citation beyond the accusation that the hearers neither see nor hear (28:26) by including a graphic description of the plight of the people (v. 27). He ends the citation with a highly significant clause which indicates that the prophetic task is to speak to the people, "that they might not see with their eyes, and hear with their ears, and understand with their heart, and turn — and I will heal them" (v. 27). These words, although couched in a negative manner, contain an implicit promise; it is still possible that people may indeed turn and thus be healed by God.

The context of the citation in the book of Isaiah supports the reading of an implicit promise in the oracle. The words were given first, not to Paul, nor to Jesus, but to Isaiah, immediately after his prophetic commissioning (Isa 6:1-8). The function of these words in this context is to strengthen the prophet for his difficult and uninviting task — the proclamation of judgment over Israel. Yet the task of the prophet is not simply to condemn Israel; rather, it is necessary that the prophet speak out so that repentance might be evoked and restoration granted. The "doom and gloom" of the prophet is required in order to bring "light and life" to whoever will pay heed. It is in this sense that Luke passes the prophetic mantle to Paul, who has become a "preacher of eschatological repentance," following the Isaianic road of warning in order to evoke fidelity among the errant people of God (Moessner 1988).

In closing this scene, Luke has Paul utter a concluding statement which bears strong marks of the author's hand: "Let it be known to you, then, that this salvation of God has been sent to the Gentiles; they will listen" (28:28). These concluding words appear to be a stark contrast to the prophetic citation; just as the Jews "hear and hear but do not understand" (v. 26), so the Gentiles "will listen" (v. 28). Paul thus articulates what has long been expected in Acts; he is to go to the Gentiles, "for they will listen" (v. 28). This final "turn to the Gentiles" is not a completely new and surprising element in the narrative. Indeed, the preparations for this "turn" stretch back before Corinth and Pisidian Antioch, even before the activities in Syrian Antioch, Caesarea, Damascus, and Samaria, right back to oracles first uttered in Jerusalem, in the days prior even to the birth of the infant Jesus. Luke has Paul end his last speech with words which demonstrate that the inclusion of the Gentiles within the salvation of God is no surprise, for it has long been expected.

The note of certainty in Paul's assertion ("Let it be known, then") invokes the persistent avowal that events in the prologue to Luke-Acts are to be "known" (Luke 1:18, 34; 2:15; cf. Luke 1:1); the same concern permeates Acts (see 2:14; 4:16; 9:42; 19:17). References to "the salvation of God" permeate the oracles of the prologue (Luke 1:47, 69, 71, 77; 2:11, 30) and continue throughout the Gospel (Luke 3:6; 7:50; 8:50; 18:42; 19:9-10) and its sequel (Acts 2:21, 47; 4:12; 11:14; 13:23, 26, 47; 15:11; 16:17, 30, 31). The claim that this salvation "has been sent to the Gentiles" has already been foreshadowed by Simeon (Luke 2:32). The affirmation that the Gentiles "will listen" places them in the same category as obedient listeners in the prologue, including Elizabeth (Luke 1:41) and the shepherds (Luke 2:20; see also Luke 1:58, 66; 2:47). Paul's declaration thus draws the Gentiles into the same arena occupied by faithful Jews in the initial stages of his narrative. Together, faithful Jews and newly obedient Gentiles now form the *laos* of God (Seccombe in Marshall and Peterson 1998: 349-72).

It is not only this final comment by Paul which harks back to the beginning of the Gospel, however (Brosend in Witherington 1996: 348-62). The conclusion to the citation also evokes a promise from the prologue to the Gospel. That the people of Israel will turn is already envisaged by the angel Gabriel in his first oracle to Zechariah, with the promise that, when the child is born to Elizabeth, "He will turn many of the sons of Israel to the Lord their God" (Luke 1:16) and the further promise that "he will go ahead . . . to turn the hearts of fathers to their children . . . and to prepare a people made ready for the Lord" (Luke 1:17). The citation from Isaiah demonstrates that God remains faithful, and so the possibility still remains that some Jews might "look . . . and listen . . . and understand . . . and turn" and so receive divine healing (Acts 28:27). Although the citation threatens final judgment, it still leaves open the possibility of including Jews within the faithful.

Then follows a final **generalizing conclusion (28:30-31)** which depicts Paul's ongoing and unfinished activity in Rome, as he continues his characteristic proclamation of God's providential sovereignty (v. 31a), especially as this is made known through Jesus (v. 31b). The Western text glosses the "all" to whom Paul preached (v. 30), adding the phrase "both Jews and Greeks." This simply makes explicit what is implicit in the Alexandrian text. This final scene is consistent with what Paul had characteristically encountered during his travels: a mixed audience of Jews and Gentiles listening to his message. The salvation of God has gone to the Gentiles; yet not all Jews are placed outside of divine salvation. The end of the work is still grappling with the issues raised in the prologue to the two volumes. And still it is within the framework of the divine activity that these issues are explored.

The fate of Paul is not reported at the end of Acts; that he died in Rome is known only from references in later writings (*1 Clem.* 5:1-7; *Acts of Paul* 11:1-7; Tertullian *De Praescriptione Haereticorum* 36; Eusebius *Hist. Eccl.* 2.22.1-8; 3.1.3). The focus of Luke's narrative at its end point thus lies elsewhere. The last sentence of Acts refocuses attention to Luke's overall program, evoking the precise phrases used in introducing the work: Paul tells of "the sovereignty of God" (28:31a; cf. 1:3; 8:12; 19:8; 20:25; 28:23) and "the things concerning the Lord Jesus Christ" (28:31b; cf. 1:1; 2:36; 4:10-12; 11:17; 20:21). Acts thus concludes with a final reference to the all-encompassing scope of God's providential activity. At the end, Paul demonstrates what it means to remain faithful to the Lukan program. He continues to preach (cf. 8:5; 9:20; 10:42; 19:13; 20:12) and to teach (cf. 2:42; 4:2; 5:21, 42; 11:26; 15:35; 18:11; 20:20), "with all boldness" (cf. 2:29; 4:13, 29, 31; 9:27-28; 13:46; 14:3; 19:8) and "without hindrance" (cf. 11:17). The story is open-ended; perhaps it offers an invitation to those who hear or read it to enter into the ongoing task of bearing witness in the midst of trials (Rosner in Marshall and Peterson 1998: 215-33)?

Bibliography. Commentaries. Barrett, C. K. 1994, 1998, *Acts,* ICC, 2 vols., Edinburgh: Clark • Conzelmann, H. 1988, *The Acts of the Apostles,* Hermeneia, Philadelphia: Fortress • Dunn, J. D. G. 1997, *The Acts of the Apostles,* Peterborough: Epworth • Fitzmyer, J. A. 1998, *The Acts of the Apostles,* AB, New York: Doubleday • Haenchen, E. 1971, *The Acts of the Apostles: A Commentary,* Philadelphia: Westminster • Johnson, L. T. 1992, *The Acts of the Apostles,* SacPag, Collegeville, Minn.: Liturgical Press • Tannehill, R. C. 1990, *The Narrative Unity of Luke-Acts: A Literary Interpretation,* vol. 2, Philadelphia: Fortress • Witherington, B. 1998, *The Acts of the Apostles: A Socio-Rhetorical Commentary,* Grand Rapids: Eerdmans.

Other Works. Bauckham, R. 1993, "James and the Jerusalem Church," in Winter and Clarke below • Bauckham, R., ed. 1995, *The Book of Acts in Its Palestinian Setting,* vol. 4 in The Book of Acts in Its First-Century Setting, Grand Rapids: Eerdmans • Brawley, R. L. 1987, *Luke-Acts and the Jews: Conflict, Apology, and Conciliation,* Atlanta: Scholars • Carroll, J. T. 1988, *Response to the End of History: Eschatology and Situation in Luke-Acts,* Atlanta: Scholars • Esler, P. F. 1987, *Community and Gospel in Luke-Acts: The Social and Political Motivations of Lucan Theology,* SNTSMS 57, Cambridge: Cambridge University • Garrett, S. R. 1989, *The Demise of the Devil: Magic and the Demonic in Luke's Writings,* Minneapolis: Fortress • Gill, D. W. J., and C. Gempf, eds. 1994, *The Book of Acts in Its Graeco-Roman Setting,* vol. 2 in The Book of Acts in Its First-Century Setting, Grand Rapids: Eerdmans • Hemer, C. J. 1989, *The Book of Acts in the Setting of Hellenistic History,* Tübingen: J. C. B. Mohr; Winona Lake, Ind.: Eisenbrauns • Hill, C. C. 1992, *Hellenists and Hebrews: Reappraising Division within the Earliest Church,* Minneapolis: Fortress • Jervell, J. 1972, *Luke and the People of God,* Minneapolis: Augsburg • Jervell, J. 1984, *The Unknown Paul: Essays on Luke-Acts and Early Christian History,* Minneapolis: Augsburg • Jervell, J. 1996, *The Theology of the Acts of the Apostles,* Cambridge: Cambridge University • Kim, K.-J. 1998, *Stewardship and Almsgiving in Luke's Theology,* Sheffield Academic • Lentz, J. C. 1993, *Luke's Portrait of Paul,* Cambridge: Cambridge University • Levinskaya, I. 1996, *The Book of Acts in Its Diaspora Setting,* vol. 5 in The Book of Acts in Its First-Century Setting, Grand Rapids: Eerdmans • Maddox, R. J. 1982, *The Purpose of Luke-Acts,* Edinburgh: T. & T. Clark • Malherbe, A. J. 1985-86, "'Not in a Corner': Early Christian Apologetic in Acts 26:26," *Second Century* 5:193-210 • Marshall, I. H., and D. Peterson, eds. 1998, *Witness to the Gospel: The Theology of Acts,* Grand Rapids: Eerdmans • Matson, D. L. 1996, *Household Conversion Narratives in Acts: Pattern and Interpretation,* Sheffield: Sheffield Academic • Moessner, D. 1988, "Paul in Acts: Preacher of Eschatological Repentance to Israel," *NTS* 34: 96-104 • Neyrey, J. H. 1991, *The Social World of*

Luke–Acts: Models for Interpretation, Peabody, Mass.: Hendrickson • Pervo, R. I. 1987, *Profit with Delight: The Literary Genre of the Acts of the Apostles,* Philadelphia: Fortress • Plymale, S. F. 1991, *The Prayer Texts of Luke-Acts,* Frankfurt am Main: Peter Lang • Rapske, B. 1994, *The Book of Acts and Paul in Roman Custody,* vol. 3 in The Book of Acts in Its First-Century Setting, Grand Rapids: Eerdmans • Reimer, I. R. 1995, *Women in the Acts of the Apostles: A Feminist Liberation Perspective,* Minneapolis: Fortress • Seim, T. K. 1994, *The Double Message: Patterns of Gender in Luke-Acts,* Edinburgh: Clark • Soards, M. 1994, *The Speeches in Acts: Their Content, Context, and Concerns,* Louisville: Westminster/John Knox • Squires, J. T. 1993, *The Plan of God in Luke-Acts,* Cambridge: Cambridge University • Squires, J. T. 1998, "The Function of Acts 8:4–12:25," *NTS* 44: 608-17 • Sterling, G. E. 1992, *Historiography and Self-Definition: Josephos, Luke-Acts and Apologetic Historiography,* Leiden: Brill • Talbert, C. H., ed. 1978, *Perspectives on Luke-Acts,* Edinburgh: Clark • Talbert, C. H., ed. 1984, *Luke-Acts: New Perspectives from the Society of Biblical Literature Seminar,* New York: Crossroads • Tiede, D. L. 1980, *Prophecy and History in Luke-Acts,* Philadelphia: Fortress • Tyson, J. 1992, *Images of Judaism in Luke-Acts,* Charleston: University of South Carolina • Wilson, S. G. 1973, *The Gentiles and the Gentile Mission in Luke-Acts,* Cambridge: Cambridge University • Winter, B. W., and A. D. Clarke, eds. 1993, *The Book of Acts in Its Ancient Literary Setting,* vol. 1 in The Book of Acts in Its First-Century Setting, Grand Rapids: Eerdmans • Witherington, B., ed. 1995, *History, Literature and Society in the Book of Acts,* Cambridge: Cambridge University.

Letters in the New Testament

Victor P. Furnish

1. Introduction

1.1. Importance

The earliest surviving Christian writings are letters. Twenty-one of the twenty-seven books of the NT canon were either specifically written as letters or handed down and incorporated into the canon as such. Collectively, the twenty-one canonical letters account for almost one-third of the text of the NT.

In addition, the book of Revelation, which is the clearest example in the NT of apocalyptic literature, may aptly be described as an apocalypse set within an epistolary framework (see 1:4-5; 22:21), and the seer's report in chs. 2–3 of what he hears the Son of Man saying to the church is formulated as seven letters addressed to seven specific congregations in the province of Asia. There are also two letters embedded within the book of Acts, one from "the apostles and elders" of the church in Jerusalem to the Christians of Antioch (15:23b-29) and the other from Claudius Lysias, the Roman tribune in Jerusalem, to Antonius Felix, the Roman procurator of Judea (23:26-30). Although the letters that stand within Revelation and Acts are the literary creations of the respective authors of these books, they nonetheless reflect certain characteristic features of actual letters known to us from the Greco-Roman world and help to show that letters were no less important in Christian circles than in society at large. Why Acts, which devotes so much attention to the missionary activities of Paul, neither portrays him writing letters nor otherwise reflects any knowledge of his letters has not yet been satisfactorily explained.

The importance of letters within Christian circles is further documented by the mention, in various places, of letters sent by congregations (the Corinthians to Paul, 1 Cor 7:1; the Ephesians to the Corinthians, Acts 18:27), carried by traveling ministers (2 Cor 3:1), or provided to others charged with some particular responsibility (1 Cor 16:3), as well as by a warning about an allegedly forged letter (2 Thess 2:2) and an instruction that neighboring churches exchange the letters they have received from Paul (Col 4:16).

1.2. Terminology

With just one exception, the Greek term employed in the NT for "letter" is *epistolē*. Because the related verb *epistellein* originally meant to convey oral instructions by means of a messenger (Herodotus 4.10.1; Thucydides 7.11.1), the noun *epistolē* (but in the earliest sources found always in the plural) was first employed with reference to what the messenger *said,* not to any document delivered. However, the verb eventually took on the added meaning of putting a message into writing, as in Acts 21:25, where the NRSV, for example, appropriately renders it as "we have sent a letter" (namely, the message from the leaders of the Jerusalem church to the believers in Antioch, ch. 15). Acts 28:21 is the only NT instance where the word *grammata* refers to a letter (the Jews of Rome tell Paul that they have received no *grammata* about him from Judea). This word points particularly to the *form* of the message — namely, one that has been set down in writing (literally, in the letters of the alphabet), whereas *epistolē* directs attention more to the manner of its *conveyance* — namely, by means of a messenger. In Hellenistic times, however, the two words were generally used interchangeably with reference to a written message, *epistolē* being the usual term and *grammata* employed mainly for variation.

The distinction still sometimes made between "letters" and "epistles" does not derive from any ancient sources but from the pioneering studies of Adolf Deissmann, who compared the letters of the NT with other letters in the ancient world. He argued that Paul's writings, like the common Greek papyrus letters that had been discovered in Egypt, are "true" or "actual" letters, whereas most of the other NT letters are not. As Deissmann described them, "true letters" are "pre-literary," "personal and intimate," "artless and unpremeditated," expressive of "the naturalness of the writer's mood," and intended neither "for the public eye" nor "for posterity." He thus reserved the term "epistle" for writings that could be called "literary letters" because even though in the form of letters they had been composed as literature, intended both "for the public of the time being" and "for the future." To this second category, according to Deissmann, belong the NT writings known as the letters of James, Peter, and Jude, as well as the so-called (and non-Pauline) letters to Timothy and Titus and the so-called letter to the Hebrews.

In its day, Deissmann's distinction served the purpose of accenting the need to understand both the historical contexts of the authentically Pauline letters and the features they shared with the ordinary Hellenistic letter. However, subsequent investigations have shown that his distinction was far too simplistically drawn. On the one hand, it takes too little account of the literary aspects of Paul's letters and of the extent to which they exhibit many of the rhetorical and stylistic conventions of his day. On the other hand, it takes too little account of the real-life settings and practical purposes of the NT writings that Deissmann called "epistles." In what follows, therefore, only the word "letter" will be used, and the adjective "epistolary" will mean simply "pertaining to a letter."

1.3. Canonical Groupings

The twenty-one NT letters are grouped together between the Gospels and Acts, which stand at the head of the NT canon, and the book of Revelation, which concludes it. Traditionally, the first fourteen (Romans through Hebrews) have been identified as constituting the "Pauline corpus" of letters (see below, 7, 10), although the status of Hebrews within this group was already regarded as problematic in the early church because it does not bear Paul's (or anyone's) name as its author (see below, 9, 10). The remaining seven letters (James through Jude) have been known collectively as the "catholic epistles" because several of them seem to have been intended for the church in general rather than for any specific person or place (see below, 8).

2. The Origins and Purposes of Letter Writing

2.1. Origins and Basic Function

Letters convey in writing what the senders would otherwise be communicating to the addressees in person and orally. Most fundamentally, therefore, the function of a letter is to substitute for a face-to-face meeting of the parties concerned and thereby begin or continue, if not actually represent, the conversation they could have had were they not separated by distance or circumstance. Thus Artemon, the editor of Aristotle's letters, was quoted as having said "that a letter ought to be written in the same manner as a dialogue" (Demetrius *On Style* 223; in Malherbe: 16-17), and Cicero commented that, "failing a *tête-à-tête* talk" with his friends, nothing gave him greater pleasure than exchanging letters with them (*Letters to His Friends* 12.30.1; in Malherbe: 26-27). Similarly, Seneca, in an essay composed as if it were a letter to his friend Lucilius, said that he preferred that his letters "should be just what my conversation would be if you and I were sitting in one another's company or taking walks together — spontaneous and easy . . ." (*Moral Epistles* 75.1-2; in Malherbe: 28-29).

Although Seneca, and before him Artemon and Cicero, were commenting on letters exchanged between friends or within a circle of friends, letters of other kinds also function to make the writer present to the reader. This is not less true of the earliest ancient Near Eastern letters known to us, including the cuneiform tablets from the Mesopotamian city of Mari, c. 1800-1760 BC, and the Canaanite town of Taanach, c. 1450 BC. Given the evidence of these very early texts, it would appear that the practice of writing letters originated with the exchange of diplomatic correspondence between ancient states as they were negotiating alliances, treaties, and other kinds of agreements, and with the official correspondence that was exchanged within states as they conducted the necessary business of government, engaged in military operations, and the like. In their earliest manifestations, therefore, letters not only substituted for oral communication but functioned more particularly to convey or acknowledge the receipt of authoritative information and injunctions.

2.2. Purposes

A letter can serve any of the three broad purposes served by oral communication in general. It may be dispatched in order to provide information, to convey requests or commands, or to sustain and deepen the relationship between the writer and recipient. More than one of these purposes may be served by the same letter, of course, and this was frequently the case in the ancient world just as it is today.

The information provided in a letter may be of any sort, ranging from everyday matters pertaining to family, business, or travel, all the way to grander matters pertaining to one's views of statecraft, the good life, and the nature of ultimate reality. Such information may be conveyed in various forms and be intended to carry more or less weight. For example, it may be offered quite informally as offhand opinion or simple hearsay, or it may be formulated very carefully as authoritative instruction.

Similarly, letters that make requests or issue commands take various forms, depending on the specific intent. Examples would include invitations requesting another's presence on a specified occasion, petitions requesting some kind of action, commendations requesting help for the bearer of the letter, letters that convey general appeals, and letters that issue very specific orders or directives.

Letters that are intended to sustain or deepen relationships are perhaps most frequently exchanged by parties of approximately equal social status, especially those who are bound by ties of family or friendship. However, letters can also play a role in affirming or strengthening relationships between persons of unequal standing, for example, parents and children, teachers and students, patrons and clients. Thus letters may convey expressions of thanks, admiration, or concern, general professions of friendship, or specific pledges of help or loyalty.

3. Letters in Ancient Israel

The letters most frequently in view in the Hebrew Bible (and Septuagint) are those represented as sent by kings, both of Israel and of Israel's neighbors, and they illustrate very well the varied purposes that royal correspondence served in the ancient world (for a catalog and analysis of the texts see Pardee). In the earliest of these, a military dispatch from David to Joab, a nephew and the commander of his army, the king arranged for the death of the letter's unsuspecting bearer, Uriah the Hittite (2 Sam 11:14-15). A quite different purpose was accomplished through the reported exchange of letters between Solomon and the king of Tyre, which resulted in the latter's pledging to help Solomon build a temple in Jerusalem (2 Chr 2:1-16). One reads also of Jehu seeking to accomplish his political aims by means of letters sent off to the leaders in Samaria (2 Kgs 10:1-6), and of Hezekiah having a letter circulated "throughout all Israel and Judah" calling the people to repentance and to keep the Passover in Jerusalem (2 Chr 30:1-9). In addition, there are letters attributed to the kings of Assyria (Sennacherib, 2 Kgs 19:9-13; Isa 37:9-13) and Babylonia (Merodach-baladan, Isa 39:1), among others.

Israel's prophets as well as her kings made use of letters — again, as a means of conveying what would be said in person if that were possible. The most important surviving example is Jeremiah's letter to the exiles in Babylonia (Jeremiah 29), in which the prophet cautions them not to expect a speedy deliverance from their captivity. His letter conveys directives to prepare for a long stay in Babylon (vv. 5-7), warns about false prophets (vv. 8-9; cf. vv. 21-23, 29-32), and offers consolation in the form of promises about God's eventual restoration of the exiles' fortunes (vv. 10-14). Here, as in his oral proclamation, Jeremiah's words are given as divine oracles, with the formula, "Thus says the LORD," occurring throughout (vv. 4, 8, 9, 10, 11, 14, etc.). This prophetic letter form is also exhibited in 2 Chr 21:12-15, where a letter supposedly written by Elijah prophesies that terrible sufferings will be visited upon Judah's King Jehoram and his people because of their unfaithfulness.

4. Letters in the Greco-Roman World

In the Greco-Roman world, letters had come to be the chief medium of written communication, not only in the conduct of affairs of state but also at every level and in every sector of society. Accordingly, there were many different types to serve the quite varied purposes for which they were written. Early Christian letters, including those in the NT, and Jewish letters from the period of the Maccabees and later share many of the formal characteristics of the usual Hellenistic letter.

4.1. Epistolary Theory and Instruction

Because of the importance of letters in Greco-Roman society, they came to play a significant role in the schooling of the youth. Early in the secondary stage of education (of boys twelve to fifteen years of age) exemplary letters were used mainly as a way of teaching proper grammar and form. Later, probably in association with the study of rhetoric and especially in the training of professional letter writers, instruction was given in such matters as choosing the type of letter best suited to one's purpose and circumstances, adopting an appropriate tone for it, and following the structural and stylistic conventions.

There is evidence from both Greek and Latin sources that by the first century BC attention was being given both to epistolary theory and to how letters should actually be written. The earliest surviving handbook of letter writing, *Typoi Epistolokoi* ("Epistolary Types," 200 BC to AD 300), falsely attributed to Demetrius of Phalerum, is probably similar to numerous others that were in circulation (Malherbe: 4 and 30-41). Pseudo-Demetrius identifies twenty-one different letter types ("friendly, commendatory, blaming, . . . admonishing, threatening, . . . inquiring, responding," etc.), briefly describing and illustrating each. For example, a congratulatory letter is written to share the joy of the addressee's good fortune and properly includes such comments as, "I did not realize that you have become a person of such consequence. . . ." A handbook from the fourth to sixth centuries AD, *Epistolimaioi Charactēres* ("Epistolary Styles"), falsely attributed to Libanius, offers brief descriptions of forty-one different kinds of letters (e.g., "the declaratory style is that in which we render and carry out harsh judgment against someone"), including the "mixed" type "which we compose from many styles" (Malherbe: 5 and 66-81).

By identifying and organizing the various kinds of letters that were typically written, handbooks like these helped to perpetuate epistolary conventions already well established and continued to be followed over the course of many centuries. Nonetheless, at least among the better educated, these conventions were not woodenly followed, but freely and creatively adapted.

4.2. The Influence of Rhetoric

Both the ancient classification of letters into various types and instruction in proper epistolary style were influenced to a certain extent by the categories and rules of classical rhetoric. Although the focus of rhetoric was public speech, its strategies were readily adaptable in letters, which continued to be viewed as substituting for what would otherwise be spoken. Three principal influences may be noted.

First, it is sometimes possible to identify a letter as representing one of the three primary species of oral discourse discussed by Aristotle (*Rhet.* 1.3). There was the deliberative (or advisory) speech, as delivered in a legislative assembly to persuade the audience about some proposed course of action; the forensic (or judicial) speech, as delivered in a courtroom to persuade the audience about events that have occurred in the past; and the epideictic (or demonstrative) speech, delivered to persuade an audience of the point of view they should be holding about something or someone (cf. Kennedy: 19-20 and chs. 2, 3, and 4).

Second, in some types of letters one may detect the influence of Aristotle's view that a speech must offer three kinds of proofs in order to be persuasive (*Rhet.* 1.2, 3-7). It must exhibit *ethos* in order to establish the credibility of the speaker, *pathos* in order to appeal to the situation and feelings of the hearers, and *logos* in order to develop a reasoned argument for the truth with which the speaker is concerned (cf. Kennedy: 14-23).

Third, Greco-Roman letters often exhibit the influence of rhetorical conventions respecting the structure and style of a speech (summarized by Kennedy: 23-30). For example, a forensic speech was to open with a *proem* (or *exordium*) that would capture the audience's attention and goodwill, and then proceed, in turn, with a *narration* of the facts, a statement of the *proposition* to be proved, the *proofs* themselves, a *refutation* of opposing views, and an *epilogue* (or *peroration*) that would summarize the argument and move the hearers to form a judgment in the matter. Many stylistic devices were quite readily transferable from oral to written discourse, ranging from relatively simple ones like metaphors, antitheses, and rhetorical questions to rather more subtle ones like hyperbole, metonymy (using a proper noun in place of a common noun), and catachresis (the intentional misuse of a word).

Despite these influences, however, most letters from the Greco-Roman world, including those in the NT, resist efforts to classify them simply or primarily according to rhetorical categories. Even the epistolary theorists recognized that conventional forms and features would often have to be freely adapted in order to produce a letter that was appropriate to the situation that occasioned its writing.

4.3. Types of Letters

The letters of Greek and Roman antiquity have been quite variously classified. A simple but very general distinction can be made between "official" and "private" letters, whereby the latter would include all types except those written by political rulers or officeholders. However, "private" letters, especially, were of so many different types and styles, depending on why, by whom, and to whom they were written, that more elaborate systems of classification are usually proposed. One of these, dependent largely on the classifications found in ancient epistolary manuals, distinguishes six types: letters of friendship, family letters, letters that praise or blame, letters that exhort or advise, letters that introduce or recommend a third party, and letters that accuse, defend, or account for some action (Stowers 1986: 49-173). This particular system has been criticized, however, because it provides no special category for official government letters and takes no account of the difference between everyday "nonliterary" letters and letters composed with more attention to their literary quality (Aune: 161-69).

Those interested primarily in understanding the letters in the NT may find it helpful to think of Hellenistic letters as belonging to one of three general classes. All letters written in the course of conducting business, to communicate more or less routine information, requests, or appeals, or to keep in touch with family or friends may be called *ordinary letters,* no matter what their individual "literary" merit. All forms of political correspondence, as well as any letters written by persons discharging official responsibilities within "private" circles, may be called *administrative letters,* no matter what the specific administrative purpose. Letters written not simply to inform but more particularly to advocate a point of view or appeal for some course of action may be classified as *edifying letters,* whether addressed to family, friends, students, members of a philosophical school, or the public at large.

Classifying a letter according to its type is often no less problematic than identifying it with one particular species of rhetoric. In part, this is because every classification scheme is artificial. Primarily, however, it is because ancient letters, by reason of their function, were inevitably shaped in significant ways by the circumstances attending their composition, including the status of the writer relative to that of the addressee.

4.4. Epistolary Conventions and Formulae

The opening and closing sections of Greco-Roman letters are highly conventional. They open with a prescript which provides the names of the sender (superscription) and addressee (adscription) and offers a word of greeting, often expanded to include some expression of goodwill. The closing (or postscript) typically includes a summary statement or appeal, a final greeting, and the date of writing. A papyrus letter from Egypt (no. 65 in White 1986: 105) is fairly representative. The prescript reads: "Isidora to her brother Asklas, greeting and may you always be well, just as I pray." In closing, Isidora writes: "If anything else should happen, I will tell you, and take care of yourself to stay well. Good-bye. Year 3, Hathyr 6 early [2 November 28 BC]."

The body of Greco-Roman letters is not so easily analyzed because how it was structured depended in large part on what the writer had to say. Moreover, by reason of its character and function, the letter form can readily assimilate a wide variety of materials and secondary forms (e.g., lists, narratives, itineraries, and reports). Nonetheless, certain epistolary formulae were often used in opening and closing the letter body and in effecting transitions from one section of it to another. For example, the body of a letter from the mid-first century AD opens with a common disclosure formula, "I want you to know" *(thelō se ginōskein),* and moves to its last point with a standard transitional formula, "Finally, then" *(loipon oun)*" (no. 91 in White 1986: 143). In addition to epistolary formulae like these, a letter body often exhibits reliance on more or less set phrases and sentiments to address such standard epistolary topics as friendship, health, and the prospects for a reunion of the writer and the addressee (Aune: 188-91).

4.5. Writing Materials, Dictation, Delivery

The widespread use of letters in the Greco-Roman world was due in part to the availability of a relatively inexpensive writing material made from the papyrus plant, which grew mainly in Egypt. Narrow strips from this plant were pasted together to form double-layered sheets that ranged from about 17 to 24 centimeters in width (6.75 to 9.75 inches), with the fibers running horizontally on one side (the *recto,* which was the side to be written on) and vertically on the other (the *verso*). After the surfaces were polished, these sheets were joined into rolls for storage, from which purchasers could secure whatever amount they needed. For most everyday correspondence a single papyrus sheet was sufficient. The standard black ink was a solution of carbon suspended in gum water, and the usual pen *(calamus)* was made by splitting the end of a reed to form a nib. (For details see Murphy-O'Connor: 2-5; White 1986: 213-14.)

Often, but not invariably, letters were dictated to an amanuensis, who could be either a professional scribe or someone else able to take dictation and produce a letter of acceptable form and in a legible hand (Longenecker: 281-88; Richards: 15-67). Dictation given at a fairly rapid rate *(vive voce)* would leave more initiative with the scribe, at least in producing the initial draft (perhaps on a waxed tablet rather than papyrus), but dictation could also be relatively slow, broken up at least into phrases if not word by word *(syllabatim).* By the first century AD this process was facilitated by the existence of shorthand systems for both Greek and Latin. It was not unusual for the closing lines or section of a letter that had been dictated to an amanuensis to be in the sender's own hand. This autographic material was generally not intended to authenticate the letter but to enhance its effectiveness in making the writer present to the addressee (Bahr: 466-68; Gamble 1995: 95-96). Even when an amanuensis was not employed, writers customarily spoke aloud the words they were themselves writing down (Gamble 1995: 204), a practice that reflects the close relationship between oral and written discourse in the ancient world.

Ordinarily the date of writing was placed at the end of a letter. The letter was then folded, secured with a fiber tie, and sealed. The outside *(verso)* was inscribed with the name of the addressee, any needed instructions about delivering the letter, and on occasion something about its contents. Sometimes multiple copies of a letter were produced so that it could be sent simultaneously to two or more places. There is evidence that some people (or their secretaries) retained copies of at least certain of the letters they wrote, but it is impossible to know how widespread this practice was. (For details see Epp; Murphy-O'Connor: 1-41; White 1984: 1738-39; White 1986: 216.)

The earliest government service for delivering letters was probably the one developed under Cyrus II of Persia in the sixth century BC, a kind of ancient "pony express" system that provided both mounted couriers and relay stations. The Roman postal service established by Augustus (the *cursus publicus*) was much the same, but enhanced with inns and mile markers. Ordinarily, however, these systems conveyed only official government mail, and private citizens were required to entrust their letters to special couriers. The well-to-do might send their letters by an employee or slave (perhaps one who had served as the amanuensis) or hire a professional courier. Others would have to rely on family members, friends, associates, or even passing strangers who were traveling to the distant place anyway. In some circumstances it was necessary to provide for the forwarding of a letter, one carrier handing it on to someone else who was able to complete the delivery. Because the sender always had to reckon with the possibility that a letter might be lost or misdelivered, two copies were sometimes sent by means of two different couriers. (For details see Epp; White 1986: 214-17; White 1988: 87-88).

It was not unusual for the person delivering a letter to read it aloud to the addressee, thereby "reanimating" the words in a way that would help to make the absent sender "present" (Stirewalt: 87; Kim: 397). Often, too, the courier was expected to expand on what the letter said (see the example in Epp: 46; see also Libanius *Letters* 753, 1429). Especially in the case of administrative correspondence, when the recipient chose to save a letter, the date of its receipt, the sender's name, and its subject might be noted on the outside in order to facilitate its retrieval from an archive (White 1986: 217).

4.6. Letter Collections

It was not unusual for prominent figures in the Greco-Roman world to plan on publishing their collected letters, although this often fell to others to accomplish after the writer's death (Aune: 170-72; Stowers 1992: 292-93). Only fragments survive of Artemon's collection of Aristotle's letters, although a few letters from other early Greek authors are extant, including Isocrates (436-338 BC), Demosthenes (384-322 BC), and Epicurus (341-270 BC). Much later the rhetorician Libanius (b. AD 314) wrote his letters intending them to have meaning even beyond the circumstances for which they were written, and a large number of them have survived. There were also Latin collections, including the 931 letters of Cicero (106-43 BC) published only after his death, although he himself had been planning publication. Pliny the Younger (AD 61-112) published 358 of his own letters, arranged in chronological order.

In the philosophical schools, especially, letters were often circulated that bore the name of the school's founder or of some other important figure in its past, even though they had been generated within the developing tradition (Stirewalt: 20-25; cf. Bauckham). Although such letters are aptly described as "fictitious" or "pseudepigraphal," they are not to be confused with forged letters, which were intended to deceive (note the warning in 2 Thess 2:2). A fictitious letter afforded the writer named — who was now and forever absent — a fresh epistolary presence within the tradition, not in order to misrepresent the alleged writer's views but for the purpose of authorizing the tradition's present formulation of them. One example is the letter supposedly written by Epicurus to his student Pythocles but actually composed after the philosopher's death by someone who condensed and combined materials drawn from several of Epicurus's writings.

5. Jewish Letters

Letters seem to have played less of a role in Jewish circles than in Greco-Roman society as a whole. Most of the Jewish letters that survive, or are referred to in the ancient sources, were written for official or administrative purposes. For example, on occasion festal letters like the one preserved in 2 Macc 1:1-9 (c. 124 BC) were sent out by Jewish officials in Jerusalem to inform Jews living in the diaspora about the appropriate way to observe a religious festival. The letter from Jonathan to the Spartans preserved in 1 Macc 12:6-18 (also from the Hasmonean period), as well as the letter Philo represents Agrippa I as sending to the Roman emperor Gaius (*Legat.* 276–329), are typical of Jewish diplomatic correspondence. The documents Paul the Pharisee is said to have carried to Damascus (Acts 9:1-2; 22:5) would have been official letters of authorization and recommendation. Most of the more than twenty letters, recovered from Judean caves, that date from Bar Kochba's campaigns against Rome (AD 132-35) may be classified as military dispatches.

The Jewish letters that survive, at least from the Hasmonean period forward, bear a certain formal resemblance to other Greco-Roman letters of the administrative type (e.g., the festal letter in 2 Macc 1:1-9). However, they do not exhibit the same degree of interest in adhering to epistolary conventions that one finds in other letters, including those in the NT.

6. Christian Letters

6.1. General Characteristics

Most of the letters in the NT have the same overall structure and component parts as the usual Greco-Roman letter. In general, there is a prescript that identifies the writer(s), specifies the addressee(s), and offers a greeting (e.g., Phlm 1-3; Jas 1:1; 2 John 1-3). In the letter body it is not unusual to find common epistolary clichés (e.g., for disclosing information, Rom 1:13; 2 Cor 1:8; Col 2:1; etc.) and sentiments (e.g., the writer's longing to be present, Gal 4:19-20; Phil 1:8; 1 Thess 3:6; Col 2:5; 2 John 12; 3 John 13-14; etc.). There is also usually a postscript, which may include brief summary statements (e.g., 1 Pet 5:12), appeals (e.g., 1 Cor 16:13-18), or specific requests (e.g., Col 4:16-17; Phlm 22), as well as a final greeting (e.g., Phlm 25). Unfortunately, no NT letter has survived with its date of writing still in place at the end of the postscript.

In one major respect, however, Christian letters are more like Jewish letters of the period — in that they reflect and seek to further the ethos and beliefs of the religious community within and for which they were written. Thus most Christian letters are addressed to congregations, not just to an individual, and they typically open and close not with the conventional "greeting" and "goodbye" of the Greek epistolary tradition, but by conveying or invoking the blessing of God or Christ (e.g., 1 Cor 1:3 and 16:23; 1 Tim 1:2 and 6:21; Jude 2 and 24-25). Similarly, where an ordinary letter might extend the opening salutation by wishing the recipient good health (see 3 John 2), NT letters more often have a paragraph that blesses or gives thanks to God for benefits already bestowed upon those addressed (e.g., Rom 1:8-15; Eph 1:3-14; 2 Thess 1:3-4; 1 Pet 1:3-9; cf. 2 Macc 1:2-6, 11-17). Also, by reason of their special aims most of the letters in the NT are significantly longer than other Greco-Roman letters, which seldom take up more than a single sheet of papyrus (only Philemon and 2 and 3 John are this short), and they incorporate from the church's traditions various types of material not usually found in letters.

Two further characteristics of NT letters are especially important. First, although in every case the sender (actual or alleged) wrote with an authority that the addressees did not share, the writers and recipients nonetheless understood themselves to be one in Christ and equal before God, brothers and sisters within the same family of faith. This accounts for the distinctive tone of the letters, which manifest the warmth and familiarity of correspondence between family members or friends even while they are establishing the absent writer as an authoritative presence with the recipients. Second, at least where the letter is accepted as that of an apostle, the writer is present with the recipients as one who has been commissioned by God. The letters in the NT, therefore, have a certain affinity with the prophetic letters in ancient Israel. Even though they do not have the form of oracular or revelatory discourse (like the letters in Jeremiah 29 and Revelation 2–3), as *apostolic address* they are distinctly different in character even from the didactic letters of the most revered philosophers (cf. Berger 1974: 1984).

6.2. Types

The letters in the NT display certain characteristics of the official or administrative letter because each was written by or in the name of someone with "official" responsibility for the welfare of the church, at least in a particular locale. Administrative concerns are most evident in the letters of the Pauline corpus (e.g., as the apostle solicits contributions to a fund for Jerusalem, 1 Cor 16:1-4; 2 Corinthians 8 and 9) and in 3 John. No less, however, the NT letters resemble the ancient philosophical letter in that they offer instruction and counsel to improve the moral and spiritual well-being of those addressed. Attempts to classify them more specifically, either with reference to ancient epistolary typologies or according to the traditional species of rhetoric, have not been particularly successful. Most are of "mixed" type and exhibit more than one kind of rhetoric. In these respects they have been shaped primarily by the occasion and the writers' specific aims and only secondarily by ancient epistolary conventions.

6.3. Dictation and Delivery

Paul dictated at least some of his letters. This is evident from Rom 16:22, where the secretary identifies himself as Tertius, and from several letters in which the apostle indicates — always near the close, as was customary — that the writing is in his own hand (1 Cor 16:21; Gal 6:11; Phlm 19; cf. 2 Thess 3:17). It would appear that Silvanus served as the secretary for the author of 1 Peter (5:12).

Christian letters were sometimes carried by delegations specifically dispatched for that purpose, as in the case of the letter drafted in Jerusalem for the church in Antioch (Acts 15:22). Probably more often, letters were carried by other Christians (or members of their households) who were traveling to the distant place anyway, perhaps on business or simply to visit. Itinerating ministers and teachers could also have served as couriers. It is likely that Paul entrusted 1 Corinthians to the three men named in 1 Cor 16:17, who had evidently brought a letter from the Corinthian congregation (1 Cor 7:1) to him, and that Philippians was carried by Epaphroditus, a member of the Philippian congregation whom Paul was sending home (Phil 2:25). We may suppose that Onesimus was the bearer of the letter to Philemon, written on his behalf (Phlm 10-17; cf. Col 4:7-9), and that Phoebe was the bearer of Romans — unless Romans 16, written on her behalf (vv. 1-2), was originally a separate letter. Paul's so-called "tearful letter" to Corinth was almost certainly carried by his associate, Titus (2 Cor 2:3-4, 9, 12-13; 7:5-16), who was later sent back with another that included an appeal for money (2 Corinthians 1–9, although ch. 9 may have been a separate letter; see 8:16-24; 9:3). When a letter was intended for more than one congregation, as were Galatians (addressed to "the churches of Galatia," 1:2) and 1 Peter (addressed to believers "in Pontus, Galatia, Cappadocia, Asia, and Bithynia," 1:1), it is possible that more than one copy was prepared and more than one courier dispatched.

Once at its destination a letter would have been read aloud, perhaps initially by the courier to whomever it was first handed over, then to all of the members of the congregation addressed whenever they were next assembled (note Paul's instruction in 1 Thess 5:27). Probably in most cases the person who had carried the letter was also expected to supplement, and perhaps even to help interpret, what it said (Col 4:7-9; cf. Eph 6:21-22).

7. Letters Bearing the Name of Paul

There is general scholarly agreement that seven of the thirteen letters bearing Paul's name are authentic, but his authorship of the other six cannot be taken for granted.

7.1. The Undisputed Letters

Romans, 1 and 2 Corinthians, Galatians, Philippians, 1 Thessalonians, and Philemon are certainly Paul's own. It is likely that 1 Thessalonians is the earliest of these, and Romans the latest. Philemon is the only one addressed primarily to an individual (but see Phlm 2), Romans is the only one addressed to a congregation that Paul had not founded or even visited, and Galatians is the only one addressed to all of the churches in a specified region (Gal 1:2; but cf. 2 Cor 1:1).

In the superscriptions of all except Romans and Galatians, Paul represents the letter as coming from himself and at least one other person: in 2 Corinthians, Philippians, and Philemon he names Timothy, in 1 Thessalonians he names both Timothy and Silvanus, and in 1 Corinthians he names Sosthenes. The naming of a cosender was not usual in other letters of the period. What role Paul's associates may have had in actually composing his letters is impossible to ascertain.

It may be that one or more of these canonical letters is actually a combination of at least two originally separate letters. This is most frequently claimed for 2 Corinthians, although partition theories have also been proposed for 1 Corinthians, Philippians, and 1 Thessalonians, and Romans 16 is sometimes identified as a separate letter. Paul's comments in 1 Cor 5:9-11 about his previous letter to Corinth provide clear-cut evidence that not all of his letters survived (see also Col 4:16, which refers to a letter written to the church in Laodicea), although it is sometimes argued that certain of his shorter letters, or fragments of his letters, have been editorially incorporated into those that have.

Despite occasional lapses and infelicities, Paul's letters are very well written. It is clear that he composed them with care, in some cases probably over a period of days (or perhaps weeks), even though he was not aiming at literary excellence. It is evident why his critics, as quoted by the apostle himself, had to concede that "his letters are weighty and strong" (2 Cor 10:10). This judgment is equally correct whether applied to the thoughts they contain or to the form in which those thoughts have been expressed.

7.2. The Disputed Letters

The so-called "Pastoral Letters," 1 and 2 Timothy and Titus, have long been regarded by most scholars as deutero-Pauline (written in Paul's name but after his death), although some have come to believe that 2 Timothy is significantly different from 1 Timothy and Titus, and likely from Paul. Ephesians is also widely regarded as deutero-Pauline. There is more scholarly support for the Pauline authorship of the other two disputed letters, Colossians and 2 Thessalonians. In all of these cases, any assessment of authorship requires consideration of both "external" and "internal" evidence. The former includes documentation of how early, how often, and by whom a given letter was accepted as Paul's. The latter involves judgments about the contents of the letter: Are the grammar, style, and vocabulary generally consistent with what one finds in the undisputed letters? Does the letter presuppose things that could not have been known or experienced by the apostle himself? Are the views expressed in it generally in accord with what we know about Paul's thought on the basis of the undisputed letters?

A judgment about the authorship of 2 Thessalonians depends in large part on how one explains the many places where its author is following the wording of 1 Thessalonians. Similarly, Colossians seems to have provided a model for the author of Ephesians. Most interpreters judge the Pastoral Letters to have been written by the same person (whether Paul or someone later), although it is not impossible that they have come from more than one hand.

Those who wrote letters in the name of Paul, or of other deceased apostles and revered leaders of the church (see below, 8), were not intent on deceit. They produced fictitious letters but not forgeries (see above, 4). Like the pseudepigraphal writings of the philosophical schools, these fictitious letters were meant to authorize and enliven new adaptations and formulations of the legacy with which the community understood itself to be entrusted.

8. The Catholic Letters

Two of the seven letters called "catholic" bear the name of Peter (1 and 2 Peter), tradition attributes three of them to John (1, 2, and 3 John), and the other two bear the names, respectively, of James and Jude. Paul identifies three of these four men — James (the brother of Jesus), Cephas (Peter), and John — as "pillars" of the Jerusalem church (Gal 2:9), with which Jude, too ("the brother of James," Jude 1), would have been associated (cf. Matt 13:55; Mark 6:3). The authenticity of the catholic letters was a matter of discussion even in the ancient church; as late as the fourth century Eusebius listed James, Jude, 2 Peter, and 2 and 3 John as disputed letters (*Hist. Eccl.* 3.25.3). In fact, 1 John was written anonymously, and the author of 2 and 3 John identifies himself only as "the elder." Most scholars today regard 2 Peter as pseudonymous, and many have reached the same conclusion about James, 1 Peter, and Jude.

The term "catholic," applied to some of these letters since at least the fourth century (Eusebius *Hist. Eccl.* 2.23.24-25), properly describes James, 1 John, 2 Peter, and Jude, which were apparently written for the church at large. None of these four is addressed to a specific person or place; indeed, 1 John has no address at all. The other three letters are not catholic in this sense, however. Second John appears to be addressed to a specific house church (vv. 1 and 10) and 3 John to an individual (Gaius, v. 1), while 1 Peter is an encyclical letter directed to Christians in several specified areas of Asia Minor (1:1).

The two letters that have come down as Peter's were almost certainly written by two different people. Whoever wrote 2 Peter drew heavily on Jude. There is no scholarly consensus on whether the three Johannine letters were written by the same person or on how they are related to the Gospel of John. Because James has no postscript and 1 John has neither a prescript nor a postscript, some interpreters describe these writings as homilies, tracts, or instructional booklets rather than letters.

The first specific citations of any of these catholic letters come from fairly late in the second century. By that time 1 John, 1 Peter, and Jude were being regarded, at least in certain circles, as canonical — although the canonical status of Jude remained somewhat questionable on down into the fourth century. The other four catholic letters gained acceptance even more slowly. Second-century sources yield relatively little evidence of the use of 2 John and 2 Peter, and no evidence of the use of 3 John or James. The acceptance of 2 and 3 John was made especially difficult because the writer's identification of himself as "the elder" *(ho presbyteros)* suggested that he did not have apostolic status. It was not until the end of the fourth century that all seven of the letters called "catholic" had a secure place in the church's canon.

9. Hebrews

Hebrews lacks a prescript, so the writing itself yields no information about its author or those for whom it was written. The title, which identifies it as "to the Hebrews," was added much later, as were the titles of the other books of the NT canon. Hebrews was doubtless written by a Jewish Christian, and probably for other Christians of Jewish heritage — but certainly not for non-Christian Jews. Hebrews exhibits no epistolary features except in ch. 13, where the mention of "our brother Timothy" in a postscript (vv. 22-23) prompted some ancient readers to include Hebrews among the letters of Paul (see below, 10).

Modern scholars agree that Hebrews could not have been written by Paul, and most identify it not as a letter (Lindars: 6-7 is an exception) but as a sermon or homily (e.g., Attridge: 14). The epistolary conclusion may have been provided in order to facilitate its distribution (Aune: 213).

10. The Pauline Letter Collection

None of the letters certainly written by Paul is addressed to the church at large, and there is no evidence that the apostle himself intended that they should ever be circulated as a group, or even that he anticipated that others might provide for their circulation after his death. Even in Romans, the most general of them, Paul deals with some issues that were quite particular to the situation of the Roman Christians (e.g., 14:1–15:13) and takes up certain topics that were also of particular moment to him as he prepared for a visit to the church in Jerusalem (e.g., chs. 9–11; see 15:25-31). Despite this, it is evident that at least one, and more likely several different collections of the apostle's letters were circulating by the beginning of the second century. At least 1 Corinthians was known to the church in Rome (*1 Clement* 47, c. AD 97), and both Ignatius (c. AD 110) and the author of 2 Peter (c. AD 125-50) knew Paul's letters as a group (Ign. *Eph.* 12:2; 2 Pet 3:16).

The evidence available does not permit firm answers to the questions when, by whom, and where the apostle's letters began to be collected and circulated. Onesimus (Phlm 10; Col 4:9) is sometimes credited with the idea, and Ephesus, Corinth, and Syrian Antioch are among the places that have been proposed. Perhaps the beginning lay in the exchange of letters by neighboring congregations (cf. Col 4:16). The production of deutero-Pauline letters — some of them well before the end of the first century — shows that quite early Paul's letters came to be valued more widely than in just the places to which they had been sent. The earliest form of the Pauline collection that can be reconstructed with any confidence seems to have contained nine (or ten) letters. However, these were presented as seven letters, probably in descending order of length: Corinthians (1 and 2 combined), Romans, Ephesians, Thessalonians (1 and 2 combined), Galatians, Philippians, Colossians (perhaps combined with Philemon) (Gamble 1995: 59-62). The formation of this *sevenfold* corpus helped to alleviate the problem posed by the particularity of Paul's letters because in antiquity the number seven symbolized wholeness and universality. This became the precedent for the seven letters to seven churches in Revelation 2–3, a sevenfold collection of the letters of Ignatius, and (by the end of the fourth century) the sevenfold collection of letters that Eusebius knew as "catholic" (see above, 8). In Marcion's canon (c. 150), which did not include Ephesians, the Pauline letters were listed in their presumed chronological sequence: Galatians, Corinthians 1–2, Romans, Thessalonians 1–2, Colossians, Philippians, and Philemon.

Most of the earliest editions of the Pauline corpus seem not to have included either the Pastoral Letters or Hebrews. The inclusion of the Pastorals within the collection is first explicitly attested by Irenaeus, late in the second century, and then by the Muratorian canon (which may be as late as the fourth century). They seem not to have been included in the Chester Beatty papyrus ($\mathfrak{p}^{46}$), the earliest surviving manuscript of the Pauline letter collection (c. 200). However, Hebrews was included in this Egyptian collection and placed immediately after Romans, which stood first. This is further evidence that Hebrews was more generally accepted as Pauline in the churches of the East than in those of the West.

Bibliography. Attridge, H. W. 1989, *The Epistle to the Hebrews,* Hermeneia, Philadelphia: Fortress • Aune, D. E. 1987, *The New Testament in Its Literary Environment,* LEC 8, Philadelphia:

Westminster, 158-225 • Bahr, G. J. 1966, "Paul and Letter Writing in the Fifth [*sic;* read "First"] Century," *CBQ* 28:465-77 • Bauckham, R. 1988, "Pseudo-Apostolic Letters," *JBL* 107:469-94 • Berger, K. 1974, "Apostelbrief und apostolische Rede," *ZNW* 65:190-231 • Berger, K. 1984, "Hellenistische Gattungen im Neuen Testament," in W. Haase and H. Temporini, eds., *ANRW* 2.25.2, Berlin and New York: de Gruyter, 1326-63 • Collins, R. F. 2000, "'I Command That This Letter Be Read': Writing as a Manner of Speaking," in K. Donfried and J. Beutler, eds., *The Thessalonians Debate: Methodological Discord or Metholological Syunthesis?* Grand Rapids: Eerdmans, 319-39 • Dahl, N. A. 1962, "The Particularity of the Pauline Epistles as a Problem in the Ancient Church," *Neotestamentica et Patristica: Eine Freundesgabe, Herrn Professor Dr. Oscar Cullmann zu seinem 60. Geburtstag überreicht,* NovTSup 6, Leiden: Brill, 261-71 • Deissmann, A. 1901, *Bible Studies,* Edinburgh: Clark, 3-59 • Epp, E. J. 1991, "New Testament Papyrus Manuscripts and Letter Carrying in Greco-Roman Times," in B. Pearson et al., eds., *The Future of Early Christianity: Essays in Honor of Helmut Koester,* Minneapolis: Fortress, 35-56 • Fitzmyer, J. A. 1981, "Aramaic Epistolography," in J. L. White, ed., *Semeia 22: Studies in Ancient Letter Writing,* Chico: Scholars Press, 25-57 • Frede, H. J. 1969, "Die Ordnung des Paulusbriefe und die Platz des Kolosserbriefs im Corpus Paulinum," in *Vetus Latine: Die Rest der altlateinischen Bibel 24/2,* Freiburg: Herder, 290-303 • Gamble, H. Y. 1995, *Books and Readers in the Early Church: A History of Early Christian Texts,* New Haven: Yale University • Gamble, H. Y. 1985, *The New Testament Canon: Its Making and Meaning,* Philadelphia: Fortress • Kennedy, G. A. 1984, *New Testament Interpretation through Rhetorical Criticism,* Chapel Hill and London: University of North Carolina • Kim, C. H. 1975, "The Papyrus Invitation," *JBL* 94:391-402 • Koester, H. 1991, "Writings and the Spirit: Authority and Politics in Ancient Christianity," *HTR* 84:353-72 • Lindars, B. 1991, *The Theology of the Letter to the Hebrews,* New Testament Theology, Cambridge: Cambridge University • Longenecker, R. N. 1974, "Ancient Amanuenses and the Pauline Epistles," in R. N. Longenecker and M. C. Tenney, eds., *New Dimensions in New Testament Study,* Grand Rapids: Zondervan, 281-97 • Malherbe, A. J. 1988, *Ancient Epistolary Theorists,* SBLSBS, Atlanta: Scholars Press • Murphy-O'Connor, J. 1995, *Paul the Letter-Writer: His World, His Options, His Skills,* Collegeville, Minn.: Liturgical Press • Pardee, D. 1982, *Handbook of Ancient Hebrew Letters,* SBLSBS 15, Missoula: Scholars Press • Richards, E. R. 1991, *The Secretary in the Letters of Paul,* WUNT 42, Tübingen: Mohr-Siebeck • Stirewalt, M. L. Jr. 1993, *Studies in Ancient Greek Epistolography,* SBLRBS 27, Atlanta: Scholars Press • Stowers, S. K. 1992, "Greek and Latin Letters," in D. N. Freedman et al., eds., *ABD* 4, New York: Doubleday, 290-93 • Stowers, S. K. 1993, *Letter Writing in Greco-Roman Antiquity,* LEC 5, Philadelphia: Westminster • White, J. L. 1988, "Ancient Greek Letters," in D. E. Aune, ed., *Greco-Roman Literature and the New Testament,* Atlanta: Scholars Press, 85-105 • White, J. L. 1984, "New Testament Epistolary Literature in the Framework of Ancient Epistolography," in W. Haase and H. Temporini, eds., *ANRW* 2.25.2, Berlin and New York: de Gruyter, 1730-56 • White, J. L. 1986, *Light from Ancient Letters,* Philadelphia: Fortress.

Romans

John Reumann

INTRODUCTION

The Letter of Paul to the Romans, as his longest extant document (7,094 words in Greek), stands for reasons besides length at the head of the Pauline corpus. Romans has overshadowed all Paul's other letters in giving voice to "the divine Apostle," as the church fathers called him, and over the centuries has proved to be, in the opinion of Luther and others, the gospel in its purest form. Its contents have again and again been decisive in the history of theology for dominant perspectives from Paul (Fitzmyer 1968: #79).

These include such classical themes as justification (3:20-26), salvation (1:16; 5:9-10; 8:24), reconciliation (5:10-11), expiation or atonement (3:25), redemption (3:24), freedom (6:20; 7:3; 8:1-2), sanctification (1:7, saints; 6:22; 15:16), transformation (12:2), new life in Christ (6:4-5, 23; 8:29), and glorification (8:18, 21, 30), not to mention gospel (1:16), sin and the human condition (3:23 as the summary of 1:18–3:20), predestination (8:29-30; 9:11-29), the Spirit (ch. 8) and spiritual charismata (1:11; 12:6-8), Israel (chs. 9–11), the law (2:12-27; 3:19-31; ch. 7; and elsewhere), life in Christian community and within the (pagan) state (chs. 12:1–15:13), and the coherent combining of such themes (8:29-30) through God's plan or "salvation history" (Adam, Abraham, Moses, Jesus Christ, and the Christ to come) and in terms of God and the divine righteousness. Indeed, the text of Romans has taken on a life of its own after leaving the hands of Paul and his scribe (16:23).

The study of Romans in this new millennium — *Anno Domini* is a confession about the significance of Jesus Christ of which Paul would have approved, though he would have reckoned the decisive turn from Jesus' death and resurrection, not Jesus' birth — often continues the theological interests of the 1,940-plus years since Paul wrote to the Christians in the empire's capital and the historical concerns of the last two hundred years or so. But now literary, sociological, and rhetorical interests also inform some recent approaches (Byrne: 2-8). Attention must therefore be given to Paul's circumstances as he wrote, the situation in Rome (insofar as we can ascertain it), and the text and its afterlife as a document that has struck readers differently over the centuries and today. These aspects so interrelate that we must move back and forth among them in introducing Romans for today.

1. Paul's Circumstances

During a stay in Greece, his work in Macedonia and Achaia well in hand (Rom 15:23, 26), Paul found the time right to begin his proposed mission to Spain, via Rome (15:24, 28). He writes to the Roman Christians while being hosted by Gaius (16:23), in Corinth (cf. 1 Cor 1:14), a city that had been a stormy center for his mission work (cf. 1 Cor 16:5-7; 2 Corinthians), along with Ephesus (Acts 19; 1 Cor 16:8). Acts 20:3 speaks of a three-month stay, probably during the winter months (likely in AD 57-58) when travel was difficult. The Pauline strategy of starting urban churches, whence the message might advance into the hinterlands, was working, with the evangelization of Macedonia and Illyricum (modern Albania, Rom 15:19), likely out of Philippi; of Achaia, out of Corinth and Cenchreae (16:1); and of the province of Asia, out of Ephesus and through converts like Philemon and his house church in the Lycus valley (Colossae, Laodicea, and Hierapolis, Col 4:13-17).

More particularly, things were in readiness to deliver to Jerusalem the collection for the poor among the Christians there (Rom 15:25-27), a project on which Paul had spent much effort over several years (1 Cor 16:1-4; 2 Corinthians 8 and 9). It went back to an agreement with the leaders in Jerusalem (Gal 2:10) but had become for Paul a way not only of sharing but also of acquainting his primarily Gentile communities with Jewish Christianity in Judea's sacred city. Gentile Christians would share material resources in thanks for spiritual blessing originating in the place where Jesus died (15:27). Paul looked on the trip to Jerusalem with certain fears, danger from unbelievers in Judea or that the gift would not be accepted (15:30-31). But this show of solidarity accomplished in Jerusalem, he hoped to go on to Rome for joyful and refreshing rest, prior to proceeding to Spain (15:32).

Thus Paul, perhaps in his early fifties, writes that "from Jerusalem and as far around as Illyricum I have fully proclaimed the good news of Christ" (15:19) — rhetorical hyperbole but reflective of his strategy of having mission teams and congregational cells advance the word in an arc across the Eastern Mediterranean. Now new ventures beckon, an ambition to preach in lands where Christ has not already been named (15:20-21). In Spain he would start afresh. But to contact Rome meant approaching a place where the foundations of Christianity were already laid. That put him in conflict with his own principle, not to encroach on others' fields of labor (2 Cor 10:14-16). Apostle to the Gentiles though he was, Paul knew it was a delicate matter to gain entrée at Rome.

2. The Situation at Rome

No one knows how Christianity in the capital city was begun or when. Perhaps it was passed on by Jewish-

Christian merchants and travelers from Palestine, among the sizable Jewish population in Rome. Acts 2:10 suggests that Jews and proselytes from Rome were in Jerusalem at Pentecost. The historian Suetonius reports that the Emperor Claudius, "since the Jews constantly made disturbances at the instigation of Chrestus, expelled them from Rome" (in AD 49; 42 on Luedemann's all-too-early chronology; *Claudius* 25.4). The reference is most likely to conflicts in the Jewish community over Christ, or perhaps among Jewish Christian groups over whether to extend their mission to Gentiles. Some of the expellees moved east, among them Aquila and Prisc(ill)a, with whom Paul worked in Corinth (Acts 18:1-3) and whose house church in Ephesus is mentioned in 1 Cor 16:19. They are among those greeted in Rome 16:3-4, now that they are back in Rome after the death of Claudius in 54. This couple provides one example of Jewish Christians from Rome whom Paul could have met in the Aegean area, and whom he could greet in Rome as he writes (16:5-15).

If many or most Jewish Christians in Rome were expelled from Rome for a time, does that mean that in the interim the Christian community there became predominantly Gentile? Proselytes in the synagogue and fresh converts from paganism then took over the church in Rome. Once Jewish Christians were allowed back, however, there was an integration problem if not a power struggle. The situation can be related to those described in Romans as "weak in faith" (14:1, 2) and "the strong" (15:1), in the main Jewish Christians and Gentile believers respectively. The former were punctilious over food, drink, and their calendars (14:2, 5, 21), the latter robust in lifestyle. Paul spends a considerable amount of papyrus on these matters (14:1–15:13) and urges the two groups to "welcome one another" (15:7). Cf. Donfried, Wiefel, Bruce, Wedderburn, and others in *The Romans Debate*.

There is another detail in Romans that has been tied to events in the empire. At 13:1-7 Christians are urged to be good citizens, subject to the state, paying direct taxes and indirect tolls. While some have seen the verses to be directed against dangers from Zealot political rebellion (but there weren't Zealots as yet), another background has been proposed. Nero, in his period of exemplary rule, gave heed to cries of protest against unjust collection of taxes by the *publicani* and was said by Tacitus (*Ann.* 13.50-51; cf. Suetonius *Nero* 10.1) to have even considered abolishing indirect taxes. This would have been in AD 58. Paul's advice, along traditional Jewish lines, urges Christians not to get caught up in the unrest of the times over taxation. Cf. Fitzmyer 1968: 30-36; Byrne: 11-13.

Such reconstructions of the situation give Romans a pertinent setting in the social, political, and ecclesial happenings of the day. To know the historical occasion clarifies passages and makes the theological content more meaningful. But others contend that theological sense does not depend on historical conjecture (Childs: 248-50, 262-63). All this relates to a broader discussion over whether Romans is a rather timeless compendium of teachings or a quite specific treatment of issues in the Rome of Paul's day (cf. Karris, Jervell, and others in *The Romans Debate*). References to the "strong" and the "weak" could simply be a replay of an earlier issue in Corinth (1 Cor 8:8-13; 10:23-30). The matters are complicated by some textual issues. On Christianity in Rome see the article by G. F. Snyder in *ABD*, 1:968-70.

3. Paul's Greek Text

It is a minor matter that very few sources omit the references to Rome in 1:7 and 15 — either by accident or deliberately to give the epistle a more general application (*TCGNT*, 505). Much more serious is the way the doxology found at 16:25-27 in most Bibles and in some of the best manuscripts appears in many manuscripts at the end of ch. 14 (see the NRSV note at 14:23); in $\mathfrak{p}^{46}$ at the end of ch. 15 (see the NRSV on 15:33); in several sources after both 14:23 and 16:23; or is omitted by some sources (*TCGNT*, 533-36). Thus Romans existed in antiquity in a short fourteen-chapter form, known to Origen and preferred by Marcion; a fifteen-chapter form, suggested by what is preserved in the Chester Beatty Papyrus, . . . 5:17–15:33 plus 16:25-27 and then 16:1-23; and the long form, through 16:27 (Fitzmyer 1968: 44-54).

This textual evidence has led to conjectures that Paul himself had, after writing chs. 1–16 to Rome, produced a shorter "general treatise," minus references to Rome and chs. 15–16 (so Lightfoot, among others, though this bisects the discussion of the strong and the weak in 14:1–15:13). More influential was the view expounded in 1948 by T. W. Manson (reprinted in *The Romans Debate*, 3-15) that a fifteen-chapter letter went to Rome and ch. 16 was sent to Ephesus as a letter of recommendation for Phoebe, along with a copy of chs. 1–15, to sum up Paul's position as he left the East. Variations of this view had wide currency in the second half of the twentieth century (Beare 1962: 113; Klein 1976: 752; Fitzmyer 1968: 53:10-11). Influential in turning the tide toward the now dominant view that all sixteen chapters were addressed to Rome was Gamble's 1977 study of the textual history of Romans. In particular he used arguments (57-95) from then emerging studies of the epistolary conclusion of Greek letter forms. Romans 16 is necessary for the elements that usually round out a Pauline letter (Fitzmyer 1993: 57-64).

Among the implications that follow from taking ch. 16 as the ending to what Paul wrote to Rome are that Phoebe (vv. 1-2) is going to Rome, likely as the bearer of the letter, and that Paul knows many more Christians in Rome by name (vv. 5-15) than just Prisca and Aquila (vv. 3-4). He would also seem to know a lot more about dissensions among Roman Christians (vv. 17-20) than is often supposed. Quite specifically, the five to seven house churches mentioned or implied in vv. 5-15 then become part of the mix of the strong and the weak, along ethnic and theological lines (Lampe in Donfried: 216-30). But it goes too far from the evidence to see two separate, hostile congregations in Rome, with Andronicus and Junia being Jewish apostolic founders (v. 7) and Prisca and Aquila being associated with "the churches of the Gentiles" (vv. 3-4) (Watson, in Donfried: 203-15 = 94-105 in Watson

1986; critique by Campbell in *SJT* 42 [1989]: 457-67). The old debate over whether Paul writes to Jewish or Gentile Christians is then resolved: the house churches were predominantly Gentile, some members were once synagogue proselytes, but there was a Jewish-Christian minority. It is not impossible that in some house churches (former house synagogues?) Jews might be present or on the fence, but Paul does not primarily address them (as Nanos has argued, seeing "the weak in faith" as people of God who had not yet recognized Jesus as the Messiah of Israel). So runs much current thinking, pointing toward specific aims on Paul's part in writing to a community of varied groups he did not found, where leaders are not identified, even in ch. 16.

4. Purpose(s)

Some aims that have been claimed in the past have receded in support in recent years. One is that Paul was in Romans providing a "last will and testament" on his theological heritage (Bornkamm 1971, in Donfried: 16-28), in part because Romans transcends the polemics in Galatians and "elevates his theology . . . into the eternally and universally valid" (28). It may, if none of the imprisonment epistles were written by Paul from Rome, turn out to be Paul's final word, but did the apostle intend it thus? For he was looking forward to joy in Rome and work in Spain, not just to the past or the eternal. Another is that the "secret addressee" of Romans was the church in Jerusalem, where Paul planned to deliver the collection but feared how it would be received; hence, it was argued, he writes what he might say to James and the others there and to line up the church in Rome as part of "the entire Gentile world" that will stand behind him in Jerusalem (e.g., Jervell, in Donfried: 53-64). Paul is concerned about Jerusalem, but he would have said more and different things about the collection and congregational representatives accompanying it if he were seeking solidarity with Jerusalem and not mutual welcome of the strong and the weak in 14:1–15:13. (Other arguments are found in Fitzmyer 1993: 74-76.)

Paul's purposes in writing to Rome were plural (cf. Wedderburn; Lung-Kwong).

1. Obviously he writes *to introduce himself and* what he calls *"my gospel"* (2:16; cf. 16:25). That means particular emphases in Paul's presentation of the good news, distinctives like justification now, in the overlap of the ages, on sufferings, or law (cf. Byrne: 22-26). As in Gal 1:1, 6, gospel and apostleship go together (Rom 1:1, 5, 9), but that does not imply that Paul thinks he must himself provide an apostolic foundation that was lacking in the Roman community, as Klein (753-54) claimed. Nor does it mean that he was confronting a sort of "truth squad" of Jewish-Christian countermissionaries who everywhere opposed his work and message (so Stuhlmacher, in Donfried: 333-45; Stuhlmacher 1994: 143). Paul must, however, answer false rumors about himself and his teaching (3:7-8; 6:1-2; 9:1-2) and thus he writes with apologetic purpose (Dunn 1988: lvi) and persuasively (Byrne: 13-18).
2. Paul seeks mutual understanding and sharing (1:11-12) in order to have *support in Rome for his proposed trip to Spain* (15:14-29, esp. 24, 28-29) (Jewett 1988 and in Donfried: 266; Dunn 1988: lv: the missionary purpose helps account for the universal emphases).
3. As regards Jerusalem, Paul asks Roman Christians to *pray for his safety and* that *the collection* "may be acceptable to the saints there" (15:25-27, 30). That Paul seeks money or support from Rome vis-à-vis the Jerusalem authorities is not stated, and the logistics of getting funds and congregational representatives from Rome to Jerusalem in time preclude it. Besides, they would not be from a Pauline congregation.
4. The extraordinary attention to the strong and the weak in 14:1–15:13 suggests that Paul not only knows of disputes among the Roman Christians over food, drink, and special days (14:2, 5, 17, 21) but also writes to *persuade the groups in Rome to greater acceptance of each other.* "Welcome one another" (15:7). While this aim can be termed "pastoral" (Dunn: lvi-lviii), it is also ecclesial, about church unity, and goes some way toward ameliorating the absence of ecclesiology that Fitzmyer (74) laments. But did Paul have a "universal" church concept? Cf. Dunn 1997: #20.2, pp. 540-41. J. C. Miller sees Paul shaping "a community of the new age."

5. Resources

For accomplishing these tasks Paul had the Scriptures of Israel and interpretative tools, other Jewish writings and traditions, the Christian (oral) gospel and its creedal slogans, liturgical and catechetical traditions, and ethical parenesis, including at points sayings from Jesus. In addition, there were Paul's own experiences "in Christ" — call, preaching, sufferings, and reflection on his Jewish heritage in light of Christ over some twenty years. Use of the OT (Cranfield: 2:862-70) in its LXX form shapes Romans at 1:17 (Hab 2:4), 3:20 (Ps 143:2), and 4:3 (Gen 15:6) and is particularly concentrated at 3:10-18, chs. 9–11, 12:16-20, and 15:3, 9-12. The rabbinical exegetical device of *gezerah shawah,* interpreting "reckoned" in Gen 15:6 by the use of the same verb in Ps 32:1-2, is applied at Rom 4:3-8. Formulae about righteousness are quoted at 3:24-26a and 4:25 (Reumann: 35-40), along with other instances like 1:3-4. Rom 12:9-21 strikes many as preset general ethical instruction, including reflections of what Jesus taught (12:14; cf. Matt 5:44, 38-39, 43-44; 12:17). Byrne (20-26) speaks of "'knowledge' (symbolic universe)" which Paul has from Judaism (such as "the eschatological perspective of Jewish apocalypticism," stressed by Beker); "the shared Christian pattern of belief" (such as what some call the "story" or narrative about Jesus), and the "experience of the Spirit"; and Paul's own distinctives like "the eschatological 'now'" (3:21), and "'justification' associated with the great judgment" that "can already be received through Christ" now (3:24, 26).

6. Literary and Rhetorical Aspects

How has Paul cast such resources into a coherent whole? Admittedly there are sometimes breaks in the sentence structure (anacoluthon) at 2:17-24; 5:6-8, 12-14; 9:22-24, where the scribe could not keep up with the flow of words. What some a generation ago thought to be glosses inserted by a later scribe, such as 2:16 or 6:17b, now may be regarded as keys to Paul's own thought (Klein: 752). Overall, the opening (1:1-15) and closing (ch. 16) are like a typical letter. But the body of the letter is so long that some call Romans a "letter essay" (Stirewalt, in Donfried 1991: 147-71; but note the cautions at 131-32 from Wuellner). Romans is not, like the next longest Pauline epistle, 1 Corinthians, organized around a series of questions to which Paul responds. The coherence of Romans has sometimes been questioned, leading Schmithals, for example, to claim that it combines three letters (summary and response by Wedderburn, in Donfried: 195-202): in addition to ch. 16 to Ephesus, Schmithals's Letter A = 1:1–4:25; 5:12–11:36 + 15:8-13; and B = 12:1-21; 13:8-10; 14:1–15:7, 14-33 + 16:21-23 and 15:33 (the omitted verses were added much later). Typical of the reasons for seeing two letters is Schmithals's claim that the travel plans in 1:13-15 differ from those in 15:20-25. But the alleged tensions can be resolved, for example, by saying that "preach the gospel" in 15:20 denotes pioneer evangelism and at 1:15 its reiteration to believers in Rome.

Efforts to classify Romans rhetorically have led some to call it "epideictic" (Lat. *demonstrativus,* praising or blaming, strengthening the ethos of the audience), but others "deliberative" (persuasive, as in an assembly), or perhaps "juridical" (as in a court of law). Jewett made Romans an "ambassadorial letter," and others a "speech of exhortation" *(logos protreptikos)* (Donfried: lv-lxi, lxxi, 266, 278-96; and Stowers). Dunn 1988: 841 is dubious whether such categorizing helps. Byrne (4-5) declines to employ even the designations for the parts of a speech like *exordium* or introduction, *narratio* or statement of the case (such as Jewett, in Donfried: 270-76, applied). There are rhetorical devices in Romans, and on occasion some of them will be noted below, on the grounds that Paul the orator-preacher could reflect popular features of rhetoric in dictating a written communication. The diatribe is a good example at 2:1-6, 17-24 and elsewhere. Here a debate form and various rhetorical devices are used, with an interlocator or dialogue partner or opponent assumed (Donfried: 113-19, lxx, questions whether Bultmann's "diatribe form" existed in antiquity, but cf. 252-53, 273, 291, and Fitzmyer 1993: 91).

7. Outline

Outlines are often arbitrary and imposed, except where an author has provided structural clues. There is considerable agreement that Paul here, as elsewhere, employs the pattern of a "doctrinal section" (1:16–8:39 or 11:36), followed by an ethics section (parenesis, 12:1–15:13). The role of chs. 9–11 has long been debated, with some regarding them as intrusive, an excursus which interrupts the flow of the whole, and others regarding the chapters as a — or the — high point of the letter. Reference to "the problem of Israel" might sound anti-Semitic; more recent discussions have often been philo-Semitic. Key passages certainly include 1:16-17; 3:21-31; 5:12-21; ch. 8 (cf. Fitzmyer 1993: 341, 406, 481); and perhaps 12:1-2. The outline below serves as a framework for the commentary, where Romans will be treated by units of meaning, seeking to show the sense of each and the flow of the argument.

Letter Opening (**1:1-17**): Salutation (1:1-7); Thanksgiving (1:8-15); Theme (1:16-17)

The Body of the Letter (**1:18–15:13**)

- I. The Need for the Revelation of God's Righteousness (the theme put in negative terms, all humanity under the old aeon or age) (1:18–3:20)
  - A. The Gentiles Subject to God's Judgment and Wrath (1:18-32)
  - B. The Jews Also Subject to God's Judgment and Wrath (2:1–3:9)
  - C. All People Sin, Unjustified by Deeds of Law (3:10-20, scriptural proof)
- II. The Gospel of God's Righteousness Manifest in Sinners' Justification by Faith (the theme positively put, all under grace, faith, and the new age, thanks to Christ) (3:21–4:25)
  - A. All Share, without Distinction, in God's Righteousness, through Christ's Sacrificial Death (3:21-26)
  - B. Justification by Faith, Not Law (3:27-31)
  - C. A Scriptural Example: Abraham Justified by Faith, Not Works (4:1-25)
- III. What Justification and New Life in Christ Mean (Chs. 5–8)
  - A. Freed from Wrath and Death (Adam/Christ contrast) (Ch. 5)
  - B. Freed from Sin and Self (Ch. 6)
  - C. Freed from the Law (Ch. 7)
  - D. Freed for Life in the Holy Spirit and for Hope (Ch. 8)
- IV. The Gospel of God's Righteousness and the Unbelief of (Much of) Israel (Chs. 9–11)
  - A. God's Sovereignty and Promises (9:1-29)
  - B. Israel's Failure at Response (9:30–10:21)
  - C. Hopes for the Future (Ch. 11)
- V. Meaning for Everyday Life of God's Justifying Righteousness (12:1–15:13)
  - A. Exhortations for Christians in Community, with the State (13:1-7), and Looking toward "the End" (13:8-14, the command to love) (Chs. 12–13)
  - B. Mutual Acceptance among the Strong and the Weak in the Christian Community (14:1–15:13)

Letter Closing (15:14–16:23 [25-27]): Paul's Plans for Visiting Rome and a Mission to Spain (15:14-33); A Recommendation for Phoebe (16:1-2); Paul's Greetings to Christians in Rome (16:3-16); Warning (16:17-19); Greetings from Those with Paul (16:21-23), and Doxology (16:25-27). (V. 24 is omitted on textual grounds.)

8. Principal Themes

The second paragraph above listed a number of topics in Romans to be noted in the Commentary. Some are so prominent that they have at one time or another been made points of entry to the entire letter or its center. Often a theme is concentrated in particular chapters, but it is worth remembering that Paul sometimes begins a topic and then drops it till later; conclusions may be delayed for a passage later on. Christ, for example, is mentioned in passing at 1:7 and 8, and something is said about him in the formula at 1:3-4, but the talk is far more about God (views on whom were in conflict, according to Moxnes) until Christ comes to the fore in 3:24-25 and 5:6-21; cf. also 9:5; 10:4, 6-13; 15:3, 7-8, not to forget that justification has been called Paul's "functional Christology." A Pauline "theology of the cross" (as at 1 Cor 1:17-18) does not come to expression in Romans in that the word for cross *(stauros)* is never used, but one can find enough references to Jesus' death (5:6-10; 8:34; 14:15) as a means of expiation (3:25) and sin offering (8:3) to make "Golgotha" relevant in Romans (Minear 1995).

8.1. **Justification** was the new perspective on Paul that the Protestant Reformation brought (Dunn 1997: #14.2). It continues to be made emphatic in numerous commentators (Käsemann; Stuhlmacher; Lohse). Today attention to the theme is broadly ecumenical (Reumann; Wilckens; Fitzmyer). In English Bibles references to "righteousness" must also be considered. For the Latin-derived terms "just/justice/justification" and the Anglo-Saxon "right/righteousness" are both used for the single Heb. root *sdq, sedaqah* and the Gk. *dikaioō, dikaiosynē.* The OT is rich in applications to God and divine judging and delivering activity and to human actions, including morality (*ABD,* 5:724-36, J. J. Scullion; 3:1129-30, R. B. Hays). The QL has provided examples often closer to Pauline thought than rabbinical and other Jewish sources, and there is also a Greco-Roman background (*ABD,* 5:736-45, Reumann). Righteousness/justification comes initially into prominence in early Christianity to interpret the meaning of Jesus' death, often in cultic terms (Rom 3:25; *ABD,* 5:745-54). Paul also takes over and develops the theme letter by letter, but especially in Galatians and Romans (*ABD,* 5:757-68). The terms are especially concentrated in Romans in 3:21-26, chs. 4, 6, 9, and 10. Treatments emphasizing righteousness/justification often focus on Romans 1–8 or even just 1–4.

8.1.1. **"The righteousness of God"** (1:17; 3:5, 21, 22, 25, cf. 26; 10:3) has attracted particular attention as a possible technical term from Jewish apocalyptic thought. For Käsemann it represents God's power and might and God's faithfulness to the covenant, with cosmic implications, not merely the individualistic sense of a "gift from God." It is probable that the genitive "of God" has different nuances in different contexts like 1:17 and 3:5, though Dunn 1997: #14 would take the phrase regularly as "God's activity in drawing individuals into and sustaining them" in a relationship (of salvation). Schreiner's outline stresses "righteousness," but "the glory of God" is the central theme.

On righteousness/justification see *TDNT,* 2:174-225 (Quell, Schrenk); *NIDNTT,* 3:352-77 (Seebass, C. Brown); *EDNT,* 1:325-35, K. Kertelge; Fitzmyer 1993: 116-19; Dunn 1997: #14; *DPL,* 517-23 (McGrath), 827-37 (Onesti and Brauch); Spicq, *TLNT,* 1:318-47.

8.1.2. The theme is made more pervasive by its frequent connection with **"faith."** The verb *pisteuō* ("have faith") and the noun *pistis* occur at Rom 1:16-17; 3:22-31; chs. 4 and 10; and with scattered references in almost every chapter. There exists a range of meanings — faith, trust, obedience, faithfulness, reliability, loyalty, even guarantee. The Greek is often expressed in English by "believe." The terms can be used for God's faithfulness to the divine promises and for human response to what God proffers. Particularly debated is the Greek phrase *pistis Christou* or some variation thereof. It has traditionally been rendered "faith in Christ" (objective genitive), as at 3:22 (NRSV). But in the last two decades the subjective genitive, "faith of Christ," has been revived (see NRSV note) (so Hays 1983; in *Pauline Theology III,* Hays [75]; Bassler [167]; for the usual view, Lincoln [147] in the same volume, and Dunn 1997: #14.8). Cf. *TDNT,* 6:174-228 (Weiser, Bultmann); *NIDNTT,* 1:587-606 (O. Becker, Michel) and 3:1211-12; *EDNT,* 3:91-98 (G. Barth); *TLNT,* 3:110-16; *DPL,* 285-91 (L. Morris); Fitzmyer 1993: 137-38; Dunn 1997: #14.7.

8.2. **Predestination** has loomed large in patristic and some Reformation readings of Romans. While the verb occurs at 8:29-30, the theme blossoms in chs. 9–11, especially for the election of Isaac and Israel in contrast to Esau and Pharaoh (thus "double predestination," to salvation and its opposite). References to Paul and the saints at Rome as "called" (1:1, 7) ought also to be connected with the theme. In the history of interpretation (Sanday and Headlam: 269-75) one may recall Augustine versus Pelagius; Aquinas, Calvin, and Barth (Cranfield: 2:448-50). Yet F. C. Baur also made chs. 9–11 the center of Romans (Käsemann 1980: 253; unless otherwise noted references are to this work). On varied subsequent views see Fitzmyer 1993: 540-42.

8.3. **Life in the Spirit** has sometimes been seen as the high point of Romans toward which Paul moves. Thus ch. 8 or perhaps 5–8, the new life in Christ. Here Paul's concept of the Spirit (Fitzmyer 1993: 124-26) and the "in Christ" theme loom large, often broadened to "participation in" or "union with Christ" (Dunn 1997: #15.1-4, with references to Deissmann and Albert Schweitzer; and in #16, the gift of the Spirit and "charismatic Christianity").

8.4. **Ethics** (12:1–15:13), some have maintained, is what Paul really delights in, after all the theology in chs. 1–11. If a Christian "was really *hagios* — consecrated . . . , he must inevitably show it" (Enslin 1957: 64-65). Cf. 6:19, 22, "freed from sin, slaves to righteousness for sanctification." A "holiness" emphasis appeals to all Wesleyan groups. On *hagiasmos* terms cf. *TDNT,* 1:88-115 (Procksch, Kuhn); *NIDNTT,* 2:223-32 (Seebass, C. Brown); *EDNT,* 1:16-20 (Balz). On Christian conduct, Fitzmyer 1993: 141-43; Dunn 1997: #24.

8.5. Emphasis on the strong and the weak accepting one another (14:1–15:13) has led to new attention to the striking **tolerance** Paul shows to the views of both groups (cf. Jewett 1982), and in some quarters to the (local) church as "the welcoming place" (15:7: "as Christ has welcomed you"). The Christian community then becomes a place for "living with fundamental disagreements" (Dunn 1997: #24.3, "'Welcome [the weak], though not with a view to settling disputes' (14.1)" (p. 683).

8.6. No one would propose **the law** as the central theme in Romans, but the Gk. *nomos* appears some 72 times in the letter, especially in 2:12-27; 3:19-31; and, above all, in ch. 7 (but also, in order of frequency, in chs. 8, 4, 5, 6, 9, 10, 13). Usually *nomos* is rendered "law," but it may on occasion have the Greek sense of "principle" or "norm" (RSV 3:27; cf. 7:21, 23, 25; 8:2). The range of meanings is as wide as the Heb. *torah; nomos* may therefore refer to the Pentateuch (3:21: "law and prophets") or Scripture more broadly (3:19, psalms and prophets cited in vv. 10-18). But most commonly it refers to the Mosaic law (always, Dunn 1997: #6 insists, "the main subplot" of Romans, p. 131). In Romans law defines sin, condemns trespasses, and serves as the measure for God's judgment (3:19-21; 7:7; 1:32: "God's decree"; 2:12, 17-23). But there is more. For all the emphasis on believers being freed from the law (Rom 7:3-4, 6; Gal 5:1), Paul still can cite the Mosaic Torah to indicate God's will for Christians (13:8-10). Such material has led to long debates over "law," at times with anti-Semitic undertones in antilegalism, and to what Dunn calls "the new perspective on Paul" in the last quarter of the twentieth century. Here Dunn 1988: lxiii-lxxii focuses entirely on "Paul and the Law," especially in light of E. P. Sanders 1977. Indeed, Paul's aim in setting forth his gospel may include dispelling false rumors about his position on the Mosaic law (Wedderburn: 64-65). How then 10:4? On *nomos* see *TDNT,* 4:1022-91 (Kleinknecht, Gutbrod); *NIDNTT,* 2:438-56 (Esser); *EDNT,* 2:471-77 (Hübner); *DPL,* 529-44 (Thielman, Schreiner); Fitzmyer 1993: 131-35; Dunn 1997: ##6 and 23.2.

8.7. **Covenant.** The Gk. *diathēkē,* for the Heb. *berit,* occurs only twice in Romans, and one of these is in a quotation at 11:27 from Isa 59:21. The concept was pervasive in the OT and Judaism, though less frequent in the NT than one might suppose (*IDB A-D,* 714-23, Mendenhall; *ABD,* 1:1179-1202, Mendenhall and Herion). Some traditions, notably the Calvinist, have maximalized "covenant theology," and some modern interpreters assume the theme widely as background (Cranfield: 2:852-61; hence the law is not abrogated; Kaylor; N. T. Wright; Hays in *Pauline Theology III,* 71, 84).

Actually, Paul refers to "the covenants" (9:4) which Israel possessed. One model, the Mosaic or obligatory covenant, involved stipulations (exemplified in the commandments) of what the Israelites were to do in response to their delivery from Egypt by God (Exod 20:2-17, with ch. 19 as setting) (*IDBSup,* 192-97, P. A. Riemann). From Judaism's concern for the *nomos* came the pattern of "covenantal nomism" which E. P. Sanders found to characterize Palestinian Judaism. Another model was that of the Abrahamic (Genesis 15) and Davidic (2 Sam 7:8-16) covenants, promissory in nature, based on God's promise, and without conditions (such as are added in 1 Kgs 2:4; Ps 132:12; and elsewhere) (*IDBSup,* 188-92, Weinfeld). It is the Abrahamic covenant of which Paul speaks in Romans 4 (and Galatians 3), with Jesus' Davidic descent (1:3) and messiahship (9:4) suggesting the Davidic covenant. When Käsemann and others speak of the Creator's covenant fidelity to the whole creation, the first of the covenants expressly mentioned in the OT, that with Noah (Gen 9:8-17), is in mind. On *diathēkē: TDNT,* 2:104-34 (Quell, Behm); 10:1041-46; *NIDNTT,* 1:365-72 (Guhrt); *EDNT,* 1:299-301 (Hegermann); *DPL,* 179-83 (Campbell); Dunn 1988: lxvii-lxix; 1997: ##6.5, 14.2, 19.1, p. 503.

8.8. **The Two Aeons.** Two ages — one old and evil, under Satan, the other new and coming from God — are sometimes used as the eschatological context for Paul's thought (Nygren: 16-26; Achtemeier 1985: 7-15, with charts; unless otherwise noted references are to this work). The concept of "this age" and "the age to come" appears in Jewish apocalyptic (cf. also *'Abot* 2.7, "life of the age to come"). Paul speaks at Gal 1:4 of Christ's death freeing us "from the present evil age" and at Rom 12:2 of not being conformed to this age (*aiōn*). This term for "age" or "world" is rare in Paul (but cf. 1 Cor 1:20; 2:6, 8; 3:18; 2 Cor 4:4), in Romans otherwise only in the phrase "forever (and ever)" (lit. "for the age[s of ages]," 1:25; 9:5; 11:36; [16:27]). Actually Nygren associated the theme with the realms of death and life, of Adam and Christ, each the head of an age; cf. 5:14, "the age to come," 8:18, the glory to be revealed. A number of commentators avail themselves of the imagery. On *aiōn,* cf. *TDNT,* 1:197-209, especially 204-7 (Sasse); *NIDNTT,* 3:826-33 (Guhrt); *EDNT,* 1:44-46 (T. Holtz); *DPL,* 256-57 (Kreitzer).

Such themes will be referred to at pertinent points in the Commentary below.

9. The Immediate Results of Romans

Acts 21:17–28:30 describe how Paul, after leaving Greece, accompanied by what seems a group of congregational representatives (20:3-6, though Luke never mentions the collection), arrived in Jerusalem, was arrested, and eventually taken to Rome, a prisoner (28:16). The account ends with Paul living at his own expense (28:30), meeting with Jews, only some of whom believe (28:17-24), and presumably awaiting Caesar's answer to his appeal (25:12). Christian brothers and sisters met with him (28:15), but there is no reference to a letter he had written to them. The tradition is that he was eventually executed in Rome, with little or no evidence that he ever got to Spain (unless implied in *1 Clem.* 5:7, Paul reached "the boundary of the west").

Paul sheds little light on how Romans was received in Rome, even if the "imprisonment epistles" (Philippians, Colossians, and Ephesians) are taken as Paul's own and written from Rome. But if Phil 1:14-18 is from there, it indicates that, while Roman Christians preached the word, some did so to afflict Paul in his imprisonment. This seems a sign of lack of unity and animosity toward Paul. Brown 1983, who thinks that Roman Christianity was shaped by Jerusalem and that the Paul who wrote Romans was wiser and closer to Peter and James than when he had written Galatians, nonetheless holds that a minority in the church in Rome opposed Paul, as "extremists insistent on circumcision" long had. Hence the "jealous zeal and envy" (*1 Clem.* 5:4-7) that led to Paul's death (and Peter's too) in Rome. Paul's letter had hardly been a success.

1 Clement, about AD 96, also shows that Roman Christianity had presbyters with oversight (1.3; 21.6; 44.4-6) as well as "deacons" (42.4-5). It felt revulsion at the removal of established presbyters by the church in Corinth (44.3), and so wrote in their support (1.1-2). Meier 1991 sees in *1 Clement* "an attempt to legitimate a certain pattern of institutionalized leadership in the Corinthian church" (135); and Jeffers 1991 finds in *1 Clement* and *Hermas* two different emerging social groups in Rome, one (according to the latter document) more prophetic and charismatic than that depicted in *1 Clement.* From such evidence it is hard to claim that Paul's pleas in Romans 14–15 had been successful in producing a unified and tolerant church.

To this extent Romans lost out at Rome and, in the bigger picture, its "pattern of religion" ("participationalist eschatology," as E. P. Sanders called it) was replaced in Christianity by the "covenantal nomism" Sanders found to characterize Palestinian Judaism (543-56, esp. 552).

10. Romans through the Centuries

Since Paul's day Romans has invited readers into its world, with varying results (cf. *Int* 34.1, Jan. 1980). If there were at times an eclipse of Paul and an inability to grasp his thought, Paul also had his champions who gathered his letters and placed Romans at the head of a corpus that became the keystone of the NT canon. This is not to mention hyper-champions like Marcion. The divine apostle (Wiles) was the single biblical author read most consistently at Sunday worship (Romans 12–13, e.g., as a *lectio continua* in Epiphany that long survived in the Roman Missal, Book of Common Prayer, and Lutheran lectionaries). Romans attracted all sorts of commentators (the fullest listing is in Fitzmyer 1993: 173-214), among them Origen, Chrysostom, Pelagius, Abelard, Aquinas, Erasmus, numerous Reformers, and scholars and theologians to our own day.

Well known is how Augustine was converted when a voice told him to pick up Romans and read it. Paul's words at 13:13-14, ". . . not in rioting and drunkenness, not in chambering and wantonness. . . . But put on the Lord Jesus Christ . . . ," brought Augustine to faith (*Confessions,* bk. 8). Romans armed him in the struggle with Pelagius over free will and sin. Luther recorded how 1:17, about the righteousness of God, plagued him until he learned it was not there a matter of divine justice and punishment but of God's gift and faith (WA 54, 185,14–186,9). Melanchthon shaped his *Loci* and Calvin *The Institutes of the Christian Religion* around Romans. John Wesley, the Church of England priest, found his heart "strangely warmed" when Luther's Commentary on Romans was read at a Moravian meeting in Aldersgate. Karl Barth, young Reformed pastor at Safenwil in Switzerland, adrift in Protestant Liberalism, found the theology of Romans, about which he wrote in 1919, to be like the experience of a man groping in a dark church tower who reaches out to grab whatever he can — and grasps the rope that rings the bell that wakes up the entire community. Romans is read (and preached upon) on many occasions, including some sixteen Sundays in the three-year post–Vatican II *Ordo Lectionum Missae* and daughter lectionaries in Year A (2002, 2005, etc.), though, alas, in the summer in the northern hemisphere.

The symbolic world into which Paul seeks to persuade hearers and readers through the words of Romans, as a corrective to our "real world," comes out differently in various interpreters. It is a tribute to this "instrument of persuasion" (Byrne: 16) that the power of the apostle's words continue, through the Spirit. It is the task of exegesis ever to confront us with Paul and the word, refereeing among conflicting interpretations.

COMMENTARY

Letter Opening (1:1-17)

Salutation (1:1-7)

Paul had developed, in his first extant letter (1 Thess 1:1), a style of epistolary address or prescript that drew on Greek and Jewish letter forms: the sender's name (here Paul alone; but cf. 16:22 for his scribe's name), to the recipients (1:7a), and a wish of blessing that Christianized the Gk. *chairein* ("greetings," Acts 23:26, 15:23) by use of the word "grace" (*charis,* also in 1:5) together with "peace" (Heb. *shalom*). Paul introduces himself as a *doulos* ("slave," NRSV note) of his Master, Jesus Christ, and as an apostle, one sent, by God's call, one set apart like prophets of old (Gal 1:15; cf. Jer 1:5) "for the good tidings" (Isa 41:27; 52:7; cf. Matt 11:5 par. Luke 7:22; used in the plural in the imperial Roman Caesar cult). Some of the contents of this good news will be spelled out in 1:2-4, just as his apostleship will be described in v. 5. The addressees are described in OT terms as "God's beloved" (Pss 60:5; 108:6; Rom 11:28) and, like Paul, "called," in their case to be "saints" or holy, dedicated people (Lev 20:26; Ps 34:9). The word "church" is not used until 16:1 and 5, the latter for one of several house churches in Rome.

God's gospel is described as "promised" through God's prophets in Scripture (1:2) and as to contents in vv. 3-4. The two-part formula there about Jesus as God's Son likely incorporates a Jewish-Christian confession: descended from Israel's anointed King David in terms of the flesh, declared "Son of God with power" in terms of the Spirit, upon his resurrection (by God; cf. Gal 1:1), pointing, among other effects (as in 4:25), to the general resurrection of all (1 Cor 15:20, 23). The OT concepts (prophets, Davidic messiah) and Hebraisms ("spirit of holiness") served to create an ethos of goodwill with Christians whose faith came out of Jewish backgrounds. Yet Paul's apostleship especially concerns Gentiles (11:13), to bring them to commitment which is part of faith (the phrase in 1:5 is repeated in 16:26 to round out the canonical letter). "Obedience to the faith" (KJV) is out of favor as too propositional a view of faith.

Thus the salutation lifts up themes to recur later: God (4 references, 1:1, 4, 7 twice; cf. also "his" in vv. 2 and 3), Christ (4 times, in vv. 1, 4, 6, 7), grace (1:5, 7), faith (1:5), gospel (1:1), call/election (1:1, 7), and a note of Paul's apostolic commission. The flesh/Spirit contrast hints of two spheres or ages. That "Jesus is all that we are, and all that we are not" (Barrett 1977: 3) is only partly true, for he was the Messiah and we need to be offered grace, peace, and life, as will be seen.

Thanksgiving (1:8-15)

In ancient letters, a prayer of thanks to (the) god(s) regularly followed the salutation (cf. 2 Macc 1:10-11). It thanks God (1:8) and expresses petitions (vv. 10, 11b, and 13b). From rhetoric the Latin term *exordium* ("introduction") or *proem(ium)* (Gk. *prooimion*) has sometimes been used for such a unit which makes the audience well disposed by taking up "our person . . . , our hearers, and the facts . . ." (*Rhet. Her.* 1.4.8). Paul's prayer reports provide something of an agenda for the letter. Here he begins (NEB, REB; lit. "first" after a long salutation, there is no "second") with thanks for the addressees and praise for these Christians at Rome: their state of faith or obedience to the gospel (16:19) is announced all over (a bit of hyperbole as a compliment). (Matters in the capital city were often widely known.) An oath follows (cf. 1 Sam 12:5, 6; Phil 1:8) to underscore the unremitting nature of Paul's desire to come to Rome in accord with God's will. There is a cultic note in the verb "I serve" (12:1; 15:16) amounting to worship accomplished by Paul's proclamation of the gospel (1:9, 15). This is one spiritual gift (*charisma,* v. 11) that he as an apostle, through his open spirit, can bring to Rome, to deepen faith there.

There is a certain convoluted awkwardness in the way Paul speaks of somehow, at last, making it to Rome (1:10), hindered up to this point by mission work for God (15:22-23), and in the way he speaks of purpose (1:11) and results at Rome (v. 13). He is writing tactfully since he was not the founder of the communities there and because he has some awareness of problems in Rome involving disunity between the "strong" and the "weak" (14:1–15:13). Byrne (48) sees a pattern of intent to visit in vv. 9-10, 13a, and 15 (eagerness) and reasons for the visit (vv. 11-12, 13b-14, 16-17). The aim of his sharing some grace gift of the Spirit (v. 11) is diplomatically corrected in v. 12 by talk of mutual encouragement. The fresh start in v. 13 leads to the idea of reaping some harvest ("fruit," for which the prayer at Phil 1:11 also hopes; at Phil 1:22, missionary terminology). Here it could point to support for Paul's proposed campaign for Christ in Spain (15:24, 28). But he tempers any presumption with the admission that he is obligated to both kinds of people which Hellenistic society envisioned: wise Greeks and unlearned non-Greek speakers. Here Paul sees the world "through the eyes of a Gentile" (Dunn 1988: 36). To all the world — in Rome too — Paul is ready and willing to preach the gospel, which will be further defined in 1:16-17.

The prayer report thus becomes a vehicle to stress the gospel's advance (1:9, 15) and faith (vv. 8, 12) among the Gentiles (v. 13) and all humanity (v. 14), including believers at Rome.

Theme (1:16-17)

The main *propositio* for the letter employs topics already indicated, such as "gospel" in 1:1, 9, and 15 and "faith" in vv. 5, 8, and 12. The connective "for" in v. 16 begins a new point (as customarily in Paul; Harrisville: 24) and in v. 17 introduces an important phrase for the first time, "the righteousness of God." The sequence is: gospel = God's power for salvation, universally; gospel, exemplified in righteousness/justification, with validation through Hab 2:4, one of the prophetic promises about the gospel of which 1:2 had spoken. The rhetorical device of litotes, "I am not ashamed," in v. 16 really means, "my proud boast is the gospel of God" (cf. 5:11). The apostle's obligation is not just psychological or social-cultural (to present the message to proud Greeks or at Caesar's capital) but may reflect a Synoptic saying about not being ashamed of Jesus (Mark 8:38 par. Luke 9:26) and so confession of Jesus Christ.

Then in thirty-two Greek words Paul sets forth what Romans will be about. Each term will be further developed in later sections. Paul unfolds his views gradually. As yet, for example, Christ is not brought in (but cf. 1:3-4 and 3:22). Here God's gospel has to do with God's power to save everyone who believes it. "Jew first, but both Jew and Gentile" reflects how God's plan historically proceeded and the sequence Paul will reiterate in 2:9-10; 3:29; 9:24; 10:12. It is for the whole world but comes individually.

The righteousness of God (see above, Introduction, 8.1.1), that is, coming from God, is here understood in a salvatory sense, as in Deutero-Isaiah ("deliverance," parallel with salvation, 46:13; 51:5, 6, 8; 56:1; 61:10; Ps 40:9-10), "effective power active in the world . . . to bring about deliverance from . . . wrath in the final judgment and reinstatement in" God's glory (Cranfield: 89). That it "is being revealed" suggests both its eschatological nature and its ongoing availability in the gospel. This kind of righteousness comes out of God's faithfulness to past promises and results in a human response of faith. Thus, it is faith all the way. Paul quotes the Habakkuk verse without the pronouns in the Hebrew (NRSV makes 2:4 plural, "the righteous live by *their* faith") or the Greek (in the LXX God says, "out of *my* faithfulness") or in the version at Heb 10:38 ("*my* righteous one"). This bare-bones version allows the ambiguity in the NRSV's "live by faith" and its note, "righteous by faith." Both will prove correct. The citation has sometimes been viewed as providing an outline for much of Romans: the person who is "through faith righteous" (1:18–4:25) "shall live" (chs. 5–8) (so Nygren); or with v. 17a (Dunn 1988: 37):

God's righteousness to faith:
    "the righteous by faith (1:18–5:21)
    . . . shall live" (chs. 6–8)
God's righteousness from faith:
    "the righteous by God's faithfulness" (chs. 9–11)

But much of Romans remains thereby unaccounted for. Yet, under "gospel," 1:16-17 set forth terms that will dominate in 3:21–5:21 and reappear in chs. 9–11 ("faith" in chs. 12–15 and "righteousness" in chs. 2, 6, 7, and 8). They are part of an already shared universe (Byrne) with the Roman Christians, from the OT and common Christianity, that Paul's letter will seek to persuade them to enter more fully and knowingly.

The Body of the Letter (1:18–15:13)

The Need for God's Saving Righteousness (1:18–3:20)

Reference to God's righteousness as salvation in 1:16-17 raises the question of who needs such a gospel. Paul will answer that all humanity does (3:20). He proceeds in reverse order from the principle in v. 16, "Jew first, also Gentile," by taking up first the situation of the Gentile world in 1:18-32, "the human condition apart from . . . the preached gospel" (Fitzmyer 1993: 269). Jews of the day agreed with Paul's negative diagnosis for non-Jews, but the tables will then be turned to assess the Jew, who possesses Moses' law, in ch. 2. An underlying link is the here-unexpressed principle that the righteous God of justice (Deut 32:4; Jer 9:24) calls for human uprightness or justice in life (Ps 7:9; Ezek 18:5, 9). Where that is absent, judgment and divine wrath follow (Ezek 18:24). "Walk in righteousness," but "[w]hen sin . . . and injustice . . . and uncleanness . . . increase, . . . the holy Lord shall emerge with wrath" to "execute judgment upon the earth" (*1 Enoch* 91:4, 7; *OTP,* 1:72).

Gentiles under Wrath (1:18-32)

Paul may previously have used what follows in missionary sermons to pagans and in debates with Jews (Fitzmyer 1993: 271). He reflects Hellenistic-Jewish sentiments, as in Wisdom 11–15, especially ch. 13 and 14:22-31. But for the apostle this description also reflects the actual coming of God's righteousness to save in the gospel. God's power is a link (1:16, 20). Some see behind Paul's account of humans perverting their knowledge of God by rebellion a reflection of Adam in Genesis 3 (cf. Wis 2:23-24; Dunn 1988: 53, 72; 1997: #4.2-4), but Fitzmyer finds the echoes "nonexistent" (274). There is an allusion in Rom 1:23 to the story of the golden calf in Israel's history (Exodus 32) via the interweaving of Ps 106:19-20; cf. Deut 4:15-19. But such echoes or phrases do not yet draw aim on Israel.

The wrath of God (Exod 15:7; Ps 2:5; Zeph 1:15) in Paul's message (1 Thess 1:10) is neither an impersonal force like fate or nemesis operating in the world nor an affect or irrational characteristic of anger in the deity. It is the activity of a just God, usually future (Rom 2:5) but here being revealed in the present, indignation (NEB, "retribution") against the state of affairs among humans. It is not part of the gospel but comes "from heaven" against all irreligion and immorality of those who hold back the truth about God's reality self-disclosed (1:18). God is knowable as to power and deity through created things (vv. 19-20). People are culpable for not honoring God or giving thanks (v. 21). Human inexcusableness lies above all in minds become futile and the worship of creatures of the Creator (rather than the Creator) in the form of human figures (in Greek cult) or of animals (in Egyptian religion) (v. 23). The result is a downward spiral that involves lusting hearts (v. 24), degrading passions (v. 26), a debased mind, and a host of things not to be done (v. 28). The catalogue of vices (vv. 29-31; cf. 13:13) has Stoic and Jewish analogies. The Roman philosopher Seneca, too, bemoaned a world where people were not only attracted to, but also pleased by, shameful things (*Ep. Mor.* 39.6). If a "natural theology" occurs here, it accuses. Humanity has switched to other masters than Israel's Creator God.

There is a rhetorical swing to the thrice-repeated refrain, "God gave them up" to what their minds and passions led them toward (1:24, 26, 28), leaving "pagan society to stew in its own juice" (Robinson: 18). But *God* did this, though hidden and invisible — a typical Semitic way of expression. Some see a pattern of exchange: vv. 22-24 (glory exchanged for degrading of self), vv. 25-27 (exchange of truth for lies and unnatural sexual intercourse), and vv. 28-31 (they did not see fit to acknowledge God and ended up with unfit minds, v. 28), so that "there is no longer any protective dike in the cosmos" (Käsemann: 44, 49; on the "baleful exchange," see Harrisville: 35-40; Byrne: 69). Others see sin against the truth of God (vv. 19-23), against nature (vv. 24-27), and against other human beings (vv. 28-32) (Dunn 1988: 53; Fitzmyer 1993: 276).

In the three "waves" (Byrne: 66-72) that engulf humans for whom there is no excuse of ignorance, one should not miss the progression from bad theology and worship to bad ethics. The actions in 1:29-31 do not result in divine wrath; they are themselves the result of divine wrath; they stem from God's giving people over because of their prior misreading of tokens of God in the world and human failure to glorify or say thanks to God (v. 21). For readers today the reference to homosexuality and lesbianism (vv. 26-27) may attract the greatest attention. It is but one example in Paul's picture, an example at which there would have been no surprise in Israel (Lev 18:22; 20:13), Jewish polemic (*T. Naph.* 3.2-4; 4.1), Christian catechesis (1 Cor 6:9-10, not here invoked), and even Greek thought ("unnatural" = contrary to the order the Creator intends; in the OT, specifically procreation of children), yet an example prevalent in the Greek world as part of "friendship," not marriage (Fitzmyer 1993: 275-76, 285-88; Byrne [69-70] cautions on the rush to some modern conclusions).

The bottom-line summary in Rom 1:32 lifts up God's decree (*dikaiōma,* 2:26; 8:4) that those who practice the vices in vv. 29-31, of mind and action, based on idolatry and thanklessness toward God, are worthy of death. A Jewish listener, hearing this verdict, would approve, "That's exactly what they're like, sinning and applauding sinners." Paul seeks "a *pathos* of horror and revulsion" in readers (Byrne: 72). But the proud critic of others may be deluded too.

Jews, Too, under Judgment (2:1–3:9)

Paul moves to the other group in the equation, "Jew and Greek or Gentile" (1:16, ironically repeated at 2:9, 10). The style shifts from the third person plural in 1:18-32 ("they, them") to a second person singular diatribe form ("thou, O man," 2:1 KJV; "you, sir"). This rhetorical device (section 6 in the Introduction, above) clearly indicates a Jew, with Torah in 2:17–3:3, but in 2:1ff. the imaginary onlooker ("implied reader"; Byrne: 79) appears in more general terms (like "doing good" or "evil," 2:7, 9, 10), to which all can assent, even a pagan moralist without the law of Moses. Melanchthon's 1532 rhetorical analysis (373-74) saw the *accusatio gentium* continuing from 1:18 through 2:16, with the Jew accused only in 2:17-29. Some interpreters see both Gentiles and Jews in 2:1-16 (e.g., Harrisville: 41), and Bassler would include Jews even in 1:18-32. For 2:1ff., "[T]he majority of modern commentators, however, agree that the interlocutor is a Jew who judges himself superior to the pagan because of his people's privileges" (Fitzmyer 1993:297). But Paul's transition is gradual, enticing critics into what Byrne calls a "rhetorical trap" (80). Dunn (1988: 91, 108) suggests that Paul knows the arguments of the interlocutor so well because they were once his own, as Saul "the unconverted Pharisee."

Paul's argument runs thus. The God who judges all humans according to the deeds of each (2:6 = Ps 62:12; Prov 24:12; Sir 16:14) shows no partiality (2:1-11). Possession of the law of Moses guarantees nothing unless one is a doer of the law — and Gentiles may come closer to doing what it requires (vv. 12-16). Jews (vv. 17-24), for all their boast about their (covenant) relationship with God and the law, break the commands. "If you break the law," circumcision (vv. 25-29), Judaism's "sacrament" (Harrisville: 48), becomes "uncircumcision." Being a real Jew is an inward matter of the heart and spirit, as the prophets taught (Deut 10:16; Jer 4:4; 9:23-26; Ezek 36:23-28). In Rom 3:1-9 Paul takes up a series of objections regarding what advantage there is, then, for the Jew (v. 1); the justice and unjustness of God (v. 5); and the bottom-line conclusion (v. 9b), "both Jews and Greeks [neither is "first" here] are all under sin." Most translations begin a new paragraph with v. 9, but its opening phrase "What then?" repeats 3:1, forming an *inclusio* for the subsection and providing the conclusion for 2:1–3:9 (cf. also 1:18), as well as the point which Scripture will verify in 3:10-20.

God as Judge and judgment vocabulary run through the entire argument (2:1-3; v. 5, a rare word combining "righteous" and "judgment"; v. 12; v. 16, of secret thoughts as well as deeds; v. 27 [NRSV, "condemn"]; 3:4, 6-8, "condemnation"). Divine judgment, as often in biblical thought, is "inseparably linked" with justification (Käsemann 1980: 56), through the apocalyptic "day" of judgment (2:15); the justification of God as judge (3:4 = Ps 51:4); and the term "wickedess" (Gk. *adikia,* 1:18, 29; 2:8; 3:5 [NRSV, "injustice," part of the *dikaiō-* word field; KJV, "unrighteousness"]). The truth(fulness) of God is at issue (1:18, 25; 2:2, 8, 20; 3:4, 7). The theological axiom of God's impartiality (Bassler; Deut. 10:17; cf. Ps 82:2; Sir 35:15; Acts 10:34; Jas 2:5) undergirds the conclusion that divine evenhandedness allows no distinctions between Gentiles and Jews (3:22; 10:12): God will judge all by works (2:6) and save all by grace (3:23-24). Of course both the judgment and kindness of God are meant to lead to repentance those who do what they condemn others for doing (2:3-5), but the degree to which Paul goes in allowing that Gentiles apart from the law of Moses do what that law calls for (vv. 14-15) has startled many a reader.

The OT principle of retribution for deeds (2:6) is spelled out in chiastic form (vv. 7-10):

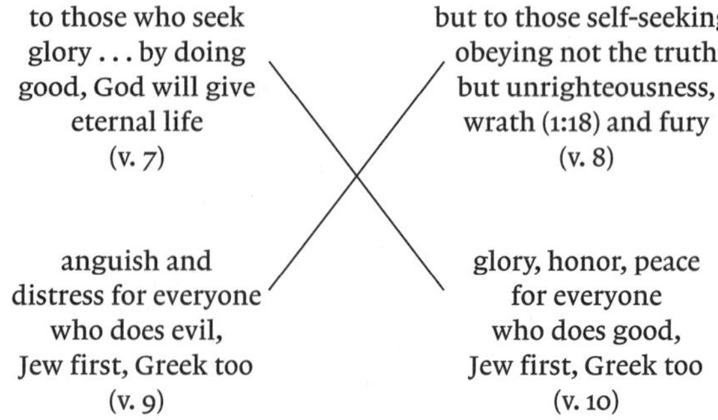

to those who seek glory . . . by doing good, God will give eternal life (v. 7)
but to those self-seeking, obeying not the truth but unrighteousness, wrath (1:18) and fury (v. 8)
anguish and distress for everyone who does evil, Jew first, Greek too (v. 9)
glory, honor, peace for everyone who does good, Jew first, Greek too (v. 10)

Then in vv. 14-16 there is talk of Gentiles, with the law written on their hearts, doing what the (Mosaic) law requires, abetted by their conscience, and so perhaps excused at the day of judgment. Who are these non-Jews who do good and end up with eternal life? Cranfield (151-52) has catalogued ten possible answers on 2:6-11; he concludes that vv. 7 and 10 must refer to Christians (a third group, then, in the section on Jews and Gentiles), "the good" their conduct that expresses faith; similarly on vv. 14-16, Gentile Christians (155-56).

These passages (2:6-11, 14-16) have long been a battleground. Käsemann (57-58) rejects notions that Paul speaks hypothetically or still reflects OT-Jewish views; or a "both/and" approach that would hold on to judgment-by-works and justification-by-faith, or some distinction between justification as a first step, followed by sanctifying works; or sacramental justification at baptism and then eschatological judgment. Rather, the judgment must for Paul be understood in light of what he will say about justification: the gift of the righteousness of God, with its power, means that one cannot live without responsibility and accountability. Similarly, Fitzmyer (297), who sees an implicit reference to Christians.

Dunn regards this view as "hardly possible." The religiosity envisioned may instead be that of some "unevangelized Gentiles," though Paul himself "found the possibility of acquittal only through . . . the gospel" (1988: 93, 106-7). There were notions in Stoicism of people being "a law to themselves" and of a law upon the heart; "conscience" is a good Greek concept, "the ability of the intelligent human being to judge one's actions in retrospect . . . or in prospect" (Fitzmyer: 310-11; cf. 128). Dunn sees Paul's aim to be "to puncture a Jewish assurance falsely based on the fact of having the law, of being the chosen people of God" (1988: 107), the sort of assurance found in Wis 15:2, "we will not sin because we know that you acknowledge us as yours." Cf. Reumann 1982: 69-72; Lincoln in *Pauline Theology III,* 142-44: being a Jew does not exempt "from the consequences of God's righteous judgment and . . . the need for the gospel."

Diatribe is not doctrine. At least for the sake of argument, however, Paul is allowing the possibility here, in some cases, at times, of a hidden human moral capacity. But in the end things will depend on grace and God's righteousness (5:17-19) and the Spirit (8:4; hinted at in 2:29 [NRSV, "spiritually," lit. "in spirit," but not yet clearly stated]; Byrne: 90).

The statements in 2:12 and 13 introduce for the first

time in Romans the terms "sin," "law," and "justified." More will be heard on each later. The picture of all peoples under sin (3:9) has been developed in 1:18–3:7 without use of the term (except for the verb in 2:12). Justification will come to the fore only at 3:21ff. as God's way of "rightwising" (to use an old Anglo-Saxon verb), God's righteousness for salvation (1:16-17). The use of "God's righteousness" at 3:5 (NRSV, "justice of God") refers to an attribute of God, as not unjust though Judge; the topic is a theodicy or defense of God's being justified in judging. But law appears in 2:12ff. some nineteen times in sixteen verses, to make the point that possession of Torah does not save. What a Jew should do in light of the law is spelled out in a series of examples in 2:17-23, each one contravened by how some disobey the precept. To "rob temples" (v. 22) may be figurative (Fitzmyer: 318), but it could mean "sale . . . of valuable artifacts purloined from pagan shrines," idols that for Jews had no real existence (Isa 44:9-20; cf. Deut 7:25-26). Circumcision (2:25) has value, as do the oracles of God (the OT revelation) entrusted to Jews (3:1-2), but external, physical circumcision and the literal or "letter" (2:29; cf. 7:6 and 2 Cor 3:3-6 on the written code and the Spirit) "misdirect" religion (Dunn 1997: #5.4). Is there a "plus" in being a Jew? According to Melanchthon the answer in 3:2-8 is in the affirmative, but in 3:9 a *responsio negativa.*

Paul concludes that Jews are under sin (3:9), and some have proved unfaithful (v. 3) in spite of God's gifts (vv. 2-3) and in contrast to God's faithfulness (v. 3; cf. 1:17). To what extent this divine faithfulness now continues will be taken up only in chs. 9–11. The form is still that of the diatribe in 3:1-9, with the questions posed in vv. 1, 3, 5, and 7 (raised by Paul, Byrne [106-7] thinks) and the answers in vv. 2, 4, and 6 (coming from the partner in the dialogue — a switch from the perception that Paul is on the attack against the interlocutor in 2:1ff.). This analysis has the advantage of suggesting that "I," "my," and "our" in 3:5 and 7 refer to Paul and that he is using a dialogical device to answer charges against his gospel — specifically, in v. 8, the slander that Paul teaches, "Do evil so that good may come" (cf. 6:1). Is this because he has stressed covenant promise, not covenantal nomism, thus breaking "the link between covenant righteousness and covenant law" (Dunn 1988: 137)? The difficult clause in 3:9b, "Are we any better off?" is better taken to mean "What then do we plead in our defense?" with reference to the attack on Paul's theology (Dunn 1988: 145-48, following Dahl 1982: 184-204, and omitting the Gk. *ou pantōs*).

All People Sin, Unjustified by Deeds of Law (3:10-20)

The conclusion to 2:1–3:8 (and 1:18-32) has already been indicated: Jews and Greeks alike, all are under Sin (3:9). It is to that proposition from the diatribe that a *testimonia* list (Fitzmyer: 91) or chain of Scripture quotations is now appended. The collection probably existed previously. The verses begin with Eccl 7:20 and draw on the Psalms (NRSV 14:2-3; 5:9; 140:3; 10:7), Isa 59:7-8, and Ps 36:1 — all loosely referred to as "the law" in 3:19. There is repetition of the phrase "There is no one . . ." five times in vv. 10-12 from Psalm 14, plus one more example of the same Gk. *ouk estin* in 3:11. Parts of the human body are singled out — throats, tongues, lips, and mouths (appropriate to v. 19b, every mouth shall shut up), but also feet, eyes, and (v. 11) "understanding." The whole person and all the world sin and are accountable! There can be no special pleading before God, even by those with the law.

The most important quotation occurs in 3:20. It comes from Ps 143:2, with the addition of (a) *sarx* as subject (NRSV, "human being," lit. "flesh"), human beings in their moral incapacitation before God (8:3; Dunn 1997: #3.3, pp. 64-65); and (b) "by works of the law" (as also at Gal 2:16; its first appearance in Romans), referring to Judaism's stance and praxis described in 2:25-29, especially of circumcision as a physical, external mark of distinctiveness and "the letter," by which the righteous elect identify their national status (Dunn 1988: 159). But Qumran usage of "works of the law" suggests a broader sense: what the Mosaic law requires (Fitzmyer: 337-39; cf. Käsemann: 88; Byrne: 120-21; cf. 117-18; Dunn 1997: #14.4, 4QMMT). Performance is called for (4:4-5), yet there has been failure to do the commands (2:17-24). There is thereby no being justified before God. What the law reveals is not our status or success but Sin; not information about Sin but the unmasking of a force that corrupts even God's holy law and kills us (7:11).

The Gospel of God's Righteousness Manifest in Sinners' Justification by Faith (3:21–4:25)

Paul returns to the theme announced in 1:17, the righteousness of God (3:21, 22, 25, 26) and faith (3:22, 25, 26, 27, 28); see 8.1.1 and 8.1.2 in the Introduction. In 3:21-26, the key and heart to Romans, this gospel is proclaimed in positive terms that provide solutions to the quandaries in the negative picture in 1:18–3:20 about the plight of Gentiles and Jews alike. From the thesis or *propositio principalis* (Melanchthon: 374) — justification or "rightwising," by God's grace, through Christ's sacrificial death, effective through faith — the argument goes on to draw consequences regarding the law of Moses in contrast to faith as God's universal way of justifying Gentiles and Jews (3:27-31). Scriptural support is offered, as at 1:17 and 3:10-18 and 20, this time in the example of Abraham, who believed and was reckoned righteous and forgiven, by faith, apart from circumcision and law (ch. 4). So for us, too, righteousness is reckoned through belief in God, who raised the crucified Jesus "for our justification" (4:24-25).

All Share, without Distinction, in God's Righteousness through Christ's Sacrificial Death (3:21-26)

From a "symbolic universe of apocalyptic Judaism" (Byrne: 122), about the day when God will judge all humanity (2:16) and a world where the wrath of God is already revealed (1:18), Paul now returns to the righteousness of God. This *dikaiosynē* could refer to justice as an attribute of God (3:5) as Judge (Isa 3:13-14; Hos 4:1-2; 12:2) that punishes injustice *(adikia)* with wrath (cf. Ps 95:10-11; 106:40; Isa 5:16). That here in 3:21ff. it refers to saving righteousness (1:16-17, "power for salvation"; Isa 33:22) becomes clear only gradually in 3:22 and 24-25. The "now" in v. 21 is not only a logical but also an eschatological transition. It refers not to a new period in human history, pure and simply, but to a new aeon (8.8 in the Introduction above) breaking in, not yet fully here but no longer the world that was. What has been "disclosed" (cf. "revealed" in 1:17 and 18) comes, shockingly for Jews accustomed to the election-covenant relationship with the Mosaic law, "apart from law," yet paradoxically witnessed to by "law and prophets." This last is forensic language. Called to testify in court are the Pentateuch (Gen 15:6, at 4:3) and Israel's prophets (1:2; 1:17 = Hab 2:4; 4:6-8, David speaking in Psalm 32; cf. 3:19 where Scripture's weight of evidence has stopped further pleas).

3:22 further delineates the ambiguous righteousness of God (Byrne: 123-24). For the first time righteousness through faith is connected with Jesus Christ, who, after references at 1:1, 4, 6, 7, and 8, has been mentioned only fleetingly at 2:16. On *pistis* plus "Christ" in the genitive, see 8.1.2 in the Introduction. The view has been revived that it means here (and some say, always in Paul) "the faith of Jesus Christ" (NRSV note). Opinions vary as to whether the sense would be how Jesus believed (in God), or was obedient unto death, or whether the (risen) Christ is meant. But does Paul indicate much interest in, or knowledge of, the historical Jesus? For "obedience" he uses a different Greek word (Rom 1:5; 5:19; Phil 2:8). What would the faith of the risen Lord mean for us? Vicarious, in our stead? Paul's own exemplar of faith is Abraham (Romans 4; Galatians 3). He never uses the verb "believe" with Jesus as subject. In Gal 2:16 Paul explains the phrase at issue by the verbal expression "we . . . believe in Christ Jesus." There is a further aspect: If Jesus' faith is involved, along with God's grace, then how does human response come into a seemingly quite external and objective process of salvation? It is believers' faith-trust-obedience that will be contrasted with their doing works of the law, not Jesus' own faith. Thus, while there is a "beguiling attractiveness" to the proposal at first glance, it rests on taking the phrase out of context (and often into one involving modern assumptions about the quest for the historical Jesus as a man who "trusted") and making it part of a narrative reconstructed by modern scholars that emphasizes the historical ministry of Jesus in a way that Paul does not (Dunn 1997: #14.8, esp. pp. 383-85). While the view is widespread in articles and monographs, commentators (Käsemann: 94, 101; Dunn 1988: 166-67, 177-78; Fitzmyer 1993: 345-46; Byrne: 130) generally adopt the long-standard NRSV text, "faith in Jesus Christ," human faith directed toward Christ.

What 3:9-20 said, vv. 22-23 reiterate: distinctions between Jews and Greeks are gone (a missionary slogan for Paul); all are under Sin (3:9). That all fail to reach the glory God intends is a commentary on the life of humanity as depicted in 1:18–3:20. If "glory" reflects the lost "image of God" in Gen 1:26-28 as interpreted in Ps 8:5 ("crowned with glory"), there may be a reflection of Genesis 3, Adam and Eve (so Käsemann [95]; the "glory of God" is "*dikaiosynē* within the horizon of the restoration of paradisaical perfection"; Dunn 1988: 168; otherwise Fitzmyer 1993: 347; Byrne: 125, "an echo"). The universal need for God's gospel is thus asserted.

Rom **3:24-26a** put the answer in the form of an earlier formula, likely Jewish-Christian (5 in the Introduction, above), about the meaning of the death of Jesus: it is a display of God's saving righteousness (*dikaiosynē,* v. 25), whereby people are being justified (v. 24, *dikaioumenoi*). The exact parameters of the earlier formulation remain debated, the question whether v. 24 was part of the piece (Reumann: 36-38, 74-77; Käsemann: 95-100, who, however, too easily makes it a eucharistic hymn; Dunn 1988: 163-64: vv. [24]25-26a). Paul's own additions likely include "by God's grace" (v. 24), "through faith" (v. 25), and v. 26 in the NRSV (which obscures the awkwardness of the Greek that suggests a tradition is redacted).

God is confessed as setting Jesus forth as a sacrifice for sin (3:25). In view is the sin offering on the Day of Atonement (Leviticus 16, esp. vv. 12-19), though some also bring in the atoning death of Maccabean martyrs (4 Macc 17:21-22). Cf. Dunn 1997: #9.2. The Gk. *hilastērion* at 3:25 has been taken as "means" or "place" (NRSV note) of propitiating (God) (KJV) or expiating (sins). Jesus' blood, thus poured out in death, becomes proof "to show" God's righteousness in connection with the way God passed over, or let go unpunished, sins in time past (v. 25; cf. Mic 7:18-20). This first of three purpose clauses in the passage serves to explain the divine forbearance (3:25) or patience (2:4) in kindly letting offenses ride, in hopes of repentance by the guilty.

The second purpose clause (3:26a) parallels the first but is Paul's comment on how, in the "now" time (v. 21), God shows forth the divine righteousness (*dikaiosynē* of God; the RSV and NRSV lose this point; better, the KJV, "to declare . . . at this time his righteousness," or the NABRNT; the NEB and REB have it as "demonstrate his justice"). This present effect of Christ's death leads on into a third purpose clause, "in order that thereby God might be both just and the justifier of [or righteous and rightwising] the person who has faith in Jesus" (v. 26b). This becomes Paul's answer to how God's justice (3:5) and saving righteousness (1:16-17; 3:24-25) can both be sustained: it is at the cost of the sacrifice God offers in Christ.

3:26 also picks up the other direction in which the formula about Christ's death moved, the justification of sinners described in v. 23, Greek and Jew alike. Paul's answer (and the formula) begins in this vein with the participle in v. 24, "being justified. . . ." The added "they" in NRSV v. 24 masks the fact that "justified" refers to "all who believe" in v. 22, the intervening vv. 22b-23 being parenthetical, an aside. Potentially, however, all sinners (v. 23) can come to be in this category, which is also described by the term "redemption." Redemption can suggest "sacred manumission" (a process whereby a slave deposited savings at a local temple bank and, when the agreed amount was there, was freed from the old master, who received the money, and the slave became the property of the temple's god, but actually free; cf. Gal 5:1) and/or Israel's liberation from Egypt or Babylon or at the end time (Fitzmyer 1993: 122-23). The phrase "in Christ Jesus" also occurs at 3:24 for the first time in Romans (6:11, 23; 8:1, 2; 9:1; 12:5; 15:17; 16:3; etc.). Here it denotes the agency ("through") and the sphere of the crucified and risen One where the redeemed live.

Thus Paul deals with the character and activity of God, just and active to justify, through Christ's sacrificial death. It is by faith in this Christ and ultimately in God that one is justified, faith being "the only requirement on the human side" (Byrne: 122), justification available for all. Implications for the Jewish view of God and the law follow.

Justification by Faith, Not Law (3:27-31)

The consequences of the universally justifying righteousness of God through faith in Christ which were elaborated in 3:21-26 are now spelled out in more polemical terms, employing the diatribe form as in 2:1–3:20. Given this gospel, what of Jewish prerogatives (touched on in 3:2; cf. 2:17-23, precepts of the law)? Here lay Judaism's identity! Paul speaks out of his own Jewish background (Fitzmyer 1993: 359; cf. Phil 3:4-6). It has been common to refer here to sinful self-reliance on, indeed arrogance over, covenant and law. Dunn (see above on 2:1–3:9; 1988: 183-86) would focus on these as sources for *national* pride and distinctive *boundary markers* that are faulted by Paul for excluding Gentiles; such a limited "self-understanding of the Jewish people" lacks universality. Others have seen *all* religiosity based on *self*-confidence as under attack (Käsemann: 102-3). There is then more to the onslaught than Jewish lack of universalism. Gentiles are in the same boat (cf. Gal 4:1-11). Byrne (137, cf. 99) sees in what Paul says "two diametrically opposed ways of regarding (and living) the law of Moses": one pursues righteousness through faithful performance of the works it commands; the other sees law from the perspective of faith, with "a verdict of 'total failure' upon all human attempts to be righteous in the sight of God" (3:19-20). Whether vv. 27-31 hit Jews only, and that for limited nationalism, or have wider human application depends in part on whether *nomos* (5 times in these verses) refers always and only to the law of Moses.

To follow the argument one needs to recall the meanings of "boasting" (3:27). It refers to glorying over what one relies on for security. Pauline usage (cf. 1 Cor 1:29-31; 2 Cor 10:17) reflects Jer 9:23-24, "Thus says the LORD, 'Do not let the wise boast in their wisdom,'" the mighty in their might, the wealthy in their wealth, "but let those who boast boast in this, that they understand and know me, that I am the LORD," acting with love, justice, and righteousness. One can therefore "boast" either in a proper sense (Gal 6:14, Christ's cross) or in a wrong way. At 3:27 the boasting by the Jew in covenant-law (2:17, 23) is meant. Such prideful glorying is now locked out. When 3:27 says, "By what law?" there is a note of irony, as in the oxymoron "'law' of faith." The answer is not Mosaic Torah but the principle (RSV, REB; *nomos;* Fitzmyer 1993: 363; 8.6 in the Introduction above) of faith.

In 3:28 Paul announces a judgment he ("we") has come to in the dispute, a judgment of faith (*TDNT,* 4:288): that a person is justified by faith (vv. 24, 25, 26b) without works of (Mosaic) law (vv. 20, 21). This pulls together and sharpens what had been said before. The contrast with "not justified by works of law" in v. 20 calls for the sense of "by faith *alone*" in v. 27, as is widely and ecumenically recognized (Käsemann: 103; Wilckens: 1:252; Fitzmyer 1993: 360-62; Dunn 1997: #14.7; Byrne: 137).

What does this mean for one's concept of God? Paul (3:30) takes Israel's credo, "God is one" (the Shema, Deut 6:4, NRSV note; *solus deus*), and asks whether this deity is God of the Jews only? Of course not. The Jews claim that the Creator is the Lord of the Gentiles too. The passage not only carries through a trend in the OT and Judaism toward universalism but also renders obsolete the function of Torah as the dividing line between Israel and "the nations" (Moxnes: 78-80). For the one God now justifies circumcised and uncircumcised alike, via faith (the use of two different prepositions, *ek* [from 1:17 and 3:26] and *dia* [3:22 and twice in v. 27]; NRSV, "on the ground of" and "through") is rhetorical variation, not doctrinal distinction). The principle of faith, not law, holds for all (v. 27).

If boasting is excluded, is then the law? *Nomos,* of course, is present as the "principle [or 'law'] of faith" (v. 27). But what of the other, OT and Jewish, senses (Introduction, 8.6) since Paul insists (v. 31), "we uphold the law"? As Scripture, and not just some reconstructed "story of salvation," Paul will continue to refer to it, indeed to the Mosaic Pentateuch, and this not only in an accusatory role (the lawcourt witnesses in 3:19-20; 7:7) but as still setting forth God's will for those who live in Christ by the Spirit (8:3-4; 13:8-10). And (reflecting 3:21, "law and prophets") he will continue to use it to undergird the principle of faith, not works of law, through the OT account of Abraham in ch. 4.

A Scriptural Example: Abraham Justified by Faith, Not Works (4:1-25)

Not Jesus but Abraham (Genesis 12–25) is used to uphold (3:31) the principle stated at Rom 3:28, "by faith, not works." Melanchthon called ch. 4 *confirmatio, argumentum de exemplo,* though "example" in 4:12 (N)RSV represents a paraphrase of "follow in the steps of the faith of Abraham." The opening diatribe question (v. 1) leads into a midrashic exposition about Abraham, unfolded in strict OT sequence, with a rabbinic interpretative device (vv. 6-8), so as to confirm what Paul has said about justification by deductions from Scripture. In the process "faith" is more fully defined — v. 5, one trusts but literally "believes in"; faith's perseverance, against all odds, vv. 18-21, without distrust (*apistia,* v. 20, lit. "disbelief"). The object of faith is God (vv. 3, 17, 20, 21), the Creator who raised Jesus to lordship (vv. 17, 24-25). *Pistis* is specifically "faith righteousness" (vv. 11, 13). Justification is seen as forgiveness and blessedness (vv. 6-9). The important term "promise" *(epangelia)* is introduced for the first time (vv. 13, 14, 16, 20; cf. ch. 9), as something that came to Abraham prior to circumcision and covenant law (vv. 13-15) and that holds for all "who share the faith of Abraham," Jew and Gentile alike (v. 16). In this way "salvation history," a continuity between Abraham and his true descendants regarding promise, is invoked to support righteousness by faith (Käsemann: 116-17; Wilckens: 1: 282-85, with Goppelt, against Klein, as in Fitzmyer 1993: 371, 377). The chapter is most simply divided into vv. 1-12 and vv. 13-25, where "promise" comes into play (Byrne), but with further subdivisions as the argument unfolds (cf. the NRSV paragraphing).

Why Abraham? Paul had to take up Israel's patriarch as a test case because, for contemporary Judaism, Abraham exemplified covenantal nomism par excellence. "Remember the deeds *(erga)* of the ancestors. . . . Was not Abraham found faithful when tested [Gen 22:1-18, in offering Isaac upon God's command to sacrifice the child], and it was reckoned to him as righteousness [Gen 15:6]?" (1 Macc 2:51-52). This interpretation, widely held in Judaism, also appears in Jas 2:22-23. "Abraham was a great father of a multitude of nations [Gen 17:5]. . . . He kept the law of the Most High and entered into a covenant with him; he certified the covenant in his flesh [Gen 17:23-24]" (Sir 44:19-20; note the sequence — law keeping, covenant, circumcision). Cf. Dunn 1988: 196-97, 200-201; on interpretations of Gen 15:6, *ABD,* 5:740-41; on promise, Moxnes: 103-206.

"What then are we to say about Abraham . . . ?" (4:1, NRSV note; on the textual problem see Fitzmyer: 371). Literally, ". . . what Abraham found" (cf. NRSV text), which might lead the diatribe partner to expect, "he found favor [in God's sight, Gen 18:3]" (Dunn 1988: 198). To call Abraham "our ancestor [lit. "forefather"] according to the flesh" (the latter derogatory, in contrast to "spirit," as at 2:29?) also fits Jewish claims (Matt 3:9 par. Luke 3:8; John 8:39). Paul's worst-case scenario (4:2) is that "if Abraham was justified by works, he had grounds for boasting" (contrast 3:27). But "not before God" *(coram deo,* Melanchthon: 123), as in the Gen 15:6 quote which follows in 4:3. This last phrase in v. 2 makes the conditional sentence contrary to fact since the text in v. 3 speaks of faith (Abraham "believed"), not works. This key text will be paraphrased in vv. 5-6 and explicitly repeated in vv. 9 and 22.

4:4 and 5 set forth a general principle: to a person who works, pay is reckoned as something due, not a favor *(kata charin);* to a person who does not work but believes *(pisteuonti),* belief or faith *(pistis)* is "reckoned as righteousness" for that person as a favor (by grace, *charis*). Abraham fits that latter category (v. 5), not the former (v. 4), for there were no "works of the law" as yet. Some are anxious to see simply an "'employment' image" here with regard to "working" (Byrne: 149), but the principle is "drawn from the particular case of Abraham" (Dunn 1988: 205). Paul indeed sharpens the issue in v. 5 by speaking of faith — "trust" (NRSV) — in the One who "justifies the ungodly." This language is a stunning reapplication to God of Israel's law in Exod 23:7 that a judge is not to acquit the guilty, LXX "not to declare righteous the ungodly" (Lincoln in *Pauline Theology III,* 151). But according to Paul God does exactly that! In Abraham's case, that he was "ungodly" rests on the fact that he was a type of pagan proselyte, from Haran, in Mesopotamia (Gen 11:31; 12:4), when called by God (12:1-3) (Dunn 1988: 205). This is another assertion of the extralegal nature of God's justifying the guilty (NEB).

A hurdle to Paul's case was the fact that "reckon" *(logizesthai)* in Gen 15:6 was a Greek bookkeeping term, "credit to an account." The device of *gezerah shawah* (5 in the Introduction, above), Hillel's second rule of interpretation, allowed explanation of "reckoned" at 15:6 by use of the same verb in Ps 32:2, "the LORD will not reckon sin" (Rom 4:8; NRSV OT, "impute no iniquity"). And since this psalm of David parallels this phrase with "iniquities forgiven, sins covered," to "reckon as righteous" in 15:6 equals to "forgive" (cf. 3:25, passing over sins). Nygren (171) calls forgiveness of sins "the essence of justification," but Paul actually makes little use of the theme, partly because he stressed Sin, not sins, and partly because forgiveness, like repentance, was for him tied up with "language of the covenant" (Dunn 1988: 207). The sense "imputed righteousness" (KJV 4:6, 8, 11, 22, 23, 24) arose from Erasmus's use of *imputatum* in his 1516 Latin rendering, which was followed by Melanchthon: 133-35 (Fitzmyer 1993:374). From "iniquities" in v. 7 came the medieval notion of concupiscence as "the tinder" for original sin (Fitzmyer 1993: 376).

Having elucidated Genesis by the use of Psalms, Paul then goes on (4:9-12) to explain Psalm 32 through the use of Genesis. Was the blessedness, mentioned in the psalm, for the circumcised only or for all peoples? The psalm does not say, but Gen 15:6 was pronounced by God prior to Genesis 17, when Abraham was first circumcised. Circumcision did not bring righteousness (2:15-29). Uncircumcised Abraham, reckoned righteous by faith, not covenant (the term is not even used) or law, is therefore, for both uncircumcised Gentiles (4:11b) and circumcised Jews who show faith as Abraham did (v. 12), "father" (NRSV, "ancestor"; the term at 4:1 is being broadened). The Greek in v. 12 is difficult. In the NRSV "the circumcised" are described by two clauses beginning with "who" (in Greek *tois*). Is this *one* group, circumcised Jews who show faith? Or *two* groups, physically circumcised Jews, of whom Abraham remains father; and Jews who believe, spiritually circumcised (2:29) (Fitzmyer 1993: 381-82)? Dunn (1988: 211) suggests that Paul is seeking "to defuse the counterargument . . . that Abraham went on to receive circumcision — so why not the same for Gentile believers now?" Because "Abraham was circumcised in order to establish his fatherhood over the circumcised," whereas he was already "father of all who believe without being circumcised" (4:11). Crystal clear is that righteousness comes by faith (vv. 11, 13), on which cf. Käsemann (107-10) and what Dunn (203) terms "lyrical . . . Lutheranism."

"Promise" (4:13ff.) introduces a term for which there is no Hebrew equivalent. In the Genesis account it refers to announcements from God to Abraham about land (12:1-3), blessing (Gen 12:7; 13:14-17; 15:7, 18-21; 17:8; etc.), and descendants ("seed," offspring; 12:7; 13:15; 15:18, 17:8; etc.). The "land" has been expanded to "the world" in Rom 4:13 (cf. Sir 44:21), a universal emphasis, possibly even "the world to come" with its salvation blessing (Byrne: 157). The question of an heir and the promise of descendants provide in Gen 15:1-5 the immediate context for 15:6, about righteousness based on faith. What Byrne (143, 152) calls "the "son/seed promise" and "the land promise" both play a role in 4:13-21.

The promised world did not come to Abraham and his descendants through the law (4:13). Indeed, if it were by law, faith and promise are null and void (v. 14). Torah brings God's wrath (1:18ff.) by laying bare transgressing of the law (4:15; 7:8; but cf. 5:13b). The two kinds of righteousness, by faith or by law (10:5-6), are mutually exclusive. Promise, like righteousness, rests on faith and God's grace, in Abraham's case and for all who are of faith (4:16). Here Paul does bring in Gen 17:5, for its phrase "father of many nations" (*ethnōn,* as at Rom 3:29, i.e., Gentiles), to press home how Abraham is "father of us all," Jews and Gentiles who believe.

Believe in what or whom? In Abraham's case, God, who is described (4:17b) as effecting two miracles: making alive the dead and creating the world out of nothing (2 Macc 7:28). Creation and resurrection are also paired in 2 Macc 2:23. Cf. also *Shemoneh 'Esreh,* the Second Benediction in synagogue liturgy; it read, "Blessed are you, Lord, who revive the dead." Rom 4:17 reflects an early Christian creedal formulation; cf. 4:24. Paul's flood of ideas at this point is overwhelming. The NRSV copes by using parentheses and a dash before picking up in v. 17b with Abraham before God (KJV; cf. 4:2). Paul now employs Gen 17:15-21, Abraham's dialogue with God about how the "son/seed promise" can possibly be fulfilled. This is no mere "reprise" (Harrisville: 67), for the verses show how faith perseveres — belief with hope in the face of a hopeless situation (4:18; Byrne: 160; Moxnes: 239-53: a healing God who creates community). Also included is not weakening in faith (4:19) but being strengthened (by God) in faith (v. 20; Nygren: 181-83). Lincoln (1992; cf. *Pauline Theology III,* 150-55) sees Paul laying initial groundwork here for dealing with "strong" and "weak" in chs. 14–15. Faith grows strong when one looks, not to self and boasting but to the promise, and when one glorifies God (4:20), wholly certain that God is able (v. 21).

Such faith, in the case of Abraham, was recorded and reckoned. So, too, with us, faith will be reckoned, for Jews and Gentiles alike who believe in the God who raised Jesus who was put to death for our trespasses and raised for our justification (another early Christian creed, reflecting Isaiah 53; Reumann: 38-39, 78). It is not a shift from "the past" through 4:22 to "the present" from v. 23 on (so Achtemeier: 89). For the past, about Jesus' death, interconnects with the future, when, at the parousia, righteousness will be reckoned to believers at the judgment (2:13; 3:20, 30). Jesus' cross and resurrection are thought of as one event, together effecting ongoing forgiveness and future acquittal, a combined result to be spelled out more fully in 5:1ff. Cf. Barth and Fletcher 1964. The last word of the section is what has dominated since 1:17, getting rightwised *(dikaiōsis).*

What Justification and New Life in Christ Mean (Chs. 5–8)

Romans 5 continues the theme of righteousness/justification from 1:17–4:25; there are eight *dikaiō-* words at 5:1, 9, 16, 17, 18 (two forms), 19, 21 (Cranfield: 253). Some, like Calvin, have therefore taken chs. 1–5 together, with chs. 6–8 treating "sanctification" (which occurs only at 6:19, 22; cf. Cranfield: 295) — a reflection of the later "orders of salvation" for the individual. Or chs. 1–5 together, with chs. 6–8 the realization of justification in daily life (Wilckens). Melanchthon (169, 374) saw 5:1-11 as an epilogue to the *disputatio* of 1:18–4:25, with 5:12–8:39 a "new book," as it were. Fitzmyer takes 5:1-11 as "Theme Announced, Justified Christians Are Reconciled to the God of Love . . . ," and 5:12–8:13 as "Theme Explained." Since Israel and the Jews are unmentioned in chs. 5–8, since the OT is rarely cited (e.g., 5:5; 7:6; 8:33, 36), and since the focus is on "Christ rather than God," Thielman, in order to link chs. 1–4 with chs. 9–11, has sought references to "the symbolical world of first-century Judaism" in chs. 5–8 (e.g., for 5:1-11 "spirit, righteousness" and "peace" as in Isa 32:15-17), but Cousar's response demurred, preferring 5:1-11 as "transitional" and vv. 12-21 as the development of it (*Pauline Theology III,* 169-95, 196-210). Dunn regards 5:1-21 as "First Conclusions: The New Perspective of Faith in Relation to the Individual [vv. 1-11] and to Humanity at Large [vv. 12-21]"; then chs. 6–11 show "The Outworking of Paul's Gospel."

Perhaps most common is to see chs. 5–8 as centered on freedom from several tyrant-kings from whom believers are liberated (Nygren; Barrett: 119-74; Fitzmyer; Byrne for 6:1–8:13, among others; section 7 in the Introduction, above). This outline holds, with several provisos. (1) The term "(set) free" actually occurs only at 6:18, 20, 22; 7:3; 8:2, 21 (twice). But cf. also "saved . . . from the wrath of God" (5:9). (2) While each of the enslaving powers is concentrated in a specific chapter, Paul often refers to them at other points:

Romans 5, freed from wrath (v. 9 only; but cf. the kerygma at 1 Thess 1:10); from death (5:17-21, but also vv. 10, 12, 14; seven times in ch. 6; 7:10, 13, 24);
Romans 6, freed from Sin (16 times, but also 15 times in ch. 7) and self (you, our old self);
Romans 7, freed from law (23 times, but also in chs. 2, 3, 4; 5:13, 20; 6:14, 15; 8:2, 4, etc.);
Romans 8, freed for life (also 5:10, 17, 18; 6:4, 21, 23), the Spirit (5:5; 7:6), and hope (4:18; 5:2, 4, 5).

For the Greek words, chapter by chapter, see Dunn 1988: 301.

(3) The most important qualification is to the impression that the believer is now, in Christ, totally free from these tyrants. The fact is that Paul often speaks in the *future* tense: we shall be saved from God's wrath (5:9, 19). Believers die, physically, even if the relationship with God survives. The Mosaic law will continue to be cited as containing God's will in 13:9-10. Sin, for all that is said about Christ's victory over it, remains "the impossible possibility" (Beker: 217). Expositors have often described believers therefore as "no longer" what they once were but "not yet" what they will be. Or by reference to the "two ages" (see Introduction, 8.8, above). Here one should rather speak of their overlap, not the full arrival of the New for us (Byrne: 162-63). Clearest evidence of the realistic view Paul has of the life of the justified is the way suffering is included (5:3; 8:18-25). One lives with confidence (5:1-2, 11), but not security; and with hope (5:2, 5; 8:24-25, thus providing a pair of bookends for chs. 5–8), but not yet sight.

Freed from Wrath and Death (Ch. 5)

Previous verses spoke of individuals like Abraham (ch. 4) and the person who has faith in Jesus (3:26). 5:1-11 continues with "us believers" (4:24), and 5:12-21 will expand the scope to "all" (humanity). Barth's theological exegesis, with a sequence of Christ (5:1-11), then Adam (5:12-21, humanity), suggested that all persons are somehow already secretly in Christ (Cranfield: 269-70, 294-95). Bultmann viewed vv. 1-11 as a Jewish, cultic Christology and vv. 12-21 as a parallel gnostic Christology, describing "the paradoxical Christian situation." Today neither view attracts much support (Käsemann: 143-44; Dunn 1988: 277-79; Fitzmyer: 407). Nygren touted 5:12-21 as the expository key to Romans, the best place to begin "for an inclusive view of the meaning of Romans" (vv. 27, 32); that reflected his emphasis on the two aeons (Introduction, 8.8, above) and the application of the words "shall live" (for 1:17) as the theme for chs. 5–8 (188-89). Fitzmyer (1993: 406) thinks that 5:12-21 is "the second most important passage" in Romans, after 3:21-26.

5:1-11 is enclosed by parallel passages at vv. 1-3 and 9-11, each beginning "having been justified," with references to "boasting" in a good sense (vv. 2, 3, 11) and the phrase "through our Lord Jesus Christ" (v. 1; cf. vv. 2, "through whom"; 9, "through him"; 10; and 11). The phrase "not only (that), but also" occurs verbatim in Greek in vv. 3 and 11 (NRSV, "more than that, we even . . ."). The rhetorical device of moving from a lesser to a greater point at vv. 9 and 10 ("much more") will also appear at vv. 15 and 17 *(a minore ad majus).* Vv. 3-5 present a syllogistic chain of reasoning — sufferings → endurance → tested character → hope, the latter an emphasis already in v. 2. Vv. 6-8 stress the death of Christ (the verb "die" occurs at the end of four consecutive sentences). Kirk (194) termed 5:6-11 "the hymn of the crucified Jesus." Christ's death, as an expression of God's love for ungodly sinners, produces the benefits of justification.

Paul's use of the past tense in 5:1 and 9, "we were justified," with reference to Christ's death (3:25), has caused some to see justification as confined to the past. But 5:19, like 4:24, points to rightwising definitively in the future, and these two points overarch a process of being justified in the present (3:24), just as salvation is past (8:24), present (1 Cor 1:18; 15:2), and future (5:9, 10; 10:9, 13). A relationship is created, lived out, and finally vindicated by God.

The specific blessings that come as a result of being in the relationship of "righteous with God" are (1) peace with God (5:1), in the place of hostility (v. 10); (2) hope, a mark of salvation (v. 2); and (3) "a share in the risen life of Christ" (v. 10) (Fitzmyer 1993: 395, 396, 401). Others add "access" to God's grace as power and position, as at a temple sanctuary or king's court (v. 2), as well as the sequence from suffering to hope in vv. 3-5, which Käsemann terms the eschatological "moral growth of the life initiated by justification" (132; Fitzmyer 1993: 397). Behind it all is God's love toward us (v. 5), poured like water on dry ground (Isa 44:3), through the Spirit given to us (communally). Experience of that love and the Spirit and the death of Christ (5:8) make believers confident they are now reconciled with God (vv. 10, 11; cf. 11:15), an image from family life or from warring forces in the Greco-Roman world; it personalizes in a different image the forensic picture of righteousness/justification.

5:12-21 can surely be read as a climactic comparison of Adam and Christ. The references may be set up in two contrasting columns (Reumann: 79), about two figures, Adam, by trespass through Sin, bringing a reign of death and condemnation upon all; the other, Christ, by his own death, bringing the free gift of righteousness, leading all to acquittal and the reign of eternal life. Achtemeier (97) sums the passage up: "Christ got us out of the mess Adam got us into. What Adam did, Christ undid; where Adam failed, Christ succeeded." The mess would involve everything from Rom 1:18 to 3:20, behind which Genesis 3 and later interpretations like Wis 2:23-24 lurk. Adam's sin (5:12) — referred to by three additional terms, transgression (v. 14), trespass (v. 15), and disobedience (v. 19) — brought death (v. 12) and condemnation (vv. 16, 18). But all over, where this mess ruled, God's grace superabounded (vv. 17, 20, the "much more" argument). The goal of the entire account is righteousness/justification, leading to the life of the coming age (v. 21).

Paul begins in 5:12 to describe how sin came through "the man" Adam, and death spread. But the construction breaks off (hence the dash in NRSV), to be resumed in vv. 18-21. The compressed expression at the end of v. 12 is, out of eleven possible construals that Fitzmyer lists (1993: 413-17), most commonly taken to mean "because." "Death spread because all have sinned." Then, as *2 Bar.* 54:19 puts it (*OTP,* 1:640), "Adam is not the cause, therefore, except only for himself, but each of us has become our own Adam." But the Vulgate rendered it (in Latin) as a reference to Adam "in whom all sinned," leading to the Western doctrine of original (hereditary) sin. What Paul meant, Fitzmyer argues after exhaustive computer search for the Greek idiom *eph' hǭ,* is "with the result that. . . ." Then sin comes from Adam as well as by each person's sinning. While Byrne (127, 183) rejects this "double causality" (though it holds true for death) as making "little sense in the context," all future exegesis will have to reckon with Fitzmyer's data.

5:13-14 intrude in the sequence to clarify the role of the law. Earlier 4:15 had said that where there was no law, as in the time between Adam and Moses, there could be no transgression (of the law). Now it is explained that, prior to Moses, sin could not be counted, but nonetheless everybody died, even those whose sins were not like that of Adam (against a clear command from God, Gen 2:17; 3:17).

5:15-17 form another digression, before getting back to where v. 12 left off. They pick up on the typology at the end of v. 14, about Adam and the one who was to come. Byrne (178-80) speaks of two "waves" of thought about "the free gift" (vv. 15, 16-17), how it is not like Adam's trespass (v. 15) or the effects of his sin (v. 16), and how grace abounds (v. 15) and brings justification (v. 16). The comparison is tied together, with repetition, in v. 17: the recipients (Christians) of Christ's gift of righteousness will reign in life.

At last 5:12 is resumed. Adam's trespass results universally in condemnation, Christ's act of righteousness in life (v. 18, cf. v. 17). The contrast in obedience in v. 19 has spawned debate: "were made sinners" and "will be made righteous" sound too deterministic, especially for relationships toward God; Kirk's "set in the way of sin" or righteousness (198) seems too weak. But need the verb mean any more than "become sinners" or "righteous" (Dunn 1997: #4.6, p. 95)? We are under the influence of one or the other of the two dominating figures in humanity's destiny, Adam and Christ (Byrne: 185). The law, last mentioned in v. 13, comes in for criticism in v. 20: it "slipped in" (cf. Gal 2:4), from Moses' day on, to make transgressions multiply (cf. Gal 3:19). It has no positive role here (but cf. 7:7-12). The answer is not law and more laws, but grace reigning, through life-giving justification.

Freed from Sin and Self (Ch. 6)

The note on which ch. 5 triumphantly concluded, that through Christ "grace has swamped sin" (Dunn 1988: 305; 5:20-21), raises a problem. Does being under grace, without the injunctions of Moses' law, encourage people to keep on sinning so that God will all the more exercise forgiveness? Do evil so that good may result on the part of God (3:8)? Paul had hinted earlier (3:5-8) at charges that his view of God's saving righteousness led to lives of unrighteousness (*adikia,* 3:5; 6:13, wickedness). Now in 6:1 and 15, he answers in diatribe style against such false inferences, "No way!"

Hope, the future aspect of faith, so prominent in 5:2-5, seems set aside till 8:20-24; in ch. 6 it yields, seemingly, to baptism and ethics. Actually many themes from ch. 5 reappear in ch. 6, especially life through righteousness/justification (5:17, 18, 21). Paul now makes clear that this life has ethical content, just as "righteousness" did in the OT (see Introduction, 8.1, above). "Paul explains the relation of Christian conduct to the status of justification and reconciliation" (Fitzmyer 1993:429). All this is part of "the celebration of the hope for salvation contained in the Christian gospel" (Byrne: 187).

The apostle makes these connections through a series of premises in 6:1-11 (dead to sin, v. 2; baptized into Jesus Christ, v. 3; united with him, v. 5; our old self crucified, v. 6; alive to God, v. 11) and then conclusions in the form of ethical exhortations in vv. 12-23 (do not let Sin reign, v. 12; present yourselves to God in the service of righteousness, vv. 13b, 16b, 18, 19). The pattern is that of "indicative" (statements of what is fact, for faith, about what God has done) and resulting "imperatives" ("consider yourselves," v. 11; "do not let . . . ," v. 12; "present yourselves," v. 19). On this important sequence in Paul see Fitzmyer 1993: 430; Käsemann: 175; Dunn 1988: 335 charts how exhortations in 5:12, 13a, 16, 19, and 21 are based on indicatives (not only in vv. 1-11 but also) in 13b, 14, 17-18, and 22; Furnish: 224-27, 262-66, 274-77, 279. Paul's more specific ethical imperatives will appear in 12:1–15:13.

This brief section at 6:12-23 on life lived out, not under law but under grace (v. 15, the solution, in contrast to law), is necessary here to show the further, fuller effects of justification: ongoing service by believers in their entirety as "instruments of righteousness" (v. 13). The imperatives are "integrated into the indicative" (Käsemann: 175) in that, in the section where exhortations are thickest, two more effects of the Christ event appear in addition to those noted in 5:1-10, namely, "freedom" from Sin (6:7, 18, 20, 22) and "sanctification" (vv. 19, 22) (Fitzmyer 1993: 441, 445). Fitzmyer (429) actually makes the primary title for all of ch. 6, "Freedom from Self . . . ," with reference to "our old self" (v. 6). But Sin (personified) or an equivalent like "things of which you are now ashamed" (v. 21) will be mentioned in sixteen of the twenty-three verses.

Exactly as in 4:1, **6:1** begins anew with a rhetorical question. The perverse charge (v. 1) about abiding in Sin is denied in v. 2, where the theme that will run throughout ch. 6 is set forth: death and life (cf. 5:21) — here, dying to Sin and not living in it. This does not mean sinlessness (cf. Dunn 1988: 307), for exhortations must be given to believers not to let Sin continue its dominion (6:12). It does mean holiness (vv. 19, 22) and conforming to what we are to be in Christ. Three short arguments, somewhat in parallel (vv. 3-4, 5-7, 8-10), lead to the conclusion in v. 11, dead in Sin, alive to God — of course, in and through Christ Jesus.

6:3-4 take up baptism as death and life. Paul could assume that in Rome, as in his own congregations, all believers have been baptized "into Christ Jesus," into Christ's Name (as at Acts 8:16; 1 Cor 6:11) or Christ's Person, and so belong to Christ instead of to their old masters. Specifically, they have been baptized into Christ's death (cf. 5:6-8), "buried with him" in the waters. Raised, Christ was. But Paul, as usual (cf. 1 Cor 15:20-23, 49; Phil 3:10-11, 21), refuses to say that Christians are already raised and instead moves the parallel into ethical language ("walk," an OT/Jewish expression for conduct, as at Deut 13:4-5), newness of life (cf. 2 Cor 5:17). The power of the resurrection life and of righteousness is at work under the seeming contraries of daily existence and the cross (6:6, crucified with Christ).

Baptism (Dunn 1988: 308-15) is only a secondary topic here. Modern theology too easily reads in "sacrament" and later concepts. There is much that Paul does not tell us in this passage about the practice, including the giving of the Spirit (1 Cor 12:13; but cf. Rom 8:9-11) and, Fitzmyer (1993: 430-31) notes, the relation of baptism to faith. But it was believers-in-Christ who were baptized. Some would speak of "baptismal justification," where the results of the Christ-event are applied to each individual at baptism and confession of faith ("you were washed, . . . you were justified," 1 Cor 6:11), but Dunn emphasizes a process of conversion-and-baptism (1988: 311-12, 327-30; 1997: #17, esp. 17.3), including conduct, after one is wrenched away "from one's native condition ('in Adam'), from one's native proclivity ('in the flesh'), and from one's ethnic background ('under the law')" (Fitzmyer 1993: 430) to be "in Christ Jesus" (5:11, the first occurrence in Romans according to some commentators, but cf. 3:24; Dunn 1988: 169, 324).

6:5-7 reiterate Christians' being knit together with Christ's death now, and their certain hope of a future resurrection. The "old self" (v. 6, lit. *anthrōpos;* KJV, "man") is terminology about the age of Adam. Existence under that age ruled by Satan is now abrogated (KJV, NRSV, "destroyed," may be overly strong), for "we" believers are no longer to keep on serving Sin (which — or who — continues). That "a person who has died is freed from sin" could simply be common sense, a rabbinic maxim, "Death pays all debts." But the verb is *dedikaiōtai.* Some commentators bring out the forensic sense, "The person who has died with Christ in baptism has been justified from sin" (Cranfield: 296, 310-11). Or ". . . declared free" (Dunn 1988: 320; cf. Acts 13:38, not Paul's usual sense). Or "acquitted of" (Fitzmyer 1993: 436-37). Through such language Paul makes clear that believers are no longer in the grasp of Sin but not yet raised up to parousia existence.

6:8-10 present another wave of the same argument, this time with more emphasis on Christ's death once for all and his resurrection as the foundation for what we Christians have already received and believe we will experience (v. 8). Thus "Christology and anthropology" are bound together as "the center of the *proprium christianum*" (Christianity's distinguishing mark; Dunn 1988: 323), with the present implication of being alive to, and living for, God.

Because of the "therefore" *(oun)* at 6:12, as at 12:1, **vv. 12-14** have usually been taken to mark the shift from indicative (vv. 1-11) to imperative (vv. 12-23). But since in v. 11 what one is to "reckon" (the same verb as in 3:28 and 4:3-11, 22-24) about one's self is already imperatival, vv. 12-14 can be taken as the parenetic conclusion of vv. 1-14 (Byrne: 188, 193-95), with its own grounding in grace (v. 14). In any case, the movement from death to life continues (v. 13), contrasting Sin, wickedness *(adikia),* and death with God, righteousness, and life (vv. 12-13). A new metaphor is the military one of the self and all one's "members" (body parts and capabilities) as "weapons" (NRSV note) of either unrighteousness or justice. To urge "let not Sin keep on ruling" suggests that it still threatens believers, "a reality to be resisted all the time" (Dunn 1988: 336). The positive formulation, "Become [in daily life] what you already are [justified in Christ, in baptism]!" is a modern attempt to balance indicative and imperative. Better is Käsemann's "Become what you can now become!" (173; Dunn 1988: 337: ". . . what you are becoming"; Fitzmyer 1993: 444).

6:15-19 begin again with the question and diatribe style of v. 1. Here it is sharpened by the reference to law (v. 14) as well as grace — as under the Abrahamic covenant of promise (ch. 4), without the Torah stipulations of the Mosaic covenant. The answer is the same, No way! But the imagery changes to that of slavery and freedom. This would have been vivid in a world where perhaps a third of a city like Corinth consisted of slaves and another third of freed ex-slaves (Dunn 1988: 341), where people in urban centers might sell themselves into slavery to survive (Fitzmyer 1993: 448), and in a community of believers as at Rome where two-thirds were likely slaves or freedpersons (Byrne: 200). What or whom you obey is your master. Paul employs the "once" (in the past) and "now" contrast, "before" and "after" God's saving righteousness. The "form of teaching" in v. 17, to which Christians have been "handed over," is likely a catechetical summary of the faith. The reference to "sanctification" (v. 19) contrasts with past impurity and iniquity. As an effect of the Christ-event, it is not a second step after justification (cf. 1 Cor 6:11, "washed, sanctified, justified") but says "the same thing under a different image": transfer to a different Lord, dedicated "to God and his awesome service" (Fitzmyer 1993: 445).

6:20-23 reiterate and sum up on Sin and righteousness, using the slave/freedom imagery. The immediate results (lit. "fruit," v. 21; RSV, "return"; NRSV, "advantage") of Sin are vices like those mentioned in 1:29-31, about which believers can now only be chagrined; of God's righteousness, the results are life and conduct marked by holiness or consecration (v. 21a). The ultimate end (*telos,* v. 21b) is (eternal) death or eternal life (Byrne: 203-4). The final verse is tersely aphoristic: death is the pay Sin doles out, but eternal life the grace-gift *(charisma)* of God, in Christ, the means and sphere for all this.

Freed from the Law (Ch. 7)

While "law" *(nomos)* dominates this chapter (23 occurrences), the flow of the argument moves on directly from ch. 6 (Harrisville: 99), with an illustration from marriage in 7:1-6, paralleling that from slavery in 6:16-22 (fuller comparisons of chs. 6 and 7 are found in Nygren [268] and Dunn 1988: 358). The parallel points are clear: set free from sin (6:18), free from the law (7:2, 3, 6). Then, after a diatribe question in v. 7 (like that at 4:1 and 6:1), Paul denies that the law itself is sin. Its functionings are vividly described in a first-person singular narrative that runs from 7:7 through v. 25. The first section (vv. 7-13) is told in the past tense ("I died"), the second (vv. 14-25) in the present tense ("I am fleshly, sold into slavery"). Some interpreters have relegated the material to an excursus. Others have traditionally paired the view here of the sinner-under-the-law with the justified-life-in-the-Spirit depicted in ch. 8, so as to provide a "before" and "after" contrast, or a picture of the Christian as both saint and sinner. Two issues among others have shaped interpretation: What is meant by "law"? Who is meant by the "I"?

The Gk. *nomos,* rendered in the NRSV as "law," can have varied senses (see the Introduction, 8.6). No consistent distinction can be made between places where the definite article is present and where it is lacking, as at 7:1, literally, "people who know law" in general, versus "*the* law" in the case of marriage. Nor is the issue settled for the chapter by what law code lies behind the comparison in vv. 2-4 to a married woman whose husband dies — generally conceded now to be Jewish, not Roman, law (Dunn 1988: 360). At issue is whether every use of *nomos* in the chapter refers to the Mosaic law (so Dunn 1988: 392-93; 1997: #6.2) or whether there are wider overtones of law systems in the Greco-Roman world, or a sense of *nomos* as "principle" at 7:21 and 23, a wordplay as at 3:27 (cf. REB; Fitzmyer 1993: 475; Byrne: 227).

Thus far in Romans Paul has used *nomos* not only for the law of Moses but also significantly for Scripture, which holds the world accountable before God (3:19-20); as a bringer of divine wrath (4:15) which threatens Gentiles and Jews alike (1:18; 2:5, 8; 3:5); and strikingly for something written on some Gentile hearts to accuse or excuse at the final judgment (2:14-16). In Galatians, where Paul dealt so severely with the law of Moses (3:19-20), the argument also saw Gentiles enslaved to "elemental spirits" and legal regulations about the calendar (4:8-10). That point is not repeated in Romans, but the scruples of "the weak" in 14:2-3, 21 may reflect legalisms in the Gentile world as well as in Judaism (Dunn 1988: 799-802). The audience in Rome, if mainly Gentile, leads one to suspect that being "under law" would for the experience of some involve more than the law of Moses. Rome had its prized legal order too (Käsemann: 187). Commentators must strain to make even "the bulk of Gentile converts" in Rome former God-fearers and synagogue adherents with "a reasonable knowledge of Torah" (Dunn 1988: 359; Byrne: 210). Some were doubtless "overconverted proselytes," but were all, especially in the years of Claudius's crackdown on Jews in Rome? Paul's principle, "Jew first, Gentile too, no distinction," makes it difficult to make freedom from law apply only to the Jewish law.

It is one of the ironies of modern scholarship that, for all the (often justified) attacks on (German) Protestant scholarship for anti-Judaism concerning the Torah (Sanders: 1-12, 33-59), those who call for "post-Lutheran" readings often know all too little about the variety of strands in Lutheran theology. In this instance, Käsemann (187, 200-202, 210) is not untypical of many broadening "law" here to cover all legalism and human piety (including that in some types of Christianity) that trusts its own ability to follow the precepts and thus obtain security.

The argument in **7:2-3** from a death in a marriage, with its implication of freedom for a new relationship (Byrne [214] has retreated from the view that a union with Christ is already meant), is applied in **vv. 4-6.** The "body of Christ" alludes to the Messiah's crucified body (cf. Gal 2:19). In 7:5 "flesh," like "our old self" at 6:6, refers to human beings in the old aeon. Sin-producing passions, spurred on by law, bring — not good ethical fruit but — death. This brief picture of life with the law and sin will be expanded in 7:7-25. The contrast in the eschatological "now" (3:21) finds believers discharged from the law (as in 7:2); "dead to what held us captive" (NABRNT), namely, the law, though Sin (6:7) and self (6:6) may also be included; and enslaved to serve (cf. 6:19, 22), a result that strikes an ethical note. The closing contrast of "letter" (paraphrased as "written code") and (Holy) Spirit picks up on 2:29 ("spiritual," not "letter-al"); "oldness" and "newness" on 6:4 and 6; and the whole on 2 Cor 3:6-9. It points forward to Romans 8. But first, in 7:7-25, the role of the law and life under it must be clarified.

At **7:7a** a new beginning is made with the same rhetorical question as at 4:1 and 6:1. How could anyone have gotten the idea that the law is Sin, a hulking menace like personified cosmic powers such as Death and Wrath? In Romans, from assertions like 3:21 on saving righteousness without the law; or 5:20, the law "slipped in," multiplying trespasses. Law, sin, and death (5:20-21) make a trio that is overcome in Christ by justification, life, and (eventually the answer will be added) the Spirit in ch. 8, reflecting the prophetic hopes of Jer 31:31-34 and Ezek 36:26-27. Paul thus now denies that the Mosaic law = sin, and will speak positively about it in 7:12 as holy, just, and good, indeed spiritual (v. 14a, from the Spirit).

The narrative begins, "I would not have known sin, except through law" (7:**7b**). Who is the "I"? Of the half-dozen explanations of *egō* (Gk. "I") in 7:7-13 (Cranfield [342], who has an even longer list for 7:14-25 on 344), the following rate consideration, though none fits every detail: (1) Paul speaks autobiographically about (a) his boyhood (including childhood and innocence; Bruce: 147-49) or (b) days as a Pharisee (Murray; L. Morris: 282). But 7:9, "I once lived apart from the law," could scarcely apply to a Jewish boy circumcised on the eighth day (Phil 3:5), and in Phil 3:4-6 Paul speaks of Saul the Pharisee as "blameless" as to righteousness under the law; cf. Gal 1:14. Some, like Beker (240-42), reply that Philippians is an objective account while Romans 7 is subjective, a Christian looking back. Theissen (234-43) believes that the "I" is "the consciousness of the pre-Christian Paul" versus what Paul became conscious of "only later" in Romans 7 (235). (2) Other commentators think the "I" is Paul as a Christian, laying bare what life is like after conversion-baptism (so Augustine, Aquinas, Luther, Calvin, Barth, and Nygren). Does such a pessimistic view, with all the references to the Mosaic law (7:7 = Exod 20:17; Deut 5:21), fit with the assertion that believers are "free from law" (7:3, 6)?

Another answer on the "I" person is (3) Adam, as is especially clear in the detail in 7:11, Sin "deceived" me — the same verb as in Gen 3:13, "The serpent tricked me" (so Dunn 1988: 404-6). Since Eve speaks there (cf. also 2 Cor 11:3), one should really argue that Eve and Adam speak in 7:7-11. Käsemann (196) overstates, "nothing in the passage . . . does not fit Adam, and everything fits Adam alone." But the command in Gen 2:16-17 = Gen 3:2-3 was not one that "promised life," as Rom 7:10 says, but aimed at preventing death. Fitzmyer (464) rejects the "Adam" approach.

Others have seen overtones of (4) Israel, receiving commands like "You shall not covet" (7:7-8) at Sinai, but then having the same experience as Adam did with the command in the garden (recall the incident of the golden calf, Exodus 32; cf. Rom 9:3 and 14, which reflect 32:32 and 33:19; Dunn 1988: 379). The Jews are then in Adam's shoes, like the rest of humankind (Byrne: 218; cf. Wright: 197). But did Judaism in Paul's day reflect thus on the law, or only Christians from the standpoint of promise and freedom instead of stipulations to stay in the covenant?

(5) In a generalizing sense, the "I" reflects Everyman or Everywoman's experience (Byrne: 217), a view that can be taken in many directions: "unregenerate humanity . . . faced with the Mosaic law" (Greek fathers; Fitzmyer [464-65] calls it "a cosmic-historical dimension"; "humanity of the race of Adam," Achtemeier: 122-24). Stowers (16-21, 264-79) finds in 7:7-25 a rhetorical form called *prosōpopoiia,* or "speech-in-character," when an author places words in the mouth of another person, earlier noted by Kümmel on Romans 7; in this case "a person who lacks self-mastery." Paul writes to argue "against Gentiles attempting to gain self-mastery by following the law" (279). Cranfield (344-46): "the experience of Christians generally," with some Pauline autobiography.

No one view has prevailed for 7:7-25. Adam's story is present in vv. 7-11. Paul's own opinion appears in v. 14 ("we know . . ."). There is wide agreement that Paul looks back as a Christian over pre-Christian existence. The personal piety reminds one of the Psalms. The "I" speaking with deep consciousness of sin is best paralleled in the QL thanksgiving hymns; cf. Fitzmyer 1993: 465-66. These verses from Paul have struck readers in a variety of ways over the centuries. Fitzmyer (465) concludes that the speaker is "unregenerate humanity faced with the Mosaic law — but as seen by a Christian," but is aware of the critique by Nygren (287-92) as to context (after 7:5, "what we once were," *and* 7:6, "what we henceforth are as Christians"), the view of "mind" *(nous)* in vv. 23, 25 (elsewhere in Paul the mind, too, is under Sin and must be transformed, 12:2), and notions about "the good" (7:19, 21; willing what is right, v. 18 — this better fits the Christian). Commentators sometimes combine several answers about the "I" who speaks.

7:7b-11, then, reflect Adam and Eve. The law makes sin known, for example, with regard to covetousness. If it is objected that "you shall not covet" comes from Sinai, not the Garden-of-Eden story, it can be replied that Jewish interpretation saw in covetousness the origin of every sin (as Eve says, in *Apoc. Mos.* 19:3); cf. Jas 1:15; Dunn 1988: 380), and that these verses are Israel's story too. The term was also used of Gentile "lusts" at 1:24. When law comes on the scene, Sin makes use of it; covetousness grows (contrary to the optimism in 4 Macc 2:1-6, that reason can control even sexual desires), and the encounter with the law ends in a person's death.

How, then, can Paul say God's holy law is good (**7:12**)? He himself is struck by the paradox that what is good brings death and answers that, for one thing, Sin is the culprit, not the law (**v. 13**). **7:14-25** will go on to speak of how the "I" is also involved. But to the question about the law, we must ask, Good for what? One function of the law is to show what sin is (vv. 7b, 13b). Read it and weep over sins (2 Kgs 22:8-13, 19; Nehemiah 8–10). Cf. Dunn 1997: #6.3 and 6.8, who adds, as a second, temporary function, "to protect and discipline Israel in the period from Moses to Christ"; and third, "to regulate and prosper life for the people chosen by God" (6.6, p. 154). This includes regulating their judgment. For according to 7:10, what was intended "for life" turned out to be "for death." To the extent that law defines sin, the verses are a defense of the law (Dunn 1988: 376-77; Fitzmyer 1993: 473). Thus its purposes and results are sorted out. But the real theme is "life under the law" as "a negative foil" to ch. 8 (Byrne: 209; Meyer: 82n.34).

Although the law is spiritual, "I" am the problem, in that we are fleshly, of Adam's epoch, and "sold into slavery under sin" (7:14b). This phrase — from Isa 50:1, sold because of sins, echoing the phrase "sold to do evil" (1 Kgs 21:25; 2 Kgs 17:1; 1 Macc 1:15); sold by God? is there an echo of Rom 1:24, 26, 28? — can stand as "a title for the argument that follows" (Käsemann: 200). The dilemma is expressed in vv. 15-17, repeated in vv. 18-20, 21-23, present tense. I, in the flesh, do not do the good I want to do (which God's good law makes clear, v. 16). Sin, resident in me, rules, as the refrain in vv. 17 and 20 makes clear. The flesh — human beings as they are without God; the world and human makeup in which justified believers still dwell, even though they seek to walk not according to the flesh but according to the Spirit (8:4) — is the workshop of Sin. A person wants salvation and creates disaster (Käsemann: 203). What "I" find to be a law (7:21, which sounds in the NRSV like a resulting principle — "the Ego learns how things stand," Fitzmyer 1993: 475; Dunn 1988: 392-93, pressing "*the* law" in Greek, argues for an encounter with Torah) is that a war results between "the law of God" and my mind, on the one hand, and a different law, that "of sin" and all other parts ("members") of me, on the other. Frustration, despair, and captivity result; rescue is needed (v. 24). A cry of thanks is heard, through Christ, who has not been mentioned throughout the chapter. V. 25 ends with a divided "I," slave to the law of God and to the law of sin.

Is all this Adam's soliloquy? Israel's? All of humanity's? There are Greco-Roman parallels to some of the poignant outcries in ch. 7, like Ovid's "Desire persuades me one way, reason another. I see the better way and approve it, but I follow the worse" (*Metamorphoses* 7.19-21), or Epictetus, "What am I? A miserable, paltry man" (*Diss.* 1.3.5; cf. 2.26.1-2, 4-5). But there are crucial differences, for the Stoic sage appeals to rationality over irrationality; right knowledge results in right actions; "you can." Cf. Theissen: 211-21.

Readers throughout the centuries have given different responses (already indicated) about Romans 7, and will continue to (Byrne: 230), often to avoid old orthodoxies or to fit current concerns (e.g., not to blacken Paul's Pharisaic past). It remains worth pondering whether the key is not eschatological ("now" in v. 6 is the same phrase as in 3:21), a tension in existence, even under Christ. Paul surely describes life under the law in the aeon of Adam, but though the new age of Christ has broken in and marks believers' lives, the old age continues on until the parousia. Thus what held fully under Sin (7:5) and what obtains now, freed from the law, in the new life of the Spirit (v. 6) — both go on in the ups and downs of believers still living in the flesh, though with redeemed mind. Even after the expression of gratitude to God for redemption (v. 25a), the "both/and" nature of existence cannot be forgotten (v. 25b). Dunn (1988: 388, 399, 407-8; 1997: #18.3) speaks of a split within the "I" of the believer — will to do and falling short, obedient yet disobeying, "flesh" and the "inmost self" (v. 22). He compares that with a "'split' in the law" in vv. 21-23 for God's gift used by Sin (chart in Dunn 1988: 398). Meyer (78, 80) speaks of the "cleavage" in the law (not the self). The worst thing is the corruption of the best *(corruptio optimi pessima)*. That is what Sin has done to the Torah. Hence Christ. But how does Torah work out in life under God's Spirit?

Freed for Life in the Holy Spirit and for Hope (Ch. 8)

Outlining Romans 5–8 by chapters may give the impression that freedom for menacing forces gets three times as much play as freedom for the life of the new aeon. Actually ch. 8 is half again as long as ch. 5, 6, or 7. A further balance: some see a break at 8:14, after freedom from Sin, death, self, and law, and the positive picture of the Christian life in 8:1-13; 8:14-39 then develops the theme of 5:1-11, hope (Fitzmyer, Byrne). "Hope" and "eager longing" do appear in 8:19-25. But the term that bursts into overwhelming prominence is *pneuma,* usually of God's Spirit (21 occurrences), after only cameo appearances at 1:4; 5:5; and 7:6; cf. 1:9 and 2:29, of Paul's spirit. Romans 8 is composed "in the key of the Spirit" (Dunn 1988: 416), a mark of the new epoch like justification by faith and the "in Christ" theme (Dunn 1997: ##14, 15, 16). The Spirit is "the key to . . . the eschatological tension in which believers find themselves" (Dunn 1988: 412).

This gift of the Spirit — to every believer (1 Cor 12:13) but not at his/her beck and call as a personal possession — required careful treatment by Paul. On the one hand, there were early Christian enthusiasts who claimed they were, through the Spirit, already completely in the new age; Paul had battled them in Corinth. On the other hand, there were those who were suspicious of all such signs and outbursts in the name of reality — believers still suffer even in this "now" time (8:18). Involved also was the matter of getting eschatology correct. In vv. 18-23 Paul will make use of a "little apocalypse" concerning creation and the end to underscore his reservations even about Christians who possess the Spirit having all God's promises in hand. Mainline churches have often had an "ecclesial reserve" toward "Spirit Christianity" (Dunn 1997: #16.1), toward Pentecostals, and toward a Lukan reading of Paul, without the apostle's balances. Romans 8 does concern the Spirit in the life of believers and the community, but we should not expect Paul's full position on God's Spirit even in this long chapter. For in addition to the blessings of the Spirit mentioned in ch. 8 — liberty (v. 2), conduct (vv. 4-6, 13-14), adoption as sons of God (vv. 15, 23), hope (vv. 24-25), and prayer (vv. 26-27) — we must look elsewhere for spiritual gifts (1 Corinthians 12–14; cf. Rom 12:6-8) and the (ethical) fruit of the Spirit (Gal 5:22-23) (Dunn 1997: #16.5).

8:1-4 begin with a bold assertion of good news: no condemnation for those of Adam (5:16) now rescued "in Christ" (5:6-11; 7:6). Freedom "from the law of sin and death" (v. 23; v. 10) has come about "in Christ" via "the 'law' of the Spirit of life." Dunn (1988: 416-19) argues for *nomos* in both cases as a reference to the Mosaic Torah. That would mean that the Torah, through the Spirit, results in life (Ezek 36:26). But did that or Christ free believers? Dunn (436-37) struggles with what he finally terms "the contradiction" of Paul's "experience" as a Jew and then as a Christian. The case is stronger for taking *nomos* in 8:2 as "principle," with ironic wordplay on Torah (Fitzmyer 1993: 482-83; Byrne [235], a "generic sense"). Given the impotence of the law because of human weakness ("flesh"), God took a new initiative, sending Jesus. The "sending" formula in v. 3 (also at Gal 4:4-5), while as close as Paul comes to speaking of an incarnation, reflects sending messengers (Isa 6:8) or wisdom (Wis 9:10). That the Son came "in the likeness of sinful flesh" suggests similarity to, but not quite total identity with, what 7:5 and 7b-11 described as the human condition. Through Christ as the "sin offering" on the cross (NRSV note; Lev 5:6-7), God condemned Sin. Torah's requirement (8:4) was fully met (by God) among us, the community — and here Paul strikes the ethical note of 6:4 — who "walk" henceforth by the Spirit, not the flesh.

Thus the contrast between flesh and Spirit that runs through **8:5-11** is introduced. The way of the flesh differs from that under God's Spirit in mind-set (v. 5), the results of one's concerns (v. 6), and one's attitude toward God and toward God's law (7), for which "flesh" is impotent. Believers are not like that because the Spirit abides among them ("you" plural, v. 9a; contrast 7:17, 18, and 20 on indwelling sin). In vv. 10 and 11 Spirit (of Christ), Christ, and Spirit of God alternate — the experience was specific, the terminology not uniform. Of course, each believer has the Spirit, a sign of belonging to Christ (v. 9b), but the stress is communal (Christ's Spirit dwells among you [plural], v. 11). Spirit and new life are included under righteousness/justification (REB; Reumann: 85).

This indicative leads in **8:12-13** to an admonition about the two ways of existing, flesh and Spirit, death and life (cf. Deut 30:15, 19; Hab 2:4 at Rom 1:17 is echoed in the closing verb "will live"). Paul here curbs enthusiast tendencies and his critics of 3:8 and 6:11 — "deeds of the body" do matter.

8:14-17, a new paragraph as in the REB, introduces the theme of "adoption" (v. 15) as sons (and daughters) of God (v. 14), children, and heirs, on the way to glory (v. 17). These important emphases are linked to the Spirit, in that the Spirit is the evidence of sonship for those who cry to God as "Abba! Father!" (vv. 15-16). In this way Paul is clarifying what 5:1-11 had spoken of as justification and reconciliation (5:1, 9-11) and "our hope of sharing the glory of God" (5:2). (The reference to sufferings in 5:3 is also brought in through the proviso at the end of 8:17, and will be clarified in 8:17-30.)

"Adoption" (*huiothesia,* 8:15, 23) was a Greco-Roman legal process (Cranfield: 397-98), but its use at 9:4, for Israel, suggests that Paul could also have had in mind OT election as God's "son" (Deut 14:1; Hos 11:1; Byrne: 249; perhaps 2 Sam 7:14a, understood not of David's descendants but the people, in eschatological restoration (Scott 1992: 96-117).

The NRSV's attempt at inclusive language blurs the meaning of *huioi* in 8:14; RSV had "sons of God," similar to Greco-Roman "sons of Zeus," etc. (Dunn 1988: 451), making the connection with Jesus as the Son of God (1:3) — hence, joint heirs with Christ, who is also heir. Believers share his Abba relationship (cf. Gal 4:6-7; Dunn 1988: 453-55; "co-heir with Christ" is "the linchpin" which holds Paul's thought together, including being "heir of the promise to Abraham" in Romans 4). Of course, in Christ women as well as male believers are included, and 8:16 uses the inclusive term "children" (*tekna*).

The family imagery should not mask the vigor of the enthusiast expression in 8:14, "*driven* by the Spirit" (cf. 1 Cor 12:2; Käsemann: 226; Dunn 1988: 450). This Paul counters with "a pilgrim theology" (Käsemann: 229): Christians are "on the way," not yet in the promised land or glory. One cannot duck the cross and suffering.

8:18-25 both continue the "anti-enthusiastic trend of v. 17c" by arguing that to possess the Spirit means waiting in hope for the glory to come (Käsemann: 230-31) and begin a sequence of three things that testify to the "new destiny" of the saints, namely, creation's groaning (vv. 19-

23), the fact of Christian hope (vv. 24-25), and the Spirit interceding for believers (vv. 26-27) (Fitzmyer 1993: 504-6, 514-15, 516-17). Byrne (255) links what often seem to be disparate segments through the "groaning" motif: creation groans with labor pains (v. 22), as do Christians with the Spirit (v. 23), and the Spirit intercedes with ineffable sighs (v. 26).

Paul begins with a settled conviction of his faith (8:18): sufferings even in the new age for those who belong to Christ are as nothing in comparison with future revealed glory (3:23). Vv. 19-22 picture in apocalyptic terms the entire nonhuman world, subjected by God to Adam at the creation (Gen 1:28-30) but, because of the disobedience of Adam and Eve, now marked by futility (cf. 1:21) and slavery to decay (dissolution, death) (Gen 3:17-19; 5:29). But this was done with hope (8:20c-21) for the freedom and glory that would come to God's children (Isa 65:17; 66:22, the apocalyptic "new heavens and earth"). The old creation/age waits longingly (8:19). So do we, Paul adds (v. 23), waiting for full "sonship" (v. 15), that is, bodily redemption at the parousia-resurrection. Saved in hope (v. 24) means waiting with patience (5:3; cf. Gal 5:5). Present "sufferings are not contrary to justification by grace through faith, but can be grace-filled" (Fitzmyer 1993: 506). And believers have the Spirit as firstfruits of the harvest to come (8:23).

8:26-27 are unparalleled in the NT. Christians do not know how to pray? This startling statement is ameliorated somewhat by the phrase "as we ought," but the real explanation lies in the "weakness" of the saints. Hence the need for help from the Spirit, who serves as intercessor. (In 8:34 it is the exalted Christ who intercedes for us, an example of how Paul thinks of the Spirit in light of Christ and in tandem with Christ.) The "sighs too deep for words" might reflect ecstatic "tongues" in Corinth (Käsemann: 241) or "our inarticulate groans" (REB), but the (N)RSV refers the phrase to the Spirit's groanings which the Searcher of hearts (God) discerns (Cranfield: 423-24).

8:28-30 move beyond groanings to the destiny of justified believers, ultimately glory. The phrase at the end of v. 27 in the NRSV about God's will (lit. "according to God") triggers this, as does reference to the divine purpose in v. 28 (cf. 9:11). What follows is an outline of God's plan for elect sinners-now-saints. Harrisville (133) calls the three verses "the hinge of the epistle," on the themes of which much of Romans turns. 8:28 is a doctrinal statement in traditional OT/Jewish terms. The phrase with which the Greek begins, "those who love God," might be expected to continue "and keep God's commandments" (Exod 20:6; Deut 6:5-6). It does not. Instead Paul will add at the end, "to those who are called according to his purpose." The core statement about all things contributing toward the good of those who are called and who love God is complicated by the addition in some manuscripts of "God" as the subject (NRSV note). But the sense is the same: God intends good even in a world in bondage (Gen 50:20; Eccl 8:12).

In **8:29-30** Paul employs a chain-link sequence, as in 5:3-4. Prior to "call" (the importance of which, in contrast to "works," will be seen at 9:12-24) were, in God's purposeful plan, "foreknowledge" and "predestination" (see ch. 9). What was decided beforehand was that those called would be conformed to the image of God's Son — Adam and (new) creation imagery (Gen 1:26-27; Rom 3:23, "glory"; 5:12-19; 8:21). The Christology of Christ as "eldest among a large family of brothers" (REB) parallels "heirs with the Heir" in 8:17. Everything after "call," including "sanctification," is covered by the term "justified." The process is so certain that even future glorification is spoken of in the past tense in this view from the endpoint of God's purpose (Dunn 1988: 485-86).

8:31-39 climax this chapter, chs. 5–8, and the body of the letter, with a lyric confession of God's triumph in Christ. The question of 4:1; 6:1; and 7:7 reappears in 8:31a. The form of what follows is a series of diatribe-like questions (including v. 34b; NRSV note). The first assertion is that "God is for us" (v. 31b), the doctrinal point made in vv. 28 and 29-30. The evidence is now (again) given: the death of God's Son (as sacrifice, 3:25; sin offering, 8:3 [NRSV note]). Here "not withholding" or "sparing" a son has suggested to many readers Abraham's proposed sacrifice of Isaac (Gen 22:16). But the "binding of Isaac" motif understood salvifically, including a "resurrection," probably arose in Judaism only in post-Christian centuries (Fitzmyer 1993: 531-32). Dunn (1988: 501) sees here Abraham's faith (4:2-3) and God's faithfulness.

8:33-34 pick up the question at the end of v. 31 and present a forensic picture of God's saving work for us. Who brings charges in the law court against us? God who justified (Isa 50:8, also in a lawsuit case)? Christ Jesus who intercedes for us? Kerygmatic language is appended about Christ's death, resurrection, and session at God's right hand.

The question, Who (or really what) will separate us from the divine love (of Christ, v. 35)? is followed by a catalogue of dangers in v. 35. "Persecution" and the "sword" are especially singled out in v. 36 with an OT quotation (Ps 44:22) to show that it is always thus with God's people. But we are winning a glorious victory through God, who loved us in Christ (a balancing phrase to 8:28, those who love God). The final statement of deep conviction is that nothing in an ad hoc list of cosmic powers — including Death, life with its dangers, angels (in Paul, often malevolent, 2 Cor 12:7 NRSV, "messenger"; Gal 3:19, derogatory), future forces, or astrological elements like height or depth — can separate us from God's love in Christ.

The Gospel of God's Righteousness and the Unbelief of (Much of) Israel (Chs. 9–11)

Paul has majestically concluded in 8:33, 38-39 that nothing can separate us, the elect, whom God has justified, from the love of God in Christ. What, then, of Israel? For missionary experience had been that more Jews rejected this gospel (or had not heard it) than accepted it, while Gentiles were coming to faith in increasing numbers, indeed had become a majority among the Christians in Rome. Paul had to take up the implications of the fact that the Jews had "not submitted to God's righteousness" (10:3) not only out of personal concern, as a Jew and an evangelist with a universal message for all, Jews and

Greeks alike, but also for the sake of his gospel and its understanding of God. Had the word of God failed (9:6a)? Have Gentiles, not striving for righteousness, attained to it through faith, while Israel, striving for righteousness based on law, did not succeed in fulfilling that law (9:30-31)? Has God therefore rejected Israel (11:1)? Paul answers, using Scripture heavily ("more than 30 percent of the whole," Dunn 1988: 520), with three interrelated points (Käsemann: 260; Byrne: 283-84, among many commentators):

1. God's sovereign power (9:17, 22) and freedom (vv. 6b-29);
2. human response, in terms of Gentile inclusion and Israel's disobedience (9:30–10:21); and
3. mercy in the end for Israel (11:1-32), God be praised (11:33-36)!

Chapters 9–11 have been regarded as marginal or central (see Introduction, section 7, above), as a philosophy of history or an essay in universalism. Older views stressed predestination (Introduction, 8.2), usually of individuals; or justification and individual responsibility to come to faith (8.1). Clearly God's righteousness (10:3) and God's people (9:25-26; 10:21; 11:1-2) are involved, as well as faith (9:30-32, in contrast to works; 10:5-11, specifically in Jesus as Lord). Dunn (1988: 519-20) sees the "problem" and "solution" in chs. 9–11 in terms of divine fidelity: "How could God be trusted to be faithful" to those in Christ (ch. 8) "if he had been unfaithful to Israel"? Hence "theodicy" enters in, defending the trustworthiness of God's promises and divine impartiality to both Jews and Gentiles (E. E. Johnson, in *Pauline Theology III*, 214-16, 220-27; cf. Moo, 241-42). Byrne (283) finds "inclusive gospel" to be the key term: Gentiles included (Romans 1–8), Israel included (chs. 9–11), so "live inclusively" (chs. 12–15, esp. 14:1–15:13). Some "salvation history" is present in chs. 9–11 (stressed by Munck and Stendahl; cf. Käsemann, 254-55), but "justification dominates" and "is the key to salvation history" (Fitzmyer 1993: 541).

Rich fare in 9–11, many interpretations (Granholm and Patte).

9:1-5 make a new beginning, with triple attestation (Christ, conscience, and the Holy Spirit) to Paul's anguish: he would so much have his Jewish brothers (NRSV note, the only time in Paul that *adelphoi* is not used for Christians) come to the faith he knows that he considers, like Moses (Exod 32:32), forfeiting his own life in Christ for their sake. Eight advantageous factors (3:1) are listed for Israel. Here Paul reverts to "Israelite" self-understanding for "the Lord's own" (Sir 17:17), compared with the term "Jew" which others might employ (Dunn 1997: #19.2). These items have sometimes been mentioned in Romans (e.g., adoption, 8:15, "sonship," cf. Exod 4:22; promise, 4:13). They are broader than the four Jewish distinctives — monotheism ("the glory" of God), covenant people, law, and temple ("worship") — which Dunn 1988: 528 notes. The patriarchs Abraham, Isaac, and Jacob will be mentioned in 9:6, 10, and 13, respectively. Does Paul call the Messiah "God"? Yes, in the NRSV note, first alternate rendering, and as a possible sense (Fitzmyer 1993: 548). No in the second alternate rendering and the NRSV text, which has cleverly applied "who is over all" to Christ, not God. Paul's argument does not need to take up the deity of Christ. It concerns the fairness of God.

God's Sovereignty and Promises (9:6-29)

A thesis that will run through this section and all of chs. 9–11 is announced in **9:6a:** God's specific word of election and promise has not failed. As 11:29 will assert, God's gifts and calling are irrevocable. But they have been misunderstood with regard to "Who is Israel?" Paul distinguished (**9:6b-7a**) "Israel" from "all those [NRSV, "Israelites"] of Israel," and "true descendants" from "all of Abraham's children" (NRSV), as the first OT example makes clear (**vv. 7b-9**): the promise was handed on through Sarah's son Isaac, not Ishmael (Gen 21:12; 18:10; contrast Gen 16). A second instance (**9:10-13**) concerns Rebecca's twins, conceived by a single act with Isaac: Jacob, not Esau, reflects God's purpose of election (Gen 25:21-24). The Pentateuch text is supported by one in the prophets (9:13 = Mal 1:2-3) This example makes clear that divine choice has nothing to do with works, good or bad; it depends entirely on the One who calls (NRSV, "his call"). That "call" defines Israel.

9:14-18 begins with questions (cf. 8:31). Is God unrighteous in proceeding thus (s)electively? A third instance, from the exodus, sharpens the issue: God's Yes of mercy to Israel was a No to the Egyptian Pharaoh, whose heart God's power "hardened" repeatedly (Exod 4:21; 7:3; 14:4, 8, 17), that is, made it unresponsive, unyielding. Here, clearly, as in the OT, is "double predestination" (Käsemann: 264-66; Dunn 1997: #19.3, pp. 512-13). But observe therewith, in 9:15 (= Exod 33:19) and the conclusion in 9:18, the note of mercy. The principle is established (v. 16) that the outcome depends not on a person's volition or exertion (lit. "running," an athletic metaphor, equally applicable to "walk" or conduct), not on the totality of human capacities, but solely on the merciful God.

This raises the objection (**9:19**), If it is God's doing, what grounds does God have for finding fault? If God is all-powerful, who has (NRSV "can") resisted his will? Paul's answer (**vv. 20-23**) is in effect the same as that of Job 40:6–42:6, but cast in terms the prophets used (Isa 29:16; 45:9; 64:7-8; Jer 18:3-6) about God the ceramist. The potter can make a lump of clay either into a fine vase or a chamber pot! Paul's strongest assertion of divine sovereignty is cast as a conditional sentence, the conclusion to which is never drawn (9:22-23; NRSV, "what if . . . ———"). Literally, "If God . . . ," and then an ominous participle, which can be taken causally, "because God wishes to show his wrath" (Cranfield: 493-96), or concessively, "although wishing . . ." (Fitzmyer: 569), and breaking off after a reference to "objects of mercy . . . prepared beforehand for glory. . . ." Throughout, as earlier in Romans, the positive and negative sides of God and the divine righteousness are seen — wrath and destruction, mercy and glory; power to judge or deliver. E. E. Johnson speaks of the "two natures" of God (*Pauline Theology III*, 221-22): faithfulness to Israel and impartiality. The order in v. 18 ("show mercy, harden") is reversed in vv. 22-23 (objects of wrath, objects of mercy) in order to attach v. 24

under the latter heading, "us whom God called." Then comes the issue.

Those effectively now called by God in Christ include not Jews only but also Gentiles (**9:24**). A church of them is implied. For Paul may be reflecting the folk etymology of *ekklēsia,* "called" *(kaleō)* "out of" *(ek)* Jews and Gentiles (Käsemann: 273). This eschatological event fits Hos 2:23; 1:9-10: those not God's people have become such, sons of the living God (**vv. 25-26**). The OT *testimonia* continues in vv. **27-28** with quotes from Isa 10:22-23 and 1:9. The prophetic idea of a "remnant" being saved out of Israel is introduced in 9:27. The term could be threatening or reassuring (Dunn 1988: 573-74). The NRSV interpretatively adds *"only"* before "a remnant." The last line from Isaiah in 9:28 (Isa 10:23, colored by Isa 28:22) looks to an accounting that at best may fulfill and curtail (promises), perhaps trimming down (to a remnant). Cf. Dunn 1988: 573-74 and Fitzmyer 1993: 574-75 on the difficult wording. **9:29** puts Israel and the Jews in the same class with Sodom and Gomorrah (Gen 19:24-25). Dunn (1997: #19.3, p. 514) speaks of "the divided 'I' of Israel." How did things come to such a pass, given God's promises?

Israel's Failure at Response (9:30–10:21)

After treating God's sovereign power to elect and call (9:6-29), Paul now goes on into Israel's failure, indeed refusal, to respond in faith to the gospel about Christ (Fitzmyer: 576-77, 594-96). Commentators employ various terms to describe the situation as Paul saw it in his day: Israel misunderstood God's righteousness and "lost the way" (Dunn 1988: 576-78), misunderstanding God's call (Dunn 1997: #19.4), in contrast to the Gentile response (9:30-31; chs. 2–4). "Israel oppos[ed] God's rightwising" (Wilckens: 6/2:209). Israel has "stumbled" (9:32-33, Byrne) and is without excuse (but there is hope, Cranfield: 503). "Israel Itself to Blame for Its Rejection" (Sanday and Headlam: 275). "Israel's Guilt and Fall," hardened by its own fault (10:14-21), makes it guilty before God (Käsemann: 276, 293).

While Paul begins afresh in 9:30 (with the diatribe question last heard at v. 14), his argument brings in familiar themes like "righteousness/justification" (11 times) and "faith/believing" (13 times, both word clusters less frequent in 3:20–5:21), plus "law" again (statistics in Dunn 1988: 577) and "(preach) gospel" (10:15-16). The unit becomes overtly christological (10:4, 6-17), bringing "salvation history" down to the moment when Paul writes, with the suggestion that it also includes *Unheilsgeschichte,* or a history of disobedience and its consequences (cf. Munck, "Israel's Unbelief" as a broader "primitive Christian problem"; Paul's view is optimistic in contrast to later ones in the Gospels).

The conclusion from ch. 9 and earlier parts of Romans is set forth as the theme for what follows in **vv. 31b-32:** Gentiles, who, outside the Mosaic covenant, do not, almost by definition, pursue covenant righteousness, have — or at least some of them have (v. 24) — obtained as a gift God's kind of righteousness through faith. Israel, however, constantly in pursuit of "the law of righteousness," did not arrive at that law. Cf. Phil 3:9. The phrase *nomos dikaiosynēs* in 9:31 is probably best not rendered as in the NRSV, "righteousness which is based on law" (Dunn 1988: 581). It could mean "law (which promises) righteousness" (Käsemann) or leads to it (Reumann: 87; Fitzmyer: 578; Byrne: 313). "Law" is front and center in Paul's phrase, in contrast to righteousness "through faith." This contrast becomes explicit in **v. 32a:** Israel saw its obligation not as faith but "as if it were works (of the law, cf. 3:20)," like circumcision and other practices which marked Jews off against Gentiles. This narrowness led to a failure to reach out to Gentiles and monopolized righteousness as "a function of Jewish identity rather than God's gracious outreach to and through faith" (Dunn 1988: 577). Actually, Judaism in Paul's day did reach out to convert Gentiles, and with some success (cf. P. F. Stuehrenberg, "Proselyte," *ABD,* 5:503-5). It is *with what,* rather than *whether,* Judaism of the day reached out to Gentiles that is at issue for Paul.

The result of "works, not faith" on Israel's part led to stumbling (**9:32b-33**). The figure comes from passages in Isa 8:14-15 where God is the stone that trips up Israel, and 28:16, a stone God lays as the foundation. This composite reference to a stone is also found in 1 Pet 2:6-7, where it is applied to Christ. At 9:32-33 the stone has been taken as the law or God (so Meyer, references in *Pauline Theology III,* 229), but more commonly as Christ (cf. 1 Cor 1:23). Since Christ, no doubt already in Paul's mind, will not be mentioned explicitly till 10:4, Fitzmyer (579) suggests that "the gospel" is meant. The final phrase in 9:33 can here be rendered "in him" (as at 10:11) or "in it." Harrisville (160-61) helpfully goes into the OT sense in this and other passages where verses are quoted; on the textual intricacies see Dunn 1988: 583-85. Israel has preferred its own way, not God's (Fitzmyer: 577).

10:1-4 begins with Paul's passionate hope that those of Israel may be saved (see 9:1-3). As in 9:4-5, there is a tribute to them, their zeal for God, to which Paul is willing to testify publicly (courtroom imagery). But this zeal becomes jealousy (*zēlos* bears both meanings) for Israel as God's distinctive people. Phineas (Num 25:6-13) had become a patron saint for Jewish ethnic purity; cf. Ps 106:31 (where Gen 15:6 is applied to his deed in the desert, halting the plague by slaying an Israelite man and his non-Israelite woman) and Sir 45:23-24.

How this national zeal worked out in Paul's day revolves around the saving righteousness of God (cf. Introduction, 8.1.1), now made known as gospel (1:17; 3:21) or justification (3:22, 25). This the Israelites disregard. Instead they seek to establish a righteousness of their own, that of covenant keepers, emphasizing nomism. They have not subjected themselves to God's new kind of righteousness. Not to be overlooked is that 10:4 defines the righteousness of God christologically (note "for" as the connective, Reumann: 88).

What seems a conclusion in **10:4** about the contrast in 9:30-31 between "faith righteousness" and "law righteousness" has traditionally been rendered "Christ [is] the end *(telos)* of the law" (KJV through NRSV). In recent years "goal of the law" has become popular, not merely as the preference of Calvinists over Lutherans (but the matter is quite complex, Cranfield: 516-18) or for interreligious reasons to speak positively of the Mosaic law. In the choice between "termination" (Nygren: 379-80; Käsemann: 282-83; Murray: 2:49-50; Stuhlmacher: 155-56) and "fulfillment" (or even "victory line" in a race course or "destination") or some combination of senses, one must ask what an interpreter means by the word chosen. Thus Fitzmyer prefers "end" (581) but questions whether "termination" suits the context and prefers "goal of the law because through him [Christ] humanity can reach . . . the goal of the law," righteousness in the sight of God (584). Byrne (315) opts for "the (true) goal of the law" but in "the sense that the law had no other purpose than to lead to Christ and the righteousness of God available to believers in him."

Actually the phrases in 10:4 will be expanded in vv. 5-13 (E. E. Johnson, *Pauline Theology III,* 228). In v. 4 itself the opening words, Christ as the *telos* of the law, must be taken with what follows, "for righteousness to everyone who believes" (KJV). That relates to 9:31-32 and 10:5, righteousness from law involving works rather than from faith. Christ is then "the end of the law as a means to righteousness for all who believe" (Dunn 1988: 589-91; 1997: #14.6, p. 369). Cf. Harrisville (162): "Christ our righteousness" (1 Cor 1:30), "the heart and core" of Romans. What Byrne (315) calls the "negative" purpose of the law, to define sin (7:13), does not end, nor does the positive use of the Mosaic lawbooks to establish Paul's message (3:21, 31; ch. 4; 10:5-21). Continuing use of the law by believers in the new age for guidance seems cut off by 6:15; 7:4, 6; but cf. 13:8-10.

In **10:5-13** the contrast begun in 9:31-32 between faith righteousness and law righteousness continues, in reverse order. 10:5 presents what Moses wrote at Lev 18:5 with regard to the latter, righteousness out of the law. Doing the things in the law of Moses will bring life. This explicates "end of the law" in 10:4 as a way to righteousness. In Gal 3:10-12 Paul emphasized doing *all* that is in the book of the law, but not here. Rom 10:5 and 2:13 refer to a "doing" kind of righteousness, arduous (Fitzmyer: 589), "beyond human capacities" (Byrne: 317). Dunn (1988: 601) shies away from such emphases, but his distinction (1997: #19.4, p. 516) between "primary righteousness" (from faith) and "secondary" righteousness (the fruit of faith) seems to come out of later theology.

Paul's contrast is between nomistic righteousness and righteousness from faith (10:6). Here what is regarded as a pesher-midrashic treatment (as in QL) of Deut 30:12-14 has faith righteousness speak. The passage is prefaced with a typically Deuteronomic phrase (8:17; 9:4), "Do not say in your heart," and is interlaced with three explanatory phrases in 10:7 and 8, beginning "this means" (in parentheses in the NRSV). Textual details are found in Dunn 1988: 603-5. The boldness of the alterations to Scripture so shocked Calvin that he could not regard it as a biblical quotation, but this is an example of treating Scripture in light of justification (Käsemann: 284, 286) or the oral gospel. Scripture can be cited against Scripture (both texts from the Pentateuch).

The overall emphasis in **10:5-10** is on the nearness of the word which Paul and other missionaries proclaim (v. 8). That message is about Christ. There is no need to bring him down from heaven, for he has been sent to us (as in 8:3, as close as Paul comes to the incarnation); or to bring him up from the dead, for God has already done that. Behind the exposition lies the figure of "wisdom" (Bar 3:29-30), applied to Christ "our wisdom" (1 Cor 1:30). How near is this word? As close as "lips" and "heart" (Deut 30:14), which Paul explicates not as a sacrament in the mouth but as the confession of faith and belief in the heart. The content of this faith goes to the center of Christian proclamation: Christ who died is risen and is Lord (in proper sequence in v. 10). The result of thus believing is to be justified.

The universal scope of this gospel is underscored in **10:11-13** by adding "everyone" to the quotation from Isa 28:16 in v. 11 (repeated from 9:33; the NRSV veils the literal sense, "Everyone who believes in him [Christ, no longer ambiguous as in 9:33] will not be put to shame"). 10:12 echoes 3:22 (there is no distinction between Jews and Gentiles as sinners) and 1:16 (both groups can be saved by the same Lord, Jesus [v. 9], who is rich in mercy; cf. 9:23, NRSV, "generous"). Joel 2:32 is used in 10:13 to confirm from the prophets and interpret what Deuteronomy had said in v. 11.

10:14-17 explain what is behind calling on the Lord Jesus, namely, messengers duly sent as Christ himself was (8:3). The sequence (cf. 5:3-4; 8:29-30) runs (reverse order in 10:14-15), those who bring good news were sent, to proclaim, so that people hear *(akouein),* thus believe, and then call upon the Lord, expressing faith. The text in v. 15b, from Isa 52:7, is better rendered, "How timely" or "welcome" (REB) these messengers. Of course, not all people have obeyed (10:16, *hypakouein,* hearing properly, a wordplay on *akouein*). Many Gentiles, especially in Rome, have obeyed, but only some Jews. But that matches what Isaiah had discovered (53:1). 10:17 sums up. Faith comes about from hearing the word that is so near (v. 8), from and concerning Christ.

Paul in first-person diatribe form goes on in **10:18-21** to strip away possible excuses. (1) Perhaps Israel has not heard the message. No, the messengers' words (the same term as in 10:8 and 17) have gone through the inhabited world, as Ps 19:4 puts it. This hyperbole reflects the world vision Paul has of the gospel in 15:19 and for Spain in 15:24. (2) Perhaps Israel did not understand (10:19). Well, Gentiles did. Moses from the outset had warned in Deut 32:21 about "those not a nation" like Israel, that is, the Gentiles, making Israel "jealous." This Pentateuchal quotation is clarified by one from the prophets in v. 20, Isa 65:1, where God says, "I have shown myself to those who did not ask for" or "seek me." This forms an *inclusio* for the section with 9:30: Gentiles, without striving, attained. Paul is underscoring the divine initiative and also, in a still obscure reference in v. 19 to making Israel "jealous," hinting at his solution (see 11:11, 14). As for Israel as Paul writes, Isa 65:2 applies — disobedient and defiant to God's continued reaching out through the very present word.

Hopes for the Future (Ch. 11)

After vigorously setting forth God's sovereignty and Israel's failure in chs. 9 and 10 — God is not unrighteous or unfaithful to his promises; the word of the gospel has not failed — Paul turns to the fate of Israel. In the face of the fact that the Jews were by and large not believing the message about Jesus as Lord (10:9, 16), though the Gentiles were accepting righteousness through faith (9:30), what now (11:7) of this eschatological inbreaking of the new age, so gloriously described in 3:21-30 and chs. 5 and 8? "Hope" is not a Greek word in ch. 11, but apocalyptic expectations control Paul's thought. It may seem too weak a term by modern definition, unless it is recalled that Paul has used "hope" to characterize the subjection of creation to futility (8:20) and our salvation (8:24); it is something not yet seen, but it calls for patient waiting (8:24-25). For ch. 11 the plural "hopes" is more accurate since Paul will deal with the future of Gentile believers (vv. 13-24) as well as that of Israel.

Talk will be primarily of God, with heavy use of the OT (see Harrisville and Dunn 1988 on OT context and textual details), not of the Spirit. Christ will come in at a crucial point in 11:27. The gospel (v. 28) will not be directly expressed in terms of righteousness/justification, but the related words "grace" and "faith" are prominent. Paul speaks in OT-Jewish terms in showing that "the history of the promise to Israel has not been broken off" (Käsemann: 298). Tersely put, Paul will claim "that Israel's disbelief is only partial (11:1-10), that it is only temporary (11:11-24), and that all Israel will be saved . . . (11:25-32)" (Fitzmyer: 602). It will take a miracle (v. 15) and a revelation from God (vv. 25-27) to effect all this.

11:1-6 begin with Paul speaking personally ("I say," 11:1 as in vv. 11, 13, and 25). His question, "Has God repudiated his people [Israel]?" is one the Israelites themselves asked (Ps 60:10) and pondered (Jer 37:31), despite promises that God would not cast them off (1 Sam 12:22; Ps 94:14). God has not, Paul answers (11:2), rejected the people whom God foreknew (8:29), God's "once-for-all choice" (Käsemann: 299). As evidence Paul cites himself (11:1b) and Jewish Christians, "a remnant chosen by grace" (v. 5). In this group Israel continues as a remnant. Paul intends his personal example to express his solidarity with all Israel. He speaks from within the Jewish heritage. The passage about Elijah (1 Kgs 19:10, 14, 18, quoted in 11:2b-4) may reflect Paul's feeling that he was, in salvation history, "the Elijah of the end-time" (Käsemann: 301). More important, the verses suggest that God kept a "remnant" by grace in Elijah's day as now. The reference to a "divine reply" in v. 4 (lit. "oracle") may point toward the revealed mystery to be unfolded in vv. 25-27 (Harrisville: 173). God's "grace" (4 times in vv. 5-6) is the common term behind both election and righteousness/justification, in contrast to "works (of the law)" (3:27-28; 4:13-16).

Israel is thus now divided, **11:7-10** go on. As a whole, it did not obtain what it sought (cf. 9:31, "law righteousness"); "the elect" did, while "the others" (NRSV, "the rest") were "hardened" (cf. 9:18; ossified, made obtuse). Who are "the elect" here? Some verses (9:30; 10:20) suggest Gentile Christians (cf. 11:17-19a). But the context calls for Jewish Christians (cf. 11:5). Likely both (Dunn 1988: 640). Within this "divided 'I' of Israel," in its eschatological tension (Dunn 1997: #19.5, pp. 521-22), Paul now makes the claim, on the basis of all three parts of the emerging Hebrew canon, that God gave the rest of Israel "eyes not to see" and "ears not to hear," right down to the present moment (Isa 29:10 plus Deut 29:4). David, as the author of Ps 69:22-23, adds in 11:9-10 a reference to "a stumbling block" (9:33) and occasion for retribution. "Eyes" in 11:10 links this quotation to the previous one. Most of Israel is blind and bowed down in slavery (cf. Cranfield: 552, but many details in these quotes Paul does not press).

11:11-12 begin a solution on the future for this large remainder of unseeing Israelites by making a distinction between "stumbling" (from v. 9) and "falling" flat on one's face. Israel's "stumbling" in 9:32-33 is now distinguished from sprawling on the ground. Some see here imagery of a foot race possible at 9:16 (KJV, "him that runneth"; cf. 9:30-31, "pursuing") and speak of "winners" (the elect) and "losers" in 11:7; then God would be tripping the latter up, "blinding, deafening, and bowing them down" (E. E. Johnson, *Pauline Theology III,* 232; 227, "God has rigged the race course") — a bit much, even in the most rugged defense of divine sovereignty and hardly "impartiality." Paul's argument moves differently. The stumbling of most of Israel has allowed salvation to come to the Gentiles. After preaching "to the Jew first," missionaries like Paul have now gone to the Gentiles with success. The point is repeated in v. 12: Israel's misstep and "defeat" (diminution) mean riches for the Gentile world, that is, a God rich toward all (10:12; NRSV, "generous"). What the NRSV calls Israel's "stumbling" in 11:11 and 12 is, as its note explains, literally "transgression" (*paraptōma,* a wordplay on the verb "stumble" in v. 11). The transgression or false step was "rejection of the gospel (10:16-21)," possibly of the cross (as the "basis of salvation") (Dunn 1988: 653, but there is no hint here, as at 1 Thess 2:14-16, that Paul thinks of "Jewish guilt" in crucifying the historical Jesus; yet cf. Munck: 79-84, 117).

Israel's stumbling thus cleared the way for salvation to come to the Gentiles. But Paul has one more turn to his argument: salvation for the Gentiles will serve "to provoke Israel to jealousy" (11:11). Paul is here applying what 10:19 had said on the basis of Deut 32:31. Now Paul, as a prophet, suggests how much more the filling up of the Jewish-Christian remnant with the rest of Israel will mean for the world. This tantalizing thesis will be amplified in 11:25-32.

In **11:13-15** Paul addresses the Gentile Christians in Rome, as the apostle to the Gentiles. There are consequences from Israel's stumbling and trespass for Paul's own ministry, which he magnifies (v. 14): he seeks to make his own flesh-and-blood Jewish kinfolk jealous, so as to save some of them (a modest, not unrealistic hope). V. 15 reiterates v. 12 in different terms. The rejection of the gospel by the Jews (a stronger possible reading is "the rejection of the Jews by God"; cf. vv. 8-10; Byrne: 339) has resulted in the message of reconciliation (5:10-11) going to the Gentile world. Jewish acceptance of the gospel (welcoming it) — or possibly God's acceptance of the rest of Israel — will be like "life from the dead!" Fitzmyer (613) would take this figuratively: the Jews involved would move from life to death (via baptism? 6:4). But most interpreters see a reference to the general resurrection at the end of time. Paul has several times referred to the resurrection of Jesus (4:17, 25; 6:4; 10:9) and that of believers (8:11) as a miraculous action by God. Paul's apocalyptic vision begins to emerge. The collection project, which was nearing completion as he wrote Romans, would take gifts and representatives from his Gentile congregations to Jerusalem and could be a means in his ministry to move some Jews in Judea to jealousy and salvation. Soon would come Christ's parousia and the conversion of "all Israel" (11:25-27) (Byrne: 339; Munck: 116-27).

As Paul moves on to consequences for Gentile Christians in Rome, the metaphors shift. **11:16** begins with cultic law (from Num 15:17-21) about how, from the firstfruits at the grain harvest, the initial dough for bread that is offered to God is holy (consecrated to God); therefore the entire batch is holy. Similarly with the root and branches of a tree. Here the reference pictures Israel as a tree of God's planting (Jer 11:16-17; Ps 92:13, of the righteous). Outcomes stem from origins. The "firstfruit" and "root" could refer to the first Jewish-Christian converts; subsequent Gentile ones would then be holy too (Barrett: 216). More likely the firstfruit is Abraham (Romans 4), followed by the patriarchs and subsequent generations. Then what? There is no appeal to the rabbinic idea of "the merits of the fathers" or to linear transmission of holiness to all of Abraham's children (cf. 9:6-8; it is a matter of promise, grace, and faith; Dunn 1988: 660).

The image of a single cultivated olive tree (Israel) interests Paul more (**11:17-24**). Branches were broken off so that wild-olive-tree shoots (Gentiles) could be grafted in. Paul uses the figure first to check Gentile-Christian presumptions. The root supports them, not vice versa (v. 18). What might sound like an anti-Jewish claim in v. 19 (displacement of Jews by Gentiles) is met with the assertion that God the arborculturist could snap off Gentile branches too (v. 21). The reason for excision: lack of faith; one stays in as part of the tree (the NRSV adds *"only"*) by faith (v. 20). The figure illustrates both God's kindness and God's judicial severity (v. 22), continued nurture or being cut away. The second use of the olive-tree image is to insist that "God is able" to graft back in those (of Israel) who have been pruned away (vv. 23-24). Indeed, more so with these original branches that for the present are fallen (v. 22) than with the "Gentile" ones (v. 24). Grace, in all cases, is the "power which overcomes unbelief and brings faith. Miracle is therefore the presupposition of faith" (Käsemann: 311). Ecclesial overtones lurk in this discussion for the house churches in Rome. In the history of God's word there can be "no church of Gentile-Christians alone," "no salvation apart from the history of Israel" (Käsemann: 309-10).

11:25-32 unveil the mystery that for Paul resolves the problems in a vision of hope. The term *mystērion* in the NT (cf. 16:25; 1 Cor 15:1 especially) has nothing to do with "mystery religions"; rather, as in Dan 2:18-19 and the QL (Dunn 1988: 678), it denotes a hidden secret made known by God. When this revelation came to Paul is not stated, hardly only as he was dictating Romans 9–11, for he has built up to it in previous references. Paul prepares for his announcement with a reminder in v. 25a about Roman Christians not claiming all wisdom for their own Jewish- or Gentile-Christian discernments (cf. 11:20; 2:17-24; 12:16b). God's revelation is that a hardening (11:7) has come on Israel until the fullness (the same term as at v. 12, the "full inclusion" of Israel) of the Gentiles comes in (to God's community). The phrase meaning "in part" (Stendahl: 38: "sort of") can be taken with "Israel" ([N]RSV, "a part of Israel," thus "the rest" in v. 7) or with "hardening" (NEB, "partial blindness," REB; Fitzmyer: 621). Either way the hardening is somewhat mitigated, and a time is set for its ending. That "all Israel will be saved" (v. 26a) means the presently elect Jewish Christians plus "the rest" of Jews in v. 7, corporately but not necessarily each individual (as in the rabbinic teaching at *m. Sanh.* 10:1, "All Israel will have a share in the world to come," but exceptions then are listed, such as the person who denies "the resurrection of the dead") (Dunn 1988: 681-82).

Behind Paul's thought is the OT idea of an eschatological pilgrimage of the nations to Mt. Zion in Jerusalem (Isa 2:2-3 = Mic 4:1-2; Isa 56:6-7; 60:3-14; Zech 14:16-17), a hope held by Jesus (Matt 8:11-12 par. Luke 13:28-29; Dunn 1988: 680-81). But Paul's use of Isa 59:20-21 in **11:26-27** changes directions from a movement *to* Zion to "those in Jacob who turn from transgression" to one of the Deliverer coming *out of* Zion, banishing impiety from Jacob and effecting God's covenant (see Introduction, 8.7) by removing their sins (v. 27b = Isa 27:9). Generally the Deliverer has been understood to be Christ. But in recent interreligious treatments some have understood the Deliverer to be God, reaffirming the everlasting covenant with Israel. This is to introduce a second way to final salvation, besides Christ, a special way for Israel (e.g., Stendahl: 39-44). For reasons to reject such "two covenants" theories see Fitzmyer: 619-20; Dunn 1988: 683; Byrne: 354-55; and E. E. Johnson, *Pauline Theology III,* 212-14, cf. 251). But the christological interpretation must decide whether Paul means (a) that "all Israel will be saved" only at the parousia – then the Jews will see that the Deliverer wears the visage of Jesus of Nazareth, so there is still a special resolution for Jews eschatologically in an apocalyptic scenario; or (b) that it will come about through the proclamation of the gospel (as in Mark 13:10) that Paul has presented throughout Romans, "that the justification of 'all' human beings depends on faith in Christ Jesus" (1:16) (Fitzmyer [620], the only tenable solution; Byrne: 351). Dunn 1988: 691-93 sees Christ's second coming in the reference, when "the split in the 'I' of Israel will be healed," but the "vagueness" of wording in 11:26-27 amounts to an invitation to "fellow Israelites to join . . . in looking for the coming of the Messiah" (1997: #19.6, p. 528).

Paul's hope for a positive response by divided Israel to the gospel and his trust in God's mercy are clear in **11:28-32.** Israelites are "beloved" "enemies" (the NRSV still adds "of God" to the latter term in v. 28, a phrase removed almost forty years ago in the Luther Bibel). The gifts (*charismata,* as listed in 3:2 and 9:4-5) and calling (in Abraham; till the present, 10:21) continue, as does disobedience (11:29, 31a). But just as disobedient Gentiles came to the obedience of faith by God's mercy, so Paul's firm hope is that Israel will come "now" in the new age of gospel proclamation (Byrne [356] wants to say "in time"). The NRSV is correct in taking "by the mercy shown to you [Gentiles]" with the final purpose clause (Fitzmyer: 627-28) rather than in connection with Israel's disobedience (REB; Dunn 1988: 687-88). The Gentiles who have received mercy will trigger Israel's receiving mercy. A concentrated assertion of predestination and grace in v. 32 concludes the vision: all, enclosed in disobedience; all, objects of God's mercy (cf. Gal 3:23).

The closing hymn to this God in **11:33-36** balances 9:1-5 but in the rhapsodic spirit of 8:31-39. Three divine attributes are lifted up: riches (9:23; 10:12; 11:12), wisdom (hidden but at work in Christ, see on 10:5-10), and knowledge (cf. 8:29; 11:2). God judges all as part of his justice, but his "ways" (as set forth in 11:25-27) can cause only exclamation by mortals. The three questions (vv. 34, 35, from Isa 40:13 and Job [cf. 35:7 and 41:3 LXX]) all expect the answer, "No one." The statement in 11:35 may reflect Greco-Roman ideas of friendship: "I give a gift to my benefactor, expecting to get a bigger one back." No *do ut des* religion ("I give in order that you may give") with God! The three relationships with God indicated in the doxology ("from, through, to") are typically Stoic in praise to the One who is sovereign over all.

The Meaning for Everyday Life of God's Justifying Righteousness (12:1–15:13)

Paul's gospel message included both "indicative" and, growing out of such proclamation about what God does, "imperative," as seen already in 6:12-14; 8:5-13; cf. 11:17-24 on the consequences for the newly added olive branches if they do not "continue" in God's generosity. "Precisely the believer is under threat" of judgment, for pride, among other things, after "justification is manifested as the grasping of our lives by Christ's lordship"; "Paul's realism can exclude neither the problem of Israel nor the dimension of the everyday" (Käsemann: 310, 323). The letter will now spend almost as many pages on "ethics" in 12:1–15:13 as on Israel in chs. 9–11. Both represent the "outworking" of the gospel (Dunn 1988).

Such moral teaching or *paraklēsis* ("exhortation, appeal, comfort," 12:1, 8, etc.) was a regular feature when Paul wrote to congregations he had founded (1 Thess 4:1–5:22; Gal 5:13–6:10). It was more difficult with Christians in a place where he had never yet visited, but there were common resources (see Introduction, section 5, above). He had to do so for any complete presentation of his Christianity. Gentile and Jewish Christians both would assess the apostle by where his gospel came out on many issues in practical life. Israel's law had said, Live by certain statutes and ordinances (Lev 18:5, cited at Rom 10:5; cf. 7:10). How do Christians live now that Mosaic legislation is no longer the norm? The three aspects of salvation which Dunn emphasizes (1997: ##14-16) — justification by faith, "in Christ," and the gift of the Spirit — are more assumed than directly mentioned in chs. 12–15. "Faith" will, however, stand out (12:3, 6; and with regard to the "weak in faith," 14:1ff.). Love will be preeminent (12:9; 13:8-10).

Readers often find the sections loosely organized. Chiastic structures have been proposed (Dunn [1988: 706] in 12:1–15:6; Fitzmyer [1993: 652] in 12:9-13), but there is little agreement. Paul begins with a transition paragraph in vv. 1-2 that is one of the most important passages in Romans, for it redefines worship and religion. Vv. 3-8 turn to existence under grace in the church community, while vv. 9-21 present exhortations for social relationships among Christians and in the world. Then 13:1-7 deal with obligations to the state. The command to love is taken up in 13:8-10, and then eschatology (13:11-14). Note the "two ages" (12:2; Introduction, 8.8). Given the apocalyptic outlook in much of Romans (e.g., 11:25-32) and Paul's strong emphasis on fulfillment only in the future, it is not easy to find a "realized eschatology" supposedly conducive to ethics (cf. Beker: ch. 13). In 14:1–15:13 Paul gets to problems of the "strong" and the "weak" in the Roman house churches (Introduction, section 2, above). Some see chs. 12–15 as the goal toward which the entire letter moves (Introduction, 8.4, above).

Exhortations for Christians in Community, with the State, and Looking toward "the End" (Chs. 12–13)

The word "therefore" *(oun)* in **12:1** points back to what Paul's exhortations rest upon, immediately 11:30-36, a glorious God from whom the brothers and sisters have received mercy, but ultimately (1:16–11:36) the gospel of God's saving righteousness and its blessings. To appeal, implore, or exhort was a recognized function in the Christian community (12:8). Paul does it here with a hint of apostolic authority, "I" (cf. 11:13). What follows is an appeal to "God's mercies" (Heb. *raḥamim,* "womb," "compassion"). The term is different from that in 11:30-32 but paralleled at 9:15 ("have compassion"). The plural suggests "the whole of salvation history as God's self-revelation" (Käsemann: 326). It can be the basis of the appeal or can go with "to present," so that offering themselves is by God's mercy (Fitzmyer: 639). The language is cultic, used for animal sacrifices in the Jerusalem temple or at pagan altars. What Christians present is "your very selves" to God (REB), though the literal "your bodies" *(sōmata)* suggests the somatic aspect of the total person, concretely, in time and space. This is for Christians "spiritual [or reasonable] worship." No one translation catches the sense of *logikēn* here, from *logos,* hence "logical" or "reasonable." In both Gentile and Jewish circles there was a revulsion against animal sacrifice and a "spiritualizing" of cult (Dunn [1988: 710-12], involving mind and spirit, as in prayer and praise, not the physical; cf. REB, "the worship offered by mind and heart"). "Worship" here is the same word used of Israel at 9:4, but now in light of the fact that Christians of Paul's day had no church buildings (the courtyard of a home or rooms in a tenement house had to do in Rome). No priests, no sacrifices — only Christ's. They appeared odd to a world where religion consisted of ritual worship and ethics (Betz 1991). Paul is redefining the heart of Christian worship/religion as voluntary self-sacrifice, and that, he will make clear, is service to one another and to others in the world (Käsemann 1969; originally 1960). No more "sacred precincts." The life of believers, who have the Spirit and grace gifts (12:8), is simultaneously "spiritualized" and "somatized" — in the Holy Spirit, in lowly tasks (NRSV note at 12:16), as situations call for it.

12:2 contrasts the age, or world, to which believers are to stop adapting themselves, with the new situation of being continually transformed through God's making new (a term found only among Christians) the mind. That is the knowing, thinking, judging faculty of a person that falls under the domination of Sin (1:28) but here is the portal through which the Spirit enters for the battle with the flesh (7:23, 25). "Conform" implies "a posture or attitude . . . changed at will," as the world changes (1 Cor 7:31); transformation "grows out of necessity from an inward condition" (Harrisville: 191; cf. 2 Cor 3:18; 4:16–5:5; Phil 3:10-11). The result is that you (plural, of the community) may discern the will of God, the norm for conduct, which is then described as "good, acceptable, and perfect" (KJV, RSV note). Or the three terms can be taken as a second object of discernment, "and to know what is good, acceptable, and mature" (REB; Fitzmyer [641], perhaps too easily, suggests "the transformed life of the Christian justified and living by faith").

In **12:3-8** Paul, to whom grace *(charis)* has been given as an apostle (1:5), addresses everyone in the community, all of whom have been given grace (12:6). They are a charismatic community, each with one grace gift or another *(charisma,* vv. 6-8). The first admonition (v. 3b) is against inflated thinking about oneself: no arrogance but sensible thought (the root *phronein,* "to think," occurs four times, in line with Paul's emphasis on rationality and discernment in vv. 1-2).

Each is to do this (12:3c) "as God has assigned 'a measure of faith.'" The interpretation of *metron pisteōs* remains disputed since the church fathers. At one extreme is "a standard by which to measure," in terms of a summary of Christian faith. At the other, a varying amount of faith with which one trusts and believes (cf. Dunn 1988: 721-22). Cranfield (613-16) lays out various combinations and decides for "a standard (by which to measure . . . self)," namely faith, not in the sense of subjective feelings but one's "God-given relation to Christ." Campbell mentions a christological foundation but then "the norm that each person is provided in the appropriation of the grace of God" (in *Pauline Theology III,* 275, 279). Reasoner (in *Pauline Theology III,* 291) refers the phrase to "the spiritual gifts that arise out of one's faith" (vv. 4-8). Byrne (371) sees the "particular gift" God allots "to each person . . . at the moment of their coming to faith." Since each of the nouns has multiple meanings, consensus is impossible. The total context suggests an individual standard for self-assessment (v. 3bc) within the community (v. 4) that includes at least two aspects of faith which Paul has stressed in Romans — belief in God/Christ/cross/resurrection, as at 10:9, and personal trust and obedience to the gospel — plus one's own particular faith gift.

12:4 and 5 bring in the body-of-Christ setting (on the several aspects of which, see Dunn 1988: 722-25 or 1997: #20). This is the place, along with the public *polis* or state, where individual and corporate activities (12:9–13:7) by Christians take place, serving one another. In vv. 6-7 follows an illustrative listing of seven charismatic activities (the last four in terms of the persons doing them). They can be organized around speaking (prophecy, teacher, exhorter) and serving *(diakonia;* NRSV, "ministry," REB "administration"!) (the giver; leader — perhaps the patron in a house church or a person who cares for the vulnerable, like an ombudsman; a person who does deeds of mercy). The phrase in v. 6, "in proportion to [the] faith," has had much the same history of interpretation as "measure of faith" in v. 3. Here it is most attractive to take it of prophecy that reflects the faith or that builds up faith.

12:9-13 employ a telegraphic style, without main verbs (see Dunn 1988: 738). The Greek participles amount to imperatives. The leitmotif is human love for one another, in light of God's love to us (5:5). Four different Greek nouns are used: *agapē* (12:9a) as a heading; "with regard to love among Christians *(philadelphia)* [show] tender family-like affection to one another" (v. 10a); hospitality; or guest friendship (v. 13). The strong words in v. 9b, "loathe evil *(ponēron),* cleave to the good," will be echoed by good/bad *(kakon)* in contrasts in vv. 17 and 21. Of these "navigation lights" (Käsemann: 345) for Christians, some verses apply specifically to the church community, such as v. 13a on "the saints," but others apply to the world (clearly in v. 17, "what is noble in the sight of *all,*" perhaps including Roman governmental officials). Some bits of advice could fit church or world (on good and evil). In v. 11 the RSV saw a reference to the Holy Spirit which in the NRSV suggests only "team spirit" or perhaps the human spirit fanned into being by God's Spirit. The textual variant in v. 11c (NRSV note) is explained in *TCGNT,* 528, as a misunderstanding of the Greek abbreviation for "Lord." There are connections between v. 12 and 8:24-27 (hope, prayer) and 5:3-5 (hope, sufferings).

In **12:14-21** we find, along with more frequent applicability to situations Christians face outside in the world — such as persecution (v. 14), peaceful relations with all people (v. 18), or vengeance (vv. 19-21) — reflections of Jesus' teachings (see Introduction, section 5, above, on v. 14). With Luke 6:27-36, compare also 12:17 and 21; or Rom 12:18 with Mark 9:50 and perhaps Matt 5:9. But Thompson (109-10, 237-40) has concluded that these echoes and allusions are not as clear as often supposed. OT material is more apparent: Prov 3:7 in 12:16 and 3:4 in 12:17; Lev 19:18 and Deut 32:35 in 12:19; and Prov 25:21-22 in 12:20. The "coals of fire" there have been taken to refer to eschatological judgment, or as symbols of shame either intensifying punishment or positively leading to repentance or even conversion. The advice in v. 16, again against haughtiness, may have Christians in Rome in mind and deal with issues of the "strong" and the "weak." "Live in harmony" is an appeal to unity (lit. "think the same thing toward one another"). All in all, "the individual" in the charismatic community "is left unusual room to maneuver within the framework of . . . abilities and weaknesses" (Käsemann: 349), under grace, with faith and love.

Few passages have been the object of such vehement swings in scholarly opinion in the twentieth century as **13:1-7** (see Wilckens [6/3: 43-66] for its fuller history). The notion that the verses are an interpolation or present a permanent "doctrine of the state" have given way to a setting in the events of Paul's day, civic unrest over Roman taxes (see Introduction, section 2, above; Byrne: 385-86). The contention of Cullmann, Karl Barth, and others, that the state has a christological basis — Christ has conquered the cosmic powers (cf. Rom 8:38; Col 2:15) which are said to stand behind the governing authorities on earth (13:1) — has now virtually disappeared from most commentaries (cf. Käsemann: 352-54; even in Cranfield [653-55], who once championed it). Rom 13:1-7 does not appeal to Jesus' teaching about Caesar (Mark 12:17 pars.). Instead Paul reflects typical OT/Jewish teaching (cf. Jer 29:7, pray for Babylon; 1 Macc 7:33) and makes use of a common theme of being good subjects (*hypotassein* terms), also found in 1 Pet 2:13-14 and part of a broader Hellenistic code for social life taken over by Jews and Christians, with modifications, in the "Tables of Household Duties" (e.g., Col 3:18–4:1). God has appointed such governing authorities (13:1b-2), but they must rule well (v. 4). (Paul is not discussing the situation when they usurp God's role.)

Such governmental servants of God have the power of the sword to execute judgment on wrongdoers (13:4). Thus "wrath" can take effect in the world prior to God's final judgment. Not only for this reason are Christians to obey but also "because of conscience" (v. 5). The Greek term here (cf. 2:15) is of the same sort as the emphasis on "rational worship" in 12:1 and discernment (12:2) on the part of Christians (how they "think" *[phronein]* at 12:3b, 16). The terms "good" and "bad," doing the former but not the latter, run through the passage (13:3-4), as at 12:9b, 17, 21. The major concern (13:7) is for Christians to pay direct tribute due from noncitizens and revenue taxes on commercial transactions, giving honor and respect, as in 12:10. So they will "live peaceably with all" in the political realm (12:18). Although Christians "live in the new aeon as a result of their justification through faith in Christ Jesus, they are still part of this aeon with its laws and order" (Fitzmyer: 663). This is part of "good missionary strategy (cf. 12:21)" (Dunn 1988: 768).

13:8-10 continue the note of obligation — "owe no one anything" (cf. REB) — found in v. 7 ("what is due"). The REB actually begins its new paragraph with v. 7. But what is now owed — indeed, the sole obligation of Christians as Christians — is to continue loving one another (v. 8b). There is a certain parallel to 12:9-13, where *agapē* was the lead theme. Is this love which is like God's to be shown to the sisters and brothers within the Christian community? It begins there (perhaps the hardest place for some in and among the house churches in Rome; note 14:15). But 13:8c broadens it to "the other" (RSV), which v. 9 equates with "the neighbor" (Lev 19:18 and Mark 12:31 pars.), suggesting all persons with whom Christians come into contact (Dunn 1988: 776). The ingenious rendering, "the one who loves has fulfilled the other law" (that of God, not the state) or "the other part of the law" (the second table of the Decalogue) has been accepted by Byrne (396), but most reject it as unlikely (e.g., Fitzmyer: 678).

Paul then quotes in 13:9 four of the Ten Commandments in a sequence different from that in Exodus 20 or Deuteronomy 5 but found in LXX manuscript B and other ancient sources (cf. Dunn 1988: 777-78 for details). These and any other commandment — and those acquainted with the 613 commands and prohibitions in the Jewish law could think of many more, while others need to be aware of anything they think of in the Roman law codes — are all summed up in the love command of Deut 19:18. Cf. Gal 5:14. To love others "as yourself" does not make self-love the starting point for ethics but indicates what the "I" is prone to do, love self, thinking of oneself more highly than one ought (12:3, 16b), apparently a greater menace among the Christians Paul knew than lack of self-respect. The self provides a standard everyone knows, to one degree or another. Cf. Phil 2:3. Wilckens (6/3:72-74) notes that love is always a miracle of God; the command seeks obedience and the help which the neighbor needs (Dunn 1988: 780). The strong and the weak will remain at odds if "self" continues and not the renewal of minds through divine self-giving love (5:5; 5:8; 15:2-3, not pleasing self but the neighbor).

The unit is rounded out in 13:10 with a "negative form of the 'golden rule'" (Dunn 1988: 780; cf. Luke 6:31 par. Matt 7:12). This negative formulation parallels the four negative commands in v. 9. The rhetorical use of litotes, a negative plus the opposite of what one wants to conclude, leads the reader to infer from Paul's understatement ("does nothing bad"), "Love does good to a neighbor" ("good/bad" as in 12:21; 13:3-4). "This love is not the *completion* but the *performance* of the law" (Barrett: 251). This is the Christian's "spiritual worship" (12:1) in daily existence and God's will for good and fulfillment (12:2).

In **13:11-14** eschatology is related to ethics. There was a negative reference at 12:2 to "this age" (NRSV note); cf. also 2:5-11. In contrast, Paul's gospel of God's saving righteousness has been set forth within the context of "the 'now' time" of the new age in which it is being revealed (3:21, "now"; 3:26, "at the present time," *kairos;* 5:9, 11, "now"; 6:22; 7:6; 8:1, 18; 11:5, 30, 31). Christians live in the overlap of these two ages, with a future fulfillment to come (e.g., 5:19; the apocalyptic imagery of 8:18-25 and 11:25-27). In 13:11 this *kairos* or "'now' time" of the new aeon is cited as a reason for practicing *agapē.* Literally, "And this, knowing the time." NRSV's "Besides this" may suggest something additional rather than what makes the love command so imperative. The NEB is better, "In all this," but its phrasing, "remember how critical the moment is," loses the connection with vv. 8-10. Supplying "do this" (Fitzmyer: 682) captures this well. It is urgent to wake up. "Sleep" denotes lethargy (Prov 6:9) or in Greek sources the overpowering of the mind (*TDNT,* 8:546-48). Since sleep usually occurs at night, the dangers of the darkness such as orgies, drunkenness, and sexual excesses (13:12, 13) enter in. One may miss the approaching day. Hence the call to wake up (v. 11) and live decently (v. 13).

What may seem simply an obvious statement in v. 11d, "our [future] salvation [at the parousia] is now closer than it was when we first came to faith" — of course, as time goes by, one is always closer to the end — acutely reflects the individual believer's interim situation between "the 'already' of commitment in conversion-initiation and the 'not yet' of salvation" (Dunn 1988: 786). But because Paul thinks more than individualistically, Fitzmyer (682) is right to see a time "between the messianic period of salvation history and its consummation," that is, between the death and resurrection of Christ and the events outlined in the revelation of 11:25-28. In this period, we are exhorted to live honorably as in the daylight (13:13). The six negative things to be cast aside include sins of the mind, strife and envy, as well as deeds of the flesh, desires which people plot to satisfy.

13:14, "Put on [like clothing] the Lord Jesus Christ," is widely seen as baptismal terminology; cf. Gal 3:27, "baptized into Christ, . . . clothed with Christ." In the Romans context it could suggest, in light of v. 12 about "the armor of light," "let[ting] Jesus Christ himself be the armor you wear" (REB). Others adduce "a theatrical background," actors putting on garments to portray a particular character (Dionysius of Halicarnassus 11.5, "play the role of Tarquin"; Dunn 1988: 790, accepted by Byrne: 400, 403). Dunn, who resists too much emphasis on baptism itself (793), also brings in the idea of a process of putting on the new [hu]man (in Eph 4:24; Col 3:9-10) and eventually the image of the heavenly, last Adam (1 Cor 15:53-54); thus, divine enabling for human responsibility. For Käsemann (363), thanks to baptism, "[e]very Christian represents his Lord on earth as a member of his body" (Rom 6:3-5; 1 Cor 12:12-13, 27). Fitzmyer goes further (684), "The baptized Christian has become another Christ." The real puzzle is why Christians, to whom this admonition is addressed, need to be told to "put on the Lord Jesus Christ." Dunn (1988: 791) sees a spiritual transformation in process, begun in conversion-initiation, but "hardly completed or final"; Käsemann (363), Christian life as "a constant return to baptism." Byrne (400-401) notes that "the 'indicative' associated with baptism" appears as an imperative in 13:11; "conformity to the risen Lord radically established in baptism is the beginning of a life-long task to allow that conformity to find expression in one's subsequent pattern of life. . . ." Ethical conduct in daily life makes clear that believers are still in the flesh and there must be constant concern not "to gratify its desires," negatively put, as in 13:10. The unspoken conclusion for hearers is this, "To exercise the same sort of provision people make for fleshly desires to living now according to God's will."

Mutual Acceptance among the Strong and Weak in Faith (14:1–15:13)

A new topic, the person "weak in faith," seems abruptly introduced. It will occupy Paul longer than any other item in the ethical section of 12:1–15:13, so it must have been important. The profile of the weak as vegetarians (14:2; apparently no meat or wine either, v. 21), with a concern for some days as more important than others (v. 5), contrasts with people who eat anything and regard all days as alike (vv. 2, 5). This second group is identified, as Christians "who are strong," only in 15:1. After asserting the problem in 14:1-2, Paul addresses the weak primarily in vv. 3-12 and the strong chiefly in 14:13–15:6. Both groups are urged to "welcome one another" in 15:7-13, as Christ has welcomed both circumcised and uncircumcised. Four scriptural verses about the Gentiles lead to a blessing that incorporates hope and themes like joy, peace, believing, and the Holy Spirit (15:13).

"The weak" as a description for people who need help appears already in Paul's first extant letter, 1 Thess 5:14. More specifically, a group designated by this term appears in 1 Corinthians 8–10, in connection with varying viewpoints about whether Christians ought to eat the main kind of meat available, from animal sacrifices at a pagan temple (in some places the alternative would have been that from a kosher butcher); cf. 1 Corinthians 8–9; especially 9:22. Of course Paul could be doing a rerun on the Corinthians dispute for those in Rome. But more likely a specific situation in Rome demands comment; see Introduction, section 2, above. Those "with robust conscience" (15:1, NEB; Kirk [237], "adaptable"; Fitzmyer [686], "progressive") formed a majority in Rome and were probably mostly Gentiles, though the Jewish-Christian Paul identified with them (15:1, "we"). The weak — Kirk calls them "rigid," Fitzmyer "conservative" — were mainly from the Jewish-Christian minority in Rome, but Gentile proselytes now Christian could have been among them. Some Christians at Rome may not have fallen into either camp. Quite likely the divisions were by house churches such as are identifiable in ch. 16; cf. "household servant belonging to another house" or master, 14:4). Few are inclined to see a split down the middle between two congregations (as Watson did, in Donfried 1991: 203-15), or Jews (Nanos) rather than Jewish Christians as "the weak" to be received.

What seems abrupt to us, as a new start in **14:1-2**, would have introduced something familiar to the audience in Rome, "the person who is weak in faith" among the hearers. This was probably a designation given by those who regarded themselves as "able" (or enabled by God) for anything. A connection with 13:14, about "putting on the Lord Jesus Christ," is implied: you are to stop making provision for "satisfying the bodily appetites" (NEB), but (there is a *de* in Greek) the person "weak" with regard to eating is in a different category. Receive that person! The verb, which implies "take into one's circle or household" (cf. Acts 28:2), provides an opening and concluding emphasis in double occurrences at 14:1, 3 and 15:7. To "welcome" also picks up on the love command at 12:9-10; 13:8-10 and on Paul's redefining of "the people of God and its corollaries" (Dunn 1988: 797). Those who believe that they can eat anything they want and those who lack such confidence are not to get together just to dispute over what is debatable. "Faith" here suggests assurance that permits one to do or not to do certain things (Fitzmyer: 689) and functions as "conscience" does in 1 Cor 8:7, 10.

In **14:3-4** Paul rather evenhandedly begins to lay out what will be his answer. One group must not belittle or judge the other. The warrant in v. 3 is that God, no less, has welcomed both into the household (of Christ; the Lord in v. 4 of the NRSV text; in 15:7 the point will clearly be put in christological terms). 14:4 plays on the point that domestic slaves are not judged by the master in another household but get status from their own master. (Is there a hint of household churches?) The Master or Lord in this case is Christ (or, in the NRSV note, "God"), who determines the standing of the servant you (in the other group) want to judge. The principle is the individual's "accountability to one Lord alone" (Byrne: 409; Dunn 1997: #24.3, p. 684). Jewish Christians especially must "leave it to the Lord."

14:5-6 bring in the case of revering certain days in the calendar, perhaps the sabbath or holy days for fasting or feasting. Here the weak show Jewish concerns. Paul poses as standards being convinced in one's own mind (v. 5) and giving thanks to God and honoring the Lord (v. 6). In these instances the person's conviction of acting out of faith (v. 23) matters, not which action is chosen. That one must be able to thank God for something sets a boundary on possible license (Dunn 1997: #24.3, pp. 687-88).

14:7-9 develop the relation to the Lord heard in v. 6. Living or dying, we belong to the Lord, not to ourselves. "We" includes both weak and strong. The creedal summary in v. 9 about Christ's death and resurrection (cf. 1 Thess 4:14 as one of many examples of this basic confession) and its result, lordship over the dead and the living (as well as the strong and the weak), calls attention to the kind of belief that matters, in contrast to disputable issues. Groundwork is also laid for 14:15. Käsemann (373) sees vv. 7-9 as the center of the section 14:1-12.

The immediate conclusion in **14:10-12** is, Why, then, do you weak pass judgment on those who eat? Or you strong belittle Christians who abstain (verbs as in v. 3)? All of us will be judged by God, bowing and confessing to the Lord (Isa 49:18; 45:23). Each will give an account for himself or herself, not the other person.

Those who think they can eat whatever they want, whatever day they want, are addressed in **14:13-23**. One of their contentions comes out in v. 14, "nothing is in itself unclean" (Heb. *kasher;* cf. Dunn 1988: 818-19 on Jewish purity laws; for Jesus, the saying in Mark 7:15). Paul agrees. But the danger is that this group puts a stumbling block in the way of Christians weak in faith by eating what the others think unclean. This is conduct that is not loving toward a sister or brother for whom Christ died (14:15). Here Paul invokes the principle of love, so strong in 12:9-10 and 13:8-10, for the only time in 14:1–15:13. He also draws out what was said earlier about Christ's atoning death (most recently in 14:9).

The arguments in this section are structured around the Greek word *oun* in 14:13, 16, and 19 ("therefore," "so," "then"). After the first argument, from love and Christ's death, urging no more judging of one another, no obstacles in the other person's path in the name of my freedom (v. 13), the second in v. 16 deals with what is "good" (cf. 12:9, 21; 13:3, 4; 15:2) for one person but proves disastrous for someone else. Opinions vary on the meaning (Cranfield: 715-17). "The good" some enjoy could simply be food or drink (Byrne: 417). Dunn (1988: 821) expands it to "all God's covenanted blessings" for Jewish and Gentile Christians (but in 1997: #24.3, pp. 685-86, he writes, conduct that "could make a bad impression on neighbours"). Fitzmyer (697) thinks "the good" is "Christian liberty." In any case, "Let it not be blasphemed" or "brought into disrepute" (REB). Again a distinction is made (as in 14:7-9) between matters of food and drink and what really matters, here the kingdom. God's kingdom means God's saving righteousness as a gift (Cranfield: 718) or divine power (Käsemann: 377), less likely the resulting righteous action by the believer (Barrett: 265). The former sense is suggested by (2) peace (Rom 5:1) and (3) joy, with which alone "in the Holy Spirit" may go, or with all three. E. Jüngel sees 14:17 as the "theological center" for chs. 12–15, "kingdom" interpreted as "righteousness" (1962: 267). The person who is Christ's servant in this way — and not in matters of eating and drinking — is "acceptable to" God (12:2) and esteemed in human society (14:18).

14:19-23 add another reason for "pursuing" (as in 1 Pet 3:11) such peace corporately; it is the "upbuilding" (*oikodomē,* edification; 14:19) of the community (in 1 Cor 8:1, what love does) together. 14:20-21 reiterate the correct theological position, in contrast to OT purity laws about foods, "all things are clean" (v. 14). But for the sake of freedom over food, we ought not to trip up another Christian (NRSV adds, "upset" or "weaken" [the weak], which Fitzmyer [1993: 698] thinks original). Such uncurtailed liberty could destroy a believer for whom Christ died and the unity of the community by insisting on what one group sees as "right(s)" and the other does not. The reference to wine, here only, in v. 21 does not readily fit Judaism; it could be hypothetical, or overscrupulosity about, for example, pagan libations (Dunn 1988: 827).

In 14:22-23 the case comes back to faith (vv. 1-2), the faith which each one has ("you" is singular). The advice is, literally, "keep it to yourself, before God" (cf. KJV). One may have convictions, but they are not to be used to make others conform on such matters as food and drink. A beatitude follows (v. 22b), blessing persons who do not condemn themselves with qualms of conscience over what they have discerned (12:2) on these issues. To have doubts or to waver (4:20, the same verb) means condemnation by one's own convictions and by God. The "weak" person who succumbs to eating (meat) because of pressure by the strong knows that (s)he has violated personal convictions — before God. For "divine condemnation follows upon any action which does not express one's creaturely dependence on God (1:19-32 . . .)," that is, which repeats "[hu]mans' fall into sin," described in 1:21 as "refusal of obedience and an offense against God's glory" (Dunn [1988: 828-29], reflecting Michel). Minear thinks a third group, "the doubters," has come into the picture, besides the "strong" and the "weak."

All groups fall under the principle, "Everything which is not 'of faith' is [an act of] sin" (14:23b). At the least, *pistis* here means "conviction" (NRSV note); so Fitzmyer (1993: 700), who would apply "the maxim" only to "indifferent matters." Can one "brush one's teeth in faith" (Byrne: 419, 422)? But it is difficult to exclude "the frame of reference of the letter as a whole," where "[f]aith refers essentially to a person's perception of relationship to God," as Byrne goes on (419). Hence Dunn 1988: 829, "*whatever* is not an expression of dependence and trust in God . . . is marked by that fatal flaw of human presumption and/or self-indulgence" seen in 1:19-32 and elsewhere in Romans. This broader sense of faith and faithfulness is also suggested by the references to Christ that follow (15:3, 7). But while "Christ remains the only measure for all," Käsemann warns (379), "No one must make his faith [cf. 12:3] a norm for others as they seek to serve Christ [cf. 12:18]."

The address to the strong continues in **15:1-6**. They are mentioned for the first time in v. 1 by the designation they preferred, *dynatoi.* Reasoner (*Pauline Theology III,* 268-69) would relate these Gentile Christians to the fixed Roman social order, those powerful in wealth and authority (*potentes*), in contrast to *inferiores.* But the household of Aristobulus (16:10), if a member of the family of Herod, would be Jewish-Christian *potentes.* The obligation (13:7, 8) that arises from being strong is to bear (with) the weaknesses of the weak (cf. Gal 6:2; Mark 8:34-36 pars.), not to strive to please self (cf. 12:2, service in daily life; 14:7-8; Phil 2:4). This is an either/or (Harrisville: 229). The result of each pleasing the neighbor (13:9-10) for "the good" is upbuilding (14:19) the community (REB, "the common life"; Byrne: 424). This may be done by edifying individuals, but the NRSV is too individualistic in adding "the neighbor" at the end of 15:2 (Dunn 1988: 838).

The phrase "please oneself" is explained in 15:3 by applying to Christ Ps 69:9b. Originally a lament by a righteous sufferer on whom reproaches against God have fallen, Psalm 69 was applied in the Gospels to Jesus (69:9 = John 2:17) and his passion (69:21b = Mark 15:36 pars.). Here Christ speaks, so identified with God's cause (as in Ps 69:7, "for your sake," and 69:9a, "zeal for your house") that insults toward God strike him. The unstated implication for the audience, since what was written previously is "for our instruction" (15:4), is that we all, thus identified with Christ, should, like Christ, not please ourselves, even when insults come regarding "strength," "weakness," or what is our own "good" (14:16, which some speak of "as evil"; 15:2). Instead, we should display "patient endurance" (vv. 4, 5; NRSV, "steadfastness") and receive, from the Scriptures and God, "encouragement" toward hope (v. 4; 5:4 — such endurance leads to proven moral character and hope) and harmonious unity (15:5). These are God-given. Paul's prayer wish is literally that all "think the same thing" (the general exhortation of 12:16 now made specific) "with one another, according to Christ Jesus," that is, the way he endured and hoped. This does not mean a single solution to a problem but a single "mind-set" (Byrne: 426). And so (15:6) "with one mind and mouth" (cf. 10:8-10) may we give glory to the God and Father of our Lord Jesus Christ, reversing 1:21. Dunn (1997: #24.3) titles it, "Living with fundamental disagreements"; better, agreement on fundamentals but deep division on some matters of practice (see Introduction, 8.5, above, "tolerance").

15:7-13 so parallels vv. 1-6 that it is usually taken as a final address to the groups in Rome, especially the strong. More broadly, the appeal of 14:1 to welcome the weak is now expanded into "welcome one another." Christ's acceptance of both Jews ("the circumcision") and Gentiles (= you = one another, v. 7) corresponds to God's welcome in v. 3 of those who eat and those who abstain. Thus, a double *inclusio* surrounding 14:1–15:13. More immediately, that all this is to God's glory (15:7, 9) reiterates v. 6. Both vv. 1-6 and 7-13 begin with an injunction (vv. 1-2, 7a); both appeal to an action of Christ (vv. 3a, 8b-9). Both cite Scripture (vv. 3b, 9b-12) and end with a prayer wish (vv. 5-6, 13) (Byrne: 428).

However, in 15:7-13 the terms "strong" and "weak" have been replaced by "the circumcised" and "Gentiles." The "quarrels," "insults" (14:1; 15:3), and unresolved differences about eating vanish. The harmony of the community is replaced by "the acceptance of the Gentiles as an eschatological miracle" (Käsemann: 384). Hence some see 15:7-13 as a "coda" to the entire "body of the letter" and a link to the personal concerns of the apostle to the Gentiles (15:16) for the Spanish mission (15:24-29) (Dunn 1988: 844-45; 1997: #19.7). Käsemann (384-85, 387) suggests that the theme of justification in Romans has not been seen by expositors in its radicality: "that Christ accepts us finds its deepest expression, with cosmic breadth, in the fact that God has had mercy on the Gentiles," the righteousness of God justifying those once regarded as "ungodly" (4:5). Fitzmyer (1993: 705) keeps the focus on communal harmony: we "see how the gospel of God's uprightness [his rendering of *dikaiosynē,* following Goodspeed's translation] unleashed in the world of humanity can seep down even into the relation of Jewish and Gentile Christians in one community."

15:8-9, about Christ, are difficult. Paul holds on to (a) the principle articulated in 1:16, "to the Jew first and also to the Greek," through reference to the historical ministry of Jesus (cf. Matt 15:24) and then that to the Gentiles, post-Easter, through commissioned heralds like Paul; but also to (b) the theme of mercy for all (11:30-32). But the parallelism is not exact. The ministry to the circumcised was "for the sake of the truth of God." Here "truth" means the covenant faithfulness of God (as in the parallelism of "true" and *pistis* at 3:3-4; cf. 7) (Käsemann: 385). That to Gentiles is "for (the sake of) God's mercy" (15:9; 11:30-31). "Mercy and truth" are, however, a regular OT hendiadys. The purpose clause about Jews, to "confirm the promises given to the patriarchs" (15:8), is only generally paralleled for the Gentiles with "to glorify God" (v. 9a), but that point is then amplified by four OT quotations, all with the terms "Gentiles" or "peoples." The "promises" (9:4) have been concentrated by Paul in that to Abraham, which in ch. 4 was applied to "all who believe," circumcised or not (4:11-12), riches in which Gentiles now share. The citations draw on the law (Deut 32:43 in 15:10, Gentiles with God's people; not "praising Israel," as in the Song of Moses), the prophets (Isa 11:10 in 15:12, Jesus of Davidic descent; cf. 1:3, the hope of the Gentiles too), and the sacred writings (Pss 18:49 in 15:9 and 117:1 in 15:11). The paean of praise triggers a final prayer (15:13) for joy and peace "as you lead the life of faith until, by the power of the Holy Spirit, you overflow with hope" (REB). Christ's service to circumcised and the Gentiles has brought them together under "promise" and "hope."

Letter Closing, 15:14–16:23 (25-27)

Paul's letters, reflecting those of the Greco-Roman world, regularly conclude, after their body, with a section on his travel plans, plus greetings and a benediction, among other items (Byrne: 15; Dunn 1988: 855). Romans is no exception (see Introduction, 3, 6, and 7 above).

The section on plans to come to Rome, often called an "apostolic *parousia*" or coming to be present (Phil 2:12, 24), is more elaborate in **15:14-33** than in most letters (e.g., Phil 2:19-24), as was true of the body of Romans. It begins with an expression of confidence in the Roman Christians (15:14): they are "full of goodness" (recall what Paul has said about "the good" at 12:9, 21; 14:16) and of knowledge and "able *(dynamenoi)* to admonish one another," strong *(dynatoi)* and weak both. This expression of goodwill (*captatio benevolentiae;* cf. 1:8) by Paul allows him then to grant, as deftly as at 1:11-12, that he has written them somewhat boldly, as an apostle (15:15-16; 1:1; 11:13). Two of Paul's purposes in the letter will come out: support for proposed evangelization in Spain (15:24, 28b-29) and prayers for his trip to Jerusalem with the collection for the Jewish Christians there (vv. 25-28a, 30-31; above, Introduction, 4 [2] and 4 [3]).

In **15:16-21** Paul provides news of himself and his work, first in cultic terms (v. 16). His priestly ministry is to proclaim the gospel. The offering (to God, REB), sanctified by the Spirit, consists of Gentiles won to the obedience of faith (v. 18). "(Very) acceptable" (to God; *TLNT,* 2:137-38) is a different word in v. 16 from that in 12:2; it may anticipate use of the same word at 15:31. About this offering Paul has grounds for boasting (in the good sense, 5:2, 3, 11) "in Christ" (15:17), for Christ has accomplished it through Paul (v. 18; lit. "I shall not dare to speak of any of [those things] which Christ did not work through me"; cf. NRSV note). These accomplishments are only through Christ. They are grace-given (*charis,* v. 15). Paul's ministering "in word and deed" can be termed "charismatic" (cf. 12:6), marked by the "power" of the Spirit and of "signs and wonders" (15:19). Actually "signs and wonders" is an OT phrase, going back to the exodus (Exod 7:3; Deut 4:34); they reflect salvation history, of which Paul is a part — another way of referring to his work. The geographical scope of the gospel's spread (see Introduction, section 1, above) is rhetorically put to make the point in 15:23 that he regards his pioneering mission work in the (north)eastern Mediterranean to be accomplished now. Going to Spain will fit with his aim to preach only where some other missionary has not already labored (v. 20; cf. 2 Cor 10:15-16). But this personal principle made approaching Roman Christians more difficult. Paul grounds the principle (15:21) in Isa 52:15, from a Servant-of-the-Lord passage (52:13–53:12), suggesting a third facet of Paul's self-understanding, as a commissioned servant sent to the Gentiles (Rom 1:1; cf. Isa 49:6).

According to **15:22-29**, the delay in Paul's plan (cf. also 1:13) because of mission in the East is about over, the desire of many years at hand, to come to Rome and then (v. 24) be "sent on his way" (a technical term, suggesting support, 1 Cor 16:6, 11), "if of you I am first somewhat filled full. . . ." 15:24 breaks off, to be completed only at v. 29, which refers to Paul's coming to Rome with the "fullness of Christ's blessing," and (v. 32) being "refreshed" together with the Romans. That much Paul permits himself to say about help for the work in Spain (but see also on 16:1-2, below).

All of this is intertwined with news in **vv. 25-28** about the collection (*koinōnia,* v. 26; ministering service, *diakonōn,* v. 25) for some of the saints who are impoverished in Jerusalem; shared "resources" (REB, "funds") from churches in two Roman provinces, including the cities of Philippi, Thessalonica, and Corinth. Paul saw this offering as more than "relief work." It is part of salvation history, perhaps reflecting passages like Isa 60:5-17 and the wealth of the nations flowing to Jerusalem, and part of his aim to stir the Jews to jealousy of the Gentile response and hence to salvation (11:13-14) (Dunn 1988: 873-74). The collection would also affirm ecclesial solidarity between regions or wings of the church (Byrne: 441-42). In 15:27 this Gentile obligation (cf. 1:14 on Paul's indebtedness) is seen as a ministry (or public service, the same root as in 15:16) of tangible resources in response to spiritual ones in which the Gentiles have shared. The literal idiom in v. 28 (see NRSV note) is commercial, to seal bags of fruit or grain with a seal of origin; cf. our phrase "signed, sealed, and delivered." The NEB translates, deliver "the proceeds under my own seal."

For the task of safely delivering this collection to Jerusalem Paul asks for the prayers of the Christians in Rome (**15:30-31**; cf. the prayer report in 1:9-10). He has two fears: Jews in Judea, "not convinced" of the gospel, who considered him an apostate, from whose hands he needed to be preserved; Jewish-Christian saints, that his *diakonia* or ministering service (some manuscripts substitute "gift-bringing," NRSV note) will not be welcome to them because it comes from Gentiles not circumcised and obeying Torah (Dunn 1988: 879-80, "nationalistic feeling," which was on the rise; Achtemeier [229-32] stresses the symbolism the offering had of "equality"). "Beware of Greeks bearing gifts" (Virgil *Aeneid* 2.49). Some think that the Jerusalem church refused the collection (cf. Achtemeier 1987: 60 and 109n.17) or that Paul was, in the prayer request, "hinting that the Roman Christians could . . . pave the way for a favourable reception in Jerusalem" (F. F. Bruce in Donfried 1991: 191-92). The first possibility "probably goes beyond the evidence," while the latter is asked at best "indirectly" (Fitzmyer 1993: 726). Paul looks to God's will to further his plans in Rome and beyond (v. 32), the third concern in joint prayers. The wish for peace through God's presence (v. 33) somewhat parallels 1:7 and is akin at this point in a letter to Phil 4:9.

16:1-2 is a letter of recommendation, typical of the period (cf. 2 Cor 3:1), for Phoebe to Rome. Cf. Introduction, section 3, above. This Gentile-Christian sister, from Cenchreae, the eastern seaport for Corinth, is described as a *diakonos* of the church there and a *prostatis* "of many," Paul included. Subsequent male-dominated churches have long blocked giving Phoebe her due. "Benefactor" (NRSV) or "patron(ess)" in 16:2 (Dunn 1988: 888-89; Fitzmyer 1993: 731) suggests a person of prominence, socially and economically, who may have provided a meeting place and status for the (house) church in Cenchreae. Too many later commentators adhere to the Eng. "deacon(ess)" (RSV). She no doubt "served" many with hospitality, but *diakonos* suggests "minister" ([N]RSV note) or even "officer in the congregation" (NEB), though her exact tasks are unstated. Paul asks those in Rome to "welcome her" (a different verb than at 15:7), as appropriate among Christians, and "assist her in whatever business she has need." This could involve commercial or legal matters of her own ("lawsuit" at 1 Cor 6:1) or "church business" (Byrne: 447-48). Once rid of notions about Romans 16 as a separate letter, we may conjecture from the context that Phoebe was Paul's "patroness for the Spanish mission," who is "to create" in Rome its "logistical base" (Jewett: 151). She may have carried Paul's letter to Rome to help bring the groups in Rome together for the mission to Spain.

Greetings to Christians in Rome begin in **16:3-5a** with Prisca and Aquila (cf. Introduction, 2 and 3, above). The form is standard in Pauline letters already in 1 Thess 5:26, "Give my greetings to . . ." (REB). Aquila came from Pontus, and this couple moved to Rome, to Corinth, to Ephesus, and now back to Rome (Acts 18:1-3, 18-19, 26-27; 1 Cor 16:19; 2 Tim 4:19). Prisca is usually mentioned first, for social status or economic reasons, in their (linen) tentmaking business. Such a pair of missionaries could have access to women and men. They "risked their necks" or fortune or status for Paul, likely at Ephesus (Acts 19:23; Paul was possibly imprisoned there; cf. 2 Cor 1:8-9). The thanks of "all the Gentile churches" is appropriate hyperbole for the apostle to the Gentiles to apply to them. This first of the house churches mentioned in Rome (16:5a) provided a place in Rome where Paul was known, possibly a "vanguard" for Paul's plans (Lampe, in Donfried: 220-21; *ABD,* 1:319-20; 5:467-68).

16:5b-16 Twenty-six Christians in Rome are greeted by name, including Prisca and Aquila; nine of them are women (so Lampe, in Donfried: 222, and Lampe's articles on the names in *ABD*). In most cases, all we know of these individuals comes from what Paul says here. Further conjectures can be made from ancient inscriptions (as to whether a name is Jewish or Greek), sociological studies, and Christian tradition, but "perhaps" must qualify most statements below. Many are singled out by some affirming or even personal note by Paul for their work in the churches: women — Prisca (vv. 3-4), Mary (v. 6), Junia (v. 7, NABRNT, REB, NRSV text), Tryphaena and Tryphosa (v. 12), Persis (v. 12), and the mother of Rufus (v. 13b); men — Aquila (vv. 3-4), Andronicus (v. 7), Urbanus (v. 9), Apelles (v. 10), and Rufus (v. 13). Especially significant are the first convert (of many) in the province of Asia, Epaenetus (v. 5), and the Jewish-Christian *apostoloi,* the husband-and-wife missionary couple, Andronicus and Junia (v. 7), believers before Paul, likely appointed by the risen Christ (1 Cor 15:7; Dunn 1988: 895). Until about 1300 *Jounian* in most manuscripts at v. 7 was taken as accusative singular of a woman's name (Fitzmyer 1993: 737-38), then down through the RSV as a man's name, Junias (NRSV note). Rufus (v. 13) might be the son of Simon of Cyrene (Mark 15:21).

Lampe (226-27) estimates that most of these individuals were active in their Christianity in Rome. But Andronicus (and Junia), imprisoned with Paul (v. 7), along with Prisca and Aquila (vv. 3-4), and Urbanus (v. 9), co-workers with Paul, had to have been active in the East. A majority of those greeted were likely not born in Rome but came from the East (e.g., Aquila, Epaenetus). Three are specifically designated as Jewish Christians (Andronicus, Junia, and Herodian, "compatriots," NRSV note, vv. 7 and 11) and are thus part of the believing remnant from Israel (11:5); the rest, Gentiles (Lampe: 224-25). Socially, two-thirds were slaves or freedpersons, reflecting society as a whole. Thus the majority were *humiliores,* a few socially elevated. Aristobulus (16:10), sometimes claimed to be a grandson of Herod the Great, and Narcissus (v. 11), if one of Claudius's aides (Dunn 1988: 896), were not themselves Christians, though members in their households were (Lampe: 222). The "many needy" suggests the necessity of social support in the community (Lampe: 229; see on 12:8).

One house church is specifically mentioned in 16:5, that of Prisca and Aquila (Jewish Christians, Acts 18:2). The believers in the households of Aristobulus (16:10) and of Narcissus (v. 11) make up two more, the former Jewish Christian, the latter Gentile. A fourth house church is reflected in v. 14 (five names of men plus "brothers and sisters with them") and a fifth in v. 15 (four names plus "all the saints with them"). From the other (fourteen) individuals named, Lampe (230) conjectures at least two more groups. All of them are to use the "sacred kiss" in greeting each other (Mark 14:45 pars.; 1 Thess 5:26; 1 Cor 16:20, perhaps prior to the Lord's Supper) as a sign of respect and endearment among equal saints (*ABD,* 4:89-92, W. Klassen). There seems to be some hyperbole in 16:16b, having "all the churches," not just Corinth and Cenchreae, greet Roman Christians, but it knits the apostle and his Gentile churches ecumenically together with each person in all the groups in Rome. The thorough greetings of vv. 3-16 provide a setting of goodwill for what unexpectedly follows.

16:17-20 are a vigorous warning about doctrinal troublemakers. The opening verb is that with which 12:1 and 15:30 initiated appeals by the apostle. Here the sense is stronger, "I adjure you [plural]" (Käsemann: 417), softened a bit by *adelphoi* and the positive compliment that the obedience (1:5; cf. 6:17) of Christians in Rome has reached the ears of all (16:19, hyperbole again; but cf. 1:8). The content of the warning is what surprises: keep your eyes peeled for those who cause divisions (Gal 5:20) and stumbling blocks (9:33; 14:13), people who serve their own belly (cf. Phil 3:19) and deceive the simple (in contrast to the clever, Prov 14:15) with fair and fine speech. Keep away from them (16:17)! These injunctions cannot fit the strong or the weak. Paul's orders are so far a cry from the broad-mindedness found in 14:1–15:13 that Jewett (1982: 18-22) sees an interpolation in 16:17-20. Others object to the way vv. 17-21 split Paul's greetings (vv. 3-16) from those of his colleagues (vv. 21-23). However, similar polemical outbursts occur at Gal 6:11-17 (where Paul takes pen in hand himself); Phil 3:18-19; and 1 Cor 16:22, an anathema formula between references to greeting one another with a holy kiss (16:20) and Paul's writing with his own hand (v. 21) and benediction (v. 23). Form-critically, 16:17-20 fit a Pauline pattern (Wilckens: 6/3:139).

Paul, then, takes over from his scribe to urge vigilance not over problems of internal unity already discussed (Dunn 1988: 901) but against false teachers who threaten from outside. Who are they? Judaizers, Zealots, Gnostics, "traveling Jewish Christians who are conducting missions after and against Paul" (Stuhlmacher: 253) have all been proposed. The data are not conclusive for settling the matter. Paul's harsh words are, in any case, directed against those teaching contrary to what the Romans have learned (6:17 — including what Paul has taught in this letter?). To keep away from them is "wisdom exhortation" (Ps 37:27; Prov 3:7; Dunn 1988: 902), as is the wish about being "wise" in 16:19b, on "the good" (cf. 12:2; 13:3). The confident prayer wish in v. 20a about the God of peace (15:33) reflects imminent apocalyptic victory over the Adversary, in which believers share. The benediction in 16:20b is usual in Paul (1 Cor 16:23; 1 Thess 5:28).

16:21-23 add the greetings of Paul's co-worker Timothy, three Jewish Christians (v. 21), his scribe (v. 22), his host Gaius, and two Corinthian Christians (v. 23). Timothy (Acts 16:1-3), co-sender with Paul for 2 Corinthians, Philippians, 1 Thessalonians, and Philemon, was not involved in writing Romans. If Lucius = Luke (Dunn 1988: 909 is more sympathetic to this than most, e.g., Fitzmyer 1993: 748), then "compatriots" (NRSV note) applies only to the last two, Jason (Acts 17:5-9?) and Sosipater (= Sopater of Berea, Acts 20:4?). Some view all three as congregational representatives sent to convey the collection to Jerusalem. Erastus (16:23), an *oikonomos* in the city of Corinth, may be the mission helper mentioned in Acts 19:22 (cf. 2 Tim 4:20) and/or the aedile mentioned in a Latin inscription for Corinth (*ABD,* 2:571, F. M. Gillman). The benediction in 16:24 adds "all" and "amen" to that in v. 20b and is assigned to the NRSV note on textual grounds (*TCGNT,* 540).

16:25-27 is a doxology ("glory to . . . ," v. 27) about God, not a benediction from Christ. Such an ascription is not demanded by the Pauline letter structure. This one is much longer than its closest analogy, Phil 4:20. The varied locations of these verses in manuscripts of Romans have been noted under Introduction, section 3, above. 16:25-27 are now generally regarded as a later addition to what Paul wrote, from the second century. Sanday and Headlam (xcv-xcviii, 433) still commented on the verses "as a genuine and original conclusion to the Epistle," but that vv. 25-27 are "inauthentic" (Käsemann: 421), "not part of Paul's original letter," is today "a virtually unanimous judgment" (Byrne: 461). Cranfield (808) thinks the doxology "was first added to a short form of Romans" (at 14:23). Childs (254) stresses 16:25-27 as canonical, "patterned after the praescript" as a final summary to the Roman church. Yes, but was it by Paul himself? For a larger audience in Christendom than the house churches in Rome of Paul's day? 16:25-27 really round out what Paul wrote, for subsequent eras and ears.

The content is structured around the pattern of "the mystery" (see on 11:25), "once hidden, now revealed." Dunn 1988: 913 offers a line-by-line arrangement and finds "the central themes of the letter" reiterated in 16:25-27. We have Paul's "gospel" (v. 25; 1:16; 2:16) in terms of "power" (1:16, 20, presented here as "God who is able . . ."; cf. 4:21). "Gospel" is equated with (*kai* means "that is to say"; Dunn 1988: 914) "the proclamation" (*kērygma*) about and from Jesus Christ. The good news is the "mystery revealed." Three participles characterize "mystery": "kept secret for aeons of time"; "but now [3:21] made manifest"; and "made known," with which all the phrases go about "prophetic scriptures," God's command, the obedience of faith, and all the Gentiles (1:5). There is no talk of justification, reconciliation, redemption, or salvation, but only of revelation, just as there is no reference to Israel or the Jews, only the Gentiles — Paul's concerns and vocabulary were no longer in view. The revelation schema combines oral proclamation (16:25) and the scriptures (v. 26) — OT and, if second century, Paul's letters and the emerging NT writings as canon.

The construction begins anew in 16:27 (anacoluthon) with the actual doxology to God through Christ. "'Paul' invites the Christians in Rome to praise God for . . . the realization of God's salvific plan . . ." (Fitzmyer 1993: 753). Some think that v. 27 was intended as a "congregational response" (Dunn 1988: 914), "the gloria for what we too have learnt" (Robinson: 147).

Bibliography. Achtemeier, P. J. 1985, *Romans,* Interpretation, Atlanta: John Knox • Achtemeier, P. J. 1987, *The Quest for Unity in the New Testament Church,* Philadelphia: Fortress • Barrett, C. K. 1957, *A Commentary on the Epistle to the Romans,* BNTC and HNTC, London: Black and New York: Harper & Row (2d ed. 1991; 1st ed. is cited) • Barrett, C. K. 1977, *Reading through Romans,* London: SCM and Philadelphia: Fortress (originally 1963, London: Epworth) • Barth, M., and V. Fletcher. 1964, *Acquittal by Resurrection,* New York: Holt, Rinehart, and Winston • Bassler, J. M. 1982, *Divine Impartiality: Paul and a Theological Axiom,* SBLDS 59, Chico, Calif.: Scholars Press • Beare, F. W. 1962, "Romans, Letter to the," *IDB R-Z,* 112-24 • Beker, J. C. 1980, *Paul the Apostle: The Triumph of God in Life and Thought,* Philadelphia: Fortress • Betz, H. D. 1991, "Christianity as Religion: Paul's Attempt at a Definition in Romans," *JR* 71:315-44, repr. in Betz, *Paulinischen Studien,* 206-39 • Brown, R. 1983, *Antioch and Rome,* New York: Paulist • Bruce, F. F. 1963, *The Epistle of Paul to the Romans,* TNTC 6, London: Tyndale and Grand Rapids: Eerdmans; 5th ed. Eerdmans 1985 • Byrne, B. 1996, *Romans,* SacPag 6, Collegeville, Minn.: Michael Glazier, Liturgical Press • Childs, B. S. 1984, *The New Testament as Canon: An Introduction,* Philadelphia: Fortress, 243-63 • Cranfield, C. E. B. 1975, 1979, *A Critical and Exegetical Commentary on the Epistle to the Romans,* ICC, 2 vols., Edinburgh: T. & T. Clark • Dahl, N. 1982, "Romans 3.9: Text and Meaning," in M. D. Hooker and S. G. Wilson, eds., *Paul and Paulinism: Essays in honour of C. K. Barrett,* London: SPCK, 184-209 • Donfried, K. P., ed. 1991, *The Romans Debate,* rev. and expanded ed., Peabody, Mass.: Hendrickson; includes essays cited by T. W. Manson, G. Bornkamm, G. Klein, Donfried, J. Jervell, R. Karris, W. Wiefel, M. L. Stirewalt, A. J. M. Wedderburn, F. Watson, P. Lampe, P. Stuhlmacher, W. S. Campbell, R. Jewett, and others • Dunn, J. D. G. 1988, *Romans 1–8, Romans 9–16,* WBC 38A-B, 2 vols., Waco: Word • Dunn, J. D. G. 1997, *The Theology of Paul the Apostle,* Grand Rapids: Eerdmans; it is specifically oriented to Romans • Enslin, M. S. 1957, *The Ethics of Paul,* Nashville/New York: Abingdon • Fitzmyer, J. 1968, "The Letter to the Romans," in R. E. Brown, J. A. Fitzmyer, and R. E. Murphy, eds., *The Jerome Bible Commentary,* Englewood Cliffs, N.J.: Prentice-Hall • Fitzmyer, J. 1990, #51 "The Letter to the

Romans," #82 "Pauline Theology," in R. E. Brown, J. A. Fitzmyer, and R. E. Murphy, eds., *The New Jerome Biblical Commentary,* Englewood Cliffs, N.J.: Prentice-Hall • Fitzmyer, J. 1993, *Romans,* AB 33, New York: Doubleday • Furnish, V. P. 1968, *Theology and Ethics of Paul,* Nashville/New York: Abingdon • Gamble, H., Jr. 1977, *The Textual History of the Letter to the Romans,* SD 42, Grand Rapids: Eerdmans • Grenholm, C., and D. Patte, eds. 2000, *Reading Israel in Romans: Legitimacy and Plausibility of Divergent Interpretations,* Romans through History and Culture, Harrisburg, Pa.: Trinity Press International • Harrisville, R. 1980, *Romans,* Augsburg Commentary on the New Testament, Minneapolis: Augsburg • Hay, D. M., and E. E. Johnson, eds. 1995, *Pauline Theology, Volume III: Romans,* Minneapolis: Fortress; pairs of essays on Romans overall and by sections for the SBL Pauline Theology Group • Hays, R. B. 1983, *The Faith of Jesus Christ,* SBLDS 56, Chico, Calif.: Scholars; 2d ed. 2002, Grand Rapids: Eerdmans • Jeffers, J. S. 1991, *Conflict at Rome: Social Order and Hierarchy in Early Christianity,* Minneapolis: Fortress • Jewett, R. 1982, *Christian Tolerance: God's Message to a Modern Church,* Philadelphia: Westminster • Jewett, R. 1988, "Paul, Phoebe, and the Spanish Mission," in J. Neusner et al., eds., *The Social World of Formative Christianity and Judaism,* Festschrift H. C. Kee, Philadelphia: Fortress, 142-61 • Jüngel, E. 1962, *Paulus und Jesus,* HUT 2, Tübingen: Mohr-Siebeck • Käsemann, E. 1969, "Worship and Everyday Life: A Note on Romans 12," in *New Testament Questions of Today,* Philadelphia: Fortress, 188-95 • Käsemann, E. 4th German ed. 1980, Eng. tr. 1980, *Commentary on Romans,* London: SCM and Grand Rapids: Eerdmans; German ed. HNT 8a, Tübingen: Mohr-Siebeck • Kaylor, R. D. 1988, *Paul's Covenant Community: Jew and Gentile in Romans,* Atlanta: John Knox • Kirk, K. E. 1937, *The Epistle to the Romans in the Revised Version,* Clarendon Bible 12, Oxford: Clarendon • Klein, G. 1976, "Romans, Letter to the," *IDBSup,* 752-54 • Lincoln, A. 1992, "Abraham Goes to Rome: Paul's Treatment of Abraham in Romans 4," in M. J. Wilkins and T. Paige, eds., *Worship, Theology, and Ministry in the Early Church: Essays in Honor of Ralph P. Martin,* Sheffield: JSOT, 163-79 • Lohse, E. 2003, *Der Brief an die Römer,* KEK 4, 15th ed., Göttingen: Vandenhoeck & Ruprecht • Luedemann, G. 1984, *Paul, Apostle to the Gentiles: Studies in Chronology,* London: SCM; Philadelphia: Fortress • Melanchthon, P. 1965. *Melanchthons Werke in Auswahl, V. Römerbrief-Kommentar 1532,* ed. R. Schäfer, Gütersloh: Gütersloher Verlagshaus Gerd Mohn • Lung-Kwong, L. 1998, *Paul's Purpose in Writing Romans: The Upbuilding of a Jewish and Gentile Christian Community in Rome,* Jian Dao Dissertation Series 6, Bible and Literature 4, Hong Kong: Alliance Bible Seminary • Meier, H. A. 1991, *The Social Setting of the Ministry as Reflected in the Writings of Hermas, Clement, and Ignatius,* Dissertations SR1, Waterloo, Ont.: Wilfrid Laurier University • Meyer, P. W. 1990, "The Worm at the Core of the Apple: Exegetical Reflections on Romans 7," in R. T. Fortna and B. R. Gaventa, eds., *The Conversation Continues: Studies in Paul and John,* Festschrift J. L. Martyn, Nashville: Abingdon, 62-84 • Miller, J. C. 2000, *The Obedience of Faith, the Eschatological People of God, and the Purpose of Romans,* SBLDS 177, Atlanta: Society of Biblical Literature • Minear, P. 1971, *The Obedience of Faith: The Purposes of Paul in the Epistle to the Romans,* SBT 2/19, London: SCM • Minear, P. 1995, *The Golgotha Earthquake: Three Witnesses,* Cleveland: Pilgrim • Moo, D. 1996, *Romans 1–8,* The Epistle to the Romans, Grand Rapids: Eerdmans • Morris, L. 1988, *The Epistle to the Romans,* Grand Rapids: Eerdmans • Moxnes, H. 1980, *Theology in Conflict: Studies in Paul's Understanding of God in Romans,* NovTSup 53, Leiden: Brill • Munck, J. 1967, *Christ & Israel: An Interpretation of Romans 9–11,* Philadelphia: Fortress; Germ. Acta Jutlandica, Theology Series 7, Copenhagen: Munksgaard, 1956 • Murray, J. 1959, 1965, *The Epistle to the Romans,* NICNT, 2 vols., Grand Rapids: Eerdmans, repr. in 1 vol. 1975 • Nanos, M. D. 1996, *The Mystery of Romans: The Jewish Context of Paul's Letter,* Minneapolis: Fortress • Nygren, A. 1949 (Swedish 1944), *Commentary on Romans,* Philadelphia: Muhlenberg; London: SCM, 1952 • Reumann, J., with J. A. Fitzmyer and J. Quinn. 1982, *"Righteousness" in the New Testament: "Justification" in the United States Lutheran–Roman Catholic Dialogue,* Philadelphia: Fortress and New York/Ramsey: Paulist • Robinson, J. A. T. 1979, *Wrestling with Romans,* London: SCM and Philadelphia: Westminster • *Romans Debate, The,* see "Donfried, K. P." • Sanday, W., and A. C. Headlam. 1895, *A Critical and Exegetical Commentary on the Epistle to the Romans,* ICC, Edinburgh: T. & T. Clark, repr. 1962 • Sanders, E. P. 1977, *Paul and Palestinian Judaism: A Comparison of Patterns of Religion,* Philadelphia: Fortress and London: SCM • Schreiner, T. R. 1998, *Romans,* Baker Exegetical Commentary on the New Testament 6, Grand Rapids: Baker • Scott, M. J. 1992, *Adoption as Sons of God,* WUNT 2/48, Tübingen: Mohr-Siebeck • Stendahl, K. 1995, *Final Account: Paul's Letter to the Romans,* Minneapolis: Fortress • Stowers, S. 1994, *A Rereading of Romans: Justice, Jews, and Gentiles,* New Haven and London: Yale University • Stuhlmacher, P. 1994, *Paul's Letter to the Romans: A Commentary,* Louisville: Westminster/John Knox; German, NTD, Göttingen: Vandenhoeck & Ruprecht, 1989 • Theissen, G. 1987, *Psychological Aspects of Pauline Theology,* Philadelphia: Fortress • Thompson, M. 1991, *Clothed with Christ: The Example and Teaching of Jesus in Romans 12.1–15.13,* JSNTSup 59, Sheffield: Sheffield Academic • Wedderburn, A. J. M. 1988, *The Reasons for Romans,* Edinburgh: T. & T. Clark • Wilckens, U. 1978, 1980, 1982, *Der Brief an die Römer,* EKKNT 6/1-3, 3 vols., Neukirchen-Vluyn: Neukirchener Verlag; Einsiedeln: Benziger • Wright, N. T. 1991, *The Climax of the Covenant: Christ and the Law in Pauline Theology,* Edinburgh: T. & T. Clark; Minneapolis: Fortress, 1992.

1 Corinthians

Stephen C. Barton

INTRODUCTION

Reading 1 Corinthians

It has been well said that reading 1 Corinthians is like reading someone else's mail. Here we have a letter from the earliest days of the Christian movement written, not for a modern readership, but for a fledgling group of "house churches" in the ancient Mediterranean city of Corinth. As we read it, we are given access to one side of a correspondence between Paul, the apostle and church founder, and members of the Corinthian church. Part of its fascination is that, as we read between the lines, the letter allows us to "lift the lid" on the life, loves, and hates of a particular church at the inception of Christianity. It also allows us to see firsthand how the great apostle exercised authority by giving guidance and responding to problems.

But the letter's fascination goes further than that. For, to a greater or lesser extent, we who read 1 Corinthians are liable to find that the life, loves, and hates to which the text bears witness are *ours as well* (Ford 1989; Craddock 1990). This is partly what we mean when we say that the biblical text is "inspired." But it is also related to the fact that 1 Corinthians has had a very significant "afterlife." By its incorporation into the canon of Christian Scripture as a work of apostolic authority, 1 Corinthians has shaped who we are as readers. Seen in this light, the text can be understood as addressed not just to the house churches of first-century Corinth but to all who share their inheritance. This embraces all members of the Christian church down the ages and all who stand in those historical traditions and cultures which have been shaped by the canon of Christian Scripture. Indeed, according to Christian belief in the inspiration of Scripture, the truth to which 1 Corinthians testifies touches all humankind. What Paul says about "Christ crucified" in ch. 1, or about the true nature of love in ch. 13, or about the resurrection of the dead in ch. 15 is testimony of universal and eternal significance. That is why it is important that our engagement with the text be a dialectical one: that we engage in a two-way process whereby it is both we who read the text and the text which "reads" us.

The implications of this for our interpretation are wide-ranging. First, we have to take with full seriousness the historical contingency of the text. We can understand Paul's letter only if we enter, imaginatively and with the aid of historical criticism in its various modes, into the world of the text itself. This involves finding out as much as possible about the values and structures of first-century city life, the thought world and common practices (Jewish, Greco-Roman and Christian) of Paul and his contemporaries, the practice of rhetoric and letter writing in the first century, the geography and archeology of Corinth, and so on. Such historical information allows us to understand the setting and content of 1 Corinthians more clearly. It also serves as a check on interpretation, on the dual assumption that the number of possible meanings is not indeterminate and that weight has to be given to what the text meant in its original context as far as that can be determined.

Second, we have to take with equal seriousness the text's continuing significance in the life of the church. The significance of 1 Corinthians cannot be restricted to what it originally meant, for that is itself a matter of ongoing interpretation. Its significance is also ongoing, as people both within and outside the church read their stories in the light of the truth of God to which 1 Corinthians bears witness (cf. Webster 1998). Our task is not just an "archeological" one, therefore. To do justice to the ecclesiological aspect of the text, in its content, its place in the canon, and its contribution to Christian worship, we have to read it as the "word of God" for the church in its mission to the world. But to do justice to its spatial and temporal horizons, we also have to read it eschatologically, as the "word of God" for the present with a view to the future consummation of all things. Reading 1 Corinthians asks of us no less than that. It is a task which invites repeated return to the text in every generation.

Author and Date

There can be no doubt that 1 Corinthians was written by the apostle Paul. What the text itself makes explicit at its beginning and end (1:1; 16:21) and what is explicit also in 2 Corinthians (1:1) is confirmed by the testimony of *1 Clement:* "Take up the epistle of the blessed Paul the apostle. . . . With true inspiration he charged you concerning himself and Cephas and Apollos, because even then you had made yourself partisans" (*1 Clem.* 47:1-3). Additional corroboration is provided by the evidence of the Acts of the Apostles, which correlates well with 1 Corinthians. For example, Acts confirms that Paul was the founder of the church at Corinth (Acts 18:1-11), that Apollos made a significant contribution to the life of the church there after Paul had moved on (Acts 18:27–19:1), and that Paul numbered people like Timothy (Acts 18:5) and Aquila and Priscilla (Acts 18:2, 18) among his fellow workers there. So we can be very confident that 1 Corinthians comes from Paul. This is important not just for reasons of historical authenticity but also for how we receive the text and respond to it in the life of the Christian church, what authority we give it. As a letter from one "called to be an apostle of Christ Jesus by the will of God" (1 Cor 1:1), it has special, canonical status, for it bears decisive witness to Christ and the truth of the gospel.

The likely date of the letter can also be established with confidence as sometime in the years AD 54-55. From Acts 18:2 we learn of Paul's partnership at Corinth in the tentmaking trade with Aquila and Priscilla, the latter having come from Italy as a result of Claudius's decree ordering the expulsion of Jews from Rome. Since the decree can be dated to 49, it is likely that Paul arrived in Corinth in about AD 50. Acts also refers to the fact that Gallio was proconsul in Achaia and had oversight of judicial proceedings which involved Paul (and Sosthenes) and which led to his departure (Acts 18:12-17). Gallio's proconsulship has been confirmed by epigraphic evidence which allows a dating of his term of office to 51-52. According to Acts 18:11, Paul stayed in Corinth for eighteen months, so we can be reasonably certain that the years of his stay were AD 50-52 (on the evidence relating to Claudius and Gallio, see Murphy-O'Connor 1983: 129-52).

After his departure, there was a substantial lapse of time during which Paul visited Jerusalem and Antioch, traveled through Galatia, and made his base for two years in Ephesus (Acts 18:22-23; 19:1-20). This was also the time when Apollos ministered in Corinth (Acts 18:27–19:1; cf. 1 Cor 16:12). Given this time lapse, it is reasonable to conclude that the letter we know as 1 Corinthians was written in Ephesus in the period AD 54-55 (see, in general, Jewett 1979).

The Occasion of the Letter

Precisely what triggered the writing of the letter is hard to determine. It is clear, nevertheless, that the letter is part of an ongoing interaction between Paul and the Corinthians, something unsurprising given the relatively close proximity of Ephesus and Corinth. We know, for example, that Paul received oral reports from visitors making him aware of scandal and division within the church (1 Cor. 4:17; 5:1; 11:18). One such report is attributed to "Chloe's people" at the letter's opening (1:11) to the effect that factions were developing between groups claiming different spiritual leaders as their respective patrons and benefactors (1:12). At the letter's close, there is also mention of a delegation made up of Stephanas, Fortunatus, and Achaicus (16:17), and it is reasonable to assume that Paul learned much about the situation at Corinth from them also.

In addition to oral reports, there is reference in 7:1 to a letter from the church itself (perhaps brought by Stephanas), asking for Paul's advice. We do not know precisely what matters were raised in the Corinthians' letter to Paul, nor in what order. However, the formula *peri de* ("Now concerning . . ."), which occurs at 7:1, 25; 8:1; 12:1; 16:1, 12, is a significant verbal indicator of the subjects about which Paul, at least, wanted to give instruction. These include: rules for the married (7:1-24) and for the unmarried (7:25-40), whether or not to eat food offered to idols (8:1–11:1), the proper exercise of "spiritual gifts" (12:1–14:40), the collection for Jerusalem (16:1-4), and the situation regarding Apollos (16:12). Included in this sequence is instruction on two other significant matters: abuses at the Lord's Supper (11:17-34) and disagreements over the resurrection of the dead (15:1-58).

We can only speculate why the Corinthian church fell victim to factionalism and why it needed instruction on such a range of fundamental issues. Some possible reasons will be explored in the commentary. Most likely, they had to do with factors both external and internal: influences upon the church from the outside world and dynamics within the church especially in the period after Paul moved on (cf. Hurd 1965). By extrapolating from Paul's response in 1 Corinthians, some have tried to reconstruct in a fairly thoroughgoing way a "Corinthian theology" manifesting itself in various ways in the church's common life. For example, some see the problem as gnosticism manifesting itself in an "overrealized" eschatology (Schmithals 1971), others detect the influence of Hellenistic-Jewish "wisdom" speculation (Pearson 1973), others identify the interests and activity of "spiritual enthusiasts" (Fee 1987), while yet others locate the problem in the beliefs and practices of a group of female prophets (Wire 1990).

Each of these suggestions may have something to commend it. But the hypothetical nature of such proposals has to be recognized given the absence of independent testimony and the difficulty of correlating a theological or religious viewpoint with any of the groups alluded to in 1:10-12. Furthermore, as Gerd Theissen (1982) has helped us to see, it may be that the causes of the various problems are as much social and cultural as "theological," and that it is Paul (rather more than his "opponents") who responds theologically and ecclesiologically. As Hays (1997: 8) puts it: "The brilliance of Paul's letter lies in his ability to diagnose the situation in theological terms and to raise the inchoate theological issues into the light of conscious reflection in light of the gospel." It is certainly providential for us that this wide range of problems did arise and that Paul gave such a comprehensive theological and ecclesiological response in his letter. It is the profundity of Paul's letter which has made it so significant in Christian moral and theological reflection down the ages.

The Unity and Structure of the Letter

There have been various scholarly arguments to the effect that apparent dislocations in the flow of the letter require us to posit a kind of partition theory according to which either the letter is a composite of several separate fragments or the letter was written in stages (cf. Hurd 1965: 43-58; de Boer 1994). The possibility that later, post-Pauline material has been interpolated into the text is also a matter of vigorous debate. The material on the place of women in the church (11:2-16; 14:33b-36) is a case in point and has obvious significance for debates in modern times about the role of women (cf. Fee 1987: 699-708).

The status of each text needs to be examined on its merits. What needs to be said here is that, whether or not such "problem texts" are deemed part of Paul's original letter and therefore part of Paul's teaching to the Corinthians, their appropriation as the "word of God for today" requires *Christian theological interpretation* within the ongoing life of the church under the guidance of the Holy Spirit (cf. Barton 1997b: 98-115).

In spite of arguments to the contrary, however, a good case can be made that 1 Corinthians is a literary unity. Study of the form and style of ancient letters has shown that the way Paul begins and ends his letter is a Christian improvisation upon a recognizable epistolary genre. Furthermore, awareness of analogies in ancient letter writing makes it possible to identify 1 Corinthians as a real and coherent letter (cf. Stowers 1986). It begins with the conventional address, greeting, and thanksgiving (1:1-9) and ends with the conventional travel plans, greetings, autograph, and benediction (16:5-23).

Perhaps even more important has been recent study of ancient rhetorical practice. The work of Margaret Mitchell (1992) in particular has shown that, from a rhetorical point of view, Paul's letter is a unity. Its content and structure conform to that form of persuasion known as "deliberative rhetoric" in which an appeal is made — based upon arguments about what is "advantageous" *(to sympheron)* and backed up by supporting examples *(paradeigmata)* — with a view to action toward a future goal, a goal which often has to do with achieving "concord" *(homonoia)*. Instead of breaking the text up into (hypothetical) fragments of previous letters or trying to achieve the impossible task of correlating the conflicting "religious" parties in Corinth with the various pastoral and theological issues Paul tackles, Mitchell argues that the common denominator which ties all the issues together is that they all contribute to factionalism, and that it is *factionalism itself* (rather than particular factions) which Paul is attempting to combat from the beginning of 1 Corinthians to its end. In this connection, Mitchell shows that many of the commonplaces found in ancient deliberative rhetoric concerned with concord are scattered throughout 1 Corinthians and bind it together (cf. the summary in 1992: 180-81). Her analysis produces the following outline of the letter's structure (1992: x-xi):

I. 1:1-3 Epistolary Prescript
II. 1:4-9 Epistolary Thanksgiving
III. 1:10–15:58 Epistolary Body
  A. 1:10 the main thesis statement *(prothesis)* of the entire letter
  B. 1:11-17 a statement of the facts *(narratio)* underlying the argument in the body of the letter
  C. 1:18–15:57 the principal argument or "proof" *(probatio)* in four sections
    1. 1:18–4:21 first section of proof: censure of Corinthian factionalism
    2. 5:1–11:1 second section of proof: the integrity of the Corinthian community against outside defilement from sexual immorality (5:1–7:40) and idol meats (8:1–11:1), with a pertinent digression or *egressio* in ch. 9
    3. 11:2–14:40 third section of proof: manifestations of Corinthian factionalism when "coming together" (divisive customs in worship, 11:2-16; divisions at the Lord's Supper, 11:17-34; spiritual gifts and unity, 12:1–14:40, with another digression or *egressio* in ch. 13)
    4. 15:1-57 fourth section of proof: the resurrection as the final goal and the need for unity in the tradition
  D. 15:58 conclusion *(peroratio)* summarizing the argument of the body of the letter
IV. 16:1-24 Epistolary Closing, including instructions on the collection (vv. 1-4), travel plans (vv. 5-12), recapitulation of the argument (vv. 13-18), greetings (vv. 19-21), and final curse and prayer for unity in love (vv. 22-24).

Mitchell's case for the unity of 1 Corinthians is impressive and has met with general approval (e.g., Witherington 1995: 73-77). Broadly speaking, it is the position taken in this commentary also. Awareness of the overall structure and unity of the letter is important primarily insofar as it contributes to our ability to read it with greater sensitivity, to identify the "real issues" it raises, and to understand the "theo-logic" of Paul's argument as a whole.

COMMENTARY

Greeting (1:1-3)

Paul begins by identifying himself, along with his brother-in-Christ Sosthenes (cf. Acts 18:17), as senders of the letter. The language Paul uses to identify and situate both himself and his addressees is significant. The focus is on what they have in common: God, Christ, and the call of God to be members of a new covenant people under the authority of Christ. This is the theological and ecclesial foundation upon which Paul wants to construct his whole argument.

Thus, in 1:1, Paul presents himself as "called" according to the will of God to be an "apostle" (or envoy) of Christ (cf. Gal 1:15-16). Therein lies his particular authority and role. He is not acting out of self-interest but in obedience to God's will and Christ's call. The Corinthians are also "called" (1:2). As in the case of Paul, their new life is grounded in grace, not in any achievement of their own. However, their call is not to apostleship but to be "saints" *(hagioi)*, individuals set apart by union with Christ — "sanctified *(hēgiasmenois)* in Christ Jesus" — who together make up a single body in one place, "the church of God that is in Corinth," and who belong at the same time to a society which is translocal, made up of "all those in every place" who acknowledge the lordship of Christ.

The call by God to be "saints" is biblical language for the election of Israel to be God's chosen people (cf. Lev 19:1-2); but here, in a way which must have been shocking to Jewish sensibilities (cf. Acts 10), it is applied to a mixed, predominantly Gentile, solidarity. This transformation of language represents a transformation of reality, the coming into being of a new covenant community. The "church of God" is a society which transcends old boundaries and brings God's grace to people previously ignorant of it. The blessing with which Paul's greeting ends (1:3) sums up this new order of things. It is an order of "grace and peace" which has been bestowed upon the Corinthians as a gift from God. But with the gift comes an implied obligation. Indebtedness to God and Christ as their heavenly benefactors places the Corinthians under obligation to practice grace and peace in their relations with one another, something which, as the letter goes on to reveal, runs against the grain.

Thanksgiving (1:4-9)

As literary and rhetorical convention dictate, Paul now proceeds, as in his other letters, from greeting to thanksgiving (cf. Rom 1:8-17; Phil 1:3-11; 1 Thess 1:2-10; 2 Thess 1:3-12; and Doty 1973: 27-47). This section — known in rhetorical terms as the *proem* — serves a twofold purpose. By praising his addressees together (but indirectly, in the form of a prayer of thanksgiving to God), he unifies them and gets them "on side" in a manner which paves the way for their more ready reception of the stern advice and correction to follow (in 1:10ff.). At the same time, as with the greeting, the thanksgiving allows him to introduce ideas which become central to his argument later on — "grace," "riches," "speech," "knowledge," "spiritual gift," "establish," "call," and "fellowship." In other words, Paul's thanksgiving is genuine, but it is also weighted toward a particular rhetorical and pedagogical goal (cf. Mitchell 1992: 194-97).

The thanksgiving begins (1:4) by picking up on the theme of the grace of God introduced already in the words of the blessing in v. 3. Although it becomes clear subsequently that Paul is concerned with the ways in which the many manifestations of God's grace among the Corinthians have been abused (e.g., 4:6-21), it is nevertheless the case that Paul's starting point is celebration: God is to be thanked "continually" for his overwhelming grace manifesting itself "in every way" in particular "graces." That God's grace can be abused is not allowed to diminish the goodness either of God or of God's gifts, even if the awareness of human fallibility in receiving and exercising those gifts opens a space for irony. As Fee (1987: 36) puts it: "The verb 'I thank' controls the whole."

The particular graces Paul mentions in the thanksgiving are two: "all speech" and "all knowledge" (1:5). From 1 Corinthians 12–14, we can identify "speech" as referring to inspired utterance such as prophecy and speaking in tongues, and "knowledge" as the understanding of heavenly mysteries and prophetic revelation. Doubtless Paul mentions these two in particular because they are the ones so highly prized by the Corinthians (as perhaps also by Paul himself). But what is noteworthy is how Paul anticipates and refuses to collude with the tendency for manifestations of grace in the church to become a ground for boasting, rivalry, and faction. He does this in four ways, each of which in its own way draws attention away from human to divine ways of seeing.

First, he stresses that the graces are given by God and are available only by being "in Christ Jesus" (1:4). Second, they are a temporary expedient to help sustain believers while they "wait for the revealing of our Lord Jesus Christ," an experience of grace far more powerful than anything they may experience in the present (v. 7). Third, the fact that the coming of the Lord is a day of judgment (v. 8) is an implicit warning against behavior which is self-centered or arises from party spirit. Fourth, and reminiscent of the words of greeting (vv. 1-3), more important than the gifts (which may divide) is the "call" from God into a new eschatological solidarity, the "fellowship" *(koinōnia)* of those who belong to Christ (v. 9). It is this larger theological and eschatological horizon — climaxing in the affirmation "God is faithful" (v. 9) — which Paul deliberately introduces and which provides the grounds for sincere thanksgiving, even in the midst of human folly.

Paul's Appeal for Unity (1:10-17)

Following the greeting and the thanksgiving comes Paul's heartfelt call for unity within the fellowship (1:10). Here we have the main theme of the entire letter addressed to a church whose unity is threatened by factionalism (1:18–4:21), disputes about social morality (5:1–11:1), divisions over worship (11:2–14:40), and disagreement about the fate of the dead (15:1-57). Responding to insider reports of "divisions" from members of Chloe's household, Paul appeals for unity in the strongest possible terms: "I appeal *(parakalō)* to you, brothers and sisters, by the name of our Lord Jesus Christ, that all of you be in agreement [lit. "speak the same"] and that there be no divisions *(schismata)* among you, but that you be united *in the same mind* and *the same purpose*" (1:10).

Important to note in passing is the fact that — given the prominence of concerns for the unity of the city-state in ancient political rhetoric and practice — Paul's letter has a goal which his addressees would recognize as practical and "political" (cf. Mitchell 1992: 81-111; Welborn 1997). What he writes is not "ivory tower theology," and his concerns as an apostle are not limited to "spiritual" matters. On the contrary, Paul is responding like the father (cf. 4:14-15) of a fragmented household or the leader of a divided people. His letter is "practical theology" in the fullest sense, aimed at promoting peace *(eirēnē)* among the new covenant people of God.

But equally important is the other side of the coin: that implicit in Paul's response to the Corinthians is the assumption that they themselves constitute a new society with its own distinctive polity, practices, and ethos. Part of the problem Paul seems to be dealing with is *the narrowness and selectiveness of the Corinthians' self-understanding as believers,* their failure to see that their new identity "in Christ" is a matter not just of the "spiritual things" *(ta pneumatika)* they prize so highly (cf. 1 Corinthians 12–14) but also (and even more) of their whole lives individual and corporate, spiritual and material (cf. Barclay 1992: 61-72). What Paul wants them to see is that, if they truly belong to the household *of God* (rather than individual households) and if they are united now under a single, new name, "the name of our Lord Jesus Christ" (1:10), they belong to a new order of things, and this requires giving up old ways in favor of new, old "politics" in favor of new.

What appears to have happened, however, is that the Corinthians have brought the political practices of the wider society into the church instead of allowing the church to be the place and time where a new kind of "politics" could develop. They have divided along primarily household lines into factions, each faction uniting under a slogan ("I belong to Paul," "I belong to Apollos," etc.) which identifies them by their allegiance to one of the "leading men" in the church's short history. Apparently, this allegiance arises both out of the high value they place on association with itinerant, sophist-type figures skilled in rhetorical display (cf. Acts 18:24-28 on Apollos; and the analysis of Winter 1997b), and out of their sense of indebtedness to the one by whom they have been baptized (cf. 1:13b-16). Somehow, the apostles' preaching and ritual practice have been subverted by the Corinthians' love of appearances and display, verbal or ritual, along with associated opportunities for rivalry and "boasting" (cf. 1:29; 3:21; 4:7). Old habits, including old social and "political" habits, die hard. Whereas Paul sees the Christian *koinōnia* (association) as a new, eschatological society oriented toward what makes for "peace" (cf. 7:15b), for some (at least) of the Corinthians it is a legitimate sphere for the extension of personal power and influence.

So Paul takes them back behind what divides them to the fundamental *reordering* of status and power which his apostolic calling and preaching represent: "For Christ did not send me to baptize but to proclaim the gospel, and not with eloquent words of wisdom [lit. "not in wisdom of word"], so that the cross of Christ might not be emptied of its power" (1:17). Here, for the first time, a fundamental contrast is drawn between two "words" *(logoi)* or "messages," two competing ways of seeing the world. On the one hand, there is Paul's gospel preaching *(euangelizesthai),* the content of which has to do with the death of the Messiah and is summed up in the phrase "the cross of Christ"; on the other is what delights the Corinthians — worldly "wisdom" *(sophia)* rhetorically displayed. This contrast underlies what Paul goes on to say in 1:18–2:5.

The point, in passing, about baptism is not that Paul is being "anti-sacramental," or exalting (what we might call) the Ministry of the Word over the Ministry of the Sacrament. Rather, in a context where both word and sacrament are being subverted by the Corinthians as occasions for human display, Paul points to the most powerful and subversive "display" of all: the cross of Christ. As previously, Paul's horizon is wholeheartedly God- and Christ-centered, and it is that horizon which he wants to persuade the Corinthians to share.

Paul's Censure of Corinthian Factionalism (1:18–4:21)

Paul now proceeds to develop this basic contrast between "the message of the cross" (1:18) and human wisdom. He does so in three steps, each of which is designed to persuade the Corinthians that the Christian gospel and Christian existence *cannot merely be added on* to the wisdom they so highly prize, as if they are just more of the same. On the contrary, they require a radical reinterpretation of wisdom as understood in Corinth.

But to understand Paul's deep ambivalence about "wisdom" we need to clarify something of its range of meanings. This has been a matter of considerable debate (cf. Dunn 1995: 34-45; also Witherington 1994: 295-319). In brief, it is a matter both of content and practice. In terms of content, *sophia* refers to ideas and values deeply rooted in the Greek tradition and highly influential in Hellenistic Judaism. Its source is twofold: it is found either in the practiced scrutiny of nature and the affairs of humankind, or it comes direct from heaven by revelation through intermediaries, especially the Spirit. Its goal is individual and corporate salvation through the acquisition of true knowledge *(gnōsis)* about the ultimate nature of reality and how to live accordingly. In terms of practice, *sophia* refers to the ability of those claiming to be philosophers (i.e., "lovers of *sophia*"), sophists, sages, or prophets to mediate and communicate such ideas in a rhetorically skillful or otherwise convincing manner, the success of which would be evident in the accumulation of a following and financial and material support from benefactors.

In consequence, wisdom in both its aspects — content and practice — tends to be hierarchical and discriminatory. It divides those who have the upbringing, learning, and leisure to pursue it from those who do not, and it divides those who follow one sophist or sage from those who follow another. Insofar as this kind of wisdom reinforces the hierarchical, patriarchal, and factional nature of ancient society as a whole, it is conservative of the status quo and, in some of its expressions, quite pessimistic. On the other hand, to the extent that a particular tradition places its emphasis on revelation and inspiration, there is the possibility that wisdom of a more innovatory and even countercultural kind may take shape. But this can be just as divisive in its own way and therefore just as conformist to wider cultural dynamics — when, as in the Corinthian fellowship, for example, those claiming to be "wise" or "spiritual" or "strong" set themselves apart from the rest. It is little wonder, therefore, that Paul strives so hard to wean the Corinthians onto a different understanding, where *wisdom is problematized and reinterpreted* by being set in the context of God's saving work in Christ at the end of time.

God's Foolishness Displayed in the Crucified Messiah (1:18-25)

Paul's first point, therefore, has to do with *the content* of the gospel. The language Paul uses is that of apocalyptic eschatology, typical of which is a series of striking antinomies designed to show that the new order of things is discontinuous with the old and turns previous wisdom on its head. Wisdom is now "foolishness," and the "foolishness" of the message of the cross is now "the power of God" *(dynamis tou theou).* This is such an astonishingly paradoxical inversion of the normal way of seeing things that for the first time in the letter Paul invokes scriptural testimony to support his understanding of God's judgment on "the wisdom of the wise" (1:19); and it is highly significant that the Scripture Paul quotes (Isa 29:14) occurs in a context which refers specifically to those in Israel who "draw near *with their mouths* and honor me *with their lips*" (Isa 29:13). True wisdom, in other words, is not to be found in weighty words pronounced by gifted speakers. It is something hidden and paradoxical, a kind of "foolishness": it is certainly not a subject for boasting.

Furthermore, humanity is divided in this scheme of things, not between Jews and Greeks — the normal way of seeing humankind, in Judaism especially — or between rich and poor, but between people who are seen now in eschatological terms as those "who are perishing" and those "who are being saved" (1:18, 23-24). On the side of "this age" or "the world" are the wise: in Jewish terms, those learned in the Torah ("the scribe"); in Greek terms, those skilled in rhetoric ("the debater"). On the other side are simply "those who believe" (vv. 20-21). Set over against the expectation of the Jews that the Messiah would perform "signs" like those done by Moses, what Paul offers is a sign of a very different kind: a crucified Messiah who, as the contradiction of Jewish eschatological hope, is a "stumbling block" *(skandalon).* Likewise, over against the quest of the Gentiles for *sophia,* the wisdom Paul offers is the opposite in human terms, something quite irrational amounting almost to madness (cf. Hengel 1977). But Paul's frame of reference is not what is constituted by human ways of seeing. His is a biblical frame of reference, whose transcendental focus is conveyed best in terms that are highly paradoxical: "For God's foolishness [i.e., the event of the cross] is wiser than human wisdom, and God's weakness is stronger than human strength" (v. 25).

God's Foolishness Displayed in the Identity of Those Called (1:26-31)

Paul's second point complements the first. If the content of the gospel is evidence of the contradiction of conventional wisdom, so are its *recipients.* For instead of being the preserve of the cultural elite, the wisdom of God finds its embodiment in a startlingly motley fellowship of people: "not many of you were wise *(sophoi)* by human standards, not many were powerful *(dynatoi),* not many of noble birth *(eugeneis)*" (1:26). This is not the most flattering way of characterizing the addressees. But it is not meant to be! Paul is trying to help the Corinthian Christians to see that their own identity as a socially and ethnically mixed group drawn mainly (though not entirely) from the bottom end of the social scale is itself a powerful testimony to God's gracious "call" (v. 26; cf. v. 2) — to the fact that in the cross of Christ God is doing something totally new which turns human values and social patterns upside down (Pickett 1997).

The language Paul uses is thoroughly biblical and the concept that of eschatological reversal. In the background are the doctrines of creation and election: "God *chose* what is foolish . . . God *chose* what is weak . . . God *chose* what is low and despised . . . things that are not . . ." (1:28). This is a statement of radical grace to a creation unable to help itself. It implies that human pride and competitive achievement are to be the basis for personal identity and sociability no longer. The anthropocentrism which pervades the Hellenistic cultural values of Corinth and sets human beings at odds with each other in a perpetual contest for dominance is placed under God's judgment and electing grace. In its place are set the three great blessings of being in covenant relationship with God — righteousness, sanctification and redemption — found now in Christ crucified as the wisdom of God "for us" (i.e., for our salvation) (1:30). And with a flourish, Paul ends this step in his argument with his second appeal to Scripture (v. 31), this time to Jeremiah's oracle of judgment on Israel, the terms of which resonate with Paul's own words to the Corinthians: "Thus says the LORD: Do not let the *wise* boast in their wisdom, do not let the *mighty* boast in their might, do not let the *wealthy* boast in their wealth; but let *those who boast* boast in this, that they understand and know me, that I am the LORD" (Jer 9:23-24).

Incidentally, the fact that the Jeremiah text has shaped Paul's argument here (cf. also 1 Sam 2:10, LXX) urges caution on attempts — of which there are many (see, e.g., Theissen 1982: 69-119; and differently, Meggitt 1998: 75-154) — to draw firm conclusions from 1:26-28 about the socioeconomic status of the Corinthian believers. Paul is not concerned to offer sociological information but to engage in theological persuasion scripturally informed. Paul's language here and elsewhere certainly reflects his sensitivity to questions of rank and status, along with the associated values of honor and shame, but only insofar as this allows him to show how the gospel of the Crucified One and the church of the "low and despised" presuppose a different order of things altogether: "God is creating a new eschatological community out of unimpressive material precisely in order to exemplify the power of his own unmerited grace. Thus, the social composition of the church is an outward and visible sign of God's paradoxical wisdom" (Hays 1999: 116-17).

God's Foolishness Displayed in Paul's Weakness as a Preacher (2:1-5)

This leads to Paul's third point. If the "shameful" content of the gospel and the social insignificance of its recipients show that the wisdom of God is incompatible with wisdom conventionally understood, then so does the style in which the gospel message was communicated to them. So he says: "I did not come proclaiming the mystery of God to you in lofty words or wisdom . . . [but] I came to you in weakness and in fear and in much trembling" (2:1, 3). In the competitive, display-oriented culture of Greco-Roman Corinth, Paul's self-confessed lack of rhetorical prowess and personal presence (cf. 2 Cor 10:10) is a damaging admission (cf. Pogoloff 1992; Litfin 1994). Who would want to associate with someone so lacking in the expected qualities of display and domination? But with a certain rhetorical finesse, Paul turns this weakness in his favor. On the one hand, his weakness (for elaborations of which see 1 Cor 4:9-13; 2 Cor 4:7-12; 6:4-10; 11:30; 12:7-10) is congruent with the gospel he preaches ("Jesus Christ and him crucified," 2:2), to which the Corinthians themselves have responded. On the other, it allows the Spirit and power *of God* to show through in such a way that the Corinthians can be confident that their faith is grounded in God alone (vv. 4-5).

Significantly, Paul's argument ends as it began. In 1:18 he identifies the central paradox of the Christian faith: that the message of the cross is "the power of God." As an effective *inclusio,* he finishes on the same note: the basis of Christian faith is not human wisdom but "the power of God" (2:5). Where the Corinthians think in terms drawn too much from the pagan society around them, Paul argues in terms set by the Scriptures and God's covenant with Israel. Where the Corinthians' thinking is primarily anthropocentric, Paul seeks to convert them to think (and act) in terms centered on God.

Wisdom Reinterpreted (2:6–3:4)

But if the gospel of the Crucified One cannot be accommodated to conventional wisdom in either content or form, that does not mean that aspects of wisdom may not be amenable to *reinterpretation in the light of the gospel* (cf. Stuhlmacher 1987). This is so especially of that type of (Hellenistic-Jewish) wisdom according to which saving knowledge comes by revelation through the Spirit and Spirit-inspired intermediaries. Indeed, given what appears to be the high regard for wisdom and the gifts of the Spirit in Corinth — a regard no doubt inspired in part by Paul himself in the period of his earlier teaching ministry there and subsequently strengthened by the teaching of Apollos — it was almost incumbent upon Paul to balance his criticism of wisdom with a reappropriation of wisdom differently understood. Otherwise, instead of "gaining" his fellow believers for a fuller commitment to the gospel by building upon what was right in their beliefs and practices (cf. 1 Cor 9:19-23), he might have offended them unnecessarily or even alienated them from the fellowship (Chadwick 1954-55).

This helps to explain the next step in what Paul writes, where he develops his argument by saying, "Yet among the mature *(en tois teleiois)* we do speak wisdom . . . God's wisdom, secret and hidden [lit. a wisdom of God hidden in a mystery], which God decreed before the ages for our glory'" (2:6-7). Paul is not here building up what he earlier tore down in 1:18–2:5. Nor is he being purely ironic, even if there are ironic touches. Rather, he seems to be taking over the language favored by the Corinthians — words like "wisdom," "the mature" and "the infants," "the spiritual" and "the unspiritual," "milk" and "solid food" — and investing it with new meaning arising out of the gospel. The character of this reinterpreted wisdom is laid out carefully and in a series of (either explicit or implied) contrasts, since Paul does not want to have any confusion between worldly wisdom and eschatological wisdom.

First, eschatological wisdom is quite other than the wisdom "of this age" which led the transient rulers "of this age" — note the repetition — to crucify the Messiah (2:6-8). Given that rulers and others of high status are understood in antiquity as people of wisdom, Paul's distinction here is quite pointed. Second, it is not a wisdom of appearance and performance, but a "secret and hidden wisdom" known previously only to God but now imparted by means of a revelation (v. 7). Third, rather than being philosophical and rhetorical, it is eschatological and soteriological in tenor, its purpose being to enable believers to share in the glory of God in accordance with God's prevenient will (vv. 7, 9). Fourth, it is mediated to all believers not through "the spirit of the world" but through the Spirit of God (vv. 10-13). Fifth, it is imparted in fulfillment of the Scriptures (vv. 9, 16). It is not, therefore, a curious novelty sprung from nowhere without credentials; rather, it springs from God's covenant love for those who are his. Sixth, it requires discernment: it is therefore hidden from those who are "unspiritual" or "natural" *(psychikos)* and received as from God by those who are "spiritual" *(pneumatikos)* — that is, those who have received the Spirit *(to pneuma)* (vv. 14-15). Finally, its effect is not to divide into competing schools of thought and practice but to unify and consolidate in a new identity and epistemology: "But we have the mind of Christ" (v. 16).

Although in the history of Christianity this passage (2:6-16) has often been taken as the scriptural basis for a doctrine and practice which distinguish levels of spiritual maturity *among believers,* it is important to point out that such an interpretation is more in line with the kind of elitism which Paul is trying to counter! For the "wisdom" of the cross which Paul commends is not one that separates believer from believer; it is, rather, what separates believer from unbeliever (*and* from those in the church who think and act like unbelievers). That is why Paul makes such heavy use of the first person plural here (cf. vv. 6, 7, 10, 12, 13, 16), whereby the "we" whom God has called are set apart from those who belong to "this age." It is also why the basic contrast (at vv. 2:10-13) is between those who have the Spirit of God (i.e., believers) and those who do not (i.e., unbelievers). Paul's whole point is that, whereas worldly wisdom creates division, rivalry, and violence, the gospel of "Christ crucified" is a wisdom of a different kind, the eschatological revelation of the power of God which brings into being a people united in the Spirit and blessed with the gifts of the Spirit.

Until the Corinthians accept this, the self-styled "spiritual ones" *(hoi pneumatikoi)* are, in Paul's eyes, no more than "fleshly ones" *(hoi sarkinoi),* "infants *(nēpioi)* in Christ," people who can be fed not solids (as they expected) but only milk (3:2)! All of which brings Paul back to his fundamental, "practical-theological" concern (cf. 1:10-17), namely, the threat to the unity of the church posed by a "wisdom" ideology which (because it is "individualistic") fosters party spirit (3:3-4). The irony, then, is that those who boast in their spiritual prowess have nothing to boast about, for in boasting they show only their immaturity — how much they still live according to the wisdom of "this age."

Leadership and Church Growth Reinterpreted (3:5-23)

Having shown that wisdom has to be reinterpreted in the light of the cross, Paul now proceeds to draw out further the implications for Corinthian factionalism: if true wisdom is identified as the revelation of God in the cross of Christ, then all human boasting, including boasting in the leadership of one apostle or teacher over another, is precluded (cf. 1:29-31). Using agricultural and architectural metaphors well known in the political rhetoric of his day (Mitchell 1992: 99-111), Paul seeks to shift the orientation of the Corinthians' social thought and practice in a radically theocentric and christocentric direction: away from divisive attachments to mere humans like Apollos or Paul or Cephas (3:5, 21; cf. 4:6) to common devotion to God and his Christ.

The first metaphor is of the Corinthian believers as "God's field" (3:5-9). This word picture, with its unitary understanding of the church as a single field and its biblical overtones of the metaphor of Israel as God's vineyard (e.g., Isa 5:1-7), allows Paul to clarify how the Corinthians are to regard their apostolic teachers in particular. Above all, they are characterized by *what they have in common:* they are both God's "servants" *(diakonoi);* their respective roles of "planting" (Paul) and "watering" (Apollos), although different, are not in conflict since both are God-given; the parts they play, although significant, are not worth boasting about since after all it is God (as Creator) who causes the Corinthians to "grow"; the parts they play are not at odds since their planting and watering has a common purpose (lit. "they are one," 3:8), and they will both be rewarded according to common criteria; and their relation to each other is as "fellow workers" — a favorite ecclesiological term of Paul's stressing unity and cooperation (cf. 2 Cor 1:24; 8:23; Phil 2:25; 4:3; 1 Thess 3:2; etc.). But most important of all, both the apostolic laborers and the field itself belong to God, something reiterated in every sentence and climaxing with the threefold genitive: "For we are *God's* servants, working together; you are *God's* field, *God's* building" (3:9).

The reference to "God's building" allows a shift to a second metaphor, this time an architectural one (3:10-15). In fact, Paul has a marked preference for architectural metaphors for the church, not least in 1 Corinthians (cf. 3:16-17; 6:19; 8:1; 10:23; 14:3-5, 12, 17, 26; 15:58; 16:13), for they allow him to explore what makes possible the "building up" *(oikodomē)* of the Corinthians' common life in the face of strong forces which threaten to tear it apart. In this first instance of the metaphor, Paul turns from characterizing himself and Apollos to what is going on in the church, developing at the same time the motif of the divine reward or retribution *(misthos)* which God will bestow on his servants at the Day of Judgment (3:8b). Thus, having identified himself in his apostolic role as "like a skilled *(sophos!)* master builder" who "by the grace of God" laid the foundation, Paul proceeds to a serious warning to those (unidentified) people who are building upon it. His warning is twofold. First, and most importantly, there is only one firm foundation: "that foundation is Jesus Christ" (v. 11). Second, those — Paul is referring no doubt to those in Corinth who exalt "wisdom," along with its corollaries and consequences — who build upon that foundation with building materials unsuited to its true nature will be judged by God (vv. 12-15).

As to the form that judgment will take, the biblical "fire" imagery Paul uses here compares well with that in Mal 4:1-2a. Paul's concern is not to impart precise instruction on "the doctrine of judgment." Rather, in line with the architectural metaphor, and drawing upon the vivid imagery of fiery judgment available to him from scriptural and apocalyptic traditions, he is recalling the Corinthians to the christological and eschatological realities in terms of which he wants them to practice their common life (cf. also 4:5). Those who build on Christ worthily — that is, with the "gold, silver, and precious stones" which in biblical times were used to build the temple (cf. 1 Chr 22:14, 16; 29:2) and which are able to withstand eschatological testing — will be rewarded; but those who build unworthily — that is, with the "wood, hay, and straw" of anthropocentric wisdom vulnerable to eschatological testing — will be judged.

This leads Paul to speak in terms of a third, climactic metaphor, also architectural, but this time of a more specialized kind: the church as God's "temple" — or, more precisely, "sanctuary," since *naos* is used rather than *hieros* (3:16-17). By virtue of its indelible associations with the biblical ideas of the presence of God with Israel and of the temple as an eschatological reality, this metaphor allows Paul to move from talking about types of leadership and practices of community formation to the nature of the community itself. Against the social and religious background of his day, with Gentiles worshiping in temples dedicated variously to a pantheon of gods and Jews worshiping "the one, true God" in the temple in Jerusalem or constituting themselves as an "alternative temple" at Qumran, what Paul says is extraordinary: "Do you [plural] not know that you are God's temple and that God's Spirit dwells in you?" (v. 16). What Paul wants this motley, mixed (and mixed-up!) group to see is that, together, they constitute nothing less than that holy place and/or people where God is present, now at the end of time, as Spirit. The main point is not a general polemic against other claims concerning where God dwells (of the kind found, e.g., in John 4:16-26). Rather, it is a specific corrective to claims by the self-styled "spiritual ones" *(hoi pneumatikoi)* in the fellowship that they alone possess the Spirit. To such as these, Paul reiterates and elaborates the eschatological warning of the immediately preceding verses: God will judge those who destroy (by their "boasting" and rivalry) the fellowship of the believers in Corinth who are "God's building . . . God's temple" (3:9, 16). God will do so because his temple is "holy" *(hagios),* and the Corinthians *in their common identity and common life founded on Christ crucified* are that holy temple (v. 17).

In the light of this warning, Paul now brings the argument begun in 1:18 to a preliminary, but powerful, conclusion (3:18-23). First, in words which recall the argument of 1:18–2:16, he returns to the issue that is threatening to destroy the holy edifice of the Corinthian fellowship: the "wisdom of this world" (3:18-20). "Let no one deceive himself," says Paul. The time has come for self-examination, discernment, and discipline. To be truly wise, those who style themselves "wise" have to become fools. Why? Because, in the light of the folly of the cross (1:18), worldly wisdom is "foolishness with God." And, as on previous occasions (cf. 1:19, 31; 2:9, 16), Paul caps his argument with an appeal to the Scriptures — this time, a twofold citation from the Writings (Job 5:13 and

Ps 94:11) common to which is the theme of God's judgment on human wisdom.

Then he addresses the related issue (cf. 3:1-9) of how the quest for wisdom leads to divisive "boasting" in human leaders rather than in God (vv. 21-23). The argument here is rhetorical and ironic. It is as if Paul is saying: Why boast about human leaders and subject yourself to one or another in factions ("I belong to Paul . . . Apollos . . . Cephas") when you should be united? For, as you so-called "wise" already know, "all things belong to you" — not just Paul or Apollos or Cephas but also the world, life, death, the present, and the future (v. 22)! And why do "all things belong to you" (v. 22b)? Because — and Paul comes to a wonderful doxological climax here — *"you belong to Christ, and Christ belongs to God"* (v. 23). The tragic irony from Paul's viewpoint is that the Corinthians' notion of wisdom, being fundamentally anthropocentric, is too narrow, its horizon too low. Set against a christological and theological horizon, however, things look different, including wisdom itself. Now the claim of the wise person (common also in Stoic and Cynic philosophy) to "possess all things" (cf. 8:1a) is true in ways about which the wise could never have dreamed: because of the saving revelation of a different kind of wisdom — the wisdom of God in the cross of Christ.

Apostleship Reinterpreted (4:1-21)

But Paul has not finished. If he has addressed the ways in which the wisdom ideology in Corinth has divided one group from another within the church itself, now he has to confront the ways in which it has divided the church from its apostle: Paul himself. What follows, then, is direct censure of the Corinthians, as of children by a parent (4:14-15, 21; cf. 3:1-2). And however painful it may have been for Paul to write and the Corinthians to receive, it provides us with unparalleled access to Paul's apostolic self-understanding — to the way in which Paul defines the nature of apostolic authority and exercises it at the same time.

The problem to which Paul is responding surfaces immediately, in 4:1-5. Paul is being "judged" — that is, in the overall game of "boasting" he is being compared unfavorably with other leader figures, most likely Apollos (his more rhetorically sophisticated "fellow worker") in particular (cf. 3:4-6, 22; 4:6). So his authority is at stake, and, along with that, the gospel and the unity of the church. Paul's response is, yet once more, theological and eschatological. Whereas the Corinthians see things primarily in terms of the human and the present, Paul offers them a vision which is transcendental.

First and most importantly, he tries to reorient the Corinthians' understanding of apostleship by offering an alternative way in which both he and Apollos should be regarded: they are not faction-leading *sophoi* after the Corinthian wisdom model but something far more significant — "servants *of Christ* and stewards *of God's mysteries*"; and what is required of them is not personal presence in front of their fellows on the human plane but trustworthiness in relation to Christ their heavenly Lord (4:1-2). This means, second, that the judgment of his apostleship is not the business of any human tribunal; so (while observing nevertheless that he has a clear conscience) Paul refuses even to judge himself (v. 3b). Rather, the only judgment that matters is eschatological. Therefore, no one will be his (and by implication, their) judge but God alone through the agency of the coming Lord (vv. 4-5).

Now, in 4:6-13, comes the censure in its most direct form. Previously (says Paul) he has been referring what he has been saying about church life to himself and Apollos (e.g., 3:5-7; 4:1) in order to teach by their example (of concord and cooperative action) the lesson of the epigram, "Nothing beyond what is written" (4:6a) — a conciliatory principle well known in ancient politics, referring to an agreement between two or more parties as a basis for reconciliation and harmonious relationship (Welborn 1997: 43-76). Hence the purpose clause which follows: "so that none of you will be puffed up *(physiousthe)* in favor of one against another" (4:6b). The verb "puffed up" occurs here for the first, but by no means the last, time (cf. 4:18-19; 5:2; 8:1; 13:4). It refers to what lies at the heart of the Corinthians' problems: the spiritual "inflation" of some (at least) in the church and its divisive consequences, including "boasting" and factional attachment to one apostle over and in opposition to another. The implication that the Corinthians have not learned (the practice of concord) leads to the devastating question of v. 7, to the effect: "Who do you think you are, anyway?" (so Fee 1987: 171). The Corinthians boast of the spiritual possessions they have received; but if they are gifts, what have they to boast about?

The threat to church unity posed by their immature boasting and partisanship is so great that it is time now for confrontation and parent-like admonition. The instrument Paul uses is irony. The irony is built around the well-known rhetorical practice of comparison *(synkrisis)* in which, in the competition between factions, one *sophos* is compared with another to establish who is superior (cf. Mitchell 1992: 219-21). In Paul's admonition, the spiritual exaltation of the Corinthians is compared and contrasted with the material and physical humiliation of their apostle. To assist in his argument, Paul uses a particular rhetorical trope: the catalogue of sufferings *(peristaseis)* cited to demonstrate the integrity and honor of the wise man and the truth of his teaching (cf. Fitzgerald 1988). Paul's purpose is twofold. On the one hand, to confront the Corinthians, in the light of the suffering of *their own* apostles (i.e., Paul himself and Apollos), with the superficiality and destructiveness of the worldly wisdom they espouse; and on the other, to provide them with an alternative and even more honorable example to imitate (cf. 4:16), the consequence of which would be to increase their solidarity with each other and their unity under the apostolic leadership of Paul himself.

The ironic comparison runs from 4:8 to 13 and is tightly organized (in groups of three) for rhetorical effect. First, the Corinthians — reflecting, perhaps, a sense that, because they have "arrived" spiritually, they have become true *sophoi* — boast of their spiritual satiety, wealth, and kingship. By comparison, all Paul can point to, in what is effectively the theme of this section, is how "God has exhibited us apostles as last of all, as though sentenced to death . . . a spectacle to the world, to angels and to mortals" (vv. 8-9). Then comes a second sequence, this time of contrasting pairs, again in a threesome: "We are fools for the sake of Christ, but you are wise in Christ. We are weak, but you are strong. You are held in honor, but we in disrepute" (v. 10). Finally, there comes a catalogue devoted solely to the apostles themselves: "To the present hour we are hungry and thirsty and poorly clothed, and beaten and homeless and weary from the work of our own hands . . ." (vv. 11-13). The use once more of threesomes (apart from the concluding summation) and careful bracketing ("To the present hour . . . to this very day") create a climactic effect and help to make Paul's most important point: *this* is the nature of a truly apostolic existence and, as such, it should be the model for Christian life in Corinth also! If the Corinthians ask why it is truly apostolic, Paul's answer, by analogy with what he has said earlier (in 1:18–2:5), is: because it conforms with the revelation of divine wisdom in the crucified Christ.

What this passage reveals about the nature of Paul's apostolic existence invites special attention (cf. Hock 1980; Meggitt 1998: 75-97), for here we have — admittedly in a rhetorical form — unique autobiographical testimony. The picture we get is one of overwhelming hardship, poverty, and vulnerability, augmented by the humiliations associated with ostracism, punishment, and persecution (4:11-13). The language Paul uses is very strong, especially in a milieu sensitive to considerations of personal honor and shame (Moxnes 1996). The other catalogues of suffering bear this picture out (cf. 2 Cor 4:8-9; 6:3-10; 11:23-29; 12:10), as does the testimony of Acts (e.g., 13:44-52; 14:1-7, 19-20; 16:19-40). No wonder that boasting (except ironically and subversively) is excluded! For the reality is nothing to boast about. In human terms, the reality is existence at the level of a slave (cf. 9:19), with an untimely and degrading death the only certainty. This is sobering; but it is also the basis for a claim to honor of a different kind. In particular, it casts apostleship and (by extension) church leadership and Christian discipleship *in the light of the cross of Christ* — something those in Corinth who boast in their superiority and the superiority of their apostle find almost impossible to acknowledge.

What Paul says next (4:14-21) concludes both the direct admonition and the first section of his argument in the letter as a whole (1:18–4:21). His words are intended to be reassuring and firm at the same time: "I am not writing this to make you ashamed, but to admonish you as my beloved children" (4:14). His authority for so doing is then made clear. Although the Corinthians may have "countless guardians," they do not have "many fathers," since he alone "fathered" them "in Christ Jesus" through the preaching of the gospel (v. 15). The metaphor of paternity here is significant and is part of a wider network of metaphors of parenting and nurturing which Paul uses elsewhere (e.g., 3:1-2; cf. 1 Thess 2:7b, 11-12). In the context of patriarchy in antiquity, it is a metaphor of authority with its consequent rights and responsibilities (cf. Pilch 1993). Its function here is basically threefold: to unify (as under one "father") a group behaving like quarrelsome children; to insure a hospitable reception for Paul's "beloved and faithful *child*" Timothy, sent to remind them of Paul's teaching and example (4:17); and also to underpin Paul's implied threat to come to discipline them (4:21) — something quite consonant with traditional wisdom teaching about the role of a father toward his children (cf. Sir 30:1-13).

At the heart of this concluding section is the command, "Be imitators of me" (4:16). It is introduced by the significant words, "I appeal to you," words which unite the end of this first part of Paul's argument with the beginning (1:10). There Paul appealed for unity; here Paul shows how unity will be attained — by the *imitation* of their fatherly apostle. Not for the last time, Paul puts himself forward as a model to be imitated, an example to follow (see 11:1; cf. also 1 Thess 1:6; 2:14). If this were arrogance on Paul's part (as some take it to be), then Paul would be undermining the very attitudes and practices he is trying to counteract. But it is something quite different (cf. Witherington 1995: 145-46 *contra* Castelli 1991). First, imitation of the wise man was recognized by contemporary moralists (like Plutarch and Seneca) as a basic way of learning wisdom; so the command to self-imitation was the *duty* of a responsible father, teacher, and leader. Second, Paul has made clear already in the "catalogue of suffering" the sacrificial nature of his apostolic lifestyle and practice; so imitation is a matter of learning, not to rule but to serve (cf. 3:5; 4:1), and it is intended for the advantage not of the few but of the many (cf. 10:31–11:1). Congruent with this, and as becomes explicit in 11:1, the imitation of Paul is of a quite particular kind: its focus is not Paul per se but Paul as himself an "imitator *of Christ*."

Finally, Paul turns to his own anticipated visit (cf. also 16:5-9). In context, this is to be understood as like the visit of a father to his children. Implied is the idea that (like the parousia of Christ) the coming of the apostle will be a time for judgment, reward, and punishment. The judgment will involve the testing of what lies at the heart of the opposition to Paul in Corinth (cf. 1:17; 2:1-5) — *logos* (i.e., worldly wisdom rhetorically displayed), as defined by those he calls the "arrogant ones" (4:18, 19; cf. 4:6). What Paul will be looking for, however, is not worldly wisdom but power *(dynamis)* as a manifestation of the eschatological reality of "the kingdom of God" (4:20; cf. 6:9-10; 15:24, 50). This is a clear warning to those who are "acting up." The choice is theirs: "What would you prefer? Am I to come to you with a stick, or with love in a spirit of gentleness?" (4:21). The "stick" is a symbol, not (as we moderns might think) of physical abuse, but of parental authority (over adult children as well as infants) and the duty of discipline. But Paul's own preference is clearly for "love in a spirit of gentleness." That is consistent with his advocacy of the way of love elsewhere in the letter as the best way both to overcome strife and division and to "build up" the Corinthians' common life (cf. 8:1; 13:1-13; 14:1; 16:14, 24).

Preserving the Holiness of the Church (5:1–11:1)

We have seen in the first major section of the letter (1:18–4:21) that Paul grapples with the threat to the church's common life arising from Corinthian factionalism, itself a manifestation of a particular, anthropocentric ideal of "wisdom." He does so by showing how God's call to be the new covenant people requires the radical transformation of wisdom in the light of the gospel, an argument he advances in both fundamental theological terms and by appeal to exemplary apostolic practice. The second major section (5:1–11:1) takes this argument a stage further. Here Paul deals with particular problems in the church's life which have come to his attention (cf. 5:1; 7:1), problems related primarily to the nature of Christian existence in the world. These he confronts, not as isolated "pastoral problems," but as specific manifestations of the same basic issue: *the transformation of individual and corporate life which living according to the gospel requires.*

To put it another way, it is not the case that chs. 1–4 lay the theological "foundations" and chs. 5–11 (or 5–16) constitute the ethical "application." It is impossible to separate Paul's theology and ethics in this way. Indeed, it is misleading and, in its tendency to reduce theology to a kind of disembodied "spiritual insight," probably has more in common with the kind of position in Corinth to which Paul is opposed. But why is it misleading? First, such a distinction is alien to the way Paul argues, where, as 1 Corinthians shows from beginning to end, talk of God and the practices of life are intertwined inextricably with a view to encouraging and shaping *a whole way of life* (cf. Engberg-Pedersen 1987). Second, such a distinction distorts our understanding of what Paul says. For example, cut off from the vocation to be the faithful people of God, what Paul says about (what we call) "sexual morality" (in 1 Corinthians 5–7) is in danger of being interpreted as a matter of personal morality in the realm of private behavior when, as we shall see, it is a matter of social morality and public witness.

The subjects Paul deals with in this section are basically twofold: how to avoid "sexual immorality" *(porneia)* (1 Corinthians 5–7) and how to avoid idolatry *(idōlolatria)* (1 Corinthians 8–10). These at first sight unrelated topics are in fact related closely, both to what Paul has said in 1 Corinthians 1–4 and to each other (cf. Mitchell 1992: 225-28). They relate to what has come before, in that sexual immorality and idolatry — apparently tolerated or at least understood differently within the more cosmopolitan "wisdom" of the Corinthians — constitute fundamental threats to the unity and growth of the Christian fellowship which Paul is doing his utmost to preserve (cf. 1:10). They relate to each other in that, within the tradition and logic of biblical law and Israelite life, avoidance of sexual immorality and idolatry is paradigmatic of what it means to be Israel, God's faithful covenant people who refrain from "whoring" after other gods (cf. Jer 3:1-5; Ezekiel 16; 23; Hos 4:12; 5:4; also Rosner 1994: 126-37). Furthermore, within the context of Paul's argument in the letter as a whole, Paul's aim in 5:1–11:1 is to encourage a marriage discipline and a cultic discipline which will strengthen both the internal cohesion of the church and the boundaries between the church and society at large (cf. Meeks 1983: 84-107). The effect of this, in turn, will be intramural and extramural: it will strengthen the unity of the church itself, and it will strengthen the witness of the church to those outside.

Marriage Discipline and the Holiness of the Church (5:1–7:40)

In 5:1–7:40, Paul addresses a range of issues: a case of incest in the fellowship (5:1-13); the practice of taking private disputes before the public courts (6:1-11); the practice of consorting with prostitutes (6:12-20); and matters relating to singleness and marriage (7:1-40). Several factors link these apparently disparate issues together. They all have to do with (1) real or potential threats to the unity and growth of the church posed by members' behavior; (2) the avoidance of *porneia* and related sins (cf. 5:1, 9-11; 6:13, 18; 7:2); (3) the "crisis of authority" in Corinth provoked by those who are "puffed up" (cf. 5:2), not least, against Paul (so Fee 1987: 194-96); and (4) regulating the boundaries of the church in such a way as to make possible, for the good of the church, the clear identification of "who's in" and "who's out."

Responding to Sex-Rule Transgression in the Church (5:1-13)

Paul turns first to a case of some notoriety: "It is actually reported that there is sexual immorality *(porneia)* among you, and of a kind that is not found even among pagans [i.e., Gentiles]; for a man is living with his father's wife. And you are arrogant!" (5:1-2a). Behind Paul's acute anxiety here lie both biblical law prohibiting incest ("Cursed be anyone who lies with his father's wife"; Deut 27:20; cf. Lev 18:8; 20:11) and prohibitions in Greco-Roman society at large (for details of which see Talbert 1987: 12-14). In relation to these prohibitions, it is clear that the offender has placed himself outside the bounds both of God's covenant with Israel as inscribed in Torah and of wider societal norms. To use Paul's own terms (cf. 10:32), he has become a cause of offense to both Jews and Greeks.

Interestingly, Paul does not dwell in his response on the sexual nature of the sin (as if it were just a matter of individual morality) but on its social character and consequences and how the society of Christians is to respond. This is characteristic of the more general point that *Paul's sexual ethics are part of his social ethics.* For Paul, the incest threatens the boundary between the church and the world. Along with the "arrogance" and "boasting" (5:2, 6) which accompany it and which reveal a lamentable vacuum in the authority of the community, the incest represents a very serious invasion of the church by destructive practices associated for Paul with demonic forces (cf. v. 5) which could undermine church life as a whole.

Thus radical surgery on the Corinthian body corporate is required. Four times Paul drives home the action he wants carried out: the offender is to be expelled from the fellowship (5:2, 5, 7, 13). This is to be done in a responsible manner in the formal gathering of believers acting (with a proper, quasi-judicial authority and with the apostle present in spirit) to ratify the decision already made by the apostle (5:3-5). Nor is any explicit provision made for the forgiveness and restitution of the offender (although cf. 2 Cor 2:5-11; also Matt 18:15-35; John 20:23). It is as if the sin of *porneia* is so serious a threat to the harmonious life and good reputation of the Christian fellowship that permanent exclusion is the only solution. It may also be that the offender is a man of wealth and status, a patron and benefactor — one of the "strong" perhaps (cf. 4:10) — whose influence, were he readmitted, is likely to be detrimental (cf. Chow 1992: 130-41; Clarke 1993: 89-107). Not that the intention of the disciplinary action is retributive only: Paul's perspective is consistently eschatological — "you are to hand this man over to Satan for the destruction of the flesh, so that his spirit may be saved in the day of the Lord" (5:5). This implies that any restitution, if it happens at all, is left to God: by expelling the man from the church into Satan's sphere of influence, the man's inclination to sin (his "flesh") will be destroyed and his life ("spirit"), thus purified, will be saved at the Day of Judgment (cf. 1 Tim 1:20).

The disciplinary action is directed not just at the individual offender, however. His failure is shared by the Corinthians as a whole on account of their easy tolerance of the incestuous relation in their midst, a tolerance which has made them complicitous. Hence: "Your boasting *(kauchēma)* is not a good thing" (5:6a; cf. 3:21; 4:7). Their attachment to "the wise" has blocked them from perceiving the threat to their common life posed by the contagious *porneia* in their midst. Their individualistic understanding of Christian freedom *(eleutheria)* (cf. 6:12; 10:29) has blunted their responsible exercise of moral discrimination. As a corrective, therefore, Paul offers (stern) fatherly instruction from the Scriptures and Jewish liturgy. The Corinthians are to see themselves in the light of the Passover, itself the biblical paradigm of *true* freedom (5:6-8). They are the batch of dough for the Passover bread from which every bit of leaven has to be excluded (cf. Exod 12:15). What is more, they have been marked out as God's chosen people by the sacrifice of Christ, "our paschal lamb" (cf. Exod 12:3-7). So they are to live as God's chosen people, not with "malice and evil," but with "sincerity and truth."

Finally, he reminds them of instruction he has given in a previous letter (which instruction some have identified with 2 Cor 6:14–7:1) on the importance of not "mixing" with people who are sexually immoral (5:9). But now he introduces a qualification: "But now I am writing to you not to associate with anyone *who bears the name of brother or sister* who is sexually immoral. . . . Do not even eat with such a one" (vv. 10-11). In terms of Paul's boundary-marking concern, this qualification is significant. Paul is drawing a boundary *around* the fellowship by drawing a line *through* it, as if to say: "Once you get your internal relations sorted out, the external ones will take care of themselves."

Interestingly, in contrast to the Qumran Covenanters who separated themselves from their fellow Jews and went to live in the desert, Paul does not advocate wholesale separation, even from Gentiles. For Paul, it is important neither to go "out of the world" (like the Qumran sect) nor to become the world (by tolerating the presence in the fellowship of a notoriously immoral person). What is important is to live counterculturally in the world *as a "mixed" society of a different kind:* where Jews and Gentiles, rich and poor, strong and weak constitute together God's new people, those whom he will describe later on as "the body of Christ" (12:27).

In sum, Paul's concern is to strengthen the unity of this radically new kind of society (the church) by clarifying its boundaries and empowering it to remove serious anomalies. The list of those to be excluded extends beyond the immediate case and is worth noting: "anyone who bears the name of brother or sister who is sexually immoral or greedy, or is an idolater, reviler, drunkard, or robber" (5:11; cf. v. 10). Here we note the linking of sexual immorality and idolatry which prepares the way for the transition later on (in 8:1–11:1) to the issue of "things offered to idols" *(eidōlothyta)*. Significant also is the sequence, according to which reference to the sexually immoral person is followed by reference to the "greedy" *(pleonektēs)* person, a connection which may help to explain the transition to matters having to do with litigation in the courts in 6:1-11, as we shall see. Also important is the resonance of this list (noted by Rosner 1994: 68-70; also Hays 1997: 87-88) with passages in the book of Deuteronomy (e.g., Deut 22:22) devoted to sins which call for capital punishment as the means to "purge the evil from your midst" (the same exclusion formula that Paul uses at the climax of his argument, in 5:13b). As with the lesson Paul draws from the symbolism of the Jewish Passover liturgy (vv. 6-8), the appeal here to vice lists which resonate with Israel's scriptures shows once again how concerted is Paul's attempt to convert the Corinthians to a different kind of wisdom expressive of a covenantal self-understanding and a holy lifestyle.

On Not Settling Private Disputes in Public (6:1-11)

Paul's handling of the case of incest presupposes that marriage rules and the avoidance of *porneia* have a paradigmatic significance for the right ordering of a society's (including the church's) common life. It also presupposes that the church itself as God's covenant people is called to exercise corporate responsibility for the correction and discipline of its members' lives. Drawing proper lines through the church in the form of rules and ordered practices is a way of drawing proper boundaries around the church such that the identity and unity of the church are preserved while at the same time its openness and witness to the world are enabled.

This helps to explain the otherwise surprising shift Paul makes from the case of incest to the issue of taking private cases before the public courts. The main connection is this: if the case of incest involves Paul in bringing the Corinthians to take responsibility for their *internal* affairs by judging and expelling the offending member (cf. 5:12b-13a), then what are they doing taking any cases at all *outside* their own jurisdiction (6:1-11)? But there is another link. A plausible case can be made for the view that the case of the incestuous marriage involves not just a sexual tie but a *property* tie as well, having to do with matters of dowry and inheritance (cf. Chow 1992: 123-41). The offender is not only immoral but greedy: he has married for financial gain and the security and social advantage that go with it. In passing, this would explain why, in the lists of vices in 5:10 and 11, "sexual immorality" (i.e., marrying within the laws of prohibited degrees) is followed immediately by "greed." It is not at all impossible, then, that the lawsuits referred to in 6:1-11 are related in some measure to conflicting property interests arising out of the case of incest and others like it.

It is significant, however, that Paul refrains from naming names and engaging with the details of particular cases — which is why, of course, attempts to reconstruct the precise situation have to remain tentative. What is important, from Paul's point of view, is how to enable the Corinthians, *with reference to a larger theological and eschatological horizon,* to evaluate and change their current practices for settling internal disputes in ways that will consolidate the authority and life of the church rather than undermine it. The way Paul does this is to argue that settling private disputes in public courts is a contradiction of who they are as believers and of what it means to be the church. It is to act as if being a Christian makes no difference to social practice; indeed, as if the church is just another sphere where worldly practices can be applied and personal advantage gained.

Thus, making deliberate use of scriptural language of separation and distinction, Paul does everything possible to persuade the Corinthians to see themselves differently: "When any of you has a grievance against another, do you dare to take it to court before the *unrighteous,* instead of taking it before the *saints?*" (6:1). As early as 1:2, Paul has addressed the Corinthians as people "called to be saints"; therefore (Paul implies), how can you make the absurd category mistake of submitting to the judgment of the *adikoi* ("unrighteous") and the *apistoi* ("unbelievers") (6:1, 6)? What is more, this lamentable lack of self-understanding is compounded by the limits of their eschatological understanding (vv. 2-3). The point here is not a matter of eschatology "in the abstract," however, but of the *authority* that their identity as "saints" and their eschatological hope bestow upon them. If they are saints and if they are to judge the world and angels, then why do they not exercise that authority already, in their own fellowship?

The issue is serious. Previously, Paul refrains from "shaming" them (4:14). But now he says, "I say this to your shame" (6:5a). The church's litigious disunity is threatening its unity as an eschatological family (or brotherhood) and compromising its witness to outsiders (cf. 14:23-25). What they should do in practice (Paul implies) is what is recommended in Scripture: appoint judges from among themselves to settle disputes (cf. Deut 1:9-18; 16:18-20). This was the practice at Qumran (cf. 1QS) and in the communities of the Jewish diaspora. It was common practice also in the cult groups and voluntary associations in the cities of the empire. That the Christians in Corinth have not adopted a similar practice shows how weak are its boundaries and sense of a common life.

But Paul goes one step further: "In fact, to have lawsuits at all with one another is already a defeat for you. Why not rather be wronged? Why not rather be defrauded?" (6:7-8). The radicalism of this challenge is easily overlooked. Lying behind what Paul says may be the well-known teaching of Socrates that it is better to suffer wrong than to do it: in which case the Corinthians are shown once again to be not as "wise" as they think they are (Hays 1997: 95-96). But also in the background is the challenge of the "hidden wisdom" of Paul's own practice — "when reviled, we bless; when persecuted, we endure; when slandered, we speak kindly" (4:12-13) — practice itself in creative fidelity with that of the crucified Christ whom Paul preaches. So the Corinthians' behavior measures up neither to the best of pagan wisdom nor to the example of Paul in imitation of Christ. Rather, what Paul implies in 6:7-10 is that by having recourse to public litigation in the courts, the Corinthians inevitably get caught up in a system which (due to the baneful influence of patronage and bribery) is corrupt and corrupting (cf. Chow 1992: 123-30; Winter 1994: 105-21).

This leads to the severe eschatological warning that "wrongdoers *(adikoi)* will not inherit the kingdom of God" (6:9; cf. v. 10b). That is how seriously Paul takes the Corinthians' practice. By going outside the fellowship for justice, they are not only denying who (eschatologically speaking) they really are; they are also becoming perpetrators of injustice in a system which is corrupt, and therefore placing themselves outside the sphere of divine grace and salvation.

The list of *adikoi* ("unrighteous") in 6:10 compares closely with the lists occurring previously in 5:10 and 11. Noteworthy additions, especially in view of the appeal to these texts in Christian discussions of sexual morality (cf. Hays 1996: 379-406; Thiselton 1997), are "male prostitutes" *(malakoi)* and "sodomites" *(arsenokoitai)* (so NRSV). The precise meaning of these terms is disputed (Winter 1997a). *Malakoi* literally means "soft ones" and may refer to young boys in pederastic relationships with older men, or to males who play the "passive" (feminine) role in a homoerotic relation. *Arsenokoitai* occurs nowhere else in extant Greek texts prior to its occurrence here (and in 1 Tim 1:10); it is almost certainly a coinage drawn from Lev 18:22 and 20:13 in the LXX ("You shall not lie with a man as with a woman [*meta arsenos koitēn gynaikos*]: it is an abomination"). It may be the antonym of *malakos* and refer to a male who plays an "active" (masculine) role in a homoerotic relation. Whatever the precise nuances, these additions clearly reflect the strong scriptural and Jewish condemnation of homoeroticism (cf. also Rom 1:24-27), a hostility shared by many in Roman society as well. Their significance here is that they constitute a way of characterizing those whose lawless behavior puts them outside the covenant community. In other words, the list is a *boundary marker* for people whose sense of boundaries is (from Paul's perspective) alarmingly weak. Its intention is to warn the Corinthians who they are in danger of becoming or reverting to (cf. 6:11a) if they get drawn (back) into public litigation and the culture surrounding it.

As a counterbalance, and to remind the Corinthians (once more — cf. 1:2, 30; 3:16-17) who they really are in virtue of their conversion and baptism, Paul states emphatically (with three strong "buts"): "But you were washed, but you were sanctified, but you were justified in the name of the Lord Jesus Christ and in the Spirit of our God" (6:11b). It is a climactic, theological, identity-transforming ending intended to act as a bulwark against the tendency of the Corinthians to revert to their old identity and former practices.

Sex-Rule Transgression Again (6:12-20)

To press home his argument, Paul turns to another practice of *porneia* which, like the case of incest and recourse to the public courts, threatens the ordered life and corporate responsibility of the church: recourse to prostitutes (for background on which see Ford 1993). That such a practice is tolerated in the church reflects the extent to which the sexual mores of the wider society continue to provide the norms for church members — especially Gentile males of means and leisure. In passing, the strong likelihood that Paul's argument in these and subsequent chapters is directed primarily (but not solely) at leading *men* in the church is worth noting, given the oft-made complaint about what Paul says to restrain the freedom of the Corinthian *women* later on (cf. 11:2-16; 14:33b-36). There as here, Paul's primary concern is the regulation and boundary maintenance of the church by the church and its apostle.

In a rhetorical style indebted to the diatribe, Paul begins by dealing with the slogans which have come to his attention, first quoting them (apparently approvingly) and then offering a further consideration which amounts to a qualification or correction (6:12-14; cf. other probable slogans in 7:1; 8:1, 4, 8; 10:23; 15:24). From what Paul says, we may infer that, in each case, the imagined interlocutors belong to the so-called "wise" and boast in a spiritual freedom which allows them to do whatever they like with their bodies. This "freedom" *(eleutheria)* may be a doctrine indebted to various philosophical schools, such as the Stoics and Epicureans. It may owe something also to an interpretation of Paul's own teaching on the believer's freedom from "the works of the law" (cf. Gal 3:10-14; and Dunn 1990: 215-41), an interpretation which, by its one-sided stress on new life "in the Spirit," leads in an antinomian (i.e., lawless) direction. Whatever the precise background, the consequences for the identity and authority of the community have been overlooked by the Corinthians, and a corrective is needed.

Hence, to those who say "all things are lawful," Paul replies, "but not all things are beneficial *(sympherei),*" that is, for the good of the individual or of the fellowship as a whole — a practical, community-building consideration common in the teaching of the sophists and used by Paul elsewhere (esp. 12:7). To those who reiterate, "all things are lawful," Paul replies (in the authoritative apostolic first person), "but I will not be dominated by anything"; that is, even if I have rights as a "free" person, I do not have to exercise them (especially if it is at some others' expense) — a point on which he will elaborate at length in 1 Corinthians 9. Then again, to those who say, "Food is meant for the stomach and the stomach for food, and God will destroy both one and the other," Paul replies, "The body is meant not for fornication *(porneia)* but for the Lord, and the Lord for the body. And God raised the Lord and will also raise us by his power"; that is, our resurrection faith — because it is founded upon the *bodily* resurrection of Christ (elaborated further in 1 Corinthians 15) — commits us to the ongoing moral value of *embodied* existence.

Paul drives this point home with three rhetorical questions beginning, "Do you not know . . . ?" (6:15, 16, 19), each of which takes further what it means to say that "the body is . . . for the Lord" (v. 13b). Underlying all three is the biblical notion of *holiness.* This becomes explicit with the metaphor of the body as a "temple of the Holy Spirit" in the third and final question (v. 19). Important in biblical holiness is the idea of not mixing categories which are incompatible (e.g., Leviticus 11; Deuteronomy 14; cf. Jenson 1992). That helps to explain the force of the first two questions. In the first, Paul asks, "If your bodies are members of Christ, how can you allow them to become members of a prostitute?" Here the Corinthians fail to take their relation to Christ seriously enough, that is, as taking precedence over all other relations and, indeed, as precluding relations which involve *porneia.* In the second question Paul asks, "How can you be united as 'one flesh' with a prostitute when you are united already as 'one spirit' to the Lord?" In this case, the Corinthians fail to understand fully the nature of the sexual relation (even with a prostitute) — namely, that (as Scripture says, in Gen 2:24) it involves the two becoming "one flesh," an intimate union incompatible with the believer's intimate, "one spirit" union with the Lord. On the grounds of this incompatibility of unions, Paul states emphatically a command fully in tune with biblical morality as a whole, "Shun fornication *(porneia)*!" (6:18a; cf. Gen 39:12).

This makes way for the climactic final question in 6:19. Previously, Paul has used the "temple" *(naos)* metaphor of the Corinthians as a body corporate (3:16-17); now he uses it of the Corinthian bodies individually. What is true of the Corinthians together is true of them individually also: their bodies are holy because they have become places where the *Holy* Spirit is present. But some of the Corinthians are behaving as if this is not so, and in so doing they are polluting and destroying the whole. So, says Paul, "You are not your own. For you were bought with a price" (6:19b-20). This is the language of slavery, used provocatively — in stark contrast with the opening slogan (of the Corinthian "strong") proclaiming freedom — to remind them to whom they belong and therefore who they really are (6:12; cf. 7:22-23; 9:19). And since God has bought them at the cost of his Son in death, they are under obligation to render to God his due: "Glorify God in your body" (6:20b). Here is the basis for a sexual morality (and therefore a social morality) which neither denigrates the body as worthless nor exalts the body as the only worthwhile thing but in which bodily relations are ordered toward their true end: the glory of the God who raised Christ bodily and will raise our bodies also "by his power."

Marriage Rules (7:1-40)

As the final stage in his instruction on how to avoid the *porneia* threatening the life of the church as a holy society (cf. 7:2), Paul turns to matters having to do with marriage and singleness, matters which have been raised in a letter from the Corinthians themselves (7:1a, 25; cf. 8:1; 12:1; 16:1). It is noteworthy that Paul deals with these matters at length. If we ask why, the answer must be Paul's awareness that, unless the Corinthians can learn stability and good order in their marital relations, the good order and witness of the church will be undermined (cf. 1 Thess 4:1-8; also 1 Pet 3:1-7). Two major traditions will have shaped this awareness (cf. Meeks 1986): the commonplace of Greco-Roman morality and politics that the health of the city-state *(polis)* depends on the health of its constituent households *(oikiai),* and the attention given in the Jewish scriptures to the practical and symbolic significance of marriage and sex rules for marking Israel off from "the nations" as God's holy people.

But what is making marriage rules an issue in the first place? In general terms, it is the impact of conversion upon every other pattern of allegiance, including that of the household (cf. Gal 3:26-28; Gordon 1997). Now the believer's allegiances, whether as married or betrothed, are "divided" (cf. 7:32-35). So questions naturally arise about how to proceed, not least in basic social matters like sex and marriage (and, as we will see later, food and meal practices). But the question in Corinth has taken a particular shape. Indicative of the problem is the slogan Paul cites at the outset: "'It is well for a man not to touch [i.e., have sexual relations with] a woman'" (7:1b). Apparently, some of the men in the fellowship are withdrawing from sexual relations with their wives. In other words, while some are expressing their spiritual "freedom" by going with prostitutes (cf. 6:12-20), others are withdrawing from sexual relations altogether, even within marriage. This seemingly contradictory behavior may have a common root. The issue at stake is *the status of the body and the material world* in the lives of Spirit-filled believers (cf. Martin 1995). Given the overwhelming reality of experiences of Spirit-possession (cf. 4:8; 12:13), the meaning of the body and bodily existence (including marriage and sexual relations) changes, becomes incidental even: so the body can be used either promiscuously or ascetically.

Several other factors are likely to have encouraged the ascetic trend in particular. First, the ideal wise man in Stoic and Cynic philosophy is one who disciplines his body by abstaining from marriage and sexual relations. By so doing, he remains "free" from the troublesome desires and worldly distractions which inhibit the pursuit and practice of wisdom. Such a model must have been attractive to the self-styled "wise" in Corinth (cf. Balch 1983; Yarbrough 1985: 31-63). Second, there are also ascetic strands in Judaism. Philo, himself influenced by Platonic body-soul dualism, speaks enthusiastically and at length about the ascetic lifestyles of the Essenes and the Therapeutae; and some, at least, of the apocalyptically minded Qumran Community refrained from marriage and adopted a life of ascetic rigor in view of the need for priestly holiness as God's elect in the "last days" (cf. Barton 1997c: 81-100). Third, there are ascetic strands in the Christian tradition itself. Jesus tradition speaks of those who "neither marry nor are given in marriage" (Luke 20:34-36) and of those who "make themselves eunuchs for the sake of the kingdom of God" (Matt 19:10-12); and, perhaps most significantly, Paul himself (in contrast to Peter and the other apostles [1 Cor 9:5]) remains unmarried and commends celibacy, as 1 Corinthians 7 itself attests (at vv. 6, 38). Little wonder, then, that influential men in the church at Corinth — and women also, especially the women prophets (cf. 11:2-16) — are pursuing the ideal of celibacy! Here is an obvious way of demonstrating their newly found freedom and authority "in the Spirit."

How does Paul respond to the threat this poses to the fellowship's common life? Most important is the way he refuses to allow the practice of the celibate elite to be imposed as the rule: he quotes their slogan (perhaps with approval) in order then to qualify the ascetic ideal in a direction accessible to the majority. Correspondingly, he does not impose his own preference for celibacy (and singleness) either (7:6-7a). What is important is not the imposition of human will (in the guise of "wisdom") but the affirmation of diversity arising out of what comes from God *as gift* (v. 7b). This is one of a number of cases where Paul insists upon legitimate diversity and the recognition of real difference within the church — something upon which he elaborates at length in terms of the metaphor of the church as "the body of Christ" in 1 Corinthians 12. Unlike some in Corinth, Paul recognizes that harmony and group cohesion are attained by fostering the diversity which comes from the Spirit, not by the egotistical imposition of uniformity. Note, then, that *Paul's pneumatology and ecclesiology play a very large part in his instructions on marriage.* It is a matter of putting the gendered, sexuate body in the right context.

Another point worth noting is that Paul enunciates as a general principle the virtue of stability (cf. *menein,* "to remain," in 7:8, 11, 20, 24, 40) and its corollary, peace (*eirēnē:* v. 15b): each church member should remain in the social (and marital) status in which God has called him or her. The widowed should not seek remarriage (7:8; cf. also vv. 32-38, 39-40). The married should not separate (vv. 10, 11b). Believers in "mixed" marriages should not leave their unbelieving partners unless forced to do so (vv. 12-16). "Virgins" (i.e., the unmarried) should remain single (vv. 25-31). And, as analogies, the circumcised should not seek to change their status as circumcised, and likewise the uncircumcised (vv. 18-19); nor should slaves be preoccupied with their status as slaves (vv. 21-23). The general principle is so important to Paul that he enunciates it three times: "let each of you lead the life that the Lord has assigned, to which God called you. This is my rule in all the churches" (v. 17; cf. vv. 20, 24). Why the principle of stability? On the one hand, this is a way of achieving order in a group threatened by disorder — or, to nuance the position slightly, this is a strategy for moderating the pace of change in a group faced with the considerable social and cultic novelty which characterized it already. On the other hand, this is a strategy consistent with Paul's strong sense of divine presence and historical contingency: since they are living at the turn of the ages (cf. vv. 29, 31), what is important is not worrying about social status (Jew/Gentile, slave/free, male/female) but devotion to Christ.

This relates to yet another feature of Paul's response: his attempt (once again) to offer a more adequate theological and eschatological framework within which the Corinthians may think and act. The elements which make up this framework are many and various. There is the warning that lack of "self-control" in sexual relations makes men and women vulnerable to satanic temptation (7:5b); appeal to dominical tradition to counter the trend toward divorce (vv. 10, 11b; cf. Mark 10:2-12); reflection on the sanctification of children effected (by God) through the believing partner in a "mixed" marriage, as a motivation for remaining together (7:14); appeal to divine providence as a "gift" and "call" in order to allay personal anxieties about identity and status (vv. 17-24); remembrance of Christ's death as what defines value in human life (vv. 22-23); focus on eschatological hope as a basis for appropriate detachment from worldly commitments (vv. 25-31); appeal to what "pleases the Lord" and life "in the Lord" as the orientation in terms of which decisions about singleness and marriage need to be made (vv. 32-35, 39-40); and, last but not least, appeal (ironic but serious also) to Spirit-possession as Paul's basis for claiming authority as a prophet and teacher in the fellowship (v. 40b).

What, then, are Paul's "marriage rules" (for detailed and different treatments, see Deming 1995 and Gordon 1997)? First, for husbands and wives (7:2-7): in view of the threat of *porneia,* they are to maintain sexual relations. They are to do so by mutual consent and in full recognition of the reciprocal "authority" *(exousia)* of the one partner in relation to the other (vv. 2-4). Any withdrawal — and this by way of concession — should be by mutual consent, for a limited time only, and for a spiritual purpose ("to devote yourselves to prayer"). But after that, "come together again, so that Satan may not tempt you because of your lack of self-control" (v. 5). Remarkable here, given the patriarchal values of Paul's day (and the modern apprehension of Paul as a misogynist), is the relatively egalitarian way in which Paul addresses both marriage partners in turn, even to the extent of saying: "likewise the husband does not have authority over his own body, but the wife does" (v. 4b). Remarkable also (again given the modern apprehension of Paul as "anti-sex") is the absence of prudery and the frank recognition of the importance of the sexual relation for the maintenance of marriage and as a prophylactic against the temptation of fornication (v. 5; cf. vv. 9b, 28).

Second, for widowers (rather than "unmarried," as the NRSV) and widows: they are to remain as they are, in imitation of Paul (a widower himself?). But if they cannot practice that "self-control" *(enkrateia)* so valued by the Stoics and apparently by Paul also, they should remarry (7:8-9). Likewise, the married should remain as they are. In obedience to the Lord's prohibition on divorce, they should not separate. But if the wife does separate from her husband, she must either remain single (and devoted to the Lord, so as not to commit *porneia*) or "be reconciled" to her husband (vv. 10-11). Even in the particularly difficult case of a "mixed" marriage, the believing partner should remain, on the ground that the believing partner "sanctifies" the other members of his or her household. But if the unbelieving partner separates, "let it be so; in such a case the brother or sister is not bound [since] it is to peace that God has called you" (vv. 12-16). In passing, it is worth noting that each time Paul enunciates a rule here, he also makes allowance for an exception (at vv. 9, 11, 15), even an exception to the dominical command prohibiting divorce (v. 11)! Just as Paul does not want the Corinthians to be enslaved by freedom (6:12), neither does he want them to be enslaved by rules.

But what of the "virgins" (*parthenoi;* RSV, "unmarried") (7:25-38)? Probably, these are unmarried young women betrothed in marriage who, together with all the other household members involved (especially the significant males — father and fiancé), are unsure how to proceed in view of their conversion, Spirit-possession and new status as "sisters" to their Christian (including affianced) "brothers." In brief, should unmarried believers proceed to marriage, in accordance with well-established cultural norms and expectations, or remain as "sisters" and "brothers" (cf. Gordon 1997)? Paul's response on the situation of the unmarried is consistent with his rulings on the married (in 7:2-16). Once again, the pattern is one of the general rule ("remain as you are") followed by allowance for an exception ("but if a virgin marries, she does not sin") (vv. 26b, 28a). This is followed by a series of arguments in favor of remaining unmarried, arguments which subtly combine Jewish-Christian imminent-end eschatology with motifs from Stoic and Cynic teaching on the need for the truly wise person to remain "undistracted" by worldly attachments and "free from care" in his or her mission as a "messenger of the gods" (vv. 29-35; and Deming 1995: 173-205). The overall thrust of Paul's advice comes at the end: "So then, he who marries his fiancée [lit. virgin] does well; and he who refrains from marriage will do better" (v. 38).

What is noteworthy about this instruction is that, while it seeks to promote what will bring "benefit" and "good order" (7:35), it is far from being socially conservative, in the sense of reverting to the patriarchal status quo. Paul's anxiety about *porneia* does not lead him to a "knee-jerk" reaction of insisting on "marriage and family life" as *the* way to live as Christians in the world. The call to "remain as you are," for example, is, in the case of the *parthenoi,* a call to remain in the socially *exceptional* state of being unmarried — hence "he who refrains from marriage will do better" (v. 38b). What Paul's views express is an underlying idea that *exceptional times require exceptional lifestyles.* Some of these may appear "conventional," as with the married who remain married and maintain sexual relations (but now with a degree of reciprocity between the sexes unusual for the times!). Others will appear "unconventional," as in the case of the apostle who refrains from going accompanied by a wife (cf. 9:5), or the widowed who remain single rather than remarrying, or the betrothed who do not proceed to marriage but remain unmarried. What is important for Paul, however, is neither conventionality nor unconventionality, but wholehearted and responsible commitment to the Lord at the turn of the ages in whatever condition and status believers find themselves. As a corollary, what is important also is resistance to pressures from the ascetically minded elite to advocate and adopt — and in the name of "wisdom" and "freedom"! — only one pattern of life as legitimate. That explains why the thrust of Paul's instruction overall is in the direction, not of reducing options, but of increasing them and (by introducing exceptions, opinions, and qualifications) making them *more complex:* always, however, within a framework of divine calling and eschatological hope.

Finally, striking in all this is the absence of (what we might call) a "systematic theology" of singleness and marriage: which is to say neither that Paul's advice is completely ad hoc, nor that what he says may not contribute to such a theology. Instead, what is most evident is Paul's determination — while remaining sensitive to limits to his own understanding (cf. 7:8, 12, 25, 40) — to give *practical guidance informed theologically* with a view to encouraging the Corinthians to act both freely and responsibly as embodied people in ways which will sustain them in a holy common life and a countercultural witness to the world.

Cultic Discipline and the Holiness of the Church (8:1–11:1)

Paul now turns to a different but closely related topic: "Now concerning food sacrificed to idols *(tōn eidōlothytōn)*" (8:1). Significantly, in the earlier lists of vices, Paul has placed sexual immorality *(porneia)* alongside idolatry *(idōlolatria)* (6:9; cf. 5:10, 11). It is concern with this latter issue which holds together all that Paul says in 8:1–11:1 (cf. 8:1, 4, 7, 10; 10:7, 14, 19). The progression from the one to the other is by no means incidental. A deep logic connects the move. (1) As indicated earlier, *porneia* and *idōlolatria* are linked in biblical and Jewish tradition with what most threatens Israel's covenantal devotion to the one true God. Paul's two parallel commands, "Flee *porneia*" and "Flee *idōlolatria*" (6:18; 10:14), show how strong is his desire for the church, as God's new covenant people, to bring its life within the parameters of biblical monotheism. Significantly, both the treatment of *porneia* in ch. 6 and of *idōlolatria* in chs. 8–10 culminate with the command to "glorify God" (6:20; 10:31). (2) Related to this, both issues bear on the question of the relation between the church and the world — how to be God's people in a pagan environment characterized by a moral and religious pluralism of "many gods and many lords" (8:5; cf. Winter 1990). Paul's position is complex and nuanced. In both spheres, Paul wants to encourage neither separation nor assimilation. To avoid separation, he draws regulatory lines through the church in order to strengthen group cohesion; to avoid assimilation, he draws lines around the church in order to strengthen group identity. (3) Another link relates to Paul's purpose as a whole. If sexual immorality threatens the unity, good order, and holiness of the Corinthian fellowship, so also does idolatry. Given Paul's overarching goal to persuade the Corinthians to avoid factionalism and party spirit (cf. 1:10), it is no surprise to find him giving instruction on whether or not to eat idol meat in pagan temples. Why? Because the church in Corinth is a mixed fellowship of Jews as well as Gentiles, "weak" as well as "strong"; and for Jews and "the weak" (the two, though almost certainly not the same, may have influenced each other), idol meat is anathema (cf. 10:31-32; also Acts 15:20, 29; 21:25). (4) Both issues have to do with the status of the body and the material world in the lives of Spirit-filled believers, first, in the primarily domestic sphere of marital relations, and second, in the more public sphere of cults, voluntary associations, and temple conviviality. Put starkly, how does life "in Christ" affect whom I sleep with (chs. 5–7) and whom I eat with (chs. 8–10)? Or, to give a different nuance, how does participation in the new "economy" *(oikonomia)* of the kingdom of God affect the "economy" of the body and of material (including sexual and social) relations as a whole? (5) Finally, and related, both issues have to do with the responsible exercise of personal "authority" *(exousia)* in a group characterized by diversity. Paul's question is: Even if we have the right to act in a certain way, are we obliged to exercise that right? That question is so important that Paul divides his treatment of idolatry into two parts and places an account of his own apostolic practice — as a model for the Corinthians to imitate — in the middle (ch. 9).

Food Rules (8:1-13)

To understand Paul's main concern about idol meat, we need to refer first to the clear admonition he gives in 8:9-11. This pinpoints what is at stake. The behavior of some church members, rather than "building up" their brothers and sisters in the faith, is causing them to fall back into idolatry. Specifically, the ones who have superior "knowledge" — that is, the ones who boast in their Spirit-imparted "wisdom" and whom, by analogy with Rom 14:1–15:6, we may call the "strong" (although they are never so called in 1 Corinthians) — are exercising their "authority" by uninhibited recourse (no doubt in the company of their pagan friends, kinsfolk, patrons, and clients) to the conviviality of temple banquets where they are eating meat that has been sacrificed to the gods (cf. 10:14, 21). This practice is causing serious harm to the common life of the church. Those converts from paganism whose consciences are "weak" by virtue of the indelible associations of idol meat and pagan temples with their former way of life (8:7) are being tempted by the practices of the "strong" to revert to their old lifestyle and are falling away from Christ. The issue is not just a matter of bad manners, of the "strong" acting in "bad taste" and thereby merely "offending" the "weak." It is much more serious than that. The behavior of the "strong" is leading the "weak" into apostasy by causing them to act against their conscience *(syneidēsis)*.

Having outlined the main issue (for more detail, cf. Theissen 1982: 121-43; Willis 1985; Winter 1994: 165-77; Horrell 1997; Cheung 1999), we are now in a better position to see how Paul responds, both in terms of what he says and how he says it. In terms of content, Paul's instructions move inexorably in the direction of prohibiting eating idol meat in explicitly idolatrous contexts like worship of the gods in pagan temples (8:1–10:22), with latitude on the question of meat from the market *(macellum)* or meat eaten as a guest at a private dinner party insofar as *conscious* association with idolatry is not an issue (10:23-30). As Dunn (1998: 704) sums it up: "The most straightforward exegesis is that Paul counseled the avoidance of meals at which it was known beforehand that idol food would be served. That effectively ruled out public or private meals within temple precincts: to participate in a temple meal would inevitably be seen by others as consenting to the idolatrous worship of the temple. Also ruled out were meals in private homes where it was clear beforehand that idol food was likely to be served." In ch. 8, Paul's argument focuses positively on what it means to love the "one God," along with its personal and social consequences; in ch. 10, it focuses negatively on the danger of provoking divine judgment by falling into idolatry.

As in his treatment of marriage rules (cf. 7:1), Paul begins by identifying the subject and then quoting with apparent approval the slogan of the spiritually elite: "Now concerning food sacrificed to idols: we know that 'all of us possess knowledge'" (8:1a). Immediately, however, he qualifies this in terms of (what amounts to) a hierarchy of virtues in which "knowledge" is subordinated to "love" *(agapē)* (8:1b). Why "love"? Because, whereas knowledge "puffs up" the individual (cf. 4:6, 18, 19; 5:2), love "builds up" the fellowship (cf. 14:3, 5, 12). To put it another way, what is important is knowledge *interpreted by love:* specifically, love *of God,* which opens the individual to a different kind of knowledge, *relational* knowledge. This is a matter not of knowing "something" (and therefore being able to boast), but of *being known* by God (which is a matter of grace and gift) (8:2-3; cf. Gal 4:9a). Paul wants the "strong" to see that Christian faith is not a special kind of esoteric "wisdom" which can just be "added on" to their previous stock of wisdom in a way that leaves lifestyle matters as they are: rather, it is entry into a love relationship (with the one true God and with those "called" by God) which changes everything. He will expand on this later, in ch. 13.

In 8:4-13, Paul goes on to apply this to idol meat. Once again the slogans of the "strong" — probably a version of teaching imparted by Paul himself when he evangelized Corinth and which sums up their *gnōsis* and justifies their eating of idol meat — are cited: "we know that 'no idol in the world really exists,' and that 'there is no God but one'" (v. 4). Once again, however, Paul moves to qualify their position by setting it in a larger moral-theological framework, in effect, developing the theme introduced in v. 3: what it means to "love God."

Yes, their monotheistic faith does mean that the gods pagans worship are only "so-called" gods, and in spite of there being "many gods and many lords" falsely worshiped in Corinth, there is "for us" only "one God, the Father, from whom are all things and for whom we exist, and one Lord, Jesus Christ, through whom are all things and through whom we exist" (8:5-6). Here is common ground expressed in the authoritative form of an early Christian confession (either pre-Pauline or composed by Paul from pre-Pauline elements; cf. Dunn 1980: 179-80). But it is common ground which provides the basis for the subsequent modification of the position of the "strong," in vv. 7-13. It does so in two ways. First, as a confession which resonates with that other great confession — the Shema — which is at the heart of the faith of Israel (cf. Deut 6:4-5), it draws the Corinthians into the orbit of a biblical monotheism whose moral life is characterized by love of the one God and abhorrence of idolatry (cf. Wright 1991: 120-36). Second, as a confession which is also distinctively christological, it draws the Corinthians toward a fuller acknowledgment of the fatherhood of God and the Lordship of Christ in their lives: the Father is the one *"for whom* we exist," and Christ is the one *"through whom* we exist." The Corinthian "strong" are not free agents (cf. 6:19-20)!

Now, significantly, Paul brings in a voice which has been silent so far. He speaks up for the "weak" (cf. 9:22a; also 1:27b): "It is not everyone, however, who has this knowledge. Since some have become so accustomed to idols until now, they still think of the food they eat as food offered to an idol; and their conscience, being weak, is defiled" (8:7). Then the "weak" are put in dialogue with the "strong," as another slogan of the "strong" is cited: "'Food will not bring us close to God. We are no worse off if we do not eat, and no better off if we do'" (v. 8). But the way has been prepared for the climax of Paul's argument. Once more the slogan is qualified, this time directly and decisively, in vv. 9-13. The "strong" are to show the kind of "authority" which is not *bound* to be exercised in a particular way. Specifically, they are to refrain from eating idol meat in idolatrous settings in order to protect the consciences (and therefore the welfare) of the "weak."

In order to persuade the "strong" to the *radical step* of changing their lifestyle on this matter — with all its potentially disturbing consequences for their patterns of sociability and networks of kinsfolk, friends, clients, and the like (cf. Barclay 1992: 56-72) — Paul provides powerful warrants (8:11-13): (a) The "weak," by being encouraged (lit. "built up"!) to revert to idolatry, are being "destroyed" (in their faith). (b) The "weak" are not insignificant: they are the Christian "brothers [and sisters]" of the "strong." (c) The "weak" are not insignificant for another reason: they, too, are people "for whom Christ died." (d) In wounding the conscience of the "weak" (and therefore dishonoring a fellow member of Christ's body; cf. ch. 12), the "strong" are sinning against Christ. (e) As on previous issues (cf. 4:16; 6:7a), there is Paul's own example to follow. With a rhetorical flourish he declares: "Therefore, if food is a cause of my brother's falling, I will never eat meat [*krea,* i.e., meat of any kind, not just idol meat], lest I cause my brother to fall" (8:13, RSV).

Leading by Example: Individual Rights and the Common Good (9:1-27)

Paul's appeal to his own proposed behavior in 8:13 takes him into an extended account of his apostolic practice in general (9:1-27; cf. Theissen 1982: 27-67; Martin 1990; Barton 1996). Certainly, this is a digression, but by no means an irrelevant one. Rather, what Paul gives is an example of his own practice of renunciation in an area *analogously controversial* to idol meat. His aim is twofold. First and foremost, he wants to persuade the Corinthians to take his personal example of renunciation and apply it to the main issue in chs. 8–10: idol meat. Second, by explaining why he refrains from exercising his "right" to material support, he wants at the same time to defuse a problem with the potential for complicating his own relations with the church (cf. 2 Cor 11:7-11).

Paul's use here of autobiographical testimony is not a one-off. We have seen similar appeals earlier in 1 Corinthians (e.g., 1:14-17; 2:1-5; 3:5-9; 4:1-5, 9-13; etc.). Its occurrence is a function, not of the apostle's ego, but of accepted philosophical and political practice, according to which the truly wise person and good leader leads and persuades by first person example (cf. Mitchell 1992: 130-38, 243-50). Furthermore, in relation to what is to come, it is important to note that (a) the autobiographical testimony in ch. 9 stands in a broadly chiastic A-B-A relation to chs. 8–10 (i.e., idol meat [ch. 8] — apostolic renunciation [ch. 9] — idol meat [ch. 10]), the effect of which is to place the apparent digression at the heart of the argument; (b) the testimony in ch. 9 stands in relation to chs. 8–10 as the testimony in ch. 13 stands in relation to chs. 12–14, the implication of which is that Paul's argument is organized in a deliberate manner to achieve maximum persuasive effect; and (c) the testimony in ch. 13 takes up and develops the testimony in ch. 9 and the surrounding material. Here the issue is the need for voluntary self-limitation out of love for the "weak" brother or sister and its implications for practices of commensality; there (in ch. 13) the issue likewise is the need for voluntary self-limitation out of love for the "weaker" and "less honorable" (12:22-23) and its implications for the practice of worship.

The argument has three main parts. In 9:1-14, Paul argues vigorously and by appeal to numerous warrants that, as a true apostle, he has the "right" *(exousia)* to receive the material support of the Corinthians. In vv. 15-23, he explains that, even though he has the right, he does not exercise it; rather, he sacrifices it for the sake of the gospel and the common good — to make the gospel "free of charge" and therefore available to as many people as possible. Finally, in vv. 24-27, with reference to the metaphor of the athletic contest, he exhorts the Corinthians to follow his example and accept the disciplines of bodily self-control that make sacrifice for the common good possible.

Paul begins his "digression" by responding to a possible accusation arising from his immediately preceding affirmation, that "if food is a cause of my ["weak"] brother's falling, I will never eat meat, lest I cause my brother to fall" (8:13, RSV). This affirmation opens Paul to the accusation (noting *anakrinein,* "to examine," in 9:3; cf. 4:3) from the cultural and spiritual elite in the church that, if he is willing so to debase himself by letting the scruples of the "weak" dictate how he acts, then he must be neither truly "free" *(eleutheros)* nor truly an apostle *(apostolos).* Hence his opening salvo of rhetorical questions in 9:1-2. Here are the qualifications of an apostle — (a) a commissioning by the Risen Lord and (b) the tangible evidence of the efficacy of divine power working through the apostle and bringing faith-communities into being — and Paul can claim both (cf. 1:1; 4:9; 12:28, 29; 15:9). So, taking the questions in reverse order: yes, he is an apostle, and (as an apostle) yes, he is "free."

On this foundation, Paul proceeds with his (slightly tongue-in-cheek) *apologia* (9:3ff.). As an apostle (and like other apostles and people of status such as Barnabas, Cephas, and "the brothers of the Lord"), Paul affirms (by means of rhetorical questions) that he most certainly does have "authority" *(exousia)* or the "right" to certain benefits: precisely what the "strong" claim for themselves (cf. 8:9) — but even more so! There is the right "to eat and drink" (precisely the issue in chs. 8 and 10!) at someone else's expense (9:4); the right to receive travel expenses and hospitality, not only for himself and Barnabas but also for an entourage including wives (v. 5; cf. 7:7a, 8); and the right to financial support (the other sensitive issue!) which makes it unnecessary to work for a living (9:6).

Not only does Paul, with the other apostles, have these rights; he can also claim strong warrants for asserting them (9:7-14). These he lists in ascending order of significance. Thus, there are warrants provided by human reason in the practice of military service, agriculture, and shepherding (v. 7). Then there is a warrant from revelation, in the form of the Mosaic law forbidding the muzzling of oxen while they are plowing, so that they can eat and work at the same time (vv. 8-12a; cf. Deut 25:4).

But now, having given good reasons for asserting his rights as an apostle, Paul springs a surprise: "Nevertheless, we have not made use of this right, but we endure anything rather than put an obstacle in the way of the gospel of Christ" (9:12b). The telltale terms "'right" *(exousia)* and "obstacle" *(enkopē)* firmly link Paul's argument here with the larger argument begun in ch. 8 (cf. *exousia* and *proskomma* in 8:9; also *aproskopoi* in 10:32). Just as Paul foregoes his right to receive financial support so as not to hinder access to salvation on the part of the poor (cf. 1:26!), so the "strong" are to forego their right to eat idol meat so as not to hinder access to salvation on the part of the "weak."

There are, however, two further warrants for asserting his apostolic right, more important than the preceding two (in 9:7-12a). The first is the precedent of employees of the temple who receive a share of the sacrificial *meat*(!) for services rendered (v. 13). The second and climactic one is the command from the Lord (Jesus) himself, "that those who proclaim the gospel should get their living by the gospel" (v. 14; cf. Matt 10:10; Luke 10:7). But neither the precedent of the temple cult in Jerusalem nor even the command of Jesus (cf. 7:10-11) is sufficient to sway Paul off his course. They establish that he has the right (to support), but they do not oblige him to exercise the right. So, for a second time, Paul affirms: "I have made no use of any of these rights" — adding, with a rhetorically emphatic flourish reminiscent of 8:13, "Indeed, I would rather die than that — no one will deprive me of my ground for boasting!" (9:15). There is a nice irony here. Paul opposes the boasting of the Corinthians (cf. 1:29; 3:21; 4:7; 5:6; and 2 Corinthians *passim*), but he boasts himself — not, however, of what he possesses but of *what he has given up* for the good of the many.

In 9:16-23, Paul proceeds to justify this position. He needs to do so because, in the culture of the time and in the view (of at least some) of the Corinthians, it is extraordinary, even shameful. Ronald Hock (1980: 52-59) has shown that the question of the means of support befitting philosophers and sophists was a matter of considerable debate. Indeed, Paul's contemporary, the Stoic philosopher Musonius Rufus, wrote a tractate on the subject, "What Means of Support Is Appropriate for a Philosopher?" There were four main options: (a) charging fees *(misthoi)*, a practice which opened the philosopher to the charge of greed and manipulation; (b) becoming a member of a rich patron's household, a practice criticized for the loss of freedom it entailed, including enslavement to the hedonistic lifestyle of the rich; (c) begging on the streets, the practice adopted by Cynic philosophers in particular, but criticized by others as shameful and demeaning; and (d) manual work at a skilled or unskilled job in order to be self-supporting, a practice advantageous in maintaining the independence *(autarkeia)* of the philosopher and his teaching, but disadvantageous in its physical demands and in the association of manual labor with low social status (cf. 4:12a). Given that the first two options were the most common means of support for respectable philosophers and sophists, in opting for the last Paul opens himself up to criticism. In particular, his refusal to accept the financial support of the Corinthians could appear as a snub (cf. 2 Cor 11:7-11), an act of social hostility in the larger context of patronage and friendship relations mediated by the giving and receiving of gifts (cf. Marshall 1987).

What, then, is Paul's defense? Overall, it is that the terms under which he operates are quite unlike those which fit a philosopher or a sophist. First, as an apostle, he is not free to do what he likes. Rather, preaching the gospel is an eschatological "obligation" or "necessity" *(anankē;* cf. 7:26) placed upon him by God (and reminiscent of the testimony of the prophets, e.g., Jeremiah [1:4-10; 20:7-9]), a necessity so serious that he is under God's curse if he does otherwise: "Woe to me if I do not preach the gospel!" (9:16). There can be no question of payment *(misthos)* for services rendered because — as Christ's servant and as a steward of God's mysteries (cf. 4:1-4) — he has been "entrusted with a commission" (9:17b). In fact, however, he does receive a reward: the paradoxical reward of *not receiving anything* in order that he can offer the gospel of true freedom "free of charge" (v. 18). Put in other words, the reward is that his practice of self-sacrifice fits the gospel he preaches and brings into its orbit people who otherwise might find themselves beyond its reach. Where the "strong" interpret freedom in terms of the advancement of their own interests, with consequences disastrous for the unity of the body, Paul illustrates from his own practice the imperative of restricting one's freedom for the common good. Nothing, not even "freedom," should be allowed to get in the way of the proclamation and reception by as many people as possible of "the gospel of Christ" (9:12, 16, 18, 23).

Paul epitomizes his overall position in 9:19-23. This famous statement probably represents Paul's response to criticism being directed at him in Corinth (cf. Marshall 1987: 306-17): that he is a slave, not free at all; that he has no will of his own but deceitfully tailors his behavior to "win" (and profit from) as many as possible; that he is inconsistent ("a Jew to Jews, a Greek to Greeks") and therefore not to be trusted; and that he is a flatterer, seeking to "please" people (10:33) for his own advantage. As several studies have shown (e.g., Malherbe 1983), Paul's language here of humility, compromise, and accommodation is well known in political and philosophical treatises which address the problem of the political chameleon and demagogue who seeks power by ingratiating himself with the masses. This explains a number of aspects of Paul's response: (a) Paul has enslaved *himself,* so he has not acted out of servility to others (9:19a). Rather, he has acted as the "slave *of Christ*" (cf. vv. 16-18; also 7:22; and Gal 1:10; Rom 1:1; Phil 1:1) — a designation not of servility but of authority. (b) Paul's enslavement to others is not a kind of self-immolation. On the contrary, it is carefully circumscribed and qualified (e.g., "though I myself am not under the law" in v. 20b). (c) The goal of his enslavement to all is to "gain" or "save" as many as possible *for the gospel,* not to increase either his own popularity or that of any one faction in the church (9:22b, 23). (d) He does not deny that his self-enslavement brings personal reward. The "payment" he receives, however, is not financial but evangelical and eschatological (v. 23).

In elaborating his practice of accommodation (9:20-22a), Paul refers to "the Jews . . . those under the law . . . those outside the law . . . [and] the weak." The precise identity of the people so designated is difficult to ascertain. Probably they refer to the same groups to whom Paul refers at the conclusion of his entire argument, when he says: "Give no offense to Jews or to Greeks or to the church of God" (10:32). The important thing to note is that these are broad *categories of difference* which are directly relevant to the mixed makeup of the Corinthian church and the problems threatening its common life (cf. 1:22-24; 7:18-19; 12:13). Important also is the repeated reference to "the law" *(ho nomos)* as a normative point of reference: variants of *nomos* occur some nine times in 9:20-21! What Paul appears to be doing here is *destabilizing "the law" as a point of Christian self-definition.* Hence he can become "*as* a Jew," "*as* one under the law," and "*as* one outside the law." The stable point of reference now is not in relation to the law but in relation to Christ: being "in-lawed to Christ" *(ennomos Christou)* (v. 21b; cf. Gal 6:2). What this means is that a new community has come into being, a community which includes those peoples previously cut off from one another by "the law." It is precisely this novel social mixture which is put at risk whenever one party or faction acts in disregard of the rest. And it is precisely the maintenance of this novel social mixture which requires of all its members — especially the "strong" — the willingness to sacrifice individual rights or the interests of particular status groups for the sake of the fellowship as a whole.

The sacrifice required is real and costly. Notice that Paul does not say that he became "*as* weak to the weak"; rather, "to the weak *I became weak,* so that I might win the weak" (9:22a; cf. 4:10b). For Paul, this means stepping down the social ladder and working with his own hands to support himself in order to make the gospel "free of charge" to the majority (i.e., the poor; cf. Hays 1997: 157 on Paul's "preferential option for the poor"; also Martin 1990). To live this way requires training. That is why Paul concludes his "digression" with a final rhetorical question inviting his readers to consider the analogy of the athletic contest (the *agōn*) (9:24-27) and to apply it to themselves ("Run!" v. 24b). Paul, like the great philosophers of his day, knows that victory in the virtuous life is not attained without bodily discipline *(askēsis)*: "I punish my body and enslave it, so that after proclaiming to others I myself should not be disqualified" (v. 27). This is not the language of the servile flatterer who has only his own interests at heart. It is the combative language of one who knows from experience the kind of rigorous self-control *(enkrateia)* necessary if the goods enjoyed by the individual or the few are to be subordinated to the higher good of the many. The lesson for those in the Corinthian church who flaunt their freedom to eat idol meat should be clear. Furthermore, the warning about the possibility of "disqualification" (v. 27b) skillfully prepares the way for the massive warning about falling back into idolatry (and in consequence being "disqualified" from the people of God) which follows in 10:1-22.

"Flee from the worship of idols!" (10:1-22)

Paul's attempt to persuade the Corinthians not to eat idol meat *(eidōlothyta)* in a context of worship of the gods *(idōlolatria)* now reaches a climax. Up to this point, his argument has taken a positive form: for the sake of the fellow believer whose conscience is "weak," it is advisable to refrain from exercising one's "right" to eat idol meat — even though this "right" is based on the *gnōsis* that idols do not really exist (ch. 8). This self-limitation is the practice of Paul himself, whose behavior in relation to the analogous issue of the apostle's "right" to receive financial support is held up as an example to imitate (ch. 9). Now, returning to the issue of idol meat, Paul's argument takes a negative form: a warning from the scriptural story of Israel in the wilderness to show the danger of falling back into idolatry associated with eating and drinking in the company of idols and idolaters.

What Paul does is to "read" the story of the Corinthians in terms of the story of Israel in the wilderness told in Exodus and Numbers. This is a kind of "applied exegesis," where the story of Israel is allowed to speak metaphorically (or better, typologically) to the situation of the church in Corinth. For Paul, the word of God has a living, contemporary, oracular quality: it is divine testimony about the past for the present (cf. 9:6, 11). Importantly, in the process of allowing themselves to be addressed by Scripture, the Corinthians are given the opportunity to *see themselves differently:* no longer as individual Corinthians who happen to have a superior "knowledge" that allows them to maintain their pagan lifestyle virtually unchanged but as spiritual descendants of the people of Israel. Importantly also, the Corinthians are given the opportunity to *see God differently:* no longer as "some abstract divine principle that sets [them] free from polytheistic superstition" (Hays 1997: 159) but as the "jealous" God of the Scriptures who refuses to share his covenant people with any other gods.

Thus, Paul begins in 10:1-4 by citing those aspects of Israel's story of liberation which speak in a typological way to the Corinthians' liberating spiritual experiences of baptism (cf. 1:13-14; 12:13) and the Lord's Supper (cf. 10:16-17; 11:17-34): "[O]ur ancestors were all under the cloud, and all passed through the sea, and all were baptized into Moses in the cloud [cf. Exod 13:12-22] and in the sea [cf. Exod 14:21-22], and all ate the same spiritual food [i.e., manna; Exod 16:1-36], and all drank the same spiritual drink [cf. Exod 17:1-7; Num 20:2-13]." For Paul, the cloud and the sea speak (respectively) of the Spirit and baptism, and the spiritual food and drink speak of the body and blood of Christ (cf. 10:16). Even the "rock" from which the Israelites drank and which, according to Jewish tradition, followed Israel on its wanderings (cf. Ps.-Philo *Bib. Ant.* 10.7; Philo *Leg. all.* 2.86) is identified as none other than Christ (v. 4). Noteworthy is the repeated "all," which occurs five times. Paul's point is that "all" the Israelites were recipients of God's liberating grace mediated sacramentally; *but* this did not prevent "most of them" from incurring God's wrath (v. 5). And (Paul implies) if that is what happened to the Corinthians' spiritual ancestors, can they themselves be complacent? As Barrett (1971: 218) puts it: "Even baptized communicants are not secure."

The next section (10:6-13) makes the analogy with the Corinthians explicit and drives home Paul's concern. Vv. 6 and 11 provide the interpretative, moral-eschatological key and bracket a series of warnings against misdirected desire addressed directly to the Corinthians. The intervening verses identify the "desires" and behavior for which the Israelites were judged. There are four such, each of which is directly relevant to the problems in Corinth.

First in the list (on account of its relevance to the immediate context) is idolatry, for which the paradigmatic case is the golden calf episode (cf. Exodus 32), associated as it was with eating, drinking, and (sexual) "play" (10:7). Second, for its relevance to Paul's other main area of concern (cf. chs. 5–7), comes "sexual immorality" (*porneia;* 10:8), as in the episode of the Israelite men and the Moabite women (cf. Num 25:1-9). Third, for its applicability overall, comes putting Christ to the test (10:9), by analogy with the episode in Num 21:4-9 where the Israelites complain to God in the wilderness about their "miserable food." Fourth, perhaps for its applicability to the Corinthians' tendency to criticize Paul, is the Israelites' constant "grumbling" against Moses (10:10; cf. Num 14). Significant overall is the fact that, in each case (in 10:7a, 8a, 9a, and 10a) — having insisted in vv. 1-4 that "all" the Israelites received the blessings of baptism and spiritual sustenance — Paul states that it is "some" of those very same people who did these things and were judged accordingly. Again, the warning against complacency is clear — thus, "if you think you are standing, watch out that you do not fall" (v. 12). At the same time, and to counter despair (the flipside of complacency), Paul complements his word of warning with a word of consolation (v. 13).

This extended argument from Scripture culminates in a single command expressing Paul's primary concern: "Flee from the worship of idols" (10:14; cf. v. 7). This recalls the earlier command, "Flee from fornication" (6:18a). *Porneia* and idolatry are the two threats from *outside* the church which, in Paul's view, are most likely to undermine the holiness and unity of the church. As we shall see when we turn to what Paul says about corporate worship in chs. 11–14, threats to the church also come from *inside.* Paul's response to the threats from outside is to seek to strengthen the church's boundaries. Thus, *porneia* and idolatry are not to be tolerated.

But Paul takes the argument a stage further: from the appeal to the testimony of Scripture to an appeal to the testimony of their own experience (10:15-22). Tongue-in-cheek he begins: "I speak as to sensible people *(phronimois)*" (10:15; cf. 4:10; also 2 Cor 11:19). Paul wants them to think again about whether their complacency over eating idol meat in temples is "sensible" after all! So he proceeds to a comparison of three types of meals: the Lord's Supper (10:16-17), the meals of the people of Israel (lit. "Israel according to the flesh") arising from the sacrificial cult (v. 18), and meals in pagan temples (vv. 19-21). The direction of his argument is that, on the basis of what he says about the first two (i.e., the Christian and Jewish) types of meals, the third type will come to be seen as out of bounds.

Thus, in a remarkable statement on the significance of the (Christian) Lord's Supper (which prepares the way for the instruction he gives in 11:17-34), Paul says, "The cup of blessing that we bless, is it not a *sharing* in the blood of Christ? The bread that we break, is it not a *sharing* in the body of Christ? Because there is *one* bread, we who are many are *one* body, for we all partake of the *one* bread." The two main emphases are clear from the repetitive use of the language of participation and unity. The Lord's Supper is a meal loaded with social meanings: it unites partakers *with Christ crucified and risen* (who is therefore *present* with his people), and it unites partakers *with each other.* It is this participation with Christ and the unity of believers that Christ makes possible that are being put at risk (cf. 11:27-34).

The point is reinforced and developed by appeal (once more) to Israel (cf. 10:1-13) and the sacrificial cult (cf. 9:13): "Consider the people of Israel; are not those who eat the sacrifices partners *(koinōnoi)* in the altar?" Paul is probably referring here both to the priests who eat the sacrificial meat (cf. Lev 7:6) and to the people as a whole who share in the tithe offerings (cf. Deut 14:22-26). Again, the point is that the cultic meal is loaded with social meaning (cf. also Philo *Spec. Leg.* 1.221). It is eaten in God's presence and it unites the people together as people of the covenant. So it is not to be taken lightly as of no real consequence. As Josephus puts it when he writes for Gentiles about sacrifices in Judaism, "Our sacrifices are not occasions for drunken self-indulgence — such practices are abhorrent to God — but for sobriety. At these sacrifices prayers for the welfare of the community must take precedence of those for ourselves; for we are born for fellowship *(koinōnia),* and he who sets its claims above his private interests is specially acceptable to God" (*Ag. Ap.* 2.196).

This brings Paul to the point at issue: eating and drinking in pagan temples. If the Lord's Supper involves the participation *(koinōnia)* of believers with Christ risen and present, and if the sacrifices of Israel involve the participation of the people with the One (i.e., God) in whose presence the sacrificial food is eaten, is table fellowship in pagan temples in the presence of idols permissible? The answer to which Paul is moving is a resounding "No!" But first he has to avoid the impression that he is contradicting the *gnōsis* he affirms in 8:4-6, that idols do not exist and that there is no God but one (10:19). He does so by quoting Scripture (not acknowledged in the NRSV): "what they sacrifice 'they sacrifice to demons and not to God'" (10:20a; cf. Deut 32:17). In its original context in the Song of Moses, this is an accusation, not against pagans, but against Israel for her unfaithfulness in falling into idolatry: "They made him jealous with strange gods. . . . They sacrificed to *demons,* not God, to deities they had not known. . . . They made me *jealous* with what is no god, provoked me with their idols" (Deut 32:16-21). This quotation provides the warrant for the shift in 10:19ff. from references to idol food and idols to references to "demons." It also provides the warrant for the introduction of the theological motif of divine "jealousy" in v. 22. So Paul concludes: "I do not want you to be partners *(koinōnous)* with demons. You cannot drink the cup of the Lord and the cup of demons. You cannot partake of the table of the Lord and the table of demons. Or are we provoking the Lord to jealousy?" (10:20b-22a).

Just as some of the Corinthians, on the basis of their *gnōsis,* are having recourse to the places where the prostitutes practice their trade, doubtless including the temples (6:12-20), some also (probably the same ones) are having recourse to the places where food and drink and conviviality are to be found, again including the temples. Likewise, just as joining with a prostitute involves *koinōnia* across forbidden boundaries — physical, social, and spiritual — by uniting a "member of Christ" with a prostitute *(pornē)* in an act of *porneia,* so eating and drinking connected with idolatry involves *koinōnia* across forbidden boundaries with (i.e., in the presence of) demons. In both cases, God's "jealous" (i.e., exclusive) covenant relationship with the ones he has called and sanctified is undermined, and, as a corollary, the unity of God's covenant people is put at risk. So to those who think they are "strong," Paul says ominously: "Are we stronger than he?" (10:22b).

But now Paul addresses a new problem: What about meat which is not consciously associated with idolatrous worship but which is bought in the meat market or offered for consumption in the context of a private dinner party (10:23–11:1)? Fascinatingly, if on the issue of *eidōlothyta* he has sided more with the "weak," here he appears to side more with the "strong" (cf. 10:25-27, 29b-30). In fact, however, appearances are deceptive. Paul's position on this new question (as previously) shows him to be siding neither with the "strong" nor with the "weak." If anything, he is seeking to "win" both (cf. 9:19) to a more mature, *other-regarding* understanding and practice.

Worth noting is the way Paul enunciates the general principle in ethical terms at the beginning and in climactic theological terms at the end, with the particular practical problems being addressed in the middle. So the pattern is broadly chiastic (A-B-A*) (Fee 1987: 478). First, and in an almost verbatim repetition of the words he uses earlier in relation to *porneia* (cf. 6:12), he twice quotes the slogan of those who are advocating total license (this time with regard to eating), only to qualify it (10:23). The exhortation here to do what is "beneficial" and what "builds up" reinforces his instruction at the beginning of this section of the letter (cf. 8:1b) and is typical of Paul's entire "social ethics" (cf. 14:3-5, 12, 17, 26; 2 Cor 12:19; 13:10). His intention is to counter the "individualism" of the Corinthians along with the disunity which follows from it. Hence, "Do not seek your own advantage, but that of the other" (10:24; cf. v. 33; also Phil 2:4).

Then he turns to specific questions from the church members (10:25-27). On whether or not to eat meat sold in the meat market, Paul's advice is: "Eat . . . without raising any question on the ground of conscience" — and he quotes Ps 24:1 in support (10:25-26). On whether or not to dine in the company of an unbeliever *(apistos)*, Paul's advice likewise is: "Eat whatever is set before you without raising any question on the ground of conscience" (v. 27). This fits with what he says earlier about *not* withdrawing from contact with outsiders (5:9-10). But once again the permission is qualified by an exception: do not eat if a fellow believer with a "weak" conscience on the matter is present and identifies the meat as having been "offered in sacrifice" *(hierothyton)*. Even though *your* conscience (i.e., sense of moral confidence) is strong and free, nevertheless abstain for the sake of the conscience of the *other* (10:28-29a). But Paul insists that such an abstention is the exception that proves the rule: it does not undermine the believer's basic freedom to eat anything with a thankful heart to the One who is Lord of all (vv. 29b-30; cf. v. 26). So if Paul does not go all the way with the "strong," neither does he go all the way with the "weak" — even if his bias, out of love (8:1-3), is clearly in their favor (cf. 9:22a).

Finally, Paul draws the threads together by reiterating what is most important for *all* the church members if they are to live in unity as God's elect (10:31–11:1). Of primary importance is precisely not what so dominates the social and moral concerns of the Corinthians, that is, eating and drinking as ways of displaying personal power (or feeling excluded from it)! Rather, it is *doing what brings glory to God* (10:31; cf. 6:20). Paul's social morality is resolutely theocentric and (as we shall see below, at 11:1) christocentric. As such, it is a firm corrective to (anthropocentric) patterns of behavior oriented on what brings glory to one group of people at the expense of another. In practice, this "giving glory to God" means, negatively, not hindering the salvation (present and ongoing) of either outsiders ("to Jews or to Greeks") or insiders ("the church of God"); positively, it means following Paul's own example of trying to "please" everyone "so that they may be saved" (10:32-33).

As in the case of the closely parallel testimony in 9:19-23, the idea of "pleasing" as many people as possible is not a matter of self-seeking servility: that is what Paul explicitly denies (10:33b). Rather, in the context of ancient treatises on political leadership, "pleasing" as many people as possible has a particular connotation: it is the sacrificial and costly business of stepping down in social status and giving up otherwise legitimate rights and privileges in order to identify with and win over the majority, that is, those at the bottom of the social scale (cf. Martin 1990). But Paul does not do this as a "party politician," for it is parties and factions which he wants the Corinthians to leave behind in their ecclesial life. He does it because he is a servant of Christ and therefore has given over his life to the imitation of Christ: "Be imitators of me *as I am of Christ*" (11:1). In his sacrificial stepping down in status and renunciation of rights, Paul is doing what Christ has done in the "foolishness" *(mōria)* of his self-giving on the cross (cf. 1:18-25; Rom 15:1-3; Phil 2:4ff.). This is the demanding, christomorphic model which Paul embodies and which he exhorts the Corinthians to embody also.

Preserving the Unity of the Church (11:2–14:40)

If the previous main section of Paul's letter (5:1–11:1) has to do with threats to church life arising out of its members' ongoing life in the wider society (i.e., issues of "Christian existence in the world"), the next main section has to do with threats which surface when church members "come together" *(synerchesthai)* for the Christian meeting (i.e., issues of "Christian community"). Previously, Paul's primary concern has been to strengthen the lines running *around* the church, to reinforce the Corinthians' rather undeveloped sense of distinctive identity. Now, in 11:2–14:40, Paul's primary concern is to strengthen the lines running *through* the church, to reinforce the order and unity of the Corinthians' common life (cf. 14:40). Broadly speaking, he deals with three issues: divisive gender innovation (11:2-16), divisive table fellowship (11:17-34), and divisive exercise of "gifts" of the Spirit (12:1–14:40), with a relevant "digression" in ch. 13 on the priority of love (cf. Mitchell 1992: 258-83).

Lying behind what Paul says on these matters is the unsurprising fact that the ingrained social behavior of the Corinthians in their everyday life is affecting significantly what happens when they "come together." The tendency toward party spirit and factionalism does not suddenly disappear. On the contrary, coming together in one place provides a regular opportunity for just such a tendency to manifest itself. Nor is this a concern unique to Paul and the first Christians. In contemporary Greco-Roman voluntary associations (cf. Kloppenborg and Wilson) strict measures were needed to foster collegiality and prevent association meetings from degenerating into faction fights. For example, the rules (c. 59-58 BC) governing the Egyptian Guild of Zeus Hypsistos include the following: "It shall not be permissible for any one of [the members] to . . . make factions, to leave the brotherhood of the president for another, or for men to enter into one another's pedigrees at the banquet, or to abuse one another at the banquet or to chatter or to indict or accuse another or to resign for the course of the year or again to bring the drinkings to nought" (Roberts 1936: 42).

Furthermore, what applies to small gatherings applies also to public assemblies and gatherings of all kinds. A good example of the threat of urban unrest when people gathered in public assembly is, in fact, in the narrative of Acts concerning events in Ephesus: "Meanwhile, some were shouting one thing, some another; for the assembly *(ekklēsia)* was in confusion, and most of them did not know why they had come together" (Acts 19:32). The urgent attempts of the town clerk to protect the assembly from the charge of rioting *(stasis)* and to restore order among the people (Acts 19:35-41) bear comparison with Paul's efforts in the more restricted sphere of the assemblies of Christians. In addition, the fact that the Corinthian meeting (like those elsewhere) is designated an *ekklēsia* (1:2; cf. 4:17; 7:17b; 10:32; etc.) — the ordinary Greek word for a public meeting of citizens — must have made it all but inevitable that the Christians there would think it permissible to behave in the Christian *ekklēsia* as they might behave in any *ekklēsia,* that is, as patrons and clients seeking their own advantage by exercising their *eleutheria* (freedom) and *exousia* (authority).

Gender Distinctions and the Unity of the Church (11:2-16)

One area where (at least some of) the Corinthians are exercising their freedom has to do with gender distinctions. When one reads between the lines, it appears that Christian women prophets — perhaps the women "holy in body and spirit" of 7:34 (so MacDonald 1990) — are expressing their new authority by disregarding conventional symbols of female identity and subordination. As people who have been remade by baptism as God's new creation where "in Christ" there is "no male and female" (Gal 3:27-28; cf. Meeks 1974), they are praying and prophesying with their heads "uncovered." Once again, therefore, the question Paul is addressing has to do with the appropriate *embodiment* (both individual and social) of Christian identity (cf. 1 Corinthians 7). In this case, the women's sense of new identity expresses itself in innovation relating to the head: specifically, letting their hair down and/or removing their veils (the matter is debated; cf. Wire 1990: 220-23), and so "uncovering" their heads (11:3-5). Because the head is a symbolic location of authority, and hairstyle is emblematic of status and group affiliation, such innovation seems to be causing contention in the church and perhaps also in the wider society. It represents a challenge to conventional patterns of authority which assume a hierarchical and patriarchal order of "headship."

But the anxiety may be related to other factors as well. Fiorenza (1983: 227), for example, points to a range of evidence showing Greek women in the mystery cults engaging in acts of worship with their heads uncovered or their hair hanging loose or both: "Such a sight of disheveled hair would be quite common in the ecstatic worship of oriental divinities. . . . Disheveled hair and head thrown back were typical for the maenads in the cult of Dionysos, in that of Cybele, the Pythia at Delphi, the Sibyl, and unbound hair was necessary for a woman to produce an effective magical incantation. . . . Flowing and unbound hair was also found in the Isis cult, which had a major center in Corinth." Against this background, Paul may be concerned that the gatherings of the Corinthians are becoming indistinguishable from those of pagan idolaters. Whatever the precise details (cf. Fee 1987: 491-530), it is clear that Paul resists this innovation and seeks to reimpose the conventional symbols of gender differentiation for the sake of good order, while at the same time providing arguments that will not detract from women's legitimate authority and, more positively still, will encourage the Corinthians as a whole in their worship, in the company of the angelic hosts, of the one true God.

What Paul says overall invites a number of comments. (a) Paul punctuates his argument with theological and christological reflection. There is the characteristic monotheism at the outset (". . . the head of Christ is God," 11:3), the appeal to the scriptural idea of the "image of God" (v. 7), the important christological and ecclesiological point of reference "in the Lord" (v. 11), and the confession that "all things come from God" toward the end (v. 12). However we judge individual points, Paul's determination to argue from theological first principles merits note.

(b) In a section comparable to his earlier treatment of gender relations in ch. 7, Paul addresses his argument to both men and women reciprocally: "Any man who prays or prophesies. . . . Any woman who prays or prophesies . . ." (11:4-5a, cf. vv. 7-12). Thus, although it is the women prophets who are the cause of anxiety (cf. vv. 13-15), Paul's response is to seek to bring both women and men within the same moral and ecclesial orbit. Why? Because the mutual interdependence of women and men is a basic building block of the unity of church members as a whole. Note, too, that Paul's argument is not just about how wives and husbands should pray and prophesy. If the main focus in ch. 7 is on wives and husbands, here it is more widely on women and men. Paul's clear assumption is that peace and good order in the *ekklēsia* depend not just on peace between wives and husbands but on peace between the female and male members in general.

(c) Paul is not objecting to women praying and prophesying. This, together with the fact that women (as well as men?) are praying and prophesying with such abandon, is important testimony to the liberating impact of Spirit-possession in the Pauline churches and in early Christianity generally (cf. Dunn 1975). Indeed, from a social-psychological point of view, one of the reasons why women were attracted to membership in the churches may have been the new identity, authority, and social participation it made possible. Given the high priority Paul attached to the gift of prophecy (cf. 12:28; 14:1-5), it is very significant that underlying what Paul says is the assumption that women as well as men are empowered by God's Spirit to pray and prophesy. Paul's basic concern is not with women's authority to prophesy but with the way they embody that authority.

(d) Specifically, Paul resists ways of embodying spiritual (or "religious") authority which blur gender distinctions. For Paul — as he goes on to argue in ch. 12 — true Christian unity is not a matter of obliterating distinctions but of acknowledging them and making space for them in ways that enable the enrichment of the whole. Just as he refuses to allow those with "knowledge" to act in ways which fail to make space for the "weak" (chs. 8–10), so now he resists ways of embodying spiritual authority which fail to respect conventional ways of symbolizing the difference between women and men.

(e) Related to the preceding, the overall thrust of Paul's argument is not to require the subordination of women; nor, however, does he require women's equality. That is why some of what he says sounds "subordinationist" (e.g., 11:7-9), while other parts of the same argument sound "egalitarian" (e.g., vv. 11-12)! Paul's agenda is different: to promote conciliation in a volatile situation. For Paul, the matter does not have to do with the equality of the sexes or "women's rights" but with how believers (women and men) are to embody their eschatological identity in everyday life in ways which are historically responsible and socially constructive. In relation to the Christian gathering, this means a practice of worship which respects the differences between the sexes (and other differences as well) and allows such differences to be incorporated into a more profound unity.

The subject is a potentially explosive one, so he begins with a word of praise, presenting in the process a little cameo of early Christian formation and the passing on of authoritative tradition (11:2). But then comes the word of correction: first in the form of an argument from shame (vv. 3-6). The Corinthians do not *know* as fully as they think: "the head of every man is Christ, the head of the woman is the man, and the head of Christ is God" (v. 3, RSV). In other words, Christian freedom (including that of the women prophets) is grounded in a divine ordering of things: it is not a license to behave willfully. This divine ordering is hierarchical and is symbolized by the metaphor of "the head" (most likely meaning "ruler" rather than "source"; cf. Fitzmyer 1993 *contra* Fee 1987: 502-5). In ascending order it goes: woman, man, Christ, God. In relation to this order, the women prophets (and their supporters) are behaving shamefully (vv. 5-6). Shame language is language related to pivotal social values often deployed to induce conformity. In this case, values having to do with the basic order of being are under threat: a man who prophesies with his head covered "disgraces his head" (i.e., Christ), and a woman who prophesies with her head uncovered "disgraces her head" (i.e., the man). The shame arises out of the failure to maintain the distinctions — of status, gender, ethnicity, and so on — around which a society organizes its common life; and for Paul, such distinctions remain important for the Christian *ekklēsia* but in a way that is transformed by the gospel.

Then Paul appeals to an argument from Scripture (11:7-12). First, to support the view that the man should not cover his head (and that the woman should), he interprets Gen 1:27 ("So God created humankind in his image . . . male and female he created them") along the lines of a tradition which accords creation in God's image to the male only and which therefore relegates the female to being the glory of the male (cf. Gen 2:18-23). The logic seems to be that the uncovered head of the man will reflect the glory of God (cf. 2 Cor 3:18) and that, since the uncovered head of the woman reflects the glory of the *man* and thus will deflect attention from the glory of *God,* the woman should go with her head covered (11:7). This is reinforced by further appeal to the creation narrative to justify the priority of male over female in the hierarchy of being: the man was created first and the woman was created from the man and, indeed, "for the sake of man" (vv. 8-9; cf. Gen 2:21-23). Then Paul makes the rather opaque statement: "For this reason a woman ought to have authority on her head, because of the angels" (11:10). In context, he probably means by this that, just as the man *ought not* to keep his head covered (v. 7), so the woman *ought* to keep hers covered (but now doing so freely, as a sign of her *exousia;* cf. 8:9), the resulting orderliness of the Christian meeting being such as will honor the divine presence represented by the angels worshiping with them and (perhaps) inspiring their prayer and prophecy (cf. Hays 1997: 187-88).

But now the argument takes a surprising new direction. The conservative thrust of the preceding instruction is qualified by instruction which sounds much more representative of the position of the women prophets and, according to D'Angelo (1988), represents an alternative, more egalitarian interpretation of the Genesis creation account. Thus, in terms strongly reminiscent of the teaching about reciprocal "rights" between wives and husbands in 7:4, he says: "Nevertheless, *in the Lord* woman is not independent of man *or man independent of woman.* For just as woman came from man [cf. Gen 2:21-23], *so man comes through woman* [i.e., in childbirth]; but *all things are from God"* (11:11-12). Here is Paul the conciliator. He brings both conservative (vv. 7-10) and radical (vv. 11-12) interpretations of Genesis into play so that the strengths of each position can be seen and the representatives of each position affirmed.

But this does not mean that Paul remains reticent about his own position: yes, "in the Lord" gender relations are transformed, in matters both of marriage rules (ch. 7) and of the corporate life of the Christian *ekklēsia* (11:2-12); no, the symbols of male-female differentiation are not to be dispensed with, even if they are no longer regarded in the way they were regarded once (cf. the famous *hōs mē* ["as though not"] in 7:29-31). To reinforce the latter, Paul ends with a battery of arguments of different kinds — from propriety (11:13), from nature (vv. 14-15), and from custom (v. 16) — all designed to constrain the women prophets from causing discord, while respecting their *exousia* to pray and prophesy. The conclusion is emphatic and shows Paul's concern as apostle and pastor to maintain church order and discipline: "But if anyone is disposed to be contentious — we have no such custom, nor do the churches of God" (v. 16).

Table Fellowship and the Unity of the Church (11:17-34)

Paul now turns to a second aspect of the practice of the Corinthians when they "come together" in assembly *(en ekklēsią):* their table fellowship (cf. Theissen 1982: 145-72). We have seen already that the Corinthians' table fellowship with *outsiders* concerns Paul on account of the threats it poses to the stability of the church (chs. 8–10). Here his concern surfaces again in an equally acute form, this time in relation to table fellowship *within* the Christian meeting itself (cf. 11:17, 18, 20, 33, 34). Significantly, both in the case of table fellowship with idols and in the present case of disordered table fellowship *en ekklēsią,* Paul appeals to the tradition of the Lord's Supper as a corrective and a control (10:14-22; 11:23-26). Appeal to the tradition of the Lord's Supper *(deipnon)* is significant not only because of its direct relevance to the way each of the Corinthians is eating his or her own meal *(to idion deipnon)* but also because it is part of the larger tradition concerning the death of Christ, which is Paul's constant point of reference for transforming the church's life (cf. 1:18–4:21).

At first sight, the shift Paul makes from the controversy over the women prophets' headcoverings/hairstyles (11:2-16) to the disorderliness of the church's meal practices (vv. 17-34) is hard to follow. But the links are threefold. First, there is a common concern with how to reconcile the freedom and authority of the individual believer and the imperative of "building up" the church as a single body. Second, there is a common concern with the role of memory in building a common life and the associated need for the right interpretation of authoritative tradition (cf. vv. 2, 23), a concern which surfaces again in ch. 15. Third, there is the social-anthropological point that, in both sections, concerns about identity and order in the church find a symbolic focus in rules governing the control of body surfaces and orifices: in the former case, the symbolic focus is the head and hair of the women prophets; in the latter, the focus is the ingestion of food and drink in the course of the common meal (cf. Neyrey 1990: 102-47).

The section has three parts: 11:17-22, 23-26, and 27-34. In vv. 17-22, Paul expresses his strong disapproval of the Corinthians' table fellowship. What should have been a ritual of incorporation and group solidarity, with members of the one body sharing their food and drink in acts of reciprocal hospitality (cf. Neyrey 1996: 159-82), seems to have degenerated into a ritual of rivalry and competitive display threatening to split the fellowship (vv. 18-21). The common meal has become anything but "common." In particular, disparities of wealth and status between members are being dramatized every time they "come together" to eat. How could this be? What is causing the breakdown into "divisions" *(schismata)* and "factions" *(haireseis)*? Vv. 21-22a provide the clue: "For when the time comes to eat, each of you goes ahead with your own supper [*to idion deipnon*], and one goes hungry and another becomes drunk. What! Do you not have homes to eat and drink in? Or do you show contempt for the church of God and humiliate those who have nothing?"

The practice presupposed here is something like a "potluck" supper. When the Christians gather they bring "their own" food and drink with them. However, whereas potluck suppers in the modern West are (ideally) democratic and egalitarian because reciprocity is fairly balanced, in antiquity they were an opportunity, via the practice of unequal reciprocity, to display social superiority and gain social advantage in a competition between rival patrons (cf. Chow 1992: 110-12). A good illustration of the way meals convey meanings of this kind comes from Pliny, describing (what he considers) the social ineptitude of a host at whose table he has dined recently: "Some very elegant dishes were served up to himself and a few more of the company; while those which were placed before the rest were cheap and paltry. He had apportioned in small flagons three different sorts of wine; but you are not to suppose it was that the guests might take their choice: on the contrary, that they might not choose at all. One was for himself and me; the next for his friends of a lower order (for, you must know, *he measures out his friendship according to the degrees of quality*); and the third for his own freedmen and mine . . ." (*Letters* 2.6, quoted in Theissen 1982: 156-57). Against this background, we can see that what is the accepted (if not always approved) meal practice in the households of the society-at-large is being carried over into the meal practice of the church. And of course, this is a tendency which is understandable given that church meetings took place, not in special, purpose-built church buildings — a later development — but in the private houses of the (presumably more prominent and wealthy) members (cf. Barton 1986; for a different view of the social stratification implied in this text, see Meggitt 1998: 118-22).

Paul's response to this serious threat to the church's common life is to appeal to the normative (and, in principle, unifying) tradition of the Lord's Supper (11:23-26; cf. Luke 22:17-19; also Matt 26:26-28; Mark 14:22-24). This tradition is not new to the Corinthians. It is authoritative tradition ("from the Lord") which Paul "handed on" to them in his original teaching (11:23) but which, by a kind of social amnesia induced by prevailing cultural norms, they seem to have forgotten. In reminding them of this Lord's Supper tradition, Paul is offering the Corinthians a framework for reordering both their common meal and the way they think about it: (a) it is "the Lord's meal" *(kyriakon deipnon),* not anyone's "own meal" *(idion deipnon)*; (b) it is a meal of solemn remembrance *(anamnēsis)* and proclamation of the sacrificial ("for you") death of Christ; (c) participation in the meal signifies participation in the "new covenant" relationship with God which the death of Christ makes possible; (d) if it follows the (Passover) pattern of the Lord's Supper, it has a clear beginning (the bread) and ending (the cup); (e) it has an eschatological dimension ("until he comes") with the corollary that it symbolizes both salvation and judgment.

On this basis, Paul calls for a major transformation in the Corinthians' common meal (11:27-34). His goal is for the meal to function as it should, not as a ritual of social enmity but as a ritual of "new covenant" incorporation which, in effect, brings three "bodies" into proper relation with each other: the bodies of individual believers, the social body of the church, and the body of Christ risen and returning (cf. also 10:16-17). That is what is signified in the injunction not to "eat the bread or drink the cup" — which comes emphatically three times (11:27, 28, 29) — without proper "discerning" *(diakrinein).* The discernment required is more than personal self-examination if that is taken in an individualistic, privatized sense. It is a discernment that tests whether or not the individual's practice of table fellowship accords with and contributes to the soteriological and covenantal nature of the meal itself. If it does not, then what is intended to be a material and symbolic instrument of salvation becomes an instrument of judgment, after the biblical pattern.

To put it another way, like holiness the meal has a dangerous quality: those who eat and drink "without discerning the body" invite divine judgment: "For this reason many of you are weak and ill, and some have died" (11:30). However strange in relation to modern sentiments, Paul assumes that there is an intimate connection (the "mechanics" of which are left unspecified, but are elucidated in Martin 1995: 190-97) between the "material" and the "spiritual," between the well-being of individual bodies and the well-being of the social body. That is why individual and corporate judgment are required (vv. 31-32). As in earlier cases (cf. 5:1-12; 6:1-11), Paul wants the church members to take more responsibility for their common life in recognition of the Lordship of Christ and of the eschatological horizon of their existence. Thus, in a final admonition which, by beginning and ending with *synerchesthai* ("to come together"), shows Paul's overarching concern with the Corinthians' pattern of common life, he says: "when you come together *(synerchomenoi)* to eat, wait for one another. If you are hungry, eat at home, so that when you come together *(synerchesthe)*, it will not be for your condemnation" (11:33-34a). Just as eating and drinking can bring either life or death, so the larger context of "coming together" can bring either life or death. The significance of the Christian gathering *en ekklēsią* is no less profound, no less open to promise or perversion, than that.

Gifts of the Spirit and the Unity of the Church (12:1–14:40)

Paul now turns his attention to what he refers to as "spiritual things" *(ta pneumatika)* (12:1; cf. 14:1). This follows from the preceding in a number of ways. First, it continues Paul's attempt to persuade the Corinthians to reorder their behavior when they "come together" as a Christian *ekklēsia* (chs. 11–14). Second, as with gender relations and table fellowship, it is another area of controversy with the potential to divide the fellowship. Third, as in the case of the controversy over idol meat, a central concern is the relation between individual freedom and authority on the one hand and solidarity with the fellowship on the other. Indeed, Paul draws attention to the continuity at this point by structuring the argument of chs. 12–14 in the same way as the argument of chs. 8–10. In both cases he addresses the same issue twice (chs. 8 and 10, 12 and 14), each time moving from a more conciliatory to a more uncompromising position; and in both cases, the two-stage argument is "interrupted" by an appeal to the overriding Christian virtue — self-renunciation (ch. 9) or love (ch. 13) — the exercise of which is to govern action on the respective issues being addressed.

Unity in Diversity in the Body of Christ (12:1-31a)

The first part of Paul's instructions, signaled by his customary formula *peri de* ("now concerning") (12:1; cf. 7:1, 25; 8:1), may be divided into four parts: an introduction on true inspiration and the Spirit (12:1-3), a discussion of the diversity of manifestations of the Spirit within the one body (vv. 4-11), an elaboration of the analogy of the body to illustrate the possibility of unity with diversity (vv. 12-26), and an application with respect to the exercise of gifts in the church as "the body of Christ" (vv. 27-31a). As Hays (1997: 206) points out, however, the goal of Paul's instructions in ch. 12 (and ch. 13) is not self-evident. Only in ch. 14 does a clearer picture of the problem emerge: certain "spiritual gifts" (glossolalia in particular), along with those who exercise them, are being exalted in ways which are detrimental to the stability and upbuilding of the church as a whole (cf. 14:5, 12, 26, 40). That Paul devotes so much attention to this problem and handles it with such care indicates (as with the idol-meat problem) how sensitive an issue it is and how vital for the preservation of the fellowship to get it right.

So Paul begins, not with the problem itself, but further back. As a skilled "pastoral theologian," he begins at the beginning: with a doctrine of the Spirit. With a touch of irony, in view of the Corinthians' confidence in their spiritual prowess, Paul tells them that in the matter of "spiritual things" he does not want them to be ignorant (12:1). He then makes a basic distinction which the Corinthian "spiritual enthusiasts" may have forgotten, to the effect that spiritual power per se is ambiguous. There is a critical difference between, on the one hand, the inspiration that led them, prior to their conversion, to worship idols (12:2; cf. 10:14-22), and since their conversion, to invoke the name of Jesus in a curse — taking *anathema Iēsous* in 12:3a as "Jesus grants a curse" (against an adversary) — and, on the other hand, the inspiration that leads them to confess that "Jesus is Lord" (cf. Winter 1990). That critical difference is identified as *the empowerment bestowed by the Holy Spirit*: "no one can say 'Jesus is Lord' except by the Holy Spirit" (v. 3b). Implicit here is the belief that discernment in the exercise of spiritual power is essential, and that, having passed into the realm of life empowered by the *Holy* Spirit (as opposed to other spirits), care is needed in order to avoid slipping back into pagan assumptions and practices. Implicit also is the belief that *everyone* who confesses the Lordship of Christ has the Spirit. "Spiritual things" are not the preserve of a select few. All of these implications are important for Paul's argument in what follows.

In 12:4-11, Paul goes on to articulate his understanding of "spiritual things" in ways designed to inform and correct the Corinthians' understanding and to counter rivalry and factionalism. We note, first, the telltale terminological shift from *pneumatika* (which is probably the Corinthians' term) to *charismata* in v. 4 (cf. vv. 9, 28, 30, 31). Something momentous is at stake here. It is a shift from understanding spiritual power as the property of the one exercising it (and therefore something to boast about) to understanding spiritual power *as a gift* of divine grace *(charis)* (and therefore something for which to thank God and to use in the service of Christ). Second, vv. 4-6 consist of a three-part, crescendoing sequence of statements which balance carefully an emphasis on the *varieties* of gifts and their *common source* in God. Paul is countering two destructive tendencies: the tendency to exalt one gift only along with those who exercise that gift, and the tendency to overlook the unifying intention of the gifts as gifts of the one God. The emphasis on diversity is conveyed with some subtlety. There is the repetition of "varieties"; the variation of terminology for the gifts themselves (as "gifts," "services," and "activities"); and the corresponding variation in terms for God ("gifts" correlates with "Spirit," "services" correlates with "Lord [Jesus]," and "activities" correlates with the [activating] "God"). The profound implication is that Christian community is not totalitarian: the gifts/services/activities are not uniform but multifarious; they are given by a God who is experienced in various (implicitly trinitarian) ways (as Spirit/Lord/God; cf. 8:6); and they are given, not to a privileged few, but to all (12:6b).

This leads to the statement which summarizes the entire argument of chs. 12–14: "To each is given the manifestation of the Spirit for the common good" (12:7). Since it is given "to each," every member of the fellowship is important and has a contribution to make. Since each one receives as a gift a "manifestation of the Spirit," what each one offers is a revelation, not of human prowess, but of the power of the divine. Finally, such manifestations are given to each, not for their own benefit, but for the benefit of all, summed up in the phrase "for the common good" *(pros to sympheron)* (cf. 6:12; 10:23).

Paul elaborates the "manifestations of the Spirit" in 12:8-10, with another summary statement in v. 11. The list he gives is representative rather than exhaustive since elsewhere the lists differ (cf. 12:28-30; Rom 12:6-8; Eph 4:11-13). It consists of nine "manifestations" which can be divided into three groups, taking our cue from the twofold use of a different Greek word for "other" *(heteros* rather than *allos).* Significantly, the first group consists of the power to speak a word of wisdom *(sophia)* or of knowledge *(gnōsis)* — precisely the things valued highly by the Corinthians (cf. chs. 1–4, 8), but represented now as given for the common good, not just the good of the few. The second group (beginning with *heterǭ,* "to another," in 12:9) consists of five gifts: faith, gifts of healing, the working of miracles, prophecy, and the discernment of spirits. The third consists, like the first, of just two gifts: various kinds of "tongues," and their interpretation. Interestingly, the gifts in the second and third groups, and especially those in the third, are the ones commented on in chs. 13–14. In other words, the list is not random. The gifts chosen are ones particularly prized by the Corinthians. But Paul wants them to understand better what the gifts mean. This is summed up in 12:11. The true benefactor in the Christian *ekklēsia* is not a wealthy patron but the Holy Spirit; and the gifts are given, not according to status or merit but in freedom by "the same Spirit." As such, they are for the building up of the church in the Spirit, not for its division into factions (i.e., a kind of spiritual elite versus the rest).

In passing, the picture implied here of what happens (or *ought* to happen) when the Corinthians "come together" is worth noting (cf. Dunn 1975: 199-342). As well as the eating together, with its Passover and eucharistic elements and its eschatological ("until he comes") ethos (10:14-21; 11:20-34), there is the exercise of a plethora of (what we have come to call) charismatic gifts, prominent among which are inspired speech of various kinds, miracle-working faith (cf. 13:2b, 13a), and gifts of healing. These connote at least two things: (a) a strong sense of the presence of the Spirit energizing all the believers and distributed in ways neither predictable nor conventional (cf. the women prophets in 11:2-16); and (b) an eschatological self-understanding according to which the life of heaven is anticipated in the Corinthians' own common life, especially in the practice of inspired speech (cf. "tongues *of angels*" in 13:1), and in the working of miracles *(dynameis)* and healings as signs of the kingdom. While not without precedent and analogy at various points — the life and traditions of Israel, the temple cult in Jerusalem, the Qumran sectaries, the Pharisaic conventicles, the Greco-Roman voluntary associations, the mystery cults, the philosophical schools, and so on — what is represented here, particularly in its urban, Roman imperial context, is a pattern of "coming together" of considerable social novelty and countercultural significance (cf. Meeks 1983: 75-84; Banks 1994). Herein lie its vitality, creativity, and witness but also its vulnerability to pressures without and within.

Not surprisingly, therefore, Paul appeals, in 12:12-26, to a metaphor well known in the political rhetoric of his day: the metaphor of society as a body. Earlier he has used this metaphor briefly to inform and regulate relations between believers and unbelievers (cf. 6:15). Now he develops it at length to inform relations within the fellowship itself. Even more than the metaphor of the building (cf. 3:10-15), it is the principal image deployed by Paul to overcome factionalism and to move church members toward unity. As Mitchell (1992: 157-64) has shown, the metaphor was used widely in antiquity in speeches calling for social harmony; and Paul uses it to this end also. The value of the metaphor lies in its potential for allowing the social imagination to conceive of the diversity (represented by the various parts of the body) between individuals and classes not as a threat to social and political unity but as making true unity possible through the contribution of the parts to the whole. What Paul does is to take this well-known political metaphor and "Christianize" it by applying it to the polity of the church. Having in the previous section emphasized that the Corinthians have a wonderful diversity of gifts which they have received from "the *same* Spirit" and "for the *common* good," he now reinforces his argument by appealing to the christological image of the *ekklēsia* as "the body *of Christ.*" The link thus established between pneumatology and Christology is worth noting. It may be that Paul is concerned lest the Corinthians' enthusiasm for the Spirit and "spiritual things" is not sufficiently informed by devotion to Christ (cf. 1:13, 17, 18-25).

This helps to make sense of the surprising way in which Paul applies the body metaphor — not directly to the church (although cf. 12:27) but to Christ: "so it is *with Christ*" (v. 12). This implies that the identity of the church is inseparable from that of Christ. The next verse indicates how this is so: "For in the one Spirit we were all baptized into one body — Jews or Greeks, slaves or free — and we were all made to drink of one Spirit" (v. 13). By baptism, the Spirit transforms the identity of disparate types of people into a new unity, the "one body" of Christ. Baptism, in other words, is a ritual of *social inte-*

gration as well as of individual empowerment. Hence the repeated use of "one" ("one Spirit" [twice!], "one body"), the powerful metaphor of ingestion ("*all* made to *drink* of *one* Spirit"; cf. John 7:37-39), and the assertion of differences of race and status (Jew/Greek, slave/free) transcended. (Significantly, the other binary, male/female, is missing; contrast Gal 3:28! In view of the conflict over gender differentiation in worship which Paul addresses a little earlier, in 11:2-26, we may attribute this omission to his concern not to complicate unnecessarily the point he is making here.)

Paul's elaboration of the body metaphor in 12:14-26 is fairly self-explanatory. The main points are as follows: (a) The overall thrust is toward the recognition of the full diversity of members as both God-given (vv. 18, 24; cf. v. 28a) and essential to the well-being of the whole. (b) In line with Paul's endeavors earlier to persuade the "strong" to set the needs of the "weak" firmly on their moral horizon (cf. chs. 8–10), he argues here that "the members of the body that seem to be weaker [*asthenestera*] are indispensable" (v. 22), and worthy therefore of greater honor. In other words, along with the acceptance of diversity (12:14-20) goes the recognition of a necessary interdependence (vv. 21-26). (c) The goal of this divine ordering of things — into what, politically speaking, is a "mixed constitution" — is "that there may be no dissension (*schisma*) in the body" (v. 25a) and, as a corollary, that members' care for one another be "the same" (v. 25b). This is to show itself in a fundamental sympathy and solidarity with fellow members in both suffering and exaltation (v. 26; cf. 13:5-6).

Finally, Paul applies the body metaphor back to the main issue: the exercise of the gifts (12:27-31a). What comes through once again is the God-given necessity of diversity (v. 28), with mutual interdependence as its corollary (vv. 29-30). Worth noting is the fact that the *charismatic polity* Paul envisages here is inclusive and participatory (all have the Spirit), but not straightforwardly democratic or egalitarian (otherwise the gifts of the Spirit would not be *gifts*): "first apostles, second prophets, third teachers; then deeds of power, then gifts of healing, forms of assistance, forms of leadership, various kinds of tongues" (v. 28). There is a ranking here (even if, significantly, it is not comprehensive), with clear precedence (cf. 14:5b) accorded those who by their proclamation of the gospel (apostles), mediation of divine revelation (prophets), and passing on of the (scriptural and Christian) tradition (teachers) bring new churches into being and sustain them in the truth. Interesting also is the inclusion of rather mundane activities like "assistance" (RSV, "helpers") and "leadership" (*kybernēsis;* lit. "steersmanship") alongside the more obviously "charismatic" activities such as miracle working and speaking in tongues. In fact, the gift of tongues is placed last three times in this chapter (at 12:10, 28, 30). This will have come as a shock to the spiritual enthusiasts for whom tongues speaking is the preeminent sign of Spirit possession; and Paul will have meant it so. To accentuate the point, he concludes with an exhortation to "strive for the *greater* gifts" (v. 31a). As we will see in ch. 14, this is a reference, not to "tongues," but to prophecy.

The Unifying Way of Love (12:31b–13:13)

Before he proceeds, however, Paul pauses for another of his rhetorically weighty "digressions." As in 9:1-27, Paul interrupts his argument to introduce the fundamental principle (or, better, *model*) which ought to govern behavior on the subject under discussion. In ch. 9 it had to do with individual self-denial for the sake of the common good; here, in ch. 13, it has to do with the positive corollary: *the priority of love for sustaining the common good.* And, as in ch. 9, Paul undertakes this elaboration by appeal to his own apostolic ministry as embodying and displaying the model he is commending. Like a good father or a good philosopher, Paul teaches by concrete, personal example. The Corinthians will learn the practice of love if they "imitate" him (cf. 11:1). Hence the sudden shift from the second person plural in 12:1-31a to the first person singular in 12:31b (cf. 8:13) — "And *I* will show you a still more excellent way" — with the return to the second person plural in 14:1.

A few general points about love (*agapē*) are worth making at the outset. (a) Love is presented as the "more excellent *way* (*hodon*)." Of course, that does not mean that it is not also a gift from the God who is the source of all love (cf. Rom 5:5, 8; 8:39). But at least here, Paul characterizes it differently: not a *charisma* but a *hodos.* As such it is a whole *way of life* (cf. 4:17; also Acts 24:14, 22) — of temperament, character, morality, belonging, ethos, habit, and practice (individual and corporate) — which is to govern the exercise of "the gifts" and which gives them their very raison d'être. (b) What Paul says here about love is concrete instruction for a specific situation (cf. 8:1b). It is not "merely rhetorical" or "sentimental" or "idealized" — as it becomes so often in the modern world when 1 Corinthians 13 is read at weddings! Rather, it is a *social praxis,* performance of which will serve as an antidote to the attitudes and behaviors in the church which are in danger of tearing it apart. (c) Whereas (some of) the Corinthians are exalting "the gifts" as eschatological realities par excellence, Paul insists that, to a degree that distinguishes it from other gifts and virtues (even "faith" and "hope"), love is *the eschatological reality.* That is why it has the primacy that it does (cf. vv. 8a, 10, 12, 13b) and why the measure of love is applied to all else.

The "digression" has three parts (13:1-3, 4-7, 8-13) and follows a chiastic pattern, with elements in the first part recurring in the third. This makes the characterization of love in vv. 4-7 the focal point. The first part (vv. 1-3) is structured around the threefold occurrence of the phrase, "but do not have love"; that is the crucial ingredient from Paul's point of view. As Holladay (1990: 92) puts it: love is "the primal impulse motivating his apostolic behavior" (cf. 2 Cor 2:4; 11:11; 12:14-15). Three times he names charismatic gifts and actions which he can claim as his own and which are also relevant to the pretensions of the spiritual enthusiasts in Corinth, only to say that, "[If I do these things] but do not have love, I am a noisy gong. . . . I am nothing. . . . I gain nothing."

The actions he lists require brief comment. First, there is the gift of "tongues of mortals and of angels" (13:1). This is a gift practiced by Paul (cf. 14:6, 18) and highly prized by the Corinthians. As a mode of inspired speech-communication with the heavenly realm (cf. 14:2; also *T. Job* 48:1-3a), it is a vivid manifestation of Spirit possession and spiritual authority. Then there is a group of three gifts, also practiced by Paul and prized by the Corinthians (13:2): prophecy, understanding of "all mysteries" and "all knowledge," and the kind of faith that moves mountains (cf., on the latter, Matt 17:19-20; 21:21). The first two of these, like "tongues," have to do with communication between heaven and earth — in particular, the mediation of revelation, especially of "secrets" *(mystēria)* about the end known already in heaven (cf. 15:51; also Dan 2:20-22). Finally, there are two charismatic actions of which (once again) Paul can speak from first-hand experience: the giving away of personal possessions (cf. 4:11; 2 Cor 6:10b) and the related act of "handing over" of his body, presumably in self-discipline or suffering on behalf of others for Jesus' sake (cf. 9:24-27; 2 Cor 4:7-12, esp. v. 11). But all of these, says Paul, however apparently impressive and important, if practiced without love (i.e., for the glory of the charismatic rather than the edification of the church), are worth "nothing."

But how is this "love" to be understood? Paul provides an answer in the focal, central section, 13:4-7. At first sight, his characterization of love appears random, moving between the positive and the negative: "Love is patient; love is kind; love is not envious or boastful. . . ." Closer inspection, however, suggests that the characteristics of love which are stated negatively ("love is not . . .") correspond with the attitudes and practices in the church of which he is critical and, conversely, that the characteristics which are stated positively ("love is . . .") correspond with how he characterizes his own apostleship. Taking the negatives first: "not jealous" recalls Paul's criticism of their jealousy in 3:3; "not boastful" and "not arrogant" (lit. "puffed up") recall his criticism of precisely these traits (cf. 1:29-31; 3:21; 4:6, 18-19; 5:2; 8:1b); and "does not insist on its own way" recalls the propensity of the "strong" to do just that, in contrast to Paul (cf. 10:24, 33b). On the positive side: "patient" and "kind" are virtues Paul claims (cf. 2 Cor 6:6); "rejoices in the truth" is echoed in Paul's testimony in 2 Cor 13:8; and "bears all things . . . endures all things" recalls his autobiographical statement in 9:12b ("we endure anything rather than put an obstacle in the way of the gospel"). The force of these correlations with the Corinthians on the one hand and with Paul on the other is considerable. They imply that, as an alternative social praxis, it is love that will unify a church which is divided, and that, as love's embodiment, Paul is the model to be imitated.

The third and final section (13:8-13) now sets the gifts spoken of at the outset in the light of the immediately preceding characterization of love. In effect, *love is made the measure of everything else,* something implicit in the *inclusio* by which references to love bracket the whole section (vv. 8a, 13b). Paul's main point is that, whereas love is the full and final eschatological reality, the gifts of the Spirit are temporary and transitory. Thus, whereas "love never ends [lit. "falls"]," prophecies and knowledge "will be brought to an end," and tongues will "cease." Contrary to the Corinthians' understanding of the gifts (cf. 4:8), their value is relative and temporary (noting the threefold occurrence of *katargēthēsetai* ["will be brought to an end"] in 13:8, 10; cf. 2:6; 6:13; 15:24-26). The *charismata* make possible what would not be possible otherwise in the time prior to the coming of the kingdom of God: anticipatory, partial sharing in the life of heaven. But when the kingdom of God comes (cf. 15:24-28), the mediation of revelation through "prophecies" and "knowledge" will not be necessary since revelation will be total and unmediated. The gift of "tongues" likewise will be unnecessary because communication will be total, "face to face" (cf. 13:12). All that will be left, all that will be necessary, will be the completeness (*to teleion,* v. 10) of relation, human and divine, which is love.

In 13:11-12 Paul drives his point home with the aid of two metaphors pertinent, as ever, to the Corinthian situation. The first is the metaphor of growth to maturity (v. 11). By appealing again to his apostolic autobiography, he challenges the Corinthians — ironically, in view of their self-estimation as mature already (cf. 3:1-4) — to grow up in their understanding and practice of the gifts by "putting an end" (*katargein* again) to "childish ways." To drive home the point that they have not yet "arrived" and that their *gnōsis* is partial only, Paul then introduces a second metaphor with an interpretative elaboration: "For now we see in a mirror, dimly [lit. "in a riddle"], but then we will see face to face. Now I know only in part; then I will know fully, even as I have been fully known" (13:12). Note the twofold contrast between "now" and "then": an eschatological distinction which the Corinthians appear to have forgotten in their claim to have "arrived" spiritually already. For Paul, direct, unmediated knowledge of God — a "knowledge" which is not narrowly "intellectual" but the moral-relational "knowledge" which is *agapē* (cf. 8:1-3) — lies still in the future, at a time when God and mortals will communicate no longer "in riddles" but as God spoke with Moses, "face to face" (cf. Num 12:6-8).

Prior to the coming of the kingdom in all its fullness, however, "faith, hope, and love abide [better: "remain"]" (13:13a). Hays (1997: 231) explains this triad of virtues in appropriate, theocentric vein: "Faith is the trust that we direct toward the God of Israel, who has kept faith with his covenant promises by putting forward Jesus for our sake and raising him to new life; hope focuses our fervent desire to see a broken world restored by God to its rightful wholeness (Rom. 8:18-39); and love is the foretaste of our ultimate union with God, graciously given to us now and shared with our brothers and sisters." But Paul does not stop there. A final statement sums up the argument as a whole: "the greatest of these is love" (13:13b). Only when they recognize this will the Corinthians *really* share in the life of the age to come. Only when they practice this will their individual and corporate lives reflect the unity and maturity of the children of God.

Unifying Speech (14:1-40)

In ch. 12 Paul argues for the unity of the church on the basis of full recognition of the diversity of gifts of the Spirit, with the (highly prized) gift of tongues as only one among many, and all given for "the common good." Then, in ch. 13, Paul elaborates on what above all else, because of its eschatological finality, will contribute to the unity of the church: the social praxis of love. With these foundations laid, he now returns to the issue of "spiritual things" *(ta pneumatika)* to show how their practice can be so ordered as to achieve what they do not achieve at present — namely, the "building up" of the fellowship as the concrete expression of love. So strong is the emphasis on what "builds up" (cf. 14:3-5, 12, 17, 26) that ch. 14 can profitably be seen as an exposition of Paul's earlier statement in 8:1b, that "knowledge puffs up, but love builds up."

The chapter has two main parts, according to the structure of Paul's argument (cf. Fee 1987: 652). In the first (14:1-25), Paul argues for the priority of gifts which are *intelligible;* in the second (vv. 26-40), he argues for an exercise of gifts which is *orderly.* The two parts of the argument are brought together skillfully at the end, as we shall see (vv. 39, 40). Paul's basic point overall is that intelligibility and orderliness will counteract present divisions and contribute to building up the church in unity. What is remarkable, in this lengthy section, is Paul's almost exclusive concentration on charismatic gifts of *speech,* especially "speaking in tongues" *(glossais lalein)* and prophecy. This is significant. First, it reminds us of the power of speech and language (of all kinds) to define a community (cf. Leach 1976). It is not coincidental, therefore, that the self-understanding of the church as a community of the eschatological Spirit should express itself in acts of inspired speech (cf. also 2:6-7, 13; 11:2-16; 12:3). Second, because speech is an act of interpersonal communication, it can consolidate communal relations or threaten them. A common or shared language is a *sine qua non* of political unity and social concord. This helps to explain why Paul addresses at length the practice of "speaking in tongues." While it may well be uniting individual "tongues" speakers with God (cf. 14:2), it is having the disastrous effect of dividing them from each other and from the fellowship as a whole. So what Paul offers here is *a morality of speech acts ordered to achieve the consolidation of the church in love.*

The first part of the argument (14:1-25) begins with a section urging that priority be given to prophesying over speaking in tongues (vv. 1-5). The primary goal of their common life, established in ch. 13, is reiterated first: "Pursue love" (14:1a). Then comes the imperative to be zealous for *ta pneumatika,* "especially that you may prophesy" (v. 1b). Why prophecy more than "tongues"? Because "tongues" is a heavenly language unintelligible to mortals. It concerns "mysteries in the Spirit" which are addressed to God alone (v. 2). Prophecy, on the other hand, is an intelligible word of revelation, given *via* a prophet for the "upbuilding and encouragement and consolation" of the fellowship (vv. 3-4). On these grounds, Paul does not hesitate to rank the two gifts and those who exercise them. At the same time he is careful not to alienate those with the gift of "tongues": "I would like you *all* to speak in tongues, but *even more* to prophesy" (v. 5a); and "tongues" are permissible in the gathering if the speaker is able then to interpret the "mystery" so communicated (v. 5b).

Paul offers basically the same argument for the priority of prophecy over "tongues" in 14:20-25, but this time with regard to the effect of the respective kinds of communication upon *outsiders (idiōtai).* This argument is significant on at least two counts. It implies that the "coming together" is not an exclusive assembly — and in this it is like the synagogue and many pagan religious gatherings but unlike the Pharisaic *ḥaburot* and the Qumran community. It also implies that the measure of love (in the form of gifts which are "upbuilding") applies not only to believers but also to unbelievers. Unfortunately, the thread of Paul's argument here is difficult to follow, especially at vv. 21-22 (on which see Dunn 1975: 230-32; Fee 1987: 680-83): although it is apparent that in describing "tongues" as "a sign not for believers *but for unbelievers,*" Paul is turning the Corinthians' evaluation of this gift on its head. What is clear from vv. 23-25, however, is that, whereas "tongues" (because they are unintelligible) will be a stumbling block to unbelievers, prophesying (because it is a clearly intelligible word of revelation) will open unbelievers up to the convicting presence of God, so that instead of saying, "You are out of your mind [like ecstatic devotees of a mystery cult]!" they will make the eschatological confession (cf. Isa 45:14; 49:23; 60:10-16), "God is really among you!"

In the intervening material (14:6-19), Paul elaborates on the limited value of the gift of tongues. He begins autobiographically (v. 6; cf. v. 19). Contrary, perhaps, to their expectations, he has not come to them speaking in tongues (cf. 2:1-2) since that would not "benefit" them. What is of benefit (because intelligible) is his speaking to them "revelation or knowledge or prophecy or teaching," an important list for the insight it gives into the kinds of communication — no less inspired than "tongues" — which according to Paul contribute most to the good of the Christian assembly. As for "tongues," they are like the sounds of a harp or flute played randomly (v. 7), or like a bugle whose summons to battle is blurred and indistinct (vv. 8-9), or like people who are foreigners *(barbaroi)* to each other because neither knows what the other is saying (vv. 10-11). The analogies are then applied to the Corinthians in terms of the overriding morality of "upbuilding": "So with yourselves; since you are eager for spiritual gifts, strive to excel in them *for building up the church*" (v. 12).

He then spells out how to apply the principle of "upbuilding" to the gatherings (14:13-19). In short, the one who speaks in tongues should seek (in prayer) the gift of the interpretation of tongues also (v. 13). The next verses (14-15) give us a fascinating glimpse into the nature of early Christian charismatic self-understanding and practice. Note especially the following: (a) The "spiritual gifts" may be prayed for (v. 13). Paul's God is one whose grace *(charis),* in response to prayer, overflows in *charismata,* manifestations of his presence as Spirit. (b) The gifts are given to promote worship. Hence Paul's specific mention of praying, singing, blessing, and giving thanks to God. (c) They enable worship at the most profound level of human being: indicated by the recurrent phrase, "with the spirit." (d) Just as Paul wants to resist a divided gathering in worship, so he seeks to resist a divided personality in worship: "with the spirit . . . *and with the mind also.*" (e) The principle of showing love for the "weaker" member (cf. chs. 8–10) remains operative; otherwise those who speak in "tongues" exclude those who cannot understand what is being said (vv. 16-17).

This latter point is reinforced by a characteristic autobiographical conclusion (14:18-19). Paul thanks God that he speaks in tongues more than all of the "spiritual enthusiasts" in Corinth, but personal advantage is not what matters (cf. 10:33). With typical hyperbole, he says, therefore: "[I]n church I would rather speak five words with my mind, *in order to instruct others also,* than ten thousand words in a tongue" (v. 19). Then, as we have seen, having applied this argument to believers, he applies it in relation to unbelievers *(apistoi)* present at the gathering (vv. 20-25). Prophecy and other gifts of inspired speech which are intelligible are given priority since they are what "build up" believers and convert unbelievers.

The second part of the chapter (14:26-40) picks up on a problem with speaking in "tongues" hinted at in v. 23 (cf. vv. 27, 33): not only is unintelligibility a barrier to harmony and growth in the assembly, but disorder is also. So what Paul gives is a kind of charismatic "order of service" for when the Corinthian Christians "come together." Throughout this passage we find Paul's most characteristic emphases: full recognition of the diversity of gifts given to each, alongside an insistence on mutual "upbuilding" as the purpose for which the gifts are given (cf. esp. vv. 26, 33, 39-40). It is precisely because these two goals may be in tension that instructions about the "order of service" are required. So the number of "tongues" speakers is restricted, and they are to speak in turn; but even then, only if they are able to interpret what they are saying. Otherwise they are to confine their practice of the gift to the domain of their private prayer (vv. 27-28). Similarly, only "two or three" prophets are to speak, taking their turn, with the remainder exercising discernment concerning the truth of the prophecies (vv. 29-30). Even though Paul can make the remarkable statement that "you can *all* prophesy one by one," he adds straightaway the crucial moral-ecclesial qualifier: "so that *all may learn* and *all be encouraged*" (v. 31). That explains why no ground is given to those in Corinth who claim that Spirit possession overrides the will of the inspired individual. Not only are "tongues" speakers told to "be silent" in the assembly if they cannot interpret; but to the prophets Paul says, "the spirits of prophets are subject to the prophets" (vv. 28, 32). All this culminates in a word of "political theology" about the nature of God: "for God is a God not of disorder but of peace" (v. 33). The church, as a kind of Christian *polis,* is a faith-community, oriented not on rivalry and division but on the eschatological reality which the "gifts" are intended to foster — namely, "peace." Nor does this apply to the Corinthians only. It applies (taking v. 33b with what precedes rather than what follows) to them "as in all the churches of the saints."

Paul concludes his argument for the orderly exercise of the "gifts" in a characteristically forceful fashion (cf. 4:18-21). First come the ironic rhetorical questions designed to put the "spiritual enthusiasts" in their place (14:36). Next, a direct assertion of the binding authority of what he is writing: it is nothing less than "a command of the Lord" — which those who are true prophets and truly "spiritual" *(pneumatikos)* will acknowledge (v. 37; cf. 3:18; 8:2), and rejection of which will lead to rejection by God (v. 38; cf. Mark 8:38). Finally, there is the recapitulation of the argument as a whole, with its dual emphasis on the priority of prophecy (and kindred gifts of revelatory utterance) over "tongues" (on grounds of intelligibility) and the right ordering of "spiritual gifts" when the Corinthians assemble so that "all things [are done] decently and in order" (vv. 39-40).

But what about the now-(in)famous rules about women speaking in the assembly in 14:34-35 (cf., in addition to the commentaries, Fiorenza 1983: 230-33; Witherington 1995; Wire 1990: 149-58)? A persuasive, but not quite water-tight, case can be made that these verses are a post-Pauline interpolation. (a) Some (Western) manuscripts place vv. 34-35 after v. 40, indicating scribal uncertainty about these verses resulting in attempts to relocate them in a more appropriate place. Certainly, omission of vv. 34-35 would iron out what appears to be something of a dislocation in the text. However, no extant manuscripts omit the verses entirely, and all the evidence indicates that, even if they are post-Pauline, they are early. (b) In terms of content, the rules themselves ("[W]omen should be silent in the churches . . .") appear to contradict the undoubted assumption in 11:2-16 that women, as well as men, pray and prophesy in the assembly. They also seem to contradict the pre-Pauline understanding of baptismal identity in Christ (cf. Gal 3:27-28) and Paul's vision of charismatic community, together with his practical partnership with both women and men in his apostolic mission. But, as we saw in relation to 11:2-16, Paul could still insist on the maintenance of symbols of gender differentiation even within the context of Spirit-inspired "coming together." (c) The rules compare favorably with the teaching of the later work of the Pauline "school," especially 1 Tim 2:11-12 (". . . I permit no woman to teach or to have authority over a man; she is to keep silent"). In this light, they are a post-Pauline interpolation of the second or third generation of Christianity, reflecting an attempt to counter the charismatic authority of Christian women by reinterpreting Paul's letter in a more conservative (i.e., patriarchal) direction. At the same time, it is quite possible that the origins of this conservative reaction lie with Paul himself (cf. his omission of "no male and female" in 12:13 in contrast to Gal 3:28), and that 1 Cor 14:34-35 is evidence of this.

If these verses are not authentically Pauline, at least they were judged authentic to the spirit of Paul's thought by an early scribe and so entered the Christian canon. Whatever the case, what is required of the interpreter — here *and at every other point* — is theological judgment historically informed. (How we interpret Pauline texts which assume the legitimacy of slavery is an obvious analogy.) Taking the verses as they stand, therefore, a few points are noteworthy. First, the command to "be silent" links 14:34-35 with the twofold command to silence in the preceding vv. 28 and 30. So the concern to restrict speech acts which disrupt the meeting is sustained here. Second, it is possible that it is *wives,* not women in general, who are the focus of concern since Paul says, "If there is anything they desire to know, let them ask *their husbands* [lit. "their own males"] at home" (v. 35a, NRSV). If so, the rules would be consistent with Paul's general support for (a "Christianized") household order (cf. ch. 7). Third, it may be that the kind of speech is not praying or prophesying, but disruptive interventions of a different kind — questions from some about the interpretation of "tongues" or prophecies, for instance. Fourth, it is evident from 11:17-34 that Paul wants to draw a line of a fairly pragmatic kind between what the Corinthians do "at home" and what they do "in church" (11:22a, 34a). The same attempt to keep household patterns and ecclesial patterns somewhat distinct is evident in relation to speech acts in 14:34-35. It is precisely because the "coming together" takes place in a household setting (cf. 16:19) that misunderstandings and strife over meal practices (11:17-34) and gender roles (11:2-16; 14:34-35) are easy to envisage (cf. Barton 1986: 229-34). In general, therefore, Paul's (not satisfactorily argued) reassertion of a modified patriarchal authority — both in 11:2-16 and 14:34-35 — may be understood as part of a pragmatic attempt to establish and maintain a framework of social order within which a Spirit-inspired common life can be built up.

Unity in the Gospel and Resurrection Faith (15:1-58)

The building up of a Spirit-inspired common life is not just a matter of an agreed "order of service," however. It is also a matter of *agreement in fundamental matters of doctrine grounded in a shared, authoritative tradition.* For matters of belief may be just as divisive as matters of practice; and, in any case, belief and practice are two sides of the same coin. Seen in this light, Paul's discussion of the resurrection of the dead in ch. 15 is by no means unrelated to his persuasive intentions in the letter as a whole. The following observations are relevant.

First, the disagreement in Corinth over the doctrine of the resurrection is understandable in the context of the times. Within Judaism, for example, there was a diversity of beliefs about the fate of the dead (cf. Josephus *J.W.* 2.119ff., 162-66; also de Boer 1988: 39-91), and such diversity could be a cause of faction and disunity. Note, for example, the terminology of "parties" and social discord surrounding resurrection belief in Acts 23:6-10. Given its potential as a source of social division in Judaism, it is no wonder that Paul attends so carefully to resurrection doctrine in the pluralistic environment of Roman Corinth where diversity of beliefs about the fate of the dead was so much greater and skepticism about the specific idea of bodily resurrection so much more likely (cf. Wedderburn 1987: 167-211; Witherington 1995: 291-98).

Second, that there is a problem does not surface immediately. Only in 14:12 does Paul ask his pointed rhetorical question: "How can some of you say there is no resurrection of the dead?" Attempts to identify this offending group and to explain their denial of the resurrection have been many and various (cf. de Boer 1988: 96-105). One widely held view is that some of the Corinthians (the *pneumatikoi*) hold to an "overrealized" eschatology according to which, through the rite of water baptism, the end-time life of the Spirit has come already and the resurrection, as the liberation of the individual into the realm of "'the spiritual," has already taken place (cf. 4:8). As a corollary, the seriousness of corporate historical existence is being trivialized and the eschatological reality and corrupting power of death *(thanatos)* are being denied. But judging from Paul's response, that does not seem to be the only problem. Given Paul's stress on belief in the resurrection as a *bodily* event, it seems likely also that the view he is trying to correct is one that denies not only a future resurrection but also a future resurrection of the body (cf. v. 35). This correlates well with issues he tackles earlier on, where (as we have seen) those who claim that they are "'spiritual" and have "knowledge" *(gnōsis)* are departing from the norms of a traditional Christian morality of embodiment in favor of a morality in which the body is a matter of indifference at best (cf. 6:12-20, esp. 13b-14).

Third, and related, whereas on some issues Paul shows a willingness to be accommodating (cf. 9:19-23), the same cannot be said for his treatment of the doctrine of the resurrection of the dead. The reason is not just pastoral or political — having to do with maintaining the unity of the Christian *ekklēsia* — though that is an issue. Even more, however, the reason is "evangelical." Christ crucified *and risen from the dead* is the very heart of Paul's gospel and apostleship (cf. 15:1-11; Gal 1:1-9). Everything else flows from that proclamation *(kērygma).* Indeed, from Paul's point of view, it is because the Corinthians have not grasped fully the meaning and significance of that kerygma, or have *reinterpreted* the kerygma in terms of an anthropology, soteriology, and Christology at odds with what they heard from Paul, that their common life is so vulnerable to dissolution. Their "coming together" does not build up because it is so unbalanced in the direction of speaking in "tongues of angels" (chs. 12–14) that matters of personal and social embodiment (including the conviction that corporeal human existence has a past and a future, not just an ecstatic present) are being neglected.

This leads to a fourth observation: Paul's teaching in ch. 15 does not stand in splendid isolation from all that has come before. On the contrary, it is related integrally to it and may be seen as the culmination of all that Paul wants to say (cf. Barth 1933). Although Paul may have made only passing reference previously to the doctrine of the resurrection (cf. 6:14), he has argued again and again for a more adequate *eschatological self-understanding;* and hope in the future bodily resurrection of the dead is part of that wider, eschatological horizon of belief. As Dunn (1995: 85) puts it: "This [eschatological] dimension of the Corinthians' existence had in effect been a subplot all along." For example, (a) Paul's teaching about the cross as the revelation of the power and wisdom of God would make no sense apart from the resurrection of the Crucified One which it presupposes (cf. 1:30). (b) The eschatological "glory" which, in the "secret and hidden" wisdom of God, is the destiny of believers (2:7) is the gift of God at the resurrection of the dead. (c) Paul's affirmation that to the Corinthians belong even "the world *or life or death* or the present or the future . . . and you belong to Christ, and Christ belongs to God" (3:22-23) presupposes an eschatological hope in the resurrection of the dead. Rather than being a self-contained treatise on the resurrection, therefore, ch. 15 is a climactic restatement of the gospel of the Lordship of the crucified and risen Christ and the sovereignty of God (cf. 15:24-28, 57). As such, it is a summons to live and die in a way that is not a denial of the body and the reality of death (*via* escape into "things spiritual") but an outworking of hope in the God who raises the dead.

Paul's argument has three main parts (15:1-11, 12-34, 35-58). In the first, Paul sets out what he wants to be understood as the common ground which unites them all: "the gospel" of Christ crucified and risen. The crucifixion and resurrection *of Christ* is the first and most important step in his argument against those who deny the resurrection of the dead (cf. v. 12). Here, as at the very beginning of his letter, Paul's argument is gospel-centered (cf. 1:17), and emphatically so: since the gospel is the eschatological power of God to overcome evil and death, a power which Paul "proclaimed," which the Corinthians "received," in which they "stand," and by which (in a process which is *not yet complete*) they "are being saved" (vv. 1-2b) — but which it is also possible to forfeit by believing "in vain" (v. 2c).

But as well as being gospel-centered, Paul's argument is also historical and ecclesial. The gospel has not originated from him. Rather, he is part of a chain of authoritative tradition (*"I handed on to you* as of first importance *what in turn I had received"*), and that tradition is a dual one of scriptural and eye-witness testimony to Christ's death and resurrection (14:3-8). As is recognized widely, Paul incorporates a very early Christian confession into his argument here: "that Christ died for our sins in accordance with the scriptures, / and that he was buried, / and that he was raised on the third day in accordance with the scriptures, / and that he appeared to Cephas, then to the twelve" (vv. 3b-5; cf. the gospel resurrection narratives). To this early tradition, Paul adds resurrection appearances to "more than five hundred brothers and sisters at one time," James (presumably the brother of Jesus), "all the apostles," and finally, "as to one untimely born [lit. "as to an aborted foetus"!]," Paul himself (vv. 6-8).

Not surprisingly, given the significance of this material for Christian faith, these verses have been the focus of enormous attention (cf. Carnley 1987; Davis et al. 1997). Here we may simply note these points: first, the phrase "in accordance with the scriptures" (twice) does not specify particular scriptural texts. Presumably these were well known (e.g., Pss 16:9-11; 110:1; Isa 53:5-6, 11-12; Hos 6:2; etc.). More important is the underlying assumption that Christ's death and resurrection are the eschatological fulfillment of God's promises to Israel and the nations. Second, the reference to the fact "that he was buried" is an emphatic statement of the reality of Christ's death. It was not avoided or foreshortened in any way. In this case, his resurrection was a bodily resurrection from death and the realm of the dead. Third, that Christ "was raised" (*egēgertai,* a perfect passive) is indicative of an act of God (cf. 15:15). Christ's resurrection is seen as an eschatological act of God, an inauguration of a new order of things, and an anticipation of the general resurrection of the dead (cf. vv. 20-28). Fourth, the recurring verb translated "he appeared" (*ōphthē*) literally means, "he [Christ] *was seen* [by so-and-so]" (vv. 5, 6, 7, 8). Some interpret this "seeing" as straightforward ocular perception, but this is hard to reconcile with the fact that the risen, transformed body of Christ was not "flesh and blood" (v. 50; cf. vv. 42-49). Others interpret it as a kind of religious "insight" into Christ's "risenness," but this view is reductionist and "psychologizing" and does not do justice to the appearance traditions. More likely, the truth lies somewhere in between: an "objective" vision of a real, differently embodied heavenly being, the Risen Christ, in identity continuous with but also different from the man of Nazareth (cf. Carnley 1987: 223-34). Fifth, the list of witnesses, including Paul, is important. In the context, it is a claim both about the verifiability of faith in Christ's bodily resurrection (cf. v. 6: "most of whom are still alive") and about the authority of the ones to whom the revelation was given.

But Paul does not stand on his apostolic dignity (15:9-11)! On the contrary, he presents his own experience as the gospel in miniature, a story of divine grace transforming evil, of resurrection power miraculously overcoming death. This has the intention of deflecting potential criticism (as one who was not one of the twelve and who "persecuted the church of God"; cf. 9:1-2). It also has the intention of serving as a pointed example to the Corinthians of God's grace not being given "in vain" but resulting instead, not only in his own conversion, but also in theirs (if they remain faithful).

Now Paul turns to the second stage in his argument (15:12-34). Having laid the gospel foundations (summed up in the conditional clause, "Now if Christ is proclaimed as raised from the dead," v. 12a), he at last broaches the point of contention: "how can some of you [i.e., you *pneumatikoi*] say there is no resurrection of the dead?" (v. 12b). Paul responds to this challenge by counterfactually allowing the position (that there is no resurrection of the dead) in order to overthrow it. He does so by pursuing two reverse lines of argument. In vv. 12-19, he argues that the position is self-defeating since it would mean that *Christ* has not been raised; and if that is so, then the apostolic preaching (*kērygma*) has been "in vain," the Corinthians' own faith likewise has been "in vain," God has been represented falsely, the Corinthians have not been saved from their sins, those who have died already are without hope, and (to cap it all) there is the shame and ignominy of knowing that "we are of all people most to be pitied." In passing, it is worth noting here that Paul does not argue for the resurrection of the dead from philosophical first principles. Rather, he argues from the integrity of Christian faith and hope grounded upon the proclamation that God raised Christ. To put it another way, if the position of the *pneumatikoi* is indebted to a philosophically informed repugnance at the idea of bodily resurrection, Paul's response comes in other terms

— terms shaped by Paul's own apocalyptic gospel (cf. Beker 1980: 163-81; de Boer 1988: 93-140).

Then, in 15:20-34, Paul takes the reverse line of argument and argues that, if Christ *has* been raised, then the future resurrection of the dead is the inevitable corollary. In a word of testimony that constitutes the central message of the whole chapter, he begins: "But in fact Christ has been raised from the dead, the first fruits *(aparchē)* of those who have died" (v. 20). This is the prelude to an elaboration of his apocalyptic gospel built in part around the antinomies of death and resurrection, Adam and Christ (vv. 21-22), in part also around an eschatological doctrine of the divine ordering of time climaxing in the triumph of Christ over all God's enemies, the last and most powerful of which is (personified) Death (vv. 23-26).

So, says Paul, summing up the totality of human history in a story of two representative humans: "For since death came through a human being, the resurrection of the dead has also come through a human being; for as in Adam all die, so all will be made alive in Christ." Unlike the Corinthians, who seem able to think only in terms of individual salvation (as release into the realm of disembodied spirit), Paul maps human experience on a universal scale, at the heart of which is the cosmic struggle between death and the resurrection power of God manifested in Christ, the "first fruits" of God's eschatological harvest. The point of the eschatological timetable in vv. 23-26 is twofold. On the one hand, it indicates the *inevitability and assured character* of what is to come (including the resurrection of those who belong to Christ), now that Christ has been raised as the "first fruits." On the other, it situates the resurrection of the Corinthians *at a point yet to come,* that is, when Christ returns. The implication of the latter is that the Corinthians are *not yet* raised from the dead (into a "spiritual" existence), as some of them seem to have believed. Nor yet do they "reign" with Christ in heaven (cf. 4:8). Rather, it is Christ who reigns (cf. 12:3b). Indeed, it is an eschatological necessity (note "he *must* . . ." in 15:25) that he reign, so that every "rule," "authority," and "power" opposed to God (including, finally, death itself) may be defeated (cf. Rom 5:12-21). Only then is the resurrection of the dead possible. But note that Christ's eschatological victory is not grounds for boasting, either on the part of Christ or on the part of those who boast in their special allegiance to Christ (cf. 1:12). For Christ is not an end unto himself (cf. 15:27-28). Rather, he is *the Son* whose mission is fulfilled only as he "hands over the kingdom to God *the Father* . . . that God may be all in all" (vv. 24, 28). As Christ finds fulfillment in a life whose ultimate goal *(telos)* is submission as the Son to the Father, so (by implication) the Corinthians will find fulfillment and concord in a life of submission to Christ and the Father.

Finally, in a return to the main problem, Paul adds further *ad hominem* arguments against those who deny the resurrection of the dead (cf. 15:12). First, the Corinthians' own ritual practice (of surrogate baptism on behalf of the dead, a suggestive analogy for which appears in 2 Macc 12:43-45) testifies against denial of the resurrection of the dead and would be rendered meaningless apart from resurrection faith (15:29). Second, and in yet another appeal to the example of his own apostleship, Paul points to the futility of his sufferings and near-death experiences on their behalf if there is no resurrection of the dead (vv. 30-32a; cf. 4:11-13; 2 Cor 4:8-12). Third, denial of the doctrine has a moral corollary. It means the end of hope, which is an invitation to the permissive morality of despair — "'Let us eat and drink, for tomorrow we die'" (15:32b, quoting Isa 22:13). But Paul wants the Corinthians to pull back from such a morality. "Do not be deceived [lit. "led astray"]," he warns, following which he quotes a proverbial saying from the Greek poet Menander: "'Bad company ruins good morals'" (15:33). What "bad company" does Paul have in mind? The answer comes in the reference to "some people who have no knowledge of God" (v. 34b) — perhaps a reference to pagan philosophies which deny a doctrine of bodily resurrection. However that may be, the characterization uncovers the fundamental issue at stake in the entire argument: the knowledge of God. For Paul, *the doctrine of the resurrection of the dead is part of the doctrine of God* since the God of Jesus Christ is the God who raises the dead. That the Corinthians could allow themselves to be so influenced by the skeptics among their contemporaries is not at all to their credit. In stern rebuke, Paul concludes (not for the first time), "I say this to your shame" (v. 34c; cf. 6:5).

Paul might well have ended at this point. Instead, in a third stage of the argument (15:35-58), he tries to get to the root of one of the main contributory factors in the Corinthians' resistance to belief in the resurrection of the dead, namely, incredulity at the idea of the resurrection of *the body* (*sōma,* a term which occurs nine times in vv. 35, 37, 38, 40, and 44). This is the force of the specifying question, posed by an imaginary interlocutor: "With what kind of body *(sōmati)* do they come?" (v. 35b). Overall, Paul's response represents a refusal to adopt a defensive posture: it is those who assume a crassly materialistic doctrine of resurrection (as the resuscitation of *corpses*) and show therefore their doubt in the creative power of God that are put on the spot (as "fools"! v. 36a; cf. Ps 14:1). By a series of arguments and analogies, Paul seeks to win the Corinthian *pneumatikoi* to a doctrine of resurrection which, rather than denying the body as an encumbrance to be sloughed off at death, affirms somatic (but not material) continuity between the present and the future on the basis of the power of God to transform the "natural" body into a "spiritual" body, an eschatological reality already revealed in the victorious resurrection of Jesus Christ.

Thus, in 15:36-44 he uses two kinds of analogies (seeds and kinds of bodies) to argue for both somatic *continuity and transformation.* First, the change from the seed which "dies" in the ground to the wheat which subsequently appears allows Paul to make the crucial theological affirmation that "*God gives it a body as he has chosen,* and to each kind of seed its own body" (v. 38). The latter point about bodies that are appropriate for different modes of existence is developed in vv. 39-41, where there is a graduation from talk about terrestrial bodies to talk about heavenly bodies, along with the different "glory" *(doxa)* that characterizes each (cf. Dan 12:2-3). These analogies are then applied to the resurrection of the dead in a series of binary oppositions — perishable/imperishable, dishonor/glory, weakness/power, "physical" body/"spiritual" body — intended to display the marvelous transformation of the body effected by God in the act of resurrection (15:42-44; cf. Phil 3:20-21).

The last of these binaries, bodies *psychikos* and *pneumatikos,* is the focal point since this is the crucial distinction Paul wants to introduce as a corrective. To those in Corinth who believe that they are *pneumatikoi* already (because they have been baptized, speak in tongues of angels, etc.), Paul is arguing for a strong "not yet" (cf. esp. 15:46). In the present, the time between the resurrection and the parousia ("coming") of Christ, believers are still "soulish" (cf. "soul," *psychē*); they are *not yet* "spiritual" (cf. *pneuma,* "spirit"). So rather than translate as (respectively) "physical" and "spiritual" (so RSV and NRSV), which seems to reinforce precisely the dichotomy which Paul is trying to move beyond, some other way of signifying the difference is required. That is why the NIV has "natural body" and "spiritual body," while the JB paraphrases v. 44 thus: "When it is sown it embodies the soul, when it is raised it embodies the spirit. If the soul has its own embodiment, so does the spirit have its own embodiment" (cf. Hays 1997: 272).

Paul elaborates and clarifies this dichotomy in 15:45-49 by referring again (cf. v. 22) to the Adam/Christ typology. Noticeable is the way Christology is never far away in Paul's pattern of persuasion. In particular, here, as in vv. 20-28, it is Christ's resurrection from the dead which serves as the critical reference point. Quoting Gen 2:7 (LXX), Paul says: "Thus it is written, 'The first man, Adam, became a living being [lit. "soul," *psychē*]'; the last Adam became a life-giving spirit *(pneuma)*" (15:45). Then, emphatically, the order of the two representative types of humanity is asserted ("But it is *not* the spiritual [or heavenly] that is first, but the natural [or soulish], and *then* the spiritual"), the clear implication being that the Corinthians have foreshortened God's eschatological work by exalting themselves as "spiritual" *(pneumatikoi)* already, the effect of which is to obliterate the very real, eschatological distinction that exists between Adam ("the man of dust") and Christ ("the man of heaven"), between believers' present as "soulish" and their glorious future as bearers of "the image of the man of heaven" (v. 49).

A final, climactic section brings the argument to a close (15:50-58). First, Paul summarizes what has gone before: "[F]lesh and blood cannot inherit the kingdom of God, nor does the perishable inherit the imperishable" (v. 50). This is so, not because the dead are not raised, but because resurrection from the dead is *a creative act of divine power which involves somatic transformation into a form of ("imperishable") personal identity appropriate to the life of heaven.* Nor is this transformation a blessing confined to those who have died, as if those still living at Christ's parousia are at a disadvantage. On the contrary, Paul has an eschatological secret to disclose: "We will not all die, *but we will all be changed* . . . the dead will be raised imperishable, *and we will be changed*" (vv. 51, 52). The nature of the change is likened to a process of being clothed, a metaphor which, again, expresses both somatic continuity and transformation: "For this perishable body must *put on* imperishability, and this mortal body must *put on* immortality." All of this is the great sign that death, the final enemy of God and God's creation, has been defeated once and for all, in fulfillment of the inscripted will of God (vv. 54b-55, quoting Isa 35:8; Hos 13:14).

The reference to the "sting" of death (15:55) brings Paul back to the present and to the *moral corollaries* of resurrection faith which the Corinthians are in danger of forgetting. Because death has not yet been finally conquered, it remains active and has powerful accomplices: sin and the law (v. 56; cf. Rom 5:12-14; 7:7-13). In consequence, believers live in a situation of eschatological tension. On the one hand, they are vulnerable to "the sting of death" and "the power of sin"; on the other, they are confident, not in themselves, but *in God,* "who gives us the victory *through our Lord Jesus Christ*" (v. 57). It is on this theological and christological basis that Paul concludes with a final, three-part exhortation on how to live, itself reminiscent of the chapter's opening: "[B]e steadfast, immovable, always excelling in the work of the Lord" (v. 58a; cf. vv. 1-2). The emphasis is on stability in their individual and common life and on devotion, not to the advancement of their own interests but to the work of the Lord. Why? Because, unlike so much of their own effort, labor done "in the [risen] Lord" is *not* "in vain" (v. 58b; cf. vv. 10, 14). To put it in other words, the death and resurrection of Christ in time past and the hope of the resurrection of the dead in time future constitute a warrant *against* futility and despair in the present and *for* the Christian "labor" of love.

By Way of Conclusion: Love in Practice (16:1-24)

The final chapter of 1 Corinthians is not just a matter of tying up loose ends. There is more to it than that. The gospel of Christ crucified and risen in fulfillment of the sovereign will of God is the basis for *a complete reordering of human energy and activity* (cf. 15:58). Implicit in these final instructions, therefore, is a multitude of ways in which the Corinthian body can demonstrate the new life arising out of its hope in the resurrection of the dead: (a) transformed economic patterns (gift-giving) (16:1-4); (b) the exercise of hospitality, especially to recognized leaders from outside (vv. 5-12); (c) growth in the individual and social virtues which maintain the body in unity and truth (vv. 13-14); (d) due recognition of local leaders in a spirit of humility (vv. 15-18); (e) accepting fraternity and interdependence within a society not restricted to one's own native territory (vv. 19-20a); (f) the practice of rituals of solidarity (v. 20b); (g) the appropriate exercise of discipline (v. 22a); and (h) living in the grace and love which come from being "in Christ Jesus" (vv. 23-24).

The structure of the chapter is as follows. The first main part (16:1-12) consists of instructions about the collection for the Jerusalem church (vv. 1-4), introduced by the now-familiar formula, "Now concerning," probably signaling that Paul is responding to an inquiry from the Corinthians. This leads to an elaboration of Paul's travel plans (vv. 5-9), as well as to instructions about the coming of Paul's co-worker Timothy (vv. 10-11). Then Paul responds to another inquiry, this time about the prospect of a visit from Apollos (v. 12). Finally, in the second main part (vv. 13-24), Paul concludes with some last words of instruction aimed at stabilizing the Corinthians' church life (vv. 13-14, 15-18), followed by words of greeting and blessing (vv. 19-24).

Ties That Bind: The Collection and Travel Plans (16:1-12)

The giving and receiving of both gifts and hospitality are two ways of building "ties that bind." Given the factional tendencies in the Corinthian church, it is not surprising, therefore, that Paul ends by touching on practical arrangements that will increase the solidarity of the church, not least by corporate action on behalf of others. The "socio-logic" may be that the church is strengthened both by looking outward and seeing itself as part of a larger whole (16:1-12, 20-21a), and by looking inward and consolidating its own common life (vv. 13-18, 20b, 21-24).

The first aspect of this "looking outward" involves gift giving: the collection which Paul is organizing for the impoverished church in Jerusalem (cf. Rom 15:25-31; 2 Corinthians 8–9; also Georgi 1992). This is *a six-way act of solidarity!* First, it involves solidarity with Jerusalem, action which acknowledges in a material way the spiritual benefit (cf. Rom 15:27) which has come to the Gentiles in Corinth (and elsewhere) from Judaism, represented by "the saints." Second, there is the solidarity between the various Pauline churches among whom the collection is being made: "follow the directions I gave to the churches of Galatia" (16:1b). Third, there is the solidarity generated within the Corinthian church itself as the members act in concert ("on the first day of every week," presumably when they "come together") and according to their respective levels of prosperity ("put aside and save whatever extra you earn") (v. 2). Fourth, there is the solidarity between the Corinthian church and the apostle Paul as they engage in this gift-giving enterprise in partnership with him (cf. vv. 3-4). Fifth, there is the solidarity between Paul and the Jerusalem church on whose behalf, and at considerable cost to himself, he is making the collection. Nor is this at the level of personal relations only, as between Paul on the one hand and James, Peter, and John on the other. It is a solidarity at the level of mission also, Paul's mission to the Gentiles and that of the Jerusalem apostolate to the Jews (cf. Gal 2:10). Finally, although not explicit here, giving to the collection expresses solidarity between believers and Christ, earth and heaven — generosity within the churches in response to the salvific generosity of God in Christ (cf. 2 Cor 8:5, 9). In short, the collection is not just a matter of relief for the poor, though it is that. It is *a medium of communication and connection,* binding participants together in multiple relations of mutual indebtedness.

Another outward-looking medium of connection is the paying and receiving of visits and the related practice of hospitality (cf. Barton 1997a: 501-7). This is bound up with the preceding since the collection has to be taken to Jerusalem by envoys. Here Paul's concern to avoid suspicion that he personally is profiting leads him to recommend in advance that the Corinthians appoint their own envoys to take the collection, accompanied either by letters of recommendation from Paul or perhaps by Paul himself (16:3-4). That naturally raises the sensitive (cf. 4:18-19; also 2 Cor 1:15–2:4!) question of Paul's own travel plans. Thus, in 16:5-9 Paul informs them of his intention, first, to stay in Ephesus (from where he is writing the present letter) until Pentecost, then to come to them to stay through the winter, but coming by way of Macedonia and the churches there.

In passing, we may note several clues to Paul's theology and practice hidden among these practical details. First, there is the breadth of Paul's missionary horizon, with mention of Jerusalem, Ephesus, Macedonia, and subsequently Asia (16:19), as well as Corinth. The problems in Corinth do not so preoccupy him that he loses sight of his vocation to preach and teach in other parts of the Gentile world. This larger vision is what he wants the Corinthians to share also. Second, there is Paul's sense of time. In part, this is related to deeply ingrained patterns of worship governed by the Jewish liturgical calendar, as the reference to Pentecost shows (v. 8). In part, it is a matter of spending time where the need for pastoral care (vv. 6-7) or the opportunity for mission (vv. 8-9) arises. Third, and related, there is Paul's openness to being guided by God. This accounts for the "vagueness" in Paul's travel plans: "I hope to spend time with you, *if the Lord permits.*" This may make Paul appear unpredictable and untrustworthy to the Corinthians (and others); but Paul seems willing to pay that price out of his prior and more fundamental allegiance to his risen Lord.

But Paul's mission involves a network of "co-workers" (*synergoi;* cf. Ellis 1970-71), and one of those is Timothy. Paul has mentioned his coming earlier (cf. 4:17). Now, in the context of potentially threatening circumstances (given the disunity in Corinth), he paves the way for a positive reception by issuing three instructions: "see that he has nothing to fear among you . . . let no one despise him . . . send him on his way in peace" (16:10-11). If the Corinthians can learn hospitality and peacemaking toward a relative outsider like Timothy, perhaps they can learn hospitality and peacemaking toward each other! What, then, about Apollos, so significant a figure for some of the Corinthians, as we have seen (cf. 1:12; 3:4-6, 22; 4:6)? Perhaps Paul has been asked about his coming (16:12a). Remarkably, in view of the potential for rivalry between the two, Paul responds positively and with generosity, in a way which is a model for potential rivals in the church in Corinth: "I strongly urged him to visit you. . . . He will come when he has the opportunity" (v. 12).

Words That Bind (16:13-24)

Paul now brings his letter to a close in a way which both conforms to conventional Pauline letter endings and is appropriate to his specific addressees in Corinth (cf. Fee 1987: 825-26). Thus there are hortatory remarks (16:13-18), greetings (vv. 19-20), a personal greeting written in Paul's own hand (rather than by the amanuensis) (v. 21), and a grace benediction (v. 23). To these conventional forms,

Paul adds here a curse warning (v. 22) and a final personal wish of love (v. 24).

The exhortations begin with a call to virtues the practice of which will achieve the goal of the letter as a whole: the unity and upbuilding of the fellowship in love. Thus, "Keep alert!" is an exhortation to eschatological vigilance in view of the coming of the risen Lord, a coming affirmed in the preceding teaching on the resurrection of the dead (cf. 15:23b; also Rom 13:11-14; 1 Thess 5:6). The command to "stand firm in the faith" is an exhortation to stability (cf. 15:1-2, 58) based on the gospel of Christ crucified and risen of which Paul has been reminding them throughout the letter. The commands to "be courageous, be strong" recall how countercultural and costly is the imitation of Christ in acts of mutual service (cf. 11:1). The last exhortation in the list is purposely so, for it sums up the message of the entire letter: "Let all that you do be done in love [*en agapę̄*]" (16:14; cf. 8:1-3; 13:1-13; 16:24).

But acting in love does not take place in a vacuum. Indeed, *it is unloving to fail to attend to the structures and practices which make love a possibility.* This is why Paul adds further exhortations with regard to the right ordering of their common life as "brothers and sisters" of one another: the Corinthians are "'urged" to submit to the authority of Stephanas and his network of "fellow workers" and "fellow laborers" (16:15-18). Noteworthy here is that Paul does not shrink from addressing questions of leadership and authority in the fellowship, and that it is the authority of *one person,* along with his associates (cf. v. 17), that is recognized. The reason for the latter may be twofold. First and foremost, acknowledging one person as leader has an obvious unifying effect, and Paul (we know) is seeking to unite a divided community. Second, since Stephanas is the likely bearer of this very letter to the Corinthians, recognition of him will guarantee a positive reception of the letter. But note also the *grounds* on which Stephanas is commended to the church as their leader. They do not have to do with speaking in "tongues of angels" or prophecy (cf. chs. 12–14); rather, they have to do with "service" (*diakonia;* cf. 12:5) — both the service of "the saints" (i.e., the believers in Corinth) and the service of their apostle (16:15b, 18a).

The exhortations are followed by the greetings (16:19-21). Like the exhortations, these are *words that bind.* They bind those who send them and those who receive them. Thus the Corinthians are held from seeing themselves in isolation. They belong to a worldwide network of fellowships under the one Lord. The unity to which Paul calls them is itself part of a larger unity. That unity includes the churches of Asia (v. 19a). It includes also those like Aquila and Prisca who were former residents in Corinth (cf. Acts 18:2-3) but whose work has taken them now to Ephesus. They, along with "the church in their house," send *warm* greetings: the use of affective language is striking. This is reinforced by the strong sense of all belonging to one family ("All the *brothers and sisters* send greetings," 16:20a), followed by the exhortation to reconciliation and mutual recognition: "Greet *one another* with a holy kiss" (v. 20b; cf. Rom 16:16; 2 Cor 13:12). Finally, there is Paul's own word of greeting, at the point where he begins the final words of the letter in his own hand (16:21).

These final four "words" are also significant. First, there is a warning curse against unnamed, intransigent opponents in Corinth — but not out of vindictiveness: even here it is "love for the Lord" which is at stake, love which involves discernment and discipline (16:22a; cf. Gal 1:8-9; 2 Thess 3:14-15). Second, there is a fervent eschatological prayer: "Our Lord, come!" (16:22b). That Paul's prayer is in Aramaic *(Marana tha)* is an indication that he is passing on to the (Greek-speaking) Corinthians primitive tradition from the worship of the earliest Aramaic-speaking Christian community. In context, the prayer fits well. It fits with the exhortation to "keep alert" (v. 13a), reinforces the immediately preceding warning curse (v. 22a), and surrounds the following benediction with eschatological hope. Third, there is the benediction itself: "The grace of the Lord Jesus be with you" (v. 23). Here the letter has come full circle (cf. 1:3, 4). The letter as a whole is about grace, but grace revealed in surprising places and people — above all in the crucified and risen Christ and in the lives of those who imitate him by giving themselves up on behalf of others for Christ's sake. The benediction is Paul's prayer to God to allow that grace to continue to flow in the church in Corinth.

But, surprisingly (cf. 2 Cor 13:13; Gal 6:18; 1 Thess 5:28; etc.), Paul adds one "word" more. In itself, it is an expression of the overflowing grace of Christ for which he has just prayed. It is an intensely personal word, the word of a father to his often-wayward spiritual children. It is an expression of the most powerful of the ties that bind: *"My love* be with all of you *in Christ Jesus"* (16:24).

Bibliography. Balch, D. L. 1983, "1 Cor 7:32-35 and Stoic Debates about Marriage, Anxiety, and Distraction," *JBL* 102/3:429-39 • Banks, R. J. 1994, *Paul's Idea of Community,* Peabody, Mass.: Hendrickson • Barclay, J. M. G. 1992, "Thessalonica and Corinth: Social Contrasts in Pauline Christianity," *JSNT* 47:49-74 • Barrett, C. K. 1971, *A Commentary on the First Epistle to the Corinthians,* London: A. & C. Black • Barth, K. 1933, *The Resurrection of the Dead,* London: Hodder & Stoughton • Barton, S. C. 1986, "Paul's Sense of Place: An Anthropological Approach to Community Formation in Corinth," *NTS* 32/2:225-46 • Barton, S. C. 1996, "'All Things to All People': Paul and the Law in the Light of 1 Corinthians 9.19-23," in J. D. G. Dunn, ed., *Paul and the Mosaic Law,* Tübingen: J. C. B. Mohr, 271-86 • Barton, S. C. 1997a, "Hospitality," in *DLNTD,* 501-7 • Barton, S. C. 1997b, *Invitation to the Bible,* London: SPCK • Barton, S. C. 1997c, "The Relativisation of Family Ties in the Jewish and Graeco-Roman Traditions," in H. Moxnes, ed., *Constructing Early Christian Families,* London: Routledge, 81-100 • Beker, J. C. 1980, *Paul the Apostle,* Edinburgh: T. & T. Clark • Carnley, P. 1987, *The Structure of Resurrection Belief,* Oxford: Clarendon • Castelli, E. A. 1991, *Imitating Paul,* Louisville: Westminster/John Knox • Chadwick, H. 1954-55, "'All Things to All Men' (I Cor. IX.22)," *NTS* 1:261-75 • Cheung, A. T. 1999, *Idol Food in Corinth,* Sheffield: Sheffield Academic • Chow, J. K. 1992, *Patronage and Power: A Study of Social Networks in Corinth,* Sheffield: Sheffield Academic • Clarke, A. D. 1993, *Secular and Christian Leadership in Corinth,* Leiden: Brill • Craddock, F. B. 1990, "Preaching to Corinthians," *Int* 44:158-

68 • D'Angelo, M. R. 1988, "The Garden: Once and Not Again," in G. A. Robbins, ed., *Genesis 1–3 in the History of Exegesis,* Lewiston: Edwin Mellen • Davis, S. et al., eds. 1997, *The Resurrection,* Oxford: Oxford University • de Boer, M. C. 1988, *The Defeat of Death,* Sheffield: Sheffield Academic • de Boer, M. C. 1994, "The Composition of 1 Corinthians," *NTS* 40:229-45 • Deming, W. 1995, *Paul on Marriage and Celibacy,* Cambridge: Cambridge University • Doty, W. 1973, *Letters in Primitive Christianity,* Philadelphia: Fortress • Dunn, J. D. G. 1975, *Jesus and the Spirit,* London: SCM • Dunn, J. D. G. 1980, *Christology in the Making,* London: SCM • Dunn, J. D. G. 1990, *Jesus, Paul and the Law,* London: SPCK • Dunn, J. D. G. 1995, *1 Corinthians,* Sheffield: Sheffield Academic • Dunn, J. D. G. 1998, *The Theology of Paul the Apostle,* Grand Rapids: Eerdmans • Ellis, E. E. 1970-71, "Paul and His Co-workers," *NTS* 17:437-52 • Engberg-Pedersen, T. 1987, "The Gospel and Social Practice According to 1 Corinthians," *NTS* 33:557-84 • Fee, G. D. 1987, *The First Epistle to the Corinthians,* Grand Rapids: Eerdmans • Fiorenza, E. S. 1983, *In Memory of Her,* London: SCM • Fitzgerald, J. T. 1988, *Cracks in an Earthen Vessel: An Examination of the Catalogues of Hardships in the Corinthian Correspondence,* Atlanta: Scholars • Fitzmyer, J. A. 1993, "*Kephalē* in I Corinthians 11:3," *Int* 47/1:52-59 • Ford, D. F. 1989, "Faith in the Cities: Corinth and the Modern City," in C. E. Gunton and D. W. Hardy, eds., *On Being the Church,* Edinburgh: T. & T. Clark, 225-56 • Ford, J. M. 1993, "Bookshelf on Prostitution," *BTB* 23/3:128-34 • Georgi, D. 1992, *Remembering the Poor,* Nashville: Abingdon • Gordon, J. D. 1997, *Sister or Wife? 1 Corinthians 7 and Cultural Anthropology,* Sheffield: Sheffield Academic • Hays, R. 1996, *The Moral Vision of the New Testament,* San Francisco: HarperCollins • Hays, R. 1997, *First Corinthians,* Louisville: Westminster/John Knox • Hays, R. 1999, "Wisdom According to Paul," in S. C. Barton, ed., *Where Shall Wisdom Be Found?,* Edinburgh: T. & T. Clark, 111-23 • Hengel, M. 1977, *Crucifixion,* London: SCM • Hock, R. F. 1980, *The Social Context of Paul's Ministry,* Philadelphia: Fortress • Holladay, C. R. 1990, "1 Corinthians 13: Paul as Apostolic Paradigm," in D. L. Balch, ed., *Greeks, Romans and Christians,* Philadelphia: Fortress, 80-98 • Horrell, D. 1997, "Theological Principle or Christological Praxis? Pauline Ethics in 1 Corinthians 8.1–11.1," *JSNT* 67:83-114 • Hurd, J. C. 1965, *The Origin of 1 Corinthians,* London: SPCK • Jenson, P. P. 1992, *Graded Holiness,* Sheffield: Sheffield Academic • Jewett, P. 1979, *Dating Paul's Life,* London: SCM • Kloppenborg, J. S., and S. G. Wilson, eds. 1996, *Voluntary Associations in the Graeco-Roman World,* London: Routledge • Leach, E. 1976, *Culture and Communication,* Cambridge: Cambridge University • Litfin, D. 1994, *St Paul's Theology of Proclamation,* Cambridge: Cambridge University • MacDonald, M. Y. 1990, "Women Holy in Body and Spirit: The Social Setting of 1 Corinthians 7," *NTS* 36:161-81 • Malherbe, A. 1983, "Antisthenes and Odysseus, and Paul at War," *HTR* 76/2:143-73 • Marshall, P. 1987, *Enmity in Corinth: Social Conventions in Paul's Relations with the Corinthians,* Tübingen: J. C. B. Mohr • Martin, D. B. 1990, *Slavery as Salvation,* New Haven: Yale University • Martin, D. B. 1995, *The Corinthian Body,* New Haven: Yale University • Meeks, W. A. 1974, "The Image of the Androgyne," *HR* 13/3:165-208 • Meeks, W. A. 1983, *The First Urban Christians,* New Haven, Conn.: Yale University • Meeks, W. A. 1986, *The Moral World of the First Christians,* London: SPCK • Meggitt, J. J. 1998, *Paul, Poverty and Survival,* Edinburgh: T. & T. Clark • Mitchell, M. M. 1992, *Paul and the Rhetoric of Reconciliation,* Louisville: Westminster/John Knox • Moxnes, H. 1996, "Honor and Shame," in R. Rohrbaugh, ed., *The Social Sciences and New Testament Interpretation,* Peabody, Mass.: Hendrickson, 19-40 • Murphy-O'Connor, J. 1983, *St. Paul's Corinth,* Wilmington: Michael Glazier • Neyrey, J. 1990, *Paul, In Other Words,* Louisville: Westminster/John Knox • Pearson, B. A. 1973, "Hellenistic-Jewish Wisdom Speculation and Paul," in R. L. Wilken, ed., *Aspects of Wisdom in Judaism and Early Christianity,* Notre Dame: University of Notre Dame, 43-66 • Pickett, R. 1997, *The Cross in Corinth,* Sheffield: Sheffield Academic • Pilch, J. J. 1993, "'Beat His Ribs While He Is Young' (Sir 30:12): A Window on the Mediterranean World," *BTB* 23/3:101-13 • Pogoloff, S. M. 1992, *Logos and Sophia: The Rhetorical Situation of 1 Corinthians,* Atlanta: Scholars • Roberts, C. 1936, "The Guild of Zeus Hypsistos," *HTR* 29:39-88 • Rosner, B. 1994, *Paul, Scripture and Ethics,* Leiden: Brill • Schmithals, W. 1971, *Gnosticism in Corinth,* New York: Abingdon • Stowers, S. K. 1986, *Letter Writing in Greco-Roman Antiquity,* Philadelphia: Westminster • Stuhlmacher, P. 1987, "The Hermeneutical Significance of 1 Cor 2:6-16," in G. F. Hawthorne and O. Betz, eds., *Tradition and Interpretation in the New Testament,* Grand Rapids: Eerdmans, 328-47 • Talbert, C. H. 1987, *Reading Corinthians,* London: SPCK • Theissen, G. 1982, *The Social Setting of Pauline Christianity,* Edinburgh: T. & T. Clark • Thiselton, A. C. 1997, "Can Hermeneutics Ease the Deadlock?" in T. Bradshaw, ed., *The Way Forward? Christian Voices on Homosexuality and the Church,* London: Hodder & Stoughton, 145-96 • Webster, J. 1998, "Hermeneutics in Modern Theology: Some Doctrinal Reflections," *SJT* 51/3:307-41 • Wedderburn, A. J. M. 1987, *Baptism and Resurrection,* Tübingen: J. C. B. Mohr • Welborn, L. L. 1997, *Politics and Rhetoric in the Corinthian Epistles,* Macon, Ga.: Mercer University • Willis, W. L. 1985, *Idol Meat in Corinth,* Chico, Calif.: Scholars • Winter, B. W. 1990, "Theological and Ethical Responses to Religious Pluralism — 1 Corinthians 8–10," *TynBul* 41/2:209-26 • Winter, B. W. 1994, *Seek the Welfare of the City,* Grand Rapids: Eerdmans • Winter, B. W. 1997a, "Homosexual Terminology in 1 Corinthians 6:9: The Roman Context and the Greek Loan-Word," in A. N. S. Lane, ed., *Interpreting the Bible,* Leicester: Apollos, 275-90 • Winter, B. W. 1997b, *Philo and Paul among the Sophists,* Cambridge: Cambridge University • Winter, B. W. 2000, *After Paul Left Corinth: The Influence of Secular Ethics and Social Change,* Grand Rapids: Eerdmans • Wire, A. C. 1990, *The Corinthian Women Prophets,* Philadelphia: Fortress • Witherington, B. 1994, *Jesus the Sage,* Minneapolis: Fortress • Witherington, B. 1995, *Conflict and Community in Corinth,* Grand Rapids: Eerdmans • Wright, N. T. 1991, *The Climax of the Covenant,* Minneapolis: Fortress • Yarbrough, O. L. 1985, *Not Like the Gentiles: Marriage Rules in the Letters of Paul,* Atlanta: Scholars.

2 Corinthians

John Barclay

INTRODUCTION

2 Corinthians is a peculiarly fascinating and puzzling document. It constitutes one of Paul's most interesting expressions of theology (on a par with Romans, Galatians, and 1 Corinthians), especially on the themes of suffering, weakness, and power. But it also poses numerous historical and literary problems and proves particularly difficult to interpret at many points. Here we will survey the most awkward historical and literary issues.

Authorship

2 Corinthians is at points written in the names of Paul and Timothy (1:1), at other points in Paul's name alone (10:1). There is no reason to doubt these ascriptions, but we may wonder to what degree the material in chs. 1–9 is really a joint production, and to what degree Paul's alone (the authorial "we" alternates with "I"). There is only one passage where some scholars suspect an interpolation of material from a source other than Paul (see on 6:14–7:1). Otherwise the emotional tone and theological content of 2 Corinthians are quintessentially Pauline.

Relationship to 1 Corinthians

2 Corinthians is clearly a sequel to 1 Corinthians and gives us fascinating glimpses into the development of Paul's relationship with the Corinthian church. Most of the moral issues addressed in 1 Corinthians, and the questions concerning communal life, have dropped into the background, such as sexual morality (1 Corinthians 5–7, alluded to only in 2 Cor 12:21), idolatry (1 Corinthians 8–10, alluded to in 2 Cor 6:14-16), and the conduct of worship (1 Corinthians 11–14). But some problems merely hinted at in the earlier letter have now come center stage, in particular the question of Paul's apostleship (1 Corinthians 1–4, the central theme of the whole of 2 Corinthians); integral to this question is Paul's nonreceipt of pay and his advocacy of the collection (1 Corinthians 9 and 16, now hugely important in 2 Corinthians 8–9 and 10–12). 2 Cor 12:21 suggests that some of the earlier problems have not disappeared but simply cannot be discussed until Paul has reestablished the authority necessary to deal with them. It appears that Paul has visited Corinth since writing 1 Corinthians, but the visit was "painful" (2 Cor 2:1) and resulted in a major affront to Paul (2:5). This same passage refers to a "tearful" letter (2:4; cf. 7:8-12) which was written in the wake of this visit, apparently containing a strong rebuke of the Corinthians. Paul's earlier fears of repudiation (1 Cor 4:18-21) had been realized, and he now has to spend all his energies in attempting to restore his standing in Corinth. Hence his refocusing of the dialogue with the Corinthian church, and hence also the reemergence of Paul's theology of the cross (1 Corinthians 1–4, developed with subtlety throughout 2 Corinthians), which reflects on the paradoxical power of God in the midst of weakness, shame, and disappointment.

Integrity: One Letter or a Collection of Letters?

Reading 2 Corinthians as a whole, one is impressed both by its thematic coherence and by its sometimes disjointed progress of thought. Several topics recur throughout, such as Paul's ministry and reliability, his commitment to the Corinthian church, protestations of honesty and openness, and interrelated financial issues. Moreover, a coherent theology undergirds the whole, concerning the life-giving grace of God amid weakness and death (Young and Ford 1987; Harvey 1996). Yet there are also abrupt shifts in the sequence of the discourse. One can finish ch. 9 without any inkling that the "tornado" of chs. 10–13 is about to arrive; the sarcastic, defensive, and almost desperate tone of those later chapters seems extraordinary after the expression of confidence in ch. 7. Less striking, but still noticeable, shifts occur between ch. 7 and ch. 8, either side of the paragraph 6:14–7:1, and between 2:13 and 2:14 (the reference to Titus and Macedonia in 2:13 being reactivated in 7:5). Even the relationship between chs. 8 and 9 is puzzling since, although the topic of the collection is the same, the latter seems to introduce it anew (9:1).

Scholars vary greatly in their assessment of these disjunctions, which can be minimized in arguing for the literary unity of the letter, or maximized in asserting that our canonical 2 Corinthians is actually a compilation of several letters (see the full discussion in the introductions to commentaries, especially those by Martin, Furnish, and Thrall). Some of the shifts noted above may be explained as Paul's careful interweaving with strategic changes of topic and tone; for instance, Paul's break in the narrative of his journey to Macedonia (2:13–2:14; cf. 7:5ff.) seems deliberately contrived to give himself space to reflect on his vulnerability and yet adequacy as an apostle, the theme which fills the intervening chapters. Other breaks in sequence seem to require at least pauses in dictation, while the gap between chs. 9 and 10 yawns extremely wide. In this latter case, the majority of scholars believe that chs. 10–13 were originally a separate letter to the Corinthians, whose opening greeting has been lost in being affixed to chs. 1–9. If this simple editorial exercise took place in a standard version of Paul's letters early in the second century, it is no surprise that later copies contain 2 Corinthians only in this composite state. (Some scholars think that Philippians is similarly stitched together, and there are many such composite texts in Jewish and Greco-Roman literature.)

Once the possibility is broached that 2 Corinthians may contain two (or more?) letters, it is legitimate to wonder if they have been preserved in their original sequence. Although we do not know how or when the Corinthian correspondence was put together, there is no reason to believe that the original chronological order was the major concern of those who assembled Paul's letters. It was not unreasonable to place the longer 2 Corinthians 1–9, with its impressive letter opening, before 2 Corinthians 10–13, although, as I shall indicate below, close attention to their contents suggests that their original order was the other way around. Thus is opened up an arena for several competing hypotheses, in which the constituent parts of 2 Corinthians can be fitted into various schemes tracing the course of Paul's dealings with Corinth. Such hypotheses are not purely speculative: they can appeal to backward or forward indications in the text, and all try to fit the correspondence around the evidence for Paul's "painful" visit to Corinth and the "tearful" letter which he subsequently wrote (referred to in 2:4; 7:8-12). The debate is significant since it makes some difference to our understanding of the text, in what order we read it, and whether, for instance, the subtle apologetic moves in chs. 1–7 come before or after the explosion of chs. 10–13. Unfortunately, none of the competing hypotheses can be secured with absolute conviction. We can only do our best to make sense of the evidence, and then interpret the text on that basis.

The Original Sequence of Material in 2 Corinthians

Leaving aside the awkward paragraph 6:14–7:1 and the relation between chs. 8 and 9 (see commentary on those texts), what are the options in reconstructing the original sequence of this Corinthian correspondence? As indicated above, the supposed gap between 2:13 and 2:14 is not as difficult as it initially appears, and (popular as this theory has been) there do not seem to be sufficient grounds for taking 2:14–7:4 as a separate letter inserted into another (1:1–2:13 plus 7:5-16). The other disjunctures, however, are more perplexing and give rise to the following three options.

Option A: Two Letters, in the Canonical Order (1–9, 10–13). At first sight, the simplest hypothesis is to take the material in 2 Corinthians in its present order. As noted above, most scholars have found the gap between ch. 9 and ch. 10 to be so large as to require that chs. 10–13 be considered a separate letter written, on this hypothesis, after chs. 1–9. It is not only the change in tone which has required this conclusion. It is also that the situation addressed in chs. 10–13, where Paul contends with more impressive "super apostles," seems far more urgent than that addressed in chs. 1–9. Thus it will not do to posit merely a "sleepless night" after dictating ch. 9, or even the arrival of fresh news (of which there is no indication in chs. 10–13); the cautious confidence of chs. 1–9 is so far banished in chs. 10–13 as to suggest a distinct letter on a different occasion. On the simple hypothesis we are presently considering (supported by, e.g., Barrett, Bruce, Furnish, Martin, and Thrall), chs. 10–13 represent a letter written after chs. 1–9, when the reconciliation between Paul and the Corinthians reported by Titus (ch. 7) is suddenly ruptured by the arrival of new figures in the church, occasioning critical comparisons with Paul and a loss of confidence in Paul's apostleship.

Although this hypothesis is straightforward, it is not without its puzzles. It requires that the reconciliation between Paul and the church effected and reported by Titus (2 Corinthians 7) was either illusory or superficial, if the relationship could fall apart again so easily soon after. Moreover, Paul's relationship with the church in Corinth would then go through a repeat cycle: breakdown at the "painful visit," restoration after the "tearful" letter and Titus's mission (reflected in 2 Corinthians 1–9), second breakdown with the arrival of "super apostles," another severe letter (2 Corinthians 10–13), and (probably) a second restoration when "Achaia" (i.e., Corinth) finally contributed to Paul's collection for Jerusalem (Rom 15:26). This is not an impossible scenario, but it is complicated, and the question remains whether a simpler solution is available. It is also odd that, in writing after the second breakdown, Paul does not censure them for relapsing nor refer back to the first rupture (i.e., there are no references in chs. 10–13 to the earlier "tearful" letter or the subsequent reconciliation). These puzzles make another solution attractive.

Option B: Chapters 10–13 as the "Tearful" Letter (2:4), Written Prior to Chapters 1–9. If chs. 10–13 are a distinct letter (missing only its opening), could they constitute the letter which Paul says he wrote after the "painful" visit, a letter written "out of much distress and anguish of heart and with many tears" (2:4)? Perhaps this letter was, as other hypotheses assert, simply lost, but perhaps we have it actually well preserved, just placed out of sequence in 2 Corinthians 10–13. The tone of 2 Corinthians 10–13 is certainly full of "anguish" and "tears" (cf. the angry tears of Phil 3:18-19), and this hypothesis would resolve the major puzzles of Option A: now we have a simple sequence of painful visit, tearful letter, and genuine reconciliation between Paul and the Corinthians. It also explains why 2 Corinthians 10–13 should be full of references to Paul's discomfort in Corinth (as a recent experience), while several verses in chs. 1–7 make best sense if they refer *back* to matching comments in this "tearful" letter (e.g., 1:23 echoes 13:2, while 2:9 echoes 10:6). This hypothesis was widely supported at the beginning of the twentieth century and has recently gained support from a powerful minority of scholars (e.g., Watson 1984; Horrell 1996: 296-312).

However, this option faces two significant difficulties. The first concerns whether the descriptions of the tearful letter in 2 Corinthians 2 and 7 really match the content of chs. 10–13. It appears from 2 Cor 2:5-11 that the tearful letter had a particular impact on an individual in the Corinthian congregation who had caused Paul some harm, and we may deduce from 7:5-12 that the rebuke in this letter was meant to effect a renewal of allegiance to Paul. The latter point matches chs. 10–13 well enough, but the former looks at first glance incompatible with Paul's verbal contest against the "super apostles" (11:5, 22-23), who are arguably new arrivals in Corinth. However, a careful scrutiny of chs. 10–13 reveals that some of Paul's rebuke there is directed against an individual (e.g., 10:7, 10-11, all singular in the Greek, despite most translations). It is plausible that the chief damage to Paul's reputation was done by someone within the church comparing him unfavorably to traveling (and transient) "super apostles." Those who object to this option point out how little is said in 2 Corinthians 1–7 about these other missionaries, but there are in fact several allusions to their style of ministry (e.g., 2 Cor 3:1-3 in connection with 10:12-18; 2:17 and 4:2 in connection with their receipt of financial support, 11:7-15), and, as 2 Corinthians 10 and 13 make clear, the prime issue for Paul was always how he stood in relation to the Corinthian church, not how he compared to other "apostles." Thus it seems that a defensible case can be made for the identification of 2 Corinthians 10–13 as the "tearful" letter.

The second difficulty with this hypothesis is that 2 Cor 12:18 refers to a past delegation of Titus and a "brother" concerned with the collection, and it is difficult to see how this could have been written (as this option maintains) *before* the dispatch of Titus and the "brothers" mentioned in 2 Cor 8:16-24. The connection between these two passages has persuaded many that 2 Corinthians 10–13 must have been written after 2 Corinthians 8 and thus must be a subsequent letter, and not the missing "tearful" one. Those who support Option B meet this problem by insisting that the two Titus delegations are not the same: in 2 Cor 12:18 only one brother is mentioned in the party, while in 2 Corinthians 8 there are two. On this view, 2 Cor 12:18 refers to an earlier Titus visit (to encourage the collection), while 2 Corinthians 8 is a subsequent one (to complete it). But then it is odd that 2 Corinthians 8 should make so little of Titus's track record on this matter (the merest allusion in 8:6), and a simpler solution would be to adopt the following modified version of Option B.

Option C: Three Letters: Chapters 8–9 (the Collection Letter), Then Chapters 10–13 (the "Tearful" Letter), Then Chapters 1–7 (the Reconciliation Letter). A recent commentary on 2 Corinthians 8 and 9 (Betz 1985) propounds a minority but defensible hypothesis that these two chapters were originally independent letters which have been tacked onto the end of 2 Corinthians 1–7. Although Titus is mentioned in both 2 Corinthians 7 and 2 Corinthians 8, there is no expressed link between the two chapters; if they originally belonged together, we would have expected in 2 Corinthians 7 some reference forward to Titus's imminent return visit, or some reference back in 2 Corinthians 8 to his recent work in Corinth. Moreover, in addressing the Corinthians in 2 Corinthians 8 and 9, Paul shows some circumspection about the collection (8:20-21) but gives no indication that their relationship has been stormy up to this point (in fact 8:7 suggests otherwise). Thus, it seems best to take 2 Corinthians 8–9 (probably together; see on 9:1) as the first piece of correspondence after 1 Corinthians: following up his appeal for the Jerusalem collection (1 Cor 16:1-4), Paul comes through Macedonia and writes out of his concern lest the Corinthians be unprepared for their donation.

The important feature of Option C (which I favor) is that 2 Corinthians 8–9 come first in the sequence of correspondence. Writing from Macedonia, on the journey promised in 1 Cor 16:5-6, Paul sends Titus and other delegates ahead to insure that the collection (the main point of the visit) will be ready when he arrives. (Sensing that it was not, he perhaps returned from Macedonia to Ephesus, as he subsequently arrived in Corinth from elsewhere, 2 Cor 1:16.) Unfortunately 2 Corinthians 8 and 9 were not well received since the Corinthians were not willing to accord Paul the "obedience" (9:13) or accreditation as "their" apostle which Paul's collection required: What right had he to demand money of them? Thus when he arrived in Corinth (intending to pick up the collection and accompany it to Jerusalem), Paul found a hostile reception in which financial issues combined with others to undermine the trust of the Corinthian congregation. Paul's physical weakness and unimpressive speech led to a showdown with an influential member of the church, who compared Paul unfavorably with other "apostles," whose powerful "signs" made a deep impression in Corinth.

Such are the main ingredients of Paul's "painful visit" to Corinth, and these are the issues which Paul addresses in 2 Corinthians 10–13, the "tearful" letter. Paul writes this letter from Macedonia, where he had staged a tactical retreat, and promises to return at once (i.e., for a third visit) to sort this matter out (12:14; 13:1). He later rationalizes this revised plan as offering Corinth a "double favor" (2 Cor 1:15-16), coming to them both before and after a journey to Macedonia, but he seems to have altered his plans again after writing 2 Corinthians 10–13, as he judges that a return visit at this stage would be too painful (2:1). He begins to regret sending the tearful letter (7:8) and wonders how it will be received (one may well doubt the pastoral wisdom of its frontal assault on the Corinthians). Since his own presence would be too inflammatory, he sends Titus to Corinth to find out what has happened. Waiting impatiently for news in Troas, he returns to Macedonia (2:12-13) and is finally delighted when Titus comes to tell him that the letter (or Titus's diplomacy) has worked, the Corinthians have rebuked the main troublemaker in Corinth (2:5-11), and they now repent of the offense they caused to Paul (7:5-16). Relieved by this comforting news, Paul writes 2 Corinthians 1–7 in which he reflects on the whole affair, taking the opportunity to deflect continuing questions about his behavior (e.g., his repeated changes of plan, 1:15-24), to reaffirm his commitment to the Corinthian church (1:13–2:4), and to put both his and their painful experiences in the larger context of God's ability to turn disaster into triumph and work life out of death (2:14–6:10). The reconciliation seems to have been sufficient to induce the Corinthians to make their much-delayed contribution to the collection (Rom 15:26), and Paul probably wrote Romans from Corinth with this awkward problem finally resolved.

The sketch just offered of the course of events remains a hypothesis like all others, and some of the clues in the text could be read differently; in truth many are ambiguous, and inferences drawn from them remain insecure. Readers might be forgiven for finding this (simplified) array of hypotheses somewhat unnerving and might wonder about its necessity. But all who engage seriously with 2 Corinthians find that they need to fit its varied contents into some sort of sequence and in relation to some narrative of Paul's relationship to the church, while the evidence is simply not strong enough to prove any hypothesis conclusively. I have set out the main options to indicate how commentators differ on these matters, but the sketch I have outlined in Option C will be the basis for the commentary to follow. Thus I have written this commentary beginning at ch. 8 (in the order 8–9, 10–13, 1–7), though I am required by the editors to set the material before you in the canonical order; this explains why, for instance, in discussing chs. 1–7, I will refer *back* to chs. 10–13. Naturally, it makes best sense to study 2 Corinthians in (what I believe to be) its original order, so readers of this commentary are encouraged to begin with me at ch. 8.

Date

For reasons outlined above, no single date can be assigned to all the material in 2 Corinthians, while competing hypotheses will reach different conclusions about the relative dating of its various parts (although none puts large intervals between them). All start from a baseline date for 1 Corinthians, which falls in the period AD 52-55. On the hypothesis just outlined (Option C), if we take 1 Corinthians as written in AD 53, 2 Corinthians 8 and 9 may date from just after Pentecost in AD 54 (cf. 1 Cor 16:5-9); we may place the "tearful" letter (2 Corinthians 10–13) only a little later, after the shock of the painful visit, and the final letter of reconciliation (2 Corinthians 1–7) either in late AD 54 or early AD 55. But these are approximations, and the evidence does not allow either precision or certainty.

The Character of the Letters

Readers who come to our letters from 1 Corinthians will find their character very different: they are simultaneously less definite — full of gaps, hints, and allusions — and more vivid in their emotional texture. The allusiveness of the letters makes them peculiarly difficult to interpret (they contain much of the most difficult material in the Pauline corpus). Paul could afford merely to allude to issues in his relationship with the Corinthians (he did not anticipate outsiders reading his correspondence), and the intimacy of that relationship also necessitated a delicate vagueness which springs from his sensitivity to previous wounds. What is more, Paul's delight in metaphor is here given free rein, and his propensity to slide one metaphor into another often leaves us baffled (e.g., in 2 Corinthians 3). Paul's complex psychological reaction to events in Corinth gives rise to a kaleidoscope of emotions, and many passages in this letter become incoherent under the influence of anger, love, relief, hurt, or longing. In letters so specifically related to historical events, we strive to pin down hints and allusions, but we constantly find ourselves frustrated by the veil which Paul's emotions draw over his experiences.

Yet 2 Corinthians represents far more than an emotional outburst. It is Paul's characteristic but still extraordinary achievement to create theology in the midst of such passionate events and to reflect theologically *about them,* in all their grubby particularity. Wounded and shamed as he was, Paul finds cause to reflect on the grace of God, which is sufficient precisely in his weakness; and, in reestablishing his standing as the Corinthians' apostle, he transmutes self-justification into renewed commitment both to the church at Corinth and to the cause of the gospel. Thus, although these letters are at one level about himself, Paul continually expresses and encourages thanksgiving to God, and turns this somewhat sordid breakdown in pastoral relations into an occasion to celebrate the grace and glory of God. In this sense, these letters are not only about the treasure of the gospel in ordinary clay jars (4:7) but also themselves constitute a theological treasure created in the midst of mundane, and somewhat defective, personal relations.

COMMENTARY

The Reconciliation Letter: 2 Corinthians 1–7

As explained above, I consider these chapters to be the third and last component of the letter collection now known as 2 Corinthians. Readers who wish to follow (what I consider to be) the original sequence of the letter are thus encouraged to start at 2 Corinthians 8–9 and come back to this point after the "tearful" letter (2 Corinthians 10–13). Many obscure remarks in chs. 1–7 can be clarified by reference to the previous letters (chs. 8–9 and 10–13); hence my references back to what is, in its canonical order, subsequent material!

The "tearful" letter (referred to here in 2:4) followed an explosive and painful visit by Paul to Corinth in which his authority was questioned and his probity impugned. He finished it with strong threats of a return visit to deal with sin and "disobedience" (12:19–13:4; cf. 10:6), and with a wounding countercharge: "if you doubt whether I am legitimate, the same question may be asked of you" (13:5-10). This letter seems to have been taken to Corinth by Titus; after sending it, Paul decided *not* to carry out his threat after all, but to bide his time, hoping that the letter, and Titus's mediation, would restore his relationship with the Corinthians. It was, he claims, an anxious wait (2:13-14; 7:5), but at last Titus returned to report that the church had "repented" of their coolness toward Paul and had repudiated the spokesman who had publicly shamed him. Hence the sigh of relief which echoes throughout chs. 1–7, the happiest of all Paul's letters to this church.

But if the wounds in the relationship had been satisfactorily healed, some scars remained. The "tearful" letter, with its biting irony and sharply pointed questions, had hit home, but at some cost; and Paul now has to reassure the Corinthians that their welfare and progress are his greatest concern. Moreover, the complex irony of that letter had left them unsure how to read Paul's letters: Could they trust that he meant what he said, or was each phrase cunningly obscure (cf. their "misunderstanding" of his earliest letter, 1 Cor 5:9-11)? Now Paul has to assure them that he means (only) what he says (1:13); indeed, this is the only one of his letters to Corinth which does not use irony, sarcasm, or other forms of double meaning. He also has to explain why his much-trumpeted third visit had not taken place, defending himself against possible charges of duplicity (1:15–2:13).

But besides these pragmatic issues, there was also a larger matter to explain. In the course of his ironic boast (11:21–12:10) Paul had presented himself as a figure of weakness, reliant on the grace of God. But he had had little chance to explain the rationale for this paradoxical greatness-through-humiliation, or how it embodied the gospel (merely hinted at in 10:1, 12:9, and 13:4). Thus he takes the opportunity of this reconciliation letter to establish his apostolic identity, with its paradoxical combination of glory and shame, weakness and power, death and life. This is his topic in the long central section of this letter (2:14–6:10), which lays the basis for his final expressions of cautious confidence in the Corinthian church (6:11–7:16).

The structure of this letter may thus be analyzed as follows:

- Prescript and Blessing, Adumbrating the Theology of the Letter (1:1-11)
- Apologetic Clarifications in the Wake of the Tearful Letter (1:12–2:13)
- The Paradoxical Character of Apostolic Ministry (2:14–6:10)
  - The grounds for its "sufficiency" (2:14–3:6)
  - The ministry of the new covenant in contrast to the old (3:7-18)
  - The open character of Paul's ministry (4:1-6)
  - The working of life in the midst of death (4:7-15)
  - The transitory present in light of the eternal future (4:16–5:10)
  - The foundation and goal of Paul's ministry (5:11–6:10)
- Securing Paul's Relationship with the Corinthians (6:11-7:17)

This is the only one of the three letters now combined in 2 Corinthians which has its opening intact, and it may have been its impressive blessing (1:3ff.) which insured its placement in the present compilation. Its ending is lost (unless preserved in 13:11-13), no doubt omitted when the three letters were combined by an editor. The structure suggested above indicates the significance of the long central discussion of apostolic ministry, but there are insufficient grounds for regarding this as itself once an independent letter; a close examination shows that it is carefully linked to its surrounding context, even if some of its ideas were originally sketched on a broader canvas.

Prescript and Blessing (1:1-11)

The letter opening corresponds closely to the greeting in 1 Cor 1:1-3, the reference to Paul's apostleship "by the will of God" foreshadowing the significance of this theme in the letter (cf. 3:4-6; 4:1). Instead of writing his usual thanksgiving, Paul offers a "blessing" (cf. Eph 1:3ff.) whose Jewish form is adapted by references to Christ. Its theme reflects both the immediate occasion of the letter and its deepest theological motif. The God who brings "consolation" (the Greek might also be translated "encouragement" or "comfort") in "all our affliction" (1:4) is the one Paul thanks for his present relief: after the trauma of the painful visit, the anguish of his letter, and the anxious wait for Titus (2:1-4, 13; 7:5, all examples of "affliction"), Paul feels flooded with "consolation" (7:4, 13). But he also recognizes this as part of a larger pattern. The servants of Christ share in his sufferings, which "overflow" from Christ to them (1:5) as they share in his "dying" and are exposed to many weaknesses "in Christ" (cf. 4:7-13; Col 1:24). But they also experience thereby the divine "consolation" which meets them in that condition. Yet the overflow principle works here too (cf. the overflow of grace in 8:1-4 and 9:8-15): God's consolation more than fills up its recipients, and overflows into the lives of those they contact and thereby help (1:5-6). This is not just about the ability of those who have suffered to empathize with other sufferers; it concerns the way God's consoling grace "spills over" beyond its immediate recipients into the lives of others. Thus Paul can see his suffering, and its resulting consolation, benefiting others (1:6), as the saving grace of God flows on through him (cf. 4:10-12 and the christological basis in 5:21; 8:9). In the wake of his recent "affliction," this letter represents the "consolation" which Paul has himself received and now passes on to those who have also been traumatized, and beyond them to all who know such suffering (1:6). The fact that the Corinthians have survived the trauma reinforces Paul's confidence that God's "consolation" is at work in them as well (1:7).

In 1:8-11 Paul offers a concrete, personal example of this principle. It appears that recently in Asia (Ephesus?) he had experienced some life-threatening trauma which brought him to the brink of death (perhaps illness or persecution). Despite the many dangers he had already encountered (11:23-33), this near-death experience clearly shook him to the core (Harvey 1996 argues that it brought to birth the new theology of suffering evidenced in this letter). What he learned from it was the lesson of vulnerability and utter dependence on God (1:9). It is in the face of death (both real and metaphorical) that the believer learns what faith is about, abandoning self-confidence to trust only in the God who gives life to the dead (cf. Rom 4:17-25; for echoes of the Psalms here and throughout 2 Corinthians, see Young and Ford 1987: 60-

69, noting allusions to Psalms 110–118). Putting the matter in these terms, Paul prepares for his description of the Christian life as "bearing the dying" and sharing the life of Christ (4:7-15). And this is no mere individual spirituality, but encompasses others in the community of faith (1:9; cf. 4:15): through their cooperation in prayer, the Corinthians share Paul's experience sufficiently to form a chorus of thanks to God for his gracious rescue of Paul (cf. the circle of grace received and thanks returned to God in 9:12-14).

Apologetic Clarifications (1:12–2:13)

As noted above, the "tearful" letter has left an aftershock and a number of issues to be resolved. 1:12-14 follows on well from the heat and anger of chs. 10–13: now that matters are more or less resolved, Paul can claim a "boast" with less awkwardness, though he makes clear again (1:12) that it is legitimated by the grace of God working in him, not by human cleverness (cf. 11:18; 12:9). With a view, perhaps, to lingering questions about his financial tactics (12:16-18) and to frustration at his complex and ironic manner of speech in chs. 10–13, Paul insists that he acts with pure sincerity (1:12) and conceals no hidden meanings between the lines (v. 13). He hopes for an end to mistrust and for mutual confidence and pride (v. 14), though he realizes that he is asking a lot for the Corinthians to boast in him: the central part of this letter will endeavor to show them that treasure can be contained in fragile jars and that Paul's paradoxical style of ministry is a fitting embodiment of the gospel (4:7; 5:12; 6:3-10).

But what of Paul's failure to return as promised, and his threat to be as fierce in person as he was by letter (10:11; 13:2)? When he withdrew from Corinth (with the collection incomplete?), Paul had promised to come back from Macedonia, a scheme here rationalized as a "double grace" (1:15-16). This was a change from the original plan announced in 1 Cor 16:5-9, but it had now been altered again since Paul had in the end sent Titus instead of coming himself. Paul knew this chopping and changing made him look unreliable, the sort of fickle figure who was characterized by human fallibility (1:17). Since that was a wounding charge, which might discredit his mission and message (cf. 10:2-3), he feels bound to give more than a merely pragmatic response. Is he the sort of person, and is his the sort of message, which says "Yes" and "No," makes promises and retracts them, at the same moment (1:17b)? (The phrase might also mean, "Is it in my power that my 'Yes' be 'Yes' and my 'No,' 'No'?" Paul would then imply that it was God who directed his travels and overruled his plans (Young and Ford 1987: 100-104). God's faithfulness is matched by the truthfulness of his spokesmen (1:18) — a crucial point for Paul's having claimed that Christ spoke through him (13:3). Thus the question of Paul's word leads into the question of his gospel message and occasions his assertion that Christ was the fulfillment and affirmation of all God's promises (1:19-20; cf. Rom 9:4; 15:8) — a fulfillment met by an equally resounding "Yes" of faith ("Amen") in the believing community. The change of travel plans has suggested uncertainty and lack of assurance, and Paul concludes by insisting that God's guarantee and "first installment" (the Spirit) are utterly secure (1:21-22; cf. 5:5; Rom 5:5; 8:23). After the unsettling questions concerning the Corinthians' Christian status in 13:5-10, this is "consolation" indeed.

So why did Paul change his plans and take back his threats? On solemn oath, he insists that it was not to spare himself embarrassment but to spare them pain (1:23, echoing 13:3 and 13:10, where he had hoped the letter would have the necessary effect). He wants to present himself not as a disciplining master but as a fellow worker (cf. 1 Cor 3:5, 21-23), and he is delighted that the question of 13:5 ("Are you living in the faith?") can be answered in the affirmative (1:24). He could not bear another sorrowful visit, in which he and the church would only hurt each other (2:1-2; cf. his reluctance to "tear down" in 10:8 and 13:10). On the principle of 1:3-7, the apostle should bring consolation and joy to his people, not pain, and Paul earnestly hoped that his tearful anguish would result in joy, not further distress (2:3-4). He didn't mean to hurt them (7:8 admits that in fact the letter had wounded) but to express his love (2:4; cf. 11:11; 12:15).

In 2:5-11 Paul alludes to the immediate cause of that "tearful" letter, an individual who had clearly caused him pain (despite 2:5) and spoiled the relationship between Paul and the congregation. Interpreters have sometimes suggested that this is the individual attacked in 1 Cor 5:1-5 (cf. the parallel references to Satan), but it is more plausible to identify this individual as the spokesman by whom Paul was wounded on the painful visit and to whom he responds in 10:10-11 ("such a person" [2:6] matches 10:11 precisely). Now it seems that the bulk of the congregation have swung back to Paul and away from this figure; and Paul, seeking now the most irenic solution, urges them to forgive and reintegrate this individual, playing down the personal offense to himself and giving the initiative as much as possible to the Corinthians themselves (2:5, 8, 10). The "super apostles" are now irrelevant since it was the church itself which Paul coveted (11:2) and now rejoices to have won back: he had written to test their obedience (cf. 10:6; 13:5-6) and was delighted they had passed the test (2:9). If Satan is still a threat, it is not through his counterfeit "apostles" but through his ability to capture a "brother" (2:11), and Paul does not wish to lose a single one.

If Paul kept away from Corinth to "spare" the Corinthian Christians, they preyed heavily on his mind in his absence. Thus he concludes this opening section with a reference to his agitation while waiting for news from Titus, the bearer of the "tearful" letter (2:12-13). Even a successful mission in Troas could not distract him; he had to press on to find Titus as quickly as possible. Such is the lot of an apostle on whose shoulders lies "the pressure of anxiety for all the churches" (11:28). It is this vulnerable role as an agent of Christ's "life-in-the-midst-of-death" which Paul will now describe in greater detail. He could offer any number of excuses for his recent behavior, but unless they grasp the divine adequacy at work in his human inadequacies, the Corinthians will never get to trust him with the confidence he craves (1:13-14).

The Paradoxical Character of Apostolic Ministry (2:14–6:10)

Interpreters have often sensed a break between 2:13 and 2:14, and the fact that the narrative of 2:13 seems to be resumed in 7:5, while the thanksgiving of 2:14 could stand at the beginning of the letter, has encouraged many to suppose that 2:14–7:4 was originally a separate letter, now inserted into another. However, this theory is now generally recognized to be unconvincing and unnecessary. It is typical of Paul to turn aside in what seems a digression in order to lay the foundations for the larger discussion (cf. the position of 1 Corinthians 9 and 1 Corinthians 13 in their respective contexts). Here, after the trauma of the painful visit and the bitterness of the tearful letter, Paul needs to supplement his early apologetic comments (1:12–2:13) with a fuller depiction of his paradoxical ministry — which is ignominious in appearance but glorious in content. This theme is now to be played through in multiple harmonic variations: in the paradox of glory in human ordinariness, of power in human weakness, and the life of Christ in human death and decay. By embodying both sides of this paradox, the apostolic ministry provides a medium of divine grace which is able to bring others life in the midst of death and eternal wealth out of shameful "poverty."

The Grounds for Its "Sufficiency" (2:14–3:6)

2:14 sets the tone for what is to follow by offering paradoxical thanks to God. The NRSV translation "who leads us in triumphal procession" might give the impression that Paul considers himself to share the victor's triumph. But the uses of this verb elsewhere in Greek literature require that it be taken to mean "who leads us as his captives [to death] as part of his triumphal procession." The metaphor draws on the Roman custom of public "triumphs," victory processions in which defeated enemies are led in public disgrace through the streets of Rome, at best into slavery, at worst to death in the course of the climactic sacrifices. The strength of this image is striking (though partially paralleled in 1 Cor 4:9): Paul portrays himself as the victim doomed to a lamentable fate (Hafemann 1986). How is this an occasion for thanksgiving? Because precisely through these circumstances God spreads the "fragrance" of the gospel (2:14-16; this metaphor may derive from the incense burned in the procession, though it links also with the incense of sacrifice). In sharing Christ's sufferings (1:5), the apostles become "the aroma of Christ to God" (2:15), though with the same double effect as the message of Christ crucified (1 Cor 1:18): to some a stench confirming their destiny in "death," to others a perfume leading to newness of life (2:16). That is clearly an awesome role to play — to embody the offense and the power of Christ crucified — and Paul naturally asks who is sufficient for this task (v. 16). That question echoes Moses' hesitations on this score (it is close to Exod 4:10 LXX, and Paul will soon compare his ministry to that of Moses (3:7-18). However, Paul is bold enough to imply: "we are." He immediately makes clear (2:17) that this is so only because "we" speak "in Christ," from God and in the presence of God, with a transparency that allows God's gracious voice to be heard through this human medium (cf. 1:12 and 3:5). And with a side glance back at the "super apostles" of chs. 10–13, Paul compares this transparency of motive with that of the "pedlars" who receive material support for their preaching (the term could imply falsification as well, a nuance which is certainly present in 4:2).

But Paul is not comfortable commending himself in this way. He has just echoed 12:19, but he does not want to rerun the awkward tactic of chs. 10–13 (alluded to in the "again" of 3:1). He has one great proof that God has used him to communicate the authentic gospel, bringing both life and death: the very existence of the Corinthian church. Thus, developing a tactic previously deployed (1 Cor 1:18–2:5; 9:1-3; 2 Cor 10:12-18), Paul claims the church itself as his conclusive "letter of recommendation": Who needs pieces of paper when you have a letter visible to all, signed by Christ and delivered (not "prepared," NRSV) by Paul — a church which he carries on his heart (cf. 7:3) like a reference authenticating his apostolic calling? It is a bold metaphor which shifts in the very course of its expression as it links with and adopts other biblical language (3:3). This writing on the heart evokes the new covenant imagery of Jer 31:31ff., while the contrast there with the law makes Paul think first of the stone tablets inscribed by the finger of God and then of Ezekiel's contrast between the hearts of stone and the new hearts of flesh, enlivened by the Spirit (Ezek 11:19; 36:26). This pastiche of allusions is not, however, random: it prepares the way for the contrast between the new and old covenants which becomes explicit in 3:5 and dominates the rest of this chapter.

If God can write such Spirit-enlivened "letters" through his ministry, Paul has grounds to be confident (3:4; cf. 1:12), though again with the proviso that his competence (lit. "sufficiency," echoing the question of 2:16) comes not from himself but from God (cf. 1 Cor 15:9-10 and the lesson learned at 1:9). As his allusions to Jeremiah 31 and Ezekiel 36 suggest, Paul recognizes in his work the signs of the promised new covenant (3:6), characterized by the life-giving power of the Spirit and in contrast to the former covenant of the "letter," whose end result is death. This contrast (cf. Rom 2:29; 7:6) does not express an antithesis between "literal" and "spiritual" (i.e., allegorical) readings of Scripture. Rather, it sets in antithesis the provision of the law as "script" — a written phenomenon exterior to the human agent, death-dealing in its inability to counter the human propensity to sin — and the transformative work of the Spirit, whose power to bring life out of death signals the presence of a new creation in which heart inscriptions are a guarantee of eternal life (cf. 1:22; 5:5, 17).

The Ministry of the New Covenant in Contrast to the Old (3:7-18)

The implied comparison with Moses (2:16) and the echoes of Jeremiah and Ezekiel (3:3) have evoked the comparison between two covenants (3:6), but why should this now be developed at such length and with extensive echoes of Exodus 34 (3:7-18)? Some scholars have suggested that this passage was pre-formed, a self-standing commentary on Exodus 34 which is inserted here by way of digression. Others speculate on the theology of Paul's Jewish-Christian rivals (cf. 11:22), suggesting that Moses' glory was important to them as precursor and model for their own glorious style of apostleship: hence Paul's need to trump their exegesis with his own (Georgi 1987). Such speculation is probably unnecessary since the passage makes sufficient sense without it. Paul's reflection on his style of ministry and its effects is entirely appropriate here, even if it had perhaps been honed over a period of time in meditation on the story of Moses and in the light of his synagogue experiences (3:14; cf. 11:24). By allusion to, and partial citation from, Exod 34:29-35, Paul compares the glory of his gospel ministry with the lesser glory of that of Moses (3:7-11) and then contrasts his unveiled preaching with the veiling practice of Moses (3:12-18). On this basis rest his boldness and confidence (v. 12) that, despite pitiful appearances, he represents and imparts a lasting glory; hence his excitement at seeing the corresponding liberation of his hearers, who, in turning to the Lord, find the Spirit transforming them into the glory they glimpse in Christ (3:16-18).

3:7-11 functions by the reasoning "if so much, how much more. . . ." Paul has reflected deeply on the passage where Moses returns from Sinai a second time, carrying the tablets of the law (Exodus 34; the first set had been smashed when he saw the golden calf). The Bible records the glowing of his face (Exod 34:29, "glorified" in the LXX), a glory which Paul recognizes but here relativizes by comparison with the greater glory of the new covenant. Moses' ministry was a "ministry of death" (3:7), probably because Paul reckons that the Mosaic law, when it meets human sinfulness, evokes death-dealing disobedience (like the golden calf; cf. Rom 7:7-25). That ministry was not without its glory — in fact, so glorious that Moses' face was unbearably bright (Exod 34:30) — but it was a glory which is "now set aside" (NRSV; better than the RSV interpretation, "fading as this was"; the biblical text makes no reference to fading, and Paul sees the Mosaic covenant being superseded now but not necessarily fading already then). If glory attended Moses' giving of the law, how much more glory must attend the gift of the life-giving Spirit (3:8), and if condemnation (the effect of the old covenant) had its glorious aspects, how much more must justification (the effect of the new, 3:9). For the old has been eclipsed, its glory not denied (Paul cannot regard Moses or the law as in error) but now outshone by a greater glory whose effects are not limited by time but destined to last forever (3:10-11; cf. 4:17-18).

In the next paragraph (3:12-18) Paul offers a rich and complex reflection on the theme of Moses' veiling (scholars continue to discuss its layers of meaning; see, e.g., Hays 1989: 122-53; Belleville 1991; Wright 1991: 175-92; Hafemann 1995). The Exodus narrative portrays Moses veiling his head when the people saw his shining face (Exod 34:29-35), and Paul finds here a suggestion of secrecy. Unlike the ministry of Moses, his is conducted with barefaced boldness since he has nothing to hide and no interest in veiling the open statement of the truth (3:12-13). Moses, Paul suggests, acted to prevent the people of Israel from gazing "at the end of what was being set aside" (some translate, "at the *goal* of what was doomed to pass away," that is, the fulfillment of the old covenant, Christ; the Greek term *telos* may include either or both senses). The ambiguities in Paul's Greek make it hard to determine what he thinks was Moses' purpose, but one possible sense is that his veil covers not just the glory on his face but also its temporary and provisional character. This is matched by a hardening of minds (v. 14), a failure to perceive, on the part of Israel, so that this same veil may also be conceived as lying over Israel's face. Exodus 34 is thus not just a past event but a continuing story ("to this very day"), for Israel continues to encounter Moses, now through the reading of the old covenant (3:14-15; since he is the author of the law, "Moses" is a natural name for the text itself). Paul had enough experience of the negative reaction of most fellow Jews to his interpretation of Scripture to consider their reading to be shrouded by a veil, an obstacle which can only be removed "in Christ." But the Exodus account does not just suggest this hermeneutical block; it also hints at the means of its removal, for Paul knows that whenever Moses talked with the Lord, he lifted the veil (Exod 34:34-35). By a selective rephrasing of Exod 34:34, Paul finds here both Moses' own experience and a possibility now open to all: when there is a "turning to the Lord," the veil can be removed (3:16).

Fittingly, it is at this point that Paul begins to unveil his own interpretation of this text (3:17-18). "The Lord" to whom one turns means (or "refers to") "the Spirit": Moses' turning is a figure for a life retuned by the Spirit, a life characterized by the freedom of those whose vision is no more restricted and whose confidence neither needs nor tolerates seclusion (v. 17). Thus, from the opening contrast between Paul and Moses (vv. 12-13) we have moved to a positive alignment of Christian experience with the story of Moses, whose unveiled experience of glory can now be taken to apply to "all of us" (v. 18). Just as Moses, in encountering the glory (of God), came himself to shine, so the community of believers can see as clearly as Moses did (and the people of Israel did not). That sight is "as though reflected in a mirror" (3:18 [NRSV], one of several possible interpretations of Paul's rare term *katoptrizomenoi*) because they see God's glory "in the face of Jesus Christ" (4:6), who is God's image (v. 4). But, like Moses, one cannot see such glory and come away unchanged: to experience God's glory in Jesus Christ is to undergo a transformation "into the same image" (cf. Rom 8:29). Believers thus become like what they see: the vision molds its viewers. The NRSV (and others) translate the penultimate phrase of 3:18 "from one degree of glory to another," but it is perhaps better read as describing a transformation which springs from glory (God's) and results in glory (ours). Such peculiarly transformative grace can be mediated only by "the Spirit of the Lord" (or "the Lord who is the Spirit," v. 18), for it is the life-giving work of the Spirit (3:6) to infuse God's beauty into human lives and to make them shine with the light of the new creation (4:6).

The Open Character of Paul's Ministry (4:1-6)

Paul now returns to the topic of his ministry (linking back to 2:14–3:6), though the intervening paragraphs have given him a new thematic contrast between hiddenness and glory. The glory of the new covenant ministry requires open proclamation, without subterfuge or concealment (4:1-2). There is doubtless a defensive element in Paul's statements here: he has been accused of "cunning" in financial matters (12:19, whose Greek closely matches 4:2) and, perhaps, of wrapping up his meaning in confusing irony (1:13) or hiding his intentions with specious promises (1:15ff.). But Paul insists that he has nothing to hide: the "open statement of the truth" is the only way in which to commend himself (4:2; cf. 1:12) and, more importantly, the only means by which the gospel's glory can shine (4:4). He allows that this may not communicate effectively to all: some ("those perishing"; cf. 2:15) have their eyes covered by "the god of this world" (a bold reference to Satan, whose temporary control of "this age" Paul never denies; cf. 1 Cor 5:5; 2 Cor 6:15). But such veils can still be penetrated by the brilliance of the gospel light, whose source is not the preacher (a mere slave of the audience, in service to the Master, 4:5; cf. 1 Cor 9:19), but the Lord being preached. Thus Paul insists again that his worth resides only in his effectiveness as a channel of (or signpost to) the grace of God in Christ (cf. 1:4; 2:14-17), and in a striking climax, alluding to both Genesis 1 and Isaiah 9, he envisages the gospel as a shaft of light, streaming from God, visible in Christ, and penetrating the human heart (4:6).

The Working of Life in the Midst of Death (4:7-15)

The glory of which Paul has spoken in 4:6 is not, he insists, hidden by his ministry; but he admits that it is present in a paradoxical form, in the midst of human weakness and suffering. Indeed, this is no mere admission on his part: it is precisely God's intention that divine glory should be present and visible not in or alongside human glory but amid the ordinary fragility of human lives. Paul here develops the theme he had first explored in chs. 11–12 (esp. 12:6-10), and which he had begun to expound in the opening blessing (1:3-11). Now he provides the climactic expression of his theology of suffering as a sharing in the suffering of Christ, a paradoxical channel of life both for the sufferer and for others.

To put treasure in clay jars (4:7) is to commit the extraordinary to disposable, cheap, and fragile containers. The contrast serves to emphasize the value of the treasure, and thus to display that the power of the gospel owes nothing to human resources or capabilities (cf. 12:8-10; 2:14). The fragility of those jars is underlined by the short catalogue of 4:8-9, which also emphasizes survival beyond all reasonable expectations (cf. 1:8-11), a resilience which can only be explained by the sustaining power of God. Thus 4:10-11 states and repeats the central thesis: we are shaped by the pattern of the death and resurrection of Jesus, sharing in his death (v. 10; Gk. *nekrōsis* could mean "his dying," the process of succumbing to death) and so also experiencing his life (cf. 13:3-4; 2:14-16). It is implied that the latter comes only through the former: just as resurrection came only from death, so "the life of Jesus" can be present, and seen to be present, only in the vulnerability of human lives, whose weakness and mortality are not an impediment to the gospel but a precondition for its full display (Savage 1996).

The turn of thought in 4:12 (death in us, but life *in you*) is a surprise only to those who have forgotten the "overflow" principle outlined in 1:3-7 (cf. 13:9): the receipt of grace ("consolation" or "life") in the midst of suffering is never only for one's own benefit but also for the sake of others who receive its abounding overflow. Hence Paul understands his suffering not merely as a means to his enrichment, effecting his inner renewal and equipping him to display the glory of the gospel; it is also, and more importantly, the medium through which the life of Christ floods on through his life into the lives of others (see also above on 2:14). Here he feels himself thoroughly in tune with the experience of the psalmist, and cites in 4:13 from the Greek version of Psalm 115 (in our English/Hebrew versions, Ps 116:10). That psalm naturally springs to Paul's mind in this context — it is full of references to suffering and death ("Precious in the sight of the LORD is the death of his faithful ones," Ps 116:15). But the particular verse Paul cites illustrates how the life of Jesus flows out through him — in "speaking," the proclamation of the gospel. Because we "believe" (i.e., "know," 4:14) that God raised Jesus and thus will raise us with him, we speak this good news and bring others into that number who experience his life and receive its future guarantee (vv. 13-14).

Thus the overflow of grace spills out to an ever-increasing range, its origin in God being recognized when its recipients complete the circle, returning thanks to God (4:15; *charis,* "grace," from God being returned as *eucharistia,* "thanksgiving," to God; cf. 9:10-15; 1:10-11). This notion of "extending to more and more" suggests that they, too, will come to share in this paradox of "life in death" which Paul has described thus far as relating to "us" (cf. 1:3-7). Indeed, although the Corinthians are somewhat ashamed by the pitiful existence of their apostle (cf. 10:1-11), Paul insists that this "clay jar" is designed precisely for their sake (4:15), both in the sense that they benefit from it and in the sense that they can see here a model for their own lives! Thus the "we" has extended to include all Christians, and from this vantage point, in retrospect, all that is said in vv. 7ff. can be taken as applicable in principle to every believer.

The Transitory Present in Light of the Eternal Future (4:16–5:10)

If the Christian life means to bear both the dying and the life of Christ (4:10-11), it may be asked where that "life" is to be seen, given that outwardly not much is visible beyond weakness and decay. The question is particularly significant for Paul since his physical weakness has created doubts concerning his apostolic role (10:10) and he is conscious of being judged adversely "in outward appearance" (5:12). Thus his thought progresses to the inner renewal effected by the life of Christ (4:16), which indicates the stamp of the eschatological Spirit (5:5) and bears with it the assurance of an eternal future. In the course of this discussion, Paul develops some of his most dualistic (indeed, "Platonist") language — contrasting transient visible things with the eternity of the invisible, the outer self with the inner person. But he wears this philosophical garb lightly since his primary purpose is not to analyze the human person or the personal impact of death but to provide grounds for his confidence that, despite appearances (5:7), human mortality is already counterbalanced by renewal, in a process which will stretch beyond death into eternal glory.

As before, the chief theme is confidence (4:16; cf. 4:1; 3:12; 5:6-8). What may look like mere decay — human mortality accelerated by the vulnerability of bearing the gospel — is accompanied by daily inner renewal (v. 16; cf. 3:18), the "decay" in fact effecting (not just "preparing us for," NRSV) an immeasurably huge "weight" of glory. (Weight is an ironic metaphor here since it is otherwise used for the crushing burden of affliction, 1:8; 5:4; Paul is looking forward to being flattened by glory!) Such is the goal to which we look — paradoxically since it cannot actually be seen (4:18).

This confidence is based on the knowledge (5:1) of an eternal house, which "we have" (already, in principle) for the moment when the present "earthly tent" is destroyed. In substance Paul seems to be thinking of the "spiritual body" which he had talked about in 1 Corinthians 15, although he never refers to it here as a "body" (in fact, he talks of leaving the body, 5:8); instead, he uses (and mixes) metaphors of housing and clothing. This passage is frequently combed for evidence of a change in Paul's expectations of the end, in comparison with 1 Corinthians 15: Does he anticipate now, after the experience of 1:8ff., the possibility of death before the parousia and, if so, is he worried about "the intermediate state" between this death and the final resurrection? There may well be some such subtle changes (Paul never offers a finished system of thought), but the basic conviction is the same as in the earlier letter — that God's purpose is to transform this mortal existence not by discarding it but by "swallowing it up" by life (5:4). The metaphor here is of layers of clothing: our present lot is a forward-looking groan, awaiting the redemption of the body (cf. Rom 8:23), which will be like donning an outer garment (5:2). The aside in v. 3 is probably meant to support this point. Although the text of this verse is uncertain and its meaning rather obscure, it should probably be translated "on the certain condition that, once having put it on, we shall never prove to be naked" (Thrall). Thus the "groaning" of vv. 2 and 4 expresses not the dreaded anticipation of an uncomfortable fate but the frustration inherent in longing for the absorption of the mortal present into the eternal future. The guarantee of this transition is the gift of the Spirit (v. 5; cf. 1:22), which has already started the irrevocable process of transformation into glory (3:18).

This future assurance places the present in a wholly different light (5:6-10). Present existence is provisional and partial, endued with a sense of not being quite "at home" (vv. 6, 8). This is the true condition of faith (v. 7) — appropriating the truth of the resurrection (4:14) even if no alternative home is yet visible. Meanwhile, even away from home, servants have a Master (Lord) to please, and Paul reminds them all of their responsibilities by invoking the future judgment (5:10). Paul takes this prospect seriously, although he can describe it in a number of ways (cf. Rom 2:16; 14:10-11; 1 Cor 3:10-15). It underlines the believers' accountability for their present bodily lives and thus serves to remind the Corinthians that their recent problems lie under the scrutiny of an ultimate judge.

The Foundation and Goal of Paul's Ministry (5:11–6:10)

The reference to the judgment seat of Christ (5:10) serves to remind Paul of a theme he has emphasized before: that he stands before Christ (or God) and is answerable first and foremost to him (12:19; 2:17). It is this "fear of the Lord" which motivates him (5:11) so that, though he aims to persuade his hearers, he cannot compromise his message to suit their values (cf. 4:2). This open and sincere "standing before the Lord" is, Paul hopes, his greatest commendation also before his church (5:11-12; cf. the closely parallel, 1:12-14), but he knows that he has had to contend there with an alternative value system which is more impressed by "outward appearance" (lit. "face," 5:12; cf. 11:6). 5:13 may allude to the ecstatic experiences which he had played down in 12:1ff.: such are best kept between himself and God, for he would rather present a sober, even if unimpressive, face to the church. (Alternatively, on a different translation, he here contrasts the "immoderate," i.e., "foolish," language of chs. 10–13 with the sober and plain speech of the present letter.)

Thus Paul finds himself on the border of two worlds, a representative of the new world restructured by the death and resurrection of Christ, but its spokesman to the old, announcing the gracious offer of salvation to a world unable to appreciate its value (5:14-19). And since the wrong kind of boasting is still attractive to this church (v. 12), Paul perceives that drawing the Corinthians from the old world into the new is an ongoing task: his appeal for reconciliation to God is not finished yet (5:20–6:2). All this is packed, with much else besides, into one of the richest and most complex theological statements in the Pauline corpus (5:14–6:2).

Paul first explains the countercultural reorientation effected by the death and resurrection of Christ (5:14-15). His life is controlled by a new force (the love of Christ) because of the realization that the death of Christ ruptures the existence of all those who share it (Rom 6:1-6; Gal 2:19-20). Here lies the heart of Paul's understanding of the cross, which is for him not only an atoning event dealing with sins but also a death in which believers participate and find their existence redefined. That dying transforms their living into a "living for Christ" (5:15) and effects a fundamental shift in their perception of the world (vv. 16-17). Now they no longer know (and judge) human life "from a human point of view" (lit. "according to the flesh," i.e., according to the standards of the old era; cf. 1:17; 10:2-4). Christ himself, once judged from this viewpoint as the epitome of folly and weakness, can now be seen with faith as the locus of God's saving power and wisdom (1 Cor 1:18-25). 5:16 is thus not an aside, discussing the relative merits of knowing the historical Jesus, but rather the pivotal statement of the passage. In coming to a different view of the crucified Christ, faith begins to see the whole world anew, so that, in Christ, a new creation begins (cf. Gal 6:14-15; Martyn 1997: 89-110). If this is what faith entails, it is easy to see why Paul is frustrated with the "fleshly" perceptions of his converts and why he had engaged so reluctantly in the "fleshly" competition of 11:21ff. (cf. 11:18). The cross has enabled a new creation by putting an end to the old, yet Paul perceives his converts still molded by the "old-world" habits of perception, impressed by power, eloquence, and visual display. As a spokesman for the new world, he cannot cease until their system of values is utterly transformed.

The metaphor by which Paul develops this thought is that of an ambassador who proclaims and offers reconciliation (5:18–6:2). The imagery is drawn from contemporary politics (see Bash 1997), although ambassadors usually sued for peace rather than offering it as an accomplished fact. The metaphor implies a previous state of enmity, a world in hostile separation from God which God draws to himself in the gracious work of Christ (5:19). As God's spokesman, Paul is not only to proclaim that event but to make it effective. Hence his proclamation, "Be reconciled to God" (v. 20), has the power to effect what it announces, spreading either life or death according to the response (2:15-16). The extraordinary identification of Christ with the human condition (lit. "made to be sin," as its representative or even embodiment) enables the equally extraordinary identification of believers with the righteousness of God in Christ (5:21). The pattern of thought here mirrors 8:9 (cf. Gal 3:13): the grace of God is evident and powerful in the humiliation of Christ and thus in those who share his death and subsequent new life (cf. Hooker 1990: 13-25, 42-55). Thus, those who share in the death of Christ (5:14-15) now "see" and "know" quite differently (vv. 12, 16-17). Paul is concerned that this process is still not consolidated in Corinth, and he regards his ambassadorial role as incomplete: the Corinthians have accepted the grace of God, but it could still come to nothing (6:1; cf. 1 Cor 15:10). The doubt is not as radical as that expressed in the devastating paragraph, 13:5-10, but the new life they enjoy has still to be firmly rooted; thus, with a citation of Isa 49:8, Paul urges them to take hold of their salvation (6:2). As 1:6 and 2:15 had made clear, "salvation" is always in process throughout the Christian life.

The Corinthians' grasp of the gospel is most clearly revealed in their attitude to Paul. Will they recognize that Christ is speaking through this ambassador (13:3-4), and that his external weaknesses are a sign that he is "working together with" the God who saves through weakness, folly, poverty, even "sin" (5:20–6:1)? That question leads Paul back to talking about his own ministry (6:3-10), not because he is obsessed with his reputation as such but because their boast in him (5:12) would reveal that they have let the grace of God take effect. Thus the following self-depiction gathers themes from the earlier letters and from this. Paul creates no obstacle (by taking no pay, 11:7) and tries to be blameless in his financial affairs (6:3; cf. 8:20). He commends himself as a servant of Christ precisely by appeal to his endurance and the humiliating deprivations he has endured (6:4-5; cf. 2:14–3:1; 11:21-29, a list here abbreviated). Throughout he conducts himself with purity and sincerity (6:6; cf. 10:1; 11:6, 11), and displays not his own strength but the powerful weapons of God (cf. 4:7-12; 10:3-6; 12:8-10). His ministry is maligned and dishonored (by those who judge "according to the flesh," 5:12, 16), but in a series of paradoxes (6:8-10) Paul affirms the hidden treasure which lies within this clay pot: outwardly he appears to be ignominious, dying, sorrowful, and poor, indeed destitute; but in reality he is honored by God, he survives, rejoices, and offers the greatest treasure on earth. Superficially this looks like the Stoic claim that the poorest man (in material goods) can be the richest (in virtue), but the echo of 8:9 (and 5:21) indicates that the basis of the Pauline paradox lies not in the superior virtue of the human mind but in sharing the fate, and therefore channeling the grace, of Christ (Fitzgerald 1988). It is only in this cruciform shape that his ministry can have any effect, and it is only on this basis that he can dare, paradoxically, to commend himself (6:4; cf. 10:12; 3:1; 4:2; 5:12). Here the foundational paradox of 12:9-10 is worked out in its multiple dimensions.

Securing Paul's Relationship with the Corinthians (6:11–7:16)

We have now met several indications of Paul's concern with the Corinthians' evaluation of his ministry (5:11-12; 4:1-6; 6:1-10), and it is therefore no surprise that he finishes this letter, as he began it (1:12–2:13), with a rehearsal of his recent dealings with the church and an attempt to secure their now warmer relationship. The tone adopted is one of confidence and relief since Paul chooses to interpret Titus's news as an indication that the Corinthians have restored their trust in him. But the pleas at the beginning of this section (6:12-13; 7:2) suggest that Paul's confidence is not quite as complete as he would like to claim (7:16).

The section begins with an assurance of honesty and openness on Paul's part (6:11; cf. 1:13; 4:2). The "widening of the heart" also suggests magnanimity, and this gives Paul cause to assure the Corinthians once more of his unswerving love (cf. 2:4) and to request reciprocation (6:12-13). The parent-child imagery recalls 12:14-15 and, as there, is employed in an appeal for a "return" not in financial but in emotional terms. Although Paul is impressed by their "obedience" (2:9), he fears that the painful visit and the tearful letter still scar his relationship to the church. He is going to need a lot of emotive language in the following passage (7:2-13) to deaden any residual pain.

But before we get to 7:2, our text contains a remarkable paragraph (6:14–7:1) which appears quite out of place. We could move from 6:13 to 7:2 without feeling an omission, and the change in tone, content, and style in 6:14–7:1 is abrupt. Why should Paul suddenly issue an appeal for separation from "unbelievers" in the midst of this delicate restoration of relationships? Further peculiarities characterize this paragraph: it contains many words and expressions not otherwise found in the Pauline letters (e.g., "mismatched," 6:14; "Beliar" as a name for Satan, 6:15; "defilement," 7:1), and the chain of quotations in 6:16-18 refers to OT texts not elsewhere cited by Paul. Indeed, such is the cluster of oddities in this short paragraph that many scholars conclude that it has been inserted from another source; and there are so many parallels in terminology and thought with the Dead Sea Scrolls that some have proposed the source to be an early Christian author influenced by Qumran theology. The chief problem with such an interpolation theory lies in explaining how the insertion took place: If it was originally not by Paul, how did it get placed so clumsily here? Of the many theories that have been, and continue to be, propounded, probably the strongest two are these:

a) The paragraph is a fragment of an earlier letter by Paul to the Corinthians, the one referred to in 1 Cor 5:9. There Paul has to correct a "misunderstanding," insisting that he did not require withdrawal from the world. This paragraph could easily lend itself to that interpretation (and set up questions such as that addressed in 1 Cor 7:12-16). It could thus represent Paul's earliest vision of the church as a pure "temple" radically distinct from its environment, a vision inspired by Palestinian Qumran-type theology but partly modified in 1 Corinthians by the lessons of experience. It is not too difficult to imagine an editor putting Paul's Corinthians letters together and slotting this fragment into its present location, the only point in 2 Corinthians 1–7 where it could possibly fit.

b) The currently most popular opinion is that this paragraph fits where it presently belongs, digressing from but not totally disrupting its surrounding context. Some take the appeal for disassociation from "unbelievers" to mean withdrawal from the influence of the "false apostles," but that would not match Pauline usage of the term "unbeliever," and the force of 6:14-16 is against associations with the non-Christian world. More plausibly, links have been proposed between the "new covenant"/ "new exodus" themes of the scriptural quotations in vv. 16-18 and the theology of the previous chapters, especially 3:1-6, 5:17, and 6:2 (if Paul models himself there on the "servant" of Isaiah 49). The passage would then constitute an appeal to embark on that new exodus, a return to the Lord parallel to their return to the apostle (Webb 1993).

It cannot be said that either of these solutions is wholly persuasive (for others see Hultgren 2003); the passage remains an enigma which may never be solved. The following comments offer some explanation of its contents but do not attempt to establish links with its present literary context.

The paragraph opens with instruction against "mismatching" with unbelievers, backed up by five rhetorical questions designed to highlight incompatibility (6:14-15). It is not clear whether the mismatch in view is specifically marital (cf. 1 Cor 7:12-16, 39) or refers to wider social partnerships (cf. 1 Cor 6:15-20; 10:14-22), but the contrasts suggest a strongly dualistic view of alternative worlds, in which unbelievers are associated with darkness, lawlessness, idolatry, and "Beliar" (= Satan, called "Belial" in the Dead Sea Scrolls). The final contrast is supported by a statement of identity as the temple of God (cf. 1 Cor 3:16; 6:19) which leads into a string of conflated quotations (6:16-18). These are carefully constructed to lead from promise (v. 16) to double command (v, 17) to further promises (vv. 17-18). The first promise is drawn from Ezek 37:27 (with Lev 26:11), a passage which refers to the "new sanctuary" in the restoration of Israel. The commands in 6:17 derive from Isa 52:11, which encourages the "new exodus" in separation from the defilement of exile. The final promises (6:17-18) are drawn from Ezek 20:34 (God's welcoming home from the exile; other texts use similar language) and 2 Sam 7:14 — the promise to David being broadened to include all believers (for "my sons and daughters"; cf. Isa 43:6). The selection suggests a theology of the people/temple of God in Christ as the fulfillment of all the covenant promises, both Davidic and post-exilic; it thus forms the basis for an exhortation to purity (7:1), strikingly applied to both "flesh" and "spirit" (cf. 1 Cor 7:34).

7:2 reasserts Paul's appeal for a full restoration of trust (cf. 6:11-13). He denies any wrongdoing on his part (with echoes of the accusations in 12:16-18) and insists that he intends no charge against them; they belong together, not in mutual antagonism but in mutual support (7:3; cf. 13:10; 1:3-7; 4:12). The reaffirmation of his "boast" in them (7:4; cf. 1:14) leads Paul into his closing expressions of relief and joy, carefully held over until this point (7:5 continues the narrative from 2:14) so that the letter can end on a note of confidence. The emotional overstatement in these verses (7:4-16) may reflect Paul's still nervous state of mind, though it also serves to banish past doubts and open a new chapter in his relationship to the Corinthian church. If my reading of the original sequence of material in 2 Corinthians is right (see the Introduction, 1354-56), this would be the final word and a hopeful sign for the future (cf. Rom 15:26); if 2 Corinthians 10–13 is a later letter, the confidence of this chapter was to prove embarrassingly misplaced.

Paul's new confidence has emerged from extreme affliction (7:4, echoing 1:3-7). The torture he endured in Macedonia (7:5) was particularly occasioned by his anxiety in waiting for Titus, who had carried the "painful letter" to Corinth and who had yet to report to Paul on its reception (vv. 6-7). Paul here recognizes the risk he took in writing that letter. He knew it would wound the church, and it might have caused a complete breach in their relationship; for a while he even regretted sending it (v. 8). But, to his enormous relief, its sting did not alienate them but spurred them into regret, repentance, and vigorous reaffirmation of their support for Paul (vv. 7, 9-11). Paul's statements here are highly allusive, but if we connect them with 2:4-11 we may build a composite picture of a figure in the church who caused considerable wrong (or "pain") to Paul and who was tolerated, if not supported, by the rest of the church. However, the rebuke in Paul's letter led to a communal change of mind, isolating (even condemning) the individual concerned and enabling Paul to pronounce them now "guiltless" in the whole affair (7:11; though the reference to "repentance" [v. 9] suggests that it was not really that simple!).

Paul chooses now not to dwell on past rights and wrongs. He declares himself satisfied that the matter has been dealt with (7:11) and represents the episode as an opportunity for the display and recognition of the Corinthians' "zeal" for Paul (7:12). At its deepest level, this is of more than merely personal significance to Paul. It indicates (for him) the Corinthians' alignment with the grace of God in its paradoxical apostolic shape, and thus their "obedience" not just to him but to the gospel (7:15; cf. 2:9; 9:13). And in this he feels vindicated before Titus as well (7:13-15). He had earlier boasted to Titus and others about the Corinthians' readiness for the collection, a symptom of their willingness to support him and his gospel (8:6-11; 9:1-5). This boast has now at last proved well founded (7:14), though for a while it appeared extremely shaky. Titus has now personally experienced, on his visit to Corinth, the welcome which Paul believes they accord to himself. After the anxieties of the collection letter (chs. 8–9) and the desperate tactics of the letter of tears (chs. 10–13), one can hear the sigh of relief in Paul's closing expression of joy and "utter confidence" (7:16).

The Collection Letter: 2 Corinthians 8–9

As explained in the Introduction (pp. 1354-56), I take 2 Corinthians 8–9 as the first of the three letters combined in our canonical 2 Corinthians — a distinct letter written from Macedonia to insure that Paul's promised visit (1 Cor 16:1-6) was a success. The main purpose of this visit was to gather the Corinthians' contribution to the Jerusalem collection, but Paul seems to have become anxious as he approached, and was perhaps informed that the money was not as ready as he had hoped. (Both the other options outlined in the Introduction take 2 Corinthians 8–9 as the conclusion to chs. 1–7: once his relationship with Corinth has been restored, Paul is in a position to renew his appeal for a Corinthian donation.)

The collection for Jerusalem was a major focus of Paul's activity at this time (see Nickle 1966; Georgi 1992). Its basis lies in a commitment made at the Jerusalem conference in the late 40s (Gal 2:10), and part of its rationale seems to have been Paul's concern that his Gentile converts remain aware of their debt to Jerusalem and Judaism (see Rom 15:25-33). By the same token, if the collection was successfully gathered and gratefully received (Paul later expresses some fears on this count, Rom 15:30-31), it would signal recognition by the Jerusalem church of what his Gentile mission had achieved. But there were also good economic reasons for the collection: those Paul calls "the poor among the saints at Jerusalem" (Rom 15:26) were in considerable need (2 Cor 8:14), perhaps because local food shortages (cf. Acts 11:27-30) were exacerbated by social discrimination against followers of Jesus. Paul had earlier given the Corinthians instructions on laying aside money for this purpose (1 Cor 16:1-4); here he claims that they were initially keen to contribute (8:10-12). But such a major, international collection was an unparalleled phenomenon, whose unusual character could occasion many doubts. It was not like the annual tax which male diaspora Jews contributed to the temple in Jerusalem, nor like the donations which wealthy Greeks and Romans might make to citizens and clients, expecting public honor in return. The fact that Paul has to use multiple arm-twisting techniques in 2 Corinthians 8–9 may indicate that the Corinthians failed to appreciate its rationale, regarded it as an unreasonable burden on their resources, and did not entirely trust Paul (who took no other pay) to deliver the money to its supposed destination (cf. 12:14-18). By here making their response a token of their commitment to the gospel (9:13) and of their love (8:7, 8, 24: to God, to others, and to him?), Paul raises the stakes and inadvertently stores up trouble for the following "painful" visit.

If the two chapters belong together (see below on 9:1), the letter is structured as two appeals around a central administrative block:

Appeal for a Corinthian contribution (8:1-15)
The collection delegates and their role (8:16–9:5)
Reasons for generosity (9:6-15)

Appeal for a Corinthian Contribution (8:1-15)

Paul's first tactic is to shame the Corinthians by citing the Macedonians' extraordinary enthusiasm for the project (8:1-5; the tactic is admitted in 8:8, while 9:1-2 suggests that he had earlier used the same method the other way around to prod the Macedonians!). References to the Macedonians' zeal are piled high: not only have they given, but they have done so despite affliction (8:2), out of extreme poverty (v. 2), beyond their means (v. 3), and voluntarily, to the extent of begging to take part (vv. 3-4). Since the Corinthian Christians clearly thought highly of themselves (cf. 1 Cor 1:4-7; 4:8-10, an opinion Paul tactfully reinforces here at 8:7), Paul implies that they should rival the Macedonians, though his request is for a level of giving far less sacrificial than the Macedonians displayed (vv. 12-15).

As these opening verses show (8:1-5), it is crucial to the theology of this letter that such human generosity is placed in the context of, and made dependent on, the grace of God in Christ. The Macedonians' response is a token of the grace (*charis*) of God (v. 1), and the multiple uses of this term (found 10 times in 2 Corinthians 8–9) tie its various appeals together. It is because of the grace of God (8:1), demonstrated in the grace of the Lord Jesus Christ (v. 9), God's indescribable gift (9:15), that believers are equipped and motivated to take their share in a "generous undertaking" such as this (8:6, Gk. *charis;* cf. v. 7, 19). And, properly undertaken, that generosity is a token not only of commitment to others but also of self-giving (back) to God (v. 5); thus God's selfgiving in Christ rebounds in Christian devotion and creates multiple ripples of generosity in a wide pool of human relationships.

Turning from Macedonia to Corinth (8:6-11), Paul affirms, perhaps with some exaggeration, their early enthusiasm for the project, initiated by Titus (v. 6) but still lacking completion (vv. 10-11). "Enthusiasm" is a repeated motif in this chapter: the Macedonians (vv. 4, 8), Titus (vv. 16-17), Paul (v. 16), and the second "brother" (v. 22) — everyone is enthusiastic for the cause, and Paul is prepared to credit that, alongside their other virtues, the Corinthians are too (v. 7). It only remains to turn that "enthusiasm" and "love" (v. 7) into action. (Here the Greek text probably read: "the love from us in you," which might mean "our love for you" [NRSV], but is better interpreted "the love which we have inspired in you"; cf. vv.

8, 24.) Such enthusiastic love can only be voluntary — hence Paul's insistence that he is not giving orders but advice (vv. 8, 10). Yet the "advice" is couched in such terms as to make it impossible to refuse without major loss of face for an eagerness unfulfilled and a task incomplete (vv. 10-11; cf. Phlm 8-9); in fact, Paul has made it *the* test of their Christian commitment (8:8). Embedded at the center of such advice is an appeal to the self-emptying grace of Christ (8:9; cf. Rom 15:3; Gal 1:4; Phil 2:6-11). The financial metaphor with which Paul describes the Christ-event is tailored to the context: if Christ impoverished himself to make others rich, it is natural for believers to participate in the dynamic of this grace in their generosity to others. As with the Macedonians (8:2), it is characteristic of God's grace that its wealth flows most richly from the depths of poverty.

However, in 8:12-15 Paul makes clear that he does not expect an unreasonable self-impoverishment from the Corinthians. He expects them to give only from what each individually has (vv. 11-12; cf. 1 Cor 16:2) — a criterion which allows for differential contributions but simultaneously lets no one off the hook. He does not intend them to be destitute (was that their excuse for nonpayment?), only that there should be a "fair balance" (lit. "equality"), of the sort envisaged in the manna collection (8:15, citing Exod 16:18), where God counteracted human greed to insure there were no extremes of plenty or want. Moreover, Paul suggests in 8:14 that this present act of "balancing" might result in future return benefits, not just spiritual blessings (cf. Rom 15:27) but also material support from Jerusalem, as and when the Corinthians needed it. The Corinthian Christians might wonder how this "mutualism" would function, whether Jerusalem would be willing to reciprocate, and whether they themselves would wish to be dependent in this way. But the ideal Paul sets forth is integral to what he understands by "sharing" (*koinōnia,* 8:4; 9:13; see Meggitt 1998: 157-80; Horrell 1995).

The Collection Delegates and Their Role (8:16–9:5)

Paul now makes clear that he is sending certain people in advance (cf. 9:3-5); they probably carry this letter with them. Of the three persons mentioned, only Titus is named. He was already known to the Corinthians (8:6), but is introduced with some care (vv. 16-17) and given special commendation for his commitment to that church (v. 23) in terms which suggest that his task is going to be particularly difficult. It might seem that Paul is sending others ahead to do his "dirty work," but he is due to come himself with the Macedonian representatives (9:4, and their money?), and by then it will be too late to start gathering Corinthian donations.

It is not clear why the two other "brothers" are unnamed. It has been suggested that their names dropped out of the text (or were suppressed), but it is more likely that Paul did not bother to name them, thereby signaling their lesser significance in his eyes. Nonetheless, Paul is happy to commend these brothers, the first of whom seems to have been specially designated by "the churches" (Paul does not specify which) to oversee and accompany the collection (8:18-19). It is important to Paul that this man should be involved since it was natural that suspicions might arise over Paul's interest in such a large sum of money (vv. 20-21, echoing Prov 3:4), and his independence helps to guarantee the probity of the collection and insure that it results in glory to Christ (8:19, 23). But both brothers are also significant as representatives of other churches (v. 23): their presence in Corinth will put the church there on display before the eyes, as it were, of a large Christian public (v. 24). And now Paul lets slip that he has already boasted to others of the Corinthians' part in the collection (v. 24; cf. v. 22; 9:2), so with the arrival of this delegation their international reputation is at stake.

Scholars have long discussed whether ch. 9 was originally an independent letter. It seems odd that Paul should keep writing about "the ministry to the saints" without reference to what he has already said, and it is strange for him to say that it is unnecessary to write about it while starting all over again! Thus it has been suggested that this is a separate letter either dispatched to Corinth soon after ch. 8 or sent simultaneously to a circuit of churches in Achaia (the province of which Corinth was capital) other than Corinth (9:2; cf. 1:1; see Betz 1985 and full discussion in the commentaries). However, there is nothing here either incompatible with ch. 8 or grossly repetitive, and the Greek wording of 9:1 actually suggests a link back to 8:24. Elsewhere, too, Paul writes what he politely calls "superfluous" instructions (1 Thess 4:9; 5:1), and we may perhaps translate here: "For it is not necessary for me to write you *like this* about the ministry to the saints." It seems best to take ch. 9 as a simple continuation and expansion of ch. 8, the length of discussion indicating Paul's anxiety on this matter.

Paul immediately expands the hint he dropped in 8:24 concerning his boast about the Corinthians. The object of that boast was the Corinthians' "eagerness" (9:2), a feature previously emphasized in 8:10-12. It now emerges that Paul had used this to stir up "most of" the Macedonians (9:2), whose commitment to the collection had thus been not quite as spontaneous or universal as 8:1-5 suggested. Paul readily employs the Greek competitive spirit — using Achaia against Macedonia, then Macedonia against Corinth (vv. 1-5) — in a worthy cause (cf. Rom 12:10). Perhaps he was correct to report at an early stage the Achaians' "eagerness," but to claim that they were "ready since last year" (9:2) seems to have been deliberately ambiguous or somewhat exaggerated, and he fears it may now rebound (v. 3). He thus explains the arrival of "the brothers" as an advance party designed to forestall embarrassment at his imminent arrival with Macedonian delegates (vv. 3-4). The fear of "humiliation" — his own and, as he delicately adds, the Corinthians' (v. 4) — ran deep in the "honor-shame" culture of his day, and Paul exploits it for all its worth. As v. 5 indicates, Paul is determined that, one way or another, he will get some money from the Corinthians, though it still matters to him that the pressure he exerts is met on the other side by a willing spirit: he wants it to be a "voluntary" and "bountiful" gift (v. 5; his term, *eulogia,* means both "gift" and "blessing").

Reasons for Generosity (9:6-15)

The notion of bounty leads Paul into his fullest exposition of the theology behind the collection. In the first place, the generosity he requires is a necessary expression of the Corinthians' relationship to God. Building on a well-worn agricultural maxim, Paul urges the benefits of a giving which blesses in its bounty (9:6, *eulogiai*), and he emphasizes the importance of a voluntary, individual, decision (cf. 1 Cor 16:2) since "God loves a cheerful giver" (9:7, based on Prov 22:9). But this divine love is not simply a reward: God loves the giver because God himself gives grace in abundance, whose overflow enables its recipients in turn to give generously to others (9:8 — the ethos of generosity is enhanced by two references to "abundance" and four uses of "all" in one sentence!). Thus when believers give, it is really God giving through them (cf. the grace given to the Macedonians, 8:1), and that ambiguity of origin is well reflected by the fact that when Paul cites Ps 112:9 in 9:9, it is not clear whether it refers to God's generosity (as v. 10a suggests, supplying seed to the sower) or human gift-giving (as in the psalm itself, and as v. 10b suggests, with "the harvest of your righteousness"). But since God and the cheerful giver are part of a continuous chain, this "giving to the poor" could well be said of either.

Moreover, God's "enrichment for generosity" is part of a larger circle of grace, as 9:11-15 now explain. By giving generously, the givers generate a response in the recipients, which consists of "thanksgiving" to God (vv. 11-12). It is no accident that this term, *eucharistia* (i.e., the giving of thanks — *charis* — to God, 9:15), is derived from the same term *charis,* which Paul has used previously of God's grace which inspires human giving (8:1, 9) and of the gift itself (8:4, 6, 7; 9:8). Paul thus depicts a *charis* circle, in which the wealth of God's grace enables an abundance of human generosity, which in turn inspires an overflow of thanks to God. We encounter here one of the deepest strands in Paul's theology, characteristically expressed while discussing mundane, practical, behavior. The *charis* which flows from God and ultimately back to God thus brings glory to God (9:13; cf. 8:19, 23). Thus, in playing their part in its onward transmission and practical expression, the Corinthians will prove their "obedience" in confession of this core feature of the gospel (9:13; cf. "the obedience of faith," Rom 1:5). Paul here alludes to the fact that, in making their contribution to Jerusalem, his Gentile converts will prove to his skeptical Jewish colleagues the validity of their faith and participation in the gospel; he thus imagines the grateful prayers of the Jerusalem church (9:14; though cf. his fears on this matter in Rom 15:31). But, on a larger scale, his depiction of their gift as "obedience" in confessing the gospel expresses his conviction that generosity is the necessary sign of Christian faith: it is as they give with generous hearts that believers indicate their submission to the power of grace which grasps and reorients their lives. Hence Paul's conclusion to the chapter is in praise of that divine gift which supplies and empowers all subsequent human giving. It, and the salvation it sets in train, are ultimately too profound for words (9:15; cf. Rom 11:33-36).

The Tearful Letter: 2 Corinthians 10–13

As noted in the Introduction, 1354-56, it is likely that these four chapters constitute a separate letter: they are a self-contained unit whose tone of anger, aggression, and irony sets them apart from the optimism of chs. 1–7 and the calculated appeal of chs. 8–9. For the reasons outlined in the Introduction, I take them to be written after the Collection Letter (chs. 8–9) but before the Reconciliation Letter (chs. 1–7). They are in fact the "tearful" letter to which Paul later refers: it caused him grief in its composition (2:3-4) and was severe enough to make him temporarily regret its dispatch (7:8-13). On this reconstruction, having sent Titus and "the brothers" ahead with the Collection Letter, Paul followed them and came to Corinth (cf. 9:3-5), a visit which proved to be disastrous and to which this Tearful Letter frequently alludes (e.g., 10:1, 10). It appears that, although Titus had succeeded in extracting some money (12:17-18), Paul's letter had been deeply resented and his reputation in the Corinthian church had suffered badly. There were already signs in 1 Corinthians that his apostolic authority was under question (1 Cor 1:10-17; 2:1-5; 4:1-6, 14-21), but now it seems that criticism had become blatant to the extent of personal affront. The collection had contributed to this deterioration in relationship (see 12:16), but that was exacerbated by the presence in Corinth of other "apostles" (11:4-5, 13-15, 22-23) in comparison with whom Paul appeared contemptible.

Scholars have long debated the identity of these other apostles (see Georgi 1987; Sumney 1990). Those whom Paul attacks as "false apostles" (11:13) are probably the same individuals he sarcastically dubs "super apostles" (11:5; 12:11). It appears from 11:22-23 that they were of Jewish origin, but it is impossible to define their geographical origins or their relationship, if any, to the apostles in Jerusalem. (Distinguishing between the false and super apostles, Barrett 1982: 60-86 and others suggest links with Peter and other Jerusalem apostles, but the evidence is uncertain.) Whoever they were, these apostles have been well received in Corinth and their presence puts Paul into the shadows. Compared to them, Paul seems weak and unimpressive — physically, in his speech and in his ability to deal with opposition face to face — although his letters were recognized to be weighty enough (10:10-11). Moreover, the other apostles have accepted the Corinthians' friendship in the form of financial support, whereas Paul's dogged refusal of Corinthian money seems both stand-offish and self-demeaning (11:5-11; 12:13-15; cf. 1 Corinthians 9). In these and other respects Paul appears such a contemptible figure as to call into question his authority in Corinth, indeed even his standing as a Christian.

While Paul is conscious of these rivals throughout, and is drawn into ironic counterboasting to prove his worth, his greatest concern is with the damage they are causing in Corinth, inculcating an inversion of gospel values (Savage 1996). Thus he directs his appeal to the Corinthian church and at times isolates in their midst an individual spokesman whose "disobedience" is in danger of infecting the rest. The letter begins and ends with the spotlight on the Corinthians themselves and is constructed in a concentric (or chiastic) pattern:

Paul's task and reputation in Corinth (10:1-18)
  Preparing the foolish boast, with focus on finance (11:1-21a)
    The foolish boast — ironically, in weakness (11:21b–12:10)
  Reflection on the boast, with finance in focus again (12:11-18)
Paul's task in Corinth on his impending visit (12:19–13:10)
Letter closing (13:11-13)

Paul's Task and Reputation in Corinth (10:1-18)

From the very first verse of this letter Paul's tone is both defensive and ironic. Admitting the contrast between his behavior face to face and his stance at a distance (10:1), he alludes to the specific criticism which he cites in v. 10: that his letters are strong but his presence weak. The contrast, which so damages his reputation, arises from his recent humiliation in Corinth, directly after the demanding tone of the Collection Letter (chs. 8–9). Paul ironically accepts that he was "humble" (cf. 11:7), but not the implication that he was servile or pusillanimous: he is now planning a return visit (cf. 12:14; 13:1), and this time he is ready to adopt a far sterner pose. But he would do that only if absolutely necessary and thus begs the Corinthians to spare both him and themselves (10:2), appealing to the character of Christ (v. 1), whose meekness explains his preference to endure abuse rather than mete it out (cf. Matt 11:29). Nonetheless, he insists he can be both "bold" and "daring" (like the other apostles, 11:20) when his ministry is impugned as being "according to human standards" (lit. "according to the flesh"). If this phrase was used against him in Corinth, it would return the charge he had leveled against them (1 Cor 3:1-4), perhaps with special reference to his weakness and inconsistency. Paul cannot allow that charge to stand since it would negate his claim that God's power was active precisely through his "humility" (10:3-4; cf. 12:9-10). He thus presents himself, weak as he might seem, as engaged in a military campaign, destroying strongholds (arguments and pride, which inhibit the spread of the knowledge of God), taking captives (every thought), and exacting punishment on the perpetrators of revolt (10:4-6). The gospel is thus portrayed as an assault on human assumptions (cf. the aggressive language of 1 Cor 1:18-31), recapturing humanity for its proper obedience to Christ (cf. 9:13; Rom 1:5). Paul is ready to turn that attack against any Corinthian Christians who have drifted into an antigospel mind-set, though he prefers to hope that their obedience will soon be restored (10:6).

The following paragraph (10:7-11) continues to respond to Corinthian criticisms, with particular reference to a single figure (v. 7 reads literally, "if anyone is confident . . . ," and v. 10, "For he says . . ."). The claim to belong to Christ may refer to some special role or some special spiritual status (cf. the party slogan of 1 Cor 1:12); in either case, questions have been raised as to whether Paul is Christ's spokesman at all (cf. 13:3). The earlier doubts about Paul's right to direct the church (cf. 1 Cor 9:1-2) have clearly grown, and Paul has had to insist on the authority he has received from the Lord (10:8). That is a boast he will never retract ("I will not be ashamed of it") since it is really a boasting in the Lord (vv. 17-18). But unlike Jeremiah (Jer 1:10), he wants to use his authority to build, not to destroy the church, and thus he does not want his letters to be taken as intended to intimidate (10:9). And now at last Paul brings to the surface the criticism which underlay the whole discussion since v. 1: that his letters are forceful (aggressively so?) while in person Paul is both physically weak (perhaps sickly and unsightly, cf. 12:7) and rhetorically pathetic (cf. 11:6; in delivery perhaps, but more likely in his lack of rhetorical polish, 1 Cor 2:1-5). Paul has thus been made to seem ridiculous, and the memory hurts: in a reprise of 1 Cor 4:18-21, he threatens that this time he really will be as strong as his word (10:11).

Paul's recent visit to Corinth had been ruined by the presence of other apostles who were more respected by the Corinthians; the latter failed to show Paul the loyalty he thought his due as the founder of this church. Thus in a complex paragraph (10:12-18), Paul sarcastically repudiates all competitive drawing of comparisons: he would not *dare* to put himself up for comparison with others since their self-manufactured standards will always have them come out on top (v. 12). What they fail to understand (v. 12) is that each is to be measured by the yardstick of God (v. 13; cf. 1 Cor 4:1-5). From that notion of yardstick Paul slides naturally into its geographical sense: he has been apportioned a territory, and that includes Corinth (10:13). Paul's ministry depends on his strong sense of commissioning as apostle to the Gentiles, a commission recognized at the Jerusalem conference (Gal 2:7-9). He is therefore ever conscious of his role as the founder of the Gentile churches, and his founding role in Corinth is the simple fact by which his authority there is legitimated (cf. 1 Cor 3:6, 10; 4:15; 9:1-2). Hence his present appeal: Corinth is not outside his sphere of authority but squarely within it since he was the first to bring the gospel (10:14). By implication, the other apostles are overstepping their limits (whatever God has assigned to them; some think that Paul alludes here to the Jerusalem apostles and their mission to Jews, but that is not clearly so). They are, in fact, trespassing on Paul's territory, and although he always works in virgin soil, in order to found new churches (vv. 15-16; cf. Rom 15:17-21), they take the softer option, reaping another's harvest — and with the cheek to boast about it as if it were their own (10:16)!

Thus Paul suggests that the Corinthian church owes allegiance primarily to him, even if he is not always present there but may be sent on, he hopes, to further mission with their support (10:15-16; cf. Rom 15:22-24: he plans to go to Rome, then to Spain). If anyone has the right to boast about the success of the gospel in Corinth it is he, though his delivery of the message and its reception indicated that the boast could only be in the Lord, not in human ability or achievement (10:17, looking back to 1 Cor 1:26–2:5, with the same citation from Jer 9:22-23). Ultimately, then, the test of approval is set and marked by the Lord: self-testing is an empty exercise (10:18). Thus

Paul dismisses the comparative boasts of the rival apostles as an irrelevant occupation, while pointing toward his final challenge to the church: you may question whether I have passed the test, but what about yourselves (13:5-10)?

Preparing the Foolish Boast (11:1-21a)

Although he has just denounced comparative boasting (10:12-18), Paul knows that his loss of face in Corinth requires him to engage in it. But he will enter this competition only if it is explicitly recognized as "foolish," a piece of folly for which he can apologize as an unfortunate necessity (cf. 12:11). Thus he pleads for indulgence in his folly in 11:1, but then delays its practice while he explains its necessity (vv. 2-15); at v. 16 he again signals the folly of this boast, but registers additional disclaimers before he finally begins in v. 21b. The false starts in vv. 1 and 16 thus dramatize his reluctance to embark on this exercise, while allowing for ironic play on the theme of his "folly" and the Corinthians' proven record of "tolerance."

The Corinthians' indulgence is first requested on the basis of Paul's selfless motivation (11:2-4). If he will boast, it is not for his sake but out of concern for them (cf. 12:19), out of his "divine jealousy" on their behalf. In line with the previous emphasis on his founding role (10:13-14; cf. 1 Cor 4:15), Paul portrays himself as their father, who is responsible for arranging the betrothal of his virgin daughter to the intended bridegroom. He has betrothed them to the one man, Christ, but fears lest they be corrupted (i.e., seduced) by a rival suitor (11:2-3). The imagery is comparable to OT notions of Israel as Yahweh's bride, but it is drawn specifically from the ancient corruption of Eve by the serpent (interpreted by many Jews as seduction by an angelic figure in disguise; cf. v. 14). No doubt the rival apostles considered themselves servants of (the same) Christ (v. 22), but Paul considers them "cunning" (v. 3; the same term has been used against him, 12:16!), leading the church not toward Christ but toward "another Jesus, another Spirit, and another gospel" (11:4). What is at stake here is not some rival christological doctrine (gnostic or otherwise), but a distortion of the gospel of Christ crucified into a glorification of human power and display. For Paul that signals another gospel altogether (cf. Gal 1:6-9), but one which is difficult to refute without playing by its rules of competition; the tactic he chooses is subversive irony, which dons the mask of his rivals only to ridicule their pretensions.

Poor as he may seem by Corinthian standards, Paul insists that he is not at all inferior to these "super apostles" (11:5; cf. 12:11). The irony is heavy and purely tactical: he will not shrink from denouncing the same people shortly as servants of Satan (11:13-15). Although he may concede inadequacies in his powers of speech (v. 6; cf. 10:10; he may exaggerate some real deficiency, using the philosopher's tactic of denouncing his opponent's "cleverness"), Paul will concede nothing in knowledge — perhaps meaning here, as in 10:5, the knowledge of God which is the essence of salvation (cf. Gal 4:8-9). It is his constant and ubiquitous concern to make this knowledge of God "evident" to his audience (11:6), and if the Corinthians claim to be Christians, it is Paul whom they must recognize as the mediator of this knowledge (cf. 1 Cor 9:2; 15:1-5).

At 11:7 Paul turns to the topic of his financial support, and its appearance in this context, with repeated echoes in 12:13-18, indicates that this had become a significant bone of contention between himself and the Corinthian church. In 1 Corinthians 9 Paul had set out at elaborate length the apostolic right to material support, only to insist that he had waived this "right" because of his commission to preach the gospel "free of charge." While Paul regarded this as a mark of his superiority (a "boast"), it could be turned against him when rival apostles were eager to score points against him. By taking no support from the Corinthian church, was Paul admitting that he was not entitled to be considered their apostle? (The rival apostles, who clearly did accept support [11:20], could claim that as a mark of their superior status.) On his first visit, and perhaps on his second, Paul's refusal of support from Corinthian converts required him to work, and his manual labor seemed to some absurdly "humbling" (v. 10; cf. 1 Cor 4:12). Moreover, he had accepted support from other churches, notably those in Macedonia, while refusing it from Corinth (11:8-9; cf. Phil 4:10-18). That surely suggested inconsistency on his part and worse: that his relationship with others was warmer than with the Corinthians. To refuse financial aid could easily be construed as a hostile act (as 11:11 suggests; see Marshall 1987). And since the Macedonians from whom he received support were also accompanying the collection (11:9; cf. 9:4), the suspicion could easily arise that Paul's collection for Jerusalem was actually an underhanded way of supporting himself (cf. 12:16-17).

It is not entirely clear why Paul took the principled line of refusing Corinthian money. Perhaps he feared that it would place him under obligation to their patronage, and he preferred to identify with the "weak" through his "demeaning" work. In any case, having made so much of his "boast" in 1 Corinthians 9, he could hardly go back on it now (11:10 echoes 1 Cor 9:15). He tries to construe this policy as an act of special benevolence ("that you might be exalted," "to serve you," to avoid "burdening you," 11:7-9; cf. 12:14), and he hints that the message of the free grace of God is best offered free of charge (11:7, whose Greek echoes 9:15). But this policy also plays a strategic role in distinguishing Paul from his rivals, in his eyes not negatively (as an inferior apostle) but positively, as one who spends himself in preaching the gospel (12:15; cf. 1 Cor 9:15-18; 15:10). In this way, he always retains an edge over his rivals (11:12), whom he now castigates with fulsome polemic (vv. 13-15). The "super apostles" are unmasked as "false," and their pretense of serving Christ is revealed as a cover for their service of Satan, that ancient master of disguises. As elsewhere, Paul "demonizes" his opponents (cf. Rom 16:17-20; Phil 3:2, 18-19) since his worldview is painted in battle colors and Satan lurks everywhere; and nothing alarms him more than the threat of deceit, whereby the church might harbor its own foes and nurture the antithesis of the gospel it is appointed to proclaim (cf. Gal 2:4-5).

Having unleashed this invective, Paul resumes his preparation for the foolish boast (11:16, echoing v. 1). He emphasizes, on the one hand, the artificiality of this exercise: don't think I am really this foolish (v. 16), I know my boast is out of order by God's standards (v. 17), and I am boasting by human standards ("according to the flesh") only because others require it (v. 18; cf. 10:2-3). On the other hand, he ironically accepts the rules of the game and demands that the Corinthians play it fair: at least you can put up with my folly, being so wise yourselves (11:16, 19; cf. the irony of 1 Cor 4:10)! With an extra jab, he lauds their tolerance — putting up with the arrogant behavior of his rivals (11:20). Like masters who use and abuse their slaves, such "apostles" are portrayed as exploiting the Corinthians (by taking their support) and, half in jest, half-serious, Paul apologizes for the "shame" of his less grasping behavior (v. 21). In truth, his refusal of support could be seen to signal a lack of confidence and authority, a "weakness" compared to the strength of others' demands; but, as the rest of this letter will show, Paul is happy to be considered "weak" so long as his power is also recognized, and attributed to Christ.

The Foolish Boast (11:21b–12:10)

Paul comes at last to the boast he has announced since 11:1, ironically claiming to pluck up his courage ("I also dare"), while twice underlining (vv. 21, 23) the madness of the exercise. It appears that his rivals have traded on their Jewish ancestry: the terms "Hebrew," "Israelite," and "descendant of Abraham" are near synonyms, with honorific connotations of membership in God's ancient elect people. (Some scholars, e.g., Barrett, have suggested a connection with Jerusalem and a policy of "Judaizing" like that of Paul's rivals in Galatia; but the context here is very different, and diaspora Jews could use their Jewish heritage for many different causes.) Paul can claim equality on each count (cf. Rom 11:1; Phil 3:5), and on the fourth claim, "ministers of Christ," he dares to bid higher (11:23).

There follows an unusually long list of labors and dangers (11:23-29; cf. 6:4-10 and 1 Cor 4:10-13), which at first looks like it might represent a claim to have achieved and endured more than any of his rivals (cf. 1 Cor 15:10). There are parallel lists of "afflictions" in Greco-Roman literature, which emphasize the wise man's endurance, tranquility, and invincibility (Fitzgerald 1988), but as Paul's list progresses it becomes clear that his aim is to highlight not his courage or strength but his vulnerability, indeed weakness (11:30). Thus he quickly turns from his "labors" to his frequent exposure to death (vv. 23-25). Five times the synagogue lashing left him bleeding and humiliated (v. 24; cf. Deut 25:2-3; it is testimony to Paul's continuing commitment to his fellow Jews that he endured this more than once); three times the Roman punishment with rods (11:25) left him near to death (if, as Acts claims, he was a Roman citizen, these were strictly illegal, but could have happened nonetheless, Acts 16:19ff.). On other occasions, shipwreck left him exposed to the elements (11:24; these took place before the shipwreck described in Acts 27). The mention of shipwrecks leads into the broader category of travel dangers (11:26), in which Paul mingles the dangers of terrain (land and sea) with the hostilities he faced on all sides, from Jews and Gentiles, from bandits, and even within the church ("false brothers and sisters"). And this perilous existence does not consist only of an occasional scare; his daily existence is marked by toil (with his hands, cf. 1 Cor 4:12), sleeplessness, and inadequate food and clothing (11:27). If the Corinthians consider Paul's bodily presence "weak" (10:2, 10), Paul will do nothing to cover such "shame"; in fact, he will glory in it as his "boast"! In truth, the struggles he has with his recalcitrant converts are also part of this paradoxical "boast" (11:28-29); as he had demonstrated in 1 Corinthians, Paul typically took the side of the vulnerable in the church against its stronger leaders, even if, as here, it cost him continuing struggles. His ensuing "weakness" might look less impressive than the arrogance of his rivals (11:20), but that was, for Paul, his proper apostolic lot.

Thus Paul has entered a competitive boast, as a necessary but foolish exercise, but succeeded in twisting it away from the familiar categories of strength into terms which emphasize his "weakness" (11:30; the strategy will continue through to 12:5 and 12:9-10; see Forbes 1986). It is unclear whether the oath of 11:31 looks backward to the catalogue (affirming the truth of all that vulnerability) or forward to the little vignette painted in vv. 32-33. The presence of this Damascus story has puzzled commentators (cf. the version in Acts 9:23-25). Does this incident merely illustrate the dangers he encounters "from Gentiles" and "in the city" (11:26), or do the details of the escape signal a particular humiliation? It is possible that an alternative, more miraculous, version of this story was in circulation among Paul's admirers (he later became the subject of considerable hagiography), and that Paul is here on oath to tell the story in its bare and somewhat inglorious truth. There may also be implied a contrast with the military prize awarded to the first to scale an enemy's walls: Paul will only boast in his ignominious descent, in secret, in order to escape!

12:1-10 indicates a further ground of boasting among Paul's rivals: in "visions and revelations of the Lord" (12:1). Such ecstatic experiences would clearly appeal to the Corinthians, with their high regard for those dramatic spiritual gifts which signal the recipients' proximity to God and their knowledge of divine "secrets" (1 Cor 2:6-16; 12:1-4). Paul cannot repudiate such experiences altogether; he has had them himself (cf. Gal 1:16, his conversion revelation; 1 Cor 14:18; Gal 2:2). But to attempt to outbid his rivals on this score would be fruitless and deeply misleading, drawing attention to himself as a superior person. Hence the complex strategy adopted here: to suggest a "vision" experience second to none but to attribute it to "a person in Christ" and to say as little about it as possible. It is clear enough from 12:6-7 that that "person" is Paul himself, but by narrating the account in the third person he can refrain from boasting about himself (v. 5) and thus turn the Corinthians' attention again to his weakness (Lincoln 1979).

The vision he recounts can be dated to a time before the Corinthians had become Christians ("fourteen years ago") and is described as a rapture to the highest ("third") heaven, the site of Paradise itself (12:2-4). Such ascents to heaven are not uncommonly recounted of

Greco-Roman mystics and Jewish seers, though usually with elaborate descriptions of the preparation, the journey, the inhabitants of the heavenly realms, and the "secrets" there learned (Tabor 1986). Paul professes — and repeats — his ignorance about the conditions of the ascent (it is not impossible for him that there should be "bodies" in heaven, 1 Cor 15:35ff.) in order to make the whole event rather impenetrable. Moreover, he finishes the account in apparent anticlimax: marvelous things were heard, but they cannot and must not be told! Thus Paul signals both his eligibility and his self-disqualification from his rivals' contest (cf. 10:12-13). He could go on like this, and truthfully, but such unverifiable claims could never compete with the evidence of the Corinthians' own eyes and ears (12:6). And if the Corinthians see a somewhat feeble body and hear a rather unimpressive voice (10:10; 11:6), so much the better, for that is the Paul he would rather have them accept as a representative of the gospel.

This preferred boast in "weakness" explains Paul's reference here to "the thorn in the flesh" (12:7). Interpreters have suggested every kind of social, psychological, and physical phenomenon to explain this mysterious phrase. It is just possible that it refers to opposition or harassment (cf. the thorns in Israel's side, Num 33:55), but it is more likely that some chronic physical ailment is in view (theories could fill a medical textbook!). Although this torment is on one level Satanic, on another it is under the Lord's control. Paul recounts his unsuccessful prayers for its removal (12:8) in what is almost a parody of a healing testimony ("I was sick, I prayed to God, and he healed me"). In this case, Paul was *not* healed, and all the accent thus falls on the Lord's word concerning grace (v. 9), whose meaning is interpreted and applied in vv. 9-10. The grace of Christ is sufficient for Paul, despite his weaknesses, in fact precisely in them; for Christ's power is "made perfect" in weakness. Thus Paul develops the paradox of power in weakness which he had expressed in 1 Corinthians 1–2 and to which he will return in 2 Cor 4:7-15 and 13:3-4. The "perfection" of Christ's power means not only its *display,* the revelation of divine power where human power is clearly missing; it means also its *actualization,* its becoming effective, in the sense that only an empty container can be filled and only a powerless human life is empty enough to receive grace. Paul applies the principle to his continual weakness: this is where he would choose to boast — in insults and injuries — since that is where the power of the Lord is at work (12:10; cf. 10:17). But he touches here also the core of his conviction about grace: that it cannot become effective among the strong and proud, only in the emptiness of those who know that they are and have nothing (cf. 1 Cor 1:26-31; 8:1-3; 4:7-15; 2 Cor 8:1-2). Thus he has turned the "foolish" boast into an expression of the gospel, and with this final paradox he subverts all the worldly values on which competitive boasting depends.

Reflection on the Boast (12:11-18)

Paul is relieved to have finished with foolishness (12:11), but he still smarts at the necessity of the exercise. As 11:1-21a had indicated, it was occasioned by the presence in Corinth of more convincing "apostles," who have soured the relationship between Paul and the church, criticizing his weakness and questioning his financial practice. Paul again insists that he is in no way inferior to such "super apostles" (12:11; cf. 11:5): he may be "nothing" in the Corinthians' eyes (10:10), or even in the Lord's (1 Cor 3:7), but they can rank no higher. 12:12 suggests that their prowess consisted in miraculous "signs" of their apostolic power (such are frequently attributed to church leaders in Acts, and even more so in later legends). Paul will not be outbid on that score (cf. Rom 15:18; Gal 3:5), though he will not claim for himself their performance (rather, "they were performed," with the implication, "by God"), and he insists that they were always accompanied by "patience" (better, "endurance" — of the trials enumerated in 11:23ff. and 12:10).

In any case, Paul has no wish to dwell on "signs." He is more exercised by the suggestion that in his financial dealings he has been unfair or deceitful to the Corinthians (12:13-18). Here two issues appear to have become entwined: (a) that he accepted no financial support from the Corinthians, suggesting that he trusted them less or regarded them less highly than others (cf. above on 11:7-12); and (b) that he had squeezed a lot of money from them for the collection, perhaps under false pretenses. On both counts, the Corinthians felt aggrieved and "worse off" than others (12:13), perhaps with the Macedonians specifically in mind (cf. 11:9 and chs. 8–9). Paul insists that he did not burden them (and ironically begs their pardon for not doing so, 12:13; cf. 11:7). He also announces a third visit when his policy will remain the same (12:14). Far from being unfriendly, he insists that his refusal of support indicates that he values them more than their money. Portraying himself once more as their "father" (cf. 11:2), he invokes the principle that parents support their children, not vice versa — thus suggesting the different status of apostles who do take pay (cf. 1 Cor 4:15, but what about Paul's acceptance of money from other churches, 11:8?). Thus what the Corinthians saw as his hostility is actually born of self-sacrificial love, and Paul has every right to feel hurt when it is misunderstood and unreciprocated (12:15). As for the accusation of deceit (v. 16), Paul can only appeal to the good character and nonthreatening manner of his delegates, Titus and "the brother" (probably the delegation announced in 8:16ff.; only the brother appointed by Paul [8:22] is mentioned, since he and Titus were Paul's own agents). Titus had successfully elicited a Corinthian contribution, but it has resulted in opprobrium and suspicion toward Paul; Paul now takes cover behind the better reputation of his delegates!

Paul's Task in Corinth on His Impending Visit (12:19–13:10)

Paul is finally finished with apologetics, though he insists that his prime audience is God (cf. 1 Cor 4:1-5) and his prime purpose not to establish his own reputation but to build up the Corinthians (12:19). This echo of 10:8 conjures up the two possibilities there canvassed: to destroy the Corinthians or to establish them. Thus Paul now closes his letter by restating these alternatives: he fears lest his impending visit might result in their destruction (12:20–13:4), but he works and prays for the better outcome, their correction (13:5-10).

First his fears: what if he finds, on his planned third visit, the same old problems of factional dispute (12:20; cf. 1 Cor 3:3-4, again perhaps with groups aligned for and against himself)? And what if the sexual immorality he had tried to eradicate through 1 Corinthians (5:1-5; 6:12-20) still remains (12:21)? It is clear that the "heaviness" of Paul's letter on this topic had not been matched by effective discipline on his recent visit to Corinth, and Paul's authority has been slighted or ignored (cf. 10:10 and the evidently unsuccessful threat of 1 Cor 4:21). This time, he promises, it will be different: not that he looks forward to wielding the stick (in fact he dreads that further "humiliation," 12:21), but too much is at stake to let matters slide any further. There have now been three warnings: in 1 Corinthians, on the second, disastrous visit, and in this letter itself. Thus the law's demand for two or three witnesses is amply fulfilled (Deut 19:15, cited in 13:1), and the time for leniency is over (13:1-2). If the Corinthians are unconvinced that Paul is the spokesman of Christ (13:3; cf. 10:7, 18), now they will find all the proof they need. Rather than naively celebrating their power in Christ (cf. 1 Cor 4:10), they will discover to their cost Christ's power among them, to examine and judge their sin (cf. 1 Cor 5:3-5). The dialectic of power-in-weakness is true both of Christ and of his representatives (13:4): Paul will happily acknowledge his weakness, modelled on the weakness of Christ, as long as the Corinthians acknowledge his strength in Christ — a strength they may have to experience all too painfully ("in dealing with you").

But Paul is not thirsting for revenge: he still wants to avoid an unhappy outcome and writes as strongly as this in the hope that he will not have to employ such destructive severity (13:10). Thus his final appeal is that the Corinthians examine and correct themselves (vv. 5-9). Even here the tone is at first ironic. The Corinthians have been setting tests to prove whether Paul is a legitimate leader (v. 3), and Paul now suggests that they test themselves (v. 5; the echo is clearer in Greek). As in 11:3, everything is at stake: whether they stand in the faith at all and know the presence of Christ. If they have questioned whether Paul is "of Christ" (10:7), he will ask the same of them, hoping that they will affirm their allegiance to Christ and thus to the gospel he preached. That affirmation would also answer their question about him, for it would prove the success of his work among them (13:6), but Paul insists that his prior concern is not his own approval but their correction (v. 7). His job is to preach the truth of the gospel, whatever it costs and whatever its results (v. 8; cf. 1 Cor 9:16). He will gladly embrace whatever weaknesses that entails (cf. 12:9-10) since it is all for the benefit of his converts (13:9). In 1 Cor 4:10, Paul had somewhat ironically compared his weakness with his converts' strength, but here his tone has finally shed all irony: he truly wants them strong in the faith since, like grace, the strength he receives in his weakness overflows to the strengthening of others. That is why he abhors the prospect of a painful showdown and writes now with sufficient sternness to insure that his visit can be more productive (13:10). As the next letter indicates (2 Corinthians 1–7), this "tearful" letter did indeed do the trick.

Letter Closing (13:11-13)

It is possible that these verses originally closed another letter in this collection (e.g., 2 Corinthians 1–7?), but they are not out of place here. The appeal to "put things in order" echoes 13:9, and the emphasis on love and peace relates both to internal dissension (cf. 12:20) and to the breakdown of relations between Paul and the church. The final grace is unusual in its triadic form (cf. 1 Cor 12:4-6), but it is not "trinitarian" in the later sense. As in 8:9, the basis of blessing is the grace of Jesus Christ, through which is experienced the love of God and the "sharing" created by the Spirit (9:13-15); it is only as they channel that grace that Paul's controversial ministry and this risky letter can be of any abiding value.

Bibliography. Commentaries. Barnett, P. 1997, *The Second Epistle to the Corinthians,* NICNT, Grand Rapids: Eerdmans • Barrett, C. K. 2d ed. 1973, *A Commentary on the Second Epistle to the Corinthians,* BNTC, London: A. & C. Black • Best, E. 1987, *Second Corinthians,* Interpretation, Atlanta: Scholars • Betz, H. D. 1985, *2 Corinthians 8 and 9,* Hermeneia, Philadelphia: Fortress • Bultmann, R. (ed. by E. Dinkler). 1985, *The Second Letter to the Corinthians,* Minneapolis: Augsburg • Furnish, V. P. 1984, *II Corinthians,* AB, New York: Doubleday • Hughes, P. E. 1962, *Paul's Second Epistle to the Corinthians,* New London Commentary, London: Marshall, Morgan & Scott • McCart, J. W. 1999, *2 Corinthians,* Readings, Sheffield: Sheffield Academic • Martin, R. P. 1986, *2 Corinthians,* WBC, Waco: Word • Talbert, C. K. 1990, *Reading Corinthians: A New Commentary for Preachers,* London: SPCK • Thrall, M. 1994, 2000, *A Critical and Exegetical Commentary on the Second Epistle to the Corinthians,* 2 vols., ICC, Edinburgh: T. & T. Clark • Witherington, B. 1995, *Conflict and Community in Corinth: A Socio-Rhetorical Commentary on 1 and 2 Corinthians,* Grand Rapids: Eerdmans; Carlisle: Paternoster.

Other Works. Barrett, C. K. 1982, *Essays on Paul,* London: SPCK • Bash, A. 1997, *Ambassadors for Christ,* Tübingen: J. C. B. Mohr (Paul Siebeck) • Belleville, L. L. 1991, *Reflections of Glory: Paul's Polemical Use of the Moses-Doxa Tradition in 2 Corinthians 3.1-18,* Sheffield: JSOT • Fitzgerald, J. T. 1988, *Cracks in an Earthen Vessel: An Examination of the Catalogues of Hardships in the Corinthian Correspondence,* Atlanta: Scholars • Forbes, C. 1986, "Comparison, Self-Praise and Irony: Paul's Boasting and the Conventions of Hellenistic Rhetoric," *NTS* 21:1-30 • Georgi, D. 1987, *The Opponents of Paul in Second Corinthians,* Edinburgh: T. & T. Clark • Georgi, D. 1992, *Remembering the Poor: The History of Paul's Collection for Jerusalem,* Nashville: Abingdon • Hafemann, S. J. 1986, *Suffering and the Spirit,* Tübingen: J. C. B. Mohr (Paul Siebeck) • Hafemann, S. J. 1995, *Paul, Moses and the History of Israel,* Tübingen: J. C. B. Mohr (Paul Siebeck) • Harvey, A. E. 1996, *Renewal through Suffering: A Study of 2 Corinthians,* Edinburgh: T. & T. Clark • Hays, R. B. 1989, *Echoes of Scripture in the Letters of Paul,* New Haven, Conn.: Yale University • Hooker, M. D. 1990, *From Adam to Christ: Essays on Paul,* Cambridge: Cambridge University • Horrell, D. G. 1995, "Paul's Collection: Resources for a Materialist Theology," *Epworth Review* 22/2:74-83 • Horrell, D. G. 1996, *The Social Ethos of the Corinthian Correspondence,* Edinburgh: T. & T. Clark • Hultgren, S. J. 2003, "2 Cor 6.14–7.1 and Rev 21.3-8: Evidence for the Ephesian Redaction of 2 Corinthians," *NTS* 49:39-56 • Lincoln, A. T. 1979, "Paul the Visionary: The Setting and Significance of the Rapture to Paradise in 2 Corinthians 12:1-10," *NTS* 25:204-20 • Marshall, P. 1987, *Enmity in Corinth: Social Conventions in Paul's Relations with the Corinthians,* Tübingen: J. C. B. Mohr (Paul Siebeck) • Martyn, J. L. 1997, *Theological Issues in the Letters of Paul,* Edinburgh: T. & T. Clark; Nashville: Abingdon • Meggitt, J. 1998, *Paul, Poverty and Survival,* Edinburgh: T. & T. Clark • Murphy-O'Connor, J. 1991, *The Theology of the Second Letter to the Corinthians,* Cambridge: Cambridge University • Nickle, K. F. 1966, *The Collection: A Study in Paul's Strategy,* London: SCM • Savage, T. B. 1996, *Power through Weakness: Paul's Understanding of the Christian Ministry in 2 Corinthians,* Cambridge: Cambridge University • Sumney, J. L. 1990, *Identifying Paul's Opponents: The Question of Method in 2 Corinthians,* Sheffield: JSOT • Tabor, J. 1986, *Things Unutterable: Paul's Ascent to Paradise in Its Graeco-Roman, Judaic, and Early Christian Contexts,* Lanham, Md.: University Press of America • Watson, F. 1984, "2 Cor. x–xiii and Paul's Painful Letter to the Corinthians," *JTS* n.s. 35:324-46 • Webb, W. J. 1993, *Returning Home: New Covenant and Second Exodus as the Context for 2 Corinthians 6.14–7.1,* Sheffield: JSOT • Wright, N. T. 1991, *The Climax of the Covenant,* Edinburgh: T. & T. Clark • Young, F., and D. F. Ford. 1987, *Meaning and Truth in 2 Corinthians,* London: SPCK.

Galatians

Beverly R. Gaventa

INTRODUCTION

Early in his letter Paul pronounces himself astonished by the behavior of his Galatian correspondents (1:6). Ironically, it is the letter itself that has astonished and perplexed readers for the many generations since Paul wrote. At first glance, rage and biting sarcasm seem to be the order of the day, as Paul berates the Galatians for their foolishness (3:1) and anticipates dire consequences for those who have misled them (5:12). The heat of the letter, however, does not prevent Paul from styling himself as the anguished mother of the Galatians (4:19) and recalling their tender concern for him during his visit (4:15).

The changes in emotional climate are not as difficult to follow as the apparent twists and turns in the argument of the letter. The central section of the letter (chs. 3 and 4) relentlessly insists that Gentiles must not follow the law of Moses; specifically, males must not submit to circumcision. Yet Paul later appeals to the "law of Christ" as he urges care for the neighbor (6:2), then finally claims that neither circumcision nor uncircumcision matters (5:6; 6:15). Puzzling through these and other questions about Galatians proves to be an endlessly fascinating task.

One of the first challenges confronting readers of Galatians is identifying the Galatians themselves. The letter makes it clear that they are Gentiles (a Jewish designation for everyone not Jewish). Paul explicitly recalls the time when they "did not know God," when they were "enslaved to beings that by nature are not gods" (4:8), statements that he would never address to a Jewish audience.

Where exactly these "Galatians" resided is a far more contested and complicated matter. "Galatia" historically referred to a region in central Asia Minor (modern Turkey) inhabited by Celts. According to what scholars call the "North Galatian" theory, Paul is writing, probably in the mid 50s, to an ethnic group residing in this area in the cities of Ancyra, Pessinus, and Tavium. In 25 BC, however, the Roman government had created a province it identified as "Galatia." This administrative province encompassed both old Galatia and territories to the south of old Galatia (including Pisidian Antioch, Iconium, and Lystra). According to the "South Galatian" theory, Paul is writing to residents of the southern area of this Roman province, probably in the early 50s.

Because the letter itself provides few clues, proponents of both views rely heavily on the narrative of the Acts of the Apostles. According to Luke, Paul travels through the areas identified by the South Galatian theory on his first missionary journey (Acts 13:4–14:28), but Luke does not refer to "Galatia" directly in this passage. Later, however, Luke does mention Paul's visits to "Galatia" in connection with a subsequent journey (16:6 and 18:23). Unfortunately, coordinating either of these accounts with data from Paul's letters is exceedingly difficult.

Scholars attempt to coordinate details from Acts with the writing of Galatians because the letter itself yields almost no evidence. One tiny clue often invoked is Paul's address of the recipients in 3:1 as "foolish Galatians," an appellation that seems more fitting for a long-standing ethnic group than for residents of a recently renamed Roman province (i.e., an argument for the "North Galatian" theory). It is also noteworthy that Paul makes no mention of Galatia when he recounts his early journeys (1:13-24); had Galatia been included in his initial mission, as Acts 13:14–14:23 suggests, it would surely have served Paul's purpose to mention that fact (Martyn 1997a: 184-86).

Happily, this debate has more bearing on reconstructing the order in which the Pauline letters were written and on coordinating those letters with the account in Acts than it does on the interpretation of the letter itself. It is sufficient to bear in mind the Gentile character of the Galatian churches, wherever they were located. In addition, on either reckoning, Paul wrote Galatians prior to Romans; that order makes it inappropriate to solve disputed problems in Galatians by referring to treatments of similar questions in the later letter.

Wherever the Galatians resided, remarkable developments took place among Christians there during Paul's absence. Another group of Christians, who may be conveniently referred to as the "Teachers" (a term preferable to the more prejudicial "Opponents" and misleading "Judaizers"; Martyn 1997a: 117), has come on the heels of Paul, presenting the Galatians with a sharply different interpretation of the gospel. The Teachers claim that the gospel of Jesus Christ makes it possible for Gentiles to be full members of the people of Israel; in order to achieve that membership, however, Gentile males should be circumcised and all Gentile converts must keep the precepts of the Mosaic law.

Paul responds with stinging invective to what he perceives to be neither a correction nor a supplement, but a perversion of the gospel. To counter the Teachers, Paul proffers a retrospective account of his own life, the experience of the Galatians themselves, and the interpretation of Scripture to recall for the Galatians that, in Jesus Christ, God has invaded "the present evil age" (1:4) and brought about "new creation" (6:15). Not only are Gentiles not obligated to observe the law of Moses; they *must* not observe it because it belongs to a past age. Following Jewish law would represent a second loyalty, a loyalty unthinkable for those who are "in Christ."

COMMENTARY

Galatians 1:1–2:21

1:1-5

The letter opens with a salutation that conforms to the letter-writing conventions of the era, including the name of the sender, the recipient, and some word of greeting. Paul identifies himself as the writer, together with unnamed fellow believers, and the "churches of Galatia" as the recipients (on the location of these Galatian churches, see the Introduction, 1374). As in the opening to Romans (1:1-7), Paul expands elements in the salutation in ways that signal some key issues in this letter.

Paul identifies himself as an apostle, one formally charged with carrying out a commission given by another (see also Rom 1:1; 1 Cor 1:1; 2 Cor 1:1). He emphasizes the origin of this commission by means of a double denial (it came neither through human means nor from a human source) and a double affirmation (it came from Jesus Christ and God the Father). Many interpreters see the double denial as evidence that Paul is on the defensive because the Teachers have undermined his authority with Galatian Christians. The Teachers have recalled that Paul was not among the followers of Jesus during his ministry, and they claim that Paul owes his apostleship to the Jerusalem church (see also 1:16-24). It may be, however, that the emphasis here is positive rather than apologetic; that is, Paul begins this letter, which so thoroughly asserts the oneness of the gospel of Jesus Christ initiated by the one God, by reminding the Galatians that his own apostleship derives singularly from Jesus and from God.

By contrast with his practice in other letters, Paul does not expand the identification of the addressees. They are simply "the churches of Galatia"; they are not "sanctified in Christ Jesus" as in 1 Cor 1:2 nor are they "God's beloved" as in Rom 1:7. Taken alone, this feature of the passage might be insignificant, but coupled with the absence of the conventional thanksgiving (see below on 1:6-10) it presages the profound crisis that makes it difficult to comment confidently on the standing of the Galatians.

Important theological assertions mark this letter opening. First, the gospel originates with God, whose will brought it into being and who raised Jesus from the dead. Second, Jesus is God's agent who "gave himself" for human sin in order to bring about the liberation of humankind. Third, the actions of God and Jesus are eschatological actions. Biblical and other Jewish writers anticipated a future time in which God would bring an end to the evil that struggles for the control of God's creation (Dan 7:23-27; CD 6:10, 14; 4 Ezra 3:1–5:20; *2 Bar.* 1:1–4:7); for Paul, that intervention has already begun in the death and resurrection of Jesus Christ.

1:6-10

In a striking deviation from his custom in other letters, Paul moves immediately from the salutation to a rebuke rather than to a thanksgiving (see, e.g., 1 Thess 1:2-10). Paul accuses the Galatians themselves of desertion, and does so in unmistakably sharp language. They are deserting the very God who called them and are turning to "a different gospel" (1:6). The harshest language, however, Paul reserves for the Teachers, who actually intend to overthrow the gospel (v. 7). Twice Paul announces that the proclamation of "another" gospel merits nothing less than a curse (vv. 8-9).

These statements stand out all the more when compared with passages in other Pauline letters. In Phil 1:15-18, for example, he concedes that some people who are proclaiming the gospel have taken advantage of his imprisonment to criticize him; nevertheless, Paul claims that such motives do not matter as long as the gospel is being preached. In Romans 14–15 he urges tolerance between Christian groups of sharply opposing views. In Galatians, however, Paul believes the issues at stake to be so crucial that such lenience is unthinkable.

1:6-10 reveal that Paul regards tolerance of the Teachers and their position as impossible, but they also provide at least a hint of why that is the case. In Paul's view, there is one gospel, the one in which God acts through the self-giving of Jesus Christ to bring about the rescue of an unworthy humankind (as summarized already in v. 4). Contrary to what they themselves may have claimed, the Teachers have not merely corrected or supplemented Paul; they have offered something so utterly different that Paul can no longer acknowledge it as the gospel. The contrast between human and divine agency that marks the opening of the letter appears again in v. 10 (note also vv. 11-12). Here, as elsewhere, Paul refers to himself as a slave of Christ (see the footnote in the NRSV; see also Rom 1:1; Phil 1:1); as such, his sole responsibility is to please God (see also 1 Thess 2:4).

1:11-24

1:11-12 expand on the assertions made in the salutation about the origin of Paul's apostleship, as Paul begins a retrospective account that extends from 1:11 through 2:21. One reason for including this autobiographical account, which has no parallel elsewhere in the Pauline letters, may be self-defense. If the Teachers have undermined Paul's authority, he must seek to reclaim it. Perhaps more important, this retrospective account also serves a parenetic function; that is, it offers instruction. As Paul will later argue that believers exist in Christ and nowhere else (3:28), and as he will urge the Galatians to trust that singular existence, he here lays the foundation for that point by reference to his own life.

Paul's claim not to have been taught the gospel apparently stands in some tension with 1 Cor 11:2 and 15:1-3, where he specifically asserts that he passed on traditions he had received. In those passages, however, Paul labors to show that his teachings about the Lord's Supper and the resurrection are consistent with what other Christian apostles have taught. Here he addresses the way in which he became an apostle, namely, by revelation either "from" or "about" Jesus Christ (the Greek is ambiguous).

Paul begins his retrospective account (1:13) by offering evidence of his earlier "Judaism," a term rare in this period; it appears in Maccabees to refer to those who remained loyal to Jewish law and custom during the persecution of Antiochus IV (2 Macc 2:21; 8:1; 14:38; 4 Macc

4:26). Paul's loyalty demonstrated itself in the attempt to destroy the church (1 Cor 15:9; Phil 3:6; and cf. Acts 8:1-3; 9:1-2; 22:3-5; 26:9-11). His zeal made him outstanding among his peers (see the similar comment of Josephus *Life* 7–11).

1:15-17 comprise one long sentence in which Paul is moved from his former life of zeal for the tradition to his new vocation as proclaimer of the gospel (cf. Rom 10:2). The language resembles that of Isa 49:1 ("The LORD called me before I was born, while I was in my mother's womb he named me") and Jer 1:4 ("Before I formed you in the womb I knew you, and before you were born I consecrated you; I appointed you a prophet to the nations"). Like Israel's prophets, Paul serves as an apostle only because God intended him to do so.

1:15-17 depict in narrative form what v. 12 has already asserted, namely, that human agents did not teach Paul the tasks of apostleship. Since he did not go to Jerusalem but to Arabia, he could not have received such instruction. "Arabia" here probably refers to the Nabatean kingdom south of the city of Damascus rather than to the entire desert peninsula.

The elusive reference to Damascus in 1:17 provides a point of contact with the story of Paul's conversion in Acts 9, although the reference itself raises questions. In Acts, Paul travels from Jerusalem, which appears to be his base of operations, to Damascus, where he plans to arrest Christians. The fact that Galatians makes no comment at this point about Jerusalem and has Paul returning to Damascus suggests that Damascus, rather than Jerusalem, may have been his starting point.

Indeed, answering any questions about Paul's conversion on the basis of these verses is exceedingly difficult. Interpreters have asked whether the conversion occurred suddenly or slowly, what was the nature of Paul's revelation, and what its immediate implications were for his theology; but here, as in Phil 3:2-11 (cf. 1 Cor 9:1-2 and 15:8-11), Paul remains silent. This account consistently draws attention to God's decision and God's action rather than recalling biographical details.

The same perspective obtains through 1:18-24, as Paul narrates his consultation with the apostles in Jerusalem. He acknowledges that eventually he did go to Jerusalem, but even this concession is downplayed by the naming of only two apostles, Cephas and James. Cephas is the Aramaic name Paul usually employs for Peter (1 Cor 1:12; 3:22; 9:5; 15:5); according to Acts, Peter and James were important figures in the Jerusalem church (see, e.g., Acts 1:15; 2:14-36; 15:6-21; 21:17-25). Paul went to Jerusalem "after three years," but it is not clear whether he means three years following the call itself (1:15) or three years after the return to Damascus (v. 17). He later went into Syria and Cilicia (v. 21), that is, into the region around Damascus.

The retrospective account of the origin of Paul's apostleship closes as it opened, with reference to his persecution of the church. Now he invokes the evidence of the Judean churches, both for his earlier persecution and for his activity as an apostle (1:23). That the Judeans glorify *God* (v. 24) serves to verify Paul's claim that his apostleship comes directly from God and not from a human source.

2:1-10

The retrospective account continues, but the focus shifts from the origin of Paul's apostolic vocation to its precise purview. Here he undertakes to demonstrate what he has already claimed in 1:16, that his specific calling was to preach the gospel among the Gentiles.

The time reference in 2:1, like the reference to "three years" in 1:18, is difficult to understand; it remains unclear whether Paul is counting fourteen years from the time of his call or from his previous trip to Jerusalem. On either calculation, these journeys to Jerusalem are important, not because they are frequent or because Paul receives instruction from the authorities but because the authorities in Jerusalem confirm the apostolic tasks Paul had already been assigned by God. Even the journey itself was taken as a result of a revelation (2:2).

Barnabas and Titus accompany Paul. In 1 Cor 9:6 Paul refers to Barnabas as one who shared his practice of supporting himself through his own labor, but the confrontation at Antioch appears to have caused a breach between the two (see below on 2:11-14 and cf. Acts 15:36-41). According to Acts, Barnabas, a resident of Cyprus, intervened in Jerusalem to testify to the authenticity of Paul's preaching and later played an important role in the mission of the Antioch church (Acts 4:36; 9:26-30; 11:19-30). Paul refers to Titus in 2 Corinthians as his respected fellow worker (see 2 Cor 2:13; 7:6, 13, 14; 8:6, 16, 23; 12:18; and cf. 2 Tim 4:10, Titus 1:4). Here his presence serves to demonstrate the acceptability of Paul's preaching since Titus is an uncircumcised Gentile and the Jerusalem faction does not demand his circumcision.

This second trip to Jerusalem involves Paul in a meeting with the Jerusalem leadership. As in 1:18-24, that leadership includes Cephas and James. It also includes John (2:9), who is among the twelve and whom Luke associates closely with Peter (see Acts 3:1–4:22; 8:14-25). The group Paul refers to as the "false brethren" remains obscure. It apparently does not include Peter, James, and John, to whom Paul does not refer so pejoratively. What exactly they are doing in Jerusalem and how they are related to the Teachers are also unknown, except that, in Paul's view, the two groups share a desire to curb Christian freedom (cf. 5:1).

Although Paul distinguishes the rightful leaders in Jerusalem from the "false brethren," he reports on this meeting in a way that emphasizes his independence from both groups. To the "false brethren" he offered no submission at all, but he also insists that even the leaders whom he acknowledged made no contribution to his understanding. At most, he placed before them the gospel as he preaches it (2:2) and received their consent for his work (v. 9).

The distinction of 2:7 between Paul's gospel "for the uncircumcised" and Peter's gospel "for the circumcised" is not a distinction in content but in audience. As v. 8 makes clear (see also 1:16), Paul and Peter address different ethnic groups. Paul's other letters confirm this point, but it stands in some tension with the narrative of Acts, which portrays Paul as preaching among Gentiles only because his message was rejected by Jewish audiences (see, e.g., Acts 13:44-47).

The only demand placed on Paul's apostleship is that he "remember the poor" (2:10), a reference to needy believers in Jerusalem (see Rom 15:26; cf. Acts 11:27-30; Josephus *Ant.* 20.51-53, 101). This demand and Paul's reported eagerness to carry it out are revealing. Jewish tradition emphasized responsibility for the disadvantaged within the community, so that care for the poor demonstrates the sense of being bound together in a familial relationship. Other letters testify to Paul's participation in the collection for Jerusalem Christians (1 Cor 16:1-4; 2 Corinthians 8 and 9) and the importance Paul placed on that collection precisely as evidence of the unity between Jewish and Gentile Christians (Rom 15:22-33).

Rhetorically, this section of the retrospective provides further support for Paul's contention that the direction of his apostleship has come from God rather than from human authorities. Even as he concedes that he sought the approval of Peter, James, and John, Paul still insists that their standing meant nothing to him (2:6) and indicates that they fully supported his work. In this way, ironically, Paul submits to the Jerusalem authorities in evidence of the validity of his preaching while simultaneously distancing himself from them.

2:11-14

Paul's second trip to Jerusalem confirmed his calling to preach among the Gentiles, but it did not resolve difficult issues regarding the conduct of social relationships between Jewish and Gentile Christians. The incident in Antioch demonstrates the continuing problem.

Paul's description of events draws attention to both the extent of the conflict and the seriousness of the issue at stake. He begins with blunt language about Cephas, and he returns to Cephas with the direct address of 2:14. Cephas is joined by some unnamed "other Jews," and even by Paul's own companion Barnabas, all of which makes the conflict more difficult. Paul voices his objections in the first person singular, which at least gives the impression that he stands completely alone (but also, in rhetorical effect, independent of them all [cf. 1:1]).

Despite the fact that Paul says Peter and the others withdrew from eating with Gentiles, it is probably not the identity of the diners but the character of the menu that proved divisive. Those who carefully followed Jewish law found eating with Gentiles difficult, not because fellowship with Gentiles was inherently objectionable but because the food offered would not conform to dietary laws.

Whatever the precise nature of the conflict, in Paul's estimation it constitutes nothing less than an assault on the gospel itself. The behavior of Cephas and the others amounts to a demand that Gentile Christians conform to Jewish food laws so that table fellowship, the sharing of meals between Jews and Gentiles, can continue. Paul resists, even if that resistance places him over against the Jerusalem leadership and his closest ally. He implicitly offers his resistance to compromise as a model to be emulated by the Galatians.

Unlike the preceding account of Paul's dealings with the Jerusalem leaders, this one does not claim that his position prevailed. That silence may mean only that he will shift now from this retrospective to a direct statement of the issues (2:15-21), but it may also mean that the Antioch incident precipitated a rupture that had lasting consequences for Paul's relationship with some other Jewish Christians.

This is Paul's only reference to Antioch in Syria (although see 2 Tim 3:11), a city that figures importantly in the story of Acts (see, e.g., Acts 11:19-30; 13:1-4; 14:21-28). Despite the emphasis on Antioch in the Acts account, Acts includes no story that is easily identified with this incident. It may be that Luke knew of the incident but declined to include it because it reveals deep divisions among early Christian leaders.

2:15-21

It is unclear where Paul's address to Cephas ends. The NRSV includes only 2:14 in the speech, but the Greek provides no quotation marks, and interpreters differ on this question. Part of the difficulty is that this passage is transitional. It both marks the conclusion to the retrospective account that began in 1:10 and introduces the contrast between faith in Jesus Christ and works of the law that will be crucial for understanding the discussion that follows in ch. 3.

At the very least, 2:15-16 appear to belong with Paul's direct address to Cephas. The "we" here consists of Paul and Cephas and the other Jews. Ironically, Paul invokes a Jewish slur against Gentiles, namely, that they are sinners who live outside the law. Even those who are born within the law, however, now know that justification comes by another means.

The contrast introduced in 2:16, that between "works of the law" and "faith in [or of] Jesus Christ," is crucial to the letter. Unfortunately, both parts of the contrast are sufficiently ambiguous to have generated heated controversy. Since the Protestant Reformation of the sixteenth century, most interpreters have understood "works of the law" to refer to anything done in order to fulfill the law of Moses. More recently, however, some scholars have argued that this is a shorthand expression not for the whole of Jewish law but for those practices that mark Jewish identity as distinctive (namely, circumcision, sabbath observance, and food laws; Dunn 1990: 183-214).

Standing in opposition to "works of the law" is a Greek phrase that may be accurately rendered either as "faith *in* Jesus Christ" or as the "faith *of* Jesus Christ." English translations customarily reflect the traditional assumption that Paul means "faith in Jesus Christ"; that is, justification or right standing with God comes about by virtue of the faith a person has in Jesus Christ. Recent scholarship has opened up the question again, with a number of scholars arguing that the phrase refers to the faithful obedience of Jesus Christ (see also 2:20; 3:22; Rom 3:22, 26; Phil 3:9; Hays 1983: 139-76; etc.).

The fundamental contrast here, however, is not between works (of whatever sort) and faith (either that of humans or of Christ) but between the law and Christ. As the argument in chs. 3 and 4 will demonstrate, Paul sees the law and Christ as mutually exclusive domains; one may live either in the law or in Christ but not in both. Paul has prepared his readers for that claim in 1:6-10 with its insistence that there is only one gospel, and he anticipates it again in this passage by the claim that the law and Christ may not be combined. Over against the Teachers, who see the law and Christ as complementary for justification, Paul asserts that they are opposed and that only Christ is powerful to save.

In 2:17-21 Paul amplifies his point, first by means of a rhetorical question: If believers, who agree that justification comes only through Christ, are judged to be sinners (because they violate Jewish food laws), does that place Christ himself in the service of sin? Rejecting that possibility again reinforces the opposition between law and Christ. First, Paul claims that, by returning to the law, he would effectively declare himself to have been sinful in breaking it. Then he moves quickly to the crucial point: he cannot return to the law because he has died to it. Previously he lived "in law," and did so successfully (see 1:13-14), but now he lives "in Christ" and Christ in him. The section closes with yet another assertion that the law and Christ are mutually exclusive: to say that justification comes through the law means that Christ died in vain.

The retrospective section of the letter culminates with Paul's insistence that he has been crucified with Christ and that Christ lives in him. These statements in 2:19-20 have given rise to considerable speculation about mystical influences in Paul, but they are better understood as theological distillations of all that Paul has said since 1:11. Everything that he once valued, including his own zeal for tradition, has died because of Jesus Christ (cf. Phil 3:2-11), and his new life is defined exclusively by Christ's loving action. The remainder of the letter demonstrates that Paul sees this radical transvaluation of values not as a purely personal matter but as something integral to the gospel itself whose effects transcend the individual believer.

Bibliography on Galatians 1:1–2:21. Dunn, J. D. G. 1990, "The New Perspective on Paul," in *Jesus, Paul and the Law,* Louisville: Westminster/John Knox • Gaventa, B. R. 1986, "Galatians 1 and 2: Autobiography as Paradigm," *NovT* 28:309-26 • Hays, R. B. 1983, *The Faith of Jesus Christ,* Chico, Calif.: Scholars; Hooker, M. D. 1989, "PISTIS CHRISTOU," *NTS* 35:321-42 • Howard, G. 1967, "Notes and Observations on the 'Faith of Christ,'" *HTR* 60:459-65 • Lyons, G. 1985, *Pauline Autobiography: Toward a New Understanding,* Chico, Calif.: Scholars • Sanders, E. P. 1990, "Jewish Association with Gentiles and Galatians 2:11-14," in *The Conversation Continues: Studies in Paul and John in Honor of J. Louis Martyn,* Nashville: Abingdon.

Galatians 3:1–5:12

3:1-5

Abruptly, Paul moves from his own experience of the gospel to a direct assault on the Galatians and a sharp reminder regarding their experience. The vivid language of 3:1 serves the rhetorical end of demanding the audience's attention. It also reflects Paul's assessment of the situation: in his view, only some outside force such as magic could render the Galatians so uncomprehending of the fact that they are already part of God's people.

3:1b provides an important clue to the content and style of Paul's preaching. Paul preaches Jesus Christ as the crucified (see also 1 Cor 1:18, 23; 2:2). Here, as elsewhere, Paul says nothing about the teachings of Jesus or his miracles. Although "the crucified" may implicitly include reference to the resurrection, what Paul places front and center is Jesus' death (see also 6:14). That Jesus was "publicly exhibited" does not mean that any of the Galatians were present for that historical event but that Paul's preaching vividly and powerfully placed it before them.

With 3:2, Paul pointedly inquires about the Galatians' own experience of the Spirit. This is the letter's first reference to the Spirit, and it is telling that Paul has no need to explain the term to the Galatians. The Spirit is already incontrovertibly a part of their experience. It is a gift granted by God (v. 5), and it is not a private experience but comes to expression in the community's life together (5:13-26).

Paul does not pause here to offer a discourse about the Spirit, however. The pressing question is not what the Spirit is and does but how the Galatians received it. Again Paul juxtaposes two phrases, both of which are ambiguous in Greek. On the phrase "works of the law," see above on 2:15-21. The second phrase can be translated as the NRSV does, "by believing what you heard," which suggests that Paul is contrasting two human activities, working and believing. However, this second phrase can also be translated "by the message of faith," which results in a contrast, like that in 2:16, between two forces, the law and faith (i.e., the content of the gospel).

3:6-18

Having appealed to the Galatians' own knowledge that they have already received the Spirit apart from the law, Paul now introduces a convoluted argument from Scripture, the first of two in the letter (see also 4:21–5:1). The argument begins with the figure of Abraham in order to demonstrate that God always planned for the salvation of the Gentiles and that God's plan for the Gentiles did not include the law.

It is curious that a letter addressed to Gentile Christians, people who were probably not well acquainted with Israel's ancestors or Israel's Scripture, makes an appeal to a key figure in Israel's history. Perhaps Paul does so because he knows that the Teachers have already instructed the Galatians about Abraham, especially about Abraham's obedience to God's demand for circumcision and God's promise to bless Abraham's offspring (for Jewish references to Abraham, see Gen 26:5; Sir 44:20-21; 1 Macc 2:52; and cf. Jas 2:23).

Paul's argument begins by quoting Gen 15:6, a passage that connects the promise of many offspring to Abraham's faithfulness; crucial for Paul's argument, Gen 15:6 never mentions circumcision. Paul immediately moves in 3:7 to the point he needs to make, that those who believe the gospel of Jesus Christ are already children of Abraham (quite apart from the law). The quotation of Gen 12:3 in 3:8 secures scriptural weight for this point; Abraham was promised that all Gentiles would be blessed through him. Paul modifies Gen 12:3 in a slight but highly significant way. Where Gen 12:3 reads that all "tribes" would be blessed, Paul substitutes the Greek word translated "nations" or "Gentiles."

The personification of Scripture in 3:8 (Scripture "foresees," and "declares") and elsewhere in the letter warrants attention (see 3:22; 4:30). Such personification is anticipated in Jewish writings, which already personified the figure of Lady Wisdom (Job 28; Proverbs 1, 8, and 9; Sirach 24; Wis 7:7–9:18). Scripture is not, in Paul's thinking, a passive repository from which readers retrieve principles and commands but an active partner in interpreting God's actions in Jesus Christ (cf. Rom 15:4). In this instance, Scripture demonstrates that God had always intended the blessing of the Gentiles through the gospel.

The expression "by faith" in 3:8 is ambiguous (similarly, see "through faith" in v. 14). Although it does not exclude the significance of the belief of Gentiles in the gospel, "by faith" also refers back to the faithfulness of Jesus. The primary, initiating act is that of Jesus' loving and faithful obedience.

By contrast with the faithfulness of Abraham, which anticipates the faithfulness of Jesus and secures blessing for Abraham's descendants, the law secures only a curse (3:10-14). Here Paul draws on several disparate passages to demonstrate the serious error involved in the Teachers' instruction that to be counted among Abraham's people the Galatians must observe the law. To begin with, in v. 10 Paul combines Deut 27:26 and 28:58, which in their original context refer to preceding lists of commandments; here, however, the combined saying serves as a warning that failure to observe all of the law results in a curse (see 5:3).

3:11-12 make a different point. The question is not whether anyone can or does obey all of the law but the mutual exclusivity that exists between the law and faith. First, the quotation of Hab 2:4b in 3:11 serves as a claim that it is faith that makes for righteousness (cf. Rom 1:17). Then the quotation of Lev 18:5 separates faith and law by insisting that the doer of the law lives in the law and, by implication, nowhere else.

3:13-14 return to the topic of the law's curse, this time not as a threat, as in v. 10, but as an established fact in the case of Christ. According to Deut 21:23, an executed criminal was supposed to be hung publicly in order to serve as a warning to others; that criminal was also under a divine curse. Paul applies that passage to Christ, carefully referring to the "curse of the law" rather than a curse from God, to argue that Christ's manner of death rendered him accursed so that he might remove the curse of the law.

Although Paul makes these statements about the curse of the law as a strategy to persuade Galatian believers not to take up observance of Jewish law, they also touch on important questions regarding early Christian interpretation of Jesus' death. Interpreters have sometimes detected in 3:13 a retort to Christian claims for the messiahship of Jesus; that is, Jews who were unconvinced by Christian preaching might have introduced Deut 21:23 as evidence that Jesus' death demonstrated that God had cursed him. Whether or not that is the case, it is clear that one of the major challenges facing Christian proclamation was the inescapable fact of Jesus' execution as a criminal. Here, as elsewhere, Paul does not attempt to silence the scandal of Jesus' death but embraces it; the cross itself, as Paul interprets it, reveals God's redemption.

3:14 returns to the question of the Gentiles and their relationship to Abraham. Christ's redemption extended beyond those under the law to include the Gentiles as well. The blessing promised to the Gentiles through Abraham has now been fulfilled, and the activity of the Spirit among the Galatians is evidence that they have received "the blessing of Abraham."

3:15-18 reinforce the argument against keeping the law by insisting that the law came only after God had established the promise to Abraham, and the promise concerned the single offspring, Christ. Paul begins by appealing to the practice of establishing a will (v. 15). In v. 17 he plays on that same Greek word, which can also be translated "covenant." A will or covenant, once made, cannot be altered, so the promise made to Abraham cannot be set aside by the law, which was given to Moses hundreds of years afterward. In other words, the promise to Abraham has priority over the law of Moses, as even the law would concede.

Having established the priority of the promise, Paul insists that the promise was made only to Abraham and his offspring. Although the Greek noun used here is a collective noun (lit. "seed"), Paul follows a conventional exegetical practice by insisting on its singular meaning; there are not "seeds" but a single "seed," and that one seed is Christ. Although he does not make explicit the logical conclusion at this point (see 3:29), the implication is clear: one becomes a child of Abraham, as the Teachers insist the Galatians must do, by and only by virtue of connection with Christ, not by keeping of the law.

3:19-25

The preceding exegetical argument necessarily raises a question about the law: If God did not intend salvation to come about through the law, then what purpose did it serve? Paul addresses the same question in Romans 7, where he insists that the law is holy and righteous and good (7:12). The very different circumstances underlying Galatians do not permit such an endorsement, and Paul's depiction of the law's role is astonishingly negative.

3:19b introduces the answer Paul will give to the question about the law's purpose: it was a temporary measure designed to protect human beings from sin. This answer begins in v. 19b with the statement that the law "was added because of transgressions." What the law has to do with transgressions is left unexplained at this point. Does the law provide a curb to transgressions (see vv. 23-25), reveal the fact of transgressions (see, e.g., Rom 3:20; 7:7-8), or even bring about transgressions (see Rom 5:20)? Given the way Paul argues just a few lines later (3:23-25), the first interpretation seems strongest in this context. The remainder of the verse introduces its temporary character. The law had a role until the arrival of "the offspring."

The notion that angels were present at Sinai does not comes from Exodus, which depicts God giving the law directly to Moses (31:18). The tradition of the angelic presence, perhaps developed from Deut 33:2 and Ps 68:17, is reflected also in Acts 7:38, 53 and Heb 2:2. The mediator involved is Moses himself (see Exod 19:7; Lev 26:46; Num 36:13). What is meant in 3:20 is quite unclear; perhaps Paul is suggesting that the involvement of a mediator itself diminishes the importance of the law when compared with the importance of the promise.

3:21 returns to the matter of the standing of the law and offers a negative answer to the question of the law's purpose; that is, it was never intended that the law should bring forth righteousness. Instead, the promise is based on "faith in [of] Jesus Christ." The "Scripture" that imprisons may refer to the will of God as revealed in Scripture, so that this verse closely resembles Rom 11:32: "For God has imprisoned all in disobedience so that he may be merciful to all."

A different and more vivid way of expressing the temporary role of the law emerges in 3:23-25. Here Paul shifts to first person plural, speaking specifically of the relationship between Israel and the law. The law was "our" disciplinarian, in Greek the *paidagōgos* or the slave who was charged with escorting young men to school and back so that they would not get into trouble. Such a figure was needed for a limited period of time only and would not be used once the young charge came of age.

Of crucial importance is the fact that Paul does not follow through on the analogy; that is, he does not say that Israel is released from the law because Israel has come of age. Instead, the contrast is between the time "before faith came" (3:23) and the time "now that faith has come." "Faith" in the Greek carries the definite article; it is "the faith" in the sense of the faithful fulfillment of the promise to Abraham and Abraham's seed in the death and resurrection of Jesus Christ (see 1:1-2; 2:20; 4:4-5).

3:26-29

This section moves away from the question of the law's purpose and take up the implications of the fact that "faith has come." One of these implications is that believers are "children of God" (see Rom 8:14-17). In addition, the gospel is for all, as emerges in the use of "all" in 3:26 and "as many of you" in v. 27.

Another implication is that believers are located in the sphere of Jesus Christ. At baptism they put on Christ-like clothing (3:27), a statement that may recall the early Christian practice of providing the one baptized with a new garment (see Rom 13:14; Eph 4:22-24; Col 3:9-10). The believer is joined with Christ so that all other relationships and values are eclipsed (see Rom 6:3-5). This union with Christ means that believers have no other identity (as in 2:19-21), and nowhere else to be.

This exclusive location of the believer in Christ comes to forceful expression in what may be an early Christian baptismal formula (3:28). The pairs (Jew or Greek, slave or free, male and female) reflect the three profound divisions among humanity, as Paul the Jew would have viewed them; the ethnic division between those who are Jews and those who are not, the economic division between slave and free, and the gender division between male and female. In Greek, the third pair differs slightly from the other two, as can be seen in the conjunction "and" rather than "or," probably because it directly quotes the Septuagint of Gen 1:27. In Christ, then, there is a new unity that subsumes these divisions. One implication of that unity, in the context of the situation in the Galatian churches, is that Gentile Christians need not observe the law in order to have unity with Jewish Christians. That unity already exists in Christ.

Whether or not he is employing an earlier baptismal formula, Paul's assertion that existence in Christ means the end of these radical divisions among humanity seems at odds with other passages in his letters. For example, what does it mean to say that there is "no longer Jew or Greek" when Paul continues to identify himself as a Jew (2:15; cf. Rom 9:1-5; Phil 3:3-6)? His comments elsewhere presuppose the continued existence of slavery (1 Cor 7:21-24). Although his letters reflect the leadership of women (Rom 16:1, 3, 6, 7) and a measure of equity in the marriage relationship (1 Cor 7:3-4, 10-11, 32-35), Paul reacts sharply when certain gender distinctions are blurred (1 Cor 11:2-16). Interpreters of Paul differ in their assessment of these apparent inconsistencies in the letters; on any assessment, however, it seems certain that Paul assigns primary, indeed exclusive, status to the location of believers "in Christ."

The final step in the argument about Abraham comes in 3:29. Those who have been baptized into Christ are already Abraham's children. Here Paul employs the singular term "offspring" with the corporate connotation he denies to it in v. 16. The clear implication is that the Galatians do not need to follow the law in order to become the offspring of Abraham.

4:1-11

These verses present an eschatological drama which depicts the Galatians' desire to follow the law as nothing less than a desire to return to slavery. As in 3:23-25, the argument begins from commonplace observations about the treatment of children: notwithstanding their connection with the family, until the arrival of the time established by the father, they have no advantage over slaves. In this instance, however, instead of comparing the law with the *paidagōgos,* Paul introduces "elemental spirits of the world," which keep the heirs in slavery.

The identity of the "elemental spirits of the world" has long been debated, with hypotheses that include the letters of the alphabet, the stars or heavenly bodies, and the physical elements of earth, air, fire, and water. More important than a precise identification of these "elemental spirits" is their universal tyranny over all humankind: Paul speaks here in the first person plural; all humankind — Jew and Gentile alike — were enslaved to these spirits.

Again, as in 3:23-24, what changes in the situation is not that humanity becomes mature but that God intervenes in the fullness of time (cf. 4:2, "the date set by the father"). God acts by sending the Son, described here with two phrases, "born of a woman" and "born under the law." Interpreters have attempted to find in the first phrase some hint of a reference to the Gospel stories of Mary's virginity, but the phrase means no more than that Jesus was born in the normal human way (cf. Matt 11:11). The second identifies Jesus as a Jew (cf. Rom 1:3; 9:4). It is precisely because Jesus is a Jew "under the law" that he can redeem others under the law (cf. 3:13).

The verb "redeem" does scant justice to the Greek here, for Paul refers to the practice that allowed slaves to obtain their freedom by purchasing it. Humanity is no longer enslaved because it has been purchased (cf. 1 Cor 6:20; 7:23); indeed, it has been adopted as children of the household. Within these children, the Spirit cries out to God as to their Father (4:6-7; cf. Rom 8:14-17). In 4:8-11 Paul moves from this depiction of the cosmic drama of salvation to press again his concern about the Galatians. They were once enslaved to "beings that by nature are not gods" (just as Jews were enslaved under the law, v. 5), and their desire to take up the observance of Jewish law constitutes nothing less than a relapse to the "elemental spirits." Paul specifically comments on their attraction to the Jewish liturgical calendar (v. 10). By equating the keeping of the law with the former religious practices of the Galatians, Paul makes an astonishing move, one possible only because he believes that the arrival of Jesus Christ has rendered all prior commitments (whether to the law or to the most outrageous example of Gentile sin [see 2:15]) equally invalid. The depth of Paul's concern comes to expression in 4:9, as he suggests that the Galatians are in the process of "converting again" ("how can you turn back . . . ?") at the crucial moment ("now") of being known by God.

4:12-20

Here Paul shifts his strategy, appealing to the relationship that had earlier obtained between himself and the Galatians. Although this appeal is undeniably personal, it also contains elements profoundly theological since Paul's understanding of his apostolic task connects that vocation with the communities in which he is involved (see 1 Cor 9:1-2).

The urgent appeal that the Galatians should imitate Paul refers to the fact that he set aside legal observance on their behalf (see 2:11-14, 17). In other letters, Paul asks readers to imitate him as he imitates Christ (1 Cor 4:16; 11:1; Phil 3:17). Only here does he speak of becoming like those in his churches (although see 1 Cor 9:19-23 and 1 Thess 1:5).

4:13-15 offer a tantalizing glimpse of Paul's initial preaching among the Galatians. Because he does not indicate the nature of his physical condition (unless v. 15 means that it involved his eyes), interpreters have speculated on it freely if not always wisely (as on the "thorn" in 2 Cor 12:7). The issue at hand, however, is not a diagnosis of Paul's health but of his relationship with the Galatians. In spite of his affliction, the Galatians received him not as a person in need of assistance or to be avoided — but as an angel of God (cf. 1:8)! That history makes Paul the more incredulous about the Galatians' apparent defection to the position of the Teachers.

In 4:19 the personal appeal culminates in a startling and convoluted metaphor in which Paul is the mother in the process of giving birth to the Galatians for a second time. On several occasions in his letters, Paul draws on maternal imagery to convey the nurturing character of apostolic work (1 Cor 3:2; 1 Thess 2:7); the specific reference to birth pangs identifies the apostle's struggle with the birth pangs of the new creation (see Rom 8:22; cf. Mark 13:8; 1 Thess 5:3). The metaphor does not develop, as logic might dictate, with the birth of the Galatians; rather, it is Christ who is to be born in them. What the gospel of Jesus Christ brings about is not mere renewal or even rebirth of the individual but nothing less than Christ's complete invasion of the individual as of the entire creation (see 2:19-21; 6:15; Gaventa 1990: 189-201).

4:21–5:1

This passage is the second extended exegetical argument in the letter (see 3:6-18 above). Both deal with Abraham, but they have very different goals; 3:6-18 addresses the disputed question of who are the rightful children of Abraham, but the present passage consolidates Paul's attack (see 4:17-18) on those Teachers who would demand that the Galatians comply with the law of Israel.

The use of allegory in this section conforms to the exegetical conventions of Paul's day, according to which texts could be searched for hidden meanings in which an element within a text corresponded to some reality outside the text. The specifics of this particular allegory are unprecedented, however, for Jewish tradition identified Hagar's child, Ishmael, with Gentiles (*Jub.* 16:17-18), while Paul identifies Ishmael with Jews or Jewish Christians.

The allegory begins with the birth of Abraham's two sons (4:22-23). The slave Hagar gave birth to Ishmael "according to the flesh"; that is, she conceived in the normal way (see Genesis 16). By contrast, Sarah gave birth to Isaac "through the promise," in the sense that the barren Sarah was able to conceive only because God was fulfilling the earlier promise (see Gen 21:1-7).

The allegory identifies the two women with two covenants. Paul identifies Hagar with Mt. Sinai and then with the present Jerusalem; Hagar continues to bear children who are enslaved along with her. By contrast, Sarah corresponds to "the Jerusalem above"; Sarah is free, as are her children. In 4:27 he quotes Isa 54:1 by way of celebrating the exaltation of the once barren Sarah among the multitude of her children. In 4:28 the focus of the allegory shifts from the two women to their children. Paul identifies the Galatians with Isaac. He then introduces a further stage in the Abraham story, one in which Ishmael "persecuted" Isaac and Hagar and Ishmael were driven out (see Gen 21:10).

Conventionally, exegetes have understood Paul's allegory to mean that Sarah and Isaac represent Christianity and its freedom from the law, while Hagar and Ishmael represent Judaism in its continuing enslavement. Recently, however, several significant problems have been noted in that interpretation of the allegory. First, earlier in the letter, references to "Jerusalem" have to do with the Jewish-Christian leadership at Jerusalem, not with Judaism as a whole (see 1:17, 17; 2:1; and cf. Rom 15:25, 26,

31). Second, 4:24 indicates that Hagar is, at the present time, bearing children into slavery. These considerations have led to the suggestion that "the present Jerusalem" refers to the Teachers and their insistence on law observance for Gentile Christians; "the Jerusalem above," then, is the law-free gospel proclaimed by Paul and his colleagues (Martyn 1997b: 191-208). When Paul quotes Gen 21:10 in 4:30, then, recalling conflict between Ishmael and Isaac, he may be doing so in order to urge the Galatians to expel the Teachers from their midst.

The strong appeal of 5:1 brings the allegory to its culmination and prepares for the discussion of the specific issue of circumcision in vv. 2-12. Believers, as children of the free woman, are themselves free and must not submit to "a yoke of slavery." Acts 15:10 refers to the law as a burdensome yoke that ought not be carried by Gentiles (see also Jer 5:5, but cf. also Matt 11:29-30).

5:2-12

For the first time in the letter, Paul addresses the specific question facing the Galatians, namely, whether males will submit to circumcision in conformity with the law of Moses. The opening statement of this passage sharply asserts what Paul has been driving at since 1:6-10; Christ and circumcision stand at such odds with one another that circumcision renders Christ "of no benefit." If there is only one gospel and believers are exclusively located "in Christ Jesus" as 3:28 insists, then following the law actually removes a person from location "in Christ Jesus."

Although 3:1–5:1 has prepared for this claim of mutual exclusion, Paul summarizes his reasoning once again in 5:2-5. Circumcision is not an isolated act but commits the individual to observance of the "entire law" (v. 3). V. 4 presses this point further, for keeping the law means being justified by the law, which means *not* being justified through grace (see 2:17-18). 5:5 then recalls 3:1-5, with its insistence that it is the Spirit — and not, by implication, the law — that ushers in hope.

5:6 appears to introduce a new point: instead of concluding what the audience might anticipate, that circumcision does not count for anything, Paul makes a far more radical claim, that *neither* uncircumcision nor circumcision counts. Paul here recasts the baptismal formula of 3:28 (see also 6:15); for those who are "in Christ," there can be no other location, so that neither being circumcised nor being uncircumcised constitutes in itself an advantage in any way.

5:7-12 bring this section of the letter to a close with an assortment of warnings, all of which presumably have the Teachers in view. As in the opening of the letter, Paul claims that what the Teachers have argued is not consistent with the Galatians' own calling (1:6). The proverbial saying about the working of yeast in 5:9 serves as a warning about the way in which the whole community can be taken over by the insidious workings of a few (cf. 1 Cor 5:6). The warnings of 5:10 and 12 are far less subtle, as might be expected from one who sees the issue involved as nothing less than "the truth" itself (v. 7).

Bibliography on Galatians 3:1–5:12. Dunn, J. D. G. 1990, "The Theology of Galatians," in *Jesus, Paul, and the Law,* Louisville: Westminster / John Knox • Gaventa, B. R. 1990, "The Maternity of Paul: An Exegetical Study of Galatians 4:19," in *The Conversation Continues: Studies in Paul and John in Honor of J. Louis Martyn,* Nashville: Abingdon • Gaventa, B. 1991, "The Singularity of the Gospel: A Reading of Galatians," in *Pauline Theology,* vol. 1, Minneapolis: Fortress • Hays, R. B. 1983, *The Faith of Jesus Christ,* Chico, Calif.: Scholars • Lull, D. J. 1986, "'The Law Was Our Pedagogue': A Study of Galatians 3:19-25," *JBL* 105:481-98 • Martyn, J. L. 1997b, *Theological Issues in the Letters of Paul,* Nashville: Abingdon.

Galatians 5:13–6:18

5:13-15

5:13 returns to the call for freedom in v. 1 and inaugurates a discussion of the freedom that characterizes life in Christian community (5:13–6:10). Although students of the letter have often treated this section as a collection of traditional ethical instructions unrelated to the earlier part of the letter, recent interpreters identify important connections between the two and suggest that Paul addresses the fear of some that Gentile Christians who do not comply with Mosaic law will be tempted to moral chaos (Barclay 1988).

Freedom from the law does not mean moral anarchy, as the warning against "self-indulgence" (lit. "flesh") makes clear. In Paul's letters, freedom is never absolute; one is always free from certain things yet enslaved to certain things (see, e.g., Rom 6:15-23). The injunction to "become slaves to one another" dramatically asserts the limitation of Christian freedom. Yet this slavery is also radically unconventional, for enslavement in Christian community is mutual rather than hierarchical.

5:14 poses a problem for interpretation; since the bulk of the letter has been concerned with persuading the Galatians that they should not conform to the law, indeed that it belongs to the age rendered ineffective by Christ, it seems odd indeed that Paul should appeal to "the whole law." The statement stands in particularly sharp contrast with 5:4, in which fulfilling the whole law is said to separate a person from Christ. The problem grows more obvious if the verb the NRSV translates as "summed up" is rendered by the more literal "fulfilled."

Commentators attempt to resolve the conflict by distinguishing between "obeying" the law in 5:3 as a means to achieving salvation and "fulfilling" (NRSV, "summed up") in v. 14 as a norm for Christian life. Romans 13:8-10 is also introduced as evidence that Paul elsewhere imagines that Christians fulfill the law through love. Neither of these steps is wholly satisfactory, however; nothing in the context permits a precise distinction between "obeying" and "fulfilling," and Paul's earlier comments in Galatians about keeping the law are so negative that it is difficult to imagine him now reintroducing any obligation to the law. An alternative possibility is that Paul refers, not to Christians' fulfilling the law but to Christ's having already fulfilled it. That is, Christ has fulfilled the law and in so doing becomes the only guideline for the community's behavior (Martyn 1996: 48-61).

The quotation "You shall love your neighbor as yourself" is from Lev 19:18. In the Gospel tradition, Jesus identifies this commandment as second only to the love of God (Matt 22:39; Mark 12:31; Luke 10:27). The epistle of James refers to it as the "royal law" (2:8), and Paul quotes it again in Rom 13:9.

5:16-26

In 5:16-26 Paul explores the dichotomy between life in the Spirit and life in the flesh. In order to see that he is not engaged in a gnostic-like polemic against the human body as such, it is important to recognize that Paul uses the term "flesh" in several ways. Flesh can refer simply to the body as it does in Rom 9:3; it can also serve as a metonym for human beings, as it does in Rom 3:20 (NRSV, "human being"). Here, however, flesh has yet another connotation, that of the self-indulgent desires of a human being when isolated from God, the values and ventures of human beings who have set themselves in opposition to God and God's will for themselves. That "flesh" here connotes no simple negation of the human body becomes especially clear when one examines the vices referred to in 5:19-21, some of which are physical acts but others of which are not (e.g., strife, jealousy, and factions).

Paul contrasts the "desires of the flesh" with life in the Spirit. Earlier in the letter Paul reminds the Galatians that they received the Spirit from God (3:1-5). It is the Spirit that enabled the Galatians to call upon God as Father (4:6; cf. Rom 8:15). As elsewhere in the NT, these remarks about the Spirit do not lend themselves readily to tidy systematization. Instead, they reflect a conviction that God supplies the Spirit to those whom God calls, and that the Spirit enables believers to live in accordance with God's will.

Each way of living may be seen in its results, which Paul depicts by means of a list of vices (5:19-21) and a list of virtues (vv. 22-23). These lists conform to a convention of Paul's day, parallels to which are found in moral philosophy as well as elsewhere in the NT (e.g., Rom 1:29-31; 1 Cor 6:9-10; 2 Pet 1:5-8). Unlike the moral philosophers, however, Paul does not imagine that philosophical knowledge will enable people to embrace virtue over vice; only God's action in the gospel is sufficiently powerful to rescue humankind from sin (see 1:3-4).

The specific vices and virtues included in this passage are many and diverse, but a concern about relationships within the community emerges as paramount. The inclusion of enmity, strife, jealousy, and anger among the vices, and love, patience, generosity, and gentleness among the virtues, taken together with the admonition in 5:13 to mutual service, suggests that the quality of community relationships was important for Paul.

Paul signals the importance of these lists by the way in which he concludes them. The vice list culminates in a warning that those who conform to the "desires of the flesh" will not be among the inheritors of God's kingdom. By invoking the category of inheritance, this warning recalls the long discussion in ch. 3 of how one becomes an heir of Abraham (3:6-29). This is one of the few times in which Paul employs the phrase "kingdom of God" (Rom 14:17; 1 Cor 4:20; 6:9-10), an expression best known from its consistent use in the Synoptic Gospels (e.g., Mark 1:15; 4:11; 12:34; Luke 4:43; 9:60; 22:16).

5:24-25 also recall important earlier stages in the letter's argument. It is not only Paul who has been crucified with Christ (2:19); all those who belong to Christ (3:28) have crucified the flesh. As recipients of the gift of God's Spirit, they live in that Spirit and nowhere else (see also 3:27).

6:1-10

This concluding section of exhortations foregrounds relationships within the Christian community. English translations obscure the fact that the exhortations alternate between use of the plural and use of the singular, that is, between exhortations concerning corporate responsibility (6:1a, 2, 6, and 9-10) and those concerning individual accountability (vv. 1b, 3-5, 7-8; Barclay 1988: 146-77). The community as a whole is responsible for restoring those who transgress (v. 1a), but each individual must take care not to succumb to temptation (v. 1b). Several of these exhortations have antecedents in biblical tradition; for example, Job 4:8 and Prov 22:8 employ the image of sowing and reaping in a way similar to 6:7-10.

The emphasis on the quality of community life does not mean that Paul sees the Galatians only as a group gathered for social purposes. He specifically identifies the Galatians as people who have "received the Spirit" (6:1). Through mutual responsibility within the community, they fulfill "the law of Christ" (v. 2; see below). They are accountable to God and will be judged by God, as the imagery of the future harvest in vv. 7-9 makes clear (see also 1 Cor 3:6-8).

Students of the letter have long and vigorously contested the meaning of the phrase "the law of Christ" in 6:2. Some see in this expression a reference to a new law that the Messiah would institute, but little evidence either in Paul's letters or elsewhere in the NT supports such a thesis. Others understand this "law" to be the commandment to love one another (5:14); Christians are not saved by keeping the law, but they are nevertheless obligated to this law of love. If 5:14 has in view Christ's own fulfillment of the law, then the "law of Christ" may be the law as Christ has taken it captive by his own loving obedience to God's will. Believers then fulfill Christ's law by acting as he did, by bearing mutual burdens.

6:11-18

With its reference to Paul's own handwriting, 6:11 signals the end of the letter. Conforming with ancient convention, a secretary had taken down the body of the letter (cf. Rom 16:22), but Paul wrote the final lines himself. This verse does more than indicate a change in handwriting, however; it also draws attention to the lines that follow, lines that bring the argument of Galatians to its forceful culmination.

6:12-13 constitute a final attack on the Teachers. Paul views them as basing their judgments on "the flesh," in the sense that they use the circumcision of Gentiles in order to enhance their own standing. Two features of this attack have given rise to discussion about the Teachers and their commitments. First, Paul charges that they urge circumcision in order to avoid being persecuted themselves (v. 12). This could mean simply that, were they to adopt Paul's understanding, they would join him in being attacked by others as they now attack Paul (see 5:11). Another possibility is that the Teachers fear the response of a zealous group of Jews who are offering resistance to Roman occupation and to Jewish acculturation to the Greco-Roman world, a group that might retaliate against Jewish Christians who claimed equal standing for Gentiles quite apart from observance of Jewish law (Jewett 1971: 198-212). Second, Paul claims that the Teachers themselves do not actually obey the law (6:13). Some scholars have read this remark as indicating that they represent a syncretistic form of Judaism for which circumcision served solely as an initiation rite; there was no effort made to live in conformity with Jewish law. Such a perspective would account for this comment, but the letter does not otherwise indicate that the Teachers are less than serious about Jewish law. Probably Paul's remark simply recalls his earlier comment about the difficulty of keeping all the law (3:10-11; cf. 5:3) and reveals little about the actual disposition of the Teachers.

In 6:14-17, Paul turns from polemic to a strong restatement of his own understanding of the gospel. He begins by contrasting his view with that of the Teachers. While they wish to boast in the flesh of the Galatians, presumably in their circumcision, Paul will boast only in the cross. As elsewhere in Paul's letters, boasting itself is a neutral activity which becomes acceptable or unacceptable by virtue of the basis on which one boasts. Only those who boast in God's actions on their behalf boast rightly (Rom 5:2; 1 Cor 1:31); all other forms of boasting are misplaced (see, e.g., Rom 3:27; 1 Cor 3:21; 2 Cor 11:16–12:10).

6:14 and 15 once again epitomize the conviction evidenced throughout the letter, that the gospel of Jesus Christ makes a singular and exclusive claim on individuals, communities, and indeed the entire world. Here "the cross of our Lord Jesus" serves as an abbreviation for the gospel, according to which Jesus' death on the cross inaugurates a new age of redemption for humankind. The "world" is a comprehensive term that includes those views and values that humanity adopts over against God's rule; all those views and values count as nothing in the face of the cross (cf. Phil 3:2-11).

That the crucifixion of the world is far more than a private experience becomes clear in 6:15. The Greek is more elusive than English translations lead readers to believe and may be rendered, "For neither circumcision nor uncircumcision is anything — but a new creation." Those who would deduce from Paul's argument in chs. 3–4 a unilateral stance against circumcision must now revise their readings; while it is true that circumcision does not count, neither does uncircumcision count. That is, nothing that human beings normally take to be criteria for assessment, evaluation, inclusion, or exclusion has any force whatsoever. There is, instead, a new creation (cf. 2 Cor 5:17).

The peace wish in 6:16 sharply contrasts with the letter's opening lines, with their curse on all who proclaim "another" gospel. Precisely for whom the benediction is intended is a question, because of the difficulty of understanding the phrase "the Israel of God." Given the letter's insistence that Christ is the single seed of Abraham (3:16), it seems unlikely that Paul here has in view the historical people of Israel (cf. Rom 11:25-32). Instead, the phrase "the Israel of God" functions as a parallel to "the law of Christ" (6:2); that is, as the law is now the law Christ fulfilled, this Israel is that which God brought into being in Abraham and brings about anew in the gospel of Jesus Christ.

In a final appeal for support of his interpretation of the gospel, Paul invokes the "marks" he bears on his own body. These marks recall the persecutions Paul has endured in the course of his labors (cf. 2 Cor 11:23-25). He proclaims in them the brand of his slavery as an apostle of Jesus Christ (see, e.g., Rom 1:1; Gal 1:10; Phil 1:1).

Bibliography on Galatians 5:13–6:18. Barclay, J. M. G. 1988, *Obeying the Truth: Paul's Ethics in Galatians,* Minneapolis: Fortress • Hays, R. B. 1987, "Christology and Ethics in Galatians: The Law of Christ," *CBQ* 49:268-90 • Jewett, R. 1971, "The Agitators and the Galatian Congregation," *NTS* 17:198-212 • Martyn, J. L. 1996, "The Crucial Event in the History of the Law (Gal 5:14)," in *Theology and Ethics in Paul and His Interpreters,* Nashville: Abingdon.

Bibliography. Betz, H. D. 1979, *Galatians,* Philadelphia: Fortress • Cousar, C. B. 1982, *Galatians,* Atlanta: John Knox • Dunn, J. D. G. 1993, *The Epistle to the Galatians,* Peabody, Mass.: Hendrickson • Martyn, J. L. 1997a, *Galatians,* Garden City, N.Y.: Doubleday • Martyn, J. L. 1997b, *Theological Issues in the Letters of Paul,* Nashville: Abingdon • Matera, F. J. 1992, *Galatians,* Collegeville, Minn.: Liturgical • Williams, S. K. 1997, *Galatians,* Nashville: Abingdon.

Ephesians

I. Howard Marshall

INTRODUCTION

What we know as the letter of Paul to the Ephesians is in some ways the most enigmatic of all the NT books. It has the normal structure of a letter: it begins with the usual Christianized form of greeting which is followed by an expression of thanks to God in the "Blessed be God . . ." form (also found in 2 Corinthians and 1 Peter); it broadly discusses doctrine in its first half and then practical Christian living in its second half (a pattern most closely followed in Romans and Colossians); it closes in the usual manner with personal references to Paul's own situation and a Christian greeting. But, although it is apparently written to a specific set of readers, it remains curiously impersonal and general in its contents, so that it is very difficult to pick up any clues that would enable us to reconstruct the situation and the identity of the recipients. In this respect it resembles the so-called "catholic" epistles, which are not addressed explicitly to identifiable audiences in specific situations. It is also very difficult to determine what the purpose of the letter as a whole is. A large proportion of the first part (chs. 1–3) is made up of material couched in the form of prayer, although what begins as prayer tends to shift into teaching addressed to the recipients of the letter. The letter is further characterized by extraordinarily long sentences, disguised in English translations which break them up into shorter units for ease in reading and understanding. The second part (chs. 4–6) is generally easier to understand, composed as it is of more practical and ethical teaching.

What, then, is going on in the letter? Basically, we may say that the first part is a celebration of the salvation which is experienced by the writer and his readers, set in a context of praising God for what he has already done (chs. 1–2) and praying for what he will do in the future (ch. 3). As is common in expressions of praise, the writer describes the nature of salvation, so that he is simultaneously teaching the readers, making them more fully aware of the nature of their experience; in doing so he clearly wishes to remind them of certain important aspects of their salvation which have practical implications and to enable them to praise God with greater understanding of the wonder of his love for them.

In the rich language of this section it may be difficult to pick out the leading ideas. But it becomes apparent that the writer is particularly concerned with the identity of his readers as Gentile believers, and he wants them to remember and recognize the dire state they were in before they were saved and to appreciate the wonderful grace of God that has saved them (cf. Titus 3:3-7). Central to his understanding is the revelation of the "mystery" (God's secret purpose now revealed) that the Gentiles have become part of the people of God which has existed from time past through the creation of the household of God in which Christ is the cornerstone. The entry of the Gentiles into this people is the great new fact brought about by God in the fulfillment of his plan, and Paul himself has been given a leading role in the execution of it. Thus the theme of the unity of Jewish and Gentile believers in God's household is particularly important. Throughout this section there is a remarkable emphasis on both the love and the power of God. The former is concerned especially with the admission of the Gentiles into a people from which they had long been excluded. The latter is associated with the idea of the Gentiles being subject to bondage to other, evil powers from which they have been delivered.

In the second part of the letter the emphasis shifts from teaching the readers about their position as Christian believers to the nature of their life. The writer begins by emphasizing the need for believers to show their unity by love for one another within the Christian community and to grow in knowledge of the truth, thanks to the help of those especially gifted to teach and care for them. This growth will be seen in a lifestyle that is progressively different from what they practiced before they became believers and is marked particularly by a new way of speaking and by behavior that is consistent with this. The need for mutual respect and love is developed at considerable length, largely in terms of reciprocal relationships within the first-century family setting. The teaching is given within the accepted structure of husbands/wives, parents/children, and masters/slaves, but it is given a new basis in obedience to the Lord, and this results in a mutuality which goes a long way toward overcoming the rigid social distinctions of the time.

There is what seems to be a sudden change of key in 6:10-20 with its developed metaphor of spiritual battle, but what is called for here is not an intensified moral struggle by individuals but a recognition that there is a cosmic power of evil at work in opposition to the church and that it can be overcome only by the superior power of God. It follows that the letter is not characterized, as some have thought, by an "overrealized eschatology," the view that believers already enjoy in full the blessings of salvation and there is no place for a future consummation; there is plenty of evidence in the letter both for the continuation of strife and imperfection in the lives of believers and for the need for hope in the consummation of God's purposes (see Best 1993: 73-76). Throughout the letter there is this dualism between the power of God and the powers of evil (see esp. Arnold 1989), and the manner of expression could leave the impression that human beings are caught up in a struggle between opposing powers in which they are mere pawns moved by their respective masters. This would be a wrong impression; for all the force of the predestinarian language, the readers are treated as responsible people with the capacity to respond to the grace of God and to praise him for what he does in their lives.

The letter is thus "pastoral rather than polemical" (Best 1993: 93) and could manifestly be significant for many different readers. It is addressed, as we have it, to Christian believers "in Ephesus"; however, this crucial phrase is found only in later MSS and is not part of the original text. Nevertheless, the similarities of the content of the letter to Colossians and the plausibility of a background in the pagan society of Ephesus suggest that the later scribes who inserted the phrase may have hit on at least part of the truth, in that the letter may have been intended for a group of churches including Ephesus.

The origin of the letter, like its destination, remains problematic. The vocabulary and the theology are observably Pauline (although some words may have slightly unusual meanings), and the letter purports to be by Paul. Nevertheless, the literary style (with the long sentences and frequent strings of nouns in genitive relationships and the piling up of lofty phrases) and certain subtleties of expression have raised strong suspicions as to whether the writer is Paul himself. The emphasis on his role as the apostle to the Gentiles and on the foundational position of "apostles and prophets" in the church has suggested that this is the work of a later writer who is attempting to deal with the problems of churches that were largely composed of Gentiles in the post-Pauline period. It is probably the majority view at present that Ephesians is the work of a later writer who has endeavored to present what he knew of Paul's teaching in a form that would speak more particularly to the needs of his situation. He drew on his detailed knowledge of Paul's letters, including especially Colossians with which there are extensive parallels in wording, although the thought is often developed differently (see, e.g., Eph 1:4/Col 1:22; Eph 1:7/Col 1:14, 20; Eph 1:15-16/Col 1:4, 9; Eph 3:1-5/Col 1:25-7; Eph 3:9/Col 1:26; Eph 4:2/Col 3:12; Eph 4:31-32/Col 3:8, 12; Eph 5:19-20/Col 3:16-17; Eph 6:21-22/Col 4:7-8). In doing so he produced a document which is a remarkable statement of the heart of Pauline theology (cf. Lincoln 1990: lxix-lxxiii; Best 1993: 16-30).

This hypothesis is beyond proof, and it has not proved to be universally convincing (Caird 1976: 11-29). The versatility of Paul himself is obvious enough from his acknowledged writings and is broad enough to accommodate the rich theology of Ephesians. The real problems are in the style and the situation. The style is certainly unusual (although there are elements of it in Colossians); it may be largely explained by the use of "liturgical" language, by which is meant nothing more than that people often speak differently when they are praying from their normal conversation. The situation is well conceivable within the lifetime of Paul. Perhaps, too, the statement in 6:21-22 is significant. Although this is close to Col 4:7-8 in wording, in both cases the question may arise whether Tychicus, as a close associate of Paul, had some share in, or was entrusted with, the actual composition of a letter that bears Paul's authority and is therefore not pseudonymous in that it is not an unauthorized attempt to deceive the readers regarding the real author. But this hypothesis may be unnecessary. In what follows we shall refer to the writer as "Paul" since he is certainly the implied author, whether or not he is the actual author.

COMMENTARY

Salutation (1:1-2)

"Paul" writes this letter with the authority of an "apostle," a term which indicates not only his role as a witness to the resurrection of Jesus, as a missionary and planter of churches (1 Cor 9:1-2), but also as the recipient of God's revelation that establishes the nature of his church (1 Cor 4:1; Gal 1:15-17). The readers are characterized as belonging to the people of God and as believers; "in Christ Jesus" indicates that they stand in a close relationship to him rather than that he is simply the object of their faith. The greeting is stereotyped, but "grace" and "peace" will become key terms in the letter, aptly summing up the love of God that creates the church (1:6-7; 2:7-8; 3:7-8) and the new life in which people experience the fruits of being reconciled to God and to one another (2:14-17; 4:3). (On "in Ephesus" see the Introduction, 1386.)

Praise to God (1:3-14)

The tone of the letter is set by this one lengthy sentence (in the Greek) which makes the whole letter virtually an expression of thanksgiving to God for salvation. Its real function is to remind the readers of what God has done and thus to lay a foundation for the further teaching and exhortation which are to follow. The statement has the form of a Jewish *berakah,* a form of words which pronounces God to be "blessed," that is, worthy of praise, because of what he is and does (cf. 2 Cor 1:3; 1 Pet 1:3). In effect, therefore, the statement is addressed to the readers as a summons: "Let us praise God because. . . ." The grounds for praising God then follow in a lengthy string which has a certain structure. The basic reason is his "blessing" of the readers, with the word here meaning that he confers benefits on them; these come through the instrumentality of Christ, who is the channel and means of all that he does for believers. "In Christ" has this particular sense frequently in the letter. God's gifts are given "in the heavenly places," an expression peculiar to this letter (1:3, 20; 2:6; 3:10; 6:12), which suggests that believers are already placed in a spiritual dimension of reality (but where both divine and evil powers are active, 6:12).

This basic statement is expanded in three stages. In the first stage (1:4-6), it is put in the setting of a plan of God with respect to "us," namely, the Christian church (including its existing members and all who will become part of it). The language stresses the initiative of God by going back to eternity past (2 Tim 1:9; 1 Pet 1:20). It may appear predestinarian — as if God has chosen certain individuals (and no others) to be saved (cf. Rom 8:29-30) — but in fact it refers collectively to his purpose in creating the church. What God does is for the good of this people, who will be blameless in his sight and not liable to condemnation and who will enjoy the privileges of belonging to his family. The section concludes with the first of three occurrences of the refrain "to the praise of his glory," which expresses the response that this people should make to his love.

In a second stage (1:7-12) this thought is developed further by using the language of deliverance and "forgiveness" (Rom 4:7; Col 1:14), which explains how believers are to be regarded as blameless by God, and again the free, unmerited divine love is stressed as the basis for this gift. But now a new element is introduced, the "wisdom and insight" that God confers on his people (1 Cor 1:24, 30). The knowledge concerns the eventual aim of God's action in Christ, which is to bring together the whole of creation in a new unity; the division between heaven and earth will be overcome (the underworld is left out of consideration!). This plan will be brought to pass in the future (*pace* Lincoln 1990: 34), but already it is partially realized in the way in which believers have become God's "property" since they have already believed in Christ. The existence of the church is thus a fact that should lead people to praise God's glory.

In the third stage (1:13-14), two things happen. The first is that Paul shifts from talking about "us" to "you," a device by which he reminds the readers themselves how they have been brought into the new people of God ("us") which was already in existence. The second is that he expresses the way in which this happened in yet another way, by describing how they heard the Christian message and believed it, and were then marked out as God's people by receiving the "Holy Spirit" of God, which is equivalent to a "seal" or stamp mark signifying divine ownership; at the same time the gift of the Spirit is the actual experience of salvation, a "pledge" or first installment of what they are going to receive from God in fuller measure when he completes his purpose in the future (2 Cor 1:22).

A Prayer for the Readers (1:15-23)

From the *berakah* it is already clear that Paul attaches great importance to his readers' knowing about what he regards as the wonderful and glorious plan of God, how he has put it into operation, and what are its consequences for believers. Such knowledge will not only give them encouragement for their prayers of thanksgiving to God but will also reveal to them and make them anxious to receive the spiritual benefits that God wants them to receive. He therefore continues to address them ("you," as in 1:13-14) as people who already have the basic characteristics of Christians. He uses the familiar Pauline device of the "prayer report" in which he tells them what he says to God in his prayers about them (1 Cor 1:4-9; Phil 1:3-11; Col 1:3-12; 1 Thess 1:2-3); thereby he encourages them with the knowledge that he intercedes for them and also instructs them further regarding what he wants them to know.

The thought of 1:8 is developed further. Knowledge of God's purpose comes from God himself. There are three objects, the future blessings to be given to God's people, the glorious character of the church that God is going to enjoy, and the enormous power of God which will bring this plan to its consummation. The third point is expanded at some length. The power of God has already been demonstrated in the twofold action of raising Christ from the dead and making him superior to whatever other powerful and authoritative being there may be in the entire universe, now and in the conceivable future. Infinite authority has been conferred on Christ, so that everything in the universe is subject to him (1 Cor 15:24-27). But this Christ is the one whom God has given (NRSV, "made") to the church in his capacity as "head" over the universe; the implication is that the church benefits from the authority of its head and shares in the results of his exaltation (Col 1:18; 2:10). So closely are Christ and the church united that the latter is described as his "body" (Rom 12:4-5; 1 Cor 10:16-17; 12:27; Col 1:24); it is filled with the power of Christ, who himself fills the universe with his power. (The last phrase is ambiguous and may equally mean that Christ is filled with the power of God.) However the difficult language be understood, it enhances the omnipotent position and influence of Christ through whom God's power is at work in the lives of believers.

How the Readers Were Saved (2:1-10)

Paul has already described the way in which God's plan of salvation and its execution have affected his readers. Now he goes over the ground again for a third time with a fresh emphasis. Previously he has been encouraging his readers to praise God for their salvation and has described the great power which is at work. Now he shows in greater detail how their salvation has been entirely due to the grace of God and has been received simply by faith (Rom 4:16; 5:20-21; 11:6; Gal 1:6; Tit 3:7). In no sense have the readers contributed anything of their own to the process; it has rested entirely on God's grace. To achieve this point he starts to paint a description of the readers ("you," 2:1) as the objects of God's action. But the thoughts tumble over one another as he finds points that he wants to stress; the result is that there is repetition in v. 5 of the description in v. 1, as he goes into greater detail than he may originally have intended about what it means to be "dead through trespasses and sins," and he has to resort to a parenthesis in v. 5b to stress another vital point. His basic purpose is to paint a black — but thoroughly realistic — picture of the situation of Gentiles in general apart from the gospel (Rom 1:28-32; 1 Cor 6:9-11; Titus 3:3). It is a picture of people who are prone to repeated acts of sinful rebellion against God; they are regarded as giving their obedience to the spiritual evil "ruler" who exercises sway over the universe. Put otherwise, they are enslaved by the temptations which arise out of human "desires" that are not subject to moral control — violence, sexual lust, material greed, and the like — and they are continually yielding to them. He sums up the situation by speaking of them as being "dead" (Col 2:13; cf. Rom 8:10) in the sense that they did not share in the new life of God and were deaf to his commands and blind to the blessings which he offered, in short, totally unresponsive to him and unaware of him. God's act of salvation can therefore be depicted in terms of a resurrection which brings life to the dead. Five points are made in developing this crucial idea.

First, once again God's initiative is traced to his "grace," expressed in terms of "mercy" to the undeserving. Second, the action of God is identified with his raising of Christ from the dead, so that in some way the raising of dead people to new life is seen as part of the raising of Jesus (cf. Rom 8:11). Third, the result of resurrection is to transfer people to the heavenly realm, so that they now live on both the physical and spiritual planes and share in Christ's lordship over the hostile powers. This thought has been considered un-Pauline by some scholars who hold that in Romans 6 believers have died with Christ and have entered into new life but have not yet been raised with him; it would be more true to say that for Paul resurrection life "has been entered on by the believer in union with Christ, yet its consummation still lies in the future" (Lincoln 1990: 105). Fourth, Paul emphasizes as strongly as possible that the action is one of divine grace, and therefore there is no sense in which the people who are saved have contributed anything to the process, no "works" of which they might be proud (Rom 3:24, 27; 2 Tim 1:9; Titus 3:5). In earlier letters (Romans; Galatians) Paul had emphasized that the Jews were not justified, or put in the right with God, by things that they did in obedience to the requirements of God's law, and that the Gentiles equally were not required to keep these Jewish observances in order to be justified (Rom 3:26-30; Gal 2:16). That thought is probably still in view here (note the reference to circumcision in 2:11!), but it has been broadened out to indicate that no human being can be put in the right with God by anything that he or she does, however good it may appear to be. But, fifth, it is made clear that there is a proper place for doing "good": part of the purpose of God in raising people to new life is precisely that they should now be active in doing good (Titus 3:8).

The Unity of Gentiles and Jews in the Church (2:11-22)

Paul has a special purpose in describing the process of salvation in the way that he has just done. He wants to show that, despite their former situation, the "Gentiles" are now an integral part of the new people of God that consists of both Gentiles and Jews. There was a certain temporal priority about the position of the Jews. Prior to the coming of Christ there was a people of God which consisted only of Jews (together with a small number of proselytes), identified by the physical mark of circumcision and sharing in the various covenants that God made over the centuries with them (e.g., with Abraham, Moses, and David) (cf. Rom 9:1-5). From this group the Gentiles were excluded, and with their exclusion from Israel there naturally resulted separation from God. There was thus a separation both from God and from his people. But the effect of God's saving act is correspondingly twofold. The saving act is identified with the death of Christ, here denoted by the term "blood" (Rom 3:25; 5:9; 1 Pet 1:2; 1 John 1:7; Rev 1:5), which brings out its character as a sacrifice and so as a means of reconciliation between sinners and God (Rom 5:10-11; 2 Cor 5:18-21; Col 1:20). The barrier between the Gentiles and God is thus removed for those who believe.

But at the same time the barrier between the Gentiles and the Jews is broken down. This barrier was the law of Moses, which separated those who accepted its authority from those who did not. But now, Paul affirms, this barrier has been removed by the death of Christ. He does not explain how this has happened; presumably he thinks that when salvation is dependent upon grace and there is no place for human works, then the function of the law of Moses in prescribing conduct no longer applies. If so, then there is no longer a division between two peoples (a division which could be defined purely in terms of whether or not people recognized the law), and there is only one people of God (cf. Rom 11:17-21). All of them, whether Gentiles or Jews, are accepted by God on the same basis, namely, faith (Rom 4:11-12). God's peace is proclaimed to people who are "near" (Jews) and to people who are "far off" (Gentiles): a startling reinterpretation of Isa 57:19 which originally referred to Jews in Israel and in exile respectively. There is now one people of God, which is based on being united with Christ, a "household" which is at the same time a "temple," that is, a structure in which God is (spiritually) present (1 Cor 3:16-17; 2 Cor 6:16; 1 Pet 2:5). On this basis the second part of the letter will appeal to the readers to demonstrate this unity (4:3-5, 13, 15-16).

Paul and the Gospel for the Gentiles (3:1-13)

Just as there was digression and parenthesis in ch. 2, so now a new thought is begun in 3:1, only to be interrupted by a lengthy digression and resumed in v. 14. Paul intends to give a second prayer report to his readers, but first of all he has more to say about the place of the Gentiles in God's plan of salvation. Although formally this is a digression, the style is presumably deliberate and perhaps is intended to draw attention to a significant point. That point is to emphasize beyond any doubt the legitimate place of the Gentiles in the church, and it may be that here we are to find one of the main grounds for the writing of the letter. Did the recipients feel that in some way they were second-class citizens in the church, perhaps because of criticisms by the Jews and Jewish Christians?

So Paul begins with the fact that, although he is a Jew, he is at present in prison, and it is obvious that his imprisonment is due to his preaching the gospel to Gentiles. Behind his missionary activity and consequent imprisonment, however, lies a divine commission to this task, and associated with that commission there is a new revelation from God. He uses the term "mystery," which refers to something that was once indeed secret and hidden but which has now been revealed to God's agents and through them to other believers (Dan 2:28-29; Luke 8:10; Rom 11:25; Col 1:26-27; 2:2; 1 Tim 3:16). What was dimly perceived in OT times had now been made clear. The revelation was not made only to Paul but to the foundational members of the church, who possessed both authority as "apostles" (cf. 1:1) and spiritual insight as "prophets" into the mind of God. Gentiles are just as much members of God's people as are Jews. They enter into their new inheritance through the gospel, and here Paul describes in detail how his commission was to go especially to the Gentiles as a preacher of the gospel (Gal 1:15-16). He comments on his unworthiness for the task, using language that parallels what he says in 2 Cor 4:7 about God committing the treasure of the gospel to earthenware jars (such as were used to store documents like the Dead Sea Scrolls). Paul's commission has a twofold effect. On the one hand, it reveals the gospel, which is like an inexhaustible treasure chest, to the Gentiles themselves. On the other hand, the resulting growth of the church makes plain to the spiritual powers how wonderful is God's wise plan. They see the new humanity being created and are forced to marvel at the wonder of God's plan, which has solved the age-long divisions in the world and overcome its sinful state.

Finally, the section is rounded off with a statement that believers can come with "confidence" into God's presence (Rom 5:1) to offer their prayers through Christ. The connection of thought is that they do not need to feel prevented by the evil powers that fill the world. The implication is that the prayers which Paul himself offers for his readers will be heard and answered. But before he reaches his prayer, Paul uses the fact of this revelation which he has received to reassure his readers that his sufferings as a prisoner are not a basis for discouragement; on the contrary, they contribute to the "glory" which will one day be theirs when God's plan is brought to completion.

A Prayer for Spiritual Strength and Knowledge (3:14-21)

With Paul's position as a servant of God in the gospel now clarified, he can go on to explain what he prays for. He regards it as important to characterize the God to whom prayer is offered as being "the Father." In biblical thought fatherhood connotes both devoted care for one's children (Ps 103:13) and the right to expect obedience from them (2 Sam 7:14). Thus the use of the metaphor of bowing the knees in prayer before a superior being to express the urgency of the request is not inconsistent with the thought of the privileged and confident access that Paul has to God (3:12) — along with all believers (1:5). At the same time, the designation of God as Father is related to the picture of the church as a "household" (2:19). "Every family" (NRSV; TNIV; not "his whole family," NIV; Gk. *patria*) takes its name from God the Father (Gk. *pater*). This does not imply that God is the Father of all people as Creator (*pace* Lincoln 1990: 203). The sense may be that God is the Father of every Christian household church (Muddiman 2001: 167).

The prayer itself is for three things. First, there is inner strength mediated by the Spirit so that believers share in the power of God himself as they face temptations to discouragement (3:13) and engage in spiritual warfare (6:10-20). Second, there is the presence of Christ in their hearts, which is a way of expressing the close union between him and believers (Gal 2:20). Third, added somewhat loosely but probably expressing the main thought in the prayer, there is the firm rooting of the readers in "love," that is, that they have a firm and secure basis for their lives in the love which God has for them; the purpose or result of this relationship will be that they in common with all the rest of God's people will understand how great is God's love for them — the four "dimensions" are a rhetorical device to express its immensity — and experience it to the full (Rom 5:5; 8:35; 1 John 4:16). To be loved in this way by God is to receive all that God can give us; there is nothing else beyond divine love.

The prayer report is followed by a doxology (3:20-21) which expresses thanks to God for the anticipated answer to the prayer. It continues the thought of the immensity of God's power which fills believers with an experience of love beyond anything they could imagine.

Maintaining the Unity (4:1-16)

The letter takes a decisive turn at this point and moves from teaching to exhortation regarding practical action (cf. Romans 11/12; Colossians 2/3), although the element of teaching to back up the exhortation is not completely absent. The main theme of the first section is the need for believers to live in ways that promote the unity in the church that represents its ideal character. An element of emotion creeps into the appeal as Paul refers again to his situation as a "prisoner." The opening part of the appeal is based on the fact that believers should live lives consistent with the fact that God has called them to be his people (1 Thess 2:12; 1 Pet 1:15-16). The qualities of mutual love and tolerance that make for unity are commended. Only here and in 4:13 is the term "unity" used in the NT to stress that the Spirit binds believers together as a united group who express their unity in sharing a common faith. What is produced by the Spirit must be worked out in practice by the people concerned.

But since they are different people with different characteristics and capabilities, Paul proceeds to stress, first, the ways in which they are one, and then how their differences harmonize. The picture of the church as a body, already used in Rom 12:4-5 and 1 Cor 12:12-27, is repeated with the implicit force that the different parts must work together in unity. The things that believers have in common and which unite them are listed. The seven items arise out of what has already been said in the letter and are associated with the God who saves and the experience of salvation. The "one Lord" is Christ; all three divine persons are thus listed in an unreflective manner. Some have found it surprising that "baptism" is included but not the Lord's Supper, but the thought is confessional and lists what is distinctively associated with becoming a believer. But despite this far-reaching common experience, individuals receive God's gifts in varying ways. All receive God's grace mediated through the ascended Lord who bestows the Spirit (Acts 2:33).

Here there is an interesting digression which arises out of the use of Ps 68:18 to back up the argument; the verse itself is reinterpreted to refer to the *giving* rather than the *receiving* of gifts, just as in rabbinic interpretation of the psalm Moses gave the law to Israel. Paul comments that the One who ascended also descended. The NRSV assumes that the descent preceded the ascent (cf. the dubious textual variant which inserts "first") and was to Hades. The NIV, probably rightly, takes it to be a descent to the earth, evidently in the incarnation. Many recent commentators prefer to see a descent subsequent to the ascent, that is, Christ descending in and through the Spirit's bestowal of gifts on the church.

However, instead of listing gifts given by the Spirit to individuals (Rom 12:6-8; 1 Cor 12:4-11; 1 Pet 4:10-11), Paul lists the kinds of gifted individuals whom Christ gives to the church. Broadly speaking, "apostles" and "prophets" represent the people who founded the church and exercise leadership (1 Cor 12:28); "evangelists, pastors, and teachers" cover the three main functions of ministry in the church (cf. 2 Tim 4:5; 1 Pet 5:1-2; 1 Tim 2:7). Since the letter comes (or purports to come) from a time when apostles and prophets were functioning, we cannot draw any conclusions from *this* passage about their continuing role in the church. There is debate whether "for the work of ministry" expresses the goal of their task of equipping the saints (NRSV), that, is, so that the latter can minister (as is clearly the case in 4:7, 16), or (perhaps less likely) is the second in a set of three phrases defining the tasks of the named functionaries (Lincoln 1990: 253-55). What is important here is the recognition that the church and its individual members need to grow toward "maturity"; there is scope for continued progress (Phil 1:9-11; 2:12-13; 2 Thess 1:3), and the initial act of salvation does not confer immediate perfection. Of particular concern is the need for individual believers to come to share the same basic belief and knowledge and not to be led astray by the jumble of other beliefs that are being hawked around. The distinction between orthodox belief, based on the gospel committed to the apostles and prophets, and heterodox views that can lead people astray, is clearly present. But upholding the "truth" must be conducted in a spirit of love (1 Pet 3:15-16), and it is to be done, not, as it were, for its own sake, but in order that the church may develop in unity, like a body in which every part has its proper role to play.

The New Life in Contrast to the Old (4:17–5:20)

Paul now gives examples of the kind of instruction to be given by teachers in order "to equip the saints." The topics covered may appear commonplace, but the amount of space given to them indicates that the points made were not necessarily obvious to readers who had been brought up in the pagan world. The connecting theme throughout the section is that the Christian way of life is different from that of pagans, and this is developed in a variety of ways. The formulation in 5:8, "once you were . . . , but now you are . . . ," controls the thought, together with the principle "Live as [what you are]."

First, a contrast is drawn between the way of life of Gentiles and that which believers have been taught (4:17-24). Paul holds to the view that behavior is related to what people know and believe. He traces the loose living of the Gentiles to the fact that they have no knowledge or belief in God; consequently, they are in the darkness of a moral maze and lack the capacity for moral perception (Rom 1:28). Although he makes sweeping statements which might seem to suggest a uniform moral depravity, it must be remembered that elsewhere the possibility of goodness and justice among Gentiles, especially in contrast to the shortcomings of Jews, is clearly recognized (Rom 2:14-15); there is no necessity to assume that here Paul is allowing for no exceptions to the general rule.

By contrast, believers have "learned Christ," which must mean that they have been taught the Christian traditions about him. It is difficult to exclude the view that this instruction included teaching about the character and actions of Jesus as a man and about the condescension that was part of the incarnation (2 Cor 8:9; Phil 2:5-11). Nevertheless, Paul goes on to explain what he means by this instruction in terms of the need to "put away" the old, pagan way of life and to "be renewed" inwardly. This basic contrast between the old way of life and the new is the essential content of the teaching. Believers have, to be sure, received the new life; they have, as it were, received a new set of clothes which make them look like God in their moral character. But they have to be taught to live out this new life.

In the second part of the instruction (4:25–5:2), therefore, they are given some very down-to-earth comments on what they are to do. The teaching largely proceeds by way of concrete contrasts between the old and the new ways: lying and speaking the truth; stealing and working honestly; evil talk and edifying conversation; angry speech and forgiveness. This is, to be sure, ethical instruction that is not distinctively Christian and which could be matched without difficulty by other writers of the time. But this in no way lowers its significance. Nevertheless, Christian motivation comes into it. Following the old way of life is said to "grieve the Spirit" (Isa 63:10), an incidental testimony to the way in which the Spirit is increasingly recognized as a personal being and not simply as a divine gift or power. Forgiving others is motivated by the forgiveness extended to sinners by God himself; and love is motivated by the love shown by Christ in his self-giving to the point of sacrifice (5:25; cf. John 13:34; 1 John 4:11). The assumption is that the joyful and thankful reception of blessings from God necessarily requires the recipient to make a like response, but directed to other people rather than simply toward God himself. God's people are to treat others in the same way that he has treated them. It is when this supreme example and motive are brought in that the quality and intensity of what is required of believers become apparent. What is important is that the purpose of the believer is not so much to please God as rather to behave like God and so to share his love with other people. Christians should aim to do good to other people for their sake rather than to promote their own standing with God.

The third part of the ethical instruction (5:3-20) follows the pattern that has already been observed. It begins with a statement of the kind of conduct which should not be found among believers. Sexual immorality, obscenity, and greed are linked together as conduct which is not acceptable; even talking about these things can become sinful when it becomes a way of enjoying acts of sin by proxy, just as Jesus commented that harboring lustful thoughts is just as much a sin as putting them into effect in immoral action (Matt 5:27-30). The practice of such sins is incompatible with enjoying membership in the kingdom of God (cf. 1 Cor 5:9-11; 6:9-10).

Various points are now made to motivate the readers to avoid such sins. They were themselves once the objects of God's wrath but have been delivered from it; to commit such sins is to return to that situation. It is to return to the darkness of sin instead of living in the searching light of God in which good flourishes. This metaphor is developed rather fully, taking up what appears to have been a traditional Christian evangelistic summons to those who are dead or asleep in sin. The light that Christ brings signifies salvation, but it also serves to show up the sinful areas of life that need to be dealt with (cf. John 3:19-21). In the end, sin is folly because it fills up the limited amount of time that believers have and which they should be using to the full in the service of God.

Finally, a contrast is drawn between the levity and sin that is associated with excessive drinking and the rich joy that comes from the inspiration of the Spirit. The parallel between being intoxicated and being enthusiastic religiously was drawn by other writers (Acts 2:13), but it is noteworthy that Paul here is not writing about religious ecstasy expressed in unusual ways (such as speaking in tongues) but about the expression of thanksgiving to God in rational language; the outward expression in music is accompanied by an inward attitude of praise to God.

Christian Relationships in the Household (5:21–6:9)

The instructions about attitudes and behavior addressed to all Christians are followed by more specific comments for the three paired types of people who formed the ancient household. This pattern of instruction was already in use among ethical teachers, and from an early date it became part of the regular teaching of the church (cf. Col 3:18–4:1; 1 Pet 2:18–3:7). There was considerable flexibility in developing the basic pattern. The form here is noteworthy in various ways.

The section begins with a call to believers for mutual submission. Although Paul goes on to require wives to submit to husbands and children and slaves to show obedience, this opening requirement applies to everybody (just as in Gal 5:13; Phil 2:3-4) and means that submission and respect are to be shown by husbands, parents, and masters, whose duties are spelled out further down. Although the mutual submission does not rule out the requirement that wives, children, and slaves show the submission which is part of the structure of their relationships as the ancient world understood them, it can be seen that a principle is being laid down which could lead in time to a reassessment of the social order. Moreover, the basis for this principle is "reverence for Christ." This suggests that submission to other people is regarded as something that is taught by Christ or has his authority behind it. It can certainly be regarded as a corollary or implication of the command to love other people as oneself.

The subjection (not obedience) of "wives" to their husbands (not of women to men in general!) is compared to the submission of the "church" to Christ as its head or leader. Here the duty expected by society is given a backing by reference to the analogy with the church's attitude to Christ. Of all the ethical statements in the NT this is the one that is probably least acceptable to Christians in the third millennium AD! Paul appears to be giving a theological rationale for patriarchalism. It can be only part of the answer that Christians were fearful of encouraging a revolution in society which could do the church no good, but it is a valid part of the answer. It is more to the point to note that the context is one of mutual submission, which does not absolve either husbands or wives from being submissive to each other.

But the major point is the instruction to "husbands." Here at considerable and, indeed, striking length their duty to "love" their wives is expounded. A theological backing is provided, again applied to the social structure of the time. If the husband is the "head" of the wife, then he must behave like the ideal head, Christ, whose love for the church is so great. Paul develops the picture by describing Christ's aim as the sanctification of the church and using the picture of "washing" (baptism; 1 Cor 6:11; Tit 3:5). Why is this point developed in this way? It does not seem to have any detailed application to husbands and wives, and it may be that Paul elaborates it for its own sake as part of his endeavor throughout the letter to develop a theology of the church. In any case, the application of the point is to the way in which husbands should lavish the same loving concern on their wives as they would on themselves. Then Paul returns to the analogy with Christ, who is likewise thought of as caring for his body and its individual members who form the church. He quotes Gen 2:24, which literally refers to human marriage, and comments that the relation of Christ to the church is a "great mystery," by which he means that this relationship is to be seen as analogous to human marriage. Thus the relationship between Christ and the church becomes the pattern for human marriage, and therefore the instruction can be concluded with a repetition of the basic injunction to husbands to love their wives and wives to respect their husbands.

It is when this husbandly duty is undertaken consistently and fully that a situation develops in which one-sided submission becomes impossible, for Christian love requires respect of and submission to the other. This insight could not be expected to develop immediately, and the NT writers should not be faulted for their failure to do so.

The command addressed to "children" is the simple one to obey their parents, which is fully in accordance with the OT command to them to honor their parents. Attention is drawn to the accompanying promise of reward in the text (Deut 5:16; cf. Exod 20:12). But the command is put in a Christian context by the fact that obedience is to be rendered "in the Lord." This phrase (and its equivalent, "in Christ") is used by Paul to characterize the situation of Christians as those whose lives are lived in the context of obedience to the Lord and his teaching (e.g., Phil 4:1-4; 1 Thess 4:1); it is the ethical equivalent to the doctrinal statements which describe Christians as people whose lives are determined by the fact that they are united by faith to Christ, who died and rose for them (e.g., Rom 8:1; 2 Cor 5:17; Phil 1:1; 1 Thess 2:14). It is significant that there are children who are fully part of the "household of faith," although the children envisaged are not just small children but include all who would still be under their parents' authority. Nobody has yet suggested that in the Christian church children should cease to obey their parents; obedience is compatible with mutual love and respect.

Next comes a balancing injunction to "fathers," who are warned against abuse of their authority; there are limits set to it, as ancient ethical teachers also stated. What is new here is the instruction to give children education and admonition that is Christian. The home is to be the place where children are taught by precept and example; in a situation of household churches nobody had yet thought of the concept of a Sunday school, but children must get instruction appropriate to their age within the context of the Christian household.

In the ancient world "slaves" were reckoned to be part of the household. They are called to serve their masters (cf. 1 Tim 6:1-2; Tit 2:9-10) with the same solicitous care and fear of failure as should characterize believers in their service of Christ (Phil 2:12). Earthly service is part of their service of the Lord, just as the governmental authorities are regarded as God's servants in Rom 13:3-4. The aim is not simply to please the "masters" and so to win favor and approval from them but rather to serve the "Lord," and to do so, therefore, with sincerity and enthusiasm. Ultimately, it is the Lord who rewards all people, whether slave or free. Again, then, the social structures are preserved, and people are urged to serve the Lord within them. Paul could hardly have told slaves that they were really free in the sight of God, and therefore they did not need to serve their masters, Christian or otherwise.

Finally, "masters" are told to "do the same" to their slaves, namely, to behave in the corresponding ways. They are not to take advantage of their position as social superiors, for they stand under the same Lord, and he will treat masters and slaves alike with utter impartiality. Once the implications of this fact are realized, the social relationship is opened up to radical revision.

The Battle against Evil (6:10-20)

The closing section is a kind of peroration in which some of the main issues of the letter are brought together in an impressive, strongly rhetorical section. There is no explicit connection with what has directly preceded, although the need for effort to live as believers in the face of temptation is there throughout the practical teaching (e.g., 4:3, 14, 17, 25-31; 5:3-7). Rather, Paul goes back to the fact of the evil domination of the world in which believers live; even the so-called "heavenly places" are not free from baneful influences (6:12). The Christian life is to be seen as a conflict in which the opposition is on this spiritual level. The implication is that the conflict is a metaphorical one, to be waged with the aid of spiritual weapons. Moreover, the battle is not simply between individuals and their enemy; Paul "addresses the whole church corporately as an army, not singular saints" (Turner 1994: 1242). Just as in Gal 5:16-26 the only remedy for the desires of the flesh is the power of the Spirit, so here the only sure defense against "the wiles of the devil" is the strength supplied by God himself. To develop the point and reinforce it, Paul takes up the picture of the armor worn by God himself (Isa 59:17; cf. 11:5; Wis 5:17-20) and makes it a picture for the spiritual resources at the disposal of the believer (cf. Rom 13:12; 1 Thess 5:8). There does not appear to be any necessary connection between the different items of armor and the spiritual qualities associated with them. The choice of weapons is partly dependent on the earlier uses of the imagery. The armor is seen as a complete set; God's warriors do not select individual items to wear but clothe themselves in the full suit. The imagery is largely that of defense, but it is a defense that wears down and defeats the enemy, so that in the end the believers stand victorious on the field. Truth, righteousness, the gospel (cf. Isa 52:7), faith, salvation, and the word of God are the items that equip believers and make them ready for combat. The result is that there is no particularly logical progression in the list. But Paul does comment on the significance of "faith" as the supreme defense against every effort of the devil to destroy the believer. He cannot bring "prayer" into the picture, and so it has special mention on its own at the end of the list. The readers are to pray for themselves and for all God's people, and to do so ceaselessly. The "theory" of prayer is never explained, but it is taken for granted that reminding the Lord of his people's needs is instrumental in causing him to act on their behalf. The mention of prayer enables Paul to slide across into the request for his readers to pray for him in his mission, which is a closing feature in several of his letters (Rom 15:30-33; 1 Thess 5:25; 2 Thess 3:1-5; cf. Phil 1:19).

The whole section thus underlines the setting of the Christian life in the conflict between good and evil, conceived as the struggle between spiritual or supernatural powers. It reflects a realization that the power of evil is something that cannot be overcome by human resources, and that human beings can gain a more than human power to enable them to win in this struggle. This interpretation of the nature of the human situation may be uncongenial to materialists and even to some Christians, but it is so fundamental to Paul that it is difficult to see how it can be rejected without rejecting the heart of his religion.

Final Greetings (6:21-24)

Personal news and greetings are the standard components of the closing of a letter, but their actual formulation need not fall into conventional forms of wording. Here the brief comment that "Tychicus," clearly the personal bearer of the letter in an age which had no postal system for ordinary people, will give fuller news about Paul and so encourage the readers is a more or less exact copy of the similar note in Col 4:7-8 where the same messenger is accompanied by Onesimus. The similarity in wording suggests either that this part of the letter is copied from Colossians by a later writer composing the kind of letter that Paul would have written or that the two letters were composed side by side. The evidence would be satisfied if Tychicus himself was responsible, at least in part, for the composition of the letter as well as for taking it to its readers.

The closing words are a prayer for the readers to receive blessings from God, and they take up in reverse order the prayer for "grace" and "peace" in the opening greeting. They constitute a promise to the readers but at the same time an exhortation to "undying love" in which all the emphasis falls on "our Lord Jesus Christ," who is the focus of this letter.

Bibliography. Arnold, C. E. 1989, *Ephesians: Power and Magic: The Concept of Power in Ephesians in Light of Its Historical Setting,* Cambridge: Cambridge University • Barth, M. 1974, *Ephesians,* New York: Doubleday • Best, E. 1993, *Ephesians,* New Testament Guides, Sheffield JSOT • Best, E. 1998, *Ephesians,* Edinburgh: T. & T. Clark • Bruce, F. F. 1984, *The Epistles to the Colossians, to Philemon and to the Ephesians,* Grand Rapids: Eerdmans • Caird, G. B. 1976, *Paul's Letters from Prison (Ephesians, Philippians, Colossians, Philemon) in the Revised Standard Version,* Oxford: Oxford University • Hoehner, H. W. 2002, *Ephesians: An Exegetical Commentary,* Grand Rapids: Baker Academic • Houlden, J. L. 1970, *Paul's Letters from Prison: Philippians, Colossians, Philemon and Ephesians,* Harmondsworth: Penguin • Kitchen, M. 1994, *Ephesians,* London: Routledge • Kreitzer, L. 1997, *The Epistle to the Ephesians,* London: Epworth • Lincoln, A. T. 1990, *Ephesians,* Dallas: Word • Lincoln, A. T., and A. J. M. Wedderburn. 1993, *The Theology of the Later Pauline Letters,* Cambridge: Cambridge University • Moritz, T. 1996, *A Profound Mystery: The Use of the Old Testament in Ephesians,* Leiden: Brill • Muddiman, J. 2001, *A Commentary on the Epistle to the Ephesians,* London and New York: Continuum • O'Brien, P. T. 1999, *The Letter to the Ephesians,* Grand Rapids: Eerdmans • Perkins, P. 1997, *Ephesians,* Nashville: Abingdon • Schnackenburg, R. 1991, *The Epistle to the Ephesians: A Commentary,* Edinburgh: T. & T. Clark • Stott, J. R. W. 1979, *God's New Society: The Message of Ephesians,* Leicester: Inter-Varsity • Turner, M. 1994, "Ephesians," in D. A. Carson, et al., eds., *New Bible Commentary: 21st Century Edition,* Leicester: Inter-Varsity Press.

Philippians

Charles A. Wanamaker

INTRODUCTION

Sometime around AD 50, the apostle Paul crossed from Asia Minor to Macedonia. He appears to have first visited the city of Philippi, establishing his first community in Europe there. As a provincial city, Philippi was unusual in that it was a Roman colony governed directly by Roman law. Its inhabitants were Roman citizens, predominantly expatriates from Italy, who were settled there in the aftermath of the Roman civil wars that followed the murder of Julius Caesar in 44 BC. Latin was the official language of the colony, though the original population, as well as many settlers from the East, would have spoken Greek. In constitution, architecture, and coinage Philippi sought to model itself on Rome (O'Brien 1991: 4). Although Paul says that his missionary work in Philippi led to considerable suffering and disgraceful mistreatment for him (Phil 1:30; 1 Thess 2:2; cf. Acts 16:16-40), it had a successful outcome. Paul's letter to the Philippians provides strong evidence that he established a vibrant Christian community which developed a special relation with him through its financial support for his subsequent missionary activity (Phil 4:15-16) and through sending one of its members, Epaphroditus, to assist him in his work (Phil 2:25-30). The community which Paul established would appear to have been predominantly, if not exclusively, Gentile in character (see Murphy-O'Connor 1996: 213-14).

Paul's Letter to the Philippians

Sometime after Paul left Philippi he wrote one or more letters to the community. A number of scholars claim that Philippians is a composite letter consisting of two or three letters written by Paul. They assume that these letters were later edited together to form the current single letter. Although several different theories exist as to which sections of Philippians formed separate letters, Murphy-O'Connor (1996: 215-20) offers a fairly typical perspective based on structure and content. He argues that Paul's first letter, found in 4:10-20, contained "an ambivalent expression of gratitude" for financial support. Paul later wrote a second letter, consisting of 1:1–3:1, during an imprisonment at Ephesus. This letter is distinguished by the theme of complacency toward pagan persecution. He then penned a third letter, 3:2–4:9, at a time when he was disturbed by the prospects of Judaizing opponents infiltrating the community.

During the 1960s and '70s, the three-letter hypothesis predominated in scholarly publications, but since the work of Garland (1985) the pendulum has swung in the opposite direction. The change in perspective has come about because Garland, Watson (1988), and Stowers (1991), among others, have examined Philippians from the perspective of Greco-Roman rhetorical and letter-writing practices. Their work has shown that theories of a composite letter are unnecessary to explain Philippians' structure and content.

Philippians does not provide any clues about how much time had elapsed between Paul's missionary visit and the writing of the letter. Paul does indicate, however, that at the time of writing he was imprisoned by Roman authorities at the official residence of the emperor, a governor, or some other political official (Phil 1:12-13; the NRSV's translation of *praitōrion* in 1:13 as "imperial guard" is misleading since the term broadly refers to the residence of a political official; cf. Acts 23:35). He also implies that some persons in the imperial service, whether soldiers, former slaves, or slaves, were Christians (4:22; on the meaning of the "imperial household" in this verse see Lightfoot 1908: 171-74). This information offers no real help in determining Paul's location at the time of writing since Rome as well as every provincial capital had a praetorium and members of the imperial service. For this reason scholars have proposed four different possibilities for Paul's location at the time of writing, with each implying a different time of composition. The traditional view holds that Paul wrote from Rome around AD 60, but a number of serious objections have been raised to this view (see Hawthorne 1983: xxxviii). Thus scholars have proposed Ephesus (AD 52-55), Caesarea Maritime (AD 57-59), and even Corinth (AD 50-51) (see Hawthorne 1983: xxxvi-xliv for a thorough discussion of the four options). We have to acknowledge that we do not know the answer to this question. Fortunately it does not have a significant impact on our interpretation of the letter.

Although the date and place of writing cannot be determined, the more important question is why Paul wrote Philippians. Watson (1988: 58-59), who undertakes a rhetorical analysis, infers from the text that Paul was confronted by the emergence of a competing gospel at Philippi. As a result he contends that Philippians is a piece of *deliberative rhetoric* in which Paul sought to persuade his converts to *decide* in favor of his version of Christian living and to *reject* that of the Judaizing Christians who offered an alternative one. Basevi and Chapa (1993: 349-56), however, show that the hortatory character of the letter identifies it as *epideictic* or *demonstrative rhetoric* since it *"demonstrates"* or in this case *confirms* how the readers should live. In any case a major question mark hangs over Watson's contention that the Philippians were threatened by Judaizing Christians, the sort who troubled the Galatians (see my discussion of 3:2).

Hawthorne (1983: xlvii-xlviii) and O'Brien (1991: 35-38) find that Paul had a variety of reasons for writing. These included: (1) to inform the Philippians of his situation and plans (1:12-24; 2:23-24); (2) to explain why he was sending Epaphroditus back (2:25-30); (3) to exhort the Philippians to unity and to faithfulness (1:27–2:18; 3:1–4:8); (4) to warn them of those who would lead them astray (3:2-21); and (5) to thank them for their financial support (4:10-20). What they do not explain well is what holds these disparate issues together.

White (1990) and Stowers (1991) correctly argue that Philippians is a hortatory letter of friendship in which the themes and virtues drawn from the Greco-Roman understanding of friendship are strongly present. Paul's purpose in writing Philippians, therefore, was to maintain the bonds of friendship with his converts in Philippi while continuing to provide Christian ethical direction for them in his absence. This helps explain what Fee (1995: 20-21) has identified as the relative rarity of Paul's technical theological vocabulary and the dearth of theological argumentation in the letter.

COMMENTARY

Greetings (1:1-2)

The greetings of Philippians are similar in form and length to those of 1 and 2 Thessalonians. Although Paul's greetings are sometimes more elaborate (e.g., Rom 1:1-7), they all follow the normal pattern of other Hellenistic letters from the period: "A to B, greetings." Paul regularly includes the names of his missionary colleagues as senders, in this case Timothy, but in Philippians, as elsewhere, the predominance of first person singular pronouns and verbal forms within the letter indicates that Paul is the real author. A unique aspect of the Philippians' salutation is the reference to the "bishops *(episkopoi)* and deacons *(diakonoi)*" in the list of addressees. The NRSV, following a long line of interpreters (e.g., Hawthorne 1983: 8-9), implies that the formal church offices of bishop and deacon already existed at Philippi, but this seems doubtful. None of the other letters of Paul from the period makes reference to such church offices. Only in the late letters of 1 and 2 Timothy and Titus do we find formal church offices bearing these names. In Greek the terms used simply mean "overseers" or "supervisors" and "servants" or "helpers." While both terms have financial, administrative, and cultic overtones in normal Greek usage, Philippians provides us with no information about how to understand the terms. What does seem probable is that the overseers (bishops) and servants (deacons) exercised some form of permanent leadership in the community based on their social function and very probably their social positions in the wider community (cf. Rom 16:1-2; see Holmberg 1980: 99-121). Those mentioned in 4:2-3, including the women Euodia and Syntyche, almost certainly come from this group, and one of them, who is unnamed, was probably the initially recipient of the letter.

Introduction (1:3-11)

Following good rhetorical practice of his day, Paul uses 1:3-11, the letter's introduction, to seek the goodwill of his readers while pointing to his main themes. The section begins with a report of Paul's thanksgiving to God for the recipients of his letter in vv. 3-6. As almost all of Paul's letters begin with a thanksgiving, scholars speak of the thanksgiving sentence in his letters as a characteristic formal structure. The important question is why he begins his letters this way.

In rhetorical terms the thanksgiving report in Philippians invokes the readers' goodwill by alluding to their friendship with Paul. Unfortunately the NRSV's translation of 1:3 obscures this. O'Brien (1991: 58-61) has shown that v. 3 should be translated: "I give thanks to my God *because of all your remembrance of me.*" This is then balanced by Paul's reciprocal remembrance of them in his prayers (v. 4) and leads to a second cause for his thanksgiving, namely, his readers' consistent "sharing" *(koinōnia)* in his missionary activities (v. 5; cf. v. 7). In antiquity sharing through reciprocity in giving and receiving both material benefits and services was a hallmark of friendship (see Marshall 1987: 1-13). In fact, Aristotle defines a friend as "one who is active in providing another with the things that he thinks are benefits to him" (*Rhet.* 1.5.16; trans. Kennedy 1991). As Paul later says in 4:15, the Philippians were the only church who "shared" *(ekoinōnēsen)* with him "in the matter of giving and receiving" in the early days of his ministry, and thus by implication they were his friends in a way in which other churches were not, for they sought to bestow benefits on him. By introducing the theme of friendship in the thanksgiving Paul sets the tone for the entire letter.

The theme of friendship, introduced in 1:3-6, is underscored in vv. 7-8 first by the elaboration of the theme of coparticipation *(synkoinōnoi)* with Paul, and second by the language of personal affection (the NRSV's "You hold me in your heart" in v. 7 is better translated "I hold you in my heart") since statements of affection were deemed particularly appropriate in ancient friendship letters (Stowers 1991: 109). V. 7, by mentioning Paul's present situation as prisoner, defender, and advocate of the gospel, and linking readers to him in these matters, also prepares readers for the discussion to follow in vv. 12-26.

Paul ends the introduction in 1:9-11 by reporting his intercessory prayer for the Philippians. In doing so Paul lays the foundation for the major theme of the letter, the exhortation of the Philippians to Christian ethical virtue in preparation for the eschatological day of Christ (cf. v. 6; 3:7–4:1). It is clear from Plutarch (*How to Tell a Flatterer from a Friend* 74C-74E) that such moral exhortation lay at the heart of ancient friendships since friends were expected to cultivate moral virtue in one another (see White 1990: 211-12).

In 1:9 Paul prays that his readers' love may overflow.

In Paul's world love (*agapē*) had more to do with "group attachment and group bonding" than with affection (Malina 1993a: 110-14). Thus Paul is actually praying for an increasing abundance of community spirit and perhaps greater attachment to God, the two things holding the Philippians together as a group (cf. Wanamaker 1990: 142-43). The importance of this theme for the letter as a whole becomes clear in 1:27–2:11, where Paul stresses the need for a common mind and spirit among the Philippians, and in 4:2-3, where it becomes clear that Paul has an actual problem in mind that was proving disruptive to the unity of the community.

Narration on Paul's Present Circumstances (1:12-26)

In 1:12-26 Paul sets out his current circumstances and reflects on their meaning for his friends, the Philippians, by showing how he had transformed adversity into advantage for the gospel. The overall function of this section is hortatory, and it divides into three paragraphs. Paul briefly rehearses his current situation in vv. 12-14, and in vv. 15-18a he praises those who support him and, by way of contrast, condemns his enemies, thereby giving the Philippians a model of how they should respond to his current misfortune. In the third paragraph, vv. 18b-26, he presents himself as an example for his friends of how a true follower of Christ overcomes personal adversity.

The public opprobrium implied by his imprisonment endangered both Paul's reputation and status with his converts since Greco-Roman society was "generally unsympathetic to losers" (Marshall 1987: 69). In addition it was axiomatically assumed that one's enemies would gloat over a person's misfortunes and attempt to take advantage of them (see Marshall 1987: 35-69). Paul writes in 1:12-14 to reassure his friends that his imprisonment has not led to his undoing nor to the impeding of his missionary activity as his enemies, who were fellow Christians, perhaps the Judaizing Christians alluded to in 3:2-4, may have hoped. Quite the contrary, he informs the Philippians that his incarceration has resulted in the advancement of the gospel in the imperial civil service (the NRSV's "imperial guard" in 1:13 is too narrow a translation), and has encouraged true brothers and sisters to speak out about the gospel with boldness. Thus Paul argues that misfortune has not had a negative impact on his work; quite the contrary, it has had a decidedly positive effect on the proclamation of the gospel. The following paragraph claims that even his enemies are assisting him in achieving his objective.

The skill of formal comparison played an important role in ancient rhetorical practice. It functioned as a device for apportioning praise and blame and as a device for invective against one's opponents (2 Cor 10:12; see Marshall 1987: 53-55). Paul undertakes just such an odious comparison through a carefully constructed antithetical parallel in 1:15-18a. He compares those in the Christian movement whose missionary activity was intended to undermine him with those whose activity supported him. One group proclaimed Christ "from envy and rivalry" (v. 15), from "selfish ambition," and from insincerity in order to intensify his troubles in his imprisonment (v. 17). Paul employs invective here to demean his opponents since he assumes that they seek to isolate him and to erode his support base. The Corinthians correspondence demonstrates just how successful the strategy of Paul's opponents could be (see Horrell 1996). By way of contrast, others proclaim Christ from goodwill toward Paul and in solidarity (see my comments on vv. 9-11 for this sense of the word "love" in v. 16) with his imprisonment for the gospel.

In 1:18a Paul rhetorically turns the negative activity of his opponents into a positive one by rejoicing that, even though their motives are devious, they, along with his friends, assist in furthering the proclamation of the gospel. By employing the antithetical comparison Paul probably intended to reassure his Philippian friends that he was still achieving his goals in spite of his adverse situation, and therefore they should not abandon him nor support those who demeaned and undermined him.

In 1:18b-26 Paul turns to his own situation in order to develop the theme of his friendship with the Philippians in preparation for the exhortation which he wishes to deliver. In the process he employs the well-known rhetorical strategy of creating identification between himself and his audience to invoke their trust, thereby establishing his *ethos* or moral character with them (see Marshall 1993: 363-66). Paul identifies himself with the Philippians by acknowledging his dependence upon their prayers for his deliverance from his imprisonment (v. 19). He does so again at the end of the paragraph when he points out that his anticipated deliverance and return to them will be grounds for their pride in Christ, presumably because their prayers will have helped bring it about (v. 26; the NRSV's translation of v. 26 is doubtful; the Greek makes Paul the grounds of their pride, not a participant with them in their pride). But the most important expression of Paul's identification with his readers relates to his choosing their interests over his own. In vv. 20-23 Paul deliberates about the meaning and significance of living and dying for Christ in the context of his current imprisonment. His own choice would be to depart from this life to be with Christ. This would be better from his perspective (vv. 21-23), but he recognizes that his remaining in this life is indispensable for his friends the Philippians. Paul, therefore, declares that he will put aside his own desire to be with Christ in favor of the Philippians' interests.

This is a profound demonstration of Paul's virtuous moral character, a key element of an individual's *ethos*. Rhetorically it also functions to invoke the *pathos* or goodwill of the readers toward Paul. But it has another significance. In Paul's world such self-abnegation for the sake of others was a hallmark of true friendship, as Lucian's story of Demetrius, a slave owner who gave up his wealth, privilege, and ultimately his freedom to serve his own slave and friend, Antiphilus (*Toxaris* 29-34), shows. Thus in 1:19-26 Paul evinces the depths of his Christ-centered friendship and commitment to the Philippians. In the process he provides a role model for the Philippians of self-abnegation which links him to Christ, who, as he will shortly show (see 2:5-11), is the ultimate example of self-abnegation. Finally, he reestablishes a basis for his readers to accept his ethical instruction.

Paul's Purpose in Writing (1:27-30)

Although Paul alludes to the important themes of the letter in the introduction (1:3-11), in vv. 27-30 he makes explicit the main concern of the letter. He wishes to offer moral instruction and encouragement in the Christian life, using Christ and himself as models for the Philippians of honorable Christian attitudes and behavior.

1:27-30 form a tightly constructed statement in which Paul employs a deductive argument known as an *enthymeme* to announce the primary theme of the letter (Watson 1988: 66). The argument runs as follows:

> Major Premise: being a good citizen in Christ's realm involves both faith and suffering (typical of enthymemes, the major premise is implied but not stated);
>
> Minor Premise: God has "graciously granted you the privilege not only of believing in Christ, but of suffering for him" (1:29);
>
> Conclusion: Therefore "live as good citizens (*politeuesthe;* the NRSV obscures the political meaning of this word by translating it as "live your lives") [of Christ's realm — see 3:20] in a manner commensurate with the values and norms of the good news of Christ" (1:27a; my translation).

Paul offers his motivation for their living as good citizens in vv. 27b-28. By placing the conclusion of the deductive argument first and abruptly introducing the first imperative of the letter ("live as good citizens") in v. 27, he emphasizes that this is the main theme of the rest of the letter (cf. Geoffrion 1993: 23-25, 179-82). Thus Paul signals his intention to spell out for them what worthy citizenship in Christ's community entails and how to achieve it.

Apart from setting out the main theme of the letter's argument, 1:27-30 have another interesting feature. The passage is replete with technical political and military language, one instance of which I have noted already. Geoffrion (1993: 54) provides compelling evidence that both the language and the concepts in these verses were associated with "*speeches* [his emphasis] of encouragement or instruction given by commanders to their troops, especially when the citizens or soldiers appear intimidated or discouraged." Thus, Paul consciously uses military metaphors (e.g., "stand firm," "strive side by side," "in no way intimidated by your opponents," "their destruction," "your salvation"), which his readers would have been familiar with as Roman citizens, to build his argument that they should "live as good citizens in a manner worthy of the good news [gospel] of Christ" (1:27) the universal and conquering Lord, whose sovereignty all humans must eventually acknowledge (2:9-11).

Amplification on How the Readers Should Live (2:1-18)

Paul begins the main body of the letter in 2:1-11 with an appeal for group solidarity based on the example of Christ. This passage has long been an interpretative crux. Interest has focused primarily upon vv. 6-11 since these verses are thought to have been an independent, poetic-like composition, perhaps an early liturgical hymn, in praise of Christ (see the classic study by Martin 1983 and later Wright 1991: 56-96). But this conception has had a negative impact on the understanding of Philippians since too little attention has been paid to vv. 1-11, the real unit of meaning from Paul's perspective.

Malina and Neyrey (1996: 186-96) have shown that Paul and his contemporaries were strongly group-oriented rather than individualistic in their outlook. For such people, creating harmony and maintaining unity in their social group was of primary importance, even if such harmony and unity were bought at the expense of the individual. Paul attempts to strengthen the in-group identity of the Philippian Christians by exhorting them to unity, humility, and service to one another (2:1-4). He then reinforces this behavior pattern by the examples of Christ (vv. 5-11) and himself (vv. 17-18; 3:4-17). Although he does not say so here, 4:2-3 disclose that the ethical exhortation of 2:1-11 was probably directed to an actual conflict in the community. Two important women were failing to put the interests of the group ahead of their own self-interest. In vv. 1-4 the language which Paul utilizes derives principally from the sphere of ancient friendship (see White 1990: 207-15; Stowers 1991: 110-12), which, along with kinship, was one of the most important sources of group solidarity in antiquity.

In good rhetorical fashion Paul solicits the *pathos* or emotional goodwill of the Philippians in 2:1-2 through the use of some highly affective language. Among other things, in v. 1 he invokes the Philippians' profound experience of Christ as the source of their encouragement in the face of opposition (the "then" links these verses back to 1:28-30), and their participation together in the Spirit, to create the basis for his appeal to his readers for Christian group solidarity in 2:2. His appeal is also based on the Philippians' loyalty to him as friends when he asks them to "make my joy complete" (v. 2) since joy was the sort of feeling which friends shared in common and strived to create for one another (see Aristotle *Rhet.* 3.4). Once again employing language from the sphere of ancient friendship in v. 2b, Paul calls for group solidarity through a common love (see comments on 1:9), will, and purpose. This constitutes an appeal to the readers to be friends with one another (see Aristotle *Nic. Eth.* 9.6). 2:3-4 spell out the practical implications of maintaining group solidarity in terms of repudiating attitudes which erode solidarity while adopting attitudes which foster it.

Two fundamentally different understandings of 2:5-11 exist. The more recent one dissociates the passage from the ethical exhortation of vv. 1-4. It sees the "hymn" (2:6-11) as a pre-Pauline statement of the salvation event in Christ Jesus which provides the basis for Christian existence (Käsemann 1968). This view seems to read into the passage a primary message about the drama of salvation which does not fit well with the ethical context in 1:27–2:18 (for further critique see O'Brien 1991: 257-62). Whatever the origins of 2:6-11, in its current context the Christ encomium, or hymn of praise, provides a powerful example of the attitude which the Philippians should adopt among themselves if their Christian solidarity is to be preserved, according to v. 5. Thus with respect to its current usage, the Christ encomium requires an "ethical interpretation" and reflects the classical rhetorical practice of praising an individual's deeds in order to present that person as a model of virtue to be imitated.

The poetic praise of Christ found in 2:6-11 presents a number of conundrums. Does the passage presuppose an Adamic Christology or a Son of God Christology? Does the word "form" (Gk. *morphē*) refer to status, to a type of existence, or to outward appearance? Was "equality with God" something Jesus refused to "exploit" (NRSV), refused to "grasp" (NIV), or declined to "hold on to"? (For a recent discussion of these issues see Wright 1991: 56-98.) When the passage is viewed as a pronouncement of praise intended to provide a definitive example for the Philippians of the type of behavior that should characterize their relations with one another, a number of these questions lose a good deal of their significance. Paul uses the story of Jesus' refusal to exploit his unique relation and status with God (v. 6), his self-abnegation from his exalted position to a position of slavery, that is, subordination to the will of others (v. 7), and finally his self-degradation in becoming obedient to the requirement of his own death on the cross (v. 8) as the prototype of Christian self-abnegation, subordination to others, and humility for the sake of the community. Having described the self-abasing deeds of Jesus in vv. 6-8, Paul concludes with the response of God to this in vv. 9-11. God bestows unparalleled honor on Jesus with the promise that all, including the enemies of Paul and of the Philippians, will be forced to acknowledge the Lordship of Christ. In christological terms vv. 9-11 are a remarkable statement because they predicate to Christ Lordship which Isa 45:23 reserves for God alone, thus suggesting that very early on Christians proclaimed Christ as the unique heir to God's sovereignty. In 3:20-21 Paul claims that he and his converts will participate in the exalted situation of Christ. Thus, 2:9-11 serves as a warrant for God's positive attitude toward those who adopted the attitude of Christ through self-abnegation and self-abasement for the sake of others.

In 2:12-18 Paul further develops the proposition from 1:27-28 that the Philippians should act as citizens in a way commensurate with the demands of the gospel. Echoing the theme of Christ's obedience from the encomium (2:8), he employs affectionate language to call upon his friends ("my beloved") to continue their obedience in his absence. The Greek does not indicate whom they are "to obey." The NRSV makes it Paul by the addition of the word "me" (v. 12). But if they are to obey Paul, it is only because he is the representative of Christ. His command for them is that they "work out" their own "salvation." O'Brien (1991: 278-80) argues that Paul is concerned with "personal salvation" in v. 12, but this runs completely against the thrust of 1:27–2:11 with its concern for solidarity within the community. Although it is possible that Paul is calling for the community "to work at its spiritual well-being" in the present (Hawthorne 1983: 99), in light of 1:28 it is more likely that he is concerned with their collectively achieving the final salvation of their community. Thus the result of their obedience imitates the result of Christ's obedience (2:9-11). Paul hastily adds, however, that this task is being accomplished in cooperation with God, who is at work in the life of the community to achieve the divine purpose of their salvation (v. 13).

In 2:14-15 Paul moves from appropriate behavior within the community for maintaining group cohesion (v. 14) to its consequence for the group's purity in a corrupt world, where their ethical behavior will mark them out as unblemished children of a pure and righteous God. Such an existence will differentiate them from those around them. Paul, therefore, engages in the socially significant activity of defining Christian group identity over against an alien and hostile environment. Simultaneously he provides motivation for their ethical conduct grounded in the reciprocity of true friendship: their loyalty to their Christian conviction, demonstrated by their blamelessness (v. 15), will supply the grounds for his claim of honor before God on the Day of Judgment (v. 16).

In keeping with the reciprocity demanded of true friendship, Paul portrays his own life metaphorically (whether he refers to his imminent martyrdom or his apostolic activity is debated) as being poured out like a libation, in response to their sacrifice and public service (probably a reference to the financial gifts and personal services given to Paul by the Philippians) which demonstrated their loyalty (faith) toward God. Thus Paul and the Philippians mutually fulfilled the demands of friendship for reciprocity in giving and receiving (2:17a), as well as through affectively sharing in one another's circumstances (vv. 17b-18), an important characteristic of ancient friendship previously noted.

Commendation of Timothy and Epaphroditus (2:19-30)

Although 2:19-30 seem to interrupt the flow of the letter, digressions were a recognized feature of ancient rhetoric. The digression found at vv. 19-30 divides into two parts. The first five verses concern Paul's assistant, Timothy, and the final six deal with Epaphroditus, the emissary of the Philippians to Paul. Whereas a number of commentators see Paul using Timothy and Epaphroditus as examples (e.g., Witherington 1994: 75), this seems to miss the point. In respect of Timothy, Paul engages in the common practice of recommendation (see Marshall 1987: 91-129). According to vv. 19 and 23 Paul intended to send Timothy to the Philippians in order to maintain his relationship with them. For Timothy to fulfill such a role it was imperative that the Philippians receive him as the accredited emissary of Paul. Therefore, Paul commends Timothy first by contrasting his sincere concern for the welfare of the Philippians (v. 20) with others who seek only their own self-interests (v. 21; cf. 1:15-17), and second by linking Timothy to himself as the one who has served him in the missionary enterprise with the loyalty and obedience of a son (v. 22). Thus Paul effectively calls on the Philippians to receive Timothy as though they were receiving Paul himself since he, too, is a true friend of theirs (cf. Stowers 1991: 114).

In the case of Epaphroditus, Paul undertakes in 2:25-30 to preserve and even enhance Epaphroditus's honor (the public acknowledgment of his worth) as part of the process of explaining why he is sending him back home to the Philippians. Epaphroditus is portrayed as having dual roles that mark him out as honorable. He stands in relation to Paul as "brother," "co-worker," and "fellow soldier" in the work of the gospel, and in relation to the Philippians as their "messenger" and "minister" to Paul (v. 25).

Sampley (1980: 54-55) suggests that Paul had actually "requested" aid from the Philippians in a time of need since the Greek word *chreia,* used here and in 4:16, can mean both "need" and "request." That they sent Epaphroditus to minister to Paul indicates that they knew of his need, probably through a request. Given the way in which Paul insisted on supporting himself to the Corinthians (1 Cor 9:18; 2 Cor 11:7-11), a request for aid from him may seem unlikely. The basis of the request, however, would have been his friendship with the Philippians, which led to their sharing with one another in giving and receiving (4:16). With this in mind, it becomes clear why Paul went to lengths to honor Epaphroditus and why he sought to explain in detail the reason for sending him back. The Philippians might have viewed this as a rejection of their "gift," an act of extreme discourteousness, or an impugning of the quality of their "gift." Paul prevents both conclusions by his praise of Epaphroditus in 2:29-30 and his explanation of why he was sending him home in vv. 26-28.

Identity and Imitation (3:1–4:1)

While a number of scholars have claimed that 3:1 concluded the original letter (e.g., Beare 1959: 100), the word translated "finally" in the NRSV is used as a transitional expression in Paul on several occasions (1 Thess 4:1; 2 Thess 3:1; cf. Garland 1985: 149), and serves this function here. Paul moves to a new topic, proper Christian identity, presented through contrasting models. This shift is marked by 3:1b. Paul indicates that what follows is for the security of readers, presumably to enable them to distinguish between true and false Christian identity. The passage makes clear that true Christian identity is closely connected to friendship with Christ.

In 3:2 the NRSV makes the common error of translating *blepete* with the expression "beware of." This seems to imply an immediate threat to the community which some scholars claim is in tension with the rest of the letter. They, therefore, conclude that 3:2–4:1 was a separate letter (e.g., Murphy-O'Connor 1996: 219-20). Kilpatrick (1968: 146-48), however, has shown that *blepete* cannot have the meaning "beware of" in 3:2 for grammatical reasons and thus should be translated "consider" or "take due note of," a sense regularly occurring in Paul's letters (cf. 1 Cor 1:26; 10:18; 2 Cor 10:7). Thus Paul is not warning about an imminent danger (Garland 1985: 166-67). Instead, as 3:3-4 reveal, Paul contrasts himself with a group about whom he is polemically critical. In Greek the reference to "those who mutilate the flesh" *(katatomē)* is a play on the word for circumcision *(peritomē)* which occurs in 3:3, and suggests that Paul has in mind Jewish-Christian missionaries who sought to coerce Gentile Christians into circumcision (cf. Galatians 5 and 2 Corinthians 10–13). In light of 3:2, 18-19, Stowers (1994: 67-70) plausibly suggests that those whom Paul castigates taught that "gentiles could learn self-mastery by association with the Jewish community and by adopting certain practices that were described as methods of self-mastery" (e.g., circumcision and dietary laws).

The three negative characterizations of 3:2, "dogs," "workers of evil," and "mutilators," are expressions intended to malign the moral character of the Judaizers (on anti-Jewish slander in antiquity see Johnson 1989) and contrast with the positive characteristics in v. 3 which apply to Paul and his readers. This leads Paul in v. 4 to stress the quality of his own Jewish pedigree in comparison to that of those whom he excoriates in v. 2 and then in vv. 5-6 to offer reasons why his Jewish identity gives him grounds for a sense of superiority to other Jewish-Christian missionaries. In terms of the personal rating system of antiquity, Paul lays claim to a higher level of honor than those with whom he compares himself by virtue of his ethnic and tribal origin and his status as a Pharisee who was both zealous and faultless with respect to the Jewish law.

In 3:6-11 Paul appears to introduce a positive comparison between himself and Christ (Malina and Neyrey 1996: 55). As Christ did not consider equality with God something to be held on to but emptied himself (2:6-7), so Paul considers all aspects of his Jewish identity as "loss" and "rubbish" (3:7-8). In short, just as Christ divested himself of his claim to equality with God, Paul divested himself of his claim to special status with God through his Jewish identity. Marshall (1993: 365-66) sees this as part of Paul's strategy to strengthen his *ethos* or his moral character with the Philippians, identifying his own life with that of Christ as portrayed in 2:6-11. Paul also emphasizes his identification with Christ through his implicit claims to friendship with Christ. His "knowing Christ Jesus my Lord" (3:8) identifies him as a friend of Christ, for it implies the intimacy that was characteristic of ancient friendship (Stowers 1991: 119). His claim to have suffered the loss of all things (3:8), including his freedom (1:13), for the sake of Christ has a similar implication since this kind of selflessness was a characteristic of true friendship (cf. Lucian *Toxaris* 29-34). This also sets Paul apart from the Jewish-Christian missionaries. They emphasized their own Jewishness as the grounds for their superiority over Gentile Christians. But for Paul knowledge of Christ as Lord was available to both Jew and Gentile and was of superior worth to identity claims based on Jewish group identity

(3:8) or righteousness (moral standing) derived from obedience to the Jewish law (v. 9). Thus Paul wants to find himself in a relation with Christ, having his moral standing (righteousness) derived from the "faithfulness or loyalty of Christ" (this translation is preferable to the NRSV's "through faith in Christ"; see Williams 1987: 431-47 on the "faithfulness of Christ" and Malina 1993b: 67-70 on "loyalty"; in favor of the NRSV's translation see Fee 1995: 324-25), who remained true to God even in his humiliation and death on the cross (2:6-8). For Paul this moral standing, coming through Christ's own faithfulness, was from God, was appropriated by imitating Christ's loyalty, and was accessible to Jews and Gentiles on the same terms (3:9; see Engberg-Pedersen 1995: 281-82).

Paul's emphasis on both his own identity with Christ and his friendship with him is encapsulated in 3:10-11, as is his theology of sharing in the suffering of Christ. He balances intimate knowledge of Christ through the power of his resurrection with participation in his suffering through conformity to his humiliating death on the cross (a reference back to 2:8) with a view to attaining the resurrection status granted by God to Christ (implied in 2:9-11). As Stowers (1994: 67) points out in relation to 3:10, "Any competent ancient reader would recognize Jesus' and Paul's behavior as examples of individuals who had shown extraordinary mastery over their passions in service of a higher purpose." This then provided a model for the conduct which Paul wished the Philippians to imitate.

Engberg-Pedersen (1995: 269-73, 280-82) argues that a strong affinity exists between Stoic ethics and Paul's language and thought in 3:12-16. As in Stoic ethics, Paul has attained knowledge (in his case of Christ Jesus, v. 8), and this directs his activity to a new goal which he describes in v. 14 as the "heavenly call of God in Christ Jesus." But in keeping with Stoic thought regarding the unattainability of the final goal of human striving, the cosmic city where like-minded people would join together in community, Paul also recognizes that he has not grasped the goal for which he strives as a Christian and cannot do so in this life, even though he now belongs to Christ (vv. 12-13a). To reinforce the point that Christian existence is goal oriented, Paul introduces the image of the footrace in athletic contests (vv. 13a-14). In races the competitors pursue the goal of victory not by focusing on the past but by pursuing the goal of victory through stretching forward (see O'Brien 1991: 428-33 on the race imagery). The prize which Paul seeks, and which his readers should seek, is described as the "heavenly call of God" (v. 14) and would seem to correspond with Christ's own exaltation in 2:9-11.

In concluding 3:12-16 Paul calls for those who consider themselves "mature" to think in the same way that he does. In essence he calls on the Philippians to agree with him and, by so doing, demonstrate their maturity. According to Paul, those holding a contrary view will have this "revealed" to them by God. Thus, either his readers agree with him and are declared to be mature, or they disagree with him and must be corrected by God so that they can become mature. Regardless of whether they agree with him or not, Paul directs them to agree together (NRSV, "hold fast") in what they have *already attained* as Christians. Thus differences should not be allowed to undermine the unity of the community, a point which takes on particular importance in 4:2-3.

The final paragraph of ch. 3 returns to the contrast with which Paul began in 3:2-6 in order to make a dramatic point about Christian identity. Paul begins by exhorting the Philippians to join together in imitating him and recognizing as worthy of honor and status those who live according to his and Timothy's (see 1:1; 2:19-23) example (3:17). Calls to personal imitation were a common feature of hortatory rhetoric (Malherbe 1986: 135-36), and at one level Paul wishes his readers to imitate his own rejection of the status and honor to which he was entitled through "birth, education, and deeds of life" (Malina and Neyrey 1996: 55; see 3:5-6), in favor of gaining an altogether different status and honor from God. The new one was to be based on imitating Christ's and Paul's loyalty to God (v. 9) and attaining self-mastery through imitating both of them in respect to suffering (v. 10). But over against vv. 18-19 Paul sets up a powerful contrast which constructs the boundary between "insiders" (true Christians) and "outsiders" (false Christians) (cf. Castelli 1991: 96-97). In the context of ch. 3 the "outsiders" are those who maintain that Jewish identity is necessary to obtain Christ's salvation and are labeled "enemies." As in v. 2, Paul vilifies his opponents in vv. 18-19. He attacks their moral character in an attempt to render identification with them absurd (Perkins 1991: 101). The "insiders" are those who join in imitating Paul and, through Paul, Christ, by rejecting status, honor, and privilege attained outside of the Christian model of loyalty to Christ and conformity to his humility. The destiny of the "outsiders" is destruction because their minds are fixed on "earthly" status, honor, and privilege (v. 19). By contrast Paul and those who imitate him are alien residents (a familiar concept in antiquity) in this world. Their citizenship is in the heavenly world, from where they await Jesus Christ, their ruler (lord), who will come as their deliverer (savior). This will result in their being transformed through the resurrection power given to Christ (cf. 2:9-11) to conform to the status and honor symbolized in his glorious body (3:21; *doxa,* the word translated as "glory," refers to honor or reputation, which is outwardly manifested in God's luminous quality; cf. 1 Cor 15:43).

The NRSV correctly indicates that 4:1 forms a conclusion to what precedes. Paul appeals to the *pathos* or emotions of his readers in v. 1 by describing them as "beloved and longed for brothers and sisters" and his own "joy and victory wreath" ("victory wreath" better renders the word which the NRSV translates as "crown" since it was the prize for those who won in athletic contests). The goal of this appeal, which picks up the theme of 1:27, is to encourage readers to remain firm in their loyalty to Christ, as citizens of his realm who await his coming as their deliverer (3:20). This clearly implies that they should not be troubled by those whom Paul describes as enemies of the cross in 3:18. More broadly 4:1 may be intended as a summary for the whole of 2:1–3:21.

Practical Unity (4:2-3)

The exhortation contained in 4:2-3 reiterates one of the main themes of the letter, the need for unity in attitude, purpose, and commitment among the members of the community (cf. 1:27; 2:1-5; 3:15), but directs it to two named individuals. This is unique in the undisputed letters of Paul since nowhere else does Paul exhort individuals by name. Although the text gives no hints regarding the nature of the problem, the hortative appeal to have the same mind in Christ suggests that a divisive dispute had occurred between Euodia and Syntyche. These women must have been important members of the community since 4:3 describes them as people who had labored with Paul in his ministry at Philippi. Perhaps like Phoebe in Rom 16:1, they were deacons or servants of the church. We probably should assume that the unnamed person (unless Gk. *syzygos* is a proper name) whom Paul describes as a "loyal companion" or, more literally, a "yokefellow" was a bishop or overseer of the community with whom Paul had some sort of special relationship. Clement and those identified as Paul's other co-workers were also probably members of the group described as bishops and deacons in the greetings of the letter. The epithet at the end of v. 3 marks the group of Paul's co-workers out as being those whom God honors through their acknowledgment in the divine register recording those whose citizenship is in heaven (cf. 3:20).

Recapitulation of the Letter's Main Themes (4:4-9)

Paul effects a transition to a recapitulation of the letter's main themes through returning to the need for his readers to rejoice (cf. 1:18; 2:17-18; 3:1). Such recapitulation was a common feature of ancient rhetoric and was used to underscore what was important.

In antiquity people were taught to accept both their social status (cf. 1 Cor 7:17-24) and the vicissitudes of life with patient endurance since everything was under the control of the divine. Paul's twice-repeated call to rejoice in 4:4 goes beyond mere patient acceptance of one's lot to a positive embracing of whatever destiny God gives, even when it entails suffering. Such an attitude goes hand in hand with Paul's instruction in v. 5. The NRSV translates *epieikes* in v. 5 as "gentleness," but Witherington (1994: 112) rightly points out that it means something more like "magnanimity" toward others, a trait that was essential in maintaining the unity of the community. The warrant for this behavior is the nearness of the Lord (v. 5b). This may refer to the physical proximity of Christ to his people or it may refer to his temporal proximity, that is, it is shorthand for the nearness of the day of the Lord. The latter seems the more likely, and in the context explains why Paul can call for magnanimity toward others: justice will be dispensed when Christ comes to exercise his God-given dominion; therefore Christians need not seek justice in relations with others in this life.

The nearness of Christ's coming (4:5) also provides the reason why the Philippians should not suffer from anxiety regarding anything (v. 6a). Within the context of the letter it seems possible that Paul may have their own current situation of suffering and struggle in mind (cf. 1:28-30). Regardless of whether this is correct, Paul adds in 4:6b that their requests to God through prayer and supplication offer a means for dealing with their anxieties. Paul concludes his line of thought by promising that the sense of wholeness and well-being which constitutes the peace of God will protect their hearts and minds in their Lord, Christ Jesus, from anxiety (v. 7). Thus vv. 5b-7 represent a closely woven meditation on dealing with the worry which the readers' situation might be engendering.

The word "finally" in 4:8 introduces a summary statement of Paul's ethical advice or exhortation to the Philippians. In vv. 8-9 the advice has two dimensions, one reflective ("think about these things," v. 8) and the other practical ("keep on doing these things," v. 9). The list of virtues in v. 8 is not uniquely Christian nor even Jewish in character. Rather, the list "espouses the highest ideals of Hellenistic virtue" (White 1990: 221). The appropriation of Hellenistic virtues by Paul has troubled some (e.g., Martin 1976: 157-58), but Paul makes no attempt to "Christianize" them. Instead he accepts what was considered ethically commendable in Hellenistic culture and tells Christians to reflect on this as a norm for their own behavior. Paul then points to his own message and example as definitive for the behavior of the Philippians in v. 9, effectively summarizing one of the main thrusts of the entire letter.

In pointing to himself as a model for the readers' behavior, Paul was drawing on the tradition of the moral philosophers of antiquity who used personal examples to illustrate ethical behavior. They considered such examples to be particularly persuasive (see Malherbe 1986: 135-36). An interesting instance of this occurs in a friendship letter of Seneca (a contemporary of Paul) in which he employs his own moral development as a paradigm for his exhortation of his protégé Lucilius (see Stowers 1986: 99-101 for the letter and a discussions of it). Seneca's letter to Lucilius is analogous to what Paul is doing in Philippians. The recipients are both Paul's friends and his protégés in the Christian faith, and he exhorts them to ethical behavior, offering himself as the paradigm for their behavior. The instructions of 4:8-9a are supported by their connection to the promise in v. 9b.

Friendship and the Giving and Receiving of Gifts (4:10-20)

A number of scholars (e.g., Craddock 1985: 76-78) have commented on Paul's seeming offhandedness and lack of real appreciation for the Philippians' gift in 4:10-20, while Sampley (1980: 52-60) claims that the passage reflects the existence of a type of business partnership between Paul and the Philippians. Given the character of Philippians as a letter of friendship, such readings are not persuasive since the theme of giving and receiving, which is reflected in Paul's discourse in vv. 10-20 (see esp. v. 15), is a hallmark of ancient friendship (see Marshall

1987: 1-34, 157-64). In Corinth Paul refused to accept financial support (cf. 1 Corinthians 9 and 2 Cor 11:7-11) because it would have imposed upon him a client relationship with the Corinthian givers, thereby compromising his apostolic freedom; however, he could accept gifts from the Philippians because they were offered in the context of the norms of friendship in which mutuality and reciprocity operated, not dependency and inferiority.

The passage 4:10-20 rests on the fact that Epaphroditus had brought gifts to Paul (v. 18), thus reviving the support which the Philippians had previously given to Paul (vv. 15-16). It was this that led Paul to rejoice (v. 10) since it indicated that his friends had not abandoned him in his imprisonment (v. 14). Although appreciative of their gifts, Paul hastened to point out that for him the gifts were a matter of personal indifference since he required nothing (v. 11a). This was because he had learned the Stoic virtue of self-sufficiency (NRSV's "to be content") whatever his material circumstances were (vv. 11-12). Unlike the Stoics, however, he had not done so simply through self-mastery. His ability to deal with every circumstance of life came from Christ, who provided the strength for him to do so (v. 13). (The NRSV's translation of v. 13 is problematic since it implies that Paul was making a general claim to the ability to accomplish anything through Christ, the one strengthening him [see O'Brien 1991: 526]; the context, however, clearly limits the claim to self-sufficiency in the face of the vicissitudes of life.) In v. 14 Paul makes the crucial point that because of his self-sufficiency through Christ, he was not dependent upon support from the Philippians in his imprisonment, but he was appreciative of it. This observation leads Paul to a brief narration of the Philippians' contributions to his ministry (vv. 15-18), with a concluding promise that God would repay them for their generosity (vv. 19-20).

The Philippians had the distinction of being the only church community to provide financial support for Paul when he left Macedonia, though their assistance had begun while he was at Thessalonica, another Macedonian city, in a situation in which he had been in need (4:16). Paul specifies that they had entered into a relation of mutual sharing through "giving and receiving" (v. 15). Although the language here and in vv. 17-18 has a strongly commercial tone (Beare 1959: 154-55), it was also used metaphorically of friendship since friendships in antiquity were often based on financial considerations (cf. Witherington 1994: 130-31). Thus, as Marshall (1987: 163) observes, the expression "shared with me in the matter of giving and receiving" (v. 15) was "an idiomatic expression indicating friendship" in which Paul was "drawing upon familiar notions of friendship to acknowledge the recent gift [of the Philippians] and to express his gratitude." Although Paul does not state it explicitly, his own giving to the Philippians consisted in his communicating the gospel of Christ to them with its promise of salvation (cf. 3:20-21).

Just as Paul sought in 4:11-13 to correct any misapprehension on the part of the Philippians that he was dependent upon their gifts to supply his needs, in v. 17 he endeavors to quash any possible innuendo that he seeks material benefit from his friendship with them. Quite the contrary, he insists that his goal is the increase of the profit accruing to their account. While he does not explain to what account he refers in v. 17, when read with vv. 18-19 the matter becomes clearer. Their gifts to Paul, based on their friendship, completely discharged their indebtedness to him for his earlier gift of Christ to them. Paul then goes on to interpret their gifts to him, as God's agent for their salvation, in terms of "a fragrant offering, a sacrifice acceptable and pleasing to God." Thus he insinuates that the gifts given to him are in fact given to God, the source of the benefit which Paul imparted to them by connecting them to God through Christ. In effect their friendship with Paul has created a friendship for them with God, and benefits accruing to them through their friendship with Paul are actually transferred to their "account" with God. Therefore, Paul asserts that God will fully satisfy their needs on a scale commensurate with his wealth (v. 19) in return for their gifts to the apostle, which were effectively given to God (v. 18). This declaration then leads Paul to a doxology or an expression of praise in v. 20 which acknowledges that glory and honor (see 3:21) belong to God at all times.

Letter Closing (4:21-23)

The closing of the letter consists of greetings from Paul and those Christians with him, followed by a distinctly Christian benediction. The brief letter closing begins with a request from Paul that the recipients greet every individual saint, or fellow Christian, on Paul's behalf. This perhaps reflects the fact that the letter was to be delivered to one or more of the overseers and church servants mentioned in 1:1, who would then be responsible for the dissemination of the letter and Paul's greetings to the wider community. Paul's own greeting is followed by a greeting from "the friends" (lit. "brothers") who were with him. This presumably refers to his co-workers such as Timothy (see 1:1) who were with him at the time of writing since in 4:22 a wider grouping of Christians are said to send their greetings, with special mention being given to those Christians who were members of the imperial household. This almost certainly is not a reference to the immediate family of the emperor or to other well-born members of his entourage, but to the slaves and freedmen who were members of the imperial civil service or even the domestic staff of the imperial household (Witherington 1994: 135-36). Nevertheless, it is noteworthy how quickly Christianity spread to the very heart of the Roman Empire.

With the exception of Romans, at least as it now stands, all of Paul's letters conclude with brief benedictions that replace the stylized conclusions of typical Hellenistic letters. The benediction of 4:23 is identical to the one occurring in Phlm 25, and both of these are very similar to the one found in Gal 6:16 in that all three call for "the grace of the Lord Jesus Christ to be with your spirit."

Most modern readers, steeped in theological language, miss the notion which lies behind Paul's benediction and more generally his and the Bible's use of the term "grace." In both the culture of ancient Israel and in Paul's world the term "grace" was associated with patron-client relations and referred to the fact that patrons by virtue of their social rank and power were in a position to offer favors or gifts to those beneath them, often in return for esteem or public praise (see Malina 1993c: 84). Thus in concluding the letter, Paul calls for the patronal favor of Christ to reside on each member of the Philippian Christian community just as the patronal favor of God resided with Israel in the OT.

Bibliography. Basevi, C., and J. Chapa. 1993, "Philippians 2:6-11: The Rhetorical Function of a Pauline 'Hymn,'" in S. E. Porter and T. H. Olbricht, eds., *Rhetoric and the New Testament: Essays from the 1992 Heidelberg Conference,* JSNTSup 90, Sheffield: Sheffield Academic, 338-55 • Beare, F. W. 1959, *A Commentary on the Epistle to the Philippians,* London: A. & C. Black • Bockmuehl, M. 1997, *The Epistle to the Philippians,* BNTC, London: A. & C. Black • Castelli, E. A. 1991, *Imitating Paul: A Discourse of Power,* Literary Currents in Biblical Interpretation, Louisville: Westminster/John Knox • Craddock, F. B. 1985, *Philippians,* IBC, Atlanta: John Knox • Engberg-Pedersen, T. 1995, "Stoicism in Philippians," in T. Engberg-Pedersen, ed., *Paul in His Hellenistic Context,* Minneapolis: Fortress, 256-90 • Engberg-Pedersen, T. 2000, *Paul and the Stoics,* Louisville: Westminster John Knox • Fee, G. D. 1995, *Paul's Letter to the Philippians,* NICNT, Grand Rapids: Eerdmans • Garland, D. E. 1985, "The Composition and Unity of Philippians: Some Neglected Literary Factors," *NovT* 27:141-73 • Geoffrion, T. C. 1993, *The Rhetorical Purpose and the Political and Military Character of Philippians: A Call to Stand Firm,* Lewiston, N.Y.: Edwin Mellen • Hawthorne, G. F. 1983, *Philippians,* WBC, Waco: Word • Holmberg, B. 1980, *Paul and Power: The Structure of Authority in the Primitive Church as Reflected in the Pauline Epistles,* Philadelphia: Fortress • Horrell, D. G. 1996, *The Social Ethos of the Corinthian Correspondence: Interests and Ideology from 1 Corinthians to 1 Clement,* Edinburgh: T. & T. Clark • Jewett, R. 1970, "Conflicting Movements in the Early Church as Reflected in Philippians," *NovT* 12:362-90 • Johnson, L. T. 1989, "The New Testament's Anti-Jewish Slander and the Conventions of Ancient Polemic," *JBL* 108:419-41 • Käsemann, E. 1968, "A Critical Analysis of Philippians 2:5-11," *JTC* 5:45-88 • Kennedy, G. A. 1991, *Aristotle's On Rhetoric: A Theory of Civic Discourse,* Oxford: Oxford University • Kilpatrick, G. D. 1968, "ΒΛΕΠΕΤΕ, Philippians 3:2," in M. Black and G. Fohrer, eds., *In Memoriam Paul Kahle,* BZAW, Berlin: A. Töpelmann, 146-48 • Lightfoot, J. B. 1908, *Saint Paul's Epistle to the Philippians,* London: Macmillan • Malherbe, A. J. 1986, *Moral Exhortation: A Greco-Roman Sourcebook,* LEC 4, Philadelphia: Westminster • Malina, B. J. 1993a, "Faith/Faithfulness," in J. J. Pilch and B. J. Malina, eds., *Biblical Social Values and Their Meaning: A Handbook,* Peabody, Mass.: Hendrickson, 67-70 • Malina, B. J. 1993b, "Grace/Favor," in J. J. Pilch and B. J. Malina, eds., *Biblical Social Values and Their Meaning: A Handbook,* Peabody, Mass.: Hendrickson, 83-86 • Malina, B. J. 1993c, "Love," in J. J. Pilch and B. J. Malina, eds., *Biblical Social Values and Their Meaning: A Handbook,* Peabody, Mass.: Hendrickson, 110-14 • Malina, B. J., and J. H. Neyrey. 1996, *Portraits of Paul: An Archaeology of Ancient Personality,* Louisville: Westminster/John Knox • Marshall, J. W. 1993, "Paul's Ethical Appeal in Philippians," in S. E. Porter and T. H. Olbricht, eds., *Rhetoric and the New Testament: Essays from the 1992 Heidelberg Conference,* JSNTSup 90, Sheffield: Sheffield Academic, 357-74 • Marshall, P. 1987, *Enmity in Corinth: Social Conventions in Paul's Relations with the Corinthians,* WUNT 2, 23, Tübingen: J. C. B. Mohr (Paul Siebeck) • Martin, R. P. 1976, *Philippians,* NCB, London: Oliphants • Martin, R. P. 2d ed., 1983, *Carmen Christi: Philippians ii.5-11 in Recent Interpretation and in the Setting of Early Christian Worship,* Grand Rapids: Eerdmans • Murphy-O'Connor, J. 1996, *Paul: A Critical Life,* Oxford: Clarendon • Oakes, P. 2001. *Philippians: From People to Letter,* SNTSMS 110, Cambridge: Cambridge University • O'Brien, P. T. 1991, *The Epistle to the Philippians: A Commentary on the Greek Text,* NIGTC, Grand Rapids: Eerdmans • Olbricht, T. H., and J. L. Sumney, eds. 2001, *Paul and Pathos,* SBLSS, Atlanta: Society of Biblical Literature • Perkins, P. 1991, "Philippians: Theology for the Heavenly Politeuma," in J. M. Bassler, ed., *Pauline Theology,* vol. 1: *Thessalonians, Philippians, Galatians, Philemon,* Minneapolis: Fortress, 89-104 • Sampley, J. P. 1980, *Pauline Partnership in Christ: Christian Community and Commitment in Light of Roman Law,* Philadelphia: Fortress • Stowers, S. K. 1986, *Letter Writing in Greco-Roman Antiquity,* LEC 5, Philadelphia: Westminster • Stowers, S. K. 1991, "Friends and Enemies in the Politics of Heaven," in J. M. Bassler, ed., *Pauline Theology,* vol. 1: *Thessalonians, Philippians, Galatians, Philemon,* Minneapolis: Fortress, 105-21 • Stowers, S. K. 1994, *A Rereading of Romans: Justice, Jews, and Gentiles,* New Haven, Conn.: Yale University • Sumney, J. L. 1999, *'Servants of Satan,' 'False Brothers' and Other Opponents of Paul,* JSOTSup, Sheffield: Sheffield Academic • Wanamaker, C. A. 1990, *The Epistles to the Thessalonians: A Commentary on the Greek Text,* NIGTC, Grand Rapids: Eerdmans • Watson, D. F. 1988, "A Rhetorical Analysis of Philippians and Its Implication for the Unity Question," *NovT* 30:57-88 • White, L. M. 1990, "Morality between Two Worlds: A Paradigm of Friendship in Philippians," in D. L. Balch, E. Ferguson, and W. A. Meeks, eds., *Greeks, Romans, and Christians: Essays in Honor of Abraham J. Malherbe,* Minneapolis: Fortress, 201-15 • Williams, S. K. 1987, "Again *pistis Christou,*" *CBQ* 49:431-47 • Witherington, B. 1994, *Friendship and Finances in Philippi: The Letter of Paul to the Philippians,* New Testament in Context, Valley Forge, Penn.: Trinity • Wright, N. T. 1991, *The Climax of the Covenant: Christ and the Law in Pauline Theology,* Edinburgh: T. & T. Clark.

Colossians

Morna D. Hooker

INTRODUCTION

Colossae was situated on the Lycus River, some one hundred miles east of Ephesus. Although its wealthy wool industry had once made it prosperous, its importance had by Paul's day apparently declined, overshadowed by nearby Laodicea and Hierapolis. Its population was mixed: native Phrygians had been joined by Greek and Syrian settlers. Considerable numbers of Jews had settled in the area c. 200 BC (Josephus *Ant.* 12.147-53), some of whom would be living in Colossae. The religion of the region was syncretistic: many deities were worshiped and cults flourished. The church in Colossae (mainly Gentile: 2:13) had been founded by Epaphras, Paul's assistant, but Paul clearly regarded himself as responsible for its welfare.

The authorship of the epistle is a matter of dispute. Many argue that its style and theology make Pauline authorship impossible. Stylistic analysis has suggested that the style is not that of the author of Romans, 1 and 2 Corinthians, and Galatians, but the issue is not clear-cut. Might use of an amanuensis explain the differences? Did Timothy (1:1) have a hand in its composition? Differences in theology are harder to analyze. When commentators argue that Colossians does not discuss the question of "righteousness" or make significant mention of the law or the Spirit, they forget that each of Paul's letters deals with particular issues. There are indeed significant developments in Paul's theology in Colosssians, and some commentators suggest that the letter's warning against "philosophy" indicates a "heresy" which developed after Paul's time (see below). Ideas are expressed which are not found in other letters: the Christology of 1:15-20 moves beyond anything he says elsewhere, his understanding of "the church" seems to have developed (v. 18), and the "household rules" of 3:18–4:1 offer a code of behavior unparalleled in the earlier epistles. The interesting point to note, however, is that there are hints of all these developments in the early Paul. Again and again we find that Colossians develops and builds on ideas which we recognize as Pauline, providing the kind of argument we would expect from Paul. And though the law is not specifically mentioned, much of the argument is based on the assumption that Christ exercises the role which Judaism once attributed to the law.

One complicating factor in the debate is the special relationship between Colossians and Ephesians: the two epistles are similar in outline and have many words and phrases in common. Most commentators believe that Ephesians is modeled on Colossians. If so, then Pauline authorship of Ephesians would entail Pauline authorship of Colossians, since Paul would hardly have used as a model a letter purporting to be his! If, as seems far more likely, Ephesians is *not* by Paul, then again Colossians is likely to be Pauline, since the author of Ephesians would have been unlikely to use a non-Pauline letter as his pattern.

Although a decision regarding authorship affects our understanding of Paul's theological contribution, it makes little difference to our understanding of Colossians. If not by Paul himself, the letter must have been by someone who understood his mind and developed his theology in an entirely appropriate way. For convenience, the author will be referred to as "Paul."

In view of its theological developments, the letter must, if it is by Paul, have been written toward the end of his ministry. Since he is in prison, this places it in Rome at the beginning of the 60s.

It is generally assumed that the primary purpose of the letter was to warn the community about the so-called "Colossian heresy." The notion of a "heresy" at this stage is an anachronism, however; what is meant is some kind of erroneous teaching. This is commonly described as a "philosophy" offering salvation through knowledge of spiritual powers and observance of religious practices, and is often understood as an early form of gnosticism, though again this term is an anachronism, since gnosticism proper was a later development (Lightfoot 1876). Other suggestions are that Christianity was being interpreted as a mystery cult (Dibelius 1917), or in terms of Hellenistic philosophy (Schweizer 1982) or Jewish mysticism (Francis 1963 and Rowland 1983). More recently, Arnold (1995) has argued that the most likely background of the "philosophy" can be found in the syncretistic atmosphere of Asia Minor and the concerns of folk religion.

The belief that this "false teaching" was posing a grave danger to the Colossian community is largely due to a common assumption that Paul wrote letters only in order to contradict views which he considered wrong, or to deal with serious pastoral problems. The tone of Colossians is very different indeed from that of Galatians and much of 2 Corinthians, where he *was* concerned to refute misunderstandings of the gospel among his readers. In Colossians, by contrast, Paul stresses the firmness of his readers' faith (1:1-8; 2:1-6). Although commentators frequently refer to "dangerous views being propagated" at Colossae and describe these as a "serious menace," it is by no means certain that anyone in the Colossian church had in fact succumbed to such teaching (Hooker 1973)!

Nevertheless, Paul thought it expedient to warn the community against certain attitudes and pressures. Whether these were a particular danger in Colossae we do not know; certainly Paul was aware from his experience elsewhere of the possible dangers facing a young Christian community. What he had in mind was apparently Jewish in origin, since he referred to various Jewish customs and regulations (2:16-23). Since he also emphasized that Christians had inherited the promises of God to Israel, there may well have been pressure from Jews who dismissed the Gentile Christians of Colossae as "outsiders" who were not members of God's people (Dunn 1995). Paul's purpose, then, was to assure his readers that they *had* been made members of Christ's kingdom (1:12-14). And since, as Gentiles, they would have believed themselves to be surrounded by hostile forces and astrological powers, the emphasis on the supremacy of Christ may have been necessary to reassure them that he was able to protect them and that there was no need to placate these alien powers.

The epistle's main impact on subsequent theology has been through the exposition of the role of Christ in 1:15-20: from this developed the idea of the "cosmic Christ," emphasizing the key role played by Christ in both creation and redemption. Also influential has been the idea found in 2:11-15 of Christ's defeat of the cosmic powers at his death: from this developed the understanding of atonement known as "Christus Victor."

COMMENTARY

Greetings (1:1-2)

The opening greeting, a Christian adaptation of those used in contemporary Greek letters, is similar to those in other Pauline letters and conveys information about both writers and recipients. As usual, Paul reminds us of his credentials as an apostle, a status not shared by his coauthor Timothy, who is a "brother," that is, a Christian. The status of the Colossians, too, is stressed, perhaps in order to reassure them: they are "saints" (i.e., God's holy people; used in the OT of Israel, this term is now applied to everyone "in Christ") and "faithful brothers [and sisters]." The greeting is in effect a prayer that the Colossians may experience the grace and peace of God.

Thanksgiving (1:3-8)

Like all of Paul's letters (except Galatians!), this one begins with thanksgiving. God is now described, not as "our Father" (1:2) but as "the Father of our Lord Jesus Christ" (v. 3), a phrase which reminds us both that it is through Christ that the benefits described in the following verses come to us and that Christ himself is obedient to God. The exalted language about Christ in vv. 15-20 must be read in this context.

Paul thanks God for what he has heard about the Colossians — about the faith which they have because they are "in Christ" (1:4), about their love for their fellow Christians, and about their hope, on which faith and love are based: this familiar triad occurs elsewhere in Paul, most notably in 1 Cor 13:13. The hope which is "laid up . . . in heaven" will be defined in 1:27 as glory, and will be spelled out in 3:1-4.

Paul reminds them that they heard of this hope when Epaphras first brought them the gospel (1:6-7), and Paul is confident that they "truly comprehended" it because "it has been bearing fruit" in their lives. As though to stress the validity of the mesage they heard, Paul describes Epaphras as "a faithful minister" (the Greek word is *diakonos,* "servant"), who had preached the gospel to the Colossians "on our behalf." This reading (NRSV mg.) is better attested and suggests that Ephaphras had gone to Colossae because Paul himself had been unable to do so. We might expect Paul to describe Epaphras as his assistant, but instead he uses "fellow servant" (Gk. *doulos* really means "slave"); apostle though he is, he regards Epaphras as a colleague.

There is no hint in these opening verses that Paul thinks there is anything amiss in the Colossian community; on the contrary, Epaphras has reported their "love in the Spirit." But the choice of language suggests that Paul may be anxious to assure them that the gospel they believed is true (1:5) — a fact proved by their own way of life (v. 6) — and to remind them of the reality of the hope which was an important part of that gospel.

Prayer for the Colossians (1:9-14)

Paul turns from thanksgiving to intercession — or, rather, to an assurance that he has prayed for the Colossians from the beginning. He prays that they may be "filled with the knowledge of God's will" — meaning insight into God's will, not knowledge of a set of rules; such knowledge will lead to spiritual wisdom and understanding.

The reference to "philosophy" in 2:8 suggests that one temptation confronting the Colossians was to pursue human wisdom and knowledge, which may explain why Paul assures them that he wants them to have the right kind; for Paul, as for all Jews, knowing God meant obeying his will (Hos 6:6). So his next prayer is that they "may lead lives worthy of the Lord" (1:10). Familiar Jewish ideas are given a Christian twist, since insight into God's will means living a life worthy of "the Lord," a term Paul now uses of Christ, through whom we comprehend God's nature and will (v. 15; cf. Phil 1:27; 2:6-11).

He prays, too, that they may be given strength by God (1:11); no doubt the Colossians, living in a world inhabited by malign forces, felt in need of divine power, but Paul sees it as operating in a paradoxical way — in endurance and patience. This was probably not how the Colossians expected divine power to manifest itself! The idea is, however, typical of Paul (cf. 1 Cor 1:23-25). This power is "glorious," that is, it reveals God's nature, which is seen both in the crucified Christ and in his resurrection (1 Cor 1:24; Rom 1:4; Phil 3:10).

They should at all times be giving thanks to God (1:12), and Paul's intercession merges straightaway into a declaration of what God has already done for them. Writing to Gentiles, Paul assures them that God has enabled them (v. 12; "you" is more probable than "us") to share in the lot of "the saints" — that is, God's people Israel (cf. Ps 105:11). There are interesting parallels in Wis 5:5; 1QS 11:7-8; 1QH 11:12. At Qumran, too, the lot of God's people is described as "light" (1QM 13:9; CD 13:12; cf. Dan 12:3). Another idea that features in the Qumran literature is a battle between light and darkness (1QM 1:1; 13:5). For the Colossians, the assurance that they had been rescued "from the power of darkness" would have been very necessary: in the kingdom of God's Son (a rare idea, but see 1 Cor 15:24) they were safe. The reference to redemption as "the forgiveness of sins" is unusual for Paul (though cf. Gal 1:4), since he normally treats Sin as an alien power enslaving humanity.

Christ's Preeminence (1:15-20)

This passage, often described as a "hymn," is rhythmic in structure, though its form is certainly not that of Greek poetry. The content is credal, spelling out the role of Christ in creation (1:15-17) and redemption (vv. 18-20). Its purpose here is perhaps to assure the Colossians of the power of their new King to protect them. The two main sections, each beginning "He is . . . ," are linked by a couplet which sums up Christ's superiority to the cosmos and the church ("And he is . . ."; two times [vv. 17, 18]). The parallelism is underlined by the use of "firstborn" in each main section, by the repetition of three identical prepositional phrases (in him, through him, for/to him), and by the phrases "in heaven" and "on earth."

Christ is described as "the image of the invisible God." Similar language is found in Jewish wisdom literature, where Wisdom is said to be the image of God and agent of creation (Prov 8:22-36; 3:19; Wis 7:22-27; 8:5-6), and is identified with the Word of God or Torah (Sirach 24; Wis 9:1-2). Philo, too, speaks of both Wisdom and God's Word as "beginning" and "image" (*Leg. all.* 1.43; *Conf. ling.* 97, 146-47; *Fug.* 101; *Somn.* 1.239). Paul has already spoken of Christ as the one through whom all things exist (1 Cor 8:6), and described him as God's image and the expression of his glory, which had been partially glimpsed in the law (2 Cor 3:7–4:6): the role which Judaism had attributed to the law was now seen as belonging to Christ (cf. also John 1:1-5; Heb 1:2-3).

The passage may be based (as suggested by Burney 1926) on an exposition, in rabbinic style, of the first word of Gen 1:1 ("in the beginning") in the light of Prov 8:22, which identifies Wisdom as "the beginning." Burney argued that it expounds every meaning of the Hebrew preposition *be* — in, by/through, into/for — and of the noun *re'shit* — beginning, sum total, head, firstfruits. If he was right, this passage identifies the divine Wisdom with Christ.

The opening statement that Christ is "the image of the invisible God" affirms, not that he is a copy of God, but that he is the manifestation of God's being. God has revealed himself through his creation, and the phrase "first-born of all creation" points to Christ's supremacy *over* creation. The reason is spelled out: all things were created in, through, and for him — the last idea goes beyond anything in wisdom literature. "All things" includes all kinds of powers, both celestial and earthly. Angelic beings were important in contemporary Jewish writings: Paul affirms that all are subservient to Christ. His Gentile readers would have needed this assurance of Christ's supremacy over hostile powers. Christ's preeminence is again affirmed in 1:17: he is "before all things," which means that they all cohere in him. This statement is balanced by v. 18a: Christ is "head of the body, the church" — and this, too, must find its coherence in him. (The idea that Christ is *head* of the body, emphasizing his preeminence, goes beyond the ideas expressed in Romans 12 and 1 Corinthians 12.)

The statement that Christ is "the beginning" (1:18b) balances v. 15a and echoes another Jewish affirmation about Wisdom, reminding us that Christ's activity in reconciliation is coherent with his work in creation: the two belong together. Again we are told that he is the "firstborn" — this time from the dead — and so has "the first place in everything." Again the reason is spelled out: it pleased "all the fullness" (i.e., "of God," an idea expressed in 2:9) to dwell in him, and to reconcile all things through him and to him. Though the NRSV understands this as "to God," God has not been mentioned since 1:15; moreover, symmetry requires that the phrase refers to Christ. But like the identical phrase in 1:16 (NRSV, "for him"), this idea is unexpected. The reference in v. 21 to the cross seems strangely abrupt; in fact, it "earths" Christ in history, in much the same way that John 1:14 does in another passage using "Wisdom" terminology.

The Implications (1:21-23)

1:21-23 point out the relevance of all this to the Colossians, for they, too, previously under the power of darkness (v. 13), have been reconciled through Christ. Reconciliation has taken place "in the body of his flesh," a reminder that Christ shared our human nature (cf. Rom 8:3); more specifically, it took place through his death, so that he might "present" the Colossians irreproachable before him, worthy subjects in his kingdom. Whether the imagery ("holy and blameless") is sacrificial or juridical, this compressed statement expresses the Pauline idea of "interchange in Christ" by which reconciliation is achieved — Christ sharing our humanity, so enabling believers to share his holiness (Hooker 1990). But they need to hold fast to the faith and to the hope promised by the gospel (v. 23). The claim that this gospel has been proclaimed throughout all creation (*sic:* the same phrase was used in v. 15) is undoubtedly an exaggeration, but it would remind the Colossian Christians that they were not alone. It is of this gospel that Paul is a "servant" or "minister" (the Greek word *diakonos* has not yet acquired the technical sense of "deacon").

Paul's Ministry (1:24–2:5)

The idea that suffering can bring joy is common in the NT. Paul rejoices because his sufferings are "for your sake," a phrase he uses elsewhere about *Christ's* sufferings: it is because he sees his sufferings as a sharing in Christ's (cf. 2 Cor 4:10; Phil 1:29; 3:10) that they can benefit others. The idea that something might be "lacking" in Christ's afflictions is puzzling, but it is obvious from 1:20 that Paul does not consider Christ's own suffering as inadequate! Paul is perhaps referring to the "messianic afflictions" which contemporary Judaism expected to precede the Day of the Lord. Christians also expected to share in this affliction (cf. Mark 13), and may have thought that there was a "quota" of suffering which had to be endured. It is Paul's share in this that needs completion (Flemington 1981). His sufferings are his contribution to what had to be endured, borne "for the sake of [Christ's] body, the church" (cf. 2 Cor 1:6; 4:12), of which he is the servant. Because all Christians are "in Christ," one member can suffer on behalf of others. Paul never imagined that Christ's sufferings and death saved Christians from physical pain and hardship; rather, Christian life meant *sharing* Christ's suffering and death.

The language of 1:26 is that of Jewish apocalyptic, reflecting the belief that God has revealed his purpose, hidden until now, to his faithful people (cf. 4 Ezra 10:38; *1 Enoch* 103:2; 106:19; 1QS 3:23); in particular, this "mystery" is hidden in Scripture (1QpHab 7:4-5). But his Gentile readers, living in a world where the "mystery religions" promised salvation to their initiates, may well have interpreted his words as a reference to a "mystery" of that kind. Paul's claim is that this mystery is Christ himself (cf. Rom 16:25) — or rather "Christ in you, the hope of glory." In Rom 11:25-26 the mystery concerns God's purpose to include the Gentiles in his people (cf. Rom 16:25-26), and since Paul is here speaking of his divine commission (to the Gentiles) to make God's word "fully known" (1:25) and of what has happened "among the Gentiles," the "you" here probably means specifically "you Gentiles."

The idea that Christ dwells in the believer (cf. Rom 8:10; Gal 2:20) is less common than that of living "in Christ," but the emphasis here is on Christ and on his transforming power, making believers like himself (Gal 4:19). It is Christ who is the basis of hope, and the object of hope is glory. In Romans, Paul tells the story of how Adam lost God's glory (1:23; 3:23) and of how believers now hope for that glory's restoration (5:2; 8:18, 30).

Paul's aim as an apostle is to "present" (an echo of 1:22) everyone as fully "mature" (or "perfect" — another word used in the mystery religions; the equivalent Hebrew term was used at Qumran of God's people) in Christ, sharing in his glory (cf. Phil 3:21). It is for this purpose that Paul preaches and teaches, toiling incessantly (1:28-29).

Paul's understanding of his ministry is firmly rooted in the christological affirmation of 1:15-20, which spelled out the "mystery" of Christ as the key to God's purposes in creation and history. It is because God's purpose was to reconcile everything to himself that men and women are restored, in Christ, to what God planned for them. The threefold use of "everyone" in v. 28 underlines the universal scope of the divine plan. The mystery concealed throughout the ages (v. 26) is now openly proclaimed.

In 2:1-5 Paul turns from this vision of the universal mission of the gospel to the needs of his readers. The struggle he is engaged in (1:29) is for them, too, together with other Christians whom he has never met. Paul is presumably referring to his constant prayers for them and to his pastoral care, even though this is exercised through others. He naturally has considerable anxieties about these young Christians whom he has not himself instructed. His concerns for them (2:2) repeat the themes of understanding, knowledge, and wisdom (1:9-10) and pick up the identification of Christ as the mystery of God (1:27). Now he emphasizes that in Christ are hidden all the riches of wisdom and knowledge — a natural deduction from 1:15-20.

2:4 introduces for the first time a note of warning: he is spelling this out lest the Colossians are deceived with plausible arguments. Although this is interpreted as evidence of a "Colossian heresy" (see Introduction, 1404), there is no indication that Paul thinks that the Colossians have succumbed to any false teaching. He is, however, well aware of the dangers! It is by no means clear whether his emphasis on what is to be found "in Christ" implies "not in the Torah," "not in other beings," or "not in some rival system." Whichever it is, the danger does not seem great, since Paul rejoices in the firmness of the Colossians' faith (v. 5).

Their Roots in Christ (2:6-15)

Paul now appeals to the Colossians to remain faithful to what they have received — that is, the gospel about Jesus Christ the Lord — by continuing to live in him (2:6). The title "Lord" is an apt reminder of 1:15-20, while the command to live in Christ picks up 1:10; once again faith and behavior are firmly bound together. Paul expresses confidence in the Colossians, who have been firmly rooted in Christ and are being built up in him, strengthened in faith and therefore overflowing with thanksgiving.

2:8 sounds another note of warning, this time a little more urgent; yet the precise danger is still unclear. The Colossians must take heed lest someone tries to capture them (out of the kingdom of Christ, 1:13) with some human philosophy or empty deceit. This vague description suggests that Paul's warning is intended to cover any belief system that challenges their Christian faith. The "elemental spirits" would certainly have included the thrones, dominions, rulers, and powers of 1:16. Jewish readers would have thought of angelic powers, Gentiles of the beings whom Paul elsewhere dismisses as "so-called gods" (1 Cor 8:5) or of the astrological forces which controlled the calendar. Paul himself may well have been thinking of them all (cf. Gal 4:3 and 9). There would be a constant temptation to assume that such forces must be acknowledged and placated. Paul's teaching is a reminder that there is no need to do so since the fullness of Deity dwells in Christ, and all these powers are therefore subject to him. This is the practical implication of 1:15-20.

2:9 repeats 1:19, making its meaning explicit. The word "fullness" is found also in John 1:16 and is a way of speaking of the name or glory or nature of God (cf. Exod

33:18-20). The affirmation that this fullness "dwells bodily" (or took bodily form) in Christ reminds us of John 1:14 ("the Word became flesh"). This means (2:10) that those who are "in him" share in his fullness and are themselves "fulfilled"; since Christ is head over every cosmic ruler and authority, the implication is that the Colossians have been freed from their power.

How this takes place is the theme of 2:11-15. Paul uses a series of vivid images to explain what has happened to the Colossians. First, they have been circumcised — a strange metaphor, we might think, for Paul to use, but this is a circumcision made without hands. It is achieved by believers sharing in Christ's own "circumcision," which here refers, not to the removal of a small piece of flesh, but to "putting off *the body* of flesh" in death. It is possible that Paul's image is a response to "Judaizers" advocating circumcision for Gentile Christians and is intended to affirm that Gentile Christians are already members of God's people. But though that may explain the origin of the image, the idea that literal circumcision is unnecessary is seemingly unimportant here. Instead, Paul uses the image to show how, by sharing Christ's circumcision (i.e., death), those who were already dead (in trespasses) and in uncircumcision were paradoxically made alive with Christ (v. 13). This happened when, in baptism, they were buried with him and raised with him (2:12). The reference to "the power of God, who raised [Christ] from the dead" is perhaps intended to remind the Colossians (who have been raised with him!) that they have nothing to fear from lesser powers. But this is not something that happened only to Gentiles! The pronouns change from "you" to "us," since what is now described applies to all Christians.

The image in 2:14 is of a legal document which lists the charges against us: its cancellation is emphasized — it has been erased, set aside, and nailed to Christ's cross. This last phrase suggests that Paul might be thinking of the accusation nailed to the cross (Mark 15:26 and pars.). With Christ's death and resurrection, the power of the charges against us has been nullified (cf. Gal 3:13-14).

The final image is unclear: if God is still the subject (as in the NRSV), then the idea is that he has stripped the cosmic forces of their power through the cross. But the margin may be correct in suggesting that Christ has stripped *himself* of these alien powers, so that it is they who are left hanging powerless on the cross. Either way, it is not the crucified Christ who is "made a public example" on the cross but the hostile powers, and the cross thus becomes the scene of triumph, an idea close to the Johannine idea that both God and Christ were "glorified" through the cross.

Specific Warnings (2:16-23)

Paul's warnings now become more precise, though whether he knows of any specific danger in the Colossian community or is merely aware of what could happen is still not clear. The Colossians must not allow anyone to pass judgment on them concerning food or drink or the observance of festivals. The list sounds Jewish, though the absence of any reference to circumcision rules out the possibility that proselytizing Judaizers are at work. Nevertheless, Paul is afraid that the Colossians may come under pressure from those Jewish Christians who believe that Gentile Christians should observe the dietary laws of Judaism and keep its holy days. The requirement which seemed appropriate to many Jewish Christians, that Gentile Christians should abstain from anything polluted by idols (Acts 15:20), would include drink as well as food. "Food and drink" are also linked together in Rom 14:17, at the conclusion of a passage where Paul urges Christians not to pass judgment on one another on this matter. Paul does not condemn Jewish Christians for continuing to observe the law; what he opposes is the attempt to make Gentile Christians conform to the Jewish law (Romans 14). New moons were important in Judaism for calculating the festivals, and the combination of festivals, new moons, and sabbaths is common (e.g., Isa 1:13-14; Hos 2:11; cf. CD 3:14-15). To Paul these things are obsolete, for they belong to the old age (Gal 4:10; cf. Rom 14:5). The idea that they are "a shadow of what is to come" (cf. Heb 10:1) has seemed to many to be Platonic, but it probably derives from Jewish apocalyptic, in which earthly events reflected heavenly realities and so pointed forward to what would happen in the age to come. The notion that the sabbath (cf. Heb. 4:9-11) and Jewish festivals (cf. John's Gospel) point forward to the messianic age is a thoroughly Jewish one; it is hardly surprising, then, if Paul declares that, in contrast to the shadow, the reality belongs to "the Messiah" (2:17), whose role in God's plan was spelled out in 1:15-20 (cf. Rom 10:4, where Christ is the goal of the law).

The warning is repeated in 2:18, but it is far from clear what dangers are in mind. Paul apparently knows of people who are placing great emphasis on (Gk. *thelōn en* means "delighting in" rather than "insisting on") certain practices. These included fasting (rather than "self-abasement"; *tapeinophrosynē,* lit. "humility" — 3:12 — often has this special sense in the LXX). The reference to angel worship is puzzling; it would be astonishing to find Jews advocating the worship of angels, though there was much speculation about them in Judaism, and they were often assigned an important role, for example, in Tob 11:14; *Jub.* 2:2; 1QSa 2:8-9; 1QM 7:6; 10:10-11; 17:5-8; 1QS 3:20-25. Paul himself speaks of the law as being given to Moses via angels (Gal 3:19), and this suggests that he sees the veneration (rather than "worship") of angels as part of the old age, no longer appropriate now that the mystery of God has been revealed to his saints (1:26). Angels are subservient to Christ (1:15-20), who alone is supreme, so that undue attention to them must deflect attention from him (2:19). The suggestion that Paul is referring to worship by angels (Francis 1963), which was perhaps part of a Jewish mystic tradition (see 4Q400-407), seems less likely. Although the meaning of 2:18 is very uncertain, it is clear that Paul's warning includes people who lay emphasis on visions; he himself is cautious about these (2 Cor 12:1-13), since claims to special revelations can lead to boasting. The idea that certain people entered heaven and saw visions was an important one in first-century Judaism (e.g., *1 Enoch; T. Levi;* Revelation 4–22), though visions were also important in the pagan world, for example, in the mystery religions. Paul dismisses all such claims as "human"; the Greek word *sarx,* literally "flesh," is his favorite one when describing human weakness in contrast to divine power. Those who belong to Christ must rely, not on these obvious religious observances, but on him. It is from Christ, the head, that the whole body receives nourishment and is held together, and so grows in accordance with God's design. Whereas the practices referred to in 2:16-18 lead to division, reliance on Christ binds the community together.

In 2:20, Paul's tone becomes more agitated. Those who have died with Christ have been set free from the power of the "elemental spirits" and now live in a new kingdom (1:13; cf. Gal 4:3-9). The NRSV, in common with most translations and commentators, assumes that some, at least, of the Colossians have succumbed to the dangers he is listing, but it is possible that Paul is still warning them not to succumb rather than reproving them for doing so. If so, we should understand him to be saying "Why live . . . ? Why submit . . . ?" rather than "Why *do you* live . . . ? Why *do you* submit . . . ?" Christians no longer belong to the world, and Paul appeals to his readers not to live as though they did. Regulations about what may be touched, tasted, or handled suggest that Paul has in mind Jewish regulations about purity. Those who touched an unclean person or ate unclean food were themselves made unclean (cf. Lev 5:2-3; 11; 15; Num 19:11-13); both the Pharisees and the members of the Qumran community were particularly concerned with questions of purity, since the people of God — his "holy" ones — must *be* holy.

The argument in 2:22 is reminiscent of Jesus' argument with the Pharisees on this very subject (Mark 7:1-23 par. Matt 15:1-20), where Isa 29:13, echoed in Colossians, is quoted in full. Remarkably, commands included in the law are regarded as "human commands" in contrast to the moral precepts of ch. 3.

The final verse is full of obscurities and rare words, but the overall sense is plain. These religious practices give the outward appearance of piety, but they are of no real value. The translation suggested in the margin, though seemingly paradoxical, may well be correct; although these regulations are all prohibitions, the fact that they are all concerned with "fleshly" matters (2:22) means that they serve only to "indulge" the flesh, which belongs to the world in which Christians no longer live (v. 20).

Raised with Christ (3:1-4)

Paul turns from the negative ("if with Christ you died . . . ," 2:20) to the positive ("So if you have been raised with Christ . . ."). He often speaks of resurrection with Christ as a future event (Rom 6:5, 8; 1 Cor 15:22-23; 1 Thess 4:16), but here (picking up 2:12-13) he emphasizes that Christians already share the risen life of Christ (cf. Rom 6:4, 11; Gal 2:19-20). Nevertheless, the tension between what has already been achieved for them and what is still to come (3:4) is clear. Christ's resurrection is interpreted as exaltation to God's right hand, an echo of Ps 110:1 and a familiar idea in the NT (e.g., Mark 14:62 and pars.; Rom 8:34).

The imagery is spatial — the earth below, and God enthroned above it — but the conviction is parallel to that expressed in 2:17 in temporal terms. In the heavenly realm, as in the age to come, God's will is already done. The implication is that Christians who share Christ's risen life are living a life that is concerned with the things that are above, where Christ now rules (see Phil 3:20 for a similar idea; cf. also Eph 2:6). Paul urges the Colossians to set their minds on these heavenly concerns (3:1, 2) in contrast to "things that are on the earth" — the things that he has disparaged in 2:20-23 as belonging to "the world" (2:20; Gk. *kosmos*), as "things that perish" (v. 22), and as "flesh" (v. 23 mg., Gk. *sarx*). He insists that they have died to these things (3:3, echoing 2:20). Although the vocabulary is different, the logic is similar to that which underlies Paul's argument in Romans 7 and Galatians 4, where the law is seen as operating in the field of the flesh, not the Spirit.

The idea that their life is hidden with Christ picks up the apocalyptic imagery used in 1:26 and 2:3. There the mystery that was hidden was Christ himself, but now it is their life that is hidden "with Christ." The language expresses vividly the tension between the idea that Christians have already in a sense been raised with Christ and yet are awaiting final resurrection. Their life is "hidden" because it belongs to the world above and will be revealed only when Christ, who is their life, is himself revealed. The imagery reminds us of Jesus' parables of seeds that are sown in the ground, where they are hidden until they burst into life (Mark 4:1-34 and pars.; cf. 1 Cor 15:35-38). The hope spoken of in 1:5, 23, 27 will be fulfilled when Christ himself is finally revealed; then God's hidden purpose that men and women should share Christ's glory will be realized. Thus the emphasis on what has already taken place ("you have been raised with Christ") is balanced by the assurance of their future glorification with Christ (cf. Rom 8:18, 21, 29; Phil 3:20-21). The parenesis that follows is based on both convictions.

Negative and Positive Teaching (3:5-17)

This section begins with negative commands. As so often, the imperative is based on the indicative: those who *have died* (3:3) must *put to death* everything in them that belongs to the earth. Lists of vices and virtues were common in both Jewish and Greek ethical teaching, and occur elsewhere in Paul, for example, in Rom 1:29-31; Gal 5:19-23. Paul here gives two lists of vices, the first (3:5) mainly sexual, the second (v. 8) chiefly concerned with personal relationships: condemnation of these particular vices is thoroughly Jewish, and there are many parallels in the OT and intertestamental writings. Although divine wrath, too, would have been familiar to those from a Gentile background, Paul's expectation is again Jewish: the wrath of God punishes both Gentile sinners (Isa 13; 34:1-4; 1 Thess 1:10) and unfaithful Jews (Zeph 1:14-18; 1QS 2:15; 5:12; Rom 2:5, 8-9). The vices that had characterized their former existence as members of a pagan society are no longer appropriate (3:7).

The metaphor now changes slightly: instead of putting sins to death (3:5), they are to put them off, lay them aside like discarded clothes (v. 8; cf. Rom 13:12). More than this, just as the Colossian believers have themselves died and been raised (2:20; 3:1), so now they are said to have stripped off the old self and put on the new (3:9-10). Although the NRSV translation disguises the link, the verb "to strip off" *(apekdyomai)* echoes what was said in 2:11 about believers "stripping off" the body of flesh in Christ's death and in 2:15 about Christ "stripping" himself of the alien powers controlling the world. Paul picks up the image here in order to remind the Colossians again of the theological basis of his ethical appeal.

Believers have stripped off "the old self." In order to recognize the significance of what Paul is saying we need to know that the Greek here is *anthrōpos,* "man"; the ideas he is using are those which he expresses elsewhere in terms of Adam and Christ. Life "in Adam" is characterized by sin, and it is "the old man" (life lived in accordance with Adam) that has been crucified with Christ (Rom 6:6) or "stripped off." But those who are "in Christ" share his righteousness (Rom 5:12-21) because they have put on "the new man" (cf. Rom 13:14 and Gal 3:27, where Christ himself is "put on") and are being conformed to the likeness of Christ (3:10).

The phrase "according to the image" is an exact echo of Gen 1:26 (LXX): a new creation is taking place (cf. 2 Cor 5:17; Gal 6:15). But the image of God (the Creator), according to whom believers are being renewed, is none other than Christ himself (1:15; 2 Cor 4:4). The idea that believers take on *his* image is found elsewhere in Paul (Rom 8:29; 1 Cor 15:49; 2 Cor 3:18), and it is always a process, not yet completed (cf. Rom 12:2; 2 Cor 4:18; Phil 3:21). When it is, they will attain full knowledge of God (cf. 1:9-10), and God's original purpose in creation will be realized.

In this new humanity (3:11; the Greek is simply *hopou,* "where") the old divisions, once so important, are no longer relevant. The reminder that the new people of God included Gentiles as well as Jews may indicate that Paul was worried that Jewish Christians might be exerting pressure on the community (cf. 2:8-23); but this inclusion of the "uncircumcised" was undoubtedly an important theme in Paul's gospel — and to him a continuing source of wonder! — whether there was opposition or not (cf. 1 Cor 12:13; Gal 3:28). Unusually, Paul includes in his list of opposing pairs two terms — "barbarian" and "Scythian" (regarded as the worst kind of barbarian) — which are almost synonymous: from the Greek point of view, *these* were the "outsiders," but they, too, can be reconciled to God and recreated in Christ, who is (as was stated in 1:15-20) "all and in all."

3:12 begins, in Greek, with the command "Put on, therefore," balancing the negative command in v. 8. Once again the imperative builds on the indicative: those who have clothed themselves with "the new self" (v. 10) must clothe themselves with the appropriate characteristics. Paul reminds the Colossians of what it means to be God's "holy" people (Gk. *hagioi* = "saints," 1:2), "chosen" and "beloved." These three terms all belonged, in Jewish tradition, to Israel.

The five virtues balance the five vices in 3:8 (for similar contrasting lists, cf. 1QS 4:3-12), being concerned, like them, with personal relationships. "Humility," disparaged in 2:18, 23, is included in the list (cf. Phil 2:3, 8), but here it denotes a modest attitude toward others, while there it referred to religious practices which led those who observed them to be "puffed up." 3:13 is a clear recognition that Christians are not yet perfect! There is an echo of Jesus' teaching in the link between forgiveness received and forgiveness offered (Matt 18:22-35; cf. 6:12, 14-15), as in the emphasis on love (Mark 12:29-31 and pars.). As elsewhere, love is of supreme importance (Rom 13:8-10; 1 Cor 13:13) because it binds the community together. Not surprisingly, then, Paul reminds the Colossians that they have been called "in the one body."

In 3:15-16 Paul prays that the peace of Christ (into whose kingdom they were transferred, 1:13, and through whom all things have been reconciled, 1:20) may rule in their hearts, and that the word of Christ may dwell richly among them. This will enable them to teach and admonish one another in all wisdom, so carrying on Paul's own proclamation of the gospel (1:28). Thankfulness (mentioned three times in 3:15-17) should characterize everything they do, not only in worship (v. 16) but also in their everyday lives since these are now lived "in the name of the Lord Jesus" (v. 17), who is "all in all" (v. 11).

Household Rules (3:18–4:1)

This passage, a somewhat humdrum list of instructions to various groups, seems to have no real connection with what surrounds it, but there is no textual evidence to support the suggestion that it is a later addition to the letter. There are similar instructions, not only in the NT (notably Eph 5:22–6:9, almost certainly based on this passage) but also in contemporary Jewish and Stoic literature. Philo, for example, interprets the fifth commandment as concerned with relations between old and young, rulers and subjects, benefactors and benefited, slaves and masters (*Decal.* 165–67; cf. Josephus *Ag. Ap.* 2.199-208). This does not mean, as is often suggested, that Paul took over a "ready-made" list. What it does indicate is that the concerns expressed here were common in his world.

Is there anything particularly "Christian" about the Colossian list? It was unusual in the Greek world to address the "inferior" partners in the relationships; here they are treated as responsible members of the community. Yet the commands addressed to the three subservient groups — to submit and to obey — hardly support the suggestion that the relationships were reciprocal! These commands offend our twenty-first-century attitudes, and so evoke criticism. Paul seems merely to be defending the status quo (cf. also 1 Cor 7:17-24) and failing to apply the radical implications of the gospel which he himself sets out elsewhere (Gal 3:28). We expect him to challenge the social structures of his age, forgetting that for him (as for Philo) they were seen as part of the divine ordering of things (cf. Rom 13:1-7). The submission he expected wives to show their husbands, and the obedience demanded from children and slaves, seemed to him appropriate attitudes in a universe in which Christ was supreme. Hence these groups are told repeatedly that what is required of them is fitting "in the Lord" (3:18, 20, 22-24). But those who exercise authority — husbands, fathers, and masters — are also under authority and must behave responsibly, for, as masters are reminded in 4:1, they have a Lord (= Master) in heaven. It is worth noting that the three terms "Husband," "Father," and "Master" (Gk. *kyrios,* "Lord") were all used in the OT to describe the relationship of God to his people; it is hardly surprising, therefore, if Paul expects these people to exercise divine authority (cf. also Eph 3:14-15).

The instructions, then, are ones with which many of Paul's contemporaries, both Jewish and Greek, would have agreed. The Christian emphasis is seen in the frequent references to "the Lord," and these give us a clue as to what the verses are doing here since in effect they spell out one way of fulfilling the command in 3:17.

One odd feature of the list is the imbalance in the attention given to the duties of slaves. Some have suggested that this teaching is aimed at Onesimus, who is referred to in 4:9 and is known to have been a slave (Phlm 16); but Onesimus was apparently a bearer of the letter rather than a recipient. This particular emphasis is probably due to the large number of slaves in the Christian community: they would be in special need of the encouragement Paul provides here, reminding them that even they will receive an inheritance from the Lord (3:24; cf. 1:12; Gal 3:28-29). Is it wrongdoers among the slaves who will be punished (3:25) or is the reference to masters? The ambiguity is perhaps deliberate since "there is no partiality," and masters, too, are answerable to the Lord in heaven (4:1).

Paul's teaching advocates the Christian attitudes that were appropriate within contemporary social structures: on the one hand, acceptance of obedience "as to the Lord," on the other, love, compassion, and justice (3:19, 21; 4:1). Yet it was the acceptance of these words into the canon which strengthened the conviction that the structures themselves were part of the divine plan and therefore could not be challenged.

Concluding Instructions (4:2-6)

Paul now addresses the whole community, urging them to persevere in prayer and reminding them, once again, to give thanks (1:12; 2:7; 3:15, 17). Just as he prayed and gave thanks for them (1:3, 9), so he expects them, in turn, to pray for him. In prison he hopes for an open door — not necessarily release but, far more important, the opportunity to proclaim the gospel.

The Colossians, too (4:5-6), must make the most of their opportunity to proclaim that gospel by their behavior to "outsiders"; the vocabulary echoes what was said in 1:9-10 and 2:6. 4:6 may be more specific than the NRSV translation suggests since it concerns "your word" (Gk. *logos,* as in v. 3). That would give more point to Paul's instructions: they need to deliver the message with charm and "salt" — that is, make it interesting — and be prepared to respond when they are questioned about their faith.

Closing Greetings (4:7-18)

The letter is conveyed to Colossae by Paul's colleague Tychicus (cf. Acts 20:4) and Onesimus (Phlm 10-21), who is from Colossae. Both are described as brothers and as faithful and beloved. The news they bring of Paul will encourage the community (cf. 2:2).

Various individuals known to the church send greetings: Aristarchus, Paul's fellow prisoner, is mentioned in Acts (19:29; 20:4; 27:2). According to Acts 15:36-41, Paul and Barnabas fell out over Mark, but the breach appears to have been healed. Nothing is known about Jesus Justus — except that, like the others, he was "of the circumcision." Paul's comment that they were the "only" Jews among his co-workers suggests regret and a sense of isolation. But if he thinks that the Colossians may come under pressure from Judaizers, then it is perhaps intended to encourage them: Paul's other co-workers are presumably Gentiles, like themselves! It is notable that, in spite of the emphasis placed on Christ in Colossians, what they are striving for is the kingdom of God. Epaphras, who first brought them the gospel (1:7), receives special commendation. 4:14 provides the information that Luke (cf. Phlm 24) was a doctor.

Paul himself sends greetings to two other churches via the Colossians: they are to exchange letters with the Laodiceans (cf. 2:1). Of this letter there is no trace; the suggestion that it was Ephesians requires that the letters were by the same author, while Philemon seems too personal to be intended for exchange (unless Paul wants support from the Colossians for the request made in that letter, and Archippus (4:17) is the key figure — see the commentary on Philemon). The reference to a "task," and the description of Archippus in Phlm 2 as Paul's fellow soldier suggest rather that Archippus had responsibility for the Laodicean church.

The conclusion in the author's own hand authenticates the letter. The reference to his chains reminds his readers of his suffering for the gospel and so of his authority. But his last word concerns God's grace.

Bibliography. Arnold, C. E. 1995, *The Colossian Syncretism,* WUNT 2.77, Tübingen: J. C. B. Mohr (Paul Siebeck) • Barclay, J. M. G. 1997, *Colossians and Philemon,* Sheffield: Sheffield Academic • Bruce, F. F. 1984, *The Epistles to the Colossians, to Philemon, and to the Ephesians,* NICNT, Grand Rapids: Eerdmans • Burney, C. F. 1926, "Christ as the APXH of Creation," *JTS* 27:160-77 • Caird, G. B. 1976, *Paul's Letters from Prison,* New Clarendon Bible, Oxford: Oxford University • Dibelius, M. 1917, "The Isis Initiation in Apuleius and Related Initiatory Rites," ET in Francis and Meeds. 1973, 61-121 • Dunn, J. D. G. 1995, "The Colossian Philosophy: A Confident Jewish Apologia," *Bib* 76:153-81; • Dunn, J. D. G. 1966, *The Epistles to the Colossians and to Philemon,* NIGTC, Grand Rapids: Eerdmans and Carlisle: Paternoster • Flemington, W. F. 1981, "On the Interpretation of Colossians 1:24" in William Horbury and Brian McNeil, eds., *Suffering and Martyrdom in the New Testament,* Cambridge: Cambridge University, 84-90 • Francis, F. O. 1963, "Humility and Angelic Worship in Col 2:18," *ST* 16:109-34; repr. in Francis and Meeks 1973, 163-95 • Francis, F. O, and W. A. Meeks, eds. 1973, *Conflict at Colossae,* SBLSBS 4, Missoula: Scholars • Hooker, M. D. 1973, "Were There False Teachers in Colossae?" in B. Lindars and S. S. Smalley, eds., *Christ and Spirit in the New Testament,* Cambridge: Cambridge University, 315-31; repr. in Hooker 1990 • Hooker, M. D. *From Adam to Christ,* Cambridge: Cambridge University • Houlden, J. L. 1970, *Paul's Letters from Prison,* Pelican Commentary, Harmondsworth: Penguin, 1970; London: SCM • Lightfoot, J. B. 1876, *St Paul's Epistles to the Colossians and to Philemon,* London: Macmillan • Lohse, E. 1968, *Colossians and Philemon,* ET, Philadelphia: Fortress • Pokorný, P. 1991, *Colossians: A Commentary,* ET, Peabody, Mass.: Hendrickson • Rowland, C. 1983, "Apocalyptic Vision and the Exaltation of Christ in the Letter to the Colossians," *JSNT* 19:73-83 • Sappington, T. J. 1991, *Revelation and Redemption at Colossae,* JSNTSup 53, Sheffield: JSOT • Schweizer, E. 1982, *The Letter to the Colossians,* ET, London: SPCK • Wedderburn, A. J. M. 1993, "The Theology of Colossians," in A. J. M. Wedderburn and A. T. Lincoln, *New Testament Theology: The Theology of the Later Pauline Letters,* ed. J. D. G. Dunn, Cambridge: Cambridge University, 3-71 • Wright, N. T. 1986, *The Epistles of Paul to the Colossians and to Philemon,* TNTC, Leicester: Inter-Varsity Press and Grand Rapids: Eerdmans • Yates, R. 1985-86, "'The Worship of Angels' (Col 2:18)," *ExpTim* 97:12-15 • Yates, R. 1993, *The Epistle to the Colossians,* Epworth Commentary, London: Epworth.

1 and 2 Thessalonians

Robert K. Jewett

INTRODUCTION

The earliest letters that we have from Paul are directed to the Thessalonian Christians. Interest has traditionally concentrated on the apocalyptic teachings contained therein, but recently there has developed a very lively discussion of the way Paul interacted with the Thessalonian audience. In the last decade or so these two small letters have become some of the most hotly debated documents in the NT. Since they reflect the earliest accessible stage of Paul's pastoral and missionary endeavors and provide our earliest glimpse into a nascent Pauline congregation, 1 and 2 Thessalonians are profoundly significant both for understanding the development of early Christianity and for nourishing faith today.

Since every commentary is based on assumptions the author draws from his or her assessment of the evidence, a brief sketch of my viewpoint may be useful. My approach combines traditional historical-critical research with insights from socio-rhetorical and theological reflection. Although some would argue to the contrary, I have concluded that both of these letters were written by Paul in their canonical sequence and that there are no interpolations or partitions that need to be taken into account. The letters were written within a short time of one another in AD 50, interacting with a rapidly developing crisis in Thessalonica caused by misunderstandings of Paul's proclamation of a new age arriving with Christ. This commentary seeks to explain Paul's responses to the congregational crisis, assuming that his letters represent one half of dialogues that took the viewpoint and situation of his congregations into account.

The first letter fits the demonstrative genre of rhetoric, attempting to clarify the congregation's orientation in the new age by a combination of thanksgiving, praise, and exhortation. In response to misunderstandings of this first letter and a deepening of the crisis, Paul writes 2 Thessalonians in the deliberative genre, reproving misconceptions about the new age and demanding strenuous responses to the congregation's troublemakers. The significant differences in tone reflect Paul's changing relationship to the developing crisis. Both letters thus contain materials that are particularly relevant for cultures and groups grappling with the promises and disappointments of brave new worlds.

The Situation of the Christian Community in Thessalonica

When Paul arrived in Thessalonica in the summer of AD 49, he found a large Roman city that had been in existence since Hellenistic times and now functioned as the capital of the province of Macedonia. The city commanded the trade routes through the Balkans, including the *Via Ignatia;* the location at the end of the Thermaic Gulf featured an important harbor that connected Thessalonica with sea routes throughout the Mediterranean. It was an important center of the Roman civic cult, with extensive evidence of honors granted to emperors and other Roman benefactors. Although Thessalonica has never been systematically excavated, lying as it does beneath the modern metropolis of Saloniki, there is evidence for the usual array of temples to the deities of the Greco-Roman mysteries (Hendrix 1992: 523-25).

A distinctive feature of Thessalonian piety was the worship of Cabirus, the benefactor of handworkers and protector of the city who was sometimes celebrated in orgiastic, phallic rites (Hemberg 1950: 203; Witt 1977: 72). His appearance on coins and public art points to a kind of "kabeiric monotheism" in Thessalonica (Witt 1977: 78; Hendrix 1984: 154). The story of this young man, depicted with a hammer in one hand and a drinking horn in the other, involved being murdered by his brothers but returning intermittently as the provider of "safety at sea, good luck in perils and ventures of various kinds, and greater righteousness" (Nock 1945: 577). This worship had apparently been incorporated into the Roman civic cult during the Augustan period, which transformed a benefactor of the laboring classes into a deity supporting an imperial establishment that benefited primarily the city elite.

Paul's references to his missionary proclamation (1 Thess 1:9) and to the congregational situation indicate that most of his converts were Greek handworkers and tradesmen. Despite references in Acts 17:4-9 and 20:4 to upper-class patrons, Paul's admonition that all the converts should work with their own hands (1 Thess 4:11) and the lack of any reference to slaves or slave owners indicate a congregation predominantly of low but free social standing. He refers in 2 Cor 8:2-4 to the "extreme poverty" of the Macedonian converts, which matches Hock's description of the penurious status of handworkers in other Roman cities (Hock 1980: 34-36). Their extraordinary response (1 Thess 1:2-9; 2:13-14) to Paul's proclamation of the crucified and resurrected Christ as an apocalyptic benefactor may reflect the religious vacuum that had been created in Thessalonica by the cooptation of the Cabirus cult.

The outbreak of civil disorder soon after Paul began his mission in Thessalonica probably was provoked by "their offensive abandonment of common Greco-Roman religion" (Barclay 1992: 514) as well as by the suspicion of subversion (Acts 17:7) because belief in Christ as a benevolent world ruler seemed to threaten Roman security (Judge 1971: 1-7). This unrest led to Paul's premature departure. Feeling that he and the congregation had been "made orphans" (1 Thess 2:17) by this enforced separation, Paul sent Timothy back as an envoy from Athens to provide encouragement (1 Thess 3:1-2) (Mitchell 1992: 660-62). Timothy's report led Paul to write 1 Thessalonians, and although its tone is encouraging, the letter reveals some serious problems:

- From 1 Thess 4:13-18 it is likely that having discounted the possibility of death in the new age, the Thessalonians were inclined to despair when members died, apparently believing they would never see them again.
- From 1 Thess 5:1-11, I infer that the congregation resisted preparedness for the parousia and appears to feel that believers should be completely secure and free from the threat of judgment in the new age.
- When 1 Thess 5:19-22 is examined in the light of 1 Thess 1:5-6; 5:6, 8, it appears that there were conflicts over charismatic manifestations in Thessalonica between those claiming that the spirit was beyond human evaluation and those who sought to stamp it out because of its disorderly potential.
- When 1 Thess 5:12-13 is viewed in the light of 1 Thess 2:1-12, I infer that there were tendencies in the congregation to disrespect the leaders Paul had left in charge and to question both them and Paul on grounds that they were not sufficiently charismatic.
- 1 Thess 4:1-8 reveals that some of the Thessalonian believers resist the traditional sexual ethic that Paul had taught and wish to justify breaking across legal and religious standards of marriage.
- In 1 Thess 5:12-14 it is clear that a group of *ataktoi* ("the disorderly ones") are abandoning their occupations and are being supported by the congregation; they resist order on principle. This is a situation that worsens over time, as indicated by 2 Thess 3:6-15.

The most comprehensive, though hotly debated, explanation for these peculiar features of the congregational situation, which are quite dissimilar to the contours of any other NT group, is that the Thessalonians were inclined toward "millenarian radicalism" (Jewett 1986: 176-78). They apparently interpreted the apocalyptic "Jesus, who rescues us from the wrath that is coming" (1 Thess 1:10), as a kind of Cabirus figure who would bring a final cessation of earthly troubles. In their ecstatic celebrations of the love feast, they felt that the new age was fully present and thus that death had been abolished and bodily responsibilities lifted. This inflated form of realized eschatology, similar in some respects to later millenarian movements, was thrown into crisis because of the continuation of persecution, the death of congregational members, and the absence of Paul. The encouraging tone of the letter, marked by the longest thanksgiving in the Pauline correspondence (1:2–3:13), does not therefore reflect an unproblematic situation. It expresses the kind of clarification and reassurance that Paul thought would most readily address this threatened collapse of faith.

The writing of 2 Thessalonians very soon afterward indicates that the congregation still failed to grasp the "already/not yet" scheme of Pauline eschatology. They misinterpreted the first letter as if Paul actually taught that "the day of the Lord has already come" (2 Thess 2:2), a conclusion so bizarre that Paul wondered whether forgery had occurred (2 Thess 2:2, 15; 3:17). When one reads 1 Thessalonians from the perspective of millennial radicalism, however, several passages could well have been misunderstood along these lines (Jewett 1986: 186-90). It is clear that sometime betweeen the writing of these two letters, some of the congregation developed the conviction that the unexpected had in fact occurred and no further vigilance was required. 2 Thessalonians was designed to refute this radically realized eschatology and to discipline the *ataktoi* who were likely responsible.

An understanding of the social circumstances of the Pauline congregation in Thessalonica is essential to understanding both letters, especially if the apocalyptic radicalism is to be taken into account. The rapid development of the crisis and the frequent allusions to the spirit (1 Thess 1:5-6; 4:8; 5:19, 23; 2 Thess 2:2, 8, 13) point to a highly intense charismatic community with a strongly familial ethos. This group is spending a great deal of time together, developing an intensity of devotion, emotional involvement, and radicality similar to modern sectarian groups. Paul recalls in 1 Thess 2:9 that he had "worked night and day, so that we might not burden any of you while we proclaimed to you the gospel of God," which indicates that the workshop was the "social setting for missionary activities. . . . During the long hours at his workbench cutting and sewing leather to make tents, Paul would not only have been supporting himself, but he would also have had opportunities to carry on missionary activity" (Hock 1979: 449-50). This correlates with other evidence in the NT that alongside house churches meeting in the houses or apartments of patrons there were "tenement churches" that met in the workshops and living spaces of the high-rise *insula* ("tenement") buildings of Roman cities (Jewett 1993a: 26-31; 1994b: 73-86). These buildings had a kind of vertical zoning, with shops and working spaces on the first floor, larger apartments for well-to-do tenants on the second and third floors, and crowded spaces for slaves and the urban underclass on the upper floors. In place of the "patriarchalism of love" that marked house churches in which patrons provided dominant leadership as well as the provisions for the love feast/Lord's Supper, tenement churches were marked by "agapaic communalism" in which the provisions for the meals came "from the sharing of the members" (Jewett 1994a: 51).

The rule for a love feast cited in 2 Thess 3:10 reveals the development of a system in which the regular evening meal was provided by contributions from the members rather than being provided by patrons (Jewett 1993a: 33-39; 1994b: 83-86). This is also reflected in 1 Thess 4:9-12, which centers on "brotherly love," implying that Christians are in some sense living together as a new fictive family, replacing their families of origin. The extraordinary weight Paul gives to the bond between members of the new Christian family is somewhat disguised by the traditional translation used by the NRSV, "for you yourselves have been taught to love one another." Paul actually refers to their being *theodidaktoi* ("God-taught") in such love, a term that likely was coined by Paul. The purpose of being "God-taught" was *philadelphia* ("brotherly love") in 4:9, which refers to the distinctive form of common life that marked early Christian congregations, namely, the love feast which replaced the pagan festivals. The sharing of resources and feeding of the poor are being accomplished here by a Christian form of brotherly love (Jewett 1993a: 39-43). The God who instructs the Thessalonian Christians about performing this kind of love is clearly the parent of Jesus Christ (1 Thess 1:10), understood to be the Lord of the Feast.

The same linkage between manual labor, eating, earning bread for the community, and brotherhood is found in 2 Thess 3:6-13, which includes the rule about not feeding persons refusing to work and ends with the admonition, "brothers, do not be weary in doing good." The "good" in this instance is not some euphemism about general responsibility; in this context it refers to supporting a community whose life centered in a love feast dependent on the contributions of each member. The translation of this passage needs to be carefully rendered so as to remove the individualistic and capitalistic slant that disguises the link to the communal meal. For instance, the admonition in the NRSV that the members should "do their work quietly and earn their own living" (2 Thess 3:12) actually should read "working with quietness, they eat their own bread" (Wanamaker 1990: 287). There is no implication in the Greek text that each person or family should be economically independent or eat separately, but rather that the community as a whole should avoid dependency. The way to do so is for each person to continue doing the "good" of contributing to the common meal. This is why the refusal of the *ataktoi* to work with their hands posed such a lethal threat to the community, rendering essential Paul's correction of the apocalyptic confusion that led to their actions.

In conclusion, to understand 1 and 2 Thessalonians, it is necessary to grasp that the apocalyptically formulated theological and ethical arguments which sound so esoteric to the modern ear were directly tied to the community's common life. The imagination of the interpreter therefore needs to be nourished not by analogies to traditional, noncharismatic mainline churches marked by distant relationships and a reluctance to share but rather by some sectarian communities where formal and informal types of communalism are practiced.

1 Thessalonians

COMMENTARY

Introduction and the Great Thanksgiving (1:1–3:13)

The communal dimensions of early church life in Thessalonica are evident in the prescript of 1:1, with three persons writing the letter (Paul, Silvanus, and Timothy) and the audience referred to as the assembly "of the Thessalonians in God . . . and . . . Christ." Alongside the other assemblies in the city, the Christians are together in a mystical association determined by the "grace and peace" that come from God and Christ. The thanksgiving of vv. 2-5 lifts up the mystical dimension of shared prayer in which Paul is "constantly remembering" the Thessalonians. If Paul habitually works "night and day" (2:9) in the workspace of a tenement building, the locale of such prayer must be the workshop itself where the common life of the community is centered.

The thanksgiving which sets the theme of the letter bears directly on the issue of inflated expectations. Paul's therapy was to begin by giving thanks for the foundation of faith, love, and hope that had already been laid in the lives of the Thessalonians. For the Thessalonian Christians had indeed been granted faith, hope, and love as a result of the gospel. The mercy of God conveyed to them in the gospel about the death and resurrection of Christ had touched a chord deep inside them, overcoming their shameful status and stirring them to a realization of their unconditional acceptance by God. So what Paul does is to clarify the active and realistic potential in what they had already experienced.

Three marvelously succinct expressions outline Paul's reality therapy for the confused Thessalonians. The first of these expressions that they had experienced is "the work of faith" (1:3). The words appear at first glance to be a contradiction: "work" seems oddly joined to its opposite, "faith." What Paul had in mind is understandable when the collapsed expectations in Thessalonica are kept in view. The "work of faith" implies an active relationship with God, a constant working through of the problems it presents. Faith for Paul is not the easy solution to the burdens of life anticipated by the millenarian radicals. Faith is the basis for living in a world where only provisional answers are available; so it is always "working," active, risk taking, and thereby capable of maturity.

The second expression Paul uses in his campaign of reality therapy is "the labor of love" (1:3). The term "labor" refers to a sensitive issue in that some of the leaders had dropped out of the tedium of labor for their daily bread. So Paul reminds them of the exhilarating activity that love had evoked in them at the beginning, before the mythic expectations of the culture had begun to filter back in again. They had spontaneously wanted to do loving acts for others and had found an amazing wellspring of activity gushing within them — actions not to quell guilt feelings but to express to others the love of God that overflowed within them as "beloved by God" (v. 4).

The third expression Paul used is equally provocative and apt. "We give thanks to God . . . remembering . . . your work of faith and labor of love and *steadfastness of hope* in our Lord Jesus Christ." The need for "steadfastness" rests on the realization that hope is something different from the expectation that whatever the heart desires will magically be provided. This addresses what the Thessalonians had discovered, leading to their despair, that antagonisms, persecutions, disease, and death remained the order of the day for Christians. The millenarian fantasy of a safe cocoon where all hopes would quickly be fulfilled did not come true. But as Paul describes it, something much more deeply satisfying had already been theirs. He thanks God that the Thessalonians had already demonstrated "the steadfastness of hope" in the transcendent Lord of history whose purposes are never flatly identical with culturally determined dreams. By placing the anchor of their hope in God, they could gain the courage to be "steadfast" under whatever pressures might unfold.

The foundation of the new life that the Thessalonians had received was their chosenness to be the beloved children of God and hence "brothers and sisters" of each other (1:4). The awareness of this new relationship of honorable, filial solidarity that includes Paul as well as the Thessalonians came as a result of the "message of the gospel" which had struck them with the convincing force of the spirit (v. 5). James Boyce refers in this connection "to the dynamic partnership of preacher and hearer, of God and God's children, of ambassador and hearer of the gospel, that enlivens and continually expresses the dynamic reality of Christian faith" (Boyce 1992: 142). The "joy inspired by the Holy Spirit" which they had shared along with Paul in the daily love feasts in tenement buildings and house churches was so powerful that word of their enthusiasm had spread to the other churches throughout the region.

As Paul goes on to narrate the grounds for his thanksgiving, it becomes even more clear that he is attempting to clarify the meaning of their faith which has recently been thrown into question. Their conversion involved turning "to God from idols, to serve a living and true God" (1:9), but this decisive alteration in worldview did not relieve them of the necessity to be steadfast in the face of ongoing difficulties as the millenarian radicals had hoped. It placed them instead in a position of needing "to wait for his Son from heaven" who alone would be able to rescue them "from the wrath that is coming" (v. 10). Meanwhile, waiting implies living with unresolved adversities while continuing to celebrate the new relationship with God and each other.

In 2:1-12 Paul clarifies the apostolic example of Christian life in a way that directly addresses the question of whether adversity should be expected to be eliminated by the presence of the new age. Although the ministry of Paul and his colleagues in Thessalonica had not been "in vain" (v. 1) in ushering in the new age, it had been preceded and accompanied by persecution. Paul had been "shamefully mistreated at Philippi" (v. 2), which correlates with Acts' account of being beaten with rods and imprisoned as ordinary criminals (Acts 16:22-40). Those whom God honors with a new identity in Christ are treated with dishonor by the world (deSilva 1996: 63). The gospel had similarly been preached in Thessalonica "in spite of great opposition" (1 Thess 2:2).

The apostolic ethos is clarified in 2:3-8 by contrasting it with other forms of leadership that were popular in the culture and were reemerging in the Thessalonian congregation in the form of the *ataktoi* (Jewett 1986: 151-57). Paul's message was not based on "deceit," a term often associated with philosophic and religious charlatans that reappears in 2 Thess 2:11 in connection with the delusory message that the day of the Lord had already arrived. The shape of this deceit is visible in the first letter as well, where Paul critiques the misguided doctrine of eschatological "peace and security" promoted by the radicals (1 Thess 5:3). That Paul had not been motivated by "impure motives," a term used elsewhere to refer to sexual behavior (1 Thess 4:7; Rom 1:24; 6:19; 2 Cor 12:21; Gal 5:19), contrasts his commitment to a disciplined life with those questioning the validity of the marital ethic (1 Thess 4:1-8). "Trickery" (2:3) was the mark of religious charlatans in the Greco-Roman world who claimed to be able to relieve the burdens of finitude through magic; Paul's contention is that such manipulations have no place in Christ.

Rather than claiming magical powers, Paul simply claims to have been "approved by God" in his preaching of the gospel, which legitimates "his right to offer parenetic instruction and to use himself as a model for his converts" (Wanamaker 1990: 96). To be "entrusted with the message of the gospel," as Paul and his colleagues were, and as the Thessalonian believers now are, meant to be set free from the culturally approved desire to "please mortals" by promising the fulfillment of wishes. The message of Christ crucified and resurrected overturned the values and expectations of the world, exposing its wishes as hostility against God. There was no further need for "flattery" (2:5), the characteristic tool of Greco-Roman rhetoric and political manipulation, whose goal was to gain "praise from mortals" (v. 6) and ultimately to line one's own pocket at the expense of others. The grace of God eliminates the need for such praise, allowing believers to face the truth. Even those filled with the spirit in the new age remain vulnerable, so any expectation of exemption from adversity is illusory.

The reminder that Paul had not used flattery as a "pretext for greed," even though he had a perfect right to make "demands as apostles of Christ" (2:5, 7), had a direct bearing on the question of whether certain members of the congregation, the *ataktoi,* could legitimately claim to be supported by others. The more accurate translation of this phrase is probably "motive of greed" (Wanamaker 1990: 97), which implies an unworthy rationale in the behavior of the Thessalonian dropouts. Rather than exploiting his fellow believers, Paul and his colleagues had been "like a nurse tenderly caring for her own children" (v. 7). Here he extends the metaphor favored by Stoic philosophers, depicting their responsible care for others (Malherbe 1970: 211-14; Gaventa 1990: 193-207), because a nurse caring for her own children is motivated by familial bonds as well as duty. Rather than seeking personal benefits from the newly emerging systems of agapaic communalism in Thessalonica, he contributed to the extent of his ability from the meager earnings of a manual laborer. As v. 8 goes on to insist, sharing the gospel meant sharing "our own selves" as members of the new Christian family. The word translated here as "selves" is *psychē*, which includes Paul's physical activities in the workshop that consume so large a part of his waking hours, providing the basis not only for his monetary contributions to the love feasts but also for his method of sharing the gospel with those visiting the workshop.

In order to make the implications of the apostolic example even clearer in relation to the *ataktoi*, Paul recalls in 2:9-12 the specific details of his lifestyle. It had been marked by "labor and toil" that extended "day and night," that is, past the normal twelve-hour workday into the period after the evening meal. As noted earlier, this term "labor" had been combined with "love" in the opening thanksgiving of the letter, and Greco-Roman hearers of this letter would have understood the emphatic implications of the repetition. The contrast with the *ataktoi* is unmistakable in Paul's reminder that he and his colleagues had not sought to "burden any of you while we proclaimed the gospel of God" (v. 9); each had contributed his own fair share to the common life of the eschatological community. This is an essential component of what constituted "pure, upright, and blameless" conduct in relation to the other believers in the church (v. 10). Paul goes on to use another familiar metaphor to describe his relationship to the congregation, "like a father with his children" (v. 11) whose task is to encourage maturity suitable for God's "own kingdom and glory" (v. 12). The eschatological concept of the new age as a time of the restoration of human glory lost in Adam's fall is clearly in view here. Paul's hope is that this argument will clarify the nature of the new age so that the escapist, antisocial behavior of the *ataktoi* will not be accepted as normative. In contrast both to biblical and and Greco-Roman utopianism, glory is defined here in terms of the labor of love rather than the achievement of blissful leisure.

In 2:13-16 Paul goes on to clarify the example of the original Christian community in Judea that suffered adversity similar to that afflicting the Thessalonians. The point in this section, which has sometimes been inappropriately identified as a non-Pauline interpolation (see the account of the debate in Jewett 1986: 36-41), is to show that the gospel does not eliminate adversity as the millenarian radicals were assuming. Paul reiterates his thanksgiving that the Thessalonians themselves confirm this truth, having accepted his preaching "as God's word" (v. 13) even though it was surrounded by violent opposition. They and all other believers are "imitators of the churches of God in Christ Jesus that are in Judea" (v. 14), which suffered persecution from its inception.

Unfortunately, the NRSV persists in adding a comma between 2:14 and 15, implying that all Jews were involved in killing "both the Lord Jesus and the prophets." As Frank Gilliard has shown, the more appropriate way to understand this passage is without the comma inserted by modern editors, thus restricting Paul's allegation to those Jews directly involved in inciting the Roman authorities to crucify Jesus and persecuting the prophets (Gilliard 1989: 498). The charge that certain Jews also "drove us out" and hindered Paul and his colleagues "from speaking to the Gentiles so that they may be saved" (vv. 15-16) reflects zealotic opposition that plagued the Pauline mission until his final trip to Jerusalem when it finally ended his public ministry (Acts 21:27-36) (Reicke 1984: 145-52). Since Paul refers in 2 Cor 11:24 to having received the ceremonial thirty-nine stripes from Jewish authorities no less than five times, there is no doubt that this opposition was real. The Jewish zealots who opposed Paul apparently believed that his mission threatened the integrity of Israel's faith and undercut the support of the Jewish cause on the part of Gentile God-fearers.

The polemical language Paul used in 2:15-16 to describe the persecution of the Nazarenes in Judea is severe enough without the burden of the mistaken comma noted above, which makes the entire Jewish population responsible for these events. This has led to the designation of this passage as "polemical hyperbole" (Schlueter 1994: 120-23). While Paul's insistence that those who hindered the preaching of the gospel "displease God and oppose everyone" employed some stock phrases of anti-Jewish propaganda in the ancient world, it is clear that his framework is informed by an apocalyptic view of history (Wanamaker 1990: 115-16). The opposition that drove Jesus to the cross was viewed as part of an end-time scheme that required "a fixed measure or amount of sin to be committed in order to bring about judgment" (Marshall 1983: 80). It remains likely that the statement "God's wrath has overtaken them at last" (v. 16) refers to the massacre in Jerusalem that occurred a year before writing 1 Thessalonians; Roman authorities were reported to have killed twenty thousand to thirty thousand Jews in response to a nationalistic uprising (Jewett 1970-71: 205; Josephus *Ant.* 20.112; *J.W.* 2.224-27).

In 2:17–3:10 Paul continues the narrative describing the basis of his thanksgiving for the faith of the Thessalonian Christians, recalling the adversities and triumphs that mark the life of the new age. Although this section is reminiscent of the philosophical topic of friendship (Malherbe 1987: 72-73; Wanamaker 1990: 119-20), the address to "brothers" (2:17; 3:7), the reference to separation as being "orphaned" (2:17), and the intense level of emotional pain at separation (v. 17; 3:1) point to the familial nature of the relationship in Paul's churches. They are a new family, derived from various families of origin yet celebrating a common life together amid adversity. The paternal feeling Paul has as a father to the Thessalonian converts is eloquently expressed by the claim that they will constitute his "glory and joy" in the parousia (2:19-20).

The reference to Satan's hindrance (2:18) fits the apocalyptic framework in which evil is expected to increase until the parousia of "our Lord Jesus" (v. 19). It seems likely that this verse was misunderstood by the Thessalonians in the sense that if Satan's activity is increasing, the day of the Lord must be very near. Paul inadvertently adds fuel to this fire by making it clear that he expects to witness the parousia in his lifetime (v. 18). But Paul's main theme is the continuation of adversity, as he moves on in 3:1 to describe his anguish at being separated from his Christian family in Thessalonica. His colleague Timothy was sent back to "strengthen and encourage you for the sake of your faith" (v. 2), a clause that succinctly reveals the rhetorical genre and purpose of 1 Thessalonians as a whole. The rhetorical situation requiring Timothy's journey and the subsequent letter is stated in the next verse, "that no one would be shaken by these persecutions." Ernst Bammel has made a compelling case that *sainesthai* ("to shake, disturb") reflects the reactions of people facing a supreme crisis, but he assumes that the final tribulations will provide such shaking (Bammel 1981: 91-100). The concerns of Paul and his colleagues reveal that the shaking was already taking place, and as reconstructed in this commentary it consisted of the ongoing presence of persecution and death in a new age when such mortal adversity was thought by some to have been abolished. That Paul feared an abandonment of their faith as a result of this disillusionment and the dishonor of public disapproval (deSilva 1996: 64-67) is perfectly plain in v. 5: "I was afraid that somehow the tempter had tempted you and that our labor had been in vain." This verse alone should be sufficient to refute the often repeated claim that there was nothing seriously amiss in Thessalonica.

The report that Timothy brought back to Paul was immensely encouraging, that their "faith and love" and affection for Paul remain intact (3:6-7). With excitement of feeling so great that the sentence is not even completed, Paul relates the impact of this report that came when he himself was facing "all our distress and persecution" (v. 7). He had felt that life itself was hanging in the balance, but "now we live, if you continue to stand firm in the Lord" (v. 8). As with any good parent, his own well-being was inextricably tied to the well-being of his children. But he also wanted to make plain that the Thessalonians "were not the only ones suffering for the sake of the gospel of Christ . . ." (Wanamaker 1990: 136). Suffering goes with the territory, despite their illusions. Paul goes on to reiterate his thanksgiving to God "for all the joy that we feel before our God because of you" (v. 10), a joy that in the light of subsequent developments turns out to have been somewhat premature. His yearning to be able to return to Thessalonica to "restore whatever is lacking in your faith" was more nearly on target. The writing of 1 Thessalonians was an effort to fill this void, but in retrospect it is worth observing that of the classical Pauline triad mentioned in 1:3, only "faith" and "love" are reported here to be in order. "Hope" is missing here because it remained muddled despite Timothy's visit. The extent of the confusion becomes apparent in the shocking misunderstandings evident in 2 Thessalonians.

The narration of the grounds for Paul's thanksgiving is brought to a conclusion by the liturgical formula of 3:11-13, which has been called a "homiletic benediction" (Jewett 1969: 18-34) or an "intercessory wish-prayer" (Wiles 1974: 22-107). It recapitulates the themes of the preceding argument and provides a framework for the second half of the letter. The request that God "direct our way to you" recapitulates 2:17-19 and 3:10; that God should "make you increase and abound in love for one another and for all" recapitulates 1:3, 6-7; 2:9-12, 14; the reminder that the Paul and his colleagues also "abound in love for you" reiterates the matter of apostolic example in vv. 9-13; and the strengthening of the "hearts" of the congregation "at the parousia of our Lord Jesus Christ" recapitulates 1:10 and 2:19. The theme for the subsequent discussion of "holiness" sets the frame for 4:1-8; the theme of mutual "love" is picked up in vv. 9-12; the theme of the parousia ("coming") "with all his saints" introduces the issues of vv. 13-18 and 5:1-11; and the matter of being "blameless" covers the last two chapters of the letter, especially the series of moral admonitions in 5:12-22, recapitulated in v. 23. Moral and intellectual accountability are offered as a replacement for the congregation's tendency toward eschatological escapism in this powerful prayer. It not only opens a "window into Paul's personal prayer life" (Wanamaker 1990: 140) but also articulates the missing theme of hope in a responsible manner.

The Issue of Marriage (4:1-8)

The second half of 1 Thessalonians contains five proofs that address the issues that Timothy apparently reported to Paul. The transition is signaled by "finally" in 4:1, which marks the beginning of the last section of the letter, just as it does in 2 Cor 13:11 and Phil 4:8. The intimate address of "brothers" is used here again, emphasizing that the believers in Thessalonica are a family (Smith 1995: 104). "As the metaphorical children of the one father Christians were themselves brothers and sisters who were to behave toward one another as family members" (Wanamaker 1990: 147). The first admonition is quite general and sets the tone for all of the succeeding proofs: that they continue to live in accordance with the familial instructions they had already received, distinguishing them from the pagan world and providing their self-identity as the church in God and Christ. The rather elaborate request that they follow these instructions "more and more," along with the reiteration in 4:2 that the instructions came "through the Lord Jesus," suggests that there were tendencies in the congregation to abandon this ethic. Otherwise the first two verses of ch. 4 would be redundant and somewhat offensive in that no one enjoys being urged to do what one is already doing. This introduction reflects the situation of the congregation shaken from its overconfidence and now questioning whether the moral example of the *ataktoi* should be followed in place of Paul's original teaching.

Paul reiterates the strict marital ethic he and his colleagues had brought to the converts in Thessalonica, based on Judaic categories such as "sanctification," abstention "from fornication," and each male "taking a vessel for himself." The metaphor of the woman as the vessel for male sexual use was characteristic of Jewish marriage contracts (Tomson 1990: 91), and it is highly unlikely that the NRSV translation "control your own body" is correct. This translation avoids the chauvinistic implications of Paul's Judaic usage but disguises the starting point of Paul's remarkable later development of an egalitarian marital ethic in 1 Corinthians (Jewett 1994b: 45-58). The antithesis to "lustful passion, like the Gentiles who do not know God" (4:5), sharply differentiates this monogamous ethic from the more relaxed sexual ethic followed by most of the pagan world. If there was an inclination in the congregation to question the sexual ethic taught by Paul, this passage aims to show that a departure from the norm moves back into paganism and out of the Christian realm of divinely sanctioned holiness.

The formulation of 4:6, to "overreach and defraud a brother in this matter," refers to males defrauding other males of their sexual rights when they commit adultery (Wanamaker 1990: 155). It is obvious that at this early stage of Christian teaching Paul had not yet developed the egalitarian sexual ethic which addresses both males and females as active agents of moral decision making (1 Corinthians 6–7). The chauvinistic ethic in Thessalonians is sidestepped by the NRSV, which refers to exploiting "a brother or sister in this matter," which is hardly consistent with Paul's earlier reference to the wife as the *skeuos* ("vessel"). I think that it is better to admit the chauvinism in this passage (Jewett 1994b: 47-48) and attend to the urgency with which Paul insists that God is an avenger of sexual transgressions (4:6) and that whoever rejects this monogamous ethic "rejects not human authority but God" (v. 8). The extraordinary sanctions Paul adduces and the coercive language he employs "suggest very strongly that Paul was dealing with a problem that had actually emerged in the community at Thessalonica" (Wanamaker 1990: 158), probably as a result of the *ataktoi* challenging the marriage ethic as merely based on human opinion and deficient in the kind of spiritual freedom that they felt they had achieved in Christ. This could well explain why Paul reiterates at the end of v. 8 that God is the one "who also gives his Holy Spirit to you." Charismatic endowment for him was not the general spiritual enthusiasm of the Greco-Roman world, resulting in amoral behavior, but the presence of the Holy Spirit who infuses believers with holy thoughts and actions.

The Issue of Communal Self Reliance in Love (4:9-12)

As noted above in the Introduction, 4:9-12 deals with *philadelphia,* "brotherly love," that binds the early Christian communities into families that care for one another in every way. Christian conversion meant turning away from former family ties to the new family of the church. The expression "God-taught" is a "Pauline creation" that claims that the community of faith "is guided by God's Spirit, whose first fruit is love . . ." (Richard 1995: 215, 210). These small groups of converts in Thessalonica are devising new ways, day after day, of pooling their resources to provide for their love feasts/Lord's Suppers and to care for the sick, the young, and the indigent. Paul's audacious formulation reflects the miracle of human transformation, taking place among the poorest of the poor as well as among groups led by patrons of house churches, replacing the normal grasping for food and station and honor with a family sense that bound all together into a single, holy destiny. They are even managing to share with others "throughout Macedonia," which is an amazing indication of the creativity and productivity of these new groups, given the extreme poverty they are facing. The accounts of, and effects of, their hospitality and generosity are rippling throughout the region, in part because it was so extraordinary for groups on this social level suddenly to develop the resources and willingness to share with others. Paul encourages the Thessalonians "to do so more and more," using the verb for abundance which implies that in these new churches the power of the Spirit and the effort of transformed humans are overcoming the ethos of scarcity.

The admonition to "aspire to live quietly, to mind your own affairs" (4:11) implies the avoidance of political agitation (Hock 1980: 46-47) and a concentration of effort on the challenging task of supporting the common life of the small house and tenement churches. Since the admonition is to "you'll," so to speak, with "you" in the plural, it certainly does not imply that each person or family should withdraw from involvement with others. That each should contribute to the common life of the love feast is clearly implied in v. 11, which says that each should "work with your hands." This expression seems close to the Jewish expression "works of one's hands," implying that everyone should contribute in some way to the provision "of personal and community needs" (Richard 1990: 220). This had apparently been part of the initial instruction of converts in Thessalonica because Paul explicitly recalls, "as we directed you." This provides additional support for the impression stated in the Introduction that most of the Christian groups in Thessalonica appear to have been tenement churches rather than house churches. It would have been the former that would suffer the most from the refusal on the part of the *ataktoi* to continue working because they would have to be supported by the rest of the community (Wanamaker 1990: 163-64). If each person contributes his or her fair share, the new community of faith will "behave properly toward outsiders and be dependent on no one" (v. 12). It is crucial to understand this not in an individualistic sense but as a description of "Paul's ideal fellowship" based on "mutual dependence and sharing among members" (Richard 1995: 221-22).

The Issue of the Dead (4:13-18)

The third proof that addresses the issues Timothy apparently reported to Paul has to do with the consternation caused by the unexpected death of Christians. In our reconstruction of the millennial radicalism of this congregation, it appears that death was thought to have been abolished with the dawning of the new age, which explains why they would grieve "as others do who have no hope." An important effort to resolve this puzzle was made by Joseph Plevnik, who suggested that an apocalyptic doctrine of assumption into paradise as a way of escaping death had been taught by Paul, which the Thessalonians erroneously took to mean that those already dead would not be caught up, or raptured (Plevnik 1984: 274-83). They are lamenting "as though there is no afterlife or resurrection" (Richard 1995: 225) because, as I would explain it, having already been resurrected by their membership in the new age, there would be no further resurrection for those who have died. In effect, the congregation thinks it has already been raptured by means of its charismatic ecstasy, placing them beyond death. This would explain both the shock at the death of loved ones and the fear that they had "believed in vain." However one explains this unprecedented confusion on the part of the Thessalonians, it is clear that they "feared their dead would lose out on the chance to be assumed to heaven at the time of the parousia" (Wanamaker 1990: 172).

Paul addresses their inconsolable grief by affirming that the resurrected Lord "will bring with him those who have died" at the time of the parousia (4:14). On this point he claims to have the authority of a "word of the Lord," probably embodied in the tradition that was later inscribed in Matt 24:29-31, 40-41, concerning the return of Christ and the reuniting of all the saints (Wanamaker 1990: 171). This tradition proves, in Paul's thinking, that those who have already died will not be left behind (4:14) because all believers will be "caught up in the clouds together with them to meet the Lord in the air" (v. 17). In fact, those who have already died in the faith "will rise first" (v. 16), a conviction that Paul urges as the basis of mutual encouragement among the grieved in Thessalonica (v. 18).

It is important to observe that these verses, which have given rise to the modern doctrine of the "rapture," actually argue against the kind of separation between believers that contemporary Fundamentalism favors. Paul's "goal was to reassure the Thessalonians that their fellow Christians who had died would participate on equal terms with them in the salvation experience accompanying the parousia of the Lord" (Wanamaker 1990: 176). It is also clear from 4:13 that Paul expected that he and most of the Thessalonians would still be alive when the parousia occurred. Since the divine wisdom of God did not see fit to fulfill that expectation, it seems absurd for modern Christians to speculate on the details of this passage in order to discover when the "rapture" is scheduled to occur. It is enough to believe that whatever the schedule, and whatever losses believers suffer in the meanwhile, they will all be together "with the Lord forever" (v. 18).

The Issue of the Eschaton (5:1-11)

Paul begins the fourth proof (see 4:1 above) with a reminder of his previous teaching that the parousia would come when least expected, "like a thief in the night" (5:2). The need to reiterate this doctrine probably derived from the millenarian radicalism that marked some members of the congregation, believing that the end of time had already in some sense arrived and that they consequently had no more need to be concerned about accountability. Paul is required by this situation to lift up "the perspective of impending judgment and the possible threat that this might pose to Christians" (Wanamaker 1990: 178). He forcefully insists that there will be "no escape" at the parousia for those who complacently claim that they already enjoy "peace and security" (v. 3). While it is likely that Paul is employing a traditional apocalyptic formula at this point (Best 1972: 207; Collins 1984: 336), the sarcastic use of political slogans of "peace" and "security" characteristic of Roman propaganda (Donfried 1985: 350; Elias 1995: 194) would not have been lost on the audience. In effect the *ataktoi* who believe they have already achieved indestructible bliss are shown to be reverting to the false promises of the Roman civic cult which their conversion should have overcome.

In 5:4-5 Paul infers from the traditional doctrine of the parousia that he had previously taught in Thessalonica that the converts are now "children of light and . . . of day" and should no longer be attracted or dominated by the propaganda or the behavior of the night. The metaphors of light and darkness are often employed in apocalyptic discourse to refer to the new and old ages, but in this instance the emphasis is upon delusion: lest the parousia "surprise you like a thief" (v. 4). This strongly suggests that the problem in Thessalonica is apocalyptic complacency: believing that the end of time has already arrived, the millenarian radicals delude themselves that the expectancy of future, divine judgment is no longer required.

The admonition in 5:6-8 is that the congregation face the parousia, the day of the Lord, with sobriety. The comparison with "others" who "fall asleep" includes the entire pagan world, unaware of "the wrath to come" (v. 6; 1:9), and again implies that the *ataktoi* have reverted to that delusionary worldview. The ethos of the night is marked by being asleep and drunk (5:7), powerful metaphors of the incapacity to maintain viligance. The defensive armor suitable for believers is faith, love, and hope, with an allusion to the breastplate and helmet of Isa 59:17 that allows him to place hope in the final place of emphasis. It is the hope of a future "salvation" that maintains a realistic sobriety in the midst of ecstatic enthusiasm.

The inference that concludes this fourth proof is that God has "destined" believers who maintain proper vigilance "not for wrath but for obtaining salvation" (5:9) in this future sense of the word. While Christians experience salvation in its provisional form in the present, it is only at the end of time that they will "obtain" it (Richard 1995: 255-56). The uncertain date of the parousia does not imply insecurity of relationship because Christ is the one who "died for us, so that whether we are awake or asleep we may live with him" (v. 10). Paul obviously intended this to reassure the Thessalonians and provide materials for their mutual "building up" (v. 11), but, as noted in the Introduction, 1414, it is likely that this passage provided one of the grounds for concluding that Paul's first letter taught that "the day of the Lord has already come" (2 Thess 2:2). Paul's shift in the metaphorical use of "sleep" in 5:10 was probably not caught by some of his congregation, predisposed toward another conclusion. They took him to mean that whether they were asleep, that is, complacent or not concerning a future parousia, they were still able to "live with" Christ in mystical union. While Paul had hoped that his counsel would aid the congregation to "encourage one another and build up each other" (v. 11), it appears that his best effort in this first of the Pauline letters was less than fully successful.

The Issues of Congregational Life (5:12-22)

The fifth and final proof (again, see 4:1) opens with a formal appeal to recognize the leaders who "labor," "have charge of you," and "admonish you." The NRSV translates the verb *eidenai* with "respect," which would produce a tautology with v. 13; the translation "acknowledge" is more likely (Wanamaker 1990: 192; Richard 1995: 268), reflecting a situation in which the established leaders are apparently being disregarded by the *ataktoi.* This could explain the emphasis on "labor," which earlier in the letter involved working with one's hands, an activity that the *ataktoi* have abandoned in their millennial enthusiasm. As 2:9 had reminded the Thessalonians, Paul had worked at his trade "night and day" so as to be able to contribute to the love feasts and not be a "burden" on others, which provided an "example" for the congregation as well as its leaders to follow (1:6). The noun used for "having charge" of the congregation *(proïstamenos)* means both being at the head of a group and being the benefactor of a group; Richard (1995: 268) points out that both connotations are visible elsewhere in the Pauline letters (Rom 12:8; 16:2). It seems likely that Paul is referring here to patrons of house churches as well as leaders of tenement churches, each of which functioned in different ways because of the different social contexts. The task of admonishing others to conform to the ethos of the group was a characteristic role for leaders in Greco-Roman and Jewish groups, and the urgent need in Thessalonica was to legitimate this role in relation to the *ataktoi* ("disorderly"), who are explicitly singled out as needing admonition in 5:14, where the NRSV provides the misleading translation "idlers."

Paul urges that such leaders be "esteemed . . . very highly" not because of the cultural habit of submitting to authority but rather because of the "love" which binds the community together and because of their "work" on behalf of the community. "In the NT church honor is not given to people because of any qualities that they may possess due to birth or social status or natural gifts but only on the basis of the spiritual task to which they are called" (Marshall 1983: 148-49; cited by Wanamaker 1990: 194-95). Once again the emphasis on labor on behalf of the congregation is at the forefront, as it has been since the opening thanksgiving of 1:3, showing the crucial importance of this issue for the congregational situation threatened by the *ataktoi.* I feel that it is highly significant that Paul moves immediately into the admonition, "Be at peace among yourselves," because the authority of established leaders stood right at the center of the conflict in Thessalonica. The term *ataktoi* implies standing against order in principle, so that the most likely interpretation of this verse is that Paul wishes to settle this conflict which is jeopardizing the future of the church in Thessalonica. He urges the entire congregation to support the leaders in this necessary admonition: "And we urge you [plural], beloved, to admonish the *ataktoi*" (5:14).

To "encourage the faint hearted" and to "help the weak" refers to the shaken confidence of the congregation, whose most radical members were contending that the end of history had arrived and death was no more, an optimism countered by the continuation of persecution and death. In the delicate task of admonishing error, encouraging faith, and defending the rights of the weak, Paul calls for being "patient with all of them" (5:14). Richard sees in this wording an echo of the egalitarian appropriation of the love ethic, in which each member should aim at "mutual encouragement and upbuilding (5:11), a goal which requires a slow temper, another divine gift or fruit of the Spirit (Gal 5:11)" (Richard 1995: 270).

Turning toward the issue of the delicate relationship between the church and the society, which has already reacted with hostility to the conversion and behavior of the church, Paul advances in 5:15 the early Christian ethic of non-retaliation that was probably based on the teaching of Jesus (Matt 5:38-42). The love of Christ compels the "beloved" (5:14) to "seek to do good to one another and to all" (v. 15), extending the hospitable mercy of God to all within reach of these small groups of believers. There is no expectation here that doing good to all will result in the conversion of all, or even in the lessening of the hostile persecution that the church of Thessalonica had experienced. Nor are these "random acts of kindness" such as current bumper stickers promote. This is the natural behavior of persons and groups who have experienced and been transformed by the unconditional love of God as conveyed through the death and resurrection of Christ. They are the "beloved of God," the "chosen" ones who have heard and responded to the gospel (1:4-5), so that Paul need provide no subsidiary motive for them to do what should come naturally.

That the new ethic of generous love toward all is grounded in the salvation event is indicated by the admonitions of 5:16-18. They are to "rejoice always," "whether in good times or in bad" (Richard 1995: 271), because Christ died for them and will rescue them "from the wrath that is coming" (1:9). They are to "pray without ceasing" and "give thanks in all circumstances" (1:17-18) because "to thank God at all times is to see God working in every situation to bring about the divine saving will" (Wanamaker 1990: 200). Rather than feeling thwarted by adversity, seeking to escape into a perfect world such as that envisioned by the *ataktoi,* they are to thank God for being with them in every trial. This brings the entire argument of the letter into focus because it is built into the most extensive thanksgiving in ancient literature. In this letter Paul attempts to provide a model for constant thanksgiving in the midst of adversity (1:2; 2:13; 3:9) because it appeared to be the best antidote to the escapist theology afflicting the Thessalonians. The crucial importance of this theme is reinforced by the second half of 5:18, "for this is the will of God in Christ Jesus for you." It is likely that this warrant includes the entire series of ethical admonitions that began in v. 12 (Wanamaker 1990: 201), thus placing the need to rejoice on the same level as the need to love neighbors and fellow members of the congregation and to admonish the *ataktoi* and the faint-hearted. While the usual, modern understanding of the Christian life would place the need of constant praise and thanksgiving on a secondary level of importance as compared with love and justice, Paul places the spiritual reinforcement of the proper relationship with God in the point of final emphasis. Worship precedes, supports, and follows ethics because the wellspring of Christian motivation is thanksgiving to God for the gift of the new relationship in Christ.

The final set of admonitions is closely related to the ecstatic piety of this congregation, which gave rise to the *ataktoi*. Paul rejects two simplistic extremes in dealing with charismatic phenomena. "Do not quench the Spirit, do not despise the words of prophets," counters the tendency in this congregation to stamp out the charismatics because of the threat they pose to good order and common sense. Although some commentators deny that there were impulses to stifle spiritual manifestations within the congregation, it seems that the wording of these admonitions would otherwise have been rhetorically offensive. No group enjoys being accused of behavior that has never in fact occurred, as the "stop beating your wife" illustration suggests. The wording of these admonitions suggests that some members of the congregation "are skeptical of or even have disdain for the powerful, ecstatic activity around them . . ." (Richard 1995: 279). Paul wishes to preserve the charismatic gifts in Thessalonica, even though they were being misused by the *ataktoi*, by insisting that the opposite danger also be avoided. In an antithetical manner marked by *de* ("but"), which remains untranslated in the NRSV, Paul is signaling that "a close link exists between the thought of vv 20 and 21" (Wanamaker 1990: 201). He wants the community "to evaluate what is said or done in the name of the Spirit or under the suppposed influence of the Spirit" (Wanamaker 1990: 203). No matter how inspired the utterance seems, it needs to be examined by all of the members of the community in the light of Christ.

It is worth observing that Paul does not locate the task of evaluation in the leaders of the congregation, some of whom may well have been involved in misleading, charismatic activity. In a remarkable expression of the democratic ethos within the early church, Paul lays this responsibility on all of the members. Since all have experienced Christ, all have been given the power of critical evaluation. The congregation replaces the philosopher and rabbi in this new age, with the apostle acting as the one who clarifies the system of life in Christ. The "criteria for true discernment" (Richard 1995: 272) in making such communal evaluations are set forth in 5:21: "hold fast to what is good; abstain from every form of evil." These criteria prevent simplistic assessments that throw out the baby with the bathwater, either abandoning the old without due cause or adopting new views without weighing their consequences. Paul formulates this same idea of democratic responsibility in a later letter (1 Cor 14:29-40), laying the groundwork for a democratic social order despite the fact that it has only infrequently been incorporated into congregational life (Jewett 1994a: 119-21).

Concluding Blessings (5:23-28)

The conclusion of 1 Thessalonians begins with a homiletic benediction or wish prayer that draws together "the themes of holiness, ethics, congregational harmony, and apocalyptic expectation. . . . In its request for God's preservation until the parousia, it serves in fact to summarize and climax the entire epistle . . ." (Jewett 1969: 24). This benediction (5:23) emphasizes that the whole person of believers, their body, soul, and spirit, must be kept in holiness and integrity until the parousia. In contrast to those who adopted the Greco-Roman mind-set, reflected in the behavior of the *ataktoi*, which tended to give the spirit priority over the body, Paul hopes for the sanctification of the whole person. If such sanctity is preserved, the Thessalonian believers will prevail in the only court of honor that is finally relevant to them (deSilva 1996: 67).

There follows an assurance formula in 5:24, affirming the faithfulness of God in preserving this wholeness despite all of the pressures the congregation is facing. The request for mutual prayer (v. 25) and the admonitions about passing on the "holy kiss" and reading the letter to all of the groups point to the extraordinary degree of familial solidarity reflected throughout this letter. The kiss was primarily a familial greeting in the Greco-Roman world, something one ordinarily did not share with nonfamily members. Since the "holy kiss" is mentioned in Rom 16:16, 1 Cor 16:20, and 2 Cor 13:12, it is clearly a regular part of the life of the Pauline churches, probably as a greeting before and after the love feast/Lord's Supper. The sudden shift in 5:27 from "we" (vv. 12, 14) and "us" (v. 25) to "I" indicates that Paul takes the pen at this point to provide an authenticating signature, so to speak, in his distinctively large handwriting (see Gal 6:11). The final greeting conveys the "grace of our Lord Jesus Christ," the source of their salvation and new life together as a family. It is a family that includes all of the believers in Thessalonica, including the *ataktoi* and Paul himself, who was temporarily separated from them "in person, not in heart" (2:17).

2 Thessalonians

COMMENTARY

The peculiar combination of different tone and similar content in 2 Thessalonians as compared with the first letter is understandable in the light of the evidence that the first letter was misunderstood. 2 Thess 2:2 refers explicitly to a false announcement supported by a "letter, as though from us," and 3:17 refers to Paul's authenticating signature in the final lines, as if there were some doubt in his mind that some other letter may have come to Thessalonica in his name. My hypothesis is: "since the millenarian radicals in Thessalonica were quoting Paul's teaching and writing to support their contention that the Day of the Lord had already come, Paul was forced to write again to clarify his argument and his intentions. He summarized his earlier argument, quite naturally with a noticeable difference in tone" (Jewett 1986: 191). This second letter has a strong tone of reproof and correction, required by the bizarre misinterpretation of the first letter and the deepening of the crisis in the congregation.

Introduction, Thanksgiving, and Prayer (1:1-12)

The prescript (1:1-2) is somewhat more expansive than that of the first letter, specifying that the "grace" and "peace" come from "our Father and the Lord Jesus Christ," thus enhancing the theme of divine patronage of the congregation (Danker and Jewett 1990: 491). As clients of this divine patron, the Thessalonians will be urged strongly to obey injunctions that convey the patron's will.

In the thanksgiving (1:3-10) and intercessory prayer (2 Thess 1:11-12) we encounter the apocalyptic tension that Paul apparently shares with his churches, which he now rehearses as the basis for the subsequent argument. The "kingdom of God" that is currently visible in the embattled suffering of believers (1:5) will soon be fully manifest with the return of Christ when vengeance is enacted against evildoers (vv. 8-10) (Bassler 1984: 502, 509). The "faith" and "endurance" of believers in the present moment of adversity, apparently consisting of adherence to the new age being ushered in through the gospel, are evidence of divine intervention for which Paul gives thanks (v. 4). As Roger Aus explains, "It is precisely in this situation of suffering that the author of 2 Thessalonians tells the addressees that he and his fellow Christians ought to give thanks to God, as is proper, because the Thessalonians' faith is growing abundantly and their love for one another is increasing; they are steadfast and are demonstrating their faith (vss. 3-4)" (Aus 1973: 438).

Both faith and love are growing in the congregation, indicating the presence of divine power (1:3). So the transformation already visible in the congregation is a direct result of "the grace of our God and the Lord Jesus Christ" (v. 12; cf. also v. 2), giving hope of future participation in the glory of the kingdom of God (vv. 10-12) (Giblin 1967: 112). The imminence of this future fulfillment is evident in the reference to those afflicted in Thessalonica who will shortly experience, along with Paul, "relief" when Christ returns (v. 7). This carries the strong implication that the *anasis* ("relief, rest," a term from which the modern brand name "Anacin" comes) is not yet available, which signals "an attempt to put a brake on their 'over-realized' expectations" (Wanamaker 1990: 225).

Paul's attitude about persecution in this text is rather stunning. He claims that the very presence of persecution is "evidence of the righteous judgment of God" and that it has the additional side effect of being "intended to make you worthy of the kingdom of God." There is a double rationale for this remarkable claim. "The trials and the way in which the readers are enduring them . . . constitute evidence of a righteous process of judgment which God is carrying out in order that he may see that they are worthy of the kingdom . . ." (Marshall 1983: 173). The reference to making Christians "worthy of the kingdom of God" implies that courageous responses to persecution help to refine and deepen the character of believers. This argument stands as a bulwark against the escapist ideology promoted by the *ataktoi.* It also addresses the most excruciating aspect of persecution, the ascription of dishonor by the society; Paul is here reinterpreting "society's attempts to disgrace Christians as actually leading toward honor within the alternative court or reputation" in divine judgment (deSilva 1996: 71).

The second part of the rationale is that retribution against persecutors will come soon, at the Day of Judgment "when the Lord Jesus is revealed from heaven with his mighty angels in flaming fire, inflicting vengeance on those who do not know God and on those who do not obey the gospel of our Lord Jesus" (1:7-8). This theme is expressed in surprisingly vindictive language: "For it is indeed just of God to repay with affliction those who afflict you" (v. 6). This strikes some modern Christians as problematic. It replaces love for the enemy, as found in the Gospels and the later Pauline letters, with a desire for their destruction. Even more problematic is the fact that this expectation of retribution assumes a return of an avenging Christ within a short time after the writing of 2 Thessalonians, which of course did not occur. But the relevance of Paul's argument for the escapist ideology currently exciting the Thessalonian churches remains clear.

Paul's prayer was that "our God will . . . fulfill by God's power every good resolve and work of faith" (1:11). This wording makes it clear that the Thessalonians were not playing the role of helpless victims in response to public pressures. They were responding with moral resolve, with deliberate decisions about how to react. Paul does not pray for happy endings but for divine power to strengthen "every good resolve and work of faith." And he does not abandon the quest for moral clarity, despite the uncertain outcome of all human action. Paul speaks here of blessing "every *good* resolve," not "every resolve." In contrast to the public monuments dedicated to prominent civic benefactors that use these terms (Danker and Jewett 1990: 492-93), this service is to the community of believers, and the standard of the service is the "good" as defined by Christ.

For Paul and the early church, there was a larger frame for the individual stories of persecution and struggle that individuals and house churches were going through. Paul refers in our text to their impact on other people. The apostle boasts of the Thessalonians' "steadfastness and faith" among the other "churches of God" (1:4). While the first letter to the Thessalonians claimed that the "word of the Lord has sounded forth from you not only in Macedonia and Achaia, but in every place your faith in God has become known (1 Thess 1:8), here he simply refers to the value of responding to "the gospel of our Lord Jesus" (2 Thess 1:8). Genuine conversion is contagious. The transformed lives of the Thessalonians and their courage under persecution are like an echo chamber, resounding throughout the region and thus advancing the gospel of Christ (Ware 1992: 127-30).

It is clear that for Paul the main strategy in responding to evil was to spread the Christian mission, creating cells of love and responsibility in the midst of a violent and corrupt world. These fragments of a transformed world glorify the name of "the Lord Jesus" (1:12) and simultaneously demonstrate for all to see that believers are recovering the glory lost in the fall of the human race. "The process of glorification begins through the Spirit working in the lives of Christians (cf. 2 Cor. 3:18) and culminated in the glorification of the believers' bodies at the parousia (cf. Rom. 8:18f; Phil. 3:20f)" (Wanamaker 1990: 235).

The Two Theses of the Letter (2:1-2)

The partitio (2:1-2) announces the two topics for discussion in rebuttal of millenarian radicalism: the true status of the parousia and the eschatological involvement of believers (Jewett 1986: 83, 86; Hughes 1988: 56-57). The false claim being made in Thessalonica was that "the day of the Lord is already here," which meant that the ultimate event in world history had occurred. That this message came "either by spirit or by word or by letter" suggests that apocalyptic prophets within the Thessalonian community announced this development, calling upon Paul's first letter as support and claiming direct revelation from the Spirit as confirmation (Danker and Jewett 1990: 494). Paul begs the Thessalonians "not to be quickly shaken in mind or alarmed" by this false message which stood in such stark variance with the doctrine he had intended to convey. It was, in fact, the most exciting message conceivable: that history had come to an end, that the last judgment had occurred, that whatever dead were going to be resurrected have been, and that heavenly bliss was now available.

The Argument That the Parousia Has Not Yet Come (2:3-12)

The first proof in 2 Thessalonians, as announced in the partitio (2:1-2), is that the day of the Lord has not arrived as the radicals had claimed (vv. 3-12). The "not yet" scheme is developed as a refutation of a contrary view cited in the partitio that "the day of the Lord has already come." Five signs must precede such an event, according to Paul's apocalyptic scenario, and their absence proves the falsity of this radically realized eschatology. The appearance of the "rebellion" (v. 3) and the "man of lawlessness" (v. 3), the removal of the "restrainer" (vv. 6-7), the destruction of the lawless one (v. 8), and finally the rise of "delusion" (vv. 11-12) are all required before anyone can think the end of history has arrived. Since the rhetorical interaction between Paul and his audience is so rarely taken into account by interpreters, this scenario is frequently understood as implying a long-term postponement of the parousia and thus as evidence of non-Pauline theology (Richard 1995: 323-54; Krentz 1992: 521-22). I agree that it is a postponement, but of an end already fallaciously announced. In the context of millenarian radicalism, the false sense of "already" needed to be countered by the "not yet," stated in thoroughly apocalyptic terms.

In addition to the theological insistence on the futurity of apocalyptic fulfillment, this proof contains language that indicates an adherence to the value of the law. The anti-Christ figure is identified as an opponent of the law (2:3, 8), and the "mystery of lawlessness" (v. 7) is depicted as already at work as a sign of the imminence of the end. The context indicates that lawlessness was thought to involve "rebellion against God" (Marshall 1983: 195), and it may well include the kind of libertinistic behavior in which the *ataktoi* were involved (Jewett 1986: 102-7; 172-75). This language assumes that there is a demonic force operating in those who oppose the law so that the "lawless" stand flatly in opposition to Christ (Best 1972: 27-32; Wanamaker 1990: 255). At this stage in Paul's theology, there is no indication of a polemical attitude toward the law that became characteristic for the later letters. As far as I can tell from 2 Thessalonians, the obligation to obey the Torah remains intact, and it appears consistent that no hint of an antithesis between law and gospel is given.

The first proof contains language implying an ambivalence between free will and predestination in connection with the phenomenon of apocalyptic delusion (2:9-12). Those who fall prey to the deception of the "lawless one" are described as having "refused to love the truth and so be saved." But this element of willful rejection of God is combined with the apocalyptic motif of the "delusion" sent by God to confirm the belief in falsehood (Aus 1977: 550). J. B. Lightfoot described the three phases of damnation implicit in this passage: first, the human rejection of the truth; second, a divinely ordained delusion; and third, the ultimate punishment (Lightfoot 1904: 117). As a more recent commentator remarks, "Whatever one may say about divine predestination, the lost carry the responsibility for their own perdition" (Marshall 1983: 203). The phrases "having faith in" and "loving the truth" (vv. 12, 10) evoke the horizon of accepting or rejecting the gospel as the key to the judgment scheme in this apocalyptic theology (Best 1972: 309).

The profile of the "lawless one" in 2:3-10 matches to some degree the superheroic model of ancient as well as modern fantasy (see Jewett 1993b: 105-17). There is a claim of divinity in v. 4, in competition with other deities, a reference to charismatic endowment in vv. 9-10, with "all power, signs, lying wonders and every kind of wicked deception," obviously aimed at gaining power through public admiration, and an innate link with "lawlessness," which in the ancient world resulted from the conception of heroes and deities as being above the law. Paul refers to the lawless one being held back by the "restrainer" (vv. 6-7), perhaps referring to the Roman Empire (Wanamaker 1990: 256-57; Richard 1995: 337-40) or angelic forces working on behalf of the gospel (Marshall 1983: 199). Paul's primary purpose in this section, however, is not to teach a new apocalyptic doctrine but to suggest that the delusion in the congregation and the "lawlessness" and "rebellion" evident in the *ataktoi*'s behavior are current signs of the influence of a demonic ideology.

The Argument That Believers Will Persist until the Parousia (2:13–3:5)

The second proof in the letter (2:13–3:5) provides assurance that believers should possess in the present moment of testing. 2:13 refers to the divine election to salvation that the Thessalonians had experienced, involving them in a process of spiritual sanctification and "faith in the truth." Paul goes on to assert that when the parousia arrives they will surely "obtain the glory of our Lord Jesus Christ" (v. 14). It is clear that in contrast to the inclinations of the *ataktoi,* such glory is not presently available to the church in a final form. This portion of Paul's "already/not yet" scheme opens with a thanksgiving concerning the election of the Thessalonian Christians to salvation and then moves on to the necessity of standing firm in faith. The close proximity of "gospel" (v. 14) and "traditions" (v. 15) suggests that, despite the use of a term often employed elsewhere for the transmission of moral teaching, Paul wishes to include the traditions about Christ as the crucified and returning Savior that had been central in his proclamation and reiterated in his earlier letter (Best 1972: 317). Christ is the supreme benefactor, restoring the glory of the creation by offering "love" and "salvation" to his adherents (v. 13) (Danker and Jewett 1990: 498). The parallel between "our gospel" in v. 14 and "the gospel of our Lord Jesus" in 1:8 indicates the substantive content of Paul's earlier christological preaching.

In the immediately following verses (2:16-17) Christ is the one who provides "comfort" and ethical firmness during the interim before the parousia. The benediction in these two verses reiterates the previous actions of Christ in providing love, comfort, and hope "through grace" (Jewett 1969: 24). Grace provides the basis for the acceptance of apocalyptic anticipation in this letter.

The request for prayerful intercession on behalf of Paul's missionary activities in 3:1-2 presupposes that Christian leaders as well as followers face continued threats from the old age. In contrast to the millenarian radicals who declared the presence of the parousia, and hence the final elimination of evil, Paul takes realistic account of adversity. What he argues in v. 3 is that Christ is capable of strengthening the faithful to resist evil and of guarding them "from the evil one," probably a demonic being (Bruce 1982: 200). Although they may suffer or die, they have the assurance that they are not finally under the power of the demonic forces. The assurance formula that Paul uses in the next sentence pertains not to their escaping the impact of malevolence but rather to their remaining faithful during testing. Hence the benediction that concludes this proof (v. 5) deals with the action of Christ to provide firm directedness on the part of Christians toward God who loves them and Christ who steadfastly stands by them through all adversity (Jewett 1969: 24).

Exhortations to the Disorderly (3:6-15)

In 3:6-15 Paul turns to the source of the millenarian confusion. In v. 6 he demands withdrawal from the *ataktoi.* In view of the discussion of work, several commentators prefer the option "loafers" to translate this term (Bruce 1982: 122; Best 1972: 230); the NRSV follows this line in the translation "idlers." But the definitive investigation of this term by Ceslaus Spicq has shown that the basic meaning of the term is "standing against the order of nature or of God." The word was typically used in military contexts to depict someone who would not keep step or follow commands. Spicq terms this group the "refractaires" (Spicq 1956: 12; 1978: 1:159), which should be rendered the "obstinate" or "insubordinate" in English (Marshall 1983: 150). Resistance against authority is therefore implied by this term, a conclusion that is strongly supported by the reference to refusing to accept the Pauline tradition in v. 6. Giblin concurs in the judgment that "the *ataktoi* are troublemakers, not just economic parasites," and, moreover, that they were "responsible for the deception on the topic of the parousia . . ." (Giblin 1967: 144, 147). In view of the likelihood that the congregation had been providing sustenance for this group of radicals, the command in v. 6 implies the withdrawal of material support.

The theological basis for Paul's command is laid out in the apostolic imitation scheme of 3:7-10. Paul had the right to demand financial support but refrained from using it in order to provide a model for economic responsibility. He goes on to provide a multileveled rationale for work: acceptance of the apostolic command, independent self-support (v. 12), and having the means to do good for others (v. 13). In vv. 12-13 Paul turns directly to the *ataktoi* themselves, urging them to begin working again to provide the resources to do "what is right" for the congregation. The formula of "command and exhort in the Lord Jesus Christ" conveys "coercive power: to reject it is to reject the Lord Jesus Christ himself and therefore to exclude oneself from the community" (Wanamaker 1990: 287).

In 3:14-15 Paul recommends that the congregation use the method of temporary exclusion should the *ataktoi* not respond to the guidelines set forth in the letter. This exclusion ought to aim to make them "ashamed" because the honor of being part of the beloved community would no longer be accessible. But they are to be treated as "believers" needing correction rather than "enemies" viewed as heretics. Paul does not desire "their complete alienation from the community" (Wanamaker 1990: 290). "God's choice and Christian commitment require restoration of wayward believers . . . and the means for this is limited association in the context of fellowship and admonition" (Richard 1995: 384).

Concluding Benediction and Greetings (3:16-18)

Second Thessalonians ends on the theme of the ethical stance required for living in the world while expecting its imminent transformation with the parousia of Christ. The already/not yet scheme appears to operate on the ethical as well as on the theological level. The "peace" that is the subject of the final benediction (3:16), in contrast to the premise of millenarian radicalism, is not the absence of adversity. It cannot be a once-and-for-all benefit, such as millenarians might expect, but rather comes "at all times in all ways" (v. 16). The peace of Christ is the constant gift of divine grace that provides sustenance for a beleaguered congregation continuing to face political as well as economic woes. As a way of coping with the suspicions of misunderstanding, even to the point of forgery, Paul adds his own greeting in his handwriting in v. 17. But he returns to the underlying matrix of the theology of 2 Thessalonians in the final words: the grace of the apocalyptic Christ will see all of them through (v. 18).

Bibliography. Aus, R. D. 1973, "The Liturgical Background of the Necessity and Propriety of Giving Thanks According to 2 Thes 1:3," *JBL* 92:433-38 • Aus, R. D. 1977, "God's Plan and God's Power: Isaiah 66 and the Restraining Factors of 2 Thess 2:6-7," *JBL* 96:537-53 • Bammel, E. 1981, "Preparation for the Perils of the Last Days: 1 Thessalonians 3:3," in W. Horbury and B. McNeil, eds., *Suffering and Martyrdom in the New Testament: Studies Presented to G. M. Styler by the Cambridge New Testament Seminar,* Cambridge: Cambridge University, 91-100 • Barclay, J. M. G. 1992, "Thessalonica and Corinth: Social Contrasts in Pauline Christianity," *JSNT* 47:49-74 • Barclay, J. M. G. 1993, "Conflict in Thessalonica," *CBQ* 55:512-30 • Bassler, J. M. 1984, "The Enigmatic Sign: 2 Thessalonians 1:5," *CBQ* 46:496-510 • Best, E. 1972, *A Commentary on the First and Second Epistles to the Thessalonians,* London: Black • Börschel, R. 2001, *Die Konstruktion einer christlichen Identität: Paulus und die Gemeinde von Thessalonich in ihrer hellenistisch-römischen Umwelt,* BBB 128, Berlin: Philo • Boyce, J. L. 1992, "Graceful Imitation: 'Imitators of Us and the Lord' (1 Thessalonians 1:6)," *WWSup* 1:139-46 • Bruce, F. F. 1982, *1 and 2 Thessalonians,* Waco, Tex.: Word • Chapa, J. 1994, "Is First Thessalonians a Letter of Consolation?" *NTS* 40:150-60 • Collins, R. F. 1980, "Tradition, Redaction and Exhortation in 1 Th 4,13–5,11," in J. Lambrecht, ed., *L'Apocalypse johannique et l'Apocalyptique dans le Nouveau Testament,* Gembloux: Duculot, 325-43 • Collins, R. F. 1984, *Studies on the First Letter to the Thessalonians,* Louvain: Peeters/Louvain University • Collins, R. F., ed. 1990, *The Thessalonian Correspondence.* Leuven: Leuven University • Danker, F., and R. Jewett. 1990, "Jesus as the Apocalyptic Benefactor in Second Thessalonians," in R. F. Collins, ed., *The Thessalonian Correspondence,* Leuven: Leuven University, 486-98 • deSilva, D. A. 1996, "'Worthy of His Kingdom': Honor Discourse and Social Engineering in 1 Thessalonians," *JSNT* 64:49-79 • Donfried, K. P. 1985, "The Cults of Thessalonica and the Thessalonian Correspondence," *NTS* 31:336-56 • Donfried, K. P. 1993a, "2 Thessalonians and the Church of Thessalonica," in B. McLean, ed., *Origins and Method: Towards a New Understanding of Judaism and Christianity: Essays in Honour of John C. Hurd,* Sheffield: JSOT, 128-44 • Donfried, K. P. 1993b, *The Theology of the Shorter Pauline Letters,* Cambridge/New York: Cambridge University • Donfried, K. P. 2000, ed., *The Thessalonians Debate: Metholological Discord or Methodological Synthesis?* Grand Rapids: Eerdmans • Elias, J. W. 1995, *1 and 2 Thessalonians,* Scottdale/Waterloo: Herald • Gaventa, B. R. 1990, "Apostles as Babes and Nurses in 1 Thessalonians 2:7," in J. Carroll et al., eds., *Faith and History: Essays in Honor of Paul W. Meyer,* Atlanta: Scholars, 193-207 • Gaventa, B. R. 1998, *First and Second Thessalonians,* Louisville: John Knox • Giblin, C. H. 1967, *The Threat to Faith: An Exegetical and Theological Reexamination of 2 Thessalonians 2,* Rome: Pontifical Biblical Institute • Gilliard, F. D. 1989, "The Problem of the Antisemitic Comma between I Thessalonians 2:14 and 15," *NTS* 35:481-502 • Hemberg, B. 1950, *Die Kabiren,* Uppsala: Almqvist & Wiksells • Hendrix, H. L. 1984, "Thessalonicans Honor Romans," Ph.D. diss., Cambridge, Mass.: Harvard University • Hendrix, H. L. 1991, "Archaeology and Eschatology at Thessalonica," in B. Pearson, ed., *The Future of Early Christianity,* Minneapolis: Augsburg, 107-18 • Hendrix, H. L. 1992, "Thessalonica," in *ABD,* 6:523-27 • Hock, R. F. 1979, "The Workshop as a Social Setting for Paul's Missionary Preaching," *CBQ* 41:438-50 • Hock, R. F. 1980, *The Social Context of Paul's Ministry: Tentmaking and Apostleship,* Philadelphia: Fortress • Holland, G. S. 1988, *The Tradition That You Received from Us: 2 Thessalonians in the Pauline Tradition,* Tübingen: Mohr [Siebeck] • Hughes, F. W. 1988, *Early Christian Rhetoric and 2 Thessalonians,* Sheffield: JSOT • Hughes, F. W. 1990, "The Rhetoric of 1 Thessalonians," in R. F. Collins, ed., *The Thessalonian Correspondence,* Leuven: Leuven University, 94-116 • Jewett, R. 1969, "The Form and Function of the Homiletic Benediction," *ATR* 51:18-34 • Jewett, R. 1970-71, "The Agitators and the Galatian Congregation," *NTS* 17:198-212 • Jewett, R. 1986, *The Thessalonian Correspondence: Pauline Rhetoric and Millenarian Piety,* Philadelphia: Fortress • Jewett, R. 1991, "A Matrix of Grace: The Theology of 2 Thessalonians as a Pauline Letter," in J. Bassler, ed., *Pauline Theology,* vol. 1: *Thessalonians, Philippians, Galatians, Philemon,* Minneapolis: Fortress, 63-70 • Jewett, R. 1993a, "Tenement Churches and Communal Meals in the Early Church: The Implications of a

Form-Critical Analysis of 2 Thess 3:10," *BR* 38:23-43 • Jewett, R. 1993b, *Saint Paul at the Movies: The Apostle's Dialogue with American Culture,* Louisville: Westminster/John Knox • Jewett, R. 1994a, "Tenement Churches and Pauline Love Feasts," *Quarterly Review: A Journal of Theological Resources for Ministry* 14.1:43-58 • Jewett, R. 1994b, *Paul the Apostle to America: Cultural Trends and Pauline Scholarship,* Louisville: Westminster/John Knox • Johanson, B. C. 1987, *To All the Brethren: A Text-Linguistic and Rhetorical Approach to I Thessalonians,* Stockholm: Almqvist & Wiksells • Judge, E. A. 1971, "The Decrees of Caesar at Thessalonica," *RTR* 30:1-7 • Krentz, E. M. 1992, "Thessalonians, First and Second Epistles to," in *ABD,* 6:515-23 • Lightfoot, J. B. 1904, *Notes on Epistles of St. Paul,* New York: Macmillan • Malherbe, A. J. 1970, "'Gentle as a Nurse': The Stoic Background to 1 Thess. II," *NovT* 12:203-17 • Malherbe, A. J. 2000, *The Letters to the Thessalonians,* AB 32B, New York: Doubleday • Malherbe, A. J. 1987, *Paul and the Thessalonians: The Philosophic Tradition of Pastoral Care,* Philadelphia: Fortress • Malherbe, A. J. 1990a, "Pastoral Care in the Thessalonian Church," *NTS* 36:375-91 • Malherbe, A. J. 1990b, "Did the Thessalonians Write to Paul?" in R. Fortna and B. Gaventa, eds., *The Conversation Continues: Studies in Paul and John in Honor of J. Louis Martyn,* Nashville: Abingdon, 246-57 • Marshall, I. H. 1983, *1 and 2 Thessalonians,* Grand Rapids: Eerdmans • Meeks, W. A. 1983, *The First Urban Christians: The Social World of the Apostle Paul,* New Haven, Conn.: Yale University Press • Meeks, W. A. 1986, *The Moral World of the First Christians,* Philadelphia: Westminster • Mitchell, M. M. 1992, "New Testament Envoys in the Context of Greco-Roman Diplomatic and Epistolary Conventions: The Example of Timothy and Titus," *JBL* 111:641-62 • Müller, P.-G. 2001, *Der erste und zweite Brief an die Thessalonicher,* Regensburg: Pustet-Verlag • Nock, A. D. 1945, "A Cabiric Rite," *AJA* 45:576-81 • Peerbolte, L. J. L. 1996, *The Antecedents of Antichrist: A Traditio-Historical Study of the Earliest Christian Views on Eschatological Opponents,* Leiden/New York/Cologne: Brill • Plevnik, J. 1979, "1 Thessalonians 5,1-11: Its Authenticity, Intention and Message," *Bib* 60:71-90 • Plevnik, J. 1984, "The Taking Up of the Faithful and the Resurrection of the Dead in 1 Thessalonians 4:13-18," *CBQ* 46:274-83 • Reicke, B. 1984, "Judaeo-Christianity and the Jewish Establishment, A.D. 33-66," in E. Bammel and C. F. D. Moule, eds., *Jesus and the Politics of His Day,* London: SCM, 145-52 • Richard, E. J. 1990, "Contemporary Research on 1 and 2 Thessalonians," *BTB* 20:107-15 • Richard, E. J. 1995, *First and Second Thessalonians,* Collegeville, Minn.: Liturgical • Schlueter, C. J. 1994, *Filling Up the Measure: Polemical Hyperbole in 1 Thessalonians 2.14-16,* Sheffield: JSOT • Smith, A. 1995, *Comfort One Another: Reconstructing the Rhetoric and Audience of 1 Thessalonians,* Louisville: Westminster/John Knox • Spicq, C. 1956, "Les Thesaloniciens 'inquiets' etaient ils des paresseux?" *ST* 10:1-13 • Spicq, C. 1978, *Notes de Lexicographie Neo-Testamentaire,* Göttingen: Vandenhoeck & Ruprecht • Still, T. D. 1999, *Conflict at Thessalonica: A Pauline Church and Its Neighbours,* JSNTSup 183, Sheffield: Sheffield Academic • Tomson, P. J. 1990, *Paul and the Jewish Law: Halakha in the Letters of the Apostle to the Gentiles,* Assen/Maastricht: Van Gorcum • Wanamaker, C. A. 1990, *The Epistles to the Thessalonians: A Commentary on the Greek Text,* Grand Rapids: Eerdmans; Exeter: Paternoster • Ware, J. 1992, "The Thessalonians as a Missionary Congregation: 1 Thessalonians 1,5-8," *ZNW* 83:126-31 • Wiles, G. P. 1974, *The Significance of the Intercessory Prayer Passages in the Letters of St. Paul,* Cambridge: Cambridge University • Witt, R. E. 1977, "The Kabeiroi in Ancient Macedonia," in B. Laourdas and C. Makaronas, eds., *Ancient Macedonia,* Thessaloniki: Institute for Balkan Studies, 2:76-80.

Pastoral Epistles

Pheme Perkins

INTRODUCTION

P. Anton referred to 1 and 2 Timothy and Titus as "pastorals" in 1726 because they direct Paul's associates, Timothy and Titus, to shepherd the churches being entrusted to them. In the early canon list, the Muratorian Canon (c. AD 200), they are described as concerned with ecclesiastical discipline. The question of how to describe the primary function of this group of letters continues to be hotly debated. On the one hand, instructions to stamp out false teachers who have infiltrated the churches (1 Tim 1:3-7; 2 Tim 2:14-19; 3:3-5; Titus 1:10-14) suggests that imposing right doctrine and communal order on churches that have been disrupted by divisive teaching is the purpose behind these letters. On the other, the virtues expected of communal leaders (1 Tim 3:1-12; 2 Tim 2:21-25; Titus 1:5-10) as well as the disciplined, orderly lives expected of members of the churches (1 Tim 2:1-4, 8-12; 5:3-16; 6:1-2, 9-10, 17-19; Titus 2:1-10; 3:1-2, 8-11) present a picture of Christianity as the "household of God" (1 Tim 3:15) within which persons are constantly exhorted to live virtuous lives. Paul's successors must serve as models and teachers of the piety which pleases God and insures a peaceful life (1 Tim 2:2-3; 4:7-8; 6:6; Titus 2:12). Some scholars understand this focus on social order, piety, and a virtuous life as evidence of the natural process by which Christianity found its place in the larger society. Others assume that such concerns are aimed at countering the influence of a radically ascetic form of Christianity, which challenged the social conventions of the time.

The emergence of historical criticism at the beginning of the nineteenth century raised a further problem about the Pastorals: Who was their actual author? Linguistic and theological divergence between these letters and the other Pauline texts requires even those who maintain Pauline authorship to invoke such hypotheses as Paul's use of a secretary, a later point in the apostle's ministry, or the fact that the Pastorals are addressed to individuals, not churches. Various mediating positions have also been proposed. Those passages which are most like other Pauline letters are treated as excerpts of the apostle's writing used by a later author. Or 2 Timothy, which is formally closer to the other Pauline epistles than 1 Timothy or Titus, is taken to be an authentic Pauline composition. This viewpoint challenges the scholarly tendency to treat the three letters as a single corpus. In part, the differences between 1 Timothy and Titus, on the one hand, and 2 Timothy, on the other, stem from the genres employed. In 1 Timothy and Titus, the apostle provides his successor with instructions for carrying out the task of guiding the churches. For 1 Timothy, the author speaks directly of a series of particular problems: women teaching (2:11-15), misuse of the order of widows (5:3-16), charges against elders (5:17-19), and possibly slaves lacking respect for their masters (6:1-2). When similar themes appear in Titus, they are treated in a more general way. Both types of letter fit the genre of administrative or mandate letter. In that type, an official writes to a subordinate about to assume administrative duties in order to instruct him. 2 Timothy fits a different pattern. Imprisoned and about to die in Rome (2 Tim 1:8, 16-17; 4:6-8), the apostle is writing a farewell testament to his trusted associate. More typical of the Pauline letters than the mandate types of 1 Timothy and Titus, 2 Timothy follows the greeting with a thanksgiving (1:3) and concludes with information about travel plans and about persons associated with the apostle, and with greetings to others in the place to which the letter is sent (4:9-21). Though Titus also concludes with travel instructions, its greetings are general, not personal (Titus 3:12-15).

Despite these elements of realism, 2 Timothy shares a number of features with 1 Timothy and Titus which support those who consider all three epistles part of a single corpus. All three are concerned with establishing continuity of faith in the Pauline tradition in the face of dissident teaching (1 Tim 6:20-21; 2 Tim 1:13-14; Titus 1:9; 2:1). This group diverges from the undisputed Pauline letters in being addressed to individuals rather than communities. For scholars who defend the Pauline authorship of the Pastorals, this difference is invoked to explain why the Pastorals are missing in the early papyrus, $\mathfrak{p}^{46}$. However, that papyrus includes Paul's letter to Philemon. Though Philemon deals with an individual matter, the apostle writes to Philemon in the setting of the larger Christian community which will serve as witness to the outcome of Paul's request. Since so much of 1 Timothy and Titus concerns communal order, one would expect Paul to address the churches as well as their leaders. In addition, the undisputed Pauline epistles all refer to co-senders with the exception of Romans, addressed to a church not founded by the apostle. Since 1 and 2 Timothy are dispatched to Ephesus, a major city in Paul's missionary activities, one would expect co-senders. Though Titus is on Crete, not a Pauline missionary foundation, the years of collaboration between Paul and Titus would suggest that had Paul composed the letter, there would have been persons around him in Rome who would have joined in greeting a fellow associate. Still another anomaly emerges in the personal references within the Pastorals. No others are mentioned as apostles than Paul.

If similarities in content and form link the three letters to one another, then it is possible to ask what generated the collection as such. Some scholars suggest that the circulation of collections of Pauline letters in the churches (explicitly 2 Pet 3:15-16; already 2 Thess 2:2; Eph 3:3-4?) provided the impetus for the Pastorals. Reading Scripture in the community was one of the obligations of the recipients (1 Tim 5:13; 2 Tim 3:15-16). The teaching which accompanies such reading must be oriented toward the healthy teaching which has been handed down from the apostle. Otherwise the churches will be open to the endless controversies being fueled by false teachers. Disputes over words destroy the faith handed down by the apostle (1 Tim 1:4-7; 6:2-4; 2 Tim 2:4; Titus 3:9).

The Jewish elements associated with false teachers in the Pastorals may be linked to interpretations of the OT. Such persons are alleged to desire status as teachers of the law (1 Tim 1:7) or engaged in debates concerning the law (Titus 3:9); to constitute "the circumcised" (Titus 1:10) and to hold "Jewish myths" (Titus 1:14; perhaps also the "myths and genealogies" of 1 Tim 1:4). However, other elements of false teaching cannot be linked clearly with a Jewish context: false claims to religious knowledge (1 Tim 6:20), ascetic rules concerning food and prohibition of marriage (1 Tim 4:1-3; Titus 1:15?), and the claim that the resurrection has already occurred (2 Tim 2:18). The last is attributed to two individuals, Hymenaeus and Philetus. 1 Tim 1:20 refers to the former as "handed over to Satan" by the apostle. In that context he is associated with Alexander, who appears in 2 Tim 4:14 as a coppersmith who had injured Paul. Though many scholars highlight the references to asceticism, knowledge, myths, and genealogies as well as realized eschatology to link the false teaching with the emergence of gnostic Christianity in the second century, distinctive marks of the latter are missing. Gnostic speculation would not contain positive references to the law or fail to challenge its depiction of God as creator. Therefore, other scholars have suggested that the syncretistic Jewish visionaries of Col 2:8–3:4 provide a better analogy for the kind of false teaching envisaged. So much of the polemical language in the Pastorals is drawn from stock motifs in the competition between philosophical schools — endless disputes, appeals to weak-minded women, general immorality, deceitful practices, desire for gain, and the like — that it is difficult to draw a clear picture of the opponents.

Some scholars even argue that such an attempt should not be made. They highlight the differences between the letters: realized eschatology in Titus and dietary rules in 1 Timothy. The conflicts within the churches may have had less to do with doctrines than with social problems of patronage, wealth, and influence in the local churches. Recent sociological studies of early Christianity have emphasized the continued proximity of Christians to the Jewish community. Continuity with an ancestral tradition plays an important role in conversion, as do personal ties to members of the group an individual is entering (Stark 1996: 18-19, 49-69). Persons who present themselves as "teachers of the law" were appealing to a tradition more venerable than that of the apostle. As for close personal ties, all scholars recognize that the Pastorals speak to churches that are organized on the model of the ancient household. Topoi from codes of behavior appropriate to the household and life in society are central to the ethical exhortation in the Pastorals (e.g., Titus 2:2-10; 3:1-2).

Some scholars assume that the emphasis on proper order in the Christian household emerged in response to pagan accusations that Christianity taught disregard for authority (as in Celsus *Contra Celsum* 3.55). Third- and fourth-century apocryphal tales depict a heroic turnaway from paternal authority, marriage, and household responsibility upon conversion to Christ. Some interpreters even detect parallels between the Pastorals and the stories of Thecla (*Acts of Paul and Thecla*), who defies even political authority to become an ascetic follower of Paul the missionary. But more mundane sociological factors may be responsible for the household ethos in the Pastorals. Studies of the spread of cults devoted to savior deities in the Greco-Roman world establish clear links between groups of worshipers and the household of a founding patron. Inscriptions specify ethical requirements for those admitted to the patron's *oikos* (household) and express the hope that those who abide by them will enjoy health, a common salvation, and a fine reputation (Kidd 1990: 123-24). In some instances, such a cult association consists entirely of persons who belong to a single household even though the inscription indicates that those incorporated include both male and female, slave and free person. As a consequence the oaths governing conduct by members bind them directly to the *paterfamilias,* whose house is also the sanctuary of the deity (White 1990: 45-47). The discussion of widows in 1 Tim 5:3-16 indicates that the Christian "household of God" drew its members from diverse households. Some are alleged to evade the responsibility of providing for widowed family members (vv. 8, 16). The good deeds which qualify an old woman for inclusion among the church's widows imply that as mistress of the household she showed hospitality to co-religionists and charity toward the poor (v. 10). Similarly, wealthy Christians demonstrate that they acknowledge God as the source of all wealth by their generosity toward others (6:17-18).

What do such persons receive as social honor and prestige in return? The case is clear for pagan cults — inscriptions attest their titular honors, special place in the community, and cultic offices. Paul's own difficulties with the Corinthians provide evidence of communal discord generated by competition for honor among the more prominent members of the community (1 Cor 1:10–4:21). The apostle administers a stinging rebuke by describing the paradoxical reversal of worldly standards of wisdom and power manifest in the crucified "Lord of glory" and in the suffering of his apostles. Indeed, he has dispatched Timothy to remind them of his own example (1 Cor 4:17). Neither the paradox of the cross nor the contrast between human and divine standards for greatness figures in the Pastorals. For some interpreters this divergence suggests increased acceptance of social commonplaces concerning honor, wealth, and virtue. Though the Pastorals never explicitly state that persons who serve as leaders in the community are its socially prominent members, the household imagery presumes that fact.

According to the Pastorals, the ideal Christian woman exhibits virtues typically extolled in inscriptions and philosophers. Though wealthy women clearly acted independently as patrons, the disjunction between such activities and the traditions of a woman's place within the household was moderated by consistently referring to the city as the family writ large. The early church created a mix of public and private space in its "household of God." The Pastorals clarify the resulting social ambiguity of the position of its prominent women benefactors by insisting that they have no authority over males (1 Tim 2:11-15) and that they remain devoted to the tasks of domestic life (5:11-14). Older women instruct the younger in such duties (Titus 2:3-5). In both cases, the author exhibits concern over the connection between women's behavior and the opinions of outsiders. This policy appears to represent a fall back from the Pauline mission. There women played prominent roles in evangelizing local communities, whether as individuals like Euodia and Syntyche (Phil 4:2-3) or as part of a husband-and-wife team like Prisca and Aquila (Rom 16:3-4). Are the Pastorals deliberate restrictions on the activity of such women "fellow workers" imposed to bring Christian communities into line with accepted gender roles? Perhaps. The lack of contextual framework for the injunctions given in the Pastorals makes it difficult to determine whether or not the prohibited activities refer to real problems or serve as stock examples.

Second- and third-century opponents of Christianity will continue to assert that it is a movement of deluded women in rebellion against the good order of society. Similar suspicions were also invoked when Roman Stoics like Musonius Rufus argued that women would benefit from the study of philosophy. Such pursuits not only went against their nature but also created women who neglected their household duties and became garrulous, quarrelsome, and aggressive in arguing with men. Musonius insisted that women require the same virtues as men: practical wisdom, control of appetite, justice, and courage. Hence both men and women should pursue philosophy, not out of love of argument but out of the desire to have a healthy soul (see Nussbaum 1994: 323-24). The Pastorals may intend a similar stock response to external critics of the early Christian movement.

Such a defense need not imply that women ascetics, prophets, or teachers were particularly well represented among the false teachers. The social demographics of early Christian churches may have been responsible for attention to gender conventions. Using average growth rates from modern examples of new religious movements, Stark estimates that at the turn of the first century there were only about 7,600 Christians in the Roman Empire (Stark 1996: 5-9). This low number coincides with the absence of identifiably Christian archeological remains until the end of the second century. By that time there may have been as many Christians in the city of Rome (= 1 percent of the city's population). The combination of higher rates of infanticide and higher mortality rates left women in short supply in the Roman world. Yet, within the Christian church the percentage of women appears to have been much higher. Paul's greetings at the end of Romans contain almost as many females (15) as males (18). Clothing stockpiled for distribution to the poor that was seized in North Africa in AD 303 was even more skewed: 16 male tunics, 82 female tunics, and 47 pairs of women's slippers. Opposition to abortion and infanticide also increased the numbers of women in early Christian circles. Eventually, the imbalance would create problems if Christians sought to marry within their own circles (cf. 1 Cor 7:39). Quite contrary to the surplus of available males in the larger culture, by the end of the second century AD Christians may have had to seek non-Christian husbands for their daughters. By permitting upper-class women to live in concubinage with lower-class males, Callistus, the Bishop of Rome, freed such Christian women from the need to seek pagan partners (Stark 1996: 97-112). The problems of exogamous marriage evident in 1 Cor 7:13-14 and 1 Pet 3:1-2 may have been the rule rather than the exception for the Pastorals as well. Note that Timothy's own faith is traced back through two generations of women (2 Tim 1:5). The eyes watching out for dishonorable or suspect behavior on the part of Christian women were not necessarily those of censorious bishops. Pagan husbands or relatives would do quite well.

Thus the Pastoral Epistles provide important evidence for the ongoing life of churches at the turn of the first century AD. Just as Timothy is encouraged to look back to the sturdy faith of his mother and grandmother, so these Christians are encouraged to remain faithful to what they have received from the apostle. Attempts to situate the letters within the lifetime of Paul himself require the assumption that he was released from the Roman imprisonment of Acts 28:14-31, that he returned to missionary activity in Asia Minor and Greece after a failed mission to Spain, and was martyred after a second Roman imprisonment. They also must assume that the false teachers referred to are the same judaizing opposition to Pauline Christianity evident in 2 Corinthians, Galatians, and Philippians (see Murphy-O'Connor 1996: 292-320). The divergence in language and theology from the undisputed Pauline letters and the few details of character and setting make this reconstruction less likely than the view of pseudonymous authorship. After the apostle's death, one of those persons connected with the Pauline mission created a handbook for community leaders in the form of the mandate epistle. Since Timothy and Titus had been two of the most trusted co-workers in the Pauline mission, they are the obvious recipients. However, it is precisely that long-term relationship with Paul which makes the Pastorals so odd as actual instructions to them. Both have already proven themselves capable of representing Paul in difficult situations at Corinth. Both routinely serve as his envoys in other contexts. They had probably continued his ministry in the region after his departure. In any event, such directions for the neophyte hardly suit what we know of them.

Unlike the earlier arguments for non-Pauline authorship which situated the Pastorals in the mid-second century AD, sometimes assuming Luke or even Polycarp as authors, we agree with defenders of Pauline authorship that these letters remain part of the apostle's own legacy.

Though they do not develop major theological imagery in that tradition as Ephesians does, for example, the Pastorals provide an instructive example of what Christians today speak of as inculturation. They shift the religious language of the apostle into culturally intelligible forms of discourse about virtue and piety. Law is now something that can be used "lawfully" (1 Tim 1:8). It does not pose a paradox in the human quest for righteousness before God that can only be resolved through faith. The terminology of faith has also shifted. It no longer designates the obedient response to God as much as a traditional set of common convictions or a virtue (1 Tim 5:8; 2 Tim 2:22; Titus 1:1). The saving event itself is no longer focused on the paradox of cross and resurrection. Instead, Christ is the Savior whose appearance marks the coming of God's grace (Titus 2:11). In the Greco-Roman world, the expression *epiphaneia* designated the intervention of a deity on behalf of his worshipers. Such manifestations might be the occasion for the founding of a new cult association. In using such terminology, the Pastorals have shifted away from the Jewish context in which the apostle spoke of justification to terms more commonly used for divine intervention. Similarly, much of the ethical exhortation in the Pastorals has been framed to show that Christianity accomplishes what the philosophers and moralists thought was only the preserve of an elite few. It promotes healthy or sound teaching that contributes to social order and stability. In order to achieve this goal, offices and patterns of authority within the local churches must be established. 1 Timothy sets forth qualifications for those who are to fill existing roles. Titus depicts the establishment of order in a newly founded church.

The interplay between speaking a commonly understood language of virtue and a theological language inherited from the Pauline tradition will be examined in discussion of individual passages. The theological and social tensions exhibited in the Pastorals reflect typical patterns of community development, not the effects of a struggle against a particular heretical school. At the same time we must exercise caution in approaching the rhetorical language of true and false teaching. The struggle for suitable boundaries in a social and religious environment about which we have fragmentary information was not as clear-cut as the polemical antitheses imply. These letters reflect one line in the development of early Christian life. Even there, they do not answer some of our most pressing questions. As we have suggested, marriage to nonbelievers appears to be a demographic requirement even as Christian leaders opposed it. How such persons from mixed households adapted the household structure of the movement to cope with that situation remains far from clear (see Osiek 1996: 14-22). Their focus on internal matters makes it easy to forget the simple demographic fact that Christianity remained a barely visible minority even into the second century AD. The sporadic persecution of leaders of the sect was fueled by local grievances, not a threatening explosive growth in numbers. So the vision of church and society crafted by the Pastorals may be most relevant today not in powerful denominations but in countries where the Christian population is a very tiny minority.

1 Timothy

COMMENTARY

Greeting (1:1-2)

The Pauline form of an ancient letter greeting typically expands the reference to the apostle sender and the secular greeting formula with a Christian substitute, "grace and peace from God our Father and the Lord Jesus Christ" (1 Cor 1:1-3). Two shifts are evident in this formula, the addition of "mercy" to the list and the title "Savior" for God. Rarely found in the earlier Pauline letters, "Savior" is characteristic of the Pastorals, where it is used both for God (1 Tim 2:3; 4:10; Titus 1:3; 3:4) and for Jesus (2 Tim 1:10; Titus 1:4; 2:13; 3:6). The LXX uses *sōtēr* ("savior") for both God (1 Sam 10:19; Isa 45:15, 21) and individuals raised up by God to rescue the people (Judg 3:9, 15). The term designates God's saving action on behalf of the righteous in Luke 1:47. Luke-Acts also employs the term for Jesus as the one who fulfills that divine promise (Luke 2:11; Acts 5:31; 13:23). In Acts the title applies to Jesus as the Messiah whom God has exalted by raising him from the dead. Paul used "Savior" for the coming Christ who delivers the faithful who belong to the heavenly citizenry (Phil 3:20). In the Greco-Roman world the expression "savior" could be used of both deities and human benefactors. When applied to the Roman emperor, it implied that his rule benefited humankind on a scale equivalent to that of a god. The repetitions of the title first for God and then for Jesus in the examples from Titus 1:3-4 and 3:4-6 indicate that the Pastorals use the expression for Jesus as the manifestation of God's saving plan for humankind. Though Christians are employing a familiar title from both religious and benefactor inscriptions, they use it uniquely of God.

The addition of "mercy" to form a triadic greeting probably points forward to the cognate verb in 1:16. The apostle himself will serve as an example of God's mercy. Where Paul's earlier formulation spoke of his apostleship as according to the will of God (1 Cor 1:1), 1 Timothy provides a more authoritative structure for Paul's mission. He has been serving at God's command. This shift corresponds with the genre of the letter as administrative mandate.

A similar shift toward criteria of public authority may be detected in the adjective used to describe the relationship between Paul and Timothy, *gnēsios* (NRSV, "loyal"). It indicates that something is genuine or authentic. Within the context of a public charge, this term supports Timothy's position as guarantor of genuine Pauline tradition. When Paul himself dispatched Timothy to represent him in the conflicts at Corinth, he referred to him as "beloved and faithful in the Lord" (1 Cor 4:17; 16:10-11). He is explicitly credited with ability to represent Paul's teaching in all the churches. His role in that conflict fits a specific ancient use of envoys. Though associated with Paul, Timothy was not attached to any of the partisan factions. Consequently, he was sent to foster reconciliation within the community (Mitchell 1992: 643). For the Pastorals, Timothy's authority over the churches has shifted from reconciling factions to determining authentic teaching and practice (1 Tim 1:3-7).

Rein in False Teachers (1:3-7)

Though a Pauline letter normally follows the greeting with an expression of thanksgiving, here it is deferred in favor of a statement which underlines the nature of the authority entrusted to Timothy. His charge is both negative, to repress false teaching (1:3), and positive, to strengthen the faith of the community (v. 5). Fitting this scenario into other versions of Paul's mission is difficult. Acts 18:18-21 has the apostle pass through Ephesus on a journey east after his departure from Corinth sometime in the summer of AD 52. The church itself appears to have been established by others already, perhaps by Prisca and Aquila. Paul probably wrote 1 Corinthians from Ephesus (1 Cor 16:19), at which point he dispatched Timothy to Corinth (16:10-11) and expects to wait for his return in Asia Minor. Timothy also functioned as Paul's representative to the churches in Macedonia (Acts 18:5; 19:22, Timothy and Erastus go to Macedonia while Paul remains in Ephesus; 1 Thess 3:2). Paul's farewell to elders from Ephesus in Acts 20:17-32 presumes that neither he nor his associates will ever see the Ephesians again. They are to assume responsibility as overseers of the church in the divisions of the last days.

1 Timothy describes the opponents as determined to "teach different doctrine" *(heterodidaskalein)* that consists in "myths and genealogies" (1:4) and their personal agenda as a desire to be "teachers of the law" *(nomodidaskaloi)*. The formulation of unusual compound words to express such concepts is one of the linguistic peculiarities of the Pastorals. As we have seen in the discussion of the opponents in the Pastorals, such details do not admit a precise description of their teaching. The characterizations "myths" and "meaningless talk" are characteristic polemic descriptions in both philosophical and comic settings (e.g., Lucian *Lover of Lies* 9). The contrasting descriptions of the impact of both forms of teaching make it clear that such teaching is not an alternative formulation of Christian faith. The Greek phrase at the end of v. 4 is ambiguous: *oikonomian theou tēn en pistei*. The NRSV gives what it thinks the author intended to say, "the divine training which is known by faith." But *oikonomia theou* is not used with the meaning "divine training" until Clement of Alexandria (d. AD 215). *Oikonomia* refers to God's plan in administering the universe or salvation. Paul refers to his own ministry as according to God's plan in that sense (Col 1:25). It is the object of Paul's preaching to show all people God's plan of salvation which has been revealed in Christ (Eph 3:9). This usage fits the theological framework of Christ as the manifestation of God's salvation found in the Pastorals. Therefore this cryptic phrase contrasts what is gained from useless speculations, probably associated with some form of interpretation of Scripture, with participation in God's plan of salvation on the part of believers. (There is nothing in the context to read *oikonomia* in its other meaning of "household management" proposed by those who treat the expression as demand for orderly behavior in the household of God.)

A triad of phrases which appear to be synonymous terms for true Christian piety describes the goal of Timothy's instruction: the "pure heart, good conscience, and sincere faith" which issue in love. The word translated "sincere" is more literally "unhypocritical," which makes a stronger polemical point. The faith alleged by false teachers is deceitful acting. Later their consciences will be described as seared or corrupt (4:2; Titus 1:15). 1 Timothy does not explain the content of the positive terms. He can presume that a Christian audience will recognize that they are standard expressions of virtue. Faith and love are nearly synonymous (1 Tim 1:14; 2 Tim 1:13, connected with healthy teaching; Titus 2:2).

Excursus on the Function of the Law (1:8-11)

1 Timothy undercuts one basis for the authority claimed by opposing teachers, the law, by employing a common topos concerning law in Hellenistic moralists, "law is not laid down for the innocent" (Gk. *dikaios*, "righteous, just"). Law serves to govern the behavior of persons not yet able to control their passions and make rational choices. Persons making progress in morality require exhortation. Greek moralists frequently speak of justice as the sum of all virtue (as Aristotle *Nic. Eth.* 5.23; 1029b). The truth of the slogan was further exhibited on stage in the new comedy (so Quinn 1990: 14). Though this line of argument is not derived from Paul's discussions of law as a paradox for humans caught under sin, 1 Timothy opens the excursus with a Pauline phrase, "we know that the law is good" (Rom 7:16).

The second step in the argument employs a list of vices to spell out the depraved character of those whose behavior must be governed by fear of legal sanctions. Recognizing that slave trading was considered a form of theft, interpreters have suggested that the list was composed to echo the Decalogue (Exod 20:12-16). However, the leadoff vices of patricide, matricide, and inclusion of sodomites and slave traders suggest a somewhat different set of associations, stock figures in tragic and comic theater or their artistic representations in painting (see Dibelius-Conzelmann 1972: 23). Rhetorically the "sound" or "healthy" teaching which conforms to the gospel can be highlighted by a collection of striking figures of human vice.

1 Tim 1:10 is the first example of a major motif in the Pastorals — the use of medical terms for health and disease to describe true and false teaching respectively. Those who follow false teaching have minds which are corrupt (1 Tim 6:5; 2 Tim 3:8). In contrast to the healthy discourse of persons who hold true faith, the useless talk of false teachers eats at a person like gangrene (2 Tim 2:17). For Stoic moralists, who considered vices and the passions which spawned them a form of disease, the philosopher's job was to serve as a physician to the soul. To those whose souls were eaten up by vice, the philosopher physician might administer the cauterizing treatment of harsh rebuke rather than the more comforting treatments of calm reason. Laws, rulers, and magistrates were also considered agents of the painful corrections necessary to remove the abnormality of a truly evil character (see Malherbe 1989: 123-30). The concluding verse shifts from the stock philosophical argument back to the true faith taught by the apostle. Elements of doxology to be picked up again in 1:17 remind readers that sound teaching did not emerge from the reasoned deliberations of philosophers. It is God's gift.

Thanksgiving, the Apostle's Example (1:12-17)

Paul typically followed the epistolary greeting with an expression of thanksgiving for the faith of his addressees. Here thanksgiving has been relocated and focused on the apostle as an example of conversion for the letter's recipients. Consequently, his own description of his prior life as vigorous persecution of the church (1 Cor 15:9; Gal 1:13-17) has been incorporated into a list of vices typical of the sinner who does not know God, the blasphemer, and the "man of violence" (*hybristēs;* Rom 1:30). This example spells out the Christian transformation of the philosophical topos in the previous section. Sinners are not rescued by philosophical action but by divine action. The christological focus of God's mercy is underlined since Jesus is the agent of both the apostle's conversion and the Lord whom he now serves. A Jewish commonplace, that God's patience with the sinner provides opportunity for repentance, has been recast with Christ as subject (1:16; Pss 86:15; 103:8).

1 Tim 1:15 introduces the first of a series of sayings designated "faithful" or "sure" (so NRSV; also 1 Tim 3:1a; 4:9; 2 Tim 2:11; Titus 3:8). In this case the brief soteriological affirmation which follows clearly constitutes the content of belief, "Christ Jesus came into the world to save sinners" (cf. Rom 5:8-9). 1 Timothy then returns to Paul as an example of Christ's power to fulfill that promise of salvation. In some cases the formula appears to refer to an affirmation of salvation that preceded it (e.g., 1 Tim 3:1a to 2:15; Titus 3:8 to 3:4-7). Finally, the thanksgiving section concludes with a doxology (cf. 1 Tim 6:15-16). Its depiction of God combines the Jewish "King of the ages" (Jer 10:10; Tob 13:7; Acts 15:3) with the more philosophical attributes, "immortal" and "invisible."

Commissioning Formula (1:18-20)

The chapter concludes by returning to the genre of a mandate epistle in which the apostle delivers the charge to his subordinate (1:18a resumes vv. 2 and 4). But just as the previous section traced Paul's authority back to the mercy of Christ which transformed a sinner into his servant, so Timothy's position is traced back to a time prior to the epistle. The prophetic utterances which pointed to Timothy presumably refer to communal discernment (cf. Acts 13:2-3). 1 Tim 4:14 places these utterances in the context of Timothy's ordination by a council of elders. This ordination is recalled to strengthen Timothy's resolve to persist in combating the false teachers. Paul commonly adopts images of military and athletic struggle to describe his mission (e.g., 1 Cor 9:24-27; 2 Cor 10:3-5; Phil 1:27-30; 3:12-14). Both the military imagery and the picture of false teachers suffering shipwreck are common in philosophical discourse. The intensity of those images is matched by the severity of the action to be taken. Individual teachers, Hymenaeus (also in 2 Tim 2:17) and Alexander (2 Tim 4:14), are to be cut off from the community. This action repeats Paul's long-distance excommunication of a Corinthian whose marriage to his stepmother was a public scandal (1 Cor 5:1-5). Neither passage explains the effect of handing a person over to Satan. If cutting a person off from the community represents the harshest remedy that the physician of the soul could take, then some hope of conversion may underlie "learn not to blaspheme."

Pray for All People (2:1-7)

The phrase "I urge" (Gk. *parakalō*) often marks the transition to community exhortation in Pauline letters (e.g., Rom 12:1; Eph 4:1; Phil 4:2). 1 Tim 2:1–3:16 detail a series of rules for the conduct of those who belong to the household of God (3:15). They are not necessarily connected with the problems of false teaching referred to in the letter opening. The household to be ordered by these instructions is first of all a gathering for prayer and worship of God, not a philosophical school. Its goal of "a quiet and peaceable life in all godliness (Gk. *eusebeia*) and dignity *(semnotēs)*" (2:2) is admittedly phrased in terms familiar in the Greco-Roman moralists. Prayer for public authorities was part of Second Temple Judaism, perhaps fostered by Persian policies connected with restoration of the temple (cf. Bar 1:10-12; 1 Esdr 6:9-10, LXX; *Ep. Arist.* 45). In the Roman period, it figures in apologetic arguments aimed at demonstrating the civic loyalty of Jews (1 Macc 7:33; Josephus *J.W.* 2.197; Philo *Legat.* 157, 317; *Flacc.* 49). The connection between a peaceable life and prayer for ruling authorities belongs to that tradition. It should not be pressed to yield a political philosophy. As capital of the Roman province of Asia, Ephesus underwent major architectural renovation from the time of Augustus on. The imperial cult made its way into the public spaces of the city, with the first of four temples built in the late first century AD. Some expression of civic piety would be required of any minority group in that context.

The terms "godliness" and "dignity" express a Greco-Roman ideal of virtuous citizenship. The repeated appeals to godliness and/or dignity in these letters (1 Tim 2:2, 10; 3:4, 8, 11, 16; 4:7, 8; 5:4; 6:3, 5, 6, 11; 2 Tim 3:12; Titus 1:1; 2:2, 7, 12) often lead to the conclusion that the Pastorals have traded in an ethic which sets itself against the prevailing culture for the ideals of the patron classes of Greco-Roman society. Here the terminology is directly associated with prayer for rulers as evidence of Christian piety. Philo argued that Jews demonstrate their godliness — and proper regard for imperial benefactions — by the prayers offered in the synagogue (*Flacc.* 48). The term "godliness" carried a wide range of meanings since it not only implied diligent performance of the rites demanded by the gods but also the inner dispositions toward divine things which motivate such activity, the desire always to please the gods.

The Christian shift occurs with 2:3b-4. Godliness is not just the cultural ideal of an upright member of the community. It is not to be had without conversion to a particular god as one's savior/benefactor. The expression "knowledge of the truth" serves as a synonym for conversion to Christianity (cf. Heb 10:26). A two-part creedal formula appeals to the unity of God and the uniqueness of Jesus as mediator in defense of this appeal for conversion (2:5-6a). The clause describing Jesus' death as a ransom echoes the formula in Mark 10:45. Since he cites a familiar formula, the author does not explain why humanity required such a mediator or to whom ransom was paid. Parallels in Hebrews would connect a mediator with the new covenant (Heb 8:6; 9:15; 12:24), but the Pastorals show no explicit interest in covenant theology. A somewhat cryptic comment tacked on to the formula in 2:6b, rendered literally "the testimony in its own times," may be aimed to answer an objection to Christian preaching. If godliness requires a specific person as mediator, why did God wait so long? The response merely hints at a stock explanation that God's providence determines the appropriate time of salvation. The reference to testimony brings the author back to the figure of the apostle himself (cf. 1 Cor 2:1; 2 Cor 1:12), who was entrusted with preaching this message to the Gentiles.

Dignity for Men and Women (2:8–3:1a)

This section poses several problems of continuity. Grammatically the instructions to women concerning dignity and godliness (2:9-10) depend upon the "I desire" of v. 8. One would expect them to deal with women and worship. Instead, 1 Timothy sketches a conventional picture of the virtuous woman. Her deportment is that of the female counterpart to the male, with hands raised up in the traditional *orans* posture. Does this segment have anything at all to do with women at prayer? That they were expected to devote themselves to prayer is clear in the description of the real widow in 5:9, though the activities of younger women are connected with their activities as mistress of the household, not prayer (5:10, 14; Titus 2:4-5). Good works are the deeds of charity and hospitality appropriate to female benefactors.

The only possible connection between this section and worship occurs in the prohibition against women teaching or having authority over males (2:11). That reading assumes that the teaching took place in the context of a community gathered for worship rather than at some other time. Nothing in the Pastorals makes that link explicitly. Teaching as evangelization took place in households, workshops, and various public spaces. The household and workshop are most likely the places within which the women who participated in the Pauline missionary efforts were active. We have seen that those who defended teaching women philosophy had to counter the objection that such education would make them figures of ridicule, neglecting home and family, seeking quarrels with men. The false teachers are described as upsetting whole households (Titus 1:11). As we have seen, women constituted a higher proportion of the early Christian churches than of the larger society. The wealth attributed to the woman in this passage suggests that she was also a person capable of exerting the influence of a rich benefactor.

To which audience is this depiction of the godly and dignified Christian woman directed? To outsiders, including pagan husbands and family, who suspect that Christianity is another oriental cult likely to involve women in the disorderly and antiauthoritarian behavior often depicted in comedy? Or to insiders, caught in the asymmetries of wealth, status, and influence that would pressure lower-status males to defer to their female patroness? The letter does not say. Women are not permitted to engage in the verbal give-and-take characteristic of the instruction of males in a rhetorical culture. To remain silent while learning automatically insures that they cannot become teachers in that setting. But 1 Tim 2:9-12 does defend instructing women. It will provide the clothing of virtue, especially modesty and self-control, to replace that of wealth (v. 9; cf. 1 Pet 3:3-6). The NRSV masks this argument somewhat by assuming that the adjectives in 2:9a refer to "suitable clothing" rather than "proper conduct" (on women's virtues see Epictetus *Disc.* 2.10; Plutarch *Bride and Groom* 26).

The section shifts from philosophical topos back to religious warrant with a striking evocation of Gen 3:13-16. Since it is the woman who was deceived by the serpent, the order in which Adam and Eve were created also points to an ontological disparity between male and female. In Philo, this gender difference is expressed in more philosophical terms. Adam represents the rational mind; Eve the power of sense perception which becomes entangled with the material world (Philo *Leg. all.* 2.24-25; *Cher.* 58–60). To gain a true perception of anything requires suppressing the power of sense perception. The identification of Eve's deception in this passage could have the sexual overtones of gnostic myths where demonic powers rape the earthly Eve. Sexual imagery seems to be encoded in both of Paul's references to this story (1 Cor 11:3-16; 2 Cor 11:3, though in this instance the whole community, men and women, is endangered by false apostles). However, a philosophical distinction like Philo's allegory makes more sense of this distinction between Adam and Eve, which otherwise makes a very odd claim that Adam was not a transgressor (contrary to Rom 5:12-14). As rational mind, Adam is not deceived about truth. Only sense perception creates that possibility.

Since 1 Timothy merely invokes the example to provide a warrant for the restriction in 2:12, one cannot determine the further implications of the image with any certainty. V. 15 rescues his argument from the suggestion that women are in some sense incapable of salvation by treating Gen 3:16 as a blessing rather than a curse. Of course, the transformation works only if the women in question continue to exhibit the virtues of faith, love, holiness, and self-control (Gk. *sōphrosynē;* NRSV, "modesty"). Since the first two are characteristic of Christian parenesis, 1 Timothy does not suggest that childbirth means salvation for all women, but only for those who retain their Christian profession of faith. Contrary to the NRSV, the "faithful saying" of 3:1a must refer back to this statement about salvation, not forward to the qualification lists in vv. 1b-13.

Qualifications of Bishops (3:1b-7)

Since the faithful saying in 3:1a refers to what precedes, the lists of qualifications for persons who are entrusted with public functions in the community continue the previous instructions. Translation of the terms *episkopos* (bishop, overseer), *diakonos* (deacon, minister, or servant) and *presbyteros* (elder, old man) is difficult both because they have both official and nonofficial meanings and because the relationships between the groups so designated and their communal functions are unclear. By the time Ignatius of Antioch (c. AD 110) writes to churches in Asia Minor a three-tier pattern of offices (bishop, presbyter, and deacon) has emerged. The bishop represents God or Jesus and is the final authority in communal teaching and discipline (*Trall.* 2:1; 3:1; *Eph.* 6:1). Given the varied problems with marriage facing the early communities, Ignatius's determination to stem exogamous marriage by requiring the bishop's consent for Christians to marry (*Pol.* 5:2) might play into the hands of those who forbade marriage (1 Tim 4:3). Such authority clearly cements the bishop's position in the community as *paterfamilias.* Though an earlier generation of scholars read the emphasis on church officers in the Pastorals as further evidence of a second-century-AD origin, nothing in the Pastorals suggests such a rigid, hierarchical structure.

Since the *episkopos* — which we will follow the NRSV in translating "bishop" even though "overseer" probably comes closer to his administrative functions — is referred to in the singular while deacons and elders are plural, supervision must have included their activities as well as those of church members in general. The terms "bishop" and "deacon" appear in Phil 1:1, where both are in the plural. The extensive financial transactions between Paul and the Philippian church (Phil 4:10-20; 2 Cor 11:9) raise the possibility that they were responsible for the material resources of the community much as the overseer in the Essene communities was (cf. CD 14:12-16). The Essene overseer was also associated with the council of the community, which may have provided the model for the relationship between the bishop and deacons being assumed in the Pastorals. Why is it necessary to declare it a "good work" to desire this office? Presumably the phrase is an indirect way of encouraging persons to come forward as communal benefactors. In the complex world of benefactors and recipients, communities often found themselves in the position of soliciting or pressuring prominent citizens to undertake civic obligations. The previous injunctions have placed severe limitations on wealthy women as potential patrons. So the author may imply that appropriate persons will have to be encouraged to undertake the task of supervising the community.

The list of virtues to be exhibited by desirable candidates holds few surprises. The bishop is to be a respected member of the larger community. His ability to care for the church has been proven by the way in which he manages his own household. The only oddity in the catalogue of virtues is the phrase "husband of one wife," which the NRSV has interpreted to mean "married only once" (3:2). When used on epitaphs honoring a deceased woman, that is clearly what the phrase means. It often indicates that she refused to remarry after the death of her husband (a practice that 5:14 would curtail). A symmetrical expression for males has not been found. The phrase would also prohibit remarriage of a divorced person (Mark 10:11; Luke 16:18), though 1 Timothy does not refer to divorce. Perhaps the expression has merely translated into the cultural idiom of honor Paul's preference for those who became single remaining so (1 Cor 7:8, 39-40).

The only qualifications that indicate the religious requirements of the position are an aptitude for teaching and an established period of life as a Christian. Lucian (b. AD 120) mocks Christians for rapidly investing a fraudulent neophyte as bishop (*Passing of Peregrinus*). Since the *paterfamilias* is responsible for the honor of all those in his household, the bishop's standing in the larger community also reflects back on the church.

Qualifications of Deacons (3:8-13)

With variations in the terminology, the list of characteristics for deacons parallels that for bishops. Omission of parallels to teaching and hospitality in the case of deacons could imply that their activities do not involve the obligations of a benefactor or patron who would be expected to put his own resources at the disposal of the church. Like the bishop, deacons must be tested to prove the genuineness of their faith (3:10). Neither the nature of the test nor the functions performed by the deacons are indicated.

Just as instructions to women were attached to those about men with the phrase "likewise" (2:9), so 3:11 contains an insertion concerning women that is attached to its context with the expression "likewise" and a grammatical form that parallels vv. 8-9 in condensed form. Who are the women in question? The view that they are wives of deacons appears to be ruled out by the fact that the topic of marriage for deacons is to be taken up in v. 12 in a form that parallels the requirement for bishops. One would also expect a possessive "their" if the women in question were married to deacons. Therefore, the structure of the passage suggests that these persons are women associated with the ministry of deacons in some way. Since deacons do not have authority over others or engage in teaching, 2:11-15 would not bar women from such service. However, the immediate return to the male deacons in 3:12 suggests that 1 Timothy does not envisage an order of women deacons. The comment may be intended to acknowledge the activities of a number of women missionaries and benefactors in the Pauline communities without establishing a particular order of female deacons. Pliny (*Ep.* 10.96-97) reports the torturing of female Christian slaves who are called deaconesses. For women in a pagan household some activities could be carried out only if the churches had women to send to them.

Digression: Reason for the Letter (3:14-16)

Before the author returns to explicit instructions directed to Timothy and the conflict against false teaching (4:1-6), he digresses to inform the reader of the purpose of the letter. Statements about the reason for writing are common in ancient letters, as are those concerning the sender's travel plans. In this case, the apostle needs to secure the faith and practice of the community. 1 Timothy has been using the expression "household" in its social, political, and religious sense. Perhaps the thought of establishing its faith led to the shift from household as a set of relationships between people to house as a building in 3:15c. Comparisons between the church and buildings occur elsewhere in Paul (e.g., 1 Cor 3:10-17; 6:19; a temple). Perhaps the imagery of a pillar and foundation was suggested by the Imperial temple building in progress at Ephesus. The word *hedraiōma,* which the NRSV translates "bulwark," is more likely a variation on *hedraios,* "foundation," since "bulwark" would confuse the metaphor even more by mixing cultic and military construction.

The section concludes with another liturgical fragment, a christological hymn that celebrates the saving work of Christ in his incarnation and resurrection/ascension to heavenly glory. Contrary to the NRSV, the translation "nations" should be adopted for Gk. *ethnē* (NRSV, "Gentiles") since the expression is in poetic parallelism with "believed in throughout the world." This triumphant hymn in honor of the exalted Christ enhances the image of temple construction in the previous verse. The confidence expressed by such poetry is all the more stunning if one remembers that this household of God had no public buildings. Like other small cultic associations, it assembled in rooms of a patron's house. The hymn itself should be set forth in a way that makes the alterations between heavenly glory and earthly manifestation clear (Bassler 1996b: 76-77). "Revealed in flesh," "proclaimed," and "believed" all take place on earth. "Vindicated in spirit," "seen by angels," and "taken up in glory" are all equivalent expressions of the same heavenly event, the exaltation of the risen Christ. Only that christological faith can sustain the Christian claim to preach God's universal plan of salvation.

False Teachers Predicted (4:1-5)

The letter suddenly shifts from exhortation and hymnic celebration to an apocalyptic prophecy concerning the end times (cf. Mark 13:5-22; Acts 20:17-38; 2 Thess 2:3-10). Predictions that many will be led astray in the end times because Satan will be working through false teachers, prophets, and messiahs are common in apocalyptic texts. Paul described the false apostles who invaded the Corinthian community as "ministers of Satan" (2 Cor 11:15). Though philosophical moralists sometimes spoke of cauterizing those who needed harsh treatment in order to reform, 1 Timothy uses the image to depict the hopeless condition of its opponents. They are now incapable of moral reform.

Though this terminology is conventional polemic, the two prohibitions attributed to the false teachers prohibiting marriage and abstinence from certain foods, appear to represent specific points at issue. Perhaps these ascetic rules were part of a larger program in which such persons claimed to achieve prophetic or visionary powers (so Goulder). The appeals to thanksgiving as a way of sanctifying food reflect Paul's use of the thanksgiving topos in the Corinthian controversy over eating meat that had been obtained from an idol sacrifice (1 Cor 10:30-33). In this case, the principle has been broadened with an echo of God's word concerning creation in Gen 1:29-31.

To Timothy on Ministry (4:6-16)

Though one might expect a sharper confrontation with the false teachers, Timothy's task is to sustain true teaching within the church. He is to avoid the useless speculations of the false teachers. Unlike the opponents with their corrupt consciences, Timothy with his athletic training in godliness provides an example for the congregation of the salvation that Christians expect from God (4:10). Athletic imagery was commonly used for the effort required to make moral progress (e.g., Epictetus *Disc.* 3.12.7; 3.22.51-52). The "sure saying" formula in 4:9 is ambiguous. It could refer back to the statement about the value of godliness for life (v. 8) which is given as the warrant for Timothy's training. Or it could refer to some part of v. 10, God as the Savior of all people. A backward reference to training in godliness makes the saying similar to that in 3:1a. A forward reference evokes the earlier affirmation that Christ came to save sinners in 1:15.

4:11 uses the imperatives (reformulated by the NRSV) "command" and "teach" in resuming the communal obligation that is the basis of Timothy's ministry. Ancient moralists regularly insist that a teacher must be the living example of his doctrine. This assumption is applied to Timothy's own efforts at training in godliness. It forms the basis of salvation for those who hear his teaching (vv. 11, 12b, 15-16). Several odd details are enclosed in this framework of conventional moral exhortation. They indicate that the author does not have the actual person Timothy in view. The recipient is described as a young man whose age might cause people to disregard his teaching (v. 12a). But Timothy was already sufficiently advanced in age, faith, and understanding of Paul's teaching to serve as his envoy during one of the first crises in Corinth sometime in the early 50s. He is co-sender of five of Paul's letters. Even at that period in his life it would have been wrong to describe Timothy himself as a young man still shaping his character and needing to take care that his progress in virtue is evident to all. Decades later Timothy has had plenty of experience in dealing with persons whose disdain had nothing to do with age but was directed at the apostle Paul himself. With his extensive missionary and ambassadorial experience in the Pauline churches, Timothy would not need to be reminded either of the gifts of ministry associated with his own selection (v. 14) or of the need to maintain reading of Scripture, preaching, and teaching in a church when the apostle is absent (v. 13).

The presumption that the apostle is about to arrive (4:13) neglects the earlier suggestion that the letter may serve to replace an apostle who may not return to Ephesus (3:14-15). Details which clash with what we know of Timothy's activities, age, character, and relationship to Paul make excellent sense if they are not intended to depict the facts of Timothy's ministry. Rather, this description serves as a verbal paradigm and authorization for those who will come after the apostles and their associates. This intent is made evident by another slip in the facade. Here the addressee is ordained by a group of elders. In 2 Tim 1:6 Paul's laying on of hands confers authority to his subordinate. The latter is more likely to have been the case. Certainly it is the apostle's authority which Timothy exercises as envoy in the churches. But the former will be the experience of all those who come after Timothy.

On Correcting Others (5:1-2)

The reference to Timothy's youth (4:12a) makes the issue of correcting those who were older, whether male or female, particularly problematic. Age aside, the question of whether gentle encouragement or harsh rebuke was the better policy appears frequently in the moralists. The preference for gentle correction would certainly prevail when addressing persons who were in some respect one's superiors. The injunction to treat various groups as one would members of one's own family was also a standard piece of advice. Emphasis on the purity required when dealing with younger women was particularly necessary since foreign cults and opposing philosophical schools were always charged with taking advantage of impressionable females, a topos that the Pastorals do not hesitate to employ against their opponents (2 Tim 3:6).

On Providing for Widows (5:3-16)

The extensive discussion of widows has created a number of puzzles for interpreters. The wealthy, independent widow was often sought after as a patron in Roman society. She was also a figure of some suspicion or envy for her actual or presumed sexual liberty. Such suspicions are clearly operative in the rules proposed for younger widows (5:11-15). Though the OT frequently speaks of caring for widows as a moral duty (Exod 22:22-23; Job 31:16; Isa 1:17, 23), the obligation to care for the widow does not appear in Greco-Roman moralists. Its appearance in the NT reflects the influence of Jewish tradition (Acts 6:1-6; Jas 1:27). The initial command (5:4) incorporates responsibilities toward the widow under the general rubric of honor owed to one's parents. Christians who refuse to provide for their own family are worse than pagans (v. 8). In this instance, the author presumes that the widows in question as well as their children and grandchildren are Christian. Even though these cases seem to represent a repudiation of the freedom exercised by some Christian women to remain single and devote themselves to the Lord (1 Cor 7:32-35, 40), the rules proposed are not particularly astonishing. They guarantee the moral propriety of the Christian community in the eyes of outsiders (5:14b; MacDonald 1996: 157-63).

The picture of the true widow, a solitary figure completely devoted to prayer, forms a sharp contrast to the popular image of the wealthy widow free to pursue her sexual desires (5:5-6). That image is also drawn with Jewish prototypes in mind (see Jdt 9:6-8; Luke 2:36-38). Again, the piety of such persons will spare the community any reproach from outsiders (5:7).

The situation becomes more complicated when the author turns from such established moral topoi to the particular difficulty of persons enrolled as widows (5:9-10, 16). These women are being supported financially by the community. In order for a woman to qualify, her earlier life must have been an exemplary model of all the virtues which the Pastorals expect of respectable Christian wives and mothers. The emphasis on the good works by which such women have benefited the church in the past establishes the charity received from the community as nothing less than the proper return owed a benefactor. Hence 1 Timothy makes appropriate use of the term "honor" to mean both remuneration and respect in the heading to the discussion (v. 3; see Kidd 1990: 103-6). Of course, the codes of reciprocity which governed ancient society never permit a gift without an obligation. Therefore, it would be more likely than not for such widows also to perform some service within the church, whether prayer (v. 5) or instruction of younger women (Titus 2:4-5). It seems unlikely that such activity constitutes them as an "order" in the formal sense in which the expression is used for bishops, deacons, or elders.

Another puzzle attaches to the age qualification. With a high rate of mortality in childbirth, women commonly died in their thirties; men, a decade or so later. How many sixty-year-old widows are there likely to be in the tiny Christian population of Ephesus? Is this in effect a way of abolishing the category? Why so drastic a response? Some scholars have pointed out that Roman texts often speak of any woman who is living independently of her husband as a widow. Consequently, a much larger number of younger women might claim that designation as a result of divorce or refusal to marry. The activities of some Christian women in Pauline missionary circles as well as Paul's own advice against remarriage (1 Cor 7:40) could also have played a role in creating this crisis (see Bassler 1984). Hence the very unusual conclusion to this set of rules. Christian women are required to provide for any other widows in their families so that the church will not be burdened with supporting them.

On Presbyters and Other Mandata (5:17-25)

As we indicated (3:1-13), the distinctions between bishop, presbyter or elder, and deacon were not yet clearly formalized. The activities for which they are to be paid by the congregation are similar to those of the bishop, though the latter appears to be an independent head of a household not in need of remuneration. Paul himself testifies to the common practice of paying those who preach the gospel — not least in the offense which his own independence caused among the Corinthians (1 Corinthians 9). The other sayings in this collection proceed from the difficulty caused by accusations against an elder. The requirement for witnesses and public rebuke of those who refuse to reform follows Jewish models (also adopted in Matt 18:15-18). A solemn oath formula in 5:21 serves to remind those who will be required to judge such cases of their responsibility to remain impartial in such proceedings.

A series of other sayings warn against hasty ordination of persons whose character may not be known (5:22, 24; cf. 3:6-7) and the promise that neither evil nor good deeds remain hidden (possibly a reference to the judgment). All of the sayings in this section are loosely related except the peculiar advice to take a little wine for the stomach (5:23). Does the author intend to correct an ascetic posture derived from the false teachers (4:3-5) or the unintended effect of his own advice (3:3)? The text does not say.

To Slaves (6:1-2)

Instructions to slaves to be respectful and obedient to their masters are a routine part of the NT adaptation of household code parenesis (so Eph 6:5-9; Col 3:22–4:1; 1 Pet 2:18-25). Unlike Colossians/Ephesians, 1 Timothy and 1 Peter lack any corresponding word to the masters against harsh and abusive treatment of the slave. 1 Peter even refers to unjust suffering at the hands of an abusive master as imitation of Christ's suffering. Reference to the reputation a slave's bad behavior might bring down on the community in 6:1 also points to a situation in which the Christian slave has a pagan master. But v. 2 shifts to slaves with Christian owners. The argument is not altogether clear. We have seen that other cults included all members of a household including its slaves under the authority of the *paterfamilias*. The cause of disrespect cannot simply be the egalitarian, familial language used for fellow believers. It must be associated with the somewhat obscure description of the masters as benefactors, "believers and beloved, who take part in works of kindness." (The NRSV makes the slaves benefactors to their masters.) In other words, the slave might abuse the beneficence of a master who is not given to harsh treatment.

Teachers: False and True (6:2b-16)

1 Timothy returns to the issue of sound teaching by sketching two pictures: that of morally depraved false teachers who are caught up in their own greed (6:3-10) and that of the man of God completely devoted to the gospel (vv. 11-16). The moral corruption and senseless arguing of the false teachers summarize the picture drawn of them throughout the epistle (1:3-11; 4:1-5; also 2 Tim 2:23; 3:6; Titus 3:9). Then the argument turns to a new element in the standard rhetoric of vilification, greed (6:5b-10). The qualifications for bishops and deacons required that such persons be free of the passion for money (3:3, 8). Among the philosophic moralists the true teacher does not seek to become rich from teaching but has genuine concern for the spiritual health of his listeners. False teachers flatter their listeners by adapting their words to whatever wins them the most popularity. One can distinguish the true teacher by his life of independent self-sufficiency. A certain austerity of conduct, dress, and other forms of consumption shows that he can do without the wealth to be gained from teaching what pleases a crowd. Paul frequently used this topos in defending the integrity of his preaching (e.g., 2 Cor 9:8; Phil 4:11-13). 6:6 alludes to this standard argument. Though the opponents think that material wealth comes from a reputation for godliness, the real wealth derived from it is self-sufficiency, the ability to be content in whatever circumstances one encounters.

6:7-8 then draw on a stock example in favor of detached indifference to one's circumstances. We come into the world with nothing and leave it with nothing (Philo *Spec. Leg.* 1.294-95; Seneca *Ep. Mor.* 102.24-25; Diogenes Laertius 6.105; and compare Matt 6:25-34). The conclusion to the argument then sharpens the picture of the destruction caused by greed (6:9-10). The proverbial "love of money is the root of all evils" (v. 10a) summarizes the point. V. 10b applies this general exhortation to the persons at hand, the false teachers.

The description of the man of God which follows (6:11-14) is the antithesis to that of the false teachers. He exhibits all the virtues of godliness as well as the endurance typical of Stoic self-sufficiency. Athletic metaphors such as "fight the good fight" (v. 12) are common in such exhortation. 1 Timothy provides a Christian framework for this standard philosophical argument by shifting from the human witnesses to Timothy's own promises when he was ordained by the elders (4:14) to the witnesses who will also be the judges of the human contest of faith, God and Jesus Christ (6:13-15a). In the only reference to Jesus' actual life in the letter, the author invokes Jesus before Pilate as an example of such heroic testimony (v. 13). The reference to God leads into an expanded doxology which combines traditional expressions for God's sovereignty with philosophical language that expresses the great distance between divine reality and human comprehension (vv. 15b-16).

Coda: To the Rich (6:17-19)

Rhetorically, the doxology should conclude the argument and the letter. However, the author takes a brief moment to correct a possible misreading of the motifs from Stoic and Cynic philosophy used in his previous argument. The severer Cynic moralists used a radically ascetic indifference to all material and social goods in stinging attacks against the rich. The author of 1 Timothy does not want to be misunderstood, so he turns to provide a series of basic instructions for wealthy Christians. They must recognize the transitory nature of possessions and show proper gratitude to God, who has given these possessions to them. Again he can rely on the cultural conventions that detailed one's obligation to respond in kind. In this instance the response is generosity in doing good works.

Letter Closing (6:20-21)

We have seen that the Pastorals depart from the format of undisputed Pauline letters. The closing of 1 Timothy is particularly sparse. The final charge serves as a rhetorical summation of the earlier argument (1:18). One would expect further information at the conclusion such as travel plans, greetings to others, or some form of benediction. Instead the letter simply ends with a rather sparse greeting.

2 Timothy

COMMENTARY

Greeting (1:1-2)

2 Timothy opens with a greeting formula similar to that in 1 Tim 1:1-2. Two slight modifications point to the shift in genre between the two letters. Instead of referring to Timothy as his "loyal" child, the author uses the term which Paul used when he dispatched Timothy as his envoy, "beloved child" (1 Cor 4:17). The formula which refers to Paul's own commissioning as an apostle also has the more characteristic "will of God" (1 Cor 1:1; 2 Cor 1:1) rather than the formal "command" (1 Tim 1:1). An additional phrase details the purpose of this apostleship, "the promise of life." A similar expression was used to encourage Timothy to continue his training in godliness in 1 Tim 4:8. The shift in genre from a mandate letter instructing Timothy to the farewell letter of the dying apostle gives this phrase a special note of pathos. Paul's own fidelity to the gospel which embodies that promise will soon cost him his life.

One should not oversentimentalize the expression "beloved child" since it could serve to designate formal and social relationships between individuals. Paul's plea on behalf of the slave Onesimus uses that terminology (Phlm 10-11). The usage there fits a cultural pattern in which old people refer to younger slaves as children or persons acting as mediators in appealing to a master for a slave adopt family terminology. In Philemon the apostle presents himself as an aged parent in need of such a child for support (see Hock). The pathos of an aging, increasingly isolated prisoner seeking contact with his "child" Timothy returns at the conclusion of the letter (4:9-15).

Thanksgiving (1:3-5)

The Pauline epistle typically uses the expression of thanksgiving to telegraph a message about the recipients' faith. It is often linked to themes in the letter's agenda as well (e.g., Rom 1:8-15). 2 Timothy injects a jarring note into the usual pattern by having the apostle affirm his own fidelity to serving God and to the faith of his ancestors. This note points forward to the prison setting of the letter. Paul's first defense has already occurred (1 Tim 4:16-17). Lacking anyone to testify on his behalf, the apostle must swear an oath by his own conscience and ancestral tradition. Timothy should understand his own faith as founded on ancestral tradition since it came through his mother (Acts 16:1) and grandmother. Honorific phrases in which a son praises his parents and grandmother appear in Greco-Roman sources (Spicq 1991). Consequently, this note also strengthens the argument that Christianity contributes to social stability and moral probity.

Paul's Example of Witness (1:6-14)

In farewell discourses, the dying patriarch typically recalls the virtues of his life while reminding his children to hold fast to the example that he has provided. Reminding Timothy to be faithful to the spirit received when he began his service with Paul and to continue to safeguard the deposit of faith entrusted to him, 2 Timothy echoes the struggle against false teaching detailed in 1 Timothy. But the rhetorical emphasis in this section lies elsewhere. The danger lies in the possibility that Paul's imprisonment, trial, and death will cause disciples like Timothy to be ashamed (1:8). Consequently the spirit received from the apostle's hands is contrasted with the cowardice which could result from such shame (v. 7). Accustomed to thinking of Paul as a heroic martyr for the faith, modern readers may have difficulty perceiving the cultural shame of imprisonment, conviction, and death as a threat to Christian faith. Paul himself was all too familiar with the potentially destructive results of imprisonment, as an earlier letter from jail in Ephesus indicates (Phil 1:12-30). Just as he called upon the Philippians to share his suffering on behalf of the gospel (Phil 1:29-30), so he expects Timothy to join his example (1:8).

1:9-10 employ the characteristic liturgical language of the Pastorals to summarize the gospel message. God's eternal plan has been revealed in Jesus Christ: to bring humanity life and immortality. Though some editors treat these verses as a hymnic fragment, they appear to be formulated for this particular passage. The final emphasis on life and immortality recalls the earlier designation of Paul's apostleship, "promise of life" (v. 1). The potential disgrace of his suffering is overcome by the divine Lord, "who abolished death" (v. 10), to whom Paul has entrusted his life.

Deserters and Loyalists (1:15-18)

"You are well aware," a stock transitional phrase in letters, enlists the reader's own experience for the final piece of this argument. Shame and honor are converted into examples of desertion and loyalty. The individuals named emerge as characters in later legends (see *Acts of Paul and Thecla*). Hermogenes is identified in 2 Tim 2:17 as a false teacher. Phil 1:12-30 shows that even when Paul was imprisoned close enough to the churches to exchange letters and envoys (a round trip from Philippi to Ephesus took one month; see Murphy O'Connor 1996: 183), divisions over teaching broke out. Now that he is in Rome fighting for his life, the situation has worsened. However, Paul can point to one example of personal loyalty in Onesiphorus, who found the imprisoned apostle in Rome. He may still be separated from his family since Paul greets his household at Ephesus, not Onesiphorus himself (4:19).

A Soldier's Service (2:1-13)

The letter returns to the legacy of courageous witness which the apostle is leaving to Timothy. Contrary to Paul's isolated situation in Rome, there are many witnesses to the apostle's life and teaching in Asia Minor. 2:2 introduces a new note into the description of Timothy's task, providing the next generation of persons who will be able to teach the faith. This subtle shift provided the basis for later Christians to convert the "chain of authoritative teachers" from the philosophical school tradition to an apostolic tradition (e.g., *1 Clem.* 42:1-4). Here it shows the churches facing a future after the death of the apostles and their immediate associates. 2:3-7 adopt three commonplaces from the philosophical moralists which Paul often used to speak of his own ministry: the soldier, the athlete, and the farmer (e.g., Epictetus *Disc.* 3.15.2-7; 4.8.35-40; 24.34-35; 1 Cor 9:7, 10, 24-25; 2 Cor 10:3-4). Instead of drawing the moral from his examples, the author presumes that the reader can do so. This delicate shift is a moralist's testimony to the mature conscience of the addressee who no longer needs the type of instruction addressed to beginners.

Both the gospel he preaches, "Jesus raised from the dead, a descendant of David" (2:8; echoing the creedal formula of Rom 1:3-4), and the apostle's own suffering (vv. 9-10) should inspire Timothy to endure the hardships of his own ministry. Reference to chains (v. 9; 1:16) once again reminds the reader of the shame attached to the apostle's situation. The author contrasts these hardships with the certainty of salvation based on God's word and promise. The faithful saying formula introduces a formulaic call to endurance (2:11-13a). It opens with parallel clauses that promise what one would expect of a judgment oracle. The faithful are rewarded with a share in Christ's heavenly reign. Those who deny him are denied (cf. Matt 12:32-33; Luke 12:8-9). But 2:13 appears to break the pattern. It does not conclude with judgment against the faithless, but a different theologoumenon, the contrast between the faithlessness of human beings and the eternal faithfulness of God (e.g., Rom 3:3-4). Why the shift? Rhetorically it focuses the reader's attention back on the major theme of the Pastorals, faithfulness (see Bassler 1996b). Just as the apostle's chains could not lock up the word of God, so the faithlessness of those who have abandoned his teaching will not destroy God's faithful ones in Asia Minor.

Working with the Word of Truth (2:14-26)

The ultimate failure of false teaching depends upon the persistence of Timothy (and others, 2:2) in reminding Christians of the truth. Once again the author turns to attack false teaching (vv. 16-18, 23). The characterizations of such teaching as senseless talk and a disease which eats away at the soul are familiar polemical topoi used frequently in the Pastorals. V. 17 charges two persons, Hymenaeus and Philetus, with claiming that the resurrection has already occurred. Some scholars use that piece of information to link the false teachers with gnostic Christians of the second century AD. But 2 Timothy shows little interest in the content of false teaching and may have no more in mind than the slogan of well-known figures. Hymenaeus appeared along with an Alexander in 1 Tim 1:20 as excommunicated by Paul's authority for shipwrecking the faith. Following the line of argument introduced in the previous section, 2 Timothy makes two new points about false teaching: it cannot succeed (2:19), and even those who have strayed may be won back to the truth (vv. 25-26).

Both possibilities depend on the continued activity of Timothy as a true teacher. His life must serve as a moral example to others (2:22). His method of correction exhibits the gentle persuasion of the philosophic physician rather than the rough, quarrelsome speech of the harsh Cynic moralist (vv. 24-25a). Typical of the Christian framework which the Pastorals provide for these philosophical commonplaces, 2 Timothy attributes the effectiveness of that ministry to God's gift, not the preacher's word (v. 25b).

2 Timothy threads these reflections together on a series of building images. Timothy comes to God as a master workman. The motif of shame echoes in the description — the master craftsman is "unashamed" (v. 15). Why? Because he is able to make a straight cut (Gk. *orthotomounta*) with his tools, in this case the word of truth. (Rather than translate the metaphor, the NRSV, "rightly explaining," interprets the activity to which it alludes.) From cutting timber, the next image focuses on the foundation (cf. 1 Tim 3:15), which guarantees that the house will stand despite the upset caused by false teachers (2:19). There two citations from Scripture (apparently a composite drawn from memory; see Num 16:5 LXX; and Num 16:26 with Sir 17:26 and Isa 26:13 or Joel 3:5, LXX) are described as a seal on that foundation. Though a seal per se would not appear on a foundation, the author may have some form of foundation inscription in mind. His final image moves inside the house to its various vessels (cf. Isa 29:16; Wis 15:7; Rom 9:19-24). Expanding the image of the house to the residence of a wealthy person, the argument presumes that its master never uses the humbler vessels of wood or clay. Consequently, anyone wishing to be of use to the master (= God) must undertake the moral training that converts a person into a finely wrought piece of gold or silver.

Wickedness in the Last Days (3:1-9)

Lest the hope of conversion held out in the previous section suggests that teaching could moderate the crisis, the author turns to the apocalyptic topos of increasing wickedness at the end of days. False teaching and prophecy are routinely taken to be on the increase in the end time (Mark 13:5-37; Acts 20:29; 1 Tim 4:1-5; 2 Pet 3:3). 3:2-4 employ a stock list of vices to depict the depravity which will overtake society in those times. Such lists were routinely used to highlight the moral disorder of those ignorant of or alienated from God (e.g., Rom 1:28-32), so that the existence of such vices is not itself a sign of the end time. The point is not in the vices as such, but in the complete moral and social breakdown that they exemplify. 2 Timothy concludes the list with the central opposition which will frame the rest of his characterization, "lovers of pleasure rather than lovers of God" (3:4). In order to gain entry among the faithful such persons cannot be overtly corrupt. They will present an outer appearance of a godliness that they do not actually teach or practice (v. 5).

The command to avoid such persons stands in some tension with the earlier hint that true teaching might convert some of the opponents. However, it echoes the expulsion order of 1 Tim 1:20. The charges that their success comes from invading households of weak and immoral women exploit a common stereotype of women in polemical literature. The ideal Christian wives, mothers, and widows depicted in 1 Timothy would be immune to such invasion (1 Tim 2:11-15; 5:3-16). Finally, the author introduces an OT example of the type of deceit such persons embody. The false teachers are like the Egyptian magicians who opposed Moses (Exod 7:11). Since 3:8 gives their names, Jannes and Jambres, 2 Timothy depends upon apocryphal traditions that were circulating in the first century AD (e.g., *Tg. Ps.-Jon.* 1:3; 7:2; CD 5:17-19). How that story demonstrates the eventual unmasking of the false teachers remains unclear. It may simply serve to reaffirm the earlier expressions of confidence in the victory of true teaching.

Equipped with Examples of Faith (3:10-17)

1 Tim 6:3-16 countered an initial description of false teachers with Timothy, the man of God, as a soldier ready to do battle for the faith. This section marks a similar transition from the false teachers to Timothy, man of God, as "fully outfitted" (3:17). The primary source of his equipment, careful observation of Paul's teaching and way of life, retrieves a convention in the ancient moralists that the student learns by imitating the example of a teacher. In this instance, both Paul's life and Timothy's own training since childhood provide salutary lessons in godliness. The geographical list, Antioch, Iconium, and Lystra (v. 11), corresponds to that in the missionary journey of Acts 13–14. According to Acts 16:1-2, Paul does not pick Timothy up until the second missionary journey. Since Timothy is recommended by persons in Lystra and Iconium, 2 Timothy may have confused the two journeys. In any event, the allusion indicates that readers of the letter would be familiar with some account of Paul's various missionary efforts and the persecutions he suffered.

Similarly, Acts 16:1-2 describes Timothy as the uncircumcised son of a Jewish mother and a pagan father. His status as a believer in the church at Lystra may have resulted from his mother's conversion but clearly represents an adult choice. 2 Tim 3:14-15 slides over the distinction between Timothy's "somewhat Jewish" childhood and his later faith. He is described as one brought up with the faith. This shift makes his family a model for those Christian women expected to train their children in godliness (1 Tim 5:10, 14). Finally, the use of Scripture to provide additional examples for teaching (2 Tim 3:16) was partially exemplified in the earlier examples of scriptural sayings on the foundation (2:19) and the more immediate reference to the story of Moses and the magicians (3:8). They spell out the charge in 1 Tim 4:13 to attend to the reading of Scripture and teaching. The inclusion of reproof and correction along with the educative function of Scripture may imply that it was to be used in refuting the false teachers, though these letters generally insist that one should avoid contentious debate.

Final Mission Charge (4:1-8)

A solemn formula which invokes God and Christ as witnesses introduces the apostle's final set of instructions

(4:1-5). Timothy's faithfulness will be determined by the judge, who will award Paul the crown he is about to win upon completing his apostleship (vv. 6-8). These instructions summarize points already made during the letter. But v. 2 gives an unusual twist to the urgency which attends Timothy's ministry. He is to persist "whether the time is favorable or unfavorable." Discussion of the appropriate time for a philosopher to speak — particularly a word of frank rebuke — was common in the moralists. One should determine whether a person was in a condition to benefit from the philosopher's admonitions. Yet v. 3 indicates that the persons to whom he must speak are suffering a chronic medical condition, an itching that drives them to seek false teaching (see Malherbe 1989: 137-45). Thus the situation is so extreme that Timothy cannot speak only to those who are well disposed to Christian teaching, though he will do that. He must also tackle persons hostile to sound teaching.

The description of Paul's impending death echoes comments made in Philippians (e.g., 1:23; 2:17). He regularly used the metaphors of boxing and the racetrack to describe his ministry (1 Cor 9:24-26). The notice of impending death concludes the farewell discourse.

Personal Information and Final Instructions (4:9-18)

Personal information, instructions to recipients, and travel plans are characteristic items in letter conclusions. Given the likelihood that Paul did not compose 2 Timothy, it is difficult to determine how much historical information about the final days of Paul's life is embedded in the persons and plans represented here (for a reconstruction that assumes 2 Timothy as Pauline see Murphy-O'Connor 1996: 357-68). Most are familiar names. Demas, Luke, Mark, and Tychicus are among a number of persons mentioned in Col 4:7-14 (also Phlm 24 for Mark, Demas, and Luke). Alexander the coppersmith may be a confusion of the Alexander from 1 Tim 1:20 with the Ephesian silversmith of Acts 19:33-34. According to Titus 1:5, Titus had been left in Crete to consolidate churches there until the arrival of Artemas or Tychicus, at which time Titus was to head for Nicopolis (Titus 3:12). Dalmatia is north of Nicopolis. Here Tychicus's arrival in Ephesus presumably makes it possible for Timothy to leave that region. If the Pastorals were always a letter collection, as we have suggested, then the scenario in 2 Timothy situates it after 1 Timothy and Titus. The movements of all the faithful associates in Paul's missionary efforts are framed by ominous references to two false brothers, Demas and Alexander. Demas was previously connected with Luke and Alexander. Neither excommunication (1 Tim 1:20) nor the curse that Paul utters prevents him from further opposition to the gospel.

The notice concerning Paul's legal situation in Rome (4:16-18) continues the ominous note set in vv. 6-8. The final expression of confidence should not be taken to mean that Paul anticipates being spared death. We have seen that expressions of confidence are characteristic of 2 Timothy. The apostle himself exhibits confidence in both death as a successful victory in his struggle and divine rescue (see Phil 1:19-26).

Final Greetings (4:19-21)

The final greetings and benediction are characteristic of the conclusions to Pauline letters. Prisca and Aquila were long-term associates whom Paul had met when he first preached in Corinth. They preceded him in evangelizing in Ephesus (Acts 18:1-3, 18-19, 26; 1 Cor 16:19). Their presence in Ephesus is somewhat puzzling if Rom 16:3 is addressed to persons in Rome. Onesiphorus, mentioned in 1:16, is apparently not with Paul nor at home in Ephesus. Erastus (Acts 19:22; Rom 16:23) and Trophimus (Acts 20:4; 21:29, with Timothy) are also familiar figures in Pauline circles. However, the names of persons from Rome who attach their greetings to the letter are not familiar. Quinn (1990: 16) speculates that they represent a person from each of the four "orders" mentioned in 1 Timothy: bishop, deacon, elder, and widow.

Titus

COMMENTARY

Greetings (1:1-4)

Unlike the other two Pastorals, Titus expands its greeting with a long statement concerning the purpose of Paul's apostolic ministry (1:1b-3). This formulation employs expressions characteristic of these letters as a group: "knowledge of truth" (1 Tim 2:4; 2 Tim 2:25; 3:7), "godliness" (1 Tim 2:2; 3:16; 4:7, 8; 6:3, 5, 6, 11; 2 Tim 3:5), "eternal life" (1 Tim 1:16; 4:8; 6:12, 19; 2 Tim 1:1, 10; Titus 3:7), "due time" (1 Tim 2:6; 6:15), "revealed" (1 Tim 3:16; 2 Tim 1:10), "Savior" (of God: 1 Tim 1:1; 2:3; 4:10; Titus 2:10; 3:4; of Jesus: 2 Tim 1:10; Titus 1:4; 2:13; 3:6). Several of these key phrases occur only in the expanded greeting of Titus. The designation "Savior" appears only for God in 1 Timothy and only for Jesus in 2 Timothy, whereas Titus 1:3-4 uses it first of God and then of Jesus. In addition, Titus 2:13 could be read to refer to Jesus as "God and Savior." This gathering of terms suggests that Titus may have been composed as a summary after the other two letters. Minus the expansion, the greeting formula employs several phrases from 1 Tim 1:1-2: command, God, our Savior, and "my loyal child in the faith."

Like Timothy, Titus had played a critical role in Paul's missionary efforts. A Gentile — evident in his non-Jewish Latin name — he was present with Paul and Barnabas during the Jerusalem Council. Despite pressure from some, Paul insists that Titus was not subjected to circumcision (Gal 2:1-3). He later served as Paul's envoy to Corinth, where he successfully calmed the crisis that had resulted from Paul's disaster visit (2 Cor 2:12-13) and later returned to complete the collection for the poor at Jerusalem which had apparently been stalemated (2 Cor 8:6-24). He does not appear elsewhere in the NT, with the exception of the notice in 2 Tim 4:10.

Establish Reliable Church Leaders (1:5-9)

The lack of an expression of thanksgiving is somewhat jarring, as is the apparent presumption that Titus would need to be told why Paul has left him on Crete. The only known visit of the apostle to Crete is the brief stop on his sea journey to Rome as a prisoner (Acts 27:8). Like other churches on busy trade routes, those on Crete must have been founded by Christians who traveled the shipping routes, probably as part of a growing Jewish community on the island (for Jews on Crete see 1 Macc 15:23; Josephus *Ant.* 17.12.1; *J.W.* 2.103; *Life* 427; Philo *Legat.* 282). As a legal expression "put in order" could imply rectifying a deficient situation, not, as the NRSV would suggest, completing unfinished work. The ordering in question involved establishing community leaders who would be able to teach the sound doctrine of apostolic preaching and correct persons who strayed. Even the brief trip around Crete in Acts 27:8-12 mentions a city and two harbor towns. The necessity of a reliable leader in each town is evident from the difficulty of travel from one to the next.

The lists of qualifications for elder and bishop are similar to those in 1 Tim 3:1-10. Use of the legal expression "unimpeachable" in Titus 1:6 might also guard against the danger of charges being lodged against a presbyter (1 Tim 5:19). Titus does not clarify the relationship between elders, referred to in the plural, and the bishop (singular). "God's steward" might imply supervision of financial resources, though Paul also used the expression of himself and Apollos in their apostolic capacity (1 Cor 4:1-2). The bishop is also the one explicitly entrusted with teaching sound doctrine and refuting those who reject it (1:9). In that task, he is to take the instructions given Titus (and Timothy) as his model.

Rebuke False Teachers (1:10-16)

The depiction of false teachers combines the stock elements of deceit, empty talk, greed, and creating turmoil in families (1:10-11) with hints of their claim to Jewish traditions, "the circumcision" (v. 10), "Jewish myths," and "commandments" (v. 14). The reference to "the circumcision" may be a biographical touch derived from Titus's connection with the controversy at the Jerusalem Council since it appears only here in the Pastorals. The reference to purity in v. 15 suggests that the commandments in question concerned purity or kosher regulations. The counterargument offered employs the topos of immorality and false teaching as evidence of a diseased mind. At the same time it reflects other NT arguments against the need to retain purity rules: nothing is created impure (Acts 10:9-15; 1 Tim 4:4); the moral state of a person's heart determines an individual's holiness (Mark 7:14-15). This combination suggests the presence of Jewish-Christian elements in the disputes over Christian faith and practice.

Titus 1:12 invokes a negative stereotype concerning Cretans to emphasize the sordid character of his opposition. The verb *krētizō*, "play the Cretan," could be used to mean "lie." The expression "Cretans are liars" appears in various forms in ancient literature. Charges of excessive tolerance for sordid gain also figures in the popular anti-Cretan slander (Polybius *Hist.* 6.46.3) and may be related to the comment in v. 11b. Cicero's variant alleges that Cretan mores are so contrary to natural social order that they even consider highway robbery honorable (*Republic* 3.9.5). Clement of Alexandria identifies the source of the hexameter in v. 12 as the sixth-century-BC Cretan sage Epimenides (*Strom.* 1.59.1-2). Aristotle referred to Epimenides as a prophet who divines what is in the past, not the future (*Rhet.* 3.17.10), perhaps the basis for the designation "prophet" in Titus 1:12. The author probably drew on an anthology of sayings about national character to produce this description of the character of the false teachers.

Rhetorically this satirical form of characterizing an opponent must exaggerate common stereotypes. Its significance in the argument of 1:10-16 is evident in the judgment which the author wants his audience to pass against such persons. They must be rebuked sharply and prohibited from teaching (vv. 11, 13). V. 13 holds out the possibility that the harsh method of moral pedagogy might restore such persons to health, but the argument from national character and the concluding "unfit for any good work" (v. 16) do not suggest that he anticipates much success.

Household Code (2:1-10)

This summary set of instructions to various members of the household constitutes healthy (NRSV, "sound") teaching as a contrast to the activities of the false teachers which caused disorder in households (1:11). Its content represents established conventions of good behavior in the Greco-Roman world. There is no particular connection to the topoi of Christian theology or to the sparse hints about the opponents' teaching in the previous section. The motivations for this teaching are stated in quite different terms. Christians must be concerned for the opinions which outsiders have of them. Immorality or insubordination would create suspicion (2:6, 8). This material may have been a set piece of parenesis. Unlike the household codes in Colossians (3:18–4:1), Ephesians (5:22–6:9), and 1 Peter (2:18–3:7), this passage has not been cast in the hierarchical pairs that address each party about its relationship with the other: wives and husbands, slaves and masters, children and parents. Instead the groups are ordered by age in the case of women and men, then slaves. Some interpreters suggest that this code develops a tradition closer to that in 1 Pet 2:18–3:7. Both have an asymmetrical word addressed to slaves and attach a related exhortation concerning obedience to civil authorities (Tit 3:1-2; 1 Pet 2:15-17; von Lips 1994). Motivational statements in 1 Peter are more specifically Christianized than those in Titus. Slaves suffer unjust abuse in imitation of Christ. Wives hope to convert an unbelieving spouse by reverent and chaste behavior which shuns external adornment.

The closest parallels to this summary remain the exhortations addressed to women, men, and slaves in 1 Timothy. For 1 Timothy, some of these traditional descriptions of dignified, sober, and reverent behavior by older men and women have been incorporated into the lists of qualifications for community leaders. 1 Timothy has shifted the original focus of such exhortations, from the household as a unit in a well-ordered society to the church understood as God's household. That pattern is less evident in the instructions on church authorities in Titus 1:5-9. This material refers only to relationships within the familial household. Therefore the requirement that older women teach the younger virtuous behavior (2:3) does not indicate that they have some teaching office within the church. Though ability to manage their households was a virtue attributed to women (Prov 31:10-31), the NRSV has inserted it into the list of virtues for young women in 2:4 by overinterpreting the Greek term *oikourgos.* The word simply means working within the household. It has no supervisory or authority implications. For younger women in a multigenerational household, it could imply not only submission to a husband's authority but that of older female relatives as well.

The particular concern for behavior among younger women may reflect the demographic situation which is explicit in 1 Peter, women with pagan husbands. Hence 2:5 concludes with the note that their behavior must protect the honor of Christianity. That motif provides the link to a comment on the behavior of young men. Unlike the instructions to women, advice to the young men is not associated with instruction by older men but with the example of behavior set by Titus himself (vv. 6-8).

As in 1 Tim 6:1-2 and 1 Pet 2:18, the instructions to slaves to be submissive to their masters have no corresponding word. The back-talking and pilfering slave was a comic stereotype of the slave character. Titus does not include the other common vices of deceitful flattery of the master, though it may be invoked by the positive items, such as to be "pleasing" (Gk. *euarestos;* NRSV, "to give satisfaction in every respect") and to demonstrate "perfect fidelity" to the master. The latter expression might be intended with more legal overtones, "give evidence of reliability" (so Quinn 1990: 149). The final motive clause (2:10b) gives an unusual twist to the concern to gain a good reputation with outsiders. Reliable Christian slaves "adorn" Christian teaching (Gk. *kosmein*). The verb was used of women's virtues in 1 Tim 2:9. The NRSV's "be an ornament to" picks up the connection with external dress rather than its metaphoric use for virtuous character. The latter is more appropriate to this argument. A translation such as "add luster to" (Quinn 1990: 127) captures both sides of the metaphor.

Virtue as God's Grace Made Manifest (2:11-15)

2:10b concludes with the phrase "doctrine of God our Savior," which provides a transition to a theological statement celebrating the manifestation of salvation (vv. 11-14). The concluding command to teach "these things" (v. 15) provides an *inclusio* with the opening of this section (v. 1) and marks a transition to final items of exhortation which follow. The theological formula comprises two parallel expressions for the appearance of salvation: (a) "the grace of God has appeared, bringing salvation . . ." (v. 11); and (b) "wait for the blessed hope and manifestation [= "appearing"] of the glory of our great God and Savior, Jesus Christ" (v. 13). The first phrase refers to the first coming of Jesus, the second to his parousia in judgment. V. 14 then explains how God's grace brought salvation, through the redeeming death of Jesus. V. 13 poses a translation problem of some importance for NT Christology. Lack of a second possessive pronoun "our" or an article "the" following the copula makes it possible to treat "Jesus Christ" in apposition to the phrase "our great God and Savior," thus clearly equating him with God. The NRSV punctuation adopts this reading. One might treat the missing word as merely a grammatical slip and supply either the pronoun or the article. However, the image is that of the risen Christ returning to manifest God's glory. For a Greco-Roman audience, the appearance of an emperor was often described in divinizing language as "epiphany." In ceremonial contexts phrases such as "god" and "savior" were also applied to the emperor. Therefore, it seems more likely that this sentence should be read as referring to Jesus as "our God and Savior."

Within this framework of high Christology, one finds the various expressions of virtuous life that the Pastorals share with the Greco-Roman moralists. Salvation is education in such a life (2:12). Possession of these virtues is the condition for inclusion in the glory of Christ's second coming (vv. 12-13). The theological premise for moral reform is stated briefly in v. 14. Humanity without Christ was alienated from God and could not have overcome its "iniquity" (Gk. *anomia,* "lawlessness"). The need for God's action to cleanse the people from lawlessness appears in several OT descriptions (e.g., Ps 129:8 LXX; Ezek 27:23). The connection between virtue and conversion will be further elaborated in 3:3-7.

Final Exhortations (3:1-11)

The concluding exhortation draws on both emphases of the letter: training in Christian virtue (3:1-8a) and countering false teachers (vv. 8b-11). The section on Christian virtue returns briefly to the type of exhortation found in the conventions of the household code. Perhaps the echoes of an imperial epiphany in the glorious appearance of Christ provided the impetus to open that list with obedience to rulers (vv. 1b-2; cf. Rom 13:1; 1 Tim 2:2 on prayer for rulers). The major focus of this section is the celebration of the religious and ethical conversion effected by the coming of salvation. This "sure saying" (3:8a) provides the only explicit reference to Christian liturgy (as distinct from Scripture reading and instruction) in the Pastorals. Cleansing from sin, washing, and renewal through the Holy Spirit all point toward a baptismal setting (vv. 5b-7). The vice list is used to depict the hopelessness of life without God (v. 3). This particular example has been organized to show the disastrous effects of the human failure to control the passions, a typical motif in Stoic moralists. Slavery to passion generates social disorders that finally break down community by causing hatred and even war (cf. Jas 4:1-4). By integrating this chain argument into the context of Christian conversion, Titus implicitly makes an argument for the importance of salvation for all humanity.

The description of God's beneficent acts in salvation (3:4) incorporates two commonplaces in Greco-Roman moral exhortation to describe human benefactors, "goodness" (Gk. *chrēstotēs*) and "lovingkindness" (Gk. *philanthrōpia*). Hellenistic Jewish authors exhort humans to imitate these attributes of God (see *Ep. Arist.* 208; Philo *Spec. Leg.* 2.141).

3:4-7 are a single long sentence in Greek which defines how God's beneficence was expressed. The possibility that human effort can achieve virtue or merit God's salvation is expressed in a Pauline phrase "not because of any works of righteousness" (v. 5; cf. Rom 3:27-28; Gal 2:16). The working of the Holy Spirit in the new life which follows upon baptism picks up another important Pauline theologoumena which has largely been absent from the Pastorals (3:5-6; Rom 5:5; 8:1-17; 12:2). This traditional formulation concludes with the consequence of the second coming of Jesus in fulfillment of that hope for eternal life (3:7; Rom 5:5; 8:15-17; 2 Cor 1:22).

The final section of exhortation returns to the internal threat posed by the false teachers (3:8b-11). The primary function of exhortation is to encourage those who are in fact capable of moral reform. That readiness is presented as the consequence of their conversion (v. 8b). The convergence between Christian virtue and the ideals of philosophical moralists reappears in the comment that such good works are "excellent and profitable to everyone." The NRSV translation "devote themselves to" masks the connotations of Gk. *proïstasthai,* which means "to take the lead." In 1 Tim 3:4, 5, 12 and 5:17, the verb is used for the activity of church leaders. Therefore the goal proposed for Christian moral instruction is not only persons devoted to doing noble (a common meaning of the Greek word *kalos*) or good deeds. Rather, such teaching should produce persons who are leaders in such activity. That requirement recalls the earlier exhortation to Titus to be the exemplar of those virtues which he teaches (2:7). It is the conviction of NT moralists that such model behavior is observed by and even benefits those outside the Christian community.

The severe sanctions against false teachers have already alerted readers to the dangers they pose for the church. 3:9-10a merely summarize earlier characterizations (e.g., 1 Tim 1:4; 6:4; 2 Tim 2:23; Titus 1:10-16). But 3:10b-11 envisage a judicial procedure taken against false teachers. The twofold admonition provides an opportunity for moral reform. Individuals who resist correction are to be excommunicated since their sin is beyond healing (cf. Matt 18:15-18). The final image of decay and corruption is used to describe such persons. The Gk. *ekstrephein,* meaning "perverted," appears in medical texts for something that has undergone a radical change. Hence Titus 3:11 implies that the condition of such persons is irreversible. Therefore the penalty in this instance seems even more severe than for those who were "turned over to Satan" in anticipation of the corrective value of such treatment (1 Tim 1:20).

Travel Plans and Final Greetings (3:12-15)

The standard letter closing included travel plans, instructions, and greetings. The greeting in 3:15 is odd in that it does not give the names of the persons with the apostle when he sends greetings. The only familiar names in the list of associates whose travels the author reports are Tychicus, an associate of Paul from Asia Minor (Acts 20:4; Eph 6:21; Col 4:7; 2 Tim 4:12), and Apollos (Acts 18:24–19:1; 1 Cor 3:5-15; 16:12). 3:13 suggests that Apollos and the otherwise unknown Zenas were bearers of the letter. Paul characteristically asks the recipients to provide them with whatever they need for the next stage of their missionary journey. Provision for traveling missionaries was one of the works of hospitality urged on early congregations. V. 14 incorporates a quotation of v. 8b to bolster that request.

Nicopolis, on the west coast of Greece, was an important transit point with roads leading across central Greece and north to the Via Egnatia. A two-hundred-mile sea journey would bring travelers to Brindisi at the heel of Italy, where one could pick up the Via Appia. Paul's intention to winter there puts the apostle at a transit point between his old mission territory of Greece and Asia Minor and the new western regions that he hoped to evangelize after visiting Christians in Rome (Rom 15:20-24). If this geographical notice were historical, one would have to assume that Paul had returned to work in the East after the Roman imprisonment of Acts 28 and undertook a second journey to the West which culminated in his death. Or that Titus 3:13 is referring to the Acts journey, but in the same fashion as the travel journal source, he chooses to neglect the fact that Paul is a prisoner at the time (so Murphy-O'Connor 1996: 353-54). However, in the Acts account (Acts 27:1-12) Paul and his party were shipwrecked trying to make a different port in Crete since the centurion did not plan to winter in Fair Havens. It would clearly be impossible for Titus to get off the island and undertake the journey across Greece to Nicopolis. As a fictive conclusion, the travel plans exhibit a general knowledge of Paul's travel habits and the use of missionary associates. They cannot be pressed for details.

Bibliography. Balch, D. 1981, *Let Wives Be Submissive: The Domestic Code in 1 Peter,* SBLDS 26, Chico: Scholars • Bassler, J. M. 1984, "The Widows' Tale: A Fresh Look at 1 Tim 5.3-16," *JBL* 103:23-41 • Bassler, J. M. 1996a, "He remains faithful" (2 Tim 2:13a)," in E. H. Lovering Jr. and J. L. Sumney, eds., *Theology and Ethics in Paul and His Interpreters: Essays in Honor of Victor Paul Furnish,* Nashville: Abingdon, 73-83 • Bassler, J. M. 1996b, *1 Timothy, 2 Timothy, Titus,* ANTC, Nashville: Abingdon • Collins, R. F. 2000, *I & II Timothy and Titus,* Louisville: Westminster John Knox • Dahl, N. A. 1995, "Euodia and Syntyche and Paul's Letter to the Philippians," in L. M. White and O. L. Yarbrough, eds., *The Social World of the First Christians: Essays in Honor of Wayne A. Meeks,* Minneapolis: Fortress, 3-15 • Dibelius, M., and H. Conzelmann. 1972, *The Pastoral Epistles,* trans. P. Buttolph and A. Yarbro, Philadelphia: Fortress • Goulder, M. 1996, "The Pastor's Wolves: Jewish Christian Visionaries behind the Pastoral Epistles," *NovT* 38:242-56 • Harris, M. J. 1980, "Titus 2:13 and the Deity of Christ," in D. A. Hagner and M. J. Harris, eds., *Pauline Studies: Essays Presented to F. F. Bruce on His 70th Birthday,* Grand Rapids: Eerdmans, 262-77 • Hock, R. F. 1995, *The Social World of the First Christians: Essays in Honor of Wayne A. Meeks,* ed. L. M. White and O. L. Yarbrough, Minneapolis: Fortress, 67-81 • Johnson, L. T. 1996, *Letters to Paul's Delegates: 1 Timothy, 2 Timothy, Titus,* Valley Forge, Penn.: Trinity Press International • Karris, R. J. 1973, "The Background and Significance of the Polemic of the Pastoral Epistles," *JBL* 92:549-64 • Kidd, R. M. 1990, *Wealth and Beneficence in the Pastoral Epistles,* SBLDS 122, Atlanta: Scholars • Knight, G. W. 1992, *Commentary on the Pastoral Epistles,* NIGTC, Grand Rapids: Eerdmans • Lee, G. M. 1980, "Epimenides in the Epistle to Titus (I,12)," *NovT* 22:96 • Lips, H. von. 1994, "Die Haustafel als 'Topos' im Rahmen der urchristlichen Paränese. Beobachtungen anhand des 1. Petrusbriefes und des Titusbriefes," *NTS* 40:261-80 • MacDonald, M. Y. 1996, *Early Christian Women and Pagan Opinion: The Power of the Hysterical Woman,* Cambridge: Cambridge University • Malherbe, A. J. 1989, *Paul and the Popular Philosophers,* Philadelphia: Fortress • Marshall, I. Howard. 1999, *The Pastoral Epistles,* ICC, Edinburgh: T. & T. Clark • Mitchell, M. M. 1992, "New Testament Envoys in the Context of Greco-Roman Diplomatic Conventions: The Example of Timothy and Titus," *JBL* 111:641-62 • Mott, S. C. 1978, "Greek Ethics and Christian Conversion: The Philonic Background of Titus 2:10-14 and 3:3-7," *NovT* 20:22-48 • Murphy-O'Connor, J. 1991, "2 Timothy Contrasted with 1 Timothy and Titus," *RB* 98:403-18 • Murphy-O'Connor, J. 1996, *Paul. A Critical Life,* Oxford: Clarendon • Nussbaum, M. C. 1994, *The Therapy of Desire: Theory and Practice in Hellenistic Ethics,* Princeton: Princeton University • Oberlinner, L. 1994, *Die Pastoralbriefe. Erste folge. Kommentar zum Ersten Timotheusbrief,* HTKNT 9/2, Freiburg: Herder • Oberlinner, L. 1995, *Die Pastoralbriefe. Zweite folge. Kommentar zum Zweiten Timotheusbrief,* HTKNT IX/2/2, Freiburg: Herder • Osiek, C. 1996, "The Family in Early Christianity: Family Values Revisited," *CBQ* 58:1-24 • Padgett, A. 1987, "Wealthy Women of Ephesus: 1 Timothy 2:8-15 in Context," *Int* 41:19-31 • Peterman, G. W. 1997, *Paul's Gift from Philippi: Conventions of Gift Exchange and Christian Giving,* SNTSMS 92, Cambridge: Cambridge University • Quinn, J. D. 1990, *The Letter to Titus,* AB 35, New York: Doubleday • Spicq, C. 1991, "Lois, Ta Grand'maman" (II Tim, I,5)," *RB* 98:362-64 • Stiefel, J. H. 1995, "Women Deacons in 1 Timothy: A Linguistic and Literary Look at 'Women Likewise . . .' (1 Tim 3.11)," *NTS* 41:442-57 • Stark, R. 1996, *The Rise of Christianity: A Sociologist Reconsiders History,* Princeton: Princeton University • Toit, A. du. 1994, "Vilification as a Pragmatic Device in Early Christian Epistolography," *Bib* 75:403-12 • Towner, P. H. 1989, *The Goal of Our Instruction: The Structure of Theology and Ethics in the Pastoral Epistles,* JSNTS 34, Sheffield: JSOT • Verner, D. C. 1983, *The Household of God: The Social World of the Pastoral Epistles,* SBLDS 71, Chico, Calif.: Scholars • White, L. M. 1990, *The Social Origins of Christian Architecture,* vol. 1: *Building God's House in the Roman World: Architectural Adaptation among Pagans, Jews and Christians,* HTS 42, Valley Forge, Penn.: Trinity Press International • Wolter, M. 1988, *Die Pastoralbriefe als Paulustradition,* FRLANT 146, Göttingen: J. C. B. Mohr • Young, F. 1994, *The Theology of the Pastoral Epistles,* Cambridge: Cambridge University.

Philemon

Morna D. Hooker

INTRODUCTION

Although the epistle to Philemon was often ignored as insignificant in the early church, few doubts have ever been raised regarding its authenticity, since no one except Paul could have had any reason to write this personal letter to an individual. It was written from prison, but there is nothing to indicate where Paul was imprisoned. The fact that Onesimus had traveled from the household of Philemon to Paul and was now returning, together with the (probably unlikely) hope expressed in v. 22 that Paul would shortly visit Philemon, suggests that the distance between them was not excessive, but this does not exclude Rome. The belief that Philemon was living in Colossae depends on the references to Onesimus and Archippus in Col 4:9 and 17, assuming these to be the persons named in Philemon. The dating of the letter also depends on the association with Colossae since the very similar lists of Paul's companions (Col 4:10-14; Phlm 23-24) imply that the letters were sent together. In Col 4:9, indeed, Onesimus is said to be accompanying the letter, though his description ("one of you") may indicate that this is a later visit than that presupposed in Philemon, which describes his recent conversion. If Colossians is not authentic, then we have no clue concerning the date or place of the letter's composition, though the references to Onesimus and Archippus in Col 4:9 and 17 still support the belief that Philemon lived in or near Colossae.

Why was the letter written? Since at least the time of Chrysostom, at the end of the fourth century, the almost universal answer has been "to plead with Philemon for clemency toward his runaway slave, Onesimus." In fact, Onesimus is never described as a runaway, and Paul makes no plea for clemency! The "clues" that have been pieced together to make this theory consist of the reference to Onesimus in v. 11 as formerly "useless," a statement in v. 15 that Onesimus has been temporarily "separated" from Philemon, and Paul's promise in v. 18 to repay Philemon if Onesimus has wronged him in any way or owes him money. None of this provides firm evidence for the theory: in v. 11 Paul is making a pun on Onesimus's name (see commentary); Onesimus's "separation" from Philemon could well have been the result of sending him on a mission, which may have included visiting Paul in prison (Winter 1987); the hypothetical injuries and debts in v. 18 which Paul promises to make good do not necessarily refer to Onesimus absconding with a sum of money. Moreover, the difficulties with this theory are overwhelming. Why does Paul not mention Onesimus's flight, repentance, and sorrow? Why does he not allude to Philemon's possible anger, and plead for forgiveness? It has been suggested that Paul is being "tactful," but we expect *some* reference to the question at issue! And how did Paul and Onesimus meet? The suggestion that they were thrown into the same prison together is sheer fantasy: Roman citizens and runaway slaves were not incarcerated together, and a chance encounter of two people who independently knew Philemon is in any case unlikely.

The obvious solution is that Onesimus had deliberately sought Paul out in prison. Why? An alternative theory suggests that, having offended his master in some way, he had, in accordance with custom, sought out a friend of his master's to ask him to intercede on his behalf (cf. esp. Lampe 1985, followed by Rapske 1991 and Dunn 1996). The frequently cited letter of Pliny to Sabinianus (though it concerns a freedman, not a slave) illustrates this situation, rather than that of the runaway. Pliny's letter is, however, very different from Paul's, since Pliny refers to Sabinianus's anger and describes the repentance of the offender and his pleas for forgiveness, while Paul makes no reference to Onesimus's offense and subsequent repentance or to Philemon's possible anger or forgiveness. There is no hint that Philemon was a harsh master who needed to be placated. Although it makes fewer assumptions than the "runaway slave" hypothesis, this theory also fails to explain the letter that we have.

So what can we say about Onesimus? It is best to begin with what the letter actually tells us. We gather that he was (or had once been) a slave (v. 16), that he had seen Paul in prison, and that he was now returning to Philemon. Most significantly of all, Paul tells us that Onesimus has recently been converted. This conversion is the central point of the letter, which suggests that it may provide the clue to its purpose. Paul makes various requests of Philemon, and they all refer to Onesimus's new status as a Christian. First, he hopes that Philemon will send Onesimus back to minister to him in prison: Paul's affection for Onesimus is directly related to the fact that he has "fathered" him in prison (v. 10). This hope, though never expressed as a clear request, is nevertheless a dominant theme (vv. 13-14, 20-21). Secondly, and explicitly, Paul wants Philemon to welcome Onesimus as a fellow Christian (v. 16): the letter serves as a testimonial to the genuineness of Onesimus's new faith. The letter's main purpose appears to be to tell Philemon that Onesimus is now a Christian (vv. 10-11) and should be welcomed as a brother — indeed, as though he were Paul himself (vv. 16-17). Third, it is possible that Paul is hinting that manumission would be the appropriate next step. If Onesimus is to be "more than a slave, a beloved brother" in the flesh as well as in the Lord, perhaps this is because his new status inevitably affects Onesimus's earthly relationships. This would mean cancelling his debts (if he had been sold into slavery) and providing the money to set him free. This is perhaps what Paul is offering to do in vv. 17-18. Even freedmen were often under obligation to their former masters, however. Onesimus could not return to Paul without Philemon's blessing.

The preservation of this letter suggests that Philemon responded positively to Paul's requests. What happened to Onesimus we do not know, but, assuming that he was about thirty years old at the time of his conversion, he *could* be the Onesimus who, according to Ignatius, was bishop of Ephesus at the beginning of the second century. John Knox (1959), who argued for this identification, went on to suggest that Onesimus's owner was not Philemon but Archippus (hence the obscure command in Col 4:17), and that Onesimus was responsible for gathering together Paul's letters and so preserving them. For these theories, however, there is no evidence whatever.

In the twenty-first century, we have problems with this letter, wondering why Paul did not condemn the whole practice of slavery and command Philemon to set Onesimus free. We forget that Greco-Roman society depended on slavery to the extent that it could not exist without it. For Philemon to release all his slaves would create huge practical problems (Barclay 1991). If Philemon released Onesimus, all his slaves were likely to announce their conversion to Christianity! Yet treating a slave as a "brother" at the "earthly" level would be well nigh impossible. Paul's special plea for Onesimus is based on the particular affection he has for him: this is why Philemon should receive him *as Paul himself.* The favor Paul requests — for Onesimus to return — is a big one, and it is hardly surprising if it is expressed so tentatively.

COMMENTARY

Greetings (1-3)

The opening salutation is unusual in two respects. First of all, Paul does not, as he often does elsewhere, describe himself as an apostle (he is not going to command, v. 8) but as "a prisoner of Christ" (v. 1). This expression (repeated in v. 9) is unusual and obscure: In what sense is Paul *Christ's* prisoner? Nevertheless, it reminds us immediately that Paul is in prison (cf. v. 13) and that his imprisonment is the result of his allegiance to Christ. Timothy's name is linked with Paul's out of courtesy. The second unusual feature is the fact that the letter is addressed primarily to individuals (v. 2) — to Philemon, Paul's coworker, and to Apphia and Archippus (possibly Philemon's wife and son). Philemon is a man of some substance since a Christian community meets in his house.

Thanksgiving (4-7)

At this point Paul switches from plural verbs and pronouns to singular, so that the "you" addressed from v. 4 to v. 22 is an individual: this is presumably the first-named addressee, Philemon. As usual, the letter begins with a prayer of thanksgiving. Paul gives thanks because he has heard (perhaps from Onesimus) of Philemon's love and faith (v. 5). In the Greek, love and faith are linked together, but the NRSV has changed the word order, perhaps on the assumption that faith toward the saints would be inappropriate. The Greek word *pistis,* however, has a wider range of meaning than our English word "faith": it includes faith, trust, faithfulness, and loyalty. Love and trust directed toward the Lord Jesus can therefore overflow in love and loyalty to the saints.

Verse 6 is the most obscure in the letter: Is Paul still giving thanks or moving into a request (as the NRSV supposes?) Perhaps both. The "sharing" of faith could refer to the fellowship in the faith which Paul and Philemon hold in common, but the word "sharing" *(koinōnia)* and its cognates often have a more practical connotation (see, e.g., 2 Cor 8:4; 9:13; Phil 1:5; 4:15). Perhaps, then, Paul is thanking God for Philemon's past generosity and praying that it will increase, as he subtly suggests that Philemon needs to be given further insight into the possibilities of doing good for Christ! Certainly there is already cause for rejoicing in what Philemon has done to "refresh" the saints in Colossae (v. 7): the benefit they have received has spilled over in joy and encouragement for Paul himself.

As often in Paul's letters, the thanksgiving contains hints of the theme of the rest of the letter. Several words used here will be picked up later: love *(agapē,* vv. 5, 7, and 9), sharing *(koinōnia,* v. 6, picked up in "partner," *koinōnos,* v. 17), good (deed) *((to) agathon,* vv. 6, 14), heart(s) *(ta splanchna,* vv. 7, 12, 20), and refresh *(anapauō,* vv. 7, 20).

Paul's Request (8-22)

Paul introduces his request with the declaration that he is not going to command Philemon to do his duty (v. 8) — an opening which nevertheless exercises considerable moral pressure! He prefers to appeal on the basis of love (v. 9). But is it also on the basis that he is an old man and a prisoner? The NRSV translation suggests that Paul is appealing to pathos: "Have pity on an old man — and in prison too!" Paul describes himself, however — with some pride — as a prisoner *of Christ.* Moreover, the word translated "old man" *(presbytēs)* may be a variant form of the word for "ambassador" *(presbeutēs).* The NRSV mg. is possibly right, therefore, in suggesting that Paul is appealing "as an ambassador — and now a prisoner — of Christ Jesus." But would this not mean that Paul was "pulling rank," something (v. 8) he has just refused to do? Not if we remember that Paul elsewhere uses the image of an ambassador to mean someone who pleads a cause and makes supplication for those whom he represents (2 Cor 5:21; cf. Bash 1997, though he interprets Phlm 9 differently). If Paul is appealing as an ambassador to Philemon, it is not on his *own* account but because he represents Christ, and the service he requests is for him. Paul refuses to command Philemon; rather, he appeals to him on the basis of love, as Christ's ambassador and prisoner.

What, then, is he requesting? The "for" in v. 10 is ambiguous: it could mean either "on behalf of" or "for." If it is the former, there is no indication as to what Paul is requesting, and we must assume that he is asking Paul to deal leniently with Onesimus. If it is the latter, then he is presumably requesting Philemon to give him or lend him Onesimus's services (Knox 1959; Winter 1987). Onesimus is described as Philemon's "child," whom he has fathered (i.e., converted) while in prison. V. 11 is a pun on the name "Onesimus," a common name for a slave since it means "useful"; but instead of using the name itself and its opposite *anonētos,* "useless," Paul plays on their synonyms, *euchrēstos* and *achrēstos.* The reason may well be that the word *achrēstos,* "useless," would *sound* exactly like *achristos,* meaning "without Christ." Onesimus, being no longer "without Christ," can now be expected to live up to his name and be truly "useful." If this is the explanation, then we should not place too much emphasis on the fact that Onesimus is described as once having been "useless": Paul's play on words may have far more to do with Onesimus's conversion than with whether or not he had been a useful slave.

Paul is sending Onesimus back to Philemon with much regret) since Onesimus has become so dear to him (v. 12). Though he longed to keep him to care for his needs in prison, he would not do so unless the initiative came from Philemon himself (vv. 13-14). Prisoners in the Roman world relied on friends and relatives to provide such assistance as nourishing food. The hint about what Philemon should do could not be broader, but at first sight vv. 15-16 seem to draw back and offer Philemon an alternative. He has been "separated" from Onesimus for a time while the latter has been away (with Paul), but now he is to "have him back forever" (v. 15). Those who think that Onesimus was a runaway naturally assume that Paul means that he will now be living and working in Philemon's household once more. If so, then Paul is clearly not expecting Philemon to accede to his request in vv. 13-14! But it is important to note how Paul continues. Philemon is to "have him back" — better, "receive him" — as a Christian brother (v. 16). The real contrast does not concern the presence or absence of Onesimus, but his status: formerly he was simply a slave, but now he is far more than a slave, since he is "a beloved brother," and this lasting relationship is unaffected by his physical whereabouts. The demand that Onesimus be received "no longer as a slave" *may* be intended as a request for manumission. If so, then this perhaps explains why, for Philemon, their new relationship applies to the sphere of "the flesh" as well as to that of "the Lord": the fact that Onesimus is now a brother will inevitably affect their everyday relationship. So while Onesimus is "especially" dear to Paul, to Philemon he is "much more" dear because the new relationship radically changes their old one. (The suggestion that they were literal brothers, and that "slave," not "brother," is the metaphorical term [Callahan 1993] seems unfounded.)

The "if" in v. 17 refers to something Philemon knows to be true: of course he regards Paul as a partner, and he is honored to do so! He should therefore welcome Onesimus as though he were Paul himself. Is the "if" in v. 18 similar? Does Paul in fact know that Onesimus *has* done wrong and that he owes Paul money? Those who believe Onesimus to be a runaway slave assume that this is the case. But slaves could be faulted for small misdemeanors, and they could be in debt to their masters without stealing from them; freedmen, too, could be in a similar position. In taking responsibility for any debts, Paul is urging Philemon to wipe the slate clean: it is perhaps another hint that Paul is hoping that, all debts discharged, Onesimus will be allowed to return to attend to his needs in prison. In writing an IOU in his own hand (v. 19), Paul declares that he will say nothing (and thereby says a great deal!) about what Philemon owes to him. The request to receive benefit from Philemon (v. 20) is a pun on the name Onesimus since the verb *(oninēmi)* is the one from which the name is derived: the benefit Paul has in mind is presumably the one hinted at in vv. 10-14. The appeal to refresh his heart echoes the expression used in v. 7; the verb *(anapauō)* is used by Ignatius of those who brought him relief in prison (*Eph.* 2:1-2; 12:1). There are in fact many echoes of Philemon in this epistle of Ignatius, which also refers to the Ephesian bishop named Onesimus (Wansink 1996: 194-97).

It may seem strange that Paul concludes by expressing his confidence in Philemon's "obedience" (v. 21) since he has refused to issue commands (v. 8). The obedience he expects is, however, to the appeal of love (v. 9); he is confident that Philemon will see the implications of his faith and the good that is open to him (v. 6). The "more" that Paul expects could include manumission, and will certainly involve allowing Onesimus to return to Paul.

Paul's request for a guest room to be prepared for him raises problems if, as seems most likely, he is writing from Rome. The journey to Colossae is a long one; moreover, Paul had originally intended to go westward from Rome — has he abandoned his plans? Even if he still hopes to take the gospel to Spain, however (Rom 15:24), he would also wish to return to strengthen the churches in the East. But the request is not an immediate one! Paul links it with the previous verse, and the introductory words *(hama de kai)* are better translated "At the same time," rather than "One thing more." At the same time that Philemon is fulfilling Paul's (unspoken) request by sending Onesimus to him in prison, he should be prepared to receive Paul himself, since Paul is still hoping to be set free. The final "you" and "your" are plural, since the prayers of the whole community are involved.

Final Greetings (23-25)

The list of those who send greetings to Philemon (the "you" is again singular) is similar to that in Colossians, though the names occur in a different order and Jesus Justus (Col 4:11) is omitted. The final grace is addressed to the whole community.

Bibliography. Bash, A. 1997, *Ambassadors for Christ,* WUNT 2.92, Tübingen: Mohr • Barclay, J. M. G. 1991, "Paul, Philemon and the Dilemma of Christian Slave-Ownership," *NTS*

37:161-86 • Barclay, J. M. G. 1997, *Colossians and Philemon,* Sheffield: Sheffield Academic • Bruce, F. F. 1984, *The Epistles to the Colossians, to Philemon, and to the Ephesians,* NICNT, Grand Rapids: Eerdmans • Callahan, A. D. 1993, "Paul's Epistle to Philemon: Toward an Alternative Argumentum," *HTR* 86:357-76 • Dunn, J. D. G. 1996, *The Epistles to the Colossians and to Philemon,* NIGTC, Grand Rapids: Eerdmans and Carlisle: Paternoster • Houlden, J. L. 1970, *Paul's Letters from Prison,* Pelican Commentary, Harmondsworth: Penguin and London: SCM • Knox, J. 2d ed. 1959, "The Epistle to Philemon," *IB* 10, New York/Nashville: Abingdon-Cokesbury • Lampe, P. 1985, "Keine 'Sklavenflucht' des Onesimus," *ZNW* 76:135-37 • Lightfoot, J. B. 2d ed. 1876, *St Paul's Epistles to the Colossians and to Philemon,* London: Macmillan • Lohse, E. 1968, *Colossians and Philemon,* ET, Philadelphia: Fortress • Nordling, J. G. 1991, "Onesimus Fugitivus: A Defense of the Runaway Slave Hypothesis in Philemon," *JSNT* 41:97-119 • Petersen, N. R. 1985, *Rediscovering Paul: Philemon,* Philadelphia: Fortress • Rapske, B. M. 1991, "The Prisoner Paul in the Eyes of Onesimus," *NTS* 37:187-203 • Wansink, C. S. 1996, *Chained in Christ,* JSNTSup 130, Sheffield: Sheffield Academic • Winter, S. 1987, "Paul's Letter to Philemon," *NTS* 33:1-15.

Hebrews

Anthony C. Thiselton

INTRODUCTION

Authorship and Place within the New Testament

Two quotations concerning Hebrews are endlessly repeated. In the early part of the third century Origen wrote, "Who it was who wrote the epistle, [only] God knows the truth" (Eusebius *Hist. Eccl.* 6.25.14). A modern writer adds, "Hebrews is in many respects the riddle of the NT. Nothing is known of its origin. . . . It stands . . . 'without father, without mother, without genealogy' . . . like . . . Melchizedek . . ." (Scott 1923: 1). The anonymity remains all the more surprising since without doubt "the author of Hebrews ranks with Paul and the Fourth Gospel as one of the three great theologians of the NT" (Lindars 1991: 1).

Speculative hypotheses about the possible or probable identity of the author abound. On grounds of language and theology, Paul is not the author (see below). Theories have been propounded about Clement of Rome, Barnabas, Luke, Stephen, Priscilla and Aquila, Apollos, Philip, and Jude, none of which can be demonstrated as seriously probable with perhaps two marginal exceptions (for a survey, cf. Ellingworth 1993: 13-21). Only Apollos and Priscilla (with Aquila) would fully explain the early anonymity of the epistle or its association with Paul. One writer argues, "there is only one person who seems to satisfy all the requirements for authorship. He is Apollos" (Montefiore 1964: 9; cf. 9-11). Apollos was of Jewish race and a person of eloquence (Acts 18:24). He had a good command of the OT scriptures and taught "accurately" (18:25). He spoke boldly, passionately, and in refutation of Jewish theology (18:25-28), and as a native of Alexandria he would use the kind of thought forms found in Hebrews (18:24). If we were also to accept Montefiore's theory that Hebrews was addressed to a group at Corinth, this would offer a convincing explanation for its anonymity since there was sensitivity about any competitive comparisons between the rhetoric of Apollos and of Paul (1 Cor 1:10–4:21). Certainly the author of our epistle was highly trained in rhetoric (Spicq 1952: 1:351-78). Montefiore was not the first to urge this theory (Manson 1949: 1-17), and Luther considered the possibility. But the arguments remain speculative.

Harnack's proposal that Priscilla (perhaps with Aquila) wrote the epistle has the merit of explaining the early anonymity more convincingly than hypotheses about Apollos. She was sufficiently learned to instruct no less a person than Apollos himself in the truth of the gospel (Acts 18:26). But apart from these two arguments, together with speculations about connections between this epistle and Rome, other arguments verge on the trivial. The mention of women of faith (Sarah and Rahab, 11:11, 31, 35) no more seriously indicates that the author was a woman than the argument that the prominence of the tabernacle suggests that the author's trade was tentmaking. We simply do not know the identity of the author.

This makes it all the more significant that Hebrews won its place within the NT. Since the earliest arguments for the canonical status of certain texts was largely bound up with beliefs about their apostolic authorship, it is scarcely surprising that certain traditions are reflected in the KJV/AV title (but not found in the earliest mss.), "The Epistle of Paul the Apostle to the Hebrews." Clement of Rome does not name an author when he writes around AD 95, even though his own writings reflect a close knowledge of the epistle. But while he recognized that the language and style were not Paul's, Clement of Alexandria (c. AD 200) attributed the composition of the content to Paul. In the West Tertullian and Hippolytus rejected Pauline authorship. Apart from eastern traditions, in the West the notion of Pauline authorship held sway only from Jerome (c. 390) and Augustine (c. 400) until Erasmus and the Reformation. Yet such was the widespread recognition of the spiritual authenticity, intellectual power, and pastoral value of the epistle that we may think of its canonicity as pointing to Hebrews as "the Letter which would not be denied. . . . Hebrews finally obtained a place in the NT because it could not be kept out" (Barclay 1965: 11). Hebrews belongs to the NT canon not because some arbitrary church committee decided what would be "in" but because the church as a whole came to recognize its authenticity as address from God through a period of testing and sifting.

To be unaware of the author's name, however, is not to be ignorant of his character, concerns, and gifts. He is "the theologian who, more diligently and successfully than any others of the NT writers, has worked at what we now describe as hermeneutics. . . . the interpretative interaction between ourselves and the originating events in which Christian faith depends . . . [including] the interrelationship between the Old and New Testaments" (Hughes 1979: 3; Leschert 1994). He "reworks" the OT by bringing "previous 'frames' . . . to function in . . . new contexts" (Hughes 1979: 125). He is a deeply learned and deeply practical scriptural expositor as well as "a pastoral theologian who adapted early Christian traditions to fashion an urgent appeal to a community in crisis . . . a gifted preacher and interpreter" (Lane 1991: li).

The Addressees: "A Community in Crisis"? Location and Date?

Does Lane's verdict about "crisis" overstate the problem which the author addresses as characterizing the situation of those to whom he writes? "The traditional view is that Hebrews is written to a group of Jewish converts who are in danger of relapsing into Judaism" (Lindars 1991: 4). If this is indeed because the group who are addressed have become seriously disillusioned with their life as Christians and have even come to doubt whether an approach to God on the basis of Christ's work fully deals with sin and guilt, it would be difficult to imagine a greater crisis. "The whole issue is a felt need on the part of the readers to resort to Jewish customs to come to terms with their sense of sin against God and need for atonement" (Lindars 1991: 10). Lindars perceives this as an inclination to return "to synagogue meals . . . to strengthen a sense of solidarity with the . . . whole sacrificial system. . . . Hebrews regards this return to Judaism as virtual apostasy (6:6 . . . cf. 10:13, 32-34). . . . The readers have lost confidence in the power of the sacrifice of Christ to deal with their consciousness of sin" (Lindars 1991: 10, 11, 12).

If Lindars is right, not only is the group addressed indeed "in crisis"; this writing also remains of paramount theological and pastoral relevance for all generations of believers. It expounds the perfect all-sufficiency of the finished work of Christ as the ground of confident approach to God. A decisive event of the past still has full and definitive efficacy.

Other writers stress the effect of persecution and external pressures on the readers rather than a spiritual lack of assurance. Manson anticipates Lindars' argument that "the Jewish means of grace are ended" but places it in a different frame: "the sin 'of the Hebrews group' was not that of abandoning Christianity for Judaism, but rather of remaining as Christians under the covert of the Jewish religion" (Manson 1951: 24). Under pressure it was tempting to portray Christianity as a *religio licita,* that is, as a recognized and permitted Jewish sect. They had already suffered ridicule and imprisonment (10:32-34; 13:3). If this reflects the situation, the "crisis" is that which, in Manson's view, Stephen and the Hellenistic Jewish Christian attack in Acts 7. "Stephen grasped and asserted the more-than-Jewish Messianic sense in which . . . Jesus [was] to be understood"; rather than slip back under the protection of past securities, they were to heed "the ever-onward call of God to his people," taking "an irreversible step" led forward by the eschatological horizons of "world-mission" (Manson 1951: 31, 35, 63). After a sympathetic but careful assessment of Manson's view, "once certain adjustments are made . . . a case exists for seeing some form of contact between the viewpoint preserved in Acts 7 and that of the *Auctor* [of Hebrews]" (Hurst 1990: 105; see 89-106 and 131-32).

This view does not exclude that of Lindars. If it is accepted, the "crisis" of the community, which may regularly apply today, is that the Christian group has lost its vision of the universal significance of Jesus Christ for world mission. In place of boldness, pilgrimage, and self-discipline, they have relapsed into a cozy, protective mind-set of "maintenance" at the expense of mission. They have tamed and domesticated the gospel into a "safe religion."

Some writers have argued that the "strange teachings" to which 13:9 alludes may reflect the kind of gnostic influences which threatened to disrupt the Colossian community. In this case the "crisis" is not so much, or not simply, doubt about the sufficiency of Christ's work but a diminishing of the cosmic status and sovereignty of his person. Thus Heb 1:3 reflects affinities with Col 1:17 that "Christ is the principle of the universe . . . 'in him all things hold together'. . . . Christ is superior to the angels. . . . Christ has overcome the elemental forces of the universe. . . . The content of Hebrews is close enough to Colossians to fit the situation of the neighbouring churches of Laodicea and Colossae in the Lycus Valley" (Jewett 1981: 6, 7; cf. 6-13). Some perceive the ascription of creation and glory to Christ as itself associated with gnostic myth (Käsemann 1984: 97-117, 130-33; Grässer 1965: 105-15, 181-84). However, this view has received decisive criticism (Hofius 1970: 5-21; Hughes 1979: 137-42; Hurst 1990: 67-75). While the community's "crisis" did indeed entail theological misunderstanding and error, to specify this as "gnostic" is narrower and more speculative than the evidence of the epistle warrants. It does, however, call attention to the universality of Christ. "Christ is all" not only in the sphere of religion but in widest reality.

We need not delay on the speculative theory that the addressees were former Jewish priests who regretted their loss of priestly status (Spicq 1952: 1:220-31). Although several passages receive special force and poignancy in this light, the specificity of the theory goes once again beyond the evidence. It does remain the case, however, that the readers betray a possible nostalgia for a status and security that was lost when they became pilgrim people, "sharing the abuse which Christ endured" (13:13; cf. deSilva 1995). True, in one sense all Christians become "outsiders" with Christ in the eyes of the world (13:13), but the "continuing city" of Christians lies ahead as an inheritance of divine promise. Clearly the addressees had come under the spell of disappointment. Despondency had led to drifting (2:1-4). Thus Hebrews is both encouragement and warning "that we do not drift off course" (Lane 1991: lv).

Discussions of the stance and attitude of the readers remain more to the point than theories about their probable location or social mix. Theories have been put forward about a group in Alexandria, Jerusalem, Qumran, the Lycus valley, Corinth, Ephesus, and Rome. Endless inconclusive debate has taken place concerning "those from Italy send you greetings" (13:24), which can be understood in various ways (Lindars 1991: 17-18 and below). Many would endorse the double comment that "Rome remains the most attractive hypothesis. . . . But this view necessarily remains only a hypothesis" (Hagner 1990 [1995]: 6-7). Even the troubles or "persecutions" associated with the edict of Claudius in AD 49, with Nero in AD 64, or with the later reign of Domitian, cannot necessarily or securely be identified with the sufferings experienced by the local community since these could be of various kinds, ranging from persecution to unofficial mob violence. The references to the tabernacle rather than to the temple reflect the author's dynamic pilgrimage theology and biblical exposition: they have no bearing on speculations about dating in relation to the destruction of the temple. The tabernacle, moreover, serves as the context for the Day of Atonement in Leviticus 16. It is therefore virtually impossible to suggest a date for Hebrews (for before AD 70, cf. Robinson 1976: 200-220). Some urge that 5:12 implies an extended history of the community and therefore a date not earlier than around AD 60. But what might represent an extended period in the context of the earliest communities? We cannot tell.

Integrity, Genre, and Distinctive Theology

In our view the internal evidence of Hebrews points to its being a sermon addressed by an author to a congregation with whom he cannot be present (Lane 1991: lxix-lxxv; Long 1997; see below on 1:1-3). Although the ms. $\mathfrak{p}^{46}$ (early third century) bears the title "To the Hebrews," there is no earlier testimony to this title, and it probably occurs on the basis of analogy with other titles (e.g., "to the Romans" . . .). 1:1-4 begins as a sermon would begin, with marvelously crafted theological declamation which serves as a multiple communicative act of creed, teaching, hymn, doxology, confession, exposition of Scripture, and acclamation (see below). Many argue for the sermon form (Lane 1991: lxix-lxxxviii and 1-9; Vanhoye 1981; against Lindars 1991: 6). The argument that Hebrews is a letter depends on the content of parts of ch. 13. But ch. 13 is clearly "an appendix. . . . It is only in this chapter that the writer speaks as though he were writing a letter" (Héring 1970: 119).

Some writers deny the integrity of Hebrews. Synge distinguishes between an expository-didactic source of material (theology) and a hortatory source (practical application) (Synge 1959: 43-52). Such a theory cannot be sustained. The unity of at least chs. 1–12 is widely accepted. Some argue that "Ch. 13 is an addition prepared for a different group. . . . The benediction [13:20-21] and 'Pauline' postscript [vv. 22-25] may have been added . . ." (Buchanan 1972: 267). But the vocabulary and especially the key themes which relate closely to issues which would face a pilgrim orientation argue for the integrity of the entire epistle (see the introduction to ch. 13; and Filson 1967: 22-29; Überlacker 1989; deSilva 1995). If the author belongs broadly to the so-called Pauline circle, or even if he does not, the "networks" of leadership and coworkers in the earliest churches make the allusion to Timothy no surprise.

Hebrews is the work of a theologian who is also a pastor and a fine expository preacher. Its theology is distinctive within the NT, although this is not to say that its foundational theology of God, Christ, and salvation fails to cohere in content with Paul, John, or the earliest apostolic preaching. But whereas, for example, Paul gives the highest possible profile to the notion of salvation as being in a relation of reconciliation with God or in a situation in which God has put things to rights, Hebrews understands Christian existence primarily in terms of an assured boldness of "approach" or "entry" into the holy presence of God on the basis of the mediatorial work of Christ as the perfect high priest and once-for-all sacrifice of self-offering (cf. 4:14-16; 6:19, 20; 7:25; 8:6; 9:12-14, 24-28; 10:12-14; Hofius 1972; Scholer 1991; Dunnill 1992). Further, although Paul does use the theme of the covenant within his theology, in Hebrews covenant becomes the dominant theme. It is the ground of a clearly defined promise according to which Christian believers know where they stand with God, through the mediation of Christ (Dunnill 1992). A major role is played by an exposition of the new covenant (9:7-13; 9:15-22; cf. Jer 31:31-34) and the role of promise (Worley 1994: 223-36).

Much of the author's theology takes the form of an exposition of Christology. One well-known volume on Hebrews bears the title *The Epistle of Priesthood* (Nairne 1913). Affinities with, for example, John 17 and Rom 8:34 come to mind, but nowhere else in the NT does this theme find such prominent and systematic exposition. Similarly, the careful and detailed reference to the Day of Atonement as an explanatory model for the finished work of Christ is distinctive: Christ's sacrifice of his own person fulfills both the prophetic demand for obedience and the priestly demand for atonement, but in contrast to the Levitical Day of Atonement and to the Aaronic or Levitical priesthood it is effective "once for all." It is a "full, perfect and sufficient oblation . . . ," in the words of one of the major traditional eucharistic prayers. This epistle, above all, provides the foundation for the emphasis of the Reformers on "the finished work of Christ" to which nothing further need be added or can be added to receive full assurance of welcome into the holy presence of God. Similarly, the emphasis on mediation, both of "descending" mediation of word and gifts "through" Christ *from* God and of "ascending" mediation of the presentation of a perfect sacrifice for sin and intercession "through" Christ *to* God, provides the clearest model of what it is to pray and to receive purification "*through* Jesus Christ our Lord."

Yet even this does not exhaust the distinctiveness of the author's Christology. In an age when many have argued that the earthly Jesus of history barely coheres with Christ of Christian theology or the creeds, Hebrews presents a more realistic portrayal of the genuine humanness of Jesus (including his weakness, tears, temptation and real need to trust God, and acceptance of abuse, 2:11-18; 4:15; 5:7-10; 13:12, 13) in close conjunction with what is probably the "highest" Christology in the NT: Christ is mediate creator of all that exists, the exact imprint of God's very being; he is "at the right hand of God"; and he is explicitly addressed as "God" (1:3, 4, 6, 8, 10-13; 4:14; 7:17; 12:2). Our commentary on 1:1-4 will show close resonances with the great ecumenical creeds. The temporal unfolding of divine purpose and the holding together of the earthly and the heavenly in the person of Christ could never find a place in Philo (Williamson 1970: 142-59 and throughout; Hurst 1990: 7-42). *Hebrews therefore provides an often neglected resource for current debates about Christology.* This is not to deny linguistic, stylistic, and conceptual resonances with the first-century Jewish Philo at very many points (Spicq 1952: 1:39-51). But this is not the place to explore them.

Hebrews remains eminently practical in its pastoral thrust. Whereas Paul tends to restrict "application" to a later section in the more "theological" of his epistles, Hebrews offers alternating panels of theological exposition and practical encouragement or warning. In a simple everyday study guide to Hebrews Barclay identifies seven "dangers" against which practical warnings are offered: (i) drifting in place of decision (2:1-4); (ii) weariness in place of endurance (10:35-38; 12:12, 13); (iii) stagnation in place of progress and growth (5:11–6:1); (iv) a search for false security and cozy comfort in place of fellowship, mutual support, and corporate worship (10:25); (vi) apostasy instead of loyalty and faithfulness (6:1-8); and (vii) looking in the wrong direction (especially backward and inward) in place of focusing on the person and work of Christ and the forward goal which lies ahead (Barclay 1965: 94-96). But encouragement remains no less prominent than warning. The Christian believer is invited to approach God "with boldness" to "receive mercy and find grace" (4:16), and to do so "in full assurance of faith" (10:22).

The finished work of Christ provides the basis for this assurance: nothing can or need be added to it; it is all-sufficient for faith, life, and pilgrimage, and it seals and affirms the promises of God which cannot be shaken (7:20-23; 9:16-22; 12:26-29). Acting in the present on the basis of divine promise is the heart of Christian faith (11:1-40), and the self-offering of Christ stands surety for the irrevocable security of the promise. Moreover, Christ's own example of the patient acceptance of constraints on the basis of God's promise of something "better" blazes the trail for all believers (2:7-15). Biblical exposition, profound theology, and incisive practical application are the marks of this writing.

Bibliography. Not listed in the main bibliography: Manson, T. W. 1949, "The Problem of the Epistle to the Heb," *BJRL* 32:1-17 • Nairne, A. 1913, *The Epistle of Priesthood*, Edinburgh: T. & T. Clark • Robinson, J. A. T. 1976, *Re-dating the New Testament*, London: SCM • Scott, E. F. 1923, *The Epistle to the Hebrews*, Edinburgh: T. & T. Clark • Synge, F. C. 1959, *Hebrews and the Scriptures*, London: SPCK • Worley, D. R. 1994, "Fleeing to Two Immutable Things: God's Oath-Taking," *ResQ* 36:222-36.

COMMENTARY

The Uniqueness of Christ in Comparison with Other Mediators between God and Humankind (1:1–4:13)

A Rhetorical Recital of Christ's Role and Rank: Revealer, Representation, Royal High Priest (1:1-4)

Revealer

Whatever the alleged problems of speaking about "revelation," our author shares with the mainline traditions of Judaism, Christianity, and Islam the conviction that "God . . . has spoken" (1:1-2). This belief is "basic to the whole argument of the epistle" (Bruce 1964: 1). Unlike the traditions of Judaism and Islam, however, the author declares that Christ alone constitutes the definitive disclosure of the nature and being of God. He articulates the reality of an otherwise unfathomable God. The Greek is bold: Christ is "the exact imprint" (Gk. *charaktēr*, "die stamp," "engraving") of "God's very being" (Gk. *tēs hypostaseōs*, "his underlying nature"). This means not that he "resembles certain aspects" of God but that as his exact representation he reveals "what it is that makes God be God" (Montefiore 1964: 35).

Christ's work as Revealer, the author urges, stands equally in *continuity with the OT revelation* through the prophets and in *contrast with* its fragmentary or varied nature. "There is . . . a conception of a longitudinal 'revelation history' . . . a continuity which allows [OT revelation] to be construed as parts of a single process"; nevertheless, we also note "discontinuity. . . . The process has . . . achieved perfection . . . in the Son" (Hughes 1979: 6). To speak only of "NT Christians" in contrast to "biblical Christians" represents a deviation known in the second century as the "heresy" of Marcion (cf. Héring 1970: 2). The Greek translated as "in many parts" *(polymeros)* has variously been rendered "in many fragments" (Weymouth) or "bit by bit" (C. B. Williams), and denotes the "formal diversity" of the OT (Attridge 1989: 37).

"These last days" (1:2; Gk. *ep' eschatou tōn hēmerōn*) reflects the Gk. LXX translation of Heb. *be'aḥarit hayyamim* (cf. Jer 23:20; Dan 10:14) to signify the well-known contrast between "the two ages" of OT expectation and of Jewish apocalyptic. The practical significance for us is that those who used this language for the coming of God's "Son" (v. 2) perceived this as nothing less than a cosmic turning point in God's dealings with the whole world, not simply for Israel's history.

These verses open a powerful sermon which is both expository (e.g., its use of Psalms 2, 8, 95, and 110) and intensely practical. The rhetoric is the most sophisticated in style in the whole NT, employing alliteration, rhythm, elegance, force, and careful artistry (cf. Gk. *polymerōs . . . polytropōs . . . palai . . . patrasin . . . prophētais . . .)*. The style, together with variations between oral and written allusions, makes it virtually certain that our "epistle" was prepared as a sermon which was committed to writing only because the congregation was in another place (Lane 1991: 1xix-1xxxviii, 1-9; Vanhoye 1981; cf. 2:5, 11; 6:9; 8:1; 9:5; but against Lindars 1991; see Introduction, 1453). These verses combine several functions at the same time: *they are sermon, creed, confession, hymn, praise, acclamation, exposition, argument, and celebration.* Much of the poverty of some preaching today derives from exclusive attention either to "teaching," "exhortation," or personal anecdote, in contrast to the richly multilayered, multilevel model of preaching, teaching, and praise seen here. This effective address sprang from scriptural learning, sensitivity to the audience, and careful and meticulous preparation (Überlacker 1989; Frankowski 1983: 183-94).

Representation

At the heart of this epistle lies the theme of *Christ as mediator:* (i) As "descending" mediator Christ represents God to humanity. He reveals who God is, reflects or radiates God's nature, and performs God's work. (ii) Later the author will expound Christ's role as "ascending" mediator: he represents humanity to God as high priest (4:14–5:8; 7:4–9:28). In 1:1-3a and 1:4 Christ represents God to humanity; v. 3b begins to anticipate Christ's high-priestly representation of humanity to God.

Christ's role and rank as representative of God also draws on OT and Jewish traditions concerning Wisdom and the Word as agents of God. "The hymn is a striking expression of Wisdom Christology. . . . In Heb 1:1-3 and Col 1:15-17 we have a way of speaking about Christ in Wisdom terms" (Dunn 1980: 206, 207). In the OT Wisdom is "beside God like a master-worker" (Prov 8:30) as God "created the worlds." Further in the Hellenistic Jewish book of Wisdom, Wisdom is described in terms which occur only here in the LXX but which are taken up in Heb 1:3: Wisdom is God's creative agent in shaping the cosmos and as such acts as a "reflection" or "radiance" (Gk. *apaugasma*) of God (Wis 9:26; cf. Wis 7:21-27 and 9:2). The image suggests a channel of effects, like the warming of the earth *by* the sun *through* its rays. NT writers (esp. John 1:1-3; 1 Cor 8:6; Col 1:16, 17; Heb 1:1-3) apply this distinction between *source of* creation (usually Gk. *ek*, "from," with the genitive) to God the Father, and *agency* of creation (usually, as here, Gk. *dia*, "through," with the genitive) to Christ.

Although Word (Gk. *logos*) is not explicit here as it is in John 1:1-14, the parallel between Word, Wisdom, and Christ is unmistakable (Lindars 1991: 31-35; cf. Hanson 1965: 48-82). The first-century Jewish writer Philo makes full use of both Wisdom and Word traditions to explain to his Greco-Roman readership how God can be active in the world. But Hebrews and John stress the flesh-and-blood humanness of Christ within time in a way which would be foreign to Philo (Williamson 1970: 142-59). The issue which Philo and Hebrews address about how a God who is "beyond" can be "real" for the world surfaces again today. Many argue that a "real" God would become a mere "object" in the world. But Hebrews insists that the enfleshed "Son," Jesus Christ, is "the exact imprint of God's very being": it is Christ who makes "real" the otherwise hidden, mysterious God who is Other and Beyond. It is thus that God becomes definitively known, even if glimpses of this reality have been anticipated by "the prophets." These verses find an echo in the ecumenical Nicene Creed: "God from God, light from light, true God from true God . . . of one being with the Father; through him [Christ] all things were made." Christ is "the Place of the Conceivability of God" (Jüngel 1983: 152). He maintains the providential government of all created existence, whether terrestrial or transterrestrial being (Lane 1991: 14; cf. Williamson 1970: 95-103; Grässer 1973: 182-230). Through Christ God keeps the cosmos from falling into the abyss of non-being.

Royal High Priest

Hebrews makes special use of the theme of "drawing near" to God or of "entering into" his presence. This liturgical picture complements Paul's social picture of reconciliation and putting things right. Hence the High Priest assumes a special role in "opening the way of approach" (Scholer 1991). Hebrews presupposes that God is not only generous in grace but also awesome in holiness. It cannot be taken for granted that human persons may "approach" God simply because they may wish to do so. However, God himself has provided a way of approach through the high-priestly work of his Son. The author emphasizes again and again that Christ's priestly work is "finished" in the sense of its reaching a perfect completion (Überlacker 1989). Hence, although the Jewish Aaronic or levitical priests continually "stand" to continue an unfinished work (10:11-14), Christ as perfect high priest "took his seat" (Gk. aorist *ekathisen*, 1:3b). This "seating" denotes both *completion* and *royal status*, for in OT tradition only the Davidic king could "be seated."

The author emphasizes Christ's being "seated at the right hand of God" (as the ecumenical creeds reaffirm). Many argue that this clause forms the centerpiece of a chiasmic structure (Ellingworth 1993: 95-98; Vanhoye 1968: 7-11, 25-76). Of greater importance is the clear use of Ps 110:4, which reappears also in 1:13 as the climax of seven quotations from the OT in 1:5-13. It has been argued that Hebrews as a whole is a "homiletical midrash based on Ps 110," citing Psalm 110 as "the primary text for the entire exposition 1:1–12:29" (Buchanan 1972: xix and 8; cf. xix-xxiii). "Christ at the right hand" constitutes a central, dominant theme (cf. Hay 1973; Loader 1978: 199-217). This is not confined to our epistle; cf. Rom 8:34; Eph 1:2; Phil 2:9-11; Col 3:1). Related themes become combined through the use of Pss 2:7, 110:1, and 110:4 (Kistemaker 1961: 116-24; Leschert 1994). These themes find expression especially in the Christology of the Reformers in terms of Christ's "office" as prophet, priest, and king whose atoning work is "finished" (Calvin [1957] 2.15.425-32). "The Son of God has accomplished something incapable of achievement by anyone else" (Bruce 1964: 7; cf. 10:14). The word "purification" (Gk. *katharismos*) is relatively rare in the NT as an exposition of Christ's atoning work (Attridge 1989: 46), but it belongs to this priestly frame of thought (Scholer 1991).

The thought moves on to the Christ's being "superior to angels" (1:4) since angels were perceived also as agents of mediation between humanity and a holy, transcendent God. The Gk. *angeloi* reflects Heb. *mal'akim*, that is, messengers who do God's bidding. But in Intertestamental Judaism the angels included especially "the angels of the [divine] Presence." Jewish tradition gave some specific names, for example, Raphael, Uriel, Phanuel, Gabriel, and Michael (Tob 1:1; *1 Enoch* 10:1; 19:1; *Sim. Enoch* 40:9; *Jub.* 1:29; cf. also Dan 12:1). Occasional allusions occur in the NT; for example, "the angel Gabriel was sent . . . to Mary" (Luke 1:26, 27), and Jesus speaks of guardian angels in Matt 18:10. But while these "angels of the Presence" convey *messages* and perform *tasks*, no angel conveys or reflects *the reality of God's own being*. In this sense, our writer insists, any revelatory or representational role assigned to angels is of a *qualitatively different order from the unique role of Christ as the one mediator* between God and humanity (cf. 8:6; 9:11-14; 10:14).

Bibliography. Deichgräber, R. 1967, *Gotteshymnus und Christushymnus in der frühen Christenheit*, SUNT 5, Göttingen: Vandenhoeck & Ruprecht • Dunn, J. D. G. 1980, *Christology in the Making,* London and Philadelphia: SCM • Frankowski, J. 1983, "Early Christian Hymns Recorded in the New Testament: A Reconsideration of the Question in the Light of Heb 1:3," *BZ* 27:183-94 • Grässer, E. 1973, "Heb 1:1-4. Ein exegetischer Versuch," in *Text und Situation,* Gütersloh: Mohn, 182-230 • Hanson, A. T. 1965, *Jesus Christ in the Old Testament,* London • Jüngel, E. 1983, *God as the Mystery of the World,* ET, Edinburgh: T. & T. Clark, 152-68 • Sanders, J. T. 1971, *The New Testament Christological Hymns,* SNTSMS 15, Cambridge: Cambridge University.

A Biblical Exposition with a Practical Warning: Christ, Angels, and Humanity (1:5–2:18)

A Chain of Seven Old Testament Passages: Christ and the Angels (1:5-14)

The writer is an expository preacher who "reworks" OT passages from the standpoint of Christian faith and Christology to bring home practical lessons to the addressees (Hughes 1979: 101-36). The use of collections of texts gathered around a single theme (often called *florilegia*) occurs for purposes of present understanding and exhortation already in contemporary Judaism in the Dead Sea Scrolls (e.g., the "messianic" use of Exod 15:17-18; 2 Sam 7:11-14; Isa 8:11; Dan 11:32 in 4QFlor [e.g., 1:18-19]), and in Philo. "Heb 1:5-13 contains passages from a florilegium on sonship, to which have been added some passages on angels . . . joined by typical midrashic introductions: 'has he ever said? . . . and again . . . it says . . .'" (Buchanan 1972: xxiii). Several of the OT passages cited already have "messianic" overtones in first-century Jewish thought. Although normally we comment more thematically, the use of seven quotations invites a comment on each separately.

(i) The first quotation (1:5a) represents the Greek LXX version of Ps 2:7. This is a standard piece of scriptural *testimonia* used by the apostolic church (e.g., Acts 4:24; 13:33). "Today" does not identify a moment in time but serves to negate the notion of sonship by physical begetting, both in the original coronation psalm itself and in its application here to the sonship of Christ. If angels are called "sons" in Jewish traditions, this is merely in a secondary and corporate sense. God appoints Christ "God's Messiah as his Son . . . in the absolute sense" (Hagner 1995 [1990]: 32).

(ii) The second quotation (1:5b) comes from 2 Sam 7:14. 2 Sam 7:11-14 is cited in 4QFlor 1:10-11 and recounts Nathan's prophecy of God's promise to David that a *son* will succeed him as king. But Solomon failed to live up to the expected ideal, as did subsequent kings of the Davidic line, and prophetic hopes began to center on the figure of an ideal future king, *the* Son of David, who would put all wrongs to right and restore well-being to God's people. This finds expression, for example, in *Psalms of Solomon* and presupposes the background of the Davidic covenant. Our epistle insists that no agent, whether prophet, king, or angel, can bring about the hopes associated with this figure except Jesus Christ as *the Son* in this preeminent eschatological sense. In Jesus Christ the covenant promise to David at last finds complete fulfillment. God's promises may be delayed (cf. 11:1-40) or have only partial actualizations in life, but they may surpass our highest hopes.

(iii) The third citation (1:6) comes from the LXX of Deut 32:43 but is a longer version not found in the standard Hebrew text. Many see an allusion to the tradition of angels giving glory at the birth of Jesus (Luke 2:13), interpreting "when he brings the firstborn into the world" (Gk. *eisagagē,* aorist subjunctive) in this way. "*Eisagō* refers to the incarnation of the Son" (Spicq 1953: 2:17). But contrary to the customary use of "again" to link scriptural citations, others regard the worship of angels as applying to the coming again of Christ (Michel 1966: 113; Andriessen 1976: 296-300). The latter seems forced (Bruce 1964: 17-18). Recently it has been argued that the verb means "He has brought Christ out of death into the glory of the heavenly assembly" (Ellingworth 1993: 118), although others argue that it means "the heavenly world of eschatological salvation" (Lane 1991: 27; cf. Attridge 1989: 56-57).

However we interpret the details, the force of the quotation is to differentiate the dignity and rank of "the firstborn" (Gk. *prōtotokos*) as the honored heir who, with the Father, is worthy of the worship of angels. Both the "Hymn of Moses" (Deuteronomy 32) and the title of Christ as "firstborn" find numerous parallels in the NT (Deuteronomy 32 in Rom 10:19; 12:19; 15:10; Heb 10:30; "firstborn" in Rom 8:29; Col 1:15, 18; Heb 11:28; 12:23; Rev 1:5). The longer LXX reading of Deut 32:43 finds an echo in Ps 97:7 and in Qumran. The NRSV correctly translates "he says," since God pronounces the imperative in Deuteronomy.

(iv) The fourth allusion (1:7) is to Ps 104:4. The context in Psalm 104 is that of contemplation on the greatness of God, who created both the celestial and terrestrial realms for his own sake; hence everything within them serves as his agent, messenger, servant, or instrument. "Angels" do not give orders but carry them out. Even if angels stand immeasurably above humanity, yet Jesus Christ stands higher still. "Winds and fire" may be swift and powerful, but they serve God's purposes. Angels bear comparison with them in both respects.

(v) The quotation of Ps 45:6-7 (in the LXX, Psalm 44) in 1:8 and 9 is remarkable. "The author must have been accustomed to the outright ascription of divinity to the Son, for he shows here not the slightest embarrassment. This is the only place in the NT where the Son is described simply as [Gk.] *ho theos* [God]" (Montefiore 1964: 47; cf. Harris 1985: 129-62; in John 1:1 Gk. *theos* occurs without the definite article *ho*). This represents a Christian reworking of Psalm 45. "The scepter" is reminiscent of a king's dispensing justice on behalf of the oppressed. "The contrast in the function which Christ and the angels perform is the contrast of ruling and serving" (Kistemaker 1961: 79). "Beyond your companions" signals the preeminence of Christ as anointed by God to rule as king. Since he "loves righteousness," the anointing of Christ is an occasion "of gladness."

(vi) The use of Ps 102:25-27 in 1:10-12 takes up the rank and role ascribed to Christ already in 1:1-4: "The quotations . . . have been purposefully arranged so that they begin and end on the note of the Son's eternal nature" (Lane 1991: 30). The doctrine of creation could not merely be taken for granted. Various first-century philosophers argued for the eternity of matter, just as today some argue for a comprehensive "explanation" of the universe in terms of cause and effect. The writer, therefore, as an article of Christian faith (see 11:3), compares creation to a "cloak" (1:12a) which can be made for a purpose and then "rolled up" when it wears out or completes its purpose. The declaration "You are the same" (Gk. *sy de ho autos ei,* v. 12b) need not be understood in Platonic terms to mean that God in Christ is entirely "outside" time or that his nature is static, for as the living God, God is ever on the move, ahead of his pilgrim people. The declaration means rather that Christ, unlike the universe or even the ministries of angels, can never become outdated or obsolete and is ever faithful to his promises. "Your years will never end" is practical as well as doctrinal: no one can "try out" God or Christ and imagine that the realities of the gospel can be "left behind" as seeming to promise nothing further for the future. This notion had seduced the addressees.

(vii) The climax of the quotations (1:13-14) returns to the key theme of Psalm 110:1 (LXX Ps 109; also quoted in 1:3; 8:1; 10:12; 12:2). The imperative "sit" occurs here in the present tense (Gk. *kathou,* NJB, "take your seat," i.e., with continuing effect). (On "being seated" and "right hand" see above on 1:3.) Remarkably, "the angelic world is not only at the service of God and of Christ but to some extent also at the service of believers . . . to aid their progress" (Héring 1970: 12). Angels *serve* Jesus in Matt 4:11. This not only underlines the contrast between angels and the Son but also adds encouragement to flagging readers. The writer does not hesitate to use the word "salvation" and to emphasize its future aspect as that which believers have still fully "to inherit."

A Practical Warning: The Danger of Drifting (2:1-4)

The greater the revelation, the author points out, the greater the responsibility of its recipients. The whole paragraph (2:1-5) turns on a contrast between "drifting away" and "paying greater attention" (v. 1). The Greek for "drift away" (*pararyōmen,* from the compound verb *pararreō*) conveys "flowing past" or "slipping away" (BAGD 1979: 622), in the case of Christian believers perhaps without fully realizing what is occurring. It denotes a state of lethargy, dullness, or inattention (cf. 5:11; 6:11-12; Vanhoye 1981). 2:3 speaks of "neglect" (Gk. *amelēsantes,* "being careless") about "salvation." The writer therefore warns the readers of the need for alert, self-aware *attention* (Gk. *prosechein,* "to give heed to," "to be alert to," BAGD 1979: 714). Drifting brings its own penalty of failing to notice when faith has "drained away."

The readers would know of the warnings attached to OT revelation. But, how much more can Christians afford to neglect "so great a salvation" as is given not "through angels" but "through the Lord" (2:2 and 3)? It was a widespread belief in first-century Judaism that the law was given through angelic mediators (cf. the LXX of Deut 33:2 and Ps 68:18), and it finds expression in Paul in Gal 3:19 as well as in Acts 7:53. Revelation "was attested" by firsthand witnesses, but "God added his testimony" by notable events and experiences through "gifts of the Spirit, distributed according to his will." This terminology has such close similarities to that of Paul in 1 Cor 12:4, 11 that some perceive it as standard descriptive vocabulary for the experience of the earliest churches. Here it underlines the involvement of every member of the community in receiving some form of gift from the Holy Spirit in the first flowering of their faith, which is now in danger of neglect or even possible extinction. They have in effect taken for granted or even spurned gifts which they formerly valued. Thereby they lose a hold on realities which they well know to be "valid" (Gk. *bebaios,* 2:2; cf. 1 Cor 1:6).

Christ the Model of Humanity as God Destined It to Be (2:5-18)

While angels serve God (even believers, 1:14) in the ordering of "the world," the act of subjection (2:5) to which Ps 110:1 refers is not performed by "angels." Even if Deut 32:8 LXX alludes to "boundaries" which angels guard or establish, this is very different from the role of "subduing" the earth. The major theme in this passage is that where humanity as represented in Adam failed, and thereby surrendered the dignity and role that God had assigned, Christ (i) bears every mark of true humanness including "sufferings" (2:10) and the need to look to God in "trust" (v. 13); and (ii) does not (like Adam) fail, but as the "pioneer" or prototype (v. 10) "destroys the one who has the power of death" (v. 14) and brings freedom (v. 15). He is "crowned . . . with glory and honor" (vv. 7, 9) and thereby regains humanity's lost destiny. Logically this passage first sets forth the major premise of God's glorious destiny for humanity: "crowned . . . with glory and honor" (v. 7). Next it concedes the apparent contradiction of a minor premise: "As it is, we do not yet see everything in subjection to them" (human beings) (v. 8b). It concludes that while humanity apart from Christ fails to reach its destined role, nevertheless "we do see Jesus, who for a little while was made lower than the angels, now crowned with glory and honor . . ." (v. 9).

The general thrust of the passage remains clear, but several details invite further explanation. On "the coming world," see under 1:6. Some allude to the background of Dan 10:13; 12:1; Sir 17:17 to argue for the meaning "heavenly" world (Ellingworth 1993: 146). But in the light of Ps 8:4-6 it is more natural to understand the phrase in 2:6-8 to denote creation as a whole perceived as "a new world-order" (Spicq 1953: 2:30; Bruce 1964: 33). However, dominion over creation (Gen 1:26-28) and eschatological reign are not mutually exclusive (Buchanan 1972: 26; Hagner 1995 [1990]: 44). Psalm 8 projects a vision of a humanity destined "to rule over all things" as vice-regent of God (Kistemaker 1961: 103). This representative Christology is well expressed in modern theology: "Jesus is man as God willed and created him. . . . The nature of the man Jesus is the key to the problem of the human. This man is *man*" (Barth 1960: 50). Paul likewise perceives the restored "image" of God in christological terms (1 Cor 15:27, 49). All this reverses a popular misunderstanding in Christology. The agenda in our epistle is not: "Was Jesus really human? Look at humanity," but: "In what lies true humanness? Look at Jesus Christ." Many writers have perceived here (cf. Phil 2:6-11) a theme of "Adam in reverse": the One who accepted vulnerability and "suffering" (2:9, 10) became "crowned . . . with glory and honor" (vv. 7, 9). The name of "Jesus" (v. 11) denotes flesh-and-blood existence (ten times in Hebrews). As Son of Man Christ not only became one with humanity as such (v. 11) but also "the pioneer of their salvation." "Pioneer" (Gk. *archēgos*) is not only a "pathfinder" or "trail-blazer" (Bruce 1964: 43; cf. Acts 3:15; 5:31; Heb 12:2), but in Greek literature also often a "hero" figure. Thus "Jesus goes in front of his redeemed host, beats down forces opposed to them, and so becomes the Founder or Inaugurator of their salvation" (Manson 1953: 103; cf. Lane 1991: 57-58; Müller 1973). This paves the way for the climax of 2:10-18, "so that through death he might destroy the one who has the power of death" (v. 14), ". . . because he himself was tested . . . he is able to help those who are being tested" (v. 18).

In modern discussions people often face confusion about whether Christ "must" die if he is to redeem humanity. The writer declares that "it was fitting" (2:10) for God to ordain this path, in other words, it was consonant with God's own nature and with the plight of humanity, given all the implications of both. Grace and love take no shortcuts. God in Christ enters fully into the human condition. Even Jesus shared the obligation to "praise" God and above all the need to "trust" God (vv. 12, 13) in the days during which he "shared flesh and blood" humanness (v. 14). Here is no mere "cardboard" humanness, but "becoming like his brothers and sisters in every respect" (v. 17; Robinson 1973). "Brother and sisters" (v. 12) draws on the language of Ps 22:22, just as the expression of "trust" (2:13) alludes to Isa 8:17. The phrase "flesh and blood" (2:14) normally denotes fragility and vulnerability in biblical contexts.

The final two verses of 2:5-18 take us to the heart of the broader argument of the epistle. If (i) God has "appointed" or ordained (v. 10) all that Christ has done, and if (ii) Christ became the paradigm case of what it is to be fully human (v. 17), and further if (iii) his self-offering of his own life in solidarity with his people constitutes "a sacrifice of atonement for the sins of the people" (v. 17), then (iv) Jesus Christ as representative human being is "merciful and faithful as their high priest before God . . . able to help those who are being tested" (vv. 17, 18). We should understand the complex language about Christ's being made "perfect through sufferings" (v. 10) specifically in this context (Gk. *teleiōsai*). "Hebrews's use of perfection language is complex and subtle. [It] is certainly not a development of his [Christ's] moral capabilities. . . . Perfection will be explicated in terms of Christ's priestly access to the transcendent realm of God's presence" (Attridge 1989: 83-87; cf. Vanhoye 1996: 321-38; Dunnill 1992: 188-226).

The translation of Gk. *hilaskesthai* (2:17b; NRSV, "to make a sacrifice of atonement for") is notoriously difficult and controversial (cf. REB and NJB, "to make expiation for, to expiate"; NIV and Weymouth, "to make atonement for, to atone for"; ASV and NIV mg., "to make propitiation for, to turn aside God's wrath"; AV/KJV, "to make reconciliation for"). Every suggestion seems to carry a positive value and a negative difficulty. "Propitiation" has the disadvantage that it may seem to ascribe to Christ the work of winning over a reluctant God on analogy with pagan religions. But it is also more personal or interpersonal than the more mechanical "expiation," which denotes the removal of sin without necessary reference to a deeply personal context. "Atone" has the advantage of alluding to sacrifice and especially the OT Day of Atonement as the context for the means of dealing with sin. The AV/KJV "to make reconciliation" draws on a more Pauline concept which is less in keeping in the imagery of Hebrews (see Introduction, 1452 and 1453).

In Hebrews the blotting out of "sins," or the means of dealing with "sin," is attributed to the perfect high-priestly work of Christ in making his one, full, perfect, covenantal "sacrifice" of himself as an offering duly ordained by God's own self-giving grace (Dunnill 1992: 115-266; Überlacker 1989). More radical scholars may describe this as a "mythological" understanding of atonement since it inescapably speaks of interpersonal acts between God as Father and Christ as Son and High Priest; more conservative scholars would usually prefer to speak of an "objective" act of atonement, which our epistle seems to reflect by the temporal adverb "once for all" (see further under 9:5).

Bibliography. Andriessen, P. 1996, "La teneur judéo-chrétienne de Hé 1:6 . . . ," *NovT* 18:293-313 • Barth, K. 1960, *CD*, 3/2, ET, Edinburgh: T. & T. Clark, sect. 43 • Harris, M. J. 1985, "The Translation and Significance of *ho theos* in Heb 1:8-9," *TynBul* 36:129-62 • Hurst, L. D. 1987, "The Christology of Heb 1 and 2," in L. D. Hurst and N. T. Wright, eds., *The Glory of Christ in the New Testament*, Oxford: Clarendon, 151-64 • Müller, P. G. 1973, *Christos Archēgos*, Bern: Lang • Robinson, J. A. T. 1973, *The Human Face of God*, London: SCM • Vanhoye, A. 1968, *Exegesis Epistulae ad Hebraeos Cap I–II*, Rome: Pontifical Biblical Institute, 81-217; • Vanhoye, A. 1996, "La *'teleiōsis'* du Christ," *NTS* 42:321-38.

Christ Compared with Moses as Son with Servant (3:1-19)

Traditional interpretations of this chapter remain valid but may need to be supplemented by a more recent emphasis. The traditional explanation makes good sense: "The stress on Jesus's full humanity [i.e., in 2:5-18] makes it necessary to prove that he is superior to Moses, since Moses was admitted to be superior to all other men" (Montefiore 1964: 71). Philo sees Moses as an inspired prophet with authority to command or to forbid (Philo *Vita Mos.* 2.2.3, 187). Josephus declares that Moses "surpassed all men that ever lived in understanding" (*Ant.* 4.8.49). In Hellenistic Judaism Moses has no equal and is even portrayed as "superhuman" or as a "divine man" (Gk. *theios anēr*).

More recently, however, this chapter has been related closely with the central chapters from 4:14 to 10:18 on Christ's high priesthood, and the comparison with Moses has been understood more specifically in terms of their respective roles as mediator and high priest (Lane 1991: 1:68-69 on literary arguments for eliminating the traditional break at 4:14). In the strands of Judaism more closely associated with apocalyptic or rabbinic traditions than with diaspora Judaism Moses is perceived as mediator of the covenant (*As. Mos.* 1:14). Traditions emerge concerning Moses' ascension into heaven in this writing (*Assumption of Moses*) which invite comparison with the high-priestly entry into the heavenly sanctuary by Christ (cf. Heb 7:14; 8:5).

In Hebrews 3 Moses and Christ alike were "faithful in all God's house" (3:5; cf. Num 12:7). But whereas Moses was faithful "as a servant" (3:5), Christ was "faithful over God's house as a son" (v. 6). The writer therefore expounds the theme that Jesus is worthy of more glory than Moses (v. 3), just as one who "builds a house" deserves more honor than what is built (v. 2). The OT accounts of Moses do indeed stress his exceptional and moving role as mediator between God and Israel. A genuine mediator (Gk. *mesitēs*, "person in the middle") identifies with both parties and hence becomes, in effect, a person "torn in two." Hence Moses acknowledges God's just judgment upon Israel's sin, but if God refuses to forgive Israel, cries: "if not, blot me out of your book" (Exod 32:32). Here indeed is an impressive model of what it is to be a mediator. In a poignant argument, therefore, the writer urges that Christ outshines even Moses as the mediator of a "better" or "new" covenant" (Heb 8:6; 9:15; 12:14). The contrast between Christ and Moses is not peculiar to Hebrews. If law came through Moses, grace came through Christ; if Moses was a channel for God's gift of transient manna, the "true" or "real" bread is Christ (John 1:17; 6:30-51). The glory of Moses was a "fading" one, but Christ radiates glory to glory (2 Cor 3:7-18). Hints of a messianic prophet "like Moses" (Deut 34:10-12) occur in the Qumran writings. But to presuppose some "Moses Christology" here is "highly unlikely" (Attridge 1989: 105). The points set forth above adequately explain the reason for the argument.

Jesus as Faithful Apostle, High Priest, and Son (3:1-6)

The name "Jesus" without qualification (3:1) calls attention to his earthly existence a second time (cf. 2:11). "Apostle" and "high priest" (v. 1) denote respectively "descending" mediation from God to humankind and "ascending" mediation from humankind to God. An "apostle" is one whom God "sends" (Gk. *apostellein*, Heb. *shaliaḥ*). Since Acts, Paul, and Hebrews provide different contexts of thought, the vast literature on "apostle" in Paul's epistles need not detain us. A "high priest" stands in full solidarity with the people to offer worship, intercession, and sacrifice to God on their behalf. Insofar as God "sent" Moses to the people and Moses spoke with God "face to face" (Exod 33:11; Num 12:8; Deut 34:10), the writer perceives Moses as sharing with Christ both aspects of mediation.

Nevertheless Moses performs these tasks within a redemptive framework already established on other grounds (he himself is part of this "house," 3:3). Christ, however, constitutes more than this: he is the very "builder" (v. 3b) by virtue of whom any "house" exists. The Gk. *oikos*, "house," has a multilayered meaning: the household of God's redeemed people, the Davidic dynasty, the created world, and especially the house of God, that is, the tabernacle, temple, or sanctuary (Moffatt 1924: 42; Attridge 1989: 109). Hence to Christ is ascribed "more glory" (Gk. *pleionos doxēs*). "Glory" is that which makes a person impressive or weighty (Heb. *kabod*), although in the case of God-in-Christ, grace and love are no less sources of glory than sheer majesty. Moses remains, like Christ, a model of "faithful" mediation (v. 5); unlike Christ, however, he does so entirely and exclusively as God's "servant" (v. 5), whereas Christ is both "builder" and above all "Son" (v. 6).

Practical Warning: Missing the Moment and Risking Loss (3:7-19)

We noted earlier (Introduction, 1452) that the writer embodies panels of practical application at regular intervals in the theological argument. 2:1-4 warned against *drifting;* the present panel warns against *missing the optimum moment to hear God's address* (cf. "today," 3:7b, 13, 15). The writer presses into the service of his warning Ps 95:7-11, "God has declared again . . . a final now, a critical last Today of salvation" (Manson 1951: 55; cf. Dunnill 1992: 134-48). The *a fortiori* nature of the argument is clear. If failure to respond to "[God's] voice" (3:7) under the old dispensation prevented many from "entering" the promised "rest" of the promised land (v. 11), how much more serious is the danger of loss if the readers fail to respond to the "today" of "God's voice" (v. 15) if the dispensation is not of Moses but of "Christ"?

The parallel between the exodus "wanderings" and the journeying pilgrimage of Christians is of fundamental importance for this epistle (Käsemann 1984: 17-96; Jewett 1981). In both cases an active response is required to the onward call of God. The emphatic "today" (Gk. *sēmeron*, 3:7, 13, 15, thrice repeated) is drawn from Ps 95:7, and "provided the writer with a catchword for bringing the biblical statement to his hearers more sharply" (Lane 1991: 87). Delay in responding to divine address (Überlacker 1989) may escalate a "hardening of the heart" (vv. 8 and 15) and risk the loss of an irretrievable opportunity. Many pastors and churchpeople recognize the phenomenon of a lost strategic moment for advance in life today. The background and meaning of "enter my rest" (Gk. *tēn katapausin mou*, v. 11; cf. v. 18) are highly complex and controversial (Hofius 1970: 33-101 versus Käsemann 1984: 97-108). Käsemann and Grässer made too much of supposed gnostic influences, as against the importance of time and timing in Hebrews (Williamson 1970: 142-59). "The living God" (v. 12) is ever on the move ahead of his pilgrim people. In his classic study Manson found affinities with the speech of Stephen (Acts 7:2-53) in which "the mobile sanctuary . . . corresponds with the idea of the ever-onward call of God . . . the static temple does not [Acts 7:48]" (Manson 1951: 35). The readers of this epistle must not neglect the onward call or they mortgage themselves to hardening, self-deception, and loss (3:12-19).

"Entering into the Rest": A Wordplay on Jesus-Joshua (4:1-13)

"Entering into [the] rest" (4:1, 3, 5, 10, 11; cf. the verb in v. 4 [= Gen 2:2], 8, 10) stands within quotation marks to indicate that in whatever way we interpret it, the phrase remains "a technical expression" (Ellingworth 1993: 234). The English of v. 8 obscures the fact that "Joshua" is the Hebrew name for which "Jesus" (Gk. *Iēsous*) is the Greek translation. "Since in Gk the names Joshua and Jesus are identical, the readers could not have avoided the implicit contrast between the 'Jesus' who failed to give them rest and the Jesus who brings the true, promised, rest to his people" (Hagner 1995 [1990]: 71). (The KJV/AV translates v. 8 as "Jesus"; NRSV, REB, ASV, NIV, and NJB as "Joshua.")

The passage 4:1-11 provides a three-stage argument: (i) It is possible to miss the opportunity of "entering" the "rest" which God has destined for his people (vv. 1-3). As in 1 Cor 10:1-13, it is possible to share in the corporate life of God's people and yet for the "message not to benefit them" (4:2). Some "failed to enter" (v. 6). (ii) Nevertheless the moment of opportunity for a positive response to God's address has not yet irrevocably passed: "Today, if you hear his voice, do not harden your hearts" (v. 7, from Ps 95:7, as in 3:7, 15; cf. 2 Cor 6:2). (iii) If Joshua had been able to provide what was entailed in "my rest" simply by leading the people physically into the promised land, it would not be the case that God's promise remained to be more completely fulfilled: God would not speak later about another day (4:8). "A sabbath rest still remains" (v. 9).

To this three-stage argument the writer adds a further comment (4:12, 13). "The word of God" itself carries no defect which leads to earlier failure. Indeed, the reverse is the case: "the word" may pierce through the lethargy of the readers to bring judgment or enabling grace. Even if their hearts are in process of hardening, "the word of God is sharper than any two-edged sword, piercing" through layers of defensive self-deception (v. 12) and exposing everything in the naked truth of judgment or grace (v. 13). The function and effect of the "word of God" is to probe and to diagnose the condition of the human heart, including the self-examination which is needed to "enter into" God's promise. Philo and Wisdom also speak of God's word as "the cutter of everything" (Philo *Her.* 130 (Gk. *tomei*); Wis 18:15-16, "Thy all-powerful word . . . the sharp sword of thy command. . . ." Further parallels abound (cf. Braun 1984: 117-20; Trompf 1971: 123-32).

The structure of the argument is clear. The most difficult problem concerns the meaning of the frequently repeated "rest" in 4:1-11 in the form of the Greek noun *katapausis* (as in 3:11) and in the verbal form *katapauein* in 4:4, 8, and 10 (together with the noun in v. 10). The initial fact that in v. 8 it refers to entry into the promised land whereas in v. 4 it refers to the sabbath rest of Gen 2:2 alerts us to the problem that "the imagery of rest is best understood as a complex symbol for the whole soteriological process that Hebrews never fully articulates" (Attridge 1989: 128; cf. 126-28; also Attridge 1980: 279-88).

One approach has been to note the concept of "sabbath rest" found in Philo and Alexandrian thought as it has been influenced by Platonic legacies. In *Post. Caini* 18 Philo interprets the sabbath of Gen 2:2 as a "heavenly" reality in the mind of God, of which earthly counterparts are but imperfect shadows or copies (cf. Moffatt 1924: 50-53; further Philo *Cher.* 87). But the view of purposive time as moving toward an end which characterizes Hebrews does not cohere with Philo's understanding of "sabbath rest" (Williamson 1970: 142-59). Käsemann's resort to gnostic influences also distracts us (Käsemann 1984: 97-108; also Theissen 1969 and Grässer 1993). The most thorough major study begins with the Hebrew concept of *menuḥah, rest,* not only in Ps 95:7 but also in apocalyptic Judaism (Hofius 1970: 33-110). Hofius convincingly concludes that the writer of Hebrews uses "rest" primarily to denote entry into the eschatological Holy of Holies, the promised "heaven" of eschatological expectation, which is God's sanctuary. This leads naturally to 4:14-16 with its assurance that on this basis Christian believers may approach the throne of grace with boldness.

Bibliography. Attridge, H. W. 1980, "Let Us Strive to Enter That Rest," *HTR* 73:279-88 • Schökel, L. 1967, *The Inspired Word,* London: Burns & Oates, 352-67 • Theissen, G. 1969, *Untersuchungen zur Hebräerbrief,* Gütersloh: Mohn • Trompf, G. 1971, "The Conception of God in Heb 4:12-13," *ST* 25:123-32.

Christ as Unique High Priest and All-Sufficient Sacrifice (4:14–10:18)

Much of the argument in these central six chapters turns on a contrast between the high priesthood of Christ as full, perfect, and sufficient in its mediation and offering and the partial and incomplete nature of the Aaronic or levitical priesthood. The mysterious Melchizedek figure (e.g., 5:6-10; 6:20; 7:1, 10-17; cf. Gen 14:18; Ps 110:4) was prominent in several strands of first-century Jewish reflection and in these chapters represents through symbol or type a different order of high priesthood from that of the Aaronic or levitical line. Whereas the levitical priests never complete their priestly work but yield an endless succession of repetition, Christ (in type or symbol anticipated by the Melchizedek figure) completes his priestly work fully and entirely.

Four essential marks of high priesthood are identified. (i) The high priest must fully share the humanity of humankind in order to represent humanity to God (cf. 3:1-6; 4:15; 5:1-5, 7-10). (ii) The priestly figure must be duly appointed by God (cf. 3:1-5; 5:5, 6). (iii) Offering sacrifice on behalf of others must not be compromised by the need to atone for the sins of the priest as well (cf. 4:15; 7:27). (iv) The offering must be so transparently full, perfect, and sufficient that the high priest has performed a finished work, without the need for further supplementation by an endless succession of further priestly acts (7:11-28; 8:8-13; 9:11-14, 25-28; 10:3, 11-18). Clearly the Aaronic or levitical priesthood fulfills the first two marks or "qualifications," but not the third and fourth. By contrast, Christ transparently fulfills all four (1:1-4; 2:5-18; 3:1-6; 4:15, 16; 5:1-10; 6:20–7:28; 8:8–10:18).

Christ Fully and Uniquely Qualified as High Priest (4:14–5:10)

Exhortation to Approach God Boldly on the Basis of Christ's Work (4:14-16)

However complex arguments about priestly figures, especially Melchizedek, become, the writer transparently draws out their practical significance for Christian faith and action. 4:14 expresses in a nutshell the central proposition about Christ's high priesthood: the "sanctuary" which Christ enters with his offering of himself is no mere earthly tabernacle or building but the immediate presence of God: "Jesus, the Son of God" (i.e., the one whose earthly work is completed and offered), "has passed through the heavens" (v. 14; i.e., entered the heavenly sanctuary of God's intimate presence). But he does not do so alone. He stands in equally intimate solidarity with our fragile humanness (v. 15). "In every respect" (v. 15) Jesus Christ has shared our humanity, even to the point of experiencing genuine human temptation or being "tested" (v. 15). The writer, however, carefully distinguishes between being "tested" (or tempted, see below) and yielding to its pull by giving in to "sin." It is fundamental to the high priesthood of Christ that he makes his sacrificial offering not for himself (for he is "without sin," v. 15) but *wholly for others.* This profound foundational theology leads to the clearest and simplest application. If Christ has achieved what is described in vv. 14 and 15, believers are urged to "approach" God "with boldness" (Gk. *parrhēsia,* "'bold frankness'. . . . In secular Gk . . . free, open speech. . . . In hellenistic Judaism . . . the term was extended to apply to speech with God" (Lane 1991: 115). Examples can be found in Josephus *Ant.* 2.52; 5.38; Philo *Her.* 5 (where Abraham speaks "frankly" to God).

The invitation to frank "boldness" has the double context of the privilege of "approach" to the awesome Majesty of the holy God, and yet also Christ's "sympathizing" (Gk. *sympathēsai,* v. 15) with our weakness and vulnerability. Although people make much of the nuance of "suffering with," the primary meaning is not psychological "feeling" (in spite of "sympathize" in the NRSV, REB, and NIV, or "feeling," NJB) but that of "showing" sympathy on the basis of common experience (BAGD 1979: 779; Lane 1991: 108; Schenk 1980: 247, 242-52). Similarly, "weakness" denotes objective ineffectiveness rather than merely feelings of inadequacy.

The NRSV places a marginal note "tempted" alongside "tested" in the main text (v. 15). The REB also has "tested" (NJB, "put to the test"), but the KJV/AV and NIV have "tempted." The Greek perfect participle *pepeirasmenon* (from *peirazein*) may mean "to put to the test" or "to tempt," depending on its context (BAGD 1979: 640). In the Synoptic Gospels the temptations which follow Christ's baptism constitute "tests" of his messianic vocation. But this epistle does not restrict the experience to these specific tests. "Tempted" coheres entirely with writer's emphasis on Jesus' sharing of what it is to be human (Ellingworth 1993: 268-69; against "tried" in Attridge 1989: 140). The two are not exclusive (Lane 1991: 114), provided that "tempted" is included: "The ability of Jesus to be tempted is much more important in Hebrews than in the Synoptics. . . . Hebrews understands the humanity of Jesus in a more comprehensive way than the Gospels . . ." (Cullmann 1963: 94; cf. 83-107). The Synoptics, however, do give us a clue about what "sin" might have been for Jesus. The messianic temptations (e.g., to perform a spectacular miracle) are toward shortcuts to the supposed good, which are not the way of God. The writer is clear that Jesus experienced the pressures and constraints of human life "in every respect . . . yet without sin." An older expositor observes: "Only one who has not yielded to sin can know the fullest degree of the strength of temptation — for he who sins yields to temptation before it has reached the greatest possible force. . . . He who falls yields before the last strain" (Westcott 1892; 3d ed. 1903: on v. 15).

Further Aspects of Christ's Qualifications as High Priest: The Melchizedek Figure (5:1-6)

5:1-5 recapitulate themes already discussed. The high priest not only stands in solidarity with "the wayward" and "weak" (v. 2) but intercedes, and "on their behalf" (v. 1). The Aaronic priests, however, are themselves among those who "must offer sacrifice for their own sins" (v. 3). Christ does not belong to this category (4:15b).

Following a second quotation of Ps 2:7 in 5:5b, a new component is introduced in v. 6, which is taken up more fully in 7:1-10. On the basis of the allusion in Ps 110:4 to the story of Melchizedek in Gen 14:17-22 it is suggested that the OT itself points to a qualitatively "better" order of priesthood than that of Aaron or Levi. In Gen 14:17-22 "Melchizedek, King of Salem . . . was priest of God Most High," and met and blessed Abraham on his return from defeating Chedorlaomer (14:17). "And Abraham gave him a tenth of everything" (14:20). In 7:1-10 the writer of Hebrews recounts this brief narrative, arguing (i) that if Abraham tithed his booty to him, Melchizedek is his "superior" and by implication is also "superior" to Abraham's descendant, Levi (7:4-7); (ii) that Melchizedek's name and office reveal him as priest-king or as royal priest (7:2; thus combining two primary messianic offices); and (iii) that his unexpected appearance in, and disappearance from, the biblical text portrays him "without father, without mother, without genealogy" (7:3). Through a combination of rabbinic hermeneutic and use of Jewish traditions (see under 7:3 and 7:1-10) this came to be associated with the notion expressed in Ps 110:4 and 5:6 that Melchizedek is a "priest forever," in contrast to the changing successions of Aaronic priests.

How important or otherwise are the nuances which surround Melchizedek in Judaism for Hebrews? Although Gen 14:18-20 and Psalm 110 provide the only allusions to Melchizedek found in the OT, this idealized figure became prominent in Intertestamental Judaism as evidenced in the fragmentary 11QMelch from Qumran, which was first published in 1965. These fragments contain a series of biblical quotations which are reworked to denote eschatological deliverance in which the Melchizedek figure contends with evil and brings kingly justice and judgment (11QMelch 3-9, 16). Some compare his role with that of Michael in 1QM 17:5-8, namely, as mediator and warrior (de Jonge and van der Woude 1966: 301-26; cf. Yadin 1965: 152-54; Fitzmyer 1967: 25-41).

But the "warrior" language of 11Q has little or nothing to do with priesthood. 11QMelch establishes not *how* Hebrews regards Melchizedek, but his importance in this period of Judaism (cf. further the many allusions to Melchizedek in Philo (e.g., *Congr.* 99; *Abr.* 235; *Leg. all.* 3.79-82; and Josephus *Ant.* 1.180). "What is remarkable is not, as is often supposed, that *Auctor* [the writer of Hebrews] makes so much out of so little, but that 'he makes so little out of so much'" (Hurst 1990: 60; cf. Hay 1973: 152 and Horton 1976). "With the combination of the two psalm quotations (Ps 2:7; Ps 110:4) the author to the Hebrews depicts Christ as king and as priest" (Kistemaker 1961: 116).

The use of Pss 2:7 and 110 looks back to 1:5-13 (Hay 1973: 114-45). At the very least, the writer argues, "the Jewish priesthood of the Aaronic or levitical order is not the last word"; but in 1:1-4 *Christ is* "the last word." In this sense Christ is priest "forever"; he has no successor. He is unsurpassed.

Christ's Full and Entire Solidarity with Humanity as High Priest (5:7-10)

Agonizing in prayer "with loud cries and tears" (5:7) is almost certainly an allusion to Gethsemane (Mark 14:32-36 par. Matt 26:36-8), although we need not assume that urgent prayer occurred only on the eve of the passion (cf. 2:14). His being "heard because of his reverent submission" (5:7b; also NIV; REB, "because of his devotion"; NJB, "by his reverence") is better than KJV/AV, "in that he feared." Since the prayer in Gethsemane did not remove the prospect of death, some argue that the verse cannot be explained (Purdy 1955: 644-45). But it is unnecessary to make such heavy weather of it; the writer is rejecting the inference that "because He was the Son of God it was different, or easier, for Him"; Jesus was not even exempt "from the common law that learning comes by suffering" (Bruce 1964: 103). The maxim "learning through suffering" (Gk. *pathein . . . mathein*) was widely known in the Greek world. Jesus accepted the human constraints of "development," and the "perfection" in question (v. 9) concerns his perfect qualification for perfect priesthood.

At once there is a practical application. Christians down the centuries have sought shortcuts and easy solutions, even in the name of "spiritual" aspirations. These may seek to avoid the very constraints that for Jesus were essential for true vocation and humanness, even if they entail "tears" (5:7) and "suffering" (v. 8). In vv. 11-14 the writer attributes the readers' lack of understanding at this point to nothing other than immaturity.

Bibliography. Cullmann, O. 2d ed. 1963, *The Christology of the New Testament,* ET, London: SCM, 83-110 • Fitzmyer, J. A. 1967, "Further Light on Melchizedek from Qumran Cave II," *JBL* 86:25-41 • Hay, D. M. 1973, *Glory at the Right Hand: Ps 110 in Early Christianity,* Nashville: Abingdon, 114-45 • Jonge, M. de, and A. S. van der Woude. 1966, "11QMelch and the NT," *NTS* 12:301-26 • Purdy, A. C. 1955, "The Epistle to the Hebrews," *IB* 11, Nashville: Abingdon, 577-763 • Schenk, W. 1980, "Hebr iv:14-16: Textlinguistik als Kommentierungspringzip," *NTS* 26:242-52 • Vanhoye, A. 1977, "Situation et signification de Hébr V:1-10," *NTS* 23:445-56 • Yadin, Y. 1965, "A Note on Melchizedek and Qumran," *IEJ* 15:152-54.

Immaturity Rebuked and Perseverance and Confidence Encouraged (5:11–6:20)

Practical Application of the Above: Immaturity Rebuked (5:11-14)

The desire to avoid constraints, discipline, and training is a symptom of immaturity, lack of initiative, and regression (5:11). "Not only have they not made progress in their understanding of faith; they have also regressed and forgotten the rudiments of Christianity" (Spicq 1953: 2:143). The Greek form for "the basic elements" (v. 12, *ta stoicheia*) has debatable meanings elsewhere in the NT, but here it means "the ABC of faith." The wish that by this time the addressees should have become "teachers" need not imply any former status as Jewish teachers or Jewish priests, as Spicq and Bornhäuser have argued. The imagery "milk" for babies and "solid food" for adults (v. 13) was widely used in Greek educational and ethical material, and it occurs in the NT in 1 Cor 3:1-3 and in 1 Pet 2:2. The context of "training" (5:14) coheres well with the analogy. Today's emphasis on spontaneity, individualism, autonomy, and postmodern hostility toward tradition and habituation risk obscuring *training* and encouraging *drifting* (2:1-5). Such seductions link the first-century addressees in their own pluralist world with that of our turn-of-the-century postmodern stances.

Moving Ahead without Falling Back or Retracing Old Ground (6:1-8)

The practical thrust of 6:1-8 is expressed in "let us go on" (v. 1a). A person who always stops building to "relay the foundation" never makes progress (v. 1b). Since the one "foundation" for believing faith is the finished work of Christ, "seeing whether I have the foundation right" betrays a gross misunderstanding of what Christian faith entails. The completeness and once-for-all nature of Christ's work are genuinely undermined if believers seek to augment or to supplement their beginnings by constant repetitions of foundation laying. Probably the six items listed as "foundational matters" in vv. 2 and 3 represent three pairs of dispositions, institutions, or events which formed the content of a catechism (Bruce 1964: 112). In some very early mss (p^{46}, B, Old Latin, Syriac) "instruction" is in apposition to "foundation," that is, "the catechetical instruction" (Lane 1991: 130 and 132n.). A larger number of early mss. read "instruction" as a genitive (Sinaiticus, A, C, D, 33); the practical difference is minor.

The plural "baptisms," however, raises a problem. For many this fatally excludes a *Christian* catechism. Hence REB translates "cleansing rites" (although the NJB and the NIV accord with the NRSV). Jewish catechetical material concerning "the two ways" appears in *T. 12 Patr.* (*T. Jud.* 20:1-5; *T. Ash.* 1:3–6:6) and in Qumran (1QS 3:18–4:26), and the Qumran community practiced rites of cleansing (plural; cf. 1QS 53:4-9). The remaining pairs are all common to Christian and Jewish catecheses. Some argue that "the list contains nothing distinctively Christian" but also "nothing exclusively Jewish" (Ellingworth 1993: 313). Probably "the writer is not asking the community to discard one aspect of Christian instruction but to build upon the solid foundation already laid for them" (Lane 1991: 140; cf. Peterson 1982: 14-21). "Baptisms" may include the relation between Christian baptism and Jewish rites of cleansing.

"Repentance" is seen in its true foundational light not in terms of the classical Gk. *metanoia* (the biblical word means more than "after-mind"), but in terms of the Hebrew word *shub,* meaning "turn" or "turning," for which the Greek is often a translation (Heb. *naḥam* in other contexts). Thus the baptismal confession "I turn to Christ" captures the meaning well, and thereby complements "faith toward God." The early church portrayed this meaning symbolically by "turning" from West to East to make the baptismal confession and to endorse this "turn" to God in the creeds (cf. 1 Thess 1:9).

The "laying on of hands" occurs in a variety of quite different contexts in the OT, rabbinic Judaism, and the NT (cf. Gen 48:13; Lev 1:4; 3:2; Num 27:18, 23; Deut 34:9; Mark 6:5; 8:23; Acts 6:6; 8:6; 1 Tim 4:14; 5:22). According to the context, the act may be associated with the bestowal of blessing, commissioning for a task (which becomes institutionalized in a specific subgroup of contexts as ordination), as a sign of succession to an office, or identification, for example, with a sacrifice or with a work of ministry. We simply do not know which of these aspects underlies this reference, but reception into the local church may have been associated with a prayer for blessing or with identification with a translocal network of leadership or communion. Unlike some catechetical instruction today, the author of Hebrews regarded "the resurrection of the dead and eternal judgment" (6:2) as fundamental elements of the most basic truths of the faith.

6:4-6 have given rise to endless distracting debates about whether a believing Christian can fall away irredeemably. This is not the key issue for the author (Hagner 1995 [1990]: 92). In his exposition of the nature of Christian faith he asserts that *either* Christian faith and discipleship are ever on the move in progress, pilgrimage, and growth (whatever temporary reversals may seem to intervene) *or* that what appears to be Christian faith is not Christian faith. "Apart from apostasy, no retrogression is possible in the Christian life. . . . The only way of recovering lost ground is to forge ahead" (Montefiore 1964: 104). "Continuance is the test of reality. . . . He is not questioning the perseverance of the saints. . . . Those who persevere are the true saints" (Bruce 1964: 118). "No means of salvation is available other than that which is . . . rejected" (Hagner 1995 [1990]: 92). In an illuminating research article the writer compares the common ethic of the time against violating commitment to a patron by renouncing one's loyalty and gratitude with the horror of apostasy (deSilva 1996: 91-116).

The author is making a pastoral and practical point rather than expounding a doctrine. Pastorally it is simply the case that some who engage with Christianity at a purely superficial level are more likely to become immunized or inoculated against it than those who leave it on one side until they undertake a more serious engagement with it. A repeated cycle of acceptance and rejection is *logically impossible:* as logically impossible as demanding a "crucifying again" of "the Son of God" when by definition the work of Christ is complete and once for all (Gk. *ephapax*). Such a notion of Christianity "holds Christ up to contempt" (6:6) since it denies the once-for-all, perfect all-sufficiency of his work.

In philosophical logic the kind of confusions often associated with these verses may be unraveled by distinguishing between *logical* possibility and possibility in life (*contingent* possibility). The writer is unpacking the logical entailments of the finished work of Christ in terms of "progress or nothing." Addressees who oscillate between retreat to Judaism and "trying out" Christian faith during favorable periods have misunderstood what Christian faith consists in. To conceive of the matter in this way is like getting married to the same person over again: either a person is married or a person is not. "The intention of the stern warning in 6:4-6, consequently, is positive. . . . God's presence and salvation are the undoubted reality of their lives. . . . That we do not choose the impossible . . . is the sum of 6:4-6" (Lane 1991: 146). The thrust is practical: "the authentic is revealed only at the end of the day" (Hagner 1995 [1990]: 93); make sure, this sermon urges, that you are among them!

The tailpiece about fruitful and unfruitful soil (6:7-8) presses home the high stakes. "Each person is held responsible for the productivity of her or his own life" (Jewett 1981: 105). If "the verge of being cursed" seems surprisingly strong, for the author apostasy is not simply a change of belief but turning against one's "covenant partner," and thereby "crucifying again the Son of God (v. 6), . . . to turn against Jesus with disdain . . ." (Jewett, 1981: 103). In fact the author retains a positive optimism about the congregation: everything has been done by Christ to enable them to produce "a useful crop" (v. 7). The imagery has multiple backgrounds (Spicq 1953: 2:154-56; Braun 1984: 173-77).

Encouragement from God's Steadfast Promise (6:9-20)

The positive understanding of 6:1-8 suggested above is confirmed by "we are confident of better things in your case" (v. 9). But this confidence rests not in the readers' capacities but in what "God" does and will do through them (v. 10). "For God is not unjust" does not imply any principle of merit but that God would not be so hardhearted as to give them a taste of new life only to abandon them to their weaknesses. Hence they may enjoy "the full assurance of hope" (v. 11).

Here a key model or paradigm case for assurance against a seemingly severely discouraging background is that of "Abraham" (6:13-20). "He received the promise and God's confirming oath after having endured the most severe trial of his faith (vv. 13-15; cf. Gen 22:1-18). The relevance of his firm faith . . . is demonstrated in vv. 16-20" (Lane 1991: 149). Thus the writer unfolds another logical argument: (i) the solemn binding force of God's speech-act of "oath" and "promise" (6:13-14, 16-18); (ii) its resolution of a difficult period in which Abraham and the addressee must "patiently endure" (v. 15); and (iii) the strong encouragement of this binding oath serves as an "anchor" which ties Christian believers irrevocably to the reality of the heavenly "inner shrine" of God's intimate presence. Christians may "enter" here following "Jesus," the "forerunner" (vv. 19-20; cf. 2:10).

The depths of Abraham's impossible situation are movingly expounded by Kierkegaard, who traces the contradiction of Abraham's being commanded to slay the very son on whom the possibility of the fulfillment of God's promise seemed to depend (Kierkegaard 1969: 9-21; cf. Gen 22:16). Ellingworth discusses textual variants and concludes, "Even human oaths are accepted as valid (v. 16). . . . God's oath is still more powerful (v. 17)" (Ellingworth 1993: 337-40). Abraham's faith was strained in two ways: the need for patience and the seeming contradiction between God's firm promise and what he was required to undergo. God's promise, however, also entailed "two unchangeable things" (v. 18): first, that although whatever God says in whatever form remains valid because God is God, God was willing to bind himself through an act of "promise" as an accommodation to human doubt; second, although any promise from God is irrevocable, as a further accommodation God doubly "guaranteed" this by an oath (v. 17). It has recently been argued that the "two unchangeable things" are God's act as oath-taker and God's act as witness (Worley 1994: 223-36). These co-jointly provide a "steadfast anchor" (v. 19) which is unshakable. Understandably Philo puzzled over the notion of God's swearing any oath (*Sacr.* 91–94; *Leg. all.* 3.203-7) since God cannot lie. Here God limits his own freedom by swearing an oath "by himself." Finally, the writer reestablishes the parallel between Abraham and Melchizedek since entry into "the inner shrine" recalls that Christ's perfect high priesthood and self-offering constitute the firm ground for the fulfillment of God's "promise." If they are suffering hostility and potential persecution, the addressees may "take refuge" in the "strong encouragement" which this "steadfast anchor" yields. They need not "drift" (2:1-4) with such an "anchor."

Bibliography. Kierkegaard, S. 1969, *Fear and Trembling,* Eng. trans., Princeton: Princeton University, 9-22 (on Genesis 22) • Worley, D. R. 1994, "Fleeing to Two Immutable Things: God's Oath-Taking," *ResQ* 36:222-36.

The Order of Melchizedek: Christ and Levitical Priests (7:1-28)

This chapter takes up the earlier references to Melchizedek in Ps 110:4 and in Gen 14:17-21 (see above under Heb 5:6, 10) in 7:1, 10, 11, 15, 17. The Aaronic or levitical priesthood of necessity carries succession, incompleteness, and thus "supercessation" (Manson 1951: 111), in contrast to the "eternal" order of high priesthood anticipated in the Melchizedek figure, fulfilled uniquely in Jesus Christ. The contrast between the two "orders" of priesthood, therefore, paves the way for a crescendo of argument in these central chapters on priesthood, sacrifice, and covenant. These establish the fully "finished" work of Christ as the ground of salvation. The chapter involves three stages: (a) the "greatness" of the Melchizedek figure in relation to levitical priests (vv. 1-10); (b) the self-confessed inadequacy of the levitical priesthood and a new order (vv. 11-19); and (c) Christ the eternal, perfect High Priest as corroborated by covenant oath (vv. 20-28).

The "Greatness" of the Melchizedek Figure Contrasted with the Levitical Priests (7:1-10)

On the writer's use of the Melchizedek episode in Gen 14:17-21, see above under 5:1-6. As in 5:1-6, the tradition is combined with Ps 110:4. However, here the argument that Melchizedek is "great" (7:4) depends on the inference that he is "without genealogy, having neither beginning of days nor end of life . . . a priest forever" (v. 3). Philo and Josephus believed that since he is the first high priest mentioned in Scripture he stands as a mythical or eternal archetype, of which levitical priests are mere imperfect instantiations (Philo *Leg. all.* 3.79; Josephus *J.W.* 6.438). We noted above the tradition found in 11QMelch 3–9, 16 that Melchizedek is a supernatural entity "resembling the Son of God" (v. 3), but also that Hebrews does not draw on the "warrior" aspects of this tradition (see above on 5:1-6 and Hurst 1990: 7-42; cf. Horton 1976).

The emphasis on time, eschatology, and purposive history in Hebrews also excludes close affinities with Philo's view of primal or "timeless" archetypes (Williamson 1970: 142-59; Barrett 1954: 369-93). Some argue that the alliteration and rhythmic style of v. 3 exhibit traces of a pre-Christian hymn to Melchizedek (Windisch 1931: 59-64). But Heb 5:1-5; 7:1-10 simply reflects the fact that whereas parentage was ordinarily of such great importance that usually no significant figure entered such a narrative as Genesis without mention of lineage, in Gen 14:17-20 the silence is significant.

These verses have been described as a typical Jewish *midrash* that interprets the Melchizedek tradition by combining Ps 110:4 and Gen 14:17-20 (Jewett 1981: 118). Nevertheless, the author's argument is distinctively christological and moves forward in four stages: (i) as priest-king Melchizedek prefigures an "order of priesthood" incompatible with that of the levitical-Aaronic priests, for these were explicitly excluded from royal office. (ii) He performed his office prior to the Mosaic law, and in his "blessing" of Abraham demonstrated his superiority to Abraham and thereby to Levi. (iii) The "order" of high priesthood represented and anticipated in Melchizedek requires no line of successors endlessly to continue the work. Hence he prefigures the priest-king Jesus Christ whose work is also complete and finished without reference to the Aaronic line of succession or requirements of the Mosaic law. (iv) Finally, an implicit contrast between *law* (as regulating priesthood in Judaism) and *promise* (the new order) is implied in the allusion to "the promises" (7:6). Vv. 9 and 10 are only superficially difficult. They press the point that the new order stands over against the whole "line" of Abraham, Levi, and the priesthood of Judaism, and this is also the point about the "tithes" (vv. 2, 4) and the "blessing" (v. 6). The author concedes that he is using imagery and resonances rather than more formal inference by the words "so to speak" (v. 9; Attridge 1989: 197).

In spite of what may seem to be an esoteric Jewish technical background, the section is clear and practical in its general force. The superiority of Christ as eternal, effective, heavenly high priest over all the transient culture and institutions of Judaism was of profoundly practical import either because the readers were suffering abuse and low esteem from others because of their Christian faith (deSilva 1995), or because their distinctiveness from Judaism exposed them to persecution and insecurity (Manson 1951), or because they had come to doubt the all-sufficiency of Christ's work (Lindars 1991). The forceful arguments of the author served as a bracing reassurance for Christ-centered faith.

The Self-Confessed Inadequacy of Levitical Priesthood: The New Order (7:11-19)

"Had the Levitical system been sufficient to the task, what need, the author asks, is there to speak of another priest (v. 11) to arise, one of the order of Melchizedek and not Aaron?" (Hagner 1995 [1990]: 103). The OT writings point beyond themselves to a new order: logically to accept the validity of the OT and Judaism entails accepting its own witness that its task is incomplete, and that it points beyond itself to a new order (cf. the parallel with Paul's two arguments in Gal 3:17, 21).

The exposition of Ps 110:4 continues as a background behind the text. Thus 7:11-13 concern the "order" of priesthood (Ps 110:4a), while 7:15-25 take up Ps 110:4b's "forever" (Kistemaker 1961: 118). God's promise persists through human "change," whether through "a change in the law" (7:12) or through changes in the fortunes of the addressees. "Forever" (v. 17; Ps 110:4) applies to Christ, not to the priests of Judaism. Further, the "new" order of Christ-Melchizedek combines the royal and the priestly offices, whereas kingly office is prohibited to Jewish priests. It therefore matters that Christ "was descended from Judah" (7:14; cf. Luke 1:32; Rom 1:3; Rev 5:5; cf. the attempt of Uzziah, 2 Chr 26:16-21, to act as priest). The allusion to "perfection" (Gk. *teleiōsis*) in 7:11 and to "perfected" in v. 19 serves as a frame around the theme of "the law," and thus marks a literary unit (an "inclusion") for vv. 11-19 within the wider argument: "The psalm's oracle shows the provisional and imperfect character of the ancient priesthood" (Vanhoye 1989: 61).

Christ the Eternal, Perfect High Priest Corroborated by Covenant (7:20-28)

The appeal to a divine "oath" (7:21) plays a major part as ch. 7 moves toward its climax. Philo expressed perplexity at the logical tautology of ascribing an "oath" to the God who does not lie (see comment above). But the allusion makes very good sense in the present context. For in vv. 18-19 our author had spoken of the "abrogation of an earlier covenant." Its abrogation introduced "a better hope." But, by the same logic, might not the introduction of the ordinance of the levitical priesthood thereby abrogate the order of priesthood represented by Melchizedek? This is inconceivable, our author explains, because God not only ordained it forever, but "confirmed it with an oath" (v. 20). Its establishment therefore remains "irrevocable."

The mention of this "oath" will lead shortly to the closely related theme of covenant. Before this is taken up, however, the writer emphasizes the contrast between the temporary nature of successive OT and Jewish priests who were "many in number" (7:23) and Jesus Christ, who (like Melchizedek) "holds his priesthood permanently, because he continues forever" (v. 24). The exposition forms a chiasmus. Part of Christ's saving work as high-priestly Mediator arises because "he always lives to make intercession" for his people (v. 25).

There is some debate about the Gk. *eis to panteles dynatai,* "he is able for all time" (NRSV), similar to the TEV and the NASB. However, Greek may denote a quality of salvation rather than its temporal permanence: KJV/AV, "to the uttermost"; NIV and REB, "completely"; NJB, "absolute." Although the debate goes back to the early centuries, many commentators favor the second view (Lane 1991: 1:189; Hagner 1990: 110). However, the writer would be well aware of the double meaning and, in view of the temporal frame of thought and emphasis on Christ's "finished" work, probably intended both nuances (Attridge 1989: 210; Ellingworth 1993: 391). The Greek terms for "approach" also remain significant. In the LXX and here they convey the double sense of "approach" in the context of worship and access to God's holy presence in a broader interpersonal sense.

The language about Christ's intercession (7:25) may also have a double meaning (cf. Rom 8:34). Since *1 Enoch* 13:4 ascribes intercession to angels, this may form part of the broader declaration that Christ's work eclipses that of angels (cf. 1:5-13). Many argue, following Cullmann, that this ministry actively occurs from the exaltation of Christ to the parousia; others view it as analogous to the way in which the blood of Abel "cries out" to God for God's action (Gen 4:10). Since the writer has not yet formally expounded the atoning effects of the work of Christ, the former views seem more likely and intercession is not restricted to the forgiveness of sins. He intercedes not only as priest but also as king for his subjects.

The climax of this part of the argument (7:26-28) turns in two clear-cut contrasts between Christ and the Aaronic priesthood: (i) the Aaronic task is continuous; the NRSV well renders Gk. *kath' hēmeran* as "day after day" in contrast to Christ's work as Gk. *ephapax,* NRSV rightly, "once for all" (v. 27); (ii) the Aaronic high priest has first to offer sacrifice for his own (Gk. *idiōn*) sins; but the single, complete, perfect self-offering of Jesus Christ is not on his own behalf. The author clearly introduces the theme of the sacrificial nature of the work of Christ. The Greek terms *heauton anenenkas* (offered himself) and the synonym *anapherein* (to offer as a sacrifice) place this beyond question. Furthermore, it is interpreted within the framework of the Day of Atonement (Lev 16:6-10; cf. Lane 1991: 193-94). Although the phrase "day after day" alludes strictly to the daily sacrifices of Leviticus and of Judaism, the Day of Atonement refers to the annual series of acts of the high priest. He makes offering first for himself, and then for the people. The sentence concerning the high priest conflates the two examples by way of succinct summary of the double point.

The third contrast of 7:28, namely, that between law and covenant promise, integrates the three themes in such a way as to form a transition to the next main argument of chs. 8 and 9, that is, the context of covenant promise. Thus the law relates to the successive activity of Aaronic priests, while covenant promise provides the framework for the completeness of the work of Christ. The respective correlations between law and "weakness," and promise and effective power resonate with Paul's epistles. Too many Christian expositions today neglect this primacy of promise in contrast to didactic information or to legislative rule following.

Bibliography. Balla, P. 1995, *The Melchizedekian Priesthood,* Budapest: Gaspar Reformed University • Demarest, B. 1976, *A History of Interpretation of Heb 7:1-10,* Tübingen: Mohr • Fitzmyer, J. A. 1969, "Further Light on Melchizedek from Qumran Case 11," *JBL* 86:25-41 • Jonge, M. de, and A. S. van der Woude. 1965-66, "11Q Melchizedek and the New Testament," *NTS* 12:301-26.

The High-Priestly Work of Christ: Sacrifice and Covenant Promise (8:1–10:18)

The style and content of 8:1-2 show that the author moves to a new stage of the argument. The allusion to "the main point" reminds the assembled readers that the author has now clearly established the qualifications of Christ as duly appointed royal high priest "forever," who also has the status of divine vice-regent "seated at the right hand" (see above on 1:3; 1:13; also Ps 110:1). Now comes a further step: the mode and medium of Christ's high-priestly ministry is not that of earthly sacrifices endlessly repeated in an earthly tabernacle but a perfect self-offering in the heavenly realm of the intimate "sanctuary" of God's holy presence. This holy shrine of God's innermost presence constitutes the "true" tabernacle (8:2; Hofius 1972).

The True "Sanctuary" to Which All Earthly Worship and Offering Points (8:1-6)

The phrase translated "the true tent" (8:2; Gk. *tēs skēnēs tēs alēthinēs*) has been the subject of considerable debate, intensified in the light of v. 5 which contrasts "a sanctuary that is a sketch and shadow" (Gk. *hypodeigmati kai skią*) to "the heavenly one." This corresponds to the ideal pattern (v. 5; Gk. *ton typon*) which constitutes the heavenly design plan which Moses was instructed to copy in the construction of the tabernacle. It is beyond dispute that Plato's contrast between eternal Ideas or Forms and the physical, contingent "copies" of these perfect Forms which we encounter in human life had long since filtered through into Alexandrian thought, and much Hellenistic thought, in the first century. It is found most strikingly and pervasively in the first-century Jewish writer Philo.

Many writers therefore believe that our epistle is heavily even if indirectly influenced by this Platonic thought. Héring urges: "The opposition between 'heavenly' and 'earthly' things is used to denigrate the Levitical cult, which is only a copy (Gk. *hypodeigma*) and shadow *(skia)* of the true cult." He adds: "Philo . . . speaks of the *'skēnē alēthinē'* ('true text', *Vita Mosis* 2; 74:15). In Platonism the suprasensible ideas are the only 'true' realities" (Héring 1970: 6; see more extensively Spicq 1952: 1:31-91; Sowers 1965).

Moffatt argued for a middle view, noting on one side that "the idea was current in Alexandrian Judaism, under the influence of Platonism, that this *skēnē* ["tent," "tabernacle"] on earth had been but a reproduction of the pre-existent heavenly sanctuary" (cf. Wis 9:8); "the phenomenal is but an imperfect, shadowy transcript of what is eternal and real"; but also noting on the other side that a significant portion of this Greek terminology can be found in the LXX or Greek translation of the OT (Moffatt 1924: 106 and xxxi). However, the notion of a correspondence between "earthly sanctuary" and "heavenly sanctuary" had acquired widespread currency in first-century Jewish sources and reflects such OT passages as Exod 25:9, 40; 26:30; 27:8; Num 8:4 (Cody 1960: 9-46).

A third group of writers attack the first view and reject the middle view. "In spite of the verbal forms used in 8:5 . . . that verse is essentially an expression of primitive Christian eschatology" (Williamson 1970: 142; cf. Hurst 1990: 7-42). Williamson emphatically rejects the view that two Platonic orders of timeless Forms and earthly copies could ever replace the eschatological contrast between the provisional, finite, creaturely realities of life in the world and the eschatological realities of the future toward which the creaturely may point. This includes the notion that the "earthly" sanctuary remains temporary and will pass away, whereas by contrast "Jesus performs his priestly service in heaven (8:1; cf. 9:11, 23-24) where the archetype *(typos)* is found" (Goppelt 1982: 166; cf. 163-70 and Ellingworth 1993: 408). An eschatological or temporal contrast accounts for the resonances with such passages as Exod 25:9, 40 or Exodus 25–31 as a whole (D'Angelo 1979: 205-27; Hurst 1990: 104; cf. Acts 7:44-50). While Williamson and Hurst make the best case, we should not underestimate the intellectual learning and conceptual resources which the author draws from Hellenistic and Alexandrian thought to express the realities of a Christian understanding.

Today some are inclined to dismiss ascribing action to this "heavenly" realm as the projection of myth "out there." But a proper understanding of creatureliness and eschatology exposes the shallowness of such an approach. The perfect high priesthood and self-offering of Christ belong to the foundation and goal of all divine action, which is based on divine promise and transcends the created order. Such an understanding of the work of Christ is not mere mythological projection but a foundational reality of which all creaturely attempts at worship are, by comparison, pale reflections.

The author clinches the point by reminding the assembled readers of his earlier argument about the grounding of the Melchizedek or "heavenly" order of high priesthood in irrevocable promise. Jesus (the name usually used for Jesus as an earthly figure) thus stands as the mediator between two orders of reality which he brings together into one as the "mediator of a better covenant" (8:6). Although the notion of mediation, or "standing in the middle between," has occurred before (e.g., the verbal form in 6:17), this is the first appearance of the very important noun "mediator" (Gk. *mesitēs*), which will reappear in 9:15 and 12:24.

The Promise of a "Better" Covenant (8:7-13)

The logic is clear: if Jer 31:31-34 witness to the importance of the promise of a "new covenant" (8:8; Gk. *diathēkēn kainēn*), which is not only a "second one" (v. 7) but also a "better covenant" (v. 6; cf. vv. 10-13), to speak of inadequacy or "fault" in the old covenant (v. 8) is to do no more than heed its own self-testimony. The contrast in vv. 1-6 between the "earthly" culture and the heavenly reality of Christ's high-priestly work finds further explication in the prophecy of Jeremiah that the new covenant will internalize God's Torah as inscribed "in their minds" and "on their hearts" (v. 10). The Greek for "mind" (here *dianoia*) denotes not merely rational capacity but also a stance or disposition which includes the mind, while the word for "heart" (Gk. *kardia*) denotes a stance or acts of will that stem from hidden depths, today associated with unconscious or preconscious. Thus the new covenant will actualize God's irrevocable promise to human persons "through-and-through." This is mediated through the work of Christ and founded on the act of God to which Jer 31:31-34 looks in joyous expectation of due fulfillment, even at the price of conceding the inadequacy or "fault" (Gk. *memphomenos,* 8:8) of the covenant of the day (Vanhoye 1976: 143-44; cf. Ezek 36:26-29).

That the first covenant is "obsolete" (8:13) provides no grounds for devaluing the OT. The author's own example (cf. Heb 1:1-13) proves that he regards OT revelation as authentic, but that the terms of its covenantal promise and its actualization have been transformed in the definitive work of Christ. "Covenant" suggests continuity; "new" also suggests contrast. The new covenant is "a linchpin"; without it this epistle would "fall apart" (Lehne 1990: 11, cf. 12-20; Hughes 1979: 36-75, 101-36). There is continuity in the "cultic categories" although the cultic "content" differs strongly (Lehne 1990: 103).

The Inadequacy of Worship and Sacrifice under the Old Covenant (9:1-10)

The declaration that through the promise of Jer 31:31-34 God implicitly "finds fault" with the old covenant order (8:8) extends to animal sacrifices. These point forward to the total adequacy of the self-offering of Christ on behalf of God's people, which will be expounded positively in 9:11-28. Meanwhile the middle section of the argument (vv. 1-10) emphasizes that in spite of the elaborate cultic detail of the old covenant tabernacle or tent of meeting, the priestly offering remains incomplete (v. 6), partial (v. 7), "unable to perfect the conscience of the worshiper," and provisional (v. 9). The argument will be resumed in 10:1-5, where the climax of the argument portrays the effect of old covenant sacrifices as a debilitating "reminder of sin year after year" (10:3).

It may be argued that the description of the details of the Jewish cultus in 9:1-10 does not correspond with what we know of Herod's temple. However, few regard this as significant since the author is discussing not the first, second, or third temple, but the tabernacle as depicted in the Pentateuch. On supposed anomalies between Heb 9:2-4 and Numbers cf. Attridge 1989: 236-38.

"In the statement concerning the high priest (v. 7) the reference to the Day of Atonement is unmistakable. The high priest alone was permitted to enter the inner sanctuary (Lev 16:32-33) . . . only once a year and then under strictly prescribed conditions (Lev 16:3-17). . . . The writer specifies . . . 'never without blood'" (Lane 1991: 222). The ritual presupposes a fundamental distinction between the two compartments within the sanctuary of "the Holy Place" (Gk. *hagia*) and the Holiest or Most Holy Place (*hagia hagiōn,* following the Heb. idiom "Holy of Holies"). In 9:1-10 our author denotes these by the terms "the first one" (vv. 2, 6, 8) and "the second" (v. 7) as respectively the holy and most holy place. Thus "the lampstand, the table, and the bread of the Presence" are located within "the first" compartment, or "Holy Place," while "behind the [second] curtain the ark of the covenant" and "the mercy seat," that is, within the "second" consecrated area, "the Holy of Holies" (Hofius 1972).

The series of partitions and entrances symbolized simultaneously the exclusive principle of *divine holiness* (lit. "that which is separate") and the inclusive principle of *divine grace* ("let us approach"; Gk. *engizō*). God has prescribed specific conditions on the basis of which he may be approached. This key model dominates the whole epistle or sermon; the Christian life is one of "drawing near" or "approaching" the holy God of grace. The Day of Atonement serves as a pointer and paradigm through the self-offering of the shed blood and priestly work of Christ. Thereby he is the mediator of God's secure covenant promise. Under the new covenant, as Jer 31:31-34 indicates in advance, the privilege of approach is no longer restricted to the high priest alone. "All" whom Christ represents as high priest may now enter the holy presence of God with Christ, since Christ (cf. 9:12) "entered once for all . . . with his own blood. . . ."

"The altar of incense" (9:4) appears on the basis of Exod 30:6 and 40:26 to be located in the outer area rather than in the holy of holies. A variety of explanations for the discrepancy have been suggested; for example, that the golden altar was placed in the inner sanctuary during a different period (1 Kgs 6:20; Lane 1991: 220); or that the author means only "that it belonged to the sanctuary" (Montefiore 1964: 145). (For six or more hypotheses cf. Ellingworth 1993: 426-28.) The other allusions to specific objects are drawn from biblical traditions: the manna, from Exod 16:32-34; Aaron's rod, from Num 17:1-11; "the tablets" of stone, from Deut 10:5; the "cherubim," from Exod 25:18-20. The author makes it clear that "detail" is not his concern (v. 5).

The noun "mercy seat" (Gk. *hilastērion,* 9:5) occurs in the NT only here and in Rom 3:25, where its more extended meaning to denote the atoning work of Christ is keenly debated. Some translations of Rom 3:23 render the term "propitiation" (KJV/AV; Phillips); others, "expiation" (RSV); others, "sacrifice of atonement" (NRSV; NIV); yet others, "sacrifice for reconciliation" (NJB). The meaning in Heb 9:5, however, is more context-specific to the Day of Atonement and the tabernacle than Rom 3:25, and "approach" remains the central concern. It is doubtful whether NIV's "atonement cover," or REB's "place of expiation," offers any improvement for Gk. *hilastērion* in 9:5 over the NRSV, ASV, and KJV/AV "mercy seat," although "throne of mercy" (Knox, NJB) also has merit.

The Once-for-All Sacrifice of Christ Inaugurates the New Covenant (9:11-28)

(i) Once-for-All Sacrifice (9:11-14). A three-stage argument emphasizes the contrast between the two orders, and the two covenants find expression, in turn, in three fundamental declarations in 9:11-12: (i) Christ's self-offering took place not in a cultic context "made with hands" (cf. Mark 14:58; Acts 7:48) but in the heavenly or eschatological realm to which earthly institutions or buildings are no more than imperfect pointers (cf. 8:5 above and 9:24 below). Second, Christ entered the "inner sanctuary" of God's immediate presence offering, not "the blood of goats and calves, but . . . his own blood" (v. 12). Third, Christ's entry as duly appointed high priest into this "Holy Place" was "once for all" (Gk. *ephapax,* v. 12), that is, a definitive, unrepeatable, complete, and perfect work in no need of any supplementation.

Each of these three terms of contrast receives some exposition and comment in the remainder of this chapter, but they are also interwoven. The heavenly sanctuary theme emerges more than once in 9:11–12:24. The contrast between the blood of Christ and animal sacrifices receives further comment in 9:14, 25, 26, and 28. The once-for-all means of approach to God finds expression in vv. 14, 22, and 28 and further in 10:19-20. Vanhoye perceives a self-contained structural unit of antithetic and complimentary parallelism of great coherent force in 9:11-28, arguing for a partial inclusion signposted by the mention of Christ in vv. 11 and 28 (Vanhoye 1976: 147-61).

A double significance attaches to "the ashes of a heifer" (9:13). After the sacrifices of a goat and a bullock on the Day of Atonement (Lev 16:6-19, 23-26) and the release of the scapegoat (Lev 16:20-22, 26a), detailed rites of purification were prescribed (Lev 16:23-28). But two factors receive attention. First, the intensity of concern about purification is demonstrated by the regulations concerning the use of "a red heifer without defect" (Num 19:2, 3), which was then burned to ash and the ashes removed (Num 19:4-10). Second, the Day of Atonement and other purification rites implied a problem of *ad infinitum* regression: What about the cleansing of those who handled the means of cleansing? Could the process ever stop? By way of answer, the author insists not only that whatever the lesser (the blood of animals) achieves, the blood of Christ achieves more (9:14) but also that Christ's self-offering excludes any *ad infinitum* process because it is *ephapax,* "once for all" (v. 12). "In the NT this is a technical term for the definitiveness and therefore the uniqueness or singularity of the death of Christ" (Stählin 1964: 383). As in Rom 6:10, the death of Christ is unrepeatable and definitive for redemption (cf. also on Heb 6:4; 7:27, above).

Of many explanations for the phrase "the eternal Spirit" (9:14, NRSV, REB, NIV, KJV/AV; cf. Knox, "the Holy Spirit") it is most likely that allusion is made to the Servant of the Lord in Isaiah 42 who yields up his life "as a guilt-offering for many . . . 'I have put my Spirit upon him' (Isa 42:1)" (Bruce 1964: 205). In contrast to animal sacrifices, Christ's holiness entailed a voluntary, rational, obedient, active self-giving, in the power of God's Spirit (against Montefiore: "man's ego or very self. It does not mean here 'the Holy Spirit'"; 1964: 154-55). The allusion to "conscience" (9:14) confirms that the thought is personal, relational, and moral rather than depending on mechanical notions of ceremony or ritual.

(ii) Mediator of the New Covenant (9:15-22). The Greek for "covenant," *diathēkē,* gives rise to a deliberate use of a double meaning since *diathēkē* means both "covenant," which defines the terms of a relationship, and "will" or testament, which defines what a deceased person bequeaths to beneficiaries. Since "the blood of Christ" (v. 14) inaugurates "a new covenant" (v. 15), Christ's death thereby bequeaths benefits like a "will" or testament, which "takes effect only at death" (v. 17). This cannot truly be said of "the first covenant" (v. 18). Most English versions translate *diathēkē* as "covenant" up to 9:15 and then translate it as "will" or "testament" in vv. 16 and 17 (NRSV, REB, NJB, NIV). The KJV/AV, however, consistently translates "testament" in vv. 15-22, which misses the use of the wordplay, while Westcott attempts with difficulty to retain "covenant" throughout. The argument is twofold. First, a covenant defines the terms of a relationship, so with the covenant God even creaturely humans can know where they stand and appropriate his warnings, promises, and assurance. Second, the author establishes the centrality of the cross by carefully arguing for the conclusion that "without the shedding of blood," and definitively that of Christ alone, "forgiveness of sins" cannot be fully and unconditionally achieved (v. 22). (On "mediator," see above, e.g., 8:6; 9:15.)

(iii) The Sacrifice in the Heavenly Sanctuary (9:23-28). Although the author did not wish to explore "details" (v. 5) from Leviticus and Numbers, enough has been said to indicate that a large variety of specified actions and objects are involved in successive rites of cleansing. All of these, however, point to the reality of the holy within the heavenly or eschatological order of reality. Hence all these varied "details" which generate concern are subsumed under the single, perfect, definitive self-offering of Christ, not in "a sanctuary made with human hands, a mere copy of the true one, but . . . heaven itself . . . the presence of God" (v. 24). "The stamp of the cross is on all of them" (Manson 1951: 140). On the question of whether the contrast between "copy" and "true" presupposes a Platonic dualism of thought, see above under 8:5 (further, Käsemann 1984: 223-25).

The author reiterates the incompleteness of the old order by a forceful rhetorical repetition of "again and again . . . year after year" (9:25). "He contrasts the sacrifice of Jesus with the limited, local, impersonal, external and forever repeated rites of the Jewish religious system" (Manson 1951: 141). The gospel of Christ proclaims a once-for-all event, not a routinized set of religious performances. Any suggestion that the work of Christ on the cross is defective in any respect would be tantamount to expecting a repetition of the crucifixion itself (v. 26). The "once for all" finality of Christ's saving work is as "final" as death itself (vv. 27, 28). Death is a single irreversible entry into a new domain which cannot be traversed a second time. Thus it offers a parallel to the once for all of Christ's work. This work will not be, and cannot be, "done over and over again" (Moffatt 1924: 132). Christian hope looks forward to Christ's "appearing" (v. 28; Gk. *pephanerōtai;* cf. 1 Pet 1:20). However, Heb 9:28 is the only example in the NT of the explicit use of Gk. *ek deuterou,* "a second time." This calls attention to the different mode and function of the promised "appearing" of Christ which is yet to occur. This public "appearing" will add nothing atoning to his once-for-all work of sacrifice. It will manifest his presence and glory, and bring to full completion the process of salvation for "those who are eagerly waiting for him" (v. 28). Nothing can stop the onward movement from the cross to Christ's final "appearing" at the consummation of the ages.

Recapitulation: Christ's Voluntary and Definitive Self-Offering (10:1-18)

Since virtually all of the themes of 8:1–9:28 are now gathered up by way of rhetorical summary, relatively little further comment need be made. On the contrast between "shadow" and "true form" (8:1) see the discussion of three views on the influence of Platonism and Philo under v. 5 and the arguments of vv. 1-6 and 9:23-28. Similarly, the contrast introduced by "continually offered" (10:1) was discussed under 9:1-10 and elsewhere, while the corollary of the need for a new order (10:2) appeared with the consideration of Jer 31:31-34 in 8:7-13.

A special comment is needed, however, on "a reminder of sin year after year" (10:3). We referred above to the problem of a perceived *ad infinitum* regress of the need for purification (9:12-14). This leaves a troubled "conscience" or insecure self-awareness (cf. Gooch 1987: 244-54) even after the elaborate ritual of the Day of Atonement. But does "reminder of sin" (Gk. *anamnēsis hamartiōn* [strictly plural, "sins"]) mean more than "brings to self-awareness"? Some see only a probable allusion to Num 5:15 and perhaps to Philo's notion of the need for a virtuous heart (Attridge 1989: 272). Others insist that *anamnēsis* (remembrance) in the biblical writings is "not a passive, psychological phenomenon, but an action which has consequences" (Ellingworth 1993: 497). Hence Ellingworth, with due logic, interprets this as the negative side of what God promises to rectify in Jer 31:31-34 when *God* will no longer "remember" sin. Commentators offer several different views (Ellingworth 1993: 494-97), but the thought may be that sacrifices without the work of Christ end up with the negative result of exposing guilt more clearly to open view.

The argument of 10:4-10 reflects the prophetic critique of sacrifice without a willing and obedient heart: "to obey is better than sacrifice" (1 Sam 15:22); "I require loving faithfulness, not sacrifice" (Hos 6:6; cf. Ps 51:16 and Ps 40:6-8, as cited in v. 7). The self-offering of Christ, however, constitutes *both* a freely given loving offering of himself in obedience and devotion *and* the definitive fulfillment of all to which the sacrificial system pointed and required in all details. Adopting the role of the figure of the Servant Songs (Isaiah 42, 52, and 53), Christ combines in himself the fulfillment of both the prophetic and priestly traditions.

The author uses Ps 40:6-8 to make this point: "I have come to do your will, O God" (10:7). The first clause of the quotation, however, "a body you have prepared for me" (v. 5b) occurs only in the LXX of Ps 40:6, not in the Hebrew MT. The literal meaning of the Hebrew, "ears have you dug" (i.e., opened), was presumably understood by the LXX translator to allude to part of the process of sculpting a body from clay in the creation of Adam (Hagner 1990: 154). Our epistle follows the LXX for the whole of the long quotation, but the difference is slight: "ears" may represent metonymy for "body" (offering of the self) or it may stress the aspect of obedience. This reflects the same concern for heart obedience as Jer 31:33. After a reiteration of the prophetic standpoint, the author points out that God "abolishes the first" (i.e., the old order, including animal sacrifices) "to establish the second" (10:9), that is, the new covenant which is inaugurated and ratified by Christ's blood and represents not only the fulfillment of the priestly tradition but no less of the prophetic tradition of Christ as "the Man for God" (Barth) and "the Man for Others" (Bonhoeffer). The logic may be compared with 7:12, 18-19 and 8:7-13.

The final subsection (10:11-17) once again summarizes and repeats the themes already expounded in 8:1–9:28. (i) The "single sacrifice" (10:12) recalls our discussions of Gk. *ephapax,* "once for all" (see on 9:11-28); (ii) the allusion to overcoming "enemies" (10:13) looks back to 1:13 (see above); the citation of Jer 31:33-34 repeats the material quoted in 8:8-12; (iv) the introductory statement recalls the contrast between the incomplete ministry of the Aaronic priest who "stands day after day" (10:11) and the finished work of Christ as the royal high priest who "takes his seat" in the heavenly presence of God (Heb 1:13, citing Ps 110:1). (v) The author concludes this summary by underlining that no "supplement" to the work of Christ remains conceivable (10:18). The promise of Jeremiah 31 is complete.

Bibliography. Cody, A. 1960, *Heavenly Sanctuary and Liturgy in the Epistle to the Hebrews,* St. Meinrad, Ind.: Grail, 9-46, 145-202 • Gooch, P. D. 1987, "'Conscience' in 1 Corinthians 8–10," *NTS* 33:244-54 • Goppelt, L. 1982, *Typos,* ET, Grand Rapids: Eerdmans, 163-70 • Hurst, L. D. 1983, "How 'Platonic' Are Heb viii:5 and ix:23F?" *JTS* 34:156-68 • Isaacs, M. E. 1992, *Sacred Space: An Approach to the Theology of the Epistle to the Hebrews,* JSNTSup 73, Sheffield: JSOT • Isaacs, M. E. 1997, "Priesthood and the Epistle to the Hebrews," *HeyJ* 38:51-62 • Lehne, S. *The New Covenant in Hebrews,* Sheffield: Sheffield Academic • Pursiful, D. J. 1993, *The Cultic Motif in the Spirituality of the Book of Hebrews,* Lewiston and Lampeter: Mellen • Sowers, S. G. 1965, *The Hermeneutics of Philo and Hebrews,* Richmond, Va., and Zurich: John Knox • Stählin, G. 1964, "Hapax, ephapax," in *TDNT,* 1:381-84.

Forward in Fearless Faith, Fellowship, and Faithfulness (10:19–13:25)

Assurance and Perseverance: The Two-Sided Implications of Covenant (10:19-39)

The invitation to enter the inner "sanctuary" of the presence of God on the basis of the covenant blood of Jesus entails approaching God with "confidence" (10:19). The covenant foundation has already provided the basis for a defined relationship of security on the part of the believer. Hence our author uses the Gk. *echontes . . . parrhēsian,* "having . . . boldness," a third time in this sermon-letter (see above on 4:16; but also cf. 3:6 and 10:35). The very security of the covenant relationship, however, has two sides. Just as covenantal marriage, for example, provides mutual commitment and security of relationship, so to betray such a relationship would be more serious and destructive than simply to terminate a more casual partnership. Logically each aspect necessarily entails the other. Hence while one side of the coin is "confidence" (10:19) and "full assurance of faith" (v. 22), inevitably any deliberate breach of such a privileged relationship constitutes a violation which, in this case, would call down "a fearful prospect of judgment" (v. 27).

Practical Implications: Assurance, Worship, Pilgrimage, Fellowship (10:19-25)

The boldness with which Christian believers are invited to approach God stands in contrast to two kinds of restrictions, each of which enhances a Christian awareness of the privilege of access to God's own presence as "the true sanctuary." First, in the view of the author Christians receive privileged access through Christ as mediator which goes beyond that of the detailed prescriptive purity regulations of the OT and Judaism. Second, Christian believers as a whole, in accordance with the new covenant promise of Jer 31:31-34, enter where before only the high priest entered on behalf of the people. The word translated "confidence" in 10:19 (NRSV, REB, NIV, NJB; Gk. *parrhēsia*; AV/KJV, "boldness") strikes a positive note as this section opens, but when the aspect of warning emerges (vv. 25-39), the negative of potential loss is seen in terms of loss of this "confidence" (v. 35). "The repetition of the key term *parrhēsian* with the change is purposeful" (Lane 1991: 279). In view of the close parallel between 10:19-39 and 5:11–6:20 the major exposition of Christ as priest and sacrifice is framed by parallel units of practical assurance and warning. 10:19-21 "spontaneously takes on a note of triumph, for Christians are in a privileged position: free of hindrances and anguish which oppressed previous generations, they can go forward with complete assurance on the way which has opened up before them" (Vanhoye 1989: 70-71).

This "way" is "new and living" because in place of the tabernacle "curtain" the very person of Jesus constitutes the open path itself into God's immediate presence. The Greek for "living way" has been understood in various ways. Almost certainly it has a double meaning: Jesus himself is "the way" (cf. John 14:6), which is "living" because Christ himself is a living mediator (rather than some impersonal "system of religion") but also "living" in the sense of leading to life (Michel 1966: 345; Lindars 1991: 102). Thus "there is a fine wordplay in this passage, with 'the way into' (Gk. *eisodos*) in v. 19 being qualified as a 'fresh and living way' (= *hodos*) in v. 20. Here the pilgrim 'way' is a 'way into' the Holy of Holies . . . ." (Jewett 1981: 174-75). The two concepts, the mediatorial and the onward-moving pilgrimage, together take up the earlier allusion to Jesus Christ as the "pioneer" or trailblazer (2:10) and prepare for the same word in 12:2. In modern theology Moltmann expounds in full this double meaning of Jesus Christ as the Way to God through his work and as "on the way" leading his people in messianic pilgrimage (Moltmann 1989). Another writer entitles his book *Hebrews: New and Living Way* (Snell 1959: 28-29, 127-30). In the light of this governing model, the exegetical debate about whether "that is, his flesh" refers to "the curtain" (Attridge 1989: 285-86; Lane 1991: 283-4; NRSV, NJB) or to "the way" (Montefiore 1964: 173; Buchanan 1972: 168; REB) perhaps represents a double meaning rather than an alternative. "Flesh" may be a metonym for Christ's full self-offering (Ellingworth 1993: 519-20), but the author may well intend yet another meaning, as indicated above.

In 10:22 "we have perhaps the supreme expression of the writer's thought of the Christian life as worshipful approach through Christ to God" (Manson 1951: 66). However, this is qualified in three ways: first, it entails a faithful commitment to "hold fast" (v. 23); second, it is a courageous venture which adopts the risks of a pilgrimage lifestyle as the messianic "way" (v. 20); third, it is not an individualist act of devotion but entails interpersonal interaction and mutual support of "one another in love" (v. 24) and "not neglecting to meet together" (v. 25).

The perfect, finished work of Christ has both objective and subjective effects. The objective effects find expression in reference to objective cleansing (10:22). "Sprinkled" (Gk. *rhantizō*) calls to mind the "sprinkling" of the blood of the covenant. The repeated use of Jer 31:31-34 confirms this. Allusions to "washing" were almost always taken as a reference to baptism in modern commentaries up to around 1970 (Manson 1951: 67), but more recently it has been forcefully argued that "washing" in the NT usually carries a broader reference than the specific rite of baptism alone, even if it includes it (Dunn 1970). "Full assurance" and "from an evil conscience" denote the subjective effects of experience. Hence the work of Christ transforms both the objective situation and subjective experience of persons who may now confidently appropriate it. Nevertheless, for the people of the new covenant there is no room for an individualistic, do-it-yourself style of life and worship. "The habit of some" (10:25) was to drift away on their own and neglect the worship assemblies of the church. This was not only a self-contradiction of their covenant status; it placed them in dire danger because thereby they also isolated themselves from the "encouraging" effects of sharing with fellow believers. They not only failed in their obligations to "encourage" others but risked extreme vulnerability in the face of pressure, temptation, and danger.

Several suggestions arise for reasons concerning failure to "meet together" on the part of some. (i) Some have pointed to the individualism of gnostic modes of thought, which may well be reflected in Paul's contrast between knowledge as inflating the self and love as concern for others in 1 Cor 8:1-13. (ii) Others argue that "some" wanted the kind of assembly where hostile powers were ritually confronted, in contrast to the assumption that these were eclipsed by Christ's work as a "living way" (Jewett 1981: 177-78). (iii) Some allude to the reference to eschatology in subsequent verses as suggesting a reference to "the regular Sunday eucharist" (Snell 1959: 129). (iv) A plausible account identifies "a group of Jewish Christians . . . under stress and disappointment . . . tempted to give up its Christian meetings, to dissolve back into the Jewish community" (cf. the use of Gk. *episynagogē;* Manson 1951: 69; cf. Schrage, *TNDT*, 7:841-43). (v) Most probably "various factors" were involved (Attridge 1989: 290). Several of these often apply today: the self-deception that a person does not need the support and fellowship of others; fastidiousness that everything in corporate worship has to be "exactly right" for the individual's wishes; fear of a public witness of faith. One writer cites all three (Moffatt 1924: 147) and adds: "either discipleship kills secrecy or secrecy kills discipleship." Thus this verse provides the transition into the dire warnings of judgment on any who "throw it all away" (10:26-39, esp. 35).

Warning against Willful Disloyalty or "Throwing Away" God's Gift (10:26-39)

To abandon a faith once begun is in effect "to profane the blood of the covenant" (10:29) and to commit an outrage against the "grace" or gift which God's Spirit mediates. It is "to treat as unholy" (NIV) the shed "blood" which in reality represents God's ultimate, unsurpassable, or "final" word and way of approach to him. Thereby it throws back into the face of God a precious gift which is then lost and abandoned irrevocably. For if God's free, sovereign acceptance of constraints through covenant is his gracious way of permitting humankind to know where they stand in a secure relationship, by the same token for human persons to play fast and loose with this solemn pledge constitutes a blasphemous betrayal.

The passage unfolds what this entails stage by stage. First, the privilege of covenant and the seriousness of deliberate, willful breach of it were made explicit under the old covenant in terms of "sin with a high hand" (in contrast to lapses, setbacks, or failures) in, for example, Num 15:30 and Deut 17:12. That "there no longer remains a sacrifice for sins" (10:26) holds under both covenants. Second, *a fortiori* to "spurn the Son of God" (cf. Mark 12:1-10; Heb 1:1, 2; 2:1-4; 3:1-9) and "profane," or count as common, his "blood" carries unthinkable consequences. In such a situation, it is indeed "fearful to fall into the hands of" the "God" whose appointed way of approach has been rejected (10:31). It is forced to insist that the conjunction of "meet together" (v. 25) and "profaning the blood of the covenant" (v. 29) must refer exhaustively to abandoning eucharistic worship, but in the light of parallel language about the Lord's Supper and "profaning" Christ's "blood" in 1 Cor 11:27 "his language . . . , while it refers to the new covenant, is [also] tinged with eucharistic overtones" (Montefiore 1964: 179; cf. Lindars 1991: 11). Such sacrilege rejects the covenant pledges along with the covenant itself, to its own devastating loss.

The argument proceeds to a third stage. Such betrayal and sacrilege would amount to "throwing away" (Gk. *apoballō,* 10:35) all of the precious gifts and privileges which Christ's blood has won. It is thereby to belittle (NIV, "to insult") God's "grace," that is, his generosity, since it throws the gift back into the face of the Giver. Since God's grace in Christ is "final," no alternative mode of approach to God is left if this is rejected (v. 26). Hence all that can remain is a "fearful prospect of judgment" (v. 27). Uniquely in this epistle v. 30 places together a double quotation from Deut 32:35 and 36, of which the first is drawn from the Hebrew text of the OT and the second (as in all other citations from the OT in this epistle) from the Greek (LXX) version of the OT. Even the Hebrew varies slightly from the received MT text, but is attested in the targums (Attridge 1989: 295, including n. 58).

On the controversial issue of whether a Christian believer can "fall away" see above on 6:4-6. But three points should be noted here. (i) These verses call attention to the logical entailment that if the work of Christ is genuinely "final" and unsurpassable, no further means of dealing with human sin is conceivable if this is willfully and consciously rejected. (ii) The strong vocabulary and OT allusions distinguish this willful rejection of God's appointed way from lapses, failures, or uncontrolled collapse. It is a deliberate revoking of a covenant pledge. (iii) As in the case of Heb 6:4-6, a note of encouragement and optimism occurs side by side with the dire warning (6:1a, 9-12; 10:32-34), reminding the readers that in fact they did "endure" (v. 32) and did not "shrink back" (v. 38) when pressures were extremely serious in "earlier days" (v. 32). They had proved their "perseverance" at least once already by continuing, even in the face of persecution (vv. 32-34).

The pilgrim path may at times make Christians "partners with the outcasts of society" (Jewett 1981: 186). But they experience a joy from the boldness with which they can enjoy the presence of God and receive, in place of the loss of transient possessions, gifts from God which are "lasting" (10:34). A similar perspective on transient suffering appears in Rom 8:18, and in 12:4 the writer reminds them that no loss of life as martyrs has as yet actually occurred. The NRSV's, REB's, NIV's, and NJB's "publicly exposed" (10:33; Gk. *theatrizomenoi*) is sometimes translated as "made a public spectacle." Some suggest that this might fit the situation described by Tacitus of Nero's persecution in AD 64 (Attridge 1989: 298-99). Most, however, decline to try to identify any specific historical episode. (See the Introduction, 1452-53.)

That the promise "will come and not delay" (10:37) is understood by many to suggest that the earlier mood of joy and endurance had reached the verge of crumbling and of turning sour because a confident hope in the imminent return of Christ in glory had been disappointed (Lindars 1991: 107, "This is precisely the problem"). The quotation from Hab 2:3 and 4 coheres with this interpretation: the prophet cries out to God for the oppressed to be vindicated and receives assurance that patient faithfulness will indeed sustain God's people until he visits them. The Greek LXX version reads, "He [God] will come," in contrast to the Hebrew OT, "It [the appointed time] will come." As usual, the author cites the LXX, and this entirely expresses his own point. Yet the promise of vindication need not be restricted to the single event of the parousia or final return of Christ. The "coming" of God in the context of the "new" stands in contrast to notions of temporal processes as repeatable "cycles" or "reversible processes." Acts of vindication by "the one who is coming" (Gk. *ho erchomenos,* v. 37) belong to a dynamic, climactic, "irreversible," purposive process which finds its ultimate fulfillment in the parousia, or "God's *final Shekinah*" (Moltmann 1996: 283 and 296, 259-95). This temporal "irreversibility" is all of a piece with the warnings and assurances concerning the finality of the way of Christ (10:20; Moltmann 1989). Meanwhile steadfast, trustful, confident "faith" is required with patient endurance and will be vindicated by the appearance of the Coming One (Barrett 1954: 382). The use of Hab 2:3-4 is not peculiar to Hebrews (cf. Rom 1:17; Gal 3:11) and may have belonged to a collection of OT material regularly used by Christians. "My righteous one" (also "my" in the REB, NIV, and NJB) rightly follows the best and earliest ms. reading ($\mathfrak{p}^{46}$, Sinaiticus, A). Hence believers do not "shrink back" (10:38) either into apostasy or into private, anonymous concealment.

Bibliography. Dunn, J. D. G. 1970, *Baptism in the Holy Spirit,* Philadelphia: Westminster • Fitzmyer, J. A. 1981, "Hab 2:3-4 and the New Testament," in *To Advance the Gospel,* New York: Crossroad, 236-46 • Koch, D. A. 1985, "Der Text von Hab 2:4b in der Sept und im NT," *ZNW* 76:68-85 • Lewis, T. W. 1975, "'. . . And if he shrinks back' (Heb 10:38b)," *NTS* 22:88-94 • Moltmann, J. 1996, *The Coming of God,* ET, London: SCM, 259-95 • Moltmann, J. 1989, *The Way of Jesus Christ,* ET, London: SCM • Snell, A. 1959, *Hebrews: New and Living Way,* London: Faith Press, 40-45, 126-34.

Faith Defined and Faith in Action (11:1-40)

Faith Defined (11:1-3)

The readers have been called to exercise bold "confidence" (10:19) and not to throw it away (v. 35). 11:1-40 now explicates what this entails, showing that what counts as faith can be seen in terms of *action.* Hence faith is defined both in general terms (vv. 1-3) and in the series of practical examples which show *in what faith consists* in specific situations.

The word order of 11:1 (Gk. *estin de pistis elpizomenōn hypostasis*... [i.e., beginning with the verb *is*]) is taken by many as indicating that the writer is giving a formal definition (against Lane 1991: 328, who calls it a "rhetorical and aphoristic... celebration of faith"; but see also Lane 325, n. a). "Faith is the assurance of..." (NRSV, ASV) is a more free translation of the Greek than REB, KJV/AV, NEB, "substance" (Gk. *hypostasis*). The Greek denotes "an underlying reality." "Assurance" is not fully adequate because it denotes "the subjective, psychological sense... [it]... never seems to have this meaning in contemporary sources" (Attridge 1989: 308, against Bruce 1964: 278 and Jewett 1981: 196). Attridge rightly argues for "the 'reality' of things hoped for" as the most accurate rendering (also Lane 1991: 328). The translation "guarantee" (NJB) is a possible but less likely alternative (Attridge 1989: 308). NIV's "being sure" implies the psychological aspect entailed by the NRSV and the ASV. The Berkeley Version has "solid ground." "Conviction" (Gk. *elenchos*) means "proof" or "conviction" in the legal, objective sense, not in the subjective sense of denoting a psychological state (BAGD, 249; Attridge 1989: 310). The linguistic evidence is decisive. Faith is an objective anchor in the realities which God has promised but which may as yet not have come to view in the present.

The contrast in imagery is primarily temporal (present versus future) but secondarily also spatial (below versus above, hidden versus openly apparent). Although many more recent thinkers could be cited in support of the view, its classic expression was formulated by Cullmann: Hebrews does not start here "from the spatial contrast between the Here and Beyond, but from the time distinction between the Formerly and Now and Then." Thus "things not seen" are unseen because they have not yet taken place (Cullmann 1951: 371; also Lane 1991: 339). The unseen are "things hoped for" (11:1; also Williamson 1970: 388). Faith is oriented here "less to the past... than to the future" (Héring 1971: 98). This dimension emerges especially in the paradigm cases of those who "died in faith without having received..." (vv. 13, 39). Thus the three most startling examples for practical application may well be (i) that of Noah's boat building under a blue sky on the basis of "events as yet unseen" (v. 7); (ii) the apparently irrational acts of "sprinkling blood" on door lintels (v. 28) and arriving at the barrier of "the Red Sea" (v. 29) on the basis of God's promised acts; and (iii) solemnly marching around "Jericho" (v. 30) in the conviction that God would act after seven days (v. 30).

Faith most clearly depends on divine promise. Christian identity and the identity of God bridge "the difference in time" between a promise and "execution of an act. The longer the period... the more constant the identity must be if the goal is to be reached. Those who make a promise that they can keep only many years later retain... time-bridging identity" (Pannenberg 1994: 202). Hence the "faith" which is instantiated in action and venture is also dependent on trust in the faithfulness of the covenant God of promise, who in turn requires the faithfulness of trustful action on the basis of confidence in the identity of God revealed through Christ (1:1-4). All that has been argued already about covenant, promise, and approach finds an integrated focus in this distinctive exposition of faith and its practical outworking in life. The temporal dimension receives primary emphasis. However, our author would agree with the Philonic principle that the "substance" *(hypostasis)* on which faith is grounded and to which it is directed is "invisible transcendent reality" (Thompson 1982: 71).

Faith also entails evaluative convictions about the nature of God and the nature of the world, that is, a Christian "worldview." Thus the doctrine of creation is a matter of faith. Creation is neither eternal nor Plato's world of appearances; Christian faith accepts the creatureliness of all things (11:3). This is no mere doctrine about a remote past event. "Faith" apprehends (unlike the secular mind) that "God" holds us from "the abyss of non-Being" (Barth 1956-75: 1/2, 388). It is faith in "the unseen creativity behind the visible universe" (Lane 1991: 330). "Worlds" (Gk. plural *tous aiōnas*) denotes not simply "world," but in modern parlance "the universe" (Hagner 1990: 181; Lane 1991: 330; against more convoluted debates in Ellingworth 1993: 569). Creation by "the word of God" (v. 3) coheres with Gen 1:3, 6, 9, 20; Ps 33:6, 9; *Jub.* 12:4; John 1:1-3; and Heb 1:2b (see above) as well as with Wisdom traditions in the OT and Judaism. "Understanding" the character of the universe (11:3) entails knowledge of God (Wis 13:1-5; cf. Rom 1:20).

These three verses form the overture to 11:4-40. The contrast between present and future (e.g., vv. 7, 13, 39), the integration of belief-conviction and evaluation (e.g., vv. 6, 13, 19), the place of venture and obedience (e.g., vv. 8, 15, 24-29), and throwing in one's lot with God's people (e.g., vv. 25, 31) in temporal history and spatial geography all play their part in elucidating faith in the following verses. (On the concept, cf. Attridge 1989: 311-14, "Excursus"; Grässer 1965: 45-63.)

Case Studies of Faith from Abel to the Patriarchs (11:4-22)

The NRSV's "more acceptable sacrifice" (11:4) glosses the Greek "greater than" (*pleiona . . . para . . .* ; also REB; cf. "better," NJB, NIV; "more excellent," KJV/AV), but thereby probably best captures the emphasis which the author wishes to place upon the narrative of Gen 4:4. Speculations about the reason for this approval have no firm ground on the basis of Gen 4:4, but haggadic traditions in Judaism have embellished the biblical account, although even these avoid differentiating the blood sacrifice from the crops in the form sometimes found in Christian pietism. The Palestinian targum on Gen 4:8 speculates about different belief systems held by Cain and Abel (also *Targum Neofiti;* cf. Vermes 1961: 81-114), while others assume that Cain had failed to present his offering in an appropriate way (Philo *Sacr.* 88; Josephus *Ant.* 1.61). Whether our author presupposes or draws on first-century traditions cannot be more than speculation. He emphasizes the link between faith, action, and God's approval.

The second example of faith, namely, Enoch (11:5-6), rests also only on inference from the OT narrative (Gen 5:24). The Hebrew "Enoch walked *(halak)* with God, and he was not because God took him" is expanded in Gen 5:24 LXX: "Enoch pleased God, and he was not found because God translated him." The Gk. *metethēn* ("to put in another place," BAGD 1979: 513) several times means "taken up to heaven" in other sources (Wis 4:10; Sir 44:16; *1 Clem.* 9:3). Heb 11:5 adds "so that he did not experience death." The argument is compressed, succinct, and implicit: intimacy with God presupposes the faith and faithfulness that pleases God. This ongoing, trustful faithfulness was so consistent and enduring that it was not interrupted even by death. In the Bible only Moses (Jude 9) and Elijah (2 Kgs 2:11) are said to be thus "taken up" also.

The general confessional content entailed in "faith" (11:6) gives the lie to the often heard maxim that that NT writers supposedly show no interest in formal assertions of the existence of God. Here, quite clearly, faith embodies the cognitive truth claim that God "exists" (Gk. *hoti estin,* "that [God] is"), and that God has interpersonal dealings with human agents as one who "rewards those who seek him." Faith acknowledges here the sovereign and just governance of the universe which belongs to God above. But faith is both cognitive (it asserts a genuine state of affairs) and self-involving (it stakes the life of the self by nailing one's colors to the mast; Neufeld 1963: 13-33 and 133-37). The first aspect declares the reality of divine governance; the second aspect commits "whoever would approach" God to a discovery of the delight of welcome, access, grace, and what it is "to please God" (v. 6a).

Noah provides a third example of faith (11:7; cf. Gen 6:9-22). In parallel "lists" Noah also follows Enoch in Sir 44:17 and in Philo. Noah provides an explicit model of the future-oriented faith of a person who acts in the present on the basis of a promised future which as yet cannot be seen. Noah's witness to the unbelieving pagan or "secular" world by his trust and integrity provided a model to believing Jews in the Greco-Roman world (Sir 44:17; Wis 10:4; Philo *Post. Caini* 173-74; *Abr.* 47; cf. *Tg. Neof.* Gen 6:9). Christian believers, our author urges, also find a fine paradigm case of faith as acting on the basis of a reality yet to appear, even if such action incurs the scorn of the world. Indeed, that Noah "built an ark" on no other basis than divine "warning" not only saved his household but thereby "condemned" the refusal of "the world" (11:7) to take his "preaching by action" seriously. The parallels with the situations of the addressees are clear, as are the inferences for today's church.

Abraham serves as the fourth example of faith over a more extended passage (11:8-19). The author draws on the Genesis narrative to make five distinct points which apply to the addressees. (i) Abraham is content to venture out, placing the future into the hands of God alone, without knowing what obedience to the onward call of God may bring: he "obeyed . . . he set out, not knowing where he was going" (v. 8). (ii) He thus embarked on a life of pilgrimage, without securities or roots within the world (vv. 8-10), "living in tents," not houses (v. 9), becoming a "stranger" in a strange land (vv. 9 and 13), and looking forward to dwelling in "the city that has foundations" in God's future time of appointing (v. 10). (iii) He trusted that God would yet fulfill his promise, even when age and health appeared to contradict the possibility (vv. 11-12). (iv) He sought no return from going onward once he had begun (vv. 15-16). (v) He trusted that God would perform his promise even though he was called to slay the very son on whose existence the promise seemed to depend (vv. 17-19).

More space is devoted to Abraham (cf. Gen 12:1–22:19) than to any other of the role models of faith. The same episodes occur in *1 Clem.* 10:1-7; 17:2; 31:2, and some argue for the possibility of a dependence of Heb 11:8-19 on *1 Clement* (c. AD 90; cf. the discussion in Hagner 1990: 184-86). But the use of Abraham for exhortation and as an example was massively widespread (cf., e.g., Philo *Abr.* 60–88; Sir 44:19-21; Wis 10:5; Acts 7:5). Whatever hypothesis we hold about sources, Abraham's "call and . . . pilgrim existence . . . provides a magnificent precedent for the . . . congregation. Rather than seeking the security of a cultic enclave or attempting to build some 'lasting city' he took up a pilgrim trek into the unknown. . . . To move courageously into the unknown is a requirement for both maturity and creativity" (Jewett 1981: 200). Although the author does locate the believing congregation within a continuing tradition and history of faith in this chapter (history and tradition are not irrelevant), this differs from drawing backward into "a futile quest for security" rather than being drawn "inexorably toward the future" (Jewett 1981: 201).

"Living in tents" (11:9) is thus the epitome of the life of faith in its pilgrim lifestyle. It is no accident that, like the author of Stephen's speech (Acts 7), the writer looks to the tabernacle, not to the temple, for his liturgical model. "The mobile sanctuary of the early days corresponds with the idea of the ever-onward call of God to his people, the static temple does not" (Manson 1951: 35; on Hebrews and Acts 7 cf. 27-46). The semantic contrast turns on the comparison with the "city" (Gk. *polis*) that has foundations. Resonances with the New Jerusalem of eschatological promise seem to be confirmed by the allusion to the heavenly Jerusalem in 12:22.

The sentence relating to Sarah (11:11) gives rise to a well-known problem. The "power of procreation" probably denotes literally the male seed in Greek (*dynamin eis katabolēn spermatos*). Most translations opt for the solution of interpreting the phrase as a transferred metaphor meaning "enabled to conceive" (REB; also NJB, ASV, KJV/AV, and Attridge 1989: 325). A less favored alternative (although accepted as verging on the probable by UBS 4th ed. *Greek Testament*) is that Gk. *steira,* "barren," was lost from the text and that the reference to Sarah is a parenthesis about her barrenness, leaving Abraham as the subject of the act of "procreation" (Metzger 1994: 602). This is followed by the NIV (for a survey of views, see Ellingworth 1993: 586-89).

Some see the reference to death in 11:13 as a contradiction of the allusion to Enoch who did not die. But if we abandon a wooden literalism, to maintain trustful faith even to the moment of death is a way of expressing the nature of faith as a habituated and sustained lifelong faithful trust, even if God has yet to fulfill his promises exhaustively. Abraham's waiting until old age and the patriarchs' vision for the future (vv. 13-16) provide a sorely needed model for patience in a church which has drawn heavily on the secular world's hunger for, and expectation of, instant satisfaction. Like the patriarchs, the Christian community does not have its "homeland" in this cultural matrix (v. 14; cf. v. 13). Pilgrimage requires patience and self-discipline, as well as resolution not to look back and confidence in the superiority of the "better country" which lies ahead (vv. 15-16).

Abraham's supreme test of faith occurs in his perceived call to "offer up Isaac" (11:17-19; cf. Gen 22:1-19). Had he dwelt upon the constraints of the human situation, he would have been dismayed by the paradox that the God who promised blessing for the world through Isaac seemingly contradicted his own word by demanding Isaac's death (v. 18). Kierkegaard presses the paradox movingly: on the human level faith is directed toward the immoral act of murder which destroys the very path to promissory grace (Kierkegaard 1969: 9-21). Yet Abraham refused to be distracted from trust in the sovereignty and grace of God to perform his word, that is, "considered . . . that God is able even to raise someone from the dead" (v. 19; cf. Rom 4:19). He left it to God how all of this could be done without God's betraying his promise. Here again the author places this trustful attitude before the addressees as their own model for faith under fire.

The remainder of the paragraph (11:20-22) demonstrates the forward-looking character of faith as instantiated in the actions of the patriarchs Isaac, Jacob, and Joseph (cf. Gen 25:19–50:26) in invoking "blessings for the future" (11:20) beyond their own individual life spans. The reference to Joseph's "bowing . . . over the top of his staff" (v. 21) calls attention either to the staff of the pilgrim traveler or more probably to the faith of people in old age who nevertheless remain trustful for a future which transcends their own part in God's purposes (cf. Gen 27:2 on Isaac's old age, 11:20; Gen 47:29 similarly to "Jacob," 11:21; and Gen 50:22-26 to Joseph's "instructions about this burial," 11:22).

From Moses to the Entry into the Land of Promise (11:23-31)

Many perceive 11:23-31 as a single unit tightly woven around the above theme (Michel 1966; D'Angelo 1979: 17-64, "a condensed life of Moses"). Five aspects of the narrative of Moses (cf. Exod 1:8–15:22) receive comment as examples of faith relevant to the addressees of this epistle.

(i) The risky but courageous venture of "his parents" in "hiding" him in contravention of Pharaoh's decree revealed that their trustful faith overcame their being "afraid" (11:23).

(ii) The author takes up his earlier exhortation about sharing together and perceives the "faith" of Moses himself as "choosing . . . to share" in solidarity "with the people of God" (11:25), even at the price of ill-treatment and suffering. He resists drifting along the easier path of retaining his worldly security in the court of Pharaoh and enjoying his old identity (v. 24). Faith entails throwing in one's lot with God's pilgrim people, whether or not they are disadvantaged and despised. The verse "directs attention to his decisive renunciation of privilege and power" (Lane 1991: 370). The exchange of courtly education for forced labor is implied by Philo *Vit. Mos.* 1.33, 40, 49-51 (cf. D'Angelo 1979: 43-45). The allusion to abuse suffered for Christ (v. 26) is difficult. The thought may be telescoped inferentially with the application formulated in 13:13: "bearing the abuse which Christ endured." Alternatively, if we accept the view that the earliest Christians applied "the reproach of the Messiah [to] . . . the pre-existent Christ" (Hanson 1974: 16; cf. 13-51), the allusion need not be "anachronistic" (Hagner 1990: 201). Most probably the verse is assimilating consciously the parallel experiences of Moses and Christ, as the readers would perceive (Lane 1991: 373).

(iii) Moses' refusal to fear "the king's anger" (11:27) is generally thought to refer not to his initial departure to Midian but to his series of encounters with Pharaoh on his return to demand the liberation of the people. This also coheres with the sustained nature of the faith under discussion as courageous trust in God over a sustained period. Thus, even when Pharaoh's heart was hardened, Moses persisted (v. 27), holding before his eyes the reality and the promise of the faithful God (cf. Exod 3:4-22; 5:1-6; 6:1-8; 7:14–11:10).

(iv) The celebration of the Passover (11:28), like Noah's building of the ark, demanded bold faith when the outcome was as yet unseen. Faith was entailed in splashing blood upon the lintel and sideposts of the doors of a half-believing people in trust for the security of Israel's first-born as the Angel of Destruction slew those of Egypt (Exod 12:1-30). For any believer to "draw back" to the illusory safety of the structures of Egypt would be folly beyond conception. The readers do not need the parallel to be explicated. There is no possibility of "re-deciding."

(v) The crossing of "the Red Sea" (11:29) or Sea of Reeds (Exod 14:13-28) embraces both the faith of Moses and the pilgrim exodus people under his leadership. Again, overcoming fear (in this case of the pursuing Egyptian army) is part of faith. It entails moral and physical courage "to go forward" (Exod 14:15). As in the case of Noah's building, Abraham's offering, and the Passover, in the eyes of the world faith to go forward when the way is blocked by an expanse of water denies common sense. Nevertheless, trust in God and faithful onward venture resulted in God's "opening the way" for them to cross the "Sea as if it were dry land" (11:29; Exod 14:22 LXX). By contrast, the Egyptian force was drowned in the attempt to replicate the external act without the framework of divine promise and believing trust in God.

The author completes this period with the entry into the land of promise to which he referred in 4:8 with the wordplay on Joshua and Jesus and the double meaning of "rest" and "promise." To attempt to capture the well-defended, walled city of Jericho without siege engines and a trained army again flies in the face of this-worldly judgments, let alone solemnly marching around the city, exposing themselves to abuse and ridicule from the top of the walls as the people of God "encircled" it "for seven days" (11:30). "Faith" again ignores the world's ridicule and shows its genuineness in trustful, sustained faithfulness to God's call. The results often surpass as well as vindicate expectation: not only was the city taken but "the walls . . . fell" (v. 30; cf. Josh 6:1-20). The next verse takes up the subplot of Rahab, which is included within the narrative in Joshua (Josh 2:1-23; 6:17). Rahab (11:31) offers a classic example of the "outsider" (as Christ was deemed to be, 13:13) whose faith is perceived in three ways: (i) believing the word concerning God's promise and God's deeds; (ii) throwing in her lot with the people of God; and (iii) acting with courage and resolution in the face of danger and apparently greater worldly forces. Again parallels with the situation of the addressees and modern life remain transparent.

From the Period of the Judges Onward: Countless Numbers (11:32-40)

"What more should I say?" (11:32) provides an ancient formula equivalent in function to the modern "etc." Space prohibits further detail, but the previous models are far from exhaustive. Four examples are drawn from the book of Judges: Gideon's ventures included especially his trust in God to face the formidable forces of Midian with a volunteer force deliberately cut down in numbers (cf. Judges 6–8); Barak (Judges 4–5) faced with courage the forces of Jabin and Sisera; Samson (Judges 12–16) led a series of raids against the Philistines, culminating in the destruction of Dagon's temple; Jephthah (Judges 11–12) led troops against Ammon. "David and Samuel are the founders respectively of the theocracy and of prophecy" (Spicq 1953: 2:362). It may be no accident that Rahab (above), Samson, Jephthah, and even David are not exempt from moral failures, even from glaring blind spots. This does not of itself invalidate a faith which elsewhere in the NT is disengaged from moral merit (esp. Rom 1:16–8:39) but which nevertheless shows itself in trustful and sustained action in response to God's promise and call in spite of lapses.

There follows a mixture of some examples which may readily be identified and some which represent countless unnamed ordinary believers who moved courageously forward whatever the odds. Thus the allusion to "lions" may include Samson (Judg 14:5-6) and David (1 Sam 17:34-7), but in the light of parallels with LXX vocabulary and its prominence in Jewish and Christian traditions it almost certainly refers especially to Daniel (Dan 6:23-24; cf 1 Macc 2:60; 3 Macc 16:3, 21; 18:13; *1 Clem.* 45:6; *Apost. Const.* 7.37.2). The "raging fire" may well reflect a movement of thought to Dan 3:19-28, where Hananiah, Azariah, and Mishael brave the wrath of the king to remain loyal to God. The "women" include not only Sarah and Rahab but also the widow of Zarephath (1 Kgs 17:17-24; cf. the faith of Elijah) and the Shunammite woman (2 Kgs 4:32-37; and Elisha). However, resurrection here refers metaphorically to return to life in the same body which is yet to die, not to resurrection in the full sense which entails transformation into a new mode of existence.

It would defeat the author's purpose to speculate in too much detail about the incidents to which he refers. Whether or not, for example, the "saw" (11:37) alludes to a tradition about Isaiah later reflected in apocalyptic (*Ascension of Isaiah*) and much later talmudic literature is not the point. Ordinary believers in countless numbers have faced the "sword" of persecutors, unjust regimes, "torture" by oppressors, or (like Stephen) "stoning," and yet have clung to trustful faith in God whatever the consequences. Wandering in "deserts . . ." also serves as a symbolic formulation of the life of pilgrimage which faith entails (Jewett 1981: 212-13; Käsemann 1984: 44-48). On one side, pilgrim believers are not "at home" in the world; on the other side, secular society did not deserve such shining witnesses: of them "the world was not worthy" (v. 38). Yet, "The exemplars of the past did not obtain the promised eternal inheritance (cf. 9:15). The writer's emphasis in v. 39 resumes v. 13" (Lane 1991: 392). This was not due to some failure in their faith; it arises from the timing of the unfolding of God's purposes for the world. To trust God is to trust that he will provide what is "better" (Gk. *kreitton*) than all human aspirations in God's own way and in God's own time. "The reference to God's final action is deliberately vague so as to suggest in an inclusive fashion the results of Christ's sacrifice" (Attridge 1989: 352).

Bibliography. Brandenburger, E. 1988, "Pistis und Soteria . . . ," *ZTK* 85:165-98 • Cullmann, O. 1951, *Christ and Time,* ET, London: SCM, 37-68 • Grässer, E. 1956, *Der Glaube im Hebräerbrief,* Marburg • Hay, D. M. 1990, "Moses through New Testament Spectacles," *Int* 44:240-52 • Hanson, A. T. 1974, *Studies in Paul's Technique and Theology,* London: SPCK, 13-51 • Hanson, A. T. 1978, "Rahab the Harlot in Early Christian Theology," *JSNT* 1:53-60 • Käsemann, E. 1971, "The Faith of Abraham," in *Perspectives on Paul,* London: SCM, 79-101 • Kierkegaard, S. 1969, *Fear and Trembling,* Princeton: Princeton University, 9-22 • Neufeld, V. H. 1963, *The Earliest Christian Confessions,* Grand Rapids: Eerdmans • Pannenberg, W. 1994, *Systematic Theology,* ET, Edinburgh: T. & T. Clark, 9-35, 181-23.

Further Call to Endurance and Faithfulness (12:1-29)

The Perfect Model of Faith: Jesus as Pioneer (12:1-3)

The people of God listed in ch. 11 entered the unknown with the risk of costly suffering, moving forward with endurance and resolution. The climactic and perfect model, however, is that of "Jesus" (v. 2). Again the author uses the name "Jesus" without further qualification to call attention to his earthly, genuinely human life of faith. Jesus "endured the cross" with its acute, dreadful suffering and "shame," especially the public disgrace and humiliation of painful, slow death by crucifixion (Hengel 1977: 22-32). Jesus represents the "pioneer" model of ultimate, unsurpassable resolution by leaving his future in the hands of God. Some interpret "for the sake of the joy" (Gk. *anti . . . charas,* v. 2) as meaning "in place of, instead of, the joy," in strict accord with the most usual meaning of Gk. *anti:* "The passage [then] refers rather to the joy of eternal sonship in heaven which Jesus renounced in order to endure a cross" (Montefiore 1964: 215). Others recognize that while this meaning is possible, "the description of joy as 'lying before him' (Gk. *prokeimenēs autǭ*) is difficult to reconcile with the image of renunciation of Christ's heavenly status. . . . The joy is in the eschatological result" (Attridge 1989: 357). While the first interpretation emphasizes the cost which faith may entail, the second underlines the divine vindication of the stance of trust, the cost of which has already been identified as the pain and shame of crucifixion. The second is more likely.

"Pioneer" is the same word (Gk. *archēgos*) as that used in 2:10 (see the comment above). If the author is borrowing Platonistic, Philonic styles of thought, this might mean *archetypal* faith; but his temporal emphasis cites "Jesus" as both defining by his deeds what faith consists in (what philosophers term a paradigm case) and inviting the addressees to follow. "Perfecter," by contrast, looks back over ch. 11 and perceives in Jesus the perfect model (climactic paradigm case) of that toward which all other models seek to correspond, even if never fully.

This should govern our understanding of a "cloud of witnesses" (12:1). The lives enumerated in ch. 11 witness to what faith is and ultimately to its perfect expression in "Jesus." In what sense, then, are we to understand "we are surrounded by so great a cloud . . ."? The verse reads literally, "having *(echontes)* placed around us [i.e. surrounding us] *(perikeimenon hēmin)*" a cloud. This phrase occurs sometimes "figuratively of a crowd of people surrounding someone" (BAGD, 647-48). But "us" is not necessarily, or even probably, the focus of their witness. Their acts have witnessed to the nature of faith and thereby preeminently by implication to Christ as its paradigm. "Cloud" may reflect a metaphor of spectators looking down from the tiered seats of a stadium at a contest taking place in the arena (Spicq 1953: 2:384), but it is doubtful whether the point is that "the witnesses . . . have an interest in our achievement" (Kistemaker 1984: 366). Rather, "By their faithful endurance [they have] given testimony to God" (Attridge 1989: 354). "It is not so much they who look at us as we who look at them — for encouragement" (Bruce 1964: 346). The parallels collected by Spicq (1953: 2:384-85) make it more likely that if any bloodied contestant in the arena remains under observation it is arguably the endurance of Jesus. "It is not towards us that these witnesses have their faces turned, but towards Jesus" (Manson 1951: 82).

The imagery of the athlete in the stadium emerges in the focused exhortation "let us run with perseverance the race that is set before us" (12:1b). This is our course, whether it be hard or not, and we cannot determine what God chooses to place "before us." Our part is to "persevere," mindful of other examples of victorious faith, and "looking to Jesus" (v. 2a). The imagery of shedding "every" excess "weight," including stripping to the minimum of clothing, is understood by every athlete: NJB helpfully renders Gk. *onkos,* "everything that weighs us down" (NIV, "everything that hinders"; also REB, "encumbrance"). The nuance of translation depends on whether excess clothing weighs us down or trips us up (BAGD, 553, "weight, burden, impediment"). "Weight" is broader since excess body weight may be included, with reference to pilgrimage discipline and training. "Sin that clings" (NJB as NRSV; cf. NIV, "that easily entangles"; REB, "that restricts"; KJV/AV, "easily beset us") translates a Greek word that occurs only here in the NT and is very rare, *euperistatos.* It may have been coined by the author (Spicq 1953: 2:385; cf. BAGD, 324). It drags down the athlete, either like undiscarded clothes which trip up the legs or like baggage which slows performance. It corresponds with a deenergizing of focus (2:1-5; 6:1-8; 10:32-36). (Some translations reflect a secondary ms. reading *euperispastos,* "easily distracting.")

The phrase "looking to Jesus" should not be removed from its context (Michel 1966: 436). The compound verb (Gk. *aphoraō*) denotes both "looking away" (Gk. *apo-*), that is, from one's own troubles, and "fixing one's eyes," that is, on Jesus (BAGD, 127; cf. Epictetus 2.19.29; 4 Macc 17:10). Moreover, this is not simply to the "person" of Jesus as such, but to the Jesus who, as a paradigm and pioneer of perfect faith, passed, bloodied, through the ring, to win victory by his faithful "endurance" of suffering and "shame" to the very end. Thereby as victor he received honor and glory from God, that is, he is "seated at God's right hand" (12:2). Our author urges: turn attention away from self-absorbed self-pity to Jesus Christ-as-trustful, enduring, crucified, and exalted: paradigm of faith vindicated. Athletes know that where they place their eye and on what they concentrate hugely affect how successfully they can make demands on themselves. This precisely defines the needs of the readers and of the Christians today.

There is a difficulty about the meaning of "hostility against himself" (12:3; REB, NIV, NJB, "opposition from sinners"; KJV/AV, "contradiction of sinners against himself"; ASV, "gainsaying of sinners"). The earliest mss. read the plural, "against themselves" (e.g., $\mathfrak{p}^{13}$, $\mathfrak{p}^{46}$, D, Sinaiticus), while only A (among the main earlier mss.) has the singular. The UBS Greek fourth edition has the singular (as does the NRSV) but with some doubt (Metzger 1994: 604-45). On grounds of sense this may be defended (Bruce 1964: 355; Ellingworth 1980: 89-96; and 1993: 643-44). But Jesus faced "the hurt that sinners do themselves" (Montefiore 1964: 216), which becomes a self-destructive structural force of the kind that precipitated the rejection, humiliation, and crucifixion of Jesus (Lane 1991: 416-17). Whichever interpretation we follow, the broader meaning remains: if we or the readers find life difficult, we face nothing approaching that which "Jesus endured" and overcame.

The Privilege of Sonship Entails Training and Discipline (12:4-17)

This section traces an argument in three stages: (i) discipline is to be perceived as a proof of God's genuine love (12:4-8); (ii) no discipline ordered by God is without some purpose and goal (vv. 9-11); (iii) hence hardship must be accepted in an appropriate spirit of trust and obedience (vv. 11-17).

(i) Discipline as a proof of God's love (12:4-8). The next verse extends the metaphor of "contest" (Gk. *agōn*) in which "struggle against" an opponent (Gk. *antagōnizomenoi*) is involved, where "the task of the afflicted is summed up in the one word *hypomonē* . . . patient endurance" (cf. Heb 10:32-36; and 4 Macc 17:14; also witness or martyr in 4 Macc 2:8-23; 5:24-34; and 7:4-23; Pfitzner 1967: 196; and *1 Clement* 5). In the arena a gladiator's glove was often spiked to draw blood (Spicq 1953: 2:390). The addressees have not yet struggled "to the point of shedding your blood" (12:4). This may be figurative ("you have not yet struggled with the utmost seriousness") or may refer to the scope of actual persecution, which had already involved imprisonment and confiscation of property (10:32-34).

Our author cites Prov 3:11-12 LXX to express the axiom that absence of corrective discipline or indulgent protectiveness toward a child on the part of a true father would imply indifference to the child's future maturity, not loving concern. The verses from Proverbs 3 are also cited by Philo (*Congr.* 177). Hardship and suffering are not a reason to "lose heart" (12:5), for regulated discipline is a sign of "accepting" parental responsibilities for an "accepted" child (v. 6). In the context of the ancient world, absence of this implied concern for the child's training would suggest that, like "illegitimate" children born outside marriage (v. 8), the child is not destined to inherit the responsibilities and privileges into which an authentic heir will enter. Earlier language about "will" or "testament" and "promise" resonates with this (9:15-17). In today's world grandparents or second-marriage "husbands" may often be more willing to indulge a child to manipulate affection than the mother or father who consciously carries responsibility for how the child's character will develop.

(ii) Discipline as directed toward a positive purpose (12:9-11). The exchange from "we" (v. 9) to "you" (v. 8) signals the author's including himself in the situation of the readers. The logic and rhetoric turn on "even more" (v. 9; also REB; Gk. *poly mallon,* "all the more," NJB). "As seemed best to them" (v. 10) may serve to make the point that we "respect" our earthly fathers even though their discipline may sometimes seem arbitrary; or it may simply call attention to a child's recognition of a parent's right to exercise discipline as he or she sees fit. Whichever meaning is accepted, the *a fortiori* argument about respecting the providential governance of an all-wise, all-loving "Father of spirits" applies. The term "Father of spirits" is very unusual in the NT and may be borrowed from a Jewish liturgical background (cf. Num 16:22; 27:16; and Attridge 1989: 362-63). The relatively "short time" of childhood discipline yields dividends "for our good" in mature adulthood, and in Christian terms it nurtures "holiness" (12:10). No one positively welcomes discipline, but it can be accepted either constructively as training (v. 11) or with misplaced resentment.

(iii) Discipline as a source of resentment or constructive training (12:12-17). The use of "therefore" (Gk. *dio*) signals the transition to the third stage of the argument of vv. 4-17. "The thought of training through discipline in v. 11 suggests . . . an athletic contest requiring flexed arms and strong knees. The members of the house church, however, are characterized by listless arms and weakened knees" (Lane 1991: 426). Hence the author borrows the words of Isa 35:3 and Prov 4:26 for strengthening muscles and for concentrating on the job at hand. The first citation is independent of both the LXX and the Heb. MT, but it faithfully reflects the thought of giving bracing encouragement to a group which feels discouraged, exhausted, and too depressed to act with resolve. The OT and NT metaphor of "drooping" (12:12) conveys the same psychosomatic state in the language of today. "Make straight paths" (v. 13) is associated in wisdom traditions with pursuing a level track in moral integrity (Spicq 1953: 2:396; Prov 4:26 LXX rather than Heb. MT). "Lame" probably refers not to disability but to the practical ef-

fects of an exhaustion which is due to misdirected energy. Those who are bitter about discipline may find themselves walking around in circles. Going straight for the goal, undeterred, leads to a reintegration of capacities, that is, being "healed" of self-inflicted incapacity.

"Peace" and "holiness" (12:14) do not come ready-made overnight without self-discipline and habituated patterns of action and work. It is an illusion to imagine that becoming a Christian is a cheap way to make life easier. Some critics may imagine this (e.g., "The 'salvation of the soul' — in plain German, 'the world revolves around me,'" Nietzsche 1909-13: 16:186, aphorism 43). But this is a distortion: it is "cheap grace. . . . The world goes on the same old way . . . forgiveness without . . . repentance, baptism without . . . discipline" (Bonhoeffer 1959: 35-36). To some this demand comes as such a shock to the system that "a root of bitterness" (v. 15) poisons all thought until they are tempted to become "like Esau, who sold his birthright" (v. 16) for some fleeting, transient pleasure (cf. Braun 1984: 426-27). Esau failed to look ahead, and "later," whatever his remorse and longing to "inherit," he had "no chance" to recommence his wasted life, even though he sought the promised blessing "with tears" (v. 17). The readers are warned that just as "a root" generates spreading growth, so seeds of "bitterness" can spread like cancer into self-destruction. Traditions about Esau's folly and regret constitute sources of warning and exhortation in, for example, Philo *Spec. Leg.* 1.102; *Ps. Sol.* 2:11, 13; *Jub.* 26:33, Josephus *Ant.* 1.274 (see Braun 1984: 426-29 further examples). "By encouraging the expectation that problems will disappear for those who become Christian, and by presenting Christ as a superheroic problem-solver rather than a pilgrim forerunner, the capacity to face adversity is diminished" (Jewett 1981: 220-21).

The Peril of Rejecting God's Warning from Heaven: Sinai and Zion (12:18-29)

The heart of this section finds expression in 12:25: "how much less will we escape if we reject the one who warns from heaven?" The two-stage argument establishes (i) the terror of Sinai as a manifestation of God's awesome holiness, and its comparison with the pilgrim's welcome to Mt. Zion, the New Jerusalem (vv. 18-24); (ii) if "trembling with fear" accompanied the manifestation of God's voice and God's word at "earthly" Sinai, how much more serious would it be to play fast and loose with the voice of God and word of God which speaks through Christ "from heaven" (vv. 25-29)?

(i) The terror of Sinai and comparison with Zion (12:18-24). The concept of the awesomeness of the holiness of God (often called "numinous" holiness in contrast to "moral" holiness) finds expression in the separateness (Heb. *qadosh*) of the holy exemplified in that which cannot "be touched" (v. 18) or a voice so majestic and fearful that hearers cannot bear to come within its sound (v. 19). "Mount" Sinai itself participated in divine majesty–holiness with such effect that even an "animal" that strayed into it should be "stoned to death" (v. 20). The string of adjectives comes from Exod 19:12-19 and Deut 4:11-14; 5:12-20. However, the use of the OT material is by way of contrast: "The terrifying atmosphere that characterized the theophany at Sinai (vv. 18-21) throws into bold relief the festive joy of Zion (vv. 22-24). The foundational experiences of Christians have been qualitatively different . . ." (Lane 1991: 459). The notion of "numinous" holiness finds expression in a classic modern study which speaks of this awesomeness as *mysterium tremendum et fascinans,* an overwhelming creature feeling of "the Other" (Otto: 1923).

We cannot discuss in detail variants which occur in the LXX text of the OT passages cited (see Childs 1974: 340-84; Katz 1958: 213-23). "The whole passage well illustrates the interplay between the author's use of scripture and his concern for the readers" (Ellingworth 1993: 670). Allegedly seven terms are not found in the OT narrative, but in some cases the author simply summarizes (e.g., by using a single adjective) an aspect of the narrative (cf. the use of what may be touched, Gk. *psēlaphōmenǭ,* found in the main mss., to which the D text adds "mountain"). The contrast between Sinai and Zion receives added point in that Moses alone was permitted "to approach" God at Sinai, just as Christ alone made the perfect high-priestly offering of himself (cf. Exod 20:19). But the whole "assembly" of God's people comes to Mt. Zion (12:22; cf. Jer 31:31-34 and Hebrews 8 and 9 [above]).

"Zion" symbolizes, therefore, the "festal gathering" (12:22) of all God's people. Indeed, where the Sinai material speaks of "frightening *things,*" Zion's celebration concerns "supportive *persons*" (Braun 1984: 435). "Zion" was originally the fortified crest of the hill of pre-Israelite Jerusalem, and subsequently the term was extended to denote the temple area, especially in the book of Psalms. It could also serve as a metonym for Jerusalem as a whole, but Jerusalem under the particular aspect of God's presence and favor; where he set his "name." Hence it is natural for the author to explicate "Zion" as God's city and the "heavenly Jerusalem" (v. 22). On the question of supposed Platonic or Philonic influences, see under 8:2-5; the new or heavenly Jerusalem is still more prominent in eschatological thinking as a purposive goal which lies ahead (Rev 3:12; 21:2; cf. Gal 4:26; *2 Bar.* 4:2-5; and above, 11:10, 16). The eschatological hope becomes more poignant and prominent in view of Jesus' language about the destruction of the "earthly" Jerusalem in conjunction with notions of "Jerusalem" as a center or source of salvation (Luke 21:20 and 24:47). The supraterrestrial glory of the city is painted in Ezekiel 40–48 (Jeremias 1974: 273-76; Buchanan 1972: 157-62; Dumbrell 1976: 154-59). The "innumerable angels" (Gk. *myriasin,* "myriads"; the highest number; cf. the hymn "Ten Thousand Times Ten Thousand . . ."). The terrifying awe inspired by the angels at Sinai is transposed into the image of the hosts of God welcoming believers in celebration of their homecoming. Blake's poetry and John Newton's "Glorious things of thee are spoken, Zion . . ." draw on the symbol of "Zion" in literature, while John Bunyan draws the pilgrim journey of Christian to a moving climax with his arrival at the celestial city, to be welcomed by "the innumerable company of angels . . . and all the bells of the city did ring." "Firstborn . . . in heaven" probably denotes believers in glory, although some interpret it to mean angels. Whereas "the blood of Abel" (12:24) cried out for vengeance, the blood of Jesus makes possible the firm assurance of acceptance and welcome.

(ii) Further warning based on the logic of "how much more?" (12:25-29). At Sinai an earthquake "shook the earth" (v. 26) as an accompaniment to the awesome "voice" of God (Exod 19:18; Ps 68:8). Yet even this will be surpassed in solemn awe when the prophecy that "yet once more" God's presence and voice "will shake" not only "the earth" but "also heaven," that is, all that is and shall be (12:27, citing Hag 2:6-7). "The earth shook when Jesus died and when he arose" (Matt 27:51; 28:2)" (Kistemaker 1984: 398). For these events represented a cosmic turning point which demanded expression in apocalyptic terms (Werner 1957: 33). But the outworking of this event will reverberate into a final, cosmic shaking up which will leave nothing as it is. If the fearful phenomena of Sinai signal urgent, high stakes, "how much more" is "everything" at stake in responding to or "rejecting" the voice of God in Christ (cf. 1:10-12; 6:4-6; 10:19-39)? The "rolling up" of all "created things" (v. 27) was introduced as a major theme in 1:10-12. Now it becomes transparent that those who seek their security in "created things" will share in the dissolution of the created order in the final shakeup, while God's pilgrim people who accept hardships in full trust in God as their security will be vindicated; theirs will be a "kingdom that cannot be shaken." "Fire" destroys what is consumable but may refine precious metals (1 Cor 3:12-15). But "our God is a consuming fire" (12:29, from Deut 4:24). The continuation of Deut 4:24 uses the term "jealous God": he gives and expects covenant faithfulness.

Bibliography. Bauckham, R. 1977, "The Eschatological Earthquake in the Apoc John," *NovT* 19:224-33 • Bonhoeffer, D. 1959, *The Cost of Discipleship,* London: SCM, 33-47 • Childs, B. S. 1974, *Exodus,* London: SCM, 340-84 • Dumbrell, W. J. 1976, "The Spirits of Just Men Made Perfect," *EvQ* 48:154-59 • Ellingworth, P. 1980, "New Testament Text and Old Testament Context in Heb 12:3," *StudBib* 3, Sheffield: JSOT, 89-96 • Elliott, J. A. 1966, *The Elect and Holy Ones,* NTSup 12, Leiden: Brill • Hamm, D. 1990, "Faith in Ep Hebs: The Jesus Factor," *CBQ* 52:270-91 • Hengel, M. 1977, *Crucifixion in the Ancient World,* Philadelphia: Fortress, 1-10, 22-32, 51-90 (also repr. 1986 as *The Cross of the Son of God,* London: SCM, 93-102, 114-24, 143-82) • Jeremias, J. 1974, "Ierousalēm," *ZNW* 65:273-76 • Katz, P. 1958, "The Quotations from Dt in Heb.," *ZNW* 49:213-23 • Nietzsche, F. 1909-13, *Works,* 18 vols., London: Allen & Unwin, vol. 16, *The Antichrist,* esp. 186 • Otto, R. 1923, *The Idea of the Holy,* ET, Oxford: Oxford University • Pfitzner, V. C. 1967, *Paul and the Agon Motif,* Leiden: Brill, 38-75, 134-53, 196-200 • Thompson, J. W. 1975, "That Which Cannot be Shaken," *JBL* 94:580-87 • Vögtle, A. 1969, "Das NT und die Zukunft des Kosmos. Heb 12:26-27 . . . ," *BibLeb* 10:239-53 • Werner, M. 1957, *The Formation of Christian Dogma,* New York: Harper, 31-40.

Appendix on Practical Attitudes Demanded by the Pilgrim Calling (13:1-25)

The powerful logical, expository, and rhetorical argument of the sermon material in chs. 1–12 has come to an end. But the author's pastoral concern spills over into a series of reminders that certain attitudes are demanded by commitment to the life of faith as a pilgrim. These are not simply pieces of "General Exhortation" (Buchanan 1972: 228), even if ch. 13 "gives the clear impression of being an appendix. . . . It is only in this chapter that the writer speaks as though he were writing a letter" (Héring 1970: 119). Theories about the relation of this material to early Christian catechetical traditions are varied, numerous, and complex (cf. Filson 1967; Thurén 1973: 49-247). Some have denied its integrity with the rest of Hebrews (see Introduction, 1453), but the themes all relate not to "general" exhortation but to that which arises in the context of pilgrimage. (a) The first four issues clearly do so (13:1-6). "Hospitality" (v. 2); concern for those whose hardships have led to "prison" (v. 3); and avoidance of "love of money" (v. 5) — all clearly belong within this context. Respect for "marriage" (v. 4) may be a necessary corrective to those who argue that true pilgrimage entails no family ties whatever. This is not to deny their place in the common Christian tradition within the NT. (b) Respect for the responsibilities of "leaders" and trust in "Jesus" (vv. 7-9) become all the more important for a group which lives in what may be a hostile environment. (c) "Strange teaching" can divert the pilgrims from their goal. They must not retreat to Judaism but share with Jesus, if necessary, abuse directed to "outsiders": they are "outside the camp" (vv. 10-17). (d) Finally, prayer, integrity, renewed purity, and active response to encouragement and exhortation all find a coherent role within this lifestyle (vv. 18-25).

Issues Typically Raised by the Call to Pilgrimage (13:1-6)

(i) As in 1 Thess 4:9, the word translated "mutual love" (Gk. *philadelphia,* 13:1; KJV/AV, "brotherly love") is the source from which more specific attitudes and actions (vv. 2-6) flow. REB, "love your fellow Christians," explicates the author's concern more clearly than NIV's "as brothers and sisters," or NJB's "love . . . like brothers." Behind the translation "let us continue" lies the continuous present imperative of Gk. *menō,* "I remain," which in turn looks back to earlier injunctions to patient, enduring loyalty. But again, since pilgrimage is never static, REB's double negative "never cease to love . . ." has much to commend it.

(ii) "Hospitality" (Gk. *philoxenia,* 13:2) "was practically an article of religion in the ancient world" (Moffatt 1924: 224). Parallel exhortations in Rom 12:13, 1 Tim 3:2, Tit 1:8 (especially pastors), and 1 Pet 4:9 may support arguments that we meet common catechetical material in this chapter. Pilgrimage of faith also meant literal physical travel for many, especially prophetic leaders and apostles, and "hospitality" above all afforded support, protection, and a safe resource for travelers or new arrivals to a city (Elliott 1981: 145-50, 165-200; Malherbe 1983: 62-68). The emphasis does not fall primarily on the reciprocal socialization of well-to-do families for mutual enjoyment (although this may help to bond the community) but on "the hungry . . . the stranger . . . those in prison" (Matt 25:35-36). "Entertain" (13:2) may be misleading. Abraham in Gen 18:1-21 (cf. also Lot in Gen 19; Tobit in Tob 12:15) "gives generous hospitality" to angelic visitors (or at least to messengers sent from heaven, Gk. *angeloi,* Heb. *melakim*), and found an unexpected, unlooked-for dividend in receiving through his guests the divine promise of the birth of Isaac. A needy guest, the author implies, may be something more in God's eyes, hence the opportunity should not be missed.

(iii) Those "in prison" (13:3) continues the thought of Matt 25:35-36. Christians are to identify with, and empathize with, those who are prisoners, "putting oneself in another's place" (Bruce 1964: 392; cf. 1 Cor 12:26); also Käsemann's reflections on writing parts of his work on Hebrews in a Nazi prison in 1937 (Käsemann 1984: 12-13; cf. 23).

(iv) Respect for "marriage" (13:4) also holds a prominent place in early Christian ethical tradition. It stands in contrast to overzealous asceticism which argues that a single state is more "spiritual," and no less in contrast to extramarital relationships (cf. 1 Cor 6:12-20; 7:1-7, 10-16; and elsewhere). In view of the strong emphasis on the importance of "covenant" in Hebrews, the culture of "cohabitation" without marriage, which in some places has infiltrated into the church, would hardly cohere with this passage. "The marriage bond . . . kept inviolate" (13:4; Gk. *hē koitē amiantos*) "is a euphemism for preserving the sexual integrity of the marriage relationship" (Lane 1991: 516; Thurén 1973: 213-25). In view of the cultic background of the term translated "inviolate," it may be argued that "sexual impurity will be a desecration *(une profanation)*" (Spicq 1953: 2:418). Hebrews, no less than Paul, warns that "God's judgment will fall" on those who habitually practice fornication (Gk. *pornous,* any illicit sexual relationship) or adultery (*moichous,* acts outside marriage by a married person). Marriage may be a support in pilgrimage, just as "assembling together" is (10:24-25).

(v) Pilgrim faith should not be distracted by "love of money" (13:5). Again, this tempts the believer to find personal security in what belongs to the world order to which the pilgrim is to sit light. What is condemned is not the responsible use of money, but "love" of it (cf. Mark 4:19; Acts 5:1; 1 Cor 6:8; 1 Tim 6:10; Jas 5:1). The same single Greek word ("free from the love of money," *aphilargyros*) occurs in 1 Tim 3:3. The author cites Deut 31:6, "he will never leave you," as a first person promise: "I will never leave you." That the Lord God, not money or possessions (cf. 10:34), constitutes the believer's security and focus for trust is corroborated by Ps 118:6, cited in 13:6.

Respect for Christian Leaders and the Steadfastness of Jesus (13:7-9a and v. 17)

There is a danger of false values which would lead pilgrims astray (13:7-16). Hence "leaders" (Gk. *hēgoumenōn*) are to offer markers for the pilgrim community both by their doctrine and their everyday conduct (v. 7). However, earthly leaders are fallible, and they come and go. Even church leaders should not usurp the trust which Jesus alone invites as the one who never "comes and goes." It is a mistake to understand "Jesus is the same" (v. 8; Gk. *ho autos*) in the sense of static timelessness: "13:8 does not embody a basically Platonic point of view. The key word that points *away* from a . . . timeless manner of thought is 'yesterday'" (Filson 1967: 32). Jesus "learned obedience . . . was made perfect" (5:8-9). The sense is that as our own life unfolds, Jesus is ever on the move with us as our utterly faithful leader who will never abandon us. Believers can rely on "his unswerving loyalty and steadfastness" (Filson 1967: 31). The theme of respect for leaders emerges again in v. 17, whose task includes "keeping watch over" the addressees in the face of doctrinal and ethical seductions and distractions. Like shepherds or soldiers they are to keep guard night and day as those who themselves will "give account" of their stewardship (cf. 1 Cor 3:8; 4:2-5).

Sharing with Jesus "Outside the Camp": The Seduction of Strange Teachings (13:9b-16)

It is widely acknowledged that "13:9-14 constitute one of the most controversial passages in Hebrews" (Lane 1991: 330; cf. 330-50). The vague allusions to objectionable doctrines and . . . 'foods' have elicited a wealth of hypothetical reconstructions" (Attridge 1989: 394; cf. his "excursus"). Since this chapter may well draw on early Christian traditions of catechesis, albeit for the author's special purpose, the allusion to "food" (Gk. *brōmasin,* v. 9b) probably refers to dietary laws retained from their former Judaism, among some Jewish Christians or among heterodox Jewish groups (cf. Mark 7:19; Rom 14:14, 17, 20; 1 Cor 8:8, 13; 1 Tim 4:3; all use Gk. *brōma*). "Jewish regulations were being commended . . . as an aid to faith . . . [But] no analogy of any kind exists between the Oblation of Christ and those Jewish sacrifices from which food was carried away for the use of ministrants or worshippers . . ." (Manson 1951: 150; cf. Lindars 1991). The way forward lies in appreciating Christ's finished work, "strengthened by grace" (13:9b).

"We have an altar" (13:10) is genuinely difficult. Some believe that it alludes to addressees who were formerly Jewish priests (see Introduction, 1452-53); some argue for a eucharistic reference. But it most probably refers to appropriation of the work of Christ. The background assumes a contrast between expiatory or atoning sacrifice (made once for all for Christ) and gift-sacrifices which offer "praise to God" (v. 15). This contrast finds expression in such liturgies as that of the Anglican Book of Common Prayer, which distinguishes Christ's "full, perfect and sufficient sacrifice, oblation and satisfaction for the sins of the whole world" from "this our sacrifice of praise and thanksgiving." Christian believers "share exclusively in the unique sacrifice of expiation" of that to which the Day of Atonement points typologically (Spicq 1953: 2:424). In this participatory sense the Lord's Supper comes to mind as a focus of the celebration and memorial of Christ's sacrifice. But the word for sacrificial "altar" (Gk. *thysiastērion*) does not serve in the NT as a synonym for the "table" at which the Lord's Supper is eaten (1 Cor 10:21; cf. Michel 1966: 502-3; and Lindars 1991). The argument, including the allusion to "altar," turns on "the typological relationship between the sacrificial ritual of the levitical priesthood and the definitive sacrifice of Christ" (Hagner 1990: 242). In terms of sin and expiation, the Christian appropriates the finished work of Christ. But doing good remains the sacrifice offered by a transformed life.

Christians thus accept the possibility of "abuse," isolation, and exile from "society" which identification with a "shameful," crucified Christ may well entail. The cross turns everything upside down (1 Cor 1:18-31; Heb 12:26-28): any seeming security "inside the walls of the city" or "the camp" is no security; to share with Christ "outside the city gate" is to belong to "the lasting city" which lies ahead, even if this "breaks ties" with the past (Filson 1967: 61).

A Plea for Prayer, Prayer of Blessing, and Greetings (13:18-25)

(i) A Plea for Prayer (13:18-19). On v. 17 see above. The author asks for the continuing "prayer" of the addressees (Gk. present imperative; cf. 1 Thess 5:25). Pastors and leaders, including the writer, need "prayer" and a "clear conscience" as they seek to perform the duties of v. 17 "honorably," especially when "caught in the crossfire of interest groups charging dishonorable conduct . . . in a tangled situation" (Jewett 1981: 238). Church life always seems to be a breeding ground for resentment against leaders (Lane 1991: 556), whether through insensitivity on one side or lack of understanding and respect (v. 17) on the other. The writer may well have been accused of provoking the addressees to take risks in his pleas for a more decisive and focused faith. A surrounding cultural pluralism expected fuzzier lines of religious allegiance. Prayer that he may be "restored" (Gk. *apokatastathō*) may denote various possibilities — perhaps release from prison or recovery from sickness but most probably the opportunity for a return visit (v. 19). Since chs. 1–12 take the form of a sermon, it is likely that the author felt frustrated by an imposed absence.

(ii) Prayer of Blessing, and Greetings (13:20-21). The whole liturgical model of "approach" (in contrast, e.g., to the Pauline social model of reconciliation) naturally concludes with a prayer of blessing which reflects a careful liturgical structure. Like a collect in church liturgies the structure of the prayer is threefold: in the first part "God" is explicated and expanded as the God "who brought back from the dead . . ." (v. 20); in the second part a main verb conveys the heart of the petition with a subordinate supplementary request; in the third part the mediation of "Jesus Christ" is again expanded with a doxology. "Amen" provides the traditional ending (v. 21).

The phrase "the God of peace" occurs frequently in NT prayers of blessing (e.g., Rom 15:33; 16:20; 2 Cor 13:11; Phil 4:9; 1 Thess 5:23; cf. Deichgräber 1967: 88-96). This is the only reference in Hebrews to resurrection (as against exaltation or implied ascension), and the writer shares the Pauline logic that "God" is the agent of Christ's resurrection (cf. Rom 8:11). Christ as Shepherd-Leader appears in 1 Pet 5:4 (cf. John 10:11), while the language of 13:20 is reminiscent of terms concerning Moses in Isa 63:11 (LXX). "The blood of the covenant" succinctly presupposes the detailed exposition of "blood" and "covenant" (see above, 7:22; 10:18; and esp. 8:7-13; 9:11-27). The direct vindication and ratification of the covenant by God are demonstrated further in God's act of resurrection (Michel 1966: 536-37), while the Gk. *anagagōn* (NRSV, "brought back," as the REB) strictly embodies the notion of "leading" *(-agō)* which underlines the role of Christ as "pioneer" of faith (2:10) and "leader" of his pilgrim people (cf. 13:12-13). Christ's covenant has "eternal" validity (cf. 9:20). The main verb of the petition is "make you complete" (v. 21). In some contexts this means "complete what is lacking" (1 Thess 3:10); but for pilgrims it also means to "put into proper condition," that is, for whatever faces them (BAGD, 417). The word matches the forward-looking nature of Christian faith and life. The KJV/AV addition "work" is based on a later, secondary, textual gloss. The "pleasing" life resonates with the "pleasing" gift-sacrifice of a life devoted to God. The syntax might suggest that "to whom" (which introduces the doxology) may refer to "Christ," but it is more likely to refer to "God" as the agent who is invoked in the whole prayer of blessing (Thurén 1973: 230-33; Lemicio 1988: 13).

(iii) A Brief Postscript (13:22-25). After the climactic prayer of blessing with its formal doxology, the last few lines can only be regarded as a postscript. Some argued in earlier years that a later hand added a postscript which embodied a reference to "our brother Timothy" (v. 23) to promote the idea that Paul was the author of the whole epistle. But most perceive it as a brief personal covering note (Vanhoye 1974: 349-80), and several argue that these verses fulfill precisely the conventions of a postscript attached as a comment following a main discourse (Überlacker 1989: 197-223). It witnesses to the author's personal pastoral concern for the addressees. "Those from Italy" (v. 24) may refer to those who live in Italy or to those who live abroad but come from Italy, perhaps where the addressees live (Lindars 1990: 1-10; cf. Introduction, 1452-53). At all events, the greetings witness to a wider network of collaboration and greetings among churches and leaders that transcends a merely local concern with "my" or "our" (local) church.

"Word of exhortation" (13:22; Gk. *logos tēs paraklēseōs*) is the cognate noun of the verb translated "I appeal" (Gk. *parakalō*), and covers a very wide range of nuances. It includes, according to context, both encouragement and exhortation, solemn appeal and "friendly request," "comfort" and "consolation" (BAGD, 618), while the verbal form ranges from "friendly request" to "calling for help," "encouraging," "comforting," "warning," and "cheering up" (BAGD, 617). Hence translations vary from "exhortation" (also NIV, KJV/AV) to "appeal" (REB), "word of encouragement" (NJB), or "words of warning" (Knox). (Cf. Bjerkelund 1967: 34-38, 188-90; Grayston 1980: 27-31.) Its primary significance for modern readers is to remind us again of the multilayered, multifunctional character of Christian communication, which, we noted in the opening section, combines praise, creed, teaching, biblical exposition, and practical application (see under 1:1-4). The author deploys a mind brimming with theological learning and overflowing with knowledge of the Scriptures, along with a mastery of powerful rhetorical strategy and conceptual translation, to serve the pastoral and practical welfare of the Christian community. His main action is to encourage his addressees gladly and boldly to place their entire trust in the finished work of Christ and to live it out as pilgrims en route to the celestial city in solidarity with Christ and Christ's people.

Bibliography. Attridge, H. W. 1990, "Paraenesis in a Homily *(logos: paraklēseōs)*," *Semeia* 50:211-26 • Bjerkelund, C. J. 1967, *Parakalô: Form, Funktion und Sinn,* Oslo: Universitetsforlaget, 34-58, 188-90 (mainly on Paul) • Deichgräber, R. 1967, *Gotteshymnus und Christushymnus in der frühen Christenheit,* SUNT 5, Göttingen: Vandenhoeck & Ruprecht • Elliott, J. 1981, *A Home for the Homeless: A Sociological Exegesis of 1 Peter,* Philadelphia: Fortress, 145-50, 165-200 • Grayston, K. 1980, "A Problem of Translation: The Meaning of *parakaleō, paraklēsis* in the New Testament," *Scripture Bulletin* 11:27-31 • Jewett, R. 1969, "Form and Function of the Homiletical Benediction," *ATR* 51:18-34 • Lemicio, E. E. 1988, "The Unifying Kerygma of the New Testament," *JSNT* 33:3-17 • Malherbe, A. 2d ed. 1983, *Social Aspects of Early Christianity,* Philadelphia: Fortress, 60-112 • Thurén, J. 1973, *Das Lobopfer der Hebräer . . . Hebr 13,* Abo: Abo Akademi • Vanhoye, A. 1974, "Discussions sur la structure de l'Épitre aux Hébreux," *Bib* 55:349-80.

Main Bibliography of Commentaries and Studies on Hebrews. Attridge, H. W. 1989, *Commentary on the Epistle to the Hebrews,* Hermeneia, Philadelphia: Fortress • Attridge, H. W. 1990, "Paraenesis in a Homily *(logos paraklēseōs)* . . . ," *Semeia* 50:211-26 • Barclay, W. 1965, *Epistle to the Hebrews,* London: Lutterworth and New York: Abingdon • Barrett, C. K. 1954, "The Eschatology of Hebrews," in W. D. Davies and D. Daube, eds., *The Background of the New Testament and Its Eschatology,* Cambridge: Cambridge University • Bornhäuser, K. 1932, *Empfänger und Verfasser des Briefes an die Hebräer,* Gütersloh: Bertelsmann • Braun, H. 1984, *An die Hebräer,* HNT 14, Tübingen: Mohr • Bruce, F. F. 1964, *The Epistle to the Hebrews,* London: Marshall and Grand Rapids: Eerdmans • Buchanan, G. W. 1972, *To the Hebrews,* AB 36, Garden City, N.Y.: Doubleday • D'Angelo, M. R. 1979, *Moses in the Letter to the Hebrews,* Missoula: Scholars • deSilva, D. A. 1995, *Despising Shame: Honor, Discourse and Community Maintenance in the Epistle to the Hebrews,* SBLDS 152, Atlanta: Scholars • deSilva, D. A. 1996, "Exchanging Favor for Wrath: Apostasy in Hebrews and Patron-Client Relationships," *JBL* 115:91-116 • Dunnill, J. 1992, *Covenant and Sacrifice in the Letter to the Hebrews,* SNTSMS 75, Cambridge: Cambridge University • Ellingworth, P. 1993, *The Epistle to the Hebrews: A Commentary on the Greek Text,* NIGTC, Grand Rapids: Eerdmans and Carlisle: Paternoster • Filson, F. V. 1967, *"Yesterday": A Study of Hebrews in the Light of Ch 13,* SBT 2.4, London: SCM • Grässer, E. 1965, *Der Glaube im Hebräerbrief,* Marburg: Elwert • Grässer, E. 1990/1993, *An die Hebräer, I, II,* EKKNT 17.1, 2, Zürich: Benziger and Neukirchen: Neukirchener: Hebr 1-6, 1990; 2, Hebr 7:1–10:18 • Guthrie, G. H. 1994, *The Structure of Hebrews,* NovTSup 73, Leiden: Brill • Hagner, D. A. 1990/1995, *Hebrews,* NIBC, Peabody, Mass.: Hendrickson and Carlisle: Paternoster • Hay, D. M. 1973, *Glory at the Right Hand: Ps 110 in Early Christianity,* Nashville: Abingdon • Héring, J. 1970, *The Epistle to the Hebrews,* ET, London: Epworth • Hofius, O. 1970, *Katapausis. Die Vorstellung vom endzeitlichen Ruheort in Hebräerbrief,* WUNT 11, Tübingen: Mohr • Hofius, O. 1972, *Der Vorhang vor dem Thron Gottes,* WUNT 14, Tübingen: Mohr • Horbury, W. 1983, "The Aaronic Priesthood in the Epistle to the Hebrews," *JSNT* 19:43-71 • Horton, F. L. Jr. 1976, *The Melchizedek Tradition,* SNTSMS 30, Cambridge: Cambridge University • Hughes, G. 1979, *Hebrews and Hermeneutics,* SNTSMS 36, Cambridge: Cambridge University • Hurst, L. D. 1990, *The Epistle to the Hebrews: Its Background of Thought,* SNTSMS 65, Cambridge: Cambridge University • Jewett, R. 1981, *Letter to Pilgrims: A Commentary on the Epistle to the Hebrews,* New York: Pilgrim • Käsemann, E. 1984, *The Wandering People of God,* ET, Minneapolis: Augsburg • Kistemaker, S. 1961, *The Psalm Citations in the Epistle to the Hebrews,* Amsterdam: Van Goest • Kistemaker, S. 1984, *Exposition of the Epistle to the Hebrews,* Welwyn: Evangelical Press and Grand Rapids: Baker • Lane, W. L. 1991, *Hebrews,* 2 vols., WBC 47A and 47B, Dallas: Word • Leschert, D. F. 1994, *Hermeneutical Foundations of Hebrews,* Lewiston and Lampeter: Mellen • Lindars, B. 1991, *The Theology of the Letter to the Hebrews,* Cambridge: Cambridge University • Loader, W. R. G. 1977-78, "Christ at the Right Hand: Ps 110:1 in the New Testament," *NTS* 24:199-217 • Long, T. G. 1997, *Hebrews,* Interpretation, Louisville: Knox • Manson, W. 1951, *The Epistle to the Hebrews,* London: Hodder & Stoughton • McCullough, J. C. 1994, "Hebrews in Recent Scholarship," *IBS* 16:66-86 • Michel, O. 1966, *Der Brief an die Hebräer,* Göttingen: Vandenhoeck & Ruprecht • Moffatt, J. 1924, *A Critical and Exegetical Commentary on the Epistle to the Hebrews,* ICC, Edinburgh: T. & T. Clark • Montefiore, H. W. 1964, *A Commentary on the Epistle to the Hebrews,* London: Black • Peterson, D. G. 1982, *Hebrews and Perfection,* Cambridge: Cambridge University • Scholer, J. M. 1991, *Proleptic Priests: Priesthood in the Epistle to the Hebrews,* JSNTSup 49, Sheffield: JSOT • Spicq, C. 1952/1953, *L'Épitre aux Hébreux,* 2 vols., Paris: Gabalda, 1, 1952; 2, 1953 • Stedman, R. C. 1992, *Hebrews,* Downers Grove and Leicester: InterVarsity • Thompson, J. W. 1982, *The Beginnings of Christian Philosophy: The Epistle to the Hebrews,* CBQMS 13, Washington D.C.: Catholic Biblical Association of America • Überlacker, W. G. 1989, *Der Hebräerbrief als Appell,* ConBNT 21, Stockholm: Almqvist & Wiksell • Vanhoye, A. 1981, *Homilie für halfbedürftige Christen,* Regensburg: Pustet • Vanhoye, A. 1989, *Structure and Message of the Epistle to the Hebrews,* Rome: Pontificio Institutio Biblico • Vanhoye, A. 1996, "La 'teleiōsis' du Christ," *NTS,* 321-38 • Westcott, B. F. 3d ed. 1903, *The Epistle to the Hebrews: The Greek Text,* London & New York: Macmillan • Williamson, R. 1970, *Philo and the Epistle to the Hebrews,* Leiden: Brill • Windisch, H. 1931, *Der Hebräerbrief,* HNT, Tübingen: J. C. B. Mohr.

James

Richard Bauckham

INTRODUCTION

Author and Audience

It is generally agreed that this work is attributed to James the brother of Jesus (see Mark 6:3; Acts 12:17; 15:13-21; 21:18-25; Gal 1:19; 2:9, 12; Jude 1), the only James who could be identified purely by the description in 1:1. Probably from some time in the 40s until his martyrdom in 62, James occupied a position of unique importance in the early Christian movement, as head of the mother church in Jerusalem which claimed authority throughout the Christian world. Whether the letter is an authentic work of James or only attributed to him has been much debated. Strongly in favor of the former is the plausibility of the epistolary situation specified in 1:1 (see comment). If James writes from the authoritative center of the Christian movement to Jewish Christians throughout the diaspora, then he writes in a Jewish tradition of such letters from the center (Jerusalem temple authorities or Pharisaic leaders) to the diaspora, of which several have survived. All that we know of the place of Jerusalem and of James in the Jewish-Christian movement makes it entirely plausible that this letter is an encyclical from the head of the mother church to all Jewish-Christian communities. There must have been such communities in many parts of the diaspora from a very early date, before Christians from Jerusalem began to take their message elsewhere (Acts 11:19), because large numbers of Jews from all over the known world were constantly visiting Jerusalem for the festivals (cf. Acts 2:5-11) and returning home. Many must have heard the Christian message from the preaching of the Jerusalem church leaders in the temple. James's letter may therefore be of very early date. That it is oblivious of the issues concerning Gentile Christians and the law which Paul's Gentile mission raised (see the comment on 2:13-26) may indicate that it was written before such matters were controversial.

The main arguments against the authenticity of the letter which have persuaded many scholars are: (1) the Greek is better and the acquaintance with Hellenistic moral philosophy greater than could be expected of a native of Nazareth. But, while it is difficult to judge what James could have learned in Nazareth, in Jerusalem he had every opportunity and good reason (preaching and teaching to visiting and resident diaspora Jews) for improving his Greek. Since even the Jewish historian Josephus, who was certainly fluent in Greek, employed secretaries to polish his literary Greek, there is no reason why James should not have done the same. The content of his letter belongs to the Jewish wisdom tradition, which was as much at home in Palestine as in the diaspora, and which was not culturally isolated from similar Hellenistic literature. The contacts with Hellenistic moral philosophy to be found in James are fairly superficial and could easily derive from Jewish tradition without firsthand acquaintance with non-Jewish literature. But even that is not to be excluded in the relatively Hellenized Jewish culture of Jerusalem.

(2) If 2:13-26 is understood as an argument against Paul's view of faith and works, then it displays serious misunderstanding of Paul, which is difficult to attribute to the historical James (cf. Gal 1:19; 2:9), though some have seen it as the latter's fierce polemic against Paul. If the author is misunderstanding Paul or attacking a distorted Paulinism rather than Paul himself, this is considered more plausible after Paul's and James's deaths. In fact, it is extremely difficult to find a situation in which this passage, which ignores the issues in the debate in Galatians and Romans (Gentile converts and the Jewish distinctives such as circumcision and food laws) and yet is verbally much closer to those letters than to Eph 2:8-9 (where the issue of faith and works is abstracted from the question of Gentiles and the Jewish law), can be plausibly understood as a response to Paulinism. In the comment below we shall show that the passage is wholly intelligible without reference to Paul.

(3) The letter shows no interest in the purity rules and cultic requirements of the law, with which it is claimed the historical James was especially concerned. In fact, there is little evidence that this is true of the historical James. If Gal 2:12 shows that he was concerned about a situation in which Jewish Christians eating with Gentiles were contravening purity rules (and this is debatable), it does not follow that he would give any particular attention to such aspects of the law in contexts (like those addressed in the letter) where no such issue arose. That Jewish Christians continued to observe the whole law (cf. Jas 2:10) was uncontroversial in most of the early Christian movement.

(4) James was slow in gaining general acceptance within the canon of the NT writings. But we should remember that Christians from the second century onward rarely had any better means than we have of judging the authenticity of a work such as James. That James appeared to contradict Paul (whose writings were among the earliest to gain general acceptance as canonical) and that it is addressed only to Jewish Christians are sufficient to explain its failure to win widespread early acceptance.

Genre and Character

Although 1:1 gives it the form of a circular letter, the rest of James is parenesis (ethical instruction) in the tradition of Jewish wisdom instruction, represented especially by Proverbs, Sirach, the wisdom texts from Qumran (1Q26, 4Q184-85, 298, 415-18, 420-21, 423, 424, 525), and Pseudo-Phocylides. Such works proffer wisdom in the sense of practical advice on the right way to live, and the later works draw on Torah and on prophetic and apocalyptic traditions as well as on the wisdom tradition itself. Their most striking formal characteristic is the short aphorism (of which there are various types: proverbial maxims, similitudes, admonitions, and others). Aphorisms are assembled in collections, sometimes largely random in order, sometimes ordered thematically or by link-words. There may also be longer passages of continuous instruction or argument, often including aphorisms which crystallize the thought. Aphorisms are often carefully crafted, memorable, and succinct. Even those which occur in connected contexts are potentially independent of their context and claim attention for their own sake, as wisdom to be considered and remembered. In order to read James correctly it is important to recognize the dominant role of aphorisms. James is not merely a collection of aphorisms. The work has an overall structure, though, as commonly in wisdom instructions, this is rather loosely conceived, and it has many passages of connected exhortation or argument. But usually the main teaching is encapsulated in aphorisms, which, instead of a train of argument leading the reader rapidly onward, invite the reader to pause and ponder.

The aphorisms of Jewish wisdom literature were not anonymous oral traditions, but were crafted by individual sages, of whom Ben Sirach (author of Sirach or Ecclesiasticus) is our most informative example. A wise man such as Ben Sirach is steeped in the wisdom of previous sages, especially an authoritative collection such as Proverbs, but is always a creative exponent of the tradition. He transmits but does not repeat. His wisdom is self-consciously his own, not only in what is substantially new but also in the way he makes the old his own, carefully formulating old insights in apt sayings which express old wisdom as his own wisdom. This should help us to understand the relation of James to the teaching of Jesus, which (in the Synoptic Gospels) often takes the form of aphoristic wisdom. That much of James resembles the teaching of Jesus in both form and content has often been recognized, but most of the contacts are not such as to be easily identified as clear allusions to sayings of Jesus, still less quotations. James's relation to the sayings of Jesus is better understood if, instead of seeking literary allusions, we recognize James as both a disciple of Jesus the sage and himself a wise teacher, who has made the wisdom of Jesus his own and re-expresses it in new formulations of his own. As Ben Sirach never repeats Proverbs, so James never repeats Jesus. He draws creatively on the wisdom of Jesus, as also on the Jewish wisdom tradition, using the teaching of Jesus as the focal point and principle that guides his appropriation of the wisdom tradition in general. This is the way in which we should understand the specifically Christian character of James. There is nothing un-Jewish in his teaching, any more than there is in that of Jesus, but the particular shape and character, emphases and concerns of James's wisdom have been determined by the corpus of the sayings of Jesus. The resemblances therefore go much further than debatable allusions.

COMMENTARY

James 1:1

This prescript follows the standard form of ancient Greek letters: X (sender) to Y (addressees): Greetings. "Servant" is here a title of authority (Neh 9:14; Ps 89:3; Rom 1:1; Phil 1:1). James does not mention his family relationship to Jesus because he does not see this as a basis for authority (cf. Mark 3:33-35). The addressees have been variously considered Jews in general in the diaspora, Jewish Christians in general in the diaspora, Jewish Christians scattered from Jerusalem (Acts 8:1), or Christians in general (understood as the new Israel). The last is most improbable: "the twelve tribes" is never elsewhere used in this way. Nor is it a suitable description of the third category. The whole phrase could hardly have been understood by any contemporary reader to mean anything other than the worldwide diaspora of the whole people of Israel (including the ten tribes in the eastern diaspora). The rest of the letter presupposes that the readers are Christians (e.g., 2:1; 5:7-8), but probably because James thinks of Jewish Christians as the nucleus of the messianic renewal of all Israel he addresses in principle all Israel, in practice the Jewish-Christian communities throughout the diaspora. His letter is an encyclical, intended to circulate widely, and so does not address specific situations but typical ones, likely to be relevant to many of his readers.

James 1:2-27

This section consists largely of some fifteen aphorisms forming nine distinct subsections. It is a mistake to look for a sequence of thought through the section as a whole. It follows the anthological style of much wisdom instruction. But it is not a random collection of aphorisms. They are collected and arranged in order to introduce the main themes of the rest of the letter. The section thus functions as an epitome of the teaching to be presented in the rest of the letter.

(1) *The testing of faith leads to perfection* (1:2-4). The reference to "trials of any kind" shows how far James is from envisaging as its audience a specific community in specific circumstances. Sooner or later any Christian community will encounter adversities of some kind, and James's advice applies to any such circumstance. This initial aphorism anticipates later treatments of faith perfected by works (2:22) and endurance to the end (5:7-11). But its appropriateness as the introductory aphorism lies especially in its adumbration of the theme of *wholeness* or integrity

which pervades the letter. That "you [plural, for this is not an individualistic matter] may be mature [*teleios*: perfect or complete] and complete" is the eschatological goal of the Christian life, to which the whole letter of James points its readers. The *teleios* word group, a favorite of James (twice in 1:4; also in 1:17, 25; 2:8, 22; 3:2), is just one of the ways in which the theme recurs. Wholeness requires wholehearted and single-minded loyalty to God (1:8; 4:8), the fulfillment of the whole law (2:8-12), not only hearing but also doing (1:22-25), not only saying but also doing (2:16), not only believing but also doing (2:22), consistency in living out all the qualities of God's grace (1:17; 3:2, 9-10, 17), as well as the wholeness of a community united by peace rather than divided by ambition (3:14–4:1, 11). The way to this comprehensive completion of God's purpose, to be fully attained only in the new creation (1:18), is the persistence of faith under all kinds of trials vv. 2-4), which should therefore be occasions for joy (v. 2).

(2) *Asking for wisdom* (1:5-8). Wisdom in James (see also 3:13-17) has the primarily practical sense it has in the Jewish wisdom tradition. It is the gift of God needed for living in faith toward perfection. It opens up that view of life and enables that practice of life which accord with God's purposes rather than with the world's values. It imparts the qualities and inspires the activities of the life of integrity (3:17, 13). Probably we should understand it also to be the wisdom of God expressed in God's creative word, engendering and empowering the new life in us (1:18, 21), and in God's word as the law by which we should live (1:22-25; 2:8-12). It thus comes close to the role of the Holy Spirit in Pauline theology, but it refers more directly to the content of understanding and instruction given by God than to their divine source.

This section reexpresses Jesus' teaching on prayer (Matt 7:7, 11; 21:21-22; Mark 11:22-24; Luke 11:9, 13), applying it to prayer for wisdom. The person with wholehearted faith in God's generosity is contrasted with the one who vacillates between trusting God and looking elsewhere. The significant term "double-minded" (used only in James in the NT) occurs also in 4:8. Behind it lies the Hebrew expression "with a double heart" (lit. "with a heart and a heart"; Ps 12:3; 1 Chr 12:33; 1QH 12:14; 4Q543 i 9; 4Q525 4:6 ["Do not seek her (Wisdom or Torah) with a double heart"]; cf. Sir 1:28; *1 Enoch* 91:4). The opposite is "with all [one's] heart" or "with all [one's] heart and with all [one's] soul" (especially Deut 4:29; see also 6:5; 2 Chr 15:12; 22:9; Ps 119:2, 10; Jer 29:13), or "with a whole heart" (1 Chr 28:9; CD 1:10; cf. 1 Kgs 8:61; 11:4; 15:3, 14), or "with a pure heart" (4Q542 i 10), or in Greek "with singleness of heart" (1 Chr 29:17 LXX; Wis 1:1; Eph 6:5). In James the opposite of "double-minded" is implied in references to wholeness (1:4; 2:22; 3:2) and purity (1:27; 3:17; 4:8). In 1:6-7 the doubt associated with double-mindedness is not intellectual but moral and motivational. Double-minded people have mixed motives and divided loyalties. Because they want to be friends with the world as well as with God (4:4), they do not truly want the wisdom they ask of God.

(3) *Reversal of status* (1:9-11). That God exalts those who are low and brings down those who are high is a common theme in the OT (1 Sam 2:7-8; Job 5:11; Ps 113:7-8; Isa 2:1; Ezek 17:24), in Jewish tradition (Sir 10:14-15; *b. 'Erub.* 13b), in the teaching of Jesus (Matt 23:12; Luke 14:12; 18:14), and elsewhere in the NT (Luke 1:52-53; 1 Cor 1:27-29; 1 Pet 5:6). James expresses it again in 4:10. In 1:9-10, as frequently, the low are the poor and the high are the rich, but more than economic condition is involved. Wealth gives privilege and status and is associated with arrogance and boasting (cf. 4:16), the false security that ignores God. The word "lowly" (also in 4:6) suggests both the economic and the social impotence of those who lack security of income and the complete trust in God of those who have no worldly support to depend on. James here refers to the Christian "brother" who is "lowly," but he does not call the rich "brother." The point is not that there are no rich Christians or that rich Christians would not be subject to this judgment, but that these verses state a general principle. In the conflict of values between God and the world, the rich exemplify the values of the world, the poor those of God.

The reversal of status is already fact in God's eyes (and should be so in the eyes of God's people; 2:5-6), but will take effect eschatologically. The parable (1:10b-11) of the judgment of the rich, echoing Isa 40:6-8, employs a common image of the transience of life, which could be used both of mortal life in general (Job 14:1; Pss 90:5-6; 103:15-16) and more specifically of the fate of wicked (Job 15:30; Ps 37:20; 1QM 15:11; 4Q185 i 10-12; *2 Apoc. Bar.* 82:7). It makes little difference whether the rich will disappear at the parousia (5:8) or through sudden death: since what they value are the goods of this world, they are vulnerable to the brevity of life as the poor are not. This section introduces the theme of rich and poor which features prominently in the rest of James (2:1-7, 14-17; 4:13–5:6).

(4) *The crown of life* (1:12). The word translated "temptation" here is translated "trials" in v. 2. Here as there it refers to outward hardships of various kinds, not to inner temptations to sin. This beatitude complements vv. 2-4 by referring to the eschatological reward of endurance under trial.

(5) *God does not tempt* (1:13-16). The verb translated "tempt" here is cognate with the noun translated "temptation" in v. 12. A shift of meaning makes "tempt" an appropriate translation, indicating interior temptation to sin. This shift is possible because of the anthological arrangement of the chapter. V. 12 and vv. 13-16 are linked by the words "temptation" and "tempt" rather than by their meaning. The meanings are connected — external trials can be the occasion for internal temptation — but, whereas God may be said to test or try the faith of believers (Gen 22:1; Exod 20:20), he cannot be said to tempt anyone to sin. Sinners cannot therefore blame God for their failure to resist temptation. In making this point James is very close to Ben Sirach (15:11-20), as he is also in attributing responsibility for temptation and sin to one's "desire" (cf. Sir 15:14), though without explicitly stressing free will as Ben Sirach does (Sir 15:15-17). Both probably refer to the "inclination" of the heart, which according to Genesis is toward evil (Gen 6:5; 8:21; cf. Deut 31:21; CD 2:14; 4Q417 2:2:12). In rabbinic theology humans are created with both a good and an evil inclination (sin lying not in the inclination itself but in yielding to it). James, like Ben Sirach, refers only to a single inclination

("desire") which entices to sin, while the power to do good he attributes to "the implanted word" (1:21). His genealogy of sin (vv. 14-15) leads to death, a contrast with "the crown of life" in v. 12. The role of the devil in all this is not mentioned, but not excluded (4:7).

(6) *God does give new birth* (1:17-18). This section is designed to contrast with the last. So far from his being responsible for evil, God's gifts are all wholly good. This beneficent generosity (cf. also v. 5) is his steadfast character and purpose, from which he never wavers. The point is made by referring to God as the creator of the heavenly bodies ("Father of lights"). Whereas they are subject to changes (v. 17 uses astrological terms for the alterations of the heavenly bodies), God as their creator is not. Whereas sin gives birth to death (v. 15), God's greatest gift is that he "gives us birth" (v. 18) to new life. The reference is probably not to creation, but to new creation, the new birth of Christian believers (cf. John 3:3-7; Titus 3:5; 1 Pet 1:3) through the word of God (1 Pet 1:23). The image of "firstfruits" refers to the first part of the harvest which is offered in sacrifice in anticipation of the full harvest to come. James must mean that Jewish Christians, the messianically renewed Israel, are the representative beginning of the new creation of all things (including the salvation of the Gentile nations). Though he addresses "the twelve tribes" (1:1), James, like all early Christians, knows that God's purpose through Jesus the Messiah extends beyond Israel to a universal goal.

(7) *Receiving the implanted word* (1:19-21). The aphorism in v. 19b is a beautifully succinct summary of advice common in the Jewish wisdom tradition but never before crystallized in a single aphorism (Prov 16:32; Eccl 7:9; Sir 5:11; 20:7; 4Q420 1 ii 1-3; *m. 'Abot* 1:15; 2:10; 5:12). It introduces the theme of speech ethics which bulks large in James (3:1-12; 4:11-12; 5:9, 12) and serves as an example of the general instruction in 1:21. "Meekness" (also 3:13) is the opposite of anger and arrogance, and is the virtue of the "lowly" (1:9; and note the two words in Matt 11:29) in their dependence on God and receptivity to his grace. Whereas in v. 18 the word was the originator of new life, here it is implanted as the continuing power of salvation. We should probably think of the law of God now written on the hearts of messianic Israel (Jer 31:33).

(8) *Hearing and doing* (1:22-25). For the implanted word to be effective for salvation, one must not only be quick to hear it (v. 19) but also put it into practice. This section adumbrates James's concern for practical — as opposed to merely professed — religion, anticipating especially 2:14-20. The parable makes precisely the same point as Jesus' parable of the two men who built their houses on rock and sand respectively (Matt 7:24-27), by similarly telling of two individuals (they are singular in the Greek) who act in parallel and contrast. James's particular choice of image is probably influenced by the Hellenistic use of the metaphor of a mirror in moral instruction. Seeing oneself in a mirror is like seeing in the law the model of the person one becomes by practicing the law. The first man's glance in the mirror has no effect because he goes away and forgets what he saw. The second man stays contemplating so that what he sees can take effect in his praxis. Only the one who practices the law truly attends to it.

The "word" (1:22, 23) is now identified as "the perfect law, the law of liberty" (v. 25; cf. 2:12: "the law of liberty"; other references to the law are 2:8-11; 4:11-12). In view of 2:8-12, it is clear that James means the law of Moses and takes for granted his readers' obligation, as Jews, to obey the whole Mosaic law. In Palestinian Jewish Christianity this was uncontroversial. The quite distinct issue of the relationship of Gentile Christians to the Torah, raised by Paul's Gentile mission, is not on the horizon of James's letter (for James's view according to Acts, see Acts 15:13-21; 21:25). But James interprets the law, following Jesus, emphasizing its moral requirements (obedience to rules of purity and cultic laws is no doubt presumed but never mentioned) and treating the love commandment as preeminent (2:8-11). This means that his teaching directed to Torah-observant Jewish Christians can, in its canonical context, be read by Gentile Christians in much the same way as they read the teaching of Jesus, also directed at Torah-observant Jews. The moral teaching of the Torah is relevant to Gentile Christians, too (cf. Gal 5:14). James calls the law "perfect" (*teleios,* as in 1:4; cf. Ps 19:7), such that obedience to it leads to perfection. The best explanation of the term "law of liberty" is probably that, like the "implanted word" (1:21), which seems to be synonymous, it refers to the new covenant of Jer 31:31-34. The law written on the heart frees one from the compulsion of sin and liberates one to fulfill its requirements, much as, even for Paul, "the law of the Spirit" frees one to fulfill the law's requirement (Rom 8:2-4).

(9) *True religion* (1:26-27). The terms "religious" (v. 26) and "religion" (vv. 26, 27) refer properly to cultic worship of a deity, while the terms "pure," "undefiled," and "unstained" (v. 27) all suggest the cultic purity required of worshipers and cultic objects in the Jewish cult. With some Jewish precedent and along with many early Christian writers, James applies language of cultic worship to ethical praxis (cf. Rom 12:2; 1 Pet 2:5) and language of cultic purity to moral purity (cf. also 4:8; Mark 7:18-25; 1 Tim 5:22; Jude 23, 24). (Since *teleios* [cf. 1:4] can mean the unblemished perfection required of a sacrifice, James's understanding of "perfection" also has this cultic connection.) So the meaning may be more precisely: "If anyone thinks he is performing divine service . . . his service of God is worthless. Divine service that is pure. . . ." The "world" here (and in 4:4; cf. Johannine usage) means the system of values and behavior opposed to God, and keeping oneself unstained by it is resisting its influence.

The three essential elements of true religion here anticipate major sections of James: bridling the tongue (cf. 3:2-3) encapsulates the theme of speech ethics (3:1-12; cf. 4:11; 5:9, 12); visiting orphans and widows, who are representative categories of the poor in Jewish literature, anticipates the insistence on practical care for the poor in ch. 2; while keeping uncorrupted by the world adumbrates the treatment of opposing values in 3:13–4:10.

James 2:1-13

In order to warn his readers against "favoritism" or "partiality" (2:1, 9) — pandering to people of wealth and status while despising the poor — James sketches a hypothetical example of the kind of situation that might occur in any Christian community. Some commentators understand the scene as a judicial one: a (Jewish or Christian) synagogue court. But in that case it would be remarkable that partiality to the rich is not illustrated by judicial decisions in their favor, rather than by the comparatively less important matter of seating arrangements (though these were important corollaries of honor and status). The reason for the judicial language in v. 4 is that James is taking a law prohibiting partiality by judges in courts (Lev 19:5) and extending its application. In the way they treat the rich and the poor who come to their meeting (*synagōgē,* 2:2, may be either the assembly of people or the place of meeting; it is the only NT use of this word for a Christian assembly), the Christians are behaving like judges condemned by this commandment. It is significant that Lev 19:5 occurs in the context of the commandment to love one's neighbor (Lev 19:18b), cited in 2:8. James seems to read the whole of the passage which concludes with that commandment (Lev 19:9-18) as instancing particular aspects of loving the neighbor. Many of its provisions underlie the text of James (Lev 19:12, cf. Jas 5:12; Lev 19:13, cf. Jas 5:4; Lev 19:15, cf. Jas 2:1, 9; Lev 19:16, cf. Jas 4:11; Lev 19:17b, cf. Jas 5:20; Lev 19:18a, cf. Jas 5:9).

James speaks of rich and poor as people other than those he addresses. This is because both terms refer to only a small segment of the social hierarchy. Most Jewish Christians would be neither rich nor poor. Even those who had a relatively secure means of supporting themselves in the mere necessities of life were not "the poor," who were those with no dependable income (cf. 1:27; 2:15; 5:4). Patronage (of inferiors by superiors on the social scale) was so pervasive a part of the social system of the time that showing special attention to a rich man who might be or might become a benefactor of the community would be virtually expected. Conversely, the poor were generally treated with contempt in the ancient world, though Jewish tradition resisted this (Prov 14:21; Sir 10:19–11:6). 2:5-6 reverse the value system of honor and shame which dominated ancient society. The contrast between "poor in [= in the eyes of] the world" and "rich in [= from the perspective of] faith" is an instance of James's sharp distinction between the values of "the world" (cf. 1:27; 3:6; 4:4) and those of God which should distinguish the Christian community from the world. God's choice of the poor as heirs of the kingdom is known from the Gospel beatitude (Matt 5:3; Luke 6:20; cf. 1 Cor 1:27-28). It means not that they are the only heirs (James does not suggest that most of his readers, not being "poor," are not heirs of the kingdom) but that they are the paradigm heirs, so that others must in some way identify with them, considering themselves of no higher status than the poor (cf. 4:10) and sharing their possessions with them (2:15-16). Whether the rich man of v. 2 is a believer or an outsider ("yourselves" in v. 4 suggests the former) is unimportant. In either case his values associate him with the rich, who are typically experienced by James's readers as oppressors, influencing courts in their favor in defiance of Lev 19:15 (2:6). God's name "invoked over" Israel is an OT expression indicating his ownership of Israel as his people. Here the name is most likely that of Jesus invoked in Christian baptism. Persecution of Christians as Christians is therefore in view, but it need not be the only form of oppression envisaged.

Since in the LXX and the NT "law" *(nomos)* only very rarely refers to an individual commandment, it is unlikely that "the royal law" (2:8) is the commandment to love the neighbor (Lev 19:18b) as one commandment among others (and "royal" as sovereign over the others). It must be understood as the commandment which summarizes the whole law (cf. Matt 22:40; Rom 13:8-10 [note that Paul, like James, instances commandments from the second table of the Decalogue]; Gal 5:14; *Sipra* Lev 19:18). The law is "royal" in that it pertains to the kingdom (2:5), and perhaps as interpreted by Jesus (with emphasis on the love commandment) in his preaching of the kingdom. James's point is that the law is a whole, summed up in Lev 19:18b, in which the prohibition of partiality is a necessary part. One cannot love one's neighbor while dishonoring the poor. One cannot pick and choose which commandments to obey and to be judged by.

A pair of aphorisms (2:13) both rounds off the section and anticipates the next, since "mercy" is the compassion which partiality denies to the poor (v. 4) and which requires practical provision for the needs of the poor (vv. 15-16; cf. Sir 29:1). The first aphorism is an example of eschatological *ius talionis* ("measure for measure"): a statement about God's eschatological judgment in which the sin or good work and the recompense are expressed in verbal and conceptual equivalence (cf. Matt 7:2). Other examples in James are 3:6, 18. In this case the principle occurs, both positively and, as here, negatively, in both Jewish tradition (Sir 28:1-4; *b. Shab.* 151b; cf. Prov 17:5 LXX) and the teaching of Jesus (Matt 5:7; 6:12, 14-15; 18:23-35; Mark 11:25). The expectation of eschatological judgment and reward functions in James to validate the values by which the readers are called to live as those of the kingdom of God which is going to prevail universally (see also 1:9-11; 3:18; 4:10; 5:1-6).

James 2:14-26

This passage is closely linked to 2:1-13 by its concern for compassionate treatment of the poor (vv. 15-16). Interpretation of it has been dominated by the question of its relationship to Pauline teaching on faith, works, and justification, but this approach does less than justice to the passage's own message in its own context. It is helpful to consider it in the first place without reference to Paul.

The passage is in the literary style of a diatribe, in which James puts possible cases to his readers ("what if someone claims to have faith but has no works?") and discusses them (2:14-17), and conducts a debate with an imagined opponent (vv. 18-20), whose hypothetical objection (v. 18) is simply a literary device ("but suppose someone were to say . . .") to help the argument along. It is quite unnecessary to suppose that James is reporting a doctrinal position taught by Christian teachers he opposed. His targets are simply people who pride themselves on their faith while neglecting practical concern for the poor. The faith in question is belief that God is one (v. 19), that is, the faith of the Shema (Deut 6:4), the nearest thing to a Jewish creed. Especially in a diaspora context, Jews were very conscious of this monotheistic profession as distinguishing them from pagans. It is easy to imagine diaspora Jews (in this case Jewish Christians) priding themselves on their monotheistic belief as though that alone were sufficient to justify them in God's sight. This need not be a doctrine at all but merely an attitude into which James knew that it was all too easy to slip. His concern is wholly to convince such people that belief in God is no substitute for practical love of the neighbor in need.

Monotheistic belief is lifeless (2:17, 26), that is, it does nothing, and unproductive (v. 20), unless "completed" by works (v. 22). To prove the point James takes the example of Abraham, who was famous as the man who renounced idols and pioneered belief in the one God. Abraham's offering of Isaac (v. 21; cf. Gen 22:1-14) was understood in Jewish tradition as the most important of the tests by which God proved Abraham's faithfulness. Gen 15:6, though prior to Genesis 22 in the Genesis narrative, was treated as the principle of all God's testing of Abraham (1 Macc 2:52), and so can be cited by James (2:23) to show that Abraham was "justified" (considered righteous by God) not by his monotheistic faith alone, but by the acts of difficult obedience to God in which he proved faithful under trial (note the parallel with Jas 1:2-4). In Jewish interpretation it was also in this way that he proved his love for God and could be called God's friend (2:23; 2 Chr 20:7; Isa 41:8; cf. Jas 4:4). The example of Rahab (2:25; Josh 2:1-21) provides not only a female parallel to Abraham but also another case of someone renouncing paganism for Israelite monotheism but demonstrating her faith in action.

The passage therefore makes its own sense without reference to Paul, and there is no need to consider it aimed either at Paul or at purveyors of a distorted Paulinism. Paul's treatment of faith, works, and justification always had in view the issue of the basis on which Gentile Christians were accepted by God as members of his people. When Paul refers to "works of the law" (a phrase not used by James) it is with special, though not exclusive, reference to the boundary markers, such as circumcision and food laws, which symbolized Jewish exclusivity. James, on the other hand, is entirely oblivious to the question of Gentile believers in Christ, and the works he has in mind are acts of neighborly love. While faith in Paul means trusting dependence on God for salvation, which Paul could not envisage as unproductive of acts of love, in James faith is belief that God is the only God, which could easily exist without practical consequences. It is notable that the closest verbal contacts between Paul and James occur in discussion of Abraham (Jas 2:18-24; Rom 3:27–4:5; with the close verbal resemblances in Jas 2:21-24; Rom 4:2-3). Since for Jews he was the classic example of faith, frequently discussed in the language of Gen 15:6, the contacts are not surprising. James's understanding of Abraham and Gen 15:6 is fully in line with Jewish tradition, while Paul's is innovatory.

James 3:1-12

Speech ethics was an important topic in the tradition of Jewish wisdom instruction, as also in Hellenistic moral instruction. The power of the tongue for good or evil (Prov 15:4; 18:21), especially its destructive force (Sir 28:14-23), and the consequent need for caution in speech (Prov 13:3; Sir 28:24-25; 4Q525 14 ii 20-27), were traditional topics, taken up here by James. But his pessimism about the human ability to control the tongue (3:8) seems unmatched elsewhere.

The opening dissuasion from becoming teachers (3:1) introduces the topic with the instance of use of the tongue which incurs the greatest temptations and can do the most harm. Because the misuse of the tongue by teachers can lead many others astray, they will be judged more strictly (v. 1). The tongue is portrayed now as the key element in attaining "perfection" (v. 2; cf. 1:4 with comment). This is intelligible if we supply the close relationship in Jewish thought between the heart (or mind) and the tongue (e.g., Ps 15:2-3; Sir 27:4-7; 4Q525 2 ii 1; Matt 12:34). The evil of the heart becomes manifest in speech. This also helps to explain the images of the tongue as the bit by which the whole horse is guided and the rudder by which the whole ship is directed (3:3-5). These images had a long history in Greek literature, in which they were mostly used to portray the mind's control of the body. James can use them of the tongue because the thoughts and intention (v. 4: "the will of the pilot directs") of the heart are expressed by the tongue. Therefore anyone who can control the tongue (cf. 1:26) can also control the whole body (3:2).

In 3:5 the emphasis shifts to the vast destructive potential of the tongue. The image of fire (vv. 5-6) derives from Jewish wisdom tradition (Prov 16:27; 26:20-21; Sir 28:10, 22; cf. *Pss. Sol.* 12:2-3). The first half of 3:6 is very obscure. Probably the text is corrupt, and it may originally have explained the image in v. 5b by identifying the fire with the tongue and the forest with "the world of iniquity." The end of v. 6 cannot, as most commentators think, mean that the tongue's destructive power derives from hell since in this period hell is never the place of the devil or the source of evil, but always the place of punishment administered by angels. What is described is an eschatological measure-for-measure punishment (see the comment on 2:13): the tongue that has set the whole wheel of existence on fire will itself be set on fire by hell.

The conclusion that the tongue is untameable (3:7-8) seems to imply that the possibility of perfection announced in v. 2b and illustrated in vv. 3-4 is unattainable. But perhaps the intention is to deny that it is attainable by unaided human power and to point forward to the need for wisdom from above (3:17) and repentance (4:7-10).

The close connection between the heart and the tongue entails a connection between the "double-minded" (1:8; see comment) and the "double-tongued" (Sir 5:9, 14; 6:1; 28:13) to whom James now implicitly refers (3:9-10). (Note that "restless"/"unstable" [the same Greek word] describes the double-minded in 1:8 and the tongue in 3:8.) It is the double-minded who bless God and curse God's human image. The inconsistency reveals duplicity. They cannot wholeheartedly intend both (cf. 4:4). The series of four parabolic images (3:11-12) move from asking whether one person can utter good and bad statements (v. 11) to asking whether a person of one kind can utter statements of another (v. 12a), to asserting that an evil person cannot utter good statements. (The images, in common Hellenistic use, are used to reexpress Jesus' teaching [Matt 12:33-35; Luke 6:43-45].) The implication is that the double-tongued reveal by their cursing that their heart is evil. This concluding parable both rounds off the section on the evil of the tongue and forms a transition to the following section, which focuses on the outward expression of what is in the heart.

James 3:13-18

In this section and the next, the contrast between God's values and those of the world is made clear, along with the need for James's readers to turn to God and to resist the influence of the world. The compromise between the two attempted by the "double-minded" is not possible. The world's attitudes and practices are competitiveness, boasting, and arrogance, resulting in conflict, whereas God's people are to align themselves with the "lowly" and their meekness, resulting in peace.

In the present section the emphasis is on wisdom, introduced in 1:5 and now characterized as the wisdom "from above" (3:15, 17), that is, the gift of God (1:17), in contrast to its worldly counterpart (3:15), which James avoids calling wisdom at all. The phrase "meekness of wisdom" (v. 13; NRSV, "gentleness born of wisdom") brings together James's two key themes of wisdom and the poor or the lowly (cf. 1:9; 2:5). The latter, as the paradigm heirs of the kingdom, model the attitude required of those instructed by wisdom from God: dependence on God and renouncing competitive ambition for status. This wisdom is further characterized by seven qualities (3:17), where seven is the number of completeness, indicating that these seven are representative of all the qualities of wisdom, contrasted with "wickedness of every kind" (v. 16). Contrasts run through this section: "from above" (vv. 15, 17) with "earthly, unspiritual, devilish" (v. 15); "peaceable" (v. 17) and "peace" (v. 18; in the biblical tradition these are strongly positive words suggesting reconciliation and wholeness) with "disorder" (v. 16); "gentle, willing to yield" (v. 17) with "envy and selfish ambition" (vv. 14, 16). That wisdom is "first pure" (v. 17) recalls 1:27 (cf. 4:8) and contrasts with "double-mindedness," as does "without a trace of hypocrisy" (3:17). The phrase "full of mercy and good fruits" (v. 17) takes up the emphasis of ch. 2 (vv. 13 and 20) into this characterization of wisdom.

The aphorism in 3:18 uses the common image of sowing now the seed which will bear fruit in the eschatological harvest, and puts it in "measure-for-measure" form (see the comment on 2:13; cf. 4Q213 5 i 7: "Whoever sows goodness, harvests good"; *2 Enoch* 42:11). Peacemakers will reap a harvest of righteousness in peace. (This is one of several points at which James is close to the Matthean beatitudes.) Once again (cf. 2:13; 3:12; 4:17) an aphorism both rounds off a section and forms a transition to the next, closely connected section, here by means of the contrast between peace and war (4:1).

James 4:1-10

Pursuing the contrast between God's values and the dominant value system in society, James now turns to prophetic denunciation of the double-minded (4:1-6) and a call to repentance (vv. 7-10). The fundamental sin at issue is envy, that is, selfish and competitive desires ("covet" in NRSV v. 2 would better be translated "envy," in line with 3:14, 16; cf. also 4:5, discussed below). Envy causes conflicts both within and between people (4:1), frustrating the "wholeness" of both individuals and the community to which God's values (especially peace: 3:17, 18) tend. The strong language of war (4:1-2) and even murder (v. 2) should probably be explained as integral to standard Hellenistic discussions of envy. It brings out the nature of envy rather than referring to actual situations. Prayers which express selfish desires of this kind are not answered because although, according to James, God is preeminently the one who gives generously (1:5, 17; 4:6), his gifts must be received in the meekness and lowliness (1:21; 4:6) of those who depend wholly on God rather than pursuing their own pleasures.

4:4 is a key statement for the dualism of value systems in James, reexpressing Jesus' teaching (Matt 6:24) in a different image. "Friendship" (cf. also Abraham as a friend of God in 2:23) has connotations of loyalty and sharing of values. Hence friendship with God and the world, both representing approaches to the whole of life, is impossible. The point is reinforced by the accusation "Adulterers!" — literally, "Adulteresses!" This presupposes the image of marriage used in the OT prophets for the covenant relation between God and his people. God's people who compromise with worldly values are like adulterous women, attempting the impossible task of combining marriage to God their husband, who requires exclusive loyalty, and liaison with another partner, the world.

4:5 presents problems which have been much debated. Probably James quotes an apocryphal work which is no longer extant. The quotation has been variously translated. The NRSV gives one possibility, which depends on taking *phthonon* in a positive sense (God's "jealousy"), although there is no precedent for such a sense of this Greek word. A possibility which gives this word its usual, negative sense ("envy"), which is appropriate to the general context (3:14, 16; 4:2) but has to presuppose a bad Greek translation of a Hebrew text is: "The Spirit God made to dwell in us abhors envy."

Those James so strongly denounces need not despair since God is the gracious and generous Giver. But he gives to the lowly, not the arrogant (4:6, quoting Prov 3:34; cf. 1 Pet 5:5-6). 4:7a, 9-10 therefore require the double-minded to renounce competitive, status-seeking arrogance and to put themselves alongside the paradigmatic heirs of the kingdom (2:5), those whose attitude to God and others reflects their needy position at the bottom of the social and economic hierarchy. Then God's favor to the lowly will also apply to the repentant (4:10; cf. 1:5). These verses also correspond to the qualities of those who are blessed as "poor in spirit" in the Matthean beatitudes (cf. Matt 5:4, 5, 8; cf. the comment on Jas 3:18 above).

4:8 uses language of cultic worship and purity, applied to moral integrity (see the comments on 1:26-27). Instead of the more usual form, "turn to God, and he will turn to you" (cf. Zech 1:3; Tob 13:6), James uses language of God's cultic presence: "draw near." In order to come into God's presence, purity is required, both of heart (intentions) and hands (actions) (cf. Ps 24:3-4).

James 4:11-12

This short warning is against slandering, in the sense of speaking maliciously about someone behind his or her back (cf. Pss 50:20; 101:5; Prov 18:8; Wis 1:11). It is based on Lev 19:16a since James is still working with the context of the commandment to love one's neighbor (see the comment on 2:1-13), and on Jesus' prohibition of judging (Matt 7:1). Slander and judging are closely related since the former involves condemning someone in secret. Since the law prohibits slander (Lev 19:16a), it is in effect a judgment on the law. The slanderer is claiming a superior position from which to judge which commandments to obey and which not to obey. But God is the only lawgiver and judge.

James 4:13-17

The parallel opening formulae of this and the following section (5:1) introduce attacks on two different categories of wealthy people. Whether the direct address is purely rhetorical or envisages such people among James's Christian readers is hard to tell (cf. 1:10-11; 2:2-3). 4:17 implies that they could be expected to know the will of God which they disregard, and so they should probably be regarded as Jewish (even if not Jewish Christian) rather than pagan. (The merchant class in Jewish Palestine was very small, but there were probably more Jewish merchants in the diaspora.) In any case, it is far more important to James that the value system they practice is that of the world, not God.

The two categories of wealthy people are condemned in quite different terms. The merchants are upbraided for their arrogant self-confidence (4:16), treating their lives as though they were entirely within their own control (v. 13), without reference to God. The passage is in the style of wisdom instruction, with a strong echo of Prov 27:1, and this is appropriate to its theme. Like the rich fool in Jesus' parable (Luke 12:13-21), which also resembles wisdom literature, the merchants are fools to think that they can make plans without reference to God's will. They lack the religious wisdom to take into account even the obvious fact that they cannot tell what will happen tomorrow. Their fate is described in an image (4:14: probably smoke rather than mist), which is used in Jewish literature very much like the parallel image in 1:10-11, both for the transience of mortal life in general (4 Ezra 4:24; *1 Clem.* 17:6) and especially for the fate of the wicked (Pss 37:20; 68:2; Hos 13:3; Wis 5:14; 1QM 15:10; 4 Ezra 7:61; *2 Apoc. Bar.* 82:6). Its stress is on the ephemerality of this life, but an overtone of God's judgment is not absent.

The aphorism in 4:17 applies to both the merchants and to the landowners condemned in 5:1-5, forming a transition like other aphorisms in this position (2:13; 3:12, 18).

James 5:1-6

By contrast with the merchants in the preceding section, the landowners are condemned in the style of a prophetic oracle (cf. Isa 13:6). They are denounced for their oppression of the poor, at whose expense they have accumulated wealth and lived in luxury. They are threatened with eschatological judgment, when justice will at last be done for the righteous they have defrauded and murdered. The past tenses in 5:2-3a are prophetic, indicating the certainty of what will occur when judgment comes and their wealth, no longer of any use to them, will in fact turn against them (v. 3b).

Specifically (5:4) they have disobeyed the commandment of Lev 19:13 (another reference to the context of Lev 19:18b; see the comment on 2:1-13) against withholding the wages of a day laborer until morning. James alludes also to Deut 24:14-15, a fuller version of that commandment, and to Isa 5:9 LXX. References to this commandment are frequent in Jewish literature (Mal 3:5; Sir 34:27; Tob 4:14; *T. Job* 12:4; Pseudo-Phocylides 19). The reason is that the day laborer was a significant category of the poor. He neither owned nor rented land, but was employed a day at a time on the estates of others and paid his wages at the end of each day's work. Of all peasant workers, he was in the most vulnerable position. His employment could be terminated at a few hours' notice. He might often be unemployed. His wages were too small to make savings possible. He and his family lived from hand to mouth, and withholding his wages even until next morning was a serious matter. An employer who did so could even be accused of murder without hyperbole (Sir 34:25-27). This may partly explain James's accusation of murder in 5:5, though (especially in view of "condemned") the reference may be to misuse of the courts in order to deprive smallholders of their land and to absorb their farms into the big estates.

5:5b alludes to Jer 12:3 (cf. 1QH 15:17; *1 Enoch* 94:9), where the rare noun "slaughter" would suggest to a Jewish exegete a connection with Jer 7:32; 19:6. The rich who have gorged themselves at the expense of the poor are depicted as food for the birds and animals at the gruesome eschatological feast of judgment (Ezek 39:17-20).

James 5:7-11

Having referred to the imminent end as the time of judgment on oppressors (5:3-5), James now addresses believers awaiting the parousia. There are three parts to his advice: (1) An encouragement to patience, illustrated by a parabolic saying (vv. 7-8). (2) A warning against lapsing into complaints against fellow believers (v. 9; cf. 4:11-12; Matt 7:1). In the frustration of enduring suffering this is a temptation, but it could incur judgment at the imminent coming of Christ, evoked in another brief parabolic saying (cf. Mark 13:29; Luke 12:35-36; Rev 3:20). (3) Biblical examples of patience and endurance are presented for emulation and encouragement (5:10-11).

Although James associates "patience" (5:7, 8, 10) and endurance (v. 11; cf. 1:2-4, 12), the terms carry different nuances. Patience is forbearance, putting up with things or people without complaint, and is frequently used of God's patience with sinners. Endurance is more like active resistance to trying circumstances, remaining steadfast, holding out to the end.

That the prophets suffered persecution (5:10) was well known in Jewish tradition, which developed this theme considerably beyond its presence in the OT itself (cf. Matt 5:12; 23:29-37; Mark 12:2-5; Heb 11:36-37). The biblical Job could hardly be said to be "patient" beyond ch. 2 of his book (cf. Job 1:21; 2:10), though he could be said to "endure" in his quest to know the truth of God and his position before God. But the *Testament of Job,* a retelling of the biblical story, makes Job a model of endurance (1:5; 4:6, etc.) and patience (26:4-5), and also ascribes Job's eventual blessing to God's compassion and mercy (26:5; 47:4; cf. Jas 5:11). The "purpose of the Lord" (5:11) may also be the "outcome" of the Lord's dealings with Job: his blessing in the end (Job 42:10-17), which provides a precedent for James's readers to expect the Lord's mercy at the parousia.

That James can speak of both Jesus (5:7, 8, 14, 15; cf. 1:1; 2:1) and God (1:8; 4:10, 15?; 5:10, 11?; cf. 5:4) indistinguishably as "the Lord" suggests a high Christology.

James 5:12

This instruction is singled out as especially important, both by its introductory words and by its standing alone without close connections to its context. It is the culmination of James's persistent concern with speech ethics (1:19; 3:1-12; 4:11-12; 5:9). It is for the sake of a demand for total truthfulness that oaths are prohibited since people who need to guarantee the truth of a particular statement by means of an oath imply thereby that other statements of theirs are unreliable. What is required is that all of a person's speech should display the truthfulness that oaths require (for Jewish parallels, see *2 Enoch* 49:1; Josephus *J.W.* 2 §135). Thus, this instruction moves from the negative warnings of James's previous comments on speech to a positive and comprehensive requirement of truthfulness. And since speech is the index of a person's whole moral being (see the comment on 3:2), this instruction can serve as the requirement of perfection (3:2). Moreover, in this instruction James comes closer than anywhere else to actually quoting a saying of Jesus (Matt 5:33-37). Probably here alone he intends an allusion which will be recognized as such, and which will indicate the coherence of all his teaching with the teaching of Jesus.

James 5:13-18

This section proffers advice on responding to God in different conditions (5:13), but focuses on sickness (vv. 14-16). While the elders of the church (the eldership was naturally adopted by Jewish-Christian communities from the synagogue) have a special responsibility to minister to the sick (v. 14), the whole community should also pray (v. 16). In common with Jewish tradition, it is assumed that sickness may often result from sin, so that confession and forgiveness have a place in healing, but it is not assumed that all sickness results from sin (vv. 15-16). The anointing (v. 14) is probably not here medicinal but a symbol of God's healing power, as in Mark 6:13. It is done "in the name of the Lord" Jesus, indicating that the elders act on his behalf, and it is Jesus who heals (5:15). The healing is envisaged thus as a continuation by the exalted Jesus of his earthly ministry of healing, as in the early chapters of Acts (3:6, 16; 4:10; 9:34). For the prayer of faith (5:15), which only "the righteous" (v. 16b), not the double-minded pray, see 1:6-7. The reference to Elijah as an example (5:17-18) depends on Jewish traditional interpretation of the OT, both in ascribing the beginning and the end of the drought to Elijah's prayer (4 Ezra 7:109; *Lives of the Prophets* 21:5) and in specifying the time period (Luke 4:25).

James 5:19-20

This section is appropriate as a conclusion because it concerns the application of James's teaching to those most in need of it: those who have strayed from the truth (cf. 1:18), that is, from the right way of living, as described by James's wise teaching. This application is a responsibility of the community as a whole, just as James has throughout addressed his readers corporately rather than (as more usually in Jewish wisdom instruction) individually. The believer who turns an erring brother or sister back (cf. Ezek 33:11) saves that person's soul (for death as the end to which sin leads, see 1:15). The last clause probably refers to the erring believer's sins, which are "covered" in the sense of forgiven (Pss 32:1; 85:2) when the sinner repents. In view of 1 Pet 4:8; *1 Clem.* 49:5; *2 Clem.* 16:4, there would seem to have been an early Christian oral tradition based on Prov 10:12, which James also reflects here, but not without attention to its context in Proverbs (10:9-12).

Bibliography. Adamson, J. B. 1989, *James: The Man and His Message,* Grand Rapids: Eerdmans • Bauckham, R. 1999, *James: Wisdom of James, Disciple of Jesus the Sage,* New Testament Readings, London: Routledge • Bauckham, R. forthcoming, *James,* New Testament Guides, Sheffield: Sheffield Academic • Chester, A. 1994, "The Theology of James," in A. Chester and R. P. Martin, *The Theology of the Letters of James, Peter, and Jude,* Cambridge: Cambridge University, 1-62 • Davids, P. H.

1982, *The Epistle of James,* NIGTC, Exeter: Paternoster and Grand Rapids: Eerdmans • Dibelius, M., and H. Greeven. 1975, *James,* Hermeneia, Philadelphia: Fortress • Johnson, L. T. 1995, *The Letter of James,* AB 37A, New York: Doubleday • Martin, R. P. 1988, *James,* WBC 48, Waco: Word • Maynard-Reid, P. U. 1987, *Poverty and Wealth in James,* New York: Orbis • Mayor, J. B. 2d ed. 1897, *The Epistle of St. James,* London: Macmillan • Penner, T. C. 1996, *The Epistle of James and Eschatology,* JSNTSup 121, Sheffield: Sheffield Academic • Tamez, E. 1992, *The Scandalous Message of James,* New York: Crossroad • Wall, R. W. 1997, *Community of the Wise: The Letter of James,* Valley Forge, Penn.: Trinity Press International, 1997.

1 Peter

Graham N. Stanton

INTRODUCTION

A Letter?

The theological richness of 1 Peter has long been recognized, as has the excellence of its Greek style. It is undeniably one of the finest literary and theological writings in the NT. What kind of writing is it? In its present form 1 Peter is a letter: both its opening and its closing verses conform closely to the conventions of ancient letter writing which are also prominent in Paul's letters. However, some of the features of the central sections of 1 Peter have been used to support theories that 1 Peter originated as a homily or even as a baptismal liturgy which was turned into a letter only at a later point.

Explanations along these lines have now been generally abandoned, as have theories which propose that two or more originally separate letters have been woven into one. 1 Peter was composed as a single circular letter addressed to Christian communities in widely scattered areas; hence it is not surprising that it is less "personal" than, say, Paul's letters to the Corinthians. The commentary which follows hopes to show that 1 Peter can be read as a single letter with an overarching theme which is related to the social circumstances of the recipients.

The First Readers

Where did the first readers live, and why was it necessary to send them such a substantial letter of encouragement? The five areas listed in 1:1 as the geographical location of the first readers were Roman provinces in Asia Minor. The order in which the provinces are listed may reflect the route to be taken by the messenger who delivered the circular letter.

The recipients of this letter are referred to in 1:1 as "exiles of the Dispersion." In 1:17 they are urged to "live in reverent fear during the time of your exile." There is a fuller reference to the first readers as "aliens and exiles" in 2:11. Who were they, and what was their social status? The answer to this question will have an important bearing on the interpretation of the letter as a whole.

These references to the first readers have been understood in three main ways. (i) In their present earthly home, Christians are aliens and exiles, for their true home is in heaven. This view was supported by Calvin, by Beare 1970, and by Best 1971, among others. A contrast between *present* earthly homes on the one hand, and *future* heavenly homes on the other, is explicit in Heb 13:14; this contrast receives its classic expression in the *Epistle to Diognetus* in the middle of the second century AD. However, our author is not concerned to contrast "earth below" and "heaven above," but the difference between *the past,* "once you were not a people," and *the present,* "now you are God's people" (2:10).

(ii) 2:11 is translated by Elliott 1981: 48 as "resident aliens and visiting strangers" and claims that these terms are to be understood literally. They identify "the addressees as a combination of displaced persons who are currently aliens permanently residing in *(paroikia, paroikoi)* or strangers temporarily visiting or passing through *(parepidēmoi)* the four provinces of Asia Minor named in the salutation (1:1)." These unusual terms refer to their status prior to their conversion: they "indicate the political, legal, social and religious limitations and estrangement which such displacement entails." While the first readers have not been forcibly exiled, their status is more ambivalent than that of those who were natives to the area. Elliott's emphasis on the importance of the social setting of the addressees for the interpretation of this letter is surely correct, but if the writer had intended to address such specific groups of displaced persons, other more common Greek words would have been used.

(iii) The preferable view, supported recently by Michaels 1988: 6-8 and Achtemeier 1996: 56 (among others), takes this phrase as another example of the writer's common practice of adapting an OT term for Israel and applying it to Christian believers — to the church, though this term is not used in 1 Peter. Abraham's self-reference in Gen 23:4, "I am an alien and a settler," is the outcome of God's call to him to leave behind the security of his home region and live in obedience to God among people where he was not at home. Similarly, God's call in Christ to the readers of this letter had radically altered their social status. They are Christians whose lifestyle marks them off as "exiles" from the society in which they live (cf. 4:3-4); they are "the scattered people of God now living as aliens" (1:1, REB).

Their ambivalent social status as Christians living in a society which was at best hostile to them, and at worst prepared to persecute them, undermined their self-confidence as Christian believers. "Having enjoyed the legal protection and social acceptance accorded the native born prior to their conversion, it was precisely their changed status to that of foreigner in their own homeland that precipitated the crisis our author addressed in this letter" (Achtemeier 1996: 174-75).

Were the first readers Jews or Gentiles? The reference in 4:3 to their pre-conversion conduct as living in "lawless idolatry" strongly suggests that the readers were Gentiles. In 2:10 a contrast is drawn between the readers' earlier lives when they were "not a people," and their standing now as God's people; this terminology would hardly be appropriate for Jews who had become Christians, but apt for Gentile converts. Although there were Jewish communities in the areas to which 1 Peter was sent, there are no passages which indicate unambiguously that any of these Jews had become Christians.

The writer is steeped in the Septuagint (LXX) and assumes that his readers are also. While this might suggest that some of the first readers were Jews, Gentiles could have been instructed in the OT within Christian communities; they may have had some acquaintance with the OT even before they became Christians.

Earlier Traditions in 1 Peter

The Old Testament

OT passages are cited at some length in nine places in 1 Peter. The LXX is normally followed closely. Variations from the LXX wording may have arisen through faulty memory, through use of a variant LXX textual tradition, or through adaptation of the text to fit the point being made. It is often difficult to decide which of these three explanations is the most likely.

The OT is quoted in order to underline the importance of the point which has just been made. Hence it is surprising that only in the first three of the nine OT quotations (1:16; 1:24-25; 2:6) is there any indication to the reader that a scriptural quotation follows. Why are the other OT quotations not prefaced by an introductory formula such as "for it stands in scripture," as in 2:6? In modern translations quotation marks indicate that the OT is being cited, but the earliest manuscripts did not contain punctuation marks. In some cases the readers of 1 Peter knew the OT passages so well that an introductory phrase was unnecessary. In other cases the vocabulary, style, and content of the OT quotation would have been a clear indication of its origin.

In as many as thirty other places OT passages are alluded to: the OT is woven more tightly into the warp and weft of this letter than in any of Paul's letters. OT phraseology and imagery used to refer to God's people are applied in this letter to Christian believers; the more striking examples will be noted in the commentary below.

Jesus Traditions

There are no explicit citations of sayings of Jesus in 1 Peter, but as many as thirty possible allusions to sayings of Jesus have been identified. Given that the author of this letter identifies himself in 1:1 as "Peter, an apostle of Jesus Christ," the extent of allusions to sayings of Jesus has played a prominent part in discussion of the apostolic authorship of 1 Peter. Are there allusions to the sayings or events in the life of Jesus which could only have come from Peter himself? Or does the paucity of personal reminiscences tell against apostolic authorship?

Gundry 1967 has argued that 1 Peter was dictated by the apostle Peter in Rome and insisted that his dictation was peppered with frequent allusions to dominical sayings which were authentic and possessive of special interest to Peter. In a response Best 1970 rejected most of the alleged allusions and concluded that contact between 1 Peter and Gospel traditions was confined very largely to two blocks, Luke 6:22-33 and 12:32-45. Several more recent writers have assessed this debate and sided largely with Best, but they have added few fresh observations.

When the writer refers to himself as a "witness of the sufferings of Christ" in 1 Pet 5:1, does he imply that he himself was an eyewitness to some of the events of the passion? Although this verse may be interpreted in this way, it should be noted that the phraseology of the references to the sufferings of Christ in 1 Pet 2:23-25 are taken from Isaiah 53, and not from eyewitness testimony.

We can be confident that the author of 1 Peter drew on several clusters of Jesus traditions which were relevant to the points he wished to make. But it is impossible to be precise about the extent of the writer's knowledge and use of Jesus traditions. In several cases allusion to Jesus traditions is possible, but the influence of other early Christian catechetical traditions cannot be ruled out. On the other hand, the writer (and perhaps his readers) may have known many more sayings of Jesus which are not alluded to in this letter simply because they were not relevant to the themes being emphasized.

Although attempts have been made from time to time to show that the author knew one or more written Gospels (especially Matthew), they have not been successful. The writer knew oral Jesus traditions rather than written Gospels; there is not enough evidence to decide whether or not he knew some form of Q.

Pauline Letters

Several Pauline passages, especially from Romans and Ephesians, are echoed in 1 Peter. The more important parallels will be noted below. Some scholars have claimed that the writer knew and used at least some of Paul's letters; a few have taken a further step and claimed that knowledge of Paul's letters rules out Petrine authorship.

However, the evidence is by no means clear-cut. The closest parallels to 1 Peter in Romans are confined to chs. 9 to 13; many of the great themes of chs. 1 to 8 are conspicuous by their absence from 1 Peter. When all the evidence is assembled, literary dependence seems less likely than shared use of catechetical traditions. The same is true of Ephesians.

Who Wrote 1 Peter — and When?

The date of the persecution of Christians referred to in 1 Peter has often been central in discussions of authorship. There is no clear evidence that Nero's persecution of Christians following the fire in Rome in AD 64 extended into any of the areas to which 1 Peter was sent. Stronger evidence for persecution comes from the reign of Domitian (AD 81-96), though it was sporadic and by no means universal. The evidence in 1 Peter for hostility toward Christians which included persecution fits this period better than any other. While the evidence that Peter was martyred under Nero in AD 64 or 65 is not quite as strong as many have supposed, it is most unlikely that Peter lived on into the reign of Domitian.

Several other arguments used in discussions of the authorship are not conclusive one way or the other. While 1 Peter uses sophisticated Greek which approaches classical standards, the apostle Peter almost certainly knew some Greek and could have allowed a co-worker or secretary (perhaps Silvanus, 5:12) to put his own thoughts into written form. Similar considerations apply to the use of the LXX in 1 Peter. And, as we have seen above, use of Jesus traditions in 1 Peter does not settle the question of authorship, though the absence of personal reminiscences does tell against Petrine authorship.

The opening reference to Peter in 1:1 is the only clear evidence in the text for associating this letter with Peter. But 1:1 is not decisive; as several scholars have noted, if this verse were not part of the letter, one would be much more likely to attribute it to Paul than to Peter! On the other hand, it is difficult to find arguments which rule out Petrine authorship completely, especially if the involvement of a co-worker or secretary in this letter's composition is posited.

When the various considerations are weighed at much greater length than is possible here, the balance of probabilities is against the close involvement of the apostle. Traditions associated with Peter may well stand behind the letter and account for the use of his name by a later pseudonymous author.

The date of the letter cannot be settled readily, but it is more likely to have been written shortly after the beginning of Domitian's reign in AD 81 than either earlier or later.

Structure

The main structural features of 1 Peter are clear: they follow the general pattern of letters in antiquity, including Paul's letters. The opening (1:1-2) and closing (5:12-14) verses both refer to the sender and to the recipients. The main central section of the letter is clearly marked by the affectionate address "beloved" or, better, "dear friends" (REB) at 2:11 and 4:12. This central section discusses Christian living in a hostile society; it is preceded and followed by lengthy introductory (1:3–2:10) and concluding sections (4:12–5:11).

COMMENTARY

Opening Greeting (1:1-2)

The literary form of the opening words is found in nearly all NT and early Christian letters: "writer to addressees, greetings." The initial reference to the writer as "an apostle of Jesus Christ" is also used by Paul at the beginning of his letters, as is the greeting "grace and peace." In other respects, however, these verses are quite distinctive.

The recipients of this letter are "exiles of the Dispersion." This phrase is to be taken metaphorically: the letter is addressed to Christians whose lifestyle now marks them off as "exiles" from the society in which they live (cf. 4:3-4); they are "the scattered people of God now living as aliens" (REB). The five named areas are Roman provinces in the northern half of Asia Minor. The order in which they are listed may reflect the route to be taken by the messenger who delivered the circular letter. (For a fuller discussion of the recipients, see the Introduction, 1493 above.)

The threefold description of the addressees in 1:2 introduces three of the letter's main themes. They have been chosen as God's "new" people, a theme developed in 1:3-12. The reference to their consecration by the Spirit anticipates 1:13-17 with its call to holy living. The outcome of the work of the Spirit is their obedience (here almost synonymous with their "faith") and sprinkling with the blood of Jesus Christ, themes developed in 1:18-25.

"Obedience" and "sprinkled with blood" recall Exod 24:7-8, where the people respond to the reading by Moses of the scroll of the covenant with the words, "We will be obedient." Moses then "dashed" the blood of the sacrificial offerings on the people, and said, "See the blood of the covenant that the LORD has made with you." Unlike Heb 9:11-22, 1 Peter has no extended comparison between the institution of the Mosaic covenant and the new covenant mediated by the death of Christ, but the further references to the blood of Christ and to obedience in 1:18 and 25 confirm that Exod 24:7-8 is in mind here.

Introduction (1:3–2:10)

Thanks Be to God (1:3-12)

This subsection contains a single elegant Greek sentence (divided grammatically at 1:6, 8, and 12) for which the NRSV uses six sentences, and most other modern translations into English even more. Although some scholars have claimed that an early Christian (baptismal) hymn lies behind these verses, this view has not been supported recently.

The opening outburst of praise to God in 1:3-5 has many OT and Jewish parallels. The customary "blessing" of God is extended by the distinctively Christian affirmation that God is "the Father of our Lord Jesus Christ," and followed by statements about what God has done through Christ for believers. The closest parallel is Eph 1:3-14 (cf. also 2 Cor 1:3-7).

The author associates himself with the recipients of his letter: God has given them "a new birth into a living hope," the features of which are explained in the clauses which follow. The verb *anagennan,* "to give new birth," is used only here and at 1:23, though the sense is close to the exhortation to Nicodemus in John 3:3, 7: "You must be born from above," that is, through God's gift of life through the Spirit. There may be a reference to baptism in 1:3, though this is by no means certain. The "living hope" given through the resurrection of Jesus Christ suggests a contrast with the hopelessness of pagan religion.

God's gift of "living hope" is linked closely to his gift of an inheritance which is free from decay and impurity; unlike the flowers of 1:24, it does not fade away. The inheritance is also closely related to God's gift of salvation at the end of time (v. 5). In the meantime the recipients of "living hope," of the inheritance, and of ultimate salvation are promised God's powerful protection. They are given this strong reassurance because of the trying ordeals they are at present undergoing (v. 6). The precise sense of the phrase "through faith" is not clear: perhaps God's protection becomes a reality through their faith or trust in him.

1:6-9 contain a movement from a present (vv. 6-7) determined by God's act of sending Christ in the past (v. 8) to a future that fulfills both past and present (vv. 7b, 9) (Achtemeier 1996:99). The gifts and promises referred to in the preceding verses ("in this," v. 6a) are the grounds for rejoicing, even though the readers are reeling under hostility of various kinds. The testing of faith is a common biblical theme (e.g., Genesis 22); it often takes place in suffering, which in turn leads to a more mature faith (cf. esp. Jas 1:2-4). The refining of gold by fire in order to remove impurities was well known in antiquity; a similar comparison of this process with suffering as a refining of faith is found in Sir 2:5. Present woes are to be set in the light of the future glory to be revealed in Christ. The themes (but not the words) of vv. 6-7 have a striking parallel in Rom 8:18: the sufferings of this present time are not worth comparing with the glory about to be revealed to us.

1:8 does not necessarily imply that while the readers have not seen Jesus Christ, the author himself was an eyewitness to the life of Jesus. The contrast and emphasis are more general: faith and love for Christ (linked closely here) far surpass sight. When will the "joy" and "rejoicing" of v. 8 be experienced? Although some exegetes and translators have taken this to refer to the future hope of believers, the NRSV correctly uses the present tense: you are receiving (now, in part) the outcome of your faith — your final salvation.

The salvation which is referred to in 1:5b and 9 is now the focus of attention in vv. 10-12. This salvation through Christ which was now being experienced by the recipients of this letter was no afterthought, for it was integral to God's plan for humankind (cf. v. 20). Although Selwyn (1947: 134, 259-68) has won some support for his claim that Christian prophets are referred to in these verses, this is unlikely. The OT prophets who testified in advance to the sufferings of Christ (v. 11) are contrasted with the evangelists ("those who brought you good news," v. 12) who have announced *now* God's purposes. Nonetheless, the continuity between the past prophetic message and the present proclamation of the Christian gospel is underlined: the prophets prophesied about "the grace that was to be *yours*" (v. 10), and the evangelists proclaimed good news *"for you"* (v. 12). In the former case this was through "the Spirit of Christ"; in the latter, "by the Holy Spirit sent from heaven."

The reference to the careful inquiry of the prophets into the *timing* of God's plan (1:11) introduces an apocalyptic motif. The more general conviction that the OT prophets spoke about the coming of Christ is found in many strands of early Christian writings (e.g., Matt 13:17 = Luke 10:24 [Q]; Luke 24:25-27; John 5:39; Acts 7:52). Although the Greek phrase *ta eis Christon pathēmata* could refer to the sufferings of believers in Christ, the context supports the NRSV, "sufferings destined for Christ." The hint that the sufferings of the recipients are related to the sufferings of Christ (1:6 and 1:11) is developed with special reference to slaves in 2:18-25.

A Call to Holy Living (1:13-16)

The opening word "therefore" links the ethical commands which follow to the references to God's acts of grace through Christ in the opening section of the letter (esp. 1:1-3). As elsewhere in the NT, and especially in Paul's letters, God's gift and God's ethical demands are linked inextricably.

The rich imagery in the Greek of the first clause of 1:13 teases translators; the two participles are often taken too readily as imperatives. Compare a literal translation, "girding up the loins of your mind, being sober . . . ," with the rather flat NRSV, "prepare your minds for action; discipline yourselves," and with the preferable but imprecise REB, "Your minds must therefore be stripped for action and fully alert." The encouragement to rigorous preparation is juxtaposed with the command to the recipients to set their hope on the grace which comes at the disclosure of Jesus Christ, a reference to future salvation which echoes 1:5 and 1:9.

Christians are to be obedient to God as children are to their parents. They are not to allow their lives to be shaped by the kind of conduct characteristic of those who do not know God, that is, those who act in ignorance of his demands (1:14). This verse has a close verbal and thematic link with Rom 12:2; both writers are probably drawing on fairly common Jewish or early Christian ethical instruction.

In all their relationships with those in the non-Christian society in which they live (1:15b), they are to reflect the holiness of the God who called them (v. 15a). The citation of Scripture in v. 16 underlines the importance of this demand. Lev 19:2 is cited; here God's people are called to a way of life which contrasts sharply with the conduct of those around them. This call is now extended to Christian believers, referred to in 2:9 as a "holy nation."

Set Your Faith and Hope in God (1:17-21)

This carefully crafted Greek sentence (usually translated as four or more sentences in English) contains a concentration of most of the themes of the letter as a whole. 1:17a may echo the opening invocation of the Lord's Prayer, but there are OT (e.g., Ps 88:27) and early Christian (Rom 8:15; Gal 4:6) parallels to calling God "Father." God's impartial judgment on the basis of deeds complements his gift of grace to those who live "in exile"; as elsewhere in 1 Peter, this refers to Christians who are at odds with the hostile society in which they live.

Their freedom or "ransom" from the former way of life they lived in that society has been bought not with money, but through the death of Christ. Their "ransom" may be contrasted with money paid for the manumission of slaves or prisoners of war. The opening words of v. 18, *"you know* that you were ransomed," probably allude to their knowledge of an early Christian tradition similar to Mark 10:45, in which the death of Christ himself is the ransom for many (cf. Michaels 1988: 63).

1:19 and 20 comment further on Christ's ransom. The comparison of Christ to a "lamb without defect or blemish" does not draw directly on the Passover lamb and Israel's redemption from Egypt, for Israel was redeemed "with God's outstretched arm" (Exod 6:6); the shed blood of that lamb was not redemptive. However, there is a clear but general background in the OT (and more widely in antiquity): the belief that Israel's sacrificial animals were to be without blemish if they were to be acceptable to God (e.g., Exod 29:1). 1:21 has a liturgical and confessional ring, as have many other verses in this letter; its reference to the resurrection and glorification of Christ as God's act has many NT parallels.

Love One Another Unwaveringly (1:22-25)

1:22-23 are like a sandwich: the central strong exhortation in v. 22b is preceded and followed by the theological reasons which make that love possible. The readers are being encouraged to love their fellow Christians ("one another"), not people in general. The NRSV translates "love deeply," but the adverb can also mean (as in the NRSV note) "constantly." In view of the emphases of the letter as a whole, the latter meaning is preferable: "love one another unwaveringly from the heart."

This demanding love is seen as the outcome of the readers' moral renewal by means of their obedience to the truth — here a reference to the truth of the Gospel. In 1:23 the readers are reminded that they have been born anew by the living word of God, a further reference to their appropriation of the proclamation of good news.

Some scholars have suggested that "having purified your souls" in 1:22a and "having been born anew" in v. 23 are references to baptism. Indeed, some have claimed that this part of 1 Peter is a baptismal liturgy: baptism took place between vv. 21 and 22! However, v. 23 explains that rebirth is through the *word* of God, so it is most unlikely that baptism is in mind.

This theme is developed in 1:24 and 25. The quotation from Isa 40:6-8 (LXX with modifications) contrasts the frailty and mortality of humanity with the abiding nature of the word of God. Achtemeier (1996: 142) notes that this quotation would be "highly appropriate for a beleaguered community of Christians facing what gave every appearance of being the permanent, even eternal, power and glory of the Roman Empire . . . the announcement that the glitter, pomp, and power of the Roman culture was as grass when compared to God's eternal word spoken in Jesus Christ . . . would give them courage to hold fast to the latter. . . ." V. 25b is a brief comment on the key point in the quotation: the enduring word of the Lord is the gospel which has been proclaimed to his readers.

Long for God's Word (2:1-3)

Although these verses introduce the second half of the opening main section of the letter which runs from 1:13 to 2:10, they continue the themes of the preceding verses. The initial exhortation can be translated as "putting off" (clothing) and understood as a reference to baptism, but the NRSV and most recent translations are probably correct to take the verb in a more general sense: "rid yourselves" of the vices which are listed. Lists of vices are common in both Jewish and Greco-Roman writings, though, unlike here, they are usually juxtaposed with a list of virtues. The author probably has in mind behavior which corrodes Christians' love for one another (1:22) rather than their relationships with non-Christians, a theme which becomes prominent from 2:12 onward.

What is the "pure spiritual milk" (2:2) which the readers are encouraged to seek with the instinctive longing of babies for their mothers' milk? In 1 Cor 3:1-2 and in Heb 5:12-14 basic Christian teaching is likened to infants' milk and contrasted with the more solid food which is appropriate for mature Christians. Here the sense is different: the context suggests that the milk which is to be sought with determination is God's word which nourishes Christian growth whose goal is eschatological salvation. The NRSV and the REB use "pure, spiritual" for the two Greek adjectives which describe "milk." Both adjectives are difficult to translate; "uncontaminated milk of the word" is a preferable translation.

The author adapts the LXX of Ps 34:8 to underline his point. His reference to "milk" has led him to recall phrases from a favorite psalm which he cites more fully in 3:10-12. The psalm's invitation, "taste and see that the LORD is good," here becomes an affirmation, "for surely you have tasted that the Lord is good" (REB). There may well be a wordplay here: the Greek adjective translated "good" *(chrēstos)* would have been pronounced in the same way as Christ *(christos)*. This is made more likely by the fact that Christ is the theme of the verses which follow.

Christ the Living Stone (2:4-10)

In these verses the imagery changes slightly awkwardly from the growth of the individual (2:1-3) to the community as a building, a "spiritual house" (vv. 4-10). The reference to the church (though the word is not used) as "living stones" is preceded by the the striking image of Christ as a "living stone." The conviction that Jesus Christ has been raised from the dead (1:3) and is alive has encouraged the use of the paradoxical phrase "living stone." The term "living" has already been used at 1:3 and 1:23 and is clearly a favorite expression of the author. Its further use here with reference to Christ and to the community as a temple (a "spiritual house") may imply a contrast with "dead" stone idols and stone temples with which the readers would have been thoroughly familiar.

Christ the "living stone" has been rejected both by his own and the author's contemporaries, but he is nonetheless "chosen by God and of great worth to him" (REB). There is a clear implication that though Christians may suffer similar rejection by those among whom they live, they too are precious in God's sight (cf. 2:6c).

If Christians constitute a "new temple" and a "holy priesthood," what are the "spiritual sacrifices" they are called to offer? No answer is given here, but the author returns to this theme in 2:9, where it is made clear that Christians as a "royal priesthood" are to proclaim the mighty acts of God who called them to be his people.

The author cites and uses Isa 28:16 in 2:6 in a way very

similar to that of Paul in Rom 9:32-33, but there are enough differences to rule out literary dependence and to suggest that both writers are using an earlier Christian collection of scriptural proof texts. This is made more probable by the use in 2:8 of Isa 8:14, which is quoted with similar wording in Rom 9:33b.

Isa 28:16 is applied in 2:6a to Christ, the "chosen and precious living stone"; the phraseology of v. 6a has already influenced v. 4a. The final clauses of the quotation, with their firm promise of the vindication of believers, would have been particularly apt for the readers of this letter, who were conscious of the hostility they faced from those among whom they lived.

In the next two verses (2:7 and 8a) this point is taken further by a reference to the fate of nonbelievers who reject Christ. Ps 118:22 is cited. This psalm is quoted in Mark 12:10-11 (and parallels) and in Acts 4:11. In these passages the builders who reject Christ the cornerstone are the Jewish authorities, whereas in 1 Peter they are the local Roman authorities. In 2:8b the writer adds a comment on the significance of the preceding scriptural quotation: rejection of the Christian message leads to "stumbling"; this is in accord with God's plan, but it does not diminish the responsibility of those who reject the cornerstone.

In 2:9 and 10 the Christian identity of the recipients is spelled out in a series of striking phrases drawn from OT references to Israel. In v. 9 Exod 19:6 and Isa 43:20-1 are woven together. Four terms are used to describe God's "new" people: since they are a chosen race *(genos)* and a holy people *(ethnos),* they are a people *(laos)* acquired by God. The precise sense of the fourth term, "royal priesthood," has been much discussed: it probably refers to the priestly functions of the whole community; Christians are "royal" because they are now under the kingly rule of God (similarly Goppelt 1993: 149).

The NRSV sets out 2:10 appropriately as four lines of a poem. The phrases are taken from Hos 1:6, 9-10; 2:1, 27, where they refer to Israel. The dramatic changes experienced by Christians called by God to be his people which are underlined in 2:9b and 10 are referred to in 1:3 as a "new birth." The relationship of Christians to God's people Israel continues to exercise Christians today, but this question is not considered at all in this passage: there is not even a hint of the supersessionism found in some early Christian writings.

2:9 and 10 sum up many of the preceding themes of the letter and prepare for the central section of the letter, which follows in 2:11 to 4:11: in the light of their calling as God's people, believers are able to face with confidence the hostility of the society in which they live.

Christian Lifestyle in a Hostile Society (2:11–4:10)

"Aliens and Exiles" (2:11-12)

The direct address in 2:11 to the readers as "beloved" (or better, as in the REB, "dear friends") marks the opening of the lengthy central section of the letter as a whole, which runs from 2:11 to 4:11. The same direct address in 4:12, "dear friends," introduces the closing section of the letter. Readers in general are addressed in 2:11-17, the opening section of the main body of the letter. In 2:18 to 3:7 the writer refers to specific groups before returning in 3:8 to 4:11 to readers in general.

The recipients are referred to as "aliens and exiles" (cf. 1:1, "exiles"). We noted above in the Introduction, 1493, that this phrase refers to the postconversion ambivalent social status of the recipients in relation to society. Because Christians are not "at home" in the society in which they live, 2:11 emphasizes that they are to resist the patterns of behavior which are taken for granted in that society, but which will destroy their Christian lives. V. 12 is more positive. It is similar in thought to Matt 5:16, "let your light shine before others, so that they may see your *good works and give glory* to your Father in heaven." Only the words in italics are shared in the Greek, so it is unlikely that 1 Peter depends on Matthew (or vice versa). Both writers seem to have quoted a similar saying of Jesus which has been adapted in the course of its transmission. The author is confident that unbelievers will glorify God "on the day of visitation." Is their ultimate conversion being referred to? Or does it refer quite specifically to the time when the readers may expect to suffer at the hands of the local authorities? The OT use of the phrase suggests that the former is more likely: the author has in mind the final judgment when unbelievers will repudiate their rejection of Christians as "evildoers."

The Household Code (2:13–3:7)

This section of the letter contains a considerable adaptation of the conventional "household code" found in a number of Greco-Roman and Jewish writings: a set of instructions to members of a household concerning their responsibilities toward one another. Several early Christian writers took over and adapted the household code for their own purposes. The conventional pattern is seen clearly in Eph 5:21–6:9 and Col 3:18–4:1, where the mutual responsibilities of wives and husbands, of children and parents, and of slaves and masters are set forth.

In 1 Peter, however, the threefold structure of the traditional household code is barely discernible. Although wives and husbands are both addressed, advice to husbands (3:7) is very much briefer than the extended advice to wives in vv. 1-6. Children and parents are not mentioned. The responsibilities of slaves are discussed at length in 2:18-25, but masters are conspicuous by their absence. In 1 Peter the extended advice concerning "internal" household relationships is preceded by comments in 2:13-17 on the attitudes Christians should adopt toward those in authority *outside* the Christian household or community. This concern for relationships between believers and the hostile society in which they lived is one of the most important emphases of the letter as a whole.

Christians and the Emperor (2:13-17)

In these verses there are striking thematic links with Rom 13:1-7, but also important differences even where similar language is used. Perhaps the most notable difference is the contrast between Rom 13:1 and 1 Pet 2:13: in the former, "all authority comes from God," but in the latter there is no reference to the *divine* authority of the emperor and governors.

The polemical nature of the encouragement to submit to the emperor for the Lord's sake can easily be missed by modern readers. At the time this letter was written, non-Christians in the area recognized the Roman emperor as a deity. For Christians, however, this was not an option; for them the emperor is a "human authority" (2:13a), as are his sundry subordinate officials ("governors") responsible for good order (v. 14). The same point is made at the end of this subsection in v. 17, where readers are urged to honor *all* people, including (almost as an afterthought) the emperor. In this way the "divine" emperor is, as it were, being cut down to size: his authority is to be respected, but there are limits to the honors he is to be accorded by Christians.

This line of thought is taken further in 2:16. The primary allegiance of all Christians is to God, not to the emperor. Christians are God's slaves who have been set free by the death of Christ (1:19), but they must not use their freedom as a pretext for evil. What form of evil is in mind? Given the social context to which the letter is addressed, it seems probable that some Christians are being tempted to conform to the religious and cultural conventions of the society in which they lived in order to avoid persecution.

Christian Slaves (2:18-25)

Unlike the cases of Eph 6:9 and Col 4:1, here advice to slaves is not juxtaposed with advice given to slave owners; presumably there were few Christian slave owners among the recipients of this letter. Slaves are urged to accept the authority of their masters "with all deference" *(en panti phobō)*. Here the NRSV translation of 2:18 is mistaken. Since the preceding verse refers to fear of God and the following verse refers to slaves' awareness of God, it is much more likely that the relationship of slaves to their masters is to be governed by their reverence *for God* rather than human deference.

In the first century some slave masters were "kind and gentle" while others were "harsh" and beat their slaves unjustly (2:18-19). Although the social and economic circumstances of slaves were often satisfactory and in some cases better than those experienced by poorer people who were not slaves, their legal rights were minimal. Their relationships to those who dominated their lives were ambivalent at best: they could never be fully "at home" even in a benign master's household. Slaves lived in uneasy tension with the dominant society, as did all the Christians addressed in this letter. So even in the advice given to slaves a wider audience is in mind.

This becomes clear in 2:20b. Those who "do right," that is, God's will, as already noted in v. 15, may suffer for their actions, but they will find favor *(charis)* with God. This encouragement, which is given explicitly to slaves in this verse, is given to all Christians in 3:14 and 17 and in 4:19.

If slaves, like all Christians, suffer unjustly, they are following the example given by Christ, whose sufferings are referred to at some length in the highly rhetorical and poetic passage which follows. Several scholars have suggested that in 2:21b to 25 the author has incorporated an early Christian hymn. These verses are set out as a poem in the most widely used edition of the Greek text but not in most modern English translations. While some features of the text seem to support this theory, neither in form nor in content are these verses comparable to NT passages which more clearly originated as hymns: Phil 2:6-11, Col 1:15-20, and 1 Tim 3:16. In the latter passages there are only a few allusions to the OT, but phrases from several verses in Isaiah 53 are quoted in 2:21b-25. Since Isaiah 53 is quoted more extensively here than elsewhere in the NT, its prominence in later Christian meditation on the death of Christ is largely due to its use in these verses.

Although imitation of Christ's sufferings became a popular theme in the later Christian tradition, this is not being encouraged here. The sufferings of Christ are a model to be *followed*. The whole of 2:22 with its double reference to the sinlessness of Christ is almost an exact quotation of Isa 53:9. Hence the NRSV's use of quotation marks is wholly appropriate, even though (in contrast to 1:24; 2:6) there is no introductory phrase to indicate that Scripture is being cited here.

The use of verbs in the imperfect tense in 2:23 suggests that the hostility endured by Christ throughout his ministry, as well as during his final days, may be in view. The NRSV supplies the object *himself* to the verb "entrust" in the final clause of v. 23, but there is no object in the Greek. But Michaels 1988: 147 notes correctly that the immediate context makes it more likely that Jesus' enemies are the implied object here, just as they are in the two preceding clauses.

2:24 weaves together Isa 53:4, 11, and 12 in a profound comment on the significance of the sufferings of Christ. The conviction that Christ suffered so that we, having parted with our sins, might live for what is right, is reminiscent of, but not necessarily dependent on, Rom 6:11.

In the final verse in this subsection the apparent abrupt change of topic is the result of reflection on Isa 53:5b-6. The shepherd to whom the straying sheep return is Christ (cf. 5:10); yet again an OT reference to God is applied to Christ. The contrast between the readers' former condition as "sheep who *were* going astray" but have *now* returned to their shepherd recalls 2:10.

Wives and Husbands (3:1-7)

The adverb "similarly" (NRSV, "in the same way") is used twice in this passage (3:1, 7) to link the instructions to wives and to husbands to the preceding instructions to slaves in 2:18, and to all Christians in 2:13. In this way the conventional structure of the household code is retained in part, though less clearly than in Eph 5:21–6:9 and Col 3:18–4:1.

The advice to wives to accept the authority of their husbands has to be set in the context of the social circumstances of the day: women, including wives, were considered inferior to men. But this passage is not a general statement either about the status of women or about the relationship of wives to husbands. It is primarily concerned with the problem which arises when a Christian wife is married to an unbelieving husband. (The reverse problem did not normally arise, for in antiquity a wife was expected to adopt the religious beliefs of her husband.)

Wives are to accept the authority of their husbands so that the latter may be won over to the word, that is, to the Christian faith (3:1). They are to do this "without a word"; this does not mean that Christian wives are to remain totally silent, but rather that they are to win over their husbands without regularly speaking about their faith, which would be counterproductive. Their conduct is to be their witness, but it does include their reverence toward God (3:2, and see above on 2:18).

The advice given negatively in 3:3 and positively in v. 4 has many Jewish and Greco-Roman parallels. In v. 5 the example of "the holy women," the matriarchs of Israel, Sarah, Rebecca, Rachel, and Leah, is referred to, and in v. 6 the obedience of Sarah to Abraham is singled out as the model to follow. Christian wives are to "do good"; this is not a bland instruction, for in 1 Peter "doing good" means "doing the will of God," as in 2:15.

The advice to husbands in 3:7 is far from conventional. They are to respect the lesser physical strength of their wives ("the weaker sex"). More importantly, they are reminded that their wives are joint heirs of God's gift of grace that consists in life. In the society in which they live, wives may be considered to be inferior in all respects to men, but in God's eyes women and men are equal, for they experience his gifts equally. The failure of husbands to appreciate the radical nature of the difference between Christian and non-Christian attitudes to wives will have profound consequences: their prayers to God will be hindered and thus of no effect.

To All Christians (3:8-12)

Specific groups of Christians, slaves (2:18), wives (3:1), and husbands (3:7), are addressed in the preceding paragraphs. These instructions were introduced in 2:13-17 with general advice for all Christians; they are now followed by general advice for all Christians (3:8-12).

Whereas 3:8 is intended to foster good relationships within the Christian communities to which this letter is addressed, v. 9 marks the transition to concern for relationships between believers and unbelievers, a concern which will be expanded in 3:13-17 and 4:1-6. Most of the phrases in 3:8 and 9 have parallels in Rom 12:9-18, though literary dependence is less likely than independent use of a catechetical tradition. In Rom 12:14 and in 1 Pet 3:9 there is a clear, strong echo of the teaching of Jesus on love of enemies (Matt 5:44 = Luke 6:27).

In 3:10-12 Ps 34:12-16a is quoted. The variations in wording from the LXX probably indicate that the psalm is quoted from memory. The psalm is concerned with God's deliverance of his oppressed people, a theme of particular interest to the writer of 1 Peter. The final line of the quotation (3:12c), with its insistence that God will ultimately triumph over evil, would have encouraged the readers who, as the next section of the letter confirms (vv. 13-17), were well aware of the hostility of the society in which they lived.

Unjust Suffering (3:13-17)

The main theme of these verses is one of the central themes of the letter as a whole. At the beginning and again at the end of this section the writer emphasizes that while there is no merit in suffering justly as a result of evil deeds, unjust suffering may be blessed by God (3:14a); it may be part of God's plan (v. 17). This theme is developed by reference to Christ's suffering (v. 18), just as it is in 2:18-25.

Matt 5:10, "blessed are those who are persecuted for righteousness' sake," is reflected in 3:14a, but there is no indication that a saying of Jesus is being quoted. As in many other cases, sayings of Jesus seem to have been absorbed into the general catechetical tradition of the early church.

3:14b and 15a use phrases from Isa 8:12-13. The NRSV translation of v. 14b is a possible but awkward rendering of the Greek; the REB is preferable: "Have no fear of other people." The negative commands of v. 14b are balanced by the positive exhortation in v. 15a to consider Christ alone as holy ("sanctify Christ").

Some of the terms used in 3:15b and 16 suggest that Christians may expect to have to defend themselves in court. We know from the Roman governor Pliny's correspondence with the Emperor Trajan that a generation or so later this did happen to Christians in part of the geographical area to which 1 Peter was written. But the encouragement to give an account of Christian hope "to anyone who asks" suggests that the charges leveled at the readers are likely to have been informal rather than legal. Unlike members of many mystery religions and quasi-religious groups whose beliefs were closely guarded secrets, the readers are to be open about their Christian faith.

Christ's Proclamation to Imprisoned Spirits (3:18-22)

This passage is one of the most baffling in the NT; it has teased interpreters down through the centuries.

The unusual stylistic features of the Greek, the awkward links between some of the clauses, and the use (esp. in 3:19-20) of several themes without clear parallels elsewhere in the NT have led many scholars to suggest that earlier traditions have been adapted somewhat clumsily to the immediate context. Some have proposed that an early Christian hymn is quoted in part, or adapted radically, but theories of this kind have failed to win wider acceptance.

The following general lines of interpretation (with numerous variations) have been proposed: (i) the preaching by Christ, "in the Spirit" (or as pre-existent), through Noah to the "imprisoned" wicked generation which lived before the flood. On this interpretation there is no reference to Christ's descent into hell. While this explanation is at least plausible for 3:18-20, it cannot account readily for vv. 21-22 or for 4:6.

(ii) The "imprisoned spirits" in 3:18 (as in 4:6) are not alive as in (i), but Noah's generation in a place of punishment after death. The preaching of the risen and exalted Christ (3:18c and vv. 21c-22) to that wicked generation by means of a descent into hell is "a particular example of a much larger truth" (Selwyn 1947: 316; similarly Goppelt 1993: 258): no one of any generation is beyond the reach of salvation through Christ.

(iii) The crucified and risen Christ (3:18c) is not announcing salvation but final judgment to the imprisoned evil angels of the time of Noah (cf. Gen 6:1-6 and related later Jewish traditions). On this view, there is no "descent into hell" in 3:19 (and 4:6 is unrelated). Christ's proclamation is "an announcement . . . of his own triumph, as the result of his death and resurrection, over all rebellious spiritual forces (vv. 19, 22)" (Achtemeier 1996: 245). Christ's triumph over all forms of evil is an encouragement to believers under threat of unjust suffering.

On balance, (iii) is preferable. This reading relates 3:18-22 to the central themes of the whole letter and accounts for what is clearly intended to be the climax of the passage in v. 22b. It also takes seriously Michaels' important reminder (1988: 196) that these verses must not be interpreted in the light either of other NT passages (including 4:6) or of later Christian doctrine. For a fuller discussion of the interpretative problems and the main solutions which have been proposed, the major recent commentaries (Achtemeier 1996, Goppelt 1993, and Michaels 1988), the invaluable Essay I in Selwyn's classic commentary (1946: 314-62), and the monographs by Reicke 1946 and Dalton 1965 should be consulted.

Christian Conduct among Unbelievers (4:1-6)

These verses are intended to encourage Christians who face unjust suffering. The opening verse, which links this section closely to 3:13-22, underlines the point made in 3:16, 18: Christians must arm themselves as if for war with the same disposition as Christ, who also suffered unjustly. Those who do so will have "finished with sin." Their lives will no longer be dominated by "human desires" (4:2); the context confirms that this is a reference to the norms of the society in which they live.

As in 2:9b and 10 (cf. "new birth" in 1:3), the pattern of their lives before they became Christians is contrasted with their present conduct; whereas they once behaved like Gentiles, they do so "no longer." The short catalogue of vices to be avoided (4:3) has parallels in both Jewish and Greco-Roman writings, but here the polemic has a distinctive edge. Idolatry is the climax to which the list of vices leads, and the reason why Christians can "no longer join with them" (NRSV), or, better, "no longer associate closely with them" (v. 4a). The refusal of Christians to conform causes acute surprise, "and so they blaspheme" (v. 4b). The latter phrase may mean, as in the NRSV footnote, "malign you"; more probably it means "blaspheme God," whose will Christians seek to do.

The lines between the recipients of this letter and the surrounding society are drawn sharply. It was not so much what Christians did or said which caused offense, but what they refused to do: that is, to join in the social and religious activities which were the very fabric of society. Surprise led to suspicion, which led in turn to hostility and eventually persecution. Hence the reminder in 4:5 that nonbelievers will one day have to face final judgment would have been a strong encouragement to believers to persevere.

How does 4:6 relate to this theme? Who proclaimed the gospel, and when? Who are "the dead"? This verse is as baffling as 3:19; the Greek is much more terse and enigmatic than most modern translations imply.

If "the dead" to whom the gospel has been proclaimed are the dead of 4:5, that is, all the dead who will face final judgment, then it is natural to assume that the verse refers to Christ's proclamation of the gospel to all who died prior to his coming. The dead are then identified with "the spirits in prison" of 3:19 to whom Christ preached. However, this view, which has been the dominant interpretation until recently, has been strongly criticized by several writers, for it carries two implications which are foreign to the NT as a whole: "the dead" are disembodied souls in Hades; they have the possibility of responding positively to Christ's proclamation of the gospel after death.

A radically different interpretation proposed by Dalton 1965 has gained some support. On this view, the verse should not be linked closely with 3:19; it refers to Christians who have died after their acceptance of the proclamation of the gospel. Although they have been judged according to human standards during their lifetimes, they will be vindicated by God in the final judgment. The strength of this interpretation is that it allows 4:6 to form the climax of the preceding sections: unjust suffering which Christians have experienced, or are now facing, will not be in vain. Its weakness is that a reference to the final judgment of "all the dead" in v. 5 is juxtaposed awkwardly with the reference in v. 6 to Christians who have died.

Conduct among Believers (4:7-11)

These verses conclude the letter's central section, which begins at 2:11. Whereas most of the preceding sections were concerned with the relationship of believers to the non-Christian society in which they lived, these verses focus on relationships within the community. Some points are developed in the closing sections of the letter which follow. Many have parallels in other NT letters, but direct literary dependence is unlikely: the writer is drawing on shared early Christian catechetical traditions.

All the instructions in these verses are to be understood in the light of the opening statement, "the end of all things is near" (NRSV). This translation fails to bring out clearly the precise nuance of the Greek: the end times are so close that they influence all aspects of present community life. The NRSV footnote, "is at hand," or the REB, "the end of all things is upon us," are preferable translations.

"Love covers a multitude of sins" (4:8) is still used as a proverb today, as it was when 1 Peter was written. Whose sins are "covered," the one who shows love for others or those who are loved? The proverb, like the parables of Jesus, is ambivalent and open-ended in order to encourage reflection. "The maxim recalls the circular movement between the love we encounter and the love we pass on, which, according to the Jesus tradition, goes forth from God (Mk. 11:25; Mt. 6:14f.; 18:35)" (Goppelt 1993: 298-99).

One wonders what little local difficulties lie behind the encouragement to extend hospitality to others "without grumbling" (4:9). In scattered Christian communities sharply at odds with the surrounding society, hospitality was even more important than it was in ancient society generally; it was an essential practical expression of "maintaining constant love for one another," whether for local or for traveling Christians (v. 8).

4:10 and 11 encourage believers to use the gift *(charisma)* given by God to serve others. These two verses are remarkably similar in theme to 1 Cor 12:4-11, but once again literary dependence is unlikely. In 1 Corinthians 12 the variety of gifts bestowed on believers are activated by the Spirit, whereas here (as in Rom 12:6) the gifts are bestowed by the grace of God.

The concluding doxology is probably addressed to God (as is usually the case elsewhere in the NT), though "to him" could refer to the immediately preceding phrase, that is, to Jesus Christ.

Concluding Exhortations (4:12–5:11)

Christian Suffering (4:12-19)

4:12 marks the beginning of the final section of the letter. It opens, as does the beginning of the lengthy central section, 2:11–4:10, with a direct affectionate address to the recipients. The final paragraphs of the letter underline several earlier themes, but, as we shall see, some new themes are introduced.

Some writers have claimed that in contrast to the earlier more general references to impending persecution, 4:12 refers to persecution now in progress; perhaps two originally separate letters have been merged to form what we now know as 1 Peter. Recent commentators, however, have abandoned such theories, noting that the "fiery ordeal" of v. 12a should be understood in the light of biblical and Qumran evidence as "a purifying fire." It is not a new situation but an enduring condition: since Christians have been called by God to suffer unjustly (2:21), the recipients' present experiences are "not something strange."

There have been several references earlier in the letter to Christians sharing Christ's suffering (2:21; 3:18; 4:1), but without the reference in 4:13 to rejoicing in the here and now, and the even greater joy promised for the future. Vv. 13 and 14 recall Matt 5:11-12 = Luke 6:22-23, though only the words "rejoice," "shout for joy," "reviled," and "blessed" are common to both passages.

Once again a contrast is drawn between suffering for wrongdoing and unjust suffering "as a Christian" (4:15 and 16; cf. 2:20 and 3:17). In 4:15 the fourth word in the list of kinds of people to be avoided is unknown in biblical or secular Greek (cf. BAGD), hence "a mischief maker" (NRSV) is no more than an intelligent guess. The word "Christian" (v. 16a) is one of only three uses in the NT (cf. Acts 11:26 and 26:28); it was probably a nickname first used by opponents before it eventually became a self-designation of followers of Jesus.

4:17 and 18 refer to the impending final judgment which will be experienced first of all by God's own people and then more harshly by unbelievers. In v. 18 Prov 11:31 is quoted almost verbatim from the LXX, but there is no introductory phrase to indicate that Scripture is being cited. 4:19 underlines an earlier point (cf. 2:15; 3:17; 4:2): the suffering being experienced by Christians "will inevitably result from following God's ways rather than those of secular society" (Achtemeier 1996: 318). In the Greek, as in the NRSV, "doing good" is the climax of this section; this is appropriate since this is such a strong emphasis throughout the letter (cf. 2:15, 20; 3:6, 17).

Christian Leaders (5:1-5)

Who are "the elders" addressed in these verses? The exhortations given to them are also relevant ("in the same way") to "you who are younger" (5:5a). So "the elders" are older men. Vv. 2-4 refer to their responsibilities as leaders but do not suggest that there was an office of elder in the Christian communities to which 1 Peter was addressed. This is in line with the evidence of the earliest Christian writings: "the elders are those who bear a title of honour, not of office" (Campbell 1994: 246 *et passim*).

The writer identifies himself as an elder and "a witness of the sufferings of Christ." Does this suggest that the writer is Peter himself? Since the Gospel traditions attest unanimously that Peter was not an eyewitness of the sufferings of Christ, the phrase must refer to "witness" in a more general sense; hence this verse neither supports nor rules out Petrine authorship.

The encouragement to "tend the flock of God" in 5:2 has deep biblical roots in OT traditions in which God is the shepherd who tends his people Israel. In vv. 2b and 3 there is a threefold antithetical pattern: the elders are *not* to exercise oversight in that way *but* in this way. In the NT Christ is referred to as "the chief shepherd" only in v. 4 and in Heb 13:20. As shepherds of their flocks, the elders are continuing the ministry of their chief shepherd.

5:5 addresses a second specific group, "those who are younger," and then exhorts all the recipients of this letter to be humble by using Prov 3:34, though once again there is no indication in the Greek that Scripture is being cited.

The God of All Grace Will Triumph (5:6-11)

"Humble yourselves" is not merely a general encouragement to adopt humility; it refers to the appropriate response "to the pressures brought by society" (Goppelt 1993: 357). The pattern of "humility–exaltation" is found in several early Christian traditions (e.g., Matt 23:12; Luke 14:11; Phil 2:8-9). Although 5:7 has often been taken by Christians to refer to all kinds of anxieties, from the letter as a whole we may infer that the hostility of the surrounding society was the recipients' primary concern.

The NRSV translation of 5:8a is too bland. "Be on the alert! Wake up!" (REB) is better. These verbs are used elsewhere in the NT in a clear eschatological sense (e.g., Mark 13:35, 37; 1 Thess 5:6, 8), and this is surely the case here. While the adversary who is threatening believers like a lion "is supernatural . . . his agents are to be thought of here as the human powers who do the bidding of the devil in persecuting Christians" (Achtemeier 1996: 541 n. 66).

There is no historical evidence which suggests that 5:9b is a reference to the outbreak of an official general persecution of Christians. The recipients are being urged to take heart from the fact that they are not alone in experiencing unjust suffering.

5:10 and 11 assure the believers that the evil one will not have the last word: four verbs are used at the end of v. 10 to refer to the actions of God on behalf of beleaguered Christians. God will triumph, hence the doxology of v. 11 (cf. 4:11).

The Close of the Letter (5:12-14)

The final verses are similar in structure and theme to the endings of Paul's letters. Silvanus is probably being commended as the bearer of the letter to the scattered communities of 1:1, though some writers take this as a reference to his role in its composition. Silvanus may be the co-worker referred to by Paul in several of his letters — the Silas of Acts, though this identification is by no means certain.

5:12b is an apt summary of the writer's primary intention: to encourage his hard-pressed readers by means of his "brief" letter — "brief" is merely conventional. The final clauses of this verse are not clear, but the writer is probably confirming that his whole letter is "true grace from God" (Michaels 1988: 309).

Who is sending greetings to the recipients of 1 Peter (5:13)? The Greek simply says, "She who is in Babylon" (as in the NRSV footnote). This could be the writer's wife, perhaps even Peter's wife (cf. 1 Cor 9:5). But the NRSV main text is preferable: "Your sister church sends greetings." "My son Mark" may be the John Mark mentioned in some of Paul's letters and in Acts, but since Mark was a common name, the Mark referred to here could be either the writer's biological son or his "son" in the faith.

The letter is not being sent from Babylon in Mesopotamia, for this famous city was in ruins in the first century. In several Jewish writings from this period "Babylon" refers to Rome, probably because Babylon, like Rome, had hounded God's people. The use of Babylon here is particularly apt: the writer indicates that his own Christian community in Babylon-Rome, like the recipients, is "in exile" (cf. 1:1).

The "kiss of love" recalls the "holy kiss" referred to at the end of four of Paul's letters (Rom 16:16; 1 Cor 16:20; 2 Cor 13:12; 1 Thess 5:26). Kissing was normally confined to family and close friends, so the final exhortation of this letter encourages the recipients to respect fellow members of the Christian family as if they were members of their own families.

Bibliography. Commentaries. Achtemeier, P. 1996, *1 Peter,* Hermeneia, Minneapolis: Fortress • Beare, F. W. 3d ed. 1970, *The First Epistle of Peter: The Greek Text with Introduction and Notes,* Oxford: Blackwell • Best, E. 1971, *1 Peter,* NCB, London: Oliphants • Davids, P. H. 1990, *The First Epistle of Peter,* NICNT, Grand Rapids: Eerdmans • Elliott, J. H. 2000, *1 Peter,* AB 37B, New York: Doubleday • Goppelt, L. 1993, *A Commentary on 1 Peter* (ET of the 1978 German edition, ed. J. A. Alsup, Grand Rapids: Eerdmans • Kelly, J. N. D. 1969, *A Commentary on the Epistles of Peter and of Jude,* London: Black • Michaels, J. R. 1988, *1 Peter,* WBC, Waco: Word • Selwyn, E. G. 1947, *The First Epistle of Peter,* London: Macmillan.

Studies. Balch, D. L. 1981, *Let Wives be Submissive: The Domestic Code in 1 Peter,* Chico: Scholars • Best, E. 1970, "I Peter and the Gospel Tradition," *NTS* 16:95-113 • Campbell, R. A. 1994, *The Elders: Seniority within Earliest Christianity,* Edinburgh: T. & T. Clark • Dalton, W. J. 1965 (2d ed. 1989), *Christ's Proclamation to the Spirits: A Study of I Peter 3:18–4:6,* Rome: Pontifical Biblical Institute • Elliott, J. H. 1966, *The Elect and the Holy: An Exegetical Examination of I Peter 2:4-10,* Leiden: Brill • Elliott, J. H. 1981, *A Home for the Homeless: A Sociological Exegesis of I Peter, Its Situation and Strategy,* Philadelphia: Fortress • Gundry, R. H. 1967, "*Verba Christi* in I Peter," *NTS* 13:336-50 • Reicke, B. 1946, *The Disobedient Spirits and Christian Baptism: A Study of 1 Pet. iii.19 and Its Context,* Copenhagen: Munksgaard.

2 Peter

Scot McKnight

INTRODUCTION

2 Peter is the last will and testament of the apostle Peter, but was probably composed within two decades after his death. No book in the Bible had more difficulty establishing itself in the canon. As late as Eusebius (d. 371) some did not consider 2 Peter to be from the Apostle or part of the canon (*Hist. Eccl.* 3.3.1-4); doubts continued for centuries (e.g., Calvin and Luther). Even if (1) early Christians rejected pseudonymous letters, (2) Peter's name begins the letter (2 Pet 1:1-2), and (3) Petrine reminscences do appear (1:16-18; cf. 3:15), the letter is actually in the form of an ancient testament, a literary form consistently connected with pseudonymity (Bauckham). This literary form was well known in the first century and, if noticed, would have led readers to suspect pseudonymity. (For other early testaments, cf. Genesis 49; Deuteronomy 31–33; Matthew 24–25; John 14–16; Acts 20:17-34; 2 Timothy; *2 Baruch* 78–86; *Testaments of the Twelve Patriarchs*.)

There is clear evidence that 2 Peter is either dependent on Jude or on a later revision of a tradition used by the author of Jude and then by the author of 2 Peter. That 2 Peter and Jude reveal some striking similarities (cf. 2 Pet 2:1-18 with Jude 4-16; 2 Pet 3:2-3 with Jude 17-18; 2 Pet 3:13-14, 18 with Jude 24-25; 2 Pet 1:5 with Jude 3; 2 Pet 1:1-2 with Jude 1-2; 2 Pet 1:12 with Jude 5; and 2 Pet 3:13-14, 18 with Jude 24-25) is not the whole story: these passages contain highly unusual terms and expressions and make dependence likely. Though the evidence is not as clear as it is in the Synoptic Gospels, a majority of scholars think 2 Peter is a reapplication of Jude (Elliott; Meade; Neyrey; Watson).

A few items in 2 Peter indicate that this "epistolary testament" was put together after the death of Peter. 2 Pet 3:4 indicates that (a) sufficient time had elapsed for doubts to arise about the parousia, suggesting a decade or two after the destruction of Jerusalem in AD 70, an event around which a large number of Jesus' prophecies centered and after which some of the early churches may well have expected the coming of the Son of Man (cf. Matt 10:23; 24:29-31; in 1 Pet 4:7 imminent expectation still dominates the horizon; cf. also 1:13; 4:17-19), and that (b) the first generation of Christians (here called "the fathers") had already died. Assuming liberally that the first "fathers" lived seventy years, we can infer that the fathers would have died by AD 80. The crisis created by the destruction of Jerusalem and the death of the apostles was no doubt serious. 2 Peter attempts to come to terms with this crisis.

Finally, the style, grammar, and theological concerns of 2 Peter are at some remove from those of 1 Peter. The vocabulary is unusual, the style of the letter is characterized by an exaggerated rhetoric and almost grotesque use of redundancy, and its theology diverges from that of 1 Peter in its concerns, center, and orientation (Elliott; Bauckham). The letter probably emerges from a Hellenistic Jewish context, possibly in Asia (Neyrey: 118-20; Webb), while 1 Peter breathes a different atmosphere. The allusion to Paul's "scriptural writings" (cf. 3:15-16) is also more probable in the later part of the first century. It is then reasonable to think that an associate of Peter later put down "Petrine" thoughts in an attempt to speak apostolically to a time that was subapostolic (Bauckham, Meade). In what follows we shall refer to the author as the "Apostle," meaning by this only that the author had an association with Peter.

The author of 2 Peter speaks prophetically against recent trends in some churches. His concerns are (1) a denial of the parousia and skepticism over the return of Christ (cf. 1:16-18; 3:4, 5-10) and (2) an ethical permissiveness not unlike that of Epicureanism (cf. 2:2, 10, 13, 18, 19-22; 3:2, 15-16; see esp. Neyrey: 122-28). The false teachers (2:1) that propagate these two ideas are causing division (2:1-3, 14, 18) and may well claim special, Spirit-inspired interpretation for their views (1:20-21; Meade: 181-83). It is possible that their views contained some heterodox beliefs about Jesus Christ (cf. 2:1, 10), and they seem to have questioned the likelihood of the final judgment (2:3-10). We must bear in mind, however, that this picture of the opponents has been drawn by the author and is in part rhetorical.

Peter's message in this context is that his readers should: (1) hold fast to the ancient faith taught since the days of the apostles (1:12-21; 3:1-2), (2) live a life of holiness and love (1:3-11; 3:11-18), and (3) be aware of the consequences of those who have repudiated the ways of God (2:1-22).

Outline: in general, the Apostle begins his letter with a typical ancient greeting formula (1:1-2), an introduction (1:3-15) *(exordium)* with both theme (1:3-11) and occasion (1:12-15), the argument itself (1:16–3:13) *(probatio),* and a conclusion (3:14-18) (*peroratio;* Watson). The following will serve as a convenient guide to the main logical sections:

1. Reply to Denial of the Parousia (1:16-18),
2. Reply to Denial of Divine Origin of Old Testament Prophecies (1:19-21),
3. Warning of False Teachers (2:1-3a),
4. Reply to Denial of Final Judgment (2:3b-10a),
5. Denunciation of the Unrighteous (2:10b-22),
6. Reply to Denial of the Return (3:1-13).

COMMENTARY

Greeting (1:1-2)

The Apostle's greeting here follows ancient custom (see White), though with clear Christian innovations. In particular, Peter serves "Jesus Christ," the recipients have a "faith . . . through the righteousness of our God and Savior Jesus Christ," and their grace and peace are "in the knowledge of God and Jesus Christ our Lord." Greetings often sound important notes that can only be heard fully when the letter has been completely read. These include (1) the apostolic connection of the letter (cf. 1:15, 19-21; 3:1-2, 15-16), (2) the importance of a faith that is "as precious as ours" (cf. 1:5-11), and (3) the value the Apostle places on true knowledge of the Savior (cf. 1:12-15, 20-21; 2:1-3a, 12, 20-22; 3:1-13, 18).

"Simeon Peter" forms a surprising combination of names. The terms "servant and apostle" are more important: (1) "servant," though in our society reflecting humility, speaks of the Apostle's exalted position (cf. Moses [Deut 34:5], Samuel [1 Sam 3:9-10], and David [2 Sam 3:18]), and (2) "apostle" evokes his special call (Matt 10:2-4) and tradition-bearing status. The Apostle's audience is comprised of "those who have received a faith as precious as ours," that is, those ordinary Christians whose faith is the same as the Apostle's (Bauckham: 167), and they have this faith either "*in* the righteousness" or "*through* the righteousness" of Jesus Christ. Because there is only one article (before "God"), it is most likely that the Apostle calls Jesus Christ "God and Savior" here (cf. 1:11; 3:18; cf. elsewhere at John 1:1; 20:28; Rom 9:5; Titus 2:13; Heb 1:8-9; Bauckham: 168-69).

Introduction (1:3-15) *(Exordium)*

The Apostle's introduction contains both a clear statement of its theme (1:3-11) and a clarification of this theme's importance in light of the situation (vv. 12-15).

Theme (1:3-11)

To find the Apostle's central theme we need to go to the end of this section and move backward: he wants his readers to enter into the eternal kingdom (1:11), but to do that they must remain faithful to their calling (v. 10) and remember their forgiveness (v. 9). Faithfulness results from the continual development of the virtues (vv. 5-8). But these virtues come from God's own nature, which he shares with believers through knowledge of God (vv. 3-4).

The Apostle begins with their *divine provision* (1:3-4). The Apostle knows no limitations to God's provision: "everything" pertaining to "life and godliness" has been granted by divine power, and this giftedness is mediated through "knowledge." Knowledge here, however, transcends mastery of facts and philosophical knowledge; rather, as 1:10-12 will make clear (cf. 1:12-15, 20-21; 2:1-3a, 12, 20-22; 3:1-13, 18), this knowledge is rooted in the apostolic tradition. Such a knowledge effectively transmits the "precious and very great promises" which enable the believers (1), negatively, to "escape" the sinfulness of their world and (2), positively, to become "participants of the divine nature." The Apostle evidently has in mind (1) those qualities of God that become attributes of his people and so permit them to ward off the evil world, (2) a mystical ecstasy through which human beings experience the divine state of being (Philo *Quaest. Exod.* 2:29), or more probably (3) the attainment of immortality after death as a result of faithfulness (4 Macc 18:3) (Bauckham: 179-82).

Because God has provided them with all they need for life and godliness, believers must *develop the disciplines associated with virtue* (1:5-9). In chain-link fashion, each virtue is supported by the next, with love as the climactic virtue. The Apostle baptizes these conventional Hellenistic philosophical terms into Christian morals by beginning with faith and ending with love. To this list are added two warnings: (1) that if his readers develop these virtues ("are yours and are increasing among you"), they will be preserved from ineffectiveness in the knowledge of the Lord Jesus Christ, and (2) that those who neglect development in these virtues have long forgotten that God has forgiven them in order that they should reflect his nature (1:3-4).

The *goal* of the Apostle's exhortation is that his readers may inherit the eternal kingdom (1:10-11). They are to "confirm their call," that is, to establish themselves in the apostolic tradition, to work out the knowledge of God and the Lord Jesus Christ by developing the virtues that lead to love. In so conforming to the apostolic tradition, they will enter into the "eternal kingdom."

Situation (1:12-15)

As a result of this section, readers in the ancient world would have recognized the letter as a testament from an authoritative figure since the letter reveals the characteristic motif (esp. Bauckham).

The Apostle begins with a *concession:* though these recipients already know these things, they need to be reminded again. "I intend" or, better yet, "I am going to" enhances the permanence of the reminder. In this letter "reminding" (cf. 1:13, 15; 3:1, 2, along with the need not to "forget" in 3:5, 8) and "established" (cf. 2:14; 3:16, 17; see also Rom 16:25; 1 Pet 5:10) have a distinct emphasis because of the testamentary nature of the communication. Consequently, an emphasis is given to "truth," a term that was constantly used in early Christian circles for the total compass of the Christian message and ethic (cf. Gal 2:5, 14; Col 1:5; 2 Tim 2:15; Jas 1:18).

Knowing that he is about to die, the Apostle claims that it is "right" (or "just") that he "refresh your memory" (1:14). Though quite typical in Platonic thought, the Apostle's use of "tent" as a metaphor for "body" was found in Christian circles as well (2 Cor 5:1-4); "tent" is used here to emphasize the transitoriness of earthly existence in comparison with the eternal state. Many scholars have pointed to John 21:18-19 as the source of Peter's knowledge (Bauckham: 200-201). Knowledge of the imminence of one's death is characteristic of ancient testaments (cf. Deut 31:2, 14, 16; Joshua 24; Acts 10:25; 2 Tim 4:6; see also John 13–17).

This reminder has a *purpose* (1:15): the Apostle wants his readers to recall his teachings and the apostolic truth when he is gone. Some scholars, however, have contended that the future tense of 1:15 ("I will make every effort . . .") refers to something after this letter, perhaps even the Gospel of Mark. But a testamentary tradition fits well here with the use of the future tense since, by nature, that sort of letter will emphasize what is to be known and done when the authoritative figure is gone (seen in the Jewish expression "my departure"; lit. "my exodus"; cf. Luke 9:31).

Argument (1:16–3:13) *(Probatio)*

At this point the Apostle begins the argument (1:16–3:13; the *probatio*). In this section he deals with various problems, beginning with a denial of the parousia (1:16-18) and continuing with responses to various situations and accusations.

Reply to the Denial of the Parousia (1:16-18)

As 3:4 states, the opponents charged the Christians with mythical beliefs by asking, "Where is the promise of his coming?" (cf. also *2 Clem.* 13:3). What the apostles divulged was the "power and coming," or "powerful coming," of our Lord Jesus Christ (cf. Mark 9:1).

In rhetorical style (Neyrey: 175-76) the Apostle counters that the apostles did not follow myths at all; in fact, they witnessed an event that had an integral connection to the enthronement of Jesus by his Father. The opponents use sharp words to describe what they perceive to be myths: "cleverly devised" (see the display of evidence in Neyrey: 175). In good rhetorical style, the Apostle rebuts the argument by appeal to (1) the eyewitness testimony and (2) an irrefutable event, the transfiguration (Neyrey: 170-71). In its more colloquial sense "eyewitness" is used of someone who has simply seen something for oneself (cf. 1 Pet 2:12; 3:2) rather than for a witness to some esoteric experience.

"His majesty" (1:16) is clarified in v. 17: the Apostle describes the transfiguration found in early Christian traditions (cf. Mark 9:2-8) but makes a different use of its significance. While the Synoptic tradition focuses on this event as foreshadowing the vindication of the rejected Messiah (cf. Mark 8:27–9:1), the Apostle uses it to convince his readers that the transfiguration was the initial revelation of the Son's enthronement as King and Judge. The parousia is defended here by the Apostle in his appeal to the transfiguration: if the latter is a fact, then surely the parousia is also a fact.

On the "holy mountain" Jesus received from the Father "honor and glory" (cf. 1 Pet 1:7). These terms together define the Father's approval (here spoken of in periphrasis: "when that voice was conveyed," "Majestic Glory") of the Son before his special followers. More importantly, the Septuagint of Ps 8:6 (ET 8:5) uses these same terms for the glorification of the son of man; and this psalm was interpreted messianically in Judaism to describe the enthronement of the Messiah. In our context the enthronement scene is anticipated in the transfiguration; in Heb 2:9 its connection is with the resurrection.

The "Majestic Glory" says, "This is my Son, my Beloved, with whom I am well pleased" (Bauckham: 218). Many have traced the roots of this statement to the enthronement psalm (Psalm 2) since the use of "holy mountain" in both 2 Pet 1:18 and Ps 2:6 confirms such a parallel. However, closer inspection of the evidence suggests that Isa 42:1 reveals even closer parallels: both "my Beloved" and "with whom I am well pleased" have direct parallels in our verse. In addition, Ps 2:7 uses "You are my son," while 2 Pet 1:17 has "This is my Son," a parallel more fitting with Isa 42:1.

The voice from heaven is typical for apocalyptic revelations like this one (cf. Dan 4:31; Rev 10:4, 8; 11:12; 14:13). Some have argued that "holy mountain" must be specific: suggestions include Mt. Sinai, Mt. Zion, and the mount on which Jesus taught (Matthew 5–7). However, it makes more sense to see here the actual mountain on which Jesus was transfigured, which, though technically not "the holy mountain" (for that would be Zion), became holy when God revealed the future glory and destiny of his Son here.

Reply to Denial of the Divine Origins of Prophecy (1:19-21)

In addition, the same opponents accuse the Christians of having a set of scriptures before them that were then subjected to self-induced interpretations. The vision, in other words, may have been divine, but the interpretation was human. The Apostle counters (1:19-21) that both the vision and the interpretation are from God and therefore provide light for a dark world.

This message about Jesus' return as Judge and King is even more sure than the eyewitnesses attest; it is also confirmed by the prophecies of the OT. That is, since God is the author of Scripture (1:20-21), since Jesus was transfigured as a prolepsis for the parousia (vv. 16-18), and since there were apostolic witnesses of the event (v. 16), the prediction of Jesus' return as Judge and King is all the more sure.

But what is this "prophetic message" specifically? Bauckham has listed six possibilities: (1) OT messianic texts, (2) the entire OT understood messianically, (3) a single OT prophecy (e.g., Num 24:17; Dan 7:13-14), (4) both OT and NT prophecies, (5) the section of 2 Peter from 1:20 to 2:19, or (6) the transfiguration understood prophetically as predicting the parousia (Bauckham: 224). Since the main topic is the parousia and the focus is especially on the final judgment and royal rule of Christ in the kingdom (cf. 2 Pet 3:10-11, 15-16), we are probably more correct to think here of interpretation (2) and to see here the Apostle appealing to the many OT prophecies that can be applied to the work of Christ. Dan 7:13-14 would be but one such passage.

Because this message is so sure, the Apostle exhorts his readers to "be attentive." The world is often likened morally to a "dark place" (cf. John 1:5; Eph 6:12; 1 Thess 5:4-5), and God's will to a "lamp" (cf. Ps 119:105; Matt 5:13-16). For the end of history, the Apostle uses an early Christian favorite: "day." Whether we look to Jesus (Matt

24:36, 42, 50; 25:13) or to an earlier apostolic witness (Rom 13:12), "day" was a term used for the final day, when God judges (2 Pet 2:9; 3:7), dissolves the earth's elements (3:10, 12), and ushers in the eternal state (3:18). That "day" will dawn like the rising of a "star," a term which here must refer to the parousia of Christ (cf. Num 24:17).

The recipients need to understand the origins of prophecy: it does not derive from human intuition; rather, God spoke through his Holy Spirit to prophets and then that same Spirit interpreted the meaning of God's revelations. The evidence from Philo and other Hellenistic Jewish and Christian sources suggests that the Apostle is not concerned with the *interpretation* of prophecy but with the *origins* of prophecy. To give one example, Philo says: "For a prophet (being a spokesman) has no utterance of his own, but all his utterances came from elsewhere, the echoes of another's voice" (*Her.?* 259, Loeb). If this evidence represents the Apostle's context (see Bauckham: 229-30), then he is saying here that prophecy does not derive from a prophet's inspired imagination but from God.

The negation of 1:20 is explained further in v. 21: prophecies do not come about by a human's will; rather, they come when "men and women are moved by the Holy Spirit." The Apostle uses here the word *pherein* ("to carry") for both the negative (v. 21a) and the positive (v. 21b). Prophets are blown forward by the forces of God's Spirit, who grants them both revelation and explanation (see Jer 20:7-12; Amos 3:7-8).

Warning of False Teachers (2:1-3a)

A characteristic of ancient testaments was the prediction and warning of the rise of false teachers. The author changes the topic from OT prophecy as confirmation to false prophets and teachers artfully. He moves from OT prophecy to the false prophets of his time, who can be reasonably compared to contemporary false teachers. The contrast between truth-bearing apostles and false teachers/false prophets could hardly be more clear (see Bauckham: 236).

The Apostle begins with a *declaration* about false prophets (2:1a). A false prophet (Deut 18:20) is one who either claims to utter a word of God without divine authorization or who utters a word of God in the name of other gods (cf. Jer 5:31). Thus, false prophets could be false either in their *claims* to be vehicles of God's communication or in the *content* of what they claimed as God's word (see Neyrey: 190; Bauckham: 238).

The *activity* of these false teachers includes (1) secretly bringing in destructive opinions and (2) denying the Master of redemption (2:1b). First, one can think either of secretly sneaking into the Christian communities for the purpose of proselytism or division or of some kind of internal deceitfulness that gradually leads people astray (Neyrey: 190). Behind "opinions" is the Greek word *hairesis,* which can mean nothing more than a school of thought (Josephus's use for the Essenes, Sadducees, and Pharisees; *J.W.* 2.118) but can also be used to denote false teachings that lead to splinter heretical movements and sectarian formations (e.g., 1 Cor 11:18-19; Gal 5:20). Final destruction preoccupies the author, who sometimes uses graphic language to describe it (cf. 2:4-10, 17, 19-20; 3:7, 10, 11-12).

Second, the false teachers deny the Master of redemption. This denial could have to do with central truths, such as the resurrection (cf. 1 Corinthians 15) or final judgment, or it could entail living contrary to the Torah or apostolic traditions. While evidence can be found to support the first view (e.g., 1:16; 2:1), in this case the Apostle more likely has in mind sinful practice, for 2:2 goes on to speak in moral rather than doctrinal categories. In using "who bought them," the Apostle assumes the language of redemption, which is the only reflection on the way Jesus saves in this letter.

The *effects* of these false teachers concern the Apostle most (2:2-3a). Because their secretive activities are so effective, many will follow (cf. 3:3-4) them in "their licentious ways" (2:2a). This style of life has been permanently memorialized on countless artifacts from the Greco-Roman world (see Lissarrague). God's name was dishonored, or maligned, whenever he did not obtain the credit and honor he rightfully deserved; this was seen most especially when his people lived in sin and suffered punishment at the hands of foreign nations. (An allusion to Isa 52:5 is almost certain.) 1 Peter develops this theme in 2:11–3:12, especially in 2:12, 17, 19-20; 3:2. While in 1 Peter the emphasis seems to be on the honor that comes through obedience, in 2 Peter the reverse is the case: it highlights the dishonor that comes through sin.

What is maligned here is the "way of truth." "Way," of course, was a favorite early Christian term for the truth and practices of those who had committed themselves to Jesus as Messiah (cf. Acts 9:2; 19:19, 23; 22:4; 24:14, 24; 1QS 3:13–4:26; 9:17-18; 10:20-21; *Did.* 1:1-2). While doctrine was certainly involved, "way" normally connoted an ethical orientation (cf. Jas 5:19-20), and this moral orientation was deeply fixed in the faith of the early Christians (Kelly: 328).

Returning to the theme of the motives of the false teachers, the Apostle accuses them of "greed" (2:3a). Early Christian authorities warned church leaders about this (1 Pet 5:2; cf. Matt 10:9-10; Acts 20:33-34; 1 Tim 3:3; Titus 1:7; *Did.* 11:12). Greed on the part of these false teachers led them to "exploit" Christians with "deceptive words."

Reply to the Denial of a Final Judgment (2:3b-10a)

A warning about the rise of false teachers leads to a prediction of their final condemnation. Since the opponents deny that there is a final judgment, however, the Apostle's warning is first a subtle general one (2:3b) and then a proof or defense of a final judgment (vv. 4-10a). But, unlike Jude 6-8 (which has several significant parallels with 2 Pet 2:3b-10a; note: angels, chains, deep darkness, judgment, Sodom and Gomorrah, and blasphemy; see Neyrey: 197-99), the Apostle focuses not on the final condemnation but on God's capacity to deliver.

The *general warning* (2:3b) refutes the opposition by denying their insinuations that God's judgment has been "idle" and "sleeping." The concern is not that God is "idle" or "asleep" but that he is not doing anything about judgment, especially in light of the timetable of some early Christian thinking. In fact, the Apostle informs his readers, the coming, imminent judgment was foreshadowed in analogous events "long ago." That is, as he will bring out in v. 6 (see the words "an example"), the judgments of God on the fallen angels (v. 4), the ancient world (v. 5), and Sodom and Gomorrah (v. 6) each foretell the final act of God against his enemies.

The Apostle selects three judgments as analogous to what he predicts will happen to the false teachers. The first, drawn from a strange collocation of ancient Jewish and Christian ideas about both sinful humans and angels from diverse texts (cf. Gen 6:1-4; *1 Enoch* 6–19; 21; 86–88; 106; 1 Pet 3:18-22; Jude 6) mixed with the Greek myth about the Titans (cf. Josephus *Ant.* 1.73), brings out the analogy between the false teachers and the fallen angels, sometimes called the Watchers (esp. in *1 Enoch*). Like those fallen angels who were thrown into Tartarus where they were chained in deep darkness, the false teachers will be damned if they continue in their ways. In contrast to 1 Pet 3:19, where the place of binding was above the earth in some sort of second heaven, here the idea appears to be that the fallen angels are in the lower regions of the underworld.

The first judgment the Apostle mentions was general; the second and third typify judgment by water (2:5) and then by fire (v. 6). The archetypal flood of Genesis 6 became fluidly connected with the final judgment in Jewish and Christian traditions (cf. *1 Enoch* 1–16; *Sib. Or.* 1:150-375; 1QH 10:35-36; Matt 24:37-39). But the Apostle's concern is not just with the punishing dimension of the flood, for God "saved Noah" through the flood. It is possible that "eight" is symbolic (Bauckham: 250). In fact, Noah was a "herald of righteousness" (cf. 1 Pet 3:18, where the ascending Christ is the "herald"; cf. *Sib. Or.* 1:148-98; *1 Clem.* 7:6; 9:4).

The third example of judgment is found in the Genesis tradition about Sodom and Gomorrah (Genesis 19; Bauckham: 251-52). Not only did God wreak vengeance on these two cities because of their sinfulness; the Apostle contends that God did this as an "example" of what God does to sinners who persist in their unfaithfulness. Thus, both water and fire are for the Apostle the means of God's judgment (cf. 2 Pet 3:5-7).

The Apostle's concern, however, is not just with judgment (but cf. Jude 6-8). While the biblical presentation of Lot is not wholly positive, the Jewish and Christian interpretative traditions tended to focus on his strength of character (e.g., Philo *Vit. Mos.* 2.58; *1 Clem.* 11:1). Contemporary Christians are to behave like Lot in another respect: "a man greatly distressed . . . was tormented in his righteous soul" (2 Pet 2:7-8). Not only are they to avoid the sins of their generation; they are also to be so vexed by sin that their very souls are tormented.

With the conditions now spelled out (from 2:4-8), the conclusion is stated: the Lord can deliver Christians from temptations, as Jesus (Matt 6:13) and Paul also promised (1 Cor 10:13). The Apostle may well have in mind the sensual sins he abhors (cf. 2:10a), but he probably is thinking on a grander scale: the assaults of the Enemy.

To this promise of deliverance the Apostle appends one more comment about judgment: God can either keep those who are presently undergoing punishment (in Tartarus?) until the final condemnation (Kelly) or he can keep those who will be finally punished until that day of condemnation (Bauckham). In light of the Petrine parallel at 1 Pet 3:19, the second option seems more probable. This punishment is especially reserved for those who are recklessly involved in sensual passions (cf. Jude 7, 8) and for those who deny the Master (2 Pet 2:1).

Denunciation of the Unrighteous (2:10b-22)

At this point the Apostle turns to a denunciation of the unrighteous (2:10b-22). It is best to describe the opponents here in terms of "unrighteousness," not just because the author does (v. 21) but also because what is attributed to these opponents pertains especially to transgressions of God's will.

The Apostle begins his section on *slander* (2:10b-13) by accusing the unrighteous of being so "bold and willful" that they are willing to "slander" the "glorious ones." He has in mind, no doubt, their utter disregard for the power of supernatural beings, even if they are demonic, to the extent that they (1) laugh at the prospect of a final judgment, which would be effected by angels (e.g., Matt 16:28), (2) pay no heed to the dangers of sin and persistent disobedience to the will of God (e.g., Deuteronomy 28), or (3) boldly deny the truths of God.

Whom they slander is a matter of some dispute; the author calls them "the glorious ones." Such a term seems almost certainly to describe angelic beings (cf. 2:11), but whether they are good angels or demonic ones is unclear to many. Since Jude 9 (or a tradition similar to Jude 9), upon which this verse seems to be based, depicts Michael not slandering the devil, some have taken this to describe the false teachers slandering demonic beings. Thus, while the opponents slander evil beings, the angels themselves are not even willing to accuse the evil beings (2:11; cf. Bauckham; but cf. Neyrey: 213-14).

Such people, the Apostle infers, are like "irrational animals," instinctual beings, devoid of mind, soul, and sense (cf. Jude 10). Since the opponents "slander" what (or "whom"; cf. Bauckham) they do not understand, they are threatened with utter destruction (2:12). Recompense, even vindication, for their slanderous activity is one of the themes of 2 Peter (cf. 2:1, 3b, 4-10a; 3:7, 10; Kelly: 339-40).

The Apostle's second concern is their *sensuality* (2:13b-16). This group of sinful teachers considers it a "pleasure" to get drunk and feast in opulence during the daytime hours (cf. Eccl. 10:16; *As. Mos.* 7:4). Reversing the Christian hope found in 3:14 ("without spot or blemish"; cf. 1 Pet 1:19), the Apostle says that these false teachers are "blots and blemishes." Using a pun, he says that they have turned the *agapē* meals into *apatē* meals, that is, from "love feasts" into "deceit feasts" (2:13b). They have slandered the name of God by turning the meal of thanksgiving into a meal of disgrace and sensuality, leaving the observer thinking that the Christian community is no different in its opulent affairs than the upper-class hedonists of Roman society (Lissarrague).

Two other sins call for comment: adultery and greed. Their eyes, certainly in a classic example of rhetorical exaggeration, are focused on their next dalliance with an adulteress because they are "insatiable for sin." Returning to a theme mentioned at 2:3a, they are "trained in greed." Because of these two sins which become stumbling blocks in the Christian community, the Apostle now calls them "accursed children." The use of "children" with some modifying description is biblical (cf. Isa 57:4; Eph 2:3; 1 Pet 1:14).

The Apostle follows these imprecations with a *general description of their fate* (2:15-16). We have already seen the term "way" used to describe a moral orientation in life (cf. v. 2); here the "road" of righteousness has been abandoned. While the text of Numbers 22–24 forms the foundation for the tradition connected with Balaam, a midrashic structure was built upon this text. In particular, the targums on Numbers emphasize his foolishness and sinfulness. That aspect of the tradition was what attracted the Apostle. Balaam, desiring to curse the Israelites, was steered by God to pronounce a eulogy upon his people. The Apostle notes that Balaam "loved the wages of doing wrong" (2:15). In Jewish tradition, Balak's offer to Balaam (Num 22:1-6) contained a promise of money, which was said to be the reason why Balaam appears in Num 31:8 with the kings of Midian, since he had gone there to collect the money (*b. Sanh.* 106a). Seizing on their greed (2:3a, 14), the Apostle denounces the false teachers for being like Balaam: loving money and leading people astray for the sake of it. Enhancing his theme of "irrational animals" (v. 12), the Apostle shows the irony of the Balaam incident: Balaam, considered to be prophet in his own religious tradition (cf. Num 22:1-6 and chs. 23–24), was actually rebuked by a "speechless donkey."

Next the Apostle gives a *warning* (2:17-22). He begins with *accusations* (vv. 17-19), likening the opponents to "waterless springs" and "mists driven by a storm." The image of darkness was used at v. 4 for the pit of chains which held demons until the final judgment; now it is used for the destination of the opponents, who will join the chained fallen angels.

The Apostle accuses the opponents of speaking "bombastic nonsense" (2:18). This is followed by a description of their sensual depravity, which they use to lead recent converts back into sin. While some have seen in this "freedom" only a special theme, it is best to see the promise as one of freedom both from moral restriction and from the consequences of the final judgment. Those who lived in such circumstance were, in effect, "slaves of corruption" (cf. 1:4) since they were bound to their sinful natures.

The *warning* form ("if . . . then") is found elsewhere in early Christianity (cf. esp. Heb 6:4-8; 10:19-39; *Herm. Sim.* 9:17:5–9:18:2). Moreover, the final state of apostates is worse than before conversion (cf. Matt 12:45; Luke 11:26). Conversion is here described as an "escape" from pollution through "knowledge" of the Lord Jesus Christ. 2:21 carries the thought about apostasy further: it would have been better never to have known the way than to know it and turn back. What they turned their back on is described in moral terms: "the holy commandment" (cf. Matthew 5–7; John 13:34-35; 1 Tim 6:14).

To finish off his denunciation, the Apostle quotes two proverbs, one from Prov 26:11 and the other from *Ahiqar* 8:15 (see Bauckham: 279-80), but the Apostle fashions them together as one "true proverb." Both proverbs illustrate how neither purging nor cleansing will have any lasting effect since the nature of beasts (read: the opponents) is irrational.

Reply to the Denial of the Parousia (3:1-13)

Latent in this entire testamentary letter of the Apostle is a response to the opponents' charge that the parousia will never take place. Now he addresses this theme directly. In essence, his final words take shape ironically: what the false teachers held to be impossible (the parousia and final judgment), the Apostle claims to be imminent.

Our section begins with a *testamentary reminder* (3:1-2). The reader will immediately recall 1:12-15 and not think of fraudulent attempts to manipulate an audience with false claims. Rather, the reader will find a venerable respect for the Petrine tradition. Just what is meant by the "second letter" is not clear. Two letters are in mind: either (1) 1 Peter and 2 Peter, (2) 2 Peter 1–2 and 2 Peter 3, (3) Jude and 2 Peter (Robinson), or (4) a lost letter and 2 Peter. To be sure, most scholars prefer option 1, but even here there is an important divergence. Some of these scholars (Bauckham, Neyrey) would contend that while 1 and 2 Peter are in mind, 2 Peter is pseudonymous and, therefore, not actually written as a second letter by the same author.

In clear testamentary fashion the Apostle states his purpose: "to arouse your sincere intention by reminding you . . ." (3:1b). As he said in 1:12-15, his purpose was to awaken in them a clear memory of the apostolic teaching, especially as it contained traditions about the parousia and the final judgment, so that they would be able to perceive the falsity of the claims of these opponents and live in true apostolic fashion.

What they are to remember are the words of the "holy prophets," most likely referring to the OT prophets (cf. 1:19-21). The words are those concerning the final judgment. Such prophecies would also include words about end-time scoffers. Thus, one thinks of Isa 5:18-23; Jer 5:12-17; Amos 9:9-10; Mal 2:17. These words of prophecy were confirmed by Jesus (cf. again 1:19a) through his "commandment," a way of putting the truth of Jesus in ethical terms (see at 2:21). This commandment was passed on to them "through your apostles"; literally, the text reads "the commandment of your apostles of the Lord and Savior."

This testamentary reminder leads to a *clarification of the denial of the parousia* on the part of the opponents (3:3-4). As with Jude 18, "scoffers" is a term used for those who violently reject the truth and will of God in both theological and moral ways. Once again the Apostle shows the connection between the theological and the moral: "indulging their own lusts." It seems unlikely that the Apostle has in mind the sensuality and greed he has previously excoriated (2:13-14, 18-19), but he does connect their false teaching with insatiable appetites.

Their sarcastic taunt is expressed in a manner typical of the OT (Ps 79:10). The taunt of the opponents expresses their utter disbelief in God's final coming; they mock the Christian's faith in God's final justice. Their argument is that since the "ancestors" died nothing has changed; in fact, everything is the same as at the beginning of creation. It is most likely that "ancestors" refers to the early Christian leaders, though some have argued that the mention of creation makes one think of the patriarchs.

These claims permit us to peer into the earliest Christian debates. In particular, the death of the earliest Christians, the apostles especially, led to somewhat of a crisis regarding the fulfillment of Jesus' prophecies. The words of Jesus now found at Matt 10:23; Mark 9:1; 13:30 seem almost certainly to have generated an enthusiastic expectation of the end. As long as the earliest founders of the faith, the apostles, were alive, such a hope could be kept alive. But when they began to die, a significant question emerged: Will these things take place as Jesus said or not?

The Apostle frames, in chiastic order (cf. 3:4 and vv. 5-10: v. 4a [time], v. 4b [creation], vv. 5-7 [creation], and vv. 8-10 [time]), two responses: (1) creation witnesses to the end of history as a judgment (vv. 5-7), and (2) time with God is not the same as time with humans (vv. 8-10).

The *first response* concerns creation (3:5-7). The gist of the first argument for the parousia is as follows: if creation is a valid idea, then judgment is as well. Thus (1) the opponents assert that things are the same as at the beginning of creation and therefore there is no final judgment; (2) since they think there was a *creation* by God, (3) they must think God made things through *water* and, therefore, (4) they must know that God used the same water to *judge* the world. (5) For the final judgment God will use *fire*. Water, therefore, is the middle factor between creation and the judgment by fire.

The Apostle recognizes a weakness in their logic: what they have "overlooked" (Bauckham) is both that God created (by his word) and how God created — by water. In the ancient world there was a belief that God created the earth out of a watery chaos. Some have argued that the "by means of water" refers to how God sustains by rain what has been created (Green: 130) or that it means "in the middle of the waters" (somewhat on the order of Pss 24:2 and 136:6; cf. Mayor: 151). Since the same expression is found in 3:6 ("through which . . ."), it is more likely that he intends "by means of water" and is arguing that God formed the earth out of water and by means of water.

In these statements God does things by the word and by something else: by the word and by water he created the world (3:5); by the word and by water he destroyed the world (v. 6); and by the word and by fire he will destroy the world (v. 7). Thus God's judgment returns the world to its chaotic, elemental forms. Interestingly, in the ancient world there was a fairly widespread idea that the world was alternately destroyed by water and fire (see Origen *Against Celsus* 4:11-12).

Moving from the past act of God's use of creation waters for judgment, the Apostle now asserts that the same word has promised that the present world will be destroyed by fire (3:7). God's judgment by fire is as old as Sodom and Gomorrah (Genesis 18–19), and that event becomes the basis for further predictions of judgment (e.g., Isa 66:15-16; see Bauckham: 300-301). That moral agents are the primary focus of this judgment, rather than nature, is seen in the final clause of 3:7: "of the godless."

The *second response* concerns time (3:8-10). Beginning with a statement (v. 8), the Apostle offers a rationale (v. 9) and then a warning (v. 10). The *statement* appears to be a quotation of a standard exegetical rule from Ps 90:4 utilized throughout Jewish exegesis: a "day" is a "thousand years." However, 3:8b shows that the author is thinking in more than simply some exegetical category, for he reverses the statement to show that time for God differs from time for humans. This needs to be seen as a profound attempt to deal with the problem of the delay of the parousia in late-first-century Christian thinking. In fact, Bauckham has found several significant pieces of evidence from Judaism that would support the direction in which the Apostle takes this statement (*Pirqe R. El.* 28; Sir 18:9-11; *2 Apoc. Bar.* 48:12-13; Ps.-Philo *Bib. Ant.* 19:13; Bauckham: 308-9) and suggests that the Apostle uses the statement of Ps 90:4 in parallel with others to show a contrast between the brevity of human life and the eternity of God's existence.

The current delay of the parousia has a *rationale:* God is giving people time to repent. (Scholars continue to debate the significance of early Christian eschatology; see Wright.) As Ps 90:4 was the basis for the Apostle's exegesis of "day," so Hab 2:3 became the same for his thoughts on God's delay of judgment. For the Apostle's testament, then, this means that, though the apostles are gone, God tarries so that people will turn from their unfaithfulness and sensuality.

This idea of God's forbearance has a parallel in 1 Pet 3:20, which says that God was patient during the days of Noah; but like then, God will come to establish his justice even if that also means punishment. God patiently waits for "all to come to repentance" (cf. 1 Tim 2:4). God's waiting for repentance was a feature of both Judaism and early Christianity (e.g., Rom 2:4). The "all" is not some universalistic hope but a call for the community to remember the apostolic tradition and return to it (Bauckham: 313).

However, the lack of repentance does not force God to wait: the Apostle seizes this promise (3:9) and warns that the Lord will come "like a thief," again drawing on an image of Jesus (Matt 24:43; Luke 12:39; cf. also 1 Thess 5:2; Rev 3:3; 16:15). When God does come, the heavens will pass away (cf. Matt 5:18; 24:35). Does the Apostle envision here total annihilation (1) of the whole earth, (2) of the heavenly bodies, or (3) of the angelic presiders over their kingdoms? While the evidence might suggest total annihilation of all physical material, the emphasis of the letter has been elsewhere: on the godless (e.g., 3:7). At that time, "everything . . . will be disclosed," that is, the truth about the human heart will be clear and manifest (Neyrey).

In light of these two arguments for a final judgment (creation and time), the Apostle now sets before his readers an option: What course will they take? An ethical application fits well with both letters and testaments. His exhortation leads the readers to two ethical qualities:

(1) holiness/godliness (3:11) and (2) faithful waiting vv. 12, 13). Waiting is a fundamentally important moral quality of those who are experiencing injustices and who think God's time to act is now (cf. Matt 24:42-43; 1 Thess 5:6; Rev 16:15). It is possible that the Apostle believes that their holiness and waiting will hasten the day of the parousia, as Jewish exegesis of Isa 60:22 might suggest (Bauckham: 325).

Conclusion (3:14-18) *(Peroratio)*

Early Christian letters normally end with some kind of doxology and greetings. There are no greetings in 2 Peter, leaving a conclusion that intensifies the ethical exhortations of the letter.

The conclusion begins with an *ethical exhortation* (3:14-15a). The Apostle roots (cf. "these things") his exhortation in the establishment of new heavens and a new earth (v. 13). While waiting (vv. 12-13), Christians are also "striving." This term is at the heart of the Apostle's concern for Christian virtue (1:10; cf. also 1:15), as it was also a feature of early Christian ethical exhortations (Eph 4:3; Heb 4:11). The idea of being found (cf. 3:10) at peace fashions a judgment scene at which time God approves of the faithful community and they are established in eternal peace.

This final state of peace will be one in which the community is found to be "without spot or blemish" (the opposite of what is found in 2:13). The expressions frequently describe the final condition of the elect people of God (cf. Eph 1:4; 5:27; Col 1:22; 1 Thess 3:13; 5:23; Jude 24), even if at times they are also used for present Christian morality (Phil 1:10; 2:15). This hope is to sustain them, and while waiting they are to consider God's gracious delay as the opportunity for their "salvation."

This appeal to wait in holiness finds *support in Paul* (3:15b-16), who was a "beloved brother" (cf. 1 Pet 5:12). While some have exaggerated the tension between Paul and Peter (see esp. Gal 2:11-14), and so see this supposed bond of affection to be a later Christian fabrication, most today would see a consistent affection between the two, with only an occasional lapse of tension (cf. Acts 15:7-11; Gal 1:18; 2:1-10). What the Apostle does here is show that his exhortations to ethical purity in light of an imminent coming of God are exactly the kinds of exhortations Paul gave to the same churches.

What the author builds on is the "wisdom" granted to Paul through his gracious calling (cf. 1 Cor 12:8; 1 Pet 4:10-11). One suspects that the Apostle here would think of Paul in prophetic terms as well (cf. 2 Pet 1:19-21). Since the text says that Paul wrote "to you," we must think of the Apostle as sending his letter to the same churches that Paul did; and in Paul's case, we must also think of churches established by him that are now being pastored in the Petrine tradition — but we cannot know which churches.

As added thoughts, the Apostle mentions the sheer difficulty of understanding some of Paul's ideas and how "ignorant and unstable" persons pervert his message. Not all misunderstand him; rather, it is a specific group who misinterprets his writings. More particularly, the false teachers are attempting to show how Paul's words about the final judgment or morality either do not mean what they appear to say or they are twisting them so they mean what the false teachers also teach. Thus it appears that the false teachers think that Paul is an ally, whereas the Apostle wants them to see that they are in fact perverters of Paul (cf. Pol. *Phil.* 7:1). In classifying Paul's writings as "scriptures," it is quite clear that the Apostle is thinking of those writings as having authority equal to that of the OT and other early Christian apostolic traditions. It ought to be noted that for this author some kind of distinction is being made between authoritative writings (Scriptures) and nonauthoritative writings. A warning is attached: those who mistreat Paul's writings do so to their own "destruction" (cf. 2:1, 3; 3:7).

Finally, the Apostle offers another *exhortation* (3:17-18a). In light of the warning he has given them, which reminds them of the true apostolic traditions (cf. 1:12-15; 3:1-2), they are to avoid being seduced by the charms of these false teachers that can jostle them away from their stable faith (1:12; 2:14). Instead, they are to "grow" in what was taught to them in the virtue list of 1:5-10. Again, "knowledge" is important, but the author steers clear from any kind of gnostic salvation (cf. 1:5-6; also 1:12, 16, 20-21; 2:2, 19-21; 3:1-2).

The Apostle's concluding *benediction,* which is typical of Christian letters (Rom 16:27; Gal 1:5; see also 1 Pet 4:11; 5:11; Jude 25), attributes glory to Christ both now and until that day, that is, the final day of judgment when the parousia occurs and God becomes Lord of all.

Bibliography. Bauckham, R. J. 1983, *Jude, 2 Peter,* WBC 50, Waco: Word • Danker, F. W. 1978, "2 Peter 1: A Solemn Decree," *CBQ* 40:64-82 • Elliott, J. H. 2000, *1 Peter: A New Translation with Introduction and Commentary,* AB 37B, New York: Doubleday • Green, M. 1968, *The Second Epistle General of Peter and the General Epistle of Jude,* TNTC, Grand Rapids: Eerdmans • Grundmann, W. 2d ed. 1979, *Der Brief des Judas und der zweite Brief des Petrus,* THKNT 15, Berlin: Evangelische Verlagsanstalt • Kelly, J. N. D. 1969, *A Commentary on the Epistles of Peter and Jude,* BNTC, London: Adam & Charles Black • Lissarrague, F. 1990, *The Aesthetics of the Greek Banquet: Images of Wine and Ritual (Un Flot d'Images),* Princeton: Princeton University • Mayor, J. B. 1907, *The Epistle of St. Jude and the Second Epistle of St. Peter: Greek Text with Introduction, Notes, and Comments,* London: Macmillan • Meade, D. G. 1986, *Pseudonymity and Canon: An Investigation into the Relationship of Authorship and Authority in Jewish and Early Christian Tradition,* WUNT 39, Tübingen: J. C. B. Mohr • Neyrey, J. H. 1993, *2 Peter, Jude,* AB 37C, New York: Doubleday • Robinson, J. A. T. 1976, *Redating the New Testament,* Philadelphia: Westminster • Von Allmen, D. 1966, "L'apocalyptique juive et le retard de la parousie en II Pierre 3:1-13," *RTP* 61:255-74 • Watson, D. F. 1988, *Invention, Arrangement, and Style: Rhetorical Criticism of Jude and 2 Peter,* SBLDS 104, Atlanta: Scholars • Webb, R. forthcoming, "The Petrine Epistles," in S. McKnight and G. R. Osborne, eds., *The Face of New Testament Studies,* Grand Rapids: Baker • White, J. 1986, *Light from Ancient Letters,* Philadelphia: Fortress; Wright, N. T. 1997, *Jesus and the Victory of God,* Minneapolis: Fortress.

1, 2, and 3 John

John Painter

INTRODUCTION

The Johannine corpus, of which the Letters form part, includes the Gospel and Revelation. The case for common authorship was first made by Irenaeus (c. AD 180). He claims to have received his information from the elders of Asia Minor, of whom he names Polycarp of Smyrna and Papias of Hierapolis (*Adv. Haer.* 3.3.3; 5.33.3-4; *Ep. ad Flor.*). The validity of this evidence has been challenged, as much on the basis of contemporary criticism as a supposed misunderstanding of the evidence by Irenaeus. He supposedly confused two Johns, one the apostle and the other the elder (Eusebius *Hist. Eccl.* 3.39.1-10). His conclusion concerning the common authorship of all five Johannine books and the identification of the author as John the son of Zebedee are far from secure. The reasons for recognizing the Johannine corpus are more secure, providing grounds for recognizing a Johannine school if not a single author. Recognition that the Gospel and Epistles share something of a common point of view is widely accepted, and recognition of Revelation as part of this corpus is not without significant supporters (Barrett 1978: 133-34; Bernard: lxviii; Brown: 56 n. 131).

Nothing in the Letters provides clear evidence of their date of composition or authorship. Theories concerning these matters arise from conclusions drawn concerning the relation of the Letters to each other, to the Gospel, and to Revelation. Once the testimony of Irenaeus has been put in question, these and many other questions are left unanswered. Nothing in the Letters *directly* links them to the Fourth Gospel or Revelation, though the Prologue of 1 John appears to be based on the Prologue of the Gospel and the language of 1 John shares the characteristic vocabulary of the Gospel.

Authorship

Nothing in the Letters *specifically* identifies the author(s). The author of 1 John presents himself as an authoritative bearer of the tradition which is from the beginning (1:1-5). In the second and third Letters the author calls himself "the elder" (2 John 1; 3 John 1), giving the impression that the same author is responsible for both letters. But this is little evidence, and we are dealing with very short works. 2 John consists of just 13 verses or 244 words, while 3 John has 15 verses or 219 words. If we were to conclude that these letters stood alone, it would be difficult to know how to read them. Most scholars conclude that, even if the three letters are not the work of a single author, they all derive from the same "school" that produced the Fourth Gospel. Some scholars continue to maintain common authorship of these works, and many would think it probable at least that the Letters had a single author.

The author's reference to himself as "the elder" *(ho presbyteros)* in 2 and 3 John could be a reference to his age or, more likely, it draws attention to his position of authority. He presents himself as an authoritative teacher and bearer of tradition. This understanding is confirmed by the references to "elders" in the Papias fragment concerning John (*Hist. Eccl.* 3.39.1-10) and in Irenaeus's treatment of the elders of Asia Minor (*Adv. Haer.* 3.3.3; 5.33.3-4; *Ep. ad Flor.*). If they are by a common author, it is a puzzle that 1 John is not addressed in the same way as the other Letters. It is more like the Letter to the Hebrews, being something of a cross between a letter and a tract. It lacks the address and signature of a letter, but it is addressed to a more specific group of readers than is normally the case with a tract. It has no personal address at the beginning, though, like Hebrews, it has something of a personal closing, "Little children, guard yourselves from idols." The personal force is reduced by recognition that "little children" is a stylized form of address.

Provenance

1 John contains direct address to the readers, not by name but in stylized collective and general terms, as "children" (*teknia,* 2:1, 12, 28; 3:7; 5:21; *paidia,* 2:14, 18), "beloved" (2:7, 15; 3:21; 4:1, 7, 11), "fathers" (2:13, 14), and "young men" (2:13, 14). There are numerous appeals introduced by "I write [wrote] to you [plural] (2:1, 7, 12, 13, 14 [3 times], 26; 5:13). In the second letter the addressees are identified as "the elect lady and her children," while the third letter is addressed to "Gaius, the beloved, whom I love in truth." A possible way of understanding this is to see 2 and 3 John as covering letters sent with 1 John, which was a circular "message" to a group of "house churches." The "elect lady" might be some notable lady, though more likely it is a personification of a local church viewed collectively. Reference to the children takes account of the church in terms of her individual members.

Just where such a circle of house churches might have been is not hinted at in the Letters. Tradition places all of the Johannine writings in Asia Minor, and this is in harmony with the milieu portrayed by Revelation. Perhaps we can say no more than that a circle of churches around Ephesus makes good sense for the Letters of John, and there is no compelling evidence suggesting any other situation.

Date and Context

Given the lack of specific evidence concerning authorship and provenance, it is not surprising that the Letters lack a clear indication of date. It would be helpful to know whether the Letters were written at the same time, which would fit the theory that 2 and 3 John were written to accompany 1 John. But when were they written? Before or after the Gospel? This is a key question. It has been argued that the Letters were written to affirm that Jesus is the Christ (Messiah) against objections that Jesus did not fulfill the messianic expectations. Thus the Letters are seen in terms of Jewish and Jewish-Christian controversy, and this is sometimes seen in relation to Cerinthus, who is understood to be a Jewish Christian (see Hengel, Lieu, and Okure). This approach owes too much to reading the Letters in the light of the Gospel and on the assumption that they were written at the same time for the same situation.

Alternatively, it is noted that there are no *quotations* from the OT in the Letters and that the final warning in 1 John, "guard yourselves from idols," is more appropriately addressed to a predominantly Gentile audience. While Gentile Christians also drew on the OT, it is less likely that a Jewish-Christian controversy would be settled without reference to the OT. Thus it seems that the Gospel, which has many quotations from and allusions to the OT, was shaped in relation to Judaism, and the Letters reflect Christianity adrift from Judaism.

Most of the evidence concerning the situation addressed comes from 1 John, where it is apparent that the Letter concerns internal problems which led to a schism (2:19). This could be evidence of the author's rhetoric rather than the reflection of an actual historical conflict. However, reference to the schism makes this unlikely, and other evidence enables us to build up a cohesive picture of the author's opponents. The author refers to what his opponents affirmed (1:6, 8, 10; 2:4, 6, 9; 4:20) and what they denied (4:1-6), and, in a series of antitheses using different syntactical constructions, he sets out the position opposed (2:29b; 3:3a, 4a, 6a, 6b, 9a, 10b, 15; 5:4, 18; 3:7, 8, 10, 14-15; 4:8; 5:6, 10, 12; 5:19; and 2:23). This conflict, evident in the text itself, should not be ignored. The cohesiveness of the position opposed by our author reveals a single group of opponents who are described as antichrists (2:18-19).

The interpreter needs to exercise caution in reading the author's unsympathetic treatment of his opponents. With caution the following can be said. They were opposed to the affirmation that Jesus Christ had come in the flesh. Minimally this means that they saw no revelatory or saving value in the humanity of Jesus. Rather, Jesus was the model of their own *experience.* As he is from above, has knowledge, and is without sin, so are they. How could such a position emerge in the Johannine community? It was a result of one reading of tradition in the Fourth Gospel. Thus the author of the Letter(s) and his opponents were separated from each other by their differing interpretations of that tradition. What led to this was the author's participation in the conflict of the Johannine community with the synagogue, which provided one context of interpretation, while the opponents, coming into the Johannine community after the breach from Judaism, interpreted the tradition from the context of their own religious experience, which was influenced by the mystery cults.

While the Gospel is the canonical culmination of a developing tradition over more than half a century, the Letters represent a single response in a moment of time to a specific problem, though each Letter deals with a specific aspect of it. It is likely that the problem had appeared before the Gospel was published. Some suggest that the schism of 1 John 2:19 is reflected in Jesus' reference to the many disciples who no longer followed him (6:60-66). This is unlikely because the controversy there concerns the bread from heaven, Jesus' heavenly origin, and his divinity, and reflects the controversy with the Jews. Those who no longer followed were the secret "believers" for whom the Gospel's presentation of Jesus as the one from above and superior to Moses did not persuade them to confront the threat of exclusion from the synagogue as a consequence of their confession of faith.

The opponents confronted by the Johannine Letters cannot be identified by name, though they have often been connected to Cerinthus, who apparently rejected the identity of Jesus as the Christ. What we know of him fits the teaching refuted in the Letters. But that falls short of proving identity. Nevertheless, we are not wrong to see the opponents as some form of Docetists. Docetism assumes that the humanity of Jesus was apparent but not real. The opponents did not take seriously the humanity of Jesus in his saving work. They also rejected the need to express their faith in terms of love for the brethren. It is not likely that this meant only a failure to love those recognized as brothers by "the elder." Rather, their religious experience made such ethical behavior irrelevant. Given the imprecise description of the opponents, it is wrong to project onto them any of the various second-century forms of docetism.

Purpose of the Letters

The purpose of the *first letter* was to refute the position of the opponents by reaffirming what the author asserted was the correct interpretation of the tradition in the Gospel. The opponents and their position are not treated sympathetically, but because their position would have been well known to the readers, the Letter is not likely to distort their views grossly. Certainly it did not aim to be flattering. Nevertheless, this polemic is not directed to the opponents. They can hardly have been the intended audience. Rather, its purpose was to persuade the author's supporters that in remaining loyal to him they were abiding in the truth of the Gospel. This was done first by a critique of the opponents. Because the controversy had unsettled even those loyal in the community, bringing uncertainty and anxiety, our author had to blend his polemic with a sensitive pastoral concern for his readers. His objective was to assure them that they were abiding in the truth, were children of God, and were walking in the light, and thus restore them to a confident relationship with the Father through faith in the Son. Because of this, 1 John manifests a literary duality of polemical and pastoral perspectives.

The *second letter* is addressed to "the elect lady and her children," which is probably a symbolic reference to a neighboring church. As a covering letter it briefly summarizes the main teaching of the first letter: the correctness of the confession of faith in Jesus Christ coming in the flesh and the outworking of faith in love for one another. This is the basis of the call for the readers to refuse hospitality to those who do not share the correct teaching (vv. 9-11).

The *third letter* is addressed to an individual named Gaius, whom the author says he loves and who was perhaps a "disciple" of the author. This letter is also about hospitality in the mission. It opposes the work of Diotrephes, who may have sided with the opponents of the author and refused hospitality to those who supported him.

There is a good case for seeing 2 and 3 John as supporting covering letters sent with 1 John. 3 John appears to have been sent to one person, while 2 John was a general covering letter accompanying 1 John. Its point was to crystallize the two main points of 1 John and to call on supporters to refuse hospitality to the opponents. 3 John indicates that the opponents and their supporters had already withdrawn hospitality to our author and his supporters.

Exegetically it is crucial that the nature and purpose of the Letters should be recognized. Only when the Letters are read as the expression of a bitter internal controversy can they be adequately appreciated. The community, born in the conflict with the synagogue, was subjected to a schism in which a large and powerful group left the Johannine community. Those who left appear to have interpreted the Johannine tradition from the perspective of the experience of the mystery religions and were on the road to what we have come to call gnosticism.

1 John

COMMENTARY

The Structure of 1 John

There are considerable problems regarding the structure of 1 John. A. E. Brooke attributed this to the "aphoristic character of the writer's meditations." Nevertheless, he recognized that Theodor Häring made the most successful attempt to show the underlying sequence of thought in the Letter and followed his analysis generally in his own commentary. A summary of Häring's analysis follows:

- I. Introduction — 1:1-4
- II. First Presentation of the Two Tests — 1:5–2:27
  Two tests of the claim to have fellowship with God (the ethical and christological theses)
  - A. The Ethical Test. Walking in the light as the true sign of fellowship with God. Refutation of the first lie — 1:5–2:17
    - 1. God Is Light and the Necessity of Walking in the Light — 1:5-10
    - 2. Christ Our Advocate — 2:1-2
    - 3. Testing the Claim to Know Him — 2:3-6
    - 4. The Paradox of the Old Commandment Which Is New — 2:7-11
    - 5. Preliminary Appeal — 2:12-14
    - 6. False Love — 2:15-17
  - B. The Christological Test. Faith in Jesus Christ as the test of the claim to have fellowship with God. Refutation of the second lie — 2:18-27
- III. Second Presentation of the Two Tests — 2:28–4:6
  Emphasizing the connection between the two tests (3:22-24)
  - A. The Ethical Test. Doing righteousness (= love of the brethren) as the sign by which we may know that we are born of God — 2:28–3:24
    - 1. Acting Righteously Is the Test of Abiding in Him — 2:28-29
    - 2. Sanctification (Separation from the Corruption of the World) Is the Test of the Claim to Be Children of God — 3:1-3
    - 3. The Incompatibility of Sin and Righteousness — 3:4-10
    - 4. The Incompatibility of Love and Hate — 3:11-18
    - 5. The Grounds for Confidence before God — 3:19-24
  - B. The Christological Test. The Spirit from God confesses Jesus Christ has come in the flesh — 4:1-6
- IV. Third Presentation of the Two Tests — 4:7–5:12
  Stressing the inseparable relation between the two tests.
  - A. Love Based on Faith in the Revelation of Love is the Proof of Knowing God and Being Born of God — 4:7-21
    - 1. God's Love Is the Source of Love for One Another — 4:7-12

2. The Spirit Is the Evidence of Abiding in God	4:13-16a
3. Abiding in Love Is the Ground of Confidence before God	4:16b-21
B. Faith Is the Basis of Love	5:1-12
1. Those Who Believe Are Begotten of God and Love One Another	5:1-3
2. Victory over the World	5:4-5
3. The Witness to the Son Is the Witness to Eternal Life	5:6-12
V. Conclusion	5:13-21
A. To Reestablish Confidence	5:13-15
B. Prayer for Those Sinning	5:16-17
C. God and the Problem of Sin	5:18-20
D. Final Exhortation	5:21

Häring's analysis of 1892 is largely followed by that of Robert Law (1909), although he appears not to have known Häring's article at the time. I have adopted the term "tests" from Law's title *The Tests of Life.* He recognized three tests, righteousness, love, and belief, whereas Häring viewed love as the expression of righteousness. Law failed to distinguish the "Conclusion" or "Epilogue" from the third cycle. Where there are substantial differences Häring's analysis is to be preferred, though Law's work remains a stimulating interpretation.

This analysis of the Letter emphasizes its controversial nature. The tests of life were necessary because our author perceived that counterfeit claims were abroad in the church. Recognition of the affirmations and denials of the opponents is important to the following interpretation, as is the evidence of the antithetical statements in which the author set his position over against that of his opponents. Their claims needed to be tested so that the true might be recognized and the false rejected.

Introduction (1:1-4)

Overlaps of language and theme between 1:1-4 and the Prologue of the Fourth Gospel (1:1-14) imply some relationship. Words shared with the Prologue are noted in the order that they appear in 1 John: "beginning," "we have seen" *(etheasametha),* "the word," "life," "to bear witness," "the Father," "Jesus Christ," and "fulfilled." All of this is found in four verses overlapping just eighteen verses of the Gospel. Yet there are important differences in the way these terms are deployed. The Gospel, with its focus on the divinity of Jesus, asserts the eternity of the divine Word. The Letter appeals to the primitive message, suggesting that a more "progressive" position is opposed. The evidence may not support a case for direct dependence but strongly suggests the diverse expression of tradition from a common (Johannine) school.

The opening sentence runs for three and a half verses, including a parenthesis on "the life" (1:2). The primitive message concerns "the word of life," or "the Word of life" (see John 14:6). Though less obviously than the "Word" *(logos)* of the Fourth Gospel, the use of "Word" in 1 John also calls for explanation. The Johannine tradition drew on Jewish Wisdom, where the creative Word of God had been identified with the law. Distinctive developments in the Johannine interpretation identified Jesus with the Word in such a way that he communicates himself in his words.

In 1 John Jesus is also present in the Word that bears witness to him, and there is a studied ambiguity concerning the message and the subject of the message. The message concerns life, and the one who is the subject of the message is himself the life. He has the words of eternal life (John 6:68; cf. 17:6-8, 14, 17). "Heard, seen, and handled" indicate an alternation between the message and its subject. The emphasis here is on having seen the subject, which is twice affirmed in 1:1. The subject is here known under the image of the "life." In the Prologue of the Gospel the *logos* is revealed as "the true light" and "the life" (John 1:4). Here the life is further elaborated as "the eternal life that was with the Father." The Letter affirms twice that the life was manifest (cf. "made flesh" in John 1:14); was seen, witnessed to, and reported. The author associates "himself" with the authoritative bearers of the tradition, while the readers are identified as the prospective recipients of it.

The purpose of the report was to bring the recipients into a sharing relationship (fellowship or *koinōnia*) with the tradition bearers. This term defines the nature of the Johannine "community." The term "church" is not used, but this word meaningfully interprets it. Priority is given to the relationship within the community before extending this to include the relationship with (God) the Father and his Son Jesus Christ. Relationship with God is dependent on relationship with the community (see 5:1-2). The theological focus of the Letter is signaled at the end of 1:3, where fellowship with the Father is mentioned before fellowship with his Son, who, characteristically of the Letter, is named "Jesus Christ" (see 1:3; 2:1, [22]; 3:23; 4:2; [5:1]; 5:6, 20 and only in John 1:17; 17:3). The purpose of the writing is expressed in terms of the fulfillment of "our ["your"] joy" (see John 15:1-11).

First Presentation of Two Tests (1:5–2:27)

The claim to have fellowship with God is now subjected to two tests, the first ethical and the second christological.

The Ethical Test (1:5–2:17)

The ethical test is first expressed in terms of walking in the light, exposing the first lie. The message is now stated as a basis for a critique of the position of the "opponents." Their position is elaborated by a series of affirmations (1:6, 8, 10; 2:4, 6, 9) and positions opposed by the Letter (2:12-17). It is likely that the opponents made claims concerning God in 1:6; 2:4, 6 which our author tests in relation to Jesus as the Christ, the revelation of God. But, as we shall see, this is precisely one of the issues contested by the opponents.

God Is Light and Fellowship with Him Involves Walking in the Light (1:5-10)

The ethical test is grounded in the character of God revealed in Jesus. Our author asserts that "we heard the message from him," apparently referring back to Jesus Christ in 1:3. The *message* (*angelia* is used here and in 3:11 only in the NT) is here tied to the "we" of the tradition bearers. In 3:11 the message is associated with the recipients of the Letter. They had received it from the tradition bearers. That message is here reported to the readers in a concentrated formulation, "God is light." While this tradition grows out of the OT (see Pss 27:1; 36:9), the dualistic opposition to the darkness reflects later developments evident also at Qumran (see, e.g., 1QS 3:13–4:26; 1QM 13:10-12), though there is no identification of God with the light at Qumran. Other relevant texts from the Hellenistic period such as the *Poimandres Tractate* (1:4-6) and the *Odes of Solomon* (11:19; 15:2; 21:3) should be noted. Jewish, Christian, and Hellenistic piety have influenced the development of the Johannine tradition.

In 1 John "God is light" is the first of two theocentric statements (see 4:8 and John 4:24). The second theocentric statement ("God is love") is associated with the second statement of the message in 3:11, which is crystallized in the command to love one another. In the Letter, focus on God became necessary because Christology was in dispute within the Johannine community. That dispute had to be settled by reference to the theological basis of Christology and by revealing the false theology, with its ethical consequences, of the opponents. That God is light is the basis of the affirmation, "in him is no darkness at all." It forms an *inclusio* with the final affirmation of the opponents in this section (2:9), where they claim "to be in the light." What emerges is that our author and his opponents have different understandings of the light. Our author has an ethical understanding in which light is opposed to darkness, and darkness is also understood in ethical terms. It becomes apparent that the light is expressed in love for the brother/sister, and the darkness is expressed in hatred (2:9-10).

The first three assertions ("lies" according to our author) are introduced by the formula, "If anyone says . . ." (1:6, 8, 10). We understand these as assertions of the opponents. The first (v. 6), the claim to have "fellowship with him," is shown by the context as a claim to have fellowship with God (not Christ). Although fellowship with God and Christ are in view in v. 3, the assertion "God is light" (v. 5) shows that fellowship with God is in view. The assertion is not impossible, not false in principle. It is shown to be a lie in the case of those who walk in the darkness. What walking in the darkness means is not explicitly spelled out at this point (but see 2:9), though it becomes clear by contrast with the way "we" who walk in the light are characterized (1:7). Here, as in 2:6, 11, "walking" is an image for the manner of living. Because "we have fellowship with one another," it is implied that the opponents do not. Minimally this means that the opponents did not have fellowship with our author and his supporters. More than likely it means that fellowship with each other was not a factor in their claim to be in the light and was not involved in fellowship with God, as it was for our author. Although the idea of the shedding of blood in an atoning sacrifice is found in the OT and Judaism as well as in the Greek and Hellenistic world, the opponents did not acknowledge cleansing from sin by the death of Jesus. Just how this could be so becomes clear in the second and third assertions (lies).

In the second the opponents asserted, "We have no sin!" (1:8). Whether sinlessness was thought to be a consequence of the relationship to God or a condition of it is unclear. Either way, they claimed that their relationship to God demonstrated their sinlessness. Such a position set aside the necessity of the purifying death of Jesus, which made the believer fit for fellowship with God. The claim to sinlessness could be made by the opponents only because they rejected the relevance of social relationships. Sinlessness was assessed solely in relation to God. Those claiming this position were lying, according to our author, and not acting truly or faithfully. Yet they were not consciously lying. Rather, there was something in the position adopted that caused them to go astray. It is as if their position, though false, was irresistibly seductive. Hence our author was concerned to provide arguments that would be persuasive *to his readers,* even though they would have been ineffective in relation to his opponents.

If the denial of sinfulness is here depicted as a lie and a failure to act faithfully, the position adopted by our author is to assert the need "to confess our sins." It is unclear whether confession to God is in view or confession to the human person(s) offended. The consequence of such confession is that God is faithful and righteous to forgive sins and to cleanse from unrighteousness. Forgiveness and cleansing might be thought of as synonyms, yet they highlight different aspects. Forgiveness means that the person is no longer held accountable, while cleansing signifies that the person is made clean. The two symbols tend to highlight first "justification" and then "sanctification," but the closer we look, the more the two symbols seem to overlap, and the traditional distinction seems to be inappropriate for our author because it is by cleansing that forgiveness is made possible.

The third lie apparently goes further than the second, asserting "We have not sinned!" This is a claim to be sinless by nature and not merely as a consequence of a relationship to God which occurred at some time in their lives. For our author, such a position is not only a lie but it makes God a liar (cf. 5:10). He does not say where, but it is assumed that God somewhere asserts universal human sinfulness and need of cleansing. It may be that he refers to the tradition of the witness of God to Jesus in the Johannine tradition (cf. John 5:32, 34, 36-40). Because this was self-evident to our author, he asserts that the *word* of God did not abide in those who claimed sinlessness (1:10; cf. John 5:38), just as he had asserted that "his truth" did not abide in those who asserted the second lie (1:8). In this way our author is led into a discussion of sin.

Christ Our Advocate (2:1-2)

For the first time our author addresses his readers in terms of familial endearment, "My little children *(teknia mou)*" (2:1 and see 2:12, 28; 3:7, 18; 4:4; 5:21); "children of God *(tekna theou)*" (3:1, 2; 5:2). This use of the diminutive is not found in the LXX, and is found in the NT only in John 13:33. For other terms of address see "children *(paidia)*" (2:14, 18) and "beloved" (2:7; 3:21; 4:1, 7). Of a different order are the distinctions among the readers, addressed as "fathers" (2:13, 14) and "young men" (2:13, 14), where the preliminary category of "little children" (first *teknia* [2:12] and then *paidia* [2:14]) is probably inclusive of all groups. On the one hand, believers are children of God (3:1, 2). Yet the readers also stand in a relationship of children to our author, who writes to them as their authoritative teacher (2:1).

Our author's use of the two terms for "children" is quite self-conscious. His use of the first (2:1) and then the second (2:18) is matched in the list of 2:12-14 where a threefold formula is repeated, with the first using *teknia* and the second *paidia*. By doing this John expresses his paternal relationship to his readers. He self-consciously indicates, "I write to you . . ." (2:1, 7, 12, 13, 14, 26; 5:13). Reminders like this show that we have a self-conscious "author" making his readers aware of the literary process. What he has written at this point is open to two readings. He tells the readers that the purpose of his letter ("these things") is "that you may not sin." Alternatively "these things" might have a more restricted sense, referring only to the words "Do not sin." The sin our author aims to prevent is the failure to love the brethren. Nevertheless, he recognizes that a lapse into sin may occur, and has a strategy to cope with this. Here he further elaborates the role of Jesus (1:7, 9), first introducing a fresh aspect in terms of his role as our "*paraclete* with the Father" and then dealing more fully with the effects of his death "for our sins," indeed, for the sins of the whole world.

Reference to Jesus as our "*paraclete* with the Father" should be seen alongside Jesus' reference to the Spirit as "another *paraclete*" (John 14:16). In the Gospel the meaning of this term is hard to tie down, but here in 1 John the meaning is "advocate." Reference to "another *paraclete*" in John 14:16 implies that Jesus was the first. Jesus promised that, although he was departing, "another *paraclete*" would come to be with the believers. One aspect of the meaning in the Gospel might be that the Spirit is Jesus' advocate with the believers. In 1 John 2:1 our author asserts that the departed Jesus was the believers' *advocate* with God (the Father). Thus the Spirit was to be Jesus' (God's) *paraclete* among the believers, while Jesus was to be the believers' *paraclete* with God. But we should not think that this implies that a compassionate Jesus saves believers from a wrathful Father. If it is Jesus Christ the righteous *(dikaion)* who takes the part of believers with the Father, it is God who is faithful and righteous *(pistos . . . dikaios)* "to forgive us our sins and cleanse us from all unrighteousness" (1:9). Clearly the death of Jesus is thought to be part of this process, "the blood of Jesus Christ his Son" (1:7). Yet we should not think that the action of the Son is in any way at odds with that of the Father. Indeed, the saying, "like father, like son," is very much to the point and probably underlies the explicit use of the Father/Son terminology in this context. Nevertheless, it is the Son who deals with the problem of the sins of the whole world.

Thus far the defilement of sin has been in view (1:7). The reference to Jesus dealing with "our sins," indeed the sins of "the whole world," should be understood in these terms. The Greek word *(hilasmos)* found here (see also 4:10 and cf. Rom 3:25) is used in the sense of propitiating angry and capricious gods in Greco-Roman religions, but here the term relates to sins and signifies the way God deals with sin by "expiation" or "atonement." In 1 John the word indicates the way sins are dealt with, removing their defiling and destructive consequences, and it is God who has dealt with the problem of human sins through his Son. The remedy for sin comes from the faithfulness and righteousness of God. Here, as in John 3:16, the universal intention of God's saving action is clear. He has dealt with the sins of the whole world.

Testing the Claim to Know Him (2:3-6)

God's action in his Son is directed to the transformation of human consciousness. He came to bring knowledge of the true God (5:20), and there is a stress on this knowledge and the assurance of it (2:3). Indeed, the opponents' claim to know *him* is the next point of contention. To prepare for this our author asserts that those who keep his (Jesus') commandments have the confirmation that they know him. Here we meet for the first time the formula "By this we know . . . ," which sets out the evidence supporting the claim to know. These appeals to evidence (see 2:3, 5; 3:10, 16, 19, 24; 4:2[6], 9, 13) show that the claims to knowledge were in dispute, especially in terms of the character of the one who was known. Keeping his commandments is the criterion of knowledge appealed to here. The primary commandment in view is to love the brother (2:7-11), though the dual command of believing and loving might be involved (3:23).

In 2:4-11 our author deals with three more assertions (lies), now introduced by "he who says" (vv. 4, 6, 9). In the first, the claim of the opponents "to know him" (Jesus) is shown to be a lie by their failure to keep his commandments (v. 4). How this relates to the central ethical criticism becomes clear in vv. 7-11. Here the argument is that those who know him would know and keep his "commandments," which is the equivalent of his "word" (v. 5). It is the nature of those commands, that word, that make(s) explicit why the love of God is fulfilled in those who keep them/it. We would expect the conclusion, "In this we know that we know him," at the end of v. 5 (see v. 3) but find, "In this we know that we are in him," because our author is making a transition to the second assertion of the opponents in this second series of lies (v. 6). They claimed "to abide in him," which our author understands as something of a synonym for the shorter "to be in him" and for the claim "to know him." In each case here "him" refers to Jesus because the example of Jesus is made the criterion of the claim to abide in him. The assumption is that the way Jesus *walked* (lived) exemplifies his commands, and this is implied by the assertion that the one who claims to abide in him *ought* to walk as he walked. Yet there were probably serious differences between our author and his opponents that would have made his arguments ineffective as far as they were concerned. It may be that the object of knowledge and abiding for them was God, not Jesus.

The language of *abiding* is characteristically Johannine, being used 40 times in the Gospel, 24 times in

1 John, and 3 times in 2 John, but only 45 times in the rest of the NT. Given the brevity of 1 John, the use of this word is concentrated there, probably reflecting the importance of it for the opponents. The first use of the term occurs in a passage where our author sets out a test for those who claim "to abide in him."

The Paradox of the Old Commandment Which Is New (2:7-11)

The clarification of the commandments is given in 2:7-11 and provides a context for the third in the second series of lies. Here, as in v. 1, our author self-consciously addresses his readers collectively. For the first time he uses "beloved" (cf. 4:1, 7, 11), reminding them of the commandment of which he has written to them. There is a strong emphasis on commandments, or more often the singular commandment, in 1 John. The word is used 14 times as against 10 times in the Gospel and 67 times in the NT as a whole. In the Johannine literature it is not used of the Mosaic commandments but of the commandment(s) of Jesus.

Given the subject of the command in 2:7, "beloved" is an appropriate form of address. If our author's command in v. 1 was negative, "Do not sin!" the present reference to a command is positive. Against the innovations of his opponents our author appeals to an old commandment, that is, one rooted in the Gospel tradition (see the command to love "one another" in John 13:34; cf. 1 John 4:11-12), where it was called a new commandment. But in what sense is the old commandment new? It is new because the reality commanded is being realized in the lives of believers. In this way the true light is shining in a world previously dominated by darkness. The characteristic Johannine dualism of light and darkness, that is, irreconcilable opposition between light and darkness, finds expression here. In this way a context is created for the next lie of the opponents.

Our author asserts that "the person who claims to be in the light and hates his brother/or sister is in the darkness until now" (2:11) Clearly *adelphos* describes the fellow believer and not just those who were men. Light and darkness are understood as ethical (not mystical religious) terms by our author. The darkness is manifest in hatred, while the light is discerned in love for the brother/sister. There is little difference for our author between the affirmation "God is light" (1:7) and "God is love" (4:8). The one who loves his brother/sister is in the light, and the one who hates his brother/sister is in the darkness. Just as those who love manifest the reality of the shining of the true light, so those who hate are blinded by the prevailing darkness of the old age.

In 1 John the character of God is revealed in the sending of his Son (4:7-10) so that Christology reveals theology. It is also true that Christology is grounded in theology. The inseparability of this connection seems to have been a point of contention between our author and his opponents.

Preliminary Appeal (2:12-14)

In 2:12-14 our author has set out stylistically two series of three addresses in which the whole community is addressed first as "children," whose sins are forgiven, who know the Father. Then sections of the community are addressed — first "fathers," then "young men." "Fathers" are twice addressed as such because "you know the one from the beginning." This might imply that they were old enough to have known Jesus, but it more likely plays on their maturity as an image of age, implying long-established and tested knowledge of the one who was "in the beginning." The reference to the young men makes use of their characteristic strength as a basis for the symbolism of victory over the evil one (the devil). The second address to them adds the explanation, "because you are strong and the word of God abides in you" (cf. 5:4). Although the inclusive term "children" is gender free, it can be used of boys and girls, but when the sectional groups are in view, women are overlooked. This is also true where the love command is expressed in terms of the "brothers" (2:11; 3:14). But "brothers" should probably be translated as a reference to believers that is not gender specific. It is the focus on loving that suggests the fraternal relationship. Language that is not gender specific would have been more appropriate.

False Love (2:15-17)

Our author now sets out a contrast between the world of darkness and those who do the will of God. The latter is now the description of those who keep the commandments of Jesus, who know him, who abide in him, who are in the light. The instruction, "Do not love the world or the things of the world," seems to break the dualism of love and hate, light and darkness. But the world is to be identified with darkness (cf. 5:19). Here we are alerted to the true and false loves, which are determined by their source, object, and manner. Earlier we learned that authentic love has its source in God. False love has its origin in darkness. It is love of the world and all that belongs to it; it is love of the darkness (see John 3:19-21) which is not an expression of the love which comes from the Father. Our author is not advocating otherworldly asceticism. The love that is opposed to God seeks to possess the world. It is expressed in lust and the desire to possess, not the love which seeks the good of the other. Thus love of the world is a false love, rooted in sensual materialism and self-glorification. It comes from the world and is opposed to the love which comes from God. The world of darkness is passing away, with all that belongs to it, because the true light is already shining. But those who do the will of God abide forever.

The Christological Test (2:18-27)

The readers are again addressed as "children" (see 2:1, 12, 14). Whereas the first lie was a manifestation of the darkness of the old age, the second lie is an expression of "the last hour." This expression is used only here in the NT. It is similar to "the last day" (see John 6:39-40, 44, 54; 11:24; 12:48 and cf. from Qumran 1QS 4:16-17; 4QpHab 7:7, 12). The difference between these two expressions seems to be that the last hour is the precursor to the last day, the day of resurrection and judgment. The last hour is announced by the appearance of the "antichrist." Though this title is used here for the first time, it is *developed* from

Jesus' prediction of those who would proclaim false Messiahs (Mark 13:6, 21-23). Here our author assumes that his readers are aware of the coming of the "antichrist," but informs them of the appearance of many "antichrists." See 2:18, 22; 4:3; 2 John 7; and Pol. *Phil.* 7:1. Their appearance now confirms that it is the last hour. What makes them "antichrists" is not their own claims to be the Christ or the prediction of the imminent appearance of the Christ at some specific place and time. Rather, it is their false (from the perspective of our author) Christology and their separation from the Johannine community (2:18-19; 4:1-6). Though the devil is the source of their power, they are distinguishable from him. On the other side, our author identifies his readers as those who know the truth, "you all know" (not "you know all things") because "you have the anointing *(chrism)* from the Holy One" (2:20, 27). The emphasis on everyone knowing counters the claim that knowledge is esoteric and restricted to a few. Yet the reference to anointing suggests that knowledge is restricted to the initiated and might be intended to exclude the opponents. The Messiah was anointed at his baptism. Anointing signifies the descent of the Spirit upon him (Mark 1:9-11; Luke 4:18 citing Isa 61:1; Acts 10:38). There is a case for thinking that the anointing is the gift of the Holy One (Holy Spirit) in the initiation of baptism so that all share this gift. But "the Holy One" might be a reference to God (see 2:27 and cf. John 17:11); or Jesus (John 6:69); or, more likely, the Holy Spirit (John 1:33; 14:26; 20:22). The anointing "abides in you" and, by implication, "teaches you." In John (5:38; 15:7) it is the word of Jesus that is to abide in the believer. In Johannine tradition there is a unity of word and Spirit (John 6:63) in an adequate understanding of the Gospel. Our author affirms that this is available to all through the gospel that initiated them to faith and was expressed in baptism.

The Letter is concerned to expose the lie and the liar (the antichrist). The lie is the denial that Jesus is the Christ (2:22). On the surface this looks like an intra-Jewish problem concerning the messianic credentials of Jesus. What follows shows this not to be the case. The liar is the antichrist "who denies the Father and the Son." This is the *Johannine interpretation* of Messiahship, the revelation of the Father in the Son so that the hidden Father is revealed in the Son. The lie is a departure from the original Johannine gospel. Consequently our author appeals to his readers to reject the innovation of the lie of the opponents, to affirm the abiding original Johannine gospel, and, by abiding in the Son, to abide in the Father also.

Second Presentation of the Two Tests (2:28–4:6)

This section is introduced by a renewed address to the readers as "children," which is appropriate because God has been characterized as Father in relation to the Son (2:22-24). While Jesus is characteristically the "Son," believers are spoken of as "children." This distinguishes believers from Jesus in relation to the Father so that their dependence on him for their relationship to the Father becomes clear. In this section the relationship between the two tests (ethical and christological) is stressed (3:22-24).

The Ethical Test (2:28–3:24)

Doing righteousness is the sign by which we may know that we are born of God. Doing righteousness and loving the brethren are clearly two ways of speaking of the one reality.

Acting Righteously Is the Test of Abiding in Him (2:28-29)

Having warned his readers of those who would lead them astray (2:18-27), our author appeals to them, "And now, little children, abide in him," that is, in the Son, as is clear from reference to his "appearance" or "coming." Only here in the Johannine literature is there a reference to the parousia (coming) of Jesus in judgment (cf. 1 Thess 2:19; 3:13; 4:15-17; 5:23). The question is, Will they have *confidence* before him at his coming or will they shrink from him in shame? Confidence *(parrhēsian)* or boldness is a key Johannine term, being used 9 times in the Gospel and 4 times in 1 John, and only 31 times in the NT as a whole. It is implied that his judgment will be based on righteousness because those who are righteous, as Jesus is righteous (2:1), may have confidence knowing that they are begotten of him. Doing righteousness (= love of the brethren) reveals those born of God.

Sanctification (Separation from the Corruption of the World) Is the Test of the Claim to Be Children of God (3:1-3)

To be begotten by the Son is to be begotten by the Father (2:23). Thus we move from a discussion of the relationship to the Son at his coming to the relationship of children to the Father (3:1). Being called children of God is rooted in the love of the Father. To be called children by the Father is to be his children. Children of the Father experience alienation from the world, which fails to recognize them as such just as it failed to recognize Jesus as the Son. The ambiguity of this reality in the eyes of the world leads to the affirmation that when the Son is manifest the reality of being children of God will be made manifest because they will see the Son as he is. This must take place at his coming, when those who see him will be like him. The assurance of this transformation, this *hope,* has an inner basis upon which is built the call for the readers to sanctify themselves as he (the Son) is holy (see John 17:15-19). Thus the Son is righteous and holy, and the readers are exhorted to be righteous and holy. That holiness is separated from the life that characterizes the world and is expressed in terms of righteousness. It is yet to become clear how our author understands righteousness.

The Incompatibility of Sin and Righteousness (3:4-10)

Clearly holiness and righteousness are opposed to sin, which is lawlessness (3:4) and which the Son came (was revealed) to remove (vv. 4-5). Consequently the reader is called to holiness and righteousness after the model or example of the Son, who, in his opposition to sin, came to take away sin. Consequently it is not a surprise when our author asserts that those who abide in him (the Son) do not sin and that everyone who sins has not seen or known him (v. 6). We would say, "no one sinning has seen or known him." On their own and in this context these views pose no problem. It is only when we recall that our author has rejected his opponents' claim to be sinless (1:8, 10) that 3:6 poses a problem. While recognizing that our author might not have been consistent or fair in his criticism of his opponents, there are important differences between them. First, their assertion of sinlessness appears to exclude their need of cleansing from sin (1:7, 9 in contrast to 1:8, 10), whereas our author's position builds on that cleansing work.

Then, when the language of 3:6-10 is carefully noted, fine distinctions of meaning emerge as *possibilities.* First, there is no suggestion of original sinlessness such as is found in the rejected assertion of 1:10. Then there is the use of the present participle with the article and the distinction of tenses in the use of the verb. Thus there is the contrast between those abiding in the Son and those sinning. To be, or to abide, in the Son is incompatible with sinning. Further, the one doing righteousness (acting righteously) is contrasted with the one doing sin, which distinguishes the children of God from the children of the devil. This stark contrast is similar to the distinction between the children of light and the children of darkness in the Qumran texts (see 1QS 1:10; 1QH 6:29-30). The devil is mentioned only in 1 John 3:8, 10. Reference to the "evil one" is more pervasive (2:13-14; 3:12; 5:18-19). Doing righteousness is interpreted in terms of loving the brother (3:10), which might imply that sinning is understood to be the failure to do so. The use of the present participle and present tense indicates continuous activity. It is in this sense that the children of the devil sin and the children of God do not *characteristically* do so. Because they are born of God, his seed (the word of God) abides in them and they are not able to live in sin, though they may slip and fall into sin. The Son of God came to destroy the works of the devil and to deal with sin, cleansing those who walk in the light and advocating their cause before the Father when they fall into sin. The distinction is between those whose lives are characterized by righteousness and those whose lives are characterized by sin. At the same time our author recognizes that the righteous fall into sin and need to be cleansed and restored (1:6–2:2).

The Incompatibility of Love and Hate (3:11-18)

The contrast between the two groups is now further clarified in terms of those who love the brothers and those who hate them (3:10, 11-18). In v. 10 we encounter the first (see vv. 16, 19, 24) of a second series (see 2:3, 5) of appeals to criteria to test the claim of the opponents. Our author seeks to test their claim to be children of God by the criterion of "doing righteousness," living faithfully, which he interprets as "loving the brother." This criterion is then related to "the message you heard from the beginning" (3:11; cf. 1:5). That message was that we should love one another (John 13:34), a command that goes back to Jesus (the beginning) in the Johannine tradition. Over against this is the example of Cain, who murdered his righteous brother (Gen 4:8), displaying, from the beginning, the conflict between the children of the devil and the children of God. This is the only allusion to the OT in 1 John. In the *Apocalypse of Abraham,* Cain is guided by satanic power. In 1 John the murderous action of Cain is taken to be typical of the world's hatred of the children of God. Interestingly, mention of the murderous action of the world leads to the highlighting of the evidence that "we have passed from death to life." The evidence is that "we love the brethren" (and sisters). Thus loving the brethren is a criterion for recognizing the children of God, who have passed from death to life, while the failure to love, which is equated with hatred and murder of the brother, reveals the children of the devil who abide in death (3:14-15).

This is our author's interpretation, and differences over the understandings of love seem to be indicated by appeal to the criterion for recognizing what love is, "In this . . . he laid down his life for us" (3:16). The example of Jesus is then made the basis for the assertion that "we ought to give our lives for the brethren" (v. 16; cf. 2:6). Our author makes clear that this example means that believers should give of their resources to those who are in need so that love cannot be understood as mere emotion or something expressed only in words. Love is to be expressed in action so that the command of Jesus finds interpretation in the manner of his life (3:17-18).

The Grounds for Confidence before God (3:19-24)

The appeal to criteria for testing claims to knowledge reflects the conflict with the opponents whose claims our author sought to repudiate. The criteria were also aimed at providing *assurance* to our author's readers. He sought to assure them that they were children of God, of the truth. Appeal to "By this . . ." probably looks back to the evidence of "loving the brethren" (and sisters). That evidence is used to calm the anxious and troubled heart. Assuming the success of this operation leads to a heart that does not accuse or condemn, something like "a clear conscience." The argument surprisingly implies that, if our heart does not condemn us, God, who is greater, will not do so either. One might have expected the argument to run, "God is greater and knows all things"; therefore, our hearts might mislead us because we are not omniscient. But for our author the fact that God knows all things means that he knows that our hearts are free from guilt. This is the ground for confidence before God. Then, in an appeal to his readers, now addressed as "beloved," the grounds for confidence are further elaborated in terms of keeping his (God's) commandments, that is, doing what is pleasing to him (3:21-22). At this point the commandments (v. 22) are reduced to a singular commandment (v. 23), although it is a two-sided one. The two sides correspond to the christological and ethical tests, and this statement of them brings out the inseparable relationship between them. Whereas the statement of the ethical test has preceded the statement of the christological test, here, where the connection between the two is made clear in terms of a singular commandment, the christological belief is stated first as the foundation of the ethical outworking.

Finally, this section asserts that the one who keeps God's commandments abides in God, and God in him. Evidence for this mutual abiding is found in the keeping of the commandments. The Letter also states that "we know that he abides in us" by the evidence of the Spirit that he has given us (3:24). After he has stated that the Spirit was evidence of God abiding in us, it soon becomes apparent that the claim to Spirit-inspired utterance was a controversial issue between our author and his opponents.

The Christological Test (4:1-6)

The Spirit of God confesses Jesus Christ come in the flesh. Our author addresses his readers as "beloved" (4:1), appropriately bridging the command to *love* one another with the new emphasis on testing the spirits. Inspiration (or ecstasy) alone is not enough. The passage implies that many spirits are manifest in inspired utterance, leading to the activity of many false prophets in the world. Because of this, the claim to be inspired needs to be tested by the confession "Jesus Christ has come in the flesh" (v. 2; cf. 1 Cor 12:3). At the very least this implies that the opponents found no significance in the humanity of Jesus. Rather, for them it was his divinity that provided them with a paradigm for understanding their own relationship to God. Their position is similar to that attributed to Cerinthus. Early tradition names him as an opponent of truth who asserted that the divine Christ came upon Jesus at his baptism and left him before his crucifixion. The opponents would not confess that Jesus was the Christ or that Jesus Christ had come in the flesh. For our author this was the truly inspired confession, while those who denied this were inspired by the spirit of the antichrist (cf. 2:22). The coming of the antichrist belongs to common expectation concerning the end time in some sectors of Judaism and was common in early Christianity (cf. Mark 13:5-6, 21-22; 2 Thess 2:1-12; 2 John 7; Revelation 13). Here the plurality of false prophets is reduced to the singular antichrist of the last day (4:3). Perhaps this is an example of representative personality, or personifying the opposition in terms of the powerful image of the antichrist.

Over against this phenomenon our author again addresses his readers as "children," an ambiguous form because it implies the relationship of the readers to himself as their authoritative teacher as well as their relationship to God as children of the Father. The latter is made explicit in the affirmation, "You are of God, children . . ." (4:4). Because of this he says, "you have conquered them," and this is explained in terms of the struggle between God and the devil. "Greater is he who is in you than he who is in the world" (v. 4; cf. 5:19). The antichrist, the false prophets, and the opponents are of the world (see 2:15-17), and the world listens to them because they speak in its terms and express its values (4:5). This reads like an explanation for the widespread success of the opponents. Over against this is our author's claim, "We are of God. The person who knows God hears us." Agreement with our author is now made the test of the claim to know God. Naturally this implies that his opponents do not. Here we meet a slight variation on the verbal formula expressing the test of claims. "From this we know the spirit of truth and the spirit of error." Formally this identifies the spirit of truth with those who agree with our author and the spirit of error with those who dissent. Alternatively, the spirit of truth is identified with the confession, "Jesus Christ is come in the flesh," and the spirit of error with those who reject this. It is notable that the opposition to the spirit of truth is not the spirit of falsehood, the natural Semitic antithesis, but the spirit of *error,* which is a thoroughly Hellenized expression. Teaching about the two spirits is found at Qumran in 1QS 3:18-19 as well as in *T. Jud.* 14:8; 19:4; 20:1; 23:1.

Third Presentation of the Two Tests (4:7–5:12)

If the connection of the two tests has been made clear, our author now insists that there is an inseparable relation between them.

Love Based on Faith Is Proof of Knowing God and Being Born of God (4:7-21)

Commencing the new cycle of tests by addressing his readers again as "beloved" (see 4:1 and note the continuation in v. 11) is altogether appropriate in a section teaching that, because God is love, those who know him and are his children will love one another.

God's Love Is the Source of Love for One Another (4:7-12)

The section begins with a call to love one another (4:7), which repeats the second part of the double command (3:23). The command is now based on the understanding that because God is love, love is from God and those who love are born of God and know God. The reverse is also true, that those who do not love do not know God (4:7-8). There are two areas that might have been contested by the opponents: the assertion that God is love and the assumption that such love necessitated love of one another. Because our author made no attempt to defend the assertion that God is love, we can only assume that this was not the storm center. Rather, the discussion moves immediately to the nature of that love. The Johannine use of love language *develops* out of its use in the LXX, but there is no precedent there for the crystallization of the message in terms of "God is love."

In 4:9-10 our author provides two statements framed in the language of his tests ("In this . . .") in which he provides evidence of what the love of God is like. First, he argues that "the love of God was revealed among us" when "God sent his only begotten Son into the world that we may live through him" (v. 9). Thus it is clear that the love of God is life-*giving.* Second, and here the negative probably identifies the position of the opponents, his characteristic formula sets out the evidence of God's love, "In this is love, *not that we loved God,* but that he loved us. . . ." Our author does not speak of human love for God but of God's love for humanity, and the response to his love is, "we ought to love one another" (v. 11). The love of God is further elaborated in the second statement. Repeating first that God sent his Son, our author now says he was sent to be "the expiation for our sins." Thus "we live through him" because he dealt with the problem of human sin. His coming involved his death by means of which he "cleanses us from all sin" (1:7); he dealt with the problem of sin (2:2).

Our author provides no rationale for the way the death of Jesus deals with sin. Clearly he understood love of one another to be the appropriate response to the revelation of the love of God. A direct response of love for God is ruled out because "No one has ever seen God." Love for one another is the evidence that he abides in us and his love is perfected in us. The presence of God is not demonstrated by some vision. It is to be found in the response of love for one another (4:11-12).

The Spirit Is the Evidence of Abiding in God (4:13-16a)

Again using the formula "By this we know . . . ," our author refers back to his opponents' claim to abide in him (2:6) and provides a test to substantiate the claim (4:13). Here the discussion concerns abiding in God, as the context shows (see vv. 7-12, 16). But there our author has taken the claim "to abide in him" to be a claim to abide in Jesus. Because our author closely identifies Jesus with God, it may be that in the earlier passage he has treated the opponents' claim to abide in God as if it were a claim to abide in Jesus so that their claim could be tested by comparison with the manner of his life. Here (v. 13) the test seems to play into their hands. First, abiding in him is expanded into a mutuality formula including his abiding "in us," the evidence of which is that "he has given us of his Spirit." "Inspiration" appears to be evidence of mutual abiding. But vv. 1-6 has already associated the Spirit of God with the confession of Jesus Christ come in the flesh, and this meaning is confirmed by the affirmation that the Father sent the Son to be the Savior of the world (v. 14), which, for our author, involved his death (1:7; 2:2). To confess that Jesus Christ is the Son of God thus becomes the test of the abiding of God and abiding in God (4:15). Recognition (to have known and believed that) of Jesus as the Son of God is the key to awareness of the love of God (4:16). The believer should recognize Jesus as the evidence of God's love for believers (for us) and for the world (v. 14), knowing that the Father sent the Son to be the Savior of the world (see John 4:42).

Abiding in Love Is the Ground of Confidence before God (4:16b-21)

The action of God in Jesus is then taken to be indicative of the being of God. Just as God was defined in terms of light (1:5), so now our author asserts, "God is love" (4:16). In terms of equations, God = love. But it does not necessarily follow that love = God. Rather, our author takes the view that love is *from* God and is defined by the character of God. Those who love abide in God, and God in them. Thus our author has reaffirmed the confession of faith and the response of love for one another as the double test of a real relationship with God.

Love is fulfilled in those who abide in love. Knowing themselves to be loved by God, they love one another (see 3:19-24). The consequence of this is confidence before God even in facing the day of judgment. Here again our author is concerned with the grounds for *assurance* and confidence in relation to God. Again he returns to the normative life of Jesus, indicated by the demonstrative "As *he* is, so are we in this world" (4:17). Those who live as he lived have proper grounds for confidence. This confidence is grounded in the experience of the love of God which banishes fear (v. 18). The priority of the love of God for us (for the world) is fundamental for this view. His love is the source of human love. In this statement no object of human love is indicated, simply "We love." The reason for that love is, "because he first loved us" (v. 19). We might have expected, "We love *him* because he first loved us." The following verses (vv. 20-21) show that responsive human love is in fact directed to the brother. The key to the argument is the assumption that love requires the seen presence of the one loved. Given the acceptance of the invisibility of God, a teaching common to Hellenistic Judaism and the Greco-Roman world, love for God is excluded. In the Gospel an exception is made for Jesus as the revealer of God (John 1:18; 5:37; 6:46; 12:49; 14:9). Thus we should understand 4:21 to mean, "This commandment we have from him, that the person who *claims* to love God should also love his brother." It is of interest that our author refers to love for the brother, not the neighbor or the enemy (Matt 5:43-45; Luke 10:27-28), as in the teaching of Jesus in the Synoptic Gospels. Love for the brother is comparable to Jesus' call for the disciples to love one another in John 13:34-35. This need not mean that love for neighbor was excluded. It certainly was not the focus. Focus on the brother (or one another) seems to be a consequence of the experience of being excluded from the synagogue (John 9:22, 35; 12:42; 16:2) and subsequently having experienced a traumatic schism (1 John 2:19). A sense of alienation from the world of the larger community accounts for preoccupation with love for members of the community, especially as this was a point of contention with those who had left the community.

Faith Is the Basis of Love (5:1-12)

Our author now sets out to show that belief in Jesus as the Christ entails love of all the children of God. The language of the argument is less than transparently clear because our author begins with the position of his opponents.

Those Who Believe Are Begotten of God and Love One Another (5:1-3)

The argument develops (5:1-2) as a response to those who claimed to love God and admitted no connection between this and the need to love those our author considered as brothers. To counter their position he asserted that every person who believes that Jesus is the Christ is born of God, is a child of God. The logic of the argument is that those who claim to love the Father should also love his children, their brothers. The test of the claim to love God, which is beyond verification in itself, is to be found in the evidence of loving God's children. This evidence is also expressed in terms of keeping his commandments (vv. 2b-3). His commandments (3:22) are reduced to the double commandment of believing in his Son Jesus Christ and loving one another (3:23). Here (5:1-

3) believing that Jesus is the Christ is the evidence of being a child of God, and loving the children of God is evidence of being born of God. Thus the two tests of 3:23 are here an expression of believing in Jesus as the Christ and a fulfillment of the commandments. The reduction of the commandments to this shows why his commandments are not burdensome (cf. Matt 11:28-30). Our author may also think that loving the brothers comes "easily" to those born of God.

Victory over the World (5:4-5)

An explanation of the implications of the nonburdensome ("easy") commandments follows in 5:4-5. One of the commandments was to believe (3:23) that "Jesus is the Christ," and those who so believe were born of God (5:1). As becomes clear in v. 5, the confession that "Jesus is the Christ" is synonymous with the confession that "Jesus is the Son of God" and, we suspect, the confession that "Jesus Christ is come in the flesh" (cf. 4:2-6). The argument now continues that everyone born of God conquers the world. The victory is linked to the confession by the affirmation that the victory is "our faith" (5:4; cf. 4:2-6), which is shorthand for saying that it is our faith that enables us to overcome the world. Naturally the world is understood (as in 2:15-17; 5:18-20) to lie in the power of "the evil one" and to express values antithetic to and violently opposed to God. Faith breaks free from the constraints and bondage of the world expressed in terms of the darkness of hatred. Consequently the victory is manifest in the love expressed by the children of God for the children of God.

The Witness to the Son Is the Witness to Eternal Life (5:6-12)

Our author further explicates the meaning of his confession as expressed in 5:1, 5 and sets out the significance of this faith, culminating in the affirmation that those who so believe have eternal life (v. 12). The confession of faith is linked to the theme of the confirming witness where contact with John 5:31-40 is evident in the exposition. He begins by using the double name "Jesus Christ," which abbreviates the confession "Jesus is the Christ" (5:1) and which was used in the confession "Jesus Christ has come in the flesh" (4:2). The double name draws attention to the uniting of the human and the divine in the flesh of Jesus. This provides a clue to the meaning of coming through water and blood. The polemic against the view that he came by water only is emphatic and draws attention to the view attributed to Cerinthus that the heavenly Christ descended on Jesus at his baptism and left him before his crucifixion. Our author does not deny the importance of the baptism of Jesus (water) but insists that he came also by blood, that is, as a real human of flesh and blood. Reference here to blood only (not flesh and blood) might be a consequence of the denial, by the opponents, of the cleansing power of the "blood" of Jesus (1:7), where blood is a symbol for the death of Jesus in its cleansing efficacy. Just how the Spirit, who descended on Jesus at his baptism, is the *witness* to *this* is unclear, though the Gospels certainly make this the event that revealed Jesus and opened his public ministry (John 1:29-34). This is a more likely interpretation than the one, on the basis of John 19:34, that takes both water and blood to refer to the circumstances of the death of Jesus. The Spirit is the truth (cf. John 14:6; 16:13) and is one of three witnesses along with the water and the blood, united in testimony to Jesus. The water of baptism united with the Spirit to reveal Jesus as the Son, and by his blood he cleanses from all sin.

The theme of witness is characteristically Johannine. The theme of the Spirit as witness finds a parallel in John 15:26-27, though it finds unique expression there. The text of 1 John 5:7-8 (the Johannine Comma) is absent from early Greek manuscripts and is a puzzling addition. The force of the addition can be seen partly in the need of multiple witnesses in the light of Deut 17:6; 19:15.

Although the witness of John the Baptist is involved (the witness of men), our author asserts that the witness of God is greater so that the role of the Spirit takes priority in revealing Jesus as the Son of God. This is emphatically reiterated as the substance of God's testimony to Jesus, confirming that this was contested by the opponents. Those who believe the witness have the assurance of God, while those who reject this are accused of calling God a liar (5:10; cf. 1:10). The object of the sending and revealing of the Son is the salvation of the world (4:14). God's witness is not simply to the Son, but to the Son as the one in whom he has given eternal life, which can be called simply "life." To have the Son, that is, to believe in him, is to have life. For our author the object of the coming of the Son was to bring eternal life.

Conclusion (5:13-21)

To Reestablish Confidence (5:13-15)

The conclusion now states the purpose of the letter, which is intimately linked to the purpose of the coming of the Son of God. The language of 5:13 should be compared with that of John 20:31. In each case the writer makes the purpose of what is written the same as the perceived purpose of Jesus in his coming. The Son came to give eternal life, and our author wrote so that his readers might *know* that they have eternal life. Since the opponents had undermined their assurance, this letter set out to reestablish the confidence of those who believed in the manner prescribed by this letter. Correct belief was crucial for our author, although he was able to vary his confessional formulae: belief that Jesus is the Christ, belief in Jesus Christ, belief that Jesus is the Son of God, belief in the name of the Son of God, belief that Jesus Christ has come in the flesh, and belief that he came by water and blood. This diversity of formulae should not lead us to think that our author was easygoing in his understanding of Jesus. Rather, the variations clarify his meaning and exclude what are considered to be the wrong views of his opponents.

The outcome of assurance is our author's concern. Grounded in this faith, the believer has the confidence of a child of God making requests of his Father (cf. 3:21-22). Again, the confidence is based in faith which involves asking according to God's will. But the point of this discussion is to bring out the bold and confident relation to God arising from the true confession of faith (5:13-15) because the opponents have threatened to undermine the faith of his readers.

Prayer for Those Sinning (5:16-17)

The Letter addresses two related problems. First, our author refutes his opponents for whom, it seems, he holds out no hope (2:19) because theirs is a mortal (to death) sin. Since there is no hope for them, our author does not ask his readers to pray for them. The notion of the unforgivable sin is found in the Gospel tradition (Mark 3:28-30), and our author attributes this sin to his opponents because they rejected the saving significance of the earthly Jesus, Jesus Christ in the flesh. Whether reference to sins which are not mortal describes specific sins is not clear. It may be that what is in mind is the faltering faith of those who have been disturbed by the opponents. Our author exhorts the faithful to pray for them, encouraging their return to an assured faith.

Second, his dominant purpose is to strengthen the flagging resistance of his readers. They were showing signs of anxiety and uncertainty under the impact of the opponents, especially the trauma of the recent schism (2:19). The refutation of the position of the opponents was an important aspect of his attempt to meet the need of his readers. The refutation was to strengthen his wavering supporters. But he also calls on the strong to help the weak, and in a spirit of brotherliness, not self-righteousness. The wavering brother is not to be treated like the opponents but caringly nurtured to reestablish him in the community. At the same time our author recognizes this wavering as sin even if it is distinguished from mortal sin. By recognizing wavering as sin he strongly discouraged it. By distinguishing it from mortal sin he encouraged the forgiveness (cf. 1:7-10; 2:1-2) and restoration of waverers (5:16-17).

God and the Problem of Sin (5:18-20)

The schism not only split the community, leading to the loss of a large group, but it destroyed the confidence of many who remained in the community. Thus the question was raised, "Is no one secure? Can anyone be shaken and ultimately lost?" Our author's urgent attention to the problem suggests that he feared the worst and acted to avert the disaster of a mass defection to the opponents. Yet teaching that unguardedly stated this would have been psychologically destructive to his very purpose of bolstering the confidence of his readers. While, humanly speaking, correct, it left God out of the equation. Thus our author's attempt to reestablish a confident faith turns attention back to God. There is also the use of the argument that the schism revealed that the opponents did not really belong to the community and that their withdrawal only revealed the true state of affairs (2:19). This is rather cheap wisdom (after the event has happened) because it does not help in the midst of doubt and despair. Nevertheless, our author argues that those who are born of God cannot live in sin. The use of the present tense implies more than a momentary failure (5:18). What is more, he appeals to his readers' awareness of this, "We know." This appeal shows that our author is working on the consciousness of his readers. He wants them to be aware that those born of God are kept by God. This does not mean that the child of God cannot waver and fall into sin. But the one born of God will not fall into mortal sin. In a hostile world, whose values threatened to overwhelm our author and his supporters, he asserted that those born of God were kept by him so that the evil one, who holds sway over the world, cannot harm them. Importantly he also appeals to his readers, "We know that we are (born) of God." On the other hand, the opponents, by their mortal sin, have demonstrated that they are not born of God. It is important to recognize that this teaching is both polemical (against the opponents) and pastoral (to build up and encourage the readers) (5:18-19).

To support his case, our author again appeals to what his readers know, "We know." This time he seeks evidence outside the readers in the story of Jesus. The way his story is known assumes the distinctive Johannine understanding and may, at this point, run very close to the claims of the opponents. There would have been disputed understandings of what the claim meant. The Son of God has come. This falls short of the assertion that he came in the flesh. Further, he is said to "have given us knowledge of the one who is true." Because he claims "We know" this, he also affirms, "We are in the one who is true," that is, the one true God who stands over against what is false and is represented by idols. The relationship between the Father and the Son means that those abiding in the Father also abide in the Son, and vice versa. To be in the one who is true is to have eternal life. The reality of the one who is true transforms the being of those who are in him.

Final Exhortation (5:21)

The epistle ends with the call, "Little children, guard yourselves from idols." The one who is true is incompatible with the falsehood of idols, and those who are in the one who is true can have nothing to do with idols, with which our author associates the false position of his opponents (5:20-21). In 1 Corinthians 10:1-13 Paul compares typologically (10:6, 11) Israel's sin in the wilderness with the situation of the Corinthians. There Israel turned to idolatry, so that many of them died. 1 John exhorts its readers to guard against idols and warns of mortal sin. The comparison with Israel allows for the eschatological situation of the Corinthians for whom the end of the ages had arrived. This is true also for 1 John, for whom the appearance of antichrists signaled the last hour.

The final warning, "Little children, guard yourselves from idols," makes more sense in a predominantly Gentile context (1 John 5:21). The suggestion that reference to idols is metaphorical is based on the Qumran expression of "the idols of his heart," found in 1QS 2:11 (thus Edwards: 43). But 1 John warns, "guard yourself from idols." There is no mention of the idols of the heart. Paul's letters remind us that idolatry was pervasive in the Roman Empire, and Jewish Christianity was concerned to avoid the contamination of idolatry (see 1 Cor 8:1–10:33 and note also Acts 15:20, 29; 21:25). Further, the wording that follows in 1QS 2:12-14 is dependent on Deut 29:17-19, where the words "I shall be safe, though I walk in the stubbornness of my heart" (see 1QS 2:13-14) are an expression of turning away to serve the gods of the nations (Deut 29:18). Thus, even in 1QS 2:11 the warning is against actual idolatry and its consequences in the community. The Jewish view that idolatry was accompanied by moral decline and the judgment of God is also to be found in Paul's letters (see Rom 1:18-32).

The pressure to find a more acceptable contemporary meaning for the warning must be held in check because of the evidence of the pervasive reality of idolatry in the Roman Empire and continued Jewish abhorrence of it. The prominence of idolatry is clear enough. It was one of the four issues forbidden to Gentile Christians in the so-called "Jerusalem decree" according to Acts 15:20, 29; 21:25. In each case the issue of idolatry is mentioned first. That this continued to be a problem is clear enough from Paul's First Letter to the Corinthians, where the subject is dealt with in a number of chapters beginning at 8:1, "Concerning food offered to idols." In what follows Paul twice directly and specifically warns against idolatry: "Do not be idolaters, as some of them were" (10:7); "Therefore, my beloved, shun the worship of idols" (10:14). This latter warning is comparable to what we have at the end of 1 John, "Little children, guard yourselves from idols."

In 1 Corinthians what follows each of these warnings is an exposition of the theme of the judgment of God on idolatry based on the example of the people of Israel who submitted to the attraction of idolatry. The warning against idolatry in 1 John 5:21 may seem to us to come unexpectedly, from out of "left court." That is because we live outside the pervasive reality of idolatry in the Roman Empire.

2 John

COMMENTARY

The Structure of 2 John

I. Opening Greeting Formula	1-3
II. Body of the Letter	4-11
A. Commendation and Call to Love One Another	4-6
B. Warning against the Opponents, the Deceivers	7-9
C. Warning against Offering Hospitality to the Opponents	10-11
III. Final Greetings	12-13

Unlike 1 John, 2 John is a genuine letter with an opening address formula and a closing greeting. Following the early Christian tradition of letter writing found in Paul's letters, these are expanded to take account of distinctive Christian themes.

Opening Greeting Formula (1-3)

The author identifies himself as "the elder." It is unlikely that this is simply a reference to his age. In 1 John the author distinguishes the older from the younger as "fathers" and "young men" (2:13-14). Rather, the title seems to apply to the authoritative tradition-bearers in the community (cf. the group designated by the "we" of 1 John 1:1-4) among whom our author may have stood out, at least in his own estimation, but also probably in the estimation of the recipients of his letter.

The Letter is addressed to "the elect lady and her children." It becomes clear from the conclusion (v. 13) that this is a reference to a sister church and its individual members. The themes of love and truth, important in the body of the letter, are introduced in the affirmation that the writer loves the recipients in truth, as do all who know the truth. This excludes the opponents. Those who know the truth and love in truth have the truth abiding in them now and forever. This is probably a variation on the theme of children *of God,* being born of God. The opening greeting concludes with good "wishes" expressed in distinctive Christian terms.

First, it is not expressed in "wishful" terms but as a statement of what will be. What will be with them is "grace, mercy, and peace." The word we translate as "grace" is characteristic of Greek greetings but has taken on a new meaning with the two other terms and in relation to the characteristically Christian understanding of the grace of God. If "grace" comes from the Greek world, "mercy and peace" are characteristically Jewish. In their company "grace" takes on a new sense but appears only in the opening greeting. It is not only by associating grace with mercy and peace that a distinctive Christian sense is given. These gifts are from the Father and his Son Jesus Christ. In this formulation the role of the Father is stressed in relation to the Son, who is named Jesus Christ, the double name being characteristic of 1 John but uncommon in the Gospel (only in 1:17; 17:3). He is the Son of the Father in truth and love.

Body of the Letter (4-11)

After commending the readers, our author calls on them to refuse hospitality to his opponents and characterizes their position as progressive and departing from the primitive gospel.

Commendation and Call to Love One Another (4-6)

The commendation concerns those children of the elect lady met by the author. The reference is to members of a neighboring church within the Johannine circle. They were commended for walking (living) in truth in accord with the commandment from the Father. Just where this command is to be found is not indicated. Our author notes this compliance in order to request the fulfillment of the command to love one another, which is expressed as not new (cf. 1 John 3:11 and contrast John 13:34). The point is that this command goes back to the Jesus tradition and is not an early Christian innovation, suggesting that the opponents were innovators. The argument of vv. 5-6 is tortuously repetitive. It does nothing to clarify what walking in love means apart from the command to love one another. It is apparently distinct from walking in truth, which therefore should be understood in terms of the confession of faith, of Jesus Christ coming in the flesh. Thus the emphasis on truth and love corresponds to the two tests of 1 John.

Warning against the Opponents, the Deceivers (7-9)

The warning concerning the many deceivers who have appeared also identifies the deceiver with the antichrist (cf. 1 John 2:18-27; 4:1-6). As in 1 John, this opposition is associated with the refusal to confess Jesus Christ *coming* in the flesh. While 2 John uses a present participle to express the coming, there is no reason to think that this is not also a reference to the historic coming of Jesus of Nazareth. Our author must have sensed the threat of the opponents, given the urgency of his warning (v. 8). Again there is evidence of the opponents being progressives who go beyond the teaching of Christ as expressed in the love command. If they did this in the name of God, our author objects that the Father and the Son are inseparably bound together so that to reject the teaching of Christ is to reject the Father. Hidden in this formulation is the opponents' objection to the identification of Jesus as the Christ, the Son of God.

Warning against Offering Hospitality to the Opponents (10-11)

Our author sets out his teaching, which corresponds to the two tests of 1 John, as the touchstone of truth. He charges his readers not to provide hospitality to traveling teachers who fail to pass these tests. To add weight to his warning he asserts that those who provide hospitality share the wickedness of the work of his opponents.

Final Greetings (12-13)

Characteristic of conclusions, our author indicates that he still has much to say to his readers but would rather do it "face to face" so that his and their joy may be complete (v. 12). Why this could not be so through his letter is unclear, though it might be that the lack of immediacy in communication by letter mitigated against the experience of joy. The author gives no reason to think that he did not expect his letter to be successful, but he thought he could do better in person. Finally, he sends greetings from the children of the elect sister of the lady to whom he has written. In all probability this is a reference to the members of his own local church.

3 John

COMMENTARY

The Structure of 3 John

I. Opening Greeting	1
II. Body of the Letter	2-12
A. Commendation for Walking in the Truth	2-4
B. Commendation for Providing Hospitality to Missionaries	5-8
C. Critique of Diotrephes	9-10
D. Commendation of Demetrius	11-12
III. Closing and Final Greeting	13-15

Opening Greeting (1)

For the author's self-identification see 2 John. This letter is addressed to an individual named Gaius. It is unclear whether this individual was a member of the church addressed by 2 John. Reference to reports of Gaius from some of the brethren might indicate another community. If so, the three letters provide evidence of a circle of churches making up the Johannine community. On the other hand, it is more likely that the brethren were traveling missionaries, and in this case they provide no evidence of Gaius's church. He is addressed as "the beloved" (see also vv. 2, 5, and 11 and cf. the use of the plural in 1 John 2:7; 3:21; 4:1, 7, 11), which fits our author's affirmation of his love for him in truth.

Body of the Letter (2-12)

Commendation for Walking in the Truth (2-4)

The first part is a transition from the opening greeting to the body of the letter. It is marked as part of the body of the letter by the rhetorical address to the reader as "beloved," a form of address repeated in vv. 2, 5, and 11. In such a brief letter this concentration alerts the reader to recognize that love for the brethren rather than truth, the confession of faith, is the major issue of this letter. First our author expresses a prayer for the well-being of Gaius, affirming at the same time that it was well with his soul. Evidence of this came to our author by way of reports from traveling brethren. Their reports confirmed that he was following the truth. Our author's concern was not, in this instance, the confession of faith. He affirms that he has no greater joy than comes from such reports of his children. Hence, as in 1 John, our author expresses a paternal spiritual relationship to his reader(s).

Commendation for Providing Hospitality to Missionaries (5-8)

Our author then commends Gaius *for occasions when* he has provided hospitality to traveling brethren, especially those who were strangers. Through these traveling "strangers" reports have reached our author. Thus they were strangers to Gaius but not to our author. They made their report to the church, not privately to our author. They were itinerant missionaries who went out "on behalf of the name," probably referring to the name of Jesus but understood in terms of the Johannine confession. The principle of hospitality upon which the mission depended probably went back to the principles of Jesus' mission (Mark 6:10-11). The principle was to accept hospitality from those who received the gospel. Here we have an early use of "the nations" or "gentiles" in the sense of "unbelievers." The section ends with an expression of the *obligation* to provide hospitality, adding the incentive that by so doing we become "fellow workers in the truth" with the missionaries.

Critique of Diotrephes (9-10)

The appeal to what was written to the church would fit 1 John. Reference to Diotrephes probably identifies one of the opponents. He did not acknowledge the "elder's" authority; rather, he put himself first. Clearly there was a leadership struggle between these two, and this might have found expression in the schism mentioned in 1 John 2:19. In the community to which the elder wrote the division might not have been so clear-cut, with Diotrephes continuing to (from our author's point of view) stir up trouble in the community. That Diotrephes continued to wield authority in the community is evidenced by his criticism of our author (which he considered slanderous), his refusal to provide hospitality to missionaries connected to our author, and his ability to prevent others from providing hospitality, putting them out of the church (excommunication!). For this reason it has been suggested that Diotrephes provides evidence of the early emergence of the single local bishop whose local authority was challenged by itinerant charismatic authority. It is also likely that Diotrephes was a leading opponent who had broken away from our author's community but who remained a dominant figure in Gaius's community.

Commendation of Demetrius (11-12)

Again addressing Gaius as "beloved," our author appeals to him to imitate, not evil but good, because good is of God. Naturally our author assumes that he and his supporters are of God. It is on this basis that he appeals on behalf of Demetrius, who was obviously one of his supporters. Thus when he appeals to the universal testimony to Demetrius, this can hardly include Diotrephes and his supporters. To bolster this testimony our author says that he has the testimony of the truth. It is unclear how this works, whether it was somehow meant to be self-authenticating or not. Appeal to his own testimony to Demetrius is bolstered by "you know my testimony is true," thus indicating that he was expecting a sympathetic hearing from readers who were his supporters, even if this letter indicates that he was worried that Diotrephes might have undermined his authority.

Closing and Final Greeting (13-15)

The closing follows the same pattern as 2 John 12-13. Both Letters indicate that the author has much to write and explain their brevity by referring to a prospective visit which was hopefully imminent in the case of 3 John. In each case these letters show a preference for face-to-face conversation. Because the complex greeting of 2 John 3 is absent from 3 John, a greeting of "peace" is given at the end. The concluding respectful greeting was expressed on behalf of his community, symbolized by "your elect sister" to the community addressed in 2 John. But 3 John was addressed to Gaius, making the conclusion more complex. First, our author identifies himself with others in greeting Gaius. He calls those associated with him "friends," though this might be an overprecise translation. The two terms translated "beloved" and "friends" might not be so clearly distinguished. In the Gospel of John the two verbs for love overlap, and this might also be true of the nouns derived from them. However we understand this, our author associates friends with himself in greeting Gaius and asks Gaius to greet the friends associated with him on our author's behalf.

From 3 John a good case can be made for looking at the three letters together, the first letter being referred to in v. 9. 2 and 3 John then seem to be written to different communities in the Johannine circle. 2 John was written to a community generally, while 3 John was written to an individual who was asked to pass on greetings to his community, by implication distinct from the community addressed in 2 John. It also appears that the schism experienced by the community from which the author of 1 John wrote was not clear-cut in the community to which 3 John was addressed. The refusal of hospitality by Diotrephes could be interpreted as a failure to love the brethren. The author of 2 John had exhorted his readers not to provide hospitality to his opponents (vv. 10-11) so that it might appear that the responses of the two groups were each the mirror image of the other. Yet it should be noted that there is no evidence that the opponents made hospitality or love for their brethren a fundamental ethical issue or a basis for mission.

Bibliography. Abbott, E. A. 1905, *Johannine Vocabulary,* London: A. & C. Black • Abbott, E. A. 1906, *Johannine Grammar,* London: A. & C. Black • Bogart, J. 1977, *Orthodox and Heretical Perfectionism,* SBLDS 33, Missoula, Mont.: Scholars • Barrett, C. K. 2d ed. 1978, *The Gospel According to St. John,* London: SPCK • Barrett, C. K. 1995, "Johannine Christianity," in *Jesus and the Word and Other Essays,* Edinburgh: T. & T. Clark • Bernard, J. H. 1928, *A Critical and Exegetical Commentary on the Gospel According to St. John,* Edinburgh: T. & T. Clark • Brooke, A. E. 1912, *A Critical and Exegetical Commentary on the Johannine Epistles,* Edinburgh: T. & T. Clark • Brown, R. E. 1982, *The Epistles of John,* AB 30, New York: Doubleday • Bultmann, R. 1973, *The Johannine Epistles,* Philadelphia: Fortress • Dodd, C. H. 1946, *The Johannine Epistles,* London: Hodder and Stoughton • Dodd, C. H. 1953, *The Interpretation of the Fourth Gospel,* Cambridge: Cambridge University • Edwards, R. B. 1996, *The Johannine Epistles,* New Testament Guides, Sheffield: Sheffield Academic • Fiorenza, E. S. 1976-77, "The Quest for the Johannine School: The Apocalypse and the Fourth Gospel," *NTS* 23:402-27 • Hengel, M. 1989, *The Johannine Question,* London: SPCK • Houlden, J. L. 1973, *A Commentary on the Johannine Epistles,* BNTC, London: A. & C. Black • Kysar, R. 1975, *The Fourth Evangelist and His Gospel,* Minneapolis: Augsburg • Law, R. 1909, *The Tests of Life,* Edinburgh: T. & T. Clark • Lieu, J. 1986, *The Second and Third Epistles of John,* Edinburgh: T. & T. Clark • Lieu, J. 1991, *The Theology of the Johannine Epistles,* Cambridge: Cambridge University • Marshall, I. H. 1978, *The Epistles of John,* NICNT, Grand Rapids: Eerdmans • Okure, T. 1988, *The Johannine Approach to Mission: A Contextual Study of John 4.1-32,* Tübingen: J. C. B. Mohr • Painter, J. 3d ed. 1986, *John: Witness and Theologian,* London: SPCK, 1975 and Melbourne: Beacon Hill • Painter, J. 1991/1993, *The Quest for the Messiah: The History, Literature and Theology of the Johannine Community,* Edinburgh: T. & T. Clark and Nashville: Abingdon • Painter, J. 1993, "Theology and Eschatology in the Prologue of John," *SJT* 46:27-42 • Schnackenburg, R. 1992, *The Johannine Epistles: A Commentary,* trans. R. and I. Fuller from the 7th German edition of 1984, London: Burns & Oates and New York: Crossroad • Schnackenburg, R. 2001, *1, 2, and 3 John,* SacPag 18, Collegeville, Minn.: Liturgical Press • Smalley, S. S. 1984, *1, 2, 3 John,* WBC, Waco: Word • Smith, D. M. 1984, *Johannine Christianity: Essays on Its Setting, Sources and Theology,* Columbia: University of South Carolina • Strecker, G. 1996, *The Johannine Letters,* Hermeneia, Minneapolis: Fortress.

Jude

Scot McKnight

INTRODUCTION

Though one of the smallest surviving letters from earliest Christianity, Jude uses a rich vocabulary efficiently and effectively (cf. Jude 10, 11-13, 24-25) to teach, to exhort, and to warn. If the author of this letter was in touch with many streams of ancient Jewish and Christian traditions, he does not seem particularly indebted to Paul or to John. His Bible was apparently the OT in Hebrew, and it was read through the lenses of many interpretive traditions. He shows an especial affinity to *1 Enoch* and the *Testament of Moses.* The Letter does not convincingly show connections to what is now called "early Catholicism" (see Dunn 1991: 341-66); instead, the Letter reflects what is best described as a form of Jewish-Christian apocalyptic (Bauckham).

Jude shows special affinities to other Christian letters, especially to James, Hebrews, 1 John, and ideas and forms found in Paul's letters. Even though Christian tradition has classified Jude as a "catholic epistle," that is, a letter with no particular church in mind but intended for the church universal, this classification is unacceptable today. The problems facing this letter do not find substantial parallels elsewhere in earliest Christianity, leaving the impression of a set of problems that were somewhat unique to that given group of Christians.

Date and Author

Some evidence in the Letter has been used to infer a later date for the Letter, that is, a date after the time of Jude the brother of Jesus. But that evidence (vv. 3, 17-18) can more naturally be explained in other ways. Accordingly, it is best to assign Jude to a period during which the brother of Jesus would have been alive, if not just after his death (e.g., AD 50-100). Bauckham's recent magisterial commentary argues for a date in the 50s. There is little to counter such a view and much in its favor. On the other hand, the author of Jude has been suggested to be either (1) the brother of Jesus or (2) a pseudonym for the brother of Jesus. The evidence for the brother of Jesus is scattered throughout the NT (Mark 6:3; Acts 1:14; 1 Cor 9:5; cf. also Mark 3:21, 31; John 7:5), but he was known well enough that it is reasonable to think that when "Jude" was mentioned, such a name would refer to the brother of Jesus unless some further description was attached (see Neyrey: 20-31). It is probable that Jude is not typical of either Jewish or Christian pseudepigraphs, which would favor the view that the brother of Jesus wrote the Letter. Thus, even if the case is hardly certain, it seems reasonable to conclude that Jude, the brother of Jesus, was the author of the Letter (Bauckham: 14-16).

Structure

It is best to see the Letter organized as follows:

Salutation (1-2)
Intention of the Author (3-4)
Context for the Appeal (5-19)
Appeal (20-23)
Doxology (24-25)

This outline, which will be used in the commentary below, requires some explanation for the "Context for the Appeal." The letter is an exhortation, and that exhortation is expressed as an appeal in vv. 20-23. What vv. 5-19 do is to set the stage for the appeal by providing a network of ideas upon which it can be constructed. While in this sense they function as preliminary, and result in the preliminary stage being longer than the act itself, the preliminary part includes appeals along the way.

In addition, the "Context for the Appeal" is characterized by a careful use of tenses: context and background find themselves expressed in past tenses (e.g., vv. 5-7), while application to the problem the church is facing with false teachers emerges from present tenses (e.g., vv. 8-10). Along with this structural observation, we also should note the repeated use of "these" as significant for interpretation (vv. 8, 10, 12, 16, and 19). Accordingly, we find the following pattern:

1. 5-7 with interpretation (8-10);
2. 11 with interpretation (12-13);
3. 14-15 with interpretation (16); and
4. 17-18 with interpretation (19).

Social Factors

If we know little about the social makeup of the author (see Neyrey: 32-41 for insights gleaned from the social sciences), we have some insight into the opponents, though we must guard against the tendency to identify Jude's rhetorical presentation of the opponents with the opponents themselves. Their stance is consistently labeled *antinomian*: they appear to the author as those who reject all moral authorities, including Jesus Christ, Moses, and angelic beings (cf. vv. 4, 8-10). The flip side of their repudiation of moral authorities is a lifestyle of sensual indulgence (vv. 6-8, 10, 23). In addition to these two clearly defined aspects of their character, Jude mentions their greed (v. 11), their self-promotion (v. 16), and possibly their ecstatic religious experiences (vv. 8, 19). Their influence on the community betrays that they are seen by some, and at least by themselves, as teachers (vv. 4, 11-13). Some have inferred from vv. 4, 8, 19, and 25 that they are gnostic, but the most recent studies have argued that the origins of the opponents lie elsewhere (Bauckham, Neyrey). One recent study has argued that the use of rhetoric in the letter makes our knowledge of the opponents much more tentative than some scholars think (Thurén).

COMMENTARY

Salutation (1-2)

As is the case with most early Christian letters, Jude Christianizes the form (White): his title is "servant of *Jesus Christ*," the addressees are "those who are called," and the blessings wished are terms rich with Christian resonance: "mercy, peace, and love."

The author's name is Jude. This could be, if one combs early Christian evidence, (1) the brother of Jesus (cf. Mark 6:3; Acts 12:17; 15:13; 21:18; 1 Cor 15:7; Gal 2:9, 12), (2) Judas brother of James (Luke 6:16; Acts 1:13), or (3) some other Jude who carried significant authority in the community. Unless Jude was written in a vacuum in which the brother of Jesus was unknown, it remains far more likely that the Jude named here is the brother of Jesus.

That he used the term "servant of Jesus Christ" for his identification reveals in one stroke his special status (Neh 9:14; Pss 89:3; 105:42; Dan 6:20). The family connection of Jude gives him "ascribed authority" (Neyrey: 47-48), but Jude makes no claim to be "apostle" (cf. v. 17). "Servant" is used in other early Christian letters (e.g., Rom 1:1; Jas 1:1; 2 Pet 1:1). (Observe that in 2 Pet 1:1, in what is probably a pseudonymous letter, "apostle" is added to "servant.") Eusebius tells us later of the continued interest in the relatives of Jesus (*Hist. Eccl.* 1.7.14; 3.20.1-6).

It is likely that Jude has Isaiah's special Servant Songs in mind when he refers to the Christians as those who are "called." Thus Isa 41:9-10; 42:5-9; and 49:1-6 each gives the call of God a special place in God's use of Israel to speak to the nations and witness to his great acts of salvation. Because they have been called by God out of their sin, they are also "beloved in God the Father." Seen most visibly in the cross as God's supreme act of self-sacrifice for the redemption of humans, God's love effectively counters sin and creates in his people the capacity to serve God in serving others. Human love is a response to God's love for humans (Morris: 1981). The Servant Songs of Isaiah use "called," "beloved," and "kept" (cf. Isa 41:9; 42:1, 6). Though some have recently argued that "in" with "God the Father" refers to the place of their love (as Paul sees Christians "in" Christ), others contend that "in" is synonymous to "by" (see Bauckham: 25-26). The blessing compounds three early Christian favorite terms: "mercy" (cf. 1 Tim 1:2; 2 Tim 1:2; 2 John 3), "peace" (Rom 1:7), and "love" (2 John 3).

Intention of the Author (3-4)

The use of "beloved" is typical in early Christian literature (cf. 1 Pet 2:11; 4:12; 2 Pet 3:1, 8, 14, 17). Jude's plan to write one kind of letter was interrupted by the need to write another. His former letter was a letter that he was "eager" to write and was either about to write (NRSV) or already doing so (see Bauckham: 29-30). His plan was to write about "the salvation we share." Salvation in earliest Christianity referred to deliverance from sin, sickness, and demonic forces through the sacrificial death of Jesus Christ (cf. Luke 1:69; Rom 1:16; Heb 2:10; Morris 1983). Such a view of salvation is found in Jude at vv. 4, 5, 20, and especially v. 25, where the doxology is offered to God "our Savior" and "through Jesus Christ our Lord."

However, owing to the disruptions generated by the false teachers, Jude interrupted that pastoral mission and wrote a letter that was more apologetic and condemnatory. Jude not only had to write to them, but he had to "appeal" to them "to contend for the faith." What he has in mind is both theological acuity and moral fidelity (cf. v. 4). The word "contend" draws upon the imagery of athletic competition (Harris) so as to evoke in his readers the effort needed to win this contest against the false teachers and the inclination to sin (cf. 1 Cor 9:24-25; Phil 1:27-30; 2 Tim 2:5). The nature of this struggle is both offensive and defensive and is spelled out in particular categories in Jude 20-23 as mutual edification, prayer, faithfulness, hope, and pastoral concern. What they are to fight for is "the faith that was once for all entrusted to the saints." While such a category has been taken by some to imply a later date when "faithfulness" had turned into a static system of "faith," such a use of the noun "faith" is found in the earliest writings of the NT (cf. Gal 1:23; see also 1 Pet 4:17; 1 Tim 3:9; 4:1, 6; 2 Tim 4:7; Dunn 1991: 341-66 with xix-xxx).

Utilizing the category so familiar in rabbinic Judaism for passing on sacred tradition, Jude refers to this faith as that which was "entrusted to the saints" (cf. Mark 7:3, 5, 13; 1 Cor 11:23; 15:1-3; Gal 1:9). Though "saints" here possibly refers only to the apostles as official tradents of the Jesus traditions (see Dunn 1991: 60-80), it is more likely that "saints" here refers to Christians in general, to those who have been made holy through Jesus Christ (Bauckham). By using "once for all" with "the faith," Jude intends to describe (1) the permanency of the apostolic faith, (2) its utter efficacy (1 Pet 3:18), and (3) its rootedness in the earliest experiences of the Spirit during the founding period.

What disrupted his plan to write an exposition of the common salvation was the rise in influence of "certain intruders" (see above, Introduction, 1529-30). However unwanted, there was a strong presence in all strands of earliest Christianity of false teachers. In light of what we know from 2 Corinthians 10–11; Gal 2:1-10 and *Didache* 11–12, some of these false teachers/prophets moved about as itinerants who obtained funds and sustenance as a result of their success in various sorts of ministries (e.g., exorcism, prophecy, teaching, and healing). Whether or not the "intruders" were from outside (itinerants) or inside (schismatics), they were dangerous to the whole community. Jude says that these intruders were prophesied "long ago," though it is unclear if he means that (1) they were destined for such activity in the plan of God, (2) such activity was predicted by the apostles (cf. Jude 17-18), or (3) they were predicted by the OT prophets (cf. Jude 5-7, 11) or *1 Enoch* 5–19. Undoubtedly, for Jude, that their activity was revealed beforehand is sufficient to make their current activity known for what it is: they "pervert the grace of God." Jude sees in some ancient prophecy an indication of their final destruction in the future judgment by God (cf. Jude 7, 15). It is because they are "ungodly" that their final punishment is certain (cf. vv. 4, 15). While Jude does not here specify what "ungodly" means, the context suggests that it is their irreverence before God, their sensual appetites, and their audacious sins (cf. vv. 8, 10, 12, 16). Their lives became the evidence for their sentence; as Bauckham has stated, it was "not theoretical atheism, but practical godlessness" that formed the basis for God's punishment (Bauckham: 38).

Such is implicit in what they effected: they "pervert the grace of God." We must steer clear of imputing to Jude a full-blown theology of grace as can be found in Paul, but, on the other hand, we are safe in seeing "grace" as a widespread early Christian term for God's salvation to undeserving sinners (cf. Rom 3:24; 5:2; Gal 5:4; Heb 4:16; 1 Pet 1:10; 2 Pet 3:18). The opponents turned grace into an opportunity for "licentiousness" (cf. also 1 Pet 4:3; 2 Pet 2:19). In so perverting the grace of God, they also "deny our only Master and Lord, Jesus Christ." The bulk of evidence for the term "Master" suggests that the "Father" would be in view here (cf. Bauckham). But 2 Pet 2:1, the grammar (one definite article is used for Master and Lord [i.e., "*the* Master and Lord"]), and the use of "slave/master" by Jesus so frequently for his relationship to his disciples (e.g., Matt 10:25) make one think that Jude has Jesus in mind here.

Context for the Appeal (5-19)

As stated in the Introduction above, 1529, Jude 5-19 functions as the context for the appeal Jude wishes to make and that appears in vv. 20-23. Jude 5-19 consists of four sections which each have a textual foundation and then an application to the current situation of Jude's readers. Each of the textual units uses past tenses, while the applications use the present tense. The word "these" also stands out (vv. 8, 10, 12, 16, and 19).

Three Ancient Jewish Types and Their Application (5-10)

Jude begins with the exodus generation (v. 5) and continues with the fallen angels (v. 6) and Sodom and Gomorrah (v. 7) before applying their typological significance to the current false teachers (vv. 8-10). What began as a letter dealing with salvation turns here into a vehement reminder of the awfulness of God's judgment. His form is a disclosure formula (cf. 2 Cor 8:1; Gal 1:11; 2 Pet 1:12; see also Jude 17).

Since they are already "fully informed" through their conversion and reception of apostolic traditions (cf. vv. 3, 17; McKnight), they need only to be reminded, as was the custom in Judaism (cf. Deut 6:4-9; 2 Pet 1:12; 3:1-2). What they needed to be reminded of was how the Lord had worked in the past: even if he saves, he also judges.

This God saved the children of Israel out of Egypt, but even after such a deliverance he "afterward destroyed those who did not believe." Their unbelief no doubt refers to their unwillingness to accept the full stipulations of God's covenant (cf. Exodus; Numbers; Deuteronomy) and not to a lack of some particular theological tenet. This God "destroyed" those unfaithful wanderers. When the children of Israel murmured about their conditions, Moses interceded; but God promised that though they would remain alive, none would live to enter the promised land (Numbers 14; 26:64-65). This rebellion and punishment by God became archetypal in Judaism (cf. Deut 1:32-33; 9:23-34; Psalm 106) and then in early Christianity (Heb 3:7–4:11). What Jude means by "afterward" is unclear: either it refers to (1) the exodus punishment and wilderness destruction or (2) the first deliverance in Egypt and then the judgment in the wilderness.

Jewish tradition about the angels of Genesis 6, also called the Watchers, led to a host of ideas about the meaning of the text. The tradition related that these angels descended, married human women, and led to the origin of evil and the magnification of sin in the world. See the ideas found in the following texts: Gen 6:1-4; *1 Enoch* 6–19; 21; 86–88; 106:13-17; *Jub.* 4:15, 22; 5:1; CD 2:17-19; 1QapGen 2:1; *Tg. Ps.-Jon.* Gen 6:1-4; *T. Reub.* 5:6-7; *T. Naph.* 3:5; see also 1 Pet 3:19-20; 2 Pet 2:4 (from Bauckham). These "angels" had a sphere of authority, whether this be seen as some place in the heavenlies which they abandoned or some locus of authority on earth (e.g., over Rome; cf. *1 Enoch* 12:4; 15:3; 82:10-20). Because of their act of sin, they were defeated, captured, and put in chains (*1 Enoch* 13:2; 54:4-5), where they are kept in "deepest darkness" (cf. *1 Enoch* 10:4-6; 1 Pet 3:19; 2 Pet 2:4; see also Matt 8:12).

Likewise, Sodom and Gomorrah (cf. Genesis 19) became another type of God's judgment on the world (cf. Jer 23:14; 49:18; 50:40; Matt 10:15; 11:24; 2 Pet 2:6; see also Deut 29:23; Ezek 38:22; Rev 14:10-11; 19:3; 20:10). While some of the precise details in the Genesis narrative are unclear, the interpreters of Genesis 19 have not been so restrained; in general, the inhabitants of Sodom and Gomorrah were guilty of sexual and sensual indulgences (cf. Gen 19:4-11 with Lev 18:22; 20:13; *T. Naph.* 3:4-5; Rom 1:26-27) as well as of inhospitality.

Changing now to his world and the present tense, Jude finds typological significance (v. 8: "in the same way . . .") in these three examples for his community as it faces the false teachers who have intruded into their midst (vv. 8-10; with v. 9 being yet another parenthetical remark). Three sins are found among the false teachers: defiling the flesh, rejecting authority, and slandering angels. Just why Jude calls the false teachers here "dreamers" has two separate consequences for interpretation. First, because he uses a present participle in so describing his opponents, one is led to two inferences: that their dreaming includes each of the three sins he lists, and that it characterizes their approach to religious matters. Second, dreaming here is probably related to an overall claim to revelation since revelation and dreams were intimately connected (cf. Isa 56:10; Jer 23:25; 36:8; Matt 1:20; 2:12-13; 2 Cor 12:1-3; Col 2:18). Of the sins listed, surely "defile the flesh" is part of his polemic against their sexual indulgences (vv. 4, 6, 7, 16, 19, and 23). That they "reject authority" not only helps to define what "dreamers" means but displays their characteristic rejection of the tradition Jude is so keen to keep before his readers (v. 3). Not only do they reject the Lord Jesus Christ (v. 4b) but they refuse to submit to either apostolic, church tradition or to angelic authorities (v. 8c; cf. Col 1:16). Their flagrant disregard for boundaries created by God and established by apostolic tradition finds its epitome in that they also "slander the glorious ones" (cf. 2 Pet 2:10). Scholars have struggled to find specific intention here, some thinking either of evil angels or the proto-gnostic angels of creation; but it is best that we see either angels in general or the angelic administration of the law (cf. Acts 7:38, 53; Gal 3:19-25; Heb 2:2; Bauckham).

The audacity of their disrespectful manner forms an amazing contrast with the demeanor of Michael, who, though the archangel, honorably kept silent and refused to lay accusations against the devil since Michael knew with whom he was dealing. Much Jewish lore developed about Michael (cf., e.g., Dan 12:1; Rev 12:7; 1QM 17) and Moses. But Michael, who came to Moses' defense, could not accuse Satan directly. Ignorant of what they are doing (v. 10), they slander what God has approved and end up destroying themselves.

Three More Ancient Types and Application (11-13)

Again, the three analogies are described in the aorist tense (v. 11b), while the application is made in the present tense (vv. 12-13). This woe, or even imprecatory, form is found in the Bible and in Judaism (cf. *1 Enoch* 92–105; Luke 6:25; 11:42-44, 46-47, 52). "Woe!" is a strong term of condemnation in the Jewish world which, in light of early Christian warnings about language (e.g., Matt 7:1-5; Jas 3:1-12), finds expression only in severe cases (cf. Matt 11:21; 23:13-16; Rev 8:13).

The three cases brought forward as analogies each deal with sinful leaders who met a decisive judgment (cf. Gen 4:11-12; Num 16:30-33; 31:8). Cain becomes the archetype sinner in Jewish tradition (cf. *T. Benj.* 7:5; Josephus *Ant.* 1:52-66; *1 Clem.* 4:7; 1 John 3:12). Balaam (see 2 Pet 2:15-16) was a mercenary prophet (cf. Num 25:1-3). Greed seems to be part of Jude's criticism of the false teachers who are threatening apostolic tradition in the community (cf. Rom 16:18; 1 Tim 3:3, 8; 6:5; 1 Pet 5:2; *Did.* 11:5-6, 12; 13:1; 15:1). Korah, on the other hand, becomes an antinomian heretic (cf. Num 16:1-35; 26:9-10; Ps 106:16-18; Sir 45:18-19). He denied either God's authority or the authority of God's messengers (cf. 2 Tim 2:19), and so was destroyed (Num 26:10).

Their "love feasts" (cf. 2 Pet 2:13), meals during which Christians were to experience both worship and socio-religious solidarity, not to mention physical provision and charity, were polluted by the presence of these "blemishes." But the false teachers polluted them through their avarice (cf. Neyrey: 74-75). They eat fearlessly (i.e., without fear of God for what they have done and are doing; cf. v. 10) and only feed themselves. This latter accusation refers either to their physical indulgence in food or their capacity to lead others into their pernicious errors.

Jude now appeals through metaphors of air, earth, water, and heaven. First, like clouds without water (cf. Prov 25:14), they do not bring the desired rain; furthermore, their instability is accentuated in that they are blown away by the sharp winds. Second, like autumn trees which are fruitless and a harvest disappointment, these false teachers are useless. Being doubly dead could be simple hyperbole (*totally* dead) or it could be an allusion to the Christian belief in a second death after a resurrection to damnation (cf. Rev 2:11; 20:6, 14). Third, like wild waves of the sea which send up frothy foam, these false teachers manifest their sinfulness and shame (cf. Isa 57:20). Fourth, they are like the fallen angels (called stars elsewhere; cf. *1 Enoch* 18:13-16; 21:3-6; 82–90) who have been assigned to places of judgment that have no light (cf. Matt 8:12; 25:30).

A Prophecy of Enoch Fulfilled (14-16)

At times Christians have been bothered by Jude's quotation of a pseudonymous writing (*1 Enoch*), but modern-day scholarship recognizes both the fluidity and diversity of early Christian thinking about a "canon" of inspired Scripture as well as the ubiquitous use of sources. Consequently, few today stumble over Jude's use of *1 Enoch* 1:9. Quoting *1 Enoch* does not nullify Jude's inspiration nor suddenly give ground for seeing *1 Enoch* as Scripture. However, the canon that is now used by Christians, whether in its Roman Catholic or Protestant form, is only a consensus; what "canon" Jude operated with is beyond our knowledge. It is possible that Jude himself, in company with others in the ancient world, considered *1 Enoch* Scripture.

Enoch, who is here described as the "seventh from Adam," referring to Gen 5:21-24, is then quoted (*1 Enoch* 1:9). The Enoch of the Genesis narrative became the ever-bearing tree of speculation since "he was not, for God took him" (Gen 5:24). In this quotation, the pseudonymous author predicts a judgment by God on all ungodly people and actions. This judgment, like the one predicted by Jesus (e.g., Matt 13:24-30, 36-43), would be administered through angels and specifically (though not exclusively) directed at those who slandered the Lord (cf. Jude 15). Three more sins become the target of his ire. First, the false teachers are like the OT Israelites in the wilderness in that they grumble and are malcontents (cf. Exod 15:24; 16:1-12; Num 14:2, 27, 29, 36). Second, they indulge their fleshly passions instead of being committed to God's pure will. Third, as previously described (cf. Jude 8, 10), they are "bombastic in speech." That is, they make arrogant claims about themselves and God's will (remember, they are called "dreamers" in v. 8). See also Dan 7:8, 20; 11:36; Rev 13:5; and from *1 Enoch* cf. 5:4; 101:3. Making this speech more emphatic, they flatter in order to seduce and convince (cf. Jude 12).

Apostolic Predictions and Application (17-19)

Jude appeals here to the apostolic traditions which predicted the very thing now occurring: latter-day apostasy. As with 2 Peter, "remember" has a specific sense: it refers to the mental and experiential recall of God's act of salvation in Christ as made known through the apostles. Whether "apostles" refers to the entire apostolic tradition (e.g., Eph 2:20) or only to the tradition made known to these specific Christians through the apostles from whom they learned (cf. 2 Tim 3:1-5; 2 Pet 3:1-4; Bauckham) is impossible to tell.

Jude quotes a text which is no longer extant as quoted, though some have seen something quite similar in 2 Tim 3:1-5. Whatever one makes of "in the last times," the writers of the NT are univocal on the three dimensions of time: the past of the OT, the present of Jesus Christ, and the future of God's coming salvation and judgment (cf. Caird and Hurst: 118-35). Prior to that future coming of God, the apostles contended, there were to be "scoffers" (cf. Ps 1:1; Prov 1:22; 9:7-8; 2 Pet 3:3) who would live sensuously and indulgently (cf. Jude 4, 16).

The Appeal (20-23)

Having set the stage for his appeal like a long-winded modern theologian, Jude finally makes his appeal to his readers (though implicitly this appeal has been clear from the beginning). These verses form the climax of the letter and are, therefore, not to be construed as an afterthought or even an insignificant pastoral application. (At this point there is a serious problem in the transmission of the text of vv. 22-23. For full discussion, see Bauckham: 108-11. We have followed the NRSV.)

Seven separate exhortations are to be found. First, the believers are to "build" themselves up by constructing both their theology and their practice "on your most holy faith." Building one's faith is either spiritual or temple-like in its background imagery (cf. 1 Cor 14:12, 26; 1 Pet 2:1-10). The image is corporate and takes place on the basis of their conversion enlightenment. Second, they are to "pray in the Holy Spirit"; in other words, they are to pray under the influence and control of God's Spirit (Gal 4:6; Eph 6:18; cf. Dunn 1975: 239-46). When such prayer is the guiding light, immoral pitfalls and heretical bypaths will be avoided.

Third, they are to persevere in the love of God (v. 21). Clearly, Jude has in mind the love God has shown in Christ and continues to show through the Spirit to his people. Those who persevere in God's love remain faithful to the truth that God made known in Jesus and so do not deny the Master (cf. Jude 4). Fourth, Jude exhorts his community to wait expectantly (cf. Isa 30:18; 49:23; 51:5; Luke 2:25, 38; 2 Pet 3:12-14) for the coming of the Lord (v. 21b). But instead of viewing the coming of the Lord in terms of judgment, Jude looks at the return of Christ from the perspective of God's mercy (cf. Matt 5:7), which will be manifested at that event and through which they will be finally redeemed for God's glory (Jude 24).

Fifth, extending the theme of mercy further, Jude urges his community to act mercifully on those "who are wavering." Surely Jude has in mind those who are being seduced by the alluring guile of the false teachers. On the other hand, it is possible that he has in mind those who are argumentative, who dispute the tradition Jude is currently advocating (cf. Bauckham). Sixth, Jude urges the Christians to save some from the fires of condemnation. Since "fire" almost certainly refers to hell, "snatch" must describe the act of redeeming others by passing on the apostolic tradition and preaching the gospel. For Jude the tradition is especially focused on Jesus Christ (cf. vv. 1, 4, 21, 25). Since Jude's language is so strong about the false teachers, it is unlikely that he has in mind saving them (cf. Jude 4, 9, 13, 14-15).

Finally, he urges a pastoral concern of mercy on yet others who have been defiled (v. 23b). But this time he appends the idea that such pastoral concern ought to be accompanied by a serious respect for the danger of sin and the potential danger of falling into sin. Even the undergarment, that which is not visible in public, of the defiled is to be detested; that is, Jude's Christians are to comprehend that sin in no form is to be tolerated. It is hard to combine the merciful, pastoral care concerns of vv. 21-22 with a total avoidance of those who have fallen into some kind of sinful disposition.

Doxology (24-25)

Jude now directs his attention to God and to Jesus Christ. Doxologies are customary at the end of homilies and early Christian exhortations. Jude's conclusion has a developed description of God: God and Jesus Christ keep them from falling (cf. 2 Thess 3:3; 1 Pet 1:5) and are capable of permitting them to stand without blemish. The community of Jude can only think that God will protect and preserve them from the pernicious ways of the false teachers. Second, Jude's praise is customary: "glory, majesty, power, and authority" (v. 25). Third, the time element about which Jude is concerned is "now" and "forever"; in addition, this praise is directed at God and Jesus Christ, who are "before all time." Jude concludes with the Aramaic term of agreement, said by all those who heard the prayer and agreed with it, "Amen." Similar doxologies can be found at Rom 16:25 and Eph 3:20.

Bibliography. Bauckham, R. J. 1983, *Jude, 2 Peter,* WBC 50, Waco: Word • Caird, G. B., and L. D. Hurst. 1994, *New Testament Theology,* Oxford: Clarendon • Dunn, J. D. G. 1975, *Jesus and the Spirit: A Study of the Religious and Charismatic Experience of Jesus and the First Christians as Reflected in the New Testament,* Philadelphia: Westminster • Dunn, J. D. G. 2d ed. 1991, *Unity and Diversity in the New Testament: An Inquiry into the Character of Earliest Christianity;* Philadelphia: Trinity Press International • Green, M. 1968, *The Second Epistle General of Peter and the General Epistle of Jude,* TNTC, Grand Rapids: Eerdmans • Grundmann, W. 2d ed. 1979, *Der Brief des Judas und der zweite Brief des Petrus,* THKNT 15, Berlin: Evangelische Verlagsanstalt • Harris, H. A. 1976, *Greek Athletics and the Jews,* Trivium Special Publications 3, Cardiff: University of Wales • Kelly, J. N. D. 1969, *A Commentary on the Epistles of Peter and*

Jude, BNTC, London: Adam & Charles Black • McKnight, S. 2002, *Turning to Jesus,* Louisville: Westminster/John Knox • Morris, L. 1981, *Testaments of Love: A Study of Love in the Bible,* Grand Rapids: Eerdmans • Morris, L. 1983, *The Atonement: Its Meaning and Significance,* Downers Grove, Ill.: InterVarsity • Neyrey, J. H. 1993, *2 Peter, Jude,* AB 37C, New York: Doubleday • Thurén, L. 1997, "Hey Jude! Asking for the Original Situation and Message of a Catholic Epistle," *NTS* 43:451-65 • White, J. 1986, *Light from Ancient Letters,* Philadelphia: Fortress.

Revelation

Loren T. Stuckenbruck

INTRODUCTION

Author

The writer of Revelation identifies himself as "John" (1:1, 4, 9; 22:8). The name itself suggests that he was a Christian of *Jewish* descent. In addition, he refers to himself as a "servant" of God (1:1) and "brother" of those to whom he addressed the work (1:4). Though he never calls himself a "prophet," it is likely that John belonged to a group of Christian prophets (10:11; 19:10; 22:6, 9, 16) and was known as such to members of the churches in Asia Minor. There is little ground, therefore, for supposing that Revelation is a pseudonymous work (see Charles 1920: 1:xxxviii-xxxix; despite Frey 1993: 415-29).

Since the second century AD many have identified the author with John the son of Zebedee, one of the twelve apostles (Justin *Dial. Tryph.* 81) and disciple of Jesus (Irenaeus *Adv. Haer.* 3.11.1-3; 5.26.1; Clement of Alexandria *Strom.* 6.106-7; Tertullian *Adv. Marc.* 3.14.24). This claim was commonly linked with an assumption that the same author wrote the Gospel of John, which was itself thought to have been written by the apostle (concerning the relationship between Revelation and John, see variously Schüssler Fiorenza 1977 and Frey 1993). Others have argued that the writer could have been John the Elder of Ephesus. This view depends partly on whether or not the tradition of Papias cited by Eusebius (*Hist. Eccl.* 3.39) was referring to someone other than the apostle. In the end, therefore, the precise identity of "John" remains unknown.

Date

The composition of Revelation is traditionally assigned to the later years of Domitian's reign (AD 81-96; on this question, see Yarbro Collins 1984: 54-83). This is claimed early on, for example, by Irenaeus in the late second century (*Adv. Haer.* 5.30.3) and implied by the statements of Clement of Alexandria (*Quis Dives* 42) and Origen (*In Matt.* 16:6) in the third century. However, some sources from the fourth century and later (cf. Charles 1920: 1:xcii) have dated John's "exile" (1:9), and by implication the work, to the reigns of Nero (AD 54-68; Jerome, who cites Tertullian), Claudius (AD 41-54; Epiphanius), and Trajan (AD 98-117; Theophylact, eleventh century). The last-mentioned date is not impossible (cf. Hengel 1989: 81), given that the most explicit evidence for the persecution of Christians in Asia Minor stems from this period (AD 112: Pliny *Ep.* 10.96-97); however, it is rendered less likely since the initial suggestion may have arisen merely as an inference based on Irenaeus's statement that John lived on into the period of Trajan's reign (Yarbro Collins 1984: 55). Attempts to date Revelation on the basis of 17:9-12 have been inconclusive. Were the identity of the sixth king ("who is," v. 10) known, the matter could be resolved. However, the identification of the seven kings which correspond to the beast's heads is fraught with difficulty. There is little agreement concerning who among the Roman emperors would have corresponded to the first king and how the succession of heads was being counted (e.g., whether the short reigns of Galba, Otho, and Vitellius are to be included). If, for instance, the line of emperors is begun with Julius Caesar (as, e.g., in Josephus *Ant.* 18.2.2; Suetonius *Vespasian*), the king "who is" could be Nero, while only a reckoning that starts with Caligula — omitting the short reigns — could bring the date to the time of Domitian (cf. Yarbro Collins 1984: 58-64; Müller 1995: 291-95).

The weight of the internal evidence is consistent with a date near the end of the first century rather than before or just after the destruction of the Jerusalem temple in AD 70 (as, e.g., argued by Robinson 1976: 238-42). The message to the Christians of Laodicea (3:14-22), which assumes that the city is flourishing economically, is hard to explain had Revelation been composed soon after the devastating earthquake there in AD 60. The symbolic interpretation of the stones on the wall of the new Jerusalem as "the twelve apostles of the Lamb" in 21:14 implies that the time of the apostles does not belong to the most recent past. More generally, the polemic against Rome as "Babylon" (14:8; 16:19; 17:5; 18:2, 10, 21; cf. Yarbro Collins 1984: 57-58) and the angel's refusal to be worshiped (19:10; 22:8-9; cf. Stuckenbruck 1995a: 103, 237-38) reflect traditions which were developing in apocalyptic literature near the end of the first century.

Details which might suggest a composition during the time of Nero remain unconvincing. Difficulties regarding 17:9-12 have been mentioned above. Furthermore, the decipherment of the beast's number "666" as a reference to Nero (13:18), along with that emperor's reputation as a persecutor of Christians (cf. Tacitus *Ann.* 15.44), need not speak against the late first century. In the years following Nero's death, rumors about his return from the East began to proliferate (*Sib. Or.* 3:63-70; 4:119-39; 5:28-34, 93-110, 361-84; *Asc. Isa.* 4:2-13; cf. Tacitus *Hist.* 1.78; Suetonius *Nero* 57); various forms of this myth may have provided the background for John's statement about the mortal wound from which the beast was healed (12:3) and his prediction of the beast's return (17:8, 11— the eighth king). Another hint at an earlier date might be 11:1-2, which refers to the Jerusalem temple as if it were still standing; however, as John is probably drawing on an earlier source from the time of the Jewish revolt against Rome (cf. Josephus *J.W.* 5.459; 6:285), the passage should not be used to date the work as a whole. Likewise, recent doubt cast on the notion of an organized persecution of Christians during the latter part of Domitian's reign (esp. Yarbro Collins 1984: 84-110; Thompson 1986) does not require a Neronian date. The language of persecution in Revelation is explicable as John's use of information about the deaths of Christians under Nero in the past to feed his expectation of a systematic persecution under Rome in the imminent future.

While the above considerations do not provide conclusive evidence for the date of composition, the internal and external evidence points toward the end of the first century, that is, to the later years of Domitian's rule.

Literary Genre

Revelation is a conflation of literary genres: it formally claims to be (a) an apocalypse, (b) a prophecy, and (c) an epistle. All three idioms of communication surface among the opening verses of the book.

(a) Unlike the other books of the NT, Revelation is distinguished by a sustained series of visions and auditions recorded as autobiographical experiences of a seer. In the opening clause the book is introduced as "the revelation *(apokalypsis)* of Jesus Christ" (1:1). As the context of this description makes apparent, John claims for his work a disclosure of divine secrets from both transcendent and future perspectives. The book is transcendent in that it imparts a message that originates with God. Since such knowledge is otherwise inaccessible, it is communicated to the seer through intermediary beings, such as Christ and heavenly angels. As the secrets in the book unfold, its recipients learn about a cosmos that is marked by a struggle between incompatible powers, a conflict through which they find their world reinterpreted. Revelation is also concerned with the future. John is convinced that the conflict between God and Satan will soon be unveiled throughout the cosmos. In anticipation of this, his visions summon the Christians of Asia Minor to a life of radical loyalty to the worship of God. At the centerpiece of John's exhortation is the revelation of Christ as the "slaughtered" Lamb (5:6), which becomes the model that determines how Christian faithfulness in a world of conflict should be expressed. In the future, the transcendent perspective on the world will culminate in the triumph of God over all evil and in the vindication of Christ's followers. As otherworldly and eschatological knowledge conveyed through mediatorial beings, Revelation shares many features with several prophetic books of the Hebrew Bible (e.g., Ezekiel, Zechariah, and Daniel) and, in particular, numerous apocalyptic Jewish writings from the Greco-Roman period (c. 300 BC to AD 200). Given the diversity of these compositions, a completely satisfactory definition of "apocalypse" as a genre remains elusive. Nevertheless, efforts to distinguish an apocalyptic idiom, where appropriate, from knowledge based on human observation, on the one hand, and from the eschatology of the Hebrew prophets, on the other hand, have succeeded in identifying the transcendent (spatial) and urgent (temporal) orientations which characterize many apocalypses. In this sense, Revelation is first of all to be regarded as an "apocalypse."

(b) Revelation, however, differs from other Jewish apocalypses in that it is not a *pseudepigraphon,* that is, it is not ascribed to someone who is not the real author. Authors of apocalyptic literature attributed their works to patriarchal figures of the distant past (e.g., Enoch, Ezra, Daniel, Baruch, and Abraham), often in order to undergird the authority of their writings and, if concerned with eschatology, to reinforce their view that the outcome of history is predetermined (Collins 1987: 30-31). In the tradition of the Hebrew prophets, John uses his own name and in several passages allows his work to be described as a "prophecy" (*prophēteia;* 1:3; 19:10; 22:7, 10, 18-19). In addition, each of the letters to the seven churches in chs. 2–3 begins with the formula "thus says," which may be understood as a prophetic oracle. Revelation may have been composed under the assumption that the author was acquainted with various circumstances of the congregations of Asia Minor and that the audience was already aware of his claim to be prophet (1:9-11). As a contemporary known to the intended recipients, John is told not to "seal up the words of this prophecy" (22:10), much in contrast to Dan 12:4. The urgent tone of his exhortations to persist in faithfulness and/or to repent thus presupposes a degree of personal accountability. John expects that there will be a measurable response among his readers to the message of the book (see 1:3; 22:7, 18-19).

(c) Revelation also understands itself in terms of an epistle. After the extended title at the beginning (1:1-3), the rest of the book is framed by the epistolary form. The text of vv. 4-5a contains formal elements that characterize standard openings of ancient letters (name of sender, identification of addressees, and a greeting); these features are followed by a doxology (vv. 5b-6) which is reminiscent of thanksgivings or benedictions found in many early Christian letters (see esp. Gal 1:5). Revelation closes in 22:21 with a benediction, as common in letters of antiquity. Although the intervening part of the book is not structured as an ancient letter, there are some indications that the author continues to be conscious of this form of communication (Karrer 1986). The epistolary address to "the seven churches that are in Asia" in 1:4 is carried further in chs. 2–3 through seven oracular messages that purport to address the individual circumstances of each of these churches. In turn, numerous details from chs. 2–3 recur throughout the apocalyptic section of the book (4:1–22:5), with the result that John's visions are endowed with a communicative character that keeps the situations of the Christian congregations in view. It is possible that John has adapted visions, some perhaps already known to his audience, into a framework that enhanced their relevance. If this is correct, the explicit and implicit epistolary features of Revelation may be said to have played an important role in John's communicative strategy.

COMMENTARY

Prologue (1:1-8)

Title: The Revelation of Jesus Christ (1:1-2)

The opening section is an extended title which (a) characterizes the work as a whole and (b) describes how the message is being conveyed to its recipients. Though "apocalyptic literature" is recognized as a widespread idiom of communication in the ancient world, scholars have yet to achieve unanimity concerning a definition of "apocalypse" as a form of literature (Collins 1987: 4). 1:1 contains the earliest use of the term *apokalypsis* as a reference to a literary composition. Here, however, the expression does not presuppose a technical sense. It signifies, rather, that the work involves the disclosure of a heavenly reality that will soon affect the author and his readers. As such, Revelation is written under the assumption that true understanding comes from God and that human beings cannot have this kind of knowledge without its being mediated to them.

The content of this *apokalypsis* is summed up in the name "Jesus Christ." It is not necessary to decide whether the revelation is *about* Christ or *from* Christ; in the book Christ functions as both subject and mediator. Nevertheless, while Revelation is distinguished by its portrait of Christ as "the Lamb" (beginning in 5:6), his position as a mediator is not consistently carried through. In 22:16 "Jesus" is identified as the one who sends his angel to John's prophetic circle, and in 4:1 it is Christ who shows John the visions which follow; in 22:6, however, Christology is at best only an implicit part of the chain of mediation (see under 22:6-9). Rev 1:1 leaves room for ambiguity. In language resembling 22:6, Christ is portrayed as the recipient of a revelation from God which he is "to show his [whose?] servants" and, as in 22:16, Christ communicates this message "by sending his angel to his servant John." However much John regards Christ as divine (note the ambiguity of "his" in v. 1), his Christology cannot dispense with a description of Christ that incorporates functions and attributes also characteristic of angels (see under 1:12-16; 4:1; 14:14).

The first human recipients of the mediated message are called "his servants" (though see 1:4); more specifically, "his servant John" (v. 1). The term *doulos* ("servant/slave") could be associated with a number of individuals or groups in Jewish and Christian tradition, for example, the prophets of the Jewish scriptures, the early Christian apostles, faithful Jews, or faithful Christians in general (Aune 1997: 13). In Revelation it is used for Moses (15:3), the Christians in Thyatira (2:20), faithful Christians in heaven (7:3; 19:2, 5; 22:3), John (1:1; see 19:10 and 22:9), and prophets (10:7; 11:18). Given the connection between 1:1 and 22:6, 16, *doulos* likely denotes John and the group of prophets to which he belongs (Schüssler Fiorenza 1985: 151) and not simply to Christians generally (against Aune 1997: 13; see further 22:9).

As a prophet-servant, John is engaged in the activity of *seeing.* Through a series of visions he has become a witness *(emartyrēsen)* to "the word of God" and "the testimony of Jesus Christ." "The word of God" (1:2) implies a claim that John stands in the tradition of the Hebrew prophets (see Jer 1:2; Joel 1:1; Hos 1:1; Jonah 1:1; etc.). Similar to "the revelation of Jesus Christ," "the testimony of Jesus Christ" may refer to the christological content of Revelation (i.e., *about* Christ); even more, and analogous to "the word of God," the phrase underscores that Christ is the source of John's visions (Donegani 1997: 376-80; see under 19:10). For John, statements about God and Christ are functionally coordinated.

Blessing on the Reception of the Book (1:3)

This is the first of seven blessings in the work (cf. 14:13; 16:15; 19:9; 20:6; 22:7, 14). The first part of the blessing suggests that John expects his work to be read aloud as Christians are gathered for worship. There is already evidence that epistles were being read in worship by the Christians in the first century (Col 4:16); given such a practice, it is possible that the blessing on the reader anticipates the epistolary form that frames the entire book to follow (1:4-6; 22:21). In the second part of the blessing, John shows a particular concern that his message be effective; what he has written should not only be heard but also *kept.* In 22:7 the blessing refers only to keeping.

John refers to his book as "the words of the prophecy." He makes no apparent distinction between a *prophēteia* and an *apokalypsis* (against, e.g., Mazzaferri 1989: 85-184). He combines the *directness* of divine communication known through the Hebrew prophets — that is, he uses his own name (1:1, 4, 9; 22:8) and openly refers to his recipients (e.g., 1:4, 11; 2:1–3:22) — with the notion that the content of his message has a hidden character that requires special mediation to be seen and understood.

Epistolary Opening (1:4-6)

The letter form frames the entire work (1:4-6 and 22:21). The form adopted in 1:4-5a is a typical example of an ancient letter. It includes (a) the name of the sender *(superscriptio),* (b) the name of the intended recipients *(adscriptio),* and (c) a greeting, commonly using the word *chairein,* "greetings" *(salutatio).* The greeting has been adapted into a Christian setting. Instead of *chairein* or merely *shalom* ("peace"), which is common in ancient Jewish letter writing, John uses the formula "grace *(charis)* to you and peace *(eirēnē).*" This greeting corresponds to early Christian practice, in particular to Pauline correspondence (e.g., Rom 1:7; 1 Cor 1:3; 2 Cor 1:2; Gal 1:3; Phil 1:2; 1 Thess 1:1; Phlm 3; cf. Eph 1:2; Col 1:2; 2 Thess 1:2).

Distinctive of 1:4b-5a is the listing of three sources for the greeting: God, seven spirits, and Christ. The designation of God as the "one who is and who was and who is to come" occurs also in 1:8 and 4:8. In 1:8 it is a first-person declaration by God, and in 4:8 it is a divine title in the heavenly liturgy. The meaning of the "seven spirits who are before his throne" is debated: either they signify the Holy Spirit (so, e.g., Bauckham 1993: 110-15) or they refer to the seven archangels of Jewish tradition (Aune 1997: 33-35; cf. Tob 12:15; *1 Enoch* 90:21). Interpreters should be wary of reading later trinitarianism into the phrase (see 3:5-6; 1 Tim 5:21; Justin Martyr *Apol.* 6). If the spirits in 1:4b are identical with the "seven spirits of God" in 3:1

and 4:5, they are subordinate to Christ and belong to the heavenly hosts which worship God (Mounce 1977: 70; cf. 19:10; 22:8-9).

The three titles of Christ correspond, respectively, to Jesus' death ("the faithful witness," *ho martys ho pistos*), resurrection ("the firstborn of the dead"), and exaltation ("the ruler of the kings of the earth"). These designations relate to themes picked up in rest of the work. The first does not merely refer to Jesus' historical death (Holtz 1971: 143) or to the exalted Christ who guarantees the truth of the revelation (Aune 1997: 37-38), but rather — like the phrases "revelation of Jesus Christ" and "testimony of Jesus Christ" in 1:1, 2 — identifies Christ as both the mediator and the content of John's message. In John's view Christ brings a message centered around the significance of Jesus' death as a way of defining the nature of Christian existence; therefore, in 2:13 the same designation can be applied to the martyr Antipas (cf. also 3:14). The second title is traditional (Col 1:18; cf. Rom 8:29). The formula intertwines Christ's death and resurrection; as in the formulations of 1:18 and 2:8, John does not refer to the resurrection without contemplating some aspect of Jesus' death (cf. Trites 1973). Less clear is whether *martys* functions for John as a technical term meaning "martyr" (cf. Vassiliades 1985: 129-34). The third title illustrates a paradox; Christ is declared "ruler over the kings of the earth" despite what John regards as the oppressive reality of Roman rule. Throughout the letters to the seven churches (chs. 2–3) and the visions (e.g., 5:5; 12:11; 21:7), social and political dimensions of the Roman Empire are criticized through a redefinition of what it means to "conquer."

In 1:5b-6 the epistolary opening concludes with a doxology (see Gal 1:5). Unlike the doxologies of other NT writings, this one focuses exclusively on Christ (see Rom 9:5), thus demonstrating the central role Christology plays in John's theology. The attributes ascribed to Christ are soteriological. The first-person plural "us," which occurs in each of the three descriptions of Christ, reflects the view that an understanding of who Christ is involves a perception that his activity relates to those who follow him. The redemption achieved by Christ is expressed in the identity of Christians as "kings" and "priests" for God (5:10; 20:6; cf. Exod 19:6). These designations are eschatological; they refer less to a present status than to a time when the faithful, because of uncompromising loyalty to God, "will rule over the earth" with Christ (see under 20:4-6; cf. 5:10; 22:5).

The character of Revelation as a letter is debated. Some argue that the epistolary framework was superimposed upon a document that was originally an apocalypse (cf. Aune 1997: cxx-cxxii), while others have attempted to show how Revelation as a whole may be interpreted in light of its epistolary character (e.g., Karrer 1986). Although the main section of the work (4:1–22:5) is not characterized by the formal features of an epistle, the significance of the letter form for Revelation should not be underestimated. The visions were collected into the book with a communicative situation in mind; thus a number of details occurring in 4:1–22:5 are coordinated with John's description of problems confronting "the seven churches that are in Asia" (see chs. 2–3).

Two Prophetic Sayings (1:7-8)

Two sayings (1:7, 8) are inserted between the opening letter formula and the first vision. They have no formal connection with each other or with the surrounding literary context. The first is an anonymous oracle which combines Dan 7:13 (v. 7a) and Zech 12:10 (v. 7b). It anticipates a future judgment when an unnamed figure (Christ) will be recognized by all, even those who have rejected him. What the author and his readers know about Christ will in the end be revealed to "all the tribes of the earth," who shall be subject to divine judgment (cf. *1 Enoch* 62:1–63:12). Since the same biblical passages are combined in Matt 24:30, the saying is taken from an early tradition (Yarbro Collins 1992: 536-47). Unlike the saying in Matthew, "the son of man" is not mentioned; the title is saved instead for the Christophany in 1:12-16, where the expression depends on Daniel 7.

The speaker of the second oracle is God, who otherwise speaks only in 21:5-8. God is "the Alpha and the Omega" (cf. 21:6), "the one who is and who was and who is coming," and "the Almighty One." In 22:13 the first of these designations is also applied to Christ. The last two titles are used exclusively for God in Revelation (esp. 1:4; 4:8; 11:17). "The one who is and who was and who is coming" picks up the designation for God in 1:4. Its significance here lies in its emphasis on God who comes; thematically, it coordinates with the coming of Christ in the previous verse. This correlation between God and Christ derives from an interpretation of Dan 7:13 (the one like a son of man *came*) and 7:22 (the ancient of days *came*); the verbs in Daniel's visions have been altered into the present tense; from John's point of view, Daniel 7 prophesies an event that lies in the near future. God's coming will manifest itself in the vindication of Christ when he comes. It may be argued that in Revelation what the author expects to happen "quickly" (*en tachei* — 1:1; 22:6; "after these things" — 1:19; 4:1) has to do with the coming of Christ "soon" (*tachy* — 22:7, 12, 20), which means blessing for the faithful (22:7, 12; see 2:25; 3:11, 20) and retribution for the wicked (22:12, 15; see 2:5, 16; 3:3).

Opening Vision (1:9-20)

Setting of the Vision and First Commission to Write (1:9-11)

Some interpreters argue that John's first vision is modeled on a prophetic call such as is found in the Hebrew scriptures (Exod 3:9-15; Jer 1:4-10; Isa 6:1-8; cf. Paul's call-conversion in Acts 9:1-6; 22:6-10; 26:9-18; Gal 1:13-17; so, e.g., Caird 1966: 9-26; Kraft 1974: 38). In such call narratives, the prophet tries to disqualify himself and undergoes a change of activity once he accepts his new role as a prophet. This cannot be said of John's commission in Revelation. John does not make any attempt to disqualify himself, nor does the vision mark any change of status. Rather, as his self-introduction "your brother and partner" (NSRV, "your brother who shares with you") suggests, he was known to the churches being addressed, and his function as bearer of a divine message is presupposed. It is even possible that some of the churches were already familiar with some of his visions and sayings found in Revelation itself. The passage thus does not record how John has become a prophet, but describes how *as a prophet* John was being called to a specific task (Aune 1997: 70; Stuckenbruck 1995a: 210). In being commissioned to write, the prophet John emphasizes his solidarity with the churches. "In Jesus" he participates with them in "the tribulation" (NSRV, "persecution"; cf. 7:14), "the kingdom," and "the patience endurance."

"I . . . was" may suggest that John's stay on the island of Patmos was only temporary. This was claimed by Eusebius (*Hist. Eccl.* 3.20.9), who thought that the exiled John was allowed to leave Patmos after the death of the emperor Domitian (Lohmeyer 1953: 15). It is not ultimately clear why John was on Patmos. "Because of the word of God and the testimony of Jesus" may allude to (a) a situation of persecution resulting in banishment to Patmos (most commentators), (b) John's wish to proclaim the gospel; or (c) an express purpose of receiving a revelation. Though the similar phrases in 6:9 and 20:4 refer to activity that results in death for the faithful (a), their combination in 1:1 may be significant, as this also refers to John's own prophetic activity (b or c). Being "in the spirit *(en pneumati)* on the Lord's day" requires no further explanation from the author; this means for receiving revelation — through spirit instead of body — is taken for granted (in Revelation see 4:2; 17:3; 21:10; Aune 1997: 83). Less satisfactory is the common view that *pneumati* simply refers to the (Holy) Spirit (as, e.g., in Harrington 1969: 78; for "the Spirit" in this sense, see, e.g., 2:7; 3:6; 14:13; 22:17). These observations suggest that, whatever the reason for being on Patmos, John claims to have received a visionary commission to write the churches while engaged in his customary prophetic activity.

John is commissioned by "a loud voice like a trumpet" to write the contents of his vision in a book to seven Christian communities. If v. 4 may be read in light of 1:1, it is likely that the "book" refers to the whole document and not just to the seven letters in chs. 2–3 (see on 1:19). The voice belongs to "one like the Son of Man" (v. 13), that is, to Christ, whose voice in 4:1 invites John to the heavenly vision.

The order in which the cities are listed (from Ephesus to Laodicea) anticipates the sequence of the letters in chs. 2–3. Since the work of William Ramsey (1904: 133-50) many have regarded these cities as main stops on a circular road used as a postal route (e.g., Hemer 1986: 14-15). This theory runs into the difficulty that a number of other cities in the Roman province of Asia Minor which had Christian communities are not included (esp. Colossae, Troas, Hierapolis, and perhaps Magnesia and Tralles; Aune 1997: 130). Concerning this list, two points may be made: (1) the choice of churches may have something to do with John's familiarity with their respective situations and (2) the number of congregations (seven) fits well with John's preference for the number as a symbol of completeness (see, e.g., 1:20; 3:1; 5:1; 10:3; 15:1; 17:9). While he no doubt knew of more churches in Asia Minor, he schematized his message into a numerical pattern that suggests he wished the revelation to be read more widely.

The Vision and Second Commission to Write (1:12-20)

John's encounter with Christ is divided into an audition (1:10-11) and vision (vv. 12-20), each of which concludes with a commission to write (vv. 11, 19). The audition is quickly overshadowed by the visionary aspect of the encounter, as in v. 11 John is told to write "what you *see*" and in v. 12 John expects to *see* "the voice" speaking with him (Charlesworth 1986; but see Yarbro Collins 1992: 552).

Christ is described as "one like the Son of Man" standing among seven golden lampstands (1:12b-13a), which John is told represent the seven churches (v. 20). The image of seven lampstands recalls the golden lampstand with seven lamps on seven branches to be placed in the most holy place of the Jewish temple (cf. Exod 25:31-40). The features of the "Son of Man" are described in 1:13-16, to which further characteristics are added in vv. 17c-18. What does the description symbolize? Many commentators have seen here evidence for the author's "high Christology," that is, John draws on scriptural tradition in order to describe Christ in terms of his divinity (e.g., Farrer 1964: 66-67; Holtz 1971: 121-22). This view, however, may be somewhat misleading. The imagery is variously taken from Ezek 1:24 ("voice [of the four living creatures] as the sound of many waters" — v. 15; see Dan 10:6 and Ezek 43:2), Ezek 9:2 (an angel "clothed in a long robe" — v. 13), Dan 10:5-6 (the angel Gabriel is "girded at the breast by a golden girdle" — v. 13; has "eyes as a flame of fire" — v. 14; "his feet as burnished bronze, refined as in a furnace" — v. 15; "appearance as the sun" — v. 16), and Dan 7:9 (the divine throne is a "flame of fire" — v. 14). The description of the humanlike figure having "his head and hair white as wool, white as snow" draws on an early Jewish interptation of Scripture which identified the "son of man" in Dan 7:13 *as* the "ancient of days" (see Stuckenbruck 1995b: 268-76); in 1:13-16 the white hair is the only feature associated *exclusively* with God. However, by the late first century this tradition, which combined Dan 7:9, 13 with 10:5-6, was being used to describe prominent angelic figures (*Jos. Asen.* 14:8-9; *Apoc. Abr.* 11:2). In addition, having "the keys of death and Hades" in 1:17c-18 is also reminiscent of functions assigned to angels in Jewish tradition (*Apoc. Abr.* 10:11; *Apoc. Zeph.* 6:15); in Revelation itself (20:1) "an angel descending from heaven" holds the key of the abyss.

The symbolism thus leaves the impression that Christ is presented as a principal angel (Rowland 1980; Yarbro Collins 1992: 558) whose appearance mediates a divine presence to the seer. Christ's angelic character is reinforced by the fact that some of the imagery is applied to angels later in the work (1:13b in 15:6; 1:15b in 14:2 and 19:6; 1:16c in 10:1; cf. 1:13a with 14:14). Some features of 1:13-18 also anticipate descriptions of Christ in the letters to the seven churches (cf. 2:1, 8, 12, 18; and 3:1). However, *none of the traits from 1:13-18 applied to angels later in Revelation occurs in chs. 2–3.* This implies that the Christ who addresses the churches is not merely an angel. Indeed, in the latter part of the vision Christ is presented as superior to the angels (1:17c-18); as God, he is also "the first and the last" (1:8; 21:6; cf. 22:13) and, unlike any of the angels, he is the one resurrected from the dead to live forever. Furthermore, in 1:16 he holds in his right hand "seven stars," identified as "the angels of the seven churches" (1:20; Karrer 1986: 176). John thus sees an "angelomorphic" Christ who both embodies characteristics ascribed to angelic mediators of Jewish tradition and is superior to them.

John's reaction to the vision ("I fell at his feet as though dead"; cf. Matt 28:4) is, significantly, more fear than worship. Though the imagery leaves the seer in no doubt about the divine presence mediated by the encounter, the vision does not represent the pinnacle of the author's Christology. In Revelation Jesus is not worshiped as a quasi-angelic being but as the "slaughtered" Lamb (5:6, 12; 7:17; 13:8; see Stuckenbruck 1994: 694-96). At the same time, John's experience is considered sufficient for purposes of his commission to write to the seven churches.

In 1:19 John is told to write (a) "the things you have seen," (b) "the things which are," and (c) "the things which are about to happen after these things." Part (a) refers to the vision of vv. 12-18, (b) to the letters to the seven churches in chs. 2–3, and (c) to the main vision in 4:1–22:5 (e.g., Müller 1995: 86). This tripartite formula covering past, present, and future corresponds to the categories of time ascribed to God in 1:4, 8. What John writes is bound up with an understanding of God as the Lord of all history, including the future. The events yet to be are hidden; the author is, however, confident that the future will unfold as a story in which the reign of God will be fully established.

Messages to the Seven Churches (2:1–3:22)

Taken as a whole, the messages from Christ to the seven churches are debated in two areas: (1) the form of communication they represent, and (2) their character as writings addressed to an "angel." Chs. 2–3 form a distinct, self-contained unit in Revelation. The seven units of this section, though addressed to different recipients, are highly stylized (esp. Hahn 1971; Müller 1995: 91-96; Aune 1990; 1997: 119-29) and formally belong together in a way that does not fit into the remainder of the work. Their conformity to a pattern suggests that they were not originally separate writings now collected but were composed at the same time and intended to be read together among the churches. The basic structural features shared by the messages are an *opening* consisting of (a) the command to write "the angel" of a given church; (b) a pronouncement formula "thus says" *(tade legei);* and (c) descriptions of Christ. This is followed by the *main body* involving (d) a description and evaluation of the circumstances faced by the church, varied in content but always beginning with "I know . . ." *(oida),* and a *conclusion* which contains (e) a summons to heed what "the Spirit says to the churches" combined with a promise to "the one who conquers" (2:7, 11, 17, 26-29; 3:5-6, 12-13, 21-22). Scholars have debated whether the style of the messages can be traced back to prophetic letters (Berger 1974), prophetic speech (Hahn 1971), prophetic sermons containing a call to repentance and a message of salvation (Müller 1975), or imperial edicts (Aune 1990: 198-203, who admits, however, that the content suggests they functioned as parenetic oracles of early Christian prophets). It is possible that the writer, though familiar with the variety of genres used in epistolary communication, has created his own form to address the various situations he perceived among the congregations, thereby endowing his message with an essential coherence (Karrer 1986: 66). To the extent that the latter is true, chs. 2–3 are highly important for establishing the communicative situation for the entire work. The distinct form of the messages should not lead one to treat them in isolation from the remainder of Revelation. Themes from each of the seven messages recur throughout the visions of 4:1–22:5. Through such thematic correspondence the recipients of Revelation find their own situations reexpressed on another, more global stage. By implication they become participants in a drama which in fact permeates the entire cosmos.

The second problem is concerned with why the messages are addressed to "angels" and not directly to the churches themselves (see Karrer 1986: 169-86; Aune 1997: 108-12). Outside the messages the other sixty-nine occurrences in Revelation of *angelos* ("angel, messenger") refer to celestial beings, whether good (most instances) or bad (9:11; 12:7, 9). Nevertheless, noting the oddity of John mediating as a scribe between Christ and heavenly beings, a number of commentators have argued that the "angel" of each congregation must be human, whether messengers or prophets sent from John or local church leaders (e.g., Kiddle 1940: 16-17; Kraft 1974: 51; Müller 1995: 87-89). Most interpreters, wishing to retain the notion of a church official, have argued that "angel" is the product of literary fiction in which an "angel" is constructed to function as a celestial counterpart to the leader or prophet in each of the congregations (e.g., Schüssler-Fiorenza 1985: 145-46). The notion of a human commissioned to write nonhumans is, however, not impossible for a Jewish apocalyptic idiom (on Enoch as a writer of God's message to fallen angels in the Qumran *Book of Giants,* see Karrer 1986: 57-59). If this mythological world may be assumed, John perhaps had in mind real angels whose relation to the churches was that of patron or guardian. The notion of angelic patrons and guardians of nations, groups, or individuals is well developed in Judaism by this time (see Dan 10:13, 20-21; 11:1; 12:1; *T. Levi* 5:5-6; *Jub.* 35:17; Tob 3:16-17; *T. Jos.* 6:7; 2 Macc. 10:29-30; *2 Bar.* 12:3 and 13:1; *2 Enoch* 19:4; *Life of Adam and Eve* 33; in early Christian texts, Matt 18:10; Acts 12:15; *Asc. Isa.* 3:15; *Herm. Sim.* 5.6). Though the messages are meant to be read by the congregations themselves (2:7, 11, 17, 29; 3:6, 13, 22), an address in the messages to angels who can be upbraided or praised may be a way of communicating that it is not enough for Christians to rely on angelic guardians in their respective circumstances. (Of the ninety-one occurrences of "you" in verbs and pronouns of the messages, only ten are plural, especially in cases in which the author is distinguishing a group from others in the congregation; see 2:10, 23-25). Just as the Christians themselves, protector angels are accountable to Christ, whose words they are to heed.

Concerning links between each of the messages and their possible background in the cities of Asia Minor see Hemer 1986 and Thompson 1990: 95-167.

Message to the Church in Ephesus (2:1-7)

Opening (2:1). The description of Christ underscores his superiority over the angels (he "holds the seven stars in his right hand"; see 1:16, 20) and his presence among the churches (he "walks among the seven golden lampstands"; see 1:13, 20).

Main Body (2:2-6). The Ephesians are commended for their persistent endurance (vv. 2a, 3), intolerance toward evildoers (v. 2b), testing for false apostles (v. 2c), and sharing with Christ a hate for "the works of the Nicolaitans" (concerning the question of their identity, see esp. Räisänen 1992). The problems confronting the congregation involve, among other things, struggles within the Christian community to identify leaders who have made fraudulent claims about themselves (cf. Paul's speech to the Ephesian elders in Acts 20:17). John does not describe the activities of the false "apostles" or the Nicolaitans, nor does he indicate whether they belong to the same or different groups. The text suggests that the apostles are within the community, while the status of the Nicolaitans is less certain (though the reference to "the teaching of the Nicolaitans" in 2:15 indicates a group within the church at Pergamum). For John the presence of false leaders both within and outside the Christian communities poses a serious threat to Christian identity and is a theme to which he returns in other messages (2:9, 14-15, 20-22; 3:9). The Ephesians' attitude toward the Nicolaitans is found commendable because it reflects Christ's own "hate" for their works. Discipleship and Christology are often intertwined by the author in such a way that they are patterned after each other. This language of correlation reinforces John's conviction that there is no room for compromise.

Though exemplary in hating what is bad, the Ephesians are criticized for having "abandoned the love you had at first" (2:4). The nature of this lost love is not explained; it is, however, understood in terms of "works" no longer being done. The situation described contrasts with that ascribed to the Thyatirans, who are criticized for a tolerant attitude while being commended for their "love" (2:19-20). One could infer that the Ephesians' problem may have been created by an atmosphere of suspicion resulting from the church's attempts to weed out troublemakers, but there is nothing to either substantiate or undermine such a conjecture. Christ's threat to remove "your lampstand" (i.e., his presence) if there is no repentance suggests that John regarded the problems in Ephesus as a threat to the very existence of the church.

Conclusion (2:7). Those who conquer are promised to eat "from the tree of life that is in the paradise of God." John may be drawing on imagery from Jewish tradition which regards the tree as a metaphor for participation in eternal life (*1 Enoch* 25:4-5; *2 Enoch* 8-9; 4 Ezra 8:52; *Tg. Neof.* to Gen 3:22, 24; *T. Levi* 18:11 — though see Aune 1997: 152). In the new Jerusalem (22:2-3) "the tree of life" is said to produce fruit "for the healing of the nations" and is no longer associated with a curse. If this tree is a veiled reference to the cross (see Gal 3:13), then the promise to eat its fruit ironically envisions death in imitation of Christ (Thompson 1990: 48-49).

Message to the Church in Smyrna (2:8-11)

Opening (2:8). The description of Christ as "the first and the last" and "who was dead and came to life" is taken from 1:17c-18a. In referring to Christ's resurrection, John uses the verb "to live" (*zaō*) in contrast to the usual words "to raise" or "to rise" (Aune 1997: 161; so also for the faithful in 20:4). John presupposes but does not focus on the death and resurrection of Jesus in history. For him these events are actually one: they are transformed into interpenetrating symbols which redefine what it means "to die" and "to live" (see v. 10c). For Christ, the way to life was death (cf. 20:4-6).

Main body (2:9-10). The Christians in Smyrna are not rebuked in this message. John attempts to redefine reality in order to interpret their circumstances: they appear afflicted and destitute, but this is a mask of the truth that they are "rich." As with the fraudulent apostles in 2:2, in Smyrna there are "those who say they are Jews and are not" (see 3:9); these have committed a "slander" (*blasphēmia*) of such gravity that they are labeled "a synagogue of Satan"; the term *blasphēmia* also occurs in 13:1, 5, 6 and 17:3, where it describes the beast's activity (Thompson 1986: 149). Most interpreters find here a reference to Jews bringing charges to the local authorities against Jewish Christians who, under the cover of Jewish privileges in the Roman Empire, were trying to circumvent obligations to participate in the emperor cult (e.g., Sweet 1979: 28-31; Hemer 1986: 8-11). Some form of social or political persecution is, however, not a necessary inference from the text. The "slander" may, more generally, presuppose a situation of mutual conflict among members of both religious communities who traded accusations in accordance with their respective interests (see Thompson 1990: 126). Significantly, John regards the so-called "Jews" as illegitimate representatives of their religion, and one may infer that he considered faithful Christians to be "real" Jews (so Schüssler Fiorenza 1985: 195; against Aune 1997: 164). In any case, for John the persecution of the faithful Christians in Smyrna lies more in the imminent future than in the past (3:10). His expectation that the Christians *will* be persecuted is not a reflection on recent tragic experience; rather, it forms part of a programmatic statement which takes Christ as the model for discipleship (v. 8). Thus he envisions the consequences of remaining faithful: imprisonment, temporary affliction, even "death." In a reversal of circumstances, those who will heed his call to suffer "until death" are promised "the crown of life" (3:11; cf. 4:4).

Conclusion (2:11). The real possibility of death for the faithful is taken seriously (cf. 13:9-10). Christians are victorious in relation to the "second death." In John's vision of a millennial reign at the end of history (20:4-6), it is the martyrs who are untouched by the second death (see also 20:14; 21:8).

Message to the Church in Pergamum (2:12-17)

Opening (2:12). The description of Christ recalls the "sharp two-edged sword" which proceeds from Christ's mouth in the inaugural vision (1:16; cf. Isa 49:2 — the servant's "sharp sword"). A sword from the mouth is also ascribed to Christ in 19:15, 21, where it functions as a symbol of divine retribution against the wicked. Its recurrence in 2:16 makes clear John's expectation that divine judgment awaits those who threaten the community with compromise.

Main body (2:13-16). John takes explicit notice of Pergamum as a place "where Satan's throne is." The expression, which alludes to the imperial cult and allied institutions (see 13:2; 16:10; Aune 1997: 182-84), serves as a caricature of the city, whose very structure is regarded as a direct threat to the life of the Christian community. This, in turn, is made the explanation for the death of Antipas (2:13 — "who was killed among you, where Satan lives"). For the author Antipas is the quintessential example of a Christian who, just like Christ (cf. 1:5), has been faithful to the point of death. While some think the killing of Antipas represents a common occurrence with which the church was familiar, others call attention to the phrase "in the days of," which suggests that the death was not a recent (and therefore infrequent) event.

Despite their fidelity during the time of Antipas, some of the Christians in Pergamum are criticized for adhering to the teaching of "Balaam" (2:14) and that of the "Nicolaitans" (v. 15; see 2:6 and bibliography cited there); both designations are figurative, perhaps referring to the same group (for *houtos,* v. 15a, "in this way . . . likewise" is preferable to NRSV's insufficiently emphatic "so also"). Balaam's teaching is essentially the same as that of "Jezebel" in the following message (2:14, 20; see Num 25:1-2). His instruction is reprehensible because it advocates eating food offered to idols and practicing "sexual immorality" *(porneuein).* Shops often sold meat remaining from temple sacrifices offered to pagan deities. John adopts a position more radical than that of Paul, who had addressed the issue in Corinth some forty years earlier (1 Cor 8:4-13; 10:14-31); for John *any* consumption of such meat is incompatible with the worship of God. This radical view, if followed by Christians, would have had economic and social consequences (Theissen 1982: 121-43). Whereas the "Nicolaitans" were probably attempting to secure the participation of Christians in social and economic life, for John religious faithfulness requires the community to adopt a separatist stance which by definition must call the Roman Empire into question (see 18:1-24). John's position does not, therefore, mean that the problem necessarily involved practices of sexual immorality within the Christian community (though this possibility cannot be entirely excluded). The emphasis of his criticism is more generally directed against an accommodating lifestyle which he regards as idolatrous. The argument thus reflects the well-established tradition in Scripture which took prostitution as a symbol for religious unfaithfulness (as in Jeremiah 2–3; Ezekiel 16; Hosea).

Conclusion (2:17). Those who reject the consumption of food from temples are promised food of their own: "some of the hidden manna." The term "manna" recalls the miraculous feeding through which the Israelites were able to survive in the wilderness (Exod 16:4-36). Here it signifies life for the faithful Christian (cf. John 6:35, 48). Unclear is the sense in which it is "hidden": is it that (a) the manna cannot be recognized by those who John thinks participate in idolatry or that (b) the manna is hidden now but will be revealed when Christ comes in judgment (2:16)? The reward of a white stone inscribed with a "new name" may symbolize the declaration of innocence to be given to the faithful who conquer. The new name could be that of a Christian who receives the stone (Hemer 1986: 96-104). If, however, the name is that of Christ (see 3:12; 14:1; 19:12, 13, 16; 22:4), the imagery may be conceived in terms of an amulet. To this extent the white stone would then represent God's protection for the one who possesses it (Aune 1997: 190-91).

Message to the Church in Thyatira (2:18-29)

Opening (2:18). Only here in Revelation is Christ called "the Son of God." The other features are taken from the opening vision ("who has eyes like a flame of fire" — 1:14b; "whose feet are like burnished bronze" — 1:15a). The imagery implies that Christ is judge, a function which is reiterated in 2:22-23. On the significance of the symbolism for the author's Christology, see under 1:12-20.

Main body (2:19-25). As in Ephesus and Pergamum, the Christians in Thyatira are praised for being reproached. The congregations in these cities are also faced by crises of leadership. John shows his familiarity with the community over a period of time through his comment that "your last works are greater than the first" (v. 19b).

The church of Thyatira is criticized for its tolerance of "that woman Jezebel, who calls herself a prophetess" (2:20a). The name "Jezebel" is used metaphorically, that is, it is taken from the non-Israelite wife of King Ahab (1 Kings 18–21). Nevertheless, John is specifically referring to a woman (NRSV misleadingly translates "prophet"!) who has wielded considerable influence in the Christian community (2:24). The problems associated with her are the same ones attributed to Balaam and the Nicolaitans in the message to Pergamum (v. 14), though here the imagery of "sexual immorality" is more explicitly developed. As one who regards himself as a true prophet, John is especially sensitive to two things: (1) other prophets (e.g., "Balaam" and "Jezebel"), whose progressive message of laxness in the social and economic spheres of life — for example, trade guilds for which Thyatira was particularly well known — poses a grave danger to the worship of God, and (2) claims which he considers false (2:2, 9, 20; 3:9; cf. 3:1b). Jezebel's teaching of *porneia* could refer literally to reprehensible sexual activity (Schüssler Fiorenza 1985: 116); however, since the author still seems to regard her as a member of the community, the term may simply refer metaphorically to eating food from the temples (Thompson 1990: 121-23). Despite the strong polemical language used, the possibility for repentance is still open to her (2:21). Significantly, for John the influence of Jezebel within the Christian community is the microcosm of a *porneia* that is taking place on a grander scale in the Roman Empire, "the great whore *(pornē)*" (17:1-2; 18:2-3; 19:2; see 14:8). Hence the false teaching could be associated with "the deep things of Satan" (2:24).

Conclusion (2:26-29). The promise of authority over the nations is taken from Ps 2:8-9. Those who conquer and persist in doing Christ's works receive such authority (5:10b; 20:4; 22:5b), just as Christ has received it from God (cf. 3:21). The promise to share in Christ's rule is elaborated by the image of receiving the "morning star," that is, Christ himself (see under 22:16).

Message to the Church in Sardis (3:1-6)

Opening (3:1a). "The seven spirits of God" are also mentioned in 1:4 and 4:5, where they are associated with the divine throne. As the "seven stars" (in 1:20; 2:1 interpreted as the seven angels of the churches), they are portrayed as subordinate to Christ.

Main body (3:1b-4). Sardis was a flourishing economic center near the end of the first century and was known for its influential Jewish community. One may infer that the Christian community was well adjusted in this setting, as the message makes no mention of either opponents or social conflict (as also the message to Laodicea, vv. 14-22). The author claims, however, that the Christians of Sardis "are dead," and not "alive" as they think (v. 1b). This pronouncement of their state is a rhetorical overstatement. In v. 2 the antithetical imagery is softened; the congregation is told to "wake up" *(grēgoreō)* since they are "on the point of death" (Yarbro Collins 1979: 24). At an earlier point than in the other messages, the Christians are called upon to repent (v. 3). To reinforce the seriousness of repentance, John draws on a Jesus tradition (Matt 24:42-44; Luke 12:39-40) which stresses the importance of being prepared because of the unexpectedness of Christ's coming to judge (cf. 1:7; 1 Thess 5:2; 2 Pet 3:10). A few in Sardis are commended for being "worthy"; they are "dressed in white" and have not ruined their "clothes." Later, language from this message (coming as a thief, being wakeful, keeping one's clothes) recurs in the form of a saying and blessing (16:15) inserted into the account of the sixth plague (16:12-16). In this way, the possibility of repentance in Sardis is placed against the backdrop of the final eschatological drama of judgment and reward.

Conclusion (3:5-6). The names of the Christians are written in "the book of life"; without repentance, however, their place in this book will be blotted out. The image of removal from such a book is a way of graphically portraying divine judgment, as in the twelfth benediction of the Jewish *Shemoneh Esreh* (Eighteen Benedictions): "Let them [the Nazarenes and the sectarians] be blotted out from the book of life, and not be written together with the righteous." In the Hebrew scriptures such a book contained a list of names of those who have survived a crisis with their lives intact (Exod 32:32-33; Isa 4:3-4; cf. Ps 69:28), and in Jewish apocalyptic literature it is a widespread motif underlining the conviction that the faithful will remembered and rewarded at the final judgment (e.g., *1 Enoch* 108:3; *Jos. Asen.* 15:4). The book of life is mentioned six more times in Revelation (13:8; 17:8; 20:12, 15; 21:27). Those whose names are not written therein are allies of the beast (13:8; 17:8) and are to be punished (20:15); on the contrary, those recorded in the book are the only ones admitted into the new Jerusalem (21:27).

The final promise that Christ will "confess" the names of Christians before "my Father and his angels" derives from a Jesus tradition variously preserved in the Gospels (Matt 10:32 — before "the Father"; Luke 12:8 — before "the angels of God"). Here Christ's confession is envisioned as a public reading of the victorious Christians' names from the book of life.

Message to the Church in Philadelphia (3:7-13)

Opening (3:7). Christ possesses "the key of David" with the authority of one who opens and shuts without the possibility of being hindered. The description (also v. 8a) draws on Isa 22:22-23, through which John emphasizes that Christ alone can make it possible, regardless of the circumstances, to enter into God's presence.

Main body (3:8-11). The message shares several features with that addressed to Smyrna (2:8-11). (a) John does not criticize any teachings or practices. Moreover, (b) the tone of both messages is to encourage the congregations in view of an imminent crisis. Finally, (c) both messages speak of opposition from the Jewish community, which is called the "synagogue of Satan" and is considered a false form of Judaism. The "open door" provided by Christ thus seems to refer less to an opportunity to do missions (as in 1 Cor 16:9; 2 Cor 2:12; so esp. Ramsey 1904: 286-93; Aune 1997: 236) than to the eschatological salvation of those who have patiently endured (e.g., Lohmeyer 1953: 33; Kraft 1974: 33). This salvation is described both in the main body of the message (3:8-11) and in the eschatological promises which follow (vv. 12-13). The Christians of Philadelphia are promised that Christ will make the false Jews "bow down" at their feet (v. 9 — *proskynēsis*). Such a role reversal can be envisioned because the Christians are promised a superior, *heavenly* Jerusalem (v. 12; cf. Isa 60:14). Their status, from a heavenly perspective, is symbolized by their possession of a "crown" which they must strive to keep (3:11; see the elders with "golden crowns" in 4:4). For John unswerving loyalty to Christ is incompatible with the political, religious, and social fabric of Roman society. This conflict is given cosmological proportions, and the inevitable outcome is "the hour of trial" which John believes will consume the entire world in the near future (3:10b). The coming of Christ "soon" will be, not to prevent the Christians from suffering, but to bring them through the anticipated crisis.

Conclusion (3:12-13). The "open door" imagery is picked up from vv. 7-8a in the eschatological promise. The one who conquers will be made into a "pillar" in God's temple (Isa 22:23 — "peg . . . in his father's house"), and upon the faithful believer shall be written the name of God, the name of the new Jerusalem (21:2; cf. 22:14), and the new name of Christ (see the comment on 2:17). The term "pillar" is a departure from the Isaiah tradition. Though a metaphorical meaning is possible as an interpretation of Isa 22:22 (so Prov 9:1; Gal 2:9; see Fekkes 1994: 133), the choice of "pillars" in the context of temple imagery suggests that the faithful Christians are promised an angelic identity (Allison 1986: 409-14, referring to 4Q403 1i, 38-46; cf. also *Jos. Asen.* 17:6).

Message to the Church in Laodicea (3:14-22)

Opening (3:14). Unlike the case in the other messages, none of the titles given to Christ is taken from the opening vision in 1:12-20. As "the faithful and true witness" (see also 1:5; 19:11), Christ has no counterpart in Laodicea (cf. 2:13). The description of Christ as "the Amen" stresses his trustworthiness in fulfilling his promises (cf. "God of Amen" in Isa 65:16). Finally, "the beginning" or "the origin *(archē)* of God's creation" is sometimes regarded as an allusion to Col 1:15 (the preexistent Christ is "the firstborn [*prōtotokos*] of all creation") since that letter was supposed to be read in Laodicea (Col 1:15; Aune 1997: 256). Both texts reflect an early Christian tradition (John 1:2-3) which, in turn, may have derived from a Jewish tradition of interpretation based on Gen 1:1 (Prov 8:22 LXX). It remains unclear whether the title regards Christ as the first creation of God or as the originator who is prior to creation.

Main body (3:15-20). As in the message to Sardis (3:1), this one contains a criticism of a community under false illusions: the Laodiceans think they are rich but are actually poor, pitiable, and "naked" (v. 17). Using terms related to wealth and, possibly, drawing on local imagery (see Hemer 1986: 178-209, esp. concerning "lukewarm" water in vv. 15-16 and "salve" in v. 18), John redefines what it means to be rich on the presumption that, despite appearances, they are actually "poor." Given their "poor" condition, they are to obtain from Christ the kind of gold that is "refined by fire," that is, John recommends that their faith be bound up with the experience of suffering (2:13) just as Christ's faithful testimony (3:14) led to his death. In addition, they need "white robes" to cover the shame of their "nakedness" and "salve" to open their blind eyes (v. 18). Whatever the appropriateness of this language for the setting in Laodicea (Hemer 1986: 199), v. 18 draws much of its inspiration from the story of Adam and Eve in paradise who, when becoming aware of their nakedness through their sin, required clothing to cover their shame (Gen 2:25; 3:6-7, 10, 21). The message thus demands repentance on the condition that (1) they are cognizant of their dire spiritual condition and, at the same time, (2) know of Christ's love for them (3:19b; cf. Prov 3:12; Heb 12:6).

3:19b-20 are somewhat gentler in tone. The motif of Christ's "coming," which recurs throughout the messages (2:5, 16; 3:3, 11, 16), is here portrayed in the image of a guest knocking on the door, though from the *outside,* waiting to be let in to eat a meal *(deipneō).* The intimacy with Christ as signified by the meal is yet to be realized. The figurative participation in a meal with Christ means sharing in the kind of witness ("faithful and true") that Christ represents (v. 14). In the apocalyptic vision fellowship with Christ is envisioned as "the marriage supper of the Lamb" (19:9); at this eschatological meal *(deipnon)* the invited guests are those who through their faithfulness are "clothed in fine linen" (19:8; cf. v. 18). The author thus lays a challenge before the Laodicean congregation to take seriously the consequences of Christ's presence. In the reading and hearing of ch. 19, the recipients of the message would have recognized that their response to John's message has eschatological implications.

Conclusion (3:21-22). Enthronement with Christ and God is promised those who conquer (cf. 2:26-27). For John this is possible for the faithful only because Christ himself has conquered through his death (5:5; 17:14). Though the theme of conquering occurs in the conclusions to each of the seven messages, this is its first mention in relation to Christ. This coordination of language shows how much the author has interwoven Christology and discipleship in Revelation. In this way the Christ event (his death followed by his exaltation) serves as a model which reorders existence to be incompatible with the social and religious realities of the Roman world.

The image of enthronement is deeply rooted in ideals associated with kingship known in ancient Israel and in the Near East. The extension of royal reign to the subjects is more rare (see 2:26-27). Among the Dead Sea texts, the author of 4Q521 expects that the pious will be honored "upon the throne of the eternal kingdom" (2ii, 7). The belief that the faithful will share Christ's reign in the end becomes a prominent theme in Revelation (1:6; 2:26-27; 5:10; 20:4, 6; 22:5; cf. Matt 19:28 = Luke 22:30). Except in 22:3, this is the clearest instance in which Christ is enthroned, whereas Christ (as the Lamb) is otherwise either described as being in the standing position (5:6) or is distinguished from God, "who is seated on the throne" (5:13; 6:16; 7:9-10; 7:17 is not clear: "the Lamb at the center of the throne"). It is possible that 3:21 already presupposes the vision of enthronement in the new Jerusalem (22:1, 3), which here is extended to include the conquering Christians (cf. 22:5).

Vision of Heavenly Worship and the Redeemer Lamb (4:1–5:14)

The beginning of ch. 4 marks a break in tone from the preceding chapters. Whereas in the messages of chs. 2–3 John acts as a scribe to address the troubles of Christian communities, the vision of heavenly worship in ch. 4 seems to transport John, now acting as seer, into "an atmosphere of perfect assurance and peace" (Charles 1920: 1:102). This shift in tone and literary form does not mean, however, that the churches of Asia Minor are forgotten in the vision as it acquired its present shape. The vision begins with an "open door," which suggests that this is neither a private nor a vicarious viewing for John, but for the communities to "see" as well (3:8; cf. 3:20). Moreover, the throne imagery, here focused so exclusively on the divine throne, picks up where the the conclusion of the seventh message leaves off (3:21) by focusing more exclusively on *God's* throne and drawing a portrait which contrasts markedly from "Satan's throne" mentioned in relation to Pergamum (2:13). The "seven spirits of God" before the throne are included in 1:4 among the sources of grace in the epistolary greeting to the churches (cf. also 3:1). Finally, it is possible to read the description of the twenty-four elders (who are clothed in "white garments" and wear "golden crowns") in such a way that it provides John's hearers and readers with a vision of what Christians are promised if they are faithful (3:4-5 — "white garments"; 2:10 — "crown of life"; cf. 3:11). In other early Jewish and Christian literature thrones, crowns, and garments are frequently metaphors for the heavenly reward awaiting the righteous (e.g., *1 Enoch* 108:12; *T. Job* 33:2-9; and the Christian *5 Ezra* 2:42-25; *Apoc. Elij.* 1:8; and *Asc. Isa.* 9:12; 11:40). Therefore, although much of the vision could be read as essentially Jewish in inspiration (Rowland 1979; see below), echoes of the literary context suggest that it has been affected to some degree by the author's Christian perspective (Hurtado 1985: 102-24).

Worship of God (4:1-11)

John's Ascent to Heaven (4:1-2a). The vision is mediated by "the first voice which I heard speaking with me like a trumpet" (v. 1; cf. 1:11), that is, Christ, whose function overlaps with that of an angel (see 17:1; 21:9, 10; 22:1, 6, 8; and the throne visions in *1 Enoch* 71:5-10; *2 Enoch* 20:3–22:3; *Apoc. Abr.* 15:2–18:14; *3 Enoch* 1:6-12). While this way of presenting Christ is sometimes explained as the activity of an editor who has tried to integrate originally separate sections of Revelation (e.g., Aune 1997: cxxiv, 282), in its present form the passage 4:1–5:14 preserves a varied portrait of Christ; on the one hand, as an angelic mediator (4:1), on the other hand, as the "Lamb" who, superior to any angel (5:2-3), is included in the worship of God (5:9-14). Such a tension might reflect the author's attempt to communicate effectively to Christians in whose lives angels may have played an important role as, for example, guardians or guides to revelation (Karrer 1986: 169-86). John opens his presentation of Christ by drawing on angelology (see also 1:13-16), but goes on to portray through rich symbolism how much more than any angel Christ actually is (chs. 2–3 and 5–22).

Once "in the spirit" (cf. 1:10), John is invited to ascend through the "open door" in order to learn "what must happen after these things" (4:1; cf. 1:1, 19; 22:16). The opening of heaven inaugurates an unfolding revelatory event (15:5-6; 19:11). Unlike some descriptions of prolonged journeys to heaven in early Jewish literature (e.g., *1 Enoch* 14; *2 Enoch* 3–22; *T. Levi* 2–3; cf. *3 Enoch* 1:1-2 and the Christian *Asc. Isa.* 6–9), the seer is rushed into the presence of the divine throne without any intermediate steps. Seen "from the top down" rather than "on the way up," the visions focus on a reality that unmasks a sharp conflict between God and institutions of the Roman Empire.

The Throne Vision (4:2b-8a). Initially, the author describes in detail the divine throne room without any mention of Christ. Though it contains motifs found in the preceding three chapters, basic elements of the vision are chiefly inspired by theophanies in the Jewish scriptures, especially Ezekiel 1 and Isaiah 6: the throne (Ezek 1:26, 28; 10:10-15; cf. 28:13; Isa 6:1); the sea of glass (4:6a; cf. Ezek 1:22); and the four living creatures, each with six wings (4:6b-8; Ezek 1:6-12, 18; cf. Isa 6:2-3: the seraphim). This creative development of biblical tradition was common in later visions of the divine throne in Jewish apocalyptic writings (*1 Enoch* 14; 71; Daniel 7; *2 Enoch* 20-22; *T. Levi* 3; *Apoc. Abr.* 18; 4Q530ii, 16-20). Significantly, whereas the throne in Ezekiel 1 moves about, the position of the divine throne seems to be fixed (4:2b) and so represents an *axis mundi,* that is, the immovable center of all reality.

Worship of God (4:8b-11). The throne room scene reaches a climax in a description of the worship of God. The worship by the living creatures takes the *trishagion* (threefold declaration of God as "holy") from Isa 6:3 as its point of departure (4:8b). The next clause corresponds to the description of God in the prologue (1:4, 8 — "who was and is and is coming"). In addition, God is praised as the creator of all things (4:11). However fixed the heavenly throne may be, the description of God as the coming one expresses the hope that the rule of God, creator of all, will manifest itself throughout the cosmos.

Throughout Isa 6:3a John stresses that the worship of the living creatures is unbroken: "day and night without ceasing" (4:8b — *kai anapausin ouk echousin hēmeras kai nyktos*). There is no speculation about what would happen in heaven were the worship of God to be temporarily interrupted (as, e.g., in *Apoc. Abr.* 18:8-11); rather, this picture of ceaseless worship (see *T. Levi* 3:8) is presented as exemplary (see 7:15). The author picks up the precise wording of 4:8b in 14:11 to stress that, in contrast to such heavenly worship, "there is no rest day or night" for the unfaithful who instead worship the beast and its image (see also 20:11). Therefore, it may be significant that the worship of the twenty-four elders (on their identity, see above) is synchronized in 4:9-10 with that of the living creatures (cf. Ezek 1:19-21).

The Redeemer Lamb (5:1-14)

In ch. 5 the mood changes dramatically with the introduction of a "scroll" with seven seals. Following the exemplary worship of ch. 4, the problem arises as to how this scroll is to be opened since no one is found worthy. The vision of the heavenly throne room is transformed into that of a heavenly court in which divine justice, predetermined from the beginning, is being put into effect. In this context, it is Christ the "Lamb" who holds the key to the execution of God's plan for creation. Despite the contrast between chs. 4 and 5, it is best to regard the whole section 4:1–5:14 as a single vision. The christological emphasis of ch. 5 develops out of the preceding vision of God's throne as John's vision comes into focus; thus "the seven spirits of God," which are visible as "seven flaming torches" in 4:5, become part of the physical features attributed to Christ the Lamb (5:6). As if he were viewing an impressionistic painting, the seer looks further into the portrait and watches an initially unrecognizable Christology emerge into full view. John regards Christ's work as essential for establishing God's purpose for the created order.

The Problem of the Scroll and the Quest to Have It Opened (5:1-5). The opening verses of ch. 5 suggest that there is a discrepancy between God's rule in heaven and the execution of God's plan for creation as a whole. The scroll, which is written inside and out, remains sealed. Perhaps analogous to double legal documents of antiquity, the scroll could be known in theory, while in the event of controversy the inside content was considered binding. In such a case the seal would have to be broken to secure its legal authority (against Prigent 1988: 94; see Holtz 1971: 31-33).

The author proceeds on the assumption that God's coming requires a mediator since the possibility of *God* breaking open the seals of the scroll is not considered. When the question in the heavenly council is posed, "Who is worthy to open the scroll?" (cf. 1 Kgs 22:20-21; Isa 6:8), John weeps because there is no mediator: "no one was found worthy to open the scroll or to look into it" (5:4). This show of emotion reflects the seer's disappointment given that all in heaven is actually not well; in the midst of a crisis in executing God's purpose, there is no solution in sight. If this is correct, his emotion may have been intended to strike a resonant chord with the feelings of at least some readers as they perceived their own suffering in the face of adversity. The elder's word of comfort, "Do not weep!" (5:5), is spoken to John, who hears on behalf of the churches. At the same time, weeping is a stock feature of visions which prepares the seer to receive a revelation of particular importance (Idel 1988: 75-88). In this case, John's revelation consists of being told about "the lion of the tribe of Judah," who as David's "root" (cf. Isa 11:1 LXX — *riza,* "root") "has conquered." These designations refer, of course, to Christ, whom John regards as the only one worthy to open the scroll. The imagery here accords with a Jewish messianic tradition (*Pss. Sol.* 17:1-42; 4 Ezra 12:32; 4Q285 fgt. 5, line 4; 4Q252v, 3-4; 4Q161iii, 18) which anticipates a military "messiah" who will triumph over Israel's political enemies and establish justice on behalf of the Jews.

Christ Commissioned as the Lamb (5:6-7). Instead of being described as one who slays the wicked (see, e.g., Isa 11:4), Christ the conqueror is introduced as a "Lamb standing as if slaughtered." He comes into focus for John "between" figures he has seen in the throne vision of ch. 4: the throne, the living creatures, and the elders. The image of a slaughtered Lamb is no doubt rooted in the sacrificial cult of Judaism known through the Hebrew scriptures. However, it remains unclear whether the imagery derives from any traditions about (a) the daily or *tamid* burnt offering (e.g., Exod 29:38-46; Num 28:3-8), (b) the Passover sacrifice which brought liberation to Israel (e.g., Exod 12:1-20; Num 9:2-5; Deut 16:1-8; 2 Chr 30:1-27), (c) a military ruler (*1 Enoch* 89:45-46, referring to David; cf. *T. Jos.* 19:8), or (d) the death of the innocent Suffering Servant of God (Isaiah 53). Since several of these elements may be recognized in the Lamb Christology of Revelation, it is possible that the author has engaged in a creative conflation of traditions. If this is correct, the Lamb symbol is meant to evoke a whole range of ideas with which John wishes his readers to identify: innocence, suffering, obedience, and rule. In relation to the Christ event the image of a sacrificed Lamb refers to his death by crucifixion (cf. John 1:29; 1 Cor 5:7). However, by locating the slaughtered victim in heaven, John goes well beyond the notion of Christ's death as an event in history; he transforms Jesus' crucifixion into a principle of cosmic significance which, in turn, serves as a starting point for understanding what it means to live faithfully in a world characterized by conflict (see under 6:9-11).

The Lamb's reception of the scroll symbolizes the commissioning of Christ with authority to bring into effect God's redemption (Aune 1997: 336-38; cf. Dan 7:13-14). The author does not make clear whether this formal act refers to a point in time when Christ can be said to have become something he was previously not. If chs. 4 and 5 are best regarded as a unified vision which does not describe successive stages in salvation history, the taking of the scroll may rather be symbolic of Christ's authority, which in one sense has existed all along (see 13:8 — "the Lamb that was slaughtered from before the foundation of the world"). Given this reality, what remains is the translation of what already stands written in the scroll into the world as yet untouched by the manifest triumph of God.

Worship of the Lamb alongside God (5:8-14). The worship following the investiture of the Lamb is modeled on the worship of God in ch. 4 (cf. 4:11; 5:9, 12-13). There are, however, two main differences. First, the Lamb is here openly acclaimed in worship (5:8-10, in the second person; vv. 12-13, in the third person). In the first worship formula, the praise of Christ to the accompaniment of harps is called "a new song" (v. 9; cf. 14:3). As a whole, this scene is the most vivid of descriptions in the NT of Christ as the object of heavenly worship (cf. Phil 2:9-11; Heb 1:6). Nevertheless, the author takes deliberate measures to insure that such an exalted view of Christ poses no threat to monotheistic belief; elsewhere, when both God and Christ are referred to together, the author strives to use singular verbs and pronouns (14:1; 20:6; 21:22; 22:3; though see 6:17) or separates them by repeating the preposition or the case following the preposition (6:16; 7:9-10; 11:15; 12:10; 14:4; 20:6; 21:22; 22:1). In any case, non-Christian Jews would have found John's exalted view of the Lamb incompatible with belief in one God (Hurtado 1988). A second difference is that the sphere of worship in ch. 5 is widened beyond the inner circle of living creatures and twenty-four elders (4:9-10; 5:8) to include the myriads of angelic beings (5:11; cf. Dan 7:9-10) and, finally, all of creation "in heaven and on earth and under the earth" (5:13; cf. Phil 2:10). For John the worship made possible through the Lamb goes hand in hand with the manifestation of God's purpose for the world. The last scenario of worship (5:13) represents an ideal picture. In the visions of judgment to follow the author stresses that any compromise of such worship is unacceptable for those who wish to participate in the blessings of the eschatological age. As in 4:9-10, the scene concludes as the elders' worship responds to that of the four living creatures (5:14).

The Seven Seals Opened (6:1–8:5)

Beginning with ch. 6 it becomes difficult to coordinate John's visions with identifiable events in history and, even more so, to determine the extent to which the visions are intended to be an orderly outline of future events. It must be remembered that Revelation was addressed to Christians who were seeking to express their faith out of a variety of circumstances regarded by John, for example, as indifference, wealth, conflict within the community, and sociopolitical oppression (cf. chs. 2–3). While the author does expect that certain events will occur in the imminent future, Revelation is first and foremost an attempt to draw a clear line of demarcation between God and Satan, between the Christian community and the contemporary world of the Roman Empire, between faithful commitment and indifferent compromise (Thompson 1990: 186-97). In short, the visions define reality from the perspective of a Lamb Christology. Whether or not the visions are concerned with a chronology of what will happen, they invite John's hearers and readers through imaginative participation to behold the full impact of God's imminent and triumphant reign.

The opening of the seven seals in 6:1–8:5 reflects the following pattern: the first four seals form a subunit containing short parallel descriptions of four horsemen and their destructive activities (6:2-8). The opened fifth seal produces a vision of martyred Christians calling for revenge against their killers (6:9-11), while the sixth opens to a vision of divine wrath (6:12-17). This is followed by an interlude consisting of two visions which depict the status of the faithful in heaven (7:1-8, 9-17). The seventh seal produces a period of silence before unleashing the seven trumpets (8:1-2). The subsequent series of seven trumpets (8:6–11:19) adopts a similar pattern with a short fourfold unit at the beginning (8:6-12) and an interlude before the seventh trumpet (10:1–11:13; Bauckham 1993: 10-13).

First Four Seals: Four Horsemen (6:1-8)

The breaking of the first four seals produces, respectively, the advent of four riders on variously colored horses (white, red, black, and pale). The vision is no doubt inspired by the four horsemen and four chariots of Zech 1:8-11 and 6:1-8 in which these groups are commissioned to traverse the earth and report on its peaceful condition. The biblical tradition is a portrait of God's judgment on the nations (the peace is only apparent), and it is this aspect which the author develops in this passage. Each of the riders responds to a divine invitation as a bringer of disaster. While there is no doubt about the nature of the second, third, and fourth riders associated with the plagues — they bring slaughter by the sword (6:4, 8), scarcity of food (vv. 6, 8), pestilence, and wild beasts (v. 8) — the identity and function of the rider on the white horse (v. 2) is debated. Some interpreters regard the conquering unleashed by the first seal as the proclamation of the gospel which, according to some accounts of apocalyptic expectation, should take place before the end (cf. Matt 24:14; Mark 13:10). Along such lines, a comparison is often drawn between 6:2 and the rider on a white horse in 19:11 who is Christ (see the bibliography in Mounce 1977: 153 n. 4). Instead, it is more likely that the first rider, only generally described as going out "conquering and to conquer," is used to introduce the evils unfurled by the following three riders, just as the catastrophes brought by the fourth rider, who is "Death" attended by "Hades" (cf. 1:18; 20:13-14), provide a summative conclusion to the events associated with the others. In this case, the image of a horseman with a bow may be reminiscent of the Parthians, who were thought to pose a military threat to the Roman Empire from the East (see also 9:14; 16:12; cf., e.g., *1 Enoch* 56:5-6). Here the allusion provides a negative counterpart to the vision of Christ in 19:11-16; as an instrument of God's purpose, it signifies John's conviction that the political stability offered under Rome is not secure. Taken together, the first four seals underscore the Roman world's vulnerability to military conquests and economic disasters. Each disaster is called forth by one of the four living creatures who worship incessantly at God's throne (4:8) and have proclaimed the Lamb worthy to open the seals (5:8-9).

How are the disasters related to the Lamb's activity as breaker of the seals? Answers which either dissociate these and other catastrophes in the book from divine purpose altogether (cf. Wis 1:13) or, conversely, ascribe them directly to God's will (cf. Ezek 5:16-17; Sir 39:29) do not do justice to the dynamic tension which John wishes to sustain between the presence of evil in the world and the reality of God's justice in creation. The vision demonstrates that the divine response to evil is not merely its eradication but rather its transformation into an instrument of God's purpose and power; hence there *is* a certain correlation between the image of the slaughtered Lamb and the first four seals. The disasters are both imminent and realistic; they are conceivable on the basis of evils which humans themselves are capable of bringing about (Caird 1966: 82-83) and as such reveal how the future judgment of God can already be seen to operate in the present world order. Divine retribution for human sin in this passage is only partial (6:8 — "a fourth of the earth," whereas "pest" and "famine" affect all of Babylon in 18:8). Apparently it is also indiscriminate, affecting people regardless of their status in relation to God. Implicitly, Christians are not spared from these disasters, for it is *through* them and the challenges they pose that faithfulness will be ultimately established.

Fifth Seal: The Victims' Complaint (6:9-11)

The first four seals produced only preliminary and indiscriminate signs of God's justice; perhaps some already correspond in some measure to experiences known to the first hearers of Revelation. Is this all the divine "coming" (1:7-8; 4:8) is supposed to bring? A cry for something more is unveiled when the fifth seal is opened. The victims of injustice take their case of complaint to God (cf., e.g., *1 Enoch* 9:1; 4Q530 6, 4). Like the Lamb in 5:6, they are "slaughtered," a description reinforced by their position underneath the heavenly altar, here a place of sacrifice (Mounce 1977: 157), but elsewhere in Revelation a place where the martyrs' prayers for vengeance are offered and demonstrably answered (8:3-5; 16:7; cf. 9:13; 14:18; cf. Bauckham 1993: 55). Whereas John is not able to provide much detail about Christian witnesses who have died for their faith (Antipas in 2:12 is the exception), he was probably aware of the persecution of Christians scapegoated under Nero after the conflagration in Rome (Tacitus *Ann.* 15.44). Such Christians would have served John as a model to show how a discipleship loyal to death is but a reflection of what characterizes Christ from the start.

The question "How long?" (6:10), adapted from biblical and apocalyptic tradition (e.g., Pss 13:1-2; 79:5; 94:3;

Jer 12:4; Dan 12:6; Hab 1:2; Zech 1:12; 4 Ezra 4:35), raises the question about the delay of divine intervention when oppression seems to go on interminably (*1 Enoch* 46:2). However, what begins as a question about God's faithful activity on behalf of his people is, as in Jewish apocalyptic tradition, transformed into a question about discipleship: the realization of divine justice against "the inhabitants of the earth," who are allied against the faithful (cf. 3:10; 6:10; 8:13; 11:10; 13:8, 12; 17:2, 8) and held responsible for their suffering, depends on the completion of the number of righteous ones predetermined by God (6:11; see *1 Enoch* 47:4; 4 Ezra 4:37; *2 Bar.* 23:4-5). Thus in Revelation the end of history is not so much preceded by a period of passive waiting as by a proactive and radical obedience through suffering and death; only when the foreordained number is complete (6:11) can salvation history be propeled forward to its conclusion. John assumes that for the loyal Christian the present life is so marked by conflict with the contemporary world that he can only express the result in terms of death (see under 20:4-6).

Throughout the remainder of Revelation, John repeatedly attempts to address the martyrs' demand for divine justice (e.g., 8:3-5; 10:3-7; 11:1-2; 14:1-3, 9-11, 13, 18; 15:1-4; 16:5-7; 18:8, 18, 20; 19:3). In the meantime, their petition is answered as each of them is given "a white robe" (6:11). White clothing, traditionally a symbol of purity, is here made the possession of believers whose heavenly status is acquired through the voluntary pursuit of an innocent death in imitation of Christ (see 3:4-5; 19:8, 14; esp. 7:9 and 22:14; cf. Dan 12:10). At the same time white robes — a motif adapted from the apocalyptic notion of special clothing reserved for the righteous in the afterlife (*1 Enoch* 62:15-16; *2 Enoch* 22:8-10; *Asc. Isa.* 1:5; 4:16-17; 8:14: there are only a set number of robes in heaven) — are also promised to all of genuine faith who, as these martyrs, conclude their earthly lives without avoiding the clash with political and economic structures encountered in daily experience (cf. 3:18). This passage raises questions to be considered in the next three visions: How will divine justice for the righteous begin to manifest itself (6:12-17), at what number will the foreordained group of martyrs be made complete (7:1-17), and how will their deaths finally be avenged (8:1-5)? Broadly, it is divine justice which becomes the burning issue that runs through many of the remaining visions.

Sixth Seal: Cosmic Signs of Divine Wrath (6:12-17)

In its context, this passage answers the martyrs' plea for God to exact vengeance against their murderers in 6:10 (for a similar sequence, see Mal 2:17–3:2). In contrast to the events unleashed through the four horsemen (6:1-8), the opening of the sixth seal produces a torrent of cosmic catastrophes. John has borrowed language from prophetic traditions about the day of the Lord in the context of holy war (Fekkes 1994: 78-80, 158-66; on v. 12b see Joel 3:4 — the sun blackened, the moon as blood; on vv. 13-14a see Isa 34:4: stars falling to the earth as figs shaken by the wind, heaven rolling up as a scroll; on vv. 15b-16, see Isa 2:10, 19, 21 — hiding from the face of God; and on v. 16a, see Hos 10:8/Luke 23:30 — the wicked calling mountains to fall on them). These signs are set into motion by a great earthquake which throws the created order into chaos (Hag 2:6 — "in a little while, I will shake the heavens and earth").

The significance of the imagery in this passage is much discussed. Does John think these images will translate into physical realities or are they to be understood as conventional language which is symbolic in some way (e.g., as divine judgment over erring celestial powers — cf. *1 Enoch* 81; as the imminent end of the world — cf. Mark 13:24-25 par., or as illustrative of social upheavals taking place on the earth)? The search for an answer is aided by the observation that final judgment is not actually reached in this passage. The language still describes a preliminary stage in which the security of representative groups in human society — kings, generals, the rich, the powerful, slave, free — is completely shattered and results in their fear of divine wrath (cf. Nah 1:6; Mal 3:2). Not until "the great supper of God" does the judgment reach its climax; then those allied with the beast (cf. 13:16; 18:3) are defeated in a final eschatological battle (19:17-21).

In this sense John allows for the development of time in his visions. However, the visions are not to be understood in terms of a linear, chronological movement from vision to vision; rather, taken as a whole, they represent different ways of communicating something about a basic theme (see under 8:1–11:19 below). In this passage the vision attempts to come to terms with the manifestation of divine wrath on behalf of the faithful. John's imaginative use of the bibical imagery underlines the principle that God will avenge the suffering of his people by bringing chaos and panic to the forces of evil in the cosmos. This view is sharpened and reinforced with more detail in 8:7–9:21; 14:14-20; 16:17-21; and 19:17-21.

The expression "the great day of *their* wrath" is a combination of two complementary phrases which occur in prophetic and apocalyptic literature: "the great day" (e.g., Joel 2:11; 3:4; Zeph 1:14; *1 Enoch* 22:11; 54:6; *2 Enoch* 18:6; cf. Jude 6) and "the day of wrath" (e.g., Zeph 1:15, 18; 2:2-3; *Jub.* 24:28, 30). The pronoun "their," the preferred reading, is the only mention in Revelation of both Christ (here the Lamb) and God using a plural form (cf. the singular forms in 11:15; 14:1; 20:6; 21:22; 22:3-4). The reference to *them* has resulted from the introduction of a statement about Christ into the second half of Isa 2:10 (LXX — "from the fear of the LORD and from the glory of his strength"), while the meaning of "the LORD" is applied to God on the throne.

The Protection of God's People from Coming Plagues (7:1-8)

This passage has sometimes been regarded as a fragment dislocated from its original context (e.g., Bousset 1906: 283-84), such as before ch. 6. Whatever the case, in its present location and content the text has been integrated with care into the narrative. The placement of an interlude between the sixth and seventh seals corresponds to the pattern applied elsewhere by the author (10:1–11:13). Furthermore, the whole of ch. 7 seems to assume the foregoing passages in ch. 6: it provides an answer to the rhetorical question in 6:17 ("Who is able to stand?"), while 7:1-8 offer a glimpse of the "complete" number anticipated in 6:11 (supplemented, though, by countless numbers in 7:9; see below). The scene thus contrasts sharply with the wicked who fear divine reprisal in 6:15-17. Whereas the breaking of the sixth seal unravels the security of the "inhabitants of the earth" (cf. 6:10), a seal is given to God's servants as protection before the onslaught of judgment being temporarily restrained by the four winds (cf. 3:10). Finally, if Zechariah 6 has influenced the scheme of the four horsemen in 6:1-8 (see above), then it is possible that the image of "four winds of the earth" (7:1) reflects a further creative use of the same passage (Zech 6:5 — the four winds of *heaven*). For the notion of "four winds" as instruments of divine judgment, see Jer 49:35-38 and Dan 7:2 (cf. further *1 Enoch* 76: eight winds from the four directions are destructive).

This "seal *(sphragis)* of the living God" (7:2) is sometimes associated with the rite of baptism: the vision of the 144,000 sealed on earth would thus illustrate the protection promised to those who through an initiatory washing are identified as God's people (so, e.g., Prigent 1988: 120). Though the language of sealing may be associated with Christian ritual (e.g. *Herm. Sim.* 9.16.4; *Odes Sol.* 8:13; *2 Clem.* 7:6; Melito *On the Passover* 15–17), John's use of it is symbolic. The seal "on their foreheads" is inspired by Ezekiel 9, in which just such a sign is placed upon those mourning the sins of Jerusalem in order that they might be protected from judgment (cf. also Rev 9:4). The scene echoes the promise of protection offered to faithful Christians in Philadelphia "from the hour of testing" (3:10). This raises the question of the nature and extent of the protection offered to the 144,000, a problem which the author addresses in later passages (11:1-14; 12:11–14:5).

By referring to the faithful as 144,000 "out of every tribe of the children of Israel" (7:4), John assumes that Christian faith is, in a profound sense, the true form of Judaism (see 2:9; 3:9; and on 7:9-17 below). The "number," though symbolic, denotes a limited group (see under 6:9-11; 14:1-5). It signifies the number of martyrs to be "completed" before the visible onset of God's final punishment of evil (6:11); perhaps there is a wordplay between the state of being "sealed" *(esphragismenos)* and the term for "slaughtered" (*esphagmenos* — 6:9; cf. 5:6).

The language of twelve tribes numbered identically has militaristic overtones since it specifically has males in view (cf. 14:4) and is reminiscent of biblical accounts which tallied the strength of Israel's army (see, e.g., Num 1:20-21, 23; 31:4-6; 1 Chr 27:1-15; cf. Boring 1989: 130-31). John reinterprets this tradition by calling, not for violent conflict, but for an "army" whose members are faithful to the point of sacrificing their lives (7:9, 14; cf. 6:9), just as the military messiah "from the stem of David" has been redefined as the slaughtered Lamb (5:5-6; Bauckham 1993: 215). As in the case of Jesus, *suffering* becomes the dominant strategy for the overthrow of evil.

Worship by the Countless Multitude (7:9-17)

The *audition* (7:4) about the 144,000 on earth is translated into a *vision* of an innumerable group in heaven representing every nation, tribe, people, and language. Without doubt the present form of the text presupposes a continuity between these two groups. Less clear, however, is their precise relationship. Does the former refer to Jewish Christians and the latter to Gentile believers (so Kraft 1974: 126-28), or do both simply refer to the faithful church, albeit from different vantage points (e.g., Sweet 1979: 150-51)? In considering the respective groups in vv. 1-8 and 9-17, it is important to note how they relate chronologically to the period of destruction, "the great tribulation" (v. 14). Whereas the author's presentation of the 144,000 fits well with the notion of preparedness for battle (see above), the multitude (vv. 9, 14) consists of those who have emerged from the conflict to stand before God's throne and worship.

The vision does not presuppose that the faithful, on account of being sealed (7:3), will have been untouched by the catastrophic signs of divine judgment. On the contrary, the author understands protection in terms of being preserved from a state of faithlessness and its eternal consequences (see under 11:1-14). Indeed, the text plays with the expectation that God's "army" of believers will suffer violent death in the eschatological crisis; their robes are only white (7:9, 13-14; cf. 3:5) because they have been "washed . . . in the blood of the Lamb" (7:14; 22:14; cf. Gen 49:11). Here the logic of imagery is sacrificed to the principle that violent death and innocence are inseparable. A spiritualizing interpretation of the robes which takes them, for instance, as a general symbol for the conquering faith and righteousness of all Christians (so, e.g., Mounce 1977: 171), does not do justice to the radical images used by the author (cf. Charles 1920: 1:201-2, 214; Boring 1989: 131). But does John think that only martyrs can be faithful Christians? At the very least, it may be said that his vision calls for imaginary participation in a future which defines the nature of Christian existence from a martyr's point of view (see under 20:4-6). To characterize faith in any other way would undermine what is at stake in John's call for the congregations to repent. Thus, beginning with the assumption that Lamb Christology and discipleship share the same reality of experience, John idealizes martyrdom as the best demonstration of Christian loyalty (cf. also 12:11). His belief that a sharp universal conflict is imminent may have led him to imagine an outcome of violent death for those who persist in faithfulness.

The state of the multitude is one of military triumph. In 7:10 their declaration that victory *(sōtēria)* belongs to God and the Lamb presupposes that the enemy has been defeated (cf. Ps 3:9). The response of the angels, four living creatures, and elders in 7:12, in which God alone is acclaimed, is reminiscent of the scenes of worship in 4:11 and 5:12. But whereas in ch. 5 the worship is described in terms which focus on Christ's unique position to open the sealed scroll, in ch. 7 the scene is also concerned with those who will find themselves able to worship God "day and night" in the heavenly temple (cf. 3:12; 4:8). Drawing on prophetic traditions from Isaiah (25:8; 49:10) and Jeremiah (31:16), John concludes the vision by expressing the nature of the promised salvation through various metaphors: no hunger, no thirst, no scorching heat from the sun, abundance of water (cf. Ps 23:2-3), and comfort from one's tears (cf. 21:4). The location of the Lamb "in the midst of the throne" (7:17) is unusual; it signifies both that the slaughtered Lamb is enthroned on the altar in the heavenly temple's most holy place and that this throne, the throne of sacrifice, is the source of living water in abundance (cf. 22:1-2; see under 3:7).

Seventh Seal: Silence in Heaven and Introduction of the Seven Trumpets (8:1-6)

The immediate result of the Lamb's breaking of the seventh seal (8:1) is unexpected. The reader may have anticipated the restrained winds of destruction to be released (7:1); moreover, the noise of heavenly worship has reached a climax (7:10 — "loud"). By contrast, the "silence in heaven for about half an hour" temporarily suspends the forward thrust of events. This does not mean, however, that all activity is brought to a halt. Indeed, heavenly "silence" is in tradition associated with the recognition of God's presence (Hab 2:20; Zech 2:13; cf. Isa 41:1), and among the *Songs of the Sabbath Sacrifice* from Qumran "divine stillness" could be understood as the "sound" that includes heavenly praise and worship (e.g., 4Q405ii, 7-13; Allison 1988: 189-97). It is therefore not surprising that in Revelation the silence is combined with two activities: (1) with the giving (not blowing; cf. 8:6–11:19) of seven trumpets to the seven angels (8:2, 6) and (2) with the priestly functions carried out by "another angel" at the heavenly altar (vv. 3-5).

The activities described in 8:2, 6, and 3-5 are formally distinct. Whereas the mention of the seven trumpets anticipates the new sequence of events in the following narrative (8:6–11:19), the ritual at the heavenly altar can be read as a self-contained unit that describes the angel-priest offering incense (e.g., Lev 10:1; 16:12; Num 16:46), while, presumably, the heavenly court waited quietly (8:1) for him to reappear (*b. Ḥag.* 12b; cf. Farrer 1964: 112, though see Bousset 1906: 294). The author has, however, merged the two units in several ways. First, the activities of receiving the trumpets and offering incense occur "before the throne" (vv. 2, 4). Second, the blowing of trumpets after the angel-priest's pouring of the censer on earth (v. 6) assumes the combination in the theophany of Exodus (Exod 19:16) of thunder peals and flashes of lightning (8:5) — these also result from the angel's priestly ritual — with the trumpet blast (cf. Isa 29:6, where the trumpet is absent). Third, and most important, both activities are intertwined with the prayers of the faithful. The function of the seven angels as mediaries of human petitions to God is traditional (e.g., Tob 12:12, 15); in Revelation it is trumpets (see 8:6-13 below) which announce God's answer to the martyrs' prayers (6:9-11). In assigning to "another angel" the task of mediating the prayers of "all the saints," John draws on a widespread tradition associated with prominent angels (e.g., *1 Enoch* 9:1-11; 15:2; 40:6, 9; 47:1-2; 99:3; 104:1; *T. Levi* 5:5-6; *T. Dan* 6:2; *3 Bar.* 11–16). Such a tradition also lies behind the judgment motif in 8:5; similarly, in Ezek 10:2 the angelic "man clothed in linen" casts the burning coals from the heavenly altar between the cherubim over Jerusalem as punishment (cf. Num 16:46). For John, the combination of the seven angels' trumpets and the priestly ritual of the angel serves to introduce something on a grander scale: signs of punishment which cover "the earth" (8:5).

The Seven Trumpet Blasts (8:7–11:19)

The sequence of seven trumpets is similar in structure to, though not fully identical with, that of the seven seals. The first four form a group of natural disasters (8:6-12) modeled on some of the plagues sent against the Egyptians before Israel's exodus (cf. Exodus 7–10). These are followed by more detailed visions produced by the fifth (9:1-11) and sixth (9:12-19) trumpet blasts. After an interlude of two visions (10:1-11: the little scroll; 11:1-13: the two witnesses; cf. 7:1-8, 9-17), the seventh trumpet is blown to announce the final triumph of God (11:14-19; cf. 11:7). The fifth and sixth trumpets are designated as the first two of three "woes" (so 8:13; 9:12; 11:14). However, it is not clear that the seventh trumpet blast (11:15-19), which focuses on the proclamation of God's victory, corresponds to the third "woe"; rather, it is likely that the trumpet blast reaches into chs. 12–13 (cf. 12:12), where the series of catastrophes reaches a climax in the advent of the Satanic dragon allied with the two beasts (e.g., Lohse 1993: 59). There is, then, a certain parallel between the seventh seal unleashing the seven trumpets and the seventh trumpet, which, in turn, inaugurates a new series of visions. If correct, this interpretation of the structure adds weight to the impression that the seven seals, trumpets, and bowls do not represent three series of chronological events, each succeeding the other. They are rather different, though increasingly intense, ways of illustrating the crisis which John expects will occur once the conflict between God's uncompromising purpose and human unfaithfulness (in the form of concessions to economic, political, and religious spheres of life) has been laid bare.

The blowing of trumpets is closely connected in early Jewish and Christian traditions with the announcement of imminent and decisive judgment (e.g., Isa 27:13; Joel 2:1-11; *Apoc. Zeph.* 12:1-8; 4 Ezra 6:23-24; 1QM 18:3-5; 1 Cor 15:52; 1 Thess 4:16). Though the context is eschatological in Revelation, the trumpets are not the ultimate means by which manifestations of divine punishment are announced; that function is saved for the "seven bowls of God's wrath" (16:1-21).

First Four Trumpets (8:7-12)

The consequences of these trumpet blasts are described in a concise and parallel form. Whereas the broken seals bring forth the horsemen to inflict violence over a *fourth* of the earth (6:8), the degree of punishment and catastrophe associated with the trumpets is more intense: they bring destruction to a *third* (cf. also 9:15) of the earth (including trees and grass), of the ocean (including sea creatures and ships), of rivers and sources of water, and of heavenly bodies (including the sun, moon, and stars). This comparison may be extended to the images reminiscent of the fifth seal (6:12-17): the removal of mountains (8:8; cf. 6:14); the falling of a star or stars (8:10; cf. 6:13); and the darkening of heavenly bodies (8:12; cf. 6:12

— sun and moon). Though differently proportioned and worse than the events produced by the broken seals, the trumpet plagues do not yet represent a complete annihilation to accompany the final judgment. Nevertheless, the chaos unleashed at this stage is a projection of the conviction that God will achieve a visible redemption that tears down the foundations of the present order (21:1). The collision between God's people and surrounding evil is such that any notion of salvation precludes a transformation of *this* world.

In 8:7, 8, and 12 — the first, second, and fourth trumpet blasts — the destructive events are in part inspired, respectively, by the seventh, first, and ninth plagues in Egypt (Exod 9:22-26; 7:17-21; 10:21-23). What, however, is limited to the Egyptians in biblical tradition is here placed within the context of the earth, throughout which the destruction seems to be evenly distributed. Not clear is whether the faithful, as Israel during the plagues, are exempted from the consequences of the first four trumpet blasts, as their protection (cf. 7:1-4) is not mentioned until 9:4 under the fifth trumpet. The Exodus plagues provide a background for the trumpets in another way: they not only represent divine punishment against the wicked (in Exodus 7–10 the plagues do not hurt the Israelites) but also serve as warning signs that allow for an opportunity to repent. As suggested in 9:20, in which the latter idea actually surfaces in the text, John expects that, just as Pharaoh could not be persuaded by the catastrophes (Exod 7:13, 22; 8:15, 32; 9:7, 12; etc.), so the unrighteous who worship false deities will not be changed when confronted by open manifestations of the one true God.

The visions of the "burning mountain" (8:8) and the fallen "burning star" (v. 10) are inspired by prophecies of Jeremiah (51:25) and Isaiah (14:12) concerning the fall of the Babylonian Empire (cf. *Sib. Or.* 5:177-78). The fallen star, which poisons the water springs of the earth, is designated "Wormwood" (8:11). The name derives from another tradition from Jeremiah (9:15; see 23:15) that describes the punishment of the idolaters of Israel in terms of drinking poisoned water (cf. also Deut 29:17; Prov 5:3-4). The combined traditions suggest that the trumpet blasts herald the fall of Rome, the new Babylon, which is expected to become the victim (being poisoned) of its own doing (idolatry; so Caird 1966: 115).

Fifth Trumpet: The First "Woe" (8:13–9:12)

Eagle's Warning (8:13; 9:12). The last three trumpets are distinguished from the first four in that they are described as "woes." Accompanied by destruction, they are directed at "the inhabitants of the earth" (3:10; 6:10; 11:10), that is, at those who have not been sealed on their foreheads (9:4; cf. 3:10; 7:3). Though the "eagle" *(aetos)* can symbolize traits such as leadership, obedience, and power (cf. *2 Bar.* 77:18-26; 4 Ezra 11–12), here the bird is a vulture, a harbinger of disaster "in mid-heaven" that symbolizes God's devouring wrath against the wicked (cf. 19:17-18; e.g., Hos 8:1 LXX — *aetos;* Matt 24:28; Luke 17:37).

Fifth Trumpet (9:1-11). The author intended the plagues of woes to be worse than the previous four. The fifth is not only more elaborate but also involves a torture that does not even allow those affected to escape through death (v. 6; 6:15-17; cf. Job 3:21-22). The author stresses that the effects of the first woe are only temporary, that is, five months (9:5, 10). The reason for this is the opportunity for repentance for those faced by the warning signs of God's imminent judgment (cf. v. 20). Therefore, the true followers of Jesus, who have been sealed with a mark on their foreheads (v. 4; see 7:1-4), are to be untouched by the plague and will not be among those trying to escape (9:5-6).

The trumpet blast produces a vision of a fallen star (cf. already 8:10-11). Here the star, which uses a "key to the shaft of the bottomless pit" to release the evils imprisoned there (9:1-3), adapts a Jewish apocalyptic tradition according to which the origin of evil is explained as the fall of rebellious angelic beings from heaven (e.g., the angel-stars in *1 Enoch* 21:6; 86:3). In the plague, the story focuses on the fall of one figure and as such is reminiscent of the story in Isa 14:12 in which the king of Babylon is portrayed as the morning star expelled from heaven. The Isaianic tradition, itself drawing on a myth originally concerned with a Canaanite deity, was later applied to the figure of Satan (Luke 10:18; cf. *1 Enoch* 86:1). The evils released from the pit (9:2-3) presuppose that demonic angels (*1 Enoch* 6–16; 86:1; *Jub.* 11:5) had been locked up as punishment for having introduced sin into the world before the flood (cf., e.g., *1 Enoch* 10; *Jub.* 10:7-14). In the vision the chains restraining demonic powers are broken, so that evil becomes worse than before (Yarbro Collins 1979: 60). In 20:1-3 the "key to the bottomless pit" is used by an "angel of heaven" to imprison these powers again. It is possible that the "angel of the bottomless pit," called "destruction" (in both Hebrew and Greek) and "king" of the hostile forces (9:11), may be identified with the fallen star at the beginning of the vision (so, e.g., Caird 1966: 120; against Müller 1995: 195).

The evil unleashed is initially described as a swarm of locusts, likened to snakelike scorpions and warhorses (9:7-10; cf. v. 19). The images are informed by Jewish interpretations of the eighth plague against the Egyptians (see Exod 10:12-20). Whereas the original tradition focuses on the punishment of Israel's enemies, in Amos (7:1-3) and especially Joel (1:4-7; 2:4-7; cf. vv. 7-9) the threat of destruction is turned on God's own people who have acted unfaithfully. Although the saints are protected from the plague (9:4), John's use of tradition signifies a warning to the Christian communities as well and is thus consistent with the calls to repentance in chs. 2–3. Being "sealed" is not a status which can be taken for granted.

Sixth Trumpet (9:13-21)

A vision of horror unfolds: a *third* (8:7-9, 12; cf. the *fourth* in 6:8) of humankind is killed by a large, fixed number (200,000,000) of menacing cavalry from the Euphrates in the East (9:14, 16-19). As in 6:2 the scene would no doubt have reminded readers of the traditional threat posed to the Roman Empire by the Parthians from the East. The elaborate details (including fire, smoke, and sulfur) associated with the vast army underscore John's concern to trace death on such a grand scale to its demonic origin (Mounce 1977: 203-4). This destruction, set to occur at a predetermined moment (9:15), is restrained until four bound angels are let loose (vv. 14-15). The command to the angel with the trumpet, which proceeds from "the golden altar" (8:3), would have reminded the readers that this destruction comes in answer to the saints' prayers. The imminent military crisis is directed exclusively at heathen humanity (as in 9:1-12). The vision assumes that the crisis is temporary since its purpose is not only to punish but also to summon people to repentance (vv. 20-21).

The opportunity for repentance, which occurs again in connection with the bowls of wrath (16:9, 11), is not for John an incidental theme. The visions of destruction in Revelation represent both comfort and challenge: they demonstrate, on the one hand, the hope that evil is essentially powerless before God and, on the other hand, make clear what is at stake when the members of the Christian communities of Asia Minor are called upon to repent (2:5, 16, 22; 3:3). The deeds singled out for vilification, except for "theft," are listed again as subject to final destruction in 21:8 and 22:15, where those who practice them are excluded from the new Jerusalem. The caricature of idolatry as the worship of lifeless objects (9:20) is a well-attested tradition in the Scriptures and writings of early Judaism (e.g., Deut 4:28; Ps 115:5-7; Isa 44:9-20; Wis 13:1–15:19; Epistle of Jeremiah; Dan 5:23; *Apoc. Abr.* 6:1–7:2); the association of idolatry with the worship of demons is also widespread (Deut 32:17; *1 Enoch* 99:6-7; cf. 1 Cor 10:20). For John idolatry is a practical problem threatening the churches (2:14, 19); his narrow definition of "idolatry" (see under 2:12-17, 18-29) does not allow his readers to hear the vision with any complacency. Given the emphasis on true worship in Revelation (Bauckham 1993: 135-40), the practices described as murder, sorcery, and theft (9:21) are considered the logical outcome of a failure to worship God (Wis 14:12, 24-27; Rom 1:18-32).

Excursus on 10:1–11:14

This section breaks the sequence between the sixth and seventh trumpet blasts (cf. 7:1-8, 9-17). One theme introduced among the sequences of seals and trumpets has been the protection of Jesus' followers through a seal marked on their foreheads (7:1-4; cf. 9:4), while the destruction brought through the fifth and sixth trumpets is targeted at a vast humankind that does not believe in God (9:4-6, 10, 20-21). The position of the faithful in relation to these calamities, however, remains ambiguous. These troubling events leave Christians neither unaffected nor unchallenged. Whereas 10:1-11 once again addresses the question of "How long?" (cf. 6:9-11), 11:1-14 exemplifies through the two witnesses what it means for followers of Jesus to remain faithful while chaos drives history to its ultimate end (cf. Beasley-Murray 1978: 168). If this is correct, then the delay of concluding the second woe until 11:14 may be a formal attempt at integrating material in which John finds a logical connection.

On the other hand, chs. 10–11 bear a significance that goes beyond the immediate context of the seven trumpet blasts; they cannot, therefore, be regarded merely as a self-contained unit analogous to 7:1-17 between the sixth and seventh seals. Although 11:15-19 proclaim the consummation of the reign of God and Christ (11:15), John is aware of further series of visions of which he has not yet made use (beginning in ch. 12). The author is thus presented with a problem of literary and theological dimensions: how to situate the followers of Jesus within the mounting clash between God and the sociopolitical structures of the world without creating the impression that the coming triumph of God is going to be delayed (Müller 1995: 199-200). While chs. 12–17 provide John's literary solution, chs. 10–11, in which the later visions are anticipated (Yarbro Collins 1979: 64-66), function to assure readers that their faithfulness in the midst of conflict will be quickly and decisively rewarded. See the discussions on 10:1-11 and 11:1-14 below.

The Little Scroll and a Further Commission (10:1-11)

The vision of "another mighty angel" shows links to both the Christophany in ch. 1 when John is first commissioned (Stuckenbruck 1995a: 229-32) and the vision in ch. 5 when the Lamb is commissioned to open the sealed book (e.g., Yarbro Collins 1979: 65-66). The angel's appearance — the rainbow above his head (cf. 4:3; Ezek 1:28), his face "like the sun" (1:16), and "legs like pillars of fire" (cf. 1:16) — combines characteristics associated by John with God and Christ, thus indicating his divine origin. If the features "wrapped in a cloud" and "pillars of fire" are allusions to Exod 14:19, 24 in the context of Israel's dangerous journey through the wilderness (cf. Exod 23:20), one may infer that the angel's commissioning of John is concerned with the promise of God's presence among the Christians in analogous circumstances (cf. Harrington 1969: 147). The book held by the angel (10:2) differs in two ways from the sealed book given to the Lamb in ch. 5: it is smaller (*bibliaridion,* a "little scroll"), and it is open. John is commissioned to "eat" this scroll in vv. 8-10.

The relation between the little scroll and 10:3-7 is not clear (so esp. Bergmeier 1985: 236-38). Despite this difficulty, it is possible to infer a logical connection. In vv. 3-7 the angel's roaring shout (cf. Amos 3:8) yields the clapping of "the seven thunders." John's wish to write (10:4) what he has heard presupposes that he has received an auditory revelation. Unlike the Lamb's task to open the sealed book (5:2, 7, 9), the open little scroll (10:4, 8-10), and the enjoinder on John to make what he has written available (22:10), this revelation is to be sealed up, that is, kept secret (cf. Dan 12:4-13). One reason for this prohibition is to reinforce the imminence of the seventh trumpet blast in which the "mystery of God will be fulfilled" (cf. 11:15-19, which in 10:7 is not identified as a "woe"), a conviction which responds again to the dead saints' complaint of "How long?" (6:9-11). Another reason for sealing the revelation may be to illustrate that the visions recorded in Revelation are an incomplete, though sufficient, record of God's message to the Christian congregations. In this case, keeping the seven thunders' revelation secret would be a rhetorical device: the addition of numerous visions (e.g., 12:1–22:5) which represent but *part* of what has been revealed to John (hence a *little scroll*) neither detracts from the imminence of God's ultimate purpose nor reduces its urgency for his readers. The legitimation of the visions following ch. 11 (i.e., 12:1–15:4) is strengthened by the commission to prophesy *again* in 10:11 (cf. vv. 8-11).

The form and content of 10:8-11 are modeled on the call of the prophet in Ezek 2:8–3:4. But whereas the scroll of woes in Ezekiel has only a sweet taste, the little scroll eaten by John has a simultaneously bitter-sweet effect: it is bitter because John is given a message about suffering, and it is sweet because the message promises victory for God's people. The protection of Jesus' followers from the events unleashed by the fifth and sixth trumpet blasts (9:1-21) should not give the impression that for them eschatological crises will be devoid of suffering; if anything, the opposite is true. Just as "conquering" in Revelation acquires a new meaning (e.g., 2:7; 5:6; 12:11), so also John redefines just what protection for the faithful means (11:5-12; 14:1-5). In 10:11 the commission of John is to "prophesy again about many peoples and nations and languages and kings." Since this task is not carried through in 11:1-14, it is likely that the *little scroll* includes the visions beginning in ch. 12 in which the "bitter" and "sweet" are likewise juxtaposed to form a series of stark contrasts (cf. Bousset 1906: 312; Yarbro Collins 1976: 26-27; 1979: 65-66).

Two Witnesses and Conclusion of the Second "Woe" (11:1-14)

Measuring the Temple (11:1-2). For the first time in Revelation, John becomes an active participant in a vision: he is given a reed to measure the temple, the altar, and those who worship there. The notion of measuring the holy city is already known through Ezekiel 40 and Zech 2:5-9; in both passages the measurements taken by an angel represent an ideal plan according to which Jerusalem, now in ruins, is to be restored (cf. 21:15-17; *New Jerusalem* document from Qumran caves 1-2, 4-5, and 11). John introduces a division between the inner temple precincts, where the altar and true worshipers are (6:9-11; 8:3-5; cf. 3:12 and *1 Enoch* 61:1-5), and the outer court, which is to be "thrown out" and given to the Gentiles (cf. Dan 8:13; 9:24; Zech 12:3; Luke 21:24). Some interpreters regard this passage as an unfulfilled prophecy taken from a literary source composed against Rome by zealots in Jerusalem during the end stages of the first Jewish war (AD 69-70); the zealots, who controlled the temple, believed that God would not allow the most holy place to be destroyed (e.g., Bousset 1906: 315-30; Charles 1920: 1:273-74). Others find therein a reference to a separation of true from false Jews, finding an allusion to the destruction of the temple by Rome in AD 70 (e.g., Rissi 1965: 77; Harrington 1969: 151-52). The language, however, is highly symbolic; analogous to the sealing in 7:1-8 and 9:4, the scene emphasizes the protection promised to loyal Christians, the new "temple" (3:12; cf. 7:15; 1 Cor 3:16-17; 2 Cor 6:16; Eph 2:19-22; 1 Pet 2:5), in the midst of the eschatological crisis (Kiddle 1940: 176-80; Prigent 1988: 160-61). In this case, the outer court would represent those claiming to follow Jesus, but whom John regards as unfaithful and subject to the vicissitudes of the Gentiles on God's people. The period of forty-two months is taken from Dan 7:25 and 12:7, where it denotes the limited time during which the righteous are allowed to suffer under an oppressive political regime (cf. 13:5). This raises a problem concerning the nature of protection promised to the faithful.

Two Witnesses (11:3-13). The issue of protection is addressed through a vision of "two witnesses." They are allowed to prophesy 1,260 days, the same duration as that of the crisis mentioned in v. 2 (cf. 12:6). The identity and purpose of the two figures are much debated. Given the graphic portrait of their activities (11:5-6), death (vv. 7-10), and resuscitation (vv. 11-12), it is frequently assumed that for John the vision refers to specific personages, whether, for example, to renowned apostles such as Peter and Paul from the recent past (Court 1994: 40-41) or to Moses and Elijah expected in the future as forerunners of Christ's return (Moses — Deut 18:15, 18; Elijah — Mal 3:23-24; Sir 48:10; John 1:21; cf. Mark 9:4 and par.; e.g., Bousset 1906: 318-19; Lohse 1993: 65). The witnesses' activities do recall traditions associated with miracles performed by Moses (Exod 7:14-19) and Elijah (1 Kgs 17–18; 2 Kgs 1:9-12; Sir 48:3; Luke 4:25; Jas 5:17). However, the witnesses have a symbolic character, as suggested by the author's borrowing in 11:4 from Zech 4:1-14 in which two anointed figures, Davidic and priestly, are identified as "olive tree branches" and "golden pipes." John's change of "golden pipes" to "two lampstands" draws on the symbolism he has applied to the seven churches in 1:20. This lends weight to the interpretation that the two witnesses' activities represent the faithful testimony to be given by loyal Christians just before the end (esp. Kiddle 1940: 181-83; Prigent 1988: 165-66).

The vulnerability of the "outer court" to the Gentiles (11:2) does not mean that those within the temple are altogether protected from harm. The witnesses' empowerment to testify does not prevent them from suffering death at the hands of "the beast" and the humiliating consequences thereof (vv. 7-10). Significantly, the account of their death is not taken from traditions associated with Moses and Elijah. Rather, they are a reflex of Christology: as in the case of Jesus (v. 8), faithful testimony in the world is bound up with death. A conventional notion of protection is thus redefined by John: being in "the temple" (v. 1) means that nothing will be able to destroy the relationship with God enjoyed by true Christians who are empowered for witness (Kiddle 1940: 180; cf. Yarbro Collins 1979: 70-71). The "outer court," trampled by the Gentiles, represents those whose adherence to Jesus will not stand the test of persecution. The beast, on the one hand, and the protection of the faithful, on the other, are motifs which anticipate the visions in the second half of Revelation (chs. 12–17).

The "temple" (11:1) and the phrase "where their Lord died" (v. 8) suggest that the events of the vision are located in Jerusalem. If, however, the two witnesses represent John's ideal of following Jesus, then the testimony of the faithful cannot be geographically limited. The allusions to Jerusalem ultimately symbolize the double character of life in the world for the Christian: power to witness, subjection to death. As "the great city," where Christ fulfilled his testimony and was crucified, Jerusalem is branded a spiritual "Sodom" and "Egypt" (cf. Trites 1977: 169-71). For John the city's character and fate are ultimately determined by its absorption into the world of Rome (16:19; Bauckham 1993: 207-8). Hence the necessity for establishing a "new Jerusalem" (21:1, 9–22:5).

The vindication of the witnesses (11:11-12) is reminiscent of the resurrection-ascension of Christ known from the Gospel tradition, except that their ascension occurs in public view before those hostile to them. This event is marked by a great earthquake which brings partial destruction and incites terror among survivors (8:5; 16:18-21; cf. 11:19). That they "gave glory to the God of heaven" (11:13) may indicate that the enemies of Christian witness are, in the end, expected to repent and be converted (esp. Bauckham 1993: 238-337; see, however, Müller 1995: 215-17). While the text says nothing about "repentance," in Revelation "fearing" or "glorifying God" can represent the virtual equivalent (16:9; cf. 11:18; 14:7; 15:4; 19:5). Given John's stringent view about what constitutes faithfulness to God, such universalism would seem surprising (cf. *1 Enoch* 62:1-13). The proclamation of the gospel to all peoples is an important secondary theme in Revelation, though it does not serve as the immediate theological point of departure for John's writing. It represents the hope in the public manifestation of God's salvation and in its recognition among all the peoples of the world (cf. 5:13; 14:6-7; 15:4). Beyond this, John does not find it necessary to specify whether this will involve conversion.

The Second Woe Concluded (11:14). One might have expected this verse at the end of ch. 9. Its location here reflects a skillful attempt to integrate 10:1-11 and 11:1-13 into the sequence of the trumpet blasts and, indeed, into the book as a whole. Each successive woe takes on an expanded form. Whereas the first consists only of one vision (9:1-12), the second woe — in the present form of the book — brings together three visions (9:13-21; 10:1-11; 11:1-13). These visions, in turn, help set the stage for themes raised in 11:15-19 (vindication, 10:3-7; 11:11-12) and the rest of book (repentance, 9:20-21; faithfulness, 11:3-6; suffering in conflict, 11:7-10), especially as developed in chs. 12–17.

Seventh Trumpet (11:15-19)

The announcement of God's manifest rule is the logical consequence of what John's hearers would have expected from the seventh trumpet blast (10:7). The designation for God as "the one who is and who was" no longer includes anything about his being "the coming one" (1:4, 8; 4:8); nothing remains to be fulfilled in time (Holtz 1980: 258). As a final celebration, the passage forms the climax of other, more proleptic scenes of worship in 4:8-11, 5:9-13, and 7:10-12. As the last of the trumpet blasts, the passage concludes the first half of Revelation. However, though the hymn of victory (11:17-18) proclaims divine judgment upon the nations and reward for all the righteous, the seventh trumpet does not sufficiently account for the third woe (see under 11:14).

Two proclamations of salvation are heard in heaven, one anonymous (11:15) and the other given by the twenty-four elders (vv. 17-18). As elsewhere in Revelation, these songs are not so much taken from the liturgy of early Christian worship as they are composed by the author at strategic points in the narrative (Jörns 1971). The hymnic proclamations are linked through their exegesis of Psalm 2. The wrath of God responds in a judgment of destruction against the raging nations (11:18; Ps 2:2, 5, 12) because of their vain plots against God and his Anointed One ("Messiah"). The consequence of judgment is the transformation of "the kingdom of this world" into "the kingdom of our Lord and of his Messiah" (11:15; cf. Ps 2:2; de Jonge 1980: 272).

The scene closes with the opening of the heavenly temple, where the ark of the covenant is made visible (11:19). Since the destruction of the first temple by Nebuchadnezzar in 587 BC (1 Kgs 25:8-10), the tradition had developed that the ark was actually hidden until it would be revealed when God regathers his people (2 Macc 2:7-8; *2 Bar.* 6:7-9). The temple and ark, which signify God's presence among the faithful, were measured with the true worshipers in 11:1. Along with the celebration of reward for the people of God, the unveiling of the temple and ark provides auditory and visionary fulfillment of the promise of protection (see under 11:1-2, 3-13).

At the same time the disclosure of the temple is punctuated by natural phenomena; in Revelation these sometimes occur at the conclusion of other sections concerned with God's judgment (cf. 8:5; 16:18). The allusion to events of the theophany at Mt. Sinai, which are accompanied by the blowing of a trumpet (Exod 19:13, 16, 18-19; 20:18), suits particularly well the end of the sequence of seven trumpets (Bauckham 1993: 203). In 15:6 the opening of the temple unleashes the last sevenfold cycle of divine punishment against evil.

Conflict between Jesus' Followers and the Powers of Evil (12:1–15:4)

The victory and eternal presence of God have been celebrated as virtual reality with the seventh trumpet blast (11:15-19). The following section, which bridges the narrative until the seven bowls of wrath are poured out (15:5–16:21), consists of a series of unnumbered visions which, in terms of structure and content, form the center of Revelation. Whereas the seven trumpets seem to be concluded at the end of ch. 11, the third eschatological woe announced in 11:14 and already anticipated in 11:7 has yet to be elaborated (see above; cf. 12:12). More so than in the seven seals and seven trumpets sequences (6:1–8:5; 8:6–11:19), the seer paints in 12:1–15:4 an uncompromising portrait of Rome as a Satanic power which threatens the very existence of loyal Christians. In ch. 12 the background to this conflict is described in mythological dimensions, while ch. 13 claims that the myth of the dragon finds concrete expression in two beasts which represent Roman rule. The beasts' oppressive activities are incompatible with Christian faith, and death is the logical outcome of resistance. At the same time, the author is convinced that the diabolical might behind Rome is already a defeated power. Its end, proclaimed in the heavenly liturgy in 12:10-12, is reinforced by the visions of judgment in 14:6-20. By contrast, in 14:1-5 John sees the final salvation of the protected followers of the Lamb on Mt. Zion, who are able to join the heavenly liturgy (cf. 15:2-4). This assurance, together with the knowledge of Satan's prior defeat, provides the basis for the intermittent challenges and exhortations for hearers to accept the consequences of being faithful (10:11; 13:9-10; 14:12). The congregations in Asia Minor thus find their local situations addressed in terms of a sharp conflict which John believes will run its course throughout the cosmos.

Defeat of Satan in Heaven and Persecution on Earth (12:1-17)

In ch. 12 John has taken up and adapted traditions perhaps familiar to some of his readers. The tensions which for him characterize Christian existence in the world derive ultimately from a clash of cosmic powers. The outcome of this conflict results in the defeat of evil which, personified as a mythical "dragon," is banished to the earth where it continues to wreak havoc on the created order by persecuting the people of God.

In one version of this story (12:7-9), the celestial battle is fought between Michael with his angels and Satan assisted by his own contingent of rebellious angels. In its present form the story is based on two myths which had been circulating among Jewish apocalyptic groups during the Second Temple period: (1) the tradition which traced the snake's deception of humanity in Eden to a prior failure to seize power in heaven (*Adam and Eve* 12–16; *2 Enoch* 31:1-6; cf. Isa 14:12-15; Luke 10:18) and (2) the variegated tradition according to which angelic forces responsible for the persistence of evil in the world are defeated by God's angels (*1 Enoch* 10:1-16; 87:1–88:3; 4Q531 17). In both instances, a primordial victory against wicked angels, sometimes expanded to include the story of the great flood, was incomplete and became a way of coming to terms with the presence of evil despite a belief in God's rule (*1 Enoch* 15–16; *Jub.* 10:1-14; cf. 1QS 3:15–4:1). Such traditions stressed — as in Revelation 12 — that the evil experienced by God's people is a defeated power whose complete annihilation is assured.

Another version of the story, adapted by John in fragmentary form (12:3-5, 13-17), goes back to an ancient "combat myth," already presupposed by some of the Jewish scriptures (Job 26:13; Ps 74:13-14; Isa 27:1; 51:9-10). According to the myth, the legitimate heir to heavenly power is threatened by a beast (on various accounts from the ancient Near East and late antiquity, cf. esp. Yarbro Collins 1976; further, Beasley-Murray 1978: 391-97). In one form of the legend the dragon Python attempts to kill the goddess Leto, who is pregnant by Zeus. Assisted by the north wind and the sea deity Poseidon (another version: the earth; cf. 12:16), she escapes from the dragon's destructive waters to safety on an island, where she gives birth to Apollo. Her child eventually returns to slay the dragon. Interpreters are agreed that, for John, the child snatched up to the throne of God (v. 5) and destined to be a shepherd over "all the nations with an iron rod" (Ps 2:9; cf. *Pss. Sol.* 18:23-24), is the exalted Christ. Given the attempts of Roman emperors to portray themselves in relation to a "golden age" of Apollo's kingship, the story of Jesus' birth could have been understood by early readers of Revelation as a challenge to their rule (Yarbro Collins 1979: 86). While the dragon in ch. 12 is the embodiment of Satan, its features connect it to Roman imperial authority (cf. 13:1 and 12:3 — seven heads, ten horns, and ten diadems).

Whatever the woman in heaven originally represented in the tradition behind 12:1 (see, e.g., Prigent 1988: 177-81; Müller 1995: 229-31), in vv. 5-6 and 14-17 she has become a symbol for God's faithful people: though they shall face the threat of being killed, they "keep the commandments of God and hold the testimony of Jesus" (cf. v. 11 and 1:9; 6:9; 19:10). Thus the woman's protection from the dragon (12:6, 14-16) does not stand in tension with the persecution of her offspring (v. 17; as, e.g., Charles 1920: 1:332), as John has not excluded suffering from his understanding of safety in the story of the two witnesses in 11:1-13.

The foreboding myth of combat, protection, and persecution is interrupted by a loud heavenly proclamation (12:10-12). The hymn of triumph, whose opening is reminiscent of 11:15, provides a clear indication of how John has interpreted his traditions (Jörns 1971: 118-20). The mythical dragon, "the accuser of our brothers" (12:10), is held responsible for the unrelenting present and future troubles faced by the community. John is so sure that, as in the case of Jesus, death will result from the conflict that it is announced as an accomplished fact (v. 11). Hand in hand with the advent of God's rule is the devil's fall to the earth (v. 10). Thus the dawning reign of God through the Christ-event (v. 5 — birth and ascension; v. 11 — death) is considered fully compatible with the deaths of the faithful whose torment is only temporary (v. 12; cf. v. 6).

The First Beast and an Exhortation to Endure (12:18–13:10)

In order to wage war against the faithful (12:17), the dragon takes its stand on the seashore. With the rise of a beast from the sea (13:1; cf. Dan 7:3), the dragon's battle plan takes effect (13:2b). The features and activities of the beast are inherited from the dragon; they are heavily indebted to visions in Daniel 7–8. With ten diadems on its ten horns (13:1; cf. Dan 7:7, 20, 24), the beast resembles the dragon (12:1) and, like the latter, is permitted to fight against and conquer the saints (13:7; cf. 11:7; Dan 7:21; 8:10-12); on the "seven heads" see under 17:7-18. The beast is a hybrid of animals (panther, bear, lion) which correspond to *different* beasts of Daniel's vision (13:2a; Dan 7:4-7). His blasphemies against God and those dwelling in heaven (13:5-6; cf. v. 1; 12:12; Dan 8:10, 12) recall the arrogant utterances ascribed to Daniel's fourth beast (i.e., Antiochus Epiphanes — Dan 7:8, 11, 20). Like Satan, whose time is short (12:12), the beast is given only temporary authority. The forty-two months (13:5), the time of persecution allowed in Dan 7:25 and 12:7, coincide with the period allotted for the protection (11:2; cf. 12:6) and empowered witness of the faithful (11:3; see under 11:1-14). The collapsing of Daniel's four-kingdom scheme into one figure creates the impression of a superbeast (i.e., Rome) which, in effect, becomes the quintessential embodiment of Satan, who, however, is already a defeated power (12:7-10). Contemporary Jewish thought likewise related the Roman Empire to the fourth beast in Daniel 7 to underscore the belief that it will succumb to divine judgment (4 Ezra 11–12).

At the same time John's caricature of the beast is a parody on Jesus. The beast, like Jesus, has horns and diadems (13:1; 5:6; 19:12), can be represented as a lion (13:2; 5:5), is delegated power (13:2; 5:12), is worshiped alongside the dragon (13:4; e.g., 5:13), and is given authority over every tribe, people, language, and nation (13:7; cf. 5:9; Dan 7:14). Most significant is that one of the beast's heads appears "as mortally slaughtered" (13:3 — *hōs esphagmenēn eis thanaton;* NRSV, "death-blow"); this is in imitation of Jesus, who in 5:6 is introduced as the Lamb standing "as slaughtered" *(hōs esphagmenon).*

The parody of Christ is not carried through consistently; the author draws on contemporary Jewish expectation that the Emperor Nero would return as an ally of Beliar to lead the faithful astray by raising the dead and performing miracles before being judged by God (esp. *Sib. Or.* 3:63-74; see *Asc. Isa.* 4:2-13), a myth which he expects to be fulfilled through imperial Roman rule (17:8; on the Nero myth: Müller 1995: 297-300; Bauckham 1993: 414-45). The wound, caused by a sword (13:14; cf. Suetonius *Nero* 49), is healed and results in a worship of the beast which parodies the true worship of God (Exod 15:11; Ps 35:10; Isa 40:25; see Jörns 1971: 121-23). For John this language helps explain why the Roman Empire, despite being Satan's prime ally, could nevertheless seem to flourish in his day. He attempts to make clear that the glory of Rome, however attractive (cf. 18:3-19), is nothing but a perversion of the truth. Those who worship the beast, the "inhabitants of the earth" (13:4, 8; cf. 8:13; 11:10), show that their names have not been destined to be recorded in "the book of life" (17:8; cf. 3:5-6).

For John reality has its starting point in the Lamb, here "slaughtered from the foundation of the world" (against the NRSV main text; Müller 1995: 250; but cf. 17:8). This view, if paradigmatic for discipleship, has serious consequences for Jesus' followers. In 13:9-10 the hearers are exhorted, not to resist the violence of the beast with violence, but to embrace suffering as it comes (following Codex Alexandrinus against Sinaiticus). In using the formula "Let anyone who has an ear listen," which occurs in each of the seven messages (see esp. 2:11), John signals the importance of nonviolent resistance to the Christian congregations.

The Second Beast (13:11-18)

A second beast emerges from the earth with "two horns like a lamb" but speaking "like a dragon." If this alludes to the two-horned ram in Dan 8:3 (Gk. *krios*), then the word "lamb" *(arnion)* is used as a deliberate parody of Christology. John expects his hearers to engage with the vision in order to discern the difference. The second beast's activities on behalf of the first are marked by deception (13:14; thus a "false prophet" in 16:13; 19:20; 20:10). His "great signs" — the calling down of fire from heaven to earth (cf. the Elijah story in 1 Kgs 18:38) and the construction of a talking statue of the first beast — are wrong, not because the author thinks they could not have happened but because their function is categorically opposed to the worship of God (Deut 13:1-3; Mark 13:22; 2 Thess 2:9; cf. Nero traditions in *Sib. Or.* 3:64-65; *Asc. Isa.* 4:5-10). It is not necessary to suppose that members of the Asia Minor congregations were being forced to participate directly in the imperial cult (Bauckham 1993: 447; against, e.g., Jones 1980: 1032-35; Sordi 1986: 42-45); the seven messages, which otherwise include so many allusions to particular circumstances, would have left more hints of such a crisis. The activity of the second beast and the killing of Christians who refuse to worship the image reflect what John thinks will happen; this is based on his probable knowledge of the Neronian persecution (cf. Tacitus *Ann.* 15.44), on the undeniable local popularity of an emperor cult (no worse under Domitian than under his predecessors; cf. Thompson 1986: 155-59), and on his conviction that the slaughtered Lamb and the powers responsible for his death are on a collision course. Thus the setting up of a statue for all to worship on the peril of death could have been taken from biblical tradition (Daniel 3) and have been combined with circulating traditions about animated statues of deities (e.g., *Ps.-Clem. Rec.* 3:47; see further Charles 1920: 1:361) to project a picture onto the imminent future.

The parody of Christ is carried over to his followers (13:16). Worshipers of the beast's image (cf. 6:15; 19:18) are given a mark "on the right hand or [20:4: and] the forehead," a counterpart to the Lamb's adherents, who are sealed on the forehead (7:1-4; Ezek 9:4). In the text, the mark (*charagma* — 13:16; 14:9, 11; 16:2; 19:20; 20:4) illustrates the unambiguous identity of the beast's worshipers, just as the seal (*sphragis* — 7:2; 9:4) distinguishes the faithful Christians. The *charagma* is symbolic of full participation in economic life, from which those with the seal are completely shut out. The mark may refer to the use of coinage imprinted with a portrait of the emperor (see Kraybill 1996: 135-41). Christians refusing to compromise are, however, assured protection from divine judgment (9:4), while those with the beast's mark will be overwhelmed by plagues (16:2) and tormented forever (14:9-11). Though the text does not link this mark directly with the death of Christians mentioned in 13:15 (Mounce 1977: 263), this does not mean that John saw no correlation. His hard line in the messages to the churches against economic participation (e.g., Nicolaitans in 2:6, 14-15; Jezebel in 2:20-23; contrast Laodiceans, 3:17-18, with Christians from Smyrna, 2:9) presupposes a worldview that does not distinguish between economic, religious, and political spheres. There is no wealth without religious compromise; conversely, there will be no Christian poverty without conflict with the beast. No less so than before, "to conquer through the blood of the Lamb" (12:11) for John's churches includes a preparedness to undergo economic ruin which, in turn, logically spirals into a situation of death. 13:17 thus builds on the premise of the slaughtered Lamb and offers a graphic portrait of the social consequences of unswerving loyalty to Christ in a world marked by conflict.

The mark is either "the name of the beast *(thērion)* or the number of his name" (13:18). These two possibilities are merged in the phrase "the number of the beast," which, in turn, is identified as the "number of a person." The number is "666." Interpreters, with few exceptions, are agreed that the number is decipherable in relation to Nero, whose myth has been adapted into John's description of the beasts (vv. 3-4, 13-15; on various solutions see Bauckham 1993: 384-407). If the person is Nero, then "666" is equal to the sum of the letters of "Nero Caesar" when spelled in Hebrew (Murabba'at text 18 in Beyer 1984: *nrwn qsr;* where n = 50, r = 200, w = 6, q = 100, s = 60); the same number is derived from the addition of the Hebrew letters transcribing the Greek word for "beast" (t = 400, r = 200, y = 10, w = 6, n = 50). The Neronic background to the number does not exclude a date of the tradition toward the end of the first century; "Nero" is a symbol for Roman rule generally, the emperor who most clearly embodied Rome's innate opposition to God's people. The procedure of deriving names from numbers, called *gematria,* was popular in antiquity (see esp. Dornseiff 1925: 91-112); for John, it is important that the discerning among his hearers be able to identify the figure and to reject what it represents (cf. 15:2).

The Lamb and His Followers on Mount Zion (14:1-5)

The full alignment between the Lamb and the 144,000 is visually portrayed on Mt. Zion (cf. the Christian passages *5 Ezra* 2:42; *6 Ezra* 13:35, 39). The 144,000, picked up from 7:1-8, are the number of martyrs required as a precondition for divine retribution to take full effect against the wicked (cf. 6:9-11). The present passage is therefore a vision of eschatological reality. At the same time the vision offers an imaginative glimpse into the present relationship of loyal Christians to God. The faithful *will* not, and therefore *do* not, stand alone in a world which operates according to another paradigm. In this light, it is not surprising that the vision takes its immediate shape from the preceding (13:11-18) and following visions (14:6–15:4). In particular, the scene provides a stark contrast to the foregoing picture of a world under Satan's control and without room for faithful Christians (Schüssler Fiorenza 1985: 188-91). Instead of bearing the mark of the beast's name (13:17), the Lamb's followers are inscribed on the forehead with the Lamb's name and the name of God (cf. 3:12; 22:4). The identifying marks are mutually exclusive. Whereas only those with the beast's mark may "buy or sell" (13:17), only the 144,000 who have been "bought from the earth" (14:3-4) have the privilege of learning a "new song" (v. 3; see under 15:1-4). The worship of the beast (13:12, 15; cf. 13:4) is offset by the induction of the faithful into the worship of heaven (14:3). While the adherents of the beast are swallowed up by a system of blasphemy and deception (13:5-6, 14; 16:11, 21; cf. 3:9; 21:7; 22:15), there is "no lie found in their mouth" (14:5; on the use of Zeph 3:13 and Isa 53:9 cf. Fekkes 1994: 191-92). The location of the 144,000 on Mt. Zion reinforces the security promised to God's covenant people (e.g., Pss 48; 78:54, 68-72; Isa 28:16; Amos 3:5; Mic 4:6-7). This passage would have left no doubt that for John people are ultimately divided into two camps: followers of the Lamb and everyone else who, by definition, participates in the Satanic system of the beast.

The character of the 144,000 is set forth in 14:4-5. Much debated is whether the description of them as male "virgins," undefiled by women, refers to the actual practice of celibacy (Bousset 1906: 379-80; Charles 1920: 2:8-9: this is added by a "monkish interpolator"), represents sexual abstinence as the ideal (Yarbro Collins 1984: 129-31; Müller 1995: 262-63), or functions as a metaphor for purity and fidelity (e.g., Schüssler Fiorenza 1985: 190-91; Prigent 1988: 220-21). A literal interpretation seems hard to maintain because it does not seriously consider the symbolic character of John's language. Though an idealization of sexual abstinence cannot be fully ruled out — see precedent for this in early Jewish and Christian sources (e.g., Philo *Hypothetica* 14 and Josephus *J.W.* 2.120-21 on the Essenes; Matt 19:12; 1 Cor 7:25-34) — there is no further indication in Revelation of its importance. At the very least, the notion of virginity is to be understood symbolically. The verb "defile" *(molynō)* also occurs as a metaphor for religious impurity in 3:5, and the reference to "women" may be a general allusion to "Jezebel" in 2:20-23, who John thought was leading Christians down the path of idolatry. The male-centered language may be explained by the fact that John presupposes a scriptural background of purity regulations designed for men who participate in holy war (e.g., Deut 20:1-9; 23:9-14; cf. further under 7:1-8).

The image of "first fruits" signals that the 144,000 are a select group that belong to God (Lev 23:9-14; cf. Exod 22:28-29; Deut 15:19-23) and should be interpreted with the phrase "redeemed [lit. "bought"] from humankind" (Müller 1995: 264; cf. 5:9). Less clear is whether "first fruits" has sacrificial overtones, referring to "untimely and violent death" (Yarbro Collins 1984: 128; Bauckham 1993: 291-92). The alliance between Christ and the faithful is expressed by the phrase "who follow the Lamb wherever he goes"; this combines the motif of discipleship known in the Gospels (Luke 9:57-62; John 10:4) with the image in Ezekiel's vision of the wheels' movements fully coordinated with the shifting position of the living creatures (Ezek 1:12, 15-21).

Three Angels Announce the Judgment (14:6-13)

The contrast between the beast's worshipers and followers of the Lamb is set forth within the context of divine judgment proclaimed by three angels. Each of their messages follows a logical progression. As a group the proclamations anticipate eschatological events that are described in chs. 18 and 19 (Müller 1995: 266). The messages of doom are announced from "mid-heaven," from where the eagle heralds the three woes in 8:13. This place corresponds to the lower regions of heaven, which some contemporary traditions believed were the location of evil powers such as Satan or the wicked angels (e.g., *2 Enoch* 7:1-5: second heaven; *Asc. Isa.* 7:9-12: firmament). The angels' unrestricted movement here may suggest that this is space vacated by Satan after his fall to earth (12:3, 9; cf. Bauckham 1993: 286).

Each heavenly messenger is called "another angel." The expression does not relate to the immediate context since the last such angel is the one who blew the seventh trumpet (11:15). It is possible, therefore, that in 14:6-11, 14-

20 John has adopted a tradition shaped originally by another context (e.g., Roloff 1984: 21-22).

The first angel bears "an eternal gospel" and announces "the hour of the day of judgment" while calling upon all nations of the world to worship God the Creator (14:6-7; cf. Ps 96:2, 7-9, 13). This summons says nothing about Christ; the term "gospel" and its verbal equivalent "to evangelize" derive more immediately from a Hebrew background (*basser;* e.g., LXX Ps 95:2; Isa 52:7; 61:1). Taken together with the theme of divine judgment, the emphasis on God as creator of "heaven and earth and sea and water sources" presupposes that revelation through nature is a sufficient basis for holding people responsible (cf. Rom 1:19-20), for even this can lead to the recognition of God's glory (Wis 13:1-9; Sir 17:8-9; see under 11:1-14).

The second angel heralds the fall of "Babylon the Great" as if it is an accomplished fact (14:8; cf. Isa 21:9). The vivid images anticipate the pronouncements against Rome in 17:2, 4 and 18:3. The use of "Babylon" as a derogatory designation for the Roman Empire is known from contemporary Jewish literature (Kraybill 1996: 142-47; e.g., *2 Bar.* 11:1; 67:7; *Sib. Or.* 5:159); the pronouncement of doom echoes the prophecy of Isaiah (21:9), who expects Babylon's destruction because of her devotion to idolatry (cf. Jer 51:8). "Fornication" *(porneia)* is introduced as a metaphor to characterize Rome's influence on the nations as defilement (contrast with 14:4); significantly, the "fornication" of Jezebel is linked with John's warning against idolatry at Thyatira (2:20-21; cf. 4 Ezra 15:48). This condemnation is supplemented by an extended metaphor "wine of wrath . . . who has made drunk all the nations," taken from Jer 51:7. The "wrath" is that of Rome (cf. 12:12; 18:3), and it is subject to the "wrath of God" (14:10; see 6:12-17; 11:18; 16:19).

The first two messages are followed by a warning of torment for worshipers of the beast (14:9-11; cf. 13:15-16). The third angel's words reveal the eschatological consequences for those who have come under the sway of Rome (cf. 14:8): they shall drink "the wine of God's anger" in undiluted form (Jer 25:15). The "fire and sulfur" correspond to the divine punishment of Sodom and Gomorrah (Gen 19:24; cf. Rev 19:20; 20:10, 14-15). Whereas the punishments envisioned in the series of seals and trumpets are temporary, God's final judgment is irreversible (14:11). The eternal "smoke of their torment" (cf. Isa 34:9-10) is a parody of the saints' prayers in 8:3-4, and by contrast provides no relief (cf. 18:8, 19; 19:3). "They have no rest day and night," referring to the beast's worshipers, is an ironic reversal of the same formula which describes the unceasing worship of God in 4:8.

A direct appeal to the faithful interrupts the vision (14:12-13). In view of the expected crisis, John exhorts his hearers to patience. At the same time the vivid imagery of judgment (vv. 11-12) may be a visual answer to the martyred saints' request that vengeance against the wicked no longer be delayed (6:10). The blessing on "those who die in the Lord from now on" reflects John's belief that death through persecution will occur on a wide scale in the near future. The "death" achieved will be rewarded by relief, the very antithesis of the punishment described in 14:11. Thus Christian conflict with the world is not ultimately bad; for John it presents an opportunity for a radical obedience which, in turn, prepares for the manifestation of God's justice.

Three Angels and the Final Judgment (14:14-20)

The sequence of angelic visions is resumed after the exhortation and blessing for John's hearers. Whereas the previous vision announces judgment (14:11-12), this one describes the execution of divine justice on the nations as commanded through the angels. The passage divides into two parts centered around the metaphors of (grain) harvest (vv. 14-16), on the one hand, and a grape harvest followed by a treading of the wine press (vv. 17-20), on the other. The author has created these short narratives on the basis of the parallel images for judgment in Joel 4:13: "Put in the sickle, for the harvest is ripe. Go in, tread, for the wine press is full. The vats overflow, for their wickedness is great." In addition, the references to "wrath" (14:19) and "blood" (v. 20) are probably influenced by Isa 63:2-3; one may compare "as high as the horse's bridle" (14:20) to *1 Enoch* 100:3 in which the extent of the final judgment is illustrated by a horse walking "through the blood of sinners up to his chest." The location of this bloodbath "outside the city" assumes the tradition from Joel 4:2, 12 (and used in *1 Enoch* 53:1), which locates the final judgment against the Gentiles in the Valley of Jehoshaphat near Jerusalem.

Whereas most scholars agree that the vision of the wine press is concerned with the punishment of the wicked, there is no unanimity about what the grain harvest signifies. Three main interpretations have been offered: it is (1) a harvest of both the righteous and the wicked (cf. Sweet 1979: 232; see Matt 13:36-43); (2) a harvest of only the righteous (Bauckham 1993: 290-96); or (3) a harvest of the wicked alone (e.g., Beasley-Murray 1978: 228; Müller 1995: 270-71; cf. 4 Ezra 4:28-32). The third option, which stresses the parallel structure of 14:14-16 with 14:17-20, is viable insofar as John has retained the original sense of the Joel passage. If the righteous are in view, then the harvest may offer the apocalyptic narrative for the image of the faithful as the "first fruits" (v. 4).

The humanlike figure "sitting on a cloud" (14:14) is not specifically identified (see esp. Stuckenbruck 1995a: 240-45; Carrell 1997: 175-95). The appearance of "another angel" in the next verse may suggest that he is an angel since contemporary Jewish traditions often represent mediating angels as human in appearance (e.g., *1 Enoch* 90:14, 17; *Jos. Asen.* 14:7-10; cf. Ezekiel 8–9). The figure alludes to the "son of man" of Dan 7:13 in the same way as the Christophany in 1:13. It is possible, therefore, that John's hearers would have thought of the coming of Christ for judgment (cf. 1:7; Matt 13:41-43; 16:27; 24:30-31; 25:31; Mark 13:26-27; 14:62 par.). Indeed, whereas the actor in 14:20a is not identified, in 19:13, 15 it is Christ himself who tramples the wine press. If v. 14 refers to Christ, then his function is comparable to that of the angels (see under 1:1-2, 12-20; 4:1-11); indeed, like the elders in 4:4, he wears "a golden crown," and like the angel of 14:17 he holds a sickle. Nevertheless, the humanlike figure's superiority to the angels may be suggested by his seated position, flanked in the narrative by three angels on either side (see Holtz 1971: 128-34).

To stress the divine authority behind the scenes of punishment, John has two of the angels come out from the heavenly temple (14:15, 17). The emergence "from the altar" by the angel with power over fire (v. 18) picks up images associated with the saints' prayers in 6:9 and 8:3-5 (Mounce 1977: 281). This underscores further that divine retribution against the wicked is envisioned as an answer to the petitions of the faithful (as in 14:11).

Anticipation of the Seven Plagues and the Conquerors' Song (15:1-4)

These verses both provide a climax for chs. 12–14 (15:2-4) and prepare (15:1) for the seven bowls of God's wrath in 15:5–16:21 (v. 1). The pattern of introducing a new section without immediately proceeding to it is also found, for example, in 8:1-5, where the blowing of the seven trumpets is postponed by a vision of the saints' prayers. Here the seven bowls of wrath are delayed by a future vision of the saints as they sing a chant declaring the justice of God's salvation. This song of triumph presupposes that the petitions of the faithful in 6:9-11 and 8:3-5 have been answered by manifestations of divine judgment over those aligned with the worship of the beast (15:2; cf. 14:9-11; 19:3).

The chant occurs at "a glass sea mixed with fire" (15:2). This setting recalls the "sea of glass, like crystal" of John's throne vision (4:6) and suggests that the liturgy takes place in the presence of God. The image of "fire" associates this body of water with judgment (cf. 14:10, 18). The chant is called both "the song of Moses, the servant of God" and "the song of the Lamb" (15:3). Though vv. 3b-4 refer to neither Moses nor the Lamb, the heavenly song is appropriate to both designations. Singing with "harps of God" in their hands, the saints are none other than the 144,000 followers of the Lamb (14:1-5), that is, the martyrs who have resisted worshiping the beast without compromise. Only they are permitted to learn and sing such a song (cf. "the new song" in 14:2-3) since the triumph of God, in the first instance, is theirs alone.

As "the song of Moses," the chant alludes to the song of deliverance sung by Moses and the Israelites at the Red Sea (Exod 15:1-18). The introduction (v. 2) thus contains elements that correspond to the story of Israel's rescue from the Egyptians: the glass sea — the Red Sea; Pharaoh and the Egyptians — the beast, his image, and his number (Müller 1995: 274). The hymn (vv. 3b-4) does not allude directly to Exodus 15, but rather stresses the universal dimension of God's rule among the nations. Whereas the Red Sea episode only strikes terror in the eyes of other nations (Exod 15:14-16), the vindication of the Lamb's followers shall be a proclamation of God's great deeds among the nations (cf. Isa 12:4); in the end, it will inspire the nations to come and worship before God in recognition that he alone is worthy to rule over them (Exod 15:11; cf. Ps 86:8-10; Jer 10:6-7; see Bauckham 1993: 296-307). This theme should not, however, be confused with the notion that all humanity will one day become the people of God. Though until the very end the opportunity to repent remains, for John there will always be people of every sort (19:18) who refuse to respond to the unmistakable signs of God's power (e.g., 16:9, 11, 21; 17:14; 19:17-21). Moreover, for John the phrase "will come and worship *(hēxousin kai proskynēsousin)* before you (God)" does not necessarily refer to repentance; in 3:9 a very similar turn of phrase *(hēxousin kai proskynēsousin)* is used to emphasize that "false" Jews will one day recognize that the faithful in Philadelphia have been the object of Christ's love. The conversion of the nations in the end thus remains an implicit theme for John (see under 11:1-14) since its full description might detract from the radical obedience enjoined on the congregations. In praising the justice of God's ways, the hymn anticipates a public and universal recognition of God's glory which is no longer hidden (cf. 15:4).

The Seven Bowls of Wrath (15:5–16:21)

The clash between the Lamb and the beast, exemplified by the conflict between the followers of each and their respective destinies, has been given a vivid description through mythical images and creative interpretation of Scripture in 12:1–15:4. This is followed by the last of the three cycles of seven visions which portray scenes of divine justice: seven seals (6:1–8:6); seven trumpets (8:7–11:19); here seven bowls of wrath (15:5–16:21). The seven bowls of wrath elaborate themes already introduced through the seven trumpets: catastrophes are imagined through language echoing some of the ten plagues against Egypt (Exodus 7–10; see under 8:7-12 and 8:13–9:12) and the people stubbornly refuse when confronted by signs of God's judgment (see 9:20-21). In comparison with the seals and trumpets, the destruction envisioned is more complete. Following the heavenly proclamation of divine justice in 15:3b-4, John's hearers would have been prepared to understand the bowl plagues both as a climactic expression of divine retribution against evil and as a final appeal to bring the nations to worship God before the end.

The Seven Angelic Emissaries of God's Anger (15:5–16:1)

The bowls of wrath are unleashed as the temple "of the tent of witness" (see Num 17:7; 18:2) is opened and seven angels emerge carrying the "seven plagues" (15:6). The bowls are further described as the "seven golden bowls filled with the wrath of God who lives forever" (v. 7; cf. 16:1). These golden bowls are probably those held by the twenty-four elders in 5:8, where they are filled with incense, "which are the prayers of the saints." Thus, like the seals and trumpets, the bowls are portrayed as an answer to the martyrs' petitions for justice (6:9-11). The theme of God's righteous anger has accompanied several of the visions of judgment thus far (6:16; 11:18; 14:10, 19). The smoke filling the temple represents the fullness of God's glory and power (Exod 40:34; cf. Isa 6:4). The overwhelming presence of God sets in motion an irreversible process which cannot be interrupted until it is carried through to completion. Though wearing clothes that symbolize royal and priestly functions, the angels are not so much acting as priests (cf. Exod 40:35; 1 Kgs 8:10-11; 2 Chr 5:13-14) but as agents of God's anger (cf. Ezek 9:2).

The description of the seven angels (15:6) is modeled on Ezek 9:2, in which six "men," each holding a "weapon for slaughter," are commissioned to dispense God's judgment upon the wicked of Jerusalem, who are not given the mark of protection (see under 7:1-8). The most prominent of these "men" is "clothed in linen" (9:2; 10:2) and has a "sapphire belt around his waist" (Ezek 9:3, 11 LXX). While Ezekiel 9 does not make clear whether this leader is one of the six or is a seventh figure, the tradition is adapted in Revelation to a seven-angel scheme. It is possible that the angelic figure of Ezekiel finds a correspondence for John in the guiding angel, one of the seven pouring out the bowls of wrath (17:1; 21:9), who accompanies John in chs. 17:1–19:10 and 21:9–22:5. The "golden sash around their chests" echoes the Ezekiel tradition (9:2; 9:3, 11 LXX; cf. *Apoc. Zeph.* 6:15), but on the level of the text it recalls the clothing of Christ in 1:13. From this it appears that John simultaneously read Ezekiel 9 in relation to angelology and Christology. As is apparent in 1:1, 1:12-20, 4:1, and 22:6-7, in appearance and function Christ is not fully distinguished from an angel (Stuckenbruck 1995a: 218-45).

First Four Bowls of Wrath (16:2-9)

First Bowl (16:2). The plague of "an evil and painful sore *(helkos)*" is inspired by the same phenomenon in the sixth plague against Egypt (Exod 9:10-11; LXX, *helkos*). Struck by the disaster are those "who have the mark of the beast and who worship his image." The promise of economic well-being symbolized by the mark of the beast (13:16) is illusory and short-lived (see under ch. 18), just as worship of the beast's image (13:15) will not go unpunished. The first bowl portrays God's punishment according to the angel's warning in 14:9-11. The text implies that, just as the Israelites in Egypt escaped the boils, this plague will not harm the faithful. Though this would be consistent with the theme of protection introduced in 7:1-8 (cf. also 9:4), it should be remembered that John attempts elsewhere to redefine what such protection actually means (see under 11:1-14).

Second and Third Bowls (16:3-4). Only one of the Egyptian plagues (7:14-25: the Nile, the first plague) and one of the seven trumpet blasts (8:8: the sea, the second trumpet) involve the transformation of water into blood. Here this becomes the subject of two of the bowl plagues. While only a third of the sea is destroyed after the second trumpet blast, all living sea creatures are killed by the "blood as of a corpse" poured from the second bowl. As in the Egyptian plague, the "springs and water sources" are bloodied (16:4), whereas they are poisoned in the third trumpet (8:10). The hymnic pieces which follow (16:5-7) reveal the reason for this emphasis on punishment by blood.

An Antiphonal Hymnic Interlude (16:5-7). The image of "pouring out" *(ekcheō)* the contents of a bowl, used throughout this cycle of plagues, finds a counterpart in this hymnic piece. The angel of the waters — that is, the waters transformed to blood in the second and third bowls — acclaims God for the justice of his punishment (Yarbro Collins 1977) against those who "shed *(ekcheō)* the blood of the saints and the prophets" (v. 6; cf. Ps 79:3). The plagues have punished like with like *(lex talionis),* as in the pattern heralded by the angels of mid-heaven in 14:8, 10. God is called "the Holy One" (16:5; cf. 15:4) instead of the one "who is coming" (1:4, 8; 4:8). Despite ongoing opportunities for repentance, God's holiness cannot be ultimately compromised; the integrity of God's character cannot allow unrepentant evil to go unpunished. As in 11:17, God is no longer the one "who is coming" because God's justice is announced as already having taken effect. The angel's proclamation of righteous judgment (16:5-6) is met by approval from "the altar" (v. 7). The altar personifies the martyrs and saints in 6:9-11 and 8:3-5 whose calls for divine justice are no longer answered in the form of proclamations (cf. 14:8-11; 15:2-4) but in the acknowledgment that God's wrath has become visibly manifest (cf. 14:18).

Fourth Bowl (16:8-9). The sun is allowed to scorch people with the magnitude of its heat; the image is intensified by the "burning with fire" of Babylon in 17:16 and 18:8. This form of punishment contrasts with the vision in 7:16 of the faithful who are promised, in a citation from Isa 49:10, that neither sun nor burning will befall them. Like the Israelites in Egypt (e.g., Exod 8:19; 9:6, 26) and the repentant of Jerusalem in Ezekiel's vision (9:6b), they are spared God's judgments (see under 16:2). Unlike the Pharaoh of Egypt, who after each of the plagues at least begged for reprieve and softened his stance against the Israelites, the effect of the plagues on the wicked illustrates how completely they are devoted to a system of deception: behind the plagues they cannot see divine justice at work. By not repenting (cf. 9:20-21) they participate in the activity of the beast (13:5-6; cf. 17:3) in that they blaspheme the name of God. The plagues highlight for John's hearers what is ultimately at stake if they themselves do not take seriously the calls for them to repent (2:5, 16, 21-22; 3:3).

Last Three Bowls of Wrath (16:10-21)

Fifth Bowl (16:10-11). This plague echoes the darkness brought upon Egypt in Exod 10:21-29. It is targeted against the beast's throne, the symbol of power invested by Satan, the dragon (13:2). The text does not describe how the darkness could manifest itself in pains and sores (Lohse 1993: 92); the latter may suggest the continuing effects of the first bowl (16:2). Imperial Rome, responsible for conditions through which members of John's congregations could enjoy economic advantages, is actually a kingdom of darkness that will result in the torture of those who participate in its institutions. As after the fourth bowl, those affected by the plague are expected to blaspheme "the God of heaven" (in contrast to 11:13; cf. Dan 2:44) without repenting "of their deeds" (cf. 2:22).

Sixth Bowl (16:12-16). Pouring, an image normally associated with fluids, has the opposite effect: the great river Euphrates is dried up. This miracle (cf. Isa 11:15; Zech 10:11; 4 Ezra 13:43-47) will ironically have disastrous consequences, as the removal of the Euphrates barrier opens up the way for an alliance of military powers openly opposed to God. This scene builds on allusions to the

Parthian threat from the borders of the empire made when the first seal is opened (6:2) and the sixth trumpet blown (9:14-16). Here, however, the might from the East, along with the gathered "kings of the whole earth," represents an alliance with Rome, not a threat, as often assumed (e.g., Yarbro Collins 1979: 114; Bauckham 1993: 382). Hence it is unlikely that the text itself alludes to the myth of Nero's return from the East (cf. *Sib. Or.* 4:119-24, 137-39), in which Nero comes to destroy Rome. The battle, for which the armies prepare, is in the first instance against God (16:14; cf. 17:12-14; 19:19-21) and ultimately portends the destruction of Rome (17:16-17). The sixth bowl thus unleashes an organized resistance against the origin of the foregoing plagues, a resistance which is doomed from the start (cf. Ps 2:2).

The assemblage is called forth by a triad of demonic spirits (cf. *1 Enoch* 56:5-6) proceeding from the mouths of the dragon, the beast, and the false prophet (i.e., the second beast of 13:11-17; cf. 19:20; 20:10). The portrayal of the unclean spirits "as frogs" (16:13; cf. Lev 11:10) recalls the second plague in Egypt (Exod 7:26–8:11), a sign which the magicians of Egypt could imitate (hence 16:14; cf. 13:13-14). On Rome as the domain of demons and unclean spirits and animals, see 18:2. The armies are to be gathered at "Harmagedon," literally "Mount Megiddo." The place name is difficult (see, e.g., Mounce 1977: 301-2): although Megiddo is known from tradition as the place of battles (Judg 5:19-20; 2 Kgs 9:27; 23:29; Wis 5:17), it is a plain (Zech 12:11), not a mountain. It is possible that John has creatively brought together different images from the Jewish scriptures: the place name Megiddo with the location on "the mountains of Israel" where Gog, Israel's enemy, is to be slaughtered (Ezek 38:1–39:21; cf. Beckwith 1919: 685).

The scene is interrupted by a word (16:15), probably spoken by Christ (see "I am coming" in 2:5; 3:4, 11; 22:7, 12). The first half of the saying is a warning that corresponds with a Jesus tradition shared by Matthew and Luke (Matt 24:42-44; Luke 12:39-40; cf. 1 Thess 5:2; 2 Pet 3:10), a tradition which had already been combined with a blessing for those who are ready (Matt 24:46; Luke 12:37). Within Revelation the saying alludes to the sharp warning in the message to the congregation at Sardis (3:4), while the second part, the blessing, alludes to the Laodicean message (3:18). As so often throughout the visions, John attempts to keep the various situations of his congregation in view (e.g., 6:11; 13:8-9; 14:1, 12-13; 18:4-5; 20:6; 21:2). It is unnecessary, then, to argue (as does, e.g., Charles 1920: 2:49) that the saying is displaced from 3:3 by a later redactor (Müller 1995: 282). In this context, the saying links the coming of Christ to the traditional motif of "the day of the Lord" widespread in the Jewish scriptures (16:14; see esp. Joel 4:11-12; Zeph 1:14-18).

Seventh Bowl (16:17-21). The final plague shares some features with the seventh trumpet in 11:15-19 and functions as a prelude to a fuller description of Rome's character and destruction in ch. 17. Of the natural catastrophes taken over from 11:19, prominence is given to the earthquake and hail (16:18, 21), drawing on language from the seventh Egyptian plague (Exod 9:17-35). The magnitude of the earthquake is without precedent (Exod 9:18, 24; cf. Dan 12:1; Joel 2:2) and supersedes the quakes described in 8:5 and 11:19 (Bauckham 1993: 202). In contrast to the general destruction in Egypt, the "great hail" (Exod 9:18, 24; also accompanying divine judgment in Isa 28:2; Ezek 38:22) is specifically targeted at wicked humanity, whose response, as in 16:9 and 11, is described in terms of blasphemy. The effect of the earthquake and hail contrasts with the acknowledgment of God's glory among survivors of the destructive earthquake of 11:13 (see under 11:1-14); this earthquake is marked by its severity and finality (16:17).

The cosmic symbolism of islands fleeing and mountains disappearing (16:20; cf. 20:11) results from the shaking of all that is not eternal (cf. Heb 12:26-27), including "the great city," "the cities of the nations," and "great Babylon" (16:19). With the seventh bowl, the announcement of Rome's fall (14:8) is fulfilled. The "cup of the fury of his wrath" is specifically directed at Rome; the expression combines, and therefore intensifies, the terms used singly to refer to God's anger against "Babylon" in 14:8, 10. "The great city" is probably Jerusalem (cf. 11:8), which in John's view will not survive divine judgment. The splitting of the city into three parts is plausibly explained as a reinterpretation of Zechariah's vision of the Lord's advent in Jerusalem (14:3-5; so esp. Sweet 1979: 250-51; Ruiz 1989: 268-69). Unlike Zechariah, however, it retains only a symbolic value, as the city itself is caught up in the system represented by the Roman Empire (see under 11:1-14); hence in the new order the city, as the dwelling of God and the Lamb, will be called "the new Jerusalem" (3:12; 21:2). John's tendency to absorb Jerusalem symbolism into that of Babylon makes it possible for him to refer to Babylon as "the great city" from now on (17:18; 18:10, 16, 19, 21; cf. Bauckham 1993: 207-8).

God's Judgment against "Babylon" (17:1–19:10)

In chs. 12–13, John has portrayed the deception of Rome and the danger it poses for Christian faith. In 17:1–19:10 this theme is elaborated within the context of visions interpreted by one of the angels who poured out the bowls of wrath. The vision of Babylon "in the spirit" (cf. 1:10; 4:2), seen from "a wilderness" (17:3a), produces a counterpart for the later vision in 21:9–22:5, seen from a "high mountain" (21:10), concerning the establishment of the new Jerusalem. The antithetical parallelism centers around the contrasting images of "the whore" of Babylon (17:1, 5, 9, 15, 18; 18:3) and "the bride of the Lamb" (21:9; already 19:8-9; 21:2). Both sections are introduced by the angel's offer of a vision to John (17:1; 21:9) and conclude with the same angel's refusal to allow John to worship him (19:10; 22:8-9; cf. Giblin 1991: 159-60). Until ch. 17 the seer's interaction with angelic beings has been minimal (5:5; 7:13-17; 10:9-10). In the contrasting parallel sections to follow such interaction is more sustained and focused on a particular, though unnamed, angel guide (17:1, 3, 6-14, 15-18; 19:9-10; see under 21:9–22:9).

This section does not actually describe new events; it provides a transition between the preparations made for the battle involving "the kings of the earth" at Harmagedon (16:12-16) and the conflict itself in 19:11-21 (Fekkes 1994: 88-91). Chronologically, it belongs before the destruction of Babylon in the seventh bowl (16:17-21). In this case, it functions analogously to the visions in 7:1-17 and 10:1–11:14, which are respectively penultimate to the seventh seal and trumpet. Chs. 17 and 18 assume that Babylon's fall, however certain (17:17; 18:2; 19:2), lies in John's future (17:11, 16; 18:8, 9, 15).

Babylon "the Whore" and the Beast with Seven Heads (17:1-18)

The Vision (17:1-6). One of the angels pouring the bowls mediates to John a vision of "the great whore" of Babylon (17:1-6; cf. 14:8; 17:18; 18:2-3) and becomes his interpreter (17:7-14, 15-18). "Whore" (vv. 1, 5) frequently occurs in the Jewish scriptures as a metaphor denoting Israel's apostasy to idolatry; in this connection it can refer to "Jerusalem" (e.g., Isa 1:21; Jer 2:24; Ezek 16:15-63; 23:1-49). The image is also used to characterize the evils associated with pagan cities (Tyre: Isa 23:15-18; Nineveh: Nah 3:4). The double identification of Rome as Babylon and a prostitute (17:5) is a contemporary development in Jewish apocalyptic tradition (cf. 4 Ezra 15:48). Both the "many waters" and intoxication by wine are associated with Babylon in Jer 51:7, 12. Hearers familiar with the message to Thyatira (2:18-29) may have recognized an attempt here to link Rome's seduction of "the kings of the earth" (17:1, 5; as a whore, *pornē,* and "mother of whores"; cf. Isa 23:17) with the dangers of idolatrous compromise posed by the prophetess Jezebel *(porneia).* John's vision of the whore's judgment in chs. 17–18 conveys an implicit warning to his readers not to be intoxicated, as "the dwellers on earth," by Rome's institutions.

In the vision itself (17:3b-6) the whore is pictured as a woman seated on "a scarlet beast, full of blasphemous names" and "with seven heads and ten horns" (cf. 13:1). The woman's features (v. 4 — purple and scarlet clothing, adorned with gold, precious stone, and pearls) anticipate the qualities of Rome decried in 18:12, 16 — these are no match for the features ascribed to "the bride of the Lamb" in 21:11-21 — while the "abominations" *(bdelygmata)* filling her golden cup (cf. Jer 51:7) may symbolize the religious "pollution" associated with false worship (Ruiz 1989: 330-31; cf. Dan 9:29; 11:31; 12:11). The "mystery" of her name invites the hearers to ponder its meaning (cf. 1:20; 13:18; 17:9). Although the vision focuses more on the description of the woman, it is the beast that dominates the angel's interpretation of the vision in 17:7-18 (Müller 1995: 286-87). "The blood of the saints and . . . the witnesses to Jesus" (cf. 6:10; 16:6; 18:24; 19:2) does not necessarily mirror a situation of widespread persecution in John's day (see under 13:11-18).

The Interpretation (17:7-18). The angel provides an eschatological interpretation for the vision. Whereas descriptions of the beast in ch. 13 have parodied Christ's death and resurrection (13:3, 13-14), here the beast represents a negative, temporary, and ultimately impotent counterpart to God's coming in judgment (esp. Bauckham 1993: 431-41). The formula in 17:8b, "was and *is not* and is to come *(parestai),*" is comparable to that describing God, "who was and *is* and is to come *(ho erchomenos)*" (4:8; cf. 1:4). For this reason, as in the parody in ch. 13, the beast will be able to gain a following among those not enrolled "in the book of life" (cf. 13:8; 3:5-6 implies a warning). The other two adaptations of the formula, however, leave no doubt that the beast's brief coming is to result in its own destruction (17:8a, 11). The image of the beast's advent (v. 8) either presupposes the legend of Nero's return in a form which envisioned his return from death (hence *"is not"*; cf. *Sib. Or.* 5:33-34, 361-80) or gives an eschatological interpretation to the beast's parody of resurrection from the dead in ch. 13. Thus, whereas ch. 13 depicts the beast in its imminent success against the faithful (e.g., 13:7; cf. 13:15-17), ch. 17 portrays the beast as one who, together with the ten horns (its royal allies), will be conquered by the Lamb (v. 14). Mention of this defeat anticipates its fuller description in 19:11-21.

The use of various symbols to denote evil powers (whore; beast's heads, beast's horns) allows the author to illustrate how Rome will become the victim of its own undoing. Unlike the case in chs. 12–13, there is no unholy alliance of a dragon and two beasts. The Nero myth assumed here, which has the former emperor return as an agent of divine judgment against the Roman Empire (*Sib. Or.* 5:367; cf. 4:130-51), is expressed through the turning of the beast and the ten kings against the whore (17:16). The "ten horns" represent a future alliance of kings with the beast (v. 13), first against the Lamb (v. 14) and then, as agents of God's wrath, against the whore (17:16-17). They are derived from the ten-horned beast in Daniel (7:7, 20, 24), where they refer to a succession of kings culminating in Antiochus Epiphanes. Here, however, they may represent provincial rulers of the empire (Kraybill 1996: 73). In John's time the fourth beast of Daniel was being interpreted as a symbol for the Roman Empire (Josephus *Ant.* 10.10.4; 4 Ezra 12:11; *2 Bar.* 39:5-6). Daniel's chronological interpretation of the horns is transferred to the image of the "seven heads" (17:10-11), which refers to successive Roman emperors (v. 9 — "seven kings"; "seven mountains"; cf., e.g., *Sib. Or.* 2:15-19 and Virgil *Aeneid* 6.782). However, the number is puzzling: only through some manipulative calculation of the line of Roman emperors can the references to the heads — the first five heads, a sixth that is, a seventh to come, and an eighth — be made to fit a dating of Revelation to the time of Domitian (e.g., Mounce 1977: 313-16; Sweet 1979: 256-58; Bauckham 1993: 405-7). Perhaps John is borrowing a tradition which itself dates to the time of Nero (if the counting of emperors begins with Augustus; cf. the Introduction above, 1535). If so, it seems best to suppose that *for John,* the number "seven" is symbolic; John communicates that the full period of Roman rule is nearly at an end; his congregations live on the verge of a crisis marked by the return of a Nero figure (17:11).

Several symbols used to portray the harlot's ruin in 17:16 anticipate expressions that occur in chs. 18 and 19: "desolate" (18:17, 19), "burn her with fire" (esp. 18:8; cf. vv. 9, 18; 19:3), and "eat her flesh" (19:18 — extended to include all the wicked). Rome's "naked" exposure corresponds to the shameful condition associated with the reprehensible wealth mentioned in the message to the Laodiceans (3:18).

Lament and Rejoicing over the Fall of Babylon (18:1–19:8)

Until 19:9-10 communication between John and the angel is suspended. After the doom of Rome is predicted in ch. 17, ch. 18 does not go on to describe the destruction itself. Instead, as if assuming Rome's downfall, 18:1–19:8 contains a series of judgment oracles (18:1-3, 6-8, 21-24), laments (18:9-10, 11-17a, 17b-19), and jubilations (18:20; 19:1-8). These subsections draw heavily on prophetic oracles (in the form of dirges spoken over a corpse to announce judgment; Yarbro Collins 1980: 192) against Tyre and Babylon in Isaiah (23; 34; 47-48), Jeremiah (25; 50–51), and Ezekiel (24; 26–27). This produces a portrait which calumniates Rome and renders the proud empire both temporary and defenseless in the face of God's wrath (Ruiz 1989: 374-504). Together, the subsections support the mandate that Christians should separate themselves from Babylon (18:4-5).

Angel's Dirge (18:1-3). As in 10:1, John has a vision of "another angel coming down from heaven." The angel's appearance illuminates the earth just as the glory of God did before entering the Jerusalem temple (Ezek 43:2). The loud voice of the heavenly messenger proclaims Rome's ruin. "Babylon the great" has "fallen, fallen" (see Isa 21:9 — Babylon's destruction is linked with idol worship; cf. also 14:8); it has become nothing more than a place where "hateful" impurities reside (Isa 13:21-22; cf. 34:11-12, 14-15). The reason for this judgment lies in what Rome does: the empire exerts an illicit sway over "all nations" in political (kings) and economic (merchants) spheres. Both areas of influence are developed in 18:9-10 and 11-19 respectively. Here the images of prostitution (Isa 23:17) and drunkenness (Jer 51:7) are used to characterize Rome's deceptive attractiveness, which itself is regarded by John as a manifestation of divine wrath (Jer 25:15; cf. 14:10; 16:19).

Summons to "Come Out" (18:4-5). A heavenly voice introduces different reactions (vv. 4-19) to the fall of Babylon proclaimed in vv. 2-3. At first, through an address to "my people," another voice declares that Christians are not immune to the influence of Babylon, the object of God's judgment (esp. Kraybill 1996: 100-101). The prophetic call to separate oneself from Babylon, which is frequent among the prophets (esp. Jer 51:45; cf. 50:8; 51:6, 9; Isa 48:20; 52:11), recognizes that the possibility of religious compromise, due to enjoyment of economic luxuries and participation in socioreligious institutions, posed a real threat both *to* and *within* John's congregations (esp. 2:9, 14, 20-23; 3:17-18). To cooperate with the sins of Babylon—that is, *not* to withdraw — is to subject oneself to the "plagues" with which she is to be judged (16:1-21; cf. 22:19). Coming out is not to be understood in a geographical sense, as in Jeremiah and Isaiah (Bauckham 1993: 377; against Boring 1989: 189). Rather than retreating, the congregations are called to lay hold of an existence in their own respective communities that clashes visibly with the predominant system.

Call for Retribution (18:6-8). The urgency of the appeal in vv. 4-5 is underscored by the certainty and imminence of Babylon's judgment. The command to execute punishment, presumably mediated by the voice of v. 4, does not specify who is being addressed. It is likely that those summoned are angels, who elsewhere in Revelation act as agents of divine judgment (e.g., the trumpet blasts, 8:6–11:19, and bowls of wrath, 14:14-20; 16:1-21; cf. Ezek 9:2, 5-7). The "plagues" to visit Babylon are appropriate to her self-indulgent behavior at the expense of others (18:6-7a). The call to exact a "double" portion for her deeds emphasizes how fully the punishment should fit the crime (Yarbro Collins 1984: 117; cf. Isa 40:2; Jer 16:18; 17:18; 50:15, 29); this principle of correlation occurs also in 13:10; 14:8, 10; and 16:5-7. Rome in her luxury is to be punished by "torment" (*basanismon;* cf. 9:5; 14:10-11; 18:15) and "grief" (*penthos;* cf. vv. 7b-8); this contrasts with her unfounded expectation that she, a "queen" and not a "widow" (Isa 47:8; cf. *Sib. Or.* 5:173), will not have to suffer "grief" (*penthos*) at all. The "plagues" of Rome, whose sudden coming recalls Isa 47:9, are further described with details that repeat the punishment just mentioned ("mourning," *penthos*) and recall the effects of the fourth seal (6:8: "hunger," "pestilence"; cf. 2:23; Ezek 5:17; 14:21) and the final punishment of Babylon (17:16, "burning with fire"; cf. 19:20 and under 16:8-9).

Kings' Lament (18:9-10). The structure of this lament — that is, the introduction of the mourners, the setting, and the pronouncement of judgment — sets the pattern for the laments to follow. As allies and dependents of Rome (cf. v. 3; 17:2), the "kings of the earth" (cf. Ps 2:2; here: provincial rulers; cf. Kraybill 1996: 73) have been economic beneficiaries. As in 17:3 and 18:3 (cf. 2:20-23), this relationship between Rome and her allies is derided as a kind of prostitution (cf. Isa 23:17). Indeed, the empire — not least, Asia Minor — was flourishing under the rule of the Flavian emperors (Magie 1950: 1:566-92). The "kings," therefore, have reason to fear God's judgment upon "the great city." The language is inspired by the dirges spoken in Ezek 26:16-17 ("princes of the coastlands"; "trembling"; "lamentation") and 27:33-35 ("kings of the earth") against the then prosperous city of Tyre. As in 18:16-17a and 19, the judgment is pronounced by Rome's friends as if it has already occurred; this, in turn, supplies the basis for the foregoing "woe" laments. From John's point of view, this punishment lies in the future (see v. 8); his use of the past tense ("your judgment has come") reflects the Hebrew prophets' use of the lament form to predict the downfall of Israel's enemies. Concerning the expression "smoke of her burning" (v. 9; cf. v. 18; 19:3), see under 14:9-11.

Merchants' Lament (18:11-17a). The structure of the lament, though generally modeled on the foregoing section (vv. 9-10), is complicated by the position of v. 14 along with the double pronouncement of judgment in vv. 14b and 17a (see Yarbro Collins 1984: 118). This form is occasioned by John's interest in cataloguing valuable goods that characterize the wealth of Rome (vv. 12-13). Therefore, the actual dirge that addresses Babylon is delayed until vv. 14 and 15-17a. Though the inclusion of a cargo list is influenced by the lament against Tyre in Ezek 27:12-24, John's choice of items is determined by contemporary knowledge of goods being imported by the city of Rome (Bauckham 1993: 350-51). Significantly, the list contains a number of items used to describe the "whore" in 17:4 (18:12: gold, jewels, pearls, purple, and scarlet), items which are likewise ascribed to "the great city" through the lament in vv. 15-16. The list concludes with a reference to slaves (literally called "bodies" — cf. Gen. 36:6 LXX; Tob 10:10 — and "human souls" — cf. Ezek 27:13 LXX). This implies a categorical rejection of slavery, in contrast to the views of some other NT authors (cf. Eph 6:5; Col 3:22; 1 Tim 6:1; Tit 2:9; 1 Pet 2:18). The destruction of Babylon will spell fiscal ruin for the mourning merchants, whose goods can no longer be purchased. This reverses the unrestricted buying and selling associated with those having the beast's mark in 13:16-17. As in 18:10 and 19, the "woes" can be pronounced because of the certainty of God's judgment (compare "has been laid waste" with the future tense in Ezek 27:32).

Mariners' Lament (18:17b-19). The mourners here consist of all those connected in some way with the maritime industry. Transport by sea was essential to maintaining Rome's food supply and importation of goods since it was less costly than traversing the trade routes by land (Kraybill 1996: 102-41). As with the kings and merchants, the mariners' economic well-being is inextricably linked to the capacity of Rome to keep shipping routes safe and to buy their goods; hence they grieve not only for Babylon but also on account of their own misfortune. The references to mariners and sailors (v. 17b) throwing dust on their heads (v. 19a) and the rhetorical question, "What city [lit. "Who"] is like the great city?" (v. 18b) are taken from the dirge spoken over Tyre in Ezekiel 27 (vv. 27, 29, 30, 35, and 32 respectively). The question implies an admission of Rome's wealth, but it does not imply admiration (against Caird 1966: 227). Rather, the magnitude of her downfall is being stressed (cf. Ezek 27:32, 34) since Rome's greatness is but an extension of her idolatrous behavior (cf. 18:7; Bauckham 1993: 344). On "the smoke of her burning" (v. 18, as in v. 9; 19:3), see under 14:9-11. "Has been laid waste" (18:19b; cf. Ezek 27:32), in the past tense, underscores John's conviction that Rome's destruction is inevitable.

Summons to Rejoice (18:20). While there is uncertainty about the identity of the speaker (whether John, as, e.g., in Bousset 1906: 423, or the "voice" of v. 4, as esp. in Caird 1966: 222-28), the change in perspective is clear: in contrast to the grief shown by collaborators with the political and economic institutions of "the great city," here the saints are to express jubilation over Rome's downfall. This summons is linked to the summons to "come out" in 18:4 through Jer 51:45, 47-48 (Müller 1995: 309), where the call to leave Babylon is followed by the prediction that, after Babylon's destruction, "heaven and earth and all that is within them" will rejoice. If the jubilation is intended as a contrast to the cries for retribution in 6:9-11, then the "saints," "apostles," and "prophets," as heavenly dwellers (cf. 12:12), could represent those martyred in John's past (cf. 18:24; so, e.g., Müller 1995: 309-10). Though the author apparently knows about the Neronian persecution (cf. 13:18 — on "apostles" as victims, see Wikenhauser 1959: 137) and is at least cognizant of the death of Antipas at Pergamum (2:13), it should be remembered that John's language is often idealistic and prescriptive. Just as the future judgment of Rome is virtually assured (18:20b), so is the jubilation of those who have and *will have* suffered death in the Christian community on her account.

Prophetic Oracle (18:21-24). A symbolic enactment of Rome's judgment is performed by "a mighty angel" (v. 21a). Followed by an announcement of judgment (vv. 21b-23a), this action is patterned after similar activities attributed to Israel's prophets (e.g., 1 Kgs 11:29-39; Isa 8:1-4; 20:1-6; Jer 19:1-15). In particular, the text recreates the scene in Jer 51:59-64, according to which Seraiah is told by Jeremiah to read a scroll of judgment against Babylon, bind it to a stone, throw it into the Euphrates, and announce, "So shall Babylon sink, to rise no more" (cf. 18:21b; further, Matt 18:6; Mark 9:42; Luke 17:2). The words of judgment in 18:22-23a, inspired by Jer 25:10 (cf. Isa 24:8; Ezek 26:13), are addressed to Rome directly. They portray fallen Rome as a place destitute of any culture.

Three reasons are given here: the high social status of Rome's merchants as "magnates of the earth" (cf. Isa 23:8); Rome's "sorcery," an illusionary power that deceives the nations (cf. Isa 47:9); and Rome's guilt of murder: "in her [against NRSV, "you"] *was found* the blood of the prophets and saints and of all those slaughtered upon the earth" (cf. Jer 51:49; *Sib. Or.* 5:155-61). In particular, the last-mentioned reason is formulated in such a way as to show how, on account of murderous activity (cf. Ezek 24:7), Rome will have forfeited her right to economic, cultural, and even social survival. For John the question of a Christian's posture toward economic institutions of the Roman Empire was not a relative or tangential matter; his sharp critique is expressed out of a conviction that the distribution of goods in the empire was usurped by a system through which Rome, not only the emperor but also city itself, was in fact being deified. Behind every commercial and social institution in the empire John sees at work a single, coherent principle which cannot be reconciled with the worship of God. Since no doubt a number of the Asia Minor congregations were confronted by some aspect of Rome in their daily lives, John's plea to "come out" from Rome (v. 4) was a demand for radical separation, even at the cost of one's own life. The dirges and oracles of judgment in ch. 18 thus assume that by religious exclusivism, the hearers will escape the violent overthrow of Rome decreed by God.

Jubilation in Heaven (19:1-8). This section is anticipated by the summons to rejoice in 18:20. It comes at the climax of the vision about God's judgment over Babylon (esp. Jörns 1971: 145-60). The passage depicts worship around a series of "Hallelujahs" (19:1, 3, 4, 6); they are not merely formulaic, as in many of the psalms (e.g., Pss 104:35; 106:1, 45; 148:1; etc.), but function as genuine calls to worship (Müller 1995: 316). As throughout Revelation, the worship is located in heaven. The acclamations are repeatedly addressed to "God" (19:1, 4, 5, 6, 7). In vv. 1-4, as in 15:4 and especially 16:7, the justice of God's retribution against Babylon "the great whore" (19:2; cf. 17:2, 4-5; 18:3) is proclaimed as true and righteous. The text singles out "the blood of his servants *(douloi)*" as the reason for Rome's guilt (cf. esp. 16:5-7; 18:24). Babylon's judgment, symbolized by "smoke" (19:3 — *kapnos*), is permanent (Isa 34:10; cf. 14:11; 18:9, 18); it stands in contrast to the "smoke" *(kapnos)* of the saints' prayers in 8:3-5. This is the last formal scene of worship in Revelation. The conclusiveness of this celebration of judgment is reinforced by the inclusion of the twenty-four elders and four living creatures among the worshipers (19:4; see 4:4, 6; 5:7; esp. 11:16-18).

Though concluding 17:1–18:24, this scene marks a transition. Whereas 19:1-4 narrate the heavenly jubilation concerning God's triumph over Babylon, vv. 5-8 include among the multitude of worshipers all God's servants *(douloi)* and those who fear him, "small and great" (v. 5; cf. 11:18; Ps 115:13). These groups refer to the believing community on earth; their praise thus participates in the angelic worship that follows in 19:6-8. Though worship is throughout the passage directed exclusively toward God, here it becomes apparent that for John Christ the Lamb provides the authentic basis for and means to this worship (Stuckenbruck 1995a: 224-26). The dawning rule of God is symbolized by the future marriage of the Lamb to his "bride" (cf. Isa 61:10-11), later identified as the "new Jerusalem" (21:2, 9; cf. 3:12). In contrast to Babylon, who wears "fine linen" associated with purple and scarlet, the bride's "fine linen" is "bright and pure" (19:8), an ideal picture of the Christian community (cf. 3:4-5, 12, 18) which, by definition, must be untainted by compromising external influences. For John the existence of such a community is not postponed to an indefinite future. It is a present reality toward which Christians are urgently exhorted to strive.

Blessing and the Angel's Refusal to Be Worshiped (19:9-10)

At the conclusion of the hymn, John is addressed by an unidentified figure, without doubt the same angel who mediated and interpreted John's vision of the whore of Babylon and the beast in ch. 17 (vv. 1, 3, 7, 15). The angel tells John to record a blessing on "those who are called to the marriage supper of the Lamb," which he declares to be "the true words of God." The blessing, like the others in Revelation (1:3; 14:13; 16:15; 20:6; 22:7, 14), has a strong parenetical force; it is an invitation to participate in the preparations required to belong to "the bride" (19:7). If Isa 25:6-8 lies in the background, the eschatological meal with the Lamb is symbolically located at Mt. Zion (cf. 14:1-5), from which death will be destroyed.

The angel's declaration is so overwhelming that John falls at his feet to worship him. The angel emphatically refuses John's gesture with an exhortation to "worship God" instead, since he himself is but a "fellow servant." In constructing this scene, John has been influenced by a tradition, attested in early Jewish and Christian sources, concerned with the rejection of inappropriate worship (cf. esp. Tob 12:16-22; *Apoc. Zeph.* 6:11-15; *Asc. Isa.* 7:18-23; 8:1-10; *2 Enoch* 20:1-4; *Jos. Asen.* 15:11-12). The occurrence of a parallel passage in 22:8-9 (v. 8 explicitly refers to an "angel") makes it unlikely that John has merely confused the angel with Christ (against Mounce 1977: 340).

Two categories of interpreting this passage should be distinguished: (1) possible situations being addressed among John's hearers and (2) John's *own* theological concerns. Concerning the first category, the main alternatives put forward have to do with angelology: the passage (a) polemicizes against a practice of angel worship (e.g., Bousset 1906: 493; Kiddle 1940: 382-83; Sweet 1979: 280); (b) corrects a view that places too much confidence in angels as agents of salvation (Karrer 1986: 169-85); or, similarly, (c) counters a real possibility of relying on angels as mediators of protection (Stuckenbruck 1995a: 232-39, 246-61).

The second category, John's own intention, is not necessarily incompatible with the first. Here it has been variously suggested that John wishes (a) to emphasize his complete rejection of idolatry (e.g., Boring 1986; Donegani 1997: 386); (b) to underscore the equality between angels and prophets, thereby reinforcing the legitimacy of John's prophetic commission and message (esp. Schüssler Fiorenza 1985: 145-46; cf. Bousset 1906: 429-30); (c) to establish that the truth of the foregoing message is *divine,* not angelic, in origin (e.g., Prigent 1989: 285-87; Müller 1995: 320, 368); (d) to emphasize that the angel is but a mediator, nothing more (Satake 1966: 104-6; Müller 1995: 320); or broadly, (e) to outline the boundaries of John's monotheistic belief to the exclusion of angels (Bauckham 1993: 133-40; Stuckenbruck 1995a: 257-62). The least likely are options 1a and 2a, b: there is little evidence for the *cultic* worship of angels by Jews in antiquity (cf. Stuckenbruck 1995a: 47-204); the passage is not merely concerned with idolatry in a conventional sense; and, if 22:8-9 is also considered, the angel's self-demotion is not merely an attempt to legitimate John's prophecy but also includes faithful believers of the churches (e.g., Müller 1995: 319-20, 368). The impossibility of excluding most of the above alternatives and, conversely, their plausibility within the context of Revelation make it likely that 19:10 and 22:8-9 reflect a convergence of concerns, respecting both John's message about the status of angels in relation to God and his interest in defining more narrowly the proper bounds of legitimate worship.

The expression "the testimony of Jesus," which occurs twice in 19:10, is bound up with John's understanding of prophecy. Jesus, not the angelic "fellow servant," is the *source* of the prophetic message given to John and his circle of prophets (Donegani 1997: 365-68). Even further, the text may hint at a criterion against which the legitimacy of Spirit-inspired prophecy is to be measured. True prophecy should somehow reflect, correspond to, or derive from the faithful testimony borne by Jesus, which for John is exemplified in "Lamb" Christology. In this sense it is Jesus' testimony which determines what it means when the angel directs John to "worship God" (see under 22:6-9).

The End of Evil (19:11–21:8)

Between 17:1–19:10 (on Babylon) and its parallel section in 21:9–22:5 (on the new Jerusalem), several visions are inserted. Structurally, they serve as a transition from the announcement of the punishment of Babylon to the visible establishment of God's rule in a transformed cosmos. Despite their transitory character, these visions are of singular importance for the interpretation of Revelation. In this section the defeat of Babylon is narrated as a victory of Christ (19:11-21). It is placed against the backdrop of a universal triumph by God over demonic evil (20:7-10). Only after Satan himself has been defeated is there a final judgment (20:11-15). Between these victories of Christ and God, John introduces a temporal, thousand-year reign in which the martyrs rule with Christ (20:1-6). At the end of all evil God's reign is established over a world transformed into a new heaven and earth (21:1-8). This complicated scenario of the end, structured around the dual notions of a "first resurrection" and a "second death" (20:5-6, 12-13), is ultimately determined by John's exhortation to Christians to model their faithfulness after the pattern set by those who die because of their faith.

Victory over the Beast and Its Allies (19:11-21)

Vision of Christ (19:11-16). For John the victory over the beast proceeds on the basis of the character attributed to the conqueror of Revelation *par excellence* (3:21; 5:5). Though unnamed, the rider on the white horse is unmistakably Christ. Features occurring here are exclusively associated with him — that is, *not* with any of the "angels" — in the rest of the book. He is "faithful and true" (19:11; 1:5; 3:7), "his eyes were as a flame of fire" (19:12; 1:14), he has a written name not known to anyone else (19:12; cf. 2:17), "from his mouth came a sharp sword" (19:15, 21; 1:16; 2:12, 16), and "he will rule over the nations with an iron rod" (19:15; 2:27; 12:5; cf. Ps 2:8). Furthermore, his robe is stained with blood (19:13; 1:5; 5:9; 7:14; cf. Isa 63:3 discussed in relation to *Tg. Pal.* to Gen. 49:11 by Fekkes 1994: 197-99), and as the victorious Lamb in 17:14 he is given the title "King of kings" and "Lord of lords" (19:16). Other features are antithetical to the beast's appearance and functions: in contrast to the latter, Christ wears "many diadems" (v. 12; cf. 13:1: "ten diadems") and "makes war" in righteousness (19:11; 11:7; 13:7; 17:14; 19:19; cf. Ps 9:9). Together these images characterize Christ's appearance from heaven as the Messiah who executes judgment against the unrepentant wicked of "the nations" (cf. Isa 11:4 and Isa 63:2-3, presupposed in 19:15b; see also 14:19-20); the correspondence between some of the features and those in the seven messages implies a warning against those who among the congregations do not repent (esp. 2:16; cf. Ps 7:12). As a "name" for Christ, "the Word of God" in 19:13b *(ho logos tou theou)* seems to contradict the mention of an unknown "name" in v. 12b and interrupts the poetic structure which otherwise presents Christ's features in pairs. Some interpreters have therefore argued that v. 13b is not from John but a later insertion into the text (see Müller 1995: 323-24). Other commentators have tried to interpret the designation as a special title for Christ influenced by Wis 18:14-16 or, more directly, by the Gospel of John 1:1, 14. Often overlooked, however, is that the same phrase occurs elsewhere in Revelation to denote God's message to which Christians are held accountable (1:2, 9 — in parallel with "the testimony of Jesus"; cf. 6:9). By using the title, then, John implies that faithfulness to "the word of God" is inseparable from loyalty to the person of Christ (cf. Carrell 1997: 214-19).

Christ is followed by an army also seated on "white horses"; their fine linen is "white" (as the saints' robes in 7:9, 13) and "pure" (as the bride's fine linen in 19:8a). In view of 17:14b, those with Christ consist of the martyred saints, who "follow the Lamb wherever he goes" (14:4) and whose garments are white because they are washed in the Lamb's blood (7:14; Sweet 1979: 283). They are allowed to participate in the defeat of the beast and his allies in 19:19-21.

Defeat of the Beast and His Allies (19:17-21). The battle is not elaborately described; in fact, as in 12:9, 12-13, details are kept to a minimum. The beast and his false prophet are "thrown" into "the fiery lake burning with sulfur" (as in 20:10, 14; cf. *1 Enoch* 21:7-10; 90:24-27), while the rest (cf. the list in 19:18) are killed by "the sword" (*1 Enoch* 91:12; *2 Bar.* 72:6; CD 19:10-11 — at the coming of "the messiah of Aaron and Israel") from Christ's mouth. The text gives the impression that the gathering of the beast and armies of "the kings of the earth," an allusion to Ps 2:2, is a vain effort from the very start (19:19). Rather than through fighting, the battle is won more on the basis of what Christ and his followers *are* (hence the detail in vv. 11-16), which contrasts with the deception attributed to the beast and his false prophet (v. 20; 13:14, 16; cf. Sweet 1979: 285). The angel's invitation to the birds of midheaven (cf. 8:13) to gather themselves for "the great supper of God" (19:17; cf. Ezek 39:17-20) provides a negative counterpart to the "marriage supper of the Lamb" introduced as an eschatological blessing for the faithful in 19:8-9. The list of the birds' prey is extensive (v. 18), reminiscent of those targeted by the sixth seal in 16:15.

The battle brings to fulfillment the preceding announcements of doom and destruction against Babylon and her allies (e.g., 14:8, 9-11; 18:2-3, 5-8, 9-19, 21-24). It is also the "military" conflict anticipated in the sixth bowl of wrath (16:12-16) and in the angel's interpretation of the vision of the whore and the beast (17:14). The present vision of Christ coming to defeat world powers builds on the expectation in Jewish tradition of an Anointed One–Messiah who would execute justice on behalf of God's people (e.g., *Pss. Sol.* 17:23-27; *Sib. Or.* 3:286-90, 652-56; 5:108-10, 414-19; 4 Ezra 13:1-50; *2 Bar.* 39:7–40:3; 72:2-6; cf. 2 Thess 1:7-8). The text does not speak of a "return" or parousia of Christ for the final judgment (Matt 25:31-46; 1 Cor 15:23; 1 Thess 2:19; 4:15; 2 Thess 2:1), which in Revelation is reserved for God (20:11-15).

The Conquerors' Millennial Reign (20:1-6)

Throughout Revelation John stresses the importance of radical loyalty to God. He does so using language that links discipleship with a Christology of the "slaughtered" Lamb. John's hearers are repeatedly exhorted not to blend their faith with the idolatrous economic and religious-political system of Rome; instead, they are to "follow" Christ in a way that stands out in sharp relief. John wants his congregations to recognize that there are two systems whose incompatibility necessarily results in death, whether at the hands of "Rome" (e.g., 13:15) or, worse, with "Babylon" at the hands of God's just retribution (e.g., 18:1-8). Here John paints a portrait to exhort his hearers about the precise advantage to be gained by the faithful for subjecting themselves to death. Concretely, this privilege consists in the promise of a "first resurrection" for the martyrs. Because of the favorable judgment on their behalf (20:4a), those who have died for the sake of "the testimony of Jesus and the word of God" (cf. 6:9) are allowed to rule over the earth with Christ for a millennium, during which they are to function as priests (20:4, 6; cf. 1:6; 5:10).

The millennial rule is set up as the immediate consequence of the destruction of Babylon and her allies (19:11-21). It provides a tangible counterpart *on earth* to Rome's seductive reign of idolatry. A court session on "thrones" (Dan 7:9; 4Q530ii, 16-20) results in a decision that the martyrs' "souls" be raised to rule with Christ (20:4; cf. 6:9) in what John calls the "first resurrection" (20:5b-6). The restriction of the "first resurrection" to the martyrs — literally, "the beheaded" — reflects how John has radicalized a contemporary Jewish tradition that envisions a resurrection for the righteous alone (Müller 1995: 339; cf. *1 Enoch* 91:10; 103:4; *T. Jud.* 25:4; *Pss. Sol.* 3:12). The martyrs are pronounced "blessed and holy" because they shall not be subject to "the second death" (2:11; 19:6, 14; cf. 14:13), that is, they are spared from the irrevocable punishment of being thrown into "the lake of fire" following the final judgment (20:14).

Given the limited duration and purpose of the millennial kingdom in John's scheme, it does not mark the end of evil itself (cf. 20:7-10, 11-15). Vv. 1-3 describe a temporary defeat. The passage opens with an angel descending from heaven holding "the key of the abyss and a great chain" (20:1); in this capacity the angel is analogous, though inferior, to Christ, who in 1:18 holds the keys of power over the ultimate bastions of evil, "Death and Hades" (cf. 20:14). This angel binds, throws, and locks up "the dragon" (called "the old serpent," "the devil," and "Satan"; cf. 12:9) in the abyss, where he is rendered impotent for a thousand years.

The scenarios in 20:1-3 and 4-6 are patterned, respectively, after two Jewish apocalyptic traditions: (1) the notion of a temporary abode for evil powers in anticipation of the final judgment (cf. Isa 24:21-22; *1 Enoch* 10:12; 21:1-10; *Jub.* 5:10; 4Q203 7, 8) and (2) the expectation of a period of messianic rule before the final judgment (cf., e.g., *1 Enoch* 91:12-16; *Sib. Or.* 3:635-701; 4 Ezra 7:26-35; *2 Bar.* 29:3–30:5). The combination of these traditions allows John to split up the eschatological judgment into two stages or resurrections, one which stresses the reward of the martyred righteous ("first resurrection") and another which stresses the judgment of the wicked ("the second death"). This, in turn, throws the spotlight on the privileges accorded to loyal Christians during a millennial reign.

Just who are these martyrs? Are they an elite group out of a larger number of Christians who are also included in 19:4 (e.g., Farrer 1964: 206-7; Mounce 1977: 356-59) or raised for the final judgment in 20:11-15 (e.g., Lohse 1993: 106; Müller 1995: 338-40, 347)? Significantly, the text makes no open statement about whether John has a place for *non-martyred faithful* Christians in either the first resurrection (vv. 4-6) or the final judgment (vv. 11-15). John may have thought that a less radical approach to faithful witness would have encouraged his congregations to seek ways to *avoid* martyrdom which, in the end, would leave them more open to the possibility of religious compromise (cf. Mealy 1992: 102-19). Only the strongest of rhetoric could impose upon the congregations a decision between two clearly defined alternatives.

Read in sequence, 20:4-6 and 11-15 could be read as an eschatological judgment occurring in two stages. What may seem to be successive stages could actually be a literary device used by John to focus singly on the vindication of the righteous martyrs and on the eradication of the wicked and evil. It is, therefore, misleading to insist that John was simply interested in chronology. Many have deliberated whether the millennial reign precedes or follows the final judgment. So formulated, this question has produced traditions of interpretation which, respectively, are labeled "premillennial" and "postmillennial." Whereas the former regards the millennium as the culmination of a gradual improvement brought about by the church in the world, the latter expects that the world will only be changed decisively when God's activity intervenes in a world in a downward spiral of evil. While it might be possible to read 19:11–20:15 either way, the passage in its present form is inconsistent. The impression is left that John, rather than being concerned primarily with the order of events to be, was attempting to draw attention to the ultimate destinies of the righteous and the wicked, that is, to show in sharpest relief that God will vindicate the faithful ones and annihilate those who are allies of Satan.

The Annihilation of Satan (20:7-10)

John describes the release of Satan to assert himself in a doomed effort. The text assumes the binding of Satan into the abyss in 20:1-3 and the millennial rule of Christ and the martyrs in vv. 4-6. The impression left is that the emergence of Satan from his imprisonment and his deception of the nations "from the four corners of the earth" follow chronologically upon the events covered by the preceding sections.

A problem, however, remains: Where do the deceived nations come from; how are they, for example, related to the millennial kingdom described in 20:4-6; who could they be if not the allies of the beast destroyed and devoured in 19:21? Since the "first resurrection" involves only the righteous, it is unlikely that John imagined that other groups would exist during the thousand years. The "rest of the dead" in 20:6 might provide a clue: these nations may have been resurrected *after* the thousand years when they fell under the sway of Satan's deception (Mealy 1992: 122-26). As "Gog and Magog," the nations are a creative allusion to Ezek 38:1–39:22 in which the monarch "Gog" from a northern mythical land of "Magog" (38:2; 39:2) was expected to pose a threat to the Israel (as in 20:9: "the encampment of the saints and the beloved city"; cf. Caird 1966: 256; Giblin 1991: 188). Through two details John betrays their connection with Satan: (1) their ascent to the surface of the earth suggests that "the four corners of the earth" from which they come represent the demonic netherworld (cf. 7:1; 9:1-11) and (2) their number, "as the sands of the seashore," alludes to the place where the dragon transmitted its great power to the beast (12:18–13:2). The siege ends in the destruction of the nations through "fire from heaven" (esp. Ezek 38:22; cf. 2 Kgs 1:10, 12), while Satan is cast into the same "lake of fire and sulfur" into which the beast and false prophet had been thrown (19:20). Described as "the second death," this destruction is permanent and corresponds to the announcement of eternal torture for Babylon in 14:11 and 19:3 (20:10; cf. Isa 34:10).

The Last Judgment and Annihilation of Death (20:11-15)

Evil's final eradication coincides with the disappearance of earth and heaven (20:11). Divine justice cannot be contained in the cosmic order as it presently exists (e.g., *1 Enoch* 1:6-7; cf. 21:1-2); this idea is already anticipated on a smaller scale in the fifth seal (6:14) and seventh bowl (16:20). In contrast to 20:4, the scene of judgment presupposes the Jewish tradition concerning the resurrection of both the wicked and the righteous for judgment (Dan 12:2; *1 Enoch* 51:1-2; 4 Ezra 7:32-35; *2 Bar.* 30:1-5). Both sides of the judgment are not equally stressed, however; aside from neutral references to the "book of life" (cf. under 3:5-6) and being judged according to one's deeds, little indicates that the righteous are here in view. In contrast to 20:4-6, which is exclusively concerned with the vindication of the martyrs, the judgment focuses on the irrevocable punishment of the wicked, that is, of the dead whom "the sea" (13:1), "Death," and "Hades" (1:18; cf. 6:7-8: the fourth horseman) have "given up" (20:14). Though the notion of "giving up" the dead refers to a general resurrection in contemporary Jewish literature (*1 Enoch* 51:1; 4 Ezra 4:41-43; 7:32; *2 Bar.* 50:2; Ps.-Philo *Bib. Ant.* 3:10), it is noteworthy that in *this context* terms for "resurrection" *(anastasis)* or coming to life (*zaō;* cf. 20:4, "they came to life") are not used. As in 13:8 and 17:8, the function of the book of life (20:12, 15) is formulated in negative terms; in it are *not* recorded names of the unrighteous. In Jewish apocalyptic visions the plural term "books" symbolizes God's judgment against the sins of the wicked (Dan 7:9-12; *1 Enoch* 90:20-19; 4Q530ii, 16-20; *2 Bar.* 24:1).

The heavenly court is conducted by the one "seated on the throne" (4:2; 5:1; 6:16; 21:5; cf. Dan 7:10). As in 20:4, the scene is reminiscent of Daniel 7, though here with a focus on the "throne" (Dan 7:10) rather than on the "thrones" (20:4; Dan 7:9). That *God* holds judgment underscores its finality (4 Ezra 6:1-10); hence it should not be interpreted as the negative side of the same event described in 20:4 (against Mealy 1991: 179-86). This scene envisions no further judgment or triumph over evil. Beyond Satan, only the very last enemy, "Death" (paired with "Hades"), is left to be destroyed (cf. 21:4; Isa 25:8; 1 Cor 15:26, 54-55).

"The lake of fire" is the destination of all (19:10: the false prophet; 20:10: the devil) whose deeds are found to be wicked. This sea is called "the second death"; it is already personified in v. 6, where it will hold no destructive power over participants in the first resurrection. Until now the lake has been a place of torment. The casting of "Death and Hades" into the lake is, however, to punish Death with death, that is, with virtual nonexistence (21:4).

The New Heaven and New Earth (21:1-8)

The end of evil has been described in an escalating series of defeats: Babylon and her allies (19:17-21); Satan and "Gog and Magog" (20:7-10); and Death and Hades, along with the rest of the wicked (20:11-15). The climax of this series is stated in 21:1: "the sea was no more" (cf. *Sib. Or.* 5:158-59; *As. Mos.* 10:6). Herewith is removed the ultimate symbol for chaos (13:1; 20:13; cf. Isa 27:1; Dan 7:3), the origin of all evil, whose antidote is a new act of creation (cf. Gen 1:2; Job 26:7-13; Isa 51:9-10). The passing of the old order coincides with the establishment of a "new heaven" and "new earth" (Isa 65:17; 66:22), whose advent is envisioned as the descent of "the holy city, the new Jerusalem." The new Jerusalem is created by God (Heb 11:10; cf. Gal 4:26; Phil 3:20; Heb 12:22). It is further described as God's people, who are adorned as a "bride" for her "husband," the Lamb (21:9; cf. 19:7, 9). This image, developed on the basis of Isaiah 54 (Fekkes 1993: 237-53; cf. further *Jos. Asen.* 4:2), symbolizes God's people who are fully and eternally reconciled to their creator, the source of all comfort and bliss. Though coming at the conclusion of a series of eschatological events, what John describes here is not merely a future reality (as in *1 Enoch* 90:28-29). The term "new" does not imply a rebuilding of the city. Like the author of 4 Ezra (esp. 10:49; see, e.g., *2 Bar.* 4:2-6), John distinguishes between the earthly temple, now in ruins, and an indestructible edifice that has been in existence from the very beginning (implied by "his tabernacle" in 13:6?). Its descent is to be *seen,* that is, *apprehended* as a new point of reference that contrasts with the old (cf. 3:12). This reality provides, in turn, the foundation for hope.

The vision thus serves as the basis for renewed parenesis, which takes the form of promises (21:3-4, 5-7) and warning (vv. 7-8). The first promises, spoken by a "loud voice from the throne," are richly endowed with motifs from the prophets Isaiah, Jeremiah, and Ezekiel that are concerned with the restoration of the Jerusalem temple after its destruction: God will dwell among his people (Ezek 37:27; 43:7; cf. Zech 2:14-15); they will be his people, and he will be their God (e.g., Ezek 11:20; 37:27; cf. Lev 26:12; Jer 7:23; 31:1); God will remove all their tears (Isa 25:8; cf. 7:17); Death will no longer exist (Isa 25:8; cf. 20:14); and there will be no further mourning, weeping (Isa 51:11; 65:19; 35:10), or labor (a reversal of Gen 3:16-19; cf. *1 Enoch* 7:3; 9:1). The list concludes with the pronouncement that the former (lit. "first") things have passed away (Isa 43:18; 65:17).

The second list of promises, along with the warning, take the form of a saying by God, "who is seated upon the throne" (4:2; 5:1; 6:16; 20:11). Though this is the second saying attributed directly to God in Revelation (cf. 1:8), only here is it *God,* the creator *par excellence* (cf. 21:5a and Isa 43:19), who commissions John to record the faithful and true words (Jesus in 1:11, 19; 2:1, 7, etc.; the heavenly voice in 14:13; the angel in 19:9; see, e.g., Giblin 1991: 194-95). The titles "the Alpha and the Omega" and "the beginning and the end" (cf. 1:8) are also attributed to Christ in 22:13, just as the function of providing the source of living water is associated with the Lamb in 7:17

(Isa 49:10; cf. Ps 23:2-3; Isa 55:1). This reinforcement of God's functional identity with Christ is picked up again in the formula at the beginning of 21:7, "to the one who conquers," which recalls the words of Jesus at the conclusion of each of the seven messages (chs. 2–3). The Davidic promise of sonship (2 Sam 7:14), applied to Christ in Heb 1:5, here describes the relation of Christians to God. In contrast to the inheritance of the faithful, the warning consists of a list of vices destined for "the lake of fire and sulfur, which is the second death" (cf. 20:6, 14). The vices, partly repeated in 22:15, identify activities condemned throughout the book (cf., e.g., 2:2, 9, 14, 20-23; 3:9; 17:2, 4; 18:23-24).

The New Jerusalem (21:9–22:9)

This is the concluding section to the main body of Revelation (4:1–22:9). It returns to interaction between John and the angel guide, the form of mediation followed in 17:1–19:10 (see the introduction there). Here, however, the angel's role is patterned after Ezekiel 40–48 (so in 21:9-10, 15, 17; 22:1, 6, 8-9). In a deliberate contrast to the idolatrous character of Babylon "the whore," this section centers on the new Jerusalem, "the bride," introduced in 21:2 (cf. 3:12) and already anticipated in 19:7, 9. The initial vision of "the holy city" (21:11-14) is supplemented by further details (vv. 15-17, 18-21) before its relation to God and the Lamb is described (21:22–22:5). As in 17:1–19:10, the vision closes with a scene in which the angelic mediator refuses to be worshiped by John (22:8-9).

Portrait of the City (21:9-21)

Jerusalem "the holy city" is to be distinguished from the earthly Jerusalem, called "the great city" in 11:8 and 16:19. Her features in 21:11-14 and 18-21 generally follow an ideal pattern inspired by eschatological descriptions of the city in Isa 54:11-12 (a general description of the foundation, walls, and gates), Ezekiel 48:30-35 (the square dimensions), and Tob 13:16-17 (jewels), traditions whose influence can be detected in a number of early Jewish writings (e.g., 11QTemple 30:4–45:12; Josephus *J.W.* 5.5.2-6 and *Ant.* 8.3.3; Eupolemus, in Eusebius *Praep. Evang.* 9.34.3-6; and the *New Jerusalem* fragments from Qumran — 1Q32; 2Q24; 4Q554–55; 5Q15; 11Q18; cf. Chyutin 1997; Fekkes 1993: 237-53). Further, some of the jewels of the twelve gates inscribed with the names of the twelve tribes (21:12b-13, 18-20) correspond to the twelve precious stones on the high priest's garments which likewise correspond to each of the twelve tribes (Exod 28:17-21; 39:10-14; Ezek 28:13 — the Adam figure of paradise). The number twelve, widespread in early Jewish tradition (tribes of Israel, the city's gates, stones decorating the wall), is further related by John to the number of angels (21:12 — identified as the twelve tribes of Israel), the apostles of the Lamb (v. 14 — associated with the twelve stones on the wall), the 12,000 stadia (v. 16 — length, width, height; the sum of all sides would be 144,000), and the length of the wall encompassing the city (v. 17 — 144,000 cubits, i.e., 12 × 12,000). The latter corresponds to the full number of martyred Christians envisioned in 7:1-8 and 14:1-5. The city is portrayed as a cube (21:16), a symbol of perfection; in the Jewish context, the shape would be reminiscent of the cubic dimensions of the holy of holies of the temple (cf. 1 Kgs 6:20), thus symbolizing the fullness of God's presence.

The setting for John's vision, "a great, high mountain" (21:10), is taken directly from Ezek 40:2. The same source accounts for the angelic tour of the city (21:9-10, 15; e.g., Ezek 40:1-2, 17, 24, 28, 32, 35; 41:1, 13; 42:1; 43:1; cf. Qumran *New Jerusalem* fragments mentioned above) and for the angel's measurements of the city's dimensions (21:15, 16, 17; e.g., Ezek 40:3, 7-9, 47; 41:1, 5, 13; cf. Zech 2:5-9; Qumran *New Jerusalem* fragments). The measuring serves as a means of describing the appearance of the city. The description is such that the new Jerusalem's superiority over Babylon is unmistakable (cf. 17:4-5; 18:16). In addition, the city represents an invitation. She not only looks attractive as a "bride" adorned for her husband, but her gates are also "open" because they do not need to protect against any outside threat (cf. 21:25, an allusion to Isa 60:11; Müller 1995: 359).

The City of God and the Lamb (21:22–22:5)

Against expectations raised by the imagery in 21:11-21, the new Jerusalem has no temple (v. 22). Nevertheless, John retains the idea through redefinition: the temple *is* "God the Almighty and the Lamb." The entire city is the innermost holy place (cf. v. 16), wherein the divine presence, unmediated, dwells among his people (cf. v. 3). In this light, the temple imagery used in the promise to those who conquer (3:12) and in the saints' heavenly worship (7:15) is no contradiction; the imagery signifies the completeness of God's presence to the faithful.

Beginning with 21:23, the section is framed by allusions to Isa 60:19: neither sun nor moon by day and night, "but *the LORD* will be your everlasting light, and *your God* will be your glory" (cf. Isa 60:1-2). Correspondingly, there shall be no night (21:25; 22:5; cf. Zech 14:7). In his reinterpretation of Isaiah, John has substituted "the Lord," which is parallel to "your God," with a reference to the Lamb (21:23; cf. v. 22); however, in 22:5, Isaiah's two designations are conflated: "the Lord God." Who, precisely, is referred to, God and/or the Lamb? The combined mention of God and the Lamb in 22:1, 3 in connection with the divine throne is elaborated through singular words (v. 3 — a verb; vv. 3-4 — four pronouns); this suggests John's concern to formulate his faith within a monotheistic framework (as in 11:15; 14:1; 20:6; however, see 6:16). If "the Lord God" ultimately refers to *both* God and the Lamb, who will be worshiped in the new Jerusalem (22:3), this reflects the extent to which for John a *Lamb* Christology has become a definitive way of talking about *God* in relation to his people.

The passage divides people into two groups. First, there are "the nations," those who "will walk" by the light of God and the Lamb and those who, together with "the kings of the earth," will bring their glory and honor to the new Jerusalem, whose gates are open to them (21:24-26; cf. Isa 60:3, 11). Mention of "the kings of the earth" is problematic since the same phrase refers to the allies of the beast which have been destroyed (19:19). Attempts to systematize these groups in Revelation might lead interpreters to suppose that the nations and kings, once worshipers of the beast, are now converted (e.g., Bauckham 1993: 313-17). It seems, however, that "the kings" is a linguistic carryover from Isaiah (60:3, 11); in this context, they would be antithetical to the "kings" in the visions concerning Babylon (17:2, 18; 18:3, 9-10). It may be that John regards them as the redeemed of the nations who participate in the new order (cf. 5:9; 7:9); they belong to those recorded in the Lamb's book of life (21:27b; cf. 3:5) and "will *reign* forever and ever" (22:5). By contrast, the second group is referred to in 21:27a. Since the new Jerusalem is "the holy city" (21:10), nothing "unclean" may defile it (Isa 35:8; 52:1; *1 Enoch* 10:20, 22; cf. 3:4-5; 17:5; 18:2); those who have practiced "abomination" (cf. 17:4; 21:8) and "falsehood" (cf. 2:2, 9, 20; 3:9; 21:8; 22:15) will be refused entry. John's mention of this group implies a warning to hearers of the vision.

The "river of the water of life" (22:1) depicts the city as paradise restored. As in Eden, there is a "tree of life," though here (unlike Gen 2:9; Ezek 47:7, 12) it is the only tree, *the* source for "healing of the nations." The text perhaps contains an allusion to the cross (cf. the comment under 2:7). The image of abundant and everlasting fruitfulness reflects Jewish expectation associated with eschatological bliss (e.g., *1 Enoch* 10:16-21; *2 Bar.* 29:5; 1Q23 fragments 1+6+22).

Two Sayings and the Angel's Refusal to Be Worshiped (22:6-9)

Following the vision, 22:6-9 form a parallel to 19:9-10: John's angel guide solemnly declares the trustworthiness and truth of "these words" (22:6; 19:9); a blessing is pronounced (22:7; 19:9); and the angel prevents John from worshiping him (22:8-9; 19:10). There are some important differences, however, which are appropriate to the conclusion of the large apocalyptic section of the book (4:1–22:5).

The angel's saying (22:6) reinforces the divine origin of "these words" by reflecting on the way in which they have been mediated. The visions come from "the Lord, the God of the spirits of the prophets," who has communicated what is about to happen to "his servants" through "his angel." The plural "prophets" and "servants" suggests that John perceives himself as part of a community of prophets which receives the visions (see under 1:1-3). The angel's function "to show" God's message to the prophets overlaps with that attributed to Christ, who mediates John's opening vision of heavenly worship (4:1).

Though not mentioned, Christ nevertheless remains an implicit part of the chain of mediation, here as the content of the message. "What must soon take place" prompts a saying in the first person by an unnamed speaker who is certainly to be identified as Christ (22:7; cf. vv. 12, 20). The event anticipated is the advent of Christ; hence the blessing is not pronounced by the angel (as in 19:9). Christ's coming spells reassurance and salvation for the faithful who "keep the words of the prophecy of this book" and, implicitly, judgment for those who do not (cf. 2:5, 16, 25; 3:3, 11).

22:8-9 repeat much of 19:10 (see the discussion under 19:9-10). Given the summary of the angel's function in 22:6, the tradition focuses more explicitly than 19:10 on the potential for misunderstanding the angel's mediatorial role (22:8 — John mentions "the angel, who showed me these things"). Whereas 19:10 makes clear that the angel is not superior to John's "brothers" (who are here identified as the prophets), 22:9 includes anyone who "keeps the words of this book." Whereas the former instance reinforces the credibility of John in his prophetic community, the latter has a parenetic force for the faithful in John's congregations: *they,* too, share the angel's status and therefore have no grounds for venerating him (cf. *Asc. Isa.* 8:3-5). Despite the angel's function in 21:9–22:5, the mediator of the vision is no substitute for the message of the vision through which the faithful experience proleptically the divine presence without mediation and worship God (see under 21:22–22:5).

Conclusion (22:10-21)

In inverted order to 1:4-8, Revelation closes with a collection of prophetic sayings attributed to the angel and Christ (22:10-20; cf. 1:7-8) and a brief epistolary closing (22:21; cf. 1:4-6). After the long section of visions, in which blessings, exhortations, and images sporadically allude to the situations addressed in the messages of the seven churches, the conclusion returns to language that reflects on the communicative significance of Revelation for John's hearers.

Prophetic Sayings (22:10-20)

22:10-11. Two sayings are united in their use of angelic sayings in Daniel 12. In contrast to Daniel (12:4), John is instructed *not* to keep secret "the words of the prophecy of this book." Daniel, as other Jewish apocalyptic literature, was attributed to a respected figure of the past; hence sealing up the content explains the passage of time between the fictive and the real author. John, however, was a contemporary to the hearers of his work; because "the time is near" there is an urgency about making his message available to the congregations (cf. 1:1, 19; 3:2, 10-11; 4:1; 22:6, 12, 20). The second saying depends on Dan 12:10. Despite the repeated summons to repent in the messages (2:5, 16, 22; 3:3, 19), the anticipated events are so close that for John the opportunity for change has virtually passed; all the more, *now* is the time to respond to his prophecy (22:14; cf. Sweet 1979: 316).

22:12-13. The words "I am coming soon" indicate that Christ is the speaker. At his coming Christ will hold people accountable for their deeds (cf., e.g., Jer 17:10; Rom 2:6; 1 Pet 1:17); as in 2:23, the emphasis is here on judgment (cf. Ps 28:4). Like God in 1:8 and 21:6, Christ identifies himself as "the Alpha and the Omega"; he is also "the first and the last" (cf. 1:17; 2:8), which is explained as "the beginning *(archē)* and the end" (see under 3:14).

22:14-15. As elsewhere (1:3; 14:13; 19:9; 22:7), the blessing functions as an exhortation to the hearers. It alludes to 2:7 (eating from the tree of life; cf. 22:2), 7:14 (washing clothes; cf. 3:4-5), and 21:25 (entry to the new Jerusalem through open gates; cf. Ps 118:19-20). The list of vices (cf. similarly 21:8, 27) characterizes those who fall "outside" the city, that is, those for whom the blessing does not apply. Some items in the list are reminiscent of caricatures applied to Babylon and parties threatening the congregations (fornicators: 2:14, 20-23; 17:1-2, 4; 18:3; sorcerers: 9:21; 18:23; 21:8; murderers: 17:5; 18:24; idolaters: 2:14, 20; cf. 13:15; and those who practice falsehood: 2:2, 9; 3:9; cf. 13:13-15; 16:13; 19:20; 20:10). The term "dogs" heads the list; as is possible in Jewish thought (e.g., Matt 7:6; 15:26; Phil 3:2; cf. Kraft 1974: 279-80), it is a label for defilement (cf. Deut 23:18 — "dogs" refers to cultic prostitution).

22:16. A saying reflects on the chain of mediation which begins with Christ (cf. 4:1; it begins with God in 1:1; 22:6), who authenticates the angel's witness. The "you" is plural and refers to John's prophetic community, which is entrusted with visions for the churches (esp. Aune 1989). Christ identifies himself as "the root and descendant of David," a messianic designation which goes back to Isa 11:1, 10 (see under 5:5). The added title "bright morning star" is promised to the faithful of Thyatira (see 2:28). It may be an allusion to the star associated with astral deities (i.e., Venus and cf. Isa 14:12); at the same time, the title has messianic overtones, especially if it alludes to Num 24:17, which was later interpreted in relation to an eschatological royal figure (e.g., in CD 7:18-20; 1QM 9:6-7; *T. Levi* 18:3; *T. Jud.* 24:1).

22:17. There are three invitations to "come," the first two of which are petitions addressed to Christ. For the faithful, Christ's advent is not a matter of dread but of eager longing (cf. v. 20b). The "one who hears" and the "one who thirsts" refer to intended recipients of Revelation (see, respectively, 1:3 and 21:6). The former refers to those who embrace what "the Spirit is saying to the churches" (2:7, 11, 17, 29; 3:6, 13, 22). For the latter, there is an invitation to "come"; those who respond seriously are promised "the water of life" (cf. 21:6; 22:1). The saying envisions a *rapprochement* between Christ and loyal believers (cf. v. 20).

22:18-19. The sayings close with a sharp warning by John against any attempt to alter the message of his prophecy. The address to "everyone who hears" indicates that the warning is directed at the recipients of the book among the congregations, not least at those who will read aloud its contents (cf. 1:3). Similar warnings are known from biblical writings (Deut 4:2; 13:1; Prov 30:6) and early Jewish literature (*Ep. Arist.* 310–11; *1 Enoch* 104:9-12; cf. van Unnik 1949: 1-36). Antithetical to the blessing upon the public reader in 1:3, the injunction takes the form of a twofold curse: those tampering with the book's content will be subject to the "plagues described in this book" and lose their portion in "the tree of life" (cf. 2:7) and "the holy city described in this book" (cf. 3:12). The warning not only underscores John's claim of authority for his prophecy but also betrays his concern that the congregations include persons and groups who will be opposed to his message (esp. 2:14-15, 20-23; cf. 2:2, 6; 3:3, 15-17).

22:20. The final saying, like v. 17a, focuses on the theme of Christ's coming. This is the last in a series of sayings attributed to Christ announcing his advent (cf. 2:5, 16, 25; 3:11; 22:7, 11). The words of Jesus are met with an antiphonal response which repeats the invitations in 22:17a. The petition is a translation into Greek of Aram. *maranatha* (in the NT, see 1 Cor 16:22), a prayer known to have been used in the Eucharist (cf. 1 Cor 11:26; esp. *Did.* 10:6).

Epistolary Closing (22:21)

The closing benediction resumes the letter framework with which the book is opened (1:4-6; cf. esp. 2 Thess 3:18; further 1 Cor 16:23; 2 Cor 13:13; Gal 6:18; Eph 6:24; etc.). The short formula focuses on "the Lord Jesus," recalling the third of the divine sources for the greetings in 1:4-5a. This focus assumes John's conviction that Christ alone, "the faithful witness" *par excellence* (1:5), is worthy to carry through the plan of God for his people in the world. Revelation is an appeal that the Christians of Asia Minor identify themselves with Christ as the Lamb and prepare for his coming to execute God's justice.

Bibliography. Allison, D. C. 1986, "*4Q403* fragm. 1, col. 1, 38-46 and the Revelation to John," *RevQ* 12:409-14 • Allison, D. C. 1988, "The Silence of Angels: Reflections on the Songs of the Sabbath Sacrifice," *RevQ* 13:189-97 • Aune, D. E. 1986, "The Apocalypse of John and the Problem of Genre," *Sem* 36:65-96 • Aune, D. E. 1989, "The Prophetic Circle of John of Patmos and the Exegesis of Revelation 22.16," *JSNT* 37:103-16 • Aune, D. E. 1990, "The Form and Function of the Proclamations to the Seven Churches (Revelation 2–3)," *NTS* 36:182-204 • Aune, D. E. 1997, *Revelation 1–5*, WBC, Dallas: Word • Bauckham, R. J. 1993, *The Climax of Prophecy: Studies on the Book of Revelation*, Edinburgh: T. & T. Clark • Beasley-Murray, G. E. 1978, *The Book of Revelation*, NCB, London: Marshall, Morgan & Scott • Beckwith, I. E. 1919, *The Apocalypse of John*, Grand Rapids: Eerdmans • Berger, K. 1974, "Apostelbrief und apostolische Rede. Zum Formular frühchristlicher Briefe," *ZNW* 65:190-231 • Bergmeier, R. 1985, "Die Buchrolle und das Lamm," *ZNW* 76:225-42 • Beyer, K. 1984, *Die aramäische Texte vom Toten Meer*, Göttingen: Vandenhoeck & Ruprecht • Boring, M. E. 1986, "The Theology of Revelation: 'The Lord Our God the Almighty Reigns,'" *Int* 40:257-69 • Boring, M. E. 1989, *Revelation*, IBC, Louisville: John Knox • Bousset, W. 1906, *Die Offenbarung Johannis*, Göttingen: Vandenhoeck & Ruprecht • Caird, G. B. 1966, *A Commentary on the Revelation of St. John the Divine*, BNTC, London: A. & C. Black • Carrell, P. R. 1997, *Jesus and the Angels: Angelology and the Christology of the Apocalypse of John*, SNTSMS, Cambridge: Cambridge University • Charles, R. H. 1920, *A Critical and Exegetical Commentary on the Revelation of St. John*, ICC, 2 vols., Edinburgh: T. & T. Clark • Charlesworth, J. H. 1986, "The Jewish Roots of Christology: The Discovery of the Hypostatic Voice," *SJT* 39:19-41 • Chyutin, M. 1997, *The New Jerusalem Scroll from Qumran: A Comprehensive Reconstruction*, JSPSS, Sheffield: Sheffield Academic • Collins, J. J. 1987, *The Apocalyptic Imagination: An Introduction to the Jewish Matrix of Christianity*, New York: Crossroad • Court, J. M. 1994, *Revelation*, NTG, Sheffield: Sheffield Academic • de Jonge, M. 1980, "The Use of the Expression *ho christos* in the Apocalypse of John," in J. Lambrecht, ed., *L'Apocalypse johannique et l'Apocalyptique dans le Nouveau Testament*, BETL, Gembloux/Leuven: Duculot/Leuven University, 267-81 • Donegani, I. 1997, *"A cause de la parole de Dieu et du témoignage de Jésus. . . ." Le* *témoignage selon l'Apocalypse de Jean,* Ebib, Paris: Gabalda • Dornseiff, F. 2d ed. 1925, *Das Alphabet in Mystik und Magie, Stoicheia* SGAW, Berlin/Leipzig: Teubner • Farrer, A. 1964, *The Revelation of St John the Divine,* Oxford: Clarendon • Fekkes, J. 1994, *Isaiah and Prophetic Traditions in the Book of Revelation,* JSNTSup, Sheffield: Sheffield Academic • Frey, J. 1993, "Erwägungen zum Verhältnis der Johannesapokalypse zu den übrigen Schriften des Corpus Johanneum," in M. Hengel, ed., *Die johanneische Frage. Ein Lösungsversuch mit einem Beitrag zur Apokalypse,* WUNT, Tübingen: J. C. B. Mohr (Paul Siebeck), 326-429 • Giblin, C. H. 1991, *The Book of Revelation,* GNS, Collegeville, Minn.: The Liturgical Press • Hahn, F. 1971, "Die Sendschreiben der Johannesapokalypse. Ein Beitrag zur Bestimmung prophetischer Redeformen," in G. Jeremias, H.-W. Kuhn, and H. Stegemann, eds., *Tradition und Glaube. Das frühe Christentum in seiner Umwelt,* Göttingen: Vandenhoeck & Ruprecht • Harrington, D. J. 1969, *Revelation,* SPS, Collegeville, Minn.: The Liturgical Press • Hemer, C. J. 1986, *The Letters to the Seven Churches of Asia in Their Local Setting,* JSNTSup, Sheffield: JSOT • Hengel, M. 1989, *The Johannine Question,* London: SCM • Holtz, T. 2d ed. 1971, *Die Christologie der Apokalypse des Johannes,* TU, Berlin: Akademie-Verlag • Holtz, T. 1980, "Gott in der Apokalypse," in J. Lambrecht, ed., *L'Apocalypse johannique et L'Apocalyptique dans le Nouveau Testament,* BETL, Gembloux/Leuven: Duculot/Leuven University • Hurtado, L. W. 1985, "Revelation 4–5 in the Light of Jewish Apocalyptic Analogies," *JSNT* 25:105-24 • Hurtado, L. W. 1988, *One God, One Lord,* Philadelphia: Fortress • Idel, M. 1988, *Kabbalah: New Perspectives,* London/New Haven: Yale University, Press • Jones, D. L. 1980, "Christianity and the Roman Imperial Cult," in W. Haase, ed., *ANRW* 23/2, Berlin/New York: Walter de Gruyter, 1023-54 • Jörns, K.-P. 1971, *Das hymnische Evangelium,* SNT, Gütersloh: Gerd Mohn • Karrer, M. 1986, *Die Johannesoffenbarung als Brief,* FRLANT, Göttingen: Vandenhoeck & Ruprecht • Kiddle, M., and M. K. Ross. 1940, *The Revelation of St. John,* MNTC, London: Hodder & Stoughton • Kraft, H. 1974, *Die Offenbarung des Johannes,* HNT, Tübingen: J. C. B. Mohr (Paul Siebeck) • Kraybill, J. N. 1996, *Imperial Cult and Commerce in John's Apocalypse,* JSNTSup, Sheffield: Sheffield Academic • Lambrecht, J. 1980, "A Structuration of Revelation 4,1–22,5," in J. Lambrecht, ed., *L'Apocalypse johannique et l'Apocalyptique dans le Nouveau Testament,* BETL, Gembloux/Leuven: Duculot/Leuven University, 77-104 • Lohmeyer, E. 1953, *Die Offenbarung des Johannes,* Tübingen: J. C. B. Mohr (Paul Siebeck) • Lohse, E. 1993, *Die Offenbarung des Johannes,* NTD, Göttingen: Vandenhoeck & Ruprecht • Magie, D. 1950, *Roman Rule in Asia Minor,* 2 vols., Princeton: Princeton University • Mazzaferri, F. D. 1989, *The Genre of the Book of Revelation from a Source-Critical Perspective,* BZNW, Berlin/New York: Walter de Gruyter • Mealy, J. W. 1992, *After the Thousand Years: Resurrection and Judgment in Revelation 20,* JSNTSup, Sheffield: Sheffield Academic • Mounce, R. H. 1977, *The Book of Revelation,* NICNT, Grand Rapids: Eerdmans • Müller, U. B. 2d ed. 1995, *Die Offenbarung des Johannes,* ÖTKNT, Gütersloh: Echter Verlag • Prigent, P. 1988, *L'Apocalypse de Saint Jean,* CNT, Lausanne: Delachaux & Niestlé • Räisänen, H. 1992, "The Nicolaitans: Apoc. 2; Acta 6," in W. Haase, ed., *ANRW* 2.26.2, 1604-44 • Ramsey, W. 1904 (repr. 1963), *The Letters to the Seven Churches of Asia,* London: Hodder & Stoughton • Rissi, M. 2d ed. 1965, *Was ist und was geschehen soll danach. Die Zeit- und Geschichtsauffassung der Offenbarung des Johannes,* ATANT, Zürich: Zwingli • Robinson, J. A. T., *Redating the New Testament,* Philadelphia: Fortress • Roloff, J. 1984, *Die Offenbarung des Johannes,* ZBKNT, Zürich: Theologischer Verlag • Rowland, C. 1979, "The Visions of God in Apocalyptic Literature," *JSJ* 10:137-54 • Rowland, C. 1980, "The Vision of the Risen Christ in Rev. I.13ff.: The Debt of an Early Christology to an Aspect of Jewish Angelology," *JTS* 31:1-11 • Rowland, C. 1982, *The Open Heaven: A Study of Apocalyptic in Judaism and Early Christianity,* London: SPCK • Ruiz, J.-P. 1989, *Ezekiel in the Apocalypse: The Transformation of Prophetic Language in Revelation 16,17–19,10,* Frankfurt/Bern/New York/Paris: Peter Lang • Satake, A. 1966, *Die Gemeindeordnung in der Johannesapokalypse,* WMANT, Neukirchen-Vluyn: Neukirchener • Schüssler Fiorenza, E. 1977, "The Quest for the Johannine School: The Apocalypse and the Fourth Gospel," *NTS* 23:402-27 • Schüssler Fiorenza, E. 1985, *The Book of Revelation: Justice and Judgment,* Philadelphia: Fortress • Sordi, M. 1986, *The Christians of the Roman Empire,* Norman/London: University of Oklahoma • Stuckenbruck, L. T. 1994, "An Angelic Refusal of Worship: The Tradition and Its Function in the Apocalypse of John," ed. E. Lovelace, SBLSP, Atlanta: Scholars, 679-96 • Stuckenbruck, L. T. 1995a, *Angel Veneration and Christology: A Study in Early Judaism and in the Christology of the Apocalypse of John,* WUNT II, Tübingen: J. C. B. Mohr (Paul Siebeck) • Stuckenbruck, L. T. 1995b, "'One like a Son of Man as the Ancient of Days' in the Old Greek Recension of Daniel 7,13: Scribal Error or Theological Translation?" *ZNW* 86:268-76 • Sweet, J. P. M. 1979, *Revelation,* TPINTC, Philadelphia: Trinity Press International • Theissen, G. 1982, *The Social Setting of Pauline Christianity,* Philadelphia: Fortress • Thompson, L. L. 1990, *The Book of Revelation: Apocalypse and Empire,* New York/Oxford: Oxford University • Trites, A. A. 1973, "*Martus* and Martyrdom in the Apocalypse: A Semantic Study," *NovT* 15:72-80 • Trites, A. A. 1977, *The New Testament Concept of Witness,* SNTSMS, Cambridge: Cambridge University • VanderKam, J. C. 1986, "The Prophetic-Sapiential Origins of Apocalyptic Thought," in J. D. Martin and P. R. Davies, eds., *A Word in Season: Essays in Honour of William McKane,* JSOTSup, Sheffield: JSOT, 63-76 • Vassiliades, P. 1985, "The Translation of MARTYRIA IESOU in Revelation," *BT* 36:129-34 • Wikenhauser, A. 3d ed. 1959, *Die Offenbarung des Johannes,* RNT, Regensburg: Pustet • Yarbro Collins, A. 1976, *The Combat Myth in the Book of Revelation,* HDR, Missoula: Scholars • Yarbro Collins, A. 1977, "The History-of-Religions Approach to Apocalypticism and the 'Angel of the Waters' (Apoc. 16:4-7)," *CBQ* 39:367-81 • Yarbro Collins, A. 1979, *The Apocalypse,* NTM, Wilmington: Glazier • Yarbro Collins, A. 1984, *Crisis and Catharsis: The Power of the Apocalypse,* Philadelphia: Westminster • Yarbro Collins, A. 1992, "The 'Son of Man' Tradition and the Book of Revelation," in J. H. Charlesworth, ed., *The Messiah: Developments in Earliest Judaism and Christianity,* Minneapolis: Fortress, 536-68.

The New Testament Apocrypha

Robert E. Van Voorst

The "New Testament Apocrypha" is a large body of approximately ninety extra–NT Christian writings from the end of the first century to the ninth. Many scholars now prefer the term "Early Christian Apocrypha" because most of these writings are only remotely related to the NT, and many of them were written before the NT canon was finalized; here we keep to the traditional term. These writings claim to have been written by the apostles or those close to them. A few, like the *Gospel of Peter,* were used in some mainstream Christian churches at first. Over time the Great Church rejected their canonicity, and these writings then became "apocryphal," or hidden. Unlike the OT Apocrypha, which many Christians accept as canonical, the NT Apocrypha is today universally rejected as a valid part of the canonical NT. The NT Apocrypha has been organized according to the NT genres that it contains: gospels, acts, letters, and apocalypses, but it has considerably more blending of genres than in the NT. The scholarly study of the NT Apocrypha is in an intermediate stage and still draws predominantly on the historical-critical method. Recently, the discovery of the Nag Hammadi literature has breathed new life into this study. The NT Apocrypha forms a main witness to Christian views of Jesus, approved and disapproved by the early mainstream church, in the formative centuries of the faith. In this article we will focus on the relationship of the NT Apocrypha to the NT itself.

We begin with a sketch of the main NT apocryphal genres. Among the gospels of the NT Apocrypha, some non-gnostic or semi-gnostic gospels feature the putative teachings of Jesus, as well as narratives about his birth, childhood, passion, descent into hell, and resurrection. These narratives often delve into areas passed over in the canonical Gospels. The gnostic gospels found at Nag Hammadi, many of which are apocryphal, are predominantly composed of secret teachings of the risen Jesus, revealed to his disciples to bring salvation by this special knowledge *(gnōsis).* Fragments of Jewish-Christian gospels are also included in the NT Apocrypha. The apocalypses of the NT Apocrypha feature visions and revelations, especially of the resurrected Jesus to his disciples. Letters such as Paul's *Epistle to the Laodiceans* and the third *Epistle to the Corinthians* continue the Pauline tradition, interpreting and applying the Pauline tradition to a new age and situation. Finally, the acts genre contains some notable works such as the *Acts of Paul and Thecla* and the *Acts of Peter, John, Andrew, Philip,* and *Thomas.* As the name of this genre implies, these works present narratives about the lives and ministries of the apostles, from when they received their apostolic calling from Jesus, continuing with their ministries, and often concluding with their martyrdoms.

Although this literature is so disparate that making generalizations about it is difficult, we can hazard a description of its general qualities. First, the NT Apocrypha is, on the whole, a mixture of orthodoxy and heterodoxy. This is important to realize because the predominant stance of the Great Church has been that these works are heretical. Second, much of the NT Apocrypha is, or at least presents itself as, an effort to "fill in the gaps" of the NT: the untreated years of Jesus' life, the background of Joseph and especially the Virgin Mary, the ministry of the apostles (most of which is ignored by the Acts of the Apostles), and so on. Third, the more orthodox literature in the NT Apocrypha shows traces of popular Christianity, in both style and content. For example, one sees legendary touches of folk religion in the treatment of Jesus' life and the apostles' ministry: punitive miracles by the boy Jesus against his playmates, talking animals, and talking crosses. Fourth, much of the NT Apocrypha centers on the apostles. In the documents that can be dated to the third century, the era of the great persecutions, the martyrdom of the apostles is stressed; in the fourth century and later, the treatment of the apostles is notably hagiographic. Finally, the NT Apocrypha is an important but long-neglected source for our knowledge of Christianity from the second century through the end of antiquity, especially of gnosticizing Christianity and folk Christianity. In what follows in this essay, we will treat two NT apocryphal works that figure largely in current NT study, the *Gospel of Thomas* and the *Gospel of Peter.*

The Gospel of Thomas

Our knowledge of the NT Apocrypha in general and gnosticism in particular has been revolutionized by the discovery in 1945 of the Nag Hammadi library. Moreover, this discovery has, to a significant extent, sparked debates about earliest Christianity. Now scholars can read what gnostics had to say for themselves about their view of Jesus and their form of Christianity, and need not depend on the limited and polemical witness about them from leaders in the Great Church. Although the gnostics themselves called most of their writings "gospels," and composed them to some extent as counterpoints to the Gospels of their opponents in the Great Church, these gospels are remarkably nonnarrative. Most fit even more closely than Q, the sayings source of Matthew and Luke, to the genre of a pure "sayings gospel." Their purpose is to convey the secret knowledge *(gnōsis)* of the risen

Christ, not to narrate the life and death of Jesus and place his teaching in that narrative context. When gnostics placed their teachings in the mouth of Jesus, it was the *risen* Jesus who spoke them, even those sayings that are attested in other gospel traditions as belonging to the *earthly* Jesus. In the NT canonical Gospels, almost all of Jesus' gospel teaching is set before his death and resurrection. Some recent scholarship has argued that the gospel tradition that culminated in the canonical Gospels had a tendency to place certain forms of the risen Christ's words given through prophets back into the earthly life of Jesus — the opposite of the gnostic tendency. For the most part, gnostics saw salvation as outside of history, so one looks in vain for any narratives, whether of Jesus' life, passion, or resurrection, in the surviving gnostic gospels. No Nag Hammadi document has proven more important for NT study, in research into both the historical Jesus and earliest Christianity, than the *Gospel of Thomas.* Indeed, probably as much scholarship in the last twenty-five years has gone into *Thomas* as into almost the entire remainder of the NT Apocrypha, and some scholars have taken to calling *Thomas* the "Fifth Gospel."

Cited occasionally by Hippolytus and Origen, the long-lost *Gospel of Thomas* was found in full among the Nag Hammadi documents. Written in Coptic, its subscription (title placed at the end) reads "The Gospel of Thomas." It begins (without a title), "These are the secret sayings which the living Jesus spoke and which Didymus Judas Thomas wrote down." This document contains, by modern scholarly division, 114 sayings of Jesus. Its sayings come in several forms: proverbs and other wisdom sayings, parables, prophetic sayings, and very brief "dialogues." About a quarter of these sayings, typically the shortest, are virtually identical to Synoptic sayings. Another one half have parallels in the canonical Gospels, in different forms or making a different point. The final approximate one quarter to one third is manifestly gnostic sayings with a different theological outlook than the rest. The sayings are organized most often by catch-words. Thomas has no christological titles, no narrative material, and no reference within its sayings to any action of Jesus or any event in his life. It is dated after 70 and before c. 140, the date archeologists have determined for its papyri. Within this range further precision is difficult, although a consensus of interpreters place its writing in the second century, understanding that many of its oral traditions are much older. Most place its composition in Syria, where traditions about Thomas, the fictional author of this book, were strong. It also shows a Jewish-Christian origin in Saying 13 with its praise of James the brother of Jesus, but it has since moved beyond this into Gentile Christianity (Saying 53 spiritualizing circumcision). Of all the extracanonical gospels, Thomas is the one most likely to have a claim to preserve a significant number of authentic sayings of Jesus.

The argument for the independence, and hence the value, of Thomas's traditions of Jesus sayings is based on three main factors. The first is genre. A collection of sayings, Thomas is in the genre in which the early Jesus material was collected and passed down, especially in Q. No collections of sayings in a similar genre are to be found later than about 150, as this genre seems to be taken into the "dialogue." So it is possible that, to judge by genre before questions of content are examined, Thomas's roots are in an early collection, most certainly in the first century. The second argument is the order of the sayings. The sayings in Thomas are completely independent of the order of the Synoptic Gospels. Occasionally Thomas and Luke agree in order against Mark, but this fact probably does not show Thomas's use of Luke; it can be explained as a variant of the Q tradition common to Luke and Thomas. Thomas's order is due to its catchword composition (typical of oral tradition and wisdom literature), completely nonnarrative structure, and other factors. The differing order makes it unlikely that Thomas was literarily dependent on the Synoptics. Third, a history-of-traditions argument states that Thomas often gives the sayings of Jesus in an earlier form than that found in the Synoptics. For example, the parables of Jesus are far less allegorized than the forms in the Synoptics, as in Saying 65, the parable of the wicked husbandman. Thomas's form is simpler and shorter than the Synoptic form (Mark 12:1-12 par.), is free of allusions to the OT (Isa 5:1-2), and shows no trace of allegory. Thus, it is arguably closer to the earliest probable form of the parable as given by Jesus.

The treatment of the sayings of Jesus in the *Gospel of Thomas* is governed by its theological aims, as are the NT canonical Gospels. Although most of the gospel books found at Nag Hammadi are fully gnostic, *Thomas* can be characterized as "semi-gnostic," that is, on the way to gnosticism but not fully there (Sayings 18, 29, 83-84). Not yet present are the formal gnostic cosmology and mythology, which will be present in later gnostic works. The short narrative contexts of a few sayings (22, 60, 100) show that *Thomas* does not have an exclusively post-resurrectional setting, as almost all other gnostic gospels do. Jesus is a revealer of secret teaching who brings salvation by his teaching alone. As the first saying of *Thomas* relates, "Anyone who finds the interpretation of these words will not taste death." The world and the human body are unqualifiedly and irredeemably evil (27, 111); femaleness is equated with fallenness, and "every woman who makes herself male will enter the kingdom of God" (114). All eschatology is "realized"; the kingdom of God is beyond time and place, and people enter it by self-knowledge (3, 49, 50, and 113). Discipleship is an individual, not a community matter; "you" in the *Gospel of Thomas* is typically singular, while in the Synoptics it is typically plural. The individual must itinerate through this life by rejecting all ties to possessions, family, sex, and religious practices like fasting, formal prayer, and circumcision (6, 14, 42, 53, 60, 89, 99, 101, and 104).

The Gospel of Peter

In 1886 a French archeological team excavating the cemetery of an ancient Pachomian monastery about fifty miles south of Cairo found a small book in a monk's grave. Pages two through ten of this book, which was dated to the seventh to ninth centuries, contain an account of the death and resurrection of Jesus that scholars soon concluded was part of the *Gospel of Peter* mentioned by early church fathers from the beginning of the third century. Scholarship at first paid close attention to the *Gospel of Peter,* but when the consensus developed that it was a popularizing and docetic adaptation of the canonical Gospels, especially Matthew, disinterest soon enveloped it. In the last few years, scholars have renewed their interest in this book. Helmut Koester and John Dominic Crossan have stirred this interest by claiming that a source of the passion narrative of the *Gospel of Peter* is also a source of the passion narratives of the canonical Gospels.

Recent study has seen the *Gospel of Peter* equally at home in the Great Church as in docetism. The *Gospel of Peter* does indeed share several characteristics of Great-Church literature of this time. It popularizes the gospel traditions with which it works; this popularizing can be seen in both style (e.g., its somewhat crude parataxis) and content. This gospel emphasizes the miraculous beyond that of the canonical Gospel traditions, making miracles into seemingly incontrovertible proofs of the faith. It has some strong connections (either oral or written) with the canonical Gospels. Like the *Acts of Pilate,* the other main passion narrative of the Great Church at this time, it has a strong anti-Jewish polemic. This may be connected with its popular origins in places where anti-Judaism probably was stronger than in official circles. Finally, the *Gospel of Peter* has a pronounced mainstream devotional element, especially seen in its consistent use of "the Lord" rather than "Jesus" or "the Savior."

However, the *Gospel of Peter* can also be read as at least incipiently gnostic and have an appeal to gnostic Christians. The phrase "as having no pain" (4:10), which could equally be understood as "as if having no pain," would appeal to gnostic Christians who downplayed or denied the suffering of Christ. The cry of dereliction, "My power, O power, you have forsaken me" (5:19), would also appeal to gnostics who held that the divine element of Jesus left him shortly before the crucifixion. That the *Gospel of Peter* could appeal to, and be used by, both orthodox and gnostic Christians in the second century should not surprise us — after all, both groups also used the Gospel of John and the letters of Paul.

The most controversial issue in current scholarship on the *Gospel of Peter* is its place in early Christian tradition. Is a source of the passion narrative of the *Gospel of Peter* also a source of the passion narratives of the Synoptic Gospels, especially Mark? Helmut Koester and John Dominic Crossan have been in the lead of those who have strongly argued for such a position. Here I offer one rather general comment on the current state of the question. Those who advocate such a source-critical position must do a much more careful job of establishing their hypotheses and defending it against criticism, which is ongoing. For example, Crossan's major statement of his hypothesis, in his *The Cross That Spoke,* features no sustained, detailed display of his source-critical efforts. Unless and until those who promote such a source hypothesis for the *Gospel of Peter* match the source-critical scope, detail, and precision of those who oppose it, this fascinating hypothesis will continue to hold a minority position. Because the passion narrative of the *Gospel of Peter* fits well in the second century, and because the argument against a precanonical source is much stronger than the argument in its favor, we must conclude for now that it does not find its source in a precanonical passion narrative.

We now must draw together the threads of this essay. First, is the source of the *Gospel of Peter* in turn a source for the canonical Gospels? This, while possible, is highly unlikely, and the consensus of current scholarship strongly inclines against it. Second, the *Gospel of Thomas* belongs in its final form among second-century gnosticizing Christians. This gnosticizing theological tendency is the context for its presentation of the sayings of Jesus. Many of its individual sayings have properly been held important in the quest for the historical Jesus. But as to the argument that the genre of *Thomas* is strong evidence to support making Jesus a sage only, even Q as a whole tends to counter this. With its John the Baptizer material, its clear references to the miracles of Jesus and narration of one miracle, and its stronger references to the death and coming of Jesus, Q distinguishes itself from *Thomas.* Despite the difference in genre and the different attitude to miracles in Q and Mark, Q is arguably closer in outlook to Mark than to *Thomas.* Third, does any historical value for our understanding of Jesus arise in the NT Apocrypha of the second and third centuries? Put another way, does this literature offer new perspectives on Jesus or tell us anything we do not already know about him with some confidence from the canonical Gospels? On the whole, probably not, although many individual pieces of data do emerge. The primary historical value of these documents is rooted in their own time and space. The same is true, of course, of the canonical Gospels, but they stand much closer to the events and were probably subject to criticism and correction by people who stood near these events. Therefore, they are of greater value in understanding the historical Jesus and the first-century church. Nevertheless, we can expect scholarly inquiry — with its characteristically sharp debate — to continue.

The NT Apocrypha gives us a rich perspective on the diversity of Christianity in the second and third centuries. It shows some variety within gnosticism on the value of the death of Jesus, the depth of popularizing tendencies in the Great Church, and the distinctive witness of Jewish Christianity. At some points it offers us some valuable information on Jesus and earliest Christianity. Despite controversial proposals that reconstruct Jesus and earliest Christianity on the basis of second-century documents, actual and hypothetical, recent scholarship in general sees the value of second- and third-century NT apocryphal works as that of being primarily witnesses to their own time. Their relationship to the NT, although an important and enduring question, is now given less attention, while their role in reconstructing the religious and social history of second- and third-century Christianity is given much more attention. In sum, to call this body of literature "Early Christian Apocrypha" is fitting after all.

Bibliography. Charlesworth, J. H. ed. 1987, *The New Testament Apocrypha and Pseudepigrapha,* Chicago: Scarecrow • Franzmann, M. 1996, *Jesus in the Nag Hammadi Writings,* Edinburgh: T. & T. Clark • Hennecke, E., and W. Schneemelcher. 2nd ed. 1991-92, *New Testament Apocrypha,* Louisville: Westminster John Knox • Meyer, M., ed. 3d ed. 1988, *The Nag Hammadi Library,* San Francisco: Harper • Tuckett, C. 1986, *Nag Hammadi and the Gospel Tradition,* Edinburgh: Clark • Van Voorst, R. 2000, *Jesus Outside the New Testament: An Introduction to the Ancient Evidence,* Grand Rapids: Eerdmans.

The Dead Sea Scrolls and the New Testament

Daniel C. Harlow

Almost immediately upon their discovery in 1947-1956, the Dead Sea Scrolls (DSS) drew the excited attention of students of the New Testament (NT). Here for the first time scholars were granted access to Jewish texts in Hebrew and Aramaic from Palestine, some of them perhaps written or copied in the time of Jesus and the early days of the movement he inspired. The Scrolls date from roughly the second century BC to AD 68. The community of Essenes who copied and composed them at Qumran thus overlapped with the early Jesus movement for a period extending about four decades. Most of the DSS, though, are pre-Christian, and all of them are non-Christian. Despite the idiosyncratic claims of a few scholars who ignore the dating of the DSS established by paleography and chemical analysis, no NT figures are mentioned or alluded to in the Scrolls. Still, the DSS have shed welcome light on the Jewish matrix of Christian origins by providing parallels to the NT in terminology, conceptuality, literary genres, biblical interpretive methods, religious practices, and theological beliefs. Together these parallels help to fill out the Palestinian Jewish context in which earliest Christianity emerged and to clarify certain passages in the Christian scriptures.

New Testament Papyri among the Dead Sea Scrolls?

In recent decades an alleged direct connection between the DSS and the NT has made headlines. In 1972 the Spanish Jesuit scholar Jose O'Callaghan hit NT scholars with the news that he had identified several Greek papyrus fragments of various NT writings among the remains of Qumran Cave 7, including portions of Mark, Acts, Romans, 1 Timothy, James, and 2 Peter. The best candidate among these fragments is 7Q5, which O'Callaghan identifies as a fragment of Mark 6:52-54 and dates to 50 BC–AD 50. If O'Callaghan were right, the presence of NT fragments in the caves near Qumran would require a radical redating of several NT writings; they would have to have been written decades earlier than most scholars think. It would also call for a major reassessment of the relationship between the Qumran Essenes and the early Christians. O'Callaghan has succeeded in convincing very few, but his cause continues to be championed. The identification of 7Q5 as a fragment of Mark is problematic for several reasons. To begin with, the scrap of papyrus is very small and preserves only a few lines of writing, with only one complete word — και, "and." Further, the date O'Callaghan assigns to the fragment is suspect. What is more, he has to contract one line of the text by omitting the words επι την γην ("to the land") in order for his reconstruction to work; the result is an otherwise unattested textual variant. Several rival transcriptions of the fragment call into question the viability of identifying the fragment with any certainty.

John the Baptist a Former Qumran Essene?

Another questionable connection between the DSS and the NT centers on John the Baptist. Even before the discovery of the Scrolls, some scholars speculated that John may have been a former Essene. Today a few maintain that John the Baptist may have lived at Qumran for a time and possibly even have grown up there. A few intriguing factors have hinted at a possible association. John was the son of elderly parents and had a priestly lineage (Luke 1:7, 18). These biographical facts are noteworthy when one recalls that according to Josephus the Essenes, a priestly group, adopted orphans (*J.W.* 2.120). According to the Gospels, John baptized in the Judean wilderness at the Jordan in an area that may have been close to Qumran. John's turn-or-burn apocalyptic preaching is compatible with Essene theology, and his baptizing ministry may have developed out of the sort of ritual immersion practiced at Qumran. Further, the Gospels apply to John Isa 40:3, a text that the Qumran covenanters applied to themselves and their move to "prepare the way of the Lord in the desert." Despite these factors, most scholars are more impressed with the differences than the alleged similarities. The suggestion that John was orphaned and then adopted is pure speculation. The site of his baptizing ministry may have been miles from Qumran in the area around the lower Jordan, not on the western shores of the Dead Sea where the Qumran Essenes lived. His rite of immersion seems to have been a one-time act performed by him on penitents who were expected to return to their normal lives, whereas immersion at Qumran was a daily, self-administered rite undertaken by members before they participated in the sacred meals of their closed community. John rejected cultivated foods like bread and wine, which the Qumran Essenes ate as staples of their diet, and he wore a camel-hair sackcloth, not the white garments of the Essenes. Finally, Isa 40:3 is appropriated rather differently in the Gospels and in the Scrolls (1QS

8:12-16). The Gospels, following the LXX, read the verse so that the words "the voice of one crying in the wilderness" go together (contrast MT: "The voice of one crying: 'In the wilderness . . .'"), and they identify John with the one crying. 1QS interprets the "way of the Lord" as the group's study of the Torah "in the desert," that is, "at Qumran."

Terms and Concepts

More secure parallels between the DSS and the NT are found in terms and concepts used by NT authors that appear in the Scrolls in their Hebrew forms. The parallels in terminology and conceptuality may not be surprising, but they are welcome nonetheless and help to uncover further the Jewish foundation of earliest Christianity. To begin with, both the Essenes of Qumran and the early Christians referred to themselves as members of "the Way" (Acts 9:2; 19:9, 23; 22:4; 24:14, 22; cf., e.g., 1QS 9:17-18; CD 1:13). The expression "(the) many/majority" (*tōn pleionōn* in 2 Cor 2:6; cf. *pollōn* in Mark 14:24 par. Matt 26:28) to designate the community or congregation appears as *ha-rabbim* several times in the community rules 1QS and CD. The word *ha-mebaqqer,* "guardian, overseer," a title found in the sectarian rule books (e.g., 1QS 6:13; CD 13:5-7; 15:5-6, 10-11), may be the Hebrew equivalent of *episkopos,* "bishop, overseer," in the NT (Acts 20:28; Phil 1:1; 1 Tim 3:2; Titus 1:7). The phrase "poor in spirit" (Matt 5:3) surfaces in 1QM 14:7 and 1QH 14:3, and the antithetical formulation "You have heard it said . . . but I say to you" in the Sermon on the Mount (Matt 5:21-48) resembles the rhetorical structure "you know . . . but we think/say" now found in 4QMMT. Furthermore, not a few expressions familiar from the letters of Paul have parallels in the Scrolls. Among them are "the righteousness of God" (Rom 1:17; 3:5, 21, 22; 10:3; 2 Cor 5:21; 1QM 14:6; 1QS 10:25; 11:12), "just judgment" (Rom 2:5-6; 1QH 1:23, 30), "spirit of holiness" (Rom 1:4; 1QS 4:21; 8:16; 9:3; CD 2:12; 1QH 7:6-7; 9:32), "sinful flesh" (Rom 8:3; 1QS 11:9; cf. 1QM 4:3), and "mystery" in the sense of divine secret (Rom 16:25; 1 Cor 2:7; 1QpHab 7:5).

"Righteousness" and "Faith"

Paul's theology of justification by grace through faith (e.g., Rom 3:21-31) is anticipated in some respects in the Scrolls. The Qumran *Rule of the Community* and *Thanksgiving Hymns* contain passages that resonate with Pauline teaching on the subject and share some of the same terminology:

> As for me, my judgment *(mishpat)* is with God. In his hand are the perfection of my way and the uprightness of my heart. He will wipe out my transgressions through his righteous acts *(beṣidqōtō)*. . . . For humankind cannot make its own way, and humanity is unable to order its steps, since to God belongs their judgment and in his hand is perfection of way. As for me, if I stagger, the mercies of God will be my salvation. If I stumble because of a sin of flesh, my judgment will be by the righteousness of God *(beṣidqat 'el)* that endures forever. . . . He will draw me near by his grace, and by His mercy will he bring my judgment. He will judge me in the righteousness of his truth, and in the greatness of his goodness he will pardon all my sins. (1QS 11:2-3, 12-14; cf. 1QH 12 [formerly col. 4]: 30-38)

Three ideas here resemble theological emphases in Paul's letters: the utter sinfulness of humanity, the provision of God's saving righteousness, and the grounding of God's judgment in mercy and grace. Of course, the Scrolls lack the distinctively Christian focus on faith in Christ as the means whereby God's saving grace works its way into the lives of believers.

The concept of faith as such has featured in discussion of the exegesis of a particular OT verse in Paul and the DSS. According to Hab 2:4b, "The righteous will live by their faith [or: faithfulness, *'emunah*]." In Galatians and Romans, Paul applies the verse to those who have faith in Christ: "The one who is righteous will live by faith" or "The one who is righteous by faith will live" (Rom 1:17; cf. Gal 3:11). The *Habakkuk Commentary* from Qumran quotes the same scriptural verse and comments on it in this way: "Interpreted, this concerns all those who observe the Torah in the house of Judah, whom God will free from the house of judgment on account of their suffering [or: their toil/work, *'amlam*] and their faith in [or: their fidelity, loyalty to: *'emunatam*] the Teacher of Righteousness" (1QpHab 8:1-3). Paul clearly understands Jesus as the object of faith, by virtue of what Christ accomplished in his saving death and resurrection. Yet for Paul faith is not some static, intellectual assent to what Christ has done but a dynamic, relational commitment to him that involves faithfulness, loyalty, or fidelity to one who himself showed his faithfulness, loyalty, or fidelity to God. Understood as loyalty or fidelity, the faith of believers in Christ may not be that much different from the Qumran sectarians' faith in the Teacher of Righteousness, insofar as both involve commitment. Two differences are notable, though. First, the Qumran text applies the Habakkuk verse to the sectarians' Torah observance, which may also be the referent of *'amlam* understood as "their observance"; this strikes a decidedly different note than Paul's emphasis on faith apart from Torah observance. Second, the Teacher of Righteousness does not seem to have been for the Essenes the sort of object of faith that Jesus was for his followers. However much they revered the Teacher, the Jews at Qumran did not attribute any saving significance to his death or see themselves as mystically united to him. The DSS therefore speak not so much of faith in the person of the Teacher of Righteousness as of faith in or fidelity to the path he had marked out for them and to the divinely revealed approach to Scripture that he had mediated to them.

"Works of the Law"

One of the most important verbal parallels provided by the Scrolls is the expression "works of the Law." Paul uses the phrase (in Greek, *ergōn nomou*) in Rom 3:20, 28;

Gal 2:16 (3x); 3:2, 10. It occurs nowhere in the Hebrew Bible or rabbinic literature, and before the discovery of the Scrolls it was considered a Pauline neologism. Now it is found in the *Florilegium* (4Q174 1-2 i 7; cf. 1QS 5:21; 6:18 for the formulation "his observances in the Law") and, most revealingly, in the halakhic document 4QMMT C 29. The abbreviation for this writing is an acronym derived from its use of the expression מקצת מעשי התורה/*miqṣat ma'aśe hattorah,* "some of the works of the Law." This document appears to be a manifesto of the Essenes or their progenitors before they left Jerusalem and before they or an offshoot of them moved to Qumran. It contains a calendar, which or may not be original to the document; a list of more than twenty legal issues on which they and their opponents disagree; and an exhortation to a person ("you") whom they try to win over to their position. Three parties are thus in view, a "we" party, a "you" [singular] party, and a "they" party. 4QMMT has been called a letter written by the Teacher of Righteousness to the Wicked Priest. Yet the document does not have the form of a letter, and the precise identity of both the senders and the recipient is unclear, although the addressee may well have been the current high priest, perhaps even the one who would become the sect's principal opponent, the so-called "Wicked Priest." Among the halakhic positions at issue in the second section of 4QMMT are matters of ritual purity, offerings brought into the temple, priestly gifts, forbidden marriages, and prohibitions on certain types of people (e.g., the blind and the deaf) entering the temple. Significantly, in both 4QMMT and Paul the expression "works of the Law" refers to matters of Jewish ritual observance. The halakhic document has therefore helped confirm what the context of Paul's usage of the phase already makes clear enough: when Paul wrote that human beings are "justified (made righteous) by faith and not from 'works of the Law,'" he was not accusing Judaism of teaching that good works earn a person's salvation. Rather, he was insisting that to be a member of God's end-time covenant people, one does not have to follow the ritual commandments of the Torah. The "works of the Law" that Paul had in mind were the ethnic boundary markers of sabbath, circumcision, and food that separated Jews as God's covenant people from Gentiles. Thus the phrase in 4QMMT and Paul is identical and deals with the same general issue — ritual observance — whereas the rhetorical function of the terminology and the precise Torah observances in view differ in each context.

Literary Forms

Beyond parallels in terminology and conceptuality, the DSS contain some of the same literary genres ensconced in the NT. *Lists of virtues and vices* are a ubiquitous feature in Greco-Roman moral philosophy and in both Jewish and Christian ethical teaching, so there has been no lack of parallels to the many such lists in the NT (e.g., Rom 1:29-31; Gal 5:16-25; Eph 4:2-3, 31; 5:3-5; Col 3:12-14; 1 Tim 3:2-4; Heb 7:26; James 3:13; 1 Pet 2:1; 4:3, 15; Rev 9:21; 21:8; 22:15). To this body of comparative material 1QS 4:3-14 makes a contribution with its list of behaviors associated with the "two ways," the way of truth and the way of falsehood, inspired by the spirit of truth and the spirit of perversity or darkness. These correspond to what Paul calls "the fruit of the Spirit" and "the works of the flesh" (Gal 5:22-23, 19-21).

Another set of related literary forms in the NT has parallels in the DSS: *testimonia, lists of blessings and curses,* and *catenae.* 4QTestimonia (4Q175) draws upon several biblical passages, including Deut 18:15, a text that is directly quoted in Acts 3:22 and 7:22; and Num 24:17, which may inform Matt 2:2 and Rev 22:16. It also contains a patterned list of blessings and curses that resembles lists in Matt 5:3-12; 23:13-36 and Luke 6:20-26. 4QCatena (4Q177) gathers a chain of citations around a common theme, and in this it resembles the catenae of scriptural quotations adduced in Rom 3:10-18 and Heb 1:5-13.

A fragmentary text from Qumran (4Q525) contains a *list of beatitudes* similar to those found in the Sermon on the Mount (Matt 5:1-12) and the Sermon on the Plain (Luke 6:20-23). The text offers a nice example of how deeply rooted some of Jesus' teachings were in the forms of early Jewish literature, and it also supplies some verbal parallels for particular beatitudes of Jesus.

> [Blessed is the one who speaks truth] with a pure heart. (4Q525 2:1)
> Blessed are the pure in heart. (Matt 5:8)
>
> Blessed are those who rejoice in her (wisdom). (4Q525 2:2)
> Blessed are you when people revile you . . . rejoice and be glad. (Matt 5:11-12)
>
> Blessed is the one who attains wisdom . . . in the meekness of his soul does not despise her (wisdom). (4Q525 2:3-6)
> In the meekness of righteousness bring forth [your] words. (4Q525 4:20)
> Blessed are the meek. (Matt. 5:5)

In both style and content the Qumran beatitudes have a pronounced sapiential or wisdom character. Jesus' ethical teaching, too, was steeped in the Jewish wisdom tradition, but many of the beatitudes attributed to him have an eschatological focus. The reconstructive and interpretive work done on 4Q525 suggests that Matthew, instead of Luke as previously thought, may preserve a more original form of Jesus' beatitudes (eight short beatitudes plus one long beatitude), or at least a structure known in earlier Jewish literature.

An Essene Interpolation in 2 Corinthians?

Parallels between the DSS and the NT extend beyond words, phrases, and genres. Remarkably, an entire paragraph of 2 Corinthians reads like it could come straight out of one of the DSS:

> 6:14 Do not be mismatched with unbelievers. For what do righteousness and lawlessness have in common? Or

> what fellowship is there between light and darkness? 6:15 What concord does Christ have with Beliar? Or what does a believer share with an unbeliever? 6:16 What agreement has the temple of God with idols? For we are the temple of the living God; as God said, "I will live in them and walk among them, and I will be their God, and they shall be my people. 6:17 Therefore come out from them, and be separate from them, says the Lord, and touch nothing unclean; then I will welcome you, 6:18 and I will be your father, and you shall be my sons and daughters, says the Lord Almighty." 7:1 Since we have these promises, beloved, let us cleanse ourselves from every defilement of body and of spirit, making holiness perfect in the fear of God. (NRSV)

These verses are widely recognized as intrusive in their surrounding context. The verses immediately preceding and following 6:14–7:1 are conciliatory in tone and deal with the relationship between Paul and his fellow apostles, on the one hand, and the Corinthians on the other. The verses in question, though, strike a decidedly negative note and deal with the relationship between the Corinthian believers and pagan unbelievers. Without the paragraph, 7:2 would follow naturally on 6:13. Although abruptness alone is not a strong enough indication of interpolation, the suspicion that the material in 6:14–7:1 was added at some point is strengthened by the fact that the passage contains many words and phrases used nowhere else in Paul's letters (*mismatched* and *have . . . in common* in 6:14; *concord, Beliar,* and *share* in 6:15; *agreement* in 6:16a; *cleanse* and *defilement* in 7:1). Further, terms that do appear in Paul's letters are used differently here *(believer, promises, making . . . perfect).* Though disruptive in its present Pauline context, the passage would be right at home in Qumran teaching. Among the Essene-looking features are the dualism of light and darkness (though not unknown in Paul); "righteousness" as a moral category set over against "lawlessness"; "Beliar" (a variant of Belial) as a name for Satan; the view of the community as God's "share" or "lot"; the catena of scriptural *testimonia* (though Paul uses the technique elsewhere); and the call for separation from what is "unclean" and for cleansing from both bodily and spiritual impurity (cf., e.g., 1QS 5:13-14; 9:8-9; CD 6:14-18). The paragraph in question, however, does have several typically Pauline words and phrases: *Do not get, unbelievers, living God, says the Lord, Therefore, having these, promises, beloved, making perfect, holiness, in the fear of God.* If the paragraph is an interpolation, who wrote it — Paul himself? An editor? An early copyist? And how is it to be regarded — as a Christian exhortation with an Essene flavor, or a Christian adaptation of an Essene text? These questions may not admit of a definitive answer, but the passage remains striking nonetheless.

Methods of Scriptural Interpretation

No NT writer undertakes the kind of systematic, verse-by-verse exegesis of extended OT passages common to many of the pesher commentaries written at Qumran. Nevertheless, the DSS and the NT share a wide variety of hermeneutical approaches to the Jewish scriptures. Of course, NT authors quote Greek forms of the Hebrew Bible, whereas the Qumran commentators cite a Hebrew text. Yet the wording of both texts, Greek and Hebrew, often differs from the Masoretic Text (MT). Another shared feature is that at times NT writers use exegetical traditions known from the later Targums (e.g., Isa 6:10 in Mark 4:12 and the *Isaiah Targum;* Ps 68:18 in Eph 4:8 and the *Psalms Targum*), a phenomenon that occurs in the DSS as well. Further, NT writers use Greek citation formulae that have Hebrew counterparts in the DSS (e.g., "for it is written"; "as it is written"; "is it not written that . . . ?"). In a noteworthy commonality, Jude 14-15 quotes as sacred scripture a verse in *1 Enoch* (1:9), an apocalypse that also enjoyed scriptural status at Qumran.

Virtually all of the exegetical methods manifest in the Scrolls are common to the NT, including *allusion without explicit citation* (e.g., virtually every page of Philippians and Revelation); *paraphrases, harmonizations, and retellings of biblical stories* (e.g., in Stephen's sermon in Acts 7); *adaptations of biblical images in new hymns and poems* (e.g., John 1:1-18; Phil 2:6-11; Col 1:15-20); *hortatory and homiletic uses of scriptural examples and statements* (e.g., Paul's midrashic exhortation in 1 Cor 10:1-13, based on passages in Exodus 13–17 and Numbers 20; Jesus' midrashic sermon on the biblical statement "He gave them bread from heaven to eat" in John 6:31-59; the midrashic sermon in Heb 3:7–4:13 warning against faithlessness, based on Ps 95:7-11 and Gen 2:2); *halakhic exegesis* (e.g., Matt 5:21-48; John 7–8); and *pesher-like exegesis* (e.g., Matthew's formulaic citations). Occasionally, the NT writings take up interpretive approaches that do not feature in the DSS, such as *typology* (e.g., Paul on Christ and Adam in Romans 5; the author of Hebrews on sacrifice and priesthood in Hebrews 7–10, esp. 8:3–10:18; and the author of 1 Peter on baptism and salvation through water in the great Flood in 1 Pet 3:18-22) and *allegory* (e.g., Paul on Hagar and Sarah in Gal 4:21–5:1). Perhaps the best general label for the favored hermeneutical approach of both the Qumran covenanters and the authors of the NT is *eschatological midrash.* Common to both is the tendency toward a contemporizing exegesis that ignores or downplays the original, contextual meaning of the biblical passage. Both the Qumran authors and the NT writers viewed themselves as living at the end of days, and both groups founds themselves in the pages of Hebrew scripture. Both interpreted their experiences as fulfillment of biblical prophecy and understood themselves as the recipients of promised blessings.

The Qumran pesharim have often been invoked in comparison with a favored mode of biblical interpretation in the Gospel of Matthew. In this Gospel, the author starts with an introductory formula (e.g., "This happened in order that what was spoken through the mouth of the prophet might be fulfilled") and follows it with an explicit biblical citation (1:22-23; 2:5-6, 15, 17-18, 23; 4:14-16; 8:17; 12:17-21; 13:35; 21:4-5; 27:9-10). Like the Qumran pesherists, Matthew largely ignores the original historical and literary contexts of the OT passages he cites, in favor of treating them as prophecies now being fulfilled. Matthew's general approach to scripture thus resembles pesher exegesis in some respects, but his particular brand of exegesis lacks the technical terms in pesher introductory formulae (פשרו/*pishro,* "its interpretation is"; פשר הדבר/*pesher ha-dabar,* "the interpretation of the passage is"). Further, Qumran pesharim start with a biblical text that becomes the point of departure for the interpretation, whereas Matthew begins with events in the life of Jesus and then finds OT proof-texts for them in an explicit scheme of prophecy-fulfillment.

The insights offered by the DSS into the NT appropriation of a single verse may be noted in the case of Paul's citation of Deut 21:23, "cursed is everyone who hangs on a tree," in Gal 3:12-13. Paul applies the verse to Jesus' crucifixion in an attempt to explain that Christ redeemed believers from the curse pronounced by the Torah on failure to keep all its commands by becoming a curse "for us." The Deuteronomy text, however, refers to the hanging of an accursed person who has already died, to make a public spectacle of him (cf. Josh 10:26-27; 2 Sam 4:12), and not to crucifixion as a mode of execution. This latter understanding, though, is reflected in two DSS, the *Temple Scroll* (11Q19 64:7-13) and the *Nahum Pesher* (4Q169 3-4 i 6-9). The pesher passage refers cryptically to Alexander Jannaeus's execution of Pharisees by "hanging them alive on the tree," and the *Temple Scroll* appeals to Deut 21:23 in its law that traitors and those guilty of capital crimes be "hung on a tree until dead."

Practices

In addition to parallels in terminology, conceptuality, and exegesis, the DSS also provide analogues to various practices reflected in the NT. Three in particular deserve attention: immersion in water, communal meals, and property sharing. The Qumran covenanters participated in self-administered ritual ablutions on a daily basis. An extensive system of aqueducts, cisterns, pools, and ritual baths *(miqva'ot)* enabled them to practice ritual immersion. Evidently, they did so primarily in order to achieve ritual purification of the body in preparation for such communal activities as meals and worship. Yet a few passages in the Scrolls associate the rite not only with external, bodily purification but inner, spiritual repentance. The *Rule of the Community* says of the person who refuses to enter the covenant of God by joining the community, "He shall not be reckoned among the perfect; he shall neither be purified by atonement, nor cleansed by purifying waters, nor sanctified by seas and rivers, nor washed clean with any ablution" (1QS 3:4-5). A passage further on speaks of the expiation of sins by the Spirit of holiness and says, "And when his flesh is sprinkled with purifying water and sanctified by cleansing water it shall be made clean by the humble submission of his soul to all the precepts of God" (1QS 3:9). These passages indicate that water immersion at Qumran resembles John's baptism insofar as both emphasize the need for repentance and good works as the evidence of it (e.g., Mark 1:4 par. Matt 3:2; Luke 3:3). And John's baptism itself may have involved an element of ritual purification. However, ritual immersion at Qumran does not resemble baptism as it developed in the Christian tradition. Already in the pages of the NT, baptism is a one-time, other-administered rite of initiation with sacramental significance — new birth and union with Christ in his dying and rising. These particular significations are naturally lacking in the Scrolls.

The *Rule of the Community* describes the meals of the Qumran group and highlights the role of the priest as the first one to stretch out his hand to bless the bread and wine (1QS 6:4-6). It also alludes to a "pure meal" and "pure drink" of which only full members of the group, who had attained the highest level of ritual purity, were allowed to partake (1QS 6:16-17). The so-called *Rule of the Congregation* or *Messianic Rule* (1QSa) describes a ritual meal to be eaten in the presence of the two messiahs of Aaron and Israel at the end of days. The cultic status of this meal at Qumran continues to be debated. Whatever its exact character, the meal does offer some striking parallels to the Lord's Supper as described in the Synoptic Gospels (Mark 14:22-25 par. Matt 26:26-29 par. Luke 22:17-20) and 1 Cor 11:27-29. Both meals feature bread and wine, both are eschatological and messianic in character, and both have an anticipatory element. However, the Lord's Supper or Eucharist has retrospective and memorializing features and came very early on to have a sacramental quality. Both of these characteristics are lacking at Qumran.

The Qumran Essenes practiced a community of goods that in some ways resembles a social experiment of the early Jesus movement in Jerusalem. The Essene practice of property sharing is noted by classical authors such as Josephus (*J.W.* 2.122), Philo (*Hypoth.* 11:4-9), and Pliny the Elder (*Nat. Hist.* 5.73). Indeed, it was the similarity of these descriptions to passages in the *Rule of the Community* that initially led, in part, to the identification of the Qumran group as Essenes (1QS 1:11-12; 6:18-23; cf. CD 14:11-16 for a different type of financial support outside Qumran). The book of Acts describes the early Christian welfare system in 2:41-47 and 4:32–5:11. The sharing of goods at Qumran and Jerusalem bears both similarities and differences. In both cases, the finances and resources of members were put at the disposal of the entire group, and members of both groups still had access to their contributed resources, at least for a while. Further, in both communities the pooling of resources was understood to fulfill biblical ideals (e.g., Lev 19:18b; Deut 6:5) and to symbolize spiritual unity. However, at Qumran the community of goods was mandatory for all full-fledged members, whereas in Jerusalem this was not the case. Also, at Qumran prospective members of the community had to go through a process of initiation, at the final stage of which their property was merged with the community's holdings. No such staggered entry procedure was in place in Jerusalem. So far, no convincing precedent or analogy for this type of social program has been found in ancient Palestine or elsewhere in the Greco-Roman world. Whether the similarities between Qumran and Jerusalem are a coincidence or indicate a connection of some sort (e.g., Essene converts to the Jesus movement) remains uncertain.

Other practices might be mentioned. The code of

communal discipline in Matthew 18 corresponds in some respects to Essene procedures, particularly in the three-stage process of rebuking a fellow member of the community (cf. Matt 18:15-17; 1QS 5:24–6:1; CD 7:2-3; 9:2-8, 16-20; 4Q477). And the practice of Christian women at Corinth covering their heads during worship "on account of the angels" (1 Cor 11:10) becomes comprehensible in light of the notion that angels were present in worship services, an idea reflected in the Scrolls (e.g., the *Angelic Liturgy* or *Songs of the Sabbath Sacrifice,* 4Q400-407; etc.).

Johannine Dualism and the Scrolls

The DSS have made major contributions to understanding the theology of the NT. One of the most notable centers on the dualistic language and conceptuality of the Gospel and Letters of John. Like the Qumran community, the Johannine community was intentionally separated from its larger Jewish milieu and developed many of the earmarks of a sect. The sectarian literature produced by the two groups abounds in the oppositional poles of heaven and earth, light and darkness, truth and falsehood, God and Satan. As in the Scrolls, so in the Johannine literature the dualism has cosmic, temporal, social, and psychological dimensions, along with a correlative determinism. One passage in particular has attracted attention, the Treatise on the Two Spirits in the Qumran *Rule of the Community* (1QS 3:13–4:26):

> From the God of knowledge comes all that is and shall be.... He has created man to govern the world and has appointed for him two spirits in which to walk until the time of visitation: the spirits of truth and injustice.... All the children of righteousness are ruled by the Prince of Light and walk in the ways of light, but those born of injustice are ruled by the Angel of Darkness and walk in all the ways of darkness.... For it is He who created the spirits of Light and Darkness and founded every action upon them and established every deed [upon] their [ways].... The nature of all the children of men is ruled by these (two spirits), and during their life all the hosts of men have a portion of their divisions and walk in (both) ways. And the whole reward for their deeds shall be, for everlasting ages, according to whether each man's portion in their two divisions is great or small. For God has established the spirits in equal measure until the final age.... Until now the spirits of truth and injustice struggle in the hearts of men and they walk in both wisdom and folly.... For God has established the two spirits in equal measure until the determined end, and until the Renewal.... (trans. Vermes)

This passage shares a stark dualistic outlook with the Johannine literature. One thinks especially of certain lines in the sermon 1 John, written in the wake of a schism within the Johannine community:

> This is the message we have heard from him and proclaim to you, that God is light and in him there is no darkness at all. If we say that we have fellowship with him while we are walking in darkness, we lie and do not do what is true.... Do not love the world or the things in the world.... for all that is in the world — the desire of the flesh, the desire of the eyes, the pride in riches — comes not from the Father but from the world. And the world and its desire are passing away, but those who do the will of God live forever.... Children, it is the last hour! As you have heard that antichrist is coming, so now many antichrists have come. From this we know that it is the last hour. They went out from us, but they did not belong to us; for if they had belonged to us, they would have remained with us. But by going out they made it plain that none of them belongs to us. But you have been anointed by the Holy One, and all of you have knowledge. I write to you, not because you do not know the truth, but because you know it, and you know that no lie comes from the truth. (1 John 1:5-6; 2:15-17, 18-21 NRSV)

Johannine dualism and determinism are oriented around a distinctive center understandably lacking at Qumran — Jesus Christ as the source and embodiment of God's truth. What Johannine theology lacks that Essene theology has is the notion that God has created good and evil *in order that* they may engage in a struggle, not only at the cosmic level, but in the very lives of individuals, each of whom has a predetermined share in both light and darkness, good and evil. Those who are among the elect, predetermined children of light — a status they cannot attain but only confirm — will be found at the last judgment to have had a greater portion in good than evil. This sort of extreme determinism and dualism goes beyond anything in the biblical tradition. Thus recognition of general similarities in terminology and worldview between John and the DSS should not disguise some very real differences. The hyper dualism of 1QS adapts ideas from ancient Persian religion (Zoroastrianism) and fuses them with Jewish apocalyptic traditions. The similarities between John and Qumran have at times been explained variously by appeal to Essene influence via John the Baptist or to Qumran converts to the Johannine community. More likely they reflect a common dependence on early Jewish traditions and an analogous sectarian consciousness.

Eschatology and Messianism

Both the Qumran Essenes and the members of the early Jesus movement that eventually became Christianity had an intense awareness that they were living in the last times (e.g., 1QpHab 2:5; 1QSa 1:1; Acts 2:17). Eschatological fervency characterized both apocalyptic movements, though with a different focus rooted in their distinctive experiences and expectations. After his death, Jesus' followers located themselves further along the eschatological time line than did the covenanters of Qumran. For the first Christians, the new age had already dawned, the kingly rule of God in the earth had already begun, the Messiah had already come. Yet both groups had a charismatic founder, and both read and interpreted Scripture in actualizing ways while seeing their respective movements as the fulfillment of biblical prophecy. Both communities thought of themselves as members of the new or renewed covenant between God and Israel, and both patterned their communal life on the experience of the people of Israel during their desert sojourn. Both could speak of themselves as children of light and of everyone else as children of darkness. Both viewed themselves as predestined by God to their elect status and their final salvation. And in both groups messianic expectation played a part.

There are, though, profound differences that distinguish the Qumran covenanters from the early Christians in the areas of eschatology and messianism and in the lifestyles that these beliefs engendered. The Essenes of Qumran revered the memory of their founder, the Teacher of Righteousness, and may even have anticipated that he would have an eschatological counterpart in a priestly messiah who would function as "Interpreter of the Law" and "teach righteousness at the end of days." But the Qumran sectarians did not regard the Teacher as a messiah, they attached no redemptive significance to his death, and they did not expect him to come back from the dead or down from heaven as God's final agent of redemption. Nor did they worship him. In each of these respects, Qumran faith differs from NT faith in Jesus. Further, most early Christians did not pull out of mainstream society and retreat to the isolation of the desert, as the Qumran Essenes did. The Christian movement was open to Jews of all persuasions and to Gentiles as well. Not so with the Qumran Essenes. The Qumran Jews were devoted to the ideals of celibacy, ritual purity, and Torah observance in a way that did not characterize most forms of Christianity. Then too, messianism was and remains much more prominent a belief in Christianity than it has ever been in Judaism or ever was at Qumran.

The DSS do indeed have messianic expectation in common with the NT, but the differences are at least as striking as the similarities. Whereas the Scrolls envisage the one coming of multiple messiahs, the NT speaks of the two comings of the one messiah. So the DSS anticipate a division of labor, whereas the NT has several messianic tasks being performed by a single figure. It is customary to speak of two messiahs at Qumran: the royal, Davidic "messiah of Israel"; and the priestly "messiah of Aaron" (e.g., 1QS 9:11; 1QSa; CD 12:23; 14:19; 19:10; 20:11). The "messiah of Israel" is also given other, biblically derived titles such as "Branch of David" (e.g., 4Q174; 4QpIsa[a]; 4Q285; 4Q252) and "Prince of the Congregation" (e.g., CD 7:19; 4Q285). His main job is to play the role of conquering warrior at the end of days. In the DSS, the priestly messiah always takes precedence over the royal messiah; his eschatological functions include providing atonement and giving instruction in and proper interpretation of the Torah; he is probably the referent of the titles "the Interpreter of the Law" (e.g., 4Q174; CD 7:18) and the one "who will teach righteousness at the end of days" (CD 6:11). Yet the Scrolls also speak about an eschatological figure known as the Prophet (1QS 9:10-11; the same figure may be in view in 11QMelch 2:18; 4QTest 5–8, citing Deut 18:18-19). And 4Q521 seems to envision an Elijah-type prophet-messiah. Further, two key scrolls invest the archangel Michael with a major role in eschatological salvation (1QM 17; 11QMelch). In view of the functions served by these various eschatological figures, then, it may be proper to speak of not two but four messiahs in Qumran expectation, even if only two of them are regularly referred to by the term *messiah*. Overall, the distinctive feature of NT messianism is that it applies variations of all four paradigms — royal, priestly, prophetic, heavenly — to a single figure of the recent past who suffered, died, rose again, and would return soon to usher in the kingdom of God that he had inaugurated during his earthly life.

Jesus and Qumran Cave 4

Among the DSS, it is the Cave 4 texts that have offered the most striking parallels with Gospel traditions. These scrolls entered the public domain of scholarship only in 1991. Although suspicions of conspiracy to suppress the Cave 4 texts attended complaints about the delay in publishing them, a decade of research has shown that they contain no bombshells and nothing to undermine the truth claims of either Judaism or Christianity. What they have offered is further strokes in the ongoing effort to sketch as fully as possible the Jewish background of NT affirmations about Jesus. The following four Cave 4 texts may be singled out as particularly important for NT study.

4Q246, The Aramaic "Son of God" Text or *Apocryphon of Daniel*. This text speaks of an eschatological figure who "will be great on earth . . . he will be called [or: call himself] grand . . . the Son of God he will be proclaimed [or: proclaim himself], and the Son of the Most High they will call him." The ongoing debate over this text centers on whether the "son of God" is a positive figure who deserves the title or a negative one who claims it for himself; and if he is a positive figure, whether or not he is a messiah. At least five different identifications have been proposed: a Syrian (Seleucid) ruler, either Antiochus Epiphanes or his son Alexander Balas; an anti-messiah; the people of Israel; the angel Michael; and a messiah. The latter two interpretations seem to make the best sense of the text; a messiah, whether heavenly or human, seems to be in view. On the one hand, an angelic figure such as Michael would make good sense in a pseudo-Daniel work. On the other, a human messiah, perhaps the Davidic messiah, would make good sense, because the title "Son of God" is never applied to Michael in the Scrolls, whereas it is given to the Davidic messiah (e.g., 4Q174). For readers of the NT, 4Q246 makes a very important contribution in its striking verbal parallels to the annunciation scene in Luke 1:30-35. If the messianic interpretation of the scroll fragment is correct, it shows that at the turn of the eras "Son of God" was a Jewish title for the messiah, not a new Christian one that could have been adapted only from Greco-Roman paganism.

4Q285, The War of the Messiah. Drawing on the language of Isa 10:34–11:1, this text speaks of the messiah as "a shoot" that will "spring from the root of Jesse." He is also called the "Branch of David" and the "Prince of the Congregation." When this text first came to light, a storm of controversy broke out when a few scholars proposed that it depicts the messiah being put to death. Virtually all scholars are now convinced that the messiah of this text does the killing, in good Davidic fashion. These rival interpretations differ most markedly in how they render the fourth line of fragment 5. Depending on how one vocalizes the verb והמיתו *(whmytw),* specifically its last letter (ו = ô or û), and on whether one identifies the Prince of the Congregation as the subject or object of the verb, the key clause can be rendered either "and they killed [or: will kill] *(hamitû)* the Prince of the Congregation, the Branch of David" or "and the Prince of the Congregation, the Branch of David, will kill [or: killed] *(hamitô)* him." The latter interpretation makes better sense of the syntax, and it has been supported by computer digital enhancement of the fragment, which has revealed a sixth line that speaks of "the corpses of the Kitians." The term "Kitians" (or "Kittim") is a label often used in the DSS in reference to the Romans. The reference to their dead bodies suggests that they are being depicted as defeated in the eschatological battle; hence, it is likely that their leader is described as being executed by the Davidic messiah. The notion of a suffering and dying messiah, then, remains unique to the NT, with no precedent in pre-Christian Judaism.

4Q491, Self-Glorification Hymn. This fascinating fragment has been regarded by some as a part of a manuscript of the *War Rule.* More recent study, though, has highlighted different versions of the hymn in 4Q471 frg. 6, 4Q427 (4QH[a]) frg. 7 col. i, and 1QH col. 26. The speaker in the first-person narration of fragment 11 of this work mentions a "powerful throne in the congregation of gods" and says of himself, "my glory is incomparable and none is exalted except me . . . I am seated in . . . in heaven . . . I am reckoned with gods and my abode is in the holy congregation. [My] des[ire] is not according to the flesh; all that is precious to me is in the glory of the holy [habi]tation. . . . Who will withstand the flow of my lips and who will advise me and be comparable to my judgments? . . . I am reckoned with the gods . . . my glory is with the sons of the king. . . ." The identity of the speaker of this text remains uncertain. The first editor of the text titled it a "canticle of Michael," yet several factors suggest that the speaker is not an angel but a human being. The implied speaker of the text is probably either the Teacher of Righteousness or else his eschatological counterpart, the priestly messiah. The former would fill the bill better if 4Q491 is related to the *Hodayot,* or Thanksgiving Hymns (1QH); the latter if it is part of the *War Rule.* For students of the NT, 4Q491 is important in light of its presumed theme of heavenly ascent (cf. Paul's ascent to paradise in 2 Cor 12:1-10) and its explicit notion of exaltation and enthronement (Jesus' resurrection).

4Q521, Messianic Apocalypse. This is perhaps the most important Cave 4 text for Gospel studies. It describes the works of the Messiah, including resurrection of the dead, in terms very similar to the Gospels' presentation of Jesus' ministry. Drawing on the language of Isa 35:5-6 and 61:1-2, 4Q521 speaks of God working, presumably through his messiah, to "heal (the) wounded, revive the dead, (and) proclaim good news to the afflicted"; and it states that "(the) [po]or he will satisfy, (the) uprooted he will guide, and on (the) hungry he will bestow riches." These words have a striking parallel in Luke 4:16-21 and Luke 7:18-23 par. Matt 11:2-6. According to the passage in Matthew, "When John heard in prison the deeds of the Messiah, he sent word by his disciples and said to him [Jesus], 'Are you the one who is to come, or are we to wait for another?' Jesus answered them, 'Go and tell John what you hear and see: the blind receive their sight, the lame walk, the lepers are cleansed, the deaf hear, the dead are raised, and the poor have good news brought to them. And blessed is anyone who takes no offense at me." The figure envisaged in the Qumran fragment fills the role of an Elijah-like prophet-messiah, which is one of the Gospels' favorite ways of understanding Jesus.

Jesus, Melchizedek, and Michael

The NT letter to the Hebrews (which is not a letter but a sermon) adds a unique perspective to NT Christology by affirming that Christ is a high priest who belongs to an eternal, spiritual priestly line superior to the historical, earthly order of levitical priesthood in ancient Israelite religion. To develop this teaching, the author of Hebrews connects Jesus' spiritual priesthood to that of Melchizedek, a figure who appears in Genesis 14 as a Canaanite priest-king to whom Abraham pays a tithe from the spoils of a war. Hebrews exploits the fact that Melchizedek appears and disappears abruptly in Genesis 14 to argue that Melchizedek was "without father, without mother, without genealogy, having neither beginning of days nor end of life, but resembling the Son of God, he remains a priest forever" (7:4). The only other place in the OT that mentions Melchizedek is Ps 110:4, "The Lord has sworn and will not change his mind, 'You [the Davidic king] are a priest forever according to the order of Melchizedek.'" Hebrews treats this statement as God's sworn oath not to an ancient Davidic king but to Jesus. In its midrash, Hebrews combines Genesis 14 and Ps 110:4 to assert that Jesus performed a priestly function in his life, death, and exaltation and that he continues to do so in his ongoing intercession for the people of God.

With the discovery of the DSS, the document known as 11QMelchizedek naturally invited comparison with Hebrews 7. The Qumran text is an eschatological midrash that combines biblical passages which mention the jubilee year and the remission of debts in sabbatical years to formulate a teaching about the eschatological release of captives from the hands of Belial. The agent of God's redemption is a figure given the symbolic name "Melchizedek." This Melchizedek, though, appears to have only a nominal relation to the figure of Genesis 14 and turns out, in fact, to be none other than the archangel Michael. As an angelic savior figure, Michael is assigned some of the same roles in eschatological salvation that the NT attributes to Jesus: forgiveness of sins, defeat of the powers of Satan, and vindication of the righteous.

11QMelchizedek, however, draws neither on Genesis 14 nor Psalm 110 in its teaching; it is therefore doubtful that the author of this text even had the OT figure of this name in mind, whereas Hebrews certainly does. In the Qumran text, Michael takes on the sobriquet "Melchizedek" because he has a wicked angelic counterpart in Satan or Belial, who in 4QAmram appears under the name "Melchiresha'."

There is a NT passage that has a better parallel in 11QMelchizedek than does Hebrews 7. It is the account of Jesus' inaugural sermon in his hometown synagogue given in Luke 4. There Jesus unrolls a scroll of Isaiah, finds a text, reads it, and in his exposition of it claims himself as its fulfillment. The text he cites is Isa 61:1-2, "The Spirit of the Lord is upon me, because he has anointed me to bring good news to the poor. He has sent me to proclaim release to the captives and recovery of sight to the blind, to let the oppressed go free, to proclaim the year of the Lord's favor." This very text is one of the key passages that 11QMelchizedek applies to the angel Michael. So both Luke 4 and the Qumran document understand the eschatological release of captives to be the work of an end-time anointed agent. The Qumran text identifies that agent with an angelic messiah figure, while Luke identifies him with the anointed prophet-messiah, Jesus.

The Final Battle and the New Jerusalem

Some final parallels between the NT and the DSS worth mentioning in a brief survey concern the last book of the Christian scriptures, the Apocalypse of John or book of Revelation. Apocalypses are writings that purport to give revelations concerning cosmic secrets and/or final events on earth mediated to a human being through an angel. The book of Revelation is the only full-fledged apocalypse in the NT and also bears the distinction of having lent its name to the wider literary genre. Although the Qumran Essenes were, like the early Christians, an apocalyptic movement, and though they composed works with apocalyptic features and copied older apocalypses such as *1 Enoch* and *Jubilees,* they evidently did not compose any full-blown apocalypses themselves. Yet one of the works found in fragments at Qumran and Masada, the *Angelic Liturgy* or *Songs of the Sabbath Sacrifice,* shares with Revelation particular themes, such as the heavenly temple and heavenly worship; and specific motifs, such as silence in heaven (Rev 8:1; 4Q403 1 i 40-46) and an animate heavenly altar (Rev 9:13-14; 4Q405 20 ii 21-22, 12-13). One of the major sectarian scrolls, the *War Rule* (1QM and Cave 4 fragments) has in common with Revelation the expectation of an end-time battle between the forces of good and evil.

The *War Scroll* envisions a forty-year war waged in seven battles between the Sons of Light under the leadership of Michael and the Sons of Darkness under the dominion of Belial. The Sons of Light, as one would expect, are members of the sect. They will prevail in the first three engagements. The Sons of Darkness, who appear under the names of Israel's ancestral foes (e.g., Edom, Moab, Ammon, the Philistines) and also include "the ungodly of the covenant" (i.e., non-Qumran Jews) will triumph in the last three. Then in the seventh, tie-breaking battle, "the mighty hand of God will bring down the army of Belial and all the angels of his kingdom" (1:13-16). The literary genre of the *War Scroll* resembles Greco-Roman military manuals or tactical treatises. After a general description of the war (cols. 1-2), the early columns of the work are taken up with descriptions of the various implements and trappings of war with their engravings — trumpets, standards, shields, spears, swords, and scabbards; the deployment of different divisions, including infantry, cavalry, and various support personnel such as plunderers, despoilers of the slain, and baggage handlers; and the various qualifications and duties of different participants in the war, including various types of soldiers, priests, and Levites (cols. 2-9). Ritual purity concerns are prominent in the holy war, and the leaders of the battle are priests and Levites. Speeches, prayers, and blessings to be delivered both before and after battle make up the central columns (10-15). These are followed in the final columns by descriptions of the seven engagements of the war (cols. 15-18), victory hymns, and a post-battle ceremony (cols. 18-19). Strikingly, none of the actual fighting is described but only events surrounding it. The battle belongs to God. The Davidic messiah is mentioned under the title "Prince of the Congregation" (5:1), but only in a passing reference to the engraving of his shield. The figure who saves the day is instead the angel Michael (col. 17; cf. Rev 12:7-9 for Michael's role in a primordial battle with Satan and his minions).

The book of Revelation describes the final battle between the forces of God and Satan at several points in its narrative, in a scheme of recapitulation with variation. Like 1QM, Revelation never depicts much of the actual fighting, but unlike 1QM it never describes the people of God participating in the battle, though a few verses (Rev 14:4; 17:14) hint that they do. For instance, in 14:1-5 John describes the followers of the Lamb as a victorious army of 144,000 celibate males who presumably have fought in a holy war (cf. 7:1-8). In Rev 16:12-16 the kings of the east team up with demonic spirits in preparing for a confrontation at [H]armagedon. In 17:9-14 a coalition of ten kings falls in line with the Beast in anticipation of making war on the Lamb, who will conquer them. Rev 19:11-21 depicts the triumph of Christ and his heavenly armies against the kings of the earth with their armies. In this scene, Christ comes down from heaven riding on a horse in true warrior fashion to judge and make war. His weapon is "a sharp sword with which to strike the nations and rule them with a rod of iron" (19:15; cf. Ps 2:9; Isa 11:4). The Beast and the False Prophet are captured and thrown alive into the lake of fire. Significantly, this is the only place in the NT where Christ fills the role of a triumphant Davidic messiah. The Gospels identify Jesus as such but never depict him in the traditional military role. Revelation applies the Davidic paradigm to Christ's second coming, but even here the warrior Christ wears a robe dipped in his own blood, and he wields the sword as one whose name is the Word of God. These features reinforce what John the seer of Revelation emphasizes in other parts of the book, that the decisive battle has already been fought and won by Jesus at Calvary. In Revelation 20 Satan is bound for a thousand years, during which time martyred believers are raised from the dead to enjoy a millennial reign with Christ. Satan is loosed again, and another final battle ensues as "the nations at the four corners of the earth, Gog and Magog," march on Jerusalem "the beloved city" and surround "the camp of the saints," only to be consumed with fire from heaven.

What follows in Revelation 21 is a vision of a new heaven and new earth. John sees "the new Jerusalem coming down out of heaven from God." The church as "the bride, the wife of the Lamb" then appears under the image of the holy city Jerusalem. The city is an enormous, perfect cube whose length, width, and height each measure 1,500 miles (c. 2,400 km.). Its wall has twelve gates, three on each side, inscribed with the names of the twelve tribes of Israel; and the wall itself rests on twelve foundations engraved with the names of the twelve apostles. John's angelic tour guide measures the city, some of whose structures are not only adorned with but built of gems and precious metals. Most significantly, the new Jerusalem is a city without a temple, "for its temple is the Lord God the Almighty and the Lamb."

Revelation's depiction of the new Jerusalem invites comparison with the *New Jerusalem* text. Several fragments of this Aramaic work were found in five of the scroll caves near Qumran. An apocalypse of pre-Qumran origin, it narrates a guided tour of the city and is modeled on Ezekiel 40–48. An anonymous tour guide, presumably an angel, surveys the future city and temple with an unnamed visionary. The work gives detailed measurements of the city, which occupies 280 square miles (736 sq. km.), and also of its wall, gates, towers, streets, and other architectural features, including a representative block of houses and a typical house. The interior of the city is laid out on a chessboard-like grid of 192 blocks.

The *New Jerusalem* text shares with the book of Revelation an extensive reliance on Ezekiel 40–48, a heavenly guide who measures the architecture and offers occasional explanations, a gargantuan size for the city, an emphasis on the twelve tribes of Israel, and an interest in precious stones and metals. The most striking difference between them is the temple. Revelation lacks one. It has no need for one, not because the people have become the eschatological dwelling place of God, an idea familiar in both the Scrolls and the NT, but because God and the Lamb have become the eternal dwelling of people.

Bibliography. Charlesworth, J. H., ed. 1992, *Jesus and the Dead Sea Scrolls,* New York, Doubleday • Charlesworth, J. H., ed. repr. 1991, *John and the Dead Sea Scrolls,* New York: Crossroad • Fitzmyer, J. A. 1999, *The Dead Sea Scrolls and Christian Origins,* Grand Rapids: Eerdmans • Flint, P. W., and J. C. VanderKam, eds. 1999, *The Dead Sea Scrolls after Fifty Years: A Comprehensive Assessment,* 2 vols., Leiden: Brill • Murphy O'Connor, J., and J. H. Charlesworth, eds. repr. 1990, *Paul and the Dead Sea Scrolls,* New York: Crossroad • Schiffman, L. H., and J. C. VanderKam, eds. 2000, *The Encyclopedia of the Dead Sea Scrolls,* 2 vols., Oxford: Oxford University • Stanton, G. 1995, *Gospel Truth? New Light on Jesus and the Gospel,* Valley Forge, Pa.: Trinity, 20-32 • Stegemann, H. 1998, *The Library of Qumran: On the Essenes, Qumran, John the Baptist, and Jesus.* Grand Rapids: Eerdmans; Leiden: Brill • Stendahl, K., with J. H. Charlesworth, eds. repr. 1992, *The Scrolls and the New Testament,* New York: Crossroad • VanderKam, J., and P. W. Flint. 2002, *The Meaning of the Dead Sea Scrolls.* San Francisco: HarperSanFrancisco • Vermes, G. 1997, *The Complete Dead Sea Scrolls in English,* London/New York: Penguin.

Index

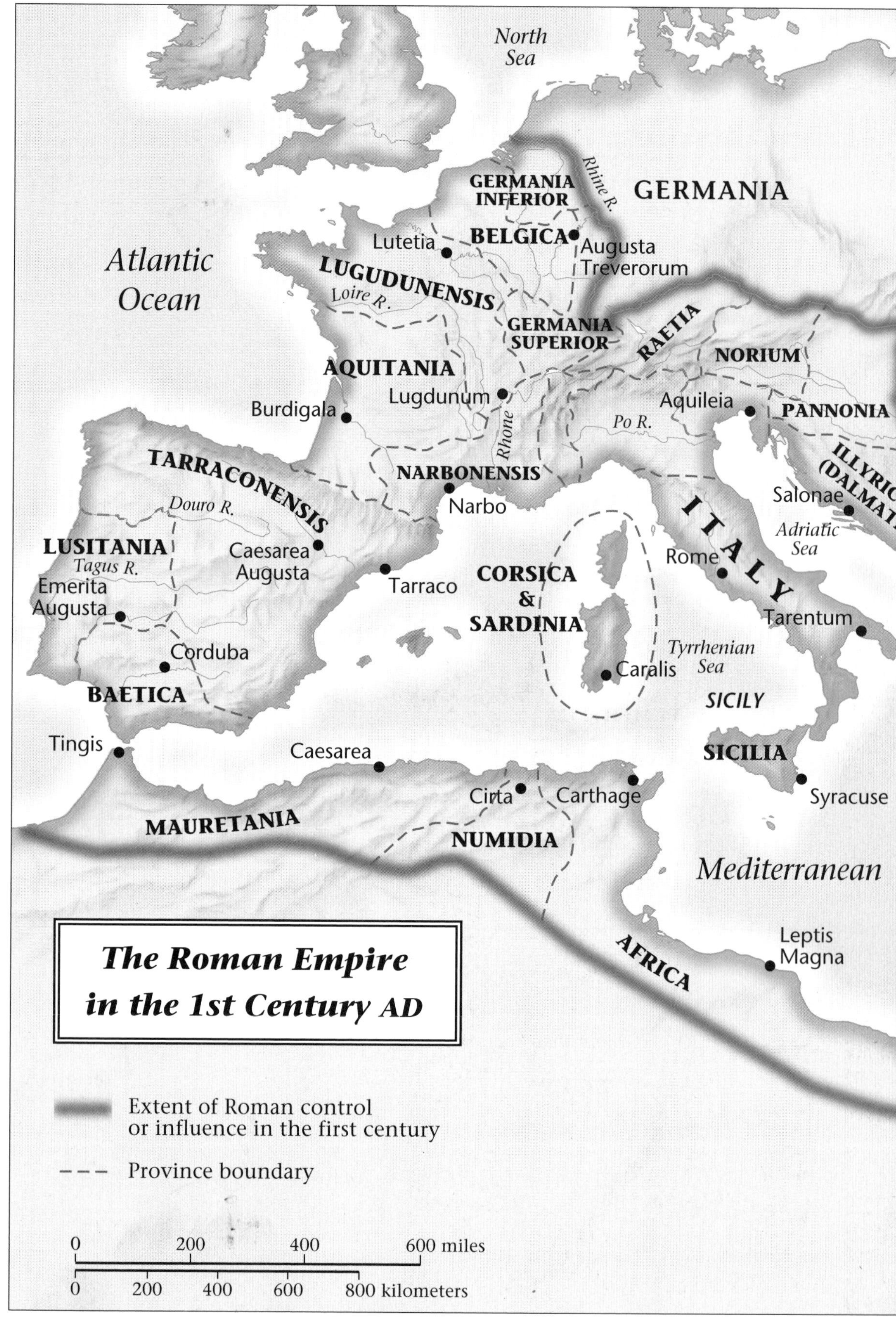
North Sea
Atlantic Ocean
GERMANIA
GERMANIA INFERIOR
Rhine R.
BELGICA
Lutetia
Augusta Treverorum
LUGUDUNENSIS
Loire R.
GERMANIA SUPERIOR
RAETIA
NORIUM
AQUITANIA
Lugdunum
Burdigala
Aquileia
PANNONIA
Po R.
Rhone
TARRACONENSIS
NARBONENSIS
Narbo
ILLYRICU (DALMATI
Salonae
Douro R.
ITALY
Adriatic Sea
LUSITANIA
Tagus R.
Caesarea Augusta
Tarraco
CORSICA & SARDINIA
Rome
Emerita Augusta
Tarentum
Corduba
Tyrrhenian Sea
Caralis
BAETICA
SICILY
SICILIA
Tingis
Caesarea
Cirta
Carthage
Syracuse
MAURETANIA
NUMIDIA
Mediterranean
AFRICA
Leptis Magna
Extent of Roman control or influence in the first century
Province boundary
0 200 400 600 miles
0 200 400 600 800 kilometers

The Roman Empire in the 1st Century AD